2005 PR

BASEBALL CARDS

DR. JAMES BECKETT

TWENTY-FIFTH EDITION

House of Collectibles
New York

Important Notice: All of the information, including valuations, in this book has been compiled from reliable sources, and efforts have been made to eliminate errors and questionable data. Nevertheless, the possibility of error, in a work of such immense scope, always exists. The publisher will not be held responsible for losses that may occur in the purchase, sale, or other transaction of items because of information contained herein. Readers who feel they have discovered errors are invited to *write* and inform us, so they may be corrected in subsequent editions. Those seeking further information on the topics covered in this book are advised to refer to the complete line of *Official Price Guides* published by the House of Collectibles.

House of Collectibles and colophon
are trademarks of Random House, Inc.

Published by:
House of Collectibles
Random House Reference
New York, New York

Distributed by Random House Reference,
an imprint of Random House, Inc.,
New York, and simultaneously in Canada by
Random House of Canada Limited, Toronto.

www.houseofcollectibles.com

Manufactured in the United States of America

ISSN: 1062-7138

ISBN: 0-375-72100-2

10 9 8 7 6 5 4 3 2 1

Twenty-fifth Edition: April 2005

Table of Contents

About the Author

Jim Beckett, the leading authority on sports card values in the United States, maintains a wide range of activities in the world of sports. He possesses one of the finest collections of sports cards and autographs in the world, has made numerous appearances on radio and television, and has been frequently cited in many national publications. He was awarded the first "Special Achievement Award" for Contributions to the Hobby by the National Sports Collectors Convention in 1980, the "Jock Jaspersen Award" for Hobby Dedication in 1983, and the "Buck Barker, Spirit of the Hobby" award in 1991.

Dr. Beckett is the author of *Beckett Baseball Card Price Guide, The Official Price Guide to Baseball Cards, Price Guide to Baseball Collectibles, The Sport Americana Baseball Memorabilia and Autograph Price Guide, Beckett Almanac of Baseball Cards and Collectibles, Beckett Football Card Price Guide, The Official Price Guide to Football Cards, Beckett Hockey Card Price Guide, The Official Price Guide to Hockey Cards, Beckett Basketball Card Price Guide, The Official Price Guide to Basketball Cards, The Beckett Baseball Card Alphabetical Checklist, The Beckett Basketball Card Alphabetical Checklist,* and *The Beckett Football Card Alphabetical Checklist.* In addition, he is the founder, publisher, and editor of *Beckett Baseball Card Monthly, Beckett Basketball Monthly, Beckett Football Card Monthly, Beckett Hockey Collector, Beckett Sports Collectibles,* and *Beckett Racing and Motorsports Marketplace.*

Jim Beckett received his Ph.D. in Statistics from Southern Methodist University in 1975. Prior to starting Beckett Publications in 1984, Dr. Beckett served as an Associate Professor of Statistics at Bowling Green State University and as a vice president of a consulting firm in Dallas, Texas.

How to Use This Book

Isn't it great? Every year this book gets better with all the new sets coming out. But even more exciting is that every year there are more options in collecting the cards we love so much. This edition has been enhanced and expanded from the previous edition. The cards you collect — who appears on them, what they look like, where they are from, and (most important to most of you) what their current values are — are enumerated within. Many of the features contained in the other *Beckett Price Guides* have been incorporated into this volume since condition grading, terminology, and many other aspects of collecting are common to the card hobby in general. We hope you find the book both interesting and useful in your collecting pursuits.

The Beckett Guide has been successful where other attempts have failed because it is complete, current, and valid. This price guide contains not just one, but three prices by condition for all the baseball cards listed. The prices were added to the card lists just prior to printing and reflect not the author's opinions or desires but the going retail prices for each card, based on the marketplace (sports memorabilia conventions and shows, sports card shops, hobby papers, current mail-order catalogs, local club meetings, auction results, and other firsthand reportings of actually realized prices).

What is the best price guide available on the market today? Of course, card sellers prefer the price guide with the highest prices, while card buyers naturally prefer the one with the lowest prices. Accuracy, however, is the true test. Use the price guide trusted by more collectors and dealers than all the others combined. Look for the Beckett® name. I won't put my name on anything I won't stake my reputation on. Not the lowest and not the highest — but the most accurate, with integrity.

To facilitate your use of this book, read the complete introductory section on the following pages before going to the pricing pages. Every collectible field has its own terminology; we've tried to capture most of these terms and definitions in our glossary. Please read carefully the section on grading and the condition of your cards, as you cannot determine which price column is appropriate for a given card without first knowing its condition.

Welcome to the world of baseball cards.

How to Collect

Each collection is personal and reflects the individuality of its owner. There are no set rules on how to collect cards. Since card collecting is a hobby or leisure pastime, what you collect, how much you collect, and how much time and money you spend collecting are entirely up to you. The funds you have available for collecting and your own personal taste should determine how you collect. Information and ideas presented here are intended to help you get the most enjoyment from this hobby.

It is impossible to collect every card ever produced. Therefore, beginners as well as intermediate and advanced collectors usually specialize in some way. One of the reasons this hobby is popular is that individual collectors can define and tailor their collecting methods to match their own tastes. To give you some idea of the various approaches to collecting, we will list some of the more popular areas of specialization.

Many collectors select complete sets from particular years. For example, they may concentrate on assembling complete sets from all the years since their birth or since they became avid sports fans. They may try to collect a card for every player during that specified period of time.

Many others wish to acquire only certain players. Usually such players are the superstars of the sport, but occasionally collectors will specialize in all the cards of players who attended a particular college or came from a certain town. Some collectors are interested in only the first cards or Rookie Cards of certain players. A handy guide for collectors interested in pursuing the hobby this way is *The Sport Americana Baseball Card Alphabetical Checklist.*

Another fun way to collect cards is by team. Most fans have a favorite team, and it is natural for that loyalty to be translated into a desire for cards of the players on that favorite team. For most of the recent years, team sets (all the cards from a given team for that year) are readily available at a reasonable price. The Sport *Americana Team Baseball Card Checklist* will open up this field to the collector.

Obtaining Cards

Several avenues are open to card collectors. Cards still can be purchased in the traditional way: by the pack at the local candy, grocery, drug, or major discount store.

But there are also thousands of card shops across the country that specialize in selling cards individually or by the pack, box, or set. Another alternative are the thousands of card shows held each month around the country, which feature anywhere from 8 to 800 tables of sports cards and memorabilia for sale.

For many years, it has been possible to purchase complete sets of baseball cards through mail-order advertisers found in traditional sports media publications, such as the *Sporting News, Baseball Digest*, and, *Street & Smith* yearbooks. These sets also are advertised in the card collecting periodicals. Many collectors will begin by subscribing to at least one of the hobby periodicals, all with good up-to-date information. In fact, subscription offers can be found in the advertising section of this book.

Most serious card collectors obtain old (and new) cards from one or more of several main sources: (1) trading or buying from other collectors or dealers; (2) responding to sale or auction ads in the hobby publications; (3) buying at a local hobby store; (4) attending sports collectibles shows or conventions; and (5) purchasing cards over the Internet.

We advise that you try all five methods since each has its own distinct advantages: (1) trading is a great way to make new friends; (2) hobby periodicals help you keep up with what's going on in the hobby (including when and where the conventions are happening); (3) stores provide the opportunity to enjoy personalized service and consider a great diversity of material in a relaxed sports-oriented atmosphere; (4) shows allow you to choose from multiple dealers and thousands of cards under one roof in a competitive situation; and (5) the Internet allows one to purchase cards in a convenient manner from almost anywhere in the world.

Preserving Your Cards

Cards are fragile. They must be handled properly in order to retain their value. Careless handling can easily result in creased or bent cards. It is, however, not recommended that tweezers or tongs be used to pick up your cards since such utensils might mar or indent card surfaces and thus reduce those cards´ conditions and values.

In general, your cards should be handled directly as little as possible. This is sometimes easier to say than to do.

Although there are still many who use custom boxes, storage trays, or even shoe boxes, plastic sheets are the preferred method of many collectors for storing cards.

A collection stored in plastic pages in a three-ring album allows you to view your collection at any time without the need to touch the card itself. Cards can also be kept in single holders (of various types and thicknesses) designed for the enjoyment of each card individually.

For a large collection, some collectors may use a combination of the above methods. When purchasing plastic sheets for your cards, be sure that you find the pocket size that fits the cards snugly. Don´t put your 1951 Bowman in a sheet designed to fit 1981 Topps.

Most hobby and collectibles shops and virtually all collectors´ conventions will have these plastic pages available in quantity for the various sizes offered, or you can purchase them directly from the advertisers in this book.

Also, remember that pocket size isn´t the only factor to consider when looking for plastic sheets. Other factors such as safety, economy, appearance, availability, or personal preference also may influence which types of sheets a collector may want to buy.

Damp, sunny, and/or hot conditions — no, this is not a weather forecast — are three elements to avoid in extremes if you are interested in preserving your collection. Too much (or too little) humidity can cause the gradual deterioration of a card. Direct, bright sun (or fluorescent light) over time will bleach out the color of a card. Extreme heat accelerates the decomposition of the card. On the other hand, many cards have lasted more than 75 years without much scientific intervention. So be cautious, even if the above factors typically present a problem only when present in the extreme. It never hurts to be prudent.

Collecting vs. Investing

Collecting individual players and collecting complete sets are both popular vehicles for investment and speculation.

Most investors and speculators stock up on complete sets or on quantities of players they think have good investment potential.

There is obviously no guarantee in this book, or anywhere else for that matter, that cards will outperform the stock market or other investment alternatives in the future. After all, baseball cards do not pay quarterly dividends and cards cannot be sold at their "current values" as easily as stocks or bonds.

Nevertheless, investors have noticed a favorable long-term trend in the past performance of baseball and other sports collectibles, and certain cards and sets have outperformed just about any other investment in some years.

Many hobbyists maintain that the best investment is and always will be the building of a collection, which traditionally has held up better than outright speculation.

Some of the obvious questions are: Which cards? When to buy? When to sell? The best investment you can make is in your own education.

The more you know about your collection and the hobby, the more informed the decisions you will be able to make. We´re not selling investment tips. We´re selling information about the current value of baseball cards. It´s up to you to use that information to your best advantage.

Terminology

Each hobby has its own language to describe its area of interest. The nomenclature traditionally used for trading cards is derived from the American Card Catalog, published in 1960 by Nostalgia Press. That catalog, written by Jefferson Burdick (who is called the "Father of Card Collecting" for his pioneering work), uses letter and number designations for each separate set of cards. The letter used in the ACC designation refers to the generic type of card. While both sport and nonsport issues are classified in the ACC, we shall confine ourselves to the sport issues. The following list defines the letters and their meanings as used by the American Card Catalog.

(none) or N - 19th Century U.S. Tobacco.
B - Blankets.
D - Bakery Inserts Including Bread.
E - Early Candy and Gum.
F - Food Inserts.
H - Advertising.
M - Periodicals.
PC - Postcards.
R - Candy and Gum since 1930.
T - Tobacco.

Following the letter prefix and an optional hyphen are one-, two-, or three-digit numbers, R(-)999. These typically represent the company or entity issuing the cards. In several cases, the ACC number is extended by an additional hyphen and another one- or two-digit numerical suffix. For example, the 1957 Topps regular-series baseball card issue carries an ACC designation of R414-11. The "R" indicates a Candy or Gum card produced since 1930. The "414" is the ACC designation for Topps Chewing Gum baseball card issues, and the "11" is the ACC designation for the 1957 regular issue (Topps´ eleventh baseball set). Like other traditional methods of identification, this system provides order to the process of cataloging cards; however, most serious collectors learn the ACC designation of the popular sets by repetition and familiarity, rather than by attempting to "figure out" what they might or should be. From 1948 forward, collectors and dealers commonly refer to all sets by their year, maker, type of issue, and any other distinguishing characteristic. For example, such a characteristic could be an unusual issue or one of several regular issues put out by a specific maker in a single year. Regional issues are usually referred to by year, maker, and sometimes by title or theme of the set.

Glossary/Legend

Our glossary defines terms used in the card collecting hobby and in this book. Many of these terms are also common to other types of sports memorabilia collecting. Some terms may have several meanings depending on use and context.

ACETATE—A transparent plastic.

AS—All-Star card. A card portraying an All-Star Player of the previous year that says "All-Star" on its face.

ATG—All-Time Great card.

ATL—All-Time Leaders card.

AU(TO)—Autographed card.

AW—Award Winner.

BB—Building Blocks.

BC—Bonus Card.

BF—Bright Futures.

BL—Blue Letters.

BNR—Banner Season.

BOX CARD—Card issued on a box (e.g., 1987 Topps Box Bottoms).

BRICK—A group of 50 or more cards having common characteristics that is intended to be bought, sold, or traded as a unit.

CABINETS—Popular and highly valuable photographs on thick card stock produced in the 19th and early 20th century.

CC—Curtain Call.

CG—Cornerstones of the Game.

CHECKLIST—A list of the cards contained in a particular set. The list is always in numerical order if the cards are numbered. Some unnumbered sets are artificially numbered in alphabetical order, by team and alphabetically within the team, or by uniform number for convenience.
CL—Checklist card. A card that lists in order the cards and players in the set or series. Older checklist cards in Mint condition that have not been marked are very desirable and command premiums.
CP—Changing Places.
CO—Coach.
COMM—Commissioner.
COMMON CARD—The typical card of any set; it has no premium value accruing from subject matter, numerical scarcity, popular demand, or anomaly.
CONVENTION—A gathering of dealers and collectors at a single location for the purpose of buying, selling, and trading sports memorabilia items. Conventions are open to the public and sometimes feature autograph guests, door prizes, contests, seminars, etc. They are frequently referred to simply as "shows."
COOP—Cooperstown.
COR—Corrected card.
CT—Cooperstown.
CY—Cy Young Award.
DD—Decade of Dominance.
DEALER—A person who engages in buying, selling, and trading sports collectibles or supplies. A dealer may also be a collector, but as a dealer, his main goal is to earn a profit.
DIE-CUT—A card with part of its stock partially cut, allowing one or more parts to be folded or removed. After removal or appropriate folding, the remaining part of the card can frequently be made to stand up.
DK—Diamond King.
DL—Division Leaders.
DP—Double Print (a card that was printed in double the quantity compared to the other cards in the same series) or a Draft Pick card.
DT—Dream Team.
DUFEX—A method of card manufacturing technology patented by Pinnacle Brands, Inc. It involves a refractive quality to a card with a foil coating.
ERA—Earned Run Average.
ERR—Error card. A card with erroneous information, spelling, or depiction on either side of the card. Most errors are not corrected by the producing card company.
FC—Fan Club.
FDP—First or First-Round Draft Pick.
FF—Future Foundation.
FOIL—Foil embossed stamp on card.
FOLD—Foldout.
FP—Franchise Player.
Fr—Franchise.
FS—Father/son card.
FS—Future Star.
FUN—Fun cards.
FY—First Year.
GL—Green Letters.
GLOSS—A card with luster; a shiny finish as in a card with UV coating.
HG—Heroes of the Game.
HIGH NUMBER—The cards in the last series of numbers in a year in which

such higher-numbered cards were printed or distributed in significantly lesser amounts than the lower-numbered cards. The high-number designation refers to a scarcity of the high-numbered cards. Not all years have high numbers in terms of this definition.

HL—Highlight card.

HOF—Hall of Fame, or a card that portrays a Hall of Famer (HOFer).

HOLOGRAM—A three-dimensional photographic image.

HH—Hometown Heroes.

HOR—Horizontal pose on card as opposed to the standard vertical orientation found on most cards.

IA—In Action card.

IF—Infielder.

INSERT—A card of a different type or any other sports collectible (typically a poster or sticker) contained and sold in the same package along with a card or cards of a major set. An insert card is either unnumbered or not numbered in the same sequence as the major set. Sometimes the inserts are randomly distributed and are not found in every pack.

INTERACTIVE—A concept that involves collector participation.

IRT—International Road Trip.

ISSUE—Synonymous with set, but usually used in conjunction with a manufacturer, e.g., a Topps issue.

JSY—means Jersey.

KM—K-Men.

LHP—Left-handed pitcher.

LL—League Leaders or large letters on card.

LUM—Lumberjack.

MAJOR SET—A set produced by a national manufacturer of cards containing a large number of cards. Usually 100 or more different cards constitute a major set.

MB—Master Blasters.

MEM—Memorial card. For example, the 1990 Donruss and Topps Bart Giamatti cards.

METALLIC—A glossy design method that enhances card features.

MG—Manager.

MI—Maximum Impact.

MINI—A small card; for example, a 1975 Topps card of identical design but smaller dimensions than the regular Topps issue of 1975.

ML—Major League.

MM—Memorable Moments.

MULTI-PLAYER CARD—A single card depicting two or more players (but not a team card).

MVP—Most Valuable Player.

NAU—No autograph on card.

NG—Next Game.

NH—No-Hitter.

NNOF—No name on front.

NOF—Name on front.

NOTCHING—The grooving of the card, usually caused by fingernails, rubber bands, or bumping card edges against other objects.

NT—Now and Then.

NV—Novato.

OF—Outfield or Outfielder.

OLY—Olympics Card.

P—Pitcher or Pitching pose.

P1—First Printing.
P2—Second Printing.
P3—Third Printing.
PACKS—A means by which cards are issued in terms of pack type (wax, cello, foil, rack, etc.) and channel of distribution (hobby, retail, etc.).
PARALLEL— A card that is similar in design to its counterpart from a basic set but offers a distinguishing quality.
PF—Profiles.
PG—Postseason Glory.
PLASTIC SHEET—A clear, plastic page that is punched for insertion into a binder (with standard three-ring spacing) containing pockets for displaying cards. Many different styles of sheets exist with pockets of varying sizes to hold the many differing card formats. Also called a display sheet or storage sheet.
PP—Power Passion.
PLATINUM—A metallic element used in the process of creating a glossy card.
PR—Printed name on back.
PREMIUM—A card, sometimes on photographic stock, that is purchased or obtained in conjunction with, or redemption for, another card or product. The premium is not packaged in the same unit as the primary item.
PRES—President.
PRISMATIC/PRISM—A glossy or bright design that refracts or disperses light.
PS—Pace Setters.
PT—Power Tools.
PUZZLE CARD—A card whose back contains a part of a picture which, when joined correctly with other puzzle cards, forms the completed picture.
PUZZLE PIECE—A die-cut piece designed to interlock with similar pieces (e.g., early 1980s Donruss).
PVC—Polyvinyl chloride, a substance used to make many of the popular card display protective sheets. Non-PVC sheets are considered preferable for long-term storage of cards by many.
RARE—A card or series of cards of very limited availability. Unfortunately, "rare" is a subjective term frequently used indiscriminately to hype value. "Rare" cards are harder to obtain than "scarce" cards.
RB—Record Breaker.
RC—Rookie Card.
REDEMPTION—A program established by multiple card manufacturers that allows collectors to mail in a special card (usually a random insert) in return for special cards, sets, or other prizes not available through conventional channels.
REFRACTORS—A card that features a design element that enhances (distorts) its color/appearance through deflecting light.
REV NEG—Reversed or flopped photo side of the card. This is a major type of error card, but only some are corrected.
RHP—Right-handed pitcher.
RHW—Rookie Home Whites.
RIF—Rifleman.
RPM—Rookie Premiere Materials.
RR—Rated Rookie.
ROO—Rookie.
ROY—Rookie of the Year.
RP—Relief pitcher.
RTC—Rookie True Colors.
SA—Super Action card.
SASE—Self-Addressed, Stamped Envelope.

SB—Scrapbook.
SB—Stolen Bases.
SCARCE—A card or series of cards of limited availability. This subjective term is sometimes used indiscriminately to hype value. "Scarce" cards are not as difficult to obtain as "rare" cards.
SCR—Script name on back.
SD—San Diego Padres.
SEMI-HIGH—A card from the next-to-last series of a sequentially issued set. It has more value than an average card and generally less value than a high number. A card is not called a semi-high unless the next-to-last series in which it exists has an additional premium attached to it.
SERIES—The entire set of cards issued by a particular producer in a particular year; e.g., the 1971 Topps series. Also, within a particular set, series can refer to a group of (consecutively numbered) cards printed at the same time, e.g., the first series of the 1957 Topps issue (#1 through #88).
SET—One each of the entire run of cards of the same type produced by a particular manufacturer during a single year. In other words, if you have a complete set of 1976 Topps then you have every card from #1 up to and including #660; i.e., all the different cards that were produced.
SF—Starflics.
SH—Season Highlight.
SHEEN—Brightness or luster emitted by card.
SKIP-NUMBERED—A set that has many unissued card numbers between the lowest number in the set and the highest number in the set, e.g., the 1948 Leaf baseball set contains 98 cards skip-numbered from #1 to #168. A major set in which a few numbers were not printed is not considered to be skip-numbered.
SP—Single or Short Print (a card that was printed in lesser quantity compared to the other cards in the same series; see also DP and TP).
SPECIAL CARD—A card that portrays something other than a single player or team, for example, a card that portrays the previous year´s statistical leaders or the results from the previous year´s World Series.
SS—Shortstop.
STANDARD SIZE—Most modern sports cards measure 2-1/2 by 3-1/2 inches. Exceptions are noted in card descriptions throughout this book.
STAR CARD—A card that portrays a player of some repute, usually determined by his ability; but sometimes referring to sheer popularity.
STOCK—The cardboard or paper on which the card is printed.
SUPERIMPOSED—To be affixed on top of something; i.e., a player photo over a solid background.
SUPERSTAR CARD—A card that portrays a superstar, e.g., a Hall of Famer or player with strong Hall of Fame potential.
TC—Team Checklist.
TEAM CARD—A card that depicts an entire team.
THREE-DIMENSIONAL (3D)—A visual image that provides an illusion of depth and perspective.
TOPICAL—A subset or group of cards that have a common theme (e.g., MVP award winners).
TP—Triple Print (a card that was printed in triple the quantity compared to the other cards in the same series).
TR—Trade reference on card.
TRANSPARENT—Clear, see-through.
UDCA—Upper Deck Classic Alumni.
UER—Uncorrected Error.
UMP—Umpire.

USA—Team USA.
UV—Ultraviolet, a glossy coating used in producing cards.
VAR—Variation card. One of two or more cards from the same series with the same number (or player with identical pose if the series is unnumbered) differing from one another by some aspect, the different feature stemming from the printing or stock of the card. This can be caused when the manufacturer of the cards notices an error in one or more of the cards, makes the changes, and then resumes the print run. In this case there will be two versions or variations of the same card. Sometimes one of the variations is relatively scarce.
VERT—Vertical pose on card.
WAS—Washington National League (1974 Topps).
WC—What´s the Call?
WL—White letters on front.
WS—World Series card.
YL—Yellow letters on front.
YT—Yellow team name on front.
*—to denote multi-sport sets.

Understanding Card Values

Determining Value

Why are some cards more valuable than others? Obviously, the economic laws of supply and demand are applicable to card collecting just as they are to any other field where a commodity is bought, sold, or traded in a free, unregulated market.

Supply (the number of cards available on the market) is less than the total number of cards originally produced since attrition diminishes that original quantity. Each year a percentage of cards is typically thrown away, destroyed, or otherwise lost to collectors. This percentage is much, much smaller today than it was in the past because more and more people have become increasingly aware of the value of their cards.

For those who collect only Mint condition cards, the supply of older cards can be quite small indeed. Until recently, collectors were not so conscious of the need to preserve the condition of their cards. For this reason, it is difficult to know exactly how many 1953 Topps are currently available, Mint or otherwise. It is generally accepted that there are fewer 1953 Topps available than 1963, 1973, or 1983 Topps cards. If demand were equal for each of these sets, the law of supply and demand would increase the price for the least available sets. Demand, however, is never equal for all sets, so price correlations can be complicated. The demand for a card is influenced by many factors. These include: (1) the age of the card; (2) the number of cards printed; (3) the player(s) portrayed on the card; (4) the attractiveness and popularity of the set; and (5) the physical condition of the card.

In general, (1) the older the card, (2) the fewer the number of the cards printed, (3) the more famous, popular, and talented the player, (4) the more attractive and popular the set, and (5) the better the condition of the card, the higher the value of the card will be. There are exceptions to all but one of these factors: the condition of the card. Given two cards similar in all respects except condition, the one in the best condition will always be valued higher.

While those guidelines help to establish the value of a card, the countless exceptions and peculiarities make any simple, direct mathematical formula to determine card values impossible.

Regional Variation

Since the market varies from region to region, card prices of local players may be higher. This is known as a regional premium. How significant the premium is — and if there is any premium at all — depends on the local popularity of the team and the player.

The largest regional premiums usually do not apply to superstars, who often are so well known nationwide that the prices of their key cards are too high for local dealers to realize a premium.

Lesser stars often command the strongest premiums. Their popularity is concentrated in their home region, creating local demand that greatly exceeds overall demand.

Regional premiums can apply to popular retired players and sometimes can be found in the areas where the players grew up or starred in college.

A regional discount is the converse of a regional premium. Regional discounts occur when a player has been so popular in his region for so long that local collectors and dealers have accumulated quantities of his key cards. The abundant supply may make the cards available in that area at the lowest prices anywhere.

Set Prices

A somewhat paradoxical situation exists in the price of a complete set versus the combined cost of the individual cards in the set. In nearly every case, the sum of the prices for the individual cards is higher than the cost for the complete set. This is prevalent especially in the cards of the last few years. The reasons for this apparent anomaly stem from the habits of collectors and from the carrying costs to dealers. Today, each card in a set normally is produced in the same quantity as all other cards in its set.

Many collectors pick up only stars, superstars, and particular teams. As a result, the dealer is left with a shortage of certain player cards and an abundance of others. He therefore incurs an expense in simply "carrying" these less desirable cards in stock. On the other hand, if he sells a complete set, he gets rid of large numbers of cards at one time. For this reason, he generally is willing to receive less money for a complete set. By doing this, he recovers all of his costs and also makes a profit.

The disparity between the price of the complete set and the sum of the individual cards also has been influenced by the fact that some of the major manufacturers now are pre-collating card sets. Since "pulling" individual cards from the sets involves a specific type of labor (and cost), the singles or star card market is not affected significantly by pre-collation.

Set prices also do not include rare card varieties, unless specifically stated. Of course, the prices for sets do include one example of each type for the given set, but this is the least expensive variety.

Scarce Series

Scarce series occur because cards issued before 1974 were made available to the public each year in several series of finite numbers of cards, rather than all cards of the set being available for purchase at one time. At some point during the year, usually toward the end of the baseball season, interest in current year baseball cards waned. Consequently, the manufacturers produced smaller numbers of these later-series cards.

Nearly all nationwide issues from post–World War II manufacturers (1948 to 1973) exhibit these series variations. In the past, Topps, for example, may have issued series consisting of many different numbers of cards, including 55, 66, 80, 88, and others. Recently, Topps has settled on what is now its standard sheet size of 132 cards, six of which constitute its 792-card set.

While the number of cards within a given series is usually the same as the number of cards on one printed sheet, this is not always the case. For example, Bowman used 36 cards on its standard printed sheets, but in 1948 substituted 12 cards during later print runs of that year's baseball cards. Twelve of the cards from the initial sheet of 36 cards were removed and replaced by 12 different cards, giving, in effect, a first series of 36 cards and a second series of 12 new cards. This replacement produced a scarcity of 24 cards — the 12 cards removed from the original sheet and the 12 new cards added to the sheet. A full sheet of 1948 Bowman cards (second printing) shows that card numbers 37 through 48 have replaced 12 of the cards on the first printing sheet.

The Topps Company also has created scarcities and/or excesses of certain cards in many of its sets. Topps, however, has most frequently gone the other direction by double printing some of the cards. Double printing causes an abundance of cards of the players who are on the same sheet more than one time. During the years from 1978 to 1981, Topps double printed 66 cards out of their large 726-card set. The Topps practice of double printing cards in earlier years is the most logical explanation for the known scarcities of particular cards in some of these Topps sets.

From 1988 through 1990, Donruss short printed and double printed certain cards in its major sets. Ostensibly this was because of its addition of bonus team MVP cards in its regular-issue wax packs.

We are always looking for information or photographs of printing sheets of cards for research. Each year, we try to update the hobby's knowledge of distribution anomalies. Please let us know at the address in this book if you have firsthand knowledge that would be helpful in this pursuit.

Grading Your Cards

Each hobby has its own grading terminology — stamps, coins, comic books, record collecting, etc. Collectors of sports cards are no exception. The one invariable criterion for determining the value of a card is its condition: The better the condition of the card, the more valuable it is. Condition grading, however, is subjective. Individual card dealers and collectors differ in the strictness of their grading, but the stated condition of a card should be determined without regard to whether it is being bought or sold.

No allowance is made for age. A 1952 card is judged by the same standards as a 1992 card. But there are specific sets and cards that are condition-sensitive (marked with "!" in the Price Guide) because of their border color, consistently poor centering, etc. Such cards and sets sometimes command premiums above the listed percentages in Mint condition.

Centering

Current centering terminology uses numbers representing the percentage of border on either side of the main design. Obviously, centering is diminished in importance for borderless cards such as Stadium Club.

Slightly Off-Center (60/40): A slightly off-center card is one that, upon close inspection, is found to have one border bigger than the opposite border. This degree once was offensive only to purists, but now some hobbyists try to avoid cards that are anything other than perfectly centered.

Off-Center (70/30): An off-center card has one border that is noticeably more than twice as wide as the opposite border.

Badly Off-Center (80/20 or worse): A badly off-center card has virtually no border on one side of the card.

Miscut: A miscut card actually shows part of the adjacent card in its larger border and consequently a corresponding amount of its card is cut off.

Corner Wear

Corner wear is the most scrutinized grading criteria in the hobby. These are the major categories of corner wear:

Corner with a slight touch of wear: The corner still is sharp, but there is a slight touch of wear showing. On a dark-bordered card, this shows as a dot of white.

Fuzzy corner: The corner still comes to a point, but the point has just begun to fray. A slightly "dinged" corner is considered the same as a fuzzy corner.

Slightly rounded corner: The fraying of the corner has increased to where there is only a hint of a point. Mild layering may be evident. A "dinged" corner is considered the same as a slightly rounded corner.

Rounded corner: The point is completely gone. Some layering is noticeable.

Badly rounded corner: The corner is completely round and rough. Severe layering is evident.

Creases

A third common defect is the crease. The degree of creasing in a card is difficult to show in a drawing or picture. On giving the specific condition of an expensive card for sale, the seller should note any creases additionally. Creases can be categorized as to severity according to the following scale:

Light Crease: A light crease is a crease that is barely noticeable upon close inspection. In fact, when cards are in plastic sheets or holders, a light crease may not be seen (until the card is taken out of the holder). A light crease on the front is much more serious than a light crease on the card back only.

Medium Crease: A medium crease is noticeable when held and studied at arm´s length by the naked eye, but does not overly detract from the appearance of the card. It is an obvious crease, but not one that breaks the picture surface of the card.

Heavy Crease: A heavy crease is one that has torn or broken through the card´s picture surface; i.e., puts a tear in the photo surface.

Alterations

Deceptive Trimming: This occurs when someone alters the card in order (1) to shave off edge wear, (2) to improve the sharpness of the corners, or (3) to improve centering — obviously their objective is to falsely increase the perceived value of the card to an unsuspecting buyer. The shrinkage usually is evident only if the trimmed card is compared to an adjacent full-size card or if the trimmed card is itself measured.

Obvious Trimming: Obvious trimming is noticeable and unfortunate. It is usually performed by noncollectors who give no thought to the present or future value of their cards.

Deceptively Retouched Borders: This occurs when the borders (especially on those cards with dark borders) are touched up on the edges and corners with magic marker or crayons of appropriate color in order to make the card appear Mint.

Categorization of Defects—Miscellaneous Flaws

The following are common minor flaws that, depending on severity, lower a card´s condition by one to four grades and often render it no better than Excellent-Mint: bubbles (lumps in surface), gum and wax stains, diamond cutting (slanted borders), notching, off-centered backs, paper wrinkles, scratched-off cartoons or puzzles on back, rubber band marks, scratches, surface impressions, and warping.

The following are common serious flaws that, depending on severity, lower a card´s condition at least four grades and often render it no better than Good: chemical or sun fading, erasure marks, mildew, miscutting (severe off-centering), holes, bleached or retouched borders, tape marks, tears, trimming, water or coffee stains, and writing.

Condition Guide

Grades

Mint (Mt)—A card with no flaws or wear. The card has four perfect corners, 60/40 or better centering from top to bottom and from left to right, original gloss, smooth edges, and original color borders. A Mint card does not have print spots or color or focus imperfections.

Near Mint-Mint (NrMt-Mt)—A card with one minor flaw. Any one of the following would lower a Mint card to Near Mint-Mint: one corner with a slight touch of wear, barely noticeable print spots, or color or focus imperfections. The card must have

60/40 or better centering in both directions, original gloss, smooth edges, and original color borders.

Near Mint (NrMt)—A card with one minor flaw. Any one of the following would lower a Mint card to Near Mint: one fuzzy corner or two to four corners with slight touches of wear, 70/30 to 60/40 centering, slightly rough edges, minor print spots, color or focus imperfections. The card must have original gloss and original color borders.

Excellent-Mint (ExMt)—A card with two or three fuzzy, but not rounded, corners and centering no worse than 80/20. The card may have no more than two of the following: slightly rough edges, very slightly discolored borders, minor print spots, color or focus imperfections. The card must have original gloss.

Excellent (Ex)—A card with four fuzzy but definitely not rounded corners and centering no worse than 80/20. The card may have a small amount of original gloss lost, rough edges, slightly discolored borders, and minor print spots or color or focus imperfections.

Very Good (Vg)—A card that has been handled but not abused: slightly rounded corners with slight layering, slight notching on edges, a significant amount of gloss lost from the surface (but no scuffing) and moderate discoloration of borders. The card may have a few light creases.

Good (G), Fair (F), Poor (P)—A well-worn, mishandled, or abused card: badly rounded and layered corners, scuffing, most or all original gloss missing, seriously discolored borders, moderate or heavy creases, and one or more serious flaws. The grade of Good, Fair, or Poor depends on the severity of wear and flaws. Good, Fair, and Poor cards generally are used only as fillers.

The most widely used grades are defined above. Obviously, many cards will not perfectly fit one of the definitions.

Therefore, categories between the major grades known as in-between grades are used, such as Good to Very Good (G-Vg), Very Good to Excellent (VgEx), and Excellent-Mint to Near Mint (ExMt-NrMt). Such grades indicate a card with all qualities of the lower category but with at least a few qualities of the higher category.

Beckett Baseball Card Price Guide lists each card and set in two grades, with the middle grade valued at about 40%–45% of the top grade.

The value of cards that fall between the listed columns can also be calculated using a percentage of the top grade. For example, a card that falls between the top and middle grades (Ex, ExMt, or NrMt in most cases) will generally be valued at anywhere from 50% to 90% of the top grade.

Similarly, a card that falls between the middle and bottom grades (G-Vg, Vg, or VgEx in most cases) will generally be valued at anywhere from 20%–40% of the top grade.

There are also cases where cards are in better condition than the top grade or worse than the bottom grade. Cards that grade worse than the lowest grade are generally valued at 5%–10% of the top grade.

When a card exceeds the top grade by one — such as NrMt-Mt when the top grade is NrMt, or Mint when the top grade is NrMt-Mt — a premium of up to 50% is possible, with 10%–20% the usual norm.

When a card exceeds the top grade by two — such as Mint when the top grade is NrMt, or NrMt-Mt when the top grade is ExMt — a premium of 25%–50% is the usual norm. But certain condition-sensitive cards or sets, particularly those from the pre-war era, can bring premiums of up to 100% or even more.

Unopened packs, boxes, and factory-collated sets are considered Mint in their unknown (and presumed perfect) state. Once opened, however, each card can be graded (and valued) in its own right by taking into account any defects that may be present in spite of the fact that the card has never been handled.

Selling Your Cards

Just about every collector sells cards or will sell cards eventually. Someday you may be interested in selling your duplicates or maybe even your whole collection. You may sell to other collectors, friends, or dealers. You may even sell cards you purchased from a certain dealer back to that same dealer. In any event, it helps to know some of the mechanics of the typical transaction between buyer and seller.

Dealers will buy cards in order to resell them to other collectors who are interested in the cards. Dealers will always pay a higher percentage for items that (in their opinion) can be resold quickly, and a much lower percentage for those items that are perceived as having low demand and hence are slow moving. In either case, dealers must buy at a price that allows for the expense of doing business and a margin for profit.

If you have cards for sale, the best advice we can give is that you get several offers for your cards — either from card shops or at a card show — and take the best offer, all things considered. Note, the "best" offer may not be the one for the highest amount. And remember, if a dealer really wants your cards, he won't let you get away without making his best competitive offer. Another alternative is to place your cards in an auction as one or several lots.

Many people think nothing of going into a department store and paying $15 for an item of clothing for which the store paid $5. But if you were selling your $15 card to a dealer and he offered you $5 for it, you might consider his markup unreasonable. To complete the analogy: Most department stores (and card dealers) that consistently pay $10 for $15 items eventually go out of business. An exception is when the dealer has lined up a willing buyer for the item(s) you are attempting to sell, or if the cards are so hot that it's likely he'll have to hold the cards for just a short period of time.

In those cases, an offer of up to 75% of book value still will allow the dealer to make a reasonable profit considering the short time he will need to hold the merchandise. In general, however, most cards and collections will bring offers in the range of 25%–50% of retail price. Also consider that most material from the last 5 to 10 years is plentiful. If that's what you're selling, don't be surprised if your best offer is well below that range.

Interesting Notes

The first card numerically of an issue is the single card most likely to obtain excessive wear.

Consequently, you typically will find the price on the #1 card (in NrMt or Mint condition) somewhat higher than might otherwise be the case.

Similarly, but to a lesser extent (because normally the less important, reverse side of the card is the one exposed), the last card numerically in an issue also is prone to abnormal wear. This extra wear and tear occurs because the first and last cards are exposed to the elements (human element included) more than any of the other cards. They are generally end cards in any brick formations and are subject to rubber bandings, stackings on wet surfaces, and like activities.

Sports cards have no intrinsic value. The value of a card, like the value of other collectibles, can be determined only by you and your enjoyment in viewing and possessing these cardboard treasures.

Remember, the buyer ultimately determines the price of each baseball card. You are the determining price factor because you have the ability to say "No" to the price of any card by not exchanging your hard-earned money for a given issue. When the cost of a trading card exceeds the enjoyment you will receive from it, your answer should be "No." We assess and report the prices. You set them!

We are always interested in receiving the price input of collectors and dealers. We happily credit major contributors.

We welcome your opinions, since your contributions assist us in ensuring a better guide each year.

If you would like to join our survey list for the next editions of this book and others authored by Dr. Beckett, please send your name and address to Dr. James Beckett, 15850 Dallas Parkway, Dallas, TX 75248.

History of Baseball Cards

Today's version of the baseball card, with its colorful and oftentimes high-tech front and back, is a far cry from its earliest predecessors. The issue remains cloudy as to which was the very first baseball card ever produced, but the institution of base-

Centering

Well-centered

Slightly Off-centered

Off-centered

Badly Off-centered

Miscut

ball cards dates from the latter half of the 19th century, more than 100 years ago. Early issues, generally printed on heavy cardboard, were of poor quality, with photographs, drawings, and printing far short of today´s standards.

Goodwin & Co., of New York, makers of Gypsy Queen, Old Judge, and other cigarette brands, is considered by many to be the first issuer of baseball and other sports cards. Its issues, predominantly sized 1-1/2 by 2-1/2 inches, generally consisted of photographs of baseball players, boxers, wrestlers, and other subjects mounted on stiff cardboard. More than 2,000 different photos of baseball players alone have been identified. These "Old Judges," a collective name commonly used for the Goodwin & Co. cards, were issued from 1886 to 1890 and are treasured parts of many collections today.

Among the other cigarette companies that issued baseball cards still attracting attention today are Allen & Ginter, D. Buchner & Co. (Gold Coin Chewing Tobacco), and P. H. Mayo & Brother. Cards from the first two companies bear colored line drawings, while the Mayos are sepia photographs on black cardboard. In addition to the small-size cards from this era, several tobacco companies issued cabinet-size baseball cards. These "cabinets" were considerably larger than the small cards, usually about 4-1/4 by 6-1/2 inches, and were printed on heavy stock. Goodwin & Co.´s Old Judge cabinets and the National Tobacco Works´ "Newsboy" baseball photos are two that remain popular today.

By 1895, the American Tobacco Company began to dominate its competition. They discontinued baseball card inserts in their cigarette packages (actually slide boxes in those days). The lack of competition in the cigarette market had made these inserts unnecessary. This marked the end of the first era of baseball cards. At the dawn of the 20th century, few baseball cards were being issued. But once again, it was the cigarette companies, particularly, the American Tobacco Company, followed to a lesser extent by the candy and gum makers that revived the practice of including baseball cards with their products. The bulk of these cards, identified in the American Card Catalog (designated hereafter as ACC) as T or E cards for 20th century "Tobacco" or "Early Candy and Gum" issues, respectively, were released from 1909 to 1915.

This romantic and popular era of baseball card collecting produced many desirable items. The most outstanding is the fabled T-206 Honus Wagner card. Other perennial favorites among collectors are the T-206 Eddie Plank card, and the T-206 Magee error card. The former was once the second most valuable card and only recently relinquished that position to a more distinctive and aesthetically pleasing Napoleon Lajoie card from the 1933–34 Goudey Gum series. The latter misspells the player´s name as "Magie"; the most famous and most valuable blooper card.

The ingenuity and distinctiveness of this era has yet to be surpassed. Highlights include:

- The T-202 Hassan triple-folders, one of the best looking and the most distinctive cards ever issued;
- The durable T-201 Mecca double-folders, one of the first sets with players´ records on the reverse;
- The T-3 Turkey Reds, the hobby´s most popular cabinet card;
- The E-145 Cracker Jacks, the only major set containing Federal League player cards; and
- The T-204 Ramlys, with their distinctive black-and-white oval photos and ornate gold borders.

These are but a few of the varieties issued during this period.

Increasing Popularity

While the American Tobacco Company dominated the field, several other tobacco companies, as well as clothing manufacturers, newspapers and periodicals, game makers, and companies whose identities remain anonymous, also issued cards during this period. In fact, the Collins-McCarthy Candy Company, makers of Zeenuts Pacific Coast League baseball cards, issued cards yearly from 1911 to 1938. Its record for continuous annual card production has been exceeded only by the Topps Chewing Gum Company. The era of the tobacco card issues closed with the onset of World War I, with the exception of the Red Man chewing tobacco sets produced from

Corner Wear

The partial cards here have been photographed at 300%. This was done in order to magnify each card's corner wear to such a degree that differences could be shown on a printed page.

The 1962 Topps Mickey Mantle card definitely has a rounded corner. Some may say that this card is badly rounded, but that is a judgment call.

The 1962 Topps Hank Aaron card has a slightly rounded corner. Note that there is definite corner wear evident by the fraying and that the corner no longer sports a sharp point.

The 1962 Topps Gil Hodges card has corner wear; it is slightly better than the Aaron card above. Nevertheless, some collectors might classify this Hodges corner as slightly rounded.

The 1962 Topps Manager's Dream card showing Mantle and Mays has slight corner wear. This is not a fuzzy corner as very slight wear is noticeable on the card's photo surface.

The 1962 Topps Don Mossi card has very slight corner wear such that it might be called a fuzzy corner. A close look at the original card shows the corner is not perfect, but almost. However, note that corner wear is somewhat academic on this card. As you can plainly see, the heavy crease going across his name breaks through the photo surface.

1952 to 1955.

The next flurry of card issues broke out in the roaring and prosperous 1920s, the era of the E card. The caramel companies (National Caramel, American Caramel, York Caramel) were the leading distributors of these E cards. In addition, the strip card, a continuous strip with several cards divided by dotted lines or other sectioning features, flourished during this time. While the E cards and the strip cards generally are considered less imaginative than the T cards or the recent candy and gum issues, they still are pursued by many advanced collectors.

Another significant event of the 1920s was the introduction of the arcade card. Taking its designation from its issuer, the Exhibit Supply Company of Chicago, it is usually known as the "Exhibit" card. Once a trademark of the penny arcades, amusement parks, and county fairs across the country, Exhibit machines dispensed nearly postcard-size photos on thick stock for one penny. These picture cards bore likenesses of a favorite cowboy, actor, actress, or baseball player. Exhibit Supply and its associated companies produced baseball cards during a longer time span, although discontinuous, than any other manufacturer. Its first cards appeared in 1921, while its last issue was in 1966. In 1979, the Exhibit Supply Company was bought and somewhat revived by a collector/dealer who has since reprinted Exhibit photos of the past.

If the T card period, from 1909 to 1915, can be designated the "Golden Age" of baseball card collecting, then perhaps the "Silver Age" commenced with the introduction of the Big League Gum series of 239 cards in 1933 (a 240th card was added in 1934). These are the forerunners of today´s baseball gum cards, and the Goudey Gum Company of Boston is responsible for their success. This era spanned the period from the Depression days of 1933 to America´s formal involvement in World War II in 1941.

Goudey´s attractive designs, with full-color line drawings on thick card stock, greatly influenced other cards being issued at that time. As a result, the most attractive and popular vintage cards in history were produced in this "Silver Age." The 1933 Goudey Big League Gum series also owes its popularity to the more than 40 Hall of Fame players in the set. These include four cards of Babe Ruth and two of Lou Gehrig. Goudey´s reign continued in 1934, when it issued a 96-card set in color, together with the single remaining card from the 1933 series, #106, the Napoleon Lajoie card.

In addition to Goudey, several other bubblegum manufacturers issued baseball cards during this era. DeLong Gum Company issued an extremely attractive set in 1933. National Chicle Company´s 192-card "Batter-Up" series of 1934-36 became the largest die-cut set in card history. In addition, that company offered the popular "Diamond Stars" series during the same period. Other popular sets included the "Tattoo Orbit" set of 60 color cards issued in 1933 and Gum Products´ 75-card "Double Play" set, featuring sepia depictions of two players per card.

In 1939, Gum Inc., which later became Bowman Gum, replaced Goudey Gum as the leading baseball card producer. In 1939 and the following year, it issued two important sets of black-and-white cards. In 1939, its "Play Ball America" set consisted of 162 cards. The larger, 240-card "Play Ball" set of 1940 still is considered by many to be the most attractive black-and-white cards ever produced. That firm introduced its only color set in 1941, consisting of 72 cards titled "Play Ball Sports Hall of Fame." Many of these were colored repeats of poses from the black-and-white 1940 series.

In addition to regular gum cards, many manufacturers distributed premium issues during the 1930s. These premiums were printed on paper or photographic stock, rather than card stock. They were much larger than the regular cards and were sold for a penny across the counter with gum (which was packaged separately from the premium). They often were redeemed at the store or through the mail in exchange for the wrappers of previously purchased gum cards, like proof-of-purchase box-top premiums today. The gum premiums are scarcer than the card issues of the 1930s and in most cases no manufacturer´s name is present.

World War II brought an end to this popular era of card collecting when paper and rubber shortages curtailed the production of bubblegum baseball cards. They were resurrected again in 1948 by the Bowman Gum Company (the direct descendent of Gum Inc.). This marked the beginning of the modern era of card collecting.

In 1948, Bowman Gum issued a 48-card set in black and white consisting of one card and one slab of gum in every 1-cent pack. That same year, the Leaf Gum Company also issued a set of cards. Although rather poor in quality, these cards were issued in color. A squabble over the rights to use players´ pictures developed between Bowman and Leaf. Eventually Leaf dropped out of the card market, but not before it had left a lasting heritage to the hobby by issuing some of the rarest cards now in existence. Leaf´s baseball card series of 1948-49 contained 98 cards, skip numbered to #168 (not all numbers were printed). Of these 98 cards, 49 are relatively plentiful; the other 49, however, are rare and quite valuable.

Bowman continued its production of cards in 1949 with a color series of 240 cards. Because there are many scarce "high numbers," this series remains the most difficult Bowman regular issue to complete. Although the set was printed in color and commands great interest due to its scarcity, it is considered aesthetically inferior to the Goudey and National Chicle issues of the 1930s. In addition to the regular issue of 1949, Bowman also produced a set of 36 Pacific Coast League players. Although this was not a regular issue, it still is prized by collectors. In fact, it has become the most valuable Bowman series.

In 1950 (representing Bowman´s one-year monopoly of the baseball card market), the company began a string of top-quality cards that continued until its demise in 1955. The 1950 series was itself something of an oddity because the low numbers, rather than the traditional high numbers, were the more difficult cards to obtain.

The year 1951 marked the beginning of the most competitive and perhaps the highest quality period of baseball card production. In that year, Topps Chewing Gum Company of Brooklyn entered the market. Topps´ 1951 series consisted of two sets of 52 cards each, one set with red backs and the other with blue backs. In addition, Topps also issued 31 insert cards, three of which remain the rarest Topps cards ("Current All-Stars" Konstanty, Roberts, and Stanky). The 1951 Topps cards were unattractive and paled in comparison to the 1951 Bowman issues. They were successful, however, and Topps has continued to produce cards ever since.

Intensified Competition

Topps issued a larger and more attractive card set in 1952. This larger size became standard for the next five years. (Bowman followed with larger-size baseball cards in 1953.) This 1952 Topps set has become, like the 1933 Goudey series and the T-206 white border series, the classic set of its era. The 407-card set is a collector´s dream of scarcities, rarities, errors, and variations. It also contains the first Topps issues of Mickey Mantle and Willie Mays.

As with Bowman and Leaf in the late 1940s, competition over player rights arose. Ensuing court battles occurred between Topps and Bowman. The market split due to stiff competition, and in January 1956, Topps bought out Bowman. (Topps, using the Bowman name, resurrected Bowman as a label in 1989.) Topps remained essentially unchallenged as the primary producer of baseball cards through 1980. So, the story of major baseball card sets from 1956 through 1980 is by and large the story of Topps´ issues. Notable exceptions include the small sets produced by Fleer Gum in 1959, 1960, 1961, and 1963, and the Kellogg´s Cereal and Hostess Cakes baseball cards issued to promote their products.

A court decision in 1980 paved the way for two other large gum companies to enter (or reenter, in Fleer´s case) the baseball card arena. Fleer, which had last made photo cards in 1963, and the Donruss Company (then a division of General Mills) secured rights to produce baseball cards of current players, thus breaking Topps´ monopoly. Each company issued major card sets in 1981 with bubblegum products.

Then a higher court decision in that year overturned the lower court ruling against Topps. It appeared that Topps had regained its sole position as a producer of baseball cards. Undaunted by the revocation ruling, Fleer and Donruss continued to issue cards in 1982 but without bubblegum or any other edible product. Fleer issued its current player baseball cards with "team logo stickers," while Donruss issued its cards with a piece of a baseball jigsaw puzzle.

Sharing the Pie

Since 1981, these three major baseball card producers all have thrived, sharing relatively equal recognition. Each has steadily increased its involvement in terms of numbers of issues per year. To the delight of collectors, their competition has generated novel, and in some cases exceptional, issues of current Major League Baseball players. Collectors also eagerly accepted the debut efforts of Score (1988) and Upper Deck (1989). These five companies were about to embark on a wild ride through the 1990s.

Upper Deck's successful entry into the market turned out to be very important. The company's card stock, photography, packaging, and marketing gave baseball cards a new standard for quality and began the "premium card" trend that continues today. The second premium baseball card set to be issued was the 1990 Leaf set, named for and issued by the parent company of Donruss. To gauge the significance of the premium card trend, one need only note that two of the most valuable post-1986 regular-issue cards in the hobby are the 1989 Upper Deck Ken Griffey Jr. and 1990 Leaf Frank Thomas Rookie Cards.

The impressive debut of Leaf in 1990 was followed by Studio, Ultra, and Stadium Club in 1991. Of those, Stadium Club with its dramatic borderless photo, uncoated card fronts made the biggest impact. In 1992, Bowman and Pinnacle joined the premium fray. In 1992, Donruss and Fleer abandoned the traditional 50-cent pack market and instead produced premium sets comparable to (and presumably designed to compete against) Upper Deck's set. Those moves, combined with the almost instantaneous spread of premium cards to the other major team sports cards, serve as strong indicators that premium cards were here to stay. Bowman had been a lower-level product from 1989 to 1991.

In 1993, Fleer, Topps, and Upper Deck produced the first "super premium" cards with Flair, Finest, and SP, respectively. The success of all three products was an indication the baseball card market was headed toward even higher price levels, and that turned out to be the case in 1994 with the introduction of Bowman's Best (a Topps hybrid of prospect-oriented Bowman and the superpremium Finest) and Leaf Limited. Other 1994 debuts included Upper Deck's entry-level Collector's Choice and Pinnacle's hobby-only Select.

Overall, inserts continued to dominate the hobby scene. Specifically, the parallel chase cards introduced in 1992 with Topps Gold became the latest major hobby trend. Topps Gold was followed by 1993 Finest Refractors (at the time the scarcest insert ever produced and still a landmark set) and the one-per-box Stadium Club First Day Issue.

Of course, the biggest on-field news of 1994 was the owner-provoked players' strike that halted the season prematurely. While the baseball card hobby suffered noticeably from the strike, there was no catastrophic market crash as some had feared. However, the strike drastically slowed down a market that was both strong and growing and contributed to a serious hobby contraction that continues to this day.

By 1995, parallel insert sets were commonplace and had taken on a new complexion: the most popular ones were those that had announced (or at least suspected) print runs of 500 or less, such as Finest Refractors and Select Artist's Proofs.

This trend continued in 1996, with several parallel inserts that were printed in quantities of 250 or less, such as Finest Gold Refractors, Fleer Circa Rave, Studio Silver Press Proofs, and three of the six Select Certified parallels. It could be argued that the high price tags on these extremely limited parallel cards (many exceeded the $1,000 plateau) were driving many single-player collectors to frustration, and even completely out of the hobby. At the same time, average pack prices soared while average number of cards per pack dropped, making the baseball card hobby increasingly expensive.

On the positive side, two trends from 1996 clearly brought in new collectors: Topps' Mickey Mantle retrospective inserts in both series of Topps and Stadium Club and Leaf's Signature Series, which included one certified autograph per pack. Although the Mantle craze following his passing seemed to be a short-term phenomenon, the inclusion of autographs in packs seemed to have more long-term significance.

In 1997 the print runs in selected sets got even lower. Both Fleer/SkyBox and

Pinnacle brands issued cards of which only one exists.

The growth in popularity of autographs also continued. Many products had autographed cards in their packs. A very positive trend was a return to basics. Many collectors bought Rookie Cards, as they understood that concept, and worked on finishing sets.

There was also an increase in international players collecting. Hideo Nomo was incredibly popular in Japan while Chan Ho Park was in demand in Korea. This bodes well for an international growth in the hobby.

Clearly, 1998 was a year of rebirth and growth for the hobby. The big boost came from the home run chase being conducted by Mark McGwire and Sammy Sosa, as well as the continued brilliance of stalwarts like Ken Griffey Jr. and Roger Clemens. The baseball card hobby received a great deal of positive publicity from the renewed interest in the game.

Rookie Cards of the key players of 1998 made significant gains in value as the hobby once again turned to Rookie Cards as the collectible of choice. Also, cards professionally graded by companies such as PSA and SGC were becoming more heavily traded in both older and newer material.

In addition, the Internet and various services such as eBay contributed to the strong growth in collecting interest over the year.

There were downsides in 1998, though. Pinnacle Brands folded, leaving a legacy of innovation and promotions not seen by other companies. In addition, there still was the problem of collectors being frustrated by the extremely short printed cards of their favorite players, making set completion almost impossible.

During 1998, Pacific received a full baseball license and added many innovations to the card market. Their 1998 OnLine set is the most comprehensive set issued in the last five years and many veteran collectors applauded Pacific´s continuing attempts to get as many players as possible into their sets.

In the last couple of years, card companies have been printing specific subsets (usually young players or Rookie Cards) in shorter supply than the regular cards. This is not in every set, but in many sets produced since 1998.

In 1999, many of the trends of the last couple of years continued to gain strength. Buying, selling, and trading cards over the Internet became a dominant factor in the secondary market. Beckett Media LP began its own Marketplace, offering the collectors a chance to search across inventory from many of the finest dealers nationwide in one comprehensive on-line database; eBay continued to flourish, while many other parties began to reap the benefits of the burgeoning online auction market. The Barry Halper collection was auctioned off, bringing many museum quality items to the market and giving the older memorabilia market a significant boost as many treasures were made available to collectors.

Also, the boom in Internet trading created a perfect fit for professionally graded cards, as buyers and sellers traded cards sight unseen with the confidence established by a third-party grader.

From a field of almost a dozen contenders, three companies emerged in 1999 to dominate the field of professional grading, BGS (Beckett Grading Services), PSA (Professional Sports Authenticator), and SGC (Sportscard Guaranty L.L.C.). In 1999 these companies made dramatic expansions in on-site grading and submissions at card shows throughout the nation. In response to the widespread acceptance of graded cards, the line of monthly Beckett Price Guides each added a separate section within the price guide area for professionally graded cards.

Similar to 1998, four licensed manufacturers (Fleer/SkyBox, Pacific, Topps, and Upper Deck) produced slightly more than fifty different products for 1999.

Perhaps the biggest hit of the 1999 card season was created by Topps. Card #220 within the basic issue first series 1999 Topps brand featured Home Run King Mark McGwire in 70 variations, one for each homer he slugged in 1998, and many collectors went after the whole set. Continuing a legacy as strong as the Yankees, the basic Topps issue was one of the most popular sets released in 1999.

Closely trailing the Topps McGwire promotion was Upper Deck´s dynamic A Piece of History bat card promotion. The card that kicked off the frenzy was the Babe Ruth A Piece of History distributed in 1999 Upper Deck series 1 packs. Upper Deck actually purchased a cracked game-used Babe Ruth bat for $24,000 and proceeded to cut it up into approximately 350-400 chips of wood to create the now famous Ruth bat card. The card instantly created polar opposites of opinion among hobbyists. Traditional collectors howled at the sacrilegious act of destroying such a historic piece of memorabilia while more open-minded collectors jumped at the opportunity to chase such an important card. The Ruth card was followed up by the cross-brand "500 Club" bat card promotion, whereby UD produced bat cards from every major league ballplayer who hit 500 or more home runs in their career (except for Mark McGwire, who hit his 500th in the midst of the 1999 season and promptly stated that he did not support Upper Deck´s promotion).

More memorabilia cards than ever were offered to collectors in 1999 as Fleer/SkyBox kicked up their efforts to match the standards set by Upper Deck in previous years. Batting gloves, hats, and shoes joined the typical bats and jerseys as pieces of game-used equipment to be featured on trading cards. Sets like E-X Century Authen-Kicks and Fleer Mystique Feel the Game typified the new offerings.

Topps only dabbled with memorabilia cards in 1999, but continued to offer some of the hottest autographed inserts, highlighted by the Topps Stars Rookie Reprint Autographs and the Topps Nolan Ryan Autographs.

Pacific made a clear decision to steer free of memorabilia and autograph inserts, instead focusing on offering collectors a wide selection of beautifully designed insert and parallel cards. Those themes worked beautifully with their established presence for making comprehensive sets, providing collectors with the necessary challenge to pursue regional stars and a favorite team in addition to the typical superstars.

An astounding total of 264 players made their first appearance on a major league licensed trading card in 1999. What may go down as the deepest class of Rookie Cards of all time features a cornucopia of talented youngsters led by Rick Ankiel, Josh Beckett, Pat Burrell, Josh Hamilton, Eric Munson, Corey Patterson, and Alfonso Soriano.

As in years past, Topps continued to provide collectors with a fistful of Rookie Cards within their Bowman, Bowman Chrome, and Bowman´s Best brands. In a trend established in 1998 by Fleer when they released their Fleer Update set (fueled largely by a J. D. Drew Rookie Card), hobbyists enjoyed a bevy of late-season sets chock full of RC´s. Fleer/SkyBox made an all-out effort by stuffing more than 100 Rookie Cards into their 1999 Fleer Update set. Topps produced their first boxed Traded set since 1994. Each 1999 Topps Traded set contained 1 of 75 different cards autographed by a rookie prospect. Considering how much wider the selection of Rookie Cards became in 1999, it´s amazing to see that so few of these RC´s were serial numbered. When one looks at the success established with serial numbered Rookie Cards in the basketball and football card markets with brands like SP Authentic and SPx Finite, one can only scratch his head when realizing that Fleer Mystique was the only brand to offer baseball collectors serial numbered RC´s. Thus, it´s not surprising to see that despite having 25 different Rookie Cards issued in 1999, Pat Burrell´s Fleer Mystique RC (#´d of 2,999) had been established as his "best" RC by year´s end.

Youngsters weren´t the only players in the limelight in 1999 as retired stars and Hall of Famers were featured on more cards than any other year in the 1990s. Upper Deck´s Century Legends brand, featuring the top 50 active and top 50 retired players of the decade as chosen by the Sporting News was a runaway hit.

Perhaps the most popular insert set of the year, outpacing all of the dazzling high-dollar memorabilia cards, was Topps Gallery Heritage. Utilizing the design and painting style of artist Gerry Dvorak from the classic 1953 Topps set, these modern masterpieces proved that insert cards can still be a hot commodity in the secondary market, albeit assuming they´re well conceived and well made, an unfortunate rarity these days.

The spate of basic issue sets with short-printed subsets continued across many brands in 1999. In reaction to many frustrated dealers and collectors struggling to complete these sets, Fleer/SkyBox created dual versions of each prospect card for the 1999 SkyBox Premium set, an action shot was short-printed and a posed shot was seeded at the same rate as other basic issue cards. The idea was well received by collectors but enjoyed a surprisingly short-lived period of active trading in the secondary market.

The year 2000 was marked by several major developments that would continue shaping the future of our hobby. First off, Pacific decided to forfeit their baseball card license on January 1st, 2000, in an effort to more sharply focus their production expenditures into football and hockey.

In a separate development, Wizards of the Coast (primarily known for their non-sport gaming cards) was granted a license to produce baseball trading cards and debuted their MLB Showdown brand. The cards proved to be quite successful in that they were collected as a set by veteran collectors and played as a game by children (and some adults) both inside and outside of the typical collecting community.

By year´s end, Fleer fazed out their SkyBox and Flair brand names in an effort to take full advantage of the historic significance and brand recognition of their flagship Fleer sets issued sporadically during the late 1950s-1970s and consistently from 1981 to the present.

Almost sixty brands of MLB-licensed cards, issued by five manufacturers, were produced in 2000. In addition, Just Minors and Team Best produced a variety of attractive minor league products. Most shop owners continued to generate their income primarily through the sales of packs and boxes of new product, and, as in years past, they had to make careful decisions as to what to keep in stock for customers and what to pass up in fear of a low sell through.

Vintage (or retro-themed) sets dominated the market highlighted by Fleer Greats of the Game, Upper Deck Yankees Legends, and the run of 3,000 hit club and Joe DiMaggio game-used cards issued by Fleer and Upper Deck. In 2001, Topps Heritage (mimicking the style of the classic ´52 Topps cards), Upper Deck Vintage (in an homage to ´63 Topps baseball), and the return of Topps Archives (after a six-year hiatus) added fuel to the fire.

Using the vintage-theme to tap into a base of wealthy consumers, Upper Deck rolled out their line of Master Collection products (which debuted in basketball a year prior with a Michael Jordan set). Both the Yankees Master Collection and Brooklyn Dodgers Master Collection sets carried initial SRP´s of $4,000 or more, marking the most expensive "factory set" of all-time. Each of these sets was serial numbered (500 Yankees and 250 Dodgers), came in a stylish wood box and contained an assortment of game-used and autograph cards from legends of days gone by.

Game-used memorabilia cards became more abundant in all products to the point where a few early 2001 releases (2001 Pacific Private Stock and 2001 SP Game Bat Edition both carrying SRP´s in the $15-$20 range) included them at a rate of one per pack. Both products enjoyed a dynamic sell through and proved to be very popular in the secondary market. The result, however, on the secondary market values of game-used memorabilia cards has been dramatic. An Alex Rodriguez or Ken Griffey Jr. game bat or game jersey card that sold for $200+ in 1999 could be had for as little as $25-$50 in early 2001.

Patch cards (a swatch of jersey that contains part of a multi-colored patch) really caught on by year´s end as the market formalized premium values on these cards. Upper Deck was the first to create separate "super-premium" jersey Patch inserts within 2000 Upper Deck 1 and 2000 Upper Deck Game Jersey Edition (aka series 2). Pacific followed suit with their Game Gear patch subset within the invincible brand.

By early 2001, Major League Baseball Properties had gotten involved with the trading card autograph and memorabilia programs. From 2001 on, all MLB-licensed trading cards produced by the manufacturers that involved an autograph or game-used memorabilia item had to have the procurement of the item witnessed by a representative of Andersen Consulting, a firm hired by MLB to oversee this historic program. Never before had consumers been provided such an effort by the league and manufacturers to be offered autographed or game-used memorabilia trading cards of such authentic provenance.

Short-printed subset cards, a trend started in 1999, continued to be a common element in most basic sets. The trend, however, evolved to the point where these short prints were now being serial numbered, autographed by the player, or incorporating an element of game-used material onto the card. The result was higher values on the key singles, but lower odds of actually finding a good RC in a pack. By year´s end, a general sentiment of frustration over not being able to pull good Rookie Cards from a box was beginning to be heard more and more often from collectors.

Rookie Cards incorporating game-used material debuted at year's end in 2000 Black Diamond Rookie Edition. Also, Rookie Cards signed by the player, introduced within the basketball and football card markets in 1999 (with Upper Deck's SPx brand), made their baseball debut in 2000 SPx. Serial-numbered Rookie Cards grew in total usage, but shrank in print run numbers as production figures reached an all-time low of 999 copies for a basic issue RC within the 2000 Pacific Omega set.

Year-end boxed sets, a trend brought back from a four-year hiatus by Fleer in 1998 with their Fleer Update set, continued to expand as Topps issued their Bowman Draft Picks and Bowman Chrome Draft Picks sets to cap the now single-series accompanying standard Bowman and Bowman Chrome products.

Fleer broke new ground by blending a 1980s "old-school" concept with some postmodern angles in their 2000 Fleer Glossy boxed set. Harkening back to the run of Glossy parallel factory sets produced from 1987 to 1989, the 2000 Fleer Glossy set included a parallel version of the complete 400-card basic 2000 Fleer set. In addition, 50 new cards (card #'s 401-450, each serial numbered to 1,000 copies) featuring a selection of prospects and rookies were created. Each Glossy factory set contained 5 of the 50 new cards, making it a real challenge to complete the Glossy set.

In a first of its kind for the baseball market, Upper Deck issued a product in December 2000 called Rookie Update that incorporated new cards for three separate popular brands (SP Authentic, SPx, and UD Pros and Prospects) into each pack of cards.

Upper Deck came to terms with Major League Baseball for a license to produce cards featuring members of past and present Team USA squads (bringing back a run of cards last seen in 1993 Topps Traded). That allowed Upper Deck the opportunity to radically expand their production of "true" Rookie Cards in year-end 2000 products, adding a spate of cards featuring heroes from the Olympics in Sydney, Australia, like Ben Sheets. Not surprisingly, the number of prospects making their Rookie Card debut in 2000 sets jumped from about 280 players in 1999 to slightly more than 350 players in 2000.

The influence of sports card dealers and collectors from the Far East (and most noticeably Japan) continued to grow in 2000 as stateside buying approached frenzied levels over scarce Hideo Nomo and Kazuhiro Sasaki cards. A much-traveled starter these days, Nomo's first-ever certified autograph card (issued within the Fleer Mystique Fresh Ink insert set) was the hottest card in the hobby for two months (initially trading for as much as $600-$800).

Not all trends were met with success this year. In particular, low-end products geared towards the youth audience (like 2000 Impact by Fleer) were roundly ignored. The hobby still faces a tough road ahead to keep new waves of collectors involved from generation to generation. Part of the Catch-22 with creating affordable brands catered to youths is that the same customers are most interested in the high-end, expensive material.

Also, Upper Deck's PowerDeck product faced an indifferent audience for a second year in a row, as collectors and even general sports enthusiasts outside the hobby failed to get excited over the CD-ROM cards. More success was met by UD's e-Card insert program, whereby collectors who pulled an e-Card from a pack of UD cards had to go to UD's Website and check the serial number printed on the card to see whether it could evolve into an autograph, game jersey, or game jersey autograph exchange.

The Internet continued to have profound ramifications on shaping the destiny of sports card collecting. By 2000, nearly every dealer (and hard-core collector) was buying or selling cards to some degree in on-line auctions. Auction sales had become so prolific that they were now having a strong effect on the secondary market sales levels of trading cards in arenas entirely outside of cyberspace, like shops, shows, and mail order.

The eBay site continued to dominate the on-line auction action, introducing what appears to be a popular "Buy It Now" option to their already established auction format. The Pit.com opened in mid-year with their concept of buying and selling a portfolio of professionally graded sports cards through their Web site. The concept is based almost exactly upon the methodology used for buying and selling stocks through a brokerage house, with daily ebbs and flows in posted buy and sell prices on your inventory.

Beckett.com made radical improvements to their Marketplace search engines and expanded their inventory of sports cards to the point where they were providing both a wider and a deeper selection of trading cards than any site on the Internet. In addition, a company-wide effort to provide daily news content on their site (coupled with a weekly newsletter sent to over 400,000 collectors) began at year's end, and the hobby has reaped the benefits ever since.

As the 2001 season approached, hobbyists waited with bated breath for seven-time Japanese batting champ Ichiro Suzuki to make his debut in the Seattle Mariner's outfield. And what a stunning debut it was. Ichiro led the league in hitting, led the Mariners to their best record ever, and walked off with the A.L. Rookie of the Year and Most Valuable Player awards. Upper Deck obtained the exclusive rights to produce his autograph cards and they hit a grand slam in midsummer by releasing his SPx Rookie Card, featuring a game jersey swatch and a cut signature autograph. In a year studded with notable cards, this one was likely the most memorable.

In the National League, 37-year-old San Francisco Giants superstar Barry Bonds captivated the nation by bashing a jaw-dropping 73 home runs, shattering Mark McGwire's 1998 single-season home run record.

Cardinals' rookie Albert Pujols emerged out of the low minor leagues to become an instant hobby superstar and walk away with N.L. Rookie of the Year honors.

The year 2001 was a tumultuous one for sports cards. Topps started the year off with a bang by celebrating their 50th anniversary producing baseball cards. Pacific forfeited its license to make baseball cards after an eight-year run to focus on football and hockey cards. Playoff, a company based out of Grand Prairie, Texas, that had earned its stripes by producing football cards in the late 1990s, purchased the rights to the much-hallowed Donruss corporate name and became a formal MLB licensee in the spring of 2001. Their entrance into the baseball card market heralded the return of benchmark brands like Donruss, Donruss Signature, and Leaf.

Competition was fiercer than ever amongst the four primary licensees (Donruss-Playoff, Fleer, Topps, and Upper Deck) as they cranked out almost 80 different products over the course of 2001.

Of all these, likely the most historically important product, Upper Deck Prospect Premieres, was widely overlooked upon release. In a bold move, Upper Deck created a set of 102 prospects, none of which had played a day in the majors. Each player was pictured, however, in the major league uniforms of their parent ballclubs and signed to individual contracts. Because no active major leaguers were featured, Upper Deck did not have to include licensing rights from the MLB Players Association, though they did get licensing from Major League Properties. The industry had never seen a major release featuring active ballplayers marketed to the mainstream audience that lacked licensing from the MLBPA. Because of its lack of historical predecessors and a mixed reception from collectors, the cards were tagged by Beckett Baseball Card Monthly as XRC's (or Extended Rookie Cards), a term that had not been used since 1989.

UD's Prospect Premieres was the first major effort by a manufacturer to level the playing field between Topps and everyone else in that Topps has exclusive rights from the MLBPA to include minor leaguers in their basic brands.

Rookie Cards continued to fascinate collectors, especially in a year with talents like Ichiro and Albert Pujols. The number of players featured on Rookie Cards in 2001 ballooned to an almost absurd figure of 505.

Exchange cards became more prevalent than ever, as manufacturers expanded their use from autograph cards that didn't get returned in time for pack out to slots within basic sets left open in brands released early in the year to fill in with late-season rookie call-ups.

Certified autograph cards remained a huge player in how brands were structured, but the quality of the players suffered greatly as autograph fees continued to spiral out of control. Signatures from superstars like Barry Bonds and Derek Jeter were now being featured on cards with miniscule print runs of 25 or 50 copies while unknown (and often aging and talentless) prospects signed their serial-numbered Rookies Cards by the hundred count.

More serial-numbered Rookie Cards were produced than ever before, but the quantities produced kept sinking lower and lower as companies tried to create secondary market value by simply limiting supply, a dangerous move to say the least. Donruss-Playoff produced the scarcest Rookie Cards of the year, a handful of Game Base cards (including Ichiro) each serial #'d to a scant 100 copies, within their Leaf Limited set.

After a six-month delay, Topps released their much awaited e-Topps program, a product sold entirely on their Web site whereby trading is conducted in a similar fashion to the buying and selling of stocks, in September.

Several products incorporated non-card memorabilia such as signed caps, bobbing head dolls, and signed baseballs with mixed results.

Memorabilia cards continued their slide into mediocrity as the number of cards featuring various bits and pieces of balls, bases, bats, jerseys, pants, shoes, seats, and whatever else could be dreamt up continued to be offered to consumers, who found the cards less appealing with each passing month. To battle consumer apathy, companies often started to offer combination memorabilia cards featuring notable teammates or several pieces of equipment from a notable star.

Retro-themed cards continued to grow in popularity, and some of the innovations seen in these sets were remarkable. Of particular note was Upper Deck's SP Legendary Cuts Autographs set, featuring 84 deceased players. The set required UD to purchase more than 3,300 autograph cuts, which were then incorporated into a windowpane card design. The result was the first certified autograph cards for legends like Roger Maris, Satchell Paige, and Jackie Robinson. Also, Topps Tribute released at year's end and carrying a hefty $40 per pack suggested retail was widely hailed as one of the most beautiful retro-themed cards ever designed, with their crystal-board fronts encasing full-color, razor-sharp photos.

Pack prices continued to escalate, but surprisingly, the public did not balk as long as they delivered value. The most notable high-end product to hit the market in 2001 was Upper Deck Ultimate Collection with a suggested retail of $100 per pack.

September 11th, 2001, is a day that will go down as one of the most devastating in the history of the United States of America. The game of baseball and the hobby of collecting sports cards were rightfully cast aside as the nation mourned the tragic loss of lives in New York, Pennsylvania, and Washington, D.C. America's economy tumbled as airline traveling ground to a near halt and threats of anthrax crippled the mail system. An economy threatening to slip into recession at the beginning of the year dove headlong into it. The sports card market, along with many other industries, felt the hit for several months. Slowly, Americans looked to move past the grief and the sports card industry, steeped in American nostalgia, provided an ideal retreat for many.

The Arizona Diamondbacks beat the New York Yankees in one of the finest World Series ever played, a much-needed diversion for a grief-stricken nation and a calling card for the dramatic power and glory of our National Pastime.

Last year was a relatively quiet one for baseball cards. Dodger's rookie pitcher Kazuhisa Ishii got off to a blazing first half start and his cards carried many releases through to the All-Star break. Ishii stumbled badly in the second half and no notable rookies were in place to pick up market interest. Cubs hurler Mark Prior created a stir, and his 2001 Rookie Cards were red hot at mid-season. For the second straight season, Barry Bonds was the most dominant star in our sport. His early cards continued to outpace all others in volume trading and professional grading submissions.

The number of players featured on Rookie Cards (or Extended Rookie Cards) reached an all-time high of 524 in 2002 as the manufacturers continued to push the envelope toward more immediate coverage of the current year draft. Though few collectors took notice at the time of release, Upper Deck's incorporation of collegiate Team USA athletes into several year-end brands may take hold and grow into a more prominent position in our industry for collegiate ballplayers. The results of these trends, however, are cards that feature a lot of talented youngsters whom most collectors, unfortunately, have never heard of and won't see in a major league uniform for several years.

To make up for the void in excitement generated by rookies and prospects, the manufacturers made some interesting innovations in product distribution and brand development. In general, base sets got noticeably bigger (including Upper Deck's 1,182 card 40-Man brand and Topps 990-card Topps Total brand). In addition, brands like Topps 206, Leaf Rookies and Stars, and Fleer Fall Classics started to incorporate variations of the base cards directly into the basic issue set (different images, switched out teams, etc.).

One of the bigger surprise hits of the year was the aforementioned Topps 206 brand, which borrowed design elements and set composition from the legendary T-206 tobacco set. Other brands continued to successfully mine from cards and eras long since passed.

Donruss continued to push the creative envelope by incorporating 8½" by 11" framed signature pieces directly into boxes of their Playoff Absolute brand. After a four-year hiatus, Fleer brought back their eponymous "Fleer" name brand with a 540-card set. Donruss introduced their wildly successful Diamond Kings brand, which featured a 150-card painted set. Fleer's Box Score brand was also a popular debut utilizing a unique box-inside-a-box distribution concept. Popular brands like SP Legendary Cuts, Leaf Certified, Topps Heritage, and Topps Tribute all received warm welcomes for their follow-ups to their successes achieved the prior year.

The 2004 season continued to bring us again a growing number of sets with price points ranging from $1.29 to $150. There were also many new heroes during the 2003 season as players such as Josh Beckett, Miguel Cabrera, and Dontrelle Willis of the World Champion Florida Marlins were very strong sellers.

Hideki Matsui, who was the most anticipated rookie for the 2003 season, had a very fine year for the American League Champion Yankees but did not draw the same interest from collectors as Ichiro Suzuki did during the 2001 season.

As we enter 2005, the nation is still struggling to dig out of recession and the sport of baseball is still working towards regaining its place as the National Pastime. For the fourth straight season, the top prospect to have a significant impact on the industry hails from Japan. This year it's legendary player Kazuo Matsui, who was perhaps the best shortstop ever in the Japanese leagues.

Despite the struggles the sport of baseball had to endure in 2003, the baseball card market has stepped back to the forefront of the card-collecting hobby, outpacing football, basketball, hockey, golf, and motor sports in volume dollars. As the hobby of collecting baseball cards evolves, we continue to face a market that is blessed with bold creativity and superlative quality and also challenged with the need to reach new consumers both in mass retail and in cyberspace to continue its growth.

Additional Reading

Each year Beckett Media LP produces comprehensive annual price guides for several sports: *Beckett Baseball Card Price Guide, Beckett Basketball Card Price Guide, Beckett Football Card Price Guide, Beckett Hockey Card Price Guide, Beckett Racing Price Guide,* and a line of *Beckett Alphabetical Checklists Books* have been released as well. The aim of these annual guides is to provide information and accurate pricing on a wide array of sports cards, ranging from main issues by the major card manufacturers to various regional, promotional, and food issues. Alphabetical checklist books are published to assist the collector in identifying all the cards of any particular player. The seasoned collector will find these tools valuable sources of information that will enable him to pursue his hobby interests.

In addition, abridged editions of the *Beckett Price Guides* have been published for each of these major sports as part of the House of Collectibles series: *The Official Price Guide to Baseball Cards, The Official Price Guide to Football Cards,* and *The Official Price Guide to Basketball Cards.* Published in a convenient mass-market paperback format, these price guides provide information and accurate pricing on all the main issues by the major card manufacturers.

Prices in this Guide

Prices found in this guide reflect current retail rates just prior to the printing of this book. They do not reflect the FOR SALE prices of the author, the publisher, the distributors, the advertisers, or any card dealers associated with this guide. No one is obligated in any way to buy, sell, or trade his or her cards based on these prices. The price listings were compiled by the author from actual buy/sell transactions at sports conventions, sports card shops, buy/sell advertisements in the hobby papers, for sale prices from dealer catalogs and price lists, and discussions with leading hobbyists in the United States and Canada. All prices are in U.S. dollars.

Acknowledgments

A great deal of diligence, hard work, and dedicated effort went into this year´s volume. However, the high standards to which we hold ourselves could not have been met without the expert input and generous amount of time contributed by many people. Our sincere thanks are extended to each and every one of you.

A complete list of these invaluable contributors appears after the **Price Guide** section.

Work in Progress

Because we intend the *Almanac* to be the most comprehensive price guide book available, we occasionally include sets with incomplete checklists and/or information. In these cases we have exhausted our resources in an attempt to fill in the missing data but have been unsuccessful. This is where you can help. We always appreciate assistance from our readers to make sure the next edition of this book is even more accurate and more complete. Write to Dr. James Beckett, 15850 Dallas Parkway, Dallas, Texas 75248.

2001 Absolute Memorabilia

	Nm-Mt	Ex-Mt
COMP.SET w/o SP's (150)	40.00	12.00
COMMON CARD (1-150)	.75	.23
COMMON RPM (151-200)	10.00	3.00
❑ 1 Alex Rodriguez	3.00	.90
❑ 2 Barry Bonds	5.00	1.50
❑ 3 Cal Ripken	6.00	1.80
❑ 4 Chipper Jones	2.00	.60
❑ 5 Derek Jeter	5.00	1.50
❑ 6 Troy Glaus	.75	.23
❑ 7 Frank Thomas	2.00	.60
❑ 8 Greg Maddux	3.00	.90
❑ 9 Ivan Rodriguez	2.00	.60
❑ 10 Jeff Bagwell	1.25	.35
❑ 11 Ryan Dempster	.75	.23
❑ 12 Todd Helton	1.25	.35
❑ 13 Ken Griffey Jr.	3.00	.90
❑ 14 Manny Ramirez	1.25	.35
❑ 15 Mark McGwire	5.00	1.50
❑ 16 Mike Piazza	3.00	.90
❑ 17 Nomar Garciaparra	3.00	.90
❑ 18 Pedro Martinez	2.00	.60
❑ 19 Randy Johnson	2.00	.60
❑ 20 Rick Ankiel	.75	.23
❑ 21 Rickey Henderson	2.00	.60
❑ 22 Roger Clemens	4.00	1.20
❑ 23 Sammy Sosa	3.00	.90
❑ 24 Tony Gwynn	2.50	.75
❑ 25 Vladimir Guerrero	2.00	.60
❑ 26 Kazuhiro Sasaki	.75	.23
❑ 27 Roberto Alomar	1.25	.35
❑ 28 Barry Zito	1.25	.35
❑ 29 Pat Burrell	.75	.23
❑ 30 Harold Baines	.75	.23
❑ 31 Carlos Delgado	.75	.23
❑ 32 J.D. Drew	.75	.23
❑ 33 Jim Edmonds	.75	.23
❑ 34 Darin Erstad	.75	.23
❑ 35 Jason Giambi	.75	.23
❑ 36 Tom Glavine	1.25	.35
❑ 37 Juan Gonzalez	1.25	.35
❑ 38 Mark Grace	1.25	.35
❑ 39 Shawn Green	.75	.23
❑ 40 Tim Hudson	.75	.23
❑ 41 Andruw Jones	.75	.23
❑ 42 David Justice	.75	.23
❑ 43 Jeff Kent	.75	.23
❑ 44 Barry Larkin	1.25	.35
❑ 45 Rafael Furcal	.75	.23
❑ 46 Mike Mussina	1.25	.35
❑ 47 Hideo Nomo	2.00	.60
❑ 48 Rafael Palmeiro	1.25	.35
❑ 49 Adam Piatt	.75	.23
❑ 50 Scott Rolen	2.00	.60
❑ 51 Gary Sheffield	.75	.23
❑ 52 Bernie Williams	1.25	.35
❑ 53 Bob Abreu	.75	.23
❑ 54 Edgardo Alfonzo	.75	.23
❑ 55 Edgar Renteria	.75	.23
❑ 56 Phil Nevin	.75	.23
❑ 57 Craig Biggio	1.25	.35
❑ 58 Andres Galarraga	.75	.23
❑ 59 Edgar Martinez	1.25	.35
❑ 60 Fred McGriff	1.25	.35
❑ 61 Magglio Ordonez	.75	.23
❑ 62 Jim Thome	2.00	.60
❑ 63 Matt Williams	.75	.23
❑ 64 Kerry Wood	2.00	.60
❑ 65 Moises Alou	.75	.23
❑ 66 Brady Anderson	.75	.23
❑ 67 Garret Anderson	.75	.23
❑ 68 Russell Branyan	.75	.23
❑ 69 Tony Batista	.75	.23
❑ 70 Vernon Wells	.75	.23
❑ 71 Carlos Beltran	1.25	.35
❑ 72 Adrian Beltre	1.25	.35
❑ 73 Kris Benson	.75	.23
❑ 74 Lance Berkman	.75	.23
❑ 75 Kevin Brown	.75	.23
❑ 76 Dee Brown	.75	.23
❑ 77 Jeromy Burnitz	.75	.23
❑ 78 Timo Perez	.75	.23
❑ 79 Sean Casey	.75	.23
❑ 80 Luis Castillo	.75	.23
❑ 81 Eric Chavez	.75	.23
❑ 82 Jeff Cirillo	.75	.23
❑ 83 Bartolo Colon	.75	.23
❑ 84 David Cone	.75	.23
❑ 85 Freddy Garcia	.75	.23
❑ 86 Johnny Damon	1.25	.35
❑ 87 Ray Durham	.75	.23
❑ 88 Jermaine Dye	.75	.23
❑ 89 Juan Encarnacion	.75	.23
❑ 90 Terrence Long	.75	.23
❑ 91 Carl Everett	.75	.23
❑ 92 Steve Finley	.75	.23
❑ 93 Cliff Floyd	.75	.23
❑ 94 Brad Fullmer	.75	.23
❑ 95 Brian Giles	.75	.23
❑ 96 Luis Gonzalez	.75	.23
❑ 97 Rusty Greer	.75	.23
❑ 98 Jeffrey Hammonds	.75	.23
❑ 99 Mike Hampton	.75	.23
❑ 100 Orlando Hernandez	.75	.23
❑ 101 Richard Hidalgo	.75	.23
❑ 102 Geoff Jenkins	.75	.23
❑ 103 Jacque Jones	.75	.23
❑ 104 Brian Jordan	.75	.23
❑ 105 Gabe Kapler	.75	.23
❑ 106 Eric Karros	.75	.23
❑ 107 Jason Kendall	.75	.23
❑ 108 Adam Kennedy	.75	.23
❑ 109 Deion Sanders	1.25	.35
❑ 110 Ryan Klesko	.75	.23
❑ 111 Chuck Knoblauch	.75	.23
❑ 112 Paul Konerko	.75	.23
❑ 113 Carlos Lee	.75	.23
❑ 114 Kenny Lofton	.75	.23
❑ 115 Javy Lopez	.75	.23
❑ 116 Tino Martinez	1.25	.35
❑ 117 Ruben Mateo	.75	.23
❑ 118 Kevin Millwood	.75	.23
❑ 119 Jimmy Rollins	.75	.23
❑ 120 Raul Mondesi	.75	.23
❑ 121 Trot Nixon	.75	.23
❑ 122 John Olerud	.75	.23
❑ 123 Paul O' Neill	1.25	.35
❑ 124 Chan Ho Park	.75	.23
❑ 125 Andy Pettitte	1.25	.35
❑ 126 Jorge Posada	1.25	.35
❑ 127 Mark Quinn	.75	.23
❑ 128 Aramis Ramirez	.75	.23
❑ 129 Mariano Rivera	1.25	.35
❑ 130 Tim Salmon	1.25	.35
❑ 131 Curt Schilling	.75	.23
❑ 132 Richie Sexson	.75	.23
❑ 133 John Smoltz	1.25	.35
❑ 134 J.T. Snow	.75	.23
❑ 135 Jay Payton	.75	.23
❑ 136 Shannon Stewart	.75	.23
❑ 137 B.J. Surhoff	.75	.23
❑ 138 Mike Sweeney	.75	.23
❑ 139 Fernando Tatis	.75	.23
❑ 140 Miguel Tejada	.75	.23
❑ 141 Jason Varitek	1.25	.35
❑ 142 Greg Vaughn	.75	.23
❑ 143 Mo Vaughn	.75	.23
❑ 144 Robin Ventura	.75	.23
❑ 145 Jose Vidro	.75	.23
❑ 146 Omar Vizquel	1.25	.35
❑ 147 Larry Walker	1.25	.35
❑ 148 David Wells	.75	.23
❑ 149 Rondell White	.75	.23
❑ 150 Preston Wilson	.75	.23
❑ 151 Bud Smith RPM RC	10.00	3.00
❑ 152 C. Aldridge RPM RC	10.00	3.00
❑ 153 W.Caceres RPM RC	10.00	3.00
❑ 154 Josh Beckett RPM	10.00	3.00
❑ 155 W.Betemit RPM RC	10.00	3.00
❑ 156 J.Michaels RPM RC	10.00	3.00
❑ 157 Albert Pujols RPM RC	100.00	30.00
❑ 158 A.Torres RPM RC	10.00	3.00
❑ 159 Jack Wilson RPM RC	15.00	4.50
❑ 160 Alex Escobar RPM	10.00	3.00
❑ 161 Ben Sheets RPM	12.00	3.60
❑ 162 R.Soriano RPM RC	12.00	3.60
❑ 163 Nate Frese RPM RC	10.00	3.00
❑ 164 C. Garcia RPM EXCH	10.00	3.00
❑ 165 B.Larson RPM RC	10.00	3.00
❑ 166 A.Gomez RPM RC	10.00	3.00
❑ 167 Jason Hart RPM	10.00	3.00
❑ 168 Nick Johnson RPM	10.00	3.00
❑ 169 Donaldo Mendez RPM	10.00	3.00
❑ 170 C. Parker RPM RC	10.00	3.00
❑ 171 Jackson Melian RPM	10.00	3.00
❑ 172 Jack Cust RPM	10.00	3.00
❑ 173 Adrian Hernandez RPM	10.00	3.00
❑ 174 Joe Crede RPM	10.00	3.00
❑ 175 Jose Mieses RPM RC	10.00	3.00
❑ 176 Roy Oswalt RPM	12.00	3.60
❑ 177 Eric Munson RPM	10.00	3.00
❑ 178 Xavier Nady RPM	10.00	3.00
❑ 179 H. Ramirez RPM RC	12.00	3.60
❑ 180 Abraham Nunez RPM	10.00	3.00
❑ 181 Jose Ortiz RPM	10.00	3.00
❑ 182 J. Owens RPM RC	10.00	3.00
❑ 183 C. Vargas RPM RC	10.00	3.00
❑ 184 Marcus Giles RPM	10.00	3.00
❑ 185 Aubrey Huff RPM	10.00	3.00
❑ 186 C.C. Sabathia RPM	10.00	3.00
❑ 187 Adam Dunn RPM	12.00	3.60
❑ 188 Adam Pettyjohn RPM	10.00	3.00
❑ 189 El. Guzman RPM RC	10.00	3.00
❑ 190 Jay Gibbons RPM RC	12.00	3.60
❑ 191 Wilkin Ruan RPM RC	10.00	3.00
❑ 192 T. Shinjo RPM RC	12.00	3.60
❑ 193 Alfonso Soriano RPM	12.00	3.60
❑ 194 Corey Patterson RPM	10.00	3.00
❑ 195 Ichiro Suzuki RPM RC	80.00	24.00
❑ 196 Billy Sylvester RPM	10.00	3.00
❑ 197 Juan Uribe RPM RC	12.00	3.60
❑ 198 J. Estrada RPM RC	12.00	3.60
❑ 199 C. Valderrama RPM RC	10.00	3.00
❑ 200 Matt White RPM	10.00	3.00

2003 Absolute Memorabilia

	MINT	NRMT
COMP.LO SET w/o SP's (150)	40.00	18.00
COMMON CARD (1-150)	.75	.35
COMMON CARD (151-208)	4.00	1.80
❑ 1 Nomar Garciaparra	3.00	1.35
❑ 2 Barry Bonds	5.00	2.20
❑ 3 Greg Maddux	3.00	1.35
❑ 4 Roger Clemens	4.00	1.80
❑ 5 Derek Jeter	5.00	2.20

❑ 6 Alex Rodriguez 3.00 1.35
❑ 7 Chipper Jones 2.00 .90
❑ 8 Sammy Sosa 3.00 1.35
❑ 9 Alfonso Soriano 1.25 .55
❑ 10 Albert Pujols 4.00 1.80
❑ 11 Adam Dunn 1.25 .55
❑ 12 Tom Glavine 1.25 .55
❑ 13 Pedro Martinez 2.00 .90
❑ 14 Jim Thome 2.00 .90
❑ 15 Hideo Nomo 2.00 .90
❑ 16 Roberto Alomar 1.25 .55
❑ 17 Barry Zito .75 .35
❑ 18 Troy Glaus .75 .35
❑ 19 Kerry Wood 2.00 .90
❑ 20 Magglio Ordonez .75 .35
❑ 21 Todd Helton 1.25 .55
❑ 22 Craig Biggio 1.25 .55
❑ 23 Roy Oswalt .75 .35
❑ 24 Torii Hunter .75 .35
❑ 25 Miquel Tejada .75 .35
❑ 26 Tsuyoshi Shinjo .75 .35
❑ 27 Scott Rolen 2.00 .90
❑ 28 Rafael Palmeiro 1.25 .55
❑ 29 Victor Martinez 1.25 .55
❑ 30 Hank Blalock 1.25 .55
❑ 31 Jason Lane .75 .35
❑ 32 Junior Spivey .75 .35
❑ 33 Gary Sheffield .75 .35
❑ 34 Corey Patterson .75 .35
❑ 35 Corky Miller .75 .35
❑ 36 Brian Tallet .75 .35
❑ 37 Cliff Lee .75 .35
❑ 38 Jason Jennings .75 .35
❑ 39 Kirk Saarloos .75 .35
❑ 40 Wade Miller .75 .35
❑ 41 Angel Berroa .75 .35
❑ 42 Mike Sweeney .75 .35
❑ 43 Paul Lo Duca .75 .35
❑ 44 A.J. Pierzynski .75 .35
❑ 45 Drew Henson .75 .35
❑ 46 Eric Chavez .75 .35
❑ 47 Tim Hudson .75 .35
❑ 48 Aramis Ramirez .75 .35
❑ 49 Jack Wilson .75 .35
❑ 50 Ryan Klesko .75 .35
❑ 51 Antonio Perez .75 .35
❑ 52 Dewon Brazelton .75 .35
❑ 53 Mark Teixeira .75 .35
❑ 54 Eric Hinske .75 .35
❑ 55 Freddy Sanchez .75 .35
❑ 56 Mike Rivera .75 .35
❑ 57 Alfredo Amezaga .75 .35
❑ 58 Cliff Floyd .75 .35
❑ 59 Brandon Larson .75 .35
❑ 60 Richard Hidalgo .75 .35
❑ 61 Cesar Izturis .75 .35
❑ 62 Richie Sexson .75 .35
❑ 63 Michael Cuddyer .75 .35
❑ 64 Javier Vazquez .75 .35
❑ 65 Brandon Claussen .75 .35
❑ 66 Carlos Rivera .75 .35
❑ 67 Vernon Wells .75 .35
❑ 68 Kenny Lofton .75 .35
❑ 69 Aubrey Huff .75 .35
❑ 70 Adam LaRoche .75 .35
❑ 71 Jeff Baker .75 .35
❑ 72 Jose Castillo .75 .35
❑ 73 Joe Borchard .75 .35
❑ 74 Walter Young .75 .35
❑ 75 Jose Morban .75 .35
❑ 76 Vinnie Chulk .75 .35
❑ 77 Christian Parker .75 .35
❑ 78 Mike Piazza 3.00 1.35
❑ 79 Ichiro Suzuki 3.00 1.35
❑ 80 Kazuhisa Ishii .75 .35
❑ 81 Rickey Henderson 2.00 .90
❑ 82 Ken Griffey Jr. 3.00 1.35
❑ 83 Jason Giambi .75 .35
❑ 84 Randy Johnson 2.00 .90
❑ 85 Curt Schilling .75 .35
❑ 86 Manny Ramirez 1.25 .55
❑ 87 Barry Larkin 1.25 .55
❑ 88 Jeff Bagwell 1.25 .55
❑ 89 Vladimir Guerrero 2.00 .90
❑ 90 Mike Mussina 1.25 .55
❑ 91 Juan Gonzalez 1.25 .55
❑ 92 Andruw Jones .75 .35
❑ 93 Frank Thomas 2.00 .90
❑ 94 Sean Casey .75 .35
❑ 95 Josh Beckett .75 .35
❑ 96 Lance Berkman .75 .35
❑ 97 Shawn Green .75 .35
❑ 98 Bernie Williams 1.25 .55
❑ 99 Pat Burrell .75 .35
❑ 100 Edgar Martinez 1.25 .55
❑ 101 Ivan Rodriguez 2.00 .90
❑ 102 Jeremy Guthrie .75 .35
❑ 103 Alexis Rios 1.25 .55
❑ 104 Nic Jackson .75 .35
❑ 105 Jason Anderson .75 .35
❑ 106 Travis Chapman .75 .35
❑ 107 Mac Suzuki .75 .35
❑ 108 Toby Hall .75 .35
❑ 109 Mark Prior 2.00 .90
❑ 110 So Taguchi .75 .35
❑ 111 Marlon Byrd .75 .35
❑ 112 Garret Anderson .75 .35
❑ 113 Luis Gonzalez .75 .35
❑ 114 Jay Gibbons .75 .35
❑ 115 Mark Buehrle .75 .35
❑ 116 Wily Mo Pena .75 .35
❑ 117 C.C. Sabathia .75 .35
❑ 118 Ricardo Rodriguez .75 .35
❑ 119 Robert Fick .75 .35
❑ 120 Rodrigo Rosario .75 .35
❑ 121 Alexis Gomez .75 .35
❑ 122 Carlos Beltran 1.25 .55
❑ 123 Joe Thurston .75 .35
❑ 124 Ben Sheets .75 .35
❑ 125 Jose Vidro .75 .35
❑ 126 Nick Johnson .75 .35
❑ 127 Mark Mulder .75 .35
❑ 128 Bobby Abreu .75 .35
❑ 129 Brian Giles .75 .35
❑ 130 Brian Lawrence .75 .35
❑ 131 Jeff Kent .75 .35
❑ 132 Chris Snelling .75 .35
❑ 133 Kevin Mench .75 .35
❑ 134 Carlos Delgado .75 .35
❑ 135 Orlando Hudson .75 .35
❑ 136 Juan Cruz .75 .35
❑ 137 Jim Edmonds .75 .35
❑ 138 Geronimo Gil .75 .35
❑ 139 Joe Crede .75 .35
❑ 140 Wilson Valdez .75 .35
❑ 141 Runelvys Hernandez .75 .35
❑ 142 Nick Neugebauer .75 .35
❑ 143 Takahito Nomura .75 .35
❑ 144 Andres Galarraga .75 .35
❑ 145 Mark Grace 1.25 .55
❑ 146 Brandon Duckworth .75 .35
❑ 147 Oliver Perez .75 .35
❑ 148 Xavier Nady .75 .35
❑ 149 Rafael Soriano .75 .35
❑ 150 Ben Kozlowski .75 .35
❑ 151 Pr. Redman ROO RC 4.00 1.80
❑ 152 Craig Brazell ROO RC 5.00 2.20
❑ 153 Nook Logan ROO RC 4.00 1.80
❑ 154 Greg Aquino ROO RC 4.00 1.80
❑ 155 Matt Kata ROO RC 5.00 2.20
❑ 156 Ian Ferguson ROO RC 4.00 1.80
❑ 157 C.Wang ROO RC 5.00 2.20
❑ 158 Beau Kemp ROO RC 4.00 1.80
❑ 159 Alej. Machado ROO RC 4.00 1.80
❑ 160 Mi. Hessman ROO RC 4.00 1.80
❑ 161 Fran. Rosario ROO RC 4.00 1.80
❑ 162 Pedro Liriano ROO 4.00 1.80
❑ 163 Rich Fischer ROO RC 4.00 1.80
❑ 164 Franklin Perez ROO RC 4.00 1.80
❑ 165 Oscar Villarreal ROO RC 4.00 1.80
❑ 166 Arnie Munoz ROO RC 4.00 1.80
❑ 167 Tim Olson ROO RC 5.00 2.20
❑ 168 Jose Contreras ROO RC 5.00 2.20
❑ 169 Fran. Cruceta ROO RC 4.00 1.80
❑ 170 Jer. Bonderman ROO RC 5.00 2.20
❑ 171 Jeremy Griffiths ROO RC 5.00 2.20
❑ 172 John Webb ROO 4.00 1.80
❑ 173 Phil Seibel ROO RC 4.00 1.80
❑ 174 Aaron Looper ROO RC 4.00 1.80
❑ 175 Brian Stokes ROO RC 4.00 1.80
❑ 176 G.Quiroz ROO RC 5.00 2.20
❑ 177 Fern. Cabrera ROO RC 4.00 1.80
❑ 178 Josh Hall ROO RC 5.00 2.20
❑ 179 D. Markwell ROO RC 4.00 1.80
❑ 180 Andrew Brown ROO RC 5.00 2.20
❑ 181 Doug Waechter ROO RC 5.00 2.20
❑ 182 Felix Sanchez ROO RC 4.00 1.80
❑ 183 Gerardo Garcia ROO 4.00 1.80
❑ 184 Matt Bruback ROO RC 4.00 1.80
❑ 185 Mi. Hernandez ROO RC 4.00 1.80
❑ 186 Rett Johnson ROO RC 5.00 2.20
❑ 187 Ryan Cameron ROO RC 4.00 1.80
❑ 188 Rob Hammock ROO RC 5.00 2.20
❑ 189 Clint Barmes ROO RC 5.00 2.20
❑ 190 Brandon Webb ROO RC 5.00 2.20
❑ 191 Jon Leicester ROO RC 4.00 1.80
❑ 192 Shane Bazzell ROO RC 4.00 1.80
❑ 193 Joe Valentine ROO RC 4.00 1.80
❑ 194 Josh Stewart ROO RC 4.00 1.80
❑ 195 Pete LaForest ROO RC 5.00 2.20
❑ 196 Shane Victorino ROO RC 4.00 1.80
❑ 197 Termel Sledge ROO RC 5.00 2.20
❑ 198 Lew Ford ROO RC 5.00 2.20
❑ 199 T.Wellemeyer ROO RC 5.00 2.20
❑ 200 Hideki Matsui ROO RC 10.00 4.50
❑ 201 Adam Loewen ROO RC 5.00 2.20
❑ 202 Ramon Nivar ROO RC 5.00 2.20
❑ 203 Dan Haren ROO RC 5.00 2.20
❑ 204 Dontrelle Willis ROO 5.00 2.20
❑ 205 Chad Gaudin ROO RC 4.00 1.80
❑ 206 Rickie Weeks ROO RC 8.00 3.60
❑ 207 Ryan Wagner ROO RC 5.00 2.20
❑ 208 Delmon Young ROO RC 10.00 4.50

2004 Absolute Memorabilia

	Nm-Mt	Ex-Mt
COMMON ACTIVE (1-200)	2.00	.60
COMMON RETIRED (1-200)	2.00	.60
1-200 PRINT RUN 1349 SERIAL #'d SETS		.00
COMMON CARD (201-250)	4.00	1.20
COMMON AU (201-250)	8.00	2.40

201-250 RANDOM INSERTS IN PACKS
201-250 NON AU PRINT RUNS 1000 #'d PER
201-250 AU PRINTS B/WN 500-700 #'d PER

❑ 1 Troy Glaus 2.00 .60
❑ 2 Garret Anderson 2.00 .60
❑ 3 Tim Salmon 2.00 .60
❑ 4 Bartolo Colon 2.00 .60
❑ 5 Troy Percival 2.00 .60
❑ 6 Nolan Ryan Angels 8.00 2.40
❑ 7 Vladimir Guerrero 3.00 .90
❑ 8 Richie Sexson 2.00 .60
❑ 9 Shea Hillenbrand 2.00 .60
❑ 10 Luis Gonzalez 2.00 .60
❑ 11 Brandon Webb 2.00 .60
❑ 12 Randy Johnson 3.00 .90
❑ 13 Robby Hammock 2.00 .60
❑ 14 Edgar Gonzalez 2.00 .60
❑ 15 Roberto Alomar 2.00 .60
❑ 16 Andruw Jones 2.00 .60
❑ 17 Chipper Jones 3.00 .90
❑ 18 Dale Murphy 2.00 .60
❑ 19 Rafael Furcal 2.00 .60
❑ 20 J.D. Drew 2.00 .60
❑ 21 Bubba Nelson 2.00 .60
❑ 22 Julio Franco 2.00 .60
❑ 23 Adam LaRoche 2.00 .60

Card	Nm-Mt	Ex-Mt
❑ 24 Michael Hessman	2.00	.60
❑ 25 Warren Spahn	2.00	.60
❑ 26 Jay Gibbons	2.00	.60
❑ 27 Cal Ripken	12.00	3.60
❑ 28 Miguel Tejada	2.00	.60
❑ 29 Adam Loewen	2.00	.60
❑ 30 Rafael Palmeiro	2.00	.60
❑ 31 Javy Lopez	2.00	.60
❑ 32 Luis Matos	2.00	.60
❑ 33 Jason Varitek	2.00	.60
❑ 34 Carl Yastrzemski	5.00	1.50
❑ 35 Manny Ramirez	2.00	.60
❑ 36 Trot Nixon	2.00	.60
❑ 37 Curt Schilling	3.00	.90
❑ 38 Pedro Martinez	3.00	.90
❑ 39 Nomar Garciaparra	5.00	1.50
❑ 40 Luis Tiant	2.00	.60
❑ 41 Kevin Youkilis	2.00	.60
❑ 42 Michel Hernandez	2.00	.60
❑ 43 Sammy Sosa	5.00	1.50
❑ 44 Greg Maddux	5.00	1.50
❑ 45 Kerry Wood	3.00	.90
❑ 46 Mark Prior	3.00	.90
❑ 47 Ernie Banks	3.00	.90
❑ 48 Aramis Ramirez	2.00	.60
❑ 49 Brendan Harris	2.00	.60
❑ 50 Todd Wellemeyer	2.00	.60
❑ 51 Frank Thomas	3.00	.90
❑ 52 Magglio Ordonez	2.00	.60
❑ 53 Carlos Lee	2.00	.60
❑ 54 Joe Crede	2.00	.60
❑ 55 Joe Borchard	2.00	.60
❑ 56 Mark Buehrle	2.00	.60
❑ 57 Sean Casey	2.00	.60
❑ 58 Adam Dunn	2.00	.60
❑ 59 Austin Kearns	2.00	.60
❑ 60 Ken Griffey Jr.	5.00	1.50
❑ 61 Barry Larkin	2.00	.60
❑ 62 Ryan Wagner	2.00	.60
❑ 63 Jody Gerut	2.00	.60
❑ 64 Jeremy Guthrie	2.00	.60
❑ 65 Travis Hafner	2.00	.60
❑ 66 Brian Tallet	2.00	.60
❑ 67 Todd Helton	2.00	.60
❑ 68 Preston Wilson	2.00	.60
❑ 69 Jeff Baker	2.00	.60
❑ 70 Clint Barmes	2.00	.60
❑ 71 Joe Kennedy	2.00	.60
❑ 72 Jack Morris	2.00	.60
❑ 73 George Kell	2.00	.60
❑ 74 Preston Larrison	2.00	.60
❑ 75 Dmitri Young	2.00	.60
❑ 76 Ivan Rodriguez	3.00	.90
❑ 77 Dontrelle Willis	2.00	.60
❑ 78 Josh Beckett	2.00	.60
❑ 79 Miguel Cabrera	2.00	.60
❑ 80 Mike Lowell	2.00	.60
❑ 81 Luis Castillo	2.00	.60
❑ 82 Juan Pierre	2.00	.60
❑ 83 Jeff Bagwell	2.00	.60
❑ 84 Jeff Kent	2.00	.60
❑ 85 Craig Biggio	2.00	.60
❑ 86 Lance Berkman	2.00	.60
❑ 87 Andy Pettitte	2.00	.60
❑ 88 Roy Oswalt	2.00	.60
❑ 89 Chris Burke	2.00	.60
❑ 90 Jason Lane	2.00	.60
❑ 91 Roger Clemens	6.00	1.80
❑ 92 Mike Sweeney	2.00	.60
❑ 93 Carlos Beltran	2.00	.60
❑ 94 Angel Berroa	2.00	.60
❑ 95 Juan Gonzalez	2.00	.60
❑ 96 Ken Harvey	2.00	.60
❑ 97 Byron Gettis	2.00	.60
❑ 98 Alexis Gomez	2.00	.60
❑ 99 Ian Ferguson	2.00	.60
❑ 100 Duke Snider	2.00	.60
❑ 101 Shawn Green	2.00	.60
❑ 102 Hideo Nomo	3.00	.90
❑ 103 Kazuhisa Ishii	2.00	.60
❑ 104 Edwin Jackson	2.00	.60
❑ 105 Fred McGriff	2.00	.60
❑ 106 Hong-Chih Kou	2.00	.60
❑ 107 Don Sutton	2.00	.60
❑ 108 Rickey Henderson	3.00	.90
❑ 109 Cesar Izturis	2.00	.60
❑ 110 Robin Ventura	2.00	.60
❑ 111 Paul Lo Duca	2.00	.60
❑ 112 Rickie Weeks	2.00	.60
❑ 113 Scott Podsednik	2.00	.60
❑ 114 Junior Spivey	2.00	.60
❑ 115 Lyle Overbay	2.00	.60
❑ 116 Tony Oliva	2.00	.60
❑ 117 Jacque Jones	2.00	.60
❑ 118 Shannon Stewart	2.00	.60
❑ 119 Torii Hunter	2.00	.60
❑ 120 Johan Santana	2.00	.60
❑ 121 J.D. Durbin	2.00	.60
❑ 122 Jason Kubel	2.00	.60
❑ 123 Michael Cuddyer	2.00	.60
❑ 124 Nick Johnson	2.00	.60
❑ 125 Jose Vidro	2.00	.60
❑ 126 Orlando Cabrera	2.00	.60
❑ 127 Zach Day	2.00	.60
❑ 128 Mike Piazza	5.00	1.50
❑ 129 Tom Glavine	2.00	.60
❑ 130 Jae Weong Seo	2.00	.60
❑ 131 Gary Carter	2.00	.60
❑ 132 Phil Seibel	2.00	.60
❑ 133 Edwin Almonte	2.00	.60
❑ 134 Aaron Boone	2.00	.60
❑ 135 Kenny Lofton	2.00	.60
❑ 136 Don Mattingly	6.00	1.80
❑ 137 Jason Giambi	2.00	.60
❑ 138 Alex Rodriguez Yanks	5.00	1.50
❑ 139 Jorge Posada	2.00	.60
❑ 140 Bernie Williams	2.00	.60
❑ 141 Hideki Matsui	5.00	1.50
❑ 142 Mike Mussina	2.00	.60
❑ 143 Mariano Rivera	2.00	.60
❑ 144 Gary Sheffield	2.00	.60
❑ 145 Derek Jeter	6.00	1.80
❑ 146 Chien-Ming Wang	2.00	.60
❑ 147 Javier Vazquez	2.00	.60
❑ 148 Jose Contreras	2.00	.60
❑ 149 Whitey Ford	2.00	.60
❑ 150 Kevin Brown	2.00	.60
❑ 151 Eric Chavez	2.00	.60
❑ 152 Barry Zito	2.00	.60
❑ 153 Mark Mulder	2.00	.60
❑ 154 Tim Hudson	2.00	.60
❑ 155 Rich Harden	2.00	.60
❑ 156 Eric Byrnes	2.00	.60
❑ 157 Jim Thome	3.00	.90
❑ 158 Bobby Abreu	2.00	.60
❑ 159 Marlon Byrd	2.00	.60
❑ 160 Lenny Dykstra	2.00	.60
❑ 161 Steve Carlton	2.00	.60
❑ 162 Ryan Howard	2.00	.60
❑ 163 Bobby Hill	2.00	.60
❑ 164 Jose Castillo	2.00	.60
❑ 165 Jay Payton	2.00	.60
❑ 166 Ryan Klesko	2.00	.60
❑ 167 Brian Giles	2.00	.60
❑ 168 Henri Stanley	2.00	.60
❑ 169 Jason Schmidt	2.00	.60
❑ 170 Jerome Williams	2.00	.60
❑ 171 J.T. Snow	2.00	.60
❑ 172 Bret Boone	2.00	.60
❑ 173 Edgar Martinez	2.00	.60
❑ 174 Ichiro Suzuki	5.00	1.50
❑ 175 Jamie Moyer	2.00	.60
❑ 176 Rich Aurilia	2.00	.60
❑ 177 Chris Snelling	2.00	.60
❑ 178 Scott Rolen	3.00	.90
❑ 179 Albert Pujols	6.00	1.80
❑ 180 Jim Edmonds	2.00	.60
❑ 181 Stan Musial	5.00	1.50
❑ 182 Dan Haren	2.00	.60
❑ 183 Red Schoendienst	2.00	.60
❑ 184 Aubrey Huff	2.00	.60
❑ 185 Delmon Young	2.00	.60
❑ 186 Rocco Baldelli	2.00	.60
❑ 187 Dewon Brazelton	2.00	.60
❑ 188 Mark Teixeira	2.00	.60
❑ 189 Hank Blalock	2.00	.60
❑ 190 Nolan Ryan Rgr	8.00	2.40
❑ 191 Alfonso Soriano	2.00	.60
❑ 192 Michael Young	2.00	.60
❑ 193 Vernon Wells	2.00	.60
❑ 194 Roy Halladay	2.00	.60
❑ 195 Carlos Delgado	2.00	.60
❑ 196 Dustin McGowan	2.00	.60
❑ 197 Josh Phelps	2.00	.60
❑ 198 Alexis Rios	2.00	.60
❑ 199 Eric Hinske	2.00	.60
❑ 200 Josh Towers	2.00	.60
❑ 201 Kazuo Matsui/1000 RC	8.00	2.40
❑ 202 Fernando Nieve AU/500 RC	8.00	2.40
❑ 203 Mike Rouse/1000 RC	4.00	1.20
❑ 204 Dennis Sarfate AU/500 RC	8.00	2.40
❑ 205 Josh Labandeira AU/500 RC	8.00	2.40
❑ 206 Chris Oxspring AU/500 RC	10.00	3.00
❑ 207 Alfredo Simon/1000 RC	4.00	1.20
❑ 208 Cory Sullivan AU/500 RC	8.00	2.40
❑ 209 Ruddy Yan AU/500	8.00	2.40
❑ 210 Jason Bartlett AU/500 RC	10.00	3.00
❑ 211 Akinori Otsuka/1000 RC	4.00	1.20
❑ 212 Lincoln Holdzkom/1000 RC	4.00	1.20
❑ 213 Justin Leone/1000 RC	5.00	1.50
❑ 214 Jorge Sequea AU/500 RC	8.00	2.40
❑ 215 John Gall/1000 RC	5.00	1.50
❑ 216 Jerome Gamble/1000 RC	4.00	1.20
❑ 217 Tim Bittner AU/500 RC	8.00	2.40
❑ 218 Ronny Cedeno AU/500 RC	8.00	2.40
❑ 219 Justin Hampson/1000 RC	4.00	1.20
❑ 220 Ryan Wing AU/500 RC	8.00	2.40
❑ 221 Mariano Gomez AU/500 RC	8.00	2.40
❑ 222 Carlos Vasquez/1000 RC	4.00	1.20
❑ 223 Casey Daigle AU/500 RC	8.00	2.40
❑ 224 Renyel Pinto AU/500 RC	10.00	3.00
❑ 225 Chris Shelton AU/500 RC	10.00	3.00
❑ 226 Mike Gosling AU/700 RC	8.00	2.40
❑ 227 Aarom Baldiris AU/700 RC	10.00	3.00
❑ 228 Ramon Ramirez AU/700 RC	8.00	2.40
❑ 229 Roberto Novoa AU/500 RC	10.00	3.00
❑ 230 Sean Henn AU/500 RC	8.00	2.40
❑ 231 Jamie Brown AU/500 RC	8.00	2.40
❑ 232 Nick Regilio AU/500 RC	8.00	2.40
❑ 233 Dave Crouthers AU/700 RC	8.00	2.40
❑ 234 Greg Dobbs AU/500 RC	8.00	2.40
❑ 235 Angel Chavez AU/500 RC	8.00	2.40
❑ 236 Willy Taveras AU/500 RC	10.00	3.00
❑ 237 Justin Knoedler AU/500 RC	8.00	2.40
❑ 238 Ian Snell AU/700 RC	10.00	3.00
❑ 239 Jason Frasor AU/500 RC	8.00	2.40
❑ 240 Jerry Gil AU/500 RC	8.00	2.40
❑ 241 Carlos Hines AU/500 RC	8.00	2.40
❑ 242 Ivan Ochoa AU/500 RC	8.00	2.40
❑ 243 Jose Capellan AU/700 RC	20.00	6.00
❑ 244 Onil Joseph AU/700 RC	8.00	2.40
❑ 245 Hector Gimenez AU/700 RC	8.00	2.40
❑ 246 Shawn Hill AU/700 RC	8.00	2.40
❑ 247 Freddy Guzman AU/700 RC	8.00	2.40
❑ 248 Graham Koonce AU/500	8.00	2.40
❑ 249 Ronald Belisario AU/500 RC	8.00	2.40
❑ 250 Merkin Valdez AU/700 RC	10.00	3.00

2000 Black Diamond Rookie Edition

	Nm-Mt	Ex-Mt
COMP.SET w/o SP's (90)	25.00	7.50
COMMON CARD (1-90)	.40	.12
COMMON GEMS (91-120)	5.00	1.50
COMMON JSY. (121-136)	8.00	2.40
COMMON USA (137-154)	8.00	2.40
❑ 1 Troy Glaus	.40	.12
❑ 2 Mo Vaughn	.40	.12

❑ 3 Darin Erstad	.40	.12
❑ 4 Jason Giambi	.40	.12
❑ 5 Tim Hudson	.40	.12
❑ 6 Ben Grieve	.40	.12
❑ 7 Eric Chavez	.40	.12
❑ 8 Tony Batista	.40	.12
❑ 9 Carlos Delgado	.40	.12
❑ 10 David Wells	.40	.12
❑ 11 Greg Vaughn	.40	.12
❑ 12 Fred McGriff	.60	.18
❑ 13 Manny Ramirez	.60	.18
❑ 14 Roberto Alomar	.60	.18
❑ 15 Jim Thome	1.00	.30
❑ 16 Alex Rodriguez	1.50	.45
❑ 17 Edgar Martinez	.60	.18
❑ 18 John Olerud	.40	.12
❑ 19 Albert Belle	.40	.12
❑ 20 Mike Mussina	.60	.18
❑ 21 Cal Ripken	3.00	.90
❑ 22 Ivan Rodriguez	1.00	.30
❑ 23 Rafael Palmeiro	.60	.18
❑ 24 Pedro Martinez	1.00	.30
❑ 25 Nomar Garciaparra	1.50	.45
❑ 26 Carl Everett	.40	.12
❑ 27 Jermaine Dye	.40	.12
❑ 28 Mike Sweeney	.40	.12
❑ 29 Juan Gonzalez	.60	.18
❑ 30 Bobby Higginson	.40	.12
❑ 31 Dean Palmer	.40	.12
❑ 32 Jacque Jones	.40	.12
❑ 33 Eric Milton	.40	.12
❑ 34 Matt Lawton	.40	.12
❑ 35 Magglio Ordonez	.40	.12
❑ 36 Paul Konerko	.40	.12
❑ 37 Frank Thomas	1.00	.30
❑ 38 Ray Durham	.40	.12
❑ 39 Roger Clemens	2.00	.60
❑ 40 Derek Jeter	2.50	.75
❑ 41 Bernie Williams	.60	.18
❑ 42 Jose Canseco	1.00	.30
❑ 43 Craig Biggio	.60	.18
❑ 44 Richard Hidalgo	.40	.12
❑ 45 Jeff Bagwell	.60	.18
❑ 46 Greg Maddux	1.50	.45
❑ 47 Chipper Jones	1.00	.30
❑ 48 Rafael Furcal	.40	.12
❑ 49 Andruw Jones	.40	.12
❑ 50 Geoff Jenkins	.40	.12
❑ 51 Jeromy Burnitz	.40	.12
❑ 52 Mark McGwire	2.50	.75
❑ 53 Rick Ankiel	.40	.12
❑ 54 Jim Edmonds	.40	.12
❑ 55 Kerry Wood	1.00	.30
❑ 56 Sammy Sosa	1.50	.45
❑ 57 Matt Williams	.40	.12
❑ 58 Randy Johnson	1.00	.30
❑ 59 Steve Finley	.40	.12
❑ 60 Curt Schilling	.40	.12
❑ 61 Kevin Brown	.40	.12
❑ 62 Gary Sheffield	.40	.12
❑ 63 Shawn Green	.40	.12
❑ 64 Jose Vidro	.40	.12
❑ 65 Vladimir Guerrero	1.00	.30
❑ 66 Jeff Kent	.40	.12
❑ 67 Barry Bonds	2.50	.75
❑ 68 Ryan Dempster	.40	.12
❑ 69 Cliff Floyd	.40	.12
❑ 70 Preston Wilson	.40	.12
❑ 71 Mike Piazza	1.50	.45
❑ 72 Al Leiter	.40	.12
❑ 73 Edgardo Alfonzo	.40	.12
❑ 74 Derek Bell	.40	.12
❑ 75 Ryan Klesko	.40	.12
❑ 76 Tony Gwynn	1.25	.35
❑ 77 Bob Abreu	.40	.12
❑ 78 Pat Burrell	.40	.12
❑ 79 Scott Rolen	1.00	.30
❑ 80 Mike Lieberthal	.40	.12
❑ 81 Jason Kendall	.40	.12
❑ 82 Brian Giles	.40	.12
❑ 83 Ken Griffey Jr.	1.50	.45
❑ 84 Pokey Reese	.40	.12
❑ 85 Dmitri Young	.40	.12
❑ 86 Sean Casey	.40	.12
❑ 87 Jeff Cirillo	.40	.12
❑ 88 Todd Helton	.60	.18
❑ 89 Jeffrey Hammonds	.40	.12
❑ 90 Larry Walker	.60	.18
❑ 91 Barry Zito RC	10.00	3.00
❑ 92 Keith Ginter RC	5.00	1.50
❑ 93 Dane Sardinha RC	5.00	1.50
❑ 94 Kenny Kelly RC	5.00	1.50
❑ 95 Ryan Kohlmeier RC	5.00	1.50
❑ 96 Leo Estrella RC	5.00	1.50
❑ 97 Danys Baez RC	5.00	1.50
❑ 98 Paul Rigdon RC	5.00	1.50
❑ 99 Mike Lamb RC	5.00	1.50
❑ 100 Aaron McNeal RC	5.00	1.50
❑ 101 Juan Pierre RC	8.00	2.40
❑ 102 Rico Washington RC	5.00	1.50
❑ 103 Luis Matos RC	5.00	1.50
❑ 104 Adam Bernero RC	5.00	1.50
❑ 105 Wascar Serrano RC	5.00	1.50
❑ 106 Chris Richard RC	5.00	1.50
❑ 107 Justin Miller RC	5.00	1.50
❑ 108 Julio Zuleta RC	5.00	1.50
❑ 109 Alex Cabrera RC	5.00	1.50
❑ 110 G.Stechschulte RC	5.00	1.50
❑ 111 Tony Mota RC	5.00	1.50
❑ 112 Tomo Ohka RC	5.00	1.50
❑ 113 Geraldo Guzman RC	5.00	1.50
❑ 114 Scott Downs RC	5.00	1.50
❑ 115 Timo Perez RC	5.00	1.50
❑ 116 Chad Durbin RC	5.00	1.50
❑ 117 Sun-Woo Kim RC	5.00	1.50
❑ 118 Tomas De la Rosa RC	5.00	1.50
❑ 119 Javier Cardona RC	5.00	1.50
❑ 120 Kazuhiro Sasaki RC	8.00	2.40
❑ 121 Brad Cresse JSY RC	8.00	2.40
❑ 122 M.Wheatland JSY RC	8.00	2.40
❑ 123 Joe Torres JSY RC	8.00	2.40
❑ 124 Dave Krynzel JSY RC	8.00	2.40
❑ 125 Ben Diggins JSY RC	8.00	2.40
❑ 126 Sean Burnett JSY RC	10.00	3.00
❑ 127 D.Espinosa JSY RC	8.00	2.40
❑ 128 Scott Heard JSY RC	8.00	2.40
❑ 129 Daylan Holt JSY RC	8.00	2.40
❑ 130 Koyie Hill JSY RC	8.00	2.40
❑ 131 Mark Buehrle JSY RC	15.00	4.50
❑ 132 Xavier Nady JSY RC	10.00	3.00
❑ 133 Mike Tonis JSY RC	8.00	2.40
❑ 134 Matt Ginter JSY RC	8.00	2.40
❑ 135 L.Barcelo JSY RC	8.00	2.40
❑ 136 Cory Vance JSY RC	8.00	2.40
❑ 137 Sean Burroughs USA	8.00	2.40
❑ 138 Todd Williams USA	8.00	2.40
❑ 139 B.Wilkerson USA RC	10.00	3.00
❑ 140 Ben Sheets USA RC	12.00	3.60
❑ 141 K.Ainsworth USA RC	8.00	2.40
❑ 142 Anthony Sanders USA	8.00	2.40
❑ 143 R.Franklin USA RC	8.00	2.40
❑ 144 S.Hearns USA RC	8.00	2.40
❑ 145 Roy Oswalt USA RC	15.00	4.50
❑ 146 Jon Rauch USA RC	8.00	2.40
❑ 147 B.Abernathy USA RC	8.00	2.40
❑ 148 Ernie Young USA	8.00	2.40
❑ 149 Chris George USA	8.00	2.40
❑ 150 Gookie Dawkins USA	8.00	2.40
❑ 151 Adam Everett USA	8.00	2.40
❑ 152 John Cotton USA RC	8.00	2.40
❑ 153 Pat Borders USA	8.00	2.40
❑ 154 D.Mientkiewicz USA	8.00	2.40

1948 Bowman

	NM	Ex
COMPLETE SET (48)	3600.00	1800.00
COMMON CARD (1-36)	20.00	10.00
COMMON CARD (37-48)	30.00	15.00
WRAPPER (5-CENT)	700.00	350.00
WRAPPER (1-CENT)		

❑ 1 Bob Elliott RC	125.00	19.00
❑ 2 Ewell Blackwell RC	60.00	30.00
❑ 3 Ralph Kiner RC	150.00	75.00
❑ 4 Johnny Mize RC	125.00	60.00
❑ 5 Bob Feller RC	250.00	125.00
❑ 6 Yogi Berra RC	500.00	250.00
❑ 7 Pete Reiser SP	125.00	60.00
❑ 8 Phil Rizzuto SP RC	350.00	180.00
❑ 9 Walker Cooper RC	20.00	10.00
❑ 10 Buddy Rosar	20.00	10.00

❑ 11 Johnny Lindell	25.00	12.50
❑ 12 Johnny Sain RC	80.00	40.00
❑ 13 Willard Marshall SP	40.00	20.00
❑ 14 Allie Reynolds RC	60.00	30.00
❑ 15 Eddie Joost	20.00	10.00
❑ 16 Jack Lohrke SP	40.00	20.00
❑ 17 Enos Slaughter RC	100.00	50.00
❑ 18 Warren Spahn RC	300.00	150.00
❑ 19 Tommy Henrich	60.00	30.00
❑ 20 Buddy Kerr SP	40.00	20.00
❑ 21 Ferris Fain RC	40.00	20.00
❑ 22 Floyd Bevens SP RC	50.00	25.00
❑ 23 Larry Jansen RC	25.00	12.50
❑ 24 Dutch Leonard SP	40.00	20.00
❑ 25 Barney McCosky	20.00	10.00
❑ 26 Frank Shea SP RC	50.00	25.00
❑ 27 Sid Gordon RC	25.00	12.50
❑ 28 Emil Verban SP	40.00	20.00
❑ 29 Joe Page SP RC	80.00	40.00
❑ 30 W.Lockman SP RC	50.00	25.00
❑ 31 Bill McCahan	20.00	10.00
❑ 32 Bill Rigney RC	20.00	10.00
❑ 33 Bill Johnson	25.00	12.50
❑ 34 Sheldon Jones SP	40.00	20.00
❑ 35 Snuffy Stirnweiss RC	40.00	20.00
❑ 36 Stan Musial RC	800.00	400.00
❑ 37 Clint Hartung RC	30.00	15.00
❑ 38 Red Schoendienst RC	200.00	100.00
❑ 39 Augie Galan	30.00	15.00
❑ 40 Marty Marion RC	80.00	40.00
❑ 41 Rex Barney RC	60.00	30.00
❑ 42 Ray Poat	30.00	15.00
❑ 43 Bruce Edwards	40.00	20.00
❑ 44 Johnny Wyrostek	30.00	15.00
❑ 45 Hank Sauer RC	60.00	30.00
❑ 46 Herman Wehmeier	30.00	15.00
❑ 47 Bobby Thomson RC	100.00	50.00
❑ 48 Dave Koslo RC	80.00	19.50

1949 Bowman

	NM	Ex
COMP. MASTER SET (252)	16000.00	8000.00
COMPLETE SET (240)	15000.00	7500.00
COMMON CARD (1-144)	15.00	7.50
COMMON (145-240)	50.00	25.00
WRAPPER (1-CENT,Rd,Wh,Bl)		
WRAP.(5-CENT,GREEN)	250.00	125.00
WRAP.(5-CENT,BLUE)	200.00	100.00

❑ 1 Vern Bickford RC	125.00	25.00

❑ 2 Whitey Lockman	40.00	20.00
❑ 3 Bob Porterfield	15.00	7.50
❑ 4A Jerry Priddy NNOF	15.00	7.50
❑ 4B Jerry Priddy NOF	50.00	25.00
❑ 5 Hank Sauer	40.00	20.00
❑ 6 Phil Cavarretta	40.00	20.00
❑ 7 Joe Dobson	15.00	7.50
❑ 8 Murry Dickson	15.00	7.50
❑ 9 Ferris Fain	40.00	20.00
❑ 10 Ted Gray	15.00	7.50
❑ 11 Lou Boudreau	80.00	40.00
❑ 12 Cass Michaels	15.00	7.50
❑ 13 Bob Chesnes	15.00	7.50
❑ 14 Curt Simmons RC	40.00	20.00
❑ 15 Ned Garver	15.00	7.50
❑ 16 Al Kozar	15.00	7.50
❑ 17 Earl Torgeson	15.00	7.50
❑ 18 Bobby Thomson	40.00	20.00
❑ 19 Bobby Brown RC	60.00	30.00
❑ 20 Gene Hermanski	15.00	7.50
❑ 21 Frank Baumholtz	25.00	12.50
❑ 22 Peanuts Lowrey	15.00	7.50
❑ 23 Bobby Doerr	80.00	40.00
❑ 24 Stan Musial	600.00	300.00
❑ 25 Carl Scheib	15.00	7.50
❑ 26 George Kell RC	80.00	40.00
❑ 27 Bob Feller	300.00	150.00
❑ 28 Don Kolloway	15.00	7.50
❑ 29 Ralph Kiner	125.00	60.00
❑ 30 Andy Seminick	40.00	20.00
❑ 31 Dick Kokos	15.00	7.50
❑ 32 Eddie Yost RC	60.00	30.00
❑ 33 Warren Spahn	200.00	100.00
❑ 34 Dave Koslo	15.00	7.50
❑ 35 Vic Raschi RC	60.00	30.00
❑ 36 Pee Wee Reese	200.00	100.00
❑ 37 Johnny Wyrostek	15.00	7.50
❑ 38 Emil Verban	15.00	7.50
❑ 39 Billy Goodman	25.00	12.50
❑ 40 George Munger	15.00	7.50
❑ 41 Lou Brissie	15.00	7.50
❑ 42 Hoot Evers	15.00	7.50
❑ 43 Dale Mitchell RC	40.00	20.00
❑ 44 Dave Philley	15.00	7.50
❑ 45 Wally Westlake	15.00	7.50
❑ 46 Robin Roberts RC	250.00	125.00
❑ 47 Johnny Sain	60.00	30.00
❑ 48 Willard Marshall	15.00	7.50
❑ 49 Frank Shea	25.00	12.50
❑ 50 Jackie Robinson RC	1200.00	600.00
❑ 51 Herman Wehmeier	15.00	7.50
❑ 52 Johnny Schmitz	15.00	7.50
❑ 53 Jack Kramer	15.00	7.50
❑ 54 Marty Marion	60.00	30.00
❑ 55 Eddie Joost	15.00	7.50
❑ 56 Pat Mullin	15.00	7.50
❑ 57 Gene Bearden	40.00	20.00
❑ 58 Bob Elliott	40.00	20.00
❑ 59 Jack Lohrke	15.00	7.50
❑ 60 Yogi Berra	300.00	150.00
❑ 61 Rex Barney	40.00	20.00
❑ 62 Grady Hatton	15.00	7.50
❑ 63 Andy Pafko	40.00	20.00
❑ 64 Dom DiMaggio	60.00	30.00
❑ 65 Enos Slaughter	80.00	40.00
❑ 66 Elmer Valo	15.00	7.50
❑ 67 Alvin Dark RC	40.00	20.00
❑ 68 Sheldon Jones	15.00	7.50
❑ 69 Tommy Henrich	40.00	20.00
❑ 70 Carl Furillo RC	125.00	60.00
❑ 71 Vern Stephens	15.00	7.50
❑ 72 Tommy Holmes	40.00	20.00
❑ 73 Billy Cox RC	40.00	20.00
❑ 74 Tom McBride	15.00	7.50
❑ 75 Eddie Mayo	15.00	7.50
❑ 76 Bill Nicholson RC	25.00	12.50
❑ 77 Ernie Bonham	15.00	7.50
❑ 78A Sam Zoldak NNOF	15.00	7.50
❑ 78B Sam Zoldak NOF	50.00	25.00
❑ 79 Ron Northey	15.00	7.50
❑ 80 Bill McCahan	15.00	7.50
❑ 81 Virgil Stallcup	15.00	7.50
❑ 82 Joe Page	60.00	30.00
❑ 83A Bob Scheffing NNOF	15.00	7.50
❑ 83B Bob Scheffing NOF	50.00	25.00
❑ 84 Roy Campanella RC	800.00	400.00
❑ 85A Johnny Mize NNOF	100.00	50.00
❑ 85B Johnny Mize NOF	150.00	75.00
❑ 86 Johnny Pesky	60.00	30.00
❑ 87 Randy Gumpert	15.00	7.50
❑ 88A Bill Salkeld NNOF	15.00	7.50
❑ 88B Bill Salkeld NOF	50.00	25.00
❑ 89 Mizell Platt	15.00	7.50
❑ 90 Gil Coan	15.00	7.50
❑ 91 Dick Wakefield	15.00	7.50
❑ 92 Willie Jones	40.00	20.00
❑ 93 Ed Stevens	15.00	7.50
❑ 94 Mickey Vernon RC	40.00	20.00
❑ 95 Howie Pollet RC	15.00	7.50
❑ 96 Taft Wright	15.00	7.50
❑ 97 Danny Litwhiler	15.00	7.50
❑ 98A Phil Rizzuto NNOF	200.00	100.00
❑ 98B Phil Rizzuto NOF	250.00	125.00
❑ 99 Frank Gustine	15.00	7.50
❑ 100 Gil Hodges RC	250.00	125.00
❑ 101 Sid Gordon	15.00	7.50
❑ 102 Stan Spence	15.00	7.50
❑ 103 Joe Tipton	15.00	7.50
❑ 104 Eddie Stanky RC	40.00	20.00
❑ 105 Bill Kennedy	15.00	7.50
❑ 106 Jake Early	15.00	7.50
❑ 107 Eddie Lake	15.00	7.50
❑ 108 Ken Heintzelman	15.00	7.50
❑ 109A Ed Fitzgerald SCR	15.00	7.50
❑ 109B Ed Fitzgerald PR	60.00	30.00
❑ 110 Early Wynn RC	150.00	75.00
❑ 111 Red Schoendienst	100.00	50.00
❑ 112 Sam Chapman	40.00	20.00
❑ 113 Ray LaManno	15.00	7.50
❑ 114 Allie Reynolds	60.00	30.00
❑ 115 Dutch Leonard	15.00	7.50
❑ 116 Joe Hatton	15.00	7.50
❑ 117 Walker Cooper	15.00	7.50
❑ 118 Sam Mele	15.00	7.50
❑ 119 Floyd Baker	15.00	7.50
❑ 120 Cliff Fannin	15.00	7.50
❑ 121 Mark Christman	15.00	7.50
❑ 122 George Vico	15.00	7.50
❑ 123 Johnny Blatnick	15.00	7.50
❑ 124A D.Murtaugh SCR RC	50.00	25.00
❑ 124B D.Murtaugh PR RC	60.00	30.00
❑ 125 Ken Keltner	25.00	12.50
❑ 126A Al Brazle SCR	15.00	7.50
❑ 126B Al Brazle PR	60.00	30.00
❑ 127A Hank Majeski SCR	15.00	7.50
❑ 127B Hank Majeski PR	60.00	30.00
❑ 128 Johnny VanderMeer	60.00	30.00
❑ 129 Bill Johnson	40.00	20.00
❑ 130 Harry Walker	15.00	7.50
❑ 131 Paul Lehner	15.00	7.50
❑ 132A Al Evans SCR	15.00	7.50
❑ 132B Al Evans PR	60.00	30.00
❑ 133 Aaron Robinson	15.00	7.50
❑ 134 Hank Borowy	15.00	7.50
❑ 135 Stan Rojek	15.00	7.50
❑ 136 Hank Edwards	15.00	7.50
❑ 137 Ted Wilks	15.00	7.50
❑ 138 Buddy Rosar	15.00	7.50
❑ 139 Hank Arft	15.00	7.50
❑ 140 Ray Scarborough	15.00	7.50
❑ 141 Tony Lupien	15.00	7.50
❑ 142 Eddie Waitkus RC	40.00	20.00
❑ 143A B.Dillinger RC SCR	25.00	12.50
❑ 143B Bob Dillinger RC PR	60.00	30.00
❑ 144 Mickey Haefner	15.00	7.50
❑ 145 Sylvester Donnelly	50.00	25.00
❑ 146 Mike McCormick	50.00	25.00
❑ 147 Bert Singleton	50.00	25.00
❑ 148 Bob Swift	50.00	25.00
❑ 149 Roy Partee	50.00	25.00
❑ 150 Allie Clark	50.00	25.00
❑ 151 Mickey Harris	50.00	25.00
❑ 152 Clarence Maddern	50.00	25.00
❑ 153 Phil Masi	50.00	25.00
❑ 154 Clint Hartung	60.00	30.00
❑ 155 Mickey Guerra	50.00	25.00
❑ 156 Al Zarilla	50.00	25.00
❑ 157 Walt Masterson	50.00	25.00
❑ 158 Harry Brecheen	60.00	30.00
❑ 159 Glen Moulder	50.00	25.00
❑ 160 Jim Blackburn	50.00	25.00
❑ 161 Jocko Thompson	50.00	25.00
❑ 162 Preacher Roe RC	125.00	60.00
❑ 163 Clyde McCullough	50.00	25.00
❑ 164 Vic Wertz RC	80.00	40.00
❑ 165 Snuffy Stirnweiss	80.00	40.00
❑ 166 Mike Tresh	50.00	25.00
❑ 167 Babe Martin	50.00	25.00
❑ 168 Doyle Lade	50.00	25.00
❑ 169 Jeff Heath	60.00	30.00
❑ 170 Bill Rigney	60.00	30.00
❑ 171 Dick Fowler	50.00	25.00
❑ 172 Eddie Pellagrini	50.00	25.00
❑ 173 Eddie Stewart	50.00	25.00
❑ 174 Terry Moore RC	80.00	40.00
❑ 175 Luke Appling	125.00	60.00
❑ 176 Ken Raffensberger	50.00	25.00
❑ 177 Stan Lopata	60.00	30.00
❑ 178 Tom Brown	60.00	30.00
❑ 179 Hugh Casey	80.00	40.00
❑ 180 Connie Berry	50.00	25.00
❑ 181 Gus Niarhos	50.00	25.00
❑ 182 Hal Peck	50.00	25.00
❑ 183 Lou Stringer	50.00	25.00
❑ 184 Bob Chipman	50.00	25.00
❑ 185 Pete Reiser	80.00	40.00
❑ 186 Buddy Kerr	50.00	25.00
❑ 187 Phil Marchildon	50.00	25.00
❑ 188 Karl Drews	50.00	25.00
❑ 189 Earl Wooten	50.00	25.00
❑ 190 Jim Hearn	50.00	25.00
❑ 191 Joe Haynes	50.00	25.00
❑ 192 Harry Gumbert	50.00	25.00
❑ 193 Ken Trinkle	50.00	25.00
❑ 194 Ralph Branca RC	100.00	50.00
❑ 195 Eddie Bockman	50.00	25.00
❑ 196 Fred Hutchinson	60.00	30.00
❑ 197 Johnny Lindell	60.00	30.00
❑ 198 Steve Gromek	50.00	25.00
❑ 199 Tex Hughson	50.00	25.00
❑ 200 Jess Dobernic	50.00	25.00
❑ 201 Sibby Sisti	50.00	25.00
❑ 202 Larry Jansen	60.00	30.00
❑ 203 Barney McCosky	50.00	25.00
❑ 204 Bob Savage	50.00	25.00
❑ 205 Dick Sisler	60.00	30.00
❑ 206 Bruce Edwards	50.00	25.00
❑ 207 Johnny Hopp	50.00	25.00
❑ 208 Dizzy Trout	60.00	30.00
❑ 209 Charlie Keller	80.00	40.00
❑ 210 Joe Gordon	80.00	40.00
❑ 211 Boo Ferriss	50.00	25.00
❑ 212 Ralph Hamner	50.00	25.00
❑ 213 Red Barrett	50.00	25.00
❑ 214 Richie Ashburn RC	600.00	300.00
❑ 215 Kirby Higbe	50.00	25.00
❑ 216 Schoolboy Rowe	60.00	30.00
❑ 217 Marino Pieretti	50.00	25.00
❑ 218 Dick Kryhoski	50.00	25.00
❑ 219 Virgil Fire Trucks	60.00	30.00
❑ 220 Johnny McCarthy	50.00	25.00
NY Giants Cap but listed as Sioux City MG		
❑ 221 Bob Muncrief	50.00	25.00
❑ 222 Alex Kellner	50.00	25.00
❑ 223 Bobby Hofman	50.00	25.00
❑ 224 Satchell Paige RC	1500.00	750.00
❑ 225 Jerry Coleman RC	80.00	40.00
❑ 226 Duke Snider RC	1000.00	500.00
❑ 227 Fritz Ostermueller	50.00	25.00
❑ 228 Jackie Mayo	50.00	25.00
❑ 229 Ed Lopat RC	125.00	60.00
❑ 230 Augie Galan	60.00	30.00
❑ 231 Earl Johnson	50.00	25.00
❑ 232 George McQuinn	60.00	30.00
❑ 233 Larry Doby RC	200.00	100.00
❑ 234 Rip Sewell	50.00	25.00
❑ 235 Jim Russell	50.00	25.00
❑ 236 Fred Sanford	50.00	25.00
❑ 237 Monte Kennedy	50.00	25.00
❑ 238 Bob Lemon RC	200.00	100.00
❑ 239 Frank McCormick	50.00	25.00
❑ 240 Babe Young UER	100.00	25.00
(Photo actually Bobby Young)		

1950 Bowman

	NM	Ex
COMPLETE SET (252)	8500.00	4200.00
COMMON CARD (1-72)	50.00	25.00
COMMON CARD (73-252)	15.00	7.50
WRAPPER (1-cent)	250.00	125.00
WRAPPER (5-cent)	250.00	125.00

Card	NM	Ex
❑ 1 Mel Parnell RC	150.00	30.00
❑ 2 Vern Stephens	60.00	30.00
❑ 3 Dom DiMaggio	80.00	40.00
❑ 4 Gus Zernial RC	60.00	30.00
❑ 5 Bob Kuzava	50.00	25.00
❑ 6 Bob Feller	300.00	150.00
❑ 7 Jim Hegan	60.00	30.00
❑ 8 George Kell	80.00	40.00
❑ 9 Vic Wertz	60.00	30.00
❑ 10 Tommy Henrich	80.00	40.00
❑ 11 Phil Rizzuto	300.00	150.00
❑ 12 Joe Page	80.00	40.00
❑ 13 Ferris Fain	60.00	30.00
❑ 14 Alex Kellner	50.00	25.00
❑ 15 Al Kozar	50.00	25.00
❑ 16 Roy Sievers RC	80.00	40.00
❑ 17 Sid Hudson	50.00	25.00
❑ 18 Eddie Robinson	50.00	25.00
❑ 19 Warren Spahn	300.00	150.00
❑ 20 Bob Elliott	60.00	30.00
❑ 21 Pee Wee Reese	300.00	150.00
❑ 22 Jackie Robinson	1200.00	600.00
❑ 23 Don Newcombe RC	150.00	75.00
❑ 24 Johnny Schmitz	50.00	25.00
❑ 25 Hank Sauer	60.00	30.00
❑ 26 Grady Hatton	50.00	25.00
❑ 27 Herman Wehmeier	50.00	25.00
❑ 28 Bobby Thomson	80.00	40.00
❑ 29 Eddie Stanky	60.00	30.00
❑ 30 Eddie Waitkus	60.00	30.00
❑ 31 Del Ennis	80.00	40.00
❑ 32 Robin Roberts	150.00	75.00
❑ 33 Ralph Kiner	100.00	50.00
❑ 34 Murry Dickson	50.00	25.00
❑ 35 Enos Slaughter	100.00	50.00
❑ 36 Eddie Kazak	60.00	30.00
❑ 37 Luke Appling	80.00	40.00
❑ 38 Bill Wight	50.00	25.00
❑ 39 Larry Doby	100.00	50.00
❑ 40 Bob Lemon	80.00	40.00
❑ 41 Hoot Evers	50.00	25.00
❑ 42 Art Houtteman	50.00	25.00
❑ 43 Bobby Doerr	80.00	40.00
❑ 44 Joe Dobson	50.00	25.00
❑ 45 Al Zarilla	50.00	25.00
❑ 46 Yogi Berra	400.00	200.00
❑ 47 Jerry Coleman	80.00	40.00
❑ 48 Lou Brissie	50.00	25.00
❑ 49 Elmer Valo	50.00	25.00
❑ 50 Dick Kokos	50.00	25.00
❑ 51 Ned Garver	60.00	30.00
❑ 52 Sam Mele	50.00	25.00
❑ 53 Clyde Vollmer	50.00	25.00
❑ 54 Gil Coan	50.00	25.00
❑ 55 Buddy Kerr	50.00	25.00
❑ 56 Del Crandall RC	60.00	30.00
❑ 57 Vern Bickford	50.00	25.00
❑ 58 Carl Furillo	80.00	40.00
❑ 59 Ralph Branca	80.00	40.00
❑ 60 Andy Pafko	60.00	30.00
❑ 61 Bob Rush	50.00	25.00
❑ 62 Ted Kluszewski	125.00	60.00
❑ 63 Ewell Blackwell	60.00	30.00
❑ 64 Alvin Dark	60.00	30.00
❑ 65 Dave Koslo	50.00	25.00
❑ 66 Larry Jansen	60.00	30.00
❑ 67 Willie Jones	60.00	30.00
❑ 68 Curt Simmons	60.00	30.00
❑ 69 Wally Westlake	50.00	25.00
❑ 70 Bob Chesnes	50.00	25.00
❑ 71 Red Schoendienst	80.00	40.00
❑ 72 Howie Pollet	50.00	25.00
❑ 73 Willard Marshall	15.00	7.50
❑ 74 Johnny Antonelli RC	60.00	30.00
❑ 75 Roy Campanella	300.00	150.00
❑ 76 Rex Barney	40.00	20.00
❑ 77 Duke Snider	300.00	150.00
❑ 78 Mickey Owen	25.00	12.50
❑ 79 Johnny VanderMeer	40.00	20.00
❑ 80 Howard Fox	15.00	7.50
❑ 81 Ron Northey	15.00	7.50
❑ 82 Whitey Lockman	25.00	12.50
❑ 83 Sheldon Jones	15.00	7.50
❑ 84 Richie Ashburn	125.00	60.00
❑ 85 Ken Heintzelman	15.00	7.50
❑ 86 Stan Rojek	15.00	7.50
❑ 87 Bill Werle	15.00	7.50
❑ 88 Marty Marion	40.00	20.00
❑ 89 George Munger	15.00	7.50
❑ 90 Harry Brecheen	40.00	20.00
❑ 91 Cass Michaels	15.00	7.50
❑ 92 Hank Majeski	15.00	7.50
❑ 93 Gene Bearden	40.00	20.00
❑ 94 Lou Boudreau	60.00	30.00
❑ 95 Aaron Robinson	15.00	7.50
❑ 96 Virgil Trucks	25.00	12.50
❑ 97 Maurice McDermott RC	15.00	7.50
❑ 98 Ted Williams	1000.00	500.00
❑ 99 Billy Goodman	25.00	12.50
❑ 100 Vic Raschi	60.00	30.00
❑ 101 Bobby Brown	60.00	30.00
❑ 102 Billy Johnson	25.00	12.50
❑ 103 Eddie Joost	15.00	7.50
❑ 104 Sam Chapman	15.00	7.50
❑ 105 Bob Dillinger	15.00	7.50
❑ 106 Cliff Fannin	15.00	7.50
❑ 107 Sam Dente	15.00	7.50
❑ 108 Ray Scarborough	15.00	7.50
❑ 109 Sid Gordon	15.00	7.50
❑ 110 Tommy Holmes	25.00	12.50
❑ 111 Walker Cooper	15.00	7.50
❑ 112 Gil Hodges	125.00	60.00
❑ 113 Gene Hermanski	15.00	7.50
❑ 114 Wayne Terwilliger RC	15.00	7.50
❑ 115 Roy Smalley	15.00	7.50
❑ 116 Virgil Stallcup	15.00	7.50
❑ 117 Bill Rigney	15.00	7.50
❑ 118 Clint Hartung	15.00	7.50
❑ 119 Dick Sisler	25.00	12.50
❑ 120 John Thompson	15.00	7.50
❑ 121 Andy Seminick	25.00	12.50
❑ 122 Johnny Hopp	25.00	12.50
❑ 123 Dino Restelli	15.00	7.50
❑ 124 Clyde McCullough	15.00	7.50
❑ 125 Del Rice	15.00	7.50
❑ 126 Al Brazle	15.00	7.50
❑ 127 Dave Philley	15.00	7.50
❑ 128 Phil Masi	15.00	7.50
❑ 129 Joe Gordon	25.00	12.50
❑ 130 Dale Mitchell	25.00	12.50
❑ 131 Steve Gromek	15.00	7.50
❑ 132 Mickey Vernon	25.00	12.50
❑ 133 Don Kolloway	15.00	7.50
❑ 134 Paul Trout	15.00	7.50
❑ 135 Pat Mullin	15.00	7.50
❑ 136 Buddy Rosar	15.00	7.50
❑ 137 Johnny Pesky	25.00	12.50
❑ 138 Allie Reynolds	60.00	30.00
❑ 139 Johnny Mize	80.00	40.00
❑ 140 Pete Suder	15.00	7.50
❑ 141 Joe Coleman	25.00	12.50
❑ 142 Sherman Lollar RC	40.00	20.00
❑ 143 Eddie Stewart	15.00	7.50
❑ 144 Al Evans	15.00	7.50
❑ 145 Jack Graham	15.00	7.50
❑ 146 Floyd Baker	15.00	7.50
❑ 147 Mike Garcia RC	40.00	20.00
❑ 148 Early Wynn	80.00	40.00
❑ 149 Bob Swift	15.00	7.50
❑ 150 George Vico	15.00	7.50
❑ 151 Fred Hutchinson	25.00	12.50
❑ 152 Ellis Kinder RC	15.00	7.50
❑ 153 Walt Masterson	15.00	7.50
❑ 154 Gus Niarhos	15.00	7.50
❑ 155 Frank Shea	25.00	12.50
❑ 156 Fred Sanford	25.00	12.50
❑ 157 Mike Guerra	15.00	7.50
❑ 158 Paul Lehner	15.00	7.50
❑ 159 Joe Tipton	15.00	7.50
❑ 160 Mickey Harris	15.00	7.50
❑ 161 Sherry Robertson	15.00	7.50
❑ 162 Eddie Yost	25.00	12.50
❑ 163 Earl Torgeson	15.00	7.50
❑ 164 Sibby Sisti	15.00	7.50
❑ 165 Bruce Edwards	15.00	7.50
❑ 166 Joe Hatton	15.00	7.50
❑ 167 Preacher Roe	60.00	30.00
❑ 168 Bob Scheffing	15.00	7.50
❑ 169 Hank Edwards	15.00	7.50
❑ 170 Dutch Leonard	15.00	7.50
❑ 171 Harry Gumbert	15.00	7.50
❑ 172 Peanuts Lowrey	15.00	7.50
❑ 173 Lloyd Merriman	15.00	7.50
❑ 174 Hank Thompson RC	40.00	20.00
❑ 175 Monte Kennedy	15.00	7.50
❑ 176 Sylvester Donnelly	15.00	7.50
❑ 177 Hank Borowy	15.00	7.50
❑ 178 Ed Fitzgerald	15.00	7.50
❑ 179 Chuck Diering	15.00	7.50
❑ 180 Harry Walker	25.00	12.50
❑ 181 Marino Pieretti	15.00	7.50
❑ 182 Sam Zoldak	15.00	7.50
❑ 183 Mickey Haefner	15.00	7.50
❑ 184 Randy Gumpert	15.00	7.50
❑ 185 Howie Judson	15.00	7.50
❑ 186 Ken Keltner	25.00	12.50
❑ 187 Lou Stringer	15.00	7.50
❑ 188 Earl Johnson	15.00	7.50
❑ 189 Owen Friend	15.00	7.50
❑ 190 Ken Wood	15.00	7.50
❑ 191 Dick Starr	15.00	7.50
❑ 192 Bob Chipman	15.00	7.50
❑ 193 Pete Reiser	40.00	20.00
❑ 194 Billy Cox	60.00	30.00
❑ 195 Phil Cavarretta	40.00	20.00
❑ 196 Doyle Lade	15.00	7.50
❑ 197 Johnny Wyrostek	15.00	7.50
❑ 198 Danny Litwhiler	15.00	7.50
❑ 199 Jack Kramer	15.00	7.50
❑ 200 Kirby Higbe	25.00	12.50
❑ 201 Pete Castiglione	15.00	7.50
❑ 202 Cliff Chambers	15.00	7.50
❑ 203 Danny Murtaugh	25.00	12.50
❑ 204 Granny Hamner RC	40.00	20.00
❑ 205 Mike Goliat	15.00	7.50
❑ 206 Stan Lopata	25.00	12.50
❑ 207 Max Lanier	15.00	7.50
❑ 208 Jim Hearn	15.00	7.50
❑ 209 Johnny Lindell	15.00	7.50
❑ 210 Ted Gray	15.00	7.50
❑ 211 Charlie Keller	40.00	20.00
❑ 212 Jerry Priddy	15.00	7.50
❑ 213 Carl Scheib	15.00	7.50
❑ 214 Dick Fowler	15.00	7.50
❑ 215 Ed Lopat	60.00	30.00
❑ 216 Bob Porterfield	25.00	12.50
❑ 217 Casey Stengel MG	125.00	60.00
❑ 218 Cliff Mapes RC	25.00	12.50
❑ 219 Hank Bauer RC	100.00	50.00
❑ 220 Leo Durocher MG	60.00	30.00
❑ 221 Don Mueller RC	40.00	20.00
❑ 222 Bobby Morgan	15.00	7.50
❑ 223 Jim Russell	15.00	7.50
❑ 224 Jack Banta	15.00	7.50
❑ 225 Eddie Sawyer MG	25.00	12.50
❑ 226 Jim Konstanty RC	60.00	30.00
❑ 227 Bob Miller	25.00	12.50
❑ 228 Bill Nicholson	25.00	12.50
❑ 229 Frank Frisch MG	60.00	30.00
❑ 230 Bill Serena	15.00	7.50
❑ 231 Preston Ward	15.00	7.50
❑ 232 Al Rosen RC	60.00	30.00
❑ 233 Allie Clark	15.00	7.50
❑ 234 Bobby Shantz RC	60.00	30.00

❑ 235 Harold Gilbert	15.00	7.50
❑ 236 Bob Cain	15.00	7.50
❑ 237 Bill Salkeld	15.00	7.50
❑ 238 Nippy Jones	15.00	7.50
❑ 239 Bill Howerton	15.00	7.50
❑ 240 Eddie Lake	15.00	7.50
❑ 241 Neil Berry	15.00	7.50
❑ 242 Dick Kryhoski	15.00	7.50
❑ 243 Johnny Groth	15.00	7.50
❑ 244 Dale Coogan	15.00	7.50
❑ 245 Al Papai	15.00	7.50
❑ 246 Walt Dropo RC	40.00	20.00
❑ 247 Irv Noren RC	25.00	12.50
❑ 248 Sam Jethroe RC	60.00	30.00
❑ 249 Snuffy Stirnweiss	25.00	12.50
❑ 250 Ray Coleman	15.00	7.50
❑ 251 Les Moss	15.00	7.50
❑ 252 Billy DeMars RC	60.00	16.50

1951 Bowman

	NM	Ex
COMPLETE SET (324)	20000.00	10000.00
COMMON CARD (1-252)	20.00	10.00
COMMON (253-324)	50.00	25.00
WRAPPER (1-cent)	200.00	100.00
WRAPPER (5-cent)	250.00	125.00

❑ 1 Whitey Ford RC	2000.00	500.00
❑ 2 Yogi Berra	400.00	200.00
❑ 3 Robin Roberts	80.00	40.00
❑ 4 Del Ennis	25.00	12.50
❑ 5 Dale Mitchell	25.00	12.50
❑ 6 Don Newcombe	60.00	30.00
❑ 7 Gil Hodges	125.00	60.00
❑ 8 Paul Lehner	20.00	10.00
❑ 9 Sam Chapman	20.00	10.00
❑ 10 Red Schoendienst	60.00	30.00
❑ 11 George Munger	20.00	10.00
❑ 12 Hank Majeski	20.00	10.00
❑ 13 Eddie Stanky	25.00	12.50
❑ 14 Alvin Dark	40.00	20.00
❑ 15 Johnny Pesky	25.00	12.50
❑ 16 Maurice McDermott	20.00	10.00
❑ 17 Pete Castiglione	20.00	10.00
❑ 18 Gil Coan	20.00	10.00
❑ 19 Sid Gordon	20.00	10.00
❑ 20 Del Crandall UER (Misspelled Crandell on card)	25.00	12.50
❑ 21 Snuffy Stirnweiss wearing St.L.Browns hat	25.00	12.50
❑ 22 Hank Sauer	25.00	12.50
❑ 23 Hoot Evers	20.00	10.00
❑ 24 Ewell Blackwell	40.00	20.00
❑ 25 Vic Raschi	60.00	30.00
❑ 26 Phil Rizzuto	125.00	60.00
❑ 27 Jim Konstanty	25.00	12.50
❑ 28 Eddie Waitkus	20.00	10.00
❑ 29 Allie Clark	20.00	10.00
❑ 30 Bob Feller	125.00	60.00
❑ 31 Roy Campanella	300.00	150.00
❑ 32 Duke Snider	250.00	125.00
❑ 33 Bob Hooper	20.00	10.00
❑ 34 Marty Marion	40.00	20.00
❑ 35 Al Zarilla	20.00	10.00
❑ 36 Joe Dobson	20.00	10.00
❑ 37 Whitey Lockman	40.00	20.00
❑ 38 Al Evans	20.00	10.00
❑ 39 Ray Scarborough	20.00	10.00
❑ 40 Gus Bell RC	60.00	30.00
❑ 41 Eddie Yost	25.00	12.50
❑ 42 Vern Bickford	20.00	10.00
❑ 43 Billy DeMars	20.00	10.00
❑ 44 Roy Smalley	20.00	10.00
❑ 45 Art Houtteman	20.00	10.00
❑ 46 George Kell 1941 UER	60.00	30.00
❑ 47 Grady Hatton	20.00	10.00
❑ 48 Ken Raffensberger	20.00	10.00
❑ 49 Jerry Coleman	25.00	12.50
❑ 50 Johnny Mize	80.00	40.00
❑ 51 Andy Seminick	20.00	10.00
❑ 52 Dick Sisler	40.00	20.00
❑ 53 Bob Lemon	60.00	30.00
❑ 54 Ray Boone RC	40.00	20.00
❑ 55 Gene Hermanski	20.00	10.00
❑ 56 Ralph Branca	60.00	30.00
❑ 57 Alex Kellner	20.00	10.00
❑ 58 Enos Slaughter	60.00	30.00
❑ 59 Randy Gumpert	20.00	10.00
❑ 60 Chico Carrasquel RC	60.00	30.00
❑ 61 Jim Hearn	25.00	12.50
❑ 62 Lou Boudreau	60.00	30.00
❑ 63 Bob Dillinger	20.00	10.00
❑ 64 Bill Werle	20.00	10.00
❑ 65 Mickey Vernon	40.00	20.00
❑ 66 Bob Elliott	25.00	12.50
❑ 67 Roy Sievers	25.00	12.50
❑ 68 Dick Kokos	20.00	10.00
❑ 69 Johnny Schmitz	20.00	10.00
❑ 70 Ron Northey	20.00	10.00
❑ 71 Jerry Priddy	20.00	10.00
❑ 72 Lloyd Merriman	20.00	10.00
❑ 73 Tommy Byrne	20.00	10.00
❑ 74 Billy Johnson	25.00	12.50
❑ 75 Russ Meyer RC	25.00	12.50
❑ 76 Stan Lopata	25.00	12.50
❑ 77 Mike Goliat	20.00	10.00
❑ 78 Early Wynn	60.00	30.00
❑ 79 Jim Hegan	25.00	12.50
❑ 80 Pee Wee Reese	200.00	100.00
❑ 81 Carl Furillo	60.00	30.00
❑ 82 Joe Tipton	20.00	10.00
❑ 83 Carl Scheib	20.00	10.00
❑ 84 Barney McCosky	20.00	10.00
❑ 85 Eddie Kazak	20.00	10.00
❑ 86 Harry Brecheen	25.00	12.50
❑ 87 Floyd Baker	20.00	10.00
❑ 88 Eddie Robinson	20.00	10.00
❑ 89 Hank Thompson	25.00	12.50
❑ 90 Dave Koslo	20.00	10.00
❑ 91 Clyde Vollmer	20.00	10.00
❑ 92 Vern Stephens	25.00	12.50
❑ 93 Danny O'Connell	20.00	10.00
❑ 94 Clyde McCullough	20.00	10.00
❑ 95 Sherry Robertson	20.00	10.00
❑ 96 Sandy Consuegra	20.00	10.00
❑ 97 Bob Kuzava	20.00	10.00
❑ 98 Willard Marshall	20.00	10.00
❑ 99 Earl Torgeson	20.00	10.00
❑ 100 Sherm Lollar	25.00	12.50
❑ 101 Owen Friend	20.00	10.00
❑ 102 Dutch Leonard	20.00	10.00
❑ 103 Andy Pafko	40.00	20.00
❑ 104 Virgil Trucks	25.00	12.50
❑ 105 Don Kolloway	20.00	10.00
❑ 106 Pat Mullin	20.00	10.00
❑ 107 Johnny Wyrostek	20.00	10.00
❑ 108 Virgil Stallcup	20.00	10.00
❑ 109 Allie Reynolds	60.00	30.00
❑ 110 Bobby Brown	40.00	20.00
❑ 111 Curt Simmons	25.00	12.50
❑ 112 Willie Jones	20.00	10.00
❑ 113 Bill Nicholson	20.00	10.00
❑ 114 Sam Zoldak Pictured in Indians uniform	20.00	10.00
❑ 115 Steve Gromek	20.00	10.00
❑ 116 Bruce Edwards	20.00	10.00
❑ 117 Eddie Miksis	20.00	10.00
❑ 118 Preacher Roe	60.00	30.00
❑ 119 Eddie Joost	20.00	10.00
❑ 120 Joe Coleman	25.00	12.50
❑ 121 Gerry Staley	20.00	10.00
❑ 122 Joe Garagiola RC	100.00	50.00
❑ 123 Howie Judson	20.00	10.00
❑ 124 Gus Niarhos	20.00	10.00
❑ 125 Bill Rigney	25.00	12.50
❑ 126 Bobby Thomson	60.00	30.00
❑ 127 Sal Maglie RC	60.00	30.00
❑ 128 Ellis Kinder	20.00	10.00
❑ 129 Matt Batts	20.00	10.00
❑ 130 Tom Saffell	20.00	10.00
❑ 131 Cliff Chambers	20.00	10.00
❑ 132 Cass Michaels	20.00	10.00
❑ 133 Sam Dente	20.00	10.00
❑ 134 Warren Spahn	125.00	60.00
❑ 135 Walker Cooper	20.00	10.00
❑ 136 Ray Coleman	20.00	10.00
❑ 137 Dick Starr	20.00	10.00
❑ 138 Phil Cavarretta	25.00	12.50
❑ 139 Doyle Lade	20.00	10.00
❑ 140 Eddie Lake	20.00	10.00
❑ 141 Fred Hutchinson	25.00	12.50
❑ 142 Aaron Robinson	20.00	10.00
❑ 143 Ted Kluszewski	80.00	40.00
❑ 144 Herman Wehmeier	20.00	10.00
❑ 145 Fred Sanford	25.00	12.50
❑ 146 Johnny Hopp	25.00	12.50
❑ 147 Ken Heintzelman	20.00	10.00
❑ 148 Granny Hamner	20.00	10.00
❑ 149 Bubba Church	20.00	10.00
❑ 150 Mike Garcia	25.00	12.50
❑ 151 Larry Doby	60.00	30.00
❑ 152 Cal Abrams	20.00	10.00
❑ 153 Rex Barney	25.00	12.50
❑ 154 Pete Suder	20.00	10.00
❑ 155 Lou Brissie	20.00	10.00
❑ 156 Del Rice	20.00	10.00
❑ 157 Al Brazle	20.00	10.00
❑ 158 Chuck Diering	20.00	10.00
❑ 159 Eddie Stewart	20.00	10.00
❑ 160 Phil Masi	20.00	10.00
❑ 161 Wes Westrum RC	20.00	10.00
❑ 162 Larry Jansen	25.00	12.50
❑ 163 Monte Kennedy	20.00	10.00
❑ 164 Bill Wight	20.00	10.00
❑ 165 Ted Williams UER Wrong birthdate	800.00	400.00
❑ 166 Stan Rojek Pictured in Pirates uniform	20.00	10.00
❑ 167 Murry Dickson	20.00	10.00
❑ 168 Sam Mele	20.00	10.00
❑ 169 Sid Hudson	20.00	10.00
❑ 170 Sibby Sisti	20.00	10.00
❑ 171 Buddy Kerr	20.00	10.00
❑ 172 Ned Garver	20.00	10.00
❑ 173 Hank Arft	20.00	10.00
❑ 174 Mickey Owen	25.00	12.50
❑ 175 Wayne Terwilliger	20.00	10.00
❑ 176 Vic Wertz	40.00	20.00
❑ 177 Charlie Keller	25.00	12.50
❑ 178 Ted Gray	20.00	10.00
❑ 179 Danny Litwhiler	20.00	10.00
❑ 180 Howie Fox	20.00	10.00
❑ 181 Casey Stengel MG	80.00	40.00
❑ 182 Tom Ferrick	20.00	10.00
❑ 183 Hank Bauer	60.00	30.00
❑ 184 Eddie Sawyer MG	40.00	20.00
❑ 185 Jimmy Bloodworth	20.00	10.00
❑ 186 Richie Ashburn	100.00	50.00
❑ 187 Al Rosen	40.00	20.00
❑ 188 Bobby Avila RC	25.00	12.50
❑ 189 Erv Palica	20.00	10.00
❑ 190 Joe Hatten	20.00	10.00
❑ 191 Billy Hitchcock	20.00	10.00
❑ 192 Hank Wyse	20.00	10.00
❑ 193 Ted Wilks	20.00	10.00
❑ 194 Peanuts Lowrey	20.00	10.00
❑ 195 Paul Richards MG (Caricature)	25.00	12.50
❑ 196 Billy Pierce RC	60.00	30.00
❑ 197 Bob Cain	20.00	10.00
❑ 198 Monte Irvin RC	100.00	50.00
❑ 199 Sheldon Jones	20.00	10.00
❑ 200 Jack Kramer Pictured in NY Giants uniform	20.00	10.00
❑ 201 Steve O'Neill MG	20.00	10.00
❑ 202 Mike Guerra	20.00	10.00
❑ 203 Vernon Law RC	60.00	30.00
❑ 204 Vic Lombardi	20.00	10.00

❑ 205 Mickey Grasso 20.00 10.00
❑ 206 Conrado Marrero 20.00 10.00
❑ 207 Billy Southworth MG 20.00 10.00
❑ 208 Blix Donnelly 20.00 10.00
❑ 209 Ken Wood 20.00 10.00
❑ 210 Les Moss 20.00 10.00
Pictured in St.L.Browns uniform
❑ 211 Hal Jeffcoat 20.00 10.00
❑ 212 Bob Rush 20.00 10.00
❑ 213 Neil Berry 20.00 10.00
❑ 214 Bob Swift 20.00 10.00
❑ 215 Ken Peterson 20.00 10.00
❑ 216 Connie Ryan 20.00 10.00
❑ 217 Joe Page 25.00 12.50
❑ 218 Ed Lopat 60.00 30.00
❑ 219 Gene Woodling RC 60.00 30.00
❑ 220 Bob Miller 20.00 10.00
❑ 221 Dick Whitman 20.00 10.00
❑ 222 Thurman Tucker 20.00 10.00
❑ 223 Johnny VanderMeer 40.00 20.00
❑ 224 Billy Cox 25.00 12.50
❑ 225 Dan Bankhead 40.00 20.00
❑ 226 Jimmy Dykes MG 20.00 10.00
❑ 227 Bobby Shantz UER 25.00 12.50
Sic, Schantz
❑ 228 Cloyd Boyer 25.00 12.50
❑ 229 Bill Howerton 20.00 10.00
Pictured in St.L.Cardinals uniform
❑ 230 Max Lanier 20.00 10.00
❑ 231 Luis Aloma 20.00 10.00
❑ 232 Nelson Fox RC 250.00 125.00
❑ 233 Leo Durocher MG 60.00 30.00
❑ 234 Clint Hartung 25.00 12.50
❑ 235 Jack Lohrke 20.00 10.00
❑ 236 Buddy Rosar 20.00 10.00
❑ 237 Billy Goodman 25.00 12.50
❑ 238 Pete Reiser 40.00 20.00
❑ 239 Bill MacDonald 20.00 10.00
❑ 240 Joe Haynes 20.00 10.00
❑ 241 Irv Noren 25.00 12.50
❑ 242 Sam Jethroe 25.00 12.50
❑ 243 Johnny Antonelli 25.00 12.50
❑ 244 Cliff Fannin 20.00 10.00
❑ 245 John Berardino RC 60.00 30.00
❑ 246 Bill Serena 20.00 10.00
❑ 247 Bob Ramazzotti 20.00 10.00
❑ 248 Johnny Klippstein 20.00 10.00
❑ 249 Johnny Groth 20.00 10.00
❑ 250 Hank Borowy 20.00 10.00
❑ 251 Willard Ramsdell 20.00 10.00
❑ 252 Dixie Howell 20.00 10.00
❑ 253 Mickey Mantle RC 8000.00 4200.00
❑ 254 Jackie Jensen RC 100.00 50.00
❑ 255 Milo Candini 50.00 25.00
❑ 256 Ken Silvestri 50.00 25.00
❑ 257 Birdie Tebbetts RC 60.00 30.00
❑ 258 Luke Easter RC 60.00 30.00
❑ 259 Chuck Dressen MG 60.00 30.00
❑ 260 Carl Erskine RC 100.00 50.00
❑ 261 Wally Moses 60.00 30.00
❑ 262 Gus Zernial 60.00 30.00
❑ 263 Howie Pollet 60.00 30.00
Pictured in Cardinals uniform
❑ 264 Don Richmond 50.00 25.00
❑ 265 Steve Bilko 50.00 25.00
❑ 266 Harry Dorish 50.00 25.00
❑ 267 Ken Holcombe 50.00 25.00
❑ 268 Don Mueller 60.00 30.00
❑ 269 Ray Noble 50.00 25.00
❑ 270 Willard Nixon 50.00 25.00
❑ 271 Tommy Wright 50.00 25.00
❑ 272 Billy Meyer MG 50.00 25.00
❑ 273 Danny Murtaugh 60.00 30.00
❑ 274 George Metkovich 50.00 25.00
❑ 275 Bucky Harris MG 80.00 40.00
❑ 276 Frank Quinn 50.00 25.00
❑ 277 Roy Hartsfield 50.00 25.00
❑ 278 Norman Roy 50.00 25.00
❑ 279 Jim Delsing 50.00 25.00
❑ 280 Frank Overmire 50.00 25.00
Pictured in Browns uniform
❑ 281 Al Widmar 50.00 25.00
❑ 282 Frank Frisch MG 100.00 50.00
❑ 283 Walt Dubiel 50.00 25.00
❑ 284 Gene Bearden 60.00 30.00
❑ 285 Johnny Lipon 50.00 25.00
❑ 286 Bob Usher 50.00 25.00
❑ 287 Jim Blackburn 50.00 25.00
❑ 288 Bobby Adams 50.00 25.00
❑ 289 Cliff Mapes 60.00 30.00
❑ 290 Bill Dickey CO 100.00 50.00
❑ 291 Tommy Henrich CO 80.00 40.00
❑ 292 Eddie Pellagrini 50.00 25.00
❑ 293 Ken Johnson 50.00 25.00
❑ 294 Jocko Thompson 50.00 25.00
❑ 295 Al Lopez MG 125.00 60.00
❑ 296 Bob Kennedy 60.00 30.00
❑ 297 Dave Philley 50.00 25.00
❑ 298 Joe Astroth 50.00 25.00
❑ 299 Clyde King 50.00 25.00
❑ 300 Hal Rice 50.00 25.00
❑ 301 Tommy Glaviano 50.00 25.00
❑ 302 Jim Busby 50.00 25.00
❑ 303 Marv Rotblatt 50.00 25.00
❑ 304 Al Gettell 50.00 25.00
❑ 305 Willie Mays RC 2500.00 1500.00
❑ 306 Jim Piersall RC 125.00 60.00
❑ 307 Walt Masterson 50.00 25.00
❑ 308 Ted Beard 50.00 25.00
❑ 309 Mel Queen 50.00 25.00
❑ 310 Erv Dusak 50.00 25.00
❑ 311 Mickey Harris 50.00 25.00
❑ 312 Gene Mauch RC 60.00 30.00
❑ 313 Ray Mueller 50.00 25.00
❑ 314 Johnny Sain 80.00 40.00
❑ 315 Zack Taylor MG 50.00 25.00
❑ 316 Duane Pillette 50.00 25.00
❑ 317 Smoky Burgess RC 80.00 40.00
❑ 318 Warren Hacker 50.00 25.00
❑ 319 Red Rolfe MG 60.00 30.00
❑ 320 Hal White 50.00 25.00
❑ 321 Earl Johnson 50.00 25.00
❑ 322 Luke Sewell MG 60.00 30.00
❑ 323 Joe Adcock RC 80.00 40.00
❑ 324 Johnny Pramesa RC 125.00 38.00

1952 Bowman

	NM	Ex
COMPLETE SET (252)	8500.00	4200.00
COMMON CARD (1-216)	15.00	6.75
COMMON (217-252)	60.00	30.00
WRAPPER (1-cent)	200.00	100.00
WRAPPER (5-cent)	100.00	50.00

❑ 1 Yogi Berra 600.00 220.00
❑ 2 Bobby Thomson 40.00 20.00
❑ 3 Fred Hutchinson 25.00 12.50
❑ 4 Robin Roberts 80.00 40.00
❑ 5 Minnie Minoso RC 125.00 60.00
❑ 6 Virgil Stallcup 15.00 7.50
❑ 7 Mike Garcia 25.00 12.50
❑ 8 Pee Wee Reese 150.00 75.00
❑ 9 Vern Stephens 25.00 12.50
❑ 10 Bob Hooper 15.00 7.50
❑ 11 Ralph Kiner 60.00 30.00
❑ 12 Max Surkont 15.00 7.50
❑ 13 Cliff Mapes 15.00 7.50
❑ 14 Cliff Chambers 15.00 7.50
❑ 15 Sam Mele 15.00 7.50
❑ 16 Turk Lown 15.00 7.50
❑ 17 Ed Lopat 40.00 20.00
❑ 18 Don Mueller 25.00 12.50
❑ 19 Bob Cain 15.00 7.50
❑ 20 Willie Jones 15.00 7.50
❑ 21 Nellie Fox 100.00 50.00
❑ 22 Willard Ramsdell 15.00 7.50
❑ 23 Bob Lemon 60.00 30.00
❑ 24 Carl Furillo 40.00 20.00
❑ 25 Mickey McDermott 15.00 7.50
❑ 26 Eddie Joost 15.00 7.50
❑ 27 Joe Garagiola 40.00 20.00
❑ 28 Roy Hartsfield 15.00 7.50
❑ 29 Ned Garver 15.00 7.50
❑ 30 Red Schoendienst 60.00 30.00
❑ 31 Eddie Yost 25.00 12.50
❑ 32 Eddie Miksis 15.00 7.50
❑ 33 Gil McDougald RC 80.00 40.00
❑ 34 Alvin Dark 25.00 12.50
❑ 35 Granny Hamner 15.00 7.50
❑ 36 Cass Michaels 15.00 7.50
❑ 37 Vic Raschi 25.00 12.50
❑ 38 Whitey Lockman 25.00 12.50
❑ 39 Vic Wertz 25.00 12.50
❑ 40 Bubba Church 15.00 7.50
❑ 41 Chico Carrasquel 25.00 12.50
❑ 42 Johnny Wyrostek 15.00 7.50
❑ 43 Bob Feller 150.00 75.00
❑ 44 Roy Campanella 250.00 125.00
❑ 45 Johnny Pesky 25.00 12.50
❑ 46 Carl Scheib 15.00 7.50
❑ 47 Pete Castiglione 15.00 7.50
❑ 48 Vern Bickford 15.00 7.50
❑ 49 Jim Hearn 15.00 7.50
❑ 50 Gerry Staley 15.00 7.50
❑ 51 Gil Coan 15.00 7.50
❑ 52 Phil Rizzuto 150.00 75.00
❑ 53 Richie Ashburn 125.00 60.00
❑ 54 Billy Pierce 25.00 12.50
❑ 55 Ken Raffensberger 15.00 7.50
❑ 56 Clyde King 25.00 12.50
❑ 57 Clyde Vollmer 15.00 7.50
❑ 58 Hank Majeski 15.00 7.50
❑ 59 Murry Dickson 15.00 7.50
❑ 60 Sid Gordon 15.00 7.50
❑ 61 Tommy Byrne 15.00 7.50
❑ 62 Joe Presko 15.00 7.50
❑ 63 Irv Noren 15.00 7.50
❑ 64 Roy Smalley 15.00 7.50
❑ 65 Hank Bauer 40.00 20.00
❑ 66 Sal Maglie 25.00 12.50
❑ 67 Johnny Groth 15.00 7.50
❑ 68 Jim Busby 15.00 7.50
❑ 69 Joe Adcock 25.00 12.50
❑ 70 Carl Erskine 40.00 20.00
❑ 71 Vernon Law 25.00 12.50
❑ 72 Earl Torgeson 15.00 7.50
❑ 73 Jerry Coleman 25.00 12.50
❑ 74 Wes Westrum 25.00 12.50
❑ 75 George Kell 60.00 30.00
❑ 76 Del Ennis 25.00 12.50
❑ 77 Eddie Robinson 15.00 7.50
❑ 78 Lloyd Merriman 15.00 7.50
❑ 79 Lou Brissie 15.00 7.50
❑ 80 Gil Hodges 100.00 50.00
❑ 81 Billy Goodman 25.00 12.50
❑ 82 Gus Zernial 25.00 12.50
❑ 83 Howie Pollet 15.00 7.50
❑ 84 Sam Jethroe 25.00 12.50
❑ 85 Marty Marion CO 25.00 12.50
❑ 86 Cal Abrams 15.00 7.50
❑ 87 Mickey Vernon 25.00 12.50
❑ 88 Bruce Edwards 15.00 7.50
❑ 89 Billy Hitchcock 15.00 7.50
❑ 90 Larry Jansen 25.00 12.50
❑ 91 Don Kolloway 15.00 7.50
❑ 92 Eddie Waitkus 25.00 12.50
❑ 93 Paul Richards MG 25.00 12.50
❑ 94 Luke Sewell MG 25.00 12.50
❑ 95 Luke Easter 25.00 12.50
❑ 96 Ralph Branca 25.00 12.50
❑ 97 Willard Marshall 15.00 7.50
❑ 98 Jimmy Dykes MG 25.00 12.50
❑ 99 Clyde McCullough 15.00 7.50
❑ 100 Sibby Sisti 15.00 7.50
❑ 101 Mickey Mantle 2500.00 1250.00
❑ 102 Peanuts Lowrey 15.00 7.50
❑ 103 Joe Haynes 15.00 7.50
❑ 104 Hal Jeffcoat 15.00 7.50
❑ 105 Bobby Brown 25.00 12.50

No.	Player	NM	Ex
106	Randy Gumpert	15.00	7.50
107	Del Rice	15.00	7.50
108	George Metkovich	15.00	7.50
109	Tom Morgan	15.00	7.50
110	Max Lanier	15.00	7.50
111	Hoot Evers	15.00	7.50
112	Smoky Burgess	25.00	12.50
113	Al Zarilla	15.00	7.50
114	Frank Hiller	15.00	7.50
115	Larry Doby	60.00	30.00
116	Duke Snider	200.00	100.00
117	Bill Wight	15.00	7.50
118	Ray Murray	15.00	7.50
119	Bill Howerton	15.00	7.50
120	Chet Nichols	15.00	7.50
121	Al Corwin	15.00	7.50
122	Billy Johnson	15.00	7.50
123	Sid Hudson	15.00	7.50
124	Birdie Tebbetts	15.00	7.50
125	Howie Fox	15.00	7.50
126	Phil Cavarretta	25.00	12.50
127	Dick Sisler	15.00	7.50
128	Don Newcombe	60.00	30.00
129	Gus Niarhos	15.00	7.50
130	Allie Clark	15.00	7.50
131	Bob Swift	15.00	7.50
132	Dave Cole	15.00	7.50
133	Dick Kryhoski	15.00	7.50
134	Al Brazle	15.00	7.50
135	Mickey Harris	15.00	7.50
136	Gene Hermanski	15.00	7.50
137	Stan Rojek	15.00	7.50
138	Ted Wilks	15.00	7.50
139	Jerry Priddy	15.00	7.50
140	Ray Scarborough	15.00	7.50
141	Hank Edwards	15.00	7.50
142	Early Wynn	60.00	30.00
143	Sandy Consuegra	15.00	7.50
144	Joe Hatton	15.00	7.50
145	Johnny Mize	60.00	30.00
146	Leo Durocher MG	60.00	30.00
147	Marlin Stuart	15.00	7.50
148	Ken Heintzelman	15.00	7.50
149	Howie Judson	15.00	7.50
150	Herman Wehmeier	15.00	7.50
151	Al Rosen	25.00	12.50
152	Billy Cox	15.00	7.50
153	Fred Hatfield	15.00	7.50
154	Ferris Fain	25.00	12.50
155	Billy Meyer MG	15.00	7.50
156	Warren Spahn	125.00	60.00
157	Jim Delsing	15.00	7.50
158	Bucky Harris MG	40.00	20.00
159	Dutch Leonard	15.00	7.50
160	Eddie Stanky	25.00	12.50
161	Jackie Jensen	40.00	20.00
162	Monte Irvin	60.00	30.00
163	Johnny Lipon	15.00	7.50
164	Connie Ryan	15.00	7.50
165	Saul Rogovin	15.00	7.50
166	Bobby Adams	15.00	7.50
167	Bobby Avila	25.00	12.50
168	Preacher Roe	25.00	12.50
169	Walt Dropo	25.00	12.50
170	Joe Astroth	15.00	7.50
171	Mel Queen	15.00	7.50
172	Ebba St.Claire	15.00	7.50
173	Gene Bearden	15.00	7.50
174	Mickey Grasso	15.00	7.50
175	Randy Jackson	15.00	7.50
176	Harry Brecheen	25.00	12.50
177	Gene Woodling	25.00	12.50
178	Dave Williams RC	25.00	12.50
179	Pete Suder	15.00	7.50
180	Ed Fitzgerald	15.00	7.50
181	Joe Collins RC	25.00	12.50
182	Dave Koslo	15.00	7.50
183	Pat Mullin	15.00	7.50
184	Curt Simmons	25.00	12.50
185	Eddie Stewart	15.00	7.50
186	Frank Smith	15.00	7.50
187	Jim Hegan	25.00	12.50
188	Chuck Dressen MG	25.00	12.50
189	Jimmy Piersall	25.00	12.50
190	Dick Fowler	15.00	7.50
191	Bob Friend RC	40.00	20.00
192	John Cusick	15.00	7.50
193	Bobby Young	15.00	7.50
194	Bob Porterfield	15.00	7.50
195	Frank Baumholtz	15.00	7.50
196	Stan Musial	500.00	300.00
197	Charlie Silvera RC	15.00	7.50
198	Chuck Diering	15.00	7.50
199	Ted Gray	15.00	7.50
200	Ken Silvestri	15.00	7.50
201	Ray Coleman	15.00	7.50
202	Harry Perkowski	15.00	7.50
203	Steve Gromek	15.00	7.50
204	Andy Pafko	25.00	12.50
205	Walt Masterson	15.00	7.50
206	Elmer Valo	15.00	7.50
207	George Strickland	15.00	7.50
208	Walker Cooper	15.00	7.50
209	Dick Littlefield	15.00	7.50
210	Archie Wilson	15.00	7.50
211	Paul Minner	15.00	7.50
212	Solly Hemus RC	15.00	7.50
213	Monte Kennedy	15.00	7.50
214	Ray Boone	15.00	7.50
215	Sheldon Jones	15.00	7.50
216	Matt Batts	15.00	7.50
217	Casey Stengel MG	150.00	75.00
218	Willie Mays	1500.00	750.00
219	Neil Berry	60.00	30.00
220	Russ Meyer	60.00	30.00
221	Lou Kretlow	60.00	30.00
222	Dixie Howell	60.00	30.00
223	Harry Simpson	60.00	30.00
224	Johnny Schmitz	60.00	30.00
225	Del Wilber	60.00	30.00
226	Alex Kellner	60.00	30.00
227	Clyde Sukeforth CO	60.00	30.00
228	Bob Chipman	60.00	30.00
229	Hank Arft	60.00	30.00
230	Frank Shea	60.00	30.00
231	Dee Fondy	60.00	30.00
232	Enos Slaughter	100.00	50.00
233	Bob Kuzava	60.00	30.00
234	Fred Fitzsimmons CO	60.00	30.00
235	Steve Souchock	60.00	30.00
236	Tommy Brown	60.00	30.00
237	Sherm Lollar	60.00	30.00
238	Roy McMillan RC	60.00	30.00
239	Dale Mitchell	60.00	30.00
240	Billy Loes RC	60.00	30.00
241	Mel Parnell	60.00	30.00
242	Everett Kell	60.00	30.00
243	George Munger	60.00	30.00
244	Lew Burdette RC	80.00	40.00
245	George Schmees	60.00	30.00
246	Jerry Snyder	60.00	30.00
247	Johnny Pramesa	60.00	30.00
248	Bill Werle Full name in signature	60.00	30.00
248A	Bill Werle Signature on front has no W	60.00	30.00
249	Hank Thompson	60.00	30.00
250	Ike Delock	60.00	30.00
251	Jack Lohrke	60.00	30.00
252	Frank Crosetti CO	125.00	31.00

1953 Bowman Color

	NM	Ex
COMPLETE SET (160)	15000.00	7500.00
COMMON CARD (1-112)	40.00	20.00
COMMON (113-128)	80.00	40.00
COMMON (129-160)	75.00	38.00
WRAPPER (1-cent)	400.00	200.00
WRAPPER (5-CENT)	300.00	150.00

No.	Player	NM	Ex
1	Dave Williams	175.00	35.00
2	Vic Wertz	50.00	25.00
3	Sam Jethroe	50.00	25.00
4	Art Houtteman	40.00	20.00
5	Sid Gordon	40.00	20.00
6	Joe Ginsberg	40.00	20.00
7	Harry Chiti	40.00	20.00
8	Al Rosen	50.00	25.00
9	Phil Rizzuto	225.00	110.00
10	Richie Ashburn	150.00	75.00
11	Bobby Shantz	50.00	25.00
12	Carl Erskine	60.00	30.00
13	Gus Zernial	50.00	25.00
14	Billy Loes	50.00	25.00
15	Jim Busby	40.00	20.00
16	Bob Friend	50.00	25.00
17	Gerry Staley	40.00	20.00
18	Nellie Fox	150.00	75.00
19	Alvin Dark	50.00	25.00
20	Don Lenhardt	40.00	20.00
21	Joe Garagiola	60.00	30.00
22	Bob Porterfield	40.00	20.00
23	Herman Wehmeier	40.00	20.00
24	Jackie Jensen	60.00	30.00
25	Hoot Evers	40.00	20.00
26	Roy McMillan	50.00	25.00
27	Vic Raschi	60.00	30.00
28	Smoky Burgess	50.00	25.00
29	Bobby Avila	50.00	25.00
30	Phil Cavarretta	50.00	25.00
31	Jimmy Dykes MG	50.00	25.00
32	Stan Musial	600.00	400.00
33	Pee Wee Reese	1000.00	500.00
34	Gil Coan	40.00	20.00
35	Maurice McDermott	40.00	20.00
36	Minnie Minoso	80.00	40.00
37	Jim Wilson	40.00	20.00
38	Harry Byrd	40.00	20.00
39	Paul Richards MG	50.00	25.00
40	Larry Doby	100.00	50.00
41	Sammy White	40.00	20.00
42	Tommy Brown	40.00	20.00
43	Mike Garcia	50.00	25.00
44	Yogi Berra Hank Bauer Mickey Mantle	800.00	400.00
45	Walt Dropo	50.00	25.00
46	Roy Campanella	350.00	180.00
47	Ned Garver	40.00	20.00
48	Hank Sauer	50.00	25.00
49	Eddie Stanky MG	50.00	25.00
50	Lou Kretlow	40.00	20.00
51	Monte Irvin	80.00	40.00
52	Marty Marion MG	50.00	25.00
53	Del Rice	40.00	20.00
54	Chico Carrasquel	40.00	20.00
55	Leo Durocher MG	80.00	40.00
56	Bob Cain	40.00	20.00
57	Lou Boudreau MG	80.00	40.00
58	Willard Marshall	40.00	20.00
59	Mickey Mantle	2000.00	1000.00
60	Granny Hamner	40.00	20.00
61	George Kell	80.00	40.00
62	Ted Kluszewski	100.00	50.00
63	Gil McDougald	80.00	40.00
64	Curt Simmons	50.00	25.00
65	Robin Roberts	125.00	60.00
66	Mel Parnell	50.00	25.00
67	Mel Clark	40.00	20.00
68	Allie Reynolds	60.00	30.00
69	Charlie Grimm MG	50.00	25.00
70	Clint Courtney	40.00	20.00
71	Paul Minner	40.00	20.00
72	Ted Gray	40.00	20.00
73	Billy Pierce	50.00	25.00
74	Don Mueller	50.00	25.00
75	Saul Rogovin	40.00	20.00
76	Jim Hearn	40.00	20.00

❑ 77 Mickey Grasso 40.00 20.00
❑ 78 Carl Furillo 60.00 30.00
❑ 79 Ray Boone 50.00 25.00
❑ 80 Ralph Kiner 100.00 50.00
❑ 81 Enos Slaughter 100.00 50.00
❑ 82 Joe Astroth 40.00 20.00
❑ 83 Jack Daniels 40.00 20.00
❑ 84 Hank Bauer 60.00 30.00
❑ 85 Solly Hemus 40.00 20.00
❑ 86 Harry Simpson 40.00 20.00
❑ 87 Harry Perkowski 40.00 20.00
❑ 88 Joe Dobson 40.00 20.00
❑ 89 Sandy Consuegra 40.00 20.00
❑ 90 Joe Nuxhall 50.00 25.00
❑ 91 Steve Souchock 40.00 20.00
❑ 92 Gil Hodges 300.00 150.00
❑ 93 Phil Rizzuto and 300.00 150.00
Billy Martin
❑ 94 Bob Addis 40.00 20.00
❑ 95 Wally Moses CO 50.00 25.00
❑ 96 Sal Maglie 50.00 25.00
❑ 97 Eddie Mathews 350.00 180.00
❑ 98 Hector Rodriguez 40.00 20.00
❑ 99 Warren Spahn 350.00 180.00
❑ 100 Bill Wight 40.00 20.00
❑ 101 Red Schoendienst 80.00 40.00
❑ 102 Jim Hegan 50.00 25.00
❑ 103 Del Ennis 50.00 25.00
❑ 104 Luke Easter 50.00 25.00
❑ 105 Eddie Joost 40.00 20.00
❑ 106 Ken Raffensberger 40.00 20.00
❑ 107 Alex Kellner 40.00 20.00
❑ 108 Bobby Adams 40.00 20.00
❑ 109 Ken Wood 40.00 20.00
❑ 110 Bob Rush 40.00 20.00
❑ 111 Jim Dyck 40.00 20.00
❑ 112 Toby Atwell 40.00 20.00
❑ 113 Karl Drews 80.00 40.00
❑ 114 Bob Feller 500.00 250.00
❑ 115 Cloyd Boyer 80.00 40.00
❑ 116 Eddie Yost 100.00 50.00
❑ 117 Duke Snider 600.00 300.00
❑ 118 Billy Martin 400.00 200.00
❑ 119 Dale Mitchell 100.00 50.00
❑ 120 Marlin Stuart 80.00 40.00
❑ 121 Yogi Berra 800.00 400.00
❑ 122 Bill Serena 80.00 40.00
❑ 123 Johnny Lipon 80.00 40.00
❑ 124 Charlie Dressen MG .. 100.00 50.00
❑ 125 Fred Hatfield 80.00 40.00
❑ 126 Al Corwin 80.00 40.00
❑ 127 Dick Kryhoski 80.00 40.00
❑ 128 Whitey Lockman 100.00 50.00
❑ 129 Russ Meyer 75.00 38.00
❑ 130 Cass Michaels 75.00 38.00
❑ 131 Connie Ryan 75.00 38.00
❑ 132 Fred Hutchinson 90.00 45.00
❑ 133 Willie Jones 75.00 38.00
❑ 134 Johnny Pesky 90.00 45.00
❑ 135 Bobby Morgan 75.00 38.00
❑ 136 Jim Brideweser 75.00 38.00
❑ 137 Sam Dente 75.00 38.00
❑ 138 Bubba Church 75.00 38.00
❑ 139 Pete Runnels 90.00 45.00
❑ 140 Al Brazle 75.00 38.00
❑ 141 Frank Shea 75.00 38.00
❑ 142 Larry Miggins 75.00 38.00
❑ 143 Al Lopez MG 110.00 55.00
❑ 144 Warren Hacker 75.00 38.00
❑ 145 George Shuba 90.00 45.00
❑ 146 Early Wynn 200.00 100.00
❑ 147 Clem Koshorek 75.00 38.00
❑ 148 Billy Goodman 90.00 45.00
❑ 149 Al Corwin 75.00 38.00
❑ 150 Carl Scheib 75.00 38.00
❑ 151 Joe Adcock 110.00 55.00
❑ 152 Clyde Vollmer 75.00 38.00
❑ 153 Whitey Ford 800.00 400.00
❑ 154 Turk Lown 75.00 38.00
❑ 155 Allie Clark 75.00 38.00
❑ 156 Max Surkont 75.00 38.00
❑ 157 Sherm Lollar 90.00 45.00
❑ 158 Howard Fox 75.00 38.00
❑ 159 Mickey Vernon UER 90.00 45.00
(Photo actually
Floyd Baker)
❑ 160 Cal Abrams 500.00 170.00

1954 Bowman

	NM	Ex
COMPLETE SET (224)	4000.00	2000.00
WRAP.(1-CENT, DATED)	150.00	75.00
WRAP.(1-CENT, UNDATED)	200.00	100.00
WRAP.(5-CENT, DATED)	150.00	75.00
WRAP.(5-CENT, UNDATED)	60.00	30.00

❑ 1 Phil Rizzuto 175.00 52.50
❑ 2 Jackie Jensen 30.00 15.00
❑ 3 Marion Fricano 12.00 6.00
❑ 4 Bob Hooper 12.00 6.00
❑ 5 Billy Hunter 12.00 6.00
❑ 6 Nellie Fox 80.00 40.00
❑ 7 Walt Dropo 20.00 10.00
❑ 8 Jim Busby 12.00 6.00
❑ 9 Dave Williams 12.00 6.00
❑ 10 Carl Erskine 20.00 10.00
❑ 11 Sid Gordon 12.00 6.00
❑ 12 Roy McMillan 20.00 10.00
❑ 13 Paul Minner 12.00 6.00
❑ 14 Gerry Staley 12.00 6.00
❑ 15 Richie Ashburn 80.00 40.00
❑ 16 Jim Wilson 12.00 6.00
❑ 17 Tom Gorman 12.00 6.00
❑ 18 Hoot Evers 12.00 6.00
❑ 19 Bobby Shantz 20.00 10.00
❑ 20 Art Houtteman 12.00 6.00
❑ 21 Vic Wertz 20.00 10.00
❑ 22 Sam Mele 12.00 6.00
❑ 23 Harvey Kuenn RC 30.00 15.00
❑ 24 Bob Porterfield 12.00 6.00
❑ 25 Wes Westrum 20.00 10.00
❑ 26 Billy Cox 20.00 10.00
❑ 27 Dick Cole 12.00 6.00
❑ 28 Jim Greengrass 12.00 6.00
❑ 29 Johnny Klippstein 12.00 6.00
❑ 30 Del Rice 12.00 6.00
❑ 31 Smoky Burgess 20.00 10.00
❑ 32 Del Crandall 20.00 10.00
❑ 33A Vic Raschi 20.00 10.00
(No mention of
trade on back)
❑ 33B Vic Raschi 30.00 15.00
(Traded to St.Louis)
❑ 34 Sammy White 12.00 6.00
❑ 35 Eddie Joost 12.00 6.00
❑ 36 George Strickland 12.00 6.00
❑ 37 Dick Kokos 12.00 6.00
❑ 38 Minnie Minoso 30.00 15.00
❑ 39 Ned Garver 12.00 6.00
❑ 40 Gil Coan 12.00 6.00
❑ 41 Alvin Dark 20.00 10.00
❑ 42 Billy Loes 20.00 10.00
❑ 43 Bob Friend 20.00 10.00
❑ 44 Harry Perkowski 12.00 6.00
❑ 45 Ralph Kiner 50.00 25.00
❑ 46 Rip Repulski 12.00 6.00
❑ 47 Granny Hamner 12.00 6.00
❑ 48 Jack Dittmer 12.00 6.00
❑ 49 Harry Byrd 12.00 6.00
❑ 50 George Kell 50.00 25.00
❑ 51 Alex Kellner 12.00 6.00
❑ 52 Joe Ginsberg 12.00 6.00
❑ 53 Don Lenhardt 12.00 6.00
❑ 54 Chico Carrasquel 12.00 6.00
❑ 55 Jim Delsing 12.00 6.00
❑ 56 Maurice McDermott 12.00 6.00
❑ 57 Hoyt Wilhelm 50.00 25.00
❑ 58 Pee Wee Reese 80.00 40.00
❑ 59 Bob Schultz 12.00 6.00
❑ 60 Fred Baczewski 12.00 6.00
❑ 61 Eddie Miksis 12.00 6.00
❑ 62 Enos Slaughter 50.00 25.00
❑ 63 Earl Torgeson 12.00 6.00
❑ 64 Eddie Mathews 80.00 40.00
❑ 65 Mickey Mantle 1500.00 750.00
❑ 66A Ted Williams 3000.00 1500.00
❑ 66B Jimmy Piersall 80.00 40.00
❑ 67 Carl Scheib 12.00 6.00
❑ 68 Bobby Avila 20.00 10.00
❑ 69 Clint Courtney 12.00 6.00
❑ 70 Willard Marshall 12.00 6.00
❑ 71 Ted Gray 12.00 6.00
❑ 72 Eddie Yost 20.00 10.00
❑ 73 Don Mueller 20.00 10.00
❑ 74 Jim Gilliam 30.00 15.00
❑ 75 Max Surkont 12.00 6.00
❑ 76 Joe Nuxhall 20.00 10.00
❑ 77 Bob Rush 12.00 6.00
❑ 78 Sal Yvars 12.00 6.00
❑ 79 Curt Simmons 20.00 10.00
❑ 80 Johnny Logan 12.00 6.00
❑ 81 Jerry Coleman 20.00 10.00
❑ 82 Billy Goodman 20.00 10.00
❑ 83 Ray Murray 12.00 6.00
❑ 84 Larry Doby 50.00 25.00
❑ 85 Jim Dyck 12.00 6.00
❑ 86 Harry Dorish 12.00 6.00
❑ 87 Don Lund 12.00 6.00
❑ 88 Tom Umphlett 12.00 6.00
❑ 89 Willie Mays 500.00 250.00
❑ 90 Roy Campanella 150.00 75.00
❑ 91 Cal Abrams 12.00 6.00
❑ 92 Ken Raffensberger 12.00 6.00
❑ 93 Bill Serena 12.00 6.00
❑ 94 Solly Hemus 12.00 6.00
❑ 95 Robin Roberts 50.00 25.00
❑ 96 Joe Adcock 20.00 10.00
❑ 97 Gil McDougald 20.00 10.00
❑ 98 Ellis Kinder 12.00 6.00
❑ 99 Pete Suder 12.00 6.00
❑ 100 Mike Garcia 20.00 10.00
❑ 101 Don Larsen RC 80.00 40.00
❑ 102 Billy Pierce 20.00 10.00
❑ 103 Steve Souchock 12.00 6.00
❑ 104 Frank Shea 12.00 6.00
❑ 105 Sal Maglie 20.00 10.00
❑ 106 Clem Labine 20.00 10.00
❑ 107 Paul LaPalme 12.00 6.00
❑ 108 Bobby Adams 12.00 6.00
❑ 109 Roy Smalley 12.00 6.00
❑ 110 Red Schoendienst 50.00 25.00
❑ 111 Murry Dickson 12.00 6.00
❑ 112 Andy Pafko 20.00 10.00
❑ 113 Allie Reynolds 20.00 10.00
❑ 114 Willard Nixon 12.00 6.00
❑ 115 Don Bollweg 12.00 6.00
❑ 116 Luke Easter 20.00 10.00
❑ 117 Dick Kryhoski 12.00 6.00
❑ 118 Bob Boyd 12.00 6.00
❑ 119 Fred Hatfield 12.00 6.00
❑ 120 Mel Hoderlein 12.00 6.00
❑ 121 Ray Katt 12.00 6.00
❑ 122 Carl Furillo 30.00 15.00
❑ 123 Toby Atwell 12.00 6.00
❑ 124 Gus Bell 20.00 10.00
❑ 125 Warren Hacker 12.00 6.00
❑ 126 Cliff Chambers 12.00 6.00
❑ 127 Del Ennis 20.00 10.00
❑ 128 Ebba St.Claire 12.00 6.00
❑ 129 Hank Bauer 30.00 15.00
❑ 130 Milt Bolling 12.00 6.00
❑ 131 Joe Astroth 12.00 6.00
❑ 132 Bob Feller 80.00 40.00
❑ 133 Duane Pillette 12.00 6.00
❑ 134 Luis Aloma 12.00 6.00
❑ 135 Johnny Pesky 20.00 10.00
❑ 136 Clyde Vollmer 12.00 6.00
❑ 137 Al Corwin 12.00 6.00
❑ 138 Gil Hodges 80.00 40.00
❑ 139 Preston Ward 12.00 6.00
❑ 140 Saul Rogovin 12.00 6.00

Card	NM	Ex
❑ 141 Joe Garagiola	30.00	15.00
❑ 142 Al Brazle	12.00	6.00
❑ 143 Willie Jones	12.00	6.00
❑ 144 Ernie Johnson RC	30.00	15.00
❑ 145 Billy Martin	80.00	40.00
❑ 146 Dick Gernert	12.00	6.00
❑ 147 Joe DeMaestri	12.00	6.00
❑ 148 Dale Mitchell	20.00	10.00
❑ 149 Bob Young	12.00	6.00
❑ 150 Cass Michaels	12.00	6.00
❑ 151 Pat Mullin	12.00	6.00
❑ 152 Mickey Vernon	20.00	10.00
❑ 153 Whitey Lockman	20.00	10.00
❑ 154 Don Newcombe	30.00	15.00
❑ 155 Frank Thomas RC	20.00	10.00
❑ 156 Rocky Bridges	12.00	6.00
❑ 157 Turk Lown	12.00	6.00
❑ 158 Stu Miller	20.00	10.00
❑ 159 Johnny Lindell	12.00	6.00
❑ 160 Danny O'Connell	12.00	6.00
❑ 161 Yogi Berra	175.00	90.00
❑ 162 Ted Lepcio	12.00	6.00
❑ 163A Dave Philley (No mention of trade on back)	20.00	10.00
❑ 163B Dave Philley (Traded to Cleveland)	30.00	15.00
❑ 164 Early Wynn	50.00	25.00
❑ 165 Johnny Groth	12.00	6.00
❑ 166 Sandy Consuegra	12.00	6.00
❑ 167 Billy Hoeft	12.00	6.00
❑ 168 Ed Fitzgerald	12.00	6.00
❑ 169 Larry Jansen	20.00	10.00
❑ 170 Duke Snider	175.00	90.00
❑ 171 Carlos Bernier	12.00	6.00
❑ 172 Andy Seminick	12.00	6.00
❑ 173 Dee Fondy	12.00	6.00
❑ 174 Pete Castiglione	12.00	6.00
❑ 175 Mel Clark	12.00	6.00
❑ 176 Vern Bickford	12.00	6.00
❑ 177 Whitey Ford	100.00	50.00
❑ 178 Del Wilber	12.00	6.00
❑ 179 Morrie Martin	12.00	6.00
❑ 180 Joe Tipton	12.00	6.00
❑ 181 Les Moss	12.00	6.00
❑ 182 Sherm Lollar	20.00	10.00
❑ 183 Matt Batts	12.00	6.00
❑ 184 Mickey Grasso	12.00	6.00
❑ 185 Daryl Spencer	12.00	6.00
❑ 186 Russ Meyer	12.00	6.00
❑ 187 Vern Law	20.00	10.00
❑ 188 Frank Smith	12.00	6.00
❑ 189 Randy Jackson	12.00	6.00
❑ 190 Joe Presko	12.00	6.00
❑ 191 Karl Drews	12.00	6.00
❑ 192 Lou Burdette	20.00	10.00
❑ 193 Eddie Robinson	12.00	6.00
❑ 194 Sid Hudson	12.00	6.00
❑ 195 Bob Cain	12.00	6.00
❑ 196 Bob Lemon	50.00	25.00
❑ 197 Lou Kretlow	12.00	6.00
❑ 198 Virgil Trucks	12.00	6.00
❑ 199 Steve Gromek	12.00	6.00
❑ 200 Conrado Marrero	12.00	6.00
❑ 201 Bobby Thomson	30.00	15.00
❑ 202 George Shuba	20.00	10.00
❑ 203 Vic Janowicz	20.00	10.00
❑ 204 Jack Collum	12.00	6.00
❑ 205 Hal Jeffcoat	12.00	6.00
❑ 206 Steve Bilko	12.00	6.00
❑ 207 Stan Lopata	12.00	6.00
❑ 208 Johnny Antonelli	20.00	10.00
❑ 209 Gene Woodling	12.00	6.00
❑ 210 Jimmy Piersall	30.00	15.00
❑ 211 Al Robertson	12.00	6.00
❑ 212 Owen Friend	12.00	6.00
❑ 213 Dick Littlefield	12.00	6.00
❑ 214 Ferris Fain	20.00	10.00
❑ 215 Johnny Bucha	12.00	6.00
❑ 216 Jerry Snyder	12.00	6.00
❑ 217 Hank Thompson	20.00	10.00
❑ 218 Preacher Roe	20.00	10.00
❑ 219 Hal Rice	12.00	6.00
❑ 220 Hobie Landrith	12.00	6.00
❑ 221 Frank Baumholtz	12.00	6.00
❑ 222 Memo Luna	12.00	6.00
❑ 223 Steve Ridzik	12.00	6.00
❑ 224 Bill Bruton	50.00	12.50

1955 Bowman

	NM	Ex
COMPLETE SET (320)	5000.00	2500.00
COMMON CARD (1-96)	12.00	6.00
COMMON CARD (97-224)	10.00	5.00
COMMON (225-320)	15.00	7.50
COMMON UMP. 225-320	30.00	15.00
WRAPPER (1-CENT)	60.00	30.00
WRAPPER (5-CENT)	60.00	30.00

Card	NM	Ex
❑ 1 Hoyt Wilhelm	100.00	22.00
❑ 2 Alvin Dark	15.00	7.50
❑ 3 Joe Coleman	15.00	7.50
❑ 4 Eddie Waitkus	15.00	7.50
❑ 5 Jim Robertson	12.00	6.00
❑ 6 Pete Suder	12.00	6.00
❑ 7 Gene Baker	12.00	6.00
❑ 8 Warren Hacker	12.00	6.00
❑ 9 Gil McDougald	20.00	10.00
❑ 10 Phil Rizzuto	125.00	60.00
❑ 11 Bill Bruton	15.00	7.50
❑ 12 Andy Pafko	15.00	7.50
❑ 13 Clyde Vollmer	12.00	6.00
❑ 14 Gus Keriazakos	12.00	6.00
❑ 15 Frank Sullivan	12.00	6.00
❑ 16 Jimmy Piersall	20.00	10.00
❑ 17 Del Ennis	15.00	7.50
❑ 18 Stan Lopata	12.00	6.00
❑ 19 Bobby Avila	15.00	7.50
❑ 20 Al Smith	15.00	7.50
❑ 21 Don Hoak	12.00	6.00
❑ 22 Roy Campanella	125.00	60.00
❑ 23 Al Kaline	150.00	75.00
❑ 24 Al Aber	12.00	6.00
❑ 25 Minnie Minoso	30.00	15.00
❑ 26 Virgil Trucks	15.00	7.50
❑ 27 Preston Ward	12.00	6.00
❑ 28 Dick Cole	12.00	6.00
❑ 29 Red Schoendienst	30.00	15.00
❑ 30 Bill Sarni	12.00	6.00
❑ 31 Johnny Temple RC	15.00	7.50
❑ 32 Wally Post	15.00	7.50
❑ 33 Nellie Fox	50.00	25.00
❑ 34 Clint Courtney	12.00	6.00
❑ 35 Bill Tuttle	12.00	6.00
❑ 36 Wayne Belardi	12.00	6.00
❑ 37 Pee Wee Reese	100.00	50.00
❑ 38 Early Wynn	30.00	15.00
❑ 39 Bob Darnell	15.00	7.50
❑ 40 Vic Wertz	15.00	7.50
❑ 41 Mel Clark	12.00	6.00
❑ 42 Bob Greenwood	12.00	6.00
❑ 43 Bob Buhl	15.00	7.50
❑ 44 Danny O'Connell	12.00	6.00
❑ 45 Tom Umphlett	12.00	6.00
❑ 46 Mickey Vernon	15.00	7.50
❑ 47 Sammy White	12.00	6.00
❑ 48A Milt Bolling ERR (Name on back is Frank Bolling)	20.00	10.00
❑ 48B Milt Bolling COR	20.00	10.00
❑ 49 Jim Greengrass	12.00	6.00
❑ 50 Hobie Landrith	12.00	6.00
❑ 51 Elvin Tappe	12.00	6.00
❑ 52 Hal Rice	12.00	6.00
❑ 53 Alex Kellner	12.00	6.00
❑ 54 Don Bollweg	12.00	6.00
❑ 55 Cal Abrams	12.00	6.00
❑ 56 Billy Cox	15.00	7.50
❑ 57 Bob Friend	15.00	7.50
❑ 58 Frank Thomas	15.00	7.50
❑ 59 Whitey Ford	100.00	50.00
❑ 60 Enos Slaughter	30.00	15.00
❑ 61 Paul LaPalme	12.00	6.00
❑ 62 Royce Lint	12.00	6.00
❑ 63 Irv Noren	15.00	7.50
❑ 64 Curt Simmons	15.00	7.50
❑ 65 Don Zimmer RC	20.00	10.00
❑ 66 George Shuba	20.00	10.00
❑ 67 Don Larsen	20.00	10.00
❑ 68 Elston Howard RC	80.00	40.00
❑ 69 Billy Hunter	12.00	6.00
❑ 70 Lou Burdette	20.00	10.00
❑ 71 Dave Jolly	12.00	6.00
❑ 72 Chet Nichols	12.00	6.00
❑ 73 Eddie Yost	15.00	7.50
❑ 74 Jerry Snyder	12.00	6.00
❑ 75 Brooks Lawrence RC	12.00	6.00
❑ 76 Tom Poholsky	12.00	6.00
❑ 77 Jim McDonald	12.00	6.00
❑ 78 Gil Coan	12.00	6.00
❑ 79 Willie Miranda	12.00	6.00
❑ 80 Lou Limmer	12.00	6.00
❑ 81 Bobby Morgan	12.00	6.00
❑ 82 Lee Walls	12.00	6.00
❑ 83 Max Surkont	12.00	6.00
❑ 84 George Freese	12.00	6.00
❑ 85 Cass Michaels	12.00	6.00
❑ 86 Ted Gray	12.00	6.00
❑ 87 Randy Jackson	12.00	6.00
❑ 88 Steve Bilko	12.00	6.00
❑ 89 Lou Boudreau MG	30.00	15.00
❑ 90 Art Ditmar	12.00	6.00
❑ 91 Dick Marlowe	12.00	6.00
❑ 92 George Zuverink	12.00	6.00
❑ 93 Andy Seminick	12.00	6.00
❑ 94 Hank Thompson	15.00	7.50
❑ 95 Sal Maglie	15.00	7.50
❑ 96 Ray Narleski RC	12.00	6.00
❑ 97 Johnny Podres	30.00	15.00
❑ 98 Jim Gilliam	20.00	10.00
❑ 99 Jerry Coleman	15.00	7.50
❑ 100 Tom Morgan	10.00	5.00
❑ 101A Don Johnson ERR (Photo actually Ernie Johnson)	20.00	10.00
❑ 101B Don Johnson COR	20.00	10.00
❑ 102 Bobby Thomson	15.00	7.50
❑ 103 Eddie Mathews	80.00	40.00
❑ 104 Bob Porterfield	10.00	5.00
❑ 105 Johnny Schmitz	10.00	5.00
❑ 106 Del Rice	10.00	5.00
❑ 107 Solly Hemus	10.00	5.00
❑ 108 Lou Kretlow	10.00	5.00
❑ 109 Vern Stephens	15.00	7.50
❑ 110 Bob Miller	10.00	5.00
❑ 111 Steve Ridzik	10.00	5.00
❑ 112 Granny Hamner	10.00	5.00
❑ 113 Bob Hall	10.00	5.00
❑ 114 Vic Janowicz	15.00	7.50
❑ 115 Roger Bowman	10.00	5.00
❑ 116 Sandy Consuegra	10.00	5.00
❑ 117 Johnny Groth	10.00	5.00
❑ 118 Bobby Adams	10.00	5.00
❑ 119 Joe Astroth	10.00	5.00
❑ 120 Ed Burtschy	10.00	5.00
❑ 121 Rufus Crawford	10.00	5.00
❑ 122 Al Corwin	10.00	5.00
❑ 123 Marv Grissom	10.00	5.00
❑ 124 Johnny Antonelli	15.00	7.50
❑ 125 Paul Giel	15.00	7.50
❑ 126 Billy Goodman	15.00	7.50
❑ 127 Hank Majeski	10.00	5.00
❑ 128 Mike Garcia	15.00	7.50
❑ 129 Hal Naragon	10.00	5.00
❑ 130 Richie Ashburn	50.00	25.00
❑ 131 Willard Marshall	10.00	5.00
❑ 132A Harvey Kueen ERR (Sic& Kuenn)	50.00	25.00

❑ 132B Harvey Kuenn COR 30.00 15.00
❑ 133 Charles King 10.00 5.00
❑ 134 Bob Feller 80.00 40.00
❑ 135 Lloyd Merriman.......... 10.00 5.00
❑ 136 Rocky Bridges.......... 10.00 5.00
❑ 137 Bob Talbot.......... 10.00 5.00
❑ 138 Davey Williams 15.00 7.50
❑ 139 Shantz Brothers.......... 15.00 7.50
Wilmer Shantz
Bobby Shantz
❑ 140 Bobby Shantz 15.00 7.50
❑ 141 Wes Westrum 15.00 7.50
❑ 142 Rudy Regalado 10.00 5.00
❑ 143 Don Newcombe.......... 30.00 15.00
❑ 144 Art Houtteman.......... 10.00 5.00
❑ 145 Bob Nieman 10.00 5.00
❑ 146 Don Liddle 10.00 5.00
❑ 147 Sam Mele 10.00 5.00
❑ 148 Bob Chakales 10.00 5.00
❑ 149 Cloyd Boyer 10.00 5.00
❑ 150 Billy Klaus.......... 10.00 5.00
❑ 151 Jim Brideweser 10.00 5.00
❑ 152 Johnny Klippstein 10.00 5.00
❑ 153 Eddie Robinson.......... 10.00 5.00
❑ 154 Frank Lary RC 15.00 7.50
❑ 155 Gerry Staley.......... 10.00 5.00
❑ 156 Jim Hughes.......... 15.00 7.50
❑ 157A Ernie Johnson ERR 20.00 10.00
(Photo actually
Don Johnson)
❑ 157B Ernie Johnson COR.... 20.00 10.00
❑ 158 Gil Hodges 50.00 25.00
❑ 159 Harry Byrd.......... 10.00 5.00
❑ 160 Bill Skowron 20.00 10.00
❑ 161 Matt Batts 10.00 5.00
❑ 162 Charlie Maxwell 10.00 5.00
❑ 163 Sid Gordon 15.00 7.50
❑ 164 Toby Atwell 10.00 5.00
❑ 165 Maurice McDermott 10.00 5.00
❑ 166 Jim Busby.......... 10.00 5.00
❑ 167 Bob Grim RC.......... 20.00 10.00
❑ 168 Yogi Berra.......... 125.00 60.00
❑ 169 Carl Furillo 30.00 15.00
❑ 170 Carl Erskine.......... 20.00 10.00
❑ 171 Robin Roberts 50.00 25.00
❑ 172 Willie Jones 10.00 5.00
❑ 173 Chico Carrasquel 10.00 5.00
❑ 174 Sherm Lollar 15.00 7.50
❑ 175 Wilmer Shantz.......... 10.00 5.00
❑ 176 Joe DeMaestri 10.00 5.00
❑ 177 Willard Nixon 10.00 5.00
❑ 178 Tom Brewer.......... 10.00 5.00
❑ 179 Hank Aaron 250.00 125.00
❑ 180 Johnny Logan 15.00 7.50
❑ 181 Eddie Miksis 10.00 5.00
❑ 182 Bob Rush 10.00 5.00
❑ 183 Ray Katt.......... 10.00 5.00
❑ 184 Willie Mays 250.00 125.00
❑ 185 Vic Raschi 10.00 5.00
❑ 186 Alex Grammas.......... 10.00 5.00
❑ 187 Fred Hatfield 10.00 5.00
❑ 188 Ned Garver 10.00 5.00
❑ 189 Jack Collum 10.00 5.00
❑ 190 Fred Baczewski 10.00 5.00
❑ 191 Bob Lemon 30.00 15.00
❑ 192 George Strickland 10.00 5.00
❑ 193 Howie Judson 10.00 5.00
❑ 194 Joe Nuxhall.......... 15.00 7.50
❑ 195A Erv Palica 15.00 7.50
(Without trade)
❑ 195B Erv Palica 40.00 20.00
(With trade)
❑ 196 Russ Meyer.......... 15.00 7.50
❑ 197 Ralph Kiner.......... 30.00 15.00
❑ 198 Dave Pope.......... 10.00 5.00
❑ 199 Vern Law.......... 15.00 7.50
❑ 200 Dick Littlefield 10.00 5.00
❑ 201 Allie Reynolds 20.00 10.00
❑ 202 Mickey Mantle UER.... 800.00 400.00
Birthdate listed as 10/30/31
Should be 10/20/31
❑ 203 Steve Gromek 10.00 5.00
❑ 204A Frank Bolling ERR...... 20.00 10.00
(Name on back is
Milt Bolling)
❑ 204B Frank Bolling COR 20.00 10.00
❑ 205 Rip Repulski 10.00 5.00
❑ 206 Ralph Beard.......... 10.00 5.00
❑ 207 Frank Shea 10.00 5.00
❑ 208 Ed Fitzgerald 10.00 5.00
❑ 209 Smoky Burgess.......... 15.00 7.50
❑ 210 Earl Torgeson 10.00 5.00
❑ 211 Sonny Dixon 10.00 5.00
❑ 212 Jack Dittmer 10.00 5.00
❑ 213 George Kell 30.00 15.00
❑ 214 Billy Pierce 15.00 7.50
❑ 215 Bob Kuzava 10.00 5.00
❑ 216 Preacher Roe.......... 20.00 10.00
❑ 217 Del Crandall 15.00 7.50
❑ 218 Joe Adcock 15.00 7.50
❑ 219 Whitey Lockman 15.00 7.50
❑ 220 Jim Hearn 10.00 5.00
❑ 221 Hector Brown 10.00 5.00
❑ 222 Russ Kemmerer.......... 10.00 5.00
❑ 223 Hal Jeffcoat 10.00 5.00
❑ 224 Dee Fondy.......... 10.00 5.00
❑ 225 Paul Richards MG 15.00 7.50
❑ 226 Bill McKinley UMP RC 30.00 15.00
❑ 227 Frank Baumholtz 15.00 7.50
❑ 228 John Phillips.......... 15.00 7.50
❑ 229 Jim Brosnan RC 20.00 10.00
❑ 230 Al Brazle 15.00 7.50
❑ 231 Jim Konstanty 20.00 10.00
❑ 232 Birdie Tebbetts MG 20.00 10.00
❑ 233 Bill Serena.......... 15.00 7.50
❑ 234 Dick Bartell CO 20.00 10.00
❑ 235 Joe Paparella UMP RC 30.00 15.00
❑ 236 Murry Dickson 15.00 7.50
❑ 237 Johnny Wyrostek.......... 15.00 7.50
❑ 238 Eddie Stanky MG.......... 20.00 10.00
❑ 239 Edwin Rommel UMP 40.00 20.00
❑ 240 Billy Loes 20.00 10.00
❑ 241 Johnny Pesky CO 20.00 10.00
❑ 242 Ernie Banks.......... 350.00 180.00
❑ 243 Gus Bell 20.00 10.00
❑ 244 Duane Pillette 15.00 7.50
❑ 245 Bill Miller 15.00 7.50
❑ 246 Hank Bauer 30.00 15.00
❑ 247 Dutch Leonard CO.......... 15.00 7.50
❑ 248 Harry Dorish 15.00 7.50
❑ 249 Billy Gardner RC 20.00 10.00
❑ 250 Larry Napp UMP RC 30.00 15.00
❑ 251 Stan Jok 15.00 7.50
❑ 252 Roy Smalley 15.00 7.50
❑ 253 Jim Wilson 15.00 7.50
❑ 254 Bennett Flowers.......... 15.00 7.50
❑ 255 Pete Runnels.......... 20.00 10.00
❑ 256 Owen Friend 15.00 7.50
❑ 257 Tom Alston 15.00 7.50
❑ 258 John Stevens UMP RC 30.00 15.00
❑ 259 Don Mossi RC.......... 30.00 15.00
❑ 260 Edwin Hurley UMP RC 30.00 15.00
❑ 261 Walt Moryn 20.00 10.00
❑ 262 Jim Lemon 15.00 7.50
❑ 263 Eddie Joost 15.00 7.50
❑ 264 Bill Henry 15.00 7.50
❑ 265 Albert Barlick UMP RC 80.00 40.00
❑ 266 Mike Fornieles 15.00 7.50
❑ 267 Jim Honochick UMP RC 80.00 40.00
❑ 268 Roy Lee Hawes 15.00 7.50
❑ 269 Joe Amalfitano RC.......... 20.00 10.00
❑ 270 Chico Fernandez 20.00 10.00
❑ 271 Bob Hooper.......... 15.00 7.50
❑ 272 John Flaherty UMP RC 30.00 15.00
❑ 273 Bubba Church 15.00 7.50
❑ 274 Jim Delsing.......... 15.00 7.50
❑ 275 William Grieve UMP RC 30.00 15.00
❑ 276 Ike Delock 15.00 7.50
❑ 277 Ed Runge UMP RC 30.00 15.00
❑ 278 Charlie Neal RC.......... 40.00 20.00
❑ 279 Hank Soar UMP RC...... 40.00 20.00
❑ 280 Clyde McCullough 15.00 7.50
❑ 281 Charles Berry UMP 40.00 20.00
❑ 282 Phil Cavarretta.......... 20.00 10.00
❑ 283 Nestor Chylak UMP RC 80.00 40.00
❑ 284 Bill Jackowski UMP RC 30.00 15.00
❑ 285 Walt Dropo 20.00 10.00
❑ 286 Frank Secory UMP RC 30.00 15.00
❑ 287 Ron Mrozinski.......... 15.00 7.50
❑ 288 Dick Smith 15.00 7.50
❑ 289 Arthur Gore UMP RC.... 30.00 15.00
❑ 290 Hershell Freeman 15.00 7.50
❑ 291 Frank Dascoli UMP RC 30.00 15.00
❑ 292 Marv Blaylock 15.00 7.50
❑ 293 Thomas Gorman UMP RC 40.00 20.00
❑ 294 Wally Moses CO 15.00 7.50
❑ 295 Lee Ballanfant UMP RC 30.00 15.00
❑ 296 Bill Virdon RC 30.00 15.00
❑ 297 Dusty Boggess UMP RC 30.00 15.00
❑ 298 Charlie Grimm MG 20.00 10.00
❑ 299 Lon Warneke UMP 40.00 20.00
❑ 300 Tommy Byrne 20.00 10.00
❑ 301 William Engeln UMP RC 30.00 15.00
❑ 302 Frank Malzone RC.......... 30.00 15.00
❑ 303 Jocko Conlan UMP 80.00 40.00
❑ 304 Harry Chiti.......... 15.00 7.50
❑ 305 Frank Umont UMP RC.. 30.00 15.00
❑ 306 Bob Cerv.......... 20.00 10.00
❑ 307 Babe Pinelli UMP 40.00 20.00
❑ 308 Al Lopez MG 50.00 25.00
❑ 309 Hal Dixon UMP RC 30.00 15.00
❑ 310 Ken Lehman 15.00 7.50
❑ 311 Lawrence Goetz UMP RC 30.00 15.00
❑ 312 Bill Wight 15.00 7.50
❑ 313 Augie Donatelli UMP RC 50.00 25.00
❑ 314 Dale Mitchell.......... 20.00 10.00
❑ 315 Cal Hubbard UMP RC .. 80.00 40.00
❑ 316 Marion Fricano 15.00 7.50
❑ 317 W. Summers UMP 20.00 10.00
❑ 318 Sid Hudson.......... 15.00 7.50
❑ 319 Al Schroll 15.00 7.50
❑ 320 George Susce RC 50.00 10.00

1989 Bowman

	Nm-Mt	Ex-Mt
COMPLETE SET (484)	25.00	10.00
COMP.FACT.SET (484)	25.00	10.00

❑ 1 Oswald Peraza.......... .05 .02
❑ 2 Brian Holton .... .05 .02
❑ 3 Jose Bautista RC.......... .10 .04
❑ 4 Pete Harnisch RC .... .25 .10
❑ 5 Dave Schmidt .... .05 .02
❑ 6 Gregg Olson RC .... .25 .10
❑ 7 Jeff Ballard .... .05 .02
❑ 8 Bob Melvin .... .05 .02
❑ 9 Cal Ripken.......... .75 .30
❑ 10 Randy Milligan .... .05 .02
❑ 11 Juan Bell RC .... .10 .04
❑ 12 Billy Ripken.......... .05 .02
❑ 13 Jim Traber.......... .05 .02
❑ 14 Pete Stanicek.......... .05 .02
❑ 15 Steve Finley RC.......... .50 .20
❑ 16 Larry Sheets .... .05 .02
❑ 17 Phil Bradley.......... .05 .02
❑ 18 Brady Anderson RC.......... .40 .16
❑ 19 Lee Smith .... .10 .04
❑ 20 Tom Fischer .... .05 .02
❑ 21 Mike Boddicker.......... .05 .02
❑ 22 Rob Murphy .... .05 .02
❑ 23 Wes Gardner .... .05 .02
❑ 24 John Dopson.......... .05 .02
❑ 25 Bob Stanley.......... .05 .02
❑ 26 Roger Clemens .... .50 .20
❑ 27 Rich Gedman.......... .05 .02
❑ 28 Marty Barrett .... .05 .02
❑ 29 Luis Rivera .... .05 .02
❑ 30 Jody Reed .... .05 .02
❑ 31 Nick Esasky.......... .05 .02

❑ 32	Wade Boggs	.15	.06
❑ 33	Jim Rice	.10	.04
❑ 34	Mike Greenwell	.05	.02
❑ 35	Dwight Evans	.10	.04
❑ 36	Ellis Burks	.10	.04
❑ 37	Chuck Finley	.10	.04
❑ 38	Kirk McCaskill	.05	.02
❑ 39	Jim Abbott RC*	.50	.20
❑ 40	Bryan Harvey RC *	.25	.10
❑ 41	Bert Blyleven	.10	.04
❑ 42	Mike Witt	.05	.02
❑ 43	Bob McClure	.05	.02
❑ 44	Bill Schroeder	.05	.02
❑ 45	Lance Parrish	.10	.04
❑ 46	Dick Schofield	.05	.02
❑ 47	Wally Joyner	.10	.04
❑ 48	Jack Howell	.05	.02
❑ 49	Johnny Ray	.05	.02
❑ 50	Chili Davis	.10	.04
❑ 51	Tony Armas	.10	.04
❑ 52	Claudell Washington	.05	.02
❑ 53	Brian Downing	.10	.04
❑ 54	Devon White	.10	.04
❑ 55	Bobby Thigpen	.05	.02
❑ 56	Bill Long	.05	.02
❑ 57	Jerry Reuss	.05	.02
❑ 58	Shawn Hillegas	.05	.02
❑ 59	Melido Perez	.05	.02
❑ 60	Jeff Bittiger	.05	.02
❑ 61	Jack McDowell	.10	.04
❑ 62	Carlton Fisk	.15	.06
❑ 63	Steve Lyons	.05	.02
❑ 64	Ozzie Guillen	.05	.02
❑ 65	Robin Ventura RC	.75	.30
❑ 66	Fred Manrique	.05	.02
❑ 67	Dan Pasqua	.05	.02
❑ 68	Ivan Calderon	.05	.02
❑ 69	Ron Kittle	.05	.02
❑ 70	Daryl Boston	.05	.02
❑ 71	Dave Gallagher	.05	.02
❑ 72	Harold Baines	.10	.04
❑ 73	Charles Nagy RC	.25	.10
❑ 74	John Farrell	.05	.02
❑ 75	Kevin Wickander	.05	.02
❑ 76	Greg Swindell	.05	.02
❑ 77	Mike Walker	.05	.02
❑ 78	Doug Jones	.05	.02
❑ 79	Rich Yett	.05	.02
❑ 80	Tom Candiotti	.05	.02
❑ 81	Jesse Orosco	.05	.02
❑ 82	Bud Black	.05	.02
❑ 83	Andy Allanson	.05	.02
❑ 84	Pete O'Brien	.05	.02
❑ 85	Jerry Browne	.05	.02
❑ 86	Brook Jacoby	.05	.02
❑ 87	Mark Lewis RC	.25	.10
❑ 88	Luis Aguayo	.05	.02
❑ 89	Cory Snyder	.05	.02
❑ 90	Oddibe McDowell	.05	.02
❑ 91	Joe Carter	.10	.04
❑ 92	Frank Tanana	.10	.04
❑ 93	Jack Morris	.10	.04
❑ 94	Doyle Alexander	.05	.02
❑ 95	Steve Searcy	.05	.02
❑ 96	Randy Bockus	.05	.02
❑ 97	Jeff M. Robinson	.05	.02
❑ 98	Mike Henneman	.05	.02
❑ 99	Paul Gibson	.05	.02
❑ 100	Frank Williams	.05	.02
❑ 101	Matt Nokes	.05	.02
❑ 102	Rico Brogna RC UER (Misspelled Ricco on card back)	.40	.16
❑ 103	Lou Whitaker	.10	.04
❑ 104	Al Pedrique	.05	.02
❑ 105	Alan Trammell	.10	.04
❑ 106	Chris Brown	.05	.02
❑ 107	Pat Sheridan	.05	.02
❑ 108	Chet Lemon	.10	.04
❑ 109	Keith Moreland	.05	.02
❑ 110	Mel Stottlemyre Jr.	.05	.02
❑ 111	Bret Saberhagen	.10	.04
❑ 112	Floyd Bannister	.05	.02
❑ 113	Jeff Montgomery	.05	.02
❑ 114	Steve Farr	.05	.02
❑ 115	Tom Gordon UER RC (Front shows autograph of Don Gordon)	.40	.16
❑ 116	Charlie Leibrandt	.05	.02
❑ 117	Mark Gubicza	.05	.02
❑ 118	Mike Macfarlane RC	.25	.10
❑ 119	Bob Boone	.10	.04
❑ 120	Kurt Stillwell	.05	.02
❑ 121	George Brett	.60	.24
❑ 122	Frank White	.10	.04
❑ 123	Kevin Seitzer	.05	.02
❑ 124	Willie Wilson	.10	.04
❑ 125	Pat Tabler	.05	.02
❑ 126	Bo Jackson	.25	.10
❑ 127	Hugh Walker RC	.10	.04
❑ 128	Danny Tartabull	.05	.02
❑ 129	Teddy Higuera	.05	.02
❑ 130	Don August	.05	.02
❑ 131	Juan Nieves	.05	.02
❑ 132	Mike Birkbeck	.05	.02
❑ 133	Dan Plesac	.05	.02
❑ 134	Chris Bosio	.05	.02
❑ 135	Bill Wegman	.05	.02
❑ 136	Chuck Crim	.05	.02
❑ 137	B.J. Surhoff	.10	.04
❑ 138	Joey Meyer	.05	.02
❑ 139	Dale Sveum	.05	.02
❑ 140	Paul Molitor	.15	.06
❑ 141	Jim Gantner	.05	.02
❑ 142	Gary Sheffield RC	1.50	.60
❑ 143	Greg Brock	.05	.02
❑ 144	Robin Yount	.40	.16
❑ 145	Glenn Braggs	.05	.02
❑ 146	Rob Deer	.05	.02
❑ 147	Fred Toliver	.05	.02
❑ 148	Jeff Reardon	.10	.04
❑ 149	Allan Anderson	.05	.02
❑ 150	Frank Viola	.10	.04
❑ 151	Shane Rawley	.05	.02
❑ 152	Juan Berenguer	.05	.02
❑ 153	Johnny Ard	.05	.02
❑ 154	Tim Laudner	.05	.02
❑ 155	Brian Harper	.05	.02
❑ 156	Al Newman	.05	.02
❑ 157	Kent Hrbek	.10	.04
❑ 158	Gary Gaetti	.10	.04
❑ 159	Wally Backman	.05	.02
❑ 160	Gene Larkin	.05	.02
❑ 161	Greg Gagne	.05	.02
❑ 162	Kirby Puckett	.25	.10
❑ 163	Dan Gladden	.05	.02
❑ 164	Randy Bush	.05	.02
❑ 165	Dave LaPoint	.05	.02
❑ 166	Andy Hawkins	.05	.02
❑ 167	Dave Righetti	.10	.04
❑ 168	Lance McCullers	.05	.02
❑ 169	Jimmy Jones	.05	.02
❑ 170	Al Leiter	.25	.10
❑ 171	John Candelaria	.05	.02
❑ 172	Don Slaught	.05	.02
❑ 173	Jamie Quirk	.05	.02
❑ 174	Rafael Santana	.05	.02
❑ 175	Mike Pagliarulo	.05	.02
❑ 176	Don Mattingly	.60	.24
❑ 177	Ken Phelps	.05	.02
❑ 178	Steve Sax	.05	.02
❑ 179	Dave Winfield	.10	.04
❑ 180	Stan Jefferson	.05	.02
❑ 181	Rickey Henderson	.25	.10
❑ 182	Bob Brower	.05	.02
❑ 183	Roberto Kelly	.05	.02
❑ 184	Curt Young	.05	.02
❑ 185	Gene Nelson	.05	.02
❑ 186	Bob Welch	.10	.04
❑ 187	Rick Honeycutt	.05	.02
❑ 188	Dave Stewart	.10	.04
❑ 189	Mike Moore	.05	.02
❑ 190	Dennis Eckersley	.15	.06
❑ 191	Eric Plunk	.05	.02
❑ 192	Storm Davis	.05	.02
❑ 193	Terry Steinbach	.10	.04
❑ 194	Ron Hassey	.05	.02
❑ 195	Stan Royer RC	.10	.04
❑ 196	Walt Weiss	.05	.02
❑ 197	Mark McGwire	1.00	.40
❑ 198	Carney Lansford	.10	.04
❑ 199	Glenn Hubbard	.05	.02
❑ 200	Dave Henderson	.05	.02
❑ 201	Jose Canseco	.25	.10
❑ 202	Dave Parker	.10	.04
❑ 203	Scott Bankhead	.05	.02
❑ 204	Tom Niedenfuer	.05	.02
❑ 205	Mark Langston	.05	.02
❑ 206	Erik Hanson RC	.25	.10
❑ 207	Mike Jackson	.05	.02
❑ 208	Dave Valle	.05	.02
❑ 209	Scott Bradley	.05	.02
❑ 210	Harold Reynolds	.10	.04
❑ 211	Tino Martinez RC	.75	.30
❑ 212	Rich Renteria	.05	.02
❑ 213	Rey Quinones	.05	.02
❑ 214	Jim Presley	.05	.02
❑ 215	Alvin Davis	.05	.02
❑ 216	Edgar Martinez	.25	.10
❑ 217	Darnell Coles	.05	.02
❑ 218	Jeffrey Leonard	.05	.02
❑ 219	Jay Buhner	.10	.04
❑ 220	Ken Griffey Jr. RC	8.00	3.20
❑ 221	Drew Hall	.05	.02
❑ 222	Bobby Witt	.05	.02
❑ 223	Jamie Moyer	.10	.04
❑ 224	Charlie Hough	.10	.04
❑ 225	Nolan Ryan	1.00	.40
❑ 226	Jeff Russell	.05	.02
❑ 227	Jim Sundberg	.10	.04
❑ 228	Julio Franco	.10	.04
❑ 229	Buddy Bell	.10	.04
❑ 230	Scott Fletcher	.05	.02
❑ 231	Jeff Kunkel	.05	.02
❑ 232	Steve Buechele	.05	.02
❑ 233	Monty Fariss	.05	.02
❑ 234	Rick Leach	.05	.02
❑ 235	Ruben Sierra	.05	.02
❑ 236	Cecil Espy	.05	.02
❑ 237	Rafael Palmeiro	.25	.10
❑ 238	Pete Incaviglia	.05	.02
❑ 239	Dave Stieb	.10	.04
❑ 240	Jeff Musselman	.05	.02
❑ 241	Mike Flanagan	.05	.02
❑ 242	Todd Stottlemyre	.05	.02
❑ 243	Jimmy Key	.10	.04
❑ 244	Tony Castillo RC	.10	.04
❑ 245	Alex Sanchez	.05	.02
❑ 246	Tom Henke	.05	.02
❑ 247	John Cerutti	.05	.02
❑ 248	Ernie Whitt	.05	.02
❑ 249	Bob Brenly	.05	.02
❑ 250	Rance Mulliniks	.05	.02
❑ 251	Kelly Gruber	.05	.02
❑ 252	Ed Sprague RC	.25	.10
❑ 253	Fred McGriff	.15	.06
❑ 254	Tony Fernandez	.05	.02
❑ 255	Tom Lawless	.05	.02
❑ 256	George Bell	.10	.04
❑ 257	Jesse Barfield	.10	.04
❑ 258	Roberto Alomar Sandy Alomar	.15	.06
❑ 259	Ken Griffey Jr. Ken Griffey Sr.	1.00	.40
❑ 260	Cal Ripken Jr. Cal Ripken Sr.	.25	.10
❑ 261	Mel Stottlemyre Jr. Mel Stottlemyre Sr.	.05	.02
❑ 262	Zane Smith	.05	.02
❑ 263	Charlie Puleo	.05	.02
❑ 264	Derek Lilliquist RC	.10	.04
❑ 265	Paul Assenmacher	.05	.02
❑ 266	John Smoltz RC	1.00	.40
❑ 267	Tom Glavine	.25	.10
❑ 268	Steve Avery RC	.25	.10
❑ 269	Pete Smith	.05	.02
❑ 270	Jody Davis	.05	.02
❑ 271	Bruce Benedict	.05	.02
❑ 272	Andres Thomas	.05	.02
❑ 273	Gerald Perry	.05	.02
❑ 274	Ron Gant	.10	.04
❑ 275	Darrell Evans	.10	.04
❑ 276	Dale Murphy	.15	.06
❑ 277	Dion James	.05	.02
❑ 278	Lonnie Smith	.05	.02
❑ 279	Geronimo Berroa	.05	.02
❑ 280	Steve Wilson RC	.10	.04
❑ 281	Rick Sutcliffe	.10	.04

❑ 282 Kevin Coffman .05 .02
❑ 283 Mitch Williams .05 .02
❑ 284 Greg Maddux .50 .20
❑ 285 Paul Kilgus .05 .02
❑ 286 Mike Harkey RC .10 .04
❑ 287 Lloyd McClendon .05 .02
❑ 288 Damon Berryhill .05 .02
❑ 289 Ty Griffin .05 .02
❑ 290 Ryne Sandberg .40 .16
❑ 291 Mark Grace .25 .10
❑ 292 Curt Wilkerson .05 .02
❑ 293 Vance Law .05 .02
❑ 294 Shawon Dunston .05 .02
❑ 295 Jerome Walton RC .25 .10
❑ 296 Mitch Webster .05 .02
❑ 297 Dwight Smith RC .25 .10
❑ 298 Andre Dawson .10 .04
❑ 299 Jeff Sellers .05 .02
❑ 300 Jose Rijo .10 .04
❑ 301 John Franco .10 .04
❑ 302 Rick Mahler .05 .02
❑ 303 Ron Robinson .05 .02
❑ 304 Danny Jackson .05 .02
❑ 305 Rob Dibble RC .50 .20
❑ 306 Tom Browning .05 .02
❑ 307 Bo Diaz .05 .02
❑ 308 Manny Trillo .05 .02
❑ 309 Chris Sabo RC * .40 .16
❑ 310 Ron Oester .05 .02
❑ 311 Barry Larkin .15 .06
❑ 312 Todd Benzinger .05 .02
❑ 313 Paul O'Neill .15 .06
❑ 314 Kal Daniels .05 .02
❑ 315 Joel Youngblood .05 .02
❑ 316 Eric Davis .10 .04
❑ 317 Dave Smith .05 .02
❑ 318 Mark Portugal .05 .02
❑ 319 Brian Meyer .05 .02
❑ 320 Jim Deshaies .05 .02
❑ 321 Juan Agosto .05 .02
❑ 322 Mike Scott .10 .04
❑ 323 Rick Rhoden .05 .02
❑ 324 Jim Clancy .05 .02
❑ 325 Larry Andersen .05 .02
❑ 326 Alex Trevino .05 .02
❑ 327 Alan Ashby .05 .02
❑ 328 Craig Reynolds .05 .02
❑ 329 Bill Doran .05 .02
❑ 330 Rafael Ramirez .05 .02
❑ 331 Glenn Davis .05 .02
❑ 332 Willie Ansley RC .10 .04
❑ 333 Gerald Young .05 .02
❑ 334 Cameron Drew .05 .02
❑ 335 Jay Howell .05 .02
❑ 336 Tim Belcher .05 .02
❑ 337 Fernando Valenzuela .10 .04
❑ 338 Ricky Horton .05 .02
❑ 339 Tim Leary .05 .02
❑ 340 Bill Bene .05 .02
❑ 341 Orel Hershiser .10 .04
❑ 342 Mike Scioscia .10 .04
❑ 343 Rick Dempsey .05 .02
❑ 344 Willie Randolph .10 .04
❑ 345 Alfredo Griffin .05 .02
❑ 346 Eddie Murray .25 .10
❑ 347 Mickey Hatcher .05 .02
❑ 348 Mike Sharperson .05 .02
❑ 349 John Shelby .05 .02
❑ 350 Mike Marshall .05 .02
❑ 351 Kirk Gibson .10 .04
❑ 352 Mike Davis .05 .02
❑ 353 Bryn Smith .05 .02
❑ 354 Pascual Perez .05 .02
❑ 355 Kevin Gross .05 .02
❑ 356 Andy McGaffigan .05 .02
❑ 357 Brian Holman RC * .10 .04
❑ 358 Dave Wainhouse RC .10 .04
❑ 359 Dennis Martinez .10 .04
❑ 360 Tim Burke .05 .02
❑ 361 Nelson Santovenia .05 .02
❑ 362 Tim Wallach .05 .02
❑ 363 Spike Owen .05 .02
❑ 364 Rex Hudler .05 .02
❑ 365 Andres Galarraga .10 .04
❑ 366 Otis Nixon .05 .02
❑ 367 Hubie Brooks .05 .02
❑ 368 Mike Aldrete .05 .02
❑ 369 Tim Raines .10 .04
❑ 370 Dave Martinez .05 .02
❑ 371 Bob Ojeda .05 .02
❑ 372 Ron Darling .10 .04
❑ 373 Wally Whitehurst RC .10 .04
❑ 374 Randy Myers .10 .04
❑ 375 David Cone .10 .04
❑ 376 Dwight Gooden .10 .04
❑ 377 Sid Fernandez .05 .02
❑ 378 Dave Proctor .05 .02
❑ 379 Gary Carter .10 .04
❑ 380 Keith Miller .05 .02
❑ 381 Gregg Jefferies .05 .02
❑ 382 Tim Teufel .05 .02
❑ 383 Kevin Elster .05 .02
❑ 384 Dave Magadan .05 .02
❑ 385 Keith Hernandez .10 .04
❑ 386 Mookie Wilson .10 .04
❑ 387 Darryl Strawberry .10 .04
❑ 388 Kevin McReynolds .05 .02
❑ 389 Mark Carreon .05 .02
❑ 390 Jeff Parrett .05 .02
❑ 391 Mike Maddux .05 .02
❑ 392 Don Carman .05 .02
❑ 393 Bruce Ruffin .05 .02
❑ 394 Ken Howell .05 .02
❑ 395 Steve Bedrosian .05 .02
❑ 396 Floyd Youmans .05 .02
❑ 397 Larry McWilliams .05 .02
❑ 398 Pat Combs RC * .10 .04
❑ 399 Steve Lake .05 .02
❑ 400 Dickie Thon .05 .02
❑ 401 Ricky Jordan RC * .25 .10
❑ 402 Mike Schmidt .50 .20
❑ 403 Tom Herr .05 .02
❑ 404 Chris James .05 .02
❑ 405 Juan Samuel .05 .02
❑ 406 Von Hayes .05 .02
❑ 407 Ron Jones .10 .04
❑ 408 Curt Ford .05 .02
❑ 409 Bob Walk .05 .02
❑ 410 Jeff D. Robinson .05 .02
❑ 411 Jim Gott .05 .02
❑ 412 Scott Medvin .05 .02
❑ 413 John Smiley .05 .02
❑ 414 Bob Kipper .05 .02
❑ 415 Brian Fisher .05 .02
❑ 416 Doug Drabek .05 .02
❑ 417 Mike LaValliere .05 .02
❑ 418 Ken Oberkfell .05 .02
❑ 419 Sid Bream .05 .02
❑ 420 Austin Manahan .05 .02
❑ 421 Jose Lind .05 .02
❑ 422 Bobby Bonilla .10 .04
❑ 423 Glenn Wilson .05 .02
❑ 424 Andy Van Slyke .10 .04
❑ 425 Gary Redus .05 .02
❑ 426 Barry Bonds 1.25 .50
❑ 427 Don Heinkel .05 .02
❑ 428 Ken Dayley .05 .02
❑ 429 Todd Worrell .05 .02
❑ 430 Brad DuVall .05 .02
❑ 431 Jose DeLeon .05 .02
❑ 432 Joe Magrane .05 .02
❑ 433 John Ericks .05 .02
❑ 434 Frank DiPino .05 .02
❑ 435 Tony Pena .05 .02
❑ 436 Ozzie Smith .40 .16
❑ 437 Terry Pendleton .10 .04
❑ 438 Jose Oquendo .05 .02
❑ 439 Tim Jones .05 .02
❑ 440 Pedro Guerrero .10 .04
❑ 441 Milt Thompson .05 .02
❑ 442 Willie McGee .10 .04
❑ 443 Vince Coleman .05 .02
❑ 444 Tom Brunansky .05 .02
❑ 445 Walt Terrell .05 .02
❑ 446 Eric Show .05 .02
❑ 447 Mark Davis .05 .02
❑ 448 Andy Benes RC .40 .16
❑ 449 Ed Whitson .05 .02
❑ 450 Dennis Rasmussen .05 .02
❑ 451 Bruce Hurst .05 .02
❑ 452 Pat Clements .05 .02
❑ 453 Benito Santiago .10 .04
❑ 454 Sandy Alomar Jr. RC .40 .16
❑ 455 Garry Templeton .10 .04
❑ 456 Jack Clark .10 .04
❑ 457 Tim Flannery .05 .02
❑ 458 Roberto Alomar .25 .10
❑ 459 Carmelo Martinez .05 .02
❑ 460 John Kruk .10 .04
❑ 461 Tony Gwynn .30 .12
❑ 462 Jerald Clark RC .10 .04
❑ 463 Don Robinson .05 .02
❑ 464 Craig Lefferts .05 .02
❑ 465 Kelly Downs .05 .02
❑ 466 Rick Reuschel .10 .04
❑ 467 Scott Garrelts .05 .02
❑ 468 Wil Tejada .05 .02
❑ 469 Kirt Manwaring .05 .02
❑ 470 Terry Kennedy .05 .02
❑ 471 Jose Uribe .05 .02
❑ 472 Royce Clayton RC .40 .16
❑ 473 Robby Thompson .05 .02
❑ 474 Kevin Mitchell .10 .04
❑ 475 Ernie Riles .05 .02
❑ 476 Will Clark .25 .10
❑ 477 Donell Nixon .05 .02
❑ 478 Candy Maldonado .05 .02
❑ 479 Tracy Jones .05 .02
❑ 480 Brett Butler .10 .04
❑ 481 Checklist 1-121 .05 .02
❑ 482 Checklist 122-242 .05 .02
❑ 483 Checklist 243-363 .05 .02
❑ 484 Checklist 364-484 .05 .02

1990 Bowman

	Nm-Mt	Ex-Mt
COMPLETE SET (528)	25.00	7.50
COMP.FACT.SET (528)	25.00	7.50

❑ 1 Tommy Greene RC .10 .03
❑ 2 Tom Glavine .15 .04
❑ 3 Andy Nezelek .05 .02
❑ 4 Mike Stanton RC .25 .07
❑ 5 Rick Luecken .05 .02
❑ 6 Kent Mercker RC .25 .07
❑ 7 Derek Lilliquist .05 .02
❑ 8 Charlie Leibrandt .05 .02
❑ 9 Steve Avery .05 .02
❑ 10 John Smoltz .25 .07
❑ 11 Mark Lemke .05 .02
❑ 12 Lonnie Smith .05 .02
❑ 13 Oddibe McDowell .05 .02
❑ 14 Tyler Houston RC .25 .07
❑ 15 Jeff Blauser .05 .02
❑ 16 Ernie Whitt .05 .02
❑ 17 Alexis Infante .05 .02
❑ 18 Jim Presley .05 .02
❑ 19 Dale Murphy .25 .07
❑ 20 Nick Esasky .05 .02
❑ 21 Rick Sutcliffe .10 .03
❑ 22 Mike Bielecki .05 .02
❑ 23 Steve Wilson .05 .02
❑ 24 Kevin Blankenship .05 .02
❑ 25 Mitch Williams .05 .02
❑ 26 Dean Wilkins .05 .02
❑ 27 Greg Maddux .40 .12
❑ 28 Mike Harkey .05 .02
❑ 29 Mark Grace .15 .04
❑ 30 Ryne Sandberg .40 .12

❑ 31	Greg Smith	.05	.02
❑ 32	Dwight Smith	.05	.02
❑ 33	Damon Berryhill	.05	.02
❑ 34	E.Cunningham UER RC (Errant * by the word "in")	.10	.03
❑ 35	Jerome Walton	.05	.02
❑ 36	Lloyd McClendon	.05	.02
❑ 37	Ty Griffin	.05	.02
❑ 38	Shawon Dunston	.05	.02
❑ 39	Andre Dawson	.10	.03
❑ 40	Luis Salazar	.05	.02
❑ 41	Tim Layana	.05	.02
❑ 42	Rob Dibble	.10	.03
❑ 43	Tom Browning	.05	.02
❑ 44	Danny Jackson	.05	.02
❑ 45	Jose Rijo	.05	.02
❑ 46	Scott Scudder	.05	.02
❑ 47	Randy Myers UER (Career ERA .274, should be 2.74)	.10	.03
❑ 48	Brian Lane RC	.10	.03
❑ 49	Paul O'Neill	.15	.04
❑ 50	Barry Larkin	.15	.04
❑ 51	Reggie Jefferson RC	.25	.07
❑ 52	Jeff Branson RC**	.10	.03
❑ 53	Chris Sabo	.05	.02
❑ 54	Joe Oliver	.05	.02
❑ 55	Todd Benzinger	.05	.02
❑ 56	Rolando Roomes	.05	.02
❑ 57	Hal Morris	.05	.02
❑ 58	Eric Davis	.10	.03
❑ 59	Scott Bryant	.05	.02
❑ 60	Ken Griffey Sr.	.10	.03
❑ 61	Darryl Kile RC	1.00	.30
❑ 62	Dave Smith	.05	.02
❑ 63	Mark Portugal	.05	.02
❑ 64	Jeff Juden RC	.10	.03
❑ 65	Bill Gullickson	.05	.02
❑ 66	Danny Darwin	.05	.02
❑ 67	Larry Andersen	.05	.02
❑ 68	Jose Cano	.05	.02
❑ 69	Dan Schatzeder	.05	.02
❑ 70	Jim Deshaies	.05	.02
❑ 71	Mike Scott	.05	.02
❑ 72	Gerald Young	.05	.02
❑ 73	Ken Caminiti	.10	.03
❑ 74	Ken Oberkfell	.05	.02
❑ 75	Dave Rohde	.05	.02
❑ 76	Bill Doran	.05	.02
❑ 77	Andujar Cedeno RC	.10	.03
❑ 78	Craig Biggio	.15	.04
❑ 79	Karl Rhodes RC	.25	.07
❑ 80	Glenn Davis	.05	.02
❑ 81	Eric Anthony RC	.10	.03
❑ 82	John Wetteland	.25	.07
❑ 83	Jay Howell	.05	.02
❑ 84	Orel Hershiser	.10	.03
❑ 85	Tim Belcher	.05	.02
❑ 86	Kiki Jones	.05	.02
❑ 87	Mike Hartley	.05	.02
❑ 88	Ramon Martinez	.05	.02
❑ 89	Mike Scioscia	.05	.02
❑ 90	Willie Randolph	.10	.03
❑ 91	Juan Samuel	.05	.02
❑ 92	Jose Offerman RC	.25	.07
❑ 93	Dave Hansen RC	.25	.07
❑ 94	Jeff Hamilton	.05	.02
❑ 95	Alfredo Griffin	.05	.02
❑ 96	Tom Goodwin RC	.25	.07
❑ 97	Kirk Gibson	.10	.03
❑ 98	Jose Vizcaino RC	.25	.07
❑ 99	Kal Daniels	.05	.02
❑ 100	Hubie Brooks	.05	.02
❑ 101	Eddie Murray	.25	.07
❑ 102	Dennis Boyd	.05	.02
❑ 103	Tim Burke	.05	.02
❑ 104	Bill Sampen	.05	.02
❑ 105	Brett Gideon	.05	.02
❑ 106	Mark Gardner RC	.10	.03
❑ 107	Howard Farmer	.05	.02
❑ 108	Mel Rojas RC	.10	.03
❑ 109	Kevin Gross	.05	.02
❑ 110	Dave Schmidt	.05	.02
❑ 111	Dennis Martinez	.10	.03
❑ 112	Jerry Goff	.05	.02
❑ 113	Andres Galarraga	.10	.03
❑ 114	Tim Wallach	.05	.02
❑ 115	Marquis Grissom RC	.50	.15
❑ 116	Spike Owen	.05	.02
❑ 117	Larry Walker RC	1.50	.45
❑ 118	Tim Raines	.10	.03
❑ 119	Delino DeShields RC	.25	.07
❑ 120	Tom Foley	.05	.02
❑ 121	Dave Martinez	.05	.02
❑ 122	Frank Viola UER (Career ERA .384 should be 3.84)	.05	.02
❑ 123	Julio Valera RC	.05	.02
❑ 124	Alejandro Pena	.05	.02
❑ 125	David Cone	.10	.03
❑ 126	Dwight Gooden	.10	.03
❑ 127	Kevin D. Brown	.05	.02
❑ 128	John Franco	.10	.03
❑ 129	Terry Bross	.05	.02
❑ 130	Blaine Beatty	.05	.02
❑ 131	Sid Fernandez	.05	.02
❑ 132	Mike Marshall	.05	.02
❑ 133	Howard Johnson	.05	.02
❑ 134	Jaime Roseboro	.05	.02
❑ 135	Alan Zinter RC	.10	.03
❑ 136	Keith Miller	.05	.02
❑ 137	Kevin Elster	.05	.02
❑ 138	Kevin McReynolds	.05	.02
❑ 139	Barry Lyons	.05	.02
❑ 140	Gregg Jefferies	.10	.03
❑ 141	Darryl Strawberry	.10	.03
❑ 142	Todd Hundley RC	.25	.07
❑ 143	Scott Service	.05	.02
❑ 144	Chuck Malone	.05	.02
❑ 145	Steve Ontiveros	.05	.02
❑ 146	Roger McDowell	.05	.02
❑ 147	Ken Howell	.05	.02
❑ 148	Pat Combs	.05	.02
❑ 149	Jeff Parrett	.05	.02
❑ 150	Chuck McElroy RC	.10	.03
❑ 151	Jason Grimsley RC	.10	.03
❑ 152	Len Dykstra	.10	.03
❑ 153	M.Morandini RC	.25	.07
❑ 154	John Kruk	.10	.03
❑ 155	Dickie Thon	.05	.02
❑ 156	Ricky Jordan	.05	.02
❑ 157	Jeff Jackson RC	.10	.03
❑ 158	Darren Daulton	.10	.03
❑ 159	Tom Herr	.05	.02
❑ 160	Von Hayes	.05	.02
❑ 161	Dave Hollins RC	.25	.07
❑ 162	Carmelo Martinez	.05	.02
❑ 163	Bob Walk	.05	.02
❑ 164	Doug Drabek	.05	.02
❑ 165	Walt Terrell	.05	.02
❑ 166	Bill Landrum	.05	.02
❑ 167	Scott Ruskin	.05	.02
❑ 168	Bob Patterson	.05	.02
❑ 169	Bobby Bonilla	.10	.03
❑ 170	Jose Lind	.05	.02
❑ 171	Andy Van Slyke	.10	.03
❑ 172	Mike LaValliere	.05	.02
❑ 173	Willie Greene RC	.10	.03
❑ 174	Jay Bell	.10	.03
❑ 175	Sid Bream	.05	.02
❑ 176	Tom Prince	.05	.02
❑ 177	Wally Backman	.05	.02
❑ 178	Moises Alou RC	.75	.23
❑ 179	Steve Carter	.05	.02
❑ 180	Gary Redus	.05	.02
❑ 181	Barry Bonds	.60	.18
❑ 182	Don Slaught UER (Card back shows headings for a pitcher)	.05	.02
❑ 183	Joe Magrane	.05	.02
❑ 184	Bryn Smith	.05	.02
❑ 185	Todd Worrell	.05	.02
❑ 186	Jose DeLeon	.05	.02
❑ 187	Frank DiPino	.05	.02
❑ 188	John Tudor	.05	.02
❑ 189	Howard Hilton	.05	.02
❑ 190	John Ericks	.05	.02
❑ 191	Ken Dayley	.05	.02
❑ 192	Ray Lankford RC	.25	.07
❑ 193	Todd Zeile	.10	.03
❑ 194	Willie McGee	.10	.03
❑ 195	Ozzie Smith	.40	.12
❑ 196	Milt Thompson	.05	.02
❑ 197	Terry Pendleton	.10	.03
❑ 198	Vince Coleman	.05	.02
❑ 199	Paul Coleman RC	.10	.03
❑ 200	Jose Oquendo	.05	.02
❑ 201	Pedro Guerrero	.05	.02
❑ 202	Tom Brunansky	.05	.02
❑ 203	Roger Smithberg	.05	.02
❑ 204	Eddie Whitson	.05	.02
❑ 205	Dennis Rasmussen	.05	.02
❑ 206	Craig Lefferts	.05	.02
❑ 207	Andy Benes	.10	.03
❑ 208	Bruce Hurst	.05	.02
❑ 209	Eric Show	.05	.02
❑ 210	Rafael Valdez	.05	.02
❑ 211	Joey Cora	.10	.03
❑ 212	Thomas Howard	.05	.02
❑ 213	Rob Nelson	.05	.02
❑ 214	Jack Clark	.10	.03
❑ 215	Garry Templeton	.05	.02
❑ 216	Fred Lynn	.05	.02
❑ 217	Tony Gwynn	.30	.09
❑ 218	Benito Santiago	.10	.03
❑ 219	Mike Pagliarulo	.05	.02
❑ 220	Joe Carter	.10	.03
❑ 221	Roberto Alomar	.15	.04
❑ 222	Bip Roberts	.05	.02
❑ 223	Rick Reuschel	.05	.02
❑ 224	Russ Swan	.05	.02
❑ 225	Eric Gunderson	.05	.02
❑ 226	Steve Bedrosian	.05	.02
❑ 227	Mike Remlinger	.05	.02
❑ 228	Scott Garrelts	.05	.02
❑ 229	Ernie Camacho	.05	.02
❑ 230	Andres Santana RC	.10	.03
❑ 231	Will Clark	.25	.07
❑ 232	Kevin Mitchell	.05	.02
❑ 233	Robby Thompson	.05	.02
❑ 234	Bill Bathe	.05	.02
❑ 235	Tony Perezchica	.05	.02
❑ 236	Gary Carter	.10	.03
❑ 237	Brett Butler	.10	.03
❑ 238	Matt Williams	.10	.03
❑ 239	Earnie Riles	.05	.02
❑ 240	Kevin Bass	.05	.02
❑ 241	Terry Kennedy	.05	.02
❑ 242	Steve Hosey RC	.10	.03
❑ 243	Ben McDonald RC	.25	.07
❑ 244	Jeff Ballard	.05	.02
❑ 245	Joe Price	.05	.02
❑ 246	Curt Schilling	1.00	.30
❑ 247	Pete Harnisch	.05	.02
❑ 248	Mark Williamson	.05	.02
❑ 249	Gregg Olson	.10	.03
❑ 250	Chris Myers	.05	.02
❑ 251	David Segui RC ERR (Missing vital stats at top of card back under name)	.25	.07
❑ 251B	David Segui COR RC	.25	.07
❑ 252	Joe Orsulak	.05	.02
❑ 253	Craig Worthington	.05	.02
❑ 254	Mickey Tettleton	.05	.02
❑ 255	Cal Ripken	.75	.23
❑ 256	Bill Ripken	.05	.02
❑ 257	Randy Milligan	.05	.02
❑ 258	Brady Anderson	.10	.03
❑ 259	Chris Hoiles RC UER Baltimore is spelled Balitmore	.25	.07
❑ 260	Mike Devereaux	.05	.02
❑ 261	Phil Bradley	.05	.02
❑ 262	Leo Gomez RC	.10	.03
❑ 263	Lee Smith	.10	.03
❑ 264	Mike Rochford	.05	.02
❑ 265	Jeff Reardon	.10	.03
❑ 266	Wes Gardner	.05	.02
❑ 267	Mike Boddicker	.05	.02
❑ 268	Roger Clemens	.50	.15
❑ 269	Rob Murphy	.05	.02
❑ 270	Mickey Pina	.05	.02
❑ 271	Tony Pena	.05	.02
❑ 272	Jody Reed	.05	.02
❑ 273	Kevin Romine	.05	.02
❑ 274	Mike Greenwell	.05	.02
❑ 275	Maurice Vaughn RC	1.00	.30

	No.	Player	Price	Price
❑	276	Danny Heep	.05	.02
❑	277	Scott Cooper RC	.10	.03
❑	278	Greg Blosser RC	.10	.03
❑	279	Dwight Evans UER (* by "1990 Team Breakdown")	.10	.03
❑	280	Ellis Burks	.15	.04
❑	281	Wade Boggs	.15	.04
❑	282	Marty Barrett	.05	.02
❑	283	Kirk McCaskill	.05	.02
❑	284	Mark Langston	.05	.02
❑	285	Bert Blyleven	.10	.03
❑	286	Mike Fetters RC	.25	.07
❑	287	Kyle Abbott	.05	.02
❑	288	Jim Abbott	.15	.04
❑	289	Chuck Finley	.10	.03
❑	290	Gary DiSarcina RC	.25	.07
❑	291	Dick Schofield	.05	.02
❑	292	Devon White	.10	.03
❑	293	Bobby Rose	.05	.02
❑	294	Brian Downing	.05	.02
❑	295	Lance Parrish	.05	.02
❑	296	Jack Howell	.05	.02
❑	297	Claudell Washington	.05	.02
❑	298	John Orton RC	.10	.03
❑	299	Wally Joyner	.10	.03
❑	300	Lee Stevens	.10	.03
❑	301	Chili Davis	.10	.03
❑	302	Johnny Ray	.05	.02
❑	303	Greg Hibbard RC	.10	.03
❑	304	Eric King	.05	.02
❑	305	Jack McDowell	.05	.02
❑	306	Bobby Thigpen	.05	.02
❑	307	Adam Peterson	.05	.02
❑	308	Scott Radinsky RC	.25	.07
❑	309	Wayne Edwards	.05	.02
❑	310	Melido Perez	.05	.02
❑	311	Robin Ventura	.25	.07
❑	312	Sammy Sosa RC	8.00	2.40
❑	313	Dan Pasqua	.05	.02
❑	314	Carlton Fisk	.15	.04
❑	315	Ozzie Guillen	.05	.02
❑	316	Ivan Calderon	.05	.02
❑	317	Daryl Boston	.05	.02
❑	318	Craig Grebeck RC	.25	.07
❑	319	Scott Fletcher	.05	.02
❑	320	Frank Thomas RC	2.00	.60
❑	321	Steve Lyons	.05	.02
❑	322	Carlos Martinez	.05	.02
❑	323	Joe Skalski	.05	.02
❑	324	Tom Candiotti	.05	.02
❑	325	Greg Swindell	.05	.02
❑	326	Steve Olin RC	.25	.07
❑	327	Kevin Wickander	.05	.02
❑	328	Doug Jones	.05	.02
❑	329	Jeff Shaw	.05	.02
❑	330	Kevin Bearse	.05	.02
❑	331	Dion James	.05	.02
❑	332	Jerry Browne	.05	.02
❑	333	Joey Belle	.25	.07
❑	334	Felix Fermin	.05	.02
❑	335	Candy Maldonado	.05	.02
❑	336	Cory Snyder	.05	.02
❑	337	Sandy Alomar Jr.	.10	.03
❑	338	Mark Lewis	.05	.02
❑	339	Carlos Baerga RC	.25	.07
❑	340	Chris James	.05	.02
❑	341	Brook Jacoby	.05	.02
❑	342	Keith Hernandez	.10	.03
❑	343	Frank Tanana	.05	.02
❑	344	Scott Aldred	.05	.02
❑	345	Mike Henneman	.05	.02
❑	346	Steve Wapnick	.05	.02
❑	347	Greg Gohr RC	.10	.03
❑	348	Eric Stone	.05	.02
❑	349	Brian DuBois	.05	.02
❑	350	Kevin Ritz	.05	.02
❑	351	Rico Brogna	.25	.07
❑	352	Mike Heath	.05	.02
❑	353	Alan Trammell	.10	.03
❑	354	Chet Lemon	.05	.02
❑	355	Dave Bergman	.05	.02
❑	356	Lou Whitaker	.10	.03
❑	357	Cecil Fielder UER * by 1990 Team Breakdown	.10	.03
❑	358	Milt Cuyler RC	.10	.03
❑	359	Tony Phillips	.05	.02
❑	360	Travis Fryman RC	.50	.15
❑	361	Ed Romero	.05	.02
❑	362	Lloyd Moseby	.05	.02
❑	363	Mark Gubicza	.05	.02
❑	364	Bret Saberhagen	.10	.03
❑	365	Tom Gordon	.10	.03
❑	366	Steve Farr	.05	.02
❑	367	Kevin Appier	.10	.03
❑	368	Storm Davis	.05	.02
❑	369	Mark Davis	.05	.02
❑	370	Jeff Montgomery	.10	.03
❑	371	Frank White	.10	.03
❑	372	Brent Mayne RC	.25	.07
❑	373	Bob Boone	.10	.03
❑	374	Jim Eisenreich	.05	.02
❑	375	Danny Tartabull	.05	.02
❑	376	Kurt Stillwell	.05	.02
❑	377	Bill Pecota	.05	.02
❑	378	Bo Jackson	.25	.07
❑	379	Bob Hamelin RC	.25	.07
❑	380	Kevin Seitzer	.05	.02
❑	381	Rey Palacios	.05	.02
❑	382	George Brett	.60	.18
❑	383	Gerald Perry	.05	.02
❑	384	Teddy Higuera	.05	.02
❑	385	Tom Filer	.05	.02
❑	386	Dan Plesac	.05	.02
❑	387	Cal Eldred RC	.25	.07
❑	388	Jaime Navarro	.05	.02
❑	389	Chris Bosio	.05	.02
❑	390	Randy Veres	.05	.02
❑	391	Gary Sheffield	.25	.07
❑	392	George Canale	.05	.02
❑	393	B.J. Surhoff	.10	.03
❑	394	Tim McIntosh	.05	.02
❑	395	Greg Brock	.05	.02
❑	396	Greg Vaughn	.05	.02
❑	397	Darryl Hamilton	.05	.02
❑	398	Dave Parker	.10	.03
❑	399	Paul Molitor	.15	.04
❑	400	Jim Gantner	.05	.02
❑	401	Rob Deer	.05	.02
❑	402	Billy Spiers	.05	.02
❑	403	Glenn Braggs	.05	.02
❑	404	Robin Yount	.40	.12
❑	405	Rick Aguilera	.10	.03
❑	406	Johnny Ard	.05	.02
❑	407	Kevin Tapani RC	.25	.07
❑	408	Park Pittman	.05	.02
❑	409	Allan Anderson	.05	.02
❑	410	Juan Berenguer	.05	.02
❑	411	Willie Banks RC	.10	.03
❑	412	Rich Yett	.05	.02
❑	413	Dave West	.05	.02
❑	414	Greg Gagne	.05	.02
❑	415	Chuck Knoblauch RC	.50	.15
❑	416	Randy Bush	.05	.02
❑	417	Gary Gaetti	.10	.03
❑	418	Kent Hrbek	.10	.03
❑	419	Al Newman	.05	.02
❑	420	Danny Gladden	.05	.02
❑	421	Paul Sorrento RC	.25	.07
❑	422	Derek Parks RC	.10	.03
❑	423	Scott Leius RC	.10	.03
❑	424	Kirby Puckett	.25	.07
❑	425	Willie Smith	.05	.02
❑	426	Dave Righetti	.05	.02
❑	427	Jeff D. Robinson	.05	.02
❑	428	Alan Mills RC	.10	.03
❑	429	Tim Leary	.05	.02
❑	430	Pascual Perez	.05	.02
❑	431	Alvaro Espinoza	.05	.02
❑	432	Dave Winfield	.10	.03
❑	433	Jesse Barfield	.05	.02
❑	434	Randy Velarde	.05	.02
❑	435	Rick Cerone	.05	.02
❑	436	Steve Balboni	.05	.02
❑	437	Mel Hall	.05	.02
❑	438	Bob Geren	.05	.02
❑	439	Bernie Williams RC	1.50	.45
❑	440	Kevin Maas RC	.25	.07
❑	441	Mike Blowers RC	.10	.03
❑	442	Steve Sax	.05	.02
❑	443	Don Mattingly	.60	.18
❑	444	Roberto Kelly	.05	.02
❑	445	Mike Moore	.05	.02
❑	446	Reggie Harris RC	.10	.03
❑	447	Scott Sanderson	.05	.02
❑	448	Dave Otto	.05	.02
❑	449	Dave Stewart	.10	.03
❑	450	Rick Honeycutt	.05	.02
❑	451	Dennis Eckersley	.10	.03
❑	452	Carney Lansford	.10	.03
❑	453	Scott Hemond RC	.10	.03
❑	454	Mark McGwire	.60	.18
❑	455	Felix Jose	.05	.02
❑	456	Terry Steinbach	.05	.02
❑	457	Rickey Henderson	.25	.07
❑	458	Dave Henderson	.05	.02
❑	459	Mike Gallego	.05	.02
❑	460	Jose Canseco	.25	.07
❑	461	Walt Weiss	.05	.02
❑	462	Ken Phelps	.05	.02
❑	463	Darren Lewis RC	.10	.03
❑	464	Ron Hassey	.05	.02
❑	465	Roger Salkeld RC	.10	.03
❑	466	Scott Bankhead	.05	.02
❑	467	Keith Comstock	.05	.02
❑	468	Randy Johnson	.50	.12
❑	469	Erik Hanson	.05	.02
❑	470	Mike Schooler	.05	.02
❑	471	Gary Eave	.05	.02
❑	472	Jeffrey Leonard	.05	.02
❑	473	Dave Valle	.05	.02
❑	474	Omar Vizquel	.25	.07
❑	475	Pete O'Brien	.05	.02
❑	476	Henry Cotto	.05	.02
❑	477	Jay Buhner	.10	.03
❑	478	Harold Reynolds	.10	.03
❑	479	Alvin Davis	.05	.02
❑	480	Darnell Coles	.05	.02
❑	481	Ken Griffey Jr.	.75	.23
❑	482	Greg Briley	.05	.02
❑	483	Scott Bradley	.05	.02
❑	484	Tino Martinez	.25	.07
❑	485	Jeff Russell	.05	.02
❑	486	Nolan Ryan	1.00	.30
❑	487	Robb Nen RC	.50	.15
❑	488	Kevin Brown	.10	.03
❑	489	Brian Bohanon RC	.10	.03
❑	490	Ruben Sierra	.05	.02
❑	491	Pete Incaviglia	.05	.02
❑	492	Juan Gonzalez RC	2.00	.60
❑	493	Steve Buechele	.05	.02
❑	494	Scott Coolbaugh	.05	.02
❑	495	Geno Petralli	.05	.02
❑	496	Rafael Palmeiro	.15	.04
❑	497	Julio Franco	.10	.03
❑	498	Gary Pettis	.05	.02
❑	499	Donald Harris	.05	.02
❑	500	Monty Fariss	.05	.02
❑	501	Harold Baines	.10	.03
❑	502	Cecil Espy	.05	.02
❑	503	Jack Daugherty	.05	.02
❑	504	Willie Blair RC	.10	.03
❑	505	Dave Stieb	.10	.03
❑	506	Tom Henke	.05	.02
❑	507	John Cerutti	.05	.02
❑	508	Paul Kilgus	.05	.02
❑	509	Jimmy Key	.10	.03
❑	510	John Olerud RC	1.00	.30
❑	511	Ed Sprague	.10	.03
❑	512	Manuel Lee	.05	.02
❑	513	Fred McGriff	.25	.07
❑	514	Glenallen Hill	.05	.02
❑	515	George Bell	.05	.02
❑	516	Mookie Wilson	.10	.03
❑	517	Luis Sojo RC	.25	.07
❑	518	Nelson Liriano	.05	.02
❑	519	Kelly Gruber	.05	.02
❑	520	Greg Myers	.05	.02
❑	521	Pat Borders	.05	.02
❑	522	Junior Felix	.05	.02
❑	523	Eddie Zosky RC	.10	.03
❑	524	Tony Fernandez	.05	.02
❑	525	Checklist 1-132 UER (No copyright mark on the back)	.05	.02
❑	526	Checklist 133-264	.05	.02
❑	527	Checklist 265-396	.05	.02
❑	528	Checklist 397-528	.05	.02

1991 Bowman

	Nm-Mt	Ex-Mt
COMPLETE SET (704)	40.00	12.00
COMP.FACT.SET (704)	40.00	12.00
❑ 1 Rod Carew I	.15	.04
❑ 2 Rod Carew II	.15	.04
❑ 3 Rod Carew III	.15	.04
❑ 4 Rod Carew IV	.15	.04
❑ 5 Rod Carew V	.15	.04
❑ 6 Willie Fraser	.05	.02
❑ 7 John Olerud	.10	.03
❑ 8 William Suero	.05	.02
❑ 9 Roberto Alomar	.15	.04
❑ 10 Todd Stottlemyre	.05	.02
❑ 11 Joe Carter	.10	.03
❑ 12 Steve Karsay RC	.50	.15
❑ 13 Mark Whiten	.05	.02
❑ 14 Pat Borders	.05	.02
❑ 15 Mike Timlin RC	.75	.23
❑ 16 Tom Henke	.05	.02
❑ 17 Eddie Zosky	.05	.02
❑ 18 Kelly Gruber	.05	.02
❑ 19 Jimmy Key	.10	.03
❑ 20 Jerry Schunk	.05	.02
❑ 21 Manuel Lee	.05	.02
❑ 22 Dave Stieb	.05	.02
❑ 23 Pat Hentgen RC	.50	.15
❑ 24 Glenallen Hill	.05	.02
❑ 25 Rene Gonzales	.05	.02
❑ 26 Ed Sprague	.05	.02
❑ 27 Ken Dayley	.05	.02
❑ 28 Pat Tabler	.05	.02
❑ 29 Denis Boucher RC	.15	.04
❑ 30 Devon White	.10	.03
❑ 31 Dante Bichette	.10	.03
❑ 32 Paul Molitor	.15	.04
❑ 33 Greg Vaughn	.05	.02
❑ 34 Dan Plesac	.05	.02
❑ 35 Chris George RC	.15	.04
❑ 36 Tim McIntosh	.05	.02
❑ 37 Franklin Stubbs	.05	.02
❑ 38 Bo Dodson RC	.15	.04
❑ 39 Ron Robinson	.05	.02
❑ 40 Ed Nunez	.05	.02
❑ 41 Greg Brock	.05	.02
❑ 42 Jaime Navarro	.05	.02
❑ 43 Chris Bosio	.05	.02
❑ 44 B.J. Surhoff	.10	.03
❑ 45 Chris Johnson	.05	.02
❑ 46 Willie Randolph	.10	.03
❑ 47 Narciso Elvira	.05	.02
❑ 48 Jim Gantner	.05	.02
❑ 49 Kevin Brown	.05	.02
❑ 50 Julio Machado	.05	.02
❑ 51 Chuck Crim	.05	.02
❑ 52 Gary Sheffield	.10	.03
❑ 53 Angel Miranda RC	.15	.04
❑ 54 Ted Higuera	.05	.02
❑ 55 Robin Yount	.40	.12
❑ 56 Cal Eldred	.05	.02
❑ 57 Sandy Alomar Jr.	.05	.02
❑ 58 Greg Swindell	.05	.02
❑ 59 Brook Jacoby	.05	.02
❑ 60 Efrain Valdez	.05	.02
❑ 61 Ever Magallanes	.05	.02
❑ 62 Tom Candiotti	.05	.02
❑ 63 Eric King	.05	.02
❑ 64 Alex Cole	.05	.02
❑ 65 Charles Nagy	.05	.02
❑ 66 Mitch Webster	.05	.02
❑ 67 Chris James	.05	.02
❑ 68 Jim Thome RC	5.00	1.50
❑ 69 Carlos Baerga	.05	.02
❑ 70 Mark Lewis	.05	.02
❑ 71 Jerry Browne	.05	.02
❑ 72 Jesse Orosco	.05	.02
❑ 73 Mike Huff	.05	.02
❑ 74 Jose Escobar	.05	.02
❑ 75 Jeff Manto	.05	.02
❑ 76 Turner Ward RC	.15	.04
❑ 77 Doug Jones	.05	.02
❑ 78 Bruce Egloff	.05	.02
❑ 79 Tim Costo RC	.15	.04
❑ 80 Beau Allred	.05	.02
❑ 81 Albert Belle	.10	.03
❑ 82 John Farrell	.05	.02
❑ 83 Glenn Davis	.05	.02
❑ 84 Joe Orsulak	.05	.02
❑ 85 Mark Williamson	.05	.02
❑ 86 Ben McDonald	.05	.02
❑ 87 Billy Ripken	.05	.02
❑ 88 Leo Gomez UER Baltimore is spelled Baltimore	.05	.02
❑ 89 Bob Melvin	.05	.02
❑ 90 Jeff M. Robinson	.05	.02
❑ 91 Jose Mesa	.05	.02
❑ 92 Gregg Olson	.05	.02
❑ 93 Mike Devereaux	.05	.02
❑ 94 Luis Mercedes RC	.15	.04
❑ 95 Arthur Rhodes RC	.50	.15
❑ 96 Juan Bell	.05	.02
❑ 97 Mike Mussina RC	2.50	.75
❑ 98 Jeff Ballard	.05	.02
❑ 99 Chris Hoiles	.05	.02
❑ 100 Brady Anderson	.10	.03
❑ 101 Bob Milacki	.05	.02
❑ 102 David Segui	.05	.02
❑ 103 Dwight Evans	.10	.03
❑ 104 Cal Ripken	.75	.23
❑ 105 Mike Linskey	.05	.02
❑ 106 Jeff Tackett RC	.15	.04
❑ 107 Jeff Reardon	.10	.03
❑ 108 Dana Kiecker	.05	.02
❑ 109 Ellis Burks	.10	.03
❑ 110 Dave Owen	.05	.02
❑ 111 Danny Darwin	.05	.02
❑ 112 Mo Vaughn	.10	.03
❑ 113 Jeff McNeely RC	.15	.04
❑ 114 Tom Bolton	.05	.02
❑ 115 Greg Blosser	.05	.02
❑ 116 Mike Greenwell	.05	.02
❑ 117 Phil Plantier RC	.15	.04
❑ 118 Roger Clemens	.50	.15
❑ 119 John Marzano	.05	.02
❑ 120 Jody Reed	.05	.02
❑ 121 Scott Taylor RC	.15	.04
❑ 122 Jack Clark	.10	.03
❑ 123 Derek Livernois	.05	.02
❑ 124 Tony Pena	.05	.02
❑ 125 Tom Brunansky	.05	.02
❑ 126 Carlos Quintana	.05	.02
❑ 127 Tim Naehring	.05	.02
❑ 128 Matt Young	.05	.02
❑ 129 Wade Boggs	.15	.04
❑ 130 Kevin Morton	.05	.02
❑ 131 Pete Incaviglia	.05	.02
❑ 132 Rob Deer	.05	.02
❑ 133 Bill Gullickson	.05	.02
❑ 134 Rico Brogna	.05	.02
❑ 135 Lloyd Moseby	.05	.02
❑ 136 Cecil Fielder	.10	.03
❑ 137 Tony Phillips	.05	.02
❑ 138 Mark Leiter RC	.15	.04
❑ 139 John Cerutti	.05	.02
❑ 140 Mickey Tettleton	.05	.02
❑ 141 Milt Cuyler	.05	.02
❑ 142 Greg Gohr	.05	.02
❑ 143 Tony Bernazard	.05	.02
❑ 144 Dan Gakeler	.05	.02
❑ 145 Travis Fryman	.10	.03
❑ 146 Dan Petry	.05	.02
❑ 147 Scott Aldred	.05	.02
❑ 148 John DeSilva	.05	.02
❑ 149 Rusty Meacham RC	.15	.04
❑ 150 Lou Whitaker	.10	.03
❑ 151 Dave Haas	.05	.02
❑ 152 Luis de los Santos	.05	.02
❑ 153 Ivan Cruz	.05	.02
❑ 154 Alan Trammell	.10	.03
❑ 155 Pat Kelly RC	.05	.02
❑ 156 Carl Everett RC	.75	.23
❑ 157 Greg Cadaret	.05	.02
❑ 158 Kevin Maas	.05	.02
❑ 159 Jeff Johnson	.05	.02
❑ 160 Willie Smith	.05	.02
❑ 161 Gerald Williams RC	.50	.15
❑ 162 Mike Humphreys RC	.15	.04
❑ 163 Alvaro Espinoza	.05	.02
❑ 164 Matt Nokes	.05	.02
❑ 165 Wade Taylor	.05	.02
❑ 166 Roberto Kelly	.05	.02
❑ 167 John Habyan	.05	.02
❑ 168 Steve Farr	.05	.02
❑ 169 Jesse Barfield	.05	.02
❑ 170 Steve Sax	.05	.02
❑ 171 Jim Leyritz	.05	.02
❑ 172 Robert Eenhoorn RC	.15	.04
❑ 173 Bernie Williams	.25	.07
❑ 174 Scott Lusader	.05	.02
❑ 175 Torey Lovullo	.05	.02
❑ 176 Chuck Cary	.05	.02
❑ 177 Scott Sanderson	.05	.02
❑ 178 Don Mattingly	.60	.18
❑ 179 Mel Hall	.05	.02
❑ 180 Juan Gonzalez	.15	.04
❑ 181 Hensley Meulens	.05	.02
❑ 182 Jose Offerman	.05	.02
❑ 183 Jeff Bagwell RC	2.00	.60
❑ 184 Jeff Conine RC	.75	.23
❑ 185 Henry Rodriguez RC	.50	.15
❑ 186 Jimmie Reese CO	.10	.03
❑ 187 Kyle Abbott	.05	.02
❑ 188 Lance Parrish	.10	.03
❑ 189 Rafael Montalvo	.05	.02
❑ 190 Floyd Bannister	.05	.02
❑ 191 Dick Schofield	.05	.02
❑ 192 Scott Lewis	.05	.02
❑ 193 Jeff D. Robinson	.05	.02
❑ 194 Kent Anderson	.05	.02
❑ 195 Wally Joyner	.10	.03
❑ 196 Chuck Finley	.10	.03
❑ 197 Luis Sojo	.05	.02
❑ 198 Jeff Richardson	.05	.02
❑ 199 Dave Parker	.10	.03
❑ 200 Jim Abbott	.15	.04
❑ 201 Junior Felix	.05	.02
❑ 202 Mark Langston	.05	.02
❑ 203 Tim Salmon RC	2.00	.60
❑ 204 Cliff Young	.05	.02
❑ 205 Scott Bailes	.05	.02
❑ 206 Bobby Rose	.05	.02
❑ 207 Gary Gaetti	.10	.03
❑ 208 Ruben Amaro RC	.15	.04
❑ 209 Luis Polonia	.05	.02
❑ 210 Dave Winfield	.10	.03
❑ 211 Bryan Harvey	.05	.02
❑ 212 Mike Moore	.05	.02
❑ 213 Rickey Henderson	.25	.07
❑ 214 Steve Chitren	.05	.02
❑ 215 Bob Welch	.05	.02
❑ 216 Terry Steinbach	.05	.02
❑ 217 Earnest Riles	.05	.02
❑ 218 Todd Van Poppel RC	.50	.15
❑ 219 Mike Gallego	.05	.02
❑ 220 Curt Young	.05	.02
❑ 221 Todd Burns	.05	.02
❑ 222 Vance Law	.05	.02
❑ 223 Eric Show	.05	.02
❑ 224 Don Peters	.05	.02
❑ 225 Dave Stewart	.10	.03
❑ 226 Dave Henderson	.05	.02
❑ 227 Jose Canseco	.25	.07
❑ 228 Walt Weiss	.05	.02
❑ 229 Dann Howitt	.05	.02
❑ 230 Willie Wilson	.05	.02
❑ 231 Harold Baines	.10	.03
❑ 232 Scott Hemond	.05	.02
❑ 233 Joe Slusarski	.05	.02

❑ 234	Mark McGwire	.60	.18
❑ 235	K.Dressendorfer RC	.15	.04
❑ 236	Craig Paquette RC	.50	.15
❑ 237	Dennis Eckersley	.10	.03
❑ 238	Dana Allison	.05	.02
❑ 239	Scott Bradley	.05	.02
❑ 240	Brian Holman	.05	.02
❑ 241	Mike Schooler	.05	.02
❑ 242	Rich DeLucia	.05	.02
❑ 243	Edgar Martinez	.15	.04
❑ 244	Henry Cotto	.05	.02
❑ 245	Omar Vizquel	.15	.04
❑ 246	Ken Griffey Jr.	.50	.15
	(See also 255)		
❑ 247	Jay Buhner	.10	.03
❑ 248	Bill Krueger	.05	.02
❑ 249	Dave Fleming RC	.15	.04
❑ 250	Patrick Lennon	.05	.02
❑ 251	Dave Valle	.05	.02
❑ 252	Harold Reynolds	.10	.03
❑ 253	Randy Johnson	.30	.09
❑ 254	Scott Bankhead	.05	.02
❑ 255	Ken Griffey Sr. UER	.05	.02
	(Card number is 246)		
❑ 256	Greg Briley	.05	.02
❑ 257	Tino Martinez	.15	.04
❑ 258	Alvin Davis	.05	.02
❑ 259	Pete O'Brien	.05	.02
❑ 260	Erik Hanson	.05	.02
❑ 261	Bret Boone RC	3.00	.90
❑ 262	Roger Salkeld	.05	.02
❑ 263	Dave Burba RC	.50	.15
❑ 264	Kerry Woodson RC	.15	.04
❑ 265	Julio Franco	.10	.03
❑ 266	Dan Peltier RC	.15	.04
❑ 267	Jeff Russell	.05	.02
❑ 268	Steve Buechele	.05	.02
❑ 269	Donald Harris	.05	.02
❑ 270	Robb Nen	.15	.04
❑ 271	Rich Gossage	.10	.03
❑ 272	Ivan Rodriguez RC	2.50	.75
❑ 273	Jeff Huson	.05	.02
❑ 274	Kevin Brown	.10	.03
❑ 275	Dan Smith RC	.15	.04
❑ 276	Gary Pettis	.05	.02
❑ 277	Jack Daugherty	.05	.02
❑ 278	Mike Jeffcoat	.05	.02
❑ 279	Brad Arnsberg	.05	.02
❑ 280	Nolan Ryan	1.00	.30
❑ 281	Eric McCray	.05	.02
❑ 282	Scott Chiamparino	.05	.02
❑ 283	Ruben Sierra	.05	.02
❑ 284	Geno Petralli	.05	.02
❑ 285	Monty Fariss	.05	.02
❑ 286	Rafael Palmeiro	.15	.04
❑ 287	Bobby Witt	.05	.02
❑ 288	Dean Palmer UER	.10	.03
	Photo is Dan Peltier		
❑ 289	Tony Scruggs	.05	.02
❑ 290	Kenny Rogers	.10	.03
❑ 291	Bret Saberhagen	.10	.03
❑ 292	Brian McRae RC	.50	.15
❑ 293	Storm Davis	.05	.02
❑ 294	Danny Tartabull	.05	.02
❑ 295	David Howard	.05	.02
❑ 296	Mike Boddicker	.05	.02
❑ 297	Joel Johnston RC	.15	.04
❑ 298	Tim Spehr	.05	.02
❑ 299	Hector Wagner	.05	.02
❑ 300	George Brett	.60	.18
❑ 301	Mike Macfarlane	.05	.02
❑ 302	Kirk Gibson	.10	.03
❑ 303	Harvey Pulliam RC	.15	.04
❑ 304	Jim Eisenreich	.05	.02
❑ 305	Kevin Seitzer	.05	.02
❑ 306	Mark Davis	.05	.02
❑ 307	Kurt Stillwell	.05	.02
❑ 308	Jeff Montgomery	.05	.02
❑ 309	Kevin Appier	.10	.03
❑ 310	Bob Hamelin	.05	.02
❑ 311	Tom Gordon	.05	.02
❑ 312	Kerwin Moore RC	.15	.04
❑ 313	Hugh Walker	.05	.02
❑ 314	Terry Shumpert	.05	.02
❑ 315	Warren Cromartie	.05	.02
❑ 316	Gary Thurman	.05	.02

❑ 317	Steve Bedrosian	.05	.02
❑ 318	Danny Gladden	.05	.02
❑ 319	Jack Morris	.10	.03
❑ 320	Kirby Puckett	.25	.07
❑ 321	Kent Hrbek	.10	.03
❑ 322	Kevin Tapani	.05	.02
❑ 323	Denny Neagle RC	.50	.15
❑ 324	Rich Garces RC	.15	.04
❑ 325	Larry Casian	.05	.02
❑ 326	Shane Mack	.05	.02
❑ 327	Allan Anderson	.05	.02
❑ 328	Junior Ortiz	.05	.02
❑ 329	Paul Abbott RC	.50	.15
❑ 330	Chuck Knoblauch	.10	.03
❑ 331	Chili Davis	.10	.03
❑ 332	Todd Ritchie RC	.50	.15
❑ 333	Brian Harper	.05	.02
❑ 334	Rick Aguilera	.10	.03
❑ 335	Scott Erickson	.05	.02
❑ 336	Pedro Munoz RC	.15	.04
❑ 337	Scott Leius	.05	.02
❑ 338	Greg Gagne	.05	.02
❑ 339	Mike Pagliarulo	.05	.02
❑ 340	Terry Leach	.05	.02
❑ 341	Willie Banks	.05	.02
❑ 342	Bobby Thigpen	.05	.02
❑ 343	R.Hernandez RC	.50	.15
❑ 344	Melido Perez	.05	.02
❑ 345	Carlton Fisk	.15	.04
❑ 346	Norberto Martin	.05	.02
❑ 347	Johnny Ruffin RC	.15	.04
❑ 348	Jeff Carter	.05	.02
❑ 349	Lance Johnson	.05	.02
❑ 350	Sammy Sosa	.50	.15
❑ 351	Alex Fernandez	.05	.02
❑ 352	Jack McDowell	.05	.02
❑ 353	Bob Wickman RC	.15	.04
❑ 354	Wilson Alvarez	.05	.02
❑ 355	Charlie Hough	.10	.03
❑ 356	Ozzie Guillen	.05	.02
❑ 357	Cory Snyder	.05	.02
❑ 358	Robin Ventura	.10	.03
❑ 359	Scott Fletcher	.05	.02
❑ 360	Cesar Bernhardt	.05	.02
❑ 361	Dan Pasqua	.05	.02
❑ 362	Tim Raines	.10	.03
❑ 363	Brian Drahman	.05	.02
❑ 364	Wayne Edwards	.05	.02
❑ 365	Scott Radinsky	.05	.02
❑ 366	Frank Thomas	.25	.07
❑ 367	Cecil Fielder SLUG	.05	.02
❑ 368	Julio Franco SLUG	.05	.02
❑ 369	Kelly Gruber SLUG	.05	.02
❑ 370	Alan Trammell SLUG	.10	.03
❑ 371	R.Henderson SLUG	.15	.04
❑ 372	Jose Canseco SLUG	.10	.03
❑ 373	Ellis Burks SLUG	.05	.02
❑ 374	Lance Parrish SLUG	.05	.02
❑ 375	Dave Parker SLUG	.05	.02
❑ 376	Eddie Murray SLUG	.15	.04
❑ 377	Ryne Sandberg SLUG	.25	.07
❑ 378	Matt Williams SLUG	.05	.02
❑ 379	Barry Larkin SLUG	.10	.03
❑ 380	Barry Bonds SLUG	.30	.09
❑ 381	Bobby Bonilla SLUG	.05	.02
❑ 382	D.Strawberry SLUG	.05	.02
❑ 383	Benny Santiago SLUG	.05	.02
❑ 384	Don Robinson SLUG	.05	.02
❑ 385	Paul Coleman	.05	.02
❑ 386	Milt Thompson	.05	.02
❑ 387	Lee Smith	.10	.03
❑ 388	Ray Lankford	.05	.02
❑ 389	Tom Pagnozzi	.05	.02
❑ 390	Ken Hill	.05	.02
❑ 391	Jamie Moyer	.10	.03
❑ 392	Greg Carmona	.05	.02
❑ 393	John Ericks	.05	.02
❑ 394	Bob Tewksbury	.05	.02
❑ 395	Jose Oquendo	.05	.02
❑ 396	Rheal Cormier RC	.15	.04
❑ 397	Mike Milchin	.05	.02
❑ 398	Ozzie Smith	.40	.12
❑ 399	Aaron Holbert RC	.15	.04
❑ 400	Jose DeLeon	.05	.02
❑ 401	Felix Jose	.05	.02
❑ 402	Juan Agosto	.05	.02

❑ 403	Pedro Guerrero	.10	.03
❑ 404	Todd Zeile	.05	.02
❑ 405	Gerald Perry	.05	.02
❑ 406	D.Osborne UER RC	.15	.04
	Card number is 410		
❑ 407	Bryn Smith	.05	.02
❑ 408	Bernard Gilkey	.05	.02
❑ 409	Rex Hudler	.05	.02
❑ 410	Bobby Thomson	.25	.07
	Ralph Branca		
	Shot Heard Round the World		
	See also 406		
❑ 411	Lance Dickson RC	.15	.04
❑ 412	Danny Jackson	.05	.02
❑ 413	Jerome Walton	.05	.02
❑ 414	Sean Cheetham	.05	.02
❑ 415	Joe Girardi	.05	.02
❑ 416	Ryne Sandberg	.40	.12
❑ 417	Mike Harkey	.05	.02
❑ 418	George Bell	.05	.02
❑ 419	Rick Wilkins RC	.15	.04
❑ 420	Earl Cunningham	.05	.02
❑ 421	H.Slocumb RC	.15	.04
❑ 422	Mike Bielecki	.05	.02
❑ 423	Jessie Hollins RC	.15	.04
❑ 424	Shawon Dunston	.05	.02
❑ 425	Dave Smith	.05	.02
❑ 426	Greg Maddux	.40	.12
❑ 427	Jose Vizcaino	.05	.02
❑ 428	Luis Salazar	.05	.02
❑ 429	Andre Dawson	.10	.03
❑ 430	Rick Sutcliffe	.10	.03
❑ 431	Paul Assenmacher	.05	.02
❑ 432	Erik Pappas	.05	.02
❑ 433	Mark Grace	.15	.04
❑ 434	Dennis Martinez	.10	.03
❑ 435	Marquis Grissom	.10	.03
❑ 436	Wil Cordero RC	.50	.15
❑ 437	Tim Wallach	.05	.02
❑ 438	Brian Barnes RC	.05	.02
❑ 439	Barry Jones	.05	.02
❑ 440	Ivan Calderon	.05	.02
❑ 441	Stan Spencer	.05	.02
❑ 442	Larry Walker	.25	.07
❑ 443	Chris Haney RC	.15	.04
❑ 444	Hector Rivera	.05	.02
❑ 445	Delino DeShields	.10	.03
❑ 446	Andres Galarraga	.10	.03
❑ 447	Gilberto Reyes	.05	.02
❑ 448	Willie Greene	.05	.02
❑ 449	Greg Colbrunn RC	.50	.15
❑ 450	Rondell White RC	.75	.23
❑ 451	Steve Frey	.05	.02
❑ 452	Shane Andrews RC	.15	.04
❑ 453	Mike Fitzgerald	.05	.02
❑ 454	Spike Owen	.05	.02
❑ 455	Dave Martinez	.05	.02
❑ 456	Dennis Boyd	.05	.02
❑ 457	Eric Bullock	.05	.02
❑ 458	Reid Cornelius RC	.15	.04
❑ 459	Chris Nabholz	.05	.02
❑ 460	David Cone	.10	.03
❑ 461	Hubie Brooks	.05	.02
❑ 462	Sid Fernandez	.05	.02
❑ 463	Doug Simons	.05	.02
❑ 464	Howard Johnson	.05	.02
❑ 465	Chris Donnels	.05	.02
❑ 466	Anthony Young RC	.15	.04
❑ 467	Todd Hundley	.05	.02
❑ 468	Rick Cerone	.05	.02
❑ 469	Kevin Elster	.05	.02
❑ 470	Wally Whitehurst	.05	.02
❑ 471	Vince Coleman	.05	.02
❑ 472	Dwight Gooden	.10	.03
❑ 473	Charlie O'Brien	.05	.02
❑ 474	Jeromy Burnitz RC	1.00	.30
❑ 475	John Franco	.10	.03
❑ 476	Daryl Boston	.05	.02
❑ 477	Frank Viola	.10	.03
❑ 478	D.J. Dozier	.05	.02
❑ 479	Kevin McReynolds	.05	.02
❑ 480	Tom Herr	.05	.02
❑ 481	Gregg Jefferies	.05	.02
❑ 482	Pete Schourek RC	.15	.04
❑ 483	Ron Darling	.05	.02
❑ 484	Dave Magadan	.05	.02

Card	Player	Nm-Mt	Ex-Mt
❑ 485	Andy Ashby RC	.50	.15
❑ 486	Dale Murphy	.25	.07
❑ 487	Von Hayes	.05	.02
❑ 488	Kim Batiste RC	.15	.04
❑ 489	Tony Longmire RC	.15	.04
❑ 490	Wally Backman	.05	.02
❑ 491	Jeff Jackson	.05	.02
❑ 492	Mickey Morandini	.05	.02
❑ 493	Darrel Akerfelds	.05	.02
❑ 494	Ricky Jordan	.05	.02
❑ 495	Randy Ready	.05	.02
❑ 496	Darrin Fletcher	.05	.02
❑ 497	Chuck Malone	.05	.02
❑ 498	Pat Combs	.05	.02
❑ 499	Dickie Thon	.05	.02
❑ 500	Roger McDowell	.05	.02
❑ 501	Len Dykstra	.10	.03
❑ 502	Joe Boever	.05	.02
❑ 503	John Kruk	.10	.03
❑ 504	Terry Mulholland	.05	.02
❑ 505	Wes Chamberlain RC	.15	.04
❑ 506	Mike Lieberthal RC	.75	.23
❑ 507	Darren Daulton	.10	.03
❑ 508	Charlie Hayes	.05	.02
❑ 509	John Smiley	.05	.02
❑ 510	Gary Varsho	.05	.02
❑ 511	Curt Wilkerson	.05	.02
❑ 512	Orlando Merced RC	.15	.04
❑ 513	Barry Bonds	.60	.18
❑ 514	Mike LaValliere	.05	.02
❑ 515	Doug Drabek	.05	.02
❑ 516	Gary Redus	.05	.02
❑ 517	W.Pennyfeather RC	.15	.04
❑ 518	Randy Tomlin RC	.05	.02
❑ 519	Mike Zimmerman RC	.15	.04
❑ 520	Jeff King	.05	.02
❑ 521	Kurt Miller RC	.15	.04
❑ 522	Jay Bell	.10	.03
❑ 523	Bill Landrum	.05	.02
❑ 524	Zane Smith	.05	.02
❑ 525	Bobby Bonilla	.10	.03
❑ 526	Bob Walk	.05	.02
❑ 527	Austin Manahan	.05	.02
❑ 528	Joe Ausanio	.05	.02
❑ 529	Andy Van Slyke	.10	.03
❑ 530	Jose Lind	.05	.02
❑ 531	Carlos Garcia RC	.15	.04
❑ 532	Don Slaught	.05	.02
❑ 533	Gen.Colin Powell	.50	.15
❑ 534	Frank Bolick RC	.15	.04
❑ 535	Gary Scott	.05	.02
❑ 536	Nikco Riesgo	.05	.02
❑ 537	Reggie Sanders RC	.75	.23
❑ 538	Tim Howard RC	.15	.04
❑ 539	Ryan Bowen RC	.15	.04
❑ 540	Eric Anthony	.05	.02
❑ 541	Jim Deshaies	.05	.02
❑ 542	Tom Nevers RC	.15	.04
❑ 543	Ken Caminiti	.10	.03
❑ 544	Karl Rhodes	.05	.02
❑ 545	Xavier Hernandez	.05	.02
❑ 546	Mike Scott	.05	.02
❑ 547	Jeff Juden	.05	.02
❑ 548	Darryl Kile	.10	.03
❑ 549	Willie Ansley	.05	.02
❑ 550	Luis Gonzalez RC	1.00	.30
❑ 551	Mike Simms	.05	.02
❑ 552	Mark Portugal	.05	.02
❑ 553	Jimmy Jones	.05	.02
❑ 554	Jim Clancy	.05	.02
❑ 555	Pete Harnisch	.05	.02
❑ 556	Craig Biggio	.15	.04
❑ 557	Eric Yelding	.05	.02
❑ 558	Dave Rohde	.05	.02
❑ 559	Casey Candaele	.05	.02
❑ 560	Curt Schilling	.25	.07
❑ 561	Steve Finley	.10	.03
❑ 562	Javier Ortiz	.05	.02
❑ 563	Andujar Cedeno	.05	.02
❑ 564	Rafael Ramirez	.05	.02
❑ 565	Kenny Lofton RC	1.00	.30
❑ 566	Steve Avery	.05	.02
❑ 567	Lonnie Smith	.05	.02
❑ 568	Kent Mercker	.05	.02
❑ 569	Chipper Jones RC	4.00	1.20
❑ 570	Terry Pendleton	.10	.03
❑ 571	Otis Nixon	.05	.02
❑ 572	Juan Berenguer	.05	.02
❑ 573	Charlie Leibrandt	.05	.02
❑ 574	David Justice	.10	.03
❑ 575	Keith Mitchell RC	.15	.04
❑ 576	Tom Glavine	.15	.04
❑ 577	Greg Olson	.05	.02
❑ 578	Rafael Belliard	.05	.02
❑ 579	Ben Rivera RC	.15	.04
❑ 580	John Smoltz	.15	.04
❑ 581	Tyler Houston	.05	.02
❑ 582	Mark Wohlers RC	.50	.15
❑ 583	Ron Gant	.10	.03
❑ 584	Ramon Caraballo RC	.15	.04
❑ 585	Sid Bream	.05	.02
❑ 586	Jeff Treadway	.05	.02
❑ 587	Javy Lopez RC	3.00	.90
❑ 588	Deion Sanders	.15	.04
❑ 589	Mike Heath	.05	.02
❑ 590	Ryan Klesko RC	1.00	.30
❑ 591	Bob Ojeda	.05	.02
❑ 592	Alfredo Griffin	.05	.02
❑ 593	Raul Mondesi RC	.75	.23
❑ 594	Greg Smith	.05	.02
❑ 595	Orel Hershiser	.10	.03
❑ 596	Juan Samuel	.05	.02
❑ 597	Brett Butler	.10	.03
❑ 598	Gary Carter	.10	.03
❑ 599	Stan Javier	.05	.02
❑ 600	Kal Daniels	.05	.02
❑ 601	Jamie McAndrew RC	.15	.04
❑ 602	Mike Sharperson	.05	.02
❑ 603	Jay Howell	.05	.02
❑ 604	Eric Karros RC	.75	.23
❑ 605	Tim Belcher	.05	.02
❑ 606	Dan Opperman	.05	.02
❑ 607	Lenny Harris	.05	.02
❑ 608	Tom Goodwin	.05	.02
❑ 609	Darryl Strawberry	.10	.03
❑ 610	Ramon Martinez	.05	.02
❑ 611	Kevin Gross	.05	.02
❑ 612	Zakary Shinall	.05	.02
❑ 613	Mike Scioscia	.05	.02
❑ 614	Eddie Murray	.25	.07
❑ 615	Ronnie Walden RC	.15	.04
❑ 616	Will Clark	.25	.07
❑ 617	Adam Hyzdu RC	.50	.15
❑ 618	Matt Williams	.10	.03
❑ 619	Don Robinson	.05	.02
❑ 620	Jeff Brantley	.05	.02
❑ 621	Greg Litton	.05	.02
❑ 622	Steve Decker	.05	.02
❑ 623	Robby Thompson	.05	.02
❑ 624	Mark Leonard	.05	.02
❑ 625	Kevin Bass	.05	.02
❑ 626	Scott Garrelts	.05	.02
❑ 627	Jose Uribe	.05	.02
❑ 628	Eric Gunderson	.05	.02
❑ 629	Steve Hosey	.05	.02
❑ 630	Trevor Wilson	.05	.02
❑ 631	Terry Kennedy	.05	.02
❑ 632	Dave Righetti	.10	.03
❑ 633	Kelly Downs	.05	.02
❑ 634	Johnny Ard	.05	.02
❑ 635	E.Christopherson RC	.15	.04
❑ 636	Kevin Mitchell	.05	.02
❑ 637	John Burkett	.05	.02
❑ 638	Kevin Rogers RC	.15	.04
❑ 639	Bud Black	.05	.02
❑ 640	Willie McGee	.10	.03
❑ 641	Royce Clayton	.05	.02
❑ 642	Tony Fernandez	.05	.02
❑ 643	Ricky Bones RC	.15	.04
❑ 644	Thomas Howard	.05	.02
❑ 645	Dave Staton RC	.15	.04
❑ 646	Jim Presley	.05	.02
❑ 647	Tony Gwynn	.30	.09
❑ 648	Marty Barrett	.05	.02
❑ 649	Scott Coolbaugh	.05	.02
❑ 650	Craig Lefferts	.05	.02
❑ 651	Eddie Whitson	.05	.02
❑ 652	Oscar Azocar	.05	.02
❑ 653	Wes Gardner	.05	.02
❑ 654	Bip Roberts	.05	.02
❑ 655	Robbie Beckett RC	.15	.04
❑ 656	Benito Santiago	.10	.03
❑ 657	Greg W.Harris	.05	.02
❑ 658	Jerald Clark	.05	.02
❑ 659	Fred McGriff	.15	.04
❑ 660	Larry Andersen	.05	.02
❑ 661	Bruce Hurst	.05	.02
❑ 662	Steve Martin UER RC Card said he pitched at Waterloo He's an outfielder	.15	.04
❑ 663	Rafael Valdez	.05	.02
❑ 664	Paul Faries	.05	.02
❑ 665	Andy Benes	.05	.02
❑ 666	Randy Myers	.05	.02
❑ 667	Rob Dibble	.10	.03
❑ 668	Glenn Sutko	.05	.02
❑ 669	Glenn Braggs	.05	.02
❑ 670	Billy Hatcher	.05	.02
❑ 671	Joe Oliver	.05	.02
❑ 672	Freddie Benavides RC	.15	.04
❑ 673	Barry Larkin	.15	.04
❑ 674	Chris Sabo	.05	.02
❑ 675	Mariano Duncan	.05	.02
❑ 676	Chris Jones RC	.05	.02
❑ 677	Gino Minutelli	.05	.02
❑ 678	Reggie Jefferson	.05	.02
❑ 679	Jack Armstrong	.05	.02
❑ 680	Chris Hammond	.05	.02
❑ 681	Jose Rijo	.05	.02
❑ 682	Bill Doran	.05	.02
❑ 683	Terry Lee	.05	.02
❑ 684	Tom Browning	.05	.02
❑ 685	Paul O'Neill	.15	.04
❑ 686	Eric Davis	.10	.03
❑ 687	Dan Wilson RC	.50	.15
❑ 688	Ted Power	.05	.02
❑ 689	Tim Layana	.05	.02
❑ 690	Norm Charlton	.05	.02
❑ 691	Hal Morris	.05	.02
❑ 692	Rickey Henderson	.15	.04
❑ 693	Sam Militello RC	.15	.04
❑ 694	Matt Mieske RC	.15	.04
❑ 695	Paul Russo RC	.15	.04
❑ 696	Domingo Mota MVP	.05	.02
❑ 697	Todd Guggiana RC	.15	.04
❑ 698	Marc Newfield RC	.15	.04
❑ 699	Checklist 1-122	.05	.02
❑ 700	Checklist 123-244	.05	.02
❑ 701	Checklist 245-366	.05	.02
❑ 702	Checklist 367-471	.05	.02
❑ 703	Checklist 472-593	.05	.02
❑ 704	Checklist 594-704	.05	.02

1992 Bowman

	Nm-Mt	Ex-Mt
COMPLETE SET (705)	150.00	45.00

Card	Player	Nm-Mt	Ex-Mt
❑ 1	Ivan Rodriguez	1.25	.35
❑ 2	Kirk McCaskill	.50	.15
❑ 3	Scott Livingstone	.50	.15
❑ 4	Salomon Torres RC	.50	.15
❑ 5	Carlos Hernandez	.50	.15
❑ 6	Dave Hollins	.50	.15
❑ 7	Scott Fletcher	.50	.15
❑ 8	Jorge Fabregas RC	.50	.15
❑ 9	Andujar Cedeno	.50	.15
❑ 10	Howard Johnson	.50	.15
❑ 11	Trevor Hoffman RC	5.00	1.50
❑ 12	Roberto Kelly	.50	.15

- ❑ 13 Gregg Jefferies .50 .15
- ❑ 14 Marquis Grissom .50 .15
- ❑ 15 Mike Ignasiak .50 .15
- ❑ 16 Jack Morris .50 .15
- ❑ 17 William Pennyfeather .50 .15
- ❑ 18 Todd Stottlemyre .50 .15
- ❑ 19 Chito Martinez .50 .15
- ❑ 20 Roberto Alomar .75 .23
- ❑ 21 Sam Militello .50 .15
- ❑ 22 Hector Fajardo RC .50 .15
- ❑ 23 Paul Quantrill RC .50 .15
- ❑ 24 Chuck Knoblauch .50 .15
- ❑ 25 Reggie Jefferson .50 .15
- ❑ 26 Jeremy McGarity RC .50 .15
- ❑ 27 Jerome Walton .50 .15
- ❑ 28 Chipper Jones 8.00 2.40
- ❑ 29 Brian Barber RC .50 .15
- ❑ 30 Ron Darling .50 .15
- ❑ 31 Roberto Petagine RC .50 .15
- ❑ 32 Chuck Finley .50 .15
- ❑ 33 Edgar Martinez .75 .23
- ❑ 34 Napoleon Robinson .50 .15
- ❑ 35 Andy Van Slyke .50 .15
- ❑ 36 Bobby Thigpen .50 .15
- ❑ 37 Travis Fryman .50 .15
- ❑ 38 Eric Christopherson .50 .15
- ❑ 39 Terry Mulholland .50 .15
- ❑ 40 Darryl Strawberry .50 .15
- ❑ 41 Manny Alexander RC .50 .15
- ❑ 42 Tracy Sanders RC .50 .15
- ❑ 43 Pete Incaviglia .50 .15
- ❑ 44 Kim Batiste .50 .15
- ❑ 45 Frank Rodriguez .50 .15
- ❑ 46 Greg Swindell .50 .15
- ❑ 47 Delino DeShields .50 .15
- ❑ 48 John Ericks .50 .15
- ❑ 49 Franklin Stubbs .50 .15
- ❑ 50 Tony Gwynn 1.50 .45
- ❑ 51 Clifton Garrett RC .50 .15
- ❑ 52 Mike Gardella .50 .15
- ❑ 53 Scott Erickson .50 .15
- ❑ 54 Gary Caraballo RC .50 .15
- ❑ 55 Jose Oliva RC .50 .15
- ❑ 56 Brook Fordyce .50 .15
- ❑ 57 Mark Whiten .50 .15
- ❑ 58 Joe Slusarski .50 .15
- ❑ 59 J.R. Phillips RC .50 .15
- ❑ 60 Barry Bonds 3.00 .90
- ❑ 61 Bob Milacki .50 .15
- ❑ 62 Keith Mitchell .50 .15
- ❑ 63 Angel Miranda .50 .15
- ❑ 64 Raul Mondesi .50 .15
- ❑ 65 Brian Koelling RC .50 .15
- ❑ 66 Brian McRae .50 .15
- ❑ 67 John Patterson RC .50 .15
- ❑ 68 John Wetteland .50 .15
- ❑ 69 Wilson Alvarez .50 .15
- ❑ 70 Wade Boggs .75 .23
- ❑ 71 Darryl Ratliff RC .50 .15
- ❑ 72 Jeff Jackson .50 .15
- ❑ 73 Jeremy Hernandez RC .50 .15
- ❑ 74 Darryl Hamilton .50 .15
- ❑ 75 Rafael Belliard .50 .15
- ❑ 76 Rick Trlicek RC .50 .15
- ❑ 77 Felipe Crespo RC .50 .15
- ❑ 78 Carney Lansford .50 .15
- ❑ 79 Ryan Long RC .50 .15
- ❑ 80 Kirby Puckett 1.25 .35
- ❑ 81 Earl Cunningham .50 .15
- ❑ 82 Pedro Martinez 10.00 3.00
- ❑ 83 Scott Hatteberg RC 1.00 .30
- ❑ 84 Juan Gonzalez UER .75 .23
  (65 doubles vs. Tigers)
- ❑ 85 Robert Nutting RC .50 .15
- ❑ 86 Pokey Reese RC 2.00 .60
- ❑ 87 Dave Silvestri .50 .15
- ❑ 88 Scott Ruffcorn RC .50 .15
- ❑ 89 Rick Aguilera .50 .15
- ❑ 90 Cecil Fielder .50 .15
- ❑ 91 Kirk Dressendorfer .50 .15
- ❑ 92 Jerry DiPoto RC .50 .15
- ❑ 93 Mike Felder .50 .15
- ❑ 94 Craig Paquette .50 .15
- ❑ 95 Elvin Paulino RC .50 .15
- ❑ 96 Donovan Osborne .50 .15
- ❑ 97 Hubie Brooks .50 .15
- ❑ 98 Derek Lowe RC 5.00 1.50
- ❑ 99 David Zancanaro .50 .15
- ❑ 100 Ken Griffey Jr. 2.00 .60
- ❑ 101 Todd Hundley .50 .15
- ❑ 102 Mike Trombley RC .50 .15
- ❑ 103 Ricky Gutierrez RC 1.00 .30
- ❑ 104 Braulio Castillo .50 .15
- ❑ 105 Craig Lefferts .50 .15
- ❑ 106 Rick Sutcliffe .50 .15
- ❑ 107 Dean Palmer .50 .15
- ❑ 108 Henry Rodriguez .50 .15
- ❑ 109 Mark Clark RC 1.00 .30
- ❑ 110 Kenny Lofton .75 .23
- ❑ 111 Mark Carreon .50 .15
- ❑ 112 J.T. Bruett .50 .15
- ❑ 113 Gerald Williams .50 .15
- ❑ 114 Frank Thomas 1.25 .35
- ❑ 115 Kevin Reimer .50 .15
- ❑ 116 Sammy Sosa 2.00 .60
- ❑ 117 Mickey Tettleton .50 .15
- ❑ 118 Reggie Sanders .50 .15
- ❑ 119 Trevor Wilson .50 .15
- ❑ 120 Cliff Brantley .50 .15
- ❑ 121 Spike Owen .50 .15
- ❑ 122 Jeff Montgomery .50 .15
- ❑ 123 Alex Sutherland .50 .15
- ❑ 124 Brien Taylor RC 1.00 .30
- ❑ 125 Brian Williams RC .50 .15
- ❑ 126 Kevin Seitzer .50 .15
- ❑ 127 Carlos Delgado RC 15.00 4.50
- ❑ 128 Gary Scott .50 .15
- ❑ 129 Scott Cooper .50 .15
- ❑ 130 Domingo Jean RC .50 .15
- ❑ 131 Pat Mahomes RC 1.00 .30
- ❑ 132 Mike Boddicker .50 .15
- ❑ 133 Roberto Hernandez .50 .15
- ❑ 134 Dave Valle .50 .15
- ❑ 135 Kurt Stillwell .50 .15
- ❑ 136 Brad Pennington RC .50 .15
- ❑ 137 Jermaine Swinton RC .50 .15
- ❑ 138 Ryan Hawblitzel RC .50 .15
- ❑ 139 Tito Navarro RC .50 .15
- ❑ 140 Sandy Alomar Jr. .50 .15
- ❑ 141 Todd Benzinger .50 .15
- ❑ 142 Danny Jackson .50 .15
- ❑ 143 Melvin Nieves RC .50 .15
- ❑ 144 Jim Campanis .50 .15
- ❑ 145 Luis Gonzalez .50 .15
- ❑ 146 D.Dooneweerd RC .50 .15
- ❑ 147 Charlie Hayes .50 .15
- ❑ 148 Greg Maddux 2.00 .60
- ❑ 149 Brian Harper .50 .15
- ❑ 150 Brent Miller RC .50 .15
- ❑ 151 Shawn Estes RC 1.00 .30
- ❑ 152 Mike Williams RC 1.00 .30
- ❑ 153 Charlie Hough .50 .15
- ❑ 154 Randy Myers .50 .15
- ❑ 155 Kevin Young RC 1.00 .30
- ❑ 156 Rick Wilkins .50 .15
- ❑ 157 Terry Shumpert .50 .15
- ❑ 158 Steve Karsay .50 .15
- ❑ 159 Gary DiSarcina .50 .15
- ❑ 160 Deion Sanders .75 .23
- ❑ 161 Tom Browning .50 .15
- ❑ 162 Dickie Thon .50 .15
- ❑ 163 Luis Mercedes .50 .15
- ❑ 164 Riccardo Ingram .50 .15
- ❑ 165 Tavo Alvarez RC .50 .15
- ❑ 166 Rickey Henderson 1.25 .35
- ❑ 167 Jaime Navarro .50 .15
- ❑ 168 Billy Ashley RC .50 .15
- ❑ 169 Phil Dauphin RC .50 .15
- ❑ 170 Ivan Cruz .50 .15
- ❑ 171 Harold Baines .50 .15
- ❑ 172 Bryan Harvey .50 .15
- ❑ 173 Alex Cole .50 .15
- ❑ 174 Curtis Shaw RC .50 .15
- ❑ 175 Matt Williams .50 .15
- ❑ 176 Felix Jose .50 .15
- ❑ 177 Sam Horn .50 .15
- ❑ 178 Randy Johnson 1.25 .35
- ❑ 179 Ivan Calderon .50 .15
- ❑ 180 Steve Avery .50 .15
- ❑ 181 William Suero .50 .15
- ❑ 182 Bill Swift .50 .15
- ❑ 183 Howard Battle RC .50 .15
- ❑ 184 Ruben Amaro .50 .15
- ❑ 185 Jim Abbott .75 .23
- ❑ 186 Mike Fitzgerald .50 .15
- ❑ 187 Bruce Hurst .50 .15
- ❑ 188 Jeff Juden .50 .15
- ❑ 189 Jeromy Burnitz .50 .15
- ❑ 190 Dave Burba .50 .15
- ❑ 191 Kevin Brown .50 .15
- ❑ 192 Patrick Lennon .50 .15
- ❑ 193 Jeff McNeely .50 .15
- ❑ 194 Wil Cordero .50 .15
- ❑ 195 Chili Davis .50 .15
- ❑ 196 Milt Cuyler .50 .15
- ❑ 197 Von Hayes .50 .15
- ❑ 198 Todd Revenig RC .50 .15
- ❑ 199 Joel Johnston .50 .15
- ❑ 200 Jeff Bagwell 1.25 .35
- ❑ 201 Alex Fernandez .50 .15
- ❑ 202 Todd Jones RC 1.00 .30
- ❑ 203 Charles Nagy .50 .15
- ❑ 204 Tim Raines .50 .15
- ❑ 205 Kevin Maas .50 .15
- ❑ 206 Julio Franco .50 .15
- ❑ 207 Randy Velarde .50 .15
- ❑ 208 Lance Johnson .50 .15
- ❑ 209 Scott Leius .50 .15
- ❑ 210 Derek Lee .50 .15
- ❑ 211 Joe Sondrini RC .50 .15
- ❑ 212 Royce Clayton .50 .15
- ❑ 213 Chris George .50 .15
- ❑ 214 Gary Sheffield .50 .15
- ❑ 215 Mark Gubicza .50 .15
- ❑ 216 Mike Moore .50 .15
- ❑ 217 Rick Huisman RC .50 .15
- ❑ 218 Jeff Russell .50 .15
- ❑ 219 D.J. Dozier .50 .15
- ❑ 220 Dave Martinez .50 .15
- ❑ 221 Alan Newman RC .50 .15
- ❑ 222 Nolan Ryan 4.00 1.20
- ❑ 223 Teddy Higuera .50 .15
- ❑ 224 Damon Buford RC .50 .15
- ❑ 225 Ruben Sierra .50 .15
- ❑ 226 Tom Nevers .50 .15
- ❑ 227 Tommy Greene .50 .15
- ❑ 228 Nigel Wilson RC .50 .15
- ❑ 229 John DeSilva .50 .15
- ❑ 230 Bobby Witt .50 .15
- ❑ 231 Greg Cadaret .50 .15
- ❑ 232 John Vander Wal RC 1.00 .30
- ❑ 233 Jack Clark .50 .15
- ❑ 234 Bill Doran .50 .15
- ❑ 235 Bobby Bonilla .50 .15
- ❑ 236 Steve Olin .50 .15
- ❑ 237 Derek Bell .50 .15
- ❑ 238 David Cone .50 .15
- ❑ 239 Victor Cole .50 .15
- ❑ 240 Rod Bolton RC .50 .15
- ❑ 241 Tom Pagnozzi .50 .15
- ❑ 242 Rob Dibble .50 .15
- ❑ 243 Michael Carter RC .50 .15
- ❑ 244 Don Peters .50 .15
- ❑ 245 Mike LaValliere .50 .15
- ❑ 246 Joe Perona RC .50 .15
- ❑ 247 Mitch Williams .50 .15
- ❑ 248 Jay Buhner .50 .15
- ❑ 249 Andy Benes .50 .15
- ❑ 250 Alex Ochoa RC 1.00 .30
- ❑ 251 Greg Blosser .50 .15
- ❑ 252 Jack Armstrong .50 .15
- ❑ 253 Juan Samuel .50 .15
- ❑ 254 Terry Pendleton .50 .15
- ❑ 255 Ramon Martinez .50 .15
- ❑ 256 Rico Brogna .50 .15
- ❑ 257 John Smiley .50 .15
- ❑ 258 Carl Everett .50 .15
- ❑ 259 Tim Salmon 1.25 .35
- ❑ 260 Will Clark 1.25 .35
- ❑ 261 Ugueth Urbina RC 1.00 .30
- ❑ 262 Jason Wood RC .50 .15
- ❑ 263 Dave Magadan .50 .15
- ❑ 264 Dante Bichette .50 .15
- ❑ 265 Jose DeLeon .50 .15
- ❑ 266 Mike Neill RC 1.00 .30
- ❑ 267 Paul O'Neill .75 .23
- ❑ 268 Anthony Young .50 .15
- ❑ 269 Greg W. Harris .50 .15

❑ 270 Todd Van Poppel .50 .15
❑ 271 Pedro Castellano RC .50 .15
❑ 272 Tony Phillips .50 .15
❑ 273 Mike Gallego .50 .15
❑ 274 Steve Cooke RC .50 .15
❑ 275 Robin Ventura .50 .15
❑ 276 Kevin Mitchell .50 .15
❑ 277 Doug Linton RC .50 .15
❑ 278 Robert Eenhoorn .50 .15
❑ 279 Gabe White RC .50 .15
❑ 280 Dave Stewart .50 .15
❑ 281 Mo Sanford .50 .15
❑ 282 Greg Perschke .50 .15
❑ 283 Kevin Flora RC .50 .15
❑ 284 Jeff Williams RC 1.00 .30
❑ 285 Keith Miller .50 .15
❑ 286 Andy Ashby .50 .15
❑ 287 Doug Dascenzo .50 .15
❑ 288 Eric Karros .50 .15
❑ 289 Glenn Murray RC .50 .15
❑ 290 Troy Percival RC 3.00 .90
❑ 291 Orlando Merced .50 .15
❑ 292 Peter Hoy .50 .15
❑ 293 Tony Fernandez .50 .15
❑ 294 Juan Guzman .50 .15
❑ 295 Jesse Barfield .50 .15
❑ 296 Sid Fernandez .50 .15
❑ 297 Scott Cepicky .50 .15
❑ 298 Garret Anderson RC 8.00 2.40
❑ 299 Cal Eldred .50 .15
❑ 300 Ryne Sandberg 2.50 .75
❑ 301 Jim Gantner .50 .15
❑ 302 Mariano Rivera RC 10.00 3.00
❑ 303 Ron Lockett RC .50 .15
❑ 304 Jose Offerman .50 .15
❑ 305 Dennis Martinez .50 .15
❑ 306 Luis Ortiz RC .50 .15
❑ 307 David Howard .50 .15
❑ 308 Russ Springer RC 1.00 .30
❑ 309 Chris Howard .50 .15
❑ 310 Kyle Abbott .50 .15
❑ 311 Aaron Sele RC 2.00 .60
❑ 312 David Justice .50 .15
❑ 313 Pete O'Brien .50 .15
❑ 314 Greg Hansell RC .50 .15
❑ 315 Dave Winfield .50 .15
❑ 316 Lance Dickson .50 .15
❑ 317 Eric King .50 .15
❑ 318 Vaughn Eshelman RC .50 .15
❑ 319 Tim Belcher .50 .15
❑ 320 Andres Galarraga .50 .15
❑ 321 Scott Bullett RC .50 .15
❑ 322 Doug Strange .50 .15
❑ 323 Jerald Clark .50 .15
❑ 324 Dave Righetti .50 .15
❑ 325 Greg Hibbard .50 .15
❑ 326 Eric Hillman RC .50 .15
❑ 327 Shane Reynolds RC 1.00 .30
❑ 328 Chris Hammond .50 .15
❑ 329 Albert Belle .50 .15
❑ 330 Rich Becker RC .50 .15
❑ 331 Eddie Williams RC .50 .15
❑ 332 Donald Harris .50 .15
❑ 333 Dave Smith .50 .15
❑ 334 Steve Fireovid .50 .15
❑ 335 Steve Buechele .50 .15
❑ 336 Mike Schooler .50 .15
❑ 337 Kevin McReynolds .50 .15
❑ 338 Hensley Meulens .50 .15
❑ 339 Benji Gil RC 1.00 .30
❑ 340 Don Mattingly 3.00 .90
❑ 341 Alvin Davis .50 .15
❑ 342 Alan Mills .50 .15
❑ 343 Kelly Downs .50 .15
❑ 344 Leo Gomez .50 .15
❑ 345 Tarrik Brock RC .50 .15
❑ 346 Ryan Turner RC .50 .15
❑ 347 John Smoltz .75 .23
❑ 348 Bill Sampen .50 .15
❑ 349 Paul Byrd RC 1.00 .30
❑ 350 Mike Bordick .50 .15
❑ 351 Jose Lind .50 .15
❑ 352 David Wells .50 .15
❑ 353 Barry Larkin .75 .23
❑ 354 Bruce Ruffin .50 .15
❑ 355 Luis Rivera .50 .15
❑ 356 Sid Bream .50 .15
❑ 357 Julian Vasquez RC .50 .15
❑ 358 Jason Bere RC 1.00 .30
❑ 359 Ben McDonald .50 .15
❑ 360 Scott Stahoviak RC .50 .15
❑ 361 Kirt Manwaring .50 .15
❑ 362 Jeff Johnson .50 .15
❑ 363 Rob Deer .50 .15
❑ 364 Tony Pena .50 .15
❑ 365 Melido Perez .50 .15
❑ 366 Clay Parker .50 .15
❑ 367 Dale Sveum .50 .15
❑ 368 Mike Scioscia .50 .15
❑ 369 Roger Salkeld .50 .15
❑ 370 Mike Stanley .50 .15
❑ 371 Jack McDowell .50 .15
❑ 372 Tim Wallach .50 .15
❑ 373 Billy Ripken .50 .15
❑ 374 Mike Christopher .50 .15
❑ 375 Paul Molitor .75 .23
❑ 376 Dave Stieb .50 .15
❑ 377 Pedro Guerrero .50 .15
❑ 378 Russ Swan .50 .15
❑ 379 Bob Ojeda .50 .15
❑ 380 Donn Pall .50 .15
❑ 381 Eddie Zosky .50 .15
❑ 382 Darnell Coles .50 .15
❑ 383 Tom Smith RC .50 .15
❑ 384 Mark McGwire 3.00 .90
❑ 385 Gary Carter .50 .15
❑ 386 Rich Amaral RC .50 .15
❑ 387 Alan Embree RC 4.00 1.20
❑ 388 Jonathan Hurst RC .50 .15
❑ 389 Bobby Jones RC 1.00 .30
❑ 390 Rico Rossy .50 .15
❑ 391 Dan Smith .50 .15
❑ 392 Terry Steinbach .50 .15
❑ 393 Jon Farrell RC .50 .15
❑ 394 Dave Anderson .50 .15
❑ 395 Benny Santiago .50 .15
❑ 396 Mark Wohlers .50 .15
❑ 397 Mo Vaughn .50 .15
❑ 398 Randy Kramer .50 .15
❑ 399 John Jaha RC 1.00 .30
❑ 400 Cal Ripken 4.00 1.20
❑ 401 Ryan Bowen .50 .15
❑ 402 Tim McIntosh .50 .15
❑ 403 Bernard Gilkey .50 .15
❑ 404 Junior Felix .50 .15
❑ 405 Cris Colon RC .50 .15
❑ 406 Marc Newfield .50 .15
❑ 407 Bernie Williams .75 .23
❑ 408 Jay Howell .50 .15
❑ 409 Zane Smith .50 .15
❑ 410 Jeff Shaw .50 .15
❑ 411 Kerry Woodson .50 .15
❑ 412 Wes Chamberlain .50 .15
❑ 413 Dave Mlicki RC 1.00 .30
❑ 414 Benny Distefano .50 .15
❑ 415 Kevin Rogers .50 .15
❑ 416 Tim Naehring .50 .15
❑ 417 Clemente Nunez RC .50 .15
❑ 418 Luis Sojo .50 .15
❑ 419 Kevin Ritz .50 .15
❑ 420 Omar Olivares .50 .15
❑ 421 Manuel Lee .50 .15
❑ 422 Julio Valera .50 .15
❑ 423 Omar Vizquel .75 .23
❑ 424 Darren Burton RC .50 .15
❑ 425 Mel Hall .50 .15
❑ 426 Dennis Powell .50 .15
❑ 427 Lee Stevens .50 .15
❑ 428 Glenn Davis .50 .15
❑ 429 Willie Greene .50 .15
❑ 430 Kevin Wickander .50 .15
❑ 431 Dennis Eckersley .50 .15
❑ 432 Joe Orsulak .50 .15
❑ 433 Eddie Murray 1.25 .35
❑ 434 Matt Stairs RC 1.00 .30
❑ 435 Wally Joyner .50 .15
❑ 436 Rondell White .50 .15
❑ 437 Rob Maurer .50 .15
❑ 438 Joe Redfield .50 .15
❑ 439 Mark Lewis .50 .15
❑ 440 Darren Daulton .50 .15
❑ 441 Mike Henneman .50 .15
❑ 442 John Cangelosi .50 .15
❑ 443 Vince Moore RC .50 .15
❑ 444 John Wehner .50 .15
❑ 445 Kent Hrbek .50 .15
❑ 446 Mark McLemore .50 .15
❑ 447 Bill Wegman .50 .15
❑ 448 Robby Thompson .50 .15
❑ 449 Mark Anthony RC .50 .15
❑ 450 Archi Cianfrocco RC .50 .15
❑ 451 Johnny Ruffin .50 .15
❑ 452 Javy Lopez 2.50 .75
❑ 453 Greg Gohr .50 .15
❑ 454 Tim Scott .50 .15
❑ 455 Stan Belinda .50 .15
❑ 456 Darrin Jackson .50 .15
❑ 457 Chris Gardner .50 .15
❑ 458 Esteban Beltre .50 .15
❑ 459 Phil Plantier .50 .15
❑ 460 Jim Thome 8.00 2.40
❑ 461 Mike Piazza RC 40.00 12.00
❑ 462 Matt Sinatro .50 .15
❑ 463 Scott Servais .50 .15
❑ 464 Brian Jordan RC 2.00 .60
❑ 465 Doug Drabek .50 .15
❑ 466 Carl Willis .50 .15
❑ 467 Bret Barberie .50 .15
❑ 468 Hal Morris .50 .15
❑ 469 Steve Sax .50 .15
❑ 470 Jerry Willard .50 .15
❑ 471 Dan Wilson .50 .15
❑ 472 Chris Hoiles .50 .15
❑ 473 Rheal Cormier .50 .15
❑ 474 John Morris .50 .15
❑ 475 Jeff Reardon .50 .15
❑ 476 Mark Leiter .50 .15
❑ 477 Tom Gordon .50 .15
❑ 478 Kent Bottenfield RC 1.00 .30
❑ 479 Gene Larkin .50 .15
❑ 480 Dwight Gooden .50 .15
❑ 481 B.J. Surhoff .50 .15
❑ 482 Andy Stankiewicz .50 .15
❑ 483 Tino Martinez .75 .23
❑ 484 Craig Biggio .75 .23
❑ 485 Denny Neagle .50 .15
❑ 486 Rusty Meacham .50 .15
❑ 487 Kal Daniels .50 .15
❑ 488 Dave Henderson .50 .15
❑ 489 Tim Costo .50 .15
❑ 490 Doug Davis .50 .15
❑ 491 Frank Viola .50 .15
❑ 492 Cory Snyder .50 .15
❑ 493 Chris Martin .50 .15
❑ 494 Dion James .50 .15
❑ 495 Randy Tomlin .50 .15
❑ 496 Greg Vaughn .50 .15
❑ 497 Dennis Cook .50 .15
❑ 498 Rosario Rodriguez .50 .15
❑ 499 Dave Staton .50 .15
❑ 500 George Brett 3.00 .90
❑ 501 Brian Barnes .50 .15
❑ 502 Butch Henry RC .50 .15
❑ 503 Harold Reynolds .50 .15
❑ 504 David Nied RC .50 .15
❑ 505 Lee Smith .50 .15
❑ 506 Steve Chitren .50 .15
❑ 507 Ken Hill .50 .15
❑ 508 Robbie Beckett .50 .15
❑ 509 Troy Afenir .50 .15
❑ 510 Kelly Gruber .50 .15
❑ 511 Bret Boone 1.25 .35
❑ 512 Jeff Branson .50 .15
❑ 513 Mike Jackson .50 .15
❑ 514 Pete Harnisch .50 .15
❑ 515 Chad Kreuter .50 .15
❑ 516 Joe Vitko RC .50 .15
❑ 517 Orel Hershiser .50 .15
❑ 518 John Doherty RC .50 .15
❑ 519 Jay Bell .50 .15
❑ 520 Mark Langston .50 .15
❑ 521 Dann Howitt .50 .15
❑ 522 Bobby Reed RC .50 .15
❑ 523 Bobby Munoz RC .50 .15
❑ 524 Todd Ritchie .50 .15
❑ 525 Bip Roberts .50 .15
❑ 526 Pat Listach RC 1.00 .30
❑ 527 Scott Brosius RC 2.00 .60

	Nm-Mt	Ex-Mt
❑ 528 John Roper RC	.50	.15
❑ 529 Phil Hiatt RC	.50	.15
❑ 530 Denny Walling	.50	.15
❑ 531 Carlos Baerga	.50	.15
❑ 532 Manny Ramirez RC	25.00	7.50
❑ 533 Pat Clements UER (Mistakenly numbered 553)	.50	.15
❑ 534 Ron Gant	.50	.15
❑ 535 Pat Kelly	.50	.15
❑ 536 Bill Spiers	.50	.15
❑ 537 Darren Reed	.50	.15
❑ 538 Ken Caminiti	.50	.15
❑ 539 Butch Huskey RC	.50	.15
❑ 540 Matt Nokes	.50	.15
❑ 541 John Kruk	.50	.15
❑ 542 John Jaha FOIL	.50	.15
❑ 543 Justin Thompson RC	.50	.15
❑ 544 Steve Hosey	.50	.15
❑ 545 Joe Kmak	.50	.15
❑ 546 John Franco	.50	.15
❑ 547 Devon White	.50	.15
❑ 548 E.Hansen FOIL RC	.50	.15
❑ 549 Ryan Klesko	1.25	.35
❑ 550 Danny Tartabull	.50	.15
❑ 551 Frank Thomas FOIL	1.25	.35
❑ 552 Kevin Tapani	.50	.15
❑ 553 Willie Banks (See also 533)	.50	.15
❑ 554 B.J. Wallace RC FOIL	.50	.15
❑ 555 Orlando Miller RC	.50	.15
❑ 556 Mark Smith RC	.50	.15
❑ 557 Tim Wallach FOIL	.50	.15
❑ 558 Bill Gullickson	.50	.15
❑ 559 Derek Bell FOIL	.50	.15
❑ 560 Joe Randa FOIL RC	1.00	.30
❑ 561 Frank Seminara RC	.50	.15
❑ 562 Mark Gardner	.50	.15
❑ 563 Rick Greene RC FOIL	.50	.15
❑ 564 Gary Gaetti	.50	.15
❑ 565 Ozzie Guillen	.50	.15
❑ 566 Charles Nagy FOIL	.50	.15
❑ 567 Mike Milchin	.50	.15
❑ 568 Ben Shelton RC	.50	.15
❑ 569 Chris Roberts FOIL	.50	.15
❑ 570 Ellis Burks	.50	.15
❑ 571 Scott Scudder	.50	.15
❑ 572 Jim Abbott FOIL	.75	.23
❑ 573 Joe Carter	.50	.15
❑ 574 Steve Finley	.50	.15
❑ 575 Jim Olander FOIL	.50	.15
❑ 576 Carlos Garcia	.50	.15
❑ 577 Gregg Olson	.50	.15
❑ 578 Greg Swindell FOIL	.50	.15
❑ 579 Matt Williams FOIL	.50	.15
❑ 580 Mark Grace	.75	.23
❑ 581 Howard House FOIL RC	.50	.15
❑ 582 Luis Polonia	.50	.15
❑ 583 Erik Hanson	.50	.15
❑ 584 Salomon Torres FOIL	.50	.15
❑ 585 Carlton Fisk	.75	.23
❑ 586 Bret Saberhagen	.50	.15
❑ 587 C.McConnell FOIL RC	.50	.15
❑ 588 Jimmy Key	.50	.15
❑ 589 Mike Macfarlane	.50	.15
❑ 590 Barry Bonds FOIL	3.00	.90
❑ 591 Jamie McAndrew	.50	.15
❑ 592 Shane Mack	.50	.15
❑ 593 Kerwin Moore	.50	.15
❑ 594 Joe Oliver	.50	.15
❑ 595 Chris Sabo	.50	.15
❑ 596 Alex Gonzalez RC	2.00	.60
❑ 597 Brett Butler	.50	.15
❑ 598 Mark Hutton RC	.50	.15
❑ 599 Andy Benes FOIL	.50	.15
❑ 600 Jose Canseco	1.25	.35
❑ 601 Darryl Kile	.50	.15
❑ 602 Matt Stairs FOIL	.50	.15
❑ 603 R.Butler RC FOIL	.50	.15
❑ 604 Willie McGee	.50	.15
❑ 605 Jack McDowell FOIL	.50	.15
❑ 606 Tom Candiotti	.50	.15
❑ 607 Ed Martel RC	.50	.15
❑ 608 Matt Mieske FOIL	.50	.15
❑ 609 Darrin Fletcher	.50	.15
❑ 610 Rafael Palmeiro	.75	.23
❑ 611 Bill Swift FOIL	.50	.15
❑ 612 Mike Mussina	1.25	.35
❑ 613 Vince Coleman	.50	.15
❑ 614 Scott Cepicky COR	.50	.15
❑ 614A S.Cepicky FOIL UER Bats: LEFLT	.50	.15
❑ 615 Mike Greenwell	.50	.15
❑ 616 Kevin McGehee RC	.50	.15
❑ 617 J.Hammonds FOIL	.50	.15
❑ 618 Scott Taylor	.50	.15
❑ 619 Dave Otto	.50	.15
❑ 620 Mark McGwire FOIL	3.00	.90
❑ 621 Kevin Tatar RC	.50	.15
❑ 622 Steve Farr	.50	.15
❑ 623 Ryan Klesko FOIL	.50	.15
❑ 624 Dave Fleming	.50	.15
❑ 625 Andre Dawson	.50	.15
❑ 626 Tino Martinez FOIL	.75	.23
❑ 627 Chad Curtis RC	1.00	.30
❑ 628 Mickey Morandini	.50	.15
❑ 629 Gregg Olson FOIL	.50	.15
❑ 630 Lou Whitaker	.50	.15
❑ 631 Arthur Rhodes	.50	.15
❑ 632 Brandon Wilson RC	.50	.15
❑ 633 Lance Jennings RC	.50	.15
❑ 634 Allen Watson RC	.50	.15
❑ 635 Len Dykstra	.50	.15
❑ 636 Joe Girardi	.50	.15
❑ 637 K.Hernandez RC FOIL	.50	.15
❑ 638 Mike Hampton RC	2.00	.60
❑ 639 Al Osuna	.50	.15
❑ 640 Kevin Appier	.50	.15
❑ 641 Rick Helling FOIL	.50	.15
❑ 642 Jody Reed	.50	.15
❑ 643 Ray Lankford	.50	.15
❑ 644 John Olerud	.50	.15
❑ 645 Paul Molitor FOIL	.75	.23
❑ 646 Pat Borders	.50	.15
❑ 647 Mike Morgan	.50	.15
❑ 648 Larry Walker	.75	.23
❑ 649 P.Castellano FOIL	.50	.15
❑ 650 Fred McGriff	.75	.23
❑ 651 Walt Weiss	.50	.15
❑ 652 C.Murray RC FOIL	1.00	.30
❑ 653 Dave Nilsson	.50	.15
❑ 654 Greg Pirkl RC	.50	.15
❑ 655 Robin Ventura FOIL	.50	.15
❑ 656 Mark Portugal	.50	.15
❑ 657 Roger McDowell	.50	.15
❑ 658 Rick Hirtensteiner FOIL RC	.50	.15
❑ 659 Glenallen Hill	.50	.15
❑ 660 Greg Gagne	.50	.15
❑ 661 Charles Johnson FOIL	.50	.15
❑ 662 Brian Hunter	.50	.15
❑ 663 Mark Lemke	.50	.15
❑ 664 Tim Belcher FOIL	.50	.15
❑ 665 Rich DeLucia	.50	.15
❑ 666 Bob Walk	.50	.15
❑ 667 Joe Carter FOIL	.50	.15
❑ 668 Jose Guzman	.50	.15
❑ 669 Otis Nixon	.50	.15
❑ 670 Phil Nevin FOIL	.75	.23
❑ 671 Eric Davis	.50	.15
❑ 672 Damion Easley RC	1.00	.30
❑ 673 Will Clark FOIL	1.25	.35
❑ 674 Mark Kiefer RC	.50	.15
❑ 675 Ozzie Smith	2.00	.60
❑ 676 Manny Ramirez FOIL	5.00	1.50
❑ 677 Gregg Olson	.50	.15
❑ 678 Cliff Floyd RC	2.00	.60
❑ 679 Duane Singleton RC	.50	.15
❑ 680 Jose Rijo	.50	.15
❑ 681 Willie Randolph	.50	.15
❑ 682 M.Tucker FOIL RC	2.00	.60
❑ 683 Darren Lewis	.50	.15
❑ 684 Dale Murphy	1.25	.35
❑ 685 Mike Pagliarulo	.50	.15
❑ 686 Paul Miller RC	.50	.15
❑ 687 Mike Robertson RC	.50	.15
❑ 688 Mike Devereaux	.50	.15
❑ 689 Pedro Astacio RC	1.00	.30
❑ 690 Alan Trammell	.50	.15
❑ 691 Roger Clemens	2.50	.75
❑ 692 Bud Black	.50	.15
❑ 693 Turk Wendell RC	1.00	.30
❑ 694 Barry Larkin FOIL	.75	.23
❑ 695 Todd Zeile	.50	.15
❑ 696 Pat Hentgen	.50	.15
❑ 697 Eddie Taubensee RC	1.00	.30
❑ 698 G.Velasquez RC	.50	.15
❑ 699 Tom Glavine	.75	.23
❑ 700 Robin Yount	2.00	.60
❑ 701 Checklist 1-141	.50	.15
❑ 702 Checklist 142-282	.50	.15
❑ 703 Checklist 283-423	.50	.15
❑ 704 Checklist 424-564	.50	.15
❑ 705 Checklist 565-705	.50	.15

1993 Bowman

	Nm-Mt	Ex-Mt
COMPLETE SET (708)	50.00	15.00
❑ 1 Glenn Davis	.15	.04
❑ 2 Hector Roa RC	.25	.07
❑ 3 Ken Ryan RC	.25	.07
❑ 4 Derek Wallace RC	.25	.07
❑ 5 Jorge Fabregas	.15	.04
❑ 6 Joe Oliver	.15	.04
❑ 7 Brandon Wilson	.15	.04
❑ 8 Mark Thompson RC	.25	.07
❑ 9 Tracy Sanders	.15	.04
❑ 10 Rich Renteria	.15	.04
❑ 11 Lou Whitaker	.30	.09
❑ 12 Brian L. Hunter RC	.50	.15
❑ 13 Joe Vitiello	.15	.04
❑ 14 Eric Karros	.30	.09
❑ 15 Joe Kmak	.15	.04
❑ 16 Tavo Alvarez	.15	.04
❑ 17 Steve Dunn RC	.25	.07
❑ 18 Tony Fernandez	.15	.04
❑ 19 Melido Perez	.15	.04
❑ 20 Mike Lieberthal	.30	.09
❑ 21 Terry Steinbach	.15	.04
❑ 22 Stan Belinda	.15	.04
❑ 23 Jay Buhner	.30	.09
❑ 24 Allen Watson	.15	.04
❑ 25 Daryl Henderson RC	.25	.07
❑ 26 Ray McDavid RC	.25	.07
❑ 27 Shawn Green	1.00	.30
❑ 28 Bud Black	.15	.04
❑ 29 Sherman Obando RC	.25	.07
❑ 30 Mike Hostetler RC	.25	.07
❑ 31 Nate Minchey RC	.25	.07
❑ 32 Randy Myers	.15	.04
❑ 33 Brian Grebeck	.15	.04
❑ 34 John Roper	.15	.04
❑ 35 Larry Thomas	.15	.04
❑ 36 Alex Cole	.15	.04
❑ 37 Tom Kramer RC	.25	.07
❑ 38 Matt Whisenant RC	.25	.07
❑ 39 Chris Gomez RC	.50	.15
❑ 40 Luis Gonzalez	.30	.09
❑ 41 Kevin Appier	.30	.09
❑ 42 Omar Daal RC	.50	.15
❑ 43 Duane Singleton	.15	.04
❑ 44 Bill Risley	.15	.04
❑ 45 Pat Meares RC	.50	.15
❑ 46 Butch Huskey	.15	.04
❑ 47 Bobby Munoz	.15	.04
❑ 48 Juan Bell	.15	.04
❑ 49 Scott Lydy RC	.25	.07
❑ 50 Dennis Moeller	.15	.04
❑ 51 Marc Newfield	.15	.04
❑ 52 Tripp Cromer RC	.25	.07

Card	Player	Price	Price
❑ 53	Kurt Miller	.15	.04
❑ 54	Jim Pena	.15	.04
❑ 55	Juan Guzman	.15	.04
❑ 56	Matt Williams	.30	.09
❑ 57	Harold Reynolds	.30	.09
❑ 58	Donnie Elliott RC	.25	.07
❑ 59	Jon Shave RC	.25	.07
❑ 60	Kevin Roberson RC	.25	.07
❑ 61	Hilly Hathaway RC	.25	.07
❑ 62	Jose Rijo	.15	.04
❑ 63	Kerry Taylor RC	.15	.04
❑ 64	Ryan Hawblitzel	.15	.04
❑ 65	Glenallen Hill	.15	.04
❑ 66	Ramon Martinez RC	.25	.07
❑ 67	Travis Fryman	.30	.09
❑ 68	Tom Nevers	.15	.04
❑ 69	Phil Hiatt	.15	.04
❑ 70	Tim Wallach	.15	.04
❑ 71	B.J. Surhoff	.30	.09
❑ 72	Rondell White	.30	.09
❑ 73	Denny Hocking RC	.50	.15
❑ 74	Mike Oquist RC	.25	.07
❑ 75	Paul O'Neill	.50	.15
❑ 76	Willie Banks	.15	.04
❑ 77	Bob Welch	.15	.04
❑ 78	Jose Sandoval RC	.25	.07
❑ 79	Bill Haselman	.15	.04
❑ 80	Rheal Cormier	.15	.04
❑ 81	Dean Palmer	.30	.09
❑ 82	Pat Gomez RC	.25	.07
❑ 83	Steve Karsay	.15	.04
❑ 84	Carl Hanselman RC	.25	.07
❑ 85	T.R. Lewis RC	.25	.07
❑ 86	Chipper Jones	.75	.23
❑ 87	Scott Hatteberg	.15	.04
❑ 88	Greg Hibbard	.15	.04
❑ 89	Lance Painter RC	.25	.07
❑ 90	Chad Mottola RC	.50	.15
❑ 91	Jason Bere	.15	.04
❑ 92	Dante Bichette	.30	.09
❑ 93	Sandy Alomar Jr.	.15	.04
❑ 94	Carl Everett	.30	.09
❑ 95	Danny Bautista RC	1.00	.30
❑ 96	Steve Finley	.30	.09
❑ 97	David Cone	.30	.09
❑ 98	Todd Hollandsworth	.15	.04
❑ 99	Matt Mieske	.15	.04
❑ 100	Larry Walker	.50	.15
❑ 101	Shane Mack	.15	.04
❑ 102	Aaron Ledesma RC	.25	.07
❑ 103	Andy Pettitte RC	8.00	2.40
❑ 104	Kevin Stocker	.15	.04
❑ 105	Mike Mohler RC	.25	.07
❑ 106	Tony Menendez	.15	.04
❑ 107	Derek Lowe	.75	.23
❑ 108	Basil Shabazz	.15	.04
❑ 109	Dan Smith	.15	.04
❑ 110	Scott Sanders RC	.50	.15
❑ 111	Todd Stottlemyre	.15	.04
❑ 112	Benji Simonton RC	.25	.07
❑ 113	Rick Sutcliffe	.30	.09
❑ 114	Lee Heath RC	.25	.07
❑ 115	Jeff Russell	.15	.04
❑ 116	Dave Stevens RC	.25	.07
❑ 117	Mark Holzemer RC	.25	.07
❑ 118	Tim Belcher	.15	.04
❑ 119	Bobby Thigpen	.15	.04
❑ 120	Roger Bailey RC	.25	.07
❑ 121	Tony Mitchell RC	.25	.07
❑ 122	Junior Felix	.15	.04
❑ 123	Rich Robertson RC	.25	.07
❑ 124	Andy Cook RC	.25	.07
❑ 125	Brian Bevil RC	.25	.07
❑ 126	Darryl Strawberry	.30	.09
❑ 127	Cal Eldred	.15	.04
❑ 128	Cliff Floyd	.30	.09
❑ 129	Alan Newman	.15	.04
❑ 130	Howard Johnson	.15	.04
❑ 131	Jim Abbott	.50	.15
❑ 132	Chad McConnell	.15	.04
❑ 133	Miguel Jimenez RC	.25	.07
❑ 134	Brett Backlund RC	.25	.07
❑ 135	John Cummings RC	.25	.07
❑ 136	Brian Barber	.15	.04
❑ 137	Rafael Palmeiro	.50	.15
❑ 138	Tim Worrell RC	.25	.07
❑ 139	Jose Pett RC	.25	.07
❑ 140	Barry Bonds	2.00	.60
❑ 141	Damon Buford	.15	.04
❑ 142	Jeff Blauser	.15	.04
❑ 143	Frankie Rodriguez	.15	.04
❑ 144	Mike Morgan	.15	.04
❑ 145	Gary DiSarcina	.15	.04
❑ 146	Pokey Reese	.15	.04
❑ 147	Johnny Ruffin	.15	.04
❑ 148	David Nied	.15	.04
❑ 149	Charles Nagy	.15	.04
❑ 150	Mike Myers RC	.25	.07
❑ 151	Kenny Carlyle RC	.25	.07
❑ 152	Eric Anthony	.15	.04
❑ 153	Jose Lind	.15	.04
❑ 154	Pedro Martinez	1.50	.45
❑ 155	Mark Kiefer	.15	.04
❑ 156	Tim Laker RC	.25	.07
❑ 157	Pat Mahomes	.15	.04
❑ 158	Bobby Bonilla	.30	.09
❑ 159	Domingo Jean	.15	.04
❑ 160	Darren Daulton	.30	.09
❑ 161	Mark McGwire	2.00	.60
❑ 162	Jason Kendall RC	1.50	.45
❑ 163	Desi Relaford	.15	.04
❑ 164	Ozzie Canseco	.15	.04
❑ 165	Rick Helling	.15	.04
❑ 166	Steve Pegues RC	.25	.07
❑ 167	Paul Molitor	.50	.15
❑ 168	Larry Carter RC	.15	.04
❑ 169	Arthur Rhodes	.15	.04
❑ 170	Damon Hollins RC	.50	.15
❑ 171	Frank Viola	.30	.09
❑ 172	Steve Trachsel RC	.50	.15
❑ 173	J.T. Snow RC	1.00	.30
❑ 174	Keith Gordon RC	.25	.07
❑ 175	Carlton Fisk	.50	.15
❑ 176	Jason Bates RC	.25	.07
❑ 177	Mike Crosby RC	.25	.07
❑ 178	Benny Santiago	.30	.09
❑ 179	Mike Moore	.15	.04
❑ 180	Jeff Juden	.15	.04
❑ 181	Darren Burton	.15	.04
❑ 182	Todd Williams RC	.50	.15
❑ 183	John Jaha	.15	.04
❑ 184	Mike Lansing RC	.50	.15
❑ 185	Pedro Grifol RC	.25	.07
❑ 186	Vince Coleman	.15	.04
❑ 187	Pat Kelly	.15	.04
❑ 188	Clemente Alvarez RC	.25	.07
❑ 189	Ron Darling	.15	.04
❑ 190	Orlando Merced	.15	.04
❑ 191	Chris Bosio	.15	.04
❑ 192	Steve Dixon RC	.25	.07
❑ 193	Doug Dascenzo	.15	.04
❑ 194	Ray Holbert RC	.25	.07
❑ 195	Howard Battle	.15	.04
❑ 196	Willie McGee	.30	.09
❑ 197	John O'Donoghue RC	.25	.07
❑ 198	Steve Avery	.15	.04
❑ 199	Greg Blosser	.15	.04
❑ 200	Ryne Sandberg	1.25	.35
❑ 201	Joe Grahe	.15	.04
❑ 202	Dan Wilson	.30	.09
❑ 203	Domingo Martinez RC	.25	.07
❑ 204	Andres Galarraga	.30	.09
❑ 205	Jamie Taylor RC	.25	.07
❑ 206	Darrell Whitmore RC	.25	.07
❑ 207	Ben Blomdahl RC	.25	.07
❑ 208	Doug Drabek	.15	.04
❑ 209	Keith Miller	.15	.04
❑ 210	Billy Ashley	.15	.04
❑ 211	Mike Farrell RC	.25	.07
❑ 212	John Wetteland	.30	.09
❑ 213	Randy Tomlin	.15	.04
❑ 214	Sid Fernandez	.15	.04
❑ 215	Quilvio Veras RC	.50	.15
❑ 216	Dave Hollins	.15	.04
❑ 217	Mike Neill	.15	.04
❑ 218	Andy Van Slyke	.30	.09
❑ 219	Bret Boone	.50	.15
❑ 220	Tom Pagnozzi	.15	.04
❑ 221	Mike Welch RC	.25	.07
❑ 222	Frank Seminara	.15	.04
❑ 223	Ron Villone	.15	.04
❑ 224	D.J. Thielen RC	.25	.07
❑ 225	Cal Ripken	2.50	.75
❑ 226	Pedro Borbon Jr. RC	.25	.07
❑ 227	Carlos Quintana	.15	.04
❑ 228	Tommy Shields	.15	.04
❑ 229	Tim Salmon	.50	.15
❑ 230	John Smiley	.15	.04
❑ 231	Ellis Burks	.30	.09
❑ 232	Pedro Castellano	.15	.04
❑ 233	Paul Byrd	.15	.04
❑ 234	Bryan Harvey	.15	.04
❑ 235	Scott Livingstone	.15	.04
❑ 236	James Mouton RC	.25	.07
❑ 237	Joe Randa	.30	.09
❑ 238	Pedro Astacio	.15	.04
❑ 239	Darryl Hamilton	.15	.04
❑ 240	Joey Eischen RC	.25	.07
❑ 241	Edgar Herrera RC	.25	.07
❑ 242	Dwight Gooden	.30	.09
❑ 243	Sam Militello	.15	.04
❑ 244	Ron Blazier RC	.25	.07
❑ 245	Ruben Sierra	.15	.04
❑ 246	Al Martin	.15	.04
❑ 247	Mike Felder	.15	.04
❑ 248	Bob Tewksbury	.15	.04
❑ 249	Craig Lefferts	.15	.04
❑ 250	Luis Lopez RC	.25	.07
❑ 251	Devon White	.30	.09
❑ 252	Will Clark	.75	.23
❑ 253	Mark Smith	.15	.04
❑ 254	Terry Pendleton	.30	.09
❑ 255	Aaron Sele	.15	.04
❑ 256	Jose Viera RC	.25	.07
❑ 257	Damion Easley	.15	.04
❑ 258	Rod Lofton RC	.25	.07
❑ 259	Chris Snopek RC	.25	.07
❑ 260	Q.McCracken RC	.50	.15
❑ 261	Mike Matthews RC	.25	.07
❑ 262	Hector Carrasco RC	.25	.07
❑ 263	Rick Greene	.15	.04
❑ 264	Chris Holt RC	.50	.15
❑ 265	George Brett	2.00	.60
❑ 266	Rick Gorecki RC	.25	.07
❑ 267	Francisco Gamez RC	.25	.07
❑ 268	Marquis Grissom	.30	.09
❑ 269	Kevin Tapani UER (Misspelled Tapan on card front)	.15	.04
❑ 270	Ryan Thompson	.15	.04
❑ 271	Gerald Williams	.15	.04
❑ 272	Paul Fletcher RC	.25	.07
❑ 273	Lance Blankenship	.15	.04
❑ 274	Marty Neff RC	.25	.07
❑ 275	Shawn Estes	.15	.04
❑ 276	Rene Arocha RC	.50	.15
❑ 277	Scott Eyre RC	.25	.07
❑ 278	Phil Plantier	.15	.04
❑ 279	Paul Spoljaric RC	.25	.07
❑ 280	Chris Gambs	.15	.04
❑ 281	Harold Baines	.30	.09
❑ 282	Jose Oliva	.15	.04
❑ 283	Matt Whiteside RC	.25	.07
❑ 284	Brant Brown RC	.50	.15
❑ 285	Russ Springer	.15	.04
❑ 286	Chris Sabo	.15	.04
❑ 287	Ozzie Guillen	.15	.04
❑ 288	Marcus Moore RC	.25	.07
❑ 289	Chad Ogea	.15	.04
❑ 290	Walt Weiss	.15	.04
❑ 291	Brian Edmondson	.15	.04
❑ 292	Jimmy Gonzalez	.15	.04
❑ 293	Danny Miceli RC	.50	.15
❑ 294	Jose Offerman	.15	.04
❑ 295	Greg Vaughn	.15	.04
❑ 296	Frank Bolick	.15	.04
❑ 297	Mike Maksudian RC	.25	.07
❑ 298	John Franco	.30	.09
❑ 299	Danny Tartabull	.15	.04
❑ 300	Len Dykstra	.30	.09
❑ 301	Bobby Witt	.15	.04
❑ 302	Trey Beamon RC	.25	.07
❑ 303	Tino Martinez	.50	.15
❑ 304	Aaron Holbert	.15	.04
❑ 305	Juan Gonzalez	.50	.15
❑ 306	Billy Hall RC	.25	.07
❑ 307	Duane Ward	.15	.04
❑ 308	Rod Beck	.15	.04

❑ 309 Jose Mercedes RC .25 .07
❑ 310 Otis Nixon .15 .04
❑ 311 Gettys Glaze RC .25 .07
❑ 312 Candy Maldonado .15 .04
❑ 313 Chad Curtis .15 .04
❑ 314 Tim Costo .15 .04
❑ 315 Mike Robertson .15 .04
❑ 316 Nigel Wilson .15 .04
❑ 317 Greg McMichael RC .50 .15
❑ 318 Scott Pose RC .25 .07
❑ 319 Ivan Cruz .15 .04
❑ 320 Greg Swindell .15 .04
❑ 321 Kevin McReynolds .15 .04
❑ 322 Tom Candiotti .15 .04
❑ 323 Rob Wishnevski RC .25 .07
❑ 324 Ken Hill .15 .04
❑ 325 Kirby Puckett .75 .23
❑ 326 Tim Bogar RC .25 .07
❑ 327 Mariano Rivera 1.00 .30
❑ 328 Mitch Williams .15 .04
❑ 329 Craig Paquette .15 .04
❑ 330 Jay Bell .30 .09
❑ 331 Jose Martinez RC .25 .07
❑ 332 Rob Deer .15 .04
❑ 333 Brook Fordyce .15 .04
❑ 334 Matt Nokes .15 .04
❑ 335 Derek Lee .15 .04
❑ 336 Paul Ellis RC .25 .07
❑ 337 Desi Wilson RC .25 .07
❑ 338 Roberto Alomar .50 .15
❑ 339 Jim Tatum FOIL RC .25 .07
❑ 340 J.T. Snow FOIL 1.00 .30
❑ 341 Tim Salmon FOIL .50 .15
❑ 342 Russ Davis FOIL RC .50 .15
❑ 343 Javy Lopez FOIL .50 .15
❑ 344 Troy O'Leary FOIL RC .50 .15
❑ 345 M.Cordova FOIL RC .50 .15
❑ 346 Bubba Smith RC FOIL .25 .07
❑ 347 Chipper Jones FOIL .75 .23
❑ 348 Jessie Hollins FOIL .15 .04
❑ 349 Willie Greene FOIL .15 .04
❑ 350 Mark Thompson FOIL .15 .04
❑ 351 Nigel Wilson FOIL .15 .04
❑ 352 Todd Jones FOIL .15 .04
❑ 353 Raul Mondesi FOIL .30 .09
❑ 354 Cliff Floyd FOIL .30 .09
❑ 355 Bobby Jones FOIL .30 .09
❑ 356 Kevin Stocker FOIL .15 .04
❑ 357 M.Cummings FOIL .15 .04
❑ 358 Allen Watson FOIL .15 .04
❑ 359 Ray McDavid FOIL .15 .04
❑ 360 Steve Hosey FOIL .15 .04
❑ 361 B.Pennington FOIL .15 .04
❑ 362 F.Rodriguez FOIL .15 .04
❑ 363 Troy Percival FOIL .50 .15
❑ 364 Jason Bere FOIL .15 .04
❑ 365 Manny Ramirez FOIL .75 .23
❑ 366 J.Thompson FOIL .15 .04
❑ 367 Joe Vitiello FOIL .15 .04
❑ 368 Tyrone Hill FOIL .15 .04
❑ 369 David McCarty FOIL .15 .04
❑ 370 Brien Taylor FOIL .15 .04
❑ 371 T.Van Poppel FOIL .15 .04
❑ 372 Marc Newfield FOIL .15 .04
❑ 373 T.Lowery RC FOIL .50 .15
❑ 374 Alex Gonzalez FOIL .15 .04
❑ 375 Ken Griffey Jr. 1.25 .35
❑ 376 Donovan Osborne .15 .04
❑ 377 Ritchie Moody RC .25 .07
❑ 378 Shane Andrews .15 .04
❑ 379 Carlos Delgado .75 .23
❑ 380 Bill Swift .15 .04
❑ 381 Leo Gomez .15 .04
❑ 382 Ron Gant .30 .09
❑ 383 Scott Fletcher .15 .04
❑ 384 Matt Walbeck RC .50 .15
❑ 385 Chuck Finley .30 .09
❑ 386 Kevin Mitchell .15 .04
❑ 387 Wilson Alvarez UER .15 .04
(Misspelled Alverez on card front)
❑ 388 John Burke RC .25 .07
❑ 389 Alan Embree .75 .23
❑ 390 Trevor Hoffman .30 .09
❑ 391 Alan Trammell .30 .09
❑ 392 Todd Jones .15 .04
❑ 393 Felix Jose .15 .04
❑ 394 Orel Hershiser .30 .09
❑ 395 Pat Listach .15 .04
❑ 396 Gabe White .15 .04
❑ 397 Dan Serafini RC .25 .07
❑ 398 Todd Hundley .15 .04
❑ 399 Wade Boggs .50 .15
❑ 400 Tyler Green .15 .04
❑ 401 Mike Bordick .15 .04
❑ 402 Scott Bullett .15 .04
❑ 403 LaGrande Russell RC .25 .07
❑ 404 Ray Lankford .15 .04
❑ 405 Nolan Ryan 3.00 .90
❑ 406 Robbie Beckett .15 .04
❑ 407 Brent Bowers RC .25 .07
❑ 408 Adell Davenport RC .25 .07
❑ 409 Brady Anderson .30 .09
❑ 410 Tom Glavine .50 .15
❑ 411 Doug Hecker RC .25 .07
❑ 412 Jose Guzman .15 .04
❑ 413 Luis Polonia .15 .04
❑ 414 Brian Williams .15 .04
❑ 415 Bo Jackson .75 .23
❑ 416 Eric Young .15 .04
❑ 417 Kenny Lofton .30 .09
❑ 418 Orestes Destrade .15 .04
❑ 419 Tony Phillips .15 .04
❑ 420 Jeff Bagwell .50 .15
❑ 421 Mark Gardner .15 .04
❑ 422 Brett Butler .30 .09
❑ 423 Graeme Lloyd RC .50 .15
❑ 424 Delino DeShields .15 .04
❑ 425 Scott Erickson .15 .04
❑ 426 Jeff Kent .75 .23
❑ 427 Jimmy Key .30 .09
❑ 428 Mickey Morandini .15 .04
❑ 429 Marcos Armas RC .25 .07
❑ 430 Don Slaught .15 .04
❑ 431 Randy Johnson .75 .23
❑ 432 Omar Olivares .15 .04
❑ 433 Charlie Leibrandt .15 .04
❑ 434 Kurt Stillwell .15 .04
❑ 435 Scott Brow RC .25 .07
❑ 436 Robby Thompson .15 .04
❑ 437 Ben McDonald .15 .04
❑ 438 Deion Sanders .50 .15
❑ 439 Tony Pena .15 .04
❑ 440 Mark Grace .50 .15
❑ 441 Eduardo Perez .15 .04
❑ 442 Tim Pugh RC .25 .07
❑ 443 Scott Ruffcorn .15 .04
❑ 444 Jay Gainer RC .25 .07
❑ 445 Albert Belle .30 .09
❑ 446 Bret Barberie .15 .04
❑ 447 Justin Mashore .15 .04
❑ 448 Pete Harnisch .15 .04
❑ 449 Greg Gagne .15 .04
❑ 450 Eric Davis .30 .09
❑ 451 Dave Mlicki .15 .04
❑ 452 Moises Alou .30 .09
❑ 453 Rick Aguilera .15 .04
❑ 454 Eddie Murray .75 .23
❑ 455 Bob Wickman .15 .04
❑ 456 Wes Chamberlain .15 .04
❑ 457 Brent Gates .15 .04
❑ 458 Paul Wagner .15 .04
❑ 459 Mike Hampton .30 .09
❑ 460 Ozzie Smith 1.25 .35
❑ 461 Tom Henke .15 .04
❑ 462 Ricky Gutierrez .15 .04
❑ 463 Jack Morris .30 .09
❑ 464 Joel Chimelis .15 .04
❑ 465 Gregg Olson .15 .04
❑ 466 Javy Lopez .50 .15
❑ 467 Scott Cooper .15 .04
❑ 468 Willie Wilson .15 .04
❑ 469 Mark Langston .15 .04
❑ 470 Barry Larkin .50 .15
❑ 471 Rod Bolton .15 .04
❑ 472 Freddie Benavides .15 .04
❑ 473 Ken Ramos RC .25 .07
❑ 474 Chuck Carr .15 .04
❑ 475 Cecil Fielder .30 .09
❑ 476 Eddie Taubensee .15 .04
❑ 477 Chris Eddy RC .25 .07
❑ 478 Greg Hansell .15 .04
❑ 479 Kevin Reimer .15 .04
❑ 480 Dennis Martinez .30 .09
❑ 481 Chuck Knoblauch .30 .09
❑ 482 Mike Draper .15 .04
❑ 483 Spike Owen .15 .04
❑ 484 Terry Mulholland .15 .04
❑ 485 Dennis Eckersley .30 .09
❑ 486 Blas Minor .15 .04
❑ 487 Dave Fleming .15 .04
❑ 488 Dan Cholowsky .15 .04
❑ 489 Ivan Rodriguez .75 .23
❑ 490 Gary Sheffield .30 .09
❑ 491 Ed Sprague .15 .04
❑ 492 Steve Hosey .15 .04
❑ 493 Jimmy Haynes RC .50 .15
❑ 494 John Smoltz .50 .15
❑ 495 Andre Dawson .30 .09
❑ 496 Rey Sanchez .15 .04
❑ 497 Ty Van Burkleo .15 .04
❑ 498 Bobby Ayala RC .25 .07
❑ 499 Tim Raines .30 .09
❑ 500 Charlie Hayes .15 .04
❑ 501 Paul Sorrento .15 .04
❑ 502 Richie Lewis RC .25 .07
❑ 503 Jason Pfaff RC .25 .07
❑ 504 Ken Caminiti .30 .09
❑ 505 Mike Macfarlane .15 .04
❑ 506 Jody Reed .15 .04
❑ 507 Bobby Hughes RC .25 .07
❑ 508 Wil Cordero .15 .04
❑ 509 George Tsamis RC .25 .07
❑ 510 Bret Saberhagen .30 .09
❑ 511 Derek Jeter RC 15.00 4.50
❑ 512 Gene Schall .15 .04
❑ 513 Curtis Shaw .15 .04
❑ 514 Steve Cooke .15 .04
❑ 515 Edgar Martinez .50 .15
❑ 516 Mike Milchin .15 .04
❑ 517 Billy Ripken .15 .04
❑ 518 Andy Benes .15 .04
❑ 519 Juan de la Rosa RC .25 .07
❑ 520 John Burkett .15 .04
❑ 521 Alex Ochoa .15 .04
❑ 522 Tony Tarasco RC .50 .15
❑ 523 Luis Ortiz .15 .04
❑ 524 Rick Wilkins .15 .04
❑ 525 Chris Turner RC .25 .07
❑ 526 Rob Dibble .30 .09
❑ 527 Jack McDowell .15 .04
❑ 528 Daryl Boston .15 .04
❑ 529 Bill Wertz RC .25 .07
❑ 530 Charlie Hough .30 .09
❑ 531 Sean Bergman .15 .04
❑ 532 Doug Jones .15 .04
❑ 533 Jeff Montgomery .15 .04
❑ 534 Roger Cedeno RC .50 .15
❑ 535 Robin Yount 1.25 .35
❑ 536 Mo Vaughn .30 .09
❑ 537 Brian Harper .15 .04
❑ 538 Juan Castillo RC .15 .04
❑ 539 Steve Farr .15 .04
❑ 540 John Kruk .30 .09
❑ 541 Troy Neel .15 .04
❑ 542 Danny Clyburn RC .25 .07
❑ 543 Jim Converse RC .25 .07
❑ 544 Gregg Jefferies .15 .04
❑ 545 Jose Canseco .75 .23
❑ 546 Julio Bruno RC .25 .07
❑ 547 Rob Butler .15 .04
❑ 548 Royce Clayton .15 .04
❑ 549 Chris Hoiles .15 .04
❑ 550 Greg Maddux 1.25 .35
❑ 551 Joe Ciccarella RC .25 .07
❑ 552 Ozzie Timmons .15 .04
❑ 553 Chili Davis .30 .09
❑ 554 Brian Koelling .15 .04
❑ 555 Frank Thomas .75 .23
❑ 556 Vinny Castilla .30 .09
❑ 557 Reggie Jefferson .15 .04
❑ 558 Rob Natal .15 .04
❑ 559 Mike Henneman .15 .04
❑ 560 Craig Biggio .50 .15
❑ 561 Billy Brewer .15 .04
❑ 562 Dan Melendez .15 .04
❑ 563 Kenny Felder RC .25 .07
❑ 564 Miguel Batista RC 1.00 .30

	No.	Player	Nm-Mt	Ex-Mt
❑	565	Dave Winfield	.30	.09
❑	566	Al Shirley	.15	.04
❑	567	Robert Eenhoorn	.15	.04
❑	568	Mike Williams	.15	.04
❑	569	Tanyon Sturtze RC	.50	.15
❑	570	Tim Wakefield	.75	.23
❑	571	Greg Pirkl	.15	.04
❑	572	Sean Lowe RC	.25	.07
❑	573	Terry Burrows RC	.25	.07
❑	574	Kevin Higgins	.15	.04
❑	575	Joe Carter	.30	.09
❑	576	Kevin Rogers	.15	.04
❑	577	Manny Alexander	.15	.04
❑	578	David Justice	.30	.09
❑	579	Brian Conroy RC	.25	.07
❑	580	Jessie Hollins	.15	.04
❑	581	Ron Watson RC	.25	.07
❑	582	Bip Roberts	.15	.04
❑	583	Tom Urbani RC	.25	.07
❑	584	Jason Hutchins RC	.25	.07
❑	585	Carlos Baerga	.15	.04
❑	586	Jeff Mutis	.15	.04
❑	587	Justin Thompson	.15	.04
❑	588	Orlando Miller	.15	.04
❑	589	Brian McRae	.15	.04
❑	590	Ramon Martinez	.15	.04
❑	591	Dave Nilsson	.15	.04
❑	592	Jose Vidro RC	1.50	.45
❑	593	Rich Becker	.15	.04
❑	594	Preston Wilson RC	1.50	.45
❑	595	Don Mattingly	2.00	.60
❑	596	Tony Longmire	.15	.04
❑	597	Kevin Seitzer	.15	.04
❑	598	Midre Cummings RC	.25	.07
❑	599	Omar Vizquel	.50	.15
❑	600	Lee Smith	.30	.09
❑	601	David Hulse RC	.25	.07
❑	602	Darrell Sherman RC	.25	.07
❑	603	Alex Gonzalez	.15	.04
❑	604	Geronimo Pena	.15	.04
❑	605	Mike Devereaux	.15	.04
❑	606	S.Hitchcock RC	.50	.15
❑	607	Mike Greenwell	.15	.04
❑	608	Steve Buechele	.15	.04
❑	609	Troy Percival	.50	.15
❑	610	Roberto Kelly	.15	.04
❑	611	James Baldwin RC	.50	.15
❑	612	Jerald Clark	.15	.04
❑	613	Albie Lopez RC	.50	.15
❑	614	Dave Magadan	.15	.04
❑	615	Mickey Tettleton	.15	.04
❑	616	Sean Runyan RC	.25	.07
❑	617	Bob Hamelin	.15	.04
❑	618	Raul Mondesi	.30	.09
❑	619	Tyrone Hill	.15	.04
❑	620	Darrin Fletcher	.15	.04
❑	621	Mike Trombley	.15	.04
❑	622	Jeromy Burnitz	.30	.09
❑	623	Bernie Williams	.50	.15
❑	624	Mike Farmer RC	.25	.07
❑	625	Rickey Henderson	.75	.23
❑	626	Carlos Garcia	.15	.04
❑	627	Jeff Darwin RC	.25	.07
❑	628	Todd Zeile	.15	.04
❑	629	Benji Gil	.15	.04
❑	630	Tony Gwynn	1.00	.30
❑	631	Aaron Small RC	.25	.07
❑	632	Joe Rosselli RC	.25	.07
❑	633	Mike Mussina	.50	.15
❑	634	Ryan Klesko	.30	.09
❑	635	Roger Clemens	1.50	.45
❑	636	Sammy Sosa	1.25	.35
❑	637	Orlando Palmeiro RC	.25	.07
❑	638	Willie Greene	.15	.04
❑	639	George Bell	.15	.04
❑	640	Garvin Alston RC	.25	.07
❑	641	Pete Janicki RC	.25	.07
❑	642	Chris Sheff RC	.25	.07
❑	643	Felipe Lira RC	.25	.07
❑	644	Roberto Petagine	.15	.04
❑	645	Wally Joyner	.30	.09
❑	646	Mike Piazza	2.00	.60
❑	647	Jaime Navarro	.15	.04
❑	648	Jeff Hartsock	.15	.04
❑	649	David McCarty	.15	.04
❑	650	Bobby Jones	.30	.09
❑	651	Mark Hutton	.15	.04
❑	652	Kyle Abbott	.15	.04
❑	653	Steve Cox RC	.50	.15
❑	654	Jeff King	.15	.04
❑	655	Norm Charlton	.15	.04
❑	656	Mike Gulan RC	.25	.07
❑	657	Julio Franco	.30	.09
❑	658	C.Cairncross RC	.25	.07
❑	659	John Olerud	.30	.09
❑	660	Salomon Torres	.15	.04
❑	661	Brad Pennington	.15	.04
❑	662	Melvin Nieves	.15	.04
❑	663	Ivan Calderon	.15	.04
❑	664	Turk Wendell	.15	.04
❑	665	Chris Pritchett	.15	.04
❑	666	Reggie Sanders	.15	.04
❑	667	Robin Ventura	.30	.09
❑	668	Joe Girardi	.15	.04
❑	669	Manny Ramirez	.75	.23
❑	670	Jeff Conine	.30	.09
❑	671	Greg Gohr	.15	.04
❑	672	Andujar Cedeno	.15	.04
❑	673	Les Norman RC	.25	.07
❑	674	Mike James RC	.25	.07
❑	675	Marshall Boze RC	.25	.07
❑	676	B.J. Wallace	.15	.04
❑	677	Kent Hrbek	.30	.09
❑	678	Jack Voigt RC	.25	.07
❑	679	Brien Taylor	.15	.04
❑	680	Curt Schilling	.30	.09
❑	681	Todd Van Poppel	.15	.04
❑	682	Kevin Young	.30	.09
❑	683	Tommy Adams	.15	.04
❑	684	Bernard Gilkey	.15	.04
❑	685	Kevin Brown	.30	.09
❑	686	Fred McGriff	.50	.15
❑	687	Pat Borders	.15	.04
❑	688	Kirt Manwaring	.15	.04
❑	689	Sid Bream	.15	.04
❑	690	John Valentin	.15	.04
❑	691	Steve Olsen RC	.25	.07
❑	692	Roberto Mejia RC	.25	.07
❑	693	Carlos Delgado FOIL	.75	.23
❑	694	S.Gibralter FOIL RC	.25	.07
❑	695	Gary Mota FOIL RC	.25	.07
❑	696	Jose Malave FOIL RC	.25	.07
❑	697	Larry Sutton FOIL RC	.25	.07
❑	698	Dan Frye FOIL RC	.25	.07
❑	699	Tim Clark FOIL RC	.25	.07
❑	700	Brian Rupp FOIL RC	.25	.07
❑	701	Felipe Alou FOIL Moises Alou	.30	.09
❑	702	Barry Bonds FOIL Bobby Bonds	.75	.23
❑	703	Ken Griffey Sr. FOIL Ken Griffey Jr.	.75	.23
❑	704	Brian McRae FOIL Hal McRae	.15	.04
❑	705	Checklist 1	.15	.04
❑	706	Checklist 2	.15	.04
❑	707	Checklist 3	.15	.04
❑	708	Checklist 4	.15	.04

1994 Bowman

	Nm-Mt	Ex-Mt
COMPLETE SET (682)	60.00	18.00

	No.	Player	Nm-Mt	Ex-Mt
❑	1	Joe Carter	.40	.12
❑	2	Marcus Moore	.25	.07
❑	3	Doug Creek RC	.50	.15
❑	4	Pedro Martinez	1.00	.30
❑	5	Ken Griffey Jr.	1.50	.45
❑	6	Greg Swindell	.25	.07
❑	7	J.J. Johnson	.25	.07
❑	8	Homer Bush RC	1.00	.30
❑	9	Arquimedez Pozo RC	.50	.15
❑	10	Bryan Harvey	.25	.07
❑	11	J.T. Snow	.40	.12
❑	12	Alan Benes RC	1.00	.30
❑	13	Chad Kreuter	.25	.07
❑	14	Eric Karros	.40	.12
❑	15	Frank Thomas	1.00	.30
❑	16	Bret Saberhagen	.40	.12
❑	17	Terrell Lowery	.25	.07
❑	18	Rod Bolton	.25	.07
❑	19	Harold Baines	.40	.12
❑	20	Matt Walbeck	.25	.07
❑	21	Tom Glavine	.60	.18
❑	22	Todd Jones	.25	.07
❑	23	Alberto Castillo RC	.50	.15
❑	24	Ruben Sierra	.25	.07
❑	25	Don Mattingly	2.50	.75
❑	26	Mike Morgan	.25	.07
❑	27	Jim Musselwhite RC	.50	.15
❑	28	Matt Brunson RC	.50	.15
❑	29	A.Meinershagen RC	.50	.15
❑	30	Joe Girardi	.25	.07
❑	31	Shane Halter	.25	.07
❑	32	Jose Paniagua RC	1.00	.30
❑	33	Paul Perkins RC	.50	.15
❑	34	John Hudek RC	.50	.15
❑	35	Frank Viola	.40	.12
❑	36	David Lamb RC	.50	.15
❑	37	Marshall Boze	.25	.07
❑	38	Jorge Posada RC	10.00	3.00
❑	39	Brian Anderson RC	1.00	.30
❑	40	Mark Whiten	.25	.07
❑	41	Sean Bergman	.25	.07
❑	42	Jose Parra RC	.50	.15
❑	43	Mike Robertson	.25	.07
❑	44	Pete Walker RC	.50	.15
❑	45	Juan Gonzalez	.60	.18
❑	46	Cleveland Ladell RC	.50	.15
❑	47	Mark Smith	.25	.07
❑	48	Kevin Jarvis UER (team listed as Yankees on back)	.50	.15
❑	49	Amaury Telemaco RC	.50	.15
❑	50	Andy Van Slyke	.40	.12
❑	51	Rikkert Faneyte RC	.50	.15
❑	52	Curtis Shaw	.25	.07
❑	53	Matt Drews RC	.50	.15
❑	54	Wilson Alvarez	.25	.07
❑	55	Manny Ramirez	.60	.18
❑	56	Bobby Munoz	.25	.07
❑	57	Ed Sprague	.25	.07
❑	58	Jamey Wright RC	1.00	.30
❑	59	Jeff Montgomery	.25	.07
❑	60	Kirk Rueter	.40	.12
❑	61	Edgar Martinez	.60	.18
❑	62	Luis Gonzalez	.40	.12
❑	63	Tim Vanegmond RC	.50	.15
❑	64	Bip Roberts	.25	.07
❑	65	John Jaha	.25	.07
❑	66	Chuck Carr	.25	.07
❑	67	Chuck Finley	.40	.12
❑	68	Aaron Holbert	.25	.07
❑	69	Cecil Fielder	.40	.12
❑	70	Tom Engle RC	.50	.15
❑	71	Ron Karkovice	.25	.07
❑	72	Joe Orsulak	.25	.07
❑	73	Duff Brumley RC	.50	.15
❑	74	Craig Clayton RC	.50	.15
❑	75	Cal Ripken	3.00	.90
❑	76	Brad Fullmer RC	1.50	.45
❑	77	Tony Tarasco	.25	.07
❑	78	Terry Farrar RC	.50	.15
❑	79	Matt Williams	.40	.12
❑	80	Rickey Henderson	1.00	.30
❑	81	Terry Mulholland	.25	.07
❑	82	Sammy Sosa	1.50	.45
❑	83	Paul Sorrento	.25	.07
❑	84	Pete Incaviglia	.25	.07
❑	85	Darren Hall RC	.50	.15

❑ 86 Scott Klingenbeck .25 .07
❑ 87 Dario Perez RC .50 .15
❑ 88 Ugueth Urbina .25 .07
❑ 89 Dave Vanhof RC .50 .15
❑ 90 Domingo Jean .25 .07
❑ 91 Otis Nixon .25 .07
❑ 92 Andres Berumen .25 .07
❑ 93 Jose Valentin .25 .07
❑ 94 Edgar Renteria RC 10.00 2.40
❑ 95 Chris Turner .25 .07
❑ 96 Ray Lankford .25 .07
❑ 97 Danny Bautista .25 .07
❑ 98 Chan Ho Park RC 1.50 .45
❑ 99 Glenn DiSarcina RC .50 .15
❑ 100 Butch Huskey .25 .07
❑ 101 Ivan Rodriguez 1.00 .30
❑ 102 Johnny Ruffin .25 .07
❑ 103 Alex Ochoa .25 .07
❑ 104 Torii Hunter RC 10.00 3.00
❑ 105 Ryan Klesko .40 .12
❑ 106 Jay Bell .40 .12
❑ 107 Kurt Peltzer RC .50 .15
❑ 108 Miguel Jimenez .25 .07
❑ 109 Russ Davis .25 .07
❑ 110 Derek Wallace .25 .07
❑ 111 Keith Lockhart RC 1.00 .30
❑ 112 Mike Lieberthal .40 .12
❑ 113 Dave Stewart .40 .12
❑ 114 Tom Schmidt .25 .07
❑ 115 Brian McRae .25 .07
❑ 116 Moises Alou .40 .12
❑ 117 Dave Fleming .25 .07
❑ 118 Jeff Bagwell .60 .18
❑ 119 Luis Ortiz .25 .07
❑ 120 Tony Gwynn 1.25 .35
❑ 121 Jaime Navarro .25 .07
❑ 122 Benito Santiago .40 .12
❑ 123 Darrell Whitmore .25 .07
❑ 124 John Mabry RC 1.00 .30
❑ 125 Mickey Tettleton .25 .07
❑ 126 Tom Candiotti .25 .07
❑ 127 Tim Raines .40 .12
❑ 128 Bobby Bonilla .40 .12
❑ 129 John Dettmer .25 .07
❑ 130 Hector Carrasco .25 .07
❑ 131 Chris Hoiles .25 .07
❑ 132 Rick Aguilera .25 .07
❑ 133 David Justice .40 .12
❑ 134 Esteban Loaiza RC 1.50 .45
❑ 135 Barry Bonds 2.50 .75
❑ 136 Bob Welch .25 .07
❑ 137 Mike Stanley .25 .07
❑ 138 Roberto Hernandez .25 .07
❑ 139 Sandy Alomar Jr. .25 .07
❑ 140 Darren Daulton .40 .12
❑ 141 Angel Martinez RC .50 .15
❑ 142 Howard Johnson .25 .07
❑ 143 Bob Hamelin UER .25 .07
(name and card number colors don't match)
❑ 144 J.J. Thobe RC .50 .15
❑ 145 Roger Salkeld .25 .07
❑ 146 Orlando Miller .25 .07
❑ 147 Dmitri Young .40 .12
❑ 148 Tim Hyers RC .50 .15
❑ 149 Mark Loretta RC 5.00 1.50
❑ 150 Chris Hammond .25 .07
❑ 151 Joel Moore RC .50 .15
❑ 152 Todd Zeile .25 .07
❑ 153 Wil Cordero .25 .07
❑ 154 Chris Smith .25 .07
❑ 155 James Baldwin .25 .07
❑ 156 Edgardo Alfonzo RC 1.50 .45
❑ 157 Kym Ashworth RC .50 .15
❑ 158 Paul Bako RC .50 .15
❑ 159 Rick Krivda RC .50 .15
❑ 160 Pat Mahomes .25 .07
❑ 161 Damon Hollins .40 .12
❑ 162 Felix Martinez RC .50 .15
❑ 163 Jason Myers RC .50 .15
❑ 164 Izzy Molina RC .50 .15
❑ 165 Brien Taylor .25 .07
❑ 166 Kevin Orie RC .50 .15
❑ 167 Casey Whitten RC .50 .15
❑ 168 Tony Longmire .25 .07
❑ 169 John Olerud .40 .12
❑ 170 Mark Thompson .25 .07
❑ 171 Jorge Fabregas .25 .07
❑ 172 John Wetteland .40 .12
❑ 173 Dan Wilson .25 .07
❑ 174 Doug Drabek .25 .07
❑ 175 Jeff McNeely .25 .07
❑ 176 Melvin Nieves .25 .07
❑ 177 Doug Glanville RC 1.00 .30
❑ 178 Javier De La Hoya RC .50 .15
❑ 179 Chad Curtis .25 .07
❑ 180 Brian Barber .25 .07
❑ 181 Mike Henneman .25 .07
❑ 182 Jose Offerman .25 .07
❑ 183 Robert Ellis RC .50 .15
❑ 184 John Franco .40 .12
❑ 185 Benji Gil .25 .07
❑ 186 Hal Morris .25 .07
❑ 187 Chris Sabo .25 .07
❑ 188 Blaise Ilsley RC .50 .15
❑ 189 Steve Avery .25 .07
❑ 190 Rick White RC .50 .15
❑ 191 Rod Beck .25 .07
❑ 192 Mark McGwire UER 2.50 .75
(No card number on back)
❑ 193 Jim Abbott .60 .18
❑ 194 Randy Myers .25 .07
❑ 195 Kenny Lofton .40 .12
❑ 196 Mariano Duncan .25 .07
❑ 197 Lee Daniels RC .50 .15
❑ 198 Armando Reynoso .25 .07
❑ 199 Joe Randa .40 .12
❑ 200 Cliff Floyd .40 .12
❑ 201 Tim Harkrider RC .50 .15
❑ 202 Kevin Gallaher RC .50 .15
❑ 203 Scott Cooper .25 .07
❑ 204 Phil Stidham RC .50 .15
❑ 205 Jeff D'Amico RC 1.00 .30
❑ 206 Matt Whisenant .25 .07
❑ 207 De Shawn Warren .25 .07
❑ 208 Rene Arocha .25 .07
❑ 209 Tony Clark RC 1.00 .30
❑ 210 Jason Jacome RC .50 .15
❑ 211 Scott Christman RC .50 .15
❑ 212 Bill Pulsipher .40 .12
❑ 213 Dean Palmer .40 .12
❑ 214 Chad Mottola .25 .07
❑ 215 Manny Alexander .25 .07
❑ 216 Rich Becker .25 .07
❑ 217 Andre King RC .50 .15
❑ 218 Carlos Garcia .25 .07
❑ 219 Ron Pezzoni RC .50 .15
❑ 220 Steve Karsay .25 .07
❑ 221 Jose Musset RC .50 .15
❑ 222 Karl Rhodes .25 .07
❑ 223 Frank Cimorelli RC .50 .15
❑ 224 Kevin Jordan RC .50 .15
❑ 225 Duane Ward .25 .07
❑ 226 John Burke .25 .07
❑ 227 Mike Macfarlane .25 .07
❑ 228 Mike Lansing .25 .07
❑ 229 Chuck Knoblauch .40 .12
❑ 230 Ken Caminiti .40 .12
❑ 231 Gar Finnvold RC .50 .15
❑ 232 Derrek Lee RC 2.50 .75
❑ 233 Brady Anderson .40 .12
❑ 234 Vic Darensbourg RC .50 .15
❑ 235 Mark Langston .25 .07
❑ 236 T.J. Mathews RC .50 .15
❑ 237 Lou Whitaker .40 .12
❑ 238 Roger Cedeno .25 .07
❑ 239 Alex Fernandez .25 .07
❑ 240 Ryan Thompson .25 .07
❑ 241 Kerry Lacy RC .50 .15
❑ 242 Reggie Sanders .25 .07
❑ 243 Brad Pennington .25 .07
❑ 244 Bryan Eversgerd RC .50 .15
❑ 245 Greg Maddux 1.50 .45
❑ 246 Jason Kendall .40 .12
❑ 247 J.R. Phillips .25 .07
❑ 248 Bobby Witt .25 .07
❑ 249 Paul O'Neill .60 .18
❑ 250 Ryne Sandberg 1.50 .45
❑ 251 Charles Nagy .25 .07
❑ 252 Kevin Stocker .25 .07
❑ 253 Shawn Green 1.00 .30
❑ 254 Charlie Hayes .25 .07
❑ 255 Donnie Elliott .25 .07
❑ 256 Rob Fitzpatrick RC .50 .15
❑ 257 Tim Davis .25 .07
❑ 258 James Mouton .25 .07
❑ 259 Mike Greenwell .25 .07
❑ 260 Ray McDavid .25 .07
❑ 261 Mike Kelly .25 .07
❑ 262 Andy Larkin RC .50 .15
❑ 263 Marquis Riley UER .25 .07
(No card number on back)
❑ 264 Bob Tewksbury .25 .07
❑ 265 Brian Edmondson .25 .07
❑ 266 Eduardo Lantigua RC .50 .15
❑ 267 Brandon Wilson .25 .07
❑ 268 Mike Welch .25 .07
❑ 269 Tom Henke .25 .07
❑ 270 Pokey Reese .25 .07
❑ 271 Greg Zaun RC 1.00 .30
❑ 272 Todd Ritchie .25 .07
❑ 273 Javier Lopez .40 .12
❑ 274 Kevin Young .25 .07
❑ 275 Kirt Manwaring .25 .07
❑ 276 Bill Taylor RC .50 .15
❑ 277 Robert Eenhoorn .25 .07
❑ 278 Jessie Hollins .25 .07
❑ 279 Julian Tavarez RC 1.00 .30
❑ 280 Gene Schall .25 .07
❑ 281 Paul Molitor .60 .18
❑ 282 Neifi Perez RC 1.00 .30
❑ 283 Greg Gagne .25 .07
❑ 284 Marquis Grissom .40 .12
❑ 285 Randy Johnson 1.00 .30
❑ 286 Pete Harnisch .25 .07
❑ 287 Joel Bennett RC .50 .15
❑ 288 Derek Bell .25 .07
❑ 289 Darryl Hamilton .25 .07
❑ 290 Gary Sheffield .40 .12
❑ 291 Eduardo Perez .25 .07
❑ 292 Basil Shabazz .25 .07
❑ 293 Eric Davis .40 .12
❑ 294 Pedro Astacio .25 .07
❑ 295 Robin Ventura .40 .12
❑ 296 Jeff Kent .40 .12
❑ 297 Rick Helling .25 .07
❑ 298 Joe Oliver .25 .07
❑ 299 Lee Smith .40 .12
❑ 300 Dave Winfield .40 .12
❑ 301 Deion Sanders .60 .18
❑ 302 R.Manzanillo RC .50 .15
❑ 303 Mark Portugal .25 .07
❑ 304 Brent Gates .25 .07
❑ 305 Wade Boggs .60 .18
❑ 306 Rick Wilkins .25 .07
❑ 307 Carlos Baerga .25 .07
❑ 308 Curt Schilling .40 .12
❑ 309 Shannon Stewart 1.00 .30
❑ 310 Darren Holmes .25 .07
❑ 311 Robert Toth RC .50 .15
❑ 312 Gabe White .25 .07
❑ 313 Mac Suzuki RC 1.00 .30
❑ 314 Alvin Morman RC .50 .15
❑ 315 Mo Vaughn .40 .12
❑ 316 Bryce Florie RC .50 .15
❑ 317 Gabby Martinez RC .50 .15
❑ 318 Carl Everett .40 .12
❑ 319 Kerwin Moore .25 .07
❑ 320 Tom Pagnozzi .25 .07
❑ 321 Chris Gomez .25 .07
❑ 322 Todd Williams .25 .07
❑ 323 Pat Hentgen .25 .07
❑ 324 Kirk Presley RC .50 .15
❑ 325 Kevin Brown .40 .12
❑ 326 J.Isringhausen RC 2.50 .75
❑ 327 Rick Forney RC .50 .15
❑ 328 Carlos Pulido RC .50 .15
❑ 329 Terrell Wade RC .50 .15
❑ 330 Al Martin .25 .07
❑ 331 Dan Carlson RC .50 .15
❑ 332 Mark Acre RC .50 .15
❑ 333 Sterling Hitchcock .25 .07
❑ 334 Jon Ratliff RC .50 .15
❑ 335 Alex Ramirez RC .50 .15
❑ 336 Phil Geisler RC .25 .07
❑ 337 E.Zambrano FOIL RC .50 .15
❑ 338 Jim Thome FOIL 1.00 .30
❑ 339 James Mouton FOIL .25 .07

❑ 340 Cliff Floyd FOIL .40 .12
❑ 341 Carlos Delgado FOIL .60 .18
❑ 342 R.Petagine FOIL .25 .07
❑ 343 Tim Clark FOIL .25 .07
❑ 344 Bubba Smith FOIL .25 .07
❑ 345 Randy Curtis FOIL RC .50 .15
❑ 346 Joe Biasucci FOIL RC .50 .15
❑ 347 D.J. Boston FOIL RC .50 .15
❑ 348 R.Rivera FOIL RC .50 .15
❑ 349 Bryan Link FOIL RC .50 .15
❑ 350 Mike Bell FOIL RC .50 .15
❑ 351 M.Watson FOIL RC .50 .15
❑ 352 Jason Myers FOIL .25 .07
❑ 353 Chipper Jones FOIL 1.00 .30
❑ 354 B.Kieschnick FOIL .25 .07
❑ 355 Pokey Reese FOIL .25 .07
❑ 356 John Burke FOIL .25 .07
❑ 357 Kurt Miller FOIL .25 .07
❑ 358 Orlando Miller FOIL .25 .07
❑ 359 T.Hollandsworth FOIL .25 .07
❑ 360 Rondell White FOIL .40 .12
❑ 361 Bill Pulsipher FOIL .40 .12
❑ 362 Tyler Green FOIL .25 .07
❑ 363 M.Cummings FOIL .25 .07
❑ 364 Brian Barber FOIL .25 .07
❑ 365 Melvin Nieves FOIL .25 .07
❑ 366 Salomon Torres FOIL .25 .07
❑ 367 Alex Ochoa FOIL .25 .07
❑ 368 F.Rodriguez FOIL .25 .07
❑ 369 Brian Anderson FOIL .40 .12
❑ 370 James Baldwin FOIL .25 .07
❑ 371 Manny Ramirez FOIL .60 .18
❑ 372 J.Thompson FOIL .25 .07
❑ 373 Johnny Damon FOIL 1.00 .30
❑ 374 Jeff D'Amico FOIL 1.00 .30
❑ 375 Rich Becker FOIL .25 .07
❑ 376 Derek Jeter FOIL 3.00 .90
❑ 377 Steve Karsay FOIL .25 .07
❑ 378 Mac Suzuki FOIL .40 .12
❑ 379 Benji Gil FOIL .25 .07
❑ 380 Alex Gonzalez FOIL .25 .07
❑ 381 Jason Bere FOIL .25 .07
❑ 382 Brett Butler FOIL .40 .12
❑ 383 Jeff Conine FOIL .40 .12
❑ 384 Darren Daulton FOIL .40 .12
❑ 385 Jeff Kent FOIL .40 .12
❑ 386 Don Mattingly FOIL 2.50 .75
❑ 387 Mike Piazza FOIL 2.00 .60
❑ 388 Ryne Sandberg FOIL 1.50 .45
❑ 389 Rich Amaral .25 .07
❑ 390 Craig Biggio .60 .18
❑ 391 Jeff Suppan RC 1.00 .30
❑ 392 Andy Benes .25 .07
❑ 393 Cal Eldred .25 .07
❑ 394 Jeff Conine .40 .12
❑ 395 Tim Salmon .60 .18
❑ 396 Ray Suplee RC .50 .15
❑ 397 Tony Phillips .25 .07
❑ 398 Ramon Martinez .25 .07
❑ 399 Julio Franco .40 .12
❑ 400 Dwight Gooden .40 .12
❑ 401 Kevin Lomon RC .50 .15
❑ 402 Jose Rijo .25 .07
❑ 403 Mike Devereaux .25 .07
❑ 404 Mike Zolecki RC .50 .15
❑ 405 Fred McGriff .60 .18
❑ 406 Danny Clyburn .25 .07
❑ 407 Robby Thompson .25 .07
❑ 408 Terry Steinbach .25 .07
❑ 409 Luis Polonia .25 .07
❑ 410 Mark Grace .60 .18
❑ 411 Albert Belle .40 .12
❑ 412 John Kruk .40 .12
❑ 413 Scott Spiezio RC 1.00 .30
❑ 414 Ellis Burks UER .40 .12
(Name spelled Elkis on front)
❑ 415 Joe Vitiello .25 .07
❑ 416 Tim Costo .25 .07
❑ 417 Marc Newfield .25 .07
❑ 418 Oscar Henriquez RC .50 .15
❑ 419 Matt Perisho RC .50 .15
❑ 420 Julio Bruno .25 .07
❑ 421 Kenny Felder .25 .07
❑ 422 Tyler Green .25 .07
❑ 423 Jim Edmonds 1.00 .30
❑ 424 Ozzie Smith 1.50 .45
❑ 425 Rick Greene .25 .07
❑ 426 Todd Hollandsworth .25 .07
❑ 427 Eddie Pearson RC .50 .15
❑ 428 Quilvio Veras .25 .07
❑ 429 Kenny Rogers .40 .12
❑ 430 Willie Greene .25 .07
❑ 431 Vaughn Eshelman .25 .07
❑ 432 Pat Meares .25 .07
❑ 433 Jermaine Dye RC 1.50 .45
❑ 434 Steve Cooke .25 .07
❑ 435 Bill Swift .25 .07
❑ 436 Fausto Cruz RC .50 .15
❑ 437 Mark Hutton .25 .07
❑ 438 B.Kieschnick RC 1.00 .30
❑ 439 Yorkis Perez .25 .07
❑ 440 Len Dykstra .40 .12
❑ 441 Pat Borders .25 .07
❑ 442 Doug Walls RC .50 .15
❑ 443 Wally Joyner .40 .12
❑ 444 Ken Hill .25 .07
❑ 445 Eric Anthony .25 .07
❑ 446 Mitch Williams .25 .07
❑ 447 Cory Bailey RC .50 .15
❑ 448 Dave Staton .25 .07
❑ 449 Greg Vaughn .25 .07
❑ 450 Dave Magadan .25 .07
❑ 451 Chili Davis .40 .12
❑ 452 Gerald Santos RC .50 .15
❑ 453 Joe Perona .25 .07
❑ 454 Delino DeShields .25 .07
❑ 455 Jack McDowell .25 .07
❑ 456 Todd Hundley .25 .07
❑ 457 Ritchie Moody .25 .07
❑ 458 Bret Boone .40 .12
❑ 459 Ben McDonald .25 .07
❑ 460 Kirby Puckett 1.00 .30
❑ 461 Gregg Olson .25 .07
❑ 462 Rich Aude RC .50 .15
❑ 463 John Burkett .25 .07
❑ 464 Troy Neel .25 .07
❑ 465 Jimmy Key .40 .12
❑ 466 Ozzie Timmons .25 .07
❑ 467 Eddie Murray 1.00 .30
❑ 468 Mark Tranberg RC .50 .15
❑ 469 Alex Gonzalez .25 .07
❑ 470 David Nied .25 .07
❑ 471 Barry Larkin .60 .18
❑ 472 Brian Looney RC .50 .15
❑ 473 Shawn Estes .25 .07
❑ 474 A.J. Sager RC .50 .15
❑ 475 Roger Clemens 2.00 .60
❑ 476 Vince Moore .25 .07
❑ 477 Scott Karl RC .50 .15
❑ 478 Kurt Miller .25 .07
❑ 479 Garret Anderson 1.00 .30
❑ 480 Allen Watson .25 .07
❑ 481 Jose Lima RC 2.50 .75
❑ 482 Rick Gorecki .25 .07
❑ 483 Jimmy Hurst RC .50 .15
❑ 484 Preston Wilson .40 .12
❑ 485 Will Clark 1.00 .30
❑ 486 Mike Ferry RC .50 .15
❑ 487 Curtis Goodwin RC .50 .15
❑ 488 Mike Myers .25 .07
❑ 489 Chipper Jones 1.00 .30
❑ 490 Jeff King .25 .07
❑ 491 W.VanLandingham RC .50 .15
❑ 492 Carlos Reyes RC .50 .15
❑ 493 Andy Pettitte 1.00 .30
❑ 494 Brant Brown .25 .07
❑ 495 Daron Kirkreit .25 .07
❑ 496 Ricky Bottalico RC 1.00 .30
❑ 497 Devon White .40 .12
❑ 498 Jason Johnson RC .50 .15
❑ 499 Vince Coleman .25 .07
❑ 500 Larry Walker .60 .18
❑ 501 Bobby Ayala .25 .07
❑ 502 Steve Finley .40 .12
❑ 503 Scott Fletcher .25 .07
❑ 504 Brad Ausmus .25 .07
❑ 505 Scott Talanoa RC .50 .15
❑ 506 Orestes Destrade .25 .07
❑ 507 Gary DiSarcina .25 .07
❑ 508 Willie Smith RC .50 .15
❑ 509 Alan Trammell .40 .12
❑ 510 Mike Piazza 2.00 .60
❑ 511 Ozzie Guillen .25 .07
❑ 512 Jeromy Burnitz .40 .12
❑ 513 Darren Oliver RC 1.00 .30
❑ 514 Kevin Mitchell .25 .07
❑ 515 Rafael Palmeiro .60 .18
❑ 516 David McCarty .25 .07
❑ 517 Jeff Blauser .25 .07
❑ 518 Trey Beamon .25 .07
❑ 519 Royce Clayton .25 .07
❑ 520 Dennis Eckersley .40 .12
❑ 521 Bernie Williams .60 .18
❑ 522 Steve Buechele .25 .07
❑ 523 Dennis Martinez .40 .12
❑ 524 Dave Hollins .25 .07
❑ 525 Joey Hamilton .25 .07
❑ 526 Andres Galarraga .40 .12
❑ 527 Jeff Granger .25 .07
❑ 528 Joey Eischen .25 .07
❑ 529 Desi Relaford .25 .07
❑ 530 Roberto Petagine .25 .07
❑ 531 Andre Dawson .40 .12
❑ 532 Ray Holbert .25 .07
❑ 533 Duane Singleton .25 .07
❑ 534 Kurt Abbott RC 1.00 .30
❑ 535 Bo Jackson 1.00 .30
❑ 536 Gregg Jefferies .25 .07
❑ 537 David Mysel .25 .07
❑ 538 Raul Mondesi .40 .12
❑ 539 Chris Snopek .25 .07
❑ 540 Brook Fordyce .25 .07
❑ 541 Ron Frazier RC .50 .15
❑ 542 Brian Koelling .25 .07
❑ 543 Jimmy Haynes .25 .07
❑ 544 Marty Cordova .25 .07
❑ 545 Jason Green RC .50 .15
❑ 546 Orlando Merced .25 .07
❑ 547 Lou Pote RC .50 .15
❑ 548 Todd Van Poppel .25 .07
❑ 549 Pat Kelly .25 .07
❑ 550 Turk Wendell .25 .07
❑ 551 Herbert Perry RC 1.00 .30
❑ 552 Ryan Karp RC .50 .15
❑ 553 Juan Guzman .25 .07
❑ 554 Bryan Rekar RC .50 .15
❑ 555 Kevin Appier .40 .12
❑ 556 Chris Schwab RC .50 .15
❑ 557 Jay Buhner .40 .12
❑ 558 Andujar Cedeno .25 .07
❑ 559 Ryan McGuire RC .50 .15
❑ 560 Ricky Gutierrez .25 .07
❑ 561 Keith Kimsey RC .50 .15
❑ 562 Tim Clark .25 .07
❑ 563 Damion Easley .25 .07
❑ 564 Clint Davis RC .50 .15
❑ 565 Mike Moore .25 .07
❑ 566 Orel Hershiser .40 .12
❑ 567 Jason Bere .25 .07
❑ 568 Kevin McReynolds .25 .07
❑ 569 Leland Macon RC .50 .15
❑ 570 John Courtright RC .50 .15
❑ 571 Sid Fernandez .25 .07
❑ 572 Chad Roper .25 .07
❑ 573 Terry Pendleton .40 .12
❑ 574 Danny Miceli .25 .07
❑ 575 Joe Rosselli .25 .07
❑ 576 Mike Bordick .25 .07
❑ 577 Danny Tartabull .25 .07
❑ 578 Jose Guzman .25 .07
❑ 579 Omar Vizquel .60 .18
❑ 580 Tommy Greene .25 .07
❑ 581 Paul Spoljaric .25 .07
❑ 582 Walt Weiss .25 .07
❑ 583 Oscar Jimenez RC .50 .15
❑ 584 Rod Henderson .25 .07
❑ 585 Derek Lowe .60 .18
❑ 586 Richard Hidalgo RC 1.50 .45
❑ 587 Shayne Bennett RC .50 .15
❑ 588 Tim Belk RC .50 .15
❑ 589 Matt Mieske .25 .07
❑ 590 Nigel Wilson .25 .07
❑ 591 Jeff Knox RC .50 .15
❑ 592 Bernard Gilkey .25 .07
❑ 593 David Cone .40 .12
❑ 594 Paul LoDuca RC 8.00 2.40
❑ 595 Scott Ruffcorn .25 .07
❑ 596 Chris Roberts .25 .07

❑ 597 Oscar Munoz RC .50 .15
❑ 598 Scott Sullivan RC .50 .15
❑ 599 Matt Jarvis RC .50 .15
❑ 600 Jose Canseco 1.00 .30
❑ 601 Tony Graffanino RC 1.00 .30
❑ 602 Don Slaught .25 .07
❑ 603 Brett King RC .50 .15
❑ 604 Jose Herrera RC .50 .15
❑ 605 Melido Perez .25 .07
❑ 606 Mike Hubbard RC .50 .15
❑ 607 Chad Ogea .25 .07
❑ 608 Wayne Gomes RC 1.00 .30
❑ 609 Roberto Alomar .60 .18
❑ 610 Angel Echevarria RC .50 .15
❑ 611 Jose Lind .25 .07
❑ 612 Darrin Fletcher .25 .07
❑ 613 Chris Bosio .25 .07
❑ 614 Darryl Kile .40 .12
❑ 615 Frankie Rodriguez .25 .07
❑ 616 Phil Plantier .25 .07
❑ 617 Pat Listach .25 .07
❑ 618 Charlie Hough .40 .12
❑ 619 Ryan Hancock RC .50 .15
❑ 620 Darrel Deak RC .50 .15
❑ 621 Travis Fryman .40 .12
❑ 622 Brett Butler .40 .12
❑ 623 Lance Johnson .25 .07
❑ 624 Pete Smith .25 .07
❑ 625 James Hurst RC .50 .15
❑ 626 Roberto Kelly .25 .07
❑ 627 Mike Mussina .60 .18
❑ 628 Kevin Tapani .25 .07
❑ 629 John Smoltz .60 .18
❑ 630 Midre Cummings .25 .07
❑ 631 Salomon Torres .25 .07
❑ 632 Willie Adams .25 .07
❑ 633 Derek Jeter 3.00 .90
❑ 634 Steve Trachsel .25 .07
❑ 635 Albie Lopez .25 .07
❑ 636 Jason Moler .25 .07
❑ 637 Carlos Delgado .60 .18
❑ 638 Roberto Mejia .25 .07
❑ 639 Darren Burton .25 .07
❑ 640 B.J. Wallace .25 .07
❑ 641 Brad Clontz RC .50 .15
❑ 642 Billy Wagner RC 2.50 .75
❑ 643 Aaron Sele .25 .07
❑ 644 Cameron Cairncross .25 .07
❑ 645 Brian Harper .25 .07
❑ 646 Marc Valdes UER .25 .07
(No card number on back)
❑ 647 Mark Ratekin .25 .07
❑ 648 Terry Bradshaw RC .50 .15
❑ 649 Justin Thompson .25 .07
❑ 650 Mike Busch RC .50 .15
❑ 651 Joe Hall RC .50 .15
❑ 652 Bobby Jones .25 .07
❑ 653 Kelly Stinnett RC 1.00 .30
❑ 654 Rod Steph RC .50 .15
❑ 655 Jay Powell RC 1.00 .30
❑ 656 K.Garagozzo RC UER .50 .15
No card number on back
❑ 657 Todd Dunn .25 .07
❑ 658 Charles Peterson RC .50 .15
❑ 659 Darren Lewis .25 .07
❑ 660 John Wasdin RC .50 .15
❑ 661 Tate Seefried RC .50 .15
❑ 662 Hector Trinidad RC .50 .15
❑ 663 John Carter RC .25 .07
❑ 664 Larry Mitchell .25 .07
❑ 665 David Catlett RC .50 .15
❑ 666 Dante Bichette .40 .12
❑ 667 Felix Jose .25 .07
❑ 668 Rondell White .40 .12
❑ 669 Tino Martinez .60 .18
❑ 670 Brian L. Hunter .25 .07
❑ 671 Jose Malave .25 .07
❑ 672 Archi Cianfrocco .25 .07
❑ 673 Mike Matheny RC 5.00 1.50
❑ 674 Bret Barberie .25 .07
❑ 675 Andrew Lorraine RC .50 .15
❑ 676 Brian Jordan .40 .12
❑ 677 Tim Belcher .25 .07
❑ 678 Antonio Osuna RC .50 .15
❑ 679 Checklist .25 .07
❑ 680 Checklist .25 .07
❑ 681 Checklist .25 .07
❑ 682 Checklist .25 .07

1995 Bowman

	Nm-Mt	Ex-Mt
COMPLETE SET (439)	150.00	45.00

❑ 1 Billy Wagner .50 .15
❑ 2 Chris Widger .25 .07
❑ 3 Brent Bowers .25 .07
❑ 4 Bob Abreu RC 6.00 1.80
❑ 5 Lou Collier RC 1.00 .30
❑ 6 Juan Acevedo RC .50 .15
❑ 7 Jason Kelley RC .50 .15
❑ 8 Brian Sackinsky .25 .07
❑ 9 Scott Christman .25 .07
❑ 10 Damon Hollins .25 .07
❑ 11 Willis Otanez RC .50 .15
❑ 12 Jason Ryan RC .50 .15
❑ 13 Jason Giambi .75 .23
❑ 14 Andy Taulbee RC .50 .15
❑ 15 Mark Thompson .25 .07
❑ 16 Hugo Pivaral RC .50 .15
❑ 17 Brien Taylor .25 .07
❑ 18 Antonio Osuna .25 .07
❑ 19 Edgardo Alfonzo .50 .15
❑ 20 Carl Everett .50 .15
❑ 21 Matt Drews .25 .07
❑ 22 Bartolo Colon RC 3.00 .90
❑ 23 Andruw Jones RC 20.00 6.00
❑ 24 Robert Person RC 1.00 .30
❑ 25 Derrek Lee .50 .15
❑ 26 John Ambrose RC .50 .15
❑ 27 Eric Knowles RC .50 .15
❑ 28 Chris Roberts .25 .07
❑ 29 Don Wengert .25 .07
❑ 30 Marcus Jensen RC 1.00 .30
❑ 31 Brian Barber .25 .07
❑ 32 Kevin Brown C .50 .15
❑ 33 Benji Gil .25 .07
❑ 34 Mike Hubbard .25 .07
❑ 35 Bart Evans RC .50 .15
❑ 36 Enrique Wilson RC .50 .15
❑ 37 Brian Buchanan RC 1.00 .30
❑ 38 Ken Ray RC .50 .15
❑ 39 Micah Franklin RC .50 .15
❑ 40 Ricky Otero RC .50 .15
❑ 41 Jason Kendall .50 .15
❑ 42 Jimmy Hurst .25 .07
❑ 43 Jerry Wolak RC .50 .15
❑ 44 Jayson Peterson RC .50 .15
❑ 45 Allen Battle RC .50 .15
❑ 46 Scott Stahoviak .25 .07
❑ 47 Steve Schrenk RC .50 .15
❑ 48 Travis Miller RC .50 .15
❑ 49 Eddie Rios RC .50 .15
❑ 50 Mike Hampton .50 .15
❑ 51 Chad Frontera RC .50 .15
❑ 52 Tom Evans .25 .07
❑ 53 C.J. Nitkowski .25 .07
❑ 54 Clay Caruthers RC .50 .15
❑ 55 Shannon Stewart .50 .15
❑ 56 Jorge Posada 1.25 .35
❑ 57 Aaron Holbert .25 .07
❑ 58 Harry Berrios RC .50 .15
❑ 59 Steve Rodriguez .25 .07
❑ 60 Shane Andrews .25 .07
❑ 61 Will Cunnane RC .50 .15
❑ 62 Richard Hidalgo .25 .07
❑ 63 Bill Selby RC .50 .15
❑ 64 Jay Cranford RC .50 .15
❑ 65 Jeff Suppan .25 .07
❑ 66 Curtis Goodwin .25 .07
❑ 67 John Thomson RC 1.00 .30
❑ 68 Justin Thompson .25 .07
❑ 69 Troy Percival .50 .15
❑ 70 Matt Wagner RC .50 .15
❑ 71 Terry Bradshaw .25 .07
❑ 72 Greg Hansell .25 .07
❑ 73 John Burke .25 .07
❑ 74 Jeff D'Amico .25 .07
❑ 75 Ernie Young .25 .07
❑ 76 Jason Bates .25 .07
❑ 77 Chris Stynes .25 .07
❑ 78 Cade Gaspar RC .50 .15
❑ 79 Melvin Nieves .25 .07
❑ 80 Rick Gorecki .25 .07
❑ 81 Felix Rodriguez RC 1.00 .30
❑ 82 Ryan Hancock .25 .07
❑ 83 Chris Carpenter RC 2.00 .60
❑ 84 Ray McDavid .25 .07
❑ 85 Chris Wimmer .25 .07
❑ 86 Doug Glanville .25 .07
❑ 87 DeShawn Warren .25 .07
❑ 88 Damian Moss RC 1.00 .30
❑ 89 Rafael Orellano RC .50 .15
❑ 90 Vladimir Guerrero RC 50.00 15.00
❑ 91 Raul Casanova RC .50 .15
❑ 92 Karim Garcia RC 1.00 .30
❑ 93 Bryce Florie .25 .07
❑ 94 Kevin Orie .25 .07
❑ 95 Ryan Nye RC .50 .15
❑ 96 Matt Sachse RC .50 .15
❑ 97 Ivan Arteaga RC .50 .15
❑ 98 Glenn Murray .25 .07
❑ 99 Stacy Hollins RC .50 .15
❑ 100 Jim Pittsley .25 .07
❑ 101 Craig Mattson RC .50 .15
❑ 102 Neifi Perez .25 .07
❑ 103 Keith Williams .25 .07
❑ 104 Roger Cedeno .25 .07
❑ 105 Tony Terry RC .50 .15
❑ 106 Jose Malave .25 .07
❑ 107 Joe Rosselli .25 .07
❑ 108 Kevin Jordan .25 .07
❑ 109 Sid Roberson RC .50 .15
❑ 110 Alan Embree .25 .07
❑ 111 Terrell Wade .25 .07
❑ 112 Bob Wolcott .25 .07
❑ 113 Carlos Perez RC 1.00 .30
❑ 114 Mike Bovee RC .50 .15
❑ 115 Tommy Davis RC .50 .15
❑ 116 Jeremey Kendall RC .50 .15
❑ 117 Rich Aude .25 .07
❑ 118 Rick Huisman .25 .07
❑ 119 Tim Belk .25 .07
❑ 120 Edgar Renteria 1.25 .23
❑ 121 Calvin Maduro RC .50 .15
❑ 122 Jerry Martin RC .50 .15
❑ 123 Ramon Fermin RC .50 .15
❑ 124 Kimera Bartee RC .50 .15
❑ 125 Mark Farris .25 .07
❑ 126 Frank Rodriguez .25 .07
❑ 127 Bobby Higginson RC 2.00 .60
❑ 128 Bret Wagner .25 .07
❑ 129 Edwin Diaz RC .50 .15
❑ 130 Jimmy Haynes .25 .07
❑ 131 Chris Weinke RC 1.00 .30
❑ 132 Damian Jackson RC 1.00 .30
❑ 133 Felix Martinez .25 .07
❑ 134 Edwin Hurtado RC .50 .15
❑ 135 Matt Raleigh RC .50 .15
❑ 136 Paul Wilson .25 .07
❑ 137 Ron Villone .25 .07
❑ 138 E.Stuckenschneider RC .50 .15
❑ 139 Tate Seefried .25 .07
❑ 140 Rey Ordonez RC 2.00 .60
❑ 141 Eddie Pearson .25 .07
❑ 142 Kevin Gallaher .25 .07
❑ 143 Torii Hunter .75 .23
❑ 144 Daron Kirkreit .25 .07
❑ 145 Craig Wilson .25 .07
❑ 146 Ugueth Urbina .25 .07

❑ 147 Chris Snopek .25 .07
❑ 148 Kym Ashworth .25 .07
❑ 149 Wayne Gomes .25 .07
❑ 150 Mark Loretta .50 .15
❑ 151 Ramon Morel RC .50 .15
❑ 152 Trot Nixon .50 .15
❑ 153 Desi Relaford .25 .07
❑ 154 Scott Sullivan .25 .07
❑ 155 Marc Barcelo .25 .07
❑ 156 Willie Adams .25 .07
❑ 157 Derrick Gibson RC .50 .15
❑ 158 Brian Meadows RC .50 .15
❑ 159 Julian Tavarez .25 .07
❑ 160 Bryan Rekar .25 .07
❑ 161 Steve Gibralter .25 .07
❑ 162 Esteban Loaiza .25 .07
❑ 163 John Wasdin .25 .07
❑ 164 Kirk Presley .25 .07
❑ 165 Mariano Rivera .75 .23
❑ 166 Andy Larkin .25 .07
❑ 167 Sean Whiteside RC .50 .15
❑ 168 Matt Apana RC .50 .15
❑ 169 Shawn Senior RC .50 .15
❑ 170 Scott Gentile .25 .07
❑ 171 Quilvio Veras .25 .07
❑ 172 Eli Marrero RC 1.50 .45
❑ 173 Mendy Lopez RC .50 .15
❑ 174 Homer Bush .25 .07
❑ 175 Brian Stephenson RC .50 .15
❑ 176 Jon Nunnally .25 .07
❑ 177 Jose Herrera .25 .07
❑ 178 Corey Avrard RC .50 .15
❑ 179 David Bell .25 .07
❑ 180 Jason Isringhausen .50 .15
❑ 181 Jamey Wright .25 .07
❑ 182 Lonell Roberts RC .25 .07
❑ 183 Marty Cordova .25 .07
❑ 184 Amaury Telemaco .25 .07
❑ 185 John Mabry .25 .07
❑ 186 Andrew Vessel RC .50 .15
❑ 187 Jim Cole RC .50 .15
❑ 188 Marquis Riley .25 .07
❑ 189 Todd Dunn .25 .07
❑ 190 John Carter .25 .07
❑ 191 Donnie Sadler RC 1.00 .30
❑ 192 Mike Bell .25 .07
❑ 193 Chris Cumberland RC .50 .15
❑ 194 Jason Schmidt 1.25 .35
❑ 195 Matt Brunson .25 .07
❑ 196 James Baldwin .25 .07
❑ 197 Bill Simas RC .50 .15
❑ 198 Gus Gandarillas .25 .07
❑ 199 Mac Suzuki .25 .07
❑ 200 Rick Holifield RC .50 .15
❑ 201 Fernando Lunar RC .50 .15
❑ 202 Kevin Jarvis .25 .07
❑ 203 Everett Stull .25 .07
❑ 204 Steve Wojciechowski .25 .07
❑ 205 Shawn Estes .25 .07
❑ 206 Jermaine Dye .50 .15
❑ 207 Marc Kroon .25 .07
❑ 208 Peter Munro RC 1.00 .30
❑ 209 Pat Watkins .25 .07
❑ 210 Matt Smith .25 .07
❑ 211 Joe Vitiello .25 .07
❑ 212 Gerald Witasick Jr. .25 .07
❑ 213 Freddy A. Garcia RC .50 .15
❑ 214 Glenn Dishman RC .50 .15
❑ 215 Jay Canizaro RC .50 .15
❑ 216 Angel Martinez .25 .07
❑ 217 Yamil Benitez RC .50 .15
❑ 218 Fausto Macey RC .50 .15
❑ 219 Eric Owens .25 .07
❑ 220 Checklist .25 .07
❑ 221 D.Hosey FOIL RC .50 .15
❑ 222 B.Woodall FOIL RC .50 .15
❑ 223 Billy Ashley FOIL .25 .07
❑ 224 M.Grudzielanek FOIL RC 1.00 .30
❑ 225 M.Johnson FOIL RC 1.00 .30
❑ 226 Tim Unroe FOIL RC .50 .15
❑ 227 Todd Greene FOIL .25 .07
❑ 228 Larry Sutton FOIL .25 .07
❑ 229 Derek Jeter FOIL 4.00 1.20
❑ 230 Sal Fasano FOIL RC .50 .15
❑ 231 Ruben Rivera FOIL .25 .07
❑ 232 Chris Truby FOIL RC .50 .15
❑ 233 John Donati FOIL .25 .07
❑ 234 D.Conner FOIL RC .50 .15
❑ 235 Sergio Nunez FOIL RC .50 .15
❑ 236 Ray Brown FOIL RC .50 .15
❑ 237 Juan Melo FOIL RC .50 .15
❑ 238 Hideo Nomo FOIL RC 5.00 1.50
❑ 239 Jamie Bluma RC FOIL .50 .15
❑ 240 Jay Payton FOIL RC 2.00 .60
❑ 241 Paul Konerko FOIL 1.00 .30
❑ 242 Scott Elarton FOIL RC 1.00 .30
❑ 243 Jeff Abbott FOIL RC 1.00 .30
❑ 244 Jim Brower FOIL RC .50 .15
❑ 245 Geoff Blum FOIL RC 1.00 .30
❑ 246 Aaron Boone FOIL RC 2.00 .60
❑ 247 J.R. Phillips FOIL .25 .07
❑ 248 Alex Ochoa FOIL .25 .07
❑ 249 N.Garciaparra FOIL 8.00 2.40
❑ 250 Garret Anderson FOIL .50 .15
❑ 251 Ray Durham FOIL .50 .15
❑ 252 Paul Shuey FOIL .25 .07
❑ 253 Tony Clark FOIL .25 .07
❑ 254 Johnny Damon FOIL .75 .23
❑ 255 Duane Singleton FOIL .25 .07
❑ 256 LaTroy Hawkins FOIL .25 .07
❑ 257 Andy Pettitte FOIL .75 .23
❑ 258 Ben Grieve FOIL .50 .15
❑ 259 Marc Newfield FOIL .25 .07
❑ 260 Terrell Lowery FOIL .25 .07
❑ 261 Shawn Green FOIL .50 .15
❑ 262 Chipper Jones FOIL 1.25 .35
❑ 263 B.Kieschnick FOIL .25 .07
❑ 264 Pokey Reese FOIL .25 .07
❑ 265 Doug Million FOIL .25 .07
❑ 266 Marc Valdes FOIL .25 .07
❑ 267 Brian L.Hunter FOIL .25 .07
❑ 268 T.Hollandsworth FOIL .25 .07
❑ 269 Rod Henderson FOIL .25 .07
❑ 270 Bill Pulsipher FOIL .25 .07
❑ 271 Scott Rolen FOIL RC 25.00 7.50
❑ 272 Trey Beamon FOIL .25 .07
❑ 273 Alan Benes FOIL .25 .07
❑ 274 D.Hermanson FOIL .25 .07
❑ 275 Ricky Bottalico .25 .07
❑ 276 Albert Belle .50 .15
❑ 277 Deion Sanders .75 .23
❑ 278 Matt Williams .50 .15
❑ 279 Jeff Bagwell .75 .23
❑ 280 Kirby Puckett 1.25 .35
❑ 281 Dave Hollins .25 .07
❑ 282 Don Mattingly 3.00 .90
❑ 283 Joey Hamilton .25 .07
❑ 284 Bobby Bonilla .50 .15
❑ 285 Moises Alou .50 .15
❑ 286 Tom Glavine .75 .23
❑ 287 Brett Butler .50 .15
❑ 288 Chris Hoiles .25 .07
❑ 289 Kenny Rogers .50 .15
❑ 290 Larry Walker .75 .23
❑ 291 Tim Raines .50 .15
❑ 292 Kevin Appier .50 .15
❑ 293 Roger Clemens 2.50 .75
❑ 294 Chuck Carr .25 .07
❑ 295 Randy Myers .25 .07
❑ 296 Dave Nilsson .25 .07
❑ 297 Joe Carter .50 .15
❑ 298 Chuck Finley .50 .15
❑ 299 Ray Lankford .25 .07
❑ 300 Roberto Kelly .25 .07
❑ 301 Jon Lieber .25 .07
❑ 302 Travis Fryman .50 .15
❑ 303 Mark McGwire 3.00 .90
❑ 304 Tony Gwynn 1.50 .45
❑ 305 Kenny Lofton .50 .15
❑ 306 Mark Whiten .25 .07
❑ 307 Doug Drabek .25 .07
❑ 308 Terry Steinbach .25 .07
❑ 309 Ryan Klesko .50 .15
❑ 310 Mike Piazza 2.00 .60
❑ 311 Ben McDonald .25 .07
❑ 312 Reggie Sanders .25 .07
❑ 313 Alex Fernandez .25 .07
❑ 314 Aaron Sele .25 .07
❑ 315 Gregg Jefferies .25 .07
❑ 316 Rickey Henderson 1.25 .35
❑ 317 Brian Anderson .25 .07
❑ 318 Jose Valentin .25 .07
❑ 319 Rod Beck .25 .07
❑ 320 Marquis Grissom .50 .15
❑ 321 Ken Griffey Jr. 2.00 .60
❑ 322 Bret Saberhagen .50 .15
❑ 323 Juan Gonzalez .75 .23
❑ 324 Paul Molitor .75 .23
❑ 325 Gary Sheffield .50 .15
❑ 326 Darren Daulton .50 .15
❑ 327 Bill Swift .25 .07
❑ 328 Brian McRae .25 .07
❑ 329 Robin Ventura .50 .15
❑ 330 Lee Smith .50 .15
❑ 331 Fred McGriff .75 .23
❑ 332 Delino DeShields .25 .07
❑ 333 Edgar Martinez .75 .23
❑ 334 Mike Mussina .75 .23
❑ 335 Orlando Merced .25 .07
❑ 336 Carlos Baerga .25 .07
❑ 337 Wil Cordero .25 .07
❑ 338 Tom Pagnozzi .25 .07
❑ 339 Pat Hentgen .25 .07
❑ 340 Chad Curtis .25 .07
❑ 341 Darren Lewis .25 .07
❑ 342 Jeff Kent .50 .15
❑ 343 Bip Roberts .25 .07
❑ 344 Ivan Rodriguez 1.25 .35
❑ 345 Jeff Montgomery .25 .07
❑ 346 Hal Morris .25 .07
❑ 347 Danny Tartabull .25 .07
❑ 348 Raul Mondesi .50 .15
❑ 349 Ken Hill .25 .07
❑ 350 Pedro Martinez 1.25 .35
❑ 351 Frank Thomas 1.25 .35
❑ 352 Manny Ramirez .75 .23
❑ 353 Tim Salmon .75 .23
❑ 354 W. VanLandingham .25 .07
❑ 355 Andres Galarraga .50 .15
❑ 356 Paul O'Neill .75 .23
❑ 357 Brady Anderson .50 .15
❑ 358 Ramon Martinez .25 .07
❑ 359 John Olerud .50 .15
❑ 360 Ruben Sierra .25 .07
❑ 361 Cal Eldred .25 .07
❑ 362 Jay Buhner .50 .15
❑ 363 Jay Bell .50 .15
❑ 364 Wally Joyner .50 .15
❑ 365 Chuck Knoblauch .50 .15
❑ 366 Len Dykstra .50 .15
❑ 367 John Wetteland .50 .15
❑ 368 Roberto Alomar .75 .23
❑ 369 Craig Biggio .75 .23
❑ 370 Ozzie Smith 2.00 .60
❑ 371 Terry Pendleton .50 .15
❑ 372 Sammy Sosa 2.00 .60
❑ 373 Carlos Garcia .25 .07
❑ 374 Jose Rijo .25 .07
❑ 375 Chris Gomez .25 .07
❑ 376 Barry Bonds 3.00 .90
❑ 377 Steve Avery .25 .07
❑ 378 Rick Wilkins .25 .07
❑ 379 Pete Harnisch .25 .07
❑ 380 Dean Palmer .50 .15
❑ 381 Bob Hamelin .25 .07
❑ 382 Jason Bere .25 .07
❑ 383 Jimmy Key .50 .15
❑ 384 Dante Bichette .50 .15
❑ 385 Rafael Palmeiro .75 .23
❑ 386 David Justice .50 .15
❑ 387 Chili Davis .50 .15
❑ 388 Mike Greenwell .25 .07
❑ 389 Todd Zeile .25 .07
❑ 390 Jeff Conine .50 .15
❑ 391 Rick Aguilera .25 .07
❑ 392 Eddie Murray 1.25 .35
❑ 393 Mike Stanley .25 .07
❑ 394 Cliff Floyd UER .50 .15
(numbered 294)
❑ 395 Randy Johnson 1.25 .35
❑ 396 David Nied .25 .07
❑ 397 Devon White .50 .15
❑ 398 Royce Clayton .25 .07
❑ 399 Andy Benes .25 .07
❑ 400 John Hudek .25 .07
❑ 401 Bobby Jones .25 .07
❑ 402 Eric Karros .50 .15
❑ 403 Will Clark 1.25 .35

Card	Nm-Mt	Ex-Mt
❑ 404 Mark Langston	.25	.07
❑ 405 Kevin Brown	.50	.15
❑ 406 Greg Maddux	2.00	.60
❑ 407 David Cone	.50	.15
❑ 408 Wade Boggs	.75	.23
❑ 409 Steve Trachsel	.25	.07
❑ 410 Greg Vaughn	.25	.07
❑ 411 Mo Vaughn	.50	.15
❑ 412 Wilson Alvarez	.25	.07
❑ 413 Cal Ripken	4.00	1.20
❑ 414 Rico Brogna	.25	.07
❑ 415 Barry Larkin	.75	.23
❑ 416 Cecil Fielder	.50	.15
❑ 417 Jose Canseco	1.25	.35
❑ 418 Jack McDowell	.25	.07
❑ 419 Mike Lieberthal	.50	.15
❑ 420 Andrew Lorraine	.25	.07
❑ 421 Rich Becker	.25	.07
❑ 422 Tony Phillips	.25	.07
❑ 423 Scott Ruffcorn	.25	.07
❑ 424 Jeff Granger	.25	.07
❑ 425 Greg Pirkl	.25	.07
❑ 426 Dennis Eckersley	.50	.15
❑ 427 Jose Lima	.25	.07
❑ 428 Russ Davis	.25	.07
❑ 429 Armando Benitez	.50	.15
❑ 430 Alex Gonzalez	.25	.07
❑ 431 Carlos Delgado	.50	.15
❑ 432 Chan Ho Park	.50	.15
❑ 433 Mickey Tettleton	.25	.07
❑ 434 Dave Winfield	.50	.15
❑ 435 John Burkett	.25	.07
❑ 436 Orlando Miller	.25	.07
❑ 437 Rondell White	.50	.15
❑ 438 Jose Oliva	.25	.07
❑ 439 Checklist	.25	.07

1996 Bowman

	Nm-Mt	Ex-Mt
COMPLETE SET (385)	60.00	18.00
❑ 1 Cal Ripken	2.50	.75
❑ 2 Ray Durham	.30	.09
❑ 3 Ivan Rodriguez	.75	.23
❑ 4 Fred McGriff	.50	.15
❑ 5 Hideo Nomo	.75	.23
❑ 6 Troy Percival	.30	.09
❑ 7 Moises Alou	.30	.09
❑ 8 Mike Stanley	.30	.09
❑ 9 Jay Buhner	.30	.09
❑ 10 Shawn Green	.30	.09
❑ 11 Ryan Klesko	.30	.09
❑ 12 Andres Galarraga	.30	.09
❑ 13 Dean Palmer	.30	.09
❑ 14 Jeff Conine	.30	.09
❑ 15 Brian L.Hunter	.30	.09
❑ 16 J.T. Snow	.30	.09
❑ 17 Larry Walker	.50	.15
❑ 18 Barry Larkin	.50	.15
❑ 19 Alex Gonzalez	.30	.09
❑ 20 Edgar Martinez	.50	.15
❑ 21 Mo Vaughn	.30	.09
❑ 22 Mark McGwire	2.00	.60
❑ 23 Jose Canseco	.75	.23
❑ 24 Jack McDowell	.30	.09
❑ 25 Dante Bichette	.30	.09
❑ 26 Wade Boggs	.50	.15
❑ 27 Mike Piazza	1.25	.35
❑ 28 Ray Lankford	.30	.09
❑ 29 Craig Biggio	.50	.15
❑ 30 Rafael Palmeiro	.50	.15
❑ 31 Ron Gant	.30	.09
❑ 32 Javy Lopez	.30	.09
❑ 33 Brian Jordan	.30	.09
❑ 34 Paul O'Neill	.50	.15
❑ 35 Mark Grace	.50	.15
❑ 36 Matt Williams	.30	.09
❑ 37 Pedro Martinez UER Wrong birthdate	.75	.23
❑ 38 Rickey Henderson	.75	.23
❑ 39 Bobby Bonilla	.30	.09
❑ 40 Todd Hollandsworth	.30	.09
❑ 41 Jim Thome	.75	.23
❑ 42 Gary Sheffield	.75	.23
❑ 43 Tim Salmon	.50	.15
❑ 44 Gregg Jefferies	.30	.09
❑ 45 Roberto Alomar	.50	.15
❑ 46 Carlos Baerga	.30	.09
❑ 47 Mark Grudzielanek	.30	.09
❑ 48 Randy Johnson	.75	.23
❑ 49 Tino Martinez	.50	.15
❑ 50 Robin Ventura	.30	.09
❑ 51 Ryne Sandberg	1.25	.35
❑ 52 Jay Bell	.30	.09
❑ 53 Jason Schmidt	.50	.15
❑ 54 Frank Thomas	.75	.23
❑ 55 Kenny Lofton	.30	.09
❑ 56 Ariel Prieto	.30	.09
❑ 57 David Cone	.30	.09
❑ 58 Reggie Sanders	.30	.09
❑ 59 Michael Tucker	.30	.09
❑ 60 Vinny Castilla	.30	.09
❑ 61 Len Dykstra	.30	.09
❑ 62 Todd Hundley	.30	.09
❑ 63 Brian McRae	.30	.09
❑ 64 Dennis Eckersley	.30	.09
❑ 65 Rondell White	.30	.09
❑ 66 Eric Karros	.30	.09
❑ 67 Greg Maddux	1.25	.35
❑ 68 Kevin Appier	.30	.09
❑ 69 Eddie Murray	.75	.23
❑ 70 John Olerud	.30	.09
❑ 71 Tony Gwynn	1.00	.30
❑ 72 David Justice	.30	.09
❑ 73 Ken Caminiti	.30	.09
❑ 74 Terry Steinbach	.30	.09
❑ 75 Alan Benes	.30	.09
❑ 76 Chipper Jones	.75	.23
❑ 77 Jeff Bagwell	.50	.15
❑ 78 Barry Bonds	2.00	.60
❑ 79 Ken Griffey Jr.	1.50	.45
❑ 80 Roger Cedeno	.30	.09
❑ 81 Joe Carter	.30	.09
❑ 82 Henry Rodriguez	.30	.09
❑ 83 Jason Isringhausen	.30	.09
❑ 84 Chuck Knoblauch	.30	.09
❑ 85 Manny Ramirez	.50	.15
❑ 86 Tom Glavine	.50	.15
❑ 87 Jeffrey Hammonds	.30	.09
❑ 88 Paul Molitor	.50	.15
❑ 89 Roger Clemens	1.50	.45
❑ 90 Greg Vaughn	.30	.09
❑ 91 Marty Cordova	.30	.09
❑ 92 Albert Belle	.30	.09
❑ 93 Mike Mussina	.50	.15
❑ 94 Garret Anderson	.30	.09
❑ 95 Juan Gonzalez	.50	.15
❑ 96 John Valentin	.30	.09
❑ 97 Jason Giambi	.30	.09
❑ 98 Kirby Puckett	.75	.23
❑ 99 Jim Edmonds	.30	.09
❑ 100 Cecil Fielder	.30	.09
❑ 101 Mike Aldrete	.30	.09
❑ 102 Marquis Grissom	.30	.09
❑ 103 Derek Bell	.30	.09
❑ 104 Raul Mondesi	.30	.09
❑ 105 Sammy Sosa	1.25	.35
❑ 106 Travis Fryman	.30	.09
❑ 107 Rico Brogna	.30	.09
❑ 108 Will Clark	.75	.23
❑ 109 Bernie Williams	.50	.15
❑ 110 Brady Anderson	.30	.09
❑ 111 Torii Hunter	.30	.09
❑ 112 Derek Jeter	2.00	.60
❑ 113 Mike Kusiewicz RC	.50	.15
❑ 114 Scott Rolen	.75	.23
❑ 115 Ramon Castro	.30	.09
❑ 116 Jose Guillen RC	3.00	.90
❑ 117 Wade Walker RC	.50	.15
❑ 118 Shawn Senior	.30	.09
❑ 119 Onan Masaoka RC	.75	.23
❑ 120 Marlon Anderson RC	1.25	.35
❑ 121 Katsuhiro Maeda RC	.75	.23
❑ 122 G.Stephenson RC	.75	.23
❑ 123 Butch Huskey	.30	.09
❑ 124 D'Angelo Jimenez RC	1.25	.35
❑ 125 Tony Mounce RC	.50	.15
❑ 126 Jay Canizaro	.30	.09
❑ 127 Juan Melo	.30	.09
❑ 128 Steve Gibralter	.30	.09
❑ 129 Freddy Garcia	.30	.09
❑ 130 Julio Santana UER Card has him born in 1993	.30	.09
❑ 131 Richard Hidalgo	.30	.09
❑ 132 Jermaine Dye	.30	.09
❑ 133 Willie Adams	.30	.09
❑ 134 Everett Stull	.30	.09
❑ 135 Ramon Morel	.30	.09
❑ 136 Chan Ho Park	.30	.09
❑ 137 Jamey Wright	.30	.09
❑ 138 Luis R.Garcia RC	.50	.15
❑ 139 Dan Serafini	.30	.09
❑ 140 Ryan Dempster RC	1.25	.35
❑ 141 Tate Seefried	.30	.09
❑ 142 Jimmy Hurst	.30	.09
❑ 143 Travis Miller	.30	.09
❑ 144 Curtis Goodwin	.30	.09
❑ 145 Rocky Coppinger RC	.50	.15
❑ 146 Enrique Wilson	.30	.09
❑ 147 Jaime Bluma	.30	.09
❑ 148 Andrew Vessel	.30	.09
❑ 149 Damian Moss	.30	.09
❑ 150 Shawn Gallagher RC	.50	.15
❑ 151 Pat Watkins	.30	.09
❑ 152 Jose Paniagua	.30	.09
❑ 153 Danny Graves	.30	.09
❑ 154 Bryon Gainey RC	.50	.15
❑ 155 Steve Soderstrom	.30	.09
❑ 156 Cliff Brumbaugh RC	.50	.15
❑ 157 Eugene Kingsale RC	.75	.23
❑ 158 Lou Collier	.30	.09
❑ 159 Todd Walker	.30	.09
❑ 160 Kris Detmers RC	.50	.15
❑ 161 Josh Booty RC	.75	.23
❑ 162 Greg Whiteman RC	.50	.15
❑ 163 Damian Jackson	.30	.09
❑ 164 Tony Clark	.30	.09
❑ 165 Jeff D'Amico	.30	.09
❑ 166 Johnny Damon	.50	.15
❑ 167 Rafael Orellano	.30	.09
❑ 168 Ruben Rivera	.30	.09
❑ 169 Alex Ochoa	.30	.09
❑ 170 Jay Powell	.30	.09
❑ 171 Tom Evans	.30	.09
❑ 172 Ron Villone	.30	.09
❑ 173 Shawn Estes	.30	.09
❑ 174 John Wasdin	.30	.09
❑ 175 Bill Simas	.30	.09
❑ 176 Kevin Brown	.30	.09
❑ 177 Shannon Stewart	.30	.09
❑ 178 Todd Greene	.30	.09
❑ 179 Bob Wolcott	.30	.09
❑ 180 Chris Snopek	.30	.09
❑ 181 Nomar Garciaparra	1.50	.45
❑ 182 Cameron Smith RC	.50	.15
❑ 183 Matt Drews	.30	.09
❑ 184 Jimmy Haynes	.30	.09
❑ 185 Chris Carpenter	.30	.09
❑ 186 Desi Relaford	.30	.09
❑ 187 Ben Grieve	.30	.09
❑ 188 Mike Bell	.30	.09
❑ 189 Luis Castillo RC	2.00	.60
❑ 190 Ugueth Urbina	.30	.09
❑ 191 Paul Wilson	.30	.09
❑ 192 Andruw Jones	.75	.23
❑ 193 Wayne Gomes	.30	.09
❑ 194 Craig Counsell RC	1.25	.35
❑ 195 Jim Cole	.30	.09
❑ 196 Brooks Kieschnick	.30	.09

❑ 197	Trey Beamon	.30	.09
❑ 198	Marino Santana RC	.50	.15
❑ 199	Bob Abreu	.30	.09
❑ 200	Pokey Reese	.30	.09
❑ 201	Dante Powell	.30	.09
❑ 202	George Arias	.30	.09
❑ 203	Jorge Velandia RC	.50	.15
❑ 204	George Lombard RC	.50	.15
❑ 205	Byron Browne RC	.50	.15
❑ 206	John Frascatore	.30	.09
❑ 207	Terry Adams	.30	.09
❑ 208	Wilson Delgado RC	.50	.15
❑ 209	Billy McMillon	.30	.09
❑ 210	Jeff Abbott	.30	.09
❑ 211	Trot Nixon	.30	.09
❑ 212	Amaury Telemaco	.30	.09
❑ 213	Scott Sullivan	.30	.09
❑ 214	Justin Thompson	.30	.09
❑ 215	Decomba Conner	.30	.09
❑ 216	Ryan McGuire	.30	.09
❑ 217	Matt Luke	.30	.09
❑ 218	Doug Million	.30	.09
❑ 219	Jason Dickson RC	.50	.15
❑ 220	Ramon Hernandez RC	1.25	.35
❑ 221	Mark Bellhorn RC	4.00	1.20
❑ 222	Eric Ludwick RC	.50	.15
❑ 223	Luke Wilcox RC	.50	.15
❑ 224	Marty Malloy RC	.50	.15
❑ 225	Gary Coffee RC	.50	.15
❑ 226	Wendell Magee RC	.50	.15
❑ 227	Brett Tomko RC	.75	.23
❑ 228	Derek Lowe	.30	.09
❑ 229	Jose Rosado RC	.50	.15
❑ 230	Steve Bourgeois RC	.50	.15
❑ 231	Neil Weber RC	.50	.15
❑ 232	Jeff Ware	.30	.09
❑ 233	Edwin Diaz	.30	.09
❑ 234	Greg Norton	.30	.09
❑ 235	Aaron Boone	.30	.09
❑ 236	Jeff Suppan	.30	.09
❑ 237	Bret Wagner	.30	.09
❑ 238	Elieser Marrero	.30	.09
❑ 239	Will Cunnane	.30	.09
❑ 240	Brian Barkley RC	.50	.15
❑ 241	Jay Payton	.30	.09
❑ 242	Marcus Jensen	.30	.09
❑ 243	Ryan Nye	.30	.09
❑ 244	Chad Mottola	.30	.09
❑ 245	Scott McClain RC	.50	.15
❑ 246	Jessie Ibarra RC	.50	.15
❑ 247	Mike Darr RC	.75	.23
❑ 248	Bobby Estalella RC	.75	.23
❑ 249	Michael Barrett	.30	.09
❑ 250	Jamie Lopiccolo RC	.50	.15
❑ 251	Shane Spencer RC	1.25	.35
❑ 252	Ben Petrick RC	.50	.15
❑ 253	Jason Bell RC	.50	.15
❑ 254	Arnold Gooch RC	.50	.15
❑ 255	T.J. Mathews	.30	.09
❑ 256	Jason Ryan	.30	.09
❑ 257	Pat Cline RC	.50	.15
❑ 258	Rafael Carmona RC	.50	.15
❑ 259	Carl Pavano RC	10.00	1.20
❑ 260	Ben Davis	.30	.09
❑ 261	Matt Lawton RC	1.25	.35
❑ 262	Kevin Sefcik RC	.50	.15
❑ 263	Chris Fussell RC	.50	.15
❑ 264	Mike Cameron RC	2.00	.60
❑ 265	Marty Janzen RC	.50	.15
❑ 266	Livan Hernandez RC	1.25	.35
❑ 267	Raul Ibanez RC	1.25	.35
❑ 268	Juan Encarnacion	.30	.09
❑ 269	David Yocum RC	.50	.15
❑ 270	Jonathan Johnson RC	.50	.15
❑ 271	Reggie Taylor	.30	.09
❑ 272	Danny Buxbaum RC	.50	.15
❑ 273	Jacob Cruz	.30	.09
❑ 274	Bobby Morris RC	.50	.15
❑ 275	Andy Fox RC	.50	.15
❑ 276	Greg Keagle	.30	.09
❑ 277	Charles Peterson	.30	.09
❑ 278	Derrek Lee	.30	.09
❑ 279	Bryant Nelson RC	.50	.15
❑ 280	Antone Williamson	.30	.09
❑ 281	Scott Elarton	.30	.09
❑ 282	Shad Williams RC	.50	.15
❑ 283	Rich Hunter RC	.50	.15
❑ 284	Chris Sheff	.30	.09
❑ 285	Derrick Gibson	.30	.09
❑ 286	Felix Rodriguez	.30	.09
❑ 287	Brian Banks RC	.50	.15
❑ 288	Jason McDonald	.30	.09
❑ 289	Glendon Rusch RC	.75	.23
❑ 290	Gary Rath	.30	.09
❑ 291	Peter Munro	.30	.09
❑ 292	Tom Fordham	.30	.09
❑ 293	Jason Kendall	.30	.09
❑ 294	Russ Johnson	.30	.09
❑ 295	Joe Long	.30	.09
❑ 296	Robert Smith RC	.75	.23
❑ 297	Jarrod Washburn RC	1.25	.35
❑ 298	Dave Coggin RC	.50	.15
❑ 299	Jeff Yoder RC	.50	.15
❑ 300	Jed Hansen RC	.50	.15
❑ 301	Matt Morris RC	3.00	.90
❑ 302	Josh Bishop RC	.50	.15
❑ 303	Dustin Hermanson	.30	.09
❑ 304	Mike Gulan	.30	.09
❑ 305	Felipe Crespo	.30	.09
❑ 306	Quinton McCracken	.30	.09
❑ 307	Jim Bonnici RC	.50	.15
❑ 308	Sal Fasano	.30	.09
❑ 309	Gabe Alvarez RC	.50	.15
❑ 310	Heath Murray RC	.50	.15
❑ 311	Javier Valentin RC	.50	.15
❑ 312	Bartolo Colon	.30	.09
❑ 313	Olmedo Saenz	.30	.09
❑ 314	Norm Hutchins RC	.50	.15
❑ 315	Chris Holt	.30	.09
❑ 316	David Doster RC	.50	.15
❑ 317	Robert Person	.30	.09
❑ 318	Donne Wall RC	.50	.15
❑ 319	Adam Riggs RC	.50	.15
❑ 320	Homer Bush	.30	.09
❑ 321	Brad Rigby RC	.50	.15
❑ 322	Lou Merloni RC	.75	.23
❑ 323	Neifi Perez	.30	.09
❑ 324	Chris Cumberland	.30	.09
❑ 325	Alvie Shepherd RC	.50	.15
❑ 326	Jarrod Patterson RC	.50	.15
❑ 327	Ray Ricken RC	.50	.15
❑ 328	Danny Klassen RC	.50	.15
❑ 329	David Miller RC	.50	.15
❑ 330	Chad Alexander RC	.50	.15
❑ 331	Matt Beaumont	.30	.09
❑ 332	Damon Hollins	.30	.09
❑ 333	Todd Dunn	.30	.09
❑ 334	Mike Sweeney RC	3.00	.90
❑ 335	Richie Sexson	.30	.09
❑ 336	Billy Wagner	.30	.09
❑ 337	Ron Wright RC	.50	.15
❑ 338	Paul Konerko	.30	.09
❑ 339	Tommy Phelps RC	.50	.15
❑ 340	Karim Garcia	.30	.09
❑ 341	Mike Grace RC	.50	.15
❑ 342	Russell Branyan RC	.75	.23
❑ 343	Randy Winn RC	1.25	.35
❑ 344	A.J. Pierzynski RC	2.00	.60
❑ 345	Mike Busby RC	.50	.15
❑ 346	Matt Beech RC	.50	.15
❑ 347	Jose Cepeda RC	.50	.15
❑ 348	Brian Stephenson	.30	.09
❑ 349	Rey Ordonez	.30	.09
❑ 350	Rich Aurilla RC	1.25	.35
❑ 351	Edgard Velazquez RC	.50	.15
❑ 352	Raul Casanova	.30	.09
❑ 353	Carlos Guillen RC	4.00	1.20
❑ 354	Bruce Aven RC	.50	.15
❑ 355	Ryan Jones RC	.50	.15
❑ 356	Derek Aucoin RC	.50	.15
❑ 357	Brian Rose RC	.50	.15
❑ 358	Richard Almanzar RC	.50	.15
❑ 359	Fletcher Bates RC	.50	.15
❑ 360	Russ Ortiz RC	3.00	.90
❑ 361	Wilton Guerrero RC	.75	.23
❑ 362	Geoff Jenkins RC	2.00	.60
❑ 363	Pete Janicki	.30	.09
❑ 364	Yamil Benitez	.30	.09
❑ 365	Aaron Holbert	.30	.09
❑ 366	Tim Belk	.30	.09
❑ 367	Terrell Wade	.30	.09
❑ 368	Terrence Long	.30	.09
❑ 369	Brad Fullmer	.30	.09
❑ 370	Matt Wagner	.30	.09
❑ 371	Craig Wilson RC	.50	.15
❑ 372	Mark Loretta	.30	.09
❑ 373	Eric Owens	.30	.09
❑ 374	Vladimir Guerrero	1.50	.45
❑ 375	Tommy Davis	.30	.09
❑ 376	Donnie Sadler	.30	.09
❑ 377	Edgar Renteria	.30	.09
❑ 378	Todd Helton	1.50	.45
❑ 379	Ralph Milliard RC	.50	.15
❑ 380	Darin Blood RC	.50	.15
❑ 381	Shayne Bennett	.30	.09
❑ 382	Mark Redman	.30	.09
❑ 383	Felix Martinez	.30	.09
❑ 384	Sean Watkins RC	.50	.15
❑ 385	Oscar Henriquez	.30	.09
❑ M20	Mickey Mantle 1952 Bowman Reprint	5.00	1.50
❑ NNO	Checklists	.30	.09

1997 Bowman

		Nm-Mt	Ex-Mt
	COMPLETE SET (441)	50.00	15.00
	COMP. SERIES 1 (221)	25.00	7.50
	COMP. SERIES 2 (220)	25.00	7.50
❑ 1	Derek Jeter	2.00	.60
❑ 2	Edgar Renteria	.30	.09
❑ 3	Chipper Jones	.75	.23
❑ 4	Hideo Nomo	.75	.23
❑ 5	Tim Salmon	.50	.15
❑ 6	Jason Giambi	.30	.09
❑ 7	Robin Ventura	.30	.09
❑ 8	Tony Clark	.30	.09
❑ 9	Barry Larkin	.50	.15
❑ 10	Paul Molitor	.50	.15
❑ 11	Bernard Gilkey	.30	.09
❑ 12	Jack McDowell	.30	.09
❑ 13	Andy Benes	.30	.09
❑ 14	Ryan Klesko	.30	.09
❑ 15	Mark McGwire	2.00	.60
❑ 16	Ken Griffey Jr.	1.25	.35
❑ 17	Robb Nen	.30	.09
❑ 18	Cal Ripken	2.50	.75
❑ 19	John Valentin	.30	.09
❑ 20	Ricky Bottalico	.30	.09
❑ 21	Mike Lansing	.30	.09
❑ 22	Ryne Sandberg	1.25	.35
❑ 23	Carlos Delgado	.30	.09
❑ 24	Craig Biggio	.50	.15
❑ 25	Eric Karros	.30	.09
❑ 26	Kevin Appier	.30	.09
❑ 27	Mariano Rivera	.50	.15
❑ 28	Vinny Castilla	.30	.09
❑ 29	Juan Gonzalez	.50	.15
❑ 30	Al Martin	.30	.09
❑ 31	Jeff Cirillo	.30	.09
❑ 32	Eddie Murray	.75	.23
❑ 33	Ray Lankford	.30	.09
❑ 34	Manny Ramirez	.50	.15
❑ 35	Roberto Alomar	.50	.15
❑ 36	Will Clark	.75	.23
❑ 37	Chuck Knoblauch	.30	.09
❑ 38	Harold Baines	.30	.09
❑ 39	Trevor Hoffman	.30	.09
❑ 40	Edgar Martinez	.50	.15

	No.	Player	Price 1	Price 2
❑	41	Geronimo Berroa	.30	.09
❑	42	Rey Ordonez	.30	.09
❑	43	Mike Stanley	.30	.09
❑	44	Mike Mussina	.50	.15
❑	45	Kevin Brown	.30	.09
❑	46	Dennis Eckersley	.30	.09
❑	47	Henry Rodriguez	.30	.09
❑	48	Tino Martinez	.50	.15
❑	49	Eric Young	.30	.09
❑	50	Bret Boone	.30	.09
❑	51	Raul Mondesi	.30	.09
❑	52	Sammy Sosa	1.25	.35
❑	53	John Smoltz	.50	.15
❑	54	Billy Wagner	.30	.09
❑	55	Jeff D'Amico	.30	.09
❑	56	Ken Caminiti	.30	.09
❑	57	Jason Kendall	.30	.09
❑	58	Wade Boggs	.50	.15
❑	59	Andres Galarraga	.30	.09
❑	60	Jeff Brantley	.30	.09
❑	61	Mel Rojas	.30	.09
❑	62	Brian L. Hunter	.30	.09
❑	63	Bobby Bonilla	.30	.09
❑	64	Roger Clemens	1.50	.45
❑	65	Jeff Kent	.30	.09
❑	66	Matt Williams	.30	.09
❑	67	Albert Belle	.30	.09
❑	68	Jeff King	.30	.09
❑	69	John Wetteland	.30	.09
❑	70	Deion Sanders	.50	.15
❑	71	Bubba Trammell RC	.50	.15
❑	72	Felix Heredia RC	.50	.15
❑	73	Billy Koch RC	.75	.23
❑	74	Sidney Ponson RC	.75	.23
❑	75	Ricky Ledee RC	.50	.15
❑	76	Brett Tomko	.30	.09
❑	77	Braden Looper RC	.50	.15
❑	78	Damian Jackson	.30	.09
❑	79	Jason Dickson	.30	.09
❑	80	Chad Green RC	.50	.15
❑	81	R.A. Dickey RC	.50	.15
❑	82	Jeff Liefer	.30	.09
❑	83	Matt Wagner	.30	.09
❑	84	Richard Hidalgo	.30	.09
❑	85	Adam Riggs	.30	.09
❑	86	Robert Smith	.30	.09
❑	87	Chad Hermansen RC	.50	.15
❑	88	Felix Martinez	.30	.09
❑	89	J.J. Johnson	.30	.09
❑	90	Todd Dunwoody	.30	.09
❑	91	Katsuhiro Maeda	.30	.09
❑	92	Darin Erstad	.30	.09
❑	93	Elieser Marrero	.30	.09
❑	94	Bartolo Colon	.30	.09
❑	95	Chris Fussell	.30	.09
❑	96	Ugueth Urbina	.30	.09
❑	97	Josh Paul RC	.50	.15
❑	98	Jaime Bluma	.30	.09
❑	99	Seth Greisinger RC	.50	.15
❑	100	Jose Cruz Jr. RC	.75	.23
❑	101	Todd Dunn	.30	.09
❑	102	Joe Young RC	.50	.15
❑	103	Jonathan Johnson	.30	.09
❑	104	Justin Towle RC	.50	.15
❑	105	Brian Rose	.30	.09
❑	106	Jose Guillen	.30	.09
❑	107	Andruw Jones	.30	.09
❑	108	Mark Kotsay RC	1.00	.30
❑	109	Wilton Guerrero	.30	.09
❑	110	Jacob Cruz	.30	.09
❑	111	Mike Sweeney	.30	.09
❑	112	Julio Mosquera	.30	.09
❑	113	Matt Morris	.30	.09
❑	114	Wendell Magee	.30	.09
❑	115	John Thomson	.30	.09
❑	116	Javier Valentin	.30	.09
❑	117	Tom Fordham	.30	.09
❑	118	Ruben Rivera	.30	.09
❑	119	Mike Drumright RC	.50	.15
❑	120	Chris Holt	.30	.09
❑	121	Sean Maloney	.30	.09
❑	122	Michael Barrett	.30	.09
❑	123	Tony Saunders RC	.50	.15
❑	124	Kevin Brown C	.30	.09
❑	125	Richard Almanzar	.30	.09
❑	126	Mark Redman	.30	.09
❑	127	Anthony Sanders RC	.50	.15
❑	128	Jeff Abbott	.30	.09
❑	129	Eugene Kingsale	.30	.09
❑	130	Paul Konerko	.30	.09
❑	131	Randall Simon RC	.50	.15
❑	132	Andy Larkin	.30	.09
❑	133	Rafael Medina	.30	.09
❑	134	Mendy Lopez	.30	.09
❑	135	Freddy Adrian Garcia	.30	.09
❑	136	Karim Garcia	.30	.09
❑	137	Larry Rodriguez RC	.50	.15
❑	138	Carlos Guillen	.30	.09
❑	139	Aaron Boone	.30	.09
❑	140	Donnie Sadler	.30	.09
❑	141	Brooks Kieschnick	.30	.09
❑	142	Scott Spiezio	.30	.09
❑	143	Everett Stull	.30	.09
❑	144	Enrique Wilson	.30	.09
❑	145	Milton Bradley RC	2.50	.75
❑	146	Kevin Orie	.30	.09
❑	147	Derek Wallace	.30	.09
❑	148	Russ Johnson	.30	.09
❑	149	Joe Lagarde RC	.50	.15
❑	150	Luis Castillo	.30	.09
❑	151	Jay Payton	.30	.09
❑	152	Joe Long	.30	.09
❑	153	Livan Hernandez	.30	.09
❑	154	Vladimir Nunez RC	.50	.15
❑	155	Pokey Reese UER Card actually numbered 156	.30	.09
❑	156	George Arias	.30	.09
❑	157	Homer Bush	.30	.09
❑	158	Chris Carpenter UER Card numbered 159	.30	.09
❑	159	Eric Milton RC	1.00	.30
❑	160	Richie Sexson	.30	.09
❑	161	Carl Pavano	1.00	.09
❑	162	Chris Gissell RC	.50	.15
❑	163	Mac Suzuki	.30	.09
❑	164	Pat Cline	.30	.09
❑	165	Ron Wright	.30	.09
❑	166	Dante Powell	.30	.09
❑	167	Mark Bellhorn	.30	.09
❑	168	George Lombard	.30	.09
❑	169	Pee Wee Lopez RC	.50	.15
❑	170	Paul Wilder RC	.50	.15
❑	171	Brad Fullmer	.30	.09
❑	172	Willie Martinez RC	.50	.15
❑	173	Dario Veras RC	.50	.15
❑	174	Dave Coggin	.30	.09
❑	175	Kris Benson RC	1.00	.30
❑	176	Torii Hunter	.30	.09
❑	177	D.T. Cromer	.30	.09
❑	178	Nelson Figueroa RC	.50	.15
❑	179	Hiram Bocachica RC	.50	.15
❑	180	Shane Monahan	.30	.09
❑	181	Jimmy Anderson RC	.50	.15
❑	182	Juan Melo	.30	.09
❑	183	Pablo Ortega RC	.50	.15
❑	184	Calvin Pickering RC	.75	.23
❑	185	Reggie Taylor	.30	.09
❑	186	Jeff Farnsworth RC	.50	.15
❑	187	Terrence Long	.30	.09
❑	188	Geoff Jenkins	.30	.09
❑	189	Steve Rain RC	.50	.15
❑	190	Nerio Rodriguez RC	.50	.15
❑	191	Derrick Gibson	.30	.09
❑	192	Darin Blood	.30	.09
❑	193	Ben Davis	.30	.09
❑	194	Adrian Beltre RC	5.00	1.50
❑	195	Damian Sapp RC UER	.50	.15
❑	196	Kerry Wood RC	8.00	2.40
❑	197	Nate Rolison RC	.50	.15
❑	198	Fernando Tatis RC	.50	.15
❑	199	Brad Penny RC	2.00	.60
❑	200	Jake Westbrook RC	1.00	.30
❑	201	Edwin Diaz	.30	.09
❑	202	Joe Fontenot RC	.50	.15
❑	203	Matt Halloran RC	.50	.15
❑	204	Blake Stein RC	.50	.15
❑	205	Onan Masaoka	.30	.09
❑	206	Ben Petrick	.30	.09
❑	207	Matt Clement RC	1.00	.30
❑	208	Todd Greene	.30	.09
❑	209	Ray Ricken	.30	.09
❑	210	Eric Chavez RC	3.00	.90
❑	211	Edgard Velazquez	.30	.09
❑	212	Bruce Chen RC	.50	.15
❑	213	Danny Patterson	.30	.09
❑	214	Jeff Yoder	.30	.09
❑	215	Luis Ordaz RC	.50	.15
❑	216	Chris Widger	.30	.09
❑	217	Jason Brester	.30	.09
❑	218	Carlton Loewer	.30	.09
❑	219	Chris Reitsma RC	.50	.15
❑	220	Neifi Perez	.30	.09
❑	221	Hideki Irabu RC	.50	.15
❑	222	Ellis Burks	.30	.09
❑	223	Pedro Martinez UER Wrong birthdate	.75	.23
❑	224	Kenny Lofton	.30	.09
❑	225	Randy Johnson	.75	.23
❑	226	Terry Steinbach	.30	.09
❑	227	Bernie Williams	.50	.15
❑	228	Dean Palmer	.30	.09
❑	229	Alan Benes	.30	.09
❑	230	Marquis Grissom	.30	.09
❑	231	Gary Sheffield	.30	.09
❑	232	Curt Schilling	.30	.09
❑	233	Reggie Sanders	.30	.09
❑	234	Bobby Higginson	.30	.09
❑	235	Moises Alou	.30	.09
❑	236	Tom Glavine	.50	.15
❑	237	Mark Grace	.50	.15
❑	238	Ramon Martinez	.30	.09
❑	239	Rafael Palmeiro	.50	.15
❑	240	John Olerud	.30	.09
❑	241	Dante Bichette	.30	.09
❑	242	Greg Vaughn	.30	.09
❑	243	Jeff Bagwell	.50	.15
❑	244	Barry Bonds	2.00	.60
❑	245	Pat Hentgen	.30	.09
❑	246	Jim Thome	.75	.23
❑	247	J.Allensworth	.30	.09
❑	248	Andy Pettitte	.50	.15
❑	249	Jay Bell	.30	.09
❑	250	John Jaha	.30	.09
❑	251	Jim Edmonds	.30	.09
❑	252	Ron Gant	.30	.09
❑	253	David Cone	.30	.09
❑	254	Jose Canseco	.75	.23
❑	255	Jay Buhner	.30	.09
❑	256	Greg Maddux	1.25	.35
❑	257	Brian McRae	.30	.09
❑	258	Lance Johnson	.30	.09
❑	259	Travis Fryman	.30	.09
❑	260	Paul O'Neill	.50	.15
❑	261	Ivan Rodriguez	.75	.23
❑	262	Gregg Jefferies	.30	.09
❑	263	Fred McGriff	.50	.15
❑	264	Derek Bell	.30	.09
❑	265	Jeff Conine	.30	.09
❑	266	Mike Piazza	1.25	.35
❑	267	Mark Grudzielanek	.30	.09
❑	268	Brady Anderson	.30	.09
❑	269	Marty Cordova	.30	.09
❑	270	Ray Durham	.30	.09
❑	271	Joe Carter	.30	.09
❑	272	Brian Jordan	.30	.09
❑	273	David Justice	.30	.09
❑	274	Tony Gwynn	1.00	.30
❑	275	Larry Walker	.50	.15
❑	276	Cecil Fielder	.30	.09
❑	277	Mo Vaughn	.30	.09
❑	278	Alex Fernandez	.30	.09
❑	279	Michael Tucker	.30	.09
❑	280	Jose Valentin	.30	.09
❑	281	Sandy Alomar Jr.	.30	.09
❑	282	Todd Hollandsworth	.30	.09
❑	283	Rico Brogna	.30	.09
❑	284	Rusty Greer	.30	.09
❑	285	Roberto Hernandez	.30	.09
❑	286	Hal Morris	.30	.09
❑	287	Johnny Damon	.50	.15
❑	288	Todd Hundley	.30	.09
❑	289	Rondell White	.30	.09
❑	290	Frank Thomas	.75	.23
❑	291	Don Denbow RC	.50	.15
❑	292	Derrek Lee	.30	.09
❑	293	Todd Walker	.30	.09
❑	294	Scott Rolen	.75	.23
❑	295	Wes Helms	.30	.09

❑ 296 Bob Abreu .30 .09
❑ 297 John Patterson RC .75 .23
❑ 298 Alex Gonzalez RC .75 .23
❑ 299 Grant Roberts RC .50 .15
❑ 300 Jeff Suppan .30 .09
❑ 301 Luke Wilcox .30 .09
❑ 302 Marlon Anderson .30 .09
❑ 303 Ray Brown .30 .09
❑ 304 Mike Caruso RC .50 .15
❑ 305 Sam Marsonek RC .50 .15
❑ 306 Brady Raggio RC .50 .15
❑ 307 Kevin McGlinchy RC .50 .15
❑ 308 Roy Halladay RC 1.00 .30
❑ 309 Jeremi Gonzalez RC .50 .15
❑ 310 Aramis Ramirez RC 2.50 .75
❑ 311 Dee Brown RC .50 .15
❑ 312 Justin Thompson .30 .09
❑ 313 Jay Tessmer RC .50 .15
❑ 314 Mike Johnson RC .50 .15
❑ 315 Danny Clyburn .30 .09
❑ 316 Bruce Aven .30 .09
❑ 317 Keith Foulke RC 4.00 1.20
❑ 318 Jimmy Osting RC .50 .15
❑ 319 Val.De Los Santos RC .50 .15
❑ 320 Shannon Stewart .30 .09
❑ 321 Willie Adams .30 .09
❑ 322 Larry Barnes RC .50 .15
❑ 323 Mark Johnson RC .50 .15
❑ 324 Chris Stowers RC .50 .15
❑ 325 Brandon Reed .30 .09
❑ 326 Randy Winn .30 .09
❑ 327 Steve Chavez RC .50 .15
❑ 328 Nomar Garciaparra 1.25 .35
❑ 329 Jacque Jones RC 1.00 .30
❑ 330 Chris Clemons .30 .09
❑ 331 Todd Helton .75 .23
❑ 332 Ryan Brannan RC .50 .15
❑ 333 Alex Sanchez RC .75 .23
❑ 334 Arnold Gooch .30 .09
❑ 335 Russell Branyan .30 .09
❑ 336 Daryle Ward .50 .15
❑ 337 John LeRoy RC .50 .15
❑ 338 Steve Cox .30 .09
❑ 339 Kevin Witt .30 .09
❑ 340 Norm Hutchins .30 .09
❑ 341 Gabby Martinez .30 .09
❑ 342 Kris Detmers .30 .09
❑ 343 Mike Villano RC .50 .15
❑ 344 Preston Wilson .30 .09
❑ 345 James Manias RC .50 .15
❑ 346 Deivi Cruz RC .50 .15
❑ 347 Donzell McDonald RC .50 .15
❑ 348 Rod Myers RC .50 .15
❑ 349 Shawn Chacon RC .75 .23
❑ 350 Elvin Hernandez RC .50 .15
❑ 351 Orlando Cabrera RC 1.50 .60
❑ 352 Brian Banks .30 .09
❑ 353 Robbie Bell .50 .15
❑ 354 Brad Rigby .30 .09
❑ 355 Scott Elarton .30 .09
❑ 356 Kevin Sweeney RC .50 .15
❑ 357 Steve Soderstrom .30 .09
❑ 358 Ryan Nye .30 .09
❑ 359 Marlon Allen RC .50 .15
❑ 360 Donny Leon RC .50 .15
❑ 361 Garrett Neubart RC .50 .15
❑ 362 Abraham Nunez RC .50 .15
❑ 363 Adam Eaton RC .50 .15
❑ 364 Octavio Dotel RC .50 .15
❑ 365 Dean Crow RC .50 .15
❑ 366 Jason Baker RC .50 .15
❑ 367 Sean Casey 1.00 .30
❑ 368 Joe Lawrence RC .50 .15
❑ 369 Adam Johnson RC .50 .15
❑ 370 S.Schoeneweis RC .50 .15
❑ 371 Gerald Witasick Jr. .30 .09
❑ 372 Ronnie Belliard RC .75 .23
❑ 373 Russ Ortiz .30 .09
❑ 374 Robert Stratton RC .50 .15
❑ 375 Bobby Estalella .30 .09
❑ 376 Corey Lee RC .50 .15
❑ 377 Carlos Beltran 3.00 .90
❑ 378 Mike Cameron .30 .09
❑ 379 Scott Randall RC .50 .15
❑ 380 Corey Erickson RC .50 .15
❑ 381 Jay Canizaro .30 .09
❑ 382 Kerry Robinson RC .50 .15
❑ 383 Todd Noel RC .50 .15
❑ 384 A.J. Zapp RC .50 .15
❑ 385 Jarrod Washburn .30 .09
❑ 386 Ben Grieve .30 .09
❑ 387 Javier Vazquez RC 1.25 .35
❑ 388 Tony Graffanino .30 .09
❑ 389 Travis Lee RC .50 .15
❑ 390 DaRond Stovall .30 .09
❑ 391 Dennis Reyes RC .50 .15
❑ 392 Danny Buxbaum .30 .09
❑ 393 Marc Lewis RC .50 .15
❑ 394 Kelvim Escobar RC .75 .23
❑ 395 Danny Klassen .30 .09
❑ 396 Ken Cloude RC .50 .15
❑ 397 Gabe Alvarez .30 .09
❑ 398 Jaret Wright RC 1.50 .30
❑ 399 Raul Casanova .30 .09
❑ 400 Clayton Bruner RC .50 .15
❑ 401 Jason Marquis RC 1.00 .30
❑ 402 Marc Kroon .30 .09
❑ 403 Jamey Wright .30 .09
❑ 404 Matt Snyder RC .50 .15
❑ 405 Josh Garrett RC .50 .15
❑ 406 Juan Encarnacion .30 .09
❑ 407 Heath Murray .30 .09
❑ 408 Brett Herbison RC .50 .15
❑ 409 Brent Butler RC .50 .15
❑ 410 Danny Peoples RC .50 .15
❑ 411 Miguel Tejada RC 4.00 1.20
❑ 412 Damian Moss .30 .09
❑ 413 Jim Pittsley .30 .09
❑ 414 Dmitri Young .30 .09
❑ 415 Glendon Rusch .30 .09
❑ 416 Vladimir Guerrero .75 .23
❑ 417 Cole Liniak RC .50 .15
❑ 418 R.Hernandez UER .30 .09
Card back says 1st Bowman card is 1997, he had a 1996 Bowman
❑ 419 Cliff Politte RC .50 .15
❑ 420 Mel Rosario RC .50 .15
❑ 421 Jorge Carrion RC .50 .15
❑ 422 John Barnes RC .50 .15
❑ 423 Chris Stowe RC .50 .15
❑ 424 Vernon Wells RC 2.00 .60
❑ 425 Brett Caradonna RC .50 .15
❑ 426 Scott Hodges RC .50 .15
❑ 427 Jon Garland RC .75 .23
❑ 428 Nathan Haynes RC .50 .15
❑ 429 Geoff Goetz RC .50 .15
❑ 430 Adam Kennedy RC .75 .23
❑ 431 T.J. Tucker RC .50 .15
❑ 432 Aaron Akin RC .50 .15
❑ 433 Jayson Werth RC 1.00 .30
❑ 434 Glenn Davis RC .50 .15
❑ 435 Mark Mangum RC .50 .15
❑ 436 Troy Cameron RC .50 .15
❑ 437 J.J. Davis RC .50 .15
❑ 438 Lance Berkman RC 5.00 1.50
❑ 439 Jason Standridge RC .50 .15
❑ 440 Jason Dellaero RC .50 .15
❑ 441 Hideki Irabu .50 .15

1998 Bowman

	Nm-Mt	Ex-Mt
COMPLETE SET (441)	50.00	15.00
COMP. SERIES 1 (221)	25.00	7.50
COMP. SERIES 2 (220)	25.00	7.50

❑ 1 Nomar Garciaparra 1.25 .35
❑ 2 Scott Rolen .75 .23
❑ 3 Andy Pettitte .50 .15
❑ 4 Ivan Rodriguez .75 .23
❑ 5 Mark McGwire 2.00 .60
❑ 6 Jason Dickson .30 .09
❑ 7 Jose Cruz Jr. .30 .09
❑ 8 Jeff Kent .30 .09
❑ 9 Mike Mussina .50 .15
❑ 10 Jason Kendall .30 .09
❑ 11 Brett Tomko .30 .09
❑ 12 Jeff King .30 .09
❑ 13 Brad Radke .30 .09
❑ 14 Robin Ventura .30 .09
❑ 15 Jeff Bagwell .50 .15
❑ 16 Greg Maddux 1.25 .35
❑ 17 John Jaha .30 .09
❑ 18 Mike Piazza 1.25 .35
❑ 19 Edgar Martinez .50 .15
❑ 20 David Justice .30 .09
❑ 21 Todd Hundley .30 .09
❑ 22 Tony Gwynn 1.00 .30
❑ 23 Larry Walker .50 .15
❑ 24 Bernie Williams .50 .15
❑ 25 Edgar Renteria .30 .09
❑ 26 Rafael Palmeiro .50 .15
❑ 27 Tim Salmon .50 .15
❑ 28 Matt Morris .30 .09
❑ 29 Shawn Estes .30 .09
❑ 30 Vladimir Guerrero .75 .23
❑ 31 Fernando Tatis .30 .09
❑ 32 Justin Thompson .30 .09
❑ 33 Ken Griffey Jr. 1.25 .35
❑ 34 Edgardo Alfonzo .30 .09
❑ 35 Mo Vaughn .30 .09
❑ 36 Marty Cordova .30 .09
❑ 37 Craig Biggio .50 .15
❑ 38 Roger Clemens 1.50 .45
❑ 39 Mark Grace .50 .15
❑ 40 Ken Caminiti .30 .09
❑ 41 Tony Womack .30 .09
❑ 42 Albert Belle .30 .09
❑ 43 Tino Martinez .50 .15
❑ 44 Sandy Alomar Jr. .30 .09
❑ 45 Jeff Cirillo .30 .09
❑ 46 Jason Giambi .30 .09
❑ 47 Darin Erstad .30 .09
❑ 48 Livan Hernandez .30 .09
❑ 49 Mark Grudzielanek .30 .09
❑ 50 Sammy Sosa 1.25 .35
❑ 51 Curt Schilling .30 .09
❑ 52 Brian Hunter .30 .09
❑ 53 Neifi Perez .30 .09
❑ 54 Todd Walker .30 .09
❑ 55 Jose Guillen .30 .09
❑ 56 Jim Thome .75 .23
❑ 57 Tom Glavine .50 .15
❑ 58 Todd Greene .30 .09
❑ 59 Rondell White .30 .09
❑ 60 Roberto Alomar .50 .15
❑ 61 Tony Clark .30 .09
❑ 62 Vinny Castilla .30 .09
❑ 63 Barry Larkin .50 .15
❑ 64 Hideki Irabu .30 .09
❑ 65 Johnny Damon .50 .15
❑ 66 Juan Gonzalez .50 .15
❑ 67 John Olerud .30 .09
❑ 68 Gary Sheffield .30 .09
❑ 69 Raul Mondesi .30 .09
❑ 70 Chipper Jones .75 .23
❑ 71 David Ortiz 1.00 .30
❑ 72 Warren Morris RC .30 .09
❑ 73 Alex Gonzalez .30 .09
❑ 74 Nick Bierbrodt .30 .09
❑ 75 Roy Halladay .30 .09
❑ 76 Danny Buxbaum .30 .09
❑ 77 Adam Kennedy .30 .09
❑ 78 Jared Sandberg .30 .09
❑ 79 Michael Barrett .30 .09
❑ 80 Gil Meche .30 .09
❑ 81 Jayson Werth .30 .09
❑ 82 Abraham Nunez .30 .09
❑ 83 Ben Petrick .30 .09
❑ 84 Brett Caradonna .30 .09

❑ 85 Mike Lowell RC 1.50 .45
❑ 86 Clayton Bruner .30 .09
❑ 87 John Curtice RC .40 .12
❑ 88 Bobby Estalella .30 .09
❑ 89 Juan Melo .30 .09
❑ 90 Arnold Gooch .30 .09
❑ 91 Kevin Millwood RC .75 .23
❑ 92 Richie Sexson .30 .09
❑ 93 Orlando Cabrera .30 .09
❑ 94 Pat Cline .30 .09
❑ 95 Anthony Sanders .30 .09
❑ 96 Russ Johnson .30 .09
❑ 97 Ben Grieve .30 .09
❑ 98 Kevin McGlinchy .30 .09
❑ 99 Paul Wilder .30 .09
❑ 100 Russ Ortiz .30 .09
❑ 101 Ryan Jackson RC .30 .09
❑ 102 Heath Murray .30 .09
❑ 103 Brian Rose .30 .09
❑ 104 R.Radmanovich RC .30 .09
❑ 105 Ricky Ledee .30 .09
❑ 106 Jeff Wallace RC .30 .09
❑ 107 Ryan Minor RC .30 .09
❑ 108 Dennis Reyes .30 .09
❑ 109 James Manias .30 .09
❑ 110 Chris Carpenter .30 .09
❑ 111 Daryle Ward .30 .09
❑ 112 Vernon Wells .30 .09
❑ 113 Chad Green .30 .09
❑ 114 Mike Stoner RC .30 .09
❑ 115 Brad Fullmer .30 .09
❑ 116 Adam Eaton .30 .09
❑ 117 Jeff Liefer .30 .09
❑ 118 Corey Koskie RC 1.00 .30
❑ 119 Todd Helton .50 .15
❑ 120 Jaime Jones RC .30 .09
❑ 121 Mel Rosario .30 .09
❑ 122 Geoff Goetz .30 .09
❑ 123 Adrian Beltre .75 .23
❑ 124 Jason Dellaero .30 .09
❑ 125 Gabe Kapler RC .50 .15
❑ 126 Scott Schoeneweis .30 .09
❑ 127 Ryan Brannan .30 .09
❑ 128 Aaron Akin .30 .09
❑ 129 Ryan Anderson RC .40 .12
❑ 130 Brad Penny .30 .09
❑ 131 Bruce Chen .30 .09
❑ 132 Eli Marrero .30 .09
❑ 133 Eric Chavez .30 .09
❑ 134 Troy Glaus RC 2.00 .60
❑ 135 Troy Cameron .30 .09
❑ 136 Brian Sikorski RC .30 .09
❑ 137 Mike Kinkade RC .30 .09
❑ 138 Braden Looper .30 .09
❑ 139 Mark Mangum .30 .09
❑ 140 Danny Peoples .30 .09
❑ 141 J.J. Davis .30 .09
❑ 142 Ben Davis .30 .09
❑ 143 Jacque Jones .30 .09
❑ 144 Derrick Gibson .30 .09
❑ 145 Bronson Arroyo .75 .23
❑ 146 L.De Los Santos RC UER .30 .09
has hitting stat line instead of pitching
❑ 147 Jeff Abbott .30 .09
❑ 148 Mike Cuddyer RC .50 .15
❑ 149 Jason Romano .30 .09
❑ 150 Shane Monahan .30 .09
❑ 151 Ntema Ndungidi RC .30 .09
❑ 152 Alex Sanchez .30 .09
❑ 153 Jack Cust RC .40 .12
❑ 154 Brent Butler .30 .09
❑ 155 Ramon Hernandez .30 .09
❑ 156 Norm Hutchins .30 .09
❑ 157 Jason Marquis .30 .09
❑ 158 Jacob Cruz .30 .09
❑ 159 Rob Burger RC .30 .09
❑ 160 Dave Coggin .30 .09
❑ 161 Preston Wilson .30 .09
❑ 162 Jason Fitzgerald RC .30 .09
❑ 163 Dan Serafini .30 .09
❑ 164 Peter Munro .30 .09
❑ 165 Trot Nixon .30 .09
❑ 166 Homer Bush .30 .09
❑ 167 Dermal Brown .30 .09
❑ 168 Chad Hermansen .30 .09
❑ 169 Julio Moreno RC .30 .09
❑ 170 John Roskos RC .30 .09
❑ 171 Grant Roberts .30 .09
❑ 172 Ken Cloude .30 .09
❑ 173 Jason Brester .30 .09
❑ 174 Jason Conti .30 .09
❑ 175 Jon Garland .30 .09
❑ 176 Robbie Bell .30 .09
❑ 177 Nathan Haynes .30 .09
❑ 178 Ramon Ortiz RC .50 .15
❑ 179 Shannon Stewart .30 .09
❑ 180 Pablo Ortega .30 .09
❑ 181 Jimmy Rollins RC .75 .23
❑ 182 Sean Casey .30 .09
❑ 183 Ted Lilly RC .50 .15
❑ 184 Chris Enochs RC .30 .09
❑ 185 M.Ordonez RC UER 2.50 .75
Front photo is Mario Valdez
❑ 186 Mike Drumright .30 .09
❑ 187 Aaron Boone .30 .09
❑ 188 Matt Clement .30 .09
❑ 189 Todd Dunwoody .30 .09
❑ 190 Larry Rodriguez .30 .09
❑ 191 Todd Noel .30 .09
❑ 192 Geoff Jenkins .30 .09
❑ 193 George Lombard .30 .09
❑ 194 Lance Berkman .50 .15
❑ 195 Marcus McCain .30 .09
❑ 196 Ryan McGuire .30 .09
❑ 197 Jhensy Sandoval .30 .09
❑ 198 Corey Lee .30 .09
❑ 199 Mario Valdez .30 .09
❑ 200 Robert Fick RC .40 .12
❑ 201 Donnie Sadler .30 .09
❑ 202 Marc Kroon .30 .09
❑ 203 David Miller .30 .09
❑ 204 Jarrod Washburn .30 .09
❑ 205 Miguel Tejada .30 .09
❑ 206 Raul Ibanez .30 .09
❑ 207 John Patterson .30 .09
❑ 208 Calvin Pickering .30 .09
❑ 209 Felix Martinez .30 .09
❑ 210 Mark Redman .30 .09
❑ 211 Scott Elarton .30 .09
❑ 212 Jose Amado RC .30 .09
❑ 213 Kerry Wood .75 .23
❑ 214 Dante Powell .30 .09
❑ 215 Aramis Ramirez .30 .09
❑ 216 A.J. Hinch .30 .09
❑ 217 Dustin Carr RC .30 .09
❑ 218 Mark Kotsay .30 .09
❑ 219 Jason Standridge .30 .09
❑ 220 Luis Ordaz .30 .09
❑ 221 O.Hernandez RC .75 .23
❑ 222 Cal Ripken 2.50 .75
❑ 223 Paul Molitor .50 .15
❑ 224 Derek Jeter 2.00 .60
❑ 225 Barry Bonds 2.00 .60
❑ 226 Jim Edmonds .30 .09
❑ 227 John Smoltz .50 .15
❑ 228 Eric Karros .30 .09
❑ 229 Ray Lankford .30 .09
❑ 230 Rey Ordonez .30 .09
❑ 231 Kenny Lofton .30 .09
❑ 232 Alex Rodriguez 1.25 .35
❑ 233 Dante Bichette .30 .09
❑ 234 Pedro Martinez .75 .23
❑ 235 Carlos Delgado .30 .09
❑ 236 Rod Beck .30 .09
❑ 237 Matt Williams .30 .09
❑ 238 Charles Johnson .30 .09
❑ 239 Rico Brogna .30 .09
❑ 240 Frank Thomas .75 .23
❑ 241 Paul O'Neill .50 .15
❑ 242 Jaret Wright .30 .09
❑ 243 Brant Brown .30 .09
❑ 244 Ryan Klesko .30 .09
❑ 245 Chuck Finley .30 .09
❑ 246 Derek Bell .30 .09
❑ 247 Delino DeShields .30 .09
❑ 248 Chan Ho Park .30 .09
❑ 249 Wade Boggs .50 .15
❑ 250 Jay Buhner .30 .09
❑ 251 Butch Huskey .30 .09
❑ 252 Steve Finley .30 .09
❑ 253 Will Clark .75 .23
❑ 254 John Valentin .30 .09
❑ 255 Bobby Higginson .30 .09
❑ 256 Darryl Strawberry .30 .09
❑ 257 Randy Johnson .75 .23
❑ 258 Al Martin .30 .09
❑ 259 Travis Fryman .30 .09
❑ 260 Fred McGriff .50 .15
❑ 261 Jose Valentin .30 .09
❑ 262 Andruw Jones .30 .09
❑ 263 Kenny Rogers .30 .09
❑ 264 Moises Alou .30 .09
❑ 265 Denny Neagle .30 .09
❑ 266 Ugueth Urbina .30 .09
❑ 267 Derrek Lee .30 .09
❑ 268 Ellis Burks .30 .09
❑ 269 Mariano Rivera .50 .15
❑ 270 Dean Palmer .30 .09
❑ 271 Eddie Taubensee .30 .09
❑ 272 Brady Anderson .30 .09
❑ 273 Brian Giles .30 .09
❑ 274 Quinton McCracken .30 .09
❑ 275 Henry Rodriguez .30 .09
❑ 276 Andres Galarraga .30 .09
❑ 277 Jose Canseco .75 .23
❑ 278 David Segui .30 .09
❑ 279 Bret Saberhagen .30 .09
❑ 280 Kevin Brown .50 .15
❑ 281 Chuck Knoblauch .30 .09
❑ 282 Jeromy Burnitz .30 .09
❑ 283 Jay Bell .30 .09
❑ 284 Manny Ramirez .50 .15
❑ 285 Rick Helling .30 .09
❑ 286 Francisco Cordova .30 .09
❑ 287 Bob Abreu .30 .09
❑ 288 J.T. Snow .30 .09
❑ 289 Hideo Nomo .75 .23
❑ 290 Brian Jordan .30 .09
❑ 291 Javy Lopez .30 .09
❑ 292 Travis Lee .30 .09
❑ 293 Russell Branyan .30 .09
❑ 294 Paul Konerko .30 .09
❑ 295 Masato Yoshii RC .50 .15
❑ 296 Kris Benson .30 .09
❑ 297 Juan Encarnacion .30 .09
❑ 298 Eric Milton .30 .09
❑ 299 Mike Caruso .30 .09
❑ 300 R.Aramboles RC .40 .12
❑ 301 Bobby Smith .30 .09
❑ 302 Billy Koch .30 .09
❑ 303 Richard Hidalgo .30 .09
❑ 304 Justin Baughman RC .30 .09
❑ 305 Chris Gissell .30 .09
❑ 306 Donnie Bridges RC .30 .09
❑ 307 Nelson Lara RC .30 .09
❑ 308 Randy Wolf RC .50 .15
❑ 309 Jason LaRue RC .40 .12
❑ 310 Jason Gooding RC .30 .09
❑ 311 Edgard Clemente .30 .09
❑ 312 Andrew Vessel .30 .09
❑ 313 Chris Reitsma .30 .09
❑ 314 Jesus Sanchez RC .30 .09
❑ 315 Buddy Carlyle RC .30 .09
❑ 316 Randy Winn .30 .09
❑ 317 Luis Rivera RC .30 .09
❑ 318 Marcus Thames RC .50 .15
❑ 319 A.J. Pierzynski .30 .09
❑ 320 Scott Randall .30 .09
❑ 321 Damian Sapp .30 .09
❑ 322 Ed Yarnall RC .30 .09
❑ 323 Luke Allen RC .40 .12
❑ 324 J.D. Smart .30 .09
❑ 325 Willie Martinez .30 .09
❑ 326 Alex Ramirez .30 .09
❑ 327 Eric DuBose RC .40 .12
❑ 328 Kevin Witt .30 .09
❑ 329 Dan McKinley RC .30 .09
❑ 330 Cliff Politte .30 .09
❑ 331 Vladimir Nunez .30 .09
❑ 332 John Halama RC .30 .09
❑ 333 Nerio Rodriguez .30 .09
❑ 334 Desi Relaford .30 .09
❑ 335 Robinson Checo .30 .09
❑ 336 John Nicholson .50 .15
❑ 337 Tom LaRosa RC .30 .09
❑ 338 Kevin Nicholson RC .30 .09
❑ 339 Javier Vazquez .30 .09
❑ 340 A.J. Zapp .30 .09

❑ 341 Tom Evans .30 .09
❑ 342 Kerry Robinson .30 .09
❑ 343 Gabe Gonzalez RC .30 .09
❑ 344 Ralph Milliard .30 .09
❑ 345 Enrique Wilson .30 .09
❑ 346 Elvin Hernandez .30 .09
❑ 347 Mike Lincoln RC .30 .09
❑ 348 Cesar King RC .30 .09
❑ 349 Cristian Guzman RC .50 .15
❑ 350 Donzell McDonald .30 .09
❑ 351 Jim Parque RC .30 .09
❑ 352 Mike Saipe RC .30 .09
❑ 353 Carlos Febles RC .40 .12
❑ 354 Dernell Stenson RC .40 .12
❑ 355 Mark Osborne RC .30 .09
❑ 356 Odalis Perez RC .75 .23
❑ 357 Jason Dewey RC .30 .09
❑ 358 Joe Fontenot .30 .09
❑ 359 Jason Grilli RC .30 .09
❑ 360 Kevin Haverbusch RC .30 .09
❑ 361 Jay Yennaco RC .30 .09
❑ 362 Brian Buchanan .30 .09
❑ 363 John Barnes .30 .09
❑ 364 Chris Fussell .30 .09
❑ 365 Kevin Gibbs RC .30 .09
❑ 366 Joe Lawrence .30 .09
❑ 367 DaRond Stovall .30 .09
❑ 368 Brian Fuentes RC .30 .09
❑ 369 Jimmy Anderson .30 .09
❑ 370 Lariel Gonzalez RC .30 .09
❑ 371 Scott Williamson RC .40 .12
❑ 372 Milton Bradley .30 .09
❑ 373 Jason Halper RC .30 .09
❑ 374 Brent Billingsley RC .30 .09
❑ 375 Joe DePastino RC .30 .09
❑ 376 Jake Westbrook .30 .09
❑ 377 Octavio Dotel .30 .09
❑ 378 Jason Williams RC .30 .09
❑ 379 Julio Ramirez RC .30 .09
❑ 380 Seth Greisinger .30 .09
❑ 381 Mike Judd RC .30 .09
❑ 382 Ben Ford RC .30 .09
❑ 383 Tom Bennett RC .30 .09
❑ 384 Adam Butler RC .30 .09
❑ 385 Wade Miller RC .50 .15
❑ 386 Kyle Peterson RC .30 .09
❑ 387 Tommy Peterman RC .30 .09
❑ 388 Onan Masaoka .30 .09
❑ 389 Jason Rakers RC .30 .09
❑ 390 Rafael Medina .30 .09
❑ 391 Luis Lopez RC .30 .09
❑ 392 Jeff Yoder .30 .09
❑ 393 Vance Wilson RC .30 .09
❑ 394 F.Seguignol RC .30 .09
❑ 395 Ron Wright .30 .09
❑ 396 Ruben Mateo RC .40 .12
❑ 397 Steve Lomasney RC .40 .12
❑ 398 Damian Jackson .30 .09
❑ 399 Mike Jerzembeck RC .30 .09
❑ 400 Luis Rivas RC .75 .23
❑ 401 Kevin Burford RC .30 .09
❑ 402 Glenn Davis .30 .09
❑ 403 Robert Luce RC .30 .09
❑ 404 Cole Liniak .30 .09
❑ 405 Matt LeCroy RC .40 .12
❑ 406 Jeremy Giambi RC .40 .12
❑ 407 Shawn Chacon .30 .09
❑ 408 Dewayne Wise RC .30 .09
❑ 409 Steve Woodard .30 .09
❑ 410 F.Cordero RC .50 .15
❑ 411 Damon Minor RC .30 .09
❑ 412 Lou Collier .30 .09
❑ 413 Justin Towle .30 .09
❑ 414 Juan LeBron .30 .09
❑ 415 Michael Coleman .30 .09
❑ 416 Felix Rodriguez .30 .09
❑ 417 Paul Ah Yat RC .30 .09
❑ 418 Kevin Barker RC .30 .09
❑ 419 Brian Meadows .30 .09
❑ 420 Darnell McDonald RC .30 .09
❑ 421 Matt Kinney RC .40 .12
❑ 422 Mike Vavrek RC .30 .09
❑ 423 Courtney Duncan RC .30 .09
❑ 424 Kevin Millar RC 3.00 .90
❑ 425 Ruben Rivera .30 .09
❑ 426 Steve Shoemaker RC .30 .09
❑ 427 Dan Reichert RC .30 .09
❑ 428 Carlos Lee RC .75 .23
❑ 429 Rod Barajas .50 .15
❑ 430 Pablo Ozuna RC .40 .12
❑ 431 Todd Belitz RC .30 .09
❑ 432 Sidney Ponson .30 .09
❑ 433 Steve Carver RC .30 .09
❑ 434 Esteban Yan RC .40 .12
❑ 435 Cedrick Bowers .30 .09
❑ 436 Marlon Anderson .30 .09
❑ 437 Carl Pavano .30 .09
❑ 438 Jae Weong Seo RC .50 .15
❑ 439 Jose Taveras RC .30 .09
❑ 440 Matt Anderson RC .40 .12
❑ 441 Darron Ingram RC .30 .09
❑ NNO S.Hasegawa '91 BBM 10.00 3.00
❑ NNO H.Irabu '91 BBM 10.00 3.00
❑ NNO H.Nomo '91 BBM 25.00 7.50

1999 Bowman

	Nm-Mt	Ex-Mt
COMPLETE SET (440)	80.00	24.00
COMP. SERIES 1 (220)	30.00	9.00
COMP. SERIES 2 (220)	50.00	15.00

❑ 1 Ben Grieve .30 .09
❑ 2 Kerry Wood .75 .23
❑ 3 Ruben Rivera .30 .09
❑ 4 Sandy Alomar Jr. .30 .09
❑ 5 Cal Ripken 2.50 .75
❑ 6 Mark McGwire 2.00 .60
❑ 7 Vladimir Guerrero .75 .23
❑ 8 Moises Alou .30 .09
❑ 9 Jim Edmonds .30 .09
❑ 10 Greg Maddux 1.25 .35
❑ 11 Gary Sheffield .30 .09
❑ 12 John Valentin .30 .09
❑ 13 Chuck Knoblauch .30 .09
❑ 14 Tony Clark .30 .09
❑ 15 Rusty Greer .30 .09
❑ 16 Al Leiter .30 .09
❑ 17 Travis Lee .30 .09
❑ 18 Jose Cruz Jr. .30 .09
❑ 19 Pedro Martinez .75 .23
❑ 20 Paul O'Neill .50 .15
❑ 21 Todd Walker .30 .09
❑ 22 Vinny Castilla .30 .09
❑ 23 Barry Larkin .50 .15
❑ 24 Curt Schilling .30 .09
❑ 25 Jason Kendall .30 .09
❑ 26 Scott Erickson .30 .09
❑ 27 Andres Galarraga .30 .09
❑ 28 Jeff Shaw .30 .09
❑ 29 John Olerud .30 .09
❑ 30 Orlando Hernandez .30 .09
❑ 31 Larry Walker .50 .15
❑ 32 Andruw Jones .30 .09
❑ 33 Jeff Cirillo .30 .09
❑ 34 Barry Bonds 2.00 .60
❑ 35 Manny Ramirez .50 .15
❑ 36 Mark Kotsay .30 .09
❑ 37 Ivan Rodriguez .75 .23
❑ 38 Jeff King .30 .09
❑ 39 Brian Hunter .30 .09
❑ 40 Ray Durham .30 .09
❑ 41 Bernie Williams .50 .15
❑ 42 Darin Erstad .30 .09
❑ 43 Chipper Jones .75 .23
❑ 44 Pat Hentgen .30 .09
❑ 45 Eric Young .30 .09
❑ 46 Jaret Wright .30 .09
❑ 47 Juan Guzman .30 .09
❑ 48 Jorge Posada .50 .15
❑ 49 Bobby Higginson .30 .09
❑ 50 Jose Guillen .30 .09
❑ 51 Trevor Hoffman .30 .09
❑ 52 Ken Griffey Jr. 1.25 .35
❑ 53 David Justice .30 .09
❑ 54 Matt Williams .30 .09
❑ 55 Eric Karros .30 .09
❑ 56 Derek Bell .30 .09
❑ 57 Ray Lankford .30 .09
❑ 58 Mariano Rivera .50 .15
❑ 59 Brett Tomko .30 .09
❑ 60 Mike Mussina .50 .15
❑ 61 Kenny Lofton .30 .09
❑ 62 Chuck Finley .30 .09
❑ 63 Alex Gonzalez .30 .09
❑ 64 Mark Grace .50 .15
❑ 65 Raul Mondesi .30 .09
❑ 66 David Cone .30 .09
❑ 67 Brad Fullmer .30 .09
❑ 68 Andy Benes .30 .09
❑ 69 John Smoltz .50 .15
❑ 70 Shane Reynolds .30 .09
❑ 71 Bruce Chen .30 .09
❑ 72 Adam Kennedy .30 .09
❑ 73 Jack Cust .30 .09
❑ 74 Matt Clement .30 .09
❑ 75 Derrick Gibson .30 .09
❑ 76 Darnell McDonald .30 .09
❑ 77 Adam Everett RC .50 .15
❑ 78 Ricardo Aramboles .30 .09
❑ 79 Mark Quinn RC .40 .12
❑ 80 Jason Rakers .30 .09
❑ 81 Seth Etherton RC .30 .09
❑ 82 Jeff Urban RC .40 .12
❑ 83 Manny Aybar .30 .09
❑ 84 Mike Nannini RC .30 .09
❑ 85 Onan Masaoka .30 .09
❑ 86 Rod Barajas .30 .09
❑ 87 Mike Frank .30 .09
❑ 88 Scott Randall .30 .09
❑ 89 Justin Bowles RC .30 .09
❑ 90 Chris Haas .30 .09
❑ 91 Arturo McDowell RC .30 .09
❑ 92 Matt Belisle RC .30 .35
❑ 93 Scott Elarton .30 .09
❑ 94 Vernon Wells .30 .09
❑ 95 Pat Cline .30 .09
❑ 96 Ryan Anderson .30 .09
❑ 97 Kevin Barker .30 .09
❑ 98 Ruben Mateo .30 .09
❑ 99 Robert Fick .30 .09
❑ 100 Corey Koskie .30 .09
❑ 101 Ricky Ledee .30 .09
❑ 102 Rick Elder RC .40 .12
❑ 103 Jack Cressend RC .30 .09
❑ 104 Joe Lawrence .30 .09
❑ 105 Mike Lincoln .30 .09
❑ 106 Kit Pellow RC .30 .09
❑ 107 Matt Burch RC .40 .12
❑ 108 Cole Liniak .30 .09
❑ 109 Jason Dewey .30 .09
❑ 110 Cesar King .30 .09
❑ 111 Julio Ramirez .30 .09
❑ 112 Jake Westbrook .30 .09
❑ 113 Eric Valent RC .40 .12
❑ 114 Roosevelt Brown RC .30 .09
❑ 115 Choo Freeman RC .40 .12
❑ 116 Juan Melo .30 .09
❑ 117 Jason Grilli .30 .09
❑ 118 Jared Sandberg .30 .09
❑ 119 Glenn Davis .30 .09
❑ 120 David Riske RC .30 .09
❑ 121 Jacque Jones .30 .09
❑ 122 Corey Lee .30 .09
❑ 123 Michael Barrett .30 .09
❑ 124 Lariel Gonzalez .30 .09
❑ 125 Mitch Meluskey .30 .09
❑ 126 Freddy Adrian Garcia .30 .09
❑ 127 Tony Torcato RC .40 .12
❑ 128 Jeff Liefer .30 .09

	No.	Player	Price	Price
❑	129	Ntema Ndungidi	.30	.09
❑	130	Andy Brown RC	.30	.09
❑	131	Ryan Mills RC	.30	.09
❑	132	Andy Abad RC	.30	.09
❑	133	Carlos Febles	.30	.09
❑	134	Jason Tyner RC	.30	.09
❑	135	Mark Osborne	.30	.09
❑	136	Phil Norton RC	.30	.09
❑	137	Nathan Haynes	.30	.09
❑	138	Roy Halladay	.30	.09
❑	139	Juan Encarnacion	.30	.09
❑	140	Brad Penny	.30	.09
❑	141	Grant Roberts	.30	.09
❑	142	Aramis Ramirez	.30	.09
❑	143	Cristian Guzman	.30	.09
❑	144	Mamon Tucker RC	.30	.09
❑	145	Ryan Bradley	.30	.09
❑	146	Brian Simmons	.30	.09
❑	147	Dan Reichert	.30	.09
❑	148	Russ Branyan	.30	.09
❑	149	Victor Valencia RC	.30	.09
❑	150	Scott Schoeneweis	.30	.09
❑	151	Sean Spencer RC	.30	.09
❑	152	Odalis Perez	.30	.09
❑	153	Joe Fontenot	.30	.09
❑	154	Milton Bradley	.30	1.30
❑	155	Josh McKinley RC	.40	.12
❑	156	Terrence Long	.30	.09
❑	157	Danny Klassen	.30	.09
❑	158	Paul Hoover RC	.40	.12
❑	159	Ron Belliard	.30	.09
❑	160	Armando Rios	.30	.09
❑	161	Ramon Hernandez	.30	.09
❑	162	Jason Conti	.30	.09
❑	163	Chad Hermansen	.30	.09
❑	164	Jason Standridge	.30	.09
❑	165	Jason Dellaero	.30	.09
❑	166	John Curtice	.30	.09
❑	167	Clayton Andrews RC	.30	.09
❑	168	Jeremy Giambi	.30	.09
❑	169	Alex Ramirez	.30	.09
❑	170	Gabe Molina RC	.30	.09
❑	171	M.Encarnacion RC	.30	.09
❑	172	Mike Zywica RC	.30	.09
❑	173	Chip Ambres RC	.30	.09
❑	174	Trot Nixon	.30	.09
❑	175	Pat Burrell RC	2.50	.75
❑	176	Jeff Yoder	.30	.09
❑	177	Chris Jones RC	.30	.09
❑	178	Kevin Witt	.30	.09
❑	179	Keith Luuloa RC	.30	.09
❑	180	Billy Koch	.30	.09
❑	181	Damaso Marte RC	.30	.09
❑	182	Ryan Glynn RC	.30	.09
❑	183	Calvin Pickering	.30	.09
❑	184	Michael Cuddyer	.30	.09
❑	185	Nick Johnson RC	.75	.23
❑	186	D.Mientkiewicz RC	.75	.23
❑	187	Nate Cornejo RC	.50	.15
❑	188	Octavio Dotel	.30	.09
❑	189	Wes Helms	.30	.09
❑	190	Nelson Lara	.30	.09
❑	191	Chuck Abbott RC	.30	.09
❑	192	Tony Armas Jr.	.30	.09
❑	193	Gil Meche	.30	.09
❑	194	Ben Petrick	.30	.09
❑	195	Chris George RC	.40	.12
❑	196	Scott Hunter RC	.30	.09
❑	197	Ryan Brannan	.30	.09
❑	198	Amaury Garcia RC	.40	.12
❑	199	Chris Gissell	.30	.09
❑	200	Austin Kearns RC	2.50	.75
❑	201	Alex Gonzalez	.30	.09
❑	202	Wade Miller	.30	.09
❑	203	Scott Williamson	.30	.09
❑	204	Chris Enochs	.30	.09
❑	205	Fernando Seguignol	.30	.09
❑	206	Marlon Anderson	.30	.09
❑	207	Todd Sears RC	.40	.12
❑	208	Nate Bump RC	.30	.09
❑	209	J.M. Gold RC	.30	.09
❑	210	Matt LeCroy	.30	.09
❑	211	Alex Hernandez	.30	.09
❑	212	Luis Rivera	.30	.09
❑	213	Troy Cameron	.30	.09
❑	214	Alex Escobar RC	.40	.12
❑	215	Jason LaRue	.30	.09
❑	216	Kyle Peterson	.30	.09
❑	217	Brent Butler	.30	.09
❑	218	Dernell Stenson	.30	.09
❑	219	Adrian Beltre	.50	.15
❑	220	Daryle Ward	.30	.09
❑	221	Jim Thome	.75	.23
❑	222	Cliff Floyd	.30	.09
❑	223	Rickey Henderson	.75	.23
❑	224	Garret Anderson	.30	.09
❑	225	Ken Caminiti	.30	.09
❑	226	Bret Boone	.30	.09
❑	227	Jeromy Burnitz	.30	.09
❑	228	Steve Finley	.30	.09
❑	229	Miguel Tejada	.30	.09
❑	230	Greg Vaughn	.30	.09
❑	231	Jose Offerman	.30	.09
❑	232	Andy Ashby	.30	.09
❑	233	Albert Belle	.30	.09
❑	234	Fernando Tatis	.30	.09
❑	235	Todd Helton	.50	.15
❑	236	Sean Casey	.30	.09
❑	237	Brian Giles	.30	.09
❑	238	Andy Pettitte	.50	.15
❑	239	Fred McGriff	.50	.15
❑	240	Roberto Alomar	.50	.15
❑	241	Edgar Martinez	.50	.15
❑	242	Lee Stevens	.30	.09
❑	243	Shawn Green	.30	.09
❑	244	Ryan Klesko	.30	.09
❑	245	Sammy Sosa	1.25	.35
❑	246	Todd Hundley	.30	.09
❑	247	Shannon Stewart	.30	.09
❑	248	Randy Johnson	.75	.23
❑	249	Rondell White	.30	.09
❑	250	Mike Piazza	1.25	.35
❑	251	Craig Biggio	.50	.15
❑	252	David Wells	.30	.09
❑	253	Brian Jordan	.30	.09
❑	254	Edgar Renteria	.30	.09
❑	255	Bartolo Colon	.30	.09
❑	256	Frank Thomas	.75	.23
❑	257	Will Clark	.75	.23
❑	258	Dean Palmer	.30	.09
❑	259	Dmitri Young	.30	.09
❑	260	Scott Rolen	.75	.23
❑	261	Jeff Kent	.30	.09
❑	262	Dante Bichette	.30	.09
❑	263	Nomar Garciaparra	1.25	.35
❑	264	Tony Gwynn	1.00	.30
❑	265	Alex Rodriguez	1.25	.35
❑	266	Jose Canseco	.75	.23
❑	267	Jason Giambi	.30	.09
❑	268	Jeff Bagwell	.50	.15
❑	269	Carlos Delgado	.30	.09
❑	270	Tom Glavine	.50	.15
❑	271	Eric Davis	.30	.09
❑	272	Edgardo Alfonzo	.30	.09
❑	273	Tim Salmon	.50	.15
❑	274	Johnny Damon	.50	.15
❑	275	Rafael Palmeiro	.50	.15
❑	276	Denny Neagle	.30	.09
❑	277	Neifi Perez	.30	.09
❑	278	Roger Clemens	1.50	.45
❑	279	Brant Brown	.30	.09
❑	280	Kevin Brown	.50	.15
❑	281	Jay Bell	.30	.09
❑	282	Jay Buhner	.30	.09
❑	283	Matt Lawton	.30	.09
❑	284	Robin Ventura	.30	.09
❑	285	Juan Gonzalez	.50	.15
❑	286	Mo Vaughn	.30	.09
❑	287	Kevin Millwood	.30	.09
❑	288	Tino Martinez	.50	.15
❑	289	Justin Thompson	.30	.09
❑	290	Derek Jeter	2.00	.60
❑	291	Ben Davis	.30	.09
❑	292	Mike Lowell	.30	.09
❑	293	Calvin Murray	.30	.09
❑	294	Micah Bowie RC	.30	.09
❑	295	Lance Berkman	.30	.09
❑	296	Jason Marquis	.30	.09
❑	297	Chad Green	.30	.09
❑	298	Dee Brown	.30	.09
❑	299	Jerry Hairston Jr.	.30	.09
❑	300	Gabe Kapler	.30	.09
❑	301	Brent Stentz RC	.40	.12
❑	302	Scott Mullen RC	.30	.09
❑	303	Brandon Reed	.30	.09
❑	304	Shea Hillenbrand RC	.75	.23
❑	305	J.D. Closser RC	.50	.15
❑	306	Gary Matthews Jr.	.30	.09
❑	307	Toby Hall RC	.40	.12
❑	308	Jason Phillips RC	.30	.09
❑	309	Jose Macias RC	.30	.09
❑	310	Jung Bong RC	.40	.12
❑	311	Ramon Soler RC	.30	.09
❑	312	Kelly Dransfeldt RC	.30	.09
❑	313	Carl. E. Hernandez RC	.40	.12
❑	314	Kevin Haverbusch	.30	.09
❑	315	Aaron Myette RC	.30	.09
❑	316	Chad Harville RC	.30	.09
❑	317	Kyle Farnsworth RC	.40	.12
❑	318	Gookie Dawkins RC	.40	.12
❑	319	Willie Martinez	.30	.09
❑	320	Carlos Lee	.30	.09
❑	321	Carlos Pena RC	.50	.15
❑	322	Peter Bergeron RC	.40	.12
❑	323	A.J. Burnett RC	.75	.23
❑	324	Bucky Jacobsen RC	4.00	1.20
❑	325	Mo Bruce RC	.30	.09
❑	326	Reggie Taylor	.30	.09
❑	327	Jackie Rexrode	.30	.09
❑	328	Alvin Morrow RC	.30	.09
❑	329	Carlos Beltran	.50	.15
❑	330	Eric Chavez	.30	.09
❑	331	John Patterson	.30	.09
❑	332	Jayson Werth	.30	.09
❑	333	Richie Sexson	.30	.09
❑	334	Randy Wolf	.30	.09
❑	335	Eli Marrero	.30	.09
❑	336	Paul LoDuca	.30	.09
❑	337	J.D Smart	.30	.09
❑	338	Ryan Minor	.30	.09
❑	339	Kris Benson	.30	.09
❑	340	George Lombard	.30	.09
❑	341	Troy Glaus	.30	.09
❑	342	Eddie Yarnall	.30	.09
❑	343	Kip Wells RC	.50	.15
❑	344	C.C. Sabathia RC	1.00	.30
❑	345	Sean Burroughs RC	1.25	.35
❑	346	Felipe Lopez RC	.40	.12
❑	347	Ryan Rupe RC	.30	.09
❑	348	Orber Moreno RC	.30	.09
❑	349	Rafael Roque RC	.30	.09
❑	350	Alfonso Soriano RC	5.00	1.50
❑	351	Pablo Ozuna	.30	.09
❑	352	Corey Patterson RC	2.00	.60
❑	353	Braden Looper	.30	.09
❑	354	Robbie Bell	.30	.09
❑	355	Mark Mulder RC	2.00	.45
❑	356	Angel Pena	.30	.09
❑	357	Kevin McGlinchy	.30	.09
❑	358	M.Restovich RC	.40	.12
❑	359	Eric DuBose	.30	.09
❑	360	Geoff Jenkins	.30	.09
❑	361	Mark Harriger RC	.30	.09
❑	362	Junior Herndon RC	.40	.12
❑	363	Tim Raines Jr. RC	.40	.12
❑	364	Rafael Furcal RC	1.00	.30
❑	365	Marcus Giles RC	1.00	.30
❑	366	Ted Lilly	.30	.09
❑	367	Jorge Toca RC	.40	.12
❑	368	David Kelton RC	.40	.12
❑	369	Adam Dunn RC	4.00	1.20
❑	370	Guillermo Mota RC	.30	.09
❑	371	Brett Laxton RC	.30	.09
❑	372	Travis Harper RC	.40	.12
❑	373	Tom Davey RC	.30	.09
❑	374	Darren Blakely RC	.30	.09
❑	375	Tim Hudson RC	2.00	.60
❑	376	Jason Romano	.30	.09
❑	377	Dan Reichert	.30	.09
❑	378	Julio Lugo RC	.40	.12
❑	379	Jose Garcia RC	.30	.09
❑	380	Erubiel Durazo RC	.50	.15
❑	381	Jose Jimenez	.30	.09
❑	382	Chris Fussell	.30	.09
❑	383	Steve Lomasney	.30	.09
❑	384	Juan Pena RC	.40	.12
❑	385	Allen Levrault RC	.30	.09
❑	386	Juan Rivera RC	.40	.12

No.	Player	Nm-Mt	Ex-Mt
387	Steve Colyer RC	.40	.12
388	Joe Nathan RC	.75	.23
389	Ron Walker RC	.30	.09
390	Nick Bierbrodt	.30	.09
391	Luke Prokopec RC	.30	.09
392	Dave Roberts RC	.50	.15
393	Mike Darr	.30	.09
394	Abraham Nunez RC	.40	.12
395	G.Chiaramonte RC	.30	.09
396	J.Van Buren RC	.30	.09
397	Mike Kusiewicz	.30	.09
398	Matt Wise RC	.30	.09
399	Joe McEwing RC	.40	.12
400	Matt Holliday RC	.75	.23
401	Willi Mo Pena RC	2.00	.60
402	Ruben Quevedo RC	.30	.09
403	Rob Ryan RC	.30	.09
404	Freddy Garcia RC	.75	.23
405	Kevin Eberwein RC	.30	.09
406	Jesus Colome RC	.30	.09
407	Chris Singleton	.30	.09
408	Bubba Crosby RC	.50	.15
409	Jesus Cordero RC	.40	.12
410	Donny Leon	.30	.09
411	G.Tomlinson RC	.40	.12
412	Jeff Winchester RC	.30	.09
413	Adam Piatt RC	.40	.12
414	Robert Stratton	.30	.09
415	T.J. Tucker	.30	.09
416	Ryan Langerhans RC	.30	.09
417	A.Shumaker RC	.30	.09
418	Matt Miller RC	.30	.09
419	Doug Clark RC	.30	.09
420	Kory DeHaan RC	.30	.09
421	David Eckstein RC	.50	.15
422	Brian Cooper RC	.30	.09
423	Brady Clark RC	.30	.09
424	Chris Magruder RC	.40	.12
425	Bobby Seay RC	.30	.09
426	Aubrey Huff RC	1.00	.30
427	Mike Jerzembeck	.30	.09
428	Matt Blank RC	.40	.12
429	Benny Agbayani RC	.40	.12
430	Kevin Beirne RC	.40	.12
431	Josh Hamilton RC	.50	.15
432	Josh Girdley RC	.30	.09
433	Kyle Snyder RC	.30	.09
434	Mike Paradis RC	.30	.09
435	Jason Jennings RC	.50	.15
436	David Walling RC	.30	.09
437	Omar Ortiz RC	.40	.12
438	Jay Gehrke RC	.40	.12
439	Casey Burns RC	.40	.12
440	Carl Crawford RC	1.50	.45

2000 Bowman

	Nm-Mt	Ex-Mt
COMPLETE SET (440)	60.00	18.00

No.	Player	Nm-Mt	Ex-Mt
1	Vladimir Guerrero	.75	.23
2	Chipper Jones	.75	.23
3	Todd Walker	.30	.09
4	Barry Larkin	.50	.15
5	Bernie Williams	.50	.15
6	Todd Helton	.50	.15
7	Jermaine Dye	.30	.09
8	Brian Giles	.30	.09
9	Freddy Garcia	.30	.09
10	Greg Vaughn	.30	.09
11	Alex Gonzalez	.30	.09
12	Luis Gonzalez	.30	.09
13	Ron Belliard	.30	.09
14	Ben Grieve	.30	.09
15	Carlos Delgado	.30	.09
16	Brian Jordan	.30	.09
17	Fernando Tatis	.30	.09
18	Ryan Rupe	.30	.09
19	Miguel Tejada	.30	.09
20	Mark Grace	.50	.15
21	Kenny Lofton	.30	.09
22	Eric Karros	.30	.09
23	Cliff Floyd	.30	.09
24	John Halama	.30	.09
25	Cristian Guzman	.30	.09
26	Scott Williamson	.30	.09
27	Mike Lieberthal	.30	.09
28	Tim Hudson	.30	.09
29	Warren Morris	.30	.09
30	Pedro Martinez	.75	.23
31	John Smoltz	.50	.15
32	Ray Durham	.30	.09
33	Chad Allen	.30	.09
34	Tony Clark	.30	.09
35	Tino Martinez	.50	.15
36	J.T. Snow	.30	.09
37	Kevin Brown	.30	.09
38	Bartolo Colon	.30	.09
39	Rey Ordonez	.30	.09
40	Jeff Bagwell	.50	.15
41	Ivan Rodriguez	.75	.23
42	Eric Chavez	.30	.09
43	Eric Milton	.30	.09
44	Jose Canseco	.75	.23
45	Shawn Green	.30	.09
46	Rich Aurilia	.30	.09
47	Roberto Alomar	.50	.15
48	Brian Daubach	.30	.09
49	Magglio Ordonez	.30	.09
50	Derek Jeter	2.00	.60
51	Kris Benson	.30	.09
52	Albert Belle	.30	.09
53	Rondell White	.30	.09
54	Justin Thompson	.30	.09
55	Nomar Garciaparra	1.25	.35
56	Chuck Finley	.30	.09
57	Omar Vizquel	.50	.15
58	Luis Castillo	.30	.09
59	Richard Hidalgo	.30	.09
60	Barry Bonds	2.00	.60
61	Craig Biggio	.50	.15
62	Doug Glanville	.30	.09
63	Gabe Kapler	.30	.09
64	Johnny Damon	.50	.15
65	Pokey Reese	.30	.09
66	Andy Pettitte	.50	.15
67	B.J. Surhoff	.30	.09
68	Richie Sexson	.30	.09
69	Javy Lopez	.30	.09
70	Raul Mondesi	.30	.09
71	Darin Erstad	.30	.09
72	Kevin Millwood	.30	.09
73	Ricky Ledee	.30	.09
74	John Olerud	.30	.09
75	Sean Casey	.30	.09
76	Carlos Febles	.30	.09
77	Paul O'Neill	.50	.15
78	Bob Abreu	.30	.09
79	Neifi Perez	.30	.09
80	Tony Gwynn	1.00	.30
81	Russ Ortiz	.30	.09
82	Matt Williams	.30	.09
83	Chris Carpenter	.30	.09
84	Roger Cedeno	.30	.09
85	Tim Salmon	.50	.15
86	Billy Koch	.30	.09
87	Jeromy Burnitz	.30	.09
88	Edgardo Alfonzo	.30	.09
89	Jay Bell	.30	.09
90	Manny Ramirez	.50	.15
91	Frank Thomas	.75	.23
92	Mike Mussina	.50	.15
93	J.D. Drew	.30	.09
94	Adrian Beltre	.50	.15
95	Alex Rodriguez	1.25	.35
96	Larry Walker	.50	.15
97	Juan Encarnacion	.30	.09
98	Mike Sweeney	.30	.09
99	Rusty Greer	.30	.09
100	Randy Johnson	.75	.23
101	Jose Vidro	.30	.09
102	Preston Wilson	.30	.09
103	Greg Maddux	1.25	.35
104	Jason Giambi	.30	.09
105	Cal Ripken	2.50	.75
106	Carlos Beltran	.50	.15
107	Vinny Castilla	.30	.09
108	Mariano Rivera	.50	.15
109	Mo Vaughn	.30	.09
110	Rafael Palmeiro	.50	.15
111	Shannon Stewart	.30	.09
112	Mike Hampton	.30	.09
113	Joe Nathan	.30	.09
114	Ben Davis	.30	.09
115	Andruw Jones	.30	.09
116	Robin Ventura	.30	.09
117	Damion Easley	.30	.09
118	Jeff Cirillo	.30	.09
119	Kerry Wood	.75	.23
120	Scott Rolen	.75	.23
121	Sammy Sosa	1.25	.35
122	Ken Griffey Jr.	1.25	.35
123	Shane Reynolds	.30	.09
124	Troy Glaus	.30	.09
125	Tom Glavine	.50	.15
126	Michael Barrett	.30	.09
127	Al Leiter	.30	.09
128	Jason Kendall	.30	.09
129	Roger Clemens	1.50	.45
130	Juan Gonzalez	.50	.15
131	Corey Koskie	.30	.09
132	Curt Schilling	.30	.09
133	Mike Piazza	1.25	.35
134	Gary Sheffield	.30	.09
135	Jim Thome	.75	.23
136	Orlando Hernandez	.30	.09
137	Ray Lankford	.30	.09
138	Geoff Jenkins	.30	.09
139	Jose Lima	.30	.09
140	Mark McGwire	2.00	.60
141	Adam Piatt	.30	.09
142	Pat Manning RC	.30	.09
143	Marcos Castillo RC	.30	.09
144	Lesli Brea RC	.30	.09
145	Humberto Cota RC	.40	.12
146	Ben Petrick	.30	.09
147	Kip Wells	.30	.09
148	Wily Pena	.30	.09
149	Chris Wakeland RC	.30	.09
150	Brad Baker RC	.40	.12
151	Robbie Morrison RC	.30	.09
152	Reggie Taylor	.30	.09
153	Matt Ginter RC	.40	.12
154	Peter Bergeron	.30	.09
155	Roosevelt Brown	.30	.09
156	Matt Cepicky RC	.30	.09
157	Ramon Castro	.30	.09
158	Brad Baisley RC	.30	.09
159	Jeff Goldbach RC	.30	.09
160	Mitch Meluskey	.30	.09
161	Chad Harville	.30	.09
162	Brian Cooper	.30	.09
163	Marcus Giles	.30	.09
164	Jim Morris	.75	.23
165	Geoff Goetz	.30	.09
166	Bobby Bradley RC	.40	.12
167	Rob Bell	.30	.09
168	Joe Crede	.30	.09
169	Michael Restovich	.30	.09
170	Quincy Foster RC	.30	.09
171	Enrique Cruz RC	.30	.09
172	Mark Quinn	.30	.09
173	Nick Johnson	.30	.09
174	Jeff Liefer	.30	.09
175	Kevin Mench RC	.75	.23
176	Steve Lomasney	.30	.09
177	Jayson Werth	.30	.09
178	Tim Drew	.30	.09
179	Chip Ambres	.30	.09
180	Ryan Anderson	.30	.09

❑	181	Matt Blank	.30	.09
❑	182	G.Chiaramonte	.30	.09
❑	183	Corey Myers RC	.40	.12
❑	184	Jeff Yoder	.30	.09
❑	185	Craig Dingman RC	.30	.09
❑	186	Jon Hamilton RC	.30	.09
❑	187	Toby Hall	.30	.09
❑	188	Russell Branyan	.30	.09
❑	189	Brian Falkenborg RC	.30	.09
❑	190	Aaron Harang RC	.40	.12
❑	191	Juan Pena	.30	.09
❑	192	Travis Thompson RC	.30	.09
❑	193	Alfonso Soriano	.75	.23
❑	194	Alejandro Diaz RC	.30	.09
❑	195	Carlos Pena	.30	.09
❑	196	Kevin Nicholson	.30	.09
❑	197	Mo Bruce	.30	.09
❑	198	C.C. Sabathia	.30	.09
❑	199	Carl Crawford	.30	.09
❑	200	Rafael Furcal	.30	.09
❑	201	Andrew Beinbrink RC	.30	.09
❑	202	Jimmy Osting	.30	.09
❑	203	Aaron McNeal RC	.40	.12
❑	204	Brett Laxton	.30	.09
❑	205	Chris George	.30	.09
❑	206	Felipe Lopez	.30	.09
❑	207	Ben Sheets RC	2.00	.60
❑	208	Mike Meyers RC	.40	.12
❑	209	Jason Conti	.30	.09
❑	210	Milton Bradley	.30	.09
❑	211	Chris Mears RC	.30	.09
❑	212	Carlos Hernandez RC	.50	.15
❑	213	Jason Romano	.30	.09
❑	214	Geofrey Tomlinson	.30	.09
❑	215	Jimmy Rollins	.30	.09
❑	216	Pablo Ozuna	.30	.09
❑	217	Steve Cox	.30	.09
❑	218	Terrence Long	.30	.09
❑	219	Jeff DaVanon RC	.40	.12
❑	220	Rick Ankiel	.30	.09
❑	221	Jason Standridge	.30	.09
❑	222	Tony Armas Jr.	.30	.09
❑	223	Jason Tyner	.30	.09
❑	224	Ramon Ortiz	.30	.09
❑	225	Daryle Ward	.30	.09
❑	226	Enger Veras RC	.30	.09
❑	227	Chris Jones	.30	.09
❑	228	Eric Cammack RC	.30	.09
❑	229	Ruben Mateo	.30	.09
❑	230	Ken Harvey RC	.75	.23
❑	231	Jake Westbrook	.30	.09
❑	232	Rob Purvis RC	.30	.09
❑	233	Choo Freeman	.30	.09
❑	234	Aramis Ramirez	.30	.09
❑	235	A.J. Burnett	.30	.09
❑	236	Kevin Barker	.30	.09
❑	237	Chance Caple RC	.30	.09
❑	238	Jarrod Washburn	.30	.09
❑	239	Lance Berkman	.30	.09
❑	240	Michael Wenner RC	.30	.09
❑	241	Alex Sanchez	.30	.09
❑	242	Pat Daneker	.30	.09
❑	243	Grant Roberts	.30	.09
❑	244	Mark Ellis RC	.40	.12
❑	245	Donny Leon	.30	.09
❑	246	David Eckstein	.30	.09
❑	247	Dicky Gonzalez RC	.30	.09
❑	248	John Patterson	.30	.09
❑	249	Chad Green	.30	.09
❑	250	Scot Shields RC	.30	.09
❑	251	Troy Cameron	.30	.09
❑	252	Jose Molina	.30	.09
❑	253	Rob Pugmire RC	.30	.09
❑	254	Rick Elder	.30	.09
❑	255	Sean Burroughs	.30	.09
❑	256	Josh Kalinowski RC	.30	.09
❑	257	Matt LeCroy	.30	.09
❑	258	Alex Graman RC	.30	.09
❑	259	Tomo Ohka RC	.40	.12
❑	260	Brady Clark	.30	.09
❑	261	Rico Washington RC	.30	.09
❑	262	Gary Matthews Jr.	.30	.09
❑	263	Matt Wise	.30	.09
❑	264	Keith Reed RC	.40	.12
❑	265	Santiago Ramirez RC	.30	.09
❑	266	Ben Broussard RC	.75	.23
❑	267	Ryan Langerhans	.30	.09
❑	268	Juan Rivera	.30	.09
❑	269	Shawn Gallagher	.30	.09
❑	270	Jorge Toca	.30	.09
❑	271	Brad Lidge	.30	.09
❑	272	Leoncio Estrella RC	.30	.09
❑	273	Ruben Quevedo	.30	.09
❑	274	Jack Cust	.30	.09
❑	275	T.J. Tucker	.30	.09
❑	276	Mike Colangelo	.30	.09
❑	277	Brian Schneider	.30	.09
❑	278	Calvin Murray	.30	.09
❑	279	Josh Girdley	.30	.09
❑	280	Mike Paradis	.30	.09
❑	281	Chad Hermansen	.30	.09
❑	282	Ty Howington RC	.40	.12
❑	283	Aaron Myette	.30	.09
❑	284	D'Angelo Jimenez	.30	.09
❑	285	Dernell Stenson	.30	.09
❑	286	Jerry Hairston Jr.	.30	.09
❑	287	Gary Majewski RC	.50	.15
❑	288	Derrin Ebert	.30	.09
❑	289	Steve Fish RC	.30	.09
❑	290	Carlos E. Hernandez	.30	.09
❑	291	Allen Levrault	.30	.09
❑	292	Sean McNally RC	.30	.09
❑	293	Randey Dorame RC	.30	.09
❑	294	Wes Anderson RC	.40	.12
❑	295	B.J. Ryan	.30	.09
❑	296	Alan Webb RC	.30	.09
❑	297	Brandon Inge RC	.40	.12
❑	298	David Walling	.30	.09
❑	299	Sun Woo Kim RC	.40	.12
❑	300	Pat Burrell	.30	.09
❑	301	Rick Guttormson RC	.30	.09
❑	302	Gil Meche	.30	.09
❑	303	Carlos Zambrano RC	3.00	.90
❑	304	Eric Byrnes UER RC Bo Porter pictured	.75	.23
❑	305	Robb Quinlan RC	.75	.23
❑	306	Jackie Rexrode	.30	.09
❑	307	Nate Bump	.30	.09
❑	308	Sean DePaula RC	.30	.09
❑	309	Matt Riley	.30	.09
❑	310	Ryan Minor	.30	.09
❑	311	J.J. Davis	.30	.09
❑	312	Randy Wolf	.30	.09
❑	313	Jason Jennings	.30	.09
❑	314	Scott Seabol RC	.30	.09
❑	315	Doug Davis	.30	.09
❑	316	Todd Moser RC	.30	.09
❑	317	Rob Ryan	.30	.09
❑	318	Bubba Crosby	.30	.09
❑	319	Ryan Knox RC	1.25	.35
❑	320	Mario Encarnacion	.30	.09
❑	321	F.Rodriguez RC	2.00	.60
❑	322	Michael Cuddyer	.30	.09
❑	323	Ed Yarnall	.30	.09
❑	324	Cesar Saba RC	.30	.09
❑	325	Gookie Dawkins	.30	.09
❑	326	Alex Escobar	.30	.09
❑	327	Julio Zuleta RC	.30	.09
❑	328	Josh Hamilton	.30	.09
❑	329	Nick Neugebauer RC	.40	.12
❑	330	Matt Belisle	.30	.09
❑	331	Kurt Ainsworth RC	.40	.12
❑	332	Tim Raines Jr.	.30	.09
❑	333	Eric Munson	.30	.09
❑	334	Donzell McDonald	.30	.09
❑	335	Larry Bigbie RC	.75	.23
❑	336	Matt Watson RC	.30	.09
❑	337	Aubrey Huff	.30	.09
❑	338	Julio Ramirez	.30	.09
❑	339	Jason Grabowski RC	.40	.12
❑	340	Jon Garland	.30	.09
❑	341	Austin Kearns	.50	.15
❑	342	Josh Pressley RC	.30	.09
❑	343	Miguel Olivo RC	.50	.15
❑	344	Julio Lugo	.30	.09
❑	345	Roberto Vaz	.30	.09
❑	346	Ramon Soler	.30	.09
❑	347	Brandon Phillips RC	.50	.15
❑	348	Vince Faison RC	.30	.09
❑	349	Mike Venafro	.30	.09
❑	350	Rick Asadoorian RC	.40	.12
❑	351	B.J. Garbe RC	.30	.09
❑	352	Dan Reichert	.30	.09
❑	353	Jason Stumm RC	.30	.09
❑	354	Ruben Salazar RC	.30	.09
❑	355	Francisco Cordero	.30	.09
❑	356	Juan Guzman RC	.30	.09
❑	357	Mike Bacsik RC	.30	.09
❑	358	Jared Sandberg	.30	.09
❑	359	Rod Barajas	.30	.09
❑	360	Junior Brignac RC	.30	.09
❑	361	J.M. Gold	.30	.09
❑	362	Octavio Dotel	.30	.09
❑	363	David Kelton	.30	.09
❑	364	Scott Morgan	.30	.09
❑	365	Wascar Serrano RC	.30	.09
❑	366	Wilton Veras	.30	.09
❑	367	Eugene Kingsale	.30	.09
❑	368	Ted Lilly	.30	.09
❑	369	George Lombard	.30	.09
❑	370	Chris Haas	.30	.09
❑	371	Wilton Pena RC	.30	.09
❑	372	Vernon Wells	.30	.09
❑	373	Jason Royer RC	.30	.09
❑	374	Jeff Heaverlo RC	.30	.09
❑	375	Calvin Pickering	.30	.09
❑	376	Mike Lamb RC	.40	.12
❑	377	Kyle Snyder	.30	.09
❑	378	Javier Cardona RC	.30	.09
❑	379	Aaron Rowand RC	1.25	.35
❑	380	Dee Brown	.30	.09
❑	381	Brett Myers RC	.50	.15
❑	382	Abraham Nunez	.30	.09
❑	383	Eric Valent	.30	.09
❑	384	Jody Gerut RC	.75	.23
❑	385	Adam Dunn	.75	.23
❑	386	Jay Gehrke	.30	.09
❑	387	Omar Ortiz	.30	.09
❑	388	Darnell McDonald	.30	.09
❑	389	Tony Schrager RC	.30	.09
	390	J.D. Closser	.30	.09
❑	391	Ben Christensen RC	.30	.09
❑	392	Adam Kennedy	.30	.09
❑	393	Nick Green RC	.75	.23
❑	394	Ramon Hernandez	.30	.09
❑	395	Roy Oswalt RC	2.50	.75
❑	396	Andy Tracy RC	.30	.09
❑	397	Eric Gagne	1.25	.35
❑	398	Michael Tejera RC	.30	.09
❑	399	Adam Everett	.30	.09
❑	400	Corey Patterson	.30	.09
❑	401	Gary Knotts RC	.30	.09
❑	402	Ryan Christianson RC	.40	.12
❑	403	Eric Ireland RC	.30	.09
❑	404	Andrew Good RC	.30	.09
❑	405	Brad Penny	.30	.09
❑	406	Jason LaRue	.30	.09
❑	407	Kit Pellow	.30	.09
❑	408	Kevin Beirne	.30	.09
❑	409	Kelly Dransfeldt	.30	.09
❑	410	Jason Grilli	.30	.09
❑	411	Scott Downs RC	.30	.09
❑	412	Jesus Colome	.30	.09
❑	413	John Sneed RC	.30	.09
❑	414	Tony McKnight	.30	.09
❑	415	Luis Rivera	.30	.09
❑	416	Adam Eaton	.30	.09
❑	417	Mike MacDougal RC	.40	.12
❑	418	Mike Nannini	.30	.09
❑	419	Barry Zito RC	2.00	.60
❑	420	DeWayne Wise	.30	.09
❑	421	Jason Dellaero	.30	.09
❑	422	Chad Moeller	.30	.09
❑	423	Jason Marquis	.30	.09
❑	424	Tim Redding RC	.40	.12
❑	425	Mark Mulder	.30	.09
❑	426	Josh Paul	.30	.09
❑	427	Chris Enochs	.30	.09
❑	428	W.Rodriguez RC	.30	.09
❑	429	Kevin Witt	.30	.09
❑	430	Scott Sobkowiak RC	.30	.09
❑	431	McKay Christensen	.30	.09
❑	432	Jung Bong	.30	.09
❑	433	Keith Evans RC	.30	.09
❑	434	Garry Maddox Jr. RC	.30	.09
❑	435	Ramon Santiago RC	.40	.12
❑	436	Alex Cora	.30	.09
❑	437	Carlos Lee	.30	.09

Card	Nm-Mt	Ex-Mt
❑ 438 Jason Repko RC	.40	.12
❑ 439 Matt Burch	.30	.09
❑ 440 Shawn Sonnier RC	.30	.09

2000 Bowman Draft Picks

	Nm-Mt	Ex-Mt
COMP.FACT.SET (111)	40.00	12.00
COMPLETE SET (110)	25.00	7.50

Card	Nm-Mt	Ex-Mt
❑ 1 Pat Burrell	.30	.09
❑ 2 Rafael Furcal	.30	.09
❑ 3 Grant Roberts	.30	.09
❑ 4 Barry Zito	1.50	.45
❑ 5 Julio Zuleta	.30	.09
❑ 6 Mark Mulder	.30	.09
❑ 7 Rob Bell	.30	.09
❑ 8 Adam Piatt	.30	.09
❑ 9 Mike Lamb	.50	.15
❑ 10 Pablo Ozuna	.30	.09
❑ 11 Jason Tyner	.30	.09
❑ 12 Jason Marquis	.30	.09
❑ 13 Eric Munson	.30	.09
❑ 14 Seth Etherton	.30	.09
❑ 15 Milton Bradley	.30	.09
❑ 16 Nick Green	.75	.23
❑ 17 Chin-Feng Chen RC	.75	.23
❑ 18 Matt Boone RC	.30	.09
❑ 19 Kevin Gregg RC	.40	.12
❑ 20 Eddy Garabito RC	.30	.09
❑ 21 Aaron Capista RC	.30	.09
❑ 22 Esteban German RC	.30	.09
❑ 23 Derek Thompson RC	.30	.09
❑ 24 Phil Merrell RC	.30	.09
❑ 25 Brian O'Connor RC	.30	.09
❑ 26 Yamid Haad	.30	.09
❑ 27 Hector Mercado RC	.30	.09
❑ 28 Jason Woolf RC	.30	.09
❑ 29 Eddy Furniss RC	.30	.09
❑ 30 Cha Sueng Baek RC	.30	.09
❑ 31 Colby Lewis RC	.40	.12
❑ 32 Pasqual Coco RC	.30	.09
❑ 33 Jorge Cantu RC	.50	.15
❑ 34 Erasmo Ramirez RC	.30	.09
❑ 35 Bobby Kielty RC	.40	.12
❑ 36 Joaquin Benoit RC	.40	.12
❑ 37 Brian Esposito RC	.30	.09
❑ 38 Michael Wenner	.30	.09
❑ 39 Juan Rincon RC	.30	.09
❑ 40 Yorvit Torrealba RC	.30	.09
❑ 41 Chad Durham RC	.30	.09
❑ 42 Jim Mann RC	.30	.09
❑ 43 Shane Loux RC	.30	.09
❑ 44 Luis Rivas	.30	.09
❑ 45 Ken Chenard RC	.30	.09
❑ 46 Mike Lockwood RC	.30	.09
❑ 47 Yovanny Lara RC	.30	.09
❑ 48 Bubba Carpenter RC	.30	.09
❑ 49 Ryan Dittfurth RC	.30	.09
❑ 50 John Stephens RC	.40	.12
❑ 51 Pedro Feliz RC	.75	.23
❑ 52 Kenny Kelly RC	.40	.12
❑ 53 Neil Jenkins RC	.30	.09
❑ 54 Mike Glendenning RC	.30	.09
❑ 55 Bo Porter	.30	.09
❑ 56 Eric Byrnes	.75	.23
❑ 57 Tony Alvarez RC	.30	.09
❑ 58 Kazuhiro Sasaki RC	.75	.23
❑ 59 Chad Durbin RC	.30	.09
❑ 60 Mike Bynum RC	.30	.09
❑ 61 Travis Wilson RC	.30	.09
❑ 62 Jose Leon RC	.30	.09
❑ 63 Ryan Vogelsong RC	.40	.12
❑ 64 Geraldo Guzman RC	.30	.09
❑ 65 Craig Anderson RC	.30	.09
❑ 66 Carlos Silva RC	.50	.15
❑ 67 Brad Thomas RC	.30	.09
❑ 68 Chin-Hui Tsao RC	.75	.23
❑ 69 Mark Buehrle RC	1.25	.35
❑ 70 Juan Salas RC	.30	.09
❑ 71 Denny Abreu RC	.30	.09
❑ 72 Keith McDonald RC	.30	.09
❑ 73 Chris Richard RC	.30	.09
❑ 74 Tomas De la Rosa RC	.30	.09
❑ 75 Vicente Padilla RC	.40	.12
❑ 76 Justin Brunette RC	.30	.09
❑ 77 Scott Linebrink RC	.30	.09
❑ 78 Jeff Sparks RC	.30	.09
❑ 79 Tike Redman RC	.50	.15
❑ 80 John Lackey RC	.75	.23
❑ 81 Joe Strong RC	.30	.09
❑ 82 Brian Tollberg RC	.30	.09
❑ 83 Steve Sisco RC	.30	.09
❑ 84 Chris Clapinski RC	.30	.09
❑ 85 Augie Ojeda RC	.30	.09
❑ 86 Adrian Gonzalez RC	1.25	.35
❑ 87 Mike Stodolka RC	.30	.09
❑ 88 Adam Johnson RC	.40	.12
❑ 89 Matt Wheatland RC	.30	.09
❑ 90 Corey Smith RC	.40	.12
❑ 91 Rocco Baldelli RC	4.00	1.20
❑ 92 Keith Bucktrot RC	.30	.09
❑ 93 Adam Wainwright RC	.75	.23
❑ 94 Blaine Boyer RC	.30	.09
❑ 95 Aaron Herr RC	.40	.12
❑ 96 Scott Thorman RC	.50	.15
❑ 97 Bryan Digby RC	.40	.12
❑ 98 Josh Shortslef RC	.30	.09
❑ 99 Sean Smith RC	.40	.12
❑ 100 Alex Cruz RC	.30	.09
❑ 101 Marc Love RC	.30	.09
❑ 102 Kevin Lee RC	.30	.09
❑ 103 Victor Ramos RC	.40	.12
❑ 104 Jason Kaanoi RC	.30	.09
❑ 105 Luis Escobar RC	.30	.09
❑ 106 Tripper Johnson RC	.40	.12
❑ 107 Phil Dumatrait RC	.40	.12
❑ 108 Bryan Edwards RC	.30	.09
❑ 109 Grady Sizemore RC	8.00	2.40
❑ 110 Thomas Mitchell RC	.30	.09

2001 Bowman

	Nm-Mt	Ex-Mt
COMPLETE SET (440)	100.00	30.00
COMMON CARD (1-440)	.30	.09
COMMON RC	.30	.09

Card	Nm-Mt	Ex-Mt
❑ 1 Jason Giambi	.30	.09
❑ 2 Rafael Furcal	.30	.09
❑ 3 Rick Ankiel	.30	.09
❑ 4 Freddy Garcia	.30	.09
❑ 5 Magglio Ordonez	.30	.09
❑ 6 Bernie Williams	.50	.15
❑ 7 Kenny Lofton	.30	.09
❑ 8 Al Leiter	.30	.09
❑ 9 Albert Belle	.30	.09
❑ 10 Craig Biggio	.50	.15
❑ 11 Mark Mulder	.30	.09
❑ 12 Carlos Delgado	.30	.09
❑ 13 Darin Erstad	.30	.09
❑ 14 Richie Sexson	.30	.09
❑ 15 Randy Johnson	.75	.23
❑ 16 Greg Maddux	1.25	.35
❑ 17 Cliff Floyd	.30	.09
❑ 18 Mark Buehrle	.30	.09
❑ 19 Chris Singleton	.30	.09
❑ 20 Orlando Hernandez	.30	.09
❑ 21 Javier Vazquez	.30	.09
❑ 22 Jeff Kent	.30	.09
❑ 23 Jim Thome	.75	.23
❑ 24 John Olerud	.30	.09
❑ 25 Jason Kendall	.30	.09
❑ 26 Scott Rolen	.75	.23
❑ 27 Tony Gwynn	1.00	.30
❑ 28 Edgardo Alfonzo	.30	.09
❑ 29 Pokey Reese	.30	.09
❑ 30 Todd Helton	.50	.15
❑ 31 Mark Quinn	.30	.09
❑ 32 Dan Tosca RC	.40	.12
❑ 33 Dean Palmer	.30	.09
❑ 34 Jacque Jones	.30	.09
❑ 35 Ray Durham	.30	.09
❑ 36 Rafael Palmeiro	.50	.15
❑ 37 Carl Everett	.30	.09
❑ 38 Ryan Dempster	.30	.09
❑ 39 Randy Wolf	.30	.09
❑ 40 Vladimir Guerrero	.75	.23
❑ 41 Livan Hernandez	.30	.09
❑ 42 Mo Vaughn	.30	.09
❑ 43 Shannon Stewart	.30	.09
❑ 44 Preston Wilson	.30	.09
❑ 45 Jose Vidro	.30	.09
❑ 46 Fred McGriff	.50	.15
❑ 47 Kevin Brown	.30	.09
❑ 48 Peter Bergeron	.30	.09
❑ 49 Miguel Tejada	.30	.09
❑ 50 Chipper Jones	.75	.23
❑ 51 Edgar Martinez	.50	.15
❑ 52 Tony Batista	.30	.09
❑ 53 Jorge Posada	.50	.15
❑ 54 Ricky Ledee	.30	.09
❑ 55 Sammy Sosa	1.25	.35
❑ 56 Steve Cox	.30	.09
❑ 57 Tony Armas Jr.	.30	.09
❑ 58 Gary Sheffield	.30	.09
❑ 59 Bartolo Colon	.30	.09
❑ 60 Pat Burrell	.30	.09
❑ 61 Jay Payton	.30	.09
❑ 62 Sean Casey	.30	.09
❑ 63 Larry Walker	.50	.15
❑ 64 Mike Mussina	.50	.15
❑ 65 Nomar Garciaparra	1.25	.35
❑ 66 Darren Dreifort	.30	.09
❑ 67 Richard Hidalgo	.30	.09
❑ 68 Troy Glaus	.30	.09
❑ 69 Ben Grieve	.30	.09
❑ 70 Jim Edmonds	.30	.09
❑ 71 Raul Mondesi	.30	.09
❑ 72 Andruw Jones	.30	.09
❑ 73 Luis Castillo	.30	.09
❑ 74 Mike Sweeney	.30	.09
❑ 75 Derek Jeter	2.00	.60
❑ 76 Ruben Mateo	.30	.09
❑ 77 Carlos Lee	.30	.09
❑ 78 Cristian Guzman	.30	.09
❑ 79 Mike Hampton	.30	.09
❑ 80 J.D. Drew	.30	.09
❑ 81 Matt Lawton	.30	.09
❑ 82 Moises Alou	.30	.09
❑ 83 Terrence Long	.30	.09
❑ 84 Geoff Jenkins	.30	.09
❑ 85 Manny Ramirez	.50	.15
❑ 86 Johnny Damon	.50	.15
❑ 87 Barry Larkin	.50	.15
❑ 88 Pedro Martinez	.75	.23
❑ 89 Juan Gonzalez	.50	.15
❑ 90 Roger Clemens	1.50	.45
❑ 91 Carlos Beltran	.50	.15
❑ 92 Brad Radke	.30	.09
❑ 93 Orlando Cabrera	.30	.09

94	Roberto Alomar	.50	.15
95	Barry Bonds	2.00	.60
96	Tim Hudson	.30	.09
97	Tom Glavine	.50	.15
98	Jeromy Burnitz	.30	.09
99	Adrian Beltre	.50	.15
100	Mike Piazza	1.25	.35
101	Kerry Wood	.75	.23
102	Steve Finley	.30	.09
103	Alex Cora	.30	.09
104	Bob Abreu	.30	.09
105	Neifi Perez	.30	.09
106	Mark Redman	.30	.09
107	Paul Konerko	.30	.09
108	Jermaine Dye	.30	.09
109	Brian Giles	.30	.09
110	Ivan Rodriguez	.75	.23
111	Vinny Castilla	.30	.09
112	Adam Kennedy	.30	.09
113	Eric Chavez	.30	.09
114	Billy Koch	.30	.09
115	Shawn Green	.30	.09
116	Matt Williams	.30	.09
117	Greg Vaughn	.30	.09
118	Gabe Kapler	.30	.09
119	Jeff Cirillo	.30	.09
120	Frank Thomas	.75	.23
121	David Justice	.30	.09
122	Cal Ripken	2.50	.75
123	Rich Aurilia	.30	.09
124	Curt Schilling	.30	.09
125	Barry Zito	.50	.15
126	Brian Jordan	.30	.09
127	Chan Ho Park	.30	.09
128	J.T. Snow	.30	.09
129	Kazuhiro Sasaki	.30	.09
130	Alex Rodriguez	1.25	.35
131	Mariano Rivera	.50	.15
132	Eric Milton	.30	.09
133	Andy Pettitte	.50	.15
134	Scott Elarton	.30	.09
135	Ken Griffey Jr.	1.25	.35
136	Bengie Molina	.30	.09
137	Jeff Bagwell	.50	.15
138	Kevin Millwood	.30	.09
139	Tino Martinez	.50	.15
140	Mark McGwire	2.00	.60
141	Larry Barnes	.30	.09
142	John Buck RC	.50	.15
143	Freddie Bynum RC	.40	.12
144	Abraham Nunez	.30	.09
145	Felix Diaz RC	.40	.12
146	Horacio Estrada	.30	.09
147	Ben Diggins	.30	.09
148	Tsuyoshi Shinjo RC	.50	.15
149	Rocco Baldelli	.50	.15
150	Rod Barajas	.30	.09
151	Luis Terrero	.30	.09
152	Milton Bradley	.30	.09
153	Kurt Ainsworth	.30	.09
154	Russell Branyan	.30	.09
155	Ryan Anderson	.30	.09
156	Mitch Jones RC	.40	.12
157	Chip Ambres	.30	.09
158	Steve Bennett RC	.30	.09
159	Ivanon Coffie	.30	.09
160	Sean Burroughs	.30	.09
161	Keith Bucktrot	.30	.09
162	Tony Alvarez	.30	.09
163	Joaquin Benoit	.30	.09
164	Rick Asadoorian	.30	.09
165	Ben Broussard	.30	.09
166	Ryan Madson RC	.75	.23
167	Dee Brown	.30	.09
168	Sergio Contreras RC	.40	.12
169	John Barnes	.30	.09
170	Ben Washburn RC	.40	.12
171	Erick Almonte RC	.40	.12
172	Shawn Fagan RC	.30	.09
173	Gary Johnson RC	.40	.12
174	Brady Clark	.30	.09
175	Grant Roberts	.30	.09
176	Tony Torcato	.30	.09
177	Ramon Castro	.30	.09
178	Esteban German	.30	.09
179	Joe Hamer RC	.40	.12
180	Nick Neugebauer	.30	.09
181	Dernell Stenson	.30	.09
182	Yhency Brazoban RC	.75	.23
183	Aaron Myette	.30	.09
184	Juan Sosa	.30	.09
185	Brandon Inge	.30	.09
186	Domingo Guante RC	.40	.12
187	Adrian Brown	.30	.09
188	Deivi Mendez RC	.40	.12
189	Luis Matos	.30	.09
190	Pedro Liriano RC	.40	.12
191	Donnie Bridges	.30	.09
192	Alex Cintron	.30	.09
193	Jace Brewer	.30	.09
194	Ron Davenport RC	.40	.12
195	Jason Belcher RC	.40	.12
196	Adrian Hernandez RC	.30	.09
197	Bobby Kielty	.30	.09
198	Reggie Griggs RC	.40	.12
199	R. Abercrombie RC	.40	.12
200	Troy Farnsworth RC	.40	.12
201	Matt Belisle	.30	.09
202	Miguel Villilo RC	.40	.12
203	Adam Everett	.30	.09
204	John Lackey	.30	.09
205	Pasqual Coco	.30	.09
206	Adam Wainwright	.30	.09
207	Matt White RC	.40	.12
208	Chin-Feng Chen	.30	.09
209	Jeff Andra RC	.40	.12
210	Willie Bloomquist	.30	.09
211	Wes Anderson	.30	.09
212	Enrique Cruz	.30	.09
213	Jerry Hairston Jr.	.30	.09
214	Mike Bynum	.30	.09
215	Brian Hitchcox RC	.40	.12
216	Ryan Christianson	.30	.09
217	J.J. Davis	.30	.09
218	Jovanny Cedeno	.30	.09
219	Elvin Nina	.30	.09
220	Alex Graman	.30	.09
221	Arturo McDowell	.30	.09
222	Deivis Santos RC	.40	.12
223	Jody Gerut	.30	.09
224	Sun Woo Kim	.30	.09
225	Jimmy Rollins	.30	.09
226	Ntema Ndungidi	.30	.09
227	Ruben Salazar	.30	.09
228	Josh Girdley	.30	.09
229	Carl Crawford	.30	.09
230	Luis Montanez RC	.40	.12
231	Ramon Carvajal RC	.40	.12
232	Matt Riley	.30	.09
233	Ben Davis	.30	.09
234	Jason Grabowski	.30	.09
235	Chris George	.30	.09
236	Hank Blalock RC	8.00	2.40
237	Roy Oswalt	.50	.15
238	Eric Reynolds RC	.40	.12
239	Brian Cole	.30	.09
240	Denny Bautista RC	.75	.23
241	Hector Garcia RC	.40	.12
242	Joe Thurston RC	.40	.12
243	Brad Cresse	.30	.09
244	Corey Patterson	.30	.09
245	Brett Evert RC	.40	.12
246	Elpidio Guzman RC	.40	.12
247	Vernon Wells	.30	.09
248	Roberto Miniel RC	.40	.12
249	Brian Bass RC	.40	.12
250	Mark Burnett RC	.40	.12
251	Juan Silvestre	.30	.09
252	Pablo Ozuna	.30	.09
253	Jayson Werth	.30	.09
254	Russ Jacobson	.30	.09
255	Chad Hermansen	.30	.09
256	Travis Hafner RC	1.50	.45
257	Brad Baker	.30	.09
258	Gookie Dawkins	.30	.09
259	Michael Cuddyer	.30	.09
260	Mark Buehrle	.30	.09
261	Ricardo Aramboles	.30	.09
262	Esix Snead RC	.40	.12
263	Wilson Betemit RC	.40	.12
264	Albert Pujols RC	50.00	15.00
265	Joe Lawrence	.30	.09
266	Ramon Ortiz	.30	.09
267	Ben Sheets	.50	.15
268	Luke Lockwood RC	.40	.12
269	Toby Hall	.30	.09
270	Jack Cust	.30	.09
271	Pedro Feliz UER	.30	.09
	No facsimile signature on card		
272	Noel Devarez RC	.40	.12
273	Josh Beckett	.30	.09
274	Alex Escobar	.30	.09
275	Doug Gredvig RC	.40	.12
276	Marcus Giles	.30	.09
277	Jon Rauch	.30	.09
278	Brian Schmitt RC	.40	.12
279	Seung Song RC	.50	.15
280	Kevin Mench	.30	.09
281	Adam Eaton	.30	.09
282	Shawn Sonnier	.30	.09
283	Andy Van Hekken RC	.40	.12
284	Aaron Rowand	.30	.09
285	Tony Blanco RC	.75	.23
286	Ryan Kohlmeier	.30	.09
287	C.C. Sabathia	.30	.09
288	Bubba Crosby	.30	.09
289	Josh Hamilton	.30	.09
290	Dee Haynes RC	.40	.12
291	Jason Marquis	.30	.09
292	Julio Zuleta	.30	.09
293	Carlos Hernandez	.30	.09
294	Matt Lecroy	.30	.09
295	Andy Beal RC	.40	.12
296	Carlos Pena	.30	.09
297	Reggie Taylor	.30	.09
298	Bob Keppel RC	.50	.15
299	Miguel Cabrera UER	1.50	.45
	Photo is Manuel Esquivia		
300	Ryan Franklin	.30	.09
301	Brandon Phillips	.30	.09
302	Victor Hall RC	.40	.12
303	Tony Pena Jr.	.30	.09
304	Jim Journell RC	.40	.12
305	Cristian Guerrero	.30	.09
306	Miguel Olivo	.30	.09
307	Jin Ho Cho	.30	.09
308	Choo Freeman	.30	.09
309	Danny Borrell RC	.40	.12
310	Doug Mientkiewicz	.30	.09
311	Aaron Herr	.30	.09
312	Keith Ginter	.30	.09
313	Felipe Lopez	.30	.09
314	Jeff Goldbach	.30	.09
315	Travis Harper	.30	.09
316	Paul LoDuca	.30	.09
317	Joe Torres	.30	.09
318	Eric Byrnes	.30	.09
319	George Lombard	.30	.09
320	Dave Krynzel	.30	.09
321	Ben Christensen	.30	.09
322	Aubrey Huff	.30	.09
323	Lyle Overbay	.30	.09
324	Sean McGowan	.30	.09
325	Jeff Heaverlo	.30	.09
326	Timo Perez	.30	.09
327	Octavio Martinez RC	.40	.12
328	Vince Faison	.30	.09
329	David Parrish RC	.40	.12
330	Bobby Bradley	.30	.09
331	Jason Miller RC	.40	.12
332	Corey Spencer RC	.40	.12
333	Craig House	.30	.09
334	Maxim St. Pierre RC	.40	.12
335	Adam Johnson	.30	.09
336	Joe Crede	.30	.09
337	Greg Nash RC	.40	.12
338	Chad Durbin	.30	.09
339	Pat Magness RC	.40	.12
340	Matt Wheatland	.30	.09
341	Julio Lugo	.30	.09
342	Grady Sizemore	.75	.23
343	Adrian Gonzalez	.30	.09
344	Tim Raines Jr.	.30	.09
345	Ranier Olmedo RC	.40	.12
346	Phil Dumatrait	.30	.09
347	Brandon Mims RC	.40	.12
348	Jason Jennings	.30	.09
349	Phil Wilson RC	.40	.12

❑ 350 Jason Hart .30 .09
❑ 351 Cesar Izturis .30 .09
❑ 352 Matt Butler RC .40 .12
❑ 353 David Kelton .30 .09
❑ 354 Luke Prokopec .30 .09
❑ 355 Corey Smith .30 .09
❑ 356 Joel Pineiro .75 .23
❑ 357 Ken Chenard .30 .09
❑ 358 Keith Reed .30 .09
❑ 359 David Walling .30 .09
❑ 360 Alexis Gomez RC .40 .12
❑ 361 Justin Morneau RC 8.00 2.40
❑ 362 Josh Fogg RC .40 .12
❑ 363 J.R. House .30 .09
❑ 364 Andy Tracy .30 .09
❑ 365 Kenny Kelly .30 .09
❑ 366 Aaron McNeal .30 .09
❑ 367 Nick Johnson .30 .09
❑ 368 Brian Esposito .30 .09
❑ 369 Charles Frazier RC .40 .12
❑ 370 Scott Heard .30 .09
❑ 371 Pat Strange .30 .09
❑ 372 Mike Meyers .30 .09
❑ 373 Ryan Ludwick RC .40 .12
❑ 374 Brad Wilkerson .30 .09
❑ 375 Allen Levrault .30 .09
❑ 376 Seth McClung RC .40 .12
❑ 377 Joe Nathan .30 .09
❑ 378 Rafael Soriano RC .50 .15
❑ 379 Chris Richard .30 .09
❑ 380 Jared Sandberg .30 .09
❑ 381 Tike Redman .30 .09
❑ 382 Adam Dunn UER .50 .15
Card lists him as a pitcher
❑ 383 Jared Abruzzo RC .40 .12
❑ 384 Jason Richardson RC .40 .12
❑ 385 Matt Holliday .30 .09
❑ 386 Darwin Cubillan RC .40 .12
❑ 387 Mike Nannini .30 .09
❑ 388 Blake Williams RC .40 .12
❑ 389 V. Pascucci RC .40 .12
❑ 390 Jon Garland .30 .09
❑ 391 Josh Pressley .30 .09
❑ 392 Jose Ortiz .30 .09
❑ 393 Ryan Hannaman RC .40 .12
❑ 394 Steve Smyth RC .40 .12
❑ 395 John Patterson .30 .09
❑ 396 Chad Petty RC .40 .12
❑ 397 Jake Peavy RC 2.00 .60
UER last name misspelled Peavey
❑ 398 Onix Mercado RC .40 .12
❑ 399 Jason Romano .30 .09
❑ 400 Luis Torres RC .40 .12
❑ 401 Casey Fossum RC .40 .12
❑ 402 Eduardo Figueroa RC .40 .12
❑ 403 Bryan Barnowski RC .40 .12
❑ 404 Tim Redding .30 .09
❑ 405 Jason Standridge .30 .09
❑ 406 Marvin Seale RC .40 .12
❑ 407 Todd Moser .30 .09
❑ 408 Alex Gordon .30 .09
❑ 409 Steve Smitherman RC .50 .15
❑ 410 Ben Petrick .30 .09
❑ 411 Eric Munson .30 .09
❑ 412 Luis Rivas .30 .09
❑ 413 Matt Ginter .30 .09
❑ 414 Alfonso Soriano .50 .15
❑ 415 Rafael Boitel RC .40 .12
❑ 416 Dany Morban RC .40 .12
❑ 417 Justin Woodrow RC .40 .12
❑ 418 Wilfredo Rodriguez .30 .09
❑ 419 Derrick Van Dusen RC .40 .12
❑ 420 Josh Spoerl RC .40 .12
❑ 421 Juan Pierre .30 .09
❑ 422 J.C. Romero .30 .09
❑ 423 Ed Rogers RC .40 .12
❑ 424 Tomo Ohka .30 .09
❑ 425 Ben Hendrickson RC .50 .15
❑ 426 Carlos Zambrano .50 .15
❑ 427 Brett Myers .30 .09
❑ 428 Scott Seabol .30 .09
❑ 429 Thomas Mitchell .30 .09
❑ 430 Jose Reyes RC 2.50 .75
❑ 431 Kip Wells .30 .09
❑ 432 Donzell McDonald .30 .09
❑ 433 Adam Pettyjohn RC .40 .12
❑ 434 Austin Kearns .30 .09
❑ 435 Rico Washington .30 .09
❑ 436 Doug Nickle RC .30 .09
❑ 437 Steve Lomasney .30 .09
❑ 438 Jason Jones RC .40 .12
❑ 439 Bobby Seay .30 .09
❑ 440 Justin Wayne RC .40 .12
❑ ROYR Kazuhiro Sasaki 25.00 7.50
Rafael Furcal ROY Jsy
❑ NNO Sean Burroughs Ball/80 40.00 12.00

2001 Bowman Draft Picks

	Nm-Mt	Ex-Mt
COMP.FACT.SET (112)	30.00	9.00
COMPLETE SET (110)	25.00	7.50

❑ BDP1 Alfredo Amezaga RC .40 .12
❑ BDP2 Andrew Good .30 .09
❑ BDP3 Kelly Johnson RC .40 .12
❑ BDP4 Larry Bigbie .30 .09
❑ BDP5 Matt Thompson RC .40 .12
❑ BDP6 Wilton Chavez RC .40 .12
❑ BDP7 Joe Borchard RC .75 .23
❑ BDP8 David Espinosa .30 .09
❑ BDP9 Zach Day RC .40 .12
❑ BDP10 Brad Hawpe RC 2.00 .60
❑ BDP11 Nate Cornejo .30 .09
❑ BDP12 Matt Cooper RC .40 .12
❑ BDP13 Brad Lidge .30 .09
❑ BDP14 Angel Berroa RC .75 .23
❑ BDP15 L. Matthews RC .40 .12
❑ BDP16 Jose Garcia .30 .09
❑ BDP17 Grant Balfour RC .30 .09
❑ BDP18 Ron Chiavacci RC .30 .09
❑ BDP19 Jae Seo .30 .09
❑ BDP20 Juan Rivera .30 .09
❑ BDP21 D'Angelo Jimenez .30 .09
❑ BDP22 Juan A.Pena RC .40 .12
❑ BDP23 Marlon Byrd RC 1.00 .30
❑ BDP24 Sean Burnett .30 .09
❑ BDP25 Josh Pearce RC .40 .12
❑ BDP26 B. Duckworth RC .40 .12
❑ BDP27 Jack Taschner RC .40 .12
❑ BDP28 Marcus Thames .30 .09
❑ BDP29 Brent Abernathy .30 .09
❑ BDP30 David Elder RC .40 .12
❑ BDP31 Scott Cassidy RC .40 .12
❑ BDP32 D. Tankersley RC .40 .12
❑ BDP33 Denny Stark .30 .09
❑ BDP34 Dave Williams RC .40 .12
❑ BDP35 Boof Bonser RC .40 .12
❑ BDP36 Kris Foster RC .30 .09
❑ BDP37 Luis Garcia RC .40 .12
❑ BDP38 Shawn Chacon .30 .09
❑ BDP39 Mike Rivera RC .40 .12
❑ BDP40 Will Smith RC .40 .12
❑ BDP41 M. Ensberg RC .75 .23
❑ BDP42 Ken Harvey .30 .09
❑ BDP43 R. Rodriguez RC .40 .12
❑ BDP44 Jose Mieses RC .40 .12
❑ BDP45 Luis Maza RC .40 .12
❑ BDP46 Julio Perez RC .40 .12
❑ BDP47 Dustan Mohr RC .40 .12
❑ BDP48 Randy Flores RC .30 .09
❑ BDP49 Covelli Crisp RC 1.50 .45
❑ BDP50 Kevin Reese RC .40 .12
❑ BDP51 Brad Thomas UER .30 .09
Card back is BDP71 Alex Herrera
❑ BDP52 Xavier Nady .30 .09
❑ BDP53 Ryan Vogelsong .30 .09
❑ BDP54 Carlos Silva .30 .09
❑ BDP55 Dan Wright .30 .09
❑ BDP56 Brent Butler .30 .09
❑ BDP57 Brandon Knight RC .30 .09
❑ BDP58 Brian Reith RC .40 .12
❑ BDP59 M. Valenzuela RC .40 .12
❑ BDP60 Bobby Hill RC .50 .15
❑ BDP61 Rich Rundles RC .40 .12
❑ BDP62 Rick Elder .30 .09
❑ BDP63 J.D. Closser .30 .09
❑ BDP64 Scot Shields .30 .09
❑ BDP65 Miguel Olivo .30 .09
❑ BDP66 Stubby Clapp RC .30 .09
❑ BDP67 J. Williams RC 2.50 .75
❑ BDP68 Jason Lane RC .40 .12
❑ BDP69 Chase Utley RC 4.00 1.20
❑ BDP70 Erik Bedard RC .40 .12
❑ BDP71 A. Herrera UER RC .30 .09
Card back is BDP51 Brad Thomas
❑ BDP72 Juan Cruz RC .40 .12
❑ BDP73 Billy Martin RC .40 .12
❑ BDP74 Ronnie Merrill RC .40 .12
❑ BDP75 Jason Kinchen RC .40 .12
❑ BDP76 Wilkin Ruan RC .40 .12
❑ BDP77 Cody Ransom RC .30 .09
❑ BDP78 Bud Smith RC .40 .12
❑ BDP79 Wily Mo Pena .30 .09
❑ BDP80 Jeff Nettles RC .40 .12
❑ BDP81 Jamal Strong RC .40 .12
❑ BDP82 Bill Ortega RC .40 .12
❑ BDP83 Mike Bell .30 .09
❑ BDP84 Ichiro Suzuki RC 10.00 3.00
❑ BDP85 F. Rodney RC .40 .12
❑ BDP86 Chris Smith RC .40 .12
❑ BDP87 J.VanBenschoten RC 1.50 .45
❑ BDP88 Bobby Crosby RC 10.00 3.00
❑ BDP89 Kenny Baugh RC .40 .12
❑ BDP90 Jake Gautreau RC .40 .12
❑ BDP91 Gabe Gross RC .50 .15
❑ BDP92 Kris Honel RC 1.50 .45
❑ BDP93 Dan Denham RC .40 .12
❑ BDP94 Aaron Heilman RC .40 .12
❑ BDP95 Irvin Guzman RC 4.00 1.20
❑ BDP96 Mike Jones RC .50 .15
❑ BDP97 J. Griffin RC .40 .12
❑ BDP98 Macay McBride RC .40 .12
❑ BDP99 J. Rheinecker RC .40 .12
❑ BDP100 B. Sardinha RC .75 .23
❑ BDP101 J. Weintraub RC .40 .12
❑ BDP102 J.D. Martin RC .40 .12
❑ BDP103 Jayson Nix RC .75 .23
❑ BDP104 Noah Lowry RC 2.50 .75
❑ BDP105 Richard Lewis RC 1.50 .45
❑ BDP106 B. Hennessey RC .75 .23
❑ BDP107 Jeff Mathis RC 2.00 .60
❑ BDP108 Jon Skaggs RC .40 .12
❑ BDP109 Justin Pope RC .40 .12
❑ BDP110 Josh Burrus RC .40 .12

2002 Bowman

	Nm-Mt	Ex-Mt
COMPLETE SET (440)	80.00	24.00
COMMON CARD (1-110)	.30	.09

Card		
COMMON CARD (111-440)	.30	.09
❑ 1 Adam Dunn	.50	.15
❑ 2 Derek Jeter	2.00	.60
❑ 3 Alex Rodriguez	1.25	.35
❑ 4 Miguel Tejada	.30	.09
❑ 5 Nomar Garciaparra	1.25	.35
❑ 6 Toby Hall	.30	.09
❑ 7 Brandon Duckworth	.30	.09
❑ 8 Paul LoDuca	.30	.09
❑ 9 Brian Giles	.30	.09
❑ 10 C.C. Sabathia	.30	.09
❑ 11 Curt Schilling	.30	.09
❑ 12 Tsuyoshi Shinjo	.30	.09
❑ 13 Ramon Hernandez	.30	.09
❑ 14 Jose Cruz Jr.	.30	.09
❑ 15 Albert Pujols	1.50	.45
❑ 16 Joe Mays	.30	.09
❑ 17 Javy Lopez	.30	.09
❑ 18 J.T. Snow	.30	.09
❑ 19 David Segui	.30	.09
❑ 20 Jorge Posada	.50	.15
❑ 21 Doug Mientkiewicz	.30	.09
❑ 22 Jerry Hairston Jr.	.30	.09
❑ 23 Bernie Williams	.50	.15
❑ 24 Mike Sweeney	.30	.09
❑ 25 Jason Giambi	.30	.09
❑ 26 Ryan Dempster	.30	.09
❑ 27 Ryan Klesko	.30	.09
❑ 28 Mark Quinn	.30	.09
❑ 29 Jeff Kent	.30	.09
❑ 30 Eric Chavez	.30	.09
❑ 31 Adrian Beltre	.50	.15
❑ 32 Andruw Jones	.30	.09
❑ 33 Alfonso Soriano	.50	.15
❑ 34 Aramis Ramirez	.30	.09
❑ 35 Greg Maddux	1.25	.35
❑ 36 Andy Pettitte	.50	.15
❑ 37 Bartolo Colon	.30	.09
❑ 38 Ben Sheets	.30	.09
❑ 39 Bobby Higginson	.30	.09
❑ 40 Ivan Rodriguez	.75	.23
❑ 41 Brad Penny	.30	.09
❑ 42 Carlos Lee	.30	.09
❑ 43 Damion Easley	.30	.09
❑ 44 Preston Wilson	.30	.09
❑ 45 Jeff Bagwell	.50	.15
❑ 46 Eric Milton	.30	.09
❑ 47 Rafael Palmeiro	.50	.15
❑ 48 Gary Sheffield	.30	.09
❑ 49 J.D. Drew	.30	.09
❑ 50 Jim Thome	.75	.23
❑ 51 Ichiro Suzuki	1.25	.35
❑ 52 Bud Smith	.30	.09
❑ 53 Chan Ho Park	.30	.09
❑ 54 D'Angelo Jimenez	.30	.09
❑ 55 Ken Griffey Jr.	1.25	.35
❑ 56 Wade Miller	.30	.09
❑ 57 Vladimir Guerrero	.75	.23
❑ 58 Troy Glaus	.30	.09
❑ 59 Shawn Green	.30	.09
❑ 60 Kerry Wood	.75	.23
❑ 61 Jack Wilson	.30	.09
❑ 62 Kevin Brown	.30	.09
❑ 63 Marcus Giles	.30	.09
❑ 64 Pat Burrell	.30	.09
❑ 65 Larry Walker	.50	.15
❑ 66 Sammy Sosa	1.25	.35
❑ 67 Raul Mondesi	.30	.09
❑ 68 Tim Hudson	.30	.09
❑ 69 Lance Berkman	.30	.09
❑ 70 Mike Mussina	.50	.15
❑ 71 Barry Zito	.30	.09
❑ 72 Jimmy Rollins	.30	.09
❑ 73 Barry Bonds	2.00	.60
❑ 74 Craig Biggio	.50	.15
❑ 75 Todd Helton	.50	.15
❑ 76 Roger Clemens	1.50	.45
❑ 77 Frank Catalanotto	.30	.09
❑ 78 Josh Towers	.30	.09
❑ 79 Roy Oswalt	.30	.09
❑ 80 Chipper Jones	.75	.23
❑ 81 Cristian Guzman	.30	.09
❑ 82 Darin Erstad	.30	.09
❑ 83 Freddy Garcia	.30	.09
❑ 84 Jason Tyner	.30	.09
❑ 85 Carlos Delgado	.30	.09
❑ 86 Jon Lieber	.30	.09
❑ 87 Juan Pierre	.30	.09
❑ 88 Matt Morris	.30	.09
❑ 89 Phil Nevin	.30	.09
❑ 90 Jim Edmonds	.30	.09
❑ 91 Magglio Ordonez	.30	.09
❑ 92 Mike Hampton	.30	.09
❑ 93 Rafael Furcal	.30	.09
❑ 94 Richie Sexson	.30	.09
❑ 95 Luis Gonzalez	.30	.09
❑ 96 Scott Rolen	.75	.23
❑ 97 Tim Redding	.30	.09
❑ 98 Moises Alou	.30	.09
❑ 99 Jose Vidro	.30	.09
❑ 100 Mike Piazza	1.25	.35
❑ 101 Pedro Martinez UER Career strikeout total incorrect	.75	.23
❑ 102 Geoff Jenkins	.30	.09
❑ 103 Johnny Damon Sox	.75	.23
❑ 104 Mike Cameron	.30	.09
❑ 105 Randy Johnson	.75	.23
❑ 106 David Eckstein	.30	.09
❑ 107 Javier Vazquez	.30	.09
❑ 108 Mark Mulder	.30	.09
❑ 109 Robert Fick	.30	.09
❑ 110 Roberto Alomar	.50	.15
❑ 111 Wilson Betemit	.30	.09
❑ 112 Chris Tritle RC	.40	.12
❑ 113 Ed Rogers	.30	.09
❑ 114 Juan Pena	.30	.09
❑ 115 Josh Beckett	.40	.12
❑ 116 Juan Cruz	.30	.09
❑ 117 Noochie Varner RC	.40	.12
❑ 118 Taylor Buchholz RC	.40	.12
❑ 119 Mike Rivera	.30	.09
❑ 120 Hank Blalock	1.00	.30
❑ 121 Hansel Izquierdo RC	.40	.12
❑ 122 Orlando Hudson	.30	.09
❑ 123 Bill Hall	.30	.09
❑ 124 Jose Reyes	.60	.18
❑ 125 Juan Rivera	.30	.09
❑ 126 Eric Valent	.30	.09
❑ 127 Scotty Layfield RC	.40	.12
❑ 128 Austin Kearns	.40	.12
❑ 129 Nic Jackson RC	.40	.12
❑ 130 Chris Baker RC	.40	.12
❑ 131 Chad Qualls RC	.40	.12
❑ 132 Marcus Thames	.30	.09
❑ 133 Nathan Haynes	.30	.09
❑ 134 Brett Evert	.30	.09
❑ 135 Joe Borchard	.30	.09
❑ 136 Ryan Christianson	.30	.09
❑ 137 Josh Hamilton	.30	.09
❑ 138 Corey Patterson	.40	.12
❑ 139 Travis Wilson	.30	.09
❑ 140 Alex Escobar	.30	.09
❑ 141 Alexis Gomez	.30	.09
❑ 142 Nick Johnson	.30	.09
❑ 143 Kenny Kelly	.30	.09
❑ 144 Marlon Byrd	.30	.09
❑ 145 Kory DeHaan	.30	.09
❑ 146 Matt Belisle	.30	.09
❑ 147 Carlos Hernandez	.30	.09
❑ 148 Sean Burroughs	.40	.12
❑ 149 Angel Berroa	.30	.09
❑ 150 Aubrey Huff	.40	.12
❑ 151 Travis Hafner	.40	.12
❑ 152 Brandon Berger	.30	.09
❑ 153 David Krynzel	.30	.09
❑ 154 Ruben Salazar	.30	.09
❑ 155 J.R. House	.30	.09
❑ 156 Juan Silvestre	.30	.09
❑ 157 Dewon Brazelton	.30	.09
❑ 158 Jayson Werth	.30	.09
❑ 159 Larry Barnes	.30	.09
❑ 160 Elvis Pena	.30	.09
❑ 161 Ruben Gotay RC	.40	.12
❑ 162 Tommy Marx RC	.40	.12
❑ 163 John Suomi RC	.40	.12
❑ 164 Javier Colina	.30	.09
❑ 165 Greg Sain RC	.50	.15
❑ 166 Robert Cosby RC	.40	.12
❑ 167 Angel Pagan RC	.40	.12
❑ 168 Ralph Santana RC	.40	.12
❑ 169 Joe Orloski RC	.40	.12
❑ 170 Shayne Wright RC	.40	.12
❑ 171 Jay Caligiuri RC	.40	.12
❑ 172 Greg Montalbano RC	.40	.12
❑ 173 Rich Harden RC	4.00	1.20
❑ 174 Rich Thompson RC	.40	.12
❑ 175 Fred Bastardo RC	.40	.12
❑ 176 Alejandro Giron RC	.40	.12
❑ 177 Jesus Medrano RC	.40	.12
❑ 178 Kevin Deaton RC	.40	.12
❑ 179 Mike Rosamond RC	.40	.12
❑ 180 Jon Guzman RC	.40	.12
❑ 181 Gerard Oakes RC	.40	.12
❑ 182 Francisco Liriano RC	.50	.15
❑ 183 Matt Allegra RC	.40	.12
❑ 184 Mike Snyder RC	.40	.12
❑ 185 James Shanks RC	.40	.12
❑ 186 Anderson Hernandez RC	.40	.12
❑ 187 Dan Trumble RC	.40	.12
❑ 188 Luis DePaula RC	.40	.12
❑ 189 Randall Shelley RC	.40	.12
❑ 190 Richard Lane RC	.40	.12
❑ 191 Antwon Rollins RC	.40	.12
❑ 192 Ryan Bukvich RC	.40	.12
❑ 193 Derrick Lewis	.30	.09
❑ 194 Eric Miller RC	.40	.12
❑ 195 Justin Schuda RC	.40	.12
❑ 196 Brian West RC	.40	.12
❑ 197 Adam Roller RC	.40	.12
❑ 198 Neal Frendling RC	.40	.12
❑ 199 Jeremy Hill RC	.40	.12
❑ 200 James Barrett RC	.40	.12
❑ 201 Brett Kay RC	.40	.12
❑ 202 Ryan Mottl RC	.40	.12
❑ 203 Brad Nelson RC	1.25	.35
❑ 204 Juan M. Gonzalez RC	.40	.12
❑ 205 Curtis Legendre RC	.40	.12
❑ 206 Ronald Acuna RC	.40	.12
❑ 207 Chris Flinn RC	.40	.12
❑ 208 Nick Alvarez RC	.40	.12
❑ 209 Jason Ellison RC	.40	.12
❑ 210 Blake McGinley RC	.40	.12
❑ 211 Dan Phillips RC	.40	.12
❑ 212 Demetrius Heath RC	.40	.12
❑ 213 Eric Bruntlett RC	.40	.12
❑ 214 Joe Jiannetti RC	.40	.12
❑ 215 Mike Hill RC	.40	.12
❑ 216 Ricardo Cordova RC	.40	.12
❑ 217 Mark Hamilton RC	.40	.12
❑ 218 David Mattox RC	.40	.12
❑ 219 Jose Morban RC	.40	.12
❑ 220 Scott Wiggins RC	.30	.09
❑ 221 Steve Green	.30	.09
❑ 222 Brian Rogers	.30	.09
❑ 223 Chin-Hui Tsao	.40	.12
❑ 224 Kenny Baugh	.30	.09
❑ 225 Nate Teut	.30	.09
❑ 226 Josh Wilson RC	.40	.12
❑ 227 Christian Parker	.30	.09
❑ 228 Tim Raines Jr.	.30	.09
❑ 229 Anastacio Martinez RC	.40	.12
❑ 230 Richard Lewis	.40	.12
❑ 231 Tim Kalita RC	.40	.12
❑ 232 Edwin Almonte RC	.40	.12
❑ 233 Hee-Seop Choi	.30	.09
❑ 234 Ty Howington	.30	.09
❑ 235 Victor Alvarez RC	.40	.12
❑ 236 Morgan Ensberg	.40	.12
❑ 237 Jeff Austin RC	.40	.12
❑ 238 Luis Terrero	.30	.09
❑ 239 Adam Wainwright	.30	.09
❑ 240 Clint Weibl RC	.30	.09
❑ 241 Eric Cyr	.30	.09
❑ 242 Marlyn Tisdale RC	.40	.12
❑ 243 John VanBenschoten	.30	.09
❑ 244 Ryan Raburn RC	.40	.12
❑ 245 Miguel Cabrera	1.50	.45
❑ 246 Jung Bong	.30	.09
❑ 247 Raul Chavez RC	.30	.09
❑ 248 Erik Bedard	.30	.09
❑ 249 Chris Snelling RC	.40	.12
❑ 250 Joe Rogers RC	.40	.12
❑ 251 Nate Field RC	.40	.12
❑ 252 Matt Herges RC	.30	.09
❑ 253 Matt Childers RC	.40	.12
❑ 254 Erick Almonte	.30	.09
❑ 255 Nick Neugebauer	.30	.09

❑ 256 Ron Calloway RC .40 .12
❑ 257 Seung Song .30 .09
❑ 258 Brandon Phillips .30 .09
❑ 259 Cole Barthel RC .40 .12
❑ 260 Jason Lane .30 .09
❑ 261 Jae Seo .30 .09
❑ 262 Randy Flores .30 .09
❑ 263 Scott Chiasson .30 .09
❑ 264 Chase Utley .60 .18
❑ 265 Tony Alvarez .30 .09
❑ 266 Ben Howard RC .40 .12
❑ 267 Nelson Castro RC .40 .12
❑ 268 Mark Lukasiewicz RC .30 .09
❑ 269 Eric Glaser RC .40 .12
❑ 270 Rob Henkel RC .40 .12
❑ 271 Jose Valverde RC .50 .15
❑ 272 Ricardo Rodriguez .30 .09
❑ 273 Chris Smith .30 .09
❑ 274 Mark Prior 2.00 .60
❑ 275 Miguel Olivo .30 .09
❑ 276 Ben Broussard .30 .09
❑ 277 Zach Sorensen .30 .09
❑ 278 Brian Mallette RC .30 .09
❑ 279 Brad Wilkerson .30 .09
❑ 280 Carl Crawford .40 .12
❑ 281 Chone Figgins RC .75 .23
❑ 282 Jimmy Alvarez RC .40 .12
❑ 283 Gavin Floyd RC 2.50 .75
❑ 284 Josh Bonifay RC .40 .12
❑ 285 Garrett Guzman RC .40 .12
❑ 286 Blake Williams .30 .09
❑ 287 Matt Holliday .30 .09
❑ 288 Ryan Madson .30 .09
❑ 289 Luis Torres .30 .09
❑ 290 Jeff Verplancke RC .40 .12
❑ 291 Nate Espy RC .40 .12
❑ 292 Jeff Lincoln RC .40 .12
❑ 293 Ryan Snare RC .40 .12
❑ 294 Jose Ortiz .30 .09
❑ 295 Eric Munson .30 .09
❑ 296 Denny Bautista .30 .09
❑ 297 Willy Aybar .30 .09
❑ 298 Kelly Johnson .30 .09
❑ 299 Justin Morneau 1.00 .30
❑ 300 Derrick Van Dusen .30 .09
❑ 301 Chad Petty .40 .12
❑ 302 Mike Restovich .30 .09
❑ 303 Shawn Fagan .30 .09
❑ 304 Yurendell DeCaster RC .40 .12
❑ 305 Justin Wayne .30 .09
❑ 306 Mike Peeples RC .30 .09
❑ 307 Joel Guzman .60 .18
❑ 308 Ryan Vogelsong .30 .09
❑ 309 Jorge Padilla RC .40 .12
❑ 310 Grady Sizemore .40 .12
❑ 311 Joe Jester RC .40 .12
❑ 312 Jim Journell .30 .09
❑ 313 Bobby Seay .30 .09
❑ 314 Ryan Church RC 1.00 .30
❑ 315 Grant Balfour .30 .09
❑ 316 Mitch Jones .30 .09
❑ 317 Travis Foley RC .40 .12
❑ 318 Bobby Crosby 1.00 .30
❑ 319 Adrian Gonzalez .40 .12
❑ 320 Ronnie Merrill .30 .09
❑ 321 Joel Pineiro .40 .12
❑ 322 John-Ford Griffin .30 .09
❑ 323 Brian Forystek RC .40 .12
❑ 324 Sean Douglass .30 .09
❑ 325 Manny Delcarmen RC .40 .12
❑ 326 Donnie Bridges .30 .09
❑ 327 Jim Kavourias RC .40 .12
❑ 328 Gabe Gross .30 .09
❑ 329 Jon Rauch .30 .09
❑ 330 Bill Ortega .30 .09
❑ 331 Joey Hammond RC .40 .12
❑ 332 Ramon Moreta RC .40 .12
❑ 333 Ron Davenport .30 .09
❑ 334 Brett Myers .30 .09
❑ 335 Carlos Pena .30 .09
❑ 336 Ezequiel Astacio RC .40 .12
❑ 337 Edwin Yan RC .40 .12
❑ 338 Josh Girdley .30 .09
❑ 339 Shaun Boyd .30 .09
❑ 340 Juan Rincon .30 .09
❑ 341 Chris Duffy RC .40 .12
❑ 342 Jason Kinchen .30 .09
❑ 343 Brad Thomas .30 .09
❑ 344 David Kelton .30 .09
❑ 345 Rafael Soriano .30 .09
❑ 346 Colin Young RC .40 .12
❑ 347 Eric Byrnes .30 .09
❑ 348 Chris Narveson RC .50 .15
❑ 349 John Rheinecker .30 .09
❑ 350 Mike Wilson RC .40 .12
❑ 351 Justin Sherrod RC .40 .12
❑ 352 Deivi Mendez .30 .09
❑ 353 Wily Mo Pena .40 .12
❑ 354 Brett Roneberg RC .40 .12
❑ 355 Trey Lunsford RC .40 .12
❑ 356 Jimmy Gobble RC .75 .23
❑ 357 Brent Butler .30 .09
❑ 358 Aaron Heilman .30 .09
❑ 359 Wilkin Ruan .30 .09
❑ 360 Brian Wolfe RC .40 .12
❑ 361 Cody Ransom .30 .09
❑ 362 Koyie Hill .30 .09
❑ 363 Scott Cassidy .30 .09
❑ 364 Tony Fontana RC .40 .12
❑ 365 Mark Teixeira .60 .18
❑ 366 Doug Sessions RC .40 .12
❑ 367 Victor Hall .30 .09
❑ 368 Josh Cisneros RC .40 .12
❑ 369 Kevin Mench .30 .09
❑ 370 Tike Redman .30 .09
❑ 371 Jeff Heaverlo .30 .09
❑ 372 Carlos Brackley RC .40 .12
❑ 373 Brad Hawpe .30 .09
❑ 374 Jesus Colome .30 .09
❑ 375 David Espinosa .30 .09
❑ 376 Jesse Foppert RC 1.00 .30
❑ 377 Ross Peeples RC .40 .12
❑ 378 Alex Requena RC .40 .12
❑ 379 Joe Mauer RC 5.00 1.50
❑ 380 Carlos Silva .30 .09
❑ 381 David Wright RC 10.00 3.00
❑ 382 Craig Kuzmic RC .40 .12
❑ 383 Pete Zamora RC .40 .12
❑ 384 Matt Parker RC .40 .12
❑ 385 Keith Ginter .30 .09
❑ 386 Gary Cates Jr. .40 .12
❑ 387 Justin Reid RC .40 .12
❑ 388 Jake Mauer RC .40 .12
❑ 389 Dennis Tankersley .30 .09
❑ 390 Josh Barfield RC 1.50 .45
❑ 391 Luis Maza .30 .09
❑ 392 Henry Pichardo RC .40 .12
❑ 393 Michael Floyd RC .40 .12
❑ 394 Clint Nageotte RC 1.00 .30
❑ 395 Raymond Cabrera RC .40 .12
❑ 396 Mauricio Lara RC .40 .12
❑ 397 Alejandro Cadena RC .40 .12
❑ 398 Jonny Gomes RC .75 .23
❑ 399 Jason Bulger RC .40 .12
❑ 400 Bobby Jenks RC .75 .23
❑ 401 David Gil RC .40 .12
❑ 402 Joel Crump RC .40 .12
❑ 403 Kazuhisa Ishii RC 1.25 .35
❑ 404 So Taguchi RC 1.25 .35
❑ 405 Ryan Doumit RC .50 .15
❑ 406 Macay McBride .30 .09
❑ 407 Brandon Claussen .30 .09
❑ 408 Chin-Feng Chen .40 .12
❑ 409 Josh Phelps .30 .09
❑ 410 Freddie Money RC .50 .15
❑ 411 Cliff Bartosh RC .40 .12
❑ 412 Josh Pearce .30 .09
❑ 413 Lyle Overbay .40 .12
❑ 414 Ryan Anderson .30 .09
❑ 415 Terrance Hill RC .40 .12
❑ 416 John Rodriguez RC .40 .12
❑ 417 Richard Stahl .30 .09
❑ 418 Brian Specht .30 .09
❑ 419 Chris Latham RC .30 .09
❑ 420 Carlos Cabrera RC .40 .12
❑ 421 Jose Bautista RC .50 .15
❑ 422 Kevin Frederick RC .40 .12
❑ 423 Jerome Williams .60 .18
❑ 424 Napoleon Calzado RC .40 .12
❑ 425 Benito Baez .30 .09
❑ 426 Xavier Nady .30 .09
❑ 427 Jason Botts RC .75 .23
❑ 428 Steve Bechler RC .40 .12
❑ 429 Reed Johnson RC .50 .15
❑ 430 Mark Outlaw RC .40 .12
❑ 431 Billy Sylvester .30 .09
❑ 432 Luke Lockwood .30 .09
❑ 433 Jake Peavy .40 .12
❑ 434 Alfredo Amezaga .30 .09
❑ 435 Aaron Cook RC .40 .12
❑ 436 Josh Shaffer RC .40 .12
❑ 437 Dan Wright .30 .09
❑ 438 Ryan Gripp RC .40 .12
❑ 439 Alex Herrera .30 .09
❑ 440 Jason Bay RC 2.50 .75

2002 Bowman Draft

	Nm-Mt	Ex-Mt
COMPLETE SET (165)	40.00	12.00

❑ BDP1 Clint Everts RC 1.50 .45
❑ BDP2 Fred Lewis RC .40 .12
❑ BDP3 Jon Broxton RC .75 .23
❑ BDP4 Jason Anderson RC .40 .12
❑ BDP5 Mike Eusebio RC .40 .12
❑ BDP6 Zack Greinke RC 3.00 .90
❑ BDP7 Joe Blanton RC 1.50 .45
❑ BDP8 Sergio Santos RC 2.00 .60
❑ BDP9 Jason Cooper RC .50 .15
❑ BDP10 Delwyn Young RC 1.25 .35
❑ BDP11 Jeremy Hermida RC 2.00 .60
❑ BDP12 Dan Ortmeier RC .75 .23
❑ BDP13 Kevin Jepsen RC 1.00 .30
❑ BDP14 Russ Adams RC 1.00 .30
❑ BDP15 Mike Nixon RC .40 .12
❑ BDP16 Nick Swisher RC 2.50 .75
❑ BDP17 Cole Hamels RC 4.00 1.20
❑ BDP18 Brian Dopirak RC 3.00 .90
❑ BDP19 James Loney RC 2.00 .60
❑ BDP20 Denard Span RC .40 .12
❑ BDP21 Billy Petrick RC .40 .12
❑ BDP22 Jared Doyle RC .40 .12
❑ BDP23 Jeff Francoeur RC 3.00 .90
❑ BDP24 Nick Bourgeois RC .40 .12
❑ BDP25 Matt Cain RC 2.50 .75
❑ BDP26 John McCurdy RC .40 .12
❑ BDP27 Mark Kiger RC .40 .12
❑ BDP28 Bill Murphy RC .50 .15
❑ BDP29 Matt Craig RC .50 .15
❑ BDP30 Mike Megrew RC 1.00 .30
❑ BDP31 Ben Crockett RC .40 .12
❑ BDP32 Luke Hagerty RC .40 .12
❑ BDP33 Matt Whitney RC .50 .15
❑ BDP34 Dan Meyer RC 1.00 .30
❑ BDP35 Jeremy Brown RC .75 .23
❑ BDP36 Doug Johnson RC .40 .12
❑ BDP37 Steve Obenchain RC .40 .12
❑ BDP38 Matt Clanton RC .40 .12
❑ BDP39 Mark Teahen RC 1.50 .45
❑ BDP40 Tom Carrow RC .40 .12
❑ BDP41 Micah Schilling RC .40 .12
❑ BDP42 Blair Johnson RC .40 .12
❑ BDP43 Jason Pridie RC 1.00 .30
❑ BDP44 Joey Votto RC 1.25 .35
❑ BDP45 Taber Lee RC .40 .12
❑ BDP46 Adam Peterson RC .40 .12
❑ BDP47 Adam Donachie RC .40 .12
❑ BDP48 Josh Murray RC .40 .12
❑ BDP49 Brent Clevlen RC 1.00 .30

Card		
❑ BDP50 Chad Pleiness RC	.40	.12
❑ BDP51 Zach Hammes RC	.40	.12
❑ BDP52 Chris Snyder RC	.75	.23
❑ BDP53 Chris Smith RC	.40	.12
❑ BDP54 Justin Maureau RC	.40	.12
❑ BDP55 David Bush RC	1.00	.30
❑ BDP56 Tim Gilhooly RC	.40	.12
❑ BDP57 Blair Barbier RC	.40	.12
❑ BDP58 Zach Segovia RC	.50	.15
❑ BDP59 Jeremy Reed RC	3.00	.90
❑ BDP60 Matt Pender RC	.40	.12
❑ BDP61 Eric Thomas RC	.40	.12
❑ BDP62 Justin Jones RC	1.25	.35
❑ BDP63 Brian Slocum RC	.40	.12
❑ BDP64 Larry Broadway RC	1.00	.30
❑ BDP65 Bo Flowers RC	.40	.12
❑ BDP66 Scott White RC	.40	.12
❑ BDP67 Steve Stanley RC	.40	.12
❑ BDP68 Alex Merricks RC	.40	.12
❑ BDP69 Josh Womack RC	.40	.12
❑ BDP70 Dave Jensen RC	.40	.12
❑ BDP71 Curtis Granderson RC	1.50	.45
❑ BDP72 Pat Osborn RC	.40	.12
❑ BDP73 Nic Carter RC	.40	.12
❑ BDP74 Mitch Talbot RC	.40	.12
❑ BDP75 Don Murphy RC	.40	.12
❑ BDP76 Val Majewski RC	1.25	.35
❑ BDP77 Javy Rodriguez RC	.40	.12
❑ BDP78 Fernando Pacheco RC	.40	.12
❑ BDP79 Steve Russell RC	.40	.12
❑ BDP80 Jon Slack RC	.40	.12
❑ BDP81 John Baker RC	.40	.12
❑ BDP82 Aaron Coonrod RC	.40	.12
❑ BDP83 Josh Johnson RC	.40	.12
❑ BDP84 Jake Blalock RC	1.50	.45
❑ BDP85 Alex Hart RC	.75	.23
❑ BDP86 Wes Bankston RC	1.25	.35
❑ BDP87 Josh Rupe RC	.40	.12
❑ BDP88 Dan Cevette RC	.40	.12
❑ BDP89 Kiel Fisher RC	.50	.15
❑ BDP90 Alan Rick RC	.40	.12
❑ BDP91 Charlie Morton RC	.40	.12
❑ BDP92 Chad Spann RC	.75	.23
❑ BDP93 Kyle Boyer RC	.40	.12
❑ BDP94 Bob Malek RC	.40	.12
❑ BDP95 Ryan Rodriguez RC	.40	.12
❑ BDP96 Jordan Renz RC	.40	.12
❑ BDP97 Randy Frye RC	.40	.12
❑ BDP98 Rich Hill RC	.40	.12
❑ BDP99 B.J. Upton RC	8.00	2.40
❑ BDP100 Dan Christensen RC	.40	.12
❑ BDP101 Casey Kotchman RC	3.00	.90
❑ BDP102 Eric Good RC	.30	.09
❑ BDP103 Mike Fontenot RC	.40	.12
❑ BDP104 John Webb RC	.40	.12
❑ BDP105 Jason Dubois RC	1.25	.35
❑ BDP106 Ryan Kibler RC	.40	.12
❑ BDP107 Jhohny Peralta RC	1.25	.35
❑ BDP108 Kirk Saarloos RC	.40	.12
❑ BDP109 Rhett Parrott RC	.40	.12
❑ BDP110 Jason Grove RC	.40	.12
❑ BDP111 Colt Griffin RC	.50	.15
❑ BDP112 Dallas McPherson RC	6.00	1.80
❑ BDP113 Oliver Perez RC	3.00	.90
❑ BDP114 Mar. McDougall RC	.40	.12
❑ BDP115 Mike Wood RC	.40	.12
❑ BDP116 Scott Hairston RC	1.50	.45
❑ BDP117 Jason Simontacchi RC	.40	.12
❑ BDP118 Taggert Bozied RC	.75	.23
❑ BDP119 Shelley Duncan RC	.40	.12
❑ BDP120 Dontrelle Willis RC	3.00	.90
❑ BDP121 Sean Burnett	.30	.09
❑ BDP122 Aaron Cook	.30	.09
❑ BDP123 Brett Evert	.30	.09
❑ BDP124 Jimmy Journell	.30	.09
❑ BDP125 Brett Myers	.30	.09
❑ BDP126 Brad Baker	.30	.09
❑ BDP127 Billy Traber RC	1.00	.30
❑ BDP128 Adam Wainwright	.30	.09
❑ BDP129 Jason Young RC	.40	.12
❑ BDP130 John Buck	.30	.09
❑ BDP131 Kevin Cash RC	.40	.12
❑ BDP132 Jason Stokes RC	3.00	.90
❑ BDP133 Drew Henson	.30	.09
❑ BDP134 Chad Tracy RC	1.50	.45
❑ BDP135 Orlando Hudson	.30	.09
❑ BDP136 Brandon Phillips	.30	.09
❑ BDP137 Joe Borchard	.30	.09
❑ BDP138 Marlon Byrd	.30	.09
❑ BDP139 Carl Crawford	.30	.09
❑ BDP140 Michael Restovich	.30	.09
❑ BDP141 Corey Hart RC	1.25	.35
❑ BDP142 Edwin Almonte	.30	.09
❑ BDP143 Francis Beltran RC	.40	.12
❑ BDP144 Jorge De La Rosa RC	.40	.12
❑ BDP145 Gerardo Garcia RC	.40	.12
❑ BDP146 Franklyn German RC	.40	.12
❑ BDP147 Francisco Liriano	.50	.15
❑ BDP148 Francisco Rodriguez	.30	.09
❑ BDP149 Ricardo Rodriguez	.30	.09
❑ BDP150 Seung Song	.30	.09
❑ BDP151 John Stephens	.30	.09
❑ BDP152 Justin Huber RC	.75	.23
❑ BDP153 Victor Martinez	.75	.23
❑ BDP154 Hee Seop Choi	.30	.09
❑ BDP155 Justin Morneau	.75	.23
❑ BDP156 Miguel Cabrera	1.25	.35
❑ BDP157 Victor Diaz RC	1.50	.45
❑ BDP158 Jose Reyes	.50	.15
❑ BDP159 Omar Infante	.30	.09
❑ BDP160 Angel Berroa	.30	.09
❑ BDP161 Tony Alvarez	.30	.09
❑ BDP162 Shin Soo Choo RC	1.25	.35
❑ BDP163 Wily Mo Pena	.30	.09
❑ BDP164 Andres Torres	.30	.09
❑ BDP165 Jose Lopez RC	3.00	.90

2003 Bowman

	Nm-Mt	Ex-Mt
COMPLETE SET (330)	80.00	24.00
COMMON CARD (1-155)	.30	.09
COMMON CARD (156-330)	.30	.09
❑ 1 Garret Anderson	.30	.09
❑ 2 Derek Jeter	2.00	.60
❑ 3 Gary Sheffield	.30	.09
❑ 4 Matt Morris	.30	.09
❑ 5 Derek Lowe	.30	.09
❑ 6 Andy Van Hekken	.30	.09
❑ 7 Sammy Sosa	1.25	.35
❑ 8 Ken Griffey Jr.	1.25	.35
❑ 9 Omar Vizquel	.50	.15
❑ 10 Jorge Posada	.50	.15
❑ 11 Lance Berkman	.30	.09
❑ 12 Mike Sweeney	.30	.09
❑ 13 Adrian Beltre	.50	.15
❑ 14 Richie Sexson	.30	.09
❑ 15 A.J. Pierzynski	.30	.09
❑ 16 Bartolo Colon	.30	.09
❑ 17 Mike Mussina	.50	.15
❑ 18 Paul Byrd	.30	.09
❑ 19 Bobby Abreu	.30	.09
❑ 20 Miguel Tejada	.30	.09
❑ 21 Aramis Ramirez	.30	.09
❑ 22 Edgardo Alfonzo	.30	.09
❑ 23 Edgar Martinez	.50	.15
❑ 24 Albert Pujols	1.50	.45
❑ 25 Carl Crawford	.30	.09
❑ 26 Eric Hinske	.30	.09
❑ 27 Tim Salmon	.50	.15
❑ 28 Luis Gonzalez	.30	.09
❑ 29 Jay Gibbons	.30	.09
❑ 30 John Smoltz	.50	.15
❑ 31 Tim Wakefield	.30	.09
❑ 32 Mark Prior	.75	.23
❑ 33 Magglio Ordonez	.30	.09
❑ 34 Adam Dunn	.50	.15
❑ 35 Larry Walker	.50	.15
❑ 36 Luis Castillo	.30	.09
❑ 37 Wade Miller	.30	.09
❑ 38 Carlos Beltran	.50	.15
❑ 39 Odalis Perez	.30	.09
❑ 40 Alex Sanchez	.30	.09
❑ 41 Torii Hunter	.30	.09
❑ 42 Cliff Floyd	.30	.09
❑ 43 Andy Pettitte	.50	.15
❑ 44 Francisco Rodriguez	.30	.09
❑ 45 Eric Chavez	.30	.09
❑ 46 Kevin Millwood	.30	.09
❑ 47 Dennis Tankersley	.30	.09
❑ 48 Hideo Nomo	.75	.23
❑ 49 Freddy Garcia	.30	.09
❑ 50 Randy Johnson	.75	.23
❑ 51 Aubrey Huff	.30	.09
❑ 52 Carlos Delgado	.30	.09
❑ 53 Troy Glaus	.30	.09
❑ 54 Junior Spivey	.30	.09
❑ 55 Mike Hampton	.30	.09
❑ 56 Sidney Ponson	.30	.09
❑ 57 Aaron Boone	.30	.09
❑ 58 Kerry Wood	.75	.23
❑ 59 Runelvys Hernandez	.30	.09
❑ 60 Nomar Garciaparra	1.25	.35
❑ 61 Todd Helton	.50	.15
❑ 62 Mike Lowell	.30	.09
❑ 63 Roy Oswalt	.30	.09
❑ 64 Raul Ibanez	.30	.09
❑ 65 Brian Jordan	.30	.09
❑ 66 Geoff Jenkins	.30	.09
❑ 67 Jermaine Dye	.30	.09
❑ 68 Tom Glavine	.50	.15
❑ 69 Bernie Williams	.50	.15
❑ 70 Vladimir Guerrero	.75	.23
❑ 71 Mark Mulder	.30	.09
❑ 72 Jimmy Rollins	.30	.09
❑ 73 Oliver Perez	.30	.09
❑ 74 Rich Aurilia	.30	.09
❑ 75 Joel Pineiro	.30	.09
❑ 76 J.D. Drew	.30	.09
❑ 77 Ivan Rodriguez	.75	.23
❑ 78 Josh Phelps	.30	.09
❑ 79 Darin Erstad	.30	.09
❑ 80 Curt Schilling	.30	.09
❑ 81 Paul Lo Duca	.30	.09
❑ 82 Marty Cordova	.30	.09
❑ 83 Manny Ramirez	.50	.15
❑ 84 Bobby Hill	.30	.09
❑ 85 Paul Konerko	.30	.09
❑ 86 Austin Kearns	.30	.09
❑ 87 Jason Jennings	.30	.09
❑ 88 Brad Penny	.30	.09
❑ 89 Jeff Bagwell	.50	.15
❑ 90 Shawn Green	.30	.09
❑ 91 Jason Schmidt	.30	.09
❑ 92 Doug Mientkiewicz	.30	.09
❑ 93 Jose Vidro	.30	.09
❑ 94 Bret Boone	.30	.09
❑ 95 Jason Giambi	.30	.09
❑ 96 Barry Zito	.30	.09
❑ 97 Roy Halladay	.30	.09
❑ 98 Pat Burrell	.30	.09
❑ 99 Sean Burroughs	.30	.09
❑ 100 Barry Bonds	2.00	.60
❑ 101 Kazuhiro Sasaki	.30	.09
❑ 102 Fernando Vina	.30	.09
❑ 103 Chan Ho Park	.30	.09
❑ 104 Andruw Jones	.30	.09
❑ 105 Adam Kennedy	.30	.09
❑ 106 Shea Hillenbrand	.30	.09
❑ 107 Greg Maddux	1.25	.35
❑ 108 Jim Edmonds	.30	.09
❑ 109 Pedro Martinez	.75	.23
❑ 110 Moises Alou	.30	.09
❑ 111 Jeff Weaver	.30	.09
❑ 112 C.C. Sabathia	.30	.09
❑ 113 Robert Fick	.30	.09
❑ 114 A.J. Burnett	.30	.09
❑ 115 Jeff Kent	.30	.09
❑ 116 Kevin Brown	.30	.09

- ❑ 117 Rafael Furcal .30 .09
- ❑ 118 Cristian Guzman .30 .09
- ❑ 119 Brad Wilkerson .30 .09
- ❑ 120 Mike Piazza 1.25 .35
- ❑ 121 Alfonso Soriano .50 .15
- ❑ 122 Mark Ellis .30 .09
- ❑ 123 Vicente Padilla .30 .09
- ❑ 124 Eric Gagne .75 .23
- ❑ 125 Ryan Klesko .30 .09
- ❑ 126 Ichiro Suzuki 1.25 .35
- ❑ 127 Tony Batista .30 .09
- ❑ 128 Roberto Alomar .50 .15
- ❑ 129 Alex Rodriguez 1.25 .35
- ❑ 130 Jim Thome .75 .23
- ❑ 131 Jarrod Washburn .30 .09
- ❑ 132 Orlando Hudson .30 .09
- ❑ 133 Chipper Jones .75 .23
- ❑ 134 Rodrigo Lopez .30 .09
- ❑ 135 Johnny Damon .75 .23
- ❑ 136 Matt Clement .30 .09
- ❑ 137 Frank Thomas .75 .23
- ❑ 138 Ellis Burks .30 .09
- ❑ 139 Carlos Pena .30 .09
- ❑ 140 Josh Beckett .30 .09
- ❑ 141 Joe Randa .30 .09
- ❑ 142 Brian Giles .30 .09
- ❑ 143 Kazuhisa Ishii .30 .09
- ❑ 144 Corey Koskie .30 .09
- ❑ 145 Orlando Cabrera .30 .09
- ❑ 146 Mark Buehrle .30 .09
- ❑ 147 Roger Clemens 1.50 .45
- ❑ 148 Tim Hudson .30 .09
- ❑ 149 Randy Wolf UER .30 .09
  resume says AL leaders,
  he pitches in NL
- ❑ 150 Josh Fogg .30 .09
- ❑ 151 Phil Nevin .30 .09
- ❑ 152 John Olerud .30 .09
- ❑ 153 Scott Rolen .75 .23
- ❑ 154 Joe Kennedy .30 .09
- ❑ 155 Rafael Palmeiro .50 .15
- ❑ 156 Chad Hutchinson .30 .09
- ❑ 157 Quincy Carter XRC .50 .15
- ❑ 158 Hee Seop Choi .30 .09
- ❑ 159 Joe Borchard .30 .09
- ❑ 160 Brandon Phillips .30 .09
- ❑ 161 Wily Mo Pena .30 .09
- ❑ 162 Victor Martinez .50 .15
- ❑ 163 Jason Stokes .50 .15
- ❑ 164 Ken Harvey .30 .09
- ❑ 165 Juan Rivera .30 .09
- ❑ 166 Jose Contreras RC 1.00 .30
- ❑ 167 Dan Haren RC .75 .23
- ❑ 168 Michel Hernandez RC .40 .12
- ❑ 169 Eider Torres RC .40 .12
- ❑ 170 Chris De La Cruz RC .40 .12
- ❑ 171 Ramon Nivar-Martinez RC .75 .23
- ❑ 172 Mike Adams RC .40 .12
- ❑ 173 Justin Arneson RC .40 .12
- ❑ 174 Jamie Athas RC .40 .12
- ❑ 175 Dwaine Bacon RC .40 .12
- ❑ 176 Clint Barmes RC .50 .15
- ❑ 177 B.J. Barns RC .40 .12
- ❑ 178 Tyler Johnson RC .40 .12
- ❑ 179 Bobby Basham RC .50 .15
- ❑ 180 T.J. Bohn RC .40 .12
- ❑ 181 J.D. Durbin RC .75 .23
- ❑ 182 Brandon Bowe RC .40 .12
- ❑ 183 Craig Brazell RC .50 .15
- ❑ 184 Dusty Brown RC .40 .12
- ❑ 185 Brian Bruney RC .50 .15
- ❑ 186 Greg Bruso RC .40 .12
- ❑ 187 Jaime Bubela RC .40 .12
- ❑ 188 Bryan Bullington RC 1.25 .35
- ❑ 189 Brian Burgamy RC .40 .12
- ❑ 190 Eny Cabreja RC .40 .12
- ❑ 191 Daniel Cabrera RC 1.00 .30
- ❑ 192 Ryan Cameron RC .40 .12
- ❑ 193 Lance Caraccioli RC .40 .12
- ❑ 194 David Cash RC .40 .12
- ❑ 195 Bernie Castro RC .40 .12
- ❑ 196 Ismael Castro RC .50 .15
- ❑ 197 Daryl Clark RC .50 .15
- ❑ 198 Jeff Clark RC .40 .12
- ❑ 199 Chris Colton RC .40 .12
- ❑ 200 Dexter Cooper RC .40 .12
- ❑ 201 Callix Crabbe RC .50 .15
- ❑ 202 Chien-Ming Wang RC 1.00 .30
- ❑ 203 Eric Crozier RC .50 .15
- ❑ 204 Nook Logan RC .40 .12
- ❑ 205 David DeJesus RC .50 .15
- ❑ 206 Matt DeMarco RC .40 .12
- ❑ 207 Chris Duncan RC .40 .12
- ❑ 208 Eric Eckenstahler .30 .09
- ❑ 209 Willie Eyre RC .40 .12
- ❑ 210 Evel Bastida-Martinez RC .40 .12
- ❑ 211 Chris Fallon RC .40 .12
- ❑ 212 Mike Flannery RC .40 .12
- ❑ 213 Mike O'Keefe RC .40 .12
- ❑ 214 Ben Francisco RC .50 .15
- ❑ 215 Kason Gabbard RC .40 .12
- ❑ 216 Mike Gallo RC .40 .12
- ❑ 217 Jairo Garcia RC .75 .23
- ❑ 218 Angel Garcia RC .50 .15
- ❑ 219 Michael Garciaparra RC .75 .23
- ❑ 220 Joey Gomes RC .40 .12
- ❑ 221 Dusty Gomon RC .50 .15
- ❑ 222 Bryan Grace RC .40 .12
- ❑ 223 Tyson Graham RC .40 .12
- ❑ 224 Henry Guerrero RC .40 .12
- ❑ 225 Franklin Gutierrez RC 2.00 .60
- ❑ 226 Carlos Guzman RC .50 .15
- ❑ 227 Matthew Hagen RC .75 .23
- ❑ 228 Josh Hall RC .50 .15
- ❑ 229 Rob Hammock RC .50 .15
- ❑ 230 Brendan Harris RC .50 .15
- ❑ 231 Gary Harris RC .40 .12
- ❑ 232 Clay Hensley RC .40 .12
- ❑ 233 Michael Hinckley RC 1.00 .30
- ❑ 234 Luis Hodge RC .40 .12
- ❑ 235 Donnie Hood RC .50 .15
- ❑ 236 Travis Ishikawa RC .40 .12
- ❑ 237 Edwin Jackson RC 2.50 .75
- ❑ 238 Ardley Jansen RC .50 .15
- ❑ 239 Ferenc Jongejan RC .40 .12
- ❑ 240 Matt Kata RC .75 .23
- ❑ 241 Kazuhiro Takeoka RC .40 .12
- ❑ 242 Beau Kemp RC .40 .12
- ❑ 243 Il Kim RC .40 .12
- ❑ 244 Brennan King RC .40 .12
- ❑ 245 Chris Kroski RC .40 .12
- ❑ 246 Jason Kubel RC 2.00 .60
- ❑ 247 Pete LaForest RC .50 .15
- ❑ 248 Wil Ledezma RC .50 .15
- ❑ 249 Jeremy Bonderman RC .75 .23
- ❑ 250 Gonzalo Lopez RC .40 .12
- ❑ 251 Brian Luderer RC .40 .12
- ❑ 252 Ruddy Lugo RC .40 .12
- ❑ 253 Wayne Lydon RC .40 .12
- ❑ 254 Mark Malaska RC .40 .12
- ❑ 255 Andy Marte RC 2.50 .75
- ❑ 256 Tyler Martin RC .40 .12
- ❑ 257 Branden Florence RC .40 .12
- ❑ 258 Aneudis Mateo RC .40 .12
- ❑ 259 Derell McCall RC .40 .12
- ❑ 260 Brian McCann RC .75 .23
- ❑ 261 Mike McNutt RC .40 .12
- ❑ 262 Jacabo Meque RC .40 .12
- ❑ 263 Derek Michaelis RC .40 .12
- ❑ 264 Aaron Miles RC 1.00 .30
- ❑ 265 Jose Morales RC .40 .12
- ❑ 266 Dustin Moseley RC .50 .15
- ❑ 267 Adrian Myers RC .40 .12
- ❑ 268 Dan Neil RC .40 .12
- ❑ 269 Jon Nelson RC .50 .15
- ❑ 270 Mike Neu RC .40 .12
- ❑ 271 Leigh Neuage RC .40 .12
- ❑ 272 Wes O'Brien RC .40 .12
- ❑ 273 Trent Oeltjen RC .50 .15
- ❑ 274 Tim Olson RC .50 .15
- ❑ 275 David Pahucki RC .40 .12
- ❑ 276 Nathan Panther RC .75 .23
- ❑ 277 Arnie Munoz RC .40 .12
- ❑ 278 Dave Pember RC .40 .12
- ❑ 279 Jason Perry RC .75 .23
- ❑ 280 Matthew Peterson RC .40 .12
- ❑ 281 Ryan Shealy RC .75 .23
- ❑ 282 Jorge Piedra RC .50 .15
- ❑ 283 Simon Pond RC .75 .23
- ❑ 284 Aaron Rakers RC .40 .12
- ❑ 285 Hanley Ramirez RC 2.00 .60
- ❑ 286 Manuel Ramirez RC .50 .15
- ❑ 287 Kevin Randel RC .40 .12
- ❑ 288 Darrell Rasner RC .40 .12
- ❑ 289 Prentice Redman RC .40 .12
- ❑ 290 Eric Reed RC .75 .23
- ❑ 291 Wilton Reynolds RC .50 .15
- ❑ 292 Eric Riggs RC .50 .15
- ❑ 293 Carlos Rijo RC .40 .12
- ❑ 294 Rajai Davis RC .50 .15
- ❑ 295 Aron Weston RC .40 .12
- ❑ 296 Arturo Rivas RC .40 .12
- ❑ 297 Kyle Roat RC .40 .12
- ❑ 298 Bubba Nelson RC .50 .15
- ❑ 299 Levi Robinson RC .40 .12
- ❑ 300 Ray Sadler RC .40 .12
- ❑ 301 Gary Schneidmiller RC .40 .12
- ❑ 302 Jon Schuerholz RC .40 .12
- ❑ 303 Corey Shafer RC .50 .15
- ❑ 304 Brian Shackelford RC .40 .12
- ❑ 305 Bill Simon RC .40 .12
- ❑ 306 Haj Turay RC .50 .15
- ❑ 307 Sean Smith RC .50 .15
- ❑ 308 Ryan Spataro RC .40 .12
- ❑ 309 Jemel Spearman RC .40 .12
- ❑ 310 Keith Stamler RC .40 .12
- ❑ 311 Luke Steidlmayer RC .40 .12
- ❑ 312 Adam Stern RC .40 .12
- ❑ 313 Jay Sitzman RC .40 .12
- ❑ 314 Thomari Story-Harden RC .50 .15
- ❑ 315 Terry Tiffee RC .75 .23
- ❑ 316 Nick Trzesniak RC .40 .12
- ❑ 317 Denny Tussen RC .40 .12
- ❑ 318 Scott Tyler RC .50 .15
- ❑ 319 Shane Victorino RC .40 .12
- ❑ 320 Doug Waechter RC .50 .15
- ❑ 321 Brandon Watson RC .40 .12
- ❑ 322 Todd Wellemeyer RC .50 .15
- ❑ 323 Eli Whiteside RC .40 .12
- ❑ 324 Josh Willingham RC .50 .15
- ❑ 325 Travis Wong RC .50 .15
- ❑ 326 Brian Wright RC .40 .12
- ❑ 327 Kevin Youkilis RC 1.50 .45
- ❑ 328 Andy Sisco RC 1.00 .30
- ❑ 329 Dustin Yount RC .50 .15
- ❑ 330 Andrew Dominique RC .40 .12
- ❑ NNO Eric Hinske Bat 15.00 4.50
  Jason Jennings Jsy
  ROY Relic

2003 Bowman Draft

	MINT	NRMT
COMPLETE SET (165)	40.00	18.00

- ❑ 1 Dontrelle Willis .50 .23
- ❑ 2 Freddy Sanchez .30 .14
- ❑ 3 Miguel Cabrera .75 .35
- ❑ 4 Ryan Ludwick .30 .14
- ❑ 5 Ty Wigginton .30 .14
- ❑ 6 Mark Teixeira .30 .14
- ❑ 7 Trey Hodges .30 .14
- ❑ 8 Laynce Nix .30 .14
- ❑ 9 Antonio Perez .30 .14
- ❑ 10 Jody Gerut .30 .14
- ❑ 11 Jae Weong Seo .30 .14
- ❑ 12 Erick Almonte .30 .14
- ❑ 13 Lyle Overbay .30 .14
- ❑ 14 Billy Traber .30 .14
- ❑ 15 Andres Torres .30 .14

❑ 16	Jose Valverde	.30	.14
❑ 17	Aaron Heilman	.30	.14
❑ 18	Brandon Larson	.30	.14
❑ 19	Jung Bong	.30	.14
❑ 20	Jesse Foppert	.30	.14
❑ 21	Angel Berroa	.30	.14
❑ 22	Jeff DaVanon	.30	.14
❑ 23	Kurt Ainsworth	.30	.14
❑ 24	Brandon Claussen	.30	.14
❑ 25	Xavier Nady	.30	.14
❑ 26	Travis Hafner	.30	.14
❑ 27	Jerome Williams	.30	.14
❑ 28	Jose Reyes	.30	.14
❑ 29	Sergio Mitre RC	.50	.23
❑ 30	Bo Hart RC	.50	.23
❑ 31	Adam Miller RC	1.50	.70
❑ 32	Brian Finch RC	.40	.18
❑ 33	Taylor Mattingly RC	1.25	.55
❑ 34	Daric Barton RC	2.50	1.10
❑ 35	Chris Ray RC	.50	.23
❑ 36	Jarrod Saltalamacchia RC	.75	.35
❑ 37	Dennis Dove RC	.50	.23
❑ 38	James Houser RC	.50	.23
❑ 39	Clint King RC	.75	.35
❑ 40	Lou Palmisano RC	1.25	.55
❑ 41	Dan Moore RC	.40	.18
❑ 42	Craig Stansberry RC	.50	.23
❑ 43	Jo Jo Reyes RC	.50	.23
❑ 44	Jake Stevens RC	1.25	.55
❑ 45	Tom Gorzelanny RC	.75	.35
❑ 46	Brian Marshall RC	.40	.18
❑ 47	Scott Beerer RC	.40	.18
❑ 48	Javi Herrera RC	.50	.23
❑ 49	Steve LeRud RC	.75	.35
❑ 50	Josh Banks RC	1.00	.45
❑ 51	Jon Papelbon RC	.40	.18
❑ 52	Juan Valdes RC	.50	.23
❑ 53	Beau Vaughan RC	.50	.23
❑ 54	Matt Chico RC	1.00	.45
❑ 55	Todd Jennings RC	.50	.23
❑ 56	Anthony Gwynn RC	1.25	.55
❑ 57	Matt Harrison RC	.75	.35
❑ 58	Aaron Marsden RC	.50	.23
❑ 59	Casey Abrams RC	.40	.18
❑ 60	Cory Stuart RC	.40	.18
❑ 61	Mike Wagner RC	.40	.18
❑ 62	Jordan Pratt RC	.50	.23
❑ 63	Andre Randolph RC	.50	.23
❑ 64	Blake Balkcom RC	.50	.23
❑ 65	Josh Muecke RC	.40	.18
❑ 66	Jamie D'Antona RC	1.50	.70
❑ 67	Cole Seifrig RC	.75	.35
❑ 68	Josh Anderson RC	1.00	.45
❑ 69	Matt Lorenzo RC	.50	.23
❑ 70	Nate Spears RC	.75	.35
❑ 71	Chris Goodman RC	.40	.18
❑ 72	Brian McFall RC	.75	.35
❑ 73	Billy Hogan RC	.50	.23
❑ 74	Jamie Romak RC	.50	.23
❑ 75	Jeff Cook RC	.50	.23
❑ 76	Brooks McNiven RC	.40	.18
❑ 77	Xavier Paul RC	1.50	.70
❑ 78	Bob Zimmermann RC	.40	.18
❑ 79	Mickey Hall RC	.50	.23
❑ 80	Shaun Marcum RC	.40	.18
❑ 81	Matt Nachreiner RC	.50	.23
❑ 82	Chris Kinsey RC	.40	.18
❑ 83	Jonathan Fulton RC	.50	.23
❑ 84	Edgardo Baez RC	.50	.23
❑ 85	Robert Valido RC	.75	.35
❑ 86	Kenny Lewis RC	.50	.23
❑ 87	Trent Peterson RC	.40	.18
❑ 88	Johnny Woodard RC	.50	.23
❑ 89	Wes Littleton RC	.50	.23
❑ 90	Sean Rodriguez RC	1.25	.55
❑ 91	Kyle Pearson RC	.40	.18
❑ 92	Josh Rainwater RC	.50	.23
❑ 93	Travis Schlichting RC	.50	.23
❑ 94	Tim Battle RC	.50	.23
❑ 95	Aaron Hill RC	1.00	.45
❑ 96	Bob McCrory RC	.40	.18
❑ 97	Rick Guarno RC	.50	.23
❑ 98	Brandon Yarbrough RC	.40	.18
❑ 99	Peter Stonard RC	.40	.18
❑ 100	Darin Downs RC	.50	.23
❑ 101	Matt Bruback RC	.30	.14
❑ 102	Danny Garcia RC	.40	.18
❑ 103	Cory Stewart RC	.40	.18
❑ 104	Ferdin Tejeda RC	.40	.18
❑ 105	Kade Johnson RC	.40	.18
❑ 106	Andrew Brown RC	.50	.23
❑ 107	Aquilino Lopez RC	.40	.18
❑ 108	Stephen Randolph RC	.40	.18
❑ 109	Dave Matranga RC	.40	.18
❑ 110	Dustin McGowan RC	.75	.35
❑ 111	Juan Camacho RC	.40	.18
❑ 112	Cliff Lee	.30	.14
❑ 113	Jeff Duncan RC	.50	.23
❑ 114	C.J. Wilson	.30	.14
❑ 115	Brandon Roberson RC	.40	.18
❑ 116	David Corrente RC	.40	.18
❑ 117	Kevin Beavers RC	.40	.18
❑ 118	Anthony Webster RC	.50	.23
❑ 119	Oscar Villarreal RC	.40	.18
❑ 120	Hong-Chih Kuo RC	.75	.35
❑ 121	Josh Barfield	.30	.14
❑ 122	Denny Bautista	.30	.14
❑ 123	Chris Burke RC	.75	.35
❑ 124	Robinson Cano RC	1.00	.45
❑ 125	Jose Castillo	.30	.14
❑ 126	Neal Cotts	.30	.14
❑ 127	Jorge De La Rosa	.30	.14
❑ 128	J.D. Durbin	.75	.35
❑ 129	Edwin Encarnacion	.30	.14
❑ 130	Gavin Floyd	.30	.14
❑ 131	Alexis Gomez	.30	.14
❑ 132	Edgar Gonzalez RC	.40	.18
❑ 133	Khalil Greene	1.50	.70
❑ 134	Zack Greinke	.50	.23
❑ 135	Franklin Gutierrez	.75	.35
❑ 136	Rich Harden	.50	.23
❑ 137	J.J. Hardy RC	1.50	.70
❑ 138	Ryan Howard RC	3.00	1.35
❑ 139	Justin Huber	.30	.14
❑ 140	David Kelton	.30	.14
❑ 141	Dave Krynzel	.30	.14
❑ 142	Pete LaForest	.50	.23
❑ 143	Adam LaRoche	.30	.14
❑ 144	Preston Larrison RC	.50	.23
❑ 145	John Maine RC	1.50	.70
❑ 146	Andy Marte	1.25	.55
❑ 147	Jeff Mathis	.30	.14
❑ 148	Joe Mauer UER Card has playing for New Haven	.75	.35
❑ 149	Clint Nageotte	.30	.14
❑ 150	Chris Narveson	.30	.14
❑ 151	Ramon Nivar	.75	.35
❑ 152	Felix Pie RC	2.00	.90
❑ 153	Guillermo Quiroz RC	.75	.35
❑ 154	Rene Reyes	.30	.14
❑ 155	Royce Ring	.30	.14
❑ 156	Alexis Rios	.50	.23
❑ 157	Grady Sizemore	.30	.14
❑ 158	Stephen Smitherman	.30	.14
❑ 159	Seung Song	.30	.14
❑ 160	Scott Thorman	.30	.14
❑ 161	Chad Tracy	.30	.14
❑ 162	Chin-Hui Tsao	.30	.14
❑ 163	John VanBenschoten	.30	.14
❑ 164	Kevin Youkilis	1.50	.70
❑ 165	Chien-Ming Wang	1.00	.45

2004 Bowman

		Nm-Mt	Ex-Mt
	COMPLETE SET (330)	80.00	24.00
	ROY ODDS 1:829 H, 1:284 HTA, 1:1632 R		
❑ 1	Garret Anderson	.30	.09
❑ 2	Larry Walker	.50	.15
❑ 3	Derek Jeter	1.50	.45
❑ 4	Curt Schilling	.75	.23
❑ 5	Carlos Zambrano	.30	.09
❑ 6	Shawn Green	.30	.09
❑ 7	Manny Ramirez	.50	.15
❑ 8	Randy Johnson	.75	.23
❑ 9	Jeremy Bonderman	.30	.09
❑ 10	Alfonso Soriano	.50	.15
❑ 11	Scott Rolen	.75	.23
❑ 12	Kerry Wood	.75	.23
❑ 13	Eric Gagne	.75	.23
❑ 14	Ryan Klesko	.30	.09
❑ 15	Kevin Millar	.30	.09
❑ 16	Ty Wigginton	.30	.09
❑ 17	David Ortiz	.75	.23
❑ 18	Luis Castillo	.30	.09
❑ 19	Bernie Williams	.50	.15
❑ 20	Edgar Renteria	.30	.09
❑ 21	Matt Kata	.30	.09
❑ 22	Bartolo Colon	.30	.09
❑ 23	Derrek Lee	.30	.09
❑ 24	Gary Sheffield	.30	.09
❑ 25	Nomar Garciaparra	1.25	.35
❑ 26	Kevin Millwood	.30	.09
❑ 27	Corey Patterson	.30	.09
❑ 28	Carlos Beltran	.50	.15
❑ 29	Mike Lieberthal	.30	.09
❑ 30	Troy Glaus	.30	.09
❑ 31	Preston Wilson	.30	.09
❑ 32	Jorge Posada	.50	.15
❑ 33	Bo Hart	.30	.09
❑ 34	Mark Prior	.75	.23
❑ 35	Hideo Nomo	.75	.23
❑ 36	Jason Kendall	.30	.09
❑ 37	Roger Clemens	1.50	.45
❑ 38	Dmitri Young	.30	.09
❑ 39	Jason Giambi	.30	.09
❑ 40	Jim Edmonds	.30	.09
❑ 41	Ryan Ludwick	.30	.09
❑ 42	Brandon Webb	.30	.09
❑ 43	Todd Helton	.50	.15
❑ 44	Jacque Jones	.30	.09
❑ 45	Jamie Moyer	.30	.09
❑ 46	Tim Salmon	.50	.15
❑ 47	Kelvim Escobar	.30	.09
❑ 48	Tony Batista	.30	.09
❑ 49	Nick Johnson	.30	.09
❑ 50	Jim Thome	.75	.23
❑ 51	Casey Blake	.30	.09
❑ 52	Trot Nixon	.30	.09
❑ 53	Luis Gonzalez	.30	.09
❑ 54	Dontrelle Willis	.30	.09
❑ 55	Mike Mussina	.50	.15
❑ 56	Carl Crawford	.30	.09
❑ 57	Mark Buehrle	.30	.09
❑ 58	Scott Podsednik	.30	.09
❑ 59	Brian Giles	.30	.09
❑ 60	Rafael Furcal	.30	.09
❑ 61	Miguel Cabrera	.50	.15
❑ 62	Rich Harden	.30	.09
❑ 63	Mark Teixeira	.30	.09
❑ 64	Frank Thomas	.75	.23
❑ 65	Johan Santana	.50	.15
❑ 66	Jason Schmidt	.30	.09
❑ 67	Aramis Ramirez	.30	.09
❑ 68	Jose Reyes	.30	.09
❑ 69	Magglio Ordonez	.30	.09
❑ 70	Mike Sweeney	.30	.09
❑ 71	Eric Chavez	.30	.09
❑ 72	Rocco Baldelli	.30	.09
❑ 73	Sammy Sosa	1.25	.35
❑ 74	Javy Lopez	.30	.09
❑ 75	Roy Oswalt	.30	.09
❑ 76	Raul Ibanez	.30	.09
❑ 77	Ivan Rodriguez	.75	.23
❑ 78	Jerome Williams	.30	.09
❑ 79	Carlos Lee	.30	.09
❑ 80	Geoff Jenkins	.30	.09
❑ 81	Sean Burroughs	.30	.09
❑ 82	Marcus Giles	.30	.09

❑ 83 Mike Lowell .30 .09
❑ 84 Barry Zito .30 .09
❑ 85 Aubrey Huff .30 .09
❑ 86 Esteban Loaiza .30 .09
❑ 87 Torii Hunter .30 .09
❑ 88 Phil Nevin .30 .09
❑ 89 Andruw Jones .30 .09
❑ 90 Josh Beckett .30 .09
❑ 91 Mark Mulder .30 .09
❑ 92 Hank Blalock .30 .09
❑ 93 Jason Phillips .30 .09
❑ 94 Russ Ortiz .30 .09
❑ 95 Juan Pierre .30 .09
❑ 96 Tom Glavine .50 .15
❑ 97 Gil Meche .30 .09
❑ 98 Ramon Ortiz .30 .09
❑ 99 Richie Sexson .30 .09
❑ 100 Albert Pujols 1.50 .45
❑ 101 Javier Vazquez .30 .09
❑ 102 Johnny Damon .75 .23
❑ 103 Alex Rodriguez Yanks 1.25 .35
❑ 104 Omar Vizquel .50 .15
❑ 105 Chipper Jones .75 .23
❑ 106 Lance Berkman .30 .09
❑ 107 Tim Hudson .30 .09
❑ 108 Carlos Delgado .30 .09
❑ 109 Austin Kearns .30 .09
❑ 110 Orlando Cabrera .30 .09
❑ 111 Edgar Martinez .50 .15
❑ 112 Melvin Mora .30 .09
❑ 113 Jeff Bagwell .50 .15
❑ 114 Marlon Byrd .30 .09
❑ 115 Vernon Wells .30 .09
❑ 116 C.C. Sabathia .30 .09
❑ 117 Cliff Floyd .30 .09
❑ 118 Ichiro Suzuki 1.25 .35
❑ 119 Miguel Olivo .30 .09
❑ 120 Mike Piazza 1.25 .35
❑ 121 Adam Dunn .50 .15
❑ 122 Paul Lo Duca .30 .09
❑ 123 Brett Myers .30 .09
❑ 124 Michael Young .30 .09
❑ 125 Sidney Ponson .30 .09
❑ 126 Greg Maddux 1.25 .35
❑ 127 Vladimir Guerrero .75 .23
❑ 128 Miguel Tejada .30 .09
❑ 129 Andy Pettitte .50 .15
❑ 130 Rafael Palmeiro .50 .15
❑ 131 Ken Griffey Jr. 1.25 .35
❑ 132 Shannon Stewart .30 .09
❑ 133 Joel Pineiro .30 .09
❑ 134 Luis Matos .30 .09
❑ 135 Jeff Kent .30 .09
❑ 136 Randy Wolf .30 .09
❑ 137 Chris Woodward .30 .09
❑ 138 Jody Gerut .30 .09
❑ 139 Jose Vidro .30 .09
❑ 140 Bret Boone .30 .09
❑ 141 Bill Mueller .30 .09
❑ 142 Angel Berroa .30 .09
❑ 143 Bobby Abreu .30 .09
❑ 144 Roy Halladay .30 .09
❑ 145 Delmon Young .50 .15
❑ 146 Jonny Gomes .30 .09
❑ 147 Rickie Weeks .30 .09
❑ 148 Edwin Jackson .30 .09
❑ 149 Neal Cotts .30 .09
❑ 150 Jason Bay .30 .09
❑ 151 Khalil Greene .75 .23
❑ 152 Joe Mauer .50 .15
❑ 153 Bobby Jenks .30 .09
❑ 154 Chin-Feng Chen .30 .09
❑ 155 Chien-Ming Wang .30 .09
❑ 156 Mickey Hall .30 .09
❑ 157 James Houser .30 .09
❑ 158 Jay Sborz .30 .09
❑ 159 Jonathan Fulton .30 .09
❑ 160 Steven Lerud .30 .09
❑ 161 Grady Sizemore .30 .09
❑ 162 Felix Pie .30 .09
❑ 163 Dustin McGowan .30 .09
❑ 164 Chris Lubanski .30 .09
❑ 165 Tom Gorzelanny .30 .09
❑ 166 Rudy Guillen FY RC 1.00 .30
❑ 167 Bobby Brownlie FY RC .75 .23
❑ 168 Conor Jackson FY RC 2.00 .60
❑ 169 Matt Moses FY RC 1.00 .30
❑ 170 Ervin Santana FY RC 1.25 .35
❑ 171 Merkin Valdez FY RC 1.00 .30
❑ 172 Erick Aybar FY RC 1.25 .35
❑ 173 Brad Sullivan FY RC .50 .15
❑ 174 David Aardsma FY RC .40 .12
❑ 175 Brad Snyder FY RC 1.00 .30
❑ 176 Alberto Callaspo FY RC .75 .23
❑ 177 Brandon Medders FY RC .30 .09
❑ 178 Zach Miner FY RC .50 .15
❑ 179 Charlie Zink FY RC .30 .09
❑ 180 Adam Greenberg FY RC .50 .15
❑ 181 Kevin Howard FY RC .50 .15
❑ 182 Wanell Severino FY RC .30 .09
❑ 183 Kevin Kouzmanoff FY RC .75 .23
❑ 184 Joel Zumaya FY RC .75 .23
❑ 185 Skip Schumaker FY RC .40 .12
❑ 186 Nic Ungs FY RC .40 .12
❑ 187 Todd Self FY RC .40 .12
❑ 188 Brian Steffek FY RC .30 .09
❑ 189 Brock Peterson FY RC .40 .12
❑ 190 Greg Thissen FY RC .40 .12
❑ 191 Frank Brooks FY RC .30 .09
❑ 192 Estee Harris FY RC .40 .12
❑ 193 Chris Mabeus FY RC .40 .12
❑ 194 Dan Giese FY RC .40 .12
❑ 195 Jared Wells FY RC .30 .09
❑ 196 Carlos Sosa FY RC .40 .12
❑ 197 Bobby Madritsch FY .75 .23
❑ 198 Calvin Hayes FY RC .50 .15
❑ 199 Omar Quintanilla FY RC 1.00 .30
❑ 200 Chris O'Riordan FY RC .40 .12
❑ 201 Tim Hutting FY RC .30 .09
❑ 202 Carlos Quentin FY RC 2.00 .60
❑ 203 Brayan Pena FY RC .40 .12
❑ 204 Jeff Salazar FY RC 1.00 .30
❑ 205 David Murphy FY RC 1.00 .30
❑ 206 Alberto Garcia FY RC .50 .15
❑ 207 Ramon Ramirez FY RC .40 .12
❑ 208 Luis Bolivar FY RC .50 .15
❑ 209 Rodney Choy Foo FY RC .30 .09
❑ 210 Kyle Sleeth FY RC 1.00 .30
❑ 211 Anthony Acevedo FY RC .40 .12
❑ 212 Chad Santos FY RC .40 .12
❑ 213 Jason Frasor FY RC .40 .12
❑ 214 Jesse Roman FY RC .30 .09
❑ 215 James Tomlin FY RC .40 .12
❑ 216 Josh Labandeira FY RC .40 .12
❑ 217 Joaquin Arias FY RC .40 .12
❑ 218 Don Sutton FY UER RC 1.00 .30
Nick Swisher pictured
❑ 219 Danny Gonzalez FY RC .30 .09
❑ 220 Javier Guzman FY RC .50 .15
❑ 221 Anthony Lerew FY RC .75 .23
❑ 222 Jon Knott FY RC .40 .12
❑ 223 Jesse English FY RC .40 .12
❑ 224 Felix Hernandez FY RC 3.00 .90
❑ 225 Travis Hanson FY RC .40 .12
❑ 226 Jesse Floyd FY RC .40 .12
❑ 227 Nick Gorneault FY RC .50 .15
❑ 228 Craig Ansman FY RC .40 .12
❑ 229 Wardell Starling FY RC .40 .12
❑ 230 Carl Loadenthal FY RC .50 .15
❑ 231 Dave Crouthers FY RC .30 .09
❑ 232 Harvey Garcia FY RC .30 .09
❑ 233 Casey Kopitzke FY RC .30 .09
❑ 234 Ricky Nolasco FY RC .40 .12
❑ 235 Miguel Perez FY RC .40 .12
❑ 236 Ryan Mulhern FY RC .30 .09
❑ 237 Chris Aguila FY RC .40 .12
❑ 238 Brooks Conrad FY RC .50 .15
❑ 239 Damaso Espino FY RC .30 .09
❑ 240 Jereme Milons FY RC .40 .12
❑ 241 Luke Hughes FY RC .30 .09
❑ 242 Kory Casto FY RC .40 .12
❑ 243 Jose Valdez FY RC .40 .12
❑ 244 J.T. Stotts FY RC .30 .09
❑ 245 Lee Gwaltney FY RC .30 .09
❑ 246 Yoann Torrealba FY RC .30 .09
❑ 247 Omar Falcon FY RC .40 .12
❑ 248 Jon Coutlangus FY RC .30 .09
❑ 249 George Sherrill FY RC .40 .12
❑ 250 John Santor FY RC .30 .09
❑ 251 Tony Richie FY RC .40 .12
❑ 252 Kevin Richardson FY RC .30 .09
❑ 253 Tim Bittner FY RC .40 .12
❑ 254 Dustin Nippert FY RC 1.25 .35
❑ 255 Jose Capellan FY RC 1.50 .45
❑ 256 Donald Levinski FY RC .30 .09
❑ 257 Jerome Gamble FY RC .30 .09
❑ 258 Jeff Keppinger FY RC .75 .23
❑ 259 Jason Szuminski FY RC .30 .09
❑ 260 Akinori Otsuka FY RC .40 .12
❑ 261 Ryan Budde FY RC .40 .12
❑ 262 Shingo Takatsu FY RC 1.00 .30
❑ 263 Jeff Allison FY RC .50 .15
❑ 264 Hector Gimenez FY RC .30 .09
❑ 265 Tim Frend FY RC .40 .12
❑ 266 Tom Farmer FY RC .30 .09
❑ 267 Shawn Hill FY RC .40 .12
❑ 268 Lastings Milledge FY RC 2.00 .60
❑ 269 Scott Proctor FY RC .50 .15
❑ 270 Jorge Mejia FY RC .40 .12
❑ 271 Terry Jones FY RC .50 .15
❑ 272 Zach Duke FY RC 1.50 .45
❑ 273 Tim Stauffer FY RC .75 .23
❑ 274 Luke Anderson FY RC .30 .09
❑ 275 Hunter Brown FY RC .30 .09
❑ 276 Matt Lemanczyk FY RC .40 .12
❑ 277 Fernando Cortez FY RC .30 .09
❑ 278 Vince Perkins FY RC .50 .15
❑ 279 Tommy Murphy FY RC .40 .12
❑ 280 Mike Gosling FY RC .30 .09
❑ 281 Paul Bacot FY RC .50 .15
❑ 282 Matt Capps FY RC .40 .12
❑ 283 Juan Gutierrez FY RC .40 .12
❑ 284 Teodoro Encarnacion FY RC .50 .15
❑ 285 Juan Cedeno FY RC .40 .12
❑ 286 Matt Creighton FY RC .40 .12
❑ 287 Ryan Hankins FY RC .30 .09
❑ 288 Leo Nunez FY RC .40 .12
❑ 289 Dave Wallace FY RC .40 .12
❑ 290 Rob Tejeda FY RC .30 .09
❑ 291 Lincoln Holdzkom FY RC .40 .12
❑ 292 Jason Hirsh FY RC .40 .12
❑ 293 Tydus Meadows FY RC .40 .12
❑ 294 Khalid Ballouli FY RC .30 .09
❑ 295 Benji DeQuin FY RC .30 .09
❑ 296 Tyler Davidson FY RC 1.50 .45
❑ 297 Brant Colamarino FY RC .75 .23
❑ 298 Marcus McBeth FY RC .30 .09
❑ 299 Brad Eldred FY RC 1.25 .35
❑ 300 David Pauley FY RC .30 .09
❑ 301 Yadier Molina FY RC 1.00 .30
❑ 302 Chris Shelton FY RC .75 .23
❑ 303 Travis Blackley FY RC .50 .15
❑ 304 Jon DeVries FY RC .40 .12
❑ 305 Sheldon Fulse FY RC .30 .09
❑ 306 Vito Chiaravalloti FY RC .75 .23
❑ 307 Warner Madrigal FY RC .75 .23
❑ 308 Reid Gorecki FY RC .40 .12
❑ 309 Sung Jung FY RC .30 .09
❑ 310 Pete Shier FY RC .30 .09
❑ 311 Michael Mooney FY RC .40 .12
❑ 312 Kenny Perez FY RC .40 .12
❑ 313 Michael Mallory FY RC .40 .12
❑ 314 Ben Himes FY RC .30 .09
❑ 315 Ivan Ochoa FY RC .40 .12
❑ 316 Donald Kelly FY RC .40 .12
❑ 317 Logan Kensing FY RC .40 .12
❑ 318 Kevin Davidson FY RC .30 .09
❑ 319 Brian Pilkington FY RC .40 .12
❑ 320 Alex Romero FY RC .40 .12
❑ 321 Chad Chop FY RC .40 .12
❑ 322 Dioner Navarro FY RC 1.25 .35
❑ 323 Casey Myers FY RC .30 .09
❑ 324 Mike Rouse FY RC .40 .12
❑ 325 Sergio Silva FY RC .30 .09
❑ 326 J.J. Furmaniak FY RC .75 .23
❑ 327 Brad Vericker FY RC .40 .12
❑ 328 Blake Hawksworth FY RC .50 .15
❑ 329 Brock Jacobsen FY RC .30 .09
❑ 330 Alec Zumwalt FY RC .30 .09
❑ BW Angel Berroa Bat 15.00 4.50
Dontrelle Willis Jsy ROY

2004 Bowman Draft

	Nm-Mt	Ex-Mt
COMPLETE SET (165)	40.00	12.00
COMMON CARD (1-165)	.30	.09
COMMON RC (1-165)	.30	.09

COMMON RC YR	.30	.09

PLATES ODDS 1:559 HOBBY
PLATES PRINT RUN 1 SERIAL #'d SET
BLACK-CYAN-MAGENTA-YELLOW EXIST
NO PLATES PRICING DUE TO SCARCITY

Card	Nm-Mt	Ex-Mt
❑ 1 Lyle Overbay	.30	.09
❑ 2 David Newhan	.30	.09
❑ 3 J.R. House	.30	.09
❑ 4 Chad Tracy	.30	.09
❑ 5 Humberto Quintero	.30	.09
❑ 6 Dave Bush	.30	.09
❑ 7 Scott Hairston	.30	.09
❑ 8 Mike Wood	.30	.09
❑ 9 Alexis Rios	.30	.09
❑ 10 Sean Burnett	.30	.09
❑ 11 Wilson Valdez	.30	.09
❑ 12 Lew Ford	.30	.09
❑ 13 Freddy Thon RC	.40	.12
❑ 14 Zack Greinke	.30	.09
❑ 15 Bucky Jacobsen	.30	.09
❑ 16 Kevin Youkilis	.30	.09
❑ 17 Grady Sizemore	.30	.09
❑ 18 Denny Bautista	.30	.09
❑ 19 David DeJesus	.30	.09
❑ 20 Casey Kotchman	.75	.23
❑ 21 David Kelton	.30	.09
❑ 22 Charles Thomas RC	.50	.15
❑ 23 Kazuhito Tadano RC	.50	.15
❑ 24 Justin Leone RC	.50	.15
❑ 25 Eduardo Villacis RC	.40	.12
❑ 26 Brian Dallimore RC	.30	.09
❑ 27 Nick Green	.30	.09
❑ 28 Sam McConnell RC	.40	.12
❑ 29 Brad Halsey RC	.50	.15
❑ 30 Roman Colon RC	.30	.09
❑ 31 Josh Fields RC	1.50	.45
❑ 32 Cody Bunkelman RC	.50	.15
❑ 33 Jay Rainville RC	1.00	.30
❑ 34 Richie Robnett RC	1.00	.30
❑ 35 Jon Poterson RC	1.00	.30
❑ 36 Huston Street RC	1.00	.30
❑ 37 Erick San Pedro RC	.40	.12
❑ 38 Cory Dunlap RC	1.25	.35
❑ 39 Kurt Suzuki RC	1.25	.35
❑ 40 Anthony Swarzak RC	.50	.15
❑ 41 Ian Desmond RC	.50	.15
❑ 42 Chris Covington RC	.50	.15
❑ 43 Christian Garcia RC	.75	.23
❑ 44 Gaby Hernandez RC	.75	.23
❑ 45 Steven Register RC	.50	.15
❑ 46 Eduardo Morlan RC	.50	.15
❑ 47 Collin Balester RC	.50	.15
❑ 48 Nathan Phillips RC	.50	.15
❑ 49 Dan Schwartzbauer RC	.50	.15
❑ 50 Rafael Gonzalez RC	.50	.15
❑ 51 K.C. Herren RC	.75	.23
❑ 52 William Susdorf RC	.40	.12
❑ 53 Rob Johnson RC	.40	.12
❑ 54 Louis Marson RC	.75	.23
❑ 55 Joe Koshansky RC	.40	.12
❑ 56 Jamar Walton RC	1.50	.45
❑ 57 Mark Lowe RC	.40	.12
❑ 58 Matt Macri RC	.75	.23
❑ 59 Donny Lucy RC	.40	.12
❑ 60 Mike Ferris RC	.50	.15
❑ 61 Mike Nickeas RC	.50	.15
❑ 62 Eric Hurley RC	.75	.23
❑ 63 Scott Elbert RC	1.00	.30
❑ 64 Blake DeWitt RC	2.00	.60
❑ 65 Danny Putnam RC	.75	.23
❑ 66 J.P. Howell RC	.75	.23
❑ 67 John Wiggins RC	.40	.12
❑ 68 Justin Orenduff RC	.75	.23
❑ 69 Ray Liotta RC	.50	.15
❑ 70 Billy Buckner RC	.50	.15
❑ 71 Eric Campbell RC	1.25	.35
❑ 72 Olin Wick RC	.40	.12
❑ 73 Sean Gamble RC	.50	.15
❑ 74 Seth Smith RC	1.25	.35
❑ 75 Wade Davis RC	.50	.15
❑ 76 Joe Jacobitz RC	.40	.12
❑ 77 J.A. Happ RC	.75	.23
❑ 78 Eric Ridener RC	.40	.12
❑ 79 Matt Tuiasosopo RC	3.00	.90
❑ 80 Brad Bergesen RC	.50	.15
❑ 81 Javy Guerra RC	.50	.15
❑ 82 Buck Shaw RC	.75	.23
❑ 83 Paul Janish RC	.50	.15
❑ 84 Sean Kazmar RC	.50	.15
❑ 85 Josh Johnson RC	.50	.15
❑ 86 Angel Salome RC	.50	.15
❑ 87 Jordan Parraz RC	.50	.15
❑ 88 Kelvin Vazquez RC	.40	.12
❑ 89 Grant Hansen RC	.40	.12
❑ 90 Matt Fox RC	.75	.23
❑ 91 Trevor Plouffe RC	1.25	.35
❑ 92 Wes Whisler RC	.50	.15
❑ 93 Curtis Thigpen RC	.75	.23
❑ 94 Donnie Smith RC	.40	.12
❑ 95 Luis Rivera RC	.50	.15
❑ 96 Jesse Hoover RC	.50	.15
❑ 97 Jason Vargas RC	.75	.23
❑ 98 Clary Carlsen RC	.40	.12
❑ 99 Mark Robinson RC	.40	.12
❑ 100 J.C. Holt RC	.75	.23
❑ 101 Chad Blackwell RC	.50	.15
❑ 102 Daryl Jones RC	.75	.23
❑ 103 Jonathan Tierce RC	.40	.12
❑ 104 Patrick Bryant RC	.40	.12
❑ 105 Eddie Prasch RC	.50	.15
❑ 106 Mitch Einertson RC	2.50	.75
❑ 107 Kyle Waldrop RC	1.00	.30
❑ 108 Jeff Marquez RC	.75	.23
❑ 109 Zach Jackson RC	.50	.15
❑ 110 Josh Wahpepah RC	.40	.12
❑ 111 Adam Lind RC	.75	.23
❑ 112 Kyle Bloom RC	.50	.15
❑ 113 Ben Harrison RC	.50	.15
❑ 114 Taylor Tankersley RC	1.00	.30
❑ 115 Steven Jackson RC	.40	.12
❑ 116 David Purcey RC	.75	.23
❑ 117 Jacob McGee RC	.50	.15
❑ 118 Lucas Harrell RC	.40	.12
❑ 119 Brandon Allen RC	.75	.23
❑ 120 Van Pope RC	.50	.15
❑ 121 Jeff Francis	.30	.09
❑ 122 Joe Blanton	.50	.15
❑ 123 Wil Ledezma	.30	.09
❑ 124 Bryan Bullington	.30	.09
❑ 125 Jairo Garcia	.30	.09
❑ 126 Matt Cain	.30	.09
❑ 127 Arnie Munoz	.30	.09
❑ 128 Clint Everts	.30	.09
❑ 129 Jesus Cota	.30	.09
❑ 130 Gavin Floyd	.30	.09
❑ 131 Edwin Encarnacion	.30	.09
❑ 132 Koyie Hill	.30	.09
❑ 133 Ruben Gotay	.30	.09
❑ 134 Jeff Mathis	.30	.09
❑ 135 Andy Marte	.30	.09
❑ 136 Dallas McPherson	.50	.15
❑ 137 Justin Morneau	.50	.15
❑ 138 Rickie Weeks	.30	.09
❑ 139 Joel Guzman	.50	.15
❑ 140 Shin Soo Choo	.30	.09
❑ 141 Yusmeiro Petit RC	2.00	.60
❑ 142 Jorge Cortes RC	.40	.12
❑ 143 Val Majewski	.30	.09
❑ 144 Felix Pie	.30	.09
❑ 145 Aaron Hill	.30	.09
❑ 146 Jose Capellan	.75	.23
❑ 147 Dioner Navarro	.50	.15
❑ 148 Fausto Carmona RC	.75	.23
❑ 149 Robinzon Diaz RC	.40	.12
❑ 150 Felix Hernandez	1.25	.35
❑ 151 Andres Blanco RC	.40	.12
❑ 152 Jason Kubel	.30	.09
❑ 153 Willy Taveras RC	.50	.15
❑ 154 Merkin Valdez	.50	.15
❑ 155 Robinson Cano	.30	.09
❑ 156 Bill Murphy	.30	.09
❑ 157 Chris Burke	.30	.09
❑ 158 Kyle Sleeth	.50	.15
❑ 159 B.J. Upton	.50	.15
❑ 160 Tim Stauffer	.50	.15
❑ 161 David Wright	.75	.23
❑ 162 Conor Jackson	.75	.23
❑ 163 Brad Thompson RC	.50	.15
❑ 164 Delmon Young	.50	.15
❑ 165 Jeremy Reed	.30	.09

1997 Bowman Chrome

	Nm-Mt	Ex-Mt
COMPLETE SET (300)	180.00	55.00
❑ 1 Derek Jeter	3.00	.90
❑ 2 Chipper Jones	1.25	.35
❑ 3 Hideo Nomo	1.25	.35
❑ 4 Tim Salmon	.75	.23
❑ 5 Robin Ventura	.50	.15
❑ 6 Tony Clark	.50	.15
❑ 7 Barry Larkin	.75	.23
❑ 8 Paul Molitor	.75	.23
❑ 9 Andy Benes	.50	.15
❑ 10 Ryan Klesko	.50	.15
❑ 11 Mark McGwire	3.00	.90
❑ 12 Ken Griffey Jr.	2.00	.60
❑ 13 Robb Nen	.50	.15
❑ 14 Cal Ripken	4.00	1.20
❑ 15 John Valentin	.50	.15
❑ 16 Ricky Bottalico	.50	.15
❑ 17 Mike Lansing	.50	.15
❑ 18 Ryne Sandberg	2.00	.60
❑ 19 Carlos Delgado	.50	.15
❑ 20 Craig Biggio	.75	.23
❑ 21 Eric Karros	.50	.15
❑ 22 Kevin Appier	.50	.15
❑ 23 Mariano Rivera	.75	.23
❑ 24 Vinny Castilla	.50	.15
❑ 25 Juan Gonzalez	.75	.23
❑ 26 Al Martin	.50	.15
❑ 27 Jeff Cirillo	.50	.15
❑ 28 Ray Lankford	.50	.15
❑ 29 Manny Ramirez	.75	.23
❑ 30 Roberto Alomar	.75	.23
❑ 31 Will Clark	1.25	.35
❑ 32 Chuck Knoblauch	.50	.15
❑ 33 Harold Baines	.50	.15
❑ 34 Edgar Martinez	.75	.23
❑ 35 Mike Mussina	.75	.23
❑ 36 Kevin Brown	.50	.15
❑ 37 Dennis Eckersley	.50	.15
❑ 38 Tino Martinez	.75	.23
❑ 39 Raul Mondesi	.50	.15
❑ 40 Sammy Sosa	2.00	.60
❑ 41 John Smoltz	.75	.23
❑ 42 Billy Wagner	.50	.15
❑ 43 Ken Caminiti	.50	.15
❑ 44 Wade Boggs	.75	.23
❑ 45 Andres Galarraga	.50	.15

❑ 46 Roger Clemens 2.50 .75
❑ 47 Matt Williams .50 .15
❑ 48 Albert Belle .50 .15
❑ 49 Jeff King .50 .15
❑ 50 John Wetteland .50 .15
❑ 51 Deion Sanders .75 .23
❑ 52 Ellis Burks .50 .15
❑ 53 Pedro Martinez 1.25 .35
❑ 54 Kenny Lofton .50 .15
❑ 55 Randy Johnson 1.25 .35
❑ 56 Bernie Williams .75 .23
❑ 57 Marquis Grissom .50 .15
❑ 58 Gary Sheffield .50 .15
❑ 59 Curt Schilling .50 .15
❑ 60 Reggie Sanders .50 .15
❑ 61 Bobby Higginson .50 .15
❑ 62 Moises Alou .50 .15
❑ 63 Tom Glavine .75 .23
❑ 64 Mark Grace .75 .23
❑ 65 Rafael Palmeiro .75 .23
❑ 66 John Olerud .50 .15
❑ 67 Dante Bichette .50 .15
❑ 68 Jeff Bagwell .75 .23
❑ 69 Barry Bonds 3.00 .90
❑ 70 Pat Hentgen .50 .15
❑ 71 Jim Thome 1.25 .35
❑ 72 Andy Pettitte .75 .23
❑ 73 Jay Bell .50 .15
❑ 74 Jim Edmonds .50 .15
❑ 75 Ron Gant .50 .15
❑ 76 David Cone .50 .15
❑ 77 Jose Canseco 1.25 .35
❑ 78 Jay Buhner .50 .15
❑ 79 Greg Maddux 2.00 .60
❑ 80 Lance Johnson .50 .15
❑ 81 Travis Fryman .50 .15
❑ 82 Paul O'Neill .75 .23
❑ 83 Ivan Rodriguez 1.25 .35
❑ 84 Fred McGriff .75 .23
❑ 85 Mike Piazza 2.00 .60
❑ 86 Brady Anderson .50 .15
❑ 87 Marty Cordova .50 .15
❑ 88 Joe Carter .50 .15
❑ 89 Brian Jordan .50 .15
❑ 90 David Justice .50 .15
❑ 91 Tony Gwynn 1.50 .45
❑ 92 Larry Walker .75 .23
❑ 93 Mo Vaughn .50 .15
❑ 94 Sandy Alomar Jr. .50 .15
❑ 95 Rusty Greer .50 .15
❑ 96 Roberto Hernandez .50 .15
❑ 97 Hal Morris .50 .15
❑ 98 Todd Hundley .50 .15
❑ 99 Rondell White .50 .15
❑ 100 Frank Thomas 1.25 .35
❑ 101 Bubba Trammell RC 1.50 .45
❑ 102 Sidney Ponson RC 2.50 .75
❑ 103 Ricky Ledee RC 1.50 .45
❑ 104 Brett Tomko .50 .15
❑ 105 Braden Looper RC 1.00 .30
❑ 106 Jason Dickson .50 .15
❑ 107 Chad Green RC 1.00 .30
❑ 108 R.A. Dickey RC 1.00 .30
❑ 109 Jeff Liefer .50 .15
❑ 110 Richard Hidalgo .50 .15
❑ 111 Chad Hermansen RC 1.50 .45
❑ 112 Felix Martinez .50 .15
❑ 113 J.J. Johnson .50 .15
❑ 114 Todd Dunwoody .50 .15
❑ 115 Katsuhiro Maeda .50 .15
❑ 116 Darin Erstad .50 .15
❑ 117 Elieser Marrero .50 .15
❑ 118 Bartolo Colon .50 .15
❑ 119 Ugueth Urbina .50 .15
❑ 120 Jaime Bluma .50 .15
❑ 121 Seth Greisinger RC 1.00 .30
❑ 122 Jose Cruz Jr. RC 2.50 .75
❑ 123 Todd Dunn .50 .15
❑ 124 Justin Towle RC 1.00 .30
❑ 125 Brian Rose .50 .15
❑ 126 Jose Guillen .50 .15
❑ 127 Andruw Jones .50 .15
❑ 128 Mark Kotsay RC 4.00 1.20
❑ 129 Wilton Guerrero .50 .15
❑ 130 Jacob Cruz .50 .15
❑ 131 Mike Sweeney .50 .15
❑ 132 Matt Morris .50 .15
❑ 133 John Thomson .50 .15
❑ 134 Javier Valentin .50 .15
❑ 135 Mike Drumright RC 1.00 .30
❑ 136 Michael Barrett .50 .15
❑ 137 Tony Saunders RC 1.00 .30
❑ 138 Kevin Brown .50 .15
❑ 139 Anthony Sanders RC 1.00 .30
❑ 140 Jeff Abbott .50 .15
❑ 141 Eugene Kingsale .50 .15
❑ 142 Paul Konerko .50 .15
❑ 143 Randall Simon RC 1.50 .45
❑ 144 Freddy Adrian Garcia .50 .15
❑ 145 Karim Garcia .50 .15
❑ 146 Carlos Guillen .50 .15
❑ 147 Aaron Boone .50 .15
❑ 148 Donnie Sadler .50 .15
❑ 149 Brooks Kieschnick .50 .15
❑ 150 Scott Spiezio .50 .15
❑ 151 Kevin Orie .50 .15
❑ 152 Russ Johnson .50 .15
❑ 153 Livan Hernandez .50 .15
❑ 154 Vladimir Nunez RC 1.00 .30
❑ 155 Pokey Reese .50 .15
❑ 156 Chris Carpenter .50 .15
❑ 157 Eric Milton RC 4.00 1.20
❑ 158 Richie Sexson .50 .15
❑ 159 Carl Pavano 1.50 .15
❑ 160 Pat Cline .50 .15
❑ 161 Ron Wright .50 .15
❑ 162 Dante Powell .50 .15
❑ 163 Mark Bellhorn .50 .15
❑ 164 George Lombard .50 .15
❑ 165 Paul Wilder RC 1.00 .30
❑ 166 Brad Fullmer .50 .15
❑ 167 Kris Benson RC 4.00 1.20
❑ 168 Torii Hunter .50 .15
❑ 169 D.T. Cromer RC 1.00 .30
❑ 170 Nelson Figueroa RC 1.00 .30
❑ 171 Hiram Bocachica RC 1.50 .45
❑ 172 Shane Monahan .50 .15
❑ 173 Juan Melo .50 .15
❑ 174 Calvin Pickering RC 2.50 .75
❑ 175 Reggie Taylor .50 .15
❑ 176 Geoff Jenkins .50 .15
❑ 177 Steve Rain RC 1.00 .30
❑ 178 Nerio Rodriguez RC 1.00 .30
❑ 179 Derrick Gibson .50 .15
❑ 180 Darin Blood .50 .15
❑ 181 Ben Davis .50 .15
❑ 182 Adrian Beltre RC 20.00 6.00
❑ 183 Kerry Wood RC 30.00 9.00
❑ 184 Nate Rolison RC 1.00 .30
❑ 185 Fernando Tatis RC 1.50 .45
❑ 186 Jake Westbrook RC 4.00 1.20
❑ 187 Edwin Diaz .50 .15
❑ 188 Joe Fontenot RC 1.00 .30
❑ 189 Matt Halloran RC 1.00 .30
❑ 190 Matt Clement RC 4.00 1.20
❑ 191 Todd Greene .50 .15
❑ 192 Eric Chavez RC 12.00 3.60
❑ 193 Edgard Velazquez .50 .15
❑ 194 Bruce Chen RC 1.50 .45
❑ 195 Jason Brester .50 .15
❑ 196 Chris Reitsma RC 1.50 .45
❑ 197 Neifi Perez .50 .15
❑ 198 Hideki Irabu RC 1.50 .45
❑ 199 Don Denbow RC 1.00 .30
❑ 200 Derrek Lee .50 .15
❑ 201 Todd Walker .50 .15
❑ 202 Scott Rolen 1.25 .35
❑ 203 Wes Helms .50 .15
❑ 204 Bob Abreu .50 .15
❑ 205 John Patterson RC 2.50 .75
❑ 206 Alex Gonzalez RC 2.50 .75
❑ 207 Grant Roberts RC 1.50 .45
❑ 208 Jeff Suppan .50 .15
❑ 209 Luke Wilcox .50 .15
❑ 210 Marlon Anderson .50 .15
❑ 211 Mike Caruso RC 1.00 .30
❑ 212 Roy Halladay RC 4.00 1.20
❑ 213 Jeremi Gonzalez RC 1.00 .30
❑ 214 Aramis Ramirez RC 10.00 3.00
❑ 215 Dee Brown RC 1.50 .45
❑ 216 Justin Thompson .50 .15
❑ 217 Danny Clyburn .50 .15
❑ 218 Bruce Aven .50 .15
❑ 219 Keith Foulke RC 5.00 1.50
❑ 220 Shannon Stewart .50 .15
❑ 221 Larry Barnes RC 1.00 .30
❑ 222 Mark Johnson RC 1.00 .30
❑ 223 Randy Winn .50 .15
❑ 224 Nomar Garciaparra 2.00 .60
❑ 225 Jacque Jones RC 4.00 1.20
❑ 226 Chris Clemons .50 .15
❑ 227 Todd Helton 1.25 .35
❑ 228 Ryan Brannan RC 1.00 .30
❑ 229 Alex Sanchez RC 2.50 .75
❑ 230 Russell Branyan .50 .15
❑ 231 Daryle Ward 1.00 .30
❑ 232 Kevin Witt .50 .15
❑ 233 Gabby Martinez .50 .15
❑ 234 Preston Wilson .50 .15
❑ 235 Donzell McDonald RC 1.00 .30
❑ 236 Orlando Cabrera RC 4.00 1.50
❑ 237 Brian Banks .50 .15
❑ 238 Robbie Bell 1.00 .30
❑ 239 Brad Rigby .50 .15
❑ 240 Scott Elarton .50 .15
❑ 241 Donny Leon RC 1.00 .30
❑ 242 Abraham Nunez RC 1.00 .30
❑ 243 Adam Eaton RC 1.50 .45
❑ 244 Octavio Dotel RC 1.50 .45
❑ 245 Sean Casey 4.00 1.20
❑ 246 Joe Lawrence RC 1.00 .30
❑ 247 Adam Johnson RC 1.00 .30
❑ 248 Ronnie Belliard RC 2.50 .75
❑ 249 Bobby Estalella .50 .15
❑ 250 Corey Lee RC 1.00 .30
❑ 251 Mike Cameron .50 .15
❑ 252 Kerry Robinson RC 1.00 .30
❑ 253 A.J. Zapp RC 1.00 .30
❑ 254 Jarrod Washburn .50 .15
❑ 255 Ben Grieve .50 .15
❑ 256 Javier Vazquez RC 5.00 1.50
❑ 257 Travis Lee RC 1.50 .45
❑ 258 Dennis Reyes RC 1.00 .30
❑ 259 Danny Buxbaum .50 .15
❑ 260 Kelvim Escobar RC 2.50 .75
❑ 261 Danny Klassen .50 .15
❑ 262 Ken Cloude RC 1.50 .45
❑ 263 Gabe Alvarez .50 .15
❑ 264 Clayton Bruner RC 1.00 .30
❑ 265 Jason Marquis RC 4.00 1.20
❑ 266 Jamey Wright .50 .15
❑ 267 Matt Snyder RC 1.00 .30
❑ 268 Josh Garrett RC 1.00 .30
❑ 269 Juan Encarnacion .50 .15
❑ 270 Heath Murray .50 .15
❑ 271 Brent Butler RC 1.50 .45
❑ 272 Danny Peoples RC 1.00 .30
❑ 273 Miguel Tejada RC 15.00 4.50
❑ 274 Jim Pittsley .50 .15
❑ 275 Dmitri Young .50 .15
❑ 276 Vladimir Guerrero 1.25 .35
❑ 277 Cole Liniak RC 1.00 .30
❑ 278 Ramon Hernandez .50 .15
❑ 279 Cliff Politte RC 1.00 .30
❑ 280 Mel Rosario RC 1.00 .30
❑ 281 Jorge Carrion RC 1.00 .30
❑ 282 John Barnes RC 1.00 .30
❑ 283 Chris Stowe RC 1.00 .30
❑ 284 Vernon Wells RC 8.00 2.40
❑ 285 Brett Caradonna RC 1.00 .30
❑ 286 Scott Hodges RC 1.00 .30
❑ 287 Jon Garland RC 2.50 .75
❑ 288 Nathan Haynes RC 1.50 .45
❑ 289 Geoff Goetz RC 1.00 .30
❑ 290 Adam Kennedy RC 2.50 .75
❑ 291 T.J. Tucker RC 1.00 .30
❑ 292 Aaron Akin RC 1.00 .30
❑ 293 Jayson Werth RC 4.00 1.20
❑ 294 Glenn Davis RC 1.00 .30
❑ 295 Mark Mangum RC 1.00 .30
❑ 296 Troy Cameron RC 1.00 .30
❑ 297 J.J. Davis RC 1.50 .45
❑ 298 Lance Berkman RC 20.00 6.00
❑ 299 Jason Standridge RC 1.50 .45
❑ 300 Jason Dellaero RC 1.00 .30

1998 Bowman Chrome

	Nm-Mt	Ex-Mt
COMPLETE SET (441)	160.00	47.50
COMP. SERIES 1 (221)	80.00	24.00
COMP. SERIES 2 (220)	80.00	24.00

#	Player	Nm-Mt	Ex-Mt
❑ 1	Nomar Garciaparra	2.00	.60
❑ 2	Scott Rolen	1.25	.35
❑ 3	Andy Pettitte	.75	.23
❑ 4	Ivan Rodriguez	1.25	.35
❑ 5	Mark McGwire	3.00	.90
❑ 6	Jason Dickson	.50	.15
❑ 7	Jose Cruz Jr.	.50	.15
❑ 8	Jeff Kent	.50	.15
❑ 9	Mike Mussina	.75	.23
❑ 10	Jason Kendall	.50	.15
❑ 11	Brett Tomko	.50	.15
❑ 12	Jeff King	.50	.15
❑ 13	Brad Radke	.50	.15
❑ 14	Robin Ventura	.50	.15
❑ 15	Jeff Bagwell	.75	.23
❑ 16	Greg Maddux	2.00	.60
❑ 17	John Jaha	.50	.15
❑ 18	Mike Piazza	2.00	.60
❑ 19	Edgar Martinez	.75	.23
❑ 20	David Justice	.50	.15
❑ 21	Todd Hundley	.50	.15
❑ 22	Tony Gwynn	1.50	.45
❑ 23	Larry Walker	.75	.23
❑ 24	Bernie Williams	.75	.23
❑ 25	Edgar Renteria	.50	.15
❑ 26	Rafael Palmeiro	.75	.23
❑ 27	Tim Salmon	.75	.23
❑ 28	Matt Morris	.50	.15
❑ 29	Shawn Estes	.50	.15
❑ 30	Vladimir Guerrero	1.25	.35
❑ 31	Fernando Tatis	.50	.15
❑ 32	Justin Thompson	.50	.15
❑ 33	Ken Griffey Jr.	2.00	.60
❑ 34	Edgardo Alfonzo	.50	.15
❑ 35	Mo Vaughn	.50	.15
❑ 36	Marty Cordova	.50	.15
❑ 37	Craig Biggio	.75	.23
❑ 38	Roger Clemens	2.50	.75
❑ 39	Mark Grace	.75	.23
❑ 40	Ken Caminiti	.50	.15
❑ 41	Tony Womack	.50	.15
❑ 42	Albert Belle	.50	.15
❑ 43	Tino Martinez	.75	.23
❑ 44	Sandy Alomar Jr.	.50	.15
❑ 45	Jeff Cirillo	.50	.15
❑ 46	Jason Giambi	.50	.15
❑ 47	Darin Erstad	.50	.15
❑ 48	Livan Hernandez	.50	.15
❑ 49	Mark Grudzielanek	.50	.15
❑ 50	Sammy Sosa	2.00	.60
❑ 51	Curt Schilling	.50	.15
❑ 52	Brian Hunter	.50	.15
❑ 53	Neifi Perez	.50	.15
❑ 54	Todd Walker	.50	.15
❑ 55	Jose Guillen	.50	.15
❑ 56	Jim Thome	1.25	.35
❑ 57	Tom Glavine	.75	.23
❑ 58	Todd Greene	.50	.15
❑ 59	Rondell White	.50	.15
❑ 60	Roberto Alomar	.75	.23
❑ 61	Tony Clark	.50	.15
❑ 62	Vinny Castilla	.50	.15
❑ 63	Barry Larkin	.75	.23
❑ 64	Hideki Irabu	.50	.15
❑ 65	Johnny Damon	.75	.23
❑ 66	Juan Gonzalez	.75	.23
❑ 67	John Olerud	.50	.15
❑ 68	Gary Sheffield	.50	.15
❑ 69	Raul Mondesi	.50	.15
❑ 70	Chipper Jones	1.25	.35
❑ 71	David Ortiz	4.00	1.20
❑ 72	Warren Morris RC	1.00	.30
❑ 73	Alex Gonzalez	.50	.15
❑ 74	Nick Bierbrodt	.50	.15
❑ 75	Roy Halladay	.50	.15
❑ 76	Danny Buxbaum	.50	.15
❑ 77	Adam Kennedy	.50	.15
❑ 78	Jared Sandberg	.50	.15
❑ 79	Michael Barrett	.50	.15
❑ 80	Gil Meche	1.00	.30
❑ 81	Jayson Werth	.50	.15
❑ 82	Abraham Nunez	.50	.15
❑ 83	Ben Petrick	.50	.15
❑ 84	Brett Caradonna	.50	.15
❑ 85	Mike Lowell RC	8.00	2.40
❑ 86	Clay Bruner	.50	.15
❑ 87	John Curtice RC	1.50	.45
❑ 88	Bobby Estalella	.50	.15
❑ 89	Juan Melo	.50	.15
❑ 90	Arnold Gooch	.50	.15
❑ 91	Kevin Millwood RC	4.00	1.20
❑ 92	Richie Sexson	.50	.15
❑ 93	Orlando Cabrera	.50	.15
❑ 94	Pat Cline	.50	.15
❑ 95	Anthony Sanders	.50	.15
❑ 96	Russ Johnson	.50	.15
❑ 97	Ben Grieve	.50	.15
❑ 98	Kevin McGlinchy	.50	.15
❑ 99	Paul Wilder	.50	.15
❑ 100	Russ Ortiz	.50	.15
❑ 101	Ryan Jackson RC	1.00	.30
❑ 102	Heath Murray	.50	.15
❑ 103	Brian Rose	.50	.15
❑ 104	R.Radmanovich RC	1.00	.30
❑ 105	Ricky Ledee	.50	.15
❑ 106	Jeff Wallace RC	1.00	.30
❑ 107	Ryan Minor RC	1.00	.30
❑ 108	Dennis Reyes	.50	.15
❑ 109	James Manias	.50	.15
❑ 110	Chris Carpenter	.50	.15
❑ 111	Daryle Ward	.50	.15
❑ 112	Vernon Wells	.50	.15
❑ 113	Chad Green	.50	.15
❑ 114	Mike Stoner RC	1.00	.30
❑ 115	Brad Fullmer	.50	.15
❑ 116	Adam Eaton	.50	.15
❑ 117	Jeff Liefer	.50	.15
❑ 118	Corey Koskie RC	5.00	1.50
❑ 119	Todd Helton	.75	.23
❑ 120	Jaime Jones RC	1.00	.30
❑ 121	Mel Rosario	.50	.15
❑ 122	Geoff Goetz	.50	.15
❑ 123	Adrian Beltre	1.25	.35
❑ 124	Jason Dellaero	.50	.15
❑ 125	Gabe Kapler RC	2.50	.75
❑ 126	Scott Schoeneweis	.50	.15
❑ 127	Ryan Brannan	.50	.15
❑ 128	Aaron Akin	.50	.15
❑ 129	Ryan Anderson RC	1.50	.45
❑ 130	Brad Penny	.50	.15
❑ 131	Bruce Chen	.50	.15
❑ 132	Eli Marrero	.50	.15
❑ 133	Eric Chavez	.50	.15
❑ 134	Troy Glaus RC	10.00	3.00
❑ 135	Troy Cameron	.50	.15
❑ 136	Brian Sikorski RC	1.00	.30
❑ 137	Mike Kinkade RC	1.00	.30
❑ 138	Braden Looper	.50	.15
❑ 139	Mark Mangum	.50	.15
❑ 140	Danny Peoples	.50	.15
❑ 141	J.J. Davis	.50	.15
❑ 142	Ben Davis	.50	.15
❑ 143	Jacque Jones	.50	.15
❑ 144	Derrick Gibson	.50	.15
❑ 145	Bronson Arroyo	4.00	1.20
❑ 146	L.De Los Santos RC	1.00	.30
❑ 147	Jeff Abbott	.50	.15
❑ 148	Mike Cuddyer RC	2.50	.75
❑ 149	Jason Romano	.50	.15
❑ 150	Shane Monahan	.50	.15
❑ 151	Ntema Ndungidi RC	1.00	.30
❑ 152	Alex Sanchez	.50	.15
❑ 153	Jack Cust RC	1.50	.45
❑ 154	Brent Butler	.50	.15
❑ 155	Ramon Hernandez	.50	.15
❑ 156	Norm Hutchins	.50	.15
❑ 157	Jason Marquis	.50	.15
❑ 158	Jacob Cruz	.50	.15
❑ 159	Rob Burger RC	1.00	.30
❑ 160	Dave Coggin	.50	.15
❑ 161	Preston Wilson	.50	.15
❑ 162	Jason Fitzgerald RC	1.00	.30
❑ 163	Dan Serafini	.50	.15
❑ 164	Pete Munro	.50	.15
❑ 165	Trot Nixon	.50	.15
❑ 166	Homer Bush	.50	.15
❑ 167	Dermal Brown	.50	.15
❑ 168	Chad Hermansen	.50	.15
❑ 169	Julio Moreno RC	1.00	.30
❑ 170	John Roskos RC	1.00	.30
❑ 171	Grant Roberts	.50	.15
❑ 172	Ken Cloude	.50	.15
❑ 173	Jason Brester	.50	.15
❑ 174	Jason Conti	.50	.15
❑ 175	Jon Garland	.50	.15
❑ 176	Robbie Bell	.50	.15
❑ 177	Nathan Haynes	.50	.15
❑ 178	Ramon Ortiz RC	2.50	.75
❑ 179	Shannon Stewart	.50	.15
❑ 180	Pablo Ortega	.50	.15
❑ 181	Jimmy Rollins RC	4.00	1.20
❑ 182	Sean Casey	.50	.15
❑ 183	Ted Lilly RC	2.50	.75
❑ 184	Chris Enochs RC	1.00	.30
❑ 185	M.Ordonez RC UER Front photo is Mario Valdez	10.00	3.00
❑ 186	Mike Drumright	.50	.15
❑ 187	Aaron Boone	.50	.15
❑ 188	Matt Clement	.50	.15
❑ 189	Todd Dunwoody	.50	.15
❑ 190	Larry Rodriguez	.50	.15
❑ 191	Todd Noel	.50	.15
❑ 192	Geoff Jenkins	.50	.15
❑ 193	George Lombard	.50	.15
❑ 194	Lance Berkman	.75	.23
❑ 195	Marcus McCain	.50	.15
❑ 196	Ryan McGuire	.50	.15
❑ 197	Jhensy Sandoval	.50	.15
❑ 198	Corey Lee	.50	.15
❑ 199	Mario Valdez	.50	.15
❑ 200	Robert Fick RC	1.50	.45
❑ 201	Donnie Sadler	.50	.15
❑ 202	Marc Kroon	.50	.15
❑ 203	David Miller	.50	.15
❑ 204	Jarrod Washburn	.50	.15
❑ 205	Miguel Tejada	.50	.15
❑ 206	Raul Ibanez	.50	.15
❑ 207	John Patterson	.50	.15
❑ 208	Calvin Pickering	.50	.15
❑ 209	Felix Martinez	.50	.15
❑ 210	Mark Redman	.50	.15
❑ 211	Scott Elarton	.50	.15
❑ 212	Jose Amado RC	1.00	.30
❑ 213	Kerry Wood	1.25	.35
❑ 214	Dante Powell	.50	.15
❑ 215	Aramis Ramirez	.50	.15
❑ 216	A.J. Hinch	.50	.15
❑ 217	Dustin Carr RC	1.00	.30
❑ 218	Mark Kotsay	.50	.15
❑ 219	Jason Standridge	.50	.15
❑ 220	Luis Ordaz	.50	.15
❑ 221	O.Hernandez RC	4.00	1.20
❑ 222	Cal Ripken	4.00	1.20
❑ 223	Paul Molitor	.75	.23
❑ 224	Derek Jeter	3.00	.90
❑ 225	Barry Bonds	3.00	.90
❑ 226	Jim Edmonds	.50	.15
❑ 227	John Smoltz	.75	.23
❑ 228	Eric Karros	.50	.15
❑ 229	Ray Lankford	.50	.15
❑ 230	Rey Ordonez	.50	.15
❑ 231	Kenny Lofton	.50	.15
❑ 232	Alex Rodriguez	2.00	.60

❑ 233 Dante Bichette .50 .15
❑ 234 Pedro Martinez 1.25 .35
❑ 235 Carlos Delgado .50 .15
❑ 236 Rod Beck .50 .15
❑ 237 Matt Williams .50 .15
❑ 238 Charles Johnson .50 .15
❑ 239 Rico Brogna .50 .15
❑ 240 Frank Thomas 1.25 .35
❑ 241 Paul O'Neill .75 .23
❑ 242 Jaret Wright .50 .15
❑ 243 Brant Brown .50 .15
❑ 244 Ryan Klesko .50 .15
❑ 245 Chuck Finley .50 .15
❑ 246 Derek Bell .50 .15
❑ 247 Delino DeShields .50 .15
❑ 248 Chan Ho Park .50 .15
❑ 249 Wade Boggs .75 .23
❑ 250 Jay Buhner .50 .15
❑ 251 Butch Huskey .50 .15
❑ 252 Steve Finley .50 .15
❑ 253 Will Clark 1.25 .35
❑ 254 John Valentin .50 .15
❑ 255 Bobby Higginson .50 .15
❑ 256 Darryl Strawberry .50 .15
❑ 257 Randy Johnson 1.25 .35
❑ 258 Al Martin .50 .15
❑ 259 Travis Fryman .50 .15
❑ 260 Fred McGriff .75 .23
❑ 261 Jose Valentin .50 .15
❑ 262 Andruw Jones .50 .15
❑ 263 Kenny Rogers .50 .15
❑ 264 Moises Alou .50 .15
❑ 265 Denny Neagle .50 .15
❑ 266 Ugueth Urbina .50 .15
❑ 267 Derrek Lee .50 .15
❑ 268 Ellis Burks .50 .15
❑ 269 Mariano Rivera .75 .23
❑ 270 Dean Palmer .50 .15
❑ 271 Eddie Taubensee .50 .15
❑ 272 Brady Anderson .50 .15
❑ 273 Brian Giles .50 .15
❑ 274 Quinton McCracken .50 .15
❑ 275 Henry Rodriguez .50 .15
❑ 276 Andres Galarraga .50 .15
❑ 277 Jose Canseco 1.25 .35
❑ 278 David Segui .50 .15
❑ 279 Bret Saberhagen .50 .15
❑ 280 Kevin Brown .75 .23
❑ 281 Chuck Knoblauch .50 .15
❑ 282 Jeromy Burnitz .50 .15
❑ 283 Jay Bell .50 .15
❑ 284 Manny Ramirez .75 .23
❑ 285 Rick Helling .50 .15
❑ 286 Francisco Cordova .50 .15
❑ 287 Bob Abreu .50 .15
❑ 288 J.T. Snow .50 .15
❑ 289 Hideo Nomo 1.25 .35
❑ 290 Brian Jordan .50 .15
❑ 291 Javy Lopez .50 .15
❑ 292 Travis Lee .50 .15
❑ 293 Russell Branyan .50 .15
❑ 294 Paul Konerko .50 .15
❑ 295 Masato Yoshii RC 2.50 .75
❑ 296 Kris Benson .50 .15
❑ 297 Juan Encarnacion .50 .15
❑ 298 Eric Milton .50 .15
❑ 299 Mike Caruso .50 .15
❑ 300 R. Aramboles RC 1.50 .45
❑ 301 Bobby Smith .50 .15
❑ 302 Billy Koch .50 .15
❑ 303 Richard Hidalgo .50 .15
❑ 304 Justin Baughman RC 1.00 .30
❑ 305 Chris Gissell .50 .15
❑ 306 Donnie Bridges RC 1.00 .30
❑ 307 Nelson Lara RC 1.00 .30
❑ 308 Randy Wolf RC 2.50 .75
❑ 309 Jason LaRue RC 1.50 .45
❑ 310 Jason Gooding RC 1.00 .30
❑ 311 Edgard Clemente .50 .15
❑ 312 Andrew Vessel .50 .15
❑ 313 Chris Reitsma .50 .15
❑ 314 Jesus Sanchez RC 1.00 .30
❑ 315 Buddy Carlyle RC 1.00 .30
❑ 316 Randy Winn .50 .15
❑ 317 Luis Rivera RC 1.00 .30
❑ 318 Marcus Thames RC 2.50 .75
❑ 319 A.J. Pierzynski .50 .15
❑ 320 Scott Randall .50 .15
❑ 321 Damian Sapp .50 .15
❑ 322 Ed Yarnall RC 1.00 .30
❑ 323 Luke Allen RC 1.50 .45
❑ 324 J.D. Smart .50 .15
❑ 325 Willie Martinez .50 .15
❑ 326 Alex Ramirez .50 .15
❑ 327 Eric DuBose RC 1.50 .45
❑ 328 Kevin Witt .50 .15
❑ 329 Dan McKinley RC 1.00 .30
❑ 330 Cliff Politte .50 .15
❑ 331 Vladimir Nunez .50 .15
❑ 332 John Halama RC 1.00 .30
❑ 333 Nerio Rodriguez .50 .15
❑ 334 Desi Relaford .50 .15
❑ 335 Robinson Checo .50 .15
❑ 336 John Nicholson .75 .23
❑ 337 Tom LaRosa RC 1.00 .30
❑ 338 Kevin Nicholson RC 1.00 .30
❑ 339 Javier Vazquez .50 .15
❑ 340 A.J. Zapp .50 .15
❑ 341 Tom Evans .50 .15
❑ 342 Kerry Robinson .50 .15
❑ 343 Gabe Gonzalez RC 1.00 .30
❑ 344 Ralph Milliard .50 .15
❑ 345 Enrique Wilson .50 .15
❑ 346 Elvin Hernandez .50 .15
❑ 347 Mike Lincoln RC 1.00 .30
❑ 348 Cesar King RC 1.00 .30
❑ 349 Cristian Guzman RC 2.50 .75
❑ 350 Donzell McDonald .50 .15
❑ 351 Jim Parque RC 1.00 .30
❑ 352 Mike Saipe RC 1.00 .30
❑ 353 Carlos Febles RC 1.50 .45
❑ 354 Dernell Stenson RC 1.50 .45
❑ 355 Mark Osborne RC 1.00 .30
❑ 356 Odalis Perez RC 4.00 1.20
❑ 357 Jason Dewey RC 1.00 .30
❑ 358 Joe Fontenot .50 .15
❑ 359 Jason Grilli RC 1.00 .30
❑ 360 Kevin Haverbusch RC 1.00 .30
❑ 361 Jay Yennaco RC 1.00 .30
❑ 362 Brian Buchanan .50 .15
❑ 363 John Barnes .50 .15
❑ 364 Chris Fussell .50 .15
❑ 365 Kevin Gibbs RC 1.00 .30
❑ 366 Joe Lawrence .50 .15
❑ 367 DaRond Stovall .50 .15
❑ 368 Brian Fuentes RC 1.00 .30
❑ 369 Jimmy Anderson .50 .15
❑ 370 Lariel Gonzalez RC 1.00 .30
❑ 371 Scott Williamson RC 1.50 .45
❑ 372 Milton Bradley .50 .15
❑ 373 Jason Halper RC 1.00 .30
❑ 374 Brent Billingsley RC 1.00 .30
❑ 375 Joe DePastino RC 1.00 .30
❑ 376 Jake Westbrook .50 .15
❑ 377 Octavio Dotel .50 .15
❑ 378 Jason Williams RC 1.00 .30
❑ 379 Julio Ramirez RC 1.00 .30
❑ 380 Seth Greisinger .50 .15
❑ 381 Mike Judd RC 1.00 .30
❑ 382 Ben Ford RC 1.00 .30
❑ 383 Tom Bennett RC 1.00 .30
❑ 384 Adam Butler RC 1.00 .30
❑ 385 Wade Miller RC 2.50 .75
❑ 386 Kyle Peterson RC 1.00 .30
❑ 387 Tommy Peterman RC 1.00 .30
❑ 388 Onan Masaoka .50 .15
❑ 389 Jason Rakers RC 1.00 .30
❑ 390 Rafael Medina .50 .15
❑ 391 Luis Lopez RC 1.00 .30
❑ 392 Jeff Yoder .50 .15
❑ 393 Vance Wilson RC 1.00 .30
❑ 394 F. Seguignol RC 1.00 .30
❑ 395 Ron Wright .50 .15
❑ 396 Ruben Mateo RC 1.50 .45
❑ 397 Steve Lomasney RC 1.50 .45
❑ 398 Damian Jackson .50 .15
❑ 399 Mike Jerzembeck RC 1.00 .30
❑ 400 Luis Rivas RC 4.00 1.20
❑ 401 Kevin Burford RC 1.00 .30
❑ 402 Glenn Davis .50 .15
❑ 403 Robert Luce RC 1.00 .30
❑ 404 Cole Liniak .50 .15
❑ 405 Matt LeCroy RC 1.50 .45
❑ 406 Jeremy Giambi RC 1.50 .45
❑ 407 Shawn Chacon .50 .15
❑ 408 Dewayne Wise RC 1.00 .30
❑ 409 Steve Woodard .50 .15
❑ 410 F.Cordero RC 2.50 .75
❑ 411 Damon Minor RC 1.00 .30
❑ 412 Lou Collier .50 .15
❑ 413 Justin Towle .50 .15
❑ 414 Juan LeBron .50 .15
❑ 415 Michael Coleman .50 .15
❑ 416 Felix Rodriguez .50 .15
❑ 417 Paul Ah Yat RC 1.00 .30
❑ 418 Kevin Barker RC 1.00 .30
❑ 419 Brian Meadows .50 .15
❑ 420 Darnell McDonald RC 1.00 .30
❑ 421 Matt Kinney RC 1.50 .45
❑ 422 Mike Vavrek RC 1.00 .30
❑ 423 Courtney Duncan RC 1.00 .30
❑ 424 Kevin Millar RC 5.00 1.50
❑ 425 Ruben Rivera .50 .15
❑ 426 Steve Shoemaker RC 1.00 .30
❑ 427 Dan Reichert RC 1.00 .30
❑ 428 Carlos Lee RC 4.00 1.20
❑ 429 Rod Barajas 2.50 .75
❑ 430 Pablo Ozuna RC 1.50 .45
❑ 431 Todd Belitz RC 1.00 .30
❑ 432 Sidney Ponson .50 .15
❑ 433 Steve Carver RC 1.00 .30
❑ 434 Esteban Yan RC 1.50 .45
❑ 435 Cedrick Bowers .50 .15
❑ 436 Marlon Anderson .50 .15
❑ 437 Carl Pavano .75 .15
❑ 438 Jae Weong Seo RC 2.50 .75
❑ 439 Jose Taveras RC 1.00 .30
❑ 440 Matt Anderson RC 1.50 .45
❑ 441 Darron Ingram RC 1.00 .30

1999 Bowman Chrome

	Nm-Mt	Ex-Mt
COMPLETE SET (440)	230.00	70.00
COMP. SERIES 1 (220)	80.00	24.00
COMP. SERIES 2 (220)	150.00	45.00

❑ 1 Ben Grieve .50 .15
❑ 2 Kerry Wood 1.25 .35
❑ 3 Ruben Rivera .50 .15
❑ 4 Sandy Alomar Jr. .50 .15
❑ 5 Cal Ripken 4.00 1.20
❑ 6 Mark McGwire 3.00 .90
❑ 7 Vladimir Guerrero 1.25 .35
❑ 8 Moises Alou .50 .15
❑ 9 Jim Edmonds .50 .15
❑ 10 Greg Maddux 2.00 .60
❑ 11 Gary Sheffield .50 .15
❑ 12 John Valentin .50 .15
❑ 13 Chuck Knoblauch .50 .15
❑ 14 Tony Clark .50 .15
❑ 15 Rusty Greer .50 .15
❑ 16 Al Leiter .50 .15
❑ 17 Travis Lee .50 .15
❑ 18 Jose Cruz Jr. .50 .15
❑ 19 Pedro Martinez 1.25 .35
❑ 20 Paul O'Neill .75 .23
❑ 21 Todd Walker .50 .15
❑ 22 Vinny Castilla .50 .15
❑ 23 Barry Larkin .75 .23

☐ 24 Curt Schilling .50 .15
☐ 25 Jason Kendall .50 .15
☐ 26 Scott Erickson .50 .15
☐ 27 Andres Galarraga .50 .15
☐ 28 Jeff Shaw .50 .15
☐ 29 John Olerud .50 .15
☐ 30 Orlando Hernandez .50 .15
☐ 31 Larry Walker .75 .23
☐ 32 Andruw Jones .50 .15
☐ 33 Jeff Cirillo .50 .15
☐ 34 Barry Bonds 3.00 .90
☐ 35 Manny Ramirez .75 .23
☐ 36 Mark Kotsay .50 .15
☐ 37 Ivan Rodriguez 1.25 .35
☐ 38 Jeff King .50 .15
☐ 39 Brian Hunter .50 .15
☐ 40 Ray Durham .50 .15
☐ 41 Bernie Williams .75 .23
☐ 42 Darin Erstad .50 .15
☐ 43 Chipper Jones 1.25 .35
☐ 44 Pat Hentgen .50 .15
☐ 45 Eric Young .50 .15
☐ 46 Jaret Wright .50 .15
☐ 47 Juan Guzman .50 .15
☐ 48 Jorge Posada .75 .23
☐ 49 Bobby Higginson .50 .15
☐ 50 Jose Guillen .50 .15
☐ 51 Trevor Hoffman .50 .15
☐ 52 Ken Griffey Jr. 2.00 .60
☐ 53 David Justice .50 .15
☐ 54 Matt Williams .50 .15
☐ 55 Eric Karros .50 .15
☐ 56 Derek Bell .50 .15
☐ 57 Ray Lankford .50 .15
☐ 58 Mariano Rivera .75 .23
☐ 59 Brett Tomko .50 .15
☐ 60 Mike Mussina .75 .23
☐ 61 Kenny Lofton .50 .15
☐ 62 Chuck Finley .50 .15
☐ 63 Alex Gonzalez .50 .15
☐ 64 Mark Grace .75 .23
☐ 65 Raul Mondesi .50 .15
☐ 66 David Cone .50 .15
☐ 67 Brad Fullmer .50 .15
☐ 68 Andy Benes .50 .15
☐ 69 John Smoltz .75 .23
☐ 70 Shane Reynolds .50 .15
☐ 71 Bruce Chen .50 .15
☐ 72 Adam Kennedy .50 .15
☐ 73 Jack Cust .50 .15
☐ 74 Matt Clement .50 .15
☐ 75 Derrick Gibson .50 .15
☐ 76 Darnell McDonald .50 .15
☐ 77 Adam Everett RC 2.50 .75
☐ 78 Ricardo Aramboles .50 .15
☐ 79 Mark Quinn RC 1.50 .45
☐ 80 Jason Rakers .50 .15
☐ 81 Seth Etherton RC 1.00 .30
☐ 82 Jeff Urban RC 1.00 .30
☐ 83 Manny Aybar .50 .15
☐ 84 Mike Nannini RC 1.00 .30
☐ 85 Onan Masaoka .50 .15
☐ 86 Rod Barajas .50 .15
☐ 87 Mike Frank .50 .15
☐ 88 Scott Randall .50 .15
☐ 89 Justin Bowles RC 1.00 .30
☐ 90 Chris Haas .50 .15
☐ 91 Arturo McDowell RC 1.00 .30
☐ 92 Matt Belisle RC 1.00 .30
☐ 93 Scott Elarton .50 .15
☐ 94 Vernon Wells .50 .15
☐ 95 Pat Cline .50 .15
☐ 96 Ryan Anderson .50 .15
☐ 97 Kevin Barker .50 .15
☐ 98 Ruben Mateo .50 .15
☐ 99 Robert Fick .50 .15
☐ 100 Corey Koskie .50 .15
☐ 101 Ricky Ledee .50 .15
☐ 102 Rick Elder RC 1.50 .45
☐ 103 Jack Cressend RC 1.00 .30
☐ 104 Joe Lawrence .50 .15
☐ 105 Mike Lincoln .50 .15
☐ 106 Kit Pellow RC 1.00 .30
☐ 107 Matt Burch RC 1.00 .30
☐ 108 Cole Liniak .50 .15
☐ 109 Jason Dewey .50 .15
☐ 110 Cesar King .50 .15
☐ 111 Julio Ramirez .50 .15
☐ 112 Jake Westbrook .50 .15
☐ 113 Eric Valent RC 1.50 .45
☐ 114 Roosevelt Brown RC 1.00 .30
☐ 115 Choo Freeman RC 1.50 .45
☐ 116 Juan Melo .50 .15
☐ 117 Jason Grilli .50 .15
☐ 118 Jared Sandberg .50 .15
☐ 119 Glenn Davis .50 .15
☐ 120 David Riske RC 1.00 .30
☐ 121 Jacque Jones .50 .15
☐ 122 Corey Lee .50 .15
☐ 123 Michael Barrett .50 .15
☐ 124 Lariel Gonzalez .50 .15
☐ 125 Mitch Meluskey .50 .15
☐ 126 Freddy Adrian Garcia .50 .15
☐ 127 Tony Torcato RC 1.50 .45
☐ 128 Jeff Liefer .50 .15
☐ 129 Ntema Ndungidi .50 .15
☐ 130 Andy Brown RC 1.00 .30
☐ 131 Ryan Mills RC 1.00 .30
☐ 132 Andy Abad RC 1.00 .30
☐ 133 Carlos Febles .50 .15
☐ 134 Jason Tyner RC 1.00 .30
☐ 135 Mark Osborne .50 .15
☐ 136 Phil Norton RC 1.00 .30
☐ 137 Nathan Haynes .50 .15
☐ 138 Roy Halladay .50 .15
☐ 139 Juan Encarnacion .50 .15
☐ 140 Brad Penny .50 .15
☐ 141 Grant Roberts .50 .15
☐ 142 Aramis Ramirez .50 .15
☐ 143 Cristian Guzman .50 .15
☐ 144 Mamon Tucker RC 1.00 .30
☐ 145 Ryan Bradley .50 .15
☐ 146 Brian Simmons .50 .15
☐ 147 Dan Reichert .50 .15
☐ 148 Russell Branyan .50 .15
☐ 149 Victor Valencia RC 1.00 .30
☐ 150 Scott Schoeneweis .50 .15
☐ 151 Sean Spencer RC 1.00 .30
☐ 152 Odalis Perez .50 .15
☐ 153 Joe Fontenot .50 .15
☐ 154 Milton Bradley .50 .15
☐ 155 Josh McKinley RC 1.50 .45
☐ 156 Terrence Long .50 .15
☐ 157 Danny Klassen .50 .15
☐ 158 Paul Hoover RC 1.00 .30
☐ 159 Ron Belliard .50 .15
☐ 160 Armando Rios .50 .15
☐ 161 Ramon Hernandez .50 .15
☐ 162 Jason Conti .50 .15
☐ 163 Chad Hermansen .50 .15
☐ 164 Jason Standridge .50 .15
☐ 165 Jason Dellaero .50 .15
☐ 166 John Curtice .50 .15
☐ 167 Clayton Andrews RC 1.00 .30
☐ 168 Jeremy Giambi .50 .15
☐ 169 Alex Ramirez .50 .15
☐ 170 Gabe Molina RC 1.00 .30
☐ 171 M.Encarnacion RC 1.00 .30
☐ 172 Mike Zywica RC 1.00 .30
☐ 173 Chip Ambres RC 1.00 .30
☐ 174 Trot Nixon .50 .15
☐ 175 Pat Burrell RC 8.00 2.40
☐ 176 Jeff Yoder .50 .15
☐ 177 Chris Jones RC 1.00 .30
☐ 178 Kevin Witt .50 .15
☐ 179 Keith Luuloa RC 1.00 .30
☐ 180 Billy Koch .50 .15
☐ 181 Damaso Marte RC 1.00 .30
☐ 182 Ryan Glynn RC 1.00 .30
☐ 183 Calvin Pickering .50 .15
☐ 184 Michael Cuddyer .50 .15
☐ 185 Nick Johnson RC 4.00 1.20
☐ 186 D.Mientkiewicz RC 4.00 1.20
☐ 187 Nate Cornejo RC 1.50 .45
☐ 188 Octavio Dotel .50 .15
☐ 189 Wes Helms .50 .15
☐ 190 Nelson Lara .50 .15
☐ 191 Chuck Abbott RC 1.00 .30
☐ 192 Tony Armas Jr. .50 .15
☐ 193 Gil Meche .50 .15
☐ 194 Ben Petrick .50 .15
☐ 195 Chris George RC 1.50 .45
☐ 196 Scott Hunter RC 1.00 .30
☐ 197 Ryan Brannan .50 .15
☐ 198 Amaury Garcia RC 1.00 .30
☐ 199 Chris Gissell .50 .15
☐ 200 Austin Kearns RC 12.00 3.60
☐ 201 Alex Gonzalez .50 .15
☐ 202 Wade Miller .50 .15
☐ 203 Scott Williamson .50 .15
☐ 204 Chris Enochs .50 .15
☐ 205 Fernando Seguignol .50 .15
☐ 206 Marlon Anderson .50 .15
☐ 207 Todd Sears RC 1.50 .45
☐ 208 Nate Bump RC 1.00 .30
☐ 209 J.M. Gold RC 1.00 .30
☐ 210 Matt LeCroy .50 .15
☐ 211 Alex Hernandez .50 .15
☐ 212 Luis Rivera .50 .15
☐ 213 Troy Cameron .50 .15
☐ 214 Alex Escobar RC 1.50 .45
☐ 215 Jason LaRue .50 .15
☐ 216 Kyle Peterson .50 .15
☐ 217 Brent Butler .50 .15
☐ 218 Dernell Stenson .50 .15
☐ 219 Adrian Beltre .75 .23
☐ 220 Daryle Ward .50 .15
☐ 221 Jim Thome 1.25 .35
☐ 222 Cliff Floyd .50 .15
☐ 223 Rickey Henderson 1.25 .35
☐ 224 Garret Anderson .50 .15
☐ 225 Ken Caminiti .50 .15
☐ 226 Bret Boone .50 .15
☐ 227 Jeromy Burnitz .50 .15
☐ 228 Steve Finley .50 .15
☐ 229 Miguel Tejada .50 .15
☐ 230 Greg Vaughn .50 .15
☐ 231 Jose Offerman .50 .15
☐ 232 Andy Ashby .50 .15
☐ 233 Albert Belle .50 .15
☐ 234 Fernando Tatis .50 .15
☐ 235 Todd Helton .75 .23
☐ 236 Sean Casey .50 .15
☐ 237 Brian Giles .50 .15
☐ 238 Andy Pettitte .75 .23
☐ 239 Fred McGriff .75 .23
☐ 240 Roberto Alomar .75 .23
☐ 241 Edgar Martinez .75 .23
☐ 242 Lee Stevens .50 .15
☐ 243 Shawn Green .50 .15
☐ 244 Ryan Klesko .50 .15
☐ 245 Sammy Sosa 2.00 .60
☐ 246 Todd Hundley .50 .15
☐ 247 Shannon Stewart .50 .15
☐ 248 Randy Johnson 1.25 .35
☐ 249 Rondell White .50 .15
☐ 250 Mike Piazza 2.00 .60
☐ 251 Craig Biggio .75 .23
☐ 252 David Wells .50 .15
☐ 253 Brian Jordan .50 .15
☐ 254 Edgar Renteria .50 .15
☐ 255 Bartolo Colon .50 .15
☐ 256 Frank Thomas 1.25 .35
☐ 257 Will Clark 1.25 .35
☐ 258 Dean Palmer .50 .15
☐ 259 Dmitri Young .50 .15
☐ 260 Scott Rolen 1.25 .35
☐ 261 Jeff Kent .50 .15
☐ 262 Dante Bichette .50 .15
☐ 263 Nomar Garciaparra 2.00 .60
☐ 264 Tony Gwynn 1.50 .45
☐ 265 Alex Rodriguez 2.00 .60
☐ 266 Jose Canseco 1.25 .35
☐ 267 Jason Giambi .50 .15
☐ 268 Jeff Bagwell .75 .23
☐ 269 Carlos Delgado .50 .15
☐ 270 Tom Glavine .75 .23
☐ 271 Eric Davis .50 .15
☐ 272 Edgardo Alfonzo .50 .15
☐ 273 Tim Salmon .75 .23
☐ 274 Johnny Damon .75 .23
☐ 275 Rafael Palmeiro .75 .23
☐ 276 Denny Neagle .50 .15
☐ 277 Neifi Perez .50 .15
☐ 278 Roger Clemens 2.50 .75
☐ 279 Brant Brown .50 .15
☐ 280 Kevin Brown .75 .23
☐ 281 Jay Bell .50 .15

	Nm-Mt	Ex-Mt
❑ 282 Jay Buhner	.50	.15
❑ 283 Matt Lawton	.50	.15
❑ 284 Robin Ventura	.50	.15
❑ 285 Juan Gonzalez	.75	.23
❑ 286 Mo Vaughn	.50	.15
❑ 287 Kevin Millwood	.50	.15
❑ 288 Tino Martinez	.75	.23
❑ 289 Justin Thompson	.50	.15
❑ 290 Derek Jeter	3.00	.90
❑ 291 Ben Davis	.50	.15
❑ 292 Mike Lowell	.50	.15
❑ 293 Calvin Murray	.50	.15
❑ 294 Micah Bowie RC	1.00	.30
❑ 295 Lance Berkman	.50	.15
❑ 296 Jason Marquis	.50	.15
❑ 297 Chad Green	.50	.15
❑ 298 Dee Brown	.50	.15
❑ 299 Jerry Hairston Jr.	.50	.15
❑ 300 Gabe Kapler	.50	.15
❑ 301 Brent Stentz RC	1.00	.30
❑ 302 Scott Mullen RC	1.00	.30
❑ 303 Brandon Reed	.50	.15
❑ 304 Shea Hillenbrand RC	4.00	1.20
❑ 305 J.D. Closser RC	2.50	.75
❑ 306 Gary Matthews Jr.	.50	.15
❑ 307 Toby Hall RC	1.50	.45
❑ 308 Jason Phillips RC	1.00	.30
❑ 309 Jose Macias RC	1.00	.30
❑ 310 Jung Bong RC	1.50	.45
❑ 311 Ramon Soler RC	1.00	.30
❑ 312 Kelly Dransfeldt RC	1.00	.30
❑ 313 Carlos E. Hernandez RC	1.50	.45
❑ 314 Kevin Haverbusch	.50	.15
❑ 315 Aaron Myette RC	1.00	.30
❑ 316 Chad Harville RC	1.00	.30
❑ 317 Kyle Farnsworth RC	1.50	.45
❑ 318 Gookie Dawkins RC	1.50	.45
❑ 319 Willie Martinez	.50	.15
❑ 320 Carlos Lee	.50	.15
❑ 321 Carlos Pena RC	2.50	.75
❑ 322 Peter Bergeron RC	1.50	.45
❑ 323 A.J. Burnett RC	4.00	1.20
❑ 324 Bucky Jacobsen RC	8.00	2.40
❑ 325 Mo Bruce RC	1.00	.30
❑ 326 Reggie Taylor	.50	.15
❑ 327 Jackie Rexrode	.50	.15
❑ 328 Alvin Morrow RC	1.00	.30
❑ 329 Carlos Beltran	.75	.23
❑ 330 Eric Chavez	.50	.15
❑ 331 John Patterson	.50	.15
❑ 332 Jayson Werth	.50	.15
❑ 333 Richie Sexson	.50	.15
❑ 334 Randy Wolf	.50	.15
❑ 335 Eli Marrero	.50	.15
❑ 336 Paul LoDuca	.50	.15
❑ 337 J.D Smart	.50	.15
❑ 338 Ryan Minor	.50	.15
❑ 339 Kris Benson	.50	.15
❑ 340 George Lombard	.50	.15
❑ 341 Troy Glaus	.50	.15
❑ 342 Eddie Yarnall	.50	.15
❑ 343 Kip Wells RC	2.50	.75
❑ 344 C.C. Sabathia RC	5.00	1.50
❑ 345 Sean Burroughs RC	6.00	1.80
❑ 346 Felipe Lopez RC	1.50	.45
❑ 347 Ryan Rupe RC	1.00	.30
❑ 348 Orber Moreno RC	1.00	.30
❑ 349 Rafael Roque RC	1.00	.30
❑ 350 Alfonso Soriano RC	25.00	7.50
❑ 351 Pablo Ozuna	.50	.15
❑ 352 Corey Patterson RC	10.00	3.00
❑ 353 Braden Looper	.50	.15
❑ 354 Robbie Bell	.50	.15
❑ 355 Mark Mulder RC	10.00	2.40
❑ 356 Angel Pena	.50	.15
❑ 357 Kevin McGlinchy	.50	.15
❑ 358 M.Restovich RC	1.50	.45
❑ 359 Eric DuBose	.50	.15
❑ 360 Geoff Jenkins	.50	.15
❑ 361 Mark Harriger RC	1.00	.30
❑ 362 Junior Herndon RC	1.50	.45
❑ 363 Tim Raines Jr. RC	1.50	.45
❑ 364 Rafael Furcal RC	5.00	1.50
❑ 365 Marcus Giles RC	5.00	1.50
❑ 366 Ted Lilly	.50	.15
❑ 367 Jorge Toca RC	1.50	.45
❑ 368 David Kelton RC	1.50	.45
❑ 369 Adam Dunn RC	20.00	6.00
❑ 370 Guillermo Mota RC	1.00	.30
❑ 371 Brett Laxton RC	1.00	.30
❑ 372 Travis Harper RC	1.00	.30
❑ 373 Tom Davey RC	1.00	.30
❑ 374 Darren Blakely RC	1.00	.30
❑ 375 Tim Hudson RC	10.00	3.00
❑ 376 Jason Romano	.50	.15
❑ 377 Dan Reichert	.50	.15
❑ 378 Julio Lugo RC	1.50	.45
❑ 379 Jose Garcia RC	1.00	.30
❑ 380 Erubiel Durazo RC	2.50	.75
❑ 381 Jose Jimenez	.50	.15
❑ 382 Chris Fussell	.50	.15
❑ 383 Steve Lomasney	.50	.15
❑ 384 Juan Pena RC	1.00	.30
❑ 385 Allen Levrault RC	1.00	.30
❑ 386 Juan Rivera RC	1.50	.45
❑ 387 Steve Colyer RC	1.50	.45
❑ 388 Joe Nathan RC	4.00	1.20
❑ 389 Ron Walker RC	1.00	.30
❑ 390 Nick Bierbrodt	.50	.15
❑ 391 Luke Prokopec RC	1.00	.30
❑ 392 Dave Roberts RC	2.50	.75
❑ 393 Mike Darr	.50	.15
❑ 394 Abraham Nunez RC	1.50	.45
❑ 395 G.Chiaramonte RC	1.00	.30
❑ 396 J.Van Buren RC	1.00	.30
❑ 397 Mike Kusiewicz	.50	.15
❑ 398 Matt Wise RC	1.00	.30
❑ 399 Joe McEwing RC	1.50	.45
❑ 400 Matt Holliday RC	4.00	1.20
❑ 401 Willi Mo Pena RC	10.00	3.00
❑ 402 Ruben Quevedo RC	1.00	.30
❑ 403 Rob Ryan RC	1.00	.30
❑ 404 Freddy Garcia RC	4.00	1.20
❑ 405 Kevin Eberwein RC	1.00	.30
❑ 406 Jesus Colome RC	1.00	.30
❑ 407 Chris Singleton	.50	.15
❑ 408 Bubba Crosby RC	2.50	.75
❑ 409 Jesus Cordero RC	1.50	.45
❑ 410 Donny Leon	.50	.15
❑ 411 G.Tomlinson RC	1.00	.30
❑ 412 Jeff Winchester RC	1.00	.30
❑ 413 Adam Piatt RC	1.50	.45
❑ 414 Robert Stratton	.50	.15
❑ 415 T.J. Tucker	.50	.15
❑ 416 Ryan Langerhans RC	1.00	.30
❑ 417 A.Shumaker RC	1.00	.30
❑ 418 Matt Miller RC	1.00	.30
❑ 419 Doug Clark RC	1.00	.30
❑ 420 Kory DeHaan RC	1.00	.30
❑ 421 David Eckstein RC	2.50	.75
❑ 422 Brian Cooper RC	1.00	.30
❑ 423 Brady Clark RC	1.00	.30
❑ 424 Chris Magruder RC	1.00	.30
❑ 425 Bobby Seay RC	1.00	.30
❑ 426 Aubrey Huff RC	5.00	1.50
❑ 427 Mike Jerzembeck	.50	.15
❑ 428 Matt Blank RC	1.00	.30
❑ 429 Benny Agbayani RC	1.50	.45
❑ 430 Kevin Beirne RC	1.50	.45
❑ 431 Josh Hamilton RC	2.50	.75
❑ 432 Josh Girdley RC	1.00	.30
❑ 433 Kyle Snyder RC	1.00	.30
❑ 434 Mike Paradis RC	1.00	.30
❑ 435 Jason Jennings RC	2.50	.75
❑ 436 David Walling RC	1.00	.30
❑ 437 Omar Ortiz RC	1.00	.30
❑ 438 Jay Gehrke RC	1.50	.45
❑ 439 Casey Burns RC	1.00	.30
❑ 440 Carl Crawford RC	8.00	2.40

2000 Bowman Chrome

	Nm-Mt	Ex-Mt
COMPLETE SET (440)	120.00	36.00
❑ 1 Vladimir Guerrero	1.25	.35
❑ 2 Chipper Jones	1.25	.35
❑ 3 Todd Walker	.50	.15
❑ 4 Barry Larkin	.75	.23
❑ 5 Bernie Williams	.75	.23
❑ 6 Todd Helton	.75	.23
❑ 7 Jermaine Dye	.50	.15

	Nm-Mt	Ex-Mt
❑ 8 Brian Giles	.50	.15
❑ 9 Freddy Garcia	.50	.15
❑ 10 Greg Vaughn	.50	.15
❑ 11 Alex Gonzalez	.50	.15
❑ 12 Luis Gonzalez	.50	.15
❑ 13 Ron Belliard	.50	.15
❑ 14 Ben Grieve	.50	.15
❑ 15 Carlos Delgado	.50	.15
❑ 16 Brian Jordan	.50	.15
❑ 17 Fernando Tatis	.50	.15
❑ 18 Ryan Rupe	.50	.15
❑ 19 Miguel Tejada	.50	.15
❑ 20 Mark Grace	.75	.23
❑ 21 Kenny Lofton	.50	.15
❑ 22 Eric Karros	.50	.15
❑ 23 Cliff Floyd	.50	.15
❑ 24 John Halama	.50	.15
❑ 25 Cristian Guzman	.50	.15
❑ 26 Scott Williamson	.50	.15
❑ 27 Mike Lieberthal	.50	.15
❑ 28 Tim Hudson	.50	.15
❑ 29 Warren Morris	.50	.15
❑ 30 Pedro Martinez	1.25	.35
❑ 31 John Smoltz	.75	.23
❑ 32 Ray Durham	.50	.15
❑ 33 Chad Allen	.50	.15
❑ 34 Tony Clark	.50	.15
❑ 35 Tino Martinez	.75	.23
❑ 36 J.T. Snow	.50	.15
❑ 37 Kevin Brown	.75	.23
❑ 38 Bartolo Colon	.50	.15
❑ 39 Rey Ordonez	.50	.15
❑ 40 Jeff Bagwell	.75	.23
❑ 41 Ivan Rodriguez	1.25	.35
❑ 42 Eric Chavez	.50	.15
❑ 43 Eric Milton	.50	.15
❑ 44 Jose Canseco	1.25	.35
❑ 45 Shawn Green	.50	.15
❑ 46 Rich Aurilia	.50	.15
❑ 47 Roberto Alomar	.75	.23
❑ 48 Brian Daubach	.50	.15
❑ 49 Magglio Ordonez	.50	.15
❑ 50 Derek Jeter	3.00	.90
❑ 51 Kris Benson	.50	.15
❑ 52 Albert Belle	.50	.15
❑ 53 Rondell White	.50	.15
❑ 54 Justin Thompson	.50	.15
❑ 55 Nomar Garciaparra	2.00	.60
❑ 56 Chuck Finley	.50	.15
❑ 57 Omar Vizquel	.75	.23
❑ 58 Luis Castillo	.50	.15
❑ 59 Richard Hidalgo	.50	.15
❑ 60 Barry Bonds	3.00	.90
❑ 61 Craig Biggio	.75	.23
❑ 62 Doug Glanville	.50	.15
❑ 63 Gabe Kapler	.50	.15
❑ 64 Johnny Damon	.75	.23
❑ 65 Pokey Reese	.50	.15
❑ 66 Andy Pettitte	.75	.23
❑ 67 B.J. Surhoff	.50	.15
❑ 68 Richie Sexson	.50	.15
❑ 69 Javy Lopez	.50	.15
❑ 70 Raul Mondesi	.50	.15
❑ 71 Darin Erstad	.50	.15
❑ 72 Kevin Millwood	.50	.15
❑ 73 Ricky Ledee	.50	.15
❑ 74 John Olerud	.50	.15
❑ 75 Sean Casey	.50	.15

❑ 76	Carlos Febles	.50	.15
❑ 77	Paul O'Neill	.75	.23
❑ 78	Bob Abreu	.50	.15
❑ 79	Neifi Perez	.50	.15
❑ 80	Tony Gwynn	1.50	.45
❑ 81	Russ Ortiz	.50	.15
❑ 82	Matt Williams	.50	.15
❑ 83	Chris Carpenter	.50	.15
❑ 84	Roger Cedeno	.50	.15
❑ 85	Tim Salmon	.75	.23
❑ 86	Billy Koch	.50	.15
❑ 87	Jeromy Burnitz	.50	.15
❑ 88	Edgardo Alfonzo	.50	.15
❑ 89	Jay Bell	.50	.15
❑ 90	Manny Ramirez	.75	.23
❑ 91	Frank Thomas	1.25	.35
❑ 92	Mike Mussina	.75	.23
❑ 93	J.D. Drew	.50	.15
❑ 94	Adrian Beltre	.75	.23
❑ 95	Alex Rodriguez	2.00	.60
❑ 96	Larry Walker	.75	.23
❑ 97	Juan Encarnacion	.50	.15
❑ 98	Mike Sweeney	.50	.15
❑ 99	Rusty Greer	.50	.15
❑ 100	Randy Johnson	1.25	.35
❑ 101	Jose Vidro	.50	.15
❑ 102	Preston Wilson	.50	.15
❑ 103	Greg Maddux	2.00	.60
❑ 104	Jason Giambi	.50	.15
❑ 105	Cal Ripken	4.00	1.20
❑ 106	Carlos Beltran	.75	.23
❑ 107	Vinny Castilla	.50	.15
❑ 108	Mariano Rivera	.75	.23
❑ 109	Mo Vaughn	.50	.15
❑ 110	Rafael Palmeiro	.75	.23
❑ 111	Shannon Stewart	.50	.15
❑ 112	Mike Hampton	.50	.15
❑ 113	Joe Nathan	.50	.15
❑ 114	Ben Davis	.50	.15
❑ 115	Andruw Jones	.50	.15
❑ 116	Robin Ventura	.50	.15
❑ 117	Damion Easley	.50	.15
❑ 118	Jeff Cirillo	.50	.15
❑ 119	Kerry Wood	1.25	.35
❑ 120	Scott Rolen	1.25	.35
❑ 121	Sammy Sosa	2.00	.60
❑ 122	Ken Griffey Jr.	2.00	.60
❑ 123	Shane Reynolds	.50	.15
❑ 124	Troy Glaus	.50	.15
❑ 125	Tom Glavine	.75	.23
❑ 126	Michael Barrett	.50	.15
❑ 127	Al Leiter	.50	.15
❑ 128	Jason Kendall	.50	.15
❑ 129	Roger Clemens	2.50	.75
❑ 130	Juan Gonzalez	.75	.23
❑ 131	Corey Koskie	.50	.15
❑ 132	Curt Schilling	.50	.15
❑ 133	Mike Piazza	2.00	.60
❑ 134	Gary Sheffield	.50	.15
❑ 135	Jim Thome	1.25	.35
❑ 136	Orlando Hernandez	.50	.15
❑ 137	Ray Lankford	.50	.15
❑ 138	Geoff Jenkins	.50	.15
❑ 139	Jose Lima	.50	.15
❑ 140	Mark McGwire	3.00	.90
❑ 141	Adam Piatt	.50	.15
❑ 142	Pat Manning RC	.75	.23
❑ 143	Marcos Castillo RC	.75	.23
❑ 144	Lesli Brea RC	.75	.23
❑ 145	Humberto Cota RC	1.25	.35
❑ 146	Ben Petrick	.50	.15
❑ 147	Kip Wells	.50	.15
❑ 148	Wily Pena	.50	.15
❑ 149	Chris Wakeland RC	.75	.23
❑ 150	Brad Baker RC	1.25	.35
❑ 151	Robbie Morrison RC	.75	.23
❑ 152	Reggie Taylor	.50	.15
❑ 153	Matt Ginter RC	1.25	.35
❑ 154	Peter Bergeron	.50	.15
❑ 155	Roosevelt Brown	.50	.15
❑ 156	Matt Cepicky RC	.75	.23
❑ 157	Ramon Castro	.50	.15
❑ 158	Brad Baisley RC	.75	.23
❑ 159	Jason Hart RC	.75	.23
❑ 160	Mitch Meluskey	.50	.15
❑ 161	Chad Harville	.50	.15
❑ 162	Brian Cooper	.50	.15
❑ 163	Marcus Giles	.50	.15
❑ 164	Jim Morris	1.25	.35
❑ 165	Geoff Goetz	.50	.15
❑ 166	Bobby Bradley RC	1.25	.35
❑ 167	Rob Bell	.50	.15
❑ 168	Joe Crede	.50	.15
❑ 169	Michael Restovich	.50	.15
❑ 170	Quincy Foster RC	.75	.23
❑ 171	Enrique Cruz RC	.75	.23
❑ 172	Mark Quinn	.50	.15
❑ 173	Nick Johnson	.50	.15
❑ 174	Jeff Liefer	.50	.15
❑ 175	Kevin Mench RC	3.00	.90
❑ 176	Steve Lomasney	.50	.15
❑ 177	Jayson Werth	.50	.15
❑ 178	Tim Drew	.50	.15
❑ 179	Chip Ambres	.50	.15
❑ 180	Ryan Anderson	.50	.15
❑ 181	Matt Blank	.50	.15
❑ 182	G. Chiaramonte	.50	.15
❑ 183	Corey Myers RC	1.25	.35
❑ 184	Jeff Yoder	.50	.15
❑ 185	Craig Dingman RC	.75	.23
❑ 186	Jon Hamilton RC	.75	.23
❑ 187	Toby Hall	.50	.15
❑ 188	Russell Branyan	.50	.15
❑ 189	Brian Falkenborg RC	.75	.23
❑ 190	Aaron Harang RC	1.25	.35
❑ 191	Juan Pena	.50	.15
❑ 192	Chin-Hui Tsao RC	3.00	.90
❑ 193	Alfonso Soriano	1.25	.35
❑ 194	Alejandro Diaz RC	.75	.23
❑ 195	Carlos Pena	.50	.15
❑ 196	Kevin Nicholson	.50	.15
❑ 197	Mo Bruce	.50	.15
❑ 198	C.C. Sabathia	.50	.15
❑ 199	Carl Crawford	.50	.15
❑ 200	Rafael Furcal	.50	.15
❑ 201	Andrew Beinbrink RC	.75	.23
❑ 202	Jimmy Osting	.50	.15
❑ 203	Aaron McNeal RC	1.25	.35
❑ 204	Brett Laxton	.50	.15
❑ 205	Chris George	.50	.15
❑ 206	Felipe Lopez	.50	.15
❑ 207	Ben Sheets RC	8.00	2.40
❑ 208	Mike Meyers RC	1.25	.35
❑ 209	Jason Conti	.50	.15
❑ 210	Milton Bradley	.50	.15
❑ 211	Chris Mears RC	.75	.23
❑ 212	Carlos Hernandez RC	1.25	.35
❑ 213	Jason Romano	.50	.15
❑ 214	Geofrey Tomlinson	.50	.15
❑ 215	Jimmy Rollins	.50	.15
❑ 216	Pablo Ozuna	.50	.15
❑ 217	Steve Cox	.50	.15
❑ 218	Terrence Long	.50	.15
❑ 219	Jeff DaVanon RC	1.25	.35
❑ 220	Rick Ankiel	.50	.15
❑ 221	Jason Standridge	.50	.15
❑ 222	Tony Armas Jr.	.50	.15
❑ 223	Jason Tyner	.50	.15
❑ 224	Ramon Ortiz	.50	.15
❑ 225	Daryle Ward	.50	.15
❑ 226	Enger Veras RC	.75	.23
❑ 227	Chris Jones	.50	.15
❑ 228	Eric Cammack RC	.75	.23
❑ 229	Ruben Mateo	.50	.15
❑ 230	Ken Harvey RC	3.00	.90
❑ 231	Jake Westbrook	.50	.15
❑ 232	Rob Purvis RC	.75	.23
❑ 233	Choo Freeman	.50	.15
❑ 234	Aramis Ramirez	.50	.15
❑ 235	A.J. Burnett	.50	.15
❑ 236	Kevin Barker	.50	.15
❑ 237	Chance Caple RC	.75	.23
❑ 238	Jarrod Washburn	.50	.15
❑ 239	Lance Berkman	.50	.15
❑ 240	Michael Wenner RC	.75	.23
❑ 241	Alex Sanchez	.50	.15
❑ 242	Pat Daneker	.50	.15
❑ 243	Grant Roberts	.50	.15
❑ 244	Mark Ellis RC	1.25	.35
❑ 245	Donny Leon	.50	.15
❑ 246	David Eckstein	.50	.15
❑ 247	Dicky Gonzalez RC	.75	.23
❑ 248	John Patterson	.50	.15
❑ 249	Chad Green	.50	.15
❑ 250	Scot Shields RC	.75	.23
❑ 251	Troy Cameron	.50	.15
❑ 252	Jose Molina	.50	.15
❑ 253	Rob Pugmire RC	.75	.23
❑ 254	Rick Elder	.50	.15
❑ 255	Sean Burroughs	.50	.15
❑ 256	Josh Kalinowski RC	.75	.23
❑ 257	Matt LeCroy	.50	.15
❑ 258	Alex Graman RC	.75	.23
❑ 259	Juan Silvestre RC	.75	.23
❑ 260	Brady Clark	.50	.15
❑ 261	Rico Washington RC	.75	.23
❑ 262	Gary Matthews Jr.	.50	.15
❑ 263	Matt Wise	.50	.15
❑ 264	Keith Reed RC	1.25	.35
❑ 265	Santiago Ramirez RC	.75	.23
❑ 266	Ben Broussard RC	3.00	.90
❑ 267	Ryan Langerhans	.50	.15
❑ 268	Juan Rivera	.50	.15
❑ 269	Shawn Gallagher	.50	.15
❑ 270	Jorge Toca	.50	.15
❑ 271	Brad Lidge	.50	.15
❑ 272	Leoncio Estrella RC	.75	.23
❑ 273	Ruben Quevedo	.50	.15
❑ 274	Jack Cust	.50	.15
❑ 275	T.J. Tucker	.50	.15
❑ 276	Mike Colangelo	.50	.15
❑ 277	Brian Schneider	.50	.15
❑ 278	Calvin Murray	.50	.15
❑ 279	Josh Girdley	.50	.15
❑ 280	Mike Paradis	.50	.15
❑ 281	Chad Hermansen	.50	.15
❑ 282	Ty Howington RC	1.25	.35
❑ 283	Aaron Myette	.50	.15
❑ 284	D'Angelo Jimenez	.50	.15
❑ 285	Dernell Stenson	.50	.15
❑ 286	Jerry Hairston Jr.	.50	.15
❑ 287	Gary Majewski RC	2.00	.60
❑ 288	Derrin Ebert	.50	.15
❑ 289	Steve Fish RC	.75	.23
❑ 290	Carlos E. Hernandez	.50	.15
❑ 291	Allen Levrault	.50	.15
❑ 292	Sean McNally RC	.75	.23
❑ 293	Randey Dorame RC	.75	.23
❑ 294	Wes Anderson RC	1.25	.35
❑ 295	B.J. Ryan	.50	.15
❑ 296	Alan Webb RC	.75	.23
❑ 297	Brandon Inge RC	1.25	.35
❑ 298	David Walling	.50	.15
❑ 299	Sun Woo Kim RC	1.25	.35
❑ 300	Pat Burrell	.50	.15
❑ 301	Rick Guttormson RC	.75	.23
❑ 302	Gil Meche	.50	.15
❑ 303	Carlos Zambrano RC	12.00	3.60
❑ 304	Eric Byrnes UER RC Bo Porter pictured	3.00	.90
❑ 305	Robb Quinlan RC	3.00	.90
❑ 306	Jackie Rexrode	.50	.15
❑ 307	Nate Bump	.50	.15
❑ 308	Sean DePaula RC	.75	.23
❑ 309	Matt Riley	.50	.15
❑ 310	Ryan Minor	.50	.15
❑ 311	J.J. Davis	.50	.15
❑ 312	Randy Wolf	.50	.15
❑ 313	Jason Jennings	.50	.15
❑ 314	Scott Seabol RC	.75	.23
❑ 315	Doug Davis	.50	.15
❑ 316	Todd Moser RC	.75	.23
❑ 317	Rob Ryan	.50	.15
❑ 318	Bubba Crosby	.50	.15
❑ 319	Lyle Overbay RC	5.00	1.50
❑ 320	Mario Encarnacion	.50	.15
❑ 321	F.Rodriguez RC	8.00	2.40
❑ 322	Michael Cuddyer	.50	.15
❑ 323	Ed Yarnall	.50	.15
❑ 324	Cesar Saba RC	.75	.23
❑ 325	Gookie Dawkins	.50	.15
❑ 326	Alex Escobar	.50	.15
❑ 327	Julio Zuleta RC	.75	.23
❑ 328	Josh Hamilton	.50	.15
❑ 329	Carlos Urquiola RC	.75	.23
❑ 330	Matt Belisle	.50	.15
❑ 331	Kurt Ainsworth RC	1.25	.35
❑ 332	Tim Raines Jr.	.50	.15

	Player	Nm-Mt	Ex-Mt
❑ 333	Eric Munson	.50	.15
❑ 334	Donzell McDonald	.50	.15
❑ 335	Larry Bigbie RC	3.00	.90
❑ 336	Matt Watson RC	.75	.23
❑ 337	Aubrey Huff	.50	.15
❑ 338	Julio Ramirez	.50	.15
❑ 339	Jason Grabowski RC	1.25	.35
❑ 340	Jon Garland	.50	.15
❑ 341	Austin Kearns	.75	.23
❑ 342	Josh Pressley RC	.75	.23
❑ 343	Miguel Olivo RC	2.00	.60
❑ 344	Julio Lugo	.50	.15
❑ 345	Roberto Vaz	.50	.15
❑ 346	Ramon Soler	.50	.15
❑ 347	Brandon Phillips RC	2.00	.60
❑ 348	Vince Faison RC	.75	.23
❑ 349	Mike Venafro	.50	.15
❑ 350	Rick Asadoorian RC	1.25	.35
❑ 351	B.J. Garbe RC	.75	.23
❑ 352	Dan Reichert	.50	.15
❑ 353	Jason Stumm RC	.75	.23
❑ 354	Ruben Salazar RC	.75	.23
❑ 355	Francisco Cordero	.50	.15
❑ 356	Juan Guzman RC	.75	.23
❑ 357	Mike Bacsik RC	.75	.23
❑ 358	Jared Sandberg	.50	.15
❑ 359	Rod Barajas	.50	.15
❑ 360	Junior Brignac RC	.75	.23
❑ 361	J.M. Gold	.50	.15
❑ 362	Octavio Dotel	.50	.15
❑ 363	David Kelton	.50	.15
❑ 364	Scott Morgan	.50	.15
❑ 365	Wascar Serrano RC	.75	.23
❑ 366	Wilton Veras	.50	.15
❑ 367	Eugene Kingsale	.50	.15
❑ 368	Ted Lilly	.50	.15
❑ 369	George Lombard	.50	.15
❑ 370	Chris Haas	.50	.15
❑ 371	Wilton Pena RC	.75	.23
❑ 372	Vernon Wells	.50	.15
❑ 373	Keith Ginter RC	.75	.23
❑ 374	Jeff Heaverlo RC	.75	.23
❑ 375	Calvin Pickering	.50	.15
❑ 376	Mike Lamb RC	1.25	.35
❑ 377	Kyle Snyder	.50	.15
❑ 378	Javier Cardona RC	.75	.23
❑ 379	Aaron Rowand RC	5.00	1.50
❑ 380	Dee Brown	.50	.15
❑ 381	Brett Myers RC	2.00	.60
❑ 382	Abraham Nunez	.50	.15
❑ 383	Eric Valent	.50	.15
❑ 384	Jody Gerut RC	3.00	.90
❑ 385	Adam Dunn	1.25	.35
❑ 386	Jay Gehrke	.50	.15
❑ 387	Omar Ortiz	.50	.15
❑ 388	Darnell McDonald	.50	.15
❑ 389	Tony Schrager RC	.75	.23
❑ 390	J.D. Closser	.50	.15
❑ 391	Ben Christensen RC	.75	.23
❑ 392	Adam Kennedy	.50	.15
❑ 393	Nick Green RC	3.00	.90
❑ 394	Ramon Hernandez	.50	.15
❑ 395	Roy Oswalt RC	10.00	3.00
❑ 396	Andy Tracy RC	.75	.23
❑ 397	Eric Gagne	2.00	.60
❑ 398	Michael Tejera RC	.75	.23
❑ 399	Adam Everett	.50	.15
❑ 400	Corey Patterson	.50	.15
❑ 401	Gary Knotts RC	.75	.23
❑ 402	Ryan Christianson RC	1.25	.35
❑ 403	Eric Ireland RC	.75	.23
❑ 404	Andrew Good RC	.75	.23
❑ 405	Brad Penny	.50	.15
❑ 406	Jason LaRue	.50	.15
❑ 407	Kit Pellow	.50	.15
❑ 408	Kevin Beirne	.50	.15
❑ 409	Kelly Dransfeldt	.50	.15
❑ 410	Jason Grilli	.50	.15
❑ 411	Scott Downs RC	.75	.23
❑ 412	Jesus Colome	.50	.15
❑ 413	John Sneed RC	.75	.23
❑ 414	Tony McKnight	.50	.15
❑ 415	Luis Rivera	.50	.15
❑ 416	Adam Eaton	.50	.15
❑ 417	Mike MacDougal RC	1.25	.35
❑ 418	Mike Nannini	.50	.15
❑ 419	Barry Zito RC	8.00	2.40
❑ 420	DeWayne Wise	.50	.15
❑ 421	Jason Dellaero	.50	.15
❑ 422	Chad Moeller	.50	.15
❑ 423	Jason Marquis	.50	.15
❑ 424	Tim Redding RC	1.25	.35
❑ 425	Mark Mulder	.50	.15
❑ 426	Josh Paul	.50	.15
❑ 427	Chris Enochs	.50	.15
❑ 428	W.Rodriguez RC	.75	.23
❑ 429	Kevin Witt	.50	.15
❑ 430	Scott Sobkowiak RC	.75	.23
❑ 431	McKay Christensen	.50	.15
❑ 432	Jung Bong	.50	.15
❑ 433	Keith Evans RC	.75	.23
❑ 434	Garry Maddox Jr. RC	.75	.23
❑ 435	Ramon Santiago RC	1.25	.35
❑ 436	Alex Cora	.50	.15
❑ 437	Carlos Lee	.50	.15
❑ 438	Jason Repko RC	1.25	.35
❑ 439	Matt Burch	.50	.15
❑ 440	Shawn Sonnier RC	.75	.23

2000 Bowman Chrome Draft Picks

	Nm-Mt	Ex-Mt
COMP.FACT.SET (110)	50.00	15.00

	Player	Nm-Mt	Ex-Mt
❑ 1	Pat Burrell	.50	.15
❑ 2	Rafael Furcal	.50	.15
❑ 3	Grant Roberts	.50	.15
❑ 4	Barry Zito	4.00	1.20
❑ 5	Julio Zuleta	.50	.15
❑ 6	Mark Mulder	.50	.15
❑ 7	Rob Bell	.50	.15
❑ 8	Adam Piatt	.50	.15
❑ 9	Mike Lamb	.75	.23
❑ 10	Pablo Ozuna	.50	.15
❑ 11	Jason Tyner	.50	.15
❑ 12	Jason Marquis	.50	.15
❑ 13	Eric Munson	.50	.15
❑ 14	Seth Etherton	.50	.15
❑ 15	Milton Bradley	.50	.15
❑ 16	Nick Green	1.25	.35
❑ 17	Chin-Feng Chen RC	2.50	.75
❑ 18	Matt Boone RC	.50	.15
❑ 19	Kevin Gregg RC	1.00	.30
❑ 20	Eddy Garabito RC	.50	.15
❑ 21	Aaron Capista RC	.50	.15
❑ 22	Esteban German RC	.50	.15
❑ 23	Derek Thompson RC	.50	.15
❑ 24	Phil Merrell RC	.50	.15
❑ 25	Brian O'Connor RC	.50	.15
❑ 26	Yamid Haad	.50	.15
❑ 27	Hector Mercado RC	.50	.15
❑ 28	Jason Woolf RC	.50	.15
❑ 29	Eddy Furniss RC	.50	.15
❑ 30	Cha Sueng Baek RC	.50	.15
❑ 31	Colby Lewis RC	1.00	.30
❑ 32	Pasqual Coco RC	.50	.15
❑ 33	Jorge Cantu RC	1.50	.45
❑ 34	Erasmo Ramirez RC	.50	.15
❑ 35	Bobby Kielty RC	1.00	.30
❑ 36	Joaquin Benoit RC	1.00	.30
❑ 37	Brian Esposito RC	.50	.15
❑ 38	Michael Wenner	.50	.15
❑ 39	Juan Rincon RC	.50	.15
❑ 40	Yorvit Torrealba RC	.50	.15
❑ 41	Chad Durham RC	.50	.15
❑ 42	Jim Mann RC	.50	.15
❑ 43	Shane Loux RC	.50	.15
❑ 44	Luis Rivas	.50	.15
❑ 45	Ken Chenard RC	.50	.15
❑ 46	Mike Lockwood RC	.50	.15
❑ 47	Yovanny Lara RC	.50	.15
❑ 48	Bubba Carpenter RC	.50	.15
❑ 49	Ryan Dittfurth RC	.50	.15
❑ 50	John Stephens RC	1.00	.30
❑ 51	Pedro Feliz RC	2.50	.75
❑ 52	Kenny Kelly RC	1.00	.30
❑ 53	Neil Jenkins RC	.50	.15
❑ 54	Mike Glendenning RC	.50	.15
❑ 55	Bo Porter	.50	.15
❑ 56	Eric Byrnes	1.25	.35
❑ 57	Tony Alvarez RC	.50	.15
❑ 58	Kazuhiro Sasaki RC	2.50	.75
❑ 59	Chad Durbin RC	.50	.15
❑ 60	Mike Bynum RC	.50	.15
❑ 61	Travis Wilson RC	.50	.15
❑ 62	Jose Leon RC	.50	.15
❑ 63	Ryan Vogelsong RC	1.00	.30
❑ 64	Geraldo Guzman RC	.50	.15
❑ 65	Craig Anderson RC	.50	.15
❑ 66	Carlos Silva RC	1.50	.45
❑ 67	Brad Thomas RC	.50	.15
❑ 68	Chin-Hui Tsao	1.25	.35
❑ 69	Mark Buehrle RC	4.00	1.20
❑ 70	Juan Salas RC	.50	.15
❑ 71	Denny Abreu RC	.50	.15
❑ 72	Keith McDonald RC	.50	.15
❑ 73	Chris Richard RC	.50	.15
❑ 74	Tomas De la Rosa RC	.50	.15
❑ 75	Vicente Padilla RC	1.00	.30
❑ 76	Justin Brunette RC	.50	.15
❑ 77	Scott Linebrink RC	.50	.15
❑ 78	Jeff Sparks RC	.50	.15
❑ 79	Tike Redman RC	1.50	.45
❑ 80	John Lackey RC	2.50	.75
❑ 81	Joe Strong RC	.50	.15
❑ 82	Brian Tollberg RC	.50	.15
❑ 83	Steve Sisco RC	.50	.15
❑ 84	Chris Clapinski RC	.50	.15
❑ 85	Augie Ojeda RC	.50	.15
❑ 86	Adrian Gonzalez RC	4.00	1.20
❑ 87	Mike Stodolka RC	.50	.15
❑ 88	Adam Johnson RC	1.00	.30
❑ 89	Matt Wheatland RC	.50	.15
❑ 90	Corey Smith RC	1.00	.30
❑ 91	Rocco Baldelli RC	12.00	3.60
❑ 92	Keith Bucktrot RC	.50	.15
❑ 93	Adam Wainwright RC	2.50	.75
❑ 94	Blaine Boyer RC	.50	.15
❑ 95	Aaron Herr RC	1.00	.30
❑ 96	Scott Thorman RC	1.00	.30
❑ 97	Bryan Digby RC	1.00	.30
❑ 98	Josh Shortslef RC	.50	.15
❑ 99	Sean Smith RC	1.00	.30
❑ 100	Alex Cruz RC	.50	.15
❑ 101	Marc Love RC	.50	.15
❑ 102	Kevin Lee RC	.50	.15
❑ 103	Timo Perez RC	1.00	.30
❑ 104	Alex Cabrera RC	1.00	.30
❑ 105	Shane Heams RC	.50	.15
❑ 106	Tripper Johnson RC	1.00	.30
❑ 107	Brent Abernathy RC	.50	.15
❑ 108	John Cotton RC	.50	.15
❑ 109	Brad Wilkerson RC	1.50	.45
❑ 110	Jon Rauch RC	1.00	.30

2001 Bowman Chrome

	Nm-Mt	Ex-Mt
COMP.SET w/o SP's (220)	50.00	15.00
COMMON (1-110/201-310)	.50	.15
COMMON (111-200/311-330)	5.00	1.50
COMMON (331-350)	30.00	9.00

	Player	Nm-Mt	Ex-Mt
❑ 1	Jason Giambi	.50	.15
❑ 2	Rafael Furcal	.50	.15
❑ 3	Bernie Williams	.75	.23
❑ 4	Kenny Lofton	.50	.15
❑ 5	Al Leiter	.50	.15
❑ 6	Albert Belle	.50	.15

No.	Player	Price	Price
❑ 7	Craig Biggio	.75	.23
❑ 8	Mark Mulder	.50	.15
❑ 9	Carlos Delgado	.50	.15
❑ 10	Darin Erstad	.50	.15
❑ 11	Richie Sexson	.50	.15
❑ 12	Randy Johnson	1.25	.35
❑ 13	Greg Maddux	2.00	.60
❑ 14	Orlando Hernandez	.50	.15
❑ 15	Javier Vazquez	.50	.15
❑ 16	Jeff Kent	.50	.15
❑ 17	Jim Thome	1.25	.35
❑ 18	John Olerud	.50	.15
❑ 19	Jason Kendall	.50	.15
❑ 20	Scott Rolen	1.25	.35
❑ 21	Tony Gwynn	1.50	.45
❑ 22	Edgardo Alfonzo	.50	.15
❑ 23	Pokey Reese	.50	.15
❑ 24	Todd Helton	.75	.23
❑ 25	Mark Quinn	.50	.15
❑ 26	Dean Palmer	.50	.15
❑ 27	Ray Durham	.50	.15
❑ 28	Rafael Palmeiro	.75	.23
❑ 29	Carl Everett	.50	.15
❑ 30	Vladimir Guerrero	1.25	.35
❑ 31	Livan Hernandez	.50	.15
❑ 32	Preston Wilson	.50	.15
❑ 33	Jose Vidro	.50	.15
❑ 34	Fred McGriff	.75	.23
❑ 35	Kevin Brown	.50	.15
❑ 36	Miguel Tejada	.50	.15
❑ 37	Chipper Jones	1.25	.35
❑ 38	Edgar Martinez	.75	.23
❑ 39	Tony Batista	.50	.15
❑ 40	Jorge Posada	.75	.23
❑ 41	Sammy Sosa	2.00	.60
❑ 42	Gary Sheffield	.50	.15
❑ 43	Bartolo Colon	.50	.15
❑ 44	Pat Burrell	.50	.15
❑ 45	Jay Payton	.50	.15
❑ 46	Mike Mussina	.75	.23
❑ 47	Nomar Garciaparra	2.00	.60
❑ 48	Darren Dreifort	.50	.15
❑ 49	Richard Hidalgo	.50	.15
❑ 50	Troy Glaus	.50	.15
❑ 51	Ben Grieve	.50	.15
❑ 52	Jim Edmonds	.50	.15
❑ 53	Raul Mondesi	.50	.15
❑ 54	Andruw Jones	.50	.15
❑ 55	Mike Sweeney	.50	.15
❑ 56	Derek Jeter	3.00	.90
❑ 57	Ruben Mateo	.50	.15
❑ 58	Cristian Guzman	.50	.15
❑ 59	Mike Hampton	.50	.15
❑ 60	J.D. Drew	.50	.15
❑ 61	Matt Lawton	.50	.15
❑ 62	Moises Alou	.50	.15
❑ 63	Terrence Long	.50	.15
❑ 64	Geoff Jenkins	.50	.15
❑ 65	Manny Ramirez	.75	.23
❑ 66	Johnny Damon	.75	.23
❑ 67	Pedro Martinez	1.25	.35
❑ 68	Juan Gonzalez	.75	.23
❑ 69	Roger Clemens	2.50	.75
❑ 70	Carlos Beltran	.75	.23
❑ 71	Roberto Alomar	.75	.23
❑ 72	Barry Bonds	3.00	.90
❑ 73	Tim Hudson	.50	.15
❑ 74	Tom Glavine	.75	.23
❑ 75	Jeromy Burnitz	.50	.15
❑ 76	Adrian Beltre	.75	.23
❑ 77	Mike Piazza	2.00	.60
❑ 78	Kerry Wood	1.25	.35
❑ 79	Steve Finley	.50	.15
❑ 80	Bob Abreu	.50	.15
❑ 81	Neifi Perez	.50	.15
❑ 82	Mark Redman	.50	.15
❑ 83	Paul Konerko	.50	.15
❑ 84	Jermaine Dye	.50	.15
❑ 85	Brian Giles	.50	.15
❑ 86	Ivan Rodriguez	1.25	.35
❑ 87	Adam Kennedy	.50	.15
❑ 88	Eric Chavez	.50	.15
❑ 89	Billy Koch	.50	.15
❑ 90	Shawn Green	.50	.15
❑ 91	Matt Williams	.50	.15
❑ 92	Greg Vaughn	.50	.15
❑ 93	Jeff Cirillo	.50	.15
❑ 94	Frank Thomas	1.25	.35
❑ 95	David Justice	.50	.15
❑ 96	Cal Ripken	4.00	1.20
❑ 97	Curt Schilling	.50	.15
❑ 98	Barry Zito	.75	.23
❑ 99	Brian Jordan	.50	.15
❑ 100	Chan Ho Park	.50	.15
❑ 101	J.T. Snow	.50	.15
❑ 102	Kazuhiro Sasaki	.50	.15
❑ 103	Alex Rodriguez	2.00	.60
❑ 104	Mariano Rivera	.75	.23
❑ 105	Eric Milton	.50	.15
❑ 106	Andy Pettitte	.75	.23
❑ 107	Ken Griffey Jr.	2.00	.60
❑ 108	Bengie Molina	.50	.15
❑ 109	Jeff Bagwell	.75	.23
❑ 110	Mark McGwire	3.00	.90
❑ 111	Dan Tosca RC	8.00	2.40
❑ 112	Sergio Contreras RC	8.00	2.40
❑ 113	Mitch Jones RC	8.00	2.40
❑ 114	Ramon Carvajal RC	8.00	2.40
❑ 115	Ryan Madson RC	10.00	3.00
❑ 116	Hank Blalock RC	70.00	21.00
❑ 117	Ben Washburn RC	8.00	2.40
❑ 118	Erick Almonte RC	8.00	2.40
❑ 119	Shawn Fagan RC	8.00	2.40
❑ 120	Gary Johnson RC	8.00	2.40
❑ 121	Brett Evert RC	8.00	2.40
❑ 122	Joe Hamer RC	8.00	2.40
❑ 123	Yhency Brazoban RC	10.00	3.00
❑ 124	Domingo Guante RC	8.00	2.40
❑ 125	Deivi Mendez RC	8.00	2.40
❑ 126	Adrian Hernandez RC	8.00	2.40
❑ 127	R. Abercrombie RC	8.00	2.40
❑ 128	Steve Bennett RC	5.00	1.50
❑ 129	Matt White RC	8.00	2.40
❑ 130	Brian Hitchcox RC	5.00	1.50
❑ 131	Deivis Santos RC	8.00	2.40
❑ 132	Luis Montanez RC	8.00	2.40
❑ 133	Eric Reynolds RC	5.00	1.50
❑ 134	Denny Bautista RC	10.00	3.00
❑ 135	Hector Garcia RC	8.00	2.40
❑ 136	Joe Thurston RC	8.00	2.40
❑ 137	Tsuyoshi Shinjo RC	10.00	3.00
❑ 138	Elpidio Guzman RC	8.00	2.40
❑ 139	Brian Bass RC	8.00	2.40
❑ 140	Mark Burnett RC	8.00	2.40
❑ 141	Russ Jacobson UER Last name misspelled Jacobsen on front	5.00	1.50
❑ 142	Travis Hafner RC	20.00	6.00
❑ 143	Wilson Betemit RC	8.00	2.40
❑ 144	Luke Lockwood RC	8.00	2.40
❑ 145	Noel Devarez RC	8.00	2.40
❑ 146	Doug Gredvig RC	8.00	2.40
❑ 147	Seung Song RC	10.00	3.00
❑ 148	Andy Van Hekken RC	8.00	2.40
❑ 149	Ryan Kohlmeier	5.00	1.50
❑ 150	Dee Haynes RC	8.00	2.40
❑ 151	Jim Journell RC	8.00	2.40
❑ 152	Chad Petty RC	8.00	2.40
❑ 153	Danny Borrell RC	8.00	2.40
❑ 154	Dave Krynzel	5.00	1.50
❑ 155	Octavio Martinez RC	8.00	2.40
❑ 156	David Parrish RC	8.00	2.40
❑ 157	Jason Miller RC	8.00	2.40
❑ 158	Corey Spencer RC	5.00	1.50
❑ 159	Maxim St. Pierre RC	8.00	2.40
❑ 160	Pat Magness RC	8.00	2.40
❑ 161	Ranier Olmedo RC	8.00	2.40
❑ 162	Brandon Mims RC	8.00	2.40
❑ 163	Phil Wilson RC	8.00	2.40
❑ 164	Jose Reyes RC	50.00	15.00
❑ 165	Matt Butler RC	8.00	2.40
❑ 166	Joel Pineiro	8.00	2.40
❑ 167	Ken Chenard	5.00	1.50
❑ 168	Alexis Gomez RC	8.00	2.40
❑ 169	Justin Morneau RC	60.00	18.00
❑ 170	Josh Fogg RC	8.00	2.40
❑ 171	Charles Frazier RC	8.00	2.40
❑ 172	Ryan Ludwick RC	8.00	2.40
❑ 173	Seth McClung RC	8.00	2.40
❑ 174	Justin Wayne RC	8.00	2.40
❑ 175	Rafael Soriano RC	10.00	3.00
❑ 176	Jared Abruzzo RC	8.00	2.40
❑ 177	Jason Richardson RC	8.00	2.40
❑ 178	Darwin Cubillan RC	5.00	1.50
❑ 179	Blake Williams RC	8.00	2.40
❑ 180	V. Pascucci RC	8.00	2.40
❑ 181	Ryan Hannaman RC	8.00	2.40
❑ 182	Steve Smyth RC	8.00	2.40
❑ 183	Jake Peavy RC	30.00	9.00
❑ 184	Onix Mercado RC	8.00	2.40
❑ 185	Luis Torres RC	8.00	2.40
❑ 186	Casey Fossum RC	8.00	2.40
❑ 187	Eduardo Figueroa RC	8.00	2.40
❑ 188	Bryan Barnowski RC	8.00	2.40
❑ 189	Jason Standridge	5.00	1.50
❑ 190	Marvin Seale RC	8.00	2.40
❑ 191	Steve Smitherman RC	10.00	3.00
❑ 192	Rafael Boitel RC	8.00	2.40
❑ 193	Dany Morban RC	8.00	2.40
❑ 194	Justin Woodrow RC	8.00	2.40
❑ 195	Ed Rogers RC	8.00	2.40
❑ 196	Ben Hendrickson RC	10.00	3.00
❑ 197	Thomas Mitchell	5.00	1.50
❑ 198	Adam Pettyjohn RC	8.00	2.40
❑ 199	Doug Nickle RC	5.00	1.50
❑ 200	Jason Jones RC	8.00	2.40
❑ 201	Larry Barnes	.50	.15
❑ 202	Ben Diggins	.50	.15
❑ 203	Dee Brown	.50	.15
❑ 204	Rocco Baldelli	.75	.23
❑ 205	Luis Terrero	.50	.15
❑ 206	Milton Bradley	.50	.15
❑ 207	Kurt Ainsworth	.50	.15
❑ 208	Sean Burroughs	.50	.15
❑ 209	Rick Asadoorian	.50	.15
❑ 210	Ramon Castro	.50	.15
❑ 211	Nick Neugebauer	.50	.15
❑ 212	Aaron Myette	.50	.15
❑ 213	Luis Matos	.50	.15
❑ 214	Donnie Bridges	.50	.15
❑ 215	Alex Cintron	.50	.15
❑ 216	Bobby Kielty	.50	.15
❑ 217	Matt Belisle	.50	.15
❑ 218	Adam Everett	.50	.15
❑ 219	John Lackey	.50	.15
❑ 220	Adam Wainwright	.50	.15
❑ 221	Jerry Hairston Jr.	.50	.15
❑ 222	Mike Bynum	.50	.15
❑ 223	Ryan Christianson	.50	.15
❑ 224	J.J. Davis	.50	.15
❑ 225	Alex Graman	.50	.15
❑ 226	Abraham Nunez	.50	.15
❑ 227	Sun Woo Kim	.50	.15
❑ 228	Jimmy Rollins	.50	.15
❑ 229	Ruben Salazar	.50	.15
❑ 230	Josh Girdley	.50	.15
❑ 231	Carl Crawford	.50	.15
❑ 232	Ben Davis	.50	.15
❑ 233	Jason Grabowski	.50	.15
❑ 234	Chris George	.50	.15
❑ 235	Roy Oswalt	.75	.23
❑ 236	Brian Cole	.50	.15
❑ 237	Corey Patterson	.50	.15
❑ 238	Vernon Wells	.50	.15
❑ 239	Brad Baker	.50	.15
❑ 240	Gookie Dawkins	.50	.15
❑ 241	Michael Cuddyer	.50	.15
❑ 242	Ricardo Aramboles	.50	.15
❑ 243	Ben Sheets	.75	.23
❑ 244	Toby Hall	.50	.15

#	Player	Nm-Mt	Ex-Mt
245	Jack Cust	.50	.15
246	Pedro Feliz	.50	.15
247	Josh Beckett	.50	.15
248	Alex Escobar	.50	.15
249	Marcus Giles	.50	.15
250	Jon Rauch	.50	.15
251	Kevin Mench	.50	.15
252	Shawn Sonnier	.50	.15
253	Aaron Rowand	.50	.15
254	C.C. Sabathia	.50	.15
255	Bubba Crosby	.50	.15
256	Josh Hamilton	.50	.15
257	Carlos Hernandez	.50	.15
258	Carlos Pena	.50	.15
259	Miguel Cabrera	4.00	1.20
260	Brandon Phillips	.50	.15
261	Tony Pena Jr.	.50	.15
262	Cristian Guerrero	.50	.15
263	Jin Ho Cho	.50	.15
264	Aaron Herr	.50	.15
265	Keith Ginter	.50	.15
266	Felipe Lopez	.50	.15
267	Travis Harper	.50	.15
268	Joe Torres	.50	.15
269	Eric Byrnes	.50	.15
270	Ben Christensen	.50	.15
271	Aubrey Huff	.50	.15
272	Lyle Overbay	.50	.15
273	Vince Faison	.50	.15
274	Bobby Bradley	.50	.15
275	Joe Crede	.50	.15
276	Matt Wheatland	.50	.15
277	Grady Sizemore	1.25	.35
278	Adrian Gonzalez	.50	.15
279	Tim Raines Jr.	.50	.15
280	Phil Dumatrait	.50	.15
281	Jason Hart	.50	.15
282	David Kelton	.50	.15
283	David Walling	.50	.15
284	J.R. House	.50	.15
285	Kenny Kelly	.50	.15
286	Aaron McNeal	.50	.15
287	Nick Johnson	.50	.15
288	Scott Heard	.50	.15
289	Brad Wilkerson	.50	.15
290	Allen Levrault	.50	.15
291	Chris Richard	.50	.15
292	Jared Sandberg	.50	.15
293	Tike Redman	.50	.15
294	Adam Dunn	.75	.23
295	Josh Pressley	.50	.15
296	Jose Ortiz	.50	.15
297	Jason Romano	.50	.15
298	Tim Redding	.50	.15
299	Alex Gordon	.50	.15
300	Ben Petrick	.50	.15
301	Eric Munson	.50	.15
302	Luis Rivas	.50	.15
303	Matt Ginter	.50	.15
304	Alfonso Soriano	.75	.23
305	Wilfredo Rodriguez	.50	.15
306	Brett Myers	.50	.15
307	Scott Seabol	.50	.15
308	Tony Alvarez	.50	.15
309	Donzell McDonald	.50	.15
310	Austin Kearns	.50	.15
311	Will Ohman RC	8.00	2.40
312	Ryan Soules RC	5.00	1.50
313	Cody Ross RC	8.00	2.40
314	Bill Whitecotton RC	8.00	2.40
315	Mike Burns RC	8.00	2.40
316	Manuel Acosta RC	8.00	2.40
317	Lance Niekro RC	8.00	2.40
318	Travis Thompson RC	8.00	2.40
319	Zach Sorensen RC	8.00	2.40
320	Austin Evans RC	5.00	1.50
321	Brad Stiles RC	8.00	2.40
322	Joe Kennedy RC	10.00	3.00
323	Luke Martin RC	8.00	2.40
324	Juan Diaz RC	8.00	2.40
325	Pat Hallmark RC	5.00	1.50
326	Christian Parker RC	5.00	1.50
327	Ronny Corona RC	8.00	2.40
328	Jermaine Clark RC	5.00	1.50
329	Scott Dunn RC	8.00	2.40
330	Scott Chiasson RC	8.00	2.40
331	Greg Nash AU RC	30.00	9.00
332	Brad Cresse AU	30.00	9.00
333	John Buck AU RC	50.00	15.00
334	Freddie Bynum AU RC	30.00	9.00
335	Felix Diaz AU RC	30.00	9.00
336	Jason Belcher AU RC	30.00	9.00
337	T.Farnsworth AU RC	30.00	9.00
338	Roberto Miniel AU RC	30.00	9.00
339	Esix Snead AU RC	30.00	9.00
340	Albert Pujols AU RC	1200.00	350.00
341	Jeff Andra AU RC	30.00	9.00
342	Victor Hall AU RC	30.00	9.00
343	Pedro Liriano AU RC	30.00	9.00
344	Andy Beal AU RC	30.00	9.00
345	Bob Keppel AU RC	50.00	15.00
346	Brian Schmitt AU RC	30.00	9.00
347	Ron Davenport AU RC	200.00	60.00
348	Tony Blanco AU RC	80.00	24.00
349	Reggie Griggs AU RC	30.00	9.00
350	D. Van Dusen AU RC	30.00	9.00
351A	I. Suzuki English RC	80.00	24.00
351B	I. Suzuki Japan RC	80.00	24.00

2002 Bowman Chrome

	Nm-Mt	Ex-Mt
COMP.RED SET (110)	40.00	12.00
COMP.BLUE w/o SP's (110)	40.00	12.00
COMMON RED (1-110)	.50	.15
COMMON BLUE (111-383)	.75	.23
COMMON AU (324B/384-405)	10.00	3.00

324B/384-405 GROUP A AUTO ODDS 1:28
403-404 GROUP B AUTO ODDS 1:1290
324B/384-405 OVERALL AUTO ODDS 1:27

#	Player	Nm-Mt	Ex-Mt
1	Adam Dunn	.75	.23
2	Derek Jeter	3.00	.90
3	Alex Rodriguez	2.00	.60
4	Miguel Tejada	.50	.15
5	Nomar Garciaparra	2.00	.60
6	Toby Hall	.50	.15
7	Brandon Duckworth	.50	.15
8	Paul LoDuca	.50	.15
9	Brian Giles	.50	.15
10	C.C. Sabathia	.50	.15
11	Curt Schilling	.50	.15
12	Tsuyoshi Shinjo	.50	.15
13	Ramon Hernandez	.50	.15
14	Jose Cruz Jr.	.50	.15
15	Albert Pujols	2.50	.75
16	Joe Mays	.50	.15
17	Javy Lopez	.50	.15
18	J.T. Snow	.50	.15
19	David Segui	.50	.15
20	Jorge Posada	.75	.23
21	Doug Mientkiewicz	.50	.15
22	Jerry Hairston Jr.	.50	.15
23	Bernie Williams	.75	.23
24	Mike Sweeney	.50	.15
25	Jason Giambi	.50	.15
26	Ryan Dempster	.50	.15
27	Ryan Klesko	.50	.15
28	Mark Quinn	.50	.15
29	Jeff Kent	.50	.15
30	Eric Chavez	.50	.15
31	Adrian Beltre	.75	.23
32	Andruw Jones	.50	.15
33	Alfonso Soriano	.75	.23
34	Aramis Ramirez	.50	.15
35	Greg Maddux	2.00	.60
36	Andy Pettitte	.75	.23
37	Bartolo Colon	.50	.15
38	Ben Sheets	.50	.15
39	Bobby Higginson	.50	.15
40	Ivan Rodriguez	1.25	.35
41	Brad Penny	.50	.15
42	Carlos Lee	.50	.15
43	Damion Easley	.50	.15
44	Preston Wilson	.50	.15
45	Jeff Bagwell	.75	.23
46	Eric Milton	.50	.15
47	Rafael Palmeiro	.75	.23
48	Gary Sheffield	.50	.15
49	J.D. Drew	.50	.15
50	Jim Thome	1.25	.35
51	Ichiro Suzuki	2.00	.60
52	Bud Smith	.50	.15
53	Chan Ho Park	.50	.15
54	D'Angelo Jimenez	.50	.15
55	Ken Griffey Jr.	2.00	.60
56	Wade Miller	.50	.15
57	Vladimir Guerrero	1.25	.35
58	Troy Glaus	.50	.15
59	Shawn Green	.50	.15
60	Kerry Wood	1.25	.35
61	Jack Wilson	.50	.15
62	Kevin Brown	.50	.15
63	Marcus Giles	.50	.15
64	Pat Burrell	.50	.15
65	Larry Walker	.75	.23
66	Sammy Sosa	2.00	.60
67	Raul Mondesi	.50	.15
68	Tim Hudson	.50	.15
69	Lance Berkman	.50	.15
70	Mike Mussina	.75	.23
71	Barry Zito	.50	.15
72	Jimmy Rollins	.50	.15
73	Barry Bonds	3.00	.90
74	Craig Biggio	.75	.23
75	Todd Helton	.75	.23
76	Roger Clemens	2.50	.75
77	Frank Catalanotto	.50	.15
78	Josh Towers	.50	.15
79	Roy Oswalt	.50	.15
80	Chipper Jones	1.25	.35
81	Cristian Guzman	.50	.15
82	Darin Erstad	.50	.15
83	Freddy Garcia	.50	.15
84	Jason Tyner	.50	.15
85	Carlos Delgado	.50	.15
86	Jon Lieber	.50	.15
87	Juan Pierre	.50	.15
88	Matt Morris	.50	.15
89	Phil Nevin	.50	.15
90	Jim Edmonds	.50	.15
91	Magglio Ordonez	.50	.15
92	Mike Hampton	.50	.15
93	Rafael Furcal	.50	.15
94	Richie Sexson	.50	.15
95	Luis Gonzalez	.50	.15
96	Scott Rolen	1.25	.35
97	Tim Redding	.50	.15
98	Moises Alou	.50	.15
99	Jose Vidro	.50	.15
100	Mike Piazza	2.00	.60
101	Pedro Martinez	1.25	.35
102	Geoff Jenkins	.50	.15
103	Johnny Damon Sox	1.25	.35
104	Mike Cameron	.50	.15
105	Randy Johnson	1.25	.35
106	David Eckstein	.50	.15
107	Javier Vazquez	.50	.15
108	Mark Mulder	.50	.15
109	Robert Fick	.50	.15
110	Roberto Alomar	.75	.23
111	Wilson Betemit	.75	.23
112	Chris Tritle SP RC	5.00	1.50
113	Ed Rogers	.75	.23
114	Juan Pena	.75	.23
115	Josh Beckett	1.25	.35
116	Juan Cruz	.75	.23
117	Noochie Varner SP RC	5.00	1.50
118	Blake Williams	.75	.23
119	Mike Rivera	.75	.23

❑ 120 Hank Blalock 3.00 .90
❑ 121 Hansel Izquierdo SP RC 5.00 1.50
❑ 122 Orlando Hudson .75 .23
❑ 123 Bill Hall SP 5.00 1.50
❑ 124 Jose Reyes 2.00 .60
❑ 125 Juan Rivera .75 .23
❑ 126 Eric Valent .75 .23
❑ 127 Scotty Layfield SP RC 5.00 1.50
❑ 128 Austin Kearns 1.25 .35
❑ 129 Nic Jackson SP RC 5.00 1.50
❑ 130 Scott Chiasson .75 .23
❑ 131 Chad Qualls SP RC 5.00 1.50
❑ 132 Marcus Thames .75 .23
❑ 133 Nathan Haynes .75 .23
❑ 134 Joe Borchard .75 .23
❑ 135 Josh Hamilton .75 .23
❑ 136 Corey Patterson 1.25 .35
❑ 137 Travis Wilson .75 .23
❑ 138 Alex Escobar .75 .23
❑ 139 Alexis Gomez .75 .23
❑ 140 Nick Johnson .75 .23
❑ 141 Marlon Byrd .75 .23
❑ 142 Kory DeHaan .75 .23
❑ 143 Carlos Hernandez .75 .23
❑ 144 Sean Burroughs 1.25 .35
❑ 145 Angel Berroa .75 .23
❑ 146 Aubrey Huff 1.25 .35
❑ 147 Travis Hafner 1.25 .35
❑ 148 Brandon Berger .75 .23
❑ 149 J.R. House .75 .23
❑ 150 Dewon Brazelton .75 .23
❑ 151 Jayson Werth .75 .23
❑ 152 Larry Barnes .75 .23
❑ 153 Ruben Gotay SP RC 5.00 1.50
❑ 154 Tommy Marx SP RC 5.00 1.50
❑ 155 John Suomi SP RC 5.00 1.50
❑ 156 Javier Colina SP 5.00 1.50
❑ 157 Greg Sain SP RC 8.00 2.40
❑ 158 Robert Cosby SP RC 5.00 1.50
❑ 159 Angel Pagan SP RC 5.00 1.50
❑ 160 Ralph Santana RC 1.25 .35
❑ 161 Joe Orloski RC 1.25 .35
❑ 162 Shayne Wright SP RC 5.00 1.50
❑ 163 Jay Caligiuri SP RC 5.00 1.50
❑ 164 Greg Montalbano SP RC 5.00 1.50
❑ 165 Rich Harden SP RC 30.00 9.00
❑ 166 Rich Thompson SP RC 5.00 1.50
❑ 167 Fred Bastardo SP RC 5.00 1.50
❑ 168 Alejandro Giron SP RC 5.00 1.50
❑ 169 Jesus Medrano SP RC 5.00 1.50
❑ 170 Kevin Deaton SP RC 5.00 1.50
❑ 171 Mike Rosamond RC 1.25 .35
❑ 172 Jon Guzman SP RC 5.00 1.50
❑ 173 Gerard Oakes SP RC 5.00 1.50
❑ 174 Francisco Liriano SP RC 8.00 2.40
❑ 175 Matt Allegra SP RC 5.00 1.50
❑ 176 Mike Snyder SP RC 5.00 1.50
❑ 177 James Shanks SP RC 5.00 1.50
❑ 178 And. Hernandez SP RC 5.00 1.50
❑ 179 Dan Trumble SP RC 5.00 1.50
❑ 180 Luis DePaula SP RC 5.00 1.50
❑ 181 Randall Shelley SP RC 5.00 1.50
❑ 182 Richard Lane SP RC 5.00 1.50
❑ 183 Antwon Rollins SP RC 5.00 1.50
❑ 184 Ryan Bukvich SP RC 5.00 1.50
❑ 185 Derrick Lewis SP 5.00 1.50
❑ 186 Eric Miller SP RC 5.00 1.50
❑ 187 Justin Schuda SP RC 5.00 1.50
❑ 188 Brian West SP RC 5.00 1.50
❑ 189 Brad Wilkerson .75 .23
❑ 190 Neal Frendling SP RC 5.00 1.50
❑ 191 Jeremy Hill SP RC 5.00 1.50
❑ 192 James Barrett SP RC 5.00 1.50
❑ 193 Brett Kay SP RC 5.00 1.50
❑ 194 Ryan Mottl SP RC 5.00 1.50
❑ 195 Brad Nelson SP RC 15.00 4.50
❑ 196 Juan M. Gonzalez SP RC 5.00 1.50
❑ 197 Curtis Legendre SP RC 5.00 1.50
❑ 198 Ronald Acuna SP RC 5.00 1.50
❑ 199 Chris Flinn SP RC 5.00 1.50
❑ 200 Nick Alvarez SP RC 5.00 1.50
❑ 201 Jason Ellison SP RC 5.00 1.50
❑ 202 Blake McGinley SP RC 5.00 1.50
❑ 203 Dan Phillips SP RC 5.00 1.50
❑ 204 Demetrius Heath SP RC 5.00 1.50
❑ 205 Eric Bruntlett SP RC 5.00 1.50
❑ 206 Joe Jiannetti SP RC 5.00 1.50
❑ 207 Mike Hill SP RC 5.00 1.50
❑ 208 Ricardo Cordova SP RC 5.00 1.50
❑ 209 Mark Hamilton SP RC 5.00 1.50
❑ 210 David Mattox SP RC 5.00 1.50
❑ 211 Jose Morban SP RC 5.00 1.50
❑ 212 Scott Wiggins SP RC 5.00 1.50
❑ 213 Steve Green .75 .23
❑ 214 Brian Rogers SP 5.00 1.50
❑ 215 Kenny Baugh .75 .23
❑ 216 Anastacio Martinez SP RC 5.00 1.50
❑ 217 Richard Lewis 1.25 .35
❑ 218 Tim Kalita SP RC 5.00 1.50
❑ 219 Edwin Almonte SP RC 5.00 1.50
❑ 220 Hee Seop Choi .75 .23
❑ 221 Ty Howington .75 .23
❑ 222 Victor Alvarez SP RC 5.00 1.50
❑ 223 Morgan Ensberg 1.25 .35
❑ 224 Jeff Austin SP RC 5.00 1.50
❑ 225 Clint Weibl SP RC 5.00 1.50
❑ 226 Eric Cyr .75 .23
❑ 227 Marlyn Tisdale SP RC 5.00 1.50
❑ 228 John VanBenschoten .75 .23
❑ 229 David Krynzel .75 .23
❑ 230 Raul Chavez SP RC 5.00 1.50
❑ 231 Brett Evert .75 .23
❑ 232 Joe Rogers SP RC 5.00 1.50
❑ 233 Adam Wainwright .75 .23
❑ 234 Matt Herges RC .75 .23
❑ 235 Matt Childers SP RC 5.00 1.50
❑ 236 Nick Neugebauer .75 .23
❑ 237 Carl Crawford 1.25 .35
❑ 238 Seung Song .75 .23
❑ 239 Randy Flores .75 .23
❑ 240 Jason Lane .75 .23
❑ 241 Chase Utley 2.00 .60
❑ 242 Ben Howard SP RC 5.00 1.50
❑ 243 Eric Glaser SP RC 5.00 1.50
❑ 244 Josh Wilson RC 1.25 .35
❑ 245 Jose Valverde SP RC 8.00 2.40
❑ 246 Chris Smith .75 .23
❑ 247 Mark Prior 8.00 2.40
❑ 248 Brian Mallette SP RC 5.00 1.50
❑ 249 Chone Figgins SP RC 10.00 3.00
❑ 250 Jimmy Alvarez SP RC 5.00 1.50
❑ 251 Luis Terrero .75 .23
❑ 252 Josh Bonifay SP RC 5.00 1.50
❑ 253 Garrett Guzman SP RC 5.00 1.50
❑ 254 Jeff Verplancke SP RC 5.00 1.50
❑ 255 Nate Espy SP RC 5.00 1.50
❑ 256 Jeff Lincoln SP RC 5.00 1.50
❑ 257 Ryan Snare SP RC 5.00 1.50
❑ 258 Jose Ortiz .75 .23
❑ 259 Denny Bautista .75 .23
❑ 260 Willy Aybar .75 .23
❑ 261 Kelly Johnson .75 .23
❑ 262 Shawn Fagan .75 .23
❑ 263 Yurendell DeCaster SP RC 5.00 1.50
❑ 264 Mike Peeples SP RC 5.00 1.50
❑ 265 Joel Guzman 2.00 .60
❑ 266 Ryan Vogelsong .75 .23
❑ 267 Jorge Padilla SP RC 5.00 1.50
❑ 268 Joe Jester SP RC 5.00 1.50
❑ 269 Ryan Church SP RC 10.00 3.00
❑ 270 Mitch Jones .75 .23
❑ 271 Travis Foley SP RC 5.00 1.50
❑ 272 Bobby Crosby 5.00 1.50
❑ 273 Adrian Gonzalez 1.25 .35
❑ 274 Ronnie Merrill .75 .23
❑ 275 Joel Pineiro 1.25 .35
❑ 276 John-Ford Griffin .75 .23
❑ 277 Brian Forystek SP RC 5.00 1.50
❑ 278 Sean Douglass .75 .23
❑ 279 Manny Delcarmen SP RC 5.00 1.50
❑ 280 Jim Kavourias SP RC 5.00 1.50
❑ 281 Gabe Gross .75 .23
❑ 282 Bill Ortega .75 .23
❑ 283 Joey Hammond SP RC 5.00 1.50
❑ 284 Brett Myers .75 .23
❑ 285 Carlos Pena .75 .23
❑ 286 Ezequiel Astacio SP RC 5.00 1.50
❑ 287 Edwin Yan SP RC 5.00 1.50
❑ 288 Chris Duffy SP RC 5.00 1.50
❑ 289 Jason Kinchen .75 .23
❑ 290 Rafael Soriano .75 .23
❑ 291 Colin Young RC 5.00 1.50
❑ 292 Eric Byrnes .75 .23
❑ 293 Chris Narveson SP RC 8.00 2.40
❑ 294 John Rheinecker .75 .23
❑ 295 Mike Wilson SP RC 5.00 1.50
❑ 296 Justin Sherrod SP RC 5.00 1.50
❑ 297 Deivi Mendez .75 .23
❑ 298 Wily Mo Pena 1.25 .35
❑ 299 Brett Roneberg SP RC 5.00 1.50
❑ 300 Trey Lunsford SP RC 5.00 1.50
❑ 301 Christian Parker .75 .23
❑ 302 Brent Butler .75 .23
❑ 303 Aaron Heilman .75 .23
❑ 304 Wilkin Ruan .75 .23
❑ 305 Kenny Kelly .75 .23
❑ 306 Cody Ransom .75 .23
❑ 307 Koyie Hill SP 5.00 1.50
❑ 308 Tony Fontana SP RC 5.00 1.50
❑ 309 Mark Teixeira 2.00 .60
❑ 310 Doug Sessions SP RC 5.00 1.50
❑ 311 Josh Cisneros SP RC 5.00 1.50
❑ 312 Carlos Brackley SP RC 5.00 1.50
❑ 313 Tim Raines Jr. .75 .23
❑ 314 Ross Peeples SP RC 5.00 1.50
❑ 315 Alex Requena SP RC 5.00 1.50
❑ 316 Chin-Hui Tsao 1.25 .35
❑ 317 Tony Alvarez .75 .23
❑ 318 Craig Kuzmic SP RC 5.00 1.50
❑ 319 Pete Zamora SP RC 5.00 1.50
❑ 320 Matt Parker SP RC 5.00 1.50
❑ 321 Keith Ginter .75 .23
❑ 322 Gary Cates Jr. SP RC 5.00 1.50
❑ 323 Matt Belisle .75 .23
❑ 324A Ben Broussard .75 .23
❑ 324B Ja.Mauer AU A RC EXCH UER 10.00 3.00
Card was mistakenly numbered as 324
❑ 325 Dennis Tankersley .75 .23
❑ 326 Juan Silvestre .75 .23
❑ 327 Henry Pichardo SP RC 5.00 1.50
❑ 328 Michael Floyd SP RC 5.00 1.50
❑ 329 Clint Nageotte SP RC 12.00 3.60
❑ 330 Raymond Cabrera SP RC 5.00 1.50
❑ 331 Mauricio Lara SP RC 5.00 1.50
❑ 332 Alejandro Cadena SP RC 5.00 1.50
❑ 333 Jonny Gomes SP RC 10.00 3.00
❑ 334 Jason Bulger SP RC 5.00 1.50
❑ 335 Nate Teut .75 .23
❑ 336 David Gil SP RC 5.00 1.50
❑ 337 Joel Crump SP RC 5.00 1.50
❑ 338 Brandon Phillips .75 .23
❑ 339 Macay McBride .75 .23
❑ 340 Brandon Claussen 5.00 1.50
❑ 341 Josh Phelps .75 .23
❑ 342 Freddie Money SP RC 5.00 1.50
❑ 343 Cliff Bartosh SP RC 5.00 1.50
❑ 344 Terrance Hill SP RC 5.00 1.50
❑ 345 John Rodriguez SP RC 5.00 1.50
❑ 346 Chris Latham SP RC 5.00 1.50
❑ 347 Carlos Cabrera SP RC 5.00 1.50
❑ 348 Jose Bautista SP RC 8.00 2.40
❑ 349 Kevin Frederick SP RC 5.00 1.50
❑ 350 Jerome Williams 2.00 .60
❑ 351 Napoleon Calzado SP RC 5.00 1.50
❑ 352 Benito Baez SP 5.00 1.50
❑ 353 Xavier Nady .75 .23
❑ 354 Jason Botts SP RC 10.00 3.00
❑ 355 Steve Bechler SP RC 5.00 1.50
❑ 356 Reed Johnson SP RC 8.00 2.40
❑ 357 Mark Outlaw SP RC 5.00 1.50
❑ 358 Jake Peavy 1.25 .35
❑ 359 Josh Shaffer SP RC 5.00 1.50
❑ 360 Dan Wright SP 5.00 1.50
❑ 361 Ryan Gripp SP RC 5.00 1.50
❑ 362 Nelson Castro SP RC 5.00 1.50
❑ 363 Jason Bay SP RC 20.00 6.00
❑ 364 Franklyn German SP RC 5.00 1.50
❑ 365 Corwin Malone SP RC 5.00 1.50
❑ 366 Kelly Ramos SP RC 5.00 1.50
❑ 367 John Ennis SP RC 5.00 1.50
❑ 368 George Perez SP 5.00 1.50
❑ 369 Rene Reyes SP RC 5.00 1.50
❑ 370 Rolando Viera SP RC 5.00 1.50
❑ 371 Earl Snyder SP RC 8.00 2.40
❑ 372 Kyle Kane SP RC 5.00 1.50
❑ 373 Mario Ramos SP RC 5.00 1.50
❑ 374 Tyler Yates SP RC 8.00 2.40
❑ 375 Jason Young SP RC 5.00 1.50

❑ 376 Chris Bootcheck SP RC..	5.00	1.50
❑ 377 Jesus Cota SP RC	5.00	1.50
❑ 378 Corky Miller SP..............	5.00	1.50
❑ 379 Matt Erickson SP RC......	5.00	1.50
❑ 380 Justin Huber SP RC	10.00	3.00
❑ 381 Felix Escalona SP RC	5.00	1.50
❑ 382 Kevin Cash SP RC..........	5.00	1.50
❑ 383 J.J. Putz SP RC..............	5.00	1.50
❑ 384 Chris Snelling AU A RC	10.00	3.00
❑ 385 David Wright AU A RC	120.00	36.00
❑ 386 Brian Wolfe AU A RC....	10.00	3.00
❑ 387 Justin Reid AU A RC	10.00	3.00
❑ 389 Ryan Raburn AU A RC..	10.00	3.00
❑ 390 Josh Barfield AU A RC	30.00	9.00
❑ 391 Joe Mauer AU A RC ..	100.00	30.00
❑ 392 Bobby Jenks AU A RC..	15.00	4.50
❑ 393 Rob Henkel AU A RC....	10.00	3.00
❑ 394 Jimmy Gobble AU A RC	15.00	4.50
❑ 395 Jesse Foppert AU A RC	20.00	6.00
❑ 396 Gavin Floyd AU A RC ..	50.00	15.00
❑ 397 Nate Field AU A RC......	10.00	3.00
❑ 398 Ryan Doumit AU A RC..	15.00	4.50
❑ 399 Ron Calloway AU A RC	10.00	3.00
❑ 400 Taylor Buchholz AU A RC	10.00	3.00
❑ 401 Adam Roller AU A RC ..	10.00	3.00
❑ 402 Cole Barthel AU A RC ..	10.00	3.00
❑ 403 Kazuhisa Ishii SP RC....	10.00	3.00
❑ 403 Kazuhisa Ishii AU B......	60.00	18.00
❑ 404 So Taguchi SP RC..........	8.00	2.40
❑ 404 So Taguchi AU B..........	40.00	12.00
❑ 405 Chris Baker AU A RC....	10.00	3.00

2002 Bowman Chrome Draft

	Nm-Mt	Ex-Mt
COMPLETE SET (175)	300.00	90.00
COMP.SET w/o AU's (165)......	175.00	52.50
COMMON CARD (1-165).............	.40	.12
COMMON CARD (166-175)......	10.00	3.00

❑ 1 Clint Everts RC	5.00	1.50
❑ 2 Fred Lewis RC..................	1.00	.30
❑ 3 Jon Broxton RC.................	2.50	.75
❑ 4 Jason Anderson RC...........	1.00	.30
❑ 5 Mike Eusebio RC...............	1.00	.30
❑ 6 Zack Greinke RC	10.00	3.00
❑ 7 Joe Blanton RC	5.00	1.50
❑ 8 Sergio Santos RC	6.00	1.80
❑ 9 Jason Cooper RC	1.50	.45
❑ 10 Delwyn Young RC	4.00	1.20
❑ 11 Jeremy Hermida RC	6.00	1.80
❑ 12 Dan Ortmeier RC..............	2.50	.75
❑ 13 Kevin Jepsen RC..............	3.00	.90
❑ 14 Russ Adams RC	3.00	.90
❑ 15 Mike Nixon RC	1.00	.30
❑ 16 Nick Swisher RC	8.00	2.40
❑ 17 Cole Hamels RC	12.00	3.60
❑ 18 Brian Dopirak RC	10.00	3.00
❑ 19 James Loney RC	6.00	1.80
❑ 20 Denard Span RC	1.00	.30
❑ 21 Billy Petrick RC...............	1.00	.30
❑ 22 Jared Doyle RC	1.00	.30
❑ 23 Jeff Francoeur RC	15.00	4.50
❑ 24 Nick Bourgeois RC	1.00	.30
❑ 25 Matt Cain RC....................	8.00	2.40
❑ 26 John McCurdy RC............	1.00	.30
❑ 27 Mark Kiger RC..................	1.00	.30
❑ 28 Bill Murphy RC	1.50	.45
❑ 29 Matt Craig RC	1.50	.45
❑ 30 Mike Megrew RC.............	3.00	.90
❑ 31 Ben Crockett RC	1.00	.30
❑ 32 Luke Hagerty RC	1.00	.30
❑ 33 Matt Whitney RC	1.50	.45
❑ 34 Dan Meyer RC..................	3.00	.90
❑ 35 Jeremy Brown RC	2.50	.75
❑ 36 Doug Johnson RC............	1.00	.30
❑ 37 Steve Obenchain RC	1.00	.30
❑ 38 Matt Clanton RC	1.00	.30
❑ 39 Mark Teahen RC	5.00	1.50
❑ 40 Tom Carrow RC................	1.00	.30
❑ 41 Micah Schilling RC	1.00	.30
❑ 42 Blair Johnson RC	1.00	.30
❑ 43 Jason Pridie RC	3.00	.90
❑ 44 Joey Votto RC	4.00	1.20
❑ 45 Taber Lee RC....................	1.00	.30
❑ 46 Adam Peterson RC	1.00	.30
❑ 47 Adam Donachie RC	1.00	.30
❑ 48 Josh Murray RC	1.00	.30
❑ 49 Brent Clevlen RC..............	3.00	.90
❑ 50 Chad Pleiness RC	1.00	.30
❑ 51 Zach Hammes RC	1.00	.30
❑ 52 Chris Snyder RC	2.50	.75
❑ 53 Chris Smith RC	1.00	.30
❑ 54 Justin Maureau RC	1.00	.30
❑ 55 David Bush RC	3.00	.90
❑ 56 Tim Gilhooly RC	1.00	.30
❑ 57 Blair Barbier RC	1.00	.30
❑ 58 Zach Segovia RC..............	1.50	.45
❑ 59 Jeremy Reed RC	10.00	3.00
❑ 60 Matt Pender RC...............	1.00	.30
❑ 61 Eric Thomas RC	1.00	.30
❑ 62 Justin Jones RC	4.00	1.20
❑ 63 Brian Slocum RC..............	1.00	.30
❑ 64 Larry Broadway RC	3.00	.90
❑ 65 Bo Flowers RC	1.00	.30
❑ 66 Scott White RC	1.00	.30
❑ 67 Steve Stanley RC..............	1.00	.30
❑ 68 Alex Merricks RC	1.00	.30
❑ 69 Josh Womack RC	1.00	.30
❑ 70 Dave Jensen RC	1.00	.30
❑ 71 Curtis Granderson RC......	5.00	1.50
❑ 72 Pat Osborn RC	1.00	.30
❑ 73 Nic Carter RC	1.00	.30
❑ 74 Mitch Talbot RC	1.00	.30
❑ 75 Don Murphy RC	1.00	.30
❑ 76 Val Majewski RC...............	4.00	1.20
❑ 77 Javy Rodriguez RC	1.00	.30
❑ 78 Fernando Pacheco RC......	1.00	.30
❑ 79 Steve Russell RC..............	1.00	.30
❑ 80 Jon Slack RC....................	1.00	.30
❑ 81 John Baker RC	1.00	.30
❑ 82 Aaron Coonrod RC	1.00	.30
❑ 83 Josh Johnson RC	1.00	.30
❑ 84 Jake Blalock RC	5.00	1.50
❑ 85 Alex Hart RC	2.50	.75
❑ 86 Wes Bankston RC	4.00	1.20
❑ 87 Josh Rupe RC...................	1.00	.30
❑ 88 Dan Cevette RC................	1.00	.30
❑ 89 Kiel Fisher RC...................	1.50	.45
❑ 90 Alan Rick RC.....................	1.00	.30
❑ 91 Charlie Morton RC	1.00	.30
❑ 92 Chad Spann RC................	2.50	.75
❑ 93 Kyle Boyer RC..................	1.00	.30
❑ 94 Bob Malek RC..................	1.00	.30
❑ 95 Ryan Rodriguez RC	1.00	.30
❑ 96 Jordan Renz RC...............	1.00	.30
❑ 97 Randy Frye RC	1.00	.30
❑ 98 Rich Hill RC	1.00	.30
❑ 99 B.J. Upton RC	25.00	7.50
❑ 100 Dan Christensen RC	1.00	.30
❑ 101 Casey Kotchman RC	10.00	3.00
❑ 102 Eric Good RC	1.00	.30
❑ 103 Mike Fontenot RC	1.00	.30
❑ 104 John Webb RC	1.00	.30
❑ 105 Jason Dubois RC	4.00	1.20
❑ 106 Ryan Kibler RC	1.00	.30
❑ 107 Jhohny Peralta RC..........	4.00	1.20
❑ 108 Kirk Saarloos RC............	1.00	.30
❑ 109 Rhett Parrott RC	1.00	.30
❑ 110 Jason Grove RC	1.00	.30
❑ 111 Colt Griffin RC................	1.50	.45
❑ 112 Dallas McPherson RC ..	20.00	6.00
❑ 113 Oliver Perez RC	10.00	3.00
❑ 114 Marshall McDougall RC	1.00	.30
❑ 115 Mike Wood RC	2.00	.60
❑ 116 Scott Hairston RC	5.00	1.50
❑ 117 Jason Simontacchi RC ..	1.00	.30
❑ 118 Taggert Bozied RC..........	2.50	.75
❑ 119 Shelley Duncan RC	1.00	.30
❑ 120 Dontrelle Willis RC	10.00	3.00
❑ 121 Sean Burnett	.40	.12
❑ 122 Aaron Cook	.60	.18
❑ 123 Brett Evert	.40	.12
❑ 124 Jimmy Journell	.40	.12
❑ 125 Brett Myers	.40	.12
❑ 126 Brad Baker.......................	.40	.12
❑ 127 Billy Traber RC	2.50	.75
❑ 128 Adam Wainwright	.40	.12
❑ 129 Jason Young	1.00	.30
❑ 130 John Buck	.40	.12
❑ 131 Kevin Cash	1.00	.30
❑ 132 Jason Stokes RC	10.00	3.00
❑ 133 Drew Henson....................	.60	.18
❑ 134 Chad Tracy RC	5.00	1.50
❑ 135 Orlando Hudson	.40	.12
❑ 136 Brandon Phillips	.40	.12
❑ 137 Joe Borchard..................	.40	.12
❑ 138 Marlon Byrd	.40	.12
❑ 139 Carl Crawford	.60	.18
❑ 140 Michael Restovich...........	.40	.12
❑ 141 Corey Hart RC................	4.00	1.20
❑ 142 Edwin Almonte	.60	.18
❑ 143 Francis Beltran RC	1.00	.30
❑ 144 Jorge De La Rosa RC	1.00	.30
❑ 145 Gerardo Garcia RC	1.00	.30
❑ 146 Franklyn German RC	1.00	.30
❑ 147 Francisco Liriano	.60	.18
❑ 148 Francisco Rodriguez	.60	.18
❑ 149 Ricardo Rodriguez...........	.40	.12
❑ 150 Seung Song	.40	.12
❑ 151 John Stephens	.40	.12
❑ 152 Justin Huber RC	2.50	.75
❑ 153 Victor Martinez	1.50	.45
❑ 154 Hee Seop Choi	.40	.12
❑ 155 Justin Morneau..............	1.50	.45
❑ 156 Miguel Cabrera	2.50	.75
❑ 157 Victor Diaz RC..............	5.00	1.50
❑ 158 Jose Reyes	1.00	.30
❑ 159 Omar Infante	.40	.12
❑ 160 Angel Berroa	.40	.12
❑ 161 Tony Alvarez	.40	.12
❑ 162 Shin Soo Choo RC	4.00	1.20
❑ 163 Wily Mo Pena	.60	.18
❑ 164 Andres Torres	.40	.12
❑ 165 Jose Lopez RC	10.00	3.00
❑ 166 Scott Moore AU RC......	15.00	4.50
❑ 167 Chris Gruler AU RC......	15.00	4.50
❑ 168 Joe Saunders AU RC....	10.00	3.00
❑ 169 Jeff Francis AU RC	40.00	12.00
❑ 170 Royce Ring AU RC	15.00	4.50
❑ 171 Greg Miller AU RC	30.00	9.00
❑ 172 Brandon Weeden AU RC	10.00	3.00
❑ 173 Drew Meyer AU RC	10.00	3.00
❑ 174 Khalil Greene AU RC	80.00	24.00
❑ 175 Mark Schramek AU RC	15.00	4.50

2003 Bowman Chrome

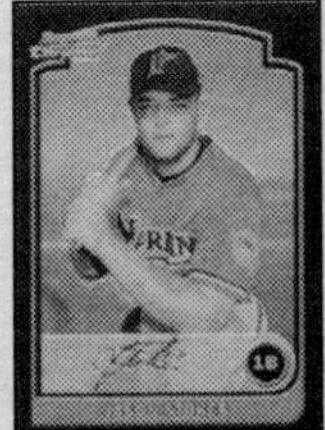

	MINT	NRMT
COMPLETE SET (351)	500.00	220.00
COMP.SET w/o AU's (331)......	150.00	70.00

COMMON CARD (1-165)	.50	.23
COMMON CARD (166-330)	.50	.23
COMMON RC (156-330)	1.00	.45

COMP.SET w/o AU'S INCLUDES 351 MAYS
MAYS AU IS NOT PART OF 351-CARD SET

❑ 1	Garret Anderson	.50	.23
❑ 2	Derek Jeter	3.00	1.35
❑ 3	Gary Sheffield	.50	.23
❑ 4	Matt Morris	.50	.23
❑ 5	Derek Lowe	.50	.23
❑ 6	Andy Van Hekken	.50	.23
❑ 7	Sammy Sosa	2.00	.90
❑ 8	Ken Griffey Jr.	2.00	.90
❑ 9	Omar Vizquel	.75	.35
❑ 10	Jorge Posada	.75	.35
❑ 11	Lance Berkman	.50	.23
❑ 12	Mike Sweeney	.50	.23
❑ 13	Adrian Beltre	.75	.35
❑ 14	Richie Sexson	.50	.23
❑ 15	A.J. Pierzynski	.50	.23
❑ 16	Bartolo Colon	.50	.23
❑ 17	Mike Mussina	.75	.35
❑ 18	Paul Byrd	.50	.23
❑ 19	Bobby Abreu	.50	.23
❑ 20	Miguel Tejada	.50	.23
❑ 21	Aramis Ramirez	.50	.23
❑ 22	Edgardo Alfonzo	.50	.23
❑ 23	Edgar Martinez	.75	.35
❑ 24	Albert Pujols	2.50	1.10
❑ 25	Carl Crawford	.50	.23
❑ 26	Eric Hinske	.50	.23
❑ 27	Tim Salmon	.75	.35
❑ 28	Luis Gonzalez	.50	.23
❑ 29	Jay Gibbons	.50	.23
❑ 30	John Smoltz	.50	.23
❑ 31	Tim Wakefield	.50	.23
❑ 32	Mark Prior	1.25	.55
❑ 33	Maggilo Ordonez	.50	.23
❑ 34	Adam Dunn	.75	.35
❑ 35	Larry Walker	.75	.35
❑ 36	Luis Castillo	.50	.23
❑ 37	Wade Miller	.50	.23
❑ 38	Carlos Beltran	.75	.35
❑ 39	Odalis Perez	.50	.23
❑ 40	Alex Sanchez	.50	.23
❑ 41	Torii Hunter	.50	.23
❑ 42	Cliff Floyd	.50	.23
❑ 43	Andy Pettitte	.75	.35
❑ 44	Francisco Rodriguez	.50	.23
❑ 45	Eric Chavez	.50	.23
❑ 46	Kevin Millwood	.50	.23
❑ 47	Dennis Tankersley	.50	.23
❑ 48	Hideo Nomo	1.25	.55
❑ 49	Freddy Garcia	.50	.23
❑ 50	Randy Johnson	1.25	.55
❑ 51	Aubrey Huff	.50	.23
❑ 52	Carlos Delgado	.50	.23
❑ 53	Troy Glaus	.50	.23
❑ 54	Junior Spivey	.50	.23
❑ 55	Mike Hampton	.50	.23
❑ 56	Sidney Ponson	.50	.23
❑ 57	Aaron Boone	.50	.23
❑ 58	Kerry Wood	1.25	.55
❑ 59	Willie Harris	.50	.23
❑ 60	Nomar Garciaparra	2.00	.90
❑ 61	Todd Helton	.75	.35
❑ 62	Mike Lowell	.50	.23
❑ 63	Roy Oswalt	.50	.23
❑ 64	Raul Ibanez	.50	.23
❑ 65	Brian Jordan	.50	.23
❑ 66	Geoff Jenkins	.50	.23
❑ 67	Jermaine Dye	.50	.23
❑ 68	Tom Glavine	.75	.35
❑ 69	Bernie Williams	.75	.35
❑ 70	Vladimir Guerrero	1.25	.55
❑ 71	Mark Mulder	.50	.23
❑ 72	Jimmy Rollins	.50	.23
❑ 73	Oliver Perez	.50	.23
❑ 74	Rich Aurilia	.50	.23
❑ 75	Joel Pineiro	.50	.23
❑ 76	J.D. Drew	.50	.23
❑ 77	Ivan Rodriguez	1.25	.55
❑ 78	Josh Phelps	.50	.23
❑ 79	Darin Erstad	.50	.23
❑ 80	Curt Schilling	.50	.23
❑ 81	Paul Lo Duca	.50	.23
❑ 82	Marty Cordova	.50	.23
❑ 83	Manny Ramirez	.75	.35
❑ 84	Bobby Hill	.50	.23
❑ 85	Paul Konerko	.50	.23
❑ 86	Austin Kearns	.50	.23
❑ 87	Jason Jennings	.50	.23
❑ 88	Brad Penny	.50	.23
❑ 89	Jeff Bagwell	.75	.35
❑ 90	Shawn Green	.50	.23
❑ 91	Jason Schmidt	.50	.23
❑ 92	Doug Mientkiewicz	.50	.23
❑ 93	Jose Vidro	.50	.23
❑ 94	Bret Boone	.50	.23
❑ 95	Jason Giambi	.50	.23
❑ 96	Barry Zito	.50	.23
❑ 97	Roy Halladay	.50	.23
❑ 98	Pat Burrell	.50	.23
❑ 99	Sean Burroughs	.50	.23
❑ 100	Barry Bonds	3.00	1.35
❑ 101	Kazuhiro Sasaki	.50	.23
❑ 102	Fernando Vina	.50	.23
❑ 103	Chan Ho Park	.50	.23
❑ 104	Andruw Jones	.50	.23
❑ 105	Adam Kennedy	.50	.23
❑ 106	Shea Hillenbrand	.50	.23
❑ 107	Greg Maddux	2.00	.90
❑ 108	Jim Edmonds	.50	.23
❑ 109	Pedro Martinez	1.25	.55
❑ 110	Moises Alou	.50	.23
❑ 111	Jeff Weaver	.50	.23
❑ 112	C.C. Sabathia	.50	.23
❑ 113	Robert Fick	.50	.23
❑ 114	A.J. Burnett	.50	.23
❑ 115	Jeff Kent	.50	.23
❑ 116	Kevin Brown	.50	.23
❑ 117	Rafael Furcal	.50	.23
❑ 118	Cristian Guzman	.50	.23
❑ 119	Brad Wilkerson	.50	.23
❑ 120	Mike Piazza	2.00	.90
❑ 121	Alfonso Soriano	.75	.35
❑ 122	Mark Ellis	.50	.23
❑ 123	Vicente Padilla	.50	.23
❑ 124	Eric Gagne	1.25	.55
❑ 125	Ryan Klesko	.50	.23
❑ 126	Ichiro Suzuki	2.00	.90
❑ 127	Tony Batista	.50	.23
❑ 128	Roberto Alomar	.75	.35
❑ 129	Alex Rodriguez	2.00	.90
❑ 130	Jim Thome	1.25	.55
❑ 131	Jarrod Washburn	.50	.23
❑ 132	Orlando Hudson	.50	.23
❑ 133	Chipper Jones	1.25	.55
❑ 134	Rodrigo Lopez	.50	.23
❑ 135	Johnny Damon	1.25	.55
❑ 136	Matt Clement	.50	.23
❑ 137	Frank Thomas	1.25	.55
❑ 138	Ellis Burks	.50	.23
❑ 139	Carlos Pena	.50	.23
❑ 140	Josh Beckett	.50	.23
❑ 141	Joe Randa	.50	.23
❑ 142	Brian Giles	.50	.23
❑ 143	Kazuhisa Ishii	.50	.23
❑ 144	Corey Koskie	.50	.23
❑ 145	Orlando Cabrera	.50	.23
❑ 146	Mark Buehrle	.50	.23
❑ 147	Roger Clemens	2.50	1.10
❑ 148	Tim Hudson	.50	.23
❑ 149	Randy Wolf	.50	.23
❑ 150	Josh Fogg	.50	.23
❑ 151	Phil Nevin	.50	.23
❑ 152	John Olerud	.50	.23
❑ 153	Scott Rolen	1.25	.55
❑ 154	Joe Kennedy	.50	.23
❑ 155	Rafael Palmeiro	.75	.35
❑ 156	Chad Hutchinson	.50	.23
❑ 157	Quincy Carter XRC	2.00	.90
❑ 158	Hee Seop Choi	.50	.23
❑ 159	Joe Borchard	.50	.23
❑ 160	Brandon Phillips	.50	.23
❑ 161	Wily Mo Pena	.50	.23
❑ 162	Victor Martinez	.75	.35
❑ 163	Jason Stokes	.75	.35
❑ 164	Ken Harvey	.50	.23
❑ 165	Juan Rivera	.50	.23
❑ 166	Joe Valentine RC	1.50	.70
❑ 167	Dan Haren RC	3.00	1.35
❑ 168	Michel Hernandez RC	1.50	.70
❑ 169	Eider Torres RC	1.50	.70
❑ 170	Chris De La Cruz RC	1.50	.70
❑ 171	Ramon Nivar-Martinez RC	3.00	1.35
❑ 172	Mike Adams RC	1.50	.70
❑ 173	Justin Arneson RC	1.50	.70
❑ 174	Jamie Athas RC	1.50	.70
❑ 175	Dwaine Bacon RC	1.50	.70
❑ 176	Clint Barmes RC	2.00	.90
❑ 177	B.J. Barns RC	1.50	.70
❑ 178	Tyler Johnson RC	1.50	.70
❑ 179	Brandon Webb RC	4.00	1.80
❑ 180	T.J. Bohn RC	1.50	.70
❑ 181	Ozzie Chavez RC	1.50	.70
❑ 182	Brandon Bowe RC	1.50	.70
❑ 183	Craig Brazell RC	2.00	.90
❑ 184	Dusty Brown RC	1.50	.70
❑ 185	Brian Bruney RC	2.00	.90
❑ 186	Greg Bruso RC	1.50	.70
❑ 187	Jaime Bubela RC	1.50	.70
❑ 188	Matt Diaz RC	2.00	.90
❑ 189	Brian Burgamy RC	1.50	.70
❑ 190	Eny Cabreja RC	1.50	.70
❑ 191	Daniel Cabrera RC	4.00	1.80
❑ 192	Ryan Cameron RC	1.50	.70
❑ 193	Lance Caracciolí RC	1.50	.70
❑ 194	David Cash RC	1.50	.70
❑ 195	Bernie Castro RC	1.50	.70
❑ 196	Ismael Castro RC	2.00	.90
❑ 197	Cory Doyne RC	1.50	.70
❑ 198	Jeff Clark RC	1.50	.70
❑ 199	Chris Colton RC	1.50	.70
❑ 200	Dexter Cooper RC	1.50	.70
❑ 201	Callix Crabbe RC	2.00	.90
❑ 202	Chien-Ming Wang RC	4.00	1.80
❑ 203	Eric Crozier RC	2.00	.90
❑ 204	Nook Logan RC	1.50	.70
❑ 205	David DeJesus RC	2.00	.90
❑ 206	Matt DeMarco RC	1.50	.70
❑ 207	Chris Duncan RC	1.50	.70
❑ 208	Eric Eckenstahler	.50	.23
❑ 209	Willie Eyre RC	1.50	.70
❑ 210	Evel Bastida-Martinez RC	1.50	.70
❑ 211	Chris Fallon RC	1.50	.70
❑ 212	Mike Flannery RC	1.50	.70
❑ 213	Mike O'Keefe RC	1.50	.70
❑ 214	Lew Ford RC	5.00	2.20
❑ 215	Kason Gabbard RC	1.50	.70
❑ 216	Mike Gallo RC	1.50	.70
❑ 217	Jairo Garcia RC	3.00	1.35
❑ 218	Angel Garcia RC	2.00	.90
❑ 219	Michael Garciaparra RC	3.00	1.35
❑ 220	Jeremy Griffiths RC	2.00	.90
❑ 221	Dusty Gomon RC	2.00	.90
❑ 222	Bryan Grace RC	1.50	.70
❑ 223	Tyson Graham RC	1.50	.70
❑ 224	Henry Guerrero RC	1.50	.70
❑ 225	Franklin Gutierrez RC	8.00	3.60
❑ 226	Carlos Guzman RC	2.00	.90
❑ 227	Matthew Hagen RC	3.00	1.35
❑ 228	Josh Hall RC	2.00	.90
❑ 229	Rob Hammock RC	2.00	.90
❑ 230	Brendan Harris RC	2.00	.90
❑ 231	Gary Harris RC	1.50	.70
❑ 232	Clay Hensley RC	1.50	.70
❑ 233	Michael Hinckley RC	4.00	1.80
❑ 234	Luis Hodge RC	1.50	.70
❑ 235	Donnie Hood RC	2.00	.90
❑ 236	Matt Hensley RC	1.50	.70
❑ 237	Edwin Jackson RC	10.00	4.50
❑ 238	Ardley Jansen RC	2.00	.90
❑ 239	Ferenc Jongejan RC	1.50	.70
❑ 240	Matt Kata RC	3.00	1.35
❑ 241	Kazuhiro Takeoka RC	1.50	.70
❑ 242	Charlie Manning RC	1.50	.70
❑ 243	Il Kim RC	1.50	.70
❑ 244	Brennan King RC	1.50	.70
❑ 245	Chris Kroski RC	1.50	.70
❑ 246	David Martinez RC	1.50	.70
❑ 247	Pete LaForest RC	2.00	.90
❑ 248	Wil Ledezma RC	2.00	.90
❑ 249	Jeremy Bonderman RC	3.00	1.35
❑ 250	Gonzalo Lopez RC	1.50	.70
❑ 251	Brian Luderer RC	1.50	.70
❑ 252	Ruddy Lugo RC	1.50	.70

❑ 253 Wayne Lydon RC 1.50 .70
❑ 254 Mark Malaska RC 1.50 .70
❑ 255 Andy Marte RC 10.00 4.50
❑ 256 Tyler Martin RC 1.50 .70
❑ 257 Branden Florence RC 1.50 .70
❑ 258 Aneudis Mateo RC 1.50 .70
❑ 259 Derell McCall RC 1.50 .70
❑ 260 Elizardo Ramirez RC 3.00 1.35
❑ 261 Mike McNutt RC 1.50 .70
❑ 262 Jacobo Meque RC 1.50 .70
❑ 263 Derek Michaelis RC 1.50 .70
❑ 264 Aaron Miles RC 4.00 1.80
❑ 265 Jose Morales RC 1.50 .70
❑ 266 Dustin Moseley RC 2.00 .90
❑ 267 Adrian Myers RC 1.50 .70
❑ 268 Dan Neil RC 1.50 .70
❑ 269 Jon Nelson RC 2.00 .90
❑ 270 Mike Neu RC 1.50 .70
❑ 271 Leigh Neuage RC 1.50 .70
❑ 272 Wes O'Brien RC 1.50 .70
❑ 273 Trent Oeltjen RC 2.00 .90
❑ 274 Tim Olson RC 2.00 .90
❑ 275 David Pahucki RC 1.50 .70
❑ 276 Nathan Panther RC 3.00 1.35
❑ 277 Arnie Munoz RC 1.50 .70
❑ 278 Dave Pember RC 1.50 .70
❑ 279 Jason Perry RC 3.00 1.35
❑ 280 Matthew Peterson RC 1.50 .70
❑ 281 Greg Aquino RC 1.50 .70
❑ 282 Jorge Piedra RC 2.00 .90
❑ 283 Simon Pond RC 3.00 1.35
❑ 284 Aaron Rakers RC 1.50 .70
❑ 285 Felix Sanchez RC 1.50 .70
❑ 286 Manuel Ramirez RC 2.00 .90
❑ 287 Kevin Randel RC 1.50 .70
❑ 288 Kelly Shoppach RC 4.00 1.80
❑ 289 Prentice Redman RC 1.50 .70
❑ 290 Eric Reed RC 3.00 1.35
❑ 291 Wilton Reynolds RC 2.00 .90
❑ 292 Eric Riggs RC 2.00 .90
❑ 293 Carlos Rijo RC 1.50 .70
❑ 294 Tyler Adamczyk RC 1.50 .70
❑ 295 Jon-Mark Sprowl RC 3.00 1.35
❑ 296 Arturo Rivas RC 1.50 .70
❑ 297 Kyle Roat RC 1.50 .70
❑ 298 Bubba Nelson RC .75 .35
❑ 299 Levi Robinson RC 1.50 .70
❑ 300 Ray Sadler RC 1.50 .70
❑ 301 Rylan Reed RC 1.50 .70
❑ 302 Jon Schuerholz RC 1.50 .70
❑ 303 Nobuaki Yoshida RC 1.50 .70
❑ 304 Brian Shackelford RC 1.50 .70
❑ 305 Bill Simon RC 1.50 .70
❑ 306 Haj Turay RC 2.00 .90
❑ 307 Sean Smith RC 2.00 .90
❑ 308 Ryan Spataro RC 1.50 .70
❑ 309 Jemel Spearman RC 1.50 .70
❑ 310 Keith Stamler RC 1.50 .70
❑ 311 Luke Steidlmayer RC 1.50 .70
❑ 312 Adam Stern RC 1.50 .70
❑ 313 Jay Sitzman RC 1.50 .70
❑ 314 Mike Wodnicki RC 1.50 .70
❑ 315 Terry Tiffee RC 3.00 1.35
❑ 316 Nick Trzesniak RC 1.50 .70
❑ 317 Denny Tussen RC 1.50 .70
❑ 318 Scott Tyler RC 2.00 .90
❑ 319 Shane Victorino RC 1.50 .70
❑ 320 Doug Waechter RC 2.00 .90
❑ 321 Brandon Watson RC 1.50 .70
❑ 322 Todd Wellemeyer RC 2.00 .90
❑ 323 Eli Whiteside RC 1.50 .70
❑ 324 Josh Willingham RC 2.00 .90
❑ 325 Travis Wong RC 2.00 .90
❑ 326 Brian Wright RC 1.50 .70
❑ 327 Felix Pie RC 8.00 3.60
❑ 328 Andy Sisco RC 4.00 1.80
❑ 329 Dustin Yount RC 2.00 .90
❑ 330 Andrew Dominique RC 1.50 .70
❑ 331 Brian McCann AU A RC 20.00 9.00
❑ 332 Jose Contreras AU B RC 200.00 90.00
❑ 333 Corey Shafer AU A RC 20.00 9.00
❑ 334 Hanley Ramirez AU A RC 50.00 22.00
❑ 335 Ryan Shealy AU A RC 20.00 9.00
❑ 336 Kevin Youkilis AU A RC 40.00 18.00
❑ 337 Jason Kubel AU A RC 50.00 22.00
❑ 338 Aron Weston AU A RC 15.00 6.75
❑ 338B Rajai Davis AU A ERR .00
❑ 339 J.D. Durbin AU A RC 20.00 9.00
❑ 340 G. Schneidmiller AU A RC 15.00 6.75
❑ 341 Travis Ishikawa AU A RC 15.00 6.75
❑ 342 Ben Francisco AU A RC 20.00 9.00
❑ 343 Bobby Basham AU A RC 20.00 9.00
❑ 344 Joey Gomes AU A RC 15.00 6.75
❑ 345 Beau Kemp AU A RC 15.00 6.75
❑ 346 T.Story-Harden AU A RC 15.00 6.75
❑ 347 Daryl Clark AU A RC 20.00 9.00
❑ 348 B.Bullington AU A RC EXCH 25.00 11.00
❑ 349 Rajai Davis AU A RC 20.00 9.00
❑ 350 Darrell Rasner AU A RC 15.00 6.75
❑ 351 Willie Mays 2.00 .90
❑ 351AU Willie Mays AU 300.00 135.00

2003 Bowman Chrome Draft

	MINT	NRMT
COMPLETE SET (176)	350.00	160.00
COMP.SET w/o AU's (165)	100.00	45.00
COMMON CARD (1-165)	.40	.18
1-165 TWO PER BOWMAN DRAFT PACK		
COMMON CARD (166-176)	15.00	6.75

166-176 STATED ODDS 1:41 H/R
168-176 ARE ALL PARTIAL LIVE/EXCH DIST
168-176 EXCH.DEADLINE 11/30/05
LUBANSKI EXCH IS AN SP BY 1000 COPIES

❑ 1 Dontrelle Willis 1.00 .45
❑ 2 Freddy Sanchez .40 .18
❑ 3 Miguel Cabrera 1.50 .70
❑ 4 Ryan Ludwick .40 .18
❑ 5 Ty Wigginton .40 .18
❑ 6 Mark Teixeira .60 .25
❑ 7 Trey Hodges .40 .18
❑ 8 Laynce Nix .60 .25
❑ 9 Antonio Perez .40 .18
❑ 10 Jody Gerut .40 .18
❑ 11 Jae Weong Seo .40 .18
❑ 12 Erick Almonte .40 .18
❑ 13 Lyle Overbay .60 .25
❑ 14 Billy Traber .40 .18
❑ 15 Andres Torres .40 .18
❑ 16 Jose Valverde .40 .18
❑ 17 Aaron Heilman .40 .18
❑ 18 Brandon Larson .40 .18
❑ 19 Jung Bong .40 .18
❑ 20 Jesse Foppert .60 .25
❑ 21 Angel Berroa .40 .18
❑ 22 Jeff DaVanon .40 .18
❑ 23 Kurt Ainsworth .40 .18
❑ 24 Brandon Claussen .40 .18
❑ 25 Xavier Nady .40 .18
❑ 26 Travis Hafner .60 .25
❑ 27 Jerome Williams .60 .25
❑ 28 Jose Reyes .60 .25
❑ 29 Sergio Mitre RC 1.50 .70
❑ 30 Bo Hart RC 1.50 .70
❑ 31 Adam Miller RC 5.00 2.20
❑ 32 Brian Finch RC 1.00 .45
❑ 33 Taylor Mattingly RC 4.00 1.80
❑ 34 Daric Barton RC 8.00 3.60
❑ 35 Chris Ray RC 1.50 .70
❑ 36 Jarrod Saltalamacchia RC 2.50 1.10
❑ 37 Dennis Dove RC 1.50 .70
❑ 38 James Houser RC 1.50 .70
❑ 39 Clint King RC 2.50 1.10
❑ 40 Lou Palmisano RC 4.00 1.80
❑ 41 Dan Moore RC 1.00 .45
❑ 42 Craig Stansberry RC 1.50 .70
❑ 43 Jo Jo Reyes RC 1.50 .70
❑ 44 Jake Stevens RC 4.00 1.80
❑ 45 Tom Gorzelanny RC 2.50 1.10
❑ 46 Brian Marshall RC 1.00 .45
❑ 47 Scott Beerer RC 1.00 .45
❑ 48 Javi Herrera RC 1.50 .70
❑ 49 Steve LeRud RC 2.50 1.10
❑ 50 Josh Banks RC 3.00 1.35
❑ 51 Jon Papelbon RC 1.00 .45
❑ 52 Juan Valdes RC 1.50 .70
❑ 53 Beau Vaughan RC 1.50 .70
❑ 54 Matt Chico RC 3.00 1.35
❑ 55 Todd Jennings RC 1.50 .70
❑ 56 Anthony Gwynn RC 4.00 1.80
❑ 57 Matt Harrison RC 2.50 1.10
❑ 58 Aaron Marsden RC 1.50 .70
❑ 59 Casey Abrams RC 1.00 .45
❑ 60 Cory Stuart RC 1.00 .45
❑ 61 Mike Wagner RC 1.00 .45
❑ 62 Jordan Pratt RC 1.50 .70
❑ 63 Andre Randolph RC 1.50 .70
❑ 64 Blake Balkcom RC 1.50 .70
❑ 65 Josh Muecke RC 1.00 .45
❑ 66 Jamie D'Antona RC 4.00 1.80
❑ 67 Cole Seifrig RC 2.50 1.10
❑ 68 Josh Anderson RC 3.00 1.35
❑ 69 Matt Lorenzo RC 1.50 .70
❑ 70 Nate Spears RC 2.50 1.10
❑ 71 Chris Goodman RC 1.00 .45
❑ 72 Brian McFall RC 2.50 1.10
❑ 73 Billy Hogan RC 1.50 .70
❑ 74 Jamie Romak RC 1.50 .70
❑ 75 Jeff Cook RC 1.50 .70
❑ 76 Brooks McNiven RC 1.00 .45
❑ 77 Xavier Paul RC 5.00 2.20
❑ 78 Bob Zimmerman RC 1.00 .45
❑ 79 Mickey Hall RC 1.50 .70
❑ 80 Shaun Marcum RC 1.00 .45
❑ 81 Matt Nachreiner RC 1.50 .70
❑ 82 Chris Kinsey RC 1.00 .45
❑ 83 Jonathan Fulton RC 1.50 .70
❑ 84 Edgardo Baez RC 1.50 .70
❑ 85 Robert Valido RC 2.50 1.10
❑ 86 Kenny Lewis RC 1.50 .70
❑ 87 Trent Peterson RC 1.00 .45
❑ 88 Johnny Woodard RC 1.50 .70
❑ 89 Wes Littleton RC 1.50 .70
❑ 90 Sean Rodriguez RC 4.00 1.80
❑ 91 Kyle Pearson RC 1.00 .45
❑ 92 Josh Rainwater RC 1.50 .70
❑ 93 Travis Schlichting RC 1.50 .70
❑ 94 Tim Battle RC 1.50 .70
❑ 95 Aaron Hill RC 3.00 1.35
❑ 96 Bob McCrory RC 1.00 .45
❑ 97 Rick Guarno RC 1.50 .70
❑ 98 Brandon Yarbrough RC 1.00 .45
❑ 99 Peter Stonard RC 1.00 .45
❑ 100 Darin Downs RC 1.50 .70
❑ 101 Matt Bruback RC 1.00 .45
❑ 102 Danny Garcia RC 1.00 .45
❑ 103 Cory Stewart RC 1.00 .45
❑ 104 Ferdin Tejeda RC 1.00 .45
❑ 105 Kade Johnson RC 1.00 .45
❑ 106 Andrew Brown RC 1.50 .70
❑ 107 Aquilino Lopez RC 1.00 .45
❑ 108 Stephen Randolph RC 1.00 .45
❑ 109 Dave Matranga RC 1.00 .45
❑ 110 Dustin McGowan RC 2.50 1.10
❑ 111 Juan Camacho RC 1.00 .45
❑ 112 Cliff Lee .40 .18
❑ 113 Jeff Duncan RC 1.50 .70
❑ 114 C.J. Wilson .40 .18
❑ 115 Brandon Roberson RC 1.00 .45
❑ 116 David Corrente RC 1.00 .45
❑ 117 Kevin Beavers RC 1.00 .45
❑ 118 Anthony Webster RC 1.50 .70
❑ 119 Oscar Villarreal RC 1.00 .45
❑ 120 Hong-Chih Kuo RC 2.50 1.10
❑ 121 Josh Barfield .60 .25
❑ 122 Denny Bautista .40 .18
❑ 123 Chris Burke RC 2.50 1.10
❑ 124 Robinson Cano RC 3.00 1.35

❑ 125 Jose Castillo .40 .18
❑ 126 Neal Cotts .60 .25
❑ 127 Jorge De La Rosa .40 .18
❑ 128 J.D. Durbin 1.50 .70
❑ 129 Edwin Encarnacion .40 .18
❑ 130 Gavin Floyd .60 .25
❑ 131 Alexis Gomez .40 .18
❑ 132 Edgar Gonzalez RC 1.00 .45
❑ 133 Khalil Greene 3.00 1.35
❑ 134 Zack Greinke 1.00 .45
❑ 135 Franklin Gutierrez 2.50 1.10
❑ 136 Rich Harden 1.00 .45
❑ 137 J.J. Hardy RC 5.00 2.20
❑ 138 Ryan Howard RC 10.00 4.50
❑ 139 Justin Huber .40 .18
❑ 140 David Kelton .40 .18
❑ 141 Dave Krynzel .40 .18
❑ 142 Pete LaForest 1.00 .45
❑ 143 Adam LaRoche .40 .18
❑ 144 Preston Larrison RC 1.00 .45
❑ 145 John Maine RC 5.00 2.20
❑ 146 Andy Marte 5.00 2.20
❑ 147 Jeff Mathis .60 .25
❑ 148 Joe Mauer 1.50 .70
❑ 149 Clint Nageotte .60 .25
❑ 150 Chris Narveson .40 .18
❑ 151 Ramon Nivar 1.50 .70
❑ 152 Felix Pie 3.00 1.35
❑ 153 Guillermo Quiroz RC 2.50 1.10
❑ 154 Rene Reyes .40 .18
❑ 155 Royce Ring .40 .18
❑ 156 Alexis Rios 2.00 .90
❑ 157 Grady Sizemore .60 .25
❑ 158 Stephen Smitherman .40 .18
❑ 159 Seung Song .40 .18
❑ 160 Scott Thorman .40 .18
❑ 161 Chad Tracy .60 .25
❑ 162 Chin-Hui Tsao .60 .25
❑ 163 John VanBenschoten .40 .18
❑ 164 Kevin Youkilis 3.00 1.35
❑ 165 Chien-Ming Wang 2.00 .90
❑ 166 Chris Lubanski AU SP RC 40.00 18.00
❑ 167 Ryan Harvey AU RC 30.00 13.50
❑ 168 Matt Murton AU RC 15.00 6.75
❑ 169 Jay Sborz AU RC 15.00 6.75
❑ 170 Brandon Wood AU RC 20.00 9.00
❑ 171 Nick Markakis AU RC 20.00 9.00
❑ 172 Rickie Weeks AU RC 50.00 22.00
❑ 173 Eric Duncan AU RC 25.00 11.00
❑ 174 Chad Billingsley AU RC 25.00 11.00
❑ 175 Ryan Wagner AU RC 20.00 9.00
❑ 176 Delmon Young AU RC 60.00 27.00

2004 Bowman Chrome

	Nm-Mt	Ex-Mt
COMPLETE SET (350)	500.00	150.00
COMP.SET w/o AU's (330)	150.00	45.00
COMMON CARD (1-150)	.50	.15
COMMON CARD (151-165)	.50	.15
COMMON AUTO (331-350)	15.00	4.50

331-350 AU'S ARE NOT SERIAL-NUMBERED
331-350 PRINT RUN PROVIDED BY TOPPS

❑ 1 Garret Anderson .50 .15
❑ 2 Larry Walker .75 .23
❑ 3 Derek Jeter 2.50 .75
❑ 4 Curt Schilling 1.25 .35
❑ 5 Carlos Zambrano .50 .15
❑ 6 Shawn Green .50 .15
❑ 7 Manny Ramirez .75 .23
❑ 8 Randy Johnson 1.25 .35
❑ 9 Jeremy Bonderman .50 .15
❑ 10 Alfonso Soriano .75 .23
❑ 11 Scott Rolen 1.25 .35
❑ 12 Kerry Wood 1.25 .35
❑ 13 Eric Gagne 1.25 .35
❑ 14 Ryan Klesko .50 .15
❑ 15 Kevin Millar .50 .15
❑ 16 Ty Wigginton .50 .15
❑ 17 David Ortiz 1.25 .35
❑ 18 Luis Castillo .50 .15
❑ 19 Bernie Williams .75 .23
❑ 20 Edgar Renteria .50 .15
❑ 21 Matt Kata .50 .15
❑ 22 Bartolo Colon .50 .15
❑ 23 Derrek Lee .50 .15
❑ 24 Gary Sheffield .50 .15
❑ 25 Nomar Garciaparra 2.00 .60
❑ 26 Kevin Millwood .50 .15
❑ 27 Corey Patterson .50 .15
❑ 28 Carlos Beltran .75 .23
❑ 29 Mike Lieberthal .50 .15
❑ 30 Troy Glaus .50 .15
❑ 31 Preston Wilson .50 .15
❑ 32 Jorge Posada .75 .23
❑ 33 Bo Hart .50 .15
❑ 34 Mark Prior 1.25 .35
❑ 35 Hideo Nomo 1.25 .35
❑ 36 Jason Kendall .50 .15
❑ 37 Roger Clemens 2.50 .75
❑ 38 Dmitri Young .50 .15
❑ 39 Jason Giambi .50 .15
❑ 40 Jim Edmonds .50 .15
❑ 41 Ryan Ludwick .50 .15
❑ 42 Brandon Webb .50 .15
❑ 43 Todd Helton .75 .23
❑ 44 Jacque Jones .50 .15
❑ 45 Jamie Moyer .50 .15
❑ 46 Tim Salmon .75 .23
❑ 47 Kelvim Escobar .50 .15
❑ 48 Tony Batista .50 .15
❑ 49 Nick Johnson .50 .15
❑ 50 Jim Thome 1.25 .35
❑ 51 Casey Blake .50 .15
❑ 52 Trot Nixon .50 .15
❑ 53 Luis Gonzalez .50 .15
❑ 54 Dontrelle Willis .50 .15
❑ 55 Mike Mussina .75 .23
❑ 56 Carl Crawford .50 .15
❑ 57 Mark Buehrle .50 .15
❑ 58 Scott Podsednik .50 .15
❑ 59 Brian Giles .50 .15
❑ 60 Rafael Furcal .50 .15
❑ 61 Miguel Cabrera .75 .23
❑ 62 Rich Harden .50 .15
❑ 63 Mark Teixeira .50 .15
❑ 64 Frank Thomas 1.25 .35
❑ 65 Johan Santana .75 .23
❑ 66 Jason Schmidt .50 .15
❑ 67 Aramis Ramirez .50 .15
❑ 68 Jose Reyes .50 .15
❑ 69 Magglio Ordonez .50 .15
❑ 70 Mike Sweeney .50 .15
❑ 71 Eric Chavez .50 .15
❑ 72 Rocco Baldelli .50 .15
❑ 73 Sammy Sosa 2.00 .60
❑ 74 Javy Lopez .50 .15
❑ 75 Roy Oswalt .50 .15
❑ 76 Raul Ibanez .50 .15
❑ 77 Ivan Rodriguez 1.25 .35
❑ 78 Jerome Williams .50 .15
❑ 79 Carlos Lee .50 .15
❑ 80 Geoff Jenkins .50 .15
❑ 81 Sean Burroughs .50 .15
❑ 82 Marcus Giles .50 .15
❑ 83 Mike Lowell .50 .15
❑ 84 Barry Zito .50 .15
❑ 85 Aubrey Huff .50 .15
❑ 86 Esteban Loaiza .50 .15
❑ 87 Torii Hunter .50 .15
❑ 88 Phil Nevin .50 .15
❑ 89 Andruw Jones .50 .15
❑ 90 Josh Beckett .50 .15
❑ 91 Mark Mulder .50 .15
❑ 92 Hank Blalock .50 .15
❑ 93 Jason Phillips .50 .15
❑ 94 Russ Ortiz .50 .15
❑ 95 Juan Pierre .50 .15
❑ 96 Tom Glavine .75 .23
❑ 97 Gil Meche .50 .15
❑ 98 Ramon Ortiz .50 .15
❑ 99 Richie Sexson .50 .15
❑ 100 Albert Pujols 2.50 .75
❑ 101 Javier Vazquez .50 .15
❑ 102 Johnny Damon 1.25 .35
❑ 103 Alex Rodriguez 2.00 .60
❑ 104 Omar Vizquel .75 .23
❑ 105 Chipper Jones 1.25 .35
❑ 106 Lance Berkman .50 .15
❑ 107 Tim Hudson .50 .15
❑ 108 Carlos Delgado .50 .15
❑ 109 Austin Kearns .50 .15
❑ 110 Orlando Cabrera .50 .15
❑ 111 Edgar Martinez .75 .23
❑ 112 Melvin Mora .50 .15
❑ 113 Jeff Bagwell .75 .23
❑ 114 Marlon Byrd .50 .15
❑ 115 Vernon Wells .50 .15
❑ 116 C.C. Sabathia .50 .15
❑ 117 Cliff Floyd .50 .15
❑ 118 Ichiro Suzuki 2.00 .60
❑ 119 Miguel Olivo .50 .15
❑ 120 Mike Piazza 2.00 .60
❑ 121 Adam Dunn .75 .23
❑ 122 Paul Lo Duca .50 .15
❑ 123 Brett Myers .50 .15
❑ 124 Michael Young .50 .15
❑ 125 Sidney Ponson .50 .15
❑ 126 Greg Maddux 2.00 .60
❑ 127 Vladimir Guerrero 1.25 .35
❑ 128 Miguel Tejada .50 .15
❑ 129 Andy Pettitte .75 .23
❑ 130 Rafael Palmeiro .75 .23
❑ 131 Ken Griffey Jr. 2.00 .60
❑ 132 Shannon Stewart .50 .15
❑ 133 Joel Pineiro .50 .15
❑ 134 Luis Matos .50 .15
❑ 135 Jeff Kent .50 .15
❑ 136 Randy Wolf .50 .15
❑ 137 Chris Woodward .50 .15
❑ 138 Jody Gerut .50 .15
❑ 139 Jose Vidro .50 .15
❑ 140 Bret Boone .50 .15
❑ 141 Bill Mueller .50 .15
❑ 142 Angel Berroa .50 .15
❑ 143 Bobby Abreu .50 .15
❑ 144 Roy Halladay .50 .15
❑ 145 Delmon Young .75 .23
❑ 146 Jonny Gomes .50 .15
❑ 147 Rickie Weeks .50 .15
❑ 148 Edwin Jackson .50 .15
❑ 149 Neal Cotts .50 .15
❑ 150 Jason Bay .50 .15
❑ 151 Khalil Greene 1.50 .45
❑ 152 Joe Mauer 1.00 .30
❑ 153 Bobby Jenks .50 .15
❑ 154 Chin-Feng Chen .50 .15
❑ 155 Chien-Ming Wang .60 .18
❑ 156 Mickey Hall .50 .15
❑ 157 James Houser .50 .15
❑ 158 Jay Sborz .50 .15
❑ 159 Jonathan Fulton .50 .15
❑ 160 Steven Lerud .50 .15
❑ 161 Grady Sizemore .60 .18
❑ 162 Felix Pie 1.50 .45
❑ 163 Dustin McGowan .50 .15
❑ 164 Chris Lubanski .60 .18
❑ 165 Tom Gorzelanny .50 .15
❑ 166 Rudy Guillen RC 4.00 1.20
❑ 167 Aarom Baldiris RC 2.00 .60
❑ 168 Conor Jackson RC 8.00 2.40
❑ 169 Matt Moses RC 4.00 1.20
❑ 170 Ervin Santana RC 5.00 1.50
❑ 171 Merkin Valdez RC 4.00 1.20
❑ 172 Erick Aybar RC 5.00 1.50
❑ 173 Brad Sullivan RC 2.00 .60
❑ 174 Joey Gathright RC 4.00 1.20
❑ 175 Brad Snyder RC 4.00 1.20
❑ 176 Alberto Callaspo RC 3.00 .90

❑ 177 Brandon Medders RC .... 1.00 .30
❑ 178 Zach Miner RC .... 2.00 .60
❑ 179 Charlie Zink RC .... 1.00 .30
❑ 180 Adam Greenberg RC ...... 2.00 .60
❑ 181 Kevin Howard RC .... 2.00 .60
❑ 182 Wanell Severino RC ...... 1.00 .30
❑ 183 Chin-Lung Hu RC 4.00 1.20
❑ 184 Joel Zumaya RC .... 3.00 .90
❑ 185 Skip Schumaker RC ...... 1.50 .45
❑ 186 Nic Ungs RC .... 1.50 .45
❑ 187 Todd Self RC .... 1.50 .45
❑ 188 Brian Steffek RC .... 1.00 .30
❑ 189 Brock Peterson RC .... 1.50 .45
❑ 190 Greg Thissen RC .... 1.50 .45
❑ 191 Frank Brooks RC .... 1.00 .30
❑ 192 Scott Olsen RC 5.00 1.50
❑ 193 Chris Mabeus RC .... 1.50 .45
❑ 194 Dan Giese RC .... 1.50 .45
❑ 195 Jared Wells RC .... 1.00 .30
❑ 196 Carlos Sosa RC .... 1.50 .45
❑ 197 Bobby Madritsch .... 3.00 .90
❑ 198 Calvin Hayes RC .... 2.00 .60
❑ 199 Omar Quintanilla RC 4.00 1.20
❑ 200 Chris O'Riordan RC .... 1.50 .45
❑ 201 Tim Hutting RC .... 1.00 .30
❑ 202 Carlos Quentin RC 8.00 2.40
❑ 203 Brayan Pena RC .... 1.50 .45
❑ 204 Jeff Salazar RC 4.00 1.20
❑ 205 David Murphy RC 4.00 1.20
❑ 206 Alberto Garcia RC .... 2.00 .60
❑ 207 Ramon Ramirez RC .... 1.50 .45
❑ 208 Luis Bolivar RC .... 1.50 .45
❑ 209 Rodney Choy Foo RC .... 1.00 .30
❑ 210 Fausto Carmona RC ...... 3.00 .90
❑ 211 Anthony Acevedo RC ...... 1.50 .45
❑ 212 Chad Santos RC .... 1.50 .45
❑ 213 Jason Frasor RC .... 1.50 .45
❑ 214 Jesse Roman RC .... 1.00 .30
❑ 215 James Tomlin RC .... 1.50 .45
❑ 216 Josh Labandeira RC ...... 1.50 .45
❑ 217 Ryan Meaux RC .... 1.50 .45
❑ 218 Don Sutton RC 4.00 1.20
❑ 219 Danny Gonzalez RC .... 1.00 .30
❑ 220 Javier Guzman RC .... 2.00 .60
❑ 221 Anthony Lerew RC .... 3.00 .90
❑ 222 Jon Connolly RC 4.00 1.20
❑ 223 Jesse English RC .... 1.50 .45
❑ 224 Hector Made RC .... 3.00 .90
❑ 225 Travis Hanson RC .... 1.50 .45
❑ 226 Jesse Floyd RC .... 1.50 .45
❑ 227 Nick Gorneault RC .... 2.00 .60
❑ 228 Craig Ansman RC .... 1.50 .45
❑ 229 Paul McAnulty RC .... 3.00 .90
❑ 230 Carl Loadenthal RC .... 2.00 .60
❑ 231 Dave Crouthers RC .... 1.00 .30
❑ 232 Harvey Garcia RC .... 1.00 .30
❑ 233 Casey Kopitzke RC .... 1.00 .30
❑ 234 Ricky Nolasco RC .... 1.50 .45
❑ 235 Miguel Perez RC .... 1.50 .45
❑ 236 Ryan Mulhern RC .... 1.00 .30
❑ 237 Chris Aguila RC .... 1.50 .45
❑ 238 Brooks Conrad RC .... 2.00 .60
❑ 239 Damaso Espino RC .... 1.00 .30
❑ 240 Jereme Milons RC .... 1.50 .45
❑ 241 Luke Hughes RC .... 1.00 .30
❑ 242 Kory Casto RC .... 1.50 .45
❑ 243 Jose Valdez RC .... 1.50 .45
❑ 244 J.T. Stotts RC .... 1.00 .30
❑ 245 Lee Gwaltney RC .... 1.00 .30
❑ 246 Yoann Torrealba RC ...... 1.00 .30
❑ 247 Omar Falcon RC .... 1.50 .45
❑ 248 Jon Coutlangus RC .... 1.00 .30
❑ 249 George Sherrill RC .... 1.50 .45
❑ 250 John Santor RC .... 1.00 .30
❑ 251 Tony Richie RC .... 1.50 .45
❑ 252 Kevin Richardson RC .... 1.00 .30
❑ 253 Tim Bittner RC .... 1.50 .45
❑ 254 Chris Saenz RC .... 1.00 .30
❑ 255 Jose Capellan RC 6.00 1.80
❑ 256 Donald Levinski RC .... 1.00 .30
❑ 257 Jerome Gamble RC .... 1.00 .30
❑ 258 Jeff Keppinger RC .... 3.00 .90
❑ 259 Jason Szuminski RC ...... 1.00 .30
❑ 260 Akinori Otsuka RC .... 1.50 .45
❑ 261 Ryan Budde RC .... 1.50 .45
❑ 262 Marland Williams RC .... 2.00 .60
❑ 263 Jeff Allison RC .... 2.00 .60
❑ 264 Hector Gimenez RC .... 1.00 .30
❑ 265 Tim Frend RC .... 1.50 .45
❑ 266 Tom Farmer RC .... 1.00 .30
❑ 267 Shawn Hill RC .... 1.50 .45
❑ 268 Mike Huggins RC .... 1.50 .45
❑ 269 Scott Proctor RC .... 2.00 .60
❑ 270 Jorge Mejia RC .... 1.50 .45
❑ 271 Terry Jones RC .... 2.00 .60
❑ 272 Zach Duke RC 6.00 1.80
❑ 273 Jesse Crain RC .... 3.00 .90
❑ 274 Luke Anderson RC .... 1.00 .30
❑ 275 Hunter Brown RC .... 1.00 .30
❑ 276 Matt Lemanczyk RC .... 1.50 .45
❑ 277 Fernando Cortez RC ...... 1.00 .30
❑ 278 Vince Perkins RC .... 2.00 .60
❑ 279 Tommy Murphy RC .... 1.50 .45
❑ 280 Mike Gosling RC .... 1.00 .30
❑ 281 Paul Bacot RC .... 2.00 .60
❑ 282 Matt Capps RC .... 1.50 .45
❑ 283 Juan Gutierrez RC .... 1.50 .45
❑ 284 Teodoro Encarnacion RC 2.00 .60
❑ 285 Chad Bentz RC .... 1.50 .45
❑ 286 Kazuo Matsui RC 5.00 1.50
❑ 287 Ryan Hankins RC .... 1.00 .30
❑ 288 Leo Nunez RC .... 1.50 .45
❑ 289 Dave Wallace RC .... 1.50 .45
❑ 290 Rob Tejeda RC .... 1.00 .30
❑ 291 Paul Maholm RC .... 3.00 .90
❑ 292 Casey Daigle RC .... 1.50 .45
❑ 293 Tydus Meadows RC ...... 1.00 .30
❑ 294 Khalid Ballouli RC .... 1.00 .30
❑ 295 Benji DeQuin RC .... 1.00 .30
❑ 296 Tyler Davidson RC .... 2.00 .60
❑ 297 Brant Colamarino RC .... 3.00 .90
❑ 298 Marcus McBeth RC .... 1.00 .30
❑ 299 Brad Eldred RC 5.00 1.50
❑ 300 David Pauley RC .... 1.00 .30
❑ 301 Yadier Molina RC 4.00 1.20
❑ 302 Chris Shelton RC .... 3.00 .90
❑ 303 Nyjer Morgan RC .... 1.00 .30
❑ 304 Jon DeVries RC .... 1.50 .45
❑ 305 Sheldon Fulse RC .... 1.00 .30
❑ 306 Vito Chiaravalloti RC ...... 3.00 .90
❑ 307 Warner Madrigal RC ...... 3.00 .90
❑ 308 Reid Gorecki RC .... 1.50 .45
❑ 309 Sung Jung RC .... 1.00 .30
❑ 310 Pete Shier RC .... 1.00 .30
❑ 311 Michael Mooney RC ...... 1.50 .45
❑ 312 Kenny Perez RC .... 1.50 .45
❑ 313 Michael Mallory RC ...... 1.50 .45
❑ 314 Ben Himes RC .... 1.00 .30
❑ 315 Ivan Ochoa RC .... 1.50 .45
❑ 316 Donald Kelly RC .... 1.50 .45
❑ 317 Tom Mastny RC .... 1.50 .45
❑ 318 Kevin Davidson RC .... 1.00 .30
❑ 319 Brian Pilkington RC ...... 1.50 .45
❑ 320 Alex Romero RC .... 1.50 .45
❑ 321 Chad Chop RC .... 1.50 .45
❑ 322 Kody Kirkland RC .... 3.00 .90
❑ 323 Casey Myers RC .... 1.00 .30
❑ 324 Mike Rouse RC .... 1.50 .45
❑ 325 Sergio Silva RC .... 1.00 .30
❑ 326 J.J. Furmaniak RC .... 3.00 .90
❑ 327 Brad Vericker RC .... 1.50 .45
❑ 328 Blake Hawksworth RC .... 2.00 .60
❑ 329 Brock Jacobsen RC .... 1.00 .30
❑ 330 Alec Zumwalt RC .... 1.00 .30
❑ 331 Wardell Starling AU RC 15.00 4.50
❑ 332 Estee Harris AU RC 15.00 4.50
❑ 333 Kyle Sleeth AU RC 25.00 7.50
❑ 334 Dioner Navarro AU RC 25.00 7.50
❑ 335 Logan Kensing AU RC.. 15.00 4.50
❑ 336 Travis Blackley AU RC.. 20.00 6.00
❑ 337 Lincoln Holdzkom AU RC 15.00 4.50
❑ 338 Jason Hirsh AU RC 15.00 4.50
❑ 339 Juan Cedeno AU RC 15.00 4.50
❑ 340 Matt Creighton AU RC.. 15.00 4.50
❑ 341 Tim Stauffer AU RC 20.00 6.00
❑ 342 Shingo Takatsu AU RC 25.00 7.50
❑ 343 Lastings Milledge AU RC 40.00 12.00
❑ 344 Dustin Nippert AU RC .. 15.00 4.50
❑ 345 Felix Hernandez AU RC 50.00 15.00
❑ 346 Joaquin Arias AU RC.... 15.00 4.50
❑ 347 Kevin Kouzmanoff AU RC 20.00 6.00
❑ 348 B.Brownlie AU RC EXCH 20.00 6.00
❑ 349 David Aardsma AU RC 15.00 4.50
❑ 350 Jon Knott AU RC 15.00 4.50

2004 Bowman Chrome Draft

	Nm-Mt	Ex-Mt
COMP.SET w/o SP's (165)	100.00	30.00
COMMON CARD (1-165)	.40	.12
COMMON RC	1.00	.30
COMMON RC YR	.40	.12

1-165 TWO PER BOWMAN DRAFT PACK
166-175 ODDS 1:60 BOWMAN DRAFT HOBBY
166-175 ODDS 1:60 BOWMAN DRAFT RETAIL
166-175 STATED PRINT RUN 1695 SETS
166-175 ARE NOT SERIAL-NUMBERED
166-175 PRINT RUN PROVIDED BY TOPPS
PLATES 1-165 ODDS 1:559 HOBBY
PLATES 166-175 ODDS 1:18,354 HOBBY
PLATES PRINT RUN 1 SERIAL #'d SET
BLACK-CYAN-MAGENTA-YELLOW EXIST
NO PLATES PRICING DUE TO SCARCITY

❑ 1 Lyle Overbay .... .60 .18
❑ 2 David Newhan .... .40 .12
❑ 3 J.R. House .... .40 .12
❑ 4 Chad Tracy .... .40 .12
❑ 5 Humberto Quintero .... .40 .12
❑ 6 Dave Bush .... .40 .12
❑ 7 Scott Hairston .... .40 .12
❑ 8 Mike Wood .... .40 .12
❑ 9 Alexis Rios .... .60 .18
❑ 10 Sean Burnett .... .40 .12
❑ 11 Wilson Valdez .... .40 .12
❑ 12 Lew Ford .... .60 .18
❑ 13 Freddy Thon RC .... 1.00 .30
❑ 14 Zack Greinke .... .60 .18
❑ 15 Bucky Jacobsen .... 1.00 .30
❑ 16 Kevin Youkilis .... .60 .18
❑ 17 Grady Sizemore .... .60 .18
❑ 18 Denny Bautista .... .40 .12
❑ 19 David DeJesus .... .40 .12
❑ 20 Casey Kotchman .... 1.50 .45
❑ 21 David Kelton .... .40 .12
❑ 22 Charles Thomas RC .... 1.50 .45
❑ 23 Kazuhito Tadano RC .... 1.50 .45
❑ 24 Justin Leone RC .... 1.50 .45
❑ 25 Eduardo Villacis RC .... 1.00 .30
❑ 26 Brian Dallimore RC .... 1.00 .30
❑ 27 Nick Green .... .40 .12
❑ 28 Sam McConnell RC .... 1.00 .30
❑ 29 Brad Halsey RC .... 1.50 .45
❑ 30 Roman Colon RC .... 1.00 .30
❑ 31 Josh Fields RC 5.00 1.50
❑ 32 Cody Bunkelman RC .... 1.50 .45
❑ 33 Jay Rainville RC .... 3.00 .90
❑ 34 Richie Robnett RC .... 3.00 .90
❑ 35 Jon Poterson RC .... 3.00 .90
❑ 36 Huston Street RC .... 3.00 .90
❑ 37 Erick San Pedro RC .... 1.00 .30
❑ 38 Cory Dunlap RC 4.00 1.20
❑ 39 Kurt Suzuki RC 4.00 1.20
❑ 40 Anthony Swarzak RC .... 1.50 .45
❑ 41 Ian Desmond RC .... 1.50 .45
❑ 42 Chris Covington RC .... 1.50 .45
❑ 43 Christian Garcia RC .... 2.50 .75
❑ 44 Gaby Hernandez RC .... 2.50 .75
❑ 45 Steven Register RC .... 1.50 .45

Card	Nm-Mt	Ex-Mt
❑ 46 Eduardo Morlan RC	1.50	.45
❑ 47 Collin Balester RC	1.50	.45
❑ 48 Nathan Phillips RC	1.50	.45
❑ 49 Dan Schwartzbauer RC	1.50	.45
❑ 50 Rafael Gonzalez RC	1.50	.45
❑ 51 K.C. Herren RC	2.50	.75
❑ 52 William Susdorf RC	1.00	.30
❑ 53 Rob Johnson RC	1.00	.30
❑ 54 Louis Marson RC	2.50	.75
❑ 55 Joe Koshansky RC	1.00	.30
❑ 56 Jamar Walton RC	5.00	1.50
❑ 57 Mark Lowe RC	1.00	.30
❑ 58 Matt Macri RC	2.50	.75
❑ 59 Donny Lucy RC	1.00	.30
❑ 60 Mike Ferris RC	1.50	.45
❑ 61 Mike Nickeas RC	1.50	.45
❑ 62 Eric Hurley RC	2.50	.75
❑ 63 Scott Elbert RC	3.00	.90
❑ 64 Blake DeWitt RC	6.00	1.80
❑ 65 Danny Putnam RC	2.50	.75
❑ 66 J.P. Howell RC	2.50	.75
❑ 67 John Wiggins RC	1.00	.30
❑ 68 Justin Orenduff RC	2.50	.75
❑ 69 Ray Liotta RC	1.50	.45
❑ 70 Billy Buckner RC	1.50	.45
❑ 71 Eric Campbell RC	4.00	1.20
❑ 72 Olin Wick RC	1.00	.30
❑ 73 Sean Gamble RC	1.50	.45
❑ 74 Seth Smith RC	4.00	1.20
❑ 75 Wade Davis RC	1.50	.45
❑ 76 Joe Jacobitz RC	1.00	.30
❑ 77 J.A. Happ RC	2.50	.75
❑ 78 Eric Ridener RC	1.00	.30
❑ 79 Matt Tuiasosopo RC	10.00	3.00
❑ 80 Brad Bergesen RC	1.50	.45
❑ 81 Javy Guerra RC	1.50	.45
❑ 82 Buck Shaw RC	2.50	.75
❑ 83 Paul Janish RC	1.50	.45
❑ 84 Sean Kazmar RC	1.50	.45
❑ 85 Josh Johnson RC	1.50	.45
❑ 86 Angel Salome RC	1.50	.45
❑ 87 Jordan Parraz RC	1.50	.45
❑ 88 Kelvin Vazquez RC	1.00	.30
❑ 89 Grant Hansen RC	1.00	.30
❑ 90 Matt Fox RC	2.50	.75
❑ 91 Trevor Plouffe RC	4.00	1.20
❑ 92 Wes Whisler RC	1.50	.45
❑ 93 Curtis Thigpen RC	2.50	.75
❑ 94 Donnie Smith RC	1.00	.30
❑ 95 Luis Rivera RC	1.50	.45
❑ 96 Jesse Hoover RC	1.50	.45
❑ 97 Jason Vargas RC	2.50	.75
❑ 98 Clary Carlsen RC	1.00	.30
❑ 99 Mark Robinson RC	1.00	.30
❑ 100 J.C. Holt RC	2.50	.75
❑ 101 Chad Blackwell RC	1.50	.45
❑ 102 Daryl Jones RC	2.50	.75
❑ 103 Jonathan Tierce RC	1.00	.30
❑ 104 Patrick Bryant RC	1.00	.30
❑ 105 Eddie Prasch RC	1.50	.45
❑ 106 Mitch Einertson RC	8.00	2.40
❑ 107 Kyle Waldrop RC	3.00	.90
❑ 108 Jeff Marquez RC	2.50	.75
❑ 109 Zach Jackson RC	1.50	.45
❑ 110 Josh Wahpepah RC	1.00	.30
❑ 111 Adam Lind RC	2.50	.75
❑ 112 Kyle Bloom RC	1.50	.45
❑ 113 Ben Harrison RC	1.50	.45
❑ 114 Taylor Tankersley RC	3.00	.90
❑ 115 Steven Jackson RC	1.00	.30
❑ 116 David Purcey RC	2.50	.75
❑ 117 Jacob McGee RC	1.50	.45
❑ 118 Lucas Harrell RC	1.00	.30
❑ 119 Brandon Allen RC	2.50	.75
❑ 120 Van Pope RC	1.50	.45
❑ 121 Jeff Francis	.60	.18
❑ 122 Joe Blanton	1.00	.30
❑ 123 Wil Ledezma	.40	.12
❑ 124 Bryan Bullington	.60	.18
❑ 125 Jairo Garcia	.60	.18
❑ 126 Matt Cain	.60	.18
❑ 127 Arnie Munoz	.40	.12
❑ 128 Clint Everts	.40	.12
❑ 129 Jesus Cota	.40	.12
❑ 130 Gavin Floyd	.60	.18
❑ 131 Edwin Encarnacion	.40	.12
❑ 132 Koyie Hill	.40	.12
❑ 133 Ruben Gotay	.40	.12
❑ 134 Jeff Mathis	.40	.12
❑ 135 Andy Marte	.60	.18
❑ 136 Dallas McPherson	1.00	.30
❑ 137 Justin Morneau	1.00	.30
❑ 138 Rickie Weeks	.60	.18
❑ 139 Joel Guzman	1.00	.30
❑ 140 Shin Soo Choo	.40	.12
❑ 141 Yusmeiro Petit RC	6.00	1.80
❑ 142 Jorge Cortes RC	1.00	.30
❑ 143 Val Majewski	.40	.12
❑ 144 Felix Pie	.60	.18
❑ 145 Aaron Hill	.40	.12
❑ 146 Jose Capellan	1.50	.45
❑ 147 Dioner Navarro	1.00	.30
❑ 148 Fausto Carmona	1.00	.30
❑ 149 Robinzon Diaz RC	1.00	.30
❑ 150 Felix Hernandez	4.00	1.20
❑ 151 Andres Blanco RC	1.00	.30
❑ 152 Jason Kubel	.60	.18
❑ 153 Willy Taveras RC	1.50	.45
❑ 154 Merkin Valdez	1.00	.30
❑ 155 Robinson Cano	.60	.18
❑ 156 Bill Murphy	.40	.12
❑ 157 Chris Burke	.40	.12
❑ 158 Kyle Sleeth	1.00	.30
❑ 159 B.J. Upton	1.00	.30
❑ 160 Tim Stauffer	1.00	.30
❑ 161 David Wright	1.50	.45
❑ 162 Conor Jackson	2.50	.75
❑ 163 Brad Thompson RC	1.50	.45
❑ 164 Delmon Young	1.00	.30
❑ 165 Jeremy Reed	.60	.18
❑ 166 Matt Bush AU RC	40.00	12.00
❑ 167 Mark Rogers AU RC	30.00	9.00
❑ 168 Thomas Diamond AU RC	25.00	7.50
❑ 169 Greg Golson AU RC	25.00	7.50
❑ 170 Homer Bailey AU RC	30.00	9.00
❑ 171 Chris Lambert AU RC	20.00	6.00
❑ 172 Neil Walker AU RC	20.00	6.00
❑ 173 Bill Bray AU RC	15.00	4.50
❑ 174 Phillip Hughes AU RC	20.00	6.00
❑ 175 Gio Gonzalez AU RC	20.00	6.00

2001 Bowman Heritage

	Nm-Mt	Ex-Mt
COMPLETE SET (440)	250.00	75.00
COMP.SET w/o SP's (330)	50.00	15.00
COMMON CARD (1-330)	.40	.12
COMMON RC (1-330)	.50	.15
COMMON (331-440)	2.00	.60

Card	Nm-Mt	Ex-Mt
❑ 1 Chipper Jones	1.00	.30
❑ 2 Pete Harnisch	.40	.12
❑ 3 Brian Giles	.75	.23
❑ 4 J.T. Snow	.75	.23
❑ 5 Bartolo Colon	.75	.23
❑ 6 Jorge Posada	.60	.18
❑ 7 Shawn Green	.75	.23
❑ 8 Derek Jeter	2.50	.75
❑ 9 Benito Santiago	.75	.23
❑ 10 Ramon Hernandez	.40	.12
❑ 11 Bernie Williams	.60	.18
❑ 12 Greg Maddux	1.50	.45
❑ 13 Barry Bonds	2.50	.75
❑ 14 Roger Clemens	2.00	.60
❑ 15 Miguel Tejada	.75	.23
❑ 16 Pedro Feliz	.40	.12
❑ 17 Jim Edmonds	.75	.23
❑ 18 Tom Glavine	.60	.18
❑ 19 David Justice	.75	.23
❑ 20 Rich Aurilia	.40	.12
❑ 21 Jason Giambi	.75	.23
❑ 22 Orlando Hernandez	.40	.12
❑ 23 Shawn Estes	.40	.12
❑ 24 Nelson Figueroa	.40	.12
❑ 25 Terrence Long	.40	.12
❑ 26 Mike Mussina	.60	.18
❑ 27 Eric Davis	.75	.23
❑ 28 Jimmy Rollins	.75	.23
❑ 29 Andy Pettitte	.60	.18
❑ 30 Shawon Dunston	.40	.12
❑ 31 Tim Hudson	.75	.23
❑ 32 Jeff Kent	.75	.23
❑ 33 Scott Brosius	.75	.23
❑ 34 Livan Hernandez	.40	.12
❑ 35 Alfonso Soriano	.60	.18
❑ 36 Mark McGwire	2.50	.75
❑ 37 Russ Ortiz	.75	.23
❑ 38 Fernando Vina	.40	.12
❑ 39 Ken Griffey Jr.	1.50	.45
❑ 40 Edgar Renteria	.75	.23
❑ 41 Kevin Brown	.75	.23
❑ 42 Robb Nen	.75	.23
❑ 43 Paul LoDuca	.75	.23
❑ 44 Bobby Abreu	.75	.23
❑ 45 Adam Dunn	.60	.18
❑ 46 Osvaldo Fernandez	.40	.12
❑ 47 Marvin Benard	.40	.12
❑ 48 Mark Gardner	.40	.12
❑ 49 Alex Rodriguez	1.50	.45
❑ 50 Preston Wilson	.75	.23
❑ 51 Roberto Alomar	.60	.18
❑ 52 Ben Davis	.40	.12
❑ 53 Derek Bell	.40	.12
❑ 54 Ken Caminiti	.75	.23
❑ 55 Barry Zito	.60	.18
❑ 56 Scott Rolen	1.00	.30
❑ 57 Geoff Jenkins	.75	.23
❑ 58 Mike Cameron	.75	.23
❑ 59 Ben Grieve	.40	.12
❑ 60 Chuck Knoblauch	.75	.23
❑ 61 Matt Lawton	.40	.12
❑ 62 Chan Ho Park	.75	.23
❑ 63 Lance Berkman	.75	.23
❑ 64 Carlos Beltran	.60	.18
❑ 65 Dean Palmer	.75	.23
❑ 66 Alex Gonzalez	.40	.12
❑ 67 Larry Walker	.60	.18
❑ 68 Magglio Ordonez	.75	.23
❑ 69 Ellis Burks	.75	.23
❑ 70 Mark Mulder	.75	.23
❑ 71 Randy Johnson	1.00	.30
❑ 72 John Smoltz	.60	.18
❑ 73 Jerry Hairston Jr.	.40	.12
❑ 74 Pedro Martinez	1.00	.30
❑ 75 Fred McGriff	.60	.18
❑ 76 Sean Casey	.75	.23
❑ 77 C.C. Sabathia	.75	.23
❑ 78 Todd Helton	.60	.18
❑ 79 Brad Penny	.40	.12
❑ 80 Mike Sweeney	.75	.23
❑ 81 Billy Wagner	.75	.23
❑ 82 Mark Buehrle	.75	.23
❑ 83 Cristian Guzman	.40	.12
❑ 84 Jose Vidro	.40	.12
❑ 85 Pat Burrell	.75	.23
❑ 86 Jermaine Dye	.75	.23
❑ 87 Brandon Inge	.40	.12
❑ 88 David Wells	.75	.23
❑ 89 Mike Piazza	1.50	.45
❑ 90 Jose Cabrera	.40	.12
❑ 91 Cliff Floyd	.75	.23
❑ 92 Matt Morris	.75	.23
❑ 93 Raul Mondesi	.75	.23
❑ 94 Joe Kennedy RC	.75	.23
❑ 95 Jack Wilson RC	2.00	.60
❑ 96 Andruw Jones	.75	.23
❑ 97 Mariano Rivera	.60	.18
❑ 98 Mike Hampton	.75	.23
❑ 99 Roger Cedeno	.40	.12
❑ 100 Jose Cruz	.40	.12

❑ 101	Mike Lowell	.75	.23
❑ 102	Pedro Astacio	.40	.12
❑ 103	Joe Mays	.40	.12
❑ 104	John Franco	.75	.23
❑ 105	Tim Redding	.40	.12
❑ 106	Sandy Alomar Jr.	.40	.12
❑ 107	Bret Boone	.75	.23
❑ 108	Josh Towers RC	.50	.15
❑ 109	Matt Stairs	.40	.12
❑ 110	Chris Truby	.40	.12
❑ 111	Jeff Suppan	.40	.12
❑ 112	J.C. Romero	.40	.12
❑ 113	Felipe Lopez	.40	.12
❑ 114	Ben Sheets	.60	.18
❑ 115	Frank Thomas	1.00	.30
❑ 116	A.J. Burnett	.40	.12
❑ 117	Tony Clark	.40	.12
❑ 118	Mac Suzuki	.40	.12
❑ 119	Brad Radke	.75	.23
❑ 120	Jeff Shaw	.40	.12
❑ 121	Nick Neugebauer	.40	.12
❑ 122	Kenny Lofton	.75	.23
❑ 123	Jacque Jones	.75	.23
❑ 124	Brent Mayne	.40	.12
❑ 125	Carlos Hernandez	.40	.12
❑ 126	Shane Spencer	.40	.12
❑ 127	John Lackey	.40	.12
❑ 128	Sterling Hitchcock	.40	.12
❑ 129	Darren Dreifort	.40	.12
❑ 130	Rusty Greer	.75	.23
❑ 131	Michael Cuddyer	.40	.12
❑ 132	Tyler Houston	.40	.12
❑ 133	Chin-Feng Chen	.75	.23
❑ 134	Ken Harvey	.40	.12
❑ 135	Marquis Grissom	.75	.23
❑ 136	Russell Branyan	.40	.12
❑ 137	Eric Karros	.75	.23
❑ 138	Josh Beckett	.75	.23
❑ 139	Todd Zeile	.75	.23
❑ 140	Corey Koskie	.75	.23
❑ 141	Steve Sparks	.40	.12
❑ 142	Bobby Seay	.40	.12
❑ 143	Tim Raines Jr.	.40	.12
❑ 144	Julio Zuleta	.40	.12
❑ 145	Jose Lima	.40	.12
❑ 146	Dante Bichette	.75	.23
❑ 147	Randy Keisler	.40	.12
❑ 148	Brent Butler	.40	.12
❑ 149	Antonio Alfonseca	.40	.12
❑ 150	Bryan Rekar	.40	.12
❑ 151	Jeffrey Hammonds	.40	.12
❑ 152	Larry Bigbie	.40	.12
❑ 153	Blake Stein	.40	.12
❑ 154	Robin Ventura	.75	.23
❑ 155	Rondell White	.75	.23
❑ 156	Juan Silvestre	.40	.12
❑ 157	Marcus Thames	.40	.12
❑ 158	Sidney Ponson	.40	.12
❑ 159	Juan A. Pena RC	.50	.15
❑ 160	C.J. Nitkowski	.40	.12
❑ 161	Adam Everett	.40	.12
❑ 162	Eric Munson	.40	.12
❑ 163	Jason Isringhausen	.75	.23
❑ 164	Brad Fullmer	.40	.12
❑ 165	Miguel Olivo	.40	.12
❑ 166	Fernando Tatis	.40	.12
❑ 167	Freddy Garcia	.75	.23
❑ 168	Tom Goodwin	.40	.12
❑ 169	Armando Benitez	.75	.23
❑ 170	Paul Konerko	.75	.23
❑ 171	Jeff Cirillo	.40	.12
❑ 172	Shane Reynolds	.40	.12
❑ 173	Kevin Tapani	.40	.12
❑ 174	Joe Crede	.40	.12
❑ 175	Omar Infante RC	2.00	.60
❑ 176	Jake Peavy RC	3.00	.90
❑ 177	Corey Patterson	.75	.23
❑ 178	Mike Penney RC	.50	.15
❑ 179	Jeromy Burnitz	.75	.23
❑ 180	David Segui	.40	.12
❑ 181	Marcus Giles	.75	.23
❑ 182	Paul O'Neill	.60	.18
❑ 183	John Olerud	.75	.23
❑ 184	Andy Benes	.40	.12
❑ 185	Brad Cresse	.40	.12
❑ 186	Ricky Ledee	.40	.12
❑ 187	Allen Levrault UER Last name misspelled Leverault	.40	.12
❑ 188	Royce Clayton	.40	.12
❑ 189	Kelly Johnson RC	.50	.15
❑ 190	Quilvio Veras	.40	.12
❑ 191	Mike Williams	.40	.12
❑ 192	Jason Lane RC	.50	.15
❑ 193	Rick Helling	.40	.12
❑ 194	Tim Wakefield	.75	.23
❑ 195	James Baldwin	.40	.12
❑ 196	Cody Ransom RC	.50	.15
❑ 197	Bobby Kielty	.40	.12
❑ 198	Bobby Jones	.40	.12
❑ 199	Steve Cox	.40	.12
❑ 200	Jamal Strong RC	.50	.15
❑ 201	Steve Lomasney	.40	.12
❑ 202	Brian Cardwell RC	.50	.15
❑ 203	Mike Matheny	.75	.23
❑ 204	Jeff Randazzo RC	.50	.15
❑ 205	Aubrey Huff	.75	.23
❑ 206	Chuck Finley	.75	.23
❑ 207	Denny Bautista RC	1.25	.35
❑ 208	Terry Mulholland	.40	.12
❑ 209	Rey Ordonez	.40	.12
❑ 210	Keith Surkont RC	.50	.15
❑ 211	Orlando Cabrera	.75	.23
❑ 212	Juan Encarnacion	.40	.12
❑ 213	Dustin Hermanson	.40	.12
❑ 214	Luis Rivas	.40	.12
❑ 215	Mark Quinn	.40	.12
❑ 216	Randy Velarde	.40	.12
❑ 217	Billy Koch	.40	.12
❑ 218	Ryan Rupe	.40	.12
❑ 219	Keith Ginter	.40	.12
❑ 220	Woody Williams	.40	.12
❑ 221	Ryan Franklin	.40	.12
❑ 222	Aaron Myette	.40	.12
❑ 223	Joe Borchard RC	1.25	.35
❑ 224	Nate Cornejo	.40	.12
❑ 225	Julian Tavarez	.40	.12
❑ 226	Kevin Millwood	.75	.23
❑ 227	Travis Hafner RC	2.50	.75
❑ 228	Charles Nagy	.40	.12
❑ 229	Mike Lieberthal	.75	.23
❑ 230	Jeff Nelson	.40	.12
❑ 231	Ryan Dempster	.40	.12
❑ 232	Andres Galarraga	.75	.23
❑ 233	Chad Durbin	.40	.12
❑ 234	Timo Perez	.40	.12
❑ 235	Troy O'Leary	.40	.12
❑ 236	Kevin Young	.40	.12
❑ 237	Gabe Kapler	.40	.12
❑ 238	Juan Cruz RC	.50	.15
❑ 239	Masato Yoshii	.40	.12
❑ 240	Aramis Ramirez	.75	.23
❑ 241	Matt Cooper RC	.50	.15
❑ 242	Randy Flores RC	.50	.15
❑ 243	Rafael Furcal	.75	.23
❑ 244	David Eckstein	.40	.12
❑ 245	Matt Clement	.40	.12
❑ 246	Craig Biggio	.60	.18
❑ 247	Rick Reed	.40	.12
❑ 248	Jose Macias	.40	.12
❑ 249	Alex Escobar	.40	.12
❑ 250	Roberto Hernandez	.40	.12
❑ 251	Andy Ashby	.40	.12
❑ 252	Tony Armas Jr.	.40	.12
❑ 253	Jamie Moyer	.75	.23
❑ 254	Jason Tyner	.40	.12
❑ 255	Charles Kegley RC	.50	.15
❑ 256	Jeff Conine	.75	.23
❑ 257	Francisco Cordova	.40	.12
❑ 258	Ted Lilly	.40	.12
❑ 259	Joe Randa	.40	.12
❑ 260	Jeff D'Amico	.40	.12
❑ 261	Albie Lopez	.40	.12
❑ 262	Kevin Appier	.75	.23
❑ 263	Richard Hidalgo	.40	.12
❑ 264	Omar Daal	.40	.12
❑ 265	Ricky Gutierrez	.40	.12
❑ 266	John Rocker	.40	.12
❑ 267	Ray Lankford	.40	.12
❑ 268	Beau Hale RC	.50	.15
❑ 269	Tony Blanco RC	1.25	.35
❑ 270	Derrek Lee UER First name misspelled Derrick	.75	.23
❑ 271	Jamey Wright	.40	.12
❑ 272	Alex Gordon	.40	.12
❑ 273	Jeff Weaver	.40	.12
❑ 274	Jaret Wright	.40	.12
❑ 275	Jose Hernandez	.40	.12
❑ 276	Bruce Chen	.40	.12
❑ 277	Todd Hollandsworth	.40	.12
❑ 278	Wade Miller	.40	.12
❑ 279	Luke Prokopec	.40	.12
❑ 280	Rafael Soriano RC	.75	.23
❑ 281	Damion Easley	.40	.12
❑ 282	Darren Oliver	.40	.12
❑ 283	B. Duckworth RC	.50	.15
❑ 284	Aaron Herr	.40	.12
❑ 285	Ray Durham	.75	.23
❑ 286	Wilmy Caceras RC	.50	.15
❑ 287	Ugueth Urbina	.40	.12
❑ 288	Scott Seabol	.40	.12
❑ 289	Lance Niekro RC	.50	.15
❑ 290	Trot Nixon	.75	.23
❑ 291	Adam Kennedy	.40	.12
❑ 292	Brian Schmitt RC	.50	.15
❑ 293	Grant Roberts	.40	.12
❑ 294	Benny Agbayani	.40	.12
❑ 295	Travis Lee	.40	.12
❑ 296	Erick Almonte RC	.50	.15
❑ 297	Jim Thome	1.00	.30
❑ 298	Eric Young	.40	.12
❑ 299	Dan Denham RC	.50	.15
❑ 300	Boof Bonser RC	.50	.15
❑ 301	Denny Neagle	.40	.12
❑ 302	Kenny Rogers	.75	.23
❑ 303	J.D. Closser	.40	.12
❑ 304	Chase Utley RC	5.00	1.50
❑ 305	Rey Sanchez	.40	.12
❑ 306	Sean McGowan	.40	.12
❑ 307	Justin Pope RC	.50	.15
❑ 308	Torii Hunter	.75	.23
❑ 309	B.J. Surhoff	.75	.23
❑ 310	Aaron Heilman RC	.50	.15
❑ 311	Gabe Gross RC	.75	.23
❑ 312	Lee Stevens	.40	.12
❑ 313	Todd Hundley	.40	.12
❑ 314	Macay McBride RC	.50	.15
❑ 315	Edgar Martinez	.60	.18
❑ 316	Omar Vizquel	.60	.18
❑ 317	Reggie Sanders	.40	.12
❑ 318	John-Ford Griffin RC	.50	.15
❑ 319	Tim Salmon UER Photo is Troy Glaus	.75	.23
❑ 320	Pokey Reese	.40	.12
❑ 321	Jay Payton	.40	.12
❑ 322	Doug Glanville	.40	.12
❑ 323	Greg Vaughn	.40	.12
❑ 324	Ruben Sierra	.40	.12
❑ 325	Kip Wells	.40	.12
❑ 326	Carl Everett	.75	.23
❑ 327	Garret Anderson	.75	.23
❑ 328	Jay Bell	.75	.23
❑ 329	Barry Larkin	.60	.18
❑ 330	Jeff Mathis RC	2.50	.75
❑ 331	Adrian Gonzalez SP	2.00	.60
❑ 332	Juan Rivera SP	2.00	.60
❑ 333	Tony Alvarez SP	2.00	.60
❑ 334	Xavier Nady SP	2.00	.60
❑ 335	Josh Hamilton SP	2.00	.60
❑ 336	Will Smith SP RC	2.00	.60
❑ 337	Israel Alcantara SP	2.00	.60
❑ 338	Chris George SP	2.00	.60
❑ 339	Sean Burroughs SP	2.00	.60
❑ 340	Jack Cust SP	2.00	.60
❑ 341	Henry Mateo SP RC	2.00	.60
❑ 342	Carlos Pena SP	2.00	.60
❑ 343	J.R. House SP	2.00	.60
❑ 344	Carlos Silva SP	2.00	.60
❑ 345	Mike Rivera SP RC	2.00	.60
❑ 346	Adam Johnson SP	2.00	.60
❑ 347	Scott Heard SP	2.00	.60
❑ 348	Alex Cintron SP	2.00	.60
❑ 349	Miguel Cabrera SP	8.00	2.40
❑ 350	Nick Johnson SP	2.00	.60
❑ 351	Albert Pujols SP RC	50.00	15.00
❑ 352	Ichiro Suzuki SP RC	40.00	12.00
❑ 353	Carlos Delgado SP	2.00	.60
❑ 354	Troy Glaus SP	2.00	.60
❑ 355	Sammy Sosa SP	5.00	1.50

No.	Player	Nm-Mt	Ex-Mt
❑ 356	Ivan Rodriguez SP	3.00	.90
❑ 357	Vladimir Guerrero SP	3.00	.90
❑ 358	Manny Ramirez SP	3.00	.90
❑ 359	Luis Gonzalez SP	2.00	.60
❑ 360	Roy Oswalt SP	3.00	.90
❑ 361	Moises Alou SP	2.00	.60
❑ 362	Juan Gonzalez SP	3.00	.90
❑ 363	Tony Gwynn SP	4.00	1.20
❑ 364	Hideo Nomo SP	3.00	.90
❑ 365	T. Shinjo SP RC	2.00	.60
❑ 366	Kazuhiro Sasaki SP	2.00	.60
❑ 367	Cal Ripken SP	10.00	3.00
❑ 368	Rafael Palmeiro SP	3.00	.90
❑ 369	J.D. Drew SP	2.00	.60
❑ 370	Doug Mientkiewicz SP	2.00	.60
❑ 371	Jeff Bagwell SP	3.00	.90
❑ 372	Darin Erstad SP	2.00	.60
❑ 373	Tom Gordon SP	2.00	.60
❑ 374	Ben Petrick SP	2.00	.60
❑ 375	Eric Milton SP	2.00	.60
❑ 376	N. Garciaparra SP	5.00	1.50
❑ 377	Julio Lugo SP	2.00	.60
❑ 378	Tino Martinez SP	3.00	.90
❑ 379	Javier Vazquez SP	2.00	.60
❑ 380	Jeremy Giambi SP	2.00	.60
❑ 381	Marty Cordova SP	2.00	.60
❑ 382	Adrian Beltre SP	3.00	.90
❑ 383	John Burkett SP	2.00	.60
❑ 384	Aaron Boone SP	2.00	.60
❑ 385	Eric Chavez SP	2.00	.60
❑ 386	Curt Schilling SP	2.00	.60
❑ 387	Cory Lidle UER First name misspelled Corey	2.00	.60
❑ 388	Jason Schmidt SP	2.00	.60
❑ 389	Johnny Damon SP	3.00	.90
❑ 390	Steve Finley SP	2.00	.60
❑ 391	Edgardo Alfonzo SP	2.00	.60
❑ 392	Jose Valentin SP	2.00	.60
❑ 393	Jose Canseco SP	3.00	.90
❑ 394	Ryan Klesko SP	2.00	.60
❑ 395	David Cone SP	2.00	.60
❑ 396	Jason Kendall UER Last name misspelled Kendell	2.00	.60
❑ 397	Placido Polanco SP	2.00	.60
❑ 398	Glendon Rusch SP	2.00	.60
❑ 399	Aaron Sele SP	2.00	.60
❑ 400	D'Angelo Jimenez SP	2.00	.60
❑ 401	Mark Grace SP	3.00	.90
❑ 402	Al Leiter SP	2.00	.60
❑ 403	Brian Jordan SP	2.00	.60
❑ 404	Phil Nevin SP	2.00	.60
❑ 405	Brent Abernathy SP	2.00	.60
❑ 406	Kerry Wood SP	3.00	.90
❑ 407	Alex Gonzalez SP	2.00	.60
❑ 408	Robert Fick SP	2.00	.60
❑ 409	Dmitri Young UER First name misspelled Dimitri	2.00	.60
❑ 410	Wes Helms SP	2.00	.60
❑ 411	Trevor Hoffman SP	2.00	.60
❑ 412	Rickey Henderson SP	3.00	.90
❑ 413	Bobby Higginson SP	2.00	.60
❑ 414	Gary Sheffield SP	2.00	.60
❑ 415	Darryl Kile SP	2.00	.60
❑ 416	Richie Sexson SP	2.00	.60
❑ 417	F. Menechino SP RC	2.00	.60
❑ 418	Javy Lopez SP	2.00	.60
❑ 419	Carlos Lee SP	2.00	.60
❑ 420	Jon Lieber SP	2.00	.60
❑ 421	Hank Blalock SP RC	15.00	4.50
❑ 422	Marlon Byrd SP RC	1.25	.35
❑ 423	Jason Kinchen SP RC	2.00	.60
❑ 424	M. Ensberg SP RC	2.00	.60
❑ 425	Greg Nash SP RC	2.00	.60
❑ 426	D. Tankersley SP RC	2.00	.60
❑ 427	Nate Murphy SP RC	2.00	.60
❑ 428	Chris Smith SP RC	2.00	.60
❑ 429	Jake Gautreau SP RC	2.00	.60
❑ 430	J. VanBenschoten SP RC	5.00	1.50
❑ 431	T.Thompson SP RC	2.00	.60
❑ 432	O.Hudson SP RC	2.00	.60
❑ 433	J.Williams SP RC	10.00	3.00
❑ 434	Kevin Reese SP RC	2.00	.60
❑ 435	Ed Rogers SP RC	2.00	.60
❑ 436	Ryan Jamison SP RC	2.00	.60
❑ 437	A. Pettyjohn SP RC	2.00	.60
❑ 438	Hee Seop Choi SP RC	2.00	.60
❑ 439	J. Morneau SP RC	15.00	4.50
❑ 440	Mitch Jones SP RC	2.00	.60

2002 Bowman Heritage

	Nm-Mt	Ex-Mt
COMP.SET w/o SP's (324)	50.00	15.00
COMMON CARD (1-439)	.40	.12
COMMON SP	2.00	.60

No.	Player	Nm-Mt	Ex-Mt
❑ 1	Brent Abernathy	.40	.12
❑ 2	Jermaine Dye	.40	.12
❑ 3	James Shanks RC	.40	.12
❑ 4	Chris Flinn RC	.40	.12
❑ 5	Mike Peeples SP RC	2.00	.60
❑ 6	Gary Sheffield	.40	.12
❑ 7	Livan Hernandez SP	2.00	.60
❑ 8	Jeff Austin RC	.40	.12
❑ 9	Jeremy Giambi	.40	.12
❑ 10	Adam Roller RC	.40	.12
❑ 11	Sandy Alomar Jr. SP	2.00	.60
❑ 12	Matt Williams SP	2.00	.60
❑ 13	Hee Seop Choi	.40	.12
❑ 14	Jose Offerman	.40	.12
❑ 15	Robin Ventura	.40	.12
❑ 16	Craig Biggio	.60	.18
❑ 17	David Wells	.40	.12
❑ 18	Rob Henkel RC	.40	.12
❑ 19	Edgar Martinez	.60	.18
❑ 20	Matt Morris SP	2.00	.60
❑ 21	Jose Valentin	.40	.12
❑ 22	Barry Bonds	2.50	.75
❑ 23	Justin Schuda RC	.40	.12
❑ 24	Josh Phelps	.40	.12
❑ 25	John Rodriguez RC	.40	.12
❑ 26	Angel Pagan RC	.40	.12
❑ 27	Aramis Ramirez	.40	.12
❑ 28	Jack Wilson	.40	.12
❑ 29	Roger Clemens	2.00	.60
❑ 30	Kazuhisa Ishii RC	1.25	.35
❑ 31	Carlos Beltran	.60	.18
❑ 32	Drew Henson SP	2.00	.60
❑ 33	Kevin Young SP	2.00	.60
❑ 34	Juan Cruz SP	2.00	.60
❑ 35	Curtis Legendre RC	.40	.12
❑ 36	Jose Morban RC	.40	.12
❑ 37	Ricardo Cordova SP RC	2.00	.60
❑ 38	Adam Everett	.40	.12
❑ 39	Mark Prior	2.00	.60
❑ 40	Jose Bautista RC	.50	.15
❑ 41	Travis Foley RC	.40	.12
❑ 42	Kerry Wood	1.00	.30
❑ 43	B.J. Surhoff	.40	.12
❑ 44	Moises Alou	.40	.12
❑ 45	Joey Hammond	.40	.12
❑ 46	Eric Bruntlett RC	.40	.12
❑ 47	Carlos Guillen	.40	.12
❑ 48	Joe Crede	.40	.12
❑ 49	Dan Phillips RC	.40	.12
❑ 50	Jason LaRue	.40	.12
❑ 51	Javy Lopez	.40	.12
❑ 52	Larry Bigbie SP	2.00	.60
❑ 53	Chris Baker RC	.40	.12
❑ 54	Marty Cordova	.40	.12
❑ 55	C.C. Sabathia	.40	.12
❑ 56	Mike Piazza	1.50	.45
❑ 57	Brian Giles	.40	.12
❑ 58	Mike Bordick SP	2.00	.60
❑ 59	Tyler Houston SP	2.00	.60
❑ 60	Gabe Kapler	.40	.12
❑ 61	Ben Broussard	.40	.12
❑ 62	Steve Finley SP	2.00	.60
❑ 63	Koyie Hill	.40	.12
❑ 64	Jeff D'Amico	.40	.12
❑ 65	Edwin Almonte RC	.40	.12
❑ 66	Pedro Martinez	1.00	.30
❑ 66B	Nomar Garciaparra 66	1.50	.45
❑ 67	Travis Fryman SP	2.00	.60
❑ 68	Brady Clark SP	2.00	.60
❑ 69	Reed Johnson SP RC	3.00	.90
❑ 70	Mark Grace SP	3.00	.90
❑ 71	Tony Batista SP	2.00	.60
❑ 72	Roy Oswalt	.40	.12
❑ 73	Pat Burrell SP	2.00	.60
❑ 74	Dennis Tankersley	.40	.12
❑ 75	Ramon Ortiz	.40	.12
❑ 76	Neal Frendling SP RC	2.00	.60
❑ 77	Omar Vizquel SP	3.00	.90
❑ 78	Hideo Nomo	1.00	.30
❑ 79	Orlando Hernandez SP	2.00	.60
❑ 80	Andy Pettitte	.60	.18
❑ 81	Cole Barthel RC	.40	.12
❑ 82	Bret Boone	.40	.12
❑ 83	Alfonso Soriano	.60	.18
❑ 84	Brandon Duckworth	.40	.12
❑ 85	Ben Grieve	.40	.12
❑ 86	Mike Rosamond SP RC	2.00	.60
❑ 87	Luke Prokopec	.40	.12
❑ 88	Chone Figgins RC	.75	.23
❑ 89	Rick Ankiel SP	2.00	.60
❑ 90	David Eckstein	.40	.12
❑ 91	Corey Koskie	.40	.12
❑ 92	David Justice	.40	.12
❑ 93	Jimmy Alvarez RC	.40	.12
❑ 94	Jason Schmidt	.40	.12
❑ 95	Reggie Sanders	.40	.12
❑ 96	Victor Alvarez RC	.40	.12
❑ 97	Brett Roneberg RC	.40	.12
❑ 98	D'Angelo Jimenez	.40	.12
❑ 99	Hank Blalock	1.00	.30
❑ 100	Juan Rivera	.40	.12
❑ 101	Mark Buehrle SP	2.00	.60
❑ 102	Juan Uribe	.40	.12
❑ 103	Royce Clayton SP	2.00	.60
❑ 104	Brett Kay RC	.40	.12
❑ 105	John Olerud	.40	.12
❑ 106	Richie Sexson	.40	.12
❑ 107	Chipper Jones	1.00	.30
❑ 108	Adam Dunn	.60	.18
❑ 109	Tim Salmon SP	3.00	.90
❑ 110	Eric Karros	.40	.12
❑ 111	Jose Vidro	.40	.12
❑ 112	Jerry Hairston Jr.	.40	.12
❑ 113	Anastacio Martinez RC	.40	.12
❑ 114	Robert Fick SP	2.00	.60
❑ 115	Randy Johnson	1.00	.30
❑ 116	Trot Nixon SP	2.00	.60
❑ 117	Nick Bierbrodt SP	2.00	.60
❑ 118	Jim Edmonds	.40	.12
❑ 119	Rafael Palmeiro	.60	.18
❑ 120	Jose Macias	.40	.12
❑ 121	Josh Beckett	.40	.12
❑ 122	Sean Douglass	.40	.12
❑ 123	Jeff Kent	.40	.12
❑ 124	Tim Redding	.40	.12
❑ 125	Xavier Nady	.40	.12
❑ 126	Carl Everett	.40	.12
❑ 127	Joe Randa	.40	.12
❑ 128	Luke Hudson SP	2.00	.60
❑ 129	Eric Miller RC	.40	.12
❑ 130	Melvin Mora	.40	.12
❑ 131	Adrian Gonzalez	.40	.12
❑ 132	Larry Walker SP	3.00	.90
❑ 133	Nic Jackson SP RC	2.00	.60
❑ 134	Mike Lowell SP	2.00	.60
❑ 135	Jim Thome	1.00	.30
❑ 136	Eric Milton	.40	.12
❑ 137	Rich Thompson SP RC	2.00	.60
❑ 138	Placido Polanco SP	2.00	.60
❑ 139	Juan Pierre	.40	.12
❑ 140	David Segui	.40	.12
❑ 141	Chuck Finley	.40	.12
❑ 142	Felipe Lopez	.40	.12
❑ 143	Toby Hall	.40	.12

❑ 144 Fred Bastardo RC .40 .12
❑ 145 Troy Glaus .40 .12
❑ 146 Todd Helton .60 .18
❑ 147 Ruben Gotay SP RC 2.00 .60
❑ 148 Darin Erstad .40 .12
❑ 149 Ryan Gripp SP RC 2.00 .60
❑ 150 Orlando Cabrera .40 .12
❑ 151 Jason Young RC .40 .12
❑ 152 Sterling Hitchcock SP 2.00 .60
❑ 153 Miguel Tejada .40 .12
❑ 154 Al Leiter .40 .12
❑ 155 Taylor Buchholz RC .40 .12
❑ 156 Juan M. Gonzalez RC .40 .12
❑ 157 Damion Easley .40 .12
❑ 158 Jimmy Gobble RC .75 .23
❑ 159 Dennis Ulacia SP RC 2.00 .60
❑ 160 Shane Reynolds SP 2.00 .60
❑ 161 Javier Colina .40 .12
❑ 162 Frank Thomas 1.00 .30
❑ 163 Chuck Knoblauch .40 .12
❑ 164 Sean Burroughs .40 .12
❑ 165 Greg Maddux 1.50 .45
❑ 166 Jason Ellison RC .40 .12
❑ 167 Tony Womack .40 .12
❑ 168 Randall Shelley SP RC 2.00 .60
❑ 169 Jason Marquis .40 .12
❑ 170 Brian Jordan .40 .12
❑ 171 Vicente Padilla .40 .12
❑ 172 Barry Zito .40 .12
❑ 173 Matt Allegra SP RC 2.00 .60
❑ 174 Ralph Santana SP RC 2.00 .60
❑ 175 Carlos Lee .40 .12
❑ 176 Richard Hidalgo SP 2.00 .60
❑ 177 Kevin Deaton RC .40 .12
❑ 178 Juan Encarnacion .40 .12
❑ 179 Mark Quinn .40 .12
❑ 180 Rafael Furcal .40 .12
❑ 181 Garret Anderson UER .40 .12
Photo is Chone Figgins
❑ 182 David Wright RC 10.00 3.00
❑ 183 Jose Reyes .60 .18
❑ 184 Mario Ramos SP RC 2.00 .60
❑ 185 J.D. Drew .40 .12
❑ 186 Juan Gonzalez .60 .18
❑ 187 Nick Neugebauer .40 .12
❑ 188 Alejandro Giron RC .40 .12
❑ 189 John Burkett .40 .12
❑ 190 Ben Sheets .40 .12
❑ 191 Vinny Castilla SP 2.00 .60
❑ 192 Cory Lidle .40 .12
❑ 193 Fernando Vina .40 .12
❑ 194 Russell Branyan SP 2.00 .60
❑ 195 Ben Davis .40 .12
❑ 196 Angel Berroa .40 .12
❑ 197 Alex Gonzalez .40 .12
❑ 198 Jared Sandberg .40 .12
❑ 199 Travis Lee SP 2.00 .60
❑ 200 Luis DePaula SP 2.00 .60
❑ 201 Ramon Hernandez SP 2.00 .60
❑ 202 Brandon Inge .40 .12
❑ 203 Aubrey Huff .40 .12
❑ 204 Mike Rivera .40 .12
❑ 205 Brad Nelson RC 1.25 .35
❑ 206 Colt Griffin SP RC 3.00 .90
❑ 207 Joel Pineiro .40 .12
❑ 208 Adam Pettyjohn .40 .12
❑ 209 Mark Redman .40 .12
❑ 210 Roberto Alomar SP 3.00 .90
❑ 211 Denny Neagle .40 .12
❑ 212 Adam Kennedy .40 .12
❑ 213 Jason Arnold SP RC 5.00 1.50
❑ 214 Jamie Moyer .40 .12
❑ 215 Aaron Boone .40 .12
❑ 216 Doug Glanville .40 .12
❑ 217 Nick Johnson SP 2.00 .60
❑ 218 Mike Cameron SP 2.00 .60
❑ 219 Tim Wakefield SP 2.00 .60
❑ 220 Todd Stottlemyre SP 2.00 .60
❑ 221 Mo Vaughn SP 2.00 .60
❑ 222 Vladimir Guerrero 1.00 .30
❑ 223 Bill Ortega .40 .12
❑ 224 Kevin Brown .40 .12
❑ 225 Peter Bergeron SP 2.00 .60
❑ 226 Shannon Stewart SP 2.00 .60
❑ 227 Eric Chavez .40 .12
❑ 228 Clint Weibl RC .40 .12
❑ 229 Todd Hollandsworth SP 2.00 .60
❑ 230 Jeff Bagwell .60 .18
❑ 231 Chad Qualls RC .40 .12
❑ 232 Ben Howard RC .40 .12
❑ 233 Rondell White SP 2.00 .60
❑ 234 Fred McGriff .60 .18
❑ 235 Steve Cox SP 2.00 .60
❑ 236 Chris Tritle RC .40 .12
❑ 237 Eric Valent .40 .12
❑ 238 Joe Mauer RC 5.00 1.50
❑ 239 Shawn Green .40 .12
❑ 240 Jimmy Rollins .40 .12
❑ 241 Edgar Renteria .40 .12
❑ 242 Edwin Yan RC .40 .12
❑ 243 Noochie Varner RC .40 .12
❑ 244 Kris Benson SP 2.00 .60
❑ 245 Mike Hampton .40 .12
❑ 246 So Taguchi RC .50 .15
❑ 247 Sammy Sosa 1.50 .45
❑ 248 Terrence Long .40 .12
❑ 249 Jason Bay RC 2.50 .75
❑ 250 Kevin Millar SP 2.00 .60
❑ 251 Albert Pujols 2.00 .60
❑ 252 Chris Latham RC .40 .12
❑ 253 Eric Byrnes .40 .12
❑ 254 Napoleon Calzado SP RC 2.00 .60
❑ 255 Bobby Higginson .40 .12
❑ 256 Ben Molina .40 .12
❑ 257 Torii Hunter SP 2.00 .60
❑ 258 Jason Giambi .40 .12
❑ 259 Bartolo Colon .40 .12
❑ 260 Benito Baez .40 .12
❑ 261 Ichiro Suzuki 1.50 .45
❑ 262 Mike Sweeney .40 .12
❑ 263 Brian West RC .40 .12
❑ 264 Brad Penny .40 .12
❑ 265 Kevin Millwood SP 2.00 .60
❑ 266 Orlando Hudson .40 .12
❑ 267 Doug Mientkiewicz .40 .12
❑ 268 Luis Gonzalez SP 2.00 .60
❑ 269 Jay Caligiuri RC .40 .12
❑ 270 Nate Cornejo SP 2.00 .60
❑ 271 Lee Stevens .40 .12
❑ 272 Eric Hinske .40 .12
❑ 273 Antwon Rollins RC .40 .12
❑ 274 Bobby Jenks RC .75 .23
❑ 275 Joe Mays .40 .12
❑ 276 Josh Shaffer RC .40 .12
❑ 277 Jonny Gomes RC .75 .23
❑ 278 Bernie Williams .60 .18
❑ 279 Ed Rogers .40 .12
❑ 280 Carlos Delgado .40 .12
❑ 281 Raul Mondesi SP 2.00 .60
❑ 282 Jose Ortiz .40 .12
❑ 283 Cesar Izturis .40 .12
❑ 284 Ryan Dempster SP 2.00 .60
❑ 285 Brian Daubach .40 .12
❑ 286 Hansel Izquierdo RC .40 .12
❑ 287 Mike Lieberthal SP 2.00 .60
❑ 288 Marcus Thames .40 .12
❑ 289 Nomar Garciaparra 1.50 .45
❑ 290 Brad Fullmer .40 .12
❑ 291 Tino Martinez .60 .18
❑ 292 James Barrett RC .40 .12
❑ 293 Jacque Jones .40 .12
❑ 294 Nick Alvarez SP RC 2.00 .60
❑ 295 Jason Grove SP RC 2.00 .60
❑ 296 Mike Wilson SP RC 2.00 .60
❑ 297 J.T. Snow .40 .12
❑ 298 Cliff Floyd .40 .12
❑ 299 Todd Hundley SP 2.00 .60
❑ 300 Tony Clark SP 2.00 .60
❑ 301 Demetrius Heath RC .40 .12
❑ 302 Morgan Ensberg .40 .12
❑ 303 Cristian Guzman .40 .12
❑ 304 Frank Catalanotto .40 .12
❑ 305 Jeff Weaver .40 .12
❑ 306 Tim Hudson .40 .12
❑ 307 Scott Wiggins SP RC 2.00 .60
❑ 308 Shea Hillenbrand SP 2.00 .60
❑ 309 Todd Walker SP 2.00 .60
❑ 310 Tsuyoshi Shinjo .40 .12
❑ 311 Adrian Beltre .60 .18
❑ 312 Craig Kuzmic RC .40 .12
❑ 313 Paul Konerko .40 .12
❑ 314 Scott Hairston RC 1.50 .45
❑ 315 Chan Ho Park .40 .12
❑ 316 Jorge Posada .60 .18
❑ 317 Chris Snelling RC .40 .12
❑ 318 Keith Foulke .40 .12
❑ 319 John Smoltz .60 .18
❑ 320 Ryan Church SP RC 5.00 1.50
❑ 321 Mike Mussina .60 .18
❑ 322 Tony Armas Jr. SP 2.00 .60
❑ 323 Craig Counsell .40 .12
❑ 324 Marcus Giles .40 .12
❑ 325 Greg Vaughn .40 .12
❑ 326 Curt Schilling .40 .12
❑ 327 Jeromy Burnitz .40 .12
❑ 328 Eric Byrnes .40 .12
❑ 329 Johnny Damon Sox 1.00 .30
❑ 330 Michael Floyd SP RC 2.00 .60
❑ 331 Edgardo Alfonzo .40 .12
❑ 332 Jeremy Hill RC .40 .12
❑ 333 Josh Bonifay RC .40 .12
❑ 334 Byung-Hyun Kim .40 .12
❑ 335 Keith Ginter .40 .12
❑ 336 Ronald Acuna SP RC 2.00 .60
❑ 337 Mike Hill SP RC 2.00 .60
❑ 338 Sean Casey .40 .12
❑ 339 Matt Anderson SP 2.00 .60
❑ 340 Dan Wright .40 .12
❑ 341 Ben Petrick .40 .12
❑ 342 Mike Sirotka SP 2.00 .60
❑ 343 Alex Rodriguez 1.50 .45
❑ 344 Einar Diaz .40 .12
❑ 345 Derek Jeter 2.50 .75
❑ 346 Jeff Conine .40 .12
❑ 347 Ray Durham SP 2.00 .60
❑ 348 Wilson Betemit SP 2.00 .60
❑ 349 Jeffrey Hammonds .40 .12
❑ 350 Dan Trumble RC .40 .12
❑ 351 Phil Nevin SP 2.00 .60
❑ 352 A.J. Burnett .40 .12
❑ 353 Bill Mueller .40 .12
❑ 354 Charles Nagy .40 .12
❑ 355 Rusty Greer SP 2.00 .60
❑ 356 Jason Botts RC .75 .23
❑ 357 Magglio Ordonez .40 .12
❑ 358 Kevin Appier .40 .12
❑ 359 Brad Radke .40 .12
❑ 360 Chris George .40 .12
❑ 361 Chris Piersoll RC .40 .12
❑ 362 Ivan Rodriguez 1.00 .30
❑ 363 Jim Kavourias RC .40 .12
❑ 364 Rick Helling SP 2.00 .60
❑ 365 Dean Palmer .40 .12
❑ 366 Rich Aurilia SP 2.00 .60
❑ 367 Ryan Vogelsong .40 .12
❑ 368 Matt Lawton .40 .12
❑ 369 Wade Miller .40 .12
❑ 370 Dustin Hermanson .40 .12
❑ 371 Craig Wilson .40 .12
❑ 372 Todd Zeile SP 2.00 .60
❑ 373 Jon Guzman RC .40 .12
❑ 374 Ellis Burks .40 .12
❑ 375 Robert Cosby SP RC 2.00 .60
❑ 376 Jason Kendall .40 .12
❑ 377 Scott Rolen SP 5.00 1.50
❑ 378 Andruw Jones .40 .12
❑ 379 Greg Sain RC .50 .15
❑ 380 Paul LoDuca .40 .12
❑ 381 Scotty Layfield RC .40 .12
❑ 382 Tomo Ohka .40 .12
❑ 383 Garrett Guzman RC .40 .12
❑ 384 Jack Cust SP 2.00 .60
❑ 385 Shayne Wright RC .40 .12
❑ 386 Derrek Lee .40 .12
❑ 387 Jesus Medrano RC .40 .12
❑ 388 Javier Vazquez .40 .12
❑ 389 Preston Wilson SP 2.00 .60
❑ 390 Gavin Floyd RC 2.50 .75
❑ 391 Sidney Ponson SP 2.00 .60
❑ 392 Jose Hernandez .40 .12
❑ 393 Scott Erickson SP 2.00 .60
❑ 394 Jose Valverde RC .50 .15
❑ 395 Mark Hamilton SP RC 2.00 .60
❑ 396 Brad Cresse .40 .12
❑ 397 Danny Bautista .40 .12
❑ 398 Ray Lankford SP 2.00 .60
❑ 399 Miguel Batista SP 2.00 .60
❑ 400 Brent Butler .40 .12

❑ 401 Manny Delcarmen SP RC 2.00 .60
❑ 402 Kyle Farnsworth SP 2.00 .60
❑ 403 Freddy Garcia .40 .12
❑ 404 Joe Jiannetti RC .40 .12
❑ 405 Josh Barfield RC 1.50 .45
❑ 406 Corey Patterson .40 .12
❑ 407 Josh Towers .40 .12
❑ 408 Carlos Pena .40 .12
❑ 409 Jeff Cirillo .40 .12
❑ 410 Jon Lieber .40 .12
❑ 411 Woody Williams SP 2.00 .60
❑ 412 Richard Lane SP RC 2.00 .60
❑ 413 Alex Gonzalez .40 .12
❑ 414 Wilkin Ruan .40 .12
❑ 415 Geoff Jenkins .40 .12
❑ 416 Carlos Hernandez .40 .12
❑ 417 Matt Clement SP 2.00 .60
❑ 418 Jose Cruz Jr. .40 .12
❑ 419 Jake Mauer RC .40 .12
❑ 420 Matt Childers RC .40 .12
❑ 421 Tom Glavine SP 3.00 .90
❑ 422 Ken Griffey Jr. 1.50 .45
❑ 423 Anderson Hernandez RC .40 .12
❑ 424 John Suomi RC .40 .12
❑ 425 Doug Sessions RC .40 .12
❑ 426 Jaret Wright .40 .12
❑ 427 Rolando Viera SP RC 2.00 .60
❑ 428 Aaron Sele .40 .12
❑ 429 Dmitri Young .40 .12
❑ 430 Ryan Klesko .40 .12
❑ 431 Kevin Tapani SP 2.00 .60
❑ 432 Joe Kennedy .40 .12
❑ 433 Austin Kearns .40 .12
❑ 434 Roger Cedeno SP 2.00 .60
❑ 435 Lance Berkman .40 .12
❑ 436 Frank Menechino .40 .12
❑ 437 Brett Myers .40 .12
❑ 438 Bob Abreu .40 .12
❑ 439 Shawn Estes SP 2.00 .60

2003 Bowman Heritage

MINT NRMT
COMPLETE SET (300) 100.00 45.00

❑ 1 Jorge Posada .60 .25
❑ 2 Todd Helton .60 .25
❑ 3 Marcus Giles .40 .18
❑ 4 Eric Chavez .40 .18
❑ 5 Edgar Martinez .60 .25
❑ 6 Luis Gonzalez .40 .18
❑ 7 Corey Patterson .40 .18
❑ 8 Preston Wilson .40 .18
❑ 9 Ryan Klesko .40 .18
❑ 10 Randy Johnson 1.00 .45
❑ 11 Jose Guillen .40 .18
❑ 12 Carlos Lee .40 .18
❑ 13 Steve Finley .40 .18
❑ 14 A.J. Pierzynski .40 .18
❑ 15 Troy Glaus .40 .18
❑ 16 Darin Erstad .40 .18
❑ 17 Moises Alou .40 .18
❑ 18 Torii Hunter .40 .18
❑ 19 Marlon Byrd .40 .18
❑ 20 Mark Prior 1.00 .45
❑ 21 Shannon Stewart .40 .18
❑ 22 Craig Biggio .60 .25
❑ 23 Johnny Damon 1.00 .45
❑ 24 Robert Fick .40 .18
❑ 25 Jason Giambi .40 .18
❑ 26 Fernando Vina .40 .18
❑ 27 Aubrey Huff .40 .18
❑ 28 Benito Santiago .40 .18
❑ 29 Jay Gibbons .40 .18
❑ 30 Ken Griffey Jr. 1.50 .70
❑ 31 Rocco Baldelli .40 .18
❑ 32 Pat Burrell .40 .18
❑ 33 A.J. Burnett .40 .18
❑ 34 Omar Vizquel .60 .25
❑ 35 Greg Maddux 1.50 .70
❑ 36 Cliff Floyd .40 .18
❑ 37 C.C. Sabathia .40 .18
❑ 38 Geoff Jenkins .40 .18
❑ 39 Ty Wigginton .40 .18
❑ 40 Jeff Kent .40 .18
❑ 41 Orlando Hudson .40 .18
❑ 42 Edgardo Alfonzo .40 .18
❑ 43 Greg Myers .40 .18
❑ 44 Melvin Mora .40 .18
❑ 45 Sammy Sosa 1.50 .70
❑ 46 Russ Ortiz .40 .18
❑ 47 Josh Beckett .40 .18
❑ 48 David Wells .40 .18
❑ 49 Woody Williams .40 .18
❑ 50 Alex Rodriguez 1.50 .70
❑ 51 Randy Wolf .40 .18
❑ 52 Carlos Beltran .60 .25
❑ 53 Austin Kearns .40 .18
❑ 54 Trot Nixon .40 .18
❑ 55 Ivan Rodriguez 1.00 .45
❑ 56 Shea Hillenbrand .40 .18
❑ 57 Roberto Alomar .60 .25
❑ 58 John Olerud .40 .18
❑ 59 Michael Young .60 .25
❑ 60 Garret Anderson .40 .18
❑ 61 Mike Lieberthal .40 .18
❑ 62 Adam Dunn .60 .25
❑ 63 Raul Ibanez .40 .18
❑ 64 Kenny Lofton .40 .18
❑ 65 Ichiro Suzuki 1.50 .70
❑ 66 Jarrod Washburn .40 .18
❑ 67 Shawn Chacon .40 .18
❑ 68 Alex Gonzalez .40 .18
❑ 69 Roy Halladay .40 .18
❑ 70 Vladimir Guerrero 1.00 .45
❑ 71 Hee Seop Choi .40 .18
❑ 72 Jody Gerut .40 .18
❑ 73 Ray Durham .40 .18
❑ 74 Mark Teixeira .40 .18
❑ 75 Hank Blalock .60 .25
❑ 76 Jerry Hairston Jr. .40 .18
❑ 77 Erubiel Durazo .40 .18
❑ 78 Frank Catalanotto .40 .18
❑ 79 Jacque Jones .40 .18
❑ 80 Bobby Abreu .40 .18
❑ 81 Mike Hampton .40 .18
❑ 82 Zach Day .40 .18
❑ 83 Jimmy Rollins .40 .18
❑ 84 Joel Pineiro .40 .18
❑ 85 Brett Myers .40 .18
❑ 86 Frank Thomas 1.00 .45
❑ 87 Aramis Ramirez .40 .18
❑ 88 Paul Lo Duca .40 .18
❑ 89 Dmitri Young .40 .18
❑ 90 Brian Giles .40 .18
❑ 91 Jose Cruz Jr. .40 .18
❑ 92 Derek Lowe .40 .18
❑ 93 Mark Buehrle .40 .18
❑ 94 Wade Miller .40 .18
❑ 95 Derek Jeter 2.50 1.10
❑ 96 Bret Boone .40 .18
❑ 97 Tony Batista .40 .18
❑ 98 Sean Casey .40 .18
❑ 99 Eric Hinske .40 .18
❑ 100 Albert Pujols 2.00 .90
❑ 101 Runelvys Hernandez .40 .18
❑ 102 Vernon Wells .40 .18
❑ 103 Kerry Wood 1.00 .45
❑ 104 Lance Berkman .40 .18
❑ 105 Alfonso Soriano .60 .25
❑ 106 Bill Mueller .40 .18
❑ 107 Bartolo Colon .40 .18
❑ 108 Andy Pettitte .60 .25
❑ 109 Rafael Furcal .40 .18
❑ 110 Dontrelle Willis .60 .25
❑ 111 Carl Crawford .40 .18
❑ 112 Scott Rolen 1.00 .45
❑ 113 Chipper Jones 1.00 .45
❑ 114 Magglio Ordonez .40 .18
❑ 115 Bernie Williams .60 .25
❑ 116 Roy Oswalt .40 .18
❑ 117 Kevin Brown .40 .18
❑ 118 Cristian Guzman .40 .18
❑ 119 Kazuhisa Ishii .40 .18
❑ 120 Larry Walker .60 .25
❑ 121 Miguel Tejada .40 .18
❑ 122 Manny Ramirez .60 .25
❑ 123 Mike Mussina .60 .25
❑ 124 Mike Lowell .40 .18
❑ 125 Scott Podsednik .40 .18
❑ 126 Aaron Boone .40 .18
❑ 127 Carlos Delgado .40 .18
❑ 128 Jose Vidro .40 .18
❑ 129 Brad Radke .40 .18
❑ 130 Rafael Palmeiro .60 .25
❑ 131 Mark Mulder .40 .18
❑ 132 Jason Schmidt .40 .18
❑ 133 Gary Sheffield .40 .18
❑ 134 Richie Sexson .40 .18
❑ 135 Barry Zito .40 .18
❑ 136 Tom Glavine .60 .25
❑ 137 Jim Edmonds .40 .18
❑ 138 Andruw Jones .40 .18
❑ 139 Pedro Martinez 1.00 .45
❑ 140 Curt Schilling .40 .18
❑ 141 Phil Nevin .40 .18
❑ 142 Nomar Garciaparra 1.50 .70
❑ 143 Vicente Padilla .40 .18
❑ 144 Kevin Millwood .40 .18
❑ 145 Shawn Green .40 .18
❑ 146 Jeff Bagwell .60 .25
❑ 147 Hideo Nomo 1.00 .45
❑ 148 Fred McGriff .60 .25
❑ 149 Matt Morris .40 .18
❑ 150 Roger Clemens 2.00 .90
❑ 151 Jerome Williams .40 .18
❑ 152 Orlando Cabrera .40 .18
❑ 153 Tim Hudson .40 .18
❑ 154 Mike Sweeney .40 .18
❑ 155 Jim Thome 1.00 .45
❑ 156 Rich Aurilia .40 .18
❑ 157 Mike Piazza 1.50 .70
❑ 158 Edgar Renteria .40 .18
❑ 159 Javy Lopez .40 .18
❑ 160 Jamie Moyer .40 .18
❑ 161 Miguel Cabrera DI 1.00 .45
❑ 162 Adam Loewen DI RC 1.25 .55
❑ 163 Jose Reyes DI .40 .18
❑ 164 Zack Greinke DI .60 .25
❑ 165 Gavin Floyd DI .40 .18
❑ 166 Jeremy Guthrie DI .40 .18
❑ 167 Victor Martinez DI .60 .25
❑ 168 Rich Harden DI .60 .25
❑ 169 Joe Mauer DI 1.00 .45
❑ 170 Khalil Greene DI 2.00 .90
❑ 171A Willie Mays 2.00 .90
❑ 171B Willie Mays DI 2.00 .90
❑ 171C Willie Mays KN 2.00 .90
❑ 172A Phil Rizzuto .60 .25
❑ 172B Phil Rizzuto DI .60 .25
❑ 172C Phil Rizzuto KN .60 .25
❑ 173A Al Kaline 1.00 .45
❑ 173B Al Kaline DI 1.00 .45
❑ 173C Al Kaline KN 1.00 .45
❑ 174A Warren Spahn .60 .25
❑ 174B Warren Spahn DI .60 .25
❑ 174C Warren Spahn KN .60 .25
❑ 175A Jimmy Piersall .40 .18
❑ 175B Jimmy Piersall DI .40 .18
❑ 175C Jimmy Piersall KN .40 .18
❑ 176A Luis Aparicio .40 .18
❑ 176B Luis Aparicio DI .40 .18
❑ 176C Luis Aparicio KN .40 .18
❑ 177A Whitey Ford .60 .25
❑ 177B Whitey Ford DI .60 .25
❑ 177C Whitey Ford KN .60 .25
❑ 178A Harmon Killebrew 1.00 .45
❑ 178B Harmon Killebrew DI 1.00 .45
❑ 178C Harmon Killebrew KN 1.00 .45
❑ 179A Duke Snider .60 .25

❑ 179B Duke Snider DI .60 .25
❑ 179C Duke Snider KN .60 .25
❑ 180A Roberto Clemente 2.50 1.10
❑ 180B Roberto Clemente DI 2.50 1.10
❑ 180C Roberto Clemente KN 2.50 1.10
❑ 181 David Martinez KN RC .40 .18
❑ 182 Felix Pie KN RC 2.50 1.10
❑ 183 Kevin Correia KN RC .40 .18
❑ 184 Brandon Webb KN RC 1.25 .55
❑ 185 Matt Diaz KN RC .60 .25
❑ 186 Lew Ford KN RC 1.50 .70
❑ 187 Jeremy Griffiths KN RC .60 .25
❑ 188 Matt Hensley KN RC .40 .18
❑ 189 Danny Garcia KN RC .40 .18
❑ 190 Elizardo Ramirez KN RC 1.00 .45
❑ 191 Greg Aquino KN RC .40 .18
❑ 192 Felix Sanchez KN RC .40 .18
❑ 193 Kelly Shoppach KN RC 1.25 .55
❑ 194 Bubba Nelson KN RC .60 .25
❑ 195 Mike O'Keefe KN RC .40 .18
❑ 196 Hanley Ramirez KN RC 2.50 1.10
❑ 197 Todd Wellemeyer KN RC .60 .25
❑ 198 Dustin Moseley KN RC .60 .25
❑ 199 Eric Crozier KN RC .60 .25
❑ 200 Ryan Shealy KN RC 1.00 .45
❑ 201 Jeremy Bonderman KN RC 1.00 .45
❑ 202 Bo Hart KN RC .60 .25
❑ 203 Dusty Brown KN RC .40 .18
❑ 204 Rob Hammock KN RC .60 .25
❑ 205 Jorge Piedra KN RC .60 .25
❑ 206 Jason Kubel KN RC 2.50 1.10
❑ 207 Stephen Randolph KN RC .40 .18
❑ 208 Andy Sisco KN RC 1.25 .55
❑ 209 Matt Kata KN RC 1.00 .45
❑ 210 Robinson Cano KN RC 1.00 .45
❑ 211 Ben Francisco KN RC .60 .25
❑ 212 Arnie Munoz KN RC .40 .18
❑ 213 Ozzie Chavez KN RC .40 .18
❑ 214 Beau Kemp KN RC .40 .18
❑ 215 Travis Wong KN RC .60 .25
❑ 216 Brian McCann KN RC 1.00 .45
❑ 217 Aquilino Lopez KN RC .40 .18
❑ 218 Bobby Basham KN RC .60 .25
❑ 219 Tim Olson KN RC .60 .25
❑ 220 Nathan Panther KN RC 1.00 .45
❑ 221 Wil Ledezma KN RC .60 .25
❑ 222 Josh Willingham KN RC .60 .25
❑ 223 David Cash KN RC .40 .18
❑ 224 Oscar Villarreal KN RC .40 .18
❑ 225 Jeff Duncan KN RC .60 .25
❑ 226 Dan Haren KN RC 1.00 .45
❑ 227 Michel Hernandez KN RC .40 .18
❑ 228 Matt Murton KN RC .40 .18
❑ 229 Clay Hensley KN RC .40 .18
❑ 230 Tyler Johnson KN RC .40 .18
❑ 231 Tyler Martin KN RC .40 .18
❑ 232 J.D. Durbin KN RC 1.00 .45
❑ 233 Shane Victorino KN RC .40 .18
❑ 234 Rajai Davis KN RC .60 .25
❑ 235 Chien-Ming Wang KN RC 1.25 .55
❑ 236 Travis Ishikawa KN RC .40 .18
❑ 237 Eric Eckenstahler KN .40 .18
❑ 238 Dustin McGowan KN RC 1.00 .45
❑ 239 Prentice Redman KN RC .40 .18
❑ 240 Haj Turay KN RC .60 .25
❑ 241 Matt DeMarco KN RC .40 .18
❑ 242 Lou Palmisano KN RC 1.50 .70
❑ 243 Eric Reed KN RC 1.00 .45
❑ 244 Willie Eyre KN RC .40 .18
❑ 245 Ferdin Tejeda KN RC .40 .18
❑ 246 Michael Garciaparra KN RC 1.00 .45
❑ 247 Michael Hinckley KN RC 1.25 .55
❑ 248 Branden Florence KN RC .40 .18
❑ 249 Trent Oeltjen KN RC .60 .25
❑ 250 Mike Neu KN RC .40 .18
❑ 251 Chris Lubanski KN RC 2.00 .90
❑ 252 Brandon Wood KN RC 1.25 .55
❑ 253 Delmon Young KN RC 4.00 1.80
❑ 254 Matt Harrison KN RC 1.00 .45
❑ 255 Chad Billingsley KN RC 1.50 .70
❑ 256 Josh Anderson KN RC 1.25 .55
❑ 257 Brian McFall KN RC 1.00 .45
❑ 258 Ryan Wagner KN RC .60 .25
❑ 259 Billy Hogan KN RC .60 .25
❑ 260 Nate Spears KN RC 1.00 .45
❑ 261 Ryan Harvey KN RC 2.00 .90
❑ 262 Wes Littleton KN RC .60 .25
❑ 263 Xavier Paul KN RC 2.00 .90
❑ 264 Sean Rodriguez KN RC 1.25 .55
❑ 265 Brian Finch KN RC .40 .18
❑ 266 Josh Rainwater KN RC .60 .25
❑ 267 Brian Snyder KN RC .60 .25
❑ 268 Eric Duncan KN RC 1.50 .70
❑ 269 Rickie Weeks KN RC 3.00 1.35
❑ 270 Tim Battle KN RC .60 .25
❑ 271 Scott Beerer KN RC .40 .18
❑ 272 Aaron Hill KN RC 1.25 .55
❑ 273 Casey Abrams KN RC .40 .18
❑ 274 Jonathan Fulton KN RC .60 .25
❑ 275 Todd Jennings KN RC .60 .25
❑ 276 Jordan Pratt KN RC .60 .25
❑ 277 Tom Gorzelanny KN RC 1.00 .45
❑ 278 Matt Lorenzo KN RC .60 .25
❑ 279 Jarrod Saltalamacchia KN RC 1.00 .45
❑ 280 Mike Wagner KN RC .40 .18

1994 Bowman's Best

	Nm-Mt	Ex-Mt
COMPLETE SET (200)	40.00	12.00

❑ B1 Chipper Jones 1.25 .35
❑ B2 Derek Jeter 4.00 1.20
❑ B3 Bill Pulsipher .50 .15
❑ B4 James Baldwin .25 .07
❑ B5 Brooks Kieschnick RC 1.00 .30
❑ B6 Justin Thompson .25 .07
❑ B7 Midre Cummings .25 .07
❑ B8 Joey Hamilton .25 .07
❑ B9 Pokey Reese .25 .07
❑ B10 Brian Barber .25 .07
❑ B11 John Burke .25 .07
❑ B12 DeShawn Warren .25 .07
❑ B13 Edgardo Alfonzo RC 1.50 .45
❑ B14 Eddie Pearson RC .50 .15
❑ B15 Jimmy Haynes .25 .07
❑ B16 Danny Bautista .25 .07
❑ B17 Roger Cedeno .25 .07
❑ B18 Jon Lieber .25 .07
❑ B19 Billy Wagner RC 2.50 .75
❑ B20 Tate Seefried RC .50 .15
❑ B21 Chad Mottola .25 .07
❑ B22 Jose Malave .25 .07
❑ B23 Terrell Wade RC .50 .15
❑ B24 Shane Andrews .25 .07
❑ B25 Chan Ho Park RC 1.50 .45
❑ B26 Kirk Presley RC .50 .15
❑ B27 Robbie Beckett .25 .07
❑ B28 Orlando Miller .25 .07
❑ B29 Jorge Posada RC 10.00 3.00
❑ B30 Frankie Rodriguez .25 .07
❑ B31 Brian L. Hunter .25 .07
❑ B32 Billy Ashley .25 .07
❑ B33 Rondell White .50 .15
❑ B34 John Roper .25 .07
❑ B35 Marc Valdes .25 .07
❑ B36 Scott Ruffcorn .25 .07
❑ B37 Rod Henderson .25 .07
❑ B38 Curtis Goodwin RC .50 .15
❑ B39 Russ Davis .25 .07
❑ B40 Rick Gorecki .25 .07
❑ B41 Johnny Damon 1.25 .35
❑ B42 Roberto Petagine .25 .07
❑ B43 Chris Snopek .25 .07
❑ B44 Mark Acre RC .50 .15
❑ B45 Todd Hollandsworth .25 .07
❑ B46 Shawn Green 1.25 .35
❑ B47 John Carter RC .50 .15
❑ B48 Jim Pittsley RC .50 .15
❑ B49 John Wasdin RC .50 .15
❑ B50 D.J. Boston RC .50 .15
❑ B51 Tim Clark .25 .07
❑ B52 Alex Ochoa .25 .07
❑ B53 Chad Roper .25 .07
❑ B54 Mike Kelly .25 .07
❑ B55 Brad Fullmer RC 1.50 .45
❑ B56 Carl Everett .50 .15
❑ B57 Tim Belk RC .50 .15
❑ B58 Jimmy Hurst RC .50 .15
❑ B59 Mac Suzuki RC 1.00 .30
❑ B60 Mike Moore .25 .07
❑ B61 Alan Benes RC .50 .15
❑ B62 Tony Clark RC 1.00 .30
❑ B63 Edgar Renteria RC 10.00 2.40
❑ B64 Trey Beamon .25 .07
❑ B65 LaTroy Hawkins RC 1.50 .45
❑ B66 Wayne Gomes RC 1.00 .30
❑ B67 Ray McDavid .25 .07
❑ B68 John Dettmer .25 .07
❑ B69 Willie Greene .25 .07
❑ B70 Dave Stevens .25 .07
❑ B71 Kevin Orie RC .25 .07
❑ B72 Chad Ogea .25 .07
❑ B73 Ben Van Ryn RC .50 .15
❑ B74 Kym Ashworth RC .50 .15
❑ B75 Dmitri Young .50 .15
❑ B76 Herbert Perry RC 1.00 .30
❑ B77 Joey Eischen .25 .07
❑ B78 Arquimedez Pozo RC .50 .15
❑ B79 Ugueth Urbina .25 .07
❑ B80 Keith Williams RC .50 .15
❑ B81 John Frascatore RC .50 .15
❑ B82 Garey Ingram RC .50 .15
❑ B83 Aaron Small .25 .07
❑ B84 Olmedo Saenz RC .50 .15
❑ B85 Jesus Tavarez RC .50 .15
❑ B86 Jose Silva RC 1.00 .30
❑ B87 Jay Witasick RC .50 .15
❑ B88 Jay Maldonado RC .50 .15
❑ B89 Keith Heberling RC .50 .15
❑ B90 Rusty Greer RC 1.50 .45
❑ R1 Paul Molitor .75 .23
❑ R2 Eddie Murray 1.25 .35
❑ R3 Ozzie Smith 2.00 .60
❑ R4 Rickey Henderson 1.25 .35
❑ R5 Lee Smith .50 .15
❑ R6 Dave Winfield .50 .15
❑ R7 Roberto Alomar .75 .23
❑ R8 Matt Williams .50 .15
❑ R9 Mark Grace .75 .23
❑ R10 Lance Johnson .25 .07
❑ R11 Darren Daulton .50 .15
❑ R12 Tom Glavine .75 .23
❑ R13 Gary Sheffield .50 .15
❑ R14 Rod Beck .25 .07
❑ R15 Fred McGriff .75 .23
❑ R16 Joe Carter .50 .15
❑ R17 Dante Bichette .50 .15
❑ R18 Danny Tartabull .25 .07
❑ R19 Juan Gonzalez .75 .23
❑ R20 Steve Avery .25 .07
❑ R21 John Wetteland .50 .15
❑ R22 Ben McDonald .25 .07
❑ R23 Jack McDowell .25 .07
❑ R24 Jose Canseco 1.25 .35
❑ R25 Tim Salmon .75 .23
❑ R26 Wilson Alvarez .25 .07
❑ R27 Gregg Jefferies .25 .07
❑ R28 John Burkett .25 .07
❑ R29 Greg Vaughn .25 .07
❑ R30 Robin Ventura .50 .15
❑ R31 Paul O'Neill .75 .23
❑ R32 Cecil Fielder .50 .15
❑ R33 Kevin Mitchell .25 .07
❑ R34 Jeff Conine .50 .15
❑ R35 Carlos Baerga .25 .07
❑ R36 Greg Maddux 2.00 .60
❑ R37 Roger Clemens 2.50 .75
❑ R38 Deion Sanders .75 .23
❑ R39 Delino DeShields .25 .07

	Card	Player	Nm-Mt	Ex-Mt
❑	R40	Ken Griffey Jr.	2.00	.60
❑	R41	Albert Belle	.50	.15
❑	R42	Wade Boggs	.75	.23
❑	R43	Andres Galarraga	.50	.15
❑	R44	Aaron Sele	.25	.07
❑	R45	Don Mattingly	3.00	.90
❑	R46	David Cone	.50	.15
❑	R47	Len Dykstra	.50	.15
❑	R48	Brett Butler	.50	.15
❑	R49	Bill Swift	.25	.07
❑	R50	Bobby Bonilla	.50	.15
❑	R51	Rafael Palmeiro	.75	.23
❑	R52	Moises Alou	.50	.15
❑	R53	Jeff Bagwell	.75	.23
❑	R54	Mike Mussina	.75	.23
❑	R55	Frank Thomas	1.25	.35
❑	R56	Jose Rijo	.25	.07
❑	R57	Ruben Sierra	.25	.07
❑	R58	Randy Myers	.25	.07
❑	R59	Barry Bonds	3.00	.90
❑	R60	Jimmy Key	.50	.15
❑	R61	Travis Fryman	.50	.15
❑	R62	John Olerud	.50	.15
❑	R63	David Justice	.50	.15
❑	R64	Ray Lankford	.25	.07
❑	R65	Bob Tewksbury	.25	.07
❑	R66	Chuck Carr	.25	.07
❑	R67	Jay Buhner	.50	.15
❑	R68	Kenny Lofton	.50	.15
❑	R69	Marquis Grissom	.50	.15
❑	R70	Sammy Sosa	2.00	.60
❑	R71	Cal Ripken	4.00	1.20
❑	R72	Ellis Burks	.50	.15
❑	R73	Jeff Montgomery	.25	.07
❑	R74	Julio Franco	.50	.15
❑	R75	Kirby Puckett	1.25	.35
❑	R76	Larry Walker	.75	.23
❑	R77	Andy Van Slyke	.50	.15
❑	R78	Tony Gwynn	1.50	.45
❑	R79	Will Clark	1.25	.35
❑	R80	Mo Vaughn	.50	.15
❑	R81	Mike Piazza	2.50	.75
❑	R82	James Mouton	.25	.07
❑	R83	Carlos Delgado	.75	.23
❑	R84	Ryan Klesko	.50	.15
❑	R85	Javier Lopez	.50	.15
❑	R86	Raul Mondesi	.50	.15
❑	R87	Cliff Floyd	.50	.15
❑	R88	Manny Ramirez	.75	.23
❑	R89	Hector Carrasco	.25	.07
❑	R90	Jeff Granger	.25	.07
❑	X91	Frank Thomas Dmitri Young	.75	.23
❑	X92	Fred McGriff Brooks Kieschnick	.50	.15
❑	X93	Matt Williams Shane Andrews	.25	.07
❑	X94	Cal Ripken Kevin Orie	2.00	.60
❑	X95	Barry Larkin Derek Jeter	2.00	.60
❑	X96	Ken Griffey Jr. Johnny Damon	1.00	.30
❑	X97	Barry Bonds Rondell White	1.50	.45
❑	X98	Albert Belle Jimmy Hurst	.50	.15
❑	X99	Raul Mondesi Ruben Rivera RC	.50	.15
❑	X100	Roger Clemens Scott Ruffcorn	1.25	.35
❑	X101	Greg Maddux John Wasdin	1.25	.35
❑	X102	Tim Salmon Chad Mottola	.75	.23
❑	X103	Carlos Baerga Arquimedez Pozo	.25	.07
❑	X104	Mike Piazza Bobby Hughes	1.25	.35
❑	X105	Carlos Delgado Melvin Nieves	.75	.23
❑	X106	Javier Lopez Jorge Posada	2.50	.75
❑	X107	Manny Ramirez Jose Malave	.75	.23
❑	X108	Travis Fryman Chipper Jones	.75	.23
❑	X109	Steve Avery Bill Pulsipher	.25	.07
❑	X110	John Olerud Shawn Green	1.25	.35

1995 Bowman's Best

	Nm-Mt	Ex-Mt
COMPLETE SET (195)	250.00	75.00
COMMON CARD (B1-R90)	.50	.15
COMMON CARD (X1-X15)	.50	.15

	Card	Player	Nm-Mt	Ex-Mt
❑	B1	Derek Jeter	3.00	.90
❑	B2	Vladimir Guerrero RC	80.00	24.00
❑	B3	Bob Abreu RC	10.00	3.00
❑	B4	Chan Ho Park	.50	.15
❑	B5	Paul Wilson	.50	.15
❑	B6	Chad Ogea	.50	.15
❑	B7	Andruw Jones RC	40.00	12.00
❑	B8	Brian Barber	.50	.15
❑	B9	Andy Larkin	.50	.15
❑	B10	Richie Sexson RC	10.00	3.00
❑	B11	Everett Stull	.50	.15
❑	B12	Brooks Kieschnick	.50	.15
❑	B13	Matt Murray	.50	.15
❑	B14	John Wasdin	.50	.15
❑	B15	Shannon Stewart	.50	.15
❑	B16	Luis Ortiz	.50	.15
❑	B17	Marc Kroon	.50	.15
❑	B18	Todd Greene	.50	.15
❑	B19	Juan Acevedo RC	1.00	.30
❑	B20	Tony Clark	.50	.15
❑	B21	Jermaine Dye	.50	.15
❑	B22	Derrek Lee	.50	.15
❑	B23	Pat Watkins	.50	.15
❑	B24	Pokey Reese	.50	.15
❑	B25	Ben Grieve	.50	.15
❑	B26	Julio Santana RC	.50	.15
❑	B27	Felix Rodriguez RC	2.00	.60
❑	B28	Paul Konerko	2.00	.60
❑	B29	Nomar Garciaparra	8.00	2.40
❑	B30	Pat Ahearne	.50	.15
❑	B31	Jason Schmidt	1.25	.35
❑	B32	Billy Wagner	.50	.15
❑	B33	Rey Ordonez RC	3.00	.90
❑	B34	Curtis Goodwin	.50	.15
❑	B35	Sergio Nunez RC	1.00	.30
❑	B36	Tim Belk	.50	.15
❑	B37	Scott Elarton RC	2.00	.60
❑	B38	Jason Isringhausen	.50	.15
❑	B39	Trot Nixon	.50	.15
❑	B40	Sid Roberson RC	1.00	.30
❑	B41	Ron Villone	.50	.15
❑	B42	Ruben Rivera	.50	.15
❑	B43	Rick Huisman	.50	.15
❑	B44	Todd Hollandsworth	.50	.15
❑	B45	Johnny Damon	.75	.23
❑	B46	Garret Anderson	.50	.15
❑	B47	Jeff D'Amico	.50	.15
❑	B48	Dustin Hermanson	.50	.15
❑	B49	Juan Encarnacion RC	3.00	.90
❑	B50	Andy Pettitte	.75	.23
❑	B51	Chris Stynes	.50	.15
❑	B52	Troy Percival	.50	.15
❑	B53	LaTroy Hawkins	.50	.15
❑	B54	Roger Cedeno	.50	.15
❑	B55	Alan Benes	.50	.15
❑	B56	Karim Garcia RC	2.00	.60
❑	B57	Andrew Lorraine	.50	.15
❑	B58	Gary Rath RC	1.00	.30
❑	B59	Bret Wagner	.50	.15
❑	B60	Jeff Suppan	.50	.15
❑	B61	Bill Pulsipher	.50	.15
❑	B62	Jay Payton RC	3.00	.90
❑	B63	Alex Ochoa	.50	.15
❑	B64	Ugueth Urbina	.50	.15
❑	B65	Armando Benitez	.50	.15
❑	B66	George Arias	.50	.15
❑	B67	Raul Casanova RC	1.00	.30
❑	B68	Matt Drews	.50	.15
❑	B69	Jimmy Haynes	.50	.15
❑	B70	Jimmy Hurst	.50	.15
❑	B71	C.J. Nitkowski	.50	.15
❑	B72	Tommy Davis RC	1.00	.30
❑	B73	Bartolo Colon RC	5.00	1.50
❑	B74	Chris Carpenter RC	3.00	.90
❑	B75	Trey Beamon	.50	.15
❑	B76	Bryan Rekar	.50	.15
❑	B77	James Baldwin	.50	.15
❑	B78	Marc Valdes	.50	.15
❑	B79	Tom Fordham RC	1.00	.30
❑	B80	Marc Newfield	.50	.15
❑	B81	Angel Martinez	.50	.15
❑	B82	Brian L. Hunter	.50	.15
❑	B83	Jose Herrera	.50	.15
❑	B84	Glenn Dishman RC	1.00	.30
❑	B85	Jacob Cruz RC	2.00	.60
❑	B86	Paul Shuey	.50	.15
❑	B87	Scott Rolen RC	40.00	12.00
❑	B88	Doug Million	.50	.15
❑	B89	Desi Relaford	.50	.15
❑	B90	Michael Tucker	.50	.15
❑	R1	Randy Johnson	1.25	.35
❑	R2	Joe Carter	.50	.15
❑	R3	Chili Davis	.50	.15
❑	R4	Moises Alou	.50	.15
❑	R5	Gary Sheffield	.50	.15
❑	R6	Kevin Appier	.50	.15
❑	R7	Denny Neagle	.50	.15
❑	R8	Ruben Sierra	.50	.15
❑	R9	Darren Daulton	.50	.15
❑	R10	Cal Ripken	4.00	1.20
❑	R11	Bobby Bonilla	.50	.15
❑	R12	Manny Ramirez	.75	.23
❑	R13	Barry Bonds	3.00	.90
❑	R14	Eric Karros	.50	.15
❑	R15	Greg Maddux	2.00	.60
❑	R16	Jeff Bagwell	.75	.23
❑	R17	Paul Molitor	.75	.23
❑	R18	Ray Lankford	.50	.15
❑	R19	Mark Grace	.75	.23
❑	R20	Kenny Lofton	.50	.15
❑	R21	Tony Gwynn	1.50	.45
❑	R22	Will Clark	1.25	.35
❑	R23	Roger Clemens	2.50	.75
❑	R24	Dante Bichette	.50	.15
❑	R25	Barry Larkin	.75	.23
❑	R26	Wade Boggs	.75	.23
❑	R27	Kirby Puckett	1.25	.35
❑	R28	Cecil Fielder	.50	.15
❑	R29	Jose Canseco	1.25	.35
❑	R30	Juan Gonzalez	.75	.23
❑	R31	David Cone	.50	.15
❑	R32	Craig Biggio	.75	.23
❑	R33	Tim Salmon	.75	.23
❑	R34	David Justice	.50	.15
❑	R35	Sammy Sosa	2.00	.60
❑	R36	Mike Piazza	2.00	.60
❑	R37	Carlos Baerga	.50	.15
❑	R38	Jeff Conine	.50	.15
❑	R39	Rafael Palmeiro	.75	.23
❑	R40	Bret Saberhagen	.50	.15
❑	R41	Len Dykstra	.50	.15
❑	R42	Mo Vaughn	.50	.15
❑	R43	Wally Joyner	.50	.15
❑	R44	Chuck Knoblauch	.50	.15
❑	R45	Robin Ventura	.50	.15
❑	R46	Don Mattingly	3.00	.90
❑	R47	Dave Hollins	.50	.15
❑	R48	Andy Benes	.50	.15
❑	R49	Ken Griffey Jr.	2.00	.60
❑	R50	Albert Belle	.50	.15
❑	R51	Matt Williams	.50	.15

❑ R52	Rondell White	.50	.15
❑ R53	Raul Mondesi	.50	.15
❑ R54	Brian Jordan	.50	.15
❑ R55	Greg Vaughn	.50	.15
❑ R56	Fred McGriff	.75	.23
❑ R57	Roberto Alomar	.75	.23
❑ R58	Dennis Eckersley	.50	.15
❑ R59	Lee Smith	.50	.15
❑ R60	Eddie Murray	1.25	.35
❑ R61	Kenny Rogers	.50	.15
❑ R62	Ron Gant	.50	.15
❑ R63	Larry Walker	.75	.23
❑ R64	Chad Curtis	.50	.15
❑ R65	Frank Thomas	1.25	.35
❑ R66	Paul O'Neill	.75	.23
❑ R67	Kevin Seitzer	.50	.15
❑ R68	Marquis Grissom	.50	.15
❑ R69	Mark McGwire	4.00	1.20
❑ R70	Travis Fryman	.50	.15
❑ R71	Andres Galarraga	.50	.15
❑ R72	Carlos Perez RC	2.00	.60
❑ R73	Tyler Green	.50	.15
❑ R74	Marty Cordova	.50	.15
❑ R75	Shawn Green	.50	.15
❑ R76	Vaughn Eshelman	.50	.15
❑ R77	John Mabry	.50	.15
❑ R78	Jason Bates	.50	.15
❑ R79	Jon Nunnally	.50	.15
❑ R80	Ray Durham	.50	.15
❑ R81	Edgardo Alfonzo	.50	.15
❑ R82	Esteban Loaiza	.50	.15
❑ R83	Hideo Nomo RC	10.00	3.00
❑ R84	Orlando Miller	.50	.15
❑ R85	Alex Gonzalez	.50	.15
❑ R86	M.Grudzielanek RC	2.00	.60
❑ R87	Julian Tavarez	.50	.15
❑ R88	Benji Gil	.50	.15
❑ R89	Quilvio Veras	.50	.15
❑ R90	Ricky Bottalico	.50	.15
❑ X1	Ben Davis RC Ivan Rodriguez	1.50	.45
❑ X2	Mark Redman RC Manny Ramirez	1.50	.45
❑ X3	Reggie Taylor RC Deion Sanders	1.50	.45
❑ X4	Ryan Jaroncyk RC Shawn Green	.50	.15
❑ X5	Juan LeBron RC Juan Gonzalez UER Card pictures Carlos Beltran instead of Juan LeBron.	5.00	1.50
❑ X6	Tony McKnight RC Craig Biggio	.50	.15
❑ X7	Michael Barrett RC Travis Fryman	1.50	.45
❑ X8	Corey Jenkins RC Mo Vaughn	.50	.15
❑ X9	Ruben Rivera Frank Thomas	1.25	.35
❑ X10	Curtis Goodwin Kenny Lofton	.50	.15
❑ X11	Brian L. Hunter Tony Gwynn	.75	.23
❑ X12	Todd Greene Ken Griffey Jr.	1.25	.35
❑ X13	Karim Garcia Matt Williams	.50	.15
❑ X14	Billy Wagner Randy Johnson	.75	.23
❑ X15	Pat Watkins Jeff Bagwell	.75	.23

1996 Bowman's Best

		Nm-Mt	Ex-Mt
COMPLETE SET (180)		40.00	12.00
❑ 1	Hideo Nomo	1.00	.30
❑ 2	Edgar Martinez	.60	.18
❑ 3	Cal Ripken	3.00	.90
❑ 4	Wade Boggs	.60	.18
❑ 5	Cecil Fielder	.40	.12
❑ 6	Albert Belle	.40	.12
❑ 7	Chipper Jones	1.00	.30
❑ 8	Ryne Sandberg	1.50	.45
❑ 9	Tim Salmon	.60	.18

❑ 10	Barry Bonds	2.50	.75
❑ 11	Ken Caminiti	.40	.12
❑ 12	Ron Gant	.40	.12
❑ 13	Frank Thomas	1.00	.30
❑ 14	Dante Bichette	.40	.12
❑ 15	Jason Kendall	.40	.12
❑ 16	Mo Vaughn	.40	.12
❑ 17	Rey Ordonez	.40	.12
❑ 18	Henry Rodriguez	.40	.12
❑ 19	Ryan Klesko	.40	.12
❑ 20	Jeff Bagwell	.60	.18
❑ 21	Randy Johnson	1.00	.30
❑ 22	Jim Edmonds	.40	.12
❑ 23	Kenny Lofton	.40	.12
❑ 24	Andy Pettitte	.60	.18
❑ 25	Brady Anderson	.40	.12
❑ 26	Mike Piazza	1.50	.45
❑ 27	Greg Vaughn	.40	.12
❑ 28	Joe Carter	.40	.12
❑ 29	Jason Giambi	.40	.12
❑ 30	Ivan Rodriguez	1.00	.30
❑ 31	Jeff Conine	.40	.12
❑ 32	Rafael Palmeiro	.60	.18
❑ 33	Roger Clemens	2.00	.60
❑ 34	Chuck Knoblauch	.40	.12
❑ 35	Reggie Sanders	.40	.12
❑ 36	Andres Galarraga	.40	.12
❑ 37	Paul O'Neill	.60	.18
❑ 38	Tony Gwynn	1.25	.35
❑ 39	Paul Wilson	.40	.12
❑ 40	Garret Anderson	.40	.12
❑ 41	David Justice	.40	.12
❑ 42	Eddie Murray	1.00	.30
❑ 43	Mike Grace RC	.50	.15
❑ 44	Marty Cordova	.40	.12
❑ 45	Kevin Appier	.40	.12
❑ 46	Raul Mondesi	.40	.12
❑ 47	Jim Thome	1.00	.30
❑ 48	Sammy Sosa	1.50	.45
❑ 49	Craig Biggio	.60	.18
❑ 50	Marquis Grissom	.40	.12
❑ 51	Alan Benes	.40	.12
❑ 52	Manny Ramirez	.60	.18
❑ 53	Gary Sheffield	.40	.12
❑ 54	Mike Mussina	.60	.18
❑ 55	Robin Ventura	.40	.12
❑ 56	Johnny Damon	.60	.18
❑ 57	Jose Canseco	1.00	.30
❑ 58	Juan Gonzalez	.60	.18
❑ 59	Tino Martinez	.60	.18
❑ 60	Brian Hunter	.40	.12
❑ 61	Fred McGriff	.60	.18
❑ 62	Jay Buhner	.40	.12
❑ 63	Carlos Delgado	.40	.12
❑ 64	Moises Alou	.40	.12
❑ 65	Roberto Alomar	.60	.18
❑ 66	Barry Larkin	.60	.18
❑ 67	Vinny Castilla	.40	.12
❑ 68	Ray Durham	.40	.12
❑ 69	Travis Fryman	.40	.12
❑ 70	Jason Isringhausen	.40	.12
❑ 71	Ken Griffey Jr.	1.50	.45
❑ 72	John Smoltz	.60	.18
❑ 73	Matt Williams	.40	.12
❑ 74	Chan Ho Park	.40	.12
❑ 75	Mark McGwire	3.00	.90
❑ 76	Jeffrey Hammonds	.40	.12
❑ 77	Will Clark	1.00	.30
❑ 78	Kirby Puckett	1.00	.30
❑ 79	Derek Jeter	2.50	.75
❑ 80	Derek Bell	.40	.12
❑ 81	Eric Karros	.40	.12
❑ 82	Len Dykstra	.40	.12
❑ 83	Larry Walker	.60	.18
❑ 84	Mark Grudzielanek	.40	.12
❑ 85	Greg Maddux	1.50	.45
❑ 86	Carlos Baerga	.40	.12
❑ 87	Paul Molitor	.60	.18
❑ 88	John Valentin	.40	.12
❑ 89	Mark Grace	.60	.18
❑ 90	Ray Lankford	.40	.12
❑ 91	Andruw Jones	1.00	.30
❑ 92	Nomar Garciaparra	2.00	.60
❑ 93	Alex Ochoa	.40	.12
❑ 94	Derrick Gibson	.40	.12
❑ 95	Jeff D'Amico	.40	.12
❑ 96	Ruben Rivera	.40	.12
❑ 97	Vladimir Guerrero	2.00	.60
❑ 98	Pokey Reese	.40	.12
❑ 99	Richard Hidalgo	.40	.12
❑ 100	Bartolo Colon	.40	.12
❑ 101	Karim Garcia	.40	.12
❑ 102	Ben Davis	.40	.12
❑ 103	Jay Powell	.40	.12
❑ 104	Chris Snopek	.40	.12
❑ 105	Glendon Rusch RC	1.00	.30
❑ 106	Enrique Wilson	.40	.12
❑ 107	A.Alfonseca RC	1.00	.30
❑ 108	Wilton Guerrero RC	1.00	.30
❑ 109	Jose Guillen RC	4.00	1.20
❑ 110	Miguel Mejia RC	.50	.15
❑ 111	Jay Payton	.40	.12
❑ 112	Scott Elarton	.40	.12
❑ 113	Brooks Kieschnick	.40	.12
❑ 114	Dustin Hermanson	.40	.12
❑ 115	Roger Cedeno	.40	.12
❑ 116	Matt Wagner	.40	.12
❑ 117	Lee Daniels	.40	.12
❑ 118	Ben Grieve	.40	.12
❑ 119	Ugueth Urbina	.40	.12
❑ 120	Danny Graves	.40	.12
❑ 121	Dan Donato RC	.50	.15
❑ 122	Matt Ruebel RC	.50	.15
❑ 123	Mark Sievert RC	.50	.15
❑ 124	Chris Stynes	.40	.12
❑ 125	Jeff Abbott	.40	.12
❑ 126	Rocky Coppinger RC	.50	.15
❑ 127	Jermaine Dye	.40	.12
❑ 128	Todd Greene	.40	.12
❑ 129	Chris Carpenter	.40	.12
❑ 130	Edgar Renteria	.40	.12
❑ 131	Matt Drews	.40	.12
❑ 132	Edgard Velazquez RC	.50	.15
❑ 133	Casey Whitten	.40	.12
❑ 134	Ryan Jones RC	.50	.15
❑ 135	Todd Walker	.40	.12
❑ 136	Geoff Jenkins RC	2.50	.75
❑ 137	Matt Morris RC	4.00	1.20
❑ 138	Richie Sexson	.40	.12
❑ 139	Todd Dunwoody RC	.50	.15
❑ 140	Gabe Alvarez RC	.50	.15
❑ 141	J.J. Johnson	.40	.12
❑ 142	Shannon Stewart	.40	.12
❑ 143	Brad Fullmer	.40	.12
❑ 144	Julio Santana	.40	.12
❑ 145	Scott Rolen	1.00	.30
❑ 146	Amaury Telemaco	.40	.12
❑ 147	Trey Beamon	.40	.12
❑ 148	Billy Wagner	.40	.12
❑ 149	Todd Hollandsworth	.40	.12
❑ 150	Doug Million	.40	.12
❑ 151	Javier Valentin RC	.50	.15
❑ 152	Wes Helms RC	1.50	.45
❑ 153	Jeff Suppan	.40	.12
❑ 154	Luis Castillo RC	2.50	.75
❑ 155	Bob Abreu	.40	.12
❑ 156	Paul Konerko	.40	.12
❑ 157	Jamey Wright	.40	.12
❑ 158	Eddie Pearson	.40	.12
❑ 159	Jimmy Haynes	.40	.12
❑ 160	Derrek Lee	.40	.12
❑ 161	Damian Moss	.40	.12
❑ 162	Carlos Guillen RC	5.00	1.50
❑ 163	Chris Fussell RC	.50	.15

	Nm-Mt	Ex-Mt
❑ 164 Mike Sweeney RC	4.00	1.20
❑ 165 Donnie Sadler	.40	.12
❑ 166 Desi Relaford	.40	.12
❑ 167 Steve Gibralter	.40	.12
❑ 168 Neifi Perez	.40	.12
❑ 169 Antone Williamson	.40	.12
❑ 170 Marty Janzen RC	.50	.15
❑ 171 Todd Helton	2.00	.60
❑ 172 Raul Ibanez RC	1.50	.45
❑ 173 Bill Selby	.40	.12
❑ 174 Shane Monahan RC	.50	.15
❑ 175 Robin Jennings	.40	.12
❑ 176 Bobby Chouinard	.40	.12
❑ 177 Einar Diaz	.40	.12
❑ 178 Jason Thompson	.40	.12
❑ 179 Rafael Medina RC	.50	.15
❑ 180 Kevin Orie	.40	.12
❑ NNO Mickey Mantle 1952 Bowman Chrome	2.50	.75
❑ NNO Mickey Mantle 1952 Bowman Atomic Ref.	10.00	3.00
❑ NNO Mickey Mantle 1952 Bowman Refractor	5.00	1.50

1997 Bowman's Best

	Nm-Mt	Ex-Mt
COMPLETE SET (200)	40.00	12.00
❑ 1 Ken Griffey Jr.	1.50	.45
❑ 2 Cecil Fielder	.40	.12
❑ 3 Albert Belle	.40	.12
❑ 4 Todd Hundley	.40	.12
❑ 5 Mike Piazza	1.50	.45
❑ 6 Matt Williams	.40	.12
❑ 7 Mo Vaughn	.40	.12
❑ 8 Ryne Sandberg	1.50	.45
❑ 9 Chipper Jones	1.00	.30
❑ 10 Edgar Martinez	.60	.18
❑ 11 Kenny Lofton	.40	.12
❑ 12 Ron Gant	.40	.12
❑ 13 Moises Alou	.40	.12
❑ 14 Pat Hentgen	.40	.12
❑ 15 Steve Finley	.40	.12
❑ 16 Mark Grace	.60	.18
❑ 17 Jay Buhner	.40	.12
❑ 18 Jeff Conine	.40	.12
❑ 19 Jim Edmonds	.40	.12
❑ 20 Todd Hollandsworth	.40	.12
❑ 21 Andy Pettitte	.60	.18
❑ 22 Jim Thome	1.00	.30
❑ 23 Eric Young	.40	.12
❑ 24 Ray Lankford	.40	.12
❑ 25 Marquis Grissom	.40	.12
❑ 26 Tony Clark	.40	.12
❑ 27 Jermaine Allensworth	.40	.12
❑ 28 Ellis Burks	.40	.12
❑ 29 Tony Gwynn	1.25	.35
❑ 30 Barry Larkin	.60	.18
❑ 31 John Olerud	.40	.12
❑ 32 Mariano Rivera	.60	.18
❑ 33 Paul Molitor	.60	.18
❑ 34 Ken Caminiti	.40	.12
❑ 35 Gary Sheffield	.40	.12
❑ 36 Al Martin	.40	.12
❑ 37 John Valentin	.40	.12
❑ 38 Frank Thomas	1.00	.30
❑ 39 John Jaha	.40	.12
❑ 40 Greg Maddux	1.50	.45
❑ 41 Alex Fernandez	.40	.12
❑ 42 Dean Palmer	.40	.12
❑ 43 Bernie Williams	.60	.18
❑ 44 Deion Sanders	.60	.18
❑ 45 Mark McGwire	3.00	.90
❑ 46 Brian Jordan	.40	.12
❑ 47 Bernard Gilkey	.40	.12
❑ 48 Will Clark	1.00	.30
❑ 49 Kevin Appier	.40	.12
❑ 50 Tom Glavine	.60	.18
❑ 51 Chuck Knoblauch	.40	.12
❑ 52 Rondell White	.40	.12
❑ 53 Greg Vaughn	.40	.12
❑ 54 Mike Mussina	.60	.18
❑ 55 Brian McRae	.40	.12
❑ 56 Chili Davis	.40	.12
❑ 57 Wade Boggs	.60	.18
❑ 58 Jeff Bagwell	.60	.18
❑ 59 Roberto Alomar	.60	.18
❑ 60 Dennis Eckersley	.40	.12
❑ 61 Ryan Klesko	.40	.12
❑ 62 Manny Ramirez	.60	.18
❑ 63 John Wetteland	.40	.12
❑ 64 Cal Ripken	3.00	.90
❑ 65 Edgar Renteria	.40	.12
❑ 66 Tino Martinez	.60	.18
❑ 67 Larry Walker	.60	.18
❑ 68 Gregg Jefferies	.40	.12
❑ 69 Lance Johnson	.40	.12
❑ 70 Carlos Delgado	.40	.12
❑ 71 Craig Biggio	.60	.18
❑ 72 Jose Canseco	1.00	.30
❑ 73 Barry Bonds	2.50	.75
❑ 74 Juan Gonzalez	.60	.18
❑ 75 Eric Karros	.40	.12
❑ 76 Reggie Sanders	.40	.12
❑ 77 Robin Ventura	.40	.12
❑ 78 Hideo Nomo	1.00	.30
❑ 79 David Justice	.40	.12
❑ 80 Vinny Castilla	.40	.12
❑ 81 Travis Fryman	.40	.12
❑ 82 Derek Jeter	2.50	.75
❑ 83 Sammy Sosa	1.50	.45
❑ 84 Ivan Rodriguez	1.00	.30
❑ 85 Rafael Palmeiro	.60	.18
❑ 86 Roger Clemens	2.00	.60
❑ 87 Jason Giambi	.40	.12
❑ 88 Andres Galarraga	.40	.12
❑ 89 Jermaine Dye	.40	.12
❑ 90 Joe Carter	.40	.12
❑ 91 Brady Anderson	.40	.12
❑ 92 Derek Bell	.40	.12
❑ 93 Randy Johnson	1.00	.30
❑ 94 Fred McGriff	.60	.18
❑ 95 John Smoltz	.60	.18
❑ 96 Harold Baines	.40	.12
❑ 97 Raul Mondesi	.40	.12
❑ 98 Tim Salmon	.60	.18
❑ 99 Carlos Baerga	.40	.12
❑ 100 Dante Bichette	.40	.12
❑ 101 Vladimir Guerrero	1.00	.30
❑ 102 Richard Hidalgo	.40	.12
❑ 103 Paul Konerko	.40	.12
❑ 104 Alex Gonzalez RC	1.00	.30
❑ 105 Jason Dickson	.40	.12
❑ 106 Jose Rosado	.40	.12
❑ 107 Todd Walker	.40	.12
❑ 108 Seth Greisinger RC	.40	.12
❑ 109 Todd Helton	1.00	.30
❑ 110 Ben Davis	.40	.12
❑ 111 Bartolo Colon	.40	.12
❑ 112 Elieser Marrero	.40	.12
❑ 113 Jeff D'Amico	.40	.12
❑ 114 Miguel Tejada RC	6.00	1.80
❑ 115 Darin Erstad	.40	.12
❑ 116 Kris Benson RC	1.50	.45
❑ 117 Adrian Beltre RC	8.00	2.40
❑ 118 Neifi Perez	.40	.12
❑ 119 Pokey Reese	.40	.12
❑ 120 Carl Pavano	1.25	.12
❑ 121 Juan Melo	.40	.12
❑ 122 Kevin McGlinchy RC	.40	.12
❑ 123 Pat Cline	.40	.12
❑ 124 Felix Heredia RC	.40	.12
❑ 125 Aaron Boone	.40	.12
❑ 126 Glendon Rusch	.40	.12
❑ 127 Mike Cameron	.40	.12
❑ 128 Justin Thompson	.40	.12
❑ 129 Chad Hermansen RC	.60	.18
❑ 130 Sidney Ponson RC	1.00	.30
❑ 131 Willie Martinez RC	.40	.12
❑ 132 Paul Wilder RC	.40	.12
❑ 133 Geoff Jenkins	.40	.12
❑ 134 Roy Halladay RC	1.50	.45
❑ 135 Carlos Guillen	.40	.12
❑ 136 Tony Batista	.40	.12
❑ 137 Todd Greene	.40	.12
❑ 138 Luis Castillo	.40	.12
❑ 139 Jimmy Anderson RC	.40	.12
❑ 140 Edgard Velazquez	.40	.12
❑ 141 Chris Snopek	.40	.12
❑ 142 Ruben Rivera	.40	.12
❑ 143 Javier Valentin	.40	.12
❑ 144 Brian Rose	.40	.12
❑ 145 Fernando Tatis RC	.60	.18
❑ 146 Dean Crow RC	.40	.12
❑ 147 Karim Garcia	.40	.12
❑ 148 Dante Powell	.40	.12
❑ 149 Hideki Irabu RC	.60	.18
❑ 150 Matt Morris	.40	.12
❑ 151 Wes Helms	.40	.12
❑ 152 Russ Johnson	.40	.12
❑ 153 Jarrod Washburn	.40	.12
❑ 154 Kerry Wood RC	12.00	3.60
❑ 155 Joe Fontenot RC	.40	.12
❑ 156 Eugene Kingsale	.40	.12
❑ 157 Terrence Long	.40	.12
❑ 158 Calvin Maduro	.40	.12
❑ 159 Jeff Suppan	.40	.12
❑ 160 DaRond Stovall	.40	.12
❑ 161 Mark Redman	.40	.12
❑ 162 Ken Cloude RC	.60	.18
❑ 163 Bobby Estalella	.40	.12
❑ 164 Abraham Nunez RC	.40	.12
❑ 165 Derrick Gibson	.40	.12
❑ 166 Mike Drumright RC	.40	.12
❑ 167 Katsuhiro Maeda	.40	.12
❑ 168 Jeff Liefer	.40	.12
❑ 169 Ben Grieve	.40	.12
❑ 170 Bob Abreu	.40	.12
❑ 171 Shannon Stewart	.40	.12
❑ 172 Braden Looper RC	.40	.12
❑ 173 Brant Brown	.40	.12
❑ 174 Marlon Anderson	.40	.12
❑ 175 Brad Fullmer	.40	.12
❑ 176 Carlos Beltran	3.00	.90
❑ 177 Nomar Garciaparra	1.50	.45
❑ 178 Derrek Lee	.40	.12
❑ 179 Val.De Los Santos RC	.40	.12
❑ 180 Dmitri Young	.40	.12
❑ 181 Jamey Wright	.40	.12
❑ 182 Hiram Bocachica RC	.60	.18
❑ 183 Wilton Guerrero	.40	.12
❑ 184 Chris Carpenter	.40	.12
❑ 185 Scott Spiezio	.40	.12
❑ 186 Andruw Jones	.40	.12
❑ 187 Travis Lee RC	.60	.18
❑ 188 Jose Cruz Jr. RC	1.00	.30
❑ 189 Jose Guillen	.40	.12
❑ 190 Jeff Abbott	.40	.12
❑ 191 Ricky Ledee RC	.60	.18
❑ 192 Mike Sweeney	.40	.12
❑ 193 Donnie Sadler	.40	.12
❑ 194 Scott Rolen	1.00	.30
❑ 195 Kevin Orie	.40	.12
❑ 196 Jason Conti RC	.40	.12
❑ 197 Mark Kotsay RC	1.50	.45
❑ 198 Eric Milton RC	1.50	.45
❑ 199 Russell Branyan	.40	.12
❑ 200 Alex Sanchez RC	1.00	.30

1998 Bowman's Best

	Nm-Mt	Ex-Mt
COMPLETE SET (200)	40.00	12.00
❑ 1 Mark McGwire	2.50	.75
❑ 2 Jeromy Burnitz	.40	.12
❑ 3 Barry Bonds	2.50	.75
❑ 4 Dante Bichette	.40	.12
❑ 5 Chipper Jones	1.00	.30

Card	Nm-Mt	Ex-Mt
❑ 6 Frank Thomas	1.00	.30
❑ 7 Kevin Brown	.60	.18
❑ 8 Juan Gonzalez	.60	.18
❑ 9 Jay Buhner	.40	.12
❑ 10 Chuck Knoblauch	.40	.12
❑ 11 Cal Ripken	3.00	.90
❑ 12 Matt Williams	.40	.12
❑ 13 Jim Edmonds	.40	.12
❑ 14 Manny Ramirez	.60	.18
❑ 15 Tony Clark	.40	.12
❑ 16 Mo Vaughn	.40	.12
❑ 17 Bernie Williams	.60	.18
❑ 18 Scott Rolen	1.00	.30
❑ 19 Gary Sheffield	.40	.12
❑ 20 Albert Belle	.40	.12
❑ 21 Mike Piazza	1.50	.45
❑ 22 John Olerud	.40	.12
❑ 23 Tony Gwynn	1.25	.35
❑ 24 Jay Bell	.40	.12
❑ 25 Jose Cruz Jr.	.40	.12
❑ 26 Justin Thompson	.40	.12
❑ 27 Ken Griffey Jr.	1.50	.45
❑ 28 Sandy Alomar Jr.	.40	.12
❑ 29 Mark Grudzielanek	.40	.12
❑ 30 Mark Grace	.60	.18
❑ 31 Ron Gant	.40	.12
❑ 32 Javy Lopez	.40	.12
❑ 33 Jeff Bagwell	.60	.18
❑ 34 Fred McGriff	.60	.18
❑ 35 Rafael Palmeiro	.60	.18
❑ 36 Vinny Castilla	.40	.12
❑ 37 Andy Benes	.40	.12
❑ 38 Pedro Martinez	1.00	.30
❑ 39 Andy Pettitte	.60	.18
❑ 40 Marty Cordova	.40	.12
❑ 41 Rusty Greer	.40	.12
❑ 42 Kevin Orie	.40	.12
❑ 43 Chan Ho Park	.40	.12
❑ 44 Ryan Klesko	.40	.12
❑ 45 Alex Rodriguez	1.50	.45
❑ 46 Travis Fryman	.40	.12
❑ 47 Jeff King	.40	.12
❑ 48 Roger Clemens	2.00	.60
❑ 49 Darin Erstad	.40	.12
❑ 50 Brady Anderson	.40	.12
❑ 51 Jason Kendall	.40	.12
❑ 52 John Valentin	.40	.12
❑ 53 Ellis Burks	.40	.12
❑ 54 Brian Hunter	.40	.12
❑ 55 Paul O'Neill	.60	.18
❑ 56 Ken Caminiti	.40	.12
❑ 57 David Justice	.40	.12
❑ 58 Eric Karros	.40	.12
❑ 59 Pat Hentgen	.40	.12
❑ 60 Greg Maddux	1.50	.45
❑ 61 Craig Biggio	.60	.18
❑ 62 Edgar Martinez	.60	.18
❑ 63 Mike Mussina	.60	.18
❑ 64 Larry Walker	.60	.18
❑ 65 Tino Martinez	.60	.18
❑ 66 Jim Thome	1.00	.30
❑ 67 Tom Glavine	.60	.18
❑ 68 Raul Mondesi	.40	.12
❑ 69 Marquis Grissom	.40	.12
❑ 70 Randy Johnson	1.00	.30
❑ 71 Steve Finley	.40	.12
❑ 72 Jose Guillen	.40	.12
❑ 73 Nomar Garciaparra	1.50	.45
❑ 74 Wade Boggs	.60	.18
❑ 75 Bobby Higginson	.40	.12
❑ 76 Robin Ventura	.40	.12
❑ 77 Derek Jeter	2.50	.75
❑ 78 Andruw Jones	.40	.12
❑ 79 Ray Lankford	.40	.12
❑ 80 Vladimir Guerrero	1.00	.30
❑ 81 Kenny Lofton	.40	.12
❑ 82 Ivan Rodriguez	1.00	.30
❑ 83 Neifi Perez	.40	.12
❑ 84 John Smoltz	.60	.18
❑ 85 Tim Salmon	.60	.18
❑ 86 Carlos Delgado	.40	.12
❑ 87 Sammy Sosa	1.50	.45
❑ 88 Jaret Wright	.40	.12
❑ 89 Roberto Alomar	.60	.18
❑ 90 Paul Molitor	.60	.18
❑ 91 Dean Palmer	.40	.12
❑ 92 Barry Larkin	.60	.18
❑ 93 Jason Giambi	.40	.12
❑ 94 Curt Schilling	.40	.12
❑ 95 Eric Young	.40	.12
❑ 96 Denny Neagle	.40	.12
❑ 97 Moises Alou	.40	.12
❑ 98 Livan Hernandez	.40	.12
❑ 99 Todd Hundley	.40	.12
❑ 100 Andres Galarraga	.40	.12
❑ 101 Travis Lee	.40	.12
❑ 102 Lance Berkman	.60	.18
❑ 103 Orlando Cabrera	.40	.12
❑ 104 Mike Lowell RC	3.00	.90
❑ 105 Ben Grieve	.40	.12
❑ 106 Jae Weong Seo RC	1.00	.30
❑ 107 Richie Sexson	.40	.12
❑ 108 Eli Marrero	.40	.12
❑ 109 Aramis Ramirez	.40	.12
❑ 110 Paul Konerko	.40	.12
❑ 111 Carl Pavano	.60	.12
❑ 112 Brad Fullmer	.40	.12
❑ 113 Matt Clement	.40	.12
❑ 114 Donzell McDonald	.40	.12
❑ 115 Todd Helton	.60	.18
❑ 116 Mike Caruso	.40	.12
❑ 117 Donnie Sadler	.40	.12
❑ 118 Bruce Chen	.40	.12
❑ 119 Jarrod Washburn	.40	.12
❑ 120 Adrian Beltre	1.00	.30
❑ 121 Ryan Jackson RC	.40	.12
❑ 122 Kevin Millar RC	3.00	.90
❑ 123 Corey Koskie RC	1.50	.45
❑ 124 Dermal Brown	.40	.12
❑ 125 Kerry Wood	1.00	.30
❑ 126 Juan Melo	.40	.12
❑ 127 Ramon Hernandez	.40	.12
❑ 128 Roy Halladay	.40	.12
❑ 129 Ron Wright	.40	.12
❑ 130 Darnell McDonald RC	.60	.18
❑ 131 Odalis Perez RC	1.50	.45
❑ 132 Alex Cora RC	.60	.18
❑ 133 Justin Towle	.40	.12
❑ 134 Juan Encarnacion	.40	.12
❑ 135 Brian Rose	.40	.12
❑ 136 Russell Branyan	.40	.12
❑ 137 Cesar King RC	.40	.12
❑ 138 Ruben Rivera	.40	.12
❑ 139 Ricky Ledee	.40	.12
❑ 140 Vernon Wells	.40	.12
❑ 141 Luis Rivas RC	1.50	.45
❑ 142 Brent Butler	.40	.12
❑ 143 Karim Garcia	.40	.12
❑ 144 George Lombard	.40	.12
❑ 145 Masato Yoshii RC	1.00	.30
❑ 146 Braden Looper	.40	.12
❑ 147 Alex Sanchez	.40	.12
❑ 148 Kris Benson	.40	.12
❑ 149 Mark Kotsay	.40	.12
❑ 150 Richard Hidalgo	.40	.12
❑ 151 Scott Elarton	.40	.12
❑ 152 Ryan Minor RC	.40	.12
❑ 153 Troy Glaus RC	3.00	.90
❑ 154 Carlos Lee RC	1.50	.45
❑ 155 Michael Coleman	.40	.12
❑ 156 Jason Grilli RC	.40	.12
❑ 157 Julio Ramirez RC	.40	.12
❑ 158 Randy Wolf RC	1.00	.30
❑ 159 Ryan Brannan	.40	.12
❑ 160 Edgard Clemente	.40	.12
❑ 161 Miguel Tejada	.40	.12
❑ 162 Chad Hermansen	.40	.12
❑ 163 Ryan Anderson RC	.60	.18
❑ 164 Ben Petrick	.40	.12
❑ 165 Alex Gonzalez	.40	.12
❑ 166 Ben Davis	.40	.12
❑ 167 John Patterson	.40	.12
❑ 168 Cliff Politte	.40	.12
❑ 169 Randall Simon	.40	.12
❑ 170 Javier Vazquez	.40	.12
❑ 171 Kevin Witt	.40	.12
❑ 172 Geoff Jenkins	.40	.12
❑ 173 David Ortiz	2.00	.60
❑ 174 Derrick Gibson	.40	.12
❑ 175 Abraham Nunez	.40	.12
❑ 176 A.J. Hinch	.40	.12
❑ 177 Ruben Mateo RC	.60	.18
❑ 178 Magglio Ordonez RC	3.00	.90
❑ 179 Todd Dunwoody	.40	.12
❑ 180 Daryle Ward	.40	.12
❑ 181 Mike Kinkade RC	.40	.12
❑ 182 Willie Martinez	.40	.12
❑ 183 O.Hernandez RC	1.50	.45
❑ 184 Eric Milton	.40	.12
❑ 185 Eric Chavez	.40	.12
❑ 186 Damian Jackson	.40	.12
❑ 187 Jim Parque RC	.60	.18
❑ 188 Dan Reichert RC	.60	.18
❑ 189 Mike Drumright	.40	.12
❑ 190 Todd Walker	.40	.12
❑ 191 Shane Monahan	.40	.12
❑ 192 Derrek Lee	.40	.12
❑ 193 Jeremy Giambi RC	.60	.18
❑ 194 Dan McKinley RC	.40	.12
❑ 195 Tony Armas Jr. RC	.60	.18
❑ 196 Matt Anderson RC	.60	.18
❑ 197 Jim Chamblee RC	.40	.12
❑ 198 F.Cordero RC	1.00	.30
❑ 199 Calvin Pickering	.40	.12
❑ 200 Reggie Taylor	.40	.12

1999 Bowman's Best

	Nm-Mt	Ex-Mt
COMPLETE SET (200)	50.00	15.00
COMP.SET w/o SP's (150)	25.00	7.50
COMMON CARD (1-150)	.40	.12
COMMON (151-200)	.50	.15

Card	Nm-Mt	Ex-Mt
❑ 1 Chipper Jones	1.00	.30
❑ 2 Brian Jordan	.40	.12
❑ 3 David Justice	.40	.12
❑ 4 Jason Kendall	.40	.12
❑ 5 Mo Vaughn	.40	.12
❑ 6 Jim Edmonds	.40	.12
❑ 7 Wade Boggs	.60	.18
❑ 8 Jeromy Burnitz	.40	.12
❑ 9 Todd Hundley	.40	.12
❑ 10 Rondell White	.40	.12
❑ 11 Cliff Floyd	.40	.12
❑ 12 Sean Casey	.40	.12
❑ 13 Bernie Williams	.60	.18
❑ 14 Dante Bichette	.40	.12
❑ 15 Greg Vaughn	.40	.12
❑ 16 Andres Galarraga	.40	.12
❑ 17 Ray Durham	.40	.12
❑ 18 Jim Thome	1.00	.30

Card	Nm-Mt	Ex-Mt
❑ 19 Gary Sheffield	.40	.12
❑ 20 Frank Thomas	1.00	.30
❑ 21 Orlando Hernandez	.40	.12
❑ 22 Ivan Rodriguez	1.00	.30
❑ 23 Jose Cruz Jr.	.40	.12
❑ 24 Jason Giambi	.40	.12
❑ 25 Craig Biggio	.60	.18
❑ 26 Kerry Wood	1.00	.30
❑ 27 Manny Ramirez	.60	.18
❑ 28 Curt Schilling	.40	.12
❑ 29 Mike Mussina	.60	.18
❑ 30 Tim Salmon	.60	.18
❑ 31 Mike Piazza	1.50	.45
❑ 32 Roberto Alomar	.60	.18
❑ 33 Larry Walker	.60	.18
❑ 34 Barry Larkin	.60	.18
❑ 35 Nomar Garciaparra	1.50	.45
❑ 36 Paul O'Neill	.60	.18
❑ 37 Todd Walker	.40	.12
❑ 38 Eric Karros	.40	.12
❑ 39 Brad Fullmer	.40	.12
❑ 40 John Olerud	.40	.12
❑ 41 Todd Helton	.60	.18
❑ 42 Raul Mondesi	.40	.12
❑ 43 Jose Canseco	1.00	.30
❑ 44 Matt Williams	.40	.12
❑ 45 Ray Lankford	.40	.12
❑ 46 Carlos Delgado	.40	.12
❑ 47 Darin Erstad	.40	.12
❑ 48 Vladimir Guerrero	1.00	.30
❑ 49 Robin Ventura	.40	.12
❑ 50 Alex Rodriguez	1.50	.45
❑ 51 Vinny Castilla	.40	.12
❑ 52 Tony Clark	.40	.12
❑ 53 Pedro Martinez	1.00	.30
❑ 54 Rafael Palmeiro	.60	.18
❑ 55 Scott Rolen	1.00	.30
❑ 56 Tino Martinez	.60	.18
❑ 57 Tony Gwynn	1.25	.35
❑ 58 Barry Bonds	2.50	.75
❑ 59 Kenny Lofton	.40	.12
❑ 60 Javy Lopez	.40	.12
❑ 61 Mark Grace	.60	.18
❑ 62 Travis Lee	.40	.12
❑ 63 Kevin Brown	.60	.18
❑ 64 Al Leiter	.40	.12
❑ 65 Albert Belle	.40	.12
❑ 66 Sammy Sosa	1.50	.45
❑ 67 Greg Maddux	1.50	.45
❑ 68 Mark Kotsay	.40	.12
❑ 69 Dmitri Young	.40	.12
❑ 70 Mark McGwire	2.50	.75
❑ 71 Juan Gonzalez	.60	.18
❑ 72 Andruw Jones	.40	.12
❑ 73 Derek Jeter	2.50	.75
❑ 74 Randy Johnson	1.00	.30
❑ 75 Cal Ripken	3.00	.90
❑ 76 Shawn Green	.40	.12
❑ 77 Moises Alou	.40	.12
❑ 78 Tom Glavine	.60	.18
❑ 79 Sandy Alomar Jr.	.40	.12
❑ 80 Ken Griffey Jr.	1.50	.45
❑ 81 Ryan Klesko	.40	.12
❑ 82 Jeff Bagwell	.60	.18
❑ 83 Ben Grieve	.40	.12
❑ 84 John Smoltz	.60	.18
❑ 85 Roger Clemens	2.00	.60
❑ 86 Ken Griffey Jr. BP	1.00	.30
❑ 87 Roger Clemens BP	1.00	.30
❑ 88 Derek Jeter BP	1.25	.35
❑ 89 Nomar Garciaparra BP	.75	.23
❑ 90 Mark McGwire BP	1.25	.35
❑ 91 Sammy Sosa BP	1.00	.30
❑ 92 Alex Rodriguez BP	.75	.23
❑ 93 Greg Maddux BP	.75	.23
❑ 94 Vladimir Guerrero BP	.60	.18
❑ 95 Chipper Jones BP	.60	.18
❑ 96 Kerry Wood BP	.60	.18
❑ 97 Ben Grieve BP	.40	.12
❑ 98 Tony Gwynn BP	.60	.18
❑ 99 Juan Gonzalez BP	.40	.12
❑ 100 Mike Piazza BP	.75	.23
❑ 101 Eric Chavez	.40	.12
❑ 102 Billy Koch	.40	.12
❑ 103 Dernell Stenson	.40	.12
❑ 104 Marlon Anderson	.40	.12
❑ 105 Ron Belliard	.40	.12
❑ 106 Bruce Chen	.40	.12
❑ 107 Carlos Beltran	.60	.18
❑ 108 Chad Hermansen	.40	.12
❑ 109 Ryan Anderson	.40	.12
❑ 110 Michael Barrett	.40	.12
❑ 111 Matt Clement	.40	.12
❑ 112 Ben Davis	.40	.12
❑ 113 Calvin Pickering	.40	.12
❑ 114 Brad Penny	.40	.12
❑ 115 Paul Konerko	.40	.12
❑ 116 Alex Gonzalez	.40	.12
❑ 117 George Lombard	.40	.12
❑ 118 John Patterson	.40	.12
❑ 119 Rob Bell	.40	.12
❑ 120 Ruben Mateo	.40	.12
❑ 121 Troy Glaus	.40	.12
❑ 122 Ryan Bradley	.40	.12
❑ 123 Carlos Lee	.40	.12
❑ 124 Gabe Kapler	.40	.12
❑ 125 Ramon Hernandez	.40	.12
❑ 126 Carlos Febles	.40	.12
❑ 127 Mitch Meluskey	.40	.12
❑ 128 Michael Cuddyer	.40	.12
❑ 129 Pablo Ozuna	.40	.12
❑ 130 Jayson Werth	.40	.12
❑ 131 Ricky Ledee	.40	.12
❑ 132 Jeremy Giambi	.40	.12
❑ 133 Danny Klassen	.40	.12
❑ 134 Mark DeRosa	.40	.12
❑ 135 Randy Wolf	.40	.12
❑ 136 Roy Halladay	.40	.12
❑ 137 Derrick Gibson	.40	.12
❑ 138 Ben Petrick	.40	.12
❑ 139 Warren Morris	.40	.12
❑ 140 Lance Berkman	.40	.12
❑ 141 Russell Branyan	.40	.12
❑ 142 Adrian Beltre	.60	.18
❑ 143 Juan Encarnacion	.40	.12
❑ 144 Fernando Seguignol	.40	.12
❑ 145 Corey Koskie	.40	.12
❑ 146 Preston Wilson	.40	.12
❑ 147 Homer Bush	.40	.12
❑ 148 Daryle Ward	.40	.12
❑ 149 Joe McEwing RC	.50	.15
❑ 150 Peter Bergeron RC	.50	.15
❑ 151 Pat Burrell RC	2.50	.75
❑ 152 Choo Freeman RC	.50	.15
❑ 153 Matt Belisle RC	.50	.15
❑ 154 Carlos Pena RC	.75	.23
❑ 155 A.J. Burnett RC	1.25	.35
❑ 156 D.Mientkiewicz RC	1.25	.35
❑ 157 Sean Burroughs RC	2.00	.60
❑ 158 Mike Zywica RC	.50	.15
❑ 159 Corey Patterson RC	3.00	.90
❑ 160 Austin Kearns RC	4.00	1.20
❑ 161 Chip Ambres RC	.50	.15
❑ 162 Kelly Dransfeldt RC	.50	.15
❑ 163 Mike Nannini RC	.50	.15
❑ 164 Mark Mulder RC	3.00	.75
❑ 165 Jason Tyner RC	.50	.15
❑ 166 Bobby Seay RC	.50	.15
❑ 167 Alex Escobar RC	.50	.15
❑ 168 Nick Johnson RC	1.25	.35
❑ 169 Alfonso Soriano RC	8.00	2.40
❑ 170 Clayton Andrews RC	.50	.15
❑ 171 C.C. Sabathia RC	1.50	.45
❑ 172 Matt Holliday RC	1.25	.35
❑ 173 Brad Lidge RC	2.50	.75
❑ 174 Kit Pellow RC	.50	.15
❑ 175 J.M. Gold RC	.50	.15
❑ 176 Roosevelt Brown RC	.50	.15
❑ 177 Eric Valent RC	.50	.15
❑ 178 Adam Everett RC	.75	.23
❑ 179 Jorge Toca RC	.50	.15
❑ 180 Matt Roney RC	.50	.15
❑ 181 Andy Brown RC	.50	.15
❑ 182 Phil Norton RC	.50	.15
❑ 183 Mickey Lopez RC	.50	.15
❑ 184 Chris George RC	.50	.15
❑ 185 Arturo McDowell RC	.50	.15
❑ 186 Jose Fernandez RC	.50	.15
❑ 187 Seth Etherton RC	.50	.15
❑ 188 Josh McKinley RC	.50	.15
❑ 189 Nate Cornejo RC	.50	.15
❑ 190 G.Chiaramonte RC	.50	.15
❑ 191 Mamon Tucker RC	.50	.15
❑ 192 Ryan Mills RC	.50	.15
❑ 193 Chad Moeller RC	.50	.15
❑ 194 Tony Torcato RC	.50	.15
❑ 195 Jeff Winchester RC	.50	.15
❑ 196 Rick Elder RC	.50	.15
❑ 197 Matt Burch RC	.50	.15
❑ 198 Jeff Urban RC	.50	.15
❑ 199 Chris Jones RC	.50	.15
❑ 200 Masao Kida RC	.50	.15

2000 Bowman's Best

	Nm-Mt	Ex-Mt
COMP.SET w/o RC's (150)	40.00	12.00
COMMON CARD (1-150)	.40	.12
COMMON (151-200)	5.00	1.50

Card	Nm-Mt	Ex-Mt
❑ 1 Nomar Garciaparra	1.50	.45
❑ 2 Chipper Jones	1.00	.30
❑ 3 Tony Clark	.40	.12
❑ 4 Bernie Williams	.60	.18
❑ 5 Barry Bonds	2.50	.75
❑ 6 Jermaine Dye	.40	.12
❑ 7 John Olerud	.40	.12
❑ 8 Mike Hampton	.40	.12
❑ 9 Cal Ripken	3.00	.90
❑ 10 Jeff Bagwell	.60	.18
❑ 11 Troy Glaus	.40	.12
❑ 12 J.D. Drew	.40	.12
❑ 13 Jeromy Burnitz	.40	.12
❑ 14 Carlos Delgado	.40	.12
❑ 15 Shawn Green	.40	.12
❑ 16 Kevin Millwood	.40	.12
❑ 17 Rondell White	.40	.12
❑ 18 Scott Rolen	1.00	.30
❑ 19 Jeff Cirillo	.40	.12
❑ 20 Barry Larkin	.60	.18
❑ 21 Brian Giles	.40	.12
❑ 22 Roger Clemens	2.00	.60
❑ 23 Manny Ramirez	.60	.18
❑ 24 Alex Gonzalez	.40	.12
❑ 25 Mark Grace	.60	.18
❑ 26 Fernando Tatis	.40	.12
❑ 27 Randy Johnson	1.00	.30
❑ 28 Roger Cedeno	.40	.12
❑ 29 Brian Jordan	.40	.12
❑ 30 Kevin Brown	.40	.12
❑ 31 Greg Vaughn	.40	.12
❑ 32 Roberto Alomar	.60	.18
❑ 33 Larry Walker	.60	.18
❑ 34 Rafael Palmeiro	.60	.18
❑ 35 Curt Schilling	.40	.12
❑ 36 Orlando Hernandez	.40	.12
❑ 37 Todd Walker	.40	.12
❑ 38 Juan Gonzalez	.60	.18
❑ 39 Sean Casey	.40	.12
❑ 40 Tony Gwynn	1.25	.35
❑ 41 Albert Belle	.40	.12
❑ 42 Gary Sheffield	.40	.12
❑ 43 Michael Barrett	.40	.12
❑ 44 Preston Wilson	.40	.12
❑ 45 Jim Thome	1.00	.30
❑ 46 Shannon Stewart	.40	.12
❑ 47 Mo Vaughn	.40	.12
❑ 48 Ben Grieve	.40	.12
❑ 49 Adrian Beltre	.60	.18
❑ 50 Sammy Sosa	1.50	.45

❑ 51 Bob Abreu	.40	.12
❑ 52 Edgardo Alfonzo	.40	.12
❑ 53 Carlos Febles	.40	.12
❑ 54 Frank Thomas	1.00	.30
❑ 55 Alex Rodriguez	1.50	.45
❑ 56 Cliff Floyd	.40	.12
❑ 57 Jose Canseco	1.00	.30
❑ 58 Erubiel Durazo	.40	.12
❑ 59 Tim Hudson	.40	.12
❑ 60 Craig Biggio	.60	.18
❑ 61 Eric Karros	.40	.12
❑ 62 Mike Mussina	.60	.18
❑ 63 Robin Ventura	.40	.12
❑ 64 Carlos Beltran	.60	.18
❑ 65 Pedro Martinez	1.00	.30
❑ 66 Gabe Kapler	.40	.12
❑ 67 Jason Kendall	.40	.12
❑ 68 Derek Jeter	2.50	.75
❑ 69 Magglio Ordonez	.40	.12
❑ 70 Mike Piazza	1.50	.45
❑ 71 Mike Lieberthal	.40	.12
❑ 72 Andres Galarraga	.40	.12
❑ 73 Raul Mondesi	.40	.12
❑ 74 Eric Chavez	.40	.12
❑ 75 Greg Maddux	1.50	.45
❑ 76 Matt Williams	.40	.12
❑ 77 Kris Benson	.40	.12
❑ 78 Ivan Rodriguez	1.00	.30
❑ 79 Pokey Reese	.40	.12
❑ 80 Vladimir Guerrero	1.00	.30
❑ 81 Mark McGwire	2.50	.75
❑ 82 Vinny Castilla	.40	.12
❑ 83 Todd Helton	.60	.18
❑ 84 Andruw Jones	.40	.12
❑ 85 Ken Griffey Jr.	1.50	.45
❑ 86 Mark McGwire BP	1.25	.35
❑ 87 Derek Jeter BP	1.25	.35
❑ 88 Chipper Jones BP	.60	.18
❑ 89 Nomar Garciaparra BP	1.00	.30
❑ 90 Sammy Sosa BP	1.00	.30
❑ 91 Cal Ripken BP	1.50	.45
❑ 92 Juan Gonzalez BP	.40	.12
❑ 93 Alex Rodriguez BP	1.00	.30
❑ 94 Barry Bonds BP	1.25	.35
❑ 95 Sean Casey BP	.40	.12
❑ 96 Vladimir Guerrero BP	.60	.18
❑ 97 Mike Piazza BP	1.00	.30
❑ 98 Shawn Green BP	.40	.12
❑ 99 Jeff Bagwell BP	.40	.12
❑ 100 Ken Griffey Jr. BP	1.00	.30
❑ 101 Rick Ankiel	.40	.12
❑ 102 John Patterson	.40	.12
❑ 103 David Walling	.40	.12
❑ 104 Michael Restovich	.40	.12
❑ 105 A.J. Burnett	.40	.12
❑ 106 Pablo Ozuna	.40	.12
❑ 107 Chad Hermansen	.40	.12
❑ 108 Choo Freeman	.40	.12
❑ 109 Mark Quinn	.40	.12
❑ 110 Corey Patterson	.40	.12
❑ 111 Ramon Ortiz	.40	.12
❑ 112 Vernon Wells	.40	.12
❑ 113 Milton Bradley	.40	.12
❑ 114 Gookie Dawkins	.40	.12
❑ 115 Sean Burroughs	.40	.12
❑ 116 Wily Mo Pena	.40	.12
❑ 117 Dee Brown	.40	.12
❑ 118 C.C. Sabathia	.40	.12
❑ 119 Adam Kennedy	.40	.12
❑ 120 Octavio Dotel	.40	.12
❑ 121 Kip Wells	.40	.12
❑ 122 Ben Petrick	.40	.12
❑ 123 Mark Mulder	.40	.12
❑ 124 Jason Standridge	.40	.12
❑ 125 Adam Piatt	.40	.12
❑ 126 Steve Lomasney	.40	.12
❑ 127 Jayson Werth	.40	.12
❑ 128 Alex Escobar	.40	.12
❑ 129 Ryan Anderson	.40	.12
❑ 130 Adam Dunn	1.00	.30
❑ 131 Ted Lilly	.40	.12
❑ 132 Brad Penny	.40	.12
❑ 133 Daryle Ward	.40	.12
❑ 134 Eric Munson	.40	.12
❑ 135 Nick Johnson	.40	.12
❑ 136 Jason Jennings	.40	.12
❑ 137 Tim Raines Jr.	.40	.12
❑ 138 Ruben Mateo	.40	.12
❑ 139 Jack Cust	.40	.12
❑ 140 Rafael Furcal	.40	.12
❑ 141 Eric Gagne	1.50	.45
❑ 142 Tony Armas Jr.	.40	.12
❑ 143 Mike Paradis	.40	.12
❑ 144 Peter Bergeron	.40	.12
❑ 145 Alfonso Soriano	1.00	.30
❑ 146 Josh Hamilton	.40	.12
❑ 147 Michael Cuddyer	.40	.12
❑ 148 Jay Gehrke	.40	.12
❑ 149 Josh Girdley	.40	.12
❑ 150 Pat Burrell	.40	.12
❑ 151 Brett Myers RC	8.00	2.40
❑ 152 Scott Seabol RC	5.00	1.50
❑ 153 Keith Reed RC	5.00	1.50
❑ 154 F.Rodriguez RC	25.00	7.50
❑ 155 Barry Zito RC	20.00	6.00
❑ 156 Pat Manning RC	5.00	1.50
❑ 157 Ben Christensen RC	5.00	1.50
❑ 158 Corey Myers RC	5.00	1.50
❑ 159 Wascar Serrano RC	5.00	1.50
❑ 160 Wes Anderson RC	5.00	1.50
❑ 161 Andy Tracy RC	5.00	1.50
❑ 162 Cesar Saba RC	5.00	1.50
❑ 163 Mike Lamb RC	5.00	1.50
❑ 164 Bobby Bradley RC	5.00	1.50
❑ 165 Vince Faison RC	5.00	1.50
❑ 166 Ty Howington RC	5.00	1.50
❑ 167 Ken Harvey RC UER Card has pitching stats on the back	8.00	2.40
❑ 168 Josh Kalinowski RC	5.00	1.50
❑ 169 Ruben Salazar RC	5.00	1.50
❑ 170 Aaron Rowand RC	10.00	3.00
❑ 171 Ramon Santiago RC	5.00	1.50
❑ 172 Scott Sobkowiak RC	5.00	1.50
❑ 173 Lyle Overbay RC	10.00	3.00
❑ 174 Rico Washington RC	5.00	1.50
❑ 175 Rick Asadoorian RC	5.00	1.50
❑ 176 Matt Ginter RC	5.00	1.50
❑ 177 Jason Stumm RC	5.00	1.50
❑ 178 B.J. Garbe RC	5.00	1.50
❑ 179 Mike MacDougal RC	5.00	1.50
❑ 180 Ryan Christianson RC	5.00	1.50
❑ 181 Kurt Ainsworth RC	5.00	1.50
❑ 182 Brad Baisley RC	5.00	1.50
❑ 183 Ben Broussard RC	8.00	2.40
❑ 184 Aaron McNeal RC	5.00	1.50
❑ 185 John Sneed RC	5.00	1.50
❑ 186 Junior Brignac RC	5.00	1.50
❑ 187 Chance Caple RC	5.00	1.50
❑ 188 Scott Downs RC	5.00	1.50
❑ 189 Matt Cepicky RC	5.00	1.50
❑ 190 Chin-Feng Chen RC	25.00	7.50
❑ 191 Johan Santana RC	50.00	15.00
❑ 192 Brad Baker RC	5.00	1.50
❑ 193 Jason Repko RC	5.00	1.50
❑ 194 Craig Dingman RC	5.00	1.50
❑ 195 Chris Wakeland RC	5.00	1.50
❑ 196 Rogelio Arias RC	5.00	1.50
❑ 197 Luis Matos RC	5.00	1.50
❑ 198 Rob Ramsay	5.00	1.50
❑ 199 Willie Bloomquist RC	25.00	7.50
❑ 200 Tony Pena Jr. RC	5.00	1.50

2001 Bowman's Best

	Nm-Mt	Ex-Mt
COMP.SET w/o SP's (150)	50.00	15.00
COMMON CARD (1-150)	.40	.12
COMMON (151-200)	5.00	1.50
❑ 1 Vladimir Guerrero	1.00	.30
❑ 2 Miguel Tejada	.40	.12
❑ 3 Geoff Jenkins	.40	.12
❑ 4 Jeff Bagwell	.60	.18
❑ 5 Todd Helton	.60	.18
❑ 6 Ken Griffey Jr.	1.50	.45
❑ 7 Nomar Garciaparra	1.50	.45
❑ 8 Chipper Jones	1.00	.30
❑ 9 Darin Erstad	.40	.12
❑ 10 Frank Thomas	1.00	.30
❑ 11 Jim Thome	1.00	.30
❑ 12 Preston Wilson	.40	.12
❑ 13 Kevin Brown	.40	.12
❑ 14 Derek Jeter	2.50	.75
❑ 15 Scott Rolen	1.00	.30
❑ 16 Ryan Klesko	.40	.12
❑ 17 Jeff Kent	.40	.12
❑ 18 Raul Mondesi	.40	.12
❑ 19 Greg Vaughn	.40	.12
❑ 20 Bernie Williams	.60	.18
❑ 21 Mike Piazza	1.50	.45
❑ 22 Richard Hidalgo	.40	.12
❑ 23 Dean Palmer	.40	.12
❑ 24 Roberto Alomar	.60	.18
❑ 25 Sammy Sosa	1.50	.45
❑ 26 Randy Johnson	1.00	.30
❑ 27 Manny Ramirez	.60	.18
❑ 28 Roger Clemens	2.00	.60
❑ 29 Terrence Long	.40	.12
❑ 30 Jason Kendall	.40	.12
❑ 31 Richie Sexson	.40	.12
❑ 32 David Wells	.40	.12
❑ 33 Andruw Jones	.40	.12
❑ 34 Pokey Reese	.40	.12
❑ 35 Juan Gonzalez	.60	.18
❑ 36 Carlos Beltran	.60	.18
❑ 37 Shawn Green	.40	.12
❑ 38 Mariano Rivera	.60	.18
❑ 39 John Olerud	.40	.12
❑ 40 Jim Edmonds	.40	.12
❑ 41 Andres Galarraga	.40	.12
❑ 42 Carlos Delgado	.40	.12
❑ 43 Kris Benson	.40	.12
❑ 44 Andy Pettitte	.60	.18
❑ 45 Jeff Cirillo	.40	.12
❑ 46 Magglio Ordonez	.40	.12
❑ 47 Tom Glavine	.60	.18
❑ 48 Garret Anderson	.40	.12
❑ 49 Cal Ripken	3.00	.90
❑ 50 Pedro Martinez	1.00	.30
❑ 51 Barry Bonds	2.50	.75
❑ 52 Alex Rodriguez	1.50	.45
❑ 53 Ben Grieve	.40	.12
❑ 54 Edgar Martinez	.60	.18
❑ 55 Jason Giambi	.40	.12
❑ 56 Jeromy Burnitz	.40	.12
❑ 57 Mike Mussina	.60	.18
❑ 58 Moises Alou	.40	.12
❑ 59 Sean Casey	.40	.12
❑ 60 Greg Maddux	1.50	.45
❑ 61 Tim Hudson	.40	.12
❑ 62 Mark McGwire	2.50	.75
❑ 63 Rafael Palmeiro	.60	.18
❑ 64 Tony Batista	.40	.12
❑ 65 Kazuhiro Sasaki	.40	.12
❑ 66 Jorge Posada	.60	.18
❑ 67 Johnny Damon	.60	.18
❑ 68 Brian Giles	.40	.12
❑ 69 Jose Vidro	.40	.12
❑ 70 Jermaine Dye	.40	.12
❑ 71 Craig Biggio	.60	.18
❑ 72 Larry Walker	.60	.18
❑ 73 Eric Chavez	.40	.12
❑ 74 David Segui	.40	.12
❑ 75 Tim Salmon	.60	.18
❑ 76 Javy Lopez	.40	.12
❑ 77 Paul Konerko	.40	.12
❑ 78 Barry Larkin	.60	.18
❑ 79 Mike Hampton	.40	.12
❑ 80 Bobby Higginson	.40	.12
❑ 81 Mark Mulder	.40	.12

- ❑ 82 Pat Burrell .40 .12
- ❑ 83 Kerry Wood 1.00 .30
- ❑ 84 J.T. Snow .40 .12
- ❑ 85 Ivan Rodriguez 1.00 .30
- ❑ 86 Edgardo Alfonzo .40 .12
- ❑ 87 Orlando Hernandez .40 .12
- ❑ 88 Gary Sheffield .40 .12
- ❑ 89 Mike Sweeney .40 .12
- ❑ 90 Carlos Lee .40 .12
- ❑ 91 Rafael Furcal .40 .12
- ❑ 92 Troy Glaus .40 .12
- ❑ 93 Bartolo Colon .40 .12
- ❑ 94 Cliff Floyd .40 .12
- ❑ 95 Barry Zito .60 .18
- ❑ 96 J.D. Drew .40 .12
- ❑ 97 Eric Karros .40 .12
- ❑ 98 Jose Valentin .40 .12
- ❑ 99 Ellis Burks .40 .12
- ❑ 100 David Justice .40 .12
- ❑ 101 Larry Barnes .40 .12
- ❑ 102 Rod Barajas .40 .12
- ❑ 103 Tony Pena Jr. .40 .12
- ❑ 104 Jerry Hairston Jr. .40 .12
- ❑ 105 Keith Ginter .40 .12
- ❑ 106 Corey Patterson .40 .12
- ❑ 107 Aaron Rowand .40 .12
- ❑ 108 Miguel Olivo .40 .12
- ❑ 109 Gookie Dawkins .40 .12
- ❑ 110 C.C. Sabathia .40 .12
- ❑ 111 Ben Petrick .40 .12
- ❑ 112 Eric Munson .40 .12
- ❑ 113 Ramon Castro .40 .12
- ❑ 114 Alex Escobar .40 .12
- ❑ 115 Josh Hamilton .40 .12
- ❑ 116 Jason Marquis .40 .12
- ❑ 117 Ben Davis .40 .12
- ❑ 118 Alex Cintron .40 .12
- ❑ 119 Julio Zuleta .40 .12
- ❑ 120 Ben Broussard .40 .12
- ❑ 121 Adam Everett .40 .12
- ❑ 122 Ramon Carvajal RC .40 .12
- ❑ 123 Felipe Lopez .40 .12
- ❑ 124 Alfonso Soriano .60 .18
- ❑ 125 Jayson Werth .40 .12
- ❑ 126 Donzell McDonald .40 .12
- ❑ 127 Jason Hart .40 .12
- ❑ 128 Joe Crede .40 .12
- ❑ 129 Sean Burroughs .40 .12
- ❑ 130 Jack Cust .40 .12
- ❑ 131 Corey Smith .40 .12
- ❑ 132 Adrian Gonzalez .40 .12
- ❑ 133 J.R. House .40 .12
- ❑ 134 Steve Lomasney .40 .12
- ❑ 135 Tim Raines Jr. .40 .12
- ❑ 136 Tony Alvarez .40 .12
- ❑ 137 Doug Mientkiewicz .40 .12
- ❑ 138 Rocco Baldelli .60 .18
- ❑ 139 Jason Romano .40 .12
- ❑ 140 Vernon Wells .40 .12
- ❑ 141 Mike Bynum .40 .12
- ❑ 142 Xavier Nady .40 .12
- ❑ 143 Brad Wilkerson .40 .12
- ❑ 144 Ben Diggins .40 .12
- ❑ 145 Aubrey Huff .40 .12
- ❑ 146 Eric Byrnes .40 .12
- ❑ 147 Alex Gordon .40 .12
- ❑ 148 Roy Oswalt .60 .18
- ❑ 149 Brian Esposito .40 .12
- ❑ 150 Scott Seabol .40 .12
- ❑ 151 Erick Almonte RC 5.00 1.50
- ❑ 152 Gary Johnson RC 5.00 1.50
- ❑ 153 Pedro Liriano RC 5.00 1.50
- ❑ 154 Matt White RC 5.00 1.50
- ❑ 155 Luis Montanez RC 5.00 1.50
- ❑ 156 Brad Cresse 5.00 1.50
- ❑ 157 Wilson Betemit RC 5.00 1.50
- ❑ 158 Octavio Martinez RC 5.00 1.50
- ❑ 159 Adam Pettyjohn RC 5.00 1.50
- ❑ 160 Corey Spencer RC 5.00 1.50
- ❑ 161 Mark Burnett RC 5.00 1.50
- ❑ 162 Ichiro Suzuki RC 60.00 18.00
- ❑ 163 Alexis Gomez RC 5.00 1.50
- ❑ 164 Greg Nash RC 5.00 1.50
- ❑ 165 Roberto Miniel RC 5.00 1.50
- ❑ 166 Justin Morneau RC 30.00 9.00
- ❑ 167 Ben Washburn RC 5.00 1.50
- ❑ 168 Bob Keppel RC 8.00 2.40
- ❑ 169 Deivi Mendez RC 5.00 1.50
- ❑ 170 Tsuyoshi Shinjo RC 8.00 2.40
- ❑ 171 Jared Abruzzo RC 5.00 1.50
- ❑ 172 Derrick Van Dusen RC 5.00 1.50
- ❑ 173 Hee Seop Choi RC 8.00 2.40
- ❑ 174 Albert Pujols RC 120.00 36.00
- ❑ 175 Travis Hafner RC 15.00 4.50
- ❑ 176 Ron Davenport RC 5.00 1.50
- ❑ 177 Luis Torres RC 5.00 1.50
- ❑ 178 Jake Peavy RC 20.00 6.00
- ❑ 179 Elvis Corporan RC 5.00 1.50
- ❑ 180 Dave Krynzel 5.00 1.50
- ❑ 181 Tony Blanco RC 8.00 2.40
- ❑ 182 Elpidio Guzman RC 5.00 1.50
- ❑ 183 Matt Butler RC 5.00 1.50
- ❑ 184 Joe Thurston RC 5.00 1.50
- ❑ 185 Andy Beal RC 5.00 1.50
- ❑ 186 Kevin Nulton RC 5.00 1.50
- ❑ 187 Sneideer Santos RC 5.00 1.50
- ❑ 188 Joe Dillon RC 5.00 1.50
- ❑ 189 Jeremy Blevins RC 5.00 1.50
- ❑ 190 Chris Amador RC 5.00 1.50
- ❑ 191 Mark Hendrickson RC 5.00 1.50
- ❑ 192 Willy Aybar RC 8.00 2.40
- ❑ 193 Antoine Cameron RC 5.00 1.50
- ❑ 194 J.J. Johnson RC 5.00 1.50
- ❑ 195 Ryan Ketchner RC 10.00 3.00
- ❑ 196 Bjorn Ivy RC 5.00 1.50
- ❑ 197 Josh Kroeger RC 15.00 4.50
- ❑ 198 Ty Wigginton RC 8.00 2.40
- ❑ 199 Stubby Clapp RC 5.00 1.50
- ❑ 200 Jerrod Riggan RC 5.00 1.50

2002 Bowman's Best

	Nm-Mt	Ex-Mt
COMP.SET w/o SP's (90)	100.00	30.00
COMMON CARD (1-90)	.75	.23
COMMON AUTO A (91-180)	8.00	2.40
AUTO GROUP A ODDS 1:3	.00	
COMMON AUTO B (91-180)	10.00	3.00
AUTO GROUP B ODDS 1:19	.00	
COMMON BAT (91-180)	5.00	1.50
91-180 BAT STATED ODDS 1:5	.00	
181 ISHII BAT EXCHANGE ODDS 1:131		.00

- ❑ 1 Josh Beckett .75 .23
- ❑ 2 Derek Jeter 5.00 1.50
- ❑ 3 Alex Rodriguez 3.00 .90
- ❑ 4 Miguel Tejada .75 .23
- ❑ 5 Nomar Garciaparra 3.00 .90
- ❑ 6 Aramis Ramirez .75 .23
- ❑ 7 Jeremy Giambi .75 .23
- ❑ 8 Bernie Williams 1.25 .35
- ❑ 9 Juan Pierre .75 .23
- ❑ 10 Chipper Jones 2.00 .60
- ❑ 11 Jimmy Rollins .75 .23
- ❑ 12 Alfonso Soriano 1.25 .35
- ❑ 13 Mark Prior 3.00 .90
- ❑ 14 Paul Konerko .75 .23
- ❑ 15 Tim Hudson .75 .23
- ❑ 16 Doug Mientkiewicz .75 .23
- ❑ 17 Todd Helton 1.25 .35
- ❑ 18 Moises Alou .75 .23
- ❑ 19 Juan Gonzalez 1.25 .35
- ❑ 20 Jorge Posada 1.25 .35
- ❑ 21 Jeff Kent .75 .23
- ❑ 22 Roger Clemens 4.00 1.20
- ❑ 23 Phil Nevin .75 .23
- ❑ 24 Brian Giles .75 .23
- ❑ 25 Carlos Delgado .75 .23
- ❑ 26 Jason Giambi .75 .23
- ❑ 27 Vladimir Guerrero 2.00 .60
- ❑ 28 Cliff Floyd .75 .23
- ❑ 29 Shea Hillenbrand .75 .23
- ❑ 30 Ken Griffey Jr. 3.00 .90
- ❑ 31 Mike Piazza 3.00 .90
- ❑ 32 Carlos Pena .75 .23
- ❑ 33 Larry Walker 1.25 .35
- ❑ 34 Magglio Ordonez .75 .23
- ❑ 35 Mike Mussina 1.25 .35
- ❑ 36 Andruw Jones .75 .23
- ❑ 37 Nick Johnson .75 .23
- ❑ 38 Curt Schilling .75 .23
- ❑ 39 Eric Chavez .75 .23
- ❑ 40 Bartolo Colon .75 .23
- ❑ 41 Eric Hinske .75 .23
- ❑ 42 Sean Burroughs .75 .23
- ❑ 43 Randy Johnson 2.00 .60
- ❑ 44 Adam Dunn 1.25 .35
- ❑ 45 Pedro Martinez 2.00 .60
- ❑ 46 Garret Anderson .75 .23
- ❑ 47 Jim Thome 2.00 .60
- ❑ 48 Gary Sheffield .75 .23
- ❑ 49 Tsuyoshi Shinjo .75 .23
- ❑ 50 Albert Pujols 4.00 1.20
- ❑ 51 Ichiro Suzuki 3.00 .90
- ❑ 52 C.C. Sabathia .75 .23
- ❑ 53 Bobby Abreu .75 .23
- ❑ 54 Ivan Rodriguez 2.00 .60
- ❑ 55 J.D. Drew .75 .23
- ❑ 56 Jacque Jones .75 .23
- ❑ 57 Jason Kendall .75 .23
- ❑ 58 Javier Vazquez .75 .23
- ❑ 59 Jeff Bagwell 1.25 .35
- ❑ 60 Greg Maddux 3.00 .90
- ❑ 61 Jim Edmonds .75 .23
- ❑ 62 Hank Blalock 2.00 .60
- ❑ 63 Jose Vidro .75 .23
- ❑ 64 Kevin Brown .75 .23
- ❑ 65 Mark Teixeira 1.25 .35
- ❑ 66 Sammy Sosa 3.00 .90
- ❑ 67 Lance Berkman .75 .23
- ❑ 68 Mark Mulder .75 .23
- ❑ 69 Marty Cordova .75 .23
- ❑ 70 Frank Thomas 2.00 .60
- ❑ 71 Mike Cameron .75 .23
- ❑ 72 Mike Sweeney .75 .23
- ❑ 73 Barry Bonds 5.00 1.50
- ❑ 74 Troy Glaus .75 .23
- ❑ 75 Barry Zito .75 .23
- ❑ 76 Pat Burrell .75 .23
- ❑ 77 Paul LoDuca .75 .23
- ❑ 78 Rafael Palmeiro 1.25 .35
- ❑ 79 Austin Kearns .75 .23
- ❑ 80 Darin Erstad .75 .23
- ❑ 81 Richie Sexson .75 .23
- ❑ 82 Roberto Alomar 1.25 .35
- ❑ 83 Roy Oswalt .75 .23
- ❑ 84 Ryan Klesko .75 .23
- ❑ 85 Luis Gonzalez .75 .23
- ❑ 86 Scott Rolen 2.00 .60
- ❑ 87 Shannon Stewart .75 .23
- ❑ 88 Shawn Green .75 .23
- ❑ 89 Toby Hall .75 .23
- ❑ 90 Bret Boone .75 .23
- ❑ 91 Casey Kotchman Bat RC 15.00 3.00
- ❑ 92 Jose Valverde AU A RC 10.00 3.00
- ❑ 93 Cole Barthel Bat RC 5.00 1.50
- ❑ 94 Brad Nelson AU A RC 15.00 4.50
- ❑ 95 Mauricio Lara AU A RC 8.00 2.40
- ❑ 96 Ryan Gripp Bat RC 5.00 1.50
- ❑ 97 Brian West AU A RC 8.00 2.40
- ❑ 98 Chris Piersoll AU B RC 10.00 3.00
- ❑ 99 Ryan Church AU B RC 15.00 4.50
- ❑ 100 Javier Colina AU A 8.00 2.40
- ❑ 101 Juan M. Gonzalez AU A RC 8.00 2.40
- ❑ 102 Benito Baez AU A 8.00 2.40
- ❑ 103 Mike Hill Bat RC 5.00 1.50
- ❑ 104 Jason Grove AU B RC 10.00 3.00
- ❑ 105 Koyie Hill AU B 10.00 3.00
- ❑ 106 Mark Outlaw AU A RC 8.00 2.40
- ❑ 107 Jason Bay Bat RC 15.00 4.50

❑ 108 Jorge Padilla AU A RC .. 8.00 2.40
❑ 109 Pete Zamora AU A RC 8.00 2.40
❑ 110 Joe Mauer AU A RC 60.00 18.00
❑ 111 Franklyn German AU A RC 8.00 2.40
❑ 112 Chris Flinn AU A RC 8.00 2.40
❑ 113 David Wright Bat RC 30.00 9.00
❑ 114 An. Martinez AU A RC 8.00 2.40
❑ 115 Nic Jackson Bat RC 5.00 1.50
❑ 116 Rene Reyes AU A RC 8.00 2.40
❑ 117 Colin Young AU A RC 8.00 2.40
❑ 118 Joe Orloski AU A RC 8.00 2.40
❑ 119 Mike Wilson AU A RC 8.00 2.40
❑ 120 Rich Thompson AU A RC 8.00 2.40
❑ 121 Jake Mauer AU B RC 10.00 3.00
❑ 122 Mario Ramos AU A RC .. 8.00 2.40
❑ 123 Doug Sessions AU B RC 10.00 3.00
❑ 124 Doug Devore Bat RC 5.00 1.50
❑ 125 Travis Foley AU A RC 8.00 2.40
❑ 126 Chris Baker AU A RC 8.00 2.40
❑ 127 Michael Floyd AU A RC .. 8.00 2.40
❑ 128 Josh Barfield Bat RC 10.00 3.00
❑ 129 Jose Bautista Bat RC 8.00 2.40
❑ 130 Gavin Floyd AU A RC .. 30.00 9.00
❑ 131 Jason Botts Bat RC 8.00 2.40
❑ 132 Clint Nageotte AU A RC 12.00 3.60
❑ 133 Jesus Cota AU B RC 10.00 3.00
❑ 134 Ron Calloway Bat RC 5.00 1.50
❑ 135 Kevin Cash Bat RC 5.00 1.50
❑ 136 Jonny Gomes AU B RC 15.00 4.50
❑ 137 Dennis Ulacia AU A RC .. 8.00 2.40
❑ 138 Ryan Snare AU A RC 8.00 2.40
❑ 139 Kevin Deaton AU A RC .. 8.00 2.40
❑ 140 Bobby Jenks AU B RC .. 15.00 4.50
❑ 141 Casey Kotchman AU A RC 25.00 7.50
❑ 142 Adam Walker AU A RC .. 8.00 2.40
❑ 143 Mike Gonzalez AU A RC 8.00 2.40
❑ 144 Ruben Gotay Bat RC 5.00 1.50
❑ 145 Jason Grove Bat RC 5.00 1.50
❑ 146 Freddy Sanchez AU B RC 10.00 3.00
❑ 147 Jason Arnold AU B RC 15.00 4.50
❑ 148 Scott Hairston AU A RC 20.00 6.00
❑ 149 Jason St. Clair AU B RC 10.00 3.00
❑ 150 Chris Tritle Bat RC 5.00 1.50
❑ 151 Edwin Yan Bat RC 5.00 1.50
❑ 152 Freddy Sanchez Bat RC .. 5.00 1.50
❑ 153 Greg Sain Bat RC 8.00 2.40
❑ 154 Yurendell De Caster Bat RC 5.00 1.50
❑ 155 Noochie Varner Bat RC .. 5.00 1.50
❑ 156 Nelson Castro AU B RC 10.00 3.00
❑ 157 Randall Shelley Bat RC .. 5.00 1.50
❑ 158 Reed Johnson Bat RC 8.00 2.40
❑ 159 Ryan Raburn AU A RC 8.00 2.40
❑ 160 Jose Morban Bat RC 5.00 1.50
❑ 161 Justin Schuda AU A RC .. 8.00 2.40
❑ 162 Henry Pichardo AU A RC 8.00 2.40
❑ 163 Josh Bard AU A RC 8.00 2.40
❑ 164 Josh Bonifay AU A RC 8.00 2.40
❑ 165 Brandon League AU B RC 10.00 3.00
❑ 166 Jorge-Julio DePaula AU A RC 10.00 3.00
❑ 167 Todd Linden AU B RC .. 25.00 7.50
❑ 168 Francisco Liriano AU A RC 10.00 3.00
❑ 169 Chris Snelling AU A RC 8.00 2.40
❑ 170 Blake McGinley AU A RC 8.00 2.40
❑ 171 Cody McKay AU A RC 8.00 2.40
❑ 172 Jason Stanford AU A RC 8.00 2.40
❑ 173 Lenny Dinardo AU A RC 8.00 2.40
❑ 174 Greg Montalbano AU A RC 8.00 2.40
❑ 175 Earl Snyder AU A RC 10.00 3.00
❑ 176 Justin Huber AU A RC .. 10.00 3.00
❑ 177 Chris Narveson AU A RC 8.00 2.40
❑ 178 Jon Switzer AU A RC 8.00 2.40
❑ 179 Ronald Acuna AU A RC .. 8.00 2.40
❑ 180 Chris Duffy Bat RC 5.00 1.50
❑ 181 Kazuhisa Ishii Bat RC .. 10.00 3.00

2003 Bowman's Best

	MINT	NRMT
COMP.SET w/o SP's (50)	40.00	18.00
COMMON CARD	1.00	.45
COMMON AUTO	8.00	3.60
COMMON BAT	4.00	1.80

❑ AB Andrew Brown FY AU RC 10.00 4.50
❑ AK Austin Kearns .... 1.00 .45
❑ AM Aneudis Mateo FY AU RC 8.00 3.60

❑ AP Albert Pujols 3.00 1.35
❑ AR Alex Rodriguez 2.50 1.10
❑ AS Alfonso Soriano .... 1.00 .45
❑ AW Aron Weston FY AU RC .. 8.00 3.60
❑ BB Bryan Bullington FY AU RC 15.00 6.75
❑ BC Bernie Castro FY RC .... 1.00 .45
❑ BFL Br. Florence FY AU RC .. 8.00 3.60
❑ BFR Ben Francisco FY AU RC 10.00 4.50
❑ BH Brendan Harris FY AU RC 10.00 4.50
❑ BJH Bo Hart FY RC .... 1.50 .70
❑ BK Beau Kemp FY AU RC 8.00 3.60
❑ BLB Barry Bonds 4.00 1.80
❑ BM Brian McCann FY AU RC 10.00 4.50
❑ BSG Brian Giles .... 1.00 .45
❑ BWB Bobby Basham FY AU RC 10.00 4.50
❑ BZ Barry Zito .... 1.00 .45
❑ CAD Carlos Duran FY AU RC 8.00 3.60
❑ CDC C. De La Cruz FY AU RC 8.00 3.60
❑ CJ Chipper Jones .... 1.50 .70
❑ CJW C.J. Wilson FY AU 8.00 3.60
❑ CM Charlie Manning FY AU RC 8.00 3.60
❑ CMS Curt Schilling .... 1.00 .45
❑ CS Cory Stewart FY AU RC .. 8.00 3.60
❑ CSS Corey Shafer FY AU RC 10.00 4.50
❑ CW Chien-Ming Wang FY RC 2.00 .90
❑ CWA Chien-Ming Wang FY AU 25.00 11.00
❑ DAM D. Moseley FY AU RC 10.00 4.50
❑ DC David Cash FY AU RC 8.00 3.60
❑ DH Dan Haren FY AU RC 10.00 4.50
❑ DJ Derek Jeter 4.00 1.80
❑ DM David Martinez FY AU RC 8.00 3.60
❑ DMM D. McGowan FY AU RC 10.00 4.50
❑ DR Darrell Rasner FY AU RC 8.00 3.60
❑ DW Doug Waechter FY AU RC 10.00 4.50
❑ DY Dustin Yount FY RC .... 1.50 .70
❑ ERA El. Ramirez FY AU RC .. 10.00 4.50
❑ ERI Eric Riggs FY AU RC 10.00 4.50
❑ ET Eider Torres FY AU RC 8.00 3.60
❑ FP Felix Pie FY AU RC 25.00 11.00
❑ FS Felix Sanchez FY AU RC .. 8.00 3.60
❑ FT Ferdin Tejeda FY AU RC .. 8.00 3.60
❑ GA Greg Aquino FY AU RC .. 8.00 3.60
❑ GB Gregor Blanco FY AU RC 8.00 3.60
❑ GJA Garret Anderson .... 1.00 .45
❑ GM Greg Maddux 2.50 1.10
❑ GS G. Schneidmiller FY AU RC 8.00 3.60
❑ HR Hanley Ramirez FY AU RC 25.00 11.00
❑ HRB Hanley Ramirez FY Bat 10.00 4.50
❑ HT Haj Turay FY RC .... 1.50 .70
❑ IS Ichiro Suzuki 2.50 1.10
❑ JB Jeremy Bonderman FY RC 1.50 .70
❑ JC Jose Contreras FY RC ...... 2.00 .90
❑ JDD J.D. Durbin FY AU RC 10.00 4.50
❑ JFK Jeff Kent .... 1.00 .45
❑ JG Joey Gomes FY AU RC 8.00 3.60
❑ JGB Joey Gomes FY Bat 4.00 1.80
❑ JGG Jason Giambi .... 1.00 .45
❑ JK Jason Kubel FY AU RC .. 25.00 11.00
❑ JKB Jason Kubel FY Bat 10.00 4.50
❑ JLB Jaime Bubela FY AU RC 8.00 3.60
❑ JM Jose Morales FY AU RC .. 8.00 3.60
❑ JMS Jon-Mark Sprowl FY RC 1.50 .70
❑ JRG Jeremy Griffiths FY AU RC 10.00 4.50
❑ JT Jim Thome .... 1.50 .70
❑ JV Joe Valentine FY AU RC .. 8.00 3.60
❑ JW Josh Willingham FY AU RC 10.00 4.50
❑ KBS Kelly Shoppach FY Bat .. 6.00 2.70
❑ KG Ken Griffey Jr. 2.50 1.10
❑ KJ Kade Johnson FY AU RC .. 8.00 3.60
❑ KS Kelly Shoppach FY AU RC 12.00 5.50
❑ KY Kevin Youkilis FY AU RC 20.00 9.00
❑ KYE Kevin Youkilis FY Bat 8.00 3.60
❑ LB Lance Berkman .... 1.00 .45
❑ LF Lew Ford FY AU RC 20.00 9.00
❑ LFJ Lew Ford FY Bat 6.00 2.70
❑ LW Larry Walker .... 1.00 .45
❑ MB Matt Bruback FY RC ...... 1.00 .45
❑ MD Matt Diaz FY RC .... 1.50 .70
❑ MDA Matt Diaz FY AU 10.00 4.50
❑ MDH Matt Hensley FY AU RC 8.00 3.60
❑ MDM Mark Malaska FY AU RC 8.00 3.60
❑ MH Mi. Hernandez FY AU RC 8.00 3.60
❑ MHI Mi. Hinckley FY AU RC 12.00 5.50
❑ MJP Mike Piazza 2.50 1.10
❑ MK Matt Kata FY AU RC 10.00 4.50
❑ MNH Matt Hagen FY AU RC 10.00 4.50
❑ MO Mike O'Keefe FY RC ...... 1.00 .45
❑ MOR Magglio Ordonez .... 1.00 .45
❑ MP Mark Prior .... 1.50 .70
❑ MR Manny Ramirez .... 1.00 .45
❑ MS Mike Sweeney .... 1.00 .45
❑ MT Miguel Tejada .... 1.00 .45
❑ NG Nomar Garciaparra 2.50 1.10
❑ NL Nook Logan FY AU RC 8.00 3.60
❑ OC Ozzie Chavez FY AU RC .. 8.00 3.60
❑ PB Pat Burrell .... 1.00 .45
❑ PL Pete LaForest FY AU RC 10.00 4.50
❑ PM Pedro Martinez .... 1.50 .70
❑ PR Prentice Redman FY AU RC 8.00 3.60
❑ RC Ryan Cameron FY AU RC 8.00 3.60
❑ RD Rajai Davis FY AU RC 10.00 4.50
❑ RH Ryan Howard FY AU RC 40.00 18.00
❑ RHJ Ryan Howard FY Bat 15.00 6.75
❑ RJ Randy Johnson .... 1.50 .70
❑ RLD Rajai Davis FY Bat 5.00 2.20
❑ RM R. Nivar-Martinez FY RC 1.50 .70
❑ RS Ryan Shealy FY AU RC .. 10.00 4.50
❑ RSB Ryan Shealy FY Bat 5.00 2.20
❑ RWH Rob. Hammock FY AU RC 10.00 4.50
❑ SG Shawn Green .... 1.00 .45
❑ SS Sammy Sosa 2.50 1.10
❑ ST Scott Tyler FY AU RC 10.00 4.50
❑ SV Shane Victorino FY RC .... 1.00 .45
❑ TA Tyler Adamczyk FY AU RC 8.00 3.60
❑ TH Todd Helton .... 1.00 .45
❑ TI Travis Ishikawa FY AU RC 8.00 3.60
❑ TJ Tyler Johnson FY AU RC .. 8.00 3.60
❑ TJB T.J. Bohn FY RC .... 1.00 .45
❑ TKH Torii Hunter .... 1.00 .45
❑ TO Tim Olson FY AU RC 10.00 4.50
❑ TS T.Story-Harden FY AU RC 8.00 3.60
❑ TSB T.Story-Harden FY Bat .. 4.00 1.80
❑ TT Terry Tiffee FY RC .... 1.50 .70
❑ VG Vladimir Guerrero .... 1.50 .70
❑ WE Willie Eyre FY AU RC 8.00 3.60
❑ WL Wil Ledezma FY AU RC 10.00 4.50
❑ WRC Roger Clemens 3.00 1.35
❑ NNO Bryan Bullington 25.00 11.00
Opened Box AU
❑ NNO Bryan Bullington
Sealed Box AU

2004 Bowman's Best

	Nm-Mt	Ex-Mt
COMP.SET w/o SP'S (50)	25.00	7.50

COMMON CARD 1.00 .30
COMMON RC 1.00 .30
ONE AUTO PER HOBBY PACK
ONE RELIC PER BOX-LOADER PACK
ONE BOX-LOADER PACK PER HOBBY BOX
STAUFFER BOX RANDOM IN HOBBY CASES
OVERALL AU PLATE ODDS 1:391 HOBBY
AU PLATE PRINT RUN 1 SET PER COLOR
BLACK-CYAN-MAGENTA-YELLOW ISSUED
NO AU PLATE PRICING DUE TO SCARCITY

❑ AER Alex Rodriguez 2.50 .75
❑ AG Adam Greenberg FY AU RC 10.00 3.00
❑ AL Anthony Lerew FY RC 1.50 .45
❑ AO Akinori Otsuka FY RC 1.00 .30
❑ AP Albert Pujols 3.00 .90
❑ AS Alfonso Soriano 1.00 .30
❑ BB Bobby Brownlie FY AU RC 15.00 4.50
❑ BEM Brandon Medders FY AU RC 8.00 2.40
❑ BG Brian Giles 1.00 .30
❑ BMS Brad Snyder FY AU RC 12.00 3.60
❑ BP Brayan Pena FY AU RC 8.00 2.40
❑ BS Brad Sullivan FY AU RC 10.00 3.00
❑ CB Carlos Beltran 1.00 .30
❑ CD Carlos Delgado 1.00 .30
❑ CJ Conor Jackson FY AU RC 25.00 7.50
❑ CLH Chin-Lung Hu FY RC 2.00 .60
❑ CMA Craig Ansman FY AU RC 8.00 2.40
❑ CMS Curt Schilling 1.50 .45
❑ CZ Charlie Zink FY AU RC 8.00 2.40
❑ DA David Aardsma FY AU RC 8.00 2.40
❑ DC Dave Crouthers FY AU RC 8.00 2.40
❑ DDN Dustin Nippert FY AU RC 8.00 2.40
❑ DG Danny Gonzalez FY RC 1.00 .30
❑ DK Donald Kelly FY AU RC 8.00 2.40
❑ DL Donald Levinski FY AU RC 8.00 2.40
❑ DM David Murphy FY AU RC 12.00 3.60
❑ DN Dioner Navarro FY AU RC 15.00 4.50
❑ DS Don Sutton FY RC 2.50 .75
❑ EA Erick Aybar FY AU RC 15.00 4.50
❑ EC Eric Chavez 1.00 .30
❑ EH Estee Harris FY AU RC 8.00 2.40
❑ ES Ervin Santana FY AU RC 15.00 4.50
❑ FH Felix Hernandez FY AU RC 30.00 9.00
❑ GA Garret Anderson 1.00 .30
❑ HB Hank Blalock 1.00 .30
❑ HM Hector Made FY RC 1.50 .45
❑ IR Ivan Rodriguez 1.50 .45
❑ IS Ichiro Suzuki 2.50 .75
❑ JA Joaquin Arias FY AU RC 8.00 2.40
❑ JAV Jose Vidro 1.00 .30
❑ JC Juan Cedeno FY AU RC 8.00 2.40
❑ JDS Jason Schmidt 1.00 .30
❑ JE Jesse English FY AU RC 8.00 2.40
❑ JGG Jason Giambi 1.00 .30
❑ JH Jason Hirsh FY AU RC 8.00 2.40
❑ JJC Jon Connolly FY RC 2.00 .60
❑ JK Jon Knott FY AU RC 8.00 2.40
❑ JL Josh Labandeira FY AU RC 8.00 2.40
❑ JLO Javy Lopez 1.00 .30
❑ JP Jorge Posada 1.00 .30
❑ JRG Joey Gathright FY RC 2.00 .60
❑ JS Jeff Salazar FY AU RC 12.00 3.60
❑ JSZ Jason Szuminski FY AU RC 8.00 2.40
❑ JT Jim Thome 1.50 .45
❑ KC Kory Casto FY AU RC 8.00 2.40
❑ KK Kevin Kouzmanoff FY AU RC 10.00 3.00
❑ KM Kazuo Matsui FY Uni RC 15.00 4.50
❑ KRK Kody Kirkland FY Bat RC 8.00 2.40
❑ KS Kyle Sleeth FY RC 2.00 .60
❑ KT Kazuhito Tadano FY Jsy RC 8.00 2.40
❑ LK Logan Kensing FY AU RC 8.00 2.40
❑ LM Lastings Milledge FY AU RC 25.00 7.50
❑ LO Lyle Overbay 1.00 .30
❑ LTH Luke Hughes FY AU RC 8.00 2.40
❑ LWJ Chipper Jones 1.50 .45
❑ MAR Manny Ramirez 1.00 .30
❑ MDC Matt Creighton FY AU RC 8.00 2.40
❑ MG Mike Gosling FY RC 1.00 .30
❑ MJP Mike Piazza 2.50 .75
❑ MO Magglio Ordonez 1.00 .30
❑ MT Miguel Tejada 1.00 .30
❑ MTC Miguel Cabrera 1.00 .30
❑ MV Merkin Valdez FY AU RC 12.00 3.60
❑ MWP Mark Prior 1.50 .45
❑ MY Michael Young 1.00 .30
❑ NAG Nomar Garciaparra 2.50 .75
❑ NG Nick Gorneault FY RC 1.50 .45
❑ NU Nic Ungs FY AU RC 8.00 2.40
❑ OQ Omar Quintanilla FY AU RC 15.00 4.50
❑ PM Paul Maholm FY AU RC 10.00 3.00
❑ PMM Paul McAnulty FY RC 1.50 .45
❑ RB Ryan Budde FY AU RC 8.00 2.40
❑ RC Roger Clemens 3.00 .90
❑ RG Rudy Guillen FY AU RC 12.00 3.60
❑ RJ Randy Johnson 1.50 .45
❑ RN Ricky Nolasco FY AU RC 8.00 2.40
❑ RR Ramon Ramirez FY AU RC 8.00 2.40
❑ RS Richie Sexson 1.00 .30
❑ RT Rob Tejeda FY AU RC 8.00 2.40
❑ SH Shawn Hill FY AU RC 8.00 2.40
❑ SR Scott Rolen 1.50 .45
❑ SS Sammy Sosa 2.50 .75
❑ ST Shingo Takatsu FY Jsy RC 10.00 3.00
❑ TB Travis Blackley FY Jsy RC 8.00 2.40
❑ TD Tyler Davidson FY AU RC 10.00 3.00
❑ TJ Terry Jones FY RC 1.50 .45
❑ TJS Tim Stauffer FY AU RC 10.00 3.00
❑ TLH Todd Helton 1.00 .30
❑ TOH Travis Hanson FY AU RC 8.00 2.40
❑ TRM Tom Mastny FY AU RC 8.00 2.40
❑ TS Todd Self FY RC 1.00 .30
❑ VC Vito Chiaravalloti FY AU RC 10.00 3.00
❑ VG Vladimir Guerrero 1.50 .45
❑ WM Warner Madrigal FY RC 1.50 .45
❑ WS Wardell Starling FY AU RC 8.00 2.40
❑ YM Yadier Molina FY AU RC 20.00 6.00
❑ ZD Zach Duke FY AU RC 20.00 6.00
❑ NNO Tim Stauffer AU Box/100 25.00 7.50

1987 Classic Update Yellow

	Nm-Mt	Ex-Mt
COMP.FACT.SET (50)	30.00	12.00

❑ 101 Mike Schmidt 1.00 .40
❑ 102 Eric Davis .25 .10
❑ 103 Pete Rose 1.25 .50
❑ 104 Don Mattingly 1.25 .50
❑ 105 Wade Boggs .25 .10
❑ 106 Dale Murphy .25 .10
❑ 107 Glenn Davis .10 .04
❑ 108 Wally Joyner .25 .10
❑ 109 Bo Jackson 2.00 .80
❑ 110 Cory Snyder .10 .04
❑ 111 Jim Lindeman .15 .06
❑ 112 Kirby Puckett .40 .16
❑ 113 Barry Bonds 15.00 6.00
❑ 114 Roger Clemens 1.00 .40
❑ 115 Oddibe McDowell .10 .04
❑ 116 Bret Saberhagen .15 .06
❑ 117 Joe Magrane .10 .04
❑ 118 Scott Fletcher .10 .04
❑ 119 Mark McLemore .15 .06
❑ 120 Joe Niekro .15 .06
Who Me
❑ 121 Mark McGwire 10.00 4.00
❑ 122 Darryl Strawberry .15 .06
❑ 123 Mike Scott .15 .06
❑ 124 Andre Dawson .15 .06
❑ 125 Jose Canseco .40 .16
❑ 126 Kevin McReynolds .10 .04
❑ 127 Joe Carter .15 .06
❑ 128 Casey Candaele .10 .04
❑ 129 Matt Nokes .40 .16
❑ 130 Kal Daniels .10 .04
❑ 131 Pete Incaviglia .40 .16
❑ 132 Benito Santiago .40 .16
❑ 133 Barry Larkin 2.00 .80
❑ 134 Gary Pettis .10 .04
❑ 135 B.J. Surhoff .60 .24
❑ 136 Juan Nieves .10 .04
❑ 137 Jim Deshaies .10 .04
❑ 138 Pete O'Brien .10 .04
❑ 139 Kevin Seitzer .15 .06
❑ 140 Devon White .60 .24
❑ 141 Rob Deer .10 .04
❑ 142 Kurt Stillwell .10 .04
❑ 143 Edwin Correa .10 .04
❑ 144 Dion James .10 .04
❑ 145 Danny Tartabull .10 .04
❑ 146 Jerry Browne .15 .06
❑ 147 Ted Higuera .10 .04
❑ 148 Jack Clark .15 .06
❑ 149 Ruben Sierra 1.00 .40
❑ 150 Mark McGwire and 1.00 .40
Eric Davis

1994 Collector's Choice

	Nm-Mt	Ex-Mt
COMPLETE SET (670)	25.00	7.50
COMP.FACT.SET (675)	30.00	9.00
COMP. SERIES 1 (320)	10.00	3.00
COMP. SERIES 2 (350)	15.00	4.50

❑ 1 Rich Becker .10 .03
❑ 2 Greg Blosser .10 .03
❑ 3 Midre Cummings .10 .03
❑ 4 Carlos Delgado .30 .09
❑ 5 Steve Dreyer RC .10 .03
❑ 6 Carl Everett .20 .06
❑ 7 Cliff Floyd .20 .06
❑ 8 Alex Gonzalez .10 .03
❑ 9 Shawn Green .50 .15
❑ 10 Butch Huskey .10 .03
❑ 11 Mark Hutton .10 .03
❑ 12 Miguel Jimenez .10 .03
❑ 13 Steve Karsay .10 .03
❑ 14 Marc Newfield .10 .03
❑ 15 Luis Ortiz .10 .03
❑ 16 Manny Ramirez .30 .09
❑ 17 Johnny Ruffin .10 .03
❑ 18 Scott Stahoviak .10 .03
❑ 19 Salomon Torres .10 .03
❑ 20 Gabe White .10 .03
❑ 21 Brian Anderson RC .25 .07
❑ 22 Wayne Gomes RC .10 .03
❑ 23 Jeff Granger .10 .03
❑ 24 Steve Soderstrom RC .10 .03
❑ 25 Trot Nixon RC 1.00 .30
❑ 26 Kirk Presley RC .10 .03
❑ 27 Matt Brunson RC .10 .03
❑ 28 Brooks Kieschnick RC .25 .07
❑ 29 Billy Wagner RC .50 .15
❑ 30 Matt Drews RC .10 .03
❑ 31 Kurt Abbott RC .25 .07
❑ 32 Luis Alicea .10 .03
❑ 33 Roberto Alomar .30 .09
❑ 34 Sandy Alomar Jr. .10 .03
❑ 35 Moises Alou .20 .06

❑ 36 Wilson Alvarez .10 .03
❑ 37 Rich Amaral .10 .03
❑ 38 Eric Anthony .10 .03
❑ 39 Luis Aquino .10 .03
❑ 40 Jack Armstrong .10 .03
❑ 41 Rene Arocha .10 .03
❑ 42 Rich Aude RC .10 .03
❑ 43 Brad Ausmus .10 .03
❑ 44 Steve Avery .10 .03
❑ 45 Bob Ayrault .10 .03
❑ 46 Willie Banks .10 .03
❑ 47 Bret Barberie .10 .03
❑ 48 Kim Batiste .10 .03
❑ 49 Rod Beck .10 .03
❑ 50 Jason Bere .10 .03
❑ 51 Sean Berry .10 .03
❑ 52 Dante Bichette .20 .06
❑ 53 Jeff Blauser .10 .03
❑ 54 Mike Blowers .10 .03
❑ 55 Tim Bogar .10 .03
❑ 56 Tom Bolton .10 .03
❑ 57 Ricky Bones .10 .03
❑ 58 Bobby Bonilla .20 .06
❑ 59 Bret Boone .20 .06
❑ 60 Pat Borders .10 .03
❑ 61 Mike Bordick .10 .03
❑ 62 Daryl Boston .10 .03
❑ 63 Ryan Bowen .10 .03
❑ 64 Jeff Branson .10 .03
❑ 65 George Brett 1.25 .35
❑ 66 Steve Buechele .10 .03
❑ 67 Dave Burba .10 .03
❑ 68 John Burkett .10 .03
❑ 69 Jeromy Burnitz .20 .06
❑ 70 Brett Butler .20 .06
❑ 71 Rob Butler .10 .03
❑ 72 Ken Caminiti .20 .06
❑ 73 Cris Carpenter .10 .03
❑ 74 Vinny Castilla .20 .06
❑ 75 Andujar Cedeno .10 .03
❑ 76 Wes Chamberlain .10 .03
❑ 77 Archi Cianfrocco .10 .03
❑ 78 Dave Clark .10 .03
❑ 79 Jerald Clark .10 .03
❑ 80 Royce Clayton .10 .03
❑ 81 David Cone .20 .06
❑ 82 Jeff Conine .20 .06
❑ 83 Steve Cooke .10 .03
❑ 84 Scott Cooper .10 .03
❑ 85 Joey Cora .10 .03
❑ 86 Tim Costo .10 .03
❑ 87 Chad Curtis .10 .03
❑ 88 Ron Darling .10 .03
❑ 89 Danny Darwin .10 .03
❑ 90 Rob Deer .10 .03
❑ 91 Jim Deshaies .10 .03
❑ 92 Delino DeShields .10 .03
❑ 93 Rob Dibble .20 .06
❑ 94 Gary DiSarcina .10 .03
❑ 95 Doug Drabek .10 .03
❑ 96 Scott Erickson .10 .03
❑ 97 Rikkert Faneyte RC .10 .03
❑ 98 Jeff Fassero .10 .03
❑ 99 Alex Fernandez .10 .03
❑ 100 Cecil Fielder .20 .06
❑ 101 Dave Fleming .10 .03
❑ 102 Darrin Fletcher .10 .03
❑ 103 Scott Fletcher .10 .03
❑ 104 Mike Gallego .10 .03
❑ 105 Carlos Garcia .10 .03
❑ 106 Jeff Gardner .10 .03
❑ 107 Brent Gates .10 .03
❑ 108 Benji Gil .10 .03
❑ 109 Bernard Gilkey .10 .03
❑ 110 Chris Gomez .10 .03
❑ 111 Luis Gonzalez .20 .06
❑ 112 Tom Gordon .10 .03
❑ 113 Jim Gott .10 .03
❑ 114 Mark Grace .30 .09
❑ 115 Tommy Greene .10 .03
❑ 116 Willie Greene .10 .03
❑ 117 Ken Griffey Jr. .75 .23
❑ 118 Bill Gullickson .10 .03
❑ 119 Ricky Gutierrez .10 .03
❑ 120 Juan Guzman .10 .03
❑ 121 Chris Gwynn .10 .03
❑ 122 Tony Gwynn .60 .18
❑ 123 Jeffrey Hammonds .10 .03
❑ 124 Erik Hanson .10 .03
❑ 125 Gene Harris .10 .03
❑ 126 Greg W. Harris .10 .03
❑ 127 Bryan Harvey .10 .03
❑ 128 Billy Hatcher .10 .03
❑ 129 Hilly Hathaway .10 .03
❑ 130 Charlie Hayes .10 .03
❑ 131 Rickey Henderson .50 .15
❑ 132 Mike Henneman .10 .03
❑ 133 Pat Hentgen .10 .03
❑ 134 Roberto Hernandez .10 .03
❑ 135 Orel Hershiser .20 .06
❑ 136 Phil Hiatt .10 .03
❑ 137 Glenallen Hill .10 .03
❑ 138 Ken Hill .10 .03
❑ 139 Eric Hillman .10 .03
❑ 140 Chris Hoiles .10 .03
❑ 141 Dave Hollins .10 .03
❑ 142 David Hulse .10 .03
❑ 143 Todd Hundley .10 .03
❑ 144 Pete Incaviglia .10 .03
❑ 145 Danny Jackson .10 .03
❑ 146 John Jaha .10 .03
❑ 147 Domingo Jean .10 .03
❑ 148 Gregg Jefferies .10 .03
❑ 149 Reggie Jefferson .10 .03
❑ 150 Lance Johnson .10 .03
❑ 151 Bobby Jones .10 .03
❑ 152 Chipper Jones .50 .15
❑ 153 Todd Jones .10 .03
❑ 154 Brian Jordan .20 .06
❑ 155 Wally Joyner .20 .06
❑ 156 David Justice .20 .06
❑ 157 Ron Karkovice .10 .03
❑ 158 Eric Karros .20 .06
❑ 159 Jeff Kent .20 .06
❑ 160 Jimmy Key .20 .06
❑ 161 Mark Kiefer .10 .03
❑ 162 Darryl Kile .20 .06
❑ 163 Jeff King .10 .03
❑ 164 Wayne Kirby .10 .03
❑ 165 Ryan Klesko .20 .06
❑ 166 Chuck Knoblauch .20 .06
❑ 167 Chad Kreuter .10 .03
❑ 168 John Kruk .20 .06
❑ 169 Mark Langston .10 .03
❑ 170 Mike Lansing .10 .03
❑ 171 Barry Larkin .30 .09
❑ 172 Manuel Lee .10 .03
❑ 173 Phil Leftwich RC .10 .03
❑ 174 Darren Lewis .10 .03
❑ 175 Derek Lilliquist .10 .03
❑ 176 Jose Lind .10 .03
❑ 177 Albie Lopez .10 .03
❑ 178 Javier Lopez .20 .06
❑ 179 Torey Lovullo .10 .03
❑ 180 Scott Lydy .10 .03
❑ 181 Mike Macfarlane .10 .03
❑ 182 Shane Mack .10 .03
❑ 183 Greg Maddux .75 .23
❑ 184 Dave Magadan .10 .03
❑ 185 Joe Magrane .10 .03
❑ 186 Kirk Manwaring .10 .03
❑ 187 Al Martin .10 .03
❑ 188 Pedro A. Martinez RC .10 .03
❑ 189 Pedro Martinez .50 .15
❑ 190 Ramon Martinez .10 .03
❑ 191 Tino Martinez .30 .09
❑ 192 Don Mattingly 1.25 .35
❑ 193 Derrick May .10 .03
❑ 194 David McCarty .10 .03
❑ 195 Ben McDonald .10 .03
❑ 196 Roger McDowell .10 .03
❑ 197 Fred McGriff UER .30 .09
(Stats on back have 73 stolen bases for 1989; should be 7)
❑ 198 Mark McLemore .10 .03
❑ 199 Greg McMichael .10 .03
❑ 200 Jeff McNeely .10 .03
❑ 201 Brian McRae .10 .03
❑ 202 Pat Meares .10 .03
❑ 203 Roberto Mejia .10 .03
❑ 204 Orlando Merced .10 .03
❑ 205 Jose Mesa .10 .03
❑ 206 Blas Minor .10 .03
❑ 207 Angel Miranda .10 .03
❑ 208 Paul Molitor .30 .09
❑ 209 Raul Mondesi .20 .06
❑ 210 Jeff Montgomery .10 .03
❑ 211 Mickey Morandini .10 .03
❑ 212 Mike Morgan .10 .03
❑ 213 Jamie Moyer .20 .06
❑ 214 Bobby Munoz .10 .03
❑ 215 Troy Neel .10 .03
❑ 216 Dave Nilsson .10 .03
❑ 217 John O'Donoghue .10 .03
❑ 218 Paul O'Neill .30 .09
❑ 219 Jose Offerman .10 .03
❑ 220 Joe Oliver .10 .03
❑ 221 Greg Olson .10 .03
❑ 222 Donovan Osborne .10 .03
❑ 223 Jayhawk Owens .10 .03
❑ 224 Mike Pagliarulo .10 .03
❑ 225 Craig Paquette .10 .03
❑ 226 Roger Pavlik .10 .03
❑ 227 Brad Pennington .10 .03
❑ 228 Eduardo Perez .10 .03
❑ 229 Mike Perez .10 .03
❑ 230 Tony Phillips .10 .03
❑ 231 Hipolito Pichardo .10 .03
❑ 232 Phil Plantier .10 .03
❑ 233 Curtis Pride RC .25 .07
❑ 234 Tim Pugh .10 .03
❑ 235 Scott Radinsky .10 .03
❑ 236 Pat Rapp .10 .03
❑ 237 Kevin Reimer .10 .03
❑ 238 Armando Reynoso .10 .03
❑ 239 Jose Rijo .10 .03
❑ 240 Cal Ripken 1.50 .45
❑ 241 Kevin Roberson .10 .03
❑ 242 Kenny Rogers .20 .06
❑ 243 Kevin Rogers .10 .03
❑ 244 Mel Rojas .10 .03
❑ 245 John Roper .10 .03
❑ 246 Kirk Rueter .20 .06
❑ 247 Scott Ruffcorn .10 .03
❑ 248 Ken Ryan .10 .03
❑ 249 Nolan Ryan 2.00 .60
❑ 250 Bret Saberhagen .20 .06
❑ 251 Tim Salmon .30 .09
❑ 252 Reggie Sanders .10 .03
❑ 253 Curt Schilling .20 .06
❑ 254 David Segui .10 .03
❑ 255 Aaron Sele .10 .03
❑ 256 Scott Servais .10 .03
❑ 257 Gary Sheffield .20 .06
❑ 258 Ruben Sierra .10 .03
❑ 259 Don Slaught .10 .03
❑ 260 Lee Smith .20 .06
❑ 261 Cory Snyder .10 .03
❑ 262 Paul Sorrento .10 .03
❑ 263 Sammy Sosa .75 .23
❑ 264 Bill Spiers .10 .03
❑ 265 Mike Stanley .10 .03
❑ 266 Dave Staton .10 .03
❑ 267 Terry Steinbach .10 .03
❑ 268 Kevin Stocker .10 .03
❑ 269 Todd Stottlemyre .10 .03
❑ 270 Doug Strange .10 .03
❑ 271 Bill Swift .10 .03
❑ 272 Kevin Tapani .10 .03
❑ 273 Tony Tarasco .10 .03
❑ 274 Julian Tavarez RC .10 .03
❑ 275 Mickey Tettleton .10 .03
❑ 276 Ryan Thompson .10 .03
❑ 277 Chris Turner .10 .03
❑ 278 John Valentin .10 .03
❑ 279 Todd Van Poppel .10 .03
❑ 280 Andy Van Slyke .20 .06
❑ 281 Mo Vaughn .20 .06
❑ 282 Robin Ventura .20 .06
❑ 283 Frank Viola .20 .06
❑ 284 Jose Vizcaino .10 .03
❑ 285 Omar Vizquel .30 .09
❑ 286 Larry Walker .30 .09
❑ 287 Duane Ward .10 .03
❑ 288 Allen Watson .10 .03
❑ 289 Bill Wegman .10 .03
❑ 290 Turk Wendell .10 .03

❑ 291 Lou Whitaker .20 .06
❑ 292 Devon White .20 .06
❑ 293 Rondell White .20 .06
❑ 294 Mark Whiten .10 .03
❑ 295 Darrel Whitmore .10 .03
❑ 296 Bob Wickman .10 .03
❑ 297 Rick Wilkins .10 .03
❑ 298 Bernie Williams .30 .09
❑ 299 Matt Williams .20 .06
❑ 300 Woody Williams .20 .06
❑ 301 Nigel Wilson .10 .03
❑ 302 Dave Winfield .20 .06
❑ 303 Anthony Young .10 .03
❑ 304 Eric Young .10 .03
❑ 305 Todd Zeile .10 .03
❑ 306 Jack McDowell TP .20 .06
John Burkett
Tom Glavine
❑ 307 Randy Johnson TP .30 .09
❑ 308 Randy Myers TP .10 .03
❑ 309 Jack McDowell TP .10 .03
❑ 310 Mike Piazza TP .50 .15
❑ 311 Barry Bonds TP .60 .18
❑ 312 Andres Galarraga TP .10 .03
❑ 313 Juan Gonzalez TP .60 .18
Barry Bonds
❑ 314 Albert Belle TP .20 .06
❑ 315 Kenny Lofton TP .10 .03
❑ 316 Barry Bonds CL .60 .18
❑ 317 Ken Griffey Jr. CL .50 .15
❑ 318 Mike Piazza CL .50 .15
❑ 319 Kirby Puckett CL .30 .09
❑ 320 Nolan Ryan CL .50 .15
❑ 321 Roberto Alomar CL .20 .06
❑ 322 Roger Clemens CL .50 .15
❑ 323 Juan Gonzalez CL .20 .06
❑ 324 Ken Griffey Jr. CL .50 .15
❑ 325 David Justice CL .10 .03
❑ 326 John Kruk CL .10 .03
❑ 327 Frank Thomas CL .20 .06
❑ 328 Tim Salmon TC .20 .06
❑ 329 Jeff Bagwell TC .20 .06
❑ 330 Mark McGwire TC .60 .18
❑ 331 Roberto Alomar TC .20 .06
❑ 332 David Justice TC .10 .03
❑ 333 Pat Listach TC .10 .03
❑ 334 Ozzie Smith TC .50 .15
❑ 335 Ryne Sandberg TC .50 .15
❑ 336 Mike Piazza TC .50 .15
❑ 337 Cliff Floyd TC .10 .03
❑ 338 Barry Bonds TC .60 .18
❑ 339 Albert Belle TC .20 .06
❑ 340 Ken Griffey Jr. TC .50 .15
❑ 341 Gary Sheffield TC .10 .03
❑ 342 Dwight Gooden TC .10 .03
❑ 343 Cal Ripken TC .75 .23
❑ 344 Tony Gwynn TC .30 .09
❑ 345 Lenny Dykstra TC .10 .03
❑ 346 Andy Van Slyke TC .10 .03
❑ 347 Juan Gonzalez TC .20 .06
❑ 348 Roger Clemens TC .50 .15
❑ 349 Barry Larkin TC .20 .06
❑ 350 Andres Galarraga TC .10 .03
❑ 351 Kevin Appier TC .10 .03
❑ 352 Cecil Fielder TC .10 .03
❑ 353 Kirby Puckett TC .30 .09
❑ 354 Frank Thomas TC .30 .09
❑ 355 Don Mattingly TC .60 .18
❑ 356 Bo Jackson .50 .15
❑ 357 Randy Johnson .50 .15
❑ 358 Darren Daulton .20 .06
❑ 359 Charlie Hough .20 .06
❑ 360 Andres Galarraga .20 .06
❑ 361 Mike Felder .10 .03
❑ 362 Chris Hammond .10 .03
❑ 363 Shawon Dunston .10 .03
❑ 364 Junior Felix .10 .03
❑ 365 Ray Lankford .10 .03
❑ 366 Darryl Strawberry .20 .06
❑ 367 Dave Magadan .10 .03
❑ 368 Gregg Olson .10 .03
❑ 369 Lenny Dykstra .20 .06
❑ 370 Darrin Jackson .10 .03
❑ 371 Dave Stewart .20 .06
❑ 372 Terry Pendleton .20 .06
❑ 373 Arthur Rhodes .10 .03
❑ 374 Benito Santiago .20 .06
❑ 375 Travis Fryman .20 .06
❑ 376 Scott Brosius .20 .06
❑ 377 Stan Belinda .10 .03
❑ 378 Derek Parks .10 .03
❑ 379 Kevin Seitzer .10 .03
❑ 380 Wade Boggs .30 .09
❑ 381 Wally Whitehurst .10 .03
❑ 382 Scott Leius .10 .03
❑ 383 Danny Tartabull .10 .03
❑ 384 Harold Reynolds .20 .06
❑ 385 Tim Raines .20 .06
❑ 386 Darryl Hamilton .10 .03
❑ 387 Felix Fermin .10 .03
❑ 388 Jim Eisenreich .10 .03
❑ 389 Kurt Abbott .20 .06
❑ 390 Kevin Appier .20 .06
❑ 391 Chris Bosio .10 .03
❑ 392 Randy Tomlin .10 .03
❑ 393 Bob Hamelin .10 .03
❑ 394 Kevin Gross .10 .03
❑ 395 Wil Cordero .10 .03
❑ 396 Joe Girardi .10 .03
❑ 397 Orestes Destrade .10 .03
❑ 398 Chris Haney .10 .03
❑ 399 Xavier Hernandez .10 .03
❑ 400 Mike Piazza 1.00 .30
❑ 401 Alex Arias .10 .03
❑ 402 Tom Candiotti .10 .03
❑ 403 Kirk Gibson .20 .06
❑ 404 Chuck Carr .10 .03
❑ 405 Brady Anderson .20 .06
❑ 406 Greg Gagne .10 .03
❑ 407 Bruce Ruffin .10 .03
❑ 408 Scott Hemond .10 .03
❑ 409 Keith Miller .10 .03
❑ 410 John Wetteland .20 .06
❑ 411 Eric Anthony .10 .03
❑ 412 Andre Dawson .20 .06
❑ 413 Doug Henry .10 .03
❑ 414 John Franco .20 .06
❑ 415 Julio Franco .20 .06
❑ 416 Dave Hansen .10 .03
❑ 417 Mike Harkey .10 .03
❑ 418 Jack Armstrong .10 .03
❑ 419 Joe Orsulak .10 .03
❑ 420 John Smoltz .30 .09
❑ 421 Scott Livingstone .10 .03
❑ 422 Darren Holmes .10 .03
❑ 423 Ed Sprague .10 .03
❑ 424 Jay Buhner .20 .06
❑ 425 Kirby Puckett .50 .15
❑ 426 Phil Clark .10 .03
❑ 427 Anthony Young .10 .03
❑ 428 Reggie Jefferson .10 .03
❑ 429 Mariano Duncan .10 .03
❑ 430 Tom Glavine .30 .09
❑ 431 Dave Henderson .10 .03
❑ 432 Melido Perez .10 .03
❑ 433 Paul Wagner .10 .03
❑ 434 Tim Worrell .10 .03
❑ 435 Ozzie Guillen .10 .03
❑ 436 Mike Butcher .10 .03
❑ 437 Jim Deshaies .10 .03
❑ 438 Kevin Young .10 .03
❑ 439 Tom Browning .10 .03
❑ 440 Mike Greenwell .10 .03
❑ 441 Mike Stanton .10 .03
❑ 442 John Doherty .10 .03
❑ 443 John Dopson .10 .03
❑ 444 Carlos Baerga .10 .03
❑ 445 Jack McDowell .10 .03
❑ 446 Kent Mercker .10 .03
❑ 447 Ricky Jordan .10 .03
❑ 448 Jerry Browne .10 .03
❑ 449 Fernando Vina .10 .03
❑ 450 Jim Abbott .30 .09
❑ 451 Teddy Higuera .10 .03
❑ 452 Tim Naehring .10 .03
❑ 453 Jim Leyritz .10 .03
❑ 454 Frank Castillo .10 .03
❑ 455 Joe Carter .20 .06
❑ 456 Craig Biggio .30 .09
❑ 457 Geronimo Pena .10 .03
❑ 458 Alejandro Pena .10 .03
❑ 459 Mike Moore .10 .03
❑ 460 Randy Myers .10 .03
❑ 461 Greg Myers .10 .03
❑ 462 Greg Hibbard .10 .03
❑ 463 Jose Guzman .10 .03
❑ 464 Tom Pagnozzi .10 .03
❑ 465 Marquis Grissom .20 .06
❑ 466 Tim Wallach .10 .03
❑ 467 Joe Grahe .10 .03
❑ 468 Bob Tewksbury .10 .03
❑ 469 B.J. Surhoff .20 .06
❑ 470 Kevin Mitchell .10 .03
❑ 471 Bobby Witt .10 .03
❑ 472 Milt Thompson .10 .03
❑ 473 John Smiley .10 .03
❑ 474 Alan Trammell .20 .06
❑ 475 Mike Mussina .30 .09
❑ 476 Rick Aguilera .10 .03
❑ 477 Jose Valentin .10 .03
❑ 478 Harold Baines .20 .06
❑ 479 Bip Roberts .10 .03
❑ 480 Edgar Martinez .30 .09
❑ 481 Rheal Cormier .10 .03
❑ 482 Hal Morris .10 .03
❑ 483 Pat Kelly .10 .03
❑ 484 Roberto Kelly .10 .03
❑ 485 Chris Sabo .10 .03
❑ 486 Kent Hrbek .20 .06
❑ 487 Scott Kamieniecki .10 .03
❑ 488 Walt Weiss .10 .03
❑ 489 Karl Rhodes .10 .03
❑ 490 Derek Bell .10 .03
❑ 491 Chili Davis .20 .06
❑ 492 Brian Harper .10 .03
❑ 493 Felix Jose .10 .03
❑ 494 Trevor Hoffman .20 .06
❑ 495 Dennis Eckersley .20 .06
❑ 496 Pedro Astacio .10 .03
❑ 497 Jay Bell .20 .06
❑ 498 Randy Velarde .10 .03
❑ 499 David Wells .20 .06
❑ 500 Frank Thomas .50 .15
❑ 501 Mark Lemke .10 .03
❑ 502 Mike Devereaux .10 .03
❑ 503 Chuck McElroy .10 .03
❑ 504 Luis Polonia .10 .03
❑ 505 Damion Easley .10 .03
❑ 506 Greg A. Harris .10 .03
❑ 507 Chris James .10 .03
❑ 508 Terry Mulholland .10 .03
❑ 509 Pete Smith .10 .03
❑ 510 Rickey Henderson .50 .15
❑ 511 Sid Fernandez .10 .03
❑ 512 Al Leiter .20 .06
❑ 513 Doug Jones .10 .03
❑ 514 Steve Farr .10 .03
❑ 515 Chuck Finley .20 .06
❑ 516 Bobby Thigpen .10 .03
❑ 517 Jim Edmonds .50 .15
❑ 518 Graeme Lloyd .10 .03
❑ 519 Dwight Gooden .20 .06
❑ 520 Pat Listach .10 .03
❑ 521 Kevin Bass .10 .03
❑ 522 Willie Banks .10 .03
❑ 523 Steve Finley .20 .06
❑ 524 Delino DeShields .10 .03
❑ 525 Mark McGwire 1.25 .35
❑ 526 Greg Swindell .10 .03
❑ 527 Chris Nabholz .10 .03
❑ 528 Scott Sanders .10 .03
❑ 529 David Segui .10 .03
❑ 530 Howard Johnson .10 .03
❑ 531 Jaime Navarro .10 .03
❑ 532 Jose Vizcaino .10 .03
❑ 533 Mark Lewis .10 .03
❑ 534 Pete Harnisch .10 .03
❑ 535 Robby Thompson .10 .03
❑ 536 Marcus Moore .10 .03
❑ 537 Kevin Brown .20 .06
❑ 538 Mark Clark .10 .03
❑ 539 Sterling Hitchcock .10 .03
❑ 540 Will Clark .50 .15
❑ 541 Denis Boucher .10 .03
❑ 542 Jack Morris .20 .06
❑ 543 Pedro Munoz .10 .03
❑ 544 Bret Boone .20 .06
❑ 545 Ozzie Smith .75 .23

❑ 546 Dennis Martinez	.20	.06
❑ 547 Dan Wilson	.10	.03
❑ 548 Rick Sutcliffe	.20	.06
❑ 549 Kevin McReynolds	.10	.03
❑ 550 Roger Clemens	1.00	.30
❑ 551 Todd Benzinger	.10	.03
❑ 552 Bill Haselman	.10	.03
❑ 553 Bobby Munoz	.10	.03
❑ 554 Ellis Burks	.20	.06
❑ 555 Ryne Sandberg	.75	.23
❑ 556 Lee Smith	.20	.06
❑ 557 Danny Bautista	.10	.03
❑ 558 Rey Sanchez	.10	.03
❑ 559 Norm Charlton	.10	.03
❑ 560 Jose Canseco	.50	.15
❑ 561 Tim Belcher	.10	.03
❑ 562 Denny Neagle	.20	.06
❑ 563 Eric Davis	.20	.06
❑ 564 Jody Reed	.10	.03
❑ 565 Kenny Lofton	.20	.06
❑ 566 Gary Gaetti	.20	.06
❑ 567 Todd Worrell	.10	.03
❑ 568 Mark Portugal	.10	.03
❑ 569 Dick Schofield	.10	.03
❑ 570 Andy Benes	.10	.03
❑ 571 Zane Smith	.10	.03
❑ 572 Bobby Ayala	.10	.03
❑ 573 Chip Hale	.10	.03
❑ 574 Bob Welch	.10	.03
❑ 575 Deion Sanders	.30	.09
❑ 576 David Nied	.10	.03
❑ 577 Pat Mahomes	.10	.03
❑ 578 Charles Nagy	.10	.03
❑ 579 Otis Nixon	.10	.03
❑ 580 Dean Palmer	.20	.06
❑ 581 Roberto Petagine	.10	.03
❑ 582 Dwight Smith	.10	.03
❑ 583 Jeff Russell	.10	.03
❑ 584 Mark Dewey	.10	.03
❑ 585 Greg Vaughn	.10	.03
❑ 586 Brian Hunter	.10	.03
❑ 587 Willie McGee	.20	.06
❑ 588 Pedro Martinez	.50	.15
❑ 589 Roger Salkeld	.10	.03
❑ 590 Jeff Bagwell	.30	.09
❑ 591 Spike Owen	.10	.03
❑ 592 Jeff Reardon	.20	.06
❑ 593 Erik Pappas	.10	.03
❑ 594 Brian Williams	.10	.03
❑ 595 Eddie Murray	.50	.15
❑ 596 Henry Rodriguez	.10	.03
❑ 597 Erik Hanson	.10	.03
❑ 598 Stan Javier	.10	.03
❑ 599 Mitch Williams	.10	.03
❑ 600 John Olerud	.20	.06
❑ 601 Vince Coleman	.10	.03
❑ 602 Damon Berryhill	.10	.03
❑ 603 Tom Brunansky	.10	.03
❑ 604 Robb Nen	.20	.06
❑ 605 Rafael Palmeiro	.30	.09
❑ 606 Cal Eldred	.10	.03
❑ 607 Jeff Brantley	.10	.03
❑ 608 Alan Mills	.10	.03
❑ 609 Jeff Nelson	.10	.03
❑ 610 Barry Bonds	1.25	.35
❑ 611 Carlos Pulido RC	.10	.03
❑ 612 Tim Hyers RC	.10	.03
❑ 613 Steve Howe	.10	.03
❑ 614 Brian Turang RC	.10	.03
❑ 615 Leo Gomez	.10	.03
❑ 616 Jesse Orosco	.10	.03
❑ 617 Dan Pasqua	.10	.03
❑ 618 Marvin Freeman	.10	.03
❑ 619 Tony Fernandez	.10	.03
❑ 620 Albert Belle	.20	.06
❑ 621 Eddie Taubensee	.10	.03
❑ 622 Mike Jackson	.10	.03
❑ 623 Jose Bautista	.10	.03
❑ 624 Jim Thome	.50	.15
❑ 625 Ivan Rodriguez	.50	.15
❑ 626 Ben Rivera	.10	.03
❑ 627 Dave Valle	.10	.03
❑ 628 Tom Henke	.10	.03
❑ 629 Omar Vizquel	.30	.09
❑ 630 Juan Gonzalez	.30	.09
❑ 631 Roberto Alomar UP	.20	.06
❑ 632 Barry Bonds UP	.60	.18
❑ 633 Juan Gonzalez UP	.20	.06
❑ 634 Ken Griffey Jr. UP	.50	.15
❑ 635 Michael Jordan UP	1.50	.45
❑ 636 David Justice UP	.10	.03
❑ 637 Mike Piazza UP	.50	.15
❑ 638 Kirby Puckett UP	.30	.09
❑ 639 Tim Salmon UP	.20	.06
❑ 640 Frank Thomas UP	.30	.09
❑ 641 Alan Benes FF RC	.10	.03
❑ 642 Johnny Damon FF	.50	.15
❑ 643 Brad Fullmer FF RC	.40	.12
❑ 644 Derek Jeter FF	1.50	.45
❑ 645 Derrek Lee FF RC	.50	.15
❑ 646 Alex Ochoa	.10	.03
❑ 647 Alex Rodriguez FF RC	10.00	3.00
❑ 648 Jose Silva FF RC	.10	.03
❑ 649 Terrell Wade FF RC	.10	.03
❑ 650 Preston Wilson FF	.20	.06
❑ 651 Shane Andrews	.10	.03
❑ 652 James Baldwin	.10	.03
❑ 653 Ricky Bottalico RC	.25	.07
❑ 654 Tavo Alvarez	.10	.03
❑ 655 Donnie Elliott	.10	.03
❑ 656 Joey Eischen	.10	.03
❑ 657 Jason Giambi	.50	.15
❑ 658 Todd Hollandsworth	.10	.03
❑ 659 Brian L. Hunter	.10	.03
❑ 660 Charles Johnson	.20	.06
❑ 661 Michael Jordan RC	3.00	.90
❑ 662 Jeff Juden	.10	.03
❑ 663 Mike Kelly	.10	.03
❑ 664 James Mouton	.10	.03
❑ 665 Ray Holbert	.10	.03
❑ 666 Pokey Reese	.10	.03
❑ 667 Ruben Santana RC	.10	.03
❑ 668 Paul Spoljaric	.10	.03
❑ 669 Luis Lopez	.10	.03
❑ 670 Matt Walbeck	.10	.03
❑ P50 Ken Griffey Jr. Promo	1.00	.30

1914 Cracker Jack

	Ex-Mt	VG
COMPLETE SET (144)	45000.00	22500.00
❑ 1 Otto Knabe	250.00	125.00
❑ 2 Frank Baker	400.00	200.00
❑ 3 Joe Tinker	400.00	200.00
❑ 4 Larry Doyle	175.00	90.00
❑ 5 Ward Miller	150.00	75.00
❑ 6 Eddie Plank	600.00	300.00
Phila. AL		
❑ 7 Eddie Collins	450.00	220.00
Phila. AL		
❑ 8 Rube Oldring	150.00	75.00
❑ 9 Artie Hoffman	150.00	75.00
❑ 10 John McInnis	150.00	75.00
❑ 11 George Stovall	150.00	75.00
❑ 12 Connie Mack MG	500.00	250.00
❑ 13 Art Wilson	150.00	75.00
❑ 14 Sam Crawford	300.00	150.00
❑ 15 Reb Russell	150.00	75.00
❑ 16 Howie Camnitz	150.00	75.00
❑ 17 Roger Bresnahan	350.00	180.00
Catcher		
❑ 18 Johnny Evers	350.00	180.00
❑ 19 Chief Bender	450.00	220.00
Phila. AL		
❑ 20 Cy Falkenberg	150.00	75.00
❑ 21 Heinie Zimmerman	150.00	75.00
❑ 22 Joe Wood	300.00	150.00
❑ 23 Chas.Comiskey OWN	350.00	180.00
❑ 24 George Mullen	150.00	75.00
❑ 25 Michael Simon	150.00	75.00
❑ 26 James Scott	150.00	75.00
❑ 27 Bill Carrigan	150.00	75.00
❑ 28 Jack Barry	150.00	75.00
❑ 29 Vean Gregg	200.00	100.00
Cleveland		
❑ 30 Ty Cobb	6000.00	3000.00
❑ 31 Heinie Wagner	150.00	75.00
❑ 32 Mordecai Brown	350.00	180.00
❑ 33 Amos Strunk	150.00	75.00
❑ 34 Ira Thomas	150.00	75.00
❑ 35 Harry Hooper	300.00	150.00
❑ 36 Ed Walsh	300.00	150.00
❑ 37 Grover C. Alexander	800.00	400.00
❑ 38 Red Dooin	200.00	100.00
Phila. NL		
❑ 39 Chick Gandil	350.00	180.00
❑ 40 Jimmy Austin	200.00	100.00
St.L. AL		
❑ 41 Tommy Leach	150.00	75.00
❑ 42 Al Bridwell	150.00	75.00
❑ 43 Rube Marquard	350.00	180.00
NY NL		
❑ 44 Charles Tesreau	150.00	75.00
❑ 45 Fred Luderus	150.00	75.00
❑ 46 Bob Groom	150.00	75.00
❑ 47 Josh Devore	200.00	100.00
Phila. NL		
❑ 48 Harry Lord	250.00	125.00
❑ 49 John Miller	150.00	75.00
❑ 50 John Hummell	150.00	75.00
❑ 51 Nap Rucker	175.00	90.00
❑ 52 Zach Wheat	350.00	180.00
❑ 53 Otto Miller	150.00	75.00
❑ 54 Marty O'Toole	150.00	75.00
❑ 55 Dick Hoblitzel	200.00	100.00
Cinc.		
❑ 56 Clyde Milan	175.00	90.00
❑ 57 Walter Johnson	2000.00	1000.00
❑ 58 Wally Schang	175.00	90.00
❑ 59 Harry Gessler	150.00	75.00
❑ 60 Rollie Zeider	250.00	125.00
❑ 61 Ray Schalk	300.00	150.00
❑ 62 Jay Cashion	300.00	150.00
❑ 63 Babe Adams	175.00	90.00
❑ 64 Jimmy Archer	150.00	75.00
❑ 65 Tris Speaker	700.00	350.00
❑ 66 Napoleon Lajoie	800.00	400.00
Cleve.		
❑ 67 Otis Crandall	150.00	75.00
❑ 68 Honus Wagner	2500.00	1250.00
❑ 69 John McGraw	450.00	220.00
❑ 70 Fred Clarke	300.00	150.00
❑ 71 Chief Meyers	175.00	90.00
❑ 72 John Boehling	150.00	75.00
❑ 73 Max Carey	300.00	150.00
❑ 74 Frank Owens	150.00	75.00
❑ 75 Miller Huggins	300.00	150.00
❑ 76 Claude Hendrix	150.00	75.00
❑ 77 Hughie Jennings MG	300.00	150.00
❑ 78 Fred Merkle	200.00	100.00
❑ 79 Ping Bodie	175.00	90.00
❑ 80 Ed Ruelbach	175.00	90.00
❑ 81 Jim C. Delehanty	175.00	90.00
❑ 82 Gavvy Cravath	200.00	100.00
❑ 83 Russ Ford	150.00	75.00
❑ 84 Elmer E. Knetzer	150.00	75.00
❑ 85 Buck Herzog	150.00	75.00
❑ 86 Burt Shotton	150.00	75.00
❑ 87 Forrest Cady	150.00	75.00
❑ 88 Christy Mathewson	3000.00	1500.00
Pitching		
❑ 89 Lawrence Cheney	150.00	75.00
❑ 90 Frank Smith	150.00	75.00
❑ 91 Roger Peckinpaugh	175.00	90.00
❑ 92 Al Demaree N.Y. NL	200.00	100.00
❑ 93 Del Pratt	250.00	125.00
Throwing		
❑ 94 Eddie Cicotte	325.00	160.00
❑ 95 Ray Keating	150.00	75.00

❑ 96	Beals Becker	150.00	75.00
❑ 97	John(Rube) Benton	150.00	75.00
❑ 98	Frank LaPorte	150.00	75.00
❑ 99	Frank Chance	1500.00	750.00
❑ 100	Thomas Seaton	150.00	75.00
❑ 101	Frank Schulte	150.00	75.00
❑ 102	Ray Fisher	150.00	75.00
❑ 103	Joe Jackson	8000.00	4000.00
❑ 104	Vic Saier	150.00	75.00
❑ 105	James Lavender	150.00	75.00
❑ 106	Joe Birmingham	150.00	75.00
❑ 107	Tom Downey	150.00	75.00
❑ 108	Sherry Magee	200.00	100.00
	Phila. NL		
❑ 109	Fred Blanding	150.00	75.00
❑ 110	Bob Bescher	150.00	75.00
❑ 111	Jim Callahan	300.00	150.00
❑ 112	Ed Sweeney	150.00	75.00
❑ 113	George Suggs	150.00	75.00
❑ 114	Geo.J. Moriarty	175.00	90.00
❑ 115	Addison Brennan	150.00	75.00
❑ 116	Rollie Zeider	150.00	75.00
❑ 117	Ted Easterly	150.00	75.00
❑ 118	Ed Konetchy	200.00	100.00
	Pittsburgh		
❑ 119	George Perring	150.00	75.00
❑ 120	Mike Doolan	150.00	75.00
❑ 121	Hub Perdue	200.00	100.00
	Boston NL		
❑ 122	Owen Bush	150.00	75.00
❑ 123	Slim Sallee	150.00	75.00
❑ 124	Earl Moore	150.00	75.00
❑ 125	Bert Niehoff	200.00	100.00
❑ 126	Walter Blair	150.00	75.00
❑ 127	Butch Schmidt	150.00	75.00
❑ 128	Steve Evans	150.00	75.00
❑ 129	Ray Caldwell	150.00	75.00
❑ 130	Ivy Wingo	150.00	75.00
❑ 131	George Baumgardner	150.00	75.00
❑ 132	Les Nunamaker	150.00	75.00
❑ 133	Branch Rickey MG	450.00	220.00
❑ 134	Armando Marsans	200.00	100.00
	Cincinnati		
❑ 135	Bill Killefer	150.00	75.00
❑ 136	Rabbit Maranville	350.00	180.00
❑ 137	William Rariden	150.00	75.00
❑ 138	Hank Gowdy	150.00	75.00
❑ 139	Rebel Oakes	150.00	75.00
❑ 140	Danny Murphy	150.00	75.00
❑ 141	Cy Barger	150.00	75.00
❑ 142	Eugene Packard	150.00	75.00
❑ 143	Jake Daubert	175.00	90.00
❑ 144	James C. Walsh	200.00	100.00

1915 Cracker Jack

	Ex-Mt	VG
COMPLETE SET (176)	35000.00	17500.00
COMMON CARD (1-144)	100.00	50.00
COMM. CARD (145-176)	125.00	60.00

❑ 1	Otto Knabe	175.00	90.00
❑ 2	Frank Baker	350.00	180.00
❑ 3	Joe Tinker	350.00	180.00
❑ 4	Larry Doyle	100.00	50.00
❑ 5	Ward Miller	100.00	50.00
❑ 6	Eddie Plank	500.00	250.00
	St.L. FED		
❑ 7	Eddie Collins	350.00	180.00
	Chicago AL		
❑ 8	Rube Oldring	100.00	50.00
❑ 9	Artie Hoffman	100.00	50.00
❑ 10	John McInnis	100.00	50.00
❑ 11	George Stovall	100.00	50.00
❑ 12	Connie Mack MG	400.00	200.00
❑ 13	Art Wilson	100.00	50.00
❑ 14	Sam Crawford	300.00	150.00
❑ 15	Reb Russell	100.00	50.00
❑ 16	Howie Camnitz	100.00	50.00
❑ 17	Roger Bresnahan	300.00	150.00
❑ 18	Johnny Evers	300.00	150.00
❑ 19	Chief Bender	350.00	180.00
	Baltimore FED		
❑ 20	Cy Falkenberg	100.00	50.00
❑ 21	Heinie Zimmerman	100.00	50.00
❑ 22	Joe Wood	250.00	125.00
❑ 23	C. Comiskey OWN	300.00	150.00
❑ 24	George Mullen	100.00	50.00
❑ 25	Michael Simon	100.00	50.00
❑ 26	James Scott	100.00	50.00
❑ 27	Bill Carrigan	100.00	50.00
❑ 28	Jack Barry	100.00	50.00
❑ 29	Vean Gregg	125.00	60.00
	Boston AL		
❑ 30	Ty Cobb	4000.00	2000.00
❑ 31	Heinie Wagner	100.00	50.00
❑ 32	Mordecai Brown	300.00	150.00
❑ 33	Amos Strunk	100.00	50.00
❑ 34	Ira Thomas	100.00	50.00
❑ 35	Harry Hooper	250.00	125.00
❑ 36	Ed Walsh	300.00	150.00
❑ 37	Grover C. Alexander	600.00	300.00
❑ 38	Red Dooin	125.00	60.00
	Cincinnati		
❑ 39	Chick Gandil	300.00	150.00
❑ 40	Jimmy Austin	125.00	60.00
	Pitts. FED		
❑ 41	Tommy Leach	100.00	50.00
❑ 42	Al Bridwell	100.00	50.00
❑ 43	Rube Marquard	350.00	180.00
	Brooklyn FED		
❑ 44	Charles(Jeff) Tesreau	100.00	50.00
❑ 45	Fred Luderus	100.00	50.00
❑ 46	Bob Groom	100.00	50.00
❑ 47	Josh Devore	125.00	60.00
	Boston NL		
❑ 48	Steve O'Neill	125.00	60.00
❑ 49	John Miller	100.00	50.00
❑ 50	John Hummell	100.00	50.00
❑ 51	Nap Rucker	125.00	60.00
❑ 52	Zach Wheat	300.00	150.00
❑ 53	Otto Miller	100.00	50.00
❑ 54	Marty O'Toole	100.00	50.00
❑ 55	Dick Hoblitzel	125.00	60.00
	Boston AL		
❑ 56	Clyde Milan	125.00	60.00
❑ 57	Walter Johnson	1500.00	750.00
❑ 58	Wally Schang	125.00	60.00
❑ 59	Harry Gessler	100.00	50.00
❑ 60	Oscar Dugey	125.00	60.00
❑ 61	Ray Schalk	250.00	125.00
❑ 62	Willie Mitchell	125.00	60.00
❑ 63	Babe Adams	125.00	60.00
❑ 64	Jimmy Archer	100.00	50.00
❑ 65	Tris Speaker	600.00	300.00
❑ 66	Napoleon Lajoie	600.00	300.00
	Phila. AL		
❑ 67	Otis Crandall	100.00	50.00
❑ 68	Honus Wagner	1500.00	750.00
❑ 69	John McGraw MG	300.00	150.00
❑ 70	Fred Clarke	250.00	125.00
❑ 71	Chief Meyers	100.00	50.00
❑ 72	John Boehling	100.00	50.00
❑ 73	Max Carey	250.00	125.00
❑ 74	Frank Owens	100.00	50.00
❑ 75	Miller Huggins	300.00	150.00
❑ 76	Claude Hendrix	100.00	50.00
❑ 77	Hughie Jennings MG	300.00	150.00
❑ 78	Fred Merkle	125.00	60.00
❑ 79	Ping Bodie	125.00	60.00
❑ 80	Ed Ruelbach	125.00	60.00
❑ 81	Jim C. Delehanty	125.00	60.00
❑ 82	Gavvy Cravath	125.00	60.00
❑ 83	Russ Ford	100.00	50.00
❑ 84	Elmer E. Knetzer	100.00	50.00
❑ 85	Buck Herzog	100.00	50.00
❑ 86	Burt Shotton	100.00	50.00
❑ 87	Forrest Cady	100.00	50.00
❑ 88	Christy Mathewson	1500.00	750.00
	Portrait		
❑ 89	Lawrence Cheney	100.00	50.00
❑ 90	Frank Smith	100.00	50.00
❑ 91	Roger Peckinpaugh	125.00	60.00
❑ 92	Al Demaree	125.00	60.00
	Phila. NL		
❑ 93	Del Pratt	175.00	90.00
	Portrait		
❑ 94	Eddie Cicotte	300.00	150.00
❑ 95	Ray Keating	100.00	50.00
❑ 96	Beals Becker	100.00	50.00
❑ 97	John(Rube) Benton	100.00	50.00
❑ 98	Frank LaPorte	100.00	50.00
❑ 99	Hal Chase	300.00	150.00
❑ 100	Thomas Seaton	100.00	50.00
❑ 101	Frank Schulte	100.00	50.00
❑ 102	Ray Fisher	100.00	50.00
❑ 103	Joe Jackson	8000.00	4000.00
❑ 104	Vic Saier	100.00	50.00
❑ 105	James Lavender	100.00	50.00
❑ 106	Joe Birmingham MG	100.00	50.00
❑ 107	Thomas Downey	100.00	50.00
❑ 108	Sherry Magee	125.00	60.00
	Boston NL		
❑ 109	Fred Blanding	100.00	50.00
❑ 110	Bob Bescher	100.00	50.00
❑ 111	Herbie Moran	125.00	60.00
❑ 112	Ed Sweeney	100.00	50.00
❑ 113	George Suggs	100.00	50.00
❑ 114	Geo.J. Moriarty	125.00	60.00
❑ 115	Addison Brennan	100.00	50.00
❑ 116	Rollie Zeider	100.00	50.00
❑ 117	Ted Easterly	100.00	50.00
❑ 118	Ed Konetchy	125.00	60.00
	Pitts. FED		
❑ 119	George Perring	100.00	50.00
❑ 120	Mike Doolan	100.00	50.00
❑ 121	Hub Perdue	125.00	60.00
	St. Louis NL		
❑ 122	Owen Bush	100.00	50.00
❑ 123	Slim Sallee	100.00	50.00
❑ 124	Earl Moore	100.00	50.00
❑ 125	Bert Niehoff	125.00	60.00
	Phila. NL		
❑ 126	Walter Blair	100.00	50.00
❑ 127	Butch Schmidt	100.00	50.00
❑ 128	Steve Evans	100.00	50.00
❑ 129	Ray Caldwell	100.00	50.00
❑ 130	Ivy Wingo	100.00	50.00
❑ 131	Geo. Baumgardner	100.00	50.00
❑ 132	Les Nunamaker	100.00	50.00
❑ 133	Branch Rickey MG	300.00	150.00
❑ 134	Armando Marsans	125.00	60.00
	St.L. FED		
❑ 135	William Killefer	100.00	50.00
❑ 136	Rabbit Maranville	250.00	125.00
❑ 137	William Rariden	100.00	50.00
❑ 138	Hank Gowdy	100.00	50.00
❑ 139	Rebel Oakes	100.00	50.00
❑ 140	Danny Murphy	100.00	50.00
❑ 141	Cy Barger	100.00	50.00
❑ 142	Eugene Packard	100.00	50.00
❑ 143	Jake Daubert	100.00	50.00
❑ 144	James C. Walsh	100.00	50.00
❑ 145	Ted Cather	125.00	60.00
❑ 146	George Tyler	125.00	60.00
❑ 147	Lee Magee	125.00	60.00
❑ 148	Owen Wilson	125.00	60.00
❑ 149	Hal Janvrin	125.00	60.00
❑ 150	Doc Johnston	125.00	60.00
❑ 151	George Whitted	125.00	60.00
❑ 152	George McQuillen	125.00	60.00
❑ 153	Bill James	125.00	60.00
❑ 154	Dick Rudolph	125.00	60.00
❑ 155	Joe Connolly	125.00	60.00
❑ 156	Jean Dubuc	125.00	60.00
❑ 157	George Kaiserling	125.00	60.00
❑ 158	Fritz Maisel	125.00	60.00
❑ 159	Heinie Groh	125.00	60.00
❑ 160	Benny Kauff	125.00	60.00
❑ 161	Edd Roush	300.00	150.00

❑ 162 George Stallings MG	125.00	60.00
❑ 163 Bert Whaling	125.00	60.00
❑ 164 Bob Shawkey	125.00	60.00
❑ 165 Eddie Murphy	125.00	60.00
❑ 166 Joe Bush	125.00	60.00
❑ 167 Clark Griffith	300.00	150.00
❑ 168 Vin Campbell	125.00	60.00
❑ 169 Raymond Collins	125.00	60.00
❑ 170 Hans Lobert	125.00	60.00
❑ 171 Earl Hamilton	125.00	60.00
❑ 172 Erskine Mayer	125.00	60.00
❑ 173 Tilly Walker	125.00	60.00
❑ 174 Robert Veach	125.00	60.00
❑ 175 Joseph Benz	125.00	60.00
❑ 176 Hippo Vaughn	175.00	90.00

2002 Diamond Kings

	Nm-Mt	Ex-Mt
COMP.LOW SET (150)	200.00	60.00
COMP.LOW w/o SP's (100)	50.00	15.00
COMP.UPDATE SET (10)	40.00	12.00
COMMON CARD (1-100)	.50	.15
COMMON PROSPECT (101-150)	4.00	1.20
COMMON RETIRED (101-150)	4.00	1.20
COMMON CARD (151-160)	4.00	1.20

❑ 1 Vladimir Guerrero	1.25	.35
❑ 2 Adam Dunn	.75	.23
❑ 3 Tsuyoshi Shinjo	.50	.15
❑ 4 Adrian Beltre	.75	.23
❑ 5 Troy Glaus	.50	.15
❑ 6 Albert Pujols	2.50	.75
❑ 7 Trot Nixon	.50	.15
❑ 8 Alex Rodriguez	2.00	.60
❑ 9 Tom Glavine	.75	.23
❑ 10 Alfonso Soriano	.75	.23
❑ 11 Todd Helton	.75	.23
❑ 12 Joe Torre	1.25	.35
❑ 13 Tim Hudson	.50	.15
❑ 14 Andruw Jones	.50	.15
❑ 15 Shawn Green	.50	.15
❑ 16 Aramis Ramirez	.50	.15
❑ 17 Shannon Stewart	.50	.15
❑ 18 Barry Bonds	3.00	.90
❑ 19 Sean Casey	.50	.15
❑ 20 Barry Larkin	.75	.23
❑ 21 Scott Rolen	1.25	.35
❑ 22 Barry Zito	.50	.15
❑ 23 Sammy Sosa	2.00	.60
❑ 24 Bartolo Colon	.50	.15
❑ 25 Ryan Klesko	.50	.15
❑ 26 Ben Grieve	.50	.15
❑ 27 Roy Oswalt	.50	.15
❑ 28 Kazuhiro Sasaki	.50	.15
❑ 29 Roger Clemens	2.50	.75
❑ 30 Bernie Williams	.75	.23
❑ 31 Roberto Alomar	.75	.23
❑ 32 Bobby Abreu	.50	.15
❑ 33 Robert Fick	.50	.15
❑ 34 Bret Boone	.50	.15
❑ 35 Rickey Henderson	1.25	.35
❑ 36 Brian Giles	.50	.15
❑ 37 Richie Sexson	.50	.15
❑ 38 Bud Smith	.50	.15
❑ 39 Richard Hidalgo	.50	.15
❑ 40 C. C. Sabathia	.50	.15
❑ 41 Rich Aurilia	.50	.15
❑ 42 Carlos Beltran	.75	.23
❑ 43 Raul Mondesi	.50	.15
❑ 44 Carlos Delgado	.50	.15
❑ 45 Randy Johnson	1.25	.35
❑ 46 Chan Ho Park	.50	.15
❑ 47 Rafael Palmeiro	.75	.23
❑ 48 Chipper Jones	1.25	.35
❑ 49 Phil Nevin	.50	.15
❑ 50 Cliff Floyd	.50	.15
❑ 51 Pedro Martinez	1.25	.35
❑ 52 Craig Biggio	.75	.23
❑ 53 Paul LoDuca	.50	.15
❑ 54 Cristian Guzman	.50	.15
❑ 55 Pat Burrell	.50	.15
❑ 56 Curt Schilling	.50	.15
❑ 57 Orlando Cabrera	.50	.15
❑ 58 Darin Erstad	.50	.15
❑ 59 Omar Vizquel	.75	.23
❑ 60 Derek Jeter	3.00	.90
❑ 61 Nomar Garciaparra	2.00	.60
❑ 62 Edgar Martinez	.75	.23
❑ 63 Moises Alou	.50	.15
❑ 64 Eric Chavez	.50	.15
❑ 65 Mike Sweeney	.50	.15
❑ 66 Frank Thomas	1.25	.35
❑ 67 Mike Piazza	2.00	.60
❑ 68 Gary Sheffield	.50	.15
❑ 69 Mike Mussina	.75	.23
❑ 70 Greg Maddux	2.00	.60
❑ 71 Juan Gonzalez	.75	.23
❑ 72 Hideo Nomo	1.25	.35
❑ 73 Miguel Tejada	.50	.15
❑ 74 Ichiro Suzuki	2.00	.60
❑ 75 Matt Morris	.50	.15
❑ 76 Ivan Rodriguez	1.25	.35
❑ 77 Mark Mulder	.50	.15
❑ 78 J.D. Drew	.50	.15
❑ 79 Mark Grace	.75	.23
❑ 80 Jason Giambi	.50	.15
❑ 81 Mark Buehrle	.50	.15
❑ 82 Jose Vidro	.50	.15
❑ 83 Manny Ramirez	.75	.23
❑ 84 Jeff Bagwell	.75	.23
❑ 85 Magglio Ordonez	.50	.15
❑ 86 Ken Griffey Jr.	2.00	.60
❑ 87 Luis Gonzalez	.50	.15
❑ 88 Jim Edmonds	.50	.15
❑ 89 Larry Walker	.75	.23
❑ 90 Jim Thome	1.25	.35
❑ 91 Lance Berkman	.50	.15
❑ 92 Jorge Posada	.75	.23
❑ 93 Kevin Brown	.50	.15
❑ 94 Joe Mays	.50	.15
❑ 95 Kerry Wood	1.25	.35
❑ 96 Mark Ellis	.50	.15
❑ 97 Austin Kearns	.50	.15
❑ 98 Jorge De La Rosa RC	.50	.15
❑ 99 Brandon Berger	.50	.15
❑ 100 Ryan Ludwick	.50	.15
❑ 101 Marlon Byrd SP	4.00	1.20
❑ 102 Brandon Backe SP RC	5.00	1.50
❑ 103 Juan Cruz SP	4.00	1.20
❑ 104 Anderson Machado SP RC	4.00	1.20
❑ 105 So Taguchi SP RC	4.00	1.20
❑ 106 Dewon Brazelton SP	4.00	1.20
❑ 107 Josh Beckett SP	4.00	1.20
❑ 108 John Buck SP	4.00	1.20
❑ 109 Jorge Padilla SP RC	4.00	1.20
❑ 110 Hee Seop Choi SP	4.00	1.20
❑ 111 Angel Berroa SP	4.00	1.20
❑ 112 Mark Teixeira SP	4.00	1.20
❑ 113 Victor Martinez SP	5.00	1.50
❑ 114 Kazuhisa Ishii SP RC	6.00	1.80
❑ 115 Dennis Tankersley SP	4.00	1.20
❑ 116 Wilson Valdez SP RC	4.00	1.20
❑ 117 Antonio Perez SP	4.00	1.20
❑ 118 Ed Rogers SP	4.00	1.20
❑ 119 Wilson Betemit SP	4.00	1.20
❑ 120 Mike Rivera SP	4.00	1.20
❑ 121 Mark Prior SP	8.00	2.40
❑ 122 Roberto Clemente SP	8.00	2.40
❑ 123 Roberto Clemente SP	8.00	2.40
❑ 124 Roberto Clemente SP	8.00	2.40
❑ 125 Roberto Clemente SP	8.00	2.40
❑ 126 Roberto Clemente SP	8.00	2.40
❑ 127 Babe Ruth SP	10.00	3.00
❑ 128 Ted Williams SP	8.00	2.40
❑ 129 Andre Dawson SP	4.00	1.20
❑ 130 Eddie Murray SP	5.00	1.50
❑ 131 Juan Marichal SP	4.00	1.20
❑ 132 Kirby Puckett SP	5.00	1.50
❑ 133 Alan Trammell SP	4.00	1.20
❑ 134 Bobby Doerr SP	4.00	1.20
❑ 135 Carlton Fisk SP	4.00	1.20
❑ 136 Eddie Mathews SP	5.00	1.50
❑ 137 Mike Schmidt SP	10.00	3.00
❑ 138 Catfish Hunter SP	4.00	1.20
❑ 139 Nolan Ryan SP	12.00	3.60
❑ 140 George Brett SP	12.00	3.60
❑ 141 Gary Carter SP	4.00	1.20
❑ 142 Paul Molitor SP	4.00	1.20
❑ 143 Lou Gehrig SP	6.00	1.80
❑ 144 Ryne Sandberg SP	10.00	3.00
❑ 145 Tony Gwynn SP	6.00	1.80
❑ 146 Ron Santo SP	4.00	1.20
❑ 147 Cal Ripken SP	15.00	4.50
❑ 148 Al Kaline SP	5.00	1.50
❑ 149 Bo Jackson SP	5.00	1.50
❑ 150 Don Mattingly SP	12.00	3.60
❑ 151 Chris Snelling RC	4.00	1.20
❑ 152 Satoru Komiyama RC	4.00	1.20
❑ 153 Oliver Perez RC	8.00	2.40
❑ 154 Kirk Saarloos RC	4.00	1.20
❑ 155 Rene Reyes RC	4.00	1.20
❑ 156 Runelvys Hernandez RC	4.00	1.20
❑ 157 Rodrigo Rosario RC	4.00	1.20
❑ 158 Jason Simontacchi RC	4.00	1.20
❑ 159 Miguel Asencio RC	4.00	1.20
❑ 160 Aaron Cook RC	4.00	1.20

2003 Diamond Kings

	Nm-Mt	Ex-Mt
COMP.LO SET (176)	150.00	45.00
COMP.LO SET w/o SP's (150)	50.00	15.00
COMMON CARD (1-150)	.50	.15
COMMON CARD (151-158)	2.00	.60
COMMON CARD (159-175)	4.00	1.20
COMMON CARD (177-201)	4.00	1.20

❑ 1 Darin Erstad	.50	.15
❑ 2 Garret Anderson	.50	.15
❑ 3 Troy Glaus	.50	.15
❑ 4 David Eckstein	.50	.15
❑ 5 Jarrod Washburn	.50	.15
❑ 6 Adam Kennedy	.50	.15
❑ 7 Jay Gibbons	.50	.15
❑ 8 Tony Batista	.50	.15
❑ 9 Melvin Mora	.50	.15
❑ 10 Rodrigo Lopez	.50	.15
❑ 11 Manny Ramirez	.75	.23
❑ 12 Pedro Martinez	1.25	.35
❑ 13 Nomar Garciaparra	2.00	.60
❑ 14 Rickey Henderson	1.25	.35
❑ 15 Johnny Damon	1.25	.35
❑ 16 Derek Lowe	.50	.15
❑ 17 Cliff Floyd	.50	.15
❑ 18 Frank Thomas	1.25	.35
❑ 19 Magglio Ordonez	.50	.15
❑ 20 Paul Konerko	.50	.15
❑ 21 Mark Buehrle	.50	.15
❑ 22 C.C. Sabathia	.50	.15
❑ 23 Omar Vizquel	.75	.23
❑ 24 Jim Thome	1.25	.35

❑ 25 Ellis Burks .50 .15
❑ 26 Robert Fick .50 .15
❑ 27 Bobby Higginson .50 .15
❑ 28 Randall Simon .50 .15
❑ 29 Carlos Pena .50 .15
❑ 30 Carlos Beltran .75 .23
❑ 31 Paul Byrd .50 .15
❑ 32 Raul Ibanez .50 .15
❑ 33 Mike Sweeney .50 .15
❑ 34 Torii Hunter .50 .15
❑ 35 Corey Koskie .50 .15
❑ 36 A.J. Pierzynski .50 .15
❑ 37 Cristian Guzman .50 .15
❑ 38 Jacque Jones .50 .15
❑ 39 Derek Jeter 3.00 .90
❑ 40 Bernie Williams .75 .23
❑ 41 Roger Clemens 2.50 .75
❑ 42 Mike Mussina .75 .23
❑ 43 Jorge Posada .75 .23
❑ 44 Alfonso Soriano .75 .23
❑ 45 Jason Giambi .50 .15
❑ 46 Robin Ventura .50 .15
❑ 47 David Wells .50 .15
❑ 48 Tim Hudson .50 .15
❑ 49 Barry Zito .50 .15
❑ 50 Mark Mulder .50 .15
❑ 51 Miguel Tejada .50 .15
❑ 52 Eric Chavez .50 .15
❑ 53 Jermaine Dye .50 .15
❑ 54 Ichiro Suzuki 2.00 .60
❑ 55 Edgar Martinez .75 .23
❑ 56 John Olerud .50 .15
❑ 57 Dan Wilson .50 .15
❑ 58 Joel Pineiro .50 .15
❑ 59 Kazuhiro Sasaki .50 .15
❑ 60 Freddy Garcia .50 .15
❑ 61 Aubrey Huff .50 .15
❑ 62 Steve Cox .50 .15
❑ 63 Randy Winn .50 .15
❑ 64 Alex Rodriguez 2.00 .60
❑ 65 Juan Gonzalez .75 .23
❑ 66 Rafael Palmeiro .75 .23
❑ 67 Ivan Rodriguez 1.25 .35
❑ 68 Kenny Rogers .50 .15
❑ 69 Carlos Delgado .50 .15
❑ 70 Eric Hinske .50 .15
❑ 71 Roy Halladay .50 .15
❑ 72 Vernon Wells .50 .15
❑ 73 Shannon Stewart .50 .15
❑ 74 Curt Schilling .50 .15
❑ 75 Randy Johnson 1.25 .35
❑ 76 Luis Gonzalez .50 .15
❑ 77 Mark Grace .75 .23
❑ 78 Junior Spivey .50 .15
❑ 79 Greg Maddux 2.00 .60
❑ 80 Tom Glavine .75 .23
❑ 81 John Smoltz .75 .23
❑ 82 Chipper Jones 1.25 .35
❑ 83 Gary Sheffield .50 .15
❑ 84 Andruw Jones .50 .15
❑ 85 Kerry Wood 1.25 .35
❑ 86 Fred McGriff .75 .23
❑ 87 Sammy Sosa 2.00 .60
❑ 88 Mark Prior 1.25 .35
❑ 89 Ken Griffey Jr. 2.00 .60
❑ 90 Barry Larkin .75 .23
❑ 91 Adam Dunn .75 .23
❑ 92 Sean Casey .50 .15
❑ 93 Austin Kearns .50 .15
❑ 94 Aaron Boone .50 .15
❑ 95 Larry Walker .75 .23
❑ 96 Todd Helton .75 .23
❑ 97 Jason Jennings .50 .15
❑ 98 Jay Payton .50 .15
❑ 99 Josh Beckett .50 .15
❑ 100 Mike Lowell .50 .15
❑ 101 A.J. Burnett .50 .15
❑ 102 Jeff Bagwell .75 .23
❑ 103 Craig Biggio .75 .23
❑ 104 Lance Berkman .50 .15
❑ 105 Roy Oswalt .50 .15
❑ 106 Wade Miller .50 .15
❑ 107 Shawn Green .50 .15
❑ 108 Adrian Beltre .75 .23
❑ 109 Hideo Nomo 1.25 .35
❑ 110 Kazuhisa Ishii .50 .15
❑ 111 Odalis Perez .50 .15
❑ 112 Paul Lo Duca .50 .15
❑ 113 Ben Sheets .50 .15
❑ 114 Richie Sexson .50 .15
❑ 115 Jose Hernandez .50 .15
❑ 116 Vladimir Guerrero 1.25 .35
❑ 117 Jose Vidro .50 .15
❑ 118 Tomo Ohka .50 .15
❑ 119 Andres Galarraga .50 .15
❑ 120 Bartolo Colon .50 .15
❑ 121 Mike Piazza 2.00 .60
❑ 122 Roberto Alomar .75 .23
❑ 123 Mo Vaughn .50 .15
❑ 124 Al Leiter .50 .15
❑ 125 Edgardo Alfonzo .50 .15
❑ 126 Pat Burrell .50 .15
❑ 127 Bobby Abreu .50 .15
❑ 128 Mike Lieberthal .50 .15
❑ 129 Vicente Padilla .50 .15
❑ 130 Marlon Byrd .50 .15
❑ 131 Jason Kendall .50 .15
❑ 132 Brian Giles .50 .15
❑ 133 Aramis Ramirez .50 .15
❑ 134 Kip Wells .50 .15
❑ 135 Ryan Klesko .50 .15
❑ 136 Phil Nevin .50 .15
❑ 137 Brian Lawrence .50 .15
❑ 138 Sean Burroughs .50 .15
❑ 139 Mark Kotsay .50 .15
❑ 140 Barry Bonds 3.00 .90
❑ 141 Jeff Kent .50 .15
❑ 142 Benito Santiago .50 .15
❑ 143 Kirk Rueter .50 .15
❑ 144 Jason Schmidt .50 .15
❑ 145 Jim Edmonds .50 .15
❑ 146 J.D. Drew .50 .15
❑ 147 Albert Pujols 2.50 .75
❑ 148 Tino Martinez .75 .23
❑ 149 Matt Morris .50 .15
❑ 150 Scott Rolen 1.25 .35
❑ 151 Joe Borchard ROO 2.00 .60
❑ 152 Cliff Lee ROO 2.00 .60
❑ 153 Brian Tallet ROO 2.00 .60
❑ 154 Freddy Sanchez ROO 2.00 .60
❑ 155 Chone Figgins ROO 2.00 .60
❑ 156 Kevin Cash ROO 2.00 .60
❑ 157 Justin Wayne ROO 2.00 .60
❑ 158 Ben Kozlowski ROO 2.00 .60
❑ 159 Babe Ruth RET 10.00 3.00
❑ 160 Jackie Robinson RET 5.00 1.50
❑ 161 Ozzie Smith RET 8.00 2.40
❑ 162 Lou Gehrig RET 6.00 1.80
❑ 163 Stan Musial RET 6.00 1.80
❑ 164 Mike Schmidt RET 10.00 3.00
❑ 165 Carlton Fisk RET 5.00 1.50
❑ 166 George Brett RET 12.00 3.60
❑ 167 Dale Murphy RET 8.00 2.40
❑ 168 Cal Ripken RET 12.00 3.60
❑ 169 Tony Gwynn RET 5.00 1.50
❑ 170 Don Mattingly RET 10.00 3.00
❑ 171 Jack Morris RET 4.00 1.20
❑ 172 Ty Cobb RET 5.00 1.50
❑ 173 Nolan Ryan RET 10.00 3.00
❑ 174 Ryne Sandberg RET 8.00 2.40
❑ 175 Thurman Munson RET 5.00 1.50
❑ 176 Jose Contreras ROO RC 8.00 2.40
❑ 177 Hideki Matsui ROO RC 10.00 3.00
❑ 178 Jeremy Bonderman ROO RC 5.00 1.50
❑ 179 Brandon Webb ROO RC 5.00 1.50
❑ 180 Adam Loewen ROO RC 5.00 1.50
❑ 181 Chien-Ming Wang ROO RC 5.00 1.50
❑ 182 Hong-Chih Kuo ROO RC 5.00 1.50
❑ 183 Clint Barmes ROO RC 5.00 1.50
❑ 184 Guillermo Quiroz ROO RC 5.00 1.50
❑ 185 Edgar Gonzalez ROO RC 4.00 1.20
❑ 186 Todd Wellemeyer ROO RC 5.00 1.50
❑ 187 Dan Haren ROO RC 5.00 1.50
❑ 188 Dustin McGowan ROO RC 5.00 1.50
❑ 189 Preston Larrison ROO RC 5.00 1.50
❑ 190 Does Not Exist
❑ 191 Kevin Youkilis ROO RC 6.00 1.80
❑ 192 Bubba Nelson ROO RC 5.00 1.50
❑ 193 Chris Burke ROO RC 5.00 1.50
❑ 194 J.D. Durbin ROO RC 5.00 1.50
❑ 195 Ryan Howard ROO RC 10.00 3.00
❑ 196 Jason Kubel ROO RC 8.00 2.40
❑ 197 Brendan Harris ROO RC 5.00 1.50
❑ 198 Brian Bruney ROO RC 5.00 1.50
❑ 199 Ramon Nivar ROO RC 5.00 1.50
❑ 200 Rickie Weeks ROO RC 10.00 3.00
❑ 201 Delmon Young ROO RC 12.00 3.60

2004 Diamond Kings

	Nm-Mt	Ex-Mt
COMPLETE SET w/Sepia (200)	200.00	60.00
COMPLETE SET (175)	100.00	30.00
COMP.SET w/o SP's (150)	40.00	12.00
COMMON CARD (1-150)	.50	.15
COMMON CARD (151-175)	3.00	.90

151-175 RANDOM INSERTS IN PACKS

❑ 1 Alex Rodriguez 2.00 .60
❑ 2 Andruw Jones .50 .15
❑ 3 Nomar Garciaparra 2.00 .60
❑ 4 Kerry Wood 1.25 .35
❑ 5 Magglio Ordonez .50 .15
❑ 6 Victor Martinez .50 .15
❑ 7 Jeremy Bonderman .50 .15
❑ 8 Josh Beckett .50 .15
❑ 9 Jeff Kent .50 .15
❑ 10 Carlos Beltran .75 .23
❑ 11 Hideo Nomo 1.25 .35
❑ 12 Richie Sexson .50 .15
❑ 13 Jose Vidro .50 .15
❑ 14 Jae Weong Seo .50 .15
❑ 15 Alfonso Soriano .75 .23
❑ 16 Barry Zito .50 .15
❑ 17 Brett Myers .50 .15
❑ 18 Brian Giles .50 .15
❑ 19 Edgar Martinez .75 .23
❑ 20 Jim Edmonds .50 .15
❑ 21 Rocco Baldelli .50 .15
❑ 22 Mark Teixeira .50 .15
❑ 23 Carlos Delgado .50 .15
❑ 24 Julius Matos .50 .15
❑ 25 Jose Reyes .50 .15
❑ 26 Marlon Byrd .50 .15
❑ 27 Albert Pujols 2.50 .75
❑ 28 Vernon Wells .50 .15
❑ 29 Garret Anderson .50 .15
❑ 30 Jerome Williams .50 .15
❑ 31 Chipper Jones 1.25 .35
❑ 32 Rich Harden .50 .15
❑ 33 Manny Ramirez .75 .23
❑ 34 Derek Jeter 2.50 .75
❑ 35 Brandon Webb .50 .15
❑ 36 Mark Prior 1.25 .35
❑ 37 Roy Halladay .50 .15
❑ 38 Frank Thomas 1.25 .35
❑ 39 Rafael Palmeiro .75 .23
❑ 40 Adam Dunn .75 .23
❑ 41 Aubrey Huff .50 .15
❑ 42 Todd Helton .75 .23
❑ 43 Matt Morris .50 .15
❑ 44 Dontrelle Willis .50 .15
❑ 45 Lance Berkman .50 .15
❑ 46 Mike Sweeney .50 .15
❑ 47 Kazuhisa Ishii .50 .15
❑ 48 Torii Hunter .50 .15
❑ 49 Vladimir Guerrero 1.25 .35
❑ 50 Mike Piazza 2.00 .60
❑ 51 Alexis Rios .50 .15
❑ 52 Shannon Stewart .50 .15

❑ 53 Eric Hinske	.50	.15
❑ 54 Jason Jennings	.50	.15
❑ 55 Jason Giambi	.50	.15
❑ 56 Brandon Claussen	.50	.15
❑ 57 Joe Thurston	.50	.15
❑ 58 Ramon Nivar	.50	.15
❑ 59 Jay Gibbons	.50	.15
❑ 60 Eric Chavez	.50	.15
❑ 61 Jimmy Gobble	.50	.15
❑ 62 Walter Young	.50	.15
❑ 63 Mark Grace	.75	.23
❑ 64 Austin Kearns	.50	.15
❑ 65 Bob Abreu	.50	.15
❑ 66 Hee Seop Choi	.50	.15
❑ 67 Brandon Phillips	.50	.15
❑ 68 Rickie Weeks	.50	.15
❑ 69 Luis Gonzalez	.50	.15
❑ 70 Mariano Rivera	.75	.23
❑ 71 Jason Lane	.50	.15
❑ 72 Xavier Nady	.50	.15
❑ 73 Runelvys Hernandez	.50	.15
❑ 74 Aramis Ramirez	.50	.15
❑ 75 Ichiro Suzuki	2.00	.60
❑ 76 Cliff Lee	.50	.15
❑ 77 Chris Snelling	.50	.15
❑ 78 Ryan Wagner	.50	.15
❑ 79 Miguel Tejada	.50	.15
❑ 80 Juan Gonzalez	.75	.23
❑ 81 Joe Borchard	.50	.15
❑ 82 Gary Sheffield	.50	.15
❑ 83 Wade Miller	.50	.15
❑ 84 Jeff Bagwell	.75	.23
❑ 85 Ryan Church	.50	.15
❑ 86 Adrian Beltre	.75	.23
❑ 87 Jeff Baker	.50	.15
❑ 88 Adam Loewen	.50	.15
❑ 89 Bernie Williams	.75	.23
❑ 90 Pedro Martinez	1.25	.35
❑ 91 Carlos Rivera	.50	.15
❑ 92 Junior Spivey	.50	.15
❑ 93 Tim Hudson	.50	.15
❑ 94 Troy Glaus	.50	.15
❑ 95 Ken Griffey Jr.	2.00	.60
❑ 96 Alexis Gomez	.50	.15
❑ 97 Antonio Perez	.50	.15
❑ 98 Dan Haren	.50	.15
❑ 99 Ivan Rodriguez	1.25	.35
❑ 100 Randy Johnson	1.25	.35
❑ 101 Lyle Overbay	.50	.15
❑ 102 Oliver Perez	.50	.15
❑ 103 Miguel Cabrera	.75	.23
❑ 104 Scott Rolen	1.25	.35
❑ 105 Roger Clemens	2.50	.75
❑ 106 Brian Tallet	.50	.15
❑ 107 Nic Jackson	.50	.15
❑ 108 Angel Berroa	.50	.15
❑ 109 Hank Blalock	.50	.15
❑ 110 Ryan Klesko	.50	.15
❑ 111 Jose Castillo	.50	.15
❑ 112 Paul Konerko	.50	.15
❑ 113 Greg Maddux	2.00	.60
❑ 114 Mark Mulder	.50	.15
❑ 115 Pat Burrell	.50	.15
❑ 116 Garrett Atkins	.50	.15
❑ 117 Jeremy Guthrie	.50	.15
❑ 118 Orlando Cabrera	.50	.15
❑ 119 Nick Johnson	.50	.15
❑ 120 Tom Glavine	.75	.23
❑ 121 Morgan Ensberg	.50	.15
❑ 122 Sean Casey	.50	.15
❑ 123 Orlando Hudson	.50	.15
❑ 124 Hideki Matsui	2.00	.60
❑ 125 Craig Biggio	.75	.23
❑ 126 Adam LaRoche	.50	.15
❑ 127 Hong-Chih Kuo	.50	.15
❑ 128 Paul Lo Duca	.50	.15
❑ 129 Shawn Green	.50	.15
❑ 130 Luis Castillo	.50	.15
❑ 131 Joe Crede	.50	.15
❑ 132 Ken Harvey	.50	.15
❑ 133 Freddy Sanchez	.50	.15
❑ 134 Roy Oswalt	.50	.15
❑ 135 Curt Schilling	1.25	.35
❑ 136 Alfredo Amezaga	.50	.15
❑ 137 Chien-Ming Wang	.50	.15
❑ 138 Barry Larkin	.75	.23
❑ 139 Trot Nixon	.50	.15
❑ 140 Jim Thome	1.25	.35
❑ 141 Bret Boone	.50	.15
❑ 142 Jacque Jones	.50	.15
❑ 143 Travis Hafner	.50	.15
❑ 144 Sammy Sosa	2.00	.60
❑ 145 Mike Mussina	.75	.23
❑ 146 Vinny Chulk	.50	.15
❑ 147 Chad Gaudin	.50	.15
❑ 148 Delmon Young	.75	.23
❑ 149 Mike Lowell	.50	.15
❑ 150 Rickey Henderson	1.25	.35
❑ 151 Roger Clemens FB	6.00	1.80
❑ 152 Mark Grace FB	4.00	1.20
❑ 153 Rickey Henderson FB	4.00	1.20
❑ 154 Alex Rodriguez FB	5.00	1.50
❑ 155 Rafael Palmeiro FB	4.00	1.20
❑ 156 Greg Maddux FB	5.00	1.50
❑ 157 Mike Piazza FB	5.00	1.50
❑ 158 Mike Mussina FB	4.00	1.20
❑ 159 Dale Murphy LGD	4.00	1.20
❑ 160 Cal Ripken LGD	10.00	3.00
❑ 161 Carl Yastrzemski LGD	5.00	1.50
❑ 162 Marty Marion LGD	3.00	.90
❑ 163 Don Mattingly LGD	8.00	2.40
❑ 164 Robin Yount LGD	5.00	1.50
❑ 165 Andre Dawson LGD	3.00	.90
❑ 166 Jim Palmer LGD	3.00	.90
❑ 167 George Brett LGD	8.00	2.40
❑ 168 Whitey Ford LGD	4.00	1.20
❑ 169 Roy Campanella LGD	4.00	1.20
❑ 170 Roger Maris LGD	4.00	1.20
❑ 171 Duke Snider LGD	4.00	1.20
❑ 172 Steve Carlton LGD	3.00	.90
❑ 173 Stan Musial LGD	5.00	1.50
❑ 174 Nolan Ryan LGD	8.00	2.40
❑ 175 Deion Sanders LGD	4.00	1.20

1981 Donruss

	Nm-Mt	Ex-Mt
COMPLETE SET (605)	40.00	16.00
❑ 1 Ozzie Smith	3.00	1.20
❑ 2 Rollie Fingers	.25	.10
❑ 3 Rick Wise	.10	.04
❑ 4 Gene Richards	.10	.04
❑ 5 Alan Trammell	.50	.20
❑ 6 Tom Brookens	.10	.04
❑ 7A Duffy Dyer P1 1980 batting average has decimal point	.25	.10
❑ 7B Duffy Dyer P2 1980 batting average has no decimal point	.10	.04
❑ 8 Mark Fidrych	.25	.10
❑ 9 Dave Rozema	.10	.04
❑ 10 Ricky Peters	.10	.04
❑ 11 Mike Schmidt	2.50	1.00
❑ 12 Willie Stargell	.50	.20
❑ 13 Tim Foli	.10	.04
❑ 14 Manny Sanguillen	.25	.10
❑ 15 Grant Jackson	.10	.04
❑ 16 Eddie Solomon	.10	.04
❑ 17 Omar Moreno	.10	.04
❑ 18 Joe Morgan	.50	.20
❑ 19 Rafael Landestoy	.10	.04
❑ 20 Bruce Bochy	.10	.04
❑ 21 Joe Sambito	.10	.04
❑ 22 Manny Trillo	.10	.04
❑ 23A Dave Smith RC P1 Line box around stats is not complete	.50	.20
❑ 23B Dave Smith RC P2 Box totally encloses stats at top	.50	.20
❑ 24 Terry Puhl	.10	.04
❑ 25 Bump Wills	.10	.04
❑ 26A John Ellis P1 ERR Danny Walton photo on front	.50	.20
❑ 26B John Ellis P2 COR	.25	.10
❑ 27 Jim Kern	.10	.04
❑ 28 Richie Zisk	.10	.04
❑ 29 John Mayberry	.10	.04
❑ 30 Bob Davis	.10	.04
❑ 31 Jackson Todd	.10	.04
❑ 32 Alvis Woods	.10	.04
❑ 33 Steve Carlton	.50	.20
❑ 34 Lee Mazzilli	.25	.10
❑ 35 John Stearns	.10	.04
❑ 36 Roy Lee Jackson	.10	.04
❑ 37 Mike Scott	.25	.10
❑ 38 Lamar Johnson	.10	.04
❑ 39 Kevin Bell	.10	.04
❑ 40 Ed Farmer	.10	.04
❑ 41 Ross Baumgarten	.10	.04
❑ 42 Leo Sutherland	.10	.04
❑ 43 Dan Meyer	.10	.04
❑ 44 Ron Reed	.10	.04
❑ 45 Mario Mendoza	.10	.04
❑ 46 Rick Honeycutt	.10	.04
❑ 47 Glenn Abbott	.10	.04
❑ 48 Leon Roberts	.10	.04
❑ 49 Rod Carew	.50	.20
❑ 50 Bert Campaneris	.25	.10
❑ 51A T.Donahue P1 ERR Name on front misspelled Donahue	.25	.10
❑ 51B Tom Donohue P2 COR	.10	.04
❑ 52 Dave Frost	.10	.04
❑ 53 Ed Halicki	.10	.04
❑ 54 Dan Ford	.10	.04
❑ 55 Garry Maddox	.10	.04
❑ 56A Steve Garvey P1 Surpassed 25 HR	.25	.10
❑ 56B Steve Garvey P2 Surpassed 21 HR	.25	.10
❑ 57 Bill Russell	.25	.10
❑ 58 Don Sutton	.25	.10
❑ 59 Reggie Smith	.25	.10
❑ 60 Rick Monday	.25	.10
❑ 61 Ray Knight	.25	.10
❑ 62 Johnny Bench	1.00	.40
❑ 63 Mario Soto	.25	.10
❑ 64 Doug Bair	.10	.04
❑ 65 George Foster	.25	.10
❑ 66 Jeff Burroughs	.25	.10
❑ 67 Keith Hernandez	.25	.10
❑ 68 Tom Herr	.10	.04
❑ 69 Bob Forsch	.10	.04
❑ 70 John Fulgham	.10	.04
❑ 71A Bobby Bonds P1 ERR 986 lifetime HR	1.00	.40
❑ 71B Bobby Bonds P2 COR 326 lifetime HR	.50	.20
❑ 72A Rennie Stennett P1 Breaking broke leg	.25	.10
❑ 72B Rennie Stennett P2 Word "broke" deleted	.10	.04
❑ 73 Joe Strain	.10	.04
❑ 74 Ed Whitson	.10	.04
❑ 75 Tom Griffin	.10	.04
❑ 76 Billy North	.10	.04
❑ 77 Gene Garber	.10	.04
❑ 78 Mike Hargrove	.10	.04
❑ 79 Dave Rosello	.10	.04
❑ 80 Ron Hassey	.10	.04
❑ 81 Sid Monge	.10	.04
❑ 82A J.Charboneau P1 RC '78 highlights For some reason	1.00	.40
❑ 82B J.Charboneau P2 RC Phrase "For some reason" deleted	1.00	.40

❑ 83 Cecil Cooper .25 .10
❑ 84 Sal Bando .25 .10
❑ 85 Moose Haas .10 .04
❑ 86 Mike Caldwell .10 .04
❑ 87A Larry Hisle P1 .25 .10
'77 highlights
line ends with "28 RBI"
❑ 87B Larry Hisle P2 .10 .04
Correct line "28 HR"
❑ 88 Luis Gomez .10 .04
❑ 89 Larry Parrish .10 .04
❑ 90 Gary Carter .50 .20
❑ 91 Bill Gullickson RC .50 .20
❑ 92 Fred Norman .10 .04
❑ 93 Tommy Hutton .10 .04
❑ 94 Carl Yastrzemski 1.50 .60
❑ 95 Glenn Hoffman .10 .04
❑ 96 Dennis Eckersley .50 .20
❑ 97A Tom Burgmeier P1 .25 .10
ERR Throws: Right
❑ 97B Tom Burgmeier P2 .10 .04
COR Throws: Left
❑ 98 Win Remmerswaal .10 .04
❑ 99 Bob Horner .25 .10
❑ 100 George Brett 2.50 1.00
❑ 101 Dave Chalk .10 .04
❑ 102 Dennis Leonard .10 .04
❑ 103 Renie Martin .10 .04
❑ 104 Amos Otis .25 .10
❑ 105 Graig Nettles .25 .10
❑ 106 Eric Soderholm .10 .04
❑ 107 Tommy John .25 .10
❑ 108 Tom Underwood .10 .04
❑ 109 Lou Piniella .25 .10
❑ 110 Mickey Klutts .10 .04
❑ 111 Bobby Murcer .25 .10
❑ 112 Eddie Murray 1.50 .60
❑ 113 Rick Dempsey .10 .04
❑ 114 Scott McGregor .10 .04
❑ 115 Ken Singleton .25 .10
❑ 116 Gary Roenicke .10 .04
❑ 117 Dave Revering .10 .04
❑ 118 Mike Norris .10 .04
❑ 119 Rickey Henderson 6.00 2.40
❑ 120 Mike Heath .10 .04
❑ 121 Dave Cash .10 .04
❑ 122 Randy Jones .25 .10
❑ 123 Eric Rasmussen .10 .04
❑ 124 Jerry Mumphrey .10 .04
❑ 125 Richie Hebner .10 .04
❑ 126 Mark Wagner .10 .04
❑ 127 Jack Morris .50 .20
❑ 128 Dan Petry .10 .04
❑ 129 Bruce Robbins .10 .04
❑ 130 Champ Summers .10 .04
❑ 131 Pete Rose P1 3.00 1.20
Last line ends with
see card 251
❑ 131B Pete Rose P2 2.00 .80
Last line corrected
see card 371
❑ 132 Willie Stargell .50 .20
❑ 133 Ed Ott .10 .04
❑ 134 Jim Bibby .10 .04
❑ 135 Bert Blyleven .25 .10
❑ 136 Dave Parker .25 .10
❑ 137 Bill Robinson .10 .04
❑ 138 Enos Cabell .10 .04
❑ 139 Dave Bergman .10 .04
❑ 140 J.R. Richard .25 .10
❑ 141 Ken Forsch .10 .04
❑ 142 Larry Bowa UER .25 .10
Shortshop on front
❑ 143 Frank LaCorte UER .10 .04
Photo actually Randy Niemann
❑ 144 Denny Walling .10 .04
❑ 145 Buddy Bell .25 .10
❑ 146 Ferguson Jenkins .25 .10
❑ 147 Danny Darwin .25 .10
❑ 148 John Grubb .10 .04
❑ 149 Alfredo Griffin .10 .04
❑ 150 Jerry Garvin .10 .04
❑ 151 Paul Mirabella .10 .04
❑ 152 Rick Bosetti .10 .04
❑ 153 Dick Ruthven .10 .04
❑ 154 Frank Taveras .10 .04
❑ 155 Craig Swan .10 .04
❑ 156 Jeff Reardon RC 1.00 .40
❑ 157 Steve Henderson .10 .04
❑ 158 Jim Morrison .10 .04
❑ 159 Glenn Borgmann .10 .04
❑ 160 LaMarr Hoyt RC .50 .20
❑ 161 Rich Wortham .10 .04
❑ 162 Thad Bosley .10 .04
❑ 163 Julio Cruz .10 .04
❑ 164A Del Unser P1 .25 .10
No "3B" heading
❑ 164B Del Unser P2 .10 .04
Batting record on back
corrected "3B"
❑ 165 Jim Anderson .10 .04
❑ 166 Jim Beattie .10 .04
❑ 167 Shane Rawley .10 .04
❑ 168 Joe Simpson .10 .04
❑ 169 Rod Carew .50 .20
❑ 170 Fred Patek .10 .04
❑ 171 Frank Tanana .25 .10
❑ 172 Alfredo Martinez .10 .04
❑ 173 Chris Knapp .10 .04
❑ 174 Joe Rudi .25 .10
❑ 175 Greg Luzinski .25 .10
❑ 176 Steve Garvey .50 .20
❑ 177 Joe Ferguson .10 .04
❑ 178 Bob Welch .25 .10
❑ 179 Dusty Baker .25 .10
❑ 180 Rudy Law .10 .04
❑ 181 Dave Concepcion .25 .10
❑ 182 Johnny Bench 1.00 .40
❑ 183 Mike LaCoss .10 .04
❑ 184 Ken Griffey .25 .10
❑ 185 Dave Collins .10 .04
❑ 186 Brian Asselstine .10 .04
❑ 187 Garry Templeton .25 .10
❑ 188 Mike Phillips .10 .04
❑ 189 Pete Vuckovich .10 .04
❑ 190 John Urrea .10 .04
❑ 191 Tony Scott .10 .04
❑ 192 Darrell Evans .25 .10
❑ 193 Milt May .10 .04
❑ 194 Bob Knepper .10 .04
❑ 195 Randy Moffitt .10 .04
❑ 196 Larry Herndon .10 .04
❑ 197 Rick Camp .10 .04
❑ 198 Andre Thornton .25 .10
❑ 199 Tom Veryzer .10 .04
❑ 200 Gary Alexander .10 .04
❑ 201 Rick Waits .10 .04
❑ 202 Rick Manning .10 .04
❑ 203 Paul Molitor 1.00 .40
❑ 204 Jim Gantner .10 .04
❑ 205 Paul Mitchell .10 .04
❑ 206 Reggie Cleveland .10 .04
❑ 207 Sixto Lezcano .10 .04
❑ 208 Bruce Benedict .10 .04
❑ 209 Rodney Scott .10 .04
❑ 210 John Tamargo .10 .04
❑ 211 Bill Lee .25 .10
❑ 212 Andre Dawson UER .50 .20
Middle name Fernando
should be Nolan
❑ 213 Rowland Office .10 .04
❑ 214 Carl Yastrzemski 1.50 .60
❑ 215 Jerry Remy .10 .04
❑ 216 Mike Torrez .10 .04
❑ 217 Skip Lockwood .10 .04
❑ 218 Fred Lynn .25 .10
❑ 219 Chris Chambliss .25 .10
❑ 220 Willie Aikens .10 .04
❑ 221 John Wathan .10 .04
❑ 222 Dan Quisenberry .10 .04
❑ 223 Willie Wilson .25 .10
❑ 224 Clint Hurdle .10 .04
❑ 225 Bob Watson .10 .04
❑ 226 Jim Spencer .10 .04
❑ 227 Ron Guidry .25 .10
❑ 228 Reggie Jackson 1.00 .40
❑ 229 Oscar Gamble .10 .04
❑ 230 Jeff Cox .10 .04
❑ 231 Luis Tiant .25 .10
❑ 232 Rich Dauer .10 .04
❑ 233 Dan Graham .10 .04
❑ 234 Mike Flanagan .10 .04
❑ 235 John Lowenstein .10 .04
❑ 236 Benny Ayala .10 .04
❑ 237 Wayne Gross .10 .04
❑ 238 Rick Langford .10 .04
❑ 239 Tony Armas .25 .10
❑ 240A Bob Lacey P1 ERR .50 .20
Name misspelled Lacy
❑ 240B Bob Lacey P2 COR .10 .04
❑ 241 Gene Tenace .25 .10
❑ 242 Bob Shirley .10 .04
❑ 243 Gary Lucas .10 .04
❑ 244 Jerry Turner .10 .04
❑ 245 John Wockenfuss .10 .04
❑ 246 Stan Papi .10 .04
❑ 247 Milt Wilcox .10 .04
❑ 248 Dan Schatzeder .10 .04
❑ 249 Steve Kemp .10 .04
❑ 250 Jim Lentine .10 .04
❑ 251 Pete Rose 3.00 1.20
❑ 252 Bill Madlock .25 .10
❑ 253 Dale Berra .10 .04
❑ 254 Kent Tekulve .10 .04
❑ 255 Enrique Romo .10 .04
❑ 256 Mike Easler .10 .04
❑ 257 Chuck Tanner MG .10 .04
❑ 258 Art Howe .10 .04
❑ 259 Alan Ashby .10 .04
❑ 260 Nolan Ryan 5.00 2.00
❑ 261A Vern Ruhle P1 ERR .50 .20
Ken Forsch photo on front
❑ 261B Vern Ruhle P2 COR .25 .10
❑ 262 Bob Boone .25 .10
❑ 263 Cesar Cedeno .25 .10
❑ 264 Jeff Leonard .25 .10
❑ 265 Pat Putnam .10 .04
❑ 266 Jon Matlack .10 .04
❑ 267 Dave Rajsich .10 .04
❑ 268 Billy Sample .10 .04
❑ 269 Damaso Garcia .10 .04
❑ 270 Tom Buskey .10 .04
❑ 271 Joey McLaughlin .10 .04
❑ 272 Barry Bonnell .10 .04
❑ 273 Tug McGraw .25 .10
❑ 274 Mike Jorgensen .10 .04
❑ 275 Pat Zachry .10 .04
❑ 276 Neil Allen .10 .04
❑ 277 Joel Youngblood .10 .04
❑ 278 Greg Pryor .10 .04
❑ 279 Britt Burns .10 .04
❑ 280 Rich Dotson .10 .04
❑ 281 Chet Lemon .25 .10
❑ 282 Rusty Kuntz .10 .04
❑ 283 Ted Cox .10 .04
❑ 284 Sparky Lyle .25 .10
❑ 285 Larry Cox .10 .04
❑ 286 Floyd Bannister .10 .04
❑ 287 Byron McLaughlin .10 .04
❑ 288 Rodney Craig .10 .04
❑ 289 Bobby Grich .25 .10
❑ 290 Dickie Thon .10 .04
❑ 291 Mark Clear .10 .04
❑ 292 Dave Lemanczyk .10 .04
❑ 293 Jason Thompson .10 .04
❑ 294 Rick Miller .10 .04
❑ 295 Lonnie Smith .25 .10
❑ 296 Ron Cey .25 .10
❑ 297 Steve Yeager .25 .10
❑ 298 Bobby Castillo .10 .04
❑ 299 Manny Mota .25 .10
❑ 300 Jay Johnstone .10 .04
❑ 301 Dan Driessen .10 .04
❑ 302 Joe Nolan .10 .04
❑ 303 Paul Householder .10 .04
❑ 304 Harry Spilman .10 .04
❑ 305 Cesar Geronimo .10 .04
❑ 306A G.Mathews P1 ERR .50 .20
Name misspelled
❑ 306B G.Matthews P2 .25 .10
COR
❑ 307 Ken Reitz .10 .04
❑ 308 Ted Simmons .25 .10
❑ 309 John Littlefield .10 .04
❑ 310 George Frazier .10 .04
❑ 311 Dane Iorg .10 .04
❑ 312 Mike Ivie .10 .04
❑ 313 Dennis Littlejohn .10 .04

❑ 314 Gary Lavelle .10 .04
❑ 315 Jack Clark .25 .10
❑ 316 Jim Wohlford .10 .04
❑ 317 Rick Matula .10 .04
❑ 318 Toby Harrah .25 .10
❑ 319A D.Kuiper P1 ERR .25 .10
Name misspelled
❑ 319B D.Kuiper P2 COR .10 .04
❑ 320 Len Barker .25 .10
❑ 321 Victor Cruz .10 .04
❑ 322 Dell Alston .10 .04
❑ 323 Robin Yount 1.50 .60
❑ 324 Charlie Moore .10 .04
❑ 325 Lary Sorensen .10 .04
❑ 326A Gorman Thomas P1 .50 .20
2nd line on back:
"30 HR mark 4th"
❑ 326B Gorman Thomas P2 .25 .10
30 HR mark 3rd
❑ 327 Bob Rodgers MG .10 .04
❑ 328 Phil Niekro .25 .10
❑ 329 Chris Speier .10 .04
❑ 330A Steve Rodgers P1 .25 .10
ERR Name misspelled
❑ 330B S.Rogers P2 COR .25 .10
❑ 331 Woodie Fryman .10 .04
❑ 332 Warren Cromartie .10 .04
❑ 333 Jerry White .10 .04
❑ 334 Tony Perez .50 .20
❑ 335 Carlton Fisk .50 .20
❑ 336 Dick Drago .10 .04
❑ 337 Steve Renko .10 .04
❑ 338 Jim Rice .25 .10
❑ 339 Jerry Royster .10 .04
❑ 340 Frank White .25 .10
❑ 341 Jamie Quirk .10 .04
❑ 342A P.Spittorff P1 ERR .25 .10
Name misspelled
❑ 342B Paul Splittorff .10 .04
P2 COR
❑ 343 Marty Pattin .10 .04
❑ 344 Pete LaCock .10 .04
❑ 345 Willie Randolph .25 .10
❑ 346 Rick Cerone .10 .04
❑ 347 Rich Gossage .25 .10
❑ 348 Reggie Jackson 1.00 .40
❑ 349 Ruppert Jones .10 .04
❑ 350 Dave McKay .10 .04
❑ 351 Yogi Berra CO 1.00 .40
❑ 352 Doug DeCinces .10 .04
❑ 353 Jim Palmer .50 .20
❑ 354 Tippy Martinez .10 .04
❑ 355 Al Bumbry .10 .04
❑ 356 Earl Weaver MG .25 .10
❑ 357A Bob Picciolo P1 ERR .25 .10
Name misspelled
❑ 357B R.Picciolo P2 COR .10 .04
❑ 358 Matt Keough .10 .04
❑ 359 Dwayne Murphy .10 .04
❑ 360 Brian Kingman .10 .04
❑ 361 Bill Fahey .10 .04
❑ 362 Steve Mura .10 .04
❑ 363 Dennis Kinney .10 .04
❑ 364 Dave Winfield .50 .20
❑ 365 Lou Whitaker .50 .20
❑ 366 Lance Parrish .25 .10
❑ 367 Tim Corcoran .10 .04
❑ 368 Pat Underwood .10 .04
❑ 369 Al Cowens .10 .04
❑ 370 Sparky Anderson MG .25 .10
❑ 371 Pete Rose 3.00 1.20
❑ 372 Phil Garner .25 .10
❑ 373 Steve Nicosia .10 .04
❑ 374 John Candelaria .25 .10
❑ 375 Don Robinson .10 .04
❑ 376 Lee Lacy .10 .04
❑ 377 John Milner .10 .04
❑ 378 Craig Reynolds .10 .04
❑ 379A Luis Pujols P1 ERR .25 .10
Name misspelled Pujois
❑ 379B Luis Pujols P2 COR .10 .04
❑ 380 Joe Niekro .10 .04
❑ 381 Joaquin Andujar .25 .10
❑ 382 Keith Moreland .10 .04
❑ 383 Jose Cruz .25 .10
❑ 384 Bill Virdon MG .10 .04
❑ 385 Jim Sundberg .25 .10
❑ 386 Doc Medich .10 .04
❑ 387 Al Oliver .25 .10
❑ 388 Jim Norris .10 .04
❑ 389 Bob Bailor .10 .04
❑ 390 Ernie Whitt .10 .04
❑ 391 Otto Velez .10 .04
❑ 392 Roy Howell .10 .04
❑ 393 Bob Walk RC .50 .20
❑ 394 Doug Flynn .10 .04
❑ 395 Pete Falcone .10 .04
❑ 396 Tom Hausman .10 .04
❑ 397 Elliott Maddox .10 .04
❑ 398 Mike Squires .10 .04
❑ 399 Marvis Foley .10 .04
❑ 400 Steve Trout .10 .04
❑ 401 Wayne Nordhagen .10 .04
❑ 402 Tony LaRussa MG .25 .10
❑ 403 Bruce Bochte .10 .04
❑ 404 Bake McBride .25 .10
❑ 405 Jerry Narron .10 .04
❑ 406 Rob Dressler .10 .04
❑ 407 Dave Heaverlo .10 .04
❑ 408 Tom Paciorek .10 .04
❑ 409 Carney Lansford .25 .10
❑ 410 Brian Downing .25 .10
❑ 411 Don Aase .10 .04
❑ 412 Jim Barr .10 .04
❑ 413 Don Baylor .25 .10
❑ 414 Jim Fregosi MG .10 .04
❑ 415 Dallas Green MG .10 .04
❑ 416 Dave Lopes .25 .10
❑ 417 Jerry Reuss .10 .04
❑ 418 Rick Sutcliffe .25 .10
❑ 419 Derrel Thomas .10 .04
❑ 420 Tom Lasorda MG .50 .20
❑ 421 Charlie Leibrandt RC .50 .20
❑ 422 Tom Seaver 1.00 .40
❑ 423 Ron Oester .10 .04
❑ 424 Junior Kennedy .10 .04
❑ 425 Tom Seaver 1.00 .40
❑ 426 Bobby Cox MG .25 .10
❑ 427 Leon Durham RC .50 .20
❑ 428 Terry Kennedy .10 .04
❑ 429 Silvio Martinez .10 .04
❑ 430 George Hendrick .25 .10
❑ 431 Red Schoendienst MG .50 .20
❑ 432 Johnnie LeMaster .10 .04
❑ 433 Vida Blue .25 .10
❑ 434 John Montefusco .10 .04
❑ 435 Terry Whitfield .10 .04
❑ 436 Dave Bristol MG .10 .04
❑ 437 Dale Murphy .50 .20
❑ 438 Jerry Dybzinski .10 .04
❑ 439 Jorge Orta .10 .04
❑ 440 Wayne Garland .10 .04
❑ 441 Miguel Dilone .10 .04
❑ 442 Dave Garcia MG .10 .04
❑ 443 Don Money .10 .04
❑ 444A B.Martinez P1 ERR .25 .10
Reverse negative
❑ 444B Buck Martinez .10 .04
P2 COR
❑ 445 Jerry Augustine .10 .04
❑ 446 Ben Oglivie .25 .10
❑ 447 Jim Slaton .10 .04
❑ 448 Doyle Alexander .10 .04
❑ 449 Tony Bernazard .10 .04
❑ 450 Scott Sanderson .10 .04
❑ 451 David Palmer .10 .04
❑ 452 Stan Bahnsen .10 .04
❑ 453 Dick Williams MG .10 .04
❑ 454 Rick Burleson .10 .04
❑ 455 Gary Allenson .10 .04
❑ 456 Bob Stanley .10 .04
❑ 457A J. Tudor P1 ERR RC 1.00 .40
Lifetime W-L 9.7
❑ 457B J.Tudor P2 COR RC 1.00 .40
Lifetime W-L 9-7
❑ 458 Dwight Evans .50 .20
❑ 459 Glenn Hubbard .10 .04
❑ 460 U.L. Washington .10 .04
❑ 461 Larry Gura .10 .04
❑ 462 Rich Gale .10 .04
❑ 463 Hal McRae .25 .10
❑ 464 Jim Frey MG .10 .04
❑ 465 Bucky Dent .25 .10
❑ 466 Dennis Werth .10 .04
❑ 467 Ron Davis .10 .04
❑ 468 Reggie Jackson UER 1.00 .40
32 HR in 1970
should be 23
❑ 469 Bobby Brown .10 .04
❑ 470 Mike Davis RC .50 .20
❑ 471 Gaylord Perry .25 .10
❑ 472 Mark Belanger .10 .04
❑ 473 Jim Palmer .50 .20
❑ 474 Sammy Stewart .10 .04
❑ 475 Tim Stoddard .10 .04
❑ 476 Steve Stone .10 .04
❑ 477 Jeff Newman .10 .04
❑ 478 Steve McCatty .10 .04
❑ 479 Billy Martin MG .50 .20
❑ 480 Mitchell Page .10 .04
❑ 481 Steve Carlton CY .25 .10
❑ 482 Bill Buckner .25 .10
❑ 483A I.DeJesus P1 ERR .25 .10
Lifetime hits 702
❑ 483B I.DeJesus P2 COR .10 .04
Lifetime hits 642
❑ 484 Cliff Johnson .10 .04
❑ 485 Lenny Randle .10 .04
❑ 486 Larry Milbourne .10 .04
❑ 487 Roy Smalley .10 .04
❑ 488 John Castino .10 .04
❑ 489 Ron Jackson .10 .04
❑ 490A Dave Roberts P1 .25 .10
Career Highlights
Showed pop in
❑ 490B Dave Roberts P2 .10 .04
Declared himself
❑ 491 George Brett MVP 1.50 .60
❑ 492 Mike Cubbage .10 .04
❑ 493 Rob Wilfong .10 .04
❑ 494 Danny Goodwin .10 .04
❑ 495 Jose Morales .10 .04
❑ 496 Mickey Rivers .10 .04
❑ 497 Mike Edwards .10 .04
❑ 498 Mike Sadek .10 .04
❑ 499 Lenn Sakata .10 .04
❑ 500 Gene Michael MG .10 .04
❑ 501 Dave Roberts .10 .04
❑ 502 Steve Dillard .10 .04
❑ 503 Jim Essian .10 .04
❑ 504 Rance Mulliniks .10 .04
❑ 505 Darrell Porter .10 .04
❑ 506 Joe Torre MG .50 .20
❑ 507 Terry Crowley .10 .04
❑ 508 Bill Travers .10 .04
❑ 509 Nelson Norman .10 .04
❑ 510 Bob McClure .10 .04
❑ 511 Steve Howe RC .50 .20
❑ 512 Dave Rader .10 .04
❑ 513 Mick Kelleher .10 .04
❑ 514 Kiko Garcia .10 .04
❑ 515 Larry Biittner .10 .04
❑ 516A Willie Norwood P1 .25 .10
Career Highlights
Spent most of
❑ 516B Willie Norwood P2 .10 .04
Traded to Seattle
❑ 517 Bo Diaz .10 .04
❑ 518 Juan Beniquez .10 .04
❑ 519 Scot Thompson .10 .04
❑ 520 Jim Tracy RC 1.00 .40
❑ 521 Carlos Lezcano .10 .04
❑ 522 Joe Amalfitano MG .10 .04
❑ 523 Preston Hanna .10 .04
❑ 524A Ray Burris P1 .25 .10
Career Highlights
Went on ...
❑ 524B Ray Burris P2 .10 .04
Drafted by ...
❑ 525 Broderick Perkins .10 .04
❑ 526 Mickey Hatcher .10 .04
❑ 527 John Goryl MG .10 .04
❑ 528 Dick Davis .10 .04
❑ 529 Butch Wynegar .10 .04
❑ 530 Sal Butera .10 .04
❑ 531 Jerry Koosman .25 .10
❑ 532A Geoff Zahn P1 .25 .10
(Career Highlights

Was 2nd in
❑ 532B Geoff Zahn P2 .... .10 .04
Signed a 3 year
❑ 533 Dennis Martinez .... .25 .10
❑ 534 Gary Thomasson .... .10 .04
❑ 535 Steve Macko .... .10 .04
❑ 536 Jim Kaat .... .25 .10
❑ 537 George Brett .... 1.50 .60
Rod Carew
❑ 538 Tim Raines RC .... 1.50 .60
❑ 539 Keith Smith .... .10 .04
❑ 540 Ken Macha .... .10 .04
❑ 541 Burt Hooton .... .10 .04
❑ 542 Butch Hobson .... .10 .04
❑ 543 Bill Stein .... .10 .04
❑ 544 Dave Stapleton .... .10 .04
❑ 545 Bob Pate .... .10 .04
❑ 546 Doug Corbett .... .10 .04
❑ 547 Darrell Jackson .... .10 .04
❑ 548 Pete Redfern .... .10 .04
❑ 549 Roger Erickson .... .10 .04
❑ 550 Al Hrabosky .... .25 .10
❑ 551 Dick Tidrow .... .10 .04
❑ 552 Dave Ford .... .10 .04
❑ 553 Dave Kingman .... .25 .10
❑ 554A Mike Vail P1 .... .25 .10
Career Highlights
After two
❑ 554B Mike Vail P2 .... .10 .04
Traded to
❑ 555A Jerry Martin P1 .... .25 .10
Career Highlights
Overcame a
❑ 555B Jerry Martin P2 .... .10 .04
Traded to
❑ 556A Jesus Figueroa P1 .... .25 .10
Career Highlights
Had an
❑ 556B Jesus Figueroa P2 .... .10 .04
Traded to
❑ 557 Don Stanhouse .... .10 .04
❑ 558 Barry Foote .... .10 .04
❑ 559 Tim Blackwell .... .10 .04
❑ 560 Bruce Sutter .... .25 .10
❑ 561 Rick Reuschel .... .25 .10
❑ 562 Lynn McGlothen .... .10 .04
❑ 563A Bob Owchinko P1 .... .25 .10
Career Highlights
Traded to
❑ 563B Bob Owchinko P2 .... .10 .04
Involved in a
❑ 564 John Verhoeven .... .10 .04
❑ 565 Ken Landreaux .... .10 .04
❑ 566A Glen Adams P1 ERR ...... .25 .10
Name misspelled
❑ 566B G. Adams P2 COR .... .10 .04
❑ 567 Hosken Powell .... .10 .04
❑ 568 Dick Noles .... .10 .04
❑ 569 Danny Ainge RC .... 1.50 .60
❑ 570 Bobby Mattick MG .... .10 .04
❑ 571 Joe Lefebvre .... .10 .04
❑ 572 Bobby Clark .... .10 .04
❑ 573 Dennis Lamp .... .10 .04
❑ 574 Randy Lerch .... .10 .04
❑ 575 Mookie Wilson RC .... 1.50 .60
❑ 576 Ron LeFlore .... .25 .10
❑ 577 Jim Dwyer .... .10 .04
❑ 578 Bill Castro .... .10 .04
❑ 579 Greg Minton .... .10 .04
❑ 580 Mark Littell .... .10 .04
❑ 581 Andy Hassler .... .10 .04
❑ 582 Dave Stieb .... .25 .10
❑ 583 Ken Oberkfell .... .10 .04
❑ 584 Larry Bradford .... .10 .04
❑ 585 Fred Stanley .... .10 .04
❑ 586 Bill Caudill .... .10 .04
❑ 587 Doug Capilla .... .10 .04
❑ 588 George Riley .... .10 .04
❑ 589 Willie Hernandez .... .10 .04
❑ 590 Mike Schmidt MVP 2.50 1.00
❑ 591 Steve Stone CY .... .10 .04
❑ 592 Rick Sofield .... .10 .04
❑ 593 Bombo Rivera .... .10 .04
❑ 594 Gary Ward .... .10 .04
❑ 595A Dave Edwards P1 .... .25 .10
Career Highlights
Sidelined the
❑ 595B Dave Edwards P2 .... .10 .04
Traded to
❑ 596 Mike Proly .... .10 .04
❑ 597 Tommy Boggs .... .10 .04
❑ 598 Greg Gross .... .10 .04
❑ 599 Elias Sosa .... .10 .04
❑ 600 Pat Kelly .... .10 .04
❑ 601A Checklist 1-120 P1 .... .25 .10
ERR Unnumbered
51 Donahue
❑ 601B Checklist 1-120 P2 .... .50 .20
COR Unnumbered
51 Donohue
❑ 602 Checklist 121-240 .... .25 .10
Unnumbered
❑ 603A CL 241-360 P1 .... .25 .10
ERR Unnumbered
306 Mathews
❑ 603B CL 241-360 P2 .... .25 .10
COR Unnumbered
306 Matthews
❑ 604A CL 361-480 P1 .... .25 .10
ERR Unnumbered
379 Pujois
❑ 604B CL 361-480 P2 .... .25 .10
COR Unnumbered
379 Pujols
❑ 605A CL 481-600 P1 .... .25 .10
ERR Unnumbered
566 Glen Adams
❑ 605B CL 481-600 P2 .... .25 .10
COR Unnumbered
566 Glenn Adams

1982 Donruss

	Nm-Mt	Ex-Mt
COMPLETE SET (660)	60.00	24.00
COMP.FACT.SET (660)	60.00	24.00
COMP.RUTH PUZZLE	10.00	4.00

❑ 1 Pete Rose DK 2.50 1.00
❑ 2 Gary Carter DK .... .20 .08
❑ 3 Steve Garvey DK .... .20 .08
❑ 4 Vida Blue DK .... .20 .08
❑ 5 Alan Trammell DK .... .20 .08
COR
❑ 5A Alan Trammel DK ERR ...... .20 .08
(Name misspelled)
❑ 6 Len Barker DK .... .10 .04
❑ 7 Dwight Evans DK .... .20 .08
❑ 8 Rod Carew DK .... .40 .16
❑ 9 George Hendrick DK .... .20 .08
❑ 10 Phil Niekro DK .... .20 .08
❑ 11 Richie Zisk DK .... .10 .04
❑ 12 Dave Parker DK .... .20 .08
❑ 13 Nolan Ryan DK 4.00 1.60
❑ 14 Ivan DeJesus DK .... .10 .04
❑ 15 George Brett DK .... 2.00 .80
❑ 16 Tom Seaver DK .... .40 .16
❑ 17 Dave Kingman DK .... .20 .08
❑ 18 Dave Winfield DK .... .20 .08
❑ 19 Mike Norris DK .... .10 .04
❑ 20 Carlton Fisk DK .... .40 .16
❑ 21 Ozzie Smith DK .... 1.50 .60
❑ 22 Roy Smalley DK .... .10 .04
❑ 23 Buddy Bell DK .... .20 .08
❑ 24 Ken Singleton DK .... .20 .08
❑ 25 John Mayberry DK .... .10 .04
❑ 26 Gorman Thomas DK .... .20 .08
❑ 27 Earl Weaver MG .... .20 .08
❑ 28 Rollie Fingers .... .20 .08
❑ 29 Sparky Anderson MG .... .20 .08
❑ 30 Dennis Eckersley .... .40 .16
❑ 31 Dave Winfield .... .20 .08
❑ 32 Burt Hooton .... .10 .04
❑ 33 Rick Waits .... .10 .04
❑ 34 George Brett .... 2.00 .80
❑ 35 Steve McCatty .... .10 .04
❑ 36 Steve Rogers .... .20 .08
❑ 37 Bill Stein .... .10 .04
❑ 38 Steve Renko .... .10 .04
❑ 39 Mike Squires .... .10 .04
❑ 40 George Hendrick .... .20 .08
❑ 41 Bob Knepper .... .10 .04
❑ 42 Steve Carlton .... .40 .16
❑ 43 Larry Biittner .... .10 .04
❑ 44 Chris Welsh .... .10 .04
❑ 45 Steve Nicosia .... .10 .04
❑ 46 Jack Clark .... .20 .08
❑ 47 Chris Chambliss .... .20 .08
❑ 48 Ivan DeJesus .... .10 .04
❑ 49 Lee Mazzilli .... .20 .08
❑ 50 Julio Cruz .... .10 .04
❑ 51 Pete Redfern .... .10 .04
❑ 52 Dave Stieb .... .20 .08
❑ 53 Doug Corbett .... .10 .04
❑ 54 Jorge Bell RC .... 1.00 .40
❑ 55 Joe Simpson .... .10 .04
❑ 56 Rusty Staub .... .20 .08
❑ 57 Hector Cruz .... .10 .04
❑ 58 Claudell Washington .... .10 .04
❑ 59 Enrique Romo .... .10 .04
❑ 60 Gary Lavelle .... .10 .04
❑ 61 Tim Flannery .... .10 .04
❑ 62 Joe Nolan .... .10 .04
❑ 63 Larry Bowa .... .20 .08
❑ 64 Sixto Lezcano .... .10 .04
❑ 65 Joe Sambito .... .10 .04
❑ 66 Bruce Kison .... .10 .04
❑ 67 Wayne Nordhagen .... .10 .04
❑ 68 Woodie Fryman .... .10 .04
❑ 69 Billy Sample .... .10 .04
❑ 70 Amos Otis .... .20 .08
❑ 71 Matt Keough .... .10 .04
❑ 72 Toby Harrah .... .20 .08
❑ 73 Dave Righetti RC .... 1.50 .60
❑ 74 Carl Yastrzemski .... 1.25 .50
❑ 75 Bob Welch .... .20 .08
❑ 76 Alan Trammell COR .... .20 .08
❑ 76A Alan Trammel ERR .... .20 .08
(Name misspelled)
❑ 77 Rick Dempsey .... .10 .04
❑ 78 Paul Molitor .... .40 .16
❑ 79 Dennis Martinez .... .20 .08
❑ 80 Jim Slaton .... .10 .04
❑ 81 Champ Summers .... .10 .04
❑ 82 Carney Lansford .... .20 .08
❑ 83 Barry Foote .... .10 .04
❑ 84 Steve Garvey .... .20 .08
❑ 85 Rick Manning .... .10 .04
❑ 86 John Wathan .... .10 .04
❑ 87 Brian Kingman .... .10 .04
❑ 88 Andre Dawson UER .... .20 .08
(Middle name Fernando
should be Nolan)
❑ 89 Jim Kern .... .10 .04
❑ 90 Bobby Grich .... .20 .08
❑ 91 Bob Forsch .... .10 .04
❑ 92 Art Howe .... .10 .04
❑ 93 Marty Bystrom .... .10 .04
❑ 94 Ozzie Smith .... 1.50 .60
❑ 95 Dave Parker .... .20 .08
❑ 96 Doyle Alexander .... .10 .04
❑ 97 Al Hrabosky .... .10 .04
❑ 98 Frank Taveras .... .10 .04
❑ 99 Tim Blackwell .... .10 .04
❑ 100 Floyd Bannister .... .10 .04
❑ 101 Alfredo Griffin .... .10 .04
❑ 102 Dave Engle .... .10 .04
❑ 103 Mario Soto .... .20 .08
❑ 104 Ross Baumgarten .... .10 .04
❑ 105 Ken Singleton .... .20 .08

❑ 106 Ted Simmons .20 .08
❑ 107 Jack Morris .20 .08
❑ 108 Bob Watson .10 .04
❑ 109 Dwight Evans .20 .08
❑ 110 Tom Lasorda MG .40 .16
❑ 111 Bert Blyleven .20 .08
❑ 112 Dan Quisenberry .10 .04
❑ 113 Rickey Henderson 2.50 1.00
❑ 114 Gary Carter .20 .08
❑ 115 Brian Downing .20 .08
❑ 116 Al Oliver .20 .08
❑ 117 LaMarr Hoyt .10 .04
❑ 118 Cesar Cedeno .20 .08
❑ 119 Keith Moreland .10 .04
❑ 120 Bob Shirley .10 .04
❑ 121 Terry Kennedy .10 .04
❑ 122 Frank Pastore .10 .04
❑ 123 Gene Garber .10 .04
❑ 124 Tony Pena .20 .08
❑ 125 Allen Ripley .10 .04
❑ 126 Randy Martz .10 .04
❑ 127 Richie Zisk .10 .04
❑ 128 Mike Scott .20 .08
❑ 129 Lloyd Moseby .10 .04
❑ 130 Rob Wilfong .10 .04
❑ 131 Tim Stoddard .10 .04
❑ 132 Gorman Thomas .20 .08
❑ 133 Dan Petry .10 .04
❑ 134 Bob Stanley .10 .04
❑ 135 Lou Piniella .20 .08
❑ 136 Pedro Guerrero .20 .08
❑ 137 Len Barker .10 .04
❑ 138 Rich Gale .10 .04
❑ 139 Wayne Gross .10 .04
❑ 140 Tim Wallach RC 1.00 .40
❑ 141 Gene Mauch MG .10 .04
❑ 142 Doc Medich .10 .04
❑ 143 Tony Bernazard .10 .04
❑ 144 Bill Virdon MG .10 .04
❑ 145 John Littlefield .10 .04
❑ 146 Dave Bergman .10 .04
❑ 147 Dick Davis .10 .04
❑ 148 Tom Seaver .75 .30
❑ 149 Matt Sinatro .10 .04
❑ 150 Chuck Tanner MG .10 .04
❑ 151 Leon Durham .10 .04
❑ 152 Gene Tenace .20 .08
❑ 153 Al Bumbry .10 .04
❑ 154 Mark Brouhard .10 .04
❑ 155 Rick Peters .10 .04
❑ 156 Jerry Remy .10 .04
❑ 157 Rick Reuschel .20 .08
❑ 158 Steve Howe .10 .04
❑ 159 Alan Bannister .10 .04
❑ 160 U.L. Washington .10 .04
❑ 161 Rick Langford .10 .04
❑ 162 Bill Gullickson .10 .04
❑ 163 Mark Wagner .10 .04
❑ 164 Geoff Zahn .10 .04
❑ 165 Ron LeFlore .20 .08
❑ 166 Dane Iorg .10 .04
❑ 167 Joe Niekro .10 .04
❑ 168 Pete Rose 2.50 1.00
❑ 169 Dave Collins .10 .04
❑ 170 Rick Wise .10 .04
❑ 171 Jim Bibby .10 .04
❑ 172 Larry Herndon .10 .04
❑ 173 Bob Horner .20 .08
❑ 174 Steve Dillard .10 .04
❑ 175 Mookie Wilson .20 .08
❑ 176 Dan Meyer .10 .04
❑ 177 Fernando Arroyo .10 .04
❑ 178 Jackson Todd .10 .04
❑ 179 Darrell Jackson .10 .04
❑ 180 Alvis Woods .10 .04
❑ 181 Jim Anderson .10 .04
❑ 182 Dave Kingman .20 .08
❑ 183 Steve Henderson .10 .04
❑ 184 Brian Asselstine .10 .04
❑ 185 Rod Scurry .10 .04
❑ 186 Fred Breining .10 .04
❑ 187 Danny Boone .10 .04
❑ 188 Junior Kennedy .10 .04
❑ 189 Sparky Lyle .20 .08
❑ 190 Whitey Herzog MG .20 .08
❑ 191 Dave Smith .10 .04
❑ 192 Ed Ott .10 .04
❑ 193 Greg Luzinski .20 .08
❑ 194 Bill Lee .20 .08
❑ 195 Don Zimmer MG .20 .08
❑ 196 Hal McRae .20 .08
❑ 197 Mike Norris .10 .04
❑ 198 Duane Kuiper .10 .04
❑ 199 Rick Cerone .10 .04
❑ 200 Jim Rice .20 .08
❑ 201 Steve Yeager .20 .08
❑ 202 Tom Brookens .10 .04
❑ 203 Jose Morales .10 .04
❑ 204 Roy Howell .10 .04
❑ 205 Tippy Martinez .10 .04
❑ 206 Moose Haas .10 .04
❑ 207 Al Cowens .10 .04
❑ 208 Dave Stapleton .10 .04
❑ 209 Bucky Dent .20 .08
❑ 210 Ron Cey .20 .08
❑ 211 Jorge Orta .10 .04
❑ 212 Jamie Quirk .10 .04
❑ 213 Jeff Jones .10 .04
❑ 214 Tim Raines .40 .16
❑ 215 Jon Matlack .10 .04
❑ 216 Rod Carew .40 .16
❑ 217 Jim Kaat .20 .08
❑ 218 Joe Pittman .10 .04
❑ 219 Larry Christenson .10 .04
❑ 220 Juan Bonilla RC .15 .06
❑ 221 Mike Easler .10 .04
❑ 222 Vida Blue .20 .08
❑ 223 Rick Camp .10 .04
❑ 224 Mike Jorgensen .10 .04
❑ 225 Jody Davis .10 .04
❑ 226 Mike Parrott .10 .04
❑ 227 Jim Clancy .10 .04
❑ 228 Hosken Powell .10 .04
❑ 229 Tom Hume .10 .04
❑ 230 Britt Burns .10 .04
❑ 231 Jim Palmer .20 .08
❑ 232 Bob Rodgers MG .10 .04
❑ 233 Milt Wilcox .10 .04
❑ 234 Dave Revering .10 .04
❑ 235 Mike Torrez .10 .04
❑ 236 Robert Castillo .10 .04
❑ 237 Von Hayes RC .50 .20
❑ 238 Renie Martin .10 .04
❑ 239 Dwayne Murphy .10 .04
❑ 240 Rodney Scott .10 .04
❑ 241 Fred Patek .10 .04
❑ 242 Mickey Rivers .10 .04
❑ 243 Steve Trout .10 .04
❑ 244 Jose Cruz .20 .08
❑ 245 Manny Trillo .10 .04
❑ 246 Lary Sorensen .10 .04
❑ 247 Dave Edwards .10 .04
❑ 248 Dan Driessen .10 .04
❑ 249 Tommy Boggs .10 .04
❑ 250 Dale Berra .10 .04
❑ 251 Ed Whitson .10 .04
❑ 252 Lee Smith RC 2.00 .80
❑ 253 Tom Paciorek .10 .04
❑ 254 Pat Zachry .10 .04
❑ 255 Luis Leal .10 .04
❑ 256 John Castino .10 .04
❑ 257 Rich Dauer .10 .04
❑ 258 Cecil Cooper .20 .08
❑ 259 Dave Rozema .10 .04
❑ 260 John Tudor .20 .08
❑ 261 Jerry Mumphrey .10 .04
❑ 262 Jay Johnstone .10 .04
❑ 263 Bo Diaz .10 .04
❑ 264 Dennis Leonard .10 .04
❑ 265 Jim Spencer .10 .04
❑ 266 John Milner .10 .04
❑ 267 Don Aase .10 .04
❑ 268 Jim Sundberg .20 .08
❑ 269 Lamar Johnson .10 .04
❑ 270 Frank LaCorte .10 .04
❑ 271 Barry Evans .10 .04
❑ 272 Enos Cabell .10 .04
❑ 273 Del Unser .10 .04
❑ 274 George Foster .20 .08
❑ 275 Brett Butler RC 1.00 .40
❑ 276 Lee Lacy .10 .04
❑ 277 Ken Reitz .10 .04
❑ 278 Keith Hernandez .20 .08
❑ 279 Doug DeCinces .10 .04
❑ 280 Charlie Moore .10 .04
❑ 281 Lance Parrish .20 .08
❑ 282 Ralph Houk MG .10 .04
❑ 283 Rich Gossage .20 .08
❑ 284 Jerry Reuss .10 .04
❑ 285 Mike Stanton .10 .04
❑ 286 Frank White .20 .08
❑ 287 Bob Owchinko .10 .04
❑ 288 Scott Sanderson .10 .04
❑ 289 Bump Wills .10 .04
❑ 290 Dave Frost .10 .04
❑ 291 Chet Lemon .20 .08
❑ 292 Tito Landrum .10 .04
❑ 293 Vern Ruhle .10 .04
❑ 294 Mike Schmidt 2.00 .80
❑ 295 Sam Mejias .10 .04
❑ 296 Gary Lucas .10 .04
❑ 297 John Candelaria .10 .04
❑ 298 Jerry Martin .10 .04
❑ 299 Dale Murphy .40 .16
❑ 300 Mike Lum .10 .04
❑ 301 Tom Hausman .10 .04
❑ 302 Glenn Abbott .10 .04
❑ 303 Roger Erickson .10 .04
❑ 304 Otto Velez .10 .04
❑ 305 Danny Goodwin .10 .04
❑ 306 John Mayberry .10 .04
❑ 307 Lenny Randle .10 .04
❑ 308 Bob Bailor .10 .04
❑ 309 Jerry Morales .10 .04
❑ 310 Rufino Linares .10 .04
❑ 311 Kent Tekulve .10 .04
❑ 312 Joe Morgan .20 .08
❑ 313 John Urrea .10 .04
❑ 314 Paul Householder .10 .04
❑ 315 Garry Maddox .10 .04
❑ 316 Mike Ramsey .10 .04
❑ 317 Alan Ashby .10 .04
❑ 318 Bob Clark .10 .04
❑ 319 Tony LaRussa MG .20 .08
❑ 320 Charlie Lea .10 .04
❑ 321 Danny Darwin .10 .04
❑ 322 Cesar Geronimo .10 .04
❑ 323 Tom Underwood .10 .04
❑ 324 Andre Thornton .10 .04
❑ 325 Rudy May .10 .04
❑ 326 Frank Tanana .20 .08
❑ 327 Dave Lopes .20 .08
❑ 328 Richie Hebner .10 .04
❑ 329 Mike Flanagan .10 .04
❑ 330 Mike Caldwell .10 .04
❑ 331 Scott McGregor .10 .04
❑ 332 Jerry Augustine .10 .04
❑ 333 Stan Papi .10 .04
❑ 334 Rick Miller .10 .04
❑ 335 Graig Nettles .20 .08
❑ 336 Dusty Baker .20 .08
❑ 337 Dave Garcia MG .10 .04
❑ 338 Larry Gura .10 .04
❑ 339 Cliff Johnson .10 .04
❑ 340 Warren Cromartie .10 .04
❑ 341 Steve Comer .10 .04
❑ 342 Rick Burleson .10 .04
❑ 343 John Martin RC .15 .06
❑ 344 Craig Reynolds .10 .04
❑ 345 Mike Proly .10 .04
❑ 346 Ruppert Jones .10 .04
❑ 347 Omar Moreno .10 .04
❑ 348 Greg Minton .10 .04
❑ 349 Rick Mahler .10 .04
❑ 350 Alex Trevino .10 .04
❑ 351 Mike Krukow .10 .04
❑ 352A Shane Rawley ERR .40 .16
(Photo actually
Jim Anderson)
❑ 352B Shane Rawley COR .10 .04
❑ 353 Garth Iorg .10 .04
❑ 354 Pete Mackanin .10 .04
❑ 355 Paul Moskau .10 .04
❑ 356 Richard Dotson .10 .04
❑ 357 Steve Stone .10 .04
❑ 358 Larry Hisle .10 .04
❑ 359 Aurelio Lopez .10 .04
❑ 360 Oscar Gamble .10 .04

❑ 361 Tom Burgmeier .10 .04
❑ 362 Terry Forster .20 .08
❑ 363 Joe Charboneau .20 .08
❑ 364 Ken Brett .10 .04
❑ 365 Tony Armas .20 .08
❑ 366 Chris Speier .10 .04
❑ 367 Fred Lynn .20 .08
❑ 368 Buddy Bell .20 .08
❑ 369 Jim Essian .10 .04
❑ 370 Terry Puhl .10 .04
❑ 371 Greg Gross .10 .04
❑ 372 Bruce Sutter .20 .08
❑ 373 Joe Lefebvre .10 .04
❑ 374 Ray Knight .20 .08
❑ 375 Bruce Benedict .10 .04
❑ 376 Tim Foli .10 .04
❑ 377 Al Holland .10 .04
❑ 378 Ken Kravec .10 .04
❑ 379 Jeff Burroughs .10 .04
❑ 380 Pete Falcone .10 .04
❑ 381 Ernie Whitt .10 .04
❑ 382 Brad Havens .10 .04
❑ 383 Terry Crowley .10 .04
❑ 384 Don Money .10 .04
❑ 385 Dan Schatzeder .10 .04
❑ 386 Gary Allenson .10 .04
❑ 387 Yogi Berra CO .75 .30
❑ 388 Ken Landreaux .10 .04
❑ 389 Mike Hargrove .10 .04
❑ 390 Darryl Motley .10 .04
❑ 391 Dave McKay .10 .04
❑ 392 Stan Bahnsen .10 .04
❑ 393 Ken Forsch .10 .04
❑ 394 Mario Mendoza .10 .04
❑ 395 Jim Morrison .10 .04
❑ 396 Mike Ivie .10 .04
❑ 397 Broderick Perkins .10 .04
❑ 398 Darrell Evans .20 .08
❑ 399 Ron Reed .10 .04
❑ 400 Johnny Bench .75 .30
❑ 401 Steve Bedrosian RC .50 .20
❑ 402 Bill Robinson .10 .04
❑ 403 Bill Buckner .20 .08
❑ 404 Ken Oberkfell .10 .04
❑ 405 Cal Ripken RC 40.00 16.00
❑ 406 Jim Gantner .10 .04
❑ 407 Kirk Gibson .75 .30
❑ 408 Tony Perez .40 .16
❑ 409 Tommy John UER .20 .08
(Text says 52-56 as Yankee, should be 52-26)
❑ 410 Dave Stewart RC 1.50 .60
❑ 411 Dan Spillner .10 .04
❑ 412 Willie Aikens .10 .04
❑ 413 Mike Heath .10 .04
❑ 414 Ray Burris .10 .04
❑ 415 Leon Roberts .10 .04
❑ 416 Mike Witt .50 .20
❑ 417 Bob Molinaro .10 .04
❑ 418 Steve Braun .10 .04
❑ 419 Nolan Ryan UER 4.00 1.60
(Nisnumbering of Nolan's no-hitters on card back)
❑ 420 Tug McGraw .20 .08
❑ 421 Dave Concepcion .20 .08
❑ 422A Juan Eichelberger .40 .16
ERR (Photo actually Gary Lucas)
❑ 422B Juan Eichelberger .10 .04
COR
❑ 423 Rick Rhoden .10 .04
❑ 424 Frank Robinson MG .40 .16
❑ 425 Eddie Miller .10 .04
❑ 426 Bill Caudill .10 .04
❑ 427 Doug Flynn .10 .04
❑ 428 Larry Andersen UER .10 .04
(Misspelled Anderson on card front)
❑ 429 Al Williams .10 .04
❑ 430 Jerry Garvin .10 .04
❑ 431 Glenn Adams .10 .04
❑ 432 Barry Bonnell .10 .04
❑ 433 Jerry Narron .10 .04
❑ 434 John Stearns .10 .04
❑ 435 Mike Tyson .10 .04
❑ 436 Glenn Hubbard .10 .04
❑ 437 Eddie Solomon .10 .04
❑ 438 Jeff Leonard .10 .04
❑ 439 Randy Bass RC .50 .20
❑ 440 Mike LaCoss .10 .04
❑ 441 Gary Matthews .20 .08
❑ 442 Mark Littell .10 .04
❑ 443 Don Sutton .20 .08
❑ 444 John Harris .10 .04
❑ 445 Vada Pinson CO .20 .08
❑ 446 Elias Sosa .10 .04
❑ 447 Charlie Hough .20 .08
❑ 448 Willie Wilson .20 .08
❑ 449 Fred Stanley .10 .04
❑ 450 Tom Veryzer .10 .04
❑ 451 Ron Davis .10 .04
❑ 452 Mark Clear .10 .04
❑ 453 Bill Russell .20 .08
❑ 454 Lou Whitaker .20 .08
❑ 455 Dan Graham .10 .04
❑ 456 Reggie Cleveland .10 .04
❑ 457 Sammy Stewart .10 .04
❑ 458 Pete Vuckovich .10 .04
❑ 459 John Wockenfuss .10 .04
❑ 460 Glenn Hoffman .10 .04
❑ 461 Willie Randolph .20 .08
❑ 462 Fernando Valenzuela .75 .30
❑ 463 Ron Hassey .10 .04
❑ 464 Paul Splittorff .10 .04
❑ 465 Rob Picciolo .10 .04
❑ 466 Larry Parrish .10 .04
❑ 467 Johnny Grubb .10 .04
❑ 468 Dan Ford .10 .04
❑ 469 Silvio Martinez .10 .04
❑ 470 Kiko Garcia .10 .04
❑ 471 Bob Boone .20 .08
❑ 472 Luis Salazar .10 .04
❑ 473 Randy Niemann .10 .04
❑ 474 Tom Griffin .10 .04
❑ 475 Phil Niekro .20 .08
❑ 476 Hubie Brooks .10 .04
❑ 477 Dick Tidrow .10 .04
❑ 478 Jim Beattie .10 .04
❑ 479 Damaso Garcia .10 .04
❑ 480 Mickey Hatcher .10 .04
❑ 481 Joe Price .10 .04
❑ 482 Ed Farmer .10 .04
❑ 483 Eddie Murray .75 .30
❑ 484 Ben Oglivie .20 .08
❑ 485 Kevin Saucier .10 .04
❑ 486 Bobby Murcer .20 .08
❑ 487 Bill Campbell .10 .04
❑ 488 Reggie Smith .20 .08
❑ 489 Wayne Garland .10 .04
❑ 490 Jim Wright .10 .04
❑ 491 Billy Martin MG .40 .16
❑ 492 Jim Fanning MG .10 .04
❑ 493 Don Baylor .20 .08
❑ 494 Rick Honeycutt .10 .04
❑ 495 Carlton Fisk .40 .16
❑ 496 Denny Walling .10 .04
❑ 497 Bake McBride .20 .08
❑ 498 Darrell Porter .10 .04
❑ 499 Gene Richards .10 .04
❑ 500 Ron Oester .10 .04
❑ 501 Ken Dayley .10 .04
❑ 502 Jason Thompson .10 .04
❑ 503 Milt May .10 .04
❑ 504 Doug Bird .10 .04
❑ 505 Bruce Bochte .10 .04
❑ 506 Neil Allen .10 .04
❑ 507 Joey McLaughlin .10 .04
❑ 508 Butch Wynegar .10 .04
❑ 509 Gary Roenicke .10 .04
❑ 510 Robin Yount 1.25 .50
❑ 511 Dave Tobik .10 .04
❑ 512 Rich Gedman .50 .20
❑ 513 Gene Nelson .10 .04
❑ 514 Rick Monday .20 .08
❑ 515 Miguel Dilone .10 .04
❑ 516 Clint Hurdle .10 .04
❑ 517 Jeff Newman .10 .04
❑ 518 Grant Jackson .10 .04
❑ 519 Andy Hassler .10 .04
❑ 520 Pat Putnam .10 .04
❑ 521 Greg Pryor .10 .04
❑ 522 Tony Scott .10 .04
❑ 523 Steve Mura .10 .04
❑ 524 Johnnie LeMaster .10 .04
❑ 525 Dick Ruthven .10 .04
❑ 526 John McNamara MG .10 .04
❑ 527 Larry McWilliams .10 .04
❑ 528 Johnny Ray RC .50 .20
❑ 529 Pat Tabler .10 .04
❑ 530 Tom Herr .10 .04
❑ 531A SD Chicken 1.00 .40
ERR (Without TM)
❑ 531B San Diego Chicken 1.00 .40
COR (With TM)
❑ 532 Sal Butera .10 .04
❑ 533 Mike Griffin .10 .04
❑ 534 Kelvin Moore .10 .04
❑ 535 Reggie Jackson .40 .16
❑ 536 Ed Romero .10 .04
❑ 537 Derrel Thomas .10 .04
❑ 538 Mike O'Berry .10 .04
❑ 539 Jack O'Connor .10 .04
❑ 540 Bob Ojeda RC .50 .20
❑ 541 Roy Lee Jackson .10 .04
❑ 542 Lynn Jones .10 .04
❑ 543 Gaylord Perry .20 .08
❑ 544A Phil Garner ERR .20 .08
(Reverse negative)
❑ 544B Phil Garner COR .20 .08
❑ 545 Garry Templeton .20 .08
❑ 546 Rafael Ramirez .10 .04
❑ 547 Jeff Reardon .20 .08
❑ 548 Ron Guidry .20 .08
❑ 549 Tim Laudner .10 .04
❑ 550 John Henry Johnson .10 .04
❑ 551 Chris Bando .10 .04
❑ 552 Bobby Brown .10 .04
❑ 553 Larry Bradford .10 .04
❑ 554 Scott Fletcher RC .50 .20
❑ 555 Jerry Royster .10 .04
❑ 556 Shooty Babitt UER .10 .04
(Spelled Babbitt on front)
❑ 557 Kent Hrbek RC 1.00 .40
❑ 558 Ron Guidry .20 .08
Tommy John
❑ 559 Mark Bomback .10 .04
❑ 560 Julio Valdez .10 .04
❑ 561 Buck Martinez .10 .04
❑ 562 Mike A. Marshall RC .50 .20
❑ 563 Rennie Stennett .10 .04
❑ 564 Steve Crawford .10 .04
❑ 565 Bob Babcock .10 .04
❑ 566 Johnny Podres CO .20 .08
❑ 567 Paul Serna .10 .04
❑ 568 Harold Baines .20 .08
❑ 569 Dave LaRoche .10 .04
❑ 570 Lee May .10 .04
❑ 571 Gary Ward .10 .04
❑ 572 John Denny .10 .04
❑ 573 Roy Smalley .10 .04
❑ 574 Bob Brenly RC 1.00 .40
❑ 575 Reggie Jackson .20 .08
Dave Winfield
❑ 576 Luis Pujols .10 .04
❑ 577 Butch Hobson .10 .04
❑ 578 Harvey Kuenn MG .10 .04
❑ 579 Cal Ripken Sr. CO .20 .08
❑ 580 Juan Berenguer .10 .04
❑ 581 Benny Ayala .10 .04
❑ 582 Vance Law .10 .04
❑ 583 Rick Leach .10 .04
❑ 584 George Frazier .10 .04
❑ 585 Phillies Finest 1.50 .60
Pete Rose
Mike Schmidt
❑ 586 Joe Rudi .20 .08
❑ 587 Juan Beniquez .10 .04
❑ 588 Luis DeLeon .10 .04
❑ 589 Craig Swan .10 .04
❑ 590 Dave Chalk .10 .04
❑ 591 Billy Gardner MG .10 .04
❑ 592 Sal Bando .20 .08
❑ 593 Bert Campaneris .20 .08
❑ 594 Steve Kemp .10 .04
❑ 595A Randy Lerch ERR .40 .16

	Card	Nm-Mt	Ex-Mt
	(Braves)		
❑	595B Randy Lerch COR	.10	.04
	(Brewers)		
❑	596 Bryan Clark RC	.15	.06
❑	597 Dave Ford	.10	.04
❑	598 Mike Scioscia	.20	.08
❑	599 John Lowenstein	.10	.04
❑	600 Rene Lachemann MG	.10	.04
❑	601 Mick Kelleher	.10	.04
❑	602 Ron Jackson	.10	.04
❑	603 Jerry Koosman	.20	.08
❑	604 Dave Goltz	.10	.04
❑	605 Ellis Valentine	.10	.04
❑	606 Lonnie Smith	.10	.04
❑	607 Joaquin Andujar	.20	.08
❑	608 Garry Hancock	.10	.04
❑	609 Jerry Turner	.10	.04
❑	610 Bob Bonner	.10	.04
❑	611 Jim Dwyer	.10	.04
❑	612 Terry Bulling	.10	.04
❑	613 Joel Youngblood	.10	.04
❑	614 Larry Milbourne	.10	.04
❑	615 Gene Roof UER	.10	.04
	(Name on front is Phil Roof)		
❑	616 Keith Drumwright	.10	.04
❑	617 Dave Rosello	.10	.04
❑	618 Rickey Keeton	.10	.04
❑	619 Dennis Lamp	.10	.04
❑	620 Sid Monge	.10	.04
❑	621 Jerry White	.10	.04
❑	622 Luis Aguayo	.10	.04
❑	623 Jamie Easterly	.10	.04
❑	624 Steve Sax RC	1.00	.40
❑	625 Dave Roberts	.10	.04
❑	626 Rick Bosetti	.10	.04
❑	627 Terry Francona RC	1.50	.60
❑	628 Tom Seaver	.75	.30
	Johnny Bench		
❑	629 Paul Mirabella	.10	.04
❑	630 Rance Mulliniks	.10	.04
❑	631 Kevin Hickey RC	.15	.06
❑	632 Reid Nichols	.10	.04
❑	633 Dave Geisel	.10	.04
❑	634 Ken Griffey	.20	.08
❑	635 Bob Lemon MG	.40	.16
❑	636 Orlando Sanchez	.10	.04
❑	637 Bill Almon	.10	.04
❑	638 Danny Ainge	.20	.08
❑	639 Willie Stargell	.40	.16
❑	640 Bob Sykes	.10	.04
❑	641 Ed Lynch	.10	.04
❑	642 John Ellis	.10	.04
❑	643 Ferguson Jenkins	.20	.08
❑	644 Lenn Sakata	.10	.04
❑	645 Julio Gonzalez	.10	.04
❑	646 Jesse Orosco	.10	.04
❑	647 Jerry Dybzinski	.10	.04
❑	648 Tommy Davis CO	.20	.08
❑	649 Ron Gardenhire RC	.50	.20
❑	650 Felipe Alou CO	.20	.08
❑	651 Harvey Haddix CO	.20	.08
❑	652 Willie Upshaw	.50	.20
❑	653 Bill Madlock	.20	.08
❑	654A DK Checklist 1-26	.40	.16
	ERR (Unnumbered) (With Trammel)		
❑	654B DK Checklist 1-26	.20	.08
	COR (Unnumbered) (With Trammell)		
❑	655 Checklist 27-130	.20	.08
	(Unnumbered)		
❑	656 Checklist 131-234	.20	.08
	(Unnumbered)		
❑	657 Checklist 235-338	.20	.08
	(Unnumbered)		
❑	658 Checklist 339-442	.20	.08
	(Unnumbered)		
❑	659 Checklist 443-544	.20	.08
	(Unnumbered)		
❑	660 Checklist 545-653	.20	.08
	(Unnumbered)		

1983 Donruss

	Nm-Mt	Ex-Mt
COMPLETE SET (660)	60.00	24.00
COMP.FACT.SET (660)	80.00	32.00
COMP.COBB PUZZLE	5.00	2.00

	Card	Nm-Mt	Ex-Mt
❑	1 Fernando Valenzuela DK	.20	.08
❑	2 Rollie Fingers DK	.20	.08
❑	3 Reggie Jackson DK	.40	.16
❑	4 Jim Palmer DK	.20	.08
❑	5 Jack Morris DK	.20	.08
❑	6 George Foster DK	.20	.08
❑	7 Jim Sundberg DK	.20	.08
❑	8 Willie Stargell DK	.40	.16
❑	9 Dave Stieb DK	.20	.08
❑	10 Joe Niekro DK	.10	.04
❑	11 Rickey Henderson DK	1.50	.60
❑	12 Dale Murphy DK	.40	.16
❑	13 Toby Harrah DK	.20	.08
❑	14 Bill Buckner DK	.20	.08
❑	15 Willie Wilson DK	.20	.08
❑	16 Steve Carlton DK	.40	.16
❑	17 Ron Guidry DK	.20	.08
❑	18 Steve Rogers DK	.20	.08
❑	19 Kent Hrbek DK	.20	.08
❑	20 Keith Hernandez DK	.20	.08
❑	21 Floyd Bannister DK	.10	.04
❑	22 Johnny Bench DK	.75	.30
❑	23 Britt Burns DK	.10	.04
❑	24 Joe Morgan DK	.20	.08
❑	25 Carl Yastrzemski DK	.75	.30
❑	26 Terry Kennedy DK	.10	.04
❑	27 Gary Roenicke	.10	.04
❑	28 Dwight Bernard	.10	.04
❑	29 Pat Underwood	.10	.04
❑	30 Gary Allenson	.10	.04
❑	31 Ron Guidry	.20	.08
❑	32 Burt Hooton	.10	.04
❑	33 Chris Bando	.10	.04
❑	34 Vida Blue	.20	.08
❑	35 Rickey Henderson	1.50	.60
❑	36 Ray Burris	.10	.04
❑	37 John Butcher	.10	.04
❑	38 Don Aase	.10	.04
❑	39 Jerry Koosman	.20	.08
❑	40 Bruce Sutter	.20	.08
❑	41 Jose Cruz	.20	.08
❑	42 Pete Rose	2.50	1.00
❑	43 Cesar Cedeno	.20	.08
❑	44 Floyd Chiffer	.10	.04
❑	45 Larry McWilliams	.10	.04
❑	46 Alan Fowlkes	.10	.04
❑	47 Dale Murphy	.40	.16
❑	48 Doug Bird	.10	.04
❑	49 Hubie Brooks	.10	.04
❑	50 Floyd Bannister	.10	.04
❑	51 Jack O'Connor	.10	.04
❑	52 Steve Senteney	.10	.04
❑	53 Gary Gaetti RC	1.00	.40
❑	54 Damaso Garcia	.10	.04
❑	55 Gene Nelson	.10	.04
❑	56 Mookie Wilson	.20	.08
❑	57 Allen Ripley	.10	.04
❑	58 Bob Horner	.20	.08
❑	59 Tony Pena	.10	.04
❑	60 Gary Lavelle	.10	.04
❑	61 Tim Lollar	.10	.04
❑	62 Frank Pastore	.10	.04
❑	63 Garry Maddox	.10	.04
❑	64 Bob Forsch	.10	.04
❑	65 Harry Spilman	.10	.04
❑	66 Geoff Zahn	.10	.04
❑	67 Salome Barojas	.10	.04
❑	68 David Palmer	.10	.04
❑	69 Charlie Hough	.20	.08
❑	70 Dan Quisenberry	.10	.04
❑	71 Tony Armas	.20	.08
❑	72 Rick Sutcliffe	.20	.08
❑	73 Steve Balboni	.10	.04
❑	74 Jerry Remy	.10	.04
❑	75 Mike Scioscia	.20	.08
❑	76 John Wockenfuss	.10	.04
❑	77 Jim Palmer	.20	.08
❑	78 Rollie Fingers	.20	.08
❑	79 Joe Nolan	.10	.04
❑	80 Pete Vuckovich	.10	.04
❑	81 Rick Leach	.10	.04
❑	82 Rick Miller	.10	.04
❑	83 Graig Nettles	.20	.08
❑	84 Ron Cey	.20	.08
❑	85 Miguel Dilone	.10	.04
❑	86 John Wathan	.10	.04
❑	87 Kelvin Moore	.10	.04
❑	88A Byrn Smith ERR	.20	.08
	(Sic, Bryn)		
❑	88B Bryn Smith COR	.40	.16
❑	89 Dave Hostetler	.10	.04
❑	90 Rod Carew	.40	.16
❑	91 Lonnie Smith	.10	.04
❑	92 Bob Knepper	.10	.04
❑	93 Marty Bystrom	.10	.04
❑	94 Chris Welsh	.10	.04
❑	95 Jason Thompson	.10	.04
❑	96 Tom O'Malley	.10	.04
❑	97 Phil Niekro	.20	.08
❑	98 Neil Allen	.10	.04
❑	99 Bill Buckner	.20	.08
❑	100 Ed VandeBerg	.10	.04
❑	101 Jim Clancy	.10	.04
❑	102 Robert Castillo	.10	.04
❑	103 Bruce Berenyi	.10	.04
❑	104 Carlton Fisk	.40	.16
❑	105 Mike Flanagan	.10	.04
❑	106 Cecil Cooper	.20	.08
❑	107 Jack Morris	.20	.08
❑	108 Mike Morgan	.10	.04
❑	109 Luis Aponte	.10	.04
❑	110 Pedro Guerrero	.20	.08
❑	111 Len Barker	.10	.04
❑	112 Willie Wilson	.20	.08
❑	113 Dave Beard	.10	.04
❑	114 Mike Gates	.10	.04
❑	115 Reggie Jackson	.40	.16
❑	116 George Wright RC	.50	.20
❑	117 Vance Law	.10	.04
❑	118 Nolan Ryan	4.00	1.60
❑	119 Mike Krukow	.10	.04
❑	120 Ozzie Smith	1.25	.50
❑	121 Broderick Perkins	.10	.04
❑	122 Tom Seaver	.75	.30
❑	123 Chris Chambliss	.20	.08
❑	124 Chuck Tanner MG	.10	.04
❑	125 Johnnie LeMaster	.10	.04
❑	126 Mel Hall RC	.50	.20
❑	127 Bruce Bochte	.10	.04
❑	128 Charlie Puleo	.10	.04
❑	129 Luis Leal	.10	.04
❑	130 John Pacella	.10	.04
❑	131 Glenn Gulliver	.10	.04
❑	132 Don Money	.10	.04
❑	133 Dave Rozema	.10	.04
❑	134 Bruce Hurst	.10	.04
❑	135 Rudy May	.10	.04
❑	136 Tom Lasorda MG	.40	.16
❑	137 Dan Spillner UER	.10	.04
	(Photo actually Ed Whitson)		
❑	138 Jerry Martin	.10	.04
❑	139 Mike Norris	.10	.04
❑	140 Al Oliver	.20	.08
❑	141 Daryl Sconiers	.10	.04
❑	142 Lamar Johnson	.10	.04
❑	143 Harold Baines	.20	.08

❑ 144 Alan Ashby .10 .04
❑ 145 Garry Templeton .20 .08
❑ 146 Al Holland .10 .04
❑ 147 Bo Diaz .10 .04
❑ 148 Dave Concepcion .20 .08
❑ 149 Rick Camp .10 .04
❑ 150 Jim Morrison .10 .04
❑ 151 Randy Martz .10 .04
❑ 152 Keith Hernandez .20 .08
❑ 153 John Lowenstein .10 .04
❑ 154 Mike Caldwell .10 .04
❑ 155 Milt Wilcox .10 .04
❑ 156 Rich Gedman .10 .04
❑ 157 Rich Gossage .20 .08
❑ 158 Jerry Reuss .10 .04
❑ 159 Ron Hassey .10 .04
❑ 160 Larry Gura .10 .04
❑ 161 Dwayne Murphy .10 .04
❑ 162 Woodie Fryman .10 .04
❑ 163 Steve Comer .10 .04
❑ 164 Ken Forsch .10 .04
❑ 165 Dennis Lamp .10 .04
❑ 166 David Green RC .50 .20
❑ 167 Terry Puhl .10 .04
❑ 168 Mike Schmidt 2.00 .80
(Wearing 37 rather than 20)
❑ 169 Eddie Milner .10 .04
❑ 170 John Curtis .10 .04
❑ 171 Don Robinson .10 .04
❑ 172 Rich Gale .10 .04
❑ 173 Steve Bedrosian .10 .04
❑ 174 Willie Hernandez .10 .04
❑ 175 Ron Gardenhire .10 .04
❑ 176 Jim Beattie .10 .04
❑ 177 Tim Laudner .10 .04
❑ 178 Buck Martinez .10 .04
❑ 179 Kent Hrbek .20 .08
❑ 180 Alfredo Griffin .10 .04
❑ 181 Larry Andersen .10 .04
❑ 182 Pete Falcone .10 .04
❑ 183 Jody Davis .10 .04
❑ 184 Glenn Hubbard .10 .04
❑ 185 Dale Berra .10 .04
❑ 186 Greg Minton .10 .04
❑ 187 Gary Lucas .10 .04
❑ 188 Dave Van Gorder .10 .04
❑ 189 Bob Dernier .10 .04
❑ 190 Willie McGee RC 1.00 .40
❑ 191 Dickie Thon .10 .04
❑ 192 Bob Boone .20 .08
❑ 193 Britt Burns .10 .04
❑ 194 Jeff Reardon .20 .08
❑ 195 Jon Matlack .10 .04
❑ 196 Don Slaught RC .50 .20
❑ 197 Fred Stanley .10 .04
❑ 198 Rick Manning .10 .04
❑ 199 Dave Righetti .20 .08
❑ 200 Dave Stapleton .10 .04
❑ 201 Steve Yeager .20 .08
❑ 202 Enos Cabell .10 .04
❑ 203 Sammy Stewart .10 .04
❑ 204 Moose Haas .10 .04
❑ 205 Lenn Sakata .10 .04
❑ 206 Charlie Moore .10 .04
❑ 207 Alan Trammell .20 .08
❑ 208 Jim Rice .20 .08
❑ 209 Roy Smalley .10 .04
❑ 210 Bill Russell .20 .08
❑ 211 Andre Thornton .10 .04
❑ 212 Willie Aikens .10 .04
❑ 213 Dave McKay .10 .04
❑ 214 Tim Blackwell .10 .04
❑ 215 Buddy Bell .20 .08
❑ 216 Doug DeCinces .10 .04
❑ 217 Tom Herr .10 .04
❑ 218 Frank LaCorte .10 .04
❑ 219 Steve Carlton .40 .16
❑ 220 Terry Kennedy .10 .04
❑ 221 Mike Easler .10 .04
❑ 222 Jack Clark .20 .08
❑ 223 Gene Garber .10 .04
❑ 224 Scott Holman .10 .04
❑ 225 Mike Proly .10 .04
❑ 226 Terry Bulling .10 .04
❑ 227 Jerry Garvin .10 .04
❑ 228 Ron Davis .10 .04
❑ 229 Tom Hume .10 .04
❑ 230 Marc Hill .10 .04
❑ 231 Dennis Martinez .20 .08
❑ 232 Jim Gantner .10 .04
❑ 233 Larry Pashnick .10 .04
❑ 234 Dave Collins .10 .04
❑ 235 Tom Burgmeier .10 .04
❑ 236 Ken Landreaux .10 .04
❑ 237 John Denny .10 .04
❑ 238 Hal McRae .20 .08
❑ 239 Matt Keough .10 .04
❑ 240 Doug Flynn .10 .04
❑ 241 Fred Lynn .20 .08
❑ 242 Billy Sample .10 .04
❑ 243 Tom Paciorek .10 .04
❑ 244 Joe Sambito .10 .04
❑ 245 Sid Monge .10 .04
❑ 246 Ken Oberkfell .10 .04
❑ 247 Joe Pittman UER .10 .04
(Photo actually Juan Eichelberger)
❑ 248 Mario Soto .20 .08
❑ 249 Claudell Washington .10 .04
❑ 250 Rick Rhoden .10 .04
❑ 251 Darrell Evans .20 .08
❑ 252 Steve Henderson .10 .04
❑ 253 Manny Castillo .10 .04
❑ 254 Craig Swan .10 .04
❑ 255 Joey McLaughlin .10 .04
❑ 256 Pete Redfern .10 .04
❑ 257 Ken Singleton .20 .08
❑ 258 Robin Yount 1.25 .50
❑ 259 Elias Sosa .10 .04
❑ 260 Bob Ojeda .10 .04
❑ 261 Bobby Murcer .20 .08
❑ 262 Candy Maldonado RC .50 .20
❑ 263 Rick Waits .10 .04
❑ 264 Greg Pryor .10 .04
❑ 265 Bob Owchinko .10 .04
❑ 266 Chris Speier .10 .04
❑ 267 Bruce Kison .10 .04
❑ 268 Mark Wagner .10 .04
❑ 269 Steve Kemp .10 .04
❑ 270 Phil Garner .20 .08
❑ 271 Gene Richards .10 .04
❑ 272 Renie Martin .10 .04
❑ 273 Dave Roberts .10 .04
❑ 274 Dan Driessen .10 .04
❑ 275 Rufino Linares .10 .04
❑ 276 Lee Lacy .10 .04
❑ 277 Ryne Sandberg RC 10.00 4.00
❑ 278 Darrell Porter .10 .04
❑ 279 Cal Ripken 6.00 2.40
❑ 280 Jamie Easterly .10 .04
❑ 281 Bill Fahey .10 .04
❑ 282 Glenn Hoffman .10 .04
❑ 283 Willie Randolph .20 .08
❑ 284 Fernando Valenzuela .20 .08
❑ 285 Alan Bannister .10 .04
❑ 286 Paul Splittorff .10 .04
❑ 287 Joe Rudi .20 .08
❑ 288 Bill Gullickson .10 .04
❑ 289 Danny Darwin .10 .04
❑ 290 Andy Hassler .10 .04
❑ 291 Ernesto Escarrega .10 .04
❑ 292 Steve Mura .10 .04
❑ 293 Tony Scott .10 .04
❑ 294 Manny Trillo .10 .04
❑ 295 Greg Harris .10 .04
❑ 296 Luis DeLeon .10 .04
❑ 297 Kent Tekulve .10 .04
❑ 298 Atlee Hammaker .10 .04
❑ 299 Bruce Benedict .10 .04
❑ 300 Fergie Jenkins .20 .08
❑ 301 Dave Kingman .20 .08
❑ 302 Bill Caudill .10 .04
❑ 303 John Castino .10 .04
❑ 304 Ernie Whitt .10 .04
❑ 305 Randy Johnson .10 .04
❑ 306 Garth Iorg .10 .04
❑ 307 Gaylord Perry .20 .08
❑ 308 Ed Lynch .10 .04
❑ 309 Keith Moreland .10 .04
❑ 310 Rafael Ramirez .10 .04
❑ 311 Bill Madlock .20 .08
❑ 312 Milt May .10 .04
❑ 313 John Montefusco .10 .04
❑ 314 Wayne Krenchicki .10 .04
❑ 315 George Vukovich .10 .04
❑ 316 Joaquin Andujar .20 .08
❑ 317 Craig Reynolds .10 .04
❑ 318 Rick Burleson .10 .04
❑ 319 Richard Dotson .10 .04
❑ 320 Steve Rogers .20 .08
❑ 321 Dave Schmidt .10 .04
❑ 322 Bud Black RC .50 .20
❑ 323 Jeff Burroughs .10 .04
❑ 324 Von Hayes .10 .04
❑ 325 Butch Wynegar .10 .04
❑ 326 Carl Yastrzemski 1.25 .50
❑ 327 Ron Roenicke .10 .04
❑ 328 Howard Johnson RC 1.00 .40
❑ 329 Rick Dempsey UER .10 .04
(Posing as a left-handed batter)
❑ 330A Jim Slaton .10 .04
(Bio printed black on white)
❑ 330B Jim Slaton .20 .08
(Bio printed black on yellow)
❑ 331 Benny Ayala .10 .04
❑ 332 Ted Simmons .20 .08
❑ 333 Lou Whitaker .20 .08
❑ 334 Chuck Rainey .10 .04
❑ 335 Lou Piniella .20 .08
❑ 336 Steve Sax .20 .08
❑ 337 Toby Harrah .20 .08
❑ 338 George Brett 2.00 .80
❑ 339 Dave Lopes .20 .08
❑ 340 Gary Carter .20 .08
❑ 341 John Grubb .10 .04
❑ 342 Tim Foli .10 .04
❑ 343 Jim Kaat .20 .08
❑ 344 Mike LaCoss .10 .04
❑ 345 Larry Christenson .10 .04
❑ 346 Juan Bonilla .10 .04
❑ 347 Omar Moreno .10 .04
❑ 348 Chili Davis .20 .08
❑ 349 Tommy Boggs .10 .04
❑ 350 Rusty Staub .20 .08
❑ 351 Bump Wills .10 .04
❑ 352 Rick Sweet .10 .04
❑ 353 Jim Gott RC .50 .20
❑ 354 Terry Felton .10 .04
❑ 355 Jim Kern .10 .04
❑ 356 Bill Almon UER .10 .04
(Expos/Mets in 1983, not Padres/Mets)
❑ 357 Tippy Martinez .10 .04
❑ 358 Roy Howell .10 .04
❑ 359 Dan Petry .10 .04
❑ 360 Jerry Mumphrey .10 .04
❑ 361 Mark Clear .10 .04
❑ 362 Mike Marshall .10 .04
❑ 363 Lary Sorensen .10 .04
❑ 364 Amos Otis .20 .08
❑ 365 Rick Langford .10 .04
❑ 366 Brad Mills .10 .04
❑ 367 Brian Downing .20 .08
❑ 368 Mike Richardt .10 .04
❑ 369 Aurelio Rodriguez .10 .04
❑ 370 Dave Smith .10 .04
❑ 371 Tug McGraw .20 .08
❑ 372 Doug Bair .10 .04
❑ 373 Ruppert Jones .10 .04
❑ 374 Alex Trevino .10 .04
❑ 375 Ken Dayley .10 .04
❑ 376 Rod Scurry .10 .04
❑ 377 Bob Brenly .10 .04
❑ 378 Scot Thompson .10 .04
❑ 379 Julio Cruz .10 .04
❑ 380 John Stearns .10 .04
❑ 381 Dale Murray .10 .04
❑ 382 Frank Viola RC 1.50 .60
❑ 383 Al Bumbry .10 .04
❑ 384 Ben Oglivie .20 .08
❑ 385 Dave Tobik .10 .04
❑ 386 Bob Stanley .10 .04
❑ 387 Andre Robertson .10 .04
❑ 388 Jorge Orta .10 .04

❑ 389 Ed Whitson .10 .04
❑ 390 Don Hood .10 .04
❑ 391 Tom Underwood .10 .04
❑ 392 Tim Wallach .20 .08
❑ 393 Steve Renko .10 .04
❑ 394 Mickey Rivers .10 .04
❑ 395 Greg Luzinski .20 .08
❑ 396 Art Howe .10 .04
❑ 397 Alan Wiggins .10 .04
❑ 398 Jim Barr .10 .04
❑ 399 Ivan DeJesus .10 .04
❑ 400 Tom Lawless .10 .04
❑ 401 Bob Walk .10 .04
❑ 402 Jimmy Smith .10 .04
❑ 403 Lee Smith .40 .16
❑ 404 George Hendrick .20 .08
❑ 405 Eddie Murray .75 .30
❑ 406 Marshall Edwards .10 .04
❑ 407 Lance Parrish .20 .08
❑ 408 Carney Lansford .20 .08
❑ 409 Dave Winfield .20 .08
❑ 410 Bob Welch .20 .08
❑ 411 Larry Milbourne .10 .04
❑ 412 Dennis Leonard .10 .04
❑ 413 Dan Meyer .10 .04
❑ 414 Charlie Lea .10 .04
❑ 415 Rick Honeycutt .10 .04
❑ 416 Mike Witt .10 .04
❑ 417 Steve Trout .10 .04
❑ 418 Glenn Brummer .10 .04
❑ 419 Denny Walling .10 .04
❑ 420 Gary Matthews .20 .08
❑ 421 Charlie Leibrandt UER .10 .04
(Liebrandt on
front of card)
❑ 422 J.Eichelberger UER .10 .04
Photo actually
Joe Pittman
❑ 423 Cecilio Guante UER .10 .04
(Listed as Matt
on card)
❑ 424 Bill Laskey .10 .04
❑ 425 Jerry Royster .10 .04
❑ 426 Dickie Noles .10 .04
❑ 427 George Foster .20 .08
❑ 428 Mike Moore RC .50 .20
❑ 429 Gary Ward .10 .04
❑ 430 Barry Bonnell .10 .04
❑ 431 Ron Washington .10 .04
❑ 432 Rance Mulliniks .10 .04
❑ 433 Mike Stanton .10 .04
❑ 434 Jesse Orosco .10 .04
❑ 435 Larry Bowa .20 .08
❑ 436 Biff Pocoroba .10 .04
❑ 437 Johnny Ray .10 .04
❑ 438 Joe Morgan .20 .08
❑ 439 Eric Show RC .50 .20
❑ 440 Larry Biittner .10 .04
❑ 441 Greg Gross .10 .04
❑ 442 Gene Tenace .20 .08
❑ 443 Danny Heep .10 .04
❑ 444 Bobby Clark .10 .04
❑ 445 Kevin Hickey .10 .04
❑ 446 Scott Sanderson .10 .04
❑ 447 Frank Tanana .20 .08
❑ 448 Cesar Geronimo .10 .04
❑ 449 Jimmy Sexton .10 .04
❑ 450 Mike Hargrove .10 .04
❑ 451 Doyle Alexander .10 .04
❑ 452 Dwight Evans .20 .08
❑ 453 Terry Forster .20 .08
❑ 454 Tom Brookens .10 .04
❑ 455 Rich Dauer .10 .04
❑ 456 Rob Picciolo .10 .04
❑ 457 Terry Crowley .10 .04
❑ 458 Ned Yost .10 .04
❑ 459 Kirk Gibson .20 .08
❑ 460 Reid Nichols .10 .04
❑ 461 Oscar Gamble .10 .04
❑ 462 Dusty Baker .20 .08
❑ 463 Jack Perconte .10 .04
❑ 464 Frank White .20 .08
❑ 465 Mickey Klutts .10 .04
❑ 466 Warren Cromartie .10 .04
❑ 467 Larry Parrish .10 .04
❑ 468 Bobby Grich .20 .08
❑ 469 Dane Iorg .10 .04
❑ 470 Joe Niekro .10 .04
❑ 471 Ed Farmer .10 .04
❑ 472 Tim Flannery .10 .04
❑ 473 Dave Parker .20 .08
❑ 474 Jeff Leonard .10 .04
❑ 475 Al Hrabosky .10 .04
❑ 476 Ron Hodges .10 .04
❑ 477 Leon Durham .10 .04
❑ 478 Jim Essian .10 .04
❑ 479 Roy Lee Jackson .10 .04
❑ 480 Brad Havens .10 .04
❑ 481 Joe Price .10 .04
❑ 482 Tony Bernazard .10 .04
❑ 483 Scott McGregor .10 .04
❑ 484 Paul Molitor .40 .16
❑ 485 Mike Ivie .10 .04
❑ 486 Ken Griffey .20 .08
❑ 487 Dennis Eckersley .40 .16
❑ 488 Steve Garvey .20 .08
❑ 489 Mike Fischlin .10 .04
❑ 490 U.L. Washington .10 .04
❑ 491 Steve McCatty .10 .04
❑ 492 Roy Johnson .10 .04
❑ 493 Don Baylor .20 .08
❑ 494 Bobby Johnson .10 .04
❑ 495 Mike Squires .10 .04
❑ 496 Bert Roberge .10 .04
❑ 497 Dick Ruthven .10 .04
❑ 498 Tito Landrum .10 .04
❑ 499 Sixto Lezcano .10 .04
❑ 500 Johnny Bench .75 .30
❑ 501 Larry Whisenton .10 .04
❑ 502 Manny Sarmiento .10 .04
❑ 503 Fred Breining .10 .04
❑ 504 Bill Campbell .10 .04
❑ 505 Todd Cruz .10 .04
❑ 506 Bob Bailor .10 .04
❑ 507 Dave Stieb .20 .08
❑ 508 Al Williams .10 .04
❑ 509 Dan Ford .10 .04
❑ 510 Gorman Thomas .20 .08
❑ 511 Chet Lemon .20 .08
❑ 512 Mike Torrez .10 .04
❑ 513 Shane Rawley .10 .04
❑ 514 Mark Belanger .10 .04
❑ 515 Rodney Craig .10 .04
❑ 516 Onix Concepcion .10 .04
❑ 517 Mike Heath .10 .04
❑ 518 Andre Dawson UER .20 .08
(Middle name Fernando,
should be Nolan)
❑ 519 Luis Sanchez .10 .04
❑ 520 Terry Bogener .10 .04
❑ 521 Rudy Law .10 .04
❑ 522 Ray Knight .20 .08
❑ 523 Joe Lefebvre .10 .04
❑ 524 Jim Wohlford .10 .04
❑ 525 Julio Franco RC 1.50 .60
❑ 526 Ron Oester .10 .04
❑ 527 Rick Mahler .10 .04
❑ 528 Steve Nicosia .10 .04
❑ 529 Junior Kennedy .10 .04
❑ 530A Whitey Herzog MG .20 .08
(Bio printed
black on white)
❑ 530B Whitey Herzog MG .20 .08
(Bio printed
black on yellow)
❑ 531A Don Sutton .20 .08
(Blue border
on photo)
❑ 531B Don Sutton .20 .08
(Green border
on photo)
❑ 532 Mark Brouhard .10 .04
❑ 533A S.Anderson MG .20 .08
(Bio printed
black on white)
❑ 533B S.Anderson MG .20 .08
(Bio printed
black on yellow)
❑ 534 Roger LaFrancois .10 .04
❑ 535 George Frazier .10 .04
❑ 536 Tom Niedenfuer .10 .04
❑ 537 Ed Glynn .10 .04
❑ 538 Lee May .10 .04
❑ 539 Bob Kearney .10 .04
❑ 540 Tim Raines .20 .08
❑ 541 Paul Mirabella .10 .04
❑ 542 Luis Tiant .20 .08
❑ 543 Ron LeFlore .20 .08
❑ 544 Dave LaPoint .10 .04
❑ 545 Randy Moffitt .10 .04
❑ 546 Luis Aguayo .10 .04
❑ 547 Brad Lesley .15 .06
❑ 548 Luis Salazar .10 .04
❑ 549 John Candelaria .10 .04
❑ 550 Dave Bergman .10 .04
❑ 551 Bob Watson .10 .04
❑ 552 Pat Tabler .10 .04
❑ 553 Brent Gaff .10 .04
❑ 554 Al Cowens .10 .04
❑ 555 Tom Brunansky .20 .08
❑ 556 Lloyd Moseby .10 .04
❑ 557A Pascual Perez ERR 2.00 .80
(Twins in glove)
❑ 557B Pascual Perez COR .20 .08
(Braves in glove)
❑ 558 Willie Upshaw .10 .04
❑ 559 Richie Zisk .10 .04
❑ 560 Pat Zachry .10 .04
❑ 561 Jay Johnstone .10 .04
❑ 562 Carlos Diaz RC .15 .06
❑ 563 John Tudor .20 .08
❑ 564 Frank Robinson MG .40 .16
❑ 565 Dave Edwards .10 .04
❑ 566 Paul Householder .10 .04
❑ 567 Ron Reed .10 .04
❑ 568 Mike Ramsey .10 .04
❑ 569 Kiko Garcia .10 .04
❑ 570 Tommy John .20 .08
❑ 571 Tony LaRussa MG .20 .08
❑ 572 Joel Youngblood .10 .04
❑ 573 Wayne Tolleson .10 .04
❑ 574 Keith Creel .10 .04
❑ 575 Billy Martin MG .40 .16
❑ 576 Jerry Dybzinski .10 .04
❑ 577 Rick Cerone .10 .04
❑ 578 Tony Perez .40 .16
❑ 579 Greg Brock .10 .04
❑ 580 Glenn Wilson .50 .20
❑ 581 Tim Stoddard .10 .04
❑ 582 Bob McClure .10 .04
❑ 583 Jim Dwyer .10 .04
❑ 584 Ed Romero .10 .04
❑ 585 Larry Herndon .10 .04
❑ 586 Wade Boggs RC 8.00 3.20
❑ 587 Jay Howell .10 .04
❑ 588 Dave Stewart .20 .08
❑ 589 Bert Blyleven .20 .08
❑ 590 Dick Howser MG .10 .04
❑ 591 Wayne Gross .10 .04
❑ 592 Terry Francona .20 .08
❑ 593 Don Werner .10 .04
❑ 594 Bill Stein .10 .04
❑ 595 Jesse Barfield .20 .08
❑ 596 Bob Molinaro .10 .04
❑ 597 Mike Vail .10 .04
❑ 598 Tony Gwynn RC 15.00 6.00
❑ 599 Gary Rajsich .10 .04
❑ 600 Jerry Ujdur .10 .04
❑ 601 Cliff Johnson .10 .04
❑ 602 Jerry White .10 .04
❑ 603 Bryan Clark .10 .04
❑ 604 Joe Ferguson .10 .04
❑ 605 Guy Sularz .10 .04
❑ 606A Ozzie Virgil .20 .08
(Green border
on photo)
❑ 606B Ozzie Virgil .20 .08
(Orange border
on photo)
❑ 607 Terry Harper .10 .04
❑ 608 Harvey Kuenn MG .10 .04
❑ 609 Jim Sundberg .20 .08
❑ 610 Willie Stargell .40 .16
❑ 611 Reggie Smith .20 .08
❑ 612 Rob Wilfong .10 .04
❑ 613 Joe Niekro .20 .08
Phil Niekro
❑ 614 Lee Elia MG .10 .04

Card	Nm-Mt	Ex-Mt
❑ 615 Mickey Hatcher	.10	.04
❑ 616 Jerry Hairston	.10	.04
❑ 617 John Martin	.10	.04
❑ 618 Wally Backman	.10	.04
❑ 619 Storm Davis RC	.50	.20
❑ 620 Alan Knicely	.10	.04
❑ 621 John Stuper	.10	.04
❑ 622 Matt Sinatro	.10	.04
❑ 623 Geno Petralli	.50	.20
❑ 624 Duane Walker	.10	.04
❑ 625 Dick Williams MG	.10	.04
❑ 626 Pat Corrales MG	.10	.04
❑ 627 Vern Ruhle	.10	.04
❑ 628 Joe Torre MG	.40	.16
❑ 629 Anthony Johnson	.10	.04
❑ 630 Steve Howe	.10	.04
❑ 631 Gary Woods	.10	.04
❑ 632 LaMarr Hoyt	.10	.04
❑ 633 Steve Swisher	.10	.04
❑ 634 Terry Leach	.10	.04
❑ 635 Jeff Newman	.10	.04
❑ 636 Brett Butler	.20	.08
❑ 637 Gary Gray	.10	.04
❑ 638 Lee Mazzilli	.20	.08
❑ 639A Ron Jackson ERR (A's in glove)	20.00	8.00
❑ 639B Ron Jackson COR (Angels in glove, red border on photo)	.10	.04
❑ 639C Ron Jackson COR (Angels in glove, green border on photo)	.40	.16
❑ 640 Juan Beniquez	.10	.04
❑ 641 Dave Rucker	.10	.04
❑ 642 Luis Pujols	.10	.04
❑ 643 Rick Monday	.20	.08
❑ 644 Hosken Powell	.10	.04
❑ 645 The Chicken	.40	.16
❑ 646 Dave Engle	.10	.04
❑ 647 Dick Davis	.10	.04
❑ 648 Frank Robinson Vida Blue Joe Morgan	.40	.16
❑ 649 Al Chambers	.10	.04
❑ 650 Jesus Vega	.10	.04
❑ 651 Jeff Jones	.10	.04
❑ 652 Marvis Foley	.10	.04
❑ 653 Ty Cobb Puzzle Card	.75	.30
❑ 654A Dick Perez/Diamond King Checklist 1-26 (Unnumbered) ERR (Word "checklist" omitted from back)	.40	.16
❑ 654B Dick Perez/Diamond King Checklist 1-26 (Unnumbered) COR (Word "checklist" is on back)	.40	.16
❑ 655 Checklist 27-130 (Unnumbered)	.10	.04
❑ 656 Checklist 131-234 (Unnumbered)	.10	.04
❑ 657 Checklist 235-338 (Unnumbered)	.10	.04
❑ 658 Checklist 339-442 (Unnumbered)	.10	.04
❑ 659 Checklist 443-544 (Unnumbered)	.10	.04
❑ 660 Checklist 545-653 (Unnumbered)	.10	.04

1984 Donruss

	Nm-Mt	Ex-Mt
COMPLETE SET (660)	120.00	47.50
COMP.FACT.SET (658)	150.00	60.00
COMP.SNIDER PUZZLE	5.00	2.00
❑ 1 Robin Yount DK COR	2.50	1.00
❑ 1A Robin Yount DK ERR	5.00	2.00
❑ 2 Dave Concepcion DK COR	.75	.30
❑ 2A Dave Concepcion DK ERR (Perez Steel)	.75	.30
❑ 3 Dwayne Murphy DK COR	.25	.10
❑ 3A Dwayne Murphy DK ERR (Perez Steel)	.25	.10
❑ 4 John Castino DK COR	.25	.10
❑ 4A John Castino DK ERR (Perez Steel)	.25	.10
❑ 5 Leon Durham DK COR	.75	.30
❑ 5A Leon Durham DK ERR (Perez Steel)	.25	.10
❑ 6 Rusty Staub DK COR	.75	.30
❑ 6A Rusty Staub DK ERR (Perez Steel)	.75	.30
❑ 7 Jack Clark DK COR	.75	.30
❑ 7A Jack Clark DK ERR (Perez Steel)	.75	.30
❑ 8 Dave Dravecky DK COR	.25	.10
❑ 8A Dave Dravecky DK ERR (Perez Steel)	.25	.10
❑ 9 Al Oliver DK COR	.75	.30
❑ 9A Al Oliver DK ERR (Perez Steel)	.75	.30
❑ 10 Dave Righetti DK COR	.75	.30
❑ 10A Dave Righetti DK ERR (Perez Steel)	.75	.30
❑ 11 Hal McRae DK COR	.75	.30
❑ 11A Hal McRae DK ERR (Perez Steel)	.75	.30
❑ 12 Ray Knight DK COR	.75	.30
❑ 12A Ray Knight DK ERR (Perez Steel)	.75	.30
❑ 13 Bruce Sutter DK COR	.75	.30
❑ 13A Bruce Sutter DK ERR (Perez Steel)	.75	.30
❑ 14 Bob Horner DK COR	.75	.30
❑ 14A Bob Horner DK ERR (Perez Steel)	.75	.30
❑ 15 Lance Parrish DK COR	.75	.30
❑ 15A Lance Parrish DK ERR (Perez Steel)	.75	.30
❑ 16 Matt Young DK COR	.75	.30
❑ 16A Matt Young DK ERR (Perez Steel)	.75	.30
❑ 17 Fred Lynn DK COR	.75	.30
❑ 17A Fred Lynn DK ERR (Perez Steel) (A's logo on back	.75	.30
❑ 18 Ron Kittle DK COR	.25	.10
❑ 18A Ron Kittle DK ERR (Perez Steel)	.25	.10
❑ 19 Jim Clancy DK COR	.25	.10
❑ 19A Jim Clancy DK ERR (Perez Steel)	.25	.10
❑ 20 Bill Madlock DK COR	.75	.30
❑ 20A Bill Madlock DK ERR (Perez Steel)	.75	.30
❑ 21 Larry Parrish DK COR	.25	.10
❑ 21A Larry Parrish DK ERR (Perez Steel)	.25	.10
❑ 22 Eddie Murray DK COR	3.00	1.20
❑ 22A Eddie Murray DK ERR	3.00	1.20
❑ 23 Mike Schmidt DK COR	5.00	2.00
❑ 23A M.Schmidt DK ERR	5.00	2.00
❑ 24 Pedro Guerrero DK COR	.75	.30
❑ 24A Pedro Guerrero DK ERR (Perez Steel)	.75	.30
❑ 25 Andre Thornton DK COR	.25	.10
❑ 25A Andre Thornton DK ERR (Perez Steel)	.25	.10
❑ 26 Wade Boggs DK COR	3.00	1.20
❑ 26A Wade Boggs DK ERR	3.00	1.20
❑ 27 Joel Skinner RR RC	.25	.10
❑ 28 Tommy Dunbar RR RC	.25	.10
❑ 29A M.Stenhouse RC RR ERR No number on back	.25	.10
❑ 29B Mike Stenhouse RR COR Numbered on back	3.00	1.20
❑ 30A R.Darling RC RR ERR No number on back	1.50	.60
❑ 30B Ron Darling RR COR (Numbered on back)	3.00	1.20
❑ 31 Dion James RR RC	.25	.10
❑ 32 Tony Fernandez RR RC	1.50	.60
❑ 33 Angel Salazar RR RC	.25	.10
❑ 34 K. McReynolds RR RC	1.50	.60
❑ 35 Dick Schofield RR RC	.75	.30
❑ 36 Brad Komminsk RR RC	.25	.10
❑ 37 Tim Teufel RR RC	.75	.30
❑ 38 Doug Frobel RR RC	.25	.10
❑ 39 Greg Gagne RR RC	.75	.30
❑ 40 Mike Fuentes RR RC	.25	.10
❑ 41 Joe Carter RR RC	5.00	2.00
❑ 42 Mike Brown RC RR (Angels OF)	.25	.10
❑ 43 Mike Jeffcoat RR RC	.25	.10
❑ 44 Sid Fernandez RR RC	1.50	.60
❑ 45 Brian Dayett RR RC	.25	.10
❑ 46 Chris Smith RR RC	.25	.10
❑ 47 Eddie Murray	3.00	1.20
❑ 48 Robin Yount	5.00	2.00
❑ 49 Lance Parrish	1.50	.60
❑ 50 Jim Rice	.75	.30
❑ 51 Dave Winfield	.75	.30
❑ 52 Fernando Valenzuela	.75	.30
❑ 53 George Brett	8.00	3.20
❑ 54 Rickey Henderson	5.00	2.00
❑ 55 Gary Carter	.75	.30
❑ 56 Buddy Bell	.75	.30
❑ 57 Reggie Jackson	1.50	.60
❑ 58 Harold Baines	.75	.30
❑ 59 Ozzie Smith	5.00	2.00
❑ 60 Nolan Ryan UER (Text on back refers to 1972 as the year he struck out 383; the year was 1973)	15.00	6.00
❑ 61 Pete Rose	10.00	4.00
❑ 62 Ron Oester	.25	.10
❑ 63 Steve Garvey	.75	.30
❑ 64 Jason Thompson	.25	.10
❑ 65 Jack Clark	.75	.30
❑ 66 Dale Murphy	1.50	.60
❑ 67 Leon Durham	.25	.10
❑ 68 Darryl Strawberry RC	5.00	2.00
❑ 69 Richie Zisk	.25	.10
❑ 70 Kent Hrbek	.75	.30
❑ 71 Dave Stieb	.75	.30
❑ 72 Ken Schrom	.25	.10
❑ 73 George Bell	.75	.30
❑ 74 John Moses	.25	.10
❑ 75 Ed Lynch	.25	.10
❑ 76 Chuck Rainey	.25	.10
❑ 77 Biff Pocoroba	.25	.10
❑ 78 Cecilio Guante	.25	.10
❑ 79 Jim Barr	.25	.10
❑ 80 Kurt Bevacqua	.25	.10
❑ 81 Tom Foley	.25	.10
❑ 82 Joe Lefebvre	.25	.10
❑ 83 Andy Van Slyke RC	1.50	.60
❑ 84 Bob Lillis MG	.25	.10
❑ 85 Ricky Adams	.25	.10
❑ 86 Jerry Hairston	.25	.10
❑ 87 Bob James	.25	.10
❑ 88 Joe Altobelli MG	.25	.10
❑ 89 Ed Romero	.25	.10
❑ 90 John Grubb	.25	.10
❑ 91 John Henry Johnson	.25	.10
❑ 92 Juan Espino	.25	.10
❑ 93 Candy Maldonado	.25	.10

❑ 94	Andre Thornton	.25	.10
❑ 95	Onix Concepcion	.25	.10
❑ 96	Donnie Hill UER (Listed as P, should be 2B)	.25	.10
❑ 97	Andre Dawson UER (Wrong middle name, should be Nolan)	.75	.30
❑ 98	Frank Tanana	.75	.30
❑ 99	Curtis Wilkerson	.25	.10
❑ 100	Larry Gura	.25	.10
❑ 101	Dwayne Murphy	.25	.10
❑ 102	Tom Brennan	.25	.10
❑ 103	Dave Righetti	.75	.30
❑ 104	Steve Sax	.25	.10
❑ 105	Dan Petry	.75	.30
❑ 106	Cal Ripken	20.00	8.00
❑ 107	Paul Molitor UER ('83 stats should say .270 BA, 608 AB, and 164 hits)	1.50	.60
❑ 108	Fred Lynn	.75	.30
❑ 109	Neil Allen	.25	.10
❑ 110	Joe Niekro	.25	.10
❑ 111	Steve Carlton	1.50	.60
❑ 112	Terry Kennedy	.25	.10
❑ 113	Bill Madlock	.75	.30
❑ 114	Chili Davis	.75	.30
❑ 115	Jim Gantner	.25	.10
❑ 116	Tom Seaver	3.00	1.20
❑ 117	Bill Buckner	.75	.30
❑ 118	Bill Caudill	.25	.10
❑ 119	Jim Clancy	.25	.10
❑ 120	John Castino	.25	.10
❑ 121	Dave Concepcion	.75	.30
❑ 122	Greg Luzinski	.75	.30
❑ 123	Mike Boddicker	.25	.10
❑ 124	Pete Ladd	.25	.10
❑ 125	Juan Berenguer	.25	.10
❑ 126	John Montefusco	.25	.10
❑ 127	Ed Jurak	.25	.10
❑ 128	Tom Niedenfuer	.25	.10
❑ 129	Bert Blyleven	.75	.30
❑ 130	Bud Black	.25	.10
❑ 131	Gorman Heimueller	.25	.10
❑ 132	Dan Schatzeder	.25	.10
❑ 133	Ron Jackson	.25	.10
❑ 134	Tom Henke RC	1.50	.60
❑ 135	Kevin Hickey	.25	.10
❑ 136	Mike Scott	.75	.30
❑ 137	Bo Diaz	.25	.10
❑ 138	Glenn Brummer	.25	.10
❑ 139	Sid Monge	.25	.10
❑ 140	Rich Gale	.25	.10
❑ 141	Brett Butler	.75	.30
❑ 142	Brian Harper RC	.75	.30
❑ 143	John Rabb	.25	.10
❑ 144	Gary Woods	.25	.10
❑ 145	Pat Putnam	.25	.10
❑ 146	Jim Acker	.25	.10
❑ 147	Mickey Hatcher	.25	.10
❑ 148	Todd Cruz	.25	.10
❑ 149	Tom Tellmann	.25	.10
❑ 150	John Wockenfuss	.25	.10
❑ 151	Wade Boggs UER 1983 runs 10; should be 100	8.00	3.20
❑ 152	Don Baylor	.75	.30
❑ 153	Bob Welch	.75	.30
❑ 154	Alan Bannister	.25	.10
❑ 155	Willie Aikens	.25	.10
❑ 156	Jeff Burroughs	.25	.10
❑ 157	Bryan Little	.25	.10
❑ 158	Bob Boone	.75	.30
❑ 159	Dave Hostetler	.25	.10
❑ 160	Jerry Dybzinski	.25	.10
❑ 161	Mike Madden	.25	.10
❑ 162	Luis DeLeon	.25	.10
❑ 163	Willie Hernandez	.25	.10
❑ 164	Frank Pastore	.25	.10
❑ 165	Rick Camp	.25	.10
❑ 166	Lee Mazzilli	.75	.30
❑ 167	Scot Thompson	.25	.10
❑ 168	Bob Forsch	.25	.10
❑ 169	Mike Flanagan	.25	.10
❑ 170	Rick Manning	.25	.10
❑ 171	Chet Lemon	.75	.30
❑ 172	Jerry Remy	.25	.10
❑ 173	Ron Guidry	.75	.30
❑ 174	Pedro Guerrero	.75	.30
❑ 175	Willie Wilson	.75	.30
❑ 176	Carney Lansford	.75	.30
❑ 177	Al Oliver	.75	.30
❑ 178	Jim Sundberg	.75	.30
❑ 179	Bobby Grich	.75	.30
❑ 180	Rich Dotson	.25	.10
❑ 181	Joaquin Andujar	.75	.30
❑ 182	Jose Cruz	.75	.30
❑ 183	Mike Schmidt	8.00	3.20
❑ 184	Gary Redus RC*	.75	.30
❑ 185	Garry Templeton	.75	.30
❑ 186	Tony Pena	.25	.10
❑ 187	Greg Minton	.25	.10
❑ 188	Phil Niekro	.75	.30
❑ 189	Ferguson Jenkins	.75	.30
❑ 190	Mookie Wilson	.75	.30
❑ 191	Jim Beattie	.25	.10
❑ 192	Gary Ward	.25	.10
❑ 193	Jesse Barfield	.75	.30
❑ 194	Pete Filson	.25	.10
❑ 195	Roy Lee Jackson	.25	.10
❑ 196	Rick Sweet	.25	.10
❑ 197	Jesse Orosco	.25	.10
❑ 198	Steve Lake	.25	.10
❑ 199	Ken Dayley	.25	.10
❑ 200	Manny Sarmiento	.25	.10
❑ 201	Mark Davis	.25	.10
❑ 202	Tim Flannery	.25	.10
❑ 203	Bill Scherrer	.25	.10
❑ 204	Al Holland	.25	.10
❑ 205	Dave Von Ohlen	.25	.10
❑ 206	Mike LaCoss	.25	.10
❑ 207	Juan Beniquez	.25	.10
❑ 208	Juan Agosto	.25	.10
❑ 209	Bobby Ramos	.25	.10
❑ 210	Al Bumbry	.25	.10
❑ 211	Mark Brouhard	.25	.10
❑ 212	Howard Bailey	.25	.10
❑ 213	Bruce Hurst	.25	.10
❑ 214	Bob Shirley	.25	.10
❑ 215	Pat Zachry	.25	.10
❑ 216	Julio Franco	1.50	.60
❑ 217	Mike Armstrong	.25	.10
❑ 218	Dave Beard	.25	.10
❑ 219	Steve Rogers	.75	.30
❑ 220	John Butcher	.25	.10
❑ 221	Mike Smithson	.25	.10
❑ 222	Frank White	.75	.30
❑ 223	Mike Heath	.25	.10
❑ 224	Chris Bando	.25	.10
❑ 225	Roy Smalley	.25	.10
❑ 226	Dusty Baker	.75	.30
❑ 227	Lou Whitaker	.75	.30
❑ 228	John Lowenstein	.25	.10
❑ 229	Ben Oglivie	.75	.30
❑ 230	Doug DeCinces	.25	.10
❑ 231	Lonnie Smith	.25	.10
❑ 232	Ray Knight	.75	.30
❑ 233	Gary Matthews	.75	.30
❑ 234	Juan Bonilla	.25	.10
❑ 235	Rod Scurry	.25	.10
❑ 236	Atlee Hammaker	.25	.10
❑ 237	Mike Caldwell	.25	.10
❑ 238	Keith Hernandez	.75	.30
❑ 239	Larry Bowa	.75	.30
❑ 240	Tony Bernazard	.25	.10
❑ 241	Damaso Garcia	.25	.10
❑ 242	Tom Brunansky	.25	.10
❑ 243	Dan Driessen	.25	.10
❑ 244	Ron Kittle	.25	.10
❑ 245	Tim Stoddard	.25	.10
❑ 246	Bob L. Gibson RC (Brewers Pitcher)	.25	.10
❑ 247	Marty Castillo	.25	.10
❑ 248	D.Mattingly RC UER traiing on back	40.00	16.00
❑ 249	Jeff Newman	.25	.10
❑ 250	Alejandro Pena RC*	1.50	.60
❑ 251	Toby Harrah	.75	.30
❑ 252	Cesar Geronimo	.25	.10
❑ 253	Tom Underwood	.25	.10
❑ 254	Doug Flynn	.25	.10
❑ 255	Andy Hassler	.25	.10
❑ 256	Odell Jones	.25	.10
❑ 257	Rudy Law	.25	.10
❑ 258	Harry Spilman	.25	.10
❑ 259	Marty Bystrom	.25	.10
❑ 260	Dave Rucker	.25	.10
❑ 261	Ruppert Jones	.25	.10
❑ 262	Jeff R. Jones (Reds OF)	.25	.10
❑ 263	Gerald Perry	.75	.30
❑ 264	Gene Tenace	.75	.30
❑ 265	Brad Wellman	.25	.10
❑ 266	Dickie Noles	.25	.10
❑ 267	Jamie Allen	.25	.10
❑ 268	Jim Gott	.25	.10
❑ 269	Ron Davis	.25	.10
❑ 270	Benny Ayala	.25	.10
❑ 271	Ned Yost	.25	.10
❑ 272	Dave Rozema	.25	.10
❑ 273	Dave Stapleton	.25	.10
❑ 274	Lou Piniella	.75	.30
❑ 275	Jose Morales	.25	.10
❑ 276	Broderick Perkins	.25	.10
❑ 277	Butch Davis RC	.25	.10
❑ 278	Tony Phillips RC	1.50	.60
❑ 279	Jeff Reardon	.75	.30
❑ 280	Ken Forsch	.25	.10
❑ 281	Pete O'Brien RC*	.75	.30
❑ 282	Tom Paciorek	.25	.10
❑ 283	Frank LaCorte	.25	.10
❑ 284	Tim Lollar	.25	.10
❑ 285	Greg Gross	.25	.10
❑ 286	Alex Trevino	.25	.10
❑ 287	Gene Garber	.25	.10
❑ 288	Dave Parker	.75	.30
❑ 289	Lee Smith	.75	.30
❑ 290	Dave LaPoint	.25	.10
❑ 291	John Shelby	.25	.10
❑ 292	Charlie Moore	.25	.10
❑ 293	Alan Trammell	.75	.30
❑ 294	Tony Armas	.75	.30
❑ 295	Shane Rawley	.25	.10
❑ 296	Greg Brock	.25	.10
❑ 297	Hal McRae	.75	.30
❑ 298	Mike Davis	.25	.10
❑ 299	Tim Raines	.75	.30
❑ 300	Bucky Dent	.75	.30
❑ 301	Tommy John	.75	.30
❑ 302	Carlton Fisk	1.50	.60
❑ 303	Darrell Porter	.25	.10
❑ 304	Dickie Thon	.25	.10
❑ 305	Garry Maddox	.25	.10
❑ 306	Cesar Cedeno	.75	.30
❑ 307	Gary Lucas	.25	.10
❑ 308	Johnny Ray	.25	.10
❑ 309	Andy McGaffigan	.25	.10
❑ 310	Claudell Washington	.25	.10
❑ 311	Ryne Sandberg	12.00	4.80
❑ 312	George Foster	.75	.30
❑ 313	Spike Owen RC	.75	.30
❑ 314	Gary Gaetti	1.50	.60
❑ 315	Willie Upshaw	.25	.10
❑ 316	Al Williams	.25	.10
❑ 317	Jorge Orta	.25	.10
❑ 318	Orlando Mercado	.25	.10
❑ 319	Junior Ortiz	.25	.10
❑ 320	Mike Proly	.25	.10
❑ 321	Randy Johnson UER ('72-'82 stats are from Twins' Randy Johnson, '83 stats are from Braves' Randy Johnson)	.25	.10
❑ 322	Jim Morrison	.25	.10
❑ 323	Max Venable	.25	.10
❑ 324	Tony Gwynn	12.00	4.80
❑ 325	Duane Walker	.25	.10
❑ 326	Ozzie Virgil	.25	.10
❑ 327	Jeff Lahti	.25	.10
❑ 328	Bill Dawley	.25	.10
❑ 329	Rob Wilfong	.25	.10
❑ 330	Marc Hill	.25	.10
❑ 331	Ray Burris	.25	.10
❑ 332	Allan Ramirez	.25	.10
❑ 333	Chuck Porter	.25	.10
❑ 334	Wayne Krenchicki	.25	.10
❑ 335	Gary Allenson	.25	.10
❑ 336	Bobby Meacham	.25	.10

❑ 337 Joe Beckwith .25 .10
❑ 338 Rick Sutcliffe .75 .30
❑ 339 Mark Huismann .25 .10
❑ 340 Tim Conroy .25 .10
❑ 341 Scott Sanderson .25 .10
❑ 342 Larry Biittner .25 .10
❑ 343 Dave Stewart .75 .30
❑ 344 Darryl Motley .25 .10
❑ 345 Chris Codiroli .25 .10
❑ 346 Rich Behenna .25 .10
❑ 347 Andre Robertson .25 .10
❑ 348 Mike Marshall .25 .10
❑ 349 Larry Herndon .75 .30
❑ 350 Rich Dauer .25 .10
❑ 351 Cecil Cooper .75 .30
❑ 352 Rod Carew 1.50 .60
❑ 353 Willie McGee .75 .30
❑ 354 Phil Garner .75 .30
❑ 355 Joe Morgan .75 .30
❑ 356 Luis Salazar .25 .10
❑ 357 John Candelaria .25 .10
❑ 358 Bill Laskey .25 .10
❑ 359 Bob McClure .25 .10
❑ 360 Dave Kingman .75 .30
❑ 361 Ron Cey .75 .30
❑ 362 Matt Young RC .75 .30
❑ 363 Lloyd Moseby .25 .10
❑ 364 Frank Viola 1.50 .60
❑ 365 Eddie Milner .25 .10
❑ 366 Floyd Bannister .25 .10
❑ 367 Dan Ford .25 .10
❑ 368 Moose Haas .25 .10
❑ 369 Doug Bair .25 .10
❑ 370 Ray Fontenot .25 .10
❑ 371 Luis Aponte .25 .10
❑ 372 Jack Fimple .25 .10
❑ 373 Neal Heaton .25 .10
❑ 374 Greg Pryor .25 .10
❑ 375 Wayne Gross .25 .10
❑ 376 Charlie Lea .25 .10
❑ 377 Steve Lubratich .25 .10
❑ 378 Jon Matlack .25 .10
❑ 379 Julio Cruz .25 .10
❑ 380 John Mizerock .25 .10
❑ 381 Kevin Gross RC .75 .30
❑ 382 Mike Ramsey .25 .10
❑ 383 Doug Gwosdz .25 .10
❑ 384 Kelly Paris .25 .10
❑ 385 Pete Falcone .25 .10
❑ 386 Milt May .25 .10
❑ 387 Fred Breining .25 .10
❑ 388 Craig Lefferts RC .25 .10
❑ 389 Steve Henderson .25 .10
❑ 390 Randy Moffitt .25 .10
❑ 391 Ron Washington .25 .10
❑ 392 Gary Roenicke .25 .10
❑ 393 Tom Candiotti RC 1.50 .60
❑ 394 Larry Pashnick .25 .10
❑ 395 Dwight Evans .75 .30
❑ 396 Rich Gossage .75 .30
❑ 397 Derrel Thomas .25 .10
❑ 398 Juan Eichelberger .25 .10
❑ 399 Leon Roberts .25 .10
❑ 400 Dave Lopes .75 .30
❑ 401 Bill Gullickson .25 .10
❑ 402 Geoff Zahn .25 .10
❑ 403 Billy Sample .25 .10
❑ 404 Mike Squires .25 .10
❑ 405 Craig Reynolds .25 .10
❑ 406 Eric Show .25 .10
❑ 407 John Denny .25 .10
❑ 408 Dann Bilardello .25 .10
❑ 409 Bruce Benedict .25 .10
❑ 410 Kent Tekulve .25 .10
❑ 411 Mel Hall .75 .30
❑ 412 John Stuper .25 .10
❑ 413 Rick Dempsey .25 .10
❑ 414 Don Sutton .75 .30
❑ 415 Jack Morris .75 .30
❑ 416 John Tudor .75 .30
❑ 417 Willie Randolph .75 .30
❑ 418 Jerry Reuss .25 .10
❑ 419 Don Slaught .75 .30
❑ 420 Steve McCatty .25 .10
❑ 421 Tim Wallach .25 .10
❑ 422 Larry Parrish .25 .10
❑ 423 Brian Downing .75 .30
❑ 424 Britt Burns .25 .10
❑ 425 David Green .25 .10
❑ 426 Jerry Mumphrey .25 .10
❑ 427 Ivan DeJesus .25 .10
❑ 428 Mario Soto .75 .30
❑ 429 Gene Richards .25 .10
❑ 430 Dale Berra .25 .10
❑ 431 Darrell Evans .75 .30
❑ 432 Glenn Hubbard .25 .10
❑ 433 Jody Davis .25 .10
❑ 434 Danny Heep .25 .10
❑ 435 Ed Nunez RC .25 .10
❑ 436 Bobby Castillo .25 .10
❑ 437 Ernie Whitt .25 .10
❑ 438 Scott Ullger .25 .10
❑ 439 Doyle Alexander .25 .10
❑ 440 Domingo Ramos .25 .10
❑ 441 Craig Swan .25 .10
❑ 442 Warren Brusstar .25 .10
❑ 443 Len Barker .25 .10
❑ 444 Mike Easler .25 .10
❑ 445 Renie Martin .25 .10
❑ 446 D.Rasmussen RC .75 .30
❑ 447 Ted Power .25 .10
❑ 448 Charles Hudson .25 .10
❑ 449 Danny Cox RC .25 .10
❑ 450 Kevin Bass .25 .10
❑ 451 Daryl Sconiers .25 .10
❑ 452 Scott Fletcher .25 .10
❑ 453 Bryn Smith .25 .10
❑ 454 Jim Dwyer .25 .10
❑ 455 Rob Picciolo .25 .10
❑ 456 Enos Cabell .25 .10
❑ 457 Dennis Boyd .75 .30
❑ 458 Butch Wynegar .25 .10
❑ 459 Burt Hooton .25 .10
❑ 460 Ron Hassey .25 .10
❑ 461 Danny Jackson RC .75 .30
❑ 462 Bob Kearney .25 .10
❑ 463 Terry Francona .75 .30
❑ 464 Wayne Tolleson .25 .10
❑ 465 Mickey Rivers .25 .10
❑ 466 John Wathan .25 .10
❑ 467 Bill Almon .25 .10
❑ 468 George Vukovich .25 .10
❑ 469 Steve Kemp .25 .10
❑ 470 Ken Landreaux .25 .10
❑ 471 Milt Wilcox .25 .10
❑ 472 Tippy Martinez .25 .10
❑ 473 Ted Simmons .75 .30
❑ 474 Tim Foli .25 .10
❑ 475 George Hendrick .75 .30
❑ 476 Terry Puhl .25 .10
❑ 477 Von Hayes .25 .10
❑ 478 Bobby Brown .25 .10
❑ 479 Lee Lacy .25 .10
❑ 480 Joel Youngblood .25 .10
❑ 481 Jim Slaton .25 .10
❑ 482 Mike Fitzgerald .25 .10
❑ 483 Keith Moreland .25 .10
❑ 484 Ron Roenicke .25 .10
❑ 485 Luis Leal .25 .10
❑ 486 Bryan Oelkers .25 .10
❑ 487 Bruce Berenyi .25 .10
❑ 488 LaMarr Hoyt .25 .10
❑ 489 Joe Nolan .25 .10
❑ 490 Marshall Edwards .25 .10
❑ 491 Mike Laga .75 .30
❑ 492 Rick Cerone .25 .10
❑ 493 Rick Miller UER .25 .10
(Listed as Mike on card front)
❑ 494 Rick Honeycutt .25 .10
❑ 495 Mike Hargrove .25 .10
❑ 496 Joe Simpson .25 .10
❑ 497 Keith Atherton .25 .10
❑ 498 Chris Welsh .25 .10
❑ 499 Bruce Kison .25 .10
❑ 500 Bobby Johnson .25 .10
❑ 501 Jerry Koosman .75 .30
❑ 502 Frank DiPino .25 .10
❑ 503 Tony Perez 1.50 .60
❑ 504 Ken Oberkfell .25 .10
❑ 505 Mark Thurmond .25 .10
❑ 506 Joe Price .25 .10
❑ 507 Pascual Perez .25 .10
❑ 508 Marvell Wynne .75 .30
❑ 509 Mike Krukow .25 .10
❑ 510 Dick Ruthven .25 .10
❑ 511 Al Cowens .25 .10
❑ 512 Cliff Johnson .25 .10
❑ 513 Randy Bush .25 .10
❑ 514 Sammy Stewart .25 .10
❑ 515 Bill Schroeder .25 .10
❑ 516 Aurelio Lopez .75 .30
❑ 517 Mike C. Brown .25 .10
❑ 518 Graig Nettles .75 .30
❑ 519 Dave Sax .25 .10
❑ 520 Jerry Willard .25 .10
❑ 521 Paul Splittorff .25 .10
❑ 522 Tom Burgmeier .25 .10
❑ 523 Chris Speier .25 .10
❑ 524 Bobby Clark .25 .10
❑ 525 George Wright .25 .10
❑ 526 Dennis Lamp .25 .10
❑ 527 Tony Scott .25 .10
❑ 528 Ed Whitson .25 .10
❑ 529 Ron Reed .25 .10
❑ 530 Charlie Puleo .25 .10
❑ 531 Jerry Royster .25 .10
❑ 532 Don Robinson .25 .10
❑ 533 Steve Trout .25 .10
❑ 534 Bruce Sutter .75 .30
❑ 535 Bob Horner .75 .30
❑ 536 Pat Tabler .25 .10
❑ 537 Chris Chambliss .75 .30
❑ 538 Bob Ojeda .25 .10
❑ 539 Alan Ashby .25 .10
❑ 540 Jay Johnstone .25 .10
❑ 541 Bob Dernier .25 .10
❑ 542 Brook Jacoby .75 .30
❑ 543 U.L. Washington .25 .10
❑ 544 Danny Darwin .25 .10
❑ 545 Kiko Garcia .25 .10
❑ 546 Vance Law UER .25 .10
(Listed as P on card front)
❑ 547 Tug McGraw .75 .30
❑ 548 Dave Smith .25 .10
❑ 549 Len Matuszek .25 .10
❑ 550 Tom Hume .25 .10
❑ 551 Dave Dravecky .25 .10
❑ 552 Rick Rhoden .25 .10
❑ 553 Duane Kuiper .25 .10
❑ 554 Rusty Staub .75 .30
❑ 555 Bill Campbell .25 .10
❑ 556 Mike Torrez .25 .10
❑ 557 Dave Henderson .75 .30
❑ 558 Len Whitehouse .25 .10
❑ 559 Barry Bonnell .25 .10
❑ 560 Rick Lysander .25 .10
❑ 561 Garth Iorg .25 .10
❑ 562 Bryan Clark .25 .10
❑ 563 Brian Giles .25 .10
❑ 564 Vern Ruhle .25 .10
❑ 565 Steve Bedrosian .25 .10
❑ 566 Larry McWilliams .25 .10
❑ 567 Jeff Leonard UER .25 .10
(Listed as P on card front)
❑ 568 Alan Wiggins .25 .10
❑ 569 Jeff Russell RC .75 .30
❑ 570 Salome Barojas .25 .10
❑ 571 Dane Iorg .25 .10
❑ 572 Bob Knepper .25 .10
❑ 573 Gary Lavelle .25 .10
❑ 574 Gorman Thomas .75 .30
❑ 575 Manny Trillo .25 .10
❑ 576 Jim Palmer .75 .30
❑ 577 Dale Murray .25 .10
❑ 578 Tom Brookens .75 .30
❑ 579 Rich Gedman .25 .10
❑ 580 Bill Doran RC* .75 .30
❑ 581 Steve Yeager .75 .30
❑ 582 Dan Spillner .25 .10
❑ 583 Dan Quisenberry .25 .10
❑ 584 Rance Mulliniks .25 .10
❑ 585 Storm Davis .25 .10
❑ 586 Dave Schmidt .25 .10
❑ 587 Bill Russell .75 .30
❑ 588 Pat Sheridan .25 .10

❑ 589 Rafael Ramirez .25 .10
UER (A's on front)
❑ 590 Bud Anderson .25 .10
❑ 591 George Frazier .25 .10
❑ 592 Lee Tunnell .25 .10
❑ 593 Kirk Gibson .75 .30
❑ 594 Scott McGregor .25 .10
❑ 595 Bob Bailor .25 .10
❑ 596 Tom Herr .25 .10
❑ 597 Luis Sanchez .25 .10
❑ 598 Dave Engle .25 .10
❑ 599 Craig McMurtry .25 .10
❑ 600 Carlos Diaz .25 .10
❑ 601 Tom O'Malley .25 .10
❑ 602 Nick Esasky .25 .10
❑ 603 Ron Hodges .25 .10
❑ 604 Ed VandeBerg .25 .10
❑ 605 Alfredo Griffin .25 .10
❑ 606 Glenn Hoffman .25 .10
❑ 607 Hubie Brooks .25 .10
❑ 608 Richard Barnes UER .25 .10
(Photo actually
Neal Heaton)
❑ 609 Greg Walker .75 .30
❑ 610 Ken Singleton .75 .30
❑ 611 Mark Clear .25 .10
❑ 612 Buck Martinez .25 .10
❑ 613 Ken Griffey .75 .30
❑ 614 Reid Nichols .25 .10
❑ 615 Doug Sisk .25 .10
❑ 616 Bob Brenly .25 .10
❑ 617 Joey McLaughlin .25 .10
❑ 618 Glenn Wilson .75 .30
❑ 619 Bob Stoddard .25 .10
❑ 620 Lenn Sakata UER .25 .10
(Listed as Len
on card front)
❑ 621 Mike Young RC .25 .10
❑ 622 John Stefero .25 .10
❑ 623 Carmelo Martinez .25 .10
❑ 624 Dave Bergman .25 .10
❑ 625 Runnin' Reds UER 3.00 1.20
(Sic, Redbirds)
David Green
Willie McGee
Lonnie Smith
Ozzie Smith
❑ 626 Rudy May .25 .10
❑ 627 Matt Keough .25 .10
❑ 628 Jose DeLeon RC .75 .30
❑ 629 Jim Essian .25 .10
❑ 630 Darnell Coles RC .75 .30
❑ 631 Mike Warren .25 .10
❑ 632 Del Crandall MG .25 .10
❑ 633 Dennis Martinez .75 .30
❑ 634 Mike Moore .25 .10
❑ 635 Lary Sorensen .25 .10
❑ 636 Ricky Nelson .25 .10
❑ 637 Omar Moreno .25 .10
❑ 638 Charlie Hough .75 .30
❑ 639 Dennis Eckersley 1.50 .60
❑ 640 Walt Terrell .25 .10
❑ 641 Denny Walling .25 .10
❑ 642 Dave Anderson RC .25 .10
❑ 643 Jose Oquendo RC .75 .30
❑ 644 Bob Stanley .25 .10
❑ 645 Dave Geisel .25 .10
❑ 646 Scott Garrelts .25 .10
❑ 647 Gary Pettis .25 .10
❑ 648 Duke Snider 1.50 .60
Puzzle Card
❑ 649 Johnnie LeMaster .25 .10
❑ 650 Dave Collins .25 .10
❑ 651 The Chicken 1.50 .60
❑ 652 DK Checklist 1-26 .75 .30
(Unnumbered)
❑ 653 Checklist 27-130 .25 .10
(Unnumbered)
❑ 654 Checklist 131-234 .25 .10
(Unnumbered)
❑ 655 Checklist 235-338 .25 .10
(Unnumbered)
❑ 656 Checklist 339-442 .25 .10
(Unnumbered)
❑ 657 Checklist 443-546 .25 .10
(Unnumbered)
❑ 658 Checklist 547-651 .25 .10
(Unnumbered)
❑ A Living Legends A 2.50 1.00
Gaylord Perry
Rollie Fingers
❑ B Living Legends B 5.00 2.00
Carl Yastrzemski
Johnny Bench

1985 Donruss

	Nm-Mt	Ex-Mt
COMPLETE SET (660)	60.00	24.00
COMP.FACT.SET (660)	80.00	32.00
COMP.GEHRIG PUZZLE	4.00	1.60

❑ 1 Ryne Sandberg DK 1.25 .50
❑ 2 Doug DeCinces DK .15 .06
❑ 3 Richard Dotson DK .15 .06
❑ 4 Bert Blyleven DK .40 .16
❑ 5 Lou Whitaker DK .40 .16
❑ 6 Dan Quisenberry DK .15 .06
❑ 7 Don Mattingly DK 2.50 1.00
❑ 8 Carney Lansford DK .40 .16
❑ 9 Frank Tanana DK .40 .16
❑ 10 Willie Upshaw DK .15 .06
❑ 11 C.Washington DK .15 .06
❑ 12 Mike Marshall DK .15 .06
❑ 13 Joaquin Andujar DK .40 .16
❑ 14 Cal Ripken DK 2.50 1.00
❑ 15 Jim Rice DK .40 .16
❑ 16 Don Sutton DK .40 .16
❑ 17 Frank Viola DK .40 .16
❑ 18 Alvin Davis DK .40 .16
❑ 19 Mario Soto DK .40 .16
❑ 20 Jose Cruz DK .40 .16
❑ 21 Charlie Lea DK .15 .06
❑ 22 Jesse Orosco DK .15 .06
❑ 23 Juan Samuel DK .15 .06
❑ 24 Tony Pena DK .15 .06
❑ 25 Tony Gwynn DK 1.25 .50
❑ 26 Bob Brenly DK .15 .06
❑ 27 Danny Tartabull RR RC 1.00 .40
❑ 28 Mike Bielecki RC .25 .10
❑ 29 Steve Lyons RR RC .50 .20
❑ 30 Jeff Reed RC .25 .10
❑ 31 Tony Brewer RC .25 .10
❑ 32 John Morris RC .25 .10
❑ 33 Daryl Boston RR RC .25 .10
❑ 34 Al Pulido RR .25 .10
❑ 35 Steve Kiefer RC .25 .10
❑ 36 Larry Sheets RC .25 .10
❑ 37 Scott Bradley RC .25 .10
❑ 38 Calvin Schiraldi RC .50 .20
❑ 39 S.Dunston RR RC 1.00 .40
❑ 40 Charlie Mitchell RC .25 .10
❑ 41 Billy Hatcher RR RC .50 .20
❑ 42 Russ Stephans RC .25 .10
❑ 43 Alejandro Sanchez RC .25 .10
❑ 44 Steve Jeltz RC .25 .10
❑ 45 Jim Traber RC .25 .10
❑ 46 Doug Loman RC .25 .10
❑ 47 Eddie Murray 1.25 .50
❑ 48 Robin Yount 2.00 .80
❑ 49 Lance Parrish .40 .16
❑ 50 Jim Rice .40 .16
❑ 51 Dave Winfield .40 .16
❑ 52 Fernando Valenzuela .40 .16
❑ 53 George Brett 3.00 1.20
❑ 54 Dave Kingman .40 .16
❑ 55 Gary Carter .40 .16
❑ 56 Buddy Bell .40 .16
❑ 57 Reggie Jackson .75 .30
❑ 58 Harold Baines .40 .16
❑ 59 Ozzie Smith 2.00 .80
❑ 60 Nolan Ryan UER 6.00 2.40
(Set strikeout record
in 1973, not 1972)
❑ 61 Mike Schmidt 3.00 1.20
❑ 62 Dave Parker .40 .16
❑ 63 Tony Gwynn 2.50 1.00
❑ 64 Tony Pena .15 .06
❑ 65 Jack Clark .40 .16
❑ 66 Dale Murphy .75 .30
❑ 67 Ryne Sandberg 2.50 1.00
❑ 68 Keith Hernandez .40 .16
❑ 69 Alvin Davis RC* .50 .20
❑ 70 Kent Hrbek .40 .16
❑ 71 Willie Upshaw .15 .06
❑ 72 Dave Engle .15 .06
❑ 73 Alfredo Griffin .15 .06
❑ 74A Jack Perconte .15 .06
(Career Highlights
takes four lines)
❑ 74B Jack Perconte .15 .06
(Career Highlights
takes three lines)
❑ 75 Jesse Orosco .15 .06
❑ 76 Jody Davis .15 .06
❑ 77 Bob Horner .40 .16
❑ 78 Larry McWilliams .15 .06
❑ 79 Joel Youngblood .15 .06
❑ 80 Alan Wiggins .15 .06
❑ 81 Ron Oester .15 .06
❑ 82 Ozzie Virgil .15 .06
❑ 83 Ricky Horton .15 .06
❑ 84 Bill Doran .15 .06
❑ 85 Rod Carew .75 .30
❑ 86 LaMarr Hoyt .15 .06
❑ 87 Tim Wallach .15 .06
❑ 88 Mike Flanagan .15 .06
❑ 89 Jim Sundberg .40 .16
❑ 90 Chet Lemon .40 .16
❑ 91 Bob Stanley .15 .06
❑ 92 Willie Randolph .40 .16
❑ 93 Bill Russell .40 .16
❑ 94 Julio Franco .40 .16
❑ 95 Dan Quisenberry .15 .06
❑ 96 Bill Caudill .15 .06
❑ 97 Bill Gullickson .15 .06
❑ 98 Danny Darwin .15 .06
❑ 99 Curtis Wilkerson .15 .06
❑ 100 Bud Black .15 .06
❑ 101 Tony Phillips .15 .06
❑ 102 Tony Bernazard .15 .06
❑ 103 Jay Howell .15 .06
❑ 104 Burt Hooton .15 .06
❑ 105 Milt Wilcox .15 .06
❑ 106 Rich Dauer .15 .06
❑ 107 Don Sutton .40 .16
❑ 108 Mike Witt .15 .06
❑ 109 Bruce Sutter .40 .16
❑ 110 Enos Cabell .15 .06
❑ 111 John Denny .15 .06
❑ 112 Dave Dravecky .15 .06
❑ 113 Marvell Wynne .15 .06
❑ 114 Johnnie LeMaster .15 .06
❑ 115 Chuck Porter .15 .06
❑ 116 John Gibbons .15 .06
❑ 117 Keith Moreland .15 .06
❑ 118 Darnell Coles .15 .06
❑ 119 Dennis Lamp .15 .06
❑ 120 Ron Davis .15 .06
❑ 121 Nick Esasky .15 .06
❑ 122 Vance Law .15 .06
❑ 123 Gary Roenicke .15 .06
❑ 124 Bill Schroeder .15 .06
❑ 125 Dave Rozema .15 .06
❑ 126 Bobby Meacham .15 .06
❑ 127 Marty Barrett .15 .06
❑ 128 R.J. Reynolds .15 .06
❑ 129 Ernie Camacho UER .15 .06
(Photo actually
Rich Thompson)

❑	130	Jorge Orta	.15	.06
❑	131	Lary Sorensen	.15	.06
❑	132	Terry Francona	.40	.16
❑	133	Fred Lynn	.40	.16
❑	134	Bob Jones	.15	.06
❑	135	Jerry Hairston	.15	.06
❑	136	Kevin Bass	.15	.06
❑	137	Garry Maddox	.15	.06
❑	138	Dave LaPoint	.15	.06
❑	139	Kevin McReynolds	.40	.16
❑	140	Wayne Krenchicki	.15	.06
❑	141	Rafael Ramirez	.15	.06
❑	142	Rod Scurry	.15	.06
❑	143	Greg Minton	.15	.06
❑	144	Tim Stoddard	.15	.06
❑	145	Steve Henderson	.15	.06
❑	146	George Bell	.40	.16
❑	147	Dave Meier	.15	.06
❑	148	Sammy Stewart	.15	.06
❑	149	Mark Brouhard	.15	.06
❑	150	Larry Herndon	.15	.06
❑	151	Oil Can Boyd	.15	.06
❑	152	Brian Dayett	.15	.06
❑	153	Tom Niedenfuer	.15	.06
❑	154	Brook Jacoby	.15	.06
❑	155	Onix Concepcion	.15	.06
❑	156	Tim Conroy	.15	.06
❑	157	Joe Hesketh	.15	.06
❑	158	Brian Downing	.40	.16
❑	159	Tommy Dunbar	.15	.06
❑	160	Marc Hill	.15	.06
❑	161	Phil Garner	.40	.16
❑	162	Jerry Davis	.15	.06
❑	163	Bill Campbell	.15	.06
❑	164	John Franco RC	1.00	.40
❑	165	Len Barker	.15	.06
❑	166	Benny Distefano	.15	.06
❑	167	George Frazier	.15	.06
❑	168	Tito Landrum	.15	.06
❑	169	Cal Ripken	5.00	2.00
❑	170	Cecil Cooper	.40	.16
❑	171	Alan Trammell	.40	.16
❑	172	Wade Boggs	1.25	.50
❑	173	Don Baylor	.40	.16
❑	174	Pedro Guerrero	.40	.16
❑	175	Frank White	.40	.16
❑	176	Rickey Henderson	1.50	.60
❑	177	Charlie Lea	.15	.06
❑	178	Pete O'Brien	.15	.06
❑	179	Doug DeCinces	.15	.06
❑	180	Ron Kittle	.15	.06
❑	181	George Hendrick	.40	.16
❑	182	Joe Niekro	.15	.06
❑	183	Juan Samuel	.15	.06
❑	184	Mario Soto	.40	.16
❑	185	Rich Gossage	.40	.16
❑	186	Johnny Ray	.15	.06
❑	187	Bob Brenly	.15	.06
❑	188	Craig McMurtry	.15	.06
❑	189	Leon Durham	.15	.06
❑	190	Dwight Gooden RC	2.00	.80
❑	191	Barry Bonnell	.15	.06
❑	192	Tim Teufel	.15	.06
❑	193	Dave Stieb	.40	.16
❑	194	Mickey Hatcher	.15	.06
❑	195	Jesse Barfield	.40	.16
❑	196	Al Cowens	.15	.06
❑	197	Hubie Brooks	.15	.06
❑	198	Steve Trout	.15	.06
❑	199	Glenn Hubbard	.15	.06
❑	200	Bill Madlock	.40	.16
❑	201	Jeff D. Robinson	.15	.06
❑	202	Eric Show	.15	.06
❑	203	Dave Concepcion	.40	.16
❑	204	Ivan DeJesus	.15	.06
❑	205	Neil Allen	.15	.06
❑	206	Jerry Mumphrey	.15	.06
❑	207	Mike C. Brown	.15	.06
❑	208	Carlton Fisk	.75	.30
❑	209	Bryn Smith	.15	.06
❑	210	Tippy Martinez	.15	.06
❑	211	Dion James	.15	.06
❑	212	Willie Hernandez	.15	.06
❑	213	Mike Easler	.15	.06
❑	214	Ron Guidry	.40	.16
❑	215	Rick Honeycutt	.15	.06
❑	216	Brett Butler	.40	.16
❑	217	Larry Gura	.15	.06
❑	218	Ray Burris	.15	.06
❑	219	Steve Rogers	.40	.16
❑	220	Frank Tanana UER (Bats Left listed twice on card back)	.40	.16
❑	221	Ned Yost	.15	.06
❑	222	B.Saberhagen RC UER 18 career IP on back	1.50	.60
❑	223	Mike Davis	.15	.06
❑	224	Bert Blyleven	.40	.16
❑	225	Steve Kemp	.15	.06
❑	226	Jerry Reuss	.15	.06
❑	227	Darrell Evans UER (80 homers in 1980)	.40	.16
❑	228	Wayne Gross	.15	.06
❑	229	Jim Gantner	.15	.06
❑	230	Bob Boone	.40	.16
❑	231	Lonnie Smith	.15	.06
❑	232	Frank DiPino	.15	.06
❑	233	Jerry Koosman	.40	.16
❑	234	Graig Nettles	.40	.16
❑	235	John Tudor	.40	.16
❑	236	John Rabb	.15	.06
❑	237	Rick Manning	.15	.06
❑	238	Mike Fitzgerald	.15	.06
❑	239	Gary Matthews	.40	.16
❑	240	Jim Presley	.50	.20
❑	241	Dave Collins	.15	.06
❑	242	Gary Gaetti	.40	.16
❑	243	Dann Bilardello	.15	.06
❑	244	Rudy Law	.15	.06
❑	245	John Lowenstein	.15	.06
❑	246	Tom Tellmann	.15	.06
❑	247	Howard Johnson	.40	.16
❑	248	Ray Fontenot	.15	.06
❑	249	Tony Armas	.40	.16
❑	250	Candy Maldonado	.15	.06
❑	251	Mike Jeffcoat	.15	.06
❑	252	Dane Iorg	.15	.06
❑	253	Bruce Bochte	.15	.06
❑	254	Pete Rose Expos	4.00	1.60
❑	255	Don Aase	.15	.06
❑	256	George Wright	.15	.06
❑	257	Britt Burns	.15	.06
❑	258	Mike Scott	.40	.16
❑	259	Len Matuszek	.15	.06
❑	260	Dave Rucker	.15	.06
❑	261	Craig Lefferts	.15	.06
❑	262	Jay Tibbs	.15	.06
❑	263	Bruce Benedict	.15	.06
❑	264	Don Robinson	.15	.06
❑	265	Gary Lavelle	.15	.06
❑	266	Scott Sanderson	.15	.06
❑	267	Matt Young	.15	.06
❑	268	Ernie Whitt	.15	.06
❑	269	Houston Jimenez	.15	.06
❑	270	Ken Dixon	.15	.06
❑	271	Pete Ladd	.15	.06
❑	272	Juan Berenguer	.15	.06
❑	273	Roger Clemens RC	40.00	16.00
❑	274	Rick Cerone	.15	.06
❑	275	Dave Anderson	.15	.06
❑	276	George Vukovich	.15	.06
❑	277	Greg Pryor	.15	.06
❑	278	Mike Warren	.15	.06
❑	279	Bob James	.15	.06
❑	280	Bobby Grich	.40	.16
❑	281	Mike Mason RC	.25	.10
❑	282	Ron Reed	.15	.06
❑	283	Alan Ashby	.15	.06
❑	284	Mark Thurmond	.15	.06
❑	285	Joe Lefebvre	.15	.06
❑	286	Ted Power	.15	.06
❑	287	Chris Chambliss	.40	.16
❑	288	Lee Tunnell	.15	.06
❑	289	Rich Bordi	.15	.06
❑	290	Glenn Brummer	.15	.06
❑	291	Mike Boddicker	.15	.06
❑	292	Rollie Fingers	.40	.16
❑	293	Lou Whitaker	.40	.16
❑	294	Dwight Evans	.40	.16
❑	295	Don Mattingly	5.00	2.00
❑	296	Mike Marshall	.15	.06
❑	297	Willie Wilson	.40	.16
❑	298	Mike Heath	.15	.06
❑	299	Tim Raines	.40	.16
❑	300	Larry Parrish	.15	.06
❑	301	Geoff Zahn	.15	.06
❑	302	Rich Dotson	.15	.06
❑	303	David Green	.15	.06
❑	304	Jose Cruz	.40	.16
❑	305	Steve Carlton	.40	.16
❑	306	Gary Redus	.15	.06
❑	307	Steve Garvey	.40	.16
❑	308	Jose DeLeon	.15	.06
❑	309	Randy Lerch	.15	.06
❑	310	Claudell Washington	.15	.06
❑	311	Lee Smith	.40	.16
❑	312	Darryl Strawberry	1.25	.50
❑	313	Jim Beattie	.15	.06
❑	314	John Butcher	.15	.06
❑	315	Damaso Garcia	.15	.06
❑	316	Mike Smithson	.15	.06
❑	317	Luis Leal	.15	.06
❑	318	Ken Phelps	.15	.06
❑	319	Wally Backman	.15	.06
❑	320	Ron Cey	.40	.16
❑	321	Brad Komminsk	.15	.06
❑	322	Jason Thompson	.15	.06
❑	323	Frank Williams	.15	.06
❑	324	Tim Lollar	.15	.06
❑	325	Eric Davis RC	1.50	.60
❑	326	Von Hayes	.15	.06
❑	327	Andy Van Slyke	.40	.16
❑	328	Craig Reynolds	.15	.06
❑	329	Dick Schofield	.15	.06
❑	330	Scott Fletcher	.15	.06
❑	331	Jeff Reardon	.40	.16
❑	332	Rick Dempsey	.15	.06
❑	333	Ben Oglivie	.40	.16
❑	334	Dan Petry	.15	.06
❑	335	Jackie Gutierrez	.15	.06
❑	336	Dave Righetti	.40	.16
❑	337	Alejandro Pena	.15	.06
❑	338	Mel Hall	.15	.06
❑	339	Pat Sheridan	.15	.06
❑	340	Keith Atherton	.15	.06
❑	341	David Palmer	.15	.06
❑	342	Gary Ward	.15	.06
❑	343	Dave Stewart	.40	.16
❑	344	Mark Gubicza RC*	.50	.20
❑	345	Carney Lansford	.40	.16
❑	346	Jerry Willard	.15	.06
❑	347	Ken Griffey	.40	.16
❑	348	Franklin Stubbs	.15	.06
❑	349	Aurelio Lopez	.15	.06
❑	350	Al Bumbry	.15	.06
❑	351	Charlie Moore	.15	.06
❑	352	Luis Sanchez	.15	.06
❑	353	Darrell Porter	.15	.06
❑	354	Bill Dawley	.15	.06
❑	355	Charles Hudson	.15	.06
❑	356	Garry Templeton	.40	.16
❑	357	Cecilio Guante	.15	.06
❑	358	Jeff Leonard	.15	.06
❑	359	Paul Molitor	.75	.30
❑	360	Ron Gardenhire	.15	.06
❑	361	Larry Bowa	.40	.16
❑	362	Bob Kearney	.15	.06
❑	363	Garth Iorg	.15	.06
❑	364	Tom Brunansky	.15	.06
❑	365	Brad Gulden	.15	.06
❑	366	Greg Walker	.15	.06
❑	367	Mike Young	.15	.06
❑	368	Rick Waits	.15	.06
❑	369	Doug Bair	.15	.06
❑	370	Bob Shirley	.15	.06
❑	371	Bob Ojeda	.15	.06
❑	372	Bob Welch	.40	.16
❑	373	Neal Heaton	.15	.06
❑	374	Danny Jackson UER (Photo actually Frank Wills)	.15	.06
❑	375	Donnie Hill	.15	.06
❑	376	Mike Stenhouse	.15	.06
❑	377	Bruce Kison	.15	.06
❑	378	Wayne Tolleson	.15	.06
❑	379	Floyd Bannister	.15	.06
❑	380	Vern Ruhle	.15	.06
❑	381	Tim Corcoran	.15	.06

❑ 382 Kurt Kepshire .15 .06
❑ 383 Bobby Brown .15 .06
❑ 384 Dave Van Gorder .15 .06
❑ 385 Rick Mahler .15 .06
❑ 386 Lee Mazzilli .40 .16
❑ 387 Bill Laskey .15 .06
❑ 388 Thad Bosley .15 .06
❑ 389 Al Chambers .15 .06
❑ 390 Tony Fernandez .40 .16
❑ 391 Ron Washington .15 .06
❑ 392 Bill Swaggerty .15 .06
❑ 393 Bob L. Gibson .15 .06
❑ 394 Marty Castillo .15 .06
❑ 395 Steve Crawford .15 .06
❑ 396 Clay Christiansen .15 .06
❑ 397 Bob Bailor .15 .06
❑ 398 Mike Hargrove .15 .06
❑ 399 Charlie Leibrandt .15 .06
❑ 400 Tom Burgmeier .15 .06
❑ 401 Razor Shines .15 .06
❑ 402 Rob Wilfong .15 .06
❑ 403 Tom Henke .40 .16
❑ 404 Al Jones .15 .06
❑ 405 Mike LaCoss .15 .06
❑ 406 Luis DeLeon .15 .06
❑ 407 Greg Gross .15 .06
❑ 408 Tom Hume .15 .06
❑ 409 Rick Camp .15 .06
❑ 410 Milt May .15 .06
❑ 411 Henry Cotto RC .25 .10
❑ 412 David Von Ohlen .15 .06
❑ 413 Scott McGregor .15 .06
❑ 414 Ted Simmons .40 .16
❑ 415 Jack Morris .40 .16
❑ 416 Bill Buckner .40 .16
❑ 417 Butch Wynegar .15 .06
❑ 418 Steve Sax .15 .06
❑ 419 Steve Balboni .15 .06
❑ 420 Dwayne Murphy .15 .06
❑ 421 Andre Dawson .40 .16
❑ 422 Charlie Hough .40 .16
❑ 423 Tommy John .40 .16
❑ 424A Tom Seaver ERR .75 .30
(Photo actually
Floyd Bannister)
❑ 424B Tom Seaver COR 10.00 4.00
❑ 425 Tom Herr .15 .06
❑ 426 Terry Puhl .15 .06
❑ 427 Al Holland .15 .06
❑ 428 Eddie Milner .15 .06
❑ 429 Terry Kennedy .15 .06
❑ 430 John Candelaria .15 .06
❑ 431 Manny Trillo .15 .06
❑ 432 Ken Oberkfell .15 .06
❑ 433 Rick Sutcliffe .40 .16
❑ 434 Ron Darling .40 .16
❑ 435 Spike Owen .15 .06
❑ 436 Frank Viola .40 .16
❑ 437 Lloyd Moseby .15 .06
❑ 438 Kirby Puckett RC 10.00 4.00
❑ 439 Jim Clancy .15 .06
❑ 440 Mike Moore .15 .06
❑ 441 Doug Sisk .15 .06
❑ 442 Dennis Eckersley .75 .30
❑ 443 Gerald Perry .15 .06
❑ 444 Dale Berra .15 .06
❑ 445 Dusty Baker .40 .16
❑ 446 Ed Whitson .15 .06
❑ 447 Cesar Cedeno .40 .16
❑ 448 Rick Schu .15 .06
❑ 449 Joaquin Andujar .40 .16
❑ 450 Mark Bailey .15 .06
❑ 451 Ron Romanick .15 .06
❑ 452 Julio Cruz .15 .06
❑ 453 Miguel Dilone .15 .06
❑ 454 Storm Davis .15 .06
❑ 455 Jaime Cocanower .15 .06
❑ 456 Barbaro Garbey .15 .06
❑ 457 Rich Gedman .15 .06
❑ 458 Phil Niekro .40 .16
❑ 459 Mike Scioscia .40 .16
❑ 460 Pat Tabler .15 .06
❑ 461 Darryl Motley .15 .06
❑ 462 Chris Codiroli .15 .06
❑ 463 Doug Flynn .15 .06
❑ 464 Billy Sample .15 .06
❑ 465 Mickey Rivers .15 .06
❑ 466 John Wathan .15 .06
❑ 467 Bill Krueger .15 .06
❑ 468 Andre Thornton .15 .06
❑ 469 Rex Hudler .15 .06
❑ 470 Sid Bream RC .50 .20
❑ 471 Kirk Gibson .40 .16
❑ 472 John Shelby .15 .06
❑ 473 Moose Haas .15 .06
❑ 474 Doug Corbett .15 .06
❑ 475 Willie McGee .40 .16
❑ 476 Bob Knepper .15 .06
❑ 477 Kevin Gross .15 .06
❑ 478 Carmelo Martinez .15 .06
❑ 479 Kent Tekulve .15 .06
❑ 480 Chili Davis .40 .16
❑ 481 Bobby Clark .15 .06
❑ 482 Mookie Wilson .40 .16
❑ 483 Dave Owen .15 .06
❑ 484 Ed Nunez .15 .06
❑ 485 Rance Mulliniks .15 .06
❑ 486 Ken Schrom .15 .06
❑ 487 Jeff Russell .15 .06
❑ 488 Tom Paciorek .15 .06
❑ 489 Dan Ford .15 .06
❑ 490 Mike Caldwell .15 .06
❑ 491 Scottie Earl .15 .06
❑ 492 Jose Rijo RC 1.00 .40
❑ 493 Bruce Hurst .15 .06
❑ 494 Ken Landreaux .15 .06
❑ 495 Mike Fischlin .15 .06
❑ 496 Don Slaught .15 .06
❑ 497 Steve McCatty .15 .06
❑ 498 Gary Lucas .15 .06
❑ 499 Gary Pettis .15 .06
❑ 500 Marvis Foley .15 .06
❑ 501 Mike Squires .15 .06
❑ 502 Jim Pankovits .15 .06
❑ 503 Luis Aguayo .15 .06
❑ 504 Ralph Citarella .15 .06
❑ 505 Bruce Bochy .15 .06
❑ 506 Bob Owchinko .15 .06
❑ 507 Pascual Perez .15 .06
❑ 508 Lee Lacy .15 .06
❑ 509 Atlee Hammaker .15 .06
❑ 510 Bob Dernier .15 .06
❑ 511 Ed VandeBerg .15 .06
❑ 512 Cliff Johnson .15 .06
❑ 513 Len Whitehouse .15 .06
❑ 514 Dennis Martinez .40 .16
❑ 515 Ed Romero .15 .06
❑ 516 Rusty Kuntz .15 .06
❑ 517 Rick Miller .15 .06
❑ 518 Dennis Rasmussen .15 .06
❑ 519 Steve Yeager .40 .16
❑ 520 Chris Bando .15 .06
❑ 521 U.L. Washington .15 .06
❑ 522 Curt Young .15 .06
❑ 523 Angel Salazar .15 .06
❑ 524 Curt Kaufman .15 .06
❑ 525 Odell Jones .15 .06
❑ 526 Juan Agosto .15 .06
❑ 527 Denny Walling .15 .06
❑ 528 Andy Hawkins .15 .06
❑ 529 Sixto Lezcano .15 .06
❑ 530 Skeeter Barnes RC .25 .10
❑ 531 Randy Johnson .15 .06
❑ 532 Jim Morrison .15 .06
❑ 533 Warren Brusstar .15 .06
❑ 534A J.Pendleton ERR RC 1.00 .40
Wrong first name
❑ 534B T.Pendleton COR RC 1.00 .40
❑ 535 Vic Rodriguez .15 .06
❑ 536 Bob McClure .15 .06
❑ 537 Dave Bergman .15 .06
❑ 538 Mark Clear .15 .06
❑ 539 Mike Pagliarulo .15 .06
❑ 540 Terry Whitfield .15 .06
❑ 541 Joe Beckwith .15 .06
❑ 542 Jeff Burroughs .15 .06
❑ 543 Dan Schatzeder .15 .06
❑ 544 Donnie Scott .15 .06
❑ 545 Jim Slaton .15 .06
❑ 546 Greg Luzinski .40 .16
❑ 547 Mark Salas .15 .06
❑ 548 Dave Smith .15 .06
❑ 549 John Wockenfuss .15 .06
❑ 550 Frank Pastore .15 .06
❑ 551 Tim Flannery .15 .06
❑ 552 Rick Rhoden .15 .06
❑ 553 Mark Davis .15 .06
❑ 554 Jeff Dedmon .15 .06
❑ 555 Gary Woods .15 .06
❑ 556 Danny Heep .15 .06
❑ 557 Mark Langston RC 1.00 .40
❑ 558 Darrell Brown .15 .06
❑ 559 Jimmy Key RC 1.00 .40
❑ 560 Rick Lysander .15 .06
❑ 561 Doyle Alexander .15 .06
❑ 562 Mike Stanton .15 .06
❑ 563 Sid Fernandez .40 .16
❑ 564 Richie Hebner .15 .06
❑ 565 Alex Trevino .15 .06
❑ 566 Brian Harper .15 .06
❑ 567 Dan Gladden RC .50 .20
❑ 568 Luis Salazar .15 .06
❑ 569 Tom Foley .15 .06
❑ 570 Larry Andersen .15 .06
❑ 571 Danny Cox .15 .06
❑ 572 Joe Sambito .15 .06
❑ 573 Juan Beniquez .15 .06
❑ 574 Joel Skinner .15 .06
❑ 575 Randy St.Claire .15 .06
❑ 576 Floyd Rayford .15 .06
❑ 577 Roy Howell .15 .06
❑ 578 John Grubb .15 .06
❑ 579 Ed Jurak .15 .06
❑ 580 John Montefusco .15 .06
❑ 581 Orel Hershiser RC 1.50 .60
❑ 582 Tom Waddell .15 .06
❑ 583 Mark Huismann .15 .06
❑ 584 Joe Morgan .40 .16
❑ 585 Jim Wohlford .15 .06
❑ 586 Dave Schmidt .15 .06
❑ 587 Jeff Kunkel .15 .06
❑ 588 Hal McRae .40 .16
❑ 589 Bill Almon .15 .06
❑ 590 Carmelo Castillo .15 .06
❑ 591 Omar Moreno .15 .06
❑ 592 Ken Howell .15 .06
❑ 593 Tom Brookens .15 .06
❑ 594 Joe Nolan .15 .06
❑ 595 Willie Lozado .15 .06
❑ 596 Tom Nieto .15 .06
❑ 597 Walt Terrell .15 .06
❑ 598 Al Oliver .40 .16
❑ 599 Shane Rawley .15 .06
❑ 600 Denny Gonzalez .15 .06
❑ 601 Mark Grant .15 .06
❑ 602 Mike Armstrong .15 .06
❑ 603 George Foster .40 .16
❑ 604 Dave Lopes .40 .16
❑ 605 Salome Barojas .15 .06
❑ 606 Roy Lee Jackson .15 .06
❑ 607 Pete Filson .15 .06
❑ 608 Duane Walker .15 .06
❑ 609 Glenn Wilson .15 .06
❑ 610 Rafael Santana .15 .06
❑ 611 Roy Smith .15 .06
❑ 612 Ruppert Jones .15 .06
❑ 613 Joe Cowley .15 .06
❑ 614 Al Nipper UER .15 .06
(Photo actually
Mike Brown)
❑ 615 Gene Nelson .15 .06
❑ 616 Joe Carter 1.25 .50
❑ 617 Ray Knight .40 .16
❑ 618 Chuck Rainey .15 .06
❑ 619 Dan Driessen .15 .06
❑ 620 Daryl Sconiers .15 .06
❑ 621 Bill Stein .15 .06
❑ 622 Roy Smalley .15 .06
❑ 623 Ed Lynch .15 .06
❑ 624 Jeff Stone .15 .06
❑ 625 Bruce Berenyi .15 .06
❑ 626 Kelvin Chapman .15 .06
❑ 627 Joe Price .15 .06
❑ 628 Steve Bedrosian .15 .06
❑ 629 Vic Mata .15 .06
❑ 630 Mike Krukow .15 .06
❑ 631 Phil Bradley .50 .20
❑ 632 Jim Gott .15 .06

❑ 633 Randy Bush .15 .06
❑ 634 Tom Browning RC .50 .20
❑ 635 Lou Gehrig 1.25 .50
Puzzle Card
❑ 636 Reid Nichols .15 .06
❑ 637 Dan Pasqua RC .50 .20
❑ 638 German Rivera .15 .06
❑ 639 Don Schulze .15 .06
❑ 640A Mike Jones .15 .06
(Career Highlights, takes five lines)
❑ 640B Mike Jones .15 .06
(Career Highlights, takes four lines)
❑ 641 Pete Rose 4.00 1.60
❑ 642 Wade Rowdon .15 .06
❑ 643 Jerry Narron .15 .06
❑ 644 Darrell Miller .15 .06
❑ 645 Tim Hulett RC .25 .10
❑ 646 Andy McGaffigan .15 .06
❑ 647 Kurt Bevacqua .15 .06
❑ 648 John Russell .15 .06
❑ 649 Ron Robinson .15 .06
❑ 650 Donnie Moore .15 .06
❑ 651A Two for the Title 2.00 .80
Dave Winfield
Don Mattingly
(Yellow letters)
❑ 651B Two for the Title 5.00 2.00
Dave Winfield
Don Mattingly
(White letters)
❑ 652 Tim Laudner .15 .06
❑ 653 Steve Farr RC .50 .20
❑ 654 DK Checklist 1-26 .15 .06
(Unnumbered)
❑ 655 Checklist 27-130 .15 .06
(Unnumbered)
❑ 656 Checklist 131-234 .15 .06
(Unnumbered)
❑ 657 Checklist 235-338 .15 .06
(Unnumbered)
❑ 658 Checklist 339-442 .15 .06
(Unnumbered)
❑ 659 Checklist 443-546 .15 .06
(Unnumbered)
❑ 660 Checklist 547-653 .15 .06
(Unnumbered)

1986 Donruss

	Nm-Mt	Ex-Mt
COMPLETE SET (660)	40.00	16.00
COMP.FACT.SET (660)	40.00	16.00
COMP.AARON PUZZLE	2.00	.80

❑ 1 Kirk Gibson DK .25 .10
❑ 2 Rich Gossage DK .25 .10
❑ 3 Willie McGee DK .25 .10
❑ 4 George Bell DK .25 .10
❑ 5 Tony Armas DK .25 .10
❑ 6 Chili Davis DK .25 .10
❑ 7 Cecil Cooper DK .25 .10
❑ 8 Mike Boddicker DK .15 .06
❑ 9 Dave Lopes DK .25 .10
❑ 10 Bill Doran DK .15 .06
❑ 11 Bret Saberhagen DK .25 .10
❑ 12 Brett Butler DK .25 .10
❑ 13 Harold Baines DK .25 .10
❑ 14 Mike Davis DK .15 .06
❑ 15 Tony Perez DK .50 .20
❑ 16 Willie Randolph DK .25 .10
❑ 17 Bob Boone DK .25 .10
❑ 18 Orel Hershiser DK .25 .10
❑ 19 Johnny Ray DK .15 .06
❑ 20 Gary Ward DK .15 .06
❑ 21 Rick Mahler DK .15 .06
❑ 22 Phil Bradley DK .15 .06
❑ 23 Jerry Koosman DK .25 .10
❑ 24 Tom Brunansky DK .15 .06
❑ 25 Andre Dawson DK .15 .06
❑ 26 Dwight Gooden DK .75 .30
❑ 27 Kal Daniels RR .50 .20
❑ 28 Fred McGriff RR RC 8.00 3.20
❑ 29 Cory Snyder RR .15 .06
❑ 30 Jose Guzman RR RC .15 .06
❑ 31 Ty Gainey RC .15 .06
❑ 32 Johnny Abrego RC .15 .06
❑ 33A A.Galarraga RC RR 1.50 .60
No accent
❑ 33B A.Galarraga RC RR 1.50 .60
Accent over e
❑ 34 Dave Shipanoff RC .15 .06
❑ 35 M.McLemore RR RC 1.00 .40
❑ 36 Marty Clary RC .15 .06
❑ 37 Paul O'Neill RR RC 4.00 1.60
❑ 38 Danny Tartabull RR .25 .10
❑ 39 Jose Canseco RR RC 10.00 4.00
❑ 40 Juan Nieves RC .15 .06
❑ 41 Lance McCullers RC .15 .06
❑ 42 Rick Surhoff RC .15 .06
❑ 43 Todd Worrell RR RC .50 .20
❑ 44 Bob Kipper RC .15 .06
❑ 45 John Habyan RR RC .15 .06
❑ 46 Mike Woodard RC .15 .06
❑ 47 Mike Boddicker .15 .06
❑ 48 Robin Yount 1.25 .50
❑ 49 Lou Whitaker .25 .10
❑ 50 Oil Can Boyd .15 .06
❑ 51 Rickey Henderson .75 .30
❑ 52 Mike Marshall .15 .06
❑ 53 George Brett 2.00 .80
❑ 54 Dave Kingman .25 .10
❑ 55 Hubie Brooks .15 .06
❑ 56 Oddibe McDowell .15 .06
❑ 57 Doug DeCinces .15 .06
❑ 58 Britt Burns .15 .06
❑ 59 Ozzie Smith 1.25 .50
❑ 60 Jose Cruz .25 .10
❑ 61 Mike Schmidt 2.00 .80
❑ 62 Pete Rose 2.50 1.00
❑ 63 Steve Garvey .25 .10
❑ 64 Tony Pena .15 .06
❑ 65 Chili Davis .25 .10
❑ 66 Dale Murphy .50 .20
❑ 67 Ryne Sandberg 1.50 .60
❑ 68 Gary Carter .25 .10
❑ 69 Alvin Davis .15 .06
❑ 70 Kent Hrbek .25 .10
❑ 71 George Bell .25 .10
❑ 72 Kirby Puckett 2.00 .80
❑ 73 Lloyd Moseby .15 .06
❑ 74 Bob Kearney .15 .06
❑ 75 Dwight Gooden .75 .30
❑ 76 Gary Matthews .25 .10
❑ 77 Rick Mahler .15 .06
❑ 78 Benny Distefano .15 .06
❑ 79 Jeff Leonard .15 .06
❑ 80 Kevin McReynolds .25 .10
❑ 81 Ron Oester .15 .06
❑ 82 John Russell .15 .06
❑ 83 Tommy Herr .15 .06
❑ 84 Jerry Mumphrey .15 .06
❑ 85 Ron Romanick .15 .06
❑ 86 Daryl Boston .15 .06
❑ 87 Andre Dawson .25 .10
❑ 88 Eddie Murray .75 .30
❑ 89 Dion James .15 .06
❑ 90 Chet Lemon .25 .10
❑ 91 Bob Stanley .15 .06
❑ 92 Willie Randolph .25 .10
❑ 93 Mike Scioscia .25 .10
❑ 94 Tom Waddell .15 .06
❑ 95 Danny Jackson .15 .06
❑ 96 Mike Davis .15 .06
❑ 97 Mike Fitzgerald .15 .06
❑ 98 Gary Ward .15 .06
❑ 99 Pete O'Brien .15 .06
❑ 100 Bret Saberhagen .25 .10
❑ 101 Alfredo Griffin .15 .06
❑ 102 Brett Butler .25 .10
❑ 103 Ron Guidry .25 .10
❑ 104 Jerry Reuss .15 .06
❑ 105 Jack Morris .25 .10
❑ 106 Rick Dempsey .15 .06
❑ 107 Ray Burris .15 .06
❑ 108 Brian Downing .25 .10
❑ 109 Willie McGee .25 .10
❑ 110 Bill Doran .15 .06
❑ 111 Kent Tekulve .15 .06
❑ 112 Tony Gwynn 1.25 .50
❑ 113 Marvell Wynne .15 .06
❑ 114 David Green .15 .06
❑ 115 Jim Gantner .15 .06
❑ 116 George Foster .25 .10
❑ 117 Steve Trout .15 .06
❑ 118 Mark Langston .25 .10
❑ 119 Tony Fernandez .15 .06
❑ 120 John Butcher .15 .06
❑ 121 Ron Robinson .15 .06
❑ 122 Dan Spillner .15 .06
❑ 123 Mike Young .15 .06
❑ 124 Paul Molitor .50 .20
❑ 125 Kirk Gibson .25 .10
❑ 126 Ken Griffey .25 .10
❑ 127 Tony Armas .25 .10
❑ 128 Mariano Duncan RC* .50 .20
❑ 129 Pat Tabler .15 .06
❑ 130 Frank White .25 .10
❑ 131 Carney Lansford .25 .10
❑ 132 Vance Law .15 .06
❑ 133 Dick Schofield .15 .06
❑ 134 Wayne Tolleson .15 .06
❑ 135 Greg Walker .15 .06
❑ 136 Denny Walling .15 .06
❑ 137 Ozzie Virgil .15 .06
❑ 138 Ricky Horton .15 .06
❑ 139 LaMarr Hoyt .15 .06
❑ 140 Wayne Krenchicki .15 .06
❑ 141 Glenn Hubbard .15 .06
❑ 142 Cecilio Guante .15 .06
❑ 143 Mike Krukow .15 .06
❑ 144 Lee Smith .25 .10
❑ 145 Edwin Nunez .15 .06
❑ 146 Dave Stieb .25 .10
❑ 147 Mike Smithson .15 .06
❑ 148 Ken Dixon .15 .06
❑ 149 Danny Darwin .15 .06
❑ 150 Chris Pittaro .15 .06
❑ 151 Bill Buckner .25 .10
❑ 152 Mike Pagliarulo .15 .06
❑ 153 Bill Russell .25 .10
❑ 154 Brook Jacoby .15 .06
❑ 155 Pat Sheridan .15 .06
❑ 156 Mike Gallego RC .15 .06
❑ 157 Jim Wohlford .15 .06
❑ 158 Gary Pettis .15 .06
❑ 159 Toby Harrah .25 .10
❑ 160 Richard Dotson .15 .06
❑ 161 Bob Knepper .15 .06
❑ 162 Dave Dravecky .15 .06
❑ 163 Greg Gross .15 .06
❑ 164 Eric Davis .50 .20
❑ 165 Gerald Perry .15 .06
❑ 166 Rick Rhoden .15 .06
❑ 167 Keith Moreland .15 .06
❑ 168 Jack Clark .25 .10
❑ 169 Storm Davis .15 .06
❑ 170 Cecil Cooper .25 .10
❑ 171 Alan Trammell .25 .10
❑ 172 Roger Clemens 4.00 1.60
❑ 173 Don Mattingly 2.50 1.00
❑ 174 Pedro Guerrero .25 .10
❑ 175 Willie Wilson .25 .10
❑ 176 Dwayne Murphy .15 .06
❑ 177 Tim Raines .25 .10
❑ 178 Larry Parrish .15 .06
❑ 179 Mike Witt .15 .06
❑ 180 Harold Baines .25 .10
❑ 181 V.Coleman RC* UER 1.00 .40

BA 2.67 on back

❑	182	Jeff Heathcock	.15	.06
❑	183	Steve Carlton	.25	.10
❑	184	Mario Soto	.25	.10
❑	185	Rich Gossage	.25	.10
❑	186	Johnny Ray	.15	.06
❑	187	Dan Gladden	.15	.06
❑	188	Bob Horner	.25	.10
❑	189	Rick Sutcliffe	.25	.10
❑	190	Keith Hernandez	.25	.10
❑	191	Phil Bradley	.15	.06
❑	192	Tom Brunansky	.15	.06
❑	193	Jesse Barfield	.25	.10
❑	194	Frank Viola	.25	.10
❑	195	Willie Upshaw	.15	.06
❑	196	Jim Beattie	.15	.06
❑	197	Darryl Strawberry	.50	.20
❑	198	Ron Cey	.25	.10
❑	199	Steve Bedrosian	.15	.06
❑	200	Steve Kemp	.15	.06
❑	201	Manny Trillo	.15	.06
❑	202	Garry Templeton	.25	.10
❑	203	Dave Parker	.25	.10
❑	204	John Denny	.15	.06
❑	205	Terry Pendleton	.25	.10
❑	206	Terry Puhl	.15	.06
❑	207	Bobby Grich	.25	.10
❑	208	Ozzie Guillen RC*	.50	.20
❑	209	Jeff Reardon	.25	.10
❑	210	Cal Ripken	3.00	1.20
❑	211	Bill Schroeder	.15	.06
❑	212	Dan Petry	.15	.06
❑	213	Jim Rice	.25	.10
❑	214	Dave Righetti	.25	.10
❑	215	Fernando Valenzuela	.25	.10
❑	216	Julio Franco	.25	.10
❑	217	Darryl Motley	.15	.06
❑	218	Dave Collins	.15	.06
❑	219	Tim Wallach	.15	.06
❑	220	George Wright	.15	.06
❑	221	Tommy Dunbar	.15	.06
❑	222	Steve Balboni	.15	.06
❑	223	Jay Howell	.15	.06
❑	224	Joe Carter	.25	.10
❑	225	Ed Whitson	.15	.06
❑	226	Orel Hershiser	.50	.20
❑	227	Willie Hernandez	.15	.06
❑	228	Lee Lacy	.15	.06
❑	229	Rollie Fingers	.25	.10
❑	230	Bob Boone	.25	.10
❑	231	Joaquin Andujar	.25	.10
❑	232	Craig Reynolds	.15	.06
❑	233	Shane Rawley	.15	.06
❑	234	Eric Show	.15	.06
❑	235	Jose DeLeon	.15	.06
❑	236	Jose Uribe	.15	.06
❑	237	Moose Haas	.15	.06
❑	238	Wally Backman	.15	.06
❑	239	Dennis Eckersley	.50	.20
❑	240	Mike Moore	.15	.06
❑	241	Damaso Garcia	.15	.06
❑	242	Tim Teufel	.15	.06
❑	243	Dave Concepcion	.25	.10
❑	244	Floyd Bannister	.15	.06
❑	245	Fred Lynn	.25	.10
❑	246	Charlie Moore	.15	.06
❑	247	Walt Terrell	.15	.06
❑	248	Dave Winfield	.25	.10
❑	249	Dwight Evans	.25	.10
❑	250	Dennis Powell	.15	.06
❑	251	Andre Thornton	.15	.06
❑	252	Onix Concepcion	.15	.06
❑	253	Mike Heath	.15	.06
❑	254A	David Palmer ERR (Position 2B)	.15	.06
❑	254B	David Palmer COR (Position P)	.50	.20
❑	255	Donnie Moore	.15	.06
❑	256	Curtis Wilkerson	.15	.06
❑	257	Julio Cruz	.15	.06
❑	258	Nolan Ryan	4.00	1.60
❑	259	Jeff Stone	.15	.06
❑	260	John Tudor	.25	.10
❑	261	Mark Thurmond	.15	.06
❑	262	Jay Tibbs	.15	.06
❑	263	Rafael Ramirez	.15	.06
❑	264	Larry McWilliams	.15	.06
❑	265	Mark Davis	.15	.06
❑	266	Bob Dernier	.15	.06
❑	267	Matt Young	.15	.06
❑	268	Jim Clancy	.15	.06
❑	269	Mickey Hatcher	.15	.06
❑	270	Sammy Stewart	.15	.06
❑	271	Bob L. Gibson	.15	.06
❑	272	Nelson Simmons	.15	.06
❑	273	Rich Gedman	.15	.06
❑	274	Butch Wynegar	.15	.06
❑	275	Ken Howell	.15	.06
❑	276	Mel Hall	.15	.06
❑	277	Jim Sundberg	.25	.10
❑	278	Chris Codiroli	.15	.06
❑	279	Herm Winningham	.15	.06
❑	280	Rod Carew	.50	.20
❑	281	Don Slaught	.15	.06
❑	282	Scott Fletcher	.15	.06
❑	283	Bill Dawley	.15	.06
❑	284	Andy Hawkins	.15	.06
❑	285	Glenn Wilson	.15	.06
❑	286	Nick Esasky	.15	.06
❑	287	Claudell Washington	.15	.06
❑	288	Lee Mazzilli	.25	.10
❑	289	Jody Davis	.15	.06
❑	290	Darrell Porter	.15	.06
❑	291	Scott McGregor	.15	.06
❑	292	Ted Simmons	.25	.10
❑	293	Aurelio Lopez	.15	.06
❑	294	Marty Barrett	.15	.06
❑	295	Dale Berra	.15	.06
❑	296	Greg Brock	.15	.06
❑	297	Charlie Leibrandt	.15	.06
❑	298	Bill Krueger	.15	.06
❑	299	Bryn Smith	.15	.06
❑	300	Burt Hooton	.15	.06
❑	301	Stu Cliburn	.15	.06
❑	302	Luis Salazar	.15	.06
❑	303	Ken Dayley	.15	.06
❑	304	Frank DiPino	.15	.06
❑	305	Von Hayes	.15	.06
❑	306	Gary Redus	.15	.06
❑	307	Craig Lefferts	.15	.06
❑	308	Sammy Khalifa	.15	.06
❑	309	Scott Garrelts	.15	.06
❑	310	Rick Cerone	.15	.06
❑	311	Shawon Dunston	.25	.10
❑	312	Howard Johnson	.25	.10
❑	313	Jim Presley	.15	.06
❑	314	Gary Gaetti	.25	.10
❑	315	Luis Leal	.15	.06
❑	316	Mark Salas	.15	.06
❑	317	Bill Caudill	.15	.06
❑	318	Dave Henderson	.15	.06
❑	319	Rafael Santana	.15	.06
❑	320	Leon Durham	.15	.06
❑	321	Bruce Sutter	.25	.10
❑	322	Jason Thompson	.15	.06
❑	323	Bob Brenly	.15	.06
❑	324	Carmelo Martinez	.15	.06
❑	325	Eddie Milner	.15	.06
❑	326	Juan Samuel	.15	.06
❑	327	Tom Nieto	.15	.06
❑	328	Dave Smith	.15	.06
❑	329	Urbano Lugo	.15	.06
❑	330	Joel Skinner	.15	.06
❑	331	Bill Gullickson	.15	.06
❑	332	Floyd Rayford	.15	.06
❑	333	Ben Oglivie	.25	.10
❑	334	Lance Parrish	.25	.10
❑	335	Jackie Gutierrez	.15	.06
❑	336	Dennis Rasmussen	.15	.06
❑	337	Terry Whitfield	.15	.06
❑	338	Neal Heaton	.15	.06
❑	339	Jorge Orta	.15	.06
❑	340	Donnie Hill	.15	.06
❑	341	Joe Hesketh	.15	.06
❑	342	Charlie Hough	.25	.10
❑	343	Dave Rozema	.15	.06
❑	344	Greg Pryor	.15	.06
❑	345	Mickey Tettleton RC	.50	.20
❑	346	George Vukovich	.15	.06
❑	347	Don Baylor	.25	.10
❑	348	Carlos Diaz	.15	.06
❑	349	Barbaro Garbey	.15	.06
❑	350	Larry Sheets	.15	.06
❑	351	Ted Higuera RC*	.50	.20
❑	352	Juan Beniquez	.15	.06
❑	353	Bob Forsch	.15	.06
❑	354	Mark Bailey	.15	.06
❑	355	Larry Andersen	.15	.06
❑	356	Terry Kennedy	.15	.06
❑	357	Don Robinson	.15	.06
❑	358	Jim Gott	.15	.06
❑	359	Earnie Riles	.15	.06
❑	360	John Christensen	.15	.06
❑	361	Ray Fontenot	.15	.06
❑	362	Spike Owen	.15	.06
❑	363	Jim Acker	.15	.06
❑	364	Ron Davis	.15	.06
❑	365	Tom Hume	.15	.06
❑	366	Carlton Fisk	.50	.20
❑	367	Nate Snell	.15	.06
❑	368	Rick Manning	.15	.06
❑	369	Darrell Evans	.25	.10
❑	370	Ron Hassey	.15	.06
❑	371	Wade Boggs	.50	.20
❑	372	Rick Honeycutt	.15	.06
❑	373	Chris Bando	.15	.06
❑	374	Bud Black	.15	.06
❑	375	Steve Henderson	.15	.06
❑	376	Charlie Lea	.15	.06
❑	377	Reggie Jackson	.50	.20
❑	378	Dave Schmidt	.15	.06
❑	379	Bob James	.15	.06
❑	380	Glenn Davis	.15	.06
❑	381	Tim Corcoran	.15	.06
❑	382	Danny Cox	.15	.06
❑	383	Tim Flannery	.15	.06
❑	384	Tom Browning	.15	.06
❑	385	Rick Camp	.15	.06
❑	386	Jim Morrison	.15	.06
❑	387	Dave LaPoint	.15	.06
❑	388	Dave Lopes	.25	.10
❑	389	Al Cowens	.15	.06
❑	390	Doyle Alexander	.15	.06
❑	391	Tim Laudner	.15	.06
❑	392	Don Aase	.15	.06
❑	393	Jaime Cocanower	.15	.06
❑	394	Randy O'Neal	.15	.06
❑	395	Mike Easler	.15	.06
❑	396	Scott Bradley	.15	.06
❑	397	Tom Niedenfuer	.15	.06
❑	398	Jerry Willard	.15	.06
❑	399	Lonnie Smith	.15	.06
❑	400	Bruce Bochte	.15	.06
❑	401	Terry Francona	.25	.10
❑	402	Jim Slaton	.15	.06
❑	403	Bill Stein	.15	.06
❑	404	Tim Hulett	.15	.06
❑	405	Alan Ashby	.15	.06
❑	406	Tim Stoddard	.15	.06
❑	407	Garry Maddox	.15	.06
❑	408	Ted Power	.15	.06
❑	409	Len Barker	.15	.06
❑	410	Denny Gonzalez	.15	.06
❑	411	George Frazier	.15	.06
❑	412	Andy Van Slyke	.25	.10
❑	413	Jim Dwyer	.15	.06
❑	414	Paul Householder	.15	.06
❑	415	Alejandro Sanchez	.15	.06
❑	416	Steve Crawford	.15	.06
❑	417	Dan Pasqua	.15	.06
❑	418	Enos Cabell	.15	.06
❑	419	Mike Jones	.15	.06
❑	420	Steve Kiefer	.15	.06
❑	421	Tim Burke	.15	.06
❑	422	Mike Mason	.15	.06
❑	423	Ruppert Jones	.15	.06
❑	424	Jerry Hairston	.15	.06
❑	425	Tito Landrum	.15	.06
❑	426	Jeff Calhoun	.15	.06
❑	427	Don Carman	.15	.06
❑	428	Tony Perez	.50	.20
❑	429	Jerry Davis	.15	.06
❑	430	Bob Walk	.15	.06
❑	431	Brad Wellman	.15	.06
❑	432	Terry Forster	.25	.10
❑	433	Billy Hatcher	.15	.06
❑	434	Clint Hurdle	.15	.06
❑	435	Ivan Calderon RC*	.50	.20

❑ 436 Pete Filson .15 .06
❑ 437 Tom Henke .25 .10
❑ 438 Dave Engle .15 .06
❑ 439 Tom Filer .15 .06
❑ 440 Gorman Thomas .25 .10
❑ 441 Rick Aguilera RC .50 .20
❑ 442 Scott Sanderson .15 .06
❑ 443 Jeff Dedmon .15 .06
❑ 444 Joe Orsulak RC* .50 .20
❑ 445 Atlee Hammaker .15 .06
❑ 446 Jerry Royster .15 .06
❑ 447 Buddy Bell .25 .10
❑ 448 Dave Rucker .15 .06
❑ 449 Ivan DeJesus .15 .06
❑ 450 Jim Pankovits .15 .06
❑ 451 Jerry Narron .15 .06
❑ 452 Bryan Little .15 .06
❑ 453 Gary Lucas .15 .06
❑ 454 Dennis Martinez .25 .10
❑ 455 Ed Romero .15 .06
❑ 456 Bob Melvin .15 .06
❑ 457 Glenn Hoffman .15 .06
❑ 458 Bob Shirley .15 .06
❑ 459 Bob Welch .25 .10
❑ 460 Carmen Castillo .15 .06
❑ 461 Dave Leeper .15 .06
❑ 462 Tim Birtsas .15 .06
❑ 463 Randy St.Claire .15 .06
❑ 464 Chris Welsh .15 .06
❑ 465 Greg Harris .15 .06
❑ 466 Lynn Jones .15 .06
❑ 467 Dusty Baker .25 .10
❑ 468 Roy Smith .15 .06
❑ 469 Andre Robertson .15 .06
❑ 470 Ken Landreaux .15 .06
❑ 471 Dave Bergman .15 .06
❑ 472 Gary Roenicke .15 .06
❑ 473 Pete Vuckovich .15 .06
❑ 474 Kirk McCaskill RC .50 .20
❑ 475 Jeff Lahti .15 .06
❑ 476 Mike Scott .25 .10
❑ 477 Darren Daulton RC 1.00 .40
❑ 478 Graig Nettles .25 .10
❑ 479 Bill Almon .15 .06
❑ 480 Greg Minton .15 .06
❑ 481 Randy Ready .15 .06
❑ 482 Len Dykstra RC 1.50 .60
❑ 483 Thad Bosley .15 .06
❑ 484 Harold Reynolds RC 1.50 .60
❑ 485 Al Oliver .25 .10
❑ 486 Roy Smalley .15 .06
❑ 487 John Franco .25 .10
❑ 488 Juan Agosto .15 .06
❑ 489 Al Pardo .15 .06
❑ 490 Bill Wegman RC .15 .06
❑ 491 Frank Tanana .25 .10
❑ 492 Brian Fisher RC .15 .06
❑ 493 Mark Clear .15 .06
❑ 494 Len Matuszek .15 .06
❑ 495 Ramon Romero .15 .06
❑ 496 John Wathan .15 .06
❑ 497 Rob Picciolo .15 .06
❑ 498 U.L. Washington .15 .06
❑ 499 John Candelaria .15 .06
❑ 500 Duane Walker .15 .06
❑ 501 Gene Nelson .15 .06
❑ 502 John Mizerock .15 .06
❑ 503 Luis Aguayo .15 .06
❑ 504 Kurt Kepshire .15 .06
❑ 505 Ed Wojna .15 .06
❑ 506 Joe Price .15 .06
❑ 507 Milt Thompson RC .50 .20
❑ 508 Junior Ortiz .15 .06
❑ 509 Vida Blue .25 .10
❑ 510 Steve Engel .15 .06
❑ 511 Karl Best .15 .06
❑ 512 Cecil Fielder RC 1.50 .60
❑ 513 Frank Eufemia .15 .06
❑ 514 Tippy Martinez .15 .06
❑ 515 Billy Joe Robidoux .15 .06
❑ 516 Bill Scherrer .15 .06
❑ 517 Bruce Hurst .15 .06
❑ 518 Rich Bordi .15 .06
❑ 519 Steve Yeager .25 .10
❑ 520 Tony Bernazard .15 .06
❑ 521 Hal McRae .25 .10
❑ 522 Jose Rijo .25 .10
❑ 523 Mitch Webster .15 .06
❑ 524 Jack Howell .15 .06
❑ 525 Alan Bannister .15 .06
❑ 526 Ron Kittle .15 .06
❑ 527 Phil Garner .25 .10
❑ 528 Kurt Bevacqua .15 .06
❑ 529 Kevin Gross .15 .06
❑ 530 Bo Diaz .15 .06
❑ 531 Ken Oberkfell .15 .06
❑ 532 Rick Reuschel .25 .10
❑ 533 Ron Meridith .15 .06
❑ 534 Steve Braun .15 .06
❑ 535 Wayne Gross .15 .06
❑ 536 Ray Searage .15 .06
❑ 537 Tom Brookens .15 .06
❑ 538 Al Nipper .15 .06
❑ 539 Billy Sample .15 .06
❑ 540 Steve Sax .15 .06
❑ 541 Dan Quisenberry .15 .06
❑ 542 Tony Phillips .15 .06
❑ 543 Floyd Youmans .15 .06
❑ 544 Steve Buechele RC .50 .20
❑ 545 Craig Gerber .15 .06
❑ 546 Joe DeSa .15 .06
❑ 547 Brian Harper .15 .06
❑ 548 Kevin Bass .15 .06
❑ 549 Tom Foley .15 .06
❑ 550 Dave Van Gorder .15 .06
❑ 551 Bruce Bochy .15 .06
❑ 552 R.J. Reynolds .15 .06
❑ 553 Chris Brown .15 .06
❑ 554 Bruce Benedict .15 .06
❑ 555 Warren Brusstar .15 .06
❑ 556 Danny Heep .15 .06
❑ 557 Darnell Coles .15 .06
❑ 558 Greg Gagne .15 .06
❑ 559 Ernie Whitt .15 .06
❑ 560 Ron Washington .15 .06
❑ 561 Jimmy Key .25 .10
❑ 562 Billy Swift .15 .06
❑ 563 Ron Darling .25 .10
❑ 564 Dick Ruthven .15 .06
❑ 565 Zane Smith .15 .06
❑ 566 Sid Bream .15 .06
❑ 567A J.Youngblood ERR Position P .15 .06
❑ 567B J.Youngblood COR Position IF .50 .20
❑ 568 Mario Ramirez .15 .06
❑ 569 Tom Runnells .15 .06
❑ 570 Rick Schu .15 .06
❑ 571 Bill Campbell .15 .06
❑ 572 Dickie Thon .15 .06
❑ 573 Al Holland .15 .06
❑ 574 Reid Nichols .15 .06
❑ 575 Bert Roberge .15 .06
❑ 576 Mike Flanagan .15 .06
❑ 577 Tim Leary .15 .06
❑ 578 Mike Laga .15 .06
❑ 579 Steve Lyons .15 .06
❑ 580 Phil Niekro .25 .10
❑ 581 Gilberto Reyes .15 .06
❑ 582 Jamie Easterly .15 .06
❑ 583 Mark Gubicza .15 .06
❑ 584 Stan Javier RC .50 .20
❑ 585 Bill Laskey .15 .06
❑ 586 Jeff Russell .15 .06
❑ 587 Dickie Noles .15 .06
❑ 588 Steve Farr .15 .06
❑ 589 Steve Ontiveros RC .15 .06
❑ 590 Mike Hargrove .15 .06
❑ 591 Marty Bystrom .15 .06
❑ 592 Franklin Stubbs .15 .06
❑ 593 Larry Herndon .15 .06
❑ 594 Bill Swaggerty .15 .06
❑ 595 Carlos Ponce .15 .06
❑ 596 Pat Perry .15 .06
❑ 597 Ray Knight .25 .10
❑ 598 Steve Lombardozzi .15 .06
❑ 599 Brad Havens .15 .06
❑ 600 Pat Clements .15 .06
❑ 601 Joe Niekro .15 .06
❑ 602 Hank Aaron Puzzle Card .75 .30
❑ 603 Dwayne Henry .15 .06
❑ 604 Mookie Wilson .25 .10
❑ 605 Buddy Biancalana .15 .06
❑ 606 Rance Mulliniks .15 .06
❑ 607 Alan Wiggins .15 .06
❑ 608 Joe Cowley .15 .06
❑ 609 Tom Seaver (Green borders on name) .50 .20
❑ 609B Tom Seaver (Yellow borders on name) 2.00 .80
❑ 610 Neil Allen .15 .06
❑ 611 Don Sutton .25 .10
❑ 612 Fred Toliver .15 .06
❑ 613 Jay Baller .15 .06
❑ 614 Marc Sullivan .15 .06
❑ 615 John Grubb .15 .06
❑ 616 Bruce Kison .15 .06
❑ 617 Bill Madlock .25 .10
❑ 618 Chris Chambliss .25 .10
❑ 619 Dave Stewart .25 .10
❑ 620 Tim Lollar .15 .06
❑ 621 Gary Lavelle .15 .06
❑ 622 Charles Hudson .15 .06
❑ 623 Joel Davis .15 .06
❑ 624 Joe Johnson .15 .06
❑ 625 Sid Fernandez .15 .06
❑ 626 Dennis Lamp .15 .06
❑ 627 Terry Harper .15 .06
❑ 628 Jack Lazorko .15 .06
❑ 629 Roger McDowell RC* .50 .20
❑ 630 Mark Funderburk .15 .06
❑ 631 Ed Lynch .15 .06
❑ 632 Rudy Law .15 .06
❑ 633 Roger Mason RC .15 .06
❑ 634 Mike Felder RC .15 .06
❑ 635 Ken Schrom .15 .06
❑ 636 Bob Ojeda .15 .06
❑ 637 Ed VandeBerg .15 .06
❑ 638 Bobby Meacham .15 .06
❑ 639 Cliff Johnson .15 .06
❑ 640 Garth Iorg .15 .06
❑ 641 Dan Driessen .15 .06
❑ 642 Mike Brown OF .15 .06
❑ 643 John Shelby .15 .06
❑ 644 Pete Rose RB .75 .30
❑ 645 Phil Niekro Joe Niekro .25 .10
❑ 646 Jesse Orosco .15 .06
❑ 647 Billy Beane RC 1.00 .40
❑ 648 Cesar Cedeno .25 .10
❑ 649 Bert Blyleven .25 .10
❑ 650 Max Venable .15 .06
❑ 651 Vince Coleman Willie McGee .15 .06
❑ 652 Calvin Schiraldi .15 .06
❑ 653 Pete Rose KING .75 .30
❑ 654 Dia. Kings CL 1-26 Unnumbered .15 .06
❑ 655A CL 1: 27-130 (Unnumbered) (45 Beane ERR) .15 .06
❑ 655B CL 1: 27-130 (Unnumbered) (45 Habyan COR) .15 .06
❑ 656 CL 2: 131-234 (Unnumbered) .15 .06
❑ 657 CL 3: 235-338 (Unnumbered) .15 .06
❑ 658 CL 4: 339-442 (Unnumbered) .15 .06
❑ 659 CL 5: 443-546 (Unnumbered) .15 .06
❑ 660 CL 6: 547-653 (Unnumbered) .15 .06

1986 Donruss Rookies

	Nm-Mt	Ex-Mt
COMP.FACT.SET (56)	50.00	20.00
❑ 1 Wally Joyner XRC	1.00	.40
❑ 2 Tracy Jones	.15	.06
❑ 3 Allan Anderson	.15	.06
❑ 4 Ed Correa	.15	.06
❑ 5 Reggie Williams	.15	.06

❑ 6 Charlie Kerfeld .15 .06
❑ 7 Andres Galarraga 1.50 .60
❑ 8 Bob Tewksbury XRC .50 .20
❑ 9 Al Newman .25 .10
❑ 10 Andres Thomas .15 .06
❑ 11 Barry Bonds XRC 40.00 16.00
❑ 12 Juan Nieves .15 .06
❑ 13 Mark Eichhorn .15 .06
❑ 14 Dan Plesac XRC .50 .20
❑ 15 Cory Snyder .15 .06
❑ 16 Kelly Gruber .15 .06
❑ 17 Kevin Mitchell XRC 1.00 .40
❑ 18 Steve Lombardozzi .15 .06
❑ 19 Mitch Williams XRC .50 .20
❑ 20 John Cerutti .15 .06
❑ 21 Todd Worrell .50 .20
❑ 22 Jose Canseco 1.50 .60
❑ 23 Pete Incaviglia XRC .50 .20
❑ 24 Jose Guzman .15 .06
❑ 25 Scott Bailes .15 .06
❑ 26 Greg Mathews .15 .06
❑ 27 Eric King .15 .06
❑ 28 Paul Assenmacher .50 .20
❑ 29 Jeff Sellers .15 .06
❑ 30 Bobby Bonilla XRC 1.00 .40
❑ 31 Doug Drabek XRC 1.00 .40
❑ 32 Will Clark UER 2.00 .80
(Listed as throwing right, should be left) XRC
❑ 33 Bip Roberts XRC .50 .20
❑ 34 Jim Deshaies XRC .15 .06
❑ 35 Mike LaValliere XRC .50 .20
❑ 36 Scott Bankhead .15 .06
❑ 37 Dale Sveum .15 .06
❑ 38 Bo Jackson XRC 2.00 .80
❑ 39 Robby Thompson XRC .50 .20
❑ 40 Eric Plunk .15 .06
❑ 41 Bill Bathe .15 .06
❑ 42 John Kruk XRC 1.50 .60
❑ 43 Andy Allanson .15 .06
❑ 44 Mark Portugal XRC .50 .20
❑ 45 Danny Tartabull .25 .10
❑ 46 Bob Kipper .15 .06
❑ 47 Gene Walter .15 .06
❑ 48 Rey Quinones UER .15 .06
(Misspelled Quinonez)
❑ 49 Bobby Witt XRC .50 .20
❑ 50 Bill Mooneyham .15 .06
❑ 51 John Cangelosi .15 .06
❑ 52 Ruben Sierra XRC 1.50 .60
❑ 53 Rob Woodward .15 .06
❑ 54 Ed Hearn .15 .06
❑ 55 Joel McKeon .15 .06
❑ 56 Checklist 1-56 .15 .06

1987 Donruss

	Nm-Mt	Ex-Mt
COMPLETE SET (660)	40.00	16.00
COMP.FACT.SET (660)	50.00	20.00
COMP.CLEMENTE PUZZLE	1.50	.60

❑ 1 Wally Joyner DK .40 .16
❑ 2 Roger Clemens DK 1.00 .40
❑ 3 Dale Murphy DK .25 .10
❑ 4 Darryl Strawberry DK .15 .06
❑ 5 Ozzie Smith DK .60 .24
❑ 6 Jose Canseco DK .40 .16
❑ 7 Charlie Hough DK .15 .06
❑ 8 Brook Jacoby DK .10 .04
❑ 9 Fred Lynn DK .15 .06
❑ 10 Rick Rhoden DK .10 .04
❑ 11 Chris Brown DK .10 .04
❑ 12 Von Hayes DK .10 .04
❑ 13 Jack Morris DK .15 .06
❑ 14A Kevin McReynolds DK .40 .16
ERR (Yellow strip missing on back)
❑ 14B Kevin McReynolds DK .10 .04
COR
❑ 15 George Brett DK 1.00 .40
❑ 16 Ted Higuera DK .10 .04
❑ 17 Hubie Brooks DK .10 .04
❑ 18 Mike Scott DK .15 .06
❑ 19 Kirby Puckett DK .40 .16
❑ 20 Dave Winfield DK .15 .06
❑ 21 Lloyd Moseby DK .10 .04
❑ 22A Eric Davis DK ERR .40 .16
(Yellow strip missing on back)
❑ 22B Eric Davis DK COR .25 .10
❑ 23 Jim Presley DK .10 .04
❑ 24 Keith Moreland DK .10 .04
❑ 25A Greg Walker DK ERR .40 .16
(Yellow strip missing on back)
❑ 25B Greg Walker DK COR .10 .04
❑ 26 Steve Sax DK .10 .04
❑ 27 DK Checklist 1-26 .10 .04
❑ 28 B.J. Surhoff RR RC .60 .24
❑ 29 Randy Myers RR RC .60 .24
❑ 30 Ken Gerhart RC .15 .06
❑ 31 Benito Santiago .15 .06
❑ 32 Greg Swindell RR RC .40 .16
❑ 33 Mike Birkbeck RC .15 .06
❑ 34 Terry Steinbach RR RC .60 .24
❑ 35 Bo Jackson RR RC 1.50 .60
❑ 36 Greg Maddux UER RC 10.00 4.00
middle name misspelled "Allen"
❑ 37 Jim Lindeman RC .15 .06
❑ 38 Devon White RR RC .60 .24
❑ 39 Eric Bell RC .15 .06
❑ 40 Willie Fraser RC .15 .06
❑ 41 Jerry Browne RR RC .15 .06
❑ 42 Chris James RR RC* .15 .06
❑ 43 Rafael Palmeiro RR RC 5.00 2.00
❑ 44 Pat Dodson RC .15 .06
❑ 45 Duane Ward RR RC* .40 .16
❑ 46 Mark McGwire RR 8.00 3.20
❑ 47 Bruce Fields UER RC .15 .06
(Photo actually Darnell Coles)
❑ 48 Eddie Murray .40 .16
❑ 49 Ted Higuera .10 .04
❑ 50 Kirk Gibson .15 .06
❑ 51 Oil Can Boyd .10 .04
❑ 52 Don Mattingly 1.25 .50
❑ 53 Pedro Guerrero .15 .06
❑ 54 George Brett 1.00 .40
❑ 55 Jose Rijo .15 .06
❑ 56 Tim Raines .15 .06
❑ 57 Ed Correa .10 .04
❑ 58 Mike Witt .10 .04
❑ 59 Greg Walker .10 .04
❑ 60 Ozzie Smith .60 .24
❑ 61 Glenn Davis .10 .04
❑ 62 Glenn Wilson .10 .04
❑ 63 Tom Browning .10 .04
❑ 64 Tony Gwynn .60 .24
❑ 65 R.J. Reynolds .10 .04
❑ 66 Will Clark RC 1.50 .60
❑ 67 Ozzie Virgil .10 .04
❑ 68 Rick Sutcliffe .15 .06
❑ 69 Gary Carter .15 .06
❑ 70 Mike Moore .10 .04
❑ 71 Bert Blyleven .15 .06
❑ 72 Tony Fernandez .10 .04
❑ 73 Kent Hrbek .15 .06
❑ 74 Lloyd Moseby .10 .04
❑ 75 Alvin Davis .10 .04
❑ 76 Keith Hernandez .15 .06
❑ 77 Ryne Sandberg .75 .30
❑ 78 Dale Murphy .25 .10
❑ 79 Sid Bream .10 .04
❑ 80 Chris Brown .10 .04
❑ 81 Steve Garvey .15 .06
❑ 82 Mario Soto .15 .06
❑ 83 Shane Rawley .10 .04
❑ 84 Willie McGee .15 .06
❑ 85 Jose Cruz .15 .06
❑ 86 Brian Downing .15 .06
❑ 87 Ozzie Guillen .10 .04
❑ 88 Hubie Brooks .10 .04
❑ 89 Cal Ripken 1.50 .60
❑ 90 Juan Nieves .10 .04
❑ 91 Lance Parrish .15 .06
❑ 92 Jim Rice .15 .06
❑ 93 Ron Guidry .15 .06
❑ 94 Fernando Valenzuela .15 .06
❑ 95 Andy Allanson .10 .04
❑ 96 Willie Wilson .15 .06
❑ 97 Jose Canseco .40 .16
❑ 98 Jeff Reardon .15 .06
❑ 99 Bobby Witt RC .40 .16
❑ 100 Checklist 28-133 .10 .04
❑ 101 Jose Guzman .10 .04
❑ 102 Steve Balboni .10 .04
❑ 103 Tony Phillips .10 .04
❑ 104 Brook Jacoby .10 .04
❑ 105 Dave Winfield .15 .06
❑ 106 Orel Hershiser .15 .06
❑ 107 Lou Whitaker .15 .06
❑ 108 Fred Lynn .15 .06
❑ 109 Bill Wegman .10 .04
❑ 110 Donnie Moore .10 .04
❑ 111 Jack Clark .15 .06
❑ 112 Bob Knepper .10 .04
❑ 113 Von Hayes .10 .04
❑ 114 Bip Roberts RC* .40 .16
❑ 115 Tony Pena .10 .04
❑ 116 Scott Garrelts .10 .04
❑ 117 Paul Molitor .25 .10
❑ 118 Darryl Strawberry .15 .06
❑ 119 Shawon Dunston .10 .04
❑ 120 Jim Presley .10 .04
❑ 121 Jesse Barfield .15 .06
❑ 122 Gary Gaetti .15 .06
❑ 123 Kurt Stillwell .10 .04
❑ 124 Joel Davis .10 .04
❑ 125 Mike Boddicker .10 .04
❑ 126 Robin Yount .60 .24
❑ 127 Alan Trammell .15 .06
❑ 128 Dave Righetti .15 .06
❑ 129 Dwight Evans .15 .06
❑ 130 Mike Scioscia .15 .06
❑ 131 Julio Franco .15 .06
❑ 132 Bret Saberhagen .15 .06
❑ 133 Mike Davis .10 .04
❑ 134 Joe Hesketh .10 .04
❑ 135 Wally Joyner RC .60 .24
❑ 136 Don Slaught .10 .04
❑ 137 Daryl Boston .10 .04
❑ 138 Nolan Ryan 2.00 .80
❑ 139 Mike Schmidt 1.00 .40
❑ 140 Tommy Herr .10 .04
❑ 141 Garry Templeton .15 .06
❑ 142 Kal Daniels .10 .04
❑ 143 Billy Sample .10 .04
❑ 144 Johnny Ray .10 .04
❑ 145 Rob Thompson RC* .40 .16
❑ 146 Bob Dernier .10 .04
❑ 147 Danny Tartabull .10 .04

❑ 148 Ernie Whitt .10 .04
❑ 149 Kirby Puckett .40 .16
❑ 150 Mike Young .10 .04
❑ 151 Ernest Riles .10 .04
❑ 152 Frank Tanana .15 .06
❑ 153 Rich Gedman .10 .04
❑ 154 Willie Randolph .15 .06
❑ 155 Bill Madlock .15 .06
❑ 156 Joe Carter .15 .06
❑ 157 Danny Jackson .10 .04
❑ 158 Carney Lansford .15 .06
❑ 159 Bryn Smith .10 .04
❑ 160 Gary Pettis .10 .04
❑ 161 Oddibe McDowell .10 .04
❑ 162 John Cangelosi .10 .04
❑ 163 Mike Scott .15 .06
❑ 164 Eric Show .10 .04
❑ 165 Juan Samuel .10 .04
❑ 166 Nick Esasky .10 .04
❑ 167 Zane Smith .10 .04
❑ 168 Mike C. Brown OF .10 .04
❑ 169 Keith Moreland .10 .04
❑ 170 John Tudor .15 .06
❑ 171 Ken Dixon .10 .04
❑ 172 Jim Gantner .10 .04
❑ 173 Jack Morris .15 .06
❑ 174 Bruce Hurst .10 .04
❑ 175 Dennis Rasmussen .10 .04
❑ 176 Mike Marshall .10 .04
❑ 177 Dan Quisenberry .10 .04
❑ 178 Eric Plunk .10 .04
❑ 179 Tim Wallach .10 .04
❑ 180 Steve Buechele .10 .04
❑ 181 Don Sutton .15 .06
❑ 182 Dave Schmidt .10 .04
❑ 183 Terry Pendleton .15 .06
❑ 184 Jim Deshaies RC * .15 .06
❑ 185 Steve Bedrosian .10 .04
❑ 186 Pete Rose 1.25 .50
❑ 187 Dave Dravecky .10 .04
❑ 188 Rick Reuschel .15 .06
❑ 189 Dan Gladden .10 .04
❑ 190 Rick Mahler .10 .04
❑ 191 Thad Bosley .10 .04
❑ 192 Ron Darling .15 .06
❑ 193 Matt Young .10 .04
❑ 194 Tom Brunansky .10 .04
❑ 195 Dave Stieb .15 .06
❑ 196 Frank Viola .15 .06
❑ 197 Tom Henke .10 .04
❑ 198 Karl Best .10 .04
❑ 199 Dwight Gooden .15 .06
❑ 200 Checklist 134-239 .10 .04
❑ 201 Steve Trout .10 .04
❑ 202 Rafael Ramirez .10 .04
❑ 203 Bob Walk .10 .04
❑ 204 Roger Mason .10 .04
❑ 205 Terry Kennedy .10 .04
❑ 206 Ron Oester .10 .04
❑ 207 John Russell .10 .04
❑ 208 Greg Mathews .10 .04
❑ 209 Charlie Kerfeld .10 .04
❑ 210 Reggie Jackson .25 .10
❑ 211 Floyd Bannister .10 .04
❑ 212 Vance Law .10 .04
❑ 213 Rich Bordi .10 .04
❑ 214 Dan Plesac .10 .04
❑ 215 Dave Collins .10 .04
❑ 216 Bob Stanley .10 .04
❑ 217 Joe Niekro .10 .04
❑ 218 Tom Niedenfuer .10 .04
❑ 219 Brett Butler .15 .06
❑ 220 Charlie Leibrandt .10 .04
❑ 221 Steve Ontiveros .10 .04
❑ 222 Tim Burke .10 .04
❑ 223 Curtis Wilkerson .10 .04
❑ 224 Pete Incaviglia RC * .40 .16
❑ 225 Lonnie Smith .10 .04
❑ 226 Chris Codiroli .10 .04
❑ 227 Scott Bailes .10 .04
❑ 228 Rickey Henderson .40 .16
❑ 229 Ken Howell .10 .04
❑ 230 Darnell Coles .10 .04
❑ 231 Don Aase .10 .04
❑ 232 Tim Leary .10 .04
❑ 233 Bob Boone .15 .06
❑ 234 Ricky Horton .10 .04
❑ 235 Mark Bailey .10 .04
❑ 236 Kevin Gross .10 .04
❑ 237 Lance McCullers .10 .04
❑ 238 Cecilio Guante .10 .04
❑ 239 Bob Melvin .10 .04
❑ 240 Billy Joe Robidoux .10 .04
❑ 241 Roger McDowell .10 .04
❑ 242 Leon Durham .10 .04
❑ 243 Ed Nunez .10 .04
❑ 244 Jimmy Key .15 .06
❑ 245 Mike Smithson .10 .04
❑ 246 Bo Diaz .10 .04
❑ 247 Carlton Fisk .25 .10
❑ 248 Larry Sheets .10 .04
❑ 249 Juan Castillo RC .15 .06
❑ 250 Eric King .10 .04
❑ 251 Doug Drabek RC .60 .24
❑ 252 Wade Boggs .25 .10
❑ 253 Mariano Duncan .10 .04
❑ 254 Pat Tabler .10 .04
❑ 255 Frank White .15 .06
❑ 256 Alfredo Griffin .10 .04
❑ 257 Floyd Youmans .10 .04
❑ 258 Rob Wilfong .10 .04
❑ 259 Pete O'Brien .10 .04
❑ 260 Tim Hulett .10 .04
❑ 261 Dickie Thon .10 .04
❑ 262 Darren Daulton .15 .06
❑ 263 Vince Coleman .10 .04
❑ 264 Andy Hawkins .10 .04
❑ 265 Eric Davis .25 .10
❑ 266 Andres Thomas .10 .04
❑ 267 Mike Diaz .10 .04
❑ 268 Chili Davis .15 .06
❑ 269 Jody Davis .10 .04
❑ 270 Phil Bradley .10 .04
❑ 271 George Bell .15 .06
❑ 272 Keith Atherton .10 .04
❑ 273 Storm Davis .10 .04
❑ 274 Rob Deer .10 .04
❑ 275 Walt Terrell .10 .04
❑ 276 Roger Clemens 1.00 .40
❑ 277 Mike Easler .10 .04
❑ 278 Steve Sax .10 .04
❑ 279 Andre Thornton .10 .04
❑ 280 Jim Sundberg .15 .06
❑ 281 Bill Bathe .10 .04
❑ 282 Jay Tibbs .10 .04
❑ 283 Dick Schofield .10 .04
❑ 284 Mike Mason .10 .04
❑ 285 Jerry Hairston .10 .04
❑ 286 Bill Doran .10 .04
❑ 287 Tim Flannery .10 .04
❑ 288 Gary Redus .10 .04
❑ 289 John Franco .15 .06
❑ 290 Paul Assenmacher .40 .16
❑ 291 Joe Orsulak .10 .04
❑ 292 Lee Smith .15 .06
❑ 293 Mike Laga .10 .04
❑ 294 Rick Dempsey .10 .04
❑ 295 Mike Felder .10 .04
❑ 296 Tom Brookens .10 .04
❑ 297 Al Nipper .10 .04
❑ 298 Mike Pagliarulo .10 .04
❑ 299 Franklin Stubbs .10 .04
❑ 300 Checklist 240-345 .10 .04
❑ 301 Steve Farr .10 .04
❑ 302 Bill Mooneyham .10 .04
❑ 303 Andres Galarraga .15 .06
❑ 304 Scott Fletcher .10 .04
❑ 305 Jack Howell .10 .04
❑ 306 Russ Morman .10 .04
❑ 307 Todd Worrell .10 .04
❑ 308 Dave Smith .10 .04
❑ 309 Jeff Stone .10 .04
❑ 310 Ron Robinson .10 .04
❑ 311 Bruce Bochy .10 .04
❑ 312 Jim Winn .10 .04
❑ 313 Mark Davis .10 .04
❑ 314 Jeff Dedmon .10 .04
❑ 315 Jamie Moyer RC 1.00 .40
❑ 316 Wally Backman .10 .04
❑ 317 Ken Phelps .10 .04
❑ 318 Steve Lombardozzi .10 .04
❑ 319 Rance Mulliniks .10 .04
❑ 320 Tim Laudner .10 .04
❑ 321 Mark Eichhorn .10 .04
❑ 322 Lee Guetterman .10 .04
❑ 323 Sid Fernandez .10 .04
❑ 324 Jerry Mumphrey .10 .04
❑ 325 David Palmer .10 .04
❑ 326 Bill Almon .10 .04
❑ 327 Candy Maldonado .10 .04
❑ 328 John Kruk RC 1.00 .40
❑ 329 John Denny .10 .04
❑ 330 Milt Thompson .10 .04
❑ 331 Mike LaValliere RC * .40 .16
❑ 332 Alan Ashby .10 .04
❑ 333 Doug Corbett .10 .04
❑ 334 Ron Karkovice RC .40 .16
❑ 335 Mitch Webster .10 .04
❑ 336 Lee Lacy .10 .04
❑ 337 Glenn Braggs RC .15 .06
❑ 338 Dwight Lowry .10 .04
❑ 339 Don Baylor .15 .06
❑ 340 Brian Fisher .10 .04
❑ 341 Reggie Williams .10 .04
❑ 342 Tom Candiotti .10 .04
❑ 343 Rudy Law .10 .04
❑ 344 Curt Young .10 .04
❑ 345 Mike Fitzgerald .10 .04
❑ 346 Ruben Sierra RC 1.00 .40
❑ 347 Mitch Williams RC * .40 .16
❑ 348 Jorge Orta .10 .04
❑ 349 Mickey Tettleton .10 .04
❑ 350 Ernie Camacho .10 .04
❑ 351 Ron Kittle .10 .04
❑ 352 Ken Landreaux .10 .04
❑ 353 Chet Lemon .15 .06
❑ 354 John Shelby .10 .04
❑ 355 Mark Clear .10 .04
❑ 356 Doug DeCinces .10 .04
❑ 357 Ken Dayley .10 .04
❑ 358 Phil Garner .15 .06
❑ 359 Steve Jeltz .10 .04
❑ 360 Ed Whitson .10 .04
❑ 361 Barry Bonds RC 15.00 6.00
❑ 362 Vida Blue .15 .06
❑ 363 Cecil Cooper .15 .06
❑ 364 Bob Ojeda .10 .04
❑ 365 Dennis Eckersley .25 .10
❑ 366 Mike Morgan .10 .04
❑ 367 Willie Upshaw .10 .04
❑ 368 Allan Anderson .10 .04
❑ 369 Bill Gullickson .10 .04
❑ 370 Bobby Thigpen RC .40 .16
❑ 371 Juan Beniquez .10 .04
❑ 372 Charlie Moore .10 .04
❑ 373 Dan Petry .10 .04
❑ 374 Rod Scurry .10 .04
❑ 375 Tom Seaver .25 .10
❑ 376 Ed VandeBerg .10 .04
❑ 377 Tony Bernazard .10 .04
❑ 378 Greg Pryor .10 .04
❑ 379 Dwayne Murphy .10 .04
❑ 380 Andy McGaffigan .10 .04
❑ 381 Kirk McCaskill .10 .04
❑ 382 Greg Harris .10 .04
❑ 383 Rich Dotson .10 .04
❑ 384 Craig Reynolds .10 .04
❑ 385 Greg Gross .10 .04
❑ 386 Tito Landrum .10 .04
❑ 387 Craig Lefferts .10 .04
❑ 388 Dave Parker .15 .06
❑ 389 Bob Horner .15 .06
❑ 390 Pat Clements .10 .04
❑ 391 Jeff Leonard .10 .04
❑ 392 Chris Speier .10 .04
❑ 393 John Moses .10 .04
❑ 394 Garth Iorg .10 .04
❑ 395 Greg Gagne .10 .04
❑ 396 Nate Snell .10 .04
❑ 397 Bryan Clutterbuck .10 .04
❑ 398 Darrell Evans .15 .06
❑ 399 Steve Crawford .10 .04
❑ 400 Checklist 346-451 .10 .04
❑ 401 Phil Lombardi .10 .04
❑ 402 Rick Honeycutt .10 .04
❑ 403 Ken Schrom .10 .04
❑ 404 Bud Black .10 .04
❑ 405 Donnie Hill .10 .04

❑ 406 Wayne Krenchicki .10 .04
❑ 407 Chuck Finley RC .60 .24
❑ 408 Toby Harrah .15 .06
❑ 409 Steve Lyons .10 .04
❑ 410 Kevin Bass .10 .04
❑ 411 Marvell Wynne .10 .04
❑ 412 Ron Roenicke .10 .04
❑ 413 Tracy Jones .10 .04
❑ 414 Gene Garber .10 .04
❑ 415 Mike Bielecki .10 .04
❑ 416 Frank DiPino .10 .04
❑ 417 Andy Van Slyke .15 .06
❑ 418 Jim Dwyer .10 .04
❑ 419 Ben Oglivie .15 .06
❑ 420 Dave Bergman .10 .04
❑ 421 Joe Sambito .10 .04
❑ 422 Bob Tewksbury RC * .40 .16
❑ 423 Len Matuszek .10 .04
❑ 424 Mike Kingery RC .15 .06
❑ 425 Dave Kingman .15 .06
❑ 426 Al Newman .10 .04
❑ 427 Gary Ward .10 .04
❑ 428 Ruppert Jones .10 .04
❑ 429 Harold Baines .15 .06
❑ 430 Pat Perry .10 .04
❑ 431 Terry Puhl .10 .04
❑ 432 Don Carman .10 .04
❑ 433 Eddie Milner .10 .04
❑ 434 LaMarr Hoyt .10 .04
❑ 435 Rick Rhoden .10 .04
❑ 436 Jose Uribe .10 .04
❑ 437 Ken Oberkfell .10 .04
❑ 438 Ron Davis .10 .04
❑ 439 Jesse Orosco .10 .04
❑ 440 Scott Bradley .10 .04
❑ 441 Randy Bush .10 .04
❑ 442 John Cerutti .10 .04
❑ 443 Roy Smalley .10 .04
❑ 444 Kelly Gruber .10 .04
❑ 445 Bob Kearney .10 .04
❑ 446 Ed Hearn .10 .04
❑ 447 Scott Sanderson .10 .04
❑ 448 Bruce Benedict .10 .04
❑ 449 Junior Ortiz .10 .04
❑ 450 Mike Aldrete .10 .04
❑ 451 Kevin McReynolds .10 .04
❑ 452 Rob Murphy .10 .04
❑ 453 Kent Tekulve .10 .04
❑ 454 Curt Ford .10 .04
❑ 455 Dave Lopes .15 .06
❑ 456 Bob Grich .15 .06
❑ 457 Jose DeLeon .10 .04
❑ 458 Andre Dawson .15 .06
❑ 459 Mike Flanagan .10 .04
❑ 460 Joey Meyer .15 .06
❑ 461 Chuck Cary .10 .04
❑ 462 Bill Buckner .15 .06
❑ 463 Bob Shirley .10 .04
❑ 464 Jeff Hamilton .10 .04
❑ 465 Phil Niekro .15 .06
❑ 466 Mark Gubicza .10 .04
❑ 467 Jerry Willard .10 .04
❑ 468 Bob Sebra .10 .04
❑ 469 Larry Parrish .10 .04
❑ 470 Charlie Hough .15 .06
❑ 471 Hal McRae .15 .06
❑ 472 Dave Leiper .10 .04
❑ 473 Mel Hall .10 .04
❑ 474 Dan Pasqua .10 .04
❑ 475 Bob Welch .15 .06
❑ 476 Johnny Grubb .10 .04
❑ 477 Jim Traber .10 .04
❑ 478 Chris Bosio RC .40 .16
❑ 479 Mark McLemore .15 .06
❑ 480 John Morris .10 .04
❑ 481 Billy Hatcher .10 .04
❑ 482 Dan Schatzeder .10 .04
❑ 483 Rich Gossage .15 .06
❑ 484 Jim Morrison .10 .04
❑ 485 Bob Brenly .10 .04
❑ 486 Bill Schroeder .10 .04
❑ 487 Mookie Wilson .15 .06
❑ 488 Dave Martinez RC .40 .16
❑ 489 Harold Reynolds .15 .06
❑ 490 Jeff Hearron .10 .04
❑ 491 Mickey Hatcher .10 .04
❑ 492 Barry Larkin RC 1.50 .60
❑ 493 Bob James .10 .04
❑ 494 John Habyan .10 .04
❑ 495 Jim Adduci .10 .04
❑ 496 Mike Heath .10 .04
❑ 497 Tim Stoddard .10 .04
❑ 498 Tony Armas .15 .06
❑ 499 Dennis Powell .10 .04
❑ 500 Checklist 452-557 .10 .04
❑ 501 Chris Bando .10 .04
❑ 502 David Cone RC 1.00 .40
❑ 503 Jay Howell .10 .04
❑ 504 Tom Foley .10 .04
❑ 505 Ray Chadwick .10 .04
❑ 506 Mike Loynd RC .15 .06
❑ 507 Neil Allen .10 .04
❑ 508 Danny Darwin .10 .04
❑ 509 Rick Schu .10 .04
❑ 510 Jose Oquendo .10 .04
❑ 511 Gene Walter .10 .04
❑ 512 Terry McGriff .10 .04
❑ 513 Ken Griffey .15 .06
❑ 514 Benny Distefano .10 .04
❑ 515 Terry Mulholland RC .40 .16
❑ 516 Ed Lynch .10 .04
❑ 517 Bill Swift .10 .04
❑ 518 Manny Lee .10 .04
❑ 519 Andre David .10 .04
❑ 520 Scott McGregor .10 .04
❑ 521 Rick Manning .10 .04
❑ 522 Willie Hernandez .10 .04
❑ 523 Marty Barrett .10 .04
❑ 524 Wayne Tolleson .10 .04
❑ 525 Jose Gonzalez RC .15 .06
❑ 526 Cory Snyder .10 .04
❑ 527 Buddy Biancalana .10 .04
❑ 528 Moose Haas .10 .04
❑ 529 Wilfredo Tejada .10 .04
❑ 530 Stu Cliburn .10 .04
❑ 531 Dale Mohorcic .10 .04
❑ 532 Ron Hassey .10 .04
❑ 533 Ty Gainey .10 .04
❑ 534 Jerry Royster .10 .04
❑ 535 Mike Maddux .10 .04
❑ 536 Ted Power .10 .04
❑ 537 Ted Simmons .15 .06
❑ 538 Rafael Belliard RC .40 .16
❑ 539 Chico Walker .10 .04
❑ 540 Bob Forsch .10 .04
❑ 541 John Stefero .10 .04
❑ 542 Dale Sveum .10 .04
❑ 543 Mark Thurmond .10 .04
❑ 544 Jeff Sellers .10 .04
❑ 545 Joel Skinner .10 .04
❑ 546 Alex Trevino .10 .04
❑ 547 Randy Kutcher .10 .04
❑ 548 Joaquin Andujar .15 .06
❑ 549 Casey Candaele .10 .04
❑ 550 Jeff Russell .10 .04
❑ 551 John Candelaria .10 .04
❑ 552 Joe Cowley .10 .04
❑ 553 Danny Cox .10 .04
❑ 554 Denny Walling .10 .04
❑ 555 Bruce Ruffin RC .15 .06
❑ 556 Buddy Bell .15 .06
❑ 557 Jimmy Jones RC .15 .06
❑ 558 Bobby Bonilla RC .60 .24
❑ 559 Jeff D. Robinson .10 .04
❑ 560 Ed Olwine .10 .04
❑ 561 Glenallen Hill RC .40 .16
❑ 562 Lee Mazzilli .15 .06
❑ 563 Mike G. Brown P .10 .04
❑ 564 George Frazier .10 .04
❑ 565 Mike Sharperson RC .15 .06
❑ 566 Mark Portugal RC * .40 .16
❑ 567 Rick Leach .10 .04
❑ 568 Mark Langston .10 .04
❑ 569 Rafael Santana .10 .04
❑ 570 Manny Trillo .10 .04
❑ 571 Cliff Speck .10 .04
❑ 572 Bob Kipper .10 .04
❑ 573 Kelly Downs RC .15 .06
❑ 574 Randy Asadoor .10 .04
❑ 575 Dave Magadan RC .40 .16
❑ 576 Marvin Freeman RC .15 .06
❑ 577 Jeff Lahti .10 .04
❑ 578 Jeff Calhoun .10 .04
❑ 579 Gus Polidor .10 .04
❑ 580 Gene Nelson .10 .04
❑ 581 Tim Teufel .10 .04
❑ 582 Odell Jones .10 .04
❑ 583 Mark Ryal .10 .04
❑ 584 Randy O'Neal .10 .04
❑ 585 Mike Greenwell RC .40 .16
❑ 586 Ray Knight .15 .06
❑ 587 Ralph Bryant .10 .04
❑ 588 Carmen Castillo .10 .04
❑ 589 Ed Wojna .10 .04
❑ 590 Stan Javier .10 .04
❑ 591 Jeff Musselman .10 .04
❑ 592 Mike Stanley RC .40 .16
❑ 593 Darrell Porter .10 .04
❑ 594 Drew Hall .10 .04
❑ 595 Rob Nelson .10 .04
❑ 596 Bryan Oelkers .10 .04
❑ 597 Scott Nielsen .10 .04
❑ 598 Brian Holton .10 .04
❑ 599 Kevin Mitchell RC * .60 .24
❑ 600 Checklist 558-660 .10 .04
❑ 601 Jackie Gutierrez .10 .04
❑ 602 Barry Jones .10 .04
❑ 603 Jerry Narron .10 .04
❑ 604 Steve Lake .10 .04
❑ 605 Jim Pankovits .10 .04
❑ 606 Ed Romero .10 .04
❑ 607 Dave LaPoint .10 .04
❑ 608 Don Robinson .10 .04
❑ 609 Mike Krukow .10 .04
❑ 610 Dave Valle RC ** .15 .06
❑ 611 Len Dykstra .15 .06
❑ 612 R.Clemente PUZ .50 .20
❑ 613 Mike Trujillo .10 .04
❑ 614 Damaso Garcia .10 .04
❑ 615 Neal Heaton .10 .04
❑ 616 Juan Berenguer .10 .04
❑ 617 Steve Carlton .15 .06
❑ 618 Gary Lucas .10 .04
❑ 619 Geno Petralli .10 .04
❑ 620 Rick Aguilera .10 .04
❑ 621 Fred McGriff .75 .30
❑ 622 Dave Henderson .10 .04
❑ 623 Dave Clark RC .15 .06
❑ 624 Angel Salazar .10 .04
❑ 625 Randy Hunt .10 .04
❑ 626 John Gibbons .10 .04
❑ 627 Kevin Brown RC 2.00 .80
❑ 628 Bill Dawley .10 .04
❑ 629 Aurelio Lopez .10 .04
❑ 630 Charles Hudson .10 .04
❑ 631 Ray Soff .10 .04
❑ 632 Ray Hayward .10 .04
❑ 633 Spike Owen .10 .04
❑ 634 Glenn Hubbard .10 .04
❑ 635 Kevin Elster RC .40 .16
❑ 636 Mike LaCoss .10 .04
❑ 637 Dwayne Henry .10 .04
❑ 638 Rey Quinones .10 .04
❑ 639 Jim Clancy .10 .04
❑ 640 Larry Andersen .10 .04
❑ 641 Calvin Schiraldi .10 .04
❑ 642 Stan Jefferson .10 .04
❑ 643 Marc Sullivan .10 .04
❑ 644 Mark Grant .10 .04
❑ 645 Cliff Johnson .10 .04
❑ 646 Howard Johnson .15 .06
❑ 647 Dave Sax .10 .04
❑ 648 Dave Stewart .15 .06
❑ 649 Danny Heep .10 .04
❑ 650 Joe Johnson .10 .04
❑ 651 Bob Brower .10 .04
❑ 652 Rob Woodward .10 .04
❑ 653 John Mizerock .10 .04
❑ 654 Tim Pyznarski .10 .04
❑ 655 Luis Aquino .10 .04
❑ 656 Mickey Brantley .10 .04
❑ 657 Doyle Alexander .10 .04
❑ 658 Sammy Stewart .10 .04
❑ 659 Jim Acker .10 .04
❑ 660 Pete Ladd .10 .04

1987 Donruss Rookies

	Nm-Mt	Ex-Mt
COMP.FACT.SET (56)	25.00	10.00
❑ 1 Mark McGwire	10.00	4.00
❑ 2 Eric Bell	.15	.06
❑ 3 Mark Williamson	.10	.04
❑ 4 Mike Greenwell	.40	.16
❑ 5 Ellis Burks XRC	.60	.24
❑ 6 DeWayne Buice	.10	.04
❑ 7 Mark McLemore	.25	.10
❑ 8 Devon White	.60	.24
❑ 9 Willie Fraser	.15	.06
❑ 10 Les Lancaster	.10	.04
❑ 11 Ken Williams XRC	.10	.04
❑ 12 Matt Nokes XRC	.40	.16
❑ 13 Jeff M. Robinson	.10	.04
❑ 14 Bo Jackson	1.00	.40
❑ 15 Kevin Seitzer XRC	.40	.16
❑ 16 Billy Ripken XRC	.40	.16
❑ 17 B.J. Surhoff	.60	.24
❑ 18 Chuck Crim	.10	.04
❑ 19 Mike Birkbeck	.15	.06
❑ 20 Chris Bosio	.40	.16
❑ 21 Les Straker	.10	.04
❑ 22 Mark Davidson	.10	.04
❑ 23 Gene Larkin XRC	.40	.16
❑ 24 Ken Gerhart	.10	.04
❑ 25 Luis Polonia XRC	.40	.16
❑ 26 Terry Steinbach	.60	.24
❑ 27 Mickey Brantley	.10	.04
❑ 28 Mike Stanley	.40	.16
❑ 29 Jerry Browne	.15	.06
❑ 30 Todd Benzinger XRC	.40	.16
❑ 31 Fred McGriff	1.50	.60
❑ 32 Mike Henneman XRC	.40	.16
❑ 33 Casey Candaele	.10	.04
❑ 34 Dave Magadan	.40	.16
❑ 35 David Cone	1.00	.40
❑ 36 Mike Jackson XRC	.40	.16
❑ 37 John Mitchell XRC	.15	.06
❑ 38 Mike Dunne	.10	.04
❑ 39 John Smiley XRC	.40	.16
❑ 40 Joe Magrane XRC	.15	.06
❑ 41 Jim Lindeman	.15	.06
❑ 42 Shane Mack	.10	.04
❑ 43 Stan Jefferson	.10	.04
❑ 44 Benito Santiago	.25	.10
❑ 45 Matt Williams XRC	2.50	1.00
❑ 46 Dave Meads	.10	.04
❑ 47 Rafael Palmeiro	5.00	2.00
❑ 48 Bill Long	.10	.04
❑ 49 Bob Brower	.10	.04
❑ 50 James Steels	.10	.04
❑ 51 Paul Noce	.10	.04
❑ 52 Greg Maddux	8.00	3.20
❑ 53 Jeff Musselman	.10	.04
❑ 54 Brian Holton	.10	.04
❑ 55 Chuck Jackson	.10	.04
❑ 56 Checklist 1-56	.10	.04

1987 Donruss Opening Day

	Nm-Mt	Ex-Mt
COMP.FACT. SET (272)	50.00	20.00

❑ 1 Doug DeCinces	.10	.04
❑ 2 Mike Witt	.10	.04
❑ 3 George Hendrick	.15	.06
❑ 4 Dick Schofield	.10	.04
❑ 5 Devon White	.60	.24
❑ 6 Butch Wynegar	.10	.04
❑ 7 Wally Joyner	.25	.10
❑ 8 Mark McLemore	.15	.06
❑ 9 Brian Downing	.15	.06
❑ 10 Gary Pettis	.10	.04
❑ 11 Bill Doran	.10	.04
❑ 12 Phil Garner	.15	.06
❑ 13 Jose Cruz	.15	.06
❑ 14 Kevin Bass	.10	.04
❑ 15 Mike Scott	.15	.06
❑ 16 Glenn Davis	.10	.04
❑ 17 Alan Ashby	.10	.04
❑ 18 Billy Hatcher	.10	.04
❑ 19 Craig Reynolds	.10	.04
❑ 20 Carney Lansford	.15	.06
❑ 21 Mike Davis	.10	.04
❑ 22 Reggie Jackson	.25	.10
❑ 23 Mickey Tettleton	.10	.04
❑ 24 Jose Canseco	.40	.16
❑ 25 Rob Nelson	.10	.04
❑ 26 Tony Phillips	.10	.04
❑ 27 Dwayne Murphy	.10	.04
❑ 28 Alfredo Griffin	.10	.04
❑ 29 Curt Young	.10	.04
❑ 30 Willie Upshaw	.10	.04
❑ 31 Mike Sharperson	.10	.04
❑ 32 Rance Mulliniks	.10	.04
❑ 33 Ernie Whitt	.10	.04
❑ 34 Jesse Barfield	.15	.06
❑ 35 Tony Fernandez	.10	.04
❑ 36 Lloyd Moseby	.10	.04
❑ 37 Jimmy Key	.15	.06
❑ 38 Fred McGriff	.75	.30
❑ 39 George Bell	.15	.06
❑ 40 Dale Murphy	.25	.10
❑ 41 Rick Mahler	.10	.04
❑ 42 Ken Griffey	.15	.06
❑ 43 Andres Thomas	.10	.04
❑ 44 Dion James	.10	.04
❑ 45 Ozzie Virgil	.10	.04
❑ 46 Ken Oberkfell	.10	.04
❑ 47 Gary Roenicke	.10	.04
❑ 48 Glenn Hubbard	.10	.04
❑ 49 Bill Schroeder	.10	.04
❑ 50 Greg Brock	.10	.04
❑ 51 Billy Joe Robidoux	.10	.04
❑ 52 Glenn Braggs	.15	.06
❑ 53 Jim Gantner	.10	.04
❑ 54 Paul Molitor	.25	.10
❑ 55 Dale Sveum	.10	.04
❑ 56 Ted Higuera	.10	.04
❑ 57 Rob Deer	.10	.04
❑ 58 Robin Yount	.60	.24
❑ 59 Jim Lindeman	.15	.06
❑ 60 Vince Coleman	.10	.04
❑ 61 Tommy Herr	.10	.04
❑ 62 Terry Pendleton	.15	.06
❑ 63 John Tudor	.15	.06
❑ 64 Tony Pena	.10	.04
❑ 65 Ozzie Smith	.60	.24
❑ 66 Tito Landrum	.10	.04
❑ 67 Jack Clark	.15	.06
❑ 68 Bob Dernier	.10	.04
❑ 69 Rick Sutcliffe	.15	.06
❑ 70 Andre Dawson	.15	.06
❑ 71 Keith Moreland	.10	.04
❑ 72 Jody Davis	.10	.04
❑ 73 Brian Dayett	.10	.04
❑ 74 Leon Durham	.10	.04
❑ 75 Ryne Sandberg	.75	.30
❑ 76 Shawon Dunston	.10	.04
❑ 77 Mike Marshall	.10	.04
❑ 78 Bill Madlock	.15	.06
❑ 79 Orel Hershiser	.15	.06
❑ 80 Mike Ramsey	.10	.04
❑ 81 Ken Landreaux	.10	.04
❑ 82 Mike Scioscia	.15	.06
❑ 83 Franklin Stubbs	.10	.04
❑ 84 Mariano Duncan	.10	.04
❑ 85 Steve Sax	.10	.04
❑ 86 Mitch Webster	.10	.04
❑ 87 Reid Nichols	.10	.04
❑ 88 Tim Wallach	.10	.04
❑ 89 Floyd Youmans	.10	.04
❑ 90 Andres Galarraga	.15	.06
❑ 91 Hubie Brooks	.10	.04
❑ 92 Jeff Reed	.10	.04
❑ 93 Alonzo Powell	.10	.04
❑ 94 Vance Law	.10	.04
❑ 95 Bob Brenly	.10	.04
❑ 96 Will Clark	2.00	.80
❑ 97 Chili Davis	.15	.06
❑ 98 Mike Krukow	.10	.04
❑ 99 Jose Uribe	.10	.04
❑ 100 Chris Brown	.10	.04
❑ 101 Robby Thompson	.40	.16
❑ 102 Candy Maldonado	.10	.04
❑ 103 Jeff Leonard	.10	.04
❑ 104 Tom Candiotti	.10	.04
❑ 105 Chris Bando	.10	.04
❑ 106 Cory Snyder	.10	.04
❑ 107 Pat Tabler	.10	.04
❑ 108 Andre Thornton	.10	.04
❑ 109 Joe Carter	.15	.06
❑ 110 Tony Bernazard	.10	.04
❑ 111 Julio Franco	.15	.06
❑ 112 Brook Jacoby	.10	.04
❑ 113 Brett Butler	.15	.06
❑ 114 Donell Nixon	.10	.04
❑ 115 Alvin Davis	.10	.04
❑ 116 Mark Langston	.10	.04
❑ 117 Harold Reynolds	.15	.06
❑ 118 Ken Phelps	.10	.04
❑ 119 Mike Kingery	.15	.06
❑ 120 Dave Valle	.15	.06
❑ 121 Rey Quinones	.10	.04
❑ 122 Phil Bradley	.10	.04
❑ 123 Jim Presley	.10	.04
❑ 124 Keith Hernandez	.15	.06
❑ 125 Kevin McReynolds	.10	.04
❑ 126 Rafael Santana	.10	.04
❑ 127 Bob Ojeda	.10	.04
❑ 128 Darryl Strawberry	.15	.06
❑ 129 Mookie Wilson	.15	.06
❑ 130 Gary Carter	.15	.06
❑ 131 Tim Teufel	.10	.04
❑ 132 Howard Johnson	.15	.06
❑ 133 Cal Ripken	1.50	.60
❑ 134 Rick Burleson	.10	.04
❑ 135 Fred Lynn	.15	.06
❑ 136 Eddie Murray	.40	.16
❑ 137 Ray Knight	.15	.06
❑ 138 Alan Wiggins	.10	.04
❑ 139 John Shelby	.10	.04
❑ 140 Mike Boddicker	.10	.04
❑ 141 Ken Gerhart	.10	.04
❑ 142 Terry Kennedy	.10	.04
❑ 143 Steve Garvey	.15	.06
❑ 144 Marvell Wynne	.10	.04
❑ 145 Kevin Mitchell	.25	.10
❑ 146 Tony Gwynn	.60	.24
❑ 147 Joey Cora	.40	.16
❑ 148 Benito Santiago	.15	.06
❑ 149 Eric Show	.10	.04
❑ 150 Garry Templeton	.15	.06
❑ 151 Carmelo Martinez	.10	.04
❑ 152 Von Hayes	.10	.04
❑ 153 Lance Parrish	.15	.06
❑ 154 Milt Thompson	.10	.04

No.	Card	Nm-Mt	Ex-Mt
❑ 155	Mike Easler	.10	.04
❑ 156	Juan Samuel	.10	.04
❑ 157	Steve Jeltz	.10	.04
❑ 158	Glenn Wilson	.10	.04
❑ 159	Shane Rawley	.10	.04
❑ 160	Mike Schmidt	1.00	.40
❑ 161	Andy Van Slyke	.15	.06
❑ 162	Johnny Ray	.10	.04
❑ 163A	Barry Bonds ERR (Photo actually Johnny Ray wearing a black shirt)	300.00	120.00
❑ 163B	Barry Bonds COR	20.00	8.00
❑ 164	Junior Ortiz	.10	.04
❑ 165	Rafael Belliard	.40	.16
❑ 166	Bob Patterson	.10	.04
❑ 167	Bobby Bonilla	.60	.24
❑ 168	Sid Bream	.10	.04
❑ 169	Jim Morrison	.10	.04
❑ 170	Jerry Browne	.15	.06
❑ 171	Scott Fletcher	.10	.04
❑ 172	Ruben Sierra	1.00	.40
❑ 173	Larry Parrish	.10	.04
❑ 174	Pete O'Brien	.10	.04
❑ 175	Pete Incaviglia	.40	.16
❑ 176	Don Slaught	.10	.04
❑ 177	Oddibe McDowell	.10	.04
❑ 178	Charlie Hough	.15	.06
❑ 179	Steve Buechele	.10	.04
❑ 180	Bob Stanley	.10	.04
❑ 181	Wade Boggs	.25	.10
❑ 182	Jim Rice	.15	.06
❑ 183	Bill Buckner	.15	.06
❑ 184	Dwight Evans	.15	.06
❑ 185	Spike Owen	.10	.04
❑ 186	Don Baylor	.15	.06
❑ 187	Marc Sullivan	.10	.04
❑ 188	Marty Barrett	.10	.04
❑ 189	Dave Henderson	.10	.04
❑ 190	Bo Diaz	.10	.04
❑ 191	Barry Larkin	2.00	.80
❑ 192	Kal Daniels	.10	.04
❑ 193	Terry Francona	.15	.06
❑ 194	Tom Browning	.10	.04
❑ 195	Ron Oester	.10	.04
❑ 196	Buddy Bell	.15	.06
❑ 197	Eric Davis	.25	.10
❑ 198	Dave Parker	.15	.06
❑ 199	Steve Balboni	.10	.04
❑ 200	Danny Tartabull	.10	.04
❑ 201	Ed Hearn	.10	.04
❑ 202	Buddy Biancalana	.10	.04
❑ 203	Danny Jackson	.10	.04
❑ 204	Frank White	.15	.06
❑ 205	Bo Jackson	2.00	.80
❑ 206	George Brett	1.00	.40
❑ 207	Kevin Seitzer	.15	.06
❑ 208	Willie Wilson	.15	.06
❑ 209	Orlando Mercado	.10	.04
❑ 210	Darrell Evans	.15	.06
❑ 211	Larry Herndon	.10	.04
❑ 212	Jack Morris	.15	.06
❑ 213	Chet Lemon	.15	.06
❑ 214	Mike Heath	.10	.04
❑ 215	Darnell Coles	.10	.04
❑ 216	Alan Trammell	.15	.06
❑ 217	Terry Harper	.10	.04
❑ 218	Lou Whitaker	.15	.06
❑ 219	Gary Gaetti	.15	.06
❑ 220	Tom Nieto	.10	.04
❑ 221	Kirby Puckett	.40	.16
❑ 222	Tom Brunansky	.10	.04
❑ 223	Greg Gagne	.10	.04
❑ 224	Dan Gladden	.10	.04
❑ 225	Mark Davidson	.10	.04
❑ 226	Bert Blyleven	.15	.06
❑ 227	Steve Lombardozzi	.10	.04
❑ 228	Kent Hrbek	.15	.06
❑ 229	Gary Redus	.10	.04
❑ 230	Ivan Calderon	.10	.04
❑ 231	Tim Hulett	.10	.04
❑ 232	Carlton Fisk	.25	.10
❑ 233	Greg Walker	.10	.04
❑ 234	Ron Karkovice	.40	.16
❑ 235	Ozzie Guillen	.10	.04
❑ 236	Harold Baines	.15	.06
❑ 237	Donnie Hill	.10	.04
❑ 238	Rich Dotson	.10	.04
❑ 239	Mike Pagliarulo	.10	.04
❑ 240	Joel Skinner	.10	.04
❑ 241	Don Mattingly	1.25	.50
❑ 242	Gary Ward	.10	.04
❑ 243	Dave Winfield	.15	.06
❑ 244	Dan Pasqua	.10	.04
❑ 245	Wayne Tolleson	.10	.04
❑ 246	Willie Randolph	.15	.06
❑ 247	Dennis Rasmussen	.10	.04
❑ 248	Rickey Henderson	.40	.16
❑ 249	Angels Logo	.05	.02
❑ 250	Astros Logo	.05	.02
❑ 251	A's Logo	.05	.02
❑ 252	Blue Jays Logo	.05	.02
❑ 253	Braves Logo	.05	.02
❑ 254	Brewers Logo	.05	.02
❑ 255	Cardinals Logo	.05	.02
❑ 256	Dodgers Logo	.05	.02
❑ 257	Expos Logo	.05	.02
❑ 258	Giants Logo	.05	.02
❑ 259	Indians Logo	.05	.02
❑ 260	Mariners Logo	.05	.02
❑ 261	Orioles Logo	.05	.02
❑ 262	Padres Logo	.05	.02
❑ 263	Phillies Logo	.05	.02
❑ 264	Pirates Logo	.05	.02
❑ 265	Rangers Logo	.05	.02
❑ 266	Red Sox Logo	.05	.02
❑ 267	Reds Logo	.05	.02
❑ 268	Royals Logo	.05	.02
❑ 269	Tigers Logo	.05	.02
❑ 270	Twins Logo	.05	.02
❑ 271	Chicago Logos	.05	.02
❑ 272	New York Logos	.05	.02

1989 Donruss

	Nm-Mt	Ex-Mt
COMPLETE SET (660)	25.00	10.00
COMP.FACT.SET (672)	25.00	10.00

No.	Card	Nm-Mt	Ex-Mt
❑ 1	Mike Greenwell DK	.05	.02
❑ 2	Bobby Bonilla DK DP	.10	.04
❑ 3	Pete Incaviglia DK	.05	.02
❑ 4	Chris Sabo DK DP	.10	.04
❑ 5	Robin Yount DK	.40	.16
❑ 6	Tony Gwynn DK DP	.15	.06
❑ 7	Carlton Fisk DK UER (OF on back)	.15	.06
❑ 8	Cory Snyder DK	.05	.02
❑ 9	David Cone DK UER ("hurdlers")	.10	.04
❑ 10	Kevin Seitzer DK	.05	.02
❑ 11	Rick Reuschel DK	.10	.04
❑ 12	Johnny Ray DK	.05	.02
❑ 13	Dave Schmidt DK	.05	.02
❑ 14	Andres Galarraga DK	.10	.04
❑ 15	Kirk Gibson DK	.10	.04
❑ 16	Fred McGriff DK	.15	.06
❑ 17	Mark Grace DK	.25	.10
❑ 18	Jeff M. Robinson DK	.05	.02
❑ 19	Vince Coleman DK DP	.05	.02
❑ 20	Dave Henderson DK	.05	.02
❑ 21	Harold Reynolds DK	.10	.04
❑ 22	Gerald Perry DK	.05	.02
❑ 23	Frank Viola DK	.10	.04
❑ 24	Steve Bedrosian DK	.05	.02
❑ 25	Glenn Davis DK	.05	.02
❑ 26	Don Mattingly DK UER (Doesn't mention Don's previous DK in 1985)	.30	.12
❑ 27	DK Checklist 1-26 DP	.05	.02
❑ 28	S.Alomar Jr. RR RC	.40	.16
❑ 29	Steve Searcy RR	.05	.02
❑ 30	Cameron Drew RR	.05	.02
❑ 31	Gary Sheffield RR RC	1.50	.60
❑ 32	Erik Hanson RR RC	.25	.10
❑ 33	Ken Griffey Jr. RR RC	8.00	3.20
❑ 34	Greg W. Harris RR RC	.10	.04
❑ 35	Gregg Jefferies RR	.05	.02
❑ 36	Luis Medina RR	.05	.02
❑ 37	Carlos Quintana RR RC	.10	.04
❑ 38	Felix Jose RR RC	.10	.04
❑ 39	Cris Carpenter RR RC*	.10	.04
❑ 40	Ron Jones RR	.10	.04
❑ 41	Dave West RR RC	.10	.04
❑ 42	R.Johnson RC RR UER Card says born in 1964 he was born in 1963	4.00	1.20
❑ 43	Mike Harkey RR RC	.10	.04
❑ 44	P.Harnisch RR DP RC	.25	.10
❑ 45	Tom Gordon RR DP RC	.40	.16
❑ 46	Gregg Olson RC RR DP	.25	.10
❑ 47	Alex Sanchez RR DP	.05	.02
❑ 48	Ruben Sierra	.05	.02
❑ 49	Rafael Palmeiro	.25	.10
❑ 50	Ron Gant	.10	.04
❑ 51	Cal Ripken	.75	.30
❑ 52	Wally Joyner	.10	.04
❑ 53	Gary Carter	.10	.04
❑ 54	Andy Van Slyke	.10	.04
❑ 55	Robin Yount	.40	.16
❑ 56	Pete Incaviglia	.05	.02
❑ 57	Greg Brock	.05	.02
❑ 58	Melido Perez	.05	.02
❑ 59	Craig Lefferts	.05	.02
❑ 60	Gary Pettis	.05	.02
❑ 61	Danny Tartabull	.05	.02
❑ 62	Guillermo Hernandez	.05	.02
❑ 63	Ozzie Smith	.40	.16
❑ 64	Gary Gaetti	.10	.04
❑ 65	Mark Davis	.05	.02
❑ 66	Lee Smith	.10	.04
❑ 67	Dennis Eckersley	.15	.06
❑ 68	Wade Boggs	.15	.06
❑ 69	Mike Scott	.10	.04
❑ 70	Fred McGriff	.15	.06
❑ 71	Tom Browning	.05	.02
❑ 72	Claudell Washington	.05	.02
❑ 73	Mel Hall	.05	.02
❑ 74	Don Mattingly	.60	.24
❑ 75	Steve Bedrosian	.05	.02
❑ 76	Juan Samuel	.05	.02
❑ 77	Mike Scioscia	.10	.04
❑ 78	Dave Righetti	.10	.04
❑ 79	Alfredo Griffin	.05	.02
❑ 80	Eric Davis UER (165 games in 1988, should be 135)	.10	.04
❑ 81	Juan Berenguer	.05	.02
❑ 82	Todd Worrell	.05	.02
❑ 83	Joe Carter	.10	.04
❑ 84	Steve Sax	.05	.02
❑ 85	Frank White	.10	.04
❑ 86	John Kruk	.10	.04
❑ 87	Rance Mulliniks	.05	.02
❑ 88	Alan Ashby	.05	.02
❑ 89	Charlie Leibrandt	.05	.02
❑ 90	Frank Tanana	.10	.04
❑ 91	Jose Canseco	.25	.10
❑ 92	Barry Bonds	1.25	.50
❑ 93	Harold Reynolds	.10	.04
❑ 94	Mark McLemore	.05	.02
❑ 95	Mark McGwire	1.00	.40
❑ 96	Eddie Murray	.25	.10
❑ 97	Tim Raines	.10	.04
❑ 98	Robby Thompson	.05	.02
❑ 99	Kevin McReynolds	.05	.02
❑ 100	Checklist 28-137	.05	.02
❑ 101	Carlton Fisk	.15	.06
❑ 102	Dave Martinez	.05	.02
❑ 103	Glenn Braggs	.05	.02

☐ 104 Dale Murphy .15 .06
☐ 105 Ryne Sandberg .40 .16
☐ 106 Dennis Martinez .10 .04
☐ 107 Pete O'Brien .05 .02
☐ 108 Dick Schofield .05 .02
☐ 109 Henry Cotto .05 .02
☐ 110 Mike Marshall .05 .02
☐ 111 Keith Moreland .05 .02
☐ 112 Tom Brunansky .05 .02
☐ 113 Kelly Gruber UER .05 .02
(Wrong birthdate)
☐ 114 Brook Jacoby .05 .02
☐ 115 Keith Brown .05 .02
☐ 116 Matt Nokes .05 .02
☐ 117 Keith Hernandez .10 .04
☐ 118 Bob Forsch .05 .02
☐ 119 Bert Blyleven UER .10 .04
(... 3000 strikeouts in
1987, should be 1986)
☐ 120 Willie Wilson .10 .04
☐ 121 Tommy Gregg .05 .02
☐ 122 Jim Rice .10 .04
☐ 123 Bob Knepper .05 .02
☐ 124 Danny Jackson .05 .02
☐ 125 Eric Plunk .05 .02
☐ 126 Brian Fisher .05 .02
☐ 127 Mike Pagliarulo .05 .02
☐ 128 Tony Gwynn .30 .12
☐ 129 Lance McCullers .05 .02
☐ 130 Andres Galarraga .10 .04
☐ 131 Jose Uribe .05 .02
☐ 132 Kirk Gibson UER .10 .04
(Wrong birthdate)
☐ 133 David Palmer .05 .02
☐ 134 R.J. Reynolds .05 .02
☐ 135 Greg Walker .05 .02
☐ 136 Kirk McCaskill UER .05 .02
(Wrong birthdate)
☐ 137 Shawon Dunston .05 .02
☐ 138 Andy Allanson .05 .02
☐ 139 Rob Murphy .05 .02
☐ 140 Mike Aldrete .05 .02
☐ 141 Terry Kennedy .05 .02
☐ 142 Scott Fletcher .05 .02
☐ 143 Steve Balboni .05 .02
☐ 144 Bret Saberhagen .10 .04
☐ 145 Ozzie Virgil .05 .02
☐ 146 Dale Sveum .05 .02
☐ 147 Darryl Strawberry .10 .04
☐ 148 Harold Baines .10 .04
☐ 149 George Bell .10 .04
☐ 150 Dave Parker .10 .04
☐ 151 Bobby Bonilla .10 .04
☐ 152 Mookie Wilson .10 .04
☐ 153 Ted Power .05 .02
☐ 154 Nolan Ryan 1.00 .40
☐ 155 Jeff Reardon .10 .04
☐ 156 Tim Wallach .05 .02
☐ 157 Jamie Moyer .10 .04
☐ 158 Rich Gossage .10 .04
☐ 159 Dave Winfield .10 .04
☐ 160 Von Hayes .05 .02
☐ 161 Willie McGee .10 .04
☐ 162 Rich Gedman .05 .02
☐ 163 Tony Pena .05 .02
☐ 164 Mike Morgan .05 .02
☐ 165 Charlie Hough .10 .04
☐ 166 Mike Stanley .05 .02
☐ 167 Andre Dawson .10 .04
☐ 168 Joe Boever .05 .02
☐ 169 Pete Stanicek .05 .02
☐ 170 Bob Boone .10 .04
☐ 171 Ron Darling .10 .04
☐ 172 Bob Walk .05 .02
☐ 173 Rob Deer .05 .02
☐ 174 Steve Buechele .05 .02
☐ 175 Ted Higuera .05 .02
☐ 176 Ozzie Guillen .05 .02
☐ 177 Candy Maldonado .05 .02
☐ 178 Doyle Alexander .05 .02
☐ 179 Mark Gubicza .05 .02
☐ 180 Alan Trammell .10 .04
☐ 181 Vince Coleman .05 .02
☐ 182 Kirby Puckett .25 .10
☐ 183 Chris Brown .05 .02
☐ 184 Marty Barrett .05 .02
☐ 185 Stan Javier .05 .02
☐ 186 Mike Greenwell .05 .02
☐ 187 Billy Hatcher .05 .02
☐ 188 Jimmy Key .10 .04
☐ 189 Nick Esasky .05 .02
☐ 190 Don Slaught .05 .02
☐ 191 Cory Snyder .05 .02
☐ 192 John Candelaria .05 .02
☐ 193 Mike Schmidt .50 .20
☐ 194 Kevin Gross .05 .02
☐ 195 John Tudor .10 .04
☐ 196 Neil Allen .05 .02
☐ 197 Orel Hershiser .10 .04
☐ 198 Kal Daniels .05 .02
☐ 199 Kent Hrbek .10 .04
☐ 200 Checklist 138-247 .05 .02
☐ 201 Joe Magrane .05 .02
☐ 202 Scott Bailes .05 .02
☐ 203 Tim Belcher .05 .02
☐ 204 George Brett .60 .24
☐ 205 Benito Santiago .10 .04
☐ 206 Tony Fernandez .05 .02
☐ 207 Gerald Young .05 .02
☐ 208 Bo Jackson .25 .10
☐ 209 Chet Lemon .10 .04
☐ 210 Storm Davis .05 .02
☐ 211 Doug Drabek .05 .02
☐ 212 Mickey Brantley UER .05 .02
(Photo actually
Nelson Simmons)
☐ 213 Devon White .10 .04
☐ 214 Dave Stewart .10 .04
☐ 215 Dave Schmidt .05 .02
☐ 216 Bryn Smith .05 .02
☐ 217 Brett Butler .10 .04
☐ 218 Bob Ojeda .05 .02
☐ 219 Steve Rosenberg .05 .02
☐ 220 Hubie Brooks .05 .02
☐ 221 B.J. Surhoff .10 .04
☐ 222 Rick Mahler .05 .02
☐ 223 Rick Sutcliffe .10 .04
☐ 224 Neal Heaton .05 .02
☐ 225 Mitch Williams .05 .02
☐ 226 Chuck Finley .10 .04
☐ 227 Mark Langston .05 .02
☐ 228 Jesse Orosco .05 .02
☐ 229 Ed Whitson .05 .02
☐ 230 Terry Pendleton .10 .04
☐ 231 Lloyd Moseby .05 .02
☐ 232 Greg Swindell .05 .02
☐ 233 John Franco .10 .04
☐ 234 Jack Morris .10 .04
☐ 235 Howard Johnson .10 .04
☐ 236 Glenn Davis .05 .02
☐ 237 Frank Viola .10 .04
☐ 238 Kevin Seitzer .05 .02
☐ 239 Gerald Perry .05 .02
☐ 240 Dwight Evans .10 .04
☐ 241 Jim Deshaies .05 .02
☐ 242 Bo Diaz .05 .02
☐ 243 Carney Lansford .10 .04
☐ 244 Mike LaValliere .05 .02
☐ 245 Rickey Henderson .25 .10
☐ 246 Roberto Alomar .25 .10
☐ 247 Jimmy Jones .05 .02
☐ 248 Pascual Perez .05 .02
☐ 249 Will Clark .25 .10
☐ 250 Fernando Valenzuela .10 .04
☐ 251 Shane Rawley .05 .02
☐ 252 Sid Bream .05 .02
☐ 253 Steve Lyons .05 .02
☐ 254 Brian Downing .10 .04
☐ 255 Mark Grace .25 .10
☐ 256 Tom Candiotti .05 .02
☐ 257 Barry Larkin .15 .06
☐ 258 Mike Krukow .05 .02
☐ 259 Billy Ripken .05 .02
☐ 260 Cecilio Guante .05 .02
☐ 261 Scott Bradley .05 .02
☐ 262 Floyd Bannister .05 .02
☐ 263 Pete Smith .05 .02
☐ 264 Jim Gantner UER .05 .02
(Wrong birthdate)
☐ 265 Roger McDowell .05 .02
☐ 266 Bobby Thigpen .05 .02
☐ 267 Jim Clancy .05 .02
☐ 268 Terry Steinbach .10 .04
☐ 269 Mike Dunne .05 .02
☐ 270 Dwight Gooden .10 .04
☐ 271 Mike Heath .05 .02
☐ 272 Dave Smith .05 .02
☐ 273 Keith Atherton .05 .02
☐ 274 Tim Burke .05 .02
☐ 275 Damon Berryhill .05 .02
☐ 276 Vance Law .05 .02
☐ 277 Rich Dotson .05 .02
☐ 278 Lance Parrish .10 .04
☐ 279 Denny Walling .05 .02
☐ 280 Roger Clemens .50 .20
☐ 281 Greg Mathews .05 .02
☐ 282 Tom Niedenfuer .05 .02
☐ 283 Paul Kilgus .05 .02
☐ 284 Jose Guzman .05 .02
☐ 285 Calvin Schiraldi .05 .02
☐ 286 Charlie Puleo UER .05 .02
(Career ERA 4.24,
should be 4.23)
☐ 287 Joe Orsulak .05 .02
☐ 288 Jack Howell .05 .02
☐ 289 Kevin Elster .05 .02
☐ 290 Jose Lind .05 .02
☐ 291 Paul Molitor .15 .06
☐ 292 Cecil Espy .05 .02
☐ 293 Bill Wegman .05 .02
☐ 294 Dan Pasqua .05 .02
☐ 295 Scott Garrelts UER .05 .02
(Wrong birthdate)
☐ 296 Walt Terrell .05 .02
☐ 297 Ed Hearn .05 .02
☐ 298 Lou Whitaker .10 .04
☐ 299 Ken Dayley .05 .02
☐ 300 Checklist 248-357 .05 .02
☐ 301 Tommy Herr .05 .02
☐ 302 Mike Brumley .05 .02
☐ 303 Ellis Burks .10 .04
☐ 304 Curt Young UER .05 .02
(Wrong birthdate)
☐ 305 Jody Reed .05 .02
☐ 306 Bill Doran .05 .02
☐ 307 David Wells .10 .04
☐ 308 Ron Robinson .05 .02
☐ 309 Rafael Santana .05 .02
☐ 310 Julio Franco .10 .04
☐ 311 Jack Clark .10 .04
☐ 312 Chris James .05 .02
☐ 313 Milt Thompson .05 .02
☐ 314 John Shelby .05 .02
☐ 315 Al Leiter .25 .10
☐ 316 Mike Davis .05 .02
☐ 317 Chris Sabo RC * .40 .16
☐ 318 Greg Gagne .05 .02
☐ 319 Jose Oquendo .05 .02
☐ 320 John Farrell .05 .02
☐ 321 Franklin Stubbs .05 .02
☐ 322 Kurt Stillwell .05 .02
☐ 323 Shawn Abner .05 .02
☐ 324 Mike Flanagan .05 .02
☐ 325 Kevin Bass .05 .02
☐ 326 Pat Tabler .05 .02
☐ 327 Mike Henneman .05 .02
☐ 328 Rick Honeycutt .05 .02
☐ 329 John Smiley .05 .02
☐ 330 Rey Quinones .05 .02
☐ 331 Johnny Ray .05 .02
☐ 332 Bob Welch .10 .04
☐ 333 Larry Sheets .05 .02
☐ 334 Jeff Parrett .05 .02
☐ 335 Rick Reuschel UER .10 .04
(For Don Robinson,
should be Jeff)
☐ 336 Randy Myers .10 .04
☐ 337 Ken Williams .05 .02
☐ 338 Andy McGaffigan .05 .02
☐ 339 Joey Meyer .05 .02
☐ 340 Dion James .05 .02
☐ 341 Les Lancaster .05 .02
☐ 342 Tom Foley .05 .02
☐ 343 Geno Petralli .05 .02
☐ 344 Dan Petry .05 .02
☐ 345 Alvin Davis .05 .02
☐ 346 Mickey Hatcher .05 .02
☐ 347 Marvell Wynne .05 .02

❑ 348 Danny Cox .05 .02
❑ 349 Dave Stieb .10 .04
❑ 350 Jay Bell .10 .04
❑ 351 Jeff Treadway .05 .02
❑ 352 Luis Salazar .05 .02
❑ 353 Len Dykstra .10 .04
❑ 354 Juan Agosto .05 .02
❑ 355 Gene Larkin .05 .02
❑ 356 Steve Farr .05 .02
❑ 357 Paul Assenmacher .05 .02
❑ 358 Todd Benzinger .05 .02
❑ 359 Larry Andersen .05 .02
❑ 360 Paul O'Neill .15 .06
❑ 361 Ron Hassey .05 .02
❑ 362 Jim Gott .05 .02
❑ 363 Ken Phelps .05 .02
❑ 364 Tim Flannery .05 .02
❑ 365 Randy Ready .05 .02
❑ 366 Nelson Santovenia .05 .02
❑ 367 Kelly Downs .05 .02
❑ 368 Danny Heep .05 .02
❑ 369 Phil Bradley .05 .02
❑ 370 Jeff D. Robinson .05 .02
❑ 371 Ivan Calderon .05 .02
❑ 372 Mike Witt .05 .02
❑ 373 Greg Maddux .50 .20
❑ 374 Carmen Castillo .05 .02
❑ 375 Jose Rijo .10 .04
❑ 376 Joe Price .05 .02
❑ 377 Rene Gonzales .05 .02
❑ 378 Oddibe McDowell .05 .02
❑ 379 Jim Presley .05 .02
❑ 380 Brad Wellman .05 .02
❑ 381 Tom Glavine .25 .10
❑ 382 Dan Plesac .05 .02
❑ 383 Wally Backman .05 .02
❑ 384 Dave Gallagher .05 .02
❑ 385 Tom Henke .05 .02
❑ 386 Luis Polonia .05 .02
❑ 387 Junior Ortiz .05 .02
❑ 388 David Cone .10 .04
❑ 389 Dave Bergman .05 .02
❑ 390 Danny Darwin .05 .02
❑ 391 Dan Gladden .05 .02
❑ 392 John Dopson .05 .02
❑ 393 Frank DiPino .05 .02
❑ 394 Al Nipper .05 .02
❑ 395 Willie Randolph .10 .04
❑ 396 Don Carman .05 .02
❑ 397 Scott Terry .05 .02
❑ 398 Rick Cerone .05 .02
❑ 399 Tom Pagnozzi .05 .02
❑ 400 Checklist 358-467 .05 .02
❑ 401 Mickey Tettleton .05 .02
❑ 402 Curtis Wilkerson .05 .02
❑ 403 Jeff Russell .05 .02
❑ 404 Pat Perry .05 .02
❑ 405 Jose Alvarez RC .10 .04
❑ 406 Rick Schu .05 .02
❑ 407 Sherman Corbett .05 .02
❑ 408 Dave Magadan .05 .02
❑ 409 Bob Kipper .05 .02
❑ 410 Don August .05 .02
❑ 411 Bob Brower .05 .02
❑ 412 Chris Bosio .05 .02
❑ 413 Jerry Reuss .05 .02
❑ 414 Atlee Hammaker .05 .02
❑ 415 Jim Walewander .05 .02
❑ 416 Mike Macfarlane RC * .25 .10
❑ 417 Pat Sheridan .05 .02
❑ 418 Pedro Guerrero .10 .04
❑ 419 Allan Anderson .05 .02
❑ 420 Mark Parent .05 .02
❑ 421 Bob Stanley .05 .02
❑ 422 Mike Gallego .05 .02
❑ 423 Bruce Hurst .05 .02
❑ 424 Dave Meads .05 .02
❑ 425 Jesse Barfield .10 .04
❑ 426 Rob Dibble RC .50 .20
❑ 427 Joel Skinner .05 .02
❑ 428 Ron Kittle .05 .02
❑ 429 Rick Rhoden .05 .02
❑ 430 Bob Dernier .05 .02
❑ 431 Steve Jeltz .05 .02
❑ 432 Rick Dempsey .05 .02
❑ 433 Roberto Kelly .05 .02
❑ 434 Dave Anderson .05 .02
❑ 435 Herm Winningham .05 .02
❑ 436 Al Newman .05 .02
❑ 437 Jose DeLeon .05 .02
❑ 438 Doug Jones .05 .02
❑ 439 Brian Holton .05 .02
❑ 440 Jeff Montgomery .05 .02
❑ 441 Dickie Thon .05 .02
❑ 442 Cecil Fielder .10 .04
❑ 443 John Fishel .05 .02
❑ 444 Jerry Don Gleaton .05 .02
❑ 445 Paul Gibson .05 .02
❑ 446 Walt Weiss .05 .02
❑ 447 Glenn Wilson .05 .02
❑ 448 Mike Moore .05 .02
❑ 449 Chili Davis .10 .04
❑ 450 Dave Henderson .05 .02
❑ 451 Jose Bautista RC .10 .04
❑ 452 Rex Hudler .05 .02
❑ 453 Bob Brenly .05 .02
❑ 454 Mackey Sasser .05 .02
❑ 455 Daryl Boston .05 .02
❑ 456 Mike R. Fitzgerald .05 .02
❑ 457 Jeffrey Leonard .05 .02
❑ 458 Bruce Sutter .10 .04
❑ 459 Mitch Webster .05 .02
❑ 460 Joe Hesketh .05 .02
❑ 461 Bobby Witt .05 .02
❑ 462 Stu Cliburn .05 .02
❑ 463 Scott Bankhead .05 .02
❑ 464 Ramon Martinez RC .25 .10
❑ 465 Dave Leiper .05 .02
❑ 466 Luis Alicea RC * .25 .10
❑ 467 John Cerutti .05 .02
❑ 468 Ron Washington .05 .02
❑ 469 Jeff Reed .05 .02
❑ 470 Jeff M. Robinson .05 .02
❑ 471 Sid Fernandez .05 .02
❑ 472 Terry Puhl .05 .02
❑ 473 Charlie Lea .05 .02
❑ 474 Israel Sanchez .05 .02
❑ 475 Bruce Benedict .05 .02
❑ 476 Oil Can Boyd .05 .02
❑ 477 Craig Reynolds .05 .02
❑ 478 Frank Williams .05 .02
❑ 479 Greg Cadaret .05 .02
❑ 480 Randy Kramer .05 .02
❑ 481 Dave Eiland .05 .02
❑ 482 Eric Show .05 .02
❑ 483 Garry Templeton .10 .04
❑ 484 Wallace Johnson .05 .02
❑ 485 Kevin Mitchell .10 .04
❑ 486 Tim Crews .05 .02
❑ 487 Mike Maddux .05 .02
❑ 488 Dave LaPoint .05 .02
❑ 489 Fred Manrique .05 .02
❑ 490 Greg Minton .05 .02
❑ 491 Doug Dascenzo UER .05 .02
(Photo actually Damon Berryhill)
❑ 492 Willie Upshaw .05 .02
❑ 493 Jack Armstrong RC * .25 .10
❑ 494 Kirt Manwaring .05 .02
❑ 495 Jeff Ballard .05 .02
❑ 496 Jeff Kunkel .05 .02
❑ 497 Mike Campbell .05 .02
❑ 498 Gary Thurman .05 .02
❑ 499 Zane Smith .05 .02
❑ 500 Checklist 468-577 DP .05 .02
❑ 501 Mike Birkbeck .05 .02
❑ 502 Terry Leach .05 .02
❑ 503 Shawn Hillegas .05 .02
❑ 504 Manny Lee .05 .02
❑ 505 Doug Jennings .05 .02
❑ 506 Ken Oberkfell .05 .02
❑ 507 Tim Teufel .05 .02
❑ 508 Tom Brookens .05 .02
❑ 509 Rafael Ramirez .05 .02
❑ 510 Fred Toliver .05 .02
❑ 511 Brian Holman RC * .10 .04
❑ 512 Mike Bielecki .05 .02
❑ 513 Jeff Pico .05 .02
❑ 514 Charles Hudson .05 .02
❑ 515 Bruce Ruffin .05 .02
❑ 516 L.McWilliams UER .05 .02
New Richland, should be North Richland
❑ 517 Jeff Sellers .05 .02
❑ 518 John Costello .05 .02
❑ 519 Brady Anderson RC .40 .16
❑ 520 Craig McMurtry .05 .02
❑ 521 Ray Hayward DP .05 .02
❑ 522 Drew Hall DP .05 .02
❑ 523 Mark Lemke DP RC .40 .16
❑ 524 Oswald Peraza DP .05 .02
❑ 525 Bryan Harvey DP RC * .25 .10
❑ 526 Rick Aguilera DP .05 .02
❑ 527 Tom Prince DP .05 .02
❑ 528 Mark Clear DP .05 .02
❑ 529 Jerry Browne DP .05 .02
❑ 530 Juan Castillo DP .05 .02
❑ 531 Jack McDowell DP .10 .04
❑ 532 Chris Speier DP .05 .02
❑ 533 Darrell Evans DP .10 .04
❑ 534 Luis Aquino DP .05 .02
❑ 535 Eric King DP .05 .02
❑ 536 Ken Hill DP RC .25 .10
❑ 537 Randy Bush DP .05 .02
❑ 538 Shane Mack DP .05 .02
❑ 539 Tom Bolton DP .05 .02
❑ 540 Gene Nelson DP .05 .02
❑ 541 Wes Gardner DP .05 .02
❑ 542 Ken Caminiti DP .10 .04
❑ 543 Duane Ward DP .05 .02
❑ 544 Norm Charlton DP RC .25 .10
❑ 545 Hal Morris DP RC .25 .10
❑ 546 Rich Yett DP .05 .02
❑ 547 H.Meulens DP RC .10 .04
❑ 548 Greg A. Harris DP .05 .02
❑ 549 Darren Daulton DP .10 .04
(Posing as right-handed hitter)
❑ 550 Jeff Hamilton DP .05 .02
❑ 551 Luis Aguayo DP .05 .02
❑ 552 Tim Leary DP .05 .02
(Resembles M.Marshall)
❑ 553 Ron Oester DP .05 .02
❑ 554 S.Lombardozzi DP .05 .02
❑ 555 Tim Jones DP .05 .02
❑ 556 Bud Black DP .05 .02
❑ 557 Alejandro Pena DP .05 .02
❑ 558 Jose DeJesus DP .05 .02
❑ 559 D.Rasmussen DP .05 .02
❑ 560 Pat Borders DP RC* .25 .10
❑ 561 Craig Biggio DP RC .75 .30
❑ 562 Luis DeLosSantos DP .05 .02
❑ 563 Fred Lynn DP .10 .04
❑ 564 Todd Burns DP .05 .02
❑ 565 Felix Fermin DP .05 .02
❑ 566 Darnell Coles DP .05 .02
❑ 567 Willie Fraser DP .05 .02
❑ 568 Glenn Hubbard DP .05 .02
❑ 569 Craig Worthington DP .05 .02
❑ 570 Johnny Paredes DP .05 .02
❑ 571 Don Robinson DP .05 .02
❑ 572 Barry Lyons DP .05 .02
❑ 573 Bill Long DP .05 .02
❑ 574 Tracy Jones DP .05 .02
❑ 575 Juan Nieves DP .05 .02
❑ 576 Andres Thomas DP .05 .02
❑ 577 Rolando Roomes DP .05 .02
❑ 578 Luis Rivera UER DP .05 .02
(Wrong birthdate)
❑ 579 Chad Kreuter DP RC .25 .10
❑ 580 Tony Armas DP .10 .04
❑ 581 Jay Buhner .10 .04
❑ 582 Ricky Horton DP .05 .02
❑ 583 Andy Hawkins DP .05 .02
❑ 584 Sil Campusano .05 .02
❑ 585 Dave Clark .05 .02
❑ 586 Van Snider DP .05 .02
❑ 587 Todd Frohwirth DP .05 .02
❑ 588 W.Spahn DP PUZ .15 .06
❑ 589 William Brennan .05 .02
❑ 590 German Gonzalez .05 .02
❑ 591 Ernie Whitt DP .05 .02
❑ 592 Jeff Blauser .05 .02
❑ 593 Spike Owen DP .05 .02
❑ 594 Matt Williams .25 .10
❑ 595 Lloyd McClendon DP .05 .02
❑ 596 Steve Ontiveros .05 .02
❑ 597 Scott Medvin .05 .02

❑ 598 Hipolito Pena DP .05 .02
❑ 599 Jerald Clark DP RC .10 .04
❑ 600A CL 578-660 DP .05 .02
635 Kurt Schilling
❑ 600B CL 578-660 DP .05 .02
635 Curt Schilling;
MVP's not listed
on checklist card
❑ 600C CL 578-660 DP .05 .02
635 Curt Schilling;
MVP's listed
following 660
❑ 601 Carmelo Martinez DP .05 .02
❑ 602 Mike LaCoss .05 .02
❑ 603 Mike Devereaux .05 .02
❑ 604 Alex Madrid DP .05 .02
❑ 605 Gary Redus DP .05 .02
❑ 606 Lance Johnson .05 .02
❑ 607 Terry Clark DP .05 .02
❑ 608 Manny Trillo DP .05 .02
❑ 609 Scott Jordan RC .25 .10
❑ 610 Jay Howell DP .05 .02
❑ 611 Francisco Melendez .05 .02
❑ 612 Mike Boddicker .05 .02
❑ 613 Kevin Brown DP .25 .10
❑ 614 Dave Valle .05 .02
❑ 615 Tim Laudner DP .05 .02
❑ 616 Andy Nezelek UER .05 .02
(Wrong birthdate)
❑ 617 Chuck Crim .05 .02
❑ 618 Jack Savage DP .05 .02
❑ 619 Adam Peterson .05 .02
❑ 620 Todd Stottlemyre .05 .02
❑ 621 Lance Blankenship RC .10 .04
❑ 622 Miguel Garcia DP .05 .02
❑ 623 Keith A. Miller DP .05 .02
❑ 624 Ricky Jordan DP RC* .25 .10
❑ 625 Ernest Riles DP .05 .02
❑ 626 John Moses DP .05 .02
❑ 627 Nelson Liriano DP .05 .02
❑ 628 Mike Smithson DP .05 .02
❑ 629 Scott Sanderson .05 .02
❑ 630 Dale Mohorcic .05 .02
❑ 631 Marvin Freeman DP .05 .02
❑ 632 Mike Young DP .05 .02
❑ 633 Dennis Lamp .05 .02
❑ 634 Dante Bichette DP RC .40 .16
❑ 635 Curt Schilling DP RC 5.00 2.00
❑ 636 Scott May DP .05 .02
❑ 637 Mike Schooler .05 .02
❑ 638 Rick Leach .05 .02
❑ 639 Tom Lampkin UER .05 .02
(Throws Left, should
be Throws Right)
❑ 640 Brian Meyer .05 .02
❑ 641 Brian Harper .05 .02
❑ 642 John Smoltz RC 1.00 .40
❑ 643 Jose Canseco .15 .06
(40/40 Club)
❑ 644 Bill Schroeder .05 .02
❑ 645 Edgar Martinez .25 .10
❑ 646 Dennis Cook RC .25 .10
❑ 647 Barry Jones .05 .02
❑ 648 Orel Hershiser .10 .04
(59 and Counting)
❑ 649 Rod Nichols .05 .02
❑ 650 Jody Davis .05 .02
❑ 651 Bob Milacki .05 .02
❑ 652 Mike Jackson .05 .02
❑ 653 Derek Lilliquist RC .10 .04
❑ 654 Paul Mirabella .05 .02
❑ 655 Mike Diaz .05 .02
❑ 656 Jeff Musselman .05 .02
❑ 657 Jerry Reed .05 .02
❑ 658 Kevin Blankenship .05 .02
❑ 659 Wayne Tolleson .05 .02
❑ 660 Eric Hetzel .05 .02
❑ BC Jose Canseco 2.00 .80
Blister Pack

1989 Donruss Rookies

	Nm-Mt	Ex-Mt
COMP.FACT.SET (56)	15.00	6.00

❑ 1 Gary Sheffield 1.50 .60

❑ 2 Gregg Jefferies .10 .04
❑ 3 Ken Griffey Jr. 5.00 3.20
❑ 4 Tom Gordon .25 .10
❑ 5 Billy Spiers RC .25 .10
❑ 6 Deion Sanders RC 1.00 .40
❑ 7 Donn Pall .05 .02
❑ 8 Steve Carter .05 .02
❑ 9 Francisco Oliveras .05 .02
❑ 10 Steve Wilson RC .10 .04
❑ 11 Bob Geren RC .05 .02
❑ 12 Tony Castillo RC .10 .04
❑ 13 Kenny Rogers RC .75 .30
❑ 14 Carlos Martinez RC .10 .04
❑ 15 Edgar Martinez .25 .10
❑ 16 Jim Abbott RC .50 .20
❑ 17 Torey Lovullo RC .10 .04
❑ 18 Mark Carreon .05 .02
❑ 19 Geronimo Berroa .05 .02
❑ 20 Luis Medina .05 .02
❑ 21 Sandy Alomar Jr. .15 .06
❑ 22 Bob Milacki .05 .02
❑ 23 Joe Girardi RC .40 .16
❑ 24 German Gonzalez .05 .02
❑ 25 Craig Worthington .05 .02
❑ 26 Jerome Walton RC .25 .10
❑ 27 Gary Wayne .05 .02
❑ 28 Tim Jones .05 .02
❑ 29 Dante Bichette .15 .06
❑ 30 Alexis Infante .05 .02
❑ 31 Ken Hill .25 .10
❑ 32 Dwight Smith RC .25 .10
❑ 33 Luis de los Santos .05 .02
❑ 34 Eric Yelding .05 .02
❑ 35 Gregg Olson .25 .10
❑ 36 Phil Stephenson .05 .02
❑ 37 Ken Patterson .05 .02
❑ 38 Rick Wrona .05 .02
❑ 39 Mike Brumley .05 .02
❑ 40 Cris Carpenter .05 .02
❑ 41 Jeff Brantley RC .25 .10
❑ 42 Ron Jones .05 .02
❑ 43 Randy Johnson 2.50 .80
❑ 44 Kevin Brown .25 .10
❑ 45 Ramon Martinez .10 .04
❑ 46 Greg W.Harris .05 .02
❑ 47 Steve Finley RC .50 .20
❑ 48 Randy Kramer .05 .02
❑ 49 Erik Hanson .10 .04
❑ 50 Matt Merullo .05 .02
❑ 51 Mike Devereaux .05 .02
❑ 52 Clay Parker .05 .02
❑ 53 Omar Vizquel RC .75 .30
❑ 54 Derek Lilliquist .05 .02
❑ 55 Junior Felix RC .10 .04
❑ 56 Checklist 1-56 .05 .02

1989 Donruss Baseball's Best

	Nm-Mt	Ex-Mt
COMP.FACT.SET (336)	100.00	40.00

❑ 1 Don Mattingly 1.50 .60
❑ 2 Tom Glavine .60 .24
❑ 3 Bert Blyleven .25 .10
❑ 4 Andre Dawson .25 .10
❑ 5 Pete O'Brien .15 .06
❑ 6 Eric Davis .25 .10

❑ 7 George Brett 1.50 .60
❑ 8 Glenn Davis .15 .06
❑ 9 Ellis Burks .25 .10
❑ 10 Kirk Gibson .25 .10
❑ 11 Carlton Fisk .40 .16
❑ 12 Andres Galarraga .25 .10
❑ 13 Alan Trammell .25 .10
❑ 14 Dwight Gooden .25 .10
❑ 15 Paul Molitor .40 .16
❑ 16 Roger McDowell .15 .06
❑ 17 Doug Drabek .15 .06
❑ 18 Kent Hrbek .25 .10
❑ 19 Vince Coleman .15 .06
❑ 20 Steve Sax .15 .06
❑ 21 Roberto Alomar .60 .24
❑ 22 Carney Lansford .25 .10
❑ 23 Will Clark .60 .24
❑ 24 Alvin Davis .15 .06
❑ 25 Bobby Thigpen .15 .06
❑ 26 Ryne Sandberg 1.00 .40
❑ 27 Devon White .25 .10
❑ 28 Mike Greenwell .15 .06
❑ 29 Dale Murphy .40 .16
❑ 30 Jeff Ballard .15 .06
❑ 31 Kelly Gruber .15 .06
❑ 32 Julio Franco .25 .10
❑ 33 Bobby Bonilla .25 .10
❑ 34 Tim Wallach .15 .06
❑ 35 Lou Whitaker .25 .10
❑ 36 Jay Howell .15 .06
❑ 37 Greg Maddux 1.25 .50
❑ 38 Bill Doran .15 .06
❑ 39 Danny Tartabull .15 .06
❑ 40 Darryl Strawberry .25 .10
❑ 41 Ron Darling .25 .10
❑ 42 Tony Gwynn .75 .30
❑ 43 Mark McGwire 2.50 1.00
❑ 44 Ozzie Smith 1.00 .40
❑ 45 Andy Van Slyke .25 .10
❑ 46 Juan Berenguer .15 .06
❑ 47 Von Hayes .15 .06
❑ 48 Tony Fernandez .15 .06
❑ 49 Eric Plunk .15 .06
❑ 50 Ernest Riles .15 .06
❑ 51 Harold Reynolds .25 .10
❑ 52 Andy Hawkins .15 .06
❑ 53 Robin Yount 1.00 .40
❑ 54 Danny Jackson .15 .06
❑ 55 Nolan Ryan 2.50 1.00
❑ 56 Joe Carter .25 .10
❑ 57 Jose Canseco .60 .24
❑ 58 Jody Davis .15 .06
❑ 59 Lance Parrish .25 .10
❑ 60 Mitch Williams .15 .06
❑ 61 Brook Jacoby .15 .06
❑ 62 Tom Browning .15 .06
❑ 63 Kurt Stillwell .15 .06
❑ 64 Rafael Ramirez .15 .06
❑ 65 Roger Clemens 1.25 .50
❑ 66 Mike Scioscia .25 .10
❑ 67 Dave Gallagher .15 .06
❑ 68 Mark Langston .15 .06
❑ 69 Chet Lemon .25 .10
❑ 70 Kevin McReynolds .15 .06
❑ 71 Rob Deer .15 .06
❑ 72 Tommy Herr .15 .06
❑ 73 Barry Bonds 3.00 1.20
❑ 74 Frank Viola .25 .10

❑ 75 Pedro Guerrero .25 .10
❑ 76 Dave Righetti UER .15 .06
(ML total of 7
wins incorrect)
❑ 77 Bruce Hurst .15 .06
❑ 78 Rickey Henderson .60 .24
❑ 79 Robby Thompson .15 .06
❑ 80 Randy Johnson 8.00 3.20
❑ 81 Harold Baines .25 .10
❑ 82 Calvin Schiraldi .15 .06
❑ 83 Kirk McCaskill .15 .06
❑ 84 Lee Smith .25 .10
❑ 85 John Smoltz 2.00 .80
❑ 86 Mickey Tettleton .15 .06
❑ 87 Jimmy Key .25 .10
❑ 88 Rafael Palmeiro .60 .24
❑ 89 Sid Bream .15 .06
❑ 90 Dennis Martinez .25 .10
❑ 91 Frank Tanana .25 .10
❑ 92 Eddie Murray .60 .24
❑ 93 Shawon Dunston .15 .06
❑ 94 Mike Scott .25 .10
❑ 95 Bret Saberhagen .25 .10
❑ 96 David Cone .25 .10
❑ 97 Kevin Elster .15 .06
❑ 98 Jack Clark .25 .10
❑ 99 Dave Stewart .25 .10
❑ 100 Jose Oquendo .15 .06
❑ 101 Jose Lind .15 .06
❑ 102 Gary Gaetti .25 .10
❑ 103 Ricky Jordan .50 .20
❑ 104 Fred McGriff .40 .16
❑ 105 Don Slaught .15 .06
❑ 106 Jose Uribe .15 .06
❑ 107 Jeffrey Leonard .15 .06
❑ 108 Lee Guetterman .15 .06
❑ 109 Chris Bosio .15 .06
❑ 110 Barry Larkin .40 .16
❑ 111 Ruben Sierra .15 .06
❑ 112 Greg Swindell .15 .06
❑ 113 Gary Sheffield 3.00 1.20
❑ 114 Lonnie Smith .15 .06
❑ 115 Chili Davis .25 .10
❑ 116 Damon Berryhill .15 .06
❑ 117 Tom Candiotti .15 .06
❑ 118 Kal Daniels .15 .06
❑ 119 Mark Gubicza .15 .06
❑ 120 Jim Deshaies .15 .06
❑ 121 Dwight Evans .25 .10
❑ 122 Mike Morgan .15 .06
❑ 123 Dan Pasqua .15 .06
❑ 124 Bryn Smith .15 .06
❑ 125 Doyle Alexander .15 .06
❑ 126 Howard Johnson .25 .10
❑ 127 Chuck Crim .15 .06
❑ 128 Darren Daulton .25 .10
❑ 129 Jeff Robinson .15 .06
❑ 130 Kirby Puckett .60 .24
❑ 131 Joe Magrane .15 .06
❑ 132 Jesse Barfield .25 .10
❑ 133 Mark Davis UER .15 .06
(Photo actually
Dave Leiper)
❑ 134 Dennis Eckersley .40 .16
❑ 135 Mike Krukow .15 .06
❑ 136 Jay Buhner .25 .10
❑ 137 Ozzie Guillen .15 .06
❑ 138 Rick Sutcliffe .25 .10
❑ 139 Wally Joyner .25 .10
❑ 140 Wade Boggs .40 .16
❑ 141 Jeff Treadway .15 .06
❑ 142 Cal Ripken 2.00 .80
❑ 143 Dave Stieb .25 .10
❑ 144 Pete Incaviglia .15 .06
❑ 145 Bob Walk .15 .06
❑ 146 Nelson Santovenia .15 .06
❑ 147 Mike Heath .15 .06
❑ 148 Willie Randolph .25 .10
❑ 149 Paul Kilgus .15 .06
❑ 150 Billy Hatcher .15 .06
❑ 151 Steve Farr .15 .06
❑ 152 Gregg Jefferies .15 .06
❑ 153 Randy Myers .25 .10
❑ 154 Garry Templeton .25 .10
❑ 155 Walt Weiss .15 .06
❑ 156 Terry Pendleton .25 .10
❑ 157 John Smiley .15 .06
❑ 158 Greg Gagne .15 .06
❑ 159 Len Dykstra .25 .10
❑ 160 Nelson Liriano .15 .06
❑ 161 Alvaro Espinoza .15 .06
❑ 162 Rick Reuschel .25 .10
❑ 163 Omar Vizquel UER 1.00 .40
(Photo actually
Darnell Coles)
❑ 164 Clay Parker .15 .06
❑ 165 Dan Plesac .15 .06
❑ 166 John Franco .25 .10
❑ 167 Scott Fletcher .15 .06
❑ 168 Cory Snyder .15 .06
❑ 169 Bo Jackson .60 .24
❑ 170 Tommy Gregg .15 .06
❑ 171 Jim Abbott 1.00 .40
❑ 172 Jerome Walton .50 .20
❑ 173 Doug Jones .15 .06
❑ 174 Todd Benzinger .15 .06
❑ 175 Frank White .25 .10
❑ 176 Craig Biggio 2.00 .80
❑ 177 John Dopson .15 .06
❑ 178 Alfredo Griffin .15 .06
❑ 179 Melido Perez .15 .06
❑ 180 Tim Burke .15 .06
❑ 181 Matt Nokes .15 .06
❑ 182 Gary Carter .25 .10
❑ 183 Ted Higuera .15 .06
❑ 184 Ken Howell .15 .06
❑ 185 Rey Quinones .15 .06
❑ 186 Wally Backman .15 .06
❑ 187 Tom Brunansky .15 .06
❑ 188 Steve Balboni .15 .06
❑ 189 Marvell Wynne .15 .06
❑ 190 Dave Henderson .15 .06
❑ 191 Don Robinson .15 .06
❑ 192 Ken Griffey Jr. 15.00 8.00
❑ 193 Ivan Calderon .15 .06
❑ 194 Mike Bielecki .15 .06
❑ 195 Johnny Ray .15 .06
❑ 196 Rob Murphy .15 .06
❑ 197 Andres Thomas .15 .06
❑ 198 Phil Bradley .15 .06
❑ 199 Junior Felix .25 .10
❑ 200 Jeff Russell .15 .06
❑ 201 Mike LaValliere .15 .06
❑ 202 Kevin Gross .15 .06
❑ 203 Keith Moreland .15 .06
❑ 204 Mike Marshall .15 .06
❑ 205 Dwight Smith .50 .20
❑ 206 Jim Clancy .15 .06
❑ 207 Kevin Seitzer .15 .06
❑ 208 Keith Hernandez .25 .10
❑ 209 Bob Ojeda .15 .06
❑ 210 Ed Whitson .15 .06
❑ 211 Tony Phillips .15 .06
❑ 212 Milt Thompson .15 .06
❑ 213 Randy Kramer .15 .06
❑ 214 Randy Bush .15 .06
❑ 215 Randy Ready .15 .06
❑ 216 Duane Ward .15 .06
❑ 217 Jimmy Jones .15 .06
❑ 218 Scott Garrelts .15 .06
❑ 219 Scott Bankhead .15 .06
❑ 220 Lance McCullers .15 .06
❑ 221 B.J. Surhoff .25 .10
❑ 222 Chris Sabo .75 .30
❑ 223 Steve Buechele .15 .06
❑ 224 Joel Skinner .15 .06
❑ 225 Orel Hershiser .25 .10
❑ 226 Derek Lilliquist .25 .10
❑ 227 Claudell Washington .15 .06
❑ 228 Lloyd McClendon .15 .06
❑ 229 Felix Fermin .15 .06
❑ 230 Paul O'Neill .40 .16
❑ 231 Charlie Leibrandt .15 .06
❑ 232 Dave Smith .15 .06
❑ 233 Bob Stanley .15 .06
❑ 234 Tim Belcher .15 .06
❑ 235 Eric King .15 .06
❑ 236 Spike Owen .15 .06
❑ 237 Mike Henneman .15 .06
❑ 238 Juan Samuel .15 .06
❑ 239 Greg Brock .15 .06
❑ 240 John Kruk .25 .10
❑ 241 Glenn Wilson .15 .06
❑ 242 Jeff Reardon .25 .10
❑ 243 Todd Worrell .15 .06
❑ 244 Dave LaPoint .15 .06
❑ 245 Walt Terrell .15 .06
❑ 246 Mike Moore .15 .06
❑ 247 Kelly Downs .15 .06
❑ 248 Dave Valle .15 .06
❑ 249 Ron Kittle .15 .06
❑ 250 Steve Wilson .25 .10
❑ 251 Dick Schofield .15 .06
❑ 252 Marty Barrett .15 .06
❑ 253 Dion James .15 .06
❑ 254 Bob Milacki .15 .06
❑ 255 Ernie Whitt .15 .06
❑ 256 Kevin Brown .60 .24
❑ 257 R.J. Reynolds .15 .06
❑ 258 Tim Raines .25 .10
❑ 259 Frank Williams .15 .06
❑ 260 Jose Gonzalez .15 .06
❑ 261 Mitch Webster .15 .06
❑ 262 Ken Caminiti .25 .10
❑ 263 Bob Boone .25 .10
❑ 264 Dave Magadan .15 .06
❑ 265 Rick Aguilera .15 .06
❑ 266 Chris James .15 .06
❑ 267 Bob Welch .25 .10
❑ 268 Ken Dayley .15 .06
❑ 269 Junior Ortiz .15 .06
❑ 270 Allan Anderson .15 .06
❑ 271 Steve Jeltz .15 .06
❑ 272 George Bell .25 .10
❑ 273 Roberto Kelly .15 .06
❑ 274 Brett Butler .25 .10
❑ 275 Mike Schooler .25 .10
❑ 276 Ken Phelps .15 .06
❑ 277 Glenn Braggs .15 .06
❑ 278 Jose Rijo .25 .10
❑ 279 Bobby Witt .15 .06
❑ 280 Jerry Browne .15 .06
❑ 281 Kevin Mitchell .25 .10
❑ 282 Craig Worthington .15 .06
❑ 283 Greg Minton .15 .06
❑ 284 Nick Esasky .15 .06
❑ 285 John Farrell .15 .06
❑ 286 Rick Mahler .15 .06
❑ 287 Tom Gordon .75 .30
❑ 288 Gerald Young .15 .06
❑ 289 Jody Reed .15 .06
❑ 290 Jeff Hamilton .15 .06
❑ 291 Gerald Perry .15 .06
❑ 292 Hubie Brooks .15 .06
❑ 293 Bo Diaz .15 .06
❑ 294 Terry Puhl .15 .06
❑ 295 Jim Gantner .15 .06
❑ 296 Jeff Parrett .15 .06
❑ 297 Mike Boddicker .15 .06
❑ 298 Dan Gladden .15 .06
❑ 299 Tony Pena .15 .06
❑ 300 Checklist Card .15 .06
❑ 301 Tom Henke .15 .06
❑ 302 Pascual Perez .15 .06
❑ 303 Steve Bedrosian .15 .06
❑ 304 Ken Hill .50 .20
❑ 305 Jerry Reuss .15 .06
❑ 306 Jim Eisenreich .15 .06
❑ 307 Jack Howell .15 .06
❑ 308 Rick Cerone .15 .06
❑ 309 Tim Leary .15 .06
❑ 310 Joe Orsulak .15 .06
❑ 311 Jim Dwyer .15 .06
❑ 312 Geno Petralli .15 .06
❑ 313 Rick Honeycutt .15 .06
❑ 314 Tom Foley .15 .06
❑ 315 Kenny Rogers 1.50 .60
❑ 316 Mike Flanagan .15 .06
❑ 317 Bryan Harvey .15 .06
❑ 318 Billy Ripken .15 .06
❑ 319 Jeff Montgomery .15 .06
❑ 320 Erik Hanson .50 .20
❑ 321 Brian Downing .25 .10
❑ 322 Gregg Olson .50 .20
❑ 323 Terry Steinbach .25 .10
❑ 324 Sammy Sosa 25.00 10.00
❑ 325 Gene Harris .15 .06
❑ 326 Mike Devereaux .15 .06

Card	Nm-Mt	Ex-Mt
❑ 327 Dennis Cook	.50	.20
❑ 328 David Wells	.25	.10
❑ 329 Checklist Card	.15	.06
❑ 330 Kirt Manwaring	.15	.06
❑ 331 Jim Presley	.15	.06
❑ 332 Checklist Card	.15	.06
❑ 333 Chuck Finley	.25	.10
❑ 334 Rob Dibble	1.00	.40
❑ 335 Cecil Espy	.15	.06
❑ 336 Dave Parker	.25	.10

1990 Donruss

	Nm-Mt	Ex-Mt
COMPLETE SET (716)	15.00	4.50
COMP.FACT.SET (728)	15.00	4.50
COMP.YAZ PUZZLE	1.00	.30

Card	Nm-Mt	Ex-Mt
❑ 1 Bo Jackson DK	.15	.04
❑ 2 Steve Sax DK	.05	.02
❑ 3A Ruben Sierra DK ERR (No small line on top border on card back)	.05	.02
❑ 3B Ruben Sierra DK COR	.05	.02
❑ 4 Ken Griffey Jr. DK	.40	.12
❑ 5 Mickey Tettleton DK	.05	.02
❑ 6 Dave Stewart DK	.05	.02
❑ 7 Jim Deshaies DK DP	.05	.02
❑ 8 John Smoltz DK	.25	.07
❑ 9 Mike Bielecki DK	.05	.02
❑ 10A Brian Downing DK ERR (Reverse negative on card front)	.15	.04
❑ 10B Brian Downing DK COR	.05	.02
❑ 11 Kevin Mitchell DK	.05	.02
❑ 12 Kelly Gruber DK	.05	.02
❑ 13 Joe Magrane DK	.05	.02
❑ 14 John Franco DK	.10	.03
❑ 15 Ozzie Guillen DK	.05	.02
❑ 16 Lou Whitaker DK	.05	.02
❑ 17 John Smiley DK	.05	.02
❑ 18 Howard Johnson DK	.05	.02
❑ 19 Willie Randolph DK	.10	.03
❑ 20 Chris Bosio DK	.05	.02
❑ 21 Tommy Herr DK DP	.05	.02
❑ 22 Dan Gladden DK	.05	.02
❑ 23 Ellis Burks DK	.10	.03
❑ 24 Pete O'Brien DK	.05	.02
❑ 25 Bryn Smith DK	.05	.02
❑ 26 Ed Whitson DK DP	.05	.02
❑ 27 DK Checklist 1-27 DP (Comments on Perez-Steele on back)	.05	.02
❑ 28 Robin Ventura RR	.25	.07
❑ 29 Todd Zeile RR	.10	.03
❑ 30 Sandy Alomar Jr.	.10	.03
❑ 31 Kent Mercker RR RC	.25	.07
❑ 32 B.McDonald RC UER Middle name Benard not Benjamin	.25	.07
❑ 33A J.Gonzalez RC ERR Reverse negative	2.00	.60
❑ 33B J.Gonzalez COR RC	1.50	.45
❑ 34 Eric Anthony RR RC	.10	.03
❑ 35 Mike Fetters RR RC	.25	.07
❑ 36 Marquis Grissom RC	.40	.12
❑ 37 Greg Vaughn RR	.05	.02
❑ 38 Brian DuBois RC	.10	.03
❑ 39 Steve Avery RR UER (Born in MI, not NJ)	.05	.02
❑ 40 Mark Gardner RR RC	.10	.03
❑ 41 Andy Benes	.10	.03
❑ 42 D.DeShields RR RC	.25	.07
❑ 43 Scott Coolbaugh RC	.10	.03
❑ 44 Pat Combs DP	.05	.02
❑ 45 Alex Sanchez DP	.05	.02
❑ 46 Kelly Mann DP RC	.10	.03
❑ 47 Julio Machado DP RC	.10	.03
❑ 48 Pete Incaviglia	.05	.02
❑ 49 Shawon Dunston	.05	.02
❑ 50 Jeff Treadway	.05	.02
❑ 51 Jeff Ballard	.05	.02
❑ 52 Claudell Washington	.05	.02
❑ 53 Juan Samuel	.05	.02
❑ 54 John Smiley	.05	.02
❑ 55 Rob Deer	.05	.02
❑ 56 Geno Petralli	.05	.02
❑ 57 Chris Bosio	.05	.02
❑ 58 Carlton Fisk	.15	.04
❑ 59 Kirt Manwaring	.05	.02
❑ 60 Chet Lemon	.05	.02
❑ 61 Bo Jackson	.25	.07
❑ 62 Doyle Alexander	.05	.02
❑ 63 Pedro Guerrero	.05	.02
❑ 64 Allan Anderson	.05	.02
❑ 65 Greg W. Harris	.05	.02
❑ 66 Mike Greenwell	.05	.02
❑ 67 Walt Weiss	.05	.02
❑ 68 Wade Boggs	.15	.04
❑ 69 Jim Clancy	.05	.02
❑ 70 Junior Felix	.05	.02
❑ 71 Barry Larkin	.15	.04
❑ 72 Dave LaPoint	.05	.02
❑ 73 Joel Skinner	.05	.02
❑ 74 Jesse Barfield	.05	.02
❑ 75 Tommy Herr	.05	.02
❑ 76 Ricky Jordan	.05	.02
❑ 77 Eddie Murray	.25	.07
❑ 78 Steve Sax	.05	.02
❑ 79 Tim Belcher	.05	.02
❑ 80 Danny Jackson	.05	.02
❑ 81 Kent Hrbek	.10	.03
❑ 82 Milt Thompson	.05	.02
❑ 83 Brook Jacoby	.05	.02
❑ 84 Mike Marshall	.05	.02
❑ 85 Kevin Seitzer	.05	.02
❑ 86 Tony Gwynn	.30	.09
❑ 87 Dave Stieb	.10	.03
❑ 88 Dave Smith	.05	.02
❑ 89 Bret Saberhagen	.10	.03
❑ 90 Alan Trammell	.10	.03
❑ 91 Tony Phillips	.05	.02
❑ 92 Doug Drabek	.05	.02
❑ 93 Jeffrey Leonard	.05	.02
❑ 94 Wally Joyner	.10	.03
❑ 95 Carney Lansford	.10	.03
❑ 96 Cal Ripken	.75	.23
❑ 97 Andres Galarraga	.10	.03
❑ 98 Kevin Mitchell	.05	.02
❑ 99 Howard Johnson	.05	.02
❑ 100A Checklist 28-129	.05	.02
❑ 100B Checklist 28-125	.05	.02
❑ 101 Melido Perez	.05	.02
❑ 102 Spike Owen	.05	.02
❑ 103 Paul Molitor	.15	.04
❑ 104 Geronimo Berroa	.05	.02
❑ 105 Ryne Sandberg	.40	.12
❑ 106 Bryn Smith	.05	.02
❑ 107 Steve Buechele	.05	.02
❑ 108 Jim Abbott	.15	.04
❑ 109 Alvin Davis	.05	.02
❑ 110 Lee Smith	.10	.03
❑ 111 Roberto Alomar	.15	.04
❑ 112 Rick Reuschel	.05	.02
❑ 113A Kelly Gruber ERR (Born 2/22)	.05	.02
❑ 113B Kelly Gruber COR (Born 2/26; corrected in factory sets)	.05	.02
❑ 114 Joe Carter	.10	.03
❑ 115 Jose Rijo	.05	.02
❑ 116 Greg Minton	.05	.02
❑ 117 Bob Ojeda	.05	.02
❑ 118 Glenn Davis	.05	.02
❑ 119 Jeff Reardon	.10	.03
❑ 120 Kurt Stillwell	.05	.02
❑ 121 John Smoltz	.25	.07
❑ 122 Dwight Evans	.10	.03
❑ 123 Eric Yelding	.05	.02
❑ 124 John Franco	.10	.03
❑ 125 Jose Canseco	.25	.07
❑ 126 Barry Bonds	.60	.18
❑ 127 Lee Guetterman	.05	.02
❑ 128 Jack Clark	.10	.03
❑ 129 Dave Valle	.05	.02
❑ 130 Hubie Brooks	.05	.02
❑ 131 Ernest Riles	.05	.02
❑ 132 Mike Morgan	.05	.02
❑ 133 Steve Jeltz	.05	.02
❑ 134 Jeff D. Robinson	.05	.02
❑ 135 Ozzie Guillen	.05	.02
❑ 136 Chili Davis	.10	.03
❑ 137 Mitch Webster	.05	.02
❑ 138 Jerry Browne	.05	.02
❑ 139 Bo Diaz	.05	.02
❑ 140 Robby Thompson	.05	.02
❑ 141 Craig Worthington	.05	.02
❑ 142 Julio Franco	.10	.03
❑ 143 Brian Holman	.05	.02
❑ 144 George Brett	.60	.18
❑ 145 Tom Glavine	.15	.04
❑ 146 Robin Yount	.40	.12
❑ 147 Gary Carter	.10	.03
❑ 148 Ron Kittle	.05	.02
❑ 149 Tony Fernandez	.05	.02
❑ 150 Dave Stewart	.10	.03
❑ 151 Gary Gaetti	.10	.03
❑ 152 Kevin Elster	.05	.02
❑ 153 Gerald Perry	.05	.02
❑ 154 Jesse Orosco	.05	.02
❑ 155 Wally Backman	.05	.02
❑ 156 Dennis Martinez	.10	.03
❑ 157 Rick Sutcliffe	.10	.03
❑ 158 Greg Maddux	.40	.12
❑ 159 Andy Hawkins	.05	.02
❑ 160 John Kruk	.10	.03
❑ 161 Jose Oquendo	.05	.02
❑ 162 John Dopson	.05	.02
❑ 163 Joe Magrane	.05	.02
❑ 164 Bill Ripken	.05	.02
❑ 165 Fred Manrique	.05	.02
❑ 166 Nolan Ryan UER (Did not lead NL in K's in '89 as he was in AL in '89)	1.00	.30
❑ 167 Damon Berryhill	.05	.02
❑ 168 Dale Murphy	.25	.07
❑ 169 Mickey Tettleton	.05	.02
❑ 170A Kirk McCaskill ERR (Born 4/19)	.05	.02
❑ 170B Kirk McCaskill COR (Born 4/9; corrected in factory sets)	.05	.02
❑ 171 Dwight Gooden	.10	.03
❑ 172 Jose Lind	.05	.02
❑ 173 B.J. Surhoff	.10	.03
❑ 174 Ruben Sierra	.05	.02
❑ 175 Dan Plesac	.05	.02
❑ 176 Dan Pasqua	.05	.02
❑ 177 Kelly Downs	.05	.02
❑ 178 Matt Nokes	.05	.02
❑ 179 Luis Aquino	.05	.02
❑ 180 Frank Tanana	.05	.02
❑ 181 Tony Pena	.05	.02
❑ 182 Dan Gladden	.05	.02
❑ 183 Bruce Hurst	.05	.02
❑ 184 Roger Clemens	.50	.15
❑ 185 Mark McGwire	.60	.18
❑ 186 Rob Murphy	.05	.02
❑ 187 Jim Deshaies	.05	.02
❑ 188 Fred McGriff	.25	.07
❑ 189 Rob Dibble	.10	.03
❑ 190 Don Mattingly	.60	.18
❑ 191 Felix Fermin	.05	.02
❑ 192 Roberto Kelly	.05	.02
❑ 193 Dennis Cook	.05	.02
❑ 194 Darren Daulton	.10	.03
❑ 195 Alfredo Griffin	.05	.02
❑ 196 Eric Plunk	.05	.02

197 Orel Hershiser	.10	.03
198 Paul O'Neill	.15	.04
199 Randy Bush	.05	.02
200A Checklist 130-231	.05	.02
200B Checklist 126-223	.05	.02
201 Ozzie Smith	.40	.12
202 Pete O'Brien	.05	.02
203 Jay Howell	.05	.02
204 Mark Gubicza	.05	.02
205 Ed Whitson	.05	.02
206 George Bell	.05	.02
207 Mike Scott	.05	.02
208 Charlie Leibrandt	.05	.02
209 Mike Heath	.05	.02
210 Dennis Eckersley	.10	.03
211 Mike LaValliere	.05	.02
212 Darnell Coles	.05	.02
213 Lance Parrish	.05	.02
214 Mike Moore	.05	.02
215 Steve Finley	.10	.03
216 Tim Raines	.10	.03
217A Scott Garrelts ERR (Born 10/20)	.05	.02
217B Scott Garrelts COR (Born 10/30; corrected in factory sets)	.05	.02
218 Kevin McReynolds	.05	.02
219 Dave Gallagher	.05	.02
220 Tim Wallach	.05	.02
221 Chuck Crim	.05	.02
222 Lonnie Smith	.05	.02
223 Andre Dawson	.10	.03
224 Nelson Santovenia	.05	.02
225 Rafael Palmeiro	.15	.04
226 Devon White	.10	.03
227 Harold Reynolds	.10	.03
228 Ellis Burks	.15	.04
229 Mark Parent	.05	.02
230 Will Clark	.25	.07
231 Jimmy Key	.10	.03
232 John Farrell	.05	.02
233 Eric Davis	.10	.03
234 Johnny Ray	.05	.02
235 Darryl Strawberry	.10	.03
236 Bill Doran	.05	.02
237 Greg Gagne	.05	.02
238 Jim Eisenreich	.05	.02
239 Tommy Gregg	.05	.02
240 Marty Barrett	.05	.02
241 Rafael Ramirez	.05	.02
242 Chris Sabo	.05	.02
243 Dave Henderson	.05	.02
244 Andy Van Slyke	.10	.03
245 Alvaro Espinoza	.05	.02
246 Garry Templeton	.05	.02
247 Gene Harris	.05	.02
248 Kevin Gross	.05	.02
249 Brett Butler	.10	.03
250 Willie Randolph	.10	.03
251 Roger McDowell	.05	.02
252 Rafael Belliard	.05	.02
253 Steve Rosenberg	.05	.02
254 Jack Howell	.05	.02
255 Marvell Wynne	.05	.02
256 Tom Candiotti	.05	.02
257 Todd Benzinger	.05	.02
258 Don Robinson	.05	.02
259 Phil Bradley	.05	.02
260 Cecil Espy	.05	.02
261 Scott Bankhead	.05	.02
262 Frank White	.10	.03
263 Andres Thomas	.05	.02
264 Glenn Braggs	.05	.02
265 David Cone	.10	.03
266 Bobby Thigpen	.05	.02
267 Nelson Liriano	.05	.02
268 Terry Steinbach	.05	.02
269 Kirby Puckett UER (Back doesn't consider Joe Torre's .363 in '71)	.25	.07
270 Gregg Jefferies	.10	.03
271 Jeff Blauser	.05	.02
272 Cory Snyder	.05	.02
273 Roy Smith	.05	.02
274 Tom Foley	.05	.02
275 Mitch Williams	.05	.02

276 Paul Kilgus	.05	.02
277 Don Slaught	.05	.02
278 Von Hayes	.05	.02
279 Vince Coleman	.05	.02
280 Mike Boddicker	.05	.02
281 Ken Dayley	.05	.02
282 Mike Devereaux	.05	.02
283 Kenny Rogers	.10	.03
284 Jeff Russell	.05	.02
285 Jerome Walton	.05	.02
286 Derek Lilliquist	.05	.02
287 Joe Orsulak	.05	.02
288 Dick Schofield	.05	.02
289 Ron Darling	.05	.02
290 Bobby Bonilla	.10	.03
291 Jim Gantner	.05	.02
292 Bobby Witt	.05	.02
293 Greg Brock	.05	.02
294 Ivan Calderon	.05	.02
295 Steve Bedrosian	.05	.02
296 Mike Henneman	.05	.02
297 Tom Gordon	.10	.03
298 Lou Whitaker	.10	.03
299 Terry Pendleton	.10	.03
300A Checklist 232-333	.05	.02
300B Checklist 224-321	.05	.02
301 Juan Berenguer	.05	.02
302 Mark Davis	.05	.02
303 Nick Esasky	.05	.02
304 Rickey Henderson	.25	.07
305 Rick Cerone	.05	.02
306 Craig Biggio	.15	.04
307 Duane Ward	.05	.02
308 Tom Browning	.05	.02
309 Walt Terrell	.05	.02
310 Greg Swindell	.05	.02
311 Dave Righetti	.05	.02
312 Mike Maddux	.05	.02
313 Len Dykstra	.10	.03
314 Jose Gonzalez	.05	.02
315 Steve Balboni	.05	.02
316 Mike Scioscia	.05	.02
317 Ron Oester	.05	.02
318 Gary Wayne	.05	.02
319 Todd Worrell	.05	.02
320 Doug Jones	.05	.02
321 Jeff Hamilton	.05	.02
322 Danny Tartabull	.05	.02
323 Chris James	.05	.02
324 Mike Flanagan	.05	.02
325 Gerald Young	.05	.02
326 Bob Boone	.10	.03
327 Frank Williams	.05	.02
328 Dave Parker	.10	.03
329 Sid Bream	.05	.02
330 Mike Schooler	.05	.02
331 Bert Blyleven	.10	.03
332 Bob Welch	.05	.02
333 Bob Milacki	.05	.02
334 Tim Burke	.05	.02
335 Jose Uribe	.05	.02
336 Randy Myers	.10	.03
337 Eric King	.05	.02
338 Mark Langston	.05	.02
339 Teddy Higuera	.05	.02
340 Oddibe McDowell	.05	.02
341 Lloyd McClendon	.05	.02
342 Pascual Perez	.05	.02
343 Kevin Brown UER (Signed is misspelled as signeed on back)	.10	.03
344 Chuck Finley	.10	.03
345 Erik Hanson	.05	.02
346 Rich Gedman	.05	.02
347 Bip Roberts	.05	.02
348 Matt Williams	.10	.03
349 Tom Henke	.05	.02
350 Brad Komminsk	.05	.02
351 Jeff Reed	.05	.02
352 Brian Downing	.05	.02
353 Frank Viola	.05	.02
354 Terry Puhl	.05	.02
355 Brian Harper	.05	.02
356 Steve Farr	.05	.02
357 Joe Boever	.05	.02
358 Danny Heep	.05	.02

359 Larry Andersen	.05	.02
360 Rolando Roomes	.05	.02
361 Mike Gallego	.05	.02
362 Bob Kipper	.05	.02
363 Clay Parker	.05	.02
364 Mike Pagliarulo	.05	.02
365 Ken Griffey Jr. UER (Signed through 1990, should be 1991)	.75	.23
366 Rex Hudler	.05	.02
367 Pat Sheridan	.05	.02
368 Kirk Gibson	.10	.03
369 Jeff Parrett	.05	.02
370 Bob Walk	.05	.02
371 Ken Patterson	.05	.02
372 Bryan Harvey	.05	.02
373 Mike Bielecki	.05	.02
374 Tom Magrann	.05	.02
375 Rick Mahler	.05	.02
376 Craig Lefferts	.05	.02
377 Gregg Olson	.10	.03
378 Jamie Moyer	.10	.03
379 Randy Johnson	.50	.12
380 Jeff Montgomery	.10	.03
381 Marty Clary	.05	.02
382 Bill Spiers	.05	.02
383 Dave Magadan	.05	.02
384 Greg Hibbard RC	.10	.03
385 Ernie Whitt	.05	.02
386 Rick Honeycutt	.05	.02
387 Dave West	.05	.02
388 Keith Hernandez	.10	.03
389 Jose Alvarez	.05	.02
390 Joey Belle	.25	.07
391 Rick Aguilera	.10	.03
392 Mike Fitzgerald	.05	.02
393 Dwight Smith	.05	.02
394 Steve Wilson	.05	.02
395 Bob Geren	.05	.02
396 Randy Ready	.05	.02
397 Ken Hill	.10	.03
398 Jody Reed	.05	.02
399 Tom Brunansky	.05	.02
400A Checklist 334-435	.05	.02
400B Checklist 322-419	.05	.02
401 Rene Gonzales	.05	.02
402 Harold Baines	.10	.03
403 Cecilio Guante	.05	.02
404 Joe Girardi	.15	.04
405A Sergio Valdez ERR (Card front shows black line crossing S in Sergio)	.05	.02
405B Sergio Valdez COR	.05	.02
406 Mark Williamson	.05	.02
407 Glenn Hoffman	.05	.02
408 Jeff Innis	.05	.02
409 Randy Kramer	.05	.02
410 Charlie O'Brien	.05	.02
411 Charlie Hough	.10	.03
412 Gus Polidor	.05	.02
413 Ron Karkovice	.05	.02
414 Trevor Wilson	.05	.02
415 Kevin Ritz	.05	.02
416 Gary Thurman	.05	.02
417 Jeff M. Robinson	.05	.02
418 Scott Terry	.05	.02
419 Tim Laudner	.05	.02
420 Dennis Rasmussen	.05	.02
421 Luis Rivera	.05	.02
422 Jim Corsi	.05	.02
423 Dennis Lamp	.05	.02
424 Ken Caminiti	.10	.03
425 David Wells	.10	.03
426 Norm Charlton	.05	.02
427 Deion Sanders	.25	.07
428 Dion James	.05	.02
429 Chuck Cary	.05	.02
430 Ken Howell	.05	.02
431 Steve Lake	.05	.02
432 Kal Daniels	.05	.02
433 Lance McCullers	.05	.02
434 Lenny Harris	.05	.02
435 Scott Scudder	.05	.02
436 Gene Larkin	.05	.02
437 Dan Quisenberry	.05	.02

- ❑ 438 Steve Olin RC .25 .07
- ❑ 439 Mickey Hatcher .05 .02
- ❑ 440 Willie Wilson .05 .02
- ❑ 441 Mark Grant .05 .02
- ❑ 442 Mookie Wilson .10 .03
- ❑ 443 Alex Trevino .05 .02
- ❑ 444 Pat Tabler .05 .02
- ❑ 445 Dave Bergman .05 .02
- ❑ 446 Todd Burns .05 .02
- ❑ 447 R.J. Reynolds .05 .02
- ❑ 448 Jay Buhner .10 .03
- ❑ 449 Lee Stevens .10 .03
- ❑ 450 Ron Hassey .05 .02
- ❑ 451 Bob Melvin .05 .02
- ❑ 452 Dave Martinez .05 .02
- ❑ 453 Greg Litton .05 .02
- ❑ 454 Mark Carreon .05 .02
- ❑ 455 Scott Fletcher .05 .02
- ❑ 456 Otis Nixon .05 .02
- ❑ 457 Tony Fossas .05 .02
- ❑ 458 John Russell .05 .02
- ❑ 459 Paul Assenmacher .05 .02
- ❑ 460 Zane Smith .05 .02
- ❑ 461 Jack Daugherty .05 .02
- ❑ 462 Rich Monteleone .05 .02
- ❑ 463 Greg Briley .05 .02
- ❑ 464 Mike Smithson .05 .02
- ❑ 465 Benito Santiago .10 .03
- ❑ 466 Jeff Brantley .05 .02
- ❑ 467 Jose Nunez .05 .02
- ❑ 468 Scott Bailes .05 .02
- ❑ 469 Ken Griffey Sr. .10 .03
- ❑ 470 Bob McClure .05 .02
- ❑ 471 Mackey Sasser .05 .02
- ❑ 472 Glenn Wilson .05 .02
- ❑ 473 Kevin Tapani RC .25 .07
- ❑ 474 Bill Buckner .05 .02
- ❑ 475 Ron Gant .10 .03
- ❑ 476 Kevin Romine .05 .02
- ❑ 477 Juan Agosto .05 .02
- ❑ 478 Herm Winningham .05 .02
- ❑ 479 Storm Davis .05 .02
- ❑ 480 Jeff King .05 .02
- ❑ 481 Kevin Mmahat .05 .02
- ❑ 482 Carmelo Martinez .05 .02
- ❑ 483 Omar Vizquel .25 .07
- ❑ 484 Jim Dwyer .05 .02
- ❑ 485 Bob Knepper .05 .02
- ❑ 486 Dave Anderson .05 .02
- ❑ 487 Ron Jones .05 .02
- ❑ 488 Jay Bell .10 .03
- ❑ 489 Sammy Sosa RC 5.00 1.50
- ❑ 490 Kent Anderson .05 .02
- ❑ 491 Domingo Ramos .05 .02
- ❑ 492 Dave Clark .05 .02
- ❑ 493 Tim Birtsas .05 .02
- ❑ 494 Ken Oberkfell .05 .02
- ❑ 495 Larry Sheets .05 .02
- ❑ 496 Jeff Kunkel .05 .02
- ❑ 497 Jim Presley .05 .02
- ❑ 498 Mike Macfarlane .05 .02
- ❑ 499 Pete Smith .05 .02
- ❑ 500A Checklist 436-537 DP .05 .02
- ❑ 500B Checklist 420-517 .05 .02
- ❑ 501 Gary Sheffield .25 .07
- ❑ 502 Terry Bross .05 .02
- ❑ 503 Jerry Kutzler .05 .02
- ❑ 504 Lloyd Moseby .05 .02
- ❑ 505 Curt Young .05 .02
- ❑ 506 Al Newman .05 .02
- ❑ 507 Keith Miller .05 .02
- ❑ 508 Mike Stanton RC .25 .07
- ❑ 509 Rich Yett .05 .02
- ❑ 510 Tim Drummond .05 .02
- ❑ 511 Joe Hesketh .05 .02
- ❑ 512 Rick Wrona .05 .02
- ❑ 513 Luis Salazar .05 .02
- ❑ 514 Hal Morris .05 .02
- ❑ 515 Terry Mulholland .05 .02
- ❑ 516 John Morris .05 .02
- ❑ 517 Carlos Quintana .05 .02
- ❑ 518 Frank DiPino .05 .02
- ❑ 519 Randy Milligan .05 .02
- ❑ 520 Chad Kreuter .05 .02
- ❑ 521 Mike Jeffcoat .05 .02
- ❑ 522 Mike Harkey .05 .02
- ❑ 523A Andy Nezelek ERR .05 .02 (Wrong birth year)
- ❑ 523B Andy Nezelek COR .15 .04 (Finally corrected in factory sets)
- ❑ 524 Dave Schmidt .05 .02
- ❑ 525 Tony Armas .05 .02
- ❑ 526 Barry Lyons .05 .02
- ❑ 527 Rick Reed RC .25 .07
- ❑ 528 Jerry Reuss .05 .02
- ❑ 529 Dean Palmer RC .25 .07
- ❑ 530 Jeff Peterek .05 .02
- ❑ 531 Carlos Martinez .05 .02
- ❑ 532 Atlee Hammaker .05 .02
- ❑ 533 Mike Brumley .05 .02
- ❑ 534 Terry Leach .05 .02
- ❑ 535 Doug Strange .05 .02
- ❑ 536 Jose DeLeon .05 .02
- ❑ 537 Shane Rawley .05 .02
- ❑ 538 Joey Cora .10 .03
- ❑ 539 Eric Hetzel .05 .02
- ❑ 540 Gene Nelson .05 .02
- ❑ 541 Wes Gardner .05 .02
- ❑ 542 Mark Portugal .05 .02
- ❑ 543 Al Leiter .25 .07
- ❑ 544 Jack Armstrong .05 .02
- ❑ 545 Greg Cadaret .05 .02
- ❑ 546 Rod Nichols .05 .02
- ❑ 547 Luis Polonia .05 .02
- ❑ 548 Charlie Hayes .05 .02
- ❑ 549 Dickie Thon .05 .02
- ❑ 550 Tim Crews .05 .02
- ❑ 551 Dave Winfield .10 .03
- ❑ 552 Mike Davis .05 .02
- ❑ 553 Ron Robinson .05 .02
- ❑ 554 Carmen Castillo .05 .02
- ❑ 555 John Costello .05 .02
- ❑ 556 Bud Black .05 .02
- ❑ 557 Rick Dempsey .05 .02
- ❑ 558 Jim Acker .05 .02
- ❑ 559 Eric Show .05 .02
- ❑ 560 Pat Borders .05 .02
- ❑ 561 Danny Darwin .05 .02
- ❑ 562 Rick Luecken .05 .02
- ❑ 563 Edwin Nunez .05 .02
- ❑ 564 Felix Jose .05 .02
- ❑ 565 John Cangelosi .05 .02
- ❑ 566 Bill Swift .05 .02
- ❑ 567 Bill Schroeder .05 .02
- ❑ 568 Stan Javier .05 .02
- ❑ 569 Jim Traber .05 .02
- ❑ 570 Wallace Johnson .05 .02
- ❑ 571 Donell Nixon .05 .02
- ❑ 572 Sid Fernandez .05 .02
- ❑ 573 Lance Johnson .05 .02
- ❑ 574 Andy McGaffigan .05 .02
- ❑ 575 Mark Knudson .05 .02
- ❑ 576 Tommy Greene RC .10 .03
- ❑ 577 Mark Grace .15 .04
- ❑ 578 Larry Walker RC 1.00 .30
- ❑ 579 Mike Stanley .05 .02
- ❑ 580 Mike Witt DP .05 .02
- ❑ 581 Scott Bradley .05 .02
- ❑ 582 Greg A. Harris .05 .02
- ❑ 583A Kevin Hickey ERR .25 .07
- ❑ 583B Kevin Hickey COR .05 .02
- ❑ 584 Lee Mazzilli .05 .02
- ❑ 585 Jeff Pico .05 .02
- ❑ 586 Joe Oliver .05 .02
- ❑ 587 Willie Fraser DP .05 .02
- ❑ 588 Carl Yastrzemski .25 .07 Puzzle Card DP
- ❑ 589 Kevin Bass DP .05 .02
- ❑ 590 John Moses DP .05 .02
- ❑ 591 Tom Pagnozzi DP .05 .02
- ❑ 592 Tony Castillo DP .05 .02
- ❑ 593 Jerald Clark DP .05 .02
- ❑ 594 Dan Schatzeder .05 .02
- ❑ 595 Luis Quinones DP .05 .02
- ❑ 596 Pete Harnisch DP .05 .02
- ❑ 597 Gary Redus .05 .02
- ❑ 598 Mel Hall .05 .02
- ❑ 599 Rick Schu .05 .02
- ❑ 600A Checklist 538-639 .05 .02
- ❑ 600B Checklist 518-617 .05 .02
- ❑ 601 Mike Kingery DP .05 .02
- ❑ 602 Terry Kennedy DP .05 .02
- ❑ 603 Mike Sharperson DP .05 .02
- ❑ 604 Don Carman DP .05 .02
- ❑ 605 Jim Gott .05 .02
- ❑ 606 Donn Pall DP .05 .02
- ❑ 607 Rance Mulliniks .05 .02
- ❑ 608 Curt Wilkerson DP .05 .02
- ❑ 609 Mike Felder DP .05 .02
- ❑ 610 G.Hernandez DP .05 .02
- ❑ 611 Candy Maldonado DP .05 .02
- ❑ 612 Mark Thurmond DP .05 .02
- ❑ 613 Rick Leach DP .05 .02
- ❑ 614 Jerry Reed DP .05 .02
- ❑ 615 Franklin Stubbs .05 .02
- ❑ 616 Billy Hatcher DP .05 .02
- ❑ 617 Don August DP .05 .02
- ❑ 618 Tim Teufel .05 .02
- ❑ 619 Shawn Hillegas DP .05 .02
- ❑ 620 Manny Lee .05 .02
- ❑ 621 Gary Ward DP .05 .02
- ❑ 622 Mark Guthrie DP .05 .02
- ❑ 623 Jeff Musselman DP .05 .02
- ❑ 624 Mark Lemke DP .05 .02
- ❑ 625 Fernando Valenzuela .10 .03
- ❑ 626 Paul Sorrento DP RC .25 .07
- ❑ 627 Glenallen Hill DP .05 .02
- ❑ 628 Les Lancaster DP .05 .02
- ❑ 629 Vance Law DP .05 .02
- ❑ 630 Randy Velarde DP .05 .02
- ❑ 631 Todd Frohwirth DP .05 .02
- ❑ 632 Willie McGee .10 .03
- ❑ 633 Dennis Boyd DP .05 .02
- ❑ 634 Cris Carpenter DP .05 .02
- ❑ 635 Brian Holton .05 .02
- ❑ 636 Tracy Jones DP .05 .02
- ❑ 637A Terry Steinbach AS .05 .02 (Recent Major League Performance)
- ❑ 637B Terry Steinbach AS .05 .02 (All-Star Game Performance)
- ❑ 638 Brady Anderson .10 .03
- ❑ 639A Jack Morris ERR .10 .03 (Card front shows black line crossing J in Jack)
- ❑ 639B Jack Morris COR .10 .03
- ❑ 640 Jaime Navarro .05 .02
- ❑ 641 Darrin Jackson .05 .02
- ❑ 642 Mike Dyer RC .05 .02
- ❑ 643 Mike Schmidt .50 .15
- ❑ 644 Henry Cotto .05 .02
- ❑ 645 John Cerutti .05 .02
- ❑ 646 Francisco Cabrera .05 .02
- ❑ 647 Scott Sanderson .05 .02
- ❑ 648 Brian Meyer .05 .02
- ❑ 649 Ray Searage .05 .02
- ❑ 650A Bo Jackson AS .25 .07 (Recent Major League Performance)
- ❑ 650B Bo Jackson AS .25 .07 (All-Star Game Performance)
- ❑ 651 Steve Lyons .05 .02
- ❑ 652 Mike LaCoss .05 .02
- ❑ 653 Ted Power .05 .02
- ❑ 654A Howard Johnson AS .05 .02 (Recent Major League Performance)
- ❑ 654B Howard Johnson AS .05 .02 (All-Star Game Performance)
- ❑ 655 Mauro Gozzo .05 .02
- ❑ 656 Mike Blowers RC .10 .03
- ❑ 657 Paul Gibson .05 .02
- ❑ 658 Neal Heaton .05 .02
- ❑ 659 Nolan Ryan 5000K .50 .15 COR (Still an error as Ryan did not lead AL in K's in '75)
- ❑ 659A Nolan Ryan 5000K 1.50 .45 (665 King of Kings back) ERR
- ❑ 660A Harold Baines AS .75 .23 (Black line through star on front;

Card	Nm-Mt	Ex-Mt
Recent Major League Performance)		
❑ 660B Harold Baines AS (Black line through star on front; All-Star Game Performance)	1.00	.30
❑ 660C Harold Baines AS (Black line behind star on front; Recent Major League Performance)	.25	.07
❑ 660D Harold Baines AS (Black line behind star on front; All-Star Game Performance)	.05	.02
❑ 661 Gary Pettis	.05	.02
❑ 662 Clint Zavaras	.05	.02
❑ 663A Rick Reuschel AS (Recent Major League Performance)	.05	.02
❑ 663B Rick Reuschel AS (All-Star Game Performance)	.05	.02
❑ 664 Alejandro Pena	.05	.02
❑ 665 N.Ryan KING COR	.50	.15
❑ 665A Nolan Ryan KING (659 5000 K back) ERR	1.50	.45
❑ 665C N.Ryan KING ERR No number on back in factory sets	.75	.23
❑ 666 Ricky Horton	.05	.02
❑ 667 Curt Schilling	1.00	.30
❑ 668 Bill Landrum	.05	.02
❑ 669 Todd Stottlemyre	.10	.03
❑ 670 Tim Leary	.05	.02
❑ 671 John Wetteland	.25	.07
❑ 672 Calvin Schiraldi	.05	.02
❑ 673A Ruben Sierra AS (Recent Major League Performance)	.05	.02
❑ 673B Ruben Sierra AS (All-Star Game Performance)	.05	.02
❑ 674A Pedro Guerrero AS (Recent Major League Performance)	.05	.02
❑ 674B Pedro Guerrero AS (All-Star Game Performance)	.05	.02
❑ 675 Ken Phelps	.05	.02
❑ 676A Cal Ripken AS (All-Star Game Performance)	.40	.12
❑ 676B Cal Ripken AS (Recent Major League Performance)	.75	.23
❑ 677 Denny Walling	.05	.02
❑ 678 Goose Gossage	.10	.03
❑ 679 Gary Mielke	.05	.02
❑ 680 Bill Bathe	.05	.02
❑ 681 Tom Lawless	.05	.02
❑ 682 Xavier Hernandez RC	.05	.02
❑ 683A Kirby Puckett AS (Recent Major League Performance)	.15	.04
❑ 683B Kirby Puckett AS (All-Star Game Performance)	.15	.04
❑ 684 Mariano Duncan	.05	.02
❑ 685 Ramon Martinez	.05	.02
❑ 686 Tim Jones	.05	.02
❑ 687 Tom Filer	.05	.02
❑ 688 Steve Lombardozzi	.05	.02
❑ 689 Bernie Williams RC	1.00	.30
❑ 690 Chip Hale	.05	.02
❑ 691 Beau Allred RC	.05	.02
❑ 692A Ryne Sandberg AS (Recent Major League Performance)	.25	.07
❑ 692B Ryne Sandberg AS (All-Star Game Performance)	.25	.07
❑ 693 Jeff Huson RC	.10	.03
❑ 694 Curt Ford	.05	.02
❑ 695A Eric Davis AS (Recent Major League Performance)	.05	.02
❑ 695B Eric Davis AS (All-Star Game Performance)	.05	.02
❑ 696 Scott Lusader	.05	.02
❑ 697A Mark McGwire AS (Recent Major League Performance)	.30	.09
❑ 697B Mark McGwire AS (All-Star Game Performance)	.30	.09
❑ 698 Steve Cummings RC	.05	.02
❑ 699 George Canale	.05	.02
❑ 700A Checklist 640-715 and BC1-BC26	.25	.07
❑ 700B Checklist 640-716 and BC1-BC26	.10	.03
❑ 700C Checklist 618-716	.05	.02
❑ 701A Julio Franco AS (Recent Major League Performance)	.05	.02
❑ 701B Julio Franco AS (All-Star Game Performance)	.05	.02
❑ 702 Dave Johnson (P)	.05	.02
❑ 703A Dave Stewart AS (Recent Major League Performance)	.05	.02
❑ 703B Dave Stewart AS (All-Star Game Performance)	.05	.02
❑ 704 Dave Justice RC	.50	.15
❑ 705 Tony Gwynn AS (All-Star Game Performance)	.15	.04
❑ 705A Tony Gwynn AS (Recent Major League Performance)	.15	.04
❑ 706 Greg Myers	.05	.02
❑ 707A Will Clark AS (Recent Major League Performance)	.25	.07
❑ 707B Will Clark AS (All-Star Game Performance)	.25	.07
❑ 708A Benito Santiago AS (Recent Major League Performance)	.05	.02
❑ 708B Benito Santiago AS (All-Star Game Performance)	.05	.02
❑ 709 Larry McWilliams	.05	.02
❑ 710A Ozzie Smith AS (Recent Major League Performance)	.25	.07
❑ 710B Ozzie Smith AS Perf	.25	.07
❑ 711 John Olerud RC	.50	.15
❑ 712A Wade Boggs AS (Recent Major League Performance)	.10	.03
❑ 712B Wade Boggs AS (All-Star Game Performance)	.10	.03
❑ 713 Gary Eave	.05	.02
❑ 714 Bob Tewksbury	.05	.02
❑ 715A Kevin Mitchell AS (Recent Major League Performance)	.05	.02
❑ 715B Kevin Mitchell AS (All-Star Game Performance)	.05	.02
❑ 716 B.Giamatti COMM In Memoriam	.25	.07

1990 Donruss Best AL

	Nm-Mt	Ex-Mt
COMP.FACT.SET (144)	40.00	12.00
❑ 1 Ken Griffey Jr.	1.25	.35
❑ 2 Bob Milacki	.15	.04
❑ 3 Mike Boddicker	.15	.04
❑ 4 Bert Blyleven	.20	.06
❑ 5 Carlton Fisk	.30	.09
❑ 6 Greg Swindell	.15	.04
❑ 7 Alan Trammell	.20	.06
❑ 8 Mark Davis	.15	.04
❑ 9 Chris Bosio	.15	.04
❑ 10 Gary Gaetti	.20	.06
❑ 11 Matt Nokes	.15	.04
❑ 12 Dennis Eckersley	.20	.06
❑ 13 Kevin Brown	.20	.06
❑ 14 Tom Henke	.15	.04
❑ 15 Mickey Tettleton	.15	.04
❑ 16 Jody Reed	.15	.04
❑ 17 Mark Langston	.15	.04
❑ 18 Melido Perez UER (Listed as an Expo rather than White Sox)	.15	.04
❑ 19 John Farrell	.15	.04
❑ 20 Tony Phillips	.15	.04
❑ 21 Bret Saberhagen	.20	.06
❑ 22 Robin Yount	.75	.23
❑ 23 Kirby Puckett	.50	.15
❑ 24 Steve Sax	.15	.04
❑ 25 Dave Stewart	.20	.06
❑ 26 Alvin Davis	.15	.04
❑ 27 Geno Petralli	.15	.04
❑ 28 Mookie Wilson	.20	.06
❑ 29 Jeff Ballard	.15	.04
❑ 30 Ellis Burks	.20	.06
❑ 31 Wally Joyner	.20	.06
❑ 32 Bobby Thigpen	.15	.04
❑ 33 Keith Hernandez	.20	.06
❑ 34 Jack Morris	.20	.06
❑ 35 George Brett	1.25	.35
❑ 36 Dan Plesac	.15	.04
❑ 37 Brian Harper	.15	.04
❑ 38 Don Mattingly	1.25	.35
❑ 39 Dave Henderson	.15	.04
❑ 40 Scott Bankhead UER (Asheboro misspelled as Ashboro on card)	.15	.04
❑ 41 Rafael Palmeiro	.30	.09
❑ 42 Jimmy Key	.20	.06
❑ 43 Gregg Olson	.15	.04
❑ 44 Tony Pena	.15	.04
❑ 45 Jack Howell	.15	.04
❑ 46 Eric King	.15	.04
❑ 47 Cory Snyder	.15	.04
❑ 48 Frank Tanana	.20	.06
❑ 49 Nolan Ryan	1.50	.45
❑ 50 Bob Boone	.20	.06
❑ 51 Dave Parker	.20	.06
❑ 52 Allan Anderson	.15	.04
❑ 53 Tim Leary	.15	.04
❑ 54 Mark McGwire	1.50	.45
❑ 55 Dave Valle	.15	.04
❑ 56 Fred McGriff	.30	.09
❑ 57 Cal Ripken	1.50	.45
❑ 58 Roger Clemens	1.00	.30
❑ 59 Lance Parrish	.20	.06
❑ 60 Robin Ventura	.50	.15
❑ 61 Doug Jones	.15	.04
❑ 62 Lloyd Moseby	.15	.04
❑ 63 Bo Jackson	.50	.15
❑ 64 Paul Molitor	.30	.09
❑ 65 Kent Hrbek	.20	.06
❑ 66 Mel Hall	.15	.04
❑ 67 Bob Welch	.20	.06
❑ 68 Erik Hanson	.15	.04

❑ 69 Harold Baines .20 .06
❑ 70 Junior Felix .15 .04
❑ 71 Craig Worthington .15 .04
❑ 72 Jeff Reardon .20 .06
❑ 73 Johnny Ray .15 .04
❑ 74 Ozzie Guillen .15 .04
❑ 75 Brook Jacoby .15 .04
❑ 76 Chet Lemon .15 .04
❑ 77 Mark Gubicza .15 .04
❑ 78 B.J. Surhoff .20 .06
❑ 79 Rick Aguilera .20 .06
❑ 80 Pascual Perez .15 .04
❑ 81 Jose Canseco .50 .15
❑ 82 Mike Schooler .15 .04
❑ 83 Jeff Huson .15 .04
❑ 84 Kelly Gruber .15 .04
❑ 85 Randy Milligan .15 .04
❑ 86 Wade Boggs .30 .09
❑ 87 Dave Winfield .20 .06
❑ 88 Scott Fletcher .15 .04
❑ 89 Tom Candiotti .15 .04
❑ 90 Mike Heath .15 .04
❑ 91 Kevin Seitzer .15 .04
❑ 92 Ted Higuera .15 .04
❑ 93 Kevin Tapani .50 .15
❑ 94 Roberto Kelly .15 .04
❑ 95 Walt Weiss .15 .04
❑ 96 Checklist Card .15 .04
❑ 97 Sandy Alomar Jr. .20 .06
❑ 98 Pete O'Brien .15 .04
❑ 99 Jeff Russell .15 .04
❑ 100 John Olerud 1.50 .45
❑ 101 Pete Harnisch .15 .04
❑ 102 Dwight Evans .20 .06
❑ 103 Chuck Finley .20 .06
❑ 104 Sammy Sosa 15.00 4.50
❑ 105 Mike Henneman .15 .04
❑ 106 Kurt Stillwell .15 .04
❑ 107 Greg Vaughn .15 .04
❑ 108 Dan Gladden .15 .04
❑ 109 Jesse Barfield .15 .04
❑ 110 Willie Randolph .20 .06
❑ 111 Randy Johnson .75 .18
❑ 112 Julio Franco .20 .06
❑ 113 Tony Fernandez .15 .04
❑ 114 Ben McDonald .15 .04
❑ 115 Mike Greenwell .15 .04
❑ 116 Luis Polonia .15 .04
❑ 117 Carney Lansford .20 .06
❑ 118 Bud Black .15 .04
❑ 119 Lou Whitaker .20 .06
❑ 120 Jim Eisenreich .15 .04
❑ 121 Gary Sheffield .50 .15
❑ 122 Shane Mack .15 .04
❑ 123 Alvaro Espinoza .15 .04
❑ 124 Rickey Henderson .50 .15
❑ 125 Jeffrey Leonard .15 .04
❑ 126 Gary Pettis .15 .04
❑ 127 Dave Stieb .20 .06
❑ 128 Danny Tartabull .15 .04
❑ 129 Joe Orsulak .15 .04
❑ 130 Tom Brunansky .15 .04
❑ 131 Dick Schofield .15 .04
❑ 132 Candy Maldonado .15 .04
❑ 133 Cecil Fielder .20 .06
❑ 134 Terry Shumpert .15 .04
❑ 135 Greg Gagne .15 .04
❑ 136 Dave Righetti .20 .06
❑ 137 Terry Steinbach .15 .04
❑ 138 Harold Reynolds .20 .06
❑ 139 George Bell .15 .04
❑ 140 Carlos Quintana .15 .04
❑ 141 Ivan Calderon .15 .04
❑ 142 Greg Brock .15 .04
❑ 143 Ruben Sierra .15 .04
❑ 144 Checklist Card .15 .04

2001 Donruss

	Nm-Mt	Ex-Mt
COMP.SET w/o SP's (150)	25.00	7.50
COMMON CARD (1-150)	.30	.09
COMMON (151-200)	8.00	2.40
COMMON (201-220)	2.50	.75

❑ 1 Alex Rodriguez 1.25 .35

❑ 2 Barry Bonds 2.00 .60
❑ 3 Cal Ripken 2.50 .75
❑ 4 Chipper Jones .75 .23
❑ 5 Derek Jeter 2.00 .60
❑ 6 Troy Glaus .30 .09
❑ 7 Frank Thomas .75 .23
❑ 8 Greg Maddux 1.25 .35
❑ 9 Ivan Rodriguez .75 .23
❑ 10 Jeff Bagwell .50 .15
❑ 11 Jose Canseco .75 .23
❑ 12 Todd Helton .50 .15
❑ 13 Ken Griffey Jr. 1.25 .35
❑ 14 Manny Ramirez .50 .15
❑ 15 Mark McGwire 2.00 .60
❑ 16 Mike Piazza 1.25 .35
❑ 17 Nomar Garciaparra 1.25 .35
❑ 18 Pedro Martinez .75 .23
❑ 19 Randy Johnson .75 .23
❑ 20 Rick Ankiel .30 .09
❑ 21 Rickey Henderson .75 .23
❑ 22 Roger Clemens 1.50 .45
❑ 23 Sammy Sosa 1.25 .35
❑ 24 Tony Gwynn 1.00 .30
❑ 25 Vladimir Guerrero .75 .23
❑ 26 Eric Davis .30 .09
❑ 27 Roberto Alomar .30 .09
❑ 28 Mark Mulder .30 .09
❑ 29 Pat Burrell .30 .09
❑ 30 Harold Baines .30 .09
❑ 31 Carlos Delgado .30 .09
❑ 32 J.D. Drew .30 .09
❑ 33 Jim Edmonds .30 .09
❑ 34 Darin Erstad .30 .09
❑ 35 Jason Giambi .30 .09
❑ 36 Tom Glavine .50 .15
❑ 37 Juan Gonzalez .50 .15
❑ 38 Mark Grace .50 .15
❑ 39 Shawn Green .30 .09
❑ 40 Tim Hudson .30 .09
❑ 41 Andruw Jones .30 .09
❑ 42 David Justice .30 .09
❑ 43 Jeff Kent .30 .09
❑ 44 Barry Larkin .50 .15
❑ 45 Pokey Reese .30 .09
❑ 46 Mike Mussina .50 .15
❑ 47 Hideo Nomo .75 .23
❑ 48 Rafael Palmeiro .50 .15
❑ 49 Adam Piatt .30 .09
❑ 50 Scott Rolen .75 .23
❑ 51 Gary Sheffield .30 .09
❑ 52 Bernie Williams .50 .15
❑ 53 Bob Abreu .30 .09
❑ 54 Edgardo Alfonzo .30 .09
❑ 55 Jermaine Clark RC .50 .15
❑ 56 Albert Belle .30 .09
❑ 57 Craig Biggio .50 .15
❑ 58 Andres Galarraga .30 .09
❑ 59 Edgar Martinez .50 .15
❑ 60 Fred McGriff .50 .15
❑ 61 Magglio Ordonez .30 .09
❑ 62 Jim Thome .75 .23
❑ 63 Matt Williams .30 .09
❑ 64 Kerry Wood .75 .23
❑ 65 Moises Alou .30 .09
❑ 66 Brady Anderson .30 .09
❑ 67 Garret Anderson .30 .09
❑ 68 Tony Armas Jr. .30 .09
❑ 69 Tony Batista .30 .09
❑ 70 Jose Cruz Jr. .30 .09
❑ 71 Carlos Beltran .50 .15
❑ 72 Adrian Beltre .50 .15
❑ 73 Kris Benson .30 .09
❑ 74 Lance Berkman .30 .09
❑ 75 Kevin Brown .30 .09
❑ 76 Jay Buhner .30 .09
❑ 77 Jeromy Burnitz .30 .09
❑ 78 Ken Caminiti .30 .09
❑ 79 Sean Casey .30 .09
❑ 80 Luis Castillo .30 .09
❑ 81 Eric Chavez .30 .09
❑ 82 Jeff Cirillo .30 .09
❑ 83 Bartolo Colon .30 .09
❑ 84 David Cone .30 .09
❑ 85 Freddy Garcia .30 .09
❑ 86 Johnny Damon .50 .15
❑ 87 Ray Durham .30 .09
❑ 88 Jermaine Dye .30 .09
❑ 89 Juan Encarnacion .30 .09
❑ 90 Terrence Long .30 .09
❑ 91 Carl Everett .30 .09
❑ 92 Steve Finley .30 .09
❑ 93 Cliff Floyd .30 .09
❑ 94 Brad Fullmer .30 .09
❑ 95 Brian Giles .30 .09
❑ 96 Luis Gonzalez .30 .09
❑ 97 Rusty Greer .30 .09
❑ 98 Jeffrey Hammonds .30 .09
❑ 99 Mike Hampton .30 .09
❑ 100 Orlando Hernandez .30 .09
❑ 101 Richard Hidalgo .30 .09
❑ 102 Geoff Jenkins .30 .09
❑ 103 Jacque Jones .30 .09
❑ 104 Brian Jordan .30 .09
❑ 105 Gabe Kapler .30 .09
❑ 106 Eric Karros .30 .09
❑ 107 Jason Kendall .30 .09
❑ 108 Adam Kennedy .30 .09
❑ 109 Byung-Hyun Kim .30 .09
❑ 110 Ryan Klesko .30 .09
❑ 111 Chuck Knoblauch .30 .09
❑ 112 Paul Konerko .30 .09
❑ 113 Carlos Lee .30 .09
❑ 114 Kenny Lofton .30 .09
❑ 115 Javy Lopez .30 .09
❑ 116 Tino Martinez .50 .15
❑ 117 Ruben Mateo .30 .09
❑ 118 Kevin Millwood .30 .09
❑ 119 Ben Molina .30 .09
❑ 120 Raul Mondesi .30 .09
❑ 121 Trot Nixon .30 .09
❑ 122 John Olerud .30 .09
❑ 123 Paul O'Neill .50 .15
❑ 124 Chan Ho Park .30 .09
❑ 125 Andy Pettitte .50 .15
❑ 126 Jorge Posada .50 .15
❑ 127 Mark Quinn .30 .09
❑ 128 Aramis Ramirez .30 .09
❑ 129 Mariano Rivera .50 .15
❑ 130 Tim Salmon .50 .15
❑ 131 Curt Schilling .30 .09
❑ 132 Richie Sexson .30 .09
❑ 133 John Smoltz .50 .15
❑ 134 J.T. Snow .30 .09
❑ 135 Jay Payton .30 .09
❑ 136 Shannon Stewart .30 .09
❑ 137 B.J. Surhoff .30 .09
❑ 138 Mike Sweeney .30 .09
❑ 139 Fernando Tatis .30 .09
❑ 140 Miguel Tejada .30 .09
❑ 141 Jason Varitek .50 .15
❑ 142 Greg Vaughn .30 .09
❑ 143 Mo Vaughn .30 .09
❑ 144 Robin Ventura UER .30 .09
Listed as playing for Yankees last 2 years
Also Bat and Throw information is wrong
❑ 145 Jose Vidro .30 .09
❑ 146 Omar Vizquel .50 .15
❑ 147 Larry Walker .50 .15
❑ 148 David Wells .30 .09
❑ 149 Rondell White .30 .09
❑ 150 Preston Wilson .30 .09
❑ 151 Brent Abernathy RR 8.00 2.40

❑ 152 Cory Aldridge RR RC	8.00	2.40
❑ 153 Gene Altman RR RC	8.00	2.40
❑ 154 Josh Beckett RR	8.00	2.40
❑ 155 W. Betemit RR RC	8.00	2.40
❑ 156 A.Pujols RR/500 RC	120.00	36.00
❑ 157 Joe Crede RR	8.00	2.40
❑ 158 Jack Cust RR	8.00	2.40
❑ 159 Ben Sheets RR/500	40.00	12.00
❑ 160 Alex Escobar RR	8.00	2.40
❑ 161 A. Hernandez RR RC	8.00	2.40
❑ 162 Pedro Feliz RR	8.00	2.40
❑ 163 Nate Frese RR RC	8.00	2.40
❑ 164 Carlos Garcia RR RC	8.00	2.40
❑ 165 Marcus Giles RR	8.00	2.40
❑ 166 Alexis Gomez RR RC	8.00	2.40
❑ 167 Jason Hart RR	8.00	2.40
❑ 168 Eric Hinske RR RC	10.00	3.00
❑ 169 Cesar Izturis RR	8.00	2.40
❑ 170 Nick Johnson RR	8.00	2.40
❑ 171 Mike Young RR	10.00	3.00
❑ 172 B. Lawrence RR RC	8.00	2.40
❑ 173 Steve Lomasney RR	8.00	2.40
❑ 174 Nick Maness RR	8.00	2.40
❑ 175 Jose Mieses RR RC	8.00	2.40
❑ 176 Greg Miller RR RC	8.00	2.40
❑ 177 Eric Munson RR	8.00	2.40
❑ 178 Xavier Nady RR	8.00	2.40
❑ 179 Blaine Neal RR RC	8.00	2.40
❑ 180 Abraham Nunez RR	8.00	2.40
❑ 181 Jose Ortiz RR	8.00	2.40
❑ 182 Jeremy Owens RR RC	8.00	2.40
❑ 183 Pablo Ozuna RR	8.00	2.40
❑ 184 Corey Patterson RR	8.00	2.40
❑ 185 Carlos Pena RR	8.00	2.40
❑ 186 Wily Mo Pena RR	8.00	2.40
❑ 187 Timo Perez RR	8.00	2.40
❑ 188 A. Pettyjohn RR RC	8.00	2.40
❑ 189 Luis Rivas RR	8.00	2.40
❑ 190 J. Melian RR RC	8.00	2.40
❑ 191 Wilken Ruan RR RC	8.00	2.40
❑ 192 D. Sanchez RR RC	8.00	2.40
❑ 193 Alfonso Soriano RR	10.00	3.00
❑ 194 Rafael Soriano RR RC	10.00	3.00
❑ 195 Ichiro Suzuki RR RC	50.00	15.00
❑ 196 Billy Sylvester RR RC	8.00	2.40
❑ 197 Juan Uribe RR RC	10.00	3.00
❑ 198 Eric Valent RR	8.00	2.40
❑ 199 C.Valderrama RR RC	8.00	2.40
❑ 200 Matt White RR RC	8.00	2.40
❑ 201 Alex Rodriguez FC	6.00	1.80
❑ 202 Barry Bonds FC	10.00	3.00
❑ 203 Cal Ripken FC	12.00	3.60
❑ 204 Chipper Jones FC	4.00	1.20
❑ 205 Derek Jeter FC	10.00	3.00
❑ 206 Troy Glaus FC	2.50	.75
❑ 207 Frank Thomas FC	4.00	1.20
❑ 208 Greg Maddux FC	6.00	1.80
❑ 209 Ivan Rodriguez FC	4.00	1.20
❑ 210 Jeff Bagwell FC	2.50	.75
❑ 211 Todd Helton FC	2.50	.75
❑ 212 Ken Griffey Jr. FC	6.00	1.80
❑ 213 Manny Ramirez FC	2.50	.75
❑ 214 Mark McGwire FC	10.00	3.00
❑ 215 Mike Piazza FC	6.00	1.80
❑ 216 Pedro Martinez FC	4.00	1.20
❑ 217 Sammy Sosa FC	6.00	1.80
❑ 218 Tony Gwynn FC	5.00	1.50
❑ 219 Vladimir Guerrero FC	4.00	1.20
❑ 220 Nomar Garciaparra FC	6.00	1.80
❑ NNO BB Best Coupon	2.00	.60
❑ NNO The Rookies Coupon	.50	.15

2001 Donruss Rookies

	Nm-Mt	Ex-Mt
COMP.FACT.SET (106)	60.00	18.00
COMP.SET w/o SP's (105)	50.00	15.00
❑ R1 Adam Dunn	.75	.23
❑ R2 Ryan Drese RC	.75	.23
❑ R3 Bud Smith RC	.40	.12
❑ R4 Tsuyoshi Shinjo RC	.75	.23
❑ R5 Roy Oswalt	.75	.23
❑ R6 Wilmy Caceres RC	.40	.12
❑ R7 Willie Harris RC	.40	.12
❑ R8 Andres Torres RC	.40	.12

❑ R9 Brandon Knight RC	.40	.12
❑ R10 Horacio Ramirez RC	.75	.23
❑ R11 Benito Baez RC	.40	.12
❑ R12 Jeremy Affeldt RC	.75	.23
❑ R13 Ryan Jensen RC	.40	.12
❑ R14 Casey Fossum RC	.40	.12
❑ R15 Ramon Vazquez RC	.40	.12
❑ R16 Dustan Mohr RC	.40	.12
❑ R17 Saul Rivera RC	.40	.12
❑ R18 Zach Day RC	.40	.12
❑ R19 Erik Hiljus RC	.40	.12
❑ R20 Cesar Crespo RC	.40	.12
❑ R21 Wilson Guzman RC	.40	.12
❑ R22 Travis Hafner RC	2.50	.75
❑ R23 Grant Balfour RC	.40	.12
❑ R24 Johnny Estrada RC	1.25	.35
❑ R25 Morgan Ensberg RC	1.25	.35
❑ R26 Jack Wilson RC	2.00	.60
❑ R27 Aubrey Huff	.40	.12
❑ R28 Endy Chavez RC	.40	.12
❑ R29 Delvin James RC	.40	.12
❑ R30 Michael Cuddyer	.40	.12
❑ R31 Jason Michaels RC	.40	.12
❑ R32 Martin Vargas RC	.40	.12
❑ R33 Donaldo Mendez RC	.40	.12
❑ R34 Jorge Julio RC	.40	.12
❑ R35 T.Spooneybarger RC	.40	.12
❑ R36 Kurt Ainsworth	.40	.12
❑ R37 Josh Fogg RC	.40	.12
❑ R38 Brian Reith RC	.40	.12
❑ R39 Rick Bauer RC	.40	.12
❑ R40 Tim Redding	.40	.12
❑ R41 Erick Almonte RC	.40	.12
❑ R42 Juan A.Pena RC	.40	.12
❑ R43 Ken Harvey	.40	.12
❑ R44 David Brous RC	.40	.12
❑ R45 Kevin Olsen RC	.40	.12
❑ R46 Henry Mateo RC	.40	.12
❑ R47 Nick Neugebauer	.40	.12
❑ R48 Mike Penney RC	.40	.12
❑ R49 Jay Gibbons RC	1.25	.35
❑ R50 Tim Christman RC	.40	.12
❑ R51 B.Duckworth RC	.40	.12
❑ R52 Brett Jodie RC	.40	.12
❑ R53 Christian Parker RC	.40	.12
❑ R54 Carlos Hernandez	.40	.12
❑ R55 Brandon Larson RC	.40	.12
❑ R56 Nick Punto RC	.40	.12
❑ R57 Elpidio Guzman RC	.40	.12
❑ R58 Joe Beimel RC	.40	.12
❑ R59 Junior Spivey RC	.75	.23
❑ R60 Will Ohman RC	.40	.12
❑ R61 Brandon Lyon RC	.40	.12
❑ R62 Stubby Clapp RC	.40	.12
❑ R63 J.Duchscherer RC	.40	.12
❑ R64 Jimmy Rollins	.40	.12
❑ R65 David Williams RC	.40	.12
❑ R66 Craig Monroe RC	.40	.12
❑ R67 Jose Acevedo RC	.40	.12
❑ R68 Jason Jennings	.40	.12
❑ R69 Josh Phelps	.40	.12
❑ R70 Brian Roberts RC	.40	.12
❑ R71 Claudio Vargas RC	.40	.12
❑ R72 Adam Johnson	.40	.12
❑ R73 Bart Miadich RC	.40	.12
❑ R74 Juan Rivera	.40	.12
❑ R75 Brad Voyles RC	.40	.12
❑ R76 Nate Cornejo	.40	.12
❑ R77 Juan Moreno RC	.40	.12
❑ R78 Brian Rogers RC	.40	.12
❑ R79 R.Rodriguez RC	.40	.12
❑ R80 Geronimo Gil RC	.40	.12
❑ R81 Joe Kennedy RC	.75	.23
❑ R82 Kevin Joseph RC	.40	.12
❑ R83 Josue Perez RC	.40	.12
❑ R84 Victor Zambrano RC	.75	.23
❑ R85 Josh Towers RC	.40	.12
❑ R86 Mike Rivera RC	.40	.12
❑ R87 Mark Prior RC	15.00	4.50
❑ R88 Juan Cruz RC	.40	.12
❑ R89 Dewon Brazelton RC	.75	.23
❑ R90 Angel Berroa RC	1.25	.35
❑ R91 Mark Teixeira RC	6.00	1.80
❑ R92 Cody Ransom RC	.40	.12
❑ R93 Angel Santos RC	.40	.12
❑ R94 Corky Miller RC	.40	.12
❑ R95 Brandon Berger RC	.40	.12
❑ R96 Corey Patterson UPD	.40	.12
❑ R97 A. Pujols UPD UER Homers and RBI Stats wrong	30.00	9.00
❑ R98 Josh Beckett UPD	.40	.12
❑ R99 C.C. Sabathia UPD	.40	.12
❑ R100 A. Soriano UPD	.75	.23
❑ R101 Ben Sheets UPD	.75	.23
❑ R102 Rafael Soriano UPD	.75	.23
❑ R103 Wilson Betemit UPD	.40	.12
❑ R104 Ichiro Suzuki UPD	15.00	4.50
❑ R105 Jose Ortiz UPD	.40	.12

2002 Donruss Rookies

	Nm-Mt	Ex-Mt
COMPLETE SET (110)	25.00	7.50
❑ 1 Kazuhisa Ishii RC	1.50	.45
❑ 2 P.J. Bevis RC	.40	.12
❑ 3 Jason Simontacchi RC	.40	.12
❑ 4 John Lackey	.25	.07
❑ 5 Travis Driskill RC	.40	.12
❑ 6 Carl Sadler RC	.40	.12
❑ 7 Tim Kalita RC	.40	.12
❑ 8 Nelson Castro RC	.40	.12
❑ 9 Francis Beltran RC	.40	.12
❑ 10 So Taguchi RC	.50	.15
❑ 11 Ryan Bukvich RC	.40	.12
❑ 12 Brian Fitzgerald RC	.40	.12
❑ 13 Kevin Frederick RC	.40	.12
❑ 14 Chone Figgins RC	.75	.23
❑ 15 Marlon Byrd	.25	.07
❑ 16 Ron Calloway RC	.40	.12
❑ 17 Jason Lane	.25	.07
❑ 18 Satoru Komiyama RC	.40	.12
❑ 19 John Ennis RC	.40	.12
❑ 20 Juan Brito RC	.40	.12
❑ 21 Gustavo Chacin RC	.50	.15
❑ 22 Josh Bard RC	.40	.12
❑ 23 Brett Myers	.25	.07
❑ 24 Mike Smith RC	.40	.12
❑ 25 Eric Hinske	.25	.07
❑ 26 Jake Peavy	.40	.12
❑ 27 Todd Donovan RC	.40	.12
❑ 28 Luis Ugueto RC	.40	.12
❑ 29 Corey Thurman RC	.40	.12
❑ 30 Takahito Nomura RC	.40	.12
❑ 31 Andy Shibilo RC	.40	.12
❑ 32 Mike Crudale RC	.40	.12

	MINT	NRMT
❑ 33 Earl Snyder RC	.50	.15
❑ 34 Brian Tallet RC	.40	.12
❑ 35 Miguel Asencio RC	.40	.12
❑ 36 Felix Escalona RC	.40	.12
❑ 37 Drew Henson	.40	.12
❑ 38 Steve Kent RC	.40	.12
❑ 39 Rene Reyes RC	.40	.12
❑ 40 Edwin Almonte RC	.40	.12
❑ 41 Chris Snelling RC	.40	.12
❑ 42 Franklyn German RC	.40	.12
❑ 43 Jeriome Robertson RC	.40	.12
❑ 44 Colin Young RC	.40	.12
❑ 45 Jeremy Lambert RC	.40	.12
❑ 46 Kirk Saarloos RC	.40	.12
❑ 47 Matt Childers RC	.40	.12
❑ 48 Justin Wayne	.25	.07
❑ 49 Jose Valverde RC	.50	.15
❑ 50 Wily Mo Pena	.40	.12
❑ 51 Victor Alvarez RC	.40	.12
❑ 52 Julius Matos RC	.40	.12
❑ 53 Aaron Cook RC	.40	.12
❑ 54 Jeff Austin RC	.40	.12
❑ 55 Adrian Burnside RC	.40	.12
❑ 56 Brandon Puffer RC	.40	.12
❑ 57 Jeremy Hill RC	.40	.12
❑ 58 Jaime Cerda RC	.40	.12
❑ 59 Aaron Guiel RC	.40	.12
❑ 60 Ron Chiavacci	.25	.07
❑ 61 Kevin Cash RC	.40	.12
❑ 62 Elio Serrano RC	.40	.12
❑ 63 Julio Mateo RC	.40	.12
❑ 64 Cam Esslinger RC	.40	.12
❑ 65 Ken Huckaby RC	.40	.12
❑ 66 Will Nieves RC	.40	.12
❑ 67 Luis Martinez RC	.40	.12
❑ 68 Scotty Layfield RC	.40	.12
❑ 69 Jeremy Guthrie RC	.75	.23
❑ 70 Hansel Izquierdo RC	.40	.12
❑ 71 Shane Nance RC	.40	.12
❑ 72 Jeff Baker RC	1.50	.45
❑ 73 Cliff Bartosh RC	.40	.12
❑ 74 Mitch Wylie RC	.40	.12
❑ 75 Oliver Perez RC	3.00	.90
❑ 76 Matt Thornton RC	.40	.12
❑ 77 John Foster RC	.40	.12
❑ 78 Joe Borchard	.25	.07
❑ 79 Eric Junge RC	.40	.12
❑ 80 Jorge Sosa RC	.40	.12
❑ 81 Runelvys Hernandez RC	.40	.12
❑ 82 Kevin Mench	.25	.07
❑ 83 Ben Kozlowski RC	.40	.12
❑ 84 Trey Hodges RC	.40	.12
❑ 85 Reed Johnson RC	.50	.15
❑ 86 Eric Eckenstahler RC	.40	.12
❑ 87 Franklin Nunez RC	.40	.12
❑ 88 Victor Martinez	.75	.23
❑ 89 Kevin Gryboski RC	.40	.12
❑ 90 Jason Jennings	.25	.07
❑ 91 Jim Rushford RC	.40	.12
❑ 92 Jeremy Ward RC	.40	.12
❑ 93 Adam Walker RC	.40	.12
❑ 94 Freddy Sanchez RC	.40	.12
❑ 95 Wilson Valdez RC	.40	.12
❑ 96 Lee Gardner RC	.40	.12
❑ 97 Eric Good RC	.40	.12
❑ 98 Hank Blalock	.75	.23
❑ 99 Mark Corey RC	.40	.12
❑ 100 Jason Davis RC	.75	.23
❑ 101 Mike Gonzalez RC	.40	.12
❑ 102 David Ross RC	.40	.12
❑ 103 Tyler Yates RC	.50	.15
❑ 104 Cliff Lee RC	.75	.23
❑ 105 Mike Moriarty RC	.40	.12
❑ 106 Josh Hancock RC	.40	.12
❑ 107 Jason Beverlin RC	.40	.12
❑ 108 Clay Condrey RC	.40	.12
❑ 109 Shawn Sedlacek RC	.40	.12
❑ 110 Sean Burroughs	.40	.12

2003 Donruss Rookies

	MINT	NRMT
COMPLETE SET (65)	20.00	9.00
COMMON CARD (1-65)	.20	.09
COMMON RC	.25	.11

	MINT	NRMT
❑ 1 Jeremy Bonderman RC	.50	.23
❑ 2 Adam Loewen RC	.60	.25
❑ 3 Dan Haren RC	.50	.23
❑ 4 Jose Contreras RC	.60	.25
❑ 5 Hideki Matsui RC	2.00	.90
❑ 6 Arnie Munoz RC	.25	.11
❑ 7 Miguel Cabrera	.50	.23
❑ 8 Andrew Brown RC	.40	.18
❑ 9 Josh Hall RC	.40	.18
❑ 10 Josh Stewart RC	.25	.11
❑ 11 Clint Barmes RC	.40	.18
❑ 12 Luis Ayala RC	.25	.11
❑ 13 Brandon Webb RC	.60	.25
❑ 14 Greg Aquino RC	.25	.11
❑ 15 Chien-Ming Wang RC	.60	.25
❑ 16 Rickie Weeks RC	1.50	.70
❑ 17 Edgar Gonzalez RC	.25	.11
❑ 18 Dontrelle Willis	.30	.14
❑ 19 Bo Hart RC	.40	.18
❑ 20 Rosman Garcia RC	.25	.11
❑ 21 Jeremy Griffiths RC	.40	.18
❑ 22 Craig Brazell RC	.40	.18
❑ 23 Daniel Cabrera RC	.60	.25
❑ 24 Fernando Cabrera RC	.25	.11
❑ 25 Terrmel Sledge RC	.40	.18
❑ 26 Ramon Nivar RC	.50	.23
❑ 27 Rob Hammock RC	.40	.18
❑ 28 Francisco Rosario RC	.25	.11
❑ 29 Cory Stewart RC	.25	.11
❑ 30 Felix Sanchez RC	.25	.11
❑ 31 Jorge Cordova RC	.25	.11
❑ 32 Rocco Baldelli	.20	.09
❑ 33 Beau Kemp RC	.25	.11
❑ 34 Mike Nakamura RC	.25	.11
❑ 35 Rett Johnson RC	.40	.18
❑ 36 Guillermo Quiroz RC	.50	.23
❑ 37 Hong-Chih Kuo RC	.50	.23
❑ 38 Ian Ferguson RC	.25	.11
❑ 39 Franklin Perez RC	.25	.11
❑ 40 Tim Olson RC	.40	.18
❑ 41 Jerome Williams	.20	.09
❑ 42 Rich Fischer RC	.25	.11
❑ 43 Phil Seibel RC	.25	.11
❑ 44 Aaron Looper RC	.25	.11
❑ 45 Jae Weong Seo	.20	.09
❑ 46 Chad Gaudin RC	.25	.11
❑ 47 Matt Kata RC	.50	.23
❑ 48 Ryan Wagner RC	.40	.18
❑ 49 Michel Hernandez RC	.25	.11
❑ 50 Diegomar Markwell RC	.25	.11
❑ 51 Doug Waechter RC	.40	.18
❑ 52 Mike Nicolas RC	.25	.11
❑ 53 Prentice Redman RC	.25	.11
❑ 54 Shane Bazzell RC	.25	.11
❑ 55 Delmon Young RC	2.00	.90
❑ 56 Brian Stokes RC	.25	.11
❑ 57 Matt Bruback RC	.25	.11
❑ 58 Nook Logan RC	.25	.11
❑ 59 Oscar Villarreal RC	.25	.11
❑ 60 Pete LaForest RC	.40	.18
❑ 61 Shea Hillenbrand	.20	.09
❑ 62 Aramis Ramirez	.20	.09
❑ 63 Aaron Boone	.20	.09
❑ 64 Roberto Alomar	.30	.14
❑ 65 Rickey Henderson	.50	.23

2004 Donruss

	MINT	NRMT
COMPLETE SET (400)	150.00	70.00
COMP.SET w/o SP's (300)	25.00	11.00
COMMON CARD (71-370)	.30	.14
COMMON CARD (1-25/371-400)	2.00	.90
COMMON CARD (26-70)	2.00	.90

	MINT	NRMT
❑ 1 Derek Jeter DK	4.00	1.80
❑ 2 Greg Maddux DK	3.00	1.35
❑ 3 Albert Pujols DK	4.00	1.80
❑ 4 Ichiro Suzuki DK	3.00	1.35
❑ 5 Alex Rodriguez DK	3.00	1.35
❑ 6 Roger Clemens DK	4.00	1.80
❑ 7 Andruw Jones DK	2.00	.90
❑ 8 Barry Bonds DK	5.00	2.20
❑ 9 Jeff Bagwell DK	2.00	.90
❑ 10 Randy Johnson DK	2.00	.90
❑ 11 Scott Rolen DK	2.00	.90
❑ 12 Lance Berkman DK	2.00	.90
❑ 13 Barry Zito DK	2.00	.90
❑ 14 Manny Ramirez DK	2.00	.90
❑ 15 Carlos Delgado DK	2.00	.90
❑ 16 Alfonso Soriano DK	2.00	.90
❑ 17 Todd Helton DK	2.00	.90
❑ 18 Mike Mussina DK	2.00	.90
❑ 19 Austin Kearns DK	2.00	.90
❑ 20 Nomar Garciaparra DK	3.00	1.35
❑ 21 Chipper Jones DK	2.00	.90
❑ 22 Mark Prior DK	2.00	.90
❑ 23 Jim Thome DK	2.00	.90
❑ 24 Vladimir Guerrero DK	2.00	.90
❑ 25 Pedro Martinez DK	2.00	.90
❑ 26 Sergio Mitre RR	2.00	.90
❑ 27 Adam Loewen RR	2.00	.90
❑ 28 Alfredo Gonzalez RR	2.00	.90
❑ 29 Miguel Ojeda RR	2.00	.90
❑ 30 Rosman Garcia RR	2.00	.90
❑ 31 Arnie Munoz RR	2.00	.90
❑ 32 Andrew Brown RR	2.00	.90
❑ 33 Josh Hall RR	2.00	.90
❑ 34 Josh Stewart RR	2.00	.90
❑ 35 Clint Barmes RR	2.00	.90
❑ 36 Brandon Webb RR	2.00	.90
❑ 37 Chien-Ming Wang RR	3.00	1.35
❑ 38 Edgar Gonzalez RR	2.00	.90
❑ 39 Alejandro Machado RR	2.00	.90
❑ 40 Jeremy Griffiths RR	2.00	.90
❑ 41 Craig Brazell RR	2.00	.90
❑ 42 Daniel Cabrera RR	3.00	1.35
❑ 43 Fernando Cabrera RR	2.00	.90
❑ 44 Termel Sledge RR	2.00	.90
❑ 45 Rob Hammock RR	2.00	.90
❑ 46 Francisco Rosario RR	2.00	.90
❑ 47 Francisco Cruceta RR	2.00	.90
❑ 48 Rett Johnson RR	2.00	.90
❑ 49 Guillermo Quiroz RR	2.00	.90
❑ 50 Hong-Chih Kuo RR	3.00	1.35
❑ 51 Ian Ferguson RR	2.00	.90
❑ 52 Tim Olson RR	2.00	.90
❑ 53 Todd Wellemeyer RR	2.00	.90
❑ 54 Rich Fischer RR	2.00	.90
❑ 55 Phil Seibel RR	2.00	.90
❑ 56 Joe Valentine RR	2.00	.90
❑ 57 Matt Kata RR	2.00	.90
❑ 58 Michael Hessman RR	2.00	.90
❑ 59 Michel Hernandez RR	2.00	.90

60	Doug Waechter RR	2.00	.90
61	Prentice Redman RR	2.00	.90
62	Nook Logan RR	2.00	.90
63	Oscar Villarreal RR	2.00	.90
64	Pete LaForest RR	2.00	.90
65	Matt Bruback RR	2.00	.90
66	Dan Haren RR	2.00	.90
67	Greg Aquino RR	2.00	.90
68	Lew Ford RR	3.00	1.35
69	Jeff Duncan RR	2.00	.90
70	Ryan Wagner RR	2.00	.90
71	Bengie Molina	.30	.14
72	Brad Fullmer	.30	.14
73	Darin Erstad	.30	.14
74	David Eckstein	.30	.14
75	Garret Anderson	.30	.14
76	Jarrod Washburn	.30	.14
77	Kevin Appier	.30	.14
78	Scott Spiezio	.30	.14
79	Tim Salmon	.50	.23
80	Troy Glaus	.30	.14
81	Troy Percival	.30	.14
82	Jason Johnson	.30	.14
83	Jay Gibbons	.30	.14
84	Melvin Mora	.30	.14
85	Sidney Ponson	.30	.14
86	Tony Batista	.30	.14
87	Bill Mueller	.30	.14
88	Byung-Hyun Kim	.30	.14
89	David Ortiz	.75	.35
90	Derek Lowe	.30	.14
91	Johnny Damon	.75	.35
92	Casey Fossum	.30	.14
93	Manny Ramirez	.50	.23
94	Nomar Garciaparra	1.25	.55
95	Pedro Martinez	.75	.35
96	Todd Walker	.30	.14
97	Trot Nixon	.30	.14
98	Bartolo Colon	.30	.14
99	Carlos Lee	.30	.14
100	D'Angelo Jimenez	.30	.14
101	Esteban Loaiza	.30	.14
102	Frank Thomas	.75	.35
103	Joe Crede	.30	.14
104	Jose Valentin	.30	.14
105	Magglio Ordonez	.30	.14
106	Mark Buehrle	.30	.14
107	Paul Konerko	.30	.14
108	Brandon Phillips	.30	.14
109	C.C Sabathia	.30	.14
110	Ellis Burks	.30	.14
111	Jeremy Guthrie	.30	.14
112	Josh Bard	.30	.14
113	Matt Lawton	.30	.14
114	Milton Bradley	.30	.14
115	Omar Vizquel	.50	.23
116	Travis Hafner	.30	.14
117	Bobby Higginson	.30	.14
118	Carlos Pena	.30	.14
119	Dmitri Young	.30	.14
120	Eric Munson	.30	.14
121	Jeremy Bonderman	.30	.14
122	Nate Cornejo	.30	.14
123	Omar Infante	.30	.14
124	Ramon Santiago	.30	.14
125	Angel Berroa	.30	.14
126	Carlos Beltran	.50	.23
127	Desi Relaford	.30	.14
128	Jeremy Affeldt	.30	.14
129	Joe Randa	.30	.14
130	Ken Harvey	.30	.14
131	Mike MacDougal	.30	.14
132	Michael Tucker	.30	.14
133	Mike Sweeney	.30	.14
134	Raul Ibanez	.30	.14
135	Runelvys Hernandez	.30	.14
136	A.J. Pierzynski	.30	.14
137	Brad Radke	.30	.14
138	Corey Koskie	.30	.14
139	Cristian Guzman	.30	.14
140	Doug Mientkiewicz	.30	.14
141	Dustan Mohr	.30	.14
142	Jacque Jones	.30	.14
143	Kenny Rogers	.30	.14
144	Bobby Kielty	.30	.14
145	Kyle Lohse	.30	.14
146	Luis Rivas	.30	.14
147	Torii Hunter	.30	.14
148	Alfonso Soriano	.50	.23
149	Andy Pettitte	.50	.23
150	Bernie Williams	.50	.23
151	David Wells	.30	.14
152	Derek Jeter	1.50	.70
153	Hideki Matsui	1.25	.55
154	Jason Giambi	.30	.14
155	Jorge Posada	.50	.23
156	Jose Contreras	.30	.14
157	Mike Mussina	.50	.23
158	Nick Johnson	.30	.14
159	Robin Ventura	.30	.14
160	Roger Clemens	1.50	.70
161	Barry Zito	.30	.14
162	Chris Singleton	.30	.14
163	Eric Byrnes	.30	.14
164	Eric Chavez	.30	.14
165	Erubiel Durazo	.30	.14
166	Keith Foulke	.30	.14
167	Mark Ellis	.30	.14
168	Miguel Tejada	.30	.14
169	Mark Mulder	.30	.14
170	Ramon Hernandez	.30	.14
171	Ted Lilly	.30	.14
172	Terrence Long	.30	.14
173	Tim Hudson	.30	.14
174	Bret Boone	.30	.14
175	Carlos Guillen	.30	.14
176	Dan Wilson	.30	.14
177	Edgar Martinez	.50	.23
178	Freddy Garcia	.30	.14
179	Gil Meche	.30	.14
180	Ichiro Suzuki	1.25	.55
181	Jamie Moyer	.30	.14
182	Joel Pineiro	.30	.14
183	John Olerud	.30	.14
184	Mike Cameron	.30	.14
185	Randy Winn	.30	.14
186	Ryan Franklin	.30	.14
187	Kazuhiro Sasaki	.30	.14
188	Aubrey Huff	.30	.14
189	Carl Crawford	.30	.14
190	Joe Kennedy	.30	.14
191	Marlon Anderson	.30	.14
192	Rey Ordonez	.30	.14
193	Rocco Baldelli	.30	.14
194	Toby Hall	.30	.14
195	Travis Lee	.30	.14
196	Alex Rodriguez	1.25	.55
197	Carl Everett	.30	.14
198	Chan Ho Park	.30	.14
199	Einar Diaz	.30	.14
200	Hank Blalock	.30	.14
201	Ismael Valdes	.30	.14
202	Juan Gonzalez	.50	.23
203	Mark Teixeira	.30	.14
204	Mike Young	.30	.14
205	Rafael Palmeiro	.50	.23
206	Carlos Delgado	.30	.14
207	Kelvim Escobar	.30	.14
208	Eric Hinske	.30	.14
209	Frank Catalanotto	.30	.14
210	Josh Phelps	.30	.14
211	Orlando Hudson	.30	.14
212	Roy Halladay	.30	.14
213	Shannon Stewart	.30	.14
214	Vernon Wells	.30	.14
215	Carlos Baerga	.30	.14
216	Curt Schilling	.30	.14
217	Junior Spivey	.30	.14
218	Luis Gonzalez	.30	.14
219	Lyle Overbay	.30	.14
220	Mark Grace	.50	.23
221	Matt Williams	.30	.14
222	Randy Johnson	.75	.35
223	Shea Hillenbrand	.30	.14
224	Steve Finley	.30	.14
225	Andruw Jones	.30	.14
226	Chipper Jones	.75	.35
227	Gary Sheffield	.30	.14
228	Greg Maddux	1.25	.55
229	Javy Lopez	.30	.14
230	John Smoltz	.50	.23
231	Marcus Giles	.30	.14
232	Mike Hampton	.30	.14
233	Rafael Furcal	.30	.14
234	Robert Fick	.30	.14
235	Russ Ortiz	.30	.14
236	Alex Gonzalez	.30	.14
237	Carlos Zambrano	.30	.14
238	Corey Patterson	.30	.14
239	Hee Seop Choi	.30	.14
240	Kerry Wood	.75	.35
241	Mark Bellhorn	.30	.14
242	Mark Prior	.75	.35
243	Moises Alou	.30	.14
244	Sammy Sosa	1.25	.55
245	Aaron Boone	.30	.14
246	Adam Dunn	.50	.23
247	Austin Kearns	.30	.14
248	Barry Larkin	.50	.23
249	Felipe Lopez	.30	.14
250	Jose Guillen	.30	.14
251	Ken Griffey Jr.	1.25	.55
252	Jason LaRue	.30	.14
253	Scott Williamson	.30	.14
254	Sean Casey	.30	.14
255	Shawn Chacon	.30	.14
256	Chris Stynes	.30	.14
257	Jason Jennings	.30	.14
258	Jay Payton	.30	.14
259	Jose Hernandez	.30	.14
260	Larry Walker	.50	.23
261	Preston Wilson	.30	.14
262	Ronnie Belliard	.30	.14
263	Todd Helton	.50	.23
264	A.J. Burnett	.30	.14
265	Alex Gonzalez	.30	.14
266	Brad Penny	.30	.14
267	Derrek Lee	.30	.14
268	Ivan Rodriguez	.75	.35
269	Josh Beckett	.30	.14
270	Juan Encarnacion	.30	.14
271	Juan Pierre	.30	.14
272	Luis Castillo	.30	.14
273	Mike Lowell	.30	.14
274	Todd Hollandsworth	.30	.14
275	Billy Wagner	.30	.14
276	Brad Ausmus	.30	.14
277	Craig Biggio	.50	.23
278	Jeff Bagwell	.50	.23
279	Jeff Kent	.30	.14
280	Lance Berkman	.30	.14
281	Richard Hidalgo	.30	.14
282	Roy Oswalt	.30	.14
283	Wade Miller	.30	.14
284	Adrian Beltre	.50	.23
285	Brian Jordan	.30	.14
286	Cesar Izturis	.30	.14
287	Dave Roberts	.30	.14
288	Eric Gagne	.75	.35
289	Fred McGriff	.50	.23
290	Hideo Nomo	.75	.35
291	Kazuhisa Ishii	.30	.14
292	Kevin Brown	.30	.14
293	Paul Lo Duca	.30	.14
294	Shawn Green	.30	.14
295	Ben Sheets	.30	.14
296	Geoff Jenkins	.30	.14
297	Rey Sanchez	.30	.14
298	Richie Sexson	.30	.14
299	Wes Helms	.30	.14
300	Brad Wilkerson	.30	.14
301	Claudio Vargas	.30	.14
302	Endy Chavez	.30	.14
303	Fernando Tatis	.30	.14
304	Javier Vazquez	.30	.14
305	Jose Vidro	.30	.14
306	Michael Barrett	.30	.14
307	Orlando Cabrera	.30	.14
308	Tony Armas Jr.	.30	.14
309	Vladimir Guerrero	.75	.35
310	Zach Day	.30	.14
311	Al Leiter	.30	.14
312	Cliff Floyd	.30	.14
313	Jae Weong Seo	.30	.14
314	Jeromy Burnitz	.30	.14
315	Mike Piazza	1.25	.55
316	Mo Vaughn	.30	.14
317	Roberto Alomar	.50	.23

#	Card	Nm-Mt	Ex-Mt
❑ 318	Roger Cedeno	.30	.14
❑ 319	Tom Glavine	.50	.23
❑ 320	Jose Reyes	.30	.14
❑ 321	Bobby Abreu	.30	.14
❑ 322	Brett Myers	.30	.14
❑ 323	David Bell	.30	.14
❑ 324	Jim Thome	.75	.35
❑ 325	Jimmy Rollins	.30	.14
❑ 326	Kevin Millwood	.30	.14
❑ 327	Marlon Byrd	.30	.14
❑ 328	Mike Lieberthal	.30	.14
❑ 329	Pat Burrell	.30	.14
❑ 330	Randy Wolf	.30	.14
❑ 331	Aramis Ramirez	.30	.14
❑ 332	Brian Giles	.30	.14
❑ 333	Jason Kendall	.30	.14
❑ 334	Kenny Lofton	.30	.14
❑ 335	Kip Wells	.30	.14
❑ 336	Kris Benson	.30	.14
❑ 337	Randall Simon	.30	.14
❑ 338	Reggie Sanders	.30	.14
❑ 339	Albert Pujols	1.50	.70
❑ 340	Edgar Renteria	.30	.14
❑ 341	Fernando Vina	.30	.14
❑ 342	J.D. Drew	.30	.14
❑ 343	Jim Edmonds	.30	.14
❑ 344	Matt Morris	.30	.14
❑ 345	Mike Matheny	.30	.14
❑ 346	Scott Rolen	.75	.35
❑ 347	Tino Martinez	.50	.23
❑ 348	Woody Williams	.30	.14
❑ 349	Brian Lawrence	.30	.14
❑ 350	Mark Kotsay	.30	.14
❑ 351	Mark Loretta	.30	.14
❑ 352	Ramon Vazquez	.30	.14
❑ 353	Rondell White	.30	.14
❑ 354	Ryan Klesko	.30	.14
❑ 355	Sean Burroughs	.30	.14
❑ 356	Trevor Hoffman	.30	.14
❑ 357	Xavier Nady	.30	.14
❑ 358	Andres Galarraga	.30	.14
❑ 359	Barry Bonds	2.00	.90
❑ 360	Benito Santiago	.30	.14
❑ 361	Deivi Cruz	.30	.14
❑ 362	Edgardo Alfonzo	.30	.14
❑ 363	J.T. Snow	.30	.14
❑ 364	Jason Schmidt	.30	.14
❑ 365	Kirk Rueter	.30	.14
❑ 366	Kurt Ainsworth	.30	.14
❑ 367	Marquis Grissom	.30	.14
❑ 368	Ray Durham	.30	.14
❑ 369	Rich Aurilia	.30	.14
❑ 370	Tim Worrell	.30	.14
❑ 371	Troy Glaus TC	2.00	.90
❑ 372	Melvin Mora TC	2.00	.90
❑ 373	Nomar Garciaparra TC	3.00	1.35
❑ 374	Maggio Ordonez TC	2.00	.90
❑ 375	Omar Vizquel TC	2.00	.90
❑ 376	Dmitri Young TC	2.00	.90
❑ 377	Mike Sweeney TC	2.00	.90
❑ 378	Torii Hunter TC	2.00	.90
❑ 379	Derek Jeter TC	4.00	1.80
❑ 380	Barry Zito TC	2.00	.90
❑ 381	Ichiro Suzuki TC	3.00	1.35
❑ 382	Rocco Baldelli TC	2.00	.90
❑ 383	Alex Rodriguez TC	3.00	1.35
❑ 384	Carlos Delgado TC	2.00	.90
❑ 385	Randy Johnson TC	2.00	.90
❑ 386	Greg Maddux TC	3.00	1.35
❑ 387	Sammy Sosa TC	3.00	1.35
❑ 388	Ken Griffey Jr. TC	3.00	1.35
❑ 389	Todd Helton TC	2.00	.90
❑ 390	Ivan Rodriguez TC	2.00	.90
❑ 391	Jeff Bagwell TC	2.00	.90
❑ 392	Hideo Nomo TC	2.00	.90
❑ 393	Richie Sexson TC	2.00	.90
❑ 394	Vladimir Guerrero TC	2.00	.90
❑ 395	Mike Piazza TC	3.00	1.35
❑ 396	Jim Thome TC	2.00	.90
❑ 397	Jason Kendall TC	2.00	.90
❑ 398	Albert Pujols TC	4.00	1.80
❑ 399	Ryan Klesko TC	2.00	.90
❑ 400	Barry Bonds TC	5.00	2.20

2005 Donruss

	Nm-Mt	Ex-Mt
COMPLETE SET (400)	150.00	45.00
COMP.SET w/o SP's (300)	25.00	7.50
COMMON CARD (71-370)	.30	.09
COMMON (1-25/371-400)	2.00	.60
COMMON CARD (26-70)	2.00	.60
1-25 STATED ODDS 1:6		
26-70 STATED ODDS 1:6		
371-400 STATED ODDS 1:6		

#	Card	Nm-Mt	Ex-Mt
❑ 1	Garret Anderson DK	2.00	.60
❑ 2	Vladimir Guerrero DK	2.00	.60
❑ 3	Manny Ramirez DK	2.00	.60
❑ 4	Kerry Wood DK	2.00	.60
❑ 5	Sammy Sosa DK	3.00	.90
❑ 6	Maggio Ordonez DK	2.00	.60
❑ 7	Adam Dunn DK	2.00	.60
❑ 8	Todd Helton DK	2.00	.60
❑ 9	Josh Beckett DK	2.00	.60
❑ 10	Miguel Cabrera DK	2.00	.60
❑ 11	Lance Berkman DK	2.00	.60
❑ 12	Carlos Beltran DK	2.00	.60
❑ 13	Shawn Green DK	2.00	.60
❑ 14	Roger Clemens DK	4.00	1.20
❑ 15	Mike Piazza DK	3.00	.90
❑ 16	Alex Rodriguez DK	3.00	.90
❑ 17	Derek Jeter DK	4.00	1.20
❑ 18	Mark Mulder DK	2.00	.60
❑ 19	Jim Thome DK	2.00	.60
❑ 20	Albert Pujols DK	4.00	1.20
❑ 21	Scott Rolen DK	2.00	.60
❑ 22	Aubrey Huff DK	2.00	.60
❑ 23	Alfonso Soriano DK	2.00	.60
❑ 24	Hank Blalock DK	2.00	.60
❑ 25	Vernon Wells DK	2.00	.60
❑ 26	Kazuo Matsui RR	3.00	.90
❑ 27	B.J. Upton RR	3.00	.90
❑ 28	Charles Thomas RR	2.00	.60
❑ 29	Akinori Otsuka RR	3.00	.90
❑ 30	David Aardsma RR	2.00	.60
❑ 31	Travis Blackley RR	2.00	.60
❑ 32	Brad Halsey RR	2.00	.60
❑ 33	David Wright RR	8.00	2.40
❑ 34	Kazuhito Tadano RR	3.00	.90
❑ 35	Casey Kotchman RR	3.00	.90
❑ 36	Khalil Greene RR	5.00	1.50
❑ 37	Adrian Gonzalez RR	2.00	.60
❑ 38	Zack Greinke RR	3.00	.90
❑ 39	Chad Cordero RR	2.00	.60
❑ 40	Scott Kazmir RR	5.00	1.50
❑ 41	Jeremy Guthrie RR	2.00	.60
❑ 42	Noah Lowry RR	2.00	.60
❑ 43	Chase Utley RR	3.00	.90
❑ 44	Billy Traber RR	2.00	.60
❑ 45	Aarom Baldiris RR	2.00	.60
❑ 46	Abe Alvarez RR	2.00	.60
❑ 47	Angel Chavez RR	2.00	.60
❑ 48	Joe Mauer RR	5.00	1.50
❑ 49	Joey Gathright RR	3.00	.90
❑ 50	John Gall RR	2.00	.60
❑ 51	Ronald Belisario RR	2.00	.60
❑ 52	Ryan Wing RR	2.00	.60
❑ 53	Scott Proctor RR	2.00	.60
❑ 54	Yadier Molina RR	3.00	.90
❑ 55	Carlos Hines RR	2.00	.60
❑ 56	Frankie Francisco RR	2.00	.60
❑ 57	Graham Koonce RR	2.00	.60
❑ 58	Jake Woods RR	2.00	.60
❑ 59	Jason Bartlett RR	2.00	.60
❑ 60	Mike Rouse RR	2.00	.60
❑ 61	Phil Stockman RR	2.00	.60
❑ 62	Renyel Pinto RR	2.00	.60
❑ 63	Roberto Novoa RR	2.00	.60
❑ 64	Ryan Meaux RR	2.00	.60
❑ 65	Dave Crouthers RR	2.00	.60
❑ 66	Justin Knoedler RR	2.00	.60
❑ 67	Justin Leone RR	2.00	.60
❑ 68	Nick Regilio RR	2.00	.60
❑ 69	Mike Gosling RR	2.00	.60
❑ 70	Onil Joseph RR	2.00	.60
❑ 71	Bartolo Colon	.30	.09
❑ 72	Brad Fullmer	.30	.09
❑ 73	Chone Figgins	.30	.09
❑ 74	Darin Erstad	.30	.09
❑ 75	Francisco Rodriguez	.30	.09
❑ 76	Garret Anderson	.30	.09
❑ 77	Jarrod Washburn	.30	.09
❑ 78	John Lackey	.30	.09
❑ 79	Jose Guillen	.30	.09
❑ 80	Robb Quinlan	.30	.09
❑ 81	Tim Salmon	.50	.15
❑ 82	Troy Glaus	.30	.09
❑ 83	Troy Percival	.30	.09
❑ 84	Vladimir Guerrero	.75	.23
❑ 85	Brandon Webb	.30	.09
❑ 86	Casey Fossum	.30	.09
❑ 87	Luis Gonzalez	.30	.09
❑ 88	Randy Johnson	.75	.23
❑ 89	Richie Sexson	.30	.09
❑ 90	Robby Hammock	.30	.09
❑ 91	Roberto Alomar	.50	.15
❑ 92	Adam LaRoche	.30	.09
❑ 93	Andruw Jones	.30	.09
❑ 94	Bubba Nelson	.30	.09
❑ 95	Chipper Jones	.75	.23
❑ 96	J.D. Drew	.30	.09
❑ 97	John Smoltz	.50	.15
❑ 98	Johnny Estrada	.30	.09
❑ 99	Marcus Giles	.30	.09
❑ 100	Mike Hampton	.30	.09
❑ 101	Nick Green	.30	.09
❑ 102	Rafael Furcal	.30	.09
❑ 103	Russ Ortiz	.30	.09
❑ 104	Adam Loewen	.30	.09
❑ 105	Brian Roberts	.30	.09
❑ 106	Javy Lopez	.30	.09
❑ 107	Jay Gibbons	.30	.09
❑ 108	Larry Bigbie	.30	.09
❑ 109	Luis Matos	.30	.09
❑ 110	Melvin Mora	.30	.09
❑ 111	Miguel Tejada	.30	.09
❑ 112	Rafael Palmeiro	.50	.15
❑ 113	Rodrigo Lopez	.30	.09
❑ 114	Sidney Ponson	.30	.09
❑ 115	Bill Mueller	.30	.09
❑ 116	Byung-Hyun Kim	.30	.09
❑ 117	Curt Schilling	.75	.23
❑ 118	David Ortiz	.75	.23
❑ 119	Derek Lowe	.30	.09
❑ 120	Doug Mientkiewicz	.30	.09
❑ 121	Jason Varitek	.50	.15
❑ 122	Johnny Damon	.75	.23
❑ 123	Keith Foulke	.30	.09
❑ 124	Kevin Youkilis	.30	.09
❑ 125	Manny Ramirez	.50	.15
❑ 126	Orlando Cabrera	.30	.09
❑ 127	Pedro Martinez	.75	.23
❑ 128	Trot Nixon	.30	.09
❑ 129	Aramis Ramirez	.30	.09
❑ 130	Carlos Zambrano	.30	.09
❑ 131	Corey Patterson	.30	.09
❑ 132	Derrek Lee	.30	.09
❑ 133	Greg Maddux	1.25	.35
❑ 134	Kerry Wood	.75	.23
❑ 135	Mark Prior	.75	.23
❑ 136	Matt Clement	.30	.09
❑ 137	Moises Alou	.30	.09
❑ 138	Nomar Garciaparra	1.25	.35
❑ 139	Sammy Sosa	1.25	.35
❑ 140	Todd Walker	.30	.09
❑ 141	Angel Guzman	.30	.09
❑ 142	Billy Koch	.30	.09

❑ 143 Carlos Lee	.30	.09
❑ 144 Frank Thomas	.75	.23
❑ 145 Maggio Ordonez	.30	.09
❑ 146 Mark Buehrle	.30	.09
❑ 147 Paul Konerko	.30	.09
❑ 148 Wilson Valdez	.30	.09
❑ 149 Adam Dunn	.50	.15
❑ 150 Austin Kearns	.30	.09
❑ 151 Barry Larkin	.50	.15
❑ 152 Benito Santiago	.30	.09
❑ 153 Jason LaRue	.30	.09
❑ 154 Ken Griffey Jr.	1.25	.35
❑ 155 Ryan Wagner	.30	.09
❑ 156 Sean Casey	.30	.09
❑ 157 Brandon Phillips	.30	.09
❑ 158 Brian Tallet	.30	.09
❑ 159 C.C. Sabathia	.30	.09
❑ 160 Cliff Lee	.30	.09
❑ 161 Jeremy Guthrie	.30	.09
❑ 162 Jody Gerut	.30	.09
❑ 163 Matt Lawton	.30	.09
❑ 164 Omar Vizquel	.50	.15
❑ 165 Travis Hafner	.30	.09
❑ 166 Victor Martinez	.30	.09
❑ 167 Charles Johnson	.30	.09
❑ 168 Garrett Atkins	.30	.09
❑ 169 Jason Jennings	.30	.09
❑ 170 Jay Payton	.30	.09
❑ 171 Jeromy Burnitz	.30	.09
❑ 172 Joe Kennedy	.30	.09
❑ 173 Larry Walker	.50	.15
❑ 174 Preston Wilson	.30	.09
❑ 175 Todd Helton	.50	.15
❑ 176 Vinny Castilla	.30	.09
❑ 177 Bobby Higginson	.30	.09
❑ 178 Brandon Inge	.30	.09
❑ 179 Carlos Guillen	.30	.09
❑ 180 Carlos Pena	.30	.09
❑ 181 Craig Monroe	.30	.09
❑ 182 Dmitri Young	.30	.09
❑ 183 Eric Munson	.30	.09
❑ 184 Fernando Vina	.30	.09
❑ 185 Ivan Rodriguez	.75	.23
❑ 186 Jeremy Bonderman	.30	.09
❑ 187 Rondell White	.30	.09
❑ 188 A.J. Burnett	.30	.09
❑ 189 Dontrelle Willis	.30	.09
❑ 190 Guillermo Mota	.30	.09
❑ 191 Hee Seop Choi	.30	.09
❑ 192 Jeff Conine	.30	.09
❑ 193 Josh Beckett	.30	.09
❑ 194 Juan Encarnacion	.30	.09
❑ 195 Juan Pierre	.30	.09
❑ 196 Luis Castillo	.30	.09
❑ 197 Miguel Cabrera	.50	.15
❑ 198 Mike Lowell	.30	.09
❑ 199 Paul Lo Duca	.30	.09
❑ 200 Andy Pettitte	.50	.15
❑ 201 Brad Ausmus	.30	.09
❑ 202 Carlos Beltran	.50	.15
❑ 203 Chris Burke	.30	.09
❑ 204 Craig Biggio	.50	.15
❑ 205 Jeff Bagwell	.50	.15
❑ 206 Jeff Kent	.30	.09
❑ 207 Lance Berkman	.30	.09
❑ 208 Morgan Ensberg	.30	.09
❑ 209 Octavio Dotel	.30	.09
❑ 210 Roger Clemens	1.50	.45
❑ 211 Roy Oswalt	.30	.09
❑ 212 Tim Redding	.30	.09
❑ 213 Angel Berroa	.30	.09
❑ 214 Juan Gonzalez	.50	.15
❑ 215 Ken Harvey	.30	.09
❑ 216 Mike Sweeney	.30	.09
❑ 217 Adrian Beltre	.50	.15
❑ 218 Brad Penny	.30	.09
❑ 219 Eric Gagne	.75	.23
❑ 220 Hideo Nomo	.75	.23
❑ 221 Hong-Chih Kuo	.30	.09
❑ 222 Jeff Weaver	.30	.09
❑ 223 Kazuhisa Ishii	.30	.09
❑ 224 Milton Bradley	.30	.09
❑ 225 Shawn Green	.30	.09
❑ 226 Steve Finley	.30	.09
❑ 227 Danny Kolb	.30	.09
❑ 228 Geoff Jenkins	.30	.09
❑ 229 Junior Spivey	.30	.09
❑ 230 Lyle Overbay	.30	.09
❑ 231 Rickie Weeks	.30	.09
❑ 232 Scott Podsednik	.30	.09
❑ 233 Brad Radke	.30	.09
❑ 234 Corey Koskie	.30	.09
❑ 235 Cristian Guzman	.30	.09
❑ 236 Dustan Mohr	.30	.09
❑ 237 Eddie Guardado	.30	.09
❑ 238 J.D. Durbin	.30	.09
❑ 239 Jacque Jones	.30	.09
❑ 240 Joe Nathan	.30	.09
❑ 241 Johan Santana	.50	.15
❑ 242 Lew Ford	.30	.09
❑ 243 Michael Cuddyer	.30	.09
❑ 244 Shannon Stewart	.30	.09
❑ 245 Torii Hunter	.30	.09
❑ 246 Brad Wilkerson	.30	.09
❑ 247 Carl Everett	.30	.09
❑ 248 Jeff Fassero	.30	.09
❑ 249 Jose Vidro	.30	.09
❑ 250 Livan Hernandez	.30	.09
❑ 251 Michael Barrett	.30	.09
❑ 252 Tony Batista	.30	.09
❑ 253 Zach Day	.30	.09
❑ 254 Al Leiter	.30	.09
❑ 255 Cliff Floyd	.30	.09
❑ 256 Jae Weong Seo	.30	.09
❑ 257 John Olerud	.30	.09
❑ 258 Jose Reyes	.30	.09
❑ 259 Mike Cameron	.30	.09
❑ 260 Mike Piazza	1.25	.35
❑ 261 Richard Hidalgo	.30	.09
❑ 262 Tom Glavine	.50	.15
❑ 263 Vance Wilson	.30	.09
❑ 264 Alex Rodriguez	1.25	.35
❑ 265 Armando Benitez	.30	.09
❑ 266 Bernie Williams	.50	.15
❑ 267 Bubba Crosby	.30	.09
❑ 268 Chien-Ming Wang	.30	.09
❑ 269 Derek Jeter	1.50	.45
❑ 270 Esteban Loaiza	.30	.09
❑ 271 Gary Sheffield	.30	.09
❑ 272 Hideki Matsui	1.25	.35
❑ 273 Jason Giambi	.30	.09
❑ 274 Javier Vazquez	.30	.09
❑ 275 Jorge Posada	.50	.15
❑ 276 Jose Contreras	.30	.09
❑ 277 Kenny Lofton	.30	.09
❑ 278 Kevin Brown	.30	.09
❑ 279 Mariano Rivera	.50	.15
❑ 280 Mike Mussina	.50	.15
❑ 281 Barry Zito	.30	.09
❑ 282 Bobby Crosby	.50	.15
❑ 283 Eric Byrnes	.30	.09
❑ 284 Eric Chavez	.30	.09
❑ 285 Erubiel Durazo	.30	.09
❑ 286 Jermaine Dye	.30	.09
❑ 287 Mark Kotsay	.30	.09
❑ 288 Mark Mulder	.30	.09
❑ 289 Rich Harden	.30	.09
❑ 290 Tim Hudson	.30	.09
❑ 291 Billy Wagner	.30	.09
❑ 292 Bobby Abreu	.30	.09
❑ 293 Brett Myers	.30	.09
❑ 294 Eric Milton	.30	.09
❑ 295 Jim Thome	.75	.23
❑ 296 Jimmy Rollins	.30	.09
❑ 297 Kevin Millwood	.30	.09
❑ 298 Marlon Byrd	.30	.09
❑ 299 Mike Lieberthal	.30	.09
❑ 300 Pat Burrell	.30	.09
❑ 301 Randy Wolf	.30	.09
❑ 302 Craig Wilson	.30	.09
❑ 303 Jack Wilson	.30	.09
❑ 304 Jacob Cruz	.30	.09
❑ 305 Jason Bay	.30	.09
❑ 306 Jason Kendall	.30	.09
❑ 307 Jose Castillo	.30	.09
❑ 308 Kip Wells	.30	.09
❑ 309 Brian Giles	.30	.09
❑ 310 Brian Lawrence	.30	.09
❑ 311 Chris Oxspring	.30	.09
❑ 312 David Wells	.30	.09
❑ 313 Freddy Guzman	.30	.09
❑ 314 Jake Peavy	.30	.09
❑ 315 Mark Loretta	.30	.09
❑ 316 Ryan Klesko	.30	.09
❑ 317 Sean Burroughs	.30	.09
❑ 318 Trevor Hoffman	.30	.09
❑ 319 Xavier Nady	.30	.09
❑ 320 A.J. Pierzynski	.30	.09
❑ 321 Edgardo Alfonzo	.30	.09
❑ 322 J.T. Snow	.30	.09
❑ 323 Jason Schmidt	.30	.09
❑ 324 Jerome Williams	.30	.09
❑ 325 Kirk Rueter	.30	.09
❑ 326 Bret Boone	.30	.09
❑ 327 Bucky Jacobsen	.30	.09
❑ 328 Edgar Martinez	.50	.15
❑ 329 Freddy Garcia	.30	.09
❑ 330 Ichiro Suzuki	1.25	.35
❑ 331 Jamie Moyer	.30	.09
❑ 332 Joel Pineiro	.30	.09
❑ 333 Scott Spiezio	.30	.09
❑ 334 Shigetoshi Hasegawa	.30	.09
❑ 335 Albert Pujols	1.50	.45
❑ 336 Edgar Renteria	.30	.09
❑ 337 Jason Isringhausen	.30	.09
❑ 338 Jim Edmonds	.30	.09
❑ 339 Matt Morris	.30	.09
❑ 340 Mike Matheny	.30	.09
❑ 341 Reggie Sanders	.30	.09
❑ 342 Scott Rolen	.75	.23
❑ 343 Woody Williams	.30	.09
❑ 344 Jeff Suppan	.30	.09
❑ 345 Aubrey Huff	.30	.09
❑ 346 Carl Crawford	.30	.09
❑ 347 Chad Gaudin	.30	.09
❑ 348 Delmon Young	.30	.09
❑ 349 Dewon Brazelton	.30	.09
❑ 350 Jose Cruz Jr.	.30	.09
❑ 351 Rocco Baldelli	.30	.09
❑ 352 Tino Martinez	.50	.15
❑ 353 Toby Hall	.30	.09
❑ 354 Alfonso Soriano	.50	.15
❑ 355 Brian Jordan	.30	.09
❑ 356 Francisco Cordero	.30	.09
❑ 357 Hank Blalock	.30	.09
❑ 358 Kenny Rogers	.30	.09
❑ 359 Kevin Mench	.30	.09
❑ 360 Laynce Nix	.30	.09
❑ 361 Mark Teixeira	.30	.09
❑ 362 Michael Young	.30	.09
❑ 363 Alex S. Gonzalez	.30	.09
❑ 364 Alexis Rios	.30	.09
❑ 365 Carlos Delgado	.30	.09
❑ 366 Eric Hinske	.30	.09
❑ 367 Frank Catalanotto	.30	.09
❑ 368 Josh Phelps	.30	.09
❑ 369 Roy Halladay	.30	.09
❑ 370 Vernon Wells	.30	.09
❑ 371 Vladimir Guerrero TC	2.00	.60
❑ 372 Randy Johnson TC	2.00	.60
❑ 373 Chipper Jones TC	2.00	.60
❑ 374 Miguel Tejada TC	2.00	.60
❑ 375 Pedro Martinez TC	2.00	.60
❑ 376 Sammy Sosa TC	3.00	.90
❑ 377 Frank Thomas TC	2.00	.60
❑ 378 Ken Griffey Jr. TC	3.00	.90
❑ 379 Victor Martinez TC	2.00	.60
❑ 380 Todd Helton TC	2.00	.60
❑ 381 Ivan Rodriguez TC	2.00	.60
❑ 382 Miguel Cabrera TC	2.00	.60
❑ 383 Roger Clemens TC	4.00	1.20
❑ 384 Ken Harvey TC	2.00	.60
❑ 385 Eric Gagne TC	2.00	.60
❑ 386 Lyle Overbay TC	2.00	.60
❑ 387 Shannon Stewart TC	2.00	.60
❑ 388 Brad Wilkerson TC	2.00	.60
❑ 389 Mike Piazza TC	3.00	.90
❑ 390 Alex Rodriguez TC	3.00	.90
❑ 391 Mark Mulder TC	2.00	.60
❑ 392 Jim Thome TC	2.00	.60
❑ 393 Jack Wilson TC	2.00	.60
❑ 394 Khalil Greene TC	2.00	.60
❑ 395 Jason Schmidt TC	2.00	.60
❑ 396 Ichiro Suzuki TC	3.00	.90
❑ 397 Albert Pujols TC	4.00	1.20
❑ 398 Rocco Baldelli TC	2.00	.60
❑ 399 Alfonso Soriano TC	2.00	.60
❑ 400 Vernon Wells TC	2.00	.60

2001 Donruss Class of 2001

	Nm-Mt	Ex-Mt
COMP.SET w/o SP's (100)	25.00	7.50
COMMON CARD (1-100)	.40	.12
COMMON (101-200)	4.00	1.20
COMMON (201-300)	6.00	1.80
❑ 1 Alex Rodriguez	1.50	.45
❑ 2 Barry Bonds	2.50	.75
❑ 3 Vladimir Guerrero	1.00	.30
❑ 4 Jim Edmonds	.40	.12
❑ 5 Derek Jeter	2.50	.75
❑ 6 Jose Canseco	1.00	.30
❑ 7 Rafael Furcal	.40	.12
❑ 8 Cal Ripken	3.00	.90
❑ 9 Brad Radke	.40	.12
❑ 10 Miguel Tejada	.40	.12
❑ 11 Pat Burrell	.40	.12
❑ 12 Ken Griffey Jr.	1.50	.45
❑ 13 Cliff Floyd	.40	.12
❑ 14 Luis Gonzalez	.40	.12
❑ 15 Frank Thomas	1.00	.30
❑ 16 Mike Sweeney	.40	.12
❑ 17 Paul LoDuca	.40	.12
❑ 18 Lance Berkman	.40	.12
❑ 19 Tony Gwynn	1.25	.35
❑ 20 Chipper Jones	1.00	.30
❑ 21 Eric Chavez	.40	.12
❑ 22 Kerry Wood	1.00	.30
❑ 23 Jorge Posada	.60	.18
❑ 24 J.D. Drew	.40	.12
❑ 25 Garret Anderson	.40	.12
❑ 26 Mike Piazza	1.50	.45
❑ 27 Kenny Lofton	.40	.12
❑ 28 Mike Mussina	.60	.18
❑ 29 Paul Konerko	.40	.12
❑ 30 Bernie Williams	.60	.18
❑ 31 Eric Milton	.40	.12
❑ 32 Shawn Green	.40	.12
❑ 33 Paul O'Neill	.60	.18
❑ 34 Juan Gonzalez	.60	.18
❑ 35 Andres Galarraga	.40	.12
❑ 36 Gary Sheffield	.40	.12
❑ 37 Ben Grieve	.40	.12
❑ 38 Scott Rolen	1.00	.30
❑ 39 Mark Grace	.60	.18
❑ 40 Hideo Nomo	1.00	.30
❑ 41 Barry Zito	.60	.18
❑ 42 Edgar Martinez	.60	.18
❑ 43 Jarrod Washburn	.40	.12
❑ 44 Greg Maddux	1.50	.45
❑ 45 Mark Buehrle	.40	.12
❑ 46 Larry Walker	.60	.18
❑ 47 Trot Nixon	.40	.12
❑ 48 Nomar Garciaparra	1.50	.45
❑ 49 Robert Fick	.40	.12
❑ 50 Sean Casey	.40	.12
❑ 51 Joe Mays	.40	.12
❑ 52 Roger Clemens	2.00	.60
❑ 53 Chan Ho Park	.40	.12
❑ 54 Carlos Delgado	.40	.12
❑ 55 Phil Nevin	.40	.12
❑ 56 Jason Giambi	.40	.12
❑ 57 Raul Mondesi	.40	.12
❑ 58 Roberto Alomar	.60	.18
❑ 59 Ryan Klesko	.40	.12
❑ 60 Andruw Jones	.40	.12
❑ 61 Gabe Kapler	.40	.12
❑ 62 Darin Erstad	.40	.12
❑ 63 Cristian Guzman	.40	.12
❑ 64 Kazuhiro Sasaki	.40	.12
❑ 65 Doug Mientkiewicz	.40	.12
❑ 66 Sammy Sosa	1.50	.45
❑ 67 Mike Hampton	.40	.12
❑ 68 Rickey Henderson	1.00	.30
❑ 69 Mark Mulder	.40	.12
❑ 70 Mark McGwire	2.50	.75
❑ 71 Freddy Garcia	.40	.12
❑ 72 Ivan Rodriguez	1.00	.30
❑ 73 Terrence Long	.40	.12
❑ 74 Jeff Bagwell	.60	.18
❑ 75 Moises Alou	.40	.12
❑ 76 Todd Helton	.60	.18
❑ 77 Preston Wilson	.40	.12
❑ 78 Pedro Martinez	1.00	.30
❑ 79 Bobby Abreu	.40	.12
❑ 80 Manny Ramirez	.60	.18
❑ 81 Jose Vidro	.40	.12
❑ 82 Randy Johnson	1.00	.30
❑ 83 Richie Sexson	.40	.12
❑ 84 Troy Glaus	.40	.12
❑ 85 Kevin Brown	.40	.12
❑ 86 Carlos Lee	.40	.12
❑ 87 Adrian Beltre	.60	.18
❑ 88 Brian Giles	.40	.12
❑ 89 Jermaine Dye	.40	.12
❑ 90 Craig Biggio	.60	.18
❑ 91 Richard Hidalgo	.40	.12
❑ 92 Magglio Ordonez	.40	.12
❑ 93 Aramis Ramirez	.40	.12
❑ 94 Jeff Kent	.40	.12
❑ 95 Curt Schilling	.40	.12
❑ 96 Tim Hudson	.40	.12
❑ 97 Fred McGriff	.60	.18
❑ 98 Barry Larkin	.60	.18
❑ 99 Jim Thome	1.00	.30
❑ 100 Tom Glavine	.60	.18
❑ 101 S.Douglass/1875 RC	4.00	1.20
❑ 102 R.MacKowiak/1875 RC	6.00	1.80
❑ 103 J.Fikac/1875 RC	4.00	1.20
❑ 104 Henry Mateo/1875 RC	4.00	1.20
❑ 105 G. Gil/1875 RC	4.00	1.20
❑ 106 R. Vazquez/1875 RC	4.00	1.20
❑ 107 P. Santana/1875 RC	4.00	1.20
❑ 108 Ryan Jensen/1875 RC	4.00	1.20
❑ 109 Paul Phillips/1625 RC	4.00	1.20
❑ 110 Saul Rivera/1875 RC	4.00	1.20
❑ 111 Larry Bigbie/1875	4.00	1.20
❑ 112 Josh Phelps/1875	4.00	1.20
❑ 113 Justin Kaye/1875 RC	4.00	1.20
❑ 114 Kris Keller/1625 RC	4.00	1.20
❑ 115 Adam Bernero/1625	4.00	1.20
❑ 116 V.Zambrano/1875 RC	6.00	1.80
❑ 117 Felipe Lopez/1875	4.00	1.20
❑ 118 B.Roberts/1875 RC	4.00	1.20
❑ 119 Kurt Ainsworth/1875	4.00	1.20
❑ 120 G.Perez/1625 RC	4.00	1.20
❑ 121 W.Guzman/1875 RC	4.00	1.20
❑ 122 D.Lewis/1875 RC	4.00	1.20
❑ 123 Nate Teut/1625 RC	4.00	1.20
❑ 124 M. Vargas/1625 RC	4.00	1.20
❑ 125 Brandon Inge/1875	4.00	1.20
❑ 126 T. Phelps/1875 RC	4.00	1.20
❑ 127 Les Walrond/1625 RC	4.00	1.20
❑ 128 J. Atchley/1875 RC	4.00	1.20
❑ 129 S. Clapp/1875 RC	4.00	1.20
❑ 130 Bret Prinz/1875 RC	4.00	1.20
❑ 131 Bert Snow/1875 RC	4.00	1.20
❑ 132 Joe Crede/1625	4.00	1.20
❑ 133 Nick Punto/1875 RC	4.00	1.20
❑ 134 C. Hernandez/1875	4.00	1.20
❑ 135 Ken Vining/1875 RC	4.00	1.20
❑ 136 Luis Pineda/1875 RC	4.00	1.20
❑ 137 W. Abreu/1625 RC	4.00	1.20
❑ 138 Matt Ginter/1625	4.00	1.20
❑ 139 Jason Smith/1875 RC	4.00	1.20
❑ 140 Gene Altman/1625 RC	4.00	1.20
❑ 141 B. Rogers/1875 RC	4.00	1.20
❑ 142 M.Cuddyer/1625	4.00	1.20
❑ 143 Mike Penney/1625 RC	4.00	1.20
❑ 144 S.Podsednik/1875 RC	15.00	4.50
❑ 145 Esix Snead/1625 RC	4.00	1.20
❑ 146 S.Watkins/1875 RC	4.00	1.20
❑ 147 O.Woodards/1625 RC	4.00	1.20
❑ 148 J.Deardorff/1775 RC	4.00	1.20
❑ 149 Eric Cyr/1875 RC	4.00	1.20
❑ 150 Blaine Neal/1625 RC	4.00	1.20
❑ 151 Ben Sheets/1875	6.00	1.80
❑ 152 S.Stewart/1875 RC	4.00	1.20
❑ 153 M.Koplove/1875 RC	4.00	1.20
❑ 154 Kyle Lohse/1875 RC	6.00	1.80
❑ 155 F. Rodney/1875 RC	4.00	1.20
❑ 156 Aubrey Huff/1625	4.00	1.20
❑ 157 Pablo Ozuna/1625	4.00	1.20
❑ 158 Bill Ortega/1625 RC	4.00	1.20
❑ 159 Toby Hall/1875	4.00	1.20
❑ 160 Kevin Olsen/1625 RC	4.00	1.20
❑ 161 Will Ohman/1625 RC	4.00	1.20
❑ 162 Nate Cornejo/1875	4.00	1.20
❑ 163 Jack Cust/1625	4.00	1.20
❑ 164 Juan Rivera/1875	4.00	1.20
❑ 165 J. Riggan/1875 RC	4.00	1.20
❑ 166 D.Mohr/1875 RC	4.00	1.20
❑ 167 Doug Nickle/1875 RC	4.00	1.20
❑ 168 C.Monroe/1625 RC	4.00	1.20
❑ 169 Jason Jennings/1625	4.00	1.20
❑ 170 Bart Miadich/1875 RC	4.00	1.20
❑ 171 Luis Rivas/1625	4.00	1.20
❑ 172 T. Christman/1875 RC	4.00	1.20
❑ 173 L. Hudson/1625 RC	4.00	1.20
❑ 174 Brett Jodie/1875 RC	4.00	1.20
❑ 175 Jorge Julio/1875 RC	4.00	1.20
❑ 176 David Espinosa/1625	4.00	1.20
❑ 177 Mike Maroth/1625 RC	4.00	1.20
❑ 178 Keith Ginter/1625	4.00	1.20
❑ 179 J. Moreno/1875 RC	4.00	1.20
❑ 180 B. Knight/1875 RC	4.00	1.20
❑ 181 Steve Lomasney/1625	4.00	1.20
❑ 182 J. Grabow/1625 RC	4.00	1.20
❑ 183 Steve Green/1875 RC	4.00	1.20
❑ 185 Bob File/1875 RC	4.00	1.20
❑ 186 Brent Abernathy/1625	4.00	1.20
❑ 187 M.Ensberg/1875 RC	6.00	1.80
❑ 188 Wily Mo Pena/1625	4.00	1.20
❑ 189 Ken Harvey/1875	4.00	1.20
❑ 190 Josh Pearce/1875 RC	4.00	1.20
❑ 191 Cesar Izturis/1625	4.00	1.20
❑ 192 Eric Hinske/1625 RC	6.00	1.80
❑ 193 Joe Beimel/1875 RC	4.00	1.20
❑ 194 Timo Perez/1775	4.00	1.20
❑ 195 Troy Mattes/1875 RC	4.00	1.20
❑ 196 Eric Valent/1625	4.00	1.20
❑ 197 Ed Rogers/1875 RC	4.00	1.20
❑ 198 G.Balfour/1875 RC	4.00	1.20
❑ 199 Benito Baez/1875 RC	4.00	1.20
❑ 200 Vernon Wells/1875	4.00	1.20
❑ 201 J.Kennedy PH/525 RC	10.00	3.00
❑ 202 W.Betemit PH/525 RC	6.00	1.80
❑ 203 C.Parker PH/525 RC	6.00	1.80
❑ 204 J.Gibbons PH/525 RC	10.00	3.00
❑ 205 C.Garcia PH/425 RC	6.00	1.80
❑ 206 J.Wilson PH/525 RC	10.00	3.00
❑ 207 J.Estrada PH/425 RC	10.00	3.00
❑ 208 W.Ruan PH/425 RC	6.00	1.80
❑ 209 B.Duckworth PH/525 RC	6.00	1.80
❑ 210 W.Harris PH/625 RC	6.00	1.80
❑ 211 M.Byrd PH/525 RC	10.00	3.00
❑ 212 C.C. Sabathia PH/600	6.00	1.80
❑ 213 D.Tankersley PH/525 RC	6.00	1.80
❑ 214 B.Larson PH/425 RC	6.00	1.80
❑ 215 A.Gomez PH/425 RC	6.00	1.80
❑ 216 Bill Hall PH/525 RC	6.00	1.80
❑ 217 A.Perez PH/525 RC	6.00	1.80
❑ 218 J.Affeldt PH/425 RC	10.00	3.00
❑ 219 J.Spivey PH/625 RC	10.00	3.00
❑ 220 C.Fossum PH/425 RC	6.00	1.80
❑ 221 B.Lyon PH/625 RC	6.00	1.80
❑ 222 A.Santos PH/625 RC	6.00	1.80
❑ 223 L.Davis PH/625 RC	6.00	1.80
❑ 224 Zach Day PH/425 RC	6.00	1.80
❑ 225 D.Williams PH/425 RC	6.00	1.80
❑ 226 C.Crespo PH/625 RC	6.00	1.80
❑ 227 J.Acevedo PH/425 RC	6.00	1.80
❑ 228 T.Hafner PH/625 RC	15.00	4.50
❑ 229 O.Hudson PH/525 RC	10.00	3.00
❑ 230 J.Mieses PH/425 RC	6.00	1.80
❑ 231 R.Rodriguez PH/425 RC	6.00	1.80
❑ 232 A.Soriano PH/525	10.00	3.00

Card	Nm-Mt	Ex-Mt
❑ 233 Jason Hart PH/525	6.00	1.80
❑ 234 E.Chavez PH/425 RC	6.00	1.80
❑ 235 D.James PH/525 RC	6.00	1.80
❑ 236 R.Drese PH/625 RC	10.00	3.00
❑ 237 J.Owens PH/425 RC	6.00	1.80
❑ 238 B.Voyles PH/425 RC	6.00	1.80
❑ 239 Nate Frese PH/425 RC	6.00	1.80
❑ 240 Josh Beckett PH/600	6.00	1.80
❑ 241 Roy Oswalt PH/525	10.00	3.00
❑ 242 J.Uribe PH/475 RC	10.00	3.00
❑ 243 C.Aldridge PH/425 RC	6.00	1.80
❑ 244 Adam Dunn PH/525	10.00	3.00
❑ 245 Bud Smith PH/525 RC	6.00	1.80
❑ 246 A.Hernandez PH/525 RC	6.00	1.80
❑ 247 M.Guerrier PH/625 RC	6.00	1.80
❑ 248 J.Rollins PH/625	6.00	1.80
❑ 249 W.Caceres PH/425 RC	6.00	1.80
❑ 250 J.Michaels PH/425 RC	6.00	1.80
❑ 251 I.Suzuki PH/625 RC	60.00	18.00
❑ 252 John Buck PH/525 RC	10.00	3.00
❑ 252 Adam Johnson PH/625	6.00	1.80
❑ 253 A.Torres PH/525 RC	6.00	1.80
❑ 254 A.Amezaga PH/625 RC	6.00	1.80
❑ 255 C.Miller PH/525 RC	6.00	1.80
❑ 256 R.Soriano PH/425 RC	10.00	3.00
❑ 257 D.Mendez PH/425 RC	6.00	1.80
❑ 258 V.Martinez PH/625 RC	80.00	24.00
❑ 259 C.Patterson PH/525	6.00	1.80
❑ 260 H.Ramirez PH/425 RC	10.00	3.00
❑ 261 E.Guzman PH/425 RC	6.00	1.80
❑ 262 Juan Diaz PH/425 RC	6.00	1.80
❑ 263 M.Rivera PH/625 RC	6.00	1.80
❑ 264 B.Lawrence PH/425 RC	6.00	1.80
❑ 265 J.Perez PH/425 RC	6.00	1.80
❑ 266 J.Nunez PH/425 RC	6.00	1.80
❑ 267 E.Bedard PH/625 RC	6.00	1.80
❑ 268 A.Pujols PH/525 RC	100.00	30.00
❑ 269 D.Sanchez PH/425 RC	6.00	1.80
❑ 270 C.Ransom PH/625 RC	6.00	1.80
❑ 271 G.Miller PH/425 RC	6.00	1.80
❑ 272 A.Pettyjohn PH/425 RC	6.00	1.80
❑ 273 T.Shinjo PH/625 RC	10.00	3.00
❑ 274 C.Vargas PH/425 RC	6.00	1.80
❑ 275 J.Duchscherer PH/625 RC	6.00	1.80
❑ 276 Tim Spooneybarger PH/625 RC	6.00	1.80
❑ 277 R.Bauer PH/625 RC	6.00	1.80
❑ 278 Josh Fogg PH/625 RC	6.00	1.80
❑ 279 B.Reith PH/425 RC	6.00	1.80
❑ 280 S.MacRae PH/625 RC	6.00	1.80
❑ 281 R.Ludwick PH/625 RC	6.00	1.80
❑ 282 E.Almonte PH/625 RC	6.00	1.80
❑ 283 J.Towers PH/525 RC	6.00	1.80
❑ 284 J. A.Pena PH/625 RC	6.00	1.80
❑ 285 D. Brous PH/425 RC	6.00	1.80
❑ 286 Erik Hiljus PH/625 RC	6.00	1.80
❑ 287 N.Neugebauer PH/525	6.00	1.80
❑ 288 J.Melian PH/625 RC	6.00	1.80
❑ 289 B.Sylvester PH/425 RC	6.00	1.80
❑ 290 Carlos Valderrama PH/425 RC	6.00	1.80
❑ 291 J.Cueto PH/625 RC	6.00	1.80
❑ 292 M.White PH/425 RC	6.00	1.80
❑ 293 N.Maness PH/425 RC	6.00	1.80
❑ 294 J.Lane PH/625 RC	6.00	1.80
❑ 295 B.Berger PH/625 RC	6.00	1.80
❑ 296 A.Berroa PH/525 RC	10.00	3.00
❑ 297 Juan Cruz PH/525 RC	6.00	1.80
❑ 298 D.Brazelton PH/525 RC	10.00	3.00
❑ 299 M.Prior PH/525 RC	60.00	18.00
❑ 300 M.Teixeira PH/525 RC	40.00	12.00

2001 Donruss Classics

	Nm-Mt	Ex-Mt
COMP.SET w/o SP's (100)	25.00	7.50
COMMON CARD (1-100)	.60	.18
COMMON (101-150)	5.00	1.50
COMMON (151-200)	4.00	1.20
❑ 1 Alex Rodriguez	2.50	.75
❑ 2 Barry Bonds	4.00	1.20
❑ 3 Cal Ripken	5.00	1.50
❑ 4 Chipper Jones	1.50	.45
❑ 5 Derek Jeter	4.00	1.20
❑ 6 Troy Glaus	.60	.18

Card	Nm-Mt	Ex-Mt
❑ 7 Frank Thomas	1.50	.45
❑ 8 Greg Maddux	2.50	.75
❑ 9 Ivan Rodriguez	1.50	.45
❑ 10 Jeff Bagwell	1.00	.30
❑ 11 Cliff Floyd	.60	.18
❑ 12 Todd Helton	1.00	.30
❑ 13 Ken Griffey Jr.	2.50	.75
❑ 14 Manny Ramirez	1.00	.30
❑ 15 Mark McGwire	4.00	1.20
❑ 16 Mike Piazza	2.50	.75
❑ 17 Nomar Garciaparra	2.50	.75
❑ 18 Pedro Martinez	1.50	.45
❑ 19 Randy Johnson	1.50	.45
❑ 20 Rick Ankiel	.60	.18
❑ 21 Rickey Henderson	1.50	.45
❑ 22 Roger Clemens	3.00	.90
❑ 23 Sammy Sosa	2.50	.75
❑ 24 Tony Gwynn	2.00	.60
❑ 25 Vladimir Guerrero	1.50	.45
❑ 26 Kazuhiro Sasaki	.60	.18
❑ 27 Roberto Alomar	1.00	.30
❑ 28 Barry Zito	1.00	.30
❑ 29 Pat Burrell	.60	.18
❑ 30 Harold Baines	.60	.18
❑ 31 Carlos Delgado	.60	.18
❑ 32 J.D. Drew	.60	.18
❑ 33 Jim Edmonds	.60	.18
❑ 34 Darin Erstad	.60	.18
❑ 35 Jason Giambi	.60	.18
❑ 36 Tom Glavine	1.00	.30
❑ 37 Juan Gonzalez	1.00	.30
❑ 38 Mark Grace	1.00	.30
❑ 39 Shawn Green	.60	.18
❑ 40 Tim Hudson	.60	.18
❑ 41 Andruw Jones	.60	.18
❑ 42 Jeff Kent	.60	.18
❑ 43 Barry Larkin	1.00	.30
❑ 44 Rafael Furcal	.60	.18
❑ 45 Mike Mussina	1.00	.30
❑ 46 Hideo Nomo	1.50	.45
❑ 47 Rafael Palmeiro	1.00	.30
❑ 48 Scott Rolen	1.50	.45
❑ 49 Gary Sheffield	.60	.18
❑ 50 Bernie Williams	1.00	.30
❑ 51 Bob Abreu	.60	.18
❑ 52 Edgardo Alfonzo	.60	.18
❑ 53 Edgar Martinez	1.00	.30
❑ 54 Magglio Ordonez	.60	.18
❑ 55 Kerry Wood	1.50	.45
❑ 56 Adrian Beltre	1.00	.30
❑ 57 Lance Berkman	.60	.18
❑ 58 Kevin Brown	.60	.18
❑ 59 Sean Casey	.60	.18
❑ 60 Eric Chavez	.60	.18
❑ 61 Bartolo Colon	.60	.18
❑ 62 Johnny Damon	1.00	.30
❑ 63 Jermaine Dye	.60	.18
❑ 64 Juan Encarnacion	.60	.18
❑ 65 Carl Everett	.60	.18
❑ 66 Brian Giles	.60	.18
❑ 67 Mike Hampton	.60	.18
❑ 68 Richard Hidalgo	.60	.18
❑ 69 Geoff Jenkins	.60	.18
❑ 70 Jacque Jones	.60	.18
❑ 71 Jason Kendall	.60	.18
❑ 72 Ryan Klesko	.60	.18
❑ 73 Chan Ho Park	.60	.18
❑ 74 Richie Sexson	.60	.18
❑ 75 Mike Sweeney	.60	.18
❑ 76 Fernando Tatis	.60	.18
❑ 77 Miguel Tejada	.60	.18
❑ 78 Jose Vidro	.60	.18
❑ 79 Larry Walker	1.00	.30
❑ 80 Preston Wilson	.60	.18
❑ 81 Craig Biggio	1.00	.30
❑ 82 Fred McGriff	1.00	.30
❑ 83 Jim Thome	1.50	.45
❑ 84 Garret Anderson	.60	.18
❑ 85 Russell Branyan	.60	.18
❑ 86 Tony Batista	.60	.18
❑ 87 Terrence Long	.60	.18
❑ 88 Brad Fullmer	.60	.18
❑ 89 Rusty Greer	.60	.18
❑ 90 Orlando Hernandez	.60	.18
❑ 91 Gabe Kapler	.60	.18
❑ 92 Paul Konerko	.60	.18
❑ 93 Carlos Lee	.60	.18
❑ 94 Kenny Lofton	.60	.18
❑ 95 Raul Mondesi	.60	.18
❑ 96 Jorge Posada	1.00	.30
❑ 97 Tim Salmon	1.00	.30
❑ 98 Greg Vaughn	.60	.18
❑ 99 Mo Vaughn	.60	.18
❑ 100 Omar Vizquel	1.00	.30
❑ 101 Aubrey Huff SP	5.00	1.50
❑ 102 Jimmy Rollins SP	5.00	1.50
❑ 103 Cory Aldridge SP RC	5.00	1.50
❑ 104 Wilmy Caceres SP RC	5.00	1.50
❑ 105 Josh Beckett SP	5.00	1.50
❑ 106 Wilson Betemit SP RC	5.00	1.50
❑ 107 Timo Perez SP	5.00	1.50
❑ 108 Albert Pujols SP RC	100.00	30.00
❑ 109 Bud Smith SP RC	5.00	1.50
❑ 110 Jack Wilson SP RC	10.00	3.00
❑ 111 Alex Escobar SP	5.00	1.50
❑ 112 J. Estrada SP RC	8.00	2.40
❑ 113 Pedro Feliz SP	5.00	1.50
❑ 114 Nate Frese SP RC	5.00	1.50
❑ 115 Carlos Garcia SP RC	5.00	1.50
❑ 116 Brandon Larson SP RC	5.00	1.50
❑ 117 Alexis Gomez SP RC	5.00	1.50
❑ 118 Jason Hart SP	5.00	1.50
❑ 119 Adam Dunn SP	8.00	2.40
❑ 120 Marcus Giles SP	5.00	1.50
❑ 121 C. Parker SP RC	5.00	1.50
❑ 122 J.Melian SP RC	5.00	1.50
❑ 123 Endy Chavez SP RC	5.00	1.50
❑ 124 A.Hernandez SP RC	5.00	1.50
❑ 125 Joe Kennedy SP RC	8.00	2.40
❑ 126 Jose Mieses SP RC	5.00	1.50
❑ 127 C.C. Sabathia SP	5.00	1.50
❑ 128 Eric Munson SP	5.00	1.50
❑ 129 Xavier Nady SP	5.00	1.50
❑ 130 H. Ramirez SP RC	8.00	2.40
❑ 131 Abraham Nunez SP	5.00	1.50
❑ 132 Jose Ortiz SP	5.00	1.50
❑ 133 Jeremy Owens SP RC	5.00	1.50
❑ 134 Claudio Vargas SP RC	5.00	1.50
❑ 135 Corey Patterson SP	5.00	1.50
❑ 136 Andres Torres SP RC	5.00	1.50
❑ 137 Ben Sheets SP	8.00	2.40
❑ 138 Joe Crede SP	5.00	1.50
❑ 139 A.Pettyjohn SP RC	5.00	1.50
❑ 140 E.Guzman SP RC	5.00	1.50
❑ 141 Jay Gibbons SP RC	8.00	2.40
❑ 142 Wilkin Ruan SP RC	5.00	1.50
❑ 143 Tsuyoshi Shinjo SP RC	8.00	2.40
❑ 144 Alfonso Soriano SP	8.00	2.40
❑ 145 Nick Johnson SP	5.00	1.50
❑ 146 Ichiro Suzuki SP RC	60.00	18.00
❑ 147 Juan Uribe SP RC	8.00	2.40
❑ 148 Jack Cust SP	5.00	1.50
❑ 149 C.Valderrama SP RC	5.00	1.50
❑ 150 Matt White SP RC	5.00	1.50
❑ 151 Hank Aaron LGD	10.00	3.00
❑ 152 Ernie Banks LGD	5.00	1.50
❑ 153 Johnny Bench LGD	5.00	1.50
❑ 154 George Brett LGD	12.00	3.60
❑ 155 Lou Brock LGD	5.00	1.50
❑ 156 Rod Carew LGD	5.00	1.50
❑ 157 Steve Carlton LGD	4.00	1.20
❑ 158 Bob Feller LGD	4.00	1.20
❑ 159 Bob Gibson LGD	5.00	1.50
❑ 160 Reggie Jackson LGD	5.00	1.50

❑ 161 Al Kaline LGD 5.00 1.50
❑ 162 Sandy Koufax LGD SP .00 .00
❑ 163 Don Mattingly LGD 12.00 3.60
❑ 164 Willie Mays LGD 10.00 3.00
❑ 165 Willie McCovey LGD 4.00 1.20
❑ 166 Joe Morgan LGD 4.00 1.20
❑ 167 Stan Musial LGD 8.00 2.40
❑ 168 Jim Palmer LGD 4.00 1.20
❑ 169 Brooks Robinson LGD 5.00 1.50
❑ 170 Frank Robinson LGD 5.00 1.50
❑ 171 Nolan Ryan LGD 12.00 3.60
❑ 172 Mike Schmidt LGD 10.00 3.00
❑ 173 Tom Seaver LGD 5.00 1.50
❑ 174 Warren Spahn LGD 5.00 1.50
❑ 175 Robin Yount LGD 8.00 2.40
❑ 176 Wade Boggs LGD 5.00 1.50
❑ 177 Ty Cobb LGD 8.00 2.40
❑ 178 Lou Gehrig LGD 10.00 3.00
❑ 179 Luis Aparicio LGD 4.00 1.20
❑ 180 Babe Ruth LGD 15.00 4.50
❑ 181 Ryne Sandberg LGD 10.00 3.00
❑ 182 Yogi Berra LGD 5.00 1.50
❑ 183 R.Clemente LGD 12.00 3.60
❑ 184 Eddie Murray LGD 5.00 1.50
❑ 185 Robin Roberts LGD SP .00 .00
❑ 186 Duke Snider LGD 5.00 1.50
❑ 187 Orlando Cepeda LGD 4.00 1.20
❑ 188 Billy Williams LGD 4.00 1.20
❑ 189 Juan Marichal LGD 4.00 1.20
❑ 190 Harmon Killebrew LGD 5.00 1.50
❑ 191 Kirby Puckett LGD 5.00 1.50
❑ 192 Carlton Fisk LGD 5.00 1.50
❑ 193 Dave Winfield LGD 4.00 1.20
❑ 194 Whitey Ford LGD 5.00 1.50
❑ 195 Paul Molitor LGD 5.00 1.50
❑ 196 Tony Perez LGD 4.00 1.20
❑ 197 Ozzie Smith LGD 8.00 2.40
❑ 198 Ralph Kiner LGD 5.00 1.50
❑ 199 Fergie Jenkins LGD 4.00 1.20
❑ 200 Phil Rizzuto LGD 5.00 1.50

2002 Donruss Classics

	Nm-Mt	Ex-Mt
COMP.SET w/o SP's (100)	25.00	7.50
COMMON CARD (1-100)	.60	.18
COMMON (101-150/201-225)	4.00	1.20
COMMON CARD (151-200)	4.00	1.20

❑ 1 Alex Rodriguez 2.50 .75
❑ 2 Barry Bonds 4.00 1.20
❑ 3 C.C. Sabathia .60 .18
❑ 4 Chipper Jones 1.50 .45
❑ 5 Derek Jeter 4.00 1.20
❑ 6 Troy Glaus .60 .18
❑ 7 Frank Thomas 1.50 .45
❑ 8 Greg Maddux 2.50 .75
❑ 9 Ivan Rodriguez 1.50 .45
❑ 10 Jeff Bagwell 1.00 .30
❑ 11 Mark Buehrle .60 .18
❑ 12 Todd Helton 1.00 .30
❑ 13 Ken Griffey Jr. 2.50 .75
❑ 14 Manny Ramirez 1.00 .30
❑ 15 Brad Penny .60 .18
❑ 16 Mike Piazza 2.50 .75
❑ 17 Nomar Garciaparra 2.50 .75
❑ 18 Pedro Martinez 1.50 .45
❑ 19 Randy Johnson 1.50 .45
❑ 20 Bud Smith .60 .18
❑ 21 Rickey Henderson 1.50 .45
❑ 22 Roger Clemens 3.00 .90
❑ 23 Sammy Sosa 2.50 .75
❑ 24 Brandon Duckworth .60 .18
❑ 25 Vladimir Guerrero 1.50 .45
❑ 26 Kazuhiro Sasaki .60 .18
❑ 27 Roberto Alomar 1.00 .30
❑ 28 Barry Zito .60 .18
❑ 29 Rich Aurilia .60 .18
❑ 30 Ben Sheets .60 .18
❑ 31 Carlos Delgado .60 .18
❑ 32 J.D. Drew .60 .18
❑ 33 Jermaine Dye .60 .18
❑ 34 Darin Erstad .60 .18
❑ 35 Jason Giambi .60 .18
❑ 36 Tom Glavine 1.00 .30
❑ 37 Juan Gonzalez 1.00 .30
❑ 38 Luis Gonzalez .60 .18
❑ 39 Shawn Green .60 .18
❑ 40 Tim Hudson .60 .18
❑ 41 Andruw Jones .60 .18
❑ 42 Shannon Stewart .60 .18
❑ 43 Barry Larkin 1.00 .30
❑ 44 Wade Miller .60 .18
❑ 45 Mike Mussina 1.00 .30
❑ 46 Hideo Nomo 1.50 .45
❑ 47 Rafael Palmeiro 1.00 .30
❑ 48 Scott Rolen 1.50 .45
❑ 49 Gary Sheffield .60 .18
❑ 50 Bernie Williams 1.00 .30
❑ 51 Bob Abreu .60 .18
❑ 52 Javier Vazquez .60 .18
❑ 53 Edgar Martinez 1.00 .30
❑ 54 Magglio Ordonez .60 .18
❑ 55 Kerry Wood 1.50 .45
❑ 56 Adrian Beltre 1.00 .30
❑ 57 Lance Berkman .60 .18
❑ 58 Kevin Brown .60 .18
❑ 59 Sean Casey .60 .18
❑ 60 Eric Chavez .60 .18
❑ 61 Robert Person .60 .18
❑ 62 Jeremy Giambi .60 .18
❑ 63 Freddy Garcia .60 .18
❑ 64 Alfonso Soriano 1.00 .30
❑ 65 Doug Davis .60 .18
❑ 66 Brian Giles .60 .18
❑ 67 Moises Alou .60 .18
❑ 68 Richard Hidalgo .60 .18
❑ 69 Paul LoDuca .60 .18
❑ 70 Aramis Ramirez .60 .18
❑ 71 Andres Galarraga .60 .18
❑ 72 Ryan Klesko .60 .18
❑ 73 Chan Ho Park .60 .18
❑ 74 Richie Sexson .60 .18
❑ 75 Mike Sweeney .60 .18
❑ 76 Aubrey Huff .60 .18
❑ 77 Miguel Tejada .60 .18
❑ 78 Jose Vidro .60 .18
❑ 79 Larry Walker 1.00 .30
❑ 80 Roy Oswalt .60 .18
❑ 81 Craig Biggio 1.00 .30
❑ 82 Juan Pierre .60 .18
❑ 83 Jim Thome 1.50 .45
❑ 84 Josh Towers .60 .18
❑ 85 Alex Escobar .60 .18
❑ 86 Cliff Floyd .60 .18
❑ 87 Terrence Long .60 .18
❑ 88 Curt Schilling .60 .18
❑ 89 Carlos Beltran 1.00 .30
❑ 90 Albert Pujols 3.00 .90
❑ 91 Gabe Kapler .60 .18
❑ 92 Mark Mulder .60 .18
❑ 93 Carlos Lee .60 .18
❑ 94 Robert Fick .60 .18
❑ 95 Raul Mondesi .60 .18
❑ 96 Ichiro Suzuki 2.50 .75
❑ 97 Adam Dunn 1.00 .30
❑ 98 Corey Patterson .60 .18
❑ 99 Tsuyoshi Shinjo .60 .18
❑ 100 Joe Mays .60 .18
❑ 101 Juan Cruz ROO 4.00 1.20
❑ 102 Marlon Byrd ROO 4.00 1.20
❑ 103 Luis Garcia ROO 4.00 1.20
❑ 104 Jorge Padilla ROO RC 4.00 1.20
❑ 105 Dennis Tankersley ROO 4.00 1.20
❑ 106 Josh Pearce ROO 4.00 1.20
❑ 107 Ramon Vazquez ROO 4.00 1.20
❑ 108 Chris Baker ROO RC 4.00 1.20
❑ 109 Eric Cyr ROO 4.00 1.20
❑ 110 Reed Johnson ROO RC 5.00 1.50
❑ 111 Ryan Jamison ROO 4.00 1.20
❑ 112 Antonio Perez ROO 4.00 1.20
❑ 113 Satoru Komiyama ROO RC 4.00 1.20
❑ 114 Austin Kearns ROO 4.00 1.20
❑ 115 Juan Pena ROO 4.00 1.20
❑ 116 Orlando Hudson ROO 4.00 1.20
❑ 117 Kazuhisa Ishii ROO RC 8.00 2.40
❑ 118 Erik Bedard ROO 4.00 1.20
❑ 119 Luis Ugueto ROO RC 4.00 1.20
❑ 120 Ben Howard ROO RC 4.00 1.20
❑ 121 Morgan Ensberg ROO 4.00 1.20
❑ 122 Doug Devore ROO RC 4.00 1.20
❑ 123 Josh Phelps ROO 4.00 1.20
❑ 124 Angel Berroa ROO 4.00 1.20
❑ 125 Ed Rogers ROO 4.00 1.20
❑ 126 Takahito Nomura ROO RC 4.00 1.20
❑ 127 John Ennis ROO RC 4.00 1.20
❑ 128 Bill Hall ROO 4.00 1.20
❑ 129 Dewon Brazelton ROO 4.00 1.20
❑ 130 Hank Blalock ROO 5.00 1.50
❑ 131 So Taguchi ROO RC 5.00 1.50
❑ 132 Jorge De La Rosa ROO RC 4.00 1.20
❑ 133 Matt Thornton ROO RC 4.00 1.20
❑ 134 Brandon Backe ROO RC 5.00 1.50
❑ 135 Jeff Deardorff ROO 4.00 1.20
❑ 136 Steve Smyth ROO 4.00 1.20
❑ 137 An. Machado ROO RC 4.00 1.20
❑ 138 John Buck ROO 4.00 1.20
❑ 139 Mark Prior ROO 8.00 2.40
❑ 140 Sean Burroughs ROO 4.00 1.20
❑ 141 Alex Herrera ROO 4.00 1.20
❑ 142 Francis Beltran ROO RC 4.00 1.20
❑ 143 Jason Romano ROO 4.00 1.20
❑ 144 Michael Cuddyer ROO 4.00 1.20
❑ 145 Steve Bechler ROO RC 4.00 1.20
❑ 146 Alfredo Amezaga ROO 4.00 1.20
❑ 147 Ryan Ludwick ROO 4.00 1.20
❑ 148 Martin Vargas ROO 4.00 1.20
❑ 149 Allan Simpson ROO RC 4.00 1.20
❑ 150 Mark Teixeira ROO 5.00 1.50
❑ 151 Dale Murphy LGD 5.00 1.50
❑ 152 Ernie Banks LGD 5.00 1.50
❑ 153 Johnny Bench LGD 5.00 1.50
❑ 154 George Brett LGD 10.00 3.00
❑ 155 Lou Brock LGD 5.00 1.50
❑ 156 Rod Carew LGD 5.00 1.50
❑ 157 Steve Carlton LGD 4.00 1.20
❑ 158 Joe Torre LGD 5.00 1.50
❑ 159 Dennis Eckersley LGD 4.00 1.20
❑ 160 Reggie Jackson LGD 5.00 1.50
❑ 161 Al Kaline LGD 5.00 1.50
❑ 162 Dave Parker LGD 4.00 1.20
❑ 163 Don Mattingly LGD 10.00 3.00
❑ 164 Tony Gwynn LGD 5.00 1.50
❑ 165 Willie McCovey LGD 4.00 1.20
❑ 166 Joe Morgan LGD 4.00 1.20
❑ 167 Stan Musial LGD 6.00 1.80
❑ 168 Jim Palmer LGD 4.00 1.20
❑ 169 Brooks Robinson LGD 5.00 1.50
❑ 170 Bo Jackson LGD 5.00 1.50
❑ 171 Nolan Ryan LGD 10.00 3.00
❑ 172 Mike Schmidt LGD 8.00 2.40
❑ 173 Tom Seaver LGD 5.00 1.50
❑ 174 Cal Ripken LGD 12.00 3.60
❑ 175 Robin Yount LGD 6.00 1.80
❑ 176 Wade Boggs LGD 5.00 1.50
❑ 177 Gary Carter LGD 4.00 1.20
❑ 178 Ron Santo LGD 5.00 1.50
❑ 179 Luis Aparicio LGD 4.00 1.20
❑ 180 Bobby Doerr LGD 5.00 1.50
❑ 181 Ryne Sandberg LGD 8.00 2.40
❑ 182 Yogi Berra LGD 5.00 1.50
❑ 183 Will Clark LGD 5.00 1.50
❑ 184 Eddie Murray LGD 5.00 1.50
❑ 185 Andre Dawson LGD 4.00 1.20
❑ 186 Duke Snider LGD 5.00 1.50
❑ 187 Orlando Cepeda LGD 4.00 1.20
❑ 188 Billy Williams LGD 4.00 1.20
❑ 189 Juan Marichal LGD 4.00 1.20
❑ 190 Harmon Killebrew LGD 5.00 1.50
❑ 191 Kirby Puckett LGD 5.00 1.50

	Card	Nm-Mt	Ex-Mt
❑	192 Carlton Fisk LGD	5.00	1.50
❑	193 Dave Winfield LGD	4.00	1.20
❑	194 Alan Trammell LGD	4.00	1.20
❑	195 Paul Molitor LGD	5.00	1.50
❑	196 Tony Perez LGD	4.00	1.20
❑	197 Ozzie Smith LGD	6.00	1.80
❑	198 Ralph Kiner LGD	4.00	1.20
❑	199 Fergie Jenkins LGD	4.00	1.20
❑	200 Phil Rizzuto LGD	5.00	1.50
❑	201 Oliver Perez ROO RC	10.00	3.00
❑	202 Aaron Cook ROO RC	4.00	1.20
❑	203 Eric Junge ROO RC	4.00	1.20
❑	204 Freddy Sanchez ROO RC	4.00	1.20
❑	205 Cliff Lee ROO RC	5.00	1.50
❑	206 Run. Hernandez ROO RC	4.00	1.20
❑	207 Chone Figgins ROO RC	5.00	1.50
❑	208 Rodrigo Rosario ROO RC	4.00	1.20
❑	209 Kevin Cash ROO RC	4.00	1.20
❑	210 Josh Bard ROO RC	4.00	1.20
❑	211 Felix Escalona ROO RC	4.00	1.20
❑	212 Jer. Robertson ROO RC	4.00	1.20
❑	213 J. Simontacchi ROO RC	4.00	1.20
❑	214 Shane Nance ROO RC	4.00	1.20
❑	215 Ben Kozlowski ROO RC	4.00	1.20
❑	216 Brian Tallet ROO RC	4.00	1.20
❑	217 Earl Snyder ROO RC	5.00	1.50
❑	218 Andy Pratt ROO RC	4.00	1.20
❑	219 Trey Hodges ROO RC	4.00	1.20
❑	220 Kirk Saarloos ROO RC	4.00	1.20
❑	221 Rene Reyes ROO RC	4.00	1.20
❑	222 Joe Borchard ROO	4.00	1.20
❑	223 Wilson Valdez ROO RC	4.00	1.20
❑	224 Miguel Asencio ROO RC	4.00	1.20
❑	225 Chris Snelling ROO RC	4.00	1.20

2003 Donruss Classics

	Nm-Mt	Ex-Mt
COMP.LO SET w/o SP's (100)	25.00	7.50
COMMON CARD (1-100)	.60	.18
COMMON CARD (101-150)	4.00	1.20
COMMON CARD (151-200)	4.00	1.20
COIMMON CARD (201-211)	4.00	1.20

	Card	Nm-Mt	Ex-Mt
❑	1 Troy Glaus	.60	.18
❑	2 Barry Bonds	4.00	1.20
❑	3 Miguel Tejada	.60	.18
❑	4 Randy Johnson	1.50	.45
❑	5 Eric Hinske	.60	.18
❑	6 Barry Zito	.60	.18
❑	7 Jason Jennings	.60	.18
❑	8 Derek Jeter	4.00	1.20
❑	9 Vladimir Guerrero	1.50	.45
❑	10 Corey Patterson	.60	.18
❑	11 Manny Ramirez	1.00	.30
❑	12 Edgar Martinez	1.00	.30
❑	13 Roy Oswalt	.60	.18
❑	14 Andruw Jones	.60	.18
❑	15 Alex Rodriguez	2.50	.75
❑	16 Mark Mulder	.60	.18
❑	17 Kazuhisa Ishii	.60	.18
❑	18 Gary Sheffield	.60	.18
❑	19 Jay Gibbons	.60	.18
❑	20 Roberto Alomar	1.00	.30
❑	21 A.J. Pierzynski	.60	.18
❑	22 Eric Chavez	.60	.18
❑	23 Roger Clemens	3.00	.90
❑	24 C.C. Sabathia	.60	.18
❑	25 Jose Vidro	.60	.18
❑	26 Shannon Stewart	.60	.18
❑	27 Mark Teixeira	.60	.18
❑	28 Joe Thurston	.60	.18
❑	29 Josh Beckett	.60	.18
❑	30 Jeff Bagwell	1.00	.30
❑	31 Geronimo Gil	.60	.18
❑	32 Curt Schilling	.60	.18
❑	33 Frank Thomas	1.50	.45
❑	34 Lance Berkman	.60	.18
❑	35 Adam Dunn	1.00	.30
❑	36 Christian Parker	.60	.18
❑	37 Jim Thome	1.50	.45
❑	38 Shawn Green	.60	.18
❑	39 Drew Henson	.60	.18
❑	40 Chipper Jones	1.50	.45
❑	41 Kevin Mench	.60	.18
❑	42 Hideo Nomo	1.50	.45
❑	43 Andres Galarraga	.60	.18
❑	44 Doug Davis	.60	.18
❑	45 Mark Prior	1.50	.45
❑	46 Sean Casey	.60	.18
❑	47 Magglio Ordonez	.60	.18
❑	48 Tom Glavine	1.00	.30
❑	49 Marlon Byrd	.60	.18
❑	50 Albert Pujols	3.00	.90
❑	51 Mark Buehrle	.60	.18
❑	52 Aramis Ramirez	.60	.18
❑	53 Pat Burrell	.60	.18
❑	54 Craig Biggio	1.00	.30
❑	55 Alfonso Soriano	1.00	.30
❑	56 Kerry Wood	1.50	.45
❑	57 Wade Miller	.60	.18
❑	58 Hank Blalock	1.00	.30
❑	59 Cliff Floyd	.60	.18
❑	60 Jason Giambi	.60	.18
❑	61 Carlos Beltran	1.00	.30
❑	62 Brian Roberts	.60	.18
❑	63 Paul Lo Duca	.60	.18
❑	64 Tim Redding	.60	.18
❑	65 Sammy Sosa	2.50	.75
❑	66 Joe Borchard	.60	.18
❑	67 Ryan Klesko	.60	.18
❑	68 Richie Sexson	.60	.18
❑	69 Carlos Lee	.60	.18
❑	70 Rickey Henderson	1.50	.45
❑	71 Brian Tallet	.60	.18
❑	72 Luis Gonzalez	.60	.18
❑	73 Satoru Komiyama	.60	.18
❑	74 Tim Hudson	.60	.18
❑	75 Ken Griffey Jr.	2.50	.75
❑	76 Adam Johnson	.60	.18
❑	77 Bobby Abreu	.60	.18
❑	78 Adrian Beltre	1.00	.30
❑	79 Rafael Palmeiro	1.00	.30
❑	80 Ichiro Suzuki	2.50	.75
❑	81 Kenny Lofton	.60	.18
❑	82 Brian Giles	.60	.18
❑	83 Barry Larkin	1.00	.30
❑	84 Robert Fick	.60	.18
❑	85 Ben Sheets	.60	.18
❑	86 Scott Rolen	1.50	.45
❑	87 Nomar Garciaparra	2.50	.75
❑	88 Brandon Phillips	.60	.18
❑	89 Ben Kozlowski	.60	.18
❑	90 Bernie Williams	1.00	.30
❑	91 Pedro Martinez	1.50	.45
❑	92 Todd Helton	1.00	.30
❑	93 Jermaine Dye	.60	.18
❑	94 Carlos Delgado	.60	.18
❑	95 Mike Piazza	2.50	.75
❑	96 Junior Spivey	.60	.18
❑	97 Torii Hunter	.60	.18
❑	98 Mike Sweeney	.60	.18
❑	99 Ivan Rodriguez	1.50	.45
❑	100 Greg Maddux	2.50	.75
❑	101 Ernie Banks LGD	5.00	1.50
❑	102 Steve Garvey LGD	4.00	1.20
❑	103 George Brett LGD	10.00	3.00
❑	104 Lou Brock LGD	5.00	1.50
❑	105 Hoyt Wilhelm LGD	4.00	1.20
❑	106 Steve Carlton LGD	4.00	1.20
❑	107 Joe Torre LGD	5.00	1.50
❑	108 Dennis Eckersley LGD	4.00	1.20
❑	109 Reggie Jackson LGD	5.00	1.50
❑	110 Al Kaline LGD	5.00	1.50
❑	111 Harold Reynolds LGD	4.00	1.20
❑	112 Don Mattingly LGD	10.00	3.00
❑	113 Tony Gwynn LGD	5.00	1.50
❑	114 Willie McCovey LGD	4.00	1.20
❑	115 Joe Morgan LGD	4.00	1.20
❑	116 Stan Musial LGD	6.00	1.80
❑	117 Jim Palmer LGD	4.00	1.20
❑	118 Brooks Robinson LGD	5.00	1.50
❑	119 Don Sutton LGD	4.00	1.20
❑	120 Nolan Ryan LGD	10.00	3.00
❑	121 Mike Schmidt LGD	8.00	2.40
❑	122 Tom Seaver LGD	5.00	1.50
❑	123 Cal Ripken LGD	12.00	3.60
❑	124 Robin Yount LGD	6.00	1.80
❑	125 Bob Feller LGD	4.00	1.20
❑	126 Joe Carter LGD	4.00	1.20
❑	127 Jack Morris LGD	4.00	1.20
❑	128 Luis Aparicio LGD	4.00	1.20
❑	129 Bobby Doerr LGD	4.00	1.20
❑	130 Dave Parker LGD	4.00	1.20
❑	131 Yogi Berra LGD	5.00	1.50
❑	132 Will Clark LGD	5.00	1.50
❑	133 Fred Lynn LGD	4.00	1.20
❑	134 Andre Dawson LGD	4.00	1.20
❑	135 Duke Snider LGD	5.00	1.50
❑	136 Orlando Cepeda LGD	4.00	1.20
❑	137 Billy Williams LGD	4.00	1.20
❑	138 Dale Murphy LGD	5.00	1.50
❑	139 Harmon Killebrew LGD	5.00	1.50
❑	140 Kirby Puckett LGD	5.00	1.50
❑	141 Carlton Fisk LGD	5.00	1.50
❑	142 Eric Davis LGD	4.00	1.20
❑	143 Alan Trammell LGD	4.00	1.20
❑	144 Paul Molitor LGD	5.00	1.50
❑	145 Jose Canseco LGD	5.00	1.50
❑	146 Ozzie Smith LGD	6.00	1.80
❑	147 Ralph Kiner LGD	4.00	1.20
❑	148 Dwight Gooden LGD	4.00	1.20
❑	149 Phil Rizzuto LGD	5.00	1.50
❑	150 Lenny Dykstra LGD	4.00	1.20
❑	151 Adam LaRoche ROO	4.00	1.20
❑	152 Tim Hummel ROO	4.00	1.20
❑	153 Matt Kata ROO RC	5.00	1.50
❑	154 Jeff Baker ROO	4.00	1.20
❑	155 Josh Stewart ROO RC	4.00	1.20
❑	156 Marshall McDougall ROO	4.00	1.20
❑	157 Jhonny Peralta ROO	4.00	1.20
❑	158 Mike Nicolas ROO RC	4.00	1.20
❑	159 Jeremy Guthrie ROO	4.00	1.20
❑	160 Craig Brazell ROO RC	5.00	1.50
❑	161 Joe Valentine ROO RC	4.00	1.20
❑	162 Buddy Hernandez ROO RC	4.00	1.20
❑	163 Freddy Sanchez ROO	4.00	1.20
❑	164 Shane Victorino ROO RC	4.00	1.20
❑	165 Corwin Malone ROO	4.00	1.20
❑	166 Jason Dubois ROO	4.00	1.20
❑	167 Josh Wilson ROO	4.00	1.20
❑	168 Tim Olson ROO RC	5.00	1.50
❑	169 Cliff Bartosh ROO	4.00	1.20
❑	170 Michael Hessman ROO RC	4.00	1.20
❑	171 Ryan Church ROO	4.00	1.20
❑	172 Garrett Atkins ROO	4.00	1.20
❑	173 Jose Morban ROO	4.00	1.20
❑	174 Ryan Cameron ROO RC	4.00	1.20
❑	175 Todd Wellemeyer ROO RC	5.00	1.50
❑	176 Travis Chapman ROO	4.00	1.20
❑	177 Jason Anderson ROO	4.00	1.20
❑	178 Adam Morrissey ROO	4.00	1.20
❑	179 Jose Contreras ROO RC	5.00	1.50
❑	180 Nic Jackson ROO	4.00	1.20
❑	181 Rob Hammock ROO RC	5.00	1.50
❑	182 Carlos Rivera ROO	4.00	1.20
❑	183 Vinny Chulk ROO	4.00	1.20
❑	184 Pete LaForest ROO RC	5.00	1.50
❑	185 Jon Leicester ROO RC	4.00	1.20
❑	186 Terrmel Sledge ROO RC	5.00	1.50
❑	187 Jose Castillo ROO	4.00	1.20
❑	188 Gerald Laird ROO	4.00	1.20
❑	189 Nook Logan ROO RC	4.00	1.20
❑	190 Clint Barmes ROO RC	5.00	1.50
❑	191 Jesus Medrano ROO	4.00	1.20
❑	192 Henri Stanley ROO	4.00	1.20
❑	193 Hideki Matsui ROO RC	10.00	3.00
❑	194 Walter Young ROO	4.00	1.20
❑	195 Jon Adkins ROO	4.00	1.20
❑	196 Tommy Whiteman ROO	4.00	1.20

❑ 197 Rob Bowen ROO 4.00 1.20
❑ 198 Brandon Webb ROO RC 5.00 1.50
❑ 199 Prentice Redman ROO RC 4.00 1.20
❑ 200 Jimmy Gobble ROO........ 4.00 1.20
❑ 201 Jeremy Bonderman ROO RC 5.00 1.50
❑ 202 Adam Loewen ROO RC .. 5.00 1.50
❑ 203 Chien-Ming Wang ROO RC 5.00 1.50
❑ 204 Hong-Chih Kuo ROO RC 5.00 1.50
❑ 205 Ryan Wagner ROO RC.... 5.00 1.50
❑ 206 Dan Haren ROO RC........ 5.00 1.50
❑ 207 Dontrelle Willis ROO 5.00 1.50
❑ 208 Rickie Weeks ROO RC 8.00 2.40
❑ 209 Ramon Nivar ROO RC 5.00 1.50
❑ 210 Chad Gaudin ROO RC 4.00 1.20
❑ 211 Delmon Young ROO RC 10.00 3.00

2004 Donruss Classics

	Nm-Mt	Ex-Mt
COMP.SET w/o SP's (153)........	25.00	7.50
COMMON CARD (1-150)............	.60	.18
COMMON (151-175/206-210)....	4.00	1.20
COMMON CARD (176-205).......	4.00	1.20
COMMON CARD (211-213)........	1.00	.30

❑ 1 Albert Pujols .... 3.00 .90
❑ 2 Derek Jeter .... 3.00 .90
❑ 3 Hank Blalock.................. .60 .18
❑ 4 Shannon Stewart.............. .60 .18
❑ 5 Jason Giambi .... .60 .18
❑ 6 Carlos Lee.................... .60 .18
❑ 7 Trot Nixon.................... .60 .18
❑ 8 Bret Boone .... .60 .18
❑ 9 Mark Mulder .... .60 .18
❑ 10 Mariano Rivera .... 1.00 .30
❑ 11 Scott Podsednik .... .60 .18
❑ 12 Jim Edmonds .... .60 .18
❑ 13 Mike Lowell.................. .60 .18
❑ 14 Robin Ventura .... .60 .18
❑ 15 Brian Giles .... .60 .18
❑ 16 Jose Vidro.................... .60 .18
❑ 17 Manny Ramirez .... 1.00 .30
❑ 18 Alex Rodriguez Rgr .... 2.50 .75
❑ 19 Carlos Beltran .... 1.00 .30
❑ 20 Hideki Matsui .... 2.50 .75
❑ 21 Johan Santana................ 1.00 .30
❑ 22 Richie Sexson .... .60 .18
❑ 23 Chipper Jones................ 1.50 .45
❑ 24 Steve Finley.................. .60 .18
❑ 25 Mark Prior.................... 1.50 .45
❑ 26 Alexis Rios .... .60 .18
❑ 27 Rafael Palmeiro .... 1.00 .30
❑ 28 Jorge Posada .... 1.00 .30
❑ 29 Barry Zito .... .60 .18
❑ 30 Jamie Moyer .... .60 .18
❑ 31 Preston Wilson .... .60 .18
❑ 32 Miguel Cabrera .... 1.00 .30
❑ 33 Pedro Martinez .... 1.50 .45
❑ 34 Curt Schilling .... 1.50 .45
❑ 35 Hee Seop Choi .... .60 .18
❑ 36 Dontrelle Willis.............. .60 .18
❑ 37 Rafael Soriano................ .60 .18
❑ 38 Richard Fischer .... .60 .18
❑ 39 Brian Tallet .... .60 .18
❑ 40 Jose Castillo .... .60 .18
❑ 41 Wade Miller................... .60 .18
❑ 42 Jose Contreras .... .60 .18
❑ 43 Runelvys Hernandez .... .60 .18
❑ 44 Joe Borchard.................. .60 .18
❑ 45 Kazuhisa Ishii .... .60 .18
❑ 46 Jose Reyes .... .60 .18
❑ 47 Adam Dunn..................... 1.00 .30
❑ 48 Randy Johnson .... 1.50 .45
❑ 49 Brandon Phillips .... .60 .18
❑ 50 Scott Rolen .... 1.50 .45
❑ 51 Ken Griffey Jr. .... 2.50 .75
❑ 52 Tom Glavine .... 1.00 .30
❑ 53 Cliff Lee...................... .60 .18
❑ 54 Chien-Ming Wang............... .60 .18
❑ 55 Roy Oswalt .... .60 .18
❑ 56 Austin Kearns .... .60 .18
❑ 57 Jhonny Peralta .... .60 .18
❑ 58 Greg Maddux Braves........... 2.50 .75
❑ 59 Mark Grace .... 1.00 .30
❑ 60 Jae Weong Seo .... .60 .18
❑ 61 Nic Jackson.................... .60 .18
❑ 62 Roger Clemens .... 3.00 .90
❑ 63 Jimmy Gobble................... .60 .18
❑ 64 Travis Hafner.................. .60 .18
❑ 65 Paul Konerko................... .60 .18
❑ 66 Jerome Williams .... .60 .18
❑ 67 Ryan Klesko .... .60 .18
❑ 68 Alexis Gomez .... .60 .18
❑ 69 Omar Vizquel................... 1.00 .30
❑ 70 Zach Day .... .60 .18
❑ 71 Rickey Henderson .... 1.50 .45
❑ 72 Morgan Ensberg .... .60 .18
❑ 73 Josh Beckett .... .60 .18
❑ 74 Garrett Atkins .... .60 .18
❑ 75 Sean Casey .... .60 .18
❑ 76 Julio Franco .... .60 .18
❑ 77 Lyle Overbay .... .60 .18
❑ 78 Josh Phelps .... .60 .18
❑ 79 Juan Gonzalez.................. 1.00 .30
❑ 80 Rich Harden .... .60 .18
❑ 81 Bernie Williams................ 1.00 .30
❑ 82 Torii Hunter................... .60 .18
❑ 83 Angel Berroa .... .60 .18
❑ 84 Jody Gerut..................... .60 .18
❑ 85 Roberto Alomar .... 1.00 .30
❑ 86 Byung-Hyun Kim................ .60 .18
❑ 87 Jay Gibbons .... .60 .18
❑ 88 Chone Figgins.................. .60 .18
❑ 89 Fred McGriff .... 1.00 .30
❑ 90 Rich Aurilia .... .60 .18
❑ 91 Xavier Nady.................... .60 .18
❑ 92 Marlon Byrd .... .60 .18
❑ 93 Mike Piazza.................... 2.50 .75
❑ 94 Vladimir Guerrero .... 1.50 .45
❑ 95 Shawn Green.................... .60 .18
❑ 96 Jeff Kent .... .60 .18
❑ 97 Ivan Rodriguez .... 1.50 .45
❑ 98 Jay Payton..................... .60 .18
❑ 99 Barry Larkin................... 1.00 .30
❑ 100 Mike Sweeney .... .60 .18
❑ 101 Adrian Beltre .... 1.00 .30
❑ 102 Robby Hammock................. .60 .18
❑ 103 Orlando Hudson .... .60 .18
❑ 104 Mark Teixeira .... .60 .18
❑ 105 Hong-Chih Kuo................. .60 .18
❑ 106 Eric Chavez .... .60 .18
❑ 107 Nick Johnson .... .60 .18
❑ 108 Jacque Jones .... .60 .18
❑ 109 Ken Harvey .... .60 .18
❑ 110 Aramis Ramirez................ .60 .18
❑ 111 Victor Martinez .... .60 .18
❑ 112 Joe Crede .... .60 .18
❑ 113 Jason Varitek.................. 1.00 .30
❑ 114 Troy Glaus..................... .60 .18
❑ 115 Billy Wagner .... .60 .18
❑ 116 Kerry Wood..................... 1.50 .45
❑ 117 Hideo Nomo .... 1.50 .45
❑ 118 Brandon Webb .... .60 .18
❑ 119 Craig Biggio .... 1.00 .30
❑ 120 Orlando Cabrera .... .60 .18
❑ 121 Sammy Sosa..................... 2.50 .75
❑ 122 Bobby Abreu.................... .60 .18
❑ 123 Andruw Jones .... .60 .18
❑ 124 Jeff Bagwell.................... 1.00 .30
❑ 125 Jim Thome .... 1.50 .45
❑ 126 Javy Lopez .... .60 .18
❑ 127 Luis Castillo .... .60 .18
❑ 128 Todd Helton .... 1.00 .30
❑ 129 Roy Halladay.................... .60 .18
❑ 130 Mike Mussina .... 1.00 .30
❑ 131 Eric Byrnes .... .60 .18
❑ 132 Eric Hinske .... .60 .18
❑ 133 Nomar Garciaparra .... 2.50 .75
❑ 134 Edgar Martinez .... 1.00 .30
❑ 135 Rocco Baldelli................. .60 .18
❑ 136 Miguel Tejada .... .60 .18
❑ 137 Alfonso Soriano Yanks .... 1.00 .30
❑ 138 Carlos Delgado .... .60 .18
❑ 139 Rafael Furcal .... .60 .18
❑ 140 Ichiro Suzuki .... 2.50 .75
❑ 141 Aubrey Huff.................... .60 .18
❑ 142 Garret Anderson .... .60 .18
❑ 143 Vernon Wells................... .60 .18
❑ 144 Magglio Ordonez................ .60 .18
❑ 145 Brett Myers .... .60 .18
❑ 146 Luis Gonzalez .... .60 .18
❑ 147 Lance Berkman .... .60 .18
❑ 148 Frank Thomas .... 1.50 .45
❑ 149 Gary Sheffield .... .60 .18
❑ 150 Tim Hudson .... .60 .18
❑ 151 Duke Snider LGD 5.00 1.50
❑ 152 Carl Yastrzemski LGD 6.00 1.80
❑ 153 Whitey Ford LGD.......... 5.00 1.50
❑ 154 Cal Ripken LGD........... 12.00 3.60
❑ 155 Dwight Gooden LGD 4.00 1.20
❑ 156 Warren Spahn LGD 5.00 1.50
❑ 157 Bob Gibson LGD 5.00 1.50
❑ 158 Don Mattingly LGD 10.00 3.00
❑ 159 Jack Morris LGD........... 4.00 1.20
❑ 160 Jim Bunning LGD 5.00 1.50
❑ 161 Fergie Jenkins LGD 4.00 1.20
❑ 162 Brooks Robinson LGD.... 5.00 1.50
❑ 163 George Kell LGD 4.00 1.20
❑ 164 Darryl Strawberry LGD .. 4.00 1.20
❑ 165 Robin Roberts LGD 4.00 1.20
❑ 166 Monte Irvin LGD 4.00 1.20
❑ 167 Ernie Banks LGD 5.00 1.50
❑ 168 Wade Boggs LGD 5.00 1.50
❑ 169 Gaylord Perry LGD 4.00 1.20
❑ 170 Keith Hernandez LGD 4.00 1.20
❑ 171 Lou Brock LGD 5.00 1.50
❑ 172 Frank Robinson LGD 4.00 1.20
❑ 173 Nolan Ryan LGD 10.00 3.00
❑ 174 Stan Musial LGD........... 6.00 1.80
❑ 175 Eddie Murray LGD......... 5.00 1.50
❑ 176 Byron Gettis ROO 4.00 1.20
❑ 177 Merkin Valdez ROO RC .. 5.00 1.50
❑ 178 Rickie Weeks ROO......... 4.00 1.20
❑ 179 Akinori Otsuka ROO RC.. 4.00 1.20
❑ 180 Brian Bruney ROO 4.00 1.20
❑ 181 Freddy Guzman ROO RC 5.00 1.50
❑ 182 Brendan Harris ROO 4.00 1.20
❑ 183 John Gall ROO RC......... 5.00 1.50
❑ 184 Jason Kubel ROO 4.00 1.20
❑ 185 Delmon Young ROO 5.00 1.50
❑ 186 Ryan Howard ROO UER.. 4.00 1.20
Stat headers are for a pitcher
❑ 187 Adam Loewen ROO 4.00 1.20
❑ 188 J.D. Durbin ROO 4.00 1.20
❑ 189 Dan Haren ROO............ 4.00 1.20
❑ 190 Dustin McGowan ROO .. 4.00 1.20
❑ 191 Chad Gaudin ROO......... 4.00 1.20
❑ 192 Preston Larrison ROO 4.00 1.20
❑ 193 Ramon Nivar ROO 4.00 1.20
❑ 194 Ronald Belisario ROO RC 4.00 1.20
❑ 195 Mike Gosling ROO RC..... 4.00 1.20
❑ 196 Kevin Youkilis ROO....... 4.00 1.20
❑ 197 Ryan Wagner ROO......... 4.00 1.20
❑ 198 Bubba Nelson ROO 4.00 1.20
❑ 199 Edwin Jackson ROO 4.00 1.20
❑ 200 Chris Burke ROO.......... 4.00 1.20
❑ 201 Carlos Hines ROO RC 4.00 1.20
❑ 202 Greg Dobbs ROO RC...... 4.00 1.20
❑ 203 Jamie Brown ROO RC 4.00 1.20
❑ 204 Dave Crouthers ROO RC 4.00 1.20
❑ 205 Ian Snell ROO RC 5.00 1.50
❑ 206 Gary Carter LGD 4.00 1.20
❑ 207 Dale Murphy LGD 5.00 1.50
❑ 208 Ryne Sandberg LGD 8.00 2.40
❑ 209 Phil Niekro LGD 4.00 1.20
❑ 210 Don Sutton LGD 4.00 1.20
❑ 211 Alex Rodriguez Yanks SP 5.00 1.50
❑ 212 Alfonso Soriano Rgr SP 1.50 .45
❑ 213 Greg Maddux Cubs SP .. 4.00 1.20

2001 Donruss Elite

	Nm-Mt	Ex-Mt
COMP.SET w/o SP's (150)	25.00	7.50
COMMON CARD (1-150)	.30	.09
COMMON (151-200)	8.00	2.40
COMMON CARD (201-250)	10.00	3.00

Card	Nm-Mt	Ex-Mt
❑ 1 Alex Rodriguez	1.25	.35
❑ 2 Barry Bonds	2.00	.60
❑ 3 Cal Ripken	2.50	.75
❑ 4 Chipper Jones	.75	.23
❑ 5 Derek Jeter	2.00	.60
❑ 6 Troy Glaus	.30	.09
❑ 7 Frank Thomas	.75	.23
❑ 8 Greg Maddux	1.25	.35
❑ 9 Ivan Rodriguez	.75	.23
❑ 10 Jeff Bagwell	.50	.15
❑ 11 Jose Canseco	.75	.23
❑ 12 Todd Helton	.50	.15
❑ 13 Ken Griffey Jr.	1.25	.35
❑ 14 Manny Ramirez	.50	.15
❑ 15 Mark McGwire	2.00	.60
❑ 16 Mike Piazza	1.25	.35
❑ 17 Nomar Garciaparra	1.25	.35
❑ 18 Pedro Martinez	.75	.23
❑ 19 Randy Johnson	.75	.23
❑ 20 Rick Ankiel	.30	.09
❑ 21 Rickey Henderson	.75	.23
❑ 22 Roger Clemens	1.50	.45
❑ 23 Sammy Sosa	1.25	.35
❑ 24 Tony Gwynn	1.00	.30
❑ 25 Vladimir Guerrero	.75	.23
❑ 26 Eric Davis	.30	.09
❑ 27 Roberto Alomar	.50	.15
❑ 28 Mark Mulder	.30	.09
❑ 29 Pat Burrell	.30	.09
❑ 30 Harold Baines	.30	.09
❑ 31 Carlos Delgado	.30	.09
❑ 32 J.D. Drew	.30	.09
❑ 33 Jim Edmonds	.30	.09
❑ 34 Darin Erstad	.30	.09
❑ 35 Jason Giambi	.30	.09
❑ 36 Tom Glavine	.50	.15
❑ 37 Juan Gonzalez	.50	.15
❑ 38 Mark Grace	.50	.15
❑ 39 Shawn Green	.30	.09
❑ 40 Tim Hudson	.30	.09
❑ 41 Andruw Jones	.30	.09
❑ 42 David Justice	.30	.09
❑ 43 Jeff Kent	.30	.09
❑ 44 Barry Larkin	.50	.15
❑ 45 Pokey Reese	.30	.09
❑ 46 Mike Mussina	.50	.15
❑ 47 Hideo Nomo	.75	.23
❑ 48 Rafael Palmeiro	.50	.15
❑ 49 Adam Piatt	.30	.09
❑ 50 Scott Rolen	.75	.23
❑ 51 Gary Sheffield	.30	.09
❑ 52 Bernie Williams	.50	.15
❑ 53 Bob Abreu	.30	.09
❑ 54 Edgardo Alfonzo	.30	.09
❑ 55 Jermaine Clark RC	.75	.23
❑ 56 Albert Belle	.30	.09
❑ 57 Craig Biggio	.50	.15
❑ 58 Andres Galarraga	.30	.09
❑ 59 Edgar Martinez	.50	.15
❑ 60 Fred McGriff	.50	.15
❑ 61 Magglio Ordonez	.30	.09
❑ 62 Jim Thome	.75	.23
❑ 63 Matt Williams	.30	.09
❑ 64 Kerry Wood	.75	.23
❑ 65 Moises Alou	.30	.09
❑ 66 Brady Anderson	.30	.09
❑ 67 Garret Anderson	.30	.09
❑ 68 Tony Armas Jr.	.30	.09
❑ 69 Tony Batista	.30	.09
❑ 70 Jose Cruz Jr.	.30	.09
❑ 71 Carlos Beltran	.50	.15
❑ 72 Adrian Beltre	.50	.15
❑ 73 Kris Benson	.30	.09
❑ 74 Lance Berkman	.30	.09
❑ 75 Kevin Brown	.30	.09
❑ 76 Jay Buhner	.30	.09
❑ 77 Jeromy Burnitz	.30	.09
❑ 78 Ken Caminiti	.30	.09
❑ 79 Sean Casey	.30	.09
❑ 80 Luis Castillo	.30	.09
❑ 81 Eric Chavez	.30	.09
❑ 82 Jeff Cirillo	.30	.09
❑ 83 Bartolo Colon	.30	.09
❑ 84 David Cone	.30	.09
❑ 85 Freddy Garcia	.30	.09
❑ 86 Johnny Damon	.50	.15
❑ 87 Ray Durham	.30	.09
❑ 88 Jermaine Dye	.30	.09
❑ 89 Juan Encarnacion	.30	.09
❑ 90 Terrence Long	.30	.09
❑ 91 Carl Everett	.30	.09
❑ 92 Steve Finley	.30	.09
❑ 93 Cliff Floyd	.30	.09
❑ 94 Brad Fullmer	.30	.09
❑ 95 Brian Giles	.30	.09
❑ 96 Luis Gonzalez	.30	.09
❑ 97 Rusty Greer	.30	.09
❑ 98 Jeffrey Hammonds	.30	.09
❑ 99 Mike Hampton	.30	.09
❑ 100 Orlando Hernandez	.30	.09
❑ 101 Richard Hidalgo	.30	.09
❑ 102 Geoff Jenkins	.30	.09
❑ 103 Jacque Jones	.30	.09
❑ 104 Brian Jordan	.30	.09
❑ 105 Gabe Kapler	.30	.09
❑ 106 Eric Karros	.30	.09
❑ 107 Jason Kendall	.30	.09
❑ 108 Adam Kennedy	.30	.09
❑ 109 Byung-Hyun Kim	.30	.09
❑ 110 Ryan Klesko	.30	.09
❑ 111 Chuck Knoblauch	.30	.09
❑ 112 Paul Konerko	.30	.09
❑ 113 Carlos Lee	.30	.09
❑ 114 Kenny Lofton	.30	.09
❑ 115 Javy Lopez	.30	.09
❑ 116 Tino Martinez	.50	.15
❑ 117 Ruben Mateo	.30	.09
❑ 118 Kevin Millwood	.30	.09
❑ 119 Ben Molina	.30	.09
❑ 120 Raul Mondesi	.30	.09
❑ 121 Trot Nixon	.30	.09
❑ 122 John Olerud	.30	.09
❑ 123 Paul O'Neill	.50	.15
❑ 124 Chan Ho Park	.30	.09
❑ 125 Andy Pettitte	.50	.15
❑ 126 Jorge Posada	.50	.15
❑ 127 Mark Quinn	.30	.09
❑ 128 Aramis Ramirez	.30	.09
❑ 129 Mariano Rivera	.50	.15
❑ 130 Tim Salmon	.50	.15
❑ 131 Curt Schilling	.30	.09
❑ 132 Richie Sexson	.30	.09
❑ 133 John Smoltz	.50	.15
❑ 134 J.T. Snow	.30	.09
❑ 135 Jay Payton	.30	.09
❑ 136 Shannon Stewart	.30	.09
❑ 137 B.J. Surhoff	.30	.09
❑ 138 Mike Sweeney	.30	.09
❑ 139 Fernando Tatis	.30	.09
❑ 140 Miguel Tejada	.30	.09
❑ 141 Jason Varitek	.50	.15
❑ 142 Greg Vaughn	.30	.09
❑ 143 Mo Vaughn	.30	.09
❑ 144 Robin Ventura UER Listed as playing for Yankees last 2 years, Also Bat and Throw information is wrong	.30	.09
❑ 145 Jose Vidro	.30	.09
❑ 146 Omar Vizquel	.50	.15
❑ 147 Larry Walker	.50	.15
❑ 148 David Wells	.30	.09
❑ 149 Rondell White	.30	.09
❑ 150 Preston Wilson	.30	.09
❑ 151 Brent Abernathy SP	8.00	2.40
❑ 152 Cory Aldridge SP RC	8.00	2.40
❑ 153 Gene Altman SP RC	8.00	2.40
❑ 154 Josh Beckett SP	8.00	2.40
❑ 155 Wilson Betemit SP RC	8.00	2.40
❑ 156 Albert Pujols SP RC	300.00	90.00
❑ 157 Joe Crede SP	8.00	2.40
❑ 158 Jack Cust SP	8.00	2.40
❑ 159 Ben Sheets SP	10.00	3.00
❑ 160 Alex Escobar SP	8.00	2.40
❑ 161 A. Hernandez SP RC	8.00	2.40
❑ 162 Pedro Feliz SP	8.00	2.40
❑ 163 Nate Frese SP RC	8.00	2.40
❑ 164 Carlos Garcia SP RC	8.00	2.40
❑ 165 Marcus Giles SP	8.00	2.40
❑ 166 Alexis Gomez SP RC	8.00	2.40
❑ 167 Jason Hart SP	8.00	2.40
❑ 168 Aubrey Huff SP	8.00	2.40
❑ 169 Cesar Izturis SP	8.00	2.40
❑ 170 Nick Johnson SP	8.00	2.40
❑ 171 Jack Wilson SP RC	15.00	4.50
❑ 172 B.Lawrence SP RC	8.00	2.40
❑ 173 C. Parker SP RC	8.00	2.40
❑ 174 Nick Maness SP RC	8.00	2.40
❑ 175 Jose Mieses SP RC	8.00	2.40
❑ 176 Greg Miller SP RC	8.00	2.40
❑ 177 Eric Munson SP	8.00	2.40
❑ 178 Xavier Nady SP	8.00	2.40
❑ 179 Blaine Neal SP RC	8.00	2.40
❑ 180 Abraham Nunez SP	8.00	2.40
❑ 181 Jose Ortiz SP	8.00	2.40
❑ 182 Jeremy Owens SP RC	8.00	2.40
❑ 183 Jay Gibbons SP RC	10.00	3.00
❑ 184 Corey Patterson SP	8.00	2.40
❑ 185 Carlos Pena SP	8.00	2.40
❑ 186 C.C. Sabathia SP	8.00	2.40
❑ 187 Timo Perez SP	8.00	2.40
❑ 188 A. Pettyjohn SP RC	8.00	2.40
❑ 189 D. Mendez SP RC	8.00	2.40
❑ 190 J. Melian SP RC	8.00	2.40
❑ 191 Wilkin Ruan SP RC	8.00	2.40
❑ 192 D. Sanchez SP RC	8.00	2.40
❑ 193 Alfonso Soriano SP	10.00	3.00
❑ 194 Rafael Soriano SP RC	10.00	3.00
❑ 195 Ichiro Suzuki SP RC	120.00	36.00
❑ 196 Billy Sylvester SP RC	8.00	2.40
❑ 197 Juan Uribe SP RC	10.00	3.00
❑ 198 T. Shinjo SP RC	10.00	3.00
❑ 199 C. Valderrama SP RC	8.00	2.40
❑ 200 Matt White SP RC	8.00	2.40
❑ 201 Adam Dunn/468	15.00	4.50
❑ 202 Joe Kennedy/465 XRC	15.00	4.50
❑ 203 Mike Rivera/427 XRC	10.00	3.00
❑ 204 Erick Almonte/401 XRC	10.00	3.00
❑ 205 Bran Duckworth EXCH	10.00	3.00
❑ 206 Victor Martinez/410 XRC	180.00	55.00
❑ 207 Rick Bauer/390 XRC	10.00	3.00
❑ 208 Jeff Deardorff/396 XRC	10.00	3.00
❑ 209 Antonio Perez/448 XRC	10.00	3.00
❑ 210 Bill Hall/404 XRC	10.00	3.00
❑ 211 D. Tankersley EXCH	10.00	3.00
❑ 212 Jeremy Affeldt/386 XRC	15.00	4.50
❑ 213 Junior Spivey/377 XRC	15.00	4.50
❑ 214 Casey Fossum/393 XRC	10.00	3.00
❑ 215 Brandon Lyon/402 XRC	10.00	3.00
❑ 216 Angel Santos/408 XRC	10.00	3.00
❑ 217 Cody Ransom/404 XRC	10.00	3.00
❑ 218 Jason Lane/424 XRC	10.00	3.00
❑ 219 David Williams/408 XRC	10.00	3.00
❑ 220 Alex Herrera/405 XRC	10.00	3.00
❑ 221 Ryan Drese/378 XRC	15.00	4.50
❑ 222 Travis Hafner/419 XRC	60.00	18.00
❑ 223 Bud Smith/468 XRC	10.00	3.00
❑ 224 Johnny Estrada/415 XRC	25.00	7.50
❑ 225 R. Rodriguez EXCH	10.00	3.00
❑ 226 Brandon Berger/428 XRC	10.00	3.00
❑ 227 Claudio Vargas/395 XRC	10.00	3.00
❑ 228 Luis Garcia/438 XRC	10.00	3.00

	Card	Nm-Mt	Ex-Mt
❑ 229	Marlon Byrd/452 XRC	25.00	7.50
❑ 230	Hee Seop Choi/479 XRC	25.00	7.50
❑ 231	Corky Miller/431 XRC	10.00	3.00
❑ 232	J. Duchscherer EXCH	10.00	3.00
❑ 233	T. Spooneybarger EXCH	10.00	3.00
❑ 234	Roy Oswalt/427	15.00	4.50
❑ 235	Willie Harris/418 XRC	10.00	3.00
❑ 236	Josh Towers/437 XRC	10.00	3.00
❑ 237	Juan A.Pena/400 XRC	10.00	3.00
❑ 238	A. Amezaga EXCH	10.00	3.00
❑ 239	Geronimo Gil/396 XRC	10.00	3.00
❑ 240	Juan Cruz/489 XRC	10.00	3.00
❑ 241	Ed Rogers/429 XRC	10.00	3.00
❑ 242	Joe Thurston/420 XRC	10.00	3.00
❑ 243	O.Hudson EXCH	15.00	4.50
❑ 244	John Buck/416 XRC	15.00	4.50
❑ 245	Martin Vargas/400 XRC	10.00	3.00
❑ 246	David Brous/399 XRC	10.00	3.00
❑ 247	D. Brazelton EXCH	15.00	4.50
❑ 248	Mark Prior/556 XRC	150.00	45.00
❑ 249	Angel Berroa/420 XRC	25.00	7.50
❑ 250	Mark Teixeira/543 XRC	80.00	24.00

2002 Donruss Elite

	Nm-Mt	Ex-Mt
COMP.LO SET w/o SP's (100)	20.00	6.00
COMMON CARD (1-100)	.30	.09
COMMON CARD (101-150)	2.00	.60
COMMON CARD (151-200)	5.00	1.50
COMMON CARD (201-275)	8.00	2.40

	Card	Nm-Mt	Ex-Mt
❑ 1	Vladimir Guerrero	.75	.23
❑ 2	Bernie Williams	.50	.15
❑ 3	Ichiro Suzuki	1.25	.35
❑ 4	Roger Clemens	1.50	.45
❑ 5	Greg Maddux	1.25	.35
❑ 6	Fred McGriff	.50	.15
❑ 7	Jermaine Dye	.30	.09
❑ 8	Ken Griffey Jr.	1.25	.35
❑ 9	Todd Helton	.50	.15
❑ 10	Torii Hunter	.30	.09
❑ 11	Pat Burrell	.30	.09
❑ 12	Chipper Jones	.75	.23
❑ 13	Ivan Rodriguez	.75	.23
❑ 14	Roy Oswalt	.30	.09
❑ 15	Shannon Stewart	.30	.09
❑ 16	Magglio Ordonez	.30	.09
❑ 17	Lance Berkman	.30	.09
❑ 18	Mark Mulder	.30	.09
❑ 19	Al Leiter	.30	.09
❑ 20	Sammy Sosa	1.25	.35
❑ 21	Scott Rolen	.75	.23
❑ 22	Aramis Ramirez	.30	.09
❑ 23	Alfonso Soriano	.50	.15
❑ 24	Phil Nevin	.30	.09
❑ 25	Barry Bonds	2.00	.60
❑ 26	Joe Mays	.30	.09
❑ 27	Jeff Kent	.30	.09
❑ 28	Mark Quinn	.30	.09
❑ 29	Adrian Beltre	.50	.15
❑ 30	Freddy Garcia	.30	.09
❑ 31	Pedro Martinez	.75	.23
❑ 32	Darryl Kile	.30	.09
❑ 33	Mike Cameron	.30	.09
❑ 34	Frank Catalanotto	.30	.09
❑ 35	Jose Vidro	.30	.09
❑ 36	Jim Thome	.75	.23
❑ 37	Javy Lopez	.30	.09
❑ 38	Paul Konerko	.30	.09
❑ 39	Jeff Bagwell	.50	.15
❑ 40	Curt Schilling	.30	.09
❑ 41	Miguel Tejada	.30	.09
❑ 42	Jim Edmonds	.30	.09
❑ 43	Ellis Burks	.30	.09
❑ 44	Mark Grace	.50	.15
❑ 45	Robb Nen	.30	.09
❑ 46	Jeff Conine	.30	.09
❑ 47	Derek Jeter	2.00	.60
❑ 48	Mike Lowell	.30	.09
❑ 49	Javier Vazquez	.30	.09
❑ 50	Manny Ramirez	.50	.15
❑ 51	Bartolo Colon	.30	.09
❑ 52	Carlos Beltran	.50	.15
❑ 53	Tim Hudson	.30	.09
❑ 54	Rafael Palmeiro	.50	.15
❑ 55	Jimmy Rollins	.30	.09
❑ 56	Andruw Jones	.30	.09
❑ 57	Orlando Cabrera	.30	.09
❑ 58	Dean Palmer	.30	.09
❑ 59	Bret Boone	.30	.09
❑ 60	Carlos Febles	.30	.09
❑ 61	Ben Grieve	.30	.09
❑ 62	Richie Sexson	.30	.09
❑ 63	Alex Rodriguez	1.25	.35
❑ 64	Juan Pierre	.30	.09
❑ 65	Bobby Higginson	.30	.09
❑ 66	Barry Zito	.30	.09
❑ 67	Raul Mondesi	.30	.09
❑ 68	Albert Pujols	1.50	.45
❑ 69	Omar Vizquel	.50	.15
❑ 70	Bobby Abreu	.30	.09
❑ 71	Corey Koskie	.30	.09
❑ 72	Tom Glavine	.50	.15
❑ 73	Paul LoDuca	.30	.09
❑ 74	Terrence Long	.30	.09
❑ 75	Matt Morris	.30	.09
❑ 76	Andy Pettitte	.50	.15
❑ 77	Rich Aurilia	.30	.09
❑ 78	Todd Walker	.30	.09
❑ 79	John Olerud UER Career Header stats are those for a pitcher	.30	.09
❑ 80	Mike Sweeney	.30	.09
❑ 81	Ray Durham	.30	.09
❑ 82	Fernando Vina	.30	.09
❑ 83	Nomar Garciaparra	1.25	.35
❑ 84	Mariano Rivera	.50	.15
❑ 85	Mike Piazza	1.25	.35
❑ 86	Mark Buehrle	.30	.09
❑ 87	Adam Dunn	.50	.15
❑ 88	Luis Gonzalez	.30	.09
❑ 89	Richard Hidalgo	.30	.09
❑ 90	Brad Radke	.30	.09
❑ 91	Russ Ortiz	.30	.09
❑ 92	Brian Giles	.30	.09
❑ 93	Billy Wagner	.30	.09
❑ 94	Cliff Floyd	.30	.09
❑ 95	Eric Milton	.30	.09
❑ 96	Bud Smith	.30	.09
❑ 97	Wade Miller	.30	.09
❑ 98	Jon Lieber	.30	.09
❑ 99	Derrek Lee	.30	.09
❑ 100	Jose Cruz Jr.	.30	.09
❑ 101	Dmitri Young STAR	2.00	.60
❑ 102	Mo Vaughn STAR	2.00	.60
❑ 103	Tino Martinez STAR	3.00	.90
❑ 104	Larry Walker STAR	3.00	.90
❑ 105	Chuck Knoblauch STAR	2.00	.60
❑ 106	Troy Glaus STAR	2.00	.60
❑ 107	Jason Giambi STAR	2.00	.60
❑ 108	Travis Fryman STAR	2.00	.60
❑ 109	Josh Beckett STAR	2.00	.60
❑ 110	Edgar Martinez STAR	3.00	.90
❑ 111	Tim Salmon STAR	3.00	.90
❑ 112	C.C. Sabathia STAR	2.00	.60
❑ 113	Randy Johnson STAR	5.00	1.50
❑ 114	Juan Gonzalez STAR	3.00	.90
❑ 115	Carlos Delgado STAR	2.00	.60
❑ 116	Hideo Nomo STAR	5.00	1.50
❑ 117	Kerry Wood STAR	5.00	1.50
❑ 118	Brian Jordan STAR	2.00	.60
❑ 119	Carlos Pena STAR	2.00	.60
❑ 120	Roger Cedeno STAR	2.00	.60
❑ 121	Chan Ho Park STAR	2.00	.60
❑ 122	Rafael Furcal STAR	2.00	.60
❑ 123	Frank Thomas STAR	5.00	1.50
❑ 124	Mike Mussina STAR	3.00	.90
❑ 125	Rickey Henderson STAR	5.00	1.50
❑ 126	Sean Casey STAR	2.00	.60
❑ 127	Barry Larkin STAR	3.00	.90
❑ 128	Kazuhiro Sasaki STAR	2.00	.60
❑ 129	Moises Alou STAR	2.00	.60
❑ 130	Jeff Cirillo STAR	2.00	.60
❑ 131	Jason Kendall STAR	2.00	.60
❑ 132	Gary Sheffield STAR	2.00	.60
❑ 133	Ryan Klesko STAR	2.00	.60
❑ 134	Kevin Brown STAR	2.00	.60
❑ 135	Darin Erstad STAR	2.00	.60
❑ 136	Roberto Alomar STAR	3.00	.90
❑ 137	Brad Fullmer STAR	2.00	.60
❑ 138	Eric Chavez STAR	2.00	.60
❑ 139	Ben Sheets STAR	2.00	.60
❑ 140	Trot Nixon STAR	2.00	.60
❑ 141	Garret Anderson STAR	2.00	.60
❑ 142	Shawn Green STAR	2.00	.60
❑ 143	Troy Percival STAR	2.00	.60
❑ 144	Craig Biggio STAR	3.00	.90
❑ 145	Jorge Posada STAR	3.00	.90
❑ 146	J.D. Drew STAR	2.00	.60
❑ 147	Johnny Damon STAR	3.00	.90
❑ 148	Jeromy Burnitz STAR	2.00	.60
❑ 149	Robin Ventura STAR	2.00	.60
❑ 150	Aaron Sele STAR	2.00	.60
❑ 151	Cam Esslinger ROO RC	5.00	1.50
❑ 152	Ben Howard ROO RC	5.00	1.50
❑ 153	Brandon Backe ROO RC	8.00	2.40
❑ 154	Jorge De La Rosa ROO RC	5.00	1.50
❑ 155	Austin Kearns ROO	5.00	1.50
❑ 156	Carlos Zambrano ROO	5.00	1.50
❑ 157	Kyle Kane ROO RC	5.00	1.50
❑ 158	So Taguchi ROO RC	8.00	2.40
❑ 159	Brian Mallette ROO RC	5.00	1.50
❑ 160	Brett Jodie ROO	5.00	1.50
❑ 161	Elio Serrano ROO RC	5.00	1.50
❑ 162	Joe Thurston ROO	5.00	1.50
❑ 163	Kevin Olsen ROO	5.00	1.50
❑ 164	Rodrigo Rosario ROO RC	5.00	1.50
❑ 165	Matt Guerrier ROO	5.00	1.50
❑ 166	And. Machado ROO RC	5.00	1.50
❑ 167	Bert Snow ROO	5.00	1.50
❑ 168	Franklyn German ROO RC	5.00	1.50
❑ 169	Brandon Claussen ROO	5.00	1.50
❑ 170	Jason Romano ROO	5.00	1.50
❑ 171	Jorge Padilla ROO RC	5.00	1.50
❑ 172	Jose Cueto ROO	5.00	1.50
❑ 173	Allan Simpson ROO RC	5.00	1.50
❑ 174	Doug Devore ROO RC	5.00	1.50
❑ 175	Justin Duchscherer ROO	5.00	1.50
❑ 176	Josh Pearce ROO	5.00	1.50
❑ 177	Steve Bechler ROO RC	5.00	1.50
❑ 178	Josh Phelps ROO	5.00	1.50
❑ 179	Juan Diaz ROO	5.00	1.50
❑ 180	Victor Alvarez ROO RC	5.00	1.50
❑ 181	Ramon Vazquez ROO	5.00	1.50
❑ 182	Mike Rivera ROO	5.00	1.50
❑ 183	Kazuhisa Ishii ROO RC	10.00	3.00
❑ 184	Henry Mateo ROO	5.00	1.50
❑ 185	Travis Hughes ROO RC	5.00	1.50
❑ 186	Zach Day ROO	5.00	1.50
❑ 187	Brad Voyles ROO	5.00	1.50
❑ 188	Sean Douglass ROO	5.00	1.50
❑ 189	Nick Neugebauer ROO	5.00	1.50
❑ 190	Tom Shearn ROO RC	5.00	1.50
❑ 191	Eric Cyr ROO	5.00	1.50
❑ 192	Adam Johnson ROO	5.00	1.50
❑ 193	Michael Cuddyer ROO	5.00	1.50
❑ 194	Erik Bedard ROO	5.00	1.50
❑ 195	Mark Ellis ROO	5.00	1.50
❑ 196	Carlos Hernandez ROO	5.00	1.50
❑ 197	Deivis Santos ROO	5.00	1.50
❑ 198	Morgan Ensberg ROO	5.00	1.50
❑ 199	Ryan Jamison ROO	5.00	1.50
❑ 200	Cody Ransom ROO	5.00	1.50
❑ 201	Chris Snelling ROO RC	8.00	2.40
❑ 202	Satoru Komiyama ROO RC	8.00	2.40
❑ 203	Jas. Simontacchi ROO RC	8.00	2.40
❑ 204	Tim Kalita ROO RC	8.00	2.40
❑ 205	Run. Hernandez ROO RC	8.00	2.40
❑ 206	Kirk Saarloos ROO RC	8.00	2.40

Card	Nm-Mt	Ex-Mt
❑ 207 Aaron Cook ROO RC	8.00	2.40
❑ 208 Luis Ugueto ROO RC	8.00	2.40
❑ 209 Gustavo Chacin ROO RC	3.00	.90
❑ 210 Francis Beltran ROO RC	8.00	2.40
❑ 211 Takahito Nomura ROO RC	8.00	2.40
❑ 212 Oliver Perez ROO RC	15.00	4.50
❑ 213 Miguel Asencio ROO RC	8.00	2.40
❑ 214 Rene Reyes ROO RC	8.00	2.40
❑ 215 Jeff Baker ROO RC	25.00	7.50
❑ 216 Jon Adkins ROO RC	8.00	2.40
❑ 217 Carlos Rivera ROO RC	8.00	2.40
❑ 218 Corey Thurman ROO RC	8.00	2.40
❑ 219 Earl Snyder ROO RC	10.00	3.00
❑ 220 Felix Escalona ROO RC	8.00	2.40
❑ 221 Jeremy Guthrie ROO RC	10.00	3.00
❑ 222 Josh Hancock ROO RC	8.00	2.40
❑ 223 Ben Kozlowski ROO RC	8.00	2.40
❑ 224 Eric Good ROO RC	8.00	2.40
❑ 225 Eric Junge ROO RC	8.00	2.40
❑ 226 Andy Pratt ROO RC	8.00	2.40
❑ 227 Matt Thornton ROO RC	8.00	2.40
❑ 228 Jorge Sosa ROO RC	8.00	2.40
❑ 229 Mike Smith ROO RC	8.00	2.40
❑ 230 Mitch Wylie ROO RC	8.00	2.40
❑ 231 John Ennis ROO RC	8.00	2.40
❑ 232 Reed Johnson ROO RC	10.00	3.00
❑ 233 Joe Borchard ROO	8.00	2.40
❑ 234 Ron Calloway ROO RC	8.00	2.40
❑ 235 Brian Tallet ROO RC	8.00	2.40
❑ 236 Chris Baker ROO RC	8.00	2.40
❑ 237 Cliff Lee ROO RC	15.00	4.50
❑ 238 Matt Childers ROO RC	8.00	2.40
❑ 239 Freddy Sanchez ROO RC	8.00	2.40
❑ 240 Chone Figgins ROO RC	10.00	3.00
❑ 241 Kevin Cash ROO RC	8.00	2.40
❑ 242 Josh Bard ROO RC	8.00	2.40
❑ 243 Jer. Robertson ROO RC	8.00	2.40
❑ 244 Jeremy Hill ROO RC	8.00	2.40
❑ 245 Shane Nance ROO RC	8.00	2.40
❑ 246 Wes Obermueller ROO RC	8.00	2.40
❑ 247 Trey Hodges ROO RC	8.00	2.40
❑ 248 Eric Eckenstahler ROO RC	8.00	2.40
❑ 249 Jim Rushford ROO RC	8.00	2.40
❑ 250 Jose Castillo ROO RC	15.00	4.50
❑ 251 Garrett Atkins ROO RC	10.00	3.00
❑ 252 Alexis Rios ROO RC	80.00	24.00
❑ 253 Ryan Church ROO RC	10.00	3.00
❑ 254 Jimmy Gobble ROO RC	10.00	3.00
❑ 255 Corwin Malone ROO RC	8.00	2.40
❑ 256 Does Not Exist		
❑ 257 Nic Jackson ROO RC	8.00	2.40
❑ 258 Tommy Whiteman ROO RC	10.00	3.00
❑ 259 Mario Ramos ROO RC	8.00	2.40
❑ 260 Rob Bowen ROO RC	8.00	2.40
❑ 261 Josh Wilson ROO RC	8.00	2.40
❑ 262 Tim Hummel ROO RC	8.00	2.40
❑ 263 Does Not Exist		
❑ 264 Gerald Laird ROO RC	15.00	4.50
❑ 265 Vinny Chulk ROO RC	8.00	2.40
❑ 266 Jesus Medrano ROO RC	8.00	2.40
❑ 267 Does Not Exist		
❑ 268 Does Not Exist		
❑ 269 Does Not Exist		
❑ 270 Does Not Exist		
❑ 271 Does Not Exist		
❑ 272 Adam LaRoche ROO RC	30.00	9.00
❑ 273 Adam Morrissey ROO RC	8.00	2.40
❑ 274 Henri Stanley ROO RC	8.00	2.40
❑ 275 Walter Young ROO RC	15.00	4.50

2003 Donruss Elite

	Nm-Mt	Ex-Mt
COMP.SET w/o SP's (180)	20.00	6.00
COMMON CARD (1-180)	.30	.09
COMMON CARD (181-200)	4.00	1.20

Card	Nm-Mt	Ex-Mt
❑ 1 Darin Erstad	.30	.09
❑ 2 David Eckstein	.30	.09
❑ 3 Garret Anderson	.30	.09
❑ 4 Jarrod Washburn	.30	.09
❑ 5 Tim Salmon	.50	.15
❑ 6 Troy Glaus	.30	.09
❑ 7 Marty Cordova	.30	.09
❑ 8 Melvin Mora	.30	.09
❑ 9 Rodrigo Lopez	.30	.09

Card	Nm-Mt	Ex-Mt
❑ 10 Tony Batista	.30	.09
❑ 11 Derek Lowe	.30	.09
❑ 12 Johnny Damon	.75	.23
❑ 13 Manny Ramirez	.50	.15
❑ 14 Nomar Garciaparra	1.25	.35
❑ 15 Pedro Martinez	.75	.23
❑ 16 Shea Hillenbrand	.30	.09
❑ 17 Carlos Lee	.30	.09
❑ 18 Joe Crede	.30	.09
❑ 19 Frank Thomas	.75	.23
❑ 20 Magglio Ordonez	.30	.09
❑ 21 Mark Buehrle	.30	.09
❑ 22 Paul Konerko	.30	.09
❑ 23 C.C. Sabathia	.30	.09
❑ 24 Ellis Burks	.30	.09
❑ 25 Omar Vizquel	.50	.15
❑ 26 Brian Tallet	.30	.09
❑ 27 Bobby Higginson	.30	.09
❑ 28 Carlos Pena	.30	.09
❑ 29 Mark Redman	.30	.09
❑ 30 Steve Sparks	.30	.09
❑ 31 Carlos Beltran	.50	.15
❑ 32 Joe Randa	.30	.09
❑ 33 Mike Sweeney	.30	.09
❑ 34 Raul Ibanez	.30	.09
❑ 35 Runelvys Hernandez	.30	.09
❑ 36 Brad Radke	.30	.09
❑ 37 Corey Koskie	.30	.09
❑ 38 Cristian Guzman	.30	.09
❑ 39 David Ortiz	.50	.15
❑ 40 Doug Mientkiewicz	.30	.09
❑ 41 Jacque Jones	.30	.09
❑ 42 Torii Hunter	.30	.09
❑ 43 Alfonso Soriano	.50	.15
❑ 44 Andy Pettitte	.50	.15
❑ 45 Bernie Williams	.50	.15
❑ 46 David Wells	.30	.09
❑ 47 Derek Jeter	2.00	.60
❑ 48 Jason Giambi	.30	.09
❑ 49 Jeff Weaver	.30	.09
❑ 50 Jorge Posada	.50	.15
❑ 51 Mike Mussina	.50	.15
❑ 52 Roger Clemens	1.50	.45
❑ 53 Barry Zito	.30	.09
❑ 54 Eric Chavez	.30	.09
❑ 55 Jermaine Dye	.30	.09
❑ 56 Mark Mulder	.30	.09
❑ 57 Miguel Tejada	.30	.09
❑ 58 Tim Hudson	.30	.09
❑ 59 Bret Boone	.30	.09
❑ 60 Chris Snelling	.30	.09
❑ 61 Edgar Martinez	.50	.15
❑ 62 Freddy Garcia	.30	.09
❑ 63 Ichiro Suzuki	1.25	.35
❑ 64 Jamie Moyer	.30	.09
❑ 65 John Olerud	.30	.09
❑ 66 Kazuhiro Sasaki	.30	.09
❑ 67 Aubrey Huff	.30	.09
❑ 68 Joe Kennedy	.30	.09
❑ 69 Paul Wilson	.30	.09
❑ 70 Alex Rodriguez	1.25	.35
❑ 71 Chan Ho Park	.30	.09
❑ 72 Hank Blalock	.50	.15
❑ 73 Juan Gonzalez	.50	.15
❑ 74 Kevin Mench	.30	.09
❑ 75 Rafael Palmeiro	.50	.15
❑ 76 Carlos Delgado	.30	.09
❑ 77 Eric Hinske	.30	.09
❑ 78 Josh Phelps	.30	.09
❑ 79 Roy Halladay	.30	.09
❑ 80 Shannon Stewart	.30	.09
❑ 81 Vernon Wells	.30	.09
❑ 82 Curt Schilling	.30	.09
❑ 83 Junior Spivey	.30	.09
❑ 84 Luis Gonzalez	.30	.09
❑ 85 Mark Grace	.50	.15
❑ 86 Randy Johnson	.75	.23
❑ 87 Steve Finley	.30	.09
❑ 88 Andruw Jones	.30	.09
❑ 89 Chipper Jones	.75	.23
❑ 90 Gary Sheffield	.30	.09
❑ 91 Greg Maddux	1.25	.35
❑ 92 John Smoltz	.50	.15
❑ 93 Corey Patterson	.30	.09
❑ 94 Kerry Wood	.75	.23
❑ 95 Mark Prior	.75	.23
❑ 96 Moises Alou	.30	.09
❑ 97 Sammy Sosa	1.25	.35
❑ 98 Adam Dunn	.50	.15
❑ 99 Austin Kearns	.30	.09
❑ 100 Barry Larkin	.50	.15
❑ 101 Ken Griffey Jr.	1.25	.35
❑ 102 Sean Casey	.30	.09
❑ 103 Jason Jennings	.30	.09
❑ 104 Jay Payton	.30	.09
❑ 105 Larry Walker	.50	.15
❑ 106 Todd Helton	.50	.15
❑ 107 A.J. Burnett	.30	.09
❑ 108 Josh Beckett	.30	.09
❑ 109 Juan Encarnacion	.30	.09
❑ 110 Mike Lowell	.30	.09
❑ 111 Craig Biggio	.50	.15
❑ 112 Daryle Ward	.30	.09
❑ 113 Jeff Bagwell	.50	.15
❑ 114 Lance Berkman	.30	.09
❑ 115 Roy Oswalt	.30	.09
❑ 116 Jason Lane	.30	.09
❑ 117 Adrian Beltre	.50	.15
❑ 118 Hideo Nomo	.75	.23
❑ 119 Kazuhisa Ishii	.30	.09
❑ 120 Kevin Brown	.30	.09
❑ 121 Odalis Perez	.30	.09
❑ 122 Paul Lo Duca	.30	.09
❑ 123 Shawn Green	.30	.09
❑ 124 Ben Sheets	.30	.09
❑ 125 Jeffrey Hammonds	.30	.09
❑ 126 Jose Hernandez	.30	.09
❑ 127 Richie Sexson	.30	.09
❑ 128 Bartolo Colon	.30	.09
❑ 129 Brad Wilkerson	.30	.09
❑ 130 Javier Vazquez	.30	.09
❑ 131 Jose Vidro	.30	.09
❑ 132 Michael Barrett	.30	.09
❑ 133 Vladimir Guerrero	.75	.23
❑ 134 Al Leiter	.30	.09
❑ 135 Mike Piazza	1.25	.35
❑ 136 Mo Vaughn	.30	.09
❑ 137 Pedro Astacio	.30	.09
❑ 138 Roberto Alomar	.50	.15
❑ 139 Pat Burrell	.30	.09
❑ 140 Vicente Padilla	.30	.09
❑ 141 Jimmy Rollins	.30	.09
❑ 142 Bobby Abreu	.30	.09
❑ 143 Marlon Byrd	.30	.09
❑ 144 Brian Giles	.30	.09
❑ 145 Jason Kendall	.30	.09
❑ 146 Aramis Ramirez	.30	.09
❑ 147 Josh Fogg	.30	.09
❑ 148 Ryan Klesko	.30	.09
❑ 149 Phil Nevin	.30	.09
❑ 150 Sean Burroughs	.30	.09
❑ 151 Mark Kotsay	.30	.09
❑ 152 Barry Bonds	2.00	.60
❑ 153 Damian Moss	.30	.09
❑ 154 Jason Schmidt	.30	.09
❑ 155 Benito Santiago	.30	.09
❑ 156 Rich Aurilia	.30	.09
❑ 157 Scott Rolen	.75	.23
❑ 158 J.D. Drew	.30	.09
❑ 159 Jim Edmonds	.30	.09
❑ 160 Matt Morris	.30	.09
❑ 161 Tino Martinez	.50	.15
❑ 162 Albert Pujols	1.50	.45
❑ 163 Russ Ortiz	.30	.09

❑ 164 Rey Ordonez	.30	.09
❑ 165 Paul Byrd	.30	.09
❑ 166 Kenny Lofton	.30	.09
❑ 167 Kenny Rogers	.30	.09
❑ 168 Rickey Henderson	.75	.23
❑ 169 Fred McGriff	.50	.15
❑ 170 Charles Johnson	.30	.09
❑ 171 Mike Hampton	.30	.09
❑ 172 Jim Thome	.75	.23
❑ 173 Travis Hafner	.30	.09
❑ 174 Ivan Rodriguez	.75	.23
❑ 175 Ray Durham	.30	.09
❑ 176 Jeremy Giambi	.30	.09
❑ 177 Jeff Kent	.30	.09
❑ 178 Cliff Floyd	.30	.09
❑ 179 Kevin Millwood	.30	.09
❑ 180 Tom Glavine	.50	.15
❑ 181 Hideki Matsui ROO RC	10.00	3.00
❑ 182 Jose Contreras ROO RC	5.00	1.50
❑ 183 Terrmel Sledge ROO RC	5.00	1.50
❑ 184 Lew Ford ROO RC	5.00	1.50
❑ 185 Jhonny Peralta ROO	4.00	1.20
❑ 186 Alexis Rios ROO	5.00	1.50
❑ 187 Jeff Baker ROO	4.00	1.20
❑ 188 Jeremy Guthrie ROO	4.00	1.20
❑ 189 Jose Castillo ROO	4.00	1.20
❑ 190 Garrett Atkins ROO	4.00	1.20
❑ 191 Jer. Bonderman ROO RC	5.00	1.50
❑ 192 Adam LaRoche ROO	4.00	1.20
❑ 193 Vinny Chulk ROO	4.00	1.20
❑ 194 Walter Young ROO	4.00	1.20
❑ 195 Jimmy Gobble ROO	4.00	1.20
❑ 196 Prentice Redman ROO RC	4.00	1.20
❑ 197 Jason Anderson ROO	4.00	1.20
❑ 198 Nic Jackson ROO	4.00	1.20
❑ 199 Travis Chapman ROO	4.00	1.20
❑ 200 Shane Victorino ROO RC	4.00	1.20

2003 Donruss Elite Extra Edition

	MINT	NRMT
❑ 1 Adam Loewen RC	5.00	2.20
❑ 2 Brandon Webb RC	5.00	2.20
❑ 3 Chien-Ming Wang RC	5.00	2.20
❑ 4 Hong-Chih Kuo RC	5.00	2.20
❑ 5 Clint Barmes RC	5.00	2.20
❑ 6 Guillermo Quiroz RC	5.00	2.20
❑ 7 Edgar Gonzalez RC	4.00	1.80
❑ 8 Todd Wellemeyer RC	5.00	2.20
❑ 9 Alfredo Gonzalez RC	4.00	1.80
❑ 10 Craig Brazell RC	5.00	2.20
❑ 11 Tim Olson RC	5.00	2.20
❑ 12 Rich Fischer RC	4.00	1.80
❑ 13 Daniel Cabrera RC	8.00	3.60
❑ 14 Francisco Rosario RC	4.00	1.80
❑ 15 Francisco Cruceta RC	4.00	1.80
❑ 16 Alejandro Machado RC	4.00	1.80
❑ 17 Andrew Brown RC	5.00	2.20
❑ 18 Rob Hammock RC	5.00	2.20
❑ 19 Arnie Munoz RC	4.00	1.80
❑ 20 Felix Sanchez RC	4.00	1.80
❑ 21 Nook Logan RC	4.00	1.80
❑ 22 Cory Stewart RC	4.00	1.80
❑ 23 Michel Hernandez RC	4.00	1.80
❑ 24 Rett Johnson RC	5.00	2.20
❑ 25 Josh Hall RC	5.00	2.20
❑ 26 Doug Waechter RC	5.00	2.20
❑ 27 Matt Kata RC	5.00	2.20
❑ 28 Dan Haren RC	5.00	2.20
❑ 29 Dontrelle Willis	5.00	2.20
❑ 30 Ramon Nivar RC	5.00	2.20
❑ 31 Chad Gaudin RC	4.00	1.80
❑ 32 Rickie Weeks RC	12.00	5.50
❑ 33 Ryan Wagner RC	5.00	2.20
❑ 34 Kevin Correia RC	4.00	1.80
❑ 35 Bo Hart RC	5.00	2.20
❑ 36 Oscar Villarreal RC	4.00	1.80
❑ 37 Josh Willingham RC	5.00	2.20
❑ 38 Jeff Duncan RC	5.00	2.20
❑ 39 David DeJesus RC	5.00	2.20
❑ 40 Dustin McGowan RC	5.00	2.20
❑ 41 Preston Larrison RC	5.00	2.20
❑ 42 Does Not Exist		
❑ 43 Kevin Youkilis RC	8.00	3.60
❑ 44 Bubba Nelson RC	5.00	2.20
❑ 45 Chris Burke RC	5.00	2.20
❑ 46 J.D. Durbin RC	5.00	2.20
❑ 47 Ryan Howard RC	12.00	5.50
❑ 48 Jason Kubel RC	10.00	4.50
❑ 49 Brendan Harris RC	5.00	2.20
❑ 50 Brian Bruney RC	5.00	2.20
❑ 51 Does Not Exist		
❑ 52 Byron Gettis RC	4.00	1.80
❑ 53 Edwin Jackson RC	12.00	5.50
❑ 54 Does Not Exist		
❑ 55 Daniel Garcia RC	4.00	1.80
❑ 56 Does Not Exist		
❑ 57 Chad Cordero RC	4.00	1.80
❑ 58 Delmon Young RC	15.00	6.75

2004 Donruss Elite

	Nm-Mt	Ex-Mt
COMP.SET w/o SP's (150)	25.00	7.50
COMMON CARD 1-150	.30	.09
COMMON AUTO (151-180)	8.00	2.40
COMMON CARD (181-200)	3.00	.90

CARD NUMBER 169 DOES NOT EXIST

❑ 1 Troy Glaus	.30	.09
❑ 2 Darin Erstad	.30	.09
❑ 3 Garret Anderson	.30	.09
❑ 4 Tim Salmon	.50	.15
❑ 5 Bartolo Colon	.30	.09
❑ 6 Jose Guillen	.30	.09
❑ 7 Miguel Tejada	.30	.09
❑ 8 Adam Loewen	.30	.09
❑ 9 Jay Gibbons	.30	.09
❑ 10 Melvin Mora	.30	.09
❑ 11 Javy Lopez	.30	.09
❑ 12 Pedro Martinez	.75	.23
❑ 13 Curt Schilling	.75	.23
❑ 14 David Ortiz	.75	.23
❑ 15 Keith Foulke	.30	.09
❑ 16 Nomar Garciaparra	1.25	.35
❑ 17 Magglio Ordonez	.30	.09
❑ 18 Frank Thomas	.75	.23
❑ 19 Carlos Lee	.30	.09
❑ 20 Paul Konerko	.30	.09
❑ 21 Mark Buehrle	.30	.09
❑ 22 Jody Gerut	.30	.09
❑ 23 Victor Martinez	.30	.09
❑ 24 C.C. Sabathia	.30	.09
❑ 25 Ellis Burks	.30	.09
❑ 26 Bobby Higginson	.30	.09
❑ 27 Jeremy Bonderman	.30	.09
❑ 28 Fernando Vina	.30	.09
❑ 29 Carlos Pena	.30	.09
❑ 30 Dmitri Young	.30	.09
❑ 31 Carlos Beltran	.50	.15
❑ 32 Benito Santiago	.30	.09
❑ 33 Mike Sweeney	.30	.09
❑ 34 Angel Berroa	.30	.09
❑ 35 Runelvys Hernandez	.30	.09
❑ 36 Johan Santana	.50	.15
❑ 37 Doug Mientkiewicz	.30	.09
❑ 38 Shannon Stewart	.30	.09
❑ 39 Torii Hunter	.30	.09
❑ 40 Derek Jeter	1.50	.45
❑ 41 Jason Giambi	.30	.09
❑ 42 Bernie Williams	.50	.15
❑ 43 Alfonso Soriano	.50	.15
❑ 44 Gary Sheffield	.30	.09
❑ 45 Mike Mussina	.50	.15
❑ 46 Jorge Posada	.50	.15
❑ 47 Hideki Matsui	1.25	.35
❑ 48 Kevin Brown	.30	.09
❑ 49 Javier Vazquez	.30	.09
❑ 50 Mariano Rivera	.50	.15
❑ 51 Eric Chavez	.30	.09
❑ 52 Tim Hudson	.30	.09
❑ 53 Mark Mulder	.30	.09
❑ 54 Barry Zito	.30	.09
❑ 55 Ichiro Suzuki	1.25	.35
❑ 56 Edgar Martinez	.50	.15
❑ 57 Bret Boone	.30	.09
❑ 58 John Olerud	.30	.09
❑ 59 Scott Spiezio	.30	.09
❑ 60 Aubrey Huff	.30	.09
❑ 61 Rocco Baldelli	.30	.09
❑ 62 Jose Cruz Jr.	.30	.09
❑ 63 Delmon Young	.50	.15
❑ 64 Mark Teixeira	.30	.09
❑ 65 Hank Blalock	.30	.09
❑ 66 Michael Young	.30	.09
❑ 67 Alex Rodriguez	1.25	.35
❑ 68 Carlos Delgado	.30	.09
❑ 69 Eric Hinske	.30	.09
❑ 70 Roy Halladay	.30	.09
❑ 71 Vernon Wells	.30	.09
❑ 72 Randy Johnson	.75	.23
❑ 73 Richie Sexson	.30	.09
❑ 74 Brandon Webb	.30	.09
❑ 75 Luis Gonzalez	.30	.09
❑ 76 Steve Finley	.30	.09
❑ 77 Chipper Jones	.75	.23
❑ 78 Andruw Jones	.30	.09
❑ 79 Marcus Giles	.30	.09
❑ 80 Rafael Furcal	.30	.09
❑ 81 J.D. Drew	.30	.09
❑ 82 Sammy Sosa	1.25	.35
❑ 83 Kerry Wood	.75	.23
❑ 84 Mark Prior	.75	.23
❑ 85 Derrek Lee	.30	.09
❑ 86 Moises Alou	.30	.09
❑ 87 Corey Patterson	.30	.09
❑ 88 Ken Griffey Jr.	1.25	.35
❑ 89 Austin Kearns	.30	.09
❑ 90 Adam Dunn	.50	.15
❑ 91 Barry Larkin	.50	.15
❑ 92 Todd Helton	.50	.15
❑ 93 Larry Walker	.50	.15
❑ 94 Preston Wilson	.30	.09
❑ 95 Charles Johnson	.30	.09
❑ 96 Luis Castillo	.30	.09
❑ 97 Josh Beckett	.30	.09
❑ 98 Mike Lowell	.30	.09
❑ 99 Miguel Cabrera	.50	.15
❑ 100 Juan Pierre	.30	.09
❑ 101 Dontrelle Willis	.30	.09
❑ 102 Andy Pettitte	.50	.15
❑ 103 Wade Miller	.30	.09
❑ 104 Jeff Bagwell	.50	.15
❑ 105 Craig Biggio	.50	.15
❑ 106 Lance Berkman	.30	.09
❑ 107 Jeff Kent	.30	.09
❑ 108 Roy Oswalt	.30	.09
❑ 109 Hideo Nomo	.75	.23
❑ 110 Adrian Beltre	.50	.15
❑ 111 Paul Lo Duca	.30	.09
❑ 112 Shawn Green	.30	.09

Card	Nm-Mt	Ex-Mt
❑ 113 Fred McGriff	.50	.15
❑ 114 Eric Gagne	.75	.23
❑ 115 Geoff Jenkins	.30	.09
❑ 116 Rickie Weeks	.30	.09
❑ 117 Scott Podsednik	.30	.09
❑ 118 Nick Johnson	.30	.09
❑ 119 Orlando Cabrera	.30	.09
❑ 120 Jose Vidro	.30	.09
❑ 121 Kazuo Matsui RC	2.50	.75
❑ 122 Tom Glavine	.50	.15
❑ 123 Al Leiter	.30	.09
❑ 124 Mike Piazza	1.25	.35
❑ 125 Jose Reyes	.30	.09
❑ 126 Mike Cameron	.30	.09
❑ 127 Pat Burrell	.30	.09
❑ 128 Jim Thome	.75	.23
❑ 129 Mike Lieberthal	.30	.09
❑ 130 Bobby Abreu	.30	.09
❑ 131 Kip Wells	.30	.09
❑ 132 Jack Wilson	.30	.09
❑ 133 Pokey Reese	.30	.09
❑ 134 Brian Giles	.30	.09
❑ 135 Sean Burroughs	.30	.09
❑ 136 Ryan Klesko	.30	.09
❑ 137 Trevor Hoffman	.30	.09
❑ 138 Jason Schmidt	.30	.09
❑ 139 J.T. Snow	.30	.09
❑ 140 A.J. Pierzynski	.30	.09
❑ 141 Ray Durham	.30	.09
❑ 142 Jim Edmonds	.30	.09
❑ 143 Albert Pujols	1.50	.45
❑ 144 Edgar Renteria	.30	.09
❑ 145 Scott Rolen	.75	.23
❑ 146 Matt Morris	.30	.09
❑ 147 Ivan Rodriguez	.75	.23
❑ 148 Vladimir Guerrero	.75	.23
❑ 149 Greg Maddux	1.25	.35
❑ 150 Kevin Millwood	.30	.09
❑ 151 Hector Gimenez AU/750 RC	8.00	2.40
❑ 152 Willy Taveras AU/750 RC	10.00	3.00
❑ 153 Ruddy Yan AU/750	8.00	2.40
❑ 154 Graham Koonce AU/750	8.00	2.40
❑ 155 Jose Capellan AU/750 RC	30.00	9.00
❑ 156 Onil Joseph AU/750 RC	8.00	2.40
❑ 157 John Gall AU/1000 RC	10.00	3.00
❑ 158 Carlos Hines AU/750 RC	8.00	2.40
❑ 159 Jerry Gil AU/750 RC	8.00	2.40
❑ 160 Mike Gosling AU/750 RC	8.00	2.40
❑ 161 Jason Frasor AU/750 RC	8.00	2.40
❑ 162 Justin Knoedler AU/750 RC	8.00	2.40
❑ 163 Merkin Valdez AU/500 RC	15.00	4.50
❑ 164 Angel Chavez AU/1000 RC	8.00	2.40
❑ 165 Ivan Ochoa AU/750 RC	8.00	2.40
❑ 166 Greg Dobbs AU/750 RC	8.00	2.40
❑ 167 Ronald Belisario AU/750 RC	8.00	2.40
❑ 168 Aarom Baldiris AU/750 RC	10.00	3.00
❑ 169 Does Not Exist		
❑ 170 Dave Crouthers AU/750 RC	8.00	2.40
❑ 171 Freddy Guzman AU/750 RC	10.00	3.00
❑ 172 Akinori Otsuka AU/250 RC	40.00	12.00
❑ 173 Ian Snell AU/750 RC	10.00	3.00
❑ 174 Nick Regilio AU/1000 RC	8.00	2.40
❑ 175 Jamie Brown AU/750 RC	8.00	2.40
❑ 176 Jerome Gamble AU/750 RC	8.00	2.40
❑ 177 Roberto Novoa AU/1000 RC	10.00	3.00
❑ 178 Sean Henn AU/1000 RC	8.00	2.40
❑ 179 Ramon Ramirez AU/1000 RC	8.00	2.40
❑ 180 Jason Bartlett AU/1000 RC	10.00	3.00
❑ 181 Bob Gibson RET	4.00	1.20
❑ 182 Cal Ripken RET	10.00	3.00
❑ 183 Carl Yastrzemski RET	5.00	1.50
❑ 184 Dale Murphy RET	4.00	1.20
❑ 185 Don Mattingly RET	8.00	2.40
❑ 186 Eddie Murray RET	4.00	1.20
❑ 187 George Brett RET	8.00	2.40
❑ 188 Jackie Robinson RET	4.00	1.20
❑ 189 Jim Palmer RET	3.00	.90
❑ 190 Lou Gehrig RET	5.00	1.50
❑ 191 Mike Schmidt RET	6.00	1.80
❑ 192 Ozzie Smith RET	5.00	1.50
❑ 193 Nolan Ryan RET	8.00	2.40
❑ 194 Reggie Jackson RET	4.00	1.20
❑ 195 Roberto Clemente RET	8.00	2.40
❑ 196 Robin Yount RET	5.00	1.50
❑ 197 Stan Musial RET	5.00	1.50
❑ 198 Ted Williams RET	6.00	1.80
❑ 199 Tony Gwynn RET	4.00	1.20
❑ 200 Ty Cobb RET	4.00	1.20

1998 Donruss Signature

	Nm-Mt	Ex-Mt
COMPLETE SET (140)	50.00	15.00
❑ 1 David Justice	.40	.12
❑ 2 Derek Jeter	2.50	.75
❑ 3 Nomar Garciaparra	1.50	.45
❑ 4 Ryan Klesko	.40	.12
❑ 5 Jeff Bagwell	.60	.18
❑ 6 Dante Bichette	.40	.12
❑ 7 Ivan Rodriguez	1.00	.30
❑ 8 Albert Belle	.40	.12
❑ 9 Cal Ripken	3.00	.90
❑ 10 Craig Biggio	.60	.18
❑ 11 Barry Larkin	.60	.18
❑ 12 Jose Guillen	.40	.12
❑ 13 Will Clark	1.00	.30
❑ 14 J.T. Snow	.40	.12
❑ 15 Chuck Knoblauch	.40	.12
❑ 16 Todd Walker	.40	.12
❑ 17 Scott Rolen	1.00	.30
❑ 18 Rickey Henderson	1.00	.30
❑ 19 Juan Gonzalez	.60	.18
❑ 20 Justin Thompson	.40	.12
❑ 21 Roger Clemens	2.00	.60
❑ 22 Ray Lankford	.40	.12
❑ 23 Jose Cruz Jr.	.40	.12
❑ 24 Ken Griffey Jr.	1.50	.45
❑ 25 Andruw Jones	.40	.12
❑ 26 Darin Erstad	.40	.12
❑ 27 Jim Thome	1.00	.30
❑ 28 Wade Boggs	.60	.18
❑ 29 Ken Caminiti	.40	.12
❑ 30 Todd Hundley	.40	.12
❑ 31 Mike Piazza	1.50	.45
❑ 32 Sammy Sosa	1.50	.45
❑ 33 Larry Walker	.60	.18
❑ 34 Matt Williams	.40	.12
❑ 35 Frank Thomas	1.00	.30
❑ 36 Gary Sheffield	.40	.12
❑ 37 Alex Rodriguez	1.50	.45
❑ 38 Hideo Nomo	1.00	.30
❑ 39 Kenny Lofton	.40	.12
❑ 40 John Smoltz	.60	.18
❑ 41 Mo Vaughn	.40	.12
❑ 42 Edgar Martinez	.60	.18
❑ 43 Paul Molitor	.60	.18
❑ 44 Rafael Palmeiro	.60	.18
❑ 45 Barry Bonds	2.50	.75
❑ 46 Vladimir Guerrero	1.00	.30
❑ 47 Carlos Delgado	.40	.12
❑ 48 Bobby Higginson	.40	.12
❑ 49 Greg Maddux	1.50	.45
❑ 50 Jim Edmonds	.40	.12
❑ 51 Randy Johnson	1.00	.30
❑ 52 Mark McGwire	2.50	.75
❑ 53 Rondell White	.40	.12
❑ 54 Raul Mondesi	.40	.12
❑ 55 Manny Ramirez	.60	.18
❑ 56 Pedro Martinez	1.00	.30
❑ 57 Tim Salmon	.60	.18
❑ 58 Moises Alou	.40	.12
❑ 59 Fred McGriff	.60	.18
❑ 60 Garret Anderson	.40	.12
❑ 61 Sandy Alomar Jr.	.40	.12
❑ 62 Chan Ho Park	.40	.12
❑ 63 Mark Kotsay	.40	.12
❑ 64 Mike Mussina	.60	.18
❑ 65 Tom Glavine	.60	.18
❑ 66 Tony Clark	.40	.12
❑ 67 Mark Grace	.60	.18
❑ 68 Tony Gwynn	1.25	.35
❑ 69 Tino Martinez	.60	.18
❑ 70 Kevin Brown	.60	.18
❑ 71 Todd Greene	.40	.12
❑ 72 Andy Pettitte	.60	.18
❑ 73 Livan Hernandez	.40	.12
❑ 74 Curt Schilling	.40	.12
❑ 75 Andres Galarraga	.40	.12
❑ 76 Rusty Greer	.40	.12
❑ 77 Jay Buhner	.40	.12
❑ 78 Bobby Bonilla	.40	.12
❑ 79 Chipper Jones	1.00	.30
❑ 80 Eric Young	.40	.12
❑ 81 Jason Giambi	.40	.12
❑ 82 Javy Lopez	.40	.12
❑ 83 Roberto Alomar	.60	.18
❑ 84 Bernie Williams	.60	.18
❑ 85 A.J. Hinch	.40	.12
❑ 86 Kerry Wood	1.00	.30
❑ 87 Juan Encarnacion	.40	.12
❑ 88 Brad Fullmer	.40	.12
❑ 89 Ben Grieve	.40	.12
❑ 90 Magglio Ordonez RC	8.00	2.40
❑ 91 Todd Helton	.60	.18
❑ 92 Richard Hidalgo	.40	.12
❑ 93 Paul Konerko	.40	.12
❑ 94 Aramis Ramirez	.40	.12
❑ 95 Ricky Ledee	.40	.12
❑ 96 Derrek Lee	.40	.12
❑ 97 Travis Lee	.40	.12
❑ 98 Matt Anderson RC	.60	.18
❑ 99 Jaret Wright	.40	.12
❑ 100 David Ortiz	1.00	.30
❑ 101 Carl Pavano	.60	.12
❑ 102 O.Hernandez RC	1.50	.45
❑ 103 Fernando Tatis	.40	.12
❑ 104 Miguel Tejada	.40	.12
❑ 105 Rolando Arrojo RC	.60	.18
❑ 106 Kevin Millwood RC	1.50	.45
❑ 107 Ken Griffey Jr. CL	1.00	.30
❑ 108 Frank Thomas CL	.60	.18
❑ 109 Cal Ripken CL	1.50	.45
❑ 110 Greg Maddux CL	1.00	.30
❑ 111 John Olerud	.40	.12
❑ 112 David Cone	.40	.12
❑ 113 Vinny Castilla	.40	.12
❑ 114 Jason Kendall	.40	.12
❑ 115 Brian Jordan	.40	.12
❑ 116 Hideki Irabu	.40	.12
❑ 117 Bartolo Colon	.40	.12
❑ 118 Greg Vaughn	.40	.12
❑ 119 David Segui	.40	.12
❑ 120 Bruce Chen	.40	.12
❑ 121 Julio Ramirez RC	.40	.12
❑ 122 Troy Glaus RC	8.00	2.40
❑ 123 Jeremy Giambi RC	.60	.18
❑ 124 Ryan Minor RC	.40	.12
❑ 125 Richie Sexson	.40	.12
❑ 126 Dermal Brown	.40	.12
❑ 127 Adrian Beltre	1.00	.30
❑ 128 Eric Chavez	.40	.12
❑ 129 J.D. Drew RC	8.00	2.40
❑ 130 Gabe Kapler RC	1.00	.30
❑ 131 Masato Yoshii RC	1.00	.30
❑ 132 Mike Lowell RC	4.00	1.20
❑ 133 Jim Parque RC	.60	.18
❑ 134 Roy Halladay	.40	.12
❑ 135 Carlos Lee RC	1.50	.45
❑ 136 Jin Ho Cho RC	.40	.12
❑ 137 Michael Barrett	.40	.12
❑ 138 F.Seguignol RC	.40	.12
❑ 139 Odalis Perez RC UER Back pictures John Rocker	1.50	.45
❑ 140 Mark McGwire CL	1.25	.35

2001 Donruss Signature

	Nm-Mt	Ex-Mt
COMP.SET w/o SP'S (110)	50.00	15.00
COMMON CARD (1-110)	1.00	.30
COMMON (111-165)	10.00	3.00

COMMON AU RC (111-165) 10.00 3.00
COMMON NO AU (111-165) 8.00 2.40
COMMON (166-311) 5.00 1.50
COMMON RC (166-311) 5.00 1.50

❑ 1 Alex Rodriguez 4.00 1.20
❑ 2 Barry Bonds 6.00 1.80
❑ 3 Cal Ripken 8.00 2.40
❑ 4 Chipper Jones 2.50 .75
❑ 5 Derek Jeter 6.00 1.80
❑ 6 Troy Glaus 1.00 .30
❑ 7 Frank Thomas 2.50 .75
❑ 8 Greg Maddux 4.00 1.20
❑ 9 Ivan Rodriguez 2.50 .75
❑ 10 Jeff Bagwell 1.50 .45
❑ 11 John Olerud 1.00 .30
❑ 12 Todd Helton 1.50 .45
❑ 13 Ken Griffey Jr. 4.00 1.20
❑ 14 Manny Ramirez 1.50 .45
❑ 15 Mark McGwire 6.00 1.80
❑ 16 Mike Piazza 4.00 1.20
❑ 17 Nomar Garciaparra 4.00 1.20
❑ 18 Moises Alou 1.00 .30
❑ 19 Aramis Ramirez 1.00 .30
❑ 20 Curt Schilling 1.00 .30
❑ 21 Pat Burrell 1.00 .30
❑ 22 Doug Mientkiewicz 1.00 .30
❑ 23 Carlos Delgado 1.00 .30
❑ 24 J.D. Drew 1.00 .30
❑ 25 Cliff Floyd 1.00 .30
❑ 26 Freddy Garcia 1.00 .30
❑ 27 Roberto Alomar 1.50 .45
❑ 28 Barry Zito 1.50 .45
❑ 29 Juan Encarnacion 1.00 .30
❑ 30 Paul Konerko 1.00 .30
❑ 31 Mark Mulder 1.00 .30
❑ 32 Andy Pettitte 1.50 .45
❑ 33 Jim Edmonds 1.00 .30
❑ 34 Darin Erstad 1.00 .30
❑ 35 Jason Giambi 1.00 .30
❑ 36 Tom Glavine 1.50 .45
❑ 37 Juan Gonzalez 1.50 .45
❑ 38 Fred McGriff 1.50 .45
❑ 39 Shawn Green 1.00 .30
❑ 40 Tim Hudson 1.00 .30
❑ 41 Andruw Jones 1.00 .30
❑ 42 Jeff Kent 1.00 .30
❑ 43 Barry Larkin 1.50 .45
❑ 44 Brad Radke 1.00 .30
❑ 45 Mike Mussina 1.50 .45
❑ 46 Hideo Nomo 2.50 .75
❑ 47 Rafael Palmeiro 1.50 .45
❑ 48 Scott Rolen 2.50 .75
❑ 49 Gary Sheffield 1.00 .30
❑ 50 Bernie Williams 1.50 .45
❑ 51 Bob Abreu 1.00 .30
❑ 52 Edgardo Alfonzo 1.00 .30
❑ 53 Edgar Martinez 1.50 .45
❑ 54 Magglio Ordonez 1.00 .30
❑ 55 Kerry Wood 2.50 .75
❑ 56 Adrian Beltre 1.50 .45
❑ 57 Lance Berkman 1.00 .30
❑ 58 Kevin Brown 2.50 .75
❑ 59 Sean Casey 1.00 .30
❑ 60 Eric Chavez 1.00 .30
❑ 61 Bartolo Colon 1.00 .30
❑ 62 Sammy Sosa 4.00 1.20
❑ 63 Jermaine Dye 1.00 .30
❑ 64 Tony Gwynn 3.00 .90
❑ 65 Carl Everett 1.00 .30
❑ 66 Brian Giles 1.00 .30
❑ 67 Mike Hampton 1.00 .30
❑ 68 Richard Hidalgo 1.00 .30
❑ 69 Geoff Jenkins 1.00 .30
❑ 70 Tony Clark 1.00 .30
❑ 71 Roger Clemens 5.00 1.50
❑ 72 Ryan Klesko 1.00 .30
❑ 73 Chan Ho Park 1.00 .30
❑ 74 Richie Sexson 1.00 .30
❑ 75 Mike Sweeney 1.00 .30
❑ 76 Kazuhiro Sasaki 1.00 .30
❑ 77 Miguel Tejada 1.00 .30
❑ 78 Jose Vidro 1.00 .30
❑ 79 Larry Walker 1.50 .45
❑ 80 Preston Wilson 1.00 .30
❑ 81 Craig Biggio 1.50 .45
❑ 82 Andres Galarraga 1.00 .30
❑ 83 Jim Thome 2.50 .75
❑ 84 Vladimir Guerrero 2.50 .75
❑ 85 Rafael Furcal 1.00 .30
❑ 86 Cristian Guzman 1.00 .30
❑ 87 Terrence Long 1.00 .30
❑ 88 Bret Boone 1.00 .30
❑ 89 Wade Miller 1.00 .30
❑ 90 Eric Milton 1.00 .30
❑ 91 Gabe Kapler 1.00 .30
❑ 92 Johnny Damon 1.50 .45
❑ 93 Carlos Lee 1.00 .30
❑ 94 Kenny Lofton 1.00 .30
❑ 95 Raul Mondesi 1.00 .30
❑ 96 Jorge Posada 1.50 .45
❑ 97 Mark Grace 1.50 .45
❑ 98 Robert Fick 1.00 .30
❑ 99 Joe Mays 1.00 .30
❑ 100 Aaron Sele 1.00 .30
❑ 101 Ben Grieve 1.00 .30
❑ 102 Luis Gonzalez 1.00 .30
❑ 103 Ray Durham 1.00 .30
❑ 104 Mark Quinn 1.00 .30
❑ 105 Jose Canseco 2.50 .75
❑ 106 David Justice 1.00 .30
❑ 107 Pedro Martinez 2.50 .75
❑ 108 Randy Johnson 2.50 .75
❑ 109 Phil Nevin 1.00 .30
❑ 110 Rickey Henderson 2.50 .75
❑ 111 Alex Escobar AU 10.00 3.00
❑ 112 J.Estrada AU RC 25.00 7.50
❑ 113 Pedro Feliz AU 10.00 3.00
❑ 114 Nate Frese AU RC 10.00 3.00
❑ 115 R. Rodriguez AU RC 10.00 3.00
❑ 116 B.Larson AU RC 10.00 3.00
❑ 117 Alexis Gomez AU RC 10.00 3.00
❑ 118 Jason Hart AU 10.00 3.00
❑ 119 C.C. Sabathia AU 15.00 4.50
❑ 120 Endy Chavez AU RC 10.00 3.00
❑ 121 C.Parker AU RC 10.00 3.00
❑ 122 Jackson Melian RC 8.00 2.40
❑ 123 Joe Kennedy AU RC 15.00 4.50
❑ 124 A.Hernandez AU RC 10.00 3.00
❑ 125 Cesar Izturis AU 15.00 4.50
❑ 126 Jose Mieses AU RC 10.00 3.00
❑ 127 Roy Oswalt AU 25.00 7.50
❑ 128 Eric Munson AU 10.00 3.00
❑ 129 Xavier Nady AU 10.00 3.00
❑ 130 H.Ramirez AU RC 15.00 4.50
❑ 131 Abraham Nunez AU 10.00 3.00
❑ 132 Jose Ortiz AU 10.00 3.00
❑ 133 Jeremy Owens AU RC 10.00 3.00
❑ 134 Claudio Vargas AU RC 10.00 3.00
❑ 135 Corey Patterson AU 15.00 4.50
❑ 136 Carlos Pena 8.00 2.40
❑ 137 Bud Smith AU RC 10.00 3.00
❑ 138 Adam Dunn AU 25.00 7.50
❑ 139 A.Pettyjohn AU RC 10.00 3.00
❑ 140 E.Guzman AU RC 10.00 3.00
❑ 141 Jay Gibbons AU RC 25.00 7.50
❑ 142 Wilkin Ruan AU RC 10.00 3.00
❑ 143 Tsuyoshi Shinjo RC 10.00 3.00
❑ 144 Alfonso Soriano AU 40.00 12.00
❑ 145 Marcus Giles AU 15.00 4.50
❑ 146 Ichiro Suzuki RC 80.00 24.00
❑ 147 Juan Uribe AU RC 15.00 4.50
❑ 148 David Williams AU RC 10.00 3.00
❑ 149 C. Valderrama AU RC 10.00 3.00
❑ 150 Matt White AU RC 10.00 3.00
❑ 151 Albert Pujols AU RC 425.00 130.00
❑ 152 D.Mendez AU RC 10.00 3.00
❑ 153 Cory Aldridge AU RC 10.00 3.00
❑ 154 B. Duckworth AU RC 10.00 3.00
❑ 155 Josh Beckett AU 25.00 7.50
❑ 156 W.Betemit AU RC 10.00 3.00
❑ 157 Ben Sheets AU 25.00 7.50
❑ 158 Andres Torres AU RC 10.00 3.00
❑ 159 Aubrey Huff AU 15.00 4.50
❑ 160 Jack Wilson AU RC 40.00 12.00
❑ 161 Rafael Soriano AU RC 15.00 4.50
❑ 162 Nick Johnson AU 15.00 4.50
❑ 163 Carlos Garcia AU RC 10.00 3.00
❑ 164 Josh Towers AU RC 10.00 3.00
❑ 165 J.Michaels AU RC 10.00 3.00
❑ 166 Ryan Drese RC 8.00 2.40
❑ 167 Dewon Brazelton RC 8.00 2.40
❑ 168 Kevin Olsen RC 5.00 1.50
❑ 169 Benito Baez RC 5.00 1.50
❑ 170 Mark Prior RC 50.00 15.00
❑ 171 Wilmy Caceres RC 5.00 1.50
❑ 172 Mark Teixeira RC 30.00 9.00
❑ 173 Willie Harris RC 5.00 1.50
❑ 174 Mike Koplove RC 5.00 1.50
❑ 175 Brandon Knight RC 5.00 1.50
❑ 176 John Grabow RC 5.00 1.50
❑ 177 Jeremy Affeldt RC 8.00 2.40
❑ 178 Brandon Inge 5.00 1.50
❑ 179 Casey Fossum RC 5.00 1.50
❑ 180 Scott Stewart RC 5.00 1.50
❑ 181 Luke Hudson RC 5.00 1.50
❑ 182 Ken Vining RC 5.00 1.50
❑ 183 Toby Hall 5.00 1.50
❑ 184 Eric Knott RC 5.00 1.50
❑ 185 Kris Foster RC 5.00 1.50
❑ 186 David Brous RC 5.00 1.50
❑ 187 Roy Smith RC 5.00 1.50
❑ 188 Grant Balfour RC 5.00 1.50
❑ 189 Jeremy Fikac RC 5.00 1.50
❑ 190 Morgan Ensberg RC 8.00 2.40
❑ 191 Ryan Freel RC 5.00 1.50
❑ 192 Ryan Jensen RC 5.00 1.50
❑ 193 Lance Davis RC 5.00 1.50
❑ 194 Delvin James RC 5.00 1.50
❑ 195 Timo Perez 5.00 1.50
❑ 196 Michael Cuddyer 5.00 1.50
❑ 197 Bob File RC 5.00 1.50
❑ 198 Martin Vargas RC 5.00 1.50
❑ 199 Kris Keller RC 5.00 1.50
❑ 200 T.Spooneybarger RC 5.00 1.50
❑ 201 Adam Everett 5.00 1.50
❑ 202 Josh Fogg RC 5.00 1.50
❑ 203 Kip Wells 5.00 1.50
❑ 204 Rick Bauer RC 5.00 1.50
❑ 205 Brent Abernathy 5.00 1.50
❑ 206 Erick Almonte RC 5.00 1.50
❑ 207 Pedro Santana RC 5.00 1.50
❑ 208 Ken Harvey 5.00 1.50
❑ 209 Jerrod Riggan RC 5.00 1.50
❑ 210 Nick Punto RC 5.00 1.50
❑ 211 Steve Green RC 5.00 1.50
❑ 212 Nick Neugebauer 5.00 1.50
❑ 213 Chris George 5.00 1.50
❑ 214 Mike Penney RC 5.00 1.50
❑ 215 Bret Prinz RC 5.00 1.50
❑ 216 Tim Christman RC 5.00 1.50
❑ 217 Sean Douglass RC 5.00 1.50
❑ 218 Brett Jodie RC 5.00 1.50
❑ 219 Juan Diaz RC 5.00 1.50
❑ 220 Carlos Hernandez 5.00 1.50
❑ 221 Alex Cintron 5.00 1.50
❑ 222 Juan Cruz RC 5.00 1.50
❑ 223 Larry Bigbie 5.00 1.50
❑ 224 Junior Spivey RC 8.00 2.40
❑ 225 Luis Rivas 5.00 1.50
❑ 226 Brandon Lyon RC 5.00 1.50
❑ 227 Tony Cogan RC 5.00 1.50
❑ 228 J.Duchscherer RC 5.00 1.50
❑ 229 Tike Redman 5.00 1.50
❑ 230 Jimmy Rollins 5.00 1.50
❑ 231 Scott Podsednik RC 20.00 6.00
❑ 232 Jose Acevedo RC 5.00 1.50
❑ 233 Luis Pineda RC 5.00 1.50
❑ 234 Josh Phelps 5.00 1.50
❑ 235 Paul Phillips RC 5.00 1.50

❑ 236	Brian Roberts RC	5.00	1.50
❑ 237	O.Woodards RC	5.00	1.50
❑ 238	Bart Miadich RC	5.00	1.50
❑ 239	Les Walrond RC	5.00	1.50
❑ 240	Brad Voyles RC	5.00	1.50
❑ 241	Joe Crede	5.00	1.50
❑ 242	Juan Moreno RC	5.00	1.50
❑ 243	Matt Ginter	5.00	1.50
❑ 244	Brian Rogers RC	5.00	1.50
❑ 245	Pablo Ozuna	5.00	1.50
❑ 246	Geronimo Gil RC	5.00	1.50
❑ 247	Mike Maroth RC	5.00	1.50
❑ 248	Josue Perez RC	5.00	1.50
❑ 249	Dee Brown	5.00	1.50
❑ 250	Victor Zambrano RC	8.00	2.40
❑ 251	Nick Maness RC	5.00	1.50
❑ 252	Kyle Lohse RC	8.00	2.40
❑ 253	Greg Miller RC	5.00	1.50
❑ 254	Henry Mateo RC	5.00	1.50
❑ 255	Duaner Sanchez RC	5.00	1.50
❑ 256	Rob MacKowiak RC	8.00	2.40
❑ 257	Steve Lomasney	5.00	1.50
❑ 258	Angel Santos RC	5.00	1.50
❑ 259	Winston Abreu RC	5.00	1.50
❑ 260	Brandon Berger RC	5.00	1.50
❑ 261	Tomas De La Rosa	5.00	1.50
❑ 262	Ramon Vazquez RC	5.00	1.50
❑ 263	Mickey Callaway RC	5.00	1.50
❑ 264	Corky Miller RC	5.00	1.50
❑ 265	Keith Ginter	5.00	1.50
❑ 266	Cody Ransom RC	5.00	1.50
❑ 267	Doug Nickle RC	5.00	1.50
❑ 268	Derrick Lewis RC	5.00	1.50
❑ 269	Eric Hinske RC	8.00	2.40
❑ 270	Travis Phelps RC	5.00	1.50
❑ 271	Eric Valent	5.00	1.50
❑ 272	Michael Rivera RC	5.00	1.50
❑ 273	Esix Snead RC	5.00	1.50
❑ 274	Troy Mattes RC	5.00	1.50
❑ 275	Jermaine Clark RC	5.00	1.50
❑ 276	Nate Cornejo	5.00	1.50
❑ 277	George Perez RC	5.00	1.50
❑ 278	Juan Rivera	5.00	1.50
❑ 279	Justin Atchley RC	5.00	1.50
❑ 280	Adam Johnson	5.00	1.50
❑ 281	Gene Altman RC	5.00	1.50
❑ 282	Jason Jennings	5.00	1.50
❑ 283	Scott MacRae RC	5.00	1.50
❑ 284	Craig Monroe RC	5.00	1.50
❑ 285	Bert Snow RC	5.00	1.50
❑ 286	Stubby Clapp RC	5.00	1.50
❑ 287	Jack Cust	5.00	1.50
❑ 288	Will Ohman RC	5.00	1.50
❑ 289	Wily Mo Pena	5.00	1.50
❑ 290	Joe Beimel RC	5.00	1.50
❑ 291	Jason Karnuth RC	5.00	1.50
❑ 292	Bill Ortega RC	5.00	1.50
❑ 293	Nate Teut RC	5.00	1.50
❑ 294	Erik Hiljus RC	5.00	1.50
❑ 295	Jason Smith RC	5.00	1.50
❑ 296	Juan A.Pena RC	5.00	1.50
❑ 297	David Espinosa	5.00	1.50
❑ 298	Tim Redding	5.00	1.50
❑ 299	Brian Lawrence RC	5.00	1.50
❑ 300	Brian Reith RC	5.00	1.50
❑ 301	Chad Durbin	5.00	1.50
❑ 302	Kurt Ainsworth	5.00	1.50
❑ 303	Blaine Neal RC	5.00	1.50
❑ 304	Jorge Julio RC	5.00	1.50
❑ 305	Adam Bernero	5.00	1.50
❑ 306	Travis Hafner RC	12.00	3.60
❑ 307	Dustan Mohr RC	5.00	1.50
❑ 308	Cesar Crespo RC	5.00	1.50
❑ 309	Billy Sylvester RC	5.00	1.50
❑ 310	Zach Day RC	5.00	1.50
❑ 311	Angel Berroa RC	8.00	2.40

2003 Donruss Signature

	MINT	NRMT
COMMON CARD (1-100)	1.00	.45
COMMON CARD (101-150)	1.00	.45

❑ 1	Garret Anderson	1.00	.45
❑ 2	Tim Salmon	1.50	.70
❑ 3	Troy Glaus	1.00	.45

❑ 4	Curt Schilling	1.00	.45
❑ 5	Luis Gonzalez	1.00	.45
❑ 6	Mark Grace	1.50	.70
❑ 7	Matt Williams	1.00	.45
❑ 8	Randy Johnson	2.50	1.10
❑ 9	Andruw Jones	1.00	.45
❑ 10	Chipper Jones	2.50	1.10
❑ 11	Gary Sheffield	1.00	.45
❑ 12	Greg Maddux	4.00	1.80
❑ 13	Johnny Damon	2.50	1.10
❑ 14	Manny Ramirez	1.50	.70
❑ 15	Nomar Garciaparra	4.00	1.80
❑ 16	Pedro Martinez	2.50	1.10
❑ 17	Corey Patterson	1.00	.45
❑ 18	Kerry Wood	2.50	1.10
❑ 19	Mark Prior	2.50	1.10
❑ 20	Sammy Sosa	4.00	1.80
❑ 21	Bartolo Colon	1.00	.45
❑ 22	Frank Thomas	2.50	1.10
❑ 23	Magglio Ordonez	1.00	.45
❑ 24	Paul Konerko	1.00	.45
❑ 25	Adam Dunn	1.50	.70
❑ 26	Austin Kearns	1.00	.45
❑ 27	Barry Larkin	1.50	.70
❑ 28	Ken Griffey Jr.	4.00	1.80
❑ 29	C.C. Sabathia	1.00	.45
❑ 30	Omar Vizquel	1.50	.70
❑ 31	Larry Walker	1.50	.70
❑ 32	Todd Helton	1.50	.70
❑ 33	Ivan Rodriguez	2.50	1.10
❑ 34	Josh Beckett	1.00	.45
❑ 35	Craig Biggio	1.50	.70
❑ 36	Jeff Bagwell	1.50	.70
❑ 37	Jeff Kent	1.00	.45
❑ 38	Lance Berkman	1.00	.45
❑ 39	Richard Hidalgo	1.00	.45
❑ 40	Roy Oswalt	1.00	.45
❑ 41	Carlos Beltran	1.50	.70
❑ 42	Mike Sweeney	1.00	.45
❑ 43	Runelvys Hernandez	1.00	.45
❑ 44	Hideo Nomo	2.50	1.10
❑ 45	Kazuhisa Ishii	1.00	.45
❑ 46	Paul Lo Duca	1.00	.45
❑ 47	Shawn Green	1.00	.45
❑ 48	Ben Sheets	1.00	.45
❑ 49	Richie Sexson	1.00	.45
❑ 50	A.J. Pierzynski	1.00	.45
❑ 51	Torii Hunter	1.00	.45
❑ 52	Javier Vazquez	1.00	.45
❑ 53	Jose Vidro	1.00	.45
❑ 54	Vladimir Guerrero	2.50	1.10
❑ 55	Cliff Floyd	1.00	.45
❑ 56	David Cone	1.00	.45
❑ 57	Mike Piazza	4.00	1.80
❑ 58	Roberto Alomar	1.50	.70
❑ 59	Tom Glavine	1.50	.70
❑ 60	Alfonso Soriano	1.50	.70
❑ 61	Derek Jeter	6.00	2.70
❑ 62	Drew Henson	1.00	.45
❑ 63	Jason Giambi	1.00	.45
❑ 64	Mike Mussina	1.50	.70
❑ 65	Nick Johnson	1.00	.45
❑ 66	Roger Clemens	5.00	2.20
❑ 67	Barry Zito	1.00	.45
❑ 68	Eric Chavez	1.00	.45
❑ 69	Mark Mulder	1.00	.45
❑ 70	Miguel Tejada	1.00	.45
❑ 71	Tim Hudson	1.00	.45
❑ 72	Bobby Abreu	1.00	.45
❑ 73	Jim Thome	2.50	1.10
❑ 74	Kevin Millwood	1.00	.45
❑ 75	Pat Burrell	1.00	.45
❑ 76	Brian Giles	1.00	.45
❑ 77	Jason Kendall	1.00	.45
❑ 78	Kenny Lofton	1.00	.45
❑ 79	Phil Nevin	1.00	.45
❑ 80	Ryan Klesko	1.00	.45
❑ 81	Andres Galarraga	1.00	.45
❑ 82	Barry Bonds	6.00	2.70
❑ 83	Rich Aurilia	1.00	.45
❑ 84	Edgar Martinez	1.50	.70
❑ 85	Freddy Garcia	1.00	.45
❑ 86	Ichiro Suzuki	4.00	1.80
❑ 87	Albert Pujols	5.00	2.20
❑ 88	Jim Edmonds	1.00	.45
❑ 89	Scott Rolen	2.50	1.10
❑ 90	So Taguchi	1.00	.45
❑ 91	Rocco Baldelli	1.00	.45
❑ 92	Alex Rodriguez	4.00	1.80
❑ 93	Hank Blalock	1.50	.70
❑ 94	Juan Gonzalez	1.50	.70
❑ 95	Mark Teixeira	1.00	.45
❑ 96	Rafael Palmeiro	1.50	.70
❑ 97	Carlos Delgado	1.00	.45
❑ 98	Eric Hinske	1.00	.45
❑ 99	Roy Halladay	1.00	.45
❑ 100	Vernon Wells	1.00	.45
❑ 101	Hideki Matsui ROO RC	10.00	4.50
❑ 102	Jose Contreras ROO RC	3.00	1.35
❑ 103	Jer. Bonderman ROO RC	2.50	1.10
❑ 104	Bernie Castro ROO RC	1.00	.45
❑ 105	Alfredo Gonzalez ROO RC	1.00	.45
❑ 106	Arnie Munoz ROO RC	1.00	.45
❑ 107	Andrew Brown ROO RC	1.50	.70
❑ 108	Josh Hall ROO RC	1.50	.70
❑ 109	Josh Stewart ROO RC	1.00	.45
❑ 110	Clint Barmes ROO RC	1.50	.70
❑ 111	Brandon Webb ROO RC	3.00	1.35
❑ 112	Chien-Ming Wang ROO RC	3.00	1.35
❑ 113	Edgar Gonzalez ROO RC	1.00	.45
❑ 114	Al. Machado ROO RC	1.00	.45
❑ 115	Jeremy Griffiths ROO RC	1.50	.70
❑ 116	Craig Brazell ROO RC	1.50	.70
❑ 117	Shane Bazzell ROO RC	1.00	.45
❑ 118	Fernando Cabrera ROO RC	1.00	.45
❑ 119	Terrmel Sledge ROO RC	1.50	.70
❑ 120	Rob Hammock ROO RC	1.50	.70
❑ 121	Francisco Rosario ROO RC	1.00	.45
❑ 122	Francisco Cruceta ROO RC	1.00	.45
❑ 123	Rett Johnson ROO RC	1.50	.70
❑ 124	Guillermo Quiroz ROO RC	2.50	1.10
❑ 125	Hong-Chih Kuo ROO RC	2.50	1.10
❑ 126	Ian Ferguson ROO RC	1.00	.45
❑ 127	Tim Olson ROO RC	1.50	.70
❑ 128	Todd Wellemeyer ROO RC	1.50	.70
❑ 129	Rich Fischer ROO RC	1.00	.45
❑ 130	Phil Seibel ROO RC	1.00	.45
❑ 131	Joe Valentine ROO RC	1.00	.45
❑ 132	Matt Kata ROO RC	2.50	1.10
❑ 133	Michael Hessman ROO RC	1.00	.45
❑ 134	Michel Hernandez ROO RC	1.00	.45
❑ 135	Doug Waechter ROO RC	1.50	.70
❑ 136	Prentice Redman ROO RC	1.00	.45
❑ 137	Nook Logan ROO RC	1.00	.45
❑ 138	Oscar Villarreal ROO RC	1.00	.45
❑ 139	Pete LaForest ROO RC	1.50	.70
❑ 140	Matt Bruback ROO RC	1.00	.45
❑ 141	Dontrelle Willis ROO	1.50	.70
❑ 142	Greg Aquino ROO RC	1.00	.45
❑ 143	Lew Ford ROO RC	4.00	1.80
❑ 144	Jeff Duncan ROO RC	1.50	.70
❑ 145	Dan Haren ROO RC	2.50	1.10
❑ 146	Miguel Ojeda ROO RC	1.00	.45
❑ 147	Rosman Garcia ROO RC	1.00	.45
❑ 148	Felix Sanchez ROO RC	1.00	.45
❑ 149	Jon Leicester ROO RC	1.00	.45
❑ 150	Roger Deago ROO RC	1.00	.45

2004 Donruss World Series

	Nm-Mt	Ex-Mt
COMP.SET w/o SP's (175)	40.00	12.00
COMP.SOX CHAMPS (25)	20.00	6.00
COMMON ACTIVE (1-175)	.40	.12
COMMON RETIRED (1-175)	.50	.15
176-200: OVERALL AU-GU ODDS 5 PER BOX		.00

176-200 PRINT RUNS B/WN 487-1000 PER		.00
COMMON (201-224/WS1)	1.00	.30
201-224/WS1 ISSUED IN SOX CHAMPS SET		.00

Card	Nm-Mt	Ex-Mt
❑ 1 Bartolo Colon	.40	.12
❑ 2 Darin Erstad	.40	.12
❑ 3 Garret Anderson	.40	.12
❑ 4 Tim Salmon	.60	.18
❑ 5 Troy Glaus	.40	.12
❑ 6 Vladimir Guerrero	1.00	.30
❑ 7 Brandon Webb	.40	.12
❑ 8 Luis Gonzalez	.40	.12
❑ 9 Randy Johnson	1.00	.30
❑ 10 Roberto Alomar	.60	.18
❑ 11 Shea Hillenbrand	.40	.12
❑ 12 Steve Finley	.40	.12
❑ 13 Andruw Jones	.40	.12
❑ 14 Chipper Jones	1.00	.30
❑ 15 J.D. Drew	.40	.12
❑ 16 Marcus Giles	.40	.12
❑ 17 Rafael Furcal	.40	.12
❑ 18 Javy Lopez	.40	.12
❑ 19 Jay Gibbons	.40	.12
❑ 20 Luis Matos	.40	.12
❑ 21 Melvin Mora	.40	.12
❑ 22 Miguel Tejada	.40	.12
❑ 23 Rafael Palmeiro	.60	.18
❑ 24 Curt Schilling	1.00	.30
❑ 25 Dwight Evans	.50	.15
❑ 26 Fred Lynn	.50	.15
❑ 27 Jason Varitek	.60	.18
❑ 28 Jim Rice	.50	.15
❑ 29 Johnny Damon	1.00	.30
❑ 30 Luis Tiant	.50	.15
❑ 31 Manny Ramirez	.60	.18
❑ 32 Nomar Garciaparra	1.50	.45
❑ 33 Pedro Martinez	1.00	.30
❑ 34 Trot Nixon	.40	.12
❑ 35 Aramis Ramirez	.40	.12
❑ 36 Corey Patterson	.40	.12
❑ 37 Derrek Lee	.40	.12
❑ 38 Greg Maddux	1.50	.45
❑ 39 Kerry Wood	1.00	.30
❑ 40 Mark Prior	1.00	.30
❑ 41 Moises Alou	.40	.12
❑ 42 Sammy Sosa	1.50	.45
❑ 43 Carlos Lee	.40	.12
❑ 44 Frank Thomas	1.00	.30
❑ 45 Luis Aparicio	.50	.15
❑ 46 Magglio Ordonez	.40	.12
❑ 47 Mark Buehrle	.40	.12
❑ 48 Paul Konerko	.40	.12
❑ 49 Adam Dunn	.60	.18
❑ 50 Austin Kearns	.40	.12
❑ 51 Barry Larkin	.60	.18
❑ 52 Dave Concepcion	.50	.15
❑ 53 George Foster	.50	.15
❑ 54 Joe Morgan	.50	.15
❑ 55 Sean Casey	.40	.12
❑ 56 Tony Perez	.50	.15
❑ 57 C.C. Sabathia	.40	.12
❑ 58 Jody Gerut	.40	.12
❑ 59 Omar Vizquel	.60	.18
❑ 60 Victor Martinez	.40	.12
❑ 61 Charles Johnson	.40	.12
❑ 62 Jeromy Burnitz	.40	.12
❑ 63 Larry Walker	.60	.18
❑ 64 Preston Wilson	.40	.12
❑ 65 Todd Helton	.60	.18
❑ 66 Alan Trammell	.50	.15
❑ 67 Dmitri Young	.40	.12
❑ 68 Ivan Rodriguez	1.00	.30
❑ 69 Jeremy Bonderman	.40	.12
❑ 70 A.J. Burnett	.40	.12
❑ 71 Brad Penny	.40	.12
❑ 72 Dontrelle Willis	.40	.12
❑ 73 Josh Beckett	.40	.12
❑ 74 Juan Pierre	.40	.12
❑ 75 Luis Castillo	.40	.12
❑ 76 Miguel Cabrera	.60	.18
❑ 77 Mike Lowell	.40	.12
❑ 78 Andy Pettitte	.60	.18
❑ 79 Craig Biggio	.60	.18
❑ 80 Jeff Bagwell	.60	.18
❑ 81 Jeff Kent	.40	.12
❑ 82 Lance Berkman	.40	.12
❑ 83 Roger Clemens	2.00	.60
❑ 84 Roy Oswalt	.40	.12
❑ 85 Wade Miller	.40	.12
❑ 86 Angel Berroa	.40	.12
❑ 87 Carlos Beltran	.60	.18
❑ 88 Juan Gonzalez	.60	.18
❑ 89 Ken Harvey	.40	.12
❑ 90 Mike Sweeney	.40	.12
❑ 91 Adrian Beltre	.60	.18
❑ 92 Hideo Nomo	1.00	.30
❑ 93 Kazuhisa Ishii	.40	.12
❑ 94 Milton Bradley	.40	.12
❑ 95 Orel Hershiser	.50	.15
❑ 96 Paul Lo Duca	.40	.12
❑ 97 Shawn Green	.40	.12
❑ 98 Ben Sheets	.40	.12
❑ 99 Geoff Jenkins	.40	.12
❑ 100 Junior Spivey	.40	.12
❑ 101 Rickie Weeks	.40	.12
❑ 102 Scott Podsednik	.40	.12
❑ 103 Jack Morris	.50	.15
❑ 104 Jacque Jones	.40	.12
❑ 105 Johan Santana	.60	.18
❑ 106 Shannon Stewart	.40	.12
❑ 107 Torii Hunter	.40	.12
❑ 108 Jose Vidro	.40	.12
❑ 109 Orlando Cabrera Sox	.60	.18
❑ 110 Al Leiter	.40	.12
❑ 111 Darryl Strawberry	.50	.15
❑ 112 Dwight Gooden	.50	.15
❑ 113 Jose Reyes	.40	.12
❑ 114 Kazuo Matsui RC	2.50	.75
❑ 115 Keith Hernandez	.50	.15
❑ 116 Lenny Dykstra	.50	.15
❑ 117 Mike Piazza	1.50	.45
❑ 118 Tom Glavine	.60	.18
❑ 119 Alex Rodriguez	1.50	.45
❑ 120 Bernie Williams	.60	.18
❑ 121 Derek Jeter	2.00	.60
❑ 122 Gary Sheffield	.40	.12
❑ 123 Jason Giambi	.40	.12
❑ 124 Javier Vazquez	.40	.12
❑ 125 Jorge Posada	.60	.18
❑ 126 Kenny Lofton	.40	.12
❑ 127 Kevin Brown	.40	.12
❑ 128 Mariano Rivera	.60	.18
❑ 129 Mike Mussina	.60	.18
❑ 130 Barry Zito	.40	.12
❑ 131 Eric Chavez	.40	.12
❑ 132 Jermaine Dye	.40	.12
❑ 133 Mark Mulder	.40	.12
❑ 134 Rich Harden	.40	.12
❑ 135 Tim Hudson	.40	.12
❑ 136 Brett Myers	.40	.12
❑ 137 Jim Thome	1.00	.30
❑ 138 Kevin Millwood	.40	.12
❑ 139 Marlon Byrd	.40	.12
❑ 140 Mike Lieberthal	.40	.12
❑ 141 Pat Burrell	.40	.12
❑ 142 Steve Carlton	.50	.15
❑ 143 Dave Parker	.50	.15
❑ 144 Jason Kendall	.40	.12
❑ 145 Brian Giles	.40	.12
❑ 146 Jay Payton	.40	.12
❑ 147 Ryan Klesko	.40	.12
❑ 148 J.T. Snow	.40	.12
❑ 149 Jason Schmidt	.40	.12
❑ 150 Bret Boone	.40	.12
❑ 151 Edgar Martinez	.60	.18
❑ 152 Jamie Moyer	.40	.12
❑ 153 Rich Aurilia	.40	.12
❑ 154 Shigetoshi Hasegawa	.40	.12
❑ 155 Albert Pujols	2.00	.60
❑ 156 Dan Haren	.40	.12
❑ 157 Edgar Renteria	.40	.12
❑ 158 Fernando Vina	.40	.12
❑ 159 Jim Edmonds	.40	.12
❑ 160 Matt Morris	.40	.12
❑ 161 Scott Rolen	1.00	.30
❑ 162 Aubrey Huff	.40	.12
❑ 163 Carl Crawford	.40	.12
❑ 164 Dewon Brazelton	.40	.12
❑ 165 Fred McGriff	.60	.18
❑ 166 Rocco Baldelli	.40	.12
❑ 167 Alfonso Soriano	.60	.18
❑ 168 Hank Blalock	.40	.12
❑ 169 Kenny Rogers	.40	.12
❑ 170 Mark Teixeira	.40	.12
❑ 171 Michael Young	.40	.12
❑ 172 Carlos Delgado	.40	.12
❑ 173 Eric Hinske	.40	.12
❑ 174 Roy Halladay	.40	.12
❑ 175 Vernon Wells	.40	.12
❑ 176 Ivan Ochoa AU/487 RC	8.00	2.40
❑ 177 Jason Bartlett AU/1000 RC	10.00	3.00
❑ 178 J.Labandeira AU/703 RC	8.00	2.40
❑ 179 Phil Stockman AU/1000 RC	8.00	2.40
❑ 180 Ronny Cedeno AU/715 RC	8.00	2.40
❑ 181 Shawn Camp AU/1000 RC	8.00	2.40
❑ 182 Ruddy Yan AU/1000	8.00	2.40
❑ 183 Roberto Novoa AU/568 RC	10.00	3.00
❑ 184 Just Knoedler AU/1000 RC	8.00	2.40
❑ 185 Jesse Harper AU/1000 RC	8.00	2.40
❑ 186 Jas Szuminski AU/1000 RC	8.00	2.40
❑ 187 Jamie Brown AU/800 RC	8.00	2.40
❑ 188 Ed Rodriguez AU/1000 RC	10.00	3.00
❑ 189 Dennis Sarfate AU/1000 RC	8.00	2.40
❑ 190 Ryan Meaux AU/1000 RC	8.00	2.40
❑ 191 Ch.Thomas AU/1000 RC	15.00	4.50
❑ 192 F.Francisco AU/1000 RC	8.00	2.40
❑ 193 Orl Rodriguez AU/500 RC	8.00	2.40
❑ 194 Joey Gathright AU/1000 RC	12.00	3.60
❑ 195 Renyel Pinto AU/1000 RC	10.00	3.00
❑ 196 Justin Leone AU/1000 RC	10.00	3.00
❑ 197 Tim Bausher AU/834 RC	8.00	2.40
❑ 198 Trav Blackley AU/1000 RC	10.00	3.00
❑ 199 Yadier Molina AU/500 RC	20.00	6.00
❑ 200 Brad Halsey AU/500 RC	10.00	3.00
❑ 201 Curt Schilling WSC	3.00	.90
❑ 202 Pedro Martinez WSC	3.00	.90
❑ 203 Derek Lowe WSC	1.00	.30
❑ 204 Tim Wakefield WSC	1.00	.30
❑ 205 Bronson Arroyo WSC	1.00	.30
❑ 206 Mike Timlin WSC	1.00	.30
❑ 207 Curtis Leskanic WSC	1.00	.30
❑ 208 Mike Myers WSC	1.00	.30
❑ 209 Alan Embree WSC	1.00	.30
❑ 210 Keith Foulke WSC	2.00	.60
❑ 211 Jason Varitek WSC	2.00	.60
❑ 212 Doug Mirabelli WSC	1.00	.30
❑ 213 Doug Mientkiewicz WSC	1.00	.30
❑ 214 Mark Bellhorn WSC	2.00	.60
❑ 215 Pokey Reese WSC	1.00	.30
❑ 216 Orlando Cabrera WSC	2.00	.60
❑ 217 Bill Mueller WSC	2.00	.60
❑ 218 Kevin Youkilis WSC	1.00	.30
❑ 219 Manny Ramirez WSC	2.00	.60
❑ 220 Johnny Damon WSC	3.00	.90
❑ 221 Dave Roberts WSC	1.00	.30
❑ 222 Trot Nixon WSC	1.00	.30
❑ 223 Gabe Kapler WSC	1.00	.30
❑ 224 David Ortiz WSC	3.00	.90
❑ WS1 Pedro Martinez Curt Schilling David Ortiz	3.00	.90

2001 eTopps

	Nm-Mt	Ex-Mt
❑ 1 Nomar Garciaparra/1315		
❑ 2 Chipper Jones/674		
❑ 3 Jeff Bagwell/485		
❑ 4 Randy Johnson/1499		
❑ 7 Adam Dunn/4197		

❑ 8 J.D. Drew/767
❑ 9 Larry Walker/420
❑ 10 Edgardo Alfonzo/338
❑ 11 Lance Berkman/595
❑ 12 Tony Gwynn/828
❑ 13 Andruw Jones/908
❑ 15 Troy Glaus/862
❑ 17 Sammy Sosa/2487
❑ 21 Darin Erstad/664
❑ 22 Barry Bonds/1567
❑ 27 Derek Jeter/1041
❑ 29 Curt Schilling/2125
❑ 30 Roberto Alomar/448
❑ 31 Luis Gonzalez/1104
❑ 32 Jimmy Rollins/1307
❑ 34 Joe Crede/1050
❑ 39 Sean Casey/537
❑ 46 Alex Rodriguez/2212
❑ 47 Tom Glavine/437
❑ 50 Jose Ortiz/738
❑ 51 Cal Ripken/2201
❑ 52 Bob Abreu/677
❑ 55 Alex Escobar/931
❑ 56 Ivan Rodriguez/698
❑ 59 Jeff Kent/452
❑ 62 Rick Ankiel/752
❑ 65 Craig Biggio/410
❑ 66 Carlos Delgado/398
❑ 68 Greg Maddux/1031
❑ 69 Kerry Wood/1056
❑ 71 Todd Helton/978
❑ 72 Mariano Rivera/824
❑ 73 Jason Kendall/672
❑ 75 Scott Rolen/498
❑ 76 Kazuhiro Sasaki/5000
❑ 77 Roy Oswalt/915
❑ 78 C.C. Sabathia/1974
❑ 83 Brian Giles/400
❑ 87 Rafael Furcal/646
❑ 88 Mike Mussina/793
❑ 89 Gary Sheffield/359
❑ 92 Mark McGwire/2908
❑ 94 Tsuyoshi Shinjo/3000
❑ 99 Jose Vidro/443
❑ 100 Ichiro Suzuki/10000 .... 20.00 6.00
❑ 105 Manny Ramirez/1074
❑ 109 Juan Gonzalez/558
❑ 112 Ken Griffey Jr./2398
❑ 114 Tim Hudson/663
❑ 115 Nick Johnson/1217
❑ 118 Jason Giambi/897
❑ 122 Rafael Palmeiro/464
❑ 124 V. Guerrero/854
❑ 125 Vernon Wells/349
❑ 127 Roger Clemens/1462
❑ 128 Frank Thomas/834
❑ 129 Carlos Beltran/489
❑ 130 Pat Burrell/1253
❑ 131 Pedro Martinez/1038
❑ 132 Mike Piazza/1379
❑ 135 Luis Montanez/5000
❑ 140 Sean Burroughs/5000
❑ 141 Barry Zito/843
❑ 142 Bobby Bradley/5000
❑ 143 Albert Pujols/5000 ...... 50.00 15.00
❑ 144 Ben Sheets/1713
❑ 145 Alfonso Soriano/1699
❑ 146 Josh Hamilton/5000
❑ 147 Eric Munson/5000
❑ 150 Mark Mulder/4335

2001 E-X

	Nm-Mt	Ex-Mt
COMP.SET w/o SP's (100)	25.00	7.50
COMMON CARD (1-100)	.50	.15
COMMON (101-130)	8.00	2.40
COMMON (131-140)	10.00	3.00
❑ 1 Jason Kendall	.50	.15
❑ 2 Derek Jeter	3.00	.90
❑ 3 Greg Vaughn	.50	.15
❑ 4 Eric Chavez	.50	.15
❑ 5 Nomar Garciaparra	2.00	.60
❑ 6 Roberto Alomar	.75	.23
❑ 7 Barry Larkin	.75	.23
❑ 8 Matt Lawton	.50	.15
❑ 9 Larry Walker	.75	.23
❑ 10 Chipper Jones	1.25	.35
❑ 11 Scott Rolen	1.25	.35
❑ 12 Carlos Lee	.50	.15
❑ 13 Adrian Beltre	.75	.23
❑ 14 Ben Grieve	.50	.15
❑ 15 Mike Sweeney	.50	.15
❑ 16 John Olerud	.50	.15
❑ 17 Gabe Kapler	.50	.15
❑ 18 Brian Giles	.50	.15
❑ 19 Luis Gonzalez	.50	.15
❑ 20 Sammy Sosa	2.00	.60
❑ 21 Roger Clemens	2.50	.75
❑ 22 Vladimir Guerrero	1.25	.35
❑ 23 Ken Griffey Jr.	2.00	.60
❑ 24 Mark McGwire	3.00	.90
❑ 25 Orlando Hernandez	.50	.15
❑ 26 Shannon Stewart	.50	.15
❑ 27 Fred McGriff	.75	.23
❑ 28 Lance Berkman	.50	.15
❑ 29 Carlos Delgado	.50	.15
❑ 30 Mike Piazza	2.00	.60
❑ 31 Juan Encarnacion	.50	.15
❑ 32 David Justice	.50	.15
❑ 33 Greg Maddux	2.00	.60
❑ 34 Frank Thomas	1.25	.35
❑ 35 Jason Giambi	.50	.15
❑ 36 Ruben Mateo	.50	.15
❑ 37 Todd Helton	.75	.23
❑ 38 Jim Edmonds	.50	.15
❑ 39 Steve Finley	.50	.15
❑ 40 Tom Glavine	.75	.23
❑ 41 Mo Vaughn	.50	.15
❑ 42 Phil Nevin	.50	.15
❑ 43 Richie Sexson	.50	.15
❑ 44 Craig Biggio	.75	.23
❑ 45 Kerry Wood	1.25	.35
❑ 46 Pat Burrell	.50	.15
❑ 47 Edgar Martinez	.75	.23
❑ 48 Jim Thome	1.25	.35
❑ 49 Jeff Bagwell	.75	.23
❑ 50 Bernie Williams	.75	.23
❑ 51 Andruw Jones	.50	.15
❑ 52 Gary Sheffield	.50	.15
❑ 53 Johnny Damon	.75	.23
❑ 54 Rondell White	.50	.15
❑ 55 J.D. Drew	.50	.15
❑ 56 Tony Batista	.50	.15
❑ 57 Paul Konerko	.50	.15
❑ 58 Rafael Palmeiro	.75	.23
❑ 59 Cal Ripken	4.00	1.20
❑ 60 Darin Erstad	.50	.15
❑ 61 Ivan Rodriguez	1.25	.35
❑ 62 Barry Bonds	3.00	.90
❑ 63 Edgardo Alfonzo	.50	.15
❑ 64 Ellis Burks	.50	.15
❑ 65 Mike Lieberthal	.50	.15
❑ 66 Robin Ventura	.50	.15
❑ 67 Richard Hidalgo	.50	.15
❑ 68 Magglio Ordonez	.50	.15
❑ 69 Kazuhiro Sasaki	.50	.15
❑ 70 Miguel Tejada	.50	.15
❑ 71 David Wells	.50	.15
❑ 72 Troy Glaus	.50	.15
❑ 73 Jose Vidro	.50	.15
❑ 74 Shawn Green	.50	.15
❑ 75 Barry Zito	.75	.23
❑ 76 Jermaine Dye	.50	.15
❑ 77 Geoff Jenkins	.50	.15
❑ 78 Jeff Kent	.50	.15
❑ 79 Al Leiter	.50	.15
❑ 80 Deivi Cruz	.50	.15
❑ 81 Eric Karros	.50	.15
❑ 82 Albert Belle	.50	.15
❑ 83 Pedro Martinez	1.25	.35
❑ 84 Raul Mondesi	.50	.15
❑ 85 Preston Wilson	.50	.15
❑ 86 Rafael Furcal	.50	.15
❑ 87 Rick Ankiel	.50	.15
❑ 88 Randy Johnson	1.25	.35
❑ 89 Kevin Brown	.50	.15
❑ 90 Sean Casey	.50	.15
❑ 91 Mike Mussina	.75	.23
❑ 92 Alex Rodriguez	2.00	.60
❑ 93 Andres Galarraga	.50	.15
❑ 94 Juan Gonzalez	.75	.23
❑ 95 Manny Ramirez	.75	.23
❑ 96 Mark Grace	.75	.23
❑ 97 Carl Everett	.50	.15
❑ 98 Tony Gwynn	1.50	.45
❑ 99 Mike Hampton	.50	.15
❑ 100 Ken Caminiti	.50	.15
❑ 101 Jason Hart/1749	8.00	2.40
❑ 102 Corey Patterson/1199	8.00	2.40
❑ 103 Timo Perez/1999	8.00	2.40
❑ 104 Marcus Giles/1999	8.00	2.40
❑ 105 I. Suzuki/1999 RC	60.00	18.00
❑ 106 Aubrey Huff/1499	8.00	2.40
❑ 107 Joe Crede/1999	8.00	2.40
❑ 108 Larry Barnes/1499	8.00	2.40
❑ 109 Esix Snead/1999 RC	8.00	2.40
❑ 110 Kenny Kelly/2249	8.00	2.40
❑ 111 Justin Miller/2249	8.00	2.40
❑ 112 Jack Cust/1999	8.00	2.40
❑ 113 Xavier Nady/999	8.00	2.40
❑ 114 Eric Munson/1499	8.00	2.40
❑ 115 E. Guzman/1749 RC	8.00	2.40
❑ 116 Juan Pierre/2189	8.00	2.40
❑ 117 W. Abreu/1749 RC	8.00	2.40
❑ 118 Keith Ginter/1999	8.00	2.40
❑ 119 Jace Brewer/2699	8.00	2.40
❑ 120 P. Crawford/2249	8.00	2.40
❑ 121 Jason Tyner/2249	8.00	2.40
❑ 122 Tike Redman/1999	8.00	2.40
❑ 123 John Riedling/2499	8.00	2.40
❑ 124 Jose Ortiz/1499	8.00	2.40
❑ 125 O. Mairena/2499	8.00	2.40
❑ 126 Eric Byrnes/2249	8.00	2.40
❑ 127 Brian Cole/999	8.00	2.40
❑ 128 Adam Piatt/2249	8.00	2.40
❑ 129 Nate Rolison/2499	8.00	2.40
❑ 130 Keith McDonald/2249	8.00	2.40
❑ 131 Albert Pujols/499 RC	100.00	30.00
❑ 132 Bud Smith/499 RC	10.00	3.00
❑ 133 T.Shinjo/499 RC	15.00	4.50
❑ 134 W.Betemit/499 RC	10.00	3.00
❑ 135 A.Hernandez/499 RC	10.00	3.00
❑ 136 J.Melian/499 RC	10.00	3.00
❑ 137 Jay Gibbons/499 RC	15.00	4.50
❑ 138 J.Estrada/499 RC	15.00	4.50
❑ 139 M.Ensberg/499 RC	15.00	4.50
❑ 140 Drew Henson/499 RC	15.00	4.50
❑ NNO Derek Jeter Base Inks AU/500	150.00	45.00
❑ MM2 Derek Jeter	12.00	3.60

Monumental Moments

❑ NNO Derek Jeter	120.00	36.00

Monumental Moments AU/96

2003 E-X

	MINT	NRMT
COMP.SET w/o SP's (72)	40.00	18.00
COMMON CARD (1-72)	.50	.23
COMMON CARD (73-82)	4.00	1.80
COMMON CARD (83-86)	4.00	1.80
COMMON CARD (87-102)	4.00	1.80

❑ 1 Troy Glaus	.50	.23
❑ 2 Darin Erstad	.50	.23
❑ 3 Garret Anderson	.50	.23
❑ 4 Curt Schilling	.50	.23
❑ 5 Randy Johnson	1.25	.55
❑ 6 Luis Gonzalez	.50	.23
❑ 7 Greg Maddux	2.00	.90
❑ 8 Chipper Jones	1.25	.55
❑ 9 Andruw Jones	.50	.23
❑ 10 Melvin Mora	.50	.23
❑ 11 Jay Gibbons	.50	.23
❑ 12 Nomar Garciaparra	2.00	.90
❑ 13 Pedro Martinez	1.25	.55
❑ 14 Manny Ramirez	.75	.35
❑ 15 Sammy Sosa	2.00	.90
❑ 16 Kerry Wood	1.25	.55
❑ 17 Magglio Ordonez	.50	.23
❑ 18 Frank Thomas	1.25	.55
❑ 19 Roberto Alomar	.75	.35
❑ 20 Barry Larkin	.75	.35
❑ 21 Adam Dunn	.75	.35
❑ 22 Austin Kearns	.50	.23
❑ 23 Omar Vizquel	.75	.35
❑ 24 Larry Walker	.75	.35
❑ 25 Todd Helton	.75	.35
❑ 26 Preston Wilson	.50	.23
❑ 27 Dmitri Young	.50	.23
❑ 28 Ivan Rodriguez	1.25	.55
❑ 29 Mike Lowell	.50	.23
❑ 30 Jeff Kent	.50	.23
❑ 31 Jeff Bagwell	.75	.35
❑ 32 Roy Oswalt	.50	.23
❑ 33 Craig Biggio	.75	.35
❑ 34 Mike Sweeney	.50	.23
❑ 35 Carlos Beltran	.75	.35
❑ 36 Shawn Green	.50	.23
❑ 37 Kazuhisa Ishii	.50	.23
❑ 38 Richie Sexson	.50	.23
❑ 39 Torii Hunter	.50	.23
❑ 40 Jacque Jones	.50	.23
❑ 41 Jose Vidro	.50	.23
❑ 42 Vladimir Guerrero	1.25	.55
❑ 43 Mike Piazza	2.00	.90
❑ 44 Tom Glavine	.75	.35
❑ 45 Roger Clemens	2.50	1.10
❑ 46 Jason Giambi	.50	.23
❑ 47 Bernie Williams	.75	.35
❑ 48 Alfonso Soriano	.75	.35
❑ 49 Mike Mussina	.75	.35
❑ 50 Barry Zito	.50	.23
❑ 51 Miguel Tejada	.50	.23
❑ 52 Eric Chavez	.50	.23
❑ 53 Eric Byrnes	.50	.23
❑ 54 Jim Thome	1.25	.55
❑ 55 Kevin Millwood	.50	.23
❑ 56 Brian Giles	.50	.23
❑ 57 Xavier Nady	.50	.23
❑ 58 Barry Bonds	3.00	1.35
❑ 59 Bret Boone	.50	.23
❑ 60 Edgar Martinez	.75	.35
❑ 61 Kazuhiro Sasaki	.50	.23
❑ 62 Edgar Renteria	.50	.23
❑ 63 J.D. Drew	.50	.23
❑ 64 Scott Rolen	1.25	.55
❑ 65 Jim Edmonds	.50	.23
❑ 66 Aubrey Huff	.50	.23
❑ 67 Alex Rodriguez	2.00	.90
❑ 68 Juan Gonzalez	.75	.35
❑ 69 Hank Blalock	.75	.35
❑ 70 Mark Teixeira	.50	.23
❑ 71 Carlos Delgado	.50	.23
❑ 72 Vernon Wells	.50	.23
❑ 73 Shea Hillenbrand SP	4.00	1.80
❑ 74 Gary Sheffield SP	4.00	1.80
❑ 75 Mark Prior SP	5.00	2.20
❑ 76 Ken Griffey Jr. SP	12.00	5.50
❑ 77 Lance Berkman SP	4.00	1.80
❑ 78 Hideo Nomo SP	15.00	6.75
❑ 79 Derek Jeter SP	20.00	9.00
❑ 80 Ichiro Suzuki SP	12.00	5.50
❑ 81 Albert Pujols SP	15.00	6.75
❑ 82 Rafael Palmeiro SP	5.00	2.20
❑ 83 Jose Reyes ROO SP	4.00	1.80
❑ 84 Rocco Baldelli ROO SP	4.00	1.80
❑ 85 Hee Seop Choi ROO SP	4.00	1.80
❑ 86 Dontrelle Willis ROO SP	5.00	2.20
❑ 87 Robb Hammock ROO SP RC	5.00	2.20
❑ 88 Brandon Webb ROO SP RC	5.00	2.20
❑ 89 Matt Kata ROO SP RC	5.00	2.20
❑ 90 T.Wellemeyer ROO SP RC	5.00	2.20
❑ 91 Fran Cruceta ROO SP RC	4.00	1.80
❑ 92 Clint Barmes ROO SP RC	5.00	2.20
❑ 93 Jer Bonderman ROO SP RC	5.00	2.20
❑ 94 David Matranga ROO SP RC	4.00	1.80
❑ 95 Ryan Wagner ROO SP RC	5.00	2.20
❑ 96 Jeremy Griffiths ROO SP RC	5.00	2.20
❑ 97 Hideki Matsui ROO SP RC	15.00	6.75
❑ 98 Jose Contreras ROO SP RC	8.00	3.60
❑ 99 C.Wang ROO SP RC	5.00	2.20
❑ 100 Bo Hart ROO SP RC	5.00	2.20
❑ 101 Danny Haren ROO SP RC	5.00	2.20
❑ 102 Rickie Weeks ROO SP RC	10.00	4.50

2004 E-X

	Nm-Mt	Ex-Mt
COMMON CARD (1-40)	2.00	.60
COMMON CARD (41-65)	5.00	1.50

SEE PARALLEL SET FOR DIE CUT PRICES

❑ 1 Vladimir Guerrero	3.00	.90
❑ 2 Randy Johnson	3.00	.90
❑ 3 Chipper Jones	3.00	.90
❑ 4 Miguel Tejada	2.00	.60
❑ 5 Pedro Martinez	3.00	.90
❑ 6 Nomar Garciaparra	5.00	1.50
❑ 7 Sammy Sosa	5.00	1.50
❑ 8 Greg Maddux	5.00	1.50
❑ 9 Frank Thomas	3.00	.90
❑ 10 Ken Griffey Jr.	5.00	1.50
❑ 11 Omar Vizquel	3.00	.90
❑ 12 Todd Helton	3.00	.90
❑ 13 Ivan Rodriguez	3.00	.90
❑ 14 Miguel Cabrera	3.00	.90
❑ 15 Dontrelle Willis	2.00	.60
❑ 16 Jeff Bagwell	3.00	.90
❑ 17 Roger Clemens	6.00	1.80
❑ 18 Carlos Beltran	3.00	.90
❑ 19 Hideo Nomo	3.00	.90
❑ 20 Scott Podsednik	2.00	.60
❑ 21 Torii Hunter	2.00	.60
❑ 22 Jose Vidro	2.00	.60
❑ 23 Mike Piazza	5.00	1.50
❑ 24 Hideki Matsui	5.00	1.50
❑ 25 Alex Rodriguez	5.00	1.50
❑ 26 Derek Jeter	6.00	1.80
❑ 27 Tim Hudson	2.00	.60
❑ 28 Jim Thome	3.00	.90
❑ 29 Craig Wilson	2.00	.60
❑ 30 Brian Giles	2.00	.60
❑ 31 Jason Schmidt	2.00	.60
❑ 32 Ichiro Suzuki	5.00	1.50
❑ 33 Scott Rolen	3.00	.90
❑ 34 Albert Pujols	6.00	1.80
❑ 35 Rocco Baldelli	2.00	.60
❑ 36 Alfonso Soriano	3.00	.90
❑ 37 Carlos Delgado	2.00	.60
❑ 38 Curt Schilling	3.00	.90
❑ 39 Mark Prior	3.00	.90
❑ 40 Josh Beckett	2.00	.60
❑ 41 Merkin Valdez ROO RC	8.00	2.40
❑ 42 Akinori Otsuka ROO RC	5.00	1.50
❑ 43 Ian Snell ROO RC	8.00	2.40
❑ 44 Kaz Matsui ROO RC	15.00	4.50
❑ 45 Jason Bartlett ROO RC	8.00	2.40
❑ 46 Dennis Sarfate ROO RC	5.00	1.50
❑ 47 Sean Henn ROO RC	5.00	1.50
❑ 48 David Aardsma ROO RC	5.00	1.50
❑ 49 Casey Kotchman ROO	5.00	1.50
❑ 50 John Gall ROO RC	8.00	2.40
❑ 51 William Bergolla ROO RC	5.00	1.50
❑ 52 Angel Chavez ROO RC	5.00	1.50
❑ 53 Hector Gimenez ROO RC	5.00	1.50
❑ 54 Aaron Baldiris ROO RC	8.00	2.40
❑ 55 Justin Leone ROO RC	8.00	2.40
❑ 56 Onil Joseph ROO RC	5.00	1.50
❑ 57 Freddy Guzman ROO RC	5.00	1.50
❑ 58 Andres Blanco ROO RC	5.00	1.50
❑ 59 Greg Dobbs ROO RC	5.00	1.50
❑ 60 Joe Mauer ROO	8.00	2.40
❑ 61 Luis Gonzalez ROO RC	5.00	1.50
❑ 62 Chris Saenz ROO RC	5.00	1.50
❑ 63 Zack Greinke ROO	5.00	1.50
❑ 64 Jose Capellan ROO RC	10.00	3.00
❑ 65 Brad Halsey ROO RC	8.00	2.40

1999 Finest

	Nm-Mt	Ex-Mt
COMPLETE SET (300)	100.00	30.00
COMP.SERIES 1 (150)	50.00	15.00
COMP.SERIES 2 (150)	50.00	15.00
COMP.SER.1 w/o SP's (100)	20.00	6.00
COMP.SER.2 w/o SP's (100)	20.00	6.00
COMMON (1-100/151-250)	.40	.12
COMMON (101-150/251-300)	.50	.15

❑ 1 Darin Erstad	.40	.12
❑ 2 Javy Lopez	.40	.12
❑ 3 Vinny Castilla	.40	.12
❑ 4 Jim Thome	1.00	.30

❑ 5 Tino Martinez	.60	.18
❑ 6 Mark Grace	.60	.18
❑ 7 Shawn Green	.40	.12
❑ 8 Dustin Hermanson	.40	.12
❑ 9 Kevin Young	.40	.12
❑ 10 Tony Clark	.40	.12
❑ 11 Scott Brosius	.40	.12
❑ 12 Craig Biggio	.60	.18
❑ 13 Brian McRae	.40	.12
❑ 14 Chan Ho Park	.40	.12
❑ 15 Manny Ramirez	.60	.18
❑ 16 Chipper Jones	1.00	.30
❑ 17 Rico Brogna	.40	.12
❑ 18 Quinton McCracken	.40	.12
❑ 19 J.T. Snow	.40	.12
❑ 20 Tony Gwynn	1.25	.35
❑ 21 Juan Guzman	.40	.12
❑ 22 John Valentin	.40	.12
❑ 23 Rick Helling	.40	.12
❑ 24 Sandy Alomar Jr.	.40	.12
❑ 25 Frank Thomas	1.00	.30
❑ 26 Jorge Posada	.60	.18
❑ 27 Dmitri Young	.40	.12
❑ 28 Rick Reed	.40	.12
❑ 29 Kevin Tapani	.40	.12
❑ 30 Troy Glaus	.40	.12
❑ 31 Kenny Rogers	.40	.12
❑ 32 Jeromy Burnitz	.40	.12
❑ 33 Mark Grudzielanek	.40	.12
❑ 34 Mike Mussina	.60	.18
❑ 35 Scott Rolen	1.00	.30
❑ 36 Neifi Perez	.40	.12
❑ 37 Brad Radke	.40	.12
❑ 38 Darryl Strawberry	.40	.12
❑ 39 Robb Nen	.40	.12
❑ 40 Moises Alou	.40	.12
❑ 41 Eric Young	.40	.12
❑ 42 Livan Hernandez	.40	.12
❑ 43 John Wetteland	.40	.12
❑ 44 Matt Lawton	.40	.12
❑ 45 Ben Grieve	.40	.12
❑ 46 Fernando Tatis	.40	.12
❑ 47 Travis Fryman	.40	.12
❑ 48 David Segui	.40	.12
❑ 49 Bob Abreu	.40	.12
❑ 50 Nomar Garciaparra	1.50	.45
❑ 51 Paul O'Neill	.60	.18
❑ 52 Jeff King	.40	.12
❑ 53 Francisco Cordova	.40	.12
❑ 54 John Olerud	.40	.12
❑ 55 Vladimir Guerrero	1.00	.30
❑ 56 Fernando Vina	.40	.12
❑ 57 Shane Reynolds	.40	.12
❑ 58 Chuck Finley	.40	.12
❑ 59 Rondell White	.40	.12
❑ 60 Greg Vaughn	.40	.12
❑ 61 Ryan Minor	.40	.12
❑ 62 Tom Gordon	.40	.12
❑ 63 Damion Easley	.40	.12
❑ 64 Ray Durham	.40	.12
❑ 65 Orlando Hernandez	.40	.12
❑ 66 Bartolo Colon	.40	.12
❑ 67 Jaret Wright	.40	.12
❑ 68 Royce Clayton	.40	.12
❑ 69 Tim Salmon	.60	.18
❑ 70 Mark McGwire	2.50	.75
❑ 71 Alex Gonzalez	.40	.12
❑ 72 Tom Glavine	.60	.18
❑ 73 David Justice	.40	.12
❑ 74 Omar Vizquel	.60	.18
❑ 75 Juan Gonzalez	.60	.18
❑ 76 Bobby Higginson	.40	.12
❑ 77 Todd Walker	.40	.12
❑ 78 Dante Bichette	.40	.12
❑ 79 Kevin Millwood	.40	.12
❑ 80 Roger Clemens	2.00	.60
❑ 81 Kerry Wood	1.00	.30
❑ 82 Cal Ripken	3.00	.90
❑ 83 Jay Bell	.40	.12
❑ 84 Barry Bonds	2.50	.75
❑ 85 Alex Rodriguez	1.50	.45
❑ 86 Doug Glanville	.40	.12
❑ 87 Jason Kendall	.40	.12
❑ 88 Sean Casey	.40	.12
❑ 89 Aaron Sele	.40	.12
❑ 90 Derek Jeter	2.50	.75
❑ 91 Andy Ashby	.40	.12
❑ 92 Rusty Greer	.40	.12
❑ 93 Rod Beck	.40	.12
❑ 94 Matt Williams	.40	.12
❑ 95 Mike Piazza	1.50	.45
❑ 96 Wally Joyner	.40	.12
❑ 97 Barry Larkin	.60	.18
❑ 98 Eric Milton	.40	.12
❑ 99 Gary Sheffield	.40	.12
❑ 100 Greg Maddux	1.50	.45
❑ 101 Ken Griffey Jr. GEM	2.50	.75
❑ 102 Frank Thomas GEM	1.25	.35
❑ 103 N.Garciaparra GEM	2.50	.75
❑ 104 Mark McGwire GEM	4.00	1.20
❑ 105 Alex Rodriguez GEM	2.50	.75
❑ 106 Tony Gwynn GEM	2.00	.60
❑ 107 Juan Gonzalez GEM	.75	.23
❑ 108 Jeff Bagwell GEM	.75	.23
❑ 109 Sammy Sosa GEM	2.50	.75
❑ 110 V.Guerrero GEM	1.25	.35
❑ 111 Roger Clemens GEM	3.00	.90
❑ 112 Barry Bonds GEM	4.00	1.20
❑ 113 Darin Erstad GEM	.50	.15
❑ 114 Mike Piazza GEM	2.50	.75
❑ 115 Derek Jeter GEM	4.00	1.20
❑ 116 Chipper Jones GEM	1.25	.35
❑ 117 Larry Walker GEM	.75	.23
❑ 118 Scott Rolen GEM	1.25	.35
❑ 119 Cal Ripken GEM	5.00	1.50
❑ 120 Greg Maddux GEM	2.50	.75
❑ 121 Troy Glaus SENS	.50	.15
❑ 122 Ben Grieve SENS	.50	.15
❑ 123 Ryan Minor SENS	.50	.15
❑ 124 Kerry Wood SENS	1.25	.35
❑ 125 Travis Lee SENS	.50	.15
❑ 126 Adrian Beltre SENS	.75	.23
❑ 127 Brad Fullmer SENS	.50	.15
❑ 128 Aramis Ramirez SENS	.50	.15
❑ 129 Eric Chavez SENS	.50	.15
❑ 130 Todd Helton SENS	.75	.23
❑ 131 Pat Burrell RC	2.50	.75
❑ 132 Ryan Mills RC	.50	.15
❑ 133 Austin Kearns RC	4.00	1.20
❑ 134 Josh McKinley RC	.50	.15
❑ 135 Adam Everett RC	.75	.23
❑ 136 Marlon Anderson	.50	.15
❑ 137 Bruce Chen	.50	.15
❑ 138 Matt Clement	.50	.15
❑ 139 Alex Gonzalez	.50	.15
❑ 140 Roy Halladay	.50	.15
❑ 141 Calvin Pickering	.50	.15
❑ 142 Randy Wolf	.50	.15
❑ 143 Ryan Anderson	.50	.15
❑ 144 Ruben Mateo	.50	.15
❑ 145 Alex Escobar RC	.50	.15
❑ 146 Jeremy Giambi	.50	.15
❑ 147 Lance Berkman	.50	.15
❑ 148 Michael Barrett	.50	.15
❑ 149 Preston Wilson	.50	.15
❑ 150 Gabe Kapler	.50	.15
❑ 151 Roger Clemens	2.00	.60
❑ 152 Jay Buhner	.40	.12
❑ 153 Brad Fullmer	.40	.12
❑ 154 Ray Lankford	.40	.12
❑ 155 Jim Edmonds	.40	.12
❑ 156 Jason Giambi	.40	.12
❑ 157 Bret Boone	.40	.12
❑ 158 Jeff Cirillo	.40	.12
❑ 159 Rickey Henderson	1.00	.30
❑ 160 Edgar Martinez	.60	.18
❑ 161 Ron Gant	.40	.12
❑ 162 Mark Kotsay	.40	.12
❑ 163 Trevor Hoffman	.40	.12
❑ 164 Jason Schmidt	.40	.12
❑ 165 Brett Tomko	.40	.12
❑ 166 David Ortiz	.60	.18
❑ 167 Dean Palmer	.40	.12
❑ 168 Hideki Irabu	.40	.12
❑ 169 Mike Cameron	.40	.12
❑ 170 Pedro Martinez	1.00	.30
❑ 171 Tom Goodwin	.40	.12
❑ 172 Brian Hunter	.40	.12
❑ 173 Al Leiter	.40	.12
❑ 174 Charles Johnson	.40	.12
❑ 175 Curt Schilling	.40	.12
❑ 176 Robin Ventura	.40	.12
❑ 177 Travis Lee	.40	.12
❑ 178 Jeff Shaw	.40	.12
❑ 179 Ugueth Urbina	.40	.12
❑ 180 Roberto Alomar	.60	.18
❑ 181 Cliff Floyd	.40	.12
❑ 182 Adrian Beltre	.60	.18
❑ 183 Tony Womack	.40	.12
❑ 184 Brian Jordan	.40	.12
❑ 185 Randy Johnson	1.00	.30
❑ 186 Mickey Morandini	.40	.12
❑ 187 Todd Hundley	.40	.12
❑ 188 Jose Valentin	.40	.12
❑ 189 Eric Davis	.40	.12
❑ 190 Ken Caminiti	.40	.12
❑ 191 David Wells	.40	.12
❑ 192 Ryan Klesko	.40	.12
❑ 193 Garret Anderson	.40	.12
❑ 194 Eric Karros	.40	.12
❑ 195 Ivan Rodriguez	1.00	.30
❑ 196 Aramis Ramirez	.40	.12
❑ 197 Mike Lieberthal	.40	.12
❑ 198 Will Clark	1.00	.30
❑ 199 Rey Ordonez	.40	.12
❑ 200 Ken Griffey Jr.	1.50	.45
❑ 201 Jose Guillen	.40	.12
❑ 202 Scott Erickson	.40	.12
❑ 203 Paul Konerko	.40	.12
❑ 204 Johnny Damon	.60	.18
❑ 205 Larry Walker	.60	.18
❑ 206 Denny Neagle	.40	.12
❑ 207 Jose Offerman	.40	.12
❑ 208 Andy Pettitte	.60	.18
❑ 209 Bobby Jones	.40	.12
❑ 210 Kevin Brown	.60	.18
❑ 211 John Smoltz	.60	.18
❑ 212 Henry Rodriguez	.40	.12
❑ 213 Tim Belcher	.40	.12
❑ 214 Carlos Delgado	.40	.12
❑ 215 Andruw Jones	.40	.12
❑ 216 Andy Benes	.40	.12
❑ 217 Fred McGriff	.60	.18
❑ 218 Edgar Renteria	.40	.12
❑ 219 Miguel Tejada	.40	.12
❑ 220 Bernie Williams	.60	.18
❑ 221 Justin Thompson	.40	.12
❑ 222 Marty Cordova	.40	.12
❑ 223 Delino DeShields	.40	.12
❑ 224 Ellis Burks	.40	.12
❑ 225 Kenny Lofton	.40	.12
❑ 226 Steve Finley	.40	.12
❑ 227 Eric Chavez	.40	.12
❑ 228 Jose Cruz Jr.	.40	.12
❑ 229 Marquis Grissom	.40	.12
❑ 230 Jeff Bagwell	.60	.18
❑ 231 Jose Canseco	1.00	.30
❑ 232 Edgardo Alfonzo	.40	.12
❑ 233 Richie Sexson	.40	.12
❑ 234 Jeff Kent	.40	.12
❑ 235 Rafael Palmeiro	.60	.18
❑ 236 David Cone	.40	.12
❑ 237 Gregg Jefferies	.40	.12
❑ 238 Mike Lansing	.40	.12
❑ 239 Mariano Rivera	.60	.18
❑ 240 Albert Belle	.40	.12
❑ 241 Chuck Knoblauch	.40	.12
❑ 242 Derek Bell	.40	.12
❑ 243 Pat Hentgen	.40	.12
❑ 244 Andres Galarraga	.40	.12
❑ 245 Mo Vaughn	.40	.12
❑ 246 Wade Boggs	.60	.18
❑ 247 Devon White	.40	.12
❑ 248 Todd Helton	.60	.18
❑ 249 Raul Mondesi	.40	.12
❑ 250 Sammy Sosa	1.50	.45
❑ 251 Nomar Garciaparra ST	2.50	.75
❑ 252 Mark McGwire ST	4.00	1.20
❑ 253 Alex Rodriguez ST	2.50	.75
❑ 254 Juan Gonzalez ST	.75	.23
❑ 255 Vladimir Guerrero ST	1.25	.35
❑ 256 Ken Griffey Jr. ST	2.50	.75
❑ 257 Mike Piazza ST	2.50	.75
❑ 258 Derek Jeter ST	4.00	1.20
❑ 259 Albert Belle ST	.50	.15
❑ 260 Greg Vaughn ST	.50	.15
❑ 261 Sammy Sosa ST	2.50	.75
❑ 262 Greg Maddux ST	2.50	.75

Card	Nm-Mt	Ex-Mt
❑ 263 Frank Thomas ST	1.25	.35
❑ 264 Mark Grace ST	.75	.23
❑ 265 Ivan Rodriguez ST	1.25	.35
❑ 266 Roger Clemens GM	3.00	.90
❑ 267 Mo Vaughn GM	.50	.15
❑ 268 Jim Thome GM	1.25	.35
❑ 269 Darin Erstad GM	.50	.15
❑ 270 Chipper Jones GM	1.25	.35
❑ 271 Larry Walker GM	.75	.23
❑ 272 Cal Ripken GM	5.00	1.50
❑ 273 Scott Rolen GM	1.25	.35
❑ 274 Randy Johnson GM	1.25	.35
❑ 275 Tony Gwynn GM	2.00	.60
❑ 276 Barry Bonds GM	4.00	1.20
❑ 277 Sean Burroughs RC	2.00	.60
❑ 278 J.M. Gold RC	.50	.15
❑ 279 Carlos Lee	.50	.15
❑ 280 George Lombard	.50	.15
❑ 281 Carlos Beltran	.75	.23
❑ 282 Fernando Seguignol	.50	.15
❑ 283 Eric Chavez	.50	.15
❑ 284 Carlos Pena RC	.75	.23
❑ 285 Corey Patterson RC	3.00	.90
❑ 286 Alfonso Soriano RC	8.00	2.40
❑ 287 Nick Johnson RC	1.25	.35
❑ 288 Jorge Toca RC	.50	.15
❑ 289 A.J. Burnett RC	1.25	.35
❑ 290 Andy Brown RC	.50	.15
❑ 291 D.Mientkiewicz RC	1.25	.35
❑ 292 Bobby Seay RC	.50	.15
❑ 293 Chip Ambres RC	.50	.15
❑ 294 C.C. Sabathia RC	1.50	.45
❑ 295 Choo Freeman RC	.50	.15
❑ 296 Eric Valent RC	.50	.15
❑ 297 Matt Belisle RC	.50	.15
❑ 298 Jason Tyner RC	.50	.15
❑ 299 Masao Kida RC	.50	.15
❑ 300 Hank Aaron Mark McGwire	3.00	.90

2000 Finest

	Nm-Mt	Ex-Mt
COMP.SERIES 1 w/o SP's (100)	25.00	7.50
COMP.SERIES 2 w/o SP's (100)	25.00	7.50
COMMON (1-100/147-246)	.40	.12
COMMON (101-120)	4.00	1.20
COMMON (121-135)	1.50	.45
COMMON (136-145/277-286)	2.00	.60
COMMON (247-266)	4.00	1.20
COMMON (267-276)	1.00	.30

Card	Nm-Mt	Ex-Mt
❑ 1 Nomar Garciaparra	1.50	.45
❑ 2 Chipper Jones	1.00	.30
❑ 3 Erubiel Durazo	.40	.12
❑ 4 Robin Ventura	.60	.18
❑ 5 Garret Anderson	.40	.12
❑ 6 Dean Palmer	.40	.12
❑ 7 Mariano Rivera	.60	.18
❑ 8 Rusty Greer	.40	.12
❑ 9 Jim Thome	1.00	.30
❑ 10 Jeff Bagwell	.60	.18
❑ 11 Jason Giambi	.40	.12
❑ 12 Jeromy Burnitz	.40	.12
❑ 13 Mark Grace	.60	.18
❑ 14 Russ Ortiz	.40	.12
❑ 15 Kevin Brown	.60	.18
❑ 16 Kevin Millwood	.40	.12
❑ 17 Scott Williamson	.40	.12
❑ 18 Orlando Hernandez	.40	.12
❑ 19 Todd Walker	.40	.12
❑ 20 Carlos Beltran	.60	.18
❑ 21 Ruben Rivera	.40	.12
❑ 22 Curt Schilling	.40	.12
❑ 23 Brian Giles	.40	.12
❑ 24 Eric Karros	.40	.12
❑ 25 Preston Wilson	.40	.12
❑ 26 Al Leiter	.40	.12
❑ 27 Juan Encarnacion	.40	.12
❑ 28 Tim Salmon	.60	.18
❑ 29 B.J. Surhoff	.40	.12
❑ 30 Bernie Williams	.60	.18
❑ 31 Lee Stevens	.40	.12
❑ 32 Pokey Reese	.40	.12
❑ 33 Mike Sweeney	.40	.12
❑ 34 Corey Koskie	.40	.12
❑ 35 Roberto Alomar	.60	.18
❑ 36 Tim Hudson	.40	.12
❑ 37 Tom Glavine	.60	.18
❑ 38 Jeff Kent	.40	.12
❑ 39 Mike Lieberthal	.40	.12
❑ 40 Barry Larkin	.60	.18
❑ 41 Paul O'Neill	.60	.18
❑ 42 Rico Brogna	.40	.12
❑ 43 Brian Daubach	.40	.12
❑ 44 Rich Aurilia	.40	.12
❑ 45 Vladimir Guerrero	1.00	.30
❑ 46 Luis Castillo	.40	.12
❑ 47 Bartolo Colon	.40	.12
❑ 48 Kevin Appier	.40	.12
❑ 49 Mo Vaughn	.40	.12
❑ 50 Alex Rodriguez	1.50	.45
❑ 51 Randy Johnson	1.00	.30
❑ 52 Kris Benson	.40	.12
❑ 53 Tony Clark	.40	.12
❑ 54 Chad Allen	.40	.12
❑ 55 Larry Walker	.60	.18
❑ 56 Freddy Garcia	.40	.12
❑ 57 Paul Konerko	.40	.12
❑ 58 Edgardo Alfonzo	.40	.12
❑ 59 Brady Anderson	.40	.12
❑ 60 Derek Jeter	2.50	.75
❑ 61 John Smoltz	.60	.18
❑ 62 Doug Glanville	.40	.12
❑ 63 Shannon Stewart	.40	.12
❑ 64 Greg Maddux	1.50	.45
❑ 65 Mark McGwire	2.50	.75
❑ 66 Gary Sheffield	.40	.12
❑ 67 Kevin Young	.40	.12
❑ 68 Tony Gwynn	1.25	.35
❑ 69 Rey Ordonez	.40	.12
❑ 70 Cal Ripken	3.00	.90
❑ 71 Todd Helton	.60	.18
❑ 72 Brian Jordan	.40	.12
❑ 73 Jose Canseco	1.00	.30
❑ 74 Luis Gonzalez	.40	.12
❑ 75 Barry Bonds	2.50	.75
❑ 76 Jermaine Dye	.40	.12
❑ 77 Jose Offerman	.40	.12
❑ 78 Magglio Ordonez	.40	.12
❑ 79 Fred McGriff	.60	.18
❑ 80 Ivan Rodriguez	1.00	.30
❑ 81 Josh Hamilton	.40	.12
❑ 82 Vernon Wells	.40	.12
❑ 83 Mark Mulder	.40	.12
❑ 84 John Patterson	.40	.12
❑ 85 Nick Johnson	.40	.12
❑ 86 Pablo Ozuna	.40	.12
❑ 87 A.J. Burnett	.40	.12
❑ 88 Jack Cust	.40	.12
❑ 89 Adam Piatt	.40	.12
❑ 90 Rob Ryan	.40	.12
❑ 91 Sean Burroughs	.40	.12
❑ 92 D'Angelo Jimenez	.40	.12
❑ 93 Chad Hermansen	.40	.12
❑ 94 Robert Fick	.40	.12
❑ 95 Ruben Mateo	.40	.12
❑ 96 Alex Escobar	.40	.12
❑ 97 Wily Pena	.40	.12
❑ 98 Corey Patterson	.40	.12
❑ 99 Eric Munson	.40	.12
❑ 100 Pat Burrell	.40	.12
❑ 101 Michael Tejera RC	4.00	1.20
❑ 102 Bobby Bradley RC	4.00	1.20
❑ 103 Larry Bigbie RC	6.00	1.80
❑ 104 B.J. Garbe RC	4.00	1.20
❑ 105 Josh Kalinowski RC	4.00	1.20
❑ 106 Brett Myers RC	6.00	1.80
❑ 107 Chris Mears RC	4.00	1.20
❑ 108 Aaron Rowand RC	8.00	2.40
❑ 109 Corey Myers RC	4.00	1.20
❑ 110 John Sneed RC	4.00	1.20
❑ 111 Ryan Christianson RC	4.00	1.20
❑ 112 Kyle Snyder	4.00	1.20
❑ 113 Mike Paradis	4.00	1.20
❑ 114 Chance Caple RC	4.00	1.20
❑ 115 Ben Christensen RC	4.00	1.20
❑ 116 Brad Baker RC	4.00	1.20
❑ 117 Rob Purvis RC	4.00	1.20
❑ 118 Rick Asadoorian RC	4.00	1.20
❑ 119 Ruben Salazar RC	4.00	1.20
❑ 120 Julio Zuleta RC	4.00	1.20
❑ 121 Alex Rodriguez Ken Griffey Jr.	2.50	.75
❑ 122 Nomar Garciaparra Derek Jeter	3.00	.90
❑ 123 Mark Mcgwire Sammy Sosa	4.00	1.20
❑ 124 Randy Johnson Pedro Martinez	2.50	.75
❑ 125 Ivan Rodriguez Mike Piazza	2.50	.75
❑ 126 Manny Ramirez Roberto Alomar	1.50	.45
❑ 127 Chipper Jones Andruw Jones	2.50	.75
❑ 128 Cal Ripken Tony Gwynn	5.00	1.50
❑ 129 Jeff Bagwell Craig Biggio	1.50	.45
❑ 130 Barry Bonds Vladimir Guerrero	4.00	1.20
❑ 131 Nick Johnson Alfonso Soriano	2.50	.75
❑ 132 Josh Hamilton Pat Burrell	4.00	1.20
❑ 133 Corey Patterson Ruben Mateo	1.50	.45
❑ 134 Larry Walker Todd Helton	1.50	.45
❑ 135 Rey Ordonez Edgardo Alfonzo	1.50	.45
❑ 136 Derek Jeter GEM	8.00	2.40
❑ 137 Alex Rodriguez GEM	5.00	1.50
❑ 138 Chipper Jones GEM	5.00	1.50
❑ 139 Mike Piazza GEM	5.00	1.50
❑ 140 Mark McGwire GEM	8.00	2.40
❑ 141 Ivan Rodriguez GEM	5.00	1.50
❑ 142 Cal Ripken GEM	10.00	3.00
❑ 143 V.Guerrero GEM	5.00	1.50
❑ 144 Randy Johnson GEM	5.00	1.50
❑ 145 Jeff Bagwell GEM	3.00	.90
❑ 146 K.Griffey Jr. ACTION	1.50	.45
❑ 146A Ken Griffey Jr. PORT	1.50	.45
❑ 147 Andruw Jones	.40	.12
❑ 148 Kerry Wood	1.00	.30
❑ 149 Jim Edmonds	.40	.12
❑ 150 Pedro Martinez	1.00	.30
❑ 151 Warren Morris	.40	.12
❑ 152 Trevor Hoffman	.40	.12
❑ 153 Ryan Klesko	.40	.12
❑ 154 Andy Pettitte	.60	.18
❑ 155 Frank Thomas	1.00	.30
❑ 156 Damion Easley	.40	.12
❑ 157 Cliff Floyd	.40	.12
❑ 158 Ben Davis	.40	.12
❑ 159 John Valentin	.40	.12
❑ 160 Rafael Palmeiro	.60	.18
❑ 161 Andy Ashby	.40	.12
❑ 162 J.D. Drew	.40	.12
❑ 163 Jay Bell	.40	.12
❑ 164 Adam Kennedy	.40	.12
❑ 165 Manny Ramirez	.60	.18
❑ 166 John Halama	.40	.12
❑ 167 Octavio Dotel	.40	.12
❑ 168 Darin Erstad	.40	.12
❑ 169 Jose Lima	.40	.12
❑ 170 Andres Galarraga	.40	.12
❑ 171 Scott Rolen	1.00	.30
❑ 172 Delino DeShields	.40	.12

❑ 173 J.T. Snow .40 .12
❑ 174 Tony Womack .40 .12
❑ 175 John Olerud .40 .12
❑ 176 Jason Kendall .40 .12
❑ 177 Carlos Lee .40 .12
❑ 178 Eric Milton .40 .12
❑ 179 Jeff Cirillo .40 .12
❑ 180 Gabe Kapler .40 .12
❑ 181 Greg Vaughn .40 .12
❑ 182 Denny Neagle .40 .12
❑ 183 Tino Martinez .60 .18
❑ 184 Doug Mientkiewicz .40 .12
❑ 185 Juan Gonzalez .60 .18
❑ 186 Ellis Burks .40 .12
❑ 187 Mike Hampton .40 .12
❑ 188 Royce Clayton .40 .12
❑ 189 Mike Mussina .60 .18
❑ 190 Carlos Delgado .40 .12
❑ 191 Ben Grieve .40 .12
❑ 192 Fernando Tatis .40 .12
❑ 193 Matt Williams .40 .12
❑ 194 Rondell White .40 .12
❑ 195 Shawn Green .40 .12
❑ 196 Hideki Irabu .40 .12
❑ 197 Troy Glaus .40 .12
❑ 198 Roger Cedeno .40 .12
❑ 199 Ray Lankford .40 .12
❑ 200 Sammy Sosa 1.50 .45
❑ 201 Kenny Lofton .40 .12
❑ 202 Edgar Martinez .60 .18
❑ 203 Mark Kotsay .40 .12
❑ 204 David Wells .40 .12
❑ 205 Craig Biggio .60 .18
❑ 206 Ray Durham .40 .12
❑ 207 Troy O'Leary .40 .12
❑ 208 Rickey Henderson 1.00 .30
❑ 209 Bob Abreu .40 .12
❑ 210 Neifi Perez .40 .12
❑ 211 Carlos Febles .40 .12
❑ 212 Chuck Knoblauch .40 .12
❑ 213 Moises Alou .40 .12
❑ 214 Omar Vizquel .60 .18
❑ 215 Vinny Castilla .40 .12
❑ 216 Javy Lopez .40 .12
❑ 217 Johnny Damon .60 .18
❑ 218 Roger Clemens 2.00 .60
❑ 219 Miguel Tejada .40 .12
❑ 220 Carl Everett .40 .12
❑ 221 Matt Lawton .40 .12
❑ 222 Albert Belle .40 .12
❑ 223 Adrian Beltre .60 .18
❑ 224 Dante Bichette .40 .12
❑ 225 Raul Mondesi .40 .12
❑ 226 Mike Piazza 1.50 .45
❑ 227 Brad Penny .40 .12
❑ 228 Kip Wells .40 .12
❑ 229 Adam Everett .40 .12
❑ 230 Eddie Yarnall .40 .12
❑ 231 Matt LeCroy .40 .12
❑ 232 Jason Tyner .40 .12
❑ 233 Rick Ankiel .40 .12
❑ 234 Lance Berkman .40 .12
❑ 235 Rafael Furcal .40 .12
❑ 236 Dee Brown .40 .12
❑ 237 Gookie Dawkins .40 .12
❑ 238 Eric Valent .40 .12
❑ 239 Peter Bergeron .40 .12
❑ 240 Alfonso Soriano 1.00 .30
❑ 241 Adam Dunn 1.00 .30
❑ 242 Jorge Toca .40 .12
❑ 243 Ryan Anderson .40 .12
❑ 244 Jason Dellaero .40 .12
❑ 245 Jason Grilli .40 .12
❑ 246 Milton Bradley .40 .12
❑ 247 Scott Downs RC 4.00 1.20
❑ 248 Keith Reed RC 4.00 1.20
❑ 249 Edgar Cruz RC 4.00 1.20
❑ 250 Wes Anderson RC 4.00 1.20
❑ 251 Lyle Overbay RC 8.00 2.40
❑ 252 Mike Lamb RC 4.00 1.20
❑ 253 Vince Faison RC 4.00 1.20
❑ 254 Chad Alexander 4.00 1.20
❑ 255 Chris Wakeland RC 4.00 1.20
❑ 256 Aaron McNeal RC 4.00 1.20
❑ 257 Tomo Ohka RC 4.00 1.20
❑ 258 Ty Howington RC 4.00 1.20
❑ 259 Javier Colina RC 4.00 1.20
❑ 260 Jason Jennings 4.00 1.20
❑ 261 Ramon Santiago RC 4.00 1.20
❑ 262 Johan Santana RC 50.00 15.00
❑ 263 Quincy Foster RC 4.00 1.20
❑ 264 Junior Brignac RC 4.00 1.20
❑ 265 Rico Washington RC 4.00 1.20
❑ 266 Scott Sobkowiak RC 4.00 1.20
❑ 267 Pedro Martinez 2.50 .75
Rick Ankiel
❑ 268 Manny Ramirez 2.50 .75
Vladimir Guerrero
❑ 269 A.J.Burnett 1.00 .30
Mark Mulder
❑ 270 Mike Piazza 2.50 .75
Eric Munson
❑ 271 Josh Hamilton 1.00 .30
Corey Patterson
❑ 272 Ken Griffey Jr. 2.00 .60
Sammy Sosa
❑ 273 Derek Jeter 4.00 1.20
Alfonso Soriano
❑ 274 Mark McGwire 4.00 1.20
Pat Burrell
❑ 275 Chipper Jones 4.00 1.20
Cal Ripken
❑ 276 Nomar Garciaparra 2.50 .75
Alex Rodriguez
❑ 277 Pedro Martinez GEM 5.00 1.50
❑ 278 Tony Gwynn GEM 4.00 1.20
❑ 279 Barry Bonds GEM 8.00 2.40
❑ 280 Juan Gonzalez GEM 3.00 .90
❑ 281 Larry Walker GEM 3.00 .90
❑ 282 N.Garciaparra GEM 5.00 1.50
❑ 283 Ken Griffey Jr. GEM 5.00 1.50
❑ 284 Manny Ramirez GEM 3.00 .90
❑ 285 Shawn Green GEM 2.00 .60
❑ 286 Sammy Sosa GEM 5.00 1.50
❑ NNO Graded Gems Ser.1 EXCH/10 .00 .00
❑ NNO Graded Gems Ser.2 EXCH/10 .00

2001 Finest

	Nm-Mt	Ex-Mt
COMP.SET w/o SP's	25.00	7.50
COMMON CARD (1-110)	.40	.12
COMMON SP	10.00	3.00
COMMON (111-140)	10.00	3.00

❑ 1 Mike Piazza SP 20.00 6.00
❑ 2 Andruw Jones .40 .12
❑ 3 Jason Giambi .40 .12
❑ 4 Fred McGriff .60 .18
❑ 5 Vladimir Guerrero SP 1.00 .30
❑ 6 Adrian Gonzalez .40 .12
❑ 7 Pedro Martinez 1.00 .30
❑ 8 Mike Lieberthal .40 .12
❑ 9 Warren Morris .40 .12
❑ 10 Juan Gonzalez .60 .18
❑ 11 Jose Canseco 1.00 .30
❑ 12 Jose Valentin .40 .12
❑ 13 Jeff Cirillo .40 .12
❑ 14 Pokey Reese .40 .12
❑ 15 Scott Rolen 1.00 .30
❑ 16 Greg Maddux 1.50 .45
❑ 17 Carlos Delgado .40 .12
❑ 18 Rick Ankiel .40 .12
❑ 19 Steve Finley .40 .12
❑ 20 Shawn Green .40 .12
❑ 21 Orlando Cabrera .40 .12
❑ 22 Roberto Alomar .60 .18
❑ 23 John Olerud .40 .12
❑ 24 Albert Belle .40 .12
❑ 25 Edgardo Alfonzo .40 .12
❑ 26 Rafael Palmeiro .60 .18
❑ 27 Mike Sweeney .40 .12
❑ 28 Bernie Williams .60 .18
❑ 29 Larry Walker .60 .18
❑ 30 Barry Bonds SP 25.00 7.50
❑ 31 Orlando Hernandez .40 .12
❑ 32 Randy Johnson 1.00 .30
❑ 33 Shannon Stewart .40 .12
❑ 34 Mark Grace .60 .18
❑ 35 Alex Rodriguez SP 25.00 7.50
❑ 36 Tino Martinez .60 .18
❑ 37 Carlos Febles .40 .12
❑ 38 Al Leiter .40 .12
❑ 39 Omar Vizquel .60 .18
❑ 40 Chuck Knoblauch .40 .12
❑ 41 Tim Salmon .60 .18
❑ 42 Brian Jordan .40 .12
❑ 43 Edgar Renteria .40 .12
❑ 44 Preston Wilson .40 .12
❑ 45 Mariano Rivera .60 .18
❑ 46 Gabe Kapler .40 .12
❑ 47 Jason Kendall .40 .12
❑ 48 Rickey Henderson 1.00 .30
❑ 49 Luis Gonzalez .40 .12
❑ 50 Tom Glavine .60 .18
❑ 51 Jeromy Burnitz .40 .12
❑ 52 Garret Anderson .40 .12
❑ 53 Craig Biggio .60 .18
❑ 54 Vinny Castilla .40 .12
❑ 55 Jeff Kent .40 .12
❑ 56 Gary Sheffield .40 .12
❑ 57 Jorge Posada .60 .18
❑ 58 Sean Casey .40 .12
❑ 59 Johnny Damon .60 .18
❑ 60 Dean Palmer .40 .12
❑ 61 Todd Helton .60 .18
❑ 62 Barry Larkin .60 .18
❑ 63 Robin Ventura .40 .12
❑ 64 Kenny Lofton .40 .12
❑ 65 Sammy Sosa SP 15.00 4.50
❑ 66 Rafael Furcal .40 .12
❑ 67 Jay Bell .40 .12
❑ 68 J.T. Snow .40 .12
❑ 69 Jose Vidro .40 .12
❑ 70 Ivan Rodriguez 1.00 .30
❑ 71 Jermaine Dye .40 .12
❑ 72 Chipper Jones SP 10.00 3.00
❑ 73 Fernando Vina .40 .12
❑ 74 Ben Grieve .40 .12
❑ 75 Mark McGwire SP 25.00 7.50
❑ 76 Matt Williams .40 .12
❑ 77 Mark Grudzielanek .40 .12
❑ 78 Mike Hampton .40 .12
❑ 79 Brian Giles .40 .12
❑ 80 Tony Gwynn 1.25 .35
❑ 81 Carlos Beltran .60 .18
❑ 82 Ray Durham .40 .12
❑ 83 Brad Radke .40 .12
❑ 84 David Justice .40 .12
❑ 85 Frank Thomas 1.00 .30
❑ 86 Todd Zeile .40 .12
❑ 87 Pat Burrell .40 .12
❑ 88 Jim Thome 1.00 .30
❑ 89 Greg Vaughn .40 .12
❑ 90 Ken Griffey Jr. SP 15.00 4.50
❑ 91 Mike Mussina .60 .18
❑ 92 Magglio Ordonez .40 .12
❑ 93 Bob Abreu .40 .12
❑ 94 Alex Gonzalez .40 .12
❑ 95 Kevin Brown .40 .12
❑ 96 Jay Buhner .40 .12
❑ 97 Roger Clemens 2.00 .60
❑ 98 Nomar Garciaparra SP 15.00 4.50
❑ 99 Derrek Lee .40 .12
❑ 100 Derek Jeter SP 25.00 7.50
❑ 101 Adrian Beltre .60 .18
❑ 102 Geoff Jenkins .40 .12
❑ 103 Javy Lopez .40 .12
❑ 104 Raul Mondesi .40 .12
❑ 105 Troy Glaus .40 .12

Card	Nm-Mt	Ex-Mt
❑ 106 Jeff Bagwell	.60	.18
❑ 107 Eric Karros	.40	.12
❑ 108 Mo Vaughn	.40	.12
❑ 109 Cal Ripken	3.00	.90
❑ 110 Manny Ramirez	.60	.18
❑ 111 Scott Heard PROS	10.00	3.00
❑ 112 L. Montanez PROS RC	10.00	3.00
❑ 113 Ben Diggins PROS	10.00	3.00
❑ 114 Shaun Boyd PROS RC	10.00	3.00
❑ 115 Sean Burnett PROS	10.00	3.00
❑ 116 Carmen Cali PROS RC	10.00	3.00
❑ 117 D.Thompson PROS	10.00	3.00
❑ 118 D.Parrish PROS RC	10.00	3.00
❑ 119 D.Rich PROS RC	10.00	3.00
❑ 120 Chad Petty PROS RC	10.00	3.00
❑ 121 S.Smyth PROS RC	10.00	3.00
❑ 122 John Lackey PROS	10.00	3.00
❑ 123 M.Galante PROS RC	10.00	3.00
❑ 124 D.Borrell PROS RC	10.00	3.00
❑ 125 Bob Keppel PROS RC	15.00	4.50
❑ 126 J.Wayne PROS RC	10.00	3.00
❑ 127 J.R. House PROS	10.00	3.00
❑ 128 Brian Sellier PROS RC	10.00	3.00
❑ 129 Dan Moylan PROS RC	10.00	3.00
❑ 130 Scott Pratt PROS RC	10.00	3.00
❑ 131 Victor Hall PROS RC	10.00	3.00
❑ 132 Joel Pineiro PROS	20.00	6.00
❑ 133 J.Axelson PROS RC	10.00	3.00
❑ 134 Jose Reyes PROS RC	50.00	15.00
❑ 135 G. Runser PROS RC	10.00	3.00
❑ 136 B. Hebson PROS RC	10.00	3.00
❑ 137 S.Serrano PROS RC	10.00	3.00
❑ 138 K. Joseph PROS RC	10.00	3.00
❑ 139 J. Richardson PROS RC	10.00	3.00
❑ 140 M. Fischer PROS RC	10.00	3.00

2002 Finest

	Nm-Mt	Ex-Mt
COMP.SET w/o SP's (100)	25.00	7.50
COMMON CARD (1-100)	.50	.15
COMMON CARD (101-110)	10.00	3.00

Card	Nm-Mt	Ex-Mt
❑ 1 Mike Mussina	.75	.23
❑ 2 Steve Sparks	.50	.15
❑ 3 Randy Johnson	1.25	.35
❑ 4 Orlando Cabrera	.50	.15
❑ 5 Jeff Kent	.50	.15
❑ 6 Carlos Delgado	.50	.15
❑ 7 Ivan Rodriguez	1.25	.35
❑ 8 Jose Cruz	.50	.15
❑ 9 Jason Giambi	.50	.15
❑ 10 Brad Penny	.50	.15
❑ 11 Moises Alou	.50	.15
❑ 12 Mike Piazza	2.00	.60
❑ 13 Ben Grieve	.50	.15
❑ 14 Derek Jeter	3.00	.90
❑ 15 Roy Oswalt	.50	.15
❑ 16 Pat Burrell	.50	.15
❑ 17 Preston Wilson	.50	.15
❑ 18 Kevin Brown	.50	.15
❑ 19 Barry Bonds	3.00	.90
❑ 20 Phil Nevin	.50	.15
❑ 21 Aramis Ramirez	.50	.15
❑ 22 Carlos Beltran	.75	.23
❑ 23 Chipper Jones	1.25	.35
❑ 24 Curt Schilling	.50	.15
❑ 25 Jorge Posada	.75	.23
❑ 26 Alfonso Soriano	.75	.23
❑ 27 Cliff Floyd	.50	.15
❑ 28 Rafael Palmeiro	.75	.23
❑ 29 Terrence Long	.50	.15
❑ 30 Ken Griffey Jr.	2.00	.60
❑ 31 Jason Kendall	.50	.15
❑ 32 Jose Vidro	.50	.15
❑ 33 Jermaine Dye	.50	.15
❑ 34 Bobby Higginson	.50	.15
❑ 35 Albert Pujols	2.50	.75
❑ 36 Miguel Tejada	.50	.15
❑ 37 Jim Edmonds	.50	.15
❑ 38 Barry Zito	.50	.15
❑ 39 Jimmy Rollins	.50	.15
❑ 40 Rafael Furcal	.50	.15
❑ 41 Omar Vizquel	.75	.23
❑ 42 Kazuhiro Sasaki	.50	.15
❑ 43 Brian Giles	.50	.15
❑ 44 Darin Erstad	.50	.15
❑ 45 Mariano Rivera	.75	.23
❑ 46 Troy Percival	.50	.15
❑ 47 Mike Sweeney	.50	.15
❑ 48 Vladimir Guerrero	1.25	.35
❑ 49 Troy Glaus	.50	.15
❑ 50 So Taguchi RC	3.00	.90
❑ 51 Edgardo Alfonzo	.50	.15
❑ 52 Roger Clemens	2.50	.75
❑ 53 Eric Chavez	.50	.15
❑ 54 Alex Rodriguez	2.00	.60
❑ 55 Cristian Guzman	.50	.15
❑ 56 Jeff Bagwell	.75	.23
❑ 57 Bernie Williams	.75	.23
❑ 58 Kerry Wood	1.25	.35
❑ 59 Ryan Klesko	.50	.15
❑ 60 Ichiro Suzuki	2.00	.60
❑ 61 Larry Walker	.75	.23
❑ 62 Nomar Garciaparra	2.00	.60
❑ 63 Craig Biggio	.75	.23
❑ 64 J.D. Drew	.50	.15
❑ 65 Juan Pierre	.50	.15
❑ 66 Roberto Alomar	.75	.23
❑ 67 Luis Gonzalez	.50	.15
❑ 68 Bud Smith	.50	.15
❑ 69 Magglio Ordonez	.50	.15
❑ 70 Scott Rolen	1.25	.35
❑ 71 Tsuyoshi Shinjo	.50	.15
❑ 72 Paul Konerko	.50	.15
❑ 73 Garret Anderson	.50	.15
❑ 74 Tim Hudson	.50	.15
❑ 75 Adam Dunn	.75	.23
❑ 76 Gary Sheffield	.50	.15
❑ 77 Johnny Damon Sox	1.25	.35
❑ 78 Todd Helton	.75	.23
❑ 79 Geoff Jenkins	.50	.15
❑ 80 Shawn Green	.50	.15
❑ 81 C.C. Sabathia	.50	.15
❑ 82 Kazuhisa Ishii RC UER 2001 ERA is incorrect	4.00	1.20
❑ 83 Rich Aurilia	.50	.15
❑ 84 Mike Hampton	.50	.15
❑ 85 Ben Sheets	.50	.15
❑ 86 Andruw Jones	.50	.15
❑ 87 Richie Sexson	.50	.15
❑ 88 Jim Thome	1.25	.35
❑ 89 Sammy Sosa	2.00	.60
❑ 90 Greg Maddux	2.00	.60
❑ 91 Pedro Martinez	1.25	.35
❑ 92 Jeromy Burnitz	.50	.15
❑ 93 Raul Mondesi	.50	.15
❑ 94 Bret Boone	.50	.15
❑ 95 Jerry Hairston	.50	.15
❑ 96 Mike Rivera	.50	.15
❑ 97 Juan Cruz	.50	.15
❑ 98 Morgan Ensberg	.50	.15
❑ 99 Nathan Haynes	.50	.15
❑ 100 Xavier Nady	.50	.15
❑ 101 Nic Jackson FY AU RC	10.00	3.00
❑ 102 Mauricio Lara FY AU RC	10.00	3.00
❑ 103 Freddy Sanchez FY AU RC	10.00	3.00
❑ 104 Clint Nageotte FY AU RC	15.00	4.50
❑ 105 Beltran Perez FY AU RC	10.00	3.00
❑ 106 Garrett Gentry FY AU RC	10.00	3.00
❑ 107 Chad Qualls FY AU RC	10.00	3.00
❑ 108 Jason Bay FY AU RC	50.00	15.00
❑ 109 Michael Hill FY AU RC	10.00	3.00
❑ 110 Brian Tallet FY AU RC	10.00	3.00

2003 Finest

	Nm-Mt	Ex-Mt
COMP.SET w/o SP's (100)	25.00	7.50
COMMON CARD (1-100)	.50	.15
COMMON CARD (101-110)	15.00	4.50

Card	Nm-Mt	Ex-Mt
❑ 1 Sammy Sosa	2.00	.60
❑ 2 Paul Konerko	.50	.15
❑ 3 Todd Helton	.75	.23
❑ 4 Mike Lowell	.50	.15
❑ 5 Lance Berkman	.50	.15
❑ 6 Kazuhisa Ishii	.50	.15
❑ 7 A.J. Pierzynski	.50	.15
❑ 8 Jose Vidro	.50	.15
❑ 9 Roberto Alomar	.75	.23
❑ 10 Derek Jeter	3.00	.90
❑ 11 Barry Zito	.50	.15
❑ 12 Jimmy Rollins	.50	.15
❑ 13 Brian Giles	.50	.15
❑ 14 Ryan Klesko	.50	.15
❑ 15 Rich Aurilia	.50	.15
❑ 16 Jim Edmonds	.50	.15
❑ 17 Aubrey Huff	.50	.15
❑ 18 Ivan Rodriguez	1.25	.35
❑ 19 Eric Hinske	.50	.15
❑ 20 Barry Bonds	3.00	.90
❑ 21 Darin Erstad	.50	.15
❑ 22 Curt Schilling	.50	.15
❑ 23 Andruw Jones	.50	.15
❑ 24 Jay Gibbons	.50	.15
❑ 25 Nomar Garciaparra	2.00	.60
❑ 26 Kerry Wood	1.25	.35
❑ 27 Magglio Ordonez	.50	.15
❑ 28 Austin Kearns	.50	.15
❑ 29 Jason Jennings	.50	.15
❑ 30 Jason Giambi	.50	.15
❑ 31 Tim Hudson	.50	.15
❑ 32 Edgar Martinez	.75	.23
❑ 33 Carl Crawford	.50	.15
❑ 34 Hee Seop Choi	.50	.15
❑ 35 Vladimir Guerrero	1.25	.35
❑ 36 Jeff Kent	.50	.15
❑ 37 John Smoltz	.75	.23
❑ 38 Frank Thomas	1.25	.35
❑ 39 Cliff Floyd	.50	.15
❑ 40 Mike Piazza	2.00	.60
❑ 41 Mark Prior	1.25	.35
❑ 42 Tim Salmon	.75	.23
❑ 43 Shawn Green	.50	.15
❑ 44 Bernie Williams	.75	.23
❑ 45 Jim Thome	1.25	.35
❑ 46 John Olerud	.50	.15
❑ 47 Orlando Hudson	.50	.15
❑ 48 Mark Teixeira	.50	.15
❑ 49 Gary Sheffield	.50	.15
❑ 50 Ichiro Suzuki	2.00	.60
❑ 51 Tom Glavine	.75	.23
❑ 52 Torii Hunter	.50	.15
❑ 53 Craig Biggio	.75	.23
❑ 54 Carlos Beltran	.75	.23
❑ 55 Bartolo Colon	.50	.15
❑ 56 Jorge Posada	.75	.23
❑ 57 Pat Burrell	.50	.15
❑ 58 Edgar Renteria	.50	.15
❑ 59 Rafael Palmeiro	.75	.23
❑ 60 Alfonso Soriano	.75	.23
❑ 61 Brandon Phillips	.50	.15

Card	Nm-Mt	Ex-Mt
❑ 62 Luis Gonzalez	.50	.15
❑ 63 Manny Ramirez	.75	.23
❑ 64 Garret Anderson	.50	.15
❑ 65 Ken Griffey Jr.	2.00	.60
❑ 66 A.J. Burnett	.50	.15
❑ 67 Mike Sweeney	.50	.15
❑ 68 Doug Mientkiewicz	.50	.15
❑ 69 Eric Chavez	.50	.15
❑ 70 Adam Dunn	.75	.23
❑ 71 Shea Hillenbrand	.50	.15
❑ 72 Troy Glaus	.50	.15
❑ 73 Rodrigo Lopez	.50	.15
❑ 74 Moises Alou	.50	.15
❑ 75 Chipper Jones	1.25	.35
❑ 76 Bobby Abreu	.50	.15
❑ 77 Mark Mulder	.50	.15
❑ 78 Kevin Brown	.50	.15
❑ 79 Josh Beckett	.50	.15
❑ 80 Larry Walker	.75	.23
❑ 81 Randy Johnson	1.25	.35
❑ 82 Greg Maddux	2.00	.60
❑ 83 Johnny Damon	1.25	.35
❑ 84 Omar Vizquel	.75	.23
❑ 85 Jeff Bagwell	.75	.23
❑ 86 Carlos Pena	.50	.15
❑ 87 Roy Oswalt	.50	.15
❑ 88 Richie Sexson	.50	.15
❑ 89 Roger Clemens	2.50	.75
❑ 90 Miguel Tejada	.50	.15
❑ 91 Vicente Padilla	.50	.15
❑ 92 Phil Nevin	.50	.15
❑ 93 Edgardo Alfonzo	.50	.15
❑ 94 Bret Boone	.50	.15
❑ 95 Albert Pujols	2.50	.75
❑ 96 Carlos Delgado	.50	.15
❑ 97 Jose Contreras RC	1.50	.45
❑ 98 Scott Rolen	1.25	.35
❑ 99 Pedro Martinez	1.25	.35
❑ 100 Alex Rodriguez	2.00	.60
❑ 101 Adam LaRoche AU	15.00	4.50
❑ 102 Andy Marte AU RC	40.00	12.00
❑ 103 Daryl Clark AU RC	15.00	4.50
❑ 104 J.D. Durbin AU RC	15.00	4.50
❑ 105 Craig Brazell AU RC	15.00	4.50
❑ 106 Brian Burgamy AU RC	10.00	3.00
❑ 107 Tyler Johnson AU RC	10.00	3.00
❑ 108 Joey Gomes AU RC	10.00	3.00
❑ 109 Bryan Bullington AU RC	25.00	7.50
❑ 110 Byron Gettis AU RC	10.00	3.00

2004 Finest

	Nm-Mt	Ex-Mt
COMP.SET w/o SP's (100)	25.00	7.50
COMMON CARD (1-100)	.50	.15
COMMON CARD (101-110)	8.00	2.40
101-110 STATED ODDS 1:7 MINI-BOXES		.00
COMMON CARD (111-122)	10.00	3.00
111-122 STATED ODDS 1:3 MINI-BOXES		.00
EXCHANGE DEADLINE 04/30/06	.00	
CARD 112 EXCH UNABLE TO BE FULFILLED		.00
04 WS HL B.THOMSON AU SENT INSTEAD		.00

Card	Nm-Mt	Ex-Mt
❑ 1 Juan Pierre	.50	.15
❑ 2 Derek Jeter	2.50	.75
❑ 3 Garret Anderson	.50	.15
❑ 4 Javy Lopez	.50	.15
❑ 5 Corey Patterson	.50	.15
❑ 6 Todd Helton	.75	.23
❑ 7 Roy Oswalt	.50	.15
❑ 8 Shawn Green	.50	.15
❑ 9 Vladimir Guerrero	1.25	.35
❑ 10 Jorge Posada	.75	.23
❑ 11 Jason Kendall	.50	.15
❑ 12 Scott Rolen	1.25	.35
❑ 13 Randy Johnson	1.25	.35
❑ 14 Bill Mueller	.50	.15
❑ 15 Magglio Ordonez	.50	.15
❑ 16 Larry Walker	.75	.23
❑ 17 Lance Berkman	.50	.15
❑ 18 Richie Sexson	.50	.15
❑ 19 Orlando Cabrera	.50	.15
❑ 20 Alfonso Soriano	.75	.23
❑ 21 Kevin Millwood	.50	.15
❑ 22 Edgar Martinez	.75	.23
❑ 23 Aubrey Huff	.50	.15
❑ 24 Carlos Delgado	.50	.15
❑ 25 Vernon Wells	.50	.15
❑ 26 Mark Teixeira	.50	.15
❑ 27 Troy Glaus	.50	.15
❑ 28 Jeff Kent	.50	.15
❑ 29 Hideo Nomo	1.25	.35
❑ 30 Torii Hunter	.50	.15
❑ 31 Hank Blalock	.50	.15
❑ 32 Brandon Webb	.50	.15
❑ 33 Tony Batista	.50	.15
❑ 34 Bret Boone	.50	.15
❑ 35 Ryan Klesko	.50	.15
❑ 36 Barry Zito	.50	.15
❑ 37 Edgar Renteria	.50	.15
❑ 38 Geoff Jenkins	.50	.15
❑ 39 Jeff Bagwell	.75	.23
❑ 40 Dontrelle Willis	.50	.15
❑ 41 Adam Dunn	.75	.23
❑ 42 Mark Buehrle	.50	.15
❑ 43 Esteban Loaiza	.50	.15
❑ 44 Angel Berroa	.50	.15
❑ 45 Ivan Rodriguez	1.25	.35
❑ 46 Jose Vidro	.50	.15
❑ 47 Mark Mulder	.50	.15
❑ 48 Roger Clemens	2.50	.75
❑ 49 Jim Edmonds	.50	.15
❑ 50 Eric Gagne	1.25	.35
❑ 51 Marcus Giles	.50	.15
❑ 52 Curt Schilling	1.25	.35
❑ 53 Ken Griffey Jr.	2.00	.60
❑ 54 Jason Schmidt	.50	.15
❑ 55 Miguel Tejada	.50	.15
❑ 56 Dmitri Young	.50	.15
❑ 57 Mike Lowell	.50	.15
❑ 58 Mike Sweeney	.50	.15
❑ 59 Scott Podsednik	.50	.15
❑ 60 Miguel Cabrera	.75	.23
❑ 61 Johan Santana	.75	.23
❑ 62 Bernie Williams	.75	.23
❑ 63 Eric Chavez	.50	.15
❑ 64 Bobby Abreu	.50	.15
❑ 65 Brian Giles	.50	.15
❑ 66 Michael Young	.50	.15
❑ 67 Paul Lo Duca	.50	.15
❑ 68 Austin Kearns	.50	.15
❑ 69 Jody Gerut	.50	.15
❑ 70 Kerry Wood	1.25	.35
❑ 71 Luis Matos	.50	.15
❑ 72 Greg Maddux	2.00	.60
❑ 73 Alex Rodriguez Yanks	2.00	.60
❑ 74 Mike Lieberthal	.50	.15
❑ 75 Jim Thome	1.25	.35
❑ 76 Javier Vazquez	.50	.15
❑ 77 Bartolo Colon	.50	.15
❑ 78 Manny Ramirez	.75	.23
❑ 79 Jacque Jones	.50	.15
❑ 80 Johnny Damon	1.25	.35
❑ 81 Carlos Beltran	.75	.23
❑ 82 C.C. Sabathia	.50	.15
❑ 83 Preston Wilson	.50	.15
❑ 84 Luis Castillo	.50	.15
❑ 85 Kevin Brown	.50	.15
❑ 86 Shannon Stewart	.50	.15
❑ 87 Cliff Floyd	.50	.15
❑ 88 Mike Mussina	.75	.23
❑ 89 Rafael Furcal	.50	.15
❑ 90 Roy Halladay	.50	.15
❑ 91 Frank Thomas	1.25	.35
❑ 92 Melvin Mora	.50	.15
❑ 93 Andruw Jones	.50	.15
❑ 94 Luis Gonzalez	.50	.15
❑ 95 David Ortiz	1.25	.35
❑ 96 Gary Sheffield	.50	.15
❑ 97 Tim Hudson	.50	.15
❑ 98 Phil Nevin	.50	.15
❑ 99 Ichiro Suzuki	2.00	.60
❑ 100 Albert Pujols	2.50	.75
❑ 101 Nomar Garciaparra SR Jsy	15.00	4.50
❑ 102 Sammy Sosa SR Jsy	15.00	4.50
❑ 103 Josh Beckett SR Jsy	8.00	2.40
❑ 104 Jason Giambi SR Jsy	8.00	2.40
❑ 105 Rocco Baldelli SR Jsy	8.00	2.40
❑ 106 Jose Reyes SR Jsy	8.00	2.40
❑ 107 Chipper Jones SR Jsy	10.00	3.00
❑ 108 Pedro Martinez SR Jsy	10.00	3.00
❑ 109 Mike Piazza SR Jsy	15.00	4.50
❑ 110 Mark Prior SR Jsy	10.00	3.00
❑ 111 Craig Ansman AU RC	10.00	3.00
❑ 112 J.Allison AU RC EXCH UER	15.00	4.50
❑ 113 David Murphy AU RC EXCH	15.00	4.50
❑ 114 Jason Hirsh AU RC	10.00	3.00
❑ 115 Matt Moses AU RC	15.00	4.50
❑ 116 Estee Harris AU RC	10.00	3.00
❑ 117 Logan Kensing AU RC	10.00	3.00
❑ 118 L.Milledge AU RC EXCH	30.00	9.00
❑ 119 Merkin Valdez AU RC	15.00	4.50
❑ 120 Travis Blackley AU RC	15.00	4.50
❑ 121 Vito Chiaravalloti AU RC	15.00	4.50
❑ 122 Dioner Navarro AU RC	20.00	6.00

1994 Flair

	Nm-Mt	Ex-Mt
COMPLETE SET (450)	80.00	24.00
COMP. SERIES 1 (250)	20.00	6.00
COMP. SERIES 2 (200)	60.00	18.00

Card	Nm-Mt	Ex-Mt
❑ 1 Harold Baines	.50	.15
❑ 2 Jeffrey Hammonds	.25	.07
❑ 3 Chris Hoiles	.25	.07
❑ 4 Ben McDonald	.25	.07
❑ 5 Mark McLemore	.25	.07
❑ 6 Jamie Moyer	.50	.15
❑ 7 Jim Poole	.25	.07
❑ 8 Cal Ripken Jr.	4.00	1.20
❑ 9 Chris Sabo	.25	.07
❑ 10 Scott Bankhead	.25	.07
❑ 11 Scott Cooper	.25	.07
❑ 12 Danny Darwin	.25	.07
❑ 13 Andre Dawson	.50	.15
❑ 14 Billy Hatcher	.25	.07
❑ 15 Aaron Sele	.25	.07
❑ 16 John Valentin	.25	.07
❑ 17 Dave Valle	.25	.07
❑ 18 Mo Vaughn	.50	.15
❑ 19 Brian Anderson RC	.50	.15
❑ 20 Gary DiSarcina	.25	.07
❑ 21 Jim Edmonds	1.25	.35
❑ 22 Chuck Finley	.50	.15
❑ 23 Bo Jackson	1.25	.35
❑ 24 Mark Leiter	.25	.07
❑ 25 Greg Myers	.25	.07
❑ 26 Eduardo Perez	.25	.07
❑ 27 Tim Salmon	.75	.23
❑ 28 Wilson Alvarez	.25	.07
❑ 29 Jason Bere	.25	.07

❑ 30 Alex Fernandez .25 .07
❑ 31 Ozzie Guillen .25 .07
❑ 32 Joe Hall RC .25 .07
❑ 33 Darrin Jackson .25 .07
❑ 34 Kirk McCaskill .25 .07
❑ 35 Tim Raines .50 .15
❑ 36 Frank Thomas 1.25 .35
❑ 37 Carlos Baerga .25 .07
❑ 38 Albert Belle .50 .15
❑ 39 Mark Clark .25 .07
❑ 40 Wayne Kirby .25 .07
❑ 41 Dennis Martinez .50 .15
❑ 42 Charles Nagy .25 .07
❑ 43 Manny Ramirez .75 .23
❑ 44 Paul Sorrento .25 .07
❑ 45 Jim Thome 1.25 .35
❑ 46 Eric Davis .50 .15
❑ 47 John Doherty .25 .07
❑ 48 Junior Felix .25 .07
❑ 49 Cecil Fielder .50 .15
❑ 50 Kirk Gibson .50 .15
❑ 51 Mike Moore .25 .07
❑ 52 Tony Phillips .25 .07
❑ 53 Alan Trammell .50 .15
❑ 54 Kevin Appier .50 .15
❑ 55 Stan Belinda .25 .07
❑ 56 Vince Coleman .25 .07
❑ 57 Greg Gagne .25 .07
❑ 58 Bob Hamelin .25 .07
❑ 59 Dave Henderson .25 .07
❑ 60 Wally Joyner .50 .15
❑ 61 Mike Macfarlane .25 .07
❑ 62 Jeff Montgomery .25 .07
❑ 63 Ricky Bones .25 .07
❑ 64 Jeff Bronkey .25 .07
❑ 65 Alex Diaz RC .25 .07
❑ 66 Cal Eldred .25 .07
❑ 67 Darryl Hamilton .25 .07
❑ 68 John Jaha .25 .07
❑ 69 Mark Kiefer .25 .07
❑ 70 Kevin Seitzer .25 .07
❑ 71 Turner Ward .25 .07
❑ 72 Rich Becker .25 .07
❑ 73 Scott Erickson .25 .07
❑ 74 Keith Garagozzo RC .25 .07
❑ 75 Kent Hrbek .50 .15
❑ 76 Scott Leius .25 .07
❑ 77 Kirby Puckett 1.25 .35
❑ 78 Matt Walbeck .25 .07
❑ 79 Dave Winfield .50 .15
❑ 80 Mike Gallego .25 .07
❑ 81 Xavier Hernandez .25 .07
❑ 82 Jimmy Key .50 .15
❑ 83 Jim Leyritz .25 .07
❑ 84 Don Mattingly 3.00 .90
❑ 85 Matt Nokes .25 .07
❑ 86 Paul O'Neill .75 .23
❑ 87 Melido Perez .25 .07
❑ 88 Danny Tartabull .25 .07
❑ 89 Mike Bordick .25 .07
❑ 90 Ron Darling .25 .07
❑ 91 Dennis Eckersley .50 .15
❑ 92 Stan Javier .25 .07
❑ 93 Steve Karsay .25 .07
❑ 94 Mark McGwire 3.00 .90
❑ 95 Troy Neel .25 .07
❑ 96 Terry Steinbach .25 .07
❑ 97 Bill Taylor RC .50 .15
❑ 98 Eric Anthony .25 .07
❑ 99 Chris Bosio .25 .07
❑ 100 Tim Davis .25 .07
❑ 101 Felix Fermin .25 .07
❑ 102 Dave Fleming .25 .07
❑ 103 Ken Griffey Jr. 2.00 .60
❑ 104 Greg Hibbard .25 .07
❑ 105 Reggie Jefferson .25 .07
❑ 106 Tino Martinez .75 .23
❑ 107 Jack Armstrong .25 .07
❑ 108 Will Clark 1.25 .35
❑ 109 Juan Gonzalez .75 .23
❑ 110 Rick Helling .25 .07
❑ 111 Tom Henke .25 .07
❑ 112 David Hulse .25 .07
❑ 113 Manuel Lee .25 .07
❑ 114 Doug Strange .25 .07
❑ 115 Roberto Alomar .75 .23
❑ 116 Joe Carter .50 .15
❑ 117 Carlos Delgado .75 .23
❑ 118 Pat Hentgen .25 .07
❑ 119 Paul Molitor .75 .23
❑ 120 John Olerud .50 .15
❑ 121 Dave Stewart .50 .15
❑ 122 Todd Stottlemyre .25 .07
❑ 123 Mike Timlin .25 .07
❑ 124 Jeff Blauser .25 .07
❑ 125 Tom Glavine .75 .23
❑ 126 David Justice .50 .15
❑ 127 Mike Kelly .25 .07
❑ 128 Ryan Klesko .50 .15
❑ 129 Javier Lopez .50 .15
❑ 130 Greg Maddux 2.00 .60
❑ 131 Fred McGriff .75 .23
❑ 132 Kent Mercker .25 .07
❑ 133 Mark Wohlers .25 .07
❑ 134 Willie Banks .25 .07
❑ 135 Steve Buechele .25 .07
❑ 136 Shawon Dunston .25 .07
❑ 137 Jose Guzman .25 .07
❑ 138 Glenallen Hill .25 .07
❑ 139 Randy Myers .25 .07
❑ 140 Karl Rhodes .25 .07
❑ 141 Ryne Sandberg 2.00 .60
❑ 142 Steve Trachsel .25 .07
❑ 143 Bret Boone .50 .15
❑ 144 Tom Browning .25 .07
❑ 145 Hector Carrasco .25 .07
❑ 146 Barry Larkin .75 .23
❑ 147 Hal Morris .25 .07
❑ 148 Jose Rijo .25 .07
❑ 149 Reggie Sanders .25 .07
❑ 150 John Smiley .25 .07
❑ 151 Dante Bichette .50 .15
❑ 152 Ellis Burks .50 .15
❑ 153 Joe Girardi .25 .07
❑ 154 Mike Harkey .25 .07
❑ 155 Roberto Mejia .25 .07
❑ 156 Marcus Moore .25 .07
❑ 157 Armando Reynoso .25 .07
❑ 158 Bruce Ruffin .25 .07
❑ 159 Eric Young .25 .07
❑ 160 Kurt Abbott RC .50 .15
❑ 161 Jeff Conine .50 .15
❑ 162 Orestes Destrade .25 .07
❑ 163 Chris Hammond .25 .07
❑ 164 Bryan Harvey .25 .07
❑ 165 Dave Magadan .25 .07
❑ 166 Gary Sheffield .50 .15
❑ 167 David Weathers .25 .07
❑ 168 Andujar Cedeno .25 .07
❑ 169 Tom Edens .25 .07
❑ 170 Luis Gonzalez .50 .15
❑ 171 Pete Harnisch .25 .07
❑ 172 Todd Jones .25 .07
❑ 173 Darryl Kile .50 .15
❑ 174 James Mouton .25 .07
❑ 175 Scott Servais .25 .07
❑ 176 Mitch Williams .25 .07
❑ 177 Pedro Astacio .25 .07
❑ 178 Orel Hershiser .50 .15
❑ 179 Raul Mondesi .50 .15
❑ 180 Jose Offerman .25 .07
❑ 181 Chan Ho Park RC .75 .23
❑ 182 Mike Piazza 2.50 .75
❑ 183 Cory Snyder .25 .07
❑ 184 Tim Wallach .25 .07
❑ 185 Todd Worrell .25 .07
❑ 186 Sean Berry .25 .07
❑ 187 Wil Cordero .25 .07
❑ 188 Darrin Fletcher .25 .07
❑ 189 Cliff Floyd .50 .15
❑ 190 Marquis Grissom .50 .15
❑ 191 Rod Henderson .25 .07
❑ 192 Ken Hill .25 .07
❑ 193 Pedro Martinez 1.25 .35
❑ 194 Kirk Rueter .50 .15
❑ 195 Jeromy Burnitz .50 .15
❑ 196 John Franco .50 .15
❑ 197 Dwight Gooden .50 .15
❑ 198 Todd Hundley .25 .07
❑ 199 Bobby Jones .25 .07
❑ 200 Jeff Kent .50 .15
❑ 201 Mike Maddux .25 .07
❑ 202 Ryan Thompson .25 .07
❑ 203 Jose Vizcaino .25 .07
❑ 204 Darren Daulton .50 .15
❑ 205 Lenny Dykstra .50 .15
❑ 206 Jim Eisenreich .25 .07
❑ 207 Dave Hollins .25 .07
❑ 208 Danny Jackson .25 .07
❑ 209 Doug Jones .25 .07
❑ 210 Jeff Juden .25 .07
❑ 211 Ben Rivera .25 .07
❑ 212 Kevin Stocker .25 .07
❑ 213 Milt Thompson .25 .07
❑ 214 Jay Bell .50 .15
❑ 215 Steve Cooke .25 .07
❑ 216 Mark Dewey .25 .07
❑ 217 Al Martin .25 .07
❑ 218 Orlando Merced .25 .07
❑ 219 Don Slaught .25 .07
❑ 220 Zane Smith .25 .07
❑ 221 Rick White RC .25 .07
❑ 222 Kevin Young .25 .07
❑ 223 Rene Arocha .25 .07
❑ 224 Rheal Cormier .25 .07
❑ 225 Brian Jordan .50 .15
❑ 226 Ray Lankford .25 .07
❑ 227 Mike Perez .25 .07
❑ 228 Ozzie Smith 2.00 .60
❑ 229 Mark Whiten .25 .07
❑ 230 Todd Zeile .25 .07
❑ 231 Derek Bell .25 .07
❑ 232 Archi Cianfrocco .25 .07
❑ 233 Ricky Gutierrez .25 .07
❑ 234 Trevor Hoffman .50 .15
❑ 235 Phil Plantier .25 .07
❑ 236 Dave Staton .25 .07
❑ 237 Wally Whitehurst .25 .07
❑ 238 Todd Benzinger .25 .07
❑ 239 Barry Bonds 3.00 .90
❑ 240 John Burkett .25 .07
❑ 241 Royce Clayton .25 .07
❑ 242 Bryan Hickerson .25 .07
❑ 243 Mike Jackson .25 .07
❑ 244 Darren Lewis .25 .07
❑ 245 Kirt Manwaring .25 .07
❑ 246 Mark Portugal .25 .07
❑ 247 Salomon Torres .25 .07
❑ 248 Checklist .25 .07
❑ 249 Checklist .25 .07
❑ 250 Checklist .25 .07
❑ 251 Brady Anderson .50 .15
❑ 252 Mike Devereaux .25 .07
❑ 253 Sid Fernandez .25 .07
❑ 254 Leo Gomez .25 .07
❑ 255 Mike Mussina .75 .23
❑ 256 Mike Oquist .25 .07
❑ 257 Rafael Palmeiro .75 .23
❑ 258 Lee Smith .50 .15
❑ 259 Damon Berryhill .25 .07
❑ 260 Wes Chamberlain .25 .07
❑ 261 Roger Clemens 2.50 .75
❑ 262 Gar Finnvold RC .25 .07
❑ 263 Mike Greenwell .25 .07
❑ 264 Tim Naehring .25 .07
❑ 265 Otis Nixon .25 .07
❑ 266 Ken Ryan .25 .07
❑ 267 Chad Curtis .25 .07
❑ 268 Chili Davis .50 .15
❑ 269 Damion Easley .25 .07
❑ 270 Jorge Fabregas .25 .07
❑ 271 Mark Langston .25 .07
❑ 272 Phil Leftwich RC .25 .07
❑ 273 Harold Reynolds .50 .15
❑ 274 J.T. Snow .50 .15
❑ 275 Joey Cora .25 .07
❑ 276 Julio Franco .50 .15
❑ 277 Roberto Hernandez .25 .07
❑ 278 Lance Johnson .25 .07
❑ 279 Ron Karkovice .25 .07
❑ 280 Jack McDowell .25 .07
❑ 281 Robin Ventura .50 .15
❑ 282 Sandy Alomar Jr. .25 .07
❑ 283 Kenny Lofton .50 .15
❑ 284 Jose Mesa .25 .07
❑ 285 Jack Morris .50 .15
❑ 286 Eddie Murray 1.25 .35
❑ 287 Chad Ogea .25 .07

❑ 288 Eric Plunk .25 .07
❑ 289 Paul Shuey .25 .07
❑ 290 Omar Vizquel .75 .23
❑ 291 Danny Bautista .25 .07
❑ 292 Travis Fryman .50 .15
❑ 293 Greg Gohr .25 .07
❑ 294 Chris Gomez .25 .07
❑ 295 Mickey Tettleton .25 .07
❑ 296 Lou Whitaker .50 .15
❑ 297 David Cone .50 .15
❑ 298 Gary Gaetti .50 .15
❑ 299 Tom Gordon .25 .07
❑ 300 Felix Jose .25 .07
❑ 301 Jose Lind .25 .07
❑ 302 Brian McRae .25 .07
❑ 303 Mike Fetters .25 .07
❑ 304 Brian Harper .25 .07
❑ 305 Pat Listach .25 .07
❑ 306 Matt Mieske .25 .07
❑ 307 Dave Nilsson .25 .07
❑ 308 Jody Reed .25 .07
❑ 309 Greg Vaughn .25 .07
❑ 310 Bill Wegman .25 .07
❑ 311 Rick Aguilera .25 .07
❑ 312 Alex Cole .25 .07
❑ 313 Denny Hocking .25 .07
❑ 314 Chuck Knoblauch .50 .15
❑ 315 Shane Mack .25 .07
❑ 316 Pat Meares .25 .07
❑ 317 Kevin Tapani .25 .07
❑ 318 Jim Abbott .75 .23
❑ 319 Wade Boggs .75 .23
❑ 320 Sterling Hitchcock .25 .07
❑ 321 Pat Kelly .25 .07
❑ 322 Terry Mulholland .25 .07
❑ 323 Luis Polonia .25 .07
❑ 324 Mike Stanley .25 .07
❑ 325 Bob Wickman .25 .07
❑ 326 Bernie Williams .75 .23
❑ 327 Mark Acre RC .25 .07
❑ 328 Geronimo Berroa .25 .07
❑ 329 Scott Brosius .50 .15
❑ 330 Brent Gates .25 .07
❑ 331 Rickey Henderson 1.25 .35
❑ 332 Carlos Reyes RC .25 .07
❑ 333 Ruben Sierra .25 .07
❑ 334 Bobby Witt .25 .07
❑ 335 Bobby Ayala .25 .07
❑ 336 Jay Buhner .50 .15
❑ 337 Randy Johnson 1.25 .35
❑ 338 Edgar Martinez .75 .23
❑ 339 Bill Risley .25 .07
❑ 340 Alex Rodriguez RC 40.00 12.00
❑ 341 Roger Salkeld .25 .07
❑ 342 Dan Wilson .25 .07
❑ 343 Kevin Brown .50 .15
❑ 344 Jose Canseco 1.25 .35
❑ 345 Dean Palmer .50 .15
❑ 346 Ivan Rodriguez 1.25 .35
❑ 347 Kenny Rogers .50 .15
❑ 348 Pat Borders .25 .07
❑ 349 Juan Guzman .25 .07
❑ 350 Ed Sprague .25 .07
❑ 351 Devon White .50 .15
❑ 352 Steve Avery .25 .07
❑ 353 Roberto Kelly .25 .07
❑ 354 Mark Lemke .25 .07
❑ 355 Greg McMichael .25 .07
❑ 356 Terry Pendleton .50 .15
❑ 357 John Smoltz .75 .23
❑ 358 Mike Stanton .25 .07
❑ 359 Tony Tarasco .25 .07
❑ 360 Mark Grace .75 .23
❑ 361 Derrick May .25 .07
❑ 362 Rey Sanchez .25 .07
❑ 363 Sammy Sosa 2.00 .60
❑ 364 Rick Wilkins .25 .07
❑ 365 Jeff Brantley .25 .07
❑ 366 Tony Fernandez .25 .07
❑ 367 Chuck McElroy .25 .07
❑ 368 Kevin Mitchell .25 .07
❑ 369 John Roper .25 .07
❑ 370 Johnny Ruffin .25 .07
❑ 371 Deion Sanders .75 .23
❑ 372 Marvin Freeman .25 .07
❑ 373 Andres Galarraga .50 .15
❑ 374 Charlie Hayes .25 .07
❑ 375 Nelson Liriano .25 .07
❑ 376 David Nied .25 .07
❑ 377 Walt Weiss .25 .07
❑ 378 Bret Barberie .25 .07
❑ 379 Jerry Browne .25 .07
❑ 380 Chuck Carr .25 .07
❑ 381 Greg Colbrunn .25 .07
❑ 382 Charlie Hough .50 .15
❑ 383 Kurt Miller .25 .07
❑ 384 Benito Santiago .50 .15
❑ 385 Jeff Bagwell .75 .23
❑ 386 Craig Biggio .75 .23
❑ 387 Ken Caminiti .50 .15
❑ 388 Doug Drabek .25 .07
❑ 389 Steve Finley .50 .15
❑ 390 John Hudek RC .25 .07
❑ 391 Orlando Miller .25 .07
❑ 392 Shane Reynolds .25 .07
❑ 393 Brett Butler .50 .15
❑ 394 Tom Candiotti .25 .07
❑ 395 Delino DeShields .25 .07
❑ 396 Kevin Gross .25 .07
❑ 397 Eric Karros .50 .15
❑ 398 Ramon Martinez .25 .07
❑ 399 Henry Rodriguez .25 .07
❑ 400 Moises Alou .50 .15
❑ 401 Jeff Fassero .25 .07
❑ 402 Mike Lansing .25 .07
❑ 403 Mel Rojas .25 .07
❑ 404 Larry Walker .75 .23
❑ 405 John Wetteland .50 .15
❑ 406 Gabe White .25 .07
❑ 407 Bobby Bonilla .50 .15
❑ 408 Josias Manzanillo .25 .07
❑ 409 Bret Saberhagen .50 .15
❑ 410 David Segui .25 .07
❑ 411 Mariano Duncan .25 .07
❑ 412 Tommy Greene .25 .07
❑ 413 Billy Hatcher .25 .07
❑ 414 Ricky Jordan .25 .07
❑ 415 John Kruk .50 .15
❑ 416 Bobby Munoz .25 .07
❑ 417 Curt Schilling .50 .15
❑ 418 Fernando Valenzuela .50 .15
❑ 419 David West .25 .07
❑ 420 Carlos Garcia .25 .07
❑ 421 Brian Hunter .25 .07
❑ 422 Jeff King .25 .07
❑ 423 Jon Lieber .25 .07
❑ 424 Ravelo Manzanillo .25 .07
❑ 425 Denny Neagle .50 .15
❑ 426 Andy Van Slyke .50 .15
❑ 427 Bryan Eversgerd RC .25 .07
❑ 428 Bernard Gilkey .25 .07
❑ 429 Gregg Jefferies .25 .07
❑ 430 Tom Pagnozzi .25 .07
❑ 431 Bob Tewksbury .25 .07
❑ 432 Allen Watson .25 .07
❑ 433 Andy Ashby .25 .07
❑ 434 Andy Benes .25 .07
❑ 435 Donnie Elliott .25 .07
❑ 436 Tony Gwynn 1.50 .45
❑ 437 Joey Hamilton .25 .07
❑ 438 Tim Hyers RC .25 .07
❑ 439 Luis Lopez .25 .07
❑ 440 Bip Roberts .25 .07
❑ 441 Scott Sanders .25 .07
❑ 442 Rod Beck .25 .07
❑ 443 Dave Burba .25 .07
❑ 444 Darryl Strawberry .50 .15
❑ 445 Bill Swift .25 .07
❑ 446 Robby Thompson .25 .07
❑ 447 B.VanLandingham RC .25 .07
❑ 448 Matt Williams .50 .15
❑ 449 Checklist .25 .07
❑ 450 Checklist .25 .07
❑ P15 Aaron Sele Promo 1.00 .30

2003 Flair

	Nm-Mt	Ex-Mt
COMP.LO SET w/o SP's (90)	25.00	7.50
COMMON CARD (1-90)	.50	.15
COMMON CARD (91-135)	5.00	1.50

❑ 1 Hideo Nomo 1.25 .35
❑ 2 Derek Jeter 3.00 .90
❑ 3 Junior Spivey .50 .15
❑ 4 Rich Aurilia .50 .15
❑ 5 Luis Gonzalez .50 .15
❑ 6 Sean Burroughs .50 .15
❑ 7 Pedro Martinez 1.25 .35
❑ 8 Randy Winn .50 .15
❑ 9 Carlos Delgado .50 .15
❑ 10 Pat Burrell .50 .15
❑ 11 Barry Larkin .75 .23
❑ 12 Roberto Alomar .75 .23
❑ 13 Tony Batista .50 .15
❑ 14 Barry Bonds 3.00 .90
❑ 15 Craig Biggio .75 .23
❑ 16 Ivan Rodriguez 1.25 .35
❑ 17 Javier Vazquez .50 .15
❑ 18 Joe Borchard .50 .15
❑ 19 Josh Phelps .50 .15
❑ 20 Omar Vizquel .75 .23
❑ 21 Tom Glavine .75 .23
❑ 22 Darin Erstad .50 .15
❑ 23 Hee Seop Choi .50 .15
❑ 24 Roger Clemens 2.50 .75
❑ 25 Michael Cuddyer .50 .15
❑ 26 Mike Sweeney .50 .15
❑ 27 Phil Nevin .50 .15
❑ 28 Torii Hunter .50 .15
❑ 29 Vladimir Guerrero 1.25 .35
❑ 30 Ellis Burks .50 .15
❑ 31 Jimmy Rollins .50 .15
❑ 32 Ken Griffey Jr. 2.00 .60
❑ 33 Magglio Ordonez .50 .15
❑ 34 Mark Prior 1.25 .35
❑ 35 Mike Lieberthal .50 .15
❑ 36 Jorge Posada .75 .23
❑ 37 Rodrigo Lopez .50 .15
❑ 38 Todd Helton .75 .23
❑ 39 Adam Kennedy .50 .15
❑ 40 Curt Schilling .50 .15
❑ 41 Jim Thome 1.25 .35
❑ 42 Josh Beckett .50 .15
❑ 43 Carlos Pena .50 .15
❑ 44 Jason Kendall .50 .15
❑ 45 Sammy Sosa 2.00 .60
❑ 46 Scott Rolen 1.25 .35
❑ 47 Alex Rodriguez 2.00 .60
❑ 48 Aubrey Huff .50 .15
❑ 49 Bobby Abreu .50 .15
❑ 50 Jeff Kent .50 .15
❑ 51 Joe Randa .50 .15
❑ 52 Lance Berkman .50 .15
❑ 53 Orlando Cabrera .50 .15
❑ 54 Richie Sexson .50 .15
❑ 55 Albert Pujols 2.00 .60
❑ 56 Alfonso Soriano .75 .23
❑ 57 Greg Maddux 2.00 .60
❑ 58 Jason Giambi .50 .15
❑ 59 Jeff Bagwell .75 .23
❑ 60 Kerry Wood 1.25 .35
❑ 61 Manny Ramirez .75 .23
❑ 62 Eric Chavez .50 .15
❑ 63 Preston Wilson .50 .15
❑ 64 Shawn Green .50 .15
❑ 65 Shea Hillenbrand .50 .15
❑ 66 Austin Kearns .50 .15
❑ 67 Cliff Floyd .50 .15
❑ 68 Edgardo Alfonzo .50 .15

		Nm-Mt	Ex-Mt
❑ 69	J.D. Drew	.50	.15
❑ 70	Larry Walker	.75	.23
❑ 71	Mike Piazza	2.00	.60
❑ 72	Andruw Jones	.50	.15
❑ 73	Ben Grieve	.50	.15
❑ 74	Eric Hinske	.50	.15
❑ 75	Geoff Jenkins	.50	.15
❑ 76	Kazuhiro Sasaki	.50	.15
❑ 77	Matt Morris	.50	.15
❑ 78	Miguel Tejada	.50	.15
❑ 79	Aramis Ramirez	.50	.15
❑ 80	Troy Glaus	.50	.15
❑ 81	Ichiro Suzuki	2.00	.60
❑ 82	Mark Teixeira	.50	.15
❑ 83	Nomar Garciaparra	2.00	.60
❑ 84	Chipper Jones	1.25	.35
❑ 85	Frank Thomas	1.25	.35
❑ 86	Paul Lo Duca	.50	.15
❑ 87	Bernie Williams	.75	.23
❑ 88	Adam Dunn	.75	.23
❑ 89	Randy Johnson	1.25	.35
❑ 90	Barry Zito	.50	.15
❑ 91	Lew Ford FF RC	10.00	3.00
❑ 92	Joe Valentine FF RC	5.00	1.50
❑ 93	Jhonny Peralta FF	5.00	1.50
❑ 94	Hideki Matsui FF RC	20.00	6.00
❑ 95	Francisco Rosario FF RC	5.00	1.50
❑ 96	Adam LaRoche FF	5.00	1.50
❑ 97	Josh Hall FF RC	8.00	2.40
❑ 98	Chien-Ming Wang FF RC	10.00	3.00
❑ 99	Josh Willingham FF RC	8.00	2.40
❑ 100	Guillermo Quiroz FF RC	8.00	2.40
❑ 101	Termel Sledge FF RC	8.00	2.40
❑ 102	Prentice Redman FF RC	5.00	1.50
❑ 103	Matt Bruback FF RC	5.00	1.50
❑ 104	Alejandro Machado FF RC	5.00	1.50
❑ 105	Shane Victorino FF RC	5.00	1.50
❑ 106	Chris Waters FF RC	5.00	1.50
❑ 107	Jose Contreras FF RC	10.00	3.00
❑ 108	Pete LaForest FF RC	8.00	2.40
❑ 109	Nook Logan FF RC	5.00	1.50
❑ 110	Hector Luna FF RC	5.00	1.50
❑ 111	Daniel Cabrera FF RC	10.00	3.00
❑ 112	Matt Kata FF RC	8.00	2.40
❑ 113	Rontrez Johnson FF RC	5.00	1.50
❑ 114	Josh Stewart FF RC	5.00	1.50
❑ 115	Michael Hessman FF RC	5.00	1.50
❑ 116	Felix Sanchez FF RC	5.00	1.50
❑ 117	Michel Hernandez FF RC	5.00	1.50
❑ 118	Arnaldo Munoz FF RC	5.00	1.50
❑ 119	Ian Ferguson FF RC	5.00	1.50
❑ 120	Clint Barmes FF RC	8.00	2.40
❑ 121	Brian Stokes FF RC	5.00	1.50
❑ 122	Craig Brazell FF RC	8.00	2.40
❑ 123	John Webb FF	5.00	1.50
❑ 124	Tim Olson FF RC	8.00	2.40
❑ 125	Jeremy Bonderman FF RC	8.00	2.40
❑ 126	Jeff Duncan RC	8.00	2.40
❑ 127	Rickie Weeks RC	12.00	3.60
❑ 128	Brandon Webb RC	10.00	3.00
❑ 129	Robby Hammock RC	8.00	2.40
❑ 130	Jon Leicester RC	5.00	1.50
❑ 131	Ryan Wagner RC	8.00	2.40
❑ 132	Bo Hart RC	8.00	2.40
❑ 133	Edwin Jackson RC	12.00	3.60
❑ 134	Sergio Mitre RC	8.00	2.40
❑ 135	Delmon Young RC	15.00	4.50

2004 Flair

		Nm-Mt	Ex-Mt
	COMMON CARD (61-82)	4.00	1.20
❑ 1	Brandon Webb	1.50	.45
❑ 2	Todd Helton	2.00	.60
❑ 3	Jeff Bagwell	2.00	.60
❑ 4	Shawn Green	1.50	.45
❑ 5	Vladimir Guerrero	3.00	.90
❑ 6	Tom Glavine	2.00	.60
❑ 7	Jason Giambi	1.50	.45
❑ 8	Barry Zito	1.50	.45
❑ 9	Jason Kendall	1.50	.45
❑ 10	Carlos Delgado	1.50	.45
❑ 11	Curt Schilling	3.00	.90
❑ 12	Ken Griffey Jr.	5.00	1.50
❑ 13	Mike Piazza	5.00	1.50
❑ 14	Alfonso Soriano	2.00	.60
❑ 15	Albert Pujols	6.00	1.80
❑ 16	Chipper Jones	3.00	.90
❑ 17	Alex Rodriguez	5.00	1.50
❑ 18	Miguel Tejada	1.50	.45
❑ 19	Pedro Martinez	3.00	.90
❑ 20	Mark Prior	3.00	.90
❑ 21	Magglio Ordonez	1.50	.45
❑ 22	Scott Podsednik	1.50	.45
❑ 23	Shannon Stewart	1.50	.45
❑ 24	Rocco Baldelli	1.50	.45
❑ 25	Darin Erstad	1.50	.45
❑ 26	Omar Vizquel	2.00	.60
❑ 27	Angel Berroa	1.50	.45
❑ 28	Jose Vidro	1.50	.45
❑ 29	Rich Harden	1.50	.45
❑ 30	Andruw Jones	1.50	.45
❑ 31	Troy Glaus	1.50	.45
❑ 32	Sammy Sosa	5.00	1.50
❑ 33	Dontrelle Willis	1.50	.45
❑ 34	Ivan Rodriguez	3.00	.90
❑ 35	Nomar Garciaparra	5.00	1.50
❑ 36	Josh Beckett	1.50	.45
❑ 37	Jose Reyes	1.50	.45
❑ 38	Scott Rolen	3.00	.90
❑ 39	Greg Maddux	5.00	1.50
❑ 40	Andy Pettitte	2.00	.60
❑ 41	Jason Schmidt	1.50	.45
❑ 42	Edgar Martinez	2.00	.60
❑ 43	Manny Ramirez	2.00	.60
❑ 44	Torii Hunter	1.50	.45
❑ 45	Mark Teixeira	1.50	.45
❑ 46	Hideo Nomo	3.00	.90
❑ 47	Brian Giles	1.50	.45
❑ 48	Adam Dunn	2.00	.60
❑ 49	Fernando Vina	1.50	.45
❑ 50	Hideki Matsui	5.00	1.50
❑ 51	Jim Thome	3.00	.90
❑ 52	Hank Blalock	1.50	.45
❑ 53	Miguel Cabrera	2.00	.60
❑ 54	Randy Johnson	3.00	.90
❑ 55	Javy Lopez	1.50	.45
❑ 56	Frank Thomas	3.00	.90
❑ 57	Roger Clemens	6.00	1.80
❑ 58	Marlon Byrd	1.50	.45
❑ 59	Derek Jeter	6.00	1.80
❑ 60	Ichiro Suzuki	5.00	1.50
❑ 61	Kaz Matsui C04 RC	8.00	2.40
❑ 62	Chad Bentz C04 RC	4.00	1.20
❑ 63	Greg Dobbs C04 RC	4.00	1.20
❑ 64	John Gall C04 RC	5.00	1.50
❑ 65	Cory Sullivan C04 RC	4.00	1.20
❑ 66	Hector Gimenez C04 RC	4.00	1.20
❑ 67	Graham Koonce C04	4.00	1.20
❑ 68	Jason Bartlett C04 RC	5.00	1.50
❑ 69	Angel Chavez C04 RC	4.00	1.20
❑ 70	Ronny Cedeno C04 RC	4.00	1.20
❑ 71	Don Kelly C04 RC	4.00	1.20
❑ 72	Ivan Ochoa C04 RC	4.00	1.20
❑ 73	Ruddy Yan C04	4.00	1.20
❑ 74	Mike Gosling C04 RC	4.00	1.20
❑ 75	Alfredo Simon C04 RC	4.00	1.20
❑ 76	Jerome Gamble C04 RC	4.00	1.20
❑ 77	Chris Aguila C04 RC	4.00	1.20
❑ 78	Mike Rouse C04 RC	4.00	1.20
❑ 79	Justin Leone C04 RC	5.00	1.50
❑ 80	Merkin Valdez C04 RC	5.00	1.50
❑ 81	Aaron Baldiris C04 RC	5.00	1.50
❑ 82	Chris Shelton C04 RC	5.00	1.50

1959 Fleer Ted Williams

	NM	Ex
COMPLETE SET (80)	1800.00	900.00
WRAPPER (6-CARD)	125.00	60.00
WRAPPER (8-CARD)	150.00	75.00

❑ 1 Ted Williams 100.00 50.00
The Early Years
Choosing up sides
on the sandlots

❑ 2 Ted Williams 100.00 50.00
Babe Ruth
Meeting boyhood idol
Babe Ruth

❑ 3 Ted Williams 15.00 7.50
Practice Makes Perfect
At place practicing on the sandlots

❑ 4 Ted Williams 15.00 7.50
Learns Fine Points
Sliding at Herbert Hoover High

❑ 5 Ted Williams 15.00 7.50
Ted's Fame Spreads
At plate at Herbert Hoover High

❑ 6 Ted Williams 25.00 12.50
Ted Turns Pro
Portrait
San Diego Padres
PCL League
uniform)

❑ 7 Ted Williams 15.00 7.50
From Mound to Plate
At plate
San Diego Padres, PCL

❑ 8 Ted Williams 15.00 7.50
1937 First Full Season
Making a leaping catch

❑ 9 Ted Williams 20.00 10.00
Eddie Collins
First Step to Majors

❑ 10 Ted Williams 15.00 7.50
Gunning as Pastime
Wearing hunting gear, taking aim

❑ 11 Ted Williams 40.00 20.00
Jimmie Foxx
First Spring Training

❑ 12 Ted Williams 20.00 10.00
Burning Up Minors
Pitching for Minneapolis
American Association

❑ 13 Ted Williams 15.00 7.50
1939 Shows Will Stay
Follow-through

❑ 14 Ted Williams 15.00 7.50
Outstanding Rookie '39
Follow-through

❑ 15 Ted Williams 20.00 10.00
Licks Sophomore Jinx
Sliding into third base
for a triple

❑ 16 Ted Williams 15.00 7.50
1941 Greatest Year
Follow-through at plate

❑ 17 Ted Williams 40.00 20.00
How Ted Hit .400
Youthful Williams
as he looked in '41

❑ 18 Ted Williams 20.00 10.00

1941 All Star Hero
Crossing plate
after home run

❑ 19 Ted Williams 15.00 7.50
Wins Triple Crown
Crossing plate at Fenway Park

❑ 20 Ted Williams 15.00 7.50
On to Naval Training
In training plane
at Amherst College

❑ 21 Ted Williams 15.00 7.50
Honors for Williams
Receiving 1942 Sporting News POY

❑ 22 Ted Williams 15.00 7.50
1944 Ted Solos
In cockpit at
Pensacola, FL Navy Air Station

❑ 23 Ted Williams 15.00 7.50
Williams Wins Wings
Wearing Naval
Aviation Cadet uniform

❑ 24 Ted Williams 15.00 7.50
1945 Sharpshooter
Taking Naval eye test

❑ 25 Ted Williams 15.00 7.50
1945 Ted Discharged
In cockpit, giving
the thumbs up

❑ 26 Ted Williams 15.00 7.50
Off to Flying Start
In batters box
spring training, 1946

❑ 27 Ted Williams 15.00 7.50
7/9/46 One Man Show
Riding blooper pitch out of park

❑ 28 Ted Williams 15.00 7.50
The Williams Shift
Diagram of Cleveland Indians
position shift to defense Williams

❑ 29 Ted Williams 20.00 10.00
Ted Hits for Cycle
Close-up of follow through

❑ 30 Ted Williams 15.00 7.50
Beating Williams Shift
Crossing plate after home run

❑ 31 Ted Williams 20.00 10.00
Sox Lose Series
Sliding across plate
Sept. 14, 1946

❑ 32 Ted Williams 15.00 7.50
Joseph Cashman
Most Valuable Player
Receiving MVP Award

❑ 33 Ted Williams 15.00 7.50
Another Triple Crown
Famous Williams' Grip

❑ 34 Ted Williams 15.00 7.50
Runs Scored Record
Sliding into 2nd base
in 1947 AS Game

❑ 35 Ted Williams 15.00 7.50
Sox Miss Pennant
Checking weight on
new 36 oz. hickory bat

❑ 36 Ted Williams 15.00 7.50
Banner Year for Ted
Bunting down the
3rd base line

❑ 37 Ted Williams 15.00 7.50
1949 Sox Miss Again
Two moods: grim and determined
smiling and happy

❑ 38 Ted Williams 15.00 7.50
1949 Power Rampage
Full shot of his
batting follow through

❑ 39 Ted Williams 25.00 12.50
Joe Cronin
Eddie Collins
1950 Great Start
Signing $125,000 contract

❑ 40 Ted Williams 15.00 7.50
Ted Crashes into Wall
Making catch in
1950 All Star game
and crashing into wall

❑ 41 Ted Williams 15.00 7.50
1950 Ted Recovers
Recuperating from elbow operation
in hospital

❑ 42 Ted Williams 15.00 7.50
Tom Yawkey
Slowed by Injury

❑ 43 Ted Williams 15.00 7.50
Double Play Lead
Leaping high to
make great catch

❑ 44 Ted Williams 15.00 7.50
Back to Marines
Hanging up number 9
prior to leaving for Marines

❑ 45 Ted Williams 15.00 7.50
Farewell to Baseball
Honored at Fenway Park
prior to return to service

❑ 46 Ted Williams 15.00 7.50
Ready for Combat
Drawing jet pilot equipment
in Willow Grove

❑ 47 Ted Williams 15.00 7.50
Ted Crash Lands Jet
In flying gear
and jet he crash landed in

❑ 48 Ted Williams 20.00 10.00
Ford Frick
1953 Ted Returns
Throwing out 1st ball
at All-Star Game in Cincinnati

❑ 49 Ted Williams 15.00 7.50
Smash Return
Giving his arm
whirlpool treatment

❑ 50 Ted Williams 25.00 12.50
1954 Spring Injury
Full batting pose at plate

❑ 51 Ted Williams 15.00 7.50
Ted is Patched Up
In first workout after
fractured collar bone

❑ 52 Ted Williams 20.00 10.00
1954 Ted's Comeback
Hitting a home run
against Detroit

❑ 53 Ted Williams 15.00 7.50
Comeback is Success
Beating catcher's
tag at home plate

❑ 54 Ted Williams 15.00 7.50
Ted Hooks Big One
With prize catch
1235 lb. black marlin

❑ 55 Ted Williams 20.00 10.00
Joe Cronin
Retirement "No Go"
Returning from retirement

❑ 56 Ted Williams 15.00 7.50
2,000th Hit
8/11/55

❑ 57 Ted Williams 20.00 10.00
400th Homer
In locker room

❑ 58 Ted Williams 15.00 7.50
Williams Hits .388
Four-picture sequence
of his batting swing

❑ 59 Ted Williams 15.00 7.50
Hot September for Ted
Full shot of follow through
at plate

❑ 60 Ted Williams 15.00 7.50
More Records for Ted
Swinging and missing

❑ 61 Ted Williams 20.00 10.00
1957 Outfielder
Warming up prior
to ball game

❑ 62 Ted Williams 15.00 7.50
1958 Sixth Batting Title
Slamming pitch into stands

❑ 63 Ted Williams 80.00 40.00
Ted's All-Star Record
Portrait and facsimile autograph

❑ 64 Ted Williams 15.00 7.50
Barbara Williams
Daughter and Daddy
In uniform holding his daughter

❑ 65 Ted Williams 20.00 10.00
1958 August 30
Determination on face
connecting with ball

❑ 66 Ted Williams 15.00 7.50
1958 Powerhouse
Stance and follow through
in batters box

❑ 67 Ted Williams 40.00 20.00
Sam Snead
Two Famous Fishermen
testing fishing equipment

❑ 68 Ted Williams 700.00 350.00
Bucky Harris
Ted Signs for 1959 SP
signing contract

❑ 69 Ted Williams 15.00 7.50
A Future Ted Williams
With eager, young newcomer

❑ 70 Ted Williams 40.00 20.00
Jim Thorpe
at Sportsmen's Show

❑ 71 Ted Williams 15.00 7.50
Hitting Fund. 1
Proper gripping of
a baseball bat

❑ 72 Ted Williams 15.00 7.50
Hitting Fund. 2
Checking his swing

❑ 73 Ted Williams 15.00 7.50
Hitting Fund. 3
Stance and follow-through

❑ 74 Ted Williams 15.00 7.50
Here's How
Demonstrating in locker room
an aspect of hitting

❑ 75 Ted Williams 50.00 25.00
Eddie Collins
Babe Ruth
Williams' Value to Sox

❑ 76 Ted Williams 15.00 7.50
On Base Record
Awaiting intentional walk
to first base

❑ 77 Ted Williams 15.00 7.50
Ted Relaxes
Displaying bonefish
which he caught

❑ 78 Ted Williams 15.00 7.50
Rep. Joe Martin
Justice Earl Warren
Honors for Williams
Clark Griffith Memorial Award

❑ 79 Ted Williams 25.00 12.50
Where Ted Stands
Wielding giant eight foot bat
when honored as modern-day Paul
Bunyan

❑ 80 Ted Williams 40.00 20.00
Ted's Goals for 1959
Admiring his portrait

1963 Fleer

	NM	Ex
COMPLETE SET (67)	1500.00	800.00
WRAPPER (5-CENT)	100.00	40.00
❑ 1 Steve Barber	25.00	7.50
❑ 2 Ron Hansen	15.00	6.00
❑ 3 Milt Pappas	20.00	8.00
❑ 4 Brooks Robinson	100.00	40.00
❑ 5 Willie Mays	175.00	70.00
❑ 6 Lou Clinton	15.00	6.00
❑ 7 Bill Monbouquette	15.00	6.00
❑ 8 Carl Yastrzemski	100.00	40.00
❑ 9 Ray Herbert	15.00	6.00
❑ 10 Jim Landis	15.00	6.00
❑ 11 Dick Donovan	15.00	6.00
❑ 12 Tito Francona	15.00	6.00
❑ 13 Jerry Kindall	15.00	6.00
❑ 14 Frank Lary	20.00	8.00
❑ 15 Dick Howser	20.00	8.00
❑ 16 Jerry Lumpe	15.00	6.00
❑ 17 Norm Siebern	15.00	6.00
❑ 18 Don Lee	15.00	6.00
❑ 19 Albie Pearson	20.00	8.00
❑ 20 Bob Rodgers	20.00	8.00
❑ 21 Leon Wagner	15.00	6.00
❑ 22 Jim Kaat	25.00	10.00
❑ 23 Vic Power	20.00	8.00
❑ 24 Rich Rollins	20.00	8.00
❑ 25 Bobby Richardson	25.00	10.00
❑ 26 Ralph Terry	20.00	8.00
❑ 27 Tom Cheney	15.00	6.00
❑ 28 Chuck Cottier	15.00	6.00
❑ 29 Jimmy Piersall	20.00	8.00
❑ 30 Dave Stenhouse	15.00	6.00
❑ 31 Glen Hobbie	15.00	6.00
❑ 32 Ron Santo	25.00	10.00
❑ 33 Gene Freese	15.00	6.00
❑ 34 Vada Pinson	25.00	10.00
❑ 35 Bob Purkey	15.00	6.00
❑ 36 Joe Amalfitano	15.00	6.00
❑ 37 Bob Aspromonte	15.00	6.00
❑ 38 Dick Farrell	15.00	6.00
❑ 39 Al Spangler	15.00	6.00
❑ 40 Tommy Davis	20.00	8.00
❑ 41 Don Drysdale	80.00	32.00
❑ 42 Sandy Koufax	200.00	80.00
❑ 43 Maury Wills RC	100.00	40.00
❑ 44 Frank Bolling	15.00	6.00
❑ 45 Warren Spahn	80.00	32.00
❑ 46 Joe Adcock SP	150.00	60.00
❑ 47 Roger Craig	20.00	8.00
❑ 48 Al Jackson	20.00	8.00
❑ 49 Rod Kanehl	20.00	8.00
❑ 50 Ruben Amaro	15.00	6.00
❑ 51 Johnny Callison	20.00	8.00
❑ 52 Clay Dalrymple	15.00	6.00
❑ 53 Don Demeter	15.00	6.00
❑ 54 Art Mahaffey	15.00	6.00
❑ 55 Smoky Burgess	20.00	8.00
❑ 56 Roberto Clemente	175.00	70.00
❑ 57 Roy Face	20.00	8.00
❑ 58 Vern Law	20.00	8.00
❑ 59 Bill Mazeroski	30.00	12.00
❑ 60 Ken Boyer	25.00	10.00
❑ 61 Bob Gibson	80.00	32.00
❑ 62 Gene Oliver	15.00	6.00
❑ 63 Bill White	20.00	8.00
❑ 64 Orlando Cepeda	30.00	12.00
❑ 65 Jim Davenport	15.00	6.00
❑ 66 Billy O'Dell	25.00	7.50
❑ NNO Checklist card	500.00	160.00

1981 Fleer

	Nm-Mt	Ex-Mt
COMPLETE SET (660)	40.00	16.00
❑ 1 Pete Rose UER 270 hits in 63 should be 170	3.00	1.20
❑ 2 Larry Bowa	.25	.10
❑ 3 Manny Trillo	.10	.04
❑ 4 Bob Boone	.25	.10
❑ 5 Mike Schmidt See also 640A	2.50	1.00
❑ 6 Steve Carlton P1 Golden Arm Back 1066 Cardinals Number on back 6	.50	.20
❑ 6B Steve Carlton P2 Pitcher of Year Back 1066 Cardinals	1.50	.60
❑ 6C Steve Carlton P3 1966 Cardinals	2.00	.80
❑ 7 Tug McGraw See 657A	.25	.10
❑ 8 Larry Christenson	.10	.04
❑ 9 Bake McBride	.25	.10
❑ 10 Greg Luzinski	.25	.10
❑ 11 Ron Reed	.10	.04
❑ 12 Dickie Noles	.10	.04
❑ 13 Keith Moreland	.10	.04
❑ 14 Bob Walk RC	.50	.20
❑ 15 Lonnie Smith	.25	.10
❑ 16 Dick Ruthven	.10	.04
❑ 17 Sparky Lyle	.25	.10
❑ 18 Greg Gross	.10	.04
❑ 19 Garry Maddox	.10	.04
❑ 20 Nino Espinosa	.10	.04
❑ 21 George Vukovich	.10	.04
❑ 22 John Vukovich	.10	.04
❑ 23 Ramon Aviles	.10	.04
❑ 24A Kevin Saucier P1 Name on back Ken	.10	.04
❑ 24B Kevin Saucier P2 Name on back Ken	.10	.04
❑ 24C Kevin Saucier P3 Name on back Kevin	.50	.20
❑ 25 Randy Lerch	.10	.04
❑ 26 Del Unser	.10	.04
❑ 27 Tim McCarver	.25	.10
❑ 28 George Brett See also 655A	2.50	1.00
❑ 29 Willie Wilson See also 653A	.25	.10
❑ 30 Paul Splittorff	.10	.04
❑ 31 Dan Quisenberry	.10	.04
❑ 32A Amos Otis P1 (Batting Pose Outfield 32 on back	.25	.10
❑ 32B Amos Otis P2 Series Starter 483 on back	.25	.10
❑ 33 Steve Busby	.10	.04
❑ 34 U.L. Washington	.10	.04
❑ 35 Dave Chalk	.10	.04
❑ 36 Darrell Porter	.10	.04
❑ 37 Marty Pattin	.10	.04
❑ 38 Larry Gura	.10	.04
❑ 39 Renie Martin	.10	.04
❑ 40 Rich Gale	.10	.04
❑ 41A Hal McRae P1 (Royals on front in black letters	.50	.20
❑ 41B Hal McRae P2 (Royals on front in blue letters	.25	.10
❑ 42 Dennis Leonard	.10	.04
❑ 43 Willie Aikens	.10	.04
❑ 44 Frank White	.25	.10
❑ 45 Clint Hurdle	.10	.04
❑ 46 John Wathan	.10	.04
❑ 47 Pete LaCock	.10	.04
❑ 48 Rance Mulliniks	.10	.04
❑ 49 Jeff Twitty	.10	.04
❑ 50 Jamie Quirk	.10	.04
❑ 51 Art Howe	.10	.04
❑ 52 Ken Forsch	.10	.04
❑ 53 Vern Ruhle	.10	.04
❑ 54 Joe Niekro	.10	.04
❑ 55 Frank LaCorte	.10	.04
❑ 56 J.R. Richard	.25	.10
❑ 57 Nolan Ryan	5.00	2.00
❑ 58 Enos Cabell	.10	.04
❑ 59 Cesar Cedeno	.25	.10
❑ 60 Jose Cruz	.25	.10
❑ 61 Bill Virdon MG	.10	.04
❑ 62 Terry Puhl	.10	.04
❑ 63 Joaquin Andujar	.25	.10
❑ 64 Alan Ashby	.10	.04
❑ 65 Joe Sambito	.10	.04
❑ 66 Denny Walling	.10	.04
❑ 67 Jeff Leonard	.25	.10
❑ 68 Luis Pujols	.10	.04
❑ 69 Bruce Bochy	.10	.04
❑ 70 Rafael Landestoy	.10	.04
❑ 71 Dave Smith RC	.50	.20
❑ 72 Danny Heep	.10	.04
❑ 73 Julio Gonzalez	.10	.04
❑ 74 Craig Reynolds	.10	.04
❑ 75 Gary Woods	.10	.04
❑ 76 Dave Bergman	.10	.04
❑ 77 Randy Niemann	.10	.04
❑ 78 Joe Morgan	.50	.20
❑ 79 Reggie Jackson See also 650A	1.00	.40
❑ 80 Bucky Dent	.25	.10
❑ 81 Tommy John	.25	.10
❑ 82 Luis Tiant	.25	.10
❑ 83 Rick Cerone	.10	.04
❑ 84 Dick Howser MG	.10	.04
❑ 85 Lou Piniella	.25	.10
❑ 86 Ron Davis	.10	.04
❑ 87A Graig Nettles ERR Name on back spelled Craig	5.00	2.00
❑ 87B Graig Nettles COR Graig	.25	.10
❑ 88 Ron Guidry	.25	.10
❑ 89 Rich Gossage	.25	.10
❑ 90 Rudy May	.10	.04
❑ 91 Gaylord Perry	.25	.10
❑ 92 Eric Soderholm	.10	.04
❑ 93 Bob Watson	.10	.04
❑ 94 Bobby Murcer	.25	.10
❑ 95 Bobby Brown	.10	.04
❑ 96 Jim Spencer	.10	.04
❑ 97 Tom Underwood	.10	.04
❑ 98 Oscar Gamble	.10	.04
❑ 99 Johnny Oates	.25	.10
❑ 100 Fred Stanley	.10	.04
❑ 101 Ruppert Jones	.10	.04
❑ 102 Dennis Werth	.10	.04
❑ 103 Joe Lefebvre	.10	.04
❑ 104 Brian Doyle	.10	.04
❑ 105 Aurelio Rodriguez	.10	.04
❑ 106 Doug Bird	.10	.04
❑ 107 Mike Griffin RC	.15	.06
❑ 108 Tim Lollar	.10	.04
❑ 109 Willie Randolph	.25	.10
❑ 110 Steve Garvey	.50	.20
❑ 111 Reggie Smith	.25	.10
❑ 112 Don Sutton	.25	.10
❑ 113 Burt Hooton	.10	.04
❑ 114A Dave Lopes P1 Small hand on back	.50	.20
❑ 114B Dave Lopes P2 No hand	.25	.10
❑ 115 Dusty Baker	.25	.10
❑ 116 Tom Lasorda MG	.50	.20
❑ 117 Bill Russell	.25	.10
❑ 118 Jerry Reuss UER Home omitted	.10	.04
❑ 119 Terry Forster	.25	.10
❑ 120A Bob Welch P1 (Name on back is Bob	.25	.10
❑ 120B Bob Welch P2 Name on back is Robert	.25	.10
❑ 121 Don Stanhouse	.10	.04
❑ 122 Rick Monday	.25	.10
❑ 123 Derrel Thomas	.10	.04
❑ 124 Joe Ferguson	.10	.04
❑ 125 Rick Sutcliffe	.25	.10

❑ 126A Ron Cey P1 .25 .10
Small hand on back
❑ 126B Ron Cey P2 .25 .10
No hand
❑ 127 Dave Goltz .10 .04
❑ 128 Jay Johnstone .10 .04
❑ 129 Steve Yeager .25 .10
❑ 130 Gary Weiss .10 .04
❑ 131 Mike Scioscia RC 1.50 .60
❑ 132 Vic Davalillo .10 .04
❑ 133 Doug Rau .10 .04
❑ 134 Pepe Frias .10 .04
❑ 135 Mickey Hatcher .10 .04
❑ 136 Steve Howe RC .50 .20
❑ 137 Robert Castillo .10 .04
❑ 138 Gary Thomasson .10 .04
❑ 139 Rudy Law .10 .04
❑ 140 F.Valenzuela RC UER 2.00 .80
Misspelled Fernand on card
❑ 141 Manny Mota .25 .10
❑ 142 Gary Carter .50 .20
❑ 143 Steve Rogers .25 .10
❑ 144 Warren Cromartie .10 .04
❑ 145 Andre Dawson .50 .20
❑ 146 Larry Parrish .10 .04
❑ 147 Rowland Office .10 .04
❑ 148 Ellis Valentine .10 .04
❑ 149 Dick Williams MG .10 .04
❑ 150 Bill Gullickson RC .50 .20
❑ 151 Elias Sosa .10 .04
❑ 152 John Tamargo .10 .04
❑ 153 Chris Speier .10 .04
❑ 154 Ron LeFlore .25 .10
❑ 155 Rodney Scott .10 .04
❑ 156 Stan Bahnsen .10 .04
❑ 157 Bill Lee .25 .10
❑ 158 Fred Norman .10 .04
❑ 159 Woodie Fryman .10 .04
❑ 160 David Palmer .10 .04
❑ 161 Jerry White .10 .04
❑ 162 Roberto Ramos .10 .04
❑ 163 John D'Acquisto .10 .04
❑ 164 Tommy Hutton .10 .04
❑ 165 Charlie Lea .10 .04
❑ 166 Scott Sanderson .10 .04
❑ 167 Ken Macha .10 .04
❑ 168 Tony Bernazard .10 .04
❑ 169 Jim Palmer .50 .20
❑ 170 Steve Stone .10 .04
❑ 171 Mike Flanagan .10 .04
❑ 172 Al Bumbry .10 .04
❑ 173 Doug DeCinces .10 .04
❑ 174 Scott McGregor .10 .04
❑ 175 Mark Belanger .10 .04
❑ 176 Tim Stoddard .10 .04
❑ 177A Rick Dempsey P1 .25 .10
Small hand on front
❑ 177B Rick Dempsey P2 .10 .04
No hand
❑ 178 Earl Weaver MG .25 .10
❑ 179 Tippy Martinez .10 .04
❑ 180 Dennis Martinez .25 .10
❑ 181 Sammy Stewart .10 .04
❑ 182 Rich Dauer .10 .04
❑ 183 Lee May .10 .04
❑ 184 Eddie Murray 1.50 .60
❑ 185 Benny Ayala .10 .04
❑ 186 John Lowenstein .10 .04
❑ 187 Gary Roenicke .10 .04
❑ 188 Ken Singleton .25 .10
❑ 189 Dan Graham .10 .04
❑ 190 Terry Crowley .10 .04
❑ 191 Kiko Garcia .10 .04
❑ 192 Dave Ford .10 .04
❑ 193 Mark Corey .10 .04
❑ 194 Lenn Sakata .10 .04
❑ 195 Doug DeCinces .10 .04
❑ 196 Johnny Bench 1.00 .40
❑ 197 Dave Concepcion .25 .10
❑ 198 Ray Knight .25 .10
❑ 199 Ken Griffey .25 .10
❑ 200 Tom Seaver 1.00 .40
❑ 201 Dave Collins .10 .04
❑ 202A George Foster P1 .50 .20
Slugger
Number on back 216
❑ 202B George Foster P2 .50 .20
Slugger
Number on back 202
❑ 203 Junior Kennedy .10 .04
❑ 204 Frank Pastore .10 .04
❑ 205 Dan Driessen .10 .04
❑ 206 Hector Cruz .10 .04
❑ 207 Paul Moskau .10 .04
❑ 208 Charlie Leibrandt RC .50 .20
❑ 209 Harry Spilman .10 .04
❑ 210 Joe Price .10 .04
❑ 211 Tom Hume .10 .04
❑ 212 Joe Nolan .10 .04
❑ 213 Doug Bair .10 .04
❑ 214 Mario Soto .25 .10
❑ 215A Bill Bonham P1 .50 .20
(Small hand on back)
❑ 215B Bill Bonham P2 .10 .04
(No hand)
❑ 216 George Foster .25 .10
(See 202)
❑ 217 Paul Householder .10 .04
❑ 218 Ron Oester .10 .04
❑ 219 Sam Mejias .10 .04
❑ 220 Sheldon Burnside .10 .04
❑ 221 Carl Yastrzemski 1.50 .60
❑ 222 Jim Rice .25 .10
❑ 223 Fred Lynn .25 .10
❑ 224 Carlton Fisk .50 .20
❑ 225 Rick Burleson .10 .04
❑ 226 Dennis Eckersley .50 .20
❑ 227 Butch Hobson .10 .04
❑ 228 Tom Burgmeier .10 .04
❑ 229 Garry Hancock .10 .04
❑ 230 Don Zimmer MG .25 .10
❑ 231 Steve Renko .10 .04
❑ 232 Dwight Evans .50 .20
❑ 233 Mike Torrez .10 .04
❑ 234 Bob Stanley .10 .04
❑ 235 Jim Dwyer .10 .04
❑ 236 Dave Stapleton .10 .04
❑ 237 Glenn Hoffman .10 .04
❑ 238 Jerry Remy .10 .04
❑ 239 Dick Drago .10 .04
❑ 240 Bill Campbell .10 .04
❑ 241 Tony Perez .50 .20
❑ 242 Phil Niekro .25 .10
❑ 243 Dale Murphy .50 .20
❑ 244 Bob Horner .25 .10
❑ 245 Jeff Burroughs .25 .10
❑ 246 Rick Camp .10 .04
❑ 247 Bobby Cox MG .25 .10
❑ 248 Bruce Benedict .10 .04
❑ 249 Gene Garber .10 .04
❑ 250 Jerry Royster .10 .04
❑ 251A Gary Matthews P1 .50 .20
Small hand on back
❑ 251B Gary Matthews P2 .25 .10
No hand
❑ 252 Chris Chambliss .25 .10
❑ 253 Luis Gomez .10 .04
❑ 254 Bill Nahorodny .10 .04
❑ 255 Doyle Alexander .10 .04
❑ 256 Brian Asselstine .10 .04
❑ 257 Biff Pocoroba .10 .04
❑ 258 Mike Lum .10 .04
❑ 259 Charlie Spikes .10 .04
❑ 260 Glenn Hubbard .10 .04
❑ 261 Tommy Boggs .10 .04
❑ 262 Al Hrabosky UER .25 .10
Card lists him as 5' 1"
❑ 263 Rick Matula .10 .04
❑ 264 Preston Hanna .10 .04
❑ 265 Larry Bradford .10 .04
❑ 266 Rafael Ramirez .10 .04
❑ 267 Larry McWilliams .10 .04
❑ 268 Rod Carew .50 .20
❑ 269 Bobby Grich .25 .10
❑ 270 Carney Lansford .25 .10
❑ 271 Don Baylor .25 .10
❑ 272 Joe Rudi .25 .10
❑ 273 Dan Ford .10 .04
❑ 274 Jim Fregosi MG .10 .04
❑ 275 Dave Frost .10 .04
❑ 276 Frank Tanana .25 .10
❑ 277 Dickie Thon .10 .04
❑ 278 Jason Thompson .10 .04
❑ 279 Rick Miller .10 .04
❑ 280 Bert Campaneris .25 .10
❑ 281 Tom Donohue .10 .04
❑ 282 Brian Downing .25 .10
❑ 283 Fred Patek .10 .04
❑ 284 Bruce Kison .10 .04
❑ 285 Dave LaRoche .10 .04
❑ 286 Don Aase .10 .04
❑ 287 Jim Barr .10 .04
❑ 288 Alfredo Martinez .10 .04
❑ 289 Larry Harlow .10 .04
❑ 290 Andy Hassler .10 .04
❑ 291 Dave Kingman .25 .10
❑ 292 Bill Buckner .25 .10
❑ 293 Rick Reuschel .25 .10
❑ 294 Bruce Sutter .25 .10
❑ 295 Jerry Martin .10 .04
❑ 296 Scot Thompson .10 .04
❑ 297 Ivan DeJesus .10 .04
❑ 298 Steve Dillard .10 .04
❑ 299 Dick Tidrow .10 .04
❑ 300 Randy Martz .10 .04
❑ 301 Lenny Randle .10 .04
❑ 302 Lynn McGlothen .10 .04
❑ 303 Cliff Johnson .10 .04
❑ 304 Tim Blackwell .10 .04
❑ 305 Dennis Lamp .10 .04
❑ 306 Bill Caudill .10 .04
❑ 307 Carlos Lezcano .10 .04
❑ 308 Jim Tracy RC 1.00 .40
❑ 309 Doug Capilla UER .10 .04
Cubs on front but
Braves on back
❑ 310 Willie Hernandez .10 .04
❑ 311 Mike Vail .10 .04
❑ 312 Mike Krukow .10 .04
❑ 313 Barry Foote .10 .04
❑ 314 Larry Biittner .10 .04
❑ 315 Mike Tyson .10 .04
❑ 316 Lee Mazzilli .25 .10
❑ 317 John Stearns .10 .04
❑ 318 Alex Trevino .10 .04
❑ 319 Craig Swan .10 .04
❑ 320 Frank Taveras .10 .04
❑ 321 Steve Henderson .10 .04
❑ 322 Neil Allen .10 .04
❑ 323 Mark Bomback .10 .04
❑ 324 Mike Jorgensen .10 .04
❑ 325 Joe Torre MG .50 .20
❑ 326 Elliott Maddox .10 .04
❑ 327 Pete Falcone .10 .04
❑ 328 Ray Burris .10 .04
❑ 329 Claudell Washington .10 .04
❑ 330 Doug Flynn .10 .04
❑ 331 Joel Youngblood .10 .04
❑ 332 Bill Almon .10 .04
❑ 333 Tom Hausman .10 .04
❑ 334 Pat Zachry .10 .04
❑ 335 Jeff Reardon RC 1.00 .40
❑ 336 Wally Backman RC .50 .20
❑ 337 Dan Norman .10 .04
❑ 338 Jerry Morales .10 .04
❑ 339 Ed Farmer .10 .04
❑ 340 Bob Molinaro .10 .04
❑ 341 Todd Cruz .10 .04
❑ 342A Britt Burns P1 .50 .20
Small hand on front
❑ 342B Britt Burns P2 .25 .10
No hand
❑ 343 Kevin Bell .10 .04
❑ 344 Tony LaRussa MG .25 .10
❑ 345 Steve Trout .10 .04
❑ 346 Harold Baines RC 3.00 1.20
❑ 347 Richard Wortham .10 .04
❑ 348 Wayne Nordhagen .10 .04
❑ 349 Mike Squires .10 .04
❑ 350 Lamar Johnson .10 .04
❑ 351 Rickey Henderson 3.00 1.20
Most Stolen Bases AL
❑ 352 Francisco Barrios .10 .04
❑ 353 Thad Bosley .10 .04
❑ 354 Chet Lemon .25 .10
❑ 355 Bruce Kimm .10 .04
❑ 356 Richard Dotson .10 .04
❑ 357 Jim Morrison .10 .04

Card	Player	Price	Price
❑ 358	Mike Proly	.10	.04
❑ 359	Greg Pryor	.10	.04
❑ 360	Dave Parker	.25	.10
❑ 361	Omar Moreno	.10	.04
❑ 362A	Kent Tekulve P1 Back 1071 Waterbury and 1078 Pirates	.10	.04
❑ 362B	Kent Tekulve P2 1971 Waterbury and 1978 Pirates	.10	.04
❑ 363	Willie Stargell	.50	.20
❑ 364	Phil Garner	.25	.10
❑ 365	Ed Ott	.10	.04
❑ 366	Don Robinson	.10	.04
❑ 367	Chuck Tanner MG	.10	.04
❑ 368	Jim Rooker	.10	.04
❑ 369	Dale Berra	.10	.04
❑ 370	Jim Bibby	.10	.04
❑ 371	Steve Nicosia	.10	.04
❑ 372	Mike Easler	.10	.04
❑ 373	Bill Robinson	.10	.04
❑ 374	Lee Lacy	.10	.04
❑ 375	John Candelaria	.25	.10
❑ 376	Manny Sanguillen	.25	.10
❑ 377	Rick Rhoden	.10	.04
❑ 378	Grant Jackson	.10	.04
❑ 379	Tim Foli	.10	.04
❑ 380	Rod Scurry	.10	.04
❑ 381	Bill Madlock	.25	.10
❑ 382A	Kurt Bevacqua P1 ERR P on cap backwards	.25	.10
❑ 382B	Kurt Bevacqua P2 COR	.10	.04
❑ 383	Bert Blyleven	.25	.10
❑ 384	Eddie Solomon	.10	.04
❑ 385	Enrique Romo	.10	.04
❑ 386	John Milner	.10	.04
❑ 387	Mike Hargrove	.10	.04
❑ 388	Jorge Orta	.10	.04
❑ 389	Toby Harrah	.25	.10
❑ 390	Tom Veryzer	.10	.04
❑ 391	Miguel Dilone	.10	.04
❑ 392	Dan Spillner	.10	.04
❑ 393	Jack Brohamer	.10	.04
❑ 394	Wayne Garland	.10	.04
❑ 395	Sid Monge	.10	.04
❑ 396	Rick Waits	.10	.04
❑ 397	Joe Charboneau RC	1.00	.40
❑ 398	Gary Alexander	.10	.04
❑ 399	Jerry Dybzinski	.10	.04
❑ 400	Mike Stanton	.10	.04
❑ 401	Mike Paxton	.10	.04
❑ 402	Gary Gray	.10	.04
❑ 403	Rick Manning	.10	.04
❑ 404	Bo Diaz	.10	.04
❑ 405	Ron Hassey	.10	.04
❑ 406	Ross Grimsley	.10	.04
❑ 407	Victor Cruz	.10	.04
❑ 408	Len Barker	.25	.10
❑ 409	Bob Bailor	.10	.04
❑ 410	Otto Velez	.10	.04
❑ 411	Ernie Whitt	.10	.04
❑ 412	Jim Clancy	.10	.04
❑ 413	Barry Bonnell	.10	.04
❑ 414	Dave Stieb	.25	.10
❑ 415	Damaso Garcia	.10	.04
❑ 416	John Mayberry	.10	.04
❑ 417	Roy Howell	.10	.04
❑ 418	Danny Ainge RC	1.50	.60
❑ 419A	Jesse Jefferson P1 Back says Pirates	.10	.04
❑ 419B	Jesse Jefferson P2 Back says Pirates	.10	.04
❑ 419C	Jesse Jefferson P3 Back says Blue Jays	.50	.20
❑ 420	Joey McLaughlin	.10	.04
❑ 421	Lloyd Moseby RC	.50	.20
❑ 422	Alvis Woods	.10	.04
❑ 423	Garth Iorg	.10	.04
❑ 424	Doug Ault	.10	.04
❑ 425	Ken Schrom	.10	.04
❑ 426	Mike Willis	.10	.04
❑ 427	Steve Braun	.10	.04
❑ 428	Bob Davis	.10	.04
❑ 429	Jerry Garvin	.10	.04
❑ 430	Alfredo Griffin	.10	.04
❑ 431	Bob Mattick MG	.10	.04
❑ 432	Vida Blue	.25	.10
❑ 433	Jack Clark	.25	.10
❑ 434	Willie McCovey	.50	.20
❑ 435	Mike Ivie	.10	.04
❑ 436A	Darrel Evans P1 ERR (Name on front Darrel	.50	.20
❑ 436B	Darrell Evans P2 COR Name on front Darrell	.50	.20
❑ 437	Terry Whitfield	.10	.04
❑ 438	Rennie Stennett	.10	.04
❑ 439	John Montefusco	.10	.04
❑ 440	Jim Wohlford	.10	.04
❑ 441	Bill North	.10	.04
❑ 442	Milt May	.10	.04
❑ 443	Max Venable	.10	.04
❑ 444	Ed Whitson	.10	.04
❑ 445	Al Holland	.10	.04
❑ 446	Randy Moffitt	.10	.04
❑ 447	Bob Knepper	.10	.04
❑ 448	Gary Lavelle	.10	.04
❑ 449	Greg Minton	.10	.04
❑ 450	Johnnie LeMaster	.10	.04
❑ 451	Larry Herndon	.10	.04
❑ 452	Rich Murray	.10	.04
❑ 453	Joe Pettini	.10	.04
❑ 454	Allen Ripley	.10	.04
❑ 455	Dennis Littlejohn	.10	.04
❑ 456	Tom Griffin	.10	.04
❑ 457	Alan Hargesheimer	.10	.04
❑ 458	Joe Strain	.10	.04
❑ 459	Steve Kemp	.10	.04
❑ 460	Sparky Anderson MG	.25	.10
❑ 461	Alan Trammell	.50	.20
❑ 462	Mark Fidrych	.25	.10
❑ 463	Lou Whitaker	.50	.20
❑ 464	Dave Rozema	.10	.04
❑ 465	Milt Wilcox	.10	.04
❑ 466	Champ Summers	.10	.04
❑ 467	Lance Parrish	.25	.10
❑ 468	Dan Petry	.10	.04
❑ 469	Pat Underwood	.10	.04
❑ 470	Rick Peters	.10	.04
❑ 471	Al Cowens	.10	.04
❑ 472	John Wockenfuss	.10	.04
❑ 473	Tom Brookens	.10	.04
❑ 474	Richie Hebner	.10	.04
❑ 475	Jack Morris	.50	.20
❑ 476	Jim Lentine	.10	.04
❑ 477	Bruce Robbins	.10	.04
❑ 478	Mark Wagner	.10	.04
❑ 479	Tim Corcoran	.10	.04
❑ 480A	Stan Papi P1 Front as Pitcher	.25	.10
❑ 480B	Stan Papi P2 Front as Shortstop	.10	.04
❑ 481	Kirk Gibson RC	2.00	.80
❑ 482	Dan Schatzeder	.10	.04
❑ 483A	Amos Otis P1 See card 32	.25	.10
❑ 483B	Amos Otis P2 See card 32	.25	.10
❑ 484	Dave Winfield	.50	.20
❑ 485	Rollie Fingers	.25	.10
❑ 486	Gene Richards	.10	.04
❑ 487	Randy Jones	.10	.04
❑ 488	Ozzie Smith	3.00	1.20
❑ 489	Gene Tenace	.25	.10
❑ 490	Bill Fahey	.10	.04
❑ 491	John Curtis	.10	.04
❑ 492	Dave Cash	.10	.04
❑ 493A	Tim Flannery P1 Batting right	.25	.10
❑ 493B	Tim Flannery P2 Batting left	.10	.04
❑ 494	Jerry Mumphrey	.10	.04
❑ 495	Bob Shirley	.10	.04
❑ 496	Steve Mura	.10	.04
❑ 497	Eric Rasmussen	.10	.04
❑ 498	Broderick Perkins	.10	.04
❑ 499	Barry Evans	.10	.04
❑ 500	Chuck Baker	.10	.04
❑ 501	Luis Salazar RC	.50	.20
❑ 502	Gary Lucas	.10	.04
❑ 503	Mike Armstrong	.10	.04
❑ 504	Jerry Turner	.10	.04
❑ 505	Dennis Kinney	.10	.04
❑ 506	Willie Montanez UER Spelled Willy on card front	.10	.04
❑ 507	Gorman Thomas	.25	.10
❑ 508	Ben Oglivie	.25	.10
❑ 509	Larry Hisle	.10	.04
❑ 510	Sal Bando	.25	.10
❑ 511	Robin Yount	1.50	.60
❑ 512	Mike Caldwell	.10	.04
❑ 513	Sixto Lezcano	.10	.04
❑ 514A	Bill Travers P1 ERR Jerry Augustine with Augustine back	.25	.10
❑ 514B	Bill Travers P2 COR	.10	.04
❑ 515	Paul Molitor	1.00	.40
❑ 516	Moose Haas	.10	.04
❑ 517	Bill Castro	.10	.04
❑ 518	Jim Slaton	.10	.04
❑ 519	Lary Sorensen	.10	.04
❑ 520	Bob McClure	.10	.04
❑ 521	Charlie Moore	.10	.04
❑ 522	Jim Gantner	.10	.04
❑ 523	Reggie Cleveland	.10	.04
❑ 524	Don Money	.10	.04
❑ 525	Bill Travers	.10	.04
❑ 526	Buck Martinez	.10	.04
❑ 527	Dick Davis	.10	.04
❑ 528	Ted Simmons	.25	.10
❑ 529	Garry Templeton	.25	.10
❑ 530	Ken Reitz	.10	.04
❑ 531	Tony Scott	.10	.04
❑ 532	Ken Oberkfell	.10	.04
❑ 533	Bob Sykes	.10	.04
❑ 534	Keith Smith	.10	.04
❑ 535	John Littlefield	.10	.04
❑ 536	Jim Kaat	.25	.10
❑ 537	Bob Forsch	.10	.04
❑ 538	Mike Phillips	.10	.04
❑ 539	Terry Landrum	.10	.04
❑ 540	Leon Durham RC	.50	.20
❑ 541	Terry Kennedy	.10	.04
❑ 542	George Hendrick	.25	.10
❑ 543	Dane Iorg	.10	.04
❑ 544	Mark Littell	.10	.04
❑ 545	Keith Hernandez	.25	.10
❑ 546	Silvio Martinez	.10	.04
❑ 547A	Don Hood P1 ERR Pete Vuckovich with Vuckovich back	.25	.10
❑ 547B	Don Hood P2 COR	.10	.04
❑ 548	Bobby Bonds	.25	.10
❑ 549	Mike Ramsey RC	.15	.06
❑ 550	Tom Herr	.10	.04
❑ 551	Roy Smalley	.10	.04
❑ 552	Jerry Koosman	.25	.10
❑ 553	Ken Landreaux	.10	.04
❑ 554	John Castino	.10	.04
❑ 555	Doug Corbett	.10	.04
❑ 556	Bombo Rivera	.10	.04
❑ 557	Ron Jackson	.10	.04
❑ 558	Butch Wynegar	.10	.04
❑ 559	Hosken Powell	.10	.04
❑ 560	Pete Redfern	.10	.04
❑ 561	Roger Erickson	.10	.04
❑ 562	Glenn Adams	.10	.04
❑ 563	Rick Sofield	.10	.04
❑ 564	Geoff Zahn	.10	.04
❑ 565	Pete Mackanin	.10	.04
❑ 566	Mike Cubbage	.10	.04
❑ 567	Darrell Jackson	.10	.04
❑ 568	Dave Edwards	.10	.04
❑ 569	Rob Wilfong	.10	.04
❑ 570	Sal Butera	.10	.04
❑ 571	Jose Morales	.10	.04
❑ 572	Rick Langford	.10	.04
❑ 573	Mike Norris	.10	.04
❑ 574	Rickey Henderson	6.00	2.40
❑ 575	Tony Armas	.25	.10
❑ 576	Dave Revering	.10	.04
❑ 577	Jeff Newman	.10	.04
❑ 578	Bob Lacey	.10	.04
❑ 579	Brian Kingman	.10	.04
❑ 580	Mitchell Page	.10	.04
❑ 581	Billy Martin MG	.50	.20
❑ 582	Rob Picciolo	.10	.04

❑ 583 Mike Heath .10 .04
❑ 584 Mickey Klutts .10 .04
❑ 585 Orlando Gonzalez .10 .04
❑ 586 Mike Davis RC .50 .20
❑ 587 Wayne Gross .10 .04
❑ 588 Matt Keough .10 .04
❑ 589 Steve McCatty .10 .04
❑ 590 Dwayne Murphy .10 .04
❑ 591 Mario Guerrero .10 .04
❑ 592 Dave McKay .10 .04
❑ 593 Jim Essian .10 .04
❑ 594 Dave Heaverlo .10 .04
❑ 595 Maury Wills MG .25 .10
❑ 596 Juan Beniquez .10 .04
❑ 597 Rodney Craig .10 .04
❑ 598 Jim Anderson .10 .04
❑ 599 Floyd Bannister .10 .04
❑ 600 Bruce Bochte .10 .04
❑ 601 Julio Cruz .10 .04
❑ 602 Ted Cox .10 .04
❑ 603 Dan Meyer .10 .04
❑ 604 Larry Cox .10 .04
❑ 605 Bill Stein .10 .04
❑ 606 Steve Garvey .50 .20
Most Hits NL
❑ 607 Dave Roberts .10 .04
❑ 608 Leon Roberts .10 .04
❑ 609 Reggie Walton .10 .04
❑ 610 Dave Edler .10 .04
❑ 611 Larry Milbourne .10 .04
❑ 612 Kim Allen .10 .04
❑ 613 Mario Mendoza .10 .04
❑ 614 Tom Paciorek .10 .04
❑ 615 Glenn Abbott .10 .04
❑ 616 Joe Simpson .10 .04
❑ 617 Mickey Rivers .10 .04
❑ 618 Jim Kern .10 .04
❑ 619 Jim Sundberg .25 .10
❑ 620 Richie Zisk .10 .04
❑ 621 Jon Matlack .10 .04
❑ 622 Ferguson Jenkins .25 .10
❑ 623 Pat Corrales MG .10 .04
❑ 624 Ed Figueroa .10 .04
❑ 625 Buddy Bell .25 .10
❑ 626 Al Oliver .25 .10
❑ 627 Doc Medich .10 .04
❑ 628 Bump Wills .10 .04
❑ 629 Rusty Staub .25 .10
❑ 630 Pat Putnam .10 .04
❑ 631 John Grubb .10 .04
❑ 632 Danny Darwin .10 .04
❑ 633 Ken Clay .10 .04
❑ 634 Jim Norris .10 .04
❑ 635 John Butcher .10 .04
❑ 636 Dave Roberts .10 .04
❑ 637 Billy Sample .10 .04
❑ 638 Carl Yastrzemski 1.50 .60
❑ 639 Cecil Cooper .25 .10
❑ 640 Mike Schmidt P1 2.50 1.00
Portrait
Third Base
number on back 5
❑ 640B Mike Schmidt P2 2.50 1.00
1980 Home Run King
640 on back
❑ 641A CL: Phils/Royals P1 .25 .10
41 is Hal McRae
❑ 641B CL: Phils/Royals P2 .25 .10
41 is Hal McRae
Double Threat
❑ 642 CL: Astros/Yankees .10 .04
❑ 643 CL: Expos/Dodgers .10 .04
❑ 644A CL: Reds/Orioles P1 .25 .10
202 is George Foster
Joe Nolan pitcher
should be catcher
❑ 644B CL: Reds/Orioles P2 .25 .10
202 is Foster Slugger
Joe Nolan pitcher
should be catcher
❑ 645 Pete Rose 1.50 .60
Larry Bowa
Mike Schmidt
Triple Threat P1
No number on back
❑ 645B Pete Rose 2.50 1.00
Larry Bowa
Mike Schmidt
Triple Threat P2
Back numbered 645
❑ 646 CL: Braves/Red Sox .10 .04
❑ 647 CL: Cubs/Angels .10 .04
❑ 648 CL: Mets/White Sox .10 .04
❑ 649 CL: Indians/Pirates .10 .04
❑ 650 Reggie Jackson 1.00 .40
Mr. Baseball P1
Number on back 79
❑ 650B Reggie Jackson .50 .20
Mr. Baseball P2
Number on back 650
❑ 651 CL: Giants/Blue Jays .10 .04
❑ 652A CL:Tigers/Padres P1 .25 .10
483 is listed
❑ 652B CL:Tigers/Padres P2 .25 .10
483 is deleted
❑ 653A Willie Wilson P1 .25 .10
Most Hits Most Runs
Number on back 29
❑ 653B Willie Wilson P2 .25 .10
Most Hits Most Runs
Number on back 653
❑ 654A Checklist Brewers .25 .10
Cards P1
514 Jerry Augustine
547 Pete Vuckovich
❑ 654B Checklist Brewers .25 .10
Cards P2
514 Billy Travers
547 Don Hood
❑ 655 George Brett P1 2.50 1.00
.390 Average
Number on back 28
❑ 655B George Brett P2 2.50 1.00
.390 Average
Number on back 655
❑ 656 CL:Twins/Oakland A's .25 .10
❑ 657A Tug McGraw P1 .25 .10
Game Saver
Number on back 7
❑ 657B Tug McGraw P2 .25 .10
Game Saver
Number on back 657
❑ 658 CL: Rangers/Mariners .10 .04
❑ 659A Checklist P1 .10 .04
of Special Cards
Last lines on front
Wilson Most Hits
❑ 659B Checklist P2 .10 .04
of Special Cards
Last lines on front
Otis Series Starter
❑ 660 Steve Carlton P1 .50 .20
Golden Arm
(Number on back 660
Back 1066 Cardinals
❑ 660B Steve Carlton P2 2.00 .80
Golden Arm
1966 Cardinals

1982 Fleer

Tim Raines

	Nm-Mt	Ex-Mt
COMPLETE SET (660)	50.00	20.00

❑ 1 Dusty Baker .20 .08
❑ 2 Robert Castillo .10 .04
❑ 3 Ron Cey .20 .08
❑ 4 Terry Forster .20 .08
❑ 5 Steve Garvey .20 .08
❑ 6 Dave Goltz .10 .04
❑ 7 Pedro Guerrero .20 .08
❑ 8 Burt Hooton .10 .04
❑ 9 Steve Howe .10 .04
❑ 10 Jay Johnstone .10 .04
❑ 11 Ken Landreaux .10 .04
❑ 12 Dave Lopes .20 .08
❑ 13 Mike A. Marshall RC .50 .20
❑ 14 Bobby Mitchell .10 .04
❑ 15 Rick Monday .20 .08
❑ 16 Tom Niedenfuer RC .50 .20
❑ 17 Ted Power RC .15 .06
❑ 18 Jerry Reuss UER .10 .04
("Home:" omitted)
❑ 19 Ron Roenicke .10 .04
❑ 20 Bill Russell .20 .08
❑ 21 Steve Sax RC 1.00 .40
❑ 22 Mike Scioscia .20 .08
❑ 23 Reggie Smith .20 .08
❑ 24 Dave Stewart RC 1.50 .60
❑ 25 Rick Sutcliffe .20 .08
❑ 26 Derrel Thomas .10 .04
❑ 27 Fernando Valenzuela .75 .30
❑ 28 Bob Welch .20 .08
❑ 29 Steve Yeager .20 .08
❑ 30 Bobby Brown .10 .04
❑ 31 Rick Cerone .10 .04
❑ 32 Ron Davis .10 .04
❑ 33 Bucky Dent .20 .08
❑ 34 Barry Foote .10 .04
❑ 35 George Frazier .10 .04
❑ 36 Oscar Gamble .10 .04
❑ 37 Rich Gossage .20 .08
❑ 38 Ron Guidry .20 .08
❑ 39 Reggie Jackson .40 .16
❑ 40 Tommy John .20 .08
❑ 41 Rudy May .10 .04
❑ 42 Larry Milbourne .10 .04
❑ 43 Jerry Mumphrey .10 .04
❑ 44 Bobby Murcer .20 .08
❑ 45 Gene Nelson .10 .04
❑ 46 Graig Nettles .20 .08
❑ 47 Johnny Oates .20 .08
❑ 48 Lou Piniella .20 .08
❑ 49 Willie Randolph .20 .08
❑ 50 Rick Reuschel .20 .08
❑ 51 Dave Revering .10 .04
❑ 52 Dave Righetti RC 1.50 .60
❑ 53 Aurelio Rodriguez .10 .04
❑ 54 Bob Watson .10 .04
❑ 55 Dennis Werth .10 .04
❑ 56 Dave Winfield .20 .08
❑ 57 Johnny Bench .75 .30
❑ 58 Bruce Berenyi .10 .04
❑ 59 Larry Biittner .10 .04
❑ 60 Scott Brown .10 .04
❑ 61 Dave Collins .10 .04
❑ 62 Geoff Combe .10 .04
❑ 63 Dave Concepcion .20 .08
❑ 64 Dan Driessen .10 .04
❑ 65 Joe Edelen .10 .04
❑ 66 George Foster .20 .08
❑ 67 Ken Griffey .20 .08
❑ 68 Paul Householder .10 .04
❑ 69 Tom Hume .10 .04
❑ 70 Junior Kennedy .10 .04
❑ 71 Ray Knight .20 .08
❑ 72 Mike LaCoss .10 .04
❑ 73 Rafael Landestoy .10 .04
❑ 74 Charlie Leibrandt .10 .04
❑ 75 Sam Mejias .10 .04
❑ 76 Paul Moskau .10 .04
❑ 77 Joe Nolan .10 .04
❑ 78 Mike O'Berry .10 .04
❑ 79 Ron Oester .10 .04
❑ 80 Frank Pastore .10 .04
❑ 81 Joe Price .10 .04
❑ 82 Tom Seaver .75 .30
❑ 83 Mario Soto .20 .08
❑ 84 Mike Vail .10 .04
❑ 85 Tony Armas .20 .08

❑ 86 Shooty Babitt .10 .04
❑ 87 Dave Beard .10 .04
❑ 88 Rick Bosetti .10 .04
❑ 89 Keith Drumwright .10 .04
❑ 90 Wayne Gross .10 .04
❑ 91 Mike Heath .10 .04
❑ 92 Rickey Henderson 2.50 1.00
❑ 93 Cliff Johnson .10 .04
❑ 94 Jeff Jones .10 .04
❑ 95 Matt Keough .10 .04
❑ 96 Brian Kingman .10 .04
❑ 97 Mickey Klutts .10 .04
❑ 98 Rick Langford .10 .04
❑ 99 Steve McCatty .10 .04
❑ 100 Dave McKay .10 .04
❑ 101 Dwayne Murphy .10 .04
❑ 102 Jeff Newman .10 .04
❑ 103 Mike Norris .10 .04
❑ 104 Bob Owchinko .10 .04
❑ 105 Mitchell Page .10 .04
❑ 106 Rob Picciolo .10 .04
❑ 107 Jim Spencer .10 .04
❑ 108 Fred Stanley .10 .04
❑ 109 Tom Underwood .10 .04
❑ 110 Joaquin Andujar .20 .08
❑ 111 Steve Braun .10 .04
❑ 112 Bob Forsch .10 .04
❑ 113 George Hendrick .20 .08
❑ 114 Keith Hernandez .20 .08
❑ 115 Tom Herr .10 .04
❑ 116 Dane Iorg .10 .04
❑ 117 Jim Kaat .20 .08
❑ 118 Tito Landrum .10 .04
❑ 119 Sixto Lezcano .10 .04
❑ 120 Mark Littell .10 .04
❑ 121 John Martin RC .15 .06
❑ 122 Silvio Martinez .10 .04
❑ 123 Ken Oberkfell .10 .04
❑ 124 Darrell Porter .10 .04
❑ 125 Mike Ramsey .10 .04
❑ 126 Orlando Sanchez .10 .04
❑ 127 Bob Shirley .10 .04
❑ 128 Lary Sorensen .10 .04
❑ 129 Bruce Sutter .20 .08
❑ 130 Bob Sykes .10 .04
❑ 131 Garry Templeton .20 .08
❑ 132 Gene Tenace .20 .08
❑ 133 Jerry Augustine .10 .04
❑ 134 Sal Bando .20 .08
❑ 135 Mark Brouhard .10 .04
❑ 136 Mike Caldwell .10 .04
❑ 137 Reggie Cleveland .10 .04
❑ 138 Cecil Cooper .20 .08
❑ 139 Jamie Easterly .10 .04
❑ 140 Marshall Edwards .10 .04
❑ 141 Rollie Fingers .20 .08
❑ 142 Jim Gantner .10 .04
❑ 143 Moose Haas .10 .04
❑ 144 Larry Hisle .10 .04
❑ 145 Roy Howell .10 .04
❑ 146 Rickey Keeton .10 .04
❑ 147 Randy Lerch .10 .04
❑ 148 Paul Molitor .40 .16
❑ 149 Don Money .10 .04
❑ 150 Charlie Moore .10 .04
❑ 151 Ben Oglivie .20 .08
❑ 152 Ted Simmons .20 .08
❑ 153 Jim Slaton .10 .04
❑ 154 Gorman Thomas .20 .08
❑ 155 Robin Yount 1.25 .50
❑ 156 Pete Vuckovich .10 .04
(Should precede Yount in the team order)
❑ 157 Benny Ayala .10 .04
❑ 158 Mark Belanger .10 .04
❑ 159 Al Bumbry .10 .04
❑ 160 Terry Crowley .10 .04
❑ 161 Rich Dauer .10 .04
❑ 162 Doug DeCinces .10 .04
❑ 163 Rick Dempsey .10 .04
❑ 164 Jim Dwyer .10 .04
❑ 165 Mike Flanagan .10 .04
❑ 166 Dave Ford .10 .04
❑ 167 Dan Graham .10 .04
❑ 168 Wayne Krenchicki .10 .04
❑ 169 John Lowenstein .10 .04
❑ 170 Dennis Martinez .20 .08
❑ 171 Tippy Martinez .10 .04
❑ 172 Scott McGregor .10 .04
❑ 173 Jose Morales .10 .04
❑ 174 Eddie Murray .75 .30
❑ 175 Jim Palmer .20 .08
❑ 176 Cal Ripken RC 40.00 16.00
Fleer Ripken cards from 1982 through 1993 erroneously have 22 games played in 1981;not 23.
❑ 177 Gary Roenicke .10 .04
❑ 178 Lenn Sakata .10 .04
❑ 179 Ken Singleton .20 .08
❑ 180 Sammy Stewart .10 .04
❑ 181 Tim Stoddard .10 .04
❑ 182 Steve Stone .10 .04
❑ 183 Stan Bahnsen .10 .04
❑ 184 Ray Burris .10 .04
❑ 185 Gary Carter .20 .08
❑ 186 Warren Cromartie .10 .04
❑ 187 Andre Dawson .20 .08
❑ 188 Terry Francona RC 1.50 .60
❑ 189 Woodie Fryman .10 .04
❑ 190 Bill Gullickson .10 .04
❑ 191 Grant Jackson .10 .04
❑ 192 Wallace Johnson .10 .04
❑ 193 Charlie Lea .10 .04
❑ 194 Bill Lee .20 .08
❑ 195 Jerry Manuel .10 .04
❑ 196 Brad Mills .10 .04
❑ 197 John Milner .10 .04
❑ 198 Rowland Office .10 .04
❑ 199 David Palmer .10 .04
❑ 200 Larry Parrish .10 .04
❑ 201 Mike Phillips .10 .04
❑ 202 Tim Raines .40 .16
❑ 203 Bobby Ramos .10 .04
❑ 204 Jeff Reardon .20 .08
❑ 205 Steve Rogers .20 .08
❑ 206 Scott Sanderson .10 .04
❑ 207 Rodney Scott UER .40 .16
(Photo actually Tim Raines)
❑ 208 Elias Sosa .10 .04
❑ 209 Chris Speier .10 .04
❑ 210 Tim Wallach RC 1.00 .40
❑ 211 Jerry White .10 .04
❑ 212 Alan Ashby .10 .04
❑ 213 Cesar Cedeno .20 .08
❑ 214 Jose Cruz .20 .08
❑ 215 Kiko Garcia .10 .04
❑ 216 Phil Garner .20 .08
❑ 217 Danny Heep .10 .04
❑ 218 Art Howe .10 .04
❑ 219 Bob Knepper .10 .04
❑ 220 Frank LaCorte .10 .04
❑ 221 Joe Niekro .10 .04
❑ 222 Joe Pittman .10 .04
❑ 223 Terry Puhl .10 .04
❑ 224 Luis Pujols .10 .04
❑ 225 Craig Reynolds .10 .04
❑ 226 J.R. Richard .20 .08
❑ 227 Dave Roberts .10 .04
❑ 228 Vern Ruhle .10 .04
❑ 229 Nolan Ryan 4.00 1.60
❑ 230 Joe Sambito .10 .04
❑ 231 Tony Scott .10 .04
❑ 232 Dave Smith .10 .04
❑ 233 Harry Spilman .10 .04
❑ 234 Don Sutton .20 .08
❑ 235 Dickie Thon .10 .04
❑ 236 Denny Walling .10 .04
❑ 237 Gary Woods .10 .04
❑ 238 Luis Aguayo .10 .04
❑ 239 Ramon Aviles .10 .04
❑ 240 Bob Boone .20 .08
❑ 241 Larry Bowa .20 .08
❑ 242 Warren Brusstar .10 .04
❑ 243 Steve Carlton .40 .16
❑ 244 Larry Christenson .10 .04
❑ 245 Dick Davis .10 .04
❑ 246 Greg Gross .10 .04
❑ 247 Sparky Lyle .20 .08
❑ 248 Garry Maddox .10 .04
❑ 249 Gary Matthews .20 .08
❑ 250 Bake McBride .20 .08
❑ 251 Tug McGraw .20 .08
❑ 252 Keith Moreland .10 .04
❑ 253 Dickie Noles .10 .04
❑ 254 Mike Proly .10 .04
❑ 255 Ron Reed .10 .04
❑ 256 Pete Rose 2.50 1.00
❑ 257 Dick Ruthven .10 .04
❑ 258 Mike Schmidt 2.00 .80
❑ 259 Lonnie Smith .10 .04
❑ 260 Manny Trillo .10 .04
❑ 261 Del Unser .10 .04
❑ 262 George Vukovich .10 .04
❑ 263 Tom Brookens .10 .04
❑ 264 George Cappuzzello .10 .04
❑ 265 Marty Castillo .10 .04
❑ 266 Al Cowens .10 .04
❑ 267 Kirk Gibson .75 .30
❑ 268 Richie Hebner .10 .04
❑ 269 Ron Jackson .10 .04
❑ 270 Lynn Jones .10 .04
❑ 271 Steve Kemp .10 .04
❑ 272 Rick Leach .10 .04
❑ 273 Aurelio Lopez .10 .04
❑ 274 Jack Morris .20 .08
❑ 275 Kevin Saucier .10 .04
❑ 276 Lance Parrish .20 .08
❑ 277 Rick Peters .10 .04
❑ 278 Dan Petry .10 .04
❑ 279 Dave Rozema .10 .04
❑ 280 Stan Papi .10 .04
❑ 281 Dan Schatzeder .10 .04
❑ 282 Champ Summers .10 .04
❑ 283 Alan Trammell .20 .08
❑ 284 Lou Whitaker .20 .08
❑ 285 Milt Wilcox .10 .04
❑ 286 John Wockenfuss .10 .04
❑ 287 Gary Allenson .10 .04
❑ 288 Tom Burgmeier .10 .04
❑ 289 Bill Campbell .10 .04
❑ 290 Mark Clear .10 .04
❑ 291 Steve Crawford .10 .04
❑ 292 Dennis Eckersley .40 .16
❑ 293 Dwight Evans .20 .08
❑ 294 Rich Gedman .50 .20
❑ 295 Garry Hancock .10 .04
❑ 296 Glenn Hoffman .10 .04
❑ 297 Bruce Hurst .10 .04
❑ 298 Carney Lansford .20 .08
❑ 299 Rick Miller .10 .04
❑ 300 Reid Nichols .10 .04
❑ 301 Bob Ojeda RC .50 .20
❑ 302 Tony Perez .40 .16
❑ 303 Chuck Rainey .10 .04
❑ 304 Jerry Remy .10 .04
❑ 305 Jim Rice .20 .08
❑ 306 Joe Rudi .20 .08
❑ 307 Bob Stanley .10 .04
❑ 308 Dave Stapleton .10 .04
❑ 309 Frank Tanana .20 .08
❑ 310 Mike Torrez .10 .04
❑ 311 John Tudor .20 .08
❑ 312 Carl Yastrzemski 1.25 .50
❑ 313 Buddy Bell .20 .08
❑ 314 Steve Comer .10 .04
❑ 315 Danny Darwin .10 .04
❑ 316 John Ellis .10 .04
❑ 317 John Grubb .10 .04
❑ 318 Rick Honeycutt .10 .04
❑ 319 Charlie Hough .20 .08
❑ 320 Ferguson Jenkins .20 .08
❑ 321 John Henry Johnson .10 .04
❑ 322 Jim Kern .10 .04
❑ 323 Jon Matlack .10 .04
❑ 324 Doc Medich .10 .04
❑ 325 Mario Mendoza .10 .04
❑ 326 Al Oliver .20 .08
❑ 327 Pat Putnam .10 .04
❑ 328 Mickey Rivers .10 .04
❑ 329 Leon Roberts .10 .04
❑ 330 Billy Sample .10 .04
❑ 331 Bill Stein .10 .04
❑ 332 Jim Sundberg .20 .08
❑ 333 Mark Wagner .10 .04
❑ 334 Bump Wills .10 .04
❑ 335 Bill Almon .10 .04
❑ 336 Harold Baines .20 .08

❑ 337 Ross Baumgarten .10 .04
❑ 338 Tony Bernazard .10 .04
❑ 339 Britt Burns .10 .04
❑ 340 Richard Dotson .10 .04
❑ 341 Jim Essian .10 .04
❑ 342 Ed Farmer .10 .04
❑ 343 Carlton Fisk .40 .16
❑ 344 Kevin Hickey RC .15 .06
❑ 345 LaMarr Hoyt .10 .04
❑ 346 Lamar Johnson .10 .04
❑ 347 Jerry Koosman .20 .08
❑ 348 Rusty Kuntz .10 .04
❑ 349 Dennis Lamp .10 .04
❑ 350 Ron LeFlore .20 .08
❑ 351 Chet Lemon .20 .08
❑ 352 Greg Luzinski .20 .08
❑ 353 Bob Molinaro .10 .04
❑ 354 Jim Morrison .10 .04
❑ 355 Wayne Nordhagen .10 .04
❑ 356 Greg Pryor .10 .04
❑ 357 Mike Squires .10 .04
❑ 358 Steve Trout .10 .04
❑ 359 Alan Bannister .10 .04
❑ 360 Len Barker .10 .04
❑ 361 Bert Blyleven .20 .08
❑ 362 Joe Charboneau .20 .08
❑ 363 John Denny .10 .04
❑ 364 Bo Diaz .10 .04
❑ 365 Miguel Dilone .10 .04
❑ 366 Jerry Dybzinski .10 .04
❑ 367 Wayne Garland .10 .04
❑ 368 Mike Hargrove .10 .04
❑ 369 Toby Harrah .20 .08
❑ 370 Ron Hassey .10 .04
❑ 371 Von Hayes RC .50 .20
❑ 372 Pat Kelly .10 .04
❑ 373 Duane Kuiper .10 .04
❑ 374 Rick Manning .10 .04
❑ 375 Sid Monge .10 .04
❑ 376 Jorge Orta .10 .04
❑ 377 Dave Rosello .10 .04
❑ 378 Dan Spillner .10 .04
❑ 379 Mike Stanton .10 .04
❑ 380 Andre Thornton .10 .04
❑ 381 Tom Veryzer .10 .04
❑ 382 Rick Waits .10 .04
❑ 383 Doyle Alexander .10 .04
❑ 384 Vida Blue .20 .08
❑ 385 Fred Breining .10 .04
❑ 386 Enos Cabell .10 .04
❑ 387 Jack Clark .20 .08
❑ 388 Darrell Evans .20 .08
❑ 389 Tom Griffin .10 .04
❑ 390 Larry Herndon .10 .04
❑ 391 Al Holland .10 .04
❑ 392 Gary Lavelle .10 .04
❑ 393 Johnnie LeMaster .10 .04
❑ 394 Jerry Martin .10 .04
❑ 395 Milt May .10 .04
❑ 396 Greg Minton .10 .04
❑ 397 Joe Morgan .20 .08
❑ 398 Joe Pettini .10 .04
❑ 399 Allen Ripley .10 .04
❑ 400 Billy Smith .10 .04
❑ 401 Rennie Stennett .10 .04
❑ 402 Ed Whitson .10 .04
❑ 403 Jim Wohlford .10 .04
❑ 404 Willie Aikens .10 .04
❑ 405 George Brett 2.00 .80
❑ 406 Ken Brett .10 .04
❑ 407 Dave Chalk .10 .04
❑ 408 Rich Gale .10 .04
❑ 409 Cesar Geronimo .10 .04
❑ 410 Larry Gura .10 .04
❑ 411 Clint Hurdle .10 .04
❑ 412 Mike Jones .10 .04
❑ 413 Dennis Leonard .10 .04
❑ 414 Renie Martin .10 .04
❑ 415 Lee May .10 .04
❑ 416 Hal McRae .20 .08
❑ 417 Darryl Motley .10 .04
❑ 418 Rance Mulliniks .10 .04
❑ 419 Amos Otis .20 .08
❑ 420 Ken Phelps .10 .04
❑ 421 Jamie Quirk .10 .04
❑ 422 Dan Quisenberry .10 .04
❑ 423 Paul Splittorff .10 .04
❑ 424 U.L. Washington .10 .04
❑ 425 John Wathan .10 .04
❑ 426 Frank White .20 .08
❑ 427 Willie Wilson .20 .08
❑ 428 Brian Asselstine .10 .04
❑ 429 Bruce Benedict .10 .04
❑ 430 Tommy Boggs .10 .04
❑ 431 Larry Bradford .10 .04
❑ 432 Rick Camp .10 .04
❑ 433 Chris Chambliss .20 .08
❑ 434 Gene Garber .10 .04
❑ 435 Preston Hanna .10 .04
❑ 436 Bob Horner .20 .08
❑ 437 Glenn Hubbard .10 .04
❑ 438A All Hrabosky ERR 8.00 3.20
(Height 5'1"
All on reverse)
❑ 438B Al Hrabosky ERR .40 .16
(Height 5'1")
❑ 438C Al Hrabosky .20 .08
(Height 5'10")
❑ 439 Rufino Linares .10 .04
❑ 440 Rick Mahler .10 .04
❑ 441 Ed Miller .10 .04
❑ 442 John Montefusco .10 .04
❑ 443 Dale Murphy .40 .16
❑ 444 Phil Niekro .20 .08
❑ 445 Gaylord Perry .20 .08
❑ 446 Biff Pocoroba .10 .04
❑ 447 Rafael Ramirez .10 .04
❑ 448 Jerry Royster .10 .04
❑ 449 Claudell Washington .10 .04
❑ 450 Don Aase .10 .04
❑ 451 Don Baylor .20 .08
❑ 452 Juan Beniquez .10 .04
❑ 453 Rick Burleson .10 .04
❑ 454 Bert Campaneris .20 .08
❑ 455 Rod Carew .40 .16
❑ 456 Bob Clark .10 .04
❑ 457 Brian Downing .20 .08
❑ 458 Dan Ford .10 .04
❑ 459 Ken Forsch .10 .04
❑ 460A Dave Frost (5 mm .10 .04
space before ERA)
❑ 460B Dave Frost .10 .04
(1 mm space)
❑ 461 Bobby Grich .20 .08
❑ 462 Larry Harlow .10 .04
❑ 463 John Harris .10 .04
❑ 464 Andy Hassler .10 .04
❑ 465 Butch Hobson .10 .04
❑ 466 Jesse Jefferson .10 .04
❑ 467 Bruce Kison .10 .04
❑ 468 Fred Lynn .20 .08
❑ 469 Angel Moreno .10 .04
❑ 470 Ed Ott .10 .04
❑ 471 Fred Patek .10 .04
❑ 472 Steve Renko .10 .04
❑ 473 Mike Witt .50 .20
❑ 474 Geoff Zahn .10 .04
❑ 475 Gary Alexander .10 .04
❑ 476 Dale Berra .10 .04
❑ 477 Kurt Bevacqua .10 .04
❑ 478 Jim Bibby .10 .04
❑ 479 John Candelaria .10 .04
❑ 480 Victor Cruz .10 .04
❑ 481 Mike Easler .10 .04
❑ 482 Tim Foli .10 .04
❑ 483 Lee Lacy .10 .04
❑ 484 Vance Law .10 .04
❑ 485 Bill Madlock .20 .08
❑ 486 Willie Montanez .10 .04
❑ 487 Omar Moreno .10 .04
❑ 488 Steve Nicosia .10 .04
❑ 489 Dave Parker .20 .08
❑ 490 Tony Pena .20 .08
❑ 491 Pascual Perez .10 .04
❑ 492 Johnny Ray RC .50 .20
❑ 493 Rick Rhoden .10 .04
❑ 494 Bill Robinson .10 .04
❑ 495 Don Robinson .10 .04
❑ 496 Enrique Romo .10 .04
❑ 497 Rod Scurry .10 .04
❑ 498 Eddie Solomon .10 .04
❑ 499 Willie Stargell .40 .16
❑ 500 Kent Tekulve .10 .04
❑ 501 Jason Thompson .10 .04
❑ 502 Glenn Abbott .10 .04
❑ 503 Jim Anderson .10 .04
❑ 504 Floyd Bannister .10 .04
❑ 505 Bruce Bochte .10 .04
❑ 506 Jeff Burroughs .10 .04
❑ 507 Bryan Clark RC .15 .06
❑ 508 Ken Clay .10 .04
❑ 509 Julio Cruz .10 .04
❑ 510 Dick Drago .10 .04
❑ 511 Gary Gray .10 .04
❑ 512 Dan Meyer .10 .04
❑ 513 Jerry Narron .10 .04
❑ 514 Tom Paciorek .10 .04
❑ 515 Casey Parsons .10 .04
❑ 516 Lenny Randle .10 .04
❑ 517 Shane Rawley .10 .04
❑ 518 Joe Simpson .10 .04
❑ 519 Richie Zisk .10 .04
❑ 520 Neil Allen .10 .04
❑ 521 Bob Bailor .10 .04
❑ 522 Hubie Brooks .10 .04
❑ 523 Mike Cubbage .10 .04
❑ 524 Pete Falcone .10 .04
❑ 525 Doug Flynn .10 .04
❑ 526 Tom Hausman .10 .04
❑ 527 Ron Hodges .10 .04
❑ 528 Randy Jones .10 .04
❑ 529 Mike Jorgensen .10 .04
❑ 530 Dave Kingman .20 .08
❑ 531 Ed Lynch .10 .04
❑ 532 Mike G. Marshall .10 .04
❑ 533 Lee Mazzilli .20 .08
❑ 534 Dyar Miller .10 .04
❑ 535 Mike Scott .20 .08
❑ 536 Rusty Staub .20 .08
❑ 537 John Stearns .10 .04
❑ 538 Craig Swan .10 .04
❑ 539 Frank Taveras .10 .04
❑ 540 Alex Trevino .10 .04
❑ 541 Ellis Valentine .10 .04
❑ 542 Mookie Wilson .20 .08
❑ 543 Joel Youngblood .10 .04
❑ 544 Pat Zachry .10 .04
❑ 545 Glenn Adams .10 .04
❑ 546 Fernando Arroyo .10 .04
❑ 547 John Verhoeven .10 .04
❑ 548 Sal Butera .10 .04
❑ 549 John Castino .10 .04
❑ 550 Don Cooper .10 .04
❑ 551 Doug Corbett .10 .04
❑ 552 Dave Engle .10 .04
❑ 553 Roger Erickson .10 .04
❑ 554 Danny Goodwin .10 .04
❑ 555A Darrell Jackson .40 .16
(Black cap)
❑ 555B Darrell Jackson .20 .08
(Red cap with T)
❑ 555C Darrell Jackson 3.00 1.20
(Red cap, no emblem)
❑ 556 Pete Mackanin .10 .04
❑ 557 Jack O'Connor .10 .04
❑ 558 Hosken Powell .10 .04
❑ 559 Pete Redfern .10 .04
❑ 560 Roy Smalley .10 .04
❑ 561 Chuck Baker UER .10 .04
(Shortshop on front)
❑ 562 Gary Ward .10 .04
❑ 563 Rob Wilfong .10 .04
❑ 564 Al Williams .10 .04
❑ 565 Butch Wynegar .10 .04
❑ 566 Randy Bass RC .50 .20
❑ 567 Juan Bonilla RC .15 .06
❑ 568 Danny Boone .10 .04
❑ 569 John Curtis .10 .04
❑ 570 Juan Eichelberger .10 .04
❑ 571 Barry Evans .10 .04
❑ 572 Tim Flannery .10 .04
❑ 573 Ruppert Jones .10 .04
❑ 574 Terry Kennedy .10 .04
❑ 575 Joe Lefebvre .10 .04
❑ 576A John Littlefield ERR 150.00 60.00
(Left handed;
reverse negative)
❑ 576B John Littlefield COR .20 .08

(Right handed)
❑ 577 Gary Lucas .10 .04
❑ 578 Steve Mura .10 .04
❑ 579 Broderick Perkins .10 .04
❑ 580 Gene Richards .10 .04
❑ 581 Luis Salazar .10 .04
❑ 582 Ozzie Smith 1.50 .60
❑ 583 John Urrea .10 .04
❑ 584 Chris Welsh .10 .04
❑ 585 Rick Wise .10 .04
❑ 586 Doug Bird .10 .04
❑ 587 Tim Blackwell .10 .04
❑ 588 Bobby Bonds .20 .08
❑ 589 Bill Buckner .20 .08
❑ 590 Bill Caudill .10 .04
❑ 591 Hector Cruz .10 .04
❑ 592 Jody Davis .10 .04
❑ 593 Ivan DeJesus .10 .04
❑ 594 Steve Dillard .10 .04
❑ 595 Leon Durham .10 .04
❑ 596 Rawly Eastwick .20 .08
❑ 597 Steve Henderson .10 .04
❑ 598 Mike Krukow .10 .04
❑ 599 Mike Lum .10 .04
❑ 600 Randy Martz .10 .04
❑ 601 Jerry Morales .10 .04
❑ 602 Ken Reitz .10 .04
❑ 603 Lee Smith RC ERR 2.00 .80
(Cubs logo reversed)
❑ 603B Lee Smith RC COR 6.00 2.40
❑ 604 Dick Tidrow .10 .04
❑ 605 Jim Tracy .20 .08
❑ 606 Mike Tyson .10 .04
❑ 607 Ty Waller .10 .04
❑ 608 Danny Ainge .20 .08
❑ 609 Jorge Bell RC 1.00 .40
❑ 610 Mark Bomback .10 .04
❑ 611 Barry Bonnell .10 .04
❑ 612 Jim Clancy .10 .04
❑ 613 Damaso Garcia .10 .04
❑ 614 Jerry Garvin .10 .04
❑ 615 Alfredo Griffin .10 .04
❑ 616 Garth Iorg .10 .04
❑ 617 Luis Leal .10 .04
❑ 618 Ken Macha .10 .04
❑ 619 John Mayberry .10 .04
❑ 620 Joey McLaughlin .10 .04
❑ 621 Lloyd Moseby .10 .04
❑ 622 Dave Stieb .20 .08
❑ 623 Jackson Todd .10 .04
❑ 624 Willie Upshaw .50 .20
❑ 625 Otto Velez .10 .04
❑ 626 Ernie Whitt .10 .04
❑ 627 Alvis Woods .10 .04
❑ 628 All Star Game .20 .08
Cleveland, Ohio
❑ 629 Frank White .20 .08
Bucky Dent
❑ 630 Dan Driessen .20 .08
Dave Concepcion
George Foster
❑ 631 Bruce Sutter .10 .04
Top NL Relief Pitcher
❑ 632 Steve Carlton .20 .08
Carlton Fisk
❑ 633 Carl Yastrzemski .75 .30
3000th Game
❑ 634 Johnny Bench .75 .30
Tom Seaver
❑ 635 Fernando Valenzuela .10 .04
Gary Carter
❑ 636A Fernando Valenzuela: .40 .16
NL SO King "he" NL
❑ 636B Fernando Valenzuela: .40 .16
NL SO King "the" NL
❑ 637 Mike Schmidt .75 .30
Home Run King
❑ 638 Gary Carter .10 .04
Dave Parker
❑ 639 Perfect Game UER .20 .08
Len Barker
Bo Diaz
(Catcher actually
Ron Hassey)
❑ 640 Pete Rose .75 .30
Pete Rose Jr.
❑ 641 Lonnie Smith .75 .30
Mike Schmidt
Steve Carlton
❑ 642 Fred Lynn .20 .08
Dwight Evans
❑ 643 Rickey Henderson 1.25 .50
Most Hits and Runs
❑ 644 Rollie Fingers .20 .08
Most Saves AL
❑ 645 Tom Seaver .20 .08
Most 1981 Wins
❑ 646 Yankee Powerhouse .20 .08
Reggie Jackson
Dave Winfield
(Comma on back
after outfielder)
❑ 646B Yankee Powerhouse .20 .08
Reggie Jackson
Dave Winfield
(No comma)
❑ 647 CL: Yankees/Dodgers .10 .04
❑ 648 CL: A's/Reds .10 .04
❑ 649 CL: Cards/Brewers .10 .04
❑ 650 CL: Expos/Orioles .10 .04
❑ 651 CL: Astros/Phillies .10 .04
❑ 652 CL: Tigers/Red Sox .10 .04
❑ 653 CL: Rangers/White Sox .10 .04
❑ 654 CL: Giants/Indians .10 .04
❑ 655 CL: Royals/Braves .10 .04
❑ 656 CL: Angels/Pirates .10 .04
❑ 657 CL: Mariners/Mets .10 .04
❑ 658 CL: Padres/Twins .10 .04
❑ 659 CL: Blue Jays/Cubs .10 .04
❑ 660 Specials Checklist .10 .04

1983 Fleer

	Nm-Mt	Ex-Mt
COMPLETE SET (660)	60.00	24.00

❑ 1 Joaquin Andujar .20 .08
❑ 2 Doug Bair .10 .04
❑ 3 Steve Braun .10 .04
❑ 4 Glenn Brummer .10 .04
❑ 5 Bob Forsch .10 .04
❑ 6 David Green RC .50 .20
❑ 7 George Hendrick .20 .08
❑ 8 Keith Hernandez .20 .08
❑ 9 Tom Herr .10 .04
❑ 10 Dane Iorg .10 .04
❑ 11 Jim Kaat .20 .08
❑ 12 Jeff Lahti .10 .04
❑ 13 Tito Landrum .10 .04
❑ 14 Dave LaPoint .10 .04
❑ 15 Willie McGee RC 1.00 .40
❑ 16 Steve Mura .10 .04
❑ 17 Ken Oberkfell .10 .04
❑ 18 Darrell Porter .10 .04
❑ 19 Mike Ramsey .10 .04
❑ 20 Gene Roof .10 .04
❑ 21 Lonnie Smith .10 .04
❑ 22 Ozzie Smith 1.25 .50
❑ 23 John Stuper .10 .04
❑ 24 Bruce Sutter .20 .08
❑ 25 Gene Tenace .20 .08
❑ 26 Jerry Augustine .10 .04
❑ 27 Dwight Bernard .10 .04
❑ 28 Mark Brouhard .10 .04
❑ 29 Mike Caldwell .10 .04
❑ 30 Cecil Cooper .20 .08
❑ 31 Jamie Easterly .10 .04
❑ 32 Marshall Edwards .10 .04
❑ 33 Rollie Fingers .20 .08
❑ 34 Jim Gantner .10 .04
❑ 35 Moose Haas .10 .04
❑ 36 Roy Howell .10 .04
❑ 37 Pete Ladd .10 .04
❑ 38 Bob McClure .10 .04
❑ 39 Doc Medich .10 .04
❑ 40 Paul Molitor .40 .16
❑ 41 Don Money .10 .04
❑ 42 Charlie Moore .10 .04
❑ 43 Ben Oglivie .20 .08
❑ 44 Ed Romero .10 .04
❑ 45 Ted Simmons .20 .08
❑ 46 Jim Slaton .10 .04
❑ 47 Don Sutton .20 .08
❑ 48 Gorman Thomas .20 .08
❑ 49 Pete Vuckovich .10 .04
❑ 50 Ned Yost .10 .04
❑ 51 Robin Yount 1.25 .50
❑ 52 Benny Ayala .10 .04
❑ 53 Bob Bonner .10 .04
❑ 54 Al Bumbry .10 .04
❑ 55 Terry Crowley .10 .04
❑ 56 Storm Davis RC .50 .20
❑ 57 Rich Dauer .10 .04
❑ 58 Rick Dempsey UER .10 .04
(Posing batting lefty)
❑ 59 Jim Dwyer .10 .04
❑ 60 Mike Flanagan .10 .04
❑ 61 Dan Ford .10 .04
❑ 62 Glenn Gulliver .10 .04
❑ 63 John Lowenstein .10 .04
❑ 64 Dennis Martinez .20 .08
❑ 65 Tippy Martinez .10 .04
❑ 66 Scott McGregor .10 .04
❑ 67 Eddie Murray .75 .30
❑ 68 Joe Nolan .10 .04
❑ 69 Jim Palmer .20 .08
❑ 70 Cal Ripken 6.00 2.40
❑ 71 Gary Roenicke .10 .04
❑ 72 Lenn Sakata .10 .04
❑ 73 Ken Singleton .20 .08
❑ 74 Sammy Stewart .10 .04
❑ 75 Tim Stoddard .10 .04
❑ 76 Don Aase .10 .04
❑ 77 Don Baylor .20 .08
❑ 78 Juan Beniquez .10 .04
❑ 79 Bob Boone .20 .08
❑ 80 Rick Burleson .10 .04
❑ 81 Rod Carew .40 .16
❑ 82 Bobby Clark .10 .04
❑ 83 Doug Corbett .10 .04
❑ 84 John Curtis .10 .04
❑ 85 Doug DeCinces .10 .04
❑ 86 Brian Downing .20 .08
❑ 87 Joe Ferguson .10 .04
❑ 88 Tim Foli .10 .04
❑ 89 Ken Forsch .10 .04
❑ 90 Dave Goltz .10 .04
❑ 91 Bobby Grich .20 .08
❑ 92 Andy Hassler .10 .04
❑ 93 Reggie Jackson .40 .16
❑ 94 Ron Jackson .10 .04
❑ 95 Tommy John .20 .08
❑ 96 Bruce Kison .10 .04
❑ 97 Fred Lynn .20 .08
❑ 98 Ed Ott .10 .04
❑ 99 Steve Renko .10 .04
❑ 100 Luis Sanchez .10 .04
❑ 101 Rob Wilfong .10 .04
❑ 102 Mike Witt .10 .04
❑ 103 Geoff Zahn .10 .04
❑ 104 Willie Aikens .10 .04
❑ 105 Mike Armstrong .10 .04
❑ 106 Vida Blue .20 .08
❑ 107 Bud Black RC .50 .20
❑ 108 George Brett 2.00 .80
❑ 109 Bill Castro .10 .04
❑ 110 Onix Concepcion .10 .04
❑ 111 Dave Frost .10 .04
❑ 112 Cesar Geronimo .10 .04
❑ 113 Larry Gura .10 .04

❑ 114 Steve Hammond .10 .04
❑ 115 Don Hood .10 .04
❑ 116 Dennis Leonard .10 .04
❑ 117 Jerry Martin .10 .04
❑ 118 Lee May .10 .04
❑ 119 Hal McRae .20 .08
❑ 120 Amos Otis .20 .08
❑ 121 Greg Pryor .10 .04
❑ 122 Dan Quisenberry .10 .04
❑ 123 Don Slaught RC .50 .20
❑ 124 Paul Splittorff .10 .04
❑ 125 U.L. Washington .10 .04
❑ 126 John Wathan .10 .04
❑ 127 Frank White .20 .08
❑ 128 Willie Wilson .20 .08
❑ 129 Steve Bedrosian UER .10 .04
(Height 6'33")
❑ 130 Bruce Benedict .10 .04
❑ 131 Tommy Boggs .10 .04
❑ 132 Brett Butler .20 .08
❑ 133 Rick Camp .10 .04
❑ 134 Chris Chambliss .20 .08
❑ 135 Ken Dayley .10 .04
❑ 136 Gene Garber .10 .04
❑ 137 Terry Harper .10 .04
❑ 138 Bob Horner .20 .08
❑ 139 Glenn Hubbard .10 .04
❑ 140 Rufino Linares .10 .04
❑ 141 Rick Mahler .10 .04
❑ 142 Dale Murphy .40 .16
❑ 143 Phil Niekro .20 .08
❑ 144 Pascual Perez .10 .04
❑ 145 Biff Pocoroba .10 .04
❑ 146 Rafael Ramirez .10 .04
❑ 147 Jerry Royster .10 .04
❑ 148 Ken Smith .10 .04
❑ 149 Bob Walk .10 .04
❑ 150 Claudell Washington .10 .04
❑ 151 Bob Watson .10 .04
❑ 152 Larry Whisenton .10 .04
❑ 153 Porfirio Altamirano .10 .04
❑ 154 Marty Bystrom .10 .04
❑ 155 Steve Carlton .40 .16
❑ 156 Larry Christenson .10 .04
❑ 157 Ivan DeJesus .10 .04
❑ 158 John Denny .10 .04
❑ 159 Bob Dernier .10 .04
❑ 160 Bo Diaz .10 .04
❑ 161 Ed Farmer .10 .04
❑ 162 Greg Gross .10 .04
❑ 163 Mike Krukow .10 .04
❑ 164 Garry Maddox .10 .04
❑ 165 Gary Matthews .20 .08
❑ 166 Tug McGraw .20 .08
❑ 167 Bob Molinaro .10 .04
❑ 168 Sid Monge .10 .04
❑ 169 Ron Reed .10 .04
❑ 170 Bill Robinson .10 .04
❑ 171 Pete Rose 2.50 1.00
❑ 172 Dick Ruthven .10 .04
❑ 173 Mike Schmidt 2.00 .80
❑ 174 Manny Trillo .10 .04
❑ 175 Ozzie Virgil .10 .04
❑ 176 George Vukovich .10 .04
❑ 177 Gary Allenson .10 .04
❑ 178 Luis Aponte .10 .04
❑ 179 Wade Boggs RC 8.00 3.20
❑ 180 Tom Burgmeier .10 .04
❑ 181 Mark Clear .10 .04
❑ 182 Dennis Eckersley .40 .16
❑ 183 Dwight Evans .20 .08
❑ 184 Rich Gedman .10 .04
❑ 185 Glenn Hoffman .10 .04
❑ 186 Bruce Hurst .10 .04
❑ 187 Carney Lansford .20 .08
❑ 188 Rick Miller .10 .04
❑ 189 Reid Nichols .10 .04
❑ 190 Bob Ojeda .10 .04
❑ 191 Tony Perez .40 .16
❑ 192 Chuck Rainey .10 .04
❑ 193 Jerry Remy .10 .04
❑ 194 Jim Rice .20 .08
❑ 195 Bob Stanley .10 .04
❑ 196 Dave Stapleton .10 .04
❑ 197 Mike Torrez .10 .04
❑ 198 John Tudor .20 .08
❑ 199 Julio Valdez .10 .04
❑ 200 Carl Yastrzemski 1.25 .50
❑ 201 Dusty Baker .20 .08
❑ 202 Joe Beckwith .10 .04
❑ 203 Greg Brock .10 .04
❑ 204 Ron Cey .20 .08
❑ 205 Terry Forster .20 .08
❑ 206 Steve Garvey .20 .08
❑ 207 Pedro Guerrero .20 .08
❑ 208 Burt Hooton .10 .04
❑ 209 Steve Howe .10 .04
❑ 210 Ken Landreaux .10 .04
❑ 211 Mike Marshall .10 .04
❑ 212 Candy Maldonado RC .50 .20
❑ 213 Rick Monday .20 .08
❑ 214 Tom Niedenfuer .10 .04
❑ 215 Jorge Orta .10 .04
❑ 216 Jerry Reuss UER .10 .04
("Home:" omitted)
❑ 217 Ron Roenicke .10 .04
❑ 218 Vicente Romo .10 .04
❑ 219 Bill Russell .20 .08
❑ 220 Steve Sax .20 .08
❑ 221 Mike Scioscia .20 .08
❑ 222 Dave Stewart .20 .08
❑ 223 Derrel Thomas .10 .04
❑ 224 Fernando Valenzuela .20 .08
❑ 225 Bob Welch .20 .08
❑ 226 Ricky Wright .10 .04
❑ 227 Steve Yeager .20 .08
❑ 228 Bill Almon .10 .04
❑ 229 Harold Baines .20 .08
❑ 230 Salome Barojas .10 .04
❑ 231 Tony Bernazard .10 .04
❑ 232 Britt Burns .10 .04
❑ 233 Richard Dotson .10 .04
❑ 234 Ernesto Escarrega .10 .04
❑ 235 Carlton Fisk .40 .16
❑ 236 Jerry Hairston .10 .04
❑ 237 Kevin Hickey .10 .04
❑ 238 LaMarr Hoyt .10 .04
❑ 239 Steve Kemp .10 .04
❑ 240 Jim Kern .10 .04
❑ 241 Ron Kittle RC 1.00 .40
❑ 242 Jerry Koosman .20 .08
❑ 243 Dennis Lamp .10 .04
❑ 244 Rudy Law .10 .04
❑ 245 Vance Law .10 .04
❑ 246 Ron LeFlore .20 .08
❑ 247 Greg Luzinski .20 .08
❑ 248 Tom Paciorek .10 .04
❑ 249 Aurelio Rodriguez .10 .04
❑ 250 Mike Squires .10 .04
❑ 251 Steve Trout .10 .04
❑ 252 Jim Barr .10 .04
❑ 253 Dave Bergman .10 .04
❑ 254 Fred Breining .10 .04
❑ 255 Bob Brenly .10 .04
❑ 256 Jack Clark .20 .08
❑ 257 Chili Davis .20 .08
❑ 258 Darrell Evans .20 .08
❑ 259 Alan Fowlkes .10 .04
❑ 260 Rich Gale .10 .04
❑ 261 Atlee Hammaker .10 .04
❑ 262 Al Holland .10 .04
❑ 263 Duane Kuiper .10 .04
❑ 264 Bill Laskey .10 .04
❑ 265 Gary Lavelle .10 .04
❑ 266 Johnnie LeMaster .10 .04
❑ 267 Renie Martin .10 .04
❑ 268 Milt May .10 .04
❑ 269 Greg Minton .10 .04
❑ 270 Joe Morgan .20 .08
❑ 271 Tom O'Malley .10 .04
❑ 272 Reggie Smith .20 .08
❑ 273 Guy Sularz .10 .04
❑ 274 Champ Summers .10 .04
❑ 275 Max Venable .10 .04
❑ 276 Jim Wohlford .10 .04
❑ 277 Ray Burris .10 .04
❑ 278 Gary Carter .20 .08
❑ 279 Warren Cromartie .10 .04
❑ 280 Andre Dawson .20 .08
❑ 281 Terry Francona .20 .08
❑ 282 Doug Flynn .10 .04
❑ 283 Woodie Fryman .10 .04
❑ 284 Bill Gullickson .10 .04
❑ 285 Wallace Johnson .10 .04
❑ 286 Charlie Lea .10 .04
❑ 287 Randy Lerch .10 .04
❑ 288 Brad Mills .10 .04
❑ 289 Dan Norman .10 .04
❑ 290 Al Oliver .20 .08
❑ 291 David Palmer .10 .04
❑ 292 Tim Raines .20 .08
❑ 293 Jeff Reardon .20 .08
❑ 294 Steve Rogers .20 .08
❑ 295 Scott Sanderson .10 .04
❑ 296 Dan Schatzeder .10 .04
❑ 297 Bryn Smith .10 .04
❑ 298 Chris Speier .10 .04
❑ 299 Tim Wallach .20 .08
❑ 300 Jerry White .10 .04
❑ 301 Joel Youngblood .10 .04
❑ 302 Ross Baumgarten .10 .04
❑ 303 Dale Berra .10 .04
❑ 304 John Candelaria .10 .04
❑ 305 Dick Davis .10 .04
❑ 306 Mike Easler .10 .04
❑ 307 Richie Hebner .10 .04
❑ 308 Lee Lacy .10 .04
❑ 309 Bill Madlock .20 .08
❑ 310 Larry McWilliams .10 .04
❑ 311 John Milner .10 .04
❑ 312 Omar Moreno .10 .04
❑ 313 Jim Morrison .10 .04
❑ 314 Steve Nicosia .10 .04
❑ 315 Dave Parker .20 .08
❑ 316 Tony Pena .10 .04
❑ 317 Johnny Ray .10 .04
❑ 318 Rick Rhoden .10 .04
❑ 319 Don Robinson .10 .04
❑ 320 Enrique Romo .10 .04
❑ 321 Manny Sarmiento .10 .04
❑ 322 Rod Scurry .10 .04
❑ 323 Jimmy Smith .10 .04
❑ 324 Willie Stargell .40 .16
❑ 325 Jason Thompson .10 .04
❑ 326 Kent Tekulve .10 .04
❑ 327A Tom Brookens .10 .04
(Short .375" brown box shaded in on card back)
❑ 327B Tom Brookens .10 .04
(Longer 1.25" brown box shaded in on card back)
❑ 328 Enos Cabell .10 .04
❑ 329 Kirk Gibson .20 .08
❑ 330 Larry Herndon .10 .04
❑ 331 Mike Ivie .10 .04
❑ 332 Howard Johnson RC 1.00 .40
❑ 333 Lynn Jones .10 .04
❑ 334 Rick Leach .10 .04
❑ 335 Chet Lemon .20 .08
❑ 336 Jack Morris .20 .08
❑ 337 Lance Parrish .20 .08
❑ 338 Larry Pashnick .10 .04
❑ 339 Dan Petry .10 .04
❑ 340 Dave Rozema .10 .04
❑ 341 Dave Rucker .10 .04
❑ 342 Elias Sosa .10 .04
❑ 343 Dave Tobik .10 .04
❑ 344 Alan Trammell .20 .08
❑ 345 Jerry Turner .10 .04
❑ 346 Jerry Ujdur .10 .04
❑ 347 Pat Underwood .10 .04
❑ 348 Lou Whitaker .20 .08
❑ 349 Milt Wilcox .10 .04
❑ 350 Glenn Wilson .50 .20
❑ 351 John Wockenfuss .10 .04
❑ 352 Kurt Bevacqua .10 .04
❑ 353 Juan Bonilla .10 .04
❑ 354 Floyd Chiffer .10 .04
❑ 355 Luis DeLeon .10 .04
❑ 356 Dave Dravecky RC 1.00 .40
❑ 357 Dave Edwards .10 .04
❑ 358 Juan Eichelberger .10 .04
❑ 359 Tim Flannery .10 .04
❑ 360 Tony Gwynn RC 15.00 6.00
❑ 361 Ruppert Jones .10 .04
❑ 362 Terry Kennedy .10 .04
❑ 363 Joe Lefebvre .10 .04
❑ 364 Sixto Lezcano .10 .04

❑ 365 Tim Lollar .10 .04
❑ 366 Gary Lucas .10 .04
❑ 367 John Montefusco .10 .04
❑ 368 Broderick Perkins .10 .04
❑ 369 Joe Pittman .10 .04
❑ 370 Gene Richards .10 .04
❑ 371 Luis Salazar .10 .04
❑ 372 Eric Show RC .50 .20
❑ 373 Garry Templeton .20 .08
❑ 374 Chris Welsh .10 .04
❑ 375 Alan Wiggins .10 .04
❑ 376 Rick Cerone .10 .04
❑ 377 Dave Collins .10 .04
❑ 378 Roger Erickson .10 .04
❑ 379 George Frazier .10 .04
❑ 380 Oscar Gamble .10 .04
❑ 381 Rich Gossage .20 .08
❑ 382 Ken Griffey .20 .08
❑ 383 Ron Guidry .20 .08
❑ 384 Dave LaRoche .10 .04
❑ 385 Rudy May .10 .04
❑ 386 John Mayberry .10 .04
❑ 387 Lee Mazzilli .20 .08
❑ 388 Mike Morgan .10 .04
❑ 389 Jerry Mumphrey .10 .04
❑ 390 Bobby Murcer .20 .08
❑ 391 Graig Nettles .20 .08
❑ 392 Lou Piniella .20 .08
❑ 393 Willie Randolph .20 .08
❑ 394 Shane Rawley .10 .04
❑ 395 Dave Righetti .20 .08
❑ 396 Andre Robertson .10 .04
❑ 397 Roy Smalley .10 .04
❑ 398 Dave Winfield .20 .08
❑ 399 Butch Wynegar .10 .04
❑ 400 Chris Bando .10 .04
❑ 401 Alan Bannister .10 .04
❑ 402 Len Barker .10 .04
❑ 403 Tom Brennan .10 .04
❑ 404 Carmelo Castillo .10 .04
❑ 405 Miguel Dilone .10 .04
❑ 406 Jerry Dybzinski .10 .04
❑ 407 Mike Fischlin .10 .04
❑ 408 Ed Glynn UER .10 .04
(Photo actually
Bud Anderson)
❑ 409 Mike Hargrove .10 .04
❑ 410 Toby Harrah .20 .08
❑ 411 Ron Hassey .10 .04
❑ 412 Von Hayes .10 .04
❑ 413 Rick Manning .10 .04
❑ 414 Bake McBride .20 .08
❑ 415 Larry Milbourne .10 .04
❑ 416 Bill Nahorodny .10 .04
❑ 417 Jack Perconte .10 .04
❑ 418 Lary Sorensen .10 .04
❑ 419 Dan Spillner .10 .04
❑ 420 Rick Sutcliffe .20 .08
❑ 421 Andre Thornton .10 .04
❑ 422 Rick Waits .10 .04
❑ 423 Eddie Whitson .10 .04
❑ 424 Jesse Barfield .20 .08
❑ 425 Barry Bonnell .10 .04
❑ 426 Jim Clancy .10 .04
❑ 427 Damaso Garcia .10 .04
❑ 428 Jerry Garvin .10 .04
❑ 429 Alfredo Griffin .10 .04
❑ 430 Garth Iorg .10 .04
❑ 431 Roy Lee Jackson .10 .04
❑ 432 Luis Leal .10 .04
❑ 433 Buck Martinez .10 .04
❑ 434 Joey McLaughlin .10 .04
❑ 435 Lloyd Moseby .10 .04
❑ 436 Rance Mulliniks .10 .04
❑ 437 Dale Murray .10 .04
❑ 438 Wayne Nordhagen .10 .04
❑ 439 Geno Petralli .50 .20
❑ 440 Hosken Powell .10 .04
❑ 441 Dave Stieb .20 .08
❑ 442 Willie Upshaw .10 .04
❑ 443 Ernie Whitt .10 .04
❑ 444 Alvis Woods .10 .04
❑ 445 Alan Ashby .10 .04
❑ 446 Jose Cruz .20 .08
❑ 447 Kiko Garcia .10 .04
❑ 448 Phil Garner .20 .08
❑ 449 Danny Heep .10 .04
❑ 450 Art Howe .10 .04
❑ 451 Bob Knepper .10 .04
❑ 452 Alan Knicely .10 .04
❑ 453 Ray Knight .20 .08
❑ 454 Frank LaCorte .10 .04
❑ 455 Mike LaCoss .10 .04
❑ 456 Randy Moffitt .10 .04
❑ 457 Joe Niekro .10 .04
❑ 458 Terry Puhl .10 .04
❑ 459 Luis Pujols .10 .04
❑ 460 Craig Reynolds .10 .04
❑ 461 Bert Roberge .10 .04
❑ 462 Vern Ruhle .10 .04
❑ 463 Nolan Ryan 4.00 1.60
❑ 464 Joe Sambito .10 .04
❑ 465 Tony Scott .10 .04
❑ 466 Dave Smith .10 .04
❑ 467 Harry Spilman .10 .04
❑ 468 Dickie Thon .10 .04
❑ 469 Denny Walling .10 .04
❑ 470 Larry Andersen .10 .04
❑ 471 Floyd Bannister .10 .04
❑ 472 Jim Beattie .10 .04
❑ 473 Bruce Bochte .10 .04
❑ 474 Manny Castillo .10 .04
❑ 475 Bill Caudill .10 .04
❑ 476 Bryan Clark .10 .04
❑ 477 Al Cowens .10 .04
❑ 478 Julio Cruz .10 .04
❑ 479 Todd Cruz .10 .04
❑ 480 Gary Gray .10 .04
❑ 481 Dave Henderson .10 .04
❑ 482 Mike Moore RC .50 .20
❑ 483 Gaylord Perry .20 .08
❑ 484 Dave Revering .10 .04
❑ 485 Joe Simpson .10 .04
❑ 486 Mike Stanton .10 .04
❑ 487 Rick Sweet .10 .04
❑ 488 Ed VandeBerg .10 .04
❑ 489 Richie Zisk .10 .04
❑ 490 Doug Bird .10 .04
❑ 491 Larry Bowa .20 .08
❑ 492 Bill Buckner .20 .08
❑ 493 Bill Campbell .10 .04
❑ 494 Jody Davis .10 .04
❑ 495 Leon Durham .10 .04
❑ 496 Steve Henderson .10 .04
❑ 497 Willie Hernandez .10 .04
❑ 498 Ferguson Jenkins .20 .08
❑ 499 Jay Johnstone .10 .04
❑ 500 Junior Kennedy .10 .04
❑ 501 Randy Martz .10 .04
❑ 502 Jerry Morales .10 .04
❑ 503 Keith Moreland .10 .04
❑ 504 Dickie Noles .10 .04
❑ 505 Mike Proly .10 .04
❑ 506 Allen Ripley .10 .04
❑ 507 R.Sandberg RC UER 10.00 4.00
Should say High School
in Spokane, Washington
❑ 508 Lee Smith .40 .16
❑ 509 Pat Tabler .10 .04
❑ 510 Dick Tidrow .10 .04
❑ 511 Bump Wills .10 .04
❑ 512 Gary Woods .10 .04
❑ 513 Tony Armas .20 .08
❑ 514 Dave Beard .10 .04
❑ 515 Jeff Burroughs .10 .04
❑ 516 John D'Acquisto .10 .04
❑ 517 Wayne Gross .10 .04
❑ 518 Mike Heath .10 .04
❑ 519 R.Henderson UER 1.50 .60
Brock record listed
as 120 steals
❑ 520 Cliff Johnson .10 .04
❑ 521 Matt Keough .10 .04
❑ 522 Brian Kingman .10 .04
❑ 523 Rick Langford .10 .04
❑ 524 Dave Lopes .20 .08
❑ 525 Steve McCatty .10 .04
❑ 526 Dave McKay .10 .04
❑ 527 Dan Meyer .10 .04
❑ 528 Dwayne Murphy .10 .04
❑ 529 Jeff Newman .10 .04
❑ 530 Mike Norris .10 .04
❑ 531 Bob Owchinko .10 .04
❑ 532 Joe Rudi .20 .08
❑ 533 Jimmy Sexton .10 .04
❑ 534 Fred Stanley .10 .04
❑ 535 Tom Underwood .10 .04
❑ 536 Neil Allen .10 .04
❑ 537 Wally Backman .10 .04
❑ 538 Bob Bailor .10 .04
❑ 539 Hubie Brooks .10 .04
❑ 540 Carlos Diaz RC .25 .10
❑ 541 Pete Falcone .10 .04
❑ 542 George Foster .20 .08
❑ 543 Ron Gardenhire .10 .04
❑ 544 Brian Giles .10 .04
❑ 545 Ron Hodges .10 .04
❑ 546 Randy Jones .10 .04
❑ 547 Mike Jorgensen .10 .04
❑ 548 Dave Kingman .20 .08
❑ 549 Ed Lynch .10 .04
❑ 550 Jesse Orosco .10 .04
❑ 551 Rick Ownbey .10 .04
❑ 552 Charlie Puleo .10 .04
❑ 553 Gary Rajsich .10 .04
❑ 554 Mike Scott .20 .08
❑ 555 Rusty Staub .20 .08
❑ 556 John Stearns .10 .04
❑ 557 Craig Swan .10 .04
❑ 558 Ellis Valentine .10 .04
❑ 559 Tom Veryzer .10 .04
❑ 560 Mookie Wilson .20 .08
❑ 561 Pat Zachry .10 .04
❑ 562 Buddy Bell .20 .08
❑ 563 John Butcher .10 .04
❑ 564 Steve Comer .10 .04
❑ 565 Danny Darwin .10 .04
❑ 566 Bucky Dent .20 .08
❑ 567 John Grubb .10 .04
❑ 568 Rick Honeycutt .10 .04
❑ 569 Dave Hostetler .10 .04
❑ 570 Charlie Hough .20 .08
❑ 571 Lamar Johnson .10 .04
❑ 572 Jon Matlack .10 .04
❑ 573 Paul Mirabella .10 .04
❑ 574 Larry Parrish .10 .04
❑ 575 Mike Richardt .10 .04
❑ 576 Mickey Rivers .10 .04
❑ 577 Billy Sample .10 .04
❑ 578 Dave Schmidt .10 .04
❑ 579 Bill Stein .10 .04
❑ 580 Jim Sundberg .20 .08
❑ 581 Frank Tanana .20 .08
❑ 582 Mark Wagner .10 .04
❑ 583 George Wright RC .50 .20
❑ 584 Johnny Bench .75 .30
❑ 585 Bruce Berenyi .10 .04
❑ 586 Larry Biittner .10 .04
❑ 587 Cesar Cedeno .20 .08
❑ 588 Dave Concepcion .20 .08
❑ 589 Dan Driessen .10 .04
❑ 590 Greg Harris .10 .04
❑ 591 Ben Hayes .10 .04
❑ 592 Paul Householder .10 .04
❑ 593 Tom Hume .10 .04
❑ 594 Wayne Krenchicki .10 .04
❑ 595 Rafael Landestoy .10 .04
❑ 596 Charlie Leibrandt .10 .04
❑ 597 Eddie Milner .10 .04
❑ 598 Ron Oester .10 .04
❑ 599 Frank Pastore .10 .04
❑ 600 Joe Price .10 .04
❑ 601 Tom Seaver .75 .30
❑ 602 Bob Shirley .10 .04
❑ 603 Mario Soto .20 .08
❑ 604 Alex Trevino .10 .04
❑ 605 Mike Vail .10 .04
❑ 606 Duane Walker .10 .04
❑ 607 Tom Brunansky .20 .08
❑ 608 Bobby Castillo .10 .04
❑ 609 John Castino .10 .04
❑ 610 Ron Davis .10 .04
❑ 611 Lenny Faedo .10 .04
❑ 612 Terry Felton .10 .04
❑ 613 Gary Gaetti RC 1.00 .40
❑ 614 Mickey Hatcher .10 .04
❑ 615 Brad Havens .10 .04
❑ 616 Kent Hrbek .20 .08

❑ 617 Randy Johnson .10 .04
❑ 618 Tim Laudner .10 .04
❑ 619 Jeff Little .10 .04
❑ 620 Bobby Mitchell .10 .04
❑ 621 Jack O'Connor .10 .04
❑ 622 John Pacella .10 .04
❑ 623 Pete Redfern .10 .04
❑ 624 Jesus Vega .10 .04
❑ 625 Frank Viola RC 1.50 .60
❑ 626 Ron Washington .10 .04
❑ 627 Gary Ward .10 .04
❑ 628 Al Williams .10 .04
❑ 629 Carl Yastrzemski .75 .30
Dennis Eckersley
Mark Clear
❑ 630 Gaylord Perry .10 .04
Terry Bulling 5/6/82
❑ 631 Dave Concepcion .20 .08
Manny Trillo
❑ 632 Robin Yount .75 .30
Buddy Bell
❑ 633 Dave Winfield .10 .04
Kent Hrbek
❑ 634 Willie Stargell .75 .30
Pete Rose
❑ 635 Toby Harrah .20 .08
Andre Thornton
❑ 636 Ozzie Smith .75 .30
Lonnie Smith
❑ 637 Bo Diaz .10 .04
Gary Carter
❑ 638 Carlton Fisk .20 .08
Gary Carter
❑ 639 Rickey Henderson IA .75 .30
❑ 640 Ben Oglivie .40 .16
Reggie Jackson
❑ 641 Joel Youngblood .10 .04
August 4, 1982
❑ 642 Ron Hassey .20 .08
Len Barker
❑ 643 Black and Blue .20 .08
Vida Blue
❑ 644 Black and Blue .10 .04
Bud Black
❑ 645 Reggie Jackson Power .20 .08
❑ 646 Rickey Henderson Speed .75 .30
❑ 647 CL: Cards/Brewers .10 .04
❑ 648 CL: Orioles/Angels .10 .04
❑ 649 CL: Royals/Braves .10 .04
❑ 650 CL: Phillies/Red Sox .10 .04
❑ 651 CL: Dodgers/White Sox .10 .04
❑ 652 CL: Giants/Expos .10 .04
❑ 653 CL: Pirates/Tigers .10 .04
❑ 654 CL: Padres/Yankees .10 .04
❑ 655 CL: Indians/Blue Jays .10 .04
❑ 656 CL: Astros/Mariners .10 .04
❑ 657 CL: Cubs/A's .10 .04
❑ 658 CL: Mets/Rangers .10 .04
❑ 659 CL: Reds/Twins .10 .04
❑ 660 CL: Specials/Teams .10 .04

1984 Fleer

	Nm-Mt	Ex-Mt
COMPLETE SET (660)	50.00	20.00

❑ 1 Mike Boddicker .15 .06
❑ 2 Al Bumbry .15 .06
❑ 3 Todd Cruz .15 .06
❑ 4 Rich Dauer .15 .06
❑ 5 Storm Davis .15 .06
❑ 6 Rick Dempsey .15 .06
❑ 7 Jim Dwyer .15 .06
❑ 8 Mike Flanagan .15 .06
❑ 9 Dan Ford .15 .06
❑ 10 John Lowenstein .15 .06
❑ 11 Dennis Martinez .40 .16
❑ 12 Tippy Martinez .15 .06
❑ 13 Scott McGregor .15 .06
❑ 14 Eddie Murray 1.50 .60
❑ 15 Joe Nolan .15 .06
❑ 16 Jim Palmer .40 .16
❑ 17 Cal Ripken 10.00 4.00
❑ 18 Gary Roenicke .15 .06
❑ 19 Lenn Sakata .15 .06
❑ 20 John Shelby .15 .06
❑ 21 Ken Singleton .40 .16
❑ 22 Sammy Stewart .15 .06
❑ 23 Tim Stoddard .15 .06
❑ 24 Marty Bystrom .15 .06
❑ 25 Steve Carlton .75 .30
❑ 26 Ivan DeJesus .15 .06
❑ 27 John Denny .15 .06
❑ 28 Bob Dernier .15 .06
❑ 29 Bo Diaz .15 .06
❑ 30 Kiko Garcia .15 .06
❑ 31 Greg Gross .15 .06
❑ 32 Kevin Gross RC .50 .20
❑ 33 Von Hayes .15 .06
❑ 34 Willie Hernandez .15 .06
❑ 35 Al Holland .15 .06
❑ 36 Charles Hudson .15 .06
❑ 37 Joe Lefebvre .15 .06
❑ 38 Sixto Lezcano .15 .06
❑ 39 Garry Maddox .15 .06
❑ 40 Gary Matthews .40 .16
❑ 41 Len Matuszek .15 .06
❑ 42 Tug McGraw .40 .16
❑ 43 Joe Morgan .40 .16
❑ 44 Tony Perez .75 .30
❑ 45 Ron Reed .15 .06
❑ 46 Pete Rose 5.00 2.00
❑ 47 Juan Samuel RC 1.00 .40
❑ 48 Mike Schmidt 4.00 1.60
❑ 49 Ozzie Virgil .15 .06
❑ 50 Juan Agosto .15 .06
❑ 51 Harold Baines .40 .16
❑ 52 Floyd Bannister .15 .06
❑ 53 Salome Barojas .15 .06
❑ 54 Britt Burns .15 .06
❑ 55 Julio Cruz .15 .06
❑ 56 Richard Dotson .15 .06
❑ 57 Jerry Dybzinski .15 .06
❑ 58 Carlton Fisk .75 .30
❑ 59 Scott Fletcher .15 .06
❑ 60 Jerry Hairston .15 .06
❑ 61 Kevin Hickey .15 .06
❑ 62 Marc Hill .15 .06
❑ 63 LaMarr Hoyt .15 .06
❑ 64 Ron Kittle .15 .06
❑ 65 Jerry Koosman .40 .16
❑ 66 Dennis Lamp .15 .06
❑ 67 Rudy Law .15 .06
❑ 68 Vance Law .15 .06
❑ 69 Greg Luzinski .40 .16
❑ 70 Tom Paciorek .15 .06
❑ 71 Mike Squires .15 .06
❑ 72 Dick Tidrow .15 .06
❑ 73 Greg Walker .50 .20
❑ 74 Glenn Abbott .15 .06
❑ 75 Howard Bailey .15 .06
❑ 76 Doug Bair .15 .06
❑ 77 Juan Berenguer .15 .06
❑ 78 Tom Brookens .40 .16
❑ 79 Enos Cabell .15 .06
❑ 80 Kirk Gibson .40 .16
❑ 81 John Grubb .15 .06
❑ 82 Larry Herndon .40 .16
❑ 83 Wayne Krenchicki .15 .06
❑ 84 Rick Leach .15 .06
❑ 85 Chet Lemon .40 .16
❑ 86 Aurelio Lopez .40 .16
❑ 87 Jack Morris .40 .16
❑ 88 Lance Parrish .75 .30
❑ 89 Dan Petry .40 .16
❑ 90 Dave Rozema .15 .06
❑ 91 Alan Trammell .40 .16
❑ 92 Lou Whitaker .40 .16
❑ 93 Milt Wilcox .15 .06
❑ 94 Glenn Wilson .40 .16
❑ 95 John Wockenfuss .15 .06
❑ 96 Dusty Baker .40 .16
❑ 97 Joe Beckwith .15 .06
❑ 98 Greg Brock .15 .06
❑ 99 Jack Fimple .15 .06
❑ 100 Pedro Guerrero .40 .16
❑ 101 Rick Honeycutt .15 .06
❑ 102 Burt Hooton .15 .06
❑ 103 Steve Howe .15 .06
❑ 104 Ken Landreaux .15 .06
❑ 105 Mike Marshall .15 .06
❑ 106 Rick Monday .40 .16
❑ 107 Jose Morales .15 .06
❑ 108 Tom Niedenfuer .15 .06
❑ 109 Alejandro Pena RC* 1.00 .40
❑ 110 Jerry Reuss UER .15 .06
("Home:" omitted)
❑ 111 Bill Russell .40 .16
❑ 112 Steve Sax .15 .06
❑ 113 Mike Scioscia .40 .16
❑ 114 Derrel Thomas .15 .06
❑ 115 Fernando Valenzuela .40 .16
❑ 116 Bob Welch .40 .16
❑ 117 Steve Yeager .40 .16
❑ 118 Pat Zachry .15 .06
❑ 119 Don Baylor .40 .16
❑ 120 Bert Campaneris .40 .16
❑ 121 Rick Cerone .15 .06
❑ 122 Ray Fontenot .15 .06
❑ 123 George Frazier .15 .06
❑ 124 Oscar Gamble .15 .06
❑ 125 Rich Gossage .40 .16
❑ 126 Ken Griffey .40 .16
❑ 127 Ron Guidry .40 .16
❑ 128 Jay Howell .15 .06
❑ 129 Steve Kemp .15 .06
❑ 130 Matt Keough .15 .06
❑ 131 Don Mattingly RC 20.00 8.00
❑ 132 John Montefusco .15 .06
❑ 133 Omar Moreno .15 .06
❑ 134 Dale Murray .15 .06
❑ 135 Graig Nettles .40 .16
❑ 136 Lou Piniella .40 .16
❑ 137 Willie Randolph .40 .16
❑ 138 Shane Rawley .15 .06
❑ 139 Dave Righetti .40 .16
❑ 140 Andre Robertson .15 .06
❑ 141 Bob Shirley .15 .06
❑ 142 Roy Smalley .15 .06
❑ 143 Dave Winfield .40 .16
❑ 144 Butch Wynegar .15 .06
❑ 145 Jim Acker .15 .06
❑ 146 Doyle Alexander .15 .06
❑ 147 Jesse Barfield .40 .16
❑ 148 Jorge Bell .40 .16
❑ 149 Barry Bonnell .15 .06
❑ 150 Jim Clancy .15 .06
❑ 151 Dave Collins .15 .06
❑ 152 Tony Fernandez RC 1.00 .40
❑ 153 Damaso Garcia .15 .06
❑ 154 Dave Geisel .15 .06
❑ 155 Jim Gott .15 .06
❑ 156 Alfredo Griffin .15 .06
❑ 157 Garth Iorg .15 .06
❑ 158 Roy Lee Jackson .15 .06
❑ 159 Cliff Johnson .15 .06
❑ 160 Luis Leal .15 .06
❑ 161 Buck Martinez .15 .06
❑ 162 Joey McLaughlin .15 .06
❑ 163 Randy Moffitt .15 .06
❑ 164 Lloyd Moseby .15 .06
❑ 165 Rance Mulliniks .15 .06
❑ 166 Jorge Orta .15 .06
❑ 167 Dave Stieb .40 .16
❑ 168 Willie Upshaw .15 .06
❑ 169 Ernie Whitt .15 .06
❑ 170 Len Barker .15 .06
❑ 171 Steve Bedrosian .15 .06
❑ 172 Bruce Benedict .15 .06
❑ 173 Brett Butler .40 .16

❑ 174 Rick Camp .15 .06
❑ 175 Chris Chambliss .40 .16
❑ 176 Ken Dayley .15 .06
❑ 177 Pete Falcone .15 .06
❑ 178 Terry Forster .40 .16
❑ 179 Gene Garber .15 .06
❑ 180 Terry Harper .15 .06
❑ 181 Bob Horner .40 .16
❑ 182 Glenn Hubbard .15 .06
❑ 183 Randy Johnson .15 .06
❑ 184 Craig McMurtry .15 .06
❑ 185 Donnie Moore .15 .06
❑ 186 Dale Murphy .75 .30
❑ 187 Phil Niekro .40 .16
❑ 188 Pascual Perez .15 .06
❑ 189 Biff Pocoroba .15 .06
❑ 190 Rafael Ramirez .15 .06
❑ 191 Jerry Royster .15 .06
❑ 192 Claudell Washington .15 .06
❑ 193 Bob Watson .15 .06
❑ 194 Jerry Augustine .15 .06
❑ 195 Mark Brouhard .15 .06
❑ 196 Mike Caldwell .15 .06
❑ 197 Tom Candiotti RC 1.00 .40
❑ 198 Cecil Cooper .40 .16
❑ 199 Rollie Fingers .40 .16
❑ 200 Jim Gantner .15 .06
❑ 201 Bob L. Gibson RC .25 .10
❑ 202 Moose Haas .15 .06
❑ 203 Roy Howell .15 .06
❑ 204 Pete Ladd .15 .06
❑ 205 Rick Manning .15 .06
❑ 206 Bob McClure .15 .06
❑ 207 Paul Molitor UER .75 .30
('83 stats should say .270 BA and 608 AB)
❑ 208 Don Money .15 .06
❑ 209 Charlie Moore .15 .06
❑ 210 Ben Oglivie .40 .16
❑ 211 Chuck Porter .15 .06
❑ 212 Ed Romero .15 .06
❑ 213 Ted Simmons .40 .16
❑ 214 Jim Slaton .15 .06
❑ 215 Don Sutton .40 .16
❑ 216 Tom Tellmann .15 .06
❑ 217 Pete Vuckovich .15 .06
❑ 218 Ned Yost .15 .06
❑ 219 Robin Yount 2.50 1.00
❑ 220 Alan Ashby .15 .06
❑ 221 Kevin Bass .15 .06
❑ 222 Jose Cruz .40 .16
❑ 223 Bill Dawley .15 .06
❑ 224 Frank DiPino .15 .06
❑ 225 Bill Doran RC* .50 .20
❑ 226 Phil Garner .40 .16
❑ 227 Art Howe .15 .06
❑ 228 Bob Knepper .15 .06
❑ 229 Ray Knight .40 .16
❑ 230 Frank LaCorte .15 .06
❑ 231 Mike LaCoss .15 .06
❑ 232 Mike Madden .15 .06
❑ 233 Jerry Mumphrey .15 .06
❑ 234 Joe Niekro .15 .06
❑ 235 Terry Puhl .15 .06
❑ 236 Luis Pujols .15 .06
❑ 237 Craig Reynolds .15 .06
❑ 238 Vern Ruhle .15 .06
❑ 239 Nolan Ryan 8.00 3.20
❑ 240 Mike Scott .40 .16
❑ 241 Tony Scott .15 .06
❑ 242 Dave Smith .15 .06
❑ 243 Dickie Thon .15 .06
❑ 244 Denny Walling .15 .06
❑ 245 Dale Berra .15 .06
❑ 246 Jim Bibby .15 .06
❑ 247 John Candelaria .15 .06
❑ 248 Jose DeLeon RC .50 .20
❑ 249 Mike Easler .15 .06
❑ 250 Cecilio Guante .15 .06
❑ 251 Richie Hebner .15 .06
❑ 252 Lee Lacy .15 .06
❑ 253 Bill Madlock .40 .16
❑ 254 Milt May .15 .06
❑ 255 Lee Mazzilli .40 .16
❑ 256 Larry McWilliams .15 .06
❑ 257 Jim Morrison .15 .06
❑ 258 Dave Parker .40 .16
❑ 259 Tony Pena .15 .06
❑ 260 Johnny Ray .15 .06
❑ 261 Rick Rhoden .15 .06
❑ 262 Don Robinson .15 .06
❑ 263 Manny Sarmiento .15 .06
❑ 264 Rod Scurry .15 .06
❑ 265 Kent Tekulve .15 .06
❑ 266 Gene Tenace .40 .16
❑ 267 Jason Thompson .15 .06
❑ 268 Lee Tunnell .15 .06
❑ 269 Marvell Wynne .50 .20
❑ 270 Ray Burris .15 .06
❑ 271 Gary Carter .40 .16
❑ 272 Warren Cromartie .15 .06
❑ 273 Andre Dawson .40 .16
❑ 274 Doug Flynn .15 .06
❑ 275 Terry Francona .40 .16
❑ 276 Bill Gullickson .15 .06
❑ 277 Bob James .15 .06
❑ 278 Charlie Lea .15 .06
❑ 279 Bryan Little .15 .06
❑ 280 Al Oliver .40 .16
❑ 281 Tim Raines .40 .16
❑ 282 Bobby Ramos .15 .06
❑ 283 Jeff Reardon .40 .16
❑ 284 Steve Rogers .40 .16
❑ 285 Scott Sanderson .15 .06
❑ 286 Dan Schatzeder .15 .06
❑ 287 Bryn Smith .15 .06
❑ 288 Chris Speier .15 .06
❑ 289 Manny Trillo .15 .06
❑ 290 Mike Vail .15 .06
❑ 291 Tim Wallach .15 .06
❑ 292 Chris Welsh .15 .06
❑ 293 Jim Wohlford .15 .06
❑ 294 Kurt Bevacqua .15 .06
❑ 295 Juan Bonilla .15 .06
❑ 296 Bobby Brown .15 .06
❑ 297 Luis DeLeon .15 .06
❑ 298 Dave Dravecky .15 .06
❑ 299 Tim Flannery .15 .06
❑ 300 Steve Garvey .40 .16
❑ 301 Tony Gwynn 6.00 2.40
❑ 302 Andy Hawkins .15 .06
❑ 303 Ruppert Jones .15 .06
❑ 304 Terry Kennedy .15 .06
❑ 305 Tim Lollar .15 .06
❑ 306 Gary Lucas .15 .06
❑ 307 Kevin McReynolds RC 1.00 .40
❑ 308 Sid Monge .15 .06
❑ 309 Mario Ramirez .15 .06
❑ 310 Gene Richards .15 .06
❑ 311 Luis Salazar .15 .06
❑ 312 Eric Show .15 .06
❑ 313 Elias Sosa .15 .06
❑ 314 Garry Templeton .40 .16
❑ 315 Mark Thurmond .15 .06
❑ 316 Ed Whitson .15 .06
❑ 317 Alan Wiggins .15 .06
❑ 318 Neil Allen .15 .06
❑ 319 Joaquin Andujar .40 .16
❑ 320 Steve Braun .15 .06
❑ 321 Glenn Brummer .15 .06
❑ 322 Bob Forsch .15 .06
❑ 323 David Green .15 .06
❑ 324 George Hendrick .40 .16
❑ 325 Tom Herr .15 .06
❑ 326 Dane Iorg .15 .06
❑ 327 Jeff Lahti .15 .06
❑ 328 Dave LaPoint .15 .06
❑ 329 Willie McGee .40 .16
❑ 330 Ken Oberkfell .15 .06
❑ 331 Darrell Porter .15 .06
❑ 332 Jamie Quirk .15 .06
❑ 333 Mike Ramsey .15 .06
❑ 334 Floyd Rayford .15 .06
❑ 335 Lonnie Smith .15 .06
❑ 336 Ozzie Smith 2.50 1.00
❑ 337 John Stuper .15 .06
❑ 338 Bruce Sutter .40 .16
❑ 339 A.Van Slyke RC UER 1.00 .40
Batting and throwing both wrong on card back
❑ 340 Dave Von Ohlen .15 .06
❑ 341 Willie Aikens .15 .06
❑ 342 Mike Armstrong .15 .06
❑ 343 Bud Black .15 .06
❑ 344 George Brett 4.00 1.60
❑ 345 Onix Concepcion .15 .06
❑ 346 Keith Creel .15 .06
❑ 347 Larry Gura .15 .06
❑ 348 Don Hood .15 .06
❑ 349 Dennis Leonard .15 .06
❑ 350 Hal McRae .40 .16
❑ 351 Amos Otis .40 .16
❑ 352 Gaylord Perry .40 .16
❑ 353 Greg Pryor .15 .06
❑ 354 Dan Quisenberry .15 .06
❑ 355 Steve Renko .15 .06
❑ 356 Leon Roberts .15 .06
❑ 357 Pat Sheridan .15 .06
❑ 358 Joe Simpson .15 .06
❑ 359 Don Slaught .40 .16
❑ 360 Paul Splittorff .15 .06
❑ 361 U.L. Washington .15 .06
❑ 362 John Wathan .15 .06
❑ 363 Frank White .40 .16
❑ 364 Willie Wilson .40 .16
❑ 365 Jim Barr .15 .06
❑ 366 Dave Bergman .15 .06
❑ 367 Fred Breining .15 .06
❑ 368 Bob Brenly .15 .06
❑ 369 Jack Clark .40 .16
❑ 370 Chili Davis .40 .16
❑ 371 Mark Davis .15 .06
❑ 372 Darrell Evans .40 .16
❑ 373 Atlee Hammaker .15 .06
❑ 374 Mike Krukow .15 .06
❑ 375 Duane Kuiper .15 .06
❑ 376 Bill Laskey .15 .06
❑ 377 Gary Lavelle .15 .06
❑ 378 Johnnie LeMaster .15 .06
❑ 379 Jeff Leonard .15 .06
❑ 380 Randy Lerch .15 .06
❑ 381 Renie Martin .15 .06
❑ 382 Andy McGaffigan .15 .06
❑ 383 Greg Minton .15 .06
❑ 384 Tom O'Malley .15 .06
❑ 385 Max Venable .15 .06
❑ 386 Brad Wellman .15 .06
❑ 387 Joel Youngblood .15 .06
❑ 388 Gary Allenson .15 .06
❑ 389 Luis Aponte .15 .06
❑ 390 Tony Armas .40 .16
❑ 391 Doug Bird .15 .06
❑ 392 Wade Boggs 4.00 1.60
❑ 393 Dennis Boyd .40 .16
❑ 394 Mike Brown UER .25 .10
(shown with record of 31-104)
❑ 395 Mark Clear .15 .06
❑ 396 Dennis Eckersley .75 .30
❑ 397 Dwight Evans .40 .16
❑ 398 Rich Gedman .15 .06
❑ 399 Glenn Hoffman .15 .06
❑ 400 Bruce Hurst .15 .06
❑ 401 John Henry Johnson .15 .06
❑ 402 Ed Jurak .15 .06
❑ 403 Rick Miller .15 .06
❑ 404 Jeff Newman .15 .06
❑ 405 Reid Nichols .15 .06
❑ 406 Bob Ojeda .15 .06
❑ 407 Jerry Remy .15 .06
❑ 408 Jim Rice .40 .16
❑ 409 Bob Stanley .15 .06
❑ 410 Dave Stapleton .15 .06
❑ 411 John Tudor .40 .16
❑ 412 Carl Yastrzemski 1.50 .60
❑ 413 Buddy Bell .40 .16
❑ 414 Larry Biittner .15 .06
❑ 415 John Butcher .15 .06
❑ 416 Danny Darwin .15 .06
❑ 417 Bucky Dent .40 .16
❑ 418 Dave Hostetler .15 .06
❑ 419 Charlie Hough .40 .16
❑ 420 Bobby Johnson .15 .06
❑ 421 Odell Jones .15 .06
❑ 422 Jon Matlack .15 .06
❑ 423 Pete O'Brien RC* .50 .20
❑ 424 Larry Parrish .15 .06
❑ 425 Mickey Rivers .15 .06

❑ 426 Billy Sample .15 .06
❑ 427 Dave Schmidt .15 .06
❑ 428 Mike Smithson .15 .06
❑ 429 Bill Stein .15 .06
❑ 430 Dave Stewart .40 .16
❑ 431 Jim Sundberg .40 .16
❑ 432 Frank Tanana .40 .16
❑ 433 Dave Tobik .15 .06
❑ 434 Wayne Tolleson .15 .06
❑ 435 George Wright .15 .06
❑ 436 Bill Almon .15 .06
❑ 437 Keith Atherton .15 .06
❑ 438 Dave Beard .15 .06
❑ 439 Tom Burgmeier .15 .06
❑ 440 Jeff Burroughs .15 .06
❑ 441 Chris Codiroli .15 .06
❑ 442 Tim Conroy .15 .06
❑ 443 Mike Davis .15 .06
❑ 444 Wayne Gross .15 .06
❑ 445 Garry Hancock .15 .06
❑ 446 Mike Heath .15 .06
❑ 447 Rickey Henderson 2.50 1.00
❑ 448 Donnie Hill .15 .06
❑ 449 Bob Kearney .15 .06
❑ 450 Bill Krueger RC .25 .10
❑ 451 Rick Langford .15 .06
❑ 452 Carney Lansford .40 .16
❑ 453 Dave Lopes .40 .16
❑ 454 Steve McCatty .15 .06
❑ 455 Dan Meyer .15 .06
❑ 456 Dwayne Murphy .15 .06
❑ 457 Mike Norris .15 .06
❑ 458 Ricky Peters .15 .06
❑ 459 Tony Phillips RC 1.00 .40
❑ 460 Tom Underwood .15 .06
❑ 461 Mike Warren .15 .06
❑ 462 Johnny Bench 1.50 .60
❑ 463 Bruce Berenyi .15 .06
❑ 464 Dann Bilardello .15 .06
❑ 465 Cesar Cedeno .40 .16
❑ 466 Dave Concepcion .40 .16
❑ 467 Dan Driessen .15 .06
❑ 468 Nick Esasky .15 .06
❑ 469 Rich Gale .15 .06
❑ 470 Ben Hayes .15 .06
❑ 471 Paul Householder .15 .06
❑ 472 Tom Hume .15 .06
❑ 473 Alan Knicely .15 .06
❑ 474 Eddie Milner .15 .06
❑ 475 Ron Oester .15 .06
❑ 476 Kelly Paris .15 .06
❑ 477 Frank Pastore .15 .06
❑ 478 Ted Power .15 .06
❑ 479 Joe Price .15 .06
❑ 480 Charlie Puleo .15 .06
❑ 481 Gary Redus RC* .50 .20
❑ 482 Bill Scherrer .15 .06
❑ 483 Mario Soto .40 .16
❑ 484 Alex Trevino .15 .06
❑ 485 Duane Walker .15 .06
❑ 486 Larry Bowa .40 .16
❑ 487 Warren Brusstar .15 .06
❑ 488 Bill Buckner .40 .16
❑ 489 Bill Campbell .15 .06
❑ 490 Ron Cey .40 .16
❑ 491 Jody Davis .15 .06
❑ 492 Leon Durham .15 .06
❑ 493 Mel Hall .40 .16
❑ 494 Ferguson Jenkins .40 .16
❑ 495 Jay Johnstone .15 .06
❑ 496 Craig Lefferts RC .25 .10
❑ 497 Carmelo Martinez .15 .06
❑ 498 Jerry Morales .15 .06
❑ 499 Keith Moreland .15 .06
❑ 500 Dickie Noles .15 .06
❑ 501 Mike Proly .15 .06
❑ 502 Chuck Rainey .15 .06
❑ 503 Dick Ruthven .15 .06
❑ 504 Ryne Sandberg 6.00 2.40
❑ 505 Lee Smith .40 .16
❑ 506 Steve Trout .15 .06
❑ 507 Gary Woods .15 .06
❑ 508 Juan Beniquez .15 .06
❑ 509 Bob Boone .40 .16
❑ 510 Rick Burleson .15 .06
❑ 511 Rod Carew .75 .30
❑ 512 Bobby Clark .15 .06
❑ 513 John Curtis .15 .06
❑ 514 Doug DeCinces .15 .06
❑ 515 Brian Downing .40 .16
❑ 516 Tim Foli .15 .06
❑ 517 Ken Forsch .15 .06
❑ 518 Bobby Grich .40 .16
❑ 519 Andy Hassler .15 .06
❑ 520 Reggie Jackson .75 .30
❑ 521 Ron Jackson .15 .06
❑ 522 Tommy John .40 .16
❑ 523 Bruce Kison .15 .06
❑ 524 Steve Lubratich .15 .06
❑ 525 Fred Lynn .40 .16
❑ 526 Gary Pettis .15 .06
❑ 527 Luis Sanchez .15 .06
❑ 528 Daryl Sconiers .15 .06
❑ 529 Ellis Valentine .15 .06
❑ 530 Rob Wilfong .15 .06
❑ 531 Mike Witt .15 .06
❑ 532 Geoff Zahn .15 .06
❑ 533 Bud Anderson .15 .06
❑ 534 Chris Bando .15 .06
❑ 535 Alan Bannister .15 .06
❑ 536 Bert Blyleven .40 .16
❑ 537 Tom Brennan .15 .06
❑ 538 Jamie Easterly .15 .06
❑ 539 Juan Eichelberger .15 .06
❑ 540 Jim Essian .15 .06
❑ 541 Mike Fischlin .15 .06
❑ 542 Julio Franco .75 .30
❑ 543 Mike Hargrove .15 .06
❑ 544 Toby Harrah .40 .16
❑ 545 Ron Hassey .15 .06
❑ 546 Neal Heaton .15 .06
❑ 547 Bake McBride .40 .16
❑ 548 Broderick Perkins .15 .06
❑ 549 Lary Sorensen .15 .06
❑ 550 Dan Spillner .15 .06
❑ 551 Rick Sutcliffe .40 .16
❑ 552 Pat Tabler .15 .06
❑ 553 Gorman Thomas .40 .16
❑ 554 Andre Thornton .15 .06
❑ 555 George Vukovich .15 .06
❑ 556 Darrell Brown .15 .06
❑ 557 Tom Brunansky .15 .06
❑ 558 Randy Bush .15 .06
❑ 559 Bobby Castillo .15 .06
❑ 560 John Castino .15 .06
❑ 561 Ron Davis .15 .06
❑ 562 Dave Engle .15 .06
❑ 563 Lenny Faedo .15 .06
❑ 564 Pete Filson .15 .06
❑ 565 Gary Gaetti .75 .30
❑ 566 Mickey Hatcher .15 .06
❑ 567 Kent Hrbek .40 .16
❑ 568 Rusty Kuntz .15 .06
❑ 569 Tim Laudner .15 .06
❑ 570 Rick Lysander .15 .06
❑ 571 Bobby Mitchell .15 .06
❑ 572 Ken Schrom .15 .06
❑ 573 Ray Smith .15 .06
❑ 574 Tim Teufel RC .50 .20
❑ 575 Frank Viola .75 .30
❑ 576 Gary Ward .15 .06
❑ 577 Ron Washington .15 .06
❑ 578 Len Whitehouse .15 .06
❑ 579 Al Williams .15 .06
❑ 580 Bob Bailor .15 .06
❑ 581 Mark Bradley .15 .06
❑ 582 Hubie Brooks .15 .06
❑ 583 Carlos Diaz .15 .06
❑ 584 George Foster .40 .16
❑ 585 Brian Giles .15 .06
❑ 586 Danny Heep .15 .06
❑ 587 Keith Hernandez .40 .16
❑ 588 Ron Hodges .15 .06
❑ 589 Scott Holman .15 .06
❑ 590 Dave Kingman .40 .16
❑ 591 Ed Lynch .15 .06
❑ 592 Jose Oquendo RC .50 .20
❑ 593 Jesse Orosco .15 .06
❑ 594 Junior Ortiz .15 .06
❑ 595 Tom Seaver 1.50 .60
❑ 596 Doug Sisk .15 .06
❑ 597 Rusty Staub .40 .16
❑ 598 John Stearns .15 .06
❑ 599 Darryl Strawberry RC 3.00 1.20
❑ 600 Craig Swan .15 .06
❑ 601 Walt Terrell .15 .06
❑ 602 Mike Torrez .15 .06
❑ 603 Mookie Wilson .40 .16
❑ 604 Jamie Allen .15 .06
❑ 605 Jim Beattie .15 .06
❑ 606 Tony Bernazard .15 .06
❑ 607 Manny Castillo .15 .06
❑ 608 Bill Caudill .15 .06
❑ 609 Bryan Clark .15 .06
❑ 610 Al Cowens .15 .06
❑ 611 Dave Henderson .40 .16
❑ 612 Steve Henderson .15 .06
❑ 613 Orlando Mercado .15 .06
❑ 614 Mike Moore .15 .06
❑ 615 Ricky Nelson UER .15 .06
(Jamie Nelson's
stats on back)
❑ 616 Spike Owen RC .50 .20
❑ 617 Pat Putnam .15 .06
❑ 618 Ron Roenicke .15 .06
❑ 619 Mike Stanton .15 .06
❑ 620 Bob Stoddard .15 .06
❑ 621 Rick Sweet .15 .06
❑ 622 Roy Thomas .15 .06
❑ 623 Ed VandeBerg .15 .06
❑ 624 Matt Young RC .50 .20
❑ 625 Richie Zisk .15 .06
❑ 626 Fred Lynn IA .40 .16
❑ 627 Manny Trillo IA .15 .06
❑ 628 Steve Garvey IA .15 .06
❑ 629 Rod Carew IA .40 .16
❑ 630 Wade Boggs IA 1.50 .60
❑ 631 Tim Raines IA .15 .06
❑ 632 Al Oliver IA .40 .16
❑ 633 Steve Sax IA .15 .06
❑ 634 Dickie Thon IA .15 .06
❑ 635 Dan Quisenberry .15 .06
Tippy Martinez
❑ 636 Joe Morgan 1.50 .60
Pete Rose
Tony Perez
❑ 637 Lance Parrish .75 .30
Bob Boone
❑ 638 George Brett 2.00 .80
Gaylord Perry
❑ 639 Dave Righetti .75 .30
Mike Warren
Bob Forsch
❑ 640 Johnny Bench 1.50 .60
Carl Yastrzemski
❑ 641 Gaylord Perry IA .15 .06
❑ 642 Steve Carlton IA .40 .16
❑ 643 Joe Altobelli MG .15 .06
Paul Owens MG
❑ 644 Rick Dempsey WS .15 .06
❑ 645 Mike Boddicker WS .15 .06
❑ 646 Scott McGregor WS .15 .06
❑ 647 CL: Orioles/Royals .15 .06
Joe Altobelli MG
❑ 648 CL: Phillies/Giants .15 .06
Paul Owens MG
❑ 649 CL: White Sox/Red Sox .75 .30
Tony LaRussa MG
❑ 650 CL: Tigers/Rangers .75 .30
Sparky Anderson MG
❑ 651 CL: Dodgers/A's .75 .30
Tommy Lasorda MG
❑ 652 CL: Yankees/Reds .75 .30
Billy Martin MG
❑ 653 CL: Blue Jays/Cubs .40 .16
Bobby Cox MG
❑ 654 CL: Braves/Angels .75 .30
Joe Torre MG
❑ 655 CL: Brewers/Indians .15 .06
Rene Lachemann MG
❑ 656 CL: Astros/Twins .15 .06
Bob Lillis MG
❑ 657 CL: Pirates/Mets .15 .06
Chuck Tanner MG
❑ 658 CL: Expos/Mariners .15 .06
Bill Virdon MG
❑ 659 CL: Padres/Specials .40 .16
Dick Williams MG

	Card	Nm-Mt	Ex-Mt
❑ 660	CL: Cardinals/Teams Whitey Herzog MG	.75	.30

1984 Fleer Update

	Nm-Mt	Ex-Mt
COMP.FACT.SET (132)	350.00	140.00

#	Player	Nm-Mt	Ex-Mt
❑ 1	Willie Aikens	1.00	.40
❑ 2	Luis Aponte	1.00	.40
❑ 3	Mark Bailey	1.00	.40
❑ 4	Bob Bailor	1.00	.40
❑ 5	Dusty Baker	1.50	.60
❑ 6	Steve Balboni	1.00	.40
❑ 7	Alan Bannister	1.00	.40
❑ 8	Marty Barrett XRC	2.00	.80
❑ 9	Dave Beard	1.00	.40
❑ 10	Joe Beckwith	1.00	.40
❑ 11	Dave Bergman	1.00	.40
❑ 12	Tony Bernazard	1.00	.40
❑ 13	Bruce Bochte	1.00	.40
❑ 14	Barry Bonnell	1.00	.40
❑ 15	Phil Bradley	2.00	.80
❑ 16	Fred Breining	1.00	.40
❑ 17	Mike C. Brown	1.00	.40
❑ 18	Bill Buckner	1.50	.60
❑ 19	Ray Burris	1.00	.40
❑ 20	John Butcher	1.00	.40
❑ 21	Brett Butler	1.50	.60
❑ 22	Enos Cabell	1.00	.40
❑ 23	Bill Campbell	1.00	.40
❑ 24	Bill Caudill	1.00	.40
❑ 25	Bobby Clark	1.00	.40
❑ 26	Bryan Clark	1.00	.40
❑ 27	Roger Clemens XRC	225.00	90.00
❑ 28	Jaime Cocanower	1.00	.40
❑ 29	Ron Darling XRC*	5.00	2.00
❑ 30	Alvin Davis XRC	2.00	.80
❑ 31	Bob Dernier	1.00	.40
❑ 32	Carlos Diaz	1.00	.40
❑ 33	Mike Easler	1.00	.40
❑ 34	Dennis Eckersley	2.50	1.00
❑ 35	Jim Essian	1.00	.40
❑ 36	Darrell Evans	1.50	.60
❑ 37	Mike Fitzgerald	1.00	.40
❑ 38	Tim Foli	1.00	.40
❑ 39	John Franco XRC	5.00	2.00
❑ 40	George Frazier	1.00	.40
❑ 41	Rich Gale	1.00	.40
❑ 42	Barbaro Garbey	1.00	.40
❑ 43	Dwight Gooden XRC	15.00	6.00
❑ 44	Rich Gossage	1.50	.60
❑ 45	Wayne Gross	1.00	.40
❑ 46	Mark Gubicza XRC	2.00	.80
❑ 47	Jackie Gutierrez	1.00	.40
❑ 48	Toby Harrah	1.50	.60
❑ 49	Ron Hassey	1.00	.40
❑ 50	Richie Hebner	1.00	.40
❑ 51	Willie Hernandez	1.00	.40
❑ 52	Ed Hodge	1.00	.40
❑ 53	Ricky Horton	1.00	.40
❑ 54	Art Howe	1.00	.40
❑ 55	Dane Iorg	1.00	.40
❑ 56	Brook Jacoby	2.00	.80
❑ 57	Dion James XRC*	1.00	.40
❑ 58	Mike Jeffcoat XRC	1.00	.40
❑ 59	Ruppert Jones	1.00	.40
❑ 60	Bob Kearney	1.00	.40
❑ 61	Jimmy Key XRC	5.00	2.00
❑ 62	Dave Kingman	1.50	.60
❑ 63	Brad Komminsk XRC	1.00	.40
❑ 64	Jerry Koosman	1.50	.60
❑ 65	Wayne Krenchicki	1.00	.40
❑ 66	Rusty Kuntz	1.00	.40
❑ 67	Frank LaCorte	1.00	.40
❑ 68	Dennis Lamp	1.00	.40
❑ 69	Tito Landrum	1.00	.40
❑ 70	Mark Langston XRC	5.00	2.00
❑ 71	Rick Leach	1.00	.40
❑ 72	Craig Lefferts	1.00	.40
❑ 73	Gary Lucas	1.00	.40
❑ 74	Jerry Martin	1.00	.40
❑ 75	Carmelo Martinez	1.00	.40
❑ 76	Mike Mason XRC	1.00	.40
❑ 77	Gary Matthews	1.50	.60
❑ 78	Andy McGaffigan	1.00	.40
❑ 79	Joey McLaughlin	1.00	.40
❑ 80	Joe Morgan	1.50	.60
❑ 81	Darryl Motley	1.00	.40
❑ 82	Graig Nettles	1.50	.60
❑ 83	Phil Niekro	1.50	.60
❑ 84	Ken Oberkfell	1.00	.40
❑ 85	Al Oliver	1.50	.60
❑ 86	Jorge Orta	1.00	.40
❑ 87	Amos Otis	1.50	.60
❑ 88	Bob Owchinko	1.00	.40
❑ 89	Dave Parker	1.50	.60
❑ 90	Jack Perconte	1.00	.40
❑ 91	Tony Perez	2.50	1.00
❑ 92	Gerald Perry	2.00	.80
❑ 93	Kirby Puckett XRC	60.00	24.00
❑ 94	Shane Rawley	1.00	.40
❑ 95	Floyd Rayford	1.00	.40
❑ 96	Ron Reed	1.00	.40
❑ 97	R.J. Reynolds	1.00	.40
❑ 98	Gene Richards	1.00	.40
❑ 99	Jose Rijo XRC	5.00	2.00
❑ 100	Jeff D. Robinson	1.00	.40
❑ 101	Ron Romanick	1.00	.40
❑ 102	Pete Rose	12.00	4.80
❑ 103	Bret Saberhagen XRC	8.00	3.20
❑ 104	Scott Sanderson	1.00	.40
❑ 105	Dick Schofield XRC*	2.00	.80
❑ 106	Tom Seaver	4.00	1.60
❑ 107	Jim Slaton	1.00	.40
❑ 108	Mike Smithson	1.00	.40
❑ 109	Lary Sorensen	1.00	.40
❑ 110	Tim Stoddard	1.00	.40
❑ 111	Jeff Stone	1.00	.40
❑ 112	Champ Summers	1.00	.40
❑ 113	Jim Sundberg	1.50	.60
❑ 114	Rick Sutcliffe	1.50	.60
❑ 115	Craig Swan	1.00	.40
❑ 116	Derrel Thomas	1.00	.40
❑ 117	Gorman Thomas	1.50	.60
❑ 118	Alex Trevino	1.00	.40
❑ 119	Manny Trillo	1.00	.40
❑ 120	John Tudor	1.50	.60
❑ 121	Tom Underwood	1.00	.40
❑ 122	Mike Vail	1.00	.40
❑ 123	Tom Waddell	1.00	.40
❑ 124	Gary Ward	1.00	.40
❑ 125	Terry Whitfield	1.00	.40
❑ 126	Curtis Wilkerson	1.00	.40
❑ 127	Frank Williams	1.00	.40
❑ 128	Glenn Wilson	1.50	.60
❑ 129	John Wockenfuss	1.00	.40
❑ 130	Ned Yost	1.00	.40
❑ 131	Mike Young RC	1.00	.40
❑ 132	Checklist 1-132	1.00	.40

1985 Fleer

	Nm-Mt	Ex-Mt
COMPLETE SET (660)	80.00	32.00

#	Player	Nm-Mt	Ex-Mt
❑ 1	Doug Bair	.15	.06
❑ 2	Juan Berenguer	.15	.06
❑ 3	Dave Bergman	.15	.06
❑ 4	Tom Brookens	.15	.06
❑ 5	Marty Castillo	.15	.06
❑ 6	Darrell Evans	.40	.16
❑ 7	Barbaro Garbey	.15	.06
❑ 8	Kirk Gibson	.40	.16
❑ 9	John Grubb	.15	.06
❑ 10	Willie Hernandez	.15	.06
❑ 11	Larry Herndon	.15	.06
❑ 12	Howard Johnson	.40	.16
❑ 13	Ruppert Jones	.15	.06
❑ 14	Rusty Kuntz	.15	.06
❑ 15	Chet Lemon	.40	.16
❑ 16	Aurelio Lopez	.15	.06
❑ 17	Sid Monge	.15	.06
❑ 18	Jack Morris	.40	.16
❑ 19	Lance Parrish	.40	.16
❑ 20	Dan Petry	.15	.06
❑ 21	Dave Rozema	.15	.06
❑ 22	Bill Scherrer	.15	.06
❑ 23	Alan Trammell	.40	.16
❑ 24	Lou Whitaker	.40	.16
❑ 25	Milt Wilcox	.15	.06
❑ 26	Kurt Bevacqua	.15	.06
❑ 27	Greg Booker	.15	.06
❑ 28	Bobby Brown	.15	.06
❑ 29	Luis DeLeon	.15	.06
❑ 30	Dave Dravecky	.15	.06
❑ 31	Tim Flannery	.15	.06
❑ 32	Steve Garvey	.40	.16
❑ 33	Rich Gossage	.40	.16
❑ 34	Tony Gwynn	2.50	1.00
❑ 35	Greg Harris	.15	.06
❑ 36	Andy Hawkins	.15	.06
❑ 37	Terry Kennedy	.15	.06
❑ 38	Craig Lefferts	.15	.06
❑ 39	Tim Lollar	.15	.06
❑ 40	Carmelo Martinez	.15	.06
❑ 41	Kevin McReynolds	.40	.16
❑ 42	Graig Nettles	.40	.16
❑ 43	Luis Salazar	.15	.06
❑ 44	Eric Show	.15	.06
❑ 45	Garry Templeton	.40	.16
❑ 46	Mark Thurmond	.15	.06
❑ 47	Ed Whitson	.15	.06
❑ 48	Alan Wiggins	.15	.06
❑ 49	Rich Bordi	.15	.06
❑ 50	Larry Bowa	.40	.16
❑ 51	Warren Brusstar	.15	.06
❑ 52	Ron Cey	.40	.16
❑ 53	Henry Cotto RC	.25	.10
❑ 54	Jody Davis	.15	.06
❑ 55	Bob Dernier	.15	.06
❑ 56	Leon Durham	.15	.06
❑ 57	Dennis Eckersley	.75	.30
❑ 58	George Frazier	.15	.06
❑ 59	Richie Hebner	.15	.06
❑ 60	Dave Lopes	.40	.16
❑ 61	Gary Matthews	.40	.16
❑ 62	Keith Moreland	.15	.06
❑ 63	Rick Reuschel	.40	.16
❑ 64	Dick Ruthven	.15	.06
❑ 65	Ryne Sandberg	2.50	1.00
❑ 66	Scott Sanderson	.15	.06
❑ 67	Lee Smith	.40	.16
❑ 68	Tim Stoddard	.15	.06
❑ 69	Rick Sutcliffe	.40	.16
❑ 70	Steve Trout	.15	.06
❑ 71	Gary Woods	.15	.06
❑ 72	Wally Backman	.15	.06
❑ 73	Bruce Berenyi	.15	.06
❑ 74	Hubie Brooks UER (Kelvin Chapman's stats on card back)	.15	.06
❑ 75	Kelvin Chapman	.15	.06
❑ 76	Ron Darling	.40	.16
❑ 77	Sid Fernandez	.40	.16
❑ 78	Mike Fitzgerald	.15	.06
❑ 79	George Foster	.40	.16
❑ 80	Brent Gaff	.15	.06
❑ 81	Ron Gardenhire	.15	.06

No.	Player	Price	Price
❑ 82	Dwight Gooden RC	2.00	.80
❑ 83	Tom Gorman	.15	.06
❑ 84	Danny Heep	.15	.06
❑ 85	Keith Hernandez	.40	.16
❑ 86	Ray Knight	.40	.16
❑ 87	Ed Lynch	.15	.06
❑ 88	Jose Oquendo	.15	.06
❑ 89	Jesse Orosco	.15	.06
❑ 90	Rafael Santana	.15	.06
❑ 91	Doug Sisk	.15	.06
❑ 92	Rusty Staub	.40	.16
❑ 93	Darryl Strawberry	1.25	.50
❑ 94	Walt Terrell	.15	.06
❑ 95	Mookie Wilson	.40	.16
❑ 96	Jim Acker	.15	.06
❑ 97	Willie Aikens	.15	.06
❑ 98	Doyle Alexander	.15	.06
❑ 99	Jesse Barfield	.40	.16
❑ 100	George Bell	.40	.16
❑ 101	Jim Clancy	.15	.06
❑ 102	Dave Collins	.15	.06
❑ 103	Tony Fernandez	.40	.16
❑ 104	Damaso Garcia	.15	.06
❑ 105	Jim Gott	.15	.06
❑ 106	Alfredo Griffin	.15	.06
❑ 107	Garth Iorg	.15	.06
❑ 108	Roy Lee Jackson	.15	.06
❑ 109	Cliff Johnson	.15	.06
❑ 110	Jimmy Key RC	1.00	.40
❑ 111	Dennis Lamp	.15	.06
❑ 112	Rick Leach	.15	.06
❑ 113	Luis Leal	.15	.06
❑ 114	Buck Martinez	.15	.06
❑ 115	Lloyd Moseby	.15	.06
❑ 116	Rance Mulliniks	.15	.06
❑ 117	Dave Stieb	.40	.16
❑ 118	Willie Upshaw	.15	.06
❑ 119	Ernie Whitt	.15	.06
❑ 120	Mike Armstrong	.15	.06
❑ 121	Don Baylor	.40	.16
❑ 122	Marty Bystrom	.15	.06
❑ 123	Rick Cerone	.15	.06
❑ 124	Joe Cowley	.15	.06
❑ 125	Brian Dayett	.15	.06
❑ 126	Tim Foli	.15	.06
❑ 127	Ray Fontenot	.15	.06
❑ 128	Ken Griffey	.40	.16
❑ 129	Ron Guidry	.40	.16
❑ 130	Toby Harrah	.40	.16
❑ 131	Jay Howell	.15	.06
❑ 132	Steve Kemp	.15	.06
❑ 133	Don Mattingly	5.00	2.00
❑ 134	Bobby Meacham	.15	.06
❑ 135	John Montefusco	.15	.06
❑ 136	Omar Moreno	.15	.06
❑ 137	Dale Murray	.15	.06
❑ 138	Phil Niekro	.40	.16
❑ 139	Mike Pagliarulo	.15	.06
❑ 140	Willie Randolph	.40	.16
❑ 141	Dennis Rasmussen	.15	.06
❑ 142	Dave Righetti	.40	.16
❑ 143	Jose Rijo RC	1.00	.40
❑ 144	Andre Robertson	.15	.06
❑ 145	Bob Shirley	.15	.06
❑ 146	Dave Winfield	.40	.16
❑ 147	Butch Wynegar	.15	.06
❑ 148	Gary Allenson	.15	.06
❑ 149	Tony Armas	.40	.16
❑ 150	Marty Barrett	.15	.06
❑ 151	Wade Boggs	1.25	.50
❑ 152	Dennis Boyd	.15	.06
❑ 153	Bill Buckner	.40	.16
❑ 154	Mark Clear	.15	.06
❑ 155	Roger Clemens RC	40.00	16.00
❑ 156	Steve Crawford	.15	.06
❑ 157	Mike Easler	.15	.06
❑ 158	Dwight Evans	.40	.16
❑ 159	Rich Gedman	.15	.06
❑ 160	Jackie Gutierrez (Wade Boggs shown on deck)	.40	.16
❑ 161	Bruce Hurst	.15	.06
❑ 162	John Henry Johnson	.15	.06
❑ 163	Rick Miller	.15	.06
❑ 164	Reid Nichols	.15	.06
❑ 165	Al Nipper	.15	.06
❑ 166	Bob Ojeda	.15	.06
❑ 167	Jerry Remy	.15	.06
❑ 168	Jim Rice	.40	.16
❑ 169	Bob Stanley	.15	.06
❑ 170	Mike Boddicker	.15	.06
❑ 171	Al Bumbry	.15	.06
❑ 172	Todd Cruz	.15	.06
❑ 173	Rich Dauer	.15	.06
❑ 174	Storm Davis	.15	.06
❑ 175	Rick Dempsey	.15	.06
❑ 176	Jim Dwyer	.15	.06
❑ 177	Mike Flanagan	.15	.06
❑ 178	Dan Ford	.15	.06
❑ 179	Wayne Gross	.15	.06
❑ 180	John Lowenstein	.15	.06
❑ 181	Dennis Martinez	.40	.16
❑ 182	Tippy Martinez	.15	.06
❑ 183	Scott McGregor	.15	.06
❑ 184	Eddie Murray	1.25	.50
❑ 185	Joe Nolan	.15	.06
❑ 186	Floyd Rayford	.15	.06
❑ 187	Cal Ripken	5.00	2.00
❑ 188	Gary Roenicke	.15	.06
❑ 189	Lenn Sakata	.15	.06
❑ 190	John Shelby	.15	.06
❑ 191	Ken Singleton	.40	.16
❑ 192	Sammy Stewart	.15	.06
❑ 193	Bill Swaggerty	.15	.06
❑ 194	Tom Underwood	.15	.06
❑ 195	Mike Young	.15	.06
❑ 196	Steve Balboni	.15	.06
❑ 197	Joe Beckwith	.15	.06
❑ 198	Bud Black	.15	.06
❑ 199	George Brett	3.00	1.20
❑ 200	Onix Concepcion	.15	.06
❑ 201	Mark Gubicza RC*	.50	.20
❑ 202	Larry Gura	.15	.06
❑ 203	Mark Huismann	.15	.06
❑ 204	Dane Iorg	.15	.06
❑ 205	Danny Jackson	.15	.06
❑ 206	Charlie Leibrandt	.15	.06
❑ 207	Hal McRae	.40	.16
❑ 208	Darryl Motley	.15	.06
❑ 209	Jorge Orta	.15	.06
❑ 210	Greg Pryor	.15	.06
❑ 211	Dan Quisenberry	.15	.06
❑ 212	Bret Saberhagen RC	1.50	.60
❑ 213	Pat Sheridan	.15	.06
❑ 214	Don Slaught	.15	.06
❑ 215	U.L. Washington	.15	.06
❑ 216	John Wathan	.15	.06
❑ 217	Frank White	.40	.16
❑ 218	Willie Wilson	.40	.16
❑ 219	Neil Allen	.15	.06
❑ 220	Joaquin Andujar	.40	.16
❑ 221	Steve Braun	.15	.06
❑ 222	Danny Cox	.15	.06
❑ 223	Bob Forsch	.15	.06
❑ 224	David Green	.15	.06
❑ 225	George Hendrick	.40	.16
❑ 226	Tom Herr	.15	.06
❑ 227	Ricky Horton	.15	.06
❑ 228	Art Howe	.15	.06
❑ 229	Mike Jorgensen	.15	.06
❑ 230	Kurt Kepshire	.15	.06
❑ 231	Jeff Lahti	.15	.06
❑ 232	Tito Landrum	.15	.06
❑ 233	Dave LaPoint	.15	.06
❑ 234	Willie McGee	.40	.16
❑ 235	Tom Nieto	.15	.06
❑ 236	Terry Pendleton RC	1.00	.40
❑ 237	Darrell Porter	.15	.06
❑ 238	Dave Rucker	.15	.06
❑ 239	Lonnie Smith	.15	.06
❑ 240	Ozzie Smith	2.00	.80
❑ 241	Bruce Sutter	.40	.16
❑ 242	Andy Van Slyke UER (Bats Right, Throws Left)	.40	.16
❑ 243	Dave Von Ohlen	.15	.06
❑ 244	Larry Andersen	.15	.06
❑ 245	Bill Campbell	.15	.06
❑ 246	Steve Carlton	.40	.16
❑ 247	Tim Corcoran	.15	.06
❑ 248	Ivan DeJesus	.15	.06
❑ 249	John Denny	.15	.06
❑ 250	Bo Diaz	.15	.06
❑ 251	Greg Gross	.15	.06
❑ 252	Kevin Gross	.15	.06
❑ 253	Von Hayes	.15	.06
❑ 254	Al Holland	.15	.06
❑ 255	Charles Hudson	.15	.06
❑ 256	Jerry Koosman	.40	.16
❑ 257	Joe Lefebvre	.15	.06
❑ 258	Sixto Lezcano	.15	.06
❑ 259	Garry Maddox	.15	.06
❑ 260	Len Matuszek	.15	.06
❑ 261	Tug McGraw	.40	.16
❑ 262	Al Oliver	.40	.16
❑ 263	Shane Rawley	.15	.06
❑ 264	Juan Samuel	.15	.06
❑ 265	Mike Schmidt	3.00	1.20
❑ 266	Jeff Stone	.15	.06
❑ 267	Ozzie Virgil	.15	.06
❑ 268	Glenn Wilson	.15	.06
❑ 269	John Wockenfuss	.15	.06
❑ 270	Darrell Brown	.15	.06
❑ 271	Tom Brunansky	.15	.06
❑ 272	Randy Bush	.15	.06
❑ 273	John Butcher	.15	.06
❑ 274	Bobby Castillo	.15	.06
❑ 275	Ron Davis	.15	.06
❑ 276	Dave Engle	.15	.06
❑ 277	Pete Filson	.15	.06
❑ 278	Gary Gaetti	.40	.16
❑ 279	Mickey Hatcher	.15	.06
❑ 280	Ed Hodge	.15	.06
❑ 281	Kent Hrbek	.40	.16
❑ 282	Houston Jimenez	.15	.06
❑ 283	Tim Laudner	.15	.06
❑ 284	Rick Lysander	.15	.06
❑ 285	Dave Meier	.15	.06
❑ 286	Kirby Puckett RC	10.00	4.00
❑ 287	Pat Putnam	.15	.06
❑ 288	Ken Schrom	.15	.06
❑ 289	Mike Smithson	.15	.06
❑ 290	Tim Teufel	.15	.06
❑ 291	Frank Viola	.40	.16
❑ 292	Ron Washington	.15	.06
❑ 293	Don Aase	.15	.06
❑ 294	Juan Beniquez	.15	.06
❑ 295	Bob Boone	.40	.16
❑ 296	Mike C. Brown	.15	.06
❑ 297	Rod Carew	.75	.30
❑ 298	Doug Corbett	.15	.06
❑ 299	Doug DeCinces	.15	.06
❑ 300	Brian Downing	.40	.16
❑ 301	Ken Forsch	.15	.06
❑ 302	Bobby Grich	.40	.16
❑ 303	Reggie Jackson	.75	.30
❑ 304	Tommy John	.40	.16
❑ 305	Curt Kaufman	.15	.06
❑ 306	Bruce Kison	.15	.06
❑ 307	Fred Lynn	.40	.16
❑ 308	Gary Pettis	.15	.06
❑ 309	Ron Romanick	.15	.06
❑ 310	Luis Sanchez	.15	.06
❑ 311	Dick Schofield	.15	.06
❑ 312	Daryl Sconiers	.15	.06
❑ 313	Jim Slaton	.15	.06
❑ 314	Derrel Thomas	.15	.06
❑ 315	Rob Wilfong	.15	.06
❑ 316	Mike Witt	.15	.06
❑ 317	Geoff Zahn	.15	.06
❑ 318	Len Barker	.15	.06
❑ 319	Steve Bedrosian	.15	.06
❑ 320	Bruce Benedict	.15	.06
❑ 321	Rick Camp	.15	.06
❑ 322	Chris Chambliss	.40	.16
❑ 323	Jeff Dedmon	.15	.06
❑ 324	Terry Forster	.40	.16
❑ 325	Gene Garber	.15	.06
❑ 326	Albert Hall	.15	.06
❑ 327	Terry Harper	.15	.06
❑ 328	Bob Horner	.40	.16
❑ 329	Glenn Hubbard	.15	.06
❑ 330	Randy Johnson	.15	.06
❑ 331	Brad Komminsk	.15	.06
❑ 332	Rick Mahler	.15	.06
❑ 333	Craig McMurtry	.15	.06
❑ 334	Donnie Moore	.15	.06
❑ 335	Dale Murphy	.75	.30

❑ 336	Ken Oberkfell	.15	.06
❑ 337	Pascual Perez	.15	.06
❑ 338	Gerald Perry	.15	.06
❑ 339	Rafael Ramirez	.15	.06
❑ 340	Jerry Royster	.15	.06
❑ 341	Alex Trevino	.15	.06
❑ 342	Claudell Washington	.15	.06
❑ 343	Alan Ashby	.15	.06
❑ 344	Mark Bailey	.15	.06
❑ 345	Kevin Bass	.15	.06
❑ 346	Enos Cabell	.15	.06
❑ 347	Jose Cruz	.40	.16
❑ 348	Bill Dawley	.15	.06
❑ 349	Frank DiPino	.15	.06
❑ 350	Bill Doran	.15	.06
❑ 351	Phil Garner	.40	.16
❑ 352	Bob Knepper	.15	.06
❑ 353	Mike LaCoss	.15	.06
❑ 354	Jerry Mumphrey	.15	.06
❑ 355	Joe Niekro	.15	.06
❑ 356	Terry Puhl	.15	.06
❑ 357	Craig Reynolds	.15	.06
❑ 358	Vern Ruhle	.15	.06
❑ 359	Nolan Ryan	6.00	2.40
❑ 360	Joe Sambito	.15	.06
❑ 361	Mike Scott	.40	.16
❑ 362	Dave Smith	.15	.06
❑ 363	Julio Solano	.15	.06
❑ 364	Dickie Thon	.15	.06
❑ 365	Denny Walling	.15	.06
❑ 366	Dave Anderson	.15	.06
❑ 367	Bob Bailor	.15	.06
❑ 368	Greg Brock	.15	.06
❑ 369	Carlos Diaz	.15	.06
❑ 370	Pedro Guerrero	.40	.16
❑ 371	Orel Hershiser RC	1.50	.60
❑ 372	Rick Honeycutt	.15	.06
❑ 373	Burt Hooton	.15	.06
❑ 374	Ken Howell	.15	.06
❑ 375	Ken Landreaux	.15	.06
❑ 376	Candy Maldonado	.15	.06
❑ 377	Mike Marshall	.15	.06
❑ 378	Tom Niedenfuer	.15	.06
❑ 379	Alejandro Pena	.15	.06
❑ 380	Jerry Reuss UER ("Home:" omitted)	.15	.06
❑ 381	R.J. Reynolds	.15	.06
❑ 382	German Rivera	.15	.06
❑ 383	Bill Russell	.40	.16
❑ 384	Steve Sax	.15	.06
❑ 385	Mike Scioscia	.40	.16
❑ 386	Franklin Stubbs	.15	.06
❑ 387	Fernando Valenzuela	.40	.16
❑ 388	Bob Welch	.40	.16
❑ 389	Terry Whitfield	.15	.06
❑ 390	Steve Yeager	.40	.16
❑ 391	Pat Zachry	.15	.06
❑ 392	Fred Breining	.15	.06
❑ 393	Gary Carter	.40	.16
❑ 394	Andre Dawson	.40	.16
❑ 395	Miguel Dilone	.15	.06
❑ 396	Dan Driessen	.15	.06
❑ 397	Doug Flynn	.15	.06
❑ 398	Terry Francona	.40	.16
❑ 399	Bill Gullickson	.15	.06
❑ 400	Bob James	.15	.06
❑ 401	Charlie Lea	.15	.06
❑ 402	Bryan Little	.15	.06
❑ 403	Gary Lucas	.15	.06
❑ 404	David Palmer	.15	.06
❑ 405	Tim Raines	.40	.16
❑ 406	Mike Ramsey	.15	.06
❑ 407	Jeff Reardon	.40	.16
❑ 408	Steve Rogers	.40	.16
❑ 409	Dan Schatzeder	.15	.06
❑ 410	Bryn Smith	.15	.06
❑ 411	Mike Stenhouse	.15	.06
❑ 412	Tim Wallach	.15	.06
❑ 413	Jim Wohlford	.15	.06
❑ 414	Bill Almon	.15	.06
❑ 415	Keith Atherton	.15	.06
❑ 416	Bruce Bochte	.15	.06
❑ 417	Tom Burgmeier	.15	.06
❑ 418	Ray Burris	.15	.06
❑ 419	Bill Caudill	.15	.06
❑ 420	Chris Codiroli	.15	.06
❑ 421	Tim Conroy	.15	.06
❑ 422	Mike Davis	.15	.06
❑ 423	Jim Essian	.15	.06
❑ 424	Mike Heath	.15	.06
❑ 425	Rickey Henderson	1.50	.60
❑ 426	Donnie Hill	.15	.06
❑ 427	Dave Kingman	.40	.16
❑ 428	Bill Krueger	.15	.06
❑ 429	Carney Lansford	.40	.16
❑ 430	Steve McCatty	.15	.06
❑ 431	Joe Morgan	.40	.16
❑ 432	Dwayne Murphy	.15	.06
❑ 433	Tony Phillips	.15	.06
❑ 434	Lary Sorensen	.15	.06
❑ 435	Mike Warren	.15	.06
❑ 436	Curt Young	.15	.06
❑ 437	Luis Aponte	.15	.06
❑ 438	Chris Bando	.15	.06
❑ 439	Tony Bernazard	.15	.06
❑ 440	Bert Blyleven	.40	.16
❑ 441	Brett Butler	.40	.16
❑ 442	Ernie Camacho	.15	.06
❑ 443	Joe Carter	1.25	.50
❑ 444	Carmelo Castillo	.15	.06
❑ 445	Jamie Easterly	.15	.06
❑ 446	Steve Farr RC	.50	.20
❑ 447	Mike Fischlin	.15	.06
❑ 448	Julio Franco	.40	.16
❑ 449	Mel Hall	.15	.06
❑ 450	Mike Hargrove	.15	.06
❑ 451	Neal Heaton	.15	.06
❑ 452	Brook Jacoby	.15	.06
❑ 453	Mike Jeffcoat	.15	.06
❑ 454	Don Schulze	.15	.06
❑ 455	Roy Smith	.15	.06
❑ 456	Pat Tabler	.15	.06
❑ 457	Andre Thornton	.15	.06
❑ 458	George Vukovich	.15	.06
❑ 459	Tom Waddell	.15	.06
❑ 460	Jerry Willard	.15	.06
❑ 461	Dale Berra	.15	.06
❑ 462	John Candelaria	.15	.06
❑ 463	Jose DeLeon	.15	.06
❑ 464	Doug Frobel	.15	.06
❑ 465	Cecilio Guante	.15	.06
❑ 466	Brian Harper	.15	.06
❑ 467	Lee Lacy	.15	.06
❑ 468	Bill Madlock	.40	.16
❑ 469	Lee Mazzilli	.40	.16
❑ 470	Larry McWilliams	.15	.06
❑ 471	Jim Morrison	.15	.06
❑ 472	Tony Pena	.15	.06
❑ 473	Johnny Ray	.15	.06
❑ 474	Rick Rhoden	.15	.06
❑ 475	Don Robinson	.15	.06
❑ 476	Rod Scurry	.15	.06
❑ 477	Kent Tekulve	.15	.06
❑ 478	Jason Thompson	.15	.06
❑ 479	John Tudor	.40	.16
❑ 480	Lee Tunnell	.15	.06
❑ 481	Marvell Wynne	.15	.06
❑ 482	Salome Barojas	.15	.06
❑ 483	Dave Beard	.15	.06
❑ 484	Jim Beattie	.15	.06
❑ 485	Barry Bonnell	.15	.06
❑ 486	Phil Bradley	.50	.20
❑ 487	Al Cowens	.15	.06
❑ 488	Alvin Davis RC*	.50	.20
❑ 489	Dave Henderson	.15	.06
❑ 490	Steve Henderson	.15	.06
❑ 491	Bob Kearney	.15	.06
❑ 492	Mark Langston RC	1.00	.40
❑ 493	Larry Milbourne	.15	.06
❑ 494	Paul Mirabella	.15	.06
❑ 495	Mike Moore	.15	.06
❑ 496	Edwin Nunez	.15	.06
❑ 497	Spike Owen	.15	.06
❑ 498	Jack Perconte	.15	.06
❑ 499	Ken Phelps	.15	.06
❑ 500	Jim Presley	.50	.20
❑ 501	Mike Stanton	.15	.06
❑ 502	Bob Stoddard	.15	.06
❑ 503	Gorman Thomas	.40	.16
❑ 504	Ed VandeBerg	.15	.06
❑ 505	Matt Young	.15	.06
❑ 506	Juan Agosto	.15	.06
❑ 507	Harold Baines	.40	.16
❑ 508	Floyd Bannister	.15	.06
❑ 509	Britt Burns	.15	.06
❑ 510	Julio Cruz	.15	.06
❑ 511	Richard Dotson	.15	.06
❑ 512	Jerry Dybzinski	.15	.06
❑ 513	Carlton Fisk	.75	.30
❑ 514	Scott Fletcher	.15	.06
❑ 515	Jerry Hairston	.15	.06
❑ 516	Marc Hill	.15	.06
❑ 517	LaMarr Hoyt	.15	.06
❑ 518	Ron Kittle	.15	.06
❑ 519	Rudy Law	.15	.06
❑ 520	Vance Law	.15	.06
❑ 521	Greg Luzinski	.40	.16
❑ 522	Gene Nelson	.15	.06
❑ 523	Tom Paciorek	.15	.06
❑ 524	Ron Reed	.15	.06
❑ 525	Bert Roberge	.15	.06
❑ 526	Tom Seaver	.75	.30
❑ 527	Roy Smalley	.15	.06
❑ 528	Dan Spillner	.15	.06
❑ 529	Mike Squires	.15	.06
❑ 530	Greg Walker	.15	.06
❑ 531	Cesar Cedeno	.40	.16
❑ 532	Dave Concepcion	.40	.16
❑ 533	Eric Davis RC	1.50	.60
❑ 534	Nick Esasky	.15	.06
❑ 535	Tom Foley	.15	.06
❑ 536	John Franco UER RC (Koufax misspelled as Kofax on back)	1.00	.40
❑ 537	Brad Gulden	.15	.06
❑ 538	Tom Hume	.15	.06
❑ 539	Wayne Krenchicki	.15	.06
❑ 540	Andy McGaffigan	.15	.06
❑ 541	Eddie Milner	.15	.06
❑ 542	Ron Oester	.15	.06
❑ 543	Bob Owchinko	.15	.06
❑ 544	Dave Parker	.40	.16
❑ 545	Frank Pastore	.15	.06
❑ 546	Tony Perez	.75	.30
❑ 547	Ted Power	.15	.06
❑ 548	Joe Price	.15	.06
❑ 549	Gary Redus	.15	.06
❑ 550	Pete Rose	4.00	1.60
❑ 551	Jeff Russell	.15	.06
❑ 552	Mario Soto	.40	.16
❑ 553	Jay Tibbs	.15	.06
❑ 554	Duane Walker	.15	.06
❑ 555	Alan Bannister	.15	.06
❑ 556	Buddy Bell	.40	.16
❑ 557	Danny Darwin	.15	.06
❑ 558	Charlie Hough	.40	.16
❑ 559	Bobby Jones	.15	.06
❑ 560	Odell Jones	.15	.06
❑ 561	Jeff Kunkel	.15	.06
❑ 562	Mike Mason RC	.25	.10
❑ 563	Pete O'Brien	.15	.06
❑ 564	Larry Parrish	.15	.06
❑ 565	Mickey Rivers	.15	.06
❑ 566	Billy Sample	.15	.06
❑ 567	Dave Schmidt	.15	.06
❑ 568	Donnie Scott	.15	.06
❑ 569	Dave Stewart	.40	.16
❑ 570	Frank Tanana	.40	.16
❑ 571	Wayne Tolleson	.15	.06
❑ 572	Gary Ward	.15	.06
❑ 573	Curtis Wilkerson	.15	.06
❑ 574	George Wright	.15	.06
❑ 575	Ned Yost	.15	.06
❑ 576	Mark Brouhard	.15	.06
❑ 577	Mike Caldwell	.15	.06
❑ 578	Bobby Clark	.15	.06
❑ 579	Jaime Cocanower	.15	.06
❑ 580	Cecil Cooper	.40	.16
❑ 581	Rollie Fingers	.40	.16
❑ 582	Jim Gantner	.15	.06
❑ 583	Moose Haas	.15	.06
❑ 584	Dion James	.15	.06
❑ 585	Pete Ladd	.15	.06
❑ 586	Rick Manning	.15	.06
❑ 587	Bob McClure	.15	.06
❑ 588	Paul Molitor	.75	.30
❑ 589	Charlie Moore	.15	.06
❑ 590	Ben Oglivie	.40	.16

❑ 591 Chuck Porter .15 .06
❑ 592 Randy Ready RC* .25 .10
❑ 593 Ed Romero .15 .06
❑ 594 Bill Schroeder .15 .06
❑ 595 Ray Searage .15 .06
❑ 596 Ted Simmons .40 .16
❑ 597 Jim Sundberg .40 .16
❑ 598 Don Sutton .40 .16
❑ 599 Tom Tellmann .15 .06
❑ 600 Rick Waits .15 .06
❑ 601 Robin Yount 2.00 .80
❑ 602 Dusty Baker .40 .16
❑ 603 Bob Brenly .15 .06
❑ 604 Jack Clark .40 .16
❑ 605 Chili Davis .40 .16
❑ 606 Mark Davis .15 .06
❑ 607 Dan Gladden RC .50 .20
❑ 608 Atlee Hammaker .15 .06
❑ 609 Mike Krukow .15 .06
❑ 610 Duane Kuiper .15 .06
❑ 611 Bob Lacey .15 .06
❑ 612 Bill Laskey .15 .06
❑ 613 Gary Lavelle .15 .06
❑ 614 Johnnie LeMaster .15 .06
❑ 615 Jeff Leonard .15 .06
❑ 616 Randy Lerch .15 .06
❑ 617 Greg Minton .15 .06
❑ 618 Steve Nicosia .15 .06
❑ 619 Gene Richards .15 .06
❑ 620 Jeff D. Robinson .15 .06
❑ 621 Scot Thompson .15 .06
❑ 622 Manny Trillo .15 .06
❑ 623 Brad Wellman .15 .06
❑ 624 Frank Williams .15 .06
❑ 625 Joel Youngblood .15 .06
❑ 626 Cal Ripken IA 3.00 1.20
❑ 627 Mike Schmidt IA 1.25 .50
❑ 628 Sparky Anderson IA .40 .16
❑ 629 Dave Winfield .40 .16
Rickey Henderson
❑ 630 Mike Schmidt 2.00 .80
Ryne Sandberg
❑ 631 Darryl Strawberry 1.25 .50
Gary Carter
Steve Garvey
Ozzie Smith
❑ 632 Gary Carter .15 .06
Charlie Lea
❑ 633 Steve Garvey .40 .16
Rich Gossage
❑ 634 Dwight Gooden 1.25 .50
Juan Samuel
❑ 635 Willie Upshaw IA .15 .06
❑ 636 Lloyd Moseby IA .15 .06
❑ 637 HOLLAND: Al Holland .15 .06
❑ 638 TUNNELL .15 .06
Lee Tunnell
❑ 639 Reggie Jackson IA .40 .16
❑ 640 4000th Hit IA 1.25 .50
❑ 641 Cal Ripken Jr. 3.00 1.20
Cal Ripken Sr.
❑ 642 Cubs Division Champs .40 .16
❑ 643 Two Perfect Games .40 .16
and One No-Hitter:
Mike Witt
David Palmer
Jack Morris
❑ 644 Willie Lozado and .15 .06
Vic Mata
❑ 645 Kelly Gruber RC and .50 .20
Randy O'Neal
❑ 646 Jose Roman .15 .06
Joel Skinner
❑ 647 Steve Kiefer RC and 1.00 .40
Danny Tartabull
❑ 648 Rob Dee RC and .50 .20
Alejandro Sanchez
❑ 649 Billy Hatcher RC and 1.00 .40
Shawon Dunston
❑ 650 Ron Robinson and .15 .06
Mike Bielecki
❑ 651 Zane Smith RC and .50 .20
Paul Zuvella
❑ 652 Joe Hesketh RC and .50 .20
Glenn Davis
❑ 653 John Russell and .15 .06
Steve Jeltz
❑ 654 CL: Tigers/Padres .15 .06
and Cubs/Mets
❑ 655 CL: Blue Jays/Yankees .15 .06
and Red Sox/Orioles
❑ 656 CL: Royals/Cardinals .15 .06
and Phillies/Twins
❑ 657 CL: Angels/Braves .15 .06
and Astros/Dodgers
❑ 658 CL: Expos/A's .15 .06
and Indians/Pirates
❑ 659 CL: Mariners/White Sox .15 .06
and Reds/Rangers
❑ 660 CL: Brewers/Giants .15 .06
and Special Cards

1986 Fleer

	Nm-Mt	Ex-Mt
COMPLETE SET (660)	40.00	16.00
COMP.FACT.SET (660)	40.00	16.00

❑ 1 Steve Balboni .15 .06
❑ 2 Joe Beckwith .15 .06
❑ 3 Buddy Biancalana .15 .06
❑ 4 Bud Black .15 .06
❑ 5 George Brett 2.00 .80
❑ 6 Onix Concepcion .15 .06
❑ 7 Steve Farr .15 .06
❑ 8 Mark Gubicza .15 .06
❑ 9 Dane Iorg .15 .06
❑ 10 Danny Jackson .15 .06
❑ 11 Lynn Jones .15 .06
❑ 12 Mike Jones .15 .06
❑ 13 Charlie Leibrandt .15 .06
❑ 14 Hal McRae .25 .10
❑ 15 Omar Moreno .15 .06
❑ 16 Darryl Motley .15 .06
❑ 17 Jorge Orta .15 .06
❑ 18 Dan Quisenberry .15 .06
❑ 19 Bret Saberhagen .25 .10
❑ 20 Pat Sheridan .15 .06
❑ 21 Lonnie Smith .15 .06
❑ 22 Jim Sundberg .25 .10
❑ 23 John Wathan .15 .06
❑ 24 Frank White .25 .10
❑ 25 Willie Wilson .25 .10
❑ 26 Joaquin Andujar .25 .10
❑ 27 Steve Braun .15 .06
❑ 28 Bill Campbell .15 .06
❑ 29 Cesar Cedeno .25 .10
❑ 30 Jack Clark .25 .10
❑ 31 Vince Coleman RC* 1.00 .40
❑ 32 Danny Cox .15 .06
❑ 33 Ken Dayley .15 .06
❑ 34 Ivan DeJesus .15 .06
❑ 35 Bob Forsch .15 .06
❑ 36 Brian Harper .15 .06
❑ 37 Tom Herr .15 .06
❑ 38 Ricky Horton .15 .06
❑ 39 Kurt Kepshire .15 .06
❑ 40 Jeff Lahti .15 .06
❑ 41 Tito Landrum .15 .06
❑ 42 Willie McGee .25 .10
❑ 43 Tom Nieto .15 .06
❑ 44 Terry Pendleton .25 .10
❑ 45 Darrell Porter .15 .06
❑ 46 Ozzie Smith 1.25 .50
❑ 47 John Tudor .25 .10
❑ 48 Andy Van Slyke .25 .10
❑ 49 Todd Worrell RC .50 .20
❑ 50 Jim Acker .15 .06
❑ 51 Doyle Alexander .15 .06
❑ 52 Jesse Barfield .25 .10
❑ 53 George Bell .25 .10
❑ 54 Jeff Burroughs .15 .06
❑ 55 Bill Caudill .15 .06
❑ 56 Jim Clancy .15 .06
❑ 57 Tony Fernandez .15 .06
❑ 58 Tom Filer .15 .06
❑ 59 Damaso Garcia .15 .06
❑ 60 Tom Henke .25 .10
❑ 61 Garth Iorg .15 .06
❑ 62 Cliff Johnson .15 .06
❑ 63 Jimmy Key .25 .10
❑ 64 Dennis Lamp .15 .06
❑ 65 Gary Lavelle .15 .06
❑ 66 Buck Martinez .15 .06
❑ 67 Lloyd Moseby .15 .06
❑ 68 Rance Mulliniks .15 .06
❑ 69 Al Oliver .25 .10
❑ 70 Dave Stieb .25 .10
❑ 71 Louis Thornton .15 .06
❑ 72 Willie Upshaw .15 .06
❑ 73 Ernie Whitt .15 .06
❑ 74 Rick Aguilera RC .50 .20
❑ 75 Wally Backman .15 .06
❑ 76 Gary Carter .25 .10
❑ 77 Ron Darling .25 .10
❑ 78 Len Dykstra RC 1.50 .60
❑ 79 Sid Fernandez .15 .06
❑ 80 George Foster .25 .10
❑ 81 Dwight Gooden .75 .30
❑ 82 Tom Gorman .15 .06
❑ 83 Danny Heep .15 .06
❑ 84 Keith Hernandez .25 .10
❑ 85 Howard Johnson .25 .10
❑ 86 Ray Knight .25 .10
❑ 87 Terry Leach .15 .06
❑ 88 Ed Lynch .15 .06
❑ 89 Roger McDowell RC* .50 .20
❑ 90 Jesse Orosco .15 .06
❑ 91 Tom Paciorek .15 .06
❑ 92 Ronn Reynolds .15 .06
❑ 93 Rafael Santana .15 .06
❑ 94 Doug Sisk .15 .06
❑ 95 Rusty Staub .25 .10
❑ 96 Darryl Strawberry .50 .20
❑ 97 Mookie Wilson .25 .10
❑ 98 Neil Allen .15 .06
❑ 99 Don Baylor .25 .10
❑ 100 Dale Berra .15 .06
❑ 101 Rich Bordi .15 .06
❑ 102 Marty Bystrom .15 .06
❑ 103 Joe Cowley .15 .06
❑ 104 Brian Fisher RC .15 .06
❑ 105 Ken Griffey .25 .10
❑ 106 Ron Guidry .25 .10
❑ 107 Ron Hassey .15 .06
❑ 108 R.Henderson UER .75 .30
SB Record of 120, sic
❑ 109 Don Mattingly 2.50 1.00
❑ 110 Bobby Meacham .15 .06
❑ 111 John Montefusco .15 .06
❑ 112 Phil Niekro .25 .10
❑ 113 Mike Pagliarulo .15 .06
❑ 114 Dan Pasqua .15 .06
❑ 115 Willie Randolph .25 .10
❑ 116 Dave Righetti .25 .10
❑ 117 Andre Robertson .15 .06
❑ 118 Billy Sample .15 .06
❑ 119 Bob Shirley .15 .06
❑ 120 Ed Whitson .15 .06
❑ 121 Dave Winfield .25 .10
❑ 122 Butch Wynegar .15 .06
❑ 123 Dave Anderson .15 .06
❑ 124 Bob Bailor .15 .06
❑ 125 Greg Brock .15 .06
❑ 126 Enos Cabell .15 .06
❑ 127 Bobby Castillo .15 .06
❑ 128 Carlos Diaz .15 .06
❑ 129 Mariano Duncan RC* .50 .20
❑ 130 Pedro Guerrero .25 .10
❑ 131 Orel Hershiser .50 .20

- ❑ 132 Rick Honeycutt .15 .06
- ❑ 133 Ken Howell .15 .06
- ❑ 134 Ken Landreaux .15 .06
- ❑ 135 Bill Madlock .25 .10
- ❑ 136 Candy Maldonado .15 .06
- ❑ 137 Mike Marshall .15 .06
- ❑ 138 Len Matuszek .15 .06
- ❑ 139 Tom Niedenfuer .15 .06
- ❑ 140 Alejandro Pena .15 .06
- ❑ 141 Jerry Reuss .15 .06
- ❑ 142 Bill Russell .25 .10
- ❑ 143 Steve Sax .15 .06
- ❑ 144 Mike Scioscia .25 .10
- ❑ 145 Fernando Valenzuela .25 .10
- ❑ 146 Bob Welch .25 .10
- ❑ 147 Terry Whitfield .15 .06
- ❑ 148 Juan Beniquez .15 .06
- ❑ 149 Bob Boone .25 .10
- ❑ 150 John Candelaria .15 .06
- ❑ 151 Rod Carew .50 .20
- ❑ 152 Stu Cliburn .15 .06
- ❑ 153 Doug DeCinces .15 .06
- ❑ 154 Brian Downing .25 .10
- ❑ 155 Ken Forsch .15 .06
- ❑ 156 Craig Gerber .15 .06
- ❑ 157 Bobby Grich .25 .10
- ❑ 158 George Hendrick .25 .10
- ❑ 159 Al Holland .15 .06
- ❑ 160 Reggie Jackson .50 .20
- ❑ 161 Ruppert Jones .15 .06
- ❑ 162 Urbano Lugo .15 .06
- ❑ 163 Kirk McCaskill RC .50 .20
- ❑ 164 Donnie Moore .15 .06
- ❑ 165 Gary Pettis .15 .06
- ❑ 166 Ron Romanick .15 .06
- ❑ 167 Dick Schofield .15 .06
- ❑ 168 Daryl Sconiers .15 .06
- ❑ 169 Jim Slaton .15 .06
- ❑ 170 Don Sutton .25 .10
- ❑ 171 Mike Witt .15 .06
- ❑ 172 Buddy Bell .25 .10
- ❑ 173 Tom Browning .15 .06
- ❑ 174 Dave Concepcion .25 .10
- ❑ 175 Eric Davis .50 .20
- ❑ 176 Bo Diaz .15 .06
- ❑ 177 Nick Esasky .15 .06
- ❑ 178 John Franco .25 .10
- ❑ 179 Tom Hume .15 .06
- ❑ 180 Wayne Krenchicki .15 .06
- ❑ 181 Andy McGaffigan .15 .06
- ❑ 182 Eddie Milner .15 .06
- ❑ 183 Ron Oester .15 .06
- ❑ 184 Dave Parker .25 .10
- ❑ 185 Frank Pastore .15 .06
- ❑ 186 Tony Perez .50 .20
- ❑ 187 Ted Power .15 .06
- ❑ 188 Joe Price .15 .06
- ❑ 189 Gary Redus .15 .06
- ❑ 190 Ron Robinson .15 .06
- ❑ 191 Pete Rose 2.50 1.00
- ❑ 192 Mario Soto .25 .10
- ❑ 193 John Stuper .15 .06
- ❑ 194 Jay Tibbs .15 .06
- ❑ 195 Dave Van Gorder .15 .06
- ❑ 196 Max Venable .15 .06
- ❑ 197 Juan Agosto .15 .06
- ❑ 198 Harold Baines .25 .10
- ❑ 199 Floyd Bannister .15 .06
- ❑ 200 Britt Burns .15 .06
- ❑ 201 Julio Cruz .15 .06
- ❑ 202 Joel Davis .15 .06
- ❑ 203 Richard Dotson .15 .06
- ❑ 204 Carlton Fisk .50 .20
- ❑ 205 Scott Fletcher .15 .06
- ❑ 206 Ozzie Guillen RC* .50 .20
- ❑ 207 Jerry Hairston .15 .06
- ❑ 208 Tim Hulett .15 .06
- ❑ 209 Bob James .15 .06
- ❑ 210 Ron Kittle .15 .06
- ❑ 211 Rudy Law .15 .06
- ❑ 212 Bryan Little .15 .06
- ❑ 213 Gene Nelson .15 .06
- ❑ 214 Reid Nichols .15 .06
- ❑ 215 Luis Salazar .15 .06
- ❑ 216 Tom Seaver .50 .20
- ❑ 217 Dan Spillner .15 .06
- ❑ 218 Bruce Tanner .15 .06
- ❑ 219 Greg Walker .15 .06
- ❑ 220 Dave Wehrmeister .15 .06
- ❑ 221 Juan Berenguer .15 .06
- ❑ 222 Dave Bergman .15 .06
- ❑ 223 Tom Brookens .15 .06
- ❑ 224 Darrell Evans .25 .10
- ❑ 225 Barbaro Garbey .15 .06
- ❑ 226 Kirk Gibson .25 .10
- ❑ 227 John Grubb .15 .06
- ❑ 228 Willie Hernandez .15 .06
- ❑ 229 Larry Herndon .15 .06
- ❑ 230 Chet Lemon .25 .10
- ❑ 231 Aurelio Lopez .15 .06
- ❑ 232 Jack Morris .25 .10
- ❑ 233 Randy O'Neal .15 .06
- ❑ 234 Lance Parrish .25 .10
- ❑ 235 Dan Petry .15 .06
- ❑ 236 Alejandro Sanchez .15 .06
- ❑ 237 Bill Scherrer .15 .06
- ❑ 238 Nelson Simmons .15 .06
- ❑ 239 Frank Tanana .25 .10
- ❑ 240 Walt Terrell .15 .06
- ❑ 241 Alan Trammell .25 .10
- ❑ 242 Lou Whitaker .25 .10
- ❑ 243 Milt Wilcox .15 .06
- ❑ 244 Hubie Brooks .15 .06
- ❑ 245 Tim Burke .15 .06
- ❑ 246 Andre Dawson .25 .10
- ❑ 247 Mike Fitzgerald .15 .06
- ❑ 248 Terry Francona .25 .10
- ❑ 249 Bill Gullickson .15 .06
- ❑ 250 Joe Hesketh .15 .06
- ❑ 251 Bill Laskey .15 .06
- ❑ 252 Vance Law .15 .06
- ❑ 253 Charlie Lea .15 .06
- ❑ 254 Gary Lucas .15 .06
- ❑ 255 David Palmer .15 .06
- ❑ 256 Tim Raines .25 .10
- ❑ 257 Jeff Reardon .25 .10
- ❑ 258 Bert Roberge .15 .06
- ❑ 259 Dan Schatzeder .15 .06
- ❑ 260 Bryn Smith .15 .06
- ❑ 261 Randy St.Claire .15 .06
- ❑ 262 Scot Thompson .15 .06
- ❑ 263 Tim Wallach .15 .06
- ❑ 264 U.L. Washington .15 .06
- ❑ 265 Mitch Webster .15 .06
- ❑ 266 Herm Winningham .15 .06
- ❑ 267 Floyd Youmans .15 .06
- ❑ 268 Don Aase .15 .06
- ❑ 269 Mike Boddicker .15 .06
- ❑ 270 Rich Dauer .15 .06
- ❑ 271 Storm Davis .15 .06
- ❑ 272 Rick Dempsey .15 .06
- ❑ 273 Ken Dixon .15 .06
- ❑ 274 Jim Dwyer .15 .06
- ❑ 275 Mike Flanagan .15 .06
- ❑ 276 Wayne Gross .15 .06
- ❑ 277 Lee Lacy .15 .06
- ❑ 278 Fred Lynn .25 .10
- ❑ 279 Tippy Martinez .15 .06
- ❑ 280 Dennis Martinez .25 .10
- ❑ 281 Scott McGregor .15 .06
- ❑ 282 Eddie Murray .75 .30
- ❑ 283 Floyd Rayford .15 .06
- ❑ 284 Cal Ripken 3.00 1.20
- ❑ 285 Gary Roenicke .15 .06
- ❑ 286 Larry Sheets .15 .06
- ❑ 287 John Shelby .15 .06
- ❑ 288 Nate Snell .15 .06
- ❑ 289 Sammy Stewart .15 .06
- ❑ 290 Alan Wiggins .15 .06
- ❑ 291 Mike Young .15 .06
- ❑ 292 Alan Ashby .15 .06
- ❑ 293 Mark Bailey .15 .06
- ❑ 294 Kevin Bass .15 .06
- ❑ 295 Jeff Calhoun .15 .06
- ❑ 296 Jose Cruz .25 .10
- ❑ 297 Glenn Davis .15 .06
- ❑ 298 Bill Dawley .15 .06
- ❑ 299 Frank DiPino .15 .06
- ❑ 300 Bill Doran .15 .06
- ❑ 301 Phil Garner .25 .10
- ❑ 302 Jeff Heathcock .15 .06
- ❑ 303 Charlie Kerfeld .15 .06
- ❑ 304 Bob Knepper .15 .06
- ❑ 305 Ron Mathis .15 .06
- ❑ 306 Jerry Mumphrey .15 .06
- ❑ 307 Jim Pankovits .15 .06
- ❑ 308 Terry Puhl .15 .06
- ❑ 309 Craig Reynolds .15 .06
- ❑ 310 Nolan Ryan 4.00 1.60
- ❑ 311 Mike Scott .25 .10
- ❑ 312 Dave Smith .15 .06
- ❑ 313 Dickie Thon .15 .06
- ❑ 314 Denny Walling .15 .06
- ❑ 315 Kurt Bevacqua .15 .06
- ❑ 316 Al Bumbry .15 .06
- ❑ 317 Jerry Davis .15 .06
- ❑ 318 Luis DeLeon .15 .06
- ❑ 319 Dave Dravecky .15 .06
- ❑ 320 Tim Flannery .15 .06
- ❑ 321 Steve Garvey .25 .10
- ❑ 322 Rich Gossage .25 .10
- ❑ 323 Tony Gwynn 1.25 .50
- ❑ 324 Andy Hawkins .15 .06
- ❑ 325 LaMarr Hoyt .15 .06
- ❑ 326 Roy Lee Jackson .15 .06
- ❑ 327 Terry Kennedy .15 .06
- ❑ 328 Craig Lefferts .15 .06
- ❑ 329 Carmelo Martinez .15 .06
- ❑ 330 Lance McCullers .15 .06
- ❑ 331 Kevin McReynolds .15 .06
- ❑ 332 Graig Nettles .25 .10
- ❑ 333 Jerry Royster .15 .06
- ❑ 334 Eric Show .15 .06
- ❑ 335 Tim Stoddard .15 .06
- ❑ 336 Garry Templeton .25 .10
- ❑ 337 Mark Thurmond .15 .06
- ❑ 338 Ed Wojna .15 .06
- ❑ 339 Tony Armas .25 .10
- ❑ 340 Marty Barrett .15 .06
- ❑ 341 Wade Boggs .50 .20
- ❑ 342 Dennis Boyd .15 .06
- ❑ 343 Bill Buckner .25 .10
- ❑ 344 Mark Clear .15 .06
- ❑ 345 Roger Clemens 4.00 1.60
- ❑ 346 Steve Crawford .15 .06
- ❑ 347 Mike Easler .15 .06
- ❑ 348 Dwight Evans .25 .10
- ❑ 349 Rich Gedman .15 .06
- ❑ 350 Jackie Gutierrez .15 .06
- ❑ 351 Glenn Hoffman .15 .06
- ❑ 352 Bruce Hurst .15 .06
- ❑ 353 Bruce Kison .15 .06
- ❑ 354 Tim Lollar .15 .06
- ❑ 355 Steve Lyons .15 .06
- ❑ 356 Al Nipper .15 .06
- ❑ 357 Bob Ojeda .15 .06
- ❑ 358 Jim Rice .25 .10
- ❑ 359 Bob Stanley .15 .06
- ❑ 360 Mike Trujillo .15 .06
- ❑ 361 Thad Bosley .15 .06
- ❑ 362 Warren Brusstar .15 .06
- ❑ 363 Ron Cey .25 .10
- ❑ 364 Jody Davis .15 .06
- ❑ 365 Bob Dernier .15 .06
- ❑ 366 Shawon Dunston .25 .10
- ❑ 367 Leon Durham .15 .06
- ❑ 368 Dennis Eckersley .50 .20
- ❑ 369 Ray Fontenot .15 .06
- ❑ 370 George Frazier .15 .06
- ❑ 371 Billy Hatcher .15 .06
- ❑ 372 Dave Lopes .25 .10
- ❑ 373 Gary Matthews .25 .10
- ❑ 374 Ron Meridith .15 .06
- ❑ 375 Keith Moreland .15 .06
- ❑ 376 Reggie Patterson .15 .06
- ❑ 377 Dick Ruthven .15 .06
- ❑ 378 Ryne Sandberg 1.50 .60
- ❑ 379 Scott Sanderson .15 .06
- ❑ 380 Lee Smith .25 .10
- ❑ 381 Lary Sorensen .15 .06
- ❑ 382 Chris Speier .15 .06
- ❑ 383 Rick Sutcliffe .25 .10
- ❑ 384 Steve Trout .15 .06
- ❑ 385 Gary Woods .15 .06
- ❑ 386 Bert Blyleven .25 .10
- ❑ 387 Tom Brunansky .15 .06
- ❑ 388 Randy Bush .15 .06
- ❑ 389 John Butcher .15 .06

❑ 390 Ron Davis .15 .06
❑ 391 Dave Engle .15 .06
❑ 392 Frank Eufemia .15 .06
❑ 393 Pete Filson .15 .06
❑ 394 Gary Gaetti .25 .10
❑ 395 Greg Gagne .15 .06
❑ 396 Mickey Hatcher .15 .06
❑ 397 Kent Hrbek .25 .10
❑ 398 Tim Laudner .15 .06
❑ 399 Rick Lysander .15 .06
❑ 400 Dave Meier .15 .06
❑ 401 Kirby Puckett UER 2.00 .80
Card has him in NL,
should be AL
❑ 402 Mark Salas .15 .06
❑ 403 Ken Schrom .15 .06
❑ 404 Roy Smalley .15 .06
❑ 405 Mike Smithson .15 .06
❑ 406 Mike Stenhouse .15 .06
❑ 407 Tim Teufel .15 .06
❑ 408 Frank Viola .25 .10
❑ 409 Ron Washington .15 .06
❑ 410 Keith Atherton .15 .06
❑ 411 Dusty Baker .25 .10
❑ 412 Tim Birtsas .15 .06
❑ 413 Bruce Bochte .15 .06
❑ 414 Chris Codiroli .15 .06
❑ 415 Dave Collins .15 .06
❑ 416 Mike Davis .15 .06
❑ 417 Alfredo Griffin .15 .06
❑ 418 Mike Heath .15 .06
❑ 419 Steve Henderson .15 .06
❑ 420 Donnie Hill .15 .06
❑ 421 Jay Howell .15 .06
❑ 422 Tommy John .25 .10
❑ 423 Dave Kingman .25 .10
❑ 424 Bill Krueger .15 .06
❑ 425 Rick Langford .15 .06
❑ 426 Carney Lansford .25 .10
❑ 427 Steve McCatty .15 .06
❑ 428 Dwayne Murphy .15 .06
❑ 429 Steve Ontiveros RC .15 .06
❑ 430 Tony Phillips .15 .06
❑ 431 Jose Rijo .25 .10
❑ 432 Mickey Tettleton RC .50 .20
❑ 433 Luis Aguayo .15 .06
❑ 434 Larry Andersen .15 .06
❑ 435 Steve Carlton .25 .10
❑ 436 Don Carman .15 .06
❑ 437 Tim Corcoran .15 .06
❑ 438 Darren Daulton RC 1.00 .40
❑ 439 John Denny .15 .06
❑ 440 Tom Foley .15 .06
❑ 441 Greg Gross .15 .06
❑ 442 Kevin Gross .15 .06
❑ 443 Von Hayes .15 .06
❑ 444 Charles Hudson .15 .06
❑ 445 Garry Maddox .15 .06
❑ 446 Shane Rawley .15 .06
❑ 447 Dave Rucker .15 .06
❑ 448 John Russell .15 .06
❑ 449 Juan Samuel .15 .06
❑ 450 Mike Schmidt 2.00 .80
❑ 451 Rick Schu .15 .06
❑ 452 Dave Shipanoff .15 .06
❑ 453 Dave Stewart .25 .10
❑ 454 Jeff Stone .15 .06
❑ 455 Kent Tekulve .15 .06
❑ 456 Ozzie Virgil .15 .06
❑ 457 Glenn Wilson .15 .06
❑ 458 Jim Beattie .15 .06
❑ 459 Karl Best .15 .06
❑ 460 Barry Bonnell .15 .06
❑ 461 Phil Bradley .15 .06
❑ 462 Ivan Calderon RC* .50 .20
❑ 463 Al Cowens .15 .06
❑ 464 Alvin Davis .15 .06
❑ 465 Dave Henderson .15 .06
❑ 466 Bob Kearney .15 .06
❑ 467 Mark Langston .25 .10
❑ 468 Bob Long .15 .06
❑ 469 Mike Moore .15 .06
❑ 470 Edwin Nunez .15 .06
❑ 471 Spike Owen .15 .06
❑ 472 Jack Perconte .15 .06
❑ 473 Jim Presley .15 .06
❑ 474 Donnie Scott .15 .06
❑ 475 Bill Swift .15 .06
❑ 476 Danny Tartabull .25 .10
❑ 477 Gorman Thomas .25 .10
❑ 478 Roy Thomas .15 .06
❑ 479 Ed VandeBerg .15 .06
❑ 480 Frank Wills .15 .06
❑ 481 Matt Young .15 .06
❑ 482 Ray Burris .15 .06
❑ 483 Jaime Cocanower .15 .06
❑ 484 Cecil Cooper .25 .10
❑ 485 Danny Darwin .15 .06
❑ 486 Rollie Fingers .25 .10
❑ 487 Jim Gantner .15 .06
❑ 488 Bob L. Gibson .15 .06
❑ 489 Moose Haas .15 .06
❑ 490 Teddy Higuera RC* .50 .20
❑ 491 Paul Householder .15 .06
❑ 492 Pete Ladd .15 .06
❑ 493 Rick Manning .15 .06
❑ 494 Bob McClure .15 .06
❑ 495 Paul Molitor .50 .20
❑ 496 Charlie Moore .15 .06
❑ 497 Ben Oglivie .25 .10
❑ 498 Randy Ready .15 .06
❑ 499 Earnie Riles .15 .06
❑ 500 Ed Romero .15 .06
❑ 501 Bill Schroeder .15 .06
❑ 502 Ray Searage .15 .06
❑ 503 Ted Simmons .25 .10
❑ 504 Pete Vuckovich .15 .06
❑ 505 Rick Waits .15 .06
❑ 506 Robin Yount 1.25 .50
❑ 507 Len Barker .15 .06
❑ 508 Steve Bedrosian .15 .06
❑ 509 Bruce Benedict .15 .06
❑ 510 Rick Camp .15 .06
❑ 511 Rick Cerone .15 .06
❑ 512 Chris Chambliss .25 .10
❑ 513 Jeff Dedmon .15 .06
❑ 514 Terry Forster .25 .10
❑ 515 Gene Garber .15 .06
❑ 516 Terry Harper .15 .06
❑ 517 Bob Horner .25 .10
❑ 518 Glenn Hubbard .15 .06
❑ 519 Joe Johnson .15 .06
❑ 520 Brad Komminsk .15 .06
❑ 521 Rick Mahler .15 .06
❑ 522 Dale Murphy .50 .20
❑ 523 Ken Oberkfell .15 .06
❑ 524 Pascual Perez .15 .06
❑ 525 Gerald Perry .15 .06
❑ 526 Rafael Ramirez .15 .06
❑ 527 Steve Shields .15 .06
❑ 528 Zane Smith .15 .06
❑ 529 Bruce Sutter .25 .10
❑ 530 Milt Thompson RC .50 .20
❑ 531 Claudell Washington .15 .06
❑ 532 Paul Zuvella .15 .06
❑ 533 Vida Blue .25 .10
❑ 534 Bob Brenly .15 .06
❑ 535 Chris Brown .15 .06
❑ 536 Chili Davis .25 .10
❑ 537 Mark Davis .15 .06
❑ 538 Rob Deer .15 .06
❑ 539 Dan Driessen .15 .06
❑ 540 Scott Garrelts .15 .06
❑ 541 Dan Gladden .15 .06
❑ 542 Jim Gott .15 .06
❑ 543 David Green .15 .06
❑ 544 Atlee Hammaker .15 .06
❑ 545 Mike Jeffcoat .15 .06
❑ 546 Mike Krukow .15 .06
❑ 547 Dave LaPoint .15 .06
❑ 548 Jeff Leonard .15 .06
❑ 549 Greg Minton .15 .06
❑ 550 Alex Trevino .15 .06
❑ 551 Manny Trillo .15 .06
❑ 552 Jose Uribe .15 .06
❑ 553 Brad Wellman .15 .06
❑ 554 Frank Williams .15 .06
❑ 555 Joel Youngblood .15 .06
❑ 556 Alan Bannister .15 .06
❑ 557 Glenn Brummer .15 .06
❑ 558 Steve Buechele RC .50 .20
❑ 559 Jose Guzman RC .15 .06
❑ 560 Toby Harrah .25 .10
❑ 561 Greg Harris .15 .06
❑ 562 Dwayne Henry .15 .06
❑ 563 Burt Hooton .15 .06
❑ 564 Charlie Hough .25 .10
❑ 565 Mike Mason .15 .06
❑ 566 Oddibe McDowell .15 .06
❑ 567 Dickie Noles .15 .06
❑ 568 Pete O'Brien .15 .06
❑ 569 Larry Parrish .15 .06
❑ 570 Dave Rozema .15 .06
❑ 571 Dave Schmidt .15 .06
❑ 572 Don Slaught .15 .06
❑ 573 Wayne Tolleson .15 .06
❑ 574 Duane Walker .15 .06
❑ 575 Gary Ward .15 .06
❑ 576 Chris Welsh .15 .06
❑ 577 Curtis Wilkerson .15 .06
❑ 578 George Wright .15 .06
❑ 579 Chris Bando .15 .06
❑ 580 Tony Bernazard .15 .06
❑ 581 Brett Butler .25 .10
❑ 582 Ernie Camacho .15 .06
❑ 583 Joe Carter .25 .10
❑ 584 Carmen Castillo .15 .06
❑ 585 Jamie Easterly .15 .06
❑ 586 Julio Franco .25 .10
❑ 587 Mel Hall .15 .06
❑ 588 Mike Hargrove .15 .06
❑ 589 Neal Heaton .15 .06
❑ 590 Brook Jacoby .15 .06
❑ 591 Otis Nixon RC .50 .20
❑ 592 Jerry Reed .15 .06
❑ 593 Vern Ruhle .15 .06
❑ 594 Pat Tabler .15 .06
❑ 595 Rich Thompson .15 .06
❑ 596 Andre Thornton .15 .06
❑ 597 Dave Von Ohlen .15 .06
❑ 598 George Vukovich .15 .06
❑ 599 Tom Waddell .15 .06
❑ 600 Curt Wardle .15 .06
❑ 601 Jerry Willard .15 .06
❑ 602 Bill Almon .15 .06
❑ 603 Mike Bielecki .15 .06
❑ 604 Sid Bream .15 .06
❑ 605 Mike C. Brown .15 .06
❑ 606 Pat Clements .15 .06
❑ 607 Jose DeLeon .15 .06
❑ 608 Denny Gonzalez .15 .06
❑ 609 Cecilio Guante .15 .06
❑ 610 Steve Kemp .15 .06
❑ 611 Sammy Khalifa .15 .06
❑ 612 Lee Mazzilli .25 .10
❑ 613 Larry McWilliams .15 .06
❑ 614 Jim Morrison .15 .06
❑ 615 Joe Orsulak RC* .50 .20
❑ 616 Tony Pena .15 .06
❑ 617 Johnny Ray .15 .06
❑ 618 Rick Reuschel .25 .10
❑ 619 R.J. Reynolds .15 .06
❑ 620 Rick Rhoden .15 .06
❑ 621 Don Robinson .15 .06
❑ 622 Jason Thompson .15 .06
❑ 623 Lee Tunnell .15 .06
❑ 624 Jim Winn .15 .06
❑ 625 Marvell Wynne .15 .06
❑ 626 Dwight Gooden IA .50 .20
❑ 627 Don Mattingly IA 1.25 .50
❑ 628 Pete Rose 4192 .50 .20
❑ 629 Rod Carew 3000 Hits .25 .10
❑ 630 Tom Seaver .25 .10
Phil Niekro
❑ 631 Don Baylor Ouch .25 .10
❑ 632 Darryl Strawberry .25 .10
Tim Raines
❑ 633 Cal Ripken 1.50 .60
Alan Trammell
❑ 634 Wade Boggs 1.00 .40
George Brett
❑ 635 Bob Horner .50 .20
Dale Murphy
❑ 636 Willie McGee .25 .10
Vince Coleman
❑ 637 Vince Coleman IA .25 .10
❑ 638 Pete Rose .75 .30
Dwight Gooden

❑ 639 Wade Boggs .... 1.25 .50
Don Mattingly
❑ 640 Dale Murphy .... .50 .20
Steve Garvey
Dave Parker
❑ 641 Fernando Valenzuela .... .50 .20
Dwight Gooden
❑ 642 Jimmy Key .... .25 .10
Dave Stieb
❑ 643 Carlton Fisk .... .25 .10
Rich Gedman
❑ 644 Gene Walter RC and .... 2.00 .80
Benito Santiago
❑ 645 Mike Woodard and .... .15 .06
Colin Ward
❑ 646 Kal Daniels RC and 4.00 1.60
Paul O'Neill
❑ 647 Andres Galarraga RC .... 1.50 .60
Fred Toliver
❑ 648 Bob Kipper and .... .15 .06
Curt Ford
❑ 649 Jose Canseco RC and 8.00 3.20
Eric Plunk
❑ 650 Mark McLemore RC .... 1.00 .40
Gus Polidor
❑ 651 Rob Woodward and .... .15 .06
Mickey Brantley
❑ 652 Billy Joe Robidoux .... .15 .06
Mark Funderburk
❑ 653 Cecil Fielder RC and .... 1.50 .60
Cory Snyder
❑ 654 CL: Royals/Cardinals .... .15 .06
Blue Jays/Mets
❑ 655 CL: Yankees/Dodgers .... .15 .06
Angels/Reds UER
(168 Darly Sconiers)
❑ 656 CL: White Sox/Tigers .... .15 .06
Expos/Orioles
(279 Dennis,
280 Tippy)
❑ 657 CL: Astros/Padres .... .15 .06
Red Sox/Cubs
❑ 658 CL: Twins/A's .... .15 .06
Phillies/Mariners
❑ 659 CL: Brewers/Braves .... .15 .06
Giants/Rangers
❑ 660 CL: Indians/Pirates .... .15 .06
Special Cards

1986 Fleer Update

	Nm-Mt	Ex-Mt
COMP.FACT.SET (132)	60.00	24.00

❑ 1 Mike Aldrete .... .15 .06
❑ 2 Andy Allanson .... .15 .06
❑ 3 Neil Allen .... .15 .06
❑ 4 Joaquin Andujar .... .25 .10
❑ 5 Paul Assenmacher .... .50 .20
❑ 6 Scott Bailes .... .15 .06
❑ 7 Jay Baller .... .15 .06
❑ 8 Scott Bankhead .... .15 .06
❑ 9 Bill Bathe .... .15 .06
❑ 10 Don Baylor .... .25 .10
❑ 11 Billy Beane XRC .... 1.00 .40
❑ 12 Steve Bedrosian .... .15 .06
❑ 13 Juan Beniquez .... .15 .06
❑ 14 Barry Bonds XRC 50.00 20.00
❑ 15 Bobby Bonilla UER .... 1.00 .40
(Wrong birthday) XRC
❑ 16 Rich Bordi .... .15 .06
❑ 17 Bill Campbell .... .15 .06
❑ 18 Tom Candiotti .... .15 .06
❑ 19 John Cangelosi .... .15 .06
❑ 20 Jose Canseco UER .... 1.50 .60
(Headings on back
for a pitcher)
❑ 21 Chuck Cary .... .15 .06
❑ 22 Juan Castillo XRC .... .15 .06
❑ 23 Rick Cerone .... .15 .06
❑ 24 John Cerutti .... .15 .06
❑ 25 Will Clark XRC .... 2.00 .80
❑ 26 Mark Clear .... .15 .06
❑ 27 Darnell Coles .... .15 .06
❑ 28 Dave Collins .... .15 .06
❑ 29 Tim Conroy .... .15 .06
❑ 30 Ed Correa .... .15 .06
❑ 31 Joe Cowley .... .15 .06
❑ 32 Bill Dawley .... .15 .06
❑ 33 Rob Deer .... .15 .06
❑ 34 John Denny .... .15 .06
❑ 35 Jim Deshaies XRC .... .15 .06
❑ 36 Doug Drabek XRC .... 1.00 .40
❑ 37 Mike Easler .... .15 .06
❑ 38 Mark Eichhorn .... .15 .06
❑ 39 Dave Engle .... .15 .06
❑ 40 Mike Fischlin .... .15 .06
❑ 41 Scott Fletcher .... .15 .06
❑ 42 Terry Forster .... .25 .10
❑ 43 Terry Francona .... .25 .10
❑ 44 Andres Galarraga .... 1.50 .60
❑ 45 Lee Guetterman .... .15 .06
❑ 46 Bill Gullickson .... .15 .06
❑ 47 Jackie Gutierrez .... .15 .06
❑ 48 Moose Haas .... .15 .06
❑ 49 Billy Hatcher .... .15 .06
❑ 50 Mike Heath .... .15 .06
❑ 51 Guy Hoffman .... .15 .06
❑ 52 Tom Hume .... .15 .06
❑ 53 Pete Incaviglia XRC .... .50 .20
❑ 54 Dane Iorg .... .15 .06
❑ 55 Chris James XRC .... .15 .06
❑ 56 Stan Javier XRC* .... .50 .20
❑ 57 Tommy John .... .25 .10
❑ 58 Tracy Jones .... .15 .06
❑ 59 Wally Joyner XRC .... 1.00 .40
❑ 60 Wayne Krenchicki .... .15 .06
❑ 61 John Kruk XRC .... 1.50 .60
❑ 62 Mike LaCoss .... .15 .06
❑ 63 Pete Ladd .... .15 .06
❑ 64 Dave LaPoint .... .15 .06
❑ 65 Mike LaValliere XRC .... .50 .20
❑ 66 Rudy Law .... .15 .06
❑ 67 Dennis Leonard .... .15 .06
❑ 68 Steve Lombardozzi .... .15 .06
❑ 69 Aurelio Lopez .... .15 .06
❑ 70 Mickey Mahler .... .15 .06
❑ 71 Candy Maldonado .... .15 .06
❑ 72 Roger Mason XRC* .... .15 .06
❑ 73 Greg Mathews .... .15 .06
❑ 74 Andy McGaffigan .... .15 .06
❑ 75 Joel McKeon .... .15 .06
❑ 76 Kevin Mitchell XRC .... 1.00 .40
❑ 77 Bill Mooneyham .... .15 .06
❑ 78 Omar Moreno .... .15 .06
❑ 79 Jerry Mumphrey .... .15 .06
❑ 80 Al Newman .... .25 .10
❑ 81 Phil Niekro .... .25 .10
❑ 82 Randy Niemann .... .15 .06
❑ 83 Juan Nieves .... .15 .06
❑ 84 Bob Ojeda .... .15 .06
❑ 85 Rick Ownbey .... .15 .06
❑ 86 Tom Paciorek .... .15 .06
❑ 87 David Palmer .... .15 .06
❑ 88 Jeff Parrett XRC .... .15 .06
❑ 89 Pat Perry .... .15 .06
❑ 90 Dan Plesac .... .15 .06
❑ 91 Darrell Porter .... .15 .06
❑ 92 Luis Quinones .... .15 .06
❑ 93 Rey Quinones UER .... .15 .06
(Misspelled Quinonez)
❑ 94 Gary Redus .... .15 .06
❑ 95 Jeff Reed .... .15 .06
❑ 96 Bip Roberts XRC .... .50 .20
❑ 97 Billy Joe Robidoux .... .15 .06
❑ 98 Gary Roenicke .... .15 .06
❑ 99 Ron Roenicke .... .15 .06
❑ 100 Angel Salazar .... .15 .06
❑ 101 Joe Sambito .... .15 .06
❑ 102 Billy Sample .... .15 .06
❑ 103 Dave Schmidt .... .15 .06
❑ 104 Ken Schrom .... .15 .06
❑ 105 Ruben Sierra XRC .... 1.50 .60
❑ 106 Ted Simmons .... .25 .10
❑ 107 Sammy Stewart .... .15 .06
❑ 108 Kurt Stillwell .... .15 .06
❑ 109 Dale Sveum .... .15 .06
❑ 110 Tim Teufel .... .15 .06
❑ 111 Bob Tewksbury XRC .... .50 .20
❑ 112 Andres Thomas .... .15 .06
❑ 113 Jason Thompson .... .15 .06
❑ 114 Milt Thompson .... .50 .20
❑ 115 R. Thompson XRC .... .50 .20
❑ 116 Jay Tibbs .... .15 .06
❑ 117 Fred Toliver .... .15 .06
❑ 118 Wayne Tolleson .... .15 .06
❑ 119 Alex Trevino .... .15 .06
❑ 120 Manny Trillo .... .15 .06
❑ 121 Ed VandeBerg .... .15 .06
❑ 122 Ozzie Virgil .... .15 .06
❑ 123 Tony Walker .... .15 .06
❑ 124 Gene Walter .... .15 .06
❑ 125 Duane Ward XRC .... .50 .20
❑ 126 Jerry Willard .... .15 .06
❑ 127 Mitch Williams XRC .... .50 .20
❑ 128 Reggie Williams .... .15 .06
❑ 129 Bobby Witt XRC .... .50 .20
❑ 130 Marvell Wynne .... .15 .06
❑ 131 Steve Yeager .... .25 .10
❑ 132 Checklist 1-132 .... .15 .06

1987 Fleer

	Nm-Mt	Ex-Mt
COMPLETE SET (660)	80.00	32.00
COMP.FACT.SET (672)	80.00	32.00

❑ 1 Rick Aguilera .... .15 .06
❑ 2 Richard Anderson .... .15 .06
❑ 3 Wally Backman .... .15 .06
❑ 4 Gary Carter .... .25 .10
❑ 5 Ron Darling .... .25 .10
❑ 6 Len Dykstra .... .25 .10
❑ 7 Kevin Elster RC .... .50 .20
❑ 8 Sid Fernandez .... .15 .06
❑ 9 Dwight Gooden .... .25 .10
❑ 10 Ed Hearn .... .15 .06
❑ 11 Danny Heep .... .15 .06
❑ 12 Keith Hernandez .... .25 .10
❑ 13 Howard Johnson .... .25 .10
❑ 14 Ray Knight .... .25 .10
❑ 15 Lee Mazzilli .... .25 .10
❑ 16 Roger McDowell .... .15 .06
❑ 17 Kevin Mitchell RC * .... 1.25 .50
❑ 18 Randy Niemann .... .15 .06
❑ 19 Bob Ojeda .... .15 .06
❑ 20 Jesse Orosco .... .15 .06
❑ 21 Rafael Santana .... .15 .06
❑ 22 Doug Sisk .... .15 .06
❑ 23 Darryl Strawberry .... .25 .10
❑ 24 Tim Teufel .... .15 .06
❑ 25 Mookie Wilson .... .25 .10

❑ 26 Tony Armas .25 .10
❑ 27 Marty Barrett .15 .06
❑ 28 Don Baylor .25 .10
❑ 29 Wade Boggs .40 .16
❑ 30 Oil Can Boyd .15 .06
❑ 31 Bill Buckner .25 .10
❑ 32 Roger Clemens 1.50 .60
❑ 33 Steve Crawford .15 .06
❑ 34 Dwight Evans .25 .10
❑ 35 Rich Gedman .15 .06
❑ 36 Dave Henderson .15 .06
❑ 37 Bruce Hurst .15 .06
❑ 38 Tim Lollar .15 .06
❑ 39 Al Nipper .15 .06
❑ 40 Spike Owen .15 .06
❑ 41 Jim Rice .25 .10
❑ 42 Ed Romero .15 .06
❑ 43 Joe Sambito .15 .06
❑ 44 Calvin Schiraldi .15 .06
❑ 45 Tom Seaver UER .40 .16
Lifetime saves total 0, should be 1
❑ 46 Jeff Sellers .15 .06
❑ 47 Bob Stanley .15 .06
❑ 48 Sammy Stewart .15 .06
❑ 49 Larry Andersen .15 .06
❑ 50 Alan Ashby .15 .06
❑ 51 Kevin Bass .15 .06
❑ 52 Jeff Calhoun .15 .06
❑ 53 Jose Cruz .25 .10
❑ 54 Danny Darwin .15 .06
❑ 55 Glenn Davis .15 .06
❑ 56 Jim Deshaies RC * .25 .10
❑ 57 Bill Doran .15 .06
❑ 58 Phil Garner .25 .10
❑ 59 Billy Hatcher .15 .06
❑ 60 Charlie Kerfeld .15 .06
❑ 61 Bob Knepper .15 .06
❑ 62 Dave Lopes .25 .10
❑ 63 Aurelio Lopez .15 .06
❑ 64 Jim Pankovits .15 .06
❑ 65 Terry Puhl .15 .06
❑ 66 Craig Reynolds .15 .06
❑ 67 Nolan Ryan 3.00 1.20
❑ 68 Mike Scott .25 .10
❑ 69 Dave Smith .15 .06
❑ 70 Dickie Thon .15 .06
❑ 71 Tony Walker .15 .06
❑ 72 Denny Walling .15 .06
❑ 73 Bob Boone .25 .10
❑ 74 Rick Burleson .15 .06
❑ 75 John Candelaria .15 .06
❑ 76 Doug Corbett .15 .06
❑ 77 Doug DeCinces .15 .06
❑ 78 Brian Downing .25 .10
❑ 79 Chuck Finley RC 1.25 .50
❑ 80 Terry Forster .25 .10
❑ 81 Bob Grich .25 .10
❑ 82 George Hendrick .25 .10
❑ 83 Jack Howell .15 .06
❑ 84 Reggie Jackson .40 .16
❑ 85 Ruppert Jones .15 .06
❑ 86 Wally Joyner RC 1.25 .50
❑ 87 Gary Lucas .15 .06
❑ 88 Kirk McCaskill .15 .06
❑ 89 Donnie Moore .15 .06
❑ 90 Gary Pettis .15 .06
❑ 91 Vern Ruhle .15 .06
❑ 92 Dick Schofield .15 .06
❑ 93 Don Sutton .25 .10
❑ 94 Rob Wilfong .15 .06
❑ 95 Mike Witt .15 .06
❑ 96 Doug Drabek RC 1.25 .50
❑ 97 Mike Easler .15 .06
❑ 98 Mike Fischlin .15 .06
❑ 99 Brian Fisher .15 .06
❑ 100 Ron Guidry .25 .10
❑ 101 Rickey Henderson .60 .24
❑ 102 Tommy John .25 .10
❑ 103 Ron Kittle .15 .06
❑ 104 Don Mattingly 2.00 .80
❑ 105 Bobby Meacham .15 .06
❑ 106 Joe Niekro .15 .06
❑ 107 Mike Pagliarulo .15 .06
❑ 108 Dan Pasqua .15 .06
❑ 109 Willie Randolph .25 .10
❑ 110 Dennis Rasmussen .15 .06
❑ 111 Dave Righetti .25 .10
❑ 112 Gary Roenicke .15 .06
❑ 113 Rod Scurry .15 .06
❑ 114 Bob Shirley .15 .06
❑ 115 Joel Skinner .15 .06
❑ 116 Tim Stoddard .15 .06
❑ 117 Bob Tewksbury RC * .50 .20
❑ 118 Wayne Tolleson .15 .06
❑ 119 Claudell Washington .15 .06
❑ 120 Dave Winfield .25 .10
❑ 121 Steve Buechele .15 .06
❑ 122 Ed Correa .15 .06
❑ 123 Scott Fletcher .15 .06
❑ 124 Jose Guzman .15 .06
❑ 125 Toby Harrah .25 .10
❑ 126 Greg Harris .15 .06
❑ 127 Charlie Hough .25 .10
❑ 128 Pete Incaviglia RC * .50 .20
❑ 129 Mike Mason .15 .06
❑ 130 Oddibe McDowell .15 .06
❑ 131 Dale Mohorcic .15 .06
❑ 132 Pete O'Brien .15 .06
❑ 133 Tom Paciorek .15 .06
❑ 134 Larry Parrish .15 .06
❑ 135 Geno Petralli .15 .06
❑ 136 Darrell Porter .15 .06
❑ 137 Jeff Russell .15 .06
❑ 138 Ruben Sierra RC 2.00 .80
❑ 139 Don Slaught .15 .06
❑ 140 Gary Ward .15 .06
❑ 141 Curtis Wilkerson .15 .06
❑ 142 Mitch Williams RC * .50 .20
❑ 143 Bobby Witt RC UER .50 .20
(Tulsa misspelled as Tusla; ERA should be 6.43, not .643)
❑ 144 Dave Bergman .15 .06
❑ 145 Tom Brookens .15 .06
❑ 146 Bill Campbell .15 .06
❑ 147 Chuck Cary .15 .06
❑ 148 Darnell Coles .15 .06
❑ 149 Dave Collins .15 .06
❑ 150 Darrell Evans .25 .10
❑ 151 Kirk Gibson .25 .10
❑ 152 John Grubb .15 .06
❑ 153 Willie Hernandez .15 .06
❑ 154 Larry Herndon .15 .06
❑ 155 Eric King .15 .06
❑ 156 Chet Lemon .25 .10
❑ 157 Dwight Lowry .15 .06
❑ 158 Jack Morris .25 .10
❑ 159 Randy O'Neal .15 .06
❑ 160 Lance Parrish .25 .10
❑ 161 Dan Petry .15 .06
❑ 162 Pat Sheridan .15 .06
❑ 163 Jim Slaton .15 .06
❑ 164 Frank Tanana .25 .10
❑ 165 Walt Terrell .15 .06
❑ 166 Mark Thurmond .15 .06
❑ 167 Alan Trammell .25 .10
❑ 168 Lou Whitaker .25 .10
❑ 169 Luis Aguayo .15 .06
❑ 170 Steve Bedrosian .15 .06
❑ 171 Don Carman .15 .06
❑ 172 Darren Daulton .25 .10
❑ 173 Greg Gross .15 .06
❑ 174 Kevin Gross .15 .06
❑ 175 Von Hayes .15 .06
❑ 176 Charles Hudson .15 .06
❑ 177 Tom Hume .15 .06
❑ 178 Steve Jeltz .15 .06
❑ 179 Mike Maddux .15 .06
❑ 180 Shane Rawley .15 .06
❑ 181 Gary Redus .15 .06
❑ 182 Ron Roenicke .15 .06
❑ 183 Bruce Ruffin RC .25 .10
❑ 184 John Russell .15 .06
❑ 185 Juan Samuel .15 .06
❑ 186 Dan Schatzeder .15 .06
❑ 187 Mike Schmidt 1.50 .60
❑ 188 Rick Schu .15 .06
❑ 189 Jeff Stone .15 .06
❑ 190 Kent Tekulve .15 .06
❑ 191 Milt Thompson .15 .06
❑ 192 Glenn Wilson .15 .06
❑ 193 Buddy Bell .25 .10
❑ 194 Tom Browning .15 .06
❑ 195 Sal Butera .15 .06
❑ 196 Dave Concepcion .25 .10
❑ 197 Kal Daniels .15 .06
❑ 198 Eric Davis .40 .16
❑ 199 John Denny .15 .06
❑ 200 Bo Diaz .15 .06
❑ 201 Nick Esasky .15 .06
❑ 202 John Franco .25 .10
❑ 203 Bill Gullickson .15 .06
❑ 204 Barry Larkin RC 3.00 1.20
❑ 205 Eddie Milner .15 .06
❑ 206 Rob Murphy .15 .06
❑ 207 Ron Oester .15 .06
❑ 208 Dave Parker .25 .10
❑ 209 Tony Perez .40 .16
❑ 210 Ted Power .15 .06
❑ 211 Joe Price .15 .06
❑ 212 Ron Robinson .15 .06
❑ 213 Pete Rose 2.00 .80
❑ 214 Mario Soto .25 .10
❑ 215 Kurt Stillwell .15 .06
❑ 216 Max Venable .15 .06
❑ 217 Chris Welsh .15 .06
❑ 218 Carl Willis RC .25 .10
❑ 219 Jesse Barfield .25 .10
❑ 220 George Bell .25 .10
❑ 221 Bill Caudill .15 .06
❑ 222 John Cerutti .15 .06
❑ 223 Jim Clancy .15 .06
❑ 224 Mark Eichhorn .15 .06
❑ 225 Tony Fernandez .15 .06
❑ 226 Damaso Garcia .15 .06
❑ 227 Kelly Gruber ERR .15 .06
(Wrong birth year)
❑ 228 Tom Henke .15 .06
❑ 229 Garth Iorg .15 .06
❑ 230 Joe Johnson .15 .06
❑ 231 Cliff Johnson .15 .06
❑ 232 Jimmy Key .25 .10
❑ 233 Dennis Lamp .15 .06
❑ 234 Rick Leach .15 .06
❑ 235 Buck Martinez .15 .06
❑ 236 Lloyd Moseby .15 .06
❑ 237 Rance Mulliniks .15 .06
❑ 238 Dave Stieb .25 .10
❑ 239 Willie Upshaw .15 .06
❑ 240 Ernie Whitt .15 .06
❑ 241 Andy Allanson .15 .06
❑ 242 Scott Bailes .15 .06
❑ 243 Chris Bando .15 .06
❑ 244 Tony Bernazard .15 .06
❑ 245 John Butcher .15 .06
❑ 246 Brett Butler .25 .10
❑ 247 Ernie Camacho .15 .06
❑ 248 Tom Candiotti .15 .06
❑ 249 Joe Carter .25 .10
❑ 250 Carmen Castillo .15 .06
❑ 251 Julio Franco .25 .10
❑ 252 Mel Hall .15 .06
❑ 253 Brook Jacoby .15 .06
❑ 254 Phil Niekro .25 .10
❑ 255 Otis Nixon .15 .06
❑ 256 Dickie Noles .15 .06
❑ 257 Bryan Oelkers .15 .06
❑ 258 Ken Schrom .15 .06
❑ 259 Don Schulze .15 .06
❑ 260 Cory Snyder .15 .06
❑ 261 Pat Tabler .15 .06
❑ 262 Andre Thornton .15 .06
❑ 263 Rich Yett .15 .06
❑ 264 Mike Aldrete .15 .06
❑ 265 Juan Berenguer .15 .06
❑ 266 Vida Blue .25 .10
❑ 267 Bob Brenly .15 .06
❑ 268 Chris Brown .15 .06
❑ 269 Will Clark RC 3.00 1.20
❑ 270 Chili Davis .25 .10
❑ 271 Mark Davis .15 .06
❑ 272 Kelly Downs RC .25 .10
❑ 273 Scott Garrelts .15 .06
❑ 274 Dan Gladden .15 .06
❑ 275 Mike Krukow .15 .06
❑ 276 Randy Kutcher .15 .06
❑ 277 Mike LaCoss .15 .06
❑ 278 Jeff Leonard .15 .06

❑ 279 Candy Maldonado .15 .06
❑ 280 Roger Mason .15 .06
❑ 281 Bob Melvin .15 .06
❑ 282 Greg Minton .15 .06
❑ 283 Jeff D. Robinson .15 .06
❑ 284 Harry Spilman .15 .06
❑ 285 R.Thompson RC* .50 .20
❑ 286 Jose Uribe .15 .06
❑ 287 Frank Williams .15 .06
❑ 288 Joel Youngblood .15 .06
❑ 289 Jack Clark .25 .10
❑ 290 Vince Coleman .15 .06
❑ 291 Tim Conroy .15 .06
❑ 292 Danny Cox .15 .06
❑ 293 Ken Dayley .15 .06
❑ 294 Curt Ford .15 .06
❑ 295 Bob Forsch .15 .06
❑ 296 Tom Herr .15 .06
❑ 297 Ricky Horton .15 .06
❑ 298 Clint Hurdle .15 .06
❑ 299 Jeff Lahti .15 .06
❑ 300 Steve Lake .15 .06
❑ 301 Tito Landrum .15 .06
❑ 302 Mike LaValliere RC * .50 .20
❑ 303 Greg Mathews .15 .06
❑ 304 Willie McGee .25 .10
❑ 305 Jose Oquendo .15 .06
❑ 306 Terry Pendleton .25 .10
❑ 307 Pat Perry .15 .06
❑ 308 Ozzie Smith 1.00 .40
❑ 309 Ray Soff .15 .06
❑ 310 John Tudor .25 .10
❑ 311 Andy Van Slyke UER .25 .10
(Bats R, Throws L)
❑ 312 Todd Worrell .15 .06
❑ 313 Dann Bilardello .15 .06
❑ 314 Hubie Brooks .15 .06
❑ 315 Tim Burke .15 .06
❑ 316 Andre Dawson .25 .10
❑ 317 Mike Fitzgerald .15 .06
❑ 318 Tom Foley .15 .06
❑ 319 Andres Galarraga .25 .10
❑ 320 Joe Hesketh .15 .06
❑ 321 Wallace Johnson .15 .06
❑ 322 Wayne Krenchicki .15 .06
❑ 323 Vance Law .15 .06
❑ 324 Dennis Martinez .25 .10
❑ 325 Bob McClure .15 .06
❑ 326 Andy McGaffigan .15 .06
❑ 327 Al Newman .15 .06
❑ 328 Tim Raines .25 .10
❑ 329 Jeff Reardon .25 .10
❑ 330 Luis Rivera RC .25 .10
❑ 331 Bob Sebra .15 .06
❑ 332 Bryn Smith .15 .06
❑ 333 Jay Tibbs .15 .06
❑ 334 Tim Wallach .15 .06
❑ 335 Mitch Webster .15 .06
❑ 336 Jim Wohlford .15 .06
❑ 337 Floyd Youmans .15 .06
❑ 338 Chris Bosio RC .50 .20
❑ 339 Glenn Braggs RC .25 .10
❑ 340 Rick Cerone .15 .06
❑ 341 Mark Clear .15 .06
❑ 342 Bryan Clutterbuck .15 .06
❑ 343 Cecil Cooper .25 .10
❑ 344 Rob Deer .15 .06
❑ 345 Jim Gantner .15 .06
❑ 346 Ted Higuera .15 .06
❑ 347 John Henry Johnson .15 .06
❑ 348 Tim Leary .15 .06
❑ 349 Rick Manning .15 .06
❑ 350 Paul Molitor .40 .16
❑ 351 Charlie Moore .15 .06
❑ 352 Juan Nieves .15 .06
❑ 353 Ben Oglivie .25 .10
❑ 354 Dan Plesac .15 .06
❑ 355 Ernest Riles .15 .06
❑ 356 Billy Joe Robidoux .15 .06
❑ 357 Bill Schroeder .15 .06
❑ 358 Dale Sveum .15 .06
❑ 359 Gorman Thomas .25 .10
❑ 360 Bill Wegman .15 .06
❑ 361 Robin Yount 1.00 .40
❑ 362 Steve Balboni .15 .06
❑ 363 Scott Bankhead .15 .06
❑ 364 Buddy Biancalana .15 .06
❑ 365 Bud Black .15 .06
❑ 366 George Brett 1.50 .60
❑ 367 Steve Farr .15 .06
❑ 368 Mark Gubicza .15 .06
❑ 369 Bo Jackson RC 3.00 1.20
❑ 370 Danny Jackson .15 .06
❑ 371 Mike Kingery RC .25 .10
❑ 372 Rudy Law .15 .06
❑ 373 Charlie Leibrandt .15 .06
❑ 374 Dennis Leonard .15 .06
❑ 375 Hal McRae .25 .10
❑ 376 Jorge Orta .15 .06
❑ 377 Jamie Quirk .15 .06
❑ 378 Dan Quisenberry .15 .06
❑ 379 Bret Saberhagen .25 .10
❑ 380 Angel Salazar .15 .06
❑ 381 Lonnie Smith .15 .06
❑ 382 Jim Sundberg .25 .10
❑ 383 Frank White .25 .10
❑ 384 Willie Wilson .25 .10
❑ 385 Joaquin Andujar .25 .10
❑ 386 Doug Bair .15 .06
❑ 387 Dusty Baker .25 .10
❑ 388 Bruce Bochte .15 .06
❑ 389 Jose Canseco .60 .24
❑ 390 Chris Codiroli .15 .06
❑ 391 Mike Davis .15 .06
❑ 392 Alfredo Griffin .15 .06
❑ 393 Moose Haas .15 .06
❑ 394 Donnie Hill .15 .06
❑ 395 Jay Howell .15 .06
❑ 396 Dave Kingman .25 .10
❑ 397 Carney Lansford .25 .10
❑ 398 Dave Leiper .15 .06
❑ 399 Bill Mooneyham .15 .06
❑ 400 Dwayne Murphy .15 .06
❑ 401 Steve Ontiveros .15 .06
❑ 402 Tony Phillips .15 .06
❑ 403 Eric Plunk .15 .06
❑ 404 Jose Rijo .25 .10
❑ 405 Terry Steinbach RC 1.25 .50
❑ 406 Dave Stewart .25 .10
❑ 407 Mickey Tettleton .15 .06
❑ 408 Dave Von Ohlen .15 .06
❑ 409 Jerry Willard .15 .06
❑ 410 Curt Young .15 .06
❑ 411 Bruce Bochy .15 .06
❑ 412 Dave Dravecky .15 .06
❑ 413 Tim Flannery .15 .06
❑ 414 Steve Garvey .25 .10
❑ 415 Rich Gossage .25 .10
❑ 416 Tony Gwynn 1.00 .40
❑ 417 Andy Hawkins .15 .06
❑ 418 LaMarr Hoyt .15 .06
❑ 419 Terry Kennedy .15 .06
❑ 420 John Kruk RC 2.00 .80
❑ 421 Dave LaPoint .15 .06
❑ 422 Craig Lefferts .15 .06
❑ 423 Carmelo Martinez .15 .06
❑ 424 Lance McCullers .15 .06
❑ 425 Kevin McReynolds .15 .06
❑ 426 Graig Nettles .25 .10
❑ 427 Bip Roberts RC .50 .20
❑ 428 Jerry Royster .15 .06
❑ 429 Benito Santiago .25 .10
❑ 430 Eric Show .15 .06
❑ 431 Bob Stoddard .15 .06
❑ 432 Garry Templeton .25 .10
❑ 433 Gene Walter .15 .06
❑ 434 Ed Whitson .15 .06
❑ 435 Marvell Wynne .15 .06
❑ 436 Dave Anderson .15 .06
❑ 437 Greg Brock .15 .06
❑ 438 Enos Cabell .15 .06
❑ 439 Mariano Duncan .15 .06
❑ 440 Pedro Guerrero .25 .10
❑ 441 Orel Hershiser .25 .10
❑ 442 Rick Honeycutt .15 .06
❑ 443 Ken Howell .15 .06
❑ 444 Ken Landreaux .15 .06
❑ 445 Bill Madlock .25 .10
❑ 446 Mike Marshall .15 .06
❑ 447 Len Matuszek .15 .06
❑ 448 Tom Niedenfuer .15 .06
❑ 449 Alejandro Pena .15 .06
❑ 450 Dennis Powell .15 .06
❑ 451 Jerry Reuss .15 .06
❑ 452 Bill Russell .25 .10
❑ 453 Steve Sax .15 .06
❑ 454 Mike Scioscia .25 .10
❑ 455 Franklin Stubbs .15 .06
❑ 456 Alex Trevino .15 .06
❑ 457 Fernando Valenzuela .25 .10
❑ 458 Ed VandeBerg .15 .06
❑ 459 Bob Welch .25 .10
❑ 460 Reggie Williams .15 .06
❑ 461 Don Aase .15 .06
❑ 462 Juan Beniquez .15 .06
❑ 463 Mike Boddicker .15 .06
❑ 464 Juan Bonilla .15 .06
❑ 465 Rich Bordi .15 .06
❑ 466 Storm Davis .15 .06
❑ 467 Rick Dempsey .15 .06
❑ 468 Ken Dixon .15 .06
❑ 469 Jim Dwyer .15 .06
❑ 470 Mike Flanagan .15 .06
❑ 471 Jackie Gutierrez .15 .06
❑ 472 Brad Havens .15 .06
❑ 473 Lee Lacy .15 .06
❑ 474 Fred Lynn .25 .10
❑ 475 Scott McGregor .15 .06
❑ 476 Eddie Murray .60 .24
❑ 477 Tom O'Malley .15 .06
❑ 478 Cal Ripken Jr. 2.50 1.00
❑ 479 Larry Sheets .15 .06
❑ 480 John Shelby .15 .06
❑ 481 Nate Snell .15 .06
❑ 482 Jim Traber .15 .06
❑ 483 Mike Young .15 .06
❑ 484 Neil Allen .15 .06
❑ 485 Harold Baines .25 .10
❑ 486 Floyd Bannister .15 .06
❑ 487 Daryl Boston .15 .06
❑ 488 Ivan Calderon .15 .06
❑ 489 John Cangelosi .15 .06
❑ 490 Steve Carlton .25 .10
❑ 491 Joe Cowley .15 .06
❑ 492 Julio Cruz .15 .06
❑ 493 Bill Dawley .15 .06
❑ 494 Jose DeLeon .15 .06
❑ 495 Richard Dotson .15 .06
❑ 496 Carlton Fisk .40 .16
❑ 497 Ozzie Guillen .15 .06
❑ 498 Jerry Hairston .15 .06
❑ 499 Ron Hassey .15 .06
❑ 500 Tim Hulett .15 .06
❑ 501 Bob James .15 .06
❑ 502 Steve Lyons .15 .06
❑ 503 Joel McKeon .15 .06
❑ 504 Gene Nelson .15 .06
❑ 505 Dave Schmidt .15 .06
❑ 506 Ray Searage .15 .06
❑ 507 Bobby Thigpen RC .50 .20
❑ 508 Greg Walker .15 .06
❑ 509 Jim Acker .15 .06
❑ 510 Doyle Alexander .15 .06
❑ 511 Paul Assenmacher .50 .20
❑ 512 Bruce Benedict .15 .06
❑ 513 Chris Chambliss .25 .10
❑ 514 Jeff Dedmon .15 .06
❑ 515 Gene Garber .15 .06
❑ 516 Ken Griffey .25 .10
❑ 517 Terry Harper .15 .06
❑ 518 Bob Horner .25 .10
❑ 519 Glenn Hubbard .15 .06
❑ 520 Rick Mahler .15 .06
❑ 521 Omar Moreno .15 .06
❑ 522 Dale Murphy .40 .16
❑ 523 Ken Oberkfell .15 .06
❑ 524 Ed Olwine .15 .06
❑ 525 David Palmer .15 .06
❑ 526 Rafael Ramirez .15 .06
❑ 527 Billy Sample .15 .06
❑ 528 Ted Simmons .25 .10
❑ 529 Zane Smith .15 .06
❑ 530 Bruce Sutter .25 .10
❑ 531 Andres Thomas .15 .06
❑ 532 Ozzie Virgil .15 .06
❑ 533 Allan Anderson .15 .06
❑ 534 Keith Atherton .15 .06
❑ 535 Billy Beane .25 .10

❑ 536	Bert Blyleven	.25	.10
❑ 537	Tom Brunansky	.15	.06
❑ 538	Randy Bush	.15	.06
❑ 539	George Frazier	.15	.06
❑ 540	Gary Gaetti	.25	.10
❑ 541	Greg Gagne	.15	.06
❑ 542	Mickey Hatcher	.15	.06
❑ 543	Neal Heaton	.15	.06
❑ 544	Kent Hrbek	.25	.10
❑ 545	Roy Lee Jackson	.15	.06
❑ 546	Tim Laudner	.15	.06
❑ 547	Steve Lombardozzi	.15	.06
❑ 548	Mark Portugal RC *	.50	.20
❑ 549	Kirby Puckett	.60	.24
❑ 550	Jeff Reed	.15	.06
❑ 551	Mark Salas	.15	.06
❑ 552	Roy Smalley	.15	.06
❑ 553	Mike Smithson	.15	.06
❑ 554	Frank Viola	.25	.10
❑ 555	Thad Bosley	.15	.06
❑ 556	Ron Cey	.25	.10
❑ 557	Jody Davis	.15	.06
❑ 558	Ron Davis	.15	.06
❑ 559	Bob Dernier	.15	.06
❑ 560	Frank DiPino	.15	.06
❑ 561	Shawon Dunston UER	.15	.06
	(Wrong birth year		
	listed on card back)		
❑ 562	Leon Durham	.15	.06
❑ 563	Dennis Eckersley	.40	.16
❑ 564	Terry Francona	.25	.10
❑ 565	Dave Gumpert	.15	.06
❑ 566	Guy Hoffman	.15	.06
❑ 567	Ed Lynch	.15	.06
❑ 568	Gary Matthews	.25	.10
❑ 569	Keith Moreland	.15	.06
❑ 570	Jamie Moyer RC	2.00	.80
❑ 571	Jerry Mumphrey	.15	.06
❑ 572	Ryne Sandberg	1.25	.50
❑ 573	Scott Sanderson	.15	.06
❑ 574	Lee Smith	.25	.10
❑ 575	Chris Speier	.15	.06
❑ 576	Rick Sutcliffe	.25	.10
❑ 577	Manny Trillo	.15	.06
❑ 578	Steve Trout	.15	.06
❑ 579	Karl Best	.15	.06
❑ 580	Scott Bradley	.15	.06
❑ 581	Phil Bradley	.15	.06
❑ 582	Mickey Brantley	.15	.06
❑ 583	Mike G. Brown P	.15	.06
❑ 584	Alvin Davis	.15	.06
❑ 585	Lee Guetterman	.15	.06
❑ 586	Mark Huismann	.15	.06
❑ 587	Bob Kearney	.15	.06
❑ 588	Pete Ladd	.15	.06
❑ 589	Mark Langston	.15	.06
❑ 590	Mike Moore	.15	.06
❑ 591	Mike Morgan	.15	.06
❑ 592	John Moses	.15	.06
❑ 593	Ken Phelps	.15	.06
❑ 594	Jim Presley	.15	.06
❑ 595	Rey Quinones UER	.15	.06
	(Quinonez on front)		
❑ 596	Harold Reynolds	.25	.10
❑ 597	Billy Swift	.15	.06
❑ 598	Danny Tartabull	.15	.06
❑ 599	Steve Yeager	.25	.10
❑ 600	Matt Young	.15	.06
❑ 601	Bill Almon	.15	.06
❑ 602	Rafael Belliard RC	.50	.20
❑ 603	Mike Bielecki	.15	.06
❑ 604	Barry Bonds RC	60.00	24.00
❑ 605	Bobby Bonilla RC	1.25	.50
❑ 606	Sid Bream	.15	.06
❑ 607	Mike C. Brown	.15	.06
❑ 608	Pat Clements	.15	.06
❑ 609	Mike Diaz	.15	.06
❑ 610	Cecilio Guante	.15	.06
❑ 611	Barry Jones	.15	.06
❑ 612	Bob Kipper	.15	.06
❑ 613	Larry McWilliams	.15	.06
❑ 614	Jim Morrison	.15	.06
❑ 615	Joe Orsulak	.15	.06
❑ 616	Junior Ortiz	.15	.06
❑ 617	Tony Pena	.15	.06
❑ 618	Johnny Ray	.15	.06

❑ 619	Rick Reuschel	.25	.10
❑ 620	R.J. Reynolds	.15	.06
❑ 621	Rick Rhoden	.15	.06
❑ 622	Don Robinson	.15	.06
❑ 623	Bob Walk	.15	.06
❑ 624	Jim Winn	.15	.06
❑ 625	Pete Incaviglia	.60	.24
	Jose Canseco		
❑ 626	Don Sutton	.25	.10
	Phil Niekro		
❑ 627	Dave Righetti	.15	.06
	Don Aase		
❑ 628	Wally Joyner	.40	.16
	Jose Canseco		
❑ 629	Gary Carter	.25	.10
	Sid Fernandez		
	Dwight Gooden		
	Keith Hernandez		
	Darryl Strawberry		
❑ 630	Mike Scott	.15	.06
	Mike Krukow		
❑ 631	Fernando Valenzuela	.15	.06
	John Franco		
❑ 632	Bob Horner 4 Homers	.15	.06
❑ 633	Jose Canseco	.60	.24
	Jim Rice		
	Kirby Puckett		
❑ 634	Gary Carter	.60	.24
	Roger Clemens		
❑ 635	Steve Carlton 4000K's	.25	.10
❑ 636	Glenn Davis	.60	.24
	Eddie Murray		
❑ 637	Wade Boggs	.25	.10
	Keith Hernandez		
❑ 638	Don Mattingly	1.00	.40
	Darryl Strawberry		
❑ 639	Dave Parker	.60	.24
	Ryne Sandberg		
❑ 640	Dwight Gooden	.60	.24
	Roger Clemens		
❑ 641	Mike Witt	.15	.06
	Charlie Hough		
❑ 642	Juan Samuel	.25	.10
	Tim Raines		
❑ 643	Harold Baines	.25	.10
	Jesse Barfield		
❑ 644	Dave Clark RC and	.50	.20
	Greg Swindell		
❑ 645	Ron Karkovice RC	.50	.20
	Russ Morman		
❑ 646	Devon White RC and	1.25	.50
	Willie Fraser		
❑ 647	Mike Stanley RC and	.50	.20
	Jerry Browne		
❑ 648	Dave Magadan RC	.50	.20
	Phil Lombardi		
❑ 649	Jose Gonzalez RC	.25	.10
	Ralph Bryant		
❑ 650	Jimmy Jones RC and	.25	.10
	Randy Asadoor		
❑ 651	Tracy Jones RC and	.25	.10
	Marvin Freeman		
❑ 652	John Stefero and	.50	.20
	Kevin Seitzer RC		
❑ 653	Rob Nelson and	.25	.10
	Steve Fireovid		
❑ 654	CL: Mets/Red Sox	.15	.06
	Astros/Angels		
❑ 655	CL: Yankees/Rangers	.15	.06
	Tigers/Phillies		
❑ 656	CL: Reds/Blue Jays	.15	.06
	Indians/Giants		
	ERR (230/231 wrong)		
❑ 657	CL: Cardinals/Expos	.15	.06
	Brewers/Royals		
❑ 658	CL: A's/Padres	.15	.06
	Dodgers/Orioles		
❑ 659	CL: White Sox/Braves	.15	.06
	Twins/Cubs		
❑ 660	CL: Mariners/Pirates	.15	.06
	Special Cards		
	ER (580/581 wrong)		

1987 Fleer Update

		Nm-Mt	Ex-Mt
COMP.FACT.SET (132)		15.00	6.00
❑ 1	Scott Bankhead	.10	.04
❑ 2	Eric Bell	.15	.06
❑ 3	Juan Beniquez	.10	.04
❑ 4	Juan Berenguer	.10	.04
❑ 5	Mike Birkbeck	.15	.06
❑ 6	Randy Bockus	.10	.04
❑ 7	Rod Booker	.10	.04
❑ 8	Thad Bosley	.10	.04
❑ 9	Greg Brock	.10	.04
❑ 10	Bob Brower	.10	.04
❑ 11	Chris Brown	.10	.04
❑ 12	Jerry Browne	.15	.06
❑ 13	Ralph Bryant	.10	.04
❑ 14	DeWayne Buice	.10	.04
❑ 15	Ellis Burks XRC	.75	.30
❑ 16	Casey Candaele	.10	.04
❑ 17	Steve Carlton	.15	.06
❑ 18	Juan Castillo	.15	.06
❑ 19	Chuck Crim	.10	.04
❑ 20	Mark Davidson	.10	.04
❑ 21	Mark Davis	.10	.04
❑ 22	Storm Davis	.10	.04
❑ 23	Bill Dawley	.10	.04
❑ 24	Andre Dawson	.15	.06
❑ 25	Brian Dayett	.10	.04
❑ 26	Rick Dempsey	.10	.04
❑ 27	Ken Dowell	.10	.04
❑ 28	Dave Dravecky	.10	.04
❑ 29	Mike Dunne	.10	.04
❑ 30	Dennis Eckersley	.25	.10
❑ 31	Cecil Fielder	.15	.06
❑ 32	Brian Fisher	.10	.04
❑ 33	Willie Fraser	.15	.06
❑ 34	Ken Gerhart	.10	.04
❑ 35	Jim Gott	.10	.04
❑ 36	Dan Gladden	.10	.04
❑ 37	Mike Greenwell XRC*	.30	.12
❑ 38	Cecilio Guante	.10	.04
❑ 39	Albert Hall	.10	.04
❑ 40	Atlee Hammaker	.10	.04
❑ 41	Mickey Hatcher	.10	.04
❑ 42	Mike Heath	.10	.04
❑ 43	Neal Heaton	.10	.04
❑ 44	Mike Henneman XRC	.30	.12
❑ 45	Guy Hoffman	.10	.04
❑ 46	Charles Hudson	.10	.04
❑ 47	Chuck Jackson	.10	.04
❑ 48	Mike Jackson XRC	.30	.12
❑ 49	Reggie Jackson	.25	.10
❑ 50	Chris James	.10	.04
❑ 51	Dion James	.10	.04
❑ 52	Stan Javier	.10	.04
❑ 53	Stan Jefferson	.10	.04
❑ 54	Jimmy Jones	.15	.06
❑ 55	Tracy Jones	.10	.04
❑ 56	Terry Kennedy	.10	.04
❑ 57	Mike Kingery	.15	.06
❑ 58	Ray Knight	.15	.06
❑ 59	Gene Larkin XRC	.30	.12
❑ 60	Mike LaValliere	.30	.12
❑ 61	Jack Lazorko	.10	.04
❑ 62	Terry Leach	.10	.04
❑ 63	Rick Leach	.10	.04

❑ 64 Craig Lefferts	.10	.04
❑ 65 Jim Lindeman	.15	.06
❑ 66 Bill Long	.10	.04
❑ 67 Mike Loynd XRC	.15	.06
❑ 68 Greg Maddux XRC	8.00	3.20
❑ 69 Bill Madlock	.15	.06
❑ 70 Dave Magadan	.30	.12
❑ 71 Joe Magrane XRC	.15	.06
❑ 72 Fred Manrique	.10	.04
❑ 73 Mike Mason	.10	.04
❑ 74 Lloyd McClendon XRC	.30	.12
❑ 75 Fred McGriff	1.00	.40
❑ 76 Mark McGwire	5.00	2.00
❑ 77 Mark McLemore	.15	.06
❑ 78 Kevin McReynolds	.10	.04
❑ 79 Dave Meads	.10	.04
❑ 80 Greg Minton	.10	.04
❑ 81 John Mitchell XRC	.15	.06
❑ 82 Kevin Mitchell	.25	.10
❑ 83 John Morris	.10	.04
❑ 84 Jeff Musselman	.10	.04
❑ 85 Randy Myers XRC	.75	.30
❑ 86 Gene Nelson	.10	.04
❑ 87 Joe Niekro	.10	.04
❑ 88 Tom Nieto	.10	.04
❑ 89 Reid Nichols	.10	.04
❑ 90 Matt Nokes XRC	.30	.12
❑ 91 Dickie Noles	.10	.04
❑ 92 Edwin Nunez	.10	.04
❑ 93 Jose Nunez	.10	.04
❑ 94 Paul O'Neill	.40	.16
❑ 95 Jim Paciorek	.10	.04
❑ 96 Lance Parrish	.15	.06
❑ 97 Bill Pecota XRC	.15	.06
❑ 98 Tony Pena	.10	.04
❑ 99 Luis Polonia XRC	.30	.12
❑ 100 Randy Ready	.10	.04
❑ 101 Jeff Reardon	.15	.06
❑ 102 Gary Redus	.10	.04
❑ 103 Rick Rhoden	.10	.04
❑ 104 Wally Ritchie	.10	.04
❑ 105 Jeff M. Robinson UER (Wrong Jeff's stats on back)	.10	.04
❑ 106 Mark Salas	.10	.04
❑ 107 Dave Schmidt	.10	.04
❑ 108 Kevin Seitzer UER (Wrong birth year)	.30	.12
❑ 109 John Shelby	.10	.04
❑ 110 John Smiley XRC	.30	.12
❑ 111 Lary Sorensen	.10	.04
❑ 112 Chris Speier	.10	.04
❑ 113 Randy St.Claire	.10	.04
❑ 114 Jim Sundberg	.15	.06
❑ 115 B.J. Surhoff XRC	.75	.30
❑ 116 Greg Swindell	.30	.12
❑ 117 Danny Tartabull	.10	.04
❑ 118 Dorn Taylor	.10	.04
❑ 119 Lee Tunnell	.10	.04
❑ 120 Ed VandeBerg	.10	.04
❑ 121 Andy Van Slyke	.15	.06
❑ 122 Gary Ward	.10	.04
❑ 123 Devon White	.75	.30
❑ 124 Alan Wiggins	.10	.04
❑ 125 Bill Wilkinson	.10	.04
❑ 126 Jim Winn	.10	.04
❑ 127 Frank Williams	.10	.04
❑ 128 Ken Williams XRC	.10	.04
❑ 129 Matt Williams XRC	1.50	.60
❑ 130 Herm Winningham	.10	.04
❑ 131 Matt Young	.10	.04
❑ 132 Checklist 1-132	.10	.04

1988 Fleer

	Nm-Mt	Ex-Mt
COMPLETE SET (660)	15.00	6.00
COMP.RETAIL SET (660)	15.00	6.00
COMP.HOBBY SET (672)	15.00	6.00

❑ 1 Keith Atherton	.10	.04
❑ 2 Don Baylor	.15	.06
❑ 3 Juan Berenguer	.10	.04
❑ 4 Bert Blyleven	.15	.06
❑ 5 Tom Brunansky	.10	.04
❑ 6 Randy Bush	.10	.04
❑ 7 Steve Carlton	.15	.06
❑ 8 Mark Davidson	.10	.04
❑ 9 George Frazier	.10	.04
❑ 10 Gary Gaetti	.15	.06
❑ 11 Greg Gagne	.10	.04
❑ 12 Dan Gladden	.10	.04
❑ 13 Kent Hrbek	.15	.06
❑ 14 Gene Larkin RC*	.40	.16
❑ 15 Tim Laudner	.10	.04
❑ 16 Steve Lombardozzi	.10	.04
❑ 17 Al Newman	.10	.04
❑ 18 Joe Niekro	.10	.04
❑ 19 Kirby Puckett	.30	.12
❑ 20 Jeff Reardon	.15	.06
❑ 21A Dan Schatzeder ERR (Misspelled Schatzader on both sides of the card)	.15	.06
❑ 21B Dan Schatzeder COR	.10	.04
❑ 22 Roy Smalley	.10	.04
❑ 23 Mike Smithson	.10	.04
❑ 24 Les Straker	.10	.04
❑ 25 Frank Viola	.15	.06
❑ 26 Jack Clark	.15	.06
❑ 27 Vince Coleman	.10	.04
❑ 28 Danny Cox	.10	.04
❑ 29 Bill Dawley	.10	.04
❑ 30 Ken Dayley	.10	.04
❑ 31 Doug DeCinces	.10	.04
❑ 32 Curt Ford	.10	.04
❑ 33 Bob Forsch	.10	.04
❑ 34 David Green	.10	.04
❑ 35 Tom Herr	.10	.04
❑ 36 Ricky Horton	.10	.04
❑ 37 Lance Johnson RC	.40	.16
❑ 38 Steve Lake	.10	.04
❑ 39 Jim Lindeman	.10	.04
❑ 40 Joe Magrane RC*	.40	.16
❑ 41 Greg Mathews	.10	.04
❑ 42 Willie McGee	.15	.06
❑ 43 John Morris	.10	.04
❑ 44 Jose Oquendo	.10	.04
❑ 45 Tony Pena	.10	.04
❑ 46 Terry Pendleton	.15	.06
❑ 47 Ozzie Smith	.50	.20
❑ 48 John Tudor	.15	.06
❑ 49 Lee Tunnell	.10	.04
❑ 50 Todd Worrell	.10	.04
❑ 51 Doyle Alexander	.10	.04
❑ 52 Dave Bergman	.10	.04
❑ 53 Tom Brookens	.10	.04
❑ 54 Darrell Evans	.15	.06
❑ 55 Kirk Gibson	.30	.12
❑ 56 Mike Heath	.10	.04
❑ 57 Mike Henneman RC*	.40	.16
❑ 58 Willie Hernandez	.10	.04
❑ 59 Larry Herndon	.10	.04
❑ 60 Eric King	.10	.04
❑ 61 Chet Lemon	.15	.06
❑ 62 Scott Lusader	.10	.04
❑ 63 Bill Madlock	.15	.06
❑ 64 Jack Morris	.15	.06
❑ 65 Jim Morrison	.10	.04
❑ 66 Matt Nokes RC*	.40	.16
❑ 67 Dan Petry	.10	.04
❑ 68A Jeff M. Robinson ERR, Stats for Jeff D. Robinson on card back Born 12-13-60	.20	.08
❑ 68B Jeff M. Robinson COR, Born 12-14-61	.10	.04
❑ 69 Pat Sheridan	.10	.04
❑ 70 Nate Snell	.10	.04
❑ 71 Frank Tanana	.15	.06
❑ 72 Walt Terrell	.10	.04
❑ 73 Mark Thurmond	.10	.04
❑ 74 Alan Trammell	.15	.06
❑ 75 Lou Whitaker	.15	.06
❑ 76 Mike Aldrete	.10	.04
❑ 77 Bob Brenly	.10	.04
❑ 78 Will Clark	.30	.12
❑ 79 Chili Davis	.15	.06
❑ 80 Kelly Downs	.10	.04
❑ 81 Dave Dravecky	.10	.04
❑ 82 Scott Garrelts	.10	.04
❑ 83 Atlee Hammaker	.10	.04
❑ 84 Dave Henderson	.10	.04
❑ 85 Mike Krukow	.10	.04
❑ 86 Mike LaCoss	.10	.04
❑ 87 Craig Lefferts	.10	.04
❑ 88 Jeff Leonard	.10	.04
❑ 89 Candy Maldonado	.10	.04
❑ 90 Eddie Milner	.10	.04
❑ 91 Bob Melvin	.10	.04
❑ 92 Kevin Mitchell	.15	.06
❑ 93 Jon Perlman	.10	.04
❑ 94 Rick Reuschel	.15	.06
❑ 95 Don Robinson	.10	.04
❑ 96 Chris Speier	.10	.04
❑ 97 Harry Spilman	.10	.04
❑ 98 Robby Thompson	.10	.04
❑ 99 Jose Uribe	.10	.04
❑ 100 Mark Wasinger	.10	.04
❑ 101 Matt Williams RC	1.50	.60
❑ 102 Jesse Barfield	.15	.06
❑ 103 George Bell	.15	.06
❑ 104 Juan Beniquez	.10	.04
❑ 105 John Cerutti	.10	.04
❑ 106 Jim Clancy	.10	.04
❑ 107 Rob Ducey	.10	.04
❑ 108 Mark Eichhorn	.10	.04
❑ 109 Tony Fernandez	.10	.04
❑ 110 Cecil Fielder	.15	.06
❑ 111 Kelly Gruber	.10	.04
❑ 112 Tom Henke	.10	.04
❑ 113A Garth Iorg ERR (Misspelled Iorq on card front)	.20	.08
❑ 113B Garth Iorg COR	.10	.04
❑ 114 Jimmy Key	.15	.06
❑ 115 Rick Leach	.10	.04
❑ 116 Manny Lee	.10	.04
❑ 117 Nelson Liriano	.10	.04
❑ 118 Fred McGriff	.30	.12
❑ 119 Lloyd Moseby	.10	.04
❑ 120 Rance Mulliniks	.10	.04
❑ 121 Jeff Musselman	.10	.04
❑ 122 Jose Nunez	.10	.04
❑ 123 Dave Stieb	.15	.06
❑ 124 Willie Upshaw	.10	.04
❑ 125 Duane Ward	.10	.04
❑ 126 Ernie Whitt	.10	.04
❑ 127 Rick Aguilera	.10	.04
❑ 128 Wally Backman	.10	.04
❑ 129 Mark Carreon RC	.15	.06
❑ 130 Gary Carter	.15	.06
❑ 131 David Cone	.15	.06
❑ 132 Ron Darling	.15	.06
❑ 133 Len Dykstra	.15	.06
❑ 134 Sid Fernandez	.10	.04
❑ 135 Dwight Gooden	.15	.06
❑ 136 Keith Hernandez	.15	.06
❑ 137 Gregg Jefferies RC	.40	.16
❑ 138 Howard Johnson	.15	.06
❑ 139 Terry Leach	.10	.04
❑ 140 Barry Lyons	.10	.04
❑ 141 Dave Magadan	.10	.04
❑ 142 Roger McDowell	.10	.04
❑ 143 Kevin McReynolds	.10	.04
❑ 144 Keith A. Miller RC	.40	.16
❑ 145 John Mitchell RC	.15	.06
❑ 146 Randy Myers	.15	.06
❑ 147 Bob Ojeda	.10	.04
❑ 148 Jesse Orosco	.10	.04
❑ 149 Rafael Santana	.10	.04

❑	150	Doug Sisk	.10	.04
❑	151	Darryl Strawberry	.15	.06
❑	152	Tim Teufel	.10	.04
❑	153	Gene Walter	.10	.04
❑	154	Mookie Wilson	.15	.06
❑	155	Jay Aldrich	.10	.04
❑	156	Chris Bosio	.10	.04
❑	157	Glenn Braggs	.10	.04
❑	158	Greg Brock	.10	.04
❑	159	Juan Castillo	.10	.04
❑	160	Mark Clear	.10	.04
❑	161	Cecil Cooper	.15	.06
❑	162	Chuck Crim	.10	.04
❑	163	Rob Deer	.10	.04
❑	164	Mike Felder	.10	.04
❑	165	Jim Gantner	.10	.04
❑	166	Ted Higuera	.10	.04
❑	167	Steve Kiefer	.10	.04
❑	168	Rick Manning	.10	.04
❑	169	Paul Molitor	.20	.08
❑	170	Juan Nieves	.10	.04
❑	171	Dan Plesac	.10	.04
❑	172	Earnest Riles	.10	.04
❑	173	Bill Schroeder	.10	.04
❑	174	Steve Stanicek	.10	.04
❑	175	B.J. Surhoff	.15	.06
❑	176	Dale Sveum	.10	.04
❑	177	Bill Wegman	.10	.04
❑	178	Robin Yount	.50	.20
❑	179	Hubie Brooks	.10	.04
❑	180	Tim Burke	.10	.04
❑	181	Casey Candaele	.10	.04
❑	182	Mike Fitzgerald	.10	.04
❑	183	Tom Foley	.10	.04
❑	184	Andres Galarraga	.15	.06
❑	185	Neal Heaton	.10	.04
❑	186	Wallace Johnson	.10	.04
❑	187	Vance Law	.10	.04
❑	188	Dennis Martinez	.15	.06
❑	189	Bob McClure	.10	.04
❑	190	Andy McGaffigan	.10	.04
❑	191	Reid Nichols	.10	.04
❑	192	Pascual Perez	.10	.04
❑	193	Tim Raines	.15	.06
❑	194	Jeff Reed	.10	.04
❑	195	Bob Sebra	.10	.04
❑	196	Bryn Smith	.10	.04
❑	197	Randy St.Claire	.10	.04
❑	198	Tim Wallach	.10	.04
❑	199	Mitch Webster	.10	.04
❑	200	Herm Winningham	.10	.04
❑	201	Floyd Youmans	.10	.04
❑	202	Brad Arnsberg	.10	.04
❑	203	Rick Cerone	.10	.04
❑	204	Pat Clements	.10	.04
❑	205	Henry Cotto	.10	.04
❑	206	Mike Easler	.10	.04
❑	207	Ron Guidry	.15	.06
❑	208	Bill Gullickson	.10	.04
❑	209	Rickey Henderson	.30	.12
❑	210	Charles Hudson	.10	.04
❑	211	Tommy John	.15	.06
❑	212	Roberto Kelly RC	.40	.16
❑	213	Ron Kittle	.10	.04
❑	214	Don Mattingly	1.00	.40
❑	215	Bobby Meacham	.10	.04
❑	216	Mike Pagliarulo	.10	.04
❑	217	Dan Pasqua	.10	.04
❑	218	Willie Randolph	.15	.06
❑	219	Rick Rhoden	.10	.04
❑	220	Dave Righetti	.15	.06
❑	221	Jerry Royster	.10	.04
❑	222	Tim Stoddard	.10	.04
❑	223	Wayne Tolleson	.10	.04
❑	224	Gary Ward	.10	.04
❑	225	Claudell Washington	.10	.04
❑	226	Dave Winfield	.15	.06
❑	227	Buddy Bell	.15	.06
❑	228	Tom Browning	.10	.04
❑	229	Dave Concepcion	.15	.06
❑	230	Kal Daniels	.10	.04
❑	231	Eric Davis	.15	.06
❑	232	Bo Diaz	.10	.04
❑	233	Nick Esasky (Has a dollar sign before '87 SB totals)	.10	.04
❑	234	John Franco	.15	.06
❑	235	Guy Hoffman	.10	.04
❑	236	Tom Hume	.10	.04
❑	237	Tracy Jones	.10	.04
❑	238	Bill Landrum	.10	.04
❑	239	Barry Larkin	.20	.08
❑	240	Terry McGriff	.10	.04
❑	241	Rob Murphy	.10	.04
❑	242	Ron Oester	.10	.04
❑	243	Dave Parker	.15	.06
❑	244	Pat Perry	.10	.04
❑	245	Ted Power	.10	.04
❑	246	Dennis Rasmussen	.10	.04
❑	247	Ron Robinson	.10	.04
❑	248	Kurt Stillwell	.10	.04
❑	249	Jeff Treadway RC	.40	.16
❑	250	Frank Williams	.10	.04
❑	251	Steve Balboni	.10	.04
❑	252	Bud Black	.10	.04
❑	253	Thad Bosley	.10	.04
❑	254	George Brett	.75	.30
❑	255	John Davis	.10	.04
❑	256	Steve Farr	.10	.04
❑	257	Gene Garber	.10	.04
❑	258	Jerry Don Gleaton	.10	.04
❑	259	Mark Gubicza	.10	.04
❑	260	Bo Jackson	.30	.12
❑	261	Danny Jackson	.10	.04
❑	262	Ross Jones	.10	.04
❑	263	Charlie Leibrandt	.10	.04
❑	264	Bill Pecota RC*	.15	.06
❑	265	Melido Perez RC	.40	.16
❑	266	Jamie Quirk	.10	.04
❑	267	Dan Quisenberry	.10	.04
❑	268	Bret Saberhagen	.15	.06
❑	269	Angel Salazar	.10	.04
❑	270	Kevin Seitzer UER (Wrong birth year)	.15	.06
❑	271	Danny Tartabull	.10	.04
❑	272	Gary Thurman	.10	.04
❑	273	Frank White	.15	.06
❑	274	Willie Wilson	.15	.06
❑	275	Tony Bernazard	.10	.04
❑	276	Jose Canseco	.30	.12
❑	277	Mike Davis	.10	.04
❑	278	Storm Davis	.10	.04
❑	279	Dennis Eckersley	.20	.08
❑	280	Alfredo Griffin	.10	.04
❑	281	Rick Honeycutt	.10	.04
❑	282	Jay Howell	.10	.04
❑	283	Reggie Jackson	.20	.08
❑	284	Dennis Lamp	.10	.04
❑	285	Carney Lansford	.15	.06
❑	286	Mark McGwire	2.50	1.00
❑	287	Dwayne Murphy	.10	.04
❑	288	Gene Nelson	.10	.04
❑	289	Steve Ontiveros	.10	.04
❑	290	Tony Phillips	.10	.04
❑	291	Eric Plunk	.10	.04
❑	292	Luis Polonia RC*	.40	.16
❑	293	Rick Rodriguez	.10	.04
❑	294	Terry Steinbach	.15	.06
❑	295	Dave Stewart	.15	.06
❑	296	Curt Young	.10	.04
❑	297	Luis Aguayo	.10	.04
❑	298	Steve Bedrosian	.10	.04
❑	299	Jeff Calhoun	.10	.04
❑	300	Don Carman	.10	.04
❑	301	Todd Frohwirth	.10	.04
❑	302	Greg Gross	.10	.04
❑	303	Kevin Gross	.10	.04
❑	304	Von Hayes	.10	.04
❑	305	Keith Hughes	.10	.04
❑	306	Mike Jackson RC*	.40	.16
❑	307	Chris James	.10	.04
❑	308	Steve Jeltz	.10	.04
❑	309	Mike Maddux	.10	.04
❑	310	Lance Parrish	.15	.06
❑	311	Shane Rawley	.10	.04
❑	312	Wally Ritchie	.10	.04
❑	313	Bruce Ruffin	.10	.04
❑	314	Juan Samuel	.10	.04
❑	315	Mike Schmidt	.75	.30
❑	316	Rick Schu	.10	.04
❑	317	Jeff Stone	.10	.04
❑	318	Kent Tekulve	.10	.04
❑	319	Milt Thompson	.10	.04
❑	320	Glenn Wilson	.10	.04
❑	321	Rafael Belliard	.10	.04
❑	322	Barry Bonds	3.00	1.20
❑	323	Bobby Bonilla UER (Wrong birth year)	.15	.06
❑	324	Sid Bream	.10	.04
❑	325	John Cangelosi	.10	.04
❑	326	Mike Diaz	.10	.04
❑	327	Doug Drabek	.10	.04
❑	328	Mike Dunne	.10	.04
❑	329	Brian Fisher	.10	.04
❑	330	Brett Gideon	.10	.04
❑	331	Terry Harper	.10	.04
❑	332	Bob Kipper	.10	.04
❑	333	Mike LaValliere	.10	.04
❑	334	Jose Lind RC	.40	.16
❑	335	Junior Ortiz	.10	.04
❑	336	Vicente Palacios	.10	.04
❑	337	Bob Patterson	.10	.04
❑	338	Al Pedrique	.10	.04
❑	339	R.J. Reynolds	.10	.04
❑	340	John Smiley RC*	.40	.16
❑	341	Andy Van Slyke UER (Wrong batting and throwing listed)	.15	.06
❑	342	Bob Walk	.10	.04
❑	343	Marty Barrett	.10	.04
❑	344	Todd Benzinger RC*	.40	.16
❑	345	Wade Boggs	.20	.08
❑	346	Tom Bolton	.10	.04
❑	347	Oil Can Boyd	.10	.04
❑	348	Ellis Burks RC	.50	.20
❑	349	Roger Clemens	.75	.30
❑	350	Steve Crawford	.10	.04
❑	351	Dwight Evans	.15	.06
❑	352	Wes Gardner	.10	.04
❑	353	Rich Gedman	.10	.04
❑	354	Mike Greenwell	.10	.04
❑	355	Sam Horn RC	.15	.06
❑	356	Bruce Hurst	.10	.04
❑	357	John Marzano	.10	.04
❑	358	Al Nipper	.10	.04
❑	359	Spike Owen	.10	.04
❑	360	Jody Reed RC	.40	.16
❑	361	Jim Rice	.15	.06
❑	362	Ed Romero	.10	.04
❑	363	Kevin Romine	.10	.04
❑	364	Joe Sambito	.10	.04
❑	365	Calvin Schiraldi	.10	.04
❑	366	Jeff Sellers	.10	.04
❑	367	Bob Stanley	.10	.04
❑	368	Scott Bankhead	.10	.04
❑	369	Phil Bradley	.10	.04
❑	370	Scott Bradley	.10	.04
❑	371	Mickey Brantley	.10	.04
❑	372	Mike Campbell	.10	.04
❑	373	Alvin Davis	.10	.04
❑	374	Lee Guetterman	.10	.04
❑	375	Dave Hengel	.10	.04
❑	376	Mike Kingery	.10	.04
❑	377	Mark Langston	.10	.04
❑	378	Edgar Martinez RC	4.00	1.60
❑	379	Mike Moore	.10	.04
❑	380	Mike Morgan	.10	.04
❑	381	John Moses	.10	.04
❑	382	Donell Nixon	.10	.04
❑	383	Edwin Nunez	.10	.04
❑	384	Ken Phelps	.10	.04
❑	385	Jim Presley	.10	.04
❑	386	Rey Quinones	.10	.04
❑	387	Jerry Reed	.10	.04
❑	388	Harold Reynolds	.15	.06
❑	389	Dave Valle	.10	.04
❑	390	Bill Wilkinson	.10	.04
❑	391	Harold Baines	.15	.06
❑	392	Floyd Bannister	.10	.04
❑	393	Daryl Boston	.10	.04
❑	394	Ivan Calderon	.10	.04
❑	395	Jose DeLeon	.10	.04
❑	396	Richard Dotson	.10	.04
❑	397	Carlton Fisk	.20	.08
❑	398	Ozzie Guillen	.10	.04
❑	399	Ron Hassey	.10	.04
❑	400	Donnie Hill	.10	.04
❑	401	Bob James	.10	.04

❑ 402	Dave LaPoint	.10	.04
❑ 403	Bill Lindsey	.10	.04
❑ 404	Bill Long	.10	.04
❑ 405	Steve Lyons	.10	.04
❑ 406	Fred Manrique	.10	.04
❑ 407	Jack McDowell RC	.50	.20
❑ 408	Gary Redus	.10	.04
❑ 409	Ray Searage	.10	.04
❑ 410	Bobby Thigpen	.10	.04
❑ 411	Greg Walker	.10	.04
❑ 412	Ken Williams RC	.10	.04
❑ 413	Jim Winn	.10	.04
❑ 414	Jody Davis	.10	.04
❑ 415	Andre Dawson	.15	.06
❑ 416	Brian Dayett	.10	.04
❑ 417	Bob Dernier	.10	.04
❑ 418	Frank DiPino	.10	.04
❑ 419	Shawon Dunston	.10	.04
❑ 420	Leon Durham	.10	.04
❑ 421	Les Lancaster	.10	.04
❑ 422	Ed Lynch	.10	.04
❑ 423	Greg Maddux	1.50	.60
❑ 424	Dave Martinez	.10	.04
❑ 425A	Keith Moreland ERR (Photo actually Jody Davis)	1.50	.60
❑ 425B	Keith Moreland COR (Bat on shoulder)	.15	.06
❑ 426	Jamie Moyer	.15	.06
❑ 427	Jerry Mumphrey	.10	.04
❑ 428	Paul Noce	.10	.04
❑ 429	Rafael Palmeiro	.60	.24
❑ 430	Wade Rowdon	.10	.04
❑ 431	Ryne Sandberg	.60	.24
❑ 432	Scott Sanderson	.10	.04
❑ 433	Lee Smith	.15	.06
❑ 434	Jim Sundberg	.15	.06
❑ 435	Rick Sutcliffe	.15	.06
❑ 436	Manny Trillo	.10	.04
❑ 437	Juan Agosto	.10	.04
❑ 438	Larry Andersen	.10	.04
❑ 439	Alan Ashby	.10	.04
❑ 440	Kevin Bass	.10	.04
❑ 441	Ken Caminiti RC	1.00	.40
❑ 442	Rocky Childress	.10	.04
❑ 443	Jose Cruz	.15	.06
❑ 444	Danny Darwin	.10	.04
❑ 445	Glenn Davis	.10	.04
❑ 446	Jim Deshaies	.10	.04
❑ 447	Bill Doran	.10	.04
❑ 448	Ty Gainey	.10	.04
❑ 449	Billy Hatcher	.10	.04
❑ 450	Jeff Heathcock	.10	.04
❑ 451	Bob Knepper	.10	.04
❑ 452	Rob Mallicoat	.10	.04
❑ 453	Dave Meads	.10	.04
❑ 454	Craig Reynolds	.10	.04
❑ 455	Nolan Ryan	1.50	.60
❑ 456	Mike Scott	.15	.06
❑ 457	Dave Smith	.10	.04
❑ 458	Denny Walling	.10	.04
❑ 459	Robbie Wine	.10	.04
❑ 460	Gerald Young	.10	.04
❑ 461	Bob Brower	.10	.04
❑ 462A	Jerry Browne ERR (Photo actually Bob Brower, white player)	1.50	.60
❑ 462B	Jerry Browne COR (Black player)	.15	.06
❑ 463	Steve Buechele	.10	.04
❑ 464	Edwin Correa	.10	.04
❑ 465	Cecil Espy	.10	.04
❑ 466	Scott Fletcher	.10	.04
❑ 467	Jose Guzman	.10	.04
❑ 468	Greg Harris	.10	.04
❑ 469	Charlie Hough	.15	.06
❑ 470	Pete Incaviglia	.10	.04
❑ 471	Paul Kilgus	.10	.04
❑ 472	Mike Loynd	.10	.04
❑ 473	Oddibe McDowell	.10	.04
❑ 474	Dale Mohorcic	.10	.04
❑ 475	Pete O'Brien	.10	.04
❑ 476	Larry Parrish	.10	.04
❑ 477	Geno Petralli	.10	.04
❑ 478	Jeff Russell	.10	.04
❑ 479	Ruben Sierra	.15	.06
❑ 480	Mike Stanley	.10	.04
❑ 481	Curtis Wilkerson	.10	.04
❑ 482	Mitch Williams	.10	.04
❑ 483	Bobby Witt	.10	.04
❑ 484	Tony Armas	.15	.06
❑ 485	Bob Boone	.15	.06
❑ 486	Bill Buckner	.15	.06
❑ 487	DeWayne Buice	.10	.04
❑ 488	Brian Downing	.15	.06
❑ 489	Chuck Finley	.15	.06
❑ 490	Willie Fraser UER (Wrong bio stats, for George Hendrick)	.10	.04
❑ 491	Jack Howell	.10	.04
❑ 492	Ruppert Jones	.10	.04
❑ 493	Wally Joyner	.15	.06
❑ 494	Jack Lazorko	.10	.04
❑ 495	Gary Lucas	.10	.04
❑ 496	Kirk McCaskill	.10	.04
❑ 497	Mark McLemore	.10	.04
❑ 498	Darrell Miller	.10	.04
❑ 499	Greg Minton	.10	.04
❑ 500	Donnie Moore	.10	.04
❑ 501	Gus Polidor	.10	.04
❑ 502	Johnny Ray	.10	.04
❑ 503	Mark Ryal	.10	.04
❑ 504	Dick Schofield	.10	.04
❑ 505	Don Sutton	.15	.06
❑ 506	Devon White	.15	.06
❑ 507	Mike Witt	.10	.04
❑ 508	Dave Anderson	.10	.04
❑ 509	Tim Belcher	.10	.04
❑ 510	Ralph Bryant	.10	.04
❑ 511	Tim Crews RC	.40	.16
❑ 512	Mike Devereaux RC	.40	.16
❑ 513	Mariano Duncan	.10	.04
❑ 514	Pedro Guerrero	.15	.06
❑ 515	Jeff Hamilton	.10	.04
❑ 516	Mickey Hatcher	.10	.04
❑ 517	Brad Havens	.10	.04
❑ 518	Orel Hershiser	.15	.06
❑ 519	Shawn Hillegas	.10	.04
❑ 520	Ken Howell	.10	.04
❑ 521	Tim Leary	.10	.04
❑ 522	Mike Marshall	.10	.04
❑ 523	Steve Sax	.10	.04
❑ 524	Mike Scioscia	.15	.06
❑ 525	Mike Sharperson	.10	.04
❑ 526	John Shelby	.10	.04
❑ 527	Franklin Stubbs	.10	.04
❑ 528	Fernando Valenzuela	.15	.06
❑ 529	Bob Welch	.15	.06
❑ 530	Matt Young	.10	.04
❑ 531	Jim Acker	.10	.04
❑ 532	Paul Assenmacher	.10	.04
❑ 533	Jeff Blauser RC	.40	.16
❑ 534	Joe Boever	.10	.04
❑ 535	Martin Clary	.10	.04
❑ 536	Kevin Coffman	.10	.04
❑ 537	Jeff Dedmon	.10	.04
❑ 538	Ron Gant RC	.50	.20
❑ 539	Tom Glavine RC	3.00	1.20
❑ 540	Ken Griffey	.15	.06
❑ 541	Albert Hall	.10	.04
❑ 542	Glenn Hubbard	.10	.04
❑ 543	Dion James	.10	.04
❑ 544	Dale Murphy	.20	.08
❑ 545	Ken Oberkfell	.10	.04
❑ 546	David Palmer	.10	.04
❑ 547	Gerald Perry	.10	.04
❑ 548	Charlie Puleo	.10	.04
❑ 549	Ted Simmons	.15	.06
❑ 550	Zane Smith	.10	.04
❑ 551	Andres Thomas	.10	.04
❑ 552	Ozzie Virgil	.10	.04
❑ 553	Don Aase	.10	.04
❑ 554	Jeff Ballard	.10	.04
❑ 555	Eric Bell	.10	.04
❑ 556	Mike Boddicker	.10	.04
❑ 557	Ken Dixon	.10	.04
❑ 558	Jim Dwyer	.10	.04
❑ 559	Ken Gerhart	.10	.04
❑ 560	Rene Gonzales RC	.15	.06
❑ 561	Mike Griffin	.10	.04
❑ 562	John Habyan UER (Misspelled Hayban on both sides of card)	.10	.04
❑ 563	Terry Kennedy	.10	.04
❑ 564	Ray Knight	.15	.06
❑ 565	Lee Lacy	.10	.04
❑ 566	Fred Lynn	.15	.06
❑ 567	Eddie Murray	.30	.12
❑ 568	Tom Niedenfuer	.10	.04
❑ 569	Bill Ripken RC*	.40	.16
❑ 570	Cal Ripken	1.25	.50
❑ 571	Dave Schmidt	.10	.04
❑ 572	Larry Sheets	.10	.04
❑ 573	Pete Stanicek	.10	.04
❑ 574	Mark Williamson	.10	.04
❑ 575	Mike Young	.10	.04
❑ 576	Shawn Abner	.10	.04
❑ 577	Greg Booker	.10	.04
❑ 578	Chris Brown	.10	.04
❑ 579	Keith Comstock	.10	.04
❑ 580	Joey Cora RC	.40	.16
❑ 581	Mark Davis	.10	.04
❑ 582	Tim Flannery (With surfboard)	.20	.08
❑ 583	Goose Gossage	.15	.06
❑ 584	Mark Grant	.10	.04
❑ 585	Tony Gwynn	.50	.20
❑ 586	Andy Hawkins	.10	.04
❑ 587	Stan Jefferson	.10	.04
❑ 588	Jimmy Jones	.10	.04
❑ 589	John Kruk	.15	.06
❑ 590	Shane Mack	.10	.04
❑ 591	Carmelo Martinez	.10	.04
❑ 592	Lance McCullers UER (6'11" tall)	.10	.04
❑ 593	Eric Nolte	.10	.04
❑ 594	Randy Ready	.10	.04
❑ 595	Luis Salazar	.10	.04
❑ 596	Benito Santiago	.15	.06
❑ 597	Eric Show	.10	.04
❑ 598	Garry Templeton	.15	.06
❑ 599	Ed Whitson	.10	.04
❑ 600	Scott Bailes	.10	.04
❑ 601	Chris Bando	.10	.04
❑ 602	Jay Bell RC	.50	.20
❑ 603	Brett Butler	.15	.06
❑ 604	Tom Candiotti	.10	.04
❑ 605	Joe Carter	.15	.06
❑ 606	Carmen Castillo	.10	.04
❑ 607	Brian Dorsett	.10	.04
❑ 608	John Farrell RC	.15	.06
❑ 609	Julio Franco	.15	.06
❑ 610	Mel Hall	.10	.04
❑ 611	Tommy Hinzo	.10	.04
❑ 612	Brook Jacoby	.10	.04
❑ 613	Doug Jones RC	.40	.16
❑ 614	Ken Schrom	.10	.04
❑ 615	Cory Snyder	.10	.04
❑ 616	Sammy Stewart	.10	.04
❑ 617	Greg Swindell	.10	.04
❑ 618	Pat Tabler	.10	.04
❑ 619	Ed VandeBerg	.10	.04
❑ 620	Eddie Williams RC	.15	.06
❑ 621	Rich Yett	.10	.04
❑ 622	Wally Joyner / Cory Snyder	.15	.06
❑ 623	George Bell / Pedro Guerrero	.10	.04
❑ 624	Mark McGwire / Jose Canseco	1.00	.40
❑ 625	Dave Righetti / Dan Plesac	.10	.04
❑ 626	Bret Saberhagen / Mike Witt / Jack Morris	.15	.06
❑ 627	John Franco / Steve Bedrosian	.10	.04
❑ 628	Ozzie Smith / Ryne Sandberg	.30	.12
❑ 629	Mark McGwire HL	1.25	.50
❑ 630	Mike Greenwell / Ellis Burks / Todd Benzinger	.30	.12
❑ 631	Tony Gwynn / Tim Raines	.20	.08
❑ 632	Mike Scott / Orel Hershiser	.15	.06

❑ 633 Pat Tabler .... 1.25 .50
Mark McGwire
❑ 634 Tony Gwynn .... .20 .08
Vince Coleman
❑ 635 Tony Fernandez .... .50 .20
Cal Ripken
Alan Trammell
❑ 636 Mike Schmidt .... .30 .12
Gary Carter
❑ 637 Darryl Strawberry .... .15 .06
Eric Davis
❑ 638 Matt Nokes .... .20 .08
Kirby Puckett
❑ 639 Keith Hernandez .... .15 .06
Dale Murphy
❑ 640 Billy Ripken .... .75 .30
Cal Ripken
❑ 641 Mark Grace RC and 3.00 1.20
Darrin Jackson
❑ 642 Damon Berryhill RC .... .40 .16
Jeff Montgomery RC
❑ 643 Felix Fermin .... .15 .06
Jesse Reid RC
❑ 644 Greg Myers .... .40 .16
Greg Tabor RC
❑ 645 Joey Meyer .... .15 .06
Jim Eppard RC
❑ 646 Adam Peterson .... .40 .16
Randy Velarde RC
❑ 647 Pete Smith .... .40 .16
Chris Gwynn RC
❑ 648 Tom Newell and .... .15 .06
Greg Jelks RC
❑ 649 Mario Diaz .... .15 .06
Clay Parker RC
❑ 650 Jack Savage and .... .15 .06
Todd Simmons RC
❑ 651 John Burkett .... .40 .16
Kirt Manwaring RC
❑ 652 Dave Otto .... .50 .20
Walt Weiss RC
❑ 653 Jeff King .... .40 .16
Randell Byers RC
❑ 654 CL: Twins/Cards .... .10 .04
Tigers/Giants UER
(90 Bob Melvin,
91 Eddie Milner)
❑ 655 CL: Blue Jays/Mets .... .10 .04
Brewers/Expos UER
(Mets listed before
Blue Jays on card)
❑ 656 CL: Yankees/Reds .... .10 .04
Royals/A's
❑ 657 CL: Phillies/Pirates .... .10 .04
Red Sox/Mariners
❑ 658 CL: White Sox/Cubs .... .10 .04
Astros/Rangers
❑ 659 CL: Angels/Dodgers .... .10 .04
Braves/Orioles
❑ 660 CL: Padres/Indians .... .10 .04
Rookies/Specials

1988 Fleer Update

	Nm-Mt	Ex-Mt
COMP.FACT.SET (132)	8.00	3.20

❑ 1 Jose Bautista XRC .... .25 .10
❑ 2 Joe Orsulak .... .10 .04
❑ 3 Doug Sisk .... .10 .04
❑ 4 Craig Worthington .... .10 .04
❑ 5 Mike Boddicker .... .10 .04
❑ 6 Rick Cerone .... .10 .04
❑ 7 Larry Parrish .... .10 .04
❑ 8 Lee Smith .... .20 .08
❑ 9 Mike Smithson .... .10 .04
❑ 10 John Trautwein .... .10 .04
❑ 11 Sherman Corbett .... .10 .04
❑ 12 Chili Davis .... .20 .08
❑ 13 Jim Eppard .... .10 .04
❑ 14 Bryan Harvey XRC .... .50 .20
❑ 15 John Davis .... .10 .04
❑ 16 Dave Gallagher .... .10 .04
❑ 17 Ricky Horton .... .10 .04
❑ 18 Dan Pasqua .... .10 .04
❑ 19 Melido Perez .... .10 .04
❑ 20 Jose Segura .... .10 .04
❑ 21 Andy Allanson .... .10 .04
❑ 22 Jon Perlman .... .10 .04
❑ 23 Domingo Ramos .... .10 .04
❑ 24 Rick Rodriguez .... .10 .04
❑ 25 Willie Upshaw .... .10 .04
❑ 26 Paul Gibson .... .10 .04
❑ 27 Don Heinkel .... .10 .04
❑ 28 Ray Knight .... .20 .08
❑ 29 Gary Pettis .... .10 .04
❑ 30 Luis Salazar .... .10 .04
❑ 31 Mike Macfarlane XRC .... .50 .20
❑ 32 Jeff Montgomery .... .50 .20
❑ 33 Ted Power .... .10 .04
❑ 34 Israel Sanchez .... .10 .04
❑ 35 Kurt Stillwell .... .10 .04
❑ 36 Pat Tabler .... .10 .04
❑ 37 Don August .... .10 .04
❑ 38 Darryl Hamilton XRC .... .50 .20
❑ 39 Jeff Leonard .... .10 .04
❑ 40 Joey Meyer .... .10 .04
❑ 41 Allan Anderson .... .10 .04
❑ 42 Brian Harper .... .10 .04
❑ 43 Tom Herr .... .10 .04
❑ 44 Charlie Lea .... .10 .04
❑ 45 John Moses .... .10 .04
(Listed as Hohn on
checklist card)
❑ 46 John Candelaria .... .10 .04
❑ 47 Jack Clark .... .20 .08
❑ 48 Richard Dotson .... .10 .04
❑ 49 Al Leiter XRC* .... 1.00 .40
❑ 50 Rafael Santana .... .10 .04
❑ 51 Don Slaught .... .10 .04
❑ 52 Todd Burns .... .10 .04
❑ 53 Dave Henderson .... .10 .04
❑ 54 Doug Jennings .... .10 .04
❑ 55 Dave Parker .... .20 .08
❑ 56 Walt Weiss .... .75 .30
❑ 57 Bob Welch .... .20 .08
❑ 58 Henry Cotto .... .10 .04
❑ 59 Mario Diaz UER .... .10 .04
(Listed as Marion
on card front)
❑ 60 Mike Jackson .... .20 .08
❑ 61 Bill Swift .... .10 .04
❑ 62 Jose Cecena .... .10 .04
❑ 63 Ray Hayward .... .10 .04
❑ 64 Jim Steels UER .... .10 .04
(Listed as Jim Steele
on card back)
❑ 65 Pat Borders XRC .... .50 .20
❑ 66 Sil Campusano .... .10 .04
❑ 67 Mike Flanagan .... .10 .04
❑ 68 Todd Stottlemyre XRC .... .50 .20
❑ 69 David Wells XRC .... 1.25 .50
❑ 70 Jose Alvarez XRC .... .25 .10
❑ 71 Paul Runge .... .10 .04
❑ 72 Cesar Jimenez .... .10 .04
(Card was intended
for German Jiminez,
it's his photo)
❑ 73 Pete Smith .... .10 .04
❑ 74 John Smoltz XRC 3.00 1.20
❑ 75 Damon Berryhill .... .25 .10
❑ 76 Goose Gossage .... .20 .08
❑ 77 Mark Grace .... 1.50 .60
❑ 78 Darrin Jackson .... .25 .10
❑ 79 Vance Law .... .10 .04
❑ 80 Jeff Pico .... .10 .04
❑ 81 Gary Varsho .... .10 .04
❑ 82 Tim Birtsas .... .10 .04
❑ 83 Rob Dibble XRC .... 1.00 .40
❑ 84 Danny Jackson .... .10 .04
❑ 85 Paul O'Neill .... .30 .12
❑ 86 Jose Rijo .... .20 .08
❑ 87 Chris Sabo XRC .... .75 .30
❑ 88 John Fishel .... .10 .04
❑ 89 Craig Biggio XRC .... 2.00 .80
❑ 90 Terry Puhl .... .10 .04
❑ 91 Rafael Ramirez .... .10 .04
❑ 92 Louie Meadows .... .10 .04
❑ 93 Kirk Gibson .... .50 .20
❑ 94 Alfredo Griffin .... .10 .04
❑ 95 Jay Howell .... .10 .04
❑ 96 Jesse Orosco .... .10 .04
❑ 97 Alejandro Pena .... .10 .04
❑ 98 Tracy Woodson XRC* .... .25 .10
❑ 99 John Dopson .... .10 .04
❑ 100 Brian Holman XRC .... .25 .10
❑ 101 Rex Hudler .... .10 .04
❑ 102 Jeff Parrett .... .10 .04
❑ 103 Nelson Santovenia .... .10 .04
❑ 104 Kevin Elster .... .10 .04
❑ 105 Jeff Innis .... .10 .04
❑ 106 Mackey Sasser XRC* .... .50 .20
❑ 107 Phil Bradley .... .10 .04
❑ 108 Danny Clay .... .10 .04
❑ 109 Greg A.Harris .... .10 .04
❑ 110 Ricky Jordan XRC .... .50 .20
❑ 111 David Palmer .... .10 .04
❑ 112 Jim Gott .... .10 .04
❑ 113 Tommy Gregg UER .... .10 .04
(Photo actually
Randy Milligan)
❑ 114 Barry Jones .... .10 .04
❑ 115 Randy Milligan XRC* .... .25 .10
❑ 116 Luis Alicea XRC .... .50 .20
❑ 117 Tom Brunansky .... .10 .04
❑ 118 John Costello .... .10 .04
❑ 119 Jose DeLeon .... .10 .04
❑ 120 Bob Horner .... .20 .08
❑ 121 Scott Terry .... .10 .04
❑ 122 Roberto Alomar XRC 3.00 1.20
❑ 123 Dave Leiper .... .10 .04
❑ 124 Keith Moreland .... .10 .04
❑ 125 Mark Parent .... .10 .04
❑ 126 Dennis Rasmussen .... .10 .04
❑ 127 Randy Bockus .... .10 .04
❑ 128 Brett Butler .... .20 .08
❑ 129 Donell Nixon .... .10 .04
❑ 130 Earnest Riles .... .10 .04
❑ 131 Roger Samuels .... .10 .04
❑ 132 Checklist U1-U132 .... .10 .04

1989 Fleer

	Nm-Mt	Ex-Mt
COMPLETE SET (660)	15.00	6.00
COMP.FACT.SET (672)	15.00	6.00

❑ 1 Don Baylor .... .10 .04
❑ 2 Lance Blankenship RC .... .10 .04
❑ 3 Todd Burns UER .... .05 .02
(Wrong birthdate;
before/after All-Star

stats missing)
❑ 4 Greg Cadaret UER .05 .02
(All-Star Break stats
show 3 losses, should be 2
❑ 5 Jose Canseco .25 .10
❑ 6 Storm Davis .05 .02
❑ 7 Dennis Eckersley .15 .06
❑ 8 Mike Gallego .05 .02
❑ 9 Ron Hassey .05 .02
❑ 10 Dave Henderson .05 .02
❑ 11 Rick Honeycutt .05 .02
❑ 12 Glenn Hubbard .05 .02
❑ 13 Stan Javier .05 .02
❑ 14 Doug Jennings .05 .02
❑ 15 Felix Jose RC .10 .04
❑ 16 Carney Lansford .10 .04
❑ 17 Mark McGwire 1.00 .40
❑ 18 Gene Nelson .05 .02
❑ 19 Dave Parker .10 .04
❑ 20 Eric Plunk .05 .02
❑ 21 Luis Polonia .05 .02
❑ 22 Terry Steinbach .10 .04
❑ 23 Dave Stewart .10 .04
❑ 24 Walt Weiss .05 .02
❑ 25 Bob Welch .10 .04
❑ 26 Curt Young .05 .02
❑ 27 Rick Aguilera .05 .02
❑ 28 Wally Backman .05 .02
❑ 29 Mark Carreon UER .05 .02
(After All-Star Break
batting 7.14)
❑ 30 Gary Carter .10 .04
❑ 31 David Cone .10 .04
❑ 32 Ron Darling .10 .04
❑ 33 Len Dykstra .10 .04
❑ 34 Kevin Elster .05 .02
❑ 35 Sid Fernandez .05 .02
❑ 36 Dwight Gooden .10 .04
❑ 37 Keith Hernandez .10 .04
❑ 38 Gregg Jefferies .05 .02
❑ 39 Howard Johnson .10 .04
❑ 40 Terry Leach .05 .02
❑ 41 Dave Magadan UER .05 .02
(Bio says 15 doubles,
should be 13)
❑ 42 Bob McClure .05 .02
❑ 43 Roger McDowell UER .05 .02
(Led Mets with 58,
should be 62)
❑ 44 Kevin McReynolds .05 .02
❑ 45 Keith A. Miller .05 .02
❑ 46 Randy Myers .10 .04
❑ 47 Bob Ojeda .05 .02
❑ 48 Mackey Sasser .05 .02
❑ 49 Darryl Strawberry .10 .04
❑ 50 Tim Teufel .05 .02
❑ 51 Dave West RC .10 .04
❑ 52 Mookie Wilson .10 .04
❑ 53 Dave Anderson .05 .02
❑ 54 Tim Belcher .05 .02
❑ 55 Mike Davis .05 .02
❑ 56 Mike Devereaux .05 .02
❑ 57 Kirk Gibson .10 .04
❑ 58 Alfredo Griffin .05 .02
❑ 59 Chris Gwynn .05 .02
❑ 60 Jeff Hamilton .05 .02
❑ 61A Danny Heep ERR .25 .10
Lake Hills
❑ 61B Danny Heep COR .05 .02
San Antonio
❑ 62 Orel Hershiser .10 .04
❑ 63 Brian Holton .05 .02
❑ 64 Jay Howell .05 .02
❑ 65 Tim Leary .05 .02
❑ 66 Mike Marshall .05 .02
❑ 67 Ramon Martinez RC .25 .10
❑ 68 Jesse Orosco .05 .02
❑ 69 Alejandro Pena .05 .02
❑ 70 Steve Sax .05 .02
❑ 71 Mike Scioscia .10 .04
❑ 72 Mike Sharperson .05 .02
❑ 73 John Shelby .05 .02
❑ 74 Franklin Stubbs .05 .02
❑ 75 John Tudor .10 .04
❑ 76 Fernando Valenzuela .10 .04
❑ 77 Tracy Woodson .05 .02
❑ 78 Marty Barrett .05 .02
❑ 79 Todd Benzinger .05 .02
❑ 80 Mike Boddicker UER .05 .02
(Rochester in '76,
should be '78)
❑ 81 Wade Boggs .15 .06
❑ 82 Oil Can Boyd .05 .02
❑ 83 Ellis Burks .10 .04
❑ 84 Rick Cerone .05 .02
❑ 85 Roger Clemens .50 .20
❑ 86 Steve Curry .05 .02
❑ 87 Dwight Evans .10 .04
❑ 88 Wes Gardner .05 .02
❑ 89 Rich Gedman .05 .02
❑ 90 Mike Greenwell .05 .02
❑ 91 Bruce Hurst .05 .02
❑ 92 Dennis Lamp .05 .02
❑ 93 Spike Owen .05 .02
❑ 94 Larry Parrish UER .05 .02
(Before All-Star Break
batting 1.90)
❑ 95 Carlos Quintana RC .10 .04
❑ 96 Jody Reed .05 .02
❑ 97 Jim Rice .10 .04
❑ 98A Kevin Romine ERR .25 .10
(Photo actually
Randy Kutcher batting)
❑ 98B Kevin Romine COR .05 .02
(Arms folded)
❑ 99 Lee Smith .10 .04
❑ 100 Mike Smithson .05 .02
❑ 101 Bob Stanley .05 .02
❑ 102 Allan Anderson .05 .02
❑ 103 Keith Atherton .05 .02
❑ 104 Juan Berenguer .05 .02
❑ 105 Bert Blyleven .10 .04
❑ 106 Eric Bullock UER .05 .02
Bats/Throws Right,
should be Left
❑ 107 Randy Bush .05 .02
❑ 108 John Christensen .05 .02
❑ 109 Mark Davidson .05 .02
❑ 110 Gary Gaetti .10 .04
❑ 111 Greg Gagne .05 .02
❑ 112 Dan Gladden .05 .02
❑ 113 German Gonzalez .05 .02
❑ 114 Brian Harper .05 .02
❑ 115 Tom Herr .05 .02
❑ 116 Kent Hrbek .10 .04
❑ 117 Gene Larkin .05 .02
❑ 118 Tim Laudner .05 .02
❑ 119 Charlie Lea .05 .02
❑ 120 Steve Lombardozzi .05 .02
❑ 121A John Moses ERR .25 .10
Tempe
❑ 121B John Moses COR .05 .02
Phoenix
❑ 122 Al Newman .05 .02
❑ 123 Mark Portugal .05 .02
❑ 124 Kirby Puckett .25 .10
❑ 125 Jeff Reardon .10 .04
❑ 126 Fred Toliver .05 .02
❑ 127 Frank Viola .10 .04
❑ 128 Doyle Alexander .05 .02
❑ 129 Dave Bergman .05 .02
❑ 130A Tom Brookens ERR .75 .30
(Mike Heath back)
❑ 130B Tom Brookens COR .05 .02
❑ 131 Paul Gibson .05 .02
❑ 132A Mike Heath ERR .75 .30
(Tom Brookens back)
❑ 132B Mike Heath COR .05 .02
❑ 133 Don Heinkel .05 .02
❑ 134 Mike Henneman .05 .02
❑ 135 Guillermo Hernandez .05 .02
❑ 136 Eric King .05 .02
❑ 137 Chet Lemon .10 .04
❑ 138 Fred Lynn UER .10 .04
'74 and '75 stats missing
❑ 139 Jack Morris .10 .04
❑ 140 Matt Nokes .05 .02
❑ 141 Gary Pettis .05 .02
❑ 142 Ted Power .05 .02
❑ 143 Jeff M. Robinson .05 .02
❑ 144 Luis Salazar .05 .02
❑ 145 Steve Searcy .05 .02
❑ 146 Pat Sheridan .05 .02
❑ 147 Frank Tanana .10 .04
❑ 148 Alan Trammell .10 .04
❑ 149 Walt Terrell .05 .02
❑ 150 Jim Walewander .05 .02
❑ 151 Lou Whitaker .10 .04
❑ 152 Tim Birtsas .05 .02
❑ 153 Tom Browning .05 .02
❑ 154 Keith Brown .05 .02
❑ 155 Norm Charlton RC .25 .10
❑ 156 Dave Concepcion .10 .04
❑ 157 Kal Daniels .05 .02
❑ 158 Eric Davis .10 .04
❑ 159 Bo Diaz .05 .02
❑ 160 Rob Dibble RC .50 .20
❑ 161 Nick Esasky .05 .02
❑ 162 John Franco .10 .04
❑ 163 Danny Jackson .05 .02
❑ 164 Barry Larkin .15 .06
❑ 165 Rob Murphy .05 .02
❑ 166 Paul O'Neill .15 .06
❑ 167 Jeff Reed .05 .02
❑ 168 Jose Rijo .10 .04
❑ 169 Ron Robinson .05 .02
❑ 170 Chris Sabo RC .40 .16
❑ 171 Candy Sierra .05 .02
❑ 172 Van Snider .05 .02
❑ 173A Jeff Treadway 5.00 2.00
(Target registration
mark above head
on front in
light blue)
❑ 173B Jeff Treadway .05 .02
(No target on front)
❑ 174 Frank Williams UER .05 .02
(After All-Star Break
stats are jumbled)
❑ 175 Herm Winningham .05 .02
❑ 176 Jim Adduci .05 .02
❑ 177 Don August .05 .02
❑ 178 Mike Birkbeck .05 .02
❑ 179 Chris Bosio .05 .02
❑ 180 Glenn Braggs .05 .02
❑ 181 Greg Brock .05 .02
❑ 182 Mark Clear .05 .02
❑ 183 Chuck Crim .05 .02
❑ 184 Rob Deer .05 .02
❑ 185 Tom Filer .05 .02
❑ 186 Jim Gantner .05 .02
❑ 187 Darryl Hamilton RC .25 .10
❑ 188 Ted Higuera .05 .02
❑ 189 Odell Jones .05 .02
❑ 190 Jeffrey Leonard .05 .02
❑ 191 Joey Meyer .05 .02
❑ 192 Paul Mirabella .05 .02
❑ 193 Paul Molitor .15 .06
❑ 194 Charlie O'Brien .05 .02
❑ 195 Dan Plesac .05 .02
❑ 196 Gary Sheffield RC 1.50 .60
❑ 197 B.J. Surhoff .10 .04
❑ 198 Dale Sveum .05 .02
❑ 199 Bill Wegman .05 .02
❑ 200 Robin Yount .40 .16
❑ 201 Rafael Belliard .05 .02
❑ 202 Barry Bonds 1.25 .50
❑ 203 Bobby Bonilla .10 .04
❑ 204 Sid Bream .05 .02
❑ 205 Benny Distefano .05 .02
❑ 206 Doug Drabek .05 .02
❑ 207 Mike Dunne .05 .02
❑ 208 Felix Fermin .05 .02
❑ 209 Brian Fisher .05 .02
❑ 210 Jim Gott .05 .02
❑ 211 Bob Kipper .05 .02
❑ 212 Dave LaPoint .05 .02
❑ 213 Mike LaValliere .05 .02
❑ 214 Jose Lind .05 .02
❑ 215 Junior Ortiz .05 .02
❑ 216 Vicente Palacios .05 .02
❑ 217 Tom Prince .05 .02
❑ 218 Gary Redus .05 .02
❑ 219 R.J. Reynolds .05 .02
❑ 220 Jeff D. Robinson .05 .02
❑ 221 John Smiley .05 .02
❑ 222 Andy Van Slyke .10 .04
❑ 223 Bob Walk .05 .02

❑ 224 Glenn Wilson .05 .02
❑ 225 Jesse Barfield .10 .04
❑ 226 George Bell .10 .04
❑ 227 Pat Borders RC .25 .10
❑ 228 John Cerutti .05 .02
❑ 229 Jim Clancy .05 .02
❑ 230 Mark Eichhorn .05 .02
❑ 231 Tony Fernandez .05 .02
❑ 232 Cecil Fielder .10 .04
❑ 233 Mike Flanagan .05 .02
❑ 234 Kelly Gruber .05 .02
❑ 235 Tom Henke .05 .02
❑ 236 Jimmy Key .10 .04
❑ 237 Rick Leach .05 .02
❑ 238 Manny Lee UER .05 .02
(Bio says regular
shortstop, sic,
Tony Fernandez)
❑ 239 Nelson Liriano .05 .02
❑ 240 Fred McGriff .15 .06
❑ 241 Lloyd Moseby .05 .02
❑ 242 Rance Mulliniks .05 .02
❑ 243 Jeff Musselman .05 .02
❑ 244 Dave Stieb .10 .04
❑ 245 Todd Stottlemyre .05 .02
❑ 246 Duane Ward .05 .02
❑ 247 David Wells .10 .04
❑ 248 Ernie Whitt UER .05 .02
(HR total 21,
should be 121)
❑ 249 Luis Aguayo .05 .02
❑ 250A Neil Allen ERR .75 .30
Sarasota, FL
❑ 250B Neil Allen COR .05 .02
Syosset, NY
❑ 251 John Candelaria .05 .02
❑ 252 Jack Clark .10 .04
❑ 253 Richard Dotson .05 .02
❑ 254 Rickey Henderson .25 .10
❑ 255 Tommy John .10 .04
❑ 256 Roberto Kelly .05 .02
❑ 257 Al Leiter .25 .10
❑ 258 Don Mattingly .60 .24
❑ 259 Dale Mohorcic .05 .02
❑ 260 Hal Morris RC .25 .10
❑ 261 Scott Nielsen .05 .02
❑ 262 Mike Pagliarulo UER .05 .02
(Wrong birthdate)
❑ 263 Hipolito Pena .05 .02
❑ 264 Ken Phelps .05 .02
❑ 265 Willie Randolph .10 .04
❑ 266 Rick Rhoden .05 .02
❑ 267 Dave Righetti .10 .04
❑ 268 Rafael Santana .05 .02
❑ 269 Steve Shields .05 .02
❑ 270 Joel Skinner .05 .02
❑ 271 Don Slaught .05 .02
❑ 272 Claudell Washington .05 .02
❑ 273 Gary Ward .05 .02
❑ 274 Dave Winfield .10 .04
❑ 275 Luis Aquino .05 .02
❑ 276 Floyd Bannister .05 .02
❑ 277 George Brett .60 .24
❑ 278 Bill Buckner .10 .04
❑ 279 Nick Capra .05 .02
❑ 280 Jose DeJesus .05 .02
❑ 281 Steve Farr .05 .02
❑ 282 Jerry Don Gleaton .05 .02
❑ 283 Mark Gubicza .05 .02
❑ 284 Tom Gordon RC UER .40 .16
(16.2 innings in '88,
should be 15.2)
❑ 285 Bo Jackson .25 .10
❑ 286 Charlie Leibrandt .05 .02
❑ 287 Mike Macfarlane RC .25 .10
❑ 288 Jeff Montgomery .05 .02
❑ 289 Bill Pecota UER .05 .02
(Photo actually
Brad Wellman)
❑ 290 Jamie Quirk .05 .02
❑ 291 Bret Saberhagen .10 .04
❑ 292 Kevin Seitzer .05 .02
❑ 293 Kurt Stillwell .05 .02
❑ 294 Pat Tabler .05 .02
❑ 295 Danny Tartabull .05 .02
❑ 296 Gary Thurman .05 .02

❑ 297 Frank White .10 .04
❑ 298 Willie Wilson .10 .04
❑ 299 Roberto Alomar .25 .10
❑ 300 S.Alomar Jr. RC UER .40 .16
Wrong birthdate, says
6/16/66, should say
6/18/66
❑ 301 Chris Brown .05 .02
❑ 302 Mike Brumley UER .05 .02
(133 hits in '88,
should be 134)
❑ 303 Mark Davis .05 .02
❑ 304 Mark Grant .05 .02
❑ 305 Tony Gwynn .30 .12
❑ 306 Greg W. Harris RC .10 .04
❑ 307 Andy Hawkins .05 .02
❑ 308 Jimmy Jones .05 .02
❑ 309 John Kruk .10 .04
❑ 310 Dave Leiper .05 .02
❑ 311 Carmelo Martinez .05 .02
❑ 312 Lance McCullers .05 .02
❑ 313 Keith Moreland .05 .02
❑ 314 Dennis Rasmussen .05 .02
❑ 315 Randy Ready UER .05 .02
(1214 games in '88,
should be 114)
❑ 316 Benito Santiago .10 .04
❑ 317 Eric Show .05 .02
❑ 318 Todd Simmons .05 .02
❑ 319 Garry Templeton .10 .04
❑ 320 Dickie Thon .05 .02
❑ 321 Ed Whitson .05 .02
❑ 322 Marvell Wynne .05 .02
❑ 323 Mike Aldrete .05 .02
❑ 324 Brett Butler .10 .04
❑ 325 Will Clark UER .25 .10
(Three consecutive
100 RBI seasons)
❑ 326 Kelly Downs UER .05 .02
('88 stats missing)
❑ 327 Dave Dravecky .05 .02
❑ 328 Scott Garrelts .05 .02
❑ 329 Atlee Hammaker .05 .02
❑ 330 Charlie Hayes RC .25 .10
❑ 331 Mike Krukow .05 .02
❑ 332 Craig Lefferts .05 .02
❑ 333 Candy Maldonado .05 .02
❑ 334 Kirt Manwaring UER .05 .02
(Bats Rights)
❑ 335 Bob Melvin .05 .02
❑ 336 Kevin Mitchell .10 .04
❑ 337 Donell Nixon .05 .02
❑ 338 Tony Perezchica .05 .02
❑ 339 Joe Price .05 .02
❑ 340 Rick Reuschel .10 .04
❑ 341 Earnest Riles .05 .02
❑ 342 Don Robinson .05 .02
❑ 343 Chris Speier .05 .02
❑ 344 Robby Thompson UER .05 .02
(West Plam Beach)
❑ 345 Jose Uribe .05 .02
❑ 346 Matt Williams .25 .10
❑ 347 Trevor Wilson RC .10 .04
❑ 348 Juan Agosto .05 .02
❑ 349 Larry Andersen .05 .02
❑ 350A Alan Ashby ERR 2.00 .80
(Throws Rig)
❑ 350B Alan Ashby COR .05 .02
❑ 351 Kevin Bass .05 .02
❑ 352 Buddy Bell .10 .04
❑ 353 Craig Biggio RC .75 .30
❑ 354 Danny Darwin .05 .02
❑ 355 Glenn Davis .05 .02
❑ 356 Jim Deshaies .05 .02
❑ 357 Bill Doran .05 .02
❑ 358 John Fishel .05 .02
❑ 359 Billy Hatcher .05 .02
❑ 360 Bob Knepper .05 .02
❑ 361 L.Meadows UER .05 .02
Bio says 10 EBH's
and 6 SB's in '88,
should be 3 and 4
❑ 362 Dave Meads .05 .02
❑ 363 Jim Pankovits .05 .02
❑ 364 Terry Puhl .05 .02
❑ 365 Rafael Ramirez .05 .02

❑ 366 Craig Reynolds .05 .02
❑ 367 Mike Scott .10 .04
(Card number listed
as 368 on Astros CL)
❑ 368 Nolan Ryan 1.00 .40
(Card number listed
as 367 on Astros CL)
❑ 369 Dave Smith .05 .02
❑ 370 Gerald Young .05 .02
❑ 371 Hubie Brooks .05 .02
❑ 372 Tim Burke .05 .02
❑ 373 John Dopson .05 .02
❑ 374 Mike R. Fitzgerald .05 .02
❑ 375 Tom Foley .05 .02
❑ 376 Andres Galarraga UER .10 .04
(Home: Caracus)
❑ 377 Neal Heaton .05 .02
❑ 378 Joe Hesketh .05 .02
❑ 379 Brian Holman RC .10 .04
❑ 380 Rex Hudler .05 .02
❑ 381 R.Johnson RC UER 4.00 1.20
Innings for '85 and
'86 shown as 27 and
120, should be 27.1
and 119.2
❑ 381B R. Johnson Marlboro VAR .00
❑ 382 Wallace Johnson .05 .02
❑ 383 Tracy Jones .05 .02
❑ 384 Dave Martinez .05 .02
❑ 385 Dennis Martinez .10 .04
❑ 386 Andy McGaffigan .05 .02
❑ 387 Otis Nixon .05 .02
❑ 388 Johnny Paredes .05 .02
❑ 389 Jeff Parrett .05 .02
❑ 390 Pascual Perez .05 .02
❑ 391 Tim Raines .10 .04
❑ 392 Luis Rivera .05 .02
❑ 393 Nelson Santovenia .05 .02
❑ 394 Bryn Smith .05 .02
❑ 395 Tim Wallach .05 .02
❑ 396 Andy Allanson UER .05 .02
1214 hits in '88,
should be 114
❑ 397 Rod Allen .05 .02
❑ 398 Scott Bailes .05 .02
❑ 399 Tom Candiotti .05 .02
❑ 400 Joe Carter .10 .04
❑ 401 Carmen Castillo UER .05 .02
(After All-Star Break
batting 2.50)
❑ 402 Dave Clark UER .05 .02
(Card front shows
position as Rookie;
after All-Star Break
batting 3.14)
❑ 403 John Farrell UER .05 .02
(Typo in runs
allowed in '88)
❑ 404 Julio Franco .10 .04
❑ 405 Don Gordon .05 .02
❑ 406 Mel Hall .05 .02
❑ 407 Brad Havens .05 .02
❑ 408 Brook Jacoby .05 .02
❑ 409 Doug Jones .05 .02
❑ 410 Jeff Kaiser .05 .02
❑ 411 Luis Medina .05 .02
❑ 412 Cory Snyder .05 .02
❑ 413 Greg Swindell .05 .02
❑ 414 Ron Tingley UER .05 .02
(Hit HR in first ML
at-bat, should be
first AL at-bat)
❑ 415 Willie Upshaw .05 .02
❑ 416 Ron Washington .05 .02
❑ 417 Rich Yett .05 .02
❑ 418 Damon Berryhill .05 .02
❑ 419 Mike Bielecki .05 .02
❑ 420 Doug Dascenzo .05 .02
❑ 421 Jody Davis UER .05 .02
(Braves stats for
'88 missing)
❑ 422 Andre Dawson .10 .04
❑ 423 Frank DiPino .05 .02
❑ 424 Shawon Dunston .05 .02
❑ 425 Rich Gossage .10 .04
❑ 426 Mark Grace UER .25 .10

(Minor League stats
for '88 missing)
❑ 427 Mike Harkey RC .10 .04
❑ 428 Darrin Jackson .10 .04
❑ 429 Les Lancaster .05 .02
❑ 430 Vance Law .05 .02
❑ 431 Greg Maddux .50 .20
❑ 432 Jamie Moyer .10 .04
❑ 433 Al Nipper .05 .02
❑ 434 Rafael Palmeiro UER .25 .10
170 hits in '88,
should be 178
❑ 435 Pat Perry .05 .02
❑ 436 Jeff Pico .05 .02
❑ 437 Ryne Sandberg .40 .16
❑ 438 Calvin Schiraldi .05 .02
❑ 439 Rick Sutcliffe .10 .04
❑ 440A Manny Trillo ERR 2.00 .80
(Throws Rig)
❑ 440B Manny Trillo COR .05 .02
❑ 441 Gary Varsho UER .05 .02
(Wrong birthdate;
.303 should be .302;
11/28 should be 9/19)
❑ 442 Mitch Webster .05 .02
❑ 443 Luis Alicea RC .25 .10
❑ 444 Tom Brunansky .05 .02
❑ 445 Vince Coleman UER .05 .02
Third straight with 83
should be fourth straight with 81
❑ 446 John Costello UER .05 .02
(Home California,
should be New York)
❑ 447 Danny Cox .05 .02
❑ 448 Ken Dayley .05 .02
❑ 449 Jose DeLeon .05 .02
❑ 450 Curt Ford .05 .02
❑ 451 Pedro Guerrero .10 .04
❑ 452 Bob Horner .10 .04
❑ 453 Tim Jones .05 .02
❑ 454 Steve Lake .05 .02
❑ 455 Joe Magrane UER .05 .02
(Des Moines, IO)
❑ 456 Greg Mathews .05 .02
❑ 457 Willie McGee .10 .04
❑ 458 Larry McWilliams .05 .02
❑ 459 Jose Oquendo .05 .02
❑ 460 Tony Pena .05 .02
❑ 461 Terry Pendleton .10 .04
❑ 462 Steve Peters UER .05 .02
(Lives in Harrah,
not Harah)
❑ 463 Ozzie Smith .40 .16
❑ 464 Scott Terry .05 .02
❑ 465 Denny Walling .05 .02
❑ 466 Todd Worrell .05 .02
❑ 467 Tony Armas UER .10 .04
(Before All-Star Break
batting 2.39)
❑ 468 Dante Bichette RC .40 .16
❑ 469 Bob Boone .10 .04
❑ 470 Terry Clark .05 .02
❑ 471 Stu Cliburn .05 .02
❑ 472 Mike Cook UER .05 .02
(TM near Angels logo
missing from front)
❑ 473 Sherman Corbett .05 .02
❑ 474 Chili Davis .10 .04
❑ 475 Brian Downing .10 .04
❑ 476 Jim Eppard .05 .02
❑ 477 Chuck Finley .10 .04
❑ 478 Willie Fraser .05 .02
❑ 479 Bryan Harvey UER RC .25 .10
ML record shows 0-0,
should be 7-5
❑ 480 Jack Howell .05 .02
❑ 481 Wally Joyner UER .10 .04
(Yorba Linda, GA)
❑ 482 Jack Lazorko .05 .02
❑ 483 Kirk McCaskill .05 .02
❑ 484 Mark McLemore .05 .02
❑ 485 Greg Minton .05 .02
❑ 486 Dan Petry .05 .02
❑ 487 Johnny Ray .05 .02
❑ 488 Dick Schofield .05 .02
❑ 489 Devon White .10 .04
❑ 490 Mike Witt .05 .02
❑ 491 Harold Baines .10 .04
❑ 492 Daryl Boston .05 .02
❑ 493 Ivan Calderon UER .05 .02
('80 stats shifted)
❑ 494 Mike Diaz .05 .02
❑ 495 Carlton Fisk .15 .06
❑ 496 Dave Gallagher .05 .02
❑ 497 Ozzie Guillen .05 .02
❑ 498 Shawn Hillegas .05 .02
❑ 499 Lance Johnson .05 .02
❑ 500 Barry Jones .05 .02
❑ 501 Bill Long .05 .02
❑ 502 Steve Lyons .05 .02
❑ 503 Fred Manrique .05 .02
❑ 504 Jack McDowell .10 .04
❑ 505 Donn Pall .05 .02
❑ 506 Kelly Paris .05 .02
❑ 507 Dan Pasqua .05 .02
❑ 508 Ken Patterson .05 .02
❑ 509 Melido Perez .05 .02
❑ 510 Jerry Reuss .05 .02
❑ 511 Mark Salas .05 .02
❑ 512 Bobby Thigpen UER .05 .02
('86 ERA 4.69,
should be 4.68)
❑ 513 Mike Woodard .05 .02
❑ 514 Bob Brower .05 .02
❑ 515 Steve Buechele .05 .02
❑ 516 Jose Cecena .05 .02
❑ 517 Cecil Espy .05 .02
❑ 518 Scott Fletcher .05 .02
❑ 519 Cecilio Guante .05 .02
('87 Yankee stats
are off-centered)
❑ 520 Jose Guzman .05 .02
❑ 521 Ray Hayward .05 .02
❑ 522 Charlie Hough .10 .04
❑ 523 Pete Incaviglia .05 .02
❑ 524 Mike Jeffcoat .05 .02
❑ 525 Paul Kilgus .05 .02
❑ 526 Chad Kreuter RC .25 .10
❑ 527 Jeff Kunkel .05 .02
❑ 528 Oddibe McDowell .05 .02
❑ 529 Pete O'Brien .05 .02
❑ 530 Geno Petralli .05 .02
❑ 531 Jeff Russell .05 .02
❑ 532 Ruben Sierra .05 .02
❑ 533 Mike Stanley .05 .02
❑ 534A Ed VandeBerg ERR 2.00 .80
(Throws Lef)
❑ 534B Ed VandeBerg COR .05 .02
❑ 535 Curtis Wilkerson ERR .05 .02
(Pitcher headings
at bottom)
❑ 536 Mitch Williams .05 .02
❑ 537 Bobby Witt UER .05 .02
('85 ERA .643,
should be 6.43)
❑ 538 Steve Balboni .05 .02
❑ 539 Scott Bankhead .05 .02
❑ 540 Scott Bradley .05 .02
❑ 541 Mickey Brantley .05 .02
❑ 542 Jay Buhner .10 .04
❑ 543 Mike Campbell .05 .02
❑ 544 Darnell Coles .05 .02
❑ 545 Henry Cotto .05 .02
❑ 546 Alvin Davis .05 .02
❑ 547 Mario Diaz .05 .02
❑ 548 Ken Griffey Jr. RC 8.00 3.20
❑ 549 Erik Hanson RC .25 .10
❑ 550 Mike Jackson UER .05 .02
(Lifetime ERA 3.345,
should be 3.45)
❑ 551 Mark Langston .05 .02
❑ 552 Edgar Martinez .25 .10
❑ 553 Bill McGuire .05 .02
❑ 554 Mike Moore .05 .02
❑ 555 Jim Presley .05 .02
❑ 556 Rey Quinones .05 .02
❑ 557 Jerry Reed .05 .02
❑ 558 Harold Reynolds .10 .04
❑ 559 Mike Schooler .05 .02
❑ 560 Bill Swift .05 .02
❑ 561 Dave Valle .05 .02
❑ 562 Steve Bedrosian .05 .02
❑ 563 Phil Bradley .05 .02
❑ 564 Don Carman .05 .02
❑ 565 Bob Dernier .05 .02
❑ 566 Marvin Freeman .05 .02
❑ 567 Todd Frohwirth .05 .02
❑ 568 Greg Gross .05 .02
❑ 569 Kevin Gross .05 .02
❑ 570 Greg A. Harris .05 .02
❑ 571 Von Hayes .05 .02
❑ 572 Chris James .05 .02
❑ 573 Steve Jeltz .05 .02
❑ 574 Ron Jones UER .10 .04
(Led IL in '88 with
85, should be 75)
❑ 575 Ricky Jordan RC .25 .10
❑ 576 Mike Maddux .05 .02
❑ 577 David Palmer .05 .02
❑ 578 Lance Parrish .10 .04
❑ 579 Shane Rawley .05 .02
❑ 580 Bruce Ruffin .05 .02
❑ 581 Juan Samuel .05 .02
❑ 582 Mike Schmidt .50 .20
❑ 583 Kent Tekulve .05 .02
❑ 584 Milt Thompson UER .05 .02
(19 hits in '88,
should be 109)
❑ 585 Jose Alvarez RC .10 .04
❑ 586 Paul Assenmacher .05 .02
❑ 587 Bruce Benedict .05 .02
❑ 588 Jeff Blauser .05 .02
❑ 589 Terry Blocker .05 .02
❑ 590 Ron Gant .10 .04
❑ 591 Tom Glavine .25 .10
❑ 592 Tommy Gregg .05 .02
❑ 593 Albert Hall .05 .02
❑ 594 Dion James .05 .02
❑ 595 Rick Mahler .05 .02
❑ 596 Dale Murphy .15 .06
❑ 597 Gerald Perry .05 .02
❑ 598 Charlie Puleo .05 .02
❑ 599 Ted Simmons .10 .04
❑ 600 Pete Smith .05 .02
❑ 601 Zane Smith .05 .02
❑ 602 John Smoltz RC 1.00 .40
❑ 603 Bruce Sutter .10 .04
❑ 604 Andres Thomas .05 .02
❑ 605 Ozzie Virgil .05 .02
❑ 606 Brady Anderson RC .40 .16
❑ 607 Jeff Ballard .05 .02
❑ 608 Jose Bautista RC .10 .04
❑ 609 Ken Gerhart .05 .02
❑ 610 Terry Kennedy .05 .02
❑ 611 Eddie Murray .25 .10
❑ 612 Carl Nichols UER .05 .02
(Before All-Star Break
batting 1.88)
❑ 613 Tom Niedenfuer .05 .02
❑ 614 Joe Orsulak .05 .02
❑ 615 Oswald Peraza UER .05 .02
(Shown as Oswaldo)
❑ 616A Bill Ripken ERR 20.00 8.00
(Rick Face written
on knob of bat)
❑ 616B Bill Ripken 80.00 32.00
(Bat knob
whited out)
❑ 616C Bill Ripken 5.00 2.00
(Words on bat knob
scribbled out in White)
❑ 616D Bill Ripken 20.00 8.00
Words on Bat
scribbled out in Black
❑ 616E Bill Ripken DP .10 .04
(Black box covering
bat knob)
❑ 617 Cal Ripken .75 .30
❑ 618 Dave Schmidt .05 .02
❑ 619 Rick Schu .05 .02
❑ 620 Larry Sheets .05 .02
❑ 621 Doug Sisk .05 .02
❑ 622 Pete Stanicek .05 .02
❑ 623 Mickey Tettleton .05 .02
❑ 624 Jay Tibbs .05 .02
❑ 625 Jim Traber .05 .02
❑ 626 Mark Williamson .05 .02
❑ 627 Craig Worthington .05 .02

❑ 628 Jose Canseco 40/40 .15 .06
❑ 629 Tom Browning Perfect .05 .02
❑ 630 Roberto Alomar .25 .10
Sandy Alomar Jr. UER
(Names on card listed
in wrong order)
❑ 631 Will Clark .25 .10
Rafael Palmeiro UER
(Gallaraga, sic;
Clark 3 consecutive
100 RBI seasons;
third with 102 RBI's)
❑ 632 Darryl Strawberry .10 .04
Will Clark UER (Homeruns
should be two words)
❑ 633 Wade Boggs .10 .04
Carney Lansford UER
(Boggs hit .366 in
'86, should be '88)
❑ 634 Jose Canseco .50 .20
Terry Steinbach
Mark McGwire
❑ 635 Mark Davis .05 .02
Dwight Gooden
❑ 636 Danny Jackson .05 .02
David Cone UER
Hersheiser, sic
❑ 637 Chris Sabo .10 .04
Bobby Bonilla UER
Bobby Bonds, sic
❑ 638 Andres Galarraga UER .05 .02
(Misspelled Gallaraga
on card back)
Gerald Perry
❑ 639 Kirby Puckett .15 .06
Eric Davis
❑ 640 Steve Wilson and .05 .02
Cameron Drew
❑ 641 Kevin Brown and .25 .10
Kevin Reimer
❑ 642 Brad Pounders RC .10 .04
Jerald Clark
❑ 643 Mike Capel and .05 .02
Drew Hall
❑ 644 Joe Girardi RC and .40 .16
Rolando Roomes
❑ 645 Lenny Harris RC and .25 .10
Marty Brown
❑ 646 Luis DeLosSantos .05 .02
and Jim Campbell
❑ 647 Randy Kramer and .05 .02
Miguel Garcia
❑ 648 Torey Lovullo RC and .10 .04
Robert Palacios
❑ 649 Jim Corsi and .05 .02
Bob Milacki
❑ 650 Grady Hall and .05 .02
Mike Rochford
❑ 651 Terry Taylor RC .10 .04
Vance Lovelace
❑ 652 Ken Hill RC and .25 .10
Dennis Cook
❑ 653 Scott Service and .05 .02
Shane Turner
❑ 654 CL: Oakland/Mets .05 .02
Dodgers/Red Sox
(10 Hendersor;
68 Jess Orosco)
❑ 655A CL: Twins/Tigers ERR .05 .02
Reds/Brewers
(179 Boslo and
Twins/Tigers positions
listed)
❑ 655B CL: Twins/Tigers COR .05 .02
Reds/Brewers
(179 Boslo but
Twins/Tigers positions
not listed)
❑ 656 CL: Pirates/Blue Jays .05 .02
Yankees/Royals
(225 Jess Barfield)
❑ 657 CL: Padres/Giants .05 .02
Astros/Expos
(367/368 wrong)
❑ 658 CL: Indians/Cubs .05 .02
Cardinals/Angels
(449 Deleon)
❑ 659 CL: White Sox/Rangers .05 .02
Mariners/Phillies
❑ 660 CL: Braves/Orioles .05 .02
Specials/Checklists
(632 hyphenated diff-
erently and 650 Hali;
595 Rich Mahler;
619 Rich Schu)

1989 Fleer Update

	Nm-Mt	Ex-Mt
COMP.FACT.SET (132)	5.00	2.00

❑ 1 Phil Bradley .05 .02
❑ 2 Mike Devereaux .05 .02
❑ 3 Steve Finley RC .50 .20
❑ 4 Kevin Hickey .05 .02
❑ 5 Brian Holton .05 .02
❑ 6 Bob Milacki .05 .02
❑ 7 Randy Milligan .05 .02
❑ 8 John Dopson .05 .02
❑ 9 Nick Esasky .05 .02
❑ 10 Rob Murphy .05 .02
❑ 11 Jim Abbott RC* .50 .20
❑ 12 Bert Blyleven .10 .04
❑ 13 Jeff Manto RC .10 .04
❑ 14 Bob McClure .05 .02
❑ 15 Lance Parrish .10 .04
❑ 16 Lee Stevens RC .25 .10
❑ 17 Claudell Washington .05 .02
❑ 18 Mark Davis RC .25 .10
❑ 19 Eric King .05 .02
❑ 20 Ron Kittle .05 .02
❑ 21 Matt Merullo .05 .02
❑ 22 Steve Rosenberg .05 .02
❑ 23 Robin Ventura RC .75 .30
❑ 24 Keith Atherton .05 .02
❑ 25 Joey Belle RC 1.00 .40
❑ 26 Jerry Browne .05 .02
❑ 27 Felix Fermin .05 .02
❑ 28 Brad Komminsk .05 .02
❑ 29 Pete O'Brien .05 .02
❑ 30 Mike Brumley .05 .02
❑ 31 Tracy Jones .05 .02
❑ 32 Mike Schwabe .05 .02
❑ 33 Gary Ward .05 .02
❑ 34 Frank Williams .05 .02
❑ 35 Kevin Appier RC .50 .20
❑ 36 Bob Boone .10 .04
❑ 37 Luis DeLosSantos .05 .02
❑ 38 Jim Eisenreich .05 .02
❑ 39 Jaime Navarro RC .10 .04
❑ 40 Bill Spiers RC .25 .10
❑ 41 Greg Vaughn RC .40 .16
❑ 42 Randy Veres .05 .02
❑ 43 Wally Backman .05 .02
❑ 44 Shane Rawley .05 .02
❑ 45 Steve Balboni .05 .02
❑ 46 Jesse Barfield .10 .04
❑ 47 Alvaro Espinoza .05 .02
❑ 48 Bob Geren RC .05 .02
❑ 49 Mel Hall .05 .02
❑ 50 Andy Hawkins .05 .02
❑ 51 Hensley Meulens RC .10 .04
❑ 52 Steve Sax .05 .02
❑ 53 Deion Sanders RC 1.00 .40
❑ 54 Rickey Henderson .25 .10
❑ 55 Mike Moore .05 .02
❑ 56 Tony Phillips .05 .02
❑ 57 Greg Briley .10 .04
❑ 58 Gene Harris RC .10 .04
❑ 59 Randy Johnson 2.50 .80
❑ 60 Jeffrey Leonard .05 .02
❑ 61 Dennis Powell .05 .02
❑ 62 Omar Vizquel RC .75 .30
❑ 63 Kevin Brown .25 .10
❑ 64 Julio Franco .10 .04
❑ 65 Jamie Moyer .10 .04
❑ 66 Rafael Palmeiro .25 .10
❑ 67 Nolan Ryan 1.50 .60
❑ 68 Francisco Cabrera RC .10 .04
❑ 69 Junior Felix RC .10 .04
❑ 70 Al Leiter .25 .10
❑ 71 Alex Sanchez .05 .02
❑ 72 Geronimo Berroa .05 .02
❑ 73 Derek Lilliquist RC .10 .04
❑ 74 Lonnie Smith .05 .02
❑ 75 Jeff Treadway .05 .02
❑ 76 Paul Kilgus .05 .02
❑ 77 Lloyd McClendon .05 .02
❑ 78 Scott Sanderson .05 .02
❑ 79 Dwight Smith RC .25 .10
❑ 80 Jerome Walton RC .25 .10
❑ 81 Mitch Williams .05 .02
❑ 82 Steve Wilson .10 .04
❑ 83 Todd Benzinger .05 .02
❑ 84 Ken Griffey Sr. .10 .04
❑ 85 Rick Mahler .05 .02
❑ 86 Rolando Roomes .05 .02
❑ 87 Scott Scudder RC .10 .04
❑ 88 Jim Clancy .05 .02
❑ 89 Rick Rhoden .05 .02
❑ 90 Dan Schatzeder .05 .02
❑ 91 Mike Morgan .05 .02
❑ 92 Eddie Murray .25 .10
❑ 93 Willie Randolph .10 .04
❑ 94 Ray Searage .05 .02
❑ 95 Mike Aldrete .05 .02
❑ 96 Kevin Gross .05 .02
❑ 97 Mark Langston .05 .02
❑ 98 Spike Owen .05 .02
❑ 99 Zane Smith .05 .02
❑ 100 Don Aase .05 .02
❑ 101 Barry Lyons .05 .02
❑ 102 Juan Samuel .05 .02
❑ 103 Wally Whitehurst RC .10 .04
❑ 104 Dennis Cook .05 .02
❑ 105 Len Dykstra .10 .04
❑ 106 Charlie Hayes .25 .10
❑ 107 Tommy Herr .05 .02
❑ 108 Ken Howell .05 .02
❑ 109 John Kruk .10 .04
❑ 110 Roger McDowell .05 .02
❑ 111 Terry Mulholland .05 .02
❑ 112 Jeff Parrett .05 .02
❑ 113 Neal Heaton .05 .02
❑ 114 Jeff King .05 .02
❑ 115 Randy Kramer .05 .02
❑ 116 Bill Landrum .05 .02
❑ 117 Cris Carpenter RC * .10 .04
❑ 118 Frank DiPino .05 .02
❑ 119 Ken Hill .25 .10
❑ 120 Dan Quisenberry .05 .02
❑ 121 Milt Thompson .05 .02
❑ 122 Todd Zeile RC .40 .16
❑ 123 Jack Clark .10 .04
❑ 124 Bruce Hurst .05 .02
❑ 125 Mark Parent .05 .02
❑ 126 Bip Roberts .05 .02
❑ 127 Jeff Brantley RC UER .25 .10
(Photo actually
Joe Kmak)
❑ 128 Terry Kennedy .05 .02
❑ 129 Mike LaCoss .05 .02
❑ 130 Greg Litton .05 .02
❑ 131 Mike Schmidt .75 .30
❑ 132 Checklist 1-132 .05 .02

1990 Fleer

	Nm-Mt	Ex-Mt
COMPLETE SET (660)	15.00	4.50
COMP.RETAIL SET (660)	15.00	4.50
COMP.HOBBY SET (672)	15.00	4.50

❑ 1 Lance Blankenship .05 .02
❑ 2 Todd Burns .05 .02
❑ 3 Jose Canseco .25 .07
❑ 4 Jim Corsi .05 .02
❑ 5 Storm Davis .05 .02
❑ 6 Dennis Eckersley .10 .03
❑ 7 Mike Gallego .05 .02
❑ 8 Ron Hassey .05 .02
❑ 9 Dave Henderson .05 .02
❑ 10 Rickey Henderson .25 .07
❑ 11 Rick Honeycutt .05 .02
❑ 12 Stan Javier .05 .02
❑ 13 Felix Jose .05 .02
❑ 14 Carney Lansford .10 .03
❑ 15 Mark McGwire UER .60 .18
(1989 runs listed as 4, should be 74)
❑ 16 Mike Moore .05 .02
❑ 17 Gene Nelson .05 .02
❑ 18 Dave Parker .10 .03
❑ 19 Tony Phillips .05 .02
❑ 20 Terry Steinbach .05 .02
❑ 21 Dave Stewart .10 .03
❑ 22 Walt Weiss .05 .02
❑ 23 Bob Welch .05 .02
❑ 24 Curt Young .05 .02
❑ 25 Paul Assenmacher .05 .02
❑ 26 Damon Berryhill .05 .02
❑ 27 Mike Bielecki .05 .02
❑ 28 Kevin Blankenship .05 .02
❑ 29 Andre Dawson .10 .03
❑ 30 Shawon Dunston .05 .02
❑ 31 Joe Girardi .15 .04
❑ 32 Mark Grace .15 .04
❑ 33 Mike Harkey .05 .02
❑ 34 Paul Kilgus .05 .02
❑ 35 Les Lancaster .05 .02
❑ 36 Vance Law .05 .02
❑ 37 Greg Maddux .40 .12
❑ 38 Lloyd McClendon .05 .02
❑ 39 Jeff Pico .05 .02
❑ 40 Ryne Sandberg .40 .12
❑ 41 Scott Sanderson .05 .02
❑ 42 Dwight Smith .05 .02
❑ 43 Rick Sutcliffe .10 .03
❑ 44 Jerome Walton .05 .02
❑ 45 Mitch Webster .05 .02
❑ 46 Curt Wilkerson .05 .02
❑ 47 Dean Wilkins .05 .02
❑ 48 Mitch Williams .05 .02
❑ 49 Steve Wilson .05 .02
❑ 50 Steve Bedrosian .05 .02
❑ 51 Mike Benjamin RC .10 .03
❑ 52 Jeff Brantley .05 .02
❑ 53 Brett Butler .10 .03
❑ 54 Will Clark UER .10 .03
(Did You Know says first in runs, should say tied for first)
❑ 55 Kelly Downs .05 .02
❑ 56 Scott Garrelts .05 .02
❑ 57 Atlee Hammaker .05 .02
❑ 58 Terry Kennedy .05 .02
❑ 59 Mike LaCoss .05 .02
❑ 60 Craig Lefferts .05 .02
❑ 61 Greg Litton .05 .02
❑ 62 Candy Maldonado .05 .02
❑ 63 Kirt Manwaring UER .05 .02
(No '88 Phoenix stats as noted in box)
❑ 64 Randy McCament .05 .02
❑ 65 Kevin Mitchell .05 .02
❑ 66 Donell Nixon .05 .02
❑ 67 Ken Oberkfell .05 .02
❑ 68 Rick Reuschel .05 .02
❑ 69 Ernest Riles .05 .02
❑ 70 Don Robinson .05 .02
❑ 71 Pat Sheridan .05 .02
❑ 72 Chris Speier .05 .02
❑ 73 Robby Thompson .05 .02
❑ 74 Jose Uribe .05 .02
❑ 75 Matt Williams .10 .03
❑ 76 George Bell .05 .02
❑ 77 Pat Borders .05 .02
❑ 78 John Cerutti .05 .02
❑ 79 Junior Felix .05 .02
❑ 80 Tony Fernandez .05 .02
❑ 81 Mike Flanagan .05 .02
❑ 82 Mauro Gozzo .05 .02
❑ 83 Kelly Gruber .05 .02
❑ 84 Tom Henke .05 .02
❑ 85 Jimmy Key .10 .03
❑ 86 Manny Lee .05 .02
❑ 87 Nelson Liriano UER .05 .02
(Should say "led the IL" instead of "led the TL")
❑ 88 Lee Mazzilli .05 .02
❑ 89 Fred McGriff .25 .07
❑ 90 Lloyd Moseby .05 .02
❑ 91 Rance Mulliniks .05 .02
❑ 92 Alex Sanchez .05 .02
❑ 93 Dave Stieb .10 .03
❑ 94 Todd Stottlemyre .10 .03
❑ 95 Duane Ward UER .05 .02
(Double line of '87 Syracuse stats)
❑ 96 David Wells .10 .03
❑ 97 Ernie Whitt .05 .02
❑ 98 Frank Wills .05 .02
❑ 99 Mookie Wilson .10 .03
❑ 100 Kevin Appier .10 .03
❑ 101 Luis Aquino .05 .02
❑ 102 Bob Boone .10 .03
❑ 103 George Brett .60 .18
❑ 104 Jose DeJesus .05 .02
❑ 105 Luis De Los Santos .05 .02
❑ 106 Jim Eisenreich .05 .02
❑ 107 Steve Farr .05 .02
❑ 108 Tom Gordon .10 .03
❑ 109 Mark Gubicza .05 .02
❑ 110 Bo Jackson .25 .07
❑ 111 Terry Leach .05 .02
❑ 112 Charlie Leibrandt .05 .02
❑ 113 Rick Luecken .05 .02
❑ 114 Mike Macfarlane .05 .02
❑ 115 Jeff Montgomery .10 .03
❑ 116 Bret Saberhagen .10 .03
❑ 117 Kevin Seitzer .05 .02
❑ 118 Kurt Stillwell .05 .02
❑ 119 Pat Tabler .05 .02
❑ 120 Danny Tartabull .05 .02
❑ 121 Gary Thurman .05 .02
❑ 122 Frank White .10 .03
❑ 123 Willie Wilson .05 .02
❑ 124 Matt Winters .05 .02
❑ 125 Jim Abbott .15 .04
❑ 126 Tony Armas .05 .02
❑ 127 Dante Bichette .25 .07
❑ 128 Bert Blyleven .10 .03
❑ 129 Chili Davis .10 .03
❑ 130 Brian Downing .05 .02
❑ 131 Mike Fetters RC .25 .07
❑ 132 Chuck Finley .10 .03
❑ 133 Willie Fraser .05 .02
❑ 134 Bryan Harvey .05 .02
❑ 135 Jack Howell .05 .02
❑ 136 Wally Joyner .10 .03
❑ 137 Jeff Manto .05 .02
❑ 138 Kirk McCaskill .05 .02
❑ 139 Bob McClure .05 .02
❑ 140 Greg Minton .05 .02
❑ 141 Lance Parrish .05 .02
❑ 142 Dan Petry .05 .02
❑ 143 Johnny Ray .05 .02
❑ 144 Dick Schofield .05 .02
❑ 145 Lee Stevens .10 .03
❑ 146 Claudell Washington .05 .02
❑ 147 Devon White .10 .03
❑ 148 Mike Witt .05 .02
❑ 149 Roberto Alomar .15 .04
❑ 150 Sandy Alomar Jr. .10 .03
❑ 151 Andy Benes .10 .03
❑ 152 Jack Clark .10 .03
❑ 153 Pat Clements .05 .02
❑ 154 Joey Cora .10 .03
❑ 155 Mark Davis .05 .02
❑ 156 Mark Grant .05 .02
❑ 157 Tony Gwynn .30 .09
❑ 158 Greg W. Harris .05 .02
❑ 159 Bruce Hurst .05 .02
❑ 160 Darrin Jackson .05 .02
❑ 161 Chris James .05 .02
❑ 162 Carmelo Martinez .05 .02
❑ 163 Mike Pagliarulo .05 .02
❑ 164 Mark Parent .05 .02
❑ 165 Dennis Rasmussen .05 .02
❑ 166 Bip Roberts .05 .02
❑ 167 Benito Santiago .10 .03
❑ 168 Calvin Schiraldi .05 .02
❑ 169 Eric Show .05 .02
❑ 170 Garry Templeton .05 .02
❑ 171 Ed Whitson .05 .02
❑ 172 Brady Anderson .10 .03
❑ 173 Jeff Ballard .05 .02
❑ 174 Phil Bradley .05 .02
❑ 175 Mike Devereaux .05 .02
❑ 176 Steve Finley .10 .03
❑ 177 Pete Harnisch .05 .02
❑ 178 Kevin Hickey .05 .02
❑ 179 Brian Holton .05 .02
❑ 180 Ben McDonald RC .25 .07
❑ 181 Bob Melvin .05 .02
❑ 182 Bob Milacki .05 .02
❑ 183 Randy Milligan UER .05 .02
(Double line of '87 stats)
❑ 184 Gregg Olson .10 .03
❑ 185 Joe Orsulak .05 .02
❑ 186 Bill Ripken .05 .02
❑ 187 Cal Ripken .75 .23
❑ 188 Dave Schmidt .05 .02
❑ 189 Larry Sheets .05 .02
❑ 190 Mickey Tettleton .05 .02
❑ 191 Mark Thurmond .05 .02
❑ 192 Jay Tibbs .05 .02
❑ 193 Jim Traber .05 .02
❑ 194 Mark Williamson .05 .02
❑ 195 Craig Worthington .05 .02
❑ 196 Don Aase .05 .02
❑ 197 Blaine Beatty .05 .02
❑ 198 Mark Carreon .05 .02
❑ 199 Gary Carter .10 .03
❑ 200 David Cone .10 .03
❑ 201 Ron Darling .05 .02
❑ 202 Kevin Elster .05 .02
❑ 203 Sid Fernandez .05 .02
❑ 204 Dwight Gooden .10 .03
❑ 205 Keith Hernandez .10 .03
❑ 206 Jeff Innis .05 .02
❑ 207 Gregg Jefferies .10 .03
❑ 208 Howard Johnson .05 .02
❑ 209 Barry Lyons UER .05 .02
(Double line of '87 stats)
❑ 210 Dave Magadan .05 .02
❑ 211 Kevin McReynolds .05 .02
❑ 212 Jeff Musselman .05 .02
❑ 213 Randy Myers .10 .03
❑ 214 Bob Ojeda .05 .02
❑ 215 Juan Samuel .05 .02
❑ 216 Mackey Sasser .05 .02
❑ 217 Darryl Strawberry .10 .03
❑ 218 Tim Teufel .05 .02
❑ 219 Frank Viola .05 .02
❑ 220 Juan Agosto .05 .02
❑ 221 Larry Andersen .05 .02
❑ 222 Eric Anthony RC .10 .03
❑ 223 Kevin Bass .05 .02
❑ 224 Craig Biggio .15 .04

❑ 225 Ken Caminiti .10 .03
❑ 226 Jim Clancy .05 .02
❑ 227 Danny Darwin .05 .02
❑ 228 Glenn Davis .05 .02
❑ 229 Jim Deshaies .05 .02
❑ 230 Bill Doran .05 .02
❑ 231 Bob Forsch .05 .02
❑ 232 Brian Meyer .05 .02
❑ 233 Terry Puhl .05 .02
❑ 234 Rafael Ramirez .05 .02
❑ 235 Rick Rhoden .05 .02
❑ 236 Dan Schatzeder .05 .02
❑ 237 Mike Scott .05 .02
❑ 238 Dave Smith .05 .02
❑ 239 Alex Trevino .05 .02
❑ 240 Glenn Wilson .05 .02
❑ 241 Gerald Young .05 .02
❑ 242 Tom Brunansky .05 .02
❑ 243 Cris Carpenter .05 .02
❑ 244 Alex Cole RC .10 .03
❑ 245 Vince Coleman .05 .02
❑ 246 John Costello .05 .02
❑ 247 Ken Dayley .05 .02
❑ 248 Jose DeLeon .05 .02
❑ 249 Frank DiPino .05 .02
❑ 250 Pedro Guerrero .05 .02
❑ 251 Ken Hill .10 .03
❑ 252 Joe Magrane .05 .02
❑ 253 Willie McGee UER .10 .03
(No decimal point
before 353)
❑ 254 John Morris .05 .02
❑ 255 Jose Oquendo .05 .02
❑ 256 Tony Pena .05 .02
❑ 257 Terry Pendleton .10 .03
❑ 258 Ted Power .05 .02
❑ 259 Dan Quisenberry .05 .02
❑ 260 Ozzie Smith .40 .12
❑ 261 Scott Terry .05 .02
❑ 262 Milt Thompson .05 .02
❑ 263 Denny Walling .05 .02
❑ 264 Todd Worrell .05 .02
❑ 265 Todd Zeile .10 .03
❑ 266 Marty Barrett .05 .02
❑ 267 Mike Boddicker .05 .02
❑ 268 Wade Boggs .15 .04
❑ 269 Ellis Burks .15 .04
❑ 270 Rick Cerone .05 .02
❑ 271 Roger Clemens .50 .15
❑ 272 John Dopson .05 .02
❑ 273 Nick Esasky .05 .02
❑ 274 Dwight Evans .10 .03
❑ 275 Wes Gardner .05 .02
❑ 276 Rich Gedman .05 .02
❑ 277 Mike Greenwell .05 .02
❑ 278 Danny Heep .05 .02
❑ 279 Eric Hetzel .05 .02
❑ 280 Dennis Lamp .05 .02
❑ 281 Rob Murphy UER .05 .02
('89 stats say Reds,
should say Red Sox)
❑ 282 Joe Price .05 .02
❑ 283 Carlos Quintana .05 .02
❑ 284 Jody Reed .05 .02
❑ 285 Luis Rivera .05 .02
❑ 286 Kevin Romine .05 .02
❑ 287 Lee Smith .10 .03
❑ 288 Mike Smithson .05 .02
❑ 289 Bob Stanley .05 .02
❑ 290 Harold Baines .10 .03
❑ 291 Kevin Brown .10 .03
❑ 292 Steve Buechele .05 .02
❑ 293 Scott Coolbaugh .05 .02
❑ 294 Jack Daugherty .05 .02
❑ 295 Cecil Espy .05 .02
❑ 296 Julio Franco .10 .03
❑ 297 Juan Gonzalez RC 1.50 .45
❑ 298 Cecilio Guante .05 .02
❑ 299 Drew Hall .05 .02
❑ 300 Charlie Hough .10 .03
❑ 301 Pete Incaviglia .05 .02
❑ 302 Mike Jeffcoat .05 .02
❑ 303 Chad Kreuter .05 .02
❑ 304 Jeff Kunkel .05 .02
❑ 305 Rick Leach .05 .02
❑ 306 Fred Manrique .05 .02
❑ 307 Jamie Moyer .10 .03
❑ 308 Rafael Palmeiro .15 .04
❑ 309 Geno Petralli .05 .02
❑ 310 Kevin Reimer .05 .02
❑ 311 Kenny Rogers .10 .03
❑ 312 Jeff Russell .05 .02
❑ 313 Nolan Ryan 1.00 .30
❑ 314 Ruben Sierra .05 .02
❑ 315 Bobby Witt .05 .02
❑ 316 Chris Bosio .05 .02
❑ 317 Glenn Braggs UER .05 .02
(Stats say 111 K's,
but bio says 117 K's)
❑ 318 Greg Brock .05 .02
❑ 319 Chuck Crim .05 .02
❑ 320 Rob Deer .05 .02
❑ 321 Mike Felder .05 .02
❑ 322 Tom Filer .05 .02
❑ 323 Tony Fossas .05 .02
❑ 324 Jim Gantner .05 .02
❑ 325 Darryl Hamilton .05 .02
❑ 326 Teddy Higuera .05 .02
❑ 327 Mark Knudson .05 .02
❑ 328 Bill Krueger UER .05 .02
('86 stats missing)
❑ 329 Tim McIntosh RC .10 .03
❑ 330 Paul Molitor .15 .04
❑ 331 Jaime Navarro .05 .02
❑ 332 Charlie O'Brien .05 .02
❑ 333 Jeff Peterek .05 .02
❑ 334 Dan Plesac .05 .02
❑ 335 Jerry Reuss .05 .02
❑ 336 Gary Sheffield UER .25 .07
(Bio says played for
3 teams in '87, but
stats say in '88)
❑ 337 Bill Spiers .05 .02
❑ 338 B.J. Surhoff .10 .03
❑ 339 Greg Vaughn .05 .02
❑ 340 Robin Yount .40 .12
❑ 341 Hubie Brooks .05 .02
❑ 342 Tim Burke .05 .02
❑ 343 Mike Fitzgerald .05 .02
❑ 344 Tom Foley .05 .02
❑ 345 Andres Galarraga .10 .03
❑ 346 Damaso Garcia .05 .02
❑ 347 Marquis Grissom RC .40 .12
❑ 348 Kevin Gross .05 .02
❑ 349 Joe Hesketh .05 .02
❑ 350 Jeff Huson RC .05 .02
❑ 351 Wallace Johnson .05 .02
❑ 352 Mark Langston .05 .02
❑ 353A Dave Martinez 2.00 .60
(Yellow on front)
❑ 353B Dave Martinez .05 .02
(Red on front)
❑ 354 Dennis Martinez UER .10 .03
('87 ERA is 616,
should be 6.16)
❑ 355 Andy McGaffigan .05 .02
❑ 356 Otis Nixon .05 .02
❑ 357 Spike Owen .05 .02
❑ 358 Pascual Perez .05 .02
❑ 359 Tim Raines .10 .03
❑ 360 Nelson Santovenia .05 .02
❑ 361 Bryn Smith .05 .02
❑ 362 Zane Smith .05 .02
❑ 363 Larry Walker RC 1.00 .30
❑ 364 Tim Wallach .05 .02
❑ 365 Rick Aguilera .10 .03
❑ 366 Allan Anderson .05 .02
❑ 367 Wally Backman .05 .02
❑ 368 Doug Baker .05 .02
❑ 369 Juan Berenguer .05 .02
❑ 370 Randy Bush .05 .02
❑ 371 Carmelo Castillo .05 .02
❑ 372 Mike Dyer RC .05 .02
❑ 373 Gary Gaetti .10 .03
❑ 374 Greg Gagne .05 .02
❑ 375 Dan Gladden .05 .02
❑ 376 G.Gonzalez UER .05 .02
Bio says 31 saves in
'88, but stats say 30
❑ 377 Brian Harper .05 .02
❑ 378 Kent Hrbek .10 .03
❑ 379 Gene Larkin .05 .02
❑ 380 Tim Laudner UER .05 .02
(No decimal point
before '85 BA of 238)
❑ 381 John Moses .05 .02
❑ 382 Al Newman .05 .02
❑ 383 Kirby Puckett .25 .07
❑ 384 Shane Rawley .05 .02
❑ 385 Jeff Reardon .10 .03
❑ 386 Roy Smith .05 .02
❑ 387 Gary Wayne .05 .02
❑ 388 Dave West .05 .02
❑ 389 Tim Belcher .05 .02
❑ 390 Tim Crews UER .05 .02
(Stats say 163 IP for
'83, but bio says 136)
❑ 391 Mike Davis .05 .02
❑ 392 Rick Dempsey .05 .02
❑ 393 Kirk Gibson .10 .03
❑ 394 Jose Gonzalez .05 .02
❑ 395 Alfredo Griffin .05 .02
❑ 396 Jeff Hamilton .05 .02
❑ 397 Lenny Harris .05 .02
❑ 398 Mickey Hatcher .05 .02
❑ 399 Orel Hershiser .10 .03
❑ 400 Jay Howell .05 .02
❑ 401 Mike Marshall .05 .02
❑ 402 Ramon Martinez .05 .02
❑ 403 Mike Morgan .05 .02
❑ 404 Eddie Murray .25 .07
❑ 405 Alejandro Pena .05 .02
❑ 406 Willie Randolph .10 .03
❑ 407 Mike Scioscia .05 .02
❑ 408 Ray Searage .05 .02
❑ 409 Fernando Valenzuela .10 .03
❑ 410 Jose Vizcaino RC .25 .07
❑ 411 John Wetteland .25 .07
❑ 412 Jack Armstrong .05 .02
❑ 413 Todd Benzinger UER .05 .02
(Bio says .323 at
Pawtucket, but
stats say .321)
❑ 414 Tim Birtsas .05 .02
❑ 415 Tom Browning .05 .02
❑ 416 Norm Charlton .05 .02
❑ 417 Eric Davis .10 .03
❑ 418 Rob Dibble .10 .03
❑ 419 John Franco .10 .03
❑ 420 Ken Griffey Sr. .10 .03
❑ 421 Chris Hammond RC .10 .03
(No 1989 used for
"Did Not Play" stat,
actually did play for
Nashville in 1989)
❑ 422 Danny Jackson .05 .02
❑ 423 Barry Larkin .15 .04
❑ 424 Tim Leary .05 .02
❑ 425 Rick Mahler .05 .02
❑ 426 Joe Oliver .05 .02
❑ 427 Paul O'Neill .15 .04
❑ 428 Luis Quinones UER .05 .02
('86-'88 stats are
omitted from card but
included in totals)
❑ 429 Jeff Reed .05 .02
❑ 430 Jose Rijo .05 .02
❑ 431 Ron Robinson .05 .02
❑ 432 Rolando Roomes .05 .02
❑ 433 Chris Sabo .05 .02
❑ 434 Scott Scudder .05 .02
❑ 435 Herm Winningham .05 .02
❑ 436 Steve Balboni .05 .02
❑ 437 Jesse Barfield .05 .02
❑ 438 Mike Blowers RC .10 .03
❑ 439 Tom Brookens .05 .02
❑ 440 Greg Cadaret .05 .02
❑ 441 Alvaro Espinoza UER .05 .02
(Career games say
218, should be 219)
❑ 442 Bob Geren .05 .02
❑ 443 Lee Guetterman .05 .02
❑ 444 Mel Hall .05 .02
❑ 445 Andy Hawkins .05 .02
❑ 446 Roberto Kelly .05 .02
❑ 447 Don Mattingly .60 .18
❑ 448 Lance McCullers .05 .02
❑ 449 Hensley Meulens .05 .02

❑ 450 Dale Mohorcic .05 .02
❑ 451 Clay Parker .05 .02
❑ 452 Eric Plunk .05 .02
❑ 453 Dave Righetti .05 .02
❑ 454 Deion Sanders .25 .07
❑ 455 Steve Sax .05 .02
❑ 456 Don Slaught .05 .02
❑ 457 Walt Terrell .05 .02
❑ 458 Dave Winfield .10 .03
❑ 459 Jay Bell .10 .03
❑ 460 Rafael Belliard .05 .02
❑ 461 Barry Bonds .60 .18
❑ 462 Bobby Bonilla .10 .03
❑ 463 Sid Bream .05 .02
❑ 464 Benny Distefano .05 .02
❑ 465 Doug Drabek .05 .02
❑ 466 Jim Gott .05 .02
❑ 467 Billy Hatcher UER .05 .02
(.1 hits for Cubs
in 1984)
❑ 468 Neal Heaton .05 .02
❑ 469 Jeff King .05 .02
❑ 470 Bob Kipper .05 .02
❑ 471 Randy Kramer .05 .02
❑ 472 Bill Landrum .05 .02
❑ 473 Mike LaValliere .05 .02
❑ 474 Jose Lind .05 .02
❑ 475 Junior Ortiz .05 .02
❑ 476 Gary Redus .05 .02
❑ 477 Rick Reed RC .25 .07
❑ 478 R.J. Reynolds .05 .02
❑ 479 Jeff D. Robinson .05 .02
❑ 480 John Smiley .05 .02
❑ 481 Andy Van Slyke .10 .03
❑ 482 Bob Walk .05 .02
❑ 483 Andy Allanson .05 .02
❑ 484 Scott Bailes .05 .02
❑ 485 Joey Belle UER .25 .07
(Has Jay Bell
"Did You Know")
Later changed his name to Albert
❑ 486 Bud Black .05 .02
❑ 487 Jerry Browne .05 .02
❑ 488 Tom Candiotti .05 .02
❑ 489 Joe Carter .10 .03
❑ 490 Dave Clark .05 .02
(No '84 stats)
❑ 491 John Farrell .05 .02
❑ 492 Felix Fermin .05 .02
❑ 493 Brook Jacoby .05 .02
❑ 494 Dion James .05 .02
❑ 495 Doug Jones .05 .02
❑ 496 Brad Komminsk .05 .02
❑ 497 Rod Nichols .05 .02
❑ 498 Pete O'Brien .05 .02
❑ 499 Steve Olin RC .10 .03
❑ 500 Jesse Orosco .05 .02
❑ 501 Joel Skinner .05 .02
❑ 502 Cory Snyder .05 .02
❑ 503 Greg Swindell .05 .02
❑ 504 Rich Yett .05 .02
❑ 505 Scott Bankhead .05 .02
❑ 506 Scott Bradley .05 .02
❑ 507 Greg Briley UER .05 .02
(28 SB's in bio,
but 27 in stats)
❑ 508 Jay Buhner .10 .03
❑ 509 Darnell Coles .05 .02
❑ 510 Keith Comstock .05 .02
❑ 511 Henry Cotto .05 .02
❑ 512 Alvin Davis .05 .02
❑ 513 Ken Griffey Jr. .75 .23
❑ 514 Erik Hanson .05 .02
❑ 515 Gene Harris .05 .02
❑ 516 Brian Holman .05 .02
❑ 517 Mike Jackson .05 .02
❑ 518 Randy Johnson .50 .12
❑ 519 Jeffrey Leonard .05 .02
❑ 520 Edgar Martinez .15 .04
❑ 521 Dennis Powell .05 .02
❑ 522 Jim Presley .05 .02
❑ 523 Jerry Reed .05 .02
❑ 524 Harold Reynolds .10 .03
❑ 525 Mike Schooler .05 .02
❑ 526 Bill Swift .05 .02
❑ 527 Dave Valle .05 .02
❑ 528 Omar Vizquel .25 .07
❑ 529 Ivan Calderon .05 .02
❑ 530 Carlton Fisk UER .15 .04
(Bellow Falls, should
be Bellows Falls)
❑ 531 Scott Fletcher .05 .02
❑ 532 Dave Gallagher .05 .02
❑ 533 Ozzie Guillen .05 .02
❑ 534 Greg Hibbard RC .10 .03
❑ 535 Shawn Hillegas .05 .02
❑ 536 Lance Johnson .05 .02
❑ 537 Eric King .05 .02
❑ 538 Ron Kittle .05 .02
❑ 539 Steve Lyons .05 .02
❑ 540 Carlos Martinez .05 .02
❑ 541 Tom McCarthy .05 .02
❑ 542 Matt Merullo .05 .02
(Had 5 ML runs scored
entering '90, not 6)
❑ 543 Donn Pall UER .05 .02
(Stats say pro career
began in '85,
bio says '88)
❑ 544 Dan Pasqua .05 .02
❑ 545 Ken Patterson .05 .02
❑ 546 Melido Perez .05 .02
❑ 547 Steve Rosenberg .05 .02
❑ 548 Sammy Sosa RC 5.00 1.50
❑ 549 Bobby Thigpen .05 .02
❑ 550 Robin Ventura .25 .07
❑ 551 Greg Walker .05 .02
❑ 552 Don Carman .05 .02
❑ 553 Pat Combs .05 .02
(6 walks for Phillies
in '89 in stats,
brief bio says 4)
❑ 554 Dennis Cook .05 .02
❑ 555 Darren Daulton .10 .03
❑ 556 Len Dykstra .10 .03
❑ 557 Curt Ford .05 .02
❑ 558 Charlie Hayes .05 .02
❑ 559 Von Hayes .05 .02
❑ 560 Tommy Herr .05 .02
❑ 561 Ken Howell .05 .02
❑ 562 Steve Jeltz .05 .02
❑ 563 Ron Jones .05 .02
❑ 564 Ricky Jordan UER .05 .02
(Duplicate line of
statistics on back)
❑ 565 John Kruk .10 .03
❑ 566 Steve Lake .05 .02
❑ 567 Roger McDowell .05 .02
❑ 568 Terry Mulholland UER .05 .02
(Did You Know refers
to Dave Magadan)
❑ 569 Dwayne Murphy .05 .02
❑ 570 Jeff Parrett .05 .02
❑ 571 Randy Ready .05 .02
❑ 572 Bruce Ruffin .05 .02
❑ 573 Dickie Thon .05 .02
❑ 574 Jose Alvarez UER .05 .02
('78 and '79 stats
are reversed)
❑ 575 Geronimo Berroa .05 .02
❑ 576 Jeff Blauser .05 .02
❑ 577 Joe Boever .05 .02
❑ 578 Marty Clary UER .05 .02
(No comma between
city and state)
❑ 579 Jody Davis .05 .02
❑ 580 Mark Eichhorn .05 .02
❑ 581 Darrell Evans .10 .03
❑ 582 Ron Gant .10 .03
❑ 583 Tom Glavine .15 .04
❑ 584 Tommy Greene RC .10 .03
❑ 585 Tommy Gregg .05 .02
❑ 586 Dave Justice RC UER .50 .15
(Actually had 16 2B
in Sumter in '86)
❑ 587 Mark Lemke .05 .02
❑ 588 Derek Lilliquist .05 .02
❑ 589 Oddibe McDowell .05 .02
❑ 590 Kent Mercker RC ERA .05 .02
(Bio says 2.75 ERA,
stats say 2.68 ERA)
❑ 591 Dale Murphy .25 .07
❑ 592 Gerald Perry .05 .02
❑ 593 Lonnie Smith .05 .02
❑ 594 Pete Smith .05 .02
❑ 595 John Smoltz .25 .07
❑ 596 Mike Stanton RC UER .25 .07
(No comma between
city and state)
❑ 597 Andres Thomas .05 .02
❑ 598 Jeff Treadway .05 .02
❑ 599 Doyle Alexander .05 .02
❑ 600 Dave Bergman .05 .02
❑ 601 Brian DuBois .05 .02
❑ 602 Paul Gibson .05 .02
❑ 603 Mike Heath .05 .02
❑ 604 Mike Henneman .05 .02
❑ 605 Guillermo Hernandez .05 .02
❑ 606 Shawn Holman .05 .02
❑ 607 Tracy Jones .05 .02
❑ 608 Chet Lemon .05 .02
❑ 609 Fred Lynn .05 .02
❑ 610 Jack Morris .10 .03
❑ 611 Matt Nokes .05 .02
❑ 612 Gary Pettis .05 .02
❑ 613 Kevin Ritz .05 .02
❑ 614 Jeff M. Robinson .05 .02
('88 stats are
not in line)
❑ 615 Steve Searcy .05 .02
❑ 616 Frank Tanana .05 .02
❑ 617 Alan Trammell .10 .03
❑ 618 Gary Ward .05 .02
❑ 619 Lou Whitaker .10 .03
❑ 620 Frank Williams .05 .02
❑ 621A George Brett '80 2.00 .60
ERR (Had 10 .390
hitting seasons)
❑ 621B George Brett '80 .30 .09
COR
❑ 622 Fern.Valenzuela '81 .05 .02
❑ 623 Dale Murphy '82 .15 .04
❑ 624A Cal Ripken '83 ERR 5.00 1.50
(Misspelled Ripkin
on card back)
❑ 624B Cal Ripken '83 COR .40 .12
❑ 625 Ryne Sandberg '84 .25 .07
❑ 626 Don Mattingly '85 .20 .06
❑ 627 Roger Clemens '86 .25 .07
❑ 628 George Bell '87 .05 .02
❑ 629 J.Canseco '88 UER .10 .03
Reggie won MVP in
'83, should say '73
❑ 630A Will Clark '89 ERR 1.00 .30
(32 total bases
on card back)
❑ 630B Will Clark '89 COR .25 .07
(321 total bases;
technically still
an error, listing
only 24 runs)
❑ 631 Mark Davis .05 .02
Mitch Williams
❑ 632 Wade Boggs .10 .03
Mike Greenwell
❑ 633 Mark Gubicza .05 .02
Jeff Russell
❑ 634 Tony Fernandez .25 .07
Cal Ripken
❑ 635 Kirby Puckett .15 .04
Bo Jackson
❑ 636 Nolan Ryan .40 .12
Mike Scott
❑ 637 Will Clark .10 .03
Kevin Mitchell
❑ 638 Don Mattingly .30 .09
Mark McGwire
❑ 639 Howard Johnson .25 .07
Ryne Sandberg
❑ 640 Rudy Seanez RC .10 .03
Colin Charland
❑ 641 George Canale RC .25 .07
Kevin Maas UER
(Canale listed as INF
on front, 1B on back)
❑ 642 Kelly Mann .25 .07
and Dave Hansen RC
❑ 643 Greg Smith .10 .03

and Stu Tate
❑ 644 Tom Drees .10 .03
and Dann Howitt
❑ 645 Mike Roesler RC .10 .03
and Derrick May
❑ 646 Scott Hemond .10 .03
and Mark Gardner RC
❑ 647 John Orton .10 .03
and Scott Leius RC
❑ 648 Rich Monteleone .10 .03
and Dana Williams
❑ 649 Mike Huff .10 .03
and Steve Frey
❑ 650 Chuck McElroy .75 .23
and Moises Alou RC
❑ 651 Bobby Rose .25 .07
and Mike Hartley
❑ 652 Matt Kinzer .10 .03
and Wayne Edwards
❑ 653 Delino DeShields RC .25 .07
and Jason Grimsley
❑ 654 CL: A's/Cubs .05 .02
Giants/Blue Jays
❑ 655 CL: Royals/Angels .05 .02
Padres/Orioles
❑ 656 CL: Mets/Astros .05 .02
Cards/Red Sox
❑ 657 CL: Rangers/Brewers .05 .02
Expos/Twins
❑ 658 CL: Dodgers/Reds .05 .02
Yankees/Pirates
❑ 659 CL: Indians/Mariners .05 .02
White Sox/Phillies
❑ 660A CL: Braves/Tigers .05 .02
Specials/Checklists
(Checklist-660 in small-
er print on card front)
❑ 660B CL: Braves/Tigers .05 .02
Specials/Checklists
(Checklist-660 in nor-
mal print on card front)

1992 Fleer Update

	Nm-Mt	Ex-Mt
COMP.FACT.SET (136)	100.00	30.00
COMPLETE SET (132)	80.00	24.00

❑ 1 Todd Frohwirth .50 .15
❑ 2 Alan Mills .50 .15
❑ 3 Rick Sutcliffe 1.00 .30
❑ 4 John Valentin RC 1.50 .45
❑ 5 Frank Viola 1.00 .30
❑ 6 Bob Zupcic RC .50 .15
❑ 7 Mike Butcher .50 .15
❑ 8 Chad Curtis RC 1.50 .45
❑ 9 Damion Easley RC 1.50 .45
❑ 10 Tim Salmon 2.50 .75
❑ 11 Julio Valera .50 .15
❑ 12 George Bell .50 .15
❑ 13 Roberto Hernandez .50 .15
❑ 14 Shawn Jeter RC .50 .15
❑ 15 Thomas Howard .50 .15
❑ 16 Jesse Levis .50 .15
❑ 17 Kenny Lofton 1.50 .45
❑ 18 Paul Sorrento .50 .15
❑ 19 Rico Brogna .50 .15
❑ 20 John Doherty RC .50 .15
❑ 21 Dan Gladden .50 .15
❑ 22 Buddy Groom RC .50 .15
❑ 23 Shawn Hare RC .50 .15
❑ 24 John Kiely .50 .15
❑ 25 Kurt Knudsen .50 .15
❑ 26 Gregg Jefferies .50 .15
❑ 27 Wally Joyner 1.00 .30
❑ 28 Kevin Koslofski .50 .15
❑ 29 Kevin McReynolds .50 .15
❑ 30 Rusty Meacham .50 .15
❑ 31 Keith Miller .50 .15
❑ 32 Hipolito Pichardo RC .50 .15
❑ 33 Jim Austin .50 .15
❑ 34 Scott Fletcher .50 .15
❑ 35 John Jaha RC 1.50 .45
❑ 36 Pat Listach RC 1.50 .45
❑ 37 Dave Nilsson .50 .15
❑ 38 Kevin Seitzer .50 .15
❑ 39 Tom Edens .50 .15
❑ 40 Pat Mahomes RC 1.50 .45
❑ 41 John Smiley .50 .15
❑ 42 Charlie Hayes .50 .15
❑ 43 Sam Militello .50 .15
❑ 44 Andy Stankiewicz .50 .15
❑ 45 Danny Tartabull .50 .15
❑ 46 Bob Wickman .50 .15
❑ 47 Jerry Browne .50 .15
❑ 48 Kevin Campbell .50 .15
❑ 49 Vince Horsman .50 .15
❑ 50 Troy Neel RC .50 .15
❑ 51 Ruben Sierra .50 .15
❑ 52 Bruce Walton .50 .15
❑ 53 Willie Wilson .50 .15
❑ 54 Bret Boone 2.50 .75
❑ 55 Dave Fleming .50 .15
❑ 56 Kevin Mitchell .50 .15
❑ 57 Jeff Nelson RC 2.50 .75
❑ 58 Shane Turner .50 .15
❑ 59 Jose Canseco 2.50 .75
❑ 60 Jeff Frye RC .50 .15
❑ 61 Danny Leon .50 .15
❑ 62 Roger Pavlik RC .50 .15
❑ 63 David Cone 1.00 .30
❑ 64 Pat Hentgen .50 .15
❑ 65 Randy Knorr .50 .15
❑ 66 Jack Morris 1.00 .30
❑ 67 Dave Winfield 1.00 .30
❑ 68 David Nied RC .50 .15
❑ 69 Otis Nixon .50 .15
❑ 70 Alejandro Pena .50 .15
❑ 71 Jeff Reardon 1.00 .30
❑ 72 Alex Arias RC .50 .15
❑ 73 Jim Bullinger .50 .15
❑ 74 Mike Morgan .50 .15
❑ 75 Rey Sanchez RC 1.50 .45
❑ 76 Bob Scanlan .50 .15
❑ 77 Sammy Sosa 4.00 1.20
❑ 78 Scott Bankhead .50 .15
❑ 79 Tim Belcher .50 .15
❑ 80 Steve Foster .50 .15
❑ 81 Willie Greene .50 .15
❑ 82 Bip Roberts .50 .15
❑ 83 Scott Ruskin .50 .15
❑ 84 Greg Swindell .50 .15
❑ 85 Juan Guerrero .50 .15
❑ 86 Butch Henry .50 .15
❑ 87 Doug Jones .50 .15
❑ 88 Brian Williams RC .50 .15
❑ 89 Tom Candiotti .50 .15
❑ 90 Eric Davis 1.00 .30
❑ 91 Carlos Hernandez .50 .15
❑ 92 Mike Piazza RC 60.00 18.00
❑ 93 Mike Sharperson .50 .15
❑ 94 Eric Young RC 1.50 .45
❑ 95 Moises Alou 1.00 .30
❑ 96 Greg Colbrunn .50 .15
❑ 97 Wil Cordero .50 .15
❑ 98 Ken Hill .50 .15
❑ 99 John Vander Wal RC 1.50 .45
❑ 100 John Wetteland 1.00 .30
❑ 101 Bobby Bonilla 1.00 .30
❑ 102 Eric Hillman RC .50 .15
❑ 103 Pat Howell .50 .15
❑ 104 Jeff Kent RC 10.00 3.00
❑ 105 Dick Schofield .50 .15
❑ 106 Ryan Thompson RC .50 .15
❑ 107 Chico Walker .50 .15
❑ 108 Juan Bell .50 .15
❑ 109 Mariano Duncan .50 .15
❑ 110 Jeff Grotewold .50 .15
❑ 111 Ben Rivera .50 .15
❑ 112 Curt Schilling 1.50 .45
❑ 113 Victor Cole .50 .15
❑ 114 Al Martin RC 1.50 .45
❑ 115 Roger Mason .50 .15
❑ 116 Blas Minor .50 .15
❑ 117 Tim Wakefield RC 5.00 1.50
❑ 118 Mark Clark RC .50 .15
❑ 119 Rheal Cormier .50 .15
❑ 120 Donovan Osborne .50 .15
❑ 121 Todd Worrell .50 .15
❑ 122 Jeremy Hernandez RC .50 .15
❑ 123 Randy Myers .50 .15
❑ 124 Frank Seminara RC .50 .15
❑ 125 Gary Sheffield 1.00 .30
❑ 126 Dan Walters .50 .15
❑ 127 Steve Hosey .50 .15
❑ 128 Mike Jackson .50 .15
❑ 129 Jim Pena .50 .15
❑ 130 Cory Snyder .50 .15
❑ 131 Bill Swift .50 .15
❑ 132 Checklist U1-U132 .50 .15

1994 Fleer Update

	Nm-Mt	Ex-Mt
COMP.FACT.SET (210)	50.00	15.00
COMPLETE SET (200)	.00	.00

❑ 1 Mark Eichhorn .25 .07
❑ 2 Sid Fernandez .25 .07
❑ 3 Leo Gomez .25 .07
❑ 4 Mike Oquist .25 .07
❑ 5 Rafael Palmeiro .75 .23
❑ 6 Chris Sabo .25 .07
❑ 7 Dwight Smith .25 .07
❑ 8 Lee Smith .50 .15
❑ 9 Damon Berryhill .25 .07
❑ 10 Wes Chamberlain .25 .07
❑ 11 Gar Finnvold .25 .07
❑ 12 Chris Howard .25 .07
❑ 13 Tim Naehring .25 .07
❑ 14 Otis Nixon .25 .07
❑ 15 Brian Anderson RC .50 .15
❑ 16 Jorge Fabregas .25 .07
❑ 17 Rex Hudler .25 .07
❑ 18 Bo Jackson 1.25 .35
❑ 19 Mark Leiter .25 .07
❑ 20 Spike Owen .25 .07
❑ 21 Harold Reynolds .50 .15
❑ 22 Chris Turner .25 .07
❑ 23 Dennis Cook .25 .07
❑ 24 Jose DeLeon .25 .07
❑ 25 Julio Franco .50 .15
❑ 26 Joe Hall .25 .07
❑ 27 Darrin Jackson .25 .07
❑ 28 Dane Johnson .25 .07
❑ 29 Norberto Martin .25 .07
❑ 30 Scott Sanderson .25 .07
❑ 31 Jason Grimsley .25 .07
❑ 32 Dennis Martinez .50 .15
❑ 33 Jack Morris .50 .15
❑ 34 Eddie Murray 1.25 .35
❑ 35 Chad Ogea .25 .07

❑ 36 Tony Pena	.25	.07
❑ 37 Paul Shuey	.25	.07
❑ 38 Omar Vizquel	.75	.23
❑ 39 Danny Bautista	.25	.07
❑ 40 Tim Belcher	.25	.07
❑ 41 Joe Boever	.25	.07
❑ 42 Storm Davis	.25	.07
❑ 43 Junior Felix	.25	.07
❑ 44 Mike Gardiner	.25	.07
❑ 45 Buddy Groom	.25	.07
❑ 46 Juan Samuel	.25	.07
❑ 47 Vince Coleman	.25	.07
❑ 48 Bob Hamelin	.25	.07
❑ 49 Dave Henderson	.25	.07
❑ 50 Rusty Meacham	.25	.07
❑ 51 Terry Shumpert	.25	.07
❑ 52 Jeff Bronkey	.25	.07
❑ 53 Alex Diaz	.25	.07
❑ 54 Brian Harper	.25	.07
❑ 55 Jose Mercedes	.25	.07
❑ 56 Jody Reed	.25	.07
❑ 57 Bob Scanlan	.25	.07
❑ 58 Turner Ward	.25	.07
❑ 59 Rich Becker	.25	.07
❑ 60 Alex Cole	.25	.07
❑ 61 Denny Hocking	.25	.07
❑ 62 Scott Leius	.25	.07
❑ 63 Pat Mahomes	.25	.07
❑ 64 Carlos Pulido	.25	.07
❑ 65 Dave Stevens	.25	.07
❑ 66 Matt Walbeck	.25	.07
❑ 67 Xavier Hernandez	.25	.07
❑ 68 Sterling Hitchcock	.25	.07
❑ 69 Terry Mulholland	.25	.07
❑ 70 Luis Polonia	.25	.07
❑ 71 Gerald Williams	.25	.07
❑ 72 Mark Acre RC	.25	.07
❑ 73 Geronimo Berroa	.25	.07
❑ 74 Rickey Henderson	1.25	.35
❑ 75 Stan Javier	.25	.07
❑ 76 Steve Karsay	.25	.07
❑ 77 Carlos Reyes	.25	.07
❑ 78 Bill Taylor RC	.50	.15
❑ 79 Eric Anthony	.25	.07
❑ 80 Bobby Ayala	.25	.07
❑ 81 Tim Davis	.25	.07
❑ 82 Felix Fermin	.25	.07
❑ 83 Reggie Jefferson	.25	.07
❑ 84 Keith Mitchell	.25	.07
❑ 85 Bill Risley	.25	.07
❑ 86 Alex Rodriguez RC	40.00	12.00
❑ 87 Roger Salkeld	.25	.07
❑ 88 Dan Wilson	.25	.07
❑ 89 Cris Carpenter	.25	.07
❑ 90 Will Clark	1.25	.35
❑ 91 Jeff Frye	.25	.07
❑ 92 Rick Helling	.25	.07
❑ 93 Chris James	.25	.07
❑ 94 Oddibe McDowell	.25	.07
❑ 95 Billy Ripken	.25	.07
❑ 96 Carlos Delgado	.75	.23
❑ 97 Alex Gonzalez	.25	.07
❑ 98 Shawn Green	1.25	.35
❑ 99 Darren Hall	.25	.07
❑ 100 Mike Huff	.25	.07
❑ 101 Mike Kelly	.25	.07
❑ 102 Roberto Kelly	.25	.07
❑ 103 Charlie O'Brien	.25	.07
❑ 104 Jose Oliva	.25	.07
❑ 105 Gregg Olson	.25	.07
❑ 106 Willie Banks	.25	.07
❑ 107 Jim Bullinger	.25	.07
❑ 108 Chuck Crim	.25	.07
❑ 109 Shawon Dunston	.25	.07
❑ 110 Karl Rhodes	.25	.07
❑ 111 Steve Trachsel	.25	.07
❑ 112 Anthony Young	.25	.07
❑ 113 Eddie Zambrano	.25	.07
❑ 114 Bret Boone	.50	.15
❑ 115 Jeff Brantley	.25	.07
❑ 116 Hector Carrasco	.25	.07
❑ 117 Tony Fernandez	.25	.07
❑ 118 Tim Fortugno	.25	.07
❑ 119 Erik Hanson	.25	.07
❑ 120 Chuck McElroy	.25	.07
❑ 121 Deion Sanders	.75	.23
❑ 122 Ellis Burks	.50	.15
❑ 123 Marvin Freeman	.25	.07
❑ 124 Mike Harkey	.25	.07
❑ 125 Howard Johnson	.25	.07
❑ 126 Mike Kingery	.25	.07
❑ 127 Nelson Liriano	.25	.07
❑ 128 Marcus Moore	.25	.07
❑ 129 Mike Munoz	.25	.07
❑ 130 Kevin Ritz	.25	.07
❑ 131 Walt Weiss	.25	.07
❑ 132 Kurt Abbott RC	.50	.15
❑ 133 Jerry Browne	.25	.07
❑ 134 Greg Colbrunn	.25	.07
❑ 135 Jeremy Hernandez	.25	.07
❑ 136 Dave Magadan	.25	.07
❑ 137 Kurt Miller	.25	.07
❑ 138 Robb Nen	.50	.15
❑ 139 Jesus Tavarez RC	.25	.07
❑ 140 Sid Bream	.25	.07
❑ 141 Tom Edens	.25	.07
❑ 142 Tony Eusebio	.25	.07
❑ 143 John Hudek RC	.25	.07
❑ 144 Brian L. Hunter	.25	.07
❑ 145 Orlando Miller	.25	.07
❑ 146 James Mouton	.25	.07
❑ 147 Shane Reynolds	.25	.07
❑ 148 Rafael Bournigal	.25	.07
❑ 149 Delino DeShields	.25	.07
❑ 150 Garey Ingram RC	.25	.07
❑ 151 Chan Ho Park RC	.75	.23
❑ 152 Wil Cordero	.25	.07
❑ 153 Pedro Martinez	1.25	.35
❑ 154 Randy Milligan	.25	.07
❑ 155 Lenny Webster	.25	.07
❑ 156 Rico Brogna	.25	.07
❑ 157 Josias Manzanillo	.25	.07
❑ 158 Kevin McReynolds	.25	.07
❑ 159 Mike Remlinger	.25	.07
❑ 160 David Segui	.25	.07
❑ 161 Pete Smith	.25	.07
❑ 162 Kelly Stinnett RC	.50	.15
❑ 163 Jose Vizcaino	.25	.07
❑ 164 Billy Hatcher	.25	.07
❑ 165 Doug Jones	.25	.07
❑ 166 Mike Lieberthal	.50	.15
❑ 167 Tony Longmire	.25	.07
❑ 168 Bobby Munoz	.25	.07
❑ 169 Paul Quantrill	.25	.07
❑ 170 Heathcliff Slocumb	.25	.07
❑ 171 Fernando Valenzuela	.50	.15
❑ 172 Mark Dewey	.25	.07
❑ 173 Brian R. Hunter	.25	.07
❑ 174 Jon Lieber	.25	.07
❑ 175 Ravelo Manzanillo	.25	.07
❑ 176 Dan Miceli	.25	.07
❑ 177 Rick White	.25	.07
❑ 178 Bryan Eversgerd	.25	.07
❑ 179 John Habyan	.25	.07
❑ 180 Terry McGriff	.25	.07
❑ 181 Vicente Palacios	.25	.07
❑ 182 Rich Rodriguez	.25	.07
❑ 183 Rick Sutcliffe	.50	.15
❑ 184 Donnie Elliott	.25	.07
❑ 185 Joey Hamilton	.25	.07
❑ 186 Tim Hyers RC	.25	.07
❑ 187 Luis Lopez	.25	.07
❑ 188 Ray McDavid	.25	.07
❑ 189 Bip Roberts	.25	.07
❑ 190 Scott Sanders	.25	.07
❑ 191 Eddie Williams	.25	.07
❑ 192 Steve Frey	.25	.07
❑ 193 Pat Gomez	.25	.07
❑ 194 Rich Monteleone	.25	.07
❑ 195 Mark Portugal	.25	.07
❑ 196 Darryl Strawberry	.50	.15
❑ 197 Salomon Torres	.25	.07
❑ 198 W.VanLandingham RC	.25	.07
❑ 199 Checklist	.25	.07
❑ 200 Checklist	.25	.07

1997 Fleer

	Nm-Mt	Ex-Mt
COMPLETE SET (761)	110.00	33.00
COMP. SERIES 1 (500)	60.00	18.00
COMP. SERIES 2 (261)	50.00	15.00
COMMON CARD (1-750)	.30	.09
COMMON CARD (751-761)	.50	.15

❑ 1 Roberto Alomar	.50	.15
❑ 2 Brady Anderson	.30	.09
❑ 3 Bobby Bonilla	.30	.09
❑ 4 Rocky Coppinger	.30	.09
❑ 5 Cesar Devarez	.30	.09
❑ 6 Scott Erickson	.30	.09
❑ 7 Jeffrey Hammonds	.30	.09
❑ 8 Chris Hoiles	.30	.09
❑ 9 Eddie Murray	.75	.23
❑ 10 Mike Mussina	.50	.15
❑ 11 Randy Myers	.30	.09
❑ 12 Rafael Palmeiro	.50	.15
❑ 13 Cal Ripken	2.50	.75
❑ 14 B.J. Surhoff	.30	.09
❑ 15 David Wells	.30	.09
❑ 16 Todd Zeile	.30	.09
❑ 17 Darren Bragg	.30	.09
❑ 18 Jose Canseco	.75	.23
❑ 19 Roger Clemens	1.50	.45
❑ 20 Wil Cordero	.30	.09
❑ 21 Jeff Frye	.30	.09
❑ 22 Nomar Garciaparra	1.25	.35
❑ 23 Tom Gordon	.30	.09
❑ 24 Mike Greenwell	.30	.09
❑ 25 Reggie Jefferson	.30	.09
❑ 26 Jose Malave	.30	.09
❑ 27 Tim Naehring	.30	.09
❑ 28 Troy O'Leary	.30	.09
❑ 29 Heathcliff Slocumb	.30	.09
❑ 30 Mike Stanley	.30	.09
❑ 31 John Valentin	.30	.09
❑ 32 Mo Vaughn	.30	.09
❑ 33 Tim Wakefield	.30	.09
❑ 34 Garret Anderson	.30	.09
❑ 35 George Arias	.30	.09
❑ 36 Shawn Boskie	.30	.09
❑ 37 Chili Davis	.30	.09
❑ 38 Jason Dickson	.30	.09
❑ 39 Gary DiSarcina	.30	.09
❑ 40 Jim Edmonds	.30	.09
❑ 41 Darin Erstad	.30	.09
❑ 42 Jorge Fabregas	.30	.09
❑ 43 Chuck Finley	.30	.09
❑ 44 Todd Greene	.30	.09
❑ 45 Mike Holtz	.30	.09
❑ 46 Rex Hudler	.30	.09
❑ 47 Mike James	.30	.09
❑ 48 Mark Langston	.30	.09
❑ 49 Troy Percival	.30	.09
❑ 50 Tim Salmon	.50	.15
❑ 51 Jeff Schmidt	.30	.09
❑ 52 J.T. Snow	.30	.09
❑ 53 Randy Velarde	.30	.09
❑ 54 Wilson Alvarez	.30	.09
❑ 55 Harold Baines	.30	.09
❑ 56 James Baldwin	.30	.09
❑ 57 Jason Bere	.30	.09
❑ 58 Mike Cameron	.30	.09
❑ 59 Ray Durham	.30	.09
❑ 60 Alex Fernandez	.30	.09
❑ 61 Ozzie Guillen	.30	.09
❑ 62 Roberto Hernandez	.30	.09
❑ 63 Ron Karkovice	.30	.09
❑ 64 Darren Lewis	.30	.09
❑ 65 Dave Martinez	.30	.09
❑ 66 Lyle Mouton	.30	.09
❑ 67 Greg Norton	.30	.09
❑ 68 Tony Phillips	.30	.09

❑ 69 Chris Snopek .30 .09
❑ 70 Kevin Tapani .30 .09
❑ 71 Danny Tartabull .30 .09
❑ 72 Frank Thomas .75 .23
❑ 73 Robin Ventura .30 .09
❑ 74 Sandy Alomar Jr. .30 .09
❑ 75 Albert Belle .30 .09
❑ 76 Mark Carreon .30 .09
❑ 77 Julio Franco .30 .09
❑ 78 Brian Giles RC 1.50 .45
❑ 79 Orel Hershiser .30 .09
❑ 80 Kenny Lofton .30 .09
❑ 81 Dennis Martinez .30 .09
❑ 82 Jack McDowell .30 .09
❑ 83 Jose Mesa .30 .09
❑ 84 Charles Nagy .30 .09
❑ 85 Chad Ogea .30 .09
❑ 86 Eric Plunk .30 .09
❑ 87 Manny Ramirez .50 .15
❑ 88 Kevin Seitzer .30 .09
❑ 89 Julian Tavarez .30 .09
❑ 90 Jim Thome .75 .23
❑ 91 Jose Vizcaino .30 .09
❑ 92 Omar Vizquel .50 .15
❑ 93 Brad Ausmus .30 .09
❑ 94 Kimera Bartee .30 .09
❑ 95 Raul Casanova .30 .09
❑ 96 Tony Clark .30 .09
❑ 97 John Cummings .30 .09
❑ 98 Travis Fryman .30 .09
❑ 99 Bob Higginson .30 .09
❑ 100 Mark Lewis .30 .09
❑ 101 Felipe Lira .30 .09
❑ 102 Phil Nevin .30 .09
❑ 103 Melvin Nieves .30 .09
❑ 104 Curtis Pride .30 .09
❑ 105 A.J. Sager .30 .09
❑ 106 Ruben Sierra .30 .09
❑ 107 Justin Thompson .30 .09
❑ 108 Alan Trammell .30 .09
❑ 109 Kevin Appier .30 .09
❑ 110 Tim Belcher .30 .09
❑ 111 Jaime Bluma .30 .09
❑ 112 Johnny Damon .50 .15
❑ 113 Tom Goodwin .30 .09
❑ 114 Chris Haney .30 .09
❑ 115 Keith Lockhart .30 .09
❑ 116 Mike Macfarlane .30 .09
❑ 117 Jeff Montgomery .30 .09
❑ 118 Jose Offerman .30 .09
❑ 119 Craig Paquette .30 .09
❑ 120 Joe Randa .30 .09
❑ 121 Bip Roberts .30 .09
❑ 122 Jose Rosado .30 .09
❑ 123 Mike Sweeney .30 .09
❑ 124 Michael Tucker .30 .09
❑ 125 Jeromy Burnitz .30 .09
❑ 126 Jeff Cirillo .30 .09
❑ 127 Jeff D'Amico .30 .09
❑ 128 Mike Fetters .30 .09
❑ 129 John Jaha .30 .09
❑ 130 Scott Karl .30 .09
❑ 131 Jesse Levis .30 .09
❑ 132 Mark Loretta .30 .09
❑ 133 Mike Matheny .30 .09
❑ 134 Ben McDonald .30 .09
❑ 135 Matt Mieske .30 .09
❑ 136 Marc Newfield .30 .09
❑ 137 Dave Nilsson .30 .09
❑ 138 Jose Valentin .30 .09
❑ 139 Fernando Vina .30 .09
❑ 140 Bob Wickman .30 .09
❑ 141 Gerald Williams .30 .09
❑ 142 Rick Aguilera .30 .09
❑ 143 Rich Becker .30 .09
❑ 144 Ron Coomer .30 .09
❑ 145 Marty Cordova .30 .09
❑ 146 Roberto Kelly .30 .09
❑ 147 Chuck Knoblauch .30 .09
❑ 148 Matt Lawton .30 .09
❑ 149 Pat Meares .30 .09
❑ 150 Travis Miller .30 .09
❑ 151 Paul Molitor .50 .15
❑ 152 Greg Myers .30 .09
❑ 153 Dan Naulty .30 .09
❑ 154 Kirby Puckett .75 .23
❑ 155 Brad Radke .30 .09
❑ 156 Frank Rodriguez .30 .09
❑ 157 Scott Stahoviak .30 .09
❑ 158 Dave Stevens .30 .09
❑ 159 Matt Walbeck .30 .09
❑ 160 Todd Walker .30 .09
❑ 161 Wade Boggs .50 .15
❑ 162 David Cone .30 .09
❑ 163 Mariano Duncan .30 .09
❑ 164 Cecil Fielder .30 .09
❑ 165 Joe Girardi .30 .09
❑ 166 Dwight Gooden .30 .09
❑ 167 Charlie Hayes .30 .09
❑ 168 Derek Jeter 2.00 .60
❑ 169 Jimmy Key .30 .09
❑ 170 Jim Leyritz .30 .09
❑ 171 Tino Martinez .50 .15
❑ 172 Ramiro Mendoza RC .30 .09
❑ 173 Jeff Nelson .30 .09
❑ 174 Paul O'Neill .50 .15
❑ 175 Andy Pettitte .50 .15
❑ 176 Mariano Rivera .50 .15
❑ 177 Ruben Rivera .30 .09
❑ 178 Kenny Rogers .30 .09
❑ 179 Darryl Strawberry .30 .09
❑ 180 John Wetteland .30 .09
❑ 181 Bernie Williams .50 .15
❑ 182 Willie Adams .30 .09
❑ 183 Tony Batista .30 .09
❑ 184 Geronimo Berroa .30 .09
❑ 185 Mike Bordick .30 .09
❑ 186 Scott Brosius .30 .09
❑ 187 Bobby Chouinard .30 .09
❑ 188 Jim Corsi .30 .09
❑ 189 Brent Gates .30 .09
❑ 190 Jason Giambi .30 .09
❑ 191 Jose Herrera .30 .09
❑ 192 Damon Mashore .30 .09
❑ 193 Mark McGwire 2.00 .60
❑ 194 Mike Mohler .30 .09
❑ 195 Scott Spiezio .30 .09
❑ 196 Terry Steinbach .30 .09
❑ 197 Bill Taylor .30 .09
❑ 198 John Wasdin .30 .09
❑ 199 Steve Wojciechowski .30 .09
❑ 200 Ernie Young .30 .09
❑ 201 Rich Amaral .30 .09
❑ 202 Jay Buhner .30 .09
❑ 203 Norm Charlton .30 .09
❑ 204 Joey Cora .30 .09
❑ 205 Russ Davis .30 .09
❑ 206 Ken Griffey Jr. 1.25 .35
❑ 207 Sterling Hitchcock .30 .09
❑ 208 Brian Hunter .30 .09
❑ 209 Raul Ibanez .30 .09
❑ 210 Randy Johnson .75 .23
❑ 211 Edgar Martinez .50 .15
❑ 212 Jamie Moyer .30 .09
❑ 213 Alex Rodriguez 1.25 .35
❑ 214 Paul Sorrento .30 .09
❑ 215 Matt Wagner .30 .09
❑ 216 Bob Wells .30 .09
❑ 217 Dan Wilson .30 .09
❑ 218 Damon Buford .30 .09
❑ 219 Will Clark .75 .23
❑ 220 Kevin Elster .30 .09
❑ 221 Juan Gonzalez .50 .15
❑ 222 Rusty Greer .30 .09
❑ 223 Kevin Gross .30 .09
❑ 224 Darryl Hamilton .30 .09
❑ 225 Mike Henneman .30 .09
❑ 226 Ken Hill .30 .09
❑ 227 Mark McLemore .30 .09
❑ 228 Darren Oliver .30 .09
❑ 229 Dean Palmer .30 .09
❑ 230 Roger Pavlik .30 .09
❑ 231 Ivan Rodriguez .75 .23
❑ 232 Mickey Tettleton .30 .09
❑ 233 Bobby Witt .30 .09
❑ 234 Jacob Brumfield .30 .09
❑ 235 Joe Carter .30 .09
❑ 236 Tim Crabtree .30 .09
❑ 237 Carlos Delgado .30 .09
❑ 238 Huck Flener .30 .09
❑ 239 Alex Gonzalez .30 .09
❑ 240 Shawn Green .30 .09
❑ 241 Juan Guzman .30 .09
❑ 242 Pat Hentgen .30 .09
❑ 243 Marty Janzen .30 .09
❑ 244 Sandy Martinez .30 .09
❑ 245 Otis Nixon .30 .09
❑ 246 Charlie O'Brien .30 .09
❑ 247 John Olerud .30 .09
❑ 248 Robert Perez .30 .09
❑ 249 Ed Sprague .30 .09
❑ 250 Mike Timlin .30 .09
❑ 251 Steve Avery .30 .09
❑ 252 Jeff Blauser .30 .09
❑ 253 Brad Clontz .30 .09
❑ 254 Jermaine Dye .30 .09
❑ 255 Tom Glavine .50 .15
❑ 256 Marquis Grissom .30 .09
❑ 257 Andruw Jones .30 .09
❑ 258 Chipper Jones .75 .23
❑ 259 David Justice .30 .09
❑ 260 Ryan Klesko .30 .09
❑ 261 Mark Lemke .30 .09
❑ 262 Javier Lopez .30 .09
❑ 263 Greg Maddux 1.25 .35
❑ 264 Fred McGriff .50 .15
❑ 265 Greg McMichael .30 .09
❑ 266 Denny Neagle .30 .09
❑ 267 Terry Pendleton .30 .09
❑ 268 Eddie Perez .30 .09
❑ 269 John Smoltz .50 .15
❑ 270 Terrell Wade .30 .09
❑ 271 Mark Wohlers .30 .09
❑ 272 Terry Adams .30 .09
❑ 273 Brant Brown .30 .09
❑ 274 Leo Gomez .30 .09
❑ 275 Luis Gonzalez .30 .09
❑ 276 Mark Grace .50 .15
❑ 277 Tyler Houston .30 .09
❑ 278 Robin Jennings .30 .09
❑ 279 Brooks Kieschnick .30 .09
❑ 280 Brian McRae .30 .09
❑ 281 Jaime Navarro .30 .09
❑ 282 Ryne Sandberg 1.25 .35
❑ 283 Scott Servais .30 .09
❑ 284 Sammy Sosa 1.25 .35
❑ 285 Dave Swartzbaugh .30 .09
❑ 286 Amaury Telemaco .30 .09
❑ 287 Steve Trachsel .30 .09
❑ 288 Pedro Valdes .30 .09
❑ 289 Turk Wendell .30 .09
❑ 290 Bret Boone .30 .09
❑ 291 Jeff Branson .30 .09
❑ 292 Jeff Brantley .30 .09
❑ 293 Eric Davis .30 .09
❑ 294 Willie Greene .30 .09
❑ 295 Thomas Howard .30 .09
❑ 296 Barry Larkin .50 .15
❑ 297 Kevin Mitchell .30 .09
❑ 298 Hal Morris .30 .09
❑ 299 Chad Mottola .30 .09
❑ 300 Joe Oliver .30 .09
❑ 301 Mark Portugal .30 .09
❑ 302 Roger Salkeld .30 .09
❑ 303 Reggie Sanders .30 .09
❑ 304 Pete Schourek .30 .09
❑ 305 John Smiley .30 .09
❑ 306 Eddie Taubensee .30 .09
❑ 307 Dante Bichette .30 .09
❑ 308 Ellis Burks .30 .09
❑ 309 Vinny Castilla .30 .09
❑ 310 Andres Galarraga .30 .09
❑ 311 Curt Leskanic .30 .09
❑ 312 Quinton McCracken .30 .09
❑ 313 Neifi Perez .30 .09
❑ 314 Jeff Reed .30 .09
❑ 315 Steve Reed .30 .09
❑ 316 Armando Reynoso .30 .09
❑ 317 Kevin Ritz .30 .09
❑ 318 Bruce Ruffin .30 .09
❑ 319 Larry Walker .50 .15
❑ 320 Walt Weiss .30 .09
❑ 321 Jamey Wright .30 .09
❑ 322 Eric Young .30 .09
❑ 323 Kurt Abbott .30 .09
❑ 324 Alex Arias .30 .09
❑ 325 Kevin Brown .30 .09
❑ 326 Luis Castillo .30 .09

❑ 327	Greg Colbrunn	.30	.09
❑ 328	Jeff Conine	.30	.09
❑ 329	Andre Dawson	.30	.09
❑ 330	Charles Johnson	.30	.09
❑ 331	Al Leiter	.30	.09
❑ 332	Ralph Milliard	.30	.09
❑ 333	Robb Nen	.30	.09
❑ 334	Pat Rapp	.30	.09
❑ 335	Edgar Renteria	.30	.09
❑ 336	Gary Sheffield	.30	.09
❑ 337	Devon White	.30	.09
❑ 338	Bob Abreu	.30	.09
❑ 339	Jeff Bagwell	.50	.15
❑ 340	Derek Bell	.30	.09
❑ 341	Sean Berry	.30	.09
❑ 342	Craig Biggio	.50	.15
❑ 343	Doug Drabek	.30	.09
❑ 344	Tony Eusebio	.30	.09
❑ 345	Ricky Gutierrez	.30	.09
❑ 346	Mike Hampton	.30	.09
❑ 347	Brian Hunter	.30	.09
❑ 348	Todd Jones	.30	.09
❑ 349	Darryl Kile	.30	.09
❑ 350	Derrick May	.30	.09
❑ 351	Orlando Miller	.30	.09
❑ 352	James Mouton	.30	.09
❑ 353	Shane Reynolds	.30	.09
❑ 354	Billy Wagner	.30	.09
❑ 355	Donne Wall	.30	.09
❑ 356	Mike Blowers	.30	.09
❑ 357	Brett Butler	.30	.09
❑ 358	Roger Cedeno	.30	.09
❑ 359	Chad Curtis	.30	.09
❑ 360	Delino DeShields	.30	.09
❑ 361	Greg Gagne	.30	.09
❑ 362	Karim Garcia	.30	.09
❑ 363	Wilton Guerrero	.30	.09
❑ 364	Todd Hollandsworth	.30	.09
❑ 365	Eric Karros	.30	.09
❑ 366	Ramon Martinez	.30	.09
❑ 367	Raul Mondesi	.30	.09
❑ 368	Hideo Nomo	.75	.23
❑ 369	Antonio Osuna	.30	.09
❑ 370	Chan Ho Park	.30	.09
❑ 371	Mike Piazza	1.25	.35
❑ 372	Ismael Valdes	.30	.09
❑ 373	Todd Worrell	.30	.09
❑ 374	Moises Alou	.30	.09
❑ 375	Shane Andrews	.30	.09
❑ 376	Yamil Benitez	.30	.09
❑ 377	Jeff Fassero	.30	.09
❑ 378	Darrin Fletcher	.30	.09
❑ 379	Cliff Floyd	.30	.09
❑ 380	Mark Grudzielanek	.30	.09
❑ 381	Mike Lansing	.30	.09
❑ 382	Barry Manuel	.30	.09
❑ 383	Pedro Martinez	.75	.23
❑ 384	Henry Rodriguez	.30	.09
❑ 385	Mel Rojas	.30	.09
❑ 386	F.P. Santangelo	.30	.09
❑ 387	David Segui	.30	.09
❑ 388	Ugueth Urbina	.30	.09
❑ 389	Rondell White	.30	.09
❑ 390	Edgardo Alfonzo	.30	.09
❑ 391	Carlos Baerga	.30	.09
❑ 392	Mark Clark	.30	.09
❑ 393	Alvaro Espinoza	.30	.09
❑ 394	John Franco	.30	.09
❑ 395	Bernard Gilkey	.30	.09
❑ 396	Pete Harnisch	.30	.09
❑ 397	Todd Hundley	.30	.09
❑ 398	Butch Huskey	.30	.09
❑ 399	Jason Isringhausen	.30	.09
❑ 400	Lance Johnson	.30	.09
❑ 401	Bobby Jones	.30	.09
❑ 402	Alex Ochoa	.30	.09
❑ 403	Rey Ordonez	.30	.09
❑ 404	Robert Person	.30	.09
❑ 405	Paul Wilson	.30	.09
❑ 406	Matt Beech	.30	.09
❑ 407	Ron Blazier	.30	.09
❑ 408	Ricky Bottalico	.30	.09
❑ 409	Lenny Dykstra	.30	.09
❑ 410	Jim Eisenreich	.30	.09
❑ 411	Bobby Estalella	.30	.09
❑ 412	Mike Grace	.30	.09
❑ 413	Gregg Jefferies	.30	.09
❑ 414	Mike Lieberthal	.30	.09
❑ 415	Wendell Magee	.30	.09
❑ 416	Mickey Morandini	.30	.09
❑ 417	Ricky Otero	.30	.09
❑ 418	Scott Rolen	.75	.23
❑ 419	Ken Ryan	.30	.09
❑ 420	Benito Santiago	.30	.09
❑ 421	Curt Schilling	.30	.09
❑ 422	Kevin Sefcik	.30	.09
❑ 423	Jermaine Allensworth	.30	.09
❑ 424	Trey Beamon	.30	.09
❑ 425	Jay Bell	.30	.09
❑ 426	Francisco Cordova	.30	.09
❑ 427	Carlos Garcia	.30	.09
❑ 428	Mark Johnson	.30	.09
❑ 429	Jason Kendall	.30	.09
❑ 430	Jeff King	.30	.09
❑ 431	Jon Lieber	.30	.09
❑ 432	Al Martin	.30	.09
❑ 433	Orlando Merced	.30	.09
❑ 434	Ramon Morel	.30	.09
❑ 435	Matt Ruebel	.30	.09
❑ 436	Jason Schmidt	.30	.09
❑ 437	Marc Wilkins	.30	.09
❑ 438	Alan Benes	.30	.09
❑ 439	Andy Benes	.30	.09
❑ 440	Royce Clayton	.30	.09
❑ 441	Dennis Eckersley	.30	.09
❑ 442	Gary Gaetti	.30	.09
❑ 443	Ron Gant	.30	.09
❑ 444	Aaron Holbert	.30	.09
❑ 445	Brian Jordan	.30	.09
❑ 446	Ray Lankford	.30	.09
❑ 447	John Mabry	.30	.09
❑ 448	T.J. Mathews	.30	.09
❑ 449	Willie McGee	.30	.09
❑ 450	Donovan Osborne	.30	.09
❑ 451	Tom Pagnozzi	.30	.09
❑ 452	Ozzie Smith	1.25	.35
❑ 453	Todd Stottlemyre	.30	.09
❑ 454	Mark Sweeney	.30	.09
❑ 455	Dmitri Young	.30	.09
❑ 456	Andy Ashby	.30	.09
❑ 457	Ken Caminiti	.30	.09
❑ 458	Archi Cianfrocco	.30	.09
❑ 459	Steve Finley	.30	.09
❑ 460	John Flaherty	.30	.09
❑ 461	Chris Gomez	.30	.09
❑ 462	Tony Gwynn	1.00	.30
❑ 463	Joey Hamilton	.30	.09
❑ 464	Rickey Henderson	.75	.23
❑ 465	Trevor Hoffman	.30	.09
❑ 466	Brian Johnson	.30	.09
❑ 467	Wally Joyner	.30	.09
❑ 468	Jody Reed	.30	.09
❑ 469	Scott Sanders	.30	.09
❑ 470	Bob Tewksbury	.30	.09
❑ 471	Fernando Valenzuela	.30	.09
❑ 472	Greg Vaughn	.30	.09
❑ 473	Tim Worrell	.30	.09
❑ 474	Rich Aurilia	.30	.09
❑ 475	Rod Beck	.30	.09
❑ 476	Marvin Benard	.30	.09
❑ 477	Barry Bonds	2.00	.60
❑ 478	Jay Canizaro	.30	.09
❑ 479	Shawon Dunston	.30	.09
❑ 480	Shawn Estes	.30	.09
❑ 481	Mark Gardner	.30	.09
❑ 482	Glenallen Hill	.30	.09
❑ 483	Stan Javier	.30	.09
❑ 484	Marcus Jensen	.30	.09
❑ 485	Bill Mueller RC	3.00	.90
❑ 486	Wm. VanLandingham	.30	.09
❑ 487	Allen Watson	.30	.09
❑ 488	Rick Wilkins	.30	.09
❑ 489	Matt Williams	.30	.09
❑ 490	Desi Wilson	.30	.09
❑ 491	Albert Belle CL	.30	.09
❑ 492	Ken Griffey Jr. CL	.75	.23
❑ 493	Andruw Jones CL	.30	.09
❑ 494	Chipper Jones CL	.50	.15
❑ 495	Mark McGwire CL	1.00	.30
❑ 496	Paul Molitor CL	.30	.09
❑ 497	Mike Piazza CL	.75	.23
❑ 498	Cal Ripken CL	1.25	.35
❑ 499	Alex Rodriguez CL	.75	.23
❑ 500	Frank Thomas CL	.50	.15
❑ 501	Kenny Lofton	.30	.09
❑ 502	Carlos Perez	.30	.09
❑ 503	Tim Raines	.30	.09
❑ 504	Danny Patterson	.30	.09
❑ 505	Derrick May	.30	.09
❑ 506	Dave Hollins	.30	.09
❑ 507	Felipe Crespo	.30	.09
❑ 508	Brian Banks	.30	.09
❑ 509	Jeff Kent	.30	.09
❑ 510	Bubba Trammell RC	.40	.12
❑ 511	Robert Person	.30	.09
❑ 512	David Arias-Ortiz RC	15.00	4.50
❑ 513	Ryan Jones	.30	.09
❑ 514	David Justice	.30	.09
❑ 515	Will Cunnane	.30	.09
❑ 516	Russ Johnson	.30	.09
❑ 517	John Burkett	.30	.09
❑ 518	Robinson Checo RC	.30	.09
❑ 519	Ricardo Rincon RC	.30	.09
❑ 520	Woody Williams	.30	.09
❑ 521	Rick Helling	.30	.09
❑ 522	Jorge Posada	.50	.15
❑ 523	Kevin Orie	.30	.09
❑ 524	Fernando Tatis RC	.40	.12
❑ 525	Jermaine Dye	.30	.09
❑ 526	Brian Hunter	.30	.09
❑ 527	Greg McMichael	.30	.09
❑ 528	Matt Wagner	.30	.09
❑ 529	Richie Sexson	.30	.09
❑ 530	Scott Ruffcorn	.30	.09
❑ 531	Luis Gonzalez	.30	.09
❑ 532	Mike Johnson RC	.30	.09
❑ 533	Mark Petkovsek	.30	.09
❑ 534	Doug Drabek	.30	.09
❑ 535	Jose Canseco	.75	.23
❑ 536	Bobby Bonilla	.30	.09
❑ 537	J.T. Snow	.30	.09
❑ 538	Shawon Dunston	.30	.09
❑ 539	John Ericks	.30	.09
❑ 540	Terry Steinbach	.30	.09
❑ 541	Jay Bell	.30	.09
❑ 542	Joe Borowski RC	.30	.09
❑ 543	David Wells	.30	.09
❑ 544	Justin Towle RC	.30	.09
❑ 545	Mike Blowers	.30	.09
❑ 546	Shannon Stewart	.30	.09
❑ 547	Rudy Pemberton	.30	.09
❑ 548	Bill Swift	.30	.09
❑ 549	Osvaldo Fernandez	.30	.09
❑ 550	Eddie Murray	.75	.23
❑ 551	Don Wengert	.30	.09
❑ 552	Brad Ausmus	.30	.09
❑ 553	Carlos Garcia	.30	.09
❑ 554	Jose Guillen	.30	.09
❑ 555	Rheal Cormier	.30	.09
❑ 556	Doug Brocail	.30	.09
❑ 557	Rex Hudler	.30	.09
❑ 558	Armando Benitez	.30	.09
❑ 559	Eli Marrero	.30	.09
❑ 560	Ricky Ledee RC	.40	.12
❑ 561	Bartolo Colon	.30	.09
❑ 562	Quilvio Veras	.30	.09
❑ 563	Alex Fernandez	.30	.09
❑ 564	Darren Dreifort	.30	.09
❑ 565	Benji Gil	.30	.09
❑ 566	Kent Mercker	.30	.09
❑ 567	Glendon Rusch	.30	.09
❑ 568	Ramon Tatis RC	.30	.09
❑ 569	Roger Clemens	1.50	.45
❑ 570	Mark Lewis	.30	.09
❑ 571	Emil Brown RC	.30	.09
❑ 572	Jaime Navarro	.30	.09
❑ 573	Sherman Obando	.30	.09
❑ 574	John Wasdin	.30	.09
❑ 575	Calvin Maduro	.30	.09
❑ 576	Todd Jones	.30	.09
❑ 577	Orlando Merced	.30	.09
❑ 578	Cal Eldred	.30	.09
❑ 579	Mark Gubicza	.30	.09
❑ 580	Michael Tucker	.30	.09
❑ 581	Tony Saunders RC	.30	.09
❑ 582	Garvin Alston	.30	.09
❑ 583	Joe Roa	.30	.09
❑ 584	Brady Raggio RC	.30	.09

❑ 585 Jimmy Key .30 .09
❑ 586 Marc Sagmoen RC .30 .09
❑ 587 Jim Bullinger .30 .09
❑ 588 Yorkis Perez .30 .09
❑ 589 Jose Cruz Jr. RC .50 .15
❑ 590 Mike Stanton .30 .09
❑ 591 Deivi Cruz RC .40 .12
❑ 592 Steve Karsay .30 .09
❑ 593 Mike Trombley .30 .09
❑ 594 Doug Glanville .30 .09
❑ 595 Scott Sanders .30 .09
❑ 596 Thomas Howard .30 .09
❑ 597 T.J. Staton RC .30 .09
❑ 598 Garrett Stephenson .30 .09
❑ 599 Rico Brogna .30 .09
❑ 600 Albert Belle .30 .09
❑ 601 Jose Vizcaino .30 .09
❑ 602 Chili Davis .30 .09
❑ 603 Shane Mack .30 .09
❑ 604 Jim Eisenreich .30 .09
❑ 605 Todd Zeile .30 .09
❑ 606 Brian Boehringer RC .30 .09
❑ 607 Paul Shuey .30 .09
❑ 608 Kevin Tapani .30 .09
❑ 609 John Wetteland .30 .09
❑ 610 Jim Leyritz .30 .09
❑ 611 Ray Montgomery RC .30 .09
❑ 612 Doug Bochtler .30 .09
❑ 613 Wady Almonte RC .30 .09
❑ 614 Danny Tartabull .30 .09
❑ 615 Orlando Miller .30 .09
❑ 616 Bobby Ayala .30 .09
❑ 617 Tony Graffanino .30 .09
❑ 618 Marc Valdes .30 .09
❑ 619 Ron Villone .30 .09
❑ 620 Derrek Lee .30 .09
❑ 621 Greg Colbrunn .30 .09
❑ 622 Felix Heredia RC .40 .12
❑ 623 Carl Everett .30 .09
❑ 624 Mark Thompson .30 .09
❑ 625 Jeff Granger .30 .09
❑ 626 Damian Jackson .30 .09
❑ 627 Mark Leiter .30 .09
❑ 628 Chris Holt .30 .09
❑ 629 Dario Veras RC .30 .09
❑ 630 Dave Burba .30 .09
❑ 631 Darryl Hamilton .30 .09
❑ 632 Mark Acre .30 .09
❑ 633 F.Hernandez RC .30 .09
❑ 634 Terry Mulholland .30 .09
❑ 635 Dustin Hermanson .30 .09
❑ 636 Delino DeShields .30 .09
❑ 637 Steve Avery .30 .09
❑ 638 Tony Womack RC .50 .15
❑ 639 Mark Whiten .30 .09
❑ 640 Marquis Grissom .30 .09
❑ 641 Xavier Hernandez .30 .09
❑ 642 Eric Davis .30 .09
❑ 643 Bob Tewksbury .30 .09
❑ 644 Dante Powell .30 .09
❑ 645 Carlos Castillo RC .30 .09
❑ 646 Chris Widger .30 .09
❑ 647 Moises Alou .30 .09
❑ 648 Pat Listach .30 .09
❑ 649 Edgar Ramos RC .30 .09
❑ 650 Deion Sanders .50 .15
❑ 651 John Olerud .30 .09
❑ 652 Todd Dunwoody .30 .09
❑ 653 Randall Simon RC .40 .12
❑ 654 Dan Carlson .30 .09
❑ 655 Matt Williams .30 .09
❑ 656 Jeff King .30 .09
❑ 657 Luis Alicea .30 .09
❑ 658 Brian Moehler RC .30 .09
❑ 659 Ariel Prieto .30 .09
❑ 660 Kevin Elster .30 .09
❑ 661 Mark Hutton .30 .09
❑ 662 Aaron Sele .30 .09
❑ 663 Graeme Lloyd .30 .09
❑ 664 John Burke .30 .09
❑ 665 Mel Rojas .30 .09
❑ 666 Sid Fernandez .30 .09
❑ 667 Pedro Astacio .30 .09
❑ 668 Jeff Abbott .30 .09
❑ 669 Darren Daulton .30 .09
❑ 670 Mike Bordick .30 .09
❑ 671 Sterling Hitchcock .30 .09
❑ 672 Damion Easley .30 .09
❑ 673 Armando Reynoso .30 .09
❑ 674 Pat Cline .30 .09
❑ 675 Orlando Cabrera RC 1.25 .45
❑ 676 Alan Embree .30 .09
❑ 677 Brian Bevil .30 .09
❑ 678 David Weathers .30 .09
❑ 679 Cliff Floyd .30 .09
❑ 680 Joe Randa .30 .09
❑ 681 Bill Haselman .30 .09
❑ 682 Jeff Fassero .30 .09
❑ 683 Matt Morris .30 .09
❑ 684 Mark Portugal .30 .09
❑ 685 Lee Smith .30 .09
❑ 686 Pokey Reese .30 .09
❑ 687 Benito Santiago .30 .09
❑ 688 Brian Johnson .30 .09
❑ 689 Brent Brede RC .30 .09
❑ 690 S.Hasegawa RC .75 .23
❑ 691 Julio Santana .30 .09
❑ 692 Steve Kline .30 .09
❑ 693 Julian Tavarez .30 .09
❑ 694 John Hudek .30 .09
❑ 695 Manny Alexander .30 .09
❑ 696 Roberto Alomar ENC .30 .09
❑ 697 Jeff Bagwell ENC .30 .09
❑ 698 Barry Bonds ENC .75 .23
❑ 699 Ken Caminiti ENC .30 .09
❑ 700 Juan Gonzalez ENC .30 .09
❑ 701 Ken Griffey Jr. ENC .75 .23
❑ 702 Tony Gwynn ENC .50 .15
❑ 703 Derek Jeter ENC 1.00 .30
❑ 704 Andruw Jones ENC .30 .09
❑ 705 Chipper Jones ENC .50 .15
❑ 706 Barry Larkin ENC .30 .09
❑ 707 Greg Maddux ENC .75 .23
❑ 708 Mark McGwire ENC 1.00 .30
❑ 709 Paul Molitor ENC .30 .09
❑ 710 Hideo Nomo ENC .30 .09
❑ 711 Andy Pettitte ENC .30 .09
❑ 712 Mike Piazza ENC .75 .23
❑ 713 Manny Ramirez ENC .50 .15
❑ 714 Cal Ripken ENC 1.25 .35
❑ 715 Alex Rodriguez ENC .75 .23
❑ 716 Ryne Sandberg ENC .75 .23
❑ 717 John Smoltz ENC .30 .09
❑ 718 Frank Thomas ENC .50 .15
❑ 719 Mo Vaughn ENC .30 .09
❑ 720 Bernie Williams ENC .30 .09
❑ 721 Tim Salmon CL .30 .09
❑ 722 Greg Maddux CL .75 .23
❑ 723 Cal Ripken CL 1.25 .35
❑ 724 Mo Vaughn CL .30 .09
❑ 725 Ryne Sandberg CL .75 .23
❑ 726 Frank Thomas CL .50 .15
❑ 727 Barry Larkin CL .30 .09
❑ 728 Manny Ramirez CL .30 .09
❑ 729 Andres Galarraga CL .30 .09
❑ 730 Tony Clark CL .30 .09
❑ 731 Gary Sheffield CL .30 .09
❑ 732 Jeff Bagwell CL .30 .09
❑ 733 Kevin Appier CL .30 .09
❑ 734 Mike Piazza CL .75 .23
❑ 735 Jeff Cirillo CL .30 .09
❑ 736 Paul Molitor CL .30 .09
❑ 737 Henry Rodriguez CL .30 .09
❑ 738 Todd Hundley CL .30 .09
❑ 739 Derek Jeter CL 1.00 .30
❑ 740 Mark McGwire CL 1.00 .30
❑ 741 Curt Schilling CL .30 .09
❑ 742 Jason Kendall CL .30 .09
❑ 743 Tony Gwynn CL .50 .15
❑ 744 Barry Bonds CL .75 .23
❑ 745 Ken Griffey Jr. CL .75 .23
❑ 746 Brian Jordan CL .30 .09
❑ 747 Juan Gonzalez CL .30 .09
❑ 748 Joe Carter CL .30 .09
❑ 749 Ariz. Diamondbacks .30 .09
CL Inserts
❑ 750 Tampa Bay Devil Rays .30 .09
CL Inserts
❑ 751 Hideki Irabu RC .75 .23
❑ 752 Jeremi Gonzalez RC .50 .15
❑ 753 Mario Valdez RC .50 .15
❑ 754 Aaron Boone .75 .23
❑ 755 Brett Tomko .50 .15
❑ 756 Jaret Wright RC 2.00 .60
❑ 757 Ryan McGuire .50 .15
❑ 758 Jason McDonald .50 .15
❑ 759 Adrian Brown RC .50 .15
❑ 760 Keith Foulke RC 3.00 .90
❑ 761 Bonus Checklist .50 .15
❑ P489 M.Williams Promo 1.00 .30
❑ NNO Andruw Jones 25.00 7.50
Circa AU/200

2001 Fleer Authority

	Nm-Mt	Ex-Mt
COMP.SET w/o SP's (100)	25.00	7.50
COMMON CARD (1-100)	.40	.12
COMMON (101-150)	5.00	1.50

JETER MM'S RANDOM INSERTS IN PACKS
JETER 93 AU RANDOM INSERT IN PACKS

❑ 1 Mark Grace .60 .18
❑ 2 Paul Konerko .40 .12
❑ 3 Sean Casey .40 .12
❑ 4 Jim Thome 1.00 .30
❑ 5 Todd Helton .60 .18
❑ 6 Tony Clark .40 .12
❑ 7 Jeff Bagwell .60 .18
❑ 8 Mike Sweeney .40 .12
❑ 9 Eric Karros .40 .12
❑ 10 Richie Sexson .40 .12
❑ 11 Doug Mientkiewicz .40 .12
❑ 12 Ryan Klesko .40 .12
❑ 13 John Olerud .40 .12
❑ 14 Mark McGwire 2.50 .75
❑ 15 Fred McGriff .60 .18
❑ 16 Rafael Palmeiro .60 .18
❑ 17 Carlos Delgado .40 .12
❑ 18 Roberto Alomar .60 .18
❑ 19 Craig Biggio .60 .18
❑ 20 Jose Vidro .40 .12
❑ 21 Edgardo Alfonzo .40 .12
❑ 22 Jeff Kent .40 .12
❑ 23 Bret Boone .40 .12
❑ 24 Rafael Furcal .40 .12
❑ 25 Nomar Garciaparra 1.50 .45
❑ 26 Barry Larkin .60 .18
❑ 27 Cristian Guzman .40 .12
❑ 28 Derek Jeter 2.50 .75
❑ 29 Miguel Tejada .40 .12
❑ 30 Jimmy Rollins .40 .12
❑ 31 Rich Aurilia .40 .12
❑ 32 Alex Rodriguez 1.50 .45
❑ 33 Cal Ripken 3.00 .90
❑ 34 Troy Glaus .40 .12
❑ 35 Matt Williams .40 .12
❑ 36 Chipper Jones 1.00 .30
❑ 37 Jeff Cirillo .40 .12
❑ 38 Robin Ventura .40 .12
❑ 39 Eric Chavez .40 .12
❑ 40 Scott Rolen 1.00 .30
❑ 41 Phil Nevin .40 .12
❑ 42 Mike Piazza 1.50 .45
❑ 43 Jorge Posada .60 .18
❑ 44 Jason Kendall .40 .12
❑ 45 Ivan Rodriguez 1.00 .30
❑ 46 Frank Thomas 1.00 .30
❑ 47 Edgar Martinez .60 .18
❑ 48 Darin Erstad .40 .12

❑ 49 Tim Salmon	.60	.18
❑ 50 Luis Gonzalez	.40	.12
❑ 51 Andruw Jones	.40	.12
❑ 52 Carl Everett	.40	.12
❑ 53 Manny Ramirez	.60	.18
❑ 54 Sammy Sosa	1.50	.45
❑ 55 Rondell White	.40	.12
❑ 56 Magglio Ordonez	.40	.12
❑ 57 Ken Griffey Jr.	1.50	.45
❑ 58 Juan Gonzalez	.60	.18
❑ 59 Larry Walker	.60	.18
❑ 60 Bobby Higginson	.40	.12
❑ 61 Cliff Floyd	.40	.12
❑ 62 Preston Wilson	.40	.12
❑ 63 Moises Alou	.40	.12
❑ 64 Lance Berkman	.40	.12
❑ 65 Richard Hidalgo	.40	.12
❑ 66 Jermaine Dye	.40	.12
❑ 67 Mark Quinn	.40	.12
❑ 68 Shawn Green	.40	.12
❑ 69 Gary Sheffield	.40	.12
❑ 70 Jeromy Burnitz	.40	.12
❑ 71 Geoff Jenkins	.40	.12
❑ 72 Vladimir Guerrero	1.00	.30
❑ 73 Bernie Williams	.60	.18
❑ 74 Johnny Damon	.60	.18
❑ 75 Jason Giambi	.40	.12
❑ 76 Bobby Abreu	.40	.12
❑ 77 Pat Burrell	.40	.12
❑ 78 Brian Giles	.40	.12
❑ 79 Tony Gwynn	1.25	.35
❑ 80 Barry Bonds	2.50	.75
❑ 81 J.D. Drew	.40	.12
❑ 82 Jim Edmonds	.40	.12
❑ 83 Greg Vaughn	.40	.12
❑ 84 Raul Mondesi	.40	.12
❑ 85 Shannon Stewart	.40	.12
❑ 86 Randy Johnson	1.00	.30
❑ 87 Curt Schilling	.40	.12
❑ 88 Tom Glavine	.60	.18
❑ 89 Greg Maddux	1.50	.45
❑ 90 Pedro Martinez	1.00	.30
❑ 91 Kerry Wood	1.00	.30
❑ 92 David Wells	.40	.12
❑ 93 Bartolo Colon	.40	.12
❑ 94 Mike Hampton	.40	.12
❑ 95 Kevin Brown	.40	.12
❑ 96 Al Leiter	.40	.12
❑ 97 Roger Clemens	2.00	.60
❑ 98 Mike Mussina	.60	.18
❑ 99 Tim Hudson	.40	.12
❑ 100 Kazuhiro Sasaki	.40	.12
❑ 101 Ichiro Suzuki RC	40.00	12.00
❑ 102 Albert Pujols RC	60.00	18.00
❑ 103 Drew Henson RC	6.00	1.80
❑ 104 Adam Pettyjohn RC	5.00	1.50
❑ 105 Adrian Hernandez RC	5.00	1.50
❑ 106 Andy Morales RC	5.00	1.50
❑ 107 Tsuyoshi Shinjo RC	6.00	1.80
❑ 108 Juan Uribe RC	6.00	1.80
❑ 109 Jack Wilson RC	8.00	2.40
❑ 110 Jason Smith RC	5.00	1.50
❑ 111 Junior Spivey RC	6.00	1.80
❑ 112 Wilson Betemit RC	5.00	1.50
❑ 113 Elpidio Guzman RC	5.00	1.50
❑ 114 Esix Snead RC	5.00	1.50
❑ 115 Winston Abreu RC	5.00	1.50
❑ 116 Jeremy Owens RC	5.00	1.50
❑ 117 Jay Gibbons RC	6.00	1.80
❑ 118 Luis Lopez	5.00	1.50
❑ 119 Ryan Freel RC	5.00	1.50
❑ 120 Rafael Soriano RC	6.00	1.80
❑ 121 Johnny Estrada RC	6.00	1.80
❑ 122 Bud Smith RC	5.00	1.50
❑ 123 Jackson Melian RC	5.00	1.50
❑ 124 Matt White RC	5.00	1.50
❑ 125 Travis Hafner RC	10.00	3.00
❑ 126 Morgan Ensberg RC	6.00	1.80
❑ 127 Endy Chavez RC	5.00	1.50
❑ 128 Brett Prinz RC	5.00	1.50
❑ 129 Juan Diaz RC	5.00	1.50
❑ 130 Erick Almonte RC	5.00	1.50
❑ 131 Rob Mackowiak RC	6.00	1.80
❑ 132 Carlos Valderrama RC	5.00	1.50
❑ 133 Wilkin Ruan RC	5.00	1.50
❑ 134 Angel Berroa RC	6.00	1.80
❑ 135 Henry Mateo RC	5.00	1.50
❑ 136 Bill Ortega RC	5.00	1.50
❑ 137 Billy Sylvester RC	5.00	1.50
❑ 138 Andres Torres RC	5.00	1.50
❑ 139 Nate Frese RC	5.00	1.50
❑ 140 Casey Fossum RC	5.00	1.50
❑ 141 Ricardo Rodriguez RC	5.00	1.50
❑ 142 Brian Roberts RC	5.00	1.50
❑ 143 Carlos Garcia RC	5.00	1.50
❑ 144 Brian Lawrence RC	5.00	1.50
❑ 145 Cory Aldridge RC	5.00	1.50
❑ 146 Mark Teixeira RC	20.00	6.00
❑ 147 Juan Cruz RC	5.00	1.50
❑ 148 B. Duckworth RC	5.00	1.50
❑ 149 Dewon Brazelton RC	6.00	1.80
❑ 150 Mark Prior RC	40.00	12.00
❑ MM4 Derek Jeter MM/2000	15.00	4.50
❑ MM4AU Derek Jeter MM AU/100	150.00	45.00
❑ NNO Derek Jeter 93 AU/500	175.00	52.50

2001 Fleer Focus

	Nm-Mt	Ex-Mt
COMP.SET w/o SP's (200)	25.00	7.50
COMMON CARD (1-200)	.30	.09
COMMON (201-240)	5.00	1.50
COMMON (241-250)	10.00	3.00

Card	Nm-Mt	Ex-Mt
❑ 1 Derek Jeter	2.00	.60
❑ 2 Manny Ramirez	.50	.15
❑ 3 Ken Griffey Jr.	1.25	.35
❑ 4 Ken Caminiti	.30	.09
❑ 5 Joe Randa	.30	.09
❑ 6 Jason Kendall	.30	.09
❑ 7 Ron Coomer	.30	.09
❑ 8 Rondell White	.30	.09
❑ 9 Tino Martinez	.50	.15
❑ 10 Nomar Garciaparra	1.25	.35
❑ 11 Tony Batista	.30	.09
❑ 12 Todd Stottlemyre	.30	.09
❑ 13 Ryan Klesko	.30	.09
❑ 14 Darin Erstad	.30	.09
❑ 15 Todd Walker	.30	.09
❑ 16 Al Leiter	.30	.09
❑ 17 Carl Everett	.30	.09
❑ 18 Bobby Abreu	.30	.09
❑ 19 Raul Mondesi	.30	.09
❑ 20 Vladimir Guerrero	.75	.23
❑ 21 Mike Bordick	.30	.09
❑ 22 Aaron Sele	.30	.09
❑ 23 Ray Lankford	.30	.09
❑ 24 Roger Clemens	1.50	.45
❑ 25 Kevin Young	.30	.09
❑ 26 Brad Radke	.30	.09
❑ 27 Todd Hundley	.30	.09
❑ 28 Ellis Burks	.30	.09
❑ 29 Lee Stevens	.30	.09
❑ 30 Eric Karros	.30	.09
❑ 31 Darren Dreifort	.30	.09
❑ 32 Ivan Rodriguez	.75	.23
❑ 33 Pedro Martinez	.75	.23
❑ 34 Travis Fryman	.30	.09
❑ 35 Garret Anderson	.30	.09
❑ 36 Rafael Palmeiro	.50	.15
❑ 37 Jason Giambi	.30	.09
❑ 38 Jeromy Burnitz	.30	.09
❑ 39 Robin Ventura	.30	.09
❑ 40 Derek Bell	.30	.09
❑ 41 Carlos Guillen	.30	.09
❑ 42 Albert Belle	.30	.09
❑ 43 Henry Rodriguez	.30	.09
❑ 44 Brian Jordan	.30	.09
❑ 45 Mike Sweeney	.30	.09
❑ 46 Ruben Rivera	.30	.09
❑ 47 Greg Maddux	1.25	.35
❑ 48 Corey Koskie	.30	.09
❑ 49 Sandy Alomar Jr.	.30	.09
❑ 50 Mike Mussina	.50	.15
❑ 51 Tom Glavine	.50	.15
❑ 52 Aaron Boone	.30	.09
❑ 53 Frank Thomas	.75	.23
❑ 54 Kenny Lofton	.30	.09
❑ 55 Danny Graves	.30	.09
❑ 56 Jose Valentin	.30	.09
❑ 57 Travis Lee	.30	.09
❑ 58 Jim Edmonds	.30	.09
❑ 59 Jim Thome	.75	.23
❑ 60 Steve Finley	.30	.09
❑ 61 Shawn Green	.30	.09
❑ 62 Lance Berkman	.30	.09
❑ 63 Mark Quinn	.30	.09
❑ 64 Randy Johnson	.75	.23
❑ 65 Dmitri Young	.30	.09
❑ 66 Andy Pettitte	.50	.15
❑ 67 Paul O'Neill	.50	.15
❑ 68 Gil Heredia	.30	.09
❑ 69 Russell Branyan	.30	.09
❑ 70 Alex Rodriguez	1.25	.35
❑ 71 Geoff Jenkins	.30	.09
❑ 72 Eric Chavez	.30	.09
❑ 73 Cal Ripken	2.50	.75
❑ 74 Mark Kotsay	.30	.09
❑ 75 Jeff D'Amico	.30	.09
❑ 76 Tony Womack	.30	.09
❑ 77 Eric Milton	.30	.09
❑ 78 Joe Girardi	.30	.09
❑ 79 Peter Bergeron	.30	.09
❑ 80 Miguel Tejada	.30	.09
❑ 81 Luis Gonzalez	.30	.09
❑ 82 Doug Glanville	.30	.09
❑ 83 Gerald Williams	.30	.09
❑ 84 Troy O'Leary	.30	.09
❑ 85 Brian Giles	.30	.09
❑ 86 Miguel Cairo	.30	.09
❑ 87 Magglio Ordonez	.30	.09
❑ 88 Rick Helling	.30	.09
❑ 89 Bruce Chen	.30	.09
❑ 90 Jason Varitek	.50	.15
❑ 91 Mike Lieberthal	.30	.09
❑ 92 Shawn Estes	.30	.09
❑ 93 Rick Ankiel	.30	.09
❑ 94 Tim Salmon	.50	.15
❑ 95 Jacque Jones	.30	.09
❑ 96 Johnny Damon	.50	.15
❑ 97 Larry Walker	.50	.15
❑ 98 Ruben Mateo	.30	.09
❑ 99 Brad Fullmer	.30	.09
❑ 100 Edgardo Alfonzo	.30	.09
❑ 101 Mark Mulder	.30	.09
❑ 102 Tony Gwynn	1.00	.30
❑ 103 Mike Cameron	.30	.09
❑ 104 Richie Sexson	.30	.09
❑ 105 Barry Larkin	.50	.15
❑ 106 Mike Piazza	1.25	.35
❑ 107 Eric Young	.30	.09
❑ 108 Edgar Renteria	.30	.09
❑ 109 Todd Zeile	.30	.09
❑ 110 Luis Castillo	.30	.09
❑ 111 Sammy Sosa	1.25	.35
❑ 112 David Justice	.30	.09
❑ 113 Delino DeShields	.30	.09
❑ 114 Mariano Rivera	.50	.15
❑ 115 Edgar Martinez	.50	.15
❑ 116 Ray Durham	.30	.09
❑ 117 Brady Anderson	.30	.09
❑ 118 Eric Owens	.30	.09
❑ 119 Alex Gonzalez	.30	.09
❑ 120 Jay Buhner	.30	.09
❑ 121 Greg Vaughn	.30	.09
❑ 122 Mike Lowell	.30	.09
❑ 123 Marquis Grissom	.30	.09

Card	Nm-Mt	Ex-Mt
❑ 124 Matt Williams	.30	.09
❑ 125 Dean Palmer	.30	.09
❑ 126 Troy Glaus	.30	.09
❑ 127 Bret Boone	.30	.09
❑ 128 David Ortiz	.50	.15
❑ 129 Glenallen Hill	.30	.09
❑ 130 Chipper Jones	.75	.23
❑ 131 Tony Clark	.30	.09
❑ 132 Terrence Long	.30	.09
❑ 133 Chuck Finley	.30	.09
❑ 134 Jeff Bagwell	.50	.15
❑ 135 J.T. Snow	.30	.09
❑ 136 Andruw Jones	.30	.09
❑ 137 Carlos Delgado	.30	.09
❑ 138 Mo Vaughn	.30	.09
❑ 139 Derrek Lee	.30	.09
❑ 140 Bobby Estalella	.30	.09
❑ 141 Kerry Wood	.75	.23
❑ 142 Jose Vidro	.30	.09
❑ 143 Ben Grieve	.30	.09
❑ 144 Barry Bonds	2.00	.60
❑ 145 Javy Lopez	.30	.09
❑ 146 Adam Kennedy	.30	.09
❑ 147 Jeff Cirillo	.30	.09
❑ 148 Cliff Floyd	.30	.09
❑ 149 Carl Pavano	.30	.09
❑ 150 Bobby Higginson	.30	.09
❑ 151 Kevin Brown	.30	.09
❑ 152 Fernando Tatis	.30	.09
❑ 153 Matt Lawton	.30	.09
❑ 154 Damion Easley	.30	.09
❑ 155 Curt Schilling	.30	.09
❑ 156 Mark McGwire	2.00	.60
❑ 157 Mark Grace	.50	.15
❑ 158 Adrian Beltre	.50	.15
❑ 159 Jorge Posada	.50	.15
❑ 160 Richard Hidalgo	.30	.09
❑ 161 Vinny Castilla	.30	.09
❑ 162 Bernie Williams	.50	.15
❑ 163 John Olerud	.30	.09
❑ 164 Todd Helton	.50	.15
❑ 165 Craig Biggio	.50	.15
❑ 166 David Wells	.30	.09
❑ 167 Phil Nevin	.30	.09
❑ 168 Andres Galarraga	.30	.09
❑ 169 Moises Alou	.30	.09
❑ 170 Denny Neagle	.30	.09
❑ 171 Jeffrey Hammonds	.30	.09
❑ 172 Sean Casey	.30	.09
❑ 173 Gary Sheffield	.30	.09
❑ 174 Carlos Lee	.30	.09
❑ 175 Juan Encarnacion	.30	.09
❑ 176 Roberto Alomar	.50	.15
❑ 177 Kenny Rogers	.30	.09
❑ 178 Charles Johnson	.30	.09
❑ 179 Shannon Stewart	.30	.09
❑ 180 B.J. Surhoff	.30	.09
❑ 181 Paul Konerko	.30	.09
❑ 182 Jermaine Dye	.30	.09
❑ 183 Scott Rolen	.75	.23
❑ 184 Fred McGriff	.50	.15
❑ 185 Juan Gonzalez	.50	.15
❑ 186 Carlos Beltran	.50	.15
❑ 187 Jay Payton	.30	.09
❑ 188 Chad Hermansen	.30	.09
❑ 189 Pat Burrell	.30	.09
❑ 190 Omar Vizquel	.50	.15
❑ 191 Trot Nixon	.30	.09
❑ 192 Mike Hampton	.30	.09
❑ 193 Kris Benson	.30	.09
❑ 194 Gabe Kapler	.30	.09
❑ 195 Rickey Henderson	.75	.23
❑ 196 J.D. Drew	.30	.09
❑ 197 Pokey Reese	.30	.09
❑ 198 Jeff Kent	.30	.09
❑ 199 Jose Cruz Jr.	.30	.09
❑ 200 Preston Wilson	.30	.09
❑ 201 Eric Munson/2499	5.00	1.50
❑ 202 Alex Cabrera/2499	5.00	1.50
❑ 203 Nate Rolison/2499	5.00	1.50
❑ 204 Julio Zuleta/2499	5.00	1.50
❑ 205 Chris Richard/2499	5.00	1.50
❑ 206 Dernell Stenson/2499	5.00	1.50
❑ 207 Aaron McNeal/2499	5.00	1.50
❑ 208 Aubrey Huff/2999	5.00	1.50
❑ 209 Mike Lamb/2999	5.00	1.50
❑ 210 Xavier Nady/2999	5.00	1.50
❑ 211 Joe Crede/2999	5.00	1.50
❑ 212 Ben Petrick/3499	5.00	1.50
❑ 213 M.Burkhart/1999	5.00	1.50
❑ 214 Jason Tyner/1999	5.00	1.50
❑ 215 Juan Pierre/1999	5.00	1.50
❑ 216 Adam Dunn/1999	8.00	2.40
❑ 217 Adam Piatt/1999	5.00	1.50
❑ 218 Eric Byrnes/1999	5.00	1.50
❑ 219 Corey Patterson/1999	5.00	1.50
❑ 220 Kenny Kelly/1999	5.00	1.50
❑ 221 Tike Redman/1999	5.00	1.50
❑ 222 Luis Matos/1999	5.00	1.50
❑ 223 Timo Perez/1999	5.00	1.50
❑ 224 Vernon Wells/1999	5.00	1.50
❑ 225 Barry Zito/4999	8.00	2.40
❑ 226 Adam Bernero/4999	5.00	1.50
❑ 227 Kazuhiro Sasaki/4999	5.00	1.50
❑ 228 O.Mairena/4999	5.00	1.50
❑ 229 Mark Buehrle/4999	5.00	1.50
❑ 230 Ryan Dempster/4999	5.00	1.50
❑ 231 Tim Hudson/4999	5.00	1.50
❑ 232 Scott Downs/4999	5.00	1.50
❑ 233 A.J. Burnett/4999	5.00	1.50
❑ 234 Adam Eaton/4999	5.00	1.50
❑ 235 P.Crawford/4999	5.00	1.50
❑ 236 Jace Brewer/3999	5.00	1.50
❑ 237 Jose Ortiz/3999	5.00	1.50
❑ 238 Rafael Furcal/3999	5.00	1.50
❑ 239 Julio Lugo/3999	5.00	1.50
❑ 240 T. De la Rosa/3999	5.00	1.50
❑ 241 T. Shinjo/999 RC	10.00	3.00
❑ 242 W. Betemit/999 RC	10.00	3.00
❑ 243 J. Owens/999 RC	10.00	3.00
❑ 244 Drew Henson/999 RC	10.00	3.00
❑ 245 Albert Pujols/999 RC	60.00	18.00
❑ 246 Travis Hafner/999 RC	15.00	4.50
❑ 247 Ichiro Suzuki/999 RC	50.00	15.00
❑ 248 E. Guzman/999 RC	10.00	3.00
❑ 249 Matt White/999 RC	10.00	3.00
❑ 250 Junior Spivey/999 RC	10.00	3.00

2001 Fleer Futures

	Nm-Mt	Ex-Mt
COMPLETE SET (220)	25.00	7.50
COMMON CARD (1-220)	.30	.09
COMMON (221-230)	5.00	1.50

Card	Nm-Mt	Ex-Mt
❑ 1 Darin Erstad	.30	.09
❑ 2 Manny Ramirez	.50	.15
❑ 3 Darryl Kile	.30	.09
❑ 4 Troy O'Leary	.30	.09
❑ 5 Mark Quinn	.30	.09
❑ 6 Brian Giles	.30	.09
❑ 7 Randy Johnson	.75	.23
❑ 8 Todd Walker	.30	.09
❑ 9 Mike Piazza	1.25	.35
❑ 10 Fred McGriff	.50	.15
❑ 11 Sammy Sosa	1.25	.35
❑ 12 Chan Ho Park	.30	.09
❑ 13 John Rocker	.30	.09
❑ 14 Luis Castillo	.30	.09
❑ 15 Eric Chavez	.30	.09
❑ 16 Carlos Delgado	.30	.09
❑ 17 Sean Casey	.30	.09
❑ 18 Corey Koskie	.30	.09
❑ 19 John Olerud	.30	.09
❑ 20 Nomar Garciaparra	1.25	.35
❑ 21 Craig Biggio	.50	.15
❑ 22 Pat Burrell	.30	.09
❑ 23 Ben Molina	.30	.09
❑ 24 Jim Thome	.75	.23
❑ 25 Rey Ordonez	.30	.09
❑ 26 Fernando Tatis	.30	.09
❑ 27 Eric Young	.30	.09
❑ 28 Eric Karros	.30	.09
❑ 29 Adam Eaton	.30	.09
❑ 30 Brian Jordan	.30	.09
❑ 31 Jorge Posada	.50	.15
❑ 32 Gabe Kapler	.30	.09
❑ 33 Keith Foulke	.30	.09
❑ 34 Ron Coomer	.30	.09
❑ 35 Chipper Jones	.75	.23
❑ 36 Miguel Tejada	.30	.09
❑ 37 David Wells	.30	.09
❑ 38 Carlos Lee	.30	.09
❑ 39 Barry Bonds	2.00	.60
❑ 40 Derrek Lee	.30	.09
❑ 41 Tim Hudson	.30	.09
❑ 42 Billy Koch	.30	.09
❑ 43 Dmitri Young	.30	.09
❑ 44 Vladimir Guerrero	.75	.23
❑ 45 Rickey Henderson	.75	.23
❑ 46 Jeff Bagwell	.50	.15
❑ 47 Robert Person	.30	.09
❑ 48 Brady Anderson	.30	.09
❑ 49 Lance Berkman	.30	.09
❑ 50 Mike Lieberthal	.30	.09
❑ 51 Adam Kennedy	.30	.09
❑ 52 Russell Branyan	.30	.09
❑ 53 Robin Ventura	.30	.09
❑ 54 Mark McGwire	2.00	.60
❑ 55 Tony Gwynn	1.00	.30
❑ 56 Matt Williams	.30	.09
❑ 57 Jeff Cirillo	.30	.09
❑ 58 Roger Clemens	1.50	.45
❑ 59 Ivan Rodriguez	.75	.23
❑ 60 Brad Radke	.30	.09
❑ 61 Kazuhiro Sasaki	.30	.09
❑ 62 Cal Ripken	2.50	.75
❑ 63 Ken Caminiti	.30	.09
❑ 64 Bob Abreu	.30	.09
❑ 65 Troy Glaus	.30	.09
❑ 66 Sandy Alomar Jr.	.30	.09
❑ 67 Jose Vidro	.30	.09
❑ 68 Pedro Martinez	.75	.23
❑ 69 Kevin Young	.30	.09
❑ 70 Jay Bell	.30	.09
❑ 71 Larry Walker	.50	.15
❑ 72 Derek Jeter	2.00	.60
❑ 73 Miguel Cairo	.30	.09
❑ 74 Magglio Ordonez	.30	.09
❑ 75 Jeromy Burnitz	.30	.09
❑ 76 J.T. Snow	.30	.09
❑ 77 Andres Galarraga	.30	.09
❑ 78 Ryan Dempster	.30	.09
❑ 79 Ken Griffey Jr.	1.25	.35
❑ 80 Aaron Sele	.30	.09
❑ 81 Tom Glavine	.50	.15
❑ 82 Hideo Nomo	.75	.23
❑ 83 Orlando Hernandez	.30	.09
❑ 84 Tony Batista	.30	.09
❑ 85 Aaron Boone	.30	.09
❑ 86 Jacque Jones	.30	.09
❑ 87 Delino DeShields	.30	.09
❑ 88 Garret Anderson	.30	.09
❑ 89 Fernando Seguignol	.30	.09
❑ 90 Jim Edmonds	.30	.09
❑ 91 Frank Thomas	.75	.23
❑ 92 Adrian Beltre	.50	.15
❑ 93 Ellis Burks	.30	.09
❑ 94 Andruw Jones	.30	.09
❑ 95 Tony Clark	.30	.09
❑ 96 Danny Graves	.30	.09
❑ 97 Alex Rodriguez	1.25	.35
❑ 98 Mike Mussina	.50	.15
❑ 99 Scott Elarton	.30	.09
❑ 100 Jason Giambi	.30	.09
❑ 101 Jay Payton	.30	.09
❑ 102 Gerald Williams	.30	.09
❑ 103 Kerry Wood	.75	.23
❑ 104 Shawn Green	.30	.09
❑ 105 Greg Maddux	1.25	.35

Card	Nm-Mt	Ex-Mt
❑ 106 Juan Encarnacion	.30	.09
❑ 107 Bernie Williams	.50	.15
❑ 108 Mike Lamb	.30	.09
❑ 109 Charles Johnson	.30	.09
❑ 110 Richie Sexson	.30	.09
❑ 111 Jeff Kent	.30	.09
❑ 112 Albert Belle	.30	.09
❑ 113 Cliff Floyd	.30	.09
❑ 114 Ben Grieve	.30	.09
❑ 115 Tim Salmon	.50	.15
❑ 116 Carl Pavano	.30	.09
❑ 117 Rick Ankiel	.30	.09
❑ 118 Dante Bichette	.30	.09
❑ 119 Johnny Damon	.50	.15
❑ 120 Brian Anderson	.30	.09
❑ 121 Roberto Alomar	.50	.15
❑ 122 Mike Hampton	.30	.09
❑ 123 Greg Vaughn	.30	.09
❑ 124 Carl Everett	.30	.09
❑ 125 Moises Alou	.30	.09
❑ 126 Jason Kendall	.30	.09
❑ 127 Omar Vizquel	.50	.15
❑ 128 Mark Grace	.50	.15
❑ 129 Kevin Brown	.30	.09
❑ 130 Phil Nevin	.30	.09
❑ 131 Kevin Millwood	.30	.09
❑ 132 Bobby Higginson	.30	.09
❑ 133 Ruben Mateo	.30	.09
❑ 134 Luis Gonzalez	.30	.09
❑ 135 Dean Palmer	.30	.09
❑ 136 Mariano Rivera	.50	.15
❑ 137 Rick Helling	.30	.09
❑ 138 Paul Konerko	.30	.09
❑ 139 Marquis Grissom	.30	.09
❑ 140 Robb Nen	.30	.09
❑ 141 Javy Lopez	.30	.09
❑ 142 Preston Wilson	.30	.09
❑ 143 Terrence Long	.30	.09
❑ 144 Shannon Stewart	.30	.09
❑ 145 Barry Larkin	.50	.15
❑ 146 Cristian Guzman	.30	.09
❑ 147 Jay Buhner	.30	.09
❑ 148 Jermaine Dye	.30	.09
❑ 149 Kris Benson	.30	.09
❑ 150 Curt Schilling	.30	.09
❑ 151 Todd Helton	.50	.15
❑ 152 Paul O'Neill	.50	.15
❑ 153 Rafael Palmeiro	.50	.15
❑ 154 Ray Durham	.30	.09
❑ 155 Geoff Jenkins	.30	.09
❑ 156 Livan Hernandez	.30	.09
❑ 157 Rafael Furcal	.30	.09
❑ 158 Juan Gonzalez	.50	.15
❑ 159 Tino Martinez	.50	.15
❑ 160 Raul Mondesi	.30	.09
❑ 161 Matt Lawton	.30	.09
❑ 162 Edgar Martinez	.50	.15
❑ 163 Richard Hidalgo	.30	.09
❑ 164 Scott Rolen	.75	.23
❑ 165 Chuck Finley	.30	.09
❑ 166 Edgardo Alfonzo	.30	.09
❑ 167 J.D. Drew	.30	.09
❑ 168 Trot Nixon	.30	.09
❑ 169 Carlos Beltran	.50	.15
❑ 170 Ryan Klesko	.30	.09
❑ 171 Mo Vaughn	.30	.09
❑ 172 Kenny Lofton	.30	.09
❑ 173 Al Leiter	.30	.09
❑ 174 Rondell White	.30	.09
❑ 175 Mike Sweeney	.30	.09
❑ 176 Trevor Hoffman	.30	.09
❑ 177 Steve Finley	.30	.09
❑ 178 Jeffrey Hammonds	.30	.09
❑ 179 David Justice	.30	.09
❑ 180 Gary Sheffield	.30	.09
❑ 181 Eric Munson BF	.30	.09
❑ 182 Luis Matos BF	.30	.09
❑ 183 Alex Cabrera BF	.30	.09
❑ 184 Randy Keisler BF	.30	.09
❑ 185 Nate Rolison BF	.30	.09
❑ 186 Jason Hart BF	.30	.09
❑ 187 Timo Perez BF	.30	.09
❑ 188 Adam Bernero BF	.30	.09
❑ 189 Barry Zito BF	.50	.15
❑ 190 Ryan Kohlmeier BF	.30	.09
❑ 191 Joey Nation BF	.30	.09
❑ 192 Oswaldo Mairena BF	.30	.09
❑ 193 Aubrey Huff BF	.30	.09
❑ 194 Mark Buehrle BF	.30	.09
❑ 195 Jace Brewer BF	.30	.09
❑ 196 Julio Zuleta BF	.30	.09
❑ 197 Xavier Nady BF	.30	.09
❑ 198 Vernon Wells BF	.30	.09
❑ 199 Joe Crede BF	.30	.09
❑ 200 Scott Downs BF	.30	.09
❑ 201 Ben Petrick BF	.30	.09
❑ 202 A.J. Burnett BF	.30	.09
❑ 203 Esix Snead BF RC	.30	.09
❑ 204 Dernell Stenson BF	.30	.09
❑ 205 Jose Ortiz BF	.30	.09
❑ 206 Paxton Crawford BF	.30	.09
❑ 207 Jason Tyner BF	.30	.09
❑ 208 Jimmy Rollins BF	.30	.09
❑ 209 Juan Pierre BF	.30	.09
❑ 210 Keith Ginter BF	.30	.09
❑ 211 Adam Dunn BF	.50	.15
❑ 212 Larry Barnes BF	.30	.09
❑ 213 Adam Piatt BF	.30	.09
❑ 214 Rodney Lindsey BF	.30	.09
❑ 215 Eric Byrnes BF	.30	.09
❑ 216 Julio Lugo BF	.30	.09
❑ 217 Corey Patterson BF	.30	.09
❑ 218 Reggie Taylor BF	.30	.09
❑ 219 Kenny Kelly BF	.30	.09
❑ 220 Tike Redman BF	.30	.09
❑ 221 D.Henson/2499 RC	5.00	1.50
❑ 222 J.Estrada/2499 RC	5.00	1.50
❑ 223 E.Guzman/2499 RC	5.00	1.50
❑ 224 Albert Pujols/2499 RC	50.00	15.00
❑ 225 W.Betemit/2499 RC	5.00	1.50
❑ 226 M.Teixeira/2499 RC	15.00	4.50
❑ 227 T.Shinjo/2499 RC	5.00	1.50
❑ 228 Matt White/2499 RC	5.00	1.50
❑ 229 A.Hernandez/2499 RC	5.00	1.50
❑ 230 I.Suzuki/2499 RC	40.00	12.00

2001 Fleer Game Time

	Nm-Mt	Ex-Mt
COMP.SET w/o SP's (90)	25.00	7.50
COMMON CARD (1-90)	.40	.12
COMMON NG (91-121)	4.00	1.20

JETER MM'S RANDOMLY INSERTED IN PACKS

Card	Nm-Mt	Ex-Mt
❑ 1 Derek Jeter	2.50	.75
❑ 2 Nomar Garciaparra	1.50	.45
❑ 3 Alex Rodriguez	1.50	.45
❑ 4 Jason Kendall	.40	.12
❑ 5 Barry Bonds	2.50	.75
❑ 6 David Wells	.40	.12
❑ 7 Craig Biggio	.60	.18
❑ 8 Adrian Beltre	.60	.18
❑ 9 Pat Burrell	.40	.12
❑ 10 Rafael Palmeiro	.60	.18
❑ 11 Jim Thome	1.00	.30
❑ 12 Mike Lowell	.40	.12
❑ 13 Trevor Hoffman	.40	.12
❑ 14 Pokey Reese	.40	.12
❑ 15 Juan Encarnacion	.40	.12
❑ 16 Shawn Green	.40	.12
❑ 17 Kerry Wood	1.00	.30
❑ 18 Richard Hidalgo	.40	.12
❑ 19 Scott Rolen	1.00	.30
❑ 20 Jeff Kent	.40	.12
❑ 21 Alex Gonzalez	.40	.12
❑ 22 Matt Williams	.40	.12
❑ 23 Mike Sweeney	.40	.12
❑ 24 Edgar Martinez	.60	.18
❑ 25 Sammy Sosa	1.50	.45
❑ 26 Bobby Higginson	.40	.12
❑ 27 Kevin Brown	.40	.12
❑ 28 Mike Lieberthal	.40	.12
❑ 29 Pedro Martinez	1.00	.30
❑ 30 Jeff Weaver	.40	.12
❑ 31 Greg Maddux	1.50	.45
❑ 32 Mike Hampton	.40	.12
❑ 33 Vladimir Guerrero	1.00	.30
❑ 34 Greg Vaughn	.40	.12
❑ 35 Manny Ramirez	.60	.18
❑ 36 Carlos Beltran	.60	.18
❑ 37 Eric Chavez	.40	.12
❑ 38 Troy Glaus	.40	.12
❑ 39 Todd Helton	.60	.18
❑ 40 Gary Sheffield	.40	.12
❑ 41 Brady Anderson	.40	.12
❑ 42 Juan Gonzalez	.60	.18
❑ 43 Tim Hudson	.40	.12
❑ 44 Kenny Lofton	.40	.12
❑ 45 Al Leiter	.40	.12
❑ 46 Eric Owens	.40	.12
❑ 47 Roberto Alomar	.60	.18
❑ 48 Preston Wilson	.40	.12
❑ 49 Tony Gwynn	1.25	.35
❑ 50 Cal Ripken	3.00	.90
❑ 51 Ben Petrick	.40	.12
❑ 52 Jason Giambi	.40	.12
❑ 53 Ben Grieve	.40	.12
❑ 54 Albert Belle	.40	.12
❑ 55 Jose Vidro	.40	.12
❑ 56 Barry Zito	.60	.18
❑ 57 Ivan Rodriguez	1.00	.30
❑ 58 Jeff Bagwell	.60	.18
❑ 59 Geoff Jenkins	.40	.12
❑ 60 Roger Clemens	2.00	.60
❑ 61 John Olerud	.40	.12
❑ 62 Randy Johnson	1.00	.30
❑ 63 Matt Lawton	.40	.12
❑ 64 Mark McGwire	2.50	.75
❑ 65 Brad Radke	.40	.12
❑ 66 Frank Thomas	1.00	.30
❑ 67 Edgardo Alfonzo	.40	.12
❑ 68 Brian Giles	.40	.12
❑ 69 J.T. Snow	.40	.12
❑ 70 Carlos Delgado	.40	.12
❑ 71 Chipper Jones	1.00	.30
❑ 72 Mark Quinn	.40	.12
❑ 73 Mike Mussina	.60	.18
❑ 74 Rick Ankiel	.40	.12
❑ 75 Rafael Furcal	.40	.12
❑ 76 Jim Edmonds	.40	.12
❑ 77 Vinny Castilla	.40	.12
❑ 78 Sean Casey	.40	.12
❑ 79 Derrek Lee	.40	.12
❑ 80 Mike Piazza	1.50	.45
❑ 81 Warren Morris	.40	.12
❑ 82 Tim Salmon	.60	.18
❑ 83 Jeromy Burnitz	.40	.12
❑ 84 Freddy Garcia	.40	.12
❑ 85 Ken Griffey Jr.	1.50	.45
❑ 86 Andruw Jones	.40	.12
❑ 87 Darryl Kile	.40	.12
❑ 88 Magglio Ordonez	.40	.12
❑ 89 Bernie Williams	.60	.18
❑ 90 Timo Perez	.40	.12
❑ 91 Ichiro Suzuki NG RC	40.00	12.00
❑ 92 Larry Barnes Darin Erstad	4.00	1.20
❑ 93 J. Randolph NG RC	4.00	1.20
❑ 94 Paul Phillips NG RC	4.00	1.20
❑ 95 Esix Snead NG RC	4.00	1.20
❑ 96 Matt White NG RC	4.00	1.20
❑ 97 Ryan Freel NG RC	4.00	1.20
❑ 98 Winston Abreu NG RC	4.00	1.20
❑ 99 Junior Spivey NG RC	5.00	1.50
❑ 100 Randy Keisler Roger Clemens	8.00	2.40
❑ 101 Mike Piazza Brian Cole	6.00	1.80
❑ 102 Aubrey Huff Chipper Jones	5.00	1.50

❑ 103 Corey Patterson Sammy Sosa	5.00	1.50
❑ 104 Sun Woo Kim Pedro Martinez	5.00	1.50
❑ 105 Drew Henson NG RC	5.00	1.50
❑ 106 C. Vargas NG RC	4.00	1.20
❑ 107 Rafael Furcal Cesar Izturis	4.00	1.20
❑ 108 Paxton Crawford Pedro Martinez	5.00	1.50
❑ 109 A. Hernandez NG RC	4.00	1.20
❑ 110 Jace Brewer Derek Jeter	10.00	3.00
❑ 111 Andy Morales NG RC	4.00	1.20
❑ 112 W. Betemit NG RC	4.00	1.20
❑ 113 Juan Diaz NG RC	4.00	1.20
❑ 114 Erick Almonte NG RC	4.00	1.20
❑ 115 Nick Punto NG RC	4.00	1.20
❑ 116 T. Shinjo NG RC	5.00	1.50
❑ 117 Jay Gibbons NG RC	5.00	1.50
❑ 118 Andres Torres NG RC	4.00	1.20
❑ 119 Alexis Gomez NG RC	4.00	1.20
❑ 120 Wilkin Ruan NG RC	4.00	1.20
❑ 121 Albert Pujols NG RC	50.00	15.00
❑ MM2 Derek Jeter/1996	12.00	3.60
❑ MM2 Derek Jeter AU/96	120.00	36.00

2001 Fleer Genuine

	Nm-Mt	Ex-Mt
COMP.SET w/o SP's (90)	25.00	7.50
COMMON CARD (1-100)	.50	.15
COMMON (101-130)	5.00	1.50

JETER AU SHEET AVAIL.VIA MAIL EXCH
JETER SHEET EXCH. RANDOM IN PACKS

❑ 1 Derek Jeter	3.00	.90
❑ 2 Nomar Garciaparra	2.00	.60
❑ 3 Alex Rodriguez	2.00	.60
❑ 4 Frank Thomas	1.25	.35
❑ 5 Travis Fryman	.50	.15
❑ 6 Gary Sheffield	.50	.15
❑ 7 Jason Giambi	.50	.15
❑ 8 Trevor Hoffman	.50	.15
❑ 9 Todd Helton	.75	.23
❑ 10 Ivan Rodriguez	1.25	.35
❑ 11 Roberto Alomar	.75	.23
❑ 12 Barry Zito	.75	.23
❑ 13 Kevin Brown	.50	.15
❑ 14 Shawn Green	.50	.15
❑ 15 Kenny Lofton	.50	.15
❑ 16 Jeff Weaver	.50	.15
❑ 17 Geoff Jenkins	.50	.15
❑ 18 Carlos Delgado	.50	.15
❑ 19 Mark Grace	.75	.23
❑ 20 Ken Griffey Jr.	2.00	.60
❑ 21 David Justice	.50	.15
❑ 22 Brian Giles	.50	.15
❑ 23 Scott Williamson	.50	.15
❑ 24 Richie Sexson	.50	.15
❑ 25 John Olerud	.50	.15
❑ 26 Sammy Sosa	2.00	.60
❑ 27 Bobby Higginson	.50	.15
❑ 28 Matt Lawton	.50	.15
❑ 29 Vinny Castilla	.50	.15
❑ 30 Alex Gonzalez	.50	.15
❑ 31 Manny Ramirez	.75	.23
❑ 32 Brad Radke	.50	.15
❑ 33 Cal Ripken	4.00	1.20
❑ 34 Richard Hidalgo	.50	.15
❑ 35 Al Leiter	.50	.15
❑ 36 Freddy Garcia	.50	.15
❑ 37 Juan Encarnacion	.50	.15
❑ 38 Corey Koskie	.50	.15
❑ 39 Greg Vaughn	.50	.15
❑ 40 Rafael Palmeiro	.75	.23
❑ 41 Vladimir Guerrero	1.25	.35
❑ 42 Troy Glaus	.50	.15
❑ 43 Mike Hampton	.50	.15
❑ 44 Jose Vidro	.50	.15
❑ 45 Ryan Rupe	.50	.15
❑ 46 Troy O'Leary	.50	.15
❑ 47 Ben Petrick	.50	.15
❑ 48 Mike Lieberthal	.50	.15
❑ 49 Mike Sweeney	.50	.15
❑ 50 Scott Rolen	1.25	.35
❑ 51 Albert Belle	.75	.23
❑ 52 Mark Quinn	.50	.15
❑ 53 Mike Piazza	2.00	.60
❑ 54 Mark McGwire	3.00	.90
❑ 55 Brady Anderson	.50	.15
❑ 56 Carlos Beltran	.75	.23
❑ 57 Michael Barrett	.50	.15
❑ 58 Jason Kendall	.50	.15
❑ 59 Jim Edmonds	.50	.15
❑ 60 Matt Williams	.50	.15
❑ 61 Pokey Reese	.50	.15
❑ 62 Bernie Williams	.75	.23
❑ 63 Barry Bonds	3.00	.90
❑ 64 David Wells	.50	.15
❑ 65 Chipper Jones	1.25	.35
❑ 66 Jim Parque	.50	.15
❑ 67 Derrek Lee	.50	.15
❑ 68 Darin Erstad	.50	.15
❑ 69 Edgar Martinez	.75	.23
❑ 70 Kerry Wood	1.25	.35
❑ 71 Omar Vizquel	.75	.23
❑ 72 Jeromy Burnitz	.50	.15
❑ 73 Warren Morris	.50	.15
❑ 74 Rick Ankiel	.50	.15
❑ 75 Andruw Jones	.50	.15
❑ 76 Paul Konerko	.50	.15
❑ 77 Mike Lowell	.50	.15
❑ 78 Roger Clemens	2.50	.75
❑ 79 Tim Hudson	.50	.15
❑ 80 Rafael Furcal	.50	.15
❑ 81 Craig Biggio	.75	.23
❑ 82 Edgardo Alfonzo	.50	.15
❑ 83 Pat Burrell	.50	.15
❑ 84 Adrian Beltre	.75	.23
❑ 85 Tony Gwynn	1.50	.45
❑ 86 J.T. Snow	.50	.15
❑ 87 Randy Johnson	1.25	.35
❑ 88 Sean Casey	.50	.15
❑ 89 Preston Wilson	.50	.15
❑ 90 Mike Mussina	.75	.23
❑ 91 Eric Chavez	.50	.15
❑ 92 Tim Salmon	.75	.23
❑ 93 Pedro Martinez	1.25	.35
❑ 94 Darryl Kile	.50	.15
❑ 95 Greg Maddux	2.00	.60
❑ 96 Magglio Ordonez	.50	.15
❑ 97 Jeff Bagwell	.75	.23
❑ 98 Timo Perez	.50	.15
❑ 99 Jeff Kent	.50	.15
❑ 100 Eric Owens	.50	.15
❑ 101 Ichiro Suzuki GU RC	40.00	12.00
❑ 102 E. Guzman GU RC	5.00	1.50
❑ 103 T. Shinjo GU RC	6.00	1.80
❑ 104 Travis Hafner GU RC	10.00	3.00
❑ 105 Larry Barnes GU	5.00	1.50
❑ 106 J. Randolph GU RC	5.00	1.50
❑ 107 Paul Phillips GU RC	5.00	1.50
❑ 108 Erick Almonte GU RC	5.00	1.50
❑ 109 Nick Punto GU RC	5.00	1.50
❑ 110 Jack Wilson GU RC	8.00	2.40
❑ 111 Jeremy Owens GU RC	5.00	1.50
❑ 112 Esix Snead GU RC	5.00	1.50
❑ 113 Jay Gibbons GU RC	6.00	1.80
❑ 114 A. Hernandez GU RC	5.00	1.50
❑ 115 Matt White GU RC	5.00	1.50
❑ 116 Ryan Freel GU RC	5.00	1.50
❑ 117 Martin Vargas GU RC	5.00	1.50
❑ 118 Winston Abreu GU RC	5.00	1.50
❑ 119 Junior Spivey GU RC	6.00	1.80
❑ 120 Paxton Crawford GU	5.00	1.50
❑ 121 Randy Keisler GU	5.00	1.50
❑ 122 Juan Diaz GU RC	5.00	1.50
❑ 123 Aaron Rowand GU	5.00	1.50
❑ 124 Toby Hall GU	5.00	1.50
❑ 125 Brian Cole GU	5.00	1.50
❑ 126 Aubrey Huff GU	5.00	1.50
❑ 127 Corey Patterson GU	5.00	1.50
❑ 128 Sun Woo Kim GU	5.00	1.50
❑ 129 Jace Brewer GU	5.00	1.50
❑ 130 Cesar Izturis GU	5.00	1.50
❑ NNO Derek Jeter AU Sheet/500 EXCH	120.00	36.00

2003 Fleer Hot Prospects

	MINT	NRMT
COMP.LO SET w/o SP's (80)	30.00	13.50
COMMON CARD (1-80)	.50	.23
FS BAT/JSY PRINT RUN 1250 #'d SETS		
CUT AU PRINT RUN 500 SERIAL #'d SETS		
GG AU PRINT RUN 400 SERIAL #'d SETS		
COMMON CARD (120-127)	10.00	4.50

❑ 1 Derek Jeter	3.00	1.35
❑ 2 Ryan Klesko	.50	.23
❑ 3 Troy Glaus	.50	.23
❑ 4 Jeff Kent	.50	.23
❑ 5 Frank Thomas	1.25	.55
❑ 6 Gary Sheffield	.50	.23
❑ 7 Jim Edmonds	.50	.23
❑ 8 Pat Burrell	.50	.23
❑ 9 Jacque Jones	.50	.23
❑ 10 Jason Jennings	.50	.23
❑ 11 Pedro Martinez	1.25	.55
❑ 12 Rafael Palmeiro	.75	.35
❑ 13 Jason Kendall	.50	.23
❑ 14 Tom Glavine	.75	.35
❑ 15 Josh Beckett	.50	.23
❑ 16 Luis Gonzalez	.50	.23
❑ 17 Edgar Martinez	.75	.35
❑ 18 Miguel Tejada	.50	.23
❑ 19 Fred McGriff	.75	.35
❑ 20 Adam Dunn	.75	.35
❑ 21 Lance Berkman	.50	.23
❑ 22 Magglio Ordonez	.50	.23
❑ 23 Darin Erstad	.50	.23
❑ 24 Rich Aurilia	.50	.23
❑ 25 Mike Piazza	2.00	.90
❑ 26 Shawn Green	.50	.23
❑ 27 Larry Walker	.75	.35
❑ 28 Manny Ramirez	.75	.35
❑ 29 Juan Gonzalez	.75	.35
❑ 30 Eric Chavez	.50	.23
❑ 31 Torii Hunter	.50	.23
❑ 32 A.J. Burnett	.50	.23
❑ 33 Sammy Sosa	2.00	.90
❑ 34 Eric Hinske	.50	.23
❑ 35 Brian Giles	.50	.23
❑ 36 Mike Sweeney	.50	.23
❑ 37 Sean Casey	.50	.23
❑ 38 Chipper Jones	1.25	.55
❑ 39 Scott Rolen	1.25	.55
❑ 40 Jason Giambi	.50	.23
❑ 41 Mo Vaughn	.50	.23
❑ 42 Roy Oswalt	.50	.23

Card	Nm-Mt	Ex-Mt
❑ 43 Paul Konerko	.50	.23
❑ 44 Tim Salmon	.75	.35
❑ 45 Edgardo Alfonzo	.50	.23
❑ 46 Jermaine Dye	.50	.23
❑ 47 Ben Sheets	.50	.23
❑ 48 Todd Helton	.75	.35
❑ 49 Greg Maddux	2.00	.90
❑ 50 Albert Pujols	2.50	1.10
❑ 51 Jim Thome	1.25	.55
❑ 52 Vladimir Guerrero	1.25	.55
❑ 53 Ivan Rodriguez	1.25	.55
❑ 54 Nomar Garciaparra	2.00	.90
❑ 55 Alex Rodriguez	2.00	.90
❑ 56 Alfonso Soriano	.75	.35
❑ 57 Kazuhisa Ishii	.50	.23
❑ 58 Austin Kearns	.50	.23
❑ 59 Curt Schilling	.50	.23
❑ 60 Bret Boone	.50	.23
❑ 61 Mark Prior	1.25	.55
❑ 62 Garret Anderson	.50	.23
❑ 63 Barry Bonds	3.00	1.35
❑ 64 Roger Clemens	2.50	1.10
❑ 65 Jeff Bagwell	.75	.35
❑ 66 Omar Vizquel	.75	.35
❑ 67 Jay Gibbons	.50	.23
❑ 68 Aubrey Huff	.50	.23
❑ 69 Bobby Abreu	.50	.23
❑ 70 Richie Sexson	.50	.23
❑ 71 Bobby Higginson	.50	.23
❑ 72 Kerry Wood	1.25	.55
❑ 73 Carlos Delgado	.50	.23
❑ 74 Sean Burroughs	.50	.23
❑ 75 Jose Vidro	.50	.23
❑ 76 Ken Griffey Jr.	2.00	.90
❑ 77 Randy Johnson	1.25	.55
❑ 78 Ichiro Suzuki	2.00	.90
❑ 79 Barry Zito	.50	.23
❑ 80 Carlos Beltran	.75	.35
❑ 81 Joe Borchard FS Jsy	8.00	3.60
❑ 82 Mark Teixeira FS Bat	8.00	3.60
❑ 83 Brandon Webb FS Jsy RC	10.00	4.50
❑ 84 S.Victorino Pants AU RC	15.00	6.75
❑ 85 Hee Seop Choi FS Jsy	8.00	3.60
❑ 86 Hank Blalock FS Bat	10.00	4.50
❑ 87 Brett Myers FS Jsy	8.00	3.60
❑ 88 Does Not Exist	.00	
❑ 89 Jesse Foppert FS Jsy	8.00	3.60
❑ 90 Lyle Overbay FS Jsy	8.00	3.60
❑ 91 Brian Stokes Pants AU RC	15.00	6.75
❑ 92 Josh Hall Bat AU RC	20.00	9.00
❑ 93 Chris Waters Pants AU RC	15.00	6.75
❑ 94 Lew Ford Pants AU RC	25.00	11.00
❑ 95 Ian Ferguson AU RC	10.00	4.50
❑ 96 Does Not Exist		
❑ 97 Josh Stewart AU RC	10.00	4.50
❑ 98 Pete LaForest AU RC	15.00	6.75
❑ 99 Jose Contreras Jsy AU/300 RC	40.00	18.00
❑ 100 Terrmel Sledge AU RC	15.00	6.75
❑ 101 Guillermo Quiroz AU RC	15.00	6.75
❑ 102 Alejandro Machado AU RC	10.00	4.50
❑ 103 Nook Logan Pants AU RC	15.00	6.75
❑ 104 R.Hammock Pants AU RC	20.00	9.00
❑ 105 Hideki Matsui FS Base RC	15.00	6.75
❑ 106 Does Not Exist		
❑ 107 Rocco Baldelli FS Jsy	8.00	3.60
❑ 108 Does Not Exist		
❑ 109 T.Wellemeyer Pants AU RC	20.00	9.00
❑ 110 Mi. Hessman Pants AU RC	15.00	6.75
❑ 111 J.Bonderman Pants AU RC	20.00	9.00
❑ 112 Craig Brazell Pants AU RC	20.00	9.00
❑ 113 Franc Rosario Pants AU RC	15.00	6.75
❑ 114 Jeff Duncan Pants AU RC	20.00	9.00
❑ 115 Dan. Cabrera Pants AU RC	25.00	11.00
❑ 116 Dontrelle Willis Pants AU	20.00	9.00
❑ 117 Cory Stewart AU RC	10.00	4.50
❑ 118 Tim Olson Pants AU RC	20.00	9.00
❑ 119 C.Wang Pants AU/500 RC	40.00	18.00
❑ 120 Josh Willingham Pants RC	10.00	4.50
❑ 121 Rickie Weeks Bat RC	15.00	6.75
❑ 122 Prentice Redman Pants RC	10.00	4.50
❑ 123 Mike Ryan Pants RC	15.00	6.75
❑ 124 Oscar Villarreal Pants RC	10.00	4.50
❑ 125 Ryan Wagner Pants RC	10.00	4.50
❑ 126 Bo Hart Pants RC	10.00	4.50
❑ 127 Edwin Jackson Pants RC	15.00	6.75

2004 Fleer Hot Prospects Draft

	Nm-Mt	Ex-Mt
COMP.SET w/o RC's (60)	15.00	4.50
COMMON CARD (1-60)	.50	.15
COMMON CARD (61-70)	3.00	.90
61-70 ODDS 1:15 HOBBY, 1:120 RETAIL		
61-70 PRINT RUN 1000 SERIAL #'d SETS		
COMMON CARD (71-120)	20.00	6.00
71-120 ODDS 1:9 HOBBY, 1:990 RETAIL		
71-120 PRINT RUN 299 SERIAL #'d SETS		
CARDS 112 AND 113 DO NOT EXIST		
EXCHANGE DEADLINE INDEFINITE		

Card	Nm-Mt	Ex-Mt
❑ 1 Miguel Tejada	.50	.15
❑ 2 Jose Vidro	.50	.15
❑ 3 Hideki Matsui	2.00	.60
❑ 4 Roger Clemens	2.50	.75
❑ 5 Craig Wilson	.50	.15
❑ 6 Bobby Crosby	.75	.23
❑ 7 Pat Burrell	.50	.15
❑ 8 Mike Sweeney	.50	.15
❑ 9 Craig Biggio	.75	.23
❑ 10 Scott Rolen	1.25	.35
❑ 11 Roy Halladay	.50	.15
❑ 12 Lyle Overbay	.50	.15
❑ 13 Rocco Baldelli	.50	.15
❑ 14 Mike Piazza	2.00	.60
❑ 15 Rafael Palmeiro	.75	.23
❑ 16 Hank Blalock	.50	.15
❑ 17 Sammy Sosa	2.00	.60
❑ 18 Dontrelle Willis	.50	.15
❑ 19 Alfonso Soriano	.75	.23
❑ 20 Gary Sheffield	.50	.15
❑ 21 Jim Thome	1.25	.35
❑ 22 Ivan Rodriguez	1.25	.35
❑ 23 Adam Dunn	.75	.23
❑ 24 Kerry Wood	1.25	.35
❑ 25 Khalil Greene	1.25	.35
❑ 26 Richie Sexson	.50	.15
❑ 27 Nomar Garciaparra	2.00	.60
❑ 28 Andruw Jones	.50	.15
❑ 29 Tom Glavine	.75	.23
❑ 30 Carlos Beltran	.75	.23
❑ 31 Chipper Jones	1.25	.35
❑ 32 Jeff Bagwell	.75	.23
❑ 33 Tim Hudson	.50	.15
❑ 34 Alex Rodriguez	2.00	.60
❑ 35 Omar Vizquel	.75	.23
❑ 36 Albert Pujols	2.50	.75
❑ 37 Frank Thomas	1.25	.35
❑ 38 Ben Sheets	.50	.15
❑ 39 Jason Schmidt	.50	.15
❑ 40 Miguel Cabrera	.75	.23
❑ 41 Carlos Delgado	.50	.15
❑ 42 Ichiro Suzuki	2.00	.60
❑ 43 Curt Schilling	1.25	.35
❑ 44 Todd Helton	.75	.23
❑ 45 Ken Griffey Jr.	2.00	.60
❑ 46 Mark Prior	1.25	.35
❑ 47 Vladimir Guerrero	1.25	.35
❑ 48 Pedro Martinez	1.25	.35
❑ 49 Manny Ramirez	.75	.23
❑ 50 Joe Mauer	.75	.23
❑ 51 Jorge Posada	.75	.23
❑ 52 Troy Glaus	.50	.15
❑ 53 Randy Johnson	1.25	.35
❑ 54 Adrian Beltre	.75	.23
❑ 55 Eric Gagne	1.25	.35
❑ 56 Josh Beckett	.50	.15
❑ 57 Jason Giambi	.50	.15
❑ 58 Barry Zito	.50	.15
❑ 59 Lance Berkman	.50	.15
❑ 60 Derek Jeter	2.50	.75
❑ 61 Kaz Matsui HP RC	5.00	1.50
❑ 62 Jason Bartlett HP RC	5.00	1.50
❑ 63 John Gall HP RC	5.00	1.50
❑ 64 Chris Saenz HP RC	3.00	.90
❑ 65 Merkin Valdez HP RC	5.00	1.50
❑ 66 Akinori Otsuka HP RC	3.00	.90
❑ 67 Joey Gathright HP RC	5.00	1.50
❑ 68 Brad Halsey HP RC	5.00	1.50
❑ 69 David Aardsma HP RC	3.00	.90
❑ 70 Scott Kazmir HP RC	10.00	3.00
❑ 71 Matt Bush AU RC	60.00	18.00
❑ 72 John Bowker AU RC	20.00	6.00
❑ 73 Mike Ferris AU RC	25.00	7.50
❑ 74 Brian Bixler AU RC EXCH	20.00	6.00
❑ 75 Scott Elbert AU RC	40.00	12.00
❑ 76 Josh Fields AU RC	50.00	15.00
❑ 77 Bill Bray AU RC	20.00	6.00
❑ 78 Greg Golson AU RC	30.00	9.00
❑ 79 Neil Walker AU RC	25.00	7.50
❑ 80 Philip Hughes AU RC	25.00	7.50
❑ 81 Chris Nelson AU RC	60.00	18.00
❑ 82 Mark Rogers AU RC	60.00	18.00
❑ 83 Trevor Plouffe AU RC	40.00	12.00
❑ 84 Chris Garcia AU RC EXCH	25.00	7.50
❑ 85 Thomas Diamond AU RC	30.00	9.00
❑ 86 B.J. Szymanski AU RC	25.00	7.50
❑ 87 Richie Robnett AU RC	30.00	9.00
❑ 88 Seth Smith AU RC	30.00	9.00
❑ 89 Kyle Waldrop AU RC	40.00	12.00
❑ 90 Curtis Thigpen AU RC	25.00	7.50
❑ 91 J.P. Howell AU RC EXCH	25.00	7.50
❑ 92 Blake DeWitt AU RC	50.00	15.00
❑ 93 Taylor Tankersley AU RC	30.00	9.00
❑ 94 Zach Jackson AU RC	25.00	7.50
❑ 95 Justin Orenduff AU RC	25.00	7.50
❑ 96 Tyler Lumsden AU RC	25.00	7.50
❑ 97 Danny Putnam AU RC	25.00	7.50
❑ 98 Jon Poterson AU RC	30.00	9.00
❑ 99 Matt Fox AU RC	25.00	7.50
❑ 100 Gio Gonzalez AU RC	25.00	7.50
❑ 101 Huston Street AU RC	30.00	9.00
❑ 102 Jay Rainville AU RC	30.00	9.00
❑ 103 Matt Durkin AU RC	20.00	6.00
❑ 104 Brett Smith AU RC	25.00	7.50
❑ 105 Justin Hoyman AU RC	20.00	6.00
❑ 106 Erick San Pedro AU RC	20.00	6.00
❑ 107 Jeff Marquez AU RC	25.00	7.50
❑ 108 Hunter Pence AU RC	20.00	6.00
❑ 109 Dustin Pedroia AU RC	30.00	9.00
❑ 110 Kurt Suzuki AU RC	50.00	15.00
❑ 111 Billy Buckner AU RC	25.00	7.50
❑ 114 J.C. Holt AU RC EXCH	25.00	7.50
❑ 115 Homer Bailey AU RC	40.00	12.00
❑ 116 David Purcey AU RC	25.00	7.50
❑ 117 Jeremy Sowers AU RC	50.00	15.00
❑ 118 Chris Lambert AU RC EXCH	25.00	7.50
❑ 119 Eric Hurley AU RC	25.00	7.50
❑ 120 Grant Johnson AU RC	20.00	6.00

2004 Fleer InScribed

	Nm-Mt	Ex-Mt
COMP.SET w/o SP's (75)	25.00	7.50
COMMON CARD (1-75)	.40	.12
COMMON CARD (76-85)	4.00	1.20
COMMON CARD (86-100)	3.00	.90

86-100 ODDS 1:12 HOBBY, 1:100 RETAIL
86-100 W/ASTERISK = ACTUAL PRINT RUN
ACTUAL PRINT RUNS PROVIDED BY FLEER
SEE AUTO PARALLEL SETS FOR AU PRICES

	Nm-Mt	Ex-Mt
❑ 1 Vladimir Guerrero	1.00	.30
❑ 2 Bartolo Colon	.40	.12
❑ 3 Troy Glaus	.40	.12
❑ 4 Richie Sexson	.40	.12
❑ 5 Randy Johnson	1.00	.30
❑ 6 Luis Gonzalez	.40	.12
❑ 7 J.D. Drew	.40	.12
❑ 8 Chipper Jones	1.00	.30
❑ 9 Andruw Jones	.40	.12
❑ 10 Melvin Mora	.40	.12
❑ 11 Miguel Tejada	.40	.12
❑ 12 Curt Schilling	1.00	.30
❑ 13 Pedro Martinez	1.00	.30
❑ 14 Nomar Garciaparra	1.50	.45
❑ 15 Kerry Wood	1.00	.30
❑ 16 Mark Prior	1.00	.30
❑ 17 Sammy Sosa	1.50	.45
❑ 18 Frank Thomas	1.00	.30
❑ 19 Magglio Ordonez	.40	.12
❑ 20 Sean Casey	.40	.12
❑ 21 Ken Griffey Jr.	1.50	.45
❑ 22 Adam Dunn	.60	.18
❑ 23 Jody Gerut	.40	.12
❑ 24 Omar Vizquel	.60	.18
❑ 25 Todd Helton	.60	.18
❑ 26 Vinny Castilla	.40	.12
❑ 27 Alex Sanchez	.40	.12
❑ 28 Ivan Rodriguez	1.00	.30
❑ 29 Dontrelle Willis	.40	.12
❑ 30 Josh Beckett	.40	.12
❑ 31 Miguel Cabrera	.60	.18
❑ 32 Roger Clemens	2.00	.60
❑ 33 Andy Pettitte	.60	.18
❑ 34 Jeff Bagwell	.60	.18
❑ 35 Ken Harvey	.40	.12
❑ 36 Carlos Beltran	.60	.18
❑ 37 Shawn Green	.40	.12
❑ 38 Hideo Nomo	1.00	.30
❑ 39 Scott Podsednik	.40	.12
❑ 40 Ben Sheets	.40	.12
❑ 41 Torii Hunter	.40	.12
❑ 42 Jacque Jones	.40	.12
❑ 43 Jose Vidro	.40	.12
❑ 44 Mike Piazza	1.50	.45
❑ 45 Tom Glavine	.60	.18
❑ 46 Derek Jeter	2.00	.60
❑ 47 Alex Rodriguez	1.50	.45
❑ 48 Jason Giambi	.40	.12
❑ 49 Hideki Matsui	1.50	.45
❑ 50 Eric Chavez	.40	.12
❑ 51 Barry Zito	.40	.12
❑ 52 Tim Hudson	.40	.12
❑ 53 Mark Mulder	.40	.12
❑ 54 Jim Thome	1.00	.30
❑ 55 Pat Burrell	.40	.12
❑ 56 Chase Utley	.40	.12
❑ 57 Jason Kendall	.40	.12
❑ 58 Jack Wilson	.40	.12
❑ 59 Khalil Greene	1.00	.30
❑ 60 Brian Giles	.40	.12
❑ 61 Jason Schmidt	.40	.12
❑ 62 Marquis Grissom	.40	.12
❑ 63 Ichiro Suzuki	1.50	.45
❑ 64 Bret Boone	.40	.12
❑ 65 Albert Pujols	2.00	.60
❑ 66 Scott Rolen	1.00	.30
❑ 67 Jim Edmonds	.40	.12
❑ 68 Tino Martinez	.60	.18
❑ 69 Rocco Baldelli	.40	.12
❑ 70 Alfonso Soriano	.60	.18
❑ 71 Michael Young	.40	.12
❑ 72 Hank Blalock	.40	.12
❑ 73 Roy Halladay	.40	.12
❑ 74 Carlos Delgado	.40	.12
❑ 75 Vernon Wells	.40	.12
❑ 76 Johnny Bench RET	5.00	1.50
❑ 77 Reggie Jackson RET	5.00	1.50
❑ 78 Al Kaline RET	5.00	1.50
❑ 79 Nolan Ryan RET	12.00	3.60
❑ 80 Tom Seaver RET	5.00	1.50
❑ 81 Robin Yount RET	8.00	2.40
❑ 82 Mike Schmidt RET	10.00	3.00
❑ 83 Jim Palmer RET	4.00	1.20
❑ 84 Harmon Killebrew RET	5.00	1.50
❑ 85 Joe Morgan RET	4.00	1.20
❑ 86 Kaz Matsui ROO/675 RC *	8.00	2.40
❑ 87 L.Gonzalez ROO/435 RC *	3.00	.90
❑ 88 Yadier Molina ROO/750 RC	8.00	2.40
❑ 89 Jon Knott ROO/675 RC *	3.00	.90
❑ 90 Kevin Youkilis ROO/640 *	3.00	.90
❑ 91 Chris Saenz ROO/325 RC *	3.00	.90
❑ 92 A.Blanco ROO/675 RC *	3.00	.90
❑ 93 D.Aardsma ROO/750 RC	3.00	.90
❑ 94 Merkin Valdez ROO/500 RC *	5.00	1.50
❑ 95 Jason Bartlett ROO/675 RC *	5.00	1.50
❑ 96 John Gall ROO/325 RC *	5.00	1.50
❑ 97 Zack Greinke ROO/675 *	3.00	.90
❑ 98 Scott Hairston ROO/675 *	3.00	.90
❑ 99 Matt Holliday ROO/750	3.00	.90
❑ 100 C.Kotchman ROO/375 *	5.00	1.50

2001 Fleer Legacy

	Nm-Mt	Ex-Mt
COMP.SET w/o SP's (90)	40.00	12.00
COMMON CARD (1-90)	1.00	.30
COMMON AUTO (91-100)	10.00	3.00
COMMON CARD (101-105)	8.00	2.40

	Nm-Mt	Ex-Mt
❑ 1 Pedro Martinez	2.50	.75
❑ 2 Andruw Jones	1.00	.30
❑ 3 Mike Hampton	1.00	.30
❑ 4 Gary Sheffield	1.00	.30
❑ 5 Barry Zito	1.50	.45
❑ 6 J.D. Drew	1.00	.30
❑ 7 Charles Johnson	1.00	.30
❑ 8 David Wells	1.00	.30
❑ 9 Kazuhiro Sasaki	1.00	.30
❑ 10 Vladimir Guerrero	2.50	.75
❑ 11 Pat Burrell	1.00	.30
❑ 12 Ruben Mateo	1.00	.30
❑ 13 Greg Maddux	4.00	1.20
❑ 14 Sean Casey	1.00	.30
❑ 15 Craig Biggio	1.50	.45
❑ 16 Bernie Williams	1.50	.45
❑ 17 Jeff Kent	1.00	.30
❑ 18 Nomar Garciaparra	4.00	1.20
❑ 19 Cal Ripken	8.00	2.40
❑ 20 Larry Walker	1.50	.45
❑ 21 Adrian Beltre	1.50	.45
❑ 22 Johnny Damon	1.50	.45
❑ 23 Rick Ankiel	1.00	.30
❑ 24 Matt Williams	1.00	.30
❑ 25 Magglio Ordonez	1.00	.30
❑ 26 Richard Hidalgo	1.00	.30
❑ 27 Robin Ventura	1.00	.30
❑ 28 Jason Kendall	1.00	.30
❑ 29 Tony Batista	1.00	.30
❑ 30 Chipper Jones	2.50	.75
❑ 31 Jim Thome	2.50	.75
❑ 32 Kevin Brown	1.00	.30
❑ 33 Mike Mussina	1.50	.45
❑ 34 Mark McGwire	6.00	1.80
❑ 35 Darin Erstad	1.00	.30
❑ 36 Manny Ramirez	1.50	.45
❑ 37 Bobby Higginson	1.00	.30
❑ 38 Richie Sexson	1.00	.30
❑ 39 Jason Giambi	1.00	.30
❑ 40 Alex Rodriguez	4.00	1.20
❑ 41 Mark Grace	1.50	.45
❑ 42 Ken Griffey Jr.	4.00	1.20
❑ 43 Moises Alou	1.00	.30
❑ 44 Edgardo Alfonzo	1.00	.30
❑ 45 Phil Nevin	1.00	.30
❑ 46 Rafael Palmeiro	1.50	.45
❑ 47 Javy Lopez	1.00	.30
❑ 48 Juan Gonzalez	1.50	.45
❑ 49 Jermaine Dye	1.00	.30
❑ 50 Roger Clemens	5.00	1.50
❑ 51 Barry Bonds	6.00	1.80
❑ 52 Carl Everett	1.00	.30
❑ 53 Ben Sheets	1.50	.45
❑ 54 Juan Encarnacion	1.00	.30
❑ 55 Jeromy Burnitz	1.00	.30
❑ 56 Miguel Tejada	1.00	.30
❑ 57 Ben Grieve	1.00	.30
❑ 58 Randy Johnson	2.50	.75
❑ 59 Frank Thomas	2.50	.75
❑ 60 Preston Wilson	1.00	.30
❑ 61 Mike Piazza	4.00	1.20
❑ 62 Brian Giles	1.00	.30
❑ 63 Carlos Delgado	1.00	.30
❑ 64 Tom Glavine	1.50	.45
❑ 65 Roberto Alomar	1.50	.45
❑ 66 Mike Sweeney	1.00	.30
❑ 67 Orlando Hernandez	1.00	.30
❑ 68 Edgar Martinez	1.50	.45
❑ 69 Tim Salmon	1.50	.45
❑ 70 Kerry Wood	2.50	.75
❑ 71 Jack Wilson RC	3.00	.90
❑ 72 Matt Lawton	1.00	.30
❑ 73 Scott Rolen	2.50	.75
❑ 74 Ivan Rodriguez	2.50	.75
❑ 75 Steve Finley	1.00	.30
❑ 76 Barry Larkin	1.50	.45
❑ 77 Jeff Bagwell	1.50	.45
❑ 78 Derek Jeter	6.00	1.80
❑ 79 Tony Gwynn	3.00	.90
❑ 80 Raul Mondesi	1.00	.30
❑ 81 Rafael Furcal	1.00	.30
❑ 82 Todd Helton	1.50	.45
❑ 83 Shawn Green	1.00	.30
❑ 84 Tim Hudson	1.00	.30
❑ 85 Jim Edmonds	1.00	.30
❑ 86 Troy Glaus	1.00	.30
❑ 87 Sammy Sosa	4.00	1.20
❑ 88 Cliff Floyd	1.00	.30
❑ 89 Jose Vidro	1.00	.30
❑ 90 Bob Abreu	1.00	.30
❑ 91 Drew Henson AU RC	40.00	12.00
❑ 92 Andy Morales AU RC	10.00	3.00
❑ 93 Wilson Betemit AU RC	10.00	3.00
❑ 94 Elpidio Guzman AU RC	10.00	3.00
❑ 95 Esix Snead AU RC	10.00	3.00
❑ 96 Winston Abreu AU RC	10.00	3.00
❑ 97 Jeremy Owens AU RC	10.00	3.00
❑ 98 Does Not Exist		
❑ 99 Junior Spivey AU RC	15.00	4.50
❑ 100 J. Randolph AU RC	10.00	3.00
❑ 101 Ichiro Suzuki RC	60.00	18.00
❑ 102 Albert Pujols RC/499	120.00	36.00
❑ 102AU Albert Pujols AU/300	400.00	120.00
❑ 103 Tsuyoshi Shinjo RC	10.00	3.00
❑ 104 Jay Gibbons RC	10.00	3.00
❑ 105 Juan Uribe RC	10.00	3.00

2004 Fleer Legacy

	Nm-Mt	Ex-Mt
COMP.SET w/o SP's (60)	100.00	30.00
COMMON CARD (1-60)	2.00	.60
COMMON CARD (61-75)	5.00	1.50
61-75 ODDS 1:1 HOBBY, 1:96 RETAIL		
61-75 PRINT RUN 599 SERIAL #'d SETS		
❑ 1 Angel Berroa	2.00	.60
❑ 2 Derek Jeter	6.00	1.80
❑ 3 Jody Gerut	2.00	.60
❑ 4 Curt Schilling	3.00	.90
❑ 5 Khalil Greene	3.00	.90
❑ 6 Manny Ramirez	3.00	.90
❑ 7 Rocco Baldelli	2.00	.60
❑ 8 Sammy Sosa	5.00	1.50
❑ 9 Shawn Green	2.00	.60
❑ 10 Austin Kearns	2.00	.60
❑ 11 Frank Thomas	3.00	.90
❑ 12 Alfonso Soriano	3.00	.90
❑ 13 Alex Rodriguez	5.00	1.50
❑ 14 Carlos Delgado	2.00	.60
❑ 15 Chipper Jones	3.00	.90
❑ 16 Edgar Martinez	3.00	.90
❑ 17 Ivan Rodriguez	3.00	.90
❑ 18 Mark Prior	3.00	.90
❑ 19 Mike Piazza	5.00	1.50
❑ 20 Orlando Cabrera	3.00	.90
❑ 21 Adam Dunn	3.00	.90
❑ 22 Andruw Jones	2.00	.60
❑ 23 Eric Chavez	2.00	.60
❑ 24 Mark Teixeira	2.00	.60
❑ 25 Scott Podsednik	2.00	.60
❑ 26 Torii Hunter	2.00	.60
❑ 27 Miguel Cabrera	3.00	.90
❑ 28 Hideki Matsui	5.00	1.50
❑ 29 Jose Reyes	2.00	.60
❑ 30 Vladimir Guerrero	3.00	.90
❑ 31 Albert Pujols	6.00	1.80
❑ 32 Greg Maddux	5.00	1.50
❑ 33 Jason Giambi	2.00	.60
❑ 34 Randy Johnson	3.00	.90
❑ 35 Roger Clemens	6.00	1.80
❑ 36 Casey Kotchman	3.00	.90
❑ 37 Ken Griffey Jr.	5.00	1.50
❑ 38 Todd Helton	3.00	.90
❑ 39 Javy Lopez	2.00	.60
❑ 40 Jim Thome	3.00	.90
❑ 41 Josh Beckett	2.00	.60
❑ 42 Kerry Wood	3.00	.90
❑ 43 Scott Rolen	3.00	.90
❑ 44 Pat Burrell	2.00	.60
❑ 45 Pedro Martinez	3.00	.90
❑ 46 Barry Zito	2.00	.60
❑ 47 Hank Blalock	2.00	.60
❑ 48 Hideo Nomo	3.00	.90
❑ 49 Jeff Bagwell	3.00	.90
❑ 50 Magglio Ordonez	2.00	.60
❑ 51 Ichiro Suzuki	5.00	1.50
❑ 52 Joe Mauer	3.00	.90
❑ 53 Richie Sexson	2.00	.60
❑ 54 Shannon Stewart	2.00	.60
❑ 55 Craig Wilson	2.00	.60
❑ 56 Miguel Tejada	2.00	.60
❑ 57 Sean Casey	2.00	.60
❑ 58 Tom Glavine	3.00	.90
❑ 59 Jason Schmidt	2.00	.60
❑ 60 Nomar Garciaparra	5.00	1.50
❑ 61 Kaz Matsui FL RC	10.00	3.00
❑ 62 Justin Leone FL RC	8.00	2.40
❑ 63 Merkin Valdez FL RC	8.00	2.40
❑ 64 Shingo Takatsu FL RC	8.00	2.40
❑ 65 Andres Blanco FL RC	5.00	1.50
❑ 66 Angel Chavez FL RC	5.00	1.50
❑ 67 Hector Gimenez FL RC	5.00	1.50
❑ 68 Akinori Otsuka FL RC	5.00	1.50
❑ 69 Jason Bartlett FL RC	8.00	2.40
❑ 70 Luis Gonzalez FL RC	5.00	1.50
❑ 71 Sean Henn FL RC	5.00	1.50
❑ 72 Mike Rouse FL RC	5.00	1.50
❑ 73 Chris Aguila FL RC	5.00	1.50
❑ 74 Aarom Baldiris FL RC	8.00	2.40
❑ 75 Jerry Gil FL RC	5.00	1.50

1999 Fleer Mystique

	Nm-Mt	Ex-Mt
COMPLETE SET (160)	250.00	75.00
COMP.SHORT SET (100)	40.00	12.00
COMMON CARD (1-100)	.40	.12
COMMON SP (1-100)	1.00	.30
COMMON (101-150)	5.00	1.50
COMMON (151-160)	5.00	1.50
❑ 1 Ken Griffey Jr. SP	2.50	.75
❑ 2 Livan Hernandez	.40	.12
❑ 3 Jeff Kent	.40	.12
❑ 4 Brian Jordan	.40	.12
❑ 5 Kevin Young	.40	.12
❑ 6 Vinny Castilla	.40	.12
❑ 7 Orlando Hernandez SP	1.00	.30
❑ 8 Bobby Abreu	.40	.12
❑ 9 Vladimir Guerrero SP	1.50	.45
❑ 10 Chuck Knoblauch	.40	.12
❑ 11 Nomar Garciaparra SP	2.50	.75
❑ 12 Jeff Bagwell	.60	.18
❑ 13 Todd Walker	.40	.12
❑ 14 Johnny Damon	.60	.18
❑ 15 Mike Caruso	.40	.12
❑ 16 Cliff Floyd	.40	.12
❑ 17 Andy Pettitte	.60	.18
❑ 18 Cal Ripken SP	5.00	1.50
❑ 19 Brian Giles	.40	.12
❑ 20 Robin Ventura	.40	.12
❑ 21 Alex Gonzalez	.40	.12
❑ 22 Randy Johnson	1.00	.30
❑ 23 Raul Mondesi	.40	.12
❑ 24 Ken Caminiti	.40	.12
❑ 25 Tom Glavine	.60	.18
❑ 26 Derek Jeter SP	4.00	1.20
❑ 27 Carlos Delgado	.40	.12
❑ 28 Adrian Beltre	.60	.18
❑ 29 Tino Martinez	.60	.18
❑ 30 Todd Helton	.60	.18
❑ 31 Juan Gonzalez SP	1.00	.30
❑ 32 Henry Rodriguez	.40	.12
❑ 33 Jim Thome	1.00	.30
❑ 34 Paul O'Neill	.60	.18
❑ 35 Scott Rolen SP	1.50	.45
❑ 36 Rafael Palmeiro	.60	.18
❑ 37 Will Clark	1.00	.30
❑ 38 Todd Hundley	.40	.12
❑ 39 Andruw Jones SP	1.00	.30
❑ 40 Rolando Arrojo	.40	.12
❑ 41 Barry Larkin	.60	.18
❑ 42 Tim Salmon	.60	.18
❑ 43 Rondell White	.40	.12
❑ 44 Curt Schilling	.40	.12
❑ 45 Chipper Jones SP	1.50	.45
❑ 46 Jeromy Burnitz	.40	.12
❑ 47 Mo Vaughn	.40	.12
❑ 48 Tony Clark	.40	.12
❑ 49 Fernando Tatis	.40	.12
❑ 50 Dmitri Young	.40	.12
❑ 51 Wade Boggs	.60	.18
❑ 52 Rickey Henderson	1.00	.30
❑ 53 Manny Ramirez SP	1.00	.30
❑ 54 Edgar Martinez	.60	.18
❑ 55 Jason Giambi	.40	.12
❑ 56 Jason Kendall	.40	.12
❑ 57 Eric Karros	.40	.12
❑ 58 Jose Canseco SP	1.50	.45
❑ 59 Shawn Green	.40	.12
❑ 60 Ellis Burks	.40	.12
❑ 61 Derek Bell	.40	.12
❑ 62 Shannon Stewart	.40	.12
❑ 63 Roger Clemens SP	3.00	.90
❑ 64 Sean Casey SP	1.00	.30
❑ 65 Jose Offerman	.40	.12
❑ 66 Sammy Sosa SP	2.50	.75
❑ 67 Frank Thomas SP	1.50	.45
❑ 68 Tony Gwynn SP	1.50	.45
❑ 69 Roberto Alomar	.60	.18
❑ 70 Mark McGwire SP	4.00	1.20
❑ 71 Troy Glaus	.40	.12
❑ 72 Ray Durham	.40	.12
❑ 73 Jeff Cirillo	.40	.12
❑ 74 Alex Rodriguez SP	2.50	.75
❑ 75 Jose Cruz Jr.	.40	.12
❑ 76 Juan Encarnacion	.40	.12
❑ 77 Mark Grace	.60	.18
❑ 78 Barry Bonds SP	4.00	1.20
❑ 79 Ivan Rodriguez SP	1.50	.45
❑ 80 Greg Vaughn	.40	.12
❑ 81 Greg Maddux SP	2.50	.75
❑ 82 Albert Belle	.40	.12
❑ 83 John Olerud	.40	.12
❑ 84 Kenny Lofton	.40	.12
❑ 85 Bernie Williams	.60	.18
❑ 86 Matt Williams	.40	.12
❑ 87 Ray Lankford	.40	.12
❑ 88 Darin Erstad	.40	.12
❑ 89 Ben Grieve	.40	.12
❑ 90 Craig Biggio	.60	.18
❑ 91 Dean Palmer	.40	.12
❑ 92 Reggie Sanders	.40	.12
❑ 93 Dante Bichette	.40	.12
❑ 94 Pedro Martinez SP	1.50	.45
❑ 95 Larry Walker	.60	.18
❑ 96 David Wells	.40	.12
❑ 97 Travis Lee SP	1.00	.30
❑ 98 Mike Piazza SP	2.50	.75
❑ 99 Mike Mussina	.60	.18
❑ 100 Kevin Brown	.60	.18
❑ 101 Ruben Mateo PROS	5.00	1.50
❑ 102 Rob. Ramirez RC	5.00	1.50
❑ 103 Glen Barker PROS RC	5.00	1.50
❑ 104 C. Bellinger PROS RC	5.00	1.50
❑ 105 Carlos Guillen PROS	5.00	1.50
❑ 106 S.Schoeneweis PROS	5.00	1.50
❑ 107 C.Gubanich PROS RC	5.00	1.50
❑ 108 S.Williamson PROS	5.00	1.50
❑ 109 E.Guzman PROS RC	5.00	1.50
❑ 110 A.J. Burnett PROS RC	10.00	3.00
❑ 111 Jeremy Giambi PROS	5.00	1.50
❑ 112 Trot Nixon PROS	5.00	1.50
❑ 113 J.D. Drew PROS	5.00	1.50
❑ 114 Roy Halladay PROS	5.00	1.50
❑ 115 J.Macias PROS RC	5.00	1.50
❑ 116 Corey Koskie PROS	5.00	1.50
❑ 117 Ryan Rupe PROS RC	5.00	1.50
❑ 118 S.Hunter PROS RC	5.00	1.50
❑ 119 Rob Fick PROS	5.00	1.50
❑ 120 M.Christensen PROS	5.00	1.50
❑ 121 Carlos Febles PROS	5.00	1.50
❑ 122 Gabe Kapler PROS	5.00	1.50
❑ 123 Jeff Liefer PROS	5.00	1.50
❑ 124 Warren Morris PROS	5.00	1.50
❑ 125 Chris Pritchett PROS	5.00	1.50
❑ 126 Torii Hunter PROS	5.00	1.50
❑ 127 Armando Rios PROS	5.00	1.50
❑ 128 Ricky Ledee PROS	5.00	1.50
❑ 129 K.Dransfeldt RC	5.00	1.50
❑ 130 J.Zimmerman RC	5.00	1.50
❑ 131 Eric Chavez PROS	5.00	1.50
❑ 132 F.Garcia PROS RC	10.00	3.00
❑ 133 Jose Jimenez PROS	5.00	1.50
❑ 134 Pat Burrell PROS RC	40.00	12.00
❑ 135 J.McEwing PROS RC	5.00	1.50
❑ 136 Kris Benson PROS	5.00	1.50
❑ 137 Joe Mays PROS RC	5.00	1.50
❑ 138 R.Roque PROS RC	5.00	1.50
❑ 139 C.Guzman PROS	5.00	1.50
❑ 140 Michael Barrett PROS	5.00	1.50
❑ 141 D.Mientkiewicz RC	10.00	3.00
❑ 142 Jeff Weaver PROS RC	8.00	2.40
❑ 143 Mike Lowell PROS	5.00	1.50
❑ 144 J.Phillips PROS RC	5.00	1.50

145 M.Anderson PROS	5.00	1.50
146 B.Hinchliffe PROS RC	5.00	1.50
147 Matt Clement PROS	5.00	1.50
148 Terrence Long PROS	5.00	1.50
149 Carlos Beltran PROS	8.00	2.40
150 Preston Wilson PROS	5.00	1.50
151 Ken Griffey Jr. STAR	8.00	2.40
152 Mark McGwire STAR	12.00	3.60
153 Sammy Sosa STAR	8.00	2.40
154 Mike Piazza STAR	8.00	2.40
155 Alex Rodriguez STAR	8.00	2.40
156 N.Garciaparra STAR	8.00	2.40
157 Cal Ripken STAR	15.00	4.50
158 Greg Maddux STAR	8.00	2.40
159 Derek Jeter STAR	12.00	3.60
160 Juan Gonzalez STAR	5.00	1.50
P113 J.D. Drew Promo	1.00	.30

2000 Fleer Mystique

	Nm-Mt	Ex-Mt
COMP.SET w/o SP's (125)	40.00	12.00
COMMON CARD (1-125)	.50	.15
COMMON (126-175)	5.00	1.50

Card	Nm-Mt	Ex-Mt
1 Derek Jeter	3.00	.90
2 David Justice	.50	.15
3 Kevin Brown	.75	.23
4 Jason Giambi	.50	.15
5 Jose Canseco	1.25	.35
6 Mark Grace	.75	.23
7 Hideo Nomo	1.25	.35
8 Edgardo Alfonzo	.50	.15
9 Barry Bonds	3.00	.90
10 Pedro Martinez	1.25	.35
11 Juan Gonzalez	.75	.23
12 Vladimir Guerrero	1.25	.35
13 Chuck Finley	.50	.15
14 Brian Jordan	.50	.15
15 Richie Sexson	.50	.15
16 Chan Ho Park	.50	.15
17 Tim Hudson	.50	.15
18 Fred McGriff	.75	.23
19 Darin Erstad	.50	.15
20 Chris Singleton	.50	.15
21 Jeff Bagwell	.75	.23
22 David Cone	.50	.15
23 Edgar Martinez	.75	.23
24 Greg Maddux	2.00	.60
25 Jim Thome	1.25	.35
26 Eric Karros	.50	.15
27 Bob Abreu	.50	.15
28 Greg Vaughn	.50	.15
29 Kevin Millwood	.50	.15
30 Omar Vizquel	.75	.23
31 Marquis Grissom	.50	.15
32 Mike Lieberthal	.50	.15
33 Gabe Kapler	.50	.15
34 Brady Anderson	.50	.15
35 Jeff Cirillo	.50	.15
36 Geoff Jenkins	.50	.15
37 Scott Rolen	1.25	.35
38 Rafael Palmeiro	.75	.23
39 Randy Johnson	1.25	.35
40 Barry Larkin	.75	.23
41 Johnny Damon	.75	.23
42 Andy Pettitte	.75	.23
43 Mark McGwire	3.00	.90
44 Albert Belle	.50	.15
45 Derrick Gibson	.50	.15
46 Corey Koskie	.50	.15
47 Curt Schilling	.50	.15
48 Ivan Rodriguez	1.25	.35
49 Mike Mussina	.75	.23
50 Todd Helton	.75	.23
51 Matt Lawton	.50	.15
52 Jason Kendall	.50	.15
53 Kenny Rogers	.50	.15
54 Cal Ripken	4.00	1.20
55 Larry Walker	.75	.23
56 Eric Milton	.50	.15
57 Warren Morris	.50	.15
58 Carlos Delgado	.50	.15
59 Kerry Wood	1.25	.35
60 Cliff Floyd	.50	.15
61 Mike Piazza	2.00	.60
62 Jeff Kent	.50	.15
63 Sammy Sosa	2.00	.60
64 Alex Fernandez	.50	.15
65 Mike Hampton	.50	.15
66 Livan Hernandez	.50	.15
67 Matt Williams	.50	.15
68 Roberto Alomar	.75	.23
69 Jermaine Dye	.50	.15
70 Bernie Williams	.75	.23
71 Edgar Martinez	.75	.23
72 Tom Glavine	.75	.23
73 Bartolo Colon	.50	.15
74 Jason Varitek	.75	.23
75 Eric Chavez	.50	.15
76 Fernando Tatis	.50	.15
77 Adrian Beltre	.75	.23
78 Paul Konerko	.50	.15
79 Mike Lowell	.50	.15
80 Robin Ventura	.50	.15
81 Russ Ortiz	.50	.15
82 Troy Glaus	.50	.15
83 Frank Thomas	1.25	.35
84 Craig Biggio	.75	.23
85 Orlando Hernandez	.50	.15
86 John Olerud	.50	.15
87 Chipper Jones	1.25	.35
88 Manny Ramirez	.75	.23
89 Shawn Green	.50	.15
90 Ben Grieve	.50	.15
91 Vinny Castilla	.50	.15
92 Tim Salmon	.75	.23
93 Dante Bichette	.50	.15
94 Ken Caminiti	.50	.15
95 Andruw Jones	.50	.15
96 Alex Rodriguez	2.00	.60
97 Erubiel Durazo	.50	.15
98 Sean Casey	.50	.15
99 Carlos Beltran	.75	.23
100 Paul O'Neill	.75	.23
101 Ray Lankford	.50	.15
102 Troy O'Leary	.50	.15
103 Bobby Higginson	.50	.15
104 Rondell White	.50	.15
105 Tony Gwynn	1.50	.45
106 Jim Edmonds	.50	.15
107 Magglio Ordonez	.50	.15
108 Preston Wilson	.50	.15
109 Roger Clemens	2.50	.75
110 Ken Griffey Jr.	2.50	.75
111 Nomar Garciaparra	2.00	.60
112 Juan Encarnacion	.50	.15
113 Michael Barrett	.50	.15
114 Matt Clement	.50	.15
115 David Wells	.50	.15
116 Mo Vaughn	.50	.15
117 Mike Cameron	.50	.15
118 Jose Lima	.50	.15
119 Tino Martinez	.75	.23
120 J.D. Drew	.50	.15
121 Carl Everett	.50	.15
122 Tony Clark	.50	.15
123 Brad Radke	.50	.15
124 Kevin Young	.50	.15
125 Raul Mondesi	.50	.15
126 Cole Liniak PROS	5.00	1.50
127 A.Soriano PROS	8.00	2.40
128 Lance Berkman PROS	5.00	1.50
129 D.Young PROS RC	5.00	1.50
130 F.Cordero PROS	5.00	1.50
131 Robert Fick PROS	5.00	1.50
132 Matt LeCroy PROS	5.00	1.50
133 Adam Piatt PROS	5.00	1.50
134 D.Turnbow PROS RC	5.00	1.50
135 Mark Quinn PROS	5.00	1.50
136 Kip Wells PROS	5.00	1.50
137 Rob Bell PROS	5.00	1.50
138 Brad Penny PROS	5.00	1.50
139 Pat Burrell PROS	5.00	1.50
140 Danys Baez PROS RC	5.00	1.50
141 C.Hermansen PROS	5.00	1.50
142 S.Lomasney PROS	5.00	1.50
143 Peter Bergeron PROS	5.00	1.50
144 J.Anderson PROS	5.00	1.50
145 Mike Darr PROS	5.00	1.50
146 Jacob Cruz PROS	5.00	1.50
147 K.Sasaki PROS RC	8.00	2.40
148 Ben Petrick PROS	5.00	1.50
149 Rick Ankiel PROS	5.00	1.50
150 A.McNeal PROS RC	5.00	1.50
151 Octavio Dotel PROS	5.00	1.50
152 Juan Pena PROS	5.00	1.50
153 Nick Johnson PROS	5.00	1.50
154 Wilton Veras PROS	5.00	1.50
155 Wily Pena PROS	5.00	1.50
156 Mark Mulder PROS	5.00	1.50
157 Daryle Ward PROS	5.00	1.50
158 C.Durbin PROS RC	5.00	1.50
159 Angel Pena PROS	5.00	1.50
160 DeWayne Wise PROS	5.00	1.50
161 Tarrik Brock PROS	5.00	1.50
162 Marcus Jensen PROS	5.00	1.50
163 Kevin Barker PROS	5.00	1.50
164 B.J. Ryan PROS	5.00	1.50
165 Cesar King PROS	5.00	1.50
166 Geoff Blum PROS	5.00	1.50
167 Ruben Mateo PROS	5.00	1.50
168 Ramon Ortiz PROS	5.00	1.50
169 Eric Munson PROS	5.00	1.50
170 Josh Beckett PROS	8.00	2.40
171 Rafael Furcal PROS	5.00	1.50
172 Matt Riley PROS	5.00	1.50
173 J.Santana PROS RC	30.00	9.00
174 Mark Johnson PROS	5.00	1.50
175 Adam Kennedy PROS	5.00	1.50
P54 Cal Ripken PROMO	2.50	.75
DW1 D.Winfield Ball/20		
DW2 Dave Winfield Helmet/40	100.00	30.00

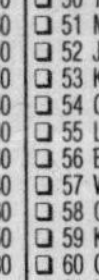

2003 Fleer Mystique

	MINT	NRMT
COMP.SET w/o SP's (80)	40.00	18.00
COMMON CARD (1-80)	.50	.23
COMMON CARD (81-130)	5.00	2.20

Card	MINT	NRMT
1 Alex Rodriguez	2.00	.90
2 Derek Jeter	3.00	1.35
3 Jose Vidro	.50	.23
4 Miguel Tejada	.50	.23
5 Albert Pujols	2.50	1.10
6 Rocco Baldelli	.50	.23
7 Jose Reyes	.50	.23
8 Hideo Nomo	1.25	.55
9 Hank Blalock	.75	.35
10 Chipper Jones	1.25	.55

❑ 11 Barry Larkin	.75	.35
❑ 12 Alfonso Soriano	.75	.35
❑ 13 Aramis Ramirez	.50	.23
❑ 14 Darin Erstad	.50	.23
❑ 15 Jim Edmonds	.50	.23
❑ 16 Garret Anderson	.50	.23
❑ 17 Todd Helton	.75	.35
❑ 18 Jason Kendall	.50	.23
❑ 19 Aubrey Huff	.50	.23
❑ 20 Troy Glaus	.50	.23
❑ 21 Sammy Sosa	2.00	.90
❑ 22 Roger Clemens	2.50	1.10
❑ 23 Mark Teixeira	.50	.23
❑ 24 Barry Bonds	3.00	1.35
❑ 25 Jim Thome	1.25	.55
❑ 26 Carlos Delgado	.50	.23
❑ 27 Vladimir Guerrero	1.25	.55
❑ 28 Austin Kearns	.50	.23
❑ 29 Pat Burrell	.50	.23
❑ 30 Ken Griffey Jr.	2.00	.90
❑ 31 Greg Maddux	2.00	.90
❑ 32 Corey Patterson	.50	.23
❑ 33 Larry Walker	.75	.35
❑ 34 Kerry Wood	1.25	.55
❑ 35 Frank Thomas	1.25	.55
❑ 36 Dontrelle Willis	.75	.35
❑ 37 Randy Johnson	1.25	.55
❑ 38 Curt Schilling	.50	.23
❑ 39 Jay Gibbons	.50	.23
❑ 40 Dmitri Young	.50	.23
❑ 41 Edgar Martinez	.75	.35
❑ 42 Kevin Brown	.50	.23
❑ 43 Scott Rolen	1.25	.55
❑ 44 Adam Dunn	.75	.35
❑ 45 Pedro Martinez	1.25	.55
❑ 46 Corey Koskie	.50	.23
❑ 47 Tom Glavine	.75	.35
❑ 48 Torii Hunter	.50	.23
❑ 49 Shawn Green	.50	.23
❑ 50 Nomar Garciaparra	2.00	.90
❑ 51 Bernie Williams	.75	.35
❑ 52 Milton Bradley	.50	.23
❑ 53 Jason Giambi	.50	.23
❑ 54 Mike Lieberthal	.50	.23
❑ 55 Jeff Bagwell	.75	.35
❑ 56 Carlos Pena	.50	.23
❑ 57 Lance Berkman	.50	.23
❑ 58 Jose Cruz Jr.	.50	.23
❑ 59 Josh Beckett	.50	.23
❑ 60 Mark Mulder	.50	.23
❑ 61 Mike Piazza	2.00	.90
❑ 62 Mark Prior	1.25	.55
❑ 63 Sean Burroughs	.50	.23
❑ 64 Angel Berroa	.50	.23
❑ 65 Geoff Jenkins	.50	.23
❑ 66 Magglio Ordonez	.50	.23
❑ 67 Craig Biggio	.75	.35
❑ 68 Roberto Alomar	.75	.35
❑ 69 Hee Seop Choi	.50	.23
❑ 70 J.D. Drew	.50	.23
❑ 71 Richie Sexson	.50	.23
❑ 72 Brian Giles	.50	.23
❑ 73 Gary Sheffield	.50	.23
❑ 74 Manny Ramirez	.75	.35
❑ 75 Barry Zito	.50	.23
❑ 76 Andruw Jones	.50	.23
❑ 77 Ivan Rodriguez	1.25	.55
❑ 78 Ichiro Suzuki	2.00	.90
❑ 79 Mike Sweeney	.50	.23
❑ 80 Vernon Wells	.50	.23
❑ 81 Craig Brazell RU RC	8.00	3.60
❑ 82 Wilfredo Ledezma RU RC	8.00	3.60
❑ 83 Josh Willingham RU RC	8.00	3.60
❑ 84 Chien-Ming Wang RU RC	8.00	3.60
❑ 85 Mike Ryan RU RC	8.00	3.60
❑ 86 Mike Gallo RU RC	5.00	2.20
❑ 87 Rickie Weeks RU RC	12.00	5.50
❑ 88 Brian Stokes RU RC	5.00	2.20
❑ 89 Humberto Quintero RU RC	5.00	2.20
❑ 90 Ramon Nivar RU RC	8.00	3.60
❑ 91 Jeremy Griffiths RU RC	8.00	3.60
❑ 92 Termel Sledge RU RC	8.00	3.60
❑ 93 Brandon Webb RU RC	8.00	3.60
❑ 94 David DeJesus RU RC	8.00	3.60
❑ 95 Doug Waechter RU RC	8.00	3.60
❑ 96 Jeremy Bonderman RU RC	8.00	3.60
❑ 97 Felix Sanchez RU RC	5.00	2.20
❑ 98 Colin Porter RU RC	5.00	2.20
❑ 99 Francisco Cruceta RU RC	5.00	2.20
❑ 100 Hideki Matsui RU RC	15.00	6.75
❑ 101 Chris Waters RU RC	5.00	2.20
❑ 102 Dan Haren RU RC	8.00	3.60
❑ 103 Lew Ford RU RC	8.00	3.60
❑ 104 Oscar Villarreal RU RC	5.00	2.20
❑ 105 Ryan Wagner RU RC	8.00	3.60
❑ 106 Prentice Redman RU RC	5.00	2.20
❑ 107 Josh Stewart RU RC	5.00	2.20
❑ 108 Carlos Mendez RU RC	5.00	2.20
❑ 109 Michael Hessman RU RC	5.00	2.20
❑ 110 Josh Hall RU RC	8.00	3.60
❑ 111 Daniel Garcia RU RC	5.00	2.20
❑ 112 Matt Kata RU RC	8.00	3.60
❑ 113 Michel Hernandez RU RC	5.00	2.20
❑ 114 Sergio Mitre RU RC	8.00	3.60
❑ 115 Pete LaForest RU RC	8.00	3.60
❑ 116 Edwin Jackson RU RC	12.00	5.50
❑ 117 Matt Diaz RU RC	8.00	3.60
❑ 118 Greg Aquino RU RC	5.00	2.20
❑ 119 Jose Contreras RU RC	8.00	3.60
❑ 120 Jeff Duncan RU RC	8.00	3.60
❑ 121 Richard Fischer RU RC	5.00	2.20
❑ 122 Todd Wellemeyer RU RC	8.00	3.60
❑ 123 Robby Hammock RU RC	8.00	3.60
❑ 124 Delmon Young RU RC	15.00	6.75
❑ 125 Clint Barmes RU RC	8.00	3.60
❑ 126 Phil Seibel RU RC	5.00	2.20
❑ 127 Bo Hart RU RC	8.00	3.60
❑ 128 Jon Leicester RU RC	5.00	2.20
❑ 129 Chad Gaudin RU RC	5.00	2.20
❑ 130 Guillermo Quiroz RU RC	8.00	3.60

2001 Fleer Platinum

	Nm-Mt	Ex-Mt
COMP. SERIES 1 (301)	200.00	60.00
COMP. SERIES 2 (300)	200.00	60.00
COMP.SER.1 w/o SP's (250)	40.00	12.00
COMP.SER.2 w/o SP's (200)	40.00	12.00
COMMON (1-250/302-501)	.30	.09
COMMON (251-280)	2.00	.60
COMMON AS (281-300)	2.00	.60
COMMON (502-601)	2.00	.60

❑ 1 Bobby Abreu	.30	.09
❑ 2 Brad Radke	.30	.09
❑ 3 Bill Mueller	.30	.09
❑ 4 Adam Eaton	.30	.09
❑ 5 Antonio Alfonseca	.30	.09
❑ 6 Manny Ramirez	.50	.15
❑ 7 Adam Kennedy	.30	.09
❑ 8 Jose Valentin	.30	.09
❑ 9 Jaret Wright	.30	.09
❑ 10 Aramis Ramirez	.30	.09
❑ 11 Jeff Kent	.30	.09
❑ 12 Juan Encarnacion	.30	.09
❑ 13 Sandy Alomar Jr.	.30	.09
❑ 14 Joe Randa	.30	.09
❑ 15 Darryl Kile	.30	.09
❑ 16 Darren Dreifort	.30	.09
❑ 17 Matt Kinney	.30	.09
❑ 18 Pokey Reese	.30	.09
❑ 19 Ryan Klesko	.30	.09
❑ 20 Shawn Estes	.30	.09
❑ 21 Moises Alou	.30	.09
❑ 22 Edgar Renteria	.30	.09
❑ 23 Chuck Knoblauch	.30	.09
❑ 24 Carl Everett	.30	.09
❑ 25 Garret Anderson	.30	.09
❑ 26 Shane Reynolds	.30	.09
❑ 27 Billy Koch	.30	.09
❑ 28 Carlos Febles	.30	.09
❑ 29 Brian Anderson	.30	.09
❑ 30 Armando Rios	.30	.09
❑ 31 Ryan Kohlmeier	.30	.09
❑ 32 Steve Finley	.30	.09
❑ 33 Brady Anderson	.30	.09
❑ 34 Cal Ripken	2.50	.75
❑ 35 Paul Konerko	.30	.09
❑ 36 Chuck Finley	.30	.09
❑ 37 Rick Ankiel	.30	.09
❑ 38 Mariano Rivera	.50	.15
❑ 39 Corey Koskie	.30	.09
❑ 40 Cliff Floyd	.30	.09
❑ 41 Kevin Appier	.30	.09
❑ 42 Henry Rodriguez	.30	.09
❑ 43 Mark Kotsay	.30	.09
❑ 44 Brook Fordyce	.30	.09
❑ 45 Brad Ausmus	.30	.09
❑ 46 Alfonso Soriano	.50	.15
❑ 47 Ray Lankford	.30	.09
❑ 48 Keith Foulke	.30	.09
❑ 49 Rich Aurilia	.30	.09
❑ 50 Alex Rodriguez	1.50	.45
❑ 51 Eric Byrnes	.30	.09
❑ 52 Travis Fryman	.30	.09
❑ 53 Jeff Bagwell	.50	.15
❑ 54 Scott Rolen	.75	.23
❑ 55 Matt Lawton	.30	.09
❑ 56 Brad Fullmer	.30	.09
❑ 57 Tony Batista	.30	.09
❑ 58 Nate Rolison	.30	.09
❑ 59 Carlos Lee	.30	.09
❑ 60 Rafael Furcal	.30	.09
❑ 61 Jay Bell	.30	.09
❑ 62 Jimmy Rollins	.30	.09
❑ 63 Derrek Lee	.30	.09
❑ 64 Andres Galarraga	.30	.09
❑ 65 Derek Bell	.30	.09
❑ 66 Tim Salmon	.50	.15
❑ 67 Travis Lee	.30	.09
❑ 68 Kevin Millwood	.30	.09
❑ 69 Albert Belle	.30	.09
❑ 70 Kazuhiro Sasaki	.30	.09
❑ 71 Al Leiter	.30	.09
❑ 72 Britt Reames	.30	.09
❑ 73 Carlos Beltran	.50	.15
❑ 74 Curt Schilling	.30	.09
❑ 75 Curtis Leskanic	.30	.09
❑ 76 Jeremy Giambi	.30	.09
❑ 77 Adrian Beltre	.50	.15
❑ 78 David Segui	.30	.09
❑ 79 Mike Lieberthal	.30	.09
❑ 80 Brian Giles	.30	.09
❑ 81 Marvin Benard	.30	.09
❑ 82 Aaron Sele	.30	.09
❑ 83 Kenny Lofton	.30	.09
❑ 84 Doug Glanville	.30	.09
❑ 85 Kris Benson	.30	.09
❑ 86 Richie Sexson	.30	.09
❑ 87 Javy Lopez	.30	.09
❑ 88 Doug Mientkiewicz	.30	.09
❑ 89 Peter Bergeron	.30	.09
❑ 90 Gary Sheffield	.30	.09
❑ 91 Derek Lowe	.30	.09
❑ 92 Tom Glavine	.50	.15
❑ 93 Lance Berkman	.30	.09
❑ 94 Chris Singleton	.30	.09
❑ 95 Mike Lowell	.30	.09
❑ 96 Luis Gonzalez	.30	.09
❑ 97 Dante Bichette	.30	.09
❑ 98 Mike Sirotka	.30	.09
❑ 99 Julio Lugo	.30	.09
❑ 100 Juan Gonzalez	.50	.15
❑ 101 Craig Biggio	.50	.15
❑ 102 Armando Benitez	.30	.09
❑ 103 Greg Maddux	1.25	.35
❑ 104 Mark Grace	.50	.15
❑ 105 John Smoltz	.50	.15
❑ 106 J.T. Snow	.30	.09
❑ 107 Al Martin	.30	.09

❑	108	Danny Graves	.30	.09
❑	109	Barry Bonds	2.00	.60
❑	110	Lee Stevens	.30	.09
❑	111	Pedro Martinez	.75	.23
❑	112	Shawn Green	.30	.09
❑	113	Bret Boone	.30	.09
❑	114	Matt Stairs	.30	.09
❑	115	Tino Martinez	.50	.15
❑	116	Rusty Greer	.30	.09
❑	117	Mike Bordick	.30	.09
❑	118	Garrett Stephenson	.30	.09
❑	119	Edgar Martinez	.50	.15
❑	120	Ben Grieve	.30	.09
❑	121	Milton Bradley	.30	.09
❑	122	Aaron Boone	.30	.09
❑	123	Ruben Mateo	.30	.09
❑	124	Ken Griffey Jr.	1.25	.35
❑	125	Russell Branyan	.30	.09
❑	126	Shannon Stewart	.30	.09
❑	127	Fred McGriff	.50	.15
❑	128	Ben Petrick	.30	.09
❑	129	Kevin Brown	.30	.09
❑	130	B.J. Surhoff	.30	.09
❑	131	Mark McGwire	2.00	.60
❑	132	Carlos Guillen	.30	.09
❑	133	Adrian Brown	.30	.09
❑	134	Mike Sweeney	.30	.09
❑	135	Eric Milton	.30	.09
❑	136	Cristian Guzman	.30	.09
❑	137	Ellis Burks	.30	.09
❑	138	Fernando Tatis	.30	.09
❑	139	Bengie Molina	.30	.09
❑	140	Tony Gwynn	1.00	.30
❑	141	Jeromy Burnitz	.30	.09
❑	142	Miguel Tejada	.30	.09
❑	143	Raul Mondesi	.30	.09
❑	144	Jeffrey Hammonds	.30	.09
❑	145	Pat Burrell	.30	.09
❑	146	Frank Thomas	.75	.23
❑	147	Eric Munson	.30	.09
❑	148	Mike Hampton	.30	.09
❑	149	Mike Cameron	.30	.09
❑	150	Jim Thome	.75	.23
❑	151	Mike Mussina	.50	.15
❑	152	Rick Helling	.30	.09
❑	153	Ken Caminiti	.30	.09
❑	154	John VanderWal	.30	.09
❑	155	Denny Neagle	.30	.09
❑	156	Robb Nen	.30	.09
❑	157	Jose Canseco	.75	.23
❑	158	Mo Vaughn	.30	.09
❑	159	Phil Nevin	.30	.09
❑	160	Pat Hentgen	.30	.09
❑	161	Sean Casey	.30	.09
❑	162	Greg Vaughn	.30	.09
❑	163	Trot Nixon	.30	.09
❑	164	Roberto Hernandez	.30	.09
❑	165	Vinny Castilla	.30	.09
❑	166	Robin Ventura	.30	.09
❑	167	Alex Ochoa	.30	.09
❑	168	Orlando Hernandez	.30	.09
❑	169	Luis Castillo	.30	.09
❑	170	Quilvio Veras	.30	.09
❑	171	Troy O'Leary	.30	.09
❑	172	Livan Hernandez	.30	.09
❑	173	Roger Cedeno	.30	.09
❑	174	Jose Vidro	.30	.09
❑	175	John Olerud	.30	.09
❑	176	Richard Hidalgo	.30	.09
❑	177	Eric Chavez	.30	.09
❑	178	Fernando Vina	.30	.09
❑	179	Chris Stynes	.30	.09
❑	180	Bobby Higginson	.30	.09
❑	181	Bruce Chen	.30	.09
❑	182	Omar Vizquel	.50	.15
❑	183	Rey Ordonez	.30	.09
❑	184	Trevor Hoffman	.30	.09
❑	185	Jeff Cirillo	.30	.09
❑	186	Billy Wagner	.30	.09
❑	187	David Ortiz	.50	.15
❑	188	Tim Hudson	.30	.09
❑	189	Tony Clark	.30	.09
❑	190	Larry Walker	.50	.15
❑	191	Eric Owens	.30	.09
❑	192	Aubrey Huff	.30	.09
❑	193	Royce Clayton	.30	.09
❑	194	Todd Walker	.30	.09
❑	195	Rafael Palmeiro	.50	.15
❑	196	Todd Hundley	.30	.09
❑	197	Roger Clemens	1.50	.45
❑	198	Jeff Weaver	.30	.09
❑	199	Dean Palmer	.30	.09
❑	200	Geoff Jenkins	.30	.09
❑	201	Matt Clement	.30	.09
❑	202	David Wells	.30	.09
❑	203	Chan Ho Park	.30	.09
❑	204	Hideo Nomo	.75	.23
❑	205	Bartolo Colon	.30	.09
❑	206	John Wetteland	.30	.09
❑	207	Corey Patterson	.30	.09
❑	208	Freddy Garcia	.30	.09
❑	209	David Cone	.30	.09
❑	210	Rondell White	.30	.09
❑	211	Carl Pavano	.30	.09
❑	212	Charles Johnson	.30	.09
❑	213	Ron Coomer	.30	.09
❑	214	Matt Williams	.30	.09
❑	215	Jay Payton	.30	.09
❑	216	Nick Johnson	.30	.09
❑	217	Deivi Cruz	.30	.09
❑	218	Scott Elarton	.30	.09
❑	219	Neifi Perez	.30	.09
❑	220	Jason Isringhausen	.30	.09
❑	221	Jose Cruz Jr.	.30	.09
❑	222	Gerald Williams	.30	.09
❑	223	Timo Perez	.30	.09
❑	224	Damion Easley	.30	.09
❑	225	Jeff D'Amico	.30	.09
❑	226	Preston Wilson	.30	.09
❑	227	Robert Person	.30	.09
❑	228	Jacque Jones	.30	.09
❑	229	Johnny Damon	.50	.15
❑	230	Tony Womack	.30	.09
❑	231	Adam Piatt	.30	.09
❑	232	Brian Jordan	.30	.09
❑	233	Ben Davis	.30	.09
❑	234	Kerry Wood	.75	.23
❑	235	Mike Piazza	1.25	.35
❑	236	David Justice	.30	.09
❑	237	Dave Veres	.30	.09
❑	238	Eric Young	.30	.09
❑	239	Juan Pierre	.30	.09
❑	240	Gabe Kapler	.30	.09
❑	241	Ryan Dempster	.30	.09
❑	242	Dmitri Young	.30	.09
❑	243	Jorge Posada	.50	.15
❑	244	Eric Karros	.30	.09
❑	245	J.D. Drew	.30	.09
❑	246	Todd Zeile	.30	.09
❑	247	Mark Quinn	.30	.09
❑	248	Kenny Kelly UER	.30	.09
		Listed as a Mariner on the front		
❑	249	Jermaine Dye	.30	.09
❑	250	Barry Zito	.50	.15
❑	251	Jason Hart	2.00	.60
		Larry Barnes		
❑	252	Ichiro Suzuki RC	25.00	7.50
		Elpidio Guzman RC		
❑	253	Tsuyoshi Shinjo RC	3.00	.90
		Brian Cole		
❑	254	John Barnes	2.00	.60
		Adrian Hernandez RC		
❑	255	Jason Tyner	2.00	.60
		Jace Brewer		
❑	256	Brian Buchanan	2.00	.60
		Luis Rivas		
❑	257	Brent Abernathy	2.00	.60
		Jose Ortiz		
❑	258	Marcus Giles	2.00	.60
		Keith Ginter		
❑	259	Tike Redman	2.00	.60
		Jaisen Randolph RC		
❑	260	Dane Sardinha	2.00	.60
		David Espinosa		
❑	261	Josh Beckett	2.00	.60
		Craig House		
❑	262	Jack Cust	2.00	.60
		Hiram Bocachica		
❑	263	Alex Escobar	2.00	.60
		Esix Snead RC		
❑	264	Chris Richard	2.00	.60
		Vernon Wells		
❑	265	Pedro Feliz	2.00	.60
		Xavier Nady		
❑	266	Brandon Inge	2.00	.60
		Joe Crede		
❑	267	Ben Sheets	3.00	.90
		Roy Oswalt		
❑	268	Drew Henson RC	4.00	1.20
		Andy Morales RC		
❑	269	C.C. Sabathia	2.00	.60
		Justin Miller		
❑	270	David Eckstein	2.00	.60
		Jason Grabowski		
❑	271	Dee Brown	2.00	.60
		Chris Wakeland		
❑	272	Junior Spivey RC	2.00	.60
		Alex Cintron		
❑	273	Elvis Pena	3.00	.90
		Juan Uribe RC		
❑	274	Carlos Pena	2.00	.60
		Jason Romano		
❑	275	Winston Abreu	2.00	.60
		Wilson Betemit		
❑	276	Jose Mieses RC	2.00	.60
		Nick Neugebauer		
❑	277	Shea Hillenbrand	2.00	.60
		Dernell Stenson		
❑	278	Jared Sandberg	2.00	.60
		Toby Hall		
❑	279	Jay Gibbons RC	4.00	1.20
		Ivanon Coffie		
❑	280	Pablo Ozuna	2.00	.60
		Santiago Perez		
❑	281	N.Garciaparra AS	8.00	2.40
❑	282	Derek Jeter AS	12.00	3.60
❑	283	Jason Giambi AS	2.00	.60
❑	284	Maggiio Ordonez AS	2.00	.60
❑	285	Ivan Rodriguez AS	5.00	1.50
❑	286	Troy Glaus AS	2.00	.60
❑	287	Carlos Delgado AS	2.00	.60
❑	288	Darin Erstad AS	2.00	.60
❑	289	Bernie Williams AS	3.00	.90
❑	290	Roberto Alomar AS	3.00	.90
❑	291	Barry Larkin AS	3.00	.90
❑	292	Chipper Jones AS	5.00	1.50
❑	293	Vladimir Guerrero AS	5.00	1.50
❑	294	Sammy Sosa AS	8.00	2.40
❑	295	Todd Helton AS	3.00	.90
❑	296	Randy Johnson AS	5.00	1.50
❑	297	Jason Kendall AS	2.00	.60
❑	298	Jim Edmonds AS	2.00	.60
❑	299	Andruw Jones AS	2.00	.60
❑	300	Edgardo Alfonzo AS	2.00	.60
❑	301	Albert Pujols RC	60.00	18.00
		Donaldo Mendez RC/1500		
❑	302	Shawn Wooten	.30	.09
❑	303	Todd Walker	.30	.09
❑	304	Brian Buchanan	.30	.09
❑	305	Jim Edmonds	.30	.09
❑	306	Jarrod Washburn	.30	.09
❑	307	Jose Rijo	.30	.09
❑	308	Tim Raines	.30	.09
❑	309	Matt Morris	.30	.09
❑	310	Troy Glaus	.30	.09
❑	311	Barry Larkin	.50	.15
❑	312	Javier Vazquez	.30	.09
❑	313	Placido Polanco	.30	.09
❑	314	Darin Erstad	.30	.09
❑	315	Marty Cordova	.30	.09
❑	316	Vladimir Guerrero	.75	.23
❑	317	Kerry Robinson	.30	.09
❑	318	Byung-Hyun Kim	.30	.09
❑	319	C.C. Sabathia	.30	.09
❑	320	Edgardo Alfonzo	.30	.09
❑	321	Jason Tyner	.30	.09
❑	322	Reggie Sanders	.30	.09
❑	323	Roberto Alomar	.50	.15
❑	324	Matt Lawton	.30	.09
❑	325	Brent Abernathy	.30	.09
❑	326	Randy Johnson	.75	.23
❑	327	Todd Helton	.50	.15
❑	328	Andy Pettitte	.50	.15
❑	329	Josh Beckett	.30	.09
❑	330	Mark DeRosa	.30	.09
❑	331	Jose Ortiz	.30	.09
❑	332	Derek Jeter	2.00	.60
❑	333	Toby Hall	.30	.09

❑ 334 Wes Helms .30 .09
❑ 335 Jose Macias .30 .09
❑ 336 Bernie Williams .50 .15
❑ 337 Ivan Rodriguez .75 .23
❑ 338 Chipper Jones .75 .23
❑ 339 Brandon Inge .30 .09
❑ 340 Jason Giambi .30 .09
❑ 341 Frank Catalanotto .30 .09
❑ 342 Andruw Jones .30 .09
❑ 343 Carlos Hernandez .30 .09
❑ 344 Jermaine Dye .30 .09
❑ 345 Mike Lamb .30 .09
❑ 346 Ken Caminiti .30 .09
❑ 347 A.J. Burnett .30 .09
❑ 348 Terrence Long .30 .09
❑ 349 Ruben Sierra .30 .09
❑ 350 Marcus Giles UER .30 .09
Listed as a pitcher on the back
❑ 351 Wade Miller .30 .09
❑ 352 Mark Mulder .30 .09
❑ 353 Carlos Delgado .30 .09
❑ 354 Chris Richard .30 .09
❑ 355 Daryle Ward .30 .09
❑ 356 Brad Penny .30 .09
❑ 357 Vernon Wells .30 .09
❑ 358 Jason Johnson .30 .09
❑ 359 Tim Redding .30 .09
❑ 360 Marlon Anderson .30 .09
❑ 361 Carlos Pena .30 .09
❑ 362 Nomar Garciaparra 1.25 .35
❑ 363 Roy Oswalt .50 .15
❑ 364 Todd Ritchie .30 .09
❑ 365 Jose Mesa .30 .09
❑ 366 Shea Hillenbrand .30 .09
❑ 367 Dee Brown .30 .09
❑ 368 Jason Kendall .30 .09
❑ 369 Vinny Castilla .30 .09
❑ 370 Fred McGriff .50 .15
❑ 371 Neifi Perez .30 .09
❑ 372 Xavier Nady .30 .09
❑ 373 Abraham Nunez .30 .09
❑ 374 Jon Lieber .30 .09
❑ 375 Paul LoDuca .30 .09
❑ 376 Bubba Trammell .30 .09
❑ 377 Brady Clark .30 .09
❑ 378 Joel Pineiro .75 .23
❑ 379 Mark Grudzielanek .30 .09
❑ 380 D'Angelo Jimenez .30 .09
❑ 381 Junior Herndon .30 .09
❑ 382 Magglio Ordonez .30 .09
❑ 383 Ben Sheets .50 .15
❑ 384 John Vander Wal .30 .09
❑ 385 Pedro Astacio .30 .09
❑ 386 Jose Canseco .75 .23
❑ 387 Jose Hernandez .30 .09
❑ 388 Eric Davis .30 .09
❑ 389 Sammy Sosa 1.25 .35
❑ 390 Mark Buehrle .30 .09
❑ 391 Mark Loretta .30 .09
❑ 392 Andres Galarraga .30 .09
❑ 393 Scott Spiezio .30 .09
❑ 394 Joe Crede .30 .09
❑ 395 Luis Rivas .30 .09
❑ 396 David Bell .30 .09
❑ 397 Einar Diaz .30 .09
❑ 398 Adam Dunn .50 .15
❑ 399 A.J. Pierzynski .30 .09
❑ 400 Jamie Moyer .30 .09
❑ 401 Nick Johnson .30 .09
❑ 402 Freddy Garcia CT SP 10.00 3.00
❑ 403 Hideo Nomo CT .30 .09
❑ 404 Mark Mulder CT .30 .09
❑ 405 Steve Sparks CT .30 .09
❑ 406 Mariano Rivera CT .30 .09
❑ 407 Mark Buehrle .30 .09
Mike Mussina CT
❑ 408 Randy Johnson CT .50 .15
❑ 409 Randy Johnson CT .50 .15
❑ 410 Curt Schilling .30 .09
Matt Morris CT
❑ 411 Greg Maddux CT .75 .23
❑ 412 Robb Nen CT .30 .09
❑ 413 Randy Johnson CT .50 .15
❑ 414 Barry Bonds CT .75 .23
❑ 415 Jason Giambi CT .30 .09
❑ 416 Ichiro Suzuki CT 5.00 1.50
❑ 417 Ichiro Suzuki CT 5.00 1.50
❑ 418 Alex Rodriguez CT .75 .23
❑ 419 Bret Boone CT .30 .09
❑ 420 Ichiro Suzuki CT 5.00 1.50
❑ 421 Alex Rodriguez CT .75 .23
❑ 422 Jason Giambi CT .30 .09
❑ 423 Alex Rodriguez CT .75 .23
❑ 424 Larry Walker CT .30 .09
❑ 425 Rich Aurilia CT .30 .09
❑ 426 Barry Bonds CT .75 .23
❑ 427 Sammy Sosa CT .75 .23
❑ 428 Jimmy Rollins .30 .09
Juan Pierre CT
❑ 429 Sammy Sosa CT .75 .23
❑ 430 Lance Berkman CT .30 .09
❑ 431 Sammy Sosa CT .75 .23
❑ 432 Carlos Delgado TL .30 .09
❑ 433 Alex Rodriguez TL .75 .23
❑ 434 Greg Vaughn TL .30 .09
❑ 435 Albert Pujols TL 15.00 4.50
❑ 436 Ichiro Suzuki TL 5.00 1.50
❑ 437 Barry Bonds TL .75 .23
❑ 438 Phil Nevin TL .30 .09
❑ 439 Brian Giles TL .30 .09
❑ 440 Bobby Abreu TL .30 .09
❑ 441 Jason Giambi TL .30 .09
❑ 442 Derek Jeter TL 1.00 .30
❑ 443 Mike Piazza TL .75 .23
❑ 444 Vladimir Guerrero TL .50 .15
❑ 445 Corey Koskie TL .30 .09
❑ 446 Richie Sexson TL .30 .09
❑ 447 Shawn Green TL .30 .09
❑ 448 Mike Sweeney TL .30 .09
❑ 449 Jeff Bagwell TL .30 .09
❑ 450 Cliff Floyd TL .30 .09
❑ 451 Roger Cedeno TL .30 .09
❑ 452 Todd Helton TL .30 .09
❑ 453 Juan Gonzalez TL .30 .09
❑ 454 Sean Casey TL .30 .09
❑ 455 Magglio Ordonez TL .30 .09
❑ 456 Sammy Sosa TL .75 .23
❑ 457 Manny Ramirez TL .30 .09
❑ 458 Jeff Conine TL .30 .09
❑ 459 Chipper Jones TL .50 .15
❑ 460 Luis Gonzalez TL .30 .09
❑ 461 Troy Glaus TL .30 .09
❑ 462 Ivan Rodriguez .50 .15
Jason Romano FF
❑ 463 Luis Gonzalez .30 .09
Jack Cust FF
❑ 464 Jim Thome .30 .09
C.C. Sabathia FF
❑ 465 Jason Giambi .30 .09
Jason Hart FF
❑ 466 Jeff Bagwell .50 .15
Roy Oswalt FF
❑ 467 Sammy Sosa .75 .23
Corey Patterson FF
❑ 468 Mike Piazza .75 .23
Alex Escobar FF
❑ 469 Ken Griffey Jr. .75 .23
Adam Dunn FF
❑ 470 Roger Clemens .75 .23
Nick Johnson FF
❑ 471 Cliff Floyd .30 .09
Josh Beckett FF
❑ 472 Cal Ripken Jr. 1.25 .35
Jerry Hairston Jr. FF
❑ 473 Phil Nevin .30 .09
Xavier Nady FF
❑ 474 Scott Rolen .50 .15
Jimmy Rollins FF
❑ 475 Barry Larkin .30 .09
David Espinosa FF
❑ 476 Larry Walker .50 .15
Jose Ortiz FF
❑ 477 Chipper Jones .50 .15
Marcus Giles FF
❑ 478 Craig Biggio .30 .09
Keith Ginter FF
❑ 479 Magglio Ordonez .30 .09
Aaron Rowand FF
❑ 480 Alex Rodriguez .75 .23
Carlos Pena FF
❑ 481 Derek Jeter 1.00 .30
Alfonso Soriano FF
❑ 482 Erubiel Durazo PG .30 .09
❑ 483 Bernie Williams PG .30 .09
❑ 484 Team Photo PG .30 .09
❑ 485 Team Photo PG .30 .09
❑ 486 Andy Pettitte PG .30 .09
❑ 487 Curt Schilling PG .30 .09
❑ 488 Randy Johnson PG .50 .15
❑ 489 Rudolph Guiliani PG .75 .23
Mayor of New York City
❑ 490 George W. Bush PG 5.00 1.50
President of United States
❑ 491 Roger Clemens PG .75 .23
❑ 492 Mariano Rivera PG .50 .15
❑ 493 Tino Martinez PG .30 .09
❑ 494 Derek Jeter PG 1.00 .30
❑ 495 Scott Brosius PG .30 .09
❑ 496 Alfonso Soriano PG .30 .09
❑ 497 Matt Williams PG .30 .09
❑ 498 Tony Womack PG .30 .09
❑ 499 Luis Gonzalez PG .30 .09
❑ 500 Arizona Diamondbacks PG .75 .23
❑ 501 Randy Johnson .50 .15
Curt Schilling
Co-MVP's PG
❑ 502 Josh Fogg RC 2.00 .60
❑ 503 Elpidio Guzman 2.00 .60
❑ 504 Corky Miller RC 2.00 .60
❑ 505 Cesar Crespo RC 2.00 .60
❑ 506 Carlos Garcia RC 2.00 .60
❑ 507 Carlos Valderrama RC 2.00 .60
❑ 508 Joe Kennedy RC 3.00 .90
❑ 509 Henry Mateo RC 2.00 .60
❑ 510 B. Duckworth RC 2.00 .60
❑ 511 Ichiro Suzuki 15.00 4.50
❑ 512 Zach Day RC 2.00 .60
❑ 513 Ryan Freel RC 2.00 .60
❑ 514 Brian Lawrence RC 2.00 .60
❑ 515 Alexis Gomez RC 2.00 .60
❑ 516 Will Ohman RC 2.00 .60
❑ 517 Juan Diaz RC 2.00 .60
❑ 518 Juan Moreno RC 2.00 .60
❑ 519 Rob Mackowiak RC 3.00 .90
❑ 520 Horacio Ramirez RC 3.00 .90
❑ 521 Albert Pujols 50.00 15.00
❑ 522 Tsuyoshi Shinjo 3.00 .90
❑ 523 Ryan Drese RC 3.00 .90
❑ 524 Angel Berroa RC 3.00 .90
❑ 525 Josh Towers RC 2.00 .60
❑ 526 Junior Spivey 3.00 .90
❑ 527 Greg Miller RC 2.00 .60
❑ 528 Esix Snead 2.00 .60
❑ 529 Mark Prior DP RC 15.00 4.50
❑ 530 Drew Henson 3.00 .90
❑ 531 Brian Reith RC 2.00 .60
❑ 532 Andres Torres RC 2.00 .60
❑ 533 Casey Fossum RC 2.00 .60
❑ 534 Wilmy Caceres RC 2.00 .60
❑ 535 Matt White RC 2.00 .60
❑ 536 Wilkin Ruan RC 2.00 .60
❑ 537 Rick Bauer RC 2.00 .60
❑ 538 Morgan Ensberg RC 3.00 .90
❑ 539 Geronimo Gil RC 2.00 .60
❑ 540 Dewon Brazelton RC 3.00 .90
❑ 541 Johnny Estrada RC 3.00 .90
❑ 542 Claudio Vargas RC 2.00 .60
❑ 543 Donaldo Mendez 2.00 .60
❑ 544 Kyle Lohse RC 3.00 .90
❑ 545 Nate Frese RC 2.00 .60
❑ 546 Christian Parker RC 2.00 .60
❑ 547 Blaine Neal RC 2.00 .60
❑ 548 Travis Hafner RC 5.00 1.50
❑ 549 Billy Sylvester RC 2.00 .60
❑ 550 Adam Pettyjohn RC 2.00 .60
❑ 551 Bill Ortega RC 2.00 .60
❑ 552 Jose Acevedo RC 2.00 .60
❑ 553 Steve Green RC 2.00 .60
❑ 554 Jay Gibbons 3.00 .90
❑ 555 Bert Snow RC 2.00 .60
❑ 556 Erick Almonte RC 2.00 .60
❑ 557 Jeremy Owens RC 2.00 .60
❑ 558 Sean Douglass RC 2.00 .60
❑ 559 Jason Smith RC 2.00 .60
❑ 560 Ricardo Rodriguez RC 2.00 .60
❑ 561 Mark Teixeira RC 12.00 3.60
❑ 562 Tyler Walker RC 2.00 .60
❑ 563 Juan Uribe 3.00 .90

❑ 564 Bud Smith RC 2.00 .60
❑ 565 Angel Santos RC 2.00 .60
❑ 566 Brandon Lyon RC 2.00 .60
❑ 567 Eric Hinske RC UER 3.00 .90
Front says he is a pitcher
❑ 568 Nick Punto RC 2.00 .60
❑ 569 Winston Abreu 2.00 .60
❑ 570 Jason Phillips RC 5.00 1.50
❑ 571 Rafael Soriano RC 3.00 .90
❑ 572 Wilson Betemit 2.00 .60
❑ 573 Endy Chavez RC 2.00 .60
❑ 574 Juan Cruz RC 2.00 .60
❑ 575 Cory Aldridge RC 2.00 .60
❑ 576 Adrian Hernandez 2.00 .60
❑ 577 Brandon Larson RC 2.00 .60
❑ 578 Bret Prinz RC 2.00 .60
❑ 579 Jackson Melian RC 2.00 .60
❑ 580 Dave Maurer RC 2.00 .60
❑ 581 Jason Michaels RC 2.00 .60
❑ 582 Travis Phelps RC 2.00 .60
❑ 583 Cody Ransom RC 2.00 .60
❑ 584 Benito Baez RC 2.00 .60
❑ 585 Brian Roberts RC 2.00 .60
❑ 586 Nate Teut RC 2.00 .60
❑ 587 Jack Wilson RC 4.00 1.20
❑ 588 Willie Harris RC 2.00 .60
❑ 589 Martin Vargas RC 2.00 .60
❑ 590 Steve Torrealba RC 2.00 .60
❑ 591 Stubby Clapp RC 2.00 .60
❑ 592 Dan Wright 2.00 .60
❑ 593 Mike Rivera RC 2.00 .60
❑ 594 Luis Pineda RC 2.00 .60
❑ 595 Lance Davis RC 2.00 .60
❑ 596 Ramon Vazquez RC 2.00 .60
❑ 597 Dustan Mohr RC 2.00 .60
❑ 598 Troy Mattes RC 2.00 .60
❑ 599 Grant Balfour RC 2.00 .60
❑ 600 Jared Fernandez RC 2.00 .60
❑ 601 Jorge Julio RC 2.00 .60

2002 Fleer Platinum

	Nm-Mt	Ex-Mt
COMPLETE SET (301)	200.00	60.00
COMP.SET w/o SP's (250)	25.00	7.50
COMMON CARD (1-250)	.30	.09
COMMON CARD (251-260)	3.00	.90
COMMON CARD (261-270)	3.00	.90
COMMON CARD (271-302)	3.00	.90

❑ 1 Garret Anderson .30 .09
❑ 2 Randy Johnson .75 .23
❑ 3 Chipper Jones .75 .23
❑ 4 David Cone .30 .09
❑ 5 Corey Patterson .30 .09
❑ 6 Carlos Lee .30 .09
❑ 7 Barry Larkin .50 .15
❑ 8 Jim Thome .75 .23
❑ 9 Larry Walker .50 .15
❑ 10 Randall Simon .30 .09
❑ 11 Charles Johnson .30 .09
❑ 12 Richard Hidalgo .30 .09
❑ 13 Mark Quinn .30 .09
❑ 14 Paul LoDuca .30 .09
❑ 15 Cristian Guzman .30 .09
❑ 16 Orlando Cabrera .30 .09
❑ 17 Al Leiter .30 .09
❑ 18 Nick Johnson .30 .09
❑ 19 Eric Chavez .30 .09
❑ 20 Miguel Tejada .30 .09
❑ 21 Mike Lieberthal .30 .09
❑ 22 Rob Mackowiak .30 .09
❑ 23 Ryan Klesko .30 .09
❑ 24 Jeff Kent .30 .09
❑ 25 Edgar Martinez .50 .15
❑ 26 Steve Kline .30 .09
❑ 27 Toby Hall .30 .09
❑ 28 Rusty Greer .30 .09
❑ 29 Jose Cruz Jr. .30 .09
❑ 30 Darin Erstad .30 .09
❑ 31 Reggie Sanders .30 .09
❑ 32 Javy Lopez .30 .09
❑ 33 Carl Everett .30 .09
❑ 34 Sammy Sosa 1.25 .35
❑ 35 Magglio Ordonez .30 .09
❑ 36 Todd Walker .30 .09
❑ 37 Omar Vizquel .50 .15
❑ 38 Matt Anderson .30 .09
❑ 39 Jeff Weaver .30 .09
❑ 40 Derrek Lee .30 .09
❑ 41 Julio Lugo .30 .09
❑ 42 Joe Randa .30 .09
❑ 43 Chan Ho Park .30 .09
❑ 44 Torii Hunter .30 .09
❑ 45 Vladimir Guerrero .75 .23
❑ 46 Rey Ordonez .30 .09
❑ 47 Tino Martinez .50 .15
❑ 48 Johnny Damon Sox .75 .23
❑ 49 Barry Zito .30 .09
❑ 50 Robert Person .30 .09
❑ 51 Aramis Ramirez .30 .09
❑ 52 Mark Kotsay .30 .09
❑ 53 Jason Schmidt .30 .09
❑ 54 Jamie Moyer .30 .09
❑ 55 David Justice .30 .09
❑ 56 Aubrey Huff .30 .09
❑ 57 Rick Helling .30 .09
❑ 58 Carlos Delgado .30 .09
❑ 59 Troy Glaus .30 .09
❑ 60 Curt Schilling .30 .09
❑ 61 Greg Maddux 1.25 .35
❑ 62 Nomar Garciaparra 1.25 .35
❑ 63 Kerry Wood .75 .23
❑ 64 Frank Thomas .75 .23
❑ 65 Dmitri Young .30 .09
❑ 66 Alex Ochoa .30 .09
❑ 67 Jose Macias .30 .09
❑ 68 Antonio Alfonseca .30 .09
❑ 69 Mike Lowell .30 .09
❑ 70 Wade Miller .30 .09
❑ 71 Mike Sweeney .30 .09
❑ 72 Gary Sheffield .30 .09
❑ 73 Corey Koskie .30 .09
❑ 74 Lee Stevens .30 .09
❑ 75 Jay Payton .30 .09
❑ 76 Mike Mussina .50 .15
❑ 77 Jermaine Dye .30 .09
❑ 78 Bobby Abreu .30 .09
❑ 79 Scott Rolen .75 .23
❑ 80 Todd Ritchie .30 .09
❑ 81 D'Angelo Jimenez .30 .09
❑ 82 Robb Nen .30 .09
❑ 83 John Olerud .30 .09
❑ 84 Matt Morris .30 .09
❑ 85 Joe Kennedy .30 .09
❑ 86 Gabe Kapler .30 .09
❑ 87 Chris Carpenter .30 .09
❑ 88 David Eckstein .30 .09
❑ 89 Matt Williams .30 .09
❑ 90 John Smoltz .50 .15
❑ 91 Pedro Martinez .75 .23
❑ 92 Eric Young .30 .09
❑ 93 Jose Valentin .30 .09
❑ 94 Erubiel Durazo .30 .09
❑ 95 Jeff Cirillo .30 .09
❑ 96 Brandon Inge .30 .09
❑ 97 Josh Beckett .30 .09
❑ 98 Preston Wilson .30 .09
❑ 99 Damian Jackson .30 .09
❑ 100 Adrian Beltre .50 .15
❑ 101 Jeromy Burnitz .30 .09
❑ 102 Joe Mays .30 .09
❑ 103 Michael Barrett .30 .09
❑ 104 Mike Piazza 1.25 .35
❑ 105 Brady Anderson .30 .09
❑ 106 Jason Giambi Yankees .30 .09
❑ 107 Marlon Anderson .30 .09
❑ 108 Jimmy Rollins .30 .09
❑ 109 Jack Wilson .30 .09
❑ 110 Brian Lawrence .30 .09
❑ 111 Russ Ortiz .30 .09
❑ 112 Kazuhiro Sasaki .30 .09
❑ 113 Placido Polanco .30 .09
❑ 114 Damian Rolls .30 .09
❑ 115 Rafael Palmeiro .50 .15
❑ 116 Brad Fullmer .30 .09
❑ 117 Tim Salmon .50 .15
❑ 118 Tony Womack .30 .09
❑ 119 Tony Batista .30 .09
❑ 120 Trot Nixon .30 .09
❑ 121 Mark Buehrle .30 .09
❑ 122 Derek Jeter 2.00 .60
❑ 123 Ellis Burks .30 .09
❑ 124 Mike Hampton .30 .09
❑ 125 Roger Cedeno .30 .09
❑ 126 A.J. Burnett .30 .09
❑ 127 Moises Alou .30 .09
❑ 128 Billy Wagner .30 .09
❑ 129 Kevin Brown .30 .09
❑ 130 Jose Hernandez .30 .09
❑ 131 Doug Mientkiewicz .30 .09
❑ 132 Javier Vazquez .30 .09
❑ 133 Tsuyoshi Shinjo .30 .09
❑ 134 Andy Pettitte .50 .15
❑ 135 Tim Hudson .30 .09
❑ 136 Pat Burrell .30 .09
❑ 137 Brian Giles .30 .09
❑ 138 Kevin Young .30 .09
❑ 139 Xavier Nady .30 .09
❑ 140 J.T. Snow .30 .09
❑ 141 Aaron Sele .30 .09
❑ 142 Albert Pujols 1.50 .45
❑ 143 Jason Tyner .30 .09
❑ 144 Ivan Rodriguez .75 .23
❑ 145 Raul Mondesi .30 .09
❑ 146 Matt Lawton .30 .09
❑ 147 Rafael Furcal .30 .09
❑ 148 Jeff Conine .30 .09
❑ 149 Hideo Nomo .75 .23
❑ 150 Jose Canseco .75 .23
❑ 151 Aaron Boone .30 .09
❑ 152 Bartolo Colon .30 .09
❑ 153 Todd Helton .50 .15
❑ 154 Tony Clark .30 .09
❑ 155 Pablo Ozuna .30 .09
❑ 156 Jeff Bagwell .50 .15
❑ 157 Carlos Beltran .50 .15
❑ 158 Shawn Green .30 .09
❑ 159 Geoff Jenkins .30 .09
❑ 160 Eric Milton .30 .09
❑ 161 Jose Vidro .30 .09
❑ 162 Robin Ventura .30 .09
❑ 163 Jorge Posada .50 .15
❑ 164 Terrence Long .30 .09
❑ 165 Brandon Duckworth .30 .09
❑ 166 Chad Hermansen .30 .09
❑ 167 Ben Davis .30 .09
❑ 168 Phil Nevin .30 .09
❑ 169 Bret Boone .30 .09
❑ 170 J.D. Drew .30 .09
❑ 171 Edgar Renteria .30 .09
❑ 172 Randy Winn .30 .09
❑ 173 Alex Rodriguez 1.25 .35
❑ 174 Shannon Stewart .30 .09
❑ 175 Steve Finley .30 .09
❑ 176 Marcus Giles .30 .09
❑ 177 Jay Gibbons .30 .09
❑ 178 Manny Ramirez .50 .15
❑ 179 Ray Durham .30 .09
❑ 180 Sean Casey .30 .09
❑ 181 Travis Fryman .30 .09
❑ 182 Denny Neagle .30 .09
❑ 183 Deivi Cruz .30 .09
❑ 184 Luis Castillo .30 .09
❑ 185 Lance Berkman .30 .09
❑ 186 Dee Brown .30 .09
❑ 187 Jeff Shaw .30 .09
❑ 188 Mark Loretta .30 .09
❑ 189 David Ortiz .50 .15
❑ 190 Edgardo Alfonzo .30 .09

	Nm-Mt	Ex-Mt
❑ 191 Roger Clemens	1.50	.45
❑ 192 Mariano Rivera	.50	.15
❑ 193 Jeremy Giambi	.30	.09
❑ 194 Johnny Estrada	.30	.09
❑ 195 Craig Wilson	.30	.09
❑ 196 Adam Eaton	.30	.09
❑ 197 Rich Aurilia	.30	.09
❑ 198 Mike Cameron	.30	.09
❑ 199 Jim Edmonds	.30	.09
❑ 200 Fernando Vina	.30	.09
❑ 201 Greg Vaughn	.30	.09
❑ 202 Mike Young	.75	.23
❑ 203 Vernon Wells	.30	.09
❑ 204 Luis Gonzalez	.30	.09
❑ 205 Tom Glavine	.50	.15
❑ 206 Chris Richard	.30	.09
❑ 207 Jon Lieber	.30	.09
❑ 208 Keith Foulke	.30	.09
❑ 209 Rondell White	.30	.09
❑ 210 Bernie Williams	.50	.15
❑ 211 Juan Pierre	.30	.09
❑ 212 Juan Encarnacion	.30	.09
❑ 213 Ryan Dempster	.30	.09
❑ 214 Tim Redding	.30	.09
❑ 215 Jeff Suppan	.30	.09
❑ 216 Mark Grudzielanek	.30	.09
❑ 217 Richie Sexson	.30	.09
❑ 218 Brad Radke	.30	.09
❑ 219 Armando Benitez	.30	.09
❑ 220 Orlando Hernandez	.30	.09
❑ 221 Alfonso Soriano	.50	.15
❑ 222 Mark Mulder	.30	.09
❑ 223 Travis Lee	.30	.09
❑ 224 Jason Kendall	.30	.09
❑ 225 Trevor Hoffman	.30	.09
❑ 226 Barry Bonds	2.00	.60
❑ 227 Freddy Garcia	.30	.09
❑ 228 Darryl Kile	.30	.09
❑ 229 Ben Grieve	.30	.09
❑ 230 Frank Catalanotto	.30	.09
❑ 231 Ruben Sierra	.30	.09
❑ 232 Homer Bush	.30	.09
❑ 233 Mark Grace	.50	.15
❑ 234 Andruw Jones	.30	.09
❑ 235 Brian Roberts	.30	.09
❑ 236 Fred McGriff	.50	.15
❑ 237 Paul Konerko	.30	.09
❑ 238 Ken Griffey Jr.	1.25	.35
❑ 239 John Burkett	.30	.09
❑ 240 Juan Uribe	.30	.09
❑ 241 Bobby Higginson	.30	.09
❑ 242 Cliff Floyd	.30	.09
❑ 243 Craig Biggio	.50	.15
❑ 244 Neifi Perez	.30	.09
❑ 245 Eric Karros	.30	.09
❑ 246 Ben Sheets	.30	.09
❑ 247 Tony Armas Jr.	.30	.09
❑ 248 Mo Vaughn	.30	.09
❑ 249 David Wells	.30	.09
❑ 250 Juan Gonzalez	.50	.15
❑ 251 Barry Bonds DD	8.00	2.40
❑ 252 Sammy Sosa DD	5.00	1.50
❑ 253 Ken Griffey Jr. DD	5.00	1.50
❑ 254 Roger Clemens DD	6.00	1.80
❑ 255 Greg Maddux DD	5.00	1.50
❑ 256 Chipper Jones DD	3.00	.90
❑ 257 Alex Rodriguez	6.00	1.80
Derek Jeter		
Nomar Garciaparra DD		
❑ 258 Roberto Alomar DD	3.00	.90
❑ 259 Jeff Bagwell DD	3.00	.90
❑ 260 Mike Piazza DD	5.00	1.50
❑ 261 Mark Teixeira BB	3.00	.90
❑ 262 Mark Prior BB	5.00	1.50
❑ 263 Alex Escobar BB	3.00	.90
❑ 264 C.C. Sabathia BB	3.00	.90
❑ 265 Drew Henson BB	3.00	.90
❑ 266 Wilson Betemit BB	3.00	.90
❑ 267 Roy Oswalt BB	3.00	.90
❑ 268 Adam Dunn BB	3.00	.90
❑ 269 Bud Smith BB	3.00	.90
❑ 270 Dewon Brazelton BB	3.00	.90
❑ 271 Brandon Backe RC	4.00	1.20
Jason Standridge		
❑ 272 Wilfredo Rodriguez	3.00	.90
Carlos Hernandez		
❑ 273 Geronimo Gil	3.00	.90
Luis Rivera		
❑ 274 Carlos Pena	3.00	.90
Jovanny Cedeno		
❑ 275 Austin Kearns	3.00	.90
Ben Broussard		
❑ 276 Jorge De La RosaRC	3.00	.90
Kenny Kelly		
❑ 277 Ryan Drese	4.00	1.20
Victor Martinez		
❑ 278 Joel Pinero	3.00	.90
Nate Cornejo		
❑ 279 David Kelton	3.00	.90
Carlos Zambrano		
❑ 280 Bill Ortega		
Satoru Komiyama ERR		
Not intended for public release		
Card features large cut out square over Komiyama image		
❑ 281 Donnie Bridges	3.00	.90
Wilkin Ruan		
❑ 282 Wily Mo Pena	3.00	.90
Brandon Claussen		
❑ 283 Jason Jennings	3.00	.90
Rene Reyes RC		
❑ 284 Steve Green	3.00	.90
Alfredo Amezaga		
❑ 285 Eric Hinske	3.00	.90
Felipe Lopez		
❑ 286 Anderson Machado RC	3.00	.90
Brad Baisley		
❑ 287 Carlos Garcia	3.00	.90
Sean Douglass		
❑ 288 Pat Strange	3.00	.90
Jae Weong Seo		
❑ 289 Marcus Thames	3.00	.90
Alex Graman		
❑ 290 Matt Childers RC	3.00	.90
Hansel Izquierdo RC		
❑ 291 Ron Calloway RC	3.00	.90
Adam Walker RC		
❑ 292 J.R. House	3.00	.90
J.J. Davis		
❑ 293 Ryan Anderson	3.00	.90
Rafael Soriano		
❑ 294 Mike Bynum	3.00	.90
Dennis Tankersley		
❑ 295 Kurt Ainsworth	3.00	.90
Carlos Valderrama		
❑ 296 Billy Hall	3.00	.90
Cristian Guerrero		
❑ 297 Miguel Olivo	3.00	.90
Danny Wright		
❑ 298 Marlon Byrd	3.00	.90
Jorge Padilla RC		
❑ 299 Juan Cruz	3.00	.90
Ben Christensen		
❑ 300 Adam Johnson	3.00	.90
Michael Restovich		
❑ 301 So Taguchi SP RC	3.00	.90
❑ 302 Kazuhisa Ishii SP RC	4.00	1.20
❑ NNO Barry Bonds 1986 AU/73	600.00	180.00

2001 Fleer Premium

	Nm-Mt	Ex-Mt
COMP.SET w/o SP's (200)	30.00	9.00
COMMON CARD (1-200)	.40	.12
COMMON (201-230)	5.00	1.50
COMMON (231-235)	8.00	2.40
❑ 1 Cal Ripken	3.00	.90
❑ 2 Derek Jeter	2.50	.75
❑ 3 Edgardo Alfonzo	.40	.12
❑ 4 Luis Castillo	.40	.12
❑ 5 Mike Lieberthal	.40	.12
❑ 6 Kazuhiro Sasaki	.40	.12
❑ 7 Jeff Kent	.40	.12
❑ 8 Eric Karros	.40	.12
❑ 9 Tom Glavine	.60	.18
❑ 10 Jeromy Burnitz	.40	.12
❑ 11 Travis Fryman	.40	.12
❑ 12 Ron Coomer	.40	.12
❑ 13 Jeff D'Amico	.40	.12
❑ 14 Carlos Febles	.40	.12
❑ 15 Kevin Brown	.40	.12
❑ 16 Deivi Cruz	.40	.12
❑ 17 Tino Martinez	.60	.18
❑ 18 Bobby Abreu	.40	.12
❑ 19 Roger Clemens	2.00	.60
❑ 20 Jeffrey Hammonds	.40	.12
❑ 21 Peter Bergeron	.40	.12
❑ 22 Ray Lankford	.40	.12
❑ 23 Scott Rolen	1.00	.30
❑ 24 Jermaine Dye	.40	.12
❑ 25 Rusty Greer	.40	.12
❑ 26 Frank Thomas	1.00	.30
❑ 27 Jeff Bagwell	.60	.18
❑ 28 Cliff Floyd	.40	.12
❑ 29 Chris Singleton	.40	.12
❑ 30 Steve Finley	.40	.12
❑ 31 Orlando Hernandez	.40	.12
❑ 32 Tom Goodwin	.40	.12
❑ 33 Larry Walker	.60	.18
❑ 34 Mike Sweeney	.40	.12
❑ 35 Tim Hudson	.40	.12
❑ 36 Kerry Wood	1.00	.30
❑ 37 Mike Lowell	.40	.12
❑ 38 Andruw Jones	.75	.23
❑ 39 Alex Gonzalez	.40	.12
❑ 40 Juan Gonzalez	.75	.23
❑ 41 J.D. Drew	.40	.12
❑ 42 Mark McLemore	.40	.12
❑ 43 Royce Clayton	.40	.12
❑ 44 Paul O'Neill	.60	.18
❑ 45 Carlos Beltran	.60	.18
❑ 46 Phil Nevin	.40	.12
❑ 47 Rondell White	.40	.12
❑ 48 Gerald Williams	.40	.12
❑ 49 Geoff Jenkins	.40	.12
❑ 50 Marvin Benard	.40	.12
❑ 51 Alex Rodriguez	1.50	.45
❑ 52 Moises Alou	.40	.12
❑ 53 Mike Lansing	.40	.12
❑ 54 Omar Vizquel	.60	.18
❑ 55 Eric Chavez	.40	.12
❑ 56 Mark Quinn	.40	.12
❑ 57 Mike Lamb	.40	.12
❑ 58 Rick Ankiel	.40	.12
❑ 59 Lance Berkman	.40	.12
❑ 60 Jeff Conine	.40	.12
❑ 61 B.J. Surhoff	.40	.12
❑ 62 Todd Helton	.60	.18
❑ 63 J.T. Snow	.40	.12
❑ 64 John VanderWal	.40	.12
❑ 65 Johnny Damon	.60	.18
❑ 66 Bobby Higginson	.40	.12
❑ 67 Carlos Delgado	.75	.23
❑ 68 Shawn Green	.40	.12
❑ 69 Mike Redmond	.40	.12
❑ 70 Mike Piazza	1.50	.45
❑ 71 Adrian Beltre	.60	.18
❑ 72 Juan Encarnacion	.40	.12
❑ 73 Chipper Jones	1.00	.30
❑ 74 Garret Anderson	.40	.12
❑ 75 Paul Konerko	.40	.12
❑ 76 Barry Larkin	.60	.18
❑ 77 Tony Gwynn	1.25	.35
❑ 78 Rafael Palmeiro	.60	.18
❑ 79 Randy Johnson	1.00	.30
❑ 80 Mark Grace	.75	.23
❑ 81 Javy Lopez	.40	.12
❑ 82 Gabe Kapler	.40	.12
❑ 83 Henry Rodriguez	.40	.12

	Nm-Mt	Ex-Mt
❑ 84 Raul Mondesi	.40	.12
❑ 85 Adam Piatt	.40	.12
❑ 86 Marquis Grissom	.40	.12
❑ 87 Charles Johnson	.40	.12
❑ 88 Sean Casey	.40	.12
❑ 89 Manny Ramirez	.60	.18
❑ 90 Curt Schilling	.40	.12
❑ 91 Fernando Tatis	.40	.12
❑ 92 Derek Bell	.40	.12
❑ 93 Tony Clark	.40	.12
❑ 94 Homer Bush	.40	.12
❑ 95 Nomar Garciaparra	1.50	.45
❑ 96 Vinny Castilla	.40	.12
❑ 97 Ben Davis	.40	.12
❑ 98 Carl Everett	.40	.12
❑ 99 Damion Easley	.40	.12
❑ 100 Craig Biggio	.60	.18
❑ 101 Todd Hollandsworth	.40	.12
❑ 102 Jay Payton	.40	.12
❑ 103 Gary Sheffield	.40	.12
❑ 104 Sandy Alomar Jr.	.40	.12
❑ 105 Doug Glanville	.40	.12
❑ 106 Barry Bonds	2.50	.75
❑ 107 Tim Salmon	.60	.18
❑ 108 Terrence Long	.40	.12
❑ 109 Jorge Posada	.60	.18
❑ 110 Jose Offerman	.40	.12
❑ 111 Edgar Martinez	.60	.18
❑ 112 Jeremy Giambi	.40	.12
❑ 113 Dean Palmer	.40	.12
❑ 114 Roberto Alomar	.75	.23
❑ 115 Aaron Boone	.40	.12
❑ 116 Adam Kennedy	.40	.12
❑ 117 Joe Randa	.40	.12
❑ 118 Jose Vidro	.40	.12
❑ 119 Tony Batista	.40	.12
❑ 120 Kevin Young	.40	.12
❑ 121 Preston Wilson	.40	.12
❑ 122 Jason Kendall	.40	.12
❑ 123 Mark Kotsay	.40	.12
❑ 124 Timo Perez	.40	.12
❑ 125 Eric Young	.40	.12
❑ 126 Greg Maddux	1.50	.45
❑ 127 Richard Hidalgo	.40	.12
❑ 128 Brian Giles	.40	.12
❑ 129 Fred McGriff	.60	.18
❑ 130 Troy Glaus	.40	.12
❑ 131 Todd Walker	.40	.12
❑ 132 Brady Anderson	.40	.12
❑ 133 Jim Edmonds	.40	.12
❑ 134 Ben Grieve	.40	.12
❑ 135 Greg Vaughn	.40	.12
❑ 136 Robin Ventura	.40	.12
❑ 137 Sammy Sosa	1.50	.45
❑ 138 Rich Aurilia	.40	.12
❑ 139 Jose Valentin	.40	.12
❑ 140 Trot Nixon	.40	.12
❑ 141 Troy Percival	.40	.12
❑ 142 Bernie Williams	.60	.18
❑ 143 Warren Morris	.40	.12
❑ 144 Jacque Jones	.40	.12
❑ 145 Danny Bautista	.40	.12
❑ 146 A.J. Pierzynski	.40	.12
❑ 147 Mark McGwire	2.50	.75
❑ 148 Rafael Furcal	.40	.12
❑ 149 Ray Durham	.40	.12
❑ 150 Mike Mussina	.75	.23
❑ 151 Jay Bell	.40	.12
❑ 152 David Wells	.40	.12
❑ 153 Ken Caminiti	.40	.12
❑ 154 Jim Thome	1.00	.30
❑ 155 Ivan Rodriguez	1.00	.30
❑ 156 Milton Bradley	.40	.12
❑ 157 Ken Griffey Jr.	1.50	.45
❑ 158 Al Leiter	.40	.12
❑ 159 Corey Koskie	.40	.12
❑ 160 Shannon Stewart	.40	.12
❑ 161 Mo Vaughn	.40	.12
❑ 162 Pedro Martinez	1.00	.30
❑ 163 Todd Hundley	.40	.12
❑ 164 Darin Erstad	.75	.23
❑ 165 Ruben Rivera	.40	.12
❑ 166 Richie Sexson	.40	.12
❑ 167 Andres Galarraga	.40	.12
❑ 168 Darryl Kile	.40	.12
❑ 169 Jose Cruz Jr.	.40	.12
❑ 170 David Justice	.40	.12
❑ 171 Vladimir Guerrero	1.00	.30
❑ 172 Jeff Cirillo	.40	.12
❑ 173 John Olerud	.40	.12
❑ 174 Devon White	.40	.12
❑ 175 Ron Belliard	.40	.12
❑ 176 Pokey Reese	.40	.12
❑ 177 Mike Hampton	.40	.12
❑ 178 David Ortiz	.60	.18
❑ 179 Maggio Ordonez	.40	.12
❑ 180 Ruben Mateo	.40	.12
❑ 181 Carlos Lee	.40	.12
❑ 182 Matt Williams	.40	.12
❑ 183 Miguel Tejada	.40	.12
❑ 184 Scott Elarton	.40	.12
❑ 185 Bret Boone	.40	.12
❑ 186 Pat Burrell	.40	.12
❑ 187 Brad Radke	.40	.12
❑ 188 Brian Jordan	.40	.12
❑ 189 Matt Lawton	.40	.12
❑ 190 Al Martin	.40	.12
❑ 191 Albert Belle	.40	.12
❑ 192 Tony Womack	.40	.12
❑ 193 Roger Cedeno	.40	.12
❑ 194 Travis Lee	.40	.12
❑ 195 Dmitri Young	.40	.12
❑ 196 Jay Buhner	.40	.12
❑ 197 Jason Giambi	.75	.23
❑ 198 Jason Tyner	.40	.12
❑ 199 Ben Petrick	.40	.12
❑ 200 Jose Canseco	.75	.23
❑ 201 Nick Johnson	5.00	1.50
❑ 202 Jace Brewer	5.00	1.50
❑ 203 Ryan Freel RC	5.00	1.50
❑ 204 Jaisen Randolph RC	5.00	1.50
❑ 205 Marcus Giles	5.00	1.50
❑ 206 Claudio Vargas RC	5.00	1.50
❑ 207 Brian Cole	5.00	1.50
❑ 208 Scott Hodges	5.00	1.50
❑ 209 Winston Abreu RC	5.00	1.50
❑ 210 Shea Hillenbrand	5.00	1.50
❑ 211 Larry Barnes	5.00	1.50
❑ 212 Paul Phillips RC	5.00	1.50
❑ 213 Pedro Santana RC	5.00	1.50
❑ 214 Ivanon Coffie	5.00	1.50
❑ 215 Junior Spivey RC	8.00	2.40
❑ 216 Donzell McDonald	5.00	1.50
❑ 217 Vernon Wells	5.00	1.50
❑ 218 Corey Patterson	5.00	1.50
❑ 219 Sang-Hoon Lee	5.00	1.50
❑ 220 Jack Cust	5.00	1.50
❑ 221 Jason Romano	5.00	1.50
❑ 222 Jack Wilson RC	10.00	3.00
❑ 223 Adam Everett	5.00	1.50
❑ 224 Esix Snead RC	5.00	1.50
❑ 225 Jason Hart	5.00	1.50
❑ 226 Joe Lawrence	5.00	1.50
❑ 227 Brandon Inge	5.00	1.50
❑ 228 Alex Escobar	5.00	1.50
❑ 229 Abraham Nunez	5.00	1.50
❑ 230 Jared Sandberg	5.00	1.50
❑ 231 Ichiro Suzuki RC	50.00	15.00
❑ 232 Tsuyoshi Shinjo RC	10.00	3.00
❑ 233 Albert Pujols RC	80.00	24.00
❑ 234 Wilson Betemit RC	8.00	2.40
❑ 235 Drew Henson RC	20.00	6.00
❑ MM1 D.Jeter MM/1995	12.00	3.60
❑ NNO D.Jeter MM AU/95 EX	120.00	36.00

2001 Fleer Showcase

	Nm-Mt	Ex-Mt
COMP.SET w/o SP's (100)	30.00	9.00
COMMON CARD (1-100)	.50	.15
COMMON (101-115)	5.00	1.50
COMMON (116-125)	10.00	3.00
COMMON (126-160)	5.00	1.50
❑ 1 Tony Gwynn	1.50	.45
❑ 2 Barry Larkin	.75	.23
❑ 3 Chan Ho Park	.50	.15
❑ 4 Darin Erstad	.50	.15
❑ 5 Rafael Furcal	.50	.15
❑ 6 Roger Cedeno	.50	.15
❑ 7 Timo Perez	.50	.15
❑ 8 Rick Ankiel	.50	.15
❑ 9 Pokey Reese	.50	.15
❑ 10 Jeromy Burnitz	.50	.15
❑ 11 Phil Nevin	.50	.15
❑ 12 Matt Williams	.50	.15
❑ 13 Mike Hampton	.50	.15
❑ 14 Fernando Tatis	.50	.15
❑ 15 Kazuhiro Sasaki	.50	.15
❑ 16 Jim Thome	1.25	.35
❑ 17 Geoff Jenkins	.50	.15
❑ 18 Jeff Kent	.50	.15
❑ 19 Tom Glavine	.75	.23
❑ 20 Dean Palmer	.50	.15
❑ 21 Todd Zeile	.50	.15
❑ 22 Edgar Renteria	.50	.15
❑ 23 Andruw Jones	.50	.15
❑ 24 Juan Encarnacion	.50	.15
❑ 25 Robin Ventura	.50	.15
❑ 26 J.D. Drew	.50	.15
❑ 27 Ray Durham	.50	.15
❑ 28 Richard Hidalgo	.50	.15
❑ 29 Eric Chavez	.50	.15
❑ 30 Rafael Palmeiro	.75	.23
❑ 31 Steve Finley	.50	.15
❑ 32 Jeff Weaver	.50	.15
❑ 33 Al Leiter	.50	.15
❑ 34 Jim Edmonds	.50	.15
❑ 35 Garret Anderson	.50	.15
❑ 36 Larry Walker	.75	.23
❑ 37 Jose Vidro	.50	.15
❑ 38 Mike Cameron	.50	.15
❑ 39 Brady Anderson	.50	.15
❑ 40 Mike Lowell	.50	.15
❑ 41 Bernie Williams	.75	.23
❑ 42 Gary Sheffield	.50	.15
❑ 43 John Smoltz	.75	.23
❑ 44 Mike Mussina	.75	.23
❑ 45 Greg Vaughn	.50	.15
❑ 46 Juan Gonzalez	.75	.23
❑ 47 Matt Lawton	.50	.15
❑ 48 Robb Nen	.50	.15
❑ 49 Brad Radke	.50	.15
❑ 50 Edgar Martinez	.75	.23
❑ 51 Mike Bordick	.50	.15
❑ 52 Shawn Green	.50	.15
❑ 53 Carl Everett	.50	.15
❑ 54 Adrian Beltre	.75	.23
❑ 55 Kerry Wood	1.25	.35
❑ 56 Kevin Brown	.50	.15
❑ 57 Brian Giles	.50	.15
❑ 58 Greg Maddux	2.00	.60
❑ 59 Preston Wilson	.50	.15
❑ 60 Orlando Hernandez	.50	.15
❑ 61 Ben Grieve	.50	.15
❑ 62 Jermaine Dye	.50	.15
❑ 63 Travis Lee	.50	.15
❑ 64 Jose Cruz Jr.	.50	.15
❑ 65 Rondell White	.50	.15
❑ 66 Carlos Beltran	.75	.23
❑ 67 Scott Rolen	1.25	.35
❑ 68 Brad Fullmer	.50	.15
❑ 69 David Wells	.50	.15
❑ 70 Mike Sweeney	.50	.15
❑ 71 Barry Zito	.75	.23
❑ 72 Tony Batista	.50	.15
❑ 73 Curt Schilling	.50	.15
❑ 74 Jeff Cirillo	.50	.15
❑ 75 Edgardo Alfonzo	.50	.15
❑ 76 John Olerud	.50	.15
❑ 77 Carlos Lee	.50	.15
❑ 78 Moises Alou	.50	.15
❑ 79 Tim Hudson	.50	.15

Card	Nm-Mt	Ex-Mt
❑ 80 Andres Galarraga	.50	.15
❑ 81 Roberto Alomar	.75	.23
❑ 82 Richie Sexson	.50	.15
❑ 83 Trevor Hoffman	.50	.15
❑ 84 Omar Vizquel	.75	.23
❑ 85 Jacque Jones	.50	.15
❑ 86 J.T. Snow	.50	.15
❑ 87 Sean Casey	.50	.15
❑ 88 Craig Biggio	.75	.23
❑ 89 Mariano Rivera	.75	.23
❑ 90 Rusty Greer	.50	.15
❑ 91 Barry Bonds	3.00	.90
❑ 92 Pedro Martinez	1.25	.35
❑ 93 Cal Ripken	4.00	1.20
❑ 94 Pat Burrell	.50	.15
❑ 95 Chipper Jones	1.25	.35
❑ 96 Magglio Ordonez	.50	.15
❑ 97 Jeff Bagwell	.75	.23
❑ 98 Randy Johnson	1.25	.35
❑ 99 Frank Thomas	1.25	.35
❑ 100 Jason Kendall	.50	.15
❑ 101 N.Garciaparra AC	12.00	3.60
❑ 102 Mark McGwire AC	20.00	6.00
❑ 103 Troy Glaus AC	5.00	1.50
❑ 104 Ivan Rodriguez AC	8.00	2.40
❑ 105 Manny Ramirez AC	5.00	1.50
❑ 106 Derek Jeter AC	20.00	6.00
❑ 107 Alex Rodriguez AC	12.00	3.60
❑ 108 Ken Griffey Jr. AC	12.00	3.60
❑ 109 Todd Helton AC	5.00	1.50
❑ 110 Sammy Sosa AC	12.00	3.60
❑ 111 Vladimir Guerrero AC	8.00	2.40
❑ 112 Mike Piazza AC	12.00	3.60
❑ 113 Roger Clemens AC	15.00	4.50
❑ 114 Jason Giambi AC	5.00	1.50
❑ 115 Carlos Delgado AC	5.00	1.50
❑ 116 Ichiro Suzuki AC RC	100.00	30.00
❑ 117 M.Ensberg AC RC	15.00	4.50
❑ 118 C. Valderrama AC RC	10.00	3.00
❑ 119 Erick Almonte AC RC	10.00	3.00
❑ 120 T.Shinjo AC RC	15.00	4.50
❑ 121 Albert Pujols AC RC	120.00	36.00
❑ 122 Wilson Betemit AC RC	10.00	3.00
❑ 123 A.Hernandez AC RC	10.00	3.00
❑ 124 J.Melian AC RC	10.00	3.00
❑ 125 Drew Henson AC RC	15.00	4.50
❑ 126 Paul Phillips RS RC	5.00	1.50
❑ 127 Esix Snead RS RC	5.00	1.50
❑ 128 Ryan Freel RS RC	5.00	1.50
❑ 129 Junior Spivey RS RC	8.00	2.40
❑ 130 E.Guzman RS RC	5.00	1.50
❑ 131 Juan Diaz RS RC	5.00	1.50
❑ 132 Andres Torres RS RC	5.00	1.50
❑ 133 Jay Gibbons RS RC	8.00	2.40
❑ 134 Bill Ortega RS RC	5.00	1.50
❑ 135 Alexis Gomez RS RC	5.00	1.50
❑ 136 Wilkin Ruan RS RC	5.00	1.50
❑ 137 Henry Mateo RS RC	5.00	1.50
❑ 138 Juan Uribe RS RC	8.00	2.40
❑ 139 J.Estrada RS RC	8.00	2.40
❑ 140 J.Randolph RS RC	5.00	1.50
❑ 141 Eric Hinske RS RC	8.00	2.40
❑ 142 Jack Wilson RS RC	10.00	3.00
❑ 143 Cody Ransom RS RC	5.00	1.50
❑ 144 Nate Frese RS RC	5.00	1.50
❑ 145 John Grabow RS RC	5.00	1.50
❑ 146 C.Parker RS RC	5.00	1.50
❑ 147 B.Lawrence RS RC	5.00	1.50
❑ 148 B. Duckworth RS RC	5.00	1.50
❑ 149 Winston Abreu RS RC	5.00	1.50
❑ 150 H.Ramirez RS RC	8.00	2.40
❑ 151 Nick Maness RS RC	5.00	1.50
❑ 152 Blaine Neal RS RC	5.00	1.50
❑ 153 Billy Sylvester RS RC	5.00	1.50
❑ 154 David Elder RS RC	5.00	1.50
❑ 155 Bert Snow RS RC	5.00	1.50
❑ 156 Claudio Vargas RS RC	5.00	1.50
❑ 157 Martin Vargas RS RC	5.00	1.50
❑ 158 Grant Balfour RS RC	5.00	1.50
❑ 159 Randy Keisler RS	5.00	1.50
❑ 160 Zach Day RS RC	5.00	1.50
❑ P1 Tony Gwynn Promo	2.00	.60
❑ MM3 D.Jeter MM/2000	12.00	3.60
❑ NNO D.Jeter MM AU/100	120.00	36.00

2004 Fleer Sweet Sigs

	Nm-Mt	Ex-Mt
COMP.SET w/o SP's (75)	25.00	7.50
COMMON CARD (1-75)	.50	.15
COMMON CARD (76-100)	3.00	.90

76-100 ODDS 1:7 HOBBY, 1:48 RETAIL
76-100 PRINT RUN 999 SERIAL #'d SETS

Card	Nm-Mt	Ex-Mt
❑ 1 Manny Ramirez	.75	.23
❑ 2 Frank Thomas	1.25	.35
❑ 3 Josh Beckett	.50	.15
❑ 4 Shawn Green	.50	.15
❑ 5 Tom Glavine	.75	.23
❑ 6 Marquis Grissom	.50	.15
❑ 7 Nomar Garciaparra	2.00	.60
❑ 8 Magglio Ordonez	.50	.15
❑ 9 Alex Rodriguez	2.00	.60
❑ 10 Chipper Jones	1.25	.35
❑ 11 Jody Gerut	.50	.15
❑ 12 Dontrelle Willis	.50	.15
❑ 13 Lance Berkman	.50	.15
❑ 14 Jose Vidro	.50	.15
❑ 15 Barry Zito	.50	.15
❑ 16 Jason Kendall	.50	.15
❑ 17 Scott Rolen	1.25	.35
❑ 18 Troy Glaus	.50	.15
❑ 19 Brandon Webb	.50	.15
❑ 20 Tim Hudson	.50	.15
❑ 21 Shannon Stewart	.50	.15
❑ 22 Darin Erstad	.50	.15
❑ 23 Curt Schilling	1.25	.35
❑ 24 Bret Boone	.50	.15
❑ 25 Richie Sexson	.50	.15
❑ 26 Hideki Matsui	2.00	.60
❑ 27 Albert Pujols	2.50	.75
❑ 28 Greg Maddux	2.00	.60
❑ 29 Austin Kearns	.50	.15
❑ 30 Todd Helton	.75	.23
❑ 31 Miguel Cabrera	.75	.23
❑ 32 Jeff Bagwell	.75	.23
❑ 33 Marlon Byrd	.50	.15
❑ 34 Ichiro Suzuki	2.00	.60
❑ 35 Rocco Baldelli	.50	.15
❑ 36 Garret Anderson	.50	.15
❑ 37 Javy Lopez	.50	.15
❑ 38 Kerry Wood	1.25	.35
❑ 39 Adam Dunn	.75	.23
❑ 40 Geoff Jenkins	.50	.15
❑ 41 Derek Jeter	2.50	.75
❑ 42 Rich Harden	.50	.15
❑ 43 Alfonso Soriano	.75	.23
❑ 44 Ken Griffey Jr.	2.00	.60
❑ 45 Ivan Rodriguez	1.25	.35
❑ 46 Pedro Martinez	1.25	.35
❑ 47 Andy Pettitte	.75	.23
❑ 48 Gary Sheffield	.50	.15
❑ 49 Brian Giles	.50	.15
❑ 50 Carlos Delgado	.50	.15
❑ 51 Mike Piazza	2.00	.60
❑ 52 Hank Blalock	.50	.15
❑ 53 Roger Clemens	2.50	.75
❑ 54 Scott Podsednik	.50	.15
❑ 55 Torii Hunter	.50	.15
❑ 56 Jose Reyes	.50	.15
❑ 57 Jim Thome	1.25	.35
❑ 58 Jason Schmidt	.50	.15
❑ 59 Jose Cruz Jr.	.50	.15
❑ 60 Mark Teixeira	.50	.15
❑ 61 Randy Johnson	1.25	.35
❑ 62 Miguel Tejada	.50	.15
❑ 63 Sammy Sosa	2.00	.60
❑ 64 Larry Walker	.75	.23
❑ 65 Carl Everett	.50	.15
❑ 66 Luis Castillo	.50	.15
❑ 67 Jason Giambi	.50	.15
❑ 68 Mike Sweeney	.50	.15
❑ 69 Andruw Jones	.50	.15
❑ 70 Vladimir Guerrero	1.25	.35
❑ 71 J.D. Drew	.50	.15
❑ 72 Mark Prior	1.25	.35
❑ 73 Angel Berroa	.50	.15
❑ 74 Hideo Nomo	1.25	.35
❑ 75 Roy Halladay	.50	.15
❑ 76 John Gall FS RC	5.00	1.50
❑ 77 Angel Chavez FS RC	3.00	.90
❑ 78 Alfredo Simon FS RC	3.00	.90
❑ 79 Merkin Valdez FS RC	5.00	1.50
❑ 80 Chad Bentz FS RC	3.00	.90
❑ 81 Justin Leone FS RC	5.00	1.50
❑ 82 Mike Rouse FS RC	3.00	.90
❑ 83 Aarom Baldiris FS RC	5.00	1.50
❑ 84 Chris Shelton FS RC	5.00	1.50
❑ 85 Akinori Otsuka FS RC	3.00	.90
❑ 86 Ruddy Yan FS	3.00	.90
❑ 87 Ramon Ramirez FS RC	3.00	.90
❑ 88 Hector Gimenez FS RC	3.00	.90
❑ 89 Mike Gosling FS RC	3.00	.90
❑ 90 Greg Dobbs FS RC	3.00	.90
❑ 91 Kaz Matsui FS RC	8.00	2.40
❑ 92 Don Kelly FS RC	3.00	.90
❑ 93 Shingo Takatsu FS RC	5.00	1.50
❑ 94 Ivan Ochoa FS RC	3.00	.90
❑ 95 Chris Aguila FS RC	3.00	.90
❑ 96 Jason Bartlett FS RC	5.00	1.50
❑ 97 Graham Koonce FS	3.00	.90
❑ 98 Ronny Cedeno FS RC	3.00	.90
❑ 99 Jerome Gamble FS RC	3.00	.90
❑ 100 Onil Joseph FS RC	3.00	.90

1998 Fleer Tradition Update

	Nm-Mt	Ex-Mt
COMP.FACT.SET (100)	20.00	6.00

Card	Nm-Mt	Ex-Mt
❑ U1 Mark McGwire HL	1.25	.35
❑ U2 Sammy Sosa HL	.75	.23
❑ U3 Roger Clemens HL	1.00	.30
❑ U4 Barry Bonds HL	1.25	.35
❑ U5 Kerry Wood HL	.50	.15
❑ U6 Paul Molitor HL	.30	.09
❑ U7 Ken Griffey Jr. HL	.75	.23
❑ U8 Cal Ripken HL	1.50	.45
❑ U9 David Wells HL	.20	.06
❑ U10 Alex Rodriguez HL	.75	.23
❑ U11 Angel Pena RC	.25	.07
❑ U12 Bruce Chen	.20	.06
❑ U13 Craig Wilson	.20	.06
❑ U14 O.Hernandez RC	1.00	.30
❑ U15 Aramis Ramirez	.20	.06
❑ U16 Aaron Boone	.20	.06
❑ U17 Bob Henley	.20	.06
❑ U18 Juan Guzman	.20	.06
❑ U19 Darryl Hamilton	.20	.06
❑ U20 Jay Payton	.20	.06

❑ U21 Jeremy Powell .20 .06
❑ U22 Ben Davis .20 .06
❑ U23 Preston Wilson .20 .06
❑ U24 Jim Parque RC .40 .12
❑ U25 Odalis Perez RC 1.00 .30
❑ U26 Ronnie Belliard .20 .06
❑ U27 Royce Clayton .20 .06
❑ U28 George Lombard .20 .06
❑ U29 Tony Phillips .20 .06
❑ U30 F.Seguignol RC .25 .07
❑ U31 Armando Rios RC .40 .12
❑ U32 Jerry Hairston Jr. RC .40 .12
❑ U33 Justin Baughman RC .25 .07
❑ U34 Seth Greisinger .20 .06
❑ U35 Alex Gonzalez .20 .06
❑ U36 Michael Barrett .20 .06
❑ U37 Carlos Beltran .75 .23
❑ U38 Ellis Burks .20 .06
❑ U39 Jose Jimenez RC .60 .18
❑ U40 Carlos Guillen .20 .06
❑ U41 Marlon Anderson .20 .06
❑ U42 Scott Elarton .20 .06
❑ U43 Glenallen Hill .20 .06
❑ U44 Shane Monahan .20 .06
❑ U45 Dennis Martinez .20 .06
❑ U46 Carlos Febles RC .40 .12
❑ U47 Carlos Perez .20 .06
❑ U48 Wilton Guerrero .20 .06
❑ U49 Randy Johnson .50 .15
❑ U50 Brian Simmons RC .25 .07
❑ U51 Carlton Loewer .20 .06
❑ U52 Mark DeRosa RC .40 .12
❑ U53 Tim Young RC .25 .07
❑ U54 Gary Gaetti .20 .06
❑ U55 Eric Chavez .20 .06
❑ U56 Carl Pavano .30 .06
❑ U57 Mike Stanley .20 .06
❑ U58 Todd Stottlemyre .20 .06
❑ U59 Gabe Kapler RC .60 .18
❑ U60 Mike Jerzembeck RC .25 .07
❑ U61 Mitch Meluskey RC .40 .12
❑ U62 Bill Pulsipher .20 .06
❑ U63 Derrick Gibson .20 .06
❑ U64 John Rocker RC .40 .12
❑ U65 Calvin Pickering .20 .06
❑ U66 Blake Stein .20 .06
❑ U67 Fernando Tatis .20 .06
❑ U68 Gabe Alvarez .20 .06
❑ U69 Jeffrey Hammonds .20 .06
❑ U70 Adrian Beltre .50 .15
❑ U71 Ryan Bradley RC .25 .07
❑ U72 Edgard Clemente .20 .06
❑ U73 Rick Croushore RC .25 .07
❑ U74 Matt Clement .20 .06
❑ U75 Dermal Brown .20 .06
❑ U76 Paul Bako .20 .06
❑ U77 Placido Polanco RC .40 .12
❑ U78 Jay Tessmer .20 .06
❑ U79 Jarrod Washburn .20 .06
❑ U80 Kevin Witt .20 .06
❑ U81 Mike Metcalfe .20 .06
❑ U82 Daryle Ward .20 .06
❑ U83 Benj Sampson RC .25 .07
❑ U84 Mike Kinkade RC .25 .07
❑ U85 Randy Winn .20 .06
❑ U86 Jeff Shaw .20 .06
❑ U87 Troy Glaus RC 3.00 .90
❑ U88 Hideo Nomo .50 .15
❑ U89 Mark Grudzielanek .20 .06
❑ U90 Mike Frank RC .25 .07
❑ U91 Bobby Howry RC .40 .12
❑ U92 Ryan Minor RC .25 .07
❑ U93 Corey Koskie RC 1.00 .30
❑ U94 Matt Anderson RC .40 .12
❑ U95 Joe Carter .20 .06
❑ U96 Paul Konerko .20 .06
❑ U97 Sidney Ponson .20 .06
❑ U98 Jeremy Giambi RC .40 .12
❑ U99 Jeff Kubenka RC .25 .07
❑ U100 J.D. Drew RC 3.00 .90

1999 Fleer Tradition Update

	Nm-Mt	Ex-Mt
COMP.FACT.SET (150)	30.00	9.00

❑ U1 Rick Ankiel RC 2.00 .60
❑ U2 Peter Bergeron RC .30 .09
❑ U3 Pat Burrell RC 1.25 .35
❑ U4 Eric Munson RC .50 .15
❑ U5 Alfonso Soriano RC 4.00 1.20
❑ U6 Tim Hudson RC 1.50 .45
❑ U7 Erubiel Durazo RC .50 .15
❑ U8 Chad Hermansen .20 .06
❑ U9 Jeff Zimmerman RC .30 .09
❑ U10 Jesus Pena RC .30 .09
❑ U11 Ramon Hernandez .30 .09
❑ U12 Trent Durrington RC .30 .09
❑ U13 Tony Armas Jr. .20 .06
❑ U14 Mike Fyhrie RC .30 .09
❑ U15 Danny Kolb RC .75 .23
❑ U16 Mike Porzio RC .30 .09
❑ U17 Will Brunson RC .30 .09
❑ U18 Mike Duvall RC .30 .09
❑ U19 D.Mientkiewicz RC .60 .18
❑ U20 Gabe Molina RC .30 .09
❑ U21 Luis Vizcaino RC .30 .09
❑ U22 Robinson Cancel RC .30 .09
❑ U23 Brett Laxton RC .30 .09
❑ U24 Joe McEwing RC .30 .09
❑ U25 Justin Speier RC .30 .09
❑ U26 Kip Wells RC .50 .15
❑ U27 Armando Almanza RC .30 .09
❑ U28 Joe Davenport RC .30 .09
❑ U29 Yamid Haad RC .30 .09
❑ U30 John Halama .20 .06
❑ U31 Adam Kennedy .20 .06
❑ U32 Micah Bowie RC .30 .09
❑ U33 Gookie Dawkins RC .30 .09
❑ U34 Ryan Rupe RC .30 .09
❑ U35 B.J. Ryan RC .30 .09
❑ U36 Chance Sanford RC .30 .09
❑ U37 A.Shumaker RC .30 .09
❑ U38 Ryan Glynn RC .30 .09
❑ U39 Roosevelt Brown RC .30 .09
❑ U40 Ben Molina RC .50 .15
❑ U41 Scott Williamson .20 .06
❑ U42 Eric Gagne RC 15.00 4.50
❑ U43 John McDonald RC .30 .09
❑ U44 Scott Sauerbeck RC .30 .09
❑ U45 Mike Venafro RC .30 .09
❑ U46 Edwards Guzman RC .30 .09
❑ U47 Richard Barker RC .30 .09
❑ U48 Braden Looper .20 .06
❑ U49 Chad Meyers RC .30 .09
❑ U50 Scott Strickland RC .30 .09
❑ U51 Billy Koch .20 .06
❑ U52 David Newhan RC 2.00 .60
❑ U53 David Riske RC .30 .09
❑ U54 Jose Santiago RC .30 .09
❑ U55 Miguel Del Toro RC .30 .09
❑ U56 Orber Moreno RC .30 .09
❑ U57 Dave Roberts RC .50 .15
❑ U58 Tim Byrdak RC .30 .09
❑ U59 David Lee RC .30 .09
❑ U60 Guillermo Mota RC .30 .09
❑ U61 Wilton Veras RC .30 .09
❑ U62 Joe Mays RC .30 .09
❑ U63 Jose Fernandez RC .30 .09
❑ U64 Ray King RC .30 .09
❑ U65 Chris Petersen RC .30 .09
❑ U66 Vernon Wells .20 .06
❑ U67 Ruben Mateo .20 .06
❑ U68 Ben Petrick .20 .06
❑ U69 Chris Tremie RC .30 .09
❑ U70 Lance Berkman .20 .06
❑ U71 Dan Smith RC .30 .09
❑ U72 Carlos E. Hernandez RC .30 .09
❑ U73 Chad Harville RC .30 .09
❑ U74 Damaso Marte RC .30 .09
❑ U75 Aaron Myette RC .30 .09
❑ U76 Willis Roberts RC .30 .09
❑ U77 Erik Sabel RC .30 .09
❑ U78 Hector Almonte RC .30 .09
❑ U79 Kris Benson .20 .06
❑ U80 Pat Daneker RC .30 .09
❑ U81 Freddy Garcia RC .60 .18
❑ U82 Byung-Hyun Kim RC .60 .18
❑ U83 Wily Pena RC 1.50 .45
❑ U84 Dan Wheeler RC .30 .09
❑ U85 Tim Harikkala RC .30 .09
❑ U86 Derrin Ebert RC .30 .09
❑ U87 Horacio Estrada RC .30 .09
❑ U88 Liu Rodriguez RC .30 .09
❑ U89 J.Zimmerman RC .30 .09
❑ U90 A.J. Burnett RC .60 .18
❑ U91 Doug Davis RC .30 .09
❑ U92 Rob Ramsay RC .30 .09
❑ U93 Clay Bellinger RC .30 .09
❑ U94 Charlie Greene RC .30 .09
❑ U95 Bo Porter RC .30 .09
❑ U96 Jorge Toca RC .30 .09
❑ U97 Casey Blake RC 2.00 .60
❑ U98 Amaury Garcia RC .30 .09
❑ U99 Jose Molina RC .30 .09
❑ U100 Melvin Mora RC 3.00 .90
❑ U101 Joe Nathan RC .60 .18
❑ U102 Juan Pena RC .30 .09
❑ U103 Dave Borkowski RC .30 .09
❑ U104 Eddie Gaillard RC .30 .09
❑ U105 Glen Barker RC .30 .09
❑ U106 Brett Hinchliffe RC .30 .09
❑ U107 Carlos Lee .20 .06
❑ U108 Rob Ryan RC .30 .09
❑ U109 Jeff Weaver RC .50 .15
❑ U110 Ed Yarnall .20 .06
❑ U111 Nelson Cruz RC .30 .09
❑ U112 C.Davidson RC .30 .09
❑ U113 Tim Kubinski RC .30 .09
❑ U114 Sean Spencer RC .30 .09
❑ U115 Joe Winkelsas RC .30 .09
❑ U116 Mike Colangelo RC .30 .09
❑ U117 Tom Davey RC .30 .09
❑ U118 Warren Morris .20 .06
❑ U119 Dan Murray RC .30 .09
❑ U120 Jose Nieves RC .30 .09
❑ U121 Mark Quinn RC .30 .09
❑ U122 Josh Beckett RC 5.00 1.50
❑ U123 Chad Allen RC .30 .09
❑ U124 Mike Figga .30 .09
❑ U125 Beiker Graterol RC .30 .09
❑ U126 Aaron Scheffer RC .30 .09
❑ U127 Wiki Gonzalez RC .30 .09
❑ U128 Ramon E.Martinez RC .30 .09
❑ U129 Matt Riley RC 1.00 .30
❑ U130 Chris Woodward RC .30 .09
❑ U131 Albert Belle .20 .06
❑ U132 Roger Cedeno .20 .06
❑ U133 Roger Clemens 1.00 .30
❑ U134 Brian Giles .20 .06
❑ U135 Rickey Henderson .50 .15
❑ U136 Randy Johnson .50 .15
❑ U137 Brian Jordan .20 .06
❑ U138 Paul Konerko .20 .06
❑ U139 Hideo Nomo .50 .15
❑ U140 Kenny Rogers .20 .06
❑ U141 Wade Boggs HL .30 .09
❑ U142 Jose Canseco HL .20 .06
❑ U143 Roger Clemens HL 1.00 .30
❑ U144 David Cone HL .20 .06
❑ U145 Tony Gwynn HL .60 .18
❑ U146 Mark McGwire HL 1.25 .35
❑ U147 Cal Ripken HL 1.50 .45
❑ U148 Alex Rodriguez HL .75 .23
❑ U149 Fernando Tatis HL .20 .06
❑ U150 Robin Ventura HL .20 .06

2000 Fleer Tradition Update

	Nm-Mt	Ex-Mt
COMP.FACT.SET (149)	20.00	6.00

❑ 1 Ken Griffey Jr. SH .75 .23
❑ 2 Cal Ripken SH 1.00 .30

❑ 3 Randy Velarde SH .30 .09
❑ 4 Fred McGriff SH .30 .09
❑ 5 Derek Jeter SH .75 .23
❑ 6 Tom Glavine SH .30 .09
❑ 7 Brent Mayne SH .30 .09
❑ 8 Alex Ochoa SH .30 .09
❑ 9 Scott Sheldon SH .30 .09
❑ 10 Randy Johnson SH .50 .15
❑ 11 Daniel Garibay RC .30 .09
❑ 12 Brad Fullmer .30 .09
❑ 13 Kazuhiro Sasaki RC 1.00 .30
❑ 14 Andy Tracy RC .30 .09
❑ 15 Bret Boone .30 .09
❑ 16 Chad Durbin RC .40 .12
❑ 17 Mark Buehrle RC 1.25 .35
❑ 18 Julio Zuleta RC .30 .09
❑ 19 Jeremy Giambi .30 .09
❑ 20 Gene Stechschulte RC .30 .09
❑ 21 Lou Pote .30 .09
Bengie Molina
❑ 22 Darrell Einertson RC .30 .09
❑ 23 Ken Griffey Jr. 1.25 .35
❑ 24 Jeff Sparks RC .30 .09
Dan Wheeler
❑ 25 Aaron Fultz RC .30 .09
❑ 26 Derek Bell .30 .09
❑ 27 Rob Bell .30 .09
D.T. Cromer
❑ 28 Robert Fick .30 .09
❑ 29 Darryl Kile .30 .09
❑ 30 Clayton Andrews .30 .09
John Bale RC
❑ 31 Dave Veres .30 .09
❑ 32 Hector Mercado RC .30 .09
❑ 33 Willie Morales RC .30 .09
❑ 34 Kelly Wunsch .30 .09
Kip Wells
❑ 35 Hideki Irabu .30 .09
❑ 36 Sean DePaula RC .30 .09
❑ 37 DeWayne Wise .30 .09
Chris Woodward
❑ 38 Curt Schilling .30 .09
❑ 39 Mark Johnson .30 .09
❑ 40 Mike Cameron .30 .09
❑ 41 Scott Sheldon .30 .09
Tom Evans
❑ 42 Brett Tomko .30 .09
❑ 43 Johan Santana RC 10.00 3.00
❑ 44 Andy Benes .30 .09
❑ 45 Matt LeCroy .30 .09
Mark Redman
❑ 46 Ryan Klesko .30 .09
❑ 47 Andy Ashby .30 .09
❑ 48 Octavio Dotel .30 .09
❑ 49 Eric Byrnes RC 1.00 .30
❑ 50 Does Not Exist .00
❑ 51 Kenny Rogers .30 .09
❑ 52 Ben Weber RC .40 .12
❑ 53 Matt Blank .30 .09
Scott Strickland
❑ 54 Tom Goodwin .30 .09
❑ 55 Jim Edmonds Cards .30 .09
❑ 56 Derrick Turnbow RC .30 .09
❑ 57 Mark Mulder .30 .09
❑ 58 Tarrick Brock .30 .09
Ruben Quevedo
❑ 59 Danny Young RC .30 .09
❑ 60 Fernando Vina .30 .09
❑ 61 Justin Brunette RC .30 .09
❑ 62 Jimmy Anderson .30 .09
❑ 63 Reggie Sanders .30 .09
❑ 64 Adam Kennedy .30 .09
❑ 65 Jesse Garcia .30 .09
B.J. Ryan
❑ 66 Al Martin .30 .09
❑ 67 Kevin Walker RC .30 .09
❑ 68 Brad Penny .30 .09
❑ 69 B.J. Surhoff .30 .09
❑ 70 Geoff Blum .30 .09
Trace Coquillette RC
❑ 71 Jose Jimenez .30 .09
❑ 72 Chuck Finley .30 .09
❑ 73 Valerio De Los Santos .30 .09
Everett Stull
❑ 74 Terry Adams .30 .09
❑ 75 Rafael Furcal .30 .09
❑ 76 John Roskos .30 .09
Mike Darr
❑ 77 Quilvio Veras .30 .09
❑ 78 Armando Almanza .30 .09
Nate Rolison
❑ 79 Greg Vaughn .30 .09
❑ 80 Keith McDonald RC .30 .09
❑ 81 Eric Cammack RC .30 .09
❑ 82 Horacio Estrada .30 .09
Ray King
❑ 83 Kory DeHaan .30 .09
❑ 84 Kevin Hodges RC .30 .09
❑ 85 Mike Lamb RC .40 .12
❑ 86 Shawn Green .30 .09
❑ 87 Dan Reichert .30 .09
Jason Rakers
❑ 88 Adam Piatt .30 .09
❑ 89 Mike Garcia .30 .09
❑ 90 Rodrigo Lopez RC .60 .18
❑ 91 John Olerud .30 .09
❑ 92 Barry Zito RC 2.00 .60
Terrence Long
❑ 93 Jimmy Rollins .30 .09
❑ 94 Denny Neagle .30 .09
❑ 95 Rickey Henderson .75 .23
❑ 96 Adam Eaton .30 .09
Buddy Carlyle
❑ 97 Brian O'Connor RC .30 .09
❑ 98 Andy Thompson RC .30 .09
❑ 99 Jason Boyd RC .30 .09
❑ 100 Joel Pineiro RC 2.00 .60
Carlos Guillen
❑ 101 Raul Gonzalez RC .30 .09
❑ 102 Brandon Kolb RC .30 .09
❑ 103 Jason Maxwell .30 .09
Mike Lincoln
❑ 104 Luis Matos RC .40 .12
❑ 105 Morgan Burkhart RC .30 .09
❑ 106 Ismael Villegas RC .30 .09
Steve Sisco RC
❑ 107 David Justice Yankees .30 .09
❑ 108 Pablo Ozuna .30 .09
❑ 109 Jose Canseco .75 .23
❑ 110 Alex Cora .30 .09
Shawn Gilbert
❑ 111 Will Clark Cardinals .75 .23
❑ 112 Keith Luuloa .30 .09
Eric Weaver
❑ 113 Bruce Chen .30 .09
❑ 114 Adam Hyzdu .30 .09
❑ 115 Scott Forster RC .30 .09
Yovanny Lara RC
❑ 116 Allen McDill RC .30 .09
Jose Macias
❑ 117 Kevin Nicholson .30 .09
❑ 118 Israel Alcantara .30 .09
Tim Young
❑ 119 Juan Alvarez RC .30 .09
❑ 120 Julio Lugo .30 .09
Mitch Meluskey
❑ 121 B.J. Waszgis RC .30 .09
❑ 122 Jeff M. D'Amico RC .30 .09
Brett Laxton
❑ 123 Ricky Ledee .30 .09
❑ 124 Mark DeRosa .30 .09
Jason Marquis
❑ 125 Alex Cabrera RC .40 .12
❑ 126 Augie Ojeda RC .30 .09
Gary Matthews Jr.
❑ 127 Richie Sexson .30 .09
❑ 128 Santiago Perez RC .30 .09
Hector Ramirez RC
❑ 129 Rondell White .30 .09
❑ 130 Craig House RC .30 .09
❑ 131 Kevin Beirne .30 .09
Jon Garland
❑ 132 Wayne Franklin RC .30 .09
❑ 133 Henry Rodriguez .30 .09
❑ 134 Jay Payton .30 .09
Jim Mann
❑ 135 Ron Gant .30 .09
❑ 136 Paxton Crawford RC .30 .09
Sang-Hoon Lee RC
❑ 137 Kent Bottenfield .30 .09
❑ 138 Rocky Biddle RC .30 .09
❑ 139 Travis Lee .30 .09
❑ 140 Ryan Vogelsong RC .40 .12
❑ 141 Jason Conti .30 .09
Geraldo Guzman RC
❑ 142 Tim Drew .30 .09
Mark Watson RC
❑ 143 John Parrish RC .30 .09
Chris Richard RC
❑ 144 Javier Cardona RC .30 .09
Brandon Villafuerte RC
❑ 145 Tike Redman RC .60 .18
Steve Sparks RC
❑ 146 Brian Schneider .30 .09
Matt Skrmetta RC
❑ 147 Pasqual Coco RC .30 .09
❑ 148 Lorenzo Barcelo RC .30 .09
Joe Crede
❑ 149 Jace Brewer RC .30 .09
❑ 150 Milton Bradley .40 .12
Tomas De La Rosa RC
❑ MP1 Mickey Mantle Jsy 200.00 60.00

2001 Fleer Tradition

	Nm-Mt	Ex-Mt
COMP.FACT.SET (485)	60.00	18.00
COMPLETE SET (450)	25.00	7.50
COMMON CARD (1-450)	.30	.09
COMMON (451-485)	.50	.15

❑ 1 Andres Galarraga .30 .09
❑ 2 Armando Rios .30 .09
❑ 3 Julio Lugo .30 .09
❑ 4 Darryl Hamilton .30 .09
❑ 5 Dave Veres .30 .09
❑ 6 Edgardo Alfonzo .30 .09
❑ 7 Brook Fordyce .30 .09
❑ 8 Eric Karros .30 .09
❑ 9 Neifi Perez .30 .09
❑ 10 Jim Edmonds .30 .09
❑ 11 Barry Larkin .50 .15
❑ 12 Trot Nixon .30 .09
❑ 13 Andy Pettitte .50 .15
❑ 14 Jose Guillen .30 .09
❑ 15 David Wells .30 .09
❑ 16 Magglio Ordonez .30 .09
❑ 17 David Segui .30 .09
❑ 17A David Segui ERR .30 .09
Card has no number on the back
❑ 18 Juan Encarnacion .30 .09
❑ 19 Robert Person .30 .09

❑ 20	Quilvio Veras	.30	.09
❑ 21	Mo Vaughn	.30	.09
❑ 22	B.J. Surhoff	.30	.09
❑ 23	Ken Caminiti	.30	.09
❑ 24	Frank Catalanotto	.30	.09
❑ 25	Luis Gonzalez	.30	.09
❑ 26	Pete Harnisch	.30	.09
❑ 27	Alex Gonzalez	.30	.09
❑ 28	Mark Quinn	.30	.09
❑ 29	Luis Castillo	.30	.09
❑ 30	Rick Helling	.30	.09
❑ 31	Barry Bonds	2.00	.60
❑ 32	Warren Morris	.30	.09
❑ 33	Aaron Boone	.30	.09
❑ 34	Ricky Gutierrez	.30	.09
❑ 35	Preston Wilson	.30	.09
❑ 36	Erubiel Durazo	.30	.09
❑ 37	Jermaine Dye	.30	.09
❑ 38	John Rocker	.30	.09
❑ 39	Mark Grudzielanek	.30	.09
❑ 40	Pedro Martinez	.75	.23
❑ 41	Phil Nevin	.30	.09
❑ 42	Luis Matos	.30	.09
❑ 43	Orlando Hernandez	.30	.09
❑ 44	Steve Cox	.30	.09
❑ 45	James Baldwin	.30	.09
❑ 46	Rafael Furcal	.30	.09
❑ 47	Todd Zeile	.30	.09
❑ 48	Elmer Dessens	.30	.09
❑ 49	Russell Branyan	.30	.09
❑ 50	Juan Gonzalez	.50	.15
❑ 51	Mac Suzuki	.30	.09
❑ 52	Adam Kennedy	.30	.09
❑ 53	Randy Velarde	.30	.09
❑ 54	David Bell	.30	.09
❑ 55	Royce Clayton	.30	.09
❑ 56	Greg Colbrunn	.30	.09
❑ 57	Rey Ordonez	.30	.09
❑ 58	Kevin Millwood	.30	.09
❑ 59	Fernando Vina	.30	.09
❑ 60	Eddie Taubensee	.30	.09
❑ 61	Enrique Wilson	.30	.09
❑ 62	Jay Bell	.30	.09
❑ 63	Brian Moehler	.30	.09
❑ 64	Brad Fullmer	.30	.09
❑ 65	Ben Petrick	.30	.09
❑ 66	Orlando Cabrera	.30	.09
❑ 67	Shane Reynolds	.30	.09
❑ 68	Mitch Meluskey	.30	.09
❑ 69	Jeff Shaw	.30	.09
❑ 70	Chipper Jones	.75	.23
❑ 71	Tomo Ohka	.30	.09
❑ 72	Ruben Rivera	.30	.09
❑ 73	Mike Sirotka	.30	.09
❑ 74	Scott Rolen	.75	.23
❑ 75	Glendon Rusch	.30	.09
❑ 76	Miguel Tejada	.30	.09
❑ 77	Brady Anderson	.30	.09
❑ 78	Bartolo Colon	.30	.09
❑ 79	Ron Coomer	.30	.09
❑ 80	Gary DiSarcina	.30	.09
❑ 81	Geoff Jenkins	.30	.09
❑ 82	Billy Koch	.30	.09
❑ 83	Mike Lamb	.30	.09
❑ 84	Alex Rodriguez	1.25	.35
❑ 85	Denny Neagle	.30	.09
❑ 86	Michael Tucker	.30	.09
❑ 87	Edgar Renteria	.30	.09
❑ 88	Brian Anderson	.30	.09
❑ 89	Glenallen Hill	.30	.09
❑ 90	Aramis Ramirez	.30	.09
❑ 91	Rondell White	.30	.09
❑ 92	Tony Womack	.30	.09
❑ 93	Jeffrey Hammonds	.30	.09
❑ 94	Freddy Garcia	.30	.09
❑ 95	Bill Mueller	.30	.09
❑ 96	Mike Lieberthal	.30	.09
❑ 97	Michael Barrett	.30	.09
❑ 98	Derrek Lee	.30	.09
❑ 99	Bill Spiers	.30	.09
❑ 100	Derek Lowe	.30	.09
❑ 101	Javy Lopez	.30	.09
❑ 102	Adrian Beltre	.50	.15
❑ 103	Jim Parque	.30	.09
❑ 104	Marquis Grissom	.30	.09
❑ 105	Eric Chavez	.30	.09
❑ 106	Todd Jones	.30	.09
❑ 107	Eric Owens	.30	.09
❑ 108	Roger Clemens	1.50	.45
❑ 109	Denny Hocking	.30	.09
❑ 110	Roberto Hernandez	.30	.09
❑ 111	Albert Belle	.30	.09
❑ 112	Troy Glaus	.30	.09
❑ 113	Ivan Rodriguez	.75	.23
❑ 114	Carlos Guillen	.30	.09
❑ 115	Chuck Finley	.30	.09
❑ 116	Dmitri Young	.30	.09
❑ 117	Paul Konerko	.30	.09
❑ 118	Damon Buford	.30	.09
❑ 119	Fernando Tatis	.30	.09
❑ 120	Larry Walker	.50	.15
❑ 121	Jason Kendall	.30	.09
❑ 122	Matt Williams	.30	.09
❑ 123	Henry Rodriguez	.30	.09
❑ 124	Placido Polanco	.30	.09
❑ 125	Bobby Estalella	.30	.09
❑ 126	Pat Burrell	.30	.09
❑ 127	Mark Loretta	.30	.09
❑ 128	Moises Alou	.30	.09
❑ 129	Tino Martinez	.50	.15
❑ 130	Milton Bradley	.30	.09
❑ 131	Todd Hundley	.30	.09
❑ 132	Keith Foulke	.30	.09
❑ 133	Robert Fick	.30	.09
❑ 134	Cristian Guzman	.30	.09
❑ 135	Rusty Greer	.30	.09
❑ 136	John Olerud	.30	.09
❑ 137	Mariano Rivera	.50	.15
❑ 138	Jeromy Burnitz	.30	.09
❑ 139	Dave Burba	.30	.09
❑ 140	Ken Griffey Jr.	1.25	.35
❑ 141	Tony Gwynn	1.00	.30
❑ 142	Carlos Delgado	.30	.09
❑ 143	Edgar Martinez	.50	.15
❑ 144	Ramon Hernandez	.30	.09
❑ 145	Pedro Astacio	.30	.09
❑ 146	Ray Lankford	.30	.09
❑ 147	Mike Mussina	.50	.15
❑ 148	Ray Durham	.30	.09
❑ 149	Lee Stevens	.30	.09
❑ 150	Jay Canizaro	.30	.09
❑ 151	Adrian Brown	.30	.09
❑ 152	Mike Piazza	1.25	.35
❑ 153	Cliff Floyd	.30	.09
❑ 154	Jose Vidro	.30	.09
❑ 155	Jason Giambi	.30	.09
❑ 156	Andruw Jones	.30	.09
❑ 157	Robin Ventura	.30	.09
❑ 158	Gary Sheffield	.30	.09
❑ 159	Jeff D'Amico	.30	.09
❑ 160	Chuck Knoblauch	.30	.09
❑ 161	Roger Cedeno	.30	.09
❑ 162	Jim Thome	.75	.23
❑ 163	Peter Bergeron	.30	.09
❑ 164	Kerry Wood	.75	.23
❑ 165	Gabe Kapler	.30	.09
❑ 166	Corey Koskie	.30	.09
❑ 167	Doug Glanville	.30	.09
❑ 168	Brent Mayne	.30	.09
❑ 169	Scott Spiezio	.30	.09
❑ 170	Steve Karsay	.30	.09
❑ 171	Al Martin	.30	.09
❑ 172	Fred McGriff	.50	.15
❑ 173	Gabe White	.30	.09
❑ 174	Alex Gonzalez	.30	.09
❑ 175	Mike Darr	.30	.09
❑ 176	Bengie Molina	.30	.09
❑ 177	Ben Grieve	.30	.09
❑ 178	Marlon Anderson	.30	.09
❑ 179	Brian Giles	.30	.09
❑ 180	Jose Valentin	.30	.09
❑ 181	Brian Jordan	.30	.09
❑ 182	Randy Johnson	.75	.23
❑ 183	Ricky Ledee	.30	.09
❑ 184	Russ Ortiz	.30	.09
❑ 185	Mike Lowell	.30	.09
❑ 186	Curtis Leskanic	.30	.09
❑ 187	Bob Abreu	.30	.09
❑ 188	Derek Jeter	2.00	.60
❑ 189	Lance Berkman	.30	.09
❑ 190	Roberto Alomar	.50	.15
❑ 191	Darin Erstad	.30	.09
❑ 192	Richie Sexson	.30	.09
❑ 193	Alex Ochoa	.30	.09
❑ 194	Carlos Febles	.30	.09
❑ 195	David Ortiz	.50	.15
❑ 196	Shawn Green	.30	.09
❑ 197	Mike Sweeney	.30	.09
❑ 198	Vladimir Guerrero	.75	.23
❑ 199	Jose Jimenez	.30	.09
❑ 200	Travis Lee	.30	.09
❑ 201	Rickey Henderson	.75	.23
❑ 202	Bob Wickman	.30	.09
❑ 203	Miguel Cairo	.30	.09
❑ 204	Steve Finley	.30	.09
❑ 205	Tony Batista	.30	.09
❑ 206	Jamey Wright	.30	.09
❑ 207	Terrence Long	.30	.09
❑ 208	Trevor Hoffman	.30	.09
❑ 209	John VanderWal	.30	.09
❑ 210	Greg Maddux	1.25	.35
❑ 211	Tim Salmon	.50	.15
❑ 212	Herbert Perry	.30	.09
❑ 213	Marvin Benard	.30	.09
❑ 214	Jose Offerman	.30	.09
❑ 215	Jay Payton	.30	.09
❑ 216	Jon Lieber	.30	.09
❑ 217	Mark Kotsay	.30	.09
❑ 218	Scott Brosius	.30	.09
❑ 219	Scott Williamson	.30	.09
❑ 220	Omar Vizquel	.50	.15
❑ 221	Mike Hampton	.30	.09
❑ 222	Richard Hidalgo	.30	.09
❑ 223	Rey Sanchez	.30	.09
❑ 224	Matt Lawton	.30	.09
❑ 225	Bruce Chen	.30	.09
❑ 226	Ryan Klesko	.30	.09
❑ 227	Garret Anderson	.30	.09
❑ 228	Kevin Brown	.30	.09
❑ 229	Mike Cameron	.30	.09
❑ 230	Tony Clark	.30	.09
❑ 231	Curt Schilling	.30	.09
❑ 232	Vinny Castilla	.30	.09
❑ 233	Carl Pavano	.30	.09
❑ 234	Eric Davis	.30	.09
❑ 235	Darrin Fletcher	.30	.09
❑ 236	Matt Stairs	.30	.09
❑ 237	Octavio Dotel	.30	.09
❑ 238	Mark Grace	.50	.15
❑ 239	John Smoltz	.50	.15
❑ 240	Matt Clement	.30	.09
❑ 241	Ellis Burks	.30	.09
❑ 242	Charles Johnson	.30	.09
❑ 243	Jeff Bagwell	.50	.15
❑ 244	Derek Bell	.30	.09
❑ 245	Nomar Garciaparra	1.25	.35
❑ 246	Jorge Posada	.50	.15
❑ 247	Ryan Dempster	.30	.09
❑ 248	J.T. Snow	.30	.09
❑ 249	Eric Young	.30	.09
❑ 250	Daryle Ward	.30	.09
❑ 251	Joe Randa	.30	.09
❑ 252	Travis Fryman	.30	.09
❑ 253	Mike Williams	.30	.09
❑ 254	Jacque Jones	.30	.09
❑ 255	Scott Elarton	.30	.09
❑ 256	Mark McGwire	2.00	.60
❑ 257	Jay Buhner	.30	.09
❑ 258	Randy Wolf	.30	.09
❑ 259	Sammy Sosa	1.25	.35
❑ 260	Chan Ho Park	.30	.09
❑ 261	Damion Easley	.30	.09
❑ 262	Rick Ankiel	.30	.09
❑ 263	Frank Thomas	.75	.23
❑ 264	Kris Benson	.30	.09
❑ 265	Luis Alicea	.30	.09
❑ 266	Jeromy Burnitz	.30	.09
❑ 267	Geoff Blum	.30	.09
❑ 268	Joe Girardi	.30	.09
❑ 269	Livan Hernandez	.30	.09
❑ 270	Jeff Conine	.30	.09
❑ 271	Danny Graves	.30	.09
❑ 272	Craig Biggio	.50	.15
❑ 273	Jose Canseco	.75	.23
❑ 274	Tom Glavine	.50	.15
❑ 275	Ruben Mateo	.30	.09
❑ 276	Jeff Kent	.30	.09
❑ 277	Kevin Young	.30	.09

No.	Card	Price	Price
❑ 278	A.J. Burnett	.30	.09
❑ 279	Dante Bichette	.30	.09
❑ 280	Sandy Alomar Jr.	.30	.09
❑ 281	John Wetteland	.30	.09
❑ 282	Torii Hunter	.30	.09
❑ 283	Jarrod Washburn	.30	.09
❑ 284	Rich Aurilia	.30	.09
❑ 285	Jeff Cirillo	.30	.09
❑ 286	Fernando Seguignol	.30	.09
❑ 287	Darren Dreifort	.30	.09
❑ 288	Deivi Cruz	.30	.09
❑ 289	Pokey Reese	.30	.09
❑ 290	Garrett Stephenson	.30	.09
❑ 291	Bret Boone	.30	.09
❑ 292	Tim Hudson	.30	.09
❑ 293	John Flaherty	.30	.09
❑ 294	Shannon Stewart	.30	.09
❑ 295	Shawn Estes	.30	.09
❑ 296	Wilton Guerrero	.30	.09
❑ 297	Delino DeShields	.30	.09
❑ 298	David Justice	.30	.09
❑ 299	Harold Baines	.30	.09
❑ 300	Al Leiter	.30	.09
❑ 301	Wil Cordero	.30	.09
❑ 302	Antonio Alfonseca	.30	.09
❑ 303	Sean Casey	.30	.09
❑ 304	Carlos Beltran	.50	.15
❑ 305	Brad Radke	.30	.09
❑ 306	Jason Varitek	.50	.15
❑ 307	Shigetoshi Hasegawa	.30	.09
❑ 308	Todd Stottlemyre	.30	.09
❑ 309	Raul Mondesi	.30	.09
❑ 310	Mike Bordick	.30	.09
❑ 311	Darryl Kile	.30	.09
❑ 312	Dean Palmer	.30	.09
❑ 313	Johnny Damon	.50	.15
❑ 314	Todd Helton	.50	.15
❑ 315	Chad Hermansen	.30	.09
❑ 316	Kevin Appier	.30	.09
❑ 317	Greg Vaughn	.30	.09
❑ 318	Robb Nen	.30	.09
❑ 319	Jose Cruz Jr.	.30	.09
❑ 320	Ron Belliard	.30	.09
❑ 321	Bernie Williams	.50	.15
❑ 322	Melvin Mora	.30	.09
❑ 323	Kenny Lofton	.30	.09
❑ 324	Armando Benitez	.30	.09
❑ 325	Carlos Lee	.30	.09
❑ 326	Damian Jackson	.30	.09
❑ 327	Eric Milton	.30	.09
❑ 328	J.D. Drew	.30	.09
❑ 329	Byung-Hyun Kim	.30	.09
❑ 330	Chris Stynes	.30	.09
❑ 331	Kazuhiro Sasaki	.30	.09
❑ 332	Troy O'Leary	.30	.09
❑ 333	Pat Hentgen	.30	.09
❑ 334	Brad Ausmus	.30	.09
❑ 335	Todd Walker	.30	.09
❑ 336	Jason Isringhausen	.30	.09
❑ 337	Gerald Williams	.30	.09
❑ 338	Aaron Sele	.30	.09
❑ 339	Paul O'Neill	.50	.15
❑ 340	Cal Ripken	2.50	.75
❑ 341	Manny Ramirez	.50	.15
❑ 342	Will Clark	.75	.23
❑ 343	Mark Redman	.30	.09
❑ 344	Bubba Trammell	.30	.09
❑ 345	Troy Percival	.30	.09
❑ 346	Chris Singleton	.30	.09
❑ 347	Rafael Palmeiro	.50	.15
❑ 348	Carl Everett	.30	.09
❑ 349	Andy Benes	.30	.09
❑ 350	Bobby Higginson	.30	.09
❑ 351	Alex Cabrera	.30	.09
❑ 352	Barry Zito	.50	.15
❑ 353	Jace Brewer	.30	.09
❑ 354	Paxton Crawford	.30	.09
❑ 355	Oswaldo Mairena	.30	.09
❑ 356	Joe Crede	.30	.09
❑ 357	A.J. Pierzynski	.30	.09
❑ 358	Daniel Garibay	.30	.09
❑ 359	Jason Tyner	.30	.09
❑ 360	Nate Rolison	.30	.09
❑ 361	Scott Downs	.30	.09
❑ 362	Keith Ginter	.30	.09
❑ 363	Juan Pierre	.30	.09
❑ 364	Adam Bernero	.30	.09
❑ 365	Chris Richard	.30	.09
❑ 366	Joey Nation	.30	.09
❑ 367	Aubrey Huff	.30	.09
❑ 368	Adam Eaton	.30	.09
❑ 369	Jose Ortiz	.30	.09
❑ 370	Eric Munson	.30	.09
❑ 371	Matt Kinney	.30	.09
❑ 372	Eric Byrnes	.30	.09
❑ 373	Keith McDonald	.30	.09
❑ 374	Matt Wise	.30	.09
❑ 375	Timo Perez	.30	.09
❑ 376	Julio Zuleta	.30	.09
❑ 377	Jimmy Rollins	.30	.09
❑ 378	Xavier Nady	.30	.09
❑ 379	Ryan Kohlmeier	.30	.09
❑ 380	Corey Patterson	.30	.09
❑ 381	Todd Helton LL	.30	.09
❑ 382	Moises Alou LL	.30	.09
❑ 383	Vladimir Guerrero LL	.50	.15
❑ 384	Luis Castillo LL	.30	.09
❑ 385	Jeffrey Hammonds LL	.30	.09
❑ 386	Nomar Garciaparra LL	.75	.23
❑ 387	Carlos Delgado LL	.30	.09
❑ 388	Darin Erstad LL	.30	.09
❑ 389	Manny Ramirez LL	.30	.09
❑ 390	Mike Sweeney LL	.30	.09
❑ 391	Sammy Sosa LL	.75	.23
❑ 392	Barry Bonds LL	.75	.23
❑ 393	Jeff Bagwell LL	.30	.09
❑ 394	Richard Hidalgo LL	.30	.09
❑ 395	Vladimir Guerrero LL	.50	.15
❑ 396	Troy Glaus LL	.30	.09
❑ 397	Frank Thomas LL	.50	.15
❑ 398	Carlos Delgado LL	.30	.09
❑ 399	David Justice LL	.30	.09
❑ 400	Jason Giambi LL	.30	.09
❑ 401	Randy Johnson LL	.50	.15
❑ 402	Kevin Brown LL	.30	.09
❑ 403	Greg Maddux LL	.75	.23
❑ 404	Al Leiter LL	.30	.09
❑ 405	Mike Hampton LL	.30	.09
❑ 406	Pedro Martinez LL	.50	.15
❑ 407	Roger Clemens LL	.75	.23
❑ 408	Mike Sirotka LL	.30	.09
❑ 409	Mike Mussina LL	.30	.09
❑ 410	Bartolo Colon LL	.30	.09
❑ 411	Subway Series WS	.50	.15
❑ 412	Jose Vizcaino WS	.50	.15
❑ 413	Jose Vizcaino WS	.50	.15
❑ 414	Roger Clemens WS	.75	.23
❑ 415	Armando Benitez	.30	.09
	Edgardo Alfonzo		
	Timo Perez WS		
❑ 416	Al Leiter WS	.50	.15
❑ 417	Luis Sojo WS	.50	.15
❑ 418	Yankees 3-Peat WS	.75	.23
❑ 419	Derek Jeter WS	1.00	.30
❑ 420	Toast of the Town WS	.50	.15
❑ 421	Rafael Furcal	.30	.09
	Chipper Jones		
	Greg Maddux		
	John Rocker		
	Tom Glavine CL		
❑ 422	Armando Benitez	.75	.23
	Mike Piazza		
	Mike Hampton		
	Al Leiter CL		
❑ 423	Ryan Dempster	.30	.09
	Luis Castillo		
	Antonio Alfonseca		
	Preston Wilson CL		
❑ 424	Robert Person	.30	.09
	Scott Rolen		
	Randy Wolf		
	Bob Abreu		
	Doug Glanville CL		
❑ 425	Vladimir Guerrero	.50	.15
	Peter Bergeron CL		
❑ 426	Fernando Vina	.30	.09
	Dave Veres		
	Jim Edmonds		
	Rick Ankiel		
	Edgar Renteria		
	Darryl Kile CL		
❑ 427	Danny Graves	.30	.09
	Ken Griffey Jr.		
	Sean Casey		
	Pokey Reese CL		
❑ 428	Jon Lieber	.50	.15
	Sammy Sosa		
	Eric Young CL		
❑ 429	Curtis Leskanic	.50	.15
	Geoff Jenkins		
	Jeff D'Amico		
	Jeromy Burnitz		
	Marquis Grissom CL		
❑ 430	Scott Elarton	.30	.09
	Jeff Bagwell		
	Octavio Dotel		
	Moises Alou		
	Roger Cedeno CL		
❑ 431	Mike Williams	.50	.15
	Jason Kendall		
	Kris Benson		
	Brian Giles CL		
❑ 432	Livan Hernandez	.30	.09
	Jeff Kent		
	Robb Nen		
	Barry Bonds		
	Marvin Benard CL		
❑ 433	Luis Gonzalez	.30	.09
	Steve Finley		
	Tony Womack		
	Randy Johnson CL		
❑ 434	Jeff Shaw	.30	.09
	Gary Sheffield		
	Kevin Brown		
	Shawn Green		
	Chan Ho Park CL UER		
	B.Shaw should be J.Shaw		
❑ 435	Jose Jimenez	.30	.09
	Todd Helton		
	Brian Bohanon		
	Tom Goodwin CL UER		
	C.Goodwin should be T.Goodwin		
❑ 436	Trevor Hoffman	.30	.09
	Phil Nevin		
	Matt Clement		
	Eric Owens CL		
❑ 437	Mariano Rivera	.75	.23
	Derek Jeter		
	Roger Clemens		
	Bernie Williams		
	Andy Pettitte CL		
❑ 438	Pedro Martinez	.50	.15
	Nomar Garciaparra		
	Derek Lowe		
	Carl Everett CL		
❑ 439	Ryan Kohlmeier	.30	.09
	Delino DeShields		
	Mike Mussina		
	Albert Belle CL		
❑ 440	David Wells	.30	.09
	Carlos Delgado		
	Billy Koch		
	Raul Mondesi CL		
❑ 441	Ramon Hernandez	.30	.09
	Fred McGriff		
	Miguel Cairo		
	Greg Vaughn CL		
❑ 442	Mike Sirotka	.50	.15
	Frank Thomas		
	Keith Foulke		
	Ray Durham CL		
❑ 443	Steve Karsay	.30	.09
	Manny Ramirez		
	Bartolo Colon		
	Roberto Alomar CL		
❑ 444	Brian Moehler	.30	.09
	Deivi Cruz		
	Juan Encarnacion		
	Todd Jones		
	Bobby Higginson CL		
❑ 445	Mac Suzuki	.30	.09
	Mike Sweeney		
	Johnny Damon		
	Jermaine Dye CL		
❑ 446	Brad Radke	.30	.09
	Matt Lawton		
	Eric Milton		
	Jacque Jones		

Cristian Guzman CL
❑ 447 Kazuhiro Sasaki .30 .09
Edgar Martinez
Aaron Sele
Rickey Henderson CL
❑ 448 Jason Isringhausen .30 .09
Jason Giambi
Tim Hudson
Randy Velarde CL
❑ 449 Shigetoshi Hasegawa .30 .09
Darin Erstad
Troy Percival
Troy Glaus CL
❑ 450 Rick Helling .30 .09
Rafael Palmeiro
John Wetteland
Luis Alicea CL
❑ 451 Albert Pujols RC 30.00 9.00
❑ 452 Ichiro Suzuki RC 15.00 4.50
❑ 453 Tsuyoshi Shinjo RC .75 .23
❑ 454 Johnny Estrada RC 1.25 .35
❑ 455 Elpidio Guzman RC .50 .15
❑ 456 Adrian Hernandez RC .50 .15
❑ 457 Rafael Soriano RC .75 .23
❑ 458 Drew Henson RC 1.25 .35
❑ 459 Juan Uribe RC .75 .23
❑ 460 Matt White RC .50 .15
❑ 461 Endy Chavez RC .50 .15
❑ 462 Bud Smith RC .50 .15
❑ 463 Morgan Ensberg RC 1.25 .35
❑ 464 Jay Gibbons RC 1.25 .35
❑ 465 Jackson Melian RC .50 .15
❑ 466 Junior Spivey RC .75 .23
❑ 467 Juan Cruz RC .50 .15
❑ 468 Wilson Betemit RC .50 .15
❑ 469 Alexis Gomez RC .50 .15
❑ 470 Mark Teixeira RC 6.00 1.80
❑ 471 Erick Almonte RC .50 .15
❑ 472 Travis Hafner RC 2.50 .75
❑ 473 Carlos Valderrama RC .50 .15
❑ 474 Brandon Duckworth RC .50 .15
❑ 475 Ryan Freel RC .50 .15
❑ 476 Wilkin Ruan RC .50 .15
❑ 477 Andres Torres RC .50 .15
❑ 478 Josh Towers RC .50 .15
❑ 479 Kyle Lohse RC .75 .23
❑ 480 Jason Michaels RC .50 .15
❑ 481 Alfonso Soriano .75 .23
❑ 482 C.C. Sabathia .50 .15
❑ 483 Roy Oswalt .75 .23
❑ 484 Ben Sheets UER .75 .23
Wrong team logo on the front
❑ 485 Adam Dunn .75 .23
❑ NNO Uncut Sheet EXCH/100 2.00 .60

2002 Fleer Tradition Update

	Nm-Mt	Ex-Mt
COMPLETE SET (400)	120.00	36.00
COMP.SET w/o SP's (300)	40.00	12.00
COMMON CARD (U101-U400)	.30	.09
COMMON CARD (U1-U100)	1.00	.30

❑ U1 P.J. Bevis SP RC 1.00 .30
❑ U2 Mike Crudale SP RC 1.00 .30
❑ U3 Ben Howard SP RC 1.00 .30
❑ U4 Travis Driskill SP RC 1.00 .30
❑ U5 Reed Johnson SP RC 1.25 .35
❑ U6 Kyle Kane SP RC 1.00 .30
❑ U7 Deivis Santos SP 1.00 .30
❑ U8 Tim Kalita SP RC 1.00 .30
❑ U9 Brandon Puffer SP RC 1.00 .30
❑ U10 Chris Snelling SP RC 1.00 .30
❑ U11 Juan Brito SP RC 1.00 .30
❑ U12 Tyler Yates SP RC 1.25 .35
❑ U13 Victor Alvarez SP RC 1.00 .30
❑ U14 Takahito Nomura SP RC 1.00 .30
❑ U15 Ron Calloway SP RC 1.00 .30
❑ U16 Satoru Komiyama SP RC 1.00 .30
❑ U17 Julius Matos SP RC 1.00 .30
❑ U18 Jorge Nunez SP RC 1.00 .30
❑ U19 Anderson Machado SP RC 1.00 .30
❑ U20 Scott Layfield SP RC 1.00 .30
❑ U21 Aaron Cook SP RC 1.00 .30
❑ U22 Alex Pelaez SP RC 1.00 .30
❑ U23 Corey Thurman SP RC 1.00 .30
❑ U24 Nelson Castro SP RC 1.00 .30
❑ U25 Jeff Austin SP RC 1.00 .30
❑ U26 Felix Escalona SP RC 1.00 .30
❑ U27 Luis Ugueto SP RC 1.00 .30
❑ U28 Jaime Cerda SP RC 1.00 .30
❑ U29 J.J. Trujillo SP RC 1.00 .30
❑ U30 Rodrigo Rosario SP RC 1.00 .30
❑ U31 Jorge Padilla SP RC 1.00 .30
❑ U32 Shawn Sedlacek SP RC 1.00 .30
❑ U33 Nate Field SP RC 1.00 .30
❑ U34 Earl Snyder SP RC 1.25 .35
❑ U35 Miguel Asencio SP RC 1.00 .30
❑ U36 Ken Huckaby SP RC 1.00 .30
❑ U37 Valentino Pascucci SP 1.00 .30
❑ U38 So Taguchi SP RC 1.25 .35
❑ U39 Brian Mallette SP RC 1.00 .30
❑ U40 Kazuhisa Ishii SP RC 3.00 .90
❑ U41 Matt Thornton SP RC 1.00 .30
❑ U42 Mark Corey SP RC 1.00 .30
❑ U43 Kirk Saarloos SP RC 1.00 .30
❑ U44 Josh Bard SP RC 1.00 .30
❑ U45 Hansel Izquierdo SP RC 1.00 .30
❑ U46 Rene Reyes SP RC 1.00 .30
❑ U47 Luis Garcia SP 1.00 .30
❑ U48 Jason Simontacchi SP RC 1.00 .30
❑ U49 John Ennis SP RC 1.00 .30
❑ U50 Franklyn German SP RC 1.00 .30
❑ U51 Aaron Guiel SP RC 1.00 .30
❑ U52 Howie Clark SP RC 1.00 .30
❑ U53 David Ross SP RC 1.00 .30
❑ U54 Jason Davis SP RC 2.00 .60
❑ U55 Francis Beltran SP RC 1.00 .30
❑ U56 Barry Wesson SP RC 1.00 .30
❑ U57 Run. Hernandez SP RC 1.00 .30
❑ U58 Oliver Perez SP RC 8.00 2.40
❑ U59 Ryan Bukvich SP RC 1.00 .30
❑ U60 Steve Kent SP RC 1.00 .30
❑ U61 Julio Mateo SP RC 1.00 .30
❑ U62 Jason Jimenez SP RC 1.00 .30
❑ U63 Jayson Durocher SP RC 1.00 .30
❑ U64 Kevin Frederick SP RC 1.00 .30
❑ U65 Kevin Gryboski SP RC 1.00 .30
❑ U66 Edwin Almonte SP RC 1.00 .30
❑ U67 John Foster SP RC 1.00 .30
❑ U68 Doug Devore SP RC 1.00 .30
❑ U69 Tom Shearn SP RC 1.00 .30
❑ U70 Colin Young SP RC 1.00 .30
❑ U71 Jon Adkins SP RC 1.00 .30
❑ U72 Wilbert Nieves SP RC 1.00 .30
❑ U73 Matt Duff SP RC 1.00 .30
❑ U74 Carl Sadler SP RC 1.00 .30
❑ U75 Jason Kershner SP RC 1.00 .30
❑ U76 Brandon Backe SP RC 2.00 .60
❑ U77 Josh Hancock SP RC 1.00 .30
❑ U78 Chris Baker SP RC 1.00 .30
❑ U79 Travis Hughes SP RC 1.00 .30
❑ U80 Steve Bechler SP RC 1.00 .30
❑ U81 Allan Simpson SP RC 1.00 .30
❑ U82 Aaron Taylor SP RC 1.00 .30
❑ U83 Kevin Cash SP RC 1.00 .30
❑ U84 Chone Figgins SP RC 2.00 .60
❑ U85 Clay Condrey SP RC 1.00 .30
❑ U86 Shane Nance SP RC 1.00 .30
❑ U87 Freddy Sanchez SP RC 1.00 .30
❑ U88 Jim Rushford SP RC 1.00 .30
❑ U89 Jeriome Robertson SP RC 1.00 .30
❑ U90 Trey Lunsford SP RC 1.00 .30
❑ U91 Cody McKay SP RC 1.00 .30
❑ U92 Trey Hodges SP RC 1.00 .30
❑ U93 Hee Seop Choi SP 1.00 .30
❑ U94 Joe Borchard SP 1.00 .30
❑ U95 Orlando Hudson SP 1.00 .30
❑ U96 Carl Crawford SP 1.00 .30
❑ U97 Mark Prior SP 4.00 1.20
❑ U98 Brett Myers SP 1.00 .30
❑ U99 Kenny Lofton SP 1.00 .30
❑ U100 Cliff Floyd SP 1.00 .30
❑ U101 Randy Winn .30 .09
❑ U102 Ryan Dempster .30 .09
❑ U103 Josh Phelps .30 .09
❑ U104 Marcus Giles .30 .09
❑ U105 Rickey Henderson .75 .23
❑ U106 Jose Leon .30 .09
❑ U107 Tino Martinez .50 .15
❑ U108 Greg Norton .30 .09
❑ U109 Odalis Perez .30 .09
❑ U110 J.C. Romero .30 .09
❑ U111 Gary Sheffield .30 .09
❑ U112 Ismael Valdes .30 .09
❑ U113 Juan Acevedo .30 .09
❑ U114 Ben Broussard .30 .09
❑ U115 Deivi Cruz .30 .09
❑ U116 Geronimo Gil .30 .09
❑ U117 Eric Hinske .30 .09
❑ U118 Ted Lilly .30 .09
❑ U119 Quinton McCracken .30 .09
❑ U120 Antonio Alfonseca .30 .09
❑ U121 Brent Abernathy .30 .09
❑ U122 Johnny Damon Sox .75 .23
❑ U123 Francisco Cordero .30 .09
❑ U124 Sterling Hitchcock .30 .09
❑ U125 Vladimir Nunez .30 .09
❑ U126 Andres Galarraga .30 .09
❑ U127 Timo Perez .30 .09
❑ U128 Tsuyoshi Shinjo .30 .09
❑ U129 Joe Girardi .30 .09
❑ U130 Roberto Alomar .50 .15
❑ U131 Ellis Burks .30 .09
❑ U132 Mike DeJean .30 .09
❑ U133 Alex Gonzalez .30 .09
❑ U134 Johan Santana 1.00 .30
❑ U135 Kenny Lofton .30 .09
❑ U136 Juan Encarnacion .30 .09
❑ U137 Dewon Brazelton .30 .09
❑ U138 Jeromy Burnitz .30 .09
❑ U139 Elmer Dessens .30 .09
❑ U140 Juan Gonzalez .50 .15
❑ U141 Todd Hundley .30 .09
❑ U142 Tomo Ohka .30 .09
❑ U143 Robin Ventura .30 .09
❑ U144 Rodrigo Lopez .30 .09
❑ U145 Ruben Sierra .30 .09
❑ U146 Jason Phillips .30 .09
❑ U147 Ryan Rupe .30 .09
❑ U148 Kevin Appier .30 .09
❑ U149 Sean Burroughs .30 .09
❑ U150 Masato Yoshii .30 .09
❑ U151 Juan Diaz .30 .09
❑ U152 Tony Graffanino .30 .09
❑ U153 Raul Ibanez .30 .09
❑ U154 Kevin Mench .30 .09
❑ U155 Pedro Astacio .30 .09
❑ U156 Brent Butler .30 .09
❑ U157 Kirk Rueter .30 .09
❑ U158 Eddie Guardado .30 .09
❑ U159 Hideki Irabu .30 .09
❑ U160 Wendell Magee .30 .09
❑ U161 Antonio Osuna .30 .09
❑ U162 Jose Vizcaino .30 .09
❑ U163 Danny Bautista .30 .09
❑ U164 Vinny Castilla .30 .09
❑ U165 Chris Singleton .30 .09
❑ U166 Mark Redman .30 .09
❑ U167 Olmedo Saenz .30 .09
❑ U168 Scott Erickson .30 .09
❑ U169 Ty Wigginton .30 .09
❑ U170 Jason Isringhausen .30 .09
❑ U171 Andy Van Hekken .30 .09
❑ U172 Chris Magruder .30 .09
❑ U173 Brandon Berger .30 .09
❑ U174 Roger Cedeno .30 .09
❑ U175 Kelvim Escobar .30 .09
❑ U176 Jose Guillen .30 .09

❑ U177 Damian Jackson .30 .09
❑ U178 Eric Owens .30 .09
❑ U179 Angel Berroa .30 .09
❑ U180 Alex Cintron .30 .09
❑ U181 Jeff Weaver .30 .09
❑ U182 Damon Minor .30 .09
❑ U183 Bobby Estalella .30 .09
❑ U184 David Justice .30 .09
❑ U185 Roy Halladay .30 .09
❑ U186 Brian Jordan .30 .09
❑ U187 Mike Maroth .30 .09
❑ U188 Pokey Reese .30 .09
❑ U189 Rey Sanchez .30 .09
❑ U190 Hank Blalock .75 .23
❑ U191 Jeff Cirillo .30 .09
❑ U192 Dmitri Young .30 .09
❑ U193 Carl Everett .30 .09
❑ U194 Joey Hamilton .30 .09
❑ U195 Jorge Julio .30 .09
❑ U196 Pablo Ozuna .30 .09
❑ U197 Jason Marquis .30 .09
❑ U198 Dustan Mohr .30 .09
❑ U199 Joe Borowski .30 .09
❑ U200 Tony Clark .30 .09
❑ U201 David Wells .30 .09
❑ U202 Josh Fogg .30 .09
❑ U203 Aaron Harang .30 .09
❑ U204 John McDonald .30 .09
❑ U205 John Stephens .30 .09
❑ U206 Chris Reitsma .30 .09
❑ U207 Alex Sanchez .30 .09
❑ U208 Milton Bradley .30 .09
❑ U209 Matt Clement .30 .09
❑ U210 Brad Fullmer .30 .09
❑ U211 Shigetoshi Hasegawa .30 .09
❑ U212 Austin Kearns .30 .09
❑ U213 Damaso Marte .30 .09
❑ U214 Vicente Padilla .30 .09
❑ U215 Raul Mondesi .30 .09
❑ U216 Russell Branyan .30 .09
❑ U217 Bartolo Colon .30 .09
❑ U218 Moises Alou .30 .09
❑ U219 Scott Hatteberg .30 .09
❑ U220 Bobby Kielty .30 .09
❑ U221 Kip Wells .30 .09
❑ U222 Scott Stewart .30 .09
❑ U223 Victor Martinez .75 .23
❑ U224 Marty Cordova .30 .09
❑ U225 Desi Relaford .30 .09
❑ U226 Reggie Sanders .30 .09
❑ U227 Jason Giambi .30 .09
❑ U228 Jimmy Haynes .30 .09
❑ U229 Billy Koch .30 .09
❑ U230 Damian Moss .30 .09
❑ U231 Chan Ho Park .30 .09
❑ U232 Cliff Floyd .30 .09
❑ U233 Todd Zeile .30 .09
❑ U234 Jeremy Giambi .30 .09
❑ U235 Rick Helling .30 .09
❑ U236 Matt Lawton .30 .09
❑ U237 Ramon Martinez .30 .09
❑ U238 Rondell White .30 .09
❑ U239 Scott Sullivan .30 .09
❑ U240 Hideo Nomo .75 .23
❑ U241 Todd Ritchie .30 .09
❑ U242 Ramon Santiago .30 .09
❑ U243 Jake Peavy .30 .09
❑ U244 Brad Wilkerson .30 .09
❑ U245 Reggie Taylor .30 .09
❑ U246 Carlos Pena .30 .09
❑ U247 Willis Roberts UER .30 .09
No U in front of card number
❑ U248 Jason Schmidt .30 .09
❑ U249 Mike Williams .30 .09
❑ U250 Alan Zinter .30 .09
❑ U251 Michael Tejera .30 .09
❑ U252 Dave Roberts .30 .09
❑ U253 Scott Schoeneweis .30 .09
❑ U254 Woody Williams .30 .09
❑ U255 John Thomson .30 .09
❑ U256 Ricardo Rodriguez .30 .09
❑ U257 Aaron Sele .30 .09
❑ U258 Paul Wilson .30 .09
❑ U259 Brett Tomko .30 .09
❑ U260 Kenny Rogers .30 .09
❑ U261 Mo Vaughn .30 .09
❑ U262 John Burkett .30 .09
❑ U263 Dennis Stark .30 .09
❑ U264 Ray Durham .30 .09
❑ U265 Scott Rolen .75 .23
❑ U266 Gabe Kapler .30 .09
❑ U267 Todd Hollandsworth .30 .09
❑ U268 Bud Smith .30 .09
❑ U269 Jay Payton .30 .09
❑ U270 Tyler Houston .30 .09
❑ U271 Brian Moehler .30 .09
❑ U272 David Espinosa .30 .09
❑ U273 Placido Polanco .30 .09
❑ U274 John Patterson .30 .09
❑ U275 Adam Hyzdu .30 .09
❑ U276 Albert Pujols DS .75 .23
❑ U277 Larry Walker DS .30 .09
❑ U278 Magglio Ordonez DS .30 .09
❑ U279 Ryan Klesko DS .30 .09
❑ U280 Darin Erstad DS .30 .09
❑ U281 Jeff Kent DS .30 .09
❑ U282 Paul Lo Duca DS .30 .09
❑ U283 Jim Edmonds DS .30 .09
❑ U284 Chipper Jones DS .50 .15
❑ U285 Bernie Williams DS .30 .09
❑ U286 Pat Burrell DS .30 .09
❑ U287 Cliff Floyd DS .30 .09
❑ U288 Troy Glaus DS .30 .09
❑ U289 Brian Giles DS .30 .09
❑ U290 Jim Thome DS .50 .15
❑ U291 Greg Maddux DS .75 .23
❑ U292 Roberto Alomar DS .30 .09
❑ U293 Jeff Bagwell DS .30 .09
❑ U294 Rafael Furcal DS .30 .09
❑ U295 Josh Beckett DS .30 .09
❑ U296 Carlos Delgado DS .30 .09
❑ U297 Ken Griffey Jr. DS .75 .23
❑ U298 Jason Giambi AS .30 .09
❑ U299 Paul Konerko AS .30 .09
❑ U300 Mike Sweeney AS .30 .09
❑ U301 Alfonso Soriano AS .30 .09
❑ U302 Shea Hillenbrand AS .30 .09
❑ U303 Tony Batista AS .30 .09
❑ U304 Robin Ventura AS .30 .09
❑ U305 Alex Rodriguez AS .75 .23
❑ U306 Nomar Garciaparra AS .75 .23
❑ U307 Derek Jeter AS 1.00 .30
❑ U308 Miguel Tejada AS .30 .09
❑ U309 Omar Vizquel AS .30 .09
❑ U310 Jorge Posada AS .30 .09
❑ U311 A.J. Pierzynski AS .30 .09
❑ U312 Ichiro Suzuki AS .75 .23
❑ U313 Manny Ramirez AS .30 .09
❑ U314 Torii Hunter AS .30 .09
❑ U315 Garret Anderson AS .30 .09
❑ U316 Robert Fick AS .30 .09
❑ U317 Randy Winn AS .30 .09
❑ U318 Mark Buehrle AS .30 .09
❑ U319 Freddy Garcia AS .30 .09
❑ U320 Eddie Guardado AS .30 .09
❑ U321 Roy Halladay AS .30 .09
❑ U322 Derek Lowe AS .30 .09
❑ U323 Pedro Martinez AS .50 .15
❑ U324 Mariano Rivera AS .30 .09
❑ U325 Kazuhiro Sasaki AS .30 .09
❑ U326 Barry Zito AS .30 .09
❑ U327 Johnny Damon Sox AS .50 .15
❑ U328 Ugueth Urbina AS .30 .09
❑ U329 Todd Helton AS .30 .09
❑ U330 Richie Sexson AS .30 .09
❑ U331 Jose Vidro AS .30 .09
❑ U332 Luis Castillo AS .30 .09
❑ U333 Junior Spivey AS .30 .09
❑ U334 Scott Rolen AS .50 .15
❑ U335 Mike Lowell AS .30 .09
❑ U336 Jimmy Rollins AS .30 .09
❑ U337 Jose Hernandez AS .30 .09
❑ U338 Mike Piazza AS .75 .23
❑ U339 Benito Santiago AS .30 .09
❑ U340 Sammy Sosa AS .75 .23
❑ U341 Barry Bonds AS 1.00 .30
❑ U342 Vladimir Guerrero AS .50 .15
❑ U343 Lance Berkman AS .30 .09
❑ U344 Adam Dunn AS .30 .09
❑ U345 Shawn Green AS .30 .09
❑ U346 Luis Gonzalez AS .30 .09
❑ U347 Eric Gagne AS .50 .15
❑ U348 Tom Glavine AS .30 .09
❑ U349 Trevor Hoffman AS .30 .09
❑ U350 Randy Johnson AS .50 .15
❑ U351 Byung-Hyun Kim AS .30 .09
❑ U352 Matt Morris AS .30 .09
❑ U353 Odalis Perez AS .30 .09
❑ U354 Curt Schilling AS .30 .09
❑ U355 John Smoltz AS .30 .09
❑ U356 Mike Williams AS .30 .09
❑ U357 Andruw Jones AS .30 .09
❑ U358 Vicente Padilla AS .30 .09
❑ U359 Mike Remlinger AS .30 .09
❑ U360 Robb Nen AS .30 .09
❑ U361 Shawn Green CC .30 .09
❑ U362 Derek Jeter CC 1.00 .30
❑ U363 Troy Glaus CC .30 .09
❑ U364 Ken Griffey Jr. CC .75 .23
❑ U365 Mike Piazza CC .75 .23
❑ U366 Jason Giambi CC .30 .09
❑ U367 Greg Maddux CC .75 .23
❑ U368 Albert Pujols CC .75 .23
❑ U369 Pedro Martinez CC .50 .15
❑ U370 Barry Zito CC .30 .09
❑ U371 Ichiro Suzuki CC .75 .23
❑ U372 Nomar Garciaparra CC .75 .23
❑ U373 Vladimir Guerrero CC .50 .15
❑ U374 Randy Johnson CC .50 .15
❑ U375 Barry Bonds CC 1.00 .30
❑ U376 Sammy Sosa CC .75 .23
❑ U377 Hideo Nomo CC .50 .15
❑ U378 Jeff Bagwell CC .30 .09
❑ U379 Curt Schilling CC .30 .09
❑ U380 Jim Thome CC .50 .15
❑ U381 Todd Helton CC .30 .09
❑ U382 Roger Clemens CC .75 .23
❑ U383 Chipper Jones CC .50 .15
❑ U384 Alex Rodriguez CC .75 .23
❑ U385 Manny Ramirez CC .30 .09
❑ U386 Barry Bonds TT 1.00 .30
❑ U387 Jim Thome TT .50 .15
❑ U388 Adam Dunn TT .30 .09
❑ U389 Alex Rodriguez TT .75 .23
❑ U390 Shawn Green TT .30 .09
❑ U391 Jason Giambi TT .30 .09
❑ U392 Lance Berkman TT .30 .09
❑ U393 Pat Burrell TT .30 .09
❑ U394 Eric Chavez TT .30 .09
❑ U395 Mike Piazza TT .75 .23
❑ U396 Vladimir Guerrero TT .50 .15
❑ U397 Paul Konerko TT .30 .09
❑ U398 Sammy Sosa TT .75 .23
❑ U399 Richie Sexson TT .30 .09
❑ U400 Torii Hunter TT .30 .09

2003 Fleer Tradition

	Nm-Mt	Ex-Mt
COMPLETE SET (485)	150.00	45.00
COMP.SET w/o SP's (385)	40.00	12.00
COMMON CARD (1-30)	1.00	.30
COMM.SP (31-66/86-100)	1.00	.30
COMMON ML (67-85)	1.50	.45
COMMON CARD (	.30	.09
COMMON PR (426-460)	.30	.09

❑ 1 Jarrod Washburn 1.00 .30
Troy Glaus
Garret Anderson

Ramon Ortiz TL SP
❑ 2 Luis Gonzalez .... 1.50 .45
Randy Johnson TL SP
❑ 3 Andruw Jones .... 1.50 .45
Chipper Jones
Tom Glavine
Kevin Millwood TL SP
❑ 4 Tony Batista .... 1.00 .30
Rodrigo Lopez TL SP
❑ 5 Manny Ramirez .... 2.50 .75
Nomar Garciaparra
Derek Lowe
Pedro Martinez TL SP
❑ 6 Sammy Sosa .... 2.50 .75
Matt Clement
Kerry Wood TL SP
❑ 7 Matt Buehrle .... 1.00 .30
Magglio Ordonez
Danny Wright TL SP
❑ 8 Adam Dunn .... 1.00 .30
Aaron Boone
Jimmy Haynes TL SP
❑ 9 C.C. Sabathia .... 1.50 .45
Jim Thome TL SP
❑ 10 Todd Helton .... 1.00 .30
Jason Jennings TL SP
❑ 11 Randall Simon .... 1.00 .30
Steve Sparks
Mark Redman TL SP
❑ 12 Derrek Lee .... 1.00 .30
Mike Lowell
A.J. Burnett TL SP
❑ 13 Lance Berkman .... 1.00 .30
Roy Oswalt TL SP
❑ 14 Paul Byrd .... 1.00 .30
Carlos Beltran TL SP
❑ 15 Shawn Green .... 1.50 .45
Hideo Nomo TL SP
❑ 16 Richie Sexson .... 1.00 .30
Ben Sheets TL SP
❑ 17 Torii Hunter .... 1.50 .45
Kyle Lohse
Johan Santana TL SP
❑ 18 Vladimir Guerrrero .... 1.50 .45
Tomo Ohka
Javier Vazquez TL SP
❑ 19 Mike Piazza .... 2.50 .75
Al Leiter TL SP
❑ 20 Jason Giambi .... 2.50 .75
David Wells
Roger Clemens TL SP
❑ 21 Eric Chavez .... 1.00 .30
Miguel Tejada
Barry Zito TL SP
❑ 22 Pat Burrell .... 1.00 .30
Vicente Padilla
Randy Wolf TL SP
❑ 23 Brian Giles .... 1.00 .30
Josh Fogg
Kip Wells TL SP
❑ 24 Ryan Klesko .... 1.00 .30
Brian Lawrence TL SP
❑ 25 Barry Bonds .... 2.50 .75
Russ Ortiz
Jason Schmidt TL SP
❑ 26 Mike Cameron .... 1.00 .30
Bret Boone
Freddy Garcia TL SP
❑ 27 Albert Pujols .... 2.50 .75
Matt Morris TL SP
❑ 28 Aubry Huff .... 1.00 .30
Randy Winn
Joe Kennedy
Tanyon Sturtze TL SP
❑ 29 Alex Rodriguez .... 2.50 .75
Kenny Rogers
Chan Ho Park TL SP
❑ 30 Carlos Delgado .... 1.00 .30
Roy Halladay TL SP
❑ 31 Greg Maddux SP 4.00 1.20
❑ 32 Nick Neugebauer SP .... 1.00 .30
❑ 33 Larry Walker SP .... 1.50 .45
❑ 34 Freddy Garcia SP .... 1.00 .30
❑ 35 Rich Aurilia SP .... 1.00 .30
❑ 36 Craig Wilson SP .... 1.00 .30
❑ 37 Jeff Suppan SP .... 1.00 .30
❑ 38 Joel Pineiro SP .... 1.00 .30
❑ 39 Pedro Feliz SP .... 1.00 .30
❑ 40 Bartolo Colon SP .... 1.00 .30
❑ 41 Pete Walker SP .... 1.00 .30
❑ 42 Mo Vaughn SP .... 1.00 .30
❑ 43 Sidney Ponson SP .... 1.00 .30
❑ 44 Jason Isringhausen SP .... 1.00 .30
❑ 45 Hideki Irabu SP .... 1.00 .30
❑ 46 Pedro Martinez SP .... 2.50 .75
❑ 47 Tom Glavine SP .... 1.50 .45
❑ 48 Matt Lawton SP .... 1.00 .30
❑ 49 Kyle Lohse SP .... 1.00 .30
❑ 50 Corey Patterson SP .... 1.00 .30
❑ 51 Ichiro Suzuki SP UER 4.00 1.20
RBI total for 2002 incorrect
❑ 52 Wade Miller SP .... 1.00 .30
❑ 53 Ben Diggins SP .... 1.00 .30
❑ 54 Jayson Werth SP .... 1.00 .30
❑ 55 Masato Yoshii SP .... 1.00 .30
❑ 56 Mark Buehrle SP .... 1.00 .30
❑ 57 Drew Henson SP .... 1.00 .30
❑ 58 Dave Williams SP .... 1.00 .30
❑ 59 Juan Rivera SP .... 1.00 .30
❑ 60 Scott Schoeneweis SP .... 1.00 .30
❑ 61 Josh Beckett SP .... 1.00 .30
❑ 62 Vinny Castilla SP .... 1.00 .30
❑ 63 Barry Zito SP .... 1.00 .30
❑ 64 Jose Valentin SP .... 1.00 .30
❑ 65 Jon Lieber SP .... 1.00 .30
❑ 66 Jorge Padilla SP .... 1.00 .30
❑ 67 Luis Aparicio ML SP .... 1.50 .45
❑ 68 Boog Powell ML SP .... 2.50 .75
❑ 69 Dick Radatz ML SP .... 1.50 .45
❑ 70 Frank Malzone ML SP .... 1.50 .45
❑ 71 Lou Brock ML SP .... 2.50 .75
❑ 72 Billy Williams ML SP .... 1.50 .45
❑ 73 Early Wynn ML SP .... 1.50 .45
❑ 74 Jim Bunning ML SP .... 2.50 .75
❑ 75 Al Kaline ML SP 4.00 1.20
❑ 76 Eddie Mathews ML SP 4.00 1.20
❑ 77 Harmon Killebrew ML SP 4.00 1.20
❑ 78 Gil Hodges ML SP .... 2.50 .75
❑ 79 Duke Snider ML SP .... 2.50 .75
❑ 80 Yogi Berra ML SP 4.00 1.20
❑ 81 Whitey Ford ML SP .... 2.50 .75
❑ 82 Willie Stargell ML SP .... 2.50 .75
❑ 83 Willie McCovey ML SP .... 1.50 .45
❑ 84 Gaylord Perry ML SP .... 1.50 .45
❑ 85 Red Schoendienst ML SP 1.50 .45
❑ 86 Luis Castillo SP .... 1.00 .30
❑ 87 Derek Jeter SP 6.00 1.80
❑ 88 Orlando Hudson SP .... 1.00 .30
❑ 89 Bobby Higginson SP .... 1.00 .30
❑ 90 Brent Butler SP .... 1.00 .30
❑ 91 Brad Wilkerson SP .... 1.00 .30
❑ 92 Craig Biggio SP .... 1.50 .45
❑ 93 Marlon Anderson SP .... 1.00 .30
❑ 94 Ty Wigginton SP .... 1.00 .30
❑ 95 Hideo Nomo SP .... 2.50 .75
❑ 96 Barry Larkin SP .... 1.50 .45
❑ 97 Roberto Alomar SP .... 1.50 .45
❑ 98 Omar Vizquel SP .... 1.50 .45
❑ 99 Andres Galarraga SP .... 1.00 .30
❑ 100 Shawn Green SP .... 1.00 .30
❑ 101 Rafael Furcal .... .30 .09
❑ 102 Bill Selby .... .30 .09
❑ 103 Brent Abernathy .... .30 .09
❑ 104 Nomar Garciaparra .... 1.25 .35
❑ 105 Michael Barrett .... .30 .09
❑ 106 Travis Hafner .... .30 .09
❑ 107 Carl Crawford .... .30 .09
❑ 108 Jeff Cirillo .... .30 .09
❑ 109 Mike Hampton .... .30 .09
❑ 110 Kip Wells .... .30 .09
❑ 111 Luis Alicea .... .30 .09
❑ 112 Ellis Burks .... .30 .09
❑ 113 Matt Anderson .... .30 .09
❑ 114 Carlos Beltran .... .50 .15
❑ 115 Paul Lo Duca .... .30 .09
❑ 116 Lance Berkman .... .30 .09
❑ 117 Moises Alou .... .30 .09
❑ 118 Roger Cedeno .... .30 .09
❑ 119 Brad Fullmer .... .30 .09
❑ 120 Sean Burroughs .... .30 .09
❑ 121 Eric Byrnes .... .30 .09
❑ 122 Milton Bradley .... .30 .09
❑ 123 Jason Giambi .... .30 .09
❑ 124 Brook Fordyce .... .30 .09
❑ 125 Kevin Appier .... .30 .09
❑ 126 Steve Cox .... .30 .09
❑ 127 Danny Bautista .... .30 .09
❑ 128 Edgardo Alfonzo .... .30 .09
❑ 129 Matt Clement .... .30 .09
❑ 130 Robb Nen .... .30 .09
❑ 131 Roy Halladay .... .30 .09
❑ 132 Brian Jordan .... .30 .09
❑ 133 A.J. Burnett .... .30 .09
❑ 134 Aaron Cook .... .30 .09
❑ 135 Paul Byrd .... .30 .09
❑ 136 Ramon Ortiz .... .30 .09
❑ 137 Adam Hyzdu .... .30 .09
❑ 138 Rafael Soriano .... .30 .09
❑ 139 Marty Cordova .... .30 .09
❑ 140 Nelson Cruz .... .30 .09
❑ 141 Jamie Moyer .... .30 .09
❑ 142 Raul Mondesi .... .30 .09
❑ 143 Josh Bard .... .30 .09
❑ 144 Elmer Dessens .... .30 .09
❑ 145 Rickey Henderson .... .75 .23
❑ 146 Joe McEwing .... .30 .09
❑ 147 Luis Rivas .... .30 .09
❑ 148 Armando Benitez .... .30 .09
❑ 149 Keith Foulke .... .30 .09
❑ 150 Zach Day .... .30 .09
❑ 151 Trey Lunsford .... .30 .09
❑ 152 Bobby Abreu .... .30 .09
❑ 153 Juan Cruz .... .30 .09
❑ 154 Ramon Hernandez .... .30 .09
❑ 155 Brandon Duckworth .... .30 .09
❑ 156 Matt Ginter .... .30 .09
❑ 157 Rob Mackowiak .... .30 .09
❑ 158 Josh Pearce .... .30 .09
❑ 159 Marlon Byrd .... .30 .09
❑ 160 Todd Walker .... .30 .09
❑ 161 Chad Hermansen .... .30 .09
❑ 162 Felix Escalona .... .30 .09
❑ 163 Ruben Mateo .... .30 .09
❑ 164 Mark Johnson .... .30 .09
❑ 165 Juan Pierre .... .30 .09
❑ 166 Gary Sheffield .... .30 .09
❑ 167 Edgar Martinez .... .50 .15
❑ 168 Randy Winn .... .30 .09
❑ 169 Pokey Reese .... .30 .09
❑ 170 Kevin Mench .... .30 .09
❑ 171 Albert Pujols .... 1.50 .45
❑ 172 J.T. Snow .... .30 .09
❑ 173 Dean Palmer .... .30 .09
❑ 174 Jay Payton .... .30 .09
❑ 175 Abraham Nunez .... .30 .09
❑ 176 Richie Sexson .... .30 .09
❑ 177 Jose Vidro .... .30 .09
❑ 178 Geoff Jenkins .... .30 .09
❑ 179 Dan Wilson .... .30 .09
❑ 180 John Olerud .... .30 .09
❑ 181 Javy Lopez .... .30 .09
❑ 182 Carl Everett .... .30 .09
❑ 183 Vernon Wells .... .30 .09
❑ 184 Juan Gonzalez .... .50 .15
❑ 185 Jorge Posada .... .50 .15
❑ 186 Mike Sweeney .... .30 .09
❑ 187 Cesar Izturis .... .30 .09
❑ 188 Jason Schmidt .... .30 .09
❑ 189 Chris Richard .... .30 .09
❑ 190 Jason Phillips .... .30 .09
❑ 191 Fred McGriff .... .50 .15
❑ 192 Shea Hillenbrand .... .30 .09
❑ 193 Ivan Rodriguez .... .75 .23
❑ 194 Mike Lowell .... .30 .09
❑ 195 Neifi Perez .... .30 .09
❑ 196 Kenny Lofton .... .30 .09
❑ 197 A.J. Pierzynski .... .30 .09
❑ 198 Larry Bigbie .... .30 .09
❑ 199 Juan Uribe .... .30 .09
❑ 200 Jeff Bagwell .... .50 .15
❑ 201 Timo Perez .... .30 .09
❑ 202 Jeremy Giambi .... .30 .09
❑ 203 Deivi Cruz .... .30 .09
❑ 204 Marquis Grissom .... .30 .09
❑ 205 Chipper Jones .... .75 .23
❑ 206 Alex Gonzalez .... .30 .09
❑ 207 Steve Finley .... .30 .09
❑ 208 Ben Davis .... .30 .09

❑ 209 Mike Bordick .30 .09
❑ 210 Casey Fossum .30 .09
❑ 211 Aramis Ramirez .30 .09
❑ 212 Aaron Boone .30 .09
❑ 213 Orlando Cabrera .30 .09
❑ 214 Hee Seop Choi .30 .09
❑ 215 Jeromy Burnitz .30 .09
❑ 216 Todd Hollandsworth .30 .09
❑ 217 Rey Sanchez .30 .09
❑ 218 Jose Cruz .30 .09
❑ 219 Roosevelt Brown .30 .09
❑ 220 Odalis Perez .30 .09
❑ 221 Carlos Delgado .30 .09
❑ 222 Orlando Hernandez .30 .09
❑ 223 Adam Everett .30 .09
❑ 224 Adrian Beltre .50 .15
❑ 225 Ken Griffey Jr. 1.25 .35
❑ 226 Brad Penny .30 .09
❑ 227 Carlos Lee .30 .09
❑ 228 J.C. Romero .30 .09
❑ 229 Ramon Martinez .30 .09
❑ 230 Matt Morris .30 .09
❑ 231 Ben Howard .30 .09
❑ 232 Damon Minor .30 .09
❑ 233 Jason Marquis .30 .09
❑ 234 Paul Wilson .30 .09
❑ 235 Ryan Dempster .30 .09
❑ 236 Jeffrey Hammonds .30 .09
❑ 237 Jaret Wright .30 .09
❑ 238 Carlos Pena .30 .09
❑ 239 Toby Hall .30 .09
❑ 240 Rick Helling .30 .09
❑ 241 Alex Escobar .30 .09
❑ 242 Trevor Hoffman .30 .09
❑ 243 Bernie Williams .50 .15
❑ 244 Jorge Julio .30 .09
❑ 245 Byung-Hyun Kim .30 .09
❑ 246 Mike Redmond .30 .09
❑ 247 Tony Armas .30 .09
❑ 248 Aaron Rowand .30 .09
❑ 249 Rusty Greer .30 .09
❑ 250 Aaron Harang .30 .09
❑ 251 Jeremy Fikac .30 .09
❑ 252 Jay Gibbons .30 .09
❑ 253 Brandon Puffer .30 .09
❑ 254 Dewayne Wise .30 .09
❑ 255 Chan Ho Park .30 .09
❑ 256 David Bell .30 .09
❑ 257 Kenny Rogers .30 .09
❑ 258 Mark Quinn .30 .09
❑ 259 Greg LaRocca .30 .09
❑ 260 Reggie Taylor .30 .09
❑ 261 Brett Tomko .30 .09
❑ 262 Jack Wilson .30 .09
❑ 263 Billy Wagner .30 .09
❑ 264 Greg Norton .30 .09
❑ 265 Tim Salmon .50 .15
❑ 266 Joe Randa .30 .09
❑ 267 Geronimo Gil .30 .09
❑ 268 Johnny Damon .75 .23
❑ 269 Robin Ventura .30 .09
❑ 270 Frank Thomas .75 .23
❑ 271 Terrence Long .30 .09
❑ 272 Mark Redman .30 .09
❑ 273 Mark Kotsay .30 .09
❑ 274 Ben Sheets .30 .09
❑ 275 Reggie Sanders .30 .09
❑ 276 Mark Grace .50 .15
❑ 277 Eddie Guardado .30 .09
❑ 278 Julio Mateo .30 .09
❑ 279 Bengie Molina .30 .09
❑ 280 Bill Hall .30 .09
❑ 281 Eric Chavez .30 .09
❑ 282 Joe Kennedy .30 .09
❑ 283 John Valentin .30 .09
❑ 284 Ray Durham .30 .09
❑ 285 Trot Nixon .30 .09
❑ 286 Rondell White .30 .09
❑ 287 Alex Gonzalez .30 .09
❑ 288 Tomas Perez .30 .09
❑ 289 Jared Sandberg .30 .09
❑ 290 Jacque Jones .30 .09
❑ 291 Cliff Floyd .30 .09
❑ 292 Ryan Klesko .30 .09
❑ 293 Morgan Ensberg .30 .09
❑ 294 Jerry Hairston .30 .09
❑ 295 Doug Mientkiewicz .30 .09
❑ 296 Darin Erstad .30 .09
❑ 297 Jeff Conine .30 .09
❑ 298 Johnny Estrada .30 .09
❑ 299 Mark Mulder .30 .09
❑ 300 Jeff Kent .30 .09
❑ 301 Roger Clemens 1.50 .45
❑ 302 Endy Chavez .30 .09
❑ 303 Joe Crede .30 .09
❑ 304 J.D. Drew .30 .09
❑ 305 David Dellucci .30 .09
❑ 306 Eli Marrero .30 .09
❑ 307 Josh Fogg .30 .09
❑ 308 Mike Crudale .30 .09
❑ 309 Bret Boone .30 .09
❑ 310 Mariano Rivera .50 .15
❑ 311 Mike Piazza 1.25 .35
❑ 312 Jason Jennings .30 .09
❑ 313 Jason Varitek .50 .15
❑ 314 Vicente Padilla .30 .09
❑ 315 Kevin Millwood .30 .09
❑ 316 Nick Johnson .30 .09
❑ 317 Shane Reynolds .30 .09
❑ 318 Joe Thurston .30 .09
❑ 319 Mike Lamb .30 .09
❑ 320 Aaron Sele .30 .09
❑ 321 Fernando Tatis .30 .09
❑ 322 Randy Wolf .30 .09
❑ 323 David Justice .30 .09
❑ 324 Andy Pettitte .50 .15
❑ 325 Freddy Sanchez .30 .09
❑ 326 Scott Spiezio .30 .09
❑ 327 Randy Johnson .75 .23
❑ 328 Karim Garcia .30 .09
❑ 329 Eric Milton .30 .09
❑ 330 Jermaine Dye .30 .09
❑ 331 Kevin Brown .30 .09
❑ 332 Adam Pettyjohn .30 .09
❑ 333 Jason Lane .30 .09
❑ 334 Mark Prior .75 .23
❑ 335 Mike Lieberthal .30 .09
❑ 336 Matt White .30 .09
❑ 337 John Patterson .30 .09
❑ 338 Marcus Giles .30 .09
❑ 339 Kazuhisa Ishii .30 .09
❑ 340 Willie Harris .30 .09
❑ 341 Travis Phelps .30 .09
❑ 342 Randall Simon .30 .09
❑ 343 Manny Ramirez .50 .15
❑ 344 Kerry Wood .75 .23
❑ 345 Shannon Stewart .30 .09
❑ 346 Mike Mussina .50 .15
❑ 347 Joe Borchard .30 .09
❑ 348 Tyler Walker .30 .09
❑ 349 Preston Wilson .30 .09
❑ 350 Damian Moss .30 .09
❑ 351 Eric Karros .30 .09
❑ 352 Bobby Kielty .30 .09
❑ 353 Jason LaRue .30 .09
❑ 354 Phil Nevin .30 .09
❑ 355 Tony Graffanino .30 .09
❑ 356 Antonio Alfonseca .30 .09
❑ 357 Eddie Taubensee .30 .09
❑ 358 Luis Ugueto .30 .09
❑ 359 Greg Vaughn .30 .09
❑ 360 Corey Thurman .30 .09
❑ 361 Omar Infante .30 .09
❑ 362 Alex Cintron .30 .09
❑ 363 Esteban Loaiza .30 .09
❑ 364 Tino Martinez .50 .15
❑ 365 David Eckstein .30 .09
❑ 366 Dave Pember RC .30 .09
❑ 367 Damian Rolls .30 .09
❑ 368 Richard Hidalgo .30 .09
❑ 369 Brad Radke .30 .09
❑ 370 Alex Sanchez .30 .09
❑ 371 Ben Grieve .30 .09
❑ 372 Brandon Inge .30 .09
❑ 373 Adam Piatt .30 .09
❑ 374 Charles Johnson .30 .09
❑ 375 Rafael Palmeiro .50 .15
❑ 376 Joe Mays .30 .09
❑ 377 Derrek Lee .30 .09
❑ 378 Fernando Vina .30 .09
❑ 379 Andruw Jones .30 .09
❑ 380 Troy Glaus .30 .09
❑ 381 Bobby Hill .30 .09
❑ 382 C.C. Sabathia .30 .09
❑ 383 Jose Hernandez .30 .09
❑ 384 Al Leiter .30 .09
❑ 385 Jarrod Washburn .30 .09
❑ 386 Cody Ransom .30 .09
❑ 387 Matt Stairs .30 .09
❑ 388 Edgar Renteria .30 .09
❑ 389 Tsuyoshi Shinjo .30 .09
❑ 390 Matt Williams .30 .09
❑ 391 Bubba Trammell .30 .09
❑ 392 Jason Kendall .30 .09
❑ 393 Scott Rolen .75 .23
❑ 394 Chuck Knoblauch .30 .09
❑ 395 Jimmy Rollins .30 .09
❑ 396 Gary Bennett .30 .09
❑ 397 David Wells .30 .09
❑ 398 Ronnie Belliard .30 .09
❑ 399 Austin Kearns .30 .09
❑ 400 Tim Hudson .30 .09
❑ 401 Andy Van Hekken .30 .09
❑ 402 Ray Lankford .30 .09
❑ 403 Todd Helton .50 .15
❑ 404 Jeff Weaver .30 .09
❑ 405 Gabe Kapler .30 .09
❑ 406 Luis Gonzalez .30 .09
❑ 407 Sean Casey .30 .09
❑ 408 Kazuhiro Sasaki .30 .09
❑ 409 Mark Teixeira .30 .09
❑ 410 Brian Giles .30 .09
❑ 411 Robert Fick .30 .09
❑ 412 Wilkin Ruan .30 .09
❑ 413 Jose Rijo .30 .09
❑ 414 Ben Broussard .30 .09
❑ 415 Aubrey Huff .30 .09
❑ 416 Magglio Ordonez .30 .09
❑ 417 Barry Bonds AW 1.00 .30
❑ 418 Miguel Tejada AW .30 .09
❑ 419 Randy Johnson AW .50 .15
❑ 420 Barry Zito AW .30 .09
❑ 421 Jason Jennings AW .30 .09
❑ 422 Eric Hinske AW .30 .09
❑ 423 Benito Santiago AW .30 .09
❑ 424 Adam Kennedy AW .30 .09
❑ 425 Troy Glaus AW .30 .09
❑ 426 Brandon Phillips PR .30 .09
❑ 427 Jake Peavy PR .30 .09
❑ 428 Jason Romano PR .30 .09
❑ 429 Jeriome Robertson PR .30 .09
❑ 430 Aaron Guiel PR .30 .09
❑ 431 Hank Blalock PR .50 .15
❑ 432 Brad Lidge PR .30 .09
❑ 433 Francisco Rodriguez PR .30 .09
❑ 434 Jaime Cerda PR .30 .09
❑ 435 Jung Bong PR .30 .09
❑ 436 Reed Johnson PR .30 .09
❑ 437 Rene Reyes PR .30 .09
❑ 438 Chris Snelling PR .30 .09
❑ 439 Miguel Olivo PR .30 .09
❑ 440 Brian Banks PR .30 .09
❑ 441 Eric Junge PR .30 .09
❑ 442 Kirk Saarloos PR .30 .09
❑ 443 Jamey Carroll PR .30 .09
❑ 444 Josh Hancock PR .30 .09
❑ 445 Michael Restovich PR .30 .09
❑ 446 Willie Bloomquist PR .30 .09
❑ 447 John Lackey PR .30 .09
❑ 448 Marcus Thames PR .30 .09
❑ 449 Victor Martinez PR .50 .15
❑ 450 Brett Myers PR .30 .09
❑ 451 Wes Obermueller PR .30 .09
❑ 452 Hansel Izquierdo PR .30 .09
❑ 453 Brian Tallet PR .30 .09
❑ 454 Craig Monroe PR .30 .09
❑ 455 Doug Devore PR .30 .09
❑ 456 John Buck PR .30 .09
❑ 457 Tony Alvarez PR .30 .09
❑ 458 Wily Mo Pena PR .30 .09
❑ 459 John Stephens PR .30 .09
❑ 460 Tony Torcato PR .30 .09
❑ 461 Adam Kennedy BNR .30 .09
❑ 462 Alex Rodriguez BNR .75 .23
❑ 463 Derek Lowe BNR .30 .09
❑ 464 Garret Anderson BNR .30 .09
❑ 465 Pat Burrell BNR .30 .09
❑ 466 Eric Gagne BNR .50 .15

Card	MINT	NRMT
❑ 467 Tomo Ohka BNR	.30	.09
❑ 468 Josh Phelps BNR	.30	.09
❑ 469 Sammy Sosa BNR	.75	.23
❑ 470 Jim Thome BNR	.50	.15
❑ 471 Vladimir Guerrero BNR	.50	.15
❑ 472 Jason Simontacchi BNR	.30	.09
❑ 473 Adam Dunn BNR	.50	.15
❑ 474 Jim Edmonds BNR	.30	.09
❑ 475 Barry Bonds BNR	1.00	.30
❑ 476 Paul Konerko BNR	.30	.09
❑ 477 Alfonso Soriano BNR	.50	.15
❑ 478 Curt Schilling BNR	.30	.09
❑ 479 John Smoltz BNR	.30	.09
❑ 480 Torii Hunter BNR	.30	.09
❑ 481 Rodrigo Lopez BNR	.30	.09
❑ 482 Miguel Tejada BNR	.30	.09
❑ 483 Eric Hinske BNR	.30	.09
❑ 484 Roy Oswalt BNR	.30	.09
❑ 485 Junior Spivey BNR	.30	.09
❑ P1 Barry Bonds Pin	8.00	2.40
❑ P87 Derek Jeter Promo	2.00	.60

2003 Fleer Tradition Update

	MINT	NRMT
COMP.SET w/o SP's (285)	40.00	18.00
COMMON CARD (1-285)	.30	.14
COMMON CARD (286-299)	1.00	.45
COMMON RC (286-299)	1.00	.45
286-299 STATED ODDS 1:4 HOB/RET		
COMMON CARD (300-398)	1.00	.45
COMMON RC (300-398)	1.00	.45
300-398 ISSUED IN MINI-BOXES		
ONE MINI-BOX PER UPDATE BOX		
25 CARDS PER MINI-BOX		

Card	MINT	NRMT
❑ 1 Aaron Boone	.30	.14
❑ 2 Carl Everett	.30	.14
❑ 3 Eduardo Perez	.30	.14
❑ 4 Jason Michaels	.30	.14
❑ 5 Karim Garcia	.30	.14
❑ 6 Rainer Olmedo	.30	.14
❑ 7 Scott Williamson	.30	.14
❑ 8 Adam Kennedy	.30	.14
❑ 9 Carl Pavano	.30	.14
❑ 10 Eli Marrero	.30	.14
❑ 11 Jason Simontacchi	.30	.14
❑ 12 Keith Foulke	.30	.14
❑ 13 Preston Wilson	.30	.14
❑ 14 Scott Hatteberg	.30	.14
❑ 15 Adam Dunn	.50	.23
❑ 16 Carlos Baerga	.30	.14
❑ 17 Elmer Dessens	.30	.14
❑ 18 Javier Vazquez	.30	.14
❑ 19 Kenny Rogers	.30	.14
❑ 20 Quinton McCracken	.30	.14
❑ 21 Shane Reynolds	.30	.14
❑ 22 Adam Eaton	.30	.14
❑ 23 Carlos Zambrano	.30	.14
❑ 24 Enrique Wilson	.30	.14
❑ 25 Jeff DaVanon	.30	.14
❑ 26 Kenny Lofton	.30	.14
❑ 27 Ramon Castro	.30	.14
❑ 28 Shannon Stewart	.30	.14
❑ 29 Al Martin	.30	.14
❑ 30 Carlos Guillen	.30	.14
❑ 31 Eric Karros	.30	.14
❑ 32 Tim Worrell	.30	.14
❑ 33 Kevin Millwood	.30	.14
❑ 34 Randall Simon	.30	.14
❑ 35 Shawn Chacon	.30	.14
❑ 36 Alex Rodriguez	1.25	.55
❑ 37 Casey Blake	.30	.14
❑ 38 Eric Munson	.30	.14
❑ 39 Jeff Kent	.30	.14
❑ 40 Kris Benson	.30	.14
❑ 41 Randy Winn	.30	.14
❑ 42 Shea Hillenbrand	.30	.14
❑ 43 Alfonso Soriano	.50	.23
❑ 44 Chris George	.30	.14
❑ 45 Eric Bruntlett	.30	.14
❑ 46 Jeromy Burnitz	.30	.14
❑ 47 Kyle Farnsworth	.30	.14
❑ 48 Torii Hunter	.30	.14
❑ 49 Sidney Ponson	.30	.14
❑ 50 Andres Galarraga	.30	.14
❑ 51 Chris Singleton	.30	.14
❑ 52 Eric Gagne	.75	.35
❑ 53 Jesse Foppert	.30	.14
❑ 54 Lance Carter	.30	.14
❑ 55 Ray Durham	.30	.14
❑ 56 Tanyon Sturtze	.30	.14
❑ 57 Andy Ashby	.30	.14
❑ 58 Cliff Floyd	.30	.14
❑ 59 Eric Young	.30	.14
❑ 60 Jhonny Peralta	.50	.23
❑ 61 Livan Hernandez	.30	.14
❑ 62 Reggie Sanders	.30	.14
❑ 63 Tim Spooneybarger	.30	.14
❑ 64 Angel Berroa	.30	.14
❑ 65 Coco Crisp	.30	.14
❑ 66 Eric Hinske	.30	.14
❑ 67 Jim Edmonds	.30	.14
❑ 68 Luis Matos	.30	.14
❑ 69 Rickey Henderson	.75	.35
❑ 70 Todd Walker	.30	.14
❑ 71 Antonio Alfonseca	.30	.14
❑ 72 Corey Koskie	.30	.14
❑ 73 Erubiel Durazo	.30	.14
❑ 74 Jim Thome	.75	.35
❑ 75 Lyle Overbay	.30	.14
❑ 76 Robert Fick	.30	.14
❑ 77 Todd Hollandsworth	.30	.14
❑ 78 Aramis Ramirez	.30	.14
❑ 79 Cristian Guzman	.30	.14
❑ 80 Esteban Loaiza	.30	.14
❑ 81 Jody Gerut	.30	.14
❑ 82 Mark Grudzielanek	.30	.14
❑ 83 Roberto Alomar	.50	.23
❑ 84 Todd Hundley	.30	.14
❑ 85 Mike Hampton	.30	.14
❑ 86 Curt Schilling	.30	.14
❑ 87 Francisco Rodriguez	.30	.14
❑ 88 John Lackey	.30	.14
❑ 89 Mark Redman	.30	.14
❑ 90 Robin Ventura	.30	.14
❑ 91 Todd Zeile	.30	.14
❑ 92 B.J. Surhoff	.30	.14
❑ 93 Raul Mondesi	.30	.14
❑ 94 Frank Catalanotto	.30	.14
❑ 95 John Smoltz	.50	.23
❑ 96 Mark Ellis	.30	.14
❑ 97 Rocco Baldelli	.30	.14
❑ 98 Todd Pratt	.30	.14
❑ 99 Barry Bonds	2.00	.90
❑ 100 Danny Graves	.30	.14
❑ 101 Fred McGriff	.50	.23
❑ 102 John Burkett	.30	.14
❑ 103 Marquis Grissom	.30	.14
❑ 104 Rocky Biddle	.30	.14
❑ 105 Tom Glavine	.50	.23
❑ 106 Bartolo Colon	.30	.14
❑ 107 Darren Bragg	.30	.14
❑ 108 Gabe Kapler	.30	.14
❑ 109 John Franco	.30	.14
❑ 110 Matt Mantei	.30	.14
❑ 111 Rod Beck	.30	.14
❑ 112 Tomo Ohka	.30	.14
❑ 113 Ben Petrick	.30	.14
❑ 114 Darren Dreifort	.30	.14
❑ 115 Garret Anderson	.30	.14
❑ 116 John Vander Wal	.30	.14
❑ 117 Melvin Mora	.30	.14
❑ 118 Rodrigo Lopez	.30	.14
❑ 119 Raul Ibanez	.30	.14
❑ 120 Benito Santiago	.30	.14
❑ 121 David Ortiz Sox	.75	.35
❑ 122 Gary Bennett	.30	.14
❑ 123 Jon Garland	.30	.14
❑ 124 Michael Young	.50	.23
❑ 125 Rodrigo Rosario	.30	.14
❑ 126 Travis Lee	.30	.14
❑ 127 Bill Mueller	.30	.14
❑ 128 Derek Lowe	.30	.14
❑ 129 Gil Meche	.30	.14
❑ 130 Jose Guillen	.30	.14
❑ 131 Miguel Cabrera	.75	.35
❑ 132 Ron Calloway	.30	.14
❑ 133 Troy Percival	.30	.14
❑ 134 Billy Koch	.30	.14
❑ 135 Dmitri Young	.30	.14
❑ 136 Glendon Rusch	.30	.14
❑ 137 Jose Jimenez	.30	.14
❑ 138 Miguel Tejada	.30	.14
❑ 139 John Thomson	.30	.14
❑ 140 Troy O'Leary	.30	.14
❑ 141 Bobby Kielty	.30	.14
❑ 142 Dontrelle Willis	.50	.23
❑ 143 Greg Myers	.30	.14
❑ 144 Jose Vizcaino	.30	.14
❑ 145 Mike MacDougal	.30	.14
❑ 146 Ronnie Belliard	.30	.14
❑ 147 Tyler Houston	.30	.14
❑ 148 Brady Clark	.30	.14
❑ 149 Edgardo Alfonzo	.30	.14
❑ 150 Guillermo Mota	.30	.14
❑ 151 Jose Lima	.30	.14
❑ 152 Mike Williams	.30	.14
❑ 153 Roy Oswalt	.30	.14
❑ 154 Scott Podsednik	5.00	2.20
❑ 155 Brandon Lyon	.30	.14
❑ 156 Henry Mateo	.30	.14
❑ 157 Jose Macias	.30	.14
❑ 158 Mike Bordick	.30	.14
❑ 159 Royce Clayton	.30	.14
❑ 160 Vance Wilson	.30	.14
❑ 161 Brent Abernathy	.30	.14
❑ 162 Horacio Ramirez	.30	.14
❑ 163 Jose Reyes	.30	.14
❑ 164 Nick Punto	.30	.14
❑ 165 Ruben Sierra	.30	.14
❑ 166 Victor Zambrano	.30	.14
❑ 167 Brett Tomko	.30	.14
❑ 168 Ivan Rodriguez	.75	.35
❑ 169 Jose Mesa	.30	.14
❑ 170 Octavio Dotel	.30	.14
❑ 171 Russ Ortiz	.30	.14
❑ 172 Vladimir Guerrero	.75	.35
❑ 173 Brian Lawrence	.30	.14
❑ 174 Jae Weong Seo	.30	.14
❑ 175 Jose Cruz Jr.	.30	.14
❑ 176 Pat Burrell	.30	.14
❑ 177 Russell Branyan	.30	.14
❑ 178 Warren Morris	.30	.14
❑ 179 Brian Boehringer	.30	.14
❑ 180 Jason Johnson	.30	.14
❑ 181 Josh Phelps	.30	.14
❑ 182 Paul Konerko	.30	.14
❑ 183 Ryan Franklin	.30	.14
❑ 184 Wes Helms	.30	.14
❑ 185 Brooks Kieschnick	.30	.14
❑ 186 Jason Davis	.30	.14
❑ 187 Juan Pierre	.30	.14
❑ 188 Paul Wilson	.30	.14
❑ 189 Sammy Sosa	1.25	.55
❑ 190 Wil Cordero	.30	.14
❑ 191 Byung-Hyun Kim	.30	.14
❑ 192 Juan Encarnacion	.30	.14
❑ 193 Placido Polanco	.30	.14
❑ 194 Sandy Alomar Jr.	.30	.14
❑ 195 Julio Lugo	.30	.14
❑ 196 Junior Spivey	.30	.14
❑ 197 Woody Williams	.30	.14
❑ 198 Xavier Nady	.30	.14
❑ 199 Mark Loretta	.30	.14
❑ 200 Deivi Cruz	.30	.14
❑ 201 Jorge Posada AS	.30	.14
❑ 202 Carlos Delgado AS	.30	.14
❑ 203 Alfonso Soriano AS	.30	.14

❑ 204 Alex Rodriguez AS .75 .35
❑ 205 Troy Glaus AS .30 .14
❑ 206 Garret Anderson AS .30 .14
❑ 207 Hideki Matsui AS 2.00 .90
❑ 208 Ichiro Suzuki AS .75 .35
❑ 209 Esteban Loaiza AS .30 .14
❑ 210 Manny Ramirez AS .30 .14
❑ 211 Roger Clemens AS .75 .35
❑ 212 Roy Halladay AS .30 .14
❑ 213 Jason Giambi AS .30 .14
❑ 214 Edgar Martinez AS .30 .14
❑ 215 Bret Boone AS .30 .14
❑ 216 Hank Blalock AS .50 .23
❑ 217 Nomar Garciaparra AS .75 .35
❑ 218 Vernon Wells AS .30 .14
❑ 219 Melvin Mora AS .30 .14
❑ 220 Magglio Ordonez AS .30 .14
❑ 221 Mike Sweeney AS .30 .14
❑ 222 Barry Zito AS .30 .14
❑ 223 Carl Everett AS .30 .14
❑ 224 Shigetoshi Hasegawa AS .30 .14
❑ 225 Jamie Moyer AS .30 .14
❑ 226 Mark Mulder AS .30 .14
❑ 227 Eddie Guardado AS .30 .14
❑ 228 Ramon Hernandez AS .30 .14
❑ 229 Keith Foulke AS .30 .14
❑ 230 Javy Lopez AS .30 .14
❑ 231 Todd Helton AS .30 .14
❑ 232 Marcus Giles AS .30 .14
❑ 233 Edgar Renteria AS .30 .14
❑ 234 Scott Rolen AS .50 .23
❑ 235 Barry Bonds AS 1.00 .45
❑ 236 Albert Pujols AS .75 .35
❑ 237 Gary Sheffield AS .30 .14
❑ 238 Jim Edmonds AS .30 .14
❑ 239 Jason Schmidt AS .30 .14
❑ 240 Mark Prior AS .50 .23
❑ 241 Dontrelle Willis AS .30 .14
❑ 242 Kerry Wood AS .50 .23
❑ 243 Kevin Brown AS .30 .14
❑ 244 Woody Williams AS .30 .14
❑ 245 Paul Lo Duca AS .30 .14
❑ 246 Richie Sexson AS .30 .14
❑ 247 Jose Vidro AS .30 .14
❑ 248 Luis Castillo AS .30 .14
❑ 249 Aaron Boone AS .30 .14
❑ 250 Mike Lowell AS .30 .14
❑ 251 Rafael Furcal AS .30 .14
❑ 252 Andruw Jones AS .30 .14
❑ 253 Preston Wilson AS .30 .14
❑ 254 John Smoltz AS .30 .14
❑ 255 Eric Gagne AS .50 .23
❑ 256 Randy Wolf AS .30 .14
❑ 257 Billy Wagner AS .30 .14
❑ 258 Luis Gonzalez AS .30 .14
❑ 259 Russ Ortiz AS .30 .14
❑ 260 Jim Thome .50 .23
Pedro Martinez IL
❑ 261 Alfonso Soriano .50 .23
Jeff Bagwell IL
❑ 262 Dontrelle Willis .30 .14
Rocco Baldelli IL
❑ 263 Carlos Delgado .50 .23
Vladimir Guerrero IL
❑ 264 Sammy Sosa .75 .35
Magglio Ordonez IL
❑ 265 Jason Giambi .30 .14
Adam Dunn IL
❑ 266 Mike Sweeney .75 .35
Albert Pujols IL
❑ 267 Barry Bonds 1.00 .45
Torii Hunter IL
❑ 268 Ichiro Suzuki .75 .35
Andruw Jones IL
❑ 269 Chipper Jones .50 .23
Hank Blalock IL
❑ 270 Mark Prior .50 .23
Vernon Wells IL
❑ 271 Nomar Garciaparra .75 .35
Scott Rolen IL
❑ 272 Alex Rodriguez .75 .35
Lance Berkman IL
❑ 273 Roger Clemens .75 .35
Kerry Wood IL
❑ 274 Derek Jeter 1.00 .45
Jose Reyes IL
❑ 275 Greg Maddux .75 .35
Barry Zito IL
❑ 276 Carlos Delgado TT .30 .14
❑ 277 J.D. Drew TT .30 .14
❑ 278 Barry Bonds TT 1.00 .45
❑ 279 Albert Pujols TT .75 .35
❑ 280 Jim Thome TT .50 .23
❑ 281 Sammy Sosa TT .75 .35
❑ 282 Alfonso Soriano TT .30 .14
❑ 283 Hideki Matsui TT 2.00 .90
❑ 284 Mike Piazza TT .75 .35
❑ 285 Vladimir Guerrero TT .50 .23
❑ 286 Rich Harden ROO 1.50 .70
❑ 287 Chin-Hui Tsao ROO 1.00 .45
❑ 288 Edwin Jackson ROO RC 5.00 2.20
❑ 289 Chien-Ming Wang ROO RC 2.50 1.10
❑ 290 Josh Willingham ROO RC 1.50 .70
❑ 291 Matt Kata ROO RC 2.50 1.10
❑ 292 Jose Contreras ROO RC 2.50 1.10
❑ 293 Chris Bootcheck ROO 1.00 .45
❑ 294 Javier Lopez ROO RC 1.00 .45
❑ 295 Delmon Young ROO RC 8.00 3.60
❑ 296 Pedro Liriano ROO 1.00 .45
❑ 297 Noah Lowry ROO 1.50 .70
❑ 298 Khalil Greene ROO 5.00 2.20
❑ 299 Rob Bowen ROO 1.00 .45
❑ 300 Bo Hart ROO RC 1.50 .70
❑ 301 Beau Kemp ROO RC 1.00 .45
❑ 302 Gerald Laird ROO 1.00 .45
❑ 303 Miguel Ojeda ROO RC 1.00 .45
❑ 304 Todd Wellemeyer ROO RC 1.50 .70
❑ 305 Ryan Wagner ROO RC 1.50 .70
❑ 306 Jeff Duncan ROO RC 1.50 .70
❑ 307 Wilfredo Ledezma ROO RC 1.50 .70
❑ 308 Wes Obermueller ROO 1.00 .45
❑ 309 Bernie Castro ROO RC 1.00 .45
❑ 310 Tim Olson ROO RC 1.50 .70
❑ 311 Colin Porter ROO RC 1.00 .45
❑ 312 Francisco Cruceta ROO RC 1.00 .45
❑ 313 Guillermo Quiroz ROO RC 2.00 .90
❑ 314 Brian Stokes ROO RC 1.00 .45
❑ 315 Robby Hammock ROO RC 1.50 .70
❑ 316 Lew Ford ROO RC 3.00 1.35
❑ 317 Todd Linden ROO 1.00 .45
❑ 318 Mike Gallo ROO RC 1.00 .45
❑ 319 Francisco Rosario ROO RC 1.00 .45
❑ 320 Rosman Garcia ROO RC 1.00 .45
❑ 321 Felix Sanchez ROO RC 1.00 .45
❑ 322 Chad Gaudin ROO RC 1.00 .45
❑ 323 Phil Seibel ROO RC 1.00 .45
❑ 324 Jason Gilfillan ROO RC 1.00 .45
❑ 325 Terrmel Sledge ROO RC 1.50 .70
❑ 326 Alfredo Gonzalez ROO RC 1.00 .45
❑ 327 Josh Stewart ROO RC 1.00 .45
❑ 328 Jeremy Griffiths ROO RC 1.50 .70
❑ 329 Cory Stewart ROO RC 1.00 .45
❑ 330 Josh Hall ROO RC 1.50 .70
❑ 331 Arnie Munoz ROO RC 1.00 .45
❑ 332 Garrett Atkins ROO 1.00 .45
❑ 333 Neal Cotts ROO 1.00 .45
❑ 334 Dan Haren ROO RC 2.00 .90
❑ 335 Shane Victorino ROO RC 1.00 .45
❑ 336 David Sanders ROO RC 1.00 .45
❑ 337 Oscar Villarreal ROO RC 1.00 .45
❑ 338 Michael Hessman ROO RC 1.00 .45
❑ 339 Andrew Brown ROO RC 1.50 .70
❑ 340 Kevin Hooper ROO 1.00 .45
❑ 341 Prentice Redman ROO RC 1.00 .45
❑ 342 Brandon Webb ROO RC 2.50 1.10
❑ 343 Jimmy Gobble ROO 1.00 .45
❑ 344 Pete LaForest ROO RC 1.50 .70
❑ 345 Chris Waters ROO RC 1.00 .45
❑ 346 Hideki Matsui ROO RC 8.00 3.60
❑ 347 Chris Capuano ROO RC 1.00 .45
❑ 348 Jon Leicester ROO RC 1.00 .45
❑ 349 Mike Nicolas ROO RC 1.00 .45
❑ 350 Nook Logan ROO RC 1.00 .45
❑ 351 Craig Brazell ROO RC 1.50 .70
❑ 352 Aaron Looper ROO RC 1.00 .45
❑ 353 D.J. Carrasco ROO RC 1.00 .45
❑ 354 Clint Barmes ROO RC 1.50 .70
❑ 355 Doug Waechter ROO RC 1.50 .70
❑ 356 Julio Manon ROO RC 1.00 .45
❑ 357 Jer. Bonderman ROO RC 2.00 .90
❑ 358 D. Markwell ROO RC 1.00 .45
❑ 359 Dave Matranga ROO RC 1.00 .45
❑ 360 Luis Ayala ROO RC 1.00 .45
❑ 361 Jason Stanford ROO 1.00 .45
❑ 362 Roger Deago ROO RC 1.00 .45
❑ 363 Geoff Geary ROO RC 1.00 .45
❑ 364 Edgar Gonzalez ROO RC 1.00 .45
❑ 365 Michel Hernandez ROO RC 1.00 .45
❑ 366 Aquilino Lopez ROO RC 1.00 .45
❑ 367 David Manning ROO 1.00 .45
❑ 368 Carlos Mendez ROO RC 1.00 .45
❑ 369 Matt Miller ROO RC 1.00 .45
❑ 370 Mi. Nakamura ROO RC 1.00 .45
❑ 371 Mike Neu ROO RC 1.00 .45
❑ 372 Ramon Nivar ROO RC 2.00 .90
❑ 373 Kevin Ohme ROO RC 1.00 .45
❑ 374 Alex Prieto ROO RC 1.00 .45
❑ 375 Stephen Randolph ROO RC 1.00 .45
❑ 376 Brian Sweeney ROO RC 1.00 .45
❑ 377 Matt Diaz ROO RC 1.50 .70
❑ 378 Mike Gonzalez ROO 1.00 .45
❑ 379 Daniel Cabrera ROO RC 2.50 1.10
❑ 380 Fernando Cabrera ROO RC 1.00 .45
❑ 381 David DeJesus ROO RC 1.50 .70
❑ 382 Mike Ryan ROO RC 1.50 .70
❑ 383 Rick Roberts ROO RC 1.00 .45
❑ 384 Seung Song ROO 1.00 .45
❑ 385 Rickie Weeks ROO RC 6.00 2.70
❑ 386 Hum. Quintero ROO RC 1.00 .45
❑ 387 Alexis Rios ROO 1.50 .70
❑ 388 Aaron Miles ROO RC 2.50 1.10
❑ 389 Tom Gregorio ROO RC 1.00 .45
❑ 390 Anthony Ferrari ROO RC 1.00 .45
❑ 391 Kevin Correia ROO RC 1.00 .45
❑ 392 Rafael Betancourt ROO RC 1.50 .70
❑ 393 Rett Johnson ROO RC 1.50 .70
❑ 394 Richard Fischer ROO RC 1.00 .45
❑ 395 Greg Aquino ROO RC 1.00 .45
❑ 396 Daniel Garcia ROO RC 1.00 .45
❑ 397 Sergio Mitre ROO RC 1.50 .70
❑ 398 Edwin Almonte ROO 1.00 .45

2004 Fleer Tradition

	Nm-Mt	Ex-Mt
COMPLETE SET (500)	150.00	45.00
COMP.SET w/o SP's (400)	40.00	12.00
COMMON CARD (1-400)	.30	.09
COMMON CARD (401-470)	1.00	.30
COMMON CARD (471-500)	1.00	.30
401-445 STATED ODDS 1:2		
446-461 STATED ODDS 1:6		
462-470 STATED ODDS 1:9		
471-500 STATED ODDS 1:3		

❑ 1 Juan Pierre WS .30 .09
❑ 2 Josh Beckett WS .30 .09
❑ 3 Ivan Rodriguez WS .75 .23
❑ 4 Miguel Cabrera WS .50 .15
❑ 5 Dontrelle Willis WS .30 .09
❑ 6 Derek Jeter WS 1.50 .45
❑ 7 Jason Giambi WS .30 .09
❑ 8 Bernie Williams WS .50 .15
❑ 9 Alfonso Soriano WS .50 .15
❑ 10 Hideki Matsui WS 1.25 .35
❑ 11 Garret Anderson .30 .09
Garret Anderson
Ramon Ortiz
John Lackey TL
❑ 12 Luis Gonzalez .30 .09

Luis Gonzalez
Brandon Webb
Curt Schilling TL
❑ 13 Javy Lopez .30 .09
Gary Sheffield
Russ Ortiz
Russ Ortiz TL
❑ 14 Tony Batista .30 .09
Jay Gibbons
Sidney Ponson
Jason Johnson TL
❑ 15 Manny Ramirez .75 .23
Nomar Garciaparra
Derek Lowe
Pedro Martinez TL
❑ 16 Sammy Sosa .75 .23
Sammy Sosa
Mark Prior
Kerry Wood TL
❑ 17 Frank Thomas .50 .15
Carlos Lee
Esteban Loaiza
Esteban Loaiza TL
❑ 18 Adam Dunn .30 .09
Sean Casey
Chris Reitsma
Paul Wilson TL
❑ 19 Jody Gerut .30 .09
Jody Gerut
C.C. Sabathia
C.C. Sabathia TL
❑ 20 Preston Wilson .30 .09
Preston Wilson
Darren Oliver
Jason Jennings TL
❑ 21 Dmitri Young .30 .09
Dmitri Young
Mike Maroth
Jeremy Bonderman TL
❑ 22 Mike Lowell .30 .09
Mike Lowell
Dontrelle Willis
Josh Beckett TL
❑ 23 Jeff Bagwell .30 .09
Jeff Bagwell
Jeriome Robertson
Wade Miller TL
❑ 24 Carlos Beltran .30 .09
Carlos Beltran
Darrell May
Darrell May TL
❑ 25 Adrian Beltre .30 .09
Shawn Green
Hideo Nomo
Kevin Brown TL
❑ 26 Richie Sexson .30 .09
Richie Sexson
Ben Sheets
Ben Sheets TL
❑ 27 Torii Hunter .50 .15
Torii Hunter
Brad Radke
Johan Santana TL
❑ 28 Vladimir Guerrero .50 .15
Orlando Cabrera
Livan Hernandez
Javier Vazquez TL
❑ 29 Cliff Floyd .30 .09
Ty Wigginton
Steve Trachsel
Al Leiter TL
❑ 30 Jason Giambi .50 .15
Jason Giambi
Andy Pettitte
Mike Mussina TL
❑ 31 Eric Chavez .30 .09
Miguel Tejada
Tim Hudson
Tim Hudson TL
❑ 32 Jim Thome .50 .15
Jim Thome
Randy Wolf
Randy Wolf TL
❑ 33 Reggie Sanders .30 .09
Reggie Sanders
Josh Fogg
Kip Wells TL
❑ 34 Ryan Klesko .30 .09
Mark Loretta
Jake Peavy
Jake Peavy TL
❑ 35 Jose Cruz Jr. .30 .09
Edgardo Alfonzo
Jason Schmidt
Jason Schmidt TL
❑ 36 Bret Boone .30 .09
Bret Boone
Jamie Moyer
Joel Pineiro TL
❑ 37 Albert Pujols .75 .23
Albert Pujols
Woody Williams
Woody Williams TL
❑ 38 Aubrey Huff .30 .09
Aubrey Huff
Victor Zambrano
Victor Zambrano TL
❑ 39 Alex Rodriguez .75 .23
Alex Rodriguez
John Thomson
John Thomson TL
❑ 40 Carlos Delgado .30 .09
Carlos Delgado
Roy Halladay
Roy Halladay TL
❑ 41 Greg Maddux 1.25 .35
❑ 42 Ben Grieve .30 .09
❑ 43 Darin Erstad .30 .09
❑ 44 Ruben Sierra .30 .09
❑ 45 Byung-Hyung Kim .30 .09
❑ 46 Freddy Garcia .30 .09
❑ 47 Richard Hidalgo .30 .09
❑ 48 Tike Redman .30 .09
❑ 49 Kevin Millwood .30 .09
❑ 50 Marquis Grissom .30 .09
❑ 51 Jae Weong Seo .30 .09
❑ 52 Wil Cordero .30 .09
❑ 53 LaTroy Hawkins .30 .09
❑ 54 Jolbert Cabrera .30 .09
❑ 55 Kevin Appier .30 .09
❑ 56 John Lackey .30 .09
❑ 57 Garret Anderson .30 .09
❑ 58 R.A. Dickey .30 .09
❑ 59 David Segui .30 .09
❑ 60 Erubiel Durazo .30 .09
❑ 61 Bobby Abreu .30 .09
❑ 62 Travis Hafner .30 .09
❑ 63 Victor Zambrano .30 .09
❑ 64 Randy Johnson .75 .23
❑ 65 Bernie Williams .50 .15
❑ 66 J.T. Snow .30 .09
❑ 67 Sammy Sosa 1.25 .35
❑ 68 Al Leiter .30 .09
❑ 69 Jason Jennings .30 .09
❑ 70 Matt Morris .30 .09
❑ 71 Mike Hampton .30 .09
❑ 72 Juan Encarnacion .30 .09
❑ 73 Alex Gonzalez .30 .09
❑ 74 Bartolo Colon .30 .09
❑ 75 Brett Myers .30 .09
❑ 76 Michael Young .30 .09
❑ 77 Ichiro Suzuki 1.25 .35
❑ 78 Jason Johnson .30 .09
❑ 79 Brad Ausmus .30 .09
❑ 80 Ted Lilly .30 .09
❑ 81 Ken Griffey Jr. 1.25 .35
❑ 82 Chone Figgins .30 .09
❑ 83 Edgar Martinez .50 .15
❑ 84 Adam Eaton .30 .09
❑ 85 Ken Harvey .30 .09
❑ 86 Francisco Rodriguez .30 .09
❑ 87 Bill Mueller .30 .09
❑ 88 Mike Maroth .30 .09
❑ 89 Charles Johnson .30 .09
❑ 90 Jhonny Peralta .30 .09
❑ 91 Kip Wells .30 .09
❑ 92 Cesar Izturis .30 .09
❑ 93 Matt Clement .30 .09
❑ 94 Lyle Overbay .30 .09
❑ 95 Kirk Rueter .30 .09
❑ 96 Cristian Guzman .30 .09
❑ 97 Garrett Stephenson .30 .09
❑ 98 Lance Berkman .30 .09
❑ 99 Brett Tomko .30 .09
❑ 100 Chris Stynes .30 .09
❑ 101 Nate Cornejo .30 .09
❑ 102 Aaron Rowand .30 .09
❑ 103 Javier Vazquez .30 .09
❑ 104 Jason Kendall .30 .09
❑ 105 Mark Redman .30 .09
❑ 106 Benito Santiago .30 .09
❑ 107 C.C. Sabathia .30 .09
❑ 108 David Wells .30 .09
❑ 109 Mark Ellis .30 .09
❑ 110 Casey Blake .30 .09
❑ 111 Sean Burroughs .30 .09
❑ 112 Carlos Beltran .50 .15
❑ 113 Ramon Hernandez .30 .09
❑ 114 Eric Hinske .30 .09
❑ 115 Luis Gonzalez .30 .09
❑ 116 Jarrod Washburn .30 .09
❑ 117 Ronnie Belliard .30 .09
❑ 118 Troy Percival .30 .09
❑ 119 Jose Valentin .30 .09
❑ 120 Chase Utley .30 .09
❑ 121 Odalis Perez .30 .09
❑ 122 Steve Finley .30 .09
❑ 123 Bret Boone .30 .09
❑ 124 Jeff Conine .30 .09
❑ 125 Josh Fogg .30 .09
❑ 126 Neifi Perez .30 .09
❑ 127 Ben Sheets .30 .09
❑ 128 Randy Winn .30 .09
❑ 129 Matt Stairs .30 .09
❑ 130 Carlos Delgado .30 .09
❑ 131 Morgan Ensberg .30 .09
❑ 132 Vinny Castilla .30 .09
❑ 133 Matt Mantei .30 .09
❑ 134 Alex Rodriguez 1.25 .35
❑ 135 Matthew LeCroy .30 .09
❑ 136 Woody Williams .30 .09
❑ 137 Frank Catalanotto .30 .09
❑ 138 Rondell White .30 .09
❑ 139 Scott Rolen .75 .23
❑ 140 Cliff Floyd .30 .09
❑ 141 Chipper Jones .75 .23
❑ 142 Robin Ventura .30 .09
❑ 143 Mariano Rivera .50 .15
❑ 144 Brady Clark .30 .09
❑ 145 Ramon Ortiz .30 .09
❑ 146 Omar Infante .30 .09
❑ 147 Mike Matheny .30 .09
❑ 148 Pedro Martinez .75 .23
❑ 149 Carlos Baerga .30 .09
❑ 150 Shannon Stewart .30 .09
❑ 151 Travis Lee .30 .09
❑ 152 Eric Byrnes .30 .09
❑ 153 Rafael Furcal .30 .09
❑ 154 B.J. Surhoff .30 .09
❑ 155 Zach Day .30 .09
❑ 156 Marlon Anderson .30 .09
❑ 157 Mark Hendrickson .30 .09
❑ 158 Mike Mussina .50 .15
❑ 159 Randall Simon .30 .09
❑ 160 Jeff DaVanon .30 .09
❑ 161 Joel Pineiro .30 .09
❑ 162 Vernon Wells .30 .09
❑ 163 Adam Kennedy .30 .09
❑ 164 Trot Nixon .30 .09
❑ 165 Rodrigo Lopez .30 .09
❑ 166 Curt Schilling .30 .09
❑ 167 Horacio Ramirez .30 .09
❑ 168 Jason Marquis .30 .09
❑ 169 Magglio Ordonez .30 .09
❑ 170 Scott Schoeneweis .30 .09
❑ 171 Andruw Jones .30 .09
❑ 172 Tino Martinez .50 .15
❑ 173 Moises Alou .30 .09
❑ 174 Kelvim Escobar .30 .09
❑ 175 Xavier Nady .30 .09
❑ 176 Ramon Martinez .30 .09
❑ 177 Pat Hentgen .30 .09
❑ 178 Austin Kearns .30 .09
❑ 179 D'Angelo Jimenez .30 .09
❑ 180 Deivi Cruz .30 .09
❑ 181 John Smoltz .50 .15
❑ 182 Toby Hall .30 .09
❑ 183 Mark Buehrle .30 .09

❑ 184 Howie Clark .30 .09
❑ 185 David Ortiz .75 .23
❑ 186 Raul Mondesi .30 .09
❑ 187 Milton Bradley .30 .09
❑ 188 Jorge Julio .30 .09
❑ 189 Victor Martinez .30 .09
❑ 190 Gabe Kapler .30 .09
❑ 191 Julio Franco .30 .09
❑ 192 Ryan Freel .30 .09
❑ 193 Brad Fullmer .30 .09
❑ 194 Joe Borowski .30 .09
❑ 195 Darren Oliver .30 .09
❑ 196 Jason Varitek .50 .15
❑ 197 Greg Myers .30 .09
❑ 198 Eric Munson .30 .09
❑ 199 Tim Wakefield .30 .09
❑ 200 Kyle Farnsworth .30 .09
❑ 201 Johnny Vander Wal .30 .09
❑ 202 Alex Escobar .30 .09
❑ 203 Sean Casey .30 .09
❑ 204 John Thomson .30 .09
❑ 205 Carlos Zambrano .30 .09
❑ 206 Kenny Lofton .30 .09
❑ 207 Marcus Giles .30 .09
❑ 208 Wade Miller .30 .09
❑ 209 Geoff Blum .30 .09
❑ 210 Jason LaRue .30 .09
❑ 211 Omar Vizquel .50 .15
❑ 212 Carlos Pena .30 .09
❑ 213 Adam Dunn .50 .15
❑ 214 Oscar Villarreal .30 .09
❑ 215 Paul Konerko .30 .09
❑ 216 Hideo Nomo .75 .23
❑ 217 Mike Sweeney .30 .09
❑ 218 Coco Crisp .30 .09
❑ 219 Shawn Chacon .30 .09
❑ 220 Brook Fordyce .30 .09
❑ 221 Josh Beckett .30 .09
❑ 222 Paul Wilson .30 .09
❑ 223 Josh Towers .30 .09
❑ 224 Geoff Jenkins .30 .09
❑ 225 Shawn Green .30 .09
❑ 226 Derrek Lee .30 .09
❑ 227 Karim Garcia .30 .09
❑ 228 Preston Wilson .30 .09
❑ 229 Dane Sardinha .30 .09
❑ 230 Aramis Ramirez .30 .09
❑ 231 Doug Mientkiewicz .30 .09
❑ 232 Jay Gibbons .30 .09
❑ 233 Adam Everett .30 .09
❑ 234 Brooks Kieschnick .30 .09
❑ 235 Dmitri Young .30 .09
❑ 236 Brad Penny .30 .09
❑ 237 Todd Zeile .30 .09
❑ 238 Eric Gagne .75 .23
❑ 239 Esteban Loaiza .30 .09
❑ 240 Billy Wagner .30 .09
❑ 241 Nomar Garciaparra 1.25 .35
❑ 242 Desi Relaford .30 .09
❑ 243 Luis Rivas .30 .09
❑ 244 Andy Pettitte .50 .15
❑ 245 Ty Wigginton .30 .09
❑ 246 Edgar Gonzalez .30 .09
❑ 247 Brian Anderson .30 .09
❑ 248 Richie Sexson .30 .09
❑ 249 Russell Branyan .30 .09
❑ 250 Jose Guillen .30 .09
❑ 251 Chin-Hui Tsao .30 .09
❑ 252 Jose Hernandez .30 .09
❑ 253 Kevin Brown .30 .09
❑ 254 Pete LaForest .30 .09
❑ 255 Adrian Beltre .50 .15
❑ 256 Jacque Jones .30 .09
❑ 257 Jimmy Rollins .30 .09
❑ 258 Brandon Phillips .30 .09
❑ 259 Derek Jeter 1.50 .45
❑ 260 Carl Everett .30 .09
❑ 261 Wes Helms .30 .09
❑ 262 Kyle Lohse .30 .09
❑ 263 Jason Phillips .30 .09
❑ 264 Jake Peavy .30 .09
❑ 265 Orlando Hernandez .30 .09
❑ 266 Keith Foulke .30 .09
❑ 267 Brad Wilkerson .30 .09
❑ 268 Corey Koskie .30 .09
❑ 269 Josh Hall .30 .09
❑ 270 Bobby Higginson .30 .09
❑ 271 Andres Galarraga .30 .09
❑ 272 Alfonso Soriano .50 .15
❑ 273 Carlos Rivera .30 .09
❑ 274 Steve Trachsel .30 .09
❑ 275 David Bell .30 .09
❑ 276 Endy Chavez .30 .09
❑ 277 Jay Payton .30 .09
❑ 278 Mark Mulder .30 .09
❑ 279 Terrence Long .30 .09
❑ 280 A.J. Burnett .30 .09
❑ 281 Pokey Reese .30 .09
❑ 282 Phil Nevin .30 .09
❑ 283 Jose Contreras .30 .09
❑ 284 Jim Thome .75 .23
❑ 285 Pat Burrell .30 .09
❑ 286 Luis Castillo .30 .09
❑ 287 Juan Uribe .30 .09
❑ 288 Raul Ibanez .30 .09
❑ 289 Sidney Ponson .30 .09
❑ 290 Scott Hatteberg .30 .09
❑ 291 Jack Wilson .30 .09
❑ 292 Reggie Sanders .30 .09
❑ 293 Brian Giles .30 .09
❑ 294 Craig Biggio .50 .15
❑ 295 Kazuhisa Ishii .30 .09
❑ 296 Jim Edmonds .30 .09
❑ 297 Trevor Hoffman .30 .09
❑ 298 Ray Durham .30 .09
❑ 299 Mike Lieberthal .30 .09
❑ 300 Tim Worrell .30 .09
❑ 301 Chris George .30 .09
❑ 302 Jamie Moyer .30 .09
❑ 303 Mike Cameron .30 .09
❑ 304 Matt Kinney .30 .09
❑ 305 Aubrey Huff .30 .09
❑ 306 Brian Lawrence .30 .09
❑ 307 Carlos Guillen .30 .09
❑ 308 J.D. Drew .30 .09
❑ 309 Paul Lo Duca .30 .09
❑ 310 Tim Salmon .50 .15
❑ 311 Jason Schmidt .30 .09
❑ 312 A.J. Pierzynski .30 .09
❑ 313 Lance Carter .30 .09
❑ 314 Julio Lugo .30 .09
❑ 315 Johan Santana .50 .15
❑ 316 Layne Nix .30 .09
❑ 317 John Olerud .30 .09
❑ 318 Robb Quinlan .30 .09
❑ 319 Scott Spiezio .30 .09
❑ 320 Tony Clark .30 .09
❑ 321 Jose Vidro .30 .09
❑ 322 Shea Hillenbrand .30 .09
❑ 323 Doug Glanville .30 .09
❑ 324 Orlando Palmeiro .30 .09
❑ 325 Juan Gonzalez .50 .15
❑ 326 Jason Giambi .30 .09
❑ 327 Junior Spivey .30 .09
❑ 328 Tom Glavine .50 .15
❑ 329 Reed Johnson .30 .09
❑ 330 David Eckstein .30 .09
❑ 331 Damian Jackson .30 .09
❑ 332 Orlando Hudson .30 .09
❑ 333 Barry Zito .30 .09
❑ 334 Robert Fick .30 .09
❑ 335 Aaron Boone .30 .09
❑ 336 Rafael Palmeiro .50 .15
❑ 337 Bobby Kielty .30 .09
❑ 338 Tony Batista .30 .09
❑ 339 Ryan Dempster .30 .09
❑ 340 Derek Lowe .30 .09
❑ 341 Alex Cintron .30 .09
❑ 342 Jermaine Dye .30 .09
❑ 343 John Burkett .30 .09
❑ 344 Javy Lopez .30 .09
❑ 345 Eric Karros .30 .09
❑ 346 Corey Patterson .30 .09
❑ 347 Josh Phelps .30 .09
❑ 348 Ryan Klesko .30 .09
❑ 349 Craig Wilson .30 .09
❑ 350 Brian Roberts .30 .09
❑ 351 Roberto Alomar .50 .15
❑ 352 Frank Thomas .75 .23
❑ 353 Gary Sheffield .30 .09
❑ 354 Alex Gonzalez .30 .09
❑ 355 Jose Cruz Jr. .30 .09
❑ 356 Jerome Williams .30 .09
❑ 357 Mark Kotsay .30 .09
❑ 358 Chris Reitsma .30 .09
❑ 359 Carlos Lee .30 .09
❑ 360 Todd Helton .50 .15
❑ 361 Gil Meche .30 .09
❑ 362 Ryan Franklin .30 .09
❑ 363 Josh Bard .30 .09
❑ 364 Juan Pierre .30 .09
❑ 365 Barry Larkin .50 .15
❑ 366 Edgar Renteria .30 .09
❑ 367 Alex Sanchez .30 .09
❑ 368 Jeff Bagwell .50 .15
❑ 369 Ben Broussard .30 .09
❑ 370 Chan-Ho Park .30 .09
❑ 371 Darrell May .30 .09
❑ 372 Roy Oswalt .30 .09
❑ 373 Craig Monroe .30 .09
❑ 374 Fred McGriff .50 .15
❑ 375 Bengie Molina .30 .09
❑ 376 Aaron Guiel .30 .09
❑ 377 Jeriome Robertson .30 .09
❑ 378 Kenny Rogers .30 .09
❑ 379 Colby Lewis .30 .09
❑ 380 Jeromy Burnitz .30 .09
❑ 381 Orlando Cabrera .30 .09
❑ 382 Joe Randa .30 .09
❑ 383 Miguel Batista .30 .09
❑ 384 Brad Radke .30 .09
❑ 385 Jeremy Giambi .30 .09
❑ 386 Vladimir Guerrero .75 .23
❑ 387 Melvin Mora .30 .09
❑ 388 Royce Clayton .30 .09
❑ 389 Danny Garcia .30 .09
❑ 390 Manny Ramirez .75 .23
❑ 391 Dave McCarty .30 .09
❑ 392 Mark Grudzielanek .30 .09
❑ 393 Mike Piazza 1.25 .35
❑ 394 Jorge Posada .50 .15
❑ 395 Tim Hudson .30 .09
❑ 396 Placido Polanco .30 .09
❑ 397 Mark Loretta .30 .09
❑ 398 Jesse Foppert .30 .09
❑ 399 Albert Pujols 1.50 .45
❑ 400 Jeremi Gonzalez .30 .09
❑ 401 Paul Bako SP 1.00 .30
❑ 402 Luis Matos SP 1.00 .30
❑ 403 Johnny Damon SP 2.50 .75
❑ 404 Kerry Wood SP 2.50 .75
❑ 405 Joe Crede SP 1.00 .30
❑ 406 Jason Davis SP 1.00 .30
❑ 407 Larry Walker SP 1.50 .45
❑ 408 Ivan Rodriguez SP 2.50 .75
❑ 409 Nick Johnson SP 1.00 .30
❑ 410 Jose Lima SP 1.00 .30
❑ 411 Brian Jordan SP 1.00 .30
❑ 412 Eddie Guardado SP 1.00 .30
❑ 413 Ron Calloway SP 1.00 .30
❑ 414 Aaron Heilman SP 1.00 .30
❑ 415 Eric Chavez SP 1.00 .30
❑ 416 Randy Wolf SP 1.00 .30
❑ 417 Jason Bay SP 1.00 .30
❑ 418 Edgardo Alfonzo SP 1.00 .30
❑ 419 Kazuhiro Sasaki SP 1.00 .30
❑ 420 Eduardo Perez SP 1.00 .30
❑ 421 Carl Crawford SP 1.00 .30
❑ 422 Troy Glaus SP 1.00 .30
❑ 423 Joaquin Benoit SP 1.00 .30
❑ 424 Russ Ortiz SP 1.00 .30
❑ 425 Larry Bigbie SP 1.00 .30
❑ 426 Todd Walker SP 1.00 .30
❑ 427 Kris Benson SP 1.00 .30
❑ 428 Sandy Alomar Jr. SP 1.00 .30
❑ 429 Jody Gerut SP 1.00 .30
❑ 430 Rene Reyes SP 1.00 .30
❑ 431 Mike Lowell SP 1.00 .30
❑ 432 Jeff Kent SP 1.00 .30
❑ 433 Mike MacDougal SP 1.00 .30
❑ 434 Dave Roberts SP 1.00 .30
❑ 435 Torii Hunter SP 1.00 .30
❑ 436 Tomo Ohka SP 1.00 .30
❑ 437 Jeremy Griffiths SP 1.00 .30
❑ 438 Miguel Tejada SP 1.00 .30
❑ 439 Vicente Padilla SP 1.00 .30
❑ 440 Bobby Hill SP 1.00 .30
❑ 441 Rich Aurilia SP 1.00 .30

❑ 442 Shigetoshi Hasegawa SP 1.00 .30
❑ 443 So Taguchi SP 1.00 .30
❑ 444 Damian Rolls SP 1.00 .30
❑ 445 Roy Halladay SP 1.00 .30
❑ 446 Rocco Baldelli SO SP 1.00 .30
❑ 447 Dontrelle Willis SO SP 1.00 .30
❑ 448 Mark Prior SO SP 2.50 .75
❑ 449 Jason Lane SO SP 1.00 .30
❑ 450 Angel Berroa SO SP 1.00 .30
❑ 451 Jose Reyes SO SP 1.00 .30
❑ 452 Ryan Wagner SO SP 1.00 .30
❑ 453 Marlon Byrd SO SP 1.00 .30
❑ 454 Hee Seop Choi SO SP 1.00 .30
❑ 455 Brandon Webb SO SP 1.00 .30
❑ 456 Bo Hart SO SP 1.00 .30
❑ 457 Hank Blalock SO SP 1.00 .30
❑ 458 Mark Teixeira SO SP 1.00 .30
❑ 459 Hideki Matsui SO SP 4.00 1.20
❑ 460 Scott Podsednik SO SP 1.00 .30
❑ 461 Miguel Cabrera SO SP 1.50 .45
❑ 462 Josh Beckett AW SP 1.00 .30
❑ 463 Mariano Rivera AW SP 1.50 .45
❑ 464 Ivan Rodriguez AW SP 2.50 .75
❑ 465 Alex Rodriguez AW SP 4.00 1.20
❑ 466 Albert Pujols AW SP 5.00 1.50
❑ 467 Roy Halladay AW SP 1.00 .30
❑ 468 Eric Gagne AW SP 2.50 .75
❑ 469 Angel Berroa AW SP 1.00 .30
❑ 470 Dontrelle Willis AW SP 1.00 .30
❑ 471 Chris Bootcheck 1.00 .30
Tom Gregorio
Richard Fischer SP
❑ 472 Matt Kata 1.00 .30
Tim Olson
Robby Hammock SP
❑ 473 Michael Hessman 1.00 .30
Chris Waters
Greg Aquino SP
❑ 474 Carlos Mendez 1.50 .45
Daniel Cabrera
Jeremy Guthrie SP
❑ 475 Edwin Almonte 1.00 .30
Phil Seibel
Felix Sanchez SP
❑ 476 Todd Wellemeyer 1.00 .30
Jon Leicester
Sergio Mitre SP
❑ 477 Josh Stewart 1.50 .45
Neal Cotts
Aaron Miles SP
❑ 478 Termel Sledge 1.00 .30
Josh Hall
Brandon Claussen SP
❑ 479 Francisco Cruceta 1.00 .30
Jason Stanford
Rafael Betancourt SP
❑ 480 Javier A.Lopez 1.00 .30
Garrett Atkins
Clint Barmes SP
❑ 481 Wilfredo Ledezma 1.00 .30
Nook Logan
Jeremy Bonderman SP
❑ 482 Josh Willingham 1.00 .30
Kevin Hooper
Rick Roberts SP
❑ 483 Colin Porter 1.00 .30
Mike Gallo
Dave Matranga SP
❑ 484 David DeJesus 1.00 .30
Jason Gilfillan
Jimmy Gobble SP
❑ 485 Koyie Hill 1.00 .30
Alfredo Gonzalez
Andrew Brown SP
❑ 486 Rickie Weeks 1.50 .45
Pedro Liriano
Wes Obermueller SP
❑ 487 Alex Prieto 1.50 .45
Mike Ryan
Lew Ford SP
❑ 488 Julio Manon 1.00 .30
Luis Ayala
Seung Song SP
❑ 489 Jeff Duncan 1.50 .45
Prentice Redman
Craig Brazell SP
❑ 490 Chien-Ming Wang 1.50 .45
Michel Hernandez
Mike Gonzalez SP
❑ 491 Rich Harden 1.50 .45
Mike Neu
Geoff Geary SP
❑ 492 Diegomar Markwell 1.00 .30
Chad Gaudin
David Sanders SP
❑ 493 Beau Kemp 1.00 .30
Micheal Nakamura
D.J. Carrasco SP
❑ 494 Khalil Greene 4.00 1.20
Miguel Ojeda
Bernie Castro SP
❑ 495 Noah Lowry 1.50 .45
Todd Linden
Kevin Correia SP
❑ 496 Aaron Looper 1.00 .30
Brian Sweeney
Rett Johnson SP
❑ 497 John Gall RC 2.50 .75
Dan Haren
Kevin Ohme SP
❑ 498 Delmon Young 2.50 .75
Doug Waechter
Matt Diaz SP
❑ 499 Gerald Laird 1.00 .30
Rosman Garcia
Ramon Nivar SP
❑ 500 Alexis Rios 1.50 .45
Guillermo Quiroz
Francisco Rosario SP

2001 Fleer Triple Crown

	Nm-Mt	Ex-Mt
COMPLETE SET (300)	30.00	9.00
COMMON CARD (1-300)	.30	.09
COMMON (301-310)	4.00	1.20

❑ 1 Derek Jeter 2.00 .60
❑ 2 Vladimir Guerrero .75 .23
❑ 3 Henry Rodriguez .30 .09
❑ 4 Jason Giambi .30 .09
❑ 5 Nomar Garciaparra 1.25 .35
❑ 6 Jeff Kent .30 .09
❑ 7 Garret Anderson .30 .09
❑ 8 Todd Helton .50 .15
❑ 9 Barry Bonds 2.00 .60
❑ 10 Preston Wilson .30 .09
❑ 11 Troy Glaus .30 .09
❑ 12 Geoff Jenkins .30 .09
❑ 13 Jim Edmonds .30 .09
❑ 14 Bobby Higginson .30 .09
❑ 15 Mark Quinn .30 .09
❑ 16 Barry Larkin .50 .15
❑ 17 Richie Sexson .30 .09
❑ 18 Fernando Tatis .30 .09
❑ 19 John VanderWal .30 .09
❑ 20 Darin Erstad .30 .09
❑ 21 Shawn Green .30 .09
❑ 22 Scott Rolen .75 .23
❑ 23 Tony Batista .30 .09
❑ 24 Phil Nevin .30 .09
❑ 25 Tim Salmon .50 .15
❑ 26 Gary Sheffield .30 .09
❑ 27 Ben Grieve .30 .09
❑ 28 Jermaine Dye .30 .09
❑ 29 Andres Galarraga .30 .09
❑ 30 Adrian Beltre .50 .15
❑ 31 Rafael Palmeiro .50 .15
❑ 32 J.T. Snow .30 .09
❑ 33 Edgardo Alfonzo .30 .09
❑ 34 Paul Konerko .30 .09
❑ 35 Jim Thome .75 .23
❑ 36 Andruw Jones .30 .09
❑ 37 Mike Sweeney .30 .09
❑ 38 Jose Cruz Jr. .30 .09
❑ 39 David Ortiz .50 .15
❑ 40 Pat Burrell .30 .09
❑ 41 Chipper Jones .75 .23
❑ 42 Jeff Bagwell .50 .15
❑ 43 Raul Mondesi .30 .09
❑ 44 Rondell White .30 .09
❑ 45 Edgar Martinez .50 .15
❑ 46 Cal Ripken 2.50 .75
❑ 47 Moises Alou .30 .09
❑ 48 Shannon Stewart .30 .09
❑ 49 Tino Martinez .50 .15
❑ 50 Jason Kendall .30 .09
❑ 51 Richard Hidalgo .30 .09
❑ 52 Albert Belle .30 .09
❑ 53 Jay Payton .30 .09
❑ 54 Cliff Floyd .30 .09
❑ 55 Rusty Greer .30 .09
❑ 56 Matt Williams .30 .09
❑ 57 Sammy Sosa 1.25 .35
❑ 58 Carl Everett .30 .09
❑ 59 Carlos Delgado .30 .09
❑ 60 Jeremy Giambi .30 .09
❑ 61 Jose Canseco .75 .23
❑ 62 David Segui .30 .09
❑ 63 Jose Vidro .30 .09
❑ 64 Matt Stairs .30 .09
❑ 65 Travis Fryman .30 .09
❑ 66 Ken Griffey Jr. 1.25 .35
❑ 67 Mike Piazza 1.25 .35
❑ 68 Mark McGwire 2.00 .60
❑ 69 Craig Biggio .50 .15
❑ 70 Eric Chavez .30 .09
❑ 71 Mo Vaughn .30 .09
❑ 72 Matt Lawton .30 .09
❑ 73 Miguel Tejada .30 .09
❑ 74 Brian Giles .30 .09
❑ 75 Sean Casey .30 .09
❑ 76 Robin Ventura .30 .09
❑ 77 Ivan Rodriguez .75 .23
❑ 78 Dean Palmer .30 .09
❑ 79 Frank Thomas .75 .23
❑ 80 Bernie Williams .50 .15
❑ 81 Juan Encarnacion .30 .09
❑ 82 John Olerud .30 .09
❑ 83 Rich Aurilia .30 .09
❑ 84 Juan Gonzalez .50 .15
❑ 85 Ray Durham .30 .09
❑ 86 Steve Finley .30 .09
❑ 87 Ken Caminiti .30 .09
❑ 88 Roberto Alomar .50 .15
❑ 89 Jeromy Burnitz .30 .09
❑ 90 J.D. Drew .30 .09
❑ 91 Lance Berkman .30 .09
❑ 92 Gabe Kapler .30 .09
❑ 93 Larry Walker .50 .15
❑ 94 Alex Rodriguez 1.25 .35
❑ 95 Jeffrey Hammonds .30 .09
❑ 96 Magglio Ordonez .30 .09
❑ 97 David Justice .30 .09
❑ 98 Eric Karros .30 .09
❑ 99 Manny Ramirez .50 .15
❑ 100 Paul O'Neill .50 .15
❑ 101 Ron Gant .30 .09
❑ 102 Erubiel Durazo .30 .09
❑ 103 Jason Varitek .50 .15
❑ 104 Chan Ho Park .30 .09
❑ 105 Corey Koskie .30 .09
❑ 106 Jeff Conine .30 .09
❑ 107 Kevin Tapani .30 .09
❑ 108 Mike Lowell .30 .09
❑ 109 Tim Hudson .30 .09
❑ 110 Bobby Abreu .30 .09
❑ 111 Bret Boone .30 .09
❑ 112 David Wells .30 .09
❑ 113 Brian Jordan .30 .09

❑ 114 Mitch Meluskey .30 .09
❑ 115 Terrence Long .30 .09
❑ 116 Matt Clement .30 .09
❑ 117 Fernando Vina .30 .09
❑ 118 Luis Alicea .30 .09
❑ 119 Jay Bell .30 .09
❑ 120 Mark Grace .50 .15
❑ 121 Carlos Febles .30 .09
❑ 122 Mark Redman .30 .09
❑ 123 Kevin Jordan .30 .09
❑ 124 Pat Meares .30 .09
❑ 125 Mark McLemore .30 .09
❑ 126 Chris Singleton .30 .09
❑ 127 Trot Nixon .30 .09
❑ 128 Carlos Beltran .50 .15
❑ 129 Lee Stevens .30 .09
❑ 130 Kris Benson .30 .09
❑ 131 Jay Buhner .30 .09
❑ 132 Greg Vaughn .30 .09
❑ 133 Eric Young .30 .09
❑ 134 Tony Womack .30 .09
❑ 135 Roger Cedeno .30 .09
❑ 136 Travis Lee .30 .09
❑ 137 Marvin Benard .30 .09
❑ 138 Aaron Sele .30 .09
❑ 139 Rick Ankiel .30 .09
❑ 140 Ruben Mateo .30 .09
❑ 141 Randy Johnson .75 .23
❑ 142 Jason Tyner .30 .09
❑ 143 Mike Redmond .30 .09
❑ 144 Ron Coomer .30 .09
❑ 145 Scott Elarton .30 .09
❑ 146 Javy Lopez .30 .09
❑ 147 Carlos Lee .30 .09
❑ 148 Tony Clark .30 .09
❑ 149 Roger Clemens 1.50 .45
❑ 150 Mike Lieberthal .30 .09
❑ 151 Shawn Estes .30 .09
❑ 152 Vinny Castilla .30 .09
❑ 153 Alex Gonzalez .30 .09
❑ 154 Troy Percival .30 .09
❑ 155 Pokey Reese .30 .09
❑ 156 Todd Hollandsworth .30 .09
❑ 157 Marquis Grissom .30 .09
❑ 158 Greg Maddux 1.25 .35
❑ 159 Dante Bichette .30 .09
❑ 160 Hideo Nomo .75 .23
❑ 161 Jacque Jones .30 .09
❑ 162 Kevin Young .30 .09
❑ 163 B.J. Surhoff .30 .09
❑ 164 Eddie Taubensee .30 .09
❑ 165 Neifi Perez .30 .09
❑ 166 Orlando Hernandez .30 .09
❑ 167 Francisco Cordova .30 .09
❑ 168 Miguel Cairo .30 .09
❑ 169 Rafael Furcal .30 .09
❑ 170 Sandy Alomar Jr. .30 .09
❑ 171 Jeff Cirillo .30 .09
❑ 172 A.J. Pierzynski .30 .09
❑ 173 Fred McGriff .50 .15
❑ 174 Mike Mussina .50 .15
❑ 175 Aaron Boone .30 .09
❑ 176 Nick Johnson .30 .09
❑ 177 Kent Bottenfield .30 .09
❑ 178 Felipe Crespo .30 .09
❑ 179 Ryan Minor .30 .09
❑ 180 Charles Johnson .30 .09
❑ 181 Damion Easley .30 .09
❑ 182 Michael Barrett .30 .09
❑ 183 Doug Glanville .30 .09
❑ 184 Ben Davis .30 .09
❑ 185 Rickey Henderson .75 .23
❑ 186 Edgard Clemente .30 .09
❑ 187 Dmitri Young .30 .09
❑ 188 Tom Goodwin .30 .09
❑ 189 Mike Hampton .30 .09
❑ 190 Gerald Williams .30 .09
❑ 191 Omar Vizquel .50 .15
❑ 192 Ben Petrick .30 .09
❑ 193 Brad Radke .30 .09
❑ 194 Russ Davis .30 .09
❑ 195 Milton Bradley .30 .09
❑ 196 John Parrish .30 .09
❑ 197 Todd Hundley .30 .09
❑ 198 Carl Pavano .30 .09
❑ 199 Bruce Chen .30 .09
❑ 200 Royce Clayton .30 .09
❑ 201 Homer Bush .30 .09
❑ 202 Mark Grudzielanek .30 .09
❑ 203 Mike Lansing .30 .09
❑ 204 Daryle Ward .30 .09
❑ 205 Jeff D'Amico .30 .09
❑ 206 Ray Lankford .30 .09
❑ 207 Curt Schilling .30 .09
❑ 208 Pedro Martinez .75 .23
❑ 209 Johnny Damon .50 .15
❑ 210 Al Leiter .30 .09
❑ 211 Ruben Rivera .30 .09
❑ 212 Kazuhiro Sasaki .30 .09
❑ 213 Will Clark .75 .23
❑ 214 Rick Helling .30 .09
❑ 215 Adam Piatt .30 .09
❑ 216 Joe Girardi .30 .09
❑ 217 A.J. Burnett .30 .09
❑ 218 Mike Bordick .30 .09
❑ 219 Mike Cameron .30 .09
❑ 220 Tony Gwynn 1.00 .30
❑ 221 Deivi Cruz .30 .09
❑ 222 Bubba Trammell .30 .09
❑ 223 Scott Erickson .30 .09
❑ 224 Kerry Wood .75 .23
❑ 225 Derrek Lee .30 .09
❑ 226 Peter Bergeron .30 .09
❑ 227 Chris Gomez .30 .09
❑ 228 Al Martin .30 .09
❑ 229 Brady Anderson .30 .09
❑ 230 Ramon Martinez .30 .09
❑ 231 Darryl Kile .30 .09
❑ 232 Devon White .30 .09
❑ 233 Charlie Hayes .30 .09
❑ 234 Aramis Ramirez .30 .09
❑ 235 Mike Lamb .30 .09
❑ 236 Tom Glavine .50 .15
❑ 237 Troy O'Leary .30 .09
❑ 238 Joe Randa .30 .09
❑ 239 Dustin Hermanson .30 .09
❑ 240 Adam Kennedy .30 .09
❑ 241 Jose Valentin .30 .09
❑ 242 Derek Bell .30 .09
❑ 243 Mark Kotsay .30 .09
❑ 244 Ron Belliard .30 .09
❑ 245 Warren Morris .30 .09
❑ 246 Ozzie Guillen .30 .09
❑ 247 Andy Ashby .30 .09
❑ 248 Jose Offerman .30 .09
❑ 249 Kevin Brown .30 .09
❑ 250 Jorge Posada .50 .15
❑ 251 Alex Cabrera .30 .09
❑ 252 Chan Perry .30 .09
❑ 253 Augie Ojeda .30 .09
❑ 254 Santiago Perez .30 .09
❑ 255 Grant Roberts .30 .09
❑ 256 Dusty Allen .30 .09
❑ 257 Elvis Pena .30 .09
❑ 258 Matt Kinney .30 .09
❑ 259 Timo Perez .30 .09
❑ 260 Adam Eaton .30 .09
❑ 261 Geraldo Guzman .30 .09
❑ 262 Damian Rolls .30 .09
❑ 263 Alfonso Soriano .50 .15
❑ 264 Corey Patterson .30 .09
❑ 265 Juan Alvarez .30 .09
❑ 266 Shawn Gilbert .30 .09
❑ 267 Adam Bernero .30 .09
❑ 268 Ben Weber .30 .09
❑ 269 Tike Redman .30 .09
❑ 270 Willie Morales .30 .09
❑ 271 Tomas De la Rosa .30 .09
❑ 272 Rodney Lindsey .30 .09
❑ 273 Carlos Casimiro .30 .09
❑ 274 Jim Mann .30 .09
❑ 275 Pasqual Coco .30 .09
❑ 276 Julio Zuleta .30 .09
❑ 277 Damon Minor .30 .09
❑ 278 Jose Ortiz .30 .09
❑ 279 Eric Munson .30 .09
❑ 280 Andy Thompson .30 .09
❑ 281 Aubrey Huff .30 .09
❑ 282 Chris Richard .30 .09
❑ 283 Ross Gload .30 .09
❑ 284 Travis Dawkins .30 .09
❑ 285 Tim Drew .30 .09
❑ 286 Barry Zito .50 .15
❑ 287 Andy Tracy .30 .09
❑ 288 Julio Lugo .30 .09
❑ 289 Greg LaRocca .30 .09
❑ 290 Keith McDonald .30 .09
❑ 291 J.C. Romero .30 .09
❑ 292 Adam Melhuse .30 .09
❑ 293 Ryan Kohlmeier .30 .09
❑ 294 John Bale .30 .09
❑ 295 Eric Cammack .30 .09
❑ 296 Morgan Burkhart .30 .09
❑ 297 Kory DeHaan .30 .09
❑ 298 Mike Mahoney .30 .09
❑ 299 Hector Ortiz .30 .09
❑ 300 Talmadge Nunnari .30 .09
❑ 301 E.Guzman/2999 RC 4.00 1.20
❑ 302 D.Henson/2999 RC 5.00 1.50
❑ 303 Bud Smith/2999 RC 4.00 1.20
❑ 304 C.Valderrama/2999 RC 4.00 1.20
❑ 305 T.Shinjo/2999 RC 5.00 1.50
❑ 306 I.Suzuki/2999 RC 30.00 9.00
❑ 307 J.Melian/2999 RC 4.00 1.20
❑ 308 M.Ensberg/2999 RC 5.00 1.50
❑ 309 Albert Pujols/2999 RC 50.00 15.00
❑ 310 J.Estrada/2999 RC 5.00 1.50

1933 Goudey

	Ex-Mt	VG
COMPLETE SET (239)	40000.00	20000.00
COMMON CARD (1-52)	75.00	38.00
COMMON (41/43/53-240)	60.00	30.00
WRAP.(1-CENT, BATTER)	100.00	50.00
WRAP.(1-CENT, AD FRONT)	175.00	90.00
❑ 1 Benny Bengough	1500.00	450.00
❑ 2 Dazzy Vance	200.00	100.00
❑ 3 Hugh Critz	75.00	38.00
❑ 4 Heinie Schuble	75.00	38.00
❑ 5 Babe Herman	75.00	38.00
❑ 6 Jimmy Dykes	75.00	38.00
❑ 7 Ted Lyons	150.00	75.00
❑ 8 Roy Johnson	75.00	38.00
❑ 9 Dave Harris	75.00	38.00
❑ 10 Glenn Myatt	75.00	38.00
❑ 11 Billy Rogell	75.00	38.00
❑ 12 George Pipgras	75.00	38.00
❑ 13 Fresco Thompson	75.00	38.00
❑ 14 Henry Johnson	75.00	38.00
❑ 15 Victor Sorrell	75.00	38.00
❑ 16 George Blaeholder	75.00	38.00
❑ 17 Watson Clark	75.00	38.00
❑ 18 Muddy Ruel	75.00	38.00
❑ 19 Bill Dickey	350.00	180.00
❑ 20 Bill Terry THROW	250.00	125.00
❑ 21 Phil Collins	75.00	38.00
❑ 22 Pie Traynor	250.00	125.00
❑ 23 Kiki Cuyler	200.00	100.00
❑ 24 Horace Ford	75.00	38.00
❑ 25 Paul Waner	200.00	100.00
❑ 26 Chalmer Cissell	75.00	38.00
❑ 27 George Connally	75.00	38.00
❑ 28 Dick Bartell	75.00	38.00
❑ 29 Jimmie Foxx	600.00	300.00
❑ 30 Frank Hogan	75.00	38.00
❑ 31 Tony Lazzeri	400.00	200.00
❑ 32 Bud Clancy	75.00	38.00
❑ 33 Ralph Kress	75.00	38.00
❑ 34 Bob O'Farrell	75.00	38.00
❑ 35 Al Simmons	350.00	180.00

	Ex-Mt	VG
❑ 36 Tommy Thevenow	75.00	38.00
❑ 37 Jimmy Wilson	75.00	38.00
❑ 38 Fred Brickell	75.00	38.00
❑ 39 Mark Koenig	75.00	38.00
❑ 40 Taylor Douthit	75.00	38.00
❑ 41 Gus Mancuso	60.00	30.00
❑ 42 Eddie Collins	150.00	75.00
❑ 43 Lew Fonseca	60.00	30.00
❑ 44 Jim Bottomley	150.00	75.00
❑ 45 Larry Benton	75.00	38.00
❑ 46 Ethan Allen	75.00	38.00
❑ 47 Heinie Manush BAT	175.00	90.00
❑ 48 Marty McManus	75.00	38.00
❑ 49 Frankie Frisch	300.00	150.00
❑ 50 Ed Brandt	75.00	38.00
❑ 51 Charlie Grimm	75.00	38.00
❑ 52 Andy Cohen	75.00	38.00
❑ 53 Babe Ruth	6000.00	3000.00
❑ 54 Ray Kremer	60.00	30.00
❑ 55 Pat Malone	60.00	30.00
❑ 56 Red Ruffing	175.00	90.00
❑ 57 Earl Clark	60.00	30.00
❑ 58 Lefty O'Doul	125.00	60.00
❑ 59 Bing Miller	60.00	30.00
❑ 60 Waite Hoyt	125.00	60.00
❑ 61 Max Bishop	60.00	30.00
❑ 62 Pepper Martin	125.00	60.00
❑ 63 Joe Cronin BAT	150.00	75.00
❑ 64 Burleigh Grimes	250.00	125.00
❑ 65 Milt Gaston	60.00	30.00
❑ 66 George Grantham	60.00	30.00
❑ 67 Guy Bush	60.00	30.00
❑ 68 Horace Lisenbee	60.00	30.00
❑ 69 Randy Moore	60.00	30.00
❑ 70 Floyd (Pete) Scott	60.00	30.00
❑ 71 Robert J. Burke	60.00	30.00
❑ 72 Owen Carroll	60.00	30.00
❑ 73 Jesse Haines	125.00	60.00
❑ 74 Eppa Rixey	150.00	75.00
❑ 75 Willie Kamm	60.00	30.00
❑ 76 Mickey Cochrane	250.00	125.00
❑ 77 Adam Comorosky	60.00	30.00
❑ 78 Jack Quinn	60.00	30.00
❑ 79 Red Faber	125.00	60.00
❑ 80 Clyde Manion	60.00	30.00
❑ 81 Sam Jones	60.00	30.00
❑ 82 Dib Williams	60.00	30.00
❑ 83 Pete Jablonowski	60.00	30.00
❑ 84 Glenn Spencer	60.00	30.00
❑ 85 Heinie Sand	60.00	30.00
❑ 86 Phil Todt	60.00	30.00
❑ 87 Frank O'Rourke	60.00	30.00
❑ 88 Russell Rollings	60.00	30.00
❑ 89 Tris Speaker RET	300.00	150.00
❑ 90 Jess Petty	60.00	30.00
❑ 91 Tom Zachary	60.00	30.00
❑ 92 Lou Gehrig	2500.00	1250.00
❑ 93 John Welch	60.00	30.00
❑ 94 Bill Walker	60.00	30.00
❑ 95 Alvin Crowder	60.00	30.00
❑ 96 Willis Hudlin	60.00	30.00
❑ 97 Joe Morrissey	60.00	30.00
❑ 98 Wally Berger	75.00	38.00
❑ 99 Tony Cuccinello	75.00	38.00
❑ 100 George Uhle	60.00	30.00
❑ 101 Richard Coffman	60.00	30.00
❑ 102 Travis Jackson	150.00	75.00
❑ 103 Earle Combs	125.00	60.00
❑ 104 Fred Marberry	60.00	30.00
❑ 105 Bernie Friberg	60.00	30.00
❑ 106 Napoleon Lajoie SP (Not issued until 1934)	25000.00	12500.00
❑ 107 Heinie Manush	125.00	60.00
❑ 108 Joe Kuhel	60.00	30.00
❑ 109 Joe Cronin	300.00	150.00
❑ 110 Goose Goslin	250.00	125.00
❑ 111 Monte Weaver	60.00	30.00
❑ 112 Fred Schulte	60.00	30.00
❑ 113 Oswald Bluege	60.00	30.00
❑ 114 Luke Sewell	75.00	38.00
❑ 115 Cliff Heathcote	60.00	30.00
❑ 116 Eddie Morgan	60.00	30.00
❑ 117 Rabbit Maranville	125.00	60.00
❑ 118 Val Picinich	60.00	30.00
❑ 119 R. Hornsby FIELD	600.00	250.00
❑ 120 Carl Reynolds	60.00	30.00
❑ 121 Walter Stewart	60.00	30.00
❑ 122 Alvin Crowder	60.00	30.00
❑ 123 Jack Russell	60.00	30.00
❑ 124 Earl Whitehill	60.00	30.00
❑ 125 Bill Terry	250.00	125.00
❑ 126 Joe Moore	60.00	30.00
❑ 127 Mel Ott	400.00	200.00
❑ 128 Chuck Klein	175.00	90.00
❑ 129 Hal Schumacher PIT	60.00	30.00
❑ 130 Fred Fitzsimmons	60.00	30.00
❑ 131 Fred Frankhouse	60.00	30.00
❑ 132 Jim Elliott	60.00	30.00
❑ 133 Fred Lindstrom	125.00	60.00
❑ 134 Sam Rice	200.00	100.00
❑ 135 Woody English	60.00	30.00
❑ 136 Flint Rhem	60.00	30.00
❑ 137 Fred(Red) Lucas	60.00	30.00
❑ 138 Herb Pennock	175.00	90.00
❑ 139 Ben Cantwell	60.00	30.00
❑ 140 Bump Hadley	60.00	30.00
❑ 141 Ray Benge	60.00	30.00
❑ 142 Paul Richards	75.00	38.00
❑ 143 Glenn Wright	60.00	30.00
❑ 144 Babe Ruth Bat DP	4000.00	2000.00
❑ 145 Rube Walberg	60.00	30.00
❑ 146 Walter Stewart PIT	60.00	30.00
❑ 147 Leo Durocher	200.00	100.00
❑ 148 Eddie Farrell	60.00	30.00
❑ 149 Babe Ruth	5000.00	2500.00
❑ 150 Ray Kolp	60.00	30.00
❑ 151 Jake Flowers	60.00	30.00
❑ 152 Zack Taylor	60.00	30.00
❑ 153 Buddy Myer	60.00	30.00
❑ 154 Jimmie Foxx	600.00	300.00
❑ 155 Joe Judge	60.00	30.00
❑ 156 Danny MacFayden	60.00	30.00
❑ 157 Sam Byrd	60.00	30.00
❑ 158 Moe Berg	400.00	200.00
❑ 159 Oswald Bluege	60.00	30.00
❑ 160 Lou Gehrig	3000.00	1500.00
❑ 161 Al Spohrer	60.00	30.00
❑ 162 Leo Mangum	60.00	30.00
❑ 163 Luke Sewell	75.00	38.00
❑ 164 Lloyd Waner	250.00	125.00
❑ 165 Joe Sewell	125.00	60.00
❑ 166 Sam West	60.00	30.00
❑ 167 Jack Russell	60.00	30.00
❑ 168 Goose Goslin	200.00	100.00
❑ 169 Al Thomas	60.00	30.00
❑ 170 Harry McCurdy	60.00	30.00
❑ 171 Charlie Jamieson	60.00	30.00
❑ 172 Billy Hargrave	60.00	30.00
❑ 173 Roscoe Holm	60.00	30.00
❑ 174 Warren(Curly) Ogden	60.00	30.00
❑ 175 Dan Howley MG	60.00	30.00
❑ 176 John Ogden	60.00	30.00
❑ 177 Walter French	60.00	30.00
❑ 178 Jackie Warner	60.00	30.00
❑ 179 Fred Leach	60.00	30.00
❑ 180 Eddie Moore	60.00	30.00
❑ 181 Babe Ruth	4000.00	2000.00
❑ 182 Andy High	60.00	30.00
❑ 183 Rube Walberg	60.00	30.00
❑ 184 Charley Berry	60.00	30.00
❑ 185 Bob Smith	60.00	30.00
❑ 186 John Schulte	60.00	30.00
❑ 187 Heinie Manush	150.00	75.00
❑ 188 Rogers Hornsby	600.00	300.00
❑ 189 Joe Cronin	200.00	100.00
❑ 190 Fred Schulte	60.00	30.00
❑ 191 Ben Chapman	75.00	38.00
❑ 192 Walter Brown	60.00	30.00
❑ 193 Lynford Lary	60.00	30.00
❑ 194 Earl Averill	200.00	100.00
❑ 195 Evar Swanson	60.00	30.00
❑ 196 Leroy Mahaffey	60.00	30.00
❑ 197 Rick Ferrell	125.00	60.00
❑ 198 Jack Burns	60.00	30.00
❑ 199 Tom Bridges	60.00	30.00
❑ 200 Bill Hallahan	60.00	30.00
❑ 201 Ernie Orsatti	60.00	30.00
❑ 202 Gabby Hartnett	250.00	125.00
❑ 203 Lon Warneke	60.00	30.00
❑ 204 Riggs Stephenson	60.00	30.00
❑ 205 Heinie Meine	60.00	30.00
❑ 206 Gus Suhr	60.00	30.00
❑ 207 Mel Ott Bat	400.00	200.00
❑ 208 Bernie James	60.00	30.00
❑ 209 Adolfo Luque	75.00	38.00
❑ 210 Spud Davis	60.00	30.00
❑ 211 Hack Wilson	400.00	200.00
❑ 212 Billy Urbanski	60.00	30.00
❑ 213 Earl Adams	60.00	30.00
❑ 214 John Kerr	60.00	30.00
❑ 215 Russ Van Atta	60.00	30.00
❑ 216 Lefty Gomez	300.00	150.00
❑ 217 Frank Crosetti	150.00	75.00
❑ 218 Wes Ferrell	75.00	38.00
❑ 219 Mule Haas UER (Name spelled Hass on front)	60.00	30.00
❑ 220 Lefty Grove	500.00	250.00
❑ 221 Dale Alexander	60.00	30.00
❑ 222 Charley Gehringer	400.00	200.00
❑ 223 Dizzy Dean	800.00	300.00
❑ 224 Frank Demaree	60.00	30.00
❑ 225 Bill Jurges	60.00	30.00
❑ 226 Charley Root	60.00	30.00
❑ 227 Billy Herman	150.00	75.00
❑ 228 Tony Piet	60.00	30.00
❑ 229 Arky Vaughan	150.00	75.00
❑ 230 Carl Hubbell PIT	400.00	150.00
❑ 231 Joe Moore FIELD	60.00	30.00
❑ 232 Lefty O'Doul	125.00	60.00
❑ 233 Johnny Vergez	60.00	30.00
❑ 234 Carl Hubbell	400.00	150.00
❑ 235 Fred Fitzsimmons	60.00	30.00
❑ 236 George Davis	60.00	30.00
❑ 237 Gus Mancuso	60.00	30.00
❑ 238 Hugh Critz	60.00	30.00
❑ 239 Leroy Parmelee	60.00	30.00
❑ 240 Hal Schumacher	125.00	60.00

1934 Goudey

	Ex-Mt	VG
COMPLETE SET (96)	16000.00	8000.00
COMMON CARD (1-48)	50.00	25.00
COMMON CARD (49-72)	75.00	38.00
COMMON CARD (73-96)	175.00	90.00
WRAP.(1-CENT, WHITE)	100.00	50.00
WRAP.(1-CENT, CLEAR)	100.00	50.00
❑ 1 Jimmie Foxx	750.00	220.00
❑ 2 Mickey Cochrane	175.00	90.00
❑ 3 Charlie Grimm	60.00	30.00
❑ 4 Woody English	50.00	25.00
❑ 5 Ed Brandt	50.00	25.00
❑ 6 Dizzy Dean	700.00	300.00
❑ 7 Leo Durocher	175.00	90.00
❑ 8 Tony Piet	50.00	25.00
❑ 9 Ben Chapman	60.00	30.00
❑ 10 Chuck Klein	150.00	75.00
❑ 11 Paul Waner	150.00	75.00
❑ 12 Carl Hubbell	175.00	90.00
❑ 13 Frankie Frisch	175.00	90.00
❑ 14 Willie Kamm	50.00	25.00
❑ 15 Alvin Crowder	50.00	25.00
❑ 16 Joe Kuhel	50.00	25.00
❑ 17 Hugh Critz	50.00	25.00
❑ 18 Heinie Manush	125.00	60.00
❑ 19 Lefty Grove	300.00	150.00
❑ 20 Frank Hogan	50.00	25.00
❑ 21 Bill Terry	200.00	100.00
❑ 22 Arky Vaughan	125.00	60.00
❑ 23 Charley Gehringer	200.00	100.00
❑ 24 Ray Benge	50.00	25.00

❑ 25	Roger Cramer	60.00	30.00
❑ 26	Gerald Walker	50.00	25.00
❑ 27	Luke Appling	150.00	75.00
❑ 28	Ed Coleman	50.00	25.00
❑ 29	Larry French	50.00	25.00
❑ 30	Julius Solters	50.00	25.00
❑ 31	Buck Jordan	50.00	25.00
❑ 32	Blondy Ryan	50.00	25.00
❑ 33	Frank Hurst	50.00	25.00
❑ 34	Chick Hafey	125.00	60.00
❑ 35	Ernie Lombardi	150.00	75.00
❑ 36	Walter Betts	50.00	25.00
❑ 37	Lou Gehrig	3000.00	1500.00
❑ 38	Oral Hildebrand	50.00	25.00
❑ 39	Fred Walker	50.00	25.00
❑ 40	John Stone	50.00	25.00
❑ 41	George Earnshaw	50.00	25.00
❑ 42	John Allen	50.00	25.00
❑ 43	Dick Porter	50.00	25.00
❑ 44	Tom Bridges	60.00	30.00
❑ 45	Oscar Melillo	50.00	25.00
❑ 46	Joe Stripp	50.00	25.00
❑ 47	John Frederick	50.00	25.00
❑ 48	Tex Carleton	50.00	25.00
❑ 49	Sam Leslie	75.00	38.00
❑ 50	Walter Beck	75.00	38.00
❑ 51	Rip Collins	75.00	38.00
❑ 52	Herman Bell	75.00	38.00
❑ 53	George Watkins	75.00	38.00
❑ 54	Wesley Schulmerich	75.00	38.00
❑ 55	Ed Holley	75.00	38.00
❑ 56	Mark Koenig	100.00	50.00
❑ 57	Bill Swift	75.00	38.00
❑ 58	Earl Grace	75.00	38.00
❑ 59	Joe Mowry	75.00	38.00
❑ 60	Lynn Nelson	75.00	38.00
❑ 61	Lou Gehrig	3000.00	1500.00
❑ 62	Hank Greenberg	700.00	300.00
❑ 63	Minter Hayes	75.00	38.00
❑ 64	Frank Grube	75.00	38.00
❑ 65	Cliff Bolton	75.00	38.00
❑ 66	Mel Harder	100.00	50.00
❑ 67	Bob Weiland	75.00	38.00
❑ 68	Bob Johnson	100.00	50.00
❑ 69	John Marcum	75.00	38.00
❑ 70	Pete Fox	75.00	38.00
❑ 71	Lyle Tinning	75.00	38.00
❑ 72	Arndt Jorgens	75.00	38.00
❑ 73	Ed Wells	175.00	90.00
❑ 74	Bob Boken	175.00	90.00
❑ 75	Bill Werber	175.00	90.00
❑ 76	Hal Trosky	200.00	100.00
❑ 77	Joe Vosmik	175.00	90.00
❑ 78	Pinky Higgins	200.00	100.00
❑ 79	Eddie Durham	175.00	90.00
❑ 80	Marty McManus CK	175.00	90.00
❑ 81	Bob Brown CK	175.00	90.00
❑ 82	Bill Hallahan CK	175.00	90.00
❑ 83	Jim Mooney CK	175.00	90.00
❑ 84	Paul Derringer CK	225.00	110.00
❑ 85	Adam Comorosky CK	175.00	90.00
❑ 86	Lloyd Johnson CK	175.00	90.00
❑ 87	George Darrow CK	175.00	90.00
❑ 88	Homer Peel CK	175.00	90.00
❑ 89	Linus Frey CK	175.00	90.00
❑ 90	KiKi Cuyler CK	350.00	180.00
❑ 91	Dolph Camilli CK	200.00	100.00
❑ 92	Steve Larkin	175.00	90.00
❑ 93	Fred Ostermueller	175.00	90.00
❑ 94	Red Rolfe	200.00	100.00
❑ 95	Myril Hoag	175.00	90.00
❑ 96	James DeShong	500.00	200.00

2004 Greats of the Game

	Nm-Mt	Ex-Mt
COMPLETE SERIES 1 (80)	40.00	12.00

❑ 1	Lou Gehrig	3.00	.90
❑ 2	Ty Cobb	2.50	.75
❑ 3	Dizzy Dean	2.00	.60
❑ 4	Jimmie Foxx	2.00	.60
❑ 5	Hank Greenberg	2.00	.60
❑ 6	Babe Ruth	5.00	1.50
❑ 7	Honus Wagner	2.00	.60
❑ 8	Mickey Cochrane	.75	.23
❑ 9	Pepper Martin	.75	.23
❑ 10	Charlie Gehringer	.75	.23
❑ 11	Carl Hubbell	1.25	.35
❑ 12	Bill Terry	.75	.23
❑ 13	Mel Ott	2.00	.60
❑ 14	Bill Dickey	1.25	.35
❑ 15	Ted Williams	4.00	1.20
❑ 16	Roger Maris Yanks	2.00	.60
❑ 17	Thurman Munson	2.00	.60
❑ 18	Phil Rizzuto	1.25	.35
❑ 19	Stan Musial	3.00	.90
❑ 20	Duke Snider Brooklyn	1.25	.35
❑ 21	Reggie Jackson Yanks	1.25	.35
❑ 22	Don Mattingly	4.00	1.20
❑ 23	Vida Blue	.75	.23
❑ 24	Harmon Killebrew	2.00	.60
❑ 25	Lou Brock	1.25	.35
❑ 26	Al Kaline	2.00	.60
❑ 27	Dave Parker	.75	.23
❑ 28	Nolan Ryan Astros	5.00	1.50
❑ 29	Jim Rice	.75	.23
❑ 30	Paul Molitor Brewers	1.25	.35
❑ 31	Dwight Evans	1.25	.35
❑ 32	Brooks Robinson	1.25	.35
❑ 33	Jose Canseco	2.00	.60
❑ 34	Alan Trammell	.75	.23
❑ 35	Johnny Bench	2.00	.60
❑ 36	Carlton Fisk R.Sox	1.25	.35
❑ 37	Jim Palmer	.75	.23
❑ 38	George Brett	5.00	1.50
❑ 39	Mike Schmidt	4.00	1.20
❑ 40	Tony Perez	.75	.23
❑ 41	Paul Blair	.50	.15
❑ 42	Fred Lynn	.75	.23
❑ 43	Carl Yastrzemski	3.00	.90
❑ 44	Steve Carlton Phils	.75	.23
❑ 45	Dennis Eckersley	1.25	.35
❑ 46	Tom Seaver Mets	1.25	.35
❑ 47	Juan Marichal	.75	.23
❑ 48	Tony Gwynn	2.50	.75
❑ 49	Moose Skowron	.75	.23
❑ 50	Bob Gibson	1.25	.35
❑ 51	Luis Tiant	.75	.23
❑ 52	Eddie Murray O's	2.00	.60
❑ 53	Frank Robinson Reds	.75	.23
❑ 54	Rocky Colavito	1.25	.35
❑ 55	Bobby Shantz	.50	.15
❑ 56	Ernie Banks	2.00	.60
❑ 57	Rod Carew Angels	1.25	.35
❑ 58	Gorman Thomas	.75	.23
❑ 59	Bernie Carbo	.50	.15
❑ 60	Joe Rudi	.50	.15
❑ 61	Graig Nettles	.75	.23
❑ 62	Ron Guidry	.75	.23
❑ 63	Whitey Ford	1.25	.35
❑ 64	George Kell	.75	.23
❑ 65	Cal Ripken	6.00	1.80
❑ 66	Willie McCovey	1.25	.35
❑ 67	Bo Jackson	2.00	.60
❑ 68	Kirby Puckett	2.00	.60
❑ 69	Ted Kluszewski	1.25	.35
❑ 70	Johnny Podres	.75	.23
❑ 71	Davey Lopes	.75	.23
❑ 72	Chris Short	.50	.15
❑ 73	Jeff Torborg	.50	.15
❑ 74	Bill Freehan	.75	.23
❑ 75	Frank Tanana	.75	.23
❑ 76	Jack Morris	.75	.23
❑ 77	Rick Dempsey	.50	.15
❑ 78	Yogi Berra	2.00	.60
❑ 79	Tim McCarver	.75	.23
❑ 80	Rusty Staub	.75	.23
❑ 81	Tony Lazzeri		
❑ 82	Al Rosen		
❑ 83	Willie McGee		
❑ 84	Preacher Roe		
❑ 85	Dave Kingman		
❑ 86	Luis Aparicio		
❑ 87	John Kruk		
❑ 88	Bing Miller		
❑ 89	Joe Charboneau		
❑ 90	Mark Fidrych		
❑ 91	Catfish Hunter		
❑ 92	Nap Lajoie		
❑ 93	Eddie Murray Indians		
❑ 94	Johnny Pesky		
❑ 95	Tom Seaver Reds		
❑ 96	Frank Robinson O's		
❑ 97	Enos Slaughter		
❑ 98	Cecil Travis		
❑ 99	Robin Yount		
❑ 100	Don Zimmer		
❑ 101	Babe Herman		
❑ 102	Ron Santo		
❑ 103	Willie Stargell		
❑ 104	Paul Molitor Jays		
❑ 105	Jimmy Piersall		
❑ 106	Johnny Sain		
❑ 107	Joe Pepitone		
❑ 108	Ryne Sandberg		
❑ 109	Jim Thorpe		
❑ 110	Steve Garvey		
❑ 111	Ray Knight		
❑ 112	Fernando Valenzuela		
❑ 113	Will Clark		
❑ 114	Tony Kubek		
❑ 115	Jim Bouton		
❑ 116	Jerry Koosman		
❑ 117	Steve Carlton Cards		
❑ 118	Richie Ashburn		
❑ 119	Roberto Clemente		
❑ 120	Paul O'Neill		
❑ 121	Reggie Jackson Angels		
❑ 122	Andre Dawson		
❑ 123	Hoyt Wilhelm		
❑ 124	Dale Murphy		
❑ 125	Dwight Gooden		
❑ 126	Roger Maris Cards		
❑ 127	Bill Mazeroski		
❑ 128	Don Newcombe		
❑ 129	Robin Roberts		
❑ 130	Duke Snider LA		
❑ 131	Eddie Mathews		
❑ 132	Wade Boggs		
❑ 133	Rollie Fingers		
❑ 134	Frankie Frisch		
❑ 135	Billy Williams		
❑ 136	Rod Carew Twins		
❑ 137	Dom DiMaggio		
❑ 138	Orel Hershiser		
❑ 139	Gary Carter		
❑ 140	Keith Hernandez		
❑ 141	Bob Lemon		
❑ 142	Nolan Ryan Angels		
❑ 143	Ozzie Smith		
❑ 144	Rick Sutcliffe		
❑ 145	Carlton Fisk W.Sox		

1949 Leaf

	NM	Ex
COMPLETE SET (98)	30000.00	15000.00
COMMON CARD (1-168)	25.00	12.50
COMMON SP's	300.00	150.00
WRAPPER (1-CENT)	160.00	80.00

❑ 1	Joe DiMaggio	3000.00	1200.00
❑ 3	Babe Ruth	2500.00	1250.00
❑ 4	Stan Musial	1000.00	500.00
❑ 5	Virgil Trucks SP RC	400.00	200.00
❑ 8	S.Paige SP RC	12000.00	6000.00
❑ 10	Dizzy Trout	40.00	20.00

❑ 11 Phil Rizzuto 350.00 180.00
❑ 13 Cass Michaels SP 300.00 150.00
❑ 14 Billy Johnson 40.00 20.00
❑ 17 Frank Overmire 25.00 12.50
❑ 19 Johnny Wyrostek SP 300.00 150.00
❑ 20 Hank Sauer SP 400.00 200.00
❑ 22 Al Evans 25.00 12.50
❑ 26 Sam Chapman 40.00 20.00
❑ 27 Mickey Harris 25.00 12.50
❑ 28 Jim Hegan RC 40.00 20.00
❑ 29 Elmer Valo RC 40.00 20.00
❑ 30 Billy Goodman SP RC .. 400.00 200.00
❑ 31 Lou Brissie 25.00 12.50
❑ 32 Warren Spahn 350.00 180.00
❑ 33 Peanuts Lowrey SP 300.00 150.00
❑ 36 Al Zarilla SP 300.00 150.00
❑ 38 Ted Kluszewski RC 200.00 100.00
❑ 39 Ewell Blackwell 60.00 30.00
❑ 42 Kent Peterson 25.00 12.50
❑ 43 Ed Stevens SP 300.00 150.00
❑ 45 Ken Keltner SP 300.00 150.00
❑ 46 Johnny Mize 100.00 50.00
❑ 47 George Vico 25.00 12.50
❑ 48 Johnny Schmitz SP 300.00 150.00
❑ 49 Del Ennis RC 60.00 30.00
❑ 50 Dick Wakefield 25.00 12.50
❑ 51 Al Dark SP RC 500.00 250.00
❑ 53 Johnny VanderMeer 100.00 50.00
❑ 54 Bobby Adams SP 300.00 150.00
❑ 55 Tommy Henrich SP 500.00 250.00
❑ 56 Larry Jansen RC UER 40.00 20.00
(Misspelled Jensen)
❑ 57 Bob McCall 25.00 12.50
❑ 59 Luke Appling 100.00 50.00
❑ 61 Jake Early 25.00 12.50
❑ 62 Eddie Joost SP 300.00 150.00
❑ 63 Barney McCosky SP 300.00 150.00
❑ 65 Robert Elliott RC UER .. 100.00 50.00
(Misspelled Elliot
on card front)
❑ 66 Orval Grove SP 300.00 150.00
❑ 68 Eddie Miller SP 300.00 150.00
❑ 70 Honus Wagner CO 350.00 180.00
❑ 72 Hank Edwards 25.00 12.50
❑ 73 Pat Seerey 25.00 12.50
❑ 75 Dom DiMaggio SP 600.00 300.00
❑ 76 Ted Williams 1200.00 600.00
❑ 77 Roy Smalley RC 25.00 12.50
❑ 78 Hoot Evers SP 300.00 150.00
❑ 79 Jackie Robinson RC .. 1500.00 750.00
❑ 81 Whitey Kurowski SP 300.00 150.00
❑ 82 Johnny Lindell 40.00 20.00
❑ 83 Bobby Doerr 100.00 50.00
❑ 84 Sid Hudson 25.00 12.50
❑ 85 Dave Philley SP RC 400.00 200.00
❑ 86 Ralph Weigel 25.00 12.50
❑ 88 Frank Gustine SP 300.00 150.00
❑ 91 Ralph Kiner 200.00 100.00
❑ 93 Bob Feller SP 2000.00 1000.00
❑ 95 George Stirnweiss RC 40.00 20.00
❑ 97 Marty Marion 60.00 30.00
❑ 98 Hal Newhouser SP RC .. 600.00 300.00
❑ 102A Gene Hermansk ERR 250.00 125.00
❑ 102B G.Hermanski COR 40.00 20.00
❑ 104 Eddie Stewart SP 300.00 150.00
❑ 106 Lou Boudreau 100.00 50.00
❑ 108 Matt Batts SP 300.00 150.00
❑ 111 Jerry Priddy 25.00 12.50
❑ 113 Dutch Leonard SP 300.00 150.00
❑ 117 Joe Gordon 40.00 20.00
❑ 120 George Kell SP RC 600.00 300.00
❑ 121 Johnny Pesky SP RC .. 400.00 200.00
❑ 123 Cliff Fannin SP 300.00 150.00
❑ 125 Andy Pafko RC 25.00 12.50
❑ 127 Enos Slaughter SP 800.00 400.00
❑ 128 Buddy Rosar 25.00 12.50
❑ 129 Kirby Higbe SP 300.00 150.00
❑ 131 Sid Gordon SP 300.00 150.00
❑ 133 Tommy Holmes SP 500.00 250.00
❑ 136A Cliff Aberson 25.00 12.50
(Full sleeve)
❑ 136B Cliff Aberson 250.00 125.00
(Short sleeve)
❑ 137 Harry Walker SP 400.00 200.00
❑ 138 Larry Doby SP RC 700.00 350.00
❑ 139 Johnny Hopp RC 25.00 12.50
❑ 142 D.Murtaugh SP RC 400.00 200.00
❑ 143 Dick Sisler SP 300.00 150.00
❑ 144 Bob Dillinger SP 300.00 150.00
❑ 146 Pete Reiser SP 500.00 250.00
❑ 149 Hank Majeski SP 300.00 150.00
❑ 153 Floyd Baker SP 300.00 150.00
❑ 158 H. Brecheen SP RC 400.00 200.00
❑ 159 Mizell Platt 25.00 12.50
❑ 160 Bob Scheffing SP 300.00 150.00
❑ 161 Vern Stephens SP RC 400.00 200.00
❑ 163 F.Hutchinson SP RC .. 400.00 200.00
❑ 165 Dale Mitchell SP RC .. 400.00 200.00
❑ 168 P.Cavarretta SP UER .. 500.00 200.00
Name spelled Cavaretta
❑ NNO Album ....

1990 Leaf

	Nm-Mt	Ex-Mt
COMPLETE SET (528)	100.00	30.00
COMPLETE SERIES 1 (264)	60.00	18.00
COMPLETE SERIES 2 (264)	40.00	12.00
COMP. BERRA PUZZLE	1.00	.30

❑ 1 Introductory Card .... .40 .12
❑ 2 Mike Henneman .... .40 .12
❑ 3 Steve Bedrosian .... .40 .12
❑ 4 Mike Scott .... .40 .12
❑ 5 Allan Anderson .... .40 .12
❑ 6 Rick Sutcliffe .... .60 .18
❑ 7 Gregg Olson .... .60 .18
❑ 8 Kevin Elster .... .40 .12
❑ 9 Pete O'Brien .... .40 .12
❑ 10 Carlton Fisk .... 1.00 .30
❑ 11 Joe Magrane .... .40 .12
❑ 12 Roger Clemens .... 3.00 .90
❑ 13 Tom Glavine .... 1.00 .30
❑ 14 Tom Gordon .... .60 .18
❑ 15 Todd Benzinger .... .40 .12
❑ 16 Hubie Brooks .... .40 .12
❑ 17 Roberto Kelly .... .40 .12
❑ 18 Barry Larkin .... 1.00 .30
❑ 19 Mike Boddicker .... .40 .12
❑ 20 Roger McDowell .... .40 .12
❑ 21 Nolan Ryan 5.00 1.50
❑ 22 John Farrell .... .40 .12
❑ 23 Bruce Hurst .... .40 .12
❑ 24 Wally Joyner .... .60 .18
❑ 25 Greg Maddux 5.00 1.50
❑ 26 Chris Bosio .... .40 .12
❑ 27 John Cerutti .... .40 .12
❑ 28 Tim Burke .... .40 .12
❑ 29 Dennis Eckersley .... .60 .18
❑ 30 Glenn Davis .... .40 .12
❑ 31 Jim Abbott .... 1.00 .30
❑ 32 Mike LaValliere .... .40 .12
❑ 33 Andres Thomas .... .40 .12
❑ 34 Lou Whitaker .... .60 .18
❑ 35 Alvin Davis .... .40 .12
❑ 36 Melido Perez .... .40 .12
❑ 37 Craig Biggio .... 1.00 .30
❑ 38 Rick Aguilera .... .60 .18
❑ 39 Pete Harnisch .... .40 .12
❑ 40 David Cone .... .60 .18
❑ 41 Scott Garrelts .... .40 .12
❑ 42 Jay Howell .... .40 .12
❑ 43 Eric King .... .40 .12
❑ 44 Pedro Guerrero .... .40 .12
❑ 45 Mike Bielecki .... .40 .12
❑ 46 Bob Boone .... .60 .18
❑ 47 Kevin Brown .... .60 .18
❑ 48 Jerry Browne .... .40 .12
❑ 49 Mike Scioscia .... .40 .12
❑ 50 Chuck Cary .... .40 .12
❑ 51 Wade Boggs .... 1.00 .30
❑ 52 Von Hayes .... .40 .12
❑ 53 Tony Fernandez .... .40 .12
❑ 54 Dennis Martinez .... .60 .18
❑ 55 Tom Candiotti .... .40 .12
❑ 56 Andy Benes .... .60 .18
❑ 57 Rob Dibble .... .60 .18
❑ 58 Chuck Crim .... .40 .12
❑ 59 John Smoltz .... 1.50 .45
❑ 60 Mike Heath .... .40 .12
❑ 61 Kevin Gross .... .40 .12
❑ 62 Mark McGwire 4.00 1.20
❑ 63 Bert Blyleven .... .60 .18
❑ 64 Bob Walk .... .40 .12
❑ 65 Mickey Tettleton .... .40 .12
❑ 66 Sid Fernandez .... .40 .12
❑ 67 Terry Kennedy .... .40 .12
❑ 68 Fernando Valenzuela .... .60 .18
❑ 69 Don Mattingly 4.00 1.20
❑ 70 Paul O'Neill .... 1.00 .30
❑ 71 Robin Yount .... 2.50 .75
❑ 72 Bret Saberhagen .... .60 .18
❑ 73 Geno Petralli .... .40 .12
❑ 74 Brook Jacoby .... .40 .12
❑ 75 Roberto Alomar .... 1.00 .30
❑ 76 Devon White .... .60 .18
❑ 77 Jose Lind .... .40 .12
❑ 78 Pat Combs .... .40 .12
❑ 79 Dave Stieb .... .60 .18
❑ 80 Tim Wallach .... .40 .12
❑ 81 Dave Stewart .... .60 .18
❑ 82 Eric Anthony RC .... .40 .12
❑ 83 Randy Bush .... .40 .12
❑ 84 Rickey Henderson CL .... .60 .18
❑ 85 Jaime Navarro .... .40 .12
❑ 86 Tommy Gregg .... .40 .12
❑ 87 Frank Tanana .... .40 .12
❑ 88 Omar Vizquel .... 1.50 .45
❑ 89 Ivan Calderon .... .40 .12
❑ 90 Vince Coleman .... .40 .12
❑ 91 Barry Bonds 4.00 1.20
❑ 92 Randy Milligan .... .40 .12
❑ 93 Frank Viola .... .40 .12
❑ 94 Matt Williams .... .60 .18
❑ 95 Alfredo Griffin .... .40 .12
❑ 96 Steve Sax .... .40 .12
❑ 97 Gary Gaetti .... .60 .18
❑ 98 Ryne Sandberg .... 3.00 .90
❑ 99 Danny Tartabull .... .40 .12
❑ 100 Rafael Palmeiro .... 1.00 .30
❑ 101 Jesse Orosco .... .40 .12
❑ 102 Garry Templeton .... .40 .12
❑ 103 Frank DiPino .... .40 .12
❑ 104 Tony Pena .... .40 .12
❑ 105 Dickie Thon .... .40 .12
❑ 106 Kelly Gruber .... .40 .12
❑ 107 Marquis Grissom RC .... 2.00 .60
❑ 108 Jose Canseco .... 1.50 .45
❑ 109 Mike Blowers RC .... .40 .12
❑ 110 Tom Browning .... .40 .12
❑ 111 Greg Vaughn .... .40 .12
❑ 112 Oddibe McDowell .... .40 .12
❑ 113 Gary Ward .... .40 .12
❑ 114 Jay Buhner .... .60 .18
❑ 115 Eric Show .... .40 .12
❑ 116 Bryan Harvey .... .40 .12
❑ 117 Andy Van Slyke .... .60 .18
❑ 118 Jeff Ballard .... .40 .12
❑ 119 Barry Lyons .... .40 .12
❑ 120 Kevin Mitchell .... .40 .12
❑ 121 Mike Gallego .... .40 .12
❑ 122 Dave Smith .... .40 .12
❑ 123 Kirby Puckett .... 1.50 .45
❑ 124 Jerome Walton .... .40 .12
❑ 125 Bo Jackson .... 1.50 .45
❑ 126 Harold Baines .... .60 .18
❑ 127 Scott Bankhead .... .40 .12
❑ 128 Ozzie Guillen .... .40 .12
❑ 129 Jose Oquendo UER .... .40 .12
(League misspelled

as Legue)
❑ 130 John Dopson .40 .12
❑ 131 Charlie Hayes .40 .12
❑ 132 Fred McGriff 1.50 .45
❑ 133 Chet Lemon .40 .12
❑ 134 Gary Carter .60 .18
❑ 135 Rafael Ramirez .40 .12
❑ 136 Shane Mack .40 .12
❑ 137 Mark Grace UER 1.00 .30
(Card back has OB:L, should be B:L)
❑ 138 Phil Bradley .40 .12
❑ 139 Dwight Gooden .60 .18
❑ 140 Harold Reynolds .60 .18
❑ 141 Scott Fletcher .40 .12
❑ 142 Ozzie Smith 2.50 .75
❑ 143 Mike Greenwell .40 .12
❑ 144 Pete Smith .40 .12
❑ 145 Mark Gubicza .40 .12
❑ 146 Chris Sabo .40 .12
❑ 147 Ramon Martinez .40 .12
❑ 148 Tim Leary .40 .12
❑ 149 Randy Myers .60 .18
❑ 150 Jody Reed .40 .12
❑ 151 Bruce Ruffin .40 .12
❑ 152 Jeff Russell .40 .12
❑ 153 Doug Jones .40 .12
❑ 154 Tony Gwynn 2.00 .60
❑ 155 Mark Langston .40 .12
❑ 156 Mitch Williams .40 .12
❑ 157 Gary Sheffield 1.50 .45
❑ 158 Tom Henke .40 .12
❑ 159 Oil Can Boyd .40 .12
❑ 160 Rickey Henderson 1.50 .45
❑ 161 Bill Doran .40 .12
❑ 162 Chuck Finley .60 .18
❑ 163 Jeff King .40 .12
❑ 164 Nick Esasky .40 .12
❑ 165 Cecil Fielder .60 .18
❑ 166 Dave Valle .40 .12
❑ 167 Robin Ventura 1.50 .45
❑ 168 Jim Deshaies .40 .12
❑ 169 Juan Berenguer .40 .12
❑ 170 Craig Worthington .40 .12
❑ 171 Gregg Jefferies .60 .18
❑ 172 Will Clark 1.50 .45
❑ 173 Kirk Gibson .60 .18
❑ 174 Carlton Fisk CL .60 .18
❑ 175 Bobby Thigpen .40 .12
❑ 176 John Tudor .40 .12
❑ 177 Andre Dawson .60 .18
❑ 178 George Brett 4.00 1.20
❑ 179 Steve Buechele .40 .12
❑ 180 Joey Belle 1.50 .45
❑ 181 Eddie Murray 1.50 .45
❑ 182 Bob Geren .40 .12
❑ 183 Rob Murphy .40 .12
❑ 184 Tom Herr .40 .12
❑ 185 George Bell .40 .12
❑ 186 Spike Owen .40 .12
❑ 187 Cory Snyder .40 .12
❑ 188 Fred Lynn .40 .12
❑ 189 Eric Davis .60 .18
❑ 190 Dave Parker .60 .18
❑ 191 Jeff Blauser .40 .12
❑ 192 Matt Nokes .40 .12
❑ 193 Delino DeShields RC 1.00 .30
❑ 194 Scott Sanderson .40 .12
❑ 195 Lance Parrish .40 .12
❑ 196 Bobby Bonilla .60 .18
❑ 197 Cal Ripken UER 5.00 1.50
(Reistertown, should be Reisterstown)
❑ 198 Kevin McReynolds .40 .12
❑ 199 Robby Thompson .40 .12
❑ 200 Tim Belcher .40 .12
❑ 201 Jesse Barfield .40 .12
❑ 202 Mariano Duncan .40 .12
❑ 203 Bill Spiers .40 .12
❑ 204 Frank White .60 .18
❑ 205 Julio Franco .60 .18
❑ 206 Greg Swindell .40 .12
❑ 207 Benito Santiago .60 .18
❑ 208 Johnny Ray .40 .12
❑ 209 Gary Redus .40 .12
❑ 210 Jeff Parrett .40 .12
❑ 211 Jimmy Key .60 .18
❑ 212 Tim Raines .60 .18
❑ 213 Carney Lansford .60 .18
❑ 214 Gerald Young .40 .12
❑ 215 Gene Larkin .40 .12
❑ 216 Dan Plesac .40 .12
❑ 217 Lonnie Smith .40 .12
❑ 218 Alan Trammell .60 .18
❑ 219 Jeffrey Leonard .40 .12
❑ 220 Sammy Sosa RC 40.00 12.00
❑ 221 Todd Zeile .60 .18
❑ 222 Bill Landrum .40 .12
❑ 223 Mike Devereaux .40 .12
❑ 224 Mike Marshall .40 .12
❑ 225 Jose Uribe .40 .12
❑ 226 Juan Samuel .40 .12
❑ 227 Mel Hall .40 .12
❑ 228 Kent Hrbek .60 .18
❑ 229 Shawon Dunston .40 .12
❑ 230 Kevin Seitzer .40 .12
❑ 231 Pete Incaviglia .40 .12
❑ 232 Sandy Alomar Jr. .60 .18
❑ 233 Bip Roberts .40 .12
❑ 234 Scott Terry .40 .12
❑ 235 Dwight Evans .60 .18
❑ 236 Ricky Jordan .40 .12
❑ 237 John Olerud RC 3.00 .90
❑ 238 Zane Smith .40 .12
❑ 239 Walt Weiss .40 .12
❑ 240 Alvaro Espinoza .40 .12
❑ 241 Billy Hatcher .40 .12
❑ 242 Paul Molitor 1.00 .30
❑ 243 Dale Murphy 1.50 .45
❑ 244 Dave Bergman .40 .12
❑ 245 Ken Griffey Jr. 5.00 1.50
❑ 246 Ed Whitson .40 .12
❑ 247 Kirk McCaskill .40 .12
❑ 248 Jay Bell .60 .18
❑ 249 Ben McDonald RC 1.00 .30
❑ 250 Darryl Strawberry .60 .18
❑ 251 Brett Butler .60 .18
❑ 252 Terry Steinbach .40 .12
❑ 253 Ken Caminiti .60 .18
❑ 254 Dan Gladden .40 .12
❑ 255 Dwight Smith .40 .12
❑ 256 Kurt Stillwell .40 .12
❑ 257 Ruben Sierra .40 .12
❑ 258 Mike Schooler .40 .12
❑ 259 Lance Johnson .40 .12
❑ 260 Terry Pendleton .60 .18
❑ 261 Ellis Burks 1.00 .30
❑ 262 Len Dykstra .60 .18
❑ 263 Mookie Wilson .60 .18
❑ 264 Nolan Ryan CL UER 1.50 .45
No TM after Ranger logo
❑ 265 Nolan Ryan 2.50 .75
No Hit King
❑ 266 Brian DuBois .40 .12
❑ 267 Don Robinson .40 .12
❑ 268 Glenn Wilson .40 .12
❑ 269 Kevin Tapani RC 1.00 .30
❑ 270 Marvell Wynne .40 .12
❑ 271 Bill Ripken .40 .12
❑ 272 Howard Johnson .40 .12
❑ 273 Brian Holman .40 .12
❑ 274 Dan Pasqua .40 .12
❑ 275 Ken Dayley .40 .12
❑ 276 Jeff Reardon .60 .18
❑ 277 Jim Presley .40 .12
❑ 278 Jim Eisenreich .40 .12
❑ 279 Danny Jackson .40 .12
❑ 280 Orel Hershiser .60 .18
❑ 281 Andy Hawkins .40 .12
❑ 282 Jose Rijo .40 .12
❑ 283 Luis Rivera .40 .12
❑ 284 John Kruk .60 .18
❑ 285 Jeff Huson RC .40 .12
❑ 286 Joel Skinner .40 .12
❑ 287 Jack Clark .60 .18
❑ 288 Chili Davis .60 .18
❑ 289 Joe Girardi 1.00 .30
❑ 290 B.J. Surhoff .60 .18
❑ 291 Luis Sojo .40 .12
❑ 292 Tom Foley .40 .12
❑ 293 Mike Moore .40 .12
❑ 294 Ken Oberkfell .40 .12
❑ 295 Luis Polonia .40 .12
❑ 296 Doug Drabek .40 .12
❑ 297 Dave Justice RC 3.00 .90
❑ 298 Paul Gibson .40 .12
❑ 299 Edgar Martinez 1.00 .30
❑ 300 F.Thomas RC UER 20.00 6.00
No B in front of birthdate
❑ 301 Eric Yelding .40 .12
❑ 302 Greg Gagne .40 .12
❑ 303 Brad Komminsk .40 .12
❑ 304 Ron Darling .40 .12
❑ 305 Kevin Bass .40 .12
❑ 306 Jeff Hamilton .40 .12
❑ 307 Ron Karkovice .40 .12
❑ 308 Milt Thompson UER .60 .18
(Ray Lankford pictured on card back)
❑ 309 Mike Harkey .40 .12
❑ 310 Mel Stottlemyre Jr. .40 .12
❑ 311 Kenny Rogers .60 .18
❑ 312 Mitch Webster .40 .12
❑ 313 Kal Daniels .40 .12
❑ 314 Matt Nokes .40 .12
❑ 315 Dennis Lamp .40 .12
❑ 316 Ken Howell .40 .12
❑ 317 Glenallen Hill .40 .12
❑ 318 Dave Martinez .40 .12
❑ 319 Chris James .40 .12
❑ 320 Mike Pagliarulo .40 .12
❑ 321 Hal Morris .40 .12
❑ 322 Rob Deer .40 .12
❑ 323 Greg Olson .40 .12
❑ 324 Tony Phillips .40 .12
❑ 325 Larry Walker RC 8.00 2.40
❑ 326 Ron Hassey .40 .12
❑ 327 Jack Howell .40 .12
❑ 328 John Smiley .40 .12
❑ 329 Steve Finley .60 .18
❑ 330 Dave Magadan .40 .12
❑ 331 Greg Litton .40 .12
❑ 332 Mickey Hatcher .40 .12
❑ 333 Lee Guetterman .40 .12
❑ 334 Norm Charlton .40 .12
❑ 335 Edgar Diaz .40 .12
❑ 336 Willie Wilson .40 .12
❑ 337 Bobby Witt .40 .12
❑ 338 Candy Maldonado .40 .12
❑ 339 Craig Lefferts .40 .12
❑ 340 Dante Bichette 1.50 .45
❑ 341 Wally Backman .40 .12
❑ 342 Dennis Cook .40 .12
❑ 343 Pat Borders .40 .12
❑ 344 Wallace Johnson .40 .12
❑ 345 Willie Randolph .60 .18
❑ 346 Danny Darwin .40 .12
❑ 347 Al Newman .40 .12
❑ 348 Mark Knudson .40 .12
❑ 349 Joe Boever .40 .12
❑ 350 Larry Sheets .40 .12
❑ 351 Mike Jackson .40 .12
❑ 352 Wayne Edwards .40 .12
❑ 353 Bernard Gilkey RC 1.00 .30
❑ 354 Don Slaught .40 .12
❑ 355 Joe Orsulak .40 .12
❑ 356 John Franco .60 .18
❑ 357 Jeff Brantley .40 .12
❑ 358 Mike Morgan .40 .12
❑ 359 Deion Sanders 1.50 .45
❑ 360 Terry Leach .40 .12
❑ 361 Les Lancaster .40 .12
❑ 362 Storm Davis .40 .12
❑ 363 Scott Coolbaugh .40 .12
❑ 364 Ozzie Smith CL 1.00 .30
❑ 365 Cecilio Guante .40 .12
❑ 366 Joey Cora .60 .18
❑ 367 Willie McGee .60 .18
❑ 368 Jerry Reed .40 .12
❑ 369 Darren Daulton .60 .18
❑ 370 Manny Lee .40 .12
❑ 371 Mark Gardner .40 .12
❑ 372 Rick Honeycutt .40 .12
❑ 373 Steve Balboni .40 .12
❑ 374 Jack Armstrong .40 .12
❑ 375 Charlie O'Brien .40 .12
❑ 376 Ron Gant .60 .18

❑ 377 Lloyd Moseby	.40	.12
❑ 378 Gene Harris	.40	.12
❑ 379 Joe Carter	.60	.18
❑ 380 Scott Bailes	.40	.12
❑ 381 R.J. Reynolds	.40	.12
❑ 382 Bob Melvin	.40	.12
❑ 383 Tim Teufel	.40	.12
❑ 384 John Burkett	.40	.12
❑ 385 Felix Jose	.40	.12
❑ 386 Larry Andersen	.40	.12
❑ 387 David West	.40	.12
❑ 388 Luis Salazar	.40	.12
❑ 389 Mike Macfarlane	.40	.12
❑ 390 Charlie Hough	.60	.18
❑ 391 Greg Briley	.40	.12
❑ 392 Donn Pall	.40	.12
❑ 393 Bryn Smith	.40	.12
❑ 394 Carlos Quintana	.40	.12
❑ 395 Steve Lake	.40	.12
❑ 396 Mark Whiten RC	1.00	.30
❑ 397 Edwin Nunez	.40	.12
❑ 398 Rick Parker	.40	.12
❑ 399 Mark Portugal	.40	.12
❑ 400 Roy Smith	.40	.12
❑ 401 Hector Villanueva	.40	.12
❑ 402 Bob Milacki	.40	.12
❑ 403 Alejandro Pena	.40	.12
❑ 404 Scott Bradley	.40	.12
❑ 405 Ron Kittle	.40	.12
❑ 406 Bob Tewksbury	.40	.12
❑ 407 Wes Gardner	.40	.12
❑ 408 Ernie Whitt	.40	.12
❑ 409 Terry Shumpert	.40	.12
❑ 410 Tim Layana	.40	.12
❑ 411 Chris Gwynn	.40	.12
❑ 412 Jeff D. Robinson	.40	.12
❑ 413 Scott Scudder	.40	.12
❑ 414 Kevin Romine	.40	.12
❑ 415 Jose DeJesus	.40	.12
❑ 416 Mike Jeffcoat	.40	.12
❑ 417 Rudy Seanez	.40	.12
❑ 418 Mike Dunne	.40	.12
❑ 419 Dick Schofield	.40	.12
❑ 420 Steve Wilson	.40	.12
❑ 421 Bill Krueger	.40	.12
❑ 422 Junior Felix	.40	.12
❑ 423 Drew Hall	.40	.12
❑ 424 Curt Young	.40	.12
❑ 425 Franklin Stubbs	.40	.12
❑ 426 Dave Winfield	.60	.18
❑ 427 Rick Reed RC	1.00	.30
❑ 428 Charlie Leibrandt	.40	.12
❑ 429 Jeff M. Robinson	.40	.12
❑ 430 Erik Hanson	.40	.12
❑ 431 Barry Jones	.40	.12
❑ 432 Alex Trevino	.40	.12
❑ 433 John Moses	.40	.12
❑ 434 Dave Johnson	.40	.12
❑ 435 Mackey Sasser	.40	.12
❑ 436 Rick Leach	.40	.12
❑ 437 Lenny Harris	.40	.12
❑ 438 Carlos Martinez	.40	.12
❑ 439 Rex Hudler	.40	.12
❑ 440 Domingo Ramos	.40	.12
❑ 441 Gerald Perry	.40	.12
❑ 442 Jeff Russell	.40	.12
❑ 443 Carlos Baerga RC	1.00	.30
❑ 444 Will Clark CL	.60	.18
❑ 445 Stan Javier	.40	.12
❑ 446 Kevin Maas RC	1.00	.30
❑ 447 Tom Brunansky	.40	.12
❑ 448 Carmelo Martinez	.40	.12
❑ 449 Willie Blair RC	.40	.12
❑ 450 Andres Galarraga	.60	.18
❑ 451 Bud Black	.40	.12
❑ 452 Greg W. Harris	.40	.12
❑ 453 Joe Oliver	.40	.12
❑ 454 Greg Brock	.40	.12
❑ 455 Jeff Treadway	.40	.12
❑ 456 Lance McCullers	.40	.12
❑ 457 Dave Schmidt	.40	.12
❑ 458 Todd Burns	.40	.12
❑ 459 Max Venable	.40	.12
❑ 460 Neal Heaton	.40	.12
❑ 461 Mark Williamson	.40	.12
❑ 462 Keith Miller	.40	.12
❑ 463 Mike LaCoss	.40	.12
❑ 464 Jose Offerman RC	1.00	.30
❑ 465 Jim Leyritz RC	1.00	.30
❑ 466 Glenn Braggs	.40	.12
❑ 467 Ron Robinson	.40	.12
❑ 468 Mark Davis	.40	.12
❑ 469 Gary Pettis	.40	.12
❑ 470 Keith Hernandez	.60	.18
❑ 471 Dennis Rasmussen	.40	.12
❑ 472 Mark Eichhorn	.40	.12
❑ 473 Ted Power	.40	.12
❑ 474 Terry Mulholland	.40	.12
❑ 475 Todd Stottlemyre	.60	.18
❑ 476 Jerry Goff	.40	.12
❑ 477 Gene Nelson	.40	.12
❑ 478 Rich Gedman	.40	.12
❑ 479 Brian Harper	.40	.12
❑ 480 Mike Felder	.40	.12
❑ 481 Steve Avery	.40	.12
❑ 482 Jack Morris	.60	.18
❑ 483 Randy Johnson	3.00	.75
❑ 484 Scott Radinsky RC	.40	.12
❑ 485 Jose DeLeon	.40	.12
❑ 486 Stan Belinda RC	.40	.12
❑ 487 Brian Holton	.40	.12
❑ 488 Mark Carreon	.40	.12
❑ 489 Trevor Wilson	.40	.12
❑ 490 Mike Sharperson	.40	.12
❑ 491 Alan Mills RC	.40	.12
❑ 492 John Candelaria	.40	.12
❑ 493 Paul Assenmacher	.40	.12
❑ 494 Steve Crawford	.40	.12
❑ 495 Brad Arnsberg	.40	.12
❑ 496 Sergio Valdez	.40	.12
❑ 497 Mark Parent	.40	.12
❑ 498 Tom Pagnozzi	.40	.12
❑ 499 Greg A. Harris	.40	.12
❑ 500 Randy Ready	.40	.12
❑ 501 Duane Ward	.40	.12
❑ 502 Nelson Santovenia	.40	.12
❑ 503 Joe Klink	.40	.12
❑ 504 Eric Plunk	.40	.12
❑ 505 Jeff Reed	.40	.12
❑ 506 Ted Higuera	.40	.12
❑ 507 Joe Hesketh	.40	.12
❑ 508 Dan Petry	.40	.12
❑ 509 Matt Young	.40	.12
❑ 510 Jerald Clark	.40	.12
❑ 511 John Orton	.40	.12
❑ 512 Scott Ruskin	.40	.12
❑ 513 Chris Hoiles RC	1.00	.30
❑ 514 Daryl Boston	.40	.12
❑ 515 Francisco Oliveras	.40	.12
❑ 516 Ozzie Canseco	.40	.12
❑ 517 Xavier Hernandez RC	.40	.12
❑ 518 Fred Manrique	.40	.12
❑ 519 Shawn Boskie RC	.40	.12
❑ 520 Jeff Montgomery	.60	.18
❑ 521 Jack Daugherty	.40	.12
❑ 522 Keith Comstock	.40	.12
❑ 523 Greg Hibbard RC	.40	.12
❑ 524 Lee Smith	.60	.18
❑ 525 Dana Kiecker	.40	.12
❑ 526 Darrel Akerfelds	.40	.12
❑ 527 Greg Myers	.40	.12
❑ 528 Ryne Sandberg CL	1.50	.45

1993 Leaf

	Nm-Mt	Ex-Mt
COMPLETE SET (550)	35.00	10.50
COMP. SERIES 1 (220)	15.00	4.50
COMP. SERIES 2 (220)	15.00	4.50
COMPLETE UPDATE (110)	5.00	1.50
❑ 1 Ben McDonald	.15	.04
❑ 2 Sid Fernandez	.15	.04
❑ 3 Juan Guzman	.15	.04
❑ 4 Curt Schilling	.30	.09
❑ 5 Ivan Rodriguez	.75	.23
❑ 6 Don Slaught	.15	.04
❑ 7 Terry Steinbach	.15	.04
❑ 8 Todd Zeile	.15	.04
❑ 9 Andy Stankiewicz	.15	.04
❑ 10 Tim Teufel	.15	.04
❑ 11 Marvin Freeman	.15	.04
❑ 12 Jim Austin	.15	.04
❑ 13 Bob Scanlan	.15	.04
❑ 14 Rusty Meacham	.15	.04
❑ 15 Casey Candaele	.15	.04
❑ 16 Travis Fryman	.30	.09
❑ 17 Jose Offerman	.15	.04
❑ 18 Albert Belle	.30	.09
❑ 19 John Vander Wal	.15	.04
❑ 20 Dan Pasqua	.15	.04
❑ 21 Frank Viola	.30	.09
❑ 22 Terry Mulholland	.15	.04
❑ 23 Gregg Olson	.15	.04
❑ 24 Randy Tomlin	.15	.04
❑ 25 Todd Stottlemyre	.15	.04
❑ 26 Jose Oquendo	.15	.04
❑ 27 Julio Franco	.30	.09
❑ 28 Tony Gwynn	1.00	.30
❑ 29 Ruben Sierra	.15	.04
❑ 30 Robby Thompson	.15	.04
❑ 31 Jim Bullinger	.15	.04
❑ 32 Rick Aguilera	.15	.04
❑ 33 Scott Servais	.15	.04
❑ 34 Cal Eldred	.15	.04
❑ 35 Mike Piazza	2.00	.60
❑ 36 Brent Mayne	.15	.04
❑ 37 Wil Cordero	.15	.04
❑ 38 Milt Cuyler	.15	.04
❑ 39 Howard Johnson	.15	.04
❑ 40 Kenny Lofton	.30	.09
❑ 41 Alex Fernandez	.15	.04
❑ 42 Denny Neagle	.30	.09
❑ 43 Tony Pena	.15	.04
❑ 44 Bob Tewksbury	.15	.04
❑ 45 Glenn Davis	.15	.04
❑ 46 Fred McGriff	.50	.15
❑ 47 John Olerud	.30	.09
❑ 48 Steve Hosey	.15	.04
❑ 49 Rafael Palmeiro	.50	.15
❑ 50 David Justice	.30	.09
❑ 51 Pete Harnisch	.15	.04
❑ 52 Sam Militello	.15	.04
❑ 53 Orel Hershiser	.30	.09
❑ 54 Pat Mahomes	.15	.04
❑ 55 Greg Colbrunn	.15	.04
❑ 56 Greg Vaughn	.15	.04
❑ 57 Vince Coleman	.15	.04
❑ 58 Brian McRae	.15	.04
❑ 59 Len Dykstra	.30	.09
❑ 60 Dan Gladden	.15	.04
❑ 61 Ted Power	.15	.04
❑ 62 Donovan Osborne	.15	.04
❑ 63 Ron Karkovice	.15	.04
❑ 64 Frank Seminara	.15	.04
❑ 65 Bob Zupcic	.15	.04
❑ 66 Kirt Manwaring	.15	.04
❑ 67 Mike Devereaux	.15	.04
❑ 68 Mark Lemke	.15	.04
❑ 69 Devon White	.30	.09
❑ 70 Sammy Sosa	1.25	.35
❑ 71 Pedro Astacio	.15	.04
❑ 72 Dennis Eckersley	.30	.09
❑ 73 Chris Nabholz	.15	.04
❑ 74 Melido Perez	.15	.04
❑ 75 Todd Hundley	.15	.04
❑ 76 Kent Hrbek	.30	.09
❑ 77 Mickey Morandini	.15	.04
❑ 78 Tim McIntosh	.15	.04
❑ 79 Andy Van Slyke	.30	.09
❑ 80 Kevin McReynolds	.15	.04

❑ 81 Mike Henneman .15 .04
❑ 82 Greg W. Harris .15 .04
❑ 83 Sandy Alomar Jr. .15 .04
❑ 84 Mike Jackson .15 .04
❑ 85 Ozzie Guillen .15 .04
❑ 86 Jeff Blauser .15 .04
❑ 87 John Valentin .15 .04
❑ 88 Rey Sanchez .15 .04
❑ 89 Rick Sutcliffe .30 .09
❑ 90 Luis Gonzalez .30 .09
❑ 91 Jeff Fassero .15 .04
❑ 92 Kenny Rogers .30 .09
❑ 93 Bret Saberhagen .30 .09
❑ 94 Bob Welch .15 .04
❑ 95 Darren Daulton .30 .09
❑ 96 Mike Gallego .15 .04
❑ 97 Orlando Merced .15 .04
❑ 98 Chuck Knoblauch .30 .09
❑ 99 Bernard Gilkey .15 .04
❑ 100 Billy Ashley .15 .04
❑ 101 Kevin Appier .30 .09
❑ 102 Jeff Brantley .15 .04
❑ 103 Bill Gullickson .15 .04
❑ 104 John Smoltz .50 .15
❑ 105 Paul Sorrento .15 .04
❑ 106 Steve Buechele .15 .04
❑ 107 Steve Sax .15 .04
❑ 108 Andujar Cedeno .15 .04
❑ 109 Billy Hatcher .15 .04
❑ 110 Checklist .15 .04
❑ 111 Alan Mills .15 .04
❑ 112 John Franco .30 .09
❑ 113 Jack Morris .30 .09
❑ 114 Mitch Williams .15 .04
❑ 115 Nolan Ryan 3.00 .90
❑ 116 Jay Bell .30 .09
❑ 117 Mike Bordick .15 .04
❑ 118 Geronimo Pena .15 .04
❑ 119 Danny Tartabull .15 .04
❑ 120 Checklist .15 .04
❑ 121 Steve Avery .15 .04
❑ 122 Ricky Bones .15 .04
❑ 123 Mike Morgan .15 .04
❑ 124 Jeff Montgomery .15 .04
❑ 125 Jeff Bagwell .50 .15
❑ 126 Tony Phillips .15 .04
❑ 127 Lenny Harris .15 .04
❑ 128 Glenallen Hill .15 .04
❑ 129 Marquis Grissom .30 .09
❑ 130 Gerald Williams UER .15 .04
(Bernie Williams
picture and stats)
❑ 131 Greg A. Harris .15 .04
❑ 132 Tommy Greene .15 .04
❑ 133 Chris Hoiles .15 .04
❑ 134 Bob Walk .15 .04
❑ 135 Duane Ward .15 .04
❑ 136 Tom Pagnozzi .15 .04
❑ 137 Jeff Huson .15 .04
❑ 138 Kurt Stillwell .15 .04
❑ 139 Dave Henderson .15 .04
❑ 140 Darrin Jackson .15 .04
❑ 141 Frank Castillo .15 .04
❑ 142 Scott Erickson .15 .04
❑ 143 Darryl Kile .30 .09
❑ 144 Bill Wegman .15 .04
❑ 145 Steve Wilson .15 .04
❑ 146 George Brett 2.00 .60
❑ 147 Moises Alou .30 .09
❑ 148 Lou Whitaker .30 .09
❑ 149 Chico Walker .15 .04
❑ 150 Jerry Browne .15 .04
❑ 151 Kirk McCaskill .15 .04
❑ 152 Zane Smith .15 .04
❑ 153 Matt Young .15 .04
❑ 154 Lee Smith .30 .09
❑ 155 Leo Gomez .15 .04
❑ 156 Dan Walters .15 .04
❑ 157 Pat Borders .15 .04
❑ 158 Matt Williams .30 .09
❑ 159 Dean Palmer .30 .09
❑ 160 John Patterson .15 .04
❑ 161 Doug Jones .15 .04
❑ 162 John Habyan .15 .04
❑ 163 Pedro Martinez 1.50 .45
❑ 164 Carl Willis .15 .04
❑ 165 Darrin Fletcher .15 .04
❑ 166 B.J. Surhoff .30 .09
❑ 167 Eddie Murray .75 .23
❑ 168 Keith Miller .15 .04
❑ 169 Ricky Jordan .15 .04
❑ 170 Juan Gonzalez .50 .15
❑ 171 Charles Nagy .15 .04
❑ 172 Mark Clark .15 .04
❑ 173 Bobby Thigpen .15 .04
❑ 174 Tim Scott .15 .04
❑ 175 Scott Cooper .15 .04
❑ 176 Royce Clayton .15 .04
❑ 177 Brady Anderson .30 .09
❑ 178 Sid Bream .15 .04
❑ 179 Derek Bell .15 .04
❑ 180 Otis Nixon .15 .04
❑ 181 Kevin Gross .15 .04
❑ 182 Ron Darling .15 .04
❑ 183 John Wetteland .30 .09
❑ 184 Mike Stanley .15 .04
❑ 185 Jeff Kent .75 .23
❑ 186 Brian Harper .15 .04
❑ 187 Mariano Duncan .15 .04
❑ 188 Robin Yount 1.25 .35
❑ 189 Al Martin .15 .04
❑ 190 Eddie Zosky .15 .04
❑ 191 Mike Munoz .15 .04
❑ 192 Andy Benes .15 .04
❑ 193 Dennis Cook .15 .04
❑ 194 Bill Swift .15 .04
❑ 195 Frank Thomas .75 .23
❑ 195A Frank Thomas 1.25 .35
Franklin visible on batting glove
❑ 196 Damon Berryhill .15 .04
❑ 197 Mike Greenwell .15 .04
❑ 198 Mark Grace .50 .15
❑ 199 Darryl Hamilton .15 .04
❑ 200 Derrick May .15 .04
❑ 201 Ken Hill .15 .04
❑ 202 Kevin Brown .30 .09
❑ 203 Dwight Gooden .30 .09
❑ 204 Bobby Witt .15 .04
❑ 205 Juan Bell .15 .04
❑ 206 Kevin Maas .15 .04
❑ 207 Jeff King .15 .04
❑ 208 Scott Leius .15 .04
❑ 209 Rheal Cormier .15 .04
❑ 210 Darryl Strawberry .30 .09
❑ 211 Tom Gordon .15 .04
❑ 212 Bud Black .15 .04
❑ 213 Mickey Tettleton .15 .04
❑ 214 Pete Smith .15 .04
❑ 215 Felix Fermin .15 .04
❑ 216 Rick Wilkins .15 .04
❑ 217 George Bell .15 .04
❑ 218 Eric Anthony .15 .04
❑ 219 Pedro Munoz .15 .04
❑ 220 Checklist .15 .04
❑ 221 Lance Blankenship .15 .04
❑ 222 Deion Sanders .50 .15
❑ 223 Craig Biggio .50 .15
❑ 224 Ryne Sandberg 1.25 .35
❑ 225 Ron Gant .30 .09
❑ 226 Tom Brunansky .15 .04
❑ 227 Chad Curtis .15 .04
❑ 228 Joe Carter .30 .09
❑ 229 Brian Jordan .30 .09
❑ 230 Brett Butler .30 .09
❑ 231 Frank Bolick .15 .04
❑ 232 Rod Beck .15 .04
❑ 233 Carlos Baerga .15 .04
❑ 234 Eric Karros .30 .09
❑ 235 Jack Armstrong .15 .04
❑ 236 Bobby Bonilla .30 .09
❑ 237 Don Mattingly 2.00 .60
❑ 238 Jeff Gardner .15 .04
❑ 239 Dave Hollins .15 .04
❑ 240 Steve Cooke .15 .04
❑ 241 Jose Canseco .75 .23
❑ 242 Ivan Calderon .15 .04
❑ 243 Tim Belcher .15 .04
❑ 244 Freddie Benavides .15 .04
❑ 245 Roberto Alomar .50 .15
❑ 246 Rob Deer .15 .04
❑ 247 Will Clark .75 .23
❑ 248 Mike Felder .15 .04
❑ 249 Harold Baines .30 .09
❑ 250 David Cone .30 .09
❑ 251 Mark Guthrie .15 .04
❑ 252 Ellis Burks .30 .09
❑ 253 Jim Abbott .50 .15
❑ 254 Chili Davis .30 .09
❑ 255 Chris Bosio .15 .04
❑ 256 Bret Barberie .15 .04
❑ 257 Hal Morris .15 .04
❑ 258 Dante Bichette .30 .09
❑ 259 Storm Davis .15 .04
❑ 260 Gary DiSarcina .15 .04
❑ 261 Ken Caminiti .30 .09
❑ 262 Paul Molitor .50 .15
❑ 263 Joe Oliver .15 .04
❑ 264 Pat Listach .15 .04
❑ 265 Gregg Jefferies .15 .04
❑ 266 Jose Guzman .15 .04
❑ 267 Eric Davis .30 .09
❑ 268 Delino DeShields .15 .04
❑ 269 Barry Bonds 2.00 .60
❑ 270 Mike Bielecki .15 .04
❑ 271 Jay Buhner .30 .09
❑ 272 Scott Pose RC .15 .04
❑ 273 Tony Fernandez .15 .04
❑ 274 Chito Martinez .15 .04
❑ 275 Phil Plantier .15 .04
❑ 276 Pete Incaviglia .15 .04
❑ 277 Carlos Garcia .15 .04
❑ 278 Tom Henke .15 .04
❑ 279 Roger Clemens 1.50 .45
❑ 280 Rob Dibble .30 .09
❑ 281 Daryl Boston .15 .04
❑ 282 Greg Gagne .15 .04
❑ 283 Cecil Fielder .30 .09
❑ 284 Carlton Fisk .50 .15
❑ 285 Wade Boggs .50 .15
❑ 286 Damion Easley .15 .04
❑ 287 Norm Charlton .15 .04
❑ 288 Jeff Conine .30 .09
❑ 289 Roberto Kelly .15 .04
❑ 290 Jerald Clark .15 .04
❑ 291 Rickey Henderson .75 .23
❑ 292 Chuck Finley .30 .09
❑ 293 Doug Drabek .15 .04
❑ 294 Dave Stewart .30 .09
❑ 295 Tom Glavine .50 .15
❑ 296 Jaime Navarro .15 .04
❑ 297 Ray Lankford .15 .04
❑ 298 Greg Hibbard .15 .04
❑ 299 Jody Reed .15 .04
❑ 300 Dennis Martinez .30 .09
❑ 301 Dave Martinez .15 .04
❑ 302 Reggie Jefferson .15 .04
❑ 303 John Cummings RC .15 .04
❑ 304 Orestes Destrade .15 .04
❑ 305 Mike Maddux .15 .04
❑ 306 David Segui .15 .04
❑ 307 Gary Sheffield .30 .09
❑ 308 Danny Jackson .15 .04
❑ 309 Craig Lefferts .15 .04
❑ 310 Andre Dawson .30 .09
❑ 311 Barry Larkin .50 .15
❑ 312 Alex Cole .15 .04
❑ 313 Mark Gardner .15 .04
❑ 314 Kirk Gibson .30 .09
❑ 315 Shane Mack .15 .04
❑ 316 Bo Jackson .75 .23
❑ 317 Jimmy Key .30 .09
❑ 318 Greg Myers .15 .04
❑ 319 Ken Griffey Jr. 1.25 .35
❑ 320 Monty Fariss .15 .04
❑ 321 Kevin Mitchell .15 .04
❑ 322 Andres Galarraga .30 .09
❑ 323 Mark McGwire 2.00 .60
❑ 324 Mark Langston .15 .04
❑ 325 Steve Finley .30 .09
❑ 326 Greg Maddux 1.25 .35
❑ 327 Dave Nilsson .15 .04
❑ 328 Ozzie Smith 1.25 .35
❑ 329 Candy Maldonado .15 .04
❑ 330 Checklist .15 .04
❑ 331 Tim Pugh RC .15 .04
❑ 332 Joe Girardi .15 .04
❑ 333 Junior Felix .15 .04
❑ 334 Greg Swindell .15 .04

❑ 335 Ramon Martinez .15 .04
❑ 336 Sean Berry .15 .04
❑ 337 Joe Orsulak .15 .04
❑ 338 Wes Chamberlain .15 .04
❑ 339 Stan Belinda .15 .04
❑ 340 Checklist UER .15 .04
(306 Luis Mercedes)
❑ 341 Bruce Hurst .15 .04
❑ 342 John Burkett .15 .04
❑ 343 Mike Mussina .50 .15
❑ 344 Scott Fletcher .15 .04
❑ 345 Rene Gonzales .15 .04
❑ 346 Roberto Hernandez .15 .04
❑ 347 Carlos Martinez .15 .04
❑ 348 Bill Krueger .15 .04
❑ 349 Felix Jose .15 .04
❑ 350 John Jaha .15 .04
❑ 351 Willie Banks .15 .04
❑ 352 Matt Nokes .15 .04
❑ 353 Kevin Seitzer .15 .04
❑ 354 Erik Hanson .15 .04
❑ 355 David Hulse RC .15 .04
❑ 356 Domingo Martinez RC .15 .04
❑ 357 Greg Olson .15 .04
❑ 358 Randy Myers .15 .04
❑ 359 Tom Browning .15 .04
❑ 360 Charlie Hayes .15 .04
❑ 361 Bryan Harvey .15 .04
❑ 362 Eddie Taubensee .15 .04
❑ 363 Tim Wallach .15 .04
❑ 364 Mel Rojas .15 .04
❑ 365 Frank Tanana .15 .04
❑ 366 John Kruk .30 .09
❑ 367 Tim Laker RC .15 .04
❑ 368 Rich Rodriguez .15 .04
❑ 369 Darren Lewis .15 .04
❑ 370 Harold Reynolds .30 .09
❑ 371 Jose Melendez .15 .04
❑ 372 Joe Grahe .15 .04
❑ 373 Lance Johnson .15 .04
❑ 374 Jose Mesa .15 .04
❑ 375 Scott Livingstone .15 .04
❑ 376 Wally Joyner .30 .09
❑ 377 Kevin Reimer .15 .04
❑ 378 Kirby Puckett .75 .23
❑ 379 Paul O'Neill .50 .15
❑ 380 Randy Johnson .75 .23
❑ 381 Manuel Lee .15 .04
❑ 382 Dick Schofield .15 .04
❑ 383 Darren Holmes .15 .04
❑ 384 Charlie Hough .30 .09
❑ 385 John Orton .15 .04
❑ 386 Edgar Martinez .50 .15
❑ 387 Terry Pendleton .30 .09
❑ 388 Dan Plesac .15 .04
❑ 389 Jeff Reardon .30 .09
❑ 390 David Nied .15 .04
❑ 391 Dave Magadan .15 .04
❑ 392 Larry Walker .50 .15
❑ 393 Ben Rivera .15 .04
❑ 394 Lonnie Smith .15 .04
❑ 395 Craig Shipley .15 .04
❑ 396 Willie McGee .30 .09
❑ 397 Arthur Rhodes .15 .04
❑ 398 Mike Stanton .15 .04
❑ 399 Luis Polonia .15 .04
❑ 400 Jack McDowell .15 .04
❑ 401 Mike Moore .15 .04
❑ 402 Jose Lind .15 .04
❑ 403 Bill Spiers .15 .04
❑ 404 Kevin Tapani .15 .04
❑ 405 Spike Owen .15 .04
❑ 406 Tino Martinez .50 .15
❑ 407 Charlie Leibrandt .15 .04
❑ 408 Ed Sprague .15 .04
❑ 409 Bryn Smith .15 .04
❑ 410 Benito Santiago .30 .09
❑ 411 Jose Rijo .15 .04
❑ 412 Pete O'Brien .15 .04
❑ 413 Willie Wilson .15 .04
❑ 414 Bip Roberts .15 .04
❑ 415 Eric Young .15 .04
❑ 416 Walt Weiss .15 .04
❑ 417 Milt Thompson .15 .04
❑ 418 Chris Sabo .15 .04
❑ 419 Scott Sanderson .15 .04
❑ 420 Tim Raines .30 .09
❑ 421 Alan Trammell .30 .09
❑ 422 Mike Macfarlane .15 .04
❑ 423 Dave Winfield .30 .09
❑ 424 Bob Wickman .15 .04
❑ 425 David Valle .15 .04
❑ 426 Gary Redus .15 .04
❑ 427 Turner Ward .15 .04
❑ 428 Reggie Sanders .15 .04
❑ 429 Todd Worrell .15 .04
❑ 430 Julio Valera .15 .04
❑ 431 Cal Ripken Jr. 2.50 .75
❑ 432 Mo Vaughn .30 .09
❑ 433 John Smiley .15 .04
❑ 434 Omar Vizquel .50 .15
❑ 435 Billy Ripken .15 .04
❑ 436 Cory Snyder .15 .04
❑ 437 Carlos Quintana .15 .04
❑ 438 Omar Olivares .15 .04
❑ 439 Robin Ventura .30 .09
❑ 440 Checklist .15 .04
❑ 441 Kevin Higgins .15 .04
❑ 442 Carlos Hernandez .15 .04
❑ 443 Dan Peltier .15 .04
❑ 444 Derek Lilliquist .15 .04
❑ 445 Tim Salmon .50 .15
❑ 446 Sherman Obando RC .15 .04
❑ 447 Pat Kelly .15 .04
❑ 448 Todd Van Poppel .15 .04
❑ 449 Mark Whiten .15 .04
❑ 450 Checklist .15 .04
❑ 451 Pat Meares RC .30 .09
❑ 452 Tony Tarasco RC .15 .04
❑ 453 Chris Gwynn .15 .04
❑ 454 Armando Reynoso .15 .04
❑ 455 Danny Darwin .15 .04
❑ 456 Willie Greene .15 .04
❑ 457 Mike Blowers .15 .04
❑ 458 Kevin Roberson RC .15 .04
❑ 459 Graeme Lloyd RC .30 .09
❑ 460 David West .15 .04
❑ 461 Joey Cora .15 .04
❑ 462 Alex Arias .15 .04
❑ 463 Chad Kreuter .15 .04
❑ 464 Mike Lansing RC .30 .09
❑ 465 Mike Timlin .15 .04
❑ 466 Paul Wagner .15 .04
❑ 467 Mark Portugal .15 .04
❑ 468 Jim Leyritz .15 .04
❑ 469 Ryan Klesko .30 .09
❑ 470 Mario Diaz .15 .04
❑ 471 Guillermo Velasquez .15 .04
❑ 472 Fernando Valenzuela .30 .09
❑ 473 Raul Mondesi .30 .09
❑ 474 Mike Pagliarulo .15 .04
❑ 475 Chris Hammond .15 .04
❑ 476 Torey Lovullo .15 .04
❑ 477 Trevor Wilson .15 .04
❑ 478 Marcos Armas RC .15 .04
❑ 479 Dave Gallagher .15 .04
❑ 480 Jeff Treadway .15 .04
❑ 481 Jeff Branson .15 .04
❑ 482 Dickie Thon .15 .04
❑ 483 Eduardo Perez .15 .04
❑ 484 David Wells .30 .09
❑ 485 Brian Williams .15 .04
❑ 486 Domingo Cedeno RC .15 .04
❑ 487 Tom Candiotti .15 .04
❑ 488 Steve Frey .15 .04
❑ 489 Greg McMichael RC .15 .04
❑ 490 Marc Newfield .15 .04
❑ 491 Larry Andersen .15 .04
❑ 492 Damon Buford .15 .04
❑ 493 Ricky Gutierrez .15 .04
❑ 494 Jeff Russell .15 .04
❑ 495 Vinny Castilla .30 .09
❑ 496 Wilson Alvarez .15 .04
❑ 497 Scott Bullett .15 .04
❑ 498 Larry Casian .15 .04
❑ 499 Jose Vizcaino .15 .04
❑ 500 J.T. Snow RC .50 .15
❑ 501 Bryan Hickerson .15 .04
❑ 502 Jeremy Hernandez .15 .04
❑ 503 Jeromy Burnitz .30 .09
❑ 504 Steve Farr .15 .04
❑ 505 J. Owens RC .15 .04
❑ 506 Craig Paquette .15 .04
❑ 507 Jim Eisenreich .15 .04
❑ 508 Matt Whiteside RC .15 .04
❑ 509 Luis Aquino .15 .04
❑ 510 Mike LaValliere .15 .04
❑ 511 Jim Gott .15 .04
❑ 512 Mark McLemore .15 .04
❑ 513 Randy Milligan .15 .04
❑ 514 Gary Gaetti .30 .09
❑ 515 Lou Frazier RC .15 .04
❑ 516 Rich Amaral .15 .04
❑ 517 Gene Harris .15 .04
❑ 518 Aaron Sele .15 .04
❑ 519 Mark Wohlers .15 .04
❑ 520 Scott Kamieniecki .15 .04
❑ 521 Kent Mercker .15 .04
❑ 522 Jim Deshaies .15 .04
❑ 523 Kevin Stocker .15 .04
❑ 524 Jason Bere .15 .04
❑ 525 Tim Bogar RC .15 .04
❑ 526 Brad Pennington .15 .04
❑ 527 Curt Leskanic RC .15 .04
❑ 528 Wayne Kirby .15 .04
❑ 529 Tim Costo .15 .04
❑ 530 Doug Henry .15 .04
❑ 531 Trevor Hoffman .30 .09
❑ 532 Kelly Gruber .15 .04
❑ 533 Mike Harkey .15 .04
❑ 534 John Doherty .15 .04
❑ 535 Erik Pappas .15 .04
❑ 536 Brent Gates .15 .04
❑ 537 Roger McDowell .15 .04
❑ 538 Chris Haney .15 .04
❑ 539 Blas Minor .15 .04
❑ 540 Pat Hentgen .15 .04
❑ 541 Chuck Carr .15 .04
❑ 542 Doug Strange .15 .04
❑ 543 Xavier Hernandez .15 .04
❑ 544 Paul Quantrill .15 .04
❑ 545 Anthony Young .15 .04
❑ 546 Bret Boone .50 .15
❑ 547 Dwight Smith .15 .04
❑ 548 Bobby Munoz .15 .04
❑ 549 Russ Springer .15 .04
❑ 550 Roger Pavlik .15 .04
❑ DW Dave Winfield 1.00 .30
3000 Hits
❑ FT Frank Thomas AU/3500 50.00 15.00
(Certified autograph)

2004 Leaf Certified Cuts

	Nm-Mt	Ex-Mt
COMP.SET w/o SP's (200)	50.00	15.00
COMMON CARD (1-200)	.75	.23
COMMON CARD (201-221)	3.00	.90
COMMON CARD (222-250)	3.00	.90
201-250 RANDOM INSERTS IN PACKS		
201-250 PRNT RUN 599 SERIAL #'d SETS		
COMMON CARD (251-300)	5.00	1.50
251-300 RANDOM INSERTS IN PACKS		
251-300 PRINT RUN 499 SERIAL #'d SETS		
OVERALL AU ODDS THREE PER BOX		
AUTO PRINT RUNS B/WN 99-499 #'d PER		
*OTSUKA JAPANESE SIG: .75X TO 2X HI		

❑ 1 Vladimir Guerrero 2.00 .60
❑ 2 Garret Anderson .75 .23

❑ 3	John Lackey	.75	.23
❑ 4	Bartolo Colon	.75	.23
❑ 5	Troy Glaus	.75	.23
❑ 6	Tim Salmon	1.25	.35
❑ 7	Shea Hillenbrand	.75	.23
❑ 8	Brandon Webb	.75	.23
❑ 9	Roberto Alomar	1.25	.35
❑ 10	Randy Johnson	2.00	.60
❑ 11	Alex Cintron	.75	.23
❑ 12	Richie Sexson	.75	.23
❑ 13	Luis Gonzalez	.75	.23
❑ 14	Adam LaRoche	.75	.23
❑ 15	Rafael Furcal	.75	.23
❑ 16	Chipper Jones	2.00	.60
❑ 17	Marcus Giles	.75	.23
❑ 18	Andruw Jones	.75	.23
❑ 19	Russ Ortiz	.75	.23
❑ 20	Rafael Palmeiro	1.25	.35
❑ 21	Melvin Mora	.75	.23
❑ 22	Luis Matos	.75	.23
❑ 23	Jay Gibbons	.75	.23
❑ 24	Adam Loewen	.75	.23
❑ 25	Larry Bigbie	.75	.23
❑ 26	Rodrigo Lopez	.75	.23
❑ 27	Javy Lopez	.75	.23
❑ 28	Miguel Tejada	.75	.23
❑ 29	Trot Nixon	.75	.23
❑ 30	Curt Schilling	2.00	.60
❑ 31	Jason Varitek	1.25	.35
❑ 32	Manny Ramirez	1.25	.35
❑ 33	Keith Foulke Sox	1.25	.35
❑ 34	Derek Lowe	.75	.23
❑ 35	Pedro Martinez	2.00	.60
❑ 36	Nomar Garciaparra	3.00	.90
❑ 37	Bill Mueller	.75	.23
❑ 38	Johnny Damon	2.00	.60
❑ 39	David Ortiz	2.00	.60
❑ 40	Mark Prior	2.00	.60
❑ 41	Kerry Wood	2.00	.60
❑ 42	Sammy Sosa	3.00	.90
❑ 43	Derrek Lee	.75	.23
❑ 44	Greg Maddux	3.00	.90
❑ 45	Aramis Ramirez	.75	.23
❑ 46	Matt Clement	.75	.23
❑ 47	Carlos Zambrano	.75	.23
❑ 48	Todd Walker	.75	.23
❑ 49	Moises Alou	.75	.23
❑ 50	Corey Patterson	.75	.23
❑ 51	Frank Thomas	2.00	.60
❑ 52	Magglio Ordonez	.75	.23
❑ 53	Carlos Lee	.75	.23
❑ 54	Mark Buehrle	.75	.23
❑ 55	Esteban Loaiza	.75	.23
❑ 56	Joe Crede	.75	.23
❑ 57	Paul Konerko	.75	.23
❑ 58	Adam Dunn	1.25	.35
❑ 59	Austin Kearns	.75	.23
❑ 60	Barry Larkin	1.25	.35
❑ 61	Ryan Wagner	.75	.23
❑ 62	Danny Graves	.75	.23
❑ 63	Sean Casey	.75	.23
❑ 64	Ken Griffey Jr.	3.00	.90
❑ 65	Jody Gerut	.75	.23
❑ 66	Cliff Lee	.75	.23
❑ 67	Victor Martinez	.75	.23
❑ 68	C.C. Sabathia	.75	.23
❑ 69	Omar Vizquel	1.25	.35
❑ 70	Travis Hafner	.75	.23
❑ 71	Todd Helton	1.25	.35
❑ 72	Preston Wilson	.75	.23
❑ 73	Jeromy Burnitz	.75	.23
❑ 74	Larry Walker	1.25	.35
❑ 75	Ivan Rodriguez	2.00	.60
❑ 76	Rondell White	.75	.23
❑ 77	Miguel Cabrera	1.25	.35
❑ 78	Luis Castillo	.75	.23
❑ 79	Josh Beckett	.75	.23
❑ 80	Mike Lowell	.75	.23
❑ 81	Dontrelle Willis	.75	.23
❑ 82	Brad Penny	.75	.23
❑ 83	Hee Seop Choi	.75	.23
❑ 84	Juan Pierre	.75	.23
❑ 85	Andy Pettitte	1.25	.35
❑ 86	Jeff Bagwell	1.25	.35
❑ 87	Roy Oswalt	.75	.23
❑ 88	Lance Berkman	.75	.23
❑ 89	Morgan Ensberg	.75	.23
❑ 90	Craig Biggio	1.25	.35
❑ 91	Octavio Dotel	.75	.23
❑ 92	Wade Miller	.75	.23
❑ 93	Jeff Kent	.75	.23
❑ 94	Richard Hidalgo	.75	.23
❑ 95	Roger Clemens	4.00	1.20
❑ 96	Carlos Beltran	1.25	.35
❑ 97	Angel Berroa	.75	.23
❑ 98	Jeremy Affeldt	.75	.23
❑ 99	Juan Gonzalez	1.25	.35
❑ 100	Mike Sweeney	.75	.23
❑ 101	Kazuhisa Ishii	.75	.23
❑ 102	Shawn Green	.75	.23
❑ 103	Milton Bradley	.75	.23
❑ 104	Paul Lo Duca	.75	.23
❑ 105	Hideo Nomo	2.00	.60
❑ 106	Eric Gagne	2.00	.60
❑ 107	Adrian Beltre	1.25	.35
❑ 108	Scott Podsednik	.75	.23
❑ 109	Rickie Weeks	.75	.23
❑ 110	Ben Sheets	.75	.23
❑ 111	Geoff Jenkins	.75	.23
❑ 112	Jacque Jones	.75	.23
❑ 113	Johan Santana	1.25	.35
❑ 114	Shannon Stewart	.75	.23
❑ 115	Corey Koskie	.75	.23
❑ 116	Lew Ford	.75	.23
❑ 117	Torii Hunter	.75	.23
❑ 118	Chad Cordero	.75	.23
❑ 119	Orlando Cabrera	.75	.23
❑ 120	Jose Vidro	.75	.23
❑ 121	Nick Johnson	.75	.23
❑ 122	Brad Wilkerson	.75	.23
❑ 123	Mike Piazza	3.00	.90
❑ 124	Jae Weong Seo	.75	.23
❑ 125	Jose Reyes	.75	.23
❑ 126	Tom Glavine	1.25	.35
❑ 127	Jorge Posada	1.25	.35
❑ 128	Gary Sheffield	.75	.23
❑ 129	Bernie Williams	1.25	.35
❑ 130	Mike Mussina	1.25	.35
❑ 131	Mariano Rivera	1.25	.35
❑ 132	Bubba Crosby	.75	.23
❑ 133	Kevin Brown	.75	.23
❑ 134	Javier Vazquez	.75	.23
❑ 135	Jason Giambi	.75	.23
❑ 136	Derek Jeter	4.00	1.20
❑ 137	Alex Rodriguez	3.00	.90
❑ 138	Hideki Matsui	3.00	.90
❑ 139	Mark Mulder	.75	.23
❑ 140	Jermaine Dye	.75	.23
❑ 141	Tim Hudson	.75	.23
❑ 142	Barry Zito	.75	.23
❑ 143	Eric Chavez	.75	.23
❑ 144	Bobby Crosby	1.25	.35
❑ 145	Eric Byrnes	.75	.23
❑ 146	Marlon Byrd	.75	.23
❑ 147	Billy Wagner	.75	.23
❑ 148	Mike Lieberthal	.75	.23
❑ 149	Jimmy Rollins	.75	.23
❑ 150	Jim Thome	2.00	.60
❑ 151	Bobby Abreu	.75	.23
❑ 152	Pat Burrell	.75	.23
❑ 153	Jose Castillo	.75	.23
❑ 154	Craig Wilson	.75	.23
❑ 155	Jason Bay	.75	.23
❑ 156	Jason Kendall	.75	.23
❑ 157	Raul Mondesi	.75	.23
❑ 158	Jay Payton	.75	.23
❑ 159	Trevor Hoffman	.75	.23
❑ 160	Jake Peavy	.75	.23
❑ 161	Sean Burroughs	.75	.23
❑ 162	Phil Nevin	.75	.23
❑ 163	Brian Giles	.75	.23
❑ 164	Ryan Klesko	.75	.23
❑ 165	Todd Linden	.75	.23
❑ 166	Jerome Williams	.75	.23
❑ 167	Jason Schmidt	.75	.23
❑ 168	Ray Durham	.75	.23
❑ 169	Marquis Grissom	.75	.23
❑ 170	Shigetoshi Hasegawa	.75	.23
❑ 171	Edgar Martinez	1.25	.35
❑ 172	Freddy Garcia	.75	.23
❑ 173	Bret Boone	.75	.23
❑ 174	Raul Ibanez	.75	.23
❑ 175	Ichiro Suzuki	3.00	.90
❑ 176	Randy Winn	.75	.23
❑ 177	Scott Rolen	2.00	.60
❑ 178	Jim Edmonds	.75	.23
❑ 179	Albert Pujols	4.00	1.20
❑ 180	Matt Morris	.75	.23
❑ 181	Edgar Renteria	.75	.23
❑ 182	Aubrey Huff	.75	.23
❑ 183	Delmon Young	.75	.23
❑ 184	Dewon Brazelton	.75	.23
❑ 185	Rocco Baldelli	.75	.23
❑ 186	Carl Crawford	.75	.23
❑ 187	Mark Teixeira	.75	.23
❑ 188	Hank Blalock	.75	.23
❑ 189	Michael Young	.75	.23
❑ 190	Laynce Nix	.75	.23
❑ 191	Alfonso Soriano	1.25	.35
❑ 192	Kevin Mench	.75	.23
❑ 193	Adrian Gonzalez	.75	.23
❑ 194	Alexis Rios	.75	.23
❑ 195	Roy Halladay	.75	.23
❑ 196	Vernon Wells	.75	.23
❑ 197	Carlos Delgado	.75	.23
❑ 198	Bill Hall	.75	.23
❑ 199	Jose Guillen	.75	.23
❑ 200	Jeremy Bonderman	.75	.23
❑ 201	Roger Clemens Yanks SP	8.00	2.40
❑ 202	Alex Rodriguez Rgr SP	8.00	2.40
❑ 203	Greg Maddux Braves SP	8.00	2.40
❑ 204	Miguel Tejada A's SP	3.00	.90
❑ 205	Alfonso Soriano Yanks SP	5.00	1.50
❑ 206	Andy Pettitte Yanks SP	5.00	1.50
❑ 207	Curt Schilling D'backs SP	3.00	.90
❑ 208	Gary Sheffield Braves SP	5.00	1.50
❑ 209	Ivan Rodriguez Marlins SP	5.00	1.50
❑ 210	Jim Thome Indians SP	5.00	1.50
❑ 211	Mike Mussina O's SP	5.00	1.50
❑ 212	Mike Piazza Dodgers SP	8.00	2.40
❑ 213	Randy Johnson M's SP	5.00	1.50
❑ 214	Roger Clemens Sox SP	8.00	2.40
❑ 215	Sammy Sosa Sox SP	8.00	2.40
❑ 216	Alex Rodriguez M's SP	8.00	2.40
❑ 217	Randy Johnson Astros SP	5.00	1.50
❑ 218	Vladimir Guerrero Expos SP	5.00	1.50
❑ 219	Rafael Palmeiro Rgr SP	5.00	1.50
❑ 220	Manny Ramirez Indians SP	5.00	1.50
❑ 221	Mike Piazza Marlins SP	8.00	2.40
❑ 222	Cal Ripken LGD	15.00	4.50
❑ 223	Ted Williams LGD	10.00	3.00
❑ 224	Duke Snider LGD	5.00	1.50
❑ 225	Ernie Banks LGD	5.00	1.50
❑ 226	Ryne Sandberg LGD	10.00	3.00
❑ 227	Mark Grace LGD	5.00	1.50
❑ 228	Andre Dawson LGD	3.00	.90
❑ 229	Bob Feller LGD	5.00	1.50
❑ 230	Ty Cobb LGD	8.00	2.40
❑ 231	George Brett LGD	10.00	3.00
❑ 232	Bo Jackson LGD	5.00	1.50
❑ 233	Robin Yount LGD	8.00	2.40
❑ 234	Harmon Killebrew LGD	5.00	1.50
❑ 235	Gary Carter LGD	3.00	.90
❑ 236	Don Mattingly LGD	10.00	3.00
❑ 237	Phil Rizzuto LGD	5.00	1.50
❑ 238	Babe Ruth LGD	10.00	3.00
❑ 239	Lou Gehrig LGD	8.00	2.40
❑ 240	Reggie Jackson LGD	5.00	1.50
❑ 241	Rickey Henderson LGD	5.00	1.50
❑ 242	Mike Schmidt LGD	10.00	3.00
❑ 243	Roberto Clemente LGD	10.00	3.00
❑ 244	Tony Gwynn LGD	8.00	2.40
❑ 245	Will Clark LGD	5.00	1.50
❑ 246	Lou Brock LGD	5.00	1.50
❑ 247	Bob Gibson LGD	5.00	1.50
❑ 248	Stan Musial LGD	8.00	2.40
❑ 249	Nolan Ryan LGD	12.00	3.60
❑ 250	Dale Murphy LGD	5.00	1.50
❑ 251	A.Baldiris ROO AU/499 RC	10.00	3.00
❑ 252	A.Otsuka ROO AU/99 RC	40.00	12.00
❑ 253	A.Blanco ROO AU/499 RC	8.00	2.40
❑ 254	A.Chavez ROO AU/499 RC	8.00	2.40
❑ 255	C.Hines ROO AU/199 RC	10.00	3.00
❑ 256	C.Vasquez ROO AU/499 RC	10.00	3.00
❑ 257	Casey Daigle ROO/499 RC	5.00	1.50
❑ 258	C.Oxspring ROO AU/499 RC	10.00	3.00
❑ 259	C.Miller ROO AU/499 RC	8.00	2.40
❑ 260	D.Crouthers ROO AU/199 RC	10.00	3.00

❑ 261 D.Kelly ROO AU/499 RC 8.00 2.40
❑ 262 E.Rodriguez ROO AU/499 RC 10.00 3.00
❑ 263 E.Sierra ROO AU/299 RC 10.00 3.00
❑ 264 E.Moreno ROO AU/499 RC 10.00 3.00
❑ 265 F.Nieve ROO AU/499 RC 8.00 2.40
❑ 266 F.Guzman ROO AU/499 RC 8.00 2.40
❑ 267 G.Dobbs ROO AU/499 RC 8.00 2.40
❑ 268 B.Halsey ROO AU/499 RC 10.00 3.00
❑ 269 H.Gimenez ROO AU/499 RC 8.00 2.40
❑ 270 I.Ochoa ROO AU/499 RC 8.00 2.40
❑ 271 J.Woods ROO AU/499 RC 8.00 2.40
❑ 272 J.Brown ROO AU/499 RC 8.00 2.40
❑ 273 J.Bartlett ROO AU/499 RC 10.00 3.00
❑ 274 J.Szuminski ROO AU/499 RC 8.00 2.40
❑ 275 John Gall ROO/499 RC .. 8.00 2.40
❑ 276 J.Vasquez ROO AU/499 RC 8.00 2.40
❑ 277 J.Labandeira ROO AU/499 RC 8.00 2.40
❑ 278 J.Hampson ROO AU/499 RC 8.00 2.40
❑ 279 Kazuo Matsui ROO/499 RC 15.00 4.50
❑ 280 K.Cave ROO AU/499 RC 10.00 3.00
❑ 281 L.Cormier ROO AU/499 RC 8.00 2.40
❑ 282 L.Holdzkom ROO AU/199 RC 10.00 3.00
❑ 283 M.Valdez ROO AU/199 RC 15.00 4.50
❑ 284 M.Wuertz ROO AU/499 RC 10.00 3.00
❑ 285 M.Johnston ROO AU/499 RC 8.00 2.40
❑ 286 M.Rouse ROO AU/329 RC 8.00 2.40
❑ 287 O.Joseph ROO AU/499 RC 8.00 2.40
❑ 288 P.Stockman ROO AU/499 RC 8.00 2.40
❑ 289 R.Novoa ROO AU/499 RC 10.00 3.00
❑ 290 R.Belisario ROO AU/499 RC 8.00 2.40
❑ 291 R.Cedeno ROO AU/499 RC 8.00 2.40
❑ 292 R.Meaux ROO AU/499 RC 8.00 2.40
❑ 293 Scott Proctor ROO/499 RC 8.00 2.40
❑ 294 S.Henn ROO AU/199 RC 10.00 3.00
❑ 295 S.Camp ROO AU/499 RC 8.00 2.40
❑ 296 S.Hill ROO AU/499 RC .. 8.00 2.40
❑ 297 S.Takatsu ROO AU/99 RC 50.00 15.00
❑ 298 T.Bittner ROO AU/199 RC 10.00 3.00
❑ 299 William Bergolla ROO/499 RC 5.00 1.50
❑ 300 Y.Molina ROO AU/499 RC 20.00 6.00

2001 Leaf Certified Materials

	Nm-Mt	Ex-Mt
COMP.SET w/o SP's (110)	40.00	12.00
COMMON CARD (1-110)	1.00	.30
COMMON (111-160)	15.00	4.50

❑ 1 Alex Rodriguez 4.00 1.20
❑ 2 Barry Bonds 6.00 1.80
❑ 3 Cal Ripken 8.00 2.40
❑ 4 Chipper Jones 2.50 .75
❑ 5 Derek Jeter 6.00 1.80
❑ 6 Troy Glaus 1.00 .30
❑ 7 Frank Thomas 2.50 .75
❑ 8 Greg Maddux 4.00 1.20
❑ 9 Ivan Rodriguez 2.50 .75
❑ 10 Jeff Bagwell 1.50 .45
❑ 11 Eric Karros 1.00 .30
❑ 12 Todd Helton 1.50 .45
❑ 13 Ken Griffey Jr. 4.00 1.20
❑ 14 Manny Ramirez 1.50 .45
❑ 15 Mark McGwire 6.00 1.80
❑ 16 Mike Piazza 4.00 1.20
❑ 17 Nomar Garciaparra 4.00 1.20
❑ 18 Pedro Martinez 2.50 .75
❑ 19 Randy Johnson 2.50 .75
❑ 20 Rick Ankiel 1.00 .30
❑ 21 Rickey Henderson 2.50 .75
❑ 22 Roger Clemens 5.00 1.50
❑ 23 Sammy Sosa 4.00 1.20
❑ 24 Tony Gwynn 3.00 .90
❑ 25 Vladimir Guerrero 2.50 .75
❑ 26 Kazuhiro Sasaki 1.00 .30
❑ 27 Roberto Alomar 1.50 .45
❑ 28 Barry Zito 1.50 .45
❑ 29 Pat Burrell 1.00 .30
❑ 30 Harold Baines 1.00 .30
❑ 31 Carlos Delgado 1.00 .30
❑ 32 J.D. Drew 1.00 .30
❑ 33 Jim Edmonds 1.00 .30
❑ 34 Darin Erstad 1.00 .30
❑ 35 Jason Giambi 1.00 .30
❑ 36 Tom Glavine 1.50 .45
❑ 37 Juan Gonzalez 1.50 .45
❑ 38 Mark Grace 1.50 .45
❑ 39 Shawn Green 1.00 .30
❑ 40 Tim Hudson 1.00 .30
❑ 41 Andruw Jones 1.00 .30
❑ 42 Jeff Kent 1.00 .30
❑ 43 Barry Larkin 1.50 .45
❑ 44 Rafael Furcal 1.00 .30
❑ 45 Mike Mussina 1.50 .45
❑ 46 Hideo Nomo 2.50 .75
❑ 47 Rafael Palmeiro 1.50 .45
❑ 48 Scott Rolen 2.50 .75
❑ 49 Gary Sheffield 1.00 .30
❑ 50 Bernie Williams 1.50 .45
❑ 51 Bob Abreu 1.00 .30
❑ 52 Edgardo Alfonzo 1.00 .30
❑ 53 Edgar Martinez 1.50 .45
❑ 54 Magglio Ordonez 1.00 .30
❑ 55 Kerry Wood 2.50 .75
❑ 56 Adrian Beltre 1.50 .45
❑ 57 Lance Berkman 1.00 .30
❑ 58 Kevin Brown 1.00 .30
❑ 59 Sean Casey 1.00 .30
❑ 60 Eric Chavez 1.00 .30
❑ 61 Bartolo Colon 1.00 .30
❑ 62 Johnny Damon 1.50 .45
❑ 63 Jermaine Dye 1.00 .30
❑ 64 Juan Encarnacion UER 1.00 .30
Card has him playing for Detroit Lions
❑ 65 Carl Everett 1.00 .30
❑ 66 Brian Giles 1.00 .30
❑ 67 Mike Hampton 1.00 .30
❑ 68 Richard Hidalgo 1.00 .30
❑ 69 Geoff Jenkins 1.00 .30
❑ 70 Jacque Jones 1.00 .30
❑ 71 Jason Kendall 1.00 .30
❑ 72 Ryan Klesko 1.00 .30
❑ 73 Chan Ho Park 1.00 .30
❑ 74 Richie Sexson 1.00 .30
❑ 75 Mike Sweeney 1.00 .30
❑ 76 Fernando Tatis 1.00 .30
❑ 77 Miguel Tejada 1.00 .30
❑ 78 Jose Vidro 1.00 .30
❑ 79 Larry Walker 1.50 .45
❑ 80 Preston Wilson 1.00 .30
❑ 81 Craig Biggio 1.50 .45
❑ 82 Fred McGriff 1.50 .45
❑ 83 Jim Thome 2.50 .75
❑ 84 Garret Anderson 1.00 .30
❑ 85 Russell Branyan 1.00 .30
❑ 86 Tony Batista 1.00 .30
❑ 87 Terrence Long 1.00 .30
❑ 88 Deion Sanders 1.50 .45
❑ 89 Rusty Greer 1.00 .30
❑ 90 Orlando Hernandez 1.00 .30
❑ 91 Gabe Kapler 1.00 .30
❑ 92 Paul Konerko 1.00 .30
❑ 93 Carlos Lee 1.00 .30
❑ 94 Kenny Lofton 1.00 .30
❑ 95 Raul Mondesi 1.00 .30
❑ 96 Jorge Posada 1.50 .45
❑ 97 Tim Salmon 1.50 .45
❑ 98 Greg Vaughn 1.00 .30
❑ 99 Mo Vaughn 1.00 .30
❑ 100 Omar Vizquel 1.50 .45
❑ 101 Ray Durham 1.00 .30
❑ 102 Jeff Cirillo 1.00 .30
❑ 103 Dean Palmer 1.00 .30
❑ 104 Ryan Dempster 1.00 .30
❑ 105 Carlos Beltran 1.50 .45
❑ 106 Timo Perez 1.00 .30
❑ 107 Robin Ventura 1.00 .30
❑ 108 Andy Pettitte 1.50 .45
❑ 109 Aramis Ramirez 1.00 .30
❑ 110 Phil Nevin 1.00 .30
❑ 111 Alex Escobar FF 15.00 4.50
❑ 112 Johnny Estrada FF RC .. 20.00 6.00
❑ 113 Pedro Feliz FF 15.00 4.50
❑ 114 Nate Frese FF RC 15.00 4.50
❑ 115 Joe Kennedy FF RC 20.00 6.00
❑ 116 B. Larson FF RC 15.00 4.50
❑ 117 Alexis Gomez FF RC 15.00 4.50
❑ 118 Jason Hart FF 15.00 4.50
❑ 119 Jason Michaels FF RC 15.00 4.50
❑ 120 Marcus Giles FF 15.00 4.50
❑ 121 C. Parker FF RC 15.00 4.50
❑ 122 Jackson Melian FF RC 15.00 4.50
❑ 123 D. Mendez FF RC 15.00 4.50
❑ 124 A. Hernandez FF RC 15.00 4.50
❑ 125 Bud Smith FF RC 15.00 4.50
❑ 126 Jose Mieses FF RC 15.00 4.50
❑ 127 Roy Oswalt FF 20.00 6.00
❑ 128 Eric Munson FF 15.00 4.50
❑ 129 Xavier Nady FF 15.00 4.50
❑ 130 H. Ramirez FF RC 20.00 6.00
❑ 131 Abraham Nunez FF 15.00 4.50
❑ 132 Jose Ortiz FF 15.00 4.50
❑ 133 Jeremy Owens FF RC .. 15.00 4.50
❑ 134 Claudio Vargas FF RC .. 15.00 4.50
❑ 135 R. Rodriguez FF RC 15.00 4.50
❑ 136 Aubrey Huff FF 15.00 4.50
❑ 137 Ben Sheets FF 20.00 6.00
❑ 138 Adam Dunn FF 20.00 6.00
❑ 139 Andres Torres FF RC 15.00 4.50
❑ 140 Elpidio Guzman FF RC 15.00 4.50
❑ 141 Jay Gibbons FF RC 20.00 6.00
❑ 142 Wilkin Ruan FF RC 15.00 4.50
❑ 143 T. Shinjo FF RC 20.00 6.00
❑ 144 Alfonso Soriano FF 20.00 6.00
❑ 145 Josh Towers FF RC 15.00 4.50
❑ 146 Ichiro Suzuki FF RC .. 150.00 45.00
❑ 147 Juan Uribe FF RC 20.00 6.00
❑ 148 Joe Crede FF 15.00 4.50
❑ 149 C. Valderrama FF RC 15.00 4.50
❑ 150 Matt White FF RC 15.00 4.50
❑ 151 Dee Brown FF 15.00 4.50
❑ 152 Juan Cruz FF RC 15.00 4.50
❑ 153 Cory Aldridge FF RC 15.00 4.50
❑ 154 Wilmy Caceres FF RC .. 15.00 4.50
❑ 155 Josh Beckett FF 15.00 4.50
❑ 156 Wilson Betemit FF RC .. 15.00 4.50
❑ 157 Corey Patterson FF 15.00 4.50
❑ 158 Albert Pujols FF RC 150.00 45.00
❑ 159 Rafael Soriano FF RC .. 20.00 6.00
❑ 160 Jack Wilson FF RC 25.00 7.50

2002 Leaf Certified

	Nm-Mt	Ex-Mt
COMP.SET w/o SP's (150)	80.00	24.00
COMMON CARD (1-150)	1.00	.30
COMMON CARD (151-200)	10.00	3.00

❑ 1 Alex Rodriguez 4.00 1.20
❑ 2 Luis Gonzalez 1.00 .30
❑ 3 Javier Vazquez 1.00 .30
❑ 4 Juan Uribe 1.00 .30

Card	Mint	NrMt
❑ 5 Ben Sheets	1.00	.30
❑ 6 George Brett	6.00	1.80
❑ 7 Magglio Ordonez	1.00	.30
❑ 8 Randy Johnson	2.50	.75
❑ 9 Joe Kennedy	1.00	.30
❑ 10 Richie Sexson	1.00	.30
❑ 11 Larry Walker	1.50	.45
❑ 12 Lance Berkman	1.00	.30
❑ 13 Jose Cruz Jr.	1.00	.30
❑ 14 Doug Davis	1.00	.30
❑ 15 Cliff Floyd	1.00	.30
❑ 16 Ryan Klesko	1.00	.30
❑ 17 Troy Glaus	1.00	.30
❑ 18 Robert Person	1.00	.30
❑ 19 Bartolo Colon	1.00	.30
❑ 20 Adam Dunn	1.50	.45
❑ 21 Kevin Brown	1.00	.30
❑ 22 John Smoltz	1.50	.45
❑ 23 Edgar Martinez	1.50	.45
❑ 24 Eric Karros	1.00	.30
❑ 25 Tony Gwynn	3.00	.90
❑ 26 Mark Mulder	1.00	.30
❑ 27 Don Mattingly	6.00	1.80
❑ 28 Brandon Duckworth	1.00	.30
❑ 29 C.C. Sabathia	1.00	.30
❑ 30 Nomar Garciaparra	4.00	1.20
❑ 31 Adam Johnson	1.00	.30
❑ 32 Miquel Tejada	1.00	.30
❑ 33 Ryne Sandberg	5.00	1.50
❑ 34 Roger Clemens	5.00	1.50
❑ 35 Edgardo Alfonzo	1.00	.30
❑ 36 Jason Jennings	1.00	.30
❑ 37 Todd Helton	1.50	.45
❑ 38 Nolan Ryan	6.00	1.80
❑ 39 Paul LoDuca	1.00	.30
❑ 40 Cal Ripken	8.00	2.40
❑ 41 Terrence Long	1.00	.30
❑ 42 Mike Sweeney	1.00	.30
❑ 43 Carlos Lee	1.00	.30
❑ 44 Ben Grieve	1.00	.30
❑ 45 Tony Armas Jr.	1.00	.30
❑ 46 Joe Mays	1.00	.30
❑ 47 Jeff Kent	1.00	.30
❑ 48 Andy Pettitte	1.50	.45
❑ 49 Kirby Puckett	2.50	.75
❑ 50 Aramis Ramirez	1.00	.30
❑ 51 Tim Redding	1.00	.30
❑ 52 Freddy Garcia	1.00	.30
❑ 53 Javy Lopez	1.00	.30
❑ 54 Mike Schmidt	6.00	1.80
❑ 55 Wade Miller	1.00	.30
❑ 56 Ramon Ortiz	1.00	.30
❑ 57 Ray Durham	1.00	.30
❑ 58 J.D. Drew	1.00	.30
❑ 59 Bret Boone	1.00	.30
❑ 60 Mark Buehrle	1.00	.30
❑ 61 Geoff Jenkins	1.00	.30
❑ 62 Greg Maddux	4.00	1.20
❑ 63 Mark Grace	1.50	.45
❑ 64 Toby Hall	1.00	.30
❑ 65 A.J. Burnett	1.00	.30
❑ 66 Bernie Williams	1.50	.45
❑ 67 Roy Oswalt	1.00	.30
❑ 68 Shannon Stewart	1.00	.30
❑ 69 Barry Zito	1.00	.30
❑ 70 Juan Pierre	1.00	.30
❑ 71 Preston Wilson	1.00	.30
❑ 72 Rafael Furcal	1.00	.30
❑ 73 Sean Casey	1.00	.30
❑ 74 John Olerud	1.00	.30
❑ 75 Paul Konerko	1.00	.30
❑ 76 Vernon Wells	1.00	.30
❑ 77 Juan Gonzalez	1.50	.45
❑ 78 Ellis Burks	1.00	.30
❑ 79 Jim Edmonds	1.00	.30
❑ 80 Robert Fick	1.00	.30
❑ 81 Michael Cuddyer	1.00	.30
❑ 82 Tim Hudson	1.00	.30
❑ 83 Phil Nevin	1.00	.30
❑ 84 Curt Schilling	1.00	.30
❑ 85 Juan Cruz	1.00	.30
❑ 86 Jeff Bagwell	1.50	.45
❑ 87 Raul Mondesi	1.00	.30
❑ 88 Bud Smith	1.00	.30
❑ 89 Omar Vizquel	1.50	.45
❑ 90 Vladimir Guerrero	2.50	.75
❑ 91 Garret Anderson	1.00	.30
❑ 92 Mike Piazza	4.00	1.20
❑ 93 Josh Beckett	1.00	.30
❑ 94 Carlos Delgado	1.00	.30
❑ 95 Kazuhiro Sasaki	1.00	.30
❑ 96 Chipper Jones	2.50	.75
❑ 97 Jacque Jones	1.00	.30
❑ 98 Pedro Martinez	2.50	.75
❑ 99 Marcus Giles	1.00	.30
❑ 100 Craig Biggio	1.50	.45
❑ 101 Orlando Cabrera	1.00	.30
❑ 102 Al Leiter	1.00	.30
❑ 103 Michael Barrett	1.00	.30
❑ 104 Hideo Nomo	2.50	.75
❑ 105 Mike Mussina	1.50	.45
❑ 106 Jeremy Giambi	1.00	.30
❑ 107 Cristian Guzman	1.00	.30
❑ 108 Frank Thomas	2.50	.75
❑ 109 Carlos Beltran	1.50	.45
❑ 110 Jorge Posada	1.50	.45
❑ 111 Roberto Alomar	1.50	.45
❑ 112 Bob Abreu	1.00	.30
❑ 113 Robin Ventura	1.00	.30
❑ 114 Pat Burrell	1.00	.30
❑ 115 Kenny Lofton	1.00	.30
❑ 116 Adrian Beltre	1.50	.45
❑ 117 Gary Sheffield	1.00	.30
❑ 118 Jermaine Dye	1.00	.30
❑ 119 Manny Ramirez	1.50	.45
❑ 120 Brian Giles	1.00	.30
❑ 121 Tsuyoshi Shinjo	1.00	.30
❑ 122 Rafael Palmeiro	1.50	.45
❑ 123 Mo Vaughn UER Yankee Logo on back	1.00	.30
❑ 124 Kerry Wood	2.50	.75
❑ 125 Moises Alou	1.00	.30
❑ 126 Rickey Henderson	2.50	.75
❑ 127 Corey Patterson	1.00	.30
❑ 128 Jim Thome	2.50	.75
❑ 129 Richard Hidalgo	1.00	.30
❑ 130 Darin Erstad	1.00	.30
❑ 131 Johnny Damon Sox	2.50	.75
❑ 132 Juan Encarnacion	1.00	.30
❑ 133 Scott Rolen	2.50	.75
❑ 134 Tom Glavine	1.50	.45
❑ 135 Ivan Rodriguez	2.50	.75
❑ 136 Jay Gibbons	1.00	.30
❑ 137 Trot Nixon	1.00	.30
❑ 138 Nick Neugebauer	1.00	.30
❑ 139 Barry Larkin	1.50	.45
❑ 140 Andruw Jones	1.00	.30
❑ 141 Shawn Green	1.00	.30
❑ 142 Jose Vidro	1.00	.30
❑ 143 Derek Jeter	6.00	1.80
❑ 144 Ichiro Suzuki	4.00	1.20
❑ 145 Ken Griffey Jr.	4.00	1.20
❑ 146 Barry Bonds	6.00	1.80
❑ 147 Albert Pujols	5.00	1.50
❑ 148 Sammy Sosa	4.00	1.20
❑ 149 Jason Giambi	1.00	.30
❑ 150 Alfonso Soriano	1.50	.45
❑ 151 Drew Henson NG Bat	10.00	3.00
❑ 152 Luis Garcia NG Bat	10.00	3.00
❑ 153 Geronimo Gil NG Jsy	10.00	3.00
❑ 154 Corky Miller NG Jsy	10.00	3.00
❑ 155 Mike Rivera NG Bat	10.00	3.00
❑ 156 Mark Ellis NG Jsy	10.00	3.00
❑ 157 Josh Pearce NG Bat	10.00	3.00
❑ 158 Ryan Ludwick NG Bat	10.00	3.00
❑ 159 So Taguchi NG Bat RC	15.00	4.50
❑ 160 Cody Ransom NG Jsy	10.00	3.00
❑ 161 Jeff Deardorff NG Bat	10.00	3.00
❑ 162 Fr. German NG Bat RC	10.00	3.00
❑ 163 Ed Rogers NG Jsy	10.00	3.00
❑ 164 Eric Cyr NG Jsy	10.00	3.00
❑ 165 Victor Alvarez NG Jsy RC	10.00	3.00
❑ 166 Victor Martinez NG Jsy	15.00	4.50
❑ 167 Brandon Berger NG Jsy	10.00	3.00
❑ 168 Juan Diaz NG Jsy	10.00	3.00
❑ 169 Kevin Frederick NG Jsy RC	10.00	3.00
❑ 170 Earl Snyder NG Bat RC	15.00	4.50
❑ 171 Morgan Ensberg NG Bat	10.00	3.00
❑ 172 Ryan Jamison NG Jsy	10.00	3.00
❑ 173 Rod. Rosario NG Jsy RC	10.00	3.00
❑ 174 Willie Harris NG Bat	10.00	3.00
❑ 175 Ramon Vazquez NG Bat	10.00	3.00
❑ 176 Kazuhisa Ishii NG Bat RC	20.00	6.00
❑ 177 Hank Blalock NG Jsy	15.00	4.50
❑ 178 Mark Prior NG Bat	20.00	6.00
❑ 179 Dewon Brazelton NG Jsy	10.00	3.00
❑ 180 Doug Devore NG Jsy RC	10.00	3.00
❑ 181 Jorge Padilla NG Bat RC	10.00	3.00
❑ 182 Mark Teixeira NG Jsy	15.00	4.50
❑ 183 Orlando Hudson NG Bat	10.00	3.00
❑ 184 John Buck NG Jsy	10.00	3.00
❑ 185 Erik Bedard NG Jsy	10.00	3.00
❑ 186 Allan Simpson NG Jsy RC	10.00	3.00
❑ 187 Travis Hafner NG Jsy	10.00	3.00
❑ 188 Jason Lane NG Jsy	10.00	3.00
❑ 189 Marlon Byrd NG Jsy	10.00	3.00
❑ 190 Joe Thurston NG Jsy	10.00	3.00
❑ 191 Brandon Backe NG Jsy RC	15.00	4.50
❑ 192 Josh Phelps NG Jsy	10.00	3.00
❑ 193 Bill Hall NG Bat	10.00	3.00
❑ 194 Chris Snelling NG Bat RC	10.00	3.00
❑ 195 Austin Kearns NG Jsy	10.00	3.00
❑ 196 Antonio Perez NG Bat	10.00	3.00
❑ 197 Angel Berroa NG Bat	10.00	3.00
❑ 198 Andy Machado NG Jsy RC	10.00	3.00
❑ 199 Alfredo Amezaga NG Jsy	10.00	3.00
❑ 200 Eric Hinske NG Bat	10.00	3.00

2003 Leaf Certified Materials

	MINT	NRMT
COMP.LO SET w/o SP's (200)	50.00	22.00
COMMON CARD (1-200)	1.00	.45
COMMON CARD (201-205)	10.00	4.50
COMMON CARD (206-250)	10.00	4.50
201-250 RANDOM INSERTS IN PACKS		.00
COM.(251-259) p/r 150-250	10.00	4.50
❑ 1 Troy Glaus	1.00	.45
❑ 2 Alfredo Amezaga	1.00	.45
❑ 3 Garret Anderson	1.00	.45
❑ 4 Nolan Ryan Angels	6.00	2.70
❑ 5 Darin Erstad	1.00	.45
❑ 6 Junior Spivey	1.00	.45
❑ 7 Randy Johnson	2.50	1.10
❑ 8 Curt Schilling	1.00	.45
❑ 9 Luis Gonzalez	1.00	.45
❑ 10 Steve Finley	1.00	.45
❑ 11 Matt Williams	1.00	.45
❑ 12 Greg Maddux	4.00	1.80
❑ 13 Chipper Jones	2.50	1.10
❑ 14 Gary Sheffield	1.00	.45
❑ 15 Adam LaRoche	1.00	.45
❑ 16 Andruw Jones	1.00	.45
❑ 17 Robert Fick	1.00	.45
❑ 18 John Smoltz	1.50	.70
❑ 19 Javy Lopez	1.00	.45
❑ 20 Jay Gibbons	1.00	.45
❑ 21 Geronimo Gil	1.00	.45
❑ 22 Cal Ripken	8.00	3.60
❑ 23 Nomar Garciaparra	4.00	1.80
❑ 24 Pedro Martinez	2.50	1.10
❑ 25 Freddy Sanchez	1.00	.45
❑ 26 Rickey Henderson	2.50	1.10
❑ 27 Manny Ramirez	1.50	.70
❑ 28 Casey Fossum	1.00	.45
❑ 29 Sammy Sosa	4.00	1.80
❑ 30 Kerry Wood	2.50	1.10
❑ 31 Corey Patterson	1.00	.45

❑ 32 Nic Jackson 1.00 .45
❑ 33 Mark Prior 2.50 1.10
❑ 34 Juan Cruz 1.00 .45
❑ 35 Steve Smyth 1.00 .45
❑ 36 Magglio Ordonez 1.00 .45
❑ 37 Joe Borchard 1.00 .45
❑ 38 Frank Thomas 2.50 1.10
❑ 39 Mark Buehrle 1.00 .45
❑ 40 Joe Crede 1.00 .45
❑ 41 Carlos Lee 1.00 .45
❑ 42 Paul Konerko 1.00 .45
❑ 43 Adam Dunn 1.50 .70
❑ 44 Corky Miller 1.00 .45
❑ 45 Brandon Larson 1.00 .45
❑ 46 Ken Griffey Jr. 4.00 1.80
❑ 47 Barry Larkin 1.50 .70
❑ 48 Sean Casey 1.00 .45
❑ 49 Wily Mo Pena 1.00 .45
❑ 50 Austin Kearns 1.00 .45
❑ 51 Victor Martinez 1.50 .70
❑ 52 Brian Tallet 1.00 .45
❑ 53 Cliff Lee 1.00 .45
❑ 54 Jeremy Guthrie 1.00 .45
❑ 55 C.C. Sabathia 1.00 .45
❑ 56 Ricardo Rodriguez 1.00 .45
❑ 57 Omar Vizquel 1.50 .70
❑ 58 Travis Hafner 1.00 .45
❑ 59 Todd Helton 1.50 .70
❑ 60 Jason Jennings 1.00 .45
❑ 61 Jeff Baker 1.00 .45
❑ 62 Larry Walker 1.50 .70
❑ 63 Travis Chapman 1.00 .45
❑ 64 Mike Maroth 1.00 .45
❑ 65 Josh Beckett 1.00 .45
❑ 66 Ivan Rodriguez 2.50 1.10
❑ 67 Brad Penny 1.00 .45
❑ 68 A.J. Burnett 1.00 .45
❑ 69 Craig Biggio 1.50 .70
❑ 70 Roy Oswalt 1.00 .45
❑ 71 Jason Lane 1.00 .45
❑ 72 Nolan Ryan Astros 6.00 2.70
❑ 73 Wade Miller 1.00 .45
❑ 74 Richard Hidalgo 1.00 .45
❑ 75 Jeff Bagwell 1.50 .70
❑ 76 Lance Berkman 1.00 .45
❑ 77 Rodrigo Rosario 1.00 .45
❑ 78 Jeff Kent 1.00 .45
❑ 79 John Buck 1.00 .45
❑ 80 Angel Berroa 1.00 .45
❑ 81 Mike Sweeney 1.00 .45
❑ 82 Mac Suzuki 1.00 .45
❑ 83 Alexis Gomez 1.00 .45
❑ 84 Carlos Beltran 1.50 .70
❑ 85 Runelvys Hernandez 1.00 .45
❑ 86 Hideo Nomo 2.50 1.10
❑ 87 Paul Lo Duca 1.00 .45
❑ 88 Cesar Izturis 1.00 .45
❑ 89 Kazuhisa Ishii 1.00 .45
❑ 90 Shawn Green 1.00 .45
❑ 91 Joe Thurston 1.00 .45
❑ 92 Adrian Beltre 1.50 .70
❑ 93 Kevin Brown 1.00 .45
❑ 94 Richie Sexson 1.00 .45
❑ 95 Ben Sheets 1.00 .45
❑ 96 Takahito Nomura 1.00 .45
❑ 97 Geoff Jenkins 1.00 .45
❑ 98 Bill Hall 1.00 .45
❑ 99 Torii Hunter 1.00 .45
❑ 100 A.J. Pierzynski 1.00 .45
❑ 101 Michael Cuddyer 1.00 .45
❑ 102 Jose Morban 1.00 .45
❑ 103 Brad Radke 1.00 .45
❑ 104 Jacque Jones 1.00 .45
❑ 105 Eric Milton 1.00 .45
❑ 106 Joe Mays 1.00 .45
❑ 107 Adam Johnson 1.00 .45
❑ 108 Javier Vazquez 1.00 .45
❑ 109 Vladimir Guerrero 2.50 1.10
❑ 110 Jose Vidro 1.00 .45
❑ 111 Michael Barrett 1.00 .45
❑ 112 Orlando Cabrera 1.00 .45
❑ 113 Tom Glavine 1.50 .70
❑ 114 Roberto Alomar 1.50 .70
❑ 115 Tsuyoshi Shinjo 1.00 .45
❑ 116 Cliff Floyd 1.00 .45
❑ 117 Mike Piazza 4.00 1.80
❑ 118 Al Leiter 1.00 .45
❑ 119 Don Mattingly 6.00 2.70
❑ 120 Roger Clemens 5.00 2.20
❑ 121 Derek Jeter 6.00 2.70
❑ 122 Alfonso Soriano 1.50 .70
❑ 123 Drew Henson 1.00 .45
❑ 124 Brandon Claussen 1.00 .45
❑ 125 Christian Parker 1.00 .45
❑ 126 Jason Giambi 1.00 .45
❑ 127 Mike Mussina 1.50 .70
❑ 128 Bernie Williams 1.50 .70
❑ 129 Jason Anderson 1.00 .45
❑ 130 Nick Johnson 1.00 .45
❑ 131 Jorge Posada 1.50 .70
❑ 132 Andy Pettitte 1.50 .70
❑ 133 Barry Zito 1.00 .45
❑ 134 Miguel Tejada 1.00 .45
❑ 135 Eric Chavez 1.00 .45
❑ 136 Tim Hudson 1.00 .45
❑ 137 Mark Mulder 1.00 .45
❑ 138 Terrence Long 1.00 .45
❑ 139 Mark Ellis 1.00 .45
❑ 140 Jim Thome 2.50 1.10
❑ 141 Pat Burrell 1.00 .45
❑ 142 Marlon Byrd 1.00 .45
❑ 143 Bobby Abreu 1.00 .45
❑ 144 Brandon Duckworth 1.00 .45
❑ 145 Robert Person 1.00 .45
❑ 146 Anderson Machado 1.00 .45
❑ 147 Aramis Ramirez 1.00 .45
❑ 148 Jack Wilson 1.00 .45
❑ 149 Carlos Rivera 1.00 .45
❑ 150 Jose Castillo 1.00 .45
❑ 151 Walter Young 1.00 .45
❑ 152 Brian Giles 1.00 .45
❑ 153 Jason Kendall 1.00 .45
❑ 154 Ryan Klesko 1.00 .45
❑ 155 Mike Rivera 1.00 .45
❑ 156 Sean Burroughs 1.00 .45
❑ 157 Brian Lawrence 1.00 .45
❑ 158 Xavier Nady 1.00 .45
❑ 159 Dennis Tankersley 1.00 .45
❑ 160 Phil Nevin 1.00 .45
❑ 161 Barry Bonds 6.00 2.70
❑ 162 Kenny Lofton 1.00 .45
❑ 163 Rich Aurilia 1.00 .45
❑ 164 Ichiro Suzuki 4.00 1.80
❑ 165 Edgar Martinez 1.50 .70
❑ 166 Chris Snelling 1.00 .45
❑ 167 Rafael Soriano 1.00 .45
❑ 168 John Olerud 1.00 .45
❑ 169 Bret Boone 1.00 .45
❑ 170 Freddy Garcia 1.00 .45
❑ 171 Aaron Sele 1.00 .45
❑ 172 Kazuhiro Sasaki 1.00 .45
❑ 173 Albert Pujols 5.00 2.20
❑ 174 Scott Rolen 2.50 1.10
❑ 175 So Taguchi 1.00 .45
❑ 176 Jim Edmonds 1.00 .45
❑ 177 Edgar Renteria 1.00 .45
❑ 178 J.D. Drew 1.00 .45
❑ 179 Antonio Perez 1.00 .45
❑ 180 Dewon Brazelton 1.00 .45
❑ 181 Aubrey Huff 1.00 .45
❑ 182 Toby Hall 1.00 .45
❑ 183 Ben Grieve 1.00 .45
❑ 184 Joe Kennedy 1.00 .45
❑ 185 Alex Rodriguez 4.00 1.80
❑ 186 Rafael Palmeiro 1.50 .70
❑ 187 Hank Blalock 1.50 .70
❑ 188 Mark Teixeira 1.00 .45
❑ 189 Juan Gonzalez 1.50 .70
❑ 190 Kevin Mench 1.00 .45
❑ 191 Nolan Ryan Rgr 6.00 2.70
❑ 192 Doug Davis 1.00 .45
❑ 193 Eric Hinske 1.00 .45
❑ 194 Vinny Chulk 1.00 .45
❑ 195 Alexis Rios 1.50 .70
❑ 196 Carlos Delgado 1.00 .45
❑ 197 Shannon Stewart 1.00 .45
❑ 198 Josh Phelps 1.00 .45
❑ 199 Vernon Wells 1.00 .45
❑ 200 Roy Halladay 1.00 .45
❑ 201 Babe Ruth RET 20.00 9.00
❑ 202 Lou Gehrig RET 12.00 5.50
❑ 203 Jackie Robinson RET 10.00 4.50
❑ 204 Ty Cobb RET 15.00 6.75
❑ 205 Thurman Munson RET 10.00 4.50
❑ 206 Pr. Redman NG AU RC 10.00 4.50
❑ 207 Craig Brazell NG AU RC 15.00 6.75
❑ 208 Nook Logan NG AU RC 10.00 4.50
❑ 209 Hong-Chih Kuo NG AU RC 25.00 11.00
❑ 210 Matt Kata NG AU RC 15.00 6.75
❑ 211 C.Wang NG AU RC 40.00 18.00
❑ 212 Alej Machado NG AU RC 10.00 4.50
❑ 213 Mike Hessman NG AU RC 10.00 4.50
❑ 214 Franc Rosario NG AU RC 10.00 4.50
❑ 215 Pedro Liriano NG AU 10.00 4.50
❑ 216 J.Bonderman NG AU RC 15.00 6.75
❑ 217 Oscar Villarreal NG AU RC 10.00 4.50
❑ 218 Arnie Munoz NG AU RC 10.00 4.50
❑ 219 Tim Olson NG AU RC 15.00 6.75
❑ 220 J.Contreras NG AU/100 RC 40.00 18.00
❑ 221 Franc Cruceta NG AU RC 10.00 4.50
❑ 222 John Webb NG AU 10.00 4.50
❑ 223 Phil Seibel NG AU RC 10.00 4.50
❑ 224 Aaron Looper NG AU RC 10.00 4.50
❑ 225 Brian Stokes NG AU RC 10.00 4.50
❑ 226 G.Quiroz NG AU RC 15.00 6.75
❑ 227 Fern Cabrera NG AU RC 10.00 4.50
❑ 228 Josh Hall NG AU RC 15.00 6.75
❑ 229 Diego Markwell NG AU RC 10.00 4.50
❑ 230 Andrew Brown NG AU RC 15.00 6.75
❑ 231 Doug Waechter NG AU RC 15.00 6.75
❑ 232 Felix Sanchez NG AU RC 10.00 4.50
❑ 233 Gerardo Garcia NG AU 10.00 4.50
❑ 234 Matt Bruback NG AU RC 10.00 4.50
❑ 235 Mi. Hernandez NG AU RC 10.00 4.50
❑ 236 Rett Johnson NG AU RC 15.00 6.75
❑ 237 Ryan Cameron NG AU RC 10.00 4.50
❑ 238 Rob Hammock NG AU RC 15.00 6.75
❑ 239 Clint Barmes NG AU RC 15.00 6.75
❑ 240 Brandon Webb NG AU RC 20.00 9.00
❑ 241 Jon Leicester NG AU RC 10.00 4.50
❑ 242 Shane Bazzell NG AU RC 10.00 4.50
❑ 243 Joe Valentine NG AU RC 10.00 4.50
❑ 244 Josh Stewart NG AU RC 10.00 4.50
❑ 245 Pete LaForest NG AU RC 15.00 6.75
❑ 246 Shane Victorino NG AU RC 10.00 4.50
❑ 247 Termel Sledge NG AU RC 15.00 6.75
❑ 248 Lew Ford NG AU RC 25.00 11.00
❑ 249 T.Wellemeyer NG AU RC 15.00 6.75
❑ 250 Hideki Matsui NG RC 15.00 6.75
❑ 251 A.Loewen NG AU/250 RC 25.00 11.00
❑ 252 Dan Haren NG AU/250 RC 20.00 9.00
❑ 253 Dontrelle Willis NG AU/150 15.00 6.75
❑ 254 Ramon Nivar NG AU/250 RC 20.00 9.00
❑ 255 Chad Gaudin NG AU/250 RC 10.00 4.50
❑ 256 Kevin Correia NG AU/150 RC 10.00 4.50
❑ 257 R.Weeks NG AU/100 RC 80.00 36.00
❑ 258 R.Wagner NG AU/250 RC 15.00 6.75
❑ 259 Del.Young NG AU/100 RC 150.00 70.00

2004 Leaf Certified Materials

	Nm-Mt	Ex-Mt
COMP.SET w/o SP's (200)	40.00	12.00
COMMON CARD (1-200)	.75	.23
COMMON CARD (201-211)	3.00	.90
201-211 STATED ODDS 1:120		
COMMON CARD (212-240)	3.00	.90
212-240 PRINT RUN 500 SERIAL #'d SETS		
COMMON NO AU (241-300)	5.00	1.50

241-300 NO AU PRINT RUN 500 #'d PER
OVERALL AU ODDS 1:10
AU PRINT RUNS B/WN 100-1000 PER
AU PRINT RUN 500 #'d PER UNLESS NOTED

❑ 1 A.J. Burnett .75 .23
❑ 2 Adam Dunn 1.25 .35
❑ 3 Adam LaRoche .75 .23
❑ 4 Adam Loewen .75 .23
❑ 5 Adrian Beltre 1.25 .35
❑ 6 Al Leiter .75 .23
❑ 7 Albert Pujols 4.00 1.20
❑ 8 Alex Rodriguez Yanks 3.00 .90
❑ 9 Alexis Rios .75 .23
❑ 10 Alfonso Soriano Rgr 1.25 .35
❑ 11 Andruw Jones .75 .23
❑ 12 Andy Pettitte 1.25 .35
❑ 13 Angel Berroa .75 .23
❑ 14 Aramis Ramirez .75 .23
❑ 15 Aubrey Huff .75 .23
❑ 16 Austin Kearns .75 .23
❑ 17 Barry Larkin 1.25 .35
❑ 18 Barry Zito .75 .23
❑ 19 Ben Sheets .75 .23
❑ 20 Bernie Williams 1.25 .35
❑ 21 Bobby Abreu .75 .23
❑ 22 Brad Penny .75 .23
❑ 23 Brad Wilkerson .75 .23
❑ 24 Brandon Webb .75 .23
❑ 25 Brendan Harris .75 .23
❑ 26 Bret Boone .75 .23
❑ 27 Brett Myers .75 .23
❑ 28 Bubba Crosby .75 .23
❑ 29 Brian Giles .75 .23
❑ 30 Chad Cordero .75 .23
❑ 31 Bubba Nelson .75 .23
❑ 32 Byron Gettis .75 .23
❑ 33 C.C. Sabathia .75 .23
❑ 34 Carl Crawford .75 .23
❑ 35 Carl Everett .75 .23
❑ 36 Carlos Beltran 1.25 .35
❑ 37 Carlos Delgado .75 .23
❑ 38 Carlos Lee .75 .23
❑ 39 Chad Gaudin .75 .23
❑ 40 Cliff Lee .75 .23
❑ 41 Chipper Jones 2.00 .60
❑ 42 Cliff Floyd .75 .23
❑ 43 Clint Barmes .75 .23
❑ 44 Corey Patterson .75 .23
❑ 45 Craig Biggio 1.25 .35
❑ 46 Curt Schilling Sox 2.00 .60
❑ 47 Dan Haren .75 .23
❑ 48 Darin Erstad .75 .23
❑ 49 David Ortiz 2.00 .60
❑ 50 Delmon Young 1.25 .35
❑ 51 Derek Jeter 4.00 1.20
❑ 52 Dewon Brazelton .75 .23
❑ 53 Dontrelle Willis .75 .23
❑ 54 Edgar Martinez 1.25 .35
❑ 55 Edgar Renteria .75 .23
❑ 56 Edwin Almonte .75 .23
❑ 57 Edwin Jackson .75 .23
❑ 58 Eric Chavez .75 .23
❑ 59 Eric Hinske .75 .23
❑ 60 Eric Munson .75 .23
❑ 61 Erubial Durazo .75 .23
❑ 62 Frank Thomas 2.00 .60
❑ 63 Fred McGriff 1.25 .35
❑ 64 Freddy Garcia .75 .23
❑ 65 Garret Anderson .75 .23
❑ 66 Garrett Atkins .75 .23
❑ 67 Gary Sheffield .75 .23
❑ 68 Geoff Jenkins .75 .23
❑ 69 Greg Maddux Cubs 3.00 .90
❑ 70 Hank Blalock .75 .23
❑ 71 Hee Seop Choi .75 .23
❑ 72 Hideki Matsui 3.00 .90
❑ 73 Hideo Nomo 2.00 .60
❑ 74 Craig Wilson .75 .23
❑ 75 Ichiro Suzuki 3.00 .90
❑ 76 Ivan Rodriguez Tigers 2.00 .60
❑ 77 J.D. Drew .75 .23
❑ 78 John Lackey .75 .23
❑ 79 Jacque Jones .75 .23
❑ 80 Jae Weong Seo .75 .23
❑ 81 Jamie Moyer .75 .23
❑ 82 Jason Giambi Yanks .75 .23
❑ 83 Jason Jennings .75 .23
❑ 84 Jason Kendall .75 .23
❑ 85 Melvin Mora .75 .23
❑ 86 Jason Varitek 1.25 .35
❑ 87 Javier Vazquez .75 .23
❑ 88 Javy Lopez .75 .23
❑ 89 Jay Gibbons .75 .23
❑ 90 Jay Payton .75 .23
❑ 91 Jeff Bagwell 1.25 .35
❑ 92 Jeff Baker .75 .23
❑ 93 Jeff Kent .75 .23
❑ 94 Jeremy Bonderman .75 .23
❑ 95 Milton Bradley .75 .23
❑ 96 Jerome Williams .75 .23
❑ 97 Jim Edmonds .75 .23
❑ 98 Jim Thome 2.00 .60
❑ 99 Jody Gerut .75 .23
❑ 100 Joe Borchard .75 .23
❑ 101 Joe Crede .75 .23
❑ 102 Johan Santana 1.25 .35
❑ 103 John Olerud .75 .23
❑ 104 John Smoltz 1.25 .35
❑ 105 Johnny Damon 2.00 .60
❑ 106 Jorge Posada 1.25 .35
❑ 107 Jose Castillo .75 .23
❑ 108 Jose Reyes .75 .23
❑ 109 Jose Vidro .75 .23
❑ 110 Josh Beckett .75 .23
❑ 111 Josh Phelps .75 .23
❑ 112 Juan Encarnacion .75 .23
❑ 113 Juan Gonzalez 1.25 .35
❑ 114 Junior Spivey .75 .23
❑ 115 Kazuhisa Ishii .75 .23
❑ 116 Kenny Lofton .75 .23
❑ 117 Kerry Wood 2.00 .60
❑ 118 Kevin Millwood .75 .23
❑ 119 Kevin Youkilis .75 .23
❑ 120 Lance Berkman .75 .23
❑ 121 Larry Bigbie .75 .23
❑ 122 Larry Walker 1.25 .35
❑ 123 Luis Castillo .75 .23
❑ 124 Luis Gonzalez .75 .23
❑ 125 Luis Matos .75 .23
❑ 126 Lyle Overbay .75 .23
❑ 127 Magglio Ordonez .75 .23
❑ 128 Manny Ramirez 1.25 .35
❑ 129 Marcus Giles .75 .23
❑ 130 Mariano Rivera 1.25 .35
❑ 131 Mark Buehrle .75 .23
❑ 132 Mark Mulder .75 .23
❑ 133 Mark Prior 2.00 .60
❑ 134 Mark Teixeira .75 .23
❑ 135 Marlon Byrd .75 .23
❑ 136 Matt Morris .75 .23
❑ 137 Miguel Cabrera 1.25 .35
❑ 138 Mike Lowell .75 .23
❑ 139 Mike Mussina 1.25 .35
❑ 140 Mike Piazza 3.00 .90
❑ 141 Mike Sweeney .75 .23
❑ 142 Morgan Ensberg .75 .23
❑ 143 Nick Johnson .75 .23
❑ 144 Nomar Garciaparra 3.00 .90
❑ 145 Omar Vizquel 1.25 .35
❑ 146 Orlando Cabrera .75 .23
❑ 147 Orlando Hudson .75 .23
❑ 148 Pat Burrell .75 .23
❑ 149 Paul Konerko .75 .23
❑ 150 Paul Lo Duca .75 .23
❑ 151 Pedro Martinez 2.00 .60
❑ 152 Jermaine Dye .75 .23
❑ 153 Preston Wilson .75 .23
❑ 154 Rafael Furcal .75 .23
❑ 155 Rafael Palmeiro O's 1.25 .35
❑ 156 Randy Johnson 2.00 .60
❑ 157 Rich Aurilia .75 .23
❑ 158 Rich Harden .75 .23
❑ 159 Richard Hidalgo .75 .23
❑ 160 Richie Sexson .75 .23
❑ 161 Rickie Weeks .75 .23
❑ 162 Roberto Alomar 1.25 .35
❑ 163 Rocco Baldelli .75 .23
❑ 164 Roger Clemens Astros 4.00 1.20
❑ 165 Roy Halladay .75 .23
❑ 166 Roy Oswalt .75 .23
❑ 167 Ryan Howard .75 .23
❑ 168 Ryan Klesko .75 .23
❑ 169 Rodrigo Lopez .75 .23
❑ 170 Sammy Sosa 3.00 .90
❑ 171 Scott Podsednik .75 .23
❑ 172 Scott Rolen 2.00 .60
❑ 173 Sean Burroughs .75 .23
❑ 174 Sean Casey .75 .23
❑ 175 Shannon Stewart .75 .23
❑ 176 Shawn Green .75 .23
❑ 177 Shea Hillenbrand .75 .23
❑ 178 Shigetoshi Hasegawa .75 .23
❑ 179 Steve Finley .75 .23
❑ 180 Tim Hudson .75 .23
❑ 181 Todd Helton 1.25 .35
❑ 182 Tom Glavine 1.25 .35
❑ 183 Torii Hunter .75 .23
❑ 184 Trot Nixon .75 .23
❑ 185 Troy Glaus .75 .23
❑ 186 Vernon Wells .75 .23
❑ 187 Victor Martinez .75 .23
❑ 188 Vladimir Guerrero Angels 2.00 .60
❑ 189 Wade Miller .75 .23
❑ 190 Brandon Larson .75 .23
❑ 191 Travis Hafner .75 .23
❑ 192 Tim Salmon 1.25 .35
❑ 193 Tim Redding .75 .23
❑ 194 Runelvys Hernandez .75 .23
❑ 195 Ramon Nivar .75 .23
❑ 196 Moises Alou .75 .23
❑ 197 Michael Young .75 .23
❑ 198 Layce Nix .75 .23
❑ 199 Tino Martinez 1.25 .35
❑ 200 Randall Simon .75 .23
❑ 201 Roger Clemens Yanks SP 8.00 2.40
❑ 202 Greg Maddux Braves SP 8.00 2.40
❑ 203 Vladimir Guerrero Expos SP 5.00 1.50
❑ 204 Miguel Tejada SP 3.00 .90
❑ 205 Kevin Brown SP 3.00 .90
❑ 206 Jason Giambi A's SP 3.00 .90
❑ 207 Curt Schilling D'backs SP 3.00 .90
❑ 208 Alex Rodriguez Rgr SP 8.00 2.40
❑ 209 Alfonso Soriano Yanks SP 5.00 1.50
❑ 210 Ivan Rodriguez Marlins SP 5.00 1.50
❑ 211 Rafael Palmeiro Rgr SP 5.00 1.50
❑ 212 Gary Carter LGD 3.00 .90
❑ 213 Duke Snider LGD 5.00 1.50
❑ 214 Whitey Ford LGD 5.00 1.50
❑ 215 Bob Feller LGD 3.00 .90
❑ 216 Reggie Jackson LGD 5.00 1.50
❑ 217 Ryne Sandberg LGD 10.00 3.00
❑ 218 Dale Murphy LGD 5.00 1.50
❑ 219 Tony Gwynn LGD 8.00 2.40
❑ 220 Don Mattingly LGD 10.00 3.00
❑ 221 Mike Schmidt LGD 10.00 3.00
❑ 222 Rickey Henderson LGD 5.00 1.50
❑ 223 Cal Ripken LGD 15.00 4.50
❑ 224 Nolan Ryan LGD 12.00 3.60
❑ 225 George Brett LGD 10.00 3.00
❑ 226 Bob Gibson LGD 5.00 1.50
❑ 227 Lou Brock LGD 5.00 1.50
❑ 228 Andre Dawson LGD 3.00 .90
❑ 229 Rod Carew LGD 5.00 1.50
❑ 230 Wade Boggs LGD 5.00 1.50
❑ 231 Roberto Clemente LGD 10.00 3.00
❑ 232 Roy Campanella LGD 5.00 1.50
❑ 233 Babe Ruth LGD 10.00 3.00
❑ 234 Lou Gehrig LGD 8.00 2.40
❑ 235 Ty Cobb LGD 8.00 2.40
❑ 236 Roger Maris LGD 5.00 1.50
❑ 237 Satchel Paige LGD 5.00 1.50
❑ 238 Ernie Banks LGD 5.00 1.50
❑ 239 Ted Williams LGD 10.00 3.00
❑ 240 Stan Musial LGD 8.00 2.40
❑ 241 Hector Gimenez NG AU RC 8.00 2.40
❑ 242 Justin Germano NG AU RC 8.00 2.40
❑ 243 Ian Snell NG AU RC 10.00 3.00
❑ 244 Graham Koonce NG AU 8.00 2.40
❑ 245 Jose Capellan NG AU RC 25.00 7.50
❑ 246 Onil Joseph NG AU RC 8.00 2.40
❑ 247 S.Takatsu NG AU/200 RC 40.00 12.00
❑ 248 Carlos Hines NG AU RC 8.00 2.40
❑ 249 Linc Holdzkom NG AU RC 8.00 2.40
❑ 250 Mike Gosling NG AU RC 8.00 2.40
❑ 251 Eduardo Sierra NG AU RC 10.00 3.00
❑ 252 Renyel Pinto NG AU RC 10.00 3.00
❑ 253 Merkin Valdez NG AU RC 15.00 4.50

❑ 254 Angel Chavez NG AU RC 8.00 2.40
❑ 255 I.Ochoa NG AU/1000 RC 8.00 2.40
❑ 256 G.Dobbs NG AU/300 RC 8.00 2.40
❑ 257 William Bergolla NG AU RC 8.00 2.40
❑ 258 Aarom Baldiris NG AU RC 10.00 3.00
❑ 259 Kazuo Matsui NG RC.... 15.00 4.50
❑ 260 Carlos Vasquez NG AU RC 10.00 3.00
❑ 261 Freddy Guzman NG AU RC 8.00 2.40
❑ 262 Aki Otsuka NG AU/200 RC 40.00 12.00
❑ 263 M.Gomez NG AU/200 RC 10.00 3.00
❑ 264 Nick Regilio NG AU RC .. 8.00 2.40
❑ 265 Jamie Brown NG AU RC 8.00 2.40
❑ 266 Shawn Hill NG AU RC.... 8.00 2.40
❑ 267 Roberto Novoa NG AU RC 10.00 3.00
❑ 268 Sean Henn NG AU RC.... 8.00 2.40
❑ 269 Ramon Ramirez NG AU RC 8.00 2.40
❑ 270 R.Cedeno NG AU/1000 RC 8.00 2.40
❑ 271 Ryan Wing NG AU/400 RC 8.00 2.40
❑ 272 Ruddy Yan NG AU......... 8.00 2.40
❑ 273 Fernando Nieve NG AU RC 8.00 2.40
❑ 274 Rusty Tucker NG AU RC 10.00 3.00
❑ 275 Jason Bartlett NG AU RC 10.00 3.00
❑ 276 Mike Rouse NG AU RC .. 8.00 2.40
❑ 277 Dennis Sarfate NG AU RC 8.00 2.40
❑ 278 Cory Sullivan NG AU RC 8.00 2.40
❑ 279 C.Daigle NG AU/250 RC 10.00 3.00
❑ 280 C.Shelton NG AU/400 RC 10.00 3.00
❑ 281 J.Harper NG AU/400 RC 8.00 2.40
❑ 282 Michael Wuertz NG AU RC 10.00 3.00
❑ 283 T.Bausher NG AU/400 RC 8.00 2.40
❑ 284 Jorge Sequea NG AU RC 8.00 2.40
❑ 285 J.Labandeira NG AU/100 RC 15.00 4.50
❑ 286 Justin Leone NG AU RC 10.00 3.00
❑ 287 Tim Bittner NG AU RC.... 8.00 2.40
❑ 288 Andres Blanco NG AU RC 8.00 2.40
❑ 289 K.Cave NG AU/1000 RC 10.00 3.00
❑ 290 M.Johnston NG AU/1000 RC 8.00 2.40
❑ 291 J.Szuminski NG AU RC .. 8.00 2.40
❑ 292 Shawn Camp NG RC...... 5.00 1.50
❑ 293 Colby Miller NG AU RC.. 8.00 2.40
❑ 294 Jake Woods NG AU RC.. 8.00 2.40
❑ 295 Ryan Meaux NG AU RC.. 8.00 2.40
❑ 296 Don Kelly NG AU RC...... 8.00 2.40
❑ 297 Edwin Moreno NG AU RC 8.00 2.40
❑ 298 Phil Stockman NG AU RC 8.00 2.40
❑ 299 Jorge Vasquez NG RC.... 8.00 2.40
❑ 300 Kaz Tadano NG AU RC 25.00 7.50

2001 Leaf Limited

	Nm-Mt	Ex-Mt
COMP.SET w/o SP'S (150)	100.00	30.00
COMMON CARD (1-150)...........	1.00	.30
COMMON HAT (326-375)	25.00	7.50
COMMON LUM/500 (151-200) ..	8.00	2.40
COMMON LUM/250 (151-200)	10.00	3.00
COMMON LUM/100 (151-200)	15.00	4.50
COMMON (201-250).................	5.00	1.50
COMMON (251-300).................	5.00	1.50
COMMON (301-325)...............	10.00	3.00
COMMON BASE (326-375)	15.00	4.50
COMMON BAT (326-375)	8.00	2.40
COMMON JSY (326-375)	8.00	2.40
COMMON PANTS (326-375)......	8.00	2.40
COMMON SPIKES (326-375)....	25.00	7.50

❑ 1 Curt Schilling .... 1.00 .30
❑ 2 Craig Biggio .... 1.50 .45
❑ 3 Brian Giles .... 1.00 .30
❑ 4 Scott Brosius...................... 1.00 .30
❑ 5 Barry Larkin........................ 1.50 .45
❑ 6 Bartolo Colon .... 1.00 .30
❑ 7 John Olerud .... 1.00 .30
❑ 8 Cal Ripken........................... 8.00 2.40
❑ 9 Moises Alou .... 1.00 .30
❑ 10 Barry Zito .... 1.50 .45
❑ 11 Ken Griffey Jr. 4.00 1.20
❑ 12 Garret Anderson .... 1.00 .30
❑ 13 Andy Pettitte .... 1.50 .45
❑ 14 Jim Edmonds .... 1.00 .30
❑ 15 Tom Glavine .... 1.50 .45
❑ 16 Jose Canseco .... 2.50 .75
❑ 17 Fred McGriff .... 1.50 .45
❑ 18 Robin Ventura .... 1.00 .30
❑ 19 Tony Gwynn .... 3.00 .90
❑ 20 Jeff Cirillo .... 1.00 .30
❑ 21 Brad Radke .... 1.00 .30
❑ 22 Ellis Burks.......................... 1.00 .30
❑ 23 Scott Rolen .... 2.50 .75
❑ 24 Rickey Henderson .... 2.50 .75
❑ 25 Edgar Martinez .... 1.50 .45
❑ 26 Kerry Wood .... 2.50 .75
❑ 27 Al Leiter.............................. 1.00 .30
❑ 28 Jose Cruz Jr....................... 1.00 .30
❑ 29 Sean Casey .... 1.00 .30
❑ 30 Eric Chavez .... 1.00 .30
❑ 31 Jarrod Washburn................ 1.00 .30
❑ 32 Gary Sheffield .... 1.00 .30
❑ 33 Jermaine Dye .... 1.00 .30
❑ 34 Bernie Williams.................. 1.50 .45
❑ 35 Tony Armas Jr. .... 1.00 .30
❑ 36 Carlos Beltran .... 1.50 .45
❑ 37 Geoff Jenkins .... 1.00 .30
❑ 38 Shawn Green...................... 1.00 .30
❑ 39 Ryan Klesko .... 1.00 .30
❑ 40 Richie Sexson .... 1.00 .30
❑ 41 Pat Burrell .... 1.00 .30
❑ 42 J.D. Drew .... 1.00 .30
❑ 43 Larry Walker .... 1.50 .45
❑ 44 Andres Galarraga................ 1.00 .30
❑ 45 Tino Martinez .... 1.50 .45
❑ 46 Rafael Furcal .... 1.00 .30
❑ 47 Cristian Guzman .... 1.00 .30
❑ 48 Omar Vizquel...................... 1.50 .45
❑ 49 Bret Boone .... 1.00 .30
❑ 50 Wade Miller.......................... 1.00 .30
❑ 51 Eric Milton .... 1.00 .30
❑ 52 Gabe Kapler........................ 1.00 .30
❑ 53 Johnny Damon .... 1.50 .45
❑ 54 Shannon Stewart................ 1.00 .30
❑ 55 Kenny Lofton .... 1.00 .30
❑ 56 Raul Mondesi .... 1.00 .30
❑ 57 Jorge Posada .... 1.50 .45
❑ 58 Mark Grace .... 1.50 .45
❑ 59 Robert Fick .... 1.00 .30
❑ 60 Phil Nevin .... 1.00 .30
❑ 61 Mike Mussina .... 1.50 .45
❑ 62 Joe Mays.............................. 1.00 .30
❑ 63 Todd Helton .... 1.50 .45
❑ 64 Tim Hudson .... 1.00 .30
❑ 65 Manny Ramirez .... 1.50 .45
❑ 66 Sammy Sosa 4.00 1.20
❑ 67 Darin Erstad .... 1.00 .30
❑ 68 Roberto Alomar.................. 1.50 .45
❑ 69 Jeff Bagwell.......................... 1.50 .45
❑ 70 Mark McGwire...................... 6.00 1.80
❑ 71 Jason Giambi .... 1.00 .30
❑ 72 Cliff Floyd .... 1.00 .30
❑ 73 Barry Bonds 6.00 1.80
❑ 74 Juan Gonzalez .... 1.50 .45
❑ 75 Jeremy Giambi .... 1.00 .30
❑ 76 Carlos Lee............................ 1.00 .30
❑ 77 Randy Johnson .... 2.50 .75
❑ 78 Frank Thomas .... 2.50 .75
❑ 79 Carlos Delgado .... 1.00 .30
❑ 80 Pedro Martinez .... 2.50 .75
❑ 81 Rusty Greer .... 1.00 .30
❑ 82 Brian Jordan .... 1.00 .30
❑ 83 Vladimir Guerrero .... 2.50 .75
❑ 84 Mike Sweeney .... 1.00 .30
❑ 85 Jose Vidro .... 1.00 .30
❑ 86 Paul LoDuca .... 1.00 .30
❑ 87 Matt Morris .... 1.00 .30
❑ 88 Adrian Beltre .... 1.50 .45
❑ 89 Aramis Ramirez .... 1.00 .30
❑ 90 Derek Jeter 6.00 1.80
❑ 91 Rich Aurilia .... 1.00 .30
❑ 92 Freddy Garcia .... 1.00 .30
❑ 93 Preston Wilson .... 1.00 .30
❑ 94 Greg Maddux 4.00 1.20
❑ 95 Miguel Tejada .... 1.00 .30
❑ 96 Luis Gonzalez .... 1.00 .30
❑ 97 Torii Hunter.......................... 1.00 .30
❑ 98 Nomar Garciaparra 4.00 1.20
❑ 99 Jamie Moyer .... 1.00 .30
❑ 100 Javier Vazquez.................. 1.00 .30
❑ 101 Ben Grieve.......................... 1.00 .30
❑ 102 Mike Piazza........................ 4.00 1.20
❑ 103 Paul O'Neill .... 1.50 .45
❑ 104 Terrence Long .... 1.00 .30
❑ 105 Charles Johnson .... 1.00 .30
❑ 106 Rafael Palmeiro .... 1.50 .45
❑ 107 David Cone .... 1.00 .30
❑ 108 Alex Rodriguez 4.00 1.20
❑ 109 John Burkett .... 1.00 .30
❑ 110 Chipper Jones.................... 2.50 .75
❑ 111 Ryan Dempster .... 1.00 .30
❑ 112 Bobby Abreu .... 1.00 .30
❑ 113 Brad Fullmer .... 1.00 .30
❑ 114 Kazuhiro Sasaki................ 1.00 .30
❑ 115 Mariano Rivera .... 1.50 .45
❑ 116 Edgardo Alfonzo .... 1.00 .30
❑ 117 Ray Durham .... 1.00 .30
❑ 118 Richard Hidalgo .... 1.00 .30
❑ 119 Jeff Weaver .... 1.00 .30
❑ 120 Paul Konerko...................... 1.00 .30
❑ 121 Jon Lieber .... 1.00 .30
❑ 122 Mike Hampton.................... 1.00 .30
❑ 123 Mike Cameron.................... 1.00 .30
❑ 124 Kevin Brown .... 1.00 .30
❑ 125 Doug Mientkiewicz .... 1.00 .30
❑ 126 Jim Thome .... 2.50 .75
❑ 127 Corey Koskie...................... 1.00 .30
❑ 128 Trot Nixon .... 1.00 .30
❑ 129 Darryl Kile .... 1.00 .30
❑ 130 Ivan Rodriguez .... 2.50 .75
❑ 131 Carl Everett .... 1.00 .30
❑ 132 Jeff Kent .... 1.00 .30
❑ 133 Rondell White .... 1.00 .30
❑ 134 Chan Ho Park .... 1.00 .30
❑ 135 Robert Person .... 1.00 .30
❑ 136 Troy Glaus.......................... 1.00 .30
❑ 137 Aaron Sele.......................... 1.00 .30
❑ 138 Roger Clemens 5.00 1.50
❑ 139 Tony Clark.......................... 1.00 .30
❑ 140 Mark Buehrle...................... 1.00 .30
❑ 141 David Justice...................... 1.00 .30
❑ 142 Magglio Ordonez................ 1.00 .30
❑ 143 Bobby Higginson .... 1.00 .30
❑ 144 Hideo Nomo .... 2.50 .75
❑ 145 Tim Salmon........................ 1.50 .45
❑ 146 Mark Mulder .... 1.00 .30
❑ 147 Troy Percival...................... 1.00 .30
❑ 148 Lance Berkman .... 1.00 .30
❑ 149 Russ Ortiz .... 1.00 .30
❑ 150 Andruw Jones .... 1.00 .30
❑ 151 Mike Piazza LUM/500 .. 15.00 4.50
❑ 152 M.Ramirez LUM/500.... 10.00 3.00
❑ 153 B.Williams LUM/500.... 10.00 3.00
❑ 154 N.Garciaparra LUM/500 15.00 4.50
❑ 155 A.Galarraga LUM/500 .... 8.00 2.40
❑ 156 K.Lofton LUM/500 .... 8.00 2.40
❑ 157 Scott Rolen LUM/250 .. 15.00 4.50
❑ 158 Jim Thome LUM/500 .. 10.00 3.00
❑ 159 Darin Erstad LUM/500 .. 8.00 2.40
❑ 160 G.Anderson LUM/500.... 8.00 2.40
❑ 161 A.Jones LUM/500.......... 8.00 2.40
❑ 162 J.Gonzalez LUM/500.... 10.00 3.00
❑ 163 R.Palmeiro LUM/500 .. 10.00 3.00
❑ 164 M.Ordonez LUM/500 .... 8.00 2.40
❑ 165 Jeff Bagwell LUM/250.. 15.00 4.50
❑ 166 Eric Chavez LUM/500 .... 8.00 2.40
❑ 167 Brian Giles LUM/500 .... 8.00 2.40
❑ 168 A.Beltre LUM/500........ 10.00 3.00
❑ 169 T.Gwynn LUM/500 .... 15.00 4.50
❑ 170 S.Green LUM/500.......... 8.00 2.40
❑ 171 Todd Helton LUM/500 10.00 3.00
❑ 172 Troy Glaus LUM/100.... 15.00 4.50
❑ 173 L.Berkman LUM/500...... 8.00 2.40
❑ 174 I.Rodriguez LUM/500 .. 10.00 3.00

❑ 175 Sean Casey LUM/500 .... 8.00 2.40
❑ 176 A.Ramirez LUM/100 .... 15.00 4.50
❑ 177 J.D. Drew LUM/500 ...... 8.00 2.40
❑ 178 Barry Bonds LUM/250 30.00 9.00
❑ 179 Barry Larkin LUM/500.. 10.00 3.00
❑ 180 Cal Ripken LUM/500.... 40.00 12.00
❑ 181 F.Thomas LUM/500 .... 10.00 3.00
❑ 182 Craig Biggio LUM/250 15.00 4.50
❑ 183 Carlos Lee LUM/500...... 8.00 2.40
❑ 184 C. Jones LUM/500 ...... 10.00 3.00
❑ 185 Miguel Tejada LUM/250 10.00 3.00
❑ 186 Jose Vidro LUM/500...... 8.00 2.40
❑ 187 T.Long LUM/500............ 8.00 2.40
❑ 188 Moises Alou LUM/500 .. 8.00 2.40
❑ 189 Trot Nixon LUM/500...... 8.00 2.40
❑ 190 S.Stewart LUM/500........ 8.00 2.40
❑ 191 Ryan Klesko LUM/500 .. 8.00 2.40
❑ 192 C.Beltran LUM/500...... 10.00 3.00
❑ 193 V.Guerrero LUM/500.... 10.00 3.00
❑ 194 E.Martinez LUM/500.... 10.00 3.00
❑ 195 L.Gonzalez LUM/500...... 8.00 2.40
❑ 196 R.Hidalgo LUM/500 ...... 8.00 2.40
❑ 197 R.Alomar LUM/500...... 10.00 3.00
❑ 198 M.Sweeney LUM/100 .. 15.00 4.50
❑ 199 B.Abreu LUM/250........ 10.00 3.00
❑ 200 Cliff Floyd LUM/500...... 8.00 2.40
❑ 201 Jackson Melian RC 5.00 1.50
❑ 202 Jason Jennings............. 5.00 1.50
❑ 203 Toby Hall....................... 5.00 1.50
❑ 204 Jason Karnuth RC 5.00 1.50
❑ 205 Jason Smith RC 5.00 1.50
❑ 206 Mike Maroth RC 5.00 1.50
❑ 207 Sean Douglass RC 5.00 1.50
❑ 208 Adam Johnson 5.00 1.50
❑ 209 Luke Hudson RC........... 5.00 1.50
❑ 210 Nick Maness RC 5.00 1.50
❑ 211 Les Walrond RC 5.00 1.50
❑ 212 Travis Phelps RC........... 5.00 1.50
❑ 213 Carlos Garcia RC........... 5.00 1.50
❑ 214 Bill Ortega RC 5.00 1.50
❑ 215 Gene Altman RC 5.00 1.50
❑ 216 Nate Frese RC 5.00 1.50
❑ 217 Bob File RC.................... 5.00 1.50
❑ 218 Steve Green RC 5.00 1.50
❑ 219 Kris Keller RC 5.00 1.50
❑ 220 Matt White RC............... 5.00 1.50
❑ 221 Nate Teut RC 5.00 1.50
❑ 222 Nick Johnson 5.00 1.50
❑ 223 Jeremy Fikac RC 5.00 1.50
❑ 224 Abraham Nunez............. 5.00 1.50
❑ 225 Mike Penney RC 5.00 1.50
❑ 226 Roy Smith RC 5.00 1.50
❑ 227 Tim Christman RC.......... 5.00 1.50
❑ 228 Carlos Pena.................. 5.00 1.50
❑ 229 Joe Beimel RC............... 5.00 1.50
❑ 230 Mike Koplove RC 5.00 1.50
❑ 231 Scott MacRae RC 5.00 1.50
❑ 232 Kyle Lohse RC................ 8.00 2.40
❑ 233 Jerrod Riggan RC 5.00 1.50
❑ 234 Scott Podsednik RC 15.00 4.50
❑ 235 Winston Abreu RC.......... 5.00 1.50
❑ 236 Ryan Freel RC 5.00 1.50
❑ 237 Ken Vining RC............... 5.00 1.50
❑ 238 Bret Prinz RC................. 5.00 1.50
❑ 239 Paul Phillips RC 5.00 1.50
❑ 240 Josh Fogg RC 5.00 1.50
❑ 241 Saul Rivera RC 5.00 1.50
❑ 242 Esix Snead RC............... 5.00 1.50
❑ 243 John Grabow RC........... 5.00 1.50
❑ 244 Tony Cogan RC............. 5.00 1.50
❑ 245 Pedro Santana RC......... 5.00 1.50
❑ 246 Jack Cust 5.00 1.50
❑ 247 Joe Crede 5.00 1.50
❑ 248 Juan Moreno RC 5.00 1.50
❑ 249 Kevin Joseph RC........... 5.00 1.50
❑ 250 Scott Stewart RC 5.00 1.50
❑ 251 Rob Mackowiak RC 8.00 2.40
❑ 252 Luis Pineda RC 5.00 1.50
❑ 253 Bert Snow RC 5.00 1.50
❑ 254 Dustan Mohr RC 5.00 1.50
❑ 255 Justin Kaye RC 5.00 1.50
❑ 256 Chad Paronto RC 5.00 1.50
❑ 257 Nick Punto RC............... 5.00 1.50
❑ 258 Brian Roberts RC........... 5.00 1.50
❑ 259 Eric Hinske RC 8.00 2.40
❑ 260 Victor Zambrano RC 8.00 2.40
❑ 261 Juan Pena RC 5.00 1.50
❑ 262 Rick Bauer RC 5.00 1.50
❑ 263 Jorge Julio RC 5.00 1.50
❑ 264 Craig Monroe RC 5.00 1.50
❑ 265 Stubby Clapp RC........... 5.00 1.50
❑ 266 Martin Vargas RC 5.00 1.50
❑ 267 Josue Perez RC............. 5.00 1.50
❑ 268 Cody Ransom RC 5.00 1.50
❑ 269 Will Ohman RC 5.00 1.50
❑ 270 Juan Diaz RC................. 5.00 1.50
❑ 271 Ramon Vazquez RC 5.00 1.50
❑ 272 Grant Balfour RC 5.00 1.50
❑ 273 Ryan Jensen RC 5.00 1.50
❑ 274 Benito Baez RC 5.00 1.50
❑ 275 Angel Santos RC 5.00 1.50
❑ 276 Brian Reith RC............... 5.00 1.50
❑ 277 Brandon Lyon RC 5.00 1.50
❑ 278 Erik Hiljus RC 5.00 1.50
❑ 279 Brandon Knight RC 5.00 1.50
❑ 280 Jose Acevedo RC 5.00 1.50
❑ 281 Cesar Crespo RC........... 5.00 1.50
❑ 282 Kevin Olsen RC............. 5.00 1.50
❑ 283 Duaner Sanchez RC........ 5.00 1.50
❑ 284 Endy Chavez RC 5.00 1.50
❑ 285 Blaine Neal RC 5.00 1.50
❑ 286 Brett Jodie RC 5.00 1.50
❑ 287 Brad Voyles RC............. 5.00 1.50
❑ 288 Doug Nickle RC............. 5.00 1.50
❑ 289 Junior Spivey RC 8.00 2.40
❑ 290 Henry Mateo RC 5.00 1.50
❑ 291 Xavier Nady................... 5.00 1.50
❑ 292 Lance Davis RC.............. 5.00 1.50
❑ 293 Willie Harris RC 5.00 1.50
❑ 294 Mark Lukasiewicz RC 5.00 1.50
❑ 295 Ryan Drese RC 8.00 2.40
❑ 296 Morgan Ensberg RC 8.00 2.40
❑ 297 Jose Mieses RC 5.00 1.50
❑ 298 Jason Michaels RC 5.00 1.50
❑ 299 Kris Foster RC............... 5.00 1.50
❑ 300 J.Duchscherer RC 5.00 1.50
❑ 301 Elpidio Guzman AU RC 10.00 3.00
❑ 302 Cory Aldridge AU RC .. 10.00 3.00
❑ 303 A.Berroa AU/500 RC 15.00 4.50
❑ 304 Travis Hafner AU RC 30.00 9.00
❑ 305 H.Ramirez AU RC 15.00 4.50
❑ 306 Juan Uribe AU RC 15.00 4.50
❑ 307 M.Prior AU/500 RC.... 175.00 52.50
❑ 308 B.Larson AU RC 10.00 3.00
❑ 309 N.Neugebauer AU/750 10.00 3.00
❑ 310 Zach Day AU/750 RC 10.00 3.00
❑ 311 Jeremy Owens AU RC .. 10.00 3.00
❑ 312 D.Brazelton AU/500 RC 15.00 4.50
❑ 313 B.Duckworth AU/750 RC 10.00 3.00
❑ 314 A.Hernandez AU RC 10.00 3.00
❑ 315 M.Teixeira AU/500 RC 100.00 30.00
❑ 316 Brian Rogers AU RC 10.00 3.00
❑ 317 D.Brous AU/750 RC 10.00 3.00
❑ 318 Geronimo Gil AU RC 10.00 3.00
❑ 319 Erick Almonte AU RC .. 10.00 3.00
❑ 320 Claudio Vargas AU RC 10.00 3.00
❑ 321 Wilkin Ruan AU RC 10.00 3.00
❑ 322 David Williams AU RC 10.00 3.00
❑ 323 Alexis Gomez AU RC.... 10.00 3.00
❑ 324 Mike Rivera AU RC 10.00 3.00
❑ 325 B.Berger AU RC............ 10.00 3.00
❑ 326 Keith Ginter Bat/125 .... 25.00 7.50
❑ 327 Brandon Inge Bat/700 .... 8.00 2.40
❑ 328 B.Abernathy Bat/700 ...... 8.00 2.40
❑ 329 B.Sylvester Bat/700 RC .. 8.00 2.40
❑ 330 B.Miadich Jsy/500 RC .. 8.00 2.40
❑ 331 T.Shinjo Jsy/500 RC 10.00 3.00
❑ 332 E.Valent Spikes/125 .... 25.00 7.50
❑ 333 Dee Brown Jsy/500 .... 8.00 2.40
❑ 334 A.Torres Spikes/125 RC 25.00 7.50
❑ 335 Timo Perez Bat/700......... 8.00 2.40
❑ 336 C.Izturis Pants/650 .... 8.00 2.40
❑ 337 P.Feliz Spikes/125 ...... 25.00 7.50
❑ 338 Jason Hart Bat/200 ...... 10.00 3.00
❑ 339 G.Miller Bat/700 RC 8.00 2.40
❑ 340 Eric Munson Bat/700 ..... 8.00 2.40
❑ 341 Aubrey Huff Jsy/450 ..... 8.00 2.40
❑ 342 W.Caceres Bat/700 RC .. 8.00 2.40
❑ 343 A.Escobar Pants/650...... 8.00 2.40
❑ 344 B.Lawrence Bat/700 RC.. 8.00 2.40
❑ 345 Adam Pettyjohn.............. 8.00 2.40
Pants/650 RC
❑ 346 D.Mendez Bat/700 RC.... 8.00 2.40
❑ 347 Carlos Valderrama........ 10.00 3.00
Jsy/250 RC
❑ 348 C.Parker Pants/650 RC .. 8.00 2.40
❑ 349 C.Miller Jsy/500 RC 8.00 2.40
❑ 350 M.Cuddyer Jsy/500........ 8.00 2.40
❑ 351 Adam Dunn Bat/500 .... 10.00 3.00
❑ 352 J.Beckett Pants/650........ 8.00 2.40
❑ 353 Juan Cruz Jsy/500 RC.... 8.00 2.40
❑ 354 Ben Sheets Jsy/400...... 10.00 3.00
❑ 355 Roy Oswalt Bat/100...... 40.00 12.00
❑ 356 R.Soriano Pants/650 RC 10.00 3.00
❑ 357 R.Rodriguez Pants/650 RC 8.00 2.40
❑ 358 J.Rollins Base/300 ...... 15.00 4.50
❑ 359 C.C. Sabathia Jsy/500.... 8.00 2.40
❑ 360 B.Smith Jsy/500 RC 8.00 2.40
❑ 361 Jose Ortiz Hat/100........ 25.00 7.50
❑ 362 Marcus Giles Jsy/400 .... 8.00 2.40
❑ 363 J.Wilson Hat/100 RC.... 40.00 12.00
❑ 364 W.Betemit Hat/100 RC 25.00 7.50
❑ 365 C.Patterson Pants/650 .. 8.00 2.40
❑ 366 J.Gibbons Spikes/125 RC 40.00 12.00
❑ 367 A.Pujols Jsy/250 RC .. 150.00 45.00
❑ 368 J.Kennedy Hat/100 RC 40.00 12.00
❑ 369 A.Soriano Hat/100........ 40.00 12.00
❑ 370 D.James Pants/650 RC .. 8.00 2.40
❑ 371 J.Towers Pants/650 RC .. 8.00 2.40
❑ 372 J.Affeldt Pants/650 RC 10.00 3.00
❑ 373 Tim Redding Jsy/500 .... 8.00 2.40
❑ 374 I.Suzuki Base/100 RC 500.00 150.00
❑ 375 J.Estrada Bat/100 RC .. 40.00 12.00

2003 Leaf Limited

	MINT	NRMT
COMMON CARD (1-151)............	3.00	1.35
1-151 PRINT RUN 999 SERIAL #'d SETS		
COMMON CARD (151-170)........	4.00	1.80
151-170 RANDOM INSERTS IN PACKS		
151-170 PRINT RUN 399 SERIAL #'d SETS		
COMMON AU GU (171-200)	20.00	9.00
AU GU 171-200 PRINT 99 SERIAL #'d SETS		
GU 174/199 PRINT RUN 99 SERIAL #'d SETS		
COMMON AU (171-204) p/r 99	15.00	6.75
AU 171-204 PRINT B/WN 49-99 COPIES PER		
171-200 RANDOM INSERTS IN PACKS		
201-204 RANDOM IN DLP R/T PACKS		
A EQUALS AWAY UNIFORM IMAGE		
H EQUALS HOME UNIFORM IMAGE		

❑ 1 Derek Jeter Btg 8.00 3.60
❑ 2 Eric Chavez 3.00 1.35
❑ 3 Alex Rodriguez Rgr A 6.00 2.70
❑ 4 Miguel Tejada Fldg 3.00 1.35
❑ 5 Nomar Garciaparra H.......... 6.00 2.70
❑ 6 Jeff Bagwell H 3.00 1.35
❑ 7 Jim Thome Phils A 4.00 1.80
❑ 8 Pat Burrell w/Bat 3.00 1.35
❑ 9 Albert Pujols H 8.00 3.60
❑ 10 Juan Gonzalez Rgr Btg 3.00 1.35
❑ 11 Shawn Green Jays........... 3.00 1.35
❑ 12 Craig Biggio H 3.00 1.35
❑ 13 Chipper Jones H 4.00 1.80
❑ 14 H.Nomo Dodgers 4.00 1.80
❑ 15 Vernon Wells.................... 3.00 1.35
❑ 16 Gary Sheffield 3.00 1.35
❑ 17 Barry Larkin...................... 3.00 1.35
❑ 18 Josh Beckett White 3.00 1.35

❑ 19 Edgar Martinez A 3.00 1.35
❑ 20 I.Rodriguez Marlins 4.00 1.80
❑ 21 Jeff Kent Astros 3.00 1.35
❑ 22 Roberto Alomar Mets A 3.00 1.35
❑ 23 Alfonso Soriano A 3.00 1.35
❑ 24 Jim Thome Indians H 4.00 1.80
❑ 25 J.Gonzalez Indians Btg 3.00 1.35
❑ 26 Carlos Beltran 3.00 1.35
❑ 27 S.Green Dodgers H 3.00 1.35
❑ 28 Tim Hudson H 3.00 1.35
❑ 29 Deion Sanders 3.00 1.35
❑ 30 Rafael Palmeiro O's 3.00 1.35
❑ 31 Todd Helton H 3.00 1.35
❑ 32 L.Berkman No Socks 3.00 1.35
❑ 33 M.Mussina Yanks H 3.00 1.35
❑ 34 Kazuhisa Ishii H 3.00 1.35
❑ 35 Pat Burrell Run 3.00 1.35
❑ 36 Miguel Tejada Btg 3.00 1.35
❑ 37 J.Gonzalez Rgr Stand 3.00 1.35
❑ 38 Roberto Alomar Mets H 3.00 1.35
❑ 39 R.Alom Indians Bunt 3.00 1.35
❑ 40 Luis Gonzalez 3.00 1.35
❑ 41 Jorge Posada 3.00 1.35
❑ 42 Mark Mulder Leg 3.00 1.35
❑ 43 Sammy Sosa H 6.00 2.70
❑ 44 Mark Prior H 4.00 1.80
❑ 45 R.Clemens Yanks H 8.00 3.60
❑ 46 Tom Glavine Mets H 3.00 1.35
❑ 47 Mark Teixeira A 3.00 1.35
❑ 48 Manny Ramirez H 3.00 1.35
❑ 49 Frank Thomas Swing 4.00 1.80
❑ 50 Troy Glaus White 3.00 1.35
❑ 51 Andruw Jones H 3.00 1.35
❑ 52 J.Giambi Yanks H 3.00 1.35
❑ 53 Jim Thome Phils H 4.00 1.80
❑ 54 Barry Bonds H 10.00 4.50
❑ 55 R.Palmeiro Rgr A 3.00 1.35
❑ 56 Edgar Martinez H 3.00 1.35
❑ 57 Vladimir Guerrero H 4.00 1.80
❑ 58 Roberto Alomar O's 3.00 1.35
❑ 59 Mike Sweeney 3.00 1.35
❑ 60 Magglio Ordonez A 3.00 1.35
❑ 61 Ken Griffey Jr. Btg 6.00 2.70
❑ 62 Craig Biggio A 3.00 1.35
❑ 63 Greg Maddux H 6.00 2.70
❑ 64 Mike Piazza Mets H 6.00 2.70
❑ 65 T.Glavine Braves A 3.00 1.35
❑ 66 Kerry Wood H 4.00 1.80
❑ 67 Frank Thomas Arms 4.00 1.80
❑ 68 M.Mussina Yanks A 3.00 1.35
❑ 69 Nick Johnson H 3.00 1.35
❑ 70 Bernie Williams H 3.00 1.35
❑ 71 Scott Rolen 4.00 1.80
❑ 72 C.Schill D'backs Leg 3.00 1.35
❑ 73 Adam Dunn A 3.00 1.35
❑ 74 Roy Oswalt A 3.00 1.35
❑ 75 P.Martinez Sox H 4.00 1.80
❑ 76 Tom Glavine Mets A 3.00 1.35
❑ 77 Torii Hunter Swing 3.00 1.35
❑ 78 Austin Kearns 3.00 1.35
❑ 79 R.Johnson D'backs A 4.00 1.80
❑ 80 Bernie Williams A 3.00 1.35
❑ 81 Ichiro Suzuki Btg 6.00 2.70
❑ 82 Kerry Wood A 4.00 1.80
❑ 83 Kazuhisa Ishii A 3.00 1.35
❑ 84 R.Johnson Astros 4.00 1.80
❑ 85 Nick Johnson A 3.00 1.35
❑ 86 J.Beckett Pinstripe 3.00 1.35
❑ 87 Curt Schilling Phils 3.00 1.35
❑ 88 Mike Mussina O's 3.00 1.35
❑ 89 P.Martinez Dodgers 4.00 1.80
❑ 90 Barry Zito A 3.00 1.35
❑ 91 Jim Edmonds 3.00 1.35
❑ 92 R.Henderson Sox 4.00 1.80
❑ 93 R.Henderson Padres 4.00 1.80
❑ 94 R.Henderson M's 4.00 1.80
❑ 95 R.Henderson Mets 4.00 1.80
❑ 96 R.Henderson Jays 4.00 1.80
❑ 97 R.Johnson M's Arm Up 4.00 1.80
❑ 98 Mark Grace 3.00 1.35
❑ 99 P.Martinez Expos 4.00 1.80
❑ 100 Hee Seop Choi 3.00 1.35
❑ 101 Ivan Rodriguez Rgr 4.00 1.80
❑ 102 Jeff Kent Giants 3.00 1.35
❑ 103 Hideo Nomo Sox 4.00 1.80
❑ 104 Hideo Nomo Mets 4.00 1.80
❑ 105 Mike Piazza Dodgers 6.00 2.70
❑ 106 T.Glavine Braves H 3.00 1.35
❑ 107 R.Alom Indians Swing 3.00 1.35
❑ 108 Roger Clemens Sox 8.00 3.60
❑ 109 Jason Giambi A's H 3.00 1.35
❑ 110 Jim Thome Indians A 4.00 1.80
❑ 111 Alex Rodriguez M's H 6.00 2.70
❑ 112 J.Gonz Indians Hands 3.00 1.35
❑ 113 Torii Hunter Crouch 3.00 1.35
❑ 114 Roy Oswalt H 3.00 1.35
❑ 115 C.Schill D'backs Throw 3.00 1.35
❑ 116 Magglio Ordonez H 3.00 1.35
❑ 117 R.Palmeiro Rgr H 3.00 1.35
❑ 118 Andruw Jones A 3.00 1.35
❑ 119 Manny Ramirez A 3.00 1.35
❑ 120 Mark Teixeira H 3.00 1.35
❑ 121 Mark Mulder Stance 3.00 1.35
❑ 122 Garret Anderson 3.00 1.35
❑ 123 Tim Hudson A 3.00 1.35
❑ 124 Todd Helton A 3.00 1.35
❑ 125 Troy Glaus Pinstripe 3.00 1.35
❑ 126 Derek Jeter Run 8.00 3.60
❑ 127 Barry Bonds A 10.00 4.50
❑ 128 Greg Maddux A 6.00 2.70
❑ 129 R.Clemens Yanks A 8.00 3.60
❑ 130 Nomar Garciaparra A 6.00 2.70
❑ 131 Mike Piazza Mets A 6.00 2.70
❑ 132 Alex Rodriguez Rgr H 6.00 2.70
❑ 133 Ichiro Suzuki Run 6.00 2.70
❑ 134 R.Johnson D'backs H 4.00 1.80
❑ 135 Sammy Sosa A 6.00 2.70
❑ 136 Ken Griffey Jr. Fldg 6.00 2.70
❑ 137 Alfonso Soriano H 3.00 1.35
❑ 138 J.Giambi Yanks A 3.00 1.35
❑ 139 Albert Pujols A 8.00 3.60
❑ 140 Chipper Jones A 4.00 1.80
❑ 141 Adam Dunn H 3.00 1.35
❑ 142 P.Martinez Sox A 4.00 1.80
❑ 143 Vladimir Guerrero A 4.00 1.80
❑ 144 Mark Prior A 4.00 1.80
❑ 145 Barry Zito H 3.00 1.35
❑ 146 Jeff Bagwell A 3.00 1.35
❑ 147 Lance Berkman Socks 3.00 1.35
❑ 148 S.Green Dodgers A 3.00 1.35
❑ 149 Jason Giambi A's A 3.00 1.35
❑ 150 R.Johnson M's Arm Out 4.00 1.80
❑ 151 Alex Rodriguez M's A 6.00 2.70
❑ 152 Babe Ruth 10.00 4.50
❑ 153 Ty Cobb 6.00 2.70
❑ 154 Jackie Robinson 5.00 2.20
❑ 155 Lou Gehrig 8.00 3.60
❑ 156 Thurman Munson 5.00 2.20
❑ 157 Roberto Clemente 12.00 5.50
❑ 158 Nolan Ryan Rgr 10.00 4.50
❑ 159 Nolan Ryan Angels 10.00 4.50
❑ 160 Nolan Ryan Astros 10.00 4.50
❑ 161 Cal Ripken 20.00 9.00
❑ 162 Don Mattingly 10.00 4.50
❑ 163 Stan Musial 8.00 3.60
❑ 164 Tony Gwynn 8.00 3.60
❑ 165 Yogi Berra 5.00 2.20
❑ 166 Johnny Bench 5.00 2.20
❑ 167 Mike Schmidt 10.00 4.50
❑ 168 George Brett 10.00 4.50
❑ 169 Ryne Sandberg 10.00 4.50
❑ 170 Ernie Banks 5.00 2.20
❑ 171 J.Bonder A PH AU Jsy RC 25.00 11.00
❑ 172 J.Contreras A PH AU RC 40.00 18.00
❑ 173 C.Wang PH AU RC 50.00 22.00
❑ 174 H.Matsui H PH Base RC 40.00 18.00
❑ 175 Hong-Chih Kuo 40.00 18.00
PH AU Bat RC
❑ 176 B.Webb A PH AU Bat RC 40.00 18.00
❑ 177 Rich Fischer PH AU RC 15.00 6.75
❑ 178 R.Hammock PH AU Bat RC 25.00 11.00
❑ 179 T.Welle Stance PH AU/49 RC 25.00 11.00
❑ 180 P.Redman PH AU Bat RC 20.00 9.00
❑ 181 Nook Logan PH AU RC 15.00 6.75
❑ 182 Craig Brazell PH AU RC 15.00 6.75
❑ 183 Tim Olson PH AU Bat RC 25.00 11.00
❑ 184 Matt Kata PH AU Bat RC 25.00 11.00
❑ 185 Alej Machado PH AU RC 15.00 6.75
❑ 186 Mike Hessman PH AU RC 15.00 6.75
❑ 187 Oscar Villarreal PH AU RC 15.00 6.75
❑ 188 G.Quiroz PH AU Bat RC 25.00 11.00
❑ 189 M.Hernandez PH AU RC 15.00 6.75
❑ 190 C.Barmes H PH AU Bat RC 25.00 11.00
❑ 191 P.LaForest PH AU Bat RC 25.00 11.00
❑ 192 Adam Loewen PH AU RC 60.00 27.00
❑ 193 T.Sledge PH AU Bat RC 25.00 11.00
❑ 194 Lew Ford PH AU Bat RC 50.00 22.00
❑ 195 T.Welle Throw PH AU/49 RC 25.00 11.00
❑ 196 C.Barmes A PH AU Bat RC 25.00 11.00
❑ 197 J.Bonder H PH AU Jsy RC 25.00 11.00
❑ 198 B.Webb H PH AU Jsy RC 40.00 18.00
❑ 199 H.Matsui A PH Base RC 40.00 18.00
❑ 200 J.Contreras H PH AU RC 40.00 18.00
❑ 201 Delmon Young PH AU RC 150.00 70.00
❑ 202 Rickie Weeks PH AU RC 100.00 45.00
❑ 203 Edwin Jackson PH AU RC 80.00 36.00
❑ 204 Dan Haren PH AU RC 20.00 9.00

2004 Leaf Limited

	Nm-Mt	Ex-Mt
COMMON CARD (1-200/230-250)	3.00	.90
COMMON CARD (201-229)	4.00	1.20
201-229 PRINT RUN 499 SERIAL #'d SETS		
COMMON AUTO (251-275)	15.00	4.50
251-275: OVERALL AU-GU ONE PER PACK		
251-275 AUTO PRINT RUN 99 #'d SETS		

❑ 1 Adam Dunn A 3.00 .90
❑ 2 Adrian Beltre 3.00 .90
❑ 3 Albert Pujols H 8.00 2.40
❑ 4 Alex Rodriguez Yanks 6.00 1.80
❑ 5 Alfonso Soriano Rgr 3.00 .90
❑ 6 Andruw Jones 3.00 .90
❑ 7 Andy Pettitte Astros 3.00 .90
❑ 8 Angel Berroa 3.00 .90
❑ 9 Aramis Ramirez 3.00 .90
❑ 10 Aubrey Huff 3.00 .90
❑ 11 Austin Kearns 3.00 .90
❑ 12 Barry Larkin 3.00 .90
❑ 13 Barry Zito H 3.00 .90
❑ 14 Bartolo Colon 3.00 .90
❑ 15 Ben Sheets 3.00 .90
❑ 16 Bernie Williams 3.00 .90
❑ 17 Bobby Abreu 3.00 .90
❑ 18 Brandon Webb 3.00 .90
❑ 19 Brian Giles 3.00 .90
❑ 20 C.C. Sabathia 3.00 .90
❑ 21 Carlos Beltran Royals A 3.00 .90
❑ 22 Carlos Delgado 3.00 .90
❑ 23 Chipper Jones H 4.00 1.20
❑ 24 Craig Biggio 3.00 .90
❑ 25 Curt Schilling Sox 4.00 1.20
❑ 26 Darin Erstad 3.00 .90
❑ 27 Delmon Young 3.00 .90
❑ 28 Derek Jeter 8.00 2.40
❑ 29 Derrek Lee 3.00 .90
❑ 30 Dontrelle Willis 3.00 .90
❑ 31 Edgar Renteria 3.00 .90
❑ 32 Eric Chavez 3.00 .90
❑ 33 Esteban Loaiza 3.00 .90
❑ 34 Frank Thomas 4.00 1.20
❑ 35 Fred McGriff 3.00 .90
❑ 36 Garret Anderson H 3.00 .90
❑ 37 Gary Sheffield Yanks 3.00 .90
❑ 38 Geoff Jenkins 3.00 .90
❑ 39 Greg Maddux Cubs 6.00 1.80
❑ 40 Hank Blalock H 3.00 .90
❑ 41 Hideki Matsui 6.00 1.80
❑ 42 Hideo Nomo Dodgers 4.00 1.20

❑ 43 Ichiro Suzuki 6.00 1.80
❑ 44 Ivan Rodriguez Tigers 4.00 1.20
❑ 45 J.D. Drew 3.00 .90
❑ 46 Jacque Jones 3.00 .90
❑ 47 Jae Weong Seo 3.00 .90
❑ 48 Jake Peavy 3.00 .90
❑ 49 Jamie Moyer 3.00 .90
❑ 50 Jason Giambi Yanks 3.00 .90
❑ 51 Jason Kendall 3.00 .90
❑ 52 Jason Schmidt 3.00 .90
❑ 53 Jason Varitek 3.00 .90
❑ 54 Javier Vazquez 3.00 .90
❑ 55 Javy Lopez 3.00 .90
❑ 56 Jay Gibbons 3.00 .90
❑ 57 Jay Payton 3.00 .90
❑ 58 Jeff Bagwell H 3.00 .90
❑ 59 Jeff Kent 3.00 .90
❑ 60 Jeremy Bonderman 3.00 .90
❑ 61 Jermaine Dye 3.00 .90
❑ 62 Jeromy Burnitz 3.00 .90
❑ 63 Jim Edmonds 3.00 .90
❑ 64 Jim Thome Phils 4.00 1.20
❑ 65 Jimmy Rollins 3.00 .90
❑ 66 Jody Gerut 3.00 .90
❑ 67 Johan Santana 3.00 .90
❑ 68 John Olerud 3.00 .90
❑ 69 John Smoltz 3.00 .90
❑ 70 Johnny Damon 4.00 1.20
❑ 71 Jorge Posada 3.00 .90
❑ 72 Jose Contreras 3.00 .90
❑ 73 Jose Reyes 3.00 .90
❑ 74 Jose Vidro 3.00 .90
❑ 75 Josh Beckett H 3.00 .90
❑ 76 Juan Gonzalez Royals 3.00 .90
❑ 77 Juan Pierre 3.00 .90
❑ 78 Junior Spivey 3.00 .90
❑ 79 Kazuhisa Ishii 3.00 .90
❑ 80 Keith Foulke Sox 3.00 .90
❑ 81 Ken Griffey Jr. Reds 6.00 1.80
❑ 82 Ken Harvey 3.00 .90
❑ 83 Kenny Rogers 3.00 .90
❑ 84 Kerry Wood 4.00 1.20
❑ 85 Kevin Brown Yanks 3.00 .90
❑ 86 Kevin Millwood 3.00 .90
❑ 87 Kip Wells 3.00 .90
❑ 88 Lance Berkman 3.00 .90
❑ 89 Larry Bigbie 3.00 .90
❑ 90 Larry Walker 3.00 .90
❑ 91 Laynce Nix 3.00 .90
❑ 92 Luis Castillo 3.00 .90
❑ 93 Luis Gonzalez 3.00 .90
❑ 94 Luis Matos 3.00 .90
❑ 95 Lyle Overbay 3.00 .90
❑ 96 Magglio Ordonez H 3.00 .90
❑ 97 Manny Ramirez Sox 3.00 .90
❑ 98 Marcus Giles 3.00 .90
❑ 99 Mark Buehrle 3.00 .90
❑ 100 Mark Mulder 3.00 .90
❑ 101 Mark Prior H 4.00 1.20
❑ 102 Mark Teixeira 3.00 .90
❑ 103 Marlon Byrd 3.00 .90
❑ 104 Matt Morris 3.00 .90
❑ 105 Melvin Mora 3.00 .90
❑ 106 Michael Young 3.00 .90
❑ 107 Miguel Cabrera Batting 3.00 .90
❑ 108 Miguel Tejada O's 3.00 .90
❑ 109 Mike Lowell 3.00 .90
❑ 110 Mike Mussina Yanks 3.00 .90
❑ 111 Mike Piazza Mets 6.00 1.80
❑ 112 Mike Sweeney 3.00 .90
❑ 113 Milton Bradley 3.00 .90
❑ 114 Moises Alou 3.00 .90
❑ 115 Morgan Ensberg 3.00 .90
❑ 116 Nick Johnson 3.00 .90
❑ 117 Nomar Garciaparra 6.00 1.80
❑ 118 Omar Vizquel 3.00 .90
❑ 119 Orlando Cabrera 3.00 .90
❑ 120 Pat Burrell 3.00 .90
❑ 121 Paul Konerko 3.00 .90
❑ 122 Paul Lo Duca 3.00 .90
❑ 123 Pedro Martinez Sox 4.00 1.20
❑ 124 Preston Wilson H 3.00 .90
❑ 125 Rafael Furcal 3.00 .90
❑ 126 Rafael Palmeiro O's 3.00 .90
❑ 127 Randy Johnson D'backs 4.00 1.20
❑ 128 Rich Harden 3.00 .90
❑ 129 Richard Hidalgo 3.00 .90
❑ 130 Richie Sexson 3.00 .90
❑ 131 Rickie Weeks 3.00 .90
❑ 132 Roberto Alomar 3.00 .90
❑ 133 Robin Ventura 3.00 .90
❑ 134 Rocco Baldelli 3.00 .90
❑ 135 Roger Clemens Astros 8.00 2.40
❑ 136 Roy Halladay 3.00 .90
❑ 137 Roy Oswalt A 3.00 .90
❑ 138 Russ Ortiz 3.00 .90
❑ 139 Ryan Klesko 3.00 .90
❑ 140 Sammy Sosa H 6.00 1.80
❑ 141 Scott Podsednik 3.00 .90
❑ 142 Scott Rolen Cards A 4.00 1.20
❑ 143 Sean Burroughs 3.00 .90
❑ 144 Sean Casey 3.00 .90
❑ 145 Shannon Stewart 3.00 .90
❑ 146 Shawn Green Dodgers 3.00 .90
❑ 147 Shigetoshi Hasegawa 3.00 .90
❑ 148 Sidney Ponson 3.00 .90
❑ 149 Steve Finley 3.00 .90
❑ 150 Tim Hudson 3.00 .90
❑ 151 Tim Salmon 3.00 .90
❑ 152 Tino Martinez 3.00 .90
❑ 153 Todd Helton H 3.00 .90
❑ 154 Tom Glavine Mets 3.00 .90
❑ 155 Torii Hunter 3.00 .90
❑ 156 Trot Nixon 3.00 .90
❑ 157 Troy Glaus 3.00 .90
❑ 158 Vernon Wells H 3.00 .90
❑ 159 Victor Martinez A 3.00 .90
❑ 160 Vinny Castilla 3.00 .90
❑ 161 Vladimir Guerrero Angels 4.00 1.20
❑ 162 Alex Rodriguez Rgr 6.00 1.80
❑ 163 Alfonso Soriano Yanks 3.00 .90
❑ 164 Andy Pettitte Yanks 3.00 .90
❑ 165 Curt Schilling D'backs 3.00 .90
❑ 166 Gary Sheffield Braves 3.00 .90
❑ 167 Greg Maddux Braves 6.00 1.80
❑ 168 Hideo Nomo Sox 4.00 1.20
❑ 169 Ivan Rodriguez Marlins 4.00 1.20
❑ 170 Jason Giambi A's 3.00 .90
❑ 171 Jim Thome Indians 4.00 1.20
❑ 172 Juan Gonzalez Rgr 3.00 .90
❑ 173 Ken Griffey Jr. M's 6.00 1.80
❑ 174 Kevin Brown Dodgers 3.00 .90
❑ 175 Manny Ramirez Indians 3.00 .90
❑ 176 Miguel Tejada A's 3.00 .90
❑ 177 Mike Mussina O's 3.00 .90
❑ 178 Mike Piazza Dodgers 6.00 1.80
❑ 179 Pedro Martinez Expos 4.00 1.20
❑ 180 Rafael Palmeiro Rgr 3.00 .90
❑ 181 Randy Johnson Astros 4.00 1.20
❑ 182 Roger Clemens Sox 8.00 2.40
❑ 183 Scott Rolen Phils 4.00 1.20
❑ 184 Shawn Green Jays 3.00 .90
❑ 185 Tom Glavine Braves 3.00 .90
❑ 186 Vladimir Guerrero Expos 4.00 1.20
❑ 187 Alex Rodriguez M's 6.00 1.80
❑ 188 Mike Piazza Marlins 6.00 1.80
❑ 189 Randy Johnson M's 4.00 1.20
❑ 190 Roger Clemens Yanks 8.00 2.40
❑ 191 Albert Pujols A 8.00 2.40
❑ 192 Barry Zito A 3.00 .90
❑ 193 Chipper Jones A 4.00 1.20
❑ 194 Garret Anderson A 3.00 .90
❑ 195 Jeff Bagwell A 3.00 .90
❑ 196 Josh Beckett A 3.00 .90
❑ 197 Magglio Ordonez A 3.00 .90
❑ 198 Mark Prior A 4.00 1.20
❑ 199 Sammy Sosa A 6.00 1.80
❑ 200 Todd Helton A 3.00 .90
❑ 201 Andre Dawson RET 4.00 1.20
❑ 202 Babe Ruth RET 10.00 3.00
❑ 203 Bob Feller RET 5.00 1.50
❑ 204 Bob Gibson RET 5.00 1.50
❑ 205 Bobby Doerr RET 4.00 1.20
❑ 206 Cal Ripken RET 20.00 6.00
❑ 207 Dale Murphy RET 5.00 1.50
❑ 208 Don Mattingly RET 10.00 3.00
❑ 209 Gary Carter RET 4.00 1.20
❑ 210 George Brett RET 10.00 3.00
❑ 211 Jackie Robinson RET 5.00 1.50
❑ 212 Lou Brock RET 5.00 1.50
❑ 213 Lou Gehrig RET 8.00 2.40
❑ 214 Mark Grace RET 5.00 1.50
❑ 215 Maury Wills RET 4.00 1.20
❑ 216 Mike Schmidt RET 10.00 3.00
❑ 217 Nolan Ryan RET 10.00 3.00
❑ 218 Orel Hershiser RET 4.00 1.20
❑ 219 Paul Molitor RET 5.00 1.50
❑ 220 Roberto Clemente RET 12.00 3.60
❑ 221 Rod Carew RET 5.00 1.50
❑ 222 Roy Campanella RET 5.00 1.50
❑ 223 Ryne Sandberg RET 10.00 3.00
❑ 224 Stan Musial RET 8.00 2.40
❑ 225 Ted Williams RET 10.00 3.00
❑ 226 Tony Gwynn RET 8.00 2.40
❑ 227 Ty Cobb RET 6.00 1.80
❑ 228 Whitey Ford RET 5.00 1.50
❑ 229 Yogi Berra RET 5.00 1.50
❑ 230 Carlos Beltran Astros H 3.00 .90
❑ 231 David Ortiz H 4.00 1.20
❑ 232 David Ortiz A 4.00 1.20
❑ 233 Carlos Zambrano 3.00 .90
❑ 234 Carlos Lee 3.00 .90
❑ 235 Travis Hafner 3.00 .90
❑ 236 Brad Penny 3.00 .90
❑ 237 Wade Miller 3.00 .90
❑ 238 Edgar Martinez 3.00 .90
❑ 239 Carl Crawford 3.00 .90
❑ 240 Roy Oswalt H 3.00 .90
❑ 241 Kazuo Matsui RC 10.00 3.00
❑ 242 Carlos Beltran Astros A 3.00 .90
❑ 243 Carlos Beltran Royals H 3.00 .90
❑ 244 Miguel Cabrera Fielding 3.00 .90
❑ 245 Scott Rolen Cards H 4.00 1.20
❑ 246 Hank Blalock A 3.00 .90
❑ 247 Vernon Wells A 3.00 .90
❑ 248 Adam Dunn H 3.00 .90
❑ 249 Preston Wilson A 3.00 .90
❑ 250 Victor Martinez H 3.00 .90
❑ 251 Aarom Baldiris PH AU RC 15.00 4.50
❑ 252 Akinori Otsuka PH AU RC 40.00 12.00
❑ 253 Andres Blanco PH AU RC 15.00 4.50
❑ 254 Brad Halsey PH AU RC 15.00 4.50
❑ 255 Joey Gathright PH AU RC 30.00 9.00
❑ 256 Colby Miller PH AU RC 15.00 4.50
❑ 257 Fernando Nieve PH AU RC 15.00 4.50
❑ 258 Freddy Guzman PH AU RC 15.00 4.50
❑ 259 Hector Gimenez PH AU RC 15.00 4.50
❑ 260 Jake Woods PH AU RC 15.00 4.50
❑ 261 Jason Bartlett PH AU RC 15.00 4.50
❑ 262 John Gall PH AU RC 15.00 4.50
❑ 263 Jose Capellan PH AU RC 40.00 12.00
❑ 264 Josh Labandeira PH AU RC 15.00 4.50
❑ 265 Justin Germano PH AU RC 15.00 4.50
❑ 266 Kazuhito Tadano PH AU RC 40.00 12.00
❑ 267 Lance Cormier PH AU RC 15.00 4.50
❑ 268 Merkin Valdez PH AU RC 25.00 7.50
❑ 269 Mike Gosling PH AU RC 15.00 4.50
❑ 270 Ramon Ramirez PH AU RC 15.00 4.50
❑ 271 Rusty Tucker PH AU RC 15.00 4.50
❑ 272 Shawn Hill PH AU RC 15.00 4.50
❑ 273 Shingo Takatsu PH AU RC 50.00 15.00
❑ 274 William Bergolla PH AU RC 15.00 4.50
❑ 275 Yadier Molina PH AU RC 30.00 9.00

1998 Leaf Rookies and Stars

	Nm-Mt	Ex-Mt
COMPLETE SET (339)	300.00	90.00
COMP.SET w/o SP's (200)	25.00	7.50

COMMON (1-130/231-300).......... .30 .09
COMMON (131-190) .... 1.00 .30
COMMON (191-230) .... 2.00 .60
COMMON RC (191-230) .... 2.50 .75
COMMON (301-339) .... 2.50 .75
COMMON RC (301-339) 4.00 1.20

❑ 2 Roberto Alomar .50 .15
❑ 3 Randy Johnson .75 .23
❑ 4 Manny Ramirez .50 .15
❑ 5 Paul Molitor .50 .15
❑ 6 Mike Mussina .50 .15
❑ 7 Jim Thome .75 .23
❑ 8 Tino Martinez .50 .15
❑ 9 Gary Sheffield .30 .09
❑ 10 Chuck Knoblauch .30 .09
❑ 11 Bernie Williams .50 .15
❑ 12 Tim Salmon .50 .15
❑ 13 Sammy Sosa 1.25 .35
❑ 14 Wade Boggs .50 .15
❑ 15 Andres Galarraga .30 .09
❑ 16 Pedro Martinez .75 .23
❑ 17 David Justice .30 .09
❑ 18 Chan Ho Park .30 .09
❑ 19 Jay Buhner .30 .09
❑ 20 Ryan Klesko .30 .09
❑ 21 Barry Larkin .50 .15
❑ 22 Will Clark .75 .23
❑ 23 Raul Mondesi .30 .09
❑ 24 Rickey Henderson .75 .23
❑ 25 Jim Edmonds .30 .09
❑ 26 Ken Griffey Jr. 1.25 .35
❑ 27 Frank Thomas .75 .23
❑ 28 Cal Ripken 2.50 .75
❑ 29 Alex Rodriguez 1.25 .35
❑ 30 Mike Piazza 1.25 .35
❑ 31 Greg Maddux 1.25 .35
❑ 32 Chipper Jones .75 .23
❑ 33 Tony Gwynn 1.00 .30
❑ 34 Derek Jeter 2.00 .60
❑ 35 Jeff Bagwell .50 .15
❑ 36 Juan Gonzalez .50 .15
❑ 37 Nomar Garciaparra 1.25 .35
❑ 38 Andruw Jones .30 .09
❑ 39 Hideo Nomo .75 .23
❑ 40 Roger Clemens 1.50 .45
❑ 41 Mark McGwire 2.00 .60
❑ 42 Scott Rolen .75 .23
❑ 43 Vladimir Guerrero .75 .23
❑ 44 Barry Bonds 2.00 .60
❑ 45 Darin Erstad .30 .09
❑ 46 Albert Belle .30 .09
❑ 47 Kenny Lofton .30 .09
❑ 48 Mo Vaughn .30 .09
❑ 49 Ivan Rodriguez .75 .23
❑ 50 Jose Cruz Jr. .30 .09
❑ 51 Tony Clark .30 .09
❑ 52 Larry Walker .50 .15
❑ 53 Mark Grace .50 .15
❑ 54 Edgar Martinez .50 .15
❑ 55 Fred McGriff .50 .15
❑ 56 Rafael Palmeiro .50 .15
❑ 57 Matt Williams .30 .09
❑ 58 Craig Biggio .50 .15
❑ 59 Ken Caminiti .30 .09
❑ 60 Jose Canseco .75 .23
❑ 61 Brady Anderson .30 .09
❑ 62 Moises Alou .30 .09
❑ 63 Justin Thompson .30 .09
❑ 64 John Smoltz .50 .15
❑ 65 Carlos Delgado .30 .09
❑ 66 J.T. Snow .30 .09
❑ 67 Jason Giambi .30 .09
❑ 68 Garret Anderson .30 .09
❑ 69 Rondell White .30 .09
❑ 70 Eric Karros .30 .09
❑ 71 Javier Lopez .30 .09
❑ 72 Pat Hentgen .30 .09
❑ 73 Dante Bichette .30 .09
❑ 74 Charles Johnson .30 .09
❑ 75 Tom Glavine .50 .15
❑ 76 Rusty Greer .30 .09
❑ 77 Travis Fryman .30 .09
❑ 78 Todd Hundley .30 .09
❑ 79 Ray Lankford .30 .09
❑ 80 Denny Neagle .30 .09
❑ 81 Henry Rodriguez .30 .09
❑ 82 Sandy Alomar Jr. .30 .09
❑ 83 Robin Ventura .30 .09
❑ 84 John Olerud .30 .09
❑ 85 Omar Vizquel .50 .15
❑ 86 Darren Dreifort .30 .09
❑ 87 Kevin Brown .30 .09
❑ 88 Curt Schilling .30 .09
❑ 89 Francisco Cordova .30 .09
❑ 90 Brad Radke .30 .09
❑ 91 David Cone .30 .09
❑ 92 Paul O'Neill .50 .15
❑ 93 Vinny Castilla .30 .09
❑ 94 Marquis Grissom .30 .09
❑ 95 Brian L.Hunter .30 .09
❑ 96 Kevin Appier .30 .09
❑ 97 Bobby Bonilla .30 .09
❑ 98 Eric Young .30 .09
❑ 99 Jason Kendall .30 .09
❑ 100 Shawn Green .30 .09
❑ 101 Edgardo Alfonzo .30 .09
❑ 102 Alan Benes .30 .09
❑ 103 Bobby Higginson .30 .09
❑ 104 Todd Greene .30 .09
❑ 105 Jose Guillen .30 .09
❑ 106 Neifi Perez .30 .09
❑ 107 Edgar Renteria .30 .09
❑ 108 Chris Stynes .30 .09
❑ 109 Todd Walker .30 .09
❑ 110 Brian Jordan .30 .09
❑ 111 Joe Carter .30 .09
❑ 112 Ellis Burks .30 .09
❑ 113 Brett Tomko .30 .09
❑ 114 Mike Cameron .30 .09
❑ 115 Shannon Stewart .30 .09
❑ 116 Kevin Orie .30 .09
❑ 117 Brian Giles .30 .09
❑ 118 Hideki Irabu .30 .09
❑ 119 Delino DeShields .30 .09
❑ 120 David Segui .30 .09
❑ 121 Dustin Hermanson .30 .09
❑ 122 Kevin Young .30 .09
❑ 123 Jay Bell .30 .09
❑ 124 Doug Glanville .30 .09
❑ 125 John Roskos RC .30 .09
❑ 126 Damon Hollins .30 .09
❑ 127 Matt Stairs .30 .09
❑ 128 Cliff Floyd .30 .09
❑ 129 Derek Bell .30 .09
❑ 130 Darryl Strawberry .30 .09
❑ 131 Ken Griffey Jr. PT SP 4.00 1.20
❑ 132 Tim Salmon PT SP 1.50 .45
❑ 133 M.Ramirez PT SP 1.50 .45
❑ 134 Paul Konerko PT SP 1.00 .30
❑ 135 Frank Thomas PT SP 2.50 .75
❑ 136 Todd Helton PT SP 1.50 .45
❑ 137 Larry Walker PT SP 1.50 .45
❑ 138 Mo Vaughn PT SP 1.00 .30
❑ 139 Travis Lee PT SP 1.00 .30
❑ 140 Ivan Rodriguez PT SP 2.50 .75
❑ 141 Ben Grieve PT SP 1.00 .30
❑ 142 Brad Fullmer PT SP 1.00 .30
❑ 143 Alex Rodriguez PT SP 4.00 1.20
❑ 144 Mike Piazza PT SP 4.00 1.20
❑ 145 Greg Maddux PT SP 4.00 1.20
❑ 146 Chipper Jones PT SP 2.50 .75
❑ 147 Kenny Lofton PT SP 1.00 .30
❑ 148 Albert Belle PT SP 1.00 .30
❑ 149 Barry Bonds PT SP 6.00 1.80
❑ 150 V.Guerrero PT SP 2.50 .75
❑ 151 Tony Gwynn PT SP 3.00 .90
❑ 152 Derek Jeter PT SP 6.00 1.80
❑ 153 Jeff Bagwell PT SP 1.50 .45
❑ 154 Juan Gonzalez PT SP 1.50 .45
❑ 155 N.Garciaparra PT SP 4.00 1.20
❑ 156 Andruw Jones PT SP 1.00 .30
❑ 157 Hideo Nomo PT SP 2.50 .75
❑ 158 Roger Clemens PT SP 5.00 1.50
❑ 159 Mark McGwire PT SP 6.00 1.80
❑ 160 Scott Rolen PT SP 2.50 .75
❑ 161 Travis Lee TLU SP 1.00 .30
❑ 162 Ben Grieve TLU SP 1.00 .30
❑ 163 Jose Guillen TLU SP 1.00 .30
❑ 164 Mike Piazza TLU SP 4.00 1.20
❑ 165 Kevin Appier TLU SP 1.00 .30
❑ 166 M.Grissom TLU SP 1.00 .30
❑ 167 Rusty Greer TLU SP 1.00 .30
❑ 168 Ken Caminiti TLU SP 1.00 .30
❑ 169 Craig Biggio TLU SP 1.50 .45
❑ 170 K.Griffey Jr. TLU SP 4.00 1.20
❑ 171 Larry Walker TLU SP 1.50 .45
❑ 172 Barry Larkin TLU SP 1.50 .45
❑ 173 A.Galarraga TLU SP 1.00 .30
❑ 174 Wade Boggs TLU SP 1.50 .45
❑ 175 Sammy Sosa TLU SP 4.00 1.20
❑ 176 T.Dunwoody TLU SP 1.00 .30
❑ 177 Jim Thome TLU SP 2.50 .75
❑ 178 Paul Molitor TLU SP 1.50 .45
❑ 179 Tony Clark TLU SP 1.00 .30
❑ 180 Jose Cruz Jr. TLU SP 1.00 .30
❑ 181 Darin Erstad TLU SP 1.00 .30
❑ 182 Barry Bonds TLU SP 6.00 1.80
❑ 183 Vlad.Guerrero TLU SP 2.50 .75
❑ 184 Scott Rolen TLU SP 2.50 .75
❑ 185 M.McGwire TLU SP 6.00 1.80
❑ 186 N.Garciaparra TLU SP 4.00 1.20
❑ 187 Gary Sheffield TLU SP 1.00 .30
❑ 188 Cal Ripken TLU SP 8.00 2.40
❑ 189 F.Thomas TLU SP 2.50 .75
❑ 190 Andy Pettitte TLU SP 1.50 .45
❑ 191 Paul Konerko SP 2.00 .60
❑ 192 Todd Helton SP 3.00 .90
❑ 193 Mark Kotsay SP 2.00 .60
❑ 194 Brad Fullmer SP 2.00 .60
❑ 195 K.Millwood SP RC 10.00 3.00
❑ 196 David Ortiz SP 8.00 2.40
❑ 197 Kerry Wood SP 5.00 1.50
❑ 198 Miguel Tejada SP 2.00 .60
❑ 199 Fernando Tatis SP 2.00 .60
❑ 200 Jaret Wright SP 2.00 .60
❑ 201 Ben Grieve SP 2.00 .60
❑ 202 Travis Lee SP 2.00 .60
❑ 203 Wes Helms SP 2.00 .60
❑ 204 Geoff Jenkins SP 10.00 3.00
❑ 205 Russell Branyan SP 2.00 .60
❑ 206 Esteban Yan SP RC 4.00 1.20
❑ 207 Ben Ford SP RC 2.50 .75
❑ 208 Rich Butler SP RC 2.50 .75
❑ 209 Ryan Jackson SP RC 2.50 .75
❑ 210 A.J. Hinch SP 2.00 .60
❑ 211 M.Ordonez SP RC 40.00 12.00
❑ 212 Dave Dellucci SP RC 6.00 1.80
❑ 213 Billy McMillon SP 2.00 .60
❑ 214 Mike Lowell SP RC 15.00 4.50
❑ 215 Todd Erdos SP RC 2.50 .75
❑ 216 C.Mendoza SP RC 2.50 .75
❑ 217 F.Catalanotto SP RC 6.00 1.80
❑ 218 Julio Ramirez SP RC 4.00 1.20
❑ 219 John Halama SP RC 4.00 1.20
❑ 220 Wilson Delgado SP 2.00 .60
❑ 221 Mike Judd SP RC 4.00 1.20
❑ 222 Rolando Arrojo SP RC 4.00 1.20
❑ 223 Jason LaRue SP RC 4.00 1.20
❑ 224 Manny Aybar SP RC 4.00 1.20
❑ 225 Jorge Velandia SP 2.00 .60
❑ 226 Mike Kinkade SP RC 4.00 1.20
❑ 227 Carlos Lee SP RC 10.00 3.00
❑ 228 Bobby Hughes SP 2.00 .60
❑ 229 R.Christenson SP RC 2.50 .75
❑ 230 Masato Yoshii SP RC 6.00 1.80
❑ 231 Richard Hidalgo .30 .09
❑ 232 Rafael Medina .30 .09
❑ 233 Damian Jackson .30 .09
❑ 234 Derek Lowe .30 .09
❑ 235 Mario Valdez .30 .09
❑ 236 Eli Marrero .30 .09
❑ 237 Juan Encarnacion .30 .09
❑ 238 Livan Hernandez .30 .09
❑ 239 Bruce Chen .30 .09
❑ 240 Eric Milton .30 .09
❑ 241 Jason Varitek .75 .23
❑ 242 Scott Elarton .30 .09
❑ 243 Manuel Barrios RC .30 .09
❑ 244 Mike Caruso .30 .09
❑ 245 Tom Evans .30 .09
❑ 246 Pat Cline .30 .09
❑ 247 Matt Clement .30 .09
❑ 248 Karim Garcia .30 .09
❑ 249 Richie Sexson .30 .09
❑ 250 Sidney Ponson .30 .09
❑ 251 Randall Simon .30 .09
❑ 252 Tony Saunders .30 .09

	Player	Nm-Mt	Ex-Mt
❑ 253	Javier Valentin	.30	.09
❑ 254	Danny Clyburn	.30	.09
❑ 255	Michael Coleman	.30	.09
❑ 256	Hanley Frias RC	.30	.09
❑ 257	Miguel Cairo	.30	.09
❑ 258	Rob Stanifer RC	.30	.09
❑ 259	Lou Collier	.30	.09
❑ 260	Abraham Nunez	.30	.09
❑ 261	Ricky Ledee	.30	.09
❑ 262	Carl Pavano	.50	.09
❑ 263	Derrek Lee	.30	.09
❑ 264	Jeff Abbott	.30	.09
❑ 265	Bob Abreu	.30	.09
❑ 266	Bartolo Colon	.30	.09
❑ 267	Mike Drumright	.30	.09
❑ 268	Daryle Ward	.30	.09
❑ 269	Gabe Alvarez	.30	.09
❑ 270	Josh Booty	.30	.09
❑ 271	Damian Moss	.30	.09
❑ 272	Brian Rose	.30	.09
❑ 273	Jarrod Washburn	.30	.09
❑ 274	Bobby Estalella	.30	.09
❑ 275	Enrique Wilson	.30	.09
❑ 276	Derrick Gibson	.30	.09
❑ 277	Ken Cloude	.30	.09
❑ 278	Kevin Witt	.30	.09
❑ 279	Donnie Sadler	.30	.09
❑ 280	Sean Casey	.30	.09
❑ 281	Jacob Cruz	.30	.09
❑ 282	Ron Wright	.30	.09
❑ 283	Jeremi Gonzalez	.30	.09
❑ 284	Desi Relaford	.30	.09
❑ 285	Bobby Smith	.30	.09
❑ 286	Javier Vazquez	.30	.09
❑ 287	Steve Woodard	.30	.09
❑ 288	Greg Norton	.30	.09
❑ 289	Cliff Politte	.30	.09
❑ 290	Felix Heredia	.30	.09
❑ 291	Braden Looper	.30	.09
❑ 292	Felix Martinez	.30	.09
❑ 293	Brian Meadows	.30	.09
❑ 294	Edwin Diaz	.30	.09
❑ 295	Pat Watkins	.30	.09
❑ 296	Marc Pisciotta RC	.30	.09
❑ 297	Rick Gorecki	.30	.09
❑ 298	DaRond Stovall	.30	.09
❑ 299	Andy Larkin	.30	.09
❑ 300	Felix Rodriguez	.30	.09
❑ 301	Blake Stein SP	2.50	.75
❑ 302	John Rocker SP RC	6.00	1.80
❑ 303	J.Baughman SP RC	4.00	1.20
❑ 304	Jesus Sanchez SP RC	6.00	1.80
❑ 305	Randy Winn SP	2.50	.75
❑ 306	Lou Merloni SP	2.50	.75
❑ 307	Jim Parque SP RC	6.00	1.80
❑ 308	Dennis Reyes SP	2.50	.75
❑ 309	O.Hernandez SP RC	15.00	4.50
❑ 310	Jason Johnson SP	2.50	.75
❑ 311	Torii Hunter SP	2.50	.75
❑ 312	M.Piazza Marlins SP	10.00	3.00
❑ 313	Mike Frank SP RC	4.00	1.20
❑ 314	Troy Glaus SP RC	80.00	24.00
❑ 315	Jin Ho Cho SP RC	6.00	1.80
❑ 316	Ruben Mateo SP RC	6.00	1.80
❑ 317	Ryan Minor SP RC	6.00	1.80
❑ 318	Aramis Ramirez SP	2.50	.75
❑ 319	Adrian Beltre SP	6.00	1.80
❑ 320	Matt Anderson SP RC	6.00	1.80
❑ 321	Gabe Kapler SP RC	10.00	3.00
❑ 322	Jeremy Giambi SP RC	6.00	1.80
❑ 323	Carlos Beltran SP	8.00	2.40
❑ 324	Dermal Brown SP	2.50	.75
❑ 325	Ben Davis SP	2.50	.75
❑ 326	Eric Chavez SP	2.50	.75
❑ 327	Bobby Howry SP RC	6.00	1.80
❑ 328	Roy Halladay SP	2.50	.75
❑ 329	George Lombard SP	2.50	.75
❑ 330	Michael Barrett SP	2.50	.75
❑ 331	F. Seguignol SP RC	4.00	1.20
❑ 332	J.D. Drew SP RC	50.00	15.00
❑ 333	Odalis Perez SP RC	15.00	4.50
❑ 334	Alex Cora SP RC	6.00	1.80
❑ 335	P.Polanco SP RC	6.00	1.80
❑ 336	Armando Rios SP RC	6.00	1.80
❑ 337	Sammy Sosa HR SP	10.00	3.00
❑ 338	Mark McGwire HR SP	15.00	4.50
❑ 339	Sammy Sosa Mark McGwire CL SP	12.00	3.60

2001 Leaf Rookies and Stars

	Nm-Mt	Ex-Mt
COMP.SET w/o SP'S (100)	20.00	6.00
COMMON CARD (1-100)	.30	.09
COMMON (101-200)	3.00	.90
COMMON (201-300)	8.00	2.40

	Player	Nm-Mt	Ex-Mt
❑ 1	Alex Rodriguez	1.25	.35
❑ 2	Derek Jeter	2.00	.60
❑ 3	Aramis Ramirez	.30	.09
❑ 4	Cliff Floyd	.30	.09
❑ 5	Nomar Garciaparra	1.25	.35
❑ 6	Craig Biggio	.50	.15
❑ 7	Ivan Rodriguez	.75	.23
❑ 8	Cal Ripken	2.50	.75
❑ 9	Fred McGriff	.50	.15
❑ 10	Chipper Jones	.75	.23
❑ 11	Roberto Alomar	.50	.15
❑ 12	Moises Alou	.30	.09
❑ 13	Freddy Garcia	.30	.09
❑ 14	Bobby Abreu	.30	.09
❑ 15	Shawn Green	.30	.09
❑ 16	Jason Giambi	.30	.09
❑ 17	Todd Helton	.50	.15
❑ 18	Robert Fick	.30	.09
❑ 19	Tony Gwynn	1.00	.30
❑ 20	Luis Gonzalez	.30	.09
❑ 21	Sean Casey	.30	.09
❑ 22	Roger Clemens	1.50	.45
❑ 23	Brian Giles	.30	.09
❑ 24	Manny Ramirez	.50	.15
❑ 25	Barry Bonds	2.00	.60
❑ 26	Richard Hidalgo	.30	.09
❑ 27	Vladimir Guerrero	.75	.23
❑ 28	Kevin Brown UER Batting headers for stats	.30	.09
❑ 29	Mike Sweeney	.30	.09
❑ 30	Ken Griffey Jr.	1.25	.35
❑ 31	Mike Piazza	1.25	.35
❑ 32	Richie Sexson	.30	.09
❑ 33	Matt Morris	.30	.09
❑ 34	Jorge Posada	.50	.15
❑ 35	Eric Chavez	.30	.09
❑ 36	Mark Buehrle	.30	.09
❑ 37	Jeff Bagwell	.50	.15
❑ 38	Curt Schilling	.30	.09
❑ 39	Bartolo Colon	.30	.09
❑ 40	Mark Quinn	.30	.09
❑ 41	Tony Clark	.30	.09
❑ 42	Brad Radke	.30	.09
❑ 43	Gary Sheffield	.30	.09
❑ 44	Doug Mientkiewicz	.30	.09
❑ 45	Pedro Martinez	.75	.23
❑ 46	Carlos Lee	.30	.09
❑ 47	Troy Glaus	.30	.09
❑ 48	Preston Wilson	.30	.09
❑ 49	Phil Nevin	.30	.09
❑ 50	Chan Ho Park	.30	.09
❑ 51	Randy Johnson	.75	.23
❑ 52	Jermaine Dye	.30	.09
❑ 53	Terrence Long	.30	.09
❑ 54	Joe Mays	.30	.09
❑ 55	Scott Rolen	.75	.23
❑ 56	Miguel Tejada	.30	.09
❑ 57	Jim Thome	.75	.23
❑ 58	Jose Vidro	.30	.09
❑ 59	Gabe Kapler	.30	.09
❑ 60	Darin Erstad	.30	.09
❑ 61	Jim Edmonds	.30	.09
❑ 62	Jarrod Washburn	.30	.09
❑ 63	Tom Glavine	.50	.15
❑ 64	Adrian Beltre	.50	.15
❑ 65	Sammy Sosa	1.25	.35
❑ 66	Juan Gonzalez	.50	.15
❑ 67	Rafael Furcal	.30	.09
❑ 68	Mike Mussina	.50	.15
❑ 69	Mark McGwire	2.00	.60
❑ 70	Ryan Klesko	.30	.09
❑ 71	Raul Mondesi	.30	.09
❑ 72	Trot Nixon	.30	.09
❑ 73	Barry Larkin	.50	.15
❑ 74	Rafael Palmeiro	.50	.15
❑ 75	Mark Mulder	.30	.09
❑ 76	Carlos Delgado	.30	.09
❑ 77	Mike Hampton	.30	.09
❑ 78	Carl Everett	.30	.09
❑ 79	Paul Konerko	.30	.09
❑ 80	Larry Walker	.50	.15
❑ 81	Kerry Wood	.75	.23
❑ 82	Frank Thomas	.75	.23
❑ 83	Andruw Jones	.30	.09
❑ 84	Eric Milton	.30	.09
❑ 85	Ben Grieve	.30	.09
❑ 86	Carlos Beltran	.50	.15
❑ 87	Tim Hudson	.30	.09
❑ 88	Hideo Nomo	.75	.23
❑ 89	Greg Maddux	1.25	.35
❑ 90	Edgar Martinez	.50	.15
❑ 91	Lance Berkman	.30	.09
❑ 92	Pat Burrell	.30	.09
❑ 93	Jeff Kent	.30	.09
❑ 94	Magglio Ordonez	.30	.09
❑ 95	Cristian Guzman	.30	.09
❑ 96	Jose Canseco	.75	.23
❑ 97	J.D. Drew	.30	.09
❑ 98	Bernie Williams	.50	.15
❑ 99	Kazuhiro Sasaki	.30	.09
❑ 100	Rickey Henderson	.75	.23
❑ 101	Wilson Guzman RC	3.00	.90
❑ 102	Nick Neugebauer	3.00	.90
❑ 103	Lance Davis RC	3.00	.90
❑ 104	Felipe Lopez	3.00	.90
❑ 105	Toby Hall	3.00	.90
❑ 106	Jack Cust	3.00	.90
❑ 107	Jason Karnuth RC	3.00	.90
❑ 108	Bart Miadich RC	3.00	.90
❑ 109	Brian Roberts RC	3.00	.90
❑ 110	Brandon Larson RC	3.00	.90
❑ 111	Sean Douglass RC	3.00	.90
❑ 112	Joe Crede	3.00	.90
❑ 113	Tim Redding	3.00	.90
❑ 114	Adam Johnson	3.00	.90
❑ 115	Marcus Giles	3.00	.90
❑ 116	Jose Ortiz	3.00	.90
❑ 117	Jose Mieses RC	3.00	.90
❑ 118	Nick Maness RC	3.00	.90
❑ 119	Les Walrond RC	3.00	.90
❑ 120	Travis Phelps RC	3.00	.90
❑ 121	Troy Mattes RC	3.00	.90
❑ 122	Carlos Garcia RC	3.00	.90
❑ 123	Bill Ortega RC	3.00	.90
❑ 124	Gene Altman RC	3.00	.90
❑ 125	Nate Frese RC	3.00	.90
❑ 126	Alfonso Soriano	5.00	1.50
❑ 127	Jose Nunez RC	3.00	.90
❑ 128	Bob File RC	3.00	.90
❑ 129	Dan Wright	3.00	.90
❑ 130	Nick Johnson	3.00	.90
❑ 131	Brent Abernathy	3.00	.90
❑ 132	Steve Green RC	3.00	.90
❑ 133	Billy Sylvester RC	3.00	.90
❑ 134	Scott MacRae RC	3.00	.90
❑ 135	Kris Keller RC	3.00	.90
❑ 136	Scott Stewart RC	3.00	.90
❑ 137	Henry Mateo RC	3.00	.90
❑ 138	Timo Perez	3.00	.90
❑ 139	Nate Teut RC	3.00	.90
❑ 140	Jason Michaels RC	3.00	.90
❑ 141	Junior Spivey RC	5.00	1.50
❑ 142	Carlos Pena	3.00	.90
❑ 143	Wilmy Caceres RC	3.00	.90
❑ 144	David Lundquist	3.00	.90

❑ 145 Jack Wilson RC 8.00 2.40
❑ 146 Jeremy Fikac RC 3.00 .90
❑ 147 Alex Escobar 3.00 .90
❑ 148 Abraham Nunez 3.00 .90
❑ 149 Xavier Nady 3.00 .90
❑ 150 Michael Cuddyer 3.00 .90
❑ 151 Greg Miller RC 3.00 .90
❑ 152 Eric Munson 3.00 .90
❑ 153 Aubrey Huff 3.00 .90
❑ 154 Tim Christman RC 3.00 .90
❑ 155 Erick Almonte RC 3.00 .90
❑ 156 Mike Penney RC 3.00 .90
❑ 157 Delvin James RC 3.00 .90
❑ 158 Ben Sheets 5.00 1.50
❑ 159 Jason Hart 3.00 .90
❑ 160 Jose Acevedo RC 3.00 .90
❑ 161 Will Ohman RC 3.00 .90
❑ 162 Erik Hiljus RC 3.00 .90
❑ 163 Juan Moreno RC 3.00 .90
❑ 164 Mike Koplove RC 3.00 .90
❑ 165 Pedro Santana RC 3.00 .90
❑ 166 Jimmy Rollins 3.00 .90
❑ 167 Matt White RC 3.00 .90
❑ 168 Cesar Crespo RC 3.00 .90
❑ 169 Carlos Hernandez 3.00 .90
❑ 170 Chris George 3.00 .90
❑ 171 Brad Voyles RC 3.00 .90
❑ 172 Luis Pineda RC 3.00 .90
❑ 173 Carlos Zambrano RC 5.00 1.50
❑ 174 Nate Cornejo 3.00 .90
❑ 175 Jason Smith RC 3.00 .90
❑ 176 Craig Monroe RC 3.00 .90
❑ 177 Cody Ransom RC 3.00 .90
❑ 178 John Grabow RC 3.00 .90
❑ 179 Pedro Feliz 3.00 .90
❑ 180 Jeremy Owens RC 3.00 .90
❑ 181 Kurt Ainsworth 3.00 .90
❑ 182 Luis Lopez 3.00 .90
❑ 183 Stubby Clapp RC 3.00 .90
❑ 184 Ryan Freel RC 3.00 .90
❑ 185 Duaner Sanchez RC 3.00 .90
❑ 186 Jason Jennings 3.00 .90
❑ 187 Kyle Lohse RC 5.00 1.50
❑ 188 Jerrod Riggan RC 3.00 .90
❑ 189 Joe Beimel RC 3.00 .90
❑ 190 Nick Punto RC 3.00 .90
❑ 191 Willie Harris RC 3.00 .90
❑ 192 Ryan Jensen RC 3.00 .90
❑ 193 Adam Pettyjohn RC 3.00 .90
❑ 194 Donaldo Mendez RC 3.00 .90
❑ 195 Bret Prinz RC 3.00 .90
❑ 196 Paul Phillips RC 3.00 .90
❑ 197 Brian Lawrence RC 3.00 .90
❑ 198 Cesar Izturis 3.00 .90
❑ 199 Blaine Neal RC 3.00 .90
❑ 200 Josh Fogg RC 8.00 2.40
❑ 201 Josh Towers RC 8.00 2.40
❑ 202 T.Spooneybarger RC 8.00 2.40
❑ 203 Michael Rivera RC 8.00 2.40
❑ 204 Juan Cruz RC 8.00 2.40
❑ 205 Albert Pujols RC 125.00 38.00
❑ 206 Josh Beckett 8.00 2.40
❑ 207 Roy Oswalt 10.00 3.00
❑ 208 Elpidio Guzman RC 8.00 2.40
❑ 209 Horacio Ramirez RC 10.00 3.00
❑ 210 Corey Patterson 8.00 2.40
❑ 211 Geronimo Gil RC 8.00 2.40
❑ 212 Jay Gibbons RC 10.00 3.00
❑ 213 O.Woodards RC 8.00 2.40
❑ 214 David Espinosa 8.00 2.40
❑ 215 Angel Berroa RC 10.00 3.00
❑ 216 B.Duckworth RC 8.00 2.40
❑ 217 Brian Reith RC 8.00 2.40
❑ 218 David Brous RC 8.00 2.40
❑ 219 Bud Smith RC 8.00 2.40
❑ 220 Ramon Vazquez RC 8.00 2.40
❑ 221 Mark Teixeira RC 50.00 15.00
❑ 222 Justin Atchley RC 8.00 2.40
❑ 223 Tony Cogan RC 8.00 2.40
❑ 224 Grant Balfour RC 8.00 2.40
❑ 225 Ricardo Rodriguez RC 8.00 2.40
❑ 226 Brian Rogers RC 8.00 2.40
❑ 227 Adam Dunn 10.00 3.00
❑ 228 Wilson Betemit RC 8.00 2.40
❑ 229 Juan Diaz RC 8.00 2.40
❑ 230 Jackson Melian RC 8.00 2.40
❑ 231 Claudio Vargas RC 8.00 2.40
❑ 232 Wilkin Ruan RC 8.00 2.40
❑ 233 J.Duchscherer RC 8.00 2.40
❑ 234 Kevin Olsen RC 8.00 2.40
❑ 235 Tony Fiore RC 8.00 2.40
❑ 236 Jeremy Affeldt RC 10.00 3.00
❑ 237 Mike Maroth RC 8.00 2.40
❑ 238 C.C. Sabathia 8.00 2.40
❑ 239 Cory Aldridge RC 8.00 2.40
❑ 240 Zach Day RC 8.00 2.40
❑ 241 Brett Jodie RC 8.00 2.40
❑ 242 Winston Abreu RC 8.00 2.40
❑ 243 Travis Hafner RC 15.00 4.50
❑ 244 Joe Kennedy RC 10.00 3.00
❑ 245 Rick Bauer RC 8.00 2.40
❑ 246 Mike Young 10.00 3.00
❑ 247 Ken Vining RC 8.00 2.40
❑ 248 Doug Nickle RC 8.00 2.40
❑ 249 Pablo Ozuna 8.00 2.40
❑ 250 Dustan Mohr RC 8.00 2.40
❑ 251 Ichiro Suzuki RC 60.00 18.00
❑ 252 Ryan Drese RC 10.00 3.00
❑ 253 Morgan Ensberg RC 10.00 3.00
❑ 254 George Perez RC 8.00 2.40
❑ 255 Roy Smith RC 8.00 2.40
❑ 256 Juan Uribe RC 10.00 3.00
❑ 257 Dewon Brazelton RC 10.00 3.00
❑ 258 Endy Chavez RC 8.00 2.40
❑ 259 Kris Foster 8.00 2.40
❑ 260 Eric Knott RC 8.00 2.40
❑ 261 Corky Miller RC 8.00 2.40
❑ 262 Larry Bigbie 8.00 2.40
❑ 263 Andres Torres RC 8.00 2.40
❑ 264 Adrian Hernandez RC 8.00 2.40
❑ 265 Johnny Estrada RC 15.00 4.50
❑ 266 David Williams RC 8.00 2.40
❑ 267 Steve Lomasney 8.00 2.40
❑ 268 Victor Zambrano RC 10.00 3.00
❑ 269 Keith Ginter 8.00 2.40
❑ 270 Casey Fossum RC 8.00 2.40
❑ 271 Josue Perez RC 8.00 2.40
❑ 272 Josh Phelps 8.00 2.40
❑ 273 Mark Prior RC 60.00 18.00
❑ 274 Brandon Berger RC 8.00 2.40
❑ 275 Scott Podsednik RC 20.00 6.00
❑ 276 Jorge Julio RC 8.00 2.40
❑ 277 Esix Snead RC 8.00 2.40
❑ 278 Brandon Knight RC 8.00 2.40
❑ 279 Saul Rivera RC 8.00 2.40
❑ 280 Benito Baez RC 8.00 2.40
❑ 281 Rob MacKowiak RC 10.00 3.00
❑ 282 Eric Hinske RC 10.00 3.00
❑ 283 Juan Rivera 8.00 2.40
❑ 284 Kevin Joseph RC 8.00 2.40
❑ 285 Juan A. Pena RC 8.00 2.40
❑ 286 Brandon Lyon RC 8.00 2.40
❑ 287 Adam Everett 8.00 2.40
❑ 288 Eric Valent 8.00 2.40
❑ 289 Ken Harvey 8.00 2.40
❑ 290 Bert Snow RC 8.00 2.40
❑ 291 Wily Mo Pena 8.00 2.40
❑ 292 Rafael Soriano RC 10.00 3.00
❑ 293 Carlos Valderrama RC 8.00 2.40
❑ 294 Christian Parker RC 8.00 2.40
❑ 295 Tsuyoshi Shinjo RC 10.00 3.00
❑ 296 Martin Vargas RC 8.00 2.40
❑ 297 Luke Hudson RC 8.00 2.40
❑ 298 Dee Brown 8.00 2.40
❑ 299 Alexis Gomez RC 8.00 2.40
❑ 300 Angel Santos RC 8.00 2.40

2004 Leather and Lumber

	Nm-Mt	Ex-Mt
COMP.SET w/o SP's (150)	40.00	12.00
COMMON CARD (1-150)	.40	.12
COMMON RETIRED (1-150)	.50	.15
COMMON AUTO (151-175)	8.00	2.40
COMMON CARD (151-175)	4.00	1.20

❑ 1 Bartolo Colon .40 .12
❑ 2 Garret Anderson .40 .12
❑ 3 Tim Salmon .60 .18
❑ 4 Troy Glaus .40 .12
❑ 5 Vladimir Guerrero 1.00 .30
❑ 6 Brandon Webb .40 .12
❑ 7 Luis Gonzalez .40 .12
❑ 8 Randy Johnson 1.00 .30
❑ 9 Richie Sexson .40 .12
❑ 10 Shea Hillenbrand .40 .12
❑ 11 Adam LaRoche .40 .12
❑ 12 Andruw Jones .40 .12
❑ 13 Chipper Jones 1.00 .30
❑ 14 Dale Murphy .75 .23
❑ 15 J.D. Drew .40 .12
❑ 16 Marcus Giles .40 .12
❑ 17 Rafael Furcal .40 .12
❑ 18 Cal Ripken 5.00 1.50
❑ 19 Javy Lopez .40 .12
❑ 20 Jay Gibbons .40 .12
❑ 21 Luis Matos .40 .12
❑ 22 Miguel Tejada .40 .12
❑ 23 Rafael Palmeiro .60 .18
❑ 24 Curt Schilling 1.00 .30
❑ 25 Jason Varitek .60 .18
❑ 26 Manny Ramirez .60 .18
❑ 27 Nomar Garciaparra 1.50 .45
❑ 28 Pedro Martinez 1.00 .30
❑ 29 Trot Nixon .40 .12
❑ 30 Greg Maddux 1.50 .45
❑ 31 Kerry Wood 1.00 .30
❑ 32 Mark Prior 1.00 .30
❑ 33 Ryne Sandberg UER 2.50 .75
Hit 267th career homer in 1977
❑ 34 Sammy Sosa 1.50 .45
❑ 35 Carlos Lee .40 .12
❑ 36 Frank Thomas 1.00 .30
❑ 37 Magglio Ordonez .40 .12
❑ 38 Paul Konerko .40 .12
❑ 39 Adam Dunn .60 .18
❑ 40 Austin Kearns .40 .12
❑ 41 Barry Larkin .60 .18
❑ 42 Ken Griffey Jr. 1.50 .45
❑ 43 Ryan Wagner .40 .12
❑ 44 C.C. Sabathia .40 .12
❑ 45 Jody Gerut .40 .12
❑ 46 Omar Vizquel .60 .18
❑ 47 Larry Walker .60 .18
❑ 48 Preston Wilson .40 .12
❑ 49 Todd Helton .60 .18
❑ 50 Alan Trammell .50 .15
❑ 51 Ivan Rodriguez 1.00 .30
❑ 52 Jeremy Bonderman .40 .12
❑ 53 Dontrelle Willis .40 .12
❑ 54 Josh Beckett .40 .12
❑ 55 Luis Castillo .40 .12
❑ 56 Miguel Cabrera .60 .18
❑ 57 Mike Lowell .40 .12
❑ 58 Andy Pettitte .60 .18
❑ 59 Craig Biggio .60 .18
❑ 60 Jeff Bagwell .60 .18
❑ 61 Jeff Kent .40 .12
❑ 62 Lance Berkman .40 .12
❑ 63 Roger Clemens 2.00 .60
❑ 64 Roy Oswalt .40 .12
❑ 65 Angel Berroa .40 .12
❑ 66 Carlos Beltran .60 .18
❑ 67 George Brett 2.50 .75
❑ 68 Juan Gonzalez .60 .18
❑ 69 Mike Sweeney .40 .12
❑ 70 Eric Gagne 1.00 .30
❑ 71 Hideo Nomo 1.00 .30
❑ 72 Kazuhisa Ishii .40 .12
❑ 73 Paul Lo Duca .40 .12
❑ 74 Shawn Green .40 .12
❑ 75 Geoff Jenkins .40 .12
❑ 76 Junior Spivey .40 .12
❑ 77 Rickie Weeks .40 .12
❑ 78 Robin Yount 2.00 .60

❑ 79 Scott Podsednik	.40	.12
❑ 80 Jacque Jones	.40	.12
❑ 81 Johan Santana	.60	.18
❑ 82 Shannon Stewart	.40	.12
❑ 83 Torii Hunter	.40	.12
❑ 84 Andre Dawson	.50	.15
❑ 85 Chad Cordero	.40	.12
❑ 86 Jose Vidro	.40	.12
❑ 87 Nick Johnson	.40	.12
❑ 88 Orlando Cabrera	.40	.12
❑ 89 Gary Carter	.50	.15
❑ 90 Jae Weong Seo	.40	.12
❑ 91 Jose Reyes	.40	.12
❑ 92 Mike Piazza	1.50	.45
❑ 93 Tom Glavine	.60	.18
❑ 94 Alex Rodriguez	1.50	.45
❑ 95 Bernie Williams	.60	.18
❑ 96 Derek Jeter	2.00	.60
❑ 97 Don Mattingly	2.50	.75
❑ 98 Gary Sheffield	.40	.12
❑ 99 Hideki Matsui	1.50	.45
❑ 100 Jason Giambi	.40	.12
❑ 101 Jorge Posada	.60	.18
❑ 102 Mike Mussina	.60	.18
❑ 103 Barry Zito	.40	.12
❑ 104 Bobby Crosby	.60	.18
❑ 105 Eric Chavez	.40	.12
❑ 106 Jermaine Dye	.40	.12
❑ 107 Mark Mulder	.40	.12
❑ 108 Rich Harden	.40	.12
❑ 109 Rickey Henderson	1.25	.35
❑ 110 Tim Hudson	.40	.12
❑ 111 Bobby Abreu	.40	.12
❑ 112 Brett Myers	.40	.12
❑ 113 Jim Thome	1.00	.30
❑ 114 Kevin Millwood	.40	.12
❑ 115 Marlon Byrd	.40	.12
❑ 116 Mike Schmidt	2.50	.75
❑ 117 Pat Burrell	.40	.12
❑ 118 Dave Parker	.50	.15
❑ 119 Jason Bay	.40	.12
❑ 120 Jason Kendall	.40	.12
❑ 121 Brian Giles	.40	.12
❑ 122 Jay Payton	.40	.12
❑ 123 Ryan Klesko	.40	.12
❑ 124 Tony Gwynn	2.00	.60
❑ 125 Edgardo Alfonzo	.40	.12
❑ 126 Jason Schmidt	.40	.12
❑ 127 Jerome Williams	.40	.12
❑ 128 Bret Boone	.40	.12
❑ 129 Edgar Martinez	.60	.18
❑ 130 Ichiro Suzuki	1.50	.45
❑ 131 Jamie Moyer	.40	.12
❑ 132 John Olerud	.40	.12
❑ 133 Albert Pujols	2.00	.60
❑ 134 Edgar Renteria	.40	.12
❑ 135 Jim Edmonds	.40	.12
❑ 136 Matt Morris	.40	.12
❑ 137 Scott Rolen	1.00	.30
❑ 138 Aubrey Huff	.40	.12
❑ 139 Carl Crawford	.40	.12
❑ 140 Delmon Young	.60	.18
❑ 141 Rocco Baldelli	.40	.12
❑ 142 Alfonso Soriano	.60	.18
❑ 143 Hank Blalock	.40	.12
❑ 144 Mark Teixeira	.40	.12
❑ 145 Michael Young	.40	.12
❑ 146 Nolan Ryan	3.00	.90
❑ 147 Carlos Delgado	.40	.12
❑ 148 Eric Hinske	.40	.12
❑ 149 Roy Halladay	.40	.12
❑ 150 Vernon Wells	.40	.12
❑ 151 Andres Blanco ROO AU RC	8.00	2.40
❑ 152 Kevin Cave ROO AU RC	10.00	3.00
❑ 153 Ryan Meaux ROO AU RC	8.00	2.40
❑ 154 Tim Bausher ROO AU RC	8.00	2.40
❑ 155 Jesse Harper ROO AU RC	8.00	2.40
❑ 156 Mike Wuertz ROO AU RC	10.00	3.00
❑ 157 Colby Miller ROO AU RC	8.00	2.40
❑ 158 Don Kelly ROO AU RC	8.00	2.40
❑ 159 Edwin Moreno ROO AU RC	10.00	3.00
❑ 160 Mike Johnston ROO AU RC	8.00	2.40
❑ 161 O.Rodriguez ROO AU RC	8.00	2.40
❑ 162 Phil Stockman ROO AU RC	8.00	2.40
❑ 163 Yadier Molina ROO RC	6.00	1.80
❑ 164 Jorge Vasquez ROO AU RC	8.00	2.40
❑ 165 Scott Proctor ROO AU RC	10.00	3.00
❑ 166 Jake Woods ROO AU RC	8.00	2.40
❑ 167 Aarom Baldiris ROO AU RC	10.00	3.00
❑ 168 Jason Bartlett ROO AU RC	10.00	3.00
❑ 169 Casey Daigle ROO AU RC	8.00	2.40
❑ 170 Dennis Sarfate ROO AU RC	8.00	2.40
❑ 171 E.Sierra ROO AU RC	10.00	3.00
❑ 172 Merkin Valdez ROO AU RC	10.00	3.00
❑ 173 E.Rodriguez ROO AU RC	10.00	3.00
❑ 174 Kazuo Matsui ROO RC	10.00	3.00
❑ 175 David Aardsma ROO RC	4.00	1.20

2000 Pacific Invincible

	Nm-Mt	Ex-Mt
COMPLETE SET (150)	100.00	30.00
❑ 1 Darin Erstad	1.25	.35
❑ 2 Troy Glaus	1.25	.35
❑ 3 Ramon Ortiz	.75	.23
❑ 4 Tim Salmon	2.00	.60
❑ 5 Mo Vaughn	1.25	.35
❑ 6 Erubiel Durazo	.75	.23
❑ 7 Luis Gonzalez	1.25	.35
❑ 8 Randy Johnson	3.00	.90
❑ 9 Matt Williams	.75	.23
❑ 10 Rafael Furcal	1.25	.35
❑ 11 Andres Galarraga	1.25	.35
❑ 12 Tom Glavine	2.00	.60
❑ 13 Andruw Jones	1.25	.35
❑ 14 Chipper Jones	3.00	.90
❑ 15 Greg Maddux	5.00	1.50
❑ 16 Kevin Millwood	1.25	.35
❑ 17 Albert Belle	1.25	.35
❑ 18 Will Clark	3.00	.90
❑ 19 Mike Mussina	2.00	.60
❑ 20 Matt Riley	.75	.23
❑ 21 Cal Ripken	10.00	3.00
❑ 22 Carl Everett	1.25	.35
❑ 23 Nomar Garciaparra	5.00	1.50
❑ 24 Steve Lomasney	.75	.23
❑ 25 Pedro Martinez	3.00	.90
❑ 26 Tomo Ohka RC	1.25	.35
❑ 27 Wilton Veras	.75	.23
❑ 28 Mark Grace	2.00	.60
❑ 29 Sammy Sosa	5.00	1.50
❑ 30 Kerry Wood	3.00	.90
❑ 31 Eric Young	.75	.23
❑ 32 Julio Zuleta RC	.75	.23
❑ 33 Paul Konerko	1.25	.35
❑ 34 Carlos Lee	1.25	.35
❑ 35 Magglio Ordonez	1.25	.35
❑ 36 Josh Paul	.75	.23
❑ 37 Frank Thomas	3.00	.90
❑ 38 Rob Bell	.75	.23
❑ 39 Dante Bichette	1.25	.35
❑ 40 Sean Casey	1.25	.35
❑ 41 Ken Griffey Jr.	5.00	1.50
❑ 42 Barry Larkin	2.00	.60
❑ 43 Pokey Reese	.75	.23
❑ 44 Roberto Alomar	2.00	.60
❑ 45 Manny Ramirez	2.00	.60
❑ 46 Richie Sexson	1.25	.35
❑ 47 Jim Thome	3.00	.90
❑ 48 Omar Vizquel	2.00	.60
❑ 49 Jeff Cirillo	.75	.23
❑ 50 Todd Helton	2.00	.60
❑ 51 Neifi Perez	.75	.23
❑ 52 Larry Walker	2.00	.60
❑ 53 Tony Clark	.75	.23
❑ 54 Juan Encarnacion	.75	.23
❑ 55 Juan Gonzalez	2.00	.60
❑ 56 Hideo Nomo	3.00	.90
❑ 57 Luis Castillo	.75	.23
❑ 58 Alex Gonzalez	.75	.23
❑ 59 Brad Penny	.75	.23
❑ 60 Preston Wilson	1.25	.35
❑ 61 Moises Alou	1.25	.35
❑ 62 Jeff Bagwell	2.00	.60
❑ 63 Lance Berkman	1.25	.35
❑ 64 Craig Biggio	2.00	.60
❑ 65 Roger Cedeno	.75	.23
❑ 66 Jose Lima	.75	.23
❑ 67 Carlos Beltran	2.00	.60
❑ 68 Johnny Damon	2.00	.60
❑ 69 Chad Durbin RC	.75	.23
❑ 70 Jermaine Dye	1.25	.35
❑ 71 Carlos Febles	.75	.23
❑ 72 Mark Quinn	.75	.23
❑ 73 Kevin Brown	1.25	.35
❑ 74 Eric Gagne	5.00	1.50
❑ 75 Shawn Green	1.25	.35
❑ 76 Eric Karros	1.25	.35
❑ 77 Gary Sheffield	1.25	.35
❑ 78 Kevin Barker	.75	.23
❑ 79 Ron Belliard	.75	.23
❑ 80 Jeromy Burnitz	1.25	.35
❑ 81 Geoff Jenkins	1.25	.35
❑ 82 Jacque Jones	1.25	.35
❑ 83 Corey Koskie	1.25	.35
❑ 84 Matt LeCroy	.75	.23
❑ 85 David Ortiz	2.00	.60
❑ 86 Johan Santana RC	15.00	4.50
❑ 87 Todd Walker	.75	.23
❑ 88 Peter Bergeron	.75	.23
❑ 89 Vladimir Guerrero	3.00	.90
❑ 90 Jose Vidro	.75	.23
❑ 91 Rondell White	1.25	.35
❑ 92 Edgardo Alfonzo	.75	.23
❑ 93 Derek Bell	.75	.23
❑ 94 Mike Hampton	1.25	.35
❑ 95 Rey Ordonez	.75	.23
❑ 96 Mike Piazza	5.00	1.50
❑ 97 Robin Ventura	1.25	.35
❑ 98 Roger Clemens	6.00	1.80
❑ 99 Orlando Hernandez	.75	.23
❑ 100 Derek Jeter	8.00	2.40
❑ 101 Alfonso Soriano	3.00	.90
❑ 102 Bernie Williams	2.00	.60
❑ 103 Eric Chavez	1.25	.35
❑ 104 Jason Giambi	1.25	.35
❑ 105 Ben Grieve	.75	.23
❑ 106 Tim Hudson	1.25	.35
❑ 107 Miguel Tejada	1.25	.35
❑ 108 Bob Abreu	1.25	.35
❑ 109 Doug Glanville	.75	.23
❑ 110 Mike Lieberthal	1.25	.35
❑ 111 Scott Rolen	3.00	.90
❑ 112 Brian Giles	1.25	.35
❑ 113 Chad Hermansen	.75	.23
❑ 114 Jason Kendall	1.25	.35
❑ 115 Warren Morris	.75	.23
❑ 116 Aramis Ramirez	1.25	.35
❑ 117 Rick Ankiel	1.25	.35
❑ 118 J.D. Drew	1.25	.35
❑ 119 Mark McGwire	8.00	2.40
❑ 120 Fernando Tatis	.75	.23
❑ 121 Fernando Vina	.75	.23
❑ 122 Bret Boone	1.25	.35
❑ 123 Ben Davis	.75	.23
❑ 124 Tony Gwynn	4.00	1.20
❑ 125 Trevor Hoffman	1.25	.35
❑ 126 Ryan Klesko	1.25	.35
❑ 127 Rich Aurilia	.75	.23
❑ 128 Barry Bonds	8.00	2.40
❑ 129 Ellis Burks	1.25	.35
❑ 130 Jeff Kent	1.25	.35
❑ 131 Freddy Garcia	1.25	.35
❑ 132 Carlos Guillen	1.25	.35
❑ 133 Edgar Martinez	2.00	.60
❑ 134 John Olerud	1.25	.35
❑ 135 Rob Ramsay	.75	.23
❑ 136 Alex Rodriguez	5.00	1.50
❑ 137 Kazuhiro Sasaki RC	3.00	.90

	Nm-Mt	Ex-Mt
❑ 138 Jose Canseco	3.00	.90
❑ 139 Vinny Castilla	1.25	.35
❑ 140 Fred McGriff	2.00	.60
❑ 141 Greg Vaughn UER Mo Vaughn is pictured	.75	.23
❑ 142 Dan Wheeler	.75	.23
❑ 143 Gabe Kapler	.75	.23
❑ 144 Ruben Mateo	.75	.23
❑ 145 Rafael Palmeiro	2.00	.60
❑ 146 Ivan Rodriguez	3.00	.90
❑ 147 Tony Batista	1.25	.35
❑ 148 Carlos Delgado	1.25	.35
❑ 149 Raul Mondesi	1.25	.35
❑ 150 Vernon Wells	1.25	.35

2000 Pacific Omega

	Nm-Mt	Ex-Mt
COMP.SET w/o SP's (150)	20.00	6.00
COMMON CARD (1-150)	.30	.09
COMMON (151-255)	5.00	1.50
❑ 1 Garret Anderson	.30	.09
❑ 2 Darin Erstad	.30	.09
❑ 3 Troy Glaus	.30	.09
❑ 4 Tim Salmon	.50	.15
❑ 5 Mo Vaughn	.30	.09
❑ 6 Jay Bell	.30	.09
❑ 7 Steve Finley	.30	.09
❑ 8 Luis Gonzalez	.30	.09
❑ 9 Randy Johnson	.75	.23
❑ 10 Matt Williams	.30	.09
❑ 11 Andres Galarraga	.30	.09
❑ 12 Andruw Jones	.30	.09
❑ 13 Chipper Jones	.75	.23
❑ 14 Brian Jordan	.30	.09
❑ 15 Greg Maddux	1.25	.35
❑ 16 B.J. Surhoff	.30	.09
❑ 17 Brady Anderson	.30	.09
❑ 18 Albert Belle	.30	.09
❑ 19 Mike Mussina	.50	.15
❑ 20 Cal Ripken	2.50	.75
❑ 21 Carl Everett	.30	.09
❑ 22 Nomar Garciaparra	1.25	.35
❑ 23 Pedro Martinez	.75	.23
❑ 24 Jason Varitek	.50	.15
❑ 25 Mark Grace	.50	.15
❑ 26 Sammy Sosa	1.25	.35
❑ 27 Rondell White	.30	.09
❑ 28 Kerry Wood	.75	.23
❑ 29 Eric Young	.30	.09
❑ 30 Ray Durham	.30	.09
❑ 31 Carlos Lee	.30	.09
❑ 32 Magglio Ordonez	.30	.09
❑ 33 Frank Thomas	.75	.23
❑ 34 Sean Casey	.30	.09
❑ 35 Ken Griffey Jr.	1.25	.35
❑ 36 Barry Larkin	.50	.15
❑ 37 Pokey Reese	.30	.09
❑ 38 Roberto Alomar	.50	.15
❑ 39 Kenny Lofton	.30	.09
❑ 40 Manny Ramirez	.50	.15
❑ 41 David Segui	.30	.09
❑ 42 Jim Thome	.75	.23
❑ 43 Omar Vizquel	.50	.15
❑ 44 Jeff Cirillo	.30	.09
❑ 45 Jeffrey Hammonds	.30	.09
❑ 46 Todd Helton	.50	.15
❑ 47 Todd Hollandsworth	.30	.09
❑ 48 Larry Walker	.50	.15
❑ 49 Tony Clark	.30	.09
❑ 50 Juan Encarnacion	.30	.09
❑ 51 Juan Gonzalez	.50	.15
❑ 52 Bobby Higginson	.30	.09
❑ 53 Hideo Nomo	.75	.23
❑ 54 Dean Palmer	.30	.09
❑ 55 Luis Castillo	.30	.09
❑ 56 Cliff Floyd	.30	.09
❑ 57 Derrek Lee	.30	.09
❑ 58 Mike Lowell	.30	.09
❑ 59 Henry Rodriguez	.30	.09
❑ 60 Preston Wilson	.30	.09
❑ 61 Moises Alou	.30	.09
❑ 62 Jeff Bagwell	.50	.15
❑ 63 Craig Biggio	.50	.15
❑ 64 Ken Caminiti	.30	.09
❑ 65 Richard Hidalgo	.30	.09
❑ 66 Carlos Beltran	.50	.15
❑ 67 Johnny Damon	.50	.15
❑ 68 Jermaine Dye	.30	.09
❑ 69 Joe Randa	.30	.09
❑ 70 Mike Sweeney	.30	.09
❑ 71 Adrian Beltre	.50	.15
❑ 72 Kevin Brown	.30	.09
❑ 73 Shawn Green	.30	.09
❑ 74 Eric Karros	.30	.09
❑ 75 Chan Ho Park	.30	.09
❑ 76 Gary Sheffield	.30	.09
❑ 77 Ron Belliard	.30	.09
❑ 78 Jeromy Burnitz	.30	.09
❑ 79 Geoff Jenkins	.30	.09
❑ 80 Richie Sexson	.30	.09
❑ 81 Ron Coomer	.30	.09
❑ 82 Jacque Jones	.30	.09
❑ 83 Corey Koskie	.30	.09
❑ 84 Matt Lawton	.30	.09
❑ 85 Vladimir Guerrero	.75	.23
❑ 86 Lee Stevens	.30	.09
❑ 87 Jose Vidro	.30	.09
❑ 88 Edgardo Alfonzo	.30	.09
❑ 89 Derek Bell	.30	.09
❑ 90 Mike Bordick	.30	.09
❑ 91 Mike Piazza	1.25	.35
❑ 92 Robin Ventura	.30	.09
❑ 93 Jose Canseco	.75	.23
❑ 94 Roger Clemens	1.50	.45
❑ 95 Orlando Hernandez	.30	.09
❑ 96 Derek Jeter	2.00	.60
❑ 97 David Justice	.30	.09
❑ 98 Tino Martinez	.50	.15
❑ 99 Jorge Posada	.50	.15
❑ 100 Bernie Williams	.50	.15
❑ 101 Eric Chavez	.30	.09
❑ 102 Jason Giambi	.30	.09
❑ 103 Ben Grieve	.30	.09
❑ 104 Miguel Tejada	.30	.09
❑ 105 Bobby Abreu	.30	.09
❑ 106 Doug Glanville	.30	.09
❑ 107 Travis Lee	.30	.09
❑ 108 Mike Lieberthal	.30	.09
❑ 109 Scott Rolen	.75	.23
❑ 110 Brian Giles	.30	.09
❑ 111 Jason Kendall	.30	.09
❑ 112 Warren Morris	.30	.09
❑ 113 Kevin Young	.30	.09
❑ 114 Will Clark	.75	.23
❑ 115 J.D. Drew	.30	.09
❑ 116 Jim Edmonds	.30	.09
❑ 117 Mark McGwire	2.00	.60
❑ 118 Edgar Renteria	.30	.09
❑ 119 Fernando Tatis	.30	.09
❑ 120 Fernando Vina	.30	.09
❑ 121 Bret Boone	.30	.09
❑ 122 Tony Gwynn	1.00	.30
❑ 123 Trevor Hoffman	.30	.09
❑ 124 Phil Nevin	.30	.09
❑ 125 Eric Owens	.30	.09
❑ 126 Barry Bonds	2.00	.60
❑ 127 Ellis Burks	.30	.09
❑ 128 Jeff Kent	.30	.09
❑ 129 J.T. Snow	.30	.09
❑ 130 Jay Buhner	.30	.09
❑ 131 Mike Cameron	.30	.09
❑ 132 Rickey Henderson	.75	.23
❑ 133 Edgar Martinez	.50	.15
❑ 134 John Olerud	.30	.09
❑ 135 Alex Rodriguez	1.25	.35
❑ 136 Kazuhiro Sasaki RC	.75	.23
❑ 137 Fred McGriff	.50	.15
❑ 138 Greg Vaughn	.30	.09
❑ 139 Gerald Williams	.30	.09
❑ 140 Rusty Greer	.30	.09
❑ 141 Gabe Kapler	.30	.09
❑ 142 Ricky Ledee	.30	.09
❑ 143 Rafael Palmeiro	.50	.15
❑ 144 Ivan Rodriguez	.75	.23
❑ 145 Tony Batista	.30	.09
❑ 146 Jose Cruz Jr.	.30	.09
❑ 147 Carlos Delgado	.30	.09
❑ 148 Brad Fullmer	.30	.09
❑ 149 Shannon Stewart	.30	.09
❑ 150 David Wells	.30	.09
❑ 151 Juan Alvarez RC Jeff DaVanon RC	5.00	1.50
❑ 152 Seth Etherton Adam Kennedy	5.00	1.50
❑ 153 Ramon Ortiz Lou Pote	5.00	1.50
❑ 154 Derrick Turnbow RC Eric Weaver	5.00	1.50
❑ 155 Rod Barajas Jason Conti	5.00	1.50
❑ 156 Byung-Hyun Kim Rob Ryan	.30	.09
❑ 157 David Cortes RC George Lombard	5.00	1.50
❑ 158 Ivanon Coffie Melvin Mora	5.00	1.50
❑ 159 Ryan Kohlmeier RC Luis Matos RC	5.00	1.50
❑ 160 Willie Morales RC John Parrish RC	5.00	1.50
❑ 161 Chris Richard RC Jay Spurgeon RC	5.00	1.50
❑ 162 Israel Alcantara Tomokazu Ohka RC	5.00	1.50
❑ 163 Paxton Crawford RC Sang-Hoon Lee RC	5.00	1.50
❑ 164 Mike Mahoney RC Wilton Veras	5.00	1.50
❑ 165 Daniel Garibay RC Ross Gload RC	5.00	1.50
❑ 166 Gary Matthews Jr. Phil Norton	5.00	1.50
❑ 167 Roosevelt Brown Ruben Quevedo	5.00	1.50
❑ 168 Lorenzo Barcelo RC Rocky Biddle RC	5.00	1.50
❑ 169 Mark Buehrle John Garland	10.00	3.00
❑ 170 Aaron Myette Josh Paul	5.00	1.50
❑ 171 Kip Wells Kelly Wunsch	5.00	1.50
❑ 172 Rob Bell Travis Dawkins	5.00	1.50
❑ 173 Hector Mercado RC John Riedling RC	5.00	1.50
❑ 174 Russell Branyan Sean DePaula RC	5.00	1.50
❑ 175 Tim Drew Mark Watson RC	5.00	1.50
❑ 176 Craig House RC Ben Petrick	5.00	1.50
❑ 177 Robert Fick Jose Macias	5.00	1.50
❑ 178 Javier Cardona RC Brandon Villafuerte RC	5.00	1.50
❑ 179 Armando Almanza A.J. Burnett	5.00	1.50
❑ 180 Ramon Castro Pablo Ozuna	5.00	1.50
❑ 181 Lance Berkman Jason Green	5.00	1.50
❑ 182 Julio Lugo Tony McKnight	5.00	1.50
❑ 183 Mitch Meluskey Wade Miller	5.00	1.50
❑ 184 Chad Durbin RC Hector Ortiz RC	5.00	1.50

❑ 185 Dermal Brown 5.00 1.50
Mark Quinn
❑ 186 Eric Gagne.................... 10.00 3.00
Mike Judd
❑ 187 Kane Davis RC 5.00 1.50
Valerio De Los Santos
❑ 188 Santiago Perez RC.......... 5.00 1.50
Paul Rigdon RC
❑ 189 Matt Kinney.................... 5.00 1.50
Matt LeCroy
❑ 190 Jason Maxwell 5.00 1.50
A.J. Pierzynski
❑ 191 J.C. Romero RC 50.00 15.00
Johan Santana RC
❑ 192 Tony Armas Jr. 5.00 1.50
Peter Bergeron
❑ 193 Matt Blank...................... 5.00 1.50
Milton Bradley
❑ 194 T.De La Rosa RC............ 5.00 1.50
Scott Forster RC
❑ 195 Yovanny Lara RC............ 5.00 1.50
Talmadge Nunnari RC
❑ 196 Brian Schneider............. 5.00 1.50
Andy Tracy RC
❑ 197 Scott Strickland............. 5.00 1.50
T.J. Tucker
❑ 198 Eric Cammack RC 5.00 1.50
Jim Mann RC
❑ 199 Grant Roberts 5.00 1.50
Jorge Toca
❑ 200 Alfonso Soriano 8.00 2.40
Jay Tessmer
❑ 201 Terrence Long................ 5.00 1.50
Mark Mulder
❑ 202 Pat Burrell..................... 5.00 1.50
Cliff Politte
❑ 203 Jimmy Anderson............ 8.00 2.40
Bronson Arroyo
❑ 204 Mike Darr 5.00 1.50
Kory DeHaan
❑ 205 Adam Eaton.................... 5.00 1.50
Wiki Gonzalez
❑ 206 Brandon Kolb RC 5.00 1.50
Kevin Walker RC
❑ 207 Damon Minor 5.00 1.50
Calvin Murray
❑ 208 Kevin Hodges RC 100.00 30.00
Joel Pineiro RC
❑ 209 Rob Ramsay 8.00 2.40
Kazuhiro Sasaki
❑ 210 Rick Ankiel 5.00 1.50
Mike Matthews
❑ 211 Steve Cox 5.00 1.50
Travis Harper
❑ 212 Kenny Kelly RC 5.00 1.50
Damian Rolls RC
❑ 213 Doug Davis..................... 5.00 1.50
Scott Sheldon
❑ 214 Brian Sikorski 5.00 1.50
Pedro Valdes
❑ 215 Francisco Cordero.......... 5.00 1.50
B.J. Waszgis RC
❑ 216 Matt DeWitt RC 8.00 2.40
Josh Phelps RC
❑ 217 Vernon Wells.................. 5.00 1.50
Dewayne Wise
❑ 218 Geraldo Guzman RC 5.00 1.50
Jason Marquis
❑ 219 Rafael Furcal.................. 5.00 1.50
Steve Sisco RC
❑ 220 B.J. Ryan........................ 5.00 1.50
Kevin Beirne
❑ 221 Matt Ginter RC 5.00 1.50
Brad Penny
❑ 222 Julio Zuleta RC 5.00 1.50
Eric Munson
❑ 223 Dan Reichert 5.00 1.50
Jeff Williams RC
❑ 224 Jason LaRue 5.00 1.50
Danny Ardoin RC
❑ 225 Ray King......................... 5.00 1.50
Mark Redman
❑ 226 Joe Crede 5.00 1.50
Mike Bell
❑ 227 Juan Pierre RC 8.00 2.40
Jay Payton
❑ 228 Wayne Franklin RC 5.00 1.50
Randy Choate RC
❑ 229 Chris Truby..................... 5.00 1.50
Adam Piatt
❑ 230 Kevin Nicholson 5.00 1.50
Chris Woodward
❑ 231 Barry Zito RC................ 15.00 4.50
Jason Boyd RC
❑ 232 Brian O'Connor RC 5.00 1.50
Miguel Del Toro
❑ 233 Carlos Guillen................ 5.00 1.50
Aubrey Huff
❑ 234 Chad Hermansen............ 5.00 1.50
Jason Tyner
❑ 235 Aaron Fultz RC 5.00 1.50
Ryan Vogelsong RC
❑ 236 Shawn Wooten 5.00 1.50
Vance Wilson
❑ 237 Danny Klassen 5.00 1.50
Mike Lamb RC
❑ 238 Chad Bradford................ 5.00 1.50
Gene Stechshulte RC
❑ 239 Ismael Villegas RC 5.00 1.50
Hector Ramirez RC
Matt T.Williams RC
Luis Vizcaino
❑ 240 Mike Garcia RC 5.00 1.50
Domingo Guzman RC
Justin Brunette RC
Pasqual Coco RC
❑ 241 Frank Charles RC 5.00 1.50
Keith McDonald RC
❑ 242 Carlos Casimiro RC 5.00 1.50
Morgan Burkhart RC
❑ 243 Raul Gonzalez RC 5.00 1.50
Shawn Gilbert
❑ 244 Darrell Einertson RC 5.00 1.50
Jeff Sparks RC
❑ 245 Augie Ojeda RC.............. 8.00 2.40
Brady Clark
Todd Belitz
Eric Byrnes RC
❑ 246 Leo Estrella RC 5.00 1.50
Charlie Greene
❑ 247 Trace Coquillette RC 8.00 2.40
Pedro Feliz RC
❑ 248 Tike Redman RC 8.00 2.40
David Newhan
❑ 249 Rodrigo Lopez RC 8.00 2.40
John Bale RC
❑ 250 Corey Patterson.............. 5.00 1.50
Jose Ortiz RC
❑ 251 Britt Reames RC 5.00 1.50
Oswaldo Mairena RC
❑ 252 Xavier Nady RC.............. 8.00 2.40
Timo Perez RC
❑ 253 Tom Jacquez RC 5.00 1.50
Vicente Padilla RC
❑ 254 Elvis Pena RC 5.00 1.50
Adam Melhuse RC
❑ 255 Ben Weber RC................ 5.00 1.50
Alex Cabrera RC

2000 Paramount Update

	Nm-Mt	Ex-Mt
COMP.FACT.SET (100)	30.00	9.00

❑ U1 Adam Kennedy .... .30 .09
❑ U2 Bengie Molina .... .30 .09
❑ U3 Derrick Turnbow RC .... .30 .09
❑ U4 Randy Johnson................. .75 .23
❑ U5 Danny Klassen .... .30 .09
❑ U6 Vicente Padilla RC .... .40 .12
❑ U7 Rafael Furcal...................... .30 .09
❑ U8 Andres Galarraga .... .30 .09
❑ U9 Chipper Jones .... .75 .23
❑ U10 Fernando Lunar .... .30 .09
❑ U11 Willie Morales RC............ .30 .09
❑ U12 Cal Ripken .... 2.50 .75
❑ U13 B.J. Ryan .... .30 .09
❑ U14 Carl Everett .... .30 .09
❑ U15 Nomar Garciaparra .... 1.25 .35
❑ U16 Pedro Martinez .... .75 .23
❑ U17 Wilton Veras..................... .30 .09
❑ U18 Scott Downs RC .... .30 .09
❑ U19 Daniel Garibay RC .... .30 .09
❑ U20 Sammy Sosa.................. 1.25 .35
❑ U21 Julio Zuleta RC................ .30 .09
❑ U22 Josh Paul .... .30 .09
❑ U23 Frank Thomas................... .75 .23
❑ U24 Rob Bell .... .30 .09
❑ U25 Dante Bichette................... .30 .09
❑ U26 Travis Dawkins .... .30 .09
❑ U27 Ken Griffey Jr................ 1.25 .35
❑ U28 Chuck Finley..................... .30 .09
❑ U29 Manny Ramirez................. .50 .15
❑ U30 Paul Rigdon RC .... .30 .09
❑ U31 Jeff Cirillo.......................... .30 .09
❑ U32 Larry Walker .... .50 .15
❑ U33 Masato Yoshii.................... .30 .09
❑ U34 Robert Fick .... .30 .09
❑ U35 Jose Macias .... .30 .09
❑ U36 Juan Gonzalez................... .50 .15
❑ U37 Hideo Nomo .... .75 .23
❑ U38 Jason Grilli......................... .30 .09
❑ U39 Pablo Ozuna .... .30 .09
❑ U40 Brad Penny......................... .30 .09
❑ U41 Jeff Bagwell .... .50 .15
❑ U42 Lance Berkman .... .30 .09
❑ U43 Roger Cedeno.................... .30 .09
❑ U44 Octavio Dotel .... .30 .09
❑ U45 Chad Durbin RC .... .30 .09
❑ U46 Eric Gagne .... 1.25 .35
❑ U47 Shawn Green .... .30 .09
❑ U48 Jose Hernandez .... .30 .09
❑ U49 Matt LeCroy .... .30 .09
❑ U50 Johan Santana RC 20.00 6.00
❑ U51 Vladimir Guerrero.............. .75 .23
❑ U52 Hideki Irabu .... .30 .09
❑ U53 Andy Tracy RC .... .30 .09
❑ U54 Derek Bell.......................... .30 .09
❑ U55 Eric Cammack RC.............. .30 .09
❑ U56 Mike Hampton .... .30 .09
❑ U57 Jay Payton .... .30 .09
❑ U58 Mike Piazza.................... 1.25 .35
❑ U59 Todd Zeile.......................... .30 .09
❑ U60 Roger Clemens .... 1.50 .45
❑ U61 Darrell Einertson RC .... .30 .09
❑ U62 Derek Jeter .... 2.00 .60
❑ U63 Jeremy Giambi .... .30 .09
❑ U64 Terrence Long.................... .30 .09
❑ U65 Mark Mulder....................... .30 .09
❑ U66 Adam Piatt .... .30 .09
❑ U67 Luis Vizcaino .... .30 .09
❑ U68 Pat Burrell.......................... .30 .09
❑ U69 Scott Rolen......................... .75 .23
❑ U70 Chad Hermansen .... .30 .09
❑ U71 Rick Ankiel .... .30 .09
❑ U72 Jim Edmonds Cards .... .30 .09
❑ U73 Mark McGwire .... 2.00 .60
❑ U74 G. Stechschulte RC .... .30 .09
❑ U75 Fernando Vina .... .30 .09
❑ U76 Bret Boone .... .30 .09
❑ U77 Tony Gwynn .... 1.00 .30
❑ U78 Ryan Klesko .... .30 .09
❑ U79 David Newhan.................... .30 .09
❑ U80 Kevin Walker RC................ .30 .09
❑ U81 Barry Bonds .... 2.00 .60
❑ U82 Aaron Fultz RC .... .30 .09
❑ U83 Ben Weber RC .... .40 .12
❑ U84 Rickey Henderson.............. .75 .23
❑ U85 Kevin Hodges RC .... .30 .09
❑ U86 John Olerud .... .30 .09
❑ U87 Rob Ramsay .... .30 .09
❑ U88 Alex Rodriguez .... 1.25 .35

❑ U89 Kazuhiro Sasaki RC 1.00 .30
❑ U90 Vinny Castilla .30 .09
❑ U91 Jeff Sparks RC .30 .09
❑ U92 Greg Vaughn .30 .09
❑ U93 Francisco Cordero .30 .09
❑ U94 Gabe Kapler .30 .09
❑ U95 Mike Lamb RC .40 .12
❑ U96 Ivan Rodriguez .75 .23
❑ U97 Clayton Andrews .30 .09
❑ U98 Brad Fullmer .30 .09
❑ U99 Raul Mondesi .30 .09
❑ U100 Dewayne Wise .30 .09

1993 Pinnacle

	Nm-Mt	Ex-Mt
COMPLETE SET (620)	40.00	12.00
COMP. SERIES 1 (310)	15.00	4.50
COMP. SERIES 2 (310)	25.00	7.50

❑ 1 Gary Sheffield .30 .09
❑ 2 Cal Eldred .15 .04
❑ 3 Larry Walker .50 .15
❑ 4 Deion Sanders .50 .15
❑ 5 Dave Fleming .15 .04
❑ 6 Carlos Baerga .15 .04
❑ 7 Bernie Williams .50 .15
❑ 8 John Kruk .30 .09
❑ 9 Jimmy Key .30 .09
❑ 10 Jeff Bagwell .50 .15
❑ 11 Jim Abbott .50 .15
❑ 12 Terry Steinbach .15 .04
❑ 13 Bob Tewksbury .15 .04
❑ 14 Eric Karros .30 .09
❑ 15 Ryne Sandberg 1.25 .35
❑ 16 Will Clark .75 .23
❑ 17 Edgar Martinez .50 .15
❑ 18 Eddie Murray .75 .23
❑ 19 Andy Van Slyke .30 .09
❑ 20 Cal Ripken Jr. 2.50 .75
❑ 21 Ivan Rodriguez .75 .23
❑ 22 Barry Larkin .50 .15
❑ 23 Don Mattingly 2.00 .60
❑ 24 Gregg Jefferies .15 .04
❑ 25 Roger Clemens 1.50 .45
❑ 26 Cecil Fielder .30 .09
❑ 27 Kent Hrbek .30 .09
❑ 28 Robin Ventura .30 .09
❑ 29 Rickey Henderson .75 .23
❑ 30 Roberto Alomar .50 .15
❑ 31 Luis Polonia .15 .04
❑ 32 Andujar Cedeno .15 .04
❑ 33 Pat Listach .15 .04
❑ 34 Mark Grace .50 .15
❑ 35 Otis Nixon .15 .04
❑ 36 Felix Jose .15 .04
❑ 37 Mike Sharperson .15 .04
❑ 38 Dennis Martinez .30 .09
❑ 39 Willie McGee .30 .09
❑ 40 Kenny Lofton .30 .09
❑ 41 Randy Johnson .75 .23
❑ 42 Andy Benes .15 .04
❑ 43 Bobby Bonilla .30 .09
❑ 44 Mike Mussina .50 .15
❑ 45 Len Dykstra .30 .09
❑ 46 Ellis Burks .30 .09
❑ 47 Chris Sabo .15 .04
❑ 48 Jay Bell .30 .09
❑ 49 Jose Canseco .75 .23
❑ 50 Craig Biggio .50 .15
❑ 51 Wally Joyner .30 .09
❑ 52 Mickey Tettleton .15 .04
❑ 53 Tim Raines .30 .09
❑ 54 Brian Harper .15 .04
❑ 55 Rene Gonzales .15 .04
❑ 56 Mark Langston .15 .04
❑ 57 Jack Morris .30 .09
❑ 58 Mark McGwire 2.00 .60
❑ 59 Ken Caminiti .30 .09
❑ 60 Terry Pendleton .30 .09
❑ 61 Dave Nilsson .15 .04
❑ 62 Tom Pagnozzi .15 .04
❑ 63 Mike Morgan .15 .04
❑ 64 Darryl Strawberry .30 .09
❑ 65 Charles Nagy .15 .04
❑ 66 Ken Hill .15 .04
❑ 67 Matt Williams .30 .09
❑ 68 Jay Buhner .30 .09
❑ 69 Vince Coleman .15 .04
❑ 70 Brady Anderson .30 .09
❑ 71 Fred McGriff .50 .15
❑ 72 Ben McDonald .15 .04
❑ 73 Terry Mulholland .15 .04
❑ 74 Randy Tomlin .15 .04
❑ 75 Nolan Ryan 3.00 .90
❑ 76 Frank Viola UER .30 .09
(Card incorrectly states he has a surgically repaired elbow)
❑ 77 Jose Rijo .15 .04
❑ 78 Shane Mack .15 .04
❑ 79 Travis Fryman .30 .09
❑ 80 Jack McDowell .15 .04
❑ 81 Mark Gubicza .15 .04
❑ 82 Matt Nokes .15 .04
❑ 83 Bert Blyleven .30 .09
❑ 84 Eric Anthony .15 .04
❑ 85 Mike Bordick .15 .04
❑ 86 John Olerud .30 .09
❑ 87 B.J. Surhoff .30 .09
❑ 88 Bernard Gilkey .15 .04
❑ 89 Shawon Dunston .15 .04
❑ 90 Tom Glavine .50 .15
❑ 91 Brett Butler .30 .09
❑ 92 Moises Alou .30 .09
❑ 93 Albert Belle .30 .09
❑ 94 Darren Lewis .15 .04
❑ 95 Omar Vizquel .50 .15
❑ 96 Dwight Gooden .30 .09
❑ 97 Gregg Olson .15 .04
❑ 98 Tony Gwynn 1.00 .30
❑ 99 Darren Daulton .30 .09
❑ 100 Dennis Eckersley .30 .09
❑ 101 Rob Dibble .30 .09
❑ 102 Mike Greenwell .15 .04
❑ 103 Jose Lind .15 .04
❑ 104 Julio Franco .30 .09
❑ 105 Tom Gordon .15 .04
❑ 106 Scott Livingstone .15 .04
❑ 107 Chuck Knoblauch .30 .09
❑ 108 Frank Thomas .75 .23
❑ 109 Melido Perez .15 .04
❑ 110 Ken Griffey Jr. 1.25 .35
❑ 111 Harold Baines .30 .09
❑ 112 Gary Gaetti .30 .09
❑ 113 Pete Harnisch .15 .04
❑ 114 David Wells .30 .09
❑ 115 Charlie Leibrandt .15 .04
❑ 116 Ray Lankford .15 .04
❑ 117 Kevin Seitzer .15 .04
❑ 118 Robin Yount 1.25 .35
❑ 119 Lenny Harris .15 .04
❑ 120 Chris James .15 .04
❑ 121 Delino DeShields .15 .04
❑ 122 Kirt Manwaring .15 .04
❑ 123 Glenallen Hill .15 .04
❑ 124 Hensley Meulens .15 .04
❑ 125 Darrin Jackson .15 .04
❑ 126 Todd Hundley .15 .04
❑ 127 Dave Hollins .15 .04
❑ 128 Sam Horn .15 .04
❑ 129 Roberto Hernandez .15 .04
❑ 130 Vicente Palacios .15 .04
❑ 131 George Brett 2.00 .60
❑ 132 Dave Martinez .15 .04
❑ 133 Kevin Appier .30 .09
❑ 134 Pat Kelly .15 .04
❑ 135 Pedro Munoz .15 .04
❑ 136 Mark Carreon .15 .04
❑ 137 Lance Johnson .15 .04
❑ 138 Devon White .30 .09
❑ 139 Julio Valera .15 .04
❑ 140 Eddie Taubensee .15 .04
❑ 141 Willie Wilson .15 .04
❑ 142 Stan Belinda .15 .04
❑ 143 John Smoltz .50 .15
❑ 144 Darryl Hamilton .15 .04
❑ 145 Sammy Sosa 1.25 .35
❑ 146 Carlos Hernandez .15 .04
❑ 147 Tom Candiotti .15 .04
❑ 148 Mike Felder .15 .04
❑ 149 Rusty Meacham .15 .04
❑ 150 Ivan Calderon .15 .04
❑ 151 Pete O'Brien .15 .04
❑ 152 Erik Hanson .15 .04
❑ 153 Billy Ripken .15 .04
❑ 154 Kurt Stillwell .15 .04
❑ 155 Jeff Kent .75 .23
❑ 156 Mickey Morandini .15 .04
❑ 157 Randy Milligan .15 .04
❑ 158 Reggie Sanders .15 .04
❑ 159 Luis Rivera .15 .04
❑ 160 Orlando Merced .15 .04
❑ 161 Dean Palmer .30 .09
❑ 162 Mike Perez .15 .04
❑ 163 Scott Erickson .15 .04
❑ 164 Kevin McReynolds .15 .04
❑ 165 Kevin Maas .15 .04
❑ 166 Ozzie Guillen .15 .04
❑ 167 Rob Deer .15 .04
❑ 168 Danny Tartabull .15 .04
❑ 169 Lee Stevens .15 .04
❑ 170 Dave Henderson .15 .04
❑ 171 Derek Bell .15 .04
❑ 172 Steve Finley .30 .09
❑ 173 Greg Olson .15 .04
❑ 174 Geronimo Pena .15 .04
❑ 175 Paul Quantrill .15 .04
❑ 176 Steve Buechele .15 .04
❑ 177 Kevin Gross .15 .04
❑ 178 Tim Wallach .15 .04
❑ 179 Dave Valle .15 .04
❑ 180 Dave Silvestri .15 .04
❑ 181 Bud Black .15 .04
❑ 182 Henry Rodriguez .15 .04
❑ 183 Tim Teufel .15 .04
❑ 184 Mark McLemore .15 .04
❑ 185 Bret Saberhagen .30 .09
❑ 186 Chris Hoiles .15 .04
❑ 187 Ricky Jordan .15 .04
❑ 188 Don Slaught .15 .04
❑ 189 Mo Vaughn .30 .09
❑ 190 Joe Oliver .15 .04
❑ 191 Juan Gonzalez .50 .15
❑ 192 Scott Leius .15 .04
❑ 193 Milt Cuyler .15 .04
❑ 194 Chris Haney .15 .04
❑ 195 Ron Karkovice .15 .04
❑ 196 Steve Farr .15 .04
❑ 197 John Orton .15 .04
❑ 198 Kelly Gruber .15 .04
❑ 199 Ron Darling .15 .04
❑ 200 Ruben Sierra .15 .04
❑ 201 Chuck Finley .30 .09
❑ 202 Mike Moore .15 .04
❑ 203 Pat Borders .15 .04
❑ 204 Sid Bream .15 .04
❑ 205 Todd Zeile .15 .04
❑ 206 Rick Wilkins .15 .04
❑ 207 Jim Gantner .15 .04
❑ 208 Frank Castillo .15 .04
❑ 209 Dave Hansen .15 .04
❑ 210 Trevor Wilson .15 .04
❑ 211 Sandy Alomar Jr. .15 .04
❑ 212 Sean Berry .15 .04
❑ 213 Tino Martinez .50 .15
❑ 214 Chito Martinez .15 .04
❑ 215 Dan Walters .15 .04
❑ 216 John Franco .30 .09
❑ 217 Glenn Davis .15 .04

❑ 218 Mariano Duncan .15 .04
❑ 219 Mike LaValliere .15 .04
❑ 220 Rafael Palmeiro .50 .15
❑ 221 Jack Clark .30 .09
❑ 222 Hal Morris .15 .04
❑ 223 Ed Sprague .15 .04
❑ 224 John Valentin .15 .04
❑ 225 Sam Militello .15 .04
❑ 226 Bob Wickman .15 .04
❑ 227 Damion Easley .15 .04
❑ 228 John Jaha .15 .04
❑ 229 Bob Ayrault .15 .04
❑ 230 Mo Sanford .15 .04
❑ 231 Walt Weiss .15 .04
❑ 232 Dante Bichette .30 .09
❑ 233 Steve Decker .15 .04
❑ 234 Jerald Clark .15 .04
❑ 235 Bryan Harvey .15 .04
❑ 236 Joe Girardi .15 .04
❑ 237 Dave Magadan .15 .04
❑ 238 David Nied .15 .04
❑ 239 Eric Wedge RC .40 .12
❑ 240 Rico Brogna .15 .04
❑ 241 J.T. Bruett .15 .04
❑ 242 Jonathan Hurst .15 .04
❑ 243 Bret Boone .50 .15
❑ 244 Manny Alexander .15 .04
❑ 245 Scooter Tucker .15 .04
❑ 246 Troy Neel .15 .04
❑ 247 Eddie Zosky .15 .04
❑ 248 Melvin Nieves .15 .04
❑ 249 Ryan Thompson .15 .04
❑ 250 Shawn Barton RC .15 .04
❑ 251 Ryan Klesko .30 .09
❑ 252 Mike Piazza 2.00 .60
❑ 253 Steve Hosey .15 .04
❑ 254 Shane Reynolds .15 .04
❑ 255 Dan Wilson .30 .09
❑ 256 Tom Marsh .15 .04
❑ 257 Barry Manuel .15 .04
❑ 258 Paul Miller .15 .04
❑ 259 Pedro Martinez 1.50 .45
❑ 260 Steve Cooke .15 .04
❑ 261 Johnny Guzman .15 .04
❑ 262 Mike Butcher .15 .04
❑ 263 Bien Figueroa .15 .04
❑ 264 Rich Rowland .15 .04
❑ 265 Shawn Jeter .15 .04
❑ 266 Gerald Williams .15 .04
❑ 267 Derek Parks .15 .04
❑ 268 Henry Mercedes .15 .04
❑ 269 David Hulse RC .15 .04
❑ 270 Tim Pugh RC .15 .04
❑ 271 William Suero .15 .04
❑ 272 Ozzie Canseco .15 .04
❑ 273 Fernando Ramsey RC .15 .04
❑ 274 Bernardo Brito .15 .04
❑ 275 Dave Mlicki .15 .04
❑ 276 Tim Salmon .50 .15
❑ 277 Mike Raczka .15 .04
❑ 278 Ken Ryan RC .40 .12
❑ 279 Rafael Bournigal .15 .04
❑ 280 Wil Cordero .15 .04
❑ 281 Billy Ashley .15 .04
❑ 282 Paul Wagner .15 .04
❑ 283 Blas Minor .15 .04
❑ 284 Rick Trlicek .15 .04
❑ 285 Willie Greene .15 .04
❑ 286 Ted Wood .15 .04
❑ 287 Phil Clark .15 .04
❑ 288 Jesse Levis .15 .04
❑ 289 Tony Gwynn NT .50 .15
❑ 290 Nolan Ryan NT 1.50 .45
❑ 291 Dennis Martinez NT .15 .04
❑ 292 Eddie Murray NT .50 .15
❑ 293 Robin Yount NT .75 .23
❑ 294 George Brett NT 1.00 .30
❑ 295 Dave Winfield NT .15 .04
❑ 296 Bert Blyleven NT .15 .04
❑ 297 Jeff Bagwell .75 .23
Carl Yastrzemski
❑ 298 John Smoltz .30 .09
Jack Morris
❑ 299 Larry Walker .50 .15
Mike Bossy
❑ 300 Gary Sheffield .30 .09
Barry Larkin
❑ 301 Ivan Rodriguez .50 .15
Carlton Fisk
❑ 302 Delino DeShields .75 .23
Malcolm X
❑ 303 Tim Salmon .50 .15
Dwight Evans
❑ 304 Bernard Gilkey HH .15 .04
❑ 305 Cal Ripken Jr. HH 1.25 .35
❑ 306 Barry Larkin HH .30 .09
❑ 307 Kent Hrbek HH .15 .04
❑ 308 Rickey Henderson HH .50 .15
❑ 309 Darryl Strawberry HH .15 .04
❑ 310 John Franco HH .15 .04
❑ 311 Todd Stottlemyre .15 .04
❑ 312 Luis Gonzalez .30 .09
❑ 313 Tommy Greene .15 .04
❑ 314 Randy Velarde .15 .04
❑ 315 Steve Avery .15 .04
❑ 316 Jose Oquendo .15 .04
❑ 317 Rey Sanchez .15 .04
❑ 318 Greg Vaughn .15 .04
❑ 319 Orel Hershiser .30 .09
❑ 320 Paul Sorrento .15 .04
❑ 321 Royce Clayton .15 .04
❑ 322 John Vander Wal .15 .04
❑ 323 Henry Cotto .15 .04
❑ 324 Pete Schourek .15 .04
❑ 325 David Segui .15 .04
❑ 326 Arthur Rhodes .15 .04
❑ 327 Bruce Hurst .15 .04
❑ 328 Wes Chamberlain .15 .04
❑ 329 Ozzie Smith 1.25 .35
❑ 330 Scott Cooper .15 .04
❑ 331 Felix Fermin .15 .04
❑ 332 Mike Macfarlane .15 .04
❑ 333 Dan Gladden .15 .04
❑ 334 Kevin Tapani .15 .04
❑ 335 Steve Sax .15 .04
❑ 336 Jeff Montgomery .15 .04
❑ 337 Gary DiSarcina .15 .04
❑ 338 Lance Blankenship .15 .04
❑ 339 Brian Williams .15 .04
❑ 340 Duane Ward .15 .04
❑ 341 Chuck McElroy .15 .04
❑ 342 Joe Magrane .15 .04
❑ 343 Jaime Navarro .15 .04
❑ 344 Dave Justice .30 .09
❑ 345 Jose Offerman .15 .04
❑ 346 Marquis Grissom .30 .09
❑ 347 Bill Swift .15 .04
❑ 348 Jim Thome .75 .23
❑ 349 Archi Cianfrocco .15 .04
❑ 350 Anthony Young .15 .04
❑ 351 Leo Gomez .15 .04
❑ 352 Bill Gullickson .15 .04
❑ 353 Alan Trammell .30 .09
❑ 354 Dan Pasqua .15 .04
❑ 355 Jeff King .15 .04
❑ 356 Kevin Brown .30 .09
❑ 357 Tim Belcher .15 .04
❑ 358 Bip Roberts .15 .04
❑ 359 Brent Mayne .15 .04
❑ 360 Rheal Cormier .15 .04
❑ 361 Mark Guthrie .15 .04
❑ 362 Craig Grebeck .15 .04
❑ 363 Andy Stankiewicz .15 .04
❑ 364 Juan Guzman .15 .04
❑ 365 Bobby Witt .15 .04
❑ 366 Mark Portugal .15 .04
❑ 367 Brian McRae .15 .04
❑ 368 Mark Lemke .15 .04
❑ 369 Bill Wegman .15 .04
❑ 370 Donovan Osborne .15 .04
❑ 371 Derrick May .15 .04
❑ 372 Carl Willis .15 .04
❑ 373 Chris Nabholz .15 .04
❑ 374 Mark Lewis .15 .04
❑ 375 John Burkett .15 .04
❑ 376 Luis Mercedes .15 .04
❑ 377 Ramon Martinez .15 .04
❑ 378 Kyle Abbott .15 .04
❑ 379 Mark Wohlers .15 .04
❑ 380 Bob Walk .15 .04
❑ 381 Kenny Rogers .30 .09
❑ 382 Tim Naehring .15 .04
❑ 383 Alex Fernandez .15 .04
❑ 384 Keith Miller .15 .04
❑ 385 Mike Henneman .15 .04
❑ 386 Rick Aguilera .15 .04
❑ 387 George Bell .15 .04
❑ 388 Mike Gallego .15 .04
❑ 389 Howard Johnson .15 .04
❑ 390 Kim Batiste .15 .04
❑ 391 Jerry Browne .15 .04
❑ 392 Damon Berryhill .15 .04
❑ 393 Ricky Bones .15 .04
❑ 394 Omar Olivares .15 .04
❑ 395 Mike Harkey .15 .04
❑ 396 Pedro Astacio .15 .04
❑ 397 John Wetteland .30 .09
❑ 398 Rod Beck .15 .04
❑ 399 Thomas Howard .15 .04
❑ 400 Mike Devereaux .15 .04
❑ 401 Tim Wakefield .75 .23
❑ 402 Curt Schilling .30 .09
❑ 403 Zane Smith .15 .04
❑ 404 Bob Zupcic .15 .04
❑ 405 Tom Browning .15 .04
❑ 406 Tony Phillips .15 .04
❑ 407 John Doherty .15 .04
❑ 408 Pat Mahomes .15 .04
❑ 409 John Habyan .15 .04
❑ 410 Steve Olin .15 .04
❑ 411 Chad Curtis .15 .04
❑ 412 Joe Grahe .15 .04
❑ 413 John Patterson .15 .04
❑ 414 Brian Hunter .15 .04
❑ 415 Doug Henry .15 .04
❑ 416 Lee Smith .30 .09
❑ 417 Bob Scanlan .15 .04
❑ 418 Kent Mercker .15 .04
❑ 419 Mel Rojas .15 .04
❑ 420 Mark Whiten .15 .04
❑ 421 Carlton Fisk .50 .15
❑ 422 Candy Maldonado .15 .04
❑ 423 Doug Drabek .15 .04
❑ 424 Wade Boggs .50 .15
❑ 425 Mark Davis .15 .04
❑ 426 Kirby Puckett .75 .23
❑ 427 Joe Carter .30 .09
❑ 428 Paul Molitor .50 .15
❑ 429 Eric Davis .30 .09
❑ 430 Darryl Kile .30 .09
❑ 431 Jeff Parrett .15 .04
❑ 432 Jeff Blauser .15 .04
❑ 433 Dan Plesac .15 .04
❑ 434 Andres Galarraga .30 .09
❑ 435 Jim Gott .15 .04
❑ 436 Jose Mesa .15 .04
❑ 437 Ben Rivera .15 .04
❑ 438 Dave Winfield .30 .09
❑ 439 Norm Charlton .15 .04
❑ 440 Chris Bosio .15 .04
❑ 441 Wilson Alvarez .15 .04
❑ 442 Dave Stewart .30 .09
❑ 443 Doug Jones .15 .04
❑ 444 Jeff Russell .15 .04
❑ 445 Ron Gant .30 .09
❑ 446 Paul O'Neill .50 .15
❑ 447 Charlie Hayes .15 .04
❑ 448 Joe Hesketh .15 .04
❑ 449 Chris Hammond .15 .04
❑ 450 Hipolito Pichardo .15 .04
❑ 451 Scott Radinsky .15 .04
❑ 452 Bobby Thigpen .15 .04
❑ 453 Xavier Hernandez .15 .04
❑ 454 Lonnie Smith .15 .04
❑ 455 Jamie Arnold DP RC .15 .04
❑ 456 B.J. Wallace DP .15 .04
❑ 457 Derek Jeter DP RC 10.00 3.00
❑ 458 Jason Kendall DP RC 1.00 .30
❑ 459 Rick Helling DP .15 .04
❑ 460 Derek Wallace DP RC .15 .04
❑ 461 Sean Lowe DP RC .15 .04
❑ 462 S. Stewart DP RC 1.00 .30
❑ 463 Benji Grigsby DP RC .15 .04
❑ 464 T. Steverson DP RC .15 .04
❑ 465 Dan Serafini DP RC .15 .04
❑ 466 Michael Tucker DP .30 .09
❑ 467 Chris Roberts DP .15 .04
❑ 468 Pete Janicki DP RC .15 .04
❑ 469 Jeff Schmidt DP RC .15 .04
❑ 470 Don Mattingly NT 1.00 .30
❑ 471 Cal Ripken Jr. NT 1.25 .35
❑ 472 Jack Morris NT .15 .04
❑ 473 Terry Pendleton NT .15 .04
❑ 474 Dennis Eckersley NT .30 .09
❑ 475 Carlton Fisk NT .30 .09
❑ 476 Wade Boggs NT .30 .09
❑ 477 Len Dykstra .30 .09

...Ken Stabler		
❑ 478 Danny Tartabull	.15	.04
Jose Tartabull		
❑ 479 Jeff Conine	.50	.15
Dale Murphy		
❑ 480 Gregg Jefferies	.15	.04
Ron Cey		
❑ 481 Paul Molitor	.30	.09
Harmon Killebrew		
❑ 482 John Valentin	.15	.04
Dave Concepcion		
❑ 483 Alex Arias	.15	.04
Dave Winfield		
❑ 484 Barry Bonds HH	1.00	.30
❑ 485 Doug Drabek HH	.15	.04
❑ 486 Dave Winfield HH	.15	.04
❑ 487 Brett Butler HH	.15	.04
❑ 488 Harold Baines HH	.15	.04
❑ 489 David Cone HH	.15	.04
❑ 490 Willie McGee HH	.15	.04
❑ 491 Robby Thompson	.15	.04
❑ 492 Pete Incaviglia	.15	.04
❑ 493 Manuel Lee	.15	.04
❑ 494 Rafael Belliard	.15	.04
❑ 495 Scott Fletcher	.15	.04
❑ 496 Jeff Frye	.15	.04
❑ 497 Andre Dawson	.30	.09
❑ 498 Mike Scioscia	.15	.04
❑ 499 Spike Owen	.15	.04
❑ 500 Sid Fernandez	.15	.04
❑ 501 Joe Orsulak	.15	.04
❑ 502 Benito Santiago	.30	.09
❑ 503 Dale Murphy	.75	.23
❑ 504 Barry Bonds	2.00	.60
❑ 505 Jose Guzman	.15	.04
❑ 506 Tony Pena	.15	.04
❑ 507 Greg Swindell	.15	.04
❑ 508 Mike Pagliarulo	.15	.04
❑ 509 Lou Whitaker	.30	.09
❑ 510 Greg Gagne	.15	.04
❑ 511 Butch Henry	.15	.04
❑ 512 Jeff Brantley	.15	.04
❑ 513 Jack Armstrong	.15	.04
❑ 514 Danny Jackson	.15	.04
❑ 515 Junior Felix	.15	.04
❑ 516 Milt Thompson	.15	.04
❑ 517 Greg Maddux	1.25	.35
❑ 518 Eric Young	.15	.04
❑ 519 Jody Reed	.15	.04
❑ 520 Roberto Kelly	.15	.04
❑ 521 Darren Holmes	.15	.04
❑ 522 Craig Lefferts	.15	.04
❑ 523 Charlie Hough	.30	.09
❑ 524 Bo Jackson	.75	.23
❑ 525 Bill Spiers	.15	.04
❑ 526 Orestes Destrade	.15	.04
❑ 527 Greg Hibbard	.15	.04
❑ 528 Roger McDowell	.15	.04
❑ 529 Cory Snyder	.15	.04
❑ 530 Harold Reynolds	.30	.09
❑ 531 Kevin Reimer	.15	.04
❑ 532 Rick Sutcliffe	.30	.09
❑ 533 Tony Fernandez	.15	.04
❑ 534 Tom Brunansky	.15	.04
❑ 535 Jeff Reardon	.30	.09
❑ 536 Chili Davis	.30	.09
❑ 537 Bob Ojeda	.15	.04
❑ 538 Greg Colbrunn	.15	.04
❑ 539 Phil Plantier	.15	.04
❑ 540 Brian Jordan	.30	.09
❑ 541 Pete Smith	.15	.04
❑ 542 Frank Tanana	.15	.04
❑ 543 John Smiley	.15	.04
❑ 544 David Cone	.30	.09
❑ 545 Daryl Boston	.15	.04
❑ 546 Tom Henke	.15	.04
❑ 547 Bill Krueger	.15	.04
❑ 548 Freddie Benavides	.15	.04
❑ 549 Randy Myers	.15	.04
❑ 550 Reggie Jefferson	.15	.04
❑ 551 Kevin Mitchell	.15	.04
❑ 552 Dave Stieb	.15	.04
❑ 553 Bret Barberie	.15	.04
❑ 554 Tim Crews	.15	.04
❑ 555 Doug Dascenzo	.15	.04
❑ 556 Alex Cole	.15	.04
❑ 557 Jeff Innis	.15	.04
❑ 558 Carlos Garcia	.15	.04
❑ 559 Steve Howe	.15	.04
❑ 560 Kirk McCaskill	.15	.04
❑ 561 Frank Seminara	.15	.04
❑ 562 Cris Carpenter	.15	.04
❑ 563 Mike Stanley	.15	.04
❑ 564 Carlos Quintana	.15	.04
❑ 565 Mitch Williams	.15	.04
❑ 566 Juan Bell	.15	.04
❑ 567 Eric Fox	.15	.04
❑ 568 Al Leiter	.30	.09
❑ 569 Mike Stanton	.15	.04
❑ 570 Scott Kamieniecki	.15	.04
❑ 571 Ryan Bowen	.15	.04
❑ 572 Andy Ashby	.15	.04
❑ 573 Bob Welch	.15	.04
❑ 574 Scott Sanderson	.15	.04
❑ 575 Joe Kmak	.15	.04
❑ 576 Scott Pose RC	.15	.04
❑ 577 Ricky Gutierrez	.15	.04
❑ 578 Mike Trombley	.15	.04
❑ 579 Sterling Hitchcock RC	.40	.12
❑ 580 Rodney Bolton	.15	.04
❑ 581 Tyler Green	.15	.04
❑ 582 Tim Costo	.15	.04
❑ 583 Tim Laker RC	.15	.04
❑ 584 Steve Reed RC	.15	.04
❑ 585 Tom Kramer RC	.15	.04
❑ 586 Robb Nen	.30	.09
❑ 587 Jim Tatum RC	.15	.04
❑ 588 Frank Bolick	.15	.04
❑ 589 Kevin Young	.30	.09
❑ 590 Matt Whiteside RC	.15	.04
❑ 591 Cesar Hernandez	.15	.04
❑ 592 Mike Mohler RC	.40	.12
❑ 593 Alan Embree	.75	.23
❑ 594 Terry Jorgensen	.15	.04
❑ 595 John Cummings RC	.15	.04
❑ 596 Domingo Martinez RC	.15	.04
❑ 597 Benji Gil	.15	.04
❑ 598 Todd Pratt RC	.40	.12
❑ 599 Rene Arocha RC	.40	.12
❑ 600 Dennis Moeller	.15	.04
❑ 601 Jeff Conine	.30	.09
❑ 602 Trevor Hoffman	.30	.09
❑ 603 Daniel Smith	.15	.04
❑ 604 Lee Tinsley	.15	.04
❑ 605 Dan Peltier	.15	.04
❑ 606 Billy Brewer	.15	.04
❑ 607 Matt Walbeck RC	.40	.12
❑ 608 Richie Lewis RC	.15	.04
❑ 609 J.T. Snow RC	.60	.18
❑ 610 Pat Gomez RC	.15	.04
❑ 611 Phil Hiatt	.15	.04
❑ 612 Alex Arias	.15	.04
❑ 613 Kevin Rogers	.15	.04
❑ 614 Al Martin	.15	.04
❑ 615 Greg Gohr	.15	.04
❑ 616 Graeme Lloyd RC	.40	.12
❑ 617 Kent Bottenfield	.15	.04
❑ 618 Chuck Carr	.15	.04
❑ 619 Darrell Sherman RC	.15	.04
❑ 620 Mike Lansing RC	.40	.12

1939 Play Ball

	Ex-Mt	VG
COMPLETE SET (161)	10000.00	5000.00
COMMON CARD (1-115)	20.00	10.00
COMMON (116-162)	75.00	38.00
WRAPPER (1-CENT)	200.00	100.00
❑ 1 Jake Powell	60.00	18.00
❑ 2 Lee Grissom	20.00	10.00
❑ 3 Red Ruffing	75.00	38.00
❑ 4 Eldon Auker	20.00	10.00
❑ 5 Luke Sewell	25.00	12.50
❑ 6 Leo Durocher	100.00	50.00
❑ 7 Bobby Doerr	75.00	38.00
❑ 8 Henry Pippen	20.00	10.00
❑ 9 James Tobin	20.00	10.00
❑ 10 James DeShong	20.00	10.00
❑ 11 Johnny Rizzo	20.00	10.00
❑ 12 Hershel Martin	20.00	10.00
❑ 13 Luke Hamlin	20.00	10.00
❑ 14 Jim Tabor	20.00	10.00
❑ 15 Paul Derringer	30.00	15.00
❑ 16 John Peacock	20.00	10.00
❑ 17 Emerson Dickman	20.00	10.00
❑ 18 Harry Danning	20.00	10.00
❑ 19 Paul Dean	40.00	20.00
❑ 20 Joe Heving	20.00	10.00
❑ 21 Dutch Leonard	30.00	15.00
❑ 22 Bucky Walters	30.00	15.00
❑ 23 Burgess Whitehead	20.00	10.00
❑ 24 Richard Coffman	20.00	10.00
❑ 25 George Selkirk	40.00	20.00
❑ 26 Joe DiMaggio	1400.00	700.00
❑ 27 Fred Ostermueller	20.00	10.00
❑ 28 Sylvester Johnson	20.00	10.00
❑ 29 John(Jack) Wilson	20.00	10.00
❑ 30 Bill Dickey	125.00	60.00
❑ 31 Sam West	20.00	10.00
❑ 32 Bob Seeds	20.00	10.00
❑ 33 Del Young	20.00	10.00
❑ 34 Frank Demaree	20.00	10.00
❑ 35 Bill Jurges	20.00	10.00
❑ 36 Frank McCormick	20.00	10.00
❑ 37 Virgil Davis	20.00	10.00
❑ 38 Billy Myers	20.00	10.00
❑ 39 Rick Ferrell	75.00	38.00
❑ 40 James Bagby Jr.	20.00	10.00
❑ 41 Lon Warneke	25.00	12.50
❑ 42 Arndt Jorgens	20.00	10.00
❑ 43 Melo Almada	25.00	12.50
❑ 44 Don Heffner	20.00	10.00
❑ 45 Merrill May	20.00	10.00
❑ 46 Morris Arnovich	20.00	10.00
❑ 47 Buddy Lewis	20.00	10.00
❑ 48 Lefty Gomez	125.00	60.00
❑ 49 Eddie Miller	20.00	10.00
❑ 50 Charley Gehringer	125.00	60.00
❑ 51 Mel Ott	125.00	60.00
❑ 52 Tommy Henrich	40.00	20.00
❑ 53 Carl Hubbell	125.00	60.00
❑ 54 Harry Gumpert	20.00	10.00
❑ 55 Arky Vaughan	75.00	38.00
❑ 56 Hank Greenberg	200.00	75.00
❑ 57 Buddy Hassett	20.00	10.00
❑ 58 Lou Chiozza	20.00	10.00
❑ 59 Ken Chase	20.00	10.00
❑ 60 Schoolboy Rowe	40.00	20.00
❑ 61 Tony Cuccinello	25.00	12.50
❑ 62 Tom Carey	20.00	10.00
❑ 63 Emmett Mueller	20.00	10.00
❑ 64 Wally Moses	25.00	12.50
❑ 65 Harry Craft	25.00	12.50
❑ 66 Jimmy Ripple	20.00	10.00
❑ 67 Ed Joost	25.00	12.50
❑ 68 Fred Sington	20.00	10.00
❑ 69 Elbie Fletcher	20.00	10.00
❑ 70 Fred Frankhouse	20.00	10.00
❑ 71 Monte Pearson	30.00	15.00
❑ 72 Debs Garms	20.00	10.00
❑ 73 Hal Schumacher	25.00	12.50
❑ 74 Cookie Lavagetto	25.00	12.50
❑ 75 Stan Bordagaray	20.00	10.00
❑ 76 Goody Rosen	20.00	10.00
❑ 77 Lew Riggs	20.00	10.00
❑ 78 Julius Solters	20.00	10.00
❑ 79 Jo Jo Moore	20.00	10.00
❑ 80 Pete Fox	20.00	10.00
❑ 81 Babe Dahlgren	30.00	15.00
❑ 82 Chuck Klein	100.00	50.00
❑ 83 Gus Suhr	20.00	10.00
❑ 84 Skeeter Newsom	20.00	10.00
❑ 85 Johnny Cooney	20.00	10.00
❑ 86 Dolph Camilli	25.00	12.50
❑ 87 Milburn Shoffner	20.00	10.00
❑ 88 Charlie Keller	40.00	20.00
❑ 89 Lloyd Waner	75.00	38.00
❑ 90 Robert Klinger	20.00	10.00
❑ 91 John Knott	20.00	10.00
❑ 92 Ted Williams	1500.00	750.00
❑ 93 Charles Gelbert	20.00	10.00
❑ 94 Heinie Manush	75.00	38.00

❑ 95 Whit Wyatt 25.00 12.50
❑ 96 Babe Phelps 20.00 10.00
❑ 97 Bob Johnson 30.00 15.00
❑ 98 Pinky Whitney 20.00 10.00
❑ 99 Wally Berger 30.00 15.00
❑ 100 Buddy Myer 25.00 12.50
❑ 101 Roger Cramer 25.00 12.50
❑ 102 Lem Young 20.00 10.00
❑ 103 Moe Berg 125.00 60.00
❑ 104 Tom Bridges 25.00 12.50
❑ 105 Rabbit McNair 20.00 10.00
❑ 106 Dolly Stark UMP 30.00 15.00
❑ 107 Joe Vosmik 20.00 10.00
❑ 108 Frank Hayes 20.00 10.00
❑ 109 Myril Hoag 20.00 10.00
❑ 110 Fred Fitzsimmons 25.00 12.50
❑ 111 Van Lingle Mungo 30.00 15.00
❑ 112 Paul Waner 100.00 50.00
❑ 113 Al Schacht 30.00 15.00
❑ 114 Cecil Travis 25.00 12.50
❑ 115 Ralph Kress 20.00 10.00
❑ 116 Gene Desautels 75.00 38.00
❑ 117 Wayne Ambler 75.00 38.00
❑ 118 Lynn Nelson 75.00 38.00
❑ 119 Will Hershberger 100.00 50.00
❑ 120 Rabbit Warstler 75.00 38.00
❑ 121 Bill Posedel 75.00 38.00
❑ 122 George McQuinn 75.00 38.00
❑ 123 Ray T. Davis 75.00 38.00
❑ 124 Walter Brown 75.00 38.00
❑ 125 Cliff Melton 75.00 38.00
❑ 126 Not issued ....
❑ 127 Gil Brack 75.00 38.00
❑ 128 Joe Bowman 75.00 38.00
❑ 129 Bill Swift 75.00 38.00
❑ 130 Bill Brubaker 75.00 38.00
❑ 131 Mort Cooper 100.00 50.00
❑ 132 Jim Brown 75.00 38.00
❑ 133 Lynn Myers 75.00 38.00
❑ 134 Tot Presnell 75.00 38.00
❑ 135 Mickey Owen 100.00 50.00
❑ 136 Roy Bell 75.00 38.00
❑ 137 Pete Appleton 75.00 38.00
❑ 138 George Case 100.00 50.00
❑ 139 Vito Tamulis 75.00 38.00
❑ 140 Ray Hayworth 75.00 38.00
❑ 141 Pete Coscarart 75.00 38.00
❑ 142 Ira Hutchinson 75.00 38.00
❑ 143 Earl Averill 175.00 90.00
❑ 144 Zeke Bonura 100.00 50.00
❑ 145 Hugh Mulcahy 75.00 38.00
❑ 146 Tom Sunkel 75.00 38.00
❑ 147 George Coffman 75.00 38.00
❑ 148 Bill Trotter 75.00 38.00
❑ 149 Max West 75.00 38.00
❑ 150 James Walkup 75.00 38.00
❑ 151 Hugh Casey 100.00 50.00
❑ 152 Roy Weatherly 75.00 38.00
❑ 153 Dizzy Trout 100.00 50.00
❑ 154 Johnny Hudson 75.00 38.00
❑ 155 Jimmy Outlaw 75.00 38.00
❑ 156 Ray Berres 75.00 38.00
❑ 157 Don Padgett 75.00 38.00
❑ 158 Bud Thomas 75.00 38.00
❑ 159 Red Evans 75.00 38.00
❑ 160 Gene Moore 75.00 38.00
❑ 161 Lonnie Frey 75.00 38.00
❑ 162 Whitey Moore 100.00 50.00

1940 Play Ball

	Ex-Mt	VG
COMPLETE SET (240)	15000.00	7500.00
COMMON CARD (1-120)	20.00	10.00
COMMON (121-180)	20.00	10.00
COMMON (181-240)	70.00	35.00
WRAP.(1-CENT, DIFF. COLORS)	800.00	400.00

❑ 1 Joe DiMaggio 2500.00 1000.00
❑ 2 Art Jorgens 25.00 12.50
❑ 3 Babe Dahlgren 25.00 12.50
❑ 4 Tommy Henrich 35.00 17.50
❑ 5 Monte Pearson 25.00 12.50
❑ 6 Lefty Gomez 150.00 75.00
❑ 7 Bill Dickey 175.00 90.00
❑ 8 George Selkirk 25.00 12.50
❑ 9 Charlie Keller 35.00 17.50
❑ 10 Red Ruffing 90.00 45.00
❑ 11 Jake Powell 25.00 12.50
❑ 12 Johnny Schulte 20.00 10.00
❑ 13 Jack Knott 20.00 10.00
❑ 14 Rabbit McNair 20.00 10.00
❑ 15 George Case 25.00 12.50
❑ 16 Cecil Travis 25.00 12.50
❑ 17 Buddy Myer 25.00 12.50
❑ 18 Charlie Gelbert 20.00 10.00
❑ 19 Ken Chase 20.00 10.00
❑ 20 Buddy Lewis 20.00 10.00
❑ 21 Rick Ferrell 80.00 40.00
❑ 22 Sammy West 20.00 10.00
❑ 23 Dutch Leonard 25.00 12.50
❑ 24 Frank Hayes 20.00 10.00
❑ 25 Bob Johnson 25.00 12.50
❑ 26 Wally Moses 25.00 12.50
❑ 27 Ted Williams 1200.00 600.00
❑ 28 Gene Desautels 20.00 10.00
❑ 29 Doc Cramer 25.00 12.50
❑ 30 Moe Berg 150.00 75.00
❑ 31 Jack Wilson 20.00 10.00
❑ 32 Jim Bagby 20.00 10.00
❑ 33 Fritz Ostermueller 20.00 10.00
❑ 34 John Peacock 20.00 10.00
❑ 35 Joe Heving 20.00 10.00
❑ 36 Jim Tabor 20.00 10.00
❑ 37 Emerson Dickman 20.00 10.00
❑ 38 Bobby Doerr 90.00 45.00
❑ 39 Tom Carey 20.00 10.00
❑ 40 Hank Greenberg 200.00 100.00
❑ 41 Charley Gehringer 150.00 75.00
❑ 42 Bud Thomas 20.00 10.00
❑ 43 Pete Fox 20.00 10.00
❑ 44 Dizzy Trout 25.00 12.50
❑ 45 Red Kress 20.00 10.00
❑ 46 Earl Averill 90.00 45.00
❑ 47 Oscar Vitt 20.00 10.00
❑ 48 Luke Sewell 25.00 12.50
❑ 49 Stormy Weatherly 20.00 10.00
❑ 50 Hal Trosky 25.00 12.50
❑ 51 Don Heffner 20.00 10.00
❑ 52 Myril Hoag 20.00 10.00
❑ 53 George McQuinn 25.00 12.50
❑ 54 Bill Trotter 20.00 10.00
❑ 55 Slick Coffman 20.00 10.00
❑ 56 Eddie Miller 25.00 12.50
❑ 57 Max West 20.00 10.00
❑ 58 Bill Posedel 20.00 10.00
❑ 59 Rabbit Warstler 20.00 10.00
❑ 60 John Cooney 20.00 10.00
❑ 61 Tony Cuccinello 25.00 12.50
❑ 62 Buddy Hassett 20.00 10.00
❑ 63 Pete Coscarart 20.00 10.00
❑ 64 Van Lingle Mungo 25.00 12.50
❑ 65 Fred Fitzsimmons 25.00 12.50
❑ 66 Babe Phelps 20.00 10.00
❑ 67 Whit Wyatt 25.00 12.50
❑ 68 Dolph Camilli 25.00 12.50
❑ 69 Cookie Lavagetto 25.00 12.50
❑ 70 Luke Hamlin (Hot Potato) 20.00 10.00
❑ 71 Mel Almada 20.00 10.00
❑ 72 Chuck Dressen 25.00 12.50
❑ 73 Bucky Walters 25.00 12.50
❑ 74 Paul(Duke) Derringer 25.00 12.50
❑ 75 Frank(Buck)McCormick 25.00 12.50
❑ 76 Lonny Frey 20.00 10.00
❑ 77 Willard Hershberger 25.00 12.50
❑ 78 Lew Riggs 20.00 10.00
❑ 79 Harry Craft 25.00 12.50
❑ 80 Billy Myers 20.00 10.00
❑ 81 Wally Berger 25.00 12.50
❑ 82 Hank Gowdy CO 25.00 12.50
❑ 83 Cliff Melton 20.00 10.00
❑ 84 Jo Jo Moore 20.00 10.00
❑ 85 Hal Schumacher 25.00 12.50
❑ 86 Harry Gumbert 20.00 10.00
❑ 87 Carl Hubbell 125.00 60.00
❑ 88 Mel Ott 175.00 90.00
❑ 89 Bill Jurges 20.00 10.00
❑ 90 Frank Demaree 20.00 10.00
❑ 91 Bob Seeds 20.00 10.00
❑ 92 Whitey Whitehead 20.00 10.00
❑ 93 Harry Danning 20.00 10.00
❑ 94 Gus Suhr 20.00 10.00
❑ 95 Hugh Mulcahy 20.00 10.00
❑ 96 Heinie Mueller 20.00 10.00
❑ 97 Morry Arnovich 20.00 10.00
❑ 98 Pinky May 20.00 10.00
❑ 99 Syl Johnson 20.00 10.00
❑ 100 Hersh Martin 20.00 10.00
❑ 101 Del Young 20.00 10.00
❑ 102 Chuck Klein 100.00 50.00
❑ 103 Elbie Fletcher 20.00 10.00
❑ 104 Paul Waner 90.00 45.00
❑ 105 Lloyd Waner 80.00 40.00
❑ 106 Pep Young 20.00 10.00
❑ 107 Arky Vaughan 80.00 40.00
❑ 108 Johnny Rizzo 20.00 10.00
❑ 109 Don Padgett 20.00 10.00
❑ 110 Tom Sunkel 20.00 10.00
❑ 111 Mickey Owen 25.00 12.50
❑ 112 Jimmy Brown 20.00 10.00
❑ 113 Mort Cooper 25.00 12.50
❑ 114 Lon Warneke 25.00 12.50
❑ 115 Mike Gonzalez CO 25.00 12.50
❑ 116 Al Schacht 25.00 12.50
❑ 117 Dolly Stark UMP 25.00 12.50
❑ 118 Waite Hoyt 90.00 45.00
❑ 119 Grover C. Alexander 175.00 90.00
❑ 120 Walter Johnson 200.00 100.00
❑ 121 Atley Donald 25.00 12.50
❑ 122 Sandy Sundra 25.00 12.50
❑ 123 Hildy Hildebrand 25.00 12.50
❑ 124 Earle Combs 100.00 50.00
❑ 125 Art Fletcher 25.00 12.50
❑ 126 Jake Solters 20.00 10.00
❑ 127 Muddy Ruel 20.00 10.00
❑ 128 Pete Appleton 20.00 10.00
❑ 129 Bucky Harris 80.00 40.00
❑ 130 Clyde Milan 25.00 12.50
❑ 131 Zeke Bonura 25.00 12.50
❑ 132 Connie Mack MG 150.00 75.00
❑ 133 Jimmie Foxx 200.00 100.00
❑ 134 Joe Cronin 100.00 50.00
❑ 135 Line Drive Nelson 20.00 10.00
❑ 136 Cotton Pippen 20.00 10.00
❑ 137 Bing Miller 20.00 10.00
❑ 138 Beau Bell 20.00 10.00
❑ 139 Elden Auker 20.00 10.00
❑ 140 Dick Coffman 20.00 10.00
❑ 141 Casey Stengel MG 175.00 90.00
❑ 142 George Kelly 90.00 45.00
❑ 143 Gene Moore 20.00 10.00
❑ 144 Joe Vosmik 20.00 10.00
❑ 145 Vito Tamulis 20.00 10.00
❑ 146 Tot Pressnell 20.00 10.00
❑ 147 Johnny Hudson 20.00 10.00
❑ 148 Hugh Casey 25.00 12.50
❑ 149 Pinky Shoffner 20.00 10.00
❑ 150 Whitey Moore 20.00 10.00
❑ 151 Edwin Joost 25.00 12.50
❑ 152 Jimmy Wilson 20.00 10.00
❑ 153 Bill McKechnie MG 80.00 40.00
❑ 154 Jumbo Brown 20.00 10.00
❑ 155 Ray Hayworth 20.00 10.00
❑ 156 Daffy Dean 35.00 17.50
❑ 157 Lou Chiozza 20.00 10.00
❑ 158 Travis Jackson 90.00 45.00
❑ 159 Pancho Snyder 20.00 10.00
❑ 160 Hans Lobert CO 20.00 10.00
❑ 161 Debs Garms 20.00 10.00
❑ 162 Joe Bowman 20.00 10.00
❑ 163 Spud Davis 20.00 10.00
❑ 164 Ray Berres 20.00 10.00
❑ 165 Bob Klinger 20.00 10.00
❑ 166 Bill Brubaker 20.00 10.00
❑ 167 Frankie Frisch MG 90.00 45.00
❑ 168 Honus Wagner CO 200.00 100.00
❑ 169 Gabby Street 20.00 10.00
❑ 170 Tris Speaker 175.00 90.00
❑ 171 Harry Heilmann 80.00 40.00
❑ 172 Chief Bender 80.00 40.00

Card	Ex-Mt	VG
❑ 173 Napoleon Lajoie	175.00	90.00
❑ 174 Johnny Evers	90.00	45.00
❑ 175 Christy Mathewson	250.00	125.00
❑ 176 Heinie Manush	90.00	45.00
❑ 177 Frank Baker	100.00	50.00
❑ 178 Max Carey	90.00	45.00
❑ 179 George Sisler	125.00	60.00
❑ 180 Mickey Cochrane	150.00	75.00
❑ 181 Spud Chandler	80.00	40.00
❑ 182 Knick Knickerbocker	70.00	35.00
❑ 183 Marvin Breuer	70.00	35.00
❑ 184 Mule Haas	70.00	35.00
❑ 185 Joe Kuhel	70.00	35.00
❑ 186 Taft Wright	70.00	35.00
❑ 187 Jimmy Dykes MG	80.00	40.00
❑ 188 Joe Krakauskas	70.00	35.00
❑ 189 Jim Bloodworth	70.00	35.00
❑ 190 Charley Berry	70.00	35.00
❑ 191 John Babich	70.00	35.00
❑ 192 Dick Siebert	70.00	35.00
❑ 193 Chubby Dean	70.00	35.00
❑ 194 Sam Chapman	70.00	35.00
❑ 195 Dee Miles	70.00	35.00
❑ 196 Red(Nonny)Nonnenkamp	70.00	35.00
❑ 197 Lou Finney	70.00	35.00
❑ 198 Denny Galehouse	70.00	35.00
❑ 199 Pinky Higgins	70.00	35.00
❑ 200 Soup Campbell	70.00	35.00
❑ 201 Barney McCosky	70.00	35.00
❑ 202 Al Milnar	70.00	35.00
❑ 203 Bad News Hale	70.00	35.00
❑ 204 Harry Eisenstat	70.00	35.00
❑ 205 Rollie Hemsley	70.00	35.00
❑ 206 Chet Laabs	70.00	35.00
❑ 207 Gus Mancuso	70.00	35.00
❑ 208 Lee Gamble	70.00	35.00
❑ 209 Hy Vandenberg	70.00	35.00
❑ 210 Bill Lohrman	70.00	35.00
❑ 211 Pop Joiner	70.00	35.00
❑ 212 Babe Young	70.00	35.00
❑ 213 John Rucker	70.00	35.00
❑ 214 Ken O'Dea	70.00	35.00
❑ 215 Johnnie McCarthy	70.00	35.00
❑ 216 Joe Marty	70.00	35.00
❑ 217 Walter Beck	70.00	35.00
❑ 218 Wally Millies	70.00	35.00
❑ 219 Russ Bauers	70.00	35.00
❑ 220 Mace Brown	70.00	35.00
❑ 221 Lee Handley	70.00	35.00
❑ 222 Max Butcher	70.00	35.00
❑ 223 Hughie Jennings	150.00	75.00
❑ 224 Pie Traynor	175.00	90.00
❑ 225 Joe Jackson	2500.00	1250.00
❑ 226 Harry Hooper	150.00	75.00
❑ 227 Jesse Haines	150.00	75.00
❑ 228 Charlie Grimm	80.00	40.00
❑ 229 Buck Herzog	70.00	35.00
❑ 230 Red Faber	175.00	90.00
❑ 231 Dolf Luque	100.00	50.00
❑ 232 Goose Goslin	150.00	75.00
❑ 233 George Earnshaw	80.00	40.00
❑ 234 Frank Chance	150.00	75.00
❑ 235 John McGraw	175.00	90.00
❑ 236 Jim Bottomley	150.00	75.00
❑ 237 Willie Keeler	175.00	90.00
❑ 238 Tony Lazzeri	175.00	90.00
❑ 239 George Uhle	70.00	35.00
❑ 240 Bill Atwood	100.00	50.00

1941 Play Ball

	Ex-Mt	VG
COMPLETE SET (72)	10000.00	5000.00
COMMON CARD (1-48)	40.00	20.00
COMMON CARD (49-72)	60.00	30.00
WRAPPER (1-CENT)	800.00	400.00
❑ 1 Eddie Miller	125.00	60.00
❑ 2 Max West	40.00	20.00
❑ 3 Bucky Walters	45.00	22.00
❑ 4 Paul Derringer	50.00	25.00
❑ 5 Frank(Buck) McCormick	45.00	22.00
❑ 6 Carl Hubbell	175.00	90.00
❑ 7 Harry Danning	40.00	20.00
❑ 8 Mel Ott	225.00	110.00
❑ 9 Pinky May	40.00	20.00
❑ 10 Arky Vaughan	100.00	50.00
❑ 11 Debs Garms	40.00	20.00
❑ 12 Jimmy Brown	40.00	20.00
❑ 13 Jimmie Foxx	300.00	150.00
❑ 14 Ted Williams	1500.00	900.00
❑ 15 Joe Cronin	125.00	60.00
❑ 16 Hal Trosky	45.00	22.00
❑ 17 Roy Weatherly	40.00	20.00
❑ 18 Hank Greenberg	300.00	150.00
❑ 19 Charley Gehringer	200.00	100.00
❑ 20 Red Ruffing	125.00	60.00
❑ 21 Charlie Keller	60.00	30.00
❑ 22 Bob Johnson	50.00	25.00
❑ 23 George McQuinn	40.00	20.00
❑ 24 Dutch Leonard	45.00	22.00
❑ 25 Gene Moore	40.00	20.00
❑ 26 Harry Gumpert	40.00	20.00
❑ 27 Babe Young	40.00	20.00
❑ 28 Joe Marty	40.00	20.00
❑ 29 Jack Wilson	40.00	20.00
❑ 30 Lou Finney	40.00	20.00
❑ 31 Joe Kuhel	40.00	20.00
❑ 32 Taft Wright	40.00	20.00
❑ 33 Al Milnar	40.00	20.00
❑ 34 Rollie Hemsley	40.00	20.00
❑ 35 Pinky Higgins	45.00	22.00
❑ 36 Barney McCosky	40.00	20.00
❑ 37 Bruce Campbell	40.00	20.00
❑ 38 Atley Donald	50.00	25.00
❑ 39 Tommy Henrich	60.00	30.00
❑ 40 John Babich	40.00	20.00
❑ 41 Frank(Blimp) Hayes	40.00	20.00
❑ 42 Wally Moses	45.00	22.00
❑ 43 Al Brancato	40.00	20.00
❑ 44 Sam Chapman	40.00	20.00
❑ 45 Eldon Auker	40.00	20.00
❑ 46 Sid Hudson	40.00	20.00
❑ 47 Buddy Lewis	40.00	20.00
❑ 48 Cecil Travis	45.00	22.00
❑ 49 Babe Dahlgren	65.00	32.00
❑ 50 Johnny Cooney	60.00	30.00
❑ 51 Dolph Camilli	65.00	32.00
❑ 52 Kirby Higbe	60.00	30.00
❑ 53 Luke Hamlin	60.00	30.00
❑ 54 Pee Wee Reese	600.00	300.00
❑ 55 Whit Wyatt	65.00	32.00
❑ 56 Johnny VanderMeer	100.00	50.00
❑ 57 Moe Arnovich	60.00	30.00
❑ 58 Frank Demaree	60.00	30.00
❑ 59 Bill Jurges	60.00	30.00
❑ 60 Chuck Klein	150.00	75.00
❑ 61 Vince DiMaggio	225.00	110.00
❑ 62 Elbie Fletcher	60.00	30.00
❑ 63 Dom DiMaggio	250.00	125.00
❑ 64 Bobby Doerr	175.00	90.00
❑ 65 Tommy Bridges	65.00	32.00
❑ 66 Harland Clift	60.00	30.00
❑ 67 Walt Judnich	60.00	30.00
❑ 68 John Knott	60.00	30.00
❑ 69 George Case	65.00	32.00
❑ 70 Bill Dickey	400.00	200.00
❑ 71 Joe DiMaggio	2500.00	1250.00
❑ 72 Lefty Gomez	475.00	240.00

2004 Playoff Honors

	Nm-Mt	Ex-Mt
COMP.SET w/o SP's (200)	50.00	15.00
COMMON ACTIVE (1-200)	.40	.12
COMMON RETIRED (1-200)	.50	.15
COMMON RC/1999 (201-250)	4.00	1.20
RC/1999 PRINT RUN 1999 SERIAL #'d SETS		.00
COMMON AUTO (201-250)	8.00	2.40
AUTO PRINT RUNS B/WN 675-1000 PER		.00
201-250 RANDOM INSERTS IN PACKS		.00

Card	Nm-Mt	Ex-Mt
❑ 1 Bartolo Colon	.40	.12
❑ 2 Garret Anderson	.40	.12
❑ 3 Tim Salmon	.60	.18
❑ 4 Troy Glaus	.40	.12
❑ 5 Vladimir Guerrero	1.00	.30
❑ 6 Brandon Webb	.40	.12
❑ 7 Brian Bruney	.40	.12
❑ 8 Luis Gonzalez	.40	.12
❑ 9 Randy Johnson	1.00	.30
❑ 10 Richie Sexson	.40	.12
❑ 11 Robby Hammock	.40	.12
❑ 12 Roberto Alomar	.60	.18
❑ 13 Shea Hillenbrand	.40	.12
❑ 14 Steve Finley	.40	.12
❑ 15 Adam LaRoche	.40	.12
❑ 16 Andruw Jones	.40	.12
❑ 17 Bubba Nelson	.40	.12
❑ 18 Chipper Jones	1.00	.30
❑ 19 Dale Murphy	.60	.18
❑ 20 J.D. Drew	.40	.12
❑ 21 John Smoltz	.60	.18
❑ 22 Marcus Giles	.40	.12
❑ 23 Rafael Furcal	.40	.12
❑ 24 Warren Spahn	.75	.23
❑ 25 Greg Maddux	1.50	.45
❑ 26 Adam Loewen	.40	.12
❑ 27 Cal Ripken	5.00	1.50
❑ 28 Javy Lopez	.40	.12
❑ 29 Jay Gibbons	.40	.12
❑ 30 Luis Matos	.40	.12
❑ 31 Miguel Tejada	.40	.12
❑ 32 Rafael Palmeiro	.40	.12
❑ 33 Bobby Doerr	.50	.15
❑ 34 Curt Schilling	1.00	.30
❑ 35 Edwin Almonte	.40	.12
❑ 36 Jason Varitek	.60	.18
❑ 37 Kevin Youkilis	.40	.12
❑ 38 Manny Ramirez	.60	.18
❑ 39 Nomar Garciaparra	1.50	.45
❑ 40 Pedro Martinez	1.00	.30
❑ 41 Trot Nixon	.40	.12
❑ 42 Andre Dawson	.50	.15
❑ 43 Aramis Ramirez	.40	.12
❑ 44 Brendan Harris	.40	.12
❑ 45 Derrek Lee	.40	.12
❑ 46 Ernie Banks	1.25	.35
❑ 47 Kerry Wood	1.00	.30
❑ 48 Mark Prior	1.00	.30
❑ 49 Ryne Sandberg	2.50	.75
❑ 50 Sammy Sosa	1.50	.45
❑ 51 Carlos Lee	.40	.12
❑ 52 Frank Thomas	1.00	.30
❑ 53 Joe Borchard	.40	.12
❑ 54 Joe Crede	.40	.12
❑ 55 Magglio Ordonez	.40	.12
❑ 56 Adam Dunn	.60	.18
❑ 57 Austin Kearns	.40	.12
❑ 58 Barry Larkin	.60	.18
❑ 59 Brandon Larson	.40	.12
❑ 60 Ken Griffey Jr.	1.50	.45
❑ 61 Ryan Wagner	.40	.12
❑ 62 Sean Casey	.40	.12
❑ 63 Bob Feller	.50	.15
❑ 64 Brian Tallet	.40	.12
❑ 65 C.C. Sabathia	.40	.12
❑ 66 Jeremy Guthrie	.40	.12
❑ 67 Jody Gerut	.40	.12
❑ 68 Clint Barmes	.40	.12
❑ 69 Jeff Baker	.40	.12
❑ 70 Joe Kennedy	.40	.12
❑ 71 Larry Walker	.60	.18

❑ 72 Preston Wilson .40 .12
❑ 73 Todd Helton .60 .18
❑ 74 Alan Trammell .50 .15
❑ 75 Dmitri Young .40 .12
❑ 76 Ivan Rodriguez 1.00 .30
❑ 77 Jeremy Bonderman .40 .12
❑ 78 Preston Larrison .40 .12
❑ 79 Dontrelle Willis .40 .12
❑ 80 Josh Beckett .40 .12
❑ 81 Juan Pierre .40 .12
❑ 82 Luis Castillo .40 .12
❑ 83 Miguel Cabrera .60 .18
❑ 84 Mike Lowell .40 .12
❑ 85 Andy Pettitte .60 .18
❑ 86 Chris Burke .40 .12
❑ 87 Craig Biggio .60 .18
❑ 88 Jeff Bagwell .60 .18
❑ 89 Jeff Kent .40 .12
❑ 90 Lance Berkman .40 .12
❑ 91 Morgan Ensberg .40 .12
❑ 92 Richard Hidalgo .40 .12
❑ 93 Roger Clemens 2.00 .60
❑ 94 Roy Oswalt .40 .12
❑ 95 Angel Berroa .40 .12
❑ 96 Byron Gettis .40 .12
❑ 97 Carlos Beltran .60 .18
❑ 98 George Brett 3.00 .90
❑ 99 Juan Gonzalez .60 .18
❑ 100 Mike Sweeney .40 .12
❑ 101 Duke Snider .75 .23
❑ 102 Edwin Jackson .40 .12
❑ 103 Eric Gagne 1.00 .30
❑ 104 Hideo Nomo 1.00 .30
❑ 105 Hong-Chih Kuo .40 .12
❑ 106 Kazuhisa Ishii .40 .12
❑ 107 Paul Lo Duca .40 .12
❑ 108 Robin Ventura .40 .12
❑ 109 Shawn Green .40 .12
❑ 110 Junior Spivey .40 .12
❑ 111 Rickie Weeks .40 .12
❑ 112 Scott Podsednik .40 .12
❑ 113 J.D. Durbin .40 .12
❑ 114 Jacque Jones .40 .12
❑ 115 Jason Kubel .40 .12
❑ 116 Johan Santana .60 .18
❑ 117 Shannon Stewart .40 .12
❑ 118 Torii Hunter .40 .12
❑ 119 Brad Wilkerson .40 .12
❑ 120 Jose Vidro .40 .12
❑ 121 Nick Johnson .40 .12
❑ 122 Orlando Cabrera .40 .12
❑ 123 Gary Carter .50 .15
❑ 124 Jae Weong Seo .40 .12
❑ 125 Lenny Dykstra .50 .15
❑ 126 Mike Piazza 1.50 .45
❑ 127 Tom Glavine .60 .18
❑ 128 Alex Rodriguez 1.50 .45
❑ 129 Bernie Williams .60 .18
❑ 130 Chien-Ming Wang .40 .12
❑ 131 Derek Jeter 2.00 .60
❑ 132 Don Mattingly 3.00 .90
❑ 133 Gary Sheffield .40 .12
❑ 134 Hideki Matsui 1.50 .45
❑ 135 Jason Giambi .40 .12
❑ 136 Javier Vazquez .40 .12
❑ 137 Jorge Posada .60 .18
❑ 138 Jose Contreras .40 .12
❑ 139 Kevin Brown .40 .12
❑ 140 Mariano Rivera .60 .18
❑ 141 Mike Mussina .60 .18
❑ 142 Whitey Ford .75 .23
❑ 143 Barry Zito .40 .12
❑ 144 Eric Chavez .40 .12
❑ 145 Mark Mulder .40 .12
❑ 146 Rich Harden .40 .12
❑ 147 Tim Hudson .40 .12
❑ 148 Reggie Jackson .75 .23
❑ 149 Rickey Henderson 1.00 .30
❑ 150 Brett Myers .40 .12
❑ 151 Bobby Abreu .40 .12
❑ 152 Jim Thome 1.00 .30
❑ 153 Kevin Millwood .40 .12
❑ 154 Marlon Byrd .40 .12
❑ 155 Mike Schmidt 2.50 .75
❑ 156 Ryan Howard .40 .12
❑ 157 Jack Wilson .40 .12
❑ 158 Jason Kendall .40 .12
❑ 159 Brian Giles .40 .12
❑ 160 David Wells .40 .12
❑ 161 Jay Payton .40 .12
❑ 162 Phil Nevin .40 .12
❑ 163 Ryan Klesko .40 .12
❑ 164 Sean Burroughs .40 .12
❑ 165 A.J. Pierzynski .40 .12
❑ 166 J.T. Snow .40 .12
❑ 167 Jason Schmidt .40 .12
❑ 168 Jerome Williams .40 .12
❑ 169 Will Clark 1.25 .35
❑ 170 Bret Boone .40 .12
❑ 171 Chris Snelling .40 .12
❑ 172 Edgar Martinez .60 .18
❑ 173 Ichiro Suzuki 1.50 .45
❑ 174 Randy Winn .40 .12
❑ 175 Rich Aurilia .40 .12
❑ 176 Shigetoshi Hasegawa .40 .12
❑ 177 Albert Pujols 2.00 .60
❑ 178 Dan Haren .40 .12
❑ 179 Edgar Renteria .40 .12
❑ 180 Jim Edmonds .40 .12
❑ 181 Matt Morris .40 .12
❑ 182 Scott Rolen 1.00 .30
❑ 183 Stan Musial 2.00 .60
❑ 184 Aubrey Huff .40 .12
❑ 185 Chad Gaudin .40 .12
❑ 186 Delmon Young .60 .18
❑ 187 Fred McGriff .60 .18
❑ 188 Rocco Baldelli .40 .12
❑ 189 Alfonso Soriano .60 .18
❑ 190 Hank Blalock .40 .12
❑ 191 Mark Teixeira .40 .12
❑ 192 Nolan Ryan 3.00 .90
❑ 193 Alexis Rios .40 .12
❑ 194 Carlos Delgado .40 .12
❑ 195 Dustin McGowan .40 .12
❑ 196 Guillermo Quiroz .40 .12
❑ 197 Josh Phelps .40 .12
❑ 198 Roy Halladay .40 .12
❑ 199 Vernon Wells .40 .12
❑ 200 Vinnie Chulk .40 .12
❑ 201 Jose Capellan/1999 RC 6.00 1.80
❑ 202 Kazuo Matsui/1999 RC 8.00 2.40
❑ 203 Dave Crouthers/1999 RC 4.00 1.20
❑ 204 Akinori Otsuka/1999 RC 4.00 1.20
❑ 205 Nick Regilio/1999 RC 4.00 1.20
❑ 206 Justin Hampson/1999 RC 4.00 1.20
❑ 207 Lincoln Holdzkom/1999 RC 4.00 1.20
❑ 208 Jorge Sequea/1999 RC 4.00 1.20
❑ 209 Justin Leone/1999 RC 5.00 1.50
❑ 210 Renyel Pinto/1999 RC 5.00 1.50
❑ 211 Mariano Gomez/1999 RC 4.00 1.20
❑ 212 Onil Joseph AU/1000 RC 8.00 2.40
❑ 213 J.Labandeira AU/1000 RC 8.00 2.40
❑ 214 Cory Sullivan/1999 RC 4.00 1.20
❑ 215 Carlos Vasquez AU/675 RC 10.00 3.00
❑ 216 Chris Shelton/1999 RC 5.00 1.50
❑ 217 Willy Taveras/1999 RC 5.00 1.50
❑ 218 John Gall/1999 RC 5.00 1.50
❑ 219 Jerry Gil/1999 RC 4.00 1.20
❑ 220 Jason Frasor/1999 RC 4.00 1.20
❑ 221 Justin Knoedler/1999 RC 4.00 1.20
❑ 222 Ronald Belisario/1999 RC 4.00 1.20
❑ 223 Mike Rouse/1999 RC 4.00 1.20
❑ 224 Dennis Sarfate/1999 RC 4.00 1.20
❑ 225 Casey Daigle/1999 RC 4.00 1.20
❑ 226 S.Takatsu AU/800 RC 25.00 7.50
❑ 227 Jason Bartlett AU/800 RC 10.00 3.00
❑ 228 Alfredo Simon AU/1000 RC 8.00 2.40
❑ 229 Chris Oxspring/1999 RC 5.00 1.50
❑ 230 Fern Nieve AU/1000 RC 8.00 2.40
❑ 231 Ruddy Yan AU/800 8.00 2.40
❑ 232 Ryan Wing/1999 RC 4.00 1.20
❑ 233 Tim Bittner AU/1000 RC 8.00 2.40
❑ 234 Ram Ramirez AU/1000 RC 8.00 2.40
❑ 235 Sean Henn AU/1000 RC 8.00 2.40
❑ 236 Roberto Novoa AU/800 RC 10.00 3.00
❑ 237 Jerome Gamble AU/800 RC 8.00 2.40
❑ 238 Jamie Brown AU/800 RC 8.00 2.40
❑ 239 Ian Snell AU/800 RC 10.00 3.00
❑ 240 Freddy Guzman AU/800 RC 8.00 2.40
❑ 241 Aarom Baldiris AU/1000 RC 10.00 3.00
❑ 242 Greg Dobbs/1999 RC 4.00 1.20
❑ 243 Ivan Ochoa/1999 RC 4.00 1.20
❑ 244 Angel Chavez AU/800 RC 8.00 2.40
❑ 245 Merkin Valdez AU/800 RC 10.00 3.00
❑ 246 Mike Gosling AU/800 RC 8.00 2.40
❑ 247 Carlos Hines AU/800 RC 8.00 2.40
❑ 248 Graham Koonce AU/1000 8.00 2.40
❑ 249 Will Bergolla AU/1000 RC 8.00 2.40
❑ 250 Hect Gimenez AU/1000 RC 8.00 2.40

2004 Prime Cuts

	MINT	NRMT
COMPLETE SET (50)	225.00	100.00

STATED PRINT RUN 949 SERIAL #'d SETS
B.RUTH SANTA STATED ODDS 1:15

❑ 1 Roger Clemens Yanks 10.00 4.50
❑ 2 Nomar Garciaparra 8.00 3.60
❑ 3 Albert Pujols 10.00 4.50
❑ 4 Sammy Sosa 8.00 3.60
❑ 5 Greg Maddux Braves 8.00 3.60
❑ 6 Jason Giambi 4.00 1.80
❑ 7 Hideo Nomo Dodgers 5.00 2.20
❑ 8 Mike Piazza Mets 8.00 3.60
❑ 9 Ichiro Suzuki 8.00 3.60
❑ 10 Jeff Bagwell 5.00 2.20
❑ 11 Derek Jeter 10.00 4.50
❑ 12 Manny Ramirez 5.00 2.20
❑ 13 R.Henderson Dodgers 5.00 2.20
❑ 14 Alex Rodriguez Rgr 8.00 3.60
❑ 15 Troy Glaus 4.00 1.80
❑ 16 Mike Mussina 5.00 2.20
❑ 17 Kerry Wood 5.00 2.20
❑ 18 Kazuhisa Ishii 4.00 1.80
❑ 19 Hideki Matsui 8.00 3.60
❑ 20 Frank Thomas 5.00 2.20
❑ 21 Barry Bonds Giants 12.00 5.50
❑ 22 Adam Dunn 5.00 2.20
❑ 23 Randy Johnson D'backs 5.00 2.20
❑ 24 Alfonso Soriano 5.00 2.20
❑ 25 Pedro Martinez Sox 5.00 2.20
❑ 26 Andruw Jones 4.00 1.80
❑ 27 Mark Prior 5.00 2.20
❑ 28 Vladimir Guerrero 5.00 2.20
❑ 29 Chipper Jones 5.00 2.20
❑ 30 Todd Helton 5.00 2.20
❑ 31 Rafael Palmeiro 5.00 2.20
❑ 32 Mark Grace 5.00 2.20
❑ 33 Pedro Martinez Dodgers 5.00 2.20
❑ 34 Randy Johnson M's 5.00 2.20
❑ 35 Randy Johnson Astros 5.00 2.20
❑ 36 Roger Clemens Sox 10.00 4.50
❑ 37 Roger Clemens Jays 10.00 4.50
❑ 38 Alex Rodriguez M's 8.00 3.60
❑ 39 Greg Maddux Cubs 8.00 3.60
❑ 40 Mike Piazza Dodgers 8.00 3.60
❑ 41 Mike Piazza Marlins 8.00 3.60
❑ 42 Hideo Nomo Mets 5.00 2.20
❑ 43 R.Henderson Yanks 5.00 2.20
❑ 44 Rickey Henderson A's 5.00 2.20
❑ 45 Barry Bonds Pirates 12.00 5.50
❑ 46 Ivan Rodriguez 5.00 2.20
❑ 47 George Brett 10.00 4.50
❑ 48 Cal Ripken 20.00 9.00
❑ 49 Nolan Ryan 12.00 5.50
❑ 50 Don Mattingly 10.00 4.50
❑ BRS1 Babe Ruth Santa 15.00 6.75

2004 Prime Cuts II

	Nm-Mt	Ex-Mt
COMMON CARD (1-91)	4.00	1.20
COMMON CARD (92-100)	4.00	1.20

❑ 1 Mark Prior 5.00 1.50

❑ 2 Derek Jeter 10.00 3.00
❑ 3 Eric Chavez 4.00 1.20
❑ 4 Carlos Delgado 4.00 1.20
❑ 5 Albert Pujols 10.00 3.00
❑ 6 Miguel Cabrera 5.00 1.50
❑ 7 Ivan Rodriguez 5.00 1.50
❑ 8 Javy Lopez 4.00 1.20
❑ 9 Hank Blalock 4.00 1.20
❑ 10 Chipper Jones 5.00 1.50
❑ 11 Gary Sheffield 4.00 1.20
❑ 12 Alfonso Soriano 5.00 1.50
❑ 13 Alex Rodriguez Yanks 8.00 2.40
❑ 14 Edgar Renteria 4.00 1.20
❑ 15 Jim Edmonds 4.00 1.20
❑ 16 Garret Anderson 4.00 1.20
❑ 17 Lance Berkman 4.00 1.20
❑ 18 Brandon Webb 4.00 1.20
❑ 19 Mike Lowell 4.00 1.20
❑ 20 Mark Mulder 4.00 1.20
❑ 21 Sammy Sosa 8.00 2.40
❑ 22 Roger Clemens Astros 8.00 2.40
❑ 23 Mark Teixeira 4.00 1.20
❑ 24 Manny Ramirez 5.00 1.50
❑ 25 Rafael Palmeiro 5.00 1.50
❑ 26 Ichiro Suzuki 8.00 2.40
❑ 27 Vladimir Guerrero 5.00 1.50
❑ 28 Austin Kearns 4.00 1.20
❑ 29 Troy Glaus 4.00 1.20
❑ 30 Ken Griffey Jr. 8.00 2.40
❑ 31 Greg Maddux 8.00 2.40
❑ 32 Roy Halladay 4.00 1.20
❑ 33 Roy Oswalt 4.00 1.20
❑ 34 Kerry Wood 5.00 1.50
❑ 35 Mike Mussina Yanks 5.00 1.50
❑ 36 Michael Young 4.00 1.20
❑ 37 Juan Gonzalez 5.00 1.50
❑ 38 Curt Schilling 5.00 1.50
❑ 39 Shannon Stewart 4.00 1.20
❑ 40 Todd Helton 5.00 1.50
❑ 41 Larry Walker 5.00 1.50
❑ 42 Mariano Rivera 5.00 1.50
❑ 43 Nomar Garciaparra 8.00 2.40
❑ 44 Adam Dunn 5.00 1.50
❑ 45 Pedro Martinez Sox 5.00 1.50
❑ 46 Bernie Williams 5.00 1.50
❑ 47 Tom Glavine 5.00 1.50
❑ 48 Torii Hunter 4.00 1.20
❑ 49 David Ortiz 5.00 1.50
❑ 50 Frank Thomas 5.00 1.50
❑ 51 Randy Johnson D'backs 5.00 1.50
❑ 52 Jason Giambi 4.00 1.20
❑ 53 Carlos Lee 4.00 1.20
❑ 54 Mike Sweeney 4.00 1.20
❑ 55 Hideki Matsui 8.00 2.40
❑ 56 Dontrelle Willis 4.00 1.20
❑ 57 Tim Hudson 4.00 1.20
❑ 58 Jose Vidro 4.00 1.20
❑ 59 Jeff Bagwell 5.00 1.50
❑ 60 Rocco Baldelli 4.00 1.20
❑ 61 Craig Biggio 5.00 1.50
❑ 62 Mike Piazza Mets 8.00 2.40
❑ 63 Magglio Ordonez 4.00 1.20
❑ 64 Hideo Nomo 5.00 1.50
❑ 65 Miguel Tejada 4.00 1.20
❑ 66 Vernon Wells 4.00 1.20
❑ 67 Barry Larkin 5.00 1.50
❑ 68 Jacque Jones 4.00 1.20
❑ 69 Scott Rolen 5.00 1.50
❑ 70 Jeff Kent 4.00 1.20
❑ 71 Steve Finley 4.00 1.20
❑ 72 Kazuo Matsui RC 8.00 2.40
❑ 73 Carlos Beltran 5.00 1.50
❑ 74 Shawn Green 4.00 1.20
❑ 75 Barry Zito 4.00 1.20
❑ 76 Aramis Ramirez 4.00 1.20
❑ 77 Paul Lo Duca 4.00 1.20
❑ 78 Kazuhisa Ishii 4.00 1.20
❑ 79 Aubrey Huff 4.00 1.20
❑ 80 Jim Thome 5.00 1.50
❑ 81 Andy Pettitte Astros 5.00 1.50
❑ 82 Andruw Jones 4.00 1.20
❑ 83 Josh Beckett 4.00 1.20
❑ 84 Sean Casey 4.00 1.20
❑ 85 Alex Rodriguez M's 8.00 2.40
❑ 86 Roger Clemens Yanks 8.00 2.40
❑ 87 Mike Mussina O's 5.00 1.50
❑ 88 Pedro Martinez Dgr 5.00 1.50
❑ 89 Randy Johnson Astros 5.00 1.50
❑ 90 Mike Piazza Dgr 8.00 2.40
❑ 91 Andy Pettitte Yanks 5.00 1.50
❑ 92 Cal Ripken 20.00 6.00
❑ 93 Dale Murphy 5.00 1.50
❑ 94 Don Mattingly 10.00 3.00
❑ 95 Gary Carter 4.00 1.20
❑ 96 George Brett 10.00 3.00
❑ 97 Nolan Ryan 12.00 3.60
❑ 98 Ozzie Smith 8.00 2.40
❑ 99 Steve Carlton 4.00 1.20
❑ 100 Tony Gwynn 8.00 2.40

2004 Reflections

	Nm-Mt	Ex-Mt
COMP.SET w/o SP's (100)	40.00	12.00
COMP.UPDATE SET (50)	30.00	9.00
COMMON CARD (1-100)	.75	.23
COMMON CARD (101-130)	4.00	1.20
COMMON CARD (131-214)	6.00	1.80
SP CL: 132/142/144/146/153/156/159		.00
SP CL: 161-162/164/178/184/186/188		.00
SP CL: 190-191/197-198/201/207/214		.00
SP INFO PROVIDED BY UPPER DECK		.00
COMMON CARD (215-298)	8.00	2.40
COMMON CARD (299-340)	25.00	7.50
COMMON CARD (341-390)	.60	.18

❑ 1 Adam Dunn .... 1.25 .35
❑ 2 Albert Pujols 4.00 1.20
❑ 3 Alex Rodriguez Yanks .... 3.00 .90
❑ 4 Alfonso Soriano .... 1.25 .35
❑ 5 Andruw Jones .... .75 .23
❑ 6 Austin Kearns .... .75 .23
❑ 7 Rafael Furcal .... .75 .23
❑ 8 Barry Zito .... .75 .23
❑ 9 Bartolo Colon .... .75 .23
❑ 10 Ben Sheets .... .75 .23
❑ 11 Bernie Williams .... 1.25 .35
❑ 12 Bobby Abreu .... .75 .23
❑ 13 Brandon Webb .... .75 .23
❑ 14 Bret Boone .... .75 .23
❑ 15 Brian Giles .... .75 .23
❑ 16 Carlos Beltran .... 1.25 .35
❑ 17 Carlos Delgado .... .75 .23
❑ 18 Carlos Lee .... .75 .23
❑ 19 Chipper Jones .... 2.00 .60
❑ 20 Corey Patterson .... .75 .23
❑ 21 Curt Schilling .... 2.00 .60
❑ 22 Delmon Young .... 1.25 .35
❑ 23 Derek Jeter 4.00 1.20
❑ 24 Dmitri Young .... .75 .23
❑ 25 Dontrelle Willis .... .75 .23
❑ 26 Edgar Martinez .... 1.25 .35
❑ 27 Edgar Renteria .... .75 .23
❑ 28 Eric Chavez .... .75 .23
❑ 29 Eric Gagne .... 2.00 .60
❑ 30 Frank Thomas .... 2.00 .60
❑ 31 Garrett Anderson .... .75 .23
❑ 32 Gary Sheffield .... .75 .23
❑ 33 Geoff Jenkins .... .75 .23
❑ 34 Greg Maddux .... 3.00 .90
❑ 35 Hank Blalock .... .75 .23
❑ 36 Hideki Matsui .... 3.00 .90
❑ 37 Hideo Nomo .... 2.00 .60
❑ 38 Ichiro Suzuki .... 3.00 .90
❑ 39 Ivan Rodriguez .... 2.00 .60
❑ 40 Jacque Jones .... .75 .23
❑ 41 Jason Giambi .... .75 .23
❑ 42 Jason Schmidt .... .75 .23
❑ 43 Javy Lopez .... .75 .23
❑ 44 Jay Gibbons .... .75 .23
❑ 45 Jeff Bagwell .... 1.25 .35
❑ 46 Jeff Kent .... .75 .23
❑ 47 Jeremy Bonderman .... .75 .23
❑ 48 Jim Edmonds .... .75 .23
❑ 49 Jim Thome .... 2.00 .60
❑ 50 Johnny Damon .... 2.00 .60
❑ 51 Jorge Posada .... 1.25 .35
❑ 52 Jose Contreras .... .75 .23
❑ 53 Jose Reyes .... .75 .23
❑ 54 Jose Vidro .... .75 .23
❑ 55 Josh Beckett .... .75 .23
❑ 56 Juan Gonzalez .... 1.25 .35
❑ 57 Ken Griffey Jr. .... 3.00 .90
❑ 58 Kerry Wood .... 2.00 .60
❑ 59 Kevin Brown .... .75 .23
❑ 60 Kevin Millwood .... .75 .23
❑ 61 Lance Berkman .... .75 .23
❑ 62 Larry Walker .... 1.25 .35
❑ 63 Luis Gonzalez .... .75 .23
❑ 64 Magglio Ordonez .... .75 .23
❑ 65 Manny Ramirez .... 1.25 .35
❑ 66 Mark Mulder .... .75 .23
❑ 67 Mark Prior .... 2.00 .60
❑ 68 Mark Teixeira .... .75 .23
❑ 69 Miguel Cabrera .... 1.25 .35
❑ 70 Miguel Tejada .... .75 .23
❑ 71 Mike Lowell .... .75 .23
❑ 72 Mike Mussina .... 1.25 .35
❑ 73 Mike Piazza .... 3.00 .90
❑ 74 Mike Sweeney .... .75 .23
❑ 75 Milton Bradley .... .75 .23
❑ 76 Nomar Garciaparra .... 3.00 .90
❑ 77 Orlando Cabrera .... .75 .23
❑ 78 Pedro Martinez .... 2.00 .60
❑ 79 Phil Nevin .... .75 .23
❑ 80 Preston Wilson .... .75 .23
❑ 81 Rafael Palmeiro .... 1.25 .35
❑ 82 Randy Johnson .... 2.00 .60
❑ 83 Rich Harden .... .75 .23
❑ 84 Richie Sexson .... .75 .23
❑ 85 Rickie Weeks .... .75 .23
❑ 86 Rocco Baldelli .... .75 .23
❑ 87 Roy Halladay .... .75 .23
❑ 88 Roy Oswalt .... .75 .23
❑ 89 Ryan Klesko .... .75 .23
❑ 90 Sammy Sosa .... 3.00 .90
❑ 91 Scott Rolen .... 2.00 .60
❑ 92 Shannon Stewart .... .75 .23
❑ 93 Shawn Green .... .75 .23
❑ 94 Tim Hudson .... .75 .23
❑ 95 Todd Helton .... 1.25 .35
❑ 96 Torii Hunter .... .75 .23
❑ 97 Trot Nixon .... .75 .23
❑ 98 Troy Glaus .... .75 .23
❑ 99 Vernon Wells .... .75 .23
❑ 100 Vladimir Guerrero .... 2.00 .60
❑ 101 Brandon Medders RC 4.00 1.20
❑ 102 Colby Miller RC 4.00 1.20
❑ 103 Dave Crouthers RC 4.00 1.20
❑ 104 Dennis Sarfate RC 4.00 1.20
❑ 105 Donnie Kelly RC 4.00 1.20
❑ 106 Alec Zumwalt RC 4.00 1.20
❑ 107 Chris Aguila RC 4.00 1.20
❑ 108 Greg Dobbs RC 4.00 1.20
❑ 109 Ian Snell RC 5.00 1.50
❑ 110 Jake Woods RC 4.00 1.20
❑ 111 Jamie Brown RC 4.00 1.20
❑ 112 Jason Frasor RC 4.00 1.20
❑ 113 Jerome Gamble RC 4.00 1.20
❑ 114 Jesse Harper RC 4.00 1.20
❑ 115 Josh Labandeira RC 4.00 1.20
❑ 116 Justin Hampson RC 4.00 1.20
❑ 117 Justin Huisman RC 4.00 1.20
❑ 118 Justin Leone RC 5.00 1.50
❑ 119 Kazuo Matsui RC 8.00 2.40

- ❑ 120 Lincoln Holdzkom RC 4.00 1.20
- ❑ 121 Mike Bumatay RC 4.00 1.20
- ❑ 122 Mike Gosling RC 4.00 1.20
- ❑ 123 Mike Johnston RC 4.00 1.20
- ❑ 124 Mike Rouse RC 4.00 1.20
- ❑ 125 Nick Regilio RC 4.00 1.20
- ❑ 126 Ryan Meaux RC 4.00 1.20
- ❑ 127 Scott Dohmann RC 4.00 1.20
- ❑ 128 Sean Henn RC 4.00 1.20
- ❑ 129 Tim Bausher RC 4.00 1.20
- ❑ 130 Tim Bittner RC 4.00 1.20
- ❑ 131 Adam Dunn Jsy L1 10.00 3.00
- ❑ 132 Andruw Jones Jsy L1 SP 8.00 2.40
- ❑ 133 Austin Kearns Jsy L1 6.00 1.80
- ❑ 134 Bartolo Colon Jsy L1 6.00 1.80
- ❑ 135 Ben Sheets Jsy L1 6.00 1.80
- ❑ 136 Bernie Williams Jsy L1 10.00 3.00
- ❑ 137 Bobby Abreu Jsy L1 6.00 1.80
- ❑ 138 Brian Giles Jsy L1 6.00 1.80
- ❑ 139 Carlos Lee Jsy L1 6.00 1.80
- ❑ 140 Chipper Jones Jsy L1 10.00 3.00
- ❑ 141 Corey Patterson Jsy L1 6.00 1.80
- ❑ 142 Darin Erstad Jsy L1 SP 8.00 2.40
- ❑ 143 Edgar Martinez Jsy L1 10.00 3.00
- ❑ 144 Vladimir Guerrero Jsy L1 SP 12.00 3.60
- ❑ 145 Eric Gagne Jsy L1 10.00 3.00
- ❑ 146 Frank Thomas Jsy L1 SP 12.00 3.60
- ❑ 147 Garret Anderson Jsy L1 6.00 1.80
- ❑ 148 Roger Clemens Jsy L1 15.00 4.50
- ❑ 149 Greg Maddux Jsy L1 10.00 3.00
- ❑ 150 Jacque Jones Jsy L1 6.00 1.80
- ❑ 151 Randy Johnson Jsy L1 10.00 3.00
- ❑ 152 Javy Lopez Jsy L1 6.00 1.80
- ❑ 153 Mike Piazza Jsy L1 SP 15.00 4.50
- ❑ 154 Albert Pujols Jsy L1 15.00 4.50
- ❑ 155 Jim Edmonds Jsy L1 6.00 1.80
- ❑ 156 Eric Milton Jsy L1 SP 8.00 2.40
- ❑ 157 Jorge Posada Jsy L1 10.00 3.00
- ❑ 158 J.D. Drew Jsy L1 6.00 1.80
- ❑ 159 Jose Vidro Jsy L1 SP 8.00 2.40
- ❑ 160 Kevin Millwood Jsy L1 6.00 1.80
- ❑ 161 Larry Walker Jsy L1 SP 12.00 3.60
- ❑ 162 Luis Gonzalez Jsy L1 SP 8.00 2.40
- ❑ 163 Mike Sweeney Jsy L1 6.00 1.80
- ❑ 164 Kerry Wood Jsy L1 SP 12.00 3.60
- ❑ 165 Mike Cameron Jsy L1 6.00 1.80
- ❑ 166 Phil Nevin Jsy L1 6.00 1.80
- ❑ 167 Rocco Baldelli Jsy L1 6.00 1.80
- ❑ 168 Ryan Klesko Jsy L1 6.00 1.80
- ❑ 169 Shannon Stewart Jsy L1 6.00 1.80
- ❑ 170 Torii Hunter Jsy L1 6.00 1.80
- ❑ 171 Trot Nixon Jsy L1 6.00 1.80
- ❑ 172 Vernon Wells Jsy L1 6.00 1.80
- ❑ 173 Alfonso Soriano Jsy L2 10.00 3.00
- ❑ 174 Andruw Jones Jsy L2 6.00 1.80
- ❑ 175 Barry Zito Jsy L2 6.00 1.80
- ❑ 176 Brandon Webb Jsy L2 6.00 1.80
- ❑ 177 Bret Boone Jsy L2 6.00 1.80
- ❑ 178 Scott Rolen Jsy L2 SP 12.00 3.60
- ❑ 179 Carlos Delgado Jsy L2 6.00 1.80
- ❑ 180 Curt Schilling Jsy L2 10.00 3.00
- ❑ 181 Dontrelle Willis Jsy L2 6.00 1.80
- ❑ 182 Eric Chavez Jsy L2 6.00 1.80
- ❑ 183 Frank Thomas Jsy L2 10.00 3.00
- ❑ 184 Gary Sheffield Jsy L2 SP 8.00 2.40
- ❑ 185 Greg Maddux Jsy L2 10.00 3.00
- ❑ 186 Hank Blalock Jsy L2 SP 8.00 2.40
- ❑ 187 Hideki Matsui Jsy L2 25.00 7.50
- ❑ 188 Hideo Nomo Jsy L2 SP 12.00 3.60
- ❑ 189 Ichiro Suzuki Jsy L2 15.00 4.50
- ❑ 190 Ivan Rodriguez Jsy L2 SP 12.00 3.60
- ❑ 191 Jason Giambi Jsy L2 SP 8.00 2.40
- ❑ 192 Rafael Furcal Jsy L2 6.00 1.80
- ❑ 193 Jeff Bagwell Jsy L2 10.00 3.00
- ❑ 194 Jeff Kent Jsy L2 6.00 1.80
- ❑ 195 Jim Thome Jsy L2 10.00 3.00
- ❑ 196 Jose Reyes Jsy L2 6.00 1.80
- ❑ 197 Josh Beckett Jsy L2 SP 8.00 2.40
- ❑ 198 Juan Gonzalez Jsy L2 SP 12.00 3.60
- ❑ 199 Ken Griffey Jr. Jsy L2 15.00 4.50
- ❑ 200 Kevin Brown Jsy L2 6.00 1.80
- ❑ 201 Lance Berkman Jsy L2 SP 8.00 2.40
- ❑ 202 Magglio Ordonez Jsy L2 6.00 1.80
- ❑ 203 Mark Mulder Jsy L2 6.00 1.80
- ❑ 204 Mark Teixeira Jsy L2 6.00 1.80
- ❑ 205 Miguel Tejada Jsy L2 6.00 1.80
- ❑ 206 Mike Mussina Jsy L2 10.00 3.00
- ❑ 207 Preston Wilson Jsy L2 SP 8.00 2.40
- ❑ 208 Rafael Palmeiro Jsy L2 10.00 3.00
- ❑ 209 Alex Rodriguez Jsy L2 15.00 4.50
- ❑ 210 Richie Sexson Jsy L2 6.00 1.80
- ❑ 211 Roy Halladay Jsy L2 6.00 1.80
- ❑ 212 Roy Oswalt Jsy L2 6.00 1.80
- ❑ 213 Tim Hudson Jsy L2 6.00 1.80
- ❑ 214 Troy Glaus Jsy L2 SP 8.00 2.40
- ❑ 215 Adam Dunn Jsy L3 12.00 3.60
- ❑ 216 Austin Kearns Jsy L3 8.00 2.40
- ❑ 217 Bartolo Colon Jsy L3 8.00 2.40
- ❑ 218 Ben Sheets Jsy L3 8.00 2.40
- ❑ 219 Bernie Williams Jsy L3 12.00 3.60
- ❑ 220 Bobby Abreu Jsy L3 8.00 2.40
- ❑ 221 Bret Boone Jsy L3 8.00 2.40
- ❑ 222 Todd Helton Jsy L3 12.00 3.60
- ❑ 223 Chipper Jones Jsy L3 12.00 3.60
- ❑ 224 Corey Patterson Jsy L3 8.00 2.40
- ❑ 225 Darin Erstad Jsy L3 8.00 2.40
- ❑ 226 Dontrelle Willis Jsy L3 8.00 2.40
- ❑ 227 Edgar Martinez Jsy L3 12.00 3.60
- ❑ 228 Eric Gagne Jsy L3 12.00 3.60
- ❑ 229 Garret Anderson Jsy L3 8.00 2.40
- ❑ 230 Roger Clemens Jsy L3 20.00 6.00
- ❑ 231 Hank Blalock Jsy L3 8.00 2.40
- ❑ 232 Jacque Jones Jsy L3 8.00 2.40
- ❑ 233 Jeff Bagwell Jsy L3 12.00 3.60
- ❑ 234 Jeff Kent Jsy L3 8.00 2.40
- ❑ 235 Jeremy Bonderman Jsy L3 8.00 2.40
- ❑ 236 Jim Edmonds Jsy L3 8.00 2.40
- ❑ 237 Jorge Posada Jsy L3 12.00 3.60
- ❑ 238 J.D. Drew Jsy L3 8.00 2.40
- ❑ 239 Jose Reyes Jsy L3 8.00 2.40
- ❑ 240 Jose Vidro Jsy L3 8.00 2.40
- ❑ 241 Kevin Millwood Jsy L3 8.00 2.40
- ❑ 242 Luis Gonzalez Jsy L3 8.00 2.40
- ❑ 243 Mike Sweeney Jsy L3 8.00 2.40
- ❑ 244 Jason Giambi Jsy L3 8.00 2.40
- ❑ 245 Manny Ramirez Jsy L3 12.00 3.60
- ❑ 246 Phil Nevin Jsy L3 8.00 2.40
- ❑ 247 Preston Wilson Jsy L3 8.00 2.40
- ❑ 248 Alex Rodriguez Jsy L3 20.00 6.00
- ❑ 249 Richie Sexson Jsy L3 8.00 2.40
- ❑ 250 Rocco Baldelli Jsy L3 8.00 2.40
- ❑ 251 Ryan Klesko Jsy L3 8.00 2.40
- ❑ 252 Sammy Sosa Jsy L3 15.00 4.50
- ❑ 253 Torii Hunter Jsy L3 8.00 2.40
- ❑ 254 Mike Lowell Jsy L3 8.00 2.40
- ❑ 255 Troy Glaus Jsy L3 8.00 2.40
- ❑ 256 Vernon Wells Jsy L3 8.00 2.40
- ❑ 257 Albert Pujols Jsy L4 25.00 7.50
- ❑ 258 Alex Rodriguez Jsy L4 20.00 6.00
- ❑ 259 Alfonso Soriano Jsy L4 12.00 3.60
- ❑ 260 Roger Clemens Jsy L4 20.00 6.00
- ❑ 261 Barry Zito Jsy L4 8.00 2.40
- ❑ 262 Brandon Webb Jsy L4 8.00 2.40
- ❑ 263 Carlos Delgado Jsy L4 8.00 2.40
- ❑ 264 Curt Schilling Jsy L4 12.00 3.60
- ❑ 265 Derek Jeter Jsy L4 30.00 9.00
- ❑ 266 Eric Chavez Jsy L4 8.00 2.40
- ❑ 267 Gary Sheffield Jsy L4 8.00 2.40
- ❑ 268 Hideki Matsui Jsy L4 30.00 9.00
- ❑ 269 Hideo Nomo Jsy L4 12.00 3.60
- ❑ 270 Ichiro Suzuki Jsy L4 25.00 7.50
- ❑ 271 Ivan Rodriguez Jsy L4 12.00 3.60
- ❑ 272 Jason Giambi Jsy L4 8.00 2.40
- ❑ 273 Jim Thome Jsy L4 12.00 3.60
- ❑ 274 Josh Beckett Jsy L4 8.00 2.40
- ❑ 275 Juan Gonzalez Jsy L4 12.00 3.60
- ❑ 276 Ken Griffey Jr. Jsy L4 20.00 6.00
- ❑ 277 Kerry Wood Jsy L4 12.00 3.60
- ❑ 278 Kevin Brown Jsy L4 8.00 2.40
- ❑ 279 Lance Berkman Jsy L4 8.00 2.40
- ❑ 280 Magglio Ordonez Jsy L4 8.00 2.40
- ❑ 281 Manny Ramirez Jsy L4 12.00 3.60
- ❑ 282 Mark Mulder Jsy L4 8.00 2.40
- ❑ 283 Mark Prior Jsy L4 12.00 3.60
- ❑ 284 Mark Teixeira Jsy L4 8.00 2.40
- ❑ 285 Miguel Tejada Jsy L4 8.00 2.40
- ❑ 286 Mike Mussina Jsy L4 12.00 3.60
- ❑ 287 Mike Piazza Jsy L4 20.00 6.00
- ❑ 288 Pedro Martinez Jsy L4 12.00 3.60
- ❑ 289 Rafael Palmeiro Jsy L4 12.00 3.60
- ❑ 290 Randy Johnson Jsy L4 12.00 3.60
- ❑ 291 Roy Halladay Jsy L4 8.00 2.40
- ❑ 292 Roy Oswalt Jsy L4 8.00 2.40
- ❑ 293 Sammy Sosa Jsy L4 20.00 6.00
- ❑ 294 Scott Rolen Jsy L4 12.00 3.60
- ❑ 295 Shawn Green Jsy L4 8.00 2.40
- ❑ 296 Tim Hudson Jsy L4 8.00 2.40
- ❑ 297 Todd Helton Jsy L4 12.00 3.60
- ❑ 298 Vladimir Guerrero Jsy L4 12.00 3.60
- ❑ 299 Bret Boone AU 40.00 12.00
- ❑ 300 Alex Rodriguez AU 200.00 60.00
- ❑ 301 Dontrelle Willis AU 40.00 12.00
- ❑ 302 Barry Larkin AU 50.00 15.00
- ❑ 303 Barry Zito AU 50.00 15.00
- ❑ 304 Eric Chavez AU 40.00 12.00
- ❑ 305 Bernie Williams AU 120.00 36.00
- ❑ 306 Brandon Webb AU 25.00 7.50
- ❑ 307 Cal Ripken AU 200.00 60.00
- ❑ 308 Carl Yastrzemski AU 80.00 24.00
- ❑ 309 Carlos Delgado AU 40.00 12.00
- ❑ 310 Shawn Green AU 40.00 12.00
- ❑ 311 Eric Gagne AU 60.00 18.00
- ❑ 312 Frank Thomas AU 60.00 18.00
- ❑ 313 Carlos Lee AU 25.00 7.50
- ❑ 314 Garret Anderson AU 40.00 12.00
- ❑ 315 Hideki Matsui AU 350.00 105.00
- ❑ 316 Jim Edmonds AU 50.00 15.00
- ❑ 317 Jeff Bagwell AU 50.00 15.00
- ❑ 318 Luis Gonzalez AU 40.00 12.00
- ❑ 319 Mike Mussina AU 50.00 15.00
- ❑ 320 John Smoltz AU 100.00 30.00
- ❑ 321 Jose Reyes AU 40.00 12.00
- ❑ 322 Josh Beckett AU 50.00 15.00
- ❑ 323 Juan Gonzalez AU 50.00 15.00
- ❑ 324 Ken Griffey Jr. AU 150.00 45.00
- ❑ 325 Rich Harden AU 25.00 7.50
- ❑ 326 Pat Burrell AU 40.00 12.00
- ❑ 327 Mark Teixeira AU 40.00 12.00
- ❑ 328 Roy Oswalt AU 40.00 12.00
- ❑ 329 Miguel Tejada AU 40.00 12.00
- ❑ 330 Mike Hampton AU 40.00 12.00
- ❑ 331 Mike Piazza AU 200.00 60.00
- ❑ 332 Nolan Ryan AU 150.00 45.00
- ❑ 333 Orlando Hernandez AU 40.00 12.00
- ❑ 334 Paul Lo Duca AU 40.00 12.00
- ❑ 335 Roberto Alomar AU 50.00 15.00
- ❑ 336 Rocco Baldelli AU 40.00 12.00
- ❑ 337 Trevor Hoffman AU 50.00 15.00
- ❑ 338 Tom Glavine AU 50.00 15.00
- ❑ 339 Tom Seaver AU 60.00 18.00
- ❑ 340 Mark Prior AU 100.00 30.00
- ❑ 341 Shingo Takatsu RC 3.00 .90
- ❑ 342 Franklyn Gracesqui RC .60 .18
- ❑ 343 Angel Chavez RC 1.00 .30
- ❑ 344 Jorge Sequea RC 1.00 .30
- ❑ 345 David Aardsma RC 1.00 .30
- ❑ 346 Ramon Ramirez RC 1.00 .30
- ❑ 347 Lino Urdaneta RC 1.00 .30
- ❑ 348 Orlando Rodriguez RC 1.00 .30
- ❑ 349 Jason Szuminski RC .60 .18
- ❑ 350 Luis A. Gonzalez RC 1.50 .45
- ❑ 351 John Gall RC 1.50 .45
- ❑ 352 Kevin Cave RC 1.50 .45
- ❑ 353 Chris Oxspring RC 1.50 .45
- ❑ 354 Freddy Guzman RC 1.00 .30
- ❑ 355 Jeff Bennett RC 1.00 .30
- ❑ 356 Jorge Vasquez RC 1.00 .30
- ❑ 357 Merkin Valdez RC 3.00 .90
- ❑ 358 Tim Hamulack RC .60 .18
- ❑ 359 Hector Gimenez RC .60 .18
- ❑ 360 Jerry Gil RC 1.00 .30
- ❑ 361 Ryan Wing RC 1.00 .30
- ❑ 362 Shawn Hill RC 1.00 .30
- ❑ 363 Jason Bartlett RC 1.50 .45
- ❑ 364 Renyel Pinto RC 1.50 .45
- ❑ 365 Carlos Vasquez RC 1.50 .45
- ❑ 366 Mike Vento RC 1.50 .45
- ❑ 367 Casey Daigle RC 1.00 .30
- ❑ 368 Chad Bentz RC 1.00 .30
- ❑ 369 Chris Saenz RC .60 .18
- ❑ 370 Shawn Camp RC .60 .18
- ❑ 371 Carlos Hines RC 1.00 .30
- ❑ 372 Edwin Moreno RC 1.00 .30
- ❑ 373 Michael Wuertz RC 1.50 .45
- ❑ 374 Aarom Baldiris RC 1.50 .45
- ❑ 375 Ronny Cedeno RC 1.00 .30
- ❑ 376 Akinori Otsuka RC 4.00 1.20
- ❑ 377 Jose Capellan RC 5.00 1.50
- ❑ 378 Justin Germano RC 1.00 .30
- ❑ 379 Justin Knoedler RC 1.00 .30
- ❑ 380 Mariano Gomez RC 1.00 .30
- ❑ 381 Fernando Nieve RC 1.00 .30
- ❑ 382 Scott Proctor RC 5.00 1.50
- ❑ 383 Roman Colon RC .60 .18
- ❑ 384 Onil Joseph RC 1.00 .30
- ❑ 385 Eddy Rodriguez RC 1.50 .45
- ❑ 386 Enemencio Pacheco RC 1.00 .30
- ❑ 387 William Bergolla RC 1.00 .30
- ❑ 388 Ivan Ochoa RC 1.00 .30
- ❑ 389 Rusty Tucker RC 1.50 .45
- ❑ 390 Roberto Novoa RC 1.50 .45
- ❑ S38 Ichiro Suzuki Promo

1988 Score Rookie/Traded

	Nm-Mt	Ex-Mt
COMP.FACT.SET (110)	40.00	16.00
❑ 1T Jack Clark	.75	.30
❑ 2T Danny Jackson	.25	.10
❑ 3T Brett Butler	.75	.30
❑ 4T Kurt Stillwell	.25	.10
❑ 5T Tom Brunansky	.25	.10
❑ 6T Dennis Lamp	.25	.10
❑ 7T Jose DeLeon	.25	.10
❑ 8T Tom Herr	.25	.10
❑ 9T Keith Moreland	.25	.10
❑ 10T Kirk Gibson	2.00	.80
❑ 11T Bud Black	.25	.10
❑ 12T Rafael Ramirez	.25	.10
❑ 13T Luis Salazar	.25	.10
❑ 14T Goose Gossage	.75	.30
❑ 15T Bob Welch	.75	.30
❑ 16T Vance Law	.25	.10
❑ 17T Ray Knight	.75	.30
❑ 18T Dan Quisenberry	.25	.10
❑ 19T Don Slaught	.25	.10
❑ 20T Lee Smith	.75	.30
❑ 21T Rick Cerone	.25	.10
❑ 22T Pat Tabler	.25	.10
❑ 23T Larry McWilliams	.25	.10
❑ 24T Ricky Horton	.25	.10
❑ 25T Graig Nettles	.75	.30
❑ 26T Dan Petry	.25	.10
❑ 27T Jose Rijo	.75	.30
❑ 28T Chili Davis	.75	.30
❑ 29T Dickie Thon	.25	.10
❑ 30T Mackey Sasser	.25	.10
❑ 31T Mickey Tettleton	.25	.10
❑ 32T Rick Dempsey	.25	.10
❑ 33T Ron Hassey	.25	.10
❑ 34T Phil Bradley	.25	.10
❑ 35T Jay Howell	.25	.10
❑ 36T Bill Buckner	.75	.30
❑ 37T Alfredo Griffin	.25	.10
❑ 38T Gary Pettis	.25	.10
❑ 39T Calvin Schiraldi	.25	.10
❑ 40T John Candelaria	.25	.10
❑ 41T Joe Orsulak	.25	.10
❑ 42T Willie Upshaw	.25	.10
❑ 43T Herm Winningham	.25	.10
❑ 44T Ron Kittle	.25	.10
❑ 45T Bob Dernier	.25	.10
❑ 46T Steve Balboni	.25	.10
❑ 47T Steve Shields	.25	.10
❑ 48T Henry Cotto	.25	.10
❑ 49T Dave Henderson	.25	.10
❑ 50T Dave Parker	.75	.30
❑ 51T Mike Young	.25	.10
❑ 52T Mark Salas	.25	.10
❑ 53T Mike Davis	.25	.10
❑ 54T Rafael Santana	.25	.10
❑ 55T Don Baylor	.75	.30
❑ 56T Dan Pasqua	.25	.10
❑ 57T Ernest Riles	.25	.10
❑ 58T Glenn Hubbard	.25	.10
❑ 59T Mike Smithson	.25	.10
❑ 60T Richard Dotson	.25	.10
❑ 61T Jerry Reuss	.25	.10
❑ 62T Mike Jackson	.75	.30
❑ 63T Floyd Bannister	.25	.10
❑ 64T Jesse Orosco	.25	.10
❑ 65T Larry Parrish	.25	.10
❑ 66T Jeff Bittiger	.25	.10
❑ 67T Ray Hayward	.25	.10
❑ 68T Ricky Jordan XRC	.75	.30
❑ 69T Tommy Gregg	.25	.10
❑ 70T Brady Anderson XRC	1.25	.50
❑ 71T Jeff Montgomery	.75	.30
❑ 72T Darryl Hamilton XRC	.75	.30
❑ 73T Cecil Espy	.25	.10
❑ 74T Greg Briley XRC	.25	.10
❑ 75T Joey Meyer	.25	.10
❑ 76T Mike Macfarlane XRC	.75	.30
❑ 77T Oswald Peraza	.25	.10
❑ 78T Jack Armstrong XRC	.25	.10
❑ 79T Don Heinkel	.25	.10
❑ 80T Mark Grace XRC	8.00	3.20
❑ 81T Steve Curry	.25	.10
❑ 82T Damon Berryhill XRC	.75	.30
❑ 83T Steve Ellsworth	.25	.10
❑ 84T Pete Smith XRC*	.25	.10
❑ 85T Jack McDowell XRC	1.25	.50
❑ 86T Rob Dibble XRC	2.00	.80
❑ 87T Bryan Harvey UER (Games Pitched 47, Innings 5) XRC	.75	.30
❑ 88T John Dopson	.25	.10
❑ 89T Dave Gallagher	.25	.10
❑ 90T Todd Stottlemyre XRC	.75	.30
❑ 91T Mike Schooler	.25	.10
❑ 92T Don Gordon	.25	.10
❑ 93T Sil Campusano	.25	.10
❑ 94T Jeff Pico	.25	.10
❑ 95T Jay Buhner XRC	2.00	.80
❑ 96T Nelson Santovenia	.25	.10
❑ 97T Al Leiter XRC*	3.00	1.20
❑ 98T Luis Alicea XRC	.75	.30
❑ 99T Pat Borders XRC	.75	.30
❑ 100T Chris Sabo XRC	1.25	.50
❑ 101T Tim Belcher	.25	.10
❑ 102T Walt Weiss XRC*	1.25	.50
❑ 103T Craig Biggio XRC	8.00	3.20
❑ 104T Don August	.25	.10
❑ 105T Roberto Alomar XRC	20.00	8.00
❑ 106T Todd Burns	.25	.10
❑ 107T John Costello	.25	.10
❑ 108T Melido Perez XRC*	.75	.30
❑ 109T Darrin Jackson XRC	.25	.10
❑ 110T O.Destrade XRC	.25	.10

1989 Score Rookie/Traded

	Nm-Mt	Ex-Mt
COMP.FACT.SET (110)	15.00	6.00
❑ 1T Rafael Palmeiro	.25	.10
❑ 2T Nolan Ryan	1.50	.60
❑ 3T Jack Clark	.10	.04
❑ 4T Dave LaPoint	.05	.02
❑ 5T Mike Moore	.05	.02
❑ 6T Pete O'Brien	.05	.02
❑ 7T Jeffrey Leonard	.05	.02
❑ 8T Rob Murphy	.05	.02
❑ 9T Tom Herr	.05	.02
❑ 10T Claudell Washington	.05	.02
❑ 11T Mike Pagliarulo	.05	.02
❑ 12T Steve Lake	.05	.02
❑ 13T Spike Owen	.05	.02
❑ 14T Andy Hawkins	.05	.02
❑ 15T Todd Benzinger	.05	.02
❑ 16T Mookie Wilson	.10	.04
❑ 17T Bert Blyleven	.10	.04
❑ 18T Jeff Treadway	.05	.02
❑ 19T Bruce Hurst	.05	.02
❑ 20T Steve Sax	.05	.02
❑ 21T Juan Samuel	.05	.02
❑ 22T Jesse Barfield	.10	.04
❑ 23T Carmen Castillo	.05	.02
❑ 24T Terry Leach	.05	.02
❑ 25T Mark Langston	.05	.02
❑ 26T Eric King	.05	.02
❑ 27T Steve Balboni	.05	.02
❑ 28T Len Dykstra	.10	.04
❑ 29T Keith Moreland	.05	.02
❑ 30T Terry Kennedy	.05	.02
❑ 31T Eddie Murray	.25	.10
❑ 32T Mitch Williams	.05	.02
❑ 33T Jeff Parrett	.05	.02
❑ 34T Wally Backman	.05	.02
❑ 35T Julio Franco	.10	.04
❑ 36T Lance Parrish	.10	.04
❑ 37T Nick Esasky	.05	.02
❑ 38T Luis Polonia	.05	.02
❑ 39T Kevin Gross	.05	.02
❑ 40T John Dopson	.05	.02
❑ 41T Willie Randolph	.10	.04
❑ 42T Jim Clancy	.05	.02
❑ 43T Tracy Jones	.05	.02
❑ 44T Phil Bradley	.05	.02
❑ 45T Milt Thompson	.05	.02
❑ 46T Chris James	.05	.02
❑ 47T Scott Fletcher	.05	.02
❑ 48T Kal Daniels	.05	.02
❑ 49T Steve Bedrosian	.05	.02
❑ 50T Rickey Henderson	.25	.10
❑ 51T Dion James	.05	.02
❑ 52T Tim Leary	.05	.02
❑ 53T Roger McDowell	.05	.02
❑ 54T Mel Hall	.05	.02
❑ 55T Dickie Thon	.05	.02
❑ 56T Zane Smith	.05	.02
❑ 57T Danny Heep	.05	.02
❑ 58T Bob McClure	.05	.02
❑ 59T Brian Holton	.05	.02
❑ 60T Randy Ready	.05	.02
❑ 61T Bob Melvin	.05	.02
❑ 62T Harold Baines	.10	.04
❑ 63T Lance McCullers	.05	.02
❑ 64T Jody Davis	.05	.02
❑ 65T Darrell Evans	.10	.04
❑ 66T Joel Youngblood	.05	.02
❑ 67T Frank Viola	.10	.04
❑ 68T Mike Aldrete	.05	.02
❑ 69T Greg Cadaret	.05	.02
❑ 70T John Kruk	.10	.04
❑ 71T Pat Sheridan	.05	.02
❑ 72T Oddibe McDowell	.05	.02
❑ 73T Tom Brookens	.05	.02
❑ 74T Bob Boone	.10	.04
❑ 75T Walt Terrell	.05	.02
❑ 76T Joel Skinner	.05	.02
❑ 77T Randy Johnson	2.50	.80
❑ 78T Felix Fermin	.05	.02
❑ 79T Rick Mahler	.05	.02
❑ 80T Richard Dotson	.05	.02
❑ 81T Cris Carpenter RC *	.10	.04
❑ 82T Bill Spiers RC	.25	.10
❑ 83T Junior Felix RC	.10	.04
❑ 84T Joe Girardi RC	.40	.16
❑ 85T Jerome Walton RC	.25	.10
❑ 86T Greg Litton	.05	.02
❑ 87T Greg W.Harris RC	.10	.04
❑ 88T Jim Abbott RC*	.50	.20
❑ 89T Kevin Brown	.25	.10
❑ 90T John Wetteland RC	.40	.16
❑ 91T Gary Wayne	.05	.02
❑ 92T Rich Monteleone	.05	.02
❑ 93T Bob Geren RC	.05	.02
❑ 94T Clay Parker	.05	.02
❑ 95T Steve Finley RC	.50	.20
❑ 96T Gregg Olson RC	.25	.10
❑ 97T Ken Patterson	.05	.02

Card	Nm-Mt	Ex-Mt
❑ 98T Ken Hill RC	.25	.10
❑ 99T Scott Scudder RC	.10	.04
❑ 100T Ken Griffey Jr. RC	8.00	3.20
❑ 101T Jeff Brantley RC	.25	.10
❑ 102T Donn Pall	.05	.02
❑ 103T Carlos Martinez RC	.10	.04
❑ 104T Joe Oliver RC	.25	.10
❑ 105T Omar Vizquel RC	.75	.30
❑ 106T Joey Belle RC	1.00	.40
❑ 107T Kenny Rogers RC	.75	.30
❑ 108T Mark Carreon	.05	.02
❑ 109T Rolando Roomes	.05	.02
❑ 110T Pete Harnisch RC	.25	.10

1990 Score

	Nm-Mt	Ex-Mt
COMPLETE SET (704)	15.00	4.50
COMP.RETAIL SET (704)	15.00	4.50
COMP.HOBBY SET (714)	15.00	4.50

Card	Nm-Mt	Ex-Mt
❑ 1 Don Mattingly	.60	.18
❑ 2 Cal Ripken	.75	.23
❑ 3 Dwight Evans	.10	.03
❑ 4 Barry Bonds	.60	.18
❑ 5 Kevin McReynolds	.05	.02
❑ 6 Ozzie Guillen	.05	.02
❑ 7 Terry Kennedy	.05	.02
❑ 8 Bryan Harvey	.05	.02
❑ 9 Alan Trammell	.10	.03
❑ 10 Cory Snyder	.05	.02
❑ 11 Jody Reed	.05	.02
❑ 12 Roberto Alomar	.15	.04
❑ 13 Pedro Guerrero	.05	.02
❑ 14 Gary Redus	.05	.02
❑ 15 Marty Barrett	.05	.02
❑ 16 Ricky Jordan	.05	.02
❑ 17 Joe Magrane	.05	.02
❑ 18 Sid Fernandez	.05	.02
❑ 19 Richard Dotson	.05	.02
❑ 20 Jack Clark	.10	.03
❑ 21 Bob Walk	.05	.02
❑ 22 Ron Karkovice	.05	.02
❑ 23 Lenny Harris	.05	.02
❑ 24 Phil Bradley	.05	.02
❑ 25 Andres Galarraga	.10	.03
❑ 26 Brian Downing	.05	.02
❑ 27 Dave Martinez	.05	.02
❑ 28 Eric King	.05	.02
❑ 29 Barry Lyons	.05	.02
❑ 30 Dave Schmidt	.05	.02
❑ 31 Mike Boddicker	.05	.02
❑ 32 Tom Foley	.05	.02
❑ 33 Brady Anderson	.10	.03
❑ 34 Jim Presley	.05	.02
❑ 35 Lance Parrish	.05	.02
❑ 36 Von Hayes	.05	.02
❑ 37 Lee Smith	.10	.03
❑ 38 Herm Winningham	.05	.02
❑ 39 Alejandro Pena	.05	.02
❑ 40 Mike Scott	.05	.02
❑ 41 Joe Orsulak	.05	.02
❑ 42 Rafael Ramirez	.05	.02
❑ 43 Gerald Young	.05	.02
❑ 44 Dick Schofield	.05	.02
❑ 45 Dave Smith	.05	.02
❑ 46 Dave Magadan	.05	.02
❑ 47 Dennis Martinez	.10	.03
❑ 48 Greg Minton	.05	.02
❑ 49 Milt Thompson	.05	.02
❑ 50 Orel Hershiser	.10	.03
❑ 51 Bip Roberts	.05	.02
❑ 52 Jerry Browne	.05	.02
❑ 53 Bob Ojeda	.05	.02
❑ 54 Fernando Valenzuela	.10	.03
❑ 55 Matt Nokes	.05	.02
❑ 56 Brook Jacoby	.05	.02
❑ 57 Frank Tanana	.05	.02
❑ 58 Scott Fletcher	.05	.02
❑ 59 Ron Oester	.05	.02
❑ 60 Bob Boone	.10	.03
❑ 61 Dan Gladden	.05	.02
❑ 62 Darnell Coles	.05	.02
❑ 63 Gregg Olson	.10	.03
❑ 64 Todd Burns	.05	.02
❑ 65 Todd Benzinger	.05	.02
❑ 66 Dale Murphy	.25	.07
❑ 67 Mike Flanagan	.05	.02
❑ 68 Jose Oquendo	.05	.02
❑ 69 Cecil Espy	.05	.02
❑ 70 Chris Sabo	.05	.02
❑ 71 Shane Rawley	.05	.02
❑ 72 Tom Brunansky	.05	.02
❑ 73 Vance Law	.05	.02
❑ 74 B.J. Surhoff	.10	.03
❑ 75 Lou Whitaker	.10	.03
❑ 76 Ken Caminiti UER Euclid and Ohio should be Hanford and California	.10	.03
❑ 77 Nelson Liriano	.05	.02
❑ 78 Tommy Gregg	.05	.02
❑ 79 Don Slaught	.05	.02
❑ 80 Eddie Murray	.25	.07
❑ 81 Joe Boever	.05	.02
❑ 82 Charlie Leibrandt	.05	.02
❑ 83 Jose Lind	.05	.02
❑ 84 Tony Phillips	.05	.02
❑ 85 Mitch Webster	.05	.02
❑ 86 Dan Plesac	.05	.02
❑ 87 Rick Mahler	.05	.02
❑ 88 Steve Lyons	.05	.02
❑ 89 Tony Fernandez	.05	.02
❑ 90 Ryne Sandberg	.40	.12
❑ 91 Nick Esasky	.05	.02
❑ 92 Luis Salazar	.05	.02
❑ 93 Pete Incaviglia	.05	.02
❑ 94 Ivan Calderon	.05	.02
❑ 95 Jeff Treadway	.05	.02
❑ 96 Kurt Stillwell	.05	.02
❑ 97 Gary Sheffield	.25	.07
❑ 98 Jeffrey Leonard	.05	.02
❑ 99 Andres Thomas	.05	.02
❑ 100 Roberto Kelly	.05	.02
❑ 101 Alvaro Espinoza	.05	.02
❑ 102 Greg Gagne	.05	.02
❑ 103 John Farrell	.05	.02
❑ 104 Willie Wilson	.05	.02
❑ 105 Glenn Braggs	.05	.02
❑ 106 Chet Lemon	.05	.02
❑ 107A Jamie Moyer ERR (Scintilating)	.10	.03
❑ 107B Jamie Moyer COR (Scintillating)	.50	.15
❑ 108 Chuck Crim	.05	.02
❑ 109 Dave Valle	.05	.02
❑ 110 Walt Weiss	.05	.02
❑ 111 Larry Sheets	.05	.02
❑ 112 Don Robinson	.05	.02
❑ 113 Danny Heep	.05	.02
❑ 114 Carmelo Martinez	.05	.02
❑ 115 Dave Gallagher	.05	.02
❑ 116 Mike LaValliere	.05	.02
❑ 117 Bob McClure	.05	.02
❑ 118 Rene Gonzales	.05	.02
❑ 119 Mark Parent	.05	.02
❑ 120 Wally Joyner	.10	.03
❑ 121 Mark Gubicza	.05	.02
❑ 122 Tony Pena	.05	.02
❑ 123 Carmelo Castillo	.05	.02
❑ 124 Howard Johnson	.05	.02
❑ 125 Steve Sax	.05	.02
❑ 126 Tim Belcher	.05	.02
❑ 127 Tim Burke	.05	.02
❑ 128 Al Newman	.05	.02
❑ 129 Dennis Rasmussen	.05	.02
❑ 130 Doug Jones	.05	.02
❑ 131 Fred Lynn	.05	.02
❑ 132 Jeff Hamilton	.05	.02
❑ 133 German Gonzalez	.05	.02
❑ 134 John Morris	.05	.02
❑ 135 Dave Parker	.10	.03
❑ 136 Gary Pettis	.05	.02
❑ 137 Dennis Boyd	.05	.02
❑ 138 Candy Maldonado	.05	.02
❑ 139 Rick Cerone	.05	.02
❑ 140 George Brett	.60	.18
❑ 141 Dave Clark	.05	.02
❑ 142 Dickie Thon	.05	.02
❑ 143 Junior Ortiz	.05	.02
❑ 144 Don August	.05	.02
❑ 145 Gary Gaetti	.10	.03
❑ 146 Kirt Manwaring	.05	.02
❑ 147 Jeff Reed	.05	.02
❑ 148 Jose Alvarez	.05	.02
❑ 149 Mike Schooler	.05	.02
❑ 150 Mark Grace	.15	.04
❑ 151 Geronimo Berroa	.05	.02
❑ 152 Barry Jones	.05	.02
❑ 153 Geno Petralli	.05	.02
❑ 154 Jim Deshaies	.05	.02
❑ 155 Barry Larkin	.15	.04
❑ 156 Alfredo Griffin	.05	.02
❑ 157 Tom Henke	.05	.02
❑ 158 Mike Jeffcoat	.05	.02
❑ 159 Bob Welch	.05	.02
❑ 160 Julio Franco	.10	.03
❑ 161 Henry Cotto	.05	.02
❑ 162 Terry Steinbach	.05	.02
❑ 163 Damon Berryhill	.05	.02
❑ 164 Tim Crews	.05	.02
❑ 165 Tom Browning	.05	.02
❑ 166 Fred Manrique	.05	.02
❑ 167 Harold Reynolds	.10	.03
❑ 168A Ron Hassey ERR (27 on back)	.05	.02
❑ 168B Ron Hassey COR (24 on back)	.50	.15
❑ 169 Shawon Dunston	.05	.02
❑ 170 Bobby Bonilla	.10	.03
❑ 171 Tommy Herr	.05	.02
❑ 172 Mike Heath	.05	.02
❑ 173 Rich Gedman	.05	.02
❑ 174 Bill Ripken	.05	.02
❑ 175 Pete O'Brien	.05	.02
❑ 176A L.McClendon ERR Uniform number on back listed as 1	.05	.02
❑ 176B L.McClendon COR Uniform number on back listed as 10	.50	.15
❑ 177 Brian Holton	.05	.02
❑ 178 Jeff Blauser	.05	.02
❑ 179 Jim Eisenreich	.05	.02
❑ 180 Bert Blyleven	.10	.03
❑ 181 Rob Murphy	.05	.02
❑ 182 Bill Doran	.05	.02
❑ 183 Curt Ford	.05	.02
❑ 184 Mike Henneman	.05	.02
❑ 185 Eric Davis	.10	.03
❑ 186 Lance McCullers	.05	.02
❑ 187 Steve Davis	.05	.02
❑ 188 Bill Wegman	.05	.02
❑ 189 Brian Harper	.05	.02
❑ 190 Mike Moore	.05	.02
❑ 191 Dale Mohorcic	.05	.02
❑ 192 Tim Wallach	.05	.02
❑ 193 Keith Hernandez	.10	.03
❑ 194 Dave Righetti	.05	.02
❑ 195A B.Saberhagen ERR Joke	.10	.03
❑ 195B B.Saberhagen COR Joker	.50	.15
❑ 196 Paul Kilgus	.05	.02
❑ 197 Bud Black	.05	.02
❑ 198 Juan Samuel	.05	.02
❑ 199 Kevin Seitzer	.05	.02
❑ 200 Darryl Strawberry	.10	.03
❑ 201 Dave Stieb	.10	.03
❑ 202 Charlie Hough	.10	.03
❑ 203 Jack Morris	.10	.03

❑ 204	Rance Mulliniks	.05	.02
❑ 205	Alvin Davis	.05	.02
❑ 206	Jack Howell	.05	.02
❑ 207	Ken Patterson	.05	.02
❑ 208	Terry Pendleton	.10	.03
❑ 209	Craig Lefferts	.05	.02
❑ 210	Kevin Brown UER (First mention of '89 Rangers should be '88)	.10	.03
❑ 211	Dan Petry	.05	.02
❑ 212	Dave Leiper	.05	.02
❑ 213	Daryl Boston	.05	.02
❑ 214	Kevin Hickey	.05	.02
❑ 215	Mike Krukow	.05	.02
❑ 216	Terry Francona	.10	.03
❑ 217	Kirk McCaskill	.05	.02
❑ 218	Scott Bailes	.05	.02
❑ 219	Bob Forsch	.05	.02
❑ 220A	Mike Aldrete ERR (25 on back)	.05	.02
❑ 220B	Mike Aldrete COR (24 on back)	.50	.15
❑ 221	Steve Buechele	.05	.02
❑ 222	Jesse Barfield	.05	.02
❑ 223	Juan Berenguer	.05	.02
❑ 224	Andy McGaffigan	.05	.02
❑ 225	Pete Smith	.05	.02
❑ 226	Mike Witt	.05	.02
❑ 227	Jay Howell	.05	.02
❑ 228	Scott Bradley	.05	.02
❑ 229	Jerome Walton	.05	.02
❑ 230	Greg Swindell	.05	.02
❑ 231	Atlee Hammaker	.05	.02
❑ 232A	Mike Devereaux ERR (RF on front)	.05	.02
❑ 232B	M.Devereaux COR CF on front	.50	.15
❑ 233	Ken Hill	.10	.03
❑ 234	Craig Worthington	.05	.02
❑ 235	Scott Terry	.05	.02
❑ 236	Brett Butler	.10	.03
❑ 237	Doyle Alexander	.05	.02
❑ 238	Dave Anderson	.05	.02
❑ 239	Bob Milacki	.05	.02
❑ 240	Dwight Smith	.05	.02
❑ 241	Otis Nixon	.05	.02
❑ 242	Pat Tabler	.05	.02
❑ 243	Derek Lilliquist	.05	.02
❑ 244	Danny Tartabull	.05	.02
❑ 245	Wade Boggs	.15	.04
❑ 246	Scott Garrelts (Should say Relief Pitcher on front)	.05	.02
❑ 247	Spike Owen	.05	.02
❑ 248	Norm Charlton	.05	.02
❑ 249	Gerald Perry	.05	.02
❑ 250	Nolan Ryan	1.00	.30
❑ 251	Kevin Gross	.05	.02
❑ 252	Randy Milligan	.05	.02
❑ 253	Mike LaCoss	.05	.02
❑ 254	Dave Bergman	.05	.02
❑ 255	Tony Gwynn	.30	.09
❑ 256	Felix Fermin	.05	.02
❑ 257	Greg W. Harris	.05	.02
❑ 258	Junior Felix	.05	.02
❑ 259	Mark Davis	.05	.02
❑ 260	Vince Coleman	.05	.02
❑ 261	Paul Gibson	.05	.02
❑ 262	Mitch Williams	.05	.02
❑ 263	Jeff Russell	.05	.02
❑ 264	Omar Vizquel	.25	.07
❑ 265	Andre Dawson	.10	.03
❑ 266	Storm Davis	.05	.02
❑ 267	Guillermo Hernandez	.05	.02
❑ 268	Mike Felder	.05	.02
❑ 269	Tom Candiotti	.05	.02
❑ 270	Bruce Hurst	.05	.02
❑ 271	Fred McGriff	.25	.07
❑ 272	Glenn Davis	.05	.02
❑ 273	John Franco	.10	.03
❑ 274	Rich Yett	.05	.02
❑ 275	Craig Biggio	.15	.04
❑ 276	Gene Larkin	.05	.02
❑ 277	Rob Dibble	.10	.03
❑ 278	Randy Bush	.05	.02
❑ 279	Kevin Bass	.05	.02
❑ 280A	Bo Jackson ERR (Watham)	.25	.07
❑ 280B	Bo Jackson COR (Wathan)	.75	.23
❑ 281	Wally Backman	.05	.02
❑ 282	Larry Andersen	.05	.02
❑ 283	Chris Bosio	.05	.02
❑ 284	Juan Agosto	.05	.02
❑ 285	Ozzie Smith	.40	.12
❑ 286	George Bell	.05	.02
❑ 287	Rex Hudler	.05	.02
❑ 288	Pat Borders	.05	.02
❑ 289	Danny Jackson	.05	.02
❑ 290	Carlton Fisk	.15	.04
❑ 291	Tracy Jones	.05	.02
❑ 292	Allan Anderson	.05	.02
❑ 293	Johnny Ray	.05	.02
❑ 294	Lee Guetterman	.05	.02
❑ 295	Paul O'Neill	.15	.04
❑ 296	Carney Lansford	.10	.03
❑ 297	Tom Brookens	.05	.02
❑ 298	Claudell Washington	.05	.02
❑ 299	Hubie Brooks	.05	.02
❑ 300	Will Clark	.25	.07
❑ 301	Kenny Rogers	.10	.03
❑ 302	Darrell Evans	.10	.03
❑ 303	Greg Briley	.05	.02
❑ 304	Donn Pall	.05	.02
❑ 305	Teddy Higuera	.05	.02
❑ 306	Dan Pasqua	.05	.02
❑ 307	Dave Winfield	.10	.03
❑ 308	Dennis Powell	.05	.02
❑ 309	Jose DeLeon	.05	.02
❑ 310	Roger Clemens UER (Dominate, should say dominant)	.50	.15
❑ 311	Melido Perez	.05	.02
❑ 312	Devon White	.10	.03
❑ 313	Dwight Gooden	.10	.03
❑ 314	Carlos Martinez	.05	.02
❑ 315	Dennis Eckersley	.10	.03
❑ 316	Clay Parker UER (Height 6'11")	.05	.02
❑ 317	Rick Honeycutt	.05	.02
❑ 318	Tim Laudner	.05	.02
❑ 319	Joe Carter	.10	.03
❑ 320	Robin Yount	.40	.12
❑ 321	Felix Jose	.05	.02
❑ 322	Mickey Tettleton	.05	.02
❑ 323	Mike Gallego	.05	.02
❑ 324	Edgar Martinez	.15	.04
❑ 325	Dave Henderson	.05	.02
❑ 326	Chili Davis	.10	.03
❑ 327	Steve Balboni	.05	.02
❑ 328	Jody Davis	.05	.02
❑ 329	Shawn Hillegas	.05	.02
❑ 330	Jim Abbott	.15	.04
❑ 331	John Dopson	.05	.02
❑ 332	Mark Williamson	.05	.02
❑ 333	Jeff D. Robinson	.05	.02
❑ 334	John Smiley	.05	.02
❑ 335	Bobby Thigpen	.05	.02
❑ 336	Garry Templeton	.05	.02
❑ 337	Marvell Wynne	.05	.02
❑ 338A	Ken Griffey Sr. ERR (Uniform number on back listed as 25)	.10	.03
❑ 338B	Ken Griffey Sr. COR (Uniform number on back listed as 30)	.50	.15
❑ 339	Steve Finley	.10	.03
❑ 340	Ellis Burks	.15	.04
❑ 341	Frank Williams	.05	.02
❑ 342	Mike Morgan	.05	.02
❑ 343	Kevin Mitchell	.05	.02
❑ 344	Joel Youngblood	.05	.02
❑ 345	Mike Greenwell	.05	.02
❑ 346	Glenn Wilson	.05	.02
❑ 347	John Costello	.05	.02
❑ 348	Wes Gardner	.05	.02
❑ 349	Jeff Ballard	.05	.02
❑ 350	Mark Thurmond UER (ERA is 192, should be 1.92)	.05	.02
❑ 351	Randy Myers	.10	.03
❑ 352	Shawn Abner	.05	.02
❑ 353	Jesse Orosco	.05	.02
❑ 354	Greg Walker	.05	.02
❑ 355	Pete Harnisch	.05	.02
❑ 356	Steve Farr	.05	.02
❑ 357	Dave LaPoint	.05	.02
❑ 358	Willie Fraser	.05	.02
❑ 359	Mickey Hatcher	.05	.02
❑ 360	Rickey Henderson	.25	.07
❑ 361	Mike Fitzgerald	.05	.02
❑ 362	Bill Schroeder	.05	.02
❑ 363	Mark Carreon	.05	.02
❑ 364	Ron Jones	.05	.02
❑ 365	Jeff Montgomery	.10	.03
❑ 366	Bill Krueger	.05	.02
❑ 367	John Cangelosi	.05	.02
❑ 368	Jose Gonzalez	.05	.02
❑ 369	Greg Hibbard RC	.10	.03
❑ 370	John Smoltz	.25	.07
❑ 371	Jeff Brantley	.05	.02
❑ 372	Frank White	.10	.03
❑ 373	Ed Whitson	.05	.02
❑ 374	Willie McGee	.10	.03
❑ 375	Jose Canseco	.25	.07
❑ 376	Randy Ready	.05	.02
❑ 377	Don Aase	.05	.02
❑ 378	Tony Armas	.05	.02
❑ 379	Steve Bedrosian	.05	.02
❑ 380	Chuck Finley	.10	.03
❑ 381	Kent Hrbek	.10	.03
❑ 382	Jim Gantner	.05	.02
❑ 383	Mel Hall	.05	.02
❑ 384	Mike Marshall	.05	.02
❑ 385	Mark McGwire	.60	.18
❑ 386	Wayne Tolleson	.05	.02
❑ 387	Brian Holman	.05	.02
❑ 388	John Wetteland	.25	.07
❑ 389	Darren Daulton	.10	.03
❑ 390	Rob Deer	.05	.02
❑ 391	John Moses	.05	.02
❑ 392	Todd Worrell	.05	.02
❑ 393	Chuck Cary	.05	.02
❑ 394	Stan Javier	.05	.02
❑ 395	Willie Randolph	.10	.03
❑ 396	Bill Buckner	.05	.02
❑ 397	Robby Thompson	.05	.02
❑ 398	Mike Scioscia	.05	.02
❑ 399	Lonnie Smith	.05	.02
❑ 400	Kirby Puckett	.25	.07
❑ 401	Mark Langston	.05	.02
❑ 402	Danny Darwin	.05	.02
❑ 403	Greg Maddux	.40	.12
❑ 404	Lloyd Moseby	.05	.02
❑ 405	Rafael Palmeiro	.15	.04
❑ 406	Chad Kreuter	.05	.02
❑ 407	Jimmy Key	.10	.03
❑ 408	Tim Birtsas	.05	.02
❑ 409	Tim Raines	.10	.03
❑ 410	Dave Stewart	.10	.03
❑ 411	Eric Yelding	.05	.02
❑ 412	Kent Anderson	.05	.02
❑ 413	Les Lancaster	.05	.02
❑ 414	Rick Dempsey	.05	.02
❑ 415	Randy Johnson	.50	.12
❑ 416	Gary Carter	.10	.03
❑ 417	Rolando Roomes	.05	.02
❑ 418	Dan Schatzeder	.05	.02
❑ 419	Bryn Smith	.05	.02
❑ 420	Ruben Sierra	.05	.02
❑ 421	Steve Jeltz	.05	.02
❑ 422	Ken Oberkfell	.05	.02
❑ 423	Sid Bream	.05	.02
❑ 424	Jim Clancy	.05	.02
❑ 425	Kelly Gruber	.05	.02
❑ 426	Rick Leach	.05	.02
❑ 427	Len Dykstra	.10	.03
❑ 428	Jeff Pico	.05	.02
❑ 429	John Cerutti	.05	.02
❑ 430	David Cone	.10	.03
❑ 431	Jeff Kunkel	.05	.02
❑ 432	Luis Aquino	.05	.02
❑ 433	Ernie Whitt	.05	.02
❑ 434	Bo Diaz	.05	.02
❑ 435	Steve Lake	.05	.02
❑ 436	Pat Perry	.05	.02
❑ 437	Mike Davis	.05	.02
❑ 438	Cecilio Guante	.05	.02

❑ 439 Duane Ward .05 .02
❑ 440 Andy Van Slyke .10 .03
❑ 441 Gene Nelson .05 .02
❑ 442 Luis Polonia .05 .02
❑ 443 Kevin Elster .05 .02
❑ 444 Keith Moreland .05 .02
❑ 445 Roger McDowell .05 .02
❑ 446 Ron Darling .05 .02
❑ 447 Ernest Riles .05 .02
❑ 448 Mookie Wilson .10 .03
❑ 449A Billy Spiers ERR .05 .02
(No birth year)
❑ 449B Billy Spiers COR .50 .15
(Born in 1966)
❑ 450 Rick Sutcliffe .10 .03
❑ 451 Nelson Santovenia .05 .02
❑ 452 Andy Allanson .05 .02
❑ 453 Bob Melvin .05 .02
❑ 454 Benito Santiago .10 .03
❑ 455 Jose Uribe .05 .02
❑ 456 Bill Landrum .05 .02
❑ 457 Bobby Witt .05 .02
❑ 458 Kevin Romine .05 .02
❑ 459 Lee Mazzilli .05 .02
❑ 460 Paul Molitor .15 .04
❑ 461 Ramon Martinez .05 .02
❑ 462 Frank DiPino .05 .02
❑ 463 Walt Terrell .05 .02
❑ 464 Bob Geren .05 .02
❑ 465 Rick Reuschel .05 .02
❑ 466 Mark Grant .05 .02
❑ 467 John Kruk .10 .03
❑ 468 Gregg Jefferies .10 .03
❑ 469 R.J. Reynolds .05 .02
❑ 470 Harold Baines .10 .03
❑ 471 Dennis Lamp .05 .02
❑ 472 Tom Gordon .10 .03
❑ 473 Terry Puhl .05 .02
❑ 474 Curt Wilkerson .05 .02
❑ 475 Dan Quisenberry .05 .02
❑ 476 Oddibe McDowell .05 .02
❑ 477A Zane Smith ERR .05 .02
(Career ERA .393)
❑ 477B Zane Smith COR .50 .15
(career ERA 3.93)
❑ 478 Franklin Stubbs .05 .02
❑ 479 Wallace Johnson .05 .02
❑ 480 Jay Tibbs .05 .02
❑ 481 Tom Glavine .15 .04
❑ 482 Manny Lee .05 .02
❑ 483 Joe Hesketh UER .05 .02
Says Rookiess on back, should say Rookies
❑ 484 Mike Bielecki .05 .02
❑ 485 Greg Brock .05 .02
❑ 486 Pascual Perez .05 .02
❑ 487 Kirk Gibson .10 .03
❑ 488 Scott Sanderson .05 .02
❑ 489 Domingo Ramos .05 .02
❑ 490 Kal Daniels .05 .02
❑ 491A David Wells ERR .10 .03
(Reverse negative photo on card back)
❑ 491B David Wells COR .50 .15
❑ 492 Jerry Reed .05 .02
❑ 493 Eric Show .05 .02
❑ 494 Mike Pagliarulo .05 .02
❑ 495 Ron Robinson .05 .02
❑ 496 Brad Komminsk .05 .02
❑ 497 Greg Litton .05 .02
❑ 498 Chris James .05 .02
❑ 499 Luis Quinones .05 .02
❑ 500 Frank Viola .05 .02
❑ 501 Tim Teufel UER .05 .02
(Twins '85, the s is lower case, should be upper case)
❑ 502 Terry Leach .05 .02
❑ 503 Matt Williams UER .10 .03
(Wearing 10 on front, listed as 9 on back)
❑ 504 Tim Leary .05 .02
❑ 505 Doug Drabek .05 .02
❑ 506 Mariano Duncan .05 .02
❑ 507 Charlie Hayes .05 .02
❑ 508 Joey Belle .15 .04
❑ 509 Pat Sheridan .05 .02
❑ 510 Mackey Sasser .05 .02
❑ 511 Jose Rijo .05 .02
❑ 512 Mike Smithson .05 .02
❑ 513 Gary Ward .05 .02
❑ 514 Dion James .05 .02
❑ 515 Jim Gott .05 .02
❑ 516 Drew Hall .05 .02
❑ 517 Doug Bair .05 .02
❑ 518 Scott Scudder .05 .02
❑ 519 Rick Aguilera .10 .03
❑ 520 Rafael Belliard .05 .02
❑ 521 Jay Buhner .10 .03
❑ 522 Jeff Reardon .10 .03
❑ 523 Steve Rosenberg .05 .02
❑ 524 Randy Velarde .05 .02
❑ 525 Jeff Musselman .05 .02
❑ 526 Bill Long .05 .02
❑ 527 Gary Wayne .05 .02
❑ 528 Dave Johnson (P) .05 .02
❑ 529 Ron Kittle .05 .02
❑ 530 Erik Hanson UER .05 .02
(5th line on back says seson, should say season)
❑ 531 Steve Wilson .05 .02
❑ 532 Joey Meyer .05 .02
❑ 533 Curt Young .05 .02
❑ 534 Kelly Downs .05 .02
❑ 535 Joe Girardi .15 .04
❑ 536 Lance Blankenship .05 .02
❑ 537 Greg Mathews .05 .02
❑ 538 Donell Nixon .05 .02
❑ 539 Mark Knudson .05 .02
❑ 540 Jeff Wetherby .05 .02
❑ 541 Darrin Jackson .05 .02
❑ 542 Terry Mulholland .05 .02
❑ 543 Eric Hetzel .05 .02
❑ 544 Rick Reed RC .25 .07
❑ 545 Dennis Cook .05 .02
❑ 546 Mike Jackson .05 .02
❑ 547 Brian Fisher .05 .02
❑ 548 Gene Harris .05 .02
❑ 549 Jeff King .05 .02
❑ 550 Dave Dravecky .25 .07
❑ 551 Randy Kutcher .05 .02
❑ 552 Mark Portugal .05 .02
❑ 553 Jim Corsi .05 .02
❑ 554 Todd Stottlemyre .10 .03
❑ 555 Scott Bankhead .05 .02
❑ 556 Ken Dayley .05 .02
❑ 557 Rick Wrona .05 .02
❑ 558 Sammy Sosa RC 5.00 1.50
❑ 559 Keith Miller .05 .02
❑ 560 Ken Griffey Jr. .75 .23
❑ 561A R.Sandberg HL ERR 8.00 2.40
Position on front listed as 3B
❑ 561B R.Sandberg HL COR .25 .07
❑ 562 Billy Hatcher .05 .02
❑ 563 Jay Bell .10 .03
❑ 564 Jack Daugherty .05 .02
❑ 565 Rich Monteleone .05 .02
❑ 566 Bo Jackson AS-MVP .10 .03
❑ 567 Tony Fossas .05 .02
❑ 568 Roy Smith .05 .02
❑ 569 Jaime Navarro .05 .02
❑ 570 Lance Johnson .05 .02
❑ 571 Mike Dyer RC .05 .02
❑ 572 Kevin Ritz .05 .02
❑ 573 Dave West .05 .02
❑ 574 Gary Mielke .05 .02
❑ 575 Scott Lusader .05 .02
❑ 576 Joe Oliver .05 .02
❑ 577 Sandy Alomar Jr. .10 .03
❑ 578 Andy Benes UER .10 .03
(Extra comma between day and year)
❑ 579 Tim Jones .05 .02
❑ 580 Randy McCament .05 .02
❑ 581 Curt Schilling 1.00 .30
❑ 582 John Orton RC .10 .03
❑ 583A Milt Cuyler ERR RC .10 .03
(998 games)
❑ 583B Milt Cuyler RC COR .50 .15
(98 games; the extra 9 was ghosted out and may still be visible)
❑ 584 Eric Anthony RC .10 .03
❑ 585 Greg Vaughn .05 .02
❑ 586 Deion Sanders .25 .07
❑ 587 Jose DeJesus .05 .02
❑ 588 Chip Hale .05 .02
❑ 589 John Olerud RC .50 .15
❑ 590 Steve Olin RC .25 .07
❑ 591 Marquis Grissom RC .40 .12
❑ 592 Moises Alou RC .75 .23
❑ 593 Mark Lemke .05 .02
❑ 594 Dean Palmer RC .25 .07
❑ 595 Robin Ventura .25 .07
❑ 596 Tino Martinez .25 .07
❑ 597 Mike Huff .05 .02
❑ 598 Scott Hemond RC .10 .03
❑ 599 Wally Whitehurst .05 .02
❑ 600 Todd Zeile .10 .03
❑ 601 Glenallen Hill .05 .02
❑ 602 Hal Morris .05 .02
❑ 603 Juan Bell .05 .02
❑ 604 Bobby Rose .05 .02
❑ 605 Matt Merullo .05 .02
❑ 606 Kevin Maas RC .25 .07
❑ 607 Randy Nosek .05 .02
❑ 608A Billy Bates .05 .02
(Text mentions 12 triples in tenth line)
❑ 608B Billy Bates .05 .02
(Text has no mention of triples)
❑ 609 Mike Stanton RC .25 .07
❑ 610 Mauro Gozzo .05 .02
❑ 611 Charles Nagy .05 .02
❑ 612 Scott Coolbaugh .05 .02
❑ 613 Jose Vizcaino RC .25 .07
❑ 614 Greg Smith .05 .02
❑ 615 Jeff Huson RC .10 .03
❑ 616 Mickey Weston .05 .02
❑ 617 John Pawlowski .05 .02
❑ 618A Joe Skalski ERR .05 .02
(27 on back)
❑ 618B Joe Skalski COR .50 .15
(67 on back)
❑ 619 Bernie Williams RC 1.00 .30
❑ 620 Shawn Holman .05 .02
❑ 621 Gary Eave .05 .02
❑ 622 Darrin Fletcher UER .10 .03
Elmherst, should be Elmhurst
❑ 623 Pat Combs .05 .02
❑ 624 Mike Blowers RC .10 .03
❑ 625 Kevin Appier .10 .03
❑ 626 Pat Austin .05 .02
❑ 627 Kelly Mann .05 .02
❑ 628 Matt Kinzer .05 .02
❑ 629 Chris Hammond RC .10 .03
❑ 630 Dean Wilkins .05 .02
❑ 631 Larry Walker RC UER 1.00 .30
Uniform number 55 on front and 33 on back; Home is Maple Ridge, not Maple River
❑ 632 Blaine Beatty .05 .02
❑ 633A Tommy Barrett ERR .05 .02
(29 on back)
❑ 633B Tommy Barrett COR .50 .15
(14 on back)
❑ 634 Stan Belinda RC .10 .03
❑ 635 Mike (Tex) Smith .05 .02
❑ 636 Hensley Meulens .05 .02
❑ 637 J.Gonzalez RC UER 1.50 .45
Sarasots on back, should be Sarasota
❑ 638 Lenny Webster RC .10 .03
❑ 639 Mark Gardner RC .10 .03
❑ 640 Tommy Greene RC .10 .03
❑ 641 Mike Hartley .05 .02
❑ 642 Phil Stephenson .05 .02
❑ 643 Kevin Mmahat .05 .02
❑ 644 Ed Whited .05 .02
❑ 645 Delino DeShields RC .25 .07
❑ 646 Kevin Blankenship .05 .02
❑ 647 Paul Sorrento RC .25 .07
❑ 648 Mike Roesler .05 .02
❑ 649 Jason Grimsley RC .10 .03

❑ 650 Dave Justice RC .50 .15
❑ 651 Scott Cooper RC .10 .03
❑ 652 Dave Eiland .05 .02
❑ 653 Mike Munoz .05 .02
❑ 654 Jeff Fischer .05 .02
❑ 655 Terry Jorgensen .05 .02
❑ 656 George Canale .05 .02
❑ 657 Brian DuBois UER .05 .02
(Misspelled Dubois on card)
❑ 658 Carlos Quintana .05 .02
❑ 659 Luis de los Santos .05 .02
❑ 660 Jerald Clark .05 .02
❑ 661 Donald Harris DC .05 .02
❑ 662 Paul Coleman DC RC .10 .03
❑ 663 Frank Thomas DC RC 2.00 .60
❑ 664 Brent Mayne DC RC .25 .07
❑ 665 Eddie Zosky DC RC .10 .03
❑ 666 Steve Hosey DC RC .10 .03
❑ 667 Scott Bryant DC .10 .03
❑ 668 Tom Goodwin DC RC .25 .07
❑ 669 Cal Eldred DC RC .25 .07
❑ 670 E.Cunningham DC RC .10 .03
❑ 671 Alan Zinter DC RC .10 .03
❑ 672 C.Knoblauch DC RC .40 .12
❑ 673 Kyle Abbott DC .05 .02
❑ 674 Roger Salkeld DC RC .05 .02
❑ 675 M.Vaughn DC RC .50 .15
❑ 676 Keith (Kiki) Jones DC .05 .02
❑ 677 Tyler Houston DC RC .25 .07
❑ 678 Jeff Jackson DC RC .10 .03
❑ 679 Greg Gohr DC RC .10 .03
❑ 680 Ben McDonald DC RC .25 .07
❑ 681 Greg Blosser DC RC .10 .03
❑ 682 W.Greene RC DC UER .25 .07
Name spelled as Green
❑ 683A W.Boggs DT ERR .10 .03
Text says 215 hits in '89, should be 205
❑ 683B W.Boggs DT COR .50 .15
Text says 205 hits in '89
❑ 684 Will Clark DT .10 .03
❑ 685 Tony Gwynn DT UER .15 .04
(Text reads battling instead of batting)
❑ 686 Rickey Henderson DT .15 .04
❑ 687 Bo Jackson DT .10 .03
❑ 688 Mark Langston DT .05 .02
❑ 689 Barry Larkin DT .10 .03
❑ 690 Kirby Puckett DT .15 .04
❑ 691 Ryne Sandberg DT .25 .07
❑ 692 Mike Scott DT .05 .02
❑ 693A Terry Steinbach DT .05 .02
ERR (cathers)
❑ 693B Terry Steinbach DT .05 .02
COR (catchers)
❑ 694 Bobby Thigpen DT .05 .02
❑ 695 Mitch Williams DT .05 .02
❑ 696 Nolan Ryan HL .40 .12
❑ 697 Bo Jackson FB/BB .50 .15
❑ 698 Rickey Henderson .15 .04
ALCS-MVP
❑ 699 Will Clark .10 .03
NLCS-MVP
❑ 700 Dave Stewart .10 .03
Mike Moore WS
❑ 701 Lights Out .25 .07
❑ 702 Carney Lansford .15 .04
Rickey Henderson
Jose Canseco
Dave Henderson WS
❑ 703 WS Game 4/Wrap-up .05 .02
❑ 704 Wade Boggs HL .10 .03

1991 Score

	Nm-Mt	Ex-Mt
COMPLETE SET (893)	20.00	6.00
COMP.FACT.SET (900)	25.00	7.50

❑ 1 Jose Canseco .25 .07
❑ 2 Ken Griffey Jr. .50 .15
❑ 3 Ryne Sandberg .40 .12
❑ 4 Nolan Ryan 1.00 .30
❑ 5 Bo Jackson .25 .07
❑ 6 Bret Saberhagen UER .05 .02
(In bio, missed misspelled as mised)
❑ 7 Will Clark .25 .07
❑ 8 Ellis Burks .10 .03
❑ 9 Joe Carter .10 .03
❑ 10 Rickey Henderson .25 .07
❑ 11 Ozzie Guillen .05 .02
❑ 12 Wade Boggs .15 .04
❑ 13 Jerome Walton .05 .02
❑ 14 John Franco .10 .03
❑ 15 Ricky Jordan UER .05 .02
(League misspelled as legue)
❑ 16 Wally Backman .05 .02
❑ 17 Rob Dibble .10 .03
❑ 18 Glenn Braggs .05 .02
❑ 19 Cory Snyder .05 .02
❑ 20 Kal Daniels .05 .02
❑ 21 Mark Langston .05 .02
❑ 22 Kevin Gross .05 .02
❑ 23 Don Mattingly UER .60 .18
First line, ' is missing from Yankee
❑ 24 Dave Righetti .10 .03
❑ 25 Roberto Alomar .15 .04
❑ 26 Robby Thompson .05 .02
❑ 27 Jack McDowell .05 .02
❑ 28 Bip Roberts UER .05 .02
(Bio reads playd)
❑ 29 Jay Howell .05 .02
❑ 30 Dave Stieb UER .05 .02
(17 wins in bio, 18 in stats)
❑ 31 Johnny Ray .05 .02
❑ 32 Steve Sax .05 .02
❑ 33 Terry Mulholland .05 .02
❑ 34 Lee Guetterman .05 .02
❑ 35 Tim Raines .10 .03
❑ 36 Scott Fletcher .05 .02
❑ 37 Lance Parrish .10 .03
❑ 38 Tony Phillips UER .05 .02
(Born 4/15 should be 4/25)
❑ 39 Todd Stottlemyre .05 .02
❑ 40 Alan Trammell .10 .03
❑ 41 Todd Burns .05 .02
❑ 42 Mookie Wilson .10 .03
❑ 43 Chris Bosio .05 .02
❑ 44 Jeffrey Leonard .05 .02
❑ 45 Doug Jones .05 .02
❑ 46 Mike Scott UER .05 .02
(In first line, dominate should read dominating)
❑ 47 Andy Hawkins .05 .02
❑ 48 Harold Reynolds .10 .03
❑ 49 Paul Molitor .15 .04
❑ 50 John Farrell .05 .02
❑ 51 Danny Darwin .05 .02
❑ 52 Jeff Blauser .05 .02
❑ 53 John Tudor UER .05 .02
(41 wins in '81)
❑ 54 Milt Thompson .05 .02
❑ 55 Dave Justice .10 .03
❑ 56 Greg Olson .05 .02
❑ 57 Willie Blair .05 .02
❑ 58 Rick Parker .05 .02
❑ 59 Shawn Boskie .05 .02
❑ 60 Kevin Tapani .05 .02
❑ 61 Dave Hollins .05 .02
❑ 62 Scott Radinsky .05 .02
❑ 63 Francisco Cabrera .05 .02
❑ 64 Tim Layana .05 .02
❑ 65 Jim Leyritz .05 .02
❑ 66 Wayne Edwards .05 .02
❑ 67 Lee Stevens .05 .02
❑ 68 Bill Sampen UER .05 .02
Fourth line, long is spelled along
❑ 69 Craig Grebeck UER .05 .02
Born in Cerritos, not Johnstown
❑ 70 John Burkett .05 .02
❑ 71 Hector Villanueva .05 .02
❑ 72 Oscar Azocar .05 .02
❑ 73 Alan Mills .05 .02
❑ 74 Carlos Baerga .05 .02
❑ 75 Charles Nagy .05 .02
❑ 76 Tim Drummond .05 .02
❑ 77 Dana Kiecker .05 .02
❑ 78 Tom Edens .05 .02
❑ 79 Kent Mercker .05 .02
❑ 80 Steve Avery .05 .02
❑ 81 Lee Smith .10 .03
❑ 82 Dave Martinez .05 .02
❑ 83 Dave Winfield .10 .03
❑ 84 Bill Spiers .05 .02
❑ 85 Dan Pasqua .05 .02
❑ 86 Randy Milligan .05 .02
❑ 87 Tracy Jones .05 .02
❑ 88 Greg Myers .05 .02
❑ 89 Keith Hernandez .10 .03
❑ 90 Todd Benzinger .05 .02
❑ 91 Mike Jackson .05 .02
❑ 92 Mike Stanley .05 .02
❑ 93 Candy Maldonado .05 .02
❑ 94 John Kruk UER .10 .03
(No decimal point before 1990 BA)
❑ 95 Cal Ripken UER .75 .23
(Genius spelled genuis)
❑ 96 Willie Fraser .05 .02
❑ 97 Mike Felder .05 .02
❑ 98 Bill Landrum .05 .02
❑ 99 Chuck Crim .05 .02
❑ 100 Chuck Finley .10 .03
❑ 101 Kirt Manwaring .05 .02
❑ 102 Jaime Navarro .05 .02
❑ 103 Dickie Thon .05 .02
❑ 104 Brian Downing .05 .02
❑ 105 Jim Abbott .15 .04
❑ 106 Tom Brookens .05 .02
❑ 107 Darryl Hamilton UER .05 .02
(Bio info is for Jeff Hamilton)
❑ 108 Bryan Harvey .05 .02
❑ 109 Greg A. Harris UER .05 .02
Shown pitching lefty, bio says righty
❑ 110 Greg Swindell .05 .02
❑ 111 Juan Berenguer .05 .02
❑ 112 Mike Heath .05 .02
❑ 113 Scott Bradley .05 .02
❑ 114 Jack Morris .10 .03
❑ 115 Barry Jones .05 .02
❑ 116 Kevin Romine .05 .02
❑ 117 Garry Templeton .05 .02
❑ 118 Scott Sanderson .05 .02
❑ 119 Roberto Kelly .05 .02
❑ 120 George Brett .60 .18
❑ 121 Oddibe McDowell .05 .02
❑ 122 Jim Acker .05 .02
❑ 123 Bill Swift UER .05 .02
(Born 12/27/61, should be 10/27)
❑ 124 Eric King .05 .02
❑ 125 Jay Buhner .10 .03
❑ 126 Matt Young .05 .02
❑ 127 Alvaro Espinoza .05 .02
❑ 128 Greg Hibbard .05 .02
❑ 129 Jeff M. Robinson .05 .02
❑ 130 Mike Greenwell .05 .02
❑ 131 Dion James .05 .02
❑ 132 Donn Pall UER .05 .02
(1988 ERA in stats 0.00)
❑ 133 Lloyd Moseby .05 .02
❑ 134 Randy Velarde .05 .02
❑ 135 Allan Anderson .05 .02

❑ 136 Mark Davis .05 .02
❑ 137 Eric Davis .10 .03
❑ 138 Phil Stephenson .05 .02
❑ 139 Felix Fermin .05 .02
❑ 140 Pedro Guerrero .10 .03
❑ 141 Charlie Hough .10 .03
❑ 142 Mike Henneman .05 .02
❑ 143 Jeff Montgomery .05 .02
❑ 144 Lenny Harris .05 .02
❑ 145 Bruce Hurst .05 .02
❑ 146 Eric Anthony .05 .02
❑ 147 Paul Assenmacher .05 .02
❑ 148 Jesse Barfield .05 .02
❑ 149 Carlos Quintana .05 .02
❑ 150 Dave Stewart .10 .03
❑ 151 Roy Smith .05 .02
❑ 152 Paul Gibson .05 .02
❑ 153 Mickey Hatcher .05 .02
❑ 154 Jim Eisenreich .05 .02
❑ 155 Kenny Rogers .10 .03
❑ 156 Dave Schmidt .05 .02
❑ 157 Lance Johnson .05 .02
❑ 158 Dave West .05 .02
❑ 159 Steve Balboni .05 .02
❑ 160 Jeff Brantley .05 .02
❑ 161 Craig Biggio .15 .04
❑ 162 Brook Jacoby .05 .02
❑ 163 Dan Gladden .05 .02
❑ 164 Jeff Reardon UER .10 .03
(Total IP shown as
943.2, should be 943.1)
❑ 165 Mark Carreon .05 .02
❑ 166 Mel Hall .05 .02
❑ 167 Gary Mielke .05 .02
❑ 168 Cecil Fielder .10 .03
❑ 169 Darrin Jackson .05 .02
❑ 170 Rick Aguilera .10 .03
❑ 171 Walt Weiss .05 .02
❑ 172 Steve Farr .05 .02
❑ 173 Jody Reed .05 .02
❑ 174 Mike Jeffcoat .05 .02
❑ 175 Mark Grace .15 .04
❑ 176 Larry Sheets .05 .02
❑ 177 Bill Gullickson .05 .02
❑ 178 Chris Gwynn .05 .02
❑ 179 Melido Perez .05 .02
❑ 180 Sid Fernandez UER .05 .02
(779 runs in 1990)
❑ 181 Tim Burke .05 .02
❑ 182 Gary Pettis .05 .02
❑ 183 Rob Murphy .05 .02
❑ 184 Craig Lefferts .05 .02
❑ 185 Howard Johnson .05 .02
❑ 186 Ken Caminiti .10 .03
❑ 187 Tim Belcher .05 .02
❑ 188 Greg Cadaret .05 .02
❑ 189 Matt Williams .10 .03
❑ 190 Dave Magadan .05 .02
❑ 191 Geno Petralli .05 .02
❑ 192 Jeff D. Robinson .05 .02
❑ 193 Jim Deshaies .05 .02
❑ 194 Willie Randolph .10 .03
❑ 195 George Bell .05 .02
❑ 196 Hubie Brooks .05 .02
❑ 197 Tom Gordon .05 .02
❑ 198 Mike Fitzgerald .05 .02
❑ 199 Mike Pagliarulo .05 .02
❑ 200 Kirby Puckett .25 .07
❑ 201 Shawon Dunston .05 .02
❑ 202 Dennis Boyd .05 .02
❑ 203 Junior Felix UER .05 .02
(Text has him in NL)
❑ 204 Alejandro Pena .05 .02
❑ 205 Pete Smith .05 .02
❑ 206 Tom Glavine UER .15 .04
(Lefty spelled leftie)
❑ 207 Luis Salazar .05 .02
❑ 208 John Smoltz .15 .04
❑ 209 Doug Dascenzo .05 .02
❑ 210 Tim Wallach .05 .02
❑ 211 Greg Gagne .05 .02
❑ 212 Mark Gubicza .05 .02
❑ 213 Mark Parent .05 .02
❑ 214 Ken Oberkfell .05 .02
❑ 215 Gary Carter .10 .03
❑ 216 Rafael Palmeiro .15 .04
❑ 217 Tom Niedenfuer .05 .02
❑ 218 Dave LaPoint .05 .02
❑ 219 Jeff Treadway .05 .02
❑ 220 Mitch Williams UER .05 .02
('89 ERA shown as 2.76,
should be 2.64)
❑ 221 Jose DeLeon .05 .02
❑ 222 Mike LaValliere .05 .02
❑ 223 Darrel Akerfelds .05 .02
❑ 224A Kent Anderson ERR .10 .03
(First line, flachy
should read flashy)
❑ 224B Kent Anderson COR .10 .03
(Corrected in
factory sets)
❑ 225 Dwight Evans .10 .03
❑ 226 Gary Redus .05 .02
❑ 227 Paul O'Neill .15 .04
❑ 228 Marty Barrett .05 .02
❑ 229 Tom Browning .05 .02
❑ 230 Terry Pendleton .10 .03
❑ 231 Jack Armstrong .05 .02
❑ 232 Mike Boddicker .05 .02
❑ 233 Neal Heaton .05 .02
❑ 234 Marquis Grissom .10 .03
❑ 235 Bert Blyleven .10 .03
❑ 236 Curt Young .05 .02
❑ 237 Don Carman .05 .02
❑ 238 Charlie Hayes .05 .02
❑ 239 Mark Knudson .05 .02
❑ 240 Todd Zeile .05 .02
❑ 241 Larry Walker UER .25 .07
(Maple River, should
be Maple Ridge)
❑ 242 Jerald Clark .05 .02
❑ 243 Jeff Ballard .05 .02
❑ 244 Jeff King .05 .02
❑ 245 Tom Brunansky .05 .02
❑ 246 Darren Daulton .10 .03
❑ 247 Scott Terry .05 .02
❑ 248 Rob Deer .05 .02
❑ 249 Brady Anderson UER .10 .03
(1990 Hagerstown 1 hit,
should say 13 hits)
❑ 250 Len Dykstra .10 .03
❑ 251 Greg W. Harris .05 .02
❑ 252 Mike Hartley .05 .02
❑ 253 Joey Cora .05 .02
❑ 254 Ivan Calderon .05 .02
❑ 255 Ted Power .05 .02
❑ 256 Sammy Sosa .50 .15
❑ 257 Steve Buechele .05 .02
❑ 258 Mike Devereaux UER .05 .02
(No comma between
city and state)
❑ 259 Brad Komminsk UER .05 .02
(Last text line,
Ba should be BA)
❑ 260 Ted Higuera .05 .02
❑ 261 Shawn Abner .05 .02
❑ 262 Dave Valle .05 .02
❑ 263 Jeff Huson .05 .02
❑ 264 Edgar Martinez .15 .04
❑ 265 Carlton Fisk .15 .04
❑ 266 Steve Finley .10 .03
❑ 267 John Wetteland .10 .03
❑ 268 Kevin Appier .10 .03
❑ 269 Steve Lyons .05 .02
❑ 270 Mickey Tettleton .05 .02
❑ 271 Luis Rivera .05 .02
❑ 272 Steve Jeltz .05 .02
❑ 273 R.J. Reynolds .05 .02
❑ 274 Carlos Martinez .05 .02
❑ 275 Dan Plesac .05 .02
❑ 276 Mike Morgan UER .05 .02
Total IP shown as
1149.1, should be 1149
❑ 277 Jeff Russell .05 .02
❑ 278 Pete Incaviglia .05 .02
❑ 279 Kevin Seitzer UER .05 .02
Bio has 200 hits twice
and .300 four times,
should be once and
three times
❑ 280 Bobby Thigpen .05 .02
❑ 281 Stan Javier UER .05 .02
(Born 1/9,
should say 9/1)
❑ 282 Henry Cotto .05 .02
❑ 283 Gary Wayne .05 .02
❑ 284 Shane Mack .05 .02
❑ 285 Brian Holman .05 .02
❑ 286 Gerald Perry .05 .02
❑ 287 Steve Crawford .05 .02
❑ 288 Nelson Liriano .05 .02
❑ 289 Don Aase .05 .02
❑ 290 Randy Johnson .30 .09
❑ 291 Harold Baines .10 .03
❑ 292 Kent Hrbek .10 .03
❑ 293A Les Lancaster ERR .05 .02
(No comma between
Dallas and Texas)
❑ 293B Les Lancaster COR .05 .02
(Corrected in
factory sets)
❑ 294 Jeff Musselman .05 .02
❑ 295 Kurt Stillwell .05 .02
❑ 296 Stan Belinda .05 .02
❑ 297 Lou Whitaker .10 .03
❑ 298 Glenn Wilson .05 .02
❑ 299 Omar Vizquel UER .15 .04
Born 5/15, should be
4/24, there is a decimal
before GP total for '90
❑ 300 Ramon Martinez .05 .02
❑ 301 Dwight Smith .05 .02
❑ 302 Tim Crews .05 .02
❑ 303 Lance Blankenship .05 .02
❑ 304 Sid Bream .05 .02
❑ 305 Rafael Ramirez .05 .02
❑ 306 Steve Wilson .05 .02
❑ 307 Mackey Sasser .05 .02
❑ 308 Franklin Stubbs .05 .02
❑ 309 Jack Daugherty UER .05 .02
(Born 6/3/60,
should say July)
❑ 310 Eddie Murray .25 .07
❑ 311 Bob Welch .05 .02
❑ 312 Brian Harper .05 .02
❑ 313 Lance McCullers .05 .02
❑ 314 Dave Smith .05 .02
❑ 315 Bobby Bonilla .10 .03
❑ 316 Jerry Don Gleaton .05 .02
❑ 317 Greg Maddux .40 .12
❑ 318 Keith Miller .05 .02
❑ 319 Mark Portugal .05 .02
❑ 320 Robin Ventura .10 .03
❑ 321 Bob Ojeda .05 .02
❑ 322 Mike Harkey .05 .02
❑ 323 Jay Bell .10 .03
❑ 324 Mark McGwire .60 .18
❑ 325 Gary Gaetti .10 .03
❑ 326 Jeff Pico .05 .02
❑ 327 Kevin McReynolds .05 .02
❑ 328 Frank Tanana .05 .02
❑ 329 Eric Yelding UER .05 .02
(Listed as 6'3"
should be 5'11")
❑ 330 Barry Bonds .60 .18
❑ 331 Brian McRae RC UER .25 .07
(No comma between
city and state)
❑ 332 Pedro Munoz RC .10 .03
❑ 333 Daryl Irvine .05 .02
❑ 334 Chris Hoiles .05 .02
❑ 335 Thomas Howard .05 .02
❑ 336 Jeff Schulz .05 .02
❑ 337 Jeff Manto .05 .02
❑ 338 Beau Allred .05 .02
❑ 339 Mike Bordick RC .40 .12
❑ 340 Todd Hundley .05 .02
❑ 341 Jim Vatcher UER .05 .02
(Height 6'9",
should be 5'9")
❑ 342 Luis Sojo .05 .02
❑ 343 Jose Offerman UER .05 .02
(Born 1969, should
say 1968)
❑ 344 Pete Coachman .05 .02
❑ 345 Mike Benjamin .05 .02
❑ 346 Ozzie Canseco .05 .02
❑ 347 Tim McIntosh .05 .02

No.	Card	Price	Price
348	Phil Plantier RC	.10	.03
349	Terry Shumpert	.05	.02
350	Darren Lewis	.05	.02
351	David Walsh RC	.05	.02
352A	Scott Chiamparino ERR Bats left, should be right	.10	.03
352B	Scott Chiamparino COR corrected in factory sets	.10	.03
353	Julio Valera UER (Progressed misspelled as progessed)	.05	.02
354	Anthony Telford	.05	.02
355	Kevin Wickander	.05	.02
356	Tim Naehring	.05	.02
357	Jim Poole	.05	.02
358	Mark Whiten UER Shown hitting lefty, bio says righty	.05	.02
359	Terry Wells	.05	.02
360	Rafael Valdez	.05	.02
361	Mel Stottlemyre Jr.	.05	.02
362	David Segui	.05	.02
363	Paul Abbott RC	.10	.03
364	Steve Howard	.05	.02
365	Karl Rhodes	.05	.02
366	Rafael Novoa	.05	.02
367	Joe Grahe RC	.05	.02
368	Darren Reed	.05	.02
369	Jeff McKnight	.05	.02
370	Scott Leius	.05	.02
371	Mark Dewey	.05	.02
372	Mark Lee UER RC (Shown hitting left, bio says righty, born in Dakota, should say North Dakota	.10	.03
373	Rosario Rodriguez UER Shown hitting lefty, bio says righty	.05	.02
374	Chuck McElroy	.05	.02
375	Mike Bell	.05	.02
376	Mickey Morandini	.05	.02
377	Bill Haselman	.05	.02
378	Dave Pavlas	.05	.02
379	Derrick May	.05	.02
380	J.Burnitz FDP RC	.50	.15
381	Donald Peters FDP	.05	.02
382	Alex Fernandez FDP	.05	.02
383	Mike Mussina FDP RC	1.25	.35
384	Dan Smith FDP RC	.10	.03
385	L.Dickson FDP RC	.10	.03
386	Carl Everett FDP RC	.40	.12
387	Tom Nevers FDP RC	.10	.03
388	Adam Hyzdu FDP RC	.25	.07
389	T.Van Poppel FDP RC	.25	.07
390	R.White FDP RC	.40	.12
391	M.Newfield FDP RC	.10	.03
392	Julio Franco AS	.05	.02
393	Wade Boggs AS	.10	.03
394	Ozzie Guillen AS	.05	.02
395	Cecil Fielder AS	.05	.02
396	Ken Griffey Jr. AS	.25	.07
397	Rickey Henderson AS	.15	.04
398	Jose Canseco AS	.10	.03
399	Roger Clemens AS	.25	.07
400	Sandy Alomar Jr. AS	.05	.02
401	Bobby Thigpen AS	.05	.02
402	Bobby Bonilla MB	.05	.02
403	Eric Davis MB	.05	.02
404	Fred McGriff MB	.10	.03
405	Glenn Davis MB	.05	.02
406	Kevin Mitchell MB	.05	.02
407	Rob Dibble KM	.05	.02
408	Ramon Martinez KM	.05	.02
409	David Cone KM	.05	.02
410	Bobby Witt KM	.05	.02
411	Mark Langston KM	.05	.02
412	Bo Jackson RIF	.10	.03
413	Shawon Dunston RIF UER In the baseball, should say in baseball	.05	.02
414	Jesse Barfield RIF	.05	.02
415	Ken Caminiti RIF	.05	.02
416	Benito Santiago RIF	.05	.02
417	Nolan Ryan HL	.50	.15
418	B.Thigpen HL UER Back refers to Hal McRae Jr., should say Brian McRae	.05	.02
419	Ramon Martinez HL	.05	.02
420	Bo Jackson HL	.10	.03
421	Carlton Fisk HL	.10	.03
422	Jimmy Key	.10	.03
423	Junior Noboa	.05	.02
424	Al Newman	.05	.02
425	Pat Borders	.05	.02
426	Von Hayes	.05	.02
427	Tim Teufel	.05	.02
428	Eric Plunk UER Text says Eric's had, no apostrophe needed	.05	.02
429	John Moses	.05	.02
430	Mike Witt	.05	.02
431	Otis Nixon	.05	.02
432	Tony Fernandez	.05	.02
433	Rance Mulliniks	.05	.02
434	Dan Petry	.05	.02
435	Bob Geren	.05	.02
436	Steve Frey	.05	.02
437	Jamie Moyer	.10	.03
438	Junior Ortiz	.05	.02
439	Tom O'Malley	.05	.02
440	Pat Combs	.05	.02
441	Jose Canseco DT	.25	.07
442	Alfredo Griffin	.05	.02
443	Andres Galarraga	.10	.03
444	Bryn Smith	.05	.02
445	Andre Dawson	.10	.03
446	Juan Samuel	.05	.02
447	Mike Aldrete	.05	.02
448	Ron Gant	.10	.03
449	Fernando Valenzuela	.10	.03
450	Vince Coleman UER Should say topped majors in steals four times, not three times	.05	.02
451	Kevin Mitchell	.05	.02
452	Spike Owen	.05	.02
453	Mike Bielecki	.05	.02
454	Dennis Martinez	.10	.03
455	Brett Butler	.10	.03
456	Ron Darling	.05	.02
457	Dennis Rasmussen	.05	.02
458	Ken Howell	.05	.02
459	Steve Bedrosian	.05	.02
460	Frank Viola	.10	.03
461	Jose Lind	.05	.02
462	Chris Sabo	.05	.02
463	Dante Bichette	.10	.03
464	Rick Mahler	.05	.02
465	John Smiley	.05	.02
466	Devon White	.10	.03
467	John Orton	.05	.02
468	Mike Stanton	.05	.02
469	Billy Hatcher	.05	.02
470	Wally Joyner	.10	.03
471	Gene Larkin	.05	.02
472	Doug Drabek	.05	.02
473	Gary Sheffield	.10	.03
474	David Wells	.10	.03
475	Andy Van Slyke	.10	.03
476	Mike Gallego	.05	.02
477	B.J. Surhoff	.10	.03
478	Gene Nelson	.05	.02
479	Mariano Duncan	.05	.02
480	Fred McGriff	.15	.04
481	Jerry Browne	.05	.02
482	Alvin Davis	.05	.02
483	Bill Wegman	.05	.02
484	Dave Parker	.10	.03
485	Dennis Eckersley	.10	.03
486	Erik Hanson UER (Basketball misspelled as baseketball)	.05	.02
487	Bill Ripken	.05	.02
488	Tom Candiotti	.05	.02
489	Mike Schooler	.05	.02
490	Gregg Olson	.05	.02
491	Chris James	.05	.02
492	Pete Harnisch	.05	.02
493	Julio Franco	.10	.03
494	Greg Briley	.05	.02
495	Ruben Sierra	.05	.02
496	Steve Olin	.05	.02
497	Mike Fetters	.05	.02
498	Mark Williamson	.05	.02
499	Bob Tewksbury	.05	.02
500	Tony Gwynn	.30	.09
501	Randy Myers	.05	.02
502	Keith Comstock	.05	.02
503	C.Worthington UER DeCinces misspelled DiCinces on back	.05	.02
504	Mark Eichhorn UER Stats incomplete, doesn't have '89 Braves stint	.05	.02
505	Barry Larkin	.15	.04
506	Dave Johnson	.05	.02
507	Bobby Witt	.05	.02
508	Joe Orsulak	.05	.02
509	Pete O'Brien	.05	.02
510	Brad Arnsberg	.05	.02
511	Storm Davis	.05	.02
512	Bob Milacki	.05	.02
513	Bill Pecota	.05	.02
514	Glenallen Hill	.05	.02
515	Danny Tartabull	.05	.02
516	Mike Moore	.05	.02
517	Ron Robinson UER (577 K's in 1990)	.05	.02
518	Mark Gardner	.05	.02
519	Rick Wrona	.05	.02
520	Mike Scioscia	.05	.02
521	Frank Wills	.05	.02
522	Greg Brock	.05	.02
523	Jack Clark	.10	.03
524	Bruce Ruffin	.05	.02
525	Robin Yount	.40	.12
526	Tom Foley	.05	.02
527	Pat Perry	.05	.02
528	Greg Vaughn	.05	.02
529	Wally Whitehurst	.05	.02
530	Norm Charlton	.05	.02
531	Marvell Wynne	.05	.02
532	Jim Gantner	.05	.02
533	Greg Litton	.05	.02
534	Manny Lee	.05	.02
535	Scott Bailes	.05	.02
536	Charlie Leibrandt	.05	.02
537	Roger McDowell	.05	.02
538	Andy Benes	.05	.02
539	Rick Honeycutt	.05	.02
540	Dwight Gooden	.10	.03
541	Scott Garrelts	.05	.02
542	Dave Clark	.05	.02
543	Lonnie Smith	.05	.02
544	Rick Reuschel	.05	.02
545	Delino DeShields UER (Rockford misspelled as Rock Ford in '88)	.10	.03
546	Mike Sharperson	.05	.02
547	Mike Kingery	.05	.02
548	Terry Kennedy	.05	.02
549	David Cone	.10	.03
550	Orel Hershiser	.10	.03
551	Matt Nokes	.05	.02
552	Eddie Williams	.05	.02
553	Frank DiPino	.05	.02
554	Fred Lynn	.05	.02
555	Alex Cole	.05	.02
556	Terry Leach	.05	.02
557	Chet Lemon	.05	.02
558	Paul Mirabella	.05	.02
559	Bill Long	.05	.02
560	Phil Bradley	.05	.02
561	Duane Ward	.05	.02
562	Dave Bergman	.05	.02
563	Eric Show	.05	.02
564	Xavier Hernandez	.05	.02
565	Jeff Parrett	.05	.02
566	Chuck Cary	.05	.02
567	Ken Hill	.05	.02
568	Bob Welch Hand (Complement should be compliment) UER	.05	.02
569	John Mitchell	.05	.02
570	Travis Fryman	.10	.03
571	Derek Lilliquist	.05	.02

❑	572	Steve Lake	.05	.02
❑	573	John Barfield	.05	.02
❑	574	Randy Bush	.05	.02
❑	575	Joe Magrane	.05	.02
❑	576	Eddie Diaz	.05	.02
❑	577	Casey Candaele	.05	.02
❑	578	Jesse Orosco	.05	.02
❑	579	Tom Henke	.05	.02
❑	580	Rick Cerone UER	.05	.02
		(Actually his third go-round with Yankees)		
❑	581	Drew Hall	.05	.02
❑	582	Tony Castillo	.05	.02
❑	583	Jimmy Jones	.05	.02
❑	584	Rick Reed	.05	.02
❑	585	Joe Girardi	.05	.02
❑	586	Jeff Gray	.05	.02
❑	587	Luis Polonia	.05	.02
❑	588	Joe Klink	.05	.02
❑	589	Rex Hudler	.05	.02
❑	590	Kirk McCaskill	.05	.02
❑	591	Juan Agosto	.05	.02
❑	592	Wes Gardner	.05	.02
❑	593	Rich Rodriguez	.05	.02
❑	594	Mitch Webster	.05	.02
❑	595	Kelly Gruber	.05	.02
❑	596	Dale Mohorcic	.05	.02
❑	597	Willie McGee	.10	.03
❑	598	Bill Krueger	.05	.02
❑	599	Bob Walk UER	.05	.02
		Cards says he's 33, but actually he's 34		
❑	600	Kevin Maas	.05	.02
❑	601	Danny Jackson	.05	.02
❑	602	Craig McMurtry UER	.05	.02
		(Anonymously misspelled anonimously)		
❑	603	Curtis Wilkerson	.05	.02
❑	604	Adam Peterson	.05	.02
❑	605	Sam Horn	.05	.02
❑	606	Tommy Gregg	.05	.02
❑	607	Ken Dayley	.05	.02
❑	608	Carmelo Castillo	.05	.02
❑	609	John Shelby	.05	.02
❑	610	Don Slaught	.05	.02
❑	611	Calvin Schiraldi	.05	.02
❑	612	Dennis Lamp	.05	.02
❑	613	Andres Thomas	.05	.02
❑	614	Jose Gonzalez	.05	.02
❑	615	Randy Ready	.05	.02
❑	616	Kevin Bass	.05	.02
❑	617	Mike Marshall	.05	.02
❑	618	Daryl Boston	.05	.02
❑	619	Andy McGaffigan	.05	.02
❑	620	Joe Oliver	.05	.02
❑	621	Jim Gott	.05	.02
❑	622	Jose Oquendo	.05	.02
❑	623	Jose DeJesus	.05	.02
❑	624	Mike Brumley	.05	.02
❑	625	John Olerud	.10	.03
❑	626	Ernest Riles	.05	.02
❑	627	Gene Harris	.05	.02
❑	628	Jose Uribe	.05	.02
❑	629	Darnell Coles	.05	.02
❑	630	Carney Lansford	.10	.03
❑	631	Tim Leary	.05	.02
❑	632	Tim Hulett	.05	.02
❑	633	Kevin Elster	.05	.02
❑	634	Tony Fossas	.05	.02
❑	635	Francisco Oliveras	.05	.02
❑	636	Bob Patterson	.05	.02
❑	637	Gary Ward	.05	.02
❑	638	Rene Gonzales	.05	.02
❑	639	Don Robinson	.05	.02
❑	640	Darryl Strawberry	.10	.03
❑	641	Dave Anderson	.05	.02
❑	642	Scott Scudder	.05	.02
❑	643	Reggie Harris UER	.05	.02
		(Hepatitis misspelled as hepititis)		
❑	644	Dave Henderson	.05	.02
❑	645	Ben McDonald	.05	.02
❑	646	Bob Kipper	.05	.02
❑	647	Hal Morris UER	.05	.02
		(It's should be its)		
❑	648	Tim Birtsas	.05	.02
❑	649	Steve Searcy	.05	.02
❑	650	Dale Murphy	.25	.07
❑	651	Ron Oester	.05	.02
❑	652	Mike LaCoss	.05	.02
❑	653	Ron Jones	.05	.02
❑	654	Kelly Downs	.05	.02
❑	655	Roger Clemens	.50	.15
❑	656	Herm Winningham	.05	.02
❑	657	Trevor Wilson	.05	.02
❑	658	Jose Rijo	.05	.02
❑	659	Dann Bilardello UER	.05	.02
		Bio has 13 games, 1 hit, and 32 AB, stats show 19, 2, and 37		
❑	660	Gregg Jefferies	.05	.02
❑	661	Doug Drabek AS UER	.05	.02
		(Through is mis-spelled though)		
❑	662	Randy Myers AS	.05	.02
❑	663	Benny Santiago AS	.05	.02
❑	664	Will Clark AS	.10	.03
❑	665	Ryne Sandberg AS	.25	.07
❑	666	Barry Larkin AS UER	.10	.03
		Line 13, coolly misspelled cooly		
❑	667	Matt Williams AS	.05	.02
❑	668	Barry Bonds AS	.30	.09
❑	669	Eric Davis AS	.05	.02
❑	670	Bobby Bonilla AS	.05	.02
❑	671	C.Jones FDP RC	4.00	1.20
❑	672	E.Christopherson RC FDP	.10	.03
❑	673	R.Beckett FDP RC	.10	.03
❑	674	S.Andrews FDP RC	.25	.07
❑	675	Steve Karsay FDP RC	.25	.07
❑	676	Aaron Holbert FDP RC	.10	.03
❑	677	D.Osborne FDP RC	.10	.03
❑	678	Todd Ritchie FDP RC	.25	.07
❑	679	Ron Walden FDP RC	.10	.03
❑	680	Tim Costo FDP RC	.10	.03
❑	681	Dan Wilson FDP RC	.25	.07
❑	682	Kurt Miller FDP RC	.10	.03
❑	683	M.Lieberthal FDP RC	.40	.12
❑	684	Roger Clemens KM	.25	.07
❑	685	Dwight Gooden KM	.05	.02
❑	686	Nolan Ryan KM	.50	.15
❑	687	Frank Viola KM	.05	.02
❑	688	Erik Hanson KM	.05	.02
❑	689	Matt Williams MB	.05	.02
❑	690	J.Canseco MB UER	.10	.03
		Mammoth misspelled as monmouth		
❑	691	Darryl Strawberry MB	.05	.02
❑	692	Bo Jackson MB	.10	.03
❑	693	Cecil Fielder MB	.05	.02
❑	694	Sandy Alomar Jr. RF	.05	.02
❑	695	Cory Snyder RF	.05	.02
❑	696	Eric Davis RF	.05	.02
❑	697	Ken Griffey Jr. RF	.25	.07
❑	698	A.Van Slyke RF UER	.05	.02
		Line 2, outfielders does not need		
❑	699	Mark Langston NH Mike Witt	.05	.02
❑	700	Randy Johnson NH	.15	.04
❑	701	Nolan Ryan NH	.50	.15
❑	702	Dave Stewart NH	.05	.02
❑	703	F.Valenzuela NH	.05	.02
❑	704	Andy Hawkins NH	.05	.02
❑	705	Melido Perez NH	.05	.02
❑	706	Terry Mulholland NH	.05	.02
❑	707	Dave Stieb NH	.05	.02
❑	708	Brian Barnes RC	.05	.02
❑	709	Bernard Gilkey	.05	.02
❑	710	Steve Decker	.05	.02
❑	711	Paul Faries	.05	.02
❑	712	Paul Marak	.05	.02
❑	713	Wes Chamberlain RC	.10	.03
❑	714	Kevin Belcher	.05	.02
❑	715	Dan Boone UER	.05	.02
		(IP adds up to 101, but card has 101.2)		
❑	716	Steve Adkins	.05	.02
❑	717	Geronimo Pena	.05	.02
❑	718	Howard Farmer	.05	.02
❑	719	Mark Leonard	.05	.02
❑	720	Tom Lampkin	.05	.02
❑	721	Mike Gardiner	.05	.02
❑	722	Jeff Conine RC	.40	.12
❑	723	Efrain Valdez	.05	.02
❑	724	Chuck Malone	.05	.02
❑	725	Leo Gomez	.05	.02
❑	726	Paul McClellan	.05	.02
❑	727	Mark Leiter RC	.10	.03
❑	728	Rich DeLucia UER	.05	.02
		(Line 2, all told is written alltold)		
❑	729	Mel Rojas	.05	.02
❑	730	Hector Wagner	.05	.02
❑	731	Ray Lankford	.05	.02
❑	732	Turner Ward RC	.10	.03
❑	733	Gerald Alexander	.05	.02
❑	734	Scott Anderson	.05	.02
❑	735	Tony Perezchica	.05	.02
❑	736	Jimmy Kremers	.05	.02
❑	737	American Flag	.25	.07
		(Pray for Peace)		
❑	738	Mike York	.05	.02
❑	739	Mike Rochford	.05	.02
❑	740	Scott Aldred	.05	.02
❑	741	Rico Brogna	.05	.02
❑	742	Dave Burba RC	.25	.07
❑	743	Ray Stephens	.05	.02
❑	744	Eric Gunderson	.05	.02
❑	745	Troy Afenir	.05	.02
❑	746	Jeff Shaw	.05	.02
❑	747	Orlando Merced RC	.10	.03
❑	748	O.Olivares UER RC	.10	.03
		Line 9, league is misspelled legaue		
❑	749	Jerry Kutzler	.05	.02
❑	750	Mo Vaughn UER	.10	.03
		(44 SB's in 1990)		
❑	751	Matt Stark	.05	.02
❑	752	Randy Hennis	.05	.02
❑	753	Andujar Cedeno	.05	.02
❑	754	Kelvin Torve	.05	.02
❑	755	Joe Kraemer	.05	.02
❑	756	Phil Clark RC	.10	.03
❑	757	Ed Vosberg	.05	.02
❑	758	Mike Perez RC	.10	.03
❑	759	Scott Lewis	.05	.02
❑	760	Steve Chitren	.05	.02
❑	761	Ray Young	.05	.02
❑	762	Andres Santana	.05	.02
❑	763	Rodney McCray	.05	.02
❑	764	Sean Berry UER RC	.10	.03
		(Name misspelled Barry on card front)		
❑	765	Brent Mayne	.05	.02
❑	766	Mike Simms	.05	.02
❑	767	Glenn Sutko	.05	.02
❑	768	Gary DiSarcina	.05	.02
❑	769	George Brett HL	.25	.07
❑	770	Cecil Fielder HL	.05	.02
❑	771	Jim Presley	.05	.02
❑	772	John Dopson	.05	.02
❑	773	Bo Jackson Breaker	.10	.03
❑	774	Brent Knackert UER	.05	.02
		Born in 1954, shown throwing righty, but bio says lefty		
❑	775	Bill Doran UER	.05	.02
		(Reds in NL East)		
❑	776	Dick Schofield	.05	.02
❑	777	Nelson Santovenia	.05	.02
❑	778	Mark Guthrie	.05	.02
❑	779	Mark Lemke	.05	.02
❑	780	Terry Steinbach	.05	.02
❑	781	Tom Bolton	.05	.02
❑	782	Randy Tomlin RC	.10	.03
❑	783	Jeff Kunkel	.05	.02
❑	784	Felix Jose	.05	.02
❑	785	Rick Sutcliffe	.10	.03
❑	786	John Cerutti	.05	.02
❑	787	Jose Vizcaino UER	.05	.02
		(Offerman, not Opperman)		
❑	788	Curt Schilling	.25	.07
❑	789	Ed Whitson	.05	.02
❑	790	Tony Pena	.05	.02
❑	791	John Candelaria	.05	.02
❑	792	Carmelo Martinez	.05	.02
❑	793	Sandy Alomar Jr. UER	.05	.02
		(Indian's should		

say Indians')
❑ 794 Jim Neidlinger .05 .02
❑ 795 Barry Larkin WS .10 .03
and Chris Sabo
❑ 796 Paul Sorrento .05 .02
❑ 797 Tom Pagnozzi .05 .02
❑ 798 Tino Martinez .15 .04
❑ 799 Scott Ruskin UER .05 .02
(Text says first three seasons but lists averages for four)
❑ 800 Kirk Gibson .10 .03
❑ 801 Walt Terrell .05 .02
❑ 802 John Russell .05 .02
❑ 803 Chili Davis .10 .03
❑ 804 Chris Nabholz .05 .02
❑ 805 Juan Gonzalez .15 .04
❑ 806 Ron Hassey .05 .02
❑ 807 Todd Worrell .05 .02
❑ 808 Tommy Greene .05 .02
❑ 809 Joel Skinner UER .05 .02
Joel, not Bob, was drafted in 1979
❑ 810 Benito Santiago .10 .03
❑ 811 Pat Tabler UER .05 .02
Line 3, always misspelled always
❑ 812 Scott Erickson UER .05 .02
(Record spelled rcord)
❑ 813 Moises Alou .10 .03
❑ 814 Dale Sveum .05 .02
❑ 815 R.Sandberg MANYR .25 .07
❑ 816 Rick Dempsey .05 .02
❑ 817 Scott Bankhead .05 .02
❑ 818 Jason Grimsley .05 .02
❑ 819 Doug Jennings .05 .02
❑ 820 Tom Herr .05 .02
❑ 821 Rob Ducey .05 .02
❑ 822 Luis Quinones .05 .02
❑ 823 Greg Minton .05 .02
❑ 824 Mark Grant .05 .02
❑ 825 Ozzie Smith UER .40 .12
(Shortstop misspelled shortsop)
❑ 826 Dave Eiland .05 .02
❑ 827 Danny Heep .05 .02
❑ 828 Hensley Meulens .05 .02
❑ 829 Charlie O'Brien .05 .02
❑ 830 Glenn Davis .05 .02
❑ 831 John Marzano UER .05 .02
(International misspelled Internaional)
❑ 832 Steve Ontiveros .05 .02
❑ 833 Ron Karkovice .05 .02
❑ 834 Jerry Goff .05 .02
❑ 835 Ken Griffey Sr. .10 .03
❑ 836 Kevin Reimer .05 .02
❑ 837 Randy Kutcher UER .05 .02
(Infectious misspelled infectous)
❑ 838 Mike Blowers .05 .02
❑ 839 Mike Macfarlane .05 .02
❑ 840 Frank Thomas UER .25 .07
1989 Sarasota stats, 15 games but 188 AB
❑ 841 Ken Griffey Jr. .40 .12
Ken Griffey Sr.
❑ 842 Jack Howell .05 .02
❑ 843 Goose Gozzo .05 .02
❑ 844 Gerald Young .05 .02
❑ 845 Zane Smith .05 .02
❑ 846 Kevin Brown .10 .03
❑ 847 Sil Campusano .05 .02
❑ 848 Larry Andersen .05 .02
❑ 849 Cal Ripken FRAN .40 .12
❑ 850 Roger Clemens FRAN .25 .07
❑ 851 S.Alomar Jr. FRAN .05 .02
❑ 852 Alan Trammell FRAN .10 .03
❑ 853 George Brett FRAN .25 .07
❑ 854 Robin Yount FRAN .25 .07
❑ 855 Kirby Puckett FRAN .15 .04
❑ 856 Don Mattingly FRAN .30 .09
❑ 857 R.Henderson FRAN .15 .04
❑ 858 Ken Griffey Jr. FRAN .25 .07
❑ 859 Ruben Sierra FRAN .05 .02
❑ 860 John Olerud FRAN .05 .02
❑ 861 Dave Justice FRAN .05 .02
❑ 862 Ryne Sandberg FRAN .25 .07
❑ 863 Eric Davis FRAN .05 .02
❑ 864 D.Strawberry FRAN .05 .02
❑ 865 Tim Wallach FRAN .05 .02
❑ 866 Dwight Gooden FRAN .05 .02
❑ 867 Len Dykstra FRAN .05 .02
❑ 868 Barry Bonds FRAN .30 .09
❑ 869 Todd Zeile FRAN UER .05 .02
(Powerful misspelled as poweful)
❑ 870 Benito Santiago FRAN .05 .02
❑ 871 Will Clark FRAN .10 .03
❑ 872 Craig Biggio FRAN .10 .03
❑ 873 Wally Joyner FRAN .05 .02
❑ 874 Frank Thomas FRAN .15 .04
❑ 875 R.Henderson MVP .15 .04
❑ 876 Barry Bonds MVP .30 .09
❑ 877 Bob Welch CY .05 .02
❑ 878 Doug Drabek CY .05 .02
❑ 879 S.Alomar Jr. ROY .05 .02
❑ 880 Dave Justice ROY .05 .02
❑ 881 Damon Berryhill .05 .02
❑ 882 Frank Viola DT .05 .02
❑ 883 Dave Stewart DT .05 .02
❑ 884 Doug Jones DT .05 .02
❑ 885 Randy Myers DT .05 .02
❑ 886 Will Clark DT .10 .03
❑ 887 Roberto Alomar DT .10 .03
❑ 888 Barry Larkin DT .10 .03
❑ 889 Wade Boggs DT .15 .04
❑ 890 Rickey Henderson DT .25 .07
❑ 891 Kirby Puckett DT .15 .04
❑ 892 Ken Griffey Jr DT .50 .15
❑ 893 Benny Santiago DT .10 .03

1993 Score

	Nm-Mt	Ex-Mt
COMPLETE SET (660)	40.00	12.00

❑ 1 Ken Griffey Jr. .75 .23
❑ 2 Gary Sheffield .20 .06
❑ 3 Frank Thomas .50 .15
❑ 4 Ryne Sandberg .75 .23
❑ 5 Larry Walker .30 .09
❑ 6 Cal Ripken Jr. 1.50 .45
❑ 7 Roger Clemens 1.00 .30
❑ 8 Bobby Bonilla .20 .06
❑ 9 Carlos Baerga .10 .03
❑ 10 Darren Daulton .20 .06
❑ 11 Travis Fryman .20 .06
❑ 12 Andy Van Slyke .20 .06
❑ 13 Jose Canseco .50 .15
❑ 14 Roberto Alomar .30 .09
❑ 15 Tom Glavine .30 .09
❑ 16 Barry Larkin .30 .09
❑ 17 Gregg Jefferies .10 .03
❑ 18 Craig Biggio .30 .09
❑ 19 Shane Mack .10 .03
❑ 20 Brett Butler .20 .06
❑ 21 Dennis Eckersley .20 .06
❑ 22 Will Clark .50 .15
❑ 23 Don Mattingly 1.25 .35
❑ 24 Tony Gwynn .60 .18
❑ 25 Ivan Rodriguez .50 .15
❑ 26 Shawon Dunston .10 .03
❑ 27 Mike Mussina .30 .09
❑ 28 Marquis Grissom .20 .06
❑ 29 Charles Nagy .10 .03
❑ 30 Len Dykstra .20 .06
❑ 31 Cecil Fielder .20 .06
❑ 32 Jay Bell .20 .06
❑ 33 B.J. Surhoff .20 .06
❑ 34 Bob Tewksbury .10 .03
❑ 35 Danny Tartabull .10 .03
❑ 36 Terry Pendleton .20 .06
❑ 37 Jack Morris .20 .06
❑ 38 Hal Morris .10 .03
❑ 39 Luis Polonia .10 .03
❑ 40 Ken Caminiti .20 .06
❑ 41 Robin Ventura .20 .06
❑ 42 Darryl Strawberry .20 .06
❑ 43 Wally Joyner .20 .06
❑ 44 Fred McGriff .30 .09
❑ 45 Kevin Tapani .10 .03
❑ 46 Matt Williams .20 .06
❑ 47 Robin Yount .75 .23
❑ 48 Ken Hill .10 .03
❑ 49 Edgar Martinez .30 .09
❑ 50 Mark Grace .30 .09
❑ 51 Juan Gonzalez .30 .09
❑ 52 Curt Schilling .20 .06
❑ 53 Dwight Gooden .20 .06
❑ 54 Chris Hoiles .10 .03
❑ 55 Frank Viola .20 .06
❑ 56 Ray Lankford .10 .03
❑ 57 George Brett 1.25 .35
❑ 58 Kenny Lofton .20 .06
❑ 59 Nolan Ryan 2.00 .60
❑ 60 Mickey Tettleton .10 .03
❑ 61 John Smoltz .30 .09
❑ 62 Howard Johnson .10 .03
❑ 63 Eric Karros .20 .06
❑ 64 Rick Aguilera .10 .03
❑ 65 Steve Finley .20 .06
❑ 66 Mark Langston .10 .03
❑ 67 Bill Swift .10 .03
❑ 68 John Olerud .20 .06
❑ 69 Kevin McReynolds .10 .03
❑ 70 Jack McDowell .10 .03
❑ 71 Rickey Henderson .50 .15
❑ 72 Brian Harper .10 .03
❑ 73 Mike Morgan .10 .03
❑ 74 Rafael Palmeiro .30 .09
❑ 75 Dennis Martinez .20 .06
❑ 76 Tino Martinez .30 .09
❑ 77 Eddie Murray .50 .15
❑ 78 Ellis Burks .20 .06
❑ 79 John Kruk .20 .06
❑ 80 Gregg Olson .10 .03
❑ 81 Bernard Gilkey .10 .03
❑ 82 Milt Cuyler .10 .03
❑ 83 Mike LaValliere .10 .03
❑ 84 Albert Belle .20 .06
❑ 85 Bip Roberts .10 .03
❑ 86 Melido Perez .10 .03
❑ 87 Otis Nixon .10 .03
❑ 88 Bill Spiers .10 .03
❑ 89 Jeff Bagwell .30 .09
❑ 90 Orel Hershiser .20 .06
❑ 91 Andy Benes .10 .03
❑ 92 Devon White .20 .06
❑ 93 Willie McGee .20 .06
❑ 94 Ozzie Guillen .10 .03
❑ 95 Ivan Calderon .10 .03
❑ 96 Keith Miller .10 .03
❑ 97 Steve Buechele .10 .03
❑ 98 Kent Hrbek .20 .06
❑ 99 Dave Hollins .10 .03
❑ 100 Mike Bordick .10 .03
❑ 101 Randy Tomlin .10 .03
❑ 102 Omar Vizquel .30 .09
❑ 103 Lee Smith .20 .06
❑ 104 Leo Gomez .10 .03
❑ 105 Jose Rijo .10 .03
❑ 106 Mark Whiten .10 .03
❑ 107 Dave Justice .20 .06
❑ 108 Eddie Taubensee .10 .03
❑ 109 Lance Johnson .10 .03
❑ 110 Felix Jose .10 .03
❑ 111 Mike Harkey .10 .03
❑ 112 Randy Milligan .10 .03
❑ 113 Anthony Young .10 .03
❑ 114 Rico Brogna .10 .03
❑ 115 Bret Saberhagen .20 .06

☐	116	Sandy Alomar Jr.	.10	.03
☐	117	Terry Mulholland	.10	.03
☐	118	Darryl Hamilton	.10	.03
☐	119	Todd Zeile	.10	.03
☐	120	Bernie Williams	.30	.09
☐	121	Zane Smith	.10	.03
☐	122	Derek Bell	.10	.03
☐	123	Deion Sanders	.30	.09
☐	124	Luis Sojo	.10	.03
☐	125	Joe Oliver	.10	.03
☐	126	Craig Grebeck	.10	.03
☐	127	Andujar Cedeno	.10	.03
☐	128	Brian McRae	.10	.03
☐	129	Jose Offerman	.10	.03
☐	130	Pedro Munoz	.10	.03
☐	131	Bud Black	.10	.03
☐	132	Mo Vaughn	.20	.06
☐	133	Bruce Hurst	.10	.03
☐	134	Dave Henderson	.10	.03
☐	135	Tom Pagnozzi	.10	.03
☐	136	Erik Hanson	.10	.03
☐	137	Orlando Merced	.10	.03
☐	138	Dean Palmer	.20	.06
☐	139	John Franco	.20	.06
☐	140	Brady Anderson	.20	.06
☐	141	Ricky Jordan	.10	.03
☐	142	Jeff Blauser	.10	.03
☐	143	Sammy Sosa	.75	.23
☐	144	Bob Walk	.10	.03
☐	145	Delino DeShields	.10	.03
☐	146	Kevin Brown	.20	.06
☐	147	Mark Lemke	.10	.03
☐	148	Chuck Knoblauch	.20	.06
☐	149	Chris Sabo	.10	.03
☐	150	Bobby Witt	.10	.03
☐	151	Luis Gonzalez	.20	.06
☐	152	Ron Karkovice	.10	.03
☐	153	Jeff Brantley	.10	.03
☐	154	Kevin Appier	.20	.06
☐	155	Darrin Jackson	.10	.03
☐	156	Kelly Gruber	.10	.03
☐	157	Royce Clayton	.10	.03
☐	158	Chuck Finley	.20	.06
☐	159	Jeff King	.10	.03
☐	160	Greg Vaughn	.10	.03
☐	161	Geronimo Pena	.10	.03
☐	162	Steve Farr	.10	.03
☐	163	Jose Oquendo	.10	.03
☐	164	Mark Lewis	.10	.03
☐	165	John Wetteland	.20	.06
☐	166	Mike Henneman	.10	.03
☐	167	Todd Hundley	.10	.03
☐	168	Wes Chamberlain	.10	.03
☐	169	Steve Avery	.10	.03
☐	170	Mike Devereaux	.10	.03
☐	171	Reggie Sanders	.10	.03
☐	172	Jay Buhner	.20	.06
☐	173	Eric Anthony	.10	.03
☐	174	John Burkett	.10	.03
☐	175	Tom Candiotti	.10	.03
☐	176	Phil Plantier	.10	.03
☐	177	Doug Henry	.10	.03
☐	178	Scott Leius	.10	.03
☐	179	Kirt Manwaring	.10	.03
☐	180	Jeff Parrett	.10	.03
☐	181	Don Slaught	.10	.03
☐	182	Scott Radinsky	.10	.03
☐	183	Luis Alicea	.10	.03
☐	184	Tom Gordon	.10	.03
☐	185	Rick Wilkins	.10	.03
☐	186	Todd Stottlemyre	.10	.03
☐	187	Moises Alou	.20	.06
☐	188	Joe Grahe	.10	.03
☐	189	Jeff Kent	.50	.15
☐	190	Bill Wegman	.10	.03
☐	191	Kim Batiste	.10	.03
☐	192	Matt Nokes	.10	.03
☐	193	Mark Wohlers	.10	.03
☐	194	Paul Sorrento	.10	.03
☐	195	Chris Hammond	.10	.03
☐	196	Scott Livingstone	.10	.03
☐	197	Doug Jones	.10	.03
☐	198	Scott Cooper	.10	.03
☐	199	Ramon Martinez	.10	.03
☐	200	Dave Valle	.10	.03
☐	201	Mariano Duncan	.10	.03
☐	202	Ben McDonald	.10	.03
☐	203	Darren Lewis	.10	.03
☐	204	Kenny Rogers	.20	.06
☐	205	Manuel Lee	.10	.03
☐	206	Scott Erickson	.10	.03
☐	207	Dan Gladden	.10	.03
☐	208	Bob Welch	.10	.03
☐	209	Greg Olson	.10	.03
☐	210	Dan Pasqua	.10	.03
☐	211	Tim Wallach	.10	.03
☐	212	Jeff Montgomery	.10	.03
☐	213	Derrick May	.10	.03
☐	214	Ed Sprague	.10	.03
☐	215	David Haas	.10	.03
☐	216	Darrin Fletcher	.10	.03
☐	217	Brian Jordan	.20	.06
☐	218	Jaime Navarro	.10	.03
☐	219	Randy Velarde	.10	.03
☐	220	Ron Gant	.20	.06
☐	221	Paul Quantrill	.10	.03
☐	222	Damion Easley	.10	.03
☐	223	Charlie Hough	.20	.06
☐	224	Brad Brink	.10	.03
☐	225	Barry Manuel	.10	.03
☐	226	Kevin Koslofski	.10	.03
☐	227	Ryan Thompson	.10	.03
☐	228	Mike Munoz	.10	.03
☐	229	Dan Wilson	.20	.06
☐	230	Peter Hoy	.10	.03
☐	231	Pedro Astacio	.10	.03
☐	232	Matt Stairs	.10	.03
☐	233	Jeff Reboulet	.10	.03
☐	234	Manny Alexander	.10	.03
☐	235	Willie Banks	.10	.03
☐	236	John Jaha	.10	.03
☐	237	Scooter Tucker	.10	.03
☐	238	Russ Springer	.10	.03
☐	239	Paul Miller	.10	.03
☐	240	Dan Peltier	.10	.03
☐	241	Ozzie Canseco	.10	.03
☐	242	Ben Rivera	.10	.03
☐	243	John Valentin	.10	.03
☐	244	Henry Rodriguez	.10	.03
☐	245	Derek Parks	.10	.03
☐	246	Carlos Garcia	.10	.03
☐	247	Tim Pugh RC	.10	.03
☐	248	Melvin Nieves	.10	.03
☐	249	Rich Amaral	.10	.03
☐	250	Willie Greene	.10	.03
☐	251	Tim Scott	.10	.03
☐	252	Dave Silvestri	.10	.03
☐	253	Rob Mallicoat	.10	.03
☐	254	Donald Harris	.10	.03
☐	255	Craig Colbert	.10	.03
☐	256	Jose Guzman	.10	.03
☐	257	Domingo Martinez RC	.10	.03
☐	258	William Suero	.10	.03
☐	259	Juan Guerrero	.10	.03
☐	260	J.T. Snow RC	.50	.15
☐	261	Tony Pena	.10	.03
☐	262	Tim Fortugno	.10	.03
☐	263	Tom Marsh	.10	.03
☐	264	Kurt Knudsen	.10	.03
☐	265	Tim Costo	.10	.03
☐	266	Steve Shifflett	.10	.03
☐	267	Billy Ashley	.10	.03
☐	268	Jerry Nielsen	.10	.03
☐	269	Pete Young	.10	.03
☐	270	Johnny Guzman	.10	.03
☐	271	Greg Colbrunn	.10	.03
☐	272	Jeff Nelson	.10	.03
☐	273	Kevin Young	.20	.06
☐	274	Jeff Frye	.10	.03
☐	275	J.T. Bruett	.10	.03
☐	276	Todd Pratt RC	.25	.07
☐	277	Mike Butcher	.10	.03
☐	278	John Flaherty	.10	.03
☐	279	John Patterson	.10	.03
☐	280	Eric Hillman	.10	.03
☐	281	Bien Figueroa	.10	.03
☐	282	Shane Reynolds	.10	.03
☐	283	Rich Rowland	.10	.03
☐	284	Steve Foster	.10	.03
☐	285	Dave Mlicki	.10	.03
☐	286	Mike Piazza	1.50	.45
☐	287	Mike Trombley	.10	.03
☐	288	Jim Pena	.10	.03
☐	289	Bob Ayrault	.10	.03
☐	290	Henry Mercedes	.10	.03
☐	291	Bob Wickman	.10	.03
☐	292	Jacob Brumfield	.10	.03
☐	293	David Hulse RC	.10	.03
☐	294	Ryan Klesko	.20	.06
☐	295	Doug Linton	.10	.03
☐	296	Steve Cooke	.10	.03
☐	297	Eddie Zosky	.10	.03
☐	298	Gerald Williams	.10	.03
☐	299	Jonathan Hurst	.10	.03
☐	300	Larry Carter RC	.10	.03
☐	301	William Pennyfeather	.10	.03
☐	302	Cesar Hernandez	.10	.03
☐	303	Steve Hosey	.10	.03
☐	304	Blas Minor	.10	.03
☐	305	Jeff Grotewald	.10	.03
☐	306	Bernardo Brito	.10	.03
☐	307	Rafael Bournigal	.10	.03
☐	308	Jeff Branson	.10	.03
☐	309	Tom Quinlan RC	.10	.03
☐	310	Pat Gomez RC	.10	.03
☐	311	Sterling Hitchcock RC	.25	.07
☐	312	Kent Bottenfield	.10	.03
☐	313	Alan Trammell	.20	.06
☐	314	Cris Colon	.10	.03
☐	315	Paul Wagner	.10	.03
☐	316	Matt Maysey	.10	.03
☐	317	Mike Stanton	.10	.03
☐	318	Rick Trlicek	.10	.03
☐	319	Kevin Rogers	.10	.03
☐	320	Mark Clark	.10	.03
☐	321	Pedro Martinez	1.00	.30
☐	322	Al Martin	.10	.03
☐	323	Mike Macfarlane	.10	.03
☐	324	Rey Sanchez	.10	.03
☐	325	Roger Pavlik	.10	.03
☐	326	Troy Neel	.10	.03
☐	327	Kerry Woodson	.10	.03
☐	328	Wayne Kirby	.10	.03
☐	329	Ken Ryan RC	.25	.07
☐	330	Jesse Levis	.10	.03
☐	331	Jim Austin	.10	.03
☐	332	Dan Walters	.10	.03
☐	333	Brian Williams	.10	.03
☐	334	Wil Cordero	.10	.03
☐	335	Bret Boone	.30	.09
☐	336	Hipolito Pichardo	.10	.03
☐	337	Pat Mahomes	.10	.03
☐	338	Andy Stankiewicz	.10	.03
☐	339	Jim Bullinger	.10	.03
☐	340	Archi Cianfrocco	.10	.03
☐	341	Ruben Amaro	.10	.03
☐	342	Frank Seminara	.10	.03
☐	343	Pat Hentgen	.10	.03
☐	344	Dave Nilsson	.10	.03
☐	345	Mike Perez	.10	.03
☐	346	Tim Salmon	.30	.09
☐	347	Tim Wakefield	.50	.15
☐	348	Carlos Hernandez	.10	.03
☐	349	Donovan Osborne	.10	.03
☐	350	Denny Neagle	.20	.06
☐	351	Sam Militello	.10	.03
☐	352	Eric Fox	.10	.03
☐	353	John Doherty	.10	.03
☐	354	Chad Curtis	.10	.03
☐	355	Jeff Tackett	.10	.03
☐	356	Dave Fleming	.10	.03
☐	357	Pat Listach	.10	.03
☐	358	Kevin Wickander	.10	.03
☐	359	John Vander Wal	.10	.03
☐	360	Arthur Rhodes	.10	.03
☐	361	Bob Scanlan	.10	.03
☐	362	Bob Zupcic	.10	.03
☐	363	Mel Rojas	.10	.03
☐	364	Jim Thome	.50	.15
☐	365	Bill Pecota	.10	.03
☐	366	Mark Carreon	.10	.03
☐	367	Mitch Williams	.10	.03
☐	368	Cal Eldred	.10	.03
☐	369	Stan Belinda	.10	.03
☐	370	Pat Kelly	.10	.03
☐	371	Rheal Cormier	.10	.03
☐	372	Juan Guzman	.10	.03
☐	373	Damon Berryhill	.10	.03

❑ 374 Gary DiSarcina .10 .03
❑ 375 Norm Charlton .10 .03
❑ 376 Roberto Hernandez .10 .03
❑ 377 Scott Kamieniecki .10 .03
❑ 378 Rusty Meacham .10 .03
❑ 379 Kurt Stillwell .10 .03
❑ 380 Lloyd McClendon .10 .03
❑ 381 Mark Leonard .10 .03
❑ 382 Jerry Browne .10 .03
❑ 383 Glenn Davis .10 .03
❑ 384 Randy Johnson .50 .15
❑ 385 Mike Greenwell .10 .03
❑ 386 Scott Chiamparino .10 .03
❑ 387 George Bell .10 .03
❑ 388 Steve Olin .10 .03
❑ 389 Chuck McElroy .10 .03
❑ 390 Mark Gardner .10 .03
❑ 391 Rod Beck .10 .03
❑ 392 Dennis Rasmussen .10 .03
❑ 393 Charlie Leibrandt .10 .03
❑ 394 Julio Franco .20 .06
❑ 395 Pete Harnisch .10 .03
❑ 396 Sid Bream .10 .03
❑ 397 Milt Thompson .10 .03
❑ 398 Glenallen Hill .10 .03
❑ 399 Chico Walker .10 .03
❑ 400 Alex Cole .10 .03
❑ 401 Trevor Wilson .10 .03
❑ 402 Jeff Conine .20 .06
❑ 403 Kyle Abbott .10 .03
❑ 404 Tom Browning .10 .03
❑ 405 Jerald Clark .10 .03
❑ 406 Vince Horsman .10 .03
❑ 407 Kevin Mitchell .10 .03
❑ 408 Pete Smith .10 .03
❑ 409 Jeff Innis .10 .03
❑ 410 Mike Timlin .10 .03
❑ 411 Charlie Hayes .10 .03
❑ 412 Alex Fernandez .10 .03
❑ 413 Jeff Russell .10 .03
❑ 414 Jody Reed .10 .03
❑ 415 Mickey Morandini .10 .03
❑ 416 Darnell Coles .10 .03
❑ 417 Xavier Hernandez .10 .03
❑ 418 Steve Sax .10 .03
❑ 419 Joe Girardi .10 .03
❑ 420 Mike Fetters .10 .03
❑ 421 Danny Jackson .10 .03
❑ 422 Jim Gott .10 .03
❑ 423 Tim Belcher .10 .03
❑ 424 Jose Mesa .10 .03
❑ 425 Junior Felix .10 .03
❑ 426 Thomas Howard .10 .03
❑ 427 Julio Valera .10 .03
❑ 428 Dante Bichette .20 .06
❑ 429 Mike Sharperson .10 .03
❑ 430 Darryl Kile .20 .06
❑ 431 Lonnie Smith .10 .03
❑ 432 Monty Fariss .10 .03
❑ 433 Reggie Jefferson .10 .03
❑ 434 Bob McClure .10 .03
❑ 435 Craig Lefferts .10 .03
❑ 436 Duane Ward .10 .03
❑ 437 Shawn Abner .10 .03
❑ 438 Roberto Kelly .10 .03
❑ 439 Paul O'Neill .30 .09
❑ 440 Alan Mills .10 .03
❑ 441 Roger Mason .10 .03
❑ 442 Gary Pettis .10 .03
❑ 443 Steve Lake .10 .03
❑ 444 Gene Larkin .10 .03
❑ 445 Larry Andersen .10 .03
❑ 446 Doug Dascenzo .10 .03
❑ 447 Daryl Boston .10 .03
❑ 448 John Candelaria .10 .03
❑ 449 Storm Davis .10 .03
❑ 450 Tom Edens .10 .03
❑ 451 Mike Maddux .10 .03
❑ 452 Tim Naehring .10 .03
❑ 453 John Orton .10 .03
❑ 454 Joey Cora .10 .03
❑ 455 Chuck Crim .10 .03
❑ 456 Dan Plesac .10 .03
❑ 457 Mike Bielecki .10 .03
❑ 458 Terry Jorgensen .10 .03
❑ 459 John Habyan .10 .03
❑ 460 Pete O'Brien .10 .03
❑ 461 Jeff Treadway .10 .03
❑ 462 Frank Castillo .10 .03
❑ 463 Jimmy Jones .10 .03
❑ 464 Tommy Greene .10 .03
❑ 465 Tracy Woodson .10 .03
❑ 466 Rich Rodriguez .10 .03
❑ 467 Joe Hesketh .10 .03
❑ 468 Greg Myers .10 .03
❑ 469 Kirk McCaskill .10 .03
❑ 470 Ricky Bones .10 .03
❑ 471 Lenny Webster .10 .03
❑ 472 Francisco Cabrera .10 .03
❑ 473 Turner Ward .10 .03
❑ 474 Dwayne Henry .10 .03
❑ 475 Al Osuna .10 .03
❑ 476 Craig Wilson .10 .03
❑ 477 Chris Nabholz .10 .03
❑ 478 Rafael Belliard .10 .03
❑ 479 Terry Leach .10 .03
❑ 480 Tim Teufel .10 .03
❑ 481 Dennis Eckersley AW .20 .06
❑ 482 Barry Bonds AW .60 .18
❑ 483 Dennis Eckersley AW .20 .06
❑ 484 Greg Maddux AW .50 .15
❑ 485 Pat Listach AW .10 .03
❑ 486 Eric Karros AW .10 .03
❑ 487 Jamie Arnold DP RC .10 .03
❑ 488 B.J. Wallace DP .10 .03
❑ 489 Derek Jeter DP RC 10.00 3.00
❑ 490 Jason Kendall DP RC .75 .23
❑ 491 Rick Helling DP .10 .03
❑ 492 Derek Wallace DP RC .10 .03
❑ 493 Sean Lowe DP RC .10 .03
❑ 494 S.Stewart DP RC .75 .23
❑ 495 Benji Grigsby DP RC .10 .03
❑ 496 T.Steverson DP RC .10 .03
❑ 497 Dan Serafini DP RC .10 .03
❑ 498 Michael Tucker DP .20 .06
❑ 499 Chris Roberts DP .10 .03
❑ 500 Pete Janicki DP RC .10 .03
❑ 501 Jeff Schmidt DP RC .10 .03
❑ 502 Edgar Martinez AS .20 .06
❑ 503 Omar Vizquel AS .20 .06
❑ 504 Ken Griffey Jr. AS .50 .15
❑ 505 Kirby Puckett AS .30 .09
❑ 506 Joe Carter AS .10 .03
❑ 507 Ivan Rodriguez AS .30 .09
❑ 508 Jack Morris AS .10 .03
❑ 509 Dennis Eckersley AS .20 .06
❑ 510 Frank Thomas AS .30 .09
❑ 511 Roberto Alomar AS .20 .06
❑ 512 Mickey Morandini AS .10 .03
❑ 513 Dennis Eckersley HL .20 .06
❑ 514 Jeff Reardon HL .10 .03
❑ 515 Danny Tartabull HL .10 .03
❑ 516 Bip Roberts HL .10 .03
❑ 517 George Brett HL .60 .18
❑ 518 Robin Yount HL .50 .15
❑ 519 Kevin Gross HL .10 .03
❑ 520 Ed Sprague WS .10 .03
❑ 521 Dave Winfield WS .10 .03
❑ 522 Ozzie Smith AS .50 .15
❑ 523 Barry Bonds AS .60 .18
❑ 524 Andy Van Slyke AS .10 .03
❑ 525 Tony Gwynn AS .30 .09
❑ 526 Darren Daulton AS .10 .03
❑ 527 Greg Maddux AS .50 .15
❑ 528 Fred McGriff AS .30 .09
❑ 529 Lee Smith AS .10 .03
❑ 530 Ryne Sandberg AS .50 .15
❑ 531 Gary Sheffield AS .10 .03
❑ 532 Ozzie Smith DT .50 .15
❑ 533 Kirby Puckett DT .30 .09
❑ 534 Gary Sheffield DT .10 .03
❑ 535 Andy Van Slyke DT .10 .03
❑ 536 Ken Griffey Jr. DT .50 .15
❑ 537 Ivan Rodriguez DT .30 .09
❑ 538 Charles Nagy DT .10 .03
❑ 539 Tom Glavine DT .20 .06
❑ 540 Dennis Eckersley DT .20 .06
❑ 541 Frank Thomas DT .30 .09
❑ 542 Roberto Alomar DT .20 .06
❑ 543 Sean Berry .10 .03
❑ 544 Mike Schooler .10 .03
❑ 545 Chuck Carr .10 .03
❑ 546 Lenny Harris .10 .03
❑ 547 Gary Scott .10 .03
❑ 548 Derek Lilliquist .10 .03
❑ 549 Brian Hunter .10 .03
❑ 550 Kirby Puckett MOY .30 .09
❑ 551 Jim Eisenreich .10 .03
❑ 552 Andre Dawson .20 .06
❑ 553 David Nied .10 .03
❑ 554 Spike Owen .10 .03
❑ 555 Greg Gagne .10 .03
❑ 556 Sid Fernandez .10 .03
❑ 557 Mark McGwire 1.25 .35
❑ 558 Bryan Harvey .10 .03
❑ 559 Harold Reynolds .20 .06
❑ 560 Barry Bonds 1.25 .35
❑ 561 Eric Wedge RC .25 .07
❑ 562 Ozzie Smith .75 .23
❑ 563 Rick Sutcliffe .20 .06
❑ 564 Jeff Reardon .20 .06
❑ 565 Alex Arias .10 .03
❑ 566 Greg Swindell .10 .03
❑ 567 Brook Jacoby .10 .03
❑ 568 Pete Incaviglia .10 .03
❑ 569 Butch Henry .10 .03
❑ 570 Eric Davis .20 .06
❑ 571 Kevin Seitzer .10 .03
❑ 572 Tony Fernandez .10 .03
❑ 573 Steve Reed RC .10 .03
❑ 574 Cory Snyder .10 .03
❑ 575 Joe Carter .20 .06
❑ 576 Greg Maddux .75 .23
❑ 577 Bert Blyleven UER .20 .06
(Should say 3701
career strikeouts)
❑ 578 Kevin Bass .10 .03
❑ 579 Carlton Fisk .30 .09
❑ 580 Doug Drabek .10 .03
❑ 581 Mark Gubicza .10 .03
❑ 582 Bobby Thigpen .10 .03
❑ 583 Chili Davis .20 .06
❑ 584 Scott Bankhead .10 .03
❑ 585 Harold Baines .20 .06
❑ 586 Eric Young .10 .03
❑ 587 Lance Parrish .20 .06
❑ 588 Juan Bell .10 .03
❑ 589 Bob Ojeda .10 .03
❑ 590 Joe Orsulak .10 .03
❑ 591 Benito Santiago .20 .06
❑ 592 Wade Boggs .30 .09
❑ 593 Robby Thompson .10 .03
❑ 594 Eric Plunk .10 .03
❑ 595 Hensley Meulens .10 .03
❑ 596 Lou Whitaker .20 .06
❑ 597 Dale Murphy .50 .15
❑ 598 Paul Molitor .30 .09
❑ 599 Greg W. Harris .10 .03
❑ 600 Darren Holmes .10 .03
❑ 601 Dave Martinez .10 .03
❑ 602 Tom Henke .10 .03
❑ 603 Mike Benjamin .10 .03
❑ 604 Rene Gonzales .10 .03
❑ 605 Roger McDowell .10 .03
❑ 606 Kirby Puckett .50 .15
❑ 607 Randy Myers .10 .03
❑ 608 Ruben Sierra .10 .03
❑ 609 Wilson Alvarez .10 .03
❑ 610 David Segui .10 .03
❑ 611 Juan Samuel .10 .03
❑ 612 Tom Brunansky .10 .03
❑ 613 Willie Randolph .20 .06
❑ 614 Tony Phillips .10 .03
❑ 615 Candy Maldonado .10 .03
❑ 616 Chris Bosio .10 .03
❑ 617 Bret Barberie .10 .03
❑ 618 Scott Sanderson .10 .03
❑ 619 Ron Darling .10 .03
❑ 620 Dave Winfield .20 .06
❑ 621 Mike Felder .10 .03
❑ 622 Greg Hibbard .10 .03
❑ 623 Mike Scioscia .10 .03
❑ 624 John Smiley .10 .03
❑ 625 Alejandro Pena .10 .03
❑ 626 Terry Steinbach .10 .03
❑ 627 Freddie Benavides .10 .03
❑ 628 Kevin Reimer .10 .03
❑ 629 Braulio Castillo .10 .03

		Nm-Mt	Ex-Mt
❑ 630	Dave Stieb	.10	.03
❑ 631	Dave Magadan	.10	.03
❑ 632	Scott Fletcher	.10	.03
❑ 633	Cris Carpenter	.10	.03
❑ 634	Kevin Maas	.10	.03
❑ 635	Todd Worrell	.10	.03
❑ 636	Rob Deer	.10	.03
❑ 637	Dwight Smith	.10	.03
❑ 638	Chito Martinez	.10	.03
❑ 639	Jimmy Key	.20	.06
❑ 640	Greg A. Harris	.10	.03
❑ 641	Mike Moore	.10	.03
❑ 642	Pat Borders	.10	.03
❑ 643	Bill Gullickson	.10	.03
❑ 644	Gary Gaetti	.20	.06
❑ 645	David Howard	.10	.03
❑ 646	Jim Abbott	.30	.09
❑ 647	Willie Wilson	.10	.03
❑ 648	David Wells	.20	.06
❑ 649	Andres Galarraga	.20	.06
❑ 650	Vince Coleman	.10	.03
❑ 651	Rob Dibble	.20	.06
❑ 652	Frank Tanana	.10	.03
❑ 653	Steve Decker	.10	.03
❑ 654	David Cone	.20	.06
❑ 655	Jack Armstrong	.10	.03
❑ 656	Dave Stewart	.20	.06
❑ 657	Billy Hatcher	.10	.03
❑ 658	Tim Raines	.20	.06
❑ 659	Walt Weiss	.10	.03
❑ 660	Jose Lind	.10	.03

1994 Score Rookie/Traded

	Nm-Mt	Ex-Mt
COMPLETE SET (165)	15.00	4.50

		Nm-Mt	Ex-Mt
❑ RT1	Will Clark	.75	.23
❑ RT2	Lee Smith	.30	.09
❑ RT3	Bo Jackson	.75	.23
❑ RT4	Ellis Burks	.30	.09
❑ RT5	Eddie Murray	.75	.23
❑ RT6	Delino DeShields	.15	.04
❑ RT7	Erik Hanson	.15	.04
❑ RT8	Rafael Palmeiro	.50	.15
❑ RT9	Luis Polonia	.15	.04
❑ RT10	Omar Vizquel	.50	.15
❑ RT11	Kurt Abbott	.30	.09
❑ RT12	Vince Coleman	.15	.04
❑ RT13	Rickey Henderson	.75	.23
❑ RT14	Terry Mulholland	.15	.04
❑ RT15	Greg Hibbard	.15	.04
❑ RT16	Walt Weiss	.15	.04
❑ RT17	Chris Sabo	.15	.04
❑ RT18	Dave Henderson	.15	.04
❑ RT19	Rick Sutcliffe	.30	.09
❑ RT20	Harold Reynolds	.30	.09
❑ RT21	Jack Morris	.30	.09
❑ RT22	Dan Wilson	.15	.04
❑ RT23	Dave Magadan	.15	.04
❑ RT24	Dennis Martinez	.30	.09
❑ RT25	Wes Chamberlain	.15	.04
❑ RT26	Otis Nixon	.15	.04
❑ RT27	Eric Anthony	.15	.04
❑ RT28	Randy Milligan	.15	.04
❑ RT29	Julio Franco	.30	.09
❑ RT30	Kevin McReynolds	.15	.04
❑ RT31	Anthony Young	.15	.04
❑ RT32	Brian Harper	.15	.04
❑ RT33	Gene Harris	.15	.04
❑ RT34	Eddie Taubensee	.15	.04
❑ RT35	David Segui	.15	.04
❑ RT36	Stan Javier	.15	.04
❑ RT37	Felix Fermin	.15	.04
❑ RT38	Darrin Jackson	.15	.04
❑ RT39	Tony Fernandez	.15	.04
❑ RT40	Jose Vizcaino	.15	.04
❑ RT41	Willie Banks	.15	.04
❑ RT42	Brian Hunter	.15	.04
❑ RT43	Reggie Jefferson	.15	.04
❑ RT44	Junior Felix	.15	.04
❑ RT45	Jack Armstrong	.15	.04
❑ RT46	Bip Roberts	.15	.04
❑ RT47	Jerry Browne	.15	.04
❑ RT48	Marvin Freeman	.15	.04
❑ RT49	Jody Reed	.15	.04
❑ RT50	Alex Cole	.15	.04
❑ RT51	Sid Fernandez	.15	.04
❑ RT52	Pete Smith	.15	.04
❑ RT53	Xavier Hernandez	.15	.04
❑ RT54	Scott Sanderson	.15	.04
❑ RT55	Turner Ward	.15	.04
❑ RT56	Rex Hudler	.15	.04
❑ RT57	Deion Sanders	.50	.15
❑ RT58	Sid Bream	.15	.04
❑ RT59	Tony Pena	.15	.04
❑ RT60	Bret Boone	.30	.09
❑ RT61	Bobby Ayala	.15	.04
❑ RT62	Pedro Martinez	.75	.23
❑ RT63	Howard Johnson	.15	.04
❑ RT64	Mark Portugal	.15	.04
❑ RT65	Roberto Kelly	.15	.04
❑ RT66	Spike Owen	.15	.04
❑ RT67	Jeff Treadway	.15	.04
❑ RT68	Mike Harkey	.15	.04
❑ RT69	Doug Jones	.15	.04
❑ RT70	Steve Farr	.15	.04
❑ RT71	Billy Taylor RC	.15	.04
❑ RT72	Manny Ramirez	.50	.15
❑ RT73	Bob Hamelin	.15	.04
❑ RT74	Steve Karsay	.15	.04
❑ RT75	Ryan Klesko	.30	.09
❑ RT76	Cliff Floyd	.30	.09
❑ RT77	Jeffrey Hammonds	.15	.04
❑ RT78	Javier Lopez	.30	.09
❑ RT79	Roger Salkeld	.15	.04
❑ RT80	Hector Carrasco	.15	.04
❑ RT81	Gerald Williams	.15	.04
❑ RT82	Raul Mondesi	.30	.09
❑ RT83	Sterling Hitchcock	.15	.04
❑ RT84	Danny Bautista	.15	.04
❑ RT85	Chris Turner	.15	.04
❑ RT86	Shane Reynolds	.15	.04
❑ RT87	Rondell White	.30	.09
❑ RT88	Salomon Torres	.15	.04
❑ RT89	Turk Wendell	.15	.04
❑ RT90	Tony Tarasco	.15	.04
❑ RT91	Shawn Green	.75	.23
❑ RT92	Greg Colbrunn	.15	.04
❑ RT93	Eddie Zambrano	.15	.04
❑ RT94	Rich Becker	.15	.04
❑ RT95	Chris Gomez	.15	.04
❑ RT96	John Patterson	.15	.04
❑ RT97	Derek Parks	.15	.04
❑ RT98	Rich Rowland	.15	.04
❑ RT99	James Mouton	.15	.04
❑ RT100	Tim Hyers RC	.15	.04
❑ RT101	Jose Valentin	.15	.04
❑ RT102	Carlos Delgado	.50	.15
❑ RT103	Robert Eenhoorn	.15	.04
❑ RT104	John Hudek RC	.15	.04
❑ RT105	Domingo Cedeno	.15	.04
❑ RT106	Denny Hocking	.15	.04
❑ RT107	Greg Pirkl	.15	.04
❑ RT108	Mark Smith	.15	.04
❑ RT109	Paul Shuey	.15	.04
❑ RT110	Jorge Fabregas	.15	.04
❑ RT111	Rikkert Faneyte RC	.15	.04
❑ RT112	Rob Butler	.15	.04
❑ RT113	Darren Oliver RC	.30	.09
❑ RT114	Troy O'Leary	.15	.04
❑ RT115	Scott Brow	.15	.04
❑ RT116	Tony Eusebio	.15	.04
❑ RT117	Carlos Reyes	.15	.04
❑ RT118	J.R. Phillips	.15	.04
❑ RT119	Alex Diaz	.15	.04
❑ RT120	Charles Johnson	.30	.09
❑ RT121	Nate Minchey	.15	.04
❑ RT122	Scott Sanders	.15	.04
❑ RT123	Daryl Boston	.15	.04
❑ RT124	Joey Hamilton	.15	.04
❑ RT125	Brian Anderson	.30	.09
❑ RT126	Dan Miceli	.15	.04
❑ RT127	Tom Brunansky	.15	.04
❑ RT128	Dave Staton	.15	.04
❑ RT129	Mike Oquist	.15	.04
❑ RT130	John Mabry RC	.30	.09
❑ RT131	Norberto Martin	.15	.04
❑ RT132	Hector Fajardo	.15	.04
❑ RT133	Mark Hutton	.15	.04
❑ RT134	Fernando Vina	.15	.04
❑ RT135	Lee Tinsley	.15	.04
❑ RT136	Chan Ho Park RC	.50	.15
❑ RT137	Paul Spoljaric	.15	.04
❑ RT138	Matias Carrillo	.15	.04
❑ RT139	Mark Kiefer	.15	.04
❑ RT140	Stan Royer	.15	.04
❑ RT141	Bryan Eversgerd	.15	.04
❑ RT142	Brian L. Hunter	.15	.04
❑ RT143	Joe Hall	.15	.04
❑ RT144	Johnny Ruffin	.15	.04
❑ RT145	Alex Gonzalez	.15	.04
❑ RT146	Keith Lockhart RC	.30	.09
❑ RT147	Tom Marsh	.15	.04
❑ RT148	Tony Longmire	.15	.04
❑ RT149	Keith Mitchell	.15	.04
❑ RT150	Melvin Nieves	.15	.04
❑ RT151	Kelly Stinnett RC	.15	.04
❑ RT152	Miguel Jimenez	.15	.04
❑ RT153	Jeff Juden	.15	.04
❑ RT154	Matt Walbeck	.15	.04
❑ RT155	Marc Newfield	.15	.04
❑ RT156	Matt Mieske	.15	.04
❑ RT157	Marcus Moore	.15	.04
❑ RT158	Jose Lima RC SP	5.00	1.50
❑ RT159	Mike Kelly	.15	.04
❑ RT160	Jim Edmonds	.75	.23
❑ RT161	Steve Trachsel	.15	.04
❑ RT162	Greg Blosser	.15	.04
❑ RT163	Marc Acre RC	.15	.04
❑ RT164	AL Checklist	.15	.04
❑ RT165	NL Checklist	.15	.04
❑ HC1	Alex Rodriguez Call-Up Redemption	400.00	120.00
❑ NNO	Sept. Call-Up Trade EXP	2.00	.60

1993 Select

	Nm-Mt	Ex-Mt
COMPLETE SET (405)	25.00	7.50

		Nm-Mt	Ex-Mt
❑ 1	Barry Bonds	1.25	.35
❑ 2	Ken Griffey Jr.	.75	.23
❑ 3	Will Clark	.50	.15
❑ 4	Kirby Puckett	.50	.15
❑ 5	Tony Gwynn	.60	.18
❑ 6	Frank Thomas	.50	.15
❑ 7	Tom Glavine	.30	.09
❑ 8	Roberto Alomar	.30	.09
❑ 9	Andre Dawson	.20	.06
❑ 10	Ron Darling	.15	.04

❑ 11 Bobby Bonilla .20 .06
❑ 12 Danny Tartabull .15 .04
❑ 13 Darren Daulton .20 .06
❑ 14 Roger Clemens 1.00 .30
❑ 15 Ozzie Smith .75 .23
❑ 16 Mark McGwire 1.25 .35
❑ 17 Terry Pendleton .20 .06
❑ 18 Cal Ripken 1.50 .45
❑ 19 Fred McGriff .30 .09
❑ 20 Cecil Fielder .20 .06
❑ 21 Darryl Strawberry .20 .06
❑ 22 Robin Yount .75 .23
❑ 23 Barry Larkin .30 .09
❑ 24 Don Mattingly 1.25 .35
❑ 25 Craig Biggio .30 .09
❑ 26 Sandy Alomar Jr. .15 .04
❑ 27 Larry Walker .30 .09
❑ 28 Junior Felix .15 .04
❑ 29 Eddie Murray .50 .15
❑ 30 Robin Ventura .20 .06
❑ 31 Greg Maddux .75 .23
❑ 32 Dave Winfield .20 .06
❑ 33 John Kruk .20 .06
❑ 34 Wally Joyner .20 .06
❑ 35 Andy Van Slyke .20 .06
❑ 36 Chuck Knoblauch .20 .06
❑ 37 Tom Pagnozzi .15 .04
❑ 38 Dennis Eckersley .20 .06
❑ 39 Dave Justice .20 .06
❑ 40 Juan Gonzalez .30 .09
❑ 41 Gary Sheffield .20 .06
❑ 42 Paul Molitor .30 .09
❑ 43 Delino DeShields .15 .04
❑ 44 Travis Fryman .20 .06
❑ 45 Hal Morris .15 .04
❑ 46 Greg Olson .15 .04
❑ 47 Ken Caminiti .20 .06
❑ 48 Wade Boggs .30 .09
❑ 49 Orel Hershiser .20 .06
❑ 50 Albert Belle .20 .06
❑ 51 Bill Swift .15 .04
❑ 52 Mark Langston .15 .04
❑ 53 Joe Girardi .15 .04
❑ 54 Keith Miller .15 .04
❑ 55 Gary Carter .20 .06
❑ 56 Brady Anderson .20 .06
❑ 57 Dwight Gooden .20 .06
❑ 58 Julio Franco .20 .06
❑ 59 Lenny Dykstra .20 .06
❑ 60 Mickey Tettleton .15 .04
❑ 61 Randy Tomlin .15 .04
❑ 62 B.J. Surhoff .20 .06
❑ 63 Todd Zeile .15 .04
❑ 64 Roberto Kelly .15 .04
❑ 65 Rob Dibble .20 .06
❑ 66 Leo Gomez .15 .04
❑ 67 Doug Jones .15 .04
❑ 68 Ellis Burks .20 .06
❑ 69 Mike Scioscia .15 .04
❑ 70 Charles Nagy .15 .04
❑ 71 Cory Snyder .15 .04
❑ 72 Devon White .20 .06
❑ 73 Mark Grace .30 .09
❑ 74 Luis Polonia .15 .04
❑ 75 John Smiley 2X .15 .04
❑ 76 Carlton Fisk .30 .09
❑ 77 Luis Sojo .15 .04
❑ 78 George Brett 1.25 .35
❑ 79 Mitch Williams .15 .04
❑ 80 Kent Hrbek .20 .06
❑ 81 Jay Bell .20 .06
❑ 82 Edgar Martinez .30 .09
❑ 83 Lee Smith .20 .06
❑ 84 Deion Sanders .30 .09
❑ 85 Bill Gullickson .15 .04
❑ 86 Paul O'Neill .30 .09
❑ 87 Kevin Seitzer .15 .04
❑ 88 Steve Finley .20 .06
❑ 89 Mel Hall .15 .04
❑ 90 Nolan Ryan 2.00 .60
❑ 91 Eric Davis .20 .06
❑ 92 Mike Mussina .30 .09
❑ 93 Tony Fernandez .15 .04
❑ 94 Frank Viola .20 .06
❑ 95 Matt Williams .20 .06
❑ 96 Joe Carter .20 .06
❑ 97 Ryne Sandberg .75 .23
❑ 98 Jim Abbott .30 .09
❑ 99 Marquis Grissom .20 .06
❑ 100 George Bell .15 .04
❑ 101 Howard Johnson .15 .04
❑ 102 Kevin Appier .20 .06
❑ 103 Dale Murphy .50 .15
❑ 104 Shane Mack .15 .04
❑ 105 Jose Lind .15 .04
❑ 106 Rickey Henderson .50 .15
❑ 107 Bob Tewksbury .15 .04
❑ 108 Kevin Mitchell .15 .04
❑ 109 Steve Avery .15 .04
❑ 110 Candy Maldonado .15 .04
❑ 111 Bip Roberts .15 .04
❑ 112 Lou Whitaker .20 .06
❑ 113 Jeff Bagwell .30 .09
❑ 114 Dante Bichette .20 .06
❑ 115 Brett Butler .20 .06
❑ 116 Melido Perez .15 .04
❑ 117 Andy Benes .15 .04
❑ 118 Randy Johnson .50 .15
❑ 119 Willie McGee .20 .06
❑ 120 Jody Reed .15 .04
❑ 121 Shawon Dunston .15 .04
❑ 122 Carlos Baerga .15 .04
❑ 123 Bret Saberhagen .20 .06
❑ 124 John Olerud .20 .06
❑ 125 Ivan Calderon .15 .04
❑ 126 Bryan Harvey .15 .04
❑ 127 Terry Mulholland .15 .04
❑ 128 Ozzie Guillen .15 .04
❑ 129 Steve Buechele .15 .04
❑ 130 Kevin Tapani .15 .04
❑ 131 Felix Jose .15 .04
❑ 132 Terry Steinbach .15 .04
❑ 133 Ron Gant .20 .06
❑ 134 Harold Reynolds .20 .06
❑ 135 Chris Sabo .15 .04
❑ 136 Ivan Rodriguez .50 .15
❑ 137 Eric Anthony .15 .04
❑ 138 Mike Henneman .15 .04
❑ 139 Robby Thompson .15 .04
❑ 140 Scott Fletcher .15 .04
❑ 141 Bruce Hurst .15 .04
❑ 142 Kevin Maas .15 .04
❑ 143 Tom Candiotti .15 .04
❑ 144 Chris Hoiles .15 .04
❑ 145 Mike Morgan .15 .04
❑ 146 Mark Whiten .15 .04
❑ 147 Dennis Martinez .20 .06
❑ 148 Tony Pena .15 .04
❑ 149 Dave Magadan .15 .04
❑ 150 Mark Lewis .15 .04
❑ 151 Mariano Duncan .15 .04
❑ 152 Gregg Jefferies .15 .04
❑ 153 Doug Drabek .15 .04
❑ 154 Brian Harper .15 .04
❑ 155 Ray Lankford .15 .04
❑ 156 Carney Lansford .20 .06
❑ 157 Mike Sharperson .15 .04
❑ 158 Jack Morris .20 .06
❑ 159 Otis Nixon .15 .04
❑ 160 Steve Sax .15 .04
❑ 161 Mark Lemke .15 .04
❑ 162 Rafael Palmeiro .30 .09
❑ 163 Jose Rijo .15 .04
❑ 164 Omar Vizquel .30 .09
❑ 165 Sammy Sosa .75 .23
❑ 166 Milt Cuyler .15 .04
❑ 167 John Franco .20 .06
❑ 168 Darryl Hamilton .15 .04
❑ 169 Ken Hill .15 .04
❑ 170 Mike Devereaux .15 .04
❑ 171 Don Slaught .15 .04
❑ 172 Steve Farr .15 .04
❑ 173 Bernard Gilkey .15 .04
❑ 174 Mike Fetters .15 .04
❑ 175 Vince Coleman .15 .04
❑ 176 Kevin McReynolds .15 .04
❑ 177 John Smoltz .30 .09
❑ 178 Greg Gagne .15 .04
❑ 179 Greg Swindell .15 .04
❑ 180 Juan Guzman .15 .04
❑ 181 Kal Daniels .15 .04
❑ 182 Rick Sutcliffe .20 .06
❑ 183 Orlando Merced .15 .04
❑ 184 Bill Wegman .15 .04
❑ 185 Mark Gardner .15 .04
❑ 186 Rob Deer .15 .04
❑ 187 Dave Hollins .15 .04
❑ 188 Jack Clark .20 .06
❑ 189 Brian Hunter .15 .04
❑ 190 Tim Wallach .15 .04
❑ 191 Tim Belcher .15 .04
❑ 192 Walt Weiss .15 .04
❑ 193 Kurt Stillwell .15 .04
❑ 194 Charlie Hayes .15 .04
❑ 195 Willie Randolph .20 .06
❑ 196 Jack McDowell .15 .04
❑ 197 Jose Offerman .15 .04
❑ 198 Chuck Finley .20 .06
❑ 199 Darrin Jackson .15 .04
❑ 200 Kelly Gruber .15 .04
❑ 201 John Wetteland .20 .06
❑ 202 Jay Buhner .20 .06
❑ 203 Mike LaValliere .15 .04
❑ 204 Kevin Brown .20 .06
❑ 205 Luis Gonzalez .20 .06
❑ 206 Rick Aguilera .15 .04
❑ 207 Norm Charlton .15 .04
❑ 208 Mike Bordick .15 .04
❑ 209 Charlie Leibrandt .15 .04
❑ 210 Tom Brunansky .15 .04
❑ 211 Tom Henke .15 .04
❑ 212 Randy Milligan .15 .04
❑ 213 Ramon Martinez .15 .04
❑ 214 Mo Vaughn .20 .06
❑ 215 Randy Myers .15 .04
❑ 216 Greg Hibbard .15 .04
❑ 217 Wes Chamberlain .15 .04
❑ 218 Tony Phillips .15 .04
❑ 219 Pete Harnisch .15 .04
❑ 220 Mike Gallego .15 .04
❑ 221 Bud Black .15 .04
❑ 222 Greg Vaughn .15 .04
❑ 223 Milt Thompson .15 .04
❑ 224 Ben McDonald .15 .04
❑ 225 Billy Hatcher .15 .04
❑ 226 Paul Sorrento .15 .04
❑ 227 Mark Gubicza .15 .04
❑ 228 Mike Greenwell .15 .04
❑ 229 Curt Schilling .20 .06
❑ 230 Alan Trammell .20 .06
❑ 231 Zane Smith .15 .04
❑ 232 Bobby Thigpen .15 .04
❑ 233 Greg Olson .15 .04
❑ 234 Joe Orsulak .15 .04
❑ 235 Joe Oliver .15 .04
❑ 236 Tim Raines .20 .06
❑ 237 Juan Samuel .15 .04
❑ 238 Chili Davis .20 .06
❑ 239 Spike Owen .15 .04
❑ 240 Dave Stewart .20 .06
❑ 241 Jim Eisenreich .15 .04
❑ 242 Phil Plantier .15 .04
❑ 243 Sid Fernandez .15 .04
❑ 244 Dan Gladden .15 .04
❑ 245 Mickey Morandini .15 .04
❑ 246 Tino Martinez .30 .09
❑ 247 Kirt Manwaring .15 .04
❑ 248 Dean Palmer .20 .06
❑ 249 Tom Browning .15 .04
❑ 250 Brian McRae .15 .04
❑ 251 Scott Leius .15 .04
❑ 252 Bert Blyleven .20 .06
❑ 253 Scott Erickson .15 .04
❑ 254 Bob Welch .15 .04
❑ 255 Pat Kelly .15 .04
❑ 256 Felix Fermin .15 .04
❑ 257 Harold Baines .20 .06
❑ 258 Duane Ward .15 .04
❑ 259 Bill Spiers .15 .04
❑ 260 Jaime Navarro .15 .04
❑ 261 Scott Sanderson .15 .04
❑ 262 Gary Gaetti .20 .06
❑ 263 Bob Ojeda .15 .04
❑ 264 Jeff Montgomery .15 .04
❑ 265 Scott Bankhead .15 .04
❑ 266 Lance Johnson .15 .04
❑ 267 Rafael Belliard .15 .04
❑ 268 Kevin Reimer .15 .04

❑ 269 Benito Santiago .20 .06
❑ 270 Mike Moore .15 .04
❑ 271 Dave Fleming .15 .04
❑ 272 Moises Alou .20 .06
❑ 273 Pat Listach .15 .04
❑ 274 Reggie Sanders .15 .04
❑ 275 Kenny Lofton .20 .06
❑ 276 Donovan Osborne .15 .04
❑ 277 Rusty Meacham .15 .04
❑ 278 Eric Karros .20 .06
❑ 279 Andy Stankiewicz .15 .04
❑ 280 Brian Jordan .20 .06
❑ 281 Gary DiSarcina .15 .04
❑ 282 Mark Wohlers .15 .04
❑ 283 Dave Nilsson .15 .04
❑ 284 Anthony Young .15 .04
❑ 285 Jim Bullinger .15 .04
❑ 286 Derek Bell .15 .04
❑ 287 Brian Williams .15 .04
❑ 288 Julio Valera .15 .04
❑ 289 Dan Walters .15 .04
❑ 290 Chad Curtis .15 .04
❑ 291 Michael Tucker DP .20 .06
❑ 292 Bob Zupcic .15 .04
❑ 293 Todd Hundley .15 .04
❑ 294 Jeff Tackett .15 .04
❑ 295 Greg Colbrunn .15 .04
❑ 296 Cal Eldred .15 .04
❑ 297 Chris Roberts DP .15 .04
❑ 298 John Doherty .15 .04
❑ 299 Denny Neagle .20 .06
❑ 300 Arthur Rhodes .15 .04
❑ 301 Mark Clark .15 .04
❑ 302 Scott Cooper .15 .04
❑ 303 Jamie Arnold DP RC .15 .04
❑ 304 Jim Thome .50 .15
❑ 305 Frank Seminara .15 .04
❑ 306 Kurt Knudsen .15 .04
❑ 307 Tim Wakefield .50 .15
❑ 308 John Jaha .15 .04
❑ 309 Pat Hentgen .15 .04
❑ 310 B.J. Wallace DP .15 .04
❑ 311 Roberto Hernandez .15 .04
❑ 312 Hipolito Pichardo .15 .04
❑ 313 Eric Fox .15 .04
❑ 314 Willie Banks .15 .04
❑ 315 Sam Militello .15 .04
❑ 316 Vince Horsman .15 .04
❑ 317 Carlos Hernandez .15 .04
❑ 318 Jeff Kent .50 .15
❑ 319 Mike Perez .15 .04
❑ 320 Scott Livingstone .15 .04
❑ 321 Jeff Conine .20 .06
❑ 322 Jim Austin .15 .04
❑ 323 John Vander Wal .15 .04
❑ 324 Pat Mahomes .15 .04
❑ 325 Pedro Astacio .15 .04
❑ 326 Bret Boone UER .30 .09
(Misspelled Brett)
❑ 327 Matt Stairs .15 .04
❑ 328 Damion Easley .15 .04
❑ 329 Ben Rivera .15 .04
❑ 330 Reggie Jefferson .15 .04
❑ 331 Luis Mercedes .15 .04
❑ 332 Kyle Abbott .15 .04
❑ 333 Eddie Taubensee .15 .04
❑ 334 Tim McIntosh .15 .04
❑ 335 Phil Clark .15 .04
❑ 336 Wil Cordero .15 .04
❑ 337 Russ Springer .15 .04
❑ 338 Craig Colbert .15 .04
❑ 339 Tim Salmon .30 .09
❑ 340 Braulio Castillo .15 .04
❑ 341 Donald Harris .15 .04
❑ 342 Eric Young .15 .04
❑ 343 Bob Wickman .15 .04
❑ 344 John Valentin .15 .04
❑ 345 Dan Wilson .20 .06
❑ 346 Steve Hosey .15 .04
❑ 347 Mike Piazza 1.50 .45
❑ 348 Willie Greene .15 .04
❑ 349 Tom Goodwin .15 .04
❑ 350 Eric Hillman .15 .04
❑ 351 Steve Reed RC .15 .04
❑ 352 Dan Serafini DP RC .15 .04
❑ 353 T.Steverson DP RC .15 .04
❑ 354 Benji Grigsby DP RC .15 .04
❑ 355 S.Stewart DP RC .75 .23
❑ 356 Sean Lowe DP RC .15 .04
❑ 357 Derek Wallace DP RC .15 .04
❑ 358 Rick Helling DP .15 .04
❑ 359 Jason Kendall DP RC .75 .23
❑ 360 Derek Jeter DP RC 10.00 3.00
❑ 361 David Cone .20 .06
❑ 362 Jeff Reardon .20 .06
❑ 363 Bobby Witt .15 .04
❑ 364 Jose Canseco .50 .15
❑ 365 Jeff Russell .15 .04
❑ 366 Ruben Sierra .15 .04
❑ 367 Alan Mills .15 .04
❑ 368 Matt Nokes .15 .04
❑ 369 Pat Borders .15 .04
❑ 370 Pedro Munoz .15 .04
❑ 371 Danny Jackson .15 .04
❑ 372 Geronimo Pena .15 .04
❑ 373 Craig Lefferts .15 .04
❑ 374 Joe Grahe .15 .04
❑ 375 Roger McDowell .15 .04
❑ 376 Jimmy Key .20 .06
❑ 377 Steve Olin .15 .04
❑ 378 Glenn Davis .15 .04
❑ 379 Rene Gonzales .15 .04
❑ 380 Manuel Lee .15 .04
❑ 381 Ron Karkovice .15 .04
❑ 382 Sid Bream .15 .04
❑ 383 Gerald Williams .15 .04
❑ 384 Lenny Harris .15 .04
❑ 385 J.T. Snow RC .50 .15
❑ 386 Dave Stieb .15 .04
❑ 387 Kirk McCaskill .15 .04
❑ 388 Lance Parrish .20 .06
❑ 389 Craig Grebeck .15 .04
❑ 390 Rick Wilkins .15 .04
❑ 391 Manny Alexander .15 .04
❑ 392 Mike Schooler .15 .04
❑ 393 Bernie Williams .30 .09
❑ 394 Kevin Koslofski .15 .04
❑ 395 Willie Wilson .15 .04
❑ 396 Jeff Parrett .15 .04
❑ 397 Mike Harkey .15 .04
❑ 398 Frank Tanana .15 .04
❑ 399 Doug Henry .15 .04
❑ 400 Royce Clayton .15 .04
❑ 401 Eric Wedge RC .25 .07
❑ 402 Derrick May .15 .04
❑ 403 Carlos Garcia .15 .04
❑ 404 Henry Rodriguez .15 .04
❑ 405 Ryan Klesko .20 .06

1993 SP

	Nm-Mt	Ex-Mt
COMPLETE SET (290)	80.00	24.00
COMMON CARD (1-270)	.50	.15
COMMON FOIL (271-290)	1.00	.30

❑ 1 Roberto Alomar AS 1.25 .35
❑ 2 Wade Boggs AS 1.25 .35
❑ 3 Joe Carter AS .50 .15
❑ 4 Ken Griffey Jr. AS 3.00 .90
❑ 5 Mark Langston AS .50 .15
❑ 6 John Olerud AS .75 .23
❑ 7 Kirby Puckett AS 2.00 .60
❑ 8 Cal Ripken Jr. AS 6.00 1.80
❑ 9 Ivan Rodriguez AS 2.00 .60
❑ 10 Barry Bonds AS 5.00 1.50
❑ 11 Darren Daulton AS .75 .23
❑ 12 Marquis Grissom AS .75 .23
❑ 13 David Justice AS .75 .23
❑ 14 John Kruk AS .75 .23
❑ 15 Barry Larkin AS 1.25 .35
❑ 16 Terry Mulholland AS .50 .15
❑ 17 Ryne Sandberg AS 3.00 .90
❑ 18 Gary Sheffield AS .75 .23
❑ 19 Chad Curtis .50 .15
❑ 20 Chili Davis .75 .23
❑ 21 Gary DiSarcina .50 .15
❑ 22 Damion Easley .50 .15
❑ 23 Chuck Finley .75 .23
❑ 24 Luis Polonia .50 .15
❑ 25 Tim Salmon 1.25 .35
❑ 26 J.T. Snow RC 1.25 .35
❑ 27 Russ Springer .50 .15
❑ 28 Jeff Bagwell 1.25 .35
❑ 29 Craig Biggio 1.25 .35
❑ 30 Ken Caminiti .75 .23
❑ 31 Andujar Cedeno .50 .15
❑ 32 Doug Drabek .50 .15
❑ 33 Steve Finley .75 .23
❑ 34 Luis Gonzalez .75 .23
❑ 35 Pete Harnisch .50 .15
❑ 36 Darryl Kile .75 .23
❑ 37 Mike Bordick .50 .15
❑ 38 Dennis Eckersley .75 .23
❑ 39 Brent Gates .50 .15
❑ 40 Rickey Henderson 2.00 .60
❑ 41 Mark McGwire 5.00 1.50
❑ 42 Craig Paquette .50 .15
❑ 43 Ruben Sierra .50 .15
❑ 44 Terry Steinbach .50 .15
❑ 45 Todd Van Poppel .50 .15
❑ 46 Pat Borders .50 .15
❑ 47 Tony Fernandez .50 .15
❑ 48 Juan Guzman .50 .15
❑ 49 Pat Hentgen .50 .15
❑ 50 Paul Molitor 1.25 .35
❑ 51 Jack Morris .75 .23
❑ 52 Ed Sprague .50 .15
❑ 53 Duane Ward .50 .15
❑ 54 Devon White .75 .23
❑ 55 Steve Avery .50 .15
❑ 56 Jeff Blauser .50 .15
❑ 57 Ron Gant .75 .23
❑ 58 Tom Glavine 1.25 .35
❑ 59 Greg Maddux 3.00 .90
❑ 60 Fred McGriff 1.25 .35
❑ 61 Terry Pendleton .75 .23
❑ 62 Deion Sanders 1.25 .35
❑ 63 John Smoltz 1.25 .35
❑ 64 Cal Eldred .50 .15
❑ 65 Darryl Hamilton .50 .15
❑ 66 John Jaha .50 .15
❑ 67 Pat Listach .50 .15
❑ 68 Jaime Navarro .50 .15
❑ 69 Kevin Reimer .50 .15
❑ 70 B.J. Surhoff .75 .23
❑ 71 Greg Vaughn .50 .15
❑ 72 Robin Yount 3.00 .90
❑ 73 Rene Arocha RC .75 .23
❑ 74 Bernard Gilkey .50 .15
❑ 75 Gregg Jefferies .50 .15
❑ 76 Ray Lankford .50 .15
❑ 77 Tom Pagnozzi .50 .15
❑ 78 Lee Smith .75 .23
❑ 79 Ozzie Smith 3.00 .90
❑ 80 Bob Tewksbury .50 .15
❑ 81 Mark Whiten .50 .15
❑ 82 Steve Buechele .50 .15
❑ 83 Mark Grace 1.25 .35
❑ 84 Jose Guzman .50 .15
❑ 85 Derrick May .50 .15
❑ 86 Mike Morgan .50 .15
❑ 87 Randy Myers .50 .15
❑ 88 Kevin Roberson RC .50 .15
❑ 89 Sammy Sosa 3.00 .90
❑ 90 Rick Wilkins .50 .15
❑ 91 Brett Butler .75 .23
❑ 92 Eric Davis .75 .23
❑ 93 Orel Hershiser .75 .23
❑ 94 Eric Karros .75 .23

Card		Nm-Mt	Ex-Mt
❑ 95	Ramon Martinez	.50	.15
❑ 96	Raul Mondesi	.75	.23
❑ 97	Jose Offerman	.50	.15
❑ 98	Mike Piazza	5.00	1.50
❑ 99	Darryl Strawberry	.75	.23
❑ 100	Moises Alou	.75	.23
❑ 101	Wil Cordero	.50	.15
❑ 102	Delino DeShields	.50	.15
❑ 103	Darrin Fletcher	.50	.15
❑ 104	Ken Hill	.50	.15
❑ 105	Mike Lansing RC	.75	.23
❑ 106	Dennis Martinez	.75	.23
❑ 107	Larry Walker	1.25	.35
❑ 108	John Wetteland	.75	.23
❑ 109	Rod Beck	.50	.15
❑ 110	John Burkett	.50	.15
❑ 111	Will Clark	2.00	.60
❑ 112	Royce Clayton	.50	.15
❑ 113	Darren Lewis	.50	.15
❑ 114	Willie McGee	.75	.23
❑ 115	Bill Swift	.50	.15
❑ 116	Robby Thompson	.50	.15
❑ 117	Matt Williams	.75	.23
❑ 118	Sandy Alomar Jr.	.50	.15
❑ 119	Carlos Baerga	.50	.15
❑ 120	Albert Belle	.75	.23
❑ 121	Reggie Jefferson	.50	.15
❑ 122	Wayne Kirby	.50	.15
❑ 123	Kenny Lofton	.75	.23
❑ 124	Carlos Martinez	.50	.15
❑ 125	Charles Nagy	.50	.15
❑ 126	Paul Sorrento	.50	.15
❑ 127	Rich Amaral	.50	.15
❑ 128	Jay Buhner	.75	.23
❑ 129	Norm Charlton	.50	.15
❑ 130	Dave Fleming	.50	.15
❑ 131	Erik Hanson	.50	.15
❑ 132	Randy Johnson	2.00	.60
❑ 133	Edgar Martinez	1.25	.35
❑ 134	Tino Martinez	1.25	.35
❑ 135	Omar Vizquel	1.25	.35
❑ 136	Bret Barberie	.50	.15
❑ 137	Chuck Carr	.50	.15
❑ 138	Jeff Conine	.75	.23
❑ 139	Orestes Destrade	.50	.15
❑ 140	Chris Hammond	.50	.15
❑ 141	Bryan Harvey	.50	.15
❑ 142	Benito Santiago	.75	.23
❑ 143	Walt Weiss	.50	.15
❑ 144	Darrell Whitmore RC	.50	.15
❑ 145	Tim Bogar RC	.50	.15
❑ 146	Bobby Bonilla	.75	.23
❑ 147	Jeromy Burnitz	.75	.23
❑ 148	Vince Coleman	.50	.15
❑ 149	Dwight Gooden	.75	.23
❑ 150	Todd Hundley	.50	.15
❑ 151	Howard Johnson	.50	.15
❑ 152	Eddie Murray	2.00	.60
❑ 153	Bret Saberhagen	.75	.23
❑ 154	Brady Anderson	.75	.23
❑ 155	Mike Devereaux	.50	.15
❑ 156	Jeffrey Hammonds	.50	.15
❑ 157	Chris Hoiles	.50	.15
❑ 158	Ben McDonald	.50	.15
❑ 159	Mark McLemore	.50	.15
❑ 160	Mike Mussina	1.25	.35
❑ 161	Gregg Olson	.50	.15
❑ 162	David Segui	.50	.15
❑ 163	Derek Bell	.50	.15
❑ 164	Andy Benes	.50	.15
❑ 165	Archi Cianfrocco	.50	.15
❑ 166	Ricky Gutierrez	.50	.15
❑ 167	Tony Gwynn	2.50	.75
❑ 168	Gene Harris	.50	.15
❑ 169	Trevor Hoffman	.75	.23
❑ 170	Ray McDavid RC	.50	.15
❑ 171	Phil Plantier	.50	.15
❑ 172	Mariano Duncan	.50	.15
❑ 173	Len Dykstra	.75	.23
❑ 174	Tommy Greene	.50	.15
❑ 175	Dave Hollins	.50	.15
❑ 176	Pete Incaviglia	.50	.15
❑ 177	Mickey Morandini	.50	.15
❑ 178	Curt Schilling	.75	.23
❑ 179	Kevin Stocker	.50	.15
❑ 180	Mitch Williams	.50	.15
❑ 181	Stan Belinda	.50	.15
❑ 182	Jay Bell	.75	.23
❑ 183	Steve Cooke	.50	.15
❑ 184	Carlos Garcia	.50	.15
❑ 185	Jeff King	.50	.15
❑ 186	Orlando Merced	.50	.15
❑ 187	Don Slaught	.50	.15
❑ 188	Andy Van Slyke	.75	.23
❑ 189	Kevin Young	.75	.23
❑ 190	Kevin Brown	.75	.23
❑ 191	Jose Canseco	2.00	.60
❑ 192	Julio Franco	.75	.23
❑ 193	Benji Gil	.50	.15
❑ 194	Juan Gonzalez	1.25	.35
❑ 195	Tom Henke	.50	.15
❑ 196	Rafael Palmeiro	1.25	.35
❑ 197	Dean Palmer	.75	.23
❑ 198	Nolan Ryan	8.00	2.40
❑ 199	Roger Clemens	4.00	1.20
❑ 200	Scott Cooper	.50	.15
❑ 201	Andre Dawson	.75	.23
❑ 202	Mike Greenwell	.50	.15
❑ 203	Carlos Quintana	.50	.15
❑ 204	Jeff Russell	.50	.15
❑ 205	Aaron Sele	.50	.15
❑ 206	Mo Vaughn	.75	.23
❑ 207	Frank Viola	.75	.23
❑ 208	Rob Dibble	.75	.23
❑ 209	Roberto Kelly	.50	.15
❑ 210	Kevin Mitchell	.50	.15
❑ 211	Hal Morris	.50	.15
❑ 212	Joe Oliver	.50	.15
❑ 213	Jose Rijo	.50	.15
❑ 214	Bip Roberts	.50	.15
❑ 215	Chris Sabo	.50	.15
❑ 216	Reggie Sanders	.50	.15
❑ 217	Dante Bichette	.75	.23
❑ 218	Jerald Clark	.50	.15
❑ 219	Alex Cole	.50	.15
❑ 220	Andres Galarraga	.75	.23
❑ 221	Joe Girardi	.50	.15
❑ 222	Charlie Hayes	.50	.15
❑ 223	Roberto Mejia RC	.50	.15
❑ 224	Armando Reynoso	.50	.15
❑ 225	Eric Young	.50	.15
❑ 226	Kevin Appier	.75	.23
❑ 227	George Brett	5.00	1.50
❑ 228	David Cone	.75	.23
❑ 229	Phil Hiatt	.50	.15
❑ 230	Felix Jose	.50	.15
❑ 231	Wally Joyner	.75	.23
❑ 232	Mike Macfarlane	.50	.15
❑ 233	Brian McRae	.50	.15
❑ 234	Jeff Montgomery	.50	.15
❑ 235	Rob Deer	.50	.15
❑ 236	Cecil Fielder	.75	.23
❑ 237	Travis Fryman	.75	.23
❑ 238	Mike Henneman	.50	.15
❑ 239	Tony Phillips	.50	.15
❑ 240	Mickey Tettleton	.50	.15
❑ 241	Alan Trammell	.75	.23
❑ 242	David Wells	.75	.23
❑ 243	Lou Whitaker	.75	.23
❑ 244	Rick Aguilera	.50	.15
❑ 245	Scott Erickson	.50	.15
❑ 246	Brian Harper	.50	.15
❑ 247	Kent Hrbek	.75	.23
❑ 248	Chuck Knoblauch	.75	.23
❑ 249	Shane Mack	.50	.15
❑ 250	David McCarty	.50	.15
❑ 251	Pedro Munoz	.50	.15
❑ 252	Dave Winfield	.75	.23
❑ 253	Alex Fernandez	.50	.15
❑ 254	Ozzie Guillen	.50	.15
❑ 255	Bo Jackson	2.00	.60
❑ 256	Lance Johnson	.50	.15
❑ 257	Ron Karkovice	.50	.15
❑ 258	Jack McDowell	.50	.15
❑ 259	Tim Raines	.75	.23
❑ 260	Frank Thomas	2.00	.60
❑ 261	Robin Ventura	.75	.23
❑ 262	Jim Abbott	1.25	.35
❑ 263	Steve Farr	.50	.15
❑ 264	Jimmy Key	.75	.23
❑ 265	Don Mattingly	5.00	1.50
❑ 266	Paul O'Neill	1.25	.35
❑ 267	Mike Stanley	.50	.15
❑ 268	Danny Tartabull	.50	.15
❑ 269	Bob Wickman	.50	.15
❑ 270	Bernie Williams	1.25	.35
❑ 271	Jason Bere FOIL	1.00	.30
❑ 272	R.Cedeno FOIL RC	1.50	.45
❑ 273	J.Damon FOIL RC	10.00	3.00
❑ 274	Russ Davis FOIL RC	1.50	.45
❑ 275	Carlos Delgado FOIL	4.00	1.20
❑ 276	Carl Everett FOIL	1.50	.45
❑ 277	Cliff Floyd FOIL	.75	.23
❑ 278	Alex Gonzalez FOIL	1.00	.30
❑ 279	Derek Jeter FOIL RC	60.00	18.00
❑ 280	Chipper Jones FOIL	4.00	1.20
❑ 281	Javier Lopez FOIL	1.25	.35
❑ 282	Chad Mottola FOIL RC	1.00	.30
❑ 283	Marc Newfield FOIL	1.00	.30
❑ 284	Eduardo Perez FOIL	1.00	.30
❑ 285	Manny Ramirez FOIL	4.00	1.20
❑ 286	T.Steverson FOIL RC	1.00	.30
❑ 287	Michael Tucker FOIL	1.50	.45
❑ 288	Allen Watson FOIL	1.00	.30
❑ 289	Rondell White FOIL	1.50	.45
❑ 290	Dmitri Young FOIL	1.50	.45

1994 SP

	Nm-Mt	Ex-Mt
COMPLETE SET (200)	100.00	30.00
COMMON CARD (21-200)	.20	.06
COMMON FOIL (1-20)	.50	.15

Card		Nm-Mt	Ex-Mt
❑ 1	Mike Bell FOIL RC	.50	.15
❑ 2	D.J. Boston FOIL RC	.50	.15
❑ 3	Johnny Damon FOIL	2.00	.60
❑ 4	Brad Fullmer FOIL RC	1.25	.35
❑ 5	Joey Hamilton FOIL	.50	.15
❑ 6	T.Hollandsworth FOIL	.50	.15
❑ 7	Brian L. Hunter FOIL	.50	.15
❑ 8	L.Hawkins FOIL RC	1.25	.35
❑ 9	B.Kieschnick FOIL RC	.75	.23
❑ 10	Derrek Lee FOIL RC	2.00	.60
❑ 11	Trot Nixon FOIL RC	2.50	.75
❑ 12	Alex Ochoa FOIL	.50	.15
❑ 13	Chan Ho Park FOIL RC	1.25	.35
❑ 14	Kirk Presley FOIL RC	.50	.15
❑ 15	A.Rodriguez FOIL RC	80.00	24.00
❑ 16	Jose Silva FOIL RC	.50	.15
❑ 17	Terrell Wade FOIL RC	.50	.15
❑ 18	Billy Wagner FOIL RC	2.00	.60
❑ 19	G.Williams FOIL RC	.50	.15
❑ 20	Preston Wilson FOIL	.75	.23
❑ 21	Brian Anderson RC	.40	.12
❑ 22	Chad Curtis	.20	.06
❑ 23	Chili Davis	.40	.12
❑ 24	Bo Jackson	1.00	.30
❑ 25	Mark Langston	.20	.06
❑ 26	Tim Salmon	.60	.18
❑ 27	Jeff Bagwell	.60	.18
❑ 28	Craig Biggio	.60	.18
❑ 29	Ken Caminiti	.40	.12
❑ 30	Doug Drabek	.20	.06
❑ 31	John Hudek RC	.20	.06
❑ 32	Greg Swindell	.20	.06
❑ 33	Brent Gates	.20	.06
❑ 34	Rickey Henderson	1.00	.30
❑ 35	Steve Karsay	.20	.06
❑ 36	Mark McGwire	2.50	.75

❑ 37 Ruben Sierra .20 .06
❑ 38 Terry Steinbach .20 .06
❑ 39 Roberto Alomar .60 .18
❑ 40 Joe Carter .40 .12
❑ 41 Carlos Delgado .60 .18
❑ 42 Alex Gonzalez .20 .06
❑ 43 Juan Guzman .20 .06
❑ 44 Paul Molitor .60 .18
❑ 45 John Olerud .40 .12
❑ 46 Devon White .40 .12
❑ 47 Steve Avery .20 .06
❑ 48 Jeff Blauser .20 .06
❑ 49 Tom Glavine .60 .18
❑ 50 David Justice .40 .12
❑ 51 Roberto Kelly .20 .06
❑ 52 Ryan Klesko .40 .12
❑ 53 Javier Lopez .40 .12
❑ 54 Greg Maddux 1.50 .45
❑ 55 Fred McGriff .60 .18
❑ 56 Ricky Bones .20 .06
❑ 57 Cal Eldred .20 .06
❑ 58 Brian Harper .20 .06
❑ 59 Pat Listach .20 .06
❑ 60 B.J. Surhoff .40 .12
❑ 61 Greg Vaughn .20 .06
❑ 62 Bernard Gilkey .20 .06
❑ 63 Gregg Jefferies .20 .06
❑ 64 Ray Lankford .20 .06
❑ 65 Ozzie Smith 1.50 .45
❑ 66 Bob Tewksbury .20 .06
❑ 67 Mark Whiten .20 .06
❑ 68 Todd Zeile .20 .06
❑ 69 Mark Grace .60 .18
❑ 70 Randy Myers .20 .06
❑ 71 Ryne Sandberg 1.50 .45
❑ 72 Sammy Sosa 1.50 .45
❑ 73 Steve Trachsel .20 .06
❑ 74 Rick Wilkins .20 .06
❑ 75 Brett Butler .40 .12
❑ 76 Delino DeShields .20 .06
❑ 77 Orel Hershiser .40 .12
❑ 78 Eric Karros .40 .12
❑ 79 Raul Mondesi .40 .12
❑ 80 Mike Piazza 2.00 .60
❑ 81 Tim Wallach .20 .06
❑ 82 Moises Alou .40 .12
❑ 83 Cliff Floyd .40 .12
❑ 84 Marquis Grissom .40 .12
❑ 85 Pedro Martinez 1.00 .30
❑ 86 Larry Walker .60 .18
❑ 87 John Wetteland .40 .12
❑ 88 Rondell White .40 .12
❑ 89 Rod Beck .20 .06
❑ 90 Barry Bonds 2.50 .75
❑ 91 John Burkett .20 .06
❑ 92 Royce Clayton .20 .06
❑ 93 Billy Swift .20 .06
❑ 94 Robby Thompson .20 .06
❑ 95 Matt Williams .40 .12
❑ 96 Carlos Baerga .20 .06
❑ 97 Albert Belle .40 .12
❑ 98 Kenny Lofton .40 .12
❑ 99 Dennis Martinez .40 .12
❑ 100 Eddie Murray 1.00 .30
❑ 101 Manny Ramirez .60 .18
❑ 102 Eric Anthony .20 .06
❑ 103 Chris Bosio .20 .06
❑ 104 Jay Buhner .40 .12
❑ 105 Ken Griffey Jr. 1.50 .45
❑ 106 Randy Johnson 1.00 .30
❑ 107 Edgar Martinez .60 .18
❑ 108 Chuck Carr .20 .06
❑ 109 Jeff Conine .40 .12
❑ 110 Carl Everett .40 .12
❑ 111 Chris Hammond .20 .06
❑ 112 Bryan Harvey .20 .06
❑ 113 Charles Johnson .40 .12
❑ 114 Gary Sheffield .40 .12
❑ 115 Bobby Bonilla .40 .12
❑ 116 Dwight Gooden .40 .12
❑ 117 Todd Hundley .20 .06
❑ 118 Bobby Jones .20 .06
❑ 119 Jeff Kent .40 .12
❑ 120 Bret Saberhagen .40 .12
❑ 121 Jeffrey Hammonds .20 .06
❑ 122 Chris Hoiles .20 .06
❑ 123 Ben McDonald .20 .06
❑ 124 Mike Mussina .60 .18
❑ 125 Rafael Palmeiro .60 .18
❑ 126 Cal Ripken Jr. 3.00 .90
❑ 127 Lee Smith .40 .12
❑ 128 Derek Bell .20 .06
❑ 129 Andy Benes .20 .06
❑ 130 Tony Gwynn 1.25 .35
❑ 131 Trevor Hoffman .40 .12
❑ 132 Phil Plantier .20 .06
❑ 133 Bip Roberts .20 .06
❑ 134 Darren Daulton .40 .12
❑ 135 Lenny Dykstra .40 .12
❑ 136 Dave Hollins .20 .06
❑ 137 Danny Jackson .20 .06
❑ 138 John Kruk .40 .12
❑ 139 Kevin Stocker .20 .06
❑ 140 Jay Bell .40 .12
❑ 141 Carlos Garcia .20 .06
❑ 142 Jeff King .20 .06
❑ 143 Orlando Merced .20 .06
❑ 144 Andy Van Slyke .40 .12
❑ 145 Rick White .20 .06
❑ 146 Jose Canseco 1.00 .30
❑ 147 Will Clark 1.00 .30
❑ 148 Juan Gonzalez .60 .18
❑ 149 Rick Helling .20 .06
❑ 150 Dean Palmer .40 .12
❑ 151 Ivan Rodriguez 1.00 .30
❑ 152 Roger Clemens 2.00 .60
❑ 153 Scott Cooper .20 .06
❑ 154 Andre Dawson .40 .12
❑ 155 Mike Greenwell .20 .06
❑ 156 Aaron Sele .20 .06
❑ 157 Mo Vaughn .40 .12
❑ 158 Bret Boone .40 .12
❑ 159 Barry Larkin .60 .18
❑ 160 Kevin Mitchell .20 .06
❑ 161 Jose Rijo .20 .06
❑ 162 Deion Sanders .60 .18
❑ 163 Reggie Sanders .20 .06
❑ 164 Dante Bichette .40 .12
❑ 165 Ellis Burks .40 .12
❑ 166 Andres Galarraga .40 .12
❑ 167 Charlie Hayes .20 .06
❑ 168 David Nied .20 .06
❑ 169 Walt Weiss .20 .06
❑ 170 Kevin Appier .40 .12
❑ 171 David Cone .40 .12
❑ 172 Jeff Granger .20 .06
❑ 173 Felix Jose .20 .06
❑ 174 Wally Joyner .40 .12
❑ 175 Brian McRae .20 .06
❑ 176 Cecil Fielder .40 .12
❑ 177 Travis Fryman .40 .12
❑ 178 Mike Henneman .20 .06
❑ 179 Tony Phillips .20 .06
❑ 180 Mickey Tettleton .20 .06
❑ 181 Alan Trammell .40 .12
❑ 182 Rick Aguilera .20 .06
❑ 183 Rich Becker .20 .06
❑ 184 Scott Erickson .20 .06
❑ 185 Chuck Knoblauch .40 .12
❑ 186 Kirby Puckett 1.00 .30
❑ 187 Dave Winfield .40 .12
❑ 188 Wilson Alvarez .20 .06
❑ 189 Jason Bere .20 .06
❑ 190 Alex Fernandez .20 .06
❑ 191 Julio Franco .40 .12
❑ 192 Jack McDowell .20 .06
❑ 193 Frank Thomas 1.00 .30
❑ 194 Robin Ventura .40 .12
❑ 195 Jim Abbott .60 .18
❑ 196 Wade Boggs .60 .18
❑ 197 Jimmy Key .40 .12
❑ 198 Don Mattingly 2.50 .75
❑ 199 Paul O'Neill .60 .18
❑ 200 Danny Tartabull .20 .06
❑ P24 Ken Griffey Jr. Promo 2.00 .60

2000 SP Authentic

	Nm-Mt	Ex-Mt
COMP.BASIC w/o SP's (90)	25.00	7.50
COMP.UPDATE w/o SP'S (30)	10.00	3.00
COMMON CARD (1-90)	.40	.12

COMMON SUP (91-105)	3.00	.90
COMMON FW (106-135)	5.00	1.50
COMMON FW (136-164)	5.00	1.50
COMMON (166-195)	.60	.18

❑ 1 Mo Vaughn .40 .12
❑ 2 Troy Glaus .40 .12
❑ 3 Jason Giambi .40 .12
❑ 4 Tim Hudson .40 .12
❑ 5 Eric Chavez .40 .12
❑ 6 Shannon Stewart .40 .12
❑ 7 Raul Mondesi .40 .12
❑ 8 Carlos Delgado .40 .12
❑ 9 Jose Canseco 1.00 .30
❑ 10 Vinny Castilla .40 .12
❑ 11 Greg Vaughn .40 .12
❑ 12 Manny Ramirez .60 .18
❑ 13 Roberto Alomar .60 .18
❑ 14 Jim Thome 1.00 .30
❑ 15 Richie Sexson .40 .12
❑ 16 Alex Rodriguez 1.50 .45
❑ 17 Freddy Garcia .40 .12
❑ 18 John Olerud .40 .12
❑ 19 Albert Belle .40 .12
❑ 20 Cal Ripken 3.00 .90
❑ 21 Mike Mussina .60 .18
❑ 22 Ivan Rodriguez 1.00 .30
❑ 23 Gabe Kapler .40 .12
❑ 24 Rafael Palmeiro .60 .18
❑ 25 Nomar Garciaparra 1.50 .45
❑ 26 Pedro Martinez 1.00 .30
❑ 27 Carl Everett .40 .12
❑ 28 Carlos Beltran .60 .18
❑ 29 Jermaine Dye .40 .12
❑ 30 Juan Gonzalez .60 .18
❑ 31 Dean Palmer .40 .12
❑ 32 Corey Koskie .40 .12
❑ 33 Jacque Jones .40 .12
❑ 34 Frank Thomas 1.00 .30
❑ 35 Paul Konerko .40 .12
❑ 36 Magglio Ordonez .40 .12
❑ 37 Bernie Williams .60 .18
❑ 38 Derek Jeter 2.50 .75
❑ 39 Roger Clemens 2.00 .60
❑ 40 Mariano Rivera .60 .18
❑ 41 Jeff Bagwell .60 .18
❑ 42 Craig Biggio .60 .18
❑ 43 Jose Lima .40 .12
❑ 44 Moises Alou .40 .12
❑ 45 Chipper Jones 1.00 .30
❑ 46 Greg Maddux 1.50 .45
❑ 47 Andruw Jones .40 .12
❑ 48 Andres Galarraga .40 .12
❑ 49 Jeromy Burnitz .40 .12
❑ 50 Geoff Jenkins .40 .12
❑ 51 Mark McGwire 2.50 .75
❑ 52 Fernando Tatis .40 .12
❑ 53 J.D. Drew .40 .12
❑ 54 Sammy Sosa 1.50 .45
❑ 55 Kerry Wood 1.00 .30
❑ 56 Mark Grace .60 .18
❑ 57 Matt Williams .40 .12
❑ 58 Randy Johnson 1.00 .30
❑ 59 Erubiel Durazo .40 .12
❑ 60 Gary Sheffield .40 .12
❑ 61 Kevin Brown .60 .18
❑ 62 Shawn Green .40 .12
❑ 63 Vladimir Guerrero 1.00 .30

Card	Nm-Mt	Ex-Mt
❑ 64 Michael Barrett	.40	.12
❑ 65 Barry Bonds	2.50	.75
❑ 66 Jeff Kent	.40	.12
❑ 67 Russ Ortiz	.40	.12
❑ 68 Preston Wilson	.40	.12
❑ 69 Mike Lowell	.40	.12
❑ 70 Mike Piazza	1.50	.45
❑ 71 Mike Hampton	.40	.12
❑ 72 Robin Ventura	.40	.12
❑ 73 Edgardo Alfonzo	.40	.12
❑ 74 Tony Gwynn	1.25	.35
❑ 75 Ryan Klesko	.40	.12
❑ 76 Trevor Hoffman	.40	.12
❑ 77 Scott Rolen	1.00	.30
❑ 78 Bob Abreu	.40	.12
❑ 79 Mike Lieberthal	.40	.12
❑ 80 Curt Schilling	.40	.12
❑ 81 Jason Kendall	.40	.12
❑ 82 Brian Giles	.40	.12
❑ 83 Kris Benson	.40	.12
❑ 84 Ken Griffey Jr.	1.50	.45
❑ 85 Sean Casey	.40	.12
❑ 86 Pokey Reese	.40	.12
❑ 87 Barry Larkin	.60	.18
❑ 88 Larry Walker	.60	.18
❑ 89 Todd Helton	.60	.18
❑ 90 Jeff Cirillo	.40	.12
❑ 91 Ken Griffey Jr. SUP	8.00	2.40
❑ 92 Mark McGwire SUP	12.00	3.60
❑ 93 Chipper Jones SUP	5.00	1.50
❑ 94 Derek Jeter SUP	12.00	3.60
❑ 95 Shawn Green SUP	3.00	.90
❑ 96 Pedro Martinez SUP	5.00	1.50
❑ 97 Mike Piazza SUP	8.00	2.40
❑ 98 Alex Rodriguez SUP	8.00	2.40
❑ 99 Jeff Bagwell SUP	3.00	.90
❑ 100 Cal Ripken SUP	15.00	4.50
❑ 101 Sammy Sosa SUP	8.00	2.40
❑ 102 Barry Bonds SUP	12.00	3.60
❑ 103 Jose Canseco SUP	5.00	1.50
❑ 104 N.Garciaparra SUP	8.00	2.40
❑ 105 Ivan Rodriguez SUP	5.00	1.50
❑ 106 Rick Ankiel FW	5.00	1.50
❑ 107 Pat Burrell FW	3.00	.90
❑ 108 Vernon Wells FW	5.00	1.50
❑ 109 Nick Johnson FW	5.00	1.50
❑ 110 Kip Wells FW	5.00	1.50
❑ 111 Matt Riley FW	5.00	1.50
❑ 112 Alfonso Soriano FW	8.00	2.40
❑ 113 Josh Beckett FW	8.00	2.40
❑ 114 Danys Baez FW RC	5.00	1.50
❑ 115 Travis Dawkins FW	5.00	1.50
❑ 116 Eric Gagne FW	15.00	4.50
❑ 117 Mike Lamb FW RC	5.00	1.50
❑ 118 Eric Munson FW	5.00	1.50
❑ 119 W.Rodriguez FW RC	5.00	1.50
❑ 120 K.Sasaki FW RC	8.00	2.40
❑ 121 Chad Hutchinson FW	5.00	1.50
❑ 122 Peter Bergeron FW	5.00	1.50
❑ 123 W.Serrano FW RC	5.00	1.50
❑ 124 Tony Armas Jr. FW	5.00	1.50
❑ 125 Ramon Ortiz FW	5.00	1.50
❑ 126 Adam Kennedy FW	5.00	1.50
❑ 127 Joe Crede FW	5.00	1.50
❑ 128 Roosevelt Brown FW	5.00	1.50
❑ 129 Mark Mulder FW	5.00	1.50
❑ 130 Brad Penny FW	5.00	1.50
❑ 131 Terrence Long FW	5.00	1.50
❑ 132 Ruben Mateo FW	5.00	1.50
❑ 133 Wily Mo Pena FW	5.00	1.50
❑ 134 Rafael Furcal FW	5.00	1.50
❑ 135 M.Encarnacion FW	5.00	1.50
❑ 136 Barry Zito FW RC	15.00	4.50
❑ 137 Aaron McNeal FW RC	5.00	1.50
❑ 138 Timo Perez FW RC	5.00	1.50
❑ 139 Sun Woo Kim FW RC	5.00	1.50
❑ 140 Xavier Nady FW RC	8.00	2.40
❑ 141 M.Wheatland FW RC	5.00	1.50
❑ 142 B.Abernathy FW RC	5.00	1.50
❑ 143 Cory Vance FW RC	5.00	1.50
❑ 144 Scott Heard FW RC	5.00	1.50
❑ 145 Mike Meyers FW RC	5.00	1.50
❑ 146 Ben Diggins FW RC	5.00	1.50
❑ 147 Luis Matos FW RC	5.00	1.50
❑ 148 Ben Sheets FW RC	15.00	4.50
❑ 149 K.Ainsworth FW RC	5.00	1.50
❑ 150 Dave Krynzel FW RC	5.00	1.50
❑ 151 Alex Cabrera FW RC	5.00	1.50
❑ 152 Mike Tonis FW RC	5.00	1.50
❑ 153 Dane Sardinha FW RC	5.00	1.50
❑ 154 Keith Ginter FW RC	5.00	1.50
❑ 155 D.Espinosa FW RC	5.00	1.50
❑ 156 Joe Torres FW RC	5.00	1.50
❑ 157 Daylan Holt FW RC	5.00	1.50
❑ 158 Koyie Hill FW RC	5.00	1.50
❑ 159 B.Wilkerson FW RC	8.00	2.40
❑ 160 Juan Pierre FW RC	8.00	2.40
❑ 161 Matt Ginter FW RC	5.00	1.50
❑ 162 Dane Artman FW RC	5.00	1.50
❑ 163 Jon Rauch FW RC	5.00	1.50
❑ 164 Sean Burnett FW RC	8.00	2.40
❑ 165 Does Not Exist	.00	
❑ 166 Darin Erstad	.60	.18
❑ 167 Ben Grieve	.60	.18
❑ 168 David Wells	.60	.18
❑ 169 Fred McGriff	1.00	.30
❑ 170 Bob Wickman	.60	.18
❑ 171 Al Martin	.60	.18
❑ 172 Melvin Mora	.60	.18
❑ 173 Ricky Ledee	.60	.18
❑ 174 Dante Bichette	.60	.18
❑ 175 Mike Sweeney	.60	.18
❑ 176 Bobby Higginson	.60	.18
❑ 177 Matt Lawton	.60	.18
❑ 178 Charles Johnson	.60	.18
❑ 179 David Justice	.60	.18
❑ 180 Richard Hidalgo	.60	.18
❑ 181 B.J. Surhoff	.60	.18
❑ 182 Richie Sexson	.60	.18
❑ 183 Jim Edmonds	.60	.18
❑ 184 Rondell White	.60	.18
❑ 185 Curt Schilling	.60	.18
❑ 186 Tom Goodwin	.60	.18
❑ 187 Jose Vidro	.60	.18
❑ 188 Ellis Burks	.60	.18
❑ 189 Henry Rodriguez	.60	.18
❑ 190 Mike Bordick	.60	.18
❑ 191 Eric Owens	.60	.18
❑ 192 Travis Lee	.60	.18
❑ 193 Kevin Young	.60	.18
❑ 194 Aaron Boone	.60	.18
❑ 195 Todd Hollandsworth	.60	.18
❑ SPA K.Griffey Jr. Sample	2.00	.60

2001 SP Authentic

	Nm-Mt	Ex-Mt
COMP.BASIC w/o SP's (90)	25.00	7.50
COMP.UPDATE w/o SP's (30)	10.00	3.00
COMMON CARD (1-90)	.40	.12
COMMON FW (91-135)	8.00	2.40
COMMON SS (136-180)	5.00	1.50
COMMON (181-210)	.60	.18
COMMON (211-240)	6.00	1.80

Card	Nm-Mt	Ex-Mt
❑ 1 Troy Glaus	.40	.12
❑ 2 Darin Erstad	.40	.12
❑ 3 Jason Giambi	.40	.12
❑ 4 Tim Hudson	.40	.12
❑ 5 Eric Chavez	.40	.12
❑ 6 Miguel Tejada	.40	.12
❑ 7 Jose Ortiz	.40	.12
❑ 8 Carlos Delgado	.40	.12
❑ 9 Tony Batista	.40	.12
❑ 10 Raul Mondesi	.40	.12
❑ 11 Aubrey Huff	.40	.12
❑ 12 Greg Vaughn	.40	.12
❑ 13 Roberto Alomar	.60	.18
❑ 14 Juan Gonzalez	.60	.18
❑ 15 Jim Thome	1.00	.30
❑ 16 Omar Vizquel	.60	.18
❑ 17 Edgar Martinez	.60	.18
❑ 18 Freddy Garcia	.40	.12
❑ 19 Cal Ripken	3.00	.90
❑ 20 Ivan Rodriguez	1.00	.30
❑ 21 Rafael Palmeiro	.60	.18
❑ 22 Alex Rodriguez	1.50	.45
❑ 23 Manny Ramirez	.60	.18
❑ 24 Pedro Martinez	1.00	.30
❑ 25 Nomar Garciaparra	1.50	.45
❑ 26 Mike Sweeney	.40	.12
❑ 27 Jermaine Dye	.40	.12
❑ 28 Bobby Higginson	.40	.12
❑ 29 Dean Palmer	.40	.12
❑ 30 Matt Lawton	.40	.12
❑ 31 Eric Milton	.40	.12
❑ 32 Frank Thomas	1.00	.30
❑ 33 Magglio Ordonez	.40	.12
❑ 34 David Wells	.40	.12
❑ 35 Paul Konerko	.40	.12
❑ 36 Derek Jeter	2.50	.75
❑ 37 Bernie Williams	.60	.18
❑ 38 Roger Clemens	2.00	.60
❑ 39 Mike Mussina	.60	.18
❑ 40 Jorge Posada	.60	.18
❑ 41 Jeff Bagwell	.60	.18
❑ 42 Richard Hidalgo	.40	.12
❑ 43 Craig Biggio	.60	.18
❑ 44 Greg Maddux	1.50	.45
❑ 45 Chipper Jones	1.00	.30
❑ 46 Andruw Jones	.40	.12
❑ 47 Rafael Furcal	.40	.12
❑ 48 Tom Glavine	.60	.18
❑ 49 Jeromy Burnitz	.40	.12
❑ 50 Jeffrey Hammonds	.40	.12
❑ 51 Mark McGwire	2.50	.75
❑ 52 Jim Edmonds	.40	.12
❑ 53 Rick Ankiel	.40	.12
❑ 54 J.D. Drew	.40	.12
❑ 55 Sammy Sosa	1.50	.45
❑ 56 Corey Patterson	.40	.12
❑ 57 Kerry Wood	1.00	.30
❑ 58 Randy Johnson	1.00	.30
❑ 59 Luis Gonzalez	.40	.12
❑ 60 Curt Schilling	.40	.12
❑ 61 Gary Sheffield	.40	.12
❑ 62 Shawn Green	.40	.12
❑ 63 Kevin Brown	.40	.12
❑ 64 Vladimir Guerrero	1.00	.30
❑ 65 Jose Vidro	.40	.12
❑ 66 Barry Bonds	2.50	.75
❑ 67 Jeff Kent	.40	.12
❑ 68 Livan Hernandez	.40	.12
❑ 69 Preston Wilson	.40	.12
❑ 70 Charles Johnson	.40	.12
❑ 71 Ryan Dempster	.40	.12
❑ 72 Mike Piazza	1.50	.45
❑ 73 Al Leiter	.40	.12
❑ 74 Edgardo Alfonzo	.40	.12
❑ 75 Robin Ventura	.40	.12
❑ 76 Tony Gwynn	1.25	.35
❑ 77 Phil Nevin	.40	.12
❑ 78 Trevor Hoffman	.40	.12
❑ 79 Scott Rolen	1.00	.30
❑ 80 Pat Burrell	.40	.12
❑ 81 Bob Abreu	.40	.12
❑ 82 Jason Kendall	.40	.12
❑ 83 Brian Giles	.40	.12
❑ 84 Kris Benson	.40	.12
❑ 85 Ken Griffey Jr.	1.50	.45
❑ 86 Barry Larkin	.60	.18
❑ 87 Sean Casey	.40	.12
❑ 88 Todd Helton	.60	.18
❑ 89 Mike Hampton	.40	.12
❑ 90 Larry Walker	.60	.18
❑ 91 Ichiro Suzuki FW RC	120.00	36.00
❑ 92 Wilson Betemit FW RC	8.00	2.40
❑ 93 A. Hernandez FW RC	8.00	2.40
❑ 94 Juan Uribe FW RC	10.00	3.00
❑ 95 Travis Hafner FW RC	20.00	6.00

❑ 96 M. Ensberg FW RC 12.00 3.60
❑ 97 Sean Douglass FW RC 8.00 2.40
❑ 98 Juan Diaz FW RC 8.00 2.40
❑ 99 Erick Almonte FW RC 8.00 2.40
❑ 100 Ryan Freel FW RC 8.00 2.40
❑ 101 E. Guzman FW RC 8.00 2.40
❑ 102 C. Parker FW RC 8.00 2.40
❑ 103 Josh Fogg FW RC 8.00 2.40
❑ 104 Bert Snow FW RC 8.00 2.40
❑ 105 H. Ramirez FW RC 10.00 3.00
❑ 106 R. Rodriguez FW RC 8.00 2.40
❑ 107 Tyler Walker FW RC 8.00 2.40
❑ 108 Jose Mieses FW RC 8.00 2.40
❑ 109 Billy Sylvester FW RC 8.00 2.40
❑ 110 Martin Vargas FW RC 8.00 2.40
❑ 111 Andres Torres FW RC 8.00 2.40
❑ 112 Greg Miller FW RC 8.00 2.40
❑ 113 Alexis Gomez FW RC 8.00 2.40
❑ 114 Grant Balfour FW RC 8.00 2.40
❑ 115 Henry Mateo FW RC 8.00 2.40
❑ 116 Esix Snead FW RC 8.00 2.40
❑ 117 J. Melian FW RC 8.00 2.40
❑ 118 Nate Teut FW RC 8.00 2.40
❑ 119 T. Shinjo FW RC 10.00 3.00
❑ 120 C. Valderrama FW RC 8.00 2.40
❑ 121 J. Estrada FW RC 20.00 6.00
❑ 122 J. Michaels FW RC 8.00 2.40
❑ 123 William Ortega FW RC 8.00 2.40
❑ 124 Jason Smith FW RC 8.00 2.40
❑ 125 B. Lawrence FW RC 8.00 2.40
❑ 126 Albert Pujols FW RC 250.00 75.00
❑ 127 Wilkin Ruan FW RC 8.00 2.40
❑ 128 Josh Towers FW RC 8.00 2.40
❑ 129 Kris Keller FW RC 8.00 2.40
❑ 130 Nick Maness FW RC 8.00 2.40
❑ 131 Jack Wilson FW RC 15.00 4.50
❑ 132 B. Duckworth FW RC 8.00 2.40
❑ 133 Mike Penney FW RC 8.00 2.40
❑ 134 Jay Gibbons FW RC 12.00 3.60
❑ 135 Cesar Crespo FW RC 8.00 2.40
❑ 136 Ken Griffey Jr. SS 10.00 3.00
❑ 137 Mark McGwire SS 15.00 4.50
❑ 138 Derek Jeter SS 15.00 4.50
❑ 139 Alex Rodriguez SS 10.00 3.00
❑ 140 Sammy Sosa SS 10.00 3.00
❑ 141 Carlos Delgado SS 5.00 1.50
❑ 142 Cal Ripken SS 20.00 6.00
❑ 143 Pedro Martinez SS 6.00 1.80
❑ 144 Frank Thomas SS 6.00 1.80
❑ 145 Juan Gonzalez SS 5.00 1.50
❑ 146 Troy Glaus SS 5.00 1.50
❑ 147 Jason Giambi SS 5.00 1.50
❑ 148 Ivan Rodriguez SS 6.00 1.80
❑ 149 Chipper Jones SS 6.00 1.80
❑ 150 Vladimir Guerrero SS 6.00 1.80
❑ 151 Mike Piazza SS 10.00 3.00
❑ 152 Jeff Bagwell SS 5.00 1.50
❑ 153 Randy Johnson SS 6.00 1.80
❑ 154 Todd Helton SS 5.00 1.50
❑ 155 Gary Sheffield SS 5.00 1.50
❑ 156 Tony Gwynn SS 8.00 2.40
❑ 157 Barry Bonds SS 15.00 4.50
❑ 158 N. Garciaparra SS 10.00 3.00
❑ 159 Bernie Williams SS 5.00 1.50
❑ 160 Greg Vaughn SS 5.00 1.50
❑ 161 David Wells SS 5.00 1.50
❑ 162 Roberto Alomar SS 5.00 1.50
❑ 163 Jermaine Dye SS 5.00 1.50
❑ 164 Rafael Palmeiro SS 5.00 1.50
❑ 165 Andruw Jones SS 5.00 1.50
❑ 166 Preston Wilson SS 5.00 1.50
❑ 167 Edgardo Alfonzo SS 5.00 1.50
❑ 168 Pat Burrell SS 5.00 1.50
❑ 169 Jim Edmonds SS 5.00 1.50
❑ 170 Mike Hampton SS 5.00 1.50
❑ 171 Jeff Kent SS 5.00 1.50
❑ 172 Kevin Brown SS 5.00 1.50
❑ 173 Manny Ramirez SS 5.00 1.50
❑ 174 Maggio Ordonez SS 5.00 1.50
❑ 175 Roger Clemens SS 12.00 3.60
❑ 176 Jim Thome SS 6.00 1.80
❑ 177 Barry Zito SS 5.00 1.50
❑ 178 Brian Giles SS 5.00 1.50
❑ 179 Rick Ankiel SS 5.00 1.50
❑ 180 Corey Patterson SS 5.00 1.50
❑ 181 Garret Anderson .60 .18
❑ 182 Jermaine Dye .60 .18
❑ 183 Shannon Stewart .60 .18
❑ 184 Ben Grieve .60 .18
❑ 185 Ellis Burks .60 .18
❑ 186 John Olerud .60 .18
❑ 187 Tony Batista .60 .18
❑ 188 Ruben Sierra .60 .18
❑ 189 Carl Everett .60 .18
❑ 190 Neifi Perez .60 .18
❑ 191 Tony Clark .60 .18
❑ 192 Doug Mientkiewicz .60 .18
❑ 193 Carlos Lee .60 .18
❑ 194 Jorge Posada 1.00 .30
❑ 195 Lance Berkman 5.00 1.50
❑ 196 Ken Caminiti .60 .18
❑ 197 Ben Sheets 1.00 .30
❑ 198 Matt Morris .60 .18
❑ 199 Fred McGriff 1.00 .30
❑ 200 Mark Grace 1.00 .30
❑ 201 Paul LoDuca .60 .18
❑ 202 Tony Armas Jr. .60 .18
❑ 203 Andres Galarraga .60 .18
❑ 204 Cliff Floyd .60 .18
❑ 205 Matt Lawton .60 .18
❑ 206 Ryan Klesko .60 .18
❑ 207 Jimmy Rollins .60 .18
❑ 208 Aramis Ramirez .60 .18
❑ 209 Aaron Boone .60 .18
❑ 210 Jose Ortiz .60 .18
❑ 211 Mark Prior FW RC 150.00 45.00
❑ 212 Mark Teixeira FW RC 60.00 18.00
❑ 213 Bud Smith FW RC 6.00 1.80
❑ 214 W.Caceres FW RC 6.00 1.80
❑ 215 Dave Williams FW RC 6.00 1.80
❑ 216 Delvin James FW RC 6.00 1.80
❑ 217 Endy Chavez FW RC 6.00 1.80
❑ 218 Doug Nickle FW RC 6.00 1.80
❑ 219 Bret Prinz FW RC 6.00 1.80
❑ 220 Troy Mattes FW RC 6.00 1.80
❑ 221 D.Sanchez FW RC 6.00 1.80
❑ 222 D.Brazelton FW RC 8.00 2.40
❑ 223 Brian Bowles FW RC 6.00 1.80
❑ 224 D.Mendez FW RC 6.00 1.80
❑ 225 Jorge Julio FW RC 6.00 1.80
❑ 226 Matt White FW RC 6.00 1.80
❑ 227 Casey Fossum FW RC 6.00 1.80
❑ 228 Mike Rivera FW RC 6.00 1.80
❑ 229 Joe Kennedy FW RC 8.00 2.40
❑ 230 Kyle Lohse FW RC 8.00 2.40
❑ 231 Juan Cruz FW RC 6.00 1.80
❑ 232 Jeremy Affeldt FW RC 8.00 2.40
❑ 233 Brandon Lyon FW RC 6.00 1.80
❑ 234 Brian Roberts FW RC 6.00 1.80
❑ 235 Willie Harris FW RC 6.00 1.80
❑ 236 Pedro Santana FW RC 6.00 1.80
❑ 237 Rafael Soriano FW RC 8.00 2.40
❑ 238 Steve Green FW RC 6.00 1.80
❑ 239 Junior Spivey FW RC 8.00 2.40
❑ 240 R.Mackowiak FW RC 8.00 2.40
❑ NNO K.Griffey Jr. Promo 2.00 .60

2002 SP Authentic

	Nm-Mt	Ex-Mt
COMP.LOW w/o SP's (90)	15.00	4.50
COMP.UPDATE w/o SP's (30)	10.00	3.00
COMMON CARD (1-90)	.40	.12
COMMON (91-135/201-230)	5.00	1.50
COMMON CARD (136-170)	15.00	4.50
COMMON CARD (171-200)	.60	.18

❑ 1 Troy Glaus .40 .12
❑ 2 Darin Erstad .40 .12
❑ 3 Barry Zito .40 .12
❑ 4 Eric Chavez .40 .12
❑ 5 Tim Hudson .40 .12
❑ 6 Miguel Tejada .40 .12
❑ 7 Carlos Delgado .40 .12
❑ 8 Shannon Stewart .40 .12
❑ 9 Ben Grieve .40 .12
❑ 10 Jim Thome 1.00 .30
❑ 11 C.C. Sabathia .40 .12
❑ 12 Ichiro Suzuki 1.50 .45
❑ 13 Freddy Garcia .40 .12
❑ 14 Edgar Martinez .60 .18
❑ 15 Bret Boone .40 .12
❑ 16 Jeff Conine .40 .12
❑ 17 Alex Rodriguez 1.50 .45
❑ 18 Juan Gonzalez .60 .18
❑ 19 Ivan Rodriguez 1.00 .30
❑ 20 Rafael Palmeiro .60 .18
❑ 21 Hank Blalock 1.00 .30
❑ 22 Pedro Martinez 1.00 .30
❑ 23 Manny Ramirez .60 .18
❑ 24 Nomar Garciaparra 1.50 .45
❑ 25 Carlos Beltran .60 .18
❑ 26 Mike Sweeney .40 .12
❑ 27 Randall Simon .40 .12
❑ 28 Dmitri Young .40 .12
❑ 29 Bobby Higginson .40 .12
❑ 30 Corey Koskie .40 .12
❑ 31 Eric Milton .40 .12
❑ 32 Torii Hunter .40 .12
❑ 33 Joe Mays .40 .12
❑ 34 Frank Thomas 1.00 .30
❑ 35 Mark Buehrle .40 .12
❑ 36 Magglio Ordonez .40 .12
❑ 37 Kenny Lofton .40 .12
❑ 38 Roger Clemens 2.00 .60
❑ 39 Derek Jeter 2.50 .75
❑ 40 Jason Giambi .40 .12
❑ 41 Bernie Williams .60 .18
❑ 42 Alfonso Soriano .60 .18
❑ 43 Lance Berkman .40 .12
❑ 44 Roy Oswalt .40 .12
❑ 45 Jeff Bagwell .60 .18
❑ 46 Craig Biggio .60 .18
❑ 47 Chipper Jones 1.00 .30
❑ 48 Greg Maddux 1.50 .45
❑ 49 Gary Sheffield .40 .12
❑ 50 Andruw Jones .40 .12
❑ 51 Ben Sheets .40 .12
❑ 52 Richie Sexson .40 .12
❑ 53 Albert Pujols 2.00 .60
❑ 54 Matt Morris .40 .12
❑ 55 J.D. Drew .40 .12
❑ 56 Sammy Sosa 1.50 .45
❑ 57 Kerry Wood 1.00 .30
❑ 58 Corey Patterson .40 .12
❑ 59 Mark Prior 1.50 .45
❑ 60 Randy Johnson 1.00 .30
❑ 61 Luis Gonzalez .40 .12
❑ 62 Curt Schilling .40 .12
❑ 63 Shawn Green .40 .12
❑ 64 Kevin Brown .40 .12
❑ 65 Hideo Nomo 1.00 .30
❑ 66 Vladimir Guerrero 1.00 .30
❑ 67 Jose Vidro .40 .12
❑ 68 Barry Bonds 2.50 .75
❑ 69 Jeff Kent .40 .12
❑ 70 Rich Aurilia .40 .12
❑ 71 Preston Wilson .40 .12
❑ 72 Josh Beckett .40 .12
❑ 73 Mike Lowell .40 .12
❑ 74 Roberto Alomar .60 .18
❑ 75 Mo Vaughn .40 .12
❑ 76 Jeromy Burnitz .40 .12
❑ 77 Mike Piazza 1.50 .45
❑ 78 Sean Burroughs .40 .12
❑ 79 Phil Nevin .40 .12
❑ 80 Bobby Abreu .40 .12
❑ 81 Pat Burrell .40 .12
❑ 82 Scott Rolen 1.00 .30
❑ 83 Jason Kendall .40 .12

No.	Player	Nm-Mt	Ex-Mt
❑ 84	Brian Giles	.40	.12
❑ 85	Ken Griffey Jr.	1.50	.45
❑ 86	Adam Dunn	.60	.18
❑ 87	Sean Casey	.40	.12
❑ 88	Todd Helton	.60	.18
❑ 89	Larry Walker	.60	.18
❑ 90	Mike Hampton	.40	.12
❑ 91	Brandon Puffer FW	5.00	1.50
❑ 92	Tom Shearn FW RC	5.00	1.50
❑ 93	Chris Baker FW RC	5.00	1.50
❑ 94	Gustavo Chacin FW RC	8.00	2.40
❑ 95	Joe Orloski FW RC	5.00	1.50
❑ 96	Mike Smith FW RC	5.00	1.50
❑ 97	John Ennis FW RC	5.00	1.50
❑ 98	John Foster FW RC	5.00	1.50
❑ 99	Kevin Gryboski FW RC	5.00	1.50
❑ 100	Brian Mallette FW RC	5.00	1.50
❑ 101	Takahito Nomura FW RC	5.00	1.50
❑ 102	So Taguchi FW RC	8.00	2.40
❑ 103	Jeremy Lambert FW RC	5.00	1.50
❑ 104	J.Simontacchi FW RC	5.00	1.50
❑ 105	Jorge Sosa FW RC	5.00	1.50
❑ 106	Brandon Backe FW RC	8.00	2.40
❑ 107	P.J. Bevis FW RC	5.00	1.50
❑ 108	Jeremy Ward FW RC	5.00	1.50
❑ 109	Doug Devore FW RC	5.00	1.50
❑ 110	Ron Chiavacci FW	5.00	1.50
❑ 111	Ron Calloway FW RC	5.00	1.50
❑ 112	Nelson Castro FW RC	5.00	1.50
❑ 113	Deivis Santos FW	5.00	1.50
❑ 114	Earl Snyder FW RC	8.00	2.40
❑ 115	Julio Mateo FW RC	5.00	1.50
❑ 116	J.J. Putz FW RC	5.00	1.50
❑ 117	Allan Simpson FW RC	5.00	1.50
❑ 118	Satoru Komiyama FW RC	5.00	1.50
❑ 119	Adam Walker FW RC	5.00	1.50
❑ 120	Oliver Perez FW RC	15.00	4.50
❑ 121	Cliff Bartosh FW RC	5.00	1.50
❑ 122	Todd Donovan FW RC	5.00	1.50
❑ 123	Elio Serrano FW RC	5.00	1.50
❑ 124	Pete Zamora FW RC	5.00	1.50
❑ 125	Mike Gonzalez FW RC	5.00	1.50
❑ 126	Travis Hughes FW RC	5.00	1.50
❑ 127	J.De La Rosa FW RC	5.00	1.50
❑ 128	An.Martinez FW RC	5.00	1.50
❑ 129	Colin Young FW RC	5.00	1.50
❑ 130	Nate Field FW RC	5.00	1.50
❑ 131	Tim Kalita FW RC	5.00	1.50
❑ 132	Julius Matos FW RC	5.00	1.50
❑ 133	Terry Pearson FW RC	5.00	1.50
❑ 134	Kyle Kane FW RC	5.00	1.50
❑ 135	Mitch Wylie FW RC	5.00	1.50
❑ 136	Rodrigo Rosario AU RC	15.00	4.50
❑ 137	Franklyn German AU RC	15.00	4.50
❑ 138	Reed Johnson AU RC	20.00	6.00
❑ 139	Luis Martinez AU RC	15.00	4.50
❑ 140	Michael Crudale AU RC	15.00	4.50
❑ 141	Francis Beltran AU RC	15.00	4.50
❑ 142	Steve Kent AU RC	15.00	4.50
❑ 143	Felix Escalona AU RC	15.00	4.50
❑ 144	Jose Valverde AU RC	20.00	6.00
❑ 145	Victor Alvarez AU RC	15.00	4.50
❑ 146	Kazuhisa Ishii AU/249 RC	50.00	15.00
❑ 147	Jorge Nunez AU RC	15.00	4.50
❑ 148	Eric Good AU RC	15.00	4.50
❑ 149	Luis Ugueto AU RC	15.00	4.50
❑ 150	Matt Thornton AU RC	15.00	4.50
❑ 151	Wilson Valdez AU RC	15.00	4.50
❑ 152	Han Izquierdo AU/249 RC	40.00	12.00
❑ 153	Jaime Cerda AU RC	15.00	4.50
❑ 154	Mark Corey AU RC	15.00	4.50
❑ 155	Tyler Yates AU RC	20.00	6.00
❑ 156	Steve Bechler AU RC	15.00	4.50
❑ 157	Ben Howard AU/249 RC	40.00	12.00
❑ 158	And. Machado AU RC	15.00	4.50
❑ 159	Jorge Padilla AU RC	15.00	4.50
❑ 160	Eric Junge AU RC	15.00	4.50
❑ 161	Adrian Burnside AU RC	15.00	4.50
❑ 162	Josh Hancock AU RC	15.00	4.50
❑ 163	Chris Booker AU RC	15.00	4.50
❑ 164	Cam Esslinger AU RC	15.00	4.50
❑ 165	Rene Reyes AU RC	15.00	4.50
❑ 166	Aaron Cook AU RC	15.00	4.50
❑ 167	Juan Brito AU RC	15.00	4.50
❑ 168	Miguel Ascencio AU RC	15.00	4.50
❑ 169	Kevin Frederick AU RC	15.00	4.50
❑ 170	Edwin Almonte AU RC	15.00	4.50
❑ 171	Erubiel Durazo	.60	.18
❑ 172	Junior Spivey	.60	.18
❑ 173	Geronimo Gil	.60	.18
❑ 174	Cliff Floyd	.60	.18
❑ 175	Brandon Larson	.60	.18
❑ 176	Aaron Boone	.60	.18
❑ 177	Shawn Estes	.60	.18
❑ 178	Austin Kearns	.60	.18
❑ 179	Joe Borchard	.60	.18
❑ 180	Russell Branyan	.60	.18
❑ 181	Jay Payton	.60	.18
❑ 182	Andres Torres	.60	.18
❑ 183	Andy Van Hekken	.60	.18
❑ 184	Alex Sanchez	.60	.18
❑ 185	Endy Chavez	.60	.18
❑ 186	Bartolo Colon	.60	.18
❑ 187	Raul Mondesi	.60	.18
❑ 188	Robin Ventura	.60	.18
❑ 189	Mike Mussina	1.00	.30
❑ 190	Jorge Posada	1.00	.30
❑ 191	Ted Lilly	.60	.18
❑ 192	Ray Durham	.60	.18
❑ 193	Brett Myers	.60	.18
❑ 194	Marlon Byrd	.60	.18
❑ 195	Vicente Padilla	.60	.18
❑ 196	Josh Fogg	.60	.18
❑ 197	Kenny Lofton	.60	.18
❑ 198	Scott Rolen	1.50	.45
❑ 199	Jason Lane	.60	.18
❑ 200	Josh Phelps	.60	.18
❑ 201	Travis Driskill FW RC	5.00	1.50
❑ 202	Howie Clark FW RC	5.00	1.50
❑ 203	Mike Mahoney FW	5.00	1.50
❑ 204	Brian Tallet FW RC	5.00	1.50
❑ 205	Kirk Saarloos FW RC	5.00	1.50
❑ 206	Barry Wesson FW RC	5.00	1.50
❑ 207	Aaron Guiel FW RC	5.00	1.50
❑ 208	Shawn Sedlacek FW RC	5.00	1.50
❑ 209	Jose Diaz FW RC	5.00	1.50
❑ 210	Jorge Nunez FW	5.00	1.50
❑ 211	Danny Mota FW RC	5.00	1.50
❑ 212	David Ross FW RC	5.00	1.50
❑ 213	Jayson Durocher FW RC	5.00	1.50
❑ 214	Shane Nance FW RC	5.00	1.50
❑ 215	Wil Nieves FW RC	5.00	1.50
❑ 216	Freddy Sanchez FW RC	5.00	1.50
❑ 217	Alex Pelaez FW RC	5.00	1.50
❑ 218	Jamey Carroll FW RC	5.00	1.50
❑ 219	J.J. Trujillo FW RC	5.00	1.50
❑ 220	Kevin Pickford FW RC	5.00	1.50
❑ 221	Clay Condrey FW RC	5.00	1.50
❑ 222	Chris Snelling FW RC	5.00	1.50
❑ 223	Cliff Lee FW RC	8.00	2.40
❑ 224	Jeremy Hill FW RC	5.00	1.50
❑ 225	Jose Rodriguez FW RC	5.00	1.50
❑ 226	Lance Carter FW RC	5.00	1.50
❑ 227	Ken Huckaby FW RC	5.00	1.50
❑ 228	Scott Wiggins FW RC	5.00	1.50
❑ 229	Corey Thurman FW RC	5.00	1.50
❑ 230	Kevin Cash FW RC	5.00	1.50
❑ RJ-D	J.DiMaggio Poster AU EX	200.00	60.00

2003 SP Authentic

	Nm-Mt	Ex-Mt
COMP.LO SET w/o SP's (90)	15.00	4.50
COMMON CARD (1-90)	.40	.12
COMMON CARD (91-123)	3.00	.90
COMMON CARD (124-150)	3.00	.90
COMMON CARD (151-180)	5.00	1.50
COMMON CARD (181-189)	15.00	4.50
91-189 RANDOM INSERTS IN PACKS		
COMMON CARD (190-239)	5.00	1.50
190-239 RANDOM IN 03 UD FINITE PACKS		
190-239 PRINT RUN 699 SERIAL #'d SETS		

No.	Player	Nm-Mt	Ex-Mt
❑ 1	Darin Erstad	.40	.12
❑ 2	Garret Anderson	.40	.12
❑ 3	Troy Glaus	.40	.12
❑ 4	Eric Chavez	.40	.12
❑ 5	Barry Zito	.40	.12
❑ 6	Miguel Tejada	.40	.12
❑ 7	Eric Hinske	.40	.12
❑ 8	Carlos Delgado	.40	.12
❑ 9	Josh Phelps	.40	.12
❑ 10	Ben Grieve	.40	.12
❑ 11	Carl Crawford	.40	.12
❑ 12	Omar Vizquel	.60	.18
❑ 13	Matt Lawton	.40	.12
❑ 14	C.C. Sabathia	.40	.12
❑ 15	Ichiro Suzuki	1.50	.45
❑ 16	John Olerud	.40	.12
❑ 17	Freddy Garcia	.40	.12
❑ 18	Jay Gibbons	.40	.12
❑ 19	Tony Batista	.40	.12
❑ 20	Melvin Mora	.40	.12
❑ 21	Alex Rodriguez	1.50	.45
❑ 22	Rafael Palmeiro	.60	.18
❑ 23	Hank Blalock	.60	.18
❑ 24	Nomar Garciaparra	1.50	.45
❑ 25	Pedro Martinez	1.00	.30
❑ 26	Johnny Damon	1.00	.30
❑ 27	Mike Sweeney	.40	.12
❑ 28	Carlos Febles	.40	.12
❑ 29	Carlos Beltran	.60	.18
❑ 30	Carlos Pena	.40	.12
❑ 31	Eric Munson	.40	.12
❑ 32	Bobby Higginson	.40	.12
❑ 33	Torii Hunter	.40	.12
❑ 34	Doug Mientkiewicz	.40	.12
❑ 35	Jacque Jones	.40	.12
❑ 36	Paul Konerko	.40	.12
❑ 37	Bartolo Colon	.40	.12
❑ 38	Magglio Ordonez	.40	.12
❑ 39	Derek Jeter	2.50	.75
❑ 40	Bernie Williams	.60	.18
❑ 41	Jason Giambi	.40	.12
❑ 42	Alfonso Soriano	.60	.18
❑ 43	Roger Clemens	2.00	.60
❑ 44	Jeff Bagwell	.60	.18
❑ 45	Jeff Kent	.40	.12
❑ 46	Lance Berkman	.40	.12
❑ 47	Chipper Jones	1.00	.30
❑ 48	Andruw Jones	.40	.12
❑ 49	Gary Sheffield	.40	.12
❑ 50	Ben Sheets	.40	.12
❑ 51	Richie Sexson	.40	.12
❑ 52	Geoff Jenkins	.40	.12
❑ 53	Jim Edmonds	.40	.12
❑ 54	Albert Pujols	2.00	.60
❑ 55	Scott Rolen	1.00	.30
❑ 56	Sammy Sosa	1.50	.45
❑ 57	Kerry Wood	1.00	.30
❑ 58	Eric Karros	.40	.12
❑ 59	Luis Gonzalez	.40	.12
❑ 60	Randy Johnson	1.00	.30
❑ 61	Curt Schilling	.40	.12
❑ 62	Fred McGriff	.60	.18
❑ 63	Shawn Green	.40	.12
❑ 64	Paul Lo Duca	.40	.12
❑ 65	Vladimir Guerrero	1.00	.30
❑ 66	Jose Vidro	.40	.12
❑ 67	Barry Bonds	2.50	.75
❑ 68	Rich Aurilia	.40	.12
❑ 69	Edgardo Alfonzo	.40	.12
❑ 70	Ivan Rodriguez	1.00	.30
❑ 71	Mike Lowell	.40	.12
❑ 72	Derrek Lee	.40	.12
❑ 73	Tom Glavine	.60	.18
❑ 74	Mike Piazza	1.50	.45
❑ 75	Roberto Alomar	.60	.18
❑ 76	Ryan Klesko	.40	.12
❑ 77	Phil Nevin	.40	.12

No.	Player	Nm-Mt	Ex-Mt
❑ 78	Mark Kotsay	.40	.12
❑ 79	Jim Thome	1.00	.30
❑ 80	Pat Burrell	.40	.12
❑ 81	Bobby Abreu	.40	.12
❑ 82	Jason Kendall	.40	.12
❑ 83	Brian Giles	.40	.12
❑ 84	Aramis Ramirez	.40	.12
❑ 85	Austin Kearns	.40	.12
❑ 86	Ken Griffey Jr.	1.50	.45
❑ 87	Adam Dunn	.60	.18
❑ 88	Larry Walker	.60	.18
❑ 89	Todd Helton	.60	.18
❑ 90	Preston Wilson	.40	.12
❑ 91	Derek Jeter RA	8.00	2.40
❑ 92	Johnny Damon RA	3.00	.90
❑ 93	Chipper Jones RA	3.00	.90
❑ 94	Manny Ramirez RA	3.00	.90
❑ 95	Trot Nixon RA	3.00	.90
❑ 96	Alex Rodriguez RA	5.00	1.50
❑ 97	Chan Ho Park RA	3.00	.90
❑ 98	Brad Fullmer RA	3.00	.90
❑ 99	Billy Wagner RA	3.00	.90
❑ 100	Hideo Nomo RA	3.00	.90
❑ 101	Freddy Garcia RA	3.00	.90
❑ 102	Darin Erstad RA	3.00	.90
❑ 103	Jose Cruz Jr. RA	3.00	.90
❑ 104	Nomar Garciaparra RA	5.00	1.50
❑ 105	Magglio Ordonez RA	3.00	.90
❑ 106	Kerry Wood RA	3.00	.90
❑ 107	Troy Glaus RA	3.00	.90
❑ 108	J.D. Drew RA	3.00	.90
❑ 109	Alfonso Soriano RA	3.00	.90
❑ 110	Danys Baez RA	3.00	.90
❑ 111	Kazuhiro Sasaki RA	3.00	.90
❑ 112	Barry Zito RA	3.00	.90
❑ 113	Brent Abernathy RA	3.00	.90
❑ 114	Ben Diggins RA	3.00	.90
❑ 115	Ben Sheets RA	3.00	.90
❑ 116	Brad Wilkerson RA	3.00	.90
❑ 117	Juan Pierre RA	3.00	.90
❑ 118	Jon Rauch RA	3.00	.90
❑ 119	Ichiro Suzuki RA	5.00	1.50
❑ 120	Albert Pujols RA	6.00	1.80
❑ 121	Mark Prior RA	3.00	.90
❑ 122	Mark Teixeira RA	3.00	.90
❑ 123	Kazuhisa Ishii RA	3.00	.90
❑ 124	Troy Glaus B93	3.00	.90
❑ 125	Randy Johnson B93	3.00	.90
❑ 126	Curt Schilling B93	3.00	.90
❑ 127	Chipper Jones B93	3.00	.90
❑ 128	Greg Maddux B93	5.00	1.50
❑ 129	Nomar Garciaparra B93	5.00	1.50
❑ 130	Pedro Martinez B93	3.00	.90
❑ 131	Sammy Sosa B93	5.00	1.50
❑ 132	Mark Prior B93	3.00	.90
❑ 133	Ken Griffey Jr. B93	5.00	1.50
❑ 134	Adam Dunn B93	3.00	.90
❑ 135	Jeff Bagwell B93	3.00	.90
❑ 136	Vladimir Guerrero B93	3.00	.90
❑ 137	Mike Piazza B93	5.00	1.50
❑ 138	Tom Glavine B93	3.00	.90
❑ 139	Derek Jeter B93	8.00	2.40
❑ 140	Roger Clemens B93	6.00	1.80
❑ 141	Jason Giambi B93	3.00	.90
❑ 142	Alfonso Soriano B93	3.00	.90
❑ 143	Miguel Tejada B93	3.00	.90
❑ 144	Barry Zito B93	3.00	.90
❑ 145	Jim Thome B93	3.00	.90
❑ 146	Barry Bonds B93	8.00	2.40
❑ 147	Ichiro Suzuki B93	5.00	1.50
❑ 148	Albert Pujols B93	6.00	1.80
❑ 149	Alex Rodriguez B93	5.00	1.50
❑ 150	Carlos Delgado B93	3.00	.90
❑ 151	Rich Fischer FW RC	5.00	1.50
❑ 152	Brandon Webb FW RC	10.00	3.00
❑ 153	Rob Hammock FW RC	8.00	2.40
❑ 154	Matt Kata FW RC	8.00	2.40
❑ 155	Tim Olson FW RC	8.00	2.40
❑ 156	Oscar Villarreal FW RC	5.00	1.50
❑ 157	Michael Hessman FW RC	5.00	1.50
❑ 158	Daniel Cabrera FW RC	8.00	2.40
❑ 159	Jon Leicester FW RC	5.00	1.50
❑ 160	Todd Wellemeyer FW RC	8.00	2.40
❑ 161	Felix Sanchez FW RC	5.00	1.50
❑ 162	David Sanders FW RC	5.00	1.50
❑ 163	Josh Stewart FW RC	5.00	1.50
❑ 164	Arnie Munoz FW RC	5.00	1.50
❑ 165	Ryan Cameron FW RC	5.00	1.50
❑ 166	Clint Barmes FW RC	8.00	2.40
❑ 167	Josh Willingham FW RC	8.00	2.40
❑ 169	Willie Eyre FW RC	5.00	1.50
❑ 170	Brent Hoard FW RC	5.00	1.50
❑ 171	Terrmel Sledge FW RC	8.00	2.40
❑ 172	Phil Seibel FW RC	5.00	1.50
❑ 173	Craig Brazell FW RC	8.00	2.40
❑ 174	Jeff Duncan FW RC	8.00	2.40
❑ 176	Bernie Castro FW RC	5.00	1.50
❑ 177	Mike Nicolas FW RC	5.00	1.50
❑ 178	Rett Johnson FW RC	8.00	2.40
❑ 179	Bobby Madritsch FW RC	15.00	4.50
❑ 180	Chris Capuano FW RC	5.00	1.50
❑ 181	Hid Matsui FW AU RC	250.00	75.00
❑ 182	J.Contreras FW AU RC	40.00	12.00
❑ 183	Lew Ford FW AU RC	40.00	12.00
❑ 184	Jer. Griffiths FW AU RC	25.00	7.50
❑ 185	G. Quiroz FW AU RC	25.00	7.50
❑ 186	Alej Machado FW AU RC	15.00	4.50
❑ 187	Fran Cruceta FW AU RC	15.00	4.50
❑ 188	Pr. Redman FW AU RC	15.00	4.50
❑ 189	S.Bazzell FW AU RC	15.00	4.50
❑ 190	Aaron Looper FW RC	5.00	1.50
❑ 191	Alex Prieto FW RC	5.00	1.50
❑ 192	Alfredo Gonzalez FW RC	5.00	1.50
❑ 193	Andrew Brown FW RC	8.00	2.40
❑ 194	Anthony Ferrari FW RC	5.00	1.50
❑ 195	Aquilino Lopez FW RC	5.00	1.50
❑ 196	Beau Kemp FW RC	5.00	1.50
❑ 197	Bo Hart FW RC	8.00	2.40
❑ 198	Chad Gaudin FW RC	5.00	1.50
❑ 199	Colin Porter FW RC	5.00	1.50
❑ 200	D.J. Carrasco FW RC	5.00	1.50
❑ 201	Dan Haren FW RC	8.00	2.40
❑ 202	Danny Garcia FW RC	5.00	1.50
❑ 203	Jon Switzer FW	5.00	1.50
❑ 204	Edwin Jackson FW RC	20.00	6.00
❑ 205	Fernando Cabrera FW RC	5.00	1.50
❑ 206	Garrett Atkins FW	5.00	1.50
❑ 207	Gerald Laird FW	5.00	1.50
❑ 208	Greg Jones FW RC	5.00	1.50
❑ 209	Ian Ferguson FW RC	5.00	1.50
❑ 210	Jason Roach FW RC	5.00	1.50
❑ 211	Jason Shiell FW RC	5.00	1.50
❑ 212	Jeremy Bonderman FW RC	8.00	2.40
❑ 213	Jeremy Wedel FW RC	5.00	1.50
❑ 214	Jhonny Peralta FW	5.00	1.50
❑ 215	Delmon Young FW RC	30.00	9.00
❑ 216	Jorge DePaula FW	5.00	1.50
❑ 217	Josh Hall FW RC	8.00	2.40
❑ 218	Julio Manon FW RC	5.00	1.50
❑ 219	Kevin Correia FW RC	5.00	1.50
❑ 220	Kevin Ohme FW RC	5.00	1.50
❑ 221	Kevin Tolar FW RC	5.00	1.50
❑ 222	Luis Ayala FW RC	5.00	1.50
❑ 223	Luis De Los Santos FW	5.00	1.50
❑ 224	Chad Cordero FW RC	5.00	1.50
❑ 225	Mark Malaska FW RC	5.00	1.50
❑ 226	Khalil Greene FW	15.00	4.50
❑ 227	Michael Nakamura FW RC	5.00	1.50
❑ 228	Michel Hernandez FW RC	5.00	1.50
❑ 229	Miguel Ojeda FW RC	5.00	1.50
❑ 230	Mike Neu FW RC	5.00	1.50
❑ 231	Nate Bland FW RC	5.00	1.50
❑ 232	Pete LaForest FW RC	8.00	2.40
❑ 233	Rickie Weeks FW RC	20.00	6.00
❑ 234	Rosman Garcia FW RC	5.00	1.50
❑ 235	Ryan Wagner FW RC	8.00	2.40
❑ 236	Lance Niekro FW	5.00	1.50
❑ 237	Tom Gregorio FW RC	5.00	1.50
❑ 238	Tommy Phelps FW	5.00	1.50
❑ 239	Wilfredo Ledezma FW RC	8.00	2.40

2004 SP Authentic

	Nm-Mt	Ex-Mt
COMP.SET w/o SP's (90)	15.00	4.50
COMMON CARD (1-90)	.40	.12
COMMON (91-132/178-191)	5.00	1.50

91-132/178-191 OVERALL FW ODDS 1:24
91-132/178-179/181-191 PRINT 704 #'d SETS
91-132/178-179/181-191 #'d FROM 296-999
CARD 180 PRINT RUN 999 #'d COPIES
CARD 180 #'d FROM 1-999

	Nm-Mt	Ex-Mt
COMMON CARD (133-177)	3.00	.90

133-177 STATED ODDS 1:24
133-177 PRINT RUN 999 SERIAL #'d SETS

No.	Player	Nm-Mt	Ex-Mt
❑ 1	Bret Boone	.40	.12
❑ 2	Gary Sheffield	.40	.12
❑ 3	Rafael Palmeiro	.60	.18
❑ 4	Jorge Posada	.60	.18
❑ 5	Derek Jeter	2.00	.60
❑ 6	Garret Anderson	.40	.12
❑ 7	Bartolo Colon	.40	.12
❑ 8	Kevin Brown	.40	.12
❑ 9	Shea Hillenbrand	.40	.12
❑ 10	Ryan Klesko	.40	.12
❑ 11	Bobby Abreu	.40	.12
❑ 12	Scott Rolen	1.00	.30
❑ 13	Alfonso Soriano	.60	.18
❑ 14	Jason Giambi	.40	.12
❑ 15	Tom Glavine	.60	.18
❑ 16	Hideo Nomo	1.00	.30
❑ 17	Johan Santana	.60	.18
❑ 18	Sammy Sosa	1.50	.45
❑ 19	Rickie Weeks	.40	.12
❑ 20	Barry Zito	.40	.12
❑ 21	Kerry Wood	1.00	.30
❑ 22	Austin Kearns	.40	.12
❑ 23	Shawn Green	.40	.12
❑ 24	Miguel Cabrera	.60	.18
❑ 25	Richard Hidalgo	.40	.12
❑ 26	Andruw Jones	.40	.12
❑ 27	Randy Wolf	.40	.12
❑ 28	David Ortiz	1.00	.30
❑ 29	Roy Oswalt	.40	.12
❑ 30	Vernon Wells	.40	.12
❑ 31	Ben Sheets	.40	.12
❑ 32	Mike Lowell	.40	.12
❑ 33	Todd Helton	.60	.18
❑ 34	Jacque Jones	.40	.12
❑ 35	Mike Sweeney	.40	.12
❑ 36	Hank Blalock	.40	.12
❑ 37	Jason Schmidt	.40	.12
❑ 38	Jeff Kent	.40	.12
❑ 39	Josh Beckett	.40	.12
❑ 40	Manny Ramirez	.60	.18
❑ 41	Torii Hunter	.40	.12
❑ 42	Brian Giles	.40	.12
❑ 43	Javier Vazquez	.40	.12
❑ 44	Jim Edmonds	.40	.12
❑ 45	Dmitri Young	.40	.12
❑ 46	Preston Wilson	.40	.12
❑ 47	Jeff Bagwell	.60	.18
❑ 48	Pedro Martinez	1.00	.30
❑ 49	Eric Chavez	.40	.12
❑ 50	Ken Griffey Jr.	1.50	.45
❑ 51	Shannon Stewart	.40	.12
❑ 52	Rafael Furcal	.40	.12
❑ 53	Brandon Webb	.40	.12
❑ 54	Juan Pierre	.40	.12
❑ 55	Roger Clemens	2.00	.60
❑ 56	Geoff Jenkins	.40	.12
❑ 57	Lance Berkman	.40	.12
❑ 58	Albert Pujols	2.00	.60
❑ 59	Frank Thomas	1.00	.30
❑ 60	Edgar Martinez	.60	.18
❑ 61	Tim Hudson	.40	.12
❑ 62	Eric Gagne	1.00	.30
❑ 63	Richie Sexson	.40	.12
❑ 64	Corey Patterson	.40	.12
❑ 65	Nomar Garciaparra	1.50	.45

❑ 66 Hideki Matsui 1.50 .45
❑ 67 Mark Teixeira .40 .12
❑ 68 Troy Glaus .40 .12
❑ 69 Carlos Lee .40 .12
❑ 70 Mike Mussina .60 .18
❑ 71 Magglio Ordonez .40 .12
❑ 72 Roy Halladay .40 .12
❑ 73 Ichiro Suzuki 1.50 .45
❑ 74 Randy Johnson 1.00 .30
❑ 75 Luis Gonzalez .40 .12
❑ 76 Mark Prior 1.00 .30
❑ 77 Carlos Beltran .60 .18
❑ 78 Ivan Rodriguez 1.00 .30
❑ 79 Alex Rodriguez 1.50 .45
❑ 80 Dontrelle Willis .40 .12
❑ 81 Mike Piazza 1.50 .45
❑ 82 Curt Schilling 1.00 .30
❑ 83 Vladimir Guerrero 1.00 .30
❑ 84 Greg Maddux 1.50 .45
❑ 85 Jim Thome 1.00 .30
❑ 86 Miguel Tejada .40 .12
❑ 87 Carlos Delgado .40 .12
❑ 88 Jose Reyes .40 .12
❑ 89 Matt Morris .40 .12
❑ 90 Mark Mulder .40 .12
❑ 91 Angel Chavez FW RC 5.00 1.50
❑ 92 Brandon Medders FW RC 5.00 1.50
❑ 93 Carlos Vasquez FW RC 8.00 2.40
❑ 94 Chris Aguila FW RC 5.00 1.50
❑ 95 Colby Miller FW RC 5.00 1.50
❑ 96 Dave Crouthers FW RC 5.00 1.50
❑ 97 Dennis Sarfate FW RC 5.00 1.50
❑ 98 Donnie Kelly FW RC 5.00 1.50
❑ 99 Merkin Valdez FW RC 8.00 2.40
❑ 100 Eddy Rodriguez FW RC 8.00 2.40
❑ 101 Edwin Moreno FW RC 5.00 1.50
❑ 102 Enemencio Pacheco FW RC 5.00 1.50
❑ 103 Roberto Novoa FW RC 8.00 2.40
❑ 104 Greg Dobbs FW RC 5.00 1.50
❑ 105 Hector Gimenez FW RC 5.00 1.50
❑ 106 Ian Snell FW RC 8.00 2.40
❑ 107 Jake Woods FW RC 5.00 1.50
❑ 108 Jamie Brown FW RC 5.00 1.50
❑ 109 Jason Frasor FW RC 5.00 1.50
❑ 110 Jerome Gamble FW RC 5.00 1.50
❑ 111 Jerry Gil FW RC 5.00 1.50
❑ 112 Jesse Harper FW RC 5.00 1.50
❑ 113 Jorge Vasquez FW RC 5.00 1.50
❑ 114 Jose Capellan FW RC 8.00 2.40
❑ 115 Josh Labandeira FW RC 5.00 1.50
❑ 116 Justin Hampson FW RC 5.00 1.50
❑ 117 Justin Huisman FW RC 5.00 1.50
❑ 118 Justin Leone FW RC 8.00 2.40
❑ 119 Lincoln Holdzkom FW RC 5.00 1.50
❑ 120 Lino Urdaneta FW RC 5.00 1.50
❑ 121 Mike Gosling FW RC 5.00 1.50
❑ 122 Mike Johnston FW RC 5.00 1.50
❑ 123 Mike Rouse FW RC 5.00 1.50
❑ 124 Scott Proctor FW RC 8.00 2.40
❑ 125 Roman Colon FW RC 5.00 1.50
❑ 126 Ronny Cedeno FW RC 5.00 1.50
❑ 127 Ryan Meaux FW RC 5.00 1.50
❑ 128 Scott Dohmann FW RC 5.00 1.50
❑ 129 Sean Henn FW RC 5.00 1.50
❑ 130 Tim Bausher FW RC 5.00 1.50
❑ 131 Tim Bittner FW RC 5.00 1.50
❑ 132 William Bergolla FW RC 5.00 1.50
❑ 133 Rick Ferrell ASM 3.00 .90
❑ 134 Joe DiMaggio ASM 5.00 1.50
❑ 135 Bob Feller ASM 3.00 .90
❑ 136 Ted Williams ASM 8.00 2.40
❑ 137 Stan Musial ASM 5.00 1.50
❑ 138 Larry Doby ASM 3.00 .90
❑ 139 Red Schoendienst ASM 3.00 .90
❑ 140 Enos Slaughter ASM 3.00 .90
❑ 141 Stan Musial ASM 5.00 1.50
❑ 142 Mickey Mantle ASM 10.00 3.00
❑ 143 Ted Williams ASM 8.00 2.40
❑ 144 Mickey Mantle ASM 10.00 3.00
❑ 145 Stan Musial ASM 5.00 1.50
❑ 146 Tom Seaver ASM 4.00 1.20
❑ 147 Willie McCovey ASM 4.00 1.20
❑ 148 Bob Gibson ASM 4.00 1.20
❑ 149 Frank Robinson ASM 3.00 .90
❑ 150 Joe Morgan ASM 3.00 .90
❑ 151 Billy Williams ASM 3.00 .90
❑ 152 Catfish Hunter ASM 4.00 1.20
❑ 153 Joe Morgan ASM 3.00 .90
❑ 154 Joe Morgan ASM 3.00 .90
❑ 155 Mike Schmidt ASM 8.00 2.40
❑ 156 Tommy Lasorda ASM 3.00 .90
❑ 157 Robin Yount ASM 5.00 1.50
❑ 158 Nolan Ryan ASM 10.00 3.00
❑ 159 John Franco ASM 3.00 .90
❑ 160 Nolan Ryan ASM 10.00 3.00
❑ 161 Ken Griffey Jr. ASM 5.00 1.50
❑ 162 Cal Ripken ASM 10.00 3.00
❑ 163 Ken Griffey Jr. ASM 5.00 1.50
❑ 164 Gary Sheffield ASM 3.00 .90
❑ 165 Fred McGriff ASM 4.00 1.20
❑ 166 Hideo Nomo ASM 4.00 1.20
❑ 167 Mike Piazza ASM 5.00 1.50
❑ 168 Sandy Alomar Jr. ASM 3.00 .90
❑ 169 Roberto Alomar ASM 4.00 1.20
❑ 170 Ted Williams ASM 8.00 2.40
❑ 171 Pedro Martinez ASM 4.00 1.20
❑ 172 Derek Jeter ASM 6.00 1.80
❑ 173 Cal Ripken ASM 10.00 3.00
❑ 174 Torii Hunter ASM 3.00 .90
❑ 175 Alfonso Soriano ASM 4.00 1.20
❑ 176 Hank Blalock ASM 3.00 .90
❑ 177 Ichiro Suzuki ASM 5.00 1.50
❑ 178 Orlando Rodriguez FW RC 5.00 1.50
❑ 179 Ramon Ramirez FW RC 5.00 1.50
❑ 180 Kazuo Matsui FW RC 10.00 3.00
❑ 181 Kevin Cave FW RC 8.00 2.40
❑ 182 John Gall FW RC 8.00 2.40
❑ 183 Freddy Guzman FW RC 5.00 1.50
❑ 184 Chris Oxspring FW RC 8.00 2.40
❑ 185 Rusty Tucker FW RC 8.00 2.40
❑ 186 Jorge Sequea FW RC 5.00 1.50
❑ 187 Carlos Hines FW RC 5.00 1.50
❑ 188 Michael Vento FW RC 8.00 2.40
❑ 189 Ryan Wing FW RC 5.00 1.50
❑ 190 Jeff Bennett FW RC 5.00 1.50
❑ 191 Luis A. Gonzalez FW RC 8.00 2.40

2001 SP Game Bat Milestone

	Nm-Mt	Ex-Mt
COMP.SET w/o SP's (90)	80.00	24.00
COMMON CARD (1-90)	1.00	.30
COMMON BAT (91-96)	8.00	2.40

❑ 1 Troy Glaus 1.00 .30
❑ 2 Darin Erstad 1.00 .30
❑ 3 Jason Giambi 1.00 .30
❑ 4 Jermaine Dye 1.00 .30
❑ 5 Eric Chavez 1.00 .30
❑ 6 Carlos Delgado 1.00 .30
❑ 7 Raul Mondesi 1.00 .30
❑ 8 Shannon Stewart 1.00 .30
❑ 9 Greg Vaughn 1.00 .30
❑ 10 Aubrey Huff 1.00 .30
❑ 11 Juan Gonzalez 1.50 .45
❑ 12 Roberto Alomar 1.50 .45
❑ 13 Jim Thome 2.50 .75
❑ 14 Omar Vizquel 1.50 .45
❑ 15 Mike Cameron 1.00 .30
❑ 16 Edgar Martinez 1.50 .45
❑ 17 John Olerud 1.00 .30
❑ 18 Bret Boone 1.00 .30
❑ 19 Cal Ripken 8.00 2.40
❑ 20 Tony Batista 1.00 .30
❑ 21 Alex Rodriguez 4.00 1.20
❑ 22 Ivan Rodriguez 2.50 .75
❑ 23 Rafael Palmeiro 1.50 .45
❑ 24 Manny Ramirez 1.50 .45
❑ 25 Pedro Martinez 2.50 .75
❑ 26 Nomar Garciaparra 4.00 1.20
❑ 27 Carl Everett 1.00 .30
❑ 28 Mike Sweeney 1.00 .30
❑ 29 Neifi Perez 1.00 .30
❑ 30 Mark Quinn 1.00 .30
❑ 31 Bobby Higginson 1.00 .30
❑ 32 Tony Clark 1.00 .30
❑ 33 Doug Mientkiewicz 1.00 .30
❑ 34 Cristian Guzman 1.00 .30
❑ 35 Joe Mays 1.00 .30
❑ 36 David Ortiz 1.50 .45
❑ 37 Frank Thomas 2.50 .75
❑ 38 Magglio Ordonez 1.00 .30
❑ 39 Carlos Lee 1.00 .30
❑ 40 Alfonso Soriano 1.50 .45
❑ 41 Bernie Williams 1.50 .45
❑ 42 Derek Jeter 6.00 1.80
❑ 43 Roger Clemens 5.00 1.50
❑ 44 Jeff Bagwell 1.50 .45
❑ 45 Richard Hidalgo 1.00 .30
❑ 46 Moises Alou 1.00 .30
❑ 47 Chipper Jones 2.50 .75
❑ 48 Greg Maddux 4.00 1.20
❑ 49 Rafael Furcal 1.00 .30
❑ 50 Andruw Jones 1.00 .30
❑ 51 Jeromy Burnitz 1.00 .30
❑ 52 Geoff Jenkins 1.00 .30
❑ 53 Richie Sexson 1.00 .30
❑ 54 Edgar Renteria 1.00 .30
❑ 55 Mark McGwire 6.00 1.80
❑ 56 Jim Edmonds 1.00 .30
❑ 57 J.D. Drew 1.00 .30
❑ 58 Sammy Sosa 4.00 1.20
❑ 59 Fred McGriff 1.50 .45
❑ 60 Luis Gonzalez 1.00 .30
❑ 61 Randy Johnson 2.50 .75
❑ 62 Gary Sheffield 1.00 .30
❑ 63 Shawn Green 1.00 .30
❑ 64 Kevin Brown 1.00 .30
❑ 65 Vladimir Guerrero 2.50 .75
❑ 66 Jose Vidro 1.00 .30
❑ 67 Fernando Tatis 1.00 .30
❑ 68 Barry Bonds 6.00 1.80
❑ 69 Jeff Kent 1.00 .30
❑ 70 Rich Aurilia 1.00 .30
❑ 71 Preston Wilson 1.00 .30
❑ 72 Charles Johnson 1.00 .30
❑ 73 Cliff Floyd 1.00 .30
❑ 74 Mike Piazza 4.00 1.20
❑ 75 Matt Lawton 1.00 .30
❑ 76 Edgardo Alfonzo 1.00 .30
❑ 77 Tony Gwynn 3.00 .90
❑ 78 Phil Nevin 1.00 .30
❑ 79 Scott Rolen 2.50 .75
❑ 80 Pat Burrell 1.00 .30
❑ 81 Bobby Abreu 1.00 .30
❑ 82 Brian Giles 1.00 .30
❑ 83 Jason Kendall 1.00 .30
❑ 84 Aramis Ramirez 1.00 .30
❑ 85 Sean Casey 1.00 .30
❑ 86 Ken Griffey Jr. 4.00 1.20
❑ 87 Barry Larkin 1.50 .45
❑ 88 Todd Helton 1.50 .45
❑ 89 Mike Hampton 1.00 .30
❑ 90 Larry Walker 1.50 .45
❑ 91 Ichiro Suzuki BAT RC 50.00 15.00
❑ 92 Albert Pujols BAT RC 60.00 18.00
❑ 93 T. Shinjo BAT RC 10.00 3.00
❑ 94 Jack Wilson BAT RC 15.00 4.50
❑ 95 D. Mendez BAT RC 8.00 2.40
❑ 96 Junior Spivey BAT RC 10.00 3.00

2001 SP Game Used Edition

	Nm-Mt	Ex-Mt
COMP.SET w/o SP's (60)	80.00	24.00
COMMON CARD (1-60)	1.25	.35
COMMON CARD (61-90)	8.00	2.40

❑ 1 Garret Anderson 1.25 .35
❑ 2 Troy Glaus 1.25 .35
❑ 3 Darin Erstad 1.25 .35
❑ 4 Jason Giambi 1.25 .35
❑ 5 Tim Hudson 1.25 .35
❑ 6 Johnny Damon 2.00 .60
❑ 7 Carlos Delgado 1.25 .35
❑ 8 Greg Vaughn 1.25 .35
❑ 9 Juan Gonzalez 2.00 .60
❑ 10 Roberto Alomar 2.00 .60
❑ 11 Jim Thome 3.00 .90
❑ 12 Edgar Martinez 2.00 .60
❑ 13 Cal Ripken 10.00 3.00
❑ 14 Andres Galarraga 1.25 .35
❑ 15 Alex Rodriguez 5.00 1.50
❑ 16 Rafael Palmeiro 2.00 .60
❑ 17 Ivan Rodriguez 3.00 .90
❑ 18 Manny Ramirez 2.00 .60
❑ 19 Nomar Garciaparra 5.00 1.50
❑ 20 Pedro Martinez 3.00 .90
❑ 21 Jermaine Dye 1.25 .35
❑ 22 Dean Palmer 1.25 .35
❑ 23 Matt Lawton 1.25 .35
❑ 24 Frank Thomas 3.00 .90
❑ 25 David Wells 1.25 .35
❑ 26 Magglio Ordonez 1.25 .35
❑ 27 Derek Jeter 8.00 2.40
❑ 28 Bernie Williams 2.00 .60
❑ 29 Roger Clemens 6.00 1.80
❑ 30 Jeff Bagwell 2.00 .60
❑ 31 Richard Hidalgo 1.25 .35
❑ 32 Chipper Jones 3.00 .90
❑ 33 Andruw Jones 1.25 .35
❑ 34 Greg Maddux 5.00 1.50
❑ 35 Jeffrey Hammonds 1.25 .35
❑ 36 Mark McGwire 8.00 2.40
❑ 37 Jim Edmonds 1.25 .35
❑ 38 Sammy Sosa 5.00 1.50
❑ 39 Corey Patterson 1.25 .35
❑ 40 Randy Johnson 3.00 .90
❑ 41 Luis Gonzalez 1.25 .35
❑ 42 Gary Sheffield 1.25 .35
❑ 43 Shawn Green 1.25 .35
❑ 44 Kevin Brown 1.25 .35
❑ 45 Vladimir Guerrero 3.00 .90
❑ 46 Barry Bonds 8.00 2.40
❑ 47 Jeff Kent 1.25 .35
❑ 48 Preston Wilson 1.25 .35
❑ 49 Charles Johnson 1.25 .35
❑ 50 Mike Piazza 5.00 1.50
❑ 51 Edgardo Alfonzo 1.25 .35
❑ 52 Tony Gwynn 4.00 1.20
❑ 53 Scott Rolen 3.00 .90
❑ 54 Pat Burrell 1.25 .35
❑ 55 Brian Giles 1.25 .35
❑ 56 Jason Kendall 1.25 .35
❑ 57 Ken Griffey Jr. 5.00 1.50
❑ 58 Mike Hampton 1.25 .35
❑ 59 Todd Helton 2.00 .60
❑ 60 Larry Walker 2.00 .60
❑ 61 Wilson Betemit RC 8.00 2.40
❑ 62 Travis Hafner RC 15.00 4.50
❑ 63 Ichiro Suzuki RC 60.00 18.00
❑ 64 Juan Diaz RC 8.00 2.40
❑ 65 Morgan Ensberg RC 10.00 3.00
❑ 66 Horacio Ramirez RC 10.00 3.00
❑ 67 Ricardo Rodriguez RC 8.00 2.40
❑ 68 Sean Douglass RC 8.00 2.40
❑ 69 Brandon Duckworth RC 8.00 2.40
❑ 70 Jackson Melian RC 8.00 2.40
❑ 71 Adrian Hernandez RC 8.00 2.40
❑ 72 Kyle Kessel RC 8.00 2.40
❑ 73 Jason Michaels RC 8.00 2.40
❑ 74 Esix Snead RC 8.00 2.40
❑ 75 Jason Smith RC 8.00 2.40
❑ 76 Tyler Walker RC 8.00 2.40
❑ 77 Juan Uribe RC 10.00 3.00
❑ 78 Adam Pettyjohn RC 8.00 2.40
❑ 79 Tsuyoshi Shinjo RC 10.00 3.00
❑ 80 Mike Penney RC 8.00 2.40
❑ 81 Josh Towers RC 8.00 2.40
❑ 82 Erick Almonte RC 8.00 2.40
❑ 83 Ryan Freel RC 8.00 2.40
❑ 84 Juan Pena 8.00 2.40
❑ 85 Albert Pujols RC 120.00 36.00
❑ 86 Henry Mateo RC 8.00 2.40
❑ 87 Greg Miller RC 8.00 2.40
❑ 88 Jose Mieses RC 8.00 2.40
❑ 89 Jack Wilson RC 12.00 3.60
❑ 90 Carlos Valderrama RC 8.00 2.40

2004 SP Game Used Patch

	Nm-Mt	Ex-Mt
COMP.UPDATE SET (50)	100.00	30.00
COMMON CARD 1-60	4.00	1.20
61-90 PRINT RUN B/WN 86-684 COPIES PER		.00
COMMON CARD (91-119)	8.00	2.40
COMMON CARD (121-135)	2.50	.75
COMMON CARD (136-170)	2.50	.75
ONE UPDATE SET PER 48 UD2 HOB.BOXES		

❑ 1 Miguel Cabrera 4.00 1.20
❑ 2 Alex Rodriguez Yanks 8.00 2.40
❑ 3 Edgar Renteria 4.00 1.20
❑ 4 Juan Gonzalez 4.00 1.20
❑ 5 Mike Lowell 4.00 1.20
❑ 6 Andruw Jones 4.00 1.20
❑ 7 Eric Chavez 4.00 1.20
❑ 8 Jim Edmonds 4.00 1.20
❑ 9 Mike Piazza 8.00 2.40
❑ 10 Angel Berroa 4.00 1.20
❑ 11 Eric Gagne 5.00 1.50
❑ 12 Jody Gerut 4.00 1.20
❑ 13 Orlando Cabrera 4.00 1.20
❑ 14 Austin Kearns 4.00 1.20
❑ 15 Frank Thomas 5.00 1.50
❑ 16 Johan Santana 4.00 1.20
❑ 17 Randy Johnson 5.00 1.50
❑ 18 Preston Wilson 4.00 1.20
❑ 19 Garret Anderson 4.00 1.20
❑ 20 Jorge Posada 4.00 1.20
❑ 21 Rich Harden 4.00 1.20
❑ 22 Barry Zito 4.00 1.20
❑ 23 Gary Sheffield 4.00 1.20
❑ 24 Jose Reyes 4.00 1.20
❑ 25 Roy Halladay 4.00 1.20
❑ 26 Ben Sheets 4.00 1.20
❑ 27 Geoff Jenkins 4.00 1.20
❑ 28 Josh Beckett 4.00 1.20
❑ 29 Roy Oswalt 4.00 1.20
❑ 30 Bobby Abreu 4.00 1.20
❑ 31 Hank Blalock 4.00 1.20
❑ 32 Kerry Wood 5.00 1.50
❑ 33 Ryan Klesko 4.00 1.20
❑ 34 Rafael Furcal 4.00 1.20
❑ 35 Tom Glavine 4.00 1.20
❑ 36 Kevin Brown 4.00 1.20
❑ 37 Scott Rolen 5.00 1.50
❑ 38 Bret Boone 4.00 1.20
❑ 39 Ichiro Suzuki 8.00 2.40
❑ 40 Lance Berkman 4.00 1.20
❑ 41 Tim Hudson 4.00 1.20
❑ 42 Carlos Delgado 4.00 1.20
❑ 43 Ivan Rodriguez 5.00 1.50
❑ 44 Luis Gonzalez 4.00 1.20
❑ 45 Torii Hunter 4.00 1.20
❑ 46 Carlos Lee 4.00 1.20
❑ 47 Jacque Jones 4.00 1.20
❑ 48 Manny Ramirez 4.00 1.20
❑ 49 Troy Glaus 4.00 1.20
❑ 50 Corey Patterson 4.00 1.20
❑ 51 Jason Schmidt 4.00 1.20
❑ 52 Mark Mulder 4.00 1.20
❑ 53 Vernon Wells 4.00 1.20
❑ 54 Curt Schilling 5.00 1.50
❑ 55 Javy Lopez 4.00 1.20
❑ 56 Mark Prior 5.00 1.50
❑ 57 Dontrelle Willis 4.00 1.20
❑ 58 Derek Jeter 10.00 3.00
❑ 59 Jeff Bagwell 4.00 1.20
❑ 60 Marlon Byrd 4.00 1.20
❑ 61 Rafael Palmeiro SN/500 5.00 1.50
❑ 62 Kevin Millwood SN/165 5.00 1.50
❑ 63 Greg Maddux SN/273 10.00 3.00
❑ 64 Adam Dunn SN/400 5.00 1.50
❑ 65 Richie Sexson SN/469 5.00 1.50
❑ 66 Magglio Ordonez SN/567 5.00 1.50
❑ 67 Hideo Nomo SN/236 6.00 1.80
❑ 68 Albert Pujols SN/194 12.00 3.60
❑ 69 Rocco Baldelli SN/368 5.00 1.50
❑ 70 Mark Teixeira SN/86 6.00 1.80
❑ 71 Jason Giambi SN/660 5.00 1.50
❑ 72 Alfonso Soriano SN/230 5.00 1.50
❑ 73 Roger Clemens SN/300 12.00 3.60
❑ 74 Miguel Tejada SN/359 5.00 1.50
❑ 75 Jeff Kent SN/684 5.00 1.50
❑ 76 Bernie Williams SN/342 5.00 1.50
❑ 77 Sammy Sosa SN/470 10.00 3.00
❑ 78 Mike Mussina SN/641 5.00 1.50
❑ 79 Jim Thome SN/334 6.00 1.80
❑ 80 Brian Giles SN/506 5.00 1.50
❑ 81 Shawn Green SN/234 5.00 1.50
❑ 82 Mike Sweeney SN/340 5.00 1.50
❑ 83 John Smoltz SN/262 5.00 1.50
❑ 84 Carlos Beltran SN/319 5.00 1.50
❑ 85 Todd Helton SN/384 5.00 1.50
❑ 86 Nomar Garciaparra SN/372 10.00 3.00
❑ 87 Ken Griffey Jr. SN/481 10.00 3.00
❑ 88 Chipper Jones SN/633 6.00 1.80
❑ 89 Vladimir Guerrero SN/226 6.00 1.80
❑ 90 Pedro Martinez SN/313 6.00 1.80
❑ 91 Brandon Medders RD RC 8.00 2.40
❑ 92 Colby Miller RD RC 8.00 2.40
❑ 93 Dave Crouthers RD RC 8.00 2.40
❑ 94 Dennis Sarfate RD RC 8.00 2.40
❑ 95 Donald Kelly RD RC 8.00 2.40
❑ 96 Alec Zumwalt RD RC 8.00 2.40
❑ 97 Chris Aguila RD RC 8.00 2.40
❑ 98 Greg Dobbs RD RC 8.00 2.40
❑ 99 Ian Snell RD RC 10.00 3.00
❑ 100 Jake Woods RD RC 8.00 2.40
❑ 101 Jamie Brown RD RC 8.00 2.40
❑ 102 Jason Frasor RD RC 8.00 2.40
❑ 103 Jerome Gamble RD RC 8.00 2.40
❑ 104 Jesse Harper RD RC 8.00 2.40
❑ 105 Josh Labandeira RD RC 8.00 2.40
❑ 106 Justin Hampson RD RC 8.00 2.40
❑ 107 Justin Huisman RD RC 8.00 2.40
❑ 108 Justin Leone RD RC 10.00 3.00
❑ 109 Lincoln Holdzkom RD RC 8.00 2.40
❑ 110 Mike Bumatay RD RC 8.00 2.40
❑ 111 Mike Gosling RD RC 8.00 2.40
❑ 112 Mike Johnston RD RC 8.00 2.40
❑ 113 Mike Rouse RD RC 8.00 2.40
❑ 114 Nick Regilio RD RC 8.00 2.40
❑ 115 Ryan Meaux RD RC 8.00 2.40
❑ 116 Scott Dohmann RD RC 8.00 2.40
❑ 117 Sean Henn RD RC 8.00 2.40
❑ 118 Tim Bausher RD RC 8.00 2.40
❑ 119 Tim Bittner RD RC 8.00 2.40

❑ 121	Richie Sexson	2.50	.75
❑ 122	Javier Vazquez	2.50	.75
❑ 123	Alex Rodriguez Yanks	8.00	2.40
❑ 124	Javy Lopez	2.50	.75
❑ 125	Miguel Tejada	2.50	.75
❑ 126	Bartolo Colon	2.50	.75
❑ 127	Ivan Rodriguez	5.00	1.50
❑ 128	Rafael Palmeiro	4.00	1.20
❑ 129	Kevin Brown	2.50	.75
❑ 130	Gary Sheffield	2.50	.75
❑ 131	Greg Maddux	8.00	2.40
❑ 132	Curt Schilling	5.00	1.50
❑ 133	Roger Clemens	10.00	3.00
❑ 134	Alfonso Soriano	4.00	1.20
❑ 135	Vladimir Guerrero	5.00	1.50
❑ 136	Carlos Vasquez RC	2.50	.75
❑ 137	Roman Colon RC	2.50	.75
❑ 138	William Bergolla RC	2.50	.75
❑ 139	Jason Bartlett RC	3.00	.90
❑ 140	Casey Daigle RC	2.50	.75
❑ 141	Ryan Wing RC	2.50	.75
❑ 142	Chris Saenz RC	2.50	.75
❑ 143	Edwin Moreno RC	2.50	.75
❑ 144	Shawn Hill RC	2.50	.75
❑ 145	Eddy Rodriguez RC	3.00	.90
❑ 146	Justin Knoedler RC	2.50	.75
❑ 147	Renyel Pinto RC	3.00	.90
❑ 148	Kevin Cave RC	3.00	.90
❑ 149	Carlos Hines RC	2.50	.75
❑ 150	Merkin Valdez RC	5.00	1.50
❑ 151	Tim Hamulack RC	2.50	.75
❑ 152	Hector Gimenez RC	2.50	.75
❑ 153	Mike Vento RC	3.00	.90
❑ 154	Scott Proctor RC	3.00	.90
❑ 155	Rusty Tucker RC	3.00	.90
❑ 156	Akinori Otsuka RC	2.50	.75
❑ 157	Ronny Cedeno RC	2.50	.75
❑ 158	Jose Capellan RC	8.00	2.40
❑ 159	Justin Germano RC	2.50	.75
❑ 160	Shingo Takatsu RC	6.00	1.80
❑ 161	Fernando Nieve RC	2.50	.75
❑ 162	Michael Wuertz RC	3.00	.90
❑ 163	Jerry Gil RC	2.50	.75
❑ 164	Jorge Vasquez RC	2.50	.75
❑ 165	Chad Bentz RC	2.50	.75
❑ 166	Luis A. Gonzalez RC	3.00	.90
❑ 167	Ivan Ochoa RC	2.50	.75
❑ 168	Onil Joseph RC	2.50	.75
❑ 169	Enemencio Pacheco RC	2.50	.75
❑ 170	Kazuo Matsui RC	10.00	3.00

1986 Sportflics Rookies

		Nm-Mt	Ex-Mt
COMP.FACT.SET (50)		25.00	10.00
❑ 1	John Kruk	.75	.30
❑ 2	Edwin Correa	.10	.04
❑ 3	Pete Incaviglia	.25	.10
❑ 4	Dale Sveum	.10	.04
❑ 5	Juan Nieves	.10	.04
❑ 6	Will Clark	2.00	.80
❑ 7	Wally Joyner	.40	.16
❑ 8	Lance McCullers	.10	.04
❑ 9	Scott Bailes	.10	.04
❑ 10	Dan Plesac	.25	.10
❑ 11	Jose Canseco	2.00	.80
❑ 12	Bobby Witt	.25	.10
❑ 13	Barry Bonds	20.00	8.00
❑ 14	Andres Thomas	.10	.04
❑ 15	Jim Deshaies	.10	.04
❑ 16	Ruben Sierra	.75	.30
❑ 17	Steve Lombardozzi	.10	.04
❑ 18	Cory Snyder	.10	.04
❑ 19	Reggie Williams	.10	.04
❑ 20	Mitch Williams	.25	.10
❑ 21	Glenn Braggs	.10	.04
❑ 22	Danny Tartabull	.25	.10
❑ 23	Charlie Kerfeld	.10	.04
❑ 24	Paul Assenmacher	.25	.10
❑ 25	Robby Thompson	.25	.10
❑ 26	Bobby Bonilla	.40	.16
❑ 27	Andres Galarraga	.75	.30
❑ 28	Billy Joe Robidoux	.10	.04
❑ 29	Bruce Ruffin	.10	.04
❑ 30	Greg Swindell	.25	.10
❑ 31	John Cangelosi	.10	.04
❑ 32	Jim Traber	.10	.04
❑ 33	Russ Morman	.10	.04
❑ 34	Barry Larkin	2.00	.80
❑ 35	Todd Worrell	.25	.10
❑ 36	John Cerutti	.10	.04
❑ 37	Mike Kingery	.10	.04
❑ 38	Mark Eichhorn	.10	.04
❑ 39	Scott Bankhead	.10	.04
❑ 40	Bo Jackson	2.00	.80
❑ 41	Greg Mathews	.10	.04
❑ 42	Eric King	.10	.04
❑ 43	Kal Daniels	.25	.10
❑ 44	Calvin Schiraldi	.10	.04
❑ 45	Mickey Brantley	.10	.04
❑ 46	Willie Mays Pete Rose Fred Lynn	.75	.30
❑ 47	Tom Seaver Fernando Valenzuela Dwight Gooden	.25	.10
❑ 48	Eddie Murray Lou Whitaker Dave Righetti Steve Sax Cal Ripken Darryl Strawberry	.75	.30
❑ 49	Kevin Mitchell	.40	.16
❑ 50	Mike Diaz	.10	.04

1990 Sportflics

		Nm-Mt	Ex-Mt
COMPLETE SET (225)		30.00	9.00
COMP. FACT.SET (225)		30.00	9.00
❑ 1	Kevin Mitchell	.20	.06
❑ 2	Wade Boggs	.50	.15
❑ 3	Cory Snyder	.20	.06
❑ 4	Paul O'Neill	.50	.15
❑ 5	Will Clark	.75	.23
❑ 6	Tony Fernandez	.20	.06
❑ 7	Ken Griffey Jr.	2.00	.60
❑ 8	Nolan Ryan	2.50	.75
❑ 9	Rafael Palmeiro	.50	.15
❑ 10	Jesse Barfield	.20	.06
❑ 11	Kirby Puckett	.75	.23
❑ 12	Steve Sax	.20	.06
❑ 13	Fred McGriff	.50	.15
❑ 14	Gregg Jefferies	.20	.06
❑ 15	Mark Grace	.50	.15
❑ 16	Ozzie Smith	1.25	.35
❑ 17	George Bell	.20	.06
❑ 18	Robin Yount	1.25	.35
❑ 19	Glenn Davis	.20	.06
❑ 20	Jeffrey Leonard	.20	.06
❑ 21	Chili Davis	.30	.09
❑ 22	Craig Biggio	.50	.15
❑ 23	Jose Canseco	.75	.23
❑ 24	Derek Lilliquist	.20	.06
❑ 25	Chris Bosio	.20	.06
❑ 26	Dave Stieb	.30	.09
❑ 27	Bobby Thigpen	.20	.06
❑ 28	Jack Clark	.30	.09
❑ 29	Kevin Ritz	.20	.06
❑ 30	Tom Gordon	.30	.09
❑ 31	Bryan Harvey	.20	.06
❑ 32	Jim Deshaies	.20	.06
❑ 33	Terry Steinbach	.20	.06
❑ 34	Tom Glavine	.50	.15
❑ 35	Bob Welch	.30	.09
❑ 36	Charlie Hayes	.20	.06
❑ 37	Jeff Reardon	.30	.09
❑ 38	Joe Orsulak	.20	.06
❑ 39	Scott Garrelts	.20	.06
❑ 40	Bob Boone	.30	.09
❑ 41	Scott Bankhead	.20	.06
❑ 42	Tom Henke	.20	.06
❑ 43	Greg Briley	.20	.06
❑ 44	Teddy Higuera	.20	.06
❑ 45	Pat Borders	.20	.06
❑ 46	Kevin Seitzer	.20	.06
❑ 47	Bruce Hurst	.20	.06
❑ 48	Ozzie Guillen	.20	.06
❑ 49	Wally Joyner	.30	.09
❑ 50	Mike Greenwell	.20	.06
❑ 51	Gary Gaetti	.30	.09
❑ 52	Gary Sheffield UER (Uniform listed as 21, should be 1)	.75	.23
❑ 53	Dennis Martinez	.30	.09
❑ 54	Ryne Sandberg	1.25	.35
❑ 55	Mike Scott	.20	.06
❑ 56	Todd Benzinger	.20	.06
❑ 57	Kelly Gruber	.20	.06
❑ 58	Jose Lind	.20	.06
❑ 59	Allan Anderson	.20	.06
❑ 60	Robby Thompson	.20	.06
❑ 61	John Smoltz	.75	.23
❑ 62	Mark Davis	.20	.06
❑ 63	Tom Herr	.20	.06
❑ 64	Randy Johnson	1.25	.30
❑ 65	Lonnie Smith	.20	.06
❑ 66	Pedro Guerrero	.30	.09
❑ 67	Jerome Walton	.20	.06
❑ 68	Ramon Martinez	.20	.06
❑ 69	Tim Raines	.30	.09
❑ 70	Matt Williams	.30	.09
❑ 71	Joe Oliver	.20	.06
❑ 72	Nick Esasky	.20	.06
❑ 73	Kevin Brown	.30	.09
❑ 74	Walt Weiss	.20	.06
❑ 75	Roger McDowell	.20	.06
❑ 76	Jose DeLeon	.20	.06
❑ 77	Brian Downing	.30	.09
❑ 78	Jay Howell	.20	.06
❑ 79	Jose Uribe	.20	.06
❑ 80	Ellis Burks	.30	.09
❑ 81	Sammy Sosa	10.00	3.00
❑ 82	Johnny Ray	.20	.06
❑ 83	Danny Darwin	.20	.06
❑ 84	Carney Lansford	.30	.09
❑ 85	Jose Oquendo	.20	.06
❑ 86	John Cerutti	.20	.06
❑ 87	Dave Winfield	.30	.09
❑ 88	Dave Righetti	.30	.09
❑ 89	Danny Jackson	.20	.06
❑ 90	Andy Benes	.30	.09
❑ 91	Tom Browning	.20	.06
❑ 92	Pete O'Brien	.20	.06
❑ 93	Roberto Alomar	.50	.15
❑ 94	Bret Saberhagen	.30	.09
❑ 95	Phil Bradley	.20	.06
❑ 96	Doug Jones	.20	.06
❑ 97	Eric Davis	.30	.09
❑ 98	Tony Gwynn	1.00	.30

❑ 99 Jim Abbott .50 .15
❑ 100 Cal Ripken 2.50 .75
❑ 101 Andy Van Slyke .30 .09
❑ 102 Dan Plesac .20 .06
❑ 103 Lou Whitaker .30 .09
❑ 104 Steve Bedrosian .20 .06
❑ 105 Dave Gallagher .20 .06
❑ 106 Keith Hernandez .30 .09
❑ 107 Duane Ward .20 .06
❑ 108 Andre Dawson .30 .09
❑ 109 Howard Johnson .20 .06
❑ 110 Mark Langston .20 .06
❑ 111 Jerry Browne .20 .06
❑ 112 Alvin Davis .20 .06
❑ 113 Sid Fernandez .20 .06
❑ 114 Mike Devereaux .20 .06
❑ 115 Benito Santiago .30 .09
❑ 116 Bip Roberts .20 .06
❑ 117 Craig Worthington .20 .06
❑ 118 Kevin Elster .20 .06
❑ 119 Harold Reynolds .30 .09
❑ 120 Joe Carter .30 .09
❑ 121 Brian Harper .20 .06
❑ 122 Frank Viola .30 .09
❑ 123 Jeff Ballard .20 .06
❑ 124 John Kruk .30 .09
❑ 125 Harold Baines .30 .09
❑ 126 Tom Candiotti .20 .06
❑ 127 Kevin McReynolds .20 .06
❑ 128 Mookie Wilson .30 .09
❑ 129 Danny Tartabull .20 .06
❑ 130 Craig Lefferts .20 .06
❑ 131 Jose DeJesus .20 .06
❑ 132 John Orton .20 .06
❑ 133 Curt Schilling 1.50 .45
❑ 134 Marquis Grissom .75 .23
❑ 135 Greg Vaughn .20 .06
❑ 136 Brett Butler .30 .09
❑ 137 Rob Deer .20 .06
❑ 138 John Franco .30 .09
❑ 139 Keith Moreland .20 .06
❑ 140 Dave Smith .20 .06
❑ 141 Mark McGwire 2.50 .75
❑ 142 Vince Coleman .20 .06
❑ 143 Barry Bonds 2.00 .60
❑ 144 Mike Henneman .20 .06
❑ 145 Dwight Gooden .30 .09
❑ 146 Darryl Strawberry .30 .09
❑ 147 Von Hayes .20 .06
❑ 148 Andres Galarraga .30 .09
❑ 149 Roger Clemens 1.50 .45
❑ 150 Don Mattingly 2.00 .60
❑ 151 Joe Magrane .20 .06
❑ 152 Dwight Smith .20 .06
❑ 153 Ricky Jordan .20 .06
❑ 154 Alan Trammell .30 .09
❑ 155 Brook Jacoby .20 .06
❑ 156 Len Dykstra .30 .09
❑ 157 Mike LaValliere .20 .06
❑ 158 Julio Franco .30 .09
❑ 159 Joey Belle .75 .23
❑ 160 Barry Larkin .50 .15
❑ 161 Rick Reuschel .20 .06
❑ 162 Nelson Santovenia .20 .06
❑ 163 Mike Scioscia .20 .06
❑ 164 Damon Berryhill .20 .06
❑ 165 Todd Worrell .20 .06
❑ 166 Jim Eisenreich .20 .06
❑ 167 Ivan Calderon .20 .06
❑ 168 Mauro Gozzo .20 .06
❑ 169 Kirk McCaskill .20 .06
❑ 170 Dennis Eckersley .30 .09
❑ 171 Mickey Tettleton .20 .06
❑ 172 Chuck Finley .30 .09
❑ 173 Dave Magadan .20 .06
❑ 174 Terry Pendleton .30 .09
❑ 175 Willie Randolph .30 .09
❑ 176 Jeff Huson .20 .06
❑ 177 Todd Zeile .30 .09
❑ 178 Steve Olin .20 .06
❑ 179 Eric Anthony .20 .06
❑ 180 Scott Coolbaugh .20 .06
❑ 181 Rick Sutcliffe .30 .09
❑ 182 Tim Wallach .20 .06
❑ 183 Paul Molitor .50 .15
❑ 184 Roberto Kelly .20 .06
❑ 185 Mike Moore .20 .06
❑ 186 Junior Felix .20 .06
❑ 187 Mike Schooler .20 .06
❑ 188 Ruben Sierra .20 .06
❑ 189 Dale Murphy .75 .23
❑ 190 Dan Gladden .20 .06
❑ 191 John Smiley .20 .06
❑ 192 Jeff Russell .20 .06
❑ 193 Bert Blyleven .30 .09
❑ 194 Dave Stewart .30 .09
❑ 195 Bobby Bonilla .30 .09
❑ 196 Mitch Williams .20 .06
❑ 197 Orel Hershiser .30 .09
❑ 198 Kevin Bass .20 .06
❑ 199 Tim Burke .20 .06
❑ 200 Bo Jackson .75 .23
❑ 201 David Cone .30 .09
❑ 202 Gary Pettis .20 .06
❑ 203 Kent Hrbek .30 .09
❑ 204 Carlton Fisk .50 .15
❑ 205 Bob Geren .20 .06
❑ 206 Bill Spiers .20 .06
❑ 207 Oddibe McDowell .20 .06
❑ 208 Rickey Henderson .75 .23
❑ 209 Ken Caminiti .30 .09
❑ 210 Devon White .30 .09
❑ 211 Greg Maddux 1.25 .35
❑ 212 Ed Whitson .20 .06
❑ 213 Carlos Martinez .20 .06
❑ 214 George Brett 2.00 .60
❑ 215 Gregg Olson .20 .06
❑ 216 Kenny Rogers .30 .09
❑ 217 Dwight Evans .30 .09
❑ 218 Pat Tabler .20 .06
❑ 219 Jeff Treadway .20 .06
❑ 220 Scott Fletcher .20 .06
❑ 221 Deion Sanders .75 .23
❑ 222 Robin Ventura .75 .23
❑ 223 Chip Hale .20 .06
❑ 224 Tommy Greene .20 .06
❑ 225 Dean Palmer .75 .23

1994 Sportflics Rookie/Traded

	Nm-Mt	Ex-Mt
COMPLETE SET (150)	25.00	7.50

❑ 1 Will Clark 1.25 .35
❑ 2 Sid Fernandez .25 .07
❑ 3 Joe Magrane .25 .07
❑ 4 Pete Smith .25 .07
❑ 5 Roberto Kelly .25 .07
❑ 6 Delino DeShields .25 .07
❑ 7 Brian Harper .25 .07
❑ 8 Darrin Jackson .25 .07
❑ 9 Omar Vizquel .75 .23
❑ 10 Luis Polonia .25 .07
❑ 11 Reggie Jefferson .25 .07
❑ 12 Geronimo Berroa .25 .07
❑ 13 Mike Harkey .25 .07
❑ 14 Bret Boone .50 .15
❑ 15 Dave Henderson .25 .07
❑ 16 Pedro Martinez 1.25 .35
❑ 17 Jose Vizcaino .25 .07
❑ 18 Xavier Hernandez .25 .07
❑ 19 Eddie Taubensee .25 .07
❑ 20 Ellis Burks .50 .15
❑ 21 Turner Ward .25 .07
❑ 22 Terry Mulholland .25 .07
❑ 23 Howard Johnson .25 .07
❑ 24 Vince Coleman .25 .07
❑ 25 Deion Sanders .75 .23
❑ 26 Rafael Palmeiro .75 .23
❑ 27 Dave Weathers .25 .07
❑ 28 Kent Mercker .25 .07
❑ 29 Gregg Olson .25 .07
❑ 30 Cory Bailey RC .25 .07
❑ 31 Brian L. Hunter .25 .07
❑ 32 Garey Ingram RC .25 .07
❑ 33 Daniel Smith .25 .07
❑ 34 Denny Hocking .25 .07
❑ 35 Charles Johnson .50 .15
❑ 36 Otis Nixon .25 .07
❑ 37 Hector Fajardo .25 .07
❑ 38 Lee Smith .50 .15
❑ 39 Phil Stidham .25 .07
❑ 40 Melvin Nieves .25 .07
❑ 41 Julio Franco .50 .15
❑ 42 Greg Gohr .25 .07
❑ 43 Steve Dunn .25 .07
❑ 44 Tony Fernandez .25 .07
❑ 45 Toby Borland RC .25 .07
❑ 46 Paul Shuey .25 .07
❑ 47 Shawn Hare .25 .07
❑ 48 Shawn Green 1.25 .35
❑ 49 Julian Tavarez RC .50 .15
❑ 50 Ernie Young RC .50 .15
❑ 51 Chris Sabo .25 .07
❑ 52 Greg O'Halloran .25 .07
❑ 53 Donnie Elliott .25 .07
❑ 54 Jim Converse .25 .07
❑ 55 Ray Holbert .25 .07
❑ 56 Keith Lockhart RC .50 .15
❑ 57 Tony Longmire .25 .07
❑ 58 Jorge Fabregas .25 .07
❑ 59 Ravelo Manzanillo .25 .07
❑ 60 Marcus Moore .25 .07
❑ 61 Carlos Rodriguez .25 .07
❑ 62 Mark Portugal .25 .07
❑ 63 Yorkis Perez .25 .07
❑ 64 Dan Miceli .25 .07
❑ 65 Chris Turner .25 .07
❑ 66 Mike Oquist .25 .07
❑ 67 Tom Quinlan .25 .07
❑ 68 Matt Walbeck .25 .07
❑ 69 Dave Staton .25 .07
❑ 70 W.VanLandingham RC .25 .07
❑ 71 Dave Stevens .25 .07
❑ 72 Domingo Cedeno .25 .07
❑ 73 Alex Diaz .25 .07
❑ 74 Darren Bragg RC .25 .07
❑ 75 James Hurst .25 .07
❑ 76 Alex Gonzalez .25 .07
❑ 77 Steve Dreyer .25 .07
❑ 78 Robert Eenhoorn .25 .07
❑ 79 Derek Parks .25 .07
❑ 80 Jose Valentin .25 .07
❑ 81 Wes Chamberlain .25 .07
❑ 82 Tony Tarasco .25 .07
❑ 83 Steve Traschel .25 .07
❑ 84 Willie Banks .25 .07
❑ 85 Rob Butler .25 .07
❑ 86 Miguel Jimenez .25 .07
❑ 87 Gerald Williams .25 .07
❑ 88 Aaron Small .25 .07
❑ 89 Matt Mieske .25 .07
❑ 90 Tim Hyers RC .25 .07
❑ 91 Eddie Murray 1.25 .35
❑ 92 Dennis Martinez .50 .15
❑ 93 Tony Eusebio .25 .07
❑ 94 Brian Anderson RC .50 .15
❑ 95 Blaise Ilsley .25 .07
❑ 96 Johnny Ruffin .25 .07
❑ 97 Carlos Reyes .25 .07
❑ 98 Greg Pirkl .25 .07
❑ 99 Jack Morris .50 .15
❑ 100 John Mabry RC .50 .15
❑ 101 Mike Kelly .25 .07
❑ 102 Rich Becker .25 .07
❑ 103 Chris Gomez .25 .07
❑ 104 Jim Edmonds 1.25 .35
❑ 105 Rich Rowland .25 .07
❑ 106 Damon Buford .25 .07

Card	Nm-Mt	Ex-Mt
❑ 107 Mark Kiefer	.25	.07
❑ 108 Matias Carrillo	.25	.07
❑ 109 James Mouton	.25	.07
❑ 110 Kelly Stinnett RC	.25	.07
❑ 111 Billy Ashley	.25	.07
❑ 112 Fausto Cruz RC	.25	.07
❑ 113 Roberto Petagine	.25	.07
❑ 114 Joe Hall	.25	.07
❑ 115 Brian Johnson RC	.25	.07
❑ 116 Kevin Jarvis	.25	.07
❑ 117 Tim Davis	.25	.07
❑ 118 John Patterson	.25	.07
❑ 119 Stan Royer	.25	.07
❑ 120 Jeff Juden	.25	.07
❑ 121 Bryan Eversgerd	.25	.07
❑ 122 Chan Ho Park RC	.75	.23
❑ 123 Shane Reynolds	.25	.07
❑ 124 Danny Bautista	.25	.07
❑ 125 Rikkert Faneyte RC	.25	.07
❑ 126 Carlos Pulido	.25	.07
❑ 127 Mike Matheny RC	2.00	.60
❑ 128 Hector Carrasco	.25	.07
❑ 129 Eddie Zambrano	.25	.07
❑ 130 Lee Tinsley	.25	.07
❑ 131 Roger Salkeld	.25	.07
❑ 132 Carlos Delgado	.75	.23
❑ 133 Troy O'Leary	.25	.07
❑ 134 Keith Mitchell	.25	.07
❑ 135 Lance Painter	.25	.07
❑ 136 Nate Minchey	.25	.07
❑ 137 Eric Anthony	.25	.07
❑ 138 Rafael Bournigal	.25	.07
❑ 139 Joey Hamilton	.25	.07
❑ 140 Bobby Munoz	.25	.07
❑ 141 Rex Hudler	.25	.07
❑ 142 Alex Cole	.25	.07
❑ 143 Stan Javier	.25	.07
❑ 144 Jose Oliva	.25	.07
❑ 145 Tom Brunansky	.25	.07
❑ 146 Greg Colbrunn	.25	.07
❑ 147 Luis Lopez	.25	.07
❑ 148 Alex Rodriguez RC	20.00	6.00
❑ 149 Darryl Strawberry	.50	.15
❑ 150 Bo Jackson	1.25	.35
❑ R01 Ryan Klesko ROY Manny Ramirez	4.00	1.20

1996 SPx

	Nm-Mt	Ex-Mt
COMPLETE SET (60)	50.00	15.00
❑ 1 Greg Maddux	3.00	.90
❑ 2 Chipper Jones	2.00	.60
❑ 3 Fred McGriff	1.25	.35
❑ 4 Tom Glavine	1.25	.35
❑ 5 Cal Ripken	6.00	1.80
❑ 6 Roberto Alomar	1.25	.35
❑ 7 Rafael Palmeiro	1.25	.35
❑ 8 Jose Canseco	2.00	.60
❑ 9 Roger Clemens	4.00	1.20
❑ 10 Mo Vaughn	.75	.23
❑ 11 Jim Edmonds	.75	.23
❑ 12 Tim Salmon	1.25	.35
❑ 13 Sammy Sosa	3.00	.90
❑ 14 Ryne Sandberg	3.00	.90
❑ 15 Mark Grace	1.25	.35
❑ 16 Frank Thomas	2.00	.60
❑ 17 Barry Larkin	1.25	.35
❑ 18 Kenny Lofton	.75	.23
❑ 19 Albert Belle	.75	.23
❑ 20 Eddie Murray	2.00	.60
❑ 21 Manny Ramirez	1.25	.35
❑ 22 Dante Bichette	.75	.23
❑ 23 Larry Walker	1.25	.35
❑ 24 Vinny Castilla	.75	.23
❑ 25 Andres Galarraga	.75	.23
❑ 26 Cecil Fielder	.75	.23
❑ 27 Gary Sheffield	.75	.23
❑ 28 Craig Biggio	1.25	.35
❑ 29 Jeff Bagwell	1.25	.35
❑ 30 Derek Bell	.75	.23
❑ 31 Johnny Damon	1.25	.35
❑ 32 Eric Karros	.75	.23
❑ 33 Mike Piazza	3.00	.90
❑ 34 Raul Mondesi	.75	.23
❑ 35 Hideo Nomo	2.00	.60
❑ 36 Kirby Puckett	2.00	.60
❑ 37 Paul Molitor	1.25	.35
❑ 38 Marty Cordova	.75	.23
❑ 39 Rondell White	.75	.23
❑ 40 Jason Isringhausen	.75	.23
❑ 41 Paul Wilson	.75	.23
❑ 42 Rey Ordonez	.75	.23
❑ 43 Derek Jeter	5.00	1.50
❑ 44 Wade Boggs	1.25	.35
❑ 45 Mark McGwire	5.00	1.50
❑ 46 Jason Kendall	.75	.23
❑ 47 Ron Gant	.75	.23
❑ 48 Ozzie Smith	3.00	.90
❑ 49 Tony Gwynn	2.50	.75
❑ 50 Ken Caminiti	.75	.23
❑ 51 Barry Bonds	5.00	1.50
❑ 52 Matt Williams	.75	.23
❑ 53 Osvaldo Fernandez	.75	.23
❑ 54 Jay Buhner	.75	.23
❑ 55 Ken Griffey Jr.	3.00	.90
❑ 56 Randy Johnson	2.00	.60
❑ 57 Alex Rodriguez	4.00	1.20
❑ 58 Juan Gonzalez	1.25	.35
❑ 59 Joe Carter	.75	.23
❑ 60 Carlos Delgado	.75	.23
❑ KG1 K.Griffey Jr. Comm.	5.00	1.50
❑ MP1 Mike Piazza Trib.	5.00	1.50
❑ KGA1 Ken Griffey Jr. Auto.	150.00	45.00
❑ MPA1 Mike Piazza Auto.	200.00	60.00

1999 SPx

	Nm-Mt	Ex-Mt
COMP.SET w/o SP's (80)	25.00	7.50
COMMON (1-10)	1.50	.45
COMMON CARD (11-80)	.50	.15
COMMON SP (81-120)	10.00	3.00
❑ 1 Mark McGwire 61	3.00	.90
❑ 2 Mark McGwire 62	3.00	.90
❑ 3 Mark McGwire 63	1.50	.45
❑ 4 Mark McGwire 64	1.50	.45
❑ 5 Mark McGwire 65	1.50	.45
❑ 6 Mark McGwire 66	1.50	.45
❑ 7 Mark McGwire 67	1.50	.45
❑ 8 Mark McGwire 68	1.50	.45
❑ 9 Mark McGwire 69	1.50	.45
❑ 10 Mark McGwire 70	4.00	1.20
❑ 11 Mo Vaughn	.50	.15
❑ 12 Darin Erstad	.50	.15
❑ 13 Travis Lee	.50	.15
❑ 14 Randy Johnson	1.25	.35
❑ 15 Matt Williams	.50	.15
❑ 16 Chipper Jones	1.25	.35
❑ 17 Greg Maddux	2.00	.60
❑ 18 Andruw Jones	.50	.15
❑ 19 Andres Galarraga	.50	.15
❑ 20 Cal Ripken	4.00	1.20
❑ 21 Albert Belle	.50	.15
❑ 22 Mike Mussina	.75	.23
❑ 23 Nomar Garciaparra	2.00	.60
❑ 24 Pedro Martinez	1.25	.35
❑ 25 John Valentin	.50	.15
❑ 26 Kerry Wood	1.25	.35
❑ 27 Sammy Sosa	2.00	.60
❑ 28 Mark Grace	.75	.23
❑ 29 Frank Thomas	1.25	.35
❑ 30 Mike Caruso	.50	.15
❑ 31 Barry Larkin	.75	.23
❑ 32 Sean Casey	.50	.15
❑ 33 Jim Thome	1.25	.35
❑ 34 Kenny Lofton	.50	.15
❑ 35 Manny Ramirez	.75	.23
❑ 36 Larry Walker	.75	.23
❑ 37 Todd Helton	.75	.23
❑ 38 Vinny Castilla	.50	.15
❑ 39 Tony Clark	.50	.15
❑ 40 Derrek Lee	.50	.15
❑ 41 Mark Kotsay	.50	.15
❑ 42 Jeff Bagwell	.75	.23
❑ 43 Craig Biggio	.75	.23
❑ 44 Moises Alou	.50	.15
❑ 45 Larry Sutton	.50	.15
❑ 46 Johnny Damon	.75	.23
❑ 47 Gary Sheffield	.50	.15
❑ 48 Raul Mondesi	.50	.15
❑ 49 Jeromy Burnitz	.50	.15
❑ 50 Todd Walker	.50	.15
❑ 51 David Ortiz	.75	.23
❑ 52 Vladimir Guerrero	1.25	.35
❑ 53 Rondell White	.50	.15
❑ 54 Mike Piazza	2.00	.60
❑ 55 Derek Jeter	3.00	.90
❑ 56 Tino Martinez	.75	.23
❑ 57 Roger Clemens	2.50	.75
❑ 58 Ben Grieve	.50	.15
❑ 59 A.J. Hinch	.50	.15
❑ 60 Scott Rolen	1.25	.35
❑ 61 Doug Glanville	.50	.15
❑ 62 Aramis Ramirez	.50	.15
❑ 63 Jose Guillen	.50	.15
❑ 64 Tony Gwynn	1.50	.45
❑ 65 Greg Vaughn	.50	.15
❑ 66 Ruben Rivera	.50	.15
❑ 67 Barry Bonds	3.00	.90
❑ 68 J.T. Snow	.50	.15
❑ 69 Alex Rodriguez	2.00	.60
❑ 70 Ken Griffey Jr.	2.00	.60
❑ 71 Jay Buhner	.50	.15
❑ 72 Mark McGwire	3.00	.90
❑ 73 Fernando Tatis	.50	.15
❑ 74 Quinton McCracken	.50	.15
❑ 75 Wade Boggs	.75	.23
❑ 76 Ivan Rodriguez	1.25	.35
❑ 77 Juan Gonzalez	.75	.23
❑ 78 Rafael Palmeiro	.75	.23
❑ 79 Jose Cruz Jr.	.50	.15
❑ 80 Carlos Delgado	.50	.15
❑ 81 Troy Glaus SP	10.00	3.00
❑ 82 Vladimir Nunez SP	10.00	3.00
❑ 83 George Lombard SP	10.00	3.00
❑ 84 Bruce Chen SP	10.00	3.00
❑ 85 Ryan Minor SP	10.00	3.00
❑ 86 Calvin Pickering SP	10.00	3.00
❑ 87 Jin Ho Cho SP	10.00	3.00
❑ 88 Russ Branyan SP	10.00	3.00
❑ 89 Derrick Gibson SP	10.00	3.00
❑ 90 Gabe Kapler SP AU	15.00	4.50
❑ 91 Matt Anderson SP	10.00	3.00
❑ 92 Robert Fick SP	10.00	3.00
❑ 93 Juan Encarnacion SP	10.00	3.00
❑ 94 Preston Wilson SP	10.00	3.00
❑ 95 Alex Gonzalez SP	10.00	3.00
❑ 96 Carlos Beltran SP	15.00	4.50
❑ 97 Jeremy Giambi SP	10.00	3.00

Card	Nm-Mt	Ex-Mt
❑ 98 Dee Brown SP	10.00	3.00
❑ 99 Adrian Beltre SP	15.00	4.50
❑ 100 Alex Cora SP	10.00	3.00
❑ 101 Angel Pena SP	10.00	3.00
❑ 102 Geoff Jenkins SP	10.00	3.00
❑ 103 Ronnie Belliard SP	10.00	3.00
❑ 104 Corey Koskie SP	10.00	3.00
❑ 105 A.J. Pierzynski SP	10.00	3.00
❑ 106 Michael Barrett SP	10.00	3.00
❑ 107 Fern.Seguignol SP	10.00	3.00
❑ 108 Mike Kinkade SP	10.00	3.00
❑ 109 Mike Lowell SP	10.00	3.00
❑ 110 Ricky Ledee SP	10.00	3.00
❑ 111 Eric Chavez SP	10.00	3.00
❑ 112 Abraham Nunez SP	10.00	3.00
❑ 113 Matt Clement SP	10.00	3.00
❑ 114 Ben Davis SP	10.00	3.00
❑ 115 Mike Darr SP	10.00	3.00
❑ 116 Ramon E.Martinez SP RC	10.00	3.00
❑ 117 Carlos Guillen SP	10.00	3.00
❑ 118 Shane Monahan SP	10.00	3.00
❑ 119 J.D. Drew SP AU	25.00	7.50
❑ 120 Kevin Witt SP	10.00	3.00
❑ 24EAST K.Griffey Jr. SAMP	2.00	.60

2000 SPx

	Nm-Mt	Ex-Mt
COMP.BASIC w/o SP's (90)	25.00	7.50
COMP.UPDATE w/o SP's (30)	10.00	3.00
COMMON CARD (1-90)	.50	.15
COMMON AU/1500 (91-120)	10.00	3.00
COMMON (121-135/182-196)	8.00	2.40
COMMON (136-151)	10.00	3.00
COMMON (152-181)	.75	.23

Card	Nm-Mt	Ex-Mt
❑ 1 Troy Glaus	.50	.15
❑ 2 Mo Vaughn	.50	.15
❑ 3 Ramon Ortiz	.50	.15
❑ 4 Jeff Bagwell	.75	.23
❑ 5 Moises Alou	.50	.15
❑ 6 Craig Biggio	.75	.23
❑ 7 Jose Lima	.50	.15
❑ 8 Jason Giambi	.50	.15
❑ 9 John Jaha	.50	.15
❑ 10 Matt Stairs	.50	.15
❑ 11 Chipper Jones	1.25	.35
❑ 12 Greg Maddux	2.00	.60
❑ 13 Andres Galarraga	.50	.15
❑ 14 Andruw Jones	.50	.15
❑ 15 Jeromy Burnitz	.50	.15
❑ 16 Ron Belliard	.50	.15
❑ 17 Carlos Delgado	.50	.15
❑ 18 David Wells	.50	.15
❑ 19 Tony Batista	.50	.15
❑ 20 Shannon Stewart	.50	.15
❑ 21 Sammy Sosa	2.00	.60
❑ 22 Mark Grace	.75	.23
❑ 23 Henry Rodriguez	.50	.15
❑ 24 Mark McGwire	3.00	.90
❑ 25 J.D. Drew	.50	.15
❑ 26 Luis Gonzalez	.50	.15
❑ 27 Randy Johnson	1.25	.35
❑ 28 Matt Williams	.50	.15
❑ 29 Steve Finley	.50	.15
❑ 30 Shawn Green	.50	.15
❑ 31 Kevin Brown	.75	.23
❑ 32 Gary Sheffield	.50	.15
❑ 33 Jose Canseco	1.25	.35
❑ 34 Greg Vaughn	.50	.15
❑ 35 Vladimir Guerrero	1.25	.35
❑ 36 Michael Barrett	.50	.15
❑ 37 Russ Ortiz	.50	.15
❑ 38 Barry Bonds	3.00	.90
❑ 39 Jeff Kent	.50	.15
❑ 40 Richie Sexson	.50	.15
❑ 41 Manny Ramirez	.75	.23
❑ 42 Jim Thome	1.25	.35
❑ 43 Roberto Alomar	.75	.23
❑ 44 Edgar Martinez	.75	.23
❑ 45 Alex Rodriguez	2.00	.60
❑ 46 John Olerud	.50	.15
❑ 47 Alex Gonzalez	.50	.15
❑ 48 Cliff Floyd	.50	.15
❑ 49 Mike Piazza	2.00	.60
❑ 50 Al Leiter	.50	.15
❑ 51 Robin Ventura	.75	.23
❑ 52 Edgardo Alfonzo	.50	.15
❑ 53 Albert Belle	.50	.15
❑ 54 Cal Ripken	4.00	1.20
❑ 55 B.J. Surhoff	.50	.15
❑ 56 Tony Gwynn	1.50	.45
❑ 57 Trevor Hoffman	.50	.15
❑ 58 Brian Giles	.50	.15
❑ 59 Jason Kendall	.50	.15
❑ 60 Kris Benson	.50	.15
❑ 61 Bob Abreu	.50	.15
❑ 62 Scott Rolen	1.25	.35
❑ 63 Curt Schilling	.50	.15
❑ 64 Mike Lieberthal	.50	.15
❑ 65 Sean Casey	.50	.15
❑ 66 Dante Bichette	.50	.15
❑ 67 Ken Griffey Jr.	2.00	.60
❑ 68 Pokey Reese	.50	.15
❑ 69 Mike Sweeney	.50	.15
❑ 70 Carlos Febles	.50	.15
❑ 71 Ivan Rodriguez	1.25	.35
❑ 72 Ruben Mateo	.50	.15
❑ 73 Rafael Palmeiro	.75	.23
❑ 74 Larry Walker	.75	.23
❑ 75 Todd Helton	.75	.23
❑ 76 Nomar Garciaparra	2.00	.60
❑ 77 Pedro Martinez	1.25	.35
❑ 78 Troy O'Leary	.50	.15
❑ 79 Jacque Jones	.50	.15
❑ 80 Corey Koskie	.50	.15
❑ 81 Juan Gonzalez	.75	.23
❑ 82 Dean Palmer	.50	.15
❑ 83 Juan Encarnacion	.50	.15
❑ 84 Frank Thomas	1.25	.35
❑ 85 Magglio Ordonez	.50	.15
❑ 86 Paul Konerko	.50	.15
❑ 87 Bernie Williams	.75	.23
❑ 88 Derek Jeter	3.00	.90
❑ 89 Roger Clemens	2.50	.75
❑ 90 Orlando Hernandez	.50	.15
❑ 91 Vernon Wells AU/1500	15.00	4.50
❑ 92 Rick Ankiel AU/1500	40.00	12.00
❑ 93 Eric Chavez AU/1500	25.00	7.50
❑ 94 A.Soriano/1500 AU	60.00	18.00
❑ 95 Eric Gagne AU/1500	100.00	30.00
❑ 96 Rob Bell AU/1500	10.00	3.00
❑ 97 Matt Riley AU/1500	15.00	4.50
❑ 98 Josh Beckett AU/1500	60.00	18.00
❑ 99 Ben Petrick AU/1500	10.00	3.00
❑ 100 Rob Ramsay AU/1500	10.00	3.00
❑ 101 Scott Williamson 1500 AU	10.00	3.00
❑ 102 Doug Davis AU/1500	10.00	3.00
❑ 103 E.Munson/1500 AU*	10.00	3.00
❑ 104 Pat Burrell AU/500	50.00	15.00
❑ 105 Jim Morris AU/1500	25.00	7.50
❑ 106 Gabe Kapler AU/500	25.00	7.50
❑ 107 Lance Berkman/1000	8.00	2.40
❑ 108 E.Durazo/1500 AU	15.00	4.50
❑ 109 Tim Hudson AU/1500	40.00	7.50
❑ 110 Ben Davis AU/1500	10.00	3.00
❑ 111 N.Johnson/1500 AU	15.00	4.50
❑ 112 O.Dotel/1500 AU	10.00	3.00
❑ 113 Jerry Hairston/1000	8.00	2.40
❑ 114 Ruben Mateo/1000	8.00	2.40
❑ 115 Chris Singleton/1000	8.00	2.40
❑ 116 Bruce Chen AU/1500	10.00	3.00
❑ 117 Derrick Gibson/1000	8.00	2.40
❑ 118 Carlos Beltran AU/500	175.00	52.50
❑ 119 F.Garcia/1500 AU	15.00	4.50
❑ 120 P.Wilson/1500 AU	15.00	4.50
❑ 121 B.Wilkerson/1600 RC	10.00	3.00
❑ 122 Roy Oswalt/1600 RC	50.00	15.00
❑ 123 W.Serrano/1600 RC	8.00	2.40
❑ 124 Sean Burnett/1600 RC	10.00	3.00
❑ 125 Alex Cabrera/1600 RC	8.00	2.40
❑ 126 Timo Perez/1600 RC	8.00	2.40
❑ 127 Juan Pierre/1600 RC	10.00	3.00
❑ 128 Daylan Holt/1600 RC	8.00	2.40
❑ 129 T.Ohka/1600 RC	8.00	2.40
❑ 130 K.Sasaki/1600 RC	10.00	3.00
❑ 131 K.Ainsworth/1600 RC	8.00	2.40
❑ 132 B.Abernathy/1600 RC	8.00	2.40
❑ 133 Danys Baez/1600 RC	8.00	2.40
❑ 134 Brad Cresse/1600 RC	8.00	2.40
❑ 135 R.Franklin/1600 RC	8.00	2.40
❑ 136 M.Lamb/1500 AU RC	10.00	3.00
❑ 137 David Espinosa 1500 AU RC	10.00	3.00
❑ 138 Matt Wheatland 1500 AU RC	10.00	3.00
❑ 139 X.Nady/1500 AU RC	15.00	4.50
❑ 140 S.Heard/1500 AU RC	10.00	3.00
❑ 141 P.Coco/1500 AU RC	10.00	3.00
Card erroneously numbered 54 instead of 141		
❑ 142 J.Miller/1500 AU RC	10.00	3.00
❑ 143 Dave Krynzel 1500 AU RC	10.00	3.00
❑ 144 Dane Sardinha 1500 AU RC	10.00	3.00
❑ 145 B.Sheets/1500 AU RC	60.00	18.00
❑ 146 L.Estrella/1500 AU RC	10.00	3.00
❑ 147 Ben Diggins 1500 AU RC	10.00	3.00
❑ 148 B.Zito/1500 AU RC	70.00	21.00
❑ 149 J.Torres/1500 AU RC	10.00	3.00
❑ 150 Mike Meyers 1500 AU RC	10.00	3.00
❑ 151 K.Wilson/1500 AU RC	10.00	3.00
❑ 152 Darin Erstad	.75	.23
❑ 153 Richard Hidalgo	.75	.23
❑ 154 Eric Chavez	.75	.23
❑ 155 B.J. Surhoff	.75	.23
❑ 156 Richie Sexson	.75	.23
❑ 157 Raul Mondesi	.75	.23
❑ 158 Rondell White	.75	.23
❑ 159 Jim Edmonds	.75	.23
❑ 160 Curt Schilling	.75	.23
❑ 161 Tom Goodwin	.75	.23
❑ 162 Fred McGriff	1.25	.35
❑ 163 Jose Vidro	.75	.23
❑ 164 Ellis Burks	.75	.23
❑ 165 David Segui	.75	.23
❑ 166 Aaron Sele	.75	.23
❑ 167 Henry Rodriguez	.75	.23
❑ 168 Mike Bordick	.75	.23
❑ 169 Mike Mussina	1.25	.35
❑ 170 Ryan Klesko	.75	.23
❑ 171 Kevin Young	.75	.23
❑ 172 Travis Lee	.75	.23
❑ 173 Aaron Boone	.75	.23
❑ 174 Jermaine Dye	.75	.23
❑ 175 Ricky Ledee	.75	.23
❑ 176 Jeffrey Hammonds	.75	.23
❑ 177 Carl Everett	.75	.23
❑ 178 Matt Lawton	.75	.23
❑ 179 Bobby Higginson	.75	.23
❑ 180 Charles Johnson	.75	.23
❑ 181 David Justice	.75	.23
❑ 182 Joey Nation/1600 RC	8.00	2.40
❑ 183 Rico Washington 1600 RC	8.00	2.40
❑ 184 Luis Matos/1600 RC	8.00	2.40
❑ 185 C.Wakeland/1600 RC	8.00	2.40
❑ 186 SW Kim/1600 RC	8.00	2.40
❑ 187 Keith Ginter/1600 RC	8.00	2.40
❑ 188 G.Guzman/1600 RC	8.00	2.40
❑ 189 J.Spurgeon/1600 RC	8.00	2.40
❑ 190 Jace Brewer/1600 RC	8.00	2.40
❑ 191 J.Guzman/1600 RC	8.00	2.40
❑ 192 Ross Gload/1600 RC	8.00	2.40
❑ 193 P.Crawford/1600 RC	8.00	2.40
❑ 194 R.Kohlmeier/1600 RC	8.00	2.40
❑ 195 Julio Zuleta/1600 RC	8.00	2.40
❑ 196 Matt Ginter/1600 RC	8.00	2.40

2001 SPx

	Nm-Mt	Ex-Mt
COMP.BASIC w/o SP's (90)	25.00	7.50
COMP.UPDATE w/o SP's (30)	10.00	3.00
COMMON CARD (1-90)	.50	.15
COMMON YS (91-120)	8.00	2.40
COMMON JSY (121-135)	10.00	3.00
COMMON (136-150)	15.00	4.50
COMMON (151-180)	.75	.23
COMMON (181-210)	5.00	1.50
❑ 1 Darin Erstad	.50	.15
❑ 2 Troy Glaus	.50	.15
❑ 3 Mo Vaughn	.50	.15
❑ 4 Johnny Damon	.75	.23
❑ 5 Jason Giambi	.50	.15
❑ 6 Tim Hudson	.50	.15
❑ 7 Miguel Tejada	.50	.15
❑ 8 Carlos Delgado	.50	.15
❑ 9 Raul Mondesi	.50	.15
❑ 10 Tony Batista	.50	.15
❑ 11 Ben Grieve	.50	.15
❑ 12 Greg Vaughn	.50	.15
❑ 13 Juan Gonzalez	.75	.23
❑ 14 Jim Thome	1.25	.35
❑ 15 Roberto Alomar	.75	.23
❑ 16 John Olerud	.50	.15
❑ 17 Edgar Martinez	.75	.23
❑ 18 Albert Belle	.50	.15
❑ 19 Cal Ripken	4.00	1.20
❑ 20 Ivan Rodriguez	1.25	.35
❑ 21 Rafael Palmeiro	.75	.23
❑ 22 Alex Rodriguez	2.00	.60
❑ 23 Nomar Garciaparra	2.00	.60
❑ 24 Pedro Martinez	1.25	.35
❑ 25 Manny Ramirez	.75	.23
❑ 26 Jermaine Dye	.50	.15
❑ 27 Mark Quinn	.50	.15
❑ 28 Carlos Beltran	.75	.23
❑ 29 Tony Clark	.50	.15
❑ 30 Bobby Higginson	.50	.15
❑ 31 Eric Milton	.50	.15
❑ 32 Matt Lawton	.50	.15
❑ 33 Frank Thomas	1.25	.35
❑ 34 Magglio Ordonez	.50	.15
❑ 35 Ray Durham	.50	.15
❑ 36 David Wells	.50	.15
❑ 37 Derek Jeter	3.00	.90
❑ 38 Bernie Williams	.75	.23
❑ 39 Roger Clemens UER Wrong uniform number on card	2.50	.75
❑ 40 David Justice	.50	.15
❑ 41 Jeff Bagwell	.75	.23
❑ 42 Richard Hidalgo	.50	.15
❑ 43 Moises Alou	.50	.15
❑ 44 Chipper Jones	1.25	.35
❑ 45 Andruw Jones	.50	.15
❑ 46 Greg Maddux	2.00	.60
❑ 47 Rafael Furcal	.50	.15
❑ 48 Jeromy Burnitz	.50	.15
❑ 49 Geoff Jenkins	.50	.15
❑ 50 Mark McGwire	3.00	.90
❑ 51 Jim Edmonds	.50	.15
❑ 52 Rick Ankiel	.50	.15
❑ 53 Edgar Renteria	.50	.15
❑ 54 Sammy Sosa	2.00	.60
❑ 55 Kerry Wood	1.25	.35
❑ 56 Rondell White	.50	.15
❑ 57 Randy Johnson	1.25	.35
❑ 58 Steve Finley	.50	.15
❑ 59 Matt Williams	.50	.15
❑ 60 Luis Gonzalez	.50	.15
❑ 61 Kevin Brown	.50	.15
❑ 62 Gary Sheffield	.50	.15
❑ 63 Shawn Green	.50	.15
❑ 64 Vladimir Guerrero	1.25	.35
❑ 65 Jose Vidro	.50	.15
❑ 66 Barry Bonds	3.00	.90
❑ 67 Jeff Kent	.50	.15
❑ 68 Livan Hernandez	.50	.15
❑ 69 Preston Wilson	.50	.15
❑ 70 Charles Johnson	.50	.15
❑ 71 Cliff Floyd	.50	.15
❑ 72 Mike Piazza	2.00	.60
❑ 73 Edgardo Alfonzo	.50	.15
❑ 74 Jay Payton	.50	.15
❑ 75 Robin Ventura	.50	.15
❑ 76 Tony Gwynn	1.50	.45
❑ 77 Phil Nevin	.50	.15
❑ 78 Ryan Klesko	.50	.15
❑ 79 Scott Rolen	1.25	.35
❑ 80 Pat Burrell	.50	.15
❑ 81 Bob Abreu	.50	.15
❑ 82 Brian Giles	.50	.15
❑ 83 Kris Benson	.50	.15
❑ 84 Jason Kendall	.50	.15
❑ 85 Ken Griffey Jr.	2.00	.60
❑ 86 Barry Larkin	.75	.23
❑ 87 Sean Casey	.50	.15
❑ 88 Todd Helton	.75	.23
❑ 89 Larry Walker	.75	.23
❑ 90 Mike Hampton	.50	.15
❑ 91 Billy Sylvester YS RC	8.00	2.40
❑ 92 Josh Towers YS RC	8.00	2.40
❑ 93 Zach Day YS RC	8.00	2.40
❑ 94 Martin Vargas YS RC	8.00	2.40
❑ 95 Adam Pettyjohn YS RC	8.00	2.40
❑ 96 Andres Torres YS RC	8.00	2.40
❑ 97 Kris Keller YS RC	8.00	2.40
❑ 98 Blaine Neal YS RC	8.00	2.40
❑ 99 Kyle Kessel YS RC	8.00	2.40
❑ 100 Greg Miller YS RC	8.00	2.40
❑ 101 Shawn Sonnier YS	8.00	2.40
❑ 102 Alexis Gomez YS RC	8.00	2.40
❑ 103 Grant Balfour YS RC	8.00	2.40
❑ 104 Henry Mateo YS RC	8.00	2.40
❑ 105 Wilken Ruan YS RC	8.00	2.40
❑ 106 Nick Maness YS RC	8.00	2.40
❑ 107 J. Michaels YS RC	8.00	2.40
❑ 108 Esix Snead YS RC	8.00	2.40
❑ 109 William Ortega YS RC	8.00	2.40
❑ 110 David Elder YS RC	8.00	2.40
❑ 111 J. Melian YS RC	8.00	2.40
❑ 112 Nate Teut YS RC	8.00	2.40
❑ 113 Jason Smith YS RC	8.00	2.40
❑ 114 Mike Penney YS RC	8.00	2.40
❑ 115 Jose Mieses YS RC	8.00	2.40
❑ 116 Juan Pena YS	8.00	2.40
❑ 117 B. Lawrence YS RC	8.00	2.40
❑ 118 Jeremy Owens YS RC	8.00	2.40
❑ 119 C. Valderrama YS RC	8.00	2.40
❑ 120 Rafael Soriano YS RC	8.00	2.40
❑ 121 H. Ramirez JSY RC	15.00	4.50
❑ 122 R. Rodriguez JSY RC	10.00	3.00
❑ 123 Juan Diaz JSY RC	10.00	3.00
❑ 124 Donnie Bridges JSY	10.00	3.00
❑ 125 Tyler Walker JSY RC	10.00	3.00
❑ 126 Erick Almonte JSY RC	10.00	3.00
❑ 127 Jesus Colome JSY	10.00	3.00
❑ 128 Ryan Freel JSY RC	10.00	3.00
❑ 129 Elpidio Guzman JSY RC	10.00	3.00
❑ 130 Jack Cust JSY	10.00	3.00
❑ 131 Eric Hinske JSY RC	15.00	4.50
❑ 132 Josh Fogg JSY RC	10.00	3.00
❑ 133 Juan Uribe JSY RC	15.00	4.50
❑ 134 Bert Snow JSY RC	10.00	3.00
❑ 135 Pedro Feliz JSY	10.00	3.00
❑ 136 W. Betemit JSY AU RC	15.00	4.50
❑ 137 S. Douglass JSY AU RC	15.00	4.50
❑ 138 D. Stenson JSY AU	15.00	4.50
❑ 139 Brandon Inge JSY AU	15.00	4.50
❑ 140 M. Ensberg JSY AU RC	25.00	7.50
❑ 141 Brian Cole JSY AU	15.00	4.50
❑ 142 A. Hernandez JSY AU RC	15.00	4.50
❑ 143 Brandon Duckworth JSY AU RC	15.00	4.50
❑ 144 J. Wilson JSY AU RC	30.00	9.00
❑ 145 T. Hafner JSY AU RC	40.00	12.00
❑ 146 Carlos Pena JSY AU	15.00	4.50
❑ 147 C. Patterson JSY AU	25.00	7.50
❑ 148 Xavier Nady JSY AU	15.00	4.50
❑ 149 Jason Hart JSY AU	15.00	4.50
❑ 150 I.Suzuki JSY AU RC	650.00	200.00
❑ 151 Garret Anderson	.75	.23
❑ 152 Jermaine Dye	.75	.23
❑ 153 Shannon Stewart	.75	.23
❑ 154 Toby Hall	.75	.23
❑ 155 C.C. Sabathia	.75	.23
❑ 156 Bret Boone	.75	.23
❑ 157 Tony Batista	.75	.23
❑ 158 Gabe Kapler	.75	.23
❑ 159 Carl Everett	.75	.23
❑ 160 Mike Sweeney	.75	.23
❑ 161 Dean Palmer	.75	.23
❑ 162 Doug Mientkiewicz	.75	.23
❑ 163 Carlos Lee	.75	.23
❑ 164 Mike Mussina	1.25	.35
❑ 165 Lance Berkman	.75	.23
❑ 166 Ken Caminiti	.75	.23
❑ 167 Ben Sheets	1.25	.35
❑ 168 Matt Morris	.75	.23
❑ 169 Fred McGriff	1.25	.35
❑ 170 Curt Schilling	.75	.23
❑ 171 Paul LoDuca	.75	.23
❑ 172 Javier Vazquez	.75	.23
❑ 173 Rich Aurilia	.75	.23
❑ 174 A.J. Burnett	.75	.23
❑ 175 Al Leiter	.75	.23
❑ 176 Mark Kotsay	.75	.23
❑ 177 Jimmy Rollins	.75	.23
❑ 178 Aramis Ramirez	.75	.23
❑ 179 Aaron Boone	.75	.23
❑ 180 Jeff Cirillo	.75	.23
❑ 181 J.Estrada YS RC	15.00	4.50
❑ 182 Dave Williams YS RC	5.00	1.50
❑ 183 D.Mendez YS RC	5.00	1.50
❑ 184 Junior Spivey YS RC	8.00	2.40
❑ 185 Jay Gibbons YS RC	8.00	2.40
❑ 186 Kyle Lohse YS RC	8.00	2.40
❑ 187 Willie Harris YS RC	5.00	1.50
❑ 188 Juan Cruz YS RC	5.00	1.50
❑ 189 Joe Kennedy YS RC	8.00	2.40
❑ 190 D.Sanchez YS RC	5.00	1.50
❑ 191 Jorge Julio YS RC	5.00	1.50
❑ 192 Cesar Crespo YS RC	5.00	1.50
❑ 193 Casey Fossum YS RC	5.00	1.50
❑ 194 Brian Roberts YS RC	5.00	1.50
❑ 195 Troy Mattes YS RC	5.00	1.50
❑ 196 R.Mackowiak YS RC	8.00	2.40
❑ 197 T.Shinjo YS RC	8.00	2.40
❑ 198 Nick Punto YS RC	5.00	1.50
❑ 199 Wilmy Caceres YS RC	5.00	1.50
❑ 200 Jeremy Affeldt YS RC	8.00	2.40
❑ 201 Bret Prinz YS RC	5.00	1.50
❑ 202 Delvin James YS RC	5.00	1.50
❑ 203 Luis Pineda YS RC	5.00	1.50
❑ 204 Matt White YS RC	5.00	1.50
❑ 205 B.Knight YS RC	5.00	1.50
❑ 206 Albert Pujols YS AU RC	400.00	120.00
❑ 207 M.Teixeira YS AU RC	100.00	30.00
❑ 208 Mark Prior YS AU RC	200.00	60.00
❑ 209 D.Brazelton YS AU RC	25.00	7.50
❑ 210 Bud Smith YS AU RC	15.00	4.50

2002 SPx

	Nm-Mt	Ex-Mt
COMP.LOW w/o SP's (90)	25.00	7.50
COMP.UPDATE w/o SP's (30)	10.00	3.00
COMMON CARD (1-90)	.50	.15
COMMON ROOKIE (91A-	8.00	2.40
COMMON CARD (121-150)	15.00	4.50
COMMON CARD (151-190)	8.00	2.40
COMMON CARD (191-220)	.75	.23
COMMON CARD (221-250)	10.00	3.00
❑ 1 Troy Glaus	.50	.15
❑ 2 Darin Erstad	.50	.15
❑ 3 David Justice	.50	.15
❑ 4 Tim Hudson	.50	.15
❑ 5 Miguel Tejada	.50	.15
❑ 6 Barry Zito	.50	.15
❑ 7 Carlos Delgado	.50	.15
❑ 8 Shannon Stewart	.50	.15
❑ 9 Greg Vaughn	.50	.15
❑ 10 Toby Hall	.50	.15
❑ 11 Jim Thome	1.25	.35
❑ 12 C.C. Sabathia	.50	.15
❑ 13 Ichiro Suzuki	2.00	.60
❑ 14 Edgar Martinez	.75	.23
❑ 15 Freddy Garcia	.50	.15
❑ 16 Mike Cameron	.50	.15
❑ 17 Jeff Conine	.50	.15
❑ 18 Tony Batista	.50	.15
❑ 19 Alex Rodriguez	2.00	.60
❑ 20 Rafael Palmeiro	.75	.23
❑ 21 Ivan Rodriguez	1.25	.35
❑ 22 Carl Everett	.50	.15
❑ 23 Pedro Martinez	1.25	.35
❑ 24 Manny Ramirez	.75	.23
❑ 25 Nomar Garciaparra	2.00	.60
❑ 26 Johnny Damon Sox	1.25	.35
❑ 27 Mike Sweeney	.50	.15
❑ 28 Carlos Beltran	.75	.23
❑ 29 Dmitri Young	.50	.15
❑ 30 Joe Mays	.50	.15
❑ 31 Doug Mientkiewicz	.50	.15
❑ 32 Cristian Guzman	.50	.15
❑ 33 Corey Koskie	.50	.15
❑ 34 Frank Thomas	1.25	.35
❑ 35 Magglio Ordonez	.50	.15
❑ 36 Mark Buehrle	.50	.15
❑ 37 Bernie Williams	.75	.23
❑ 38 Roger Clemens	2.50	.75
❑ 39 Derek Jeter	3.00	.90
❑ 40 Jason Giambi	.50	.15
❑ 41 Mike Mussina	.75	.23
❑ 42 Lance Berkman	.50	.15
❑ 43 Jeff Bagwell	.75	.23
❑ 44 Roy Oswalt	.50	.15
❑ 45 Greg Maddux	2.00	.60
❑ 46 Chipper Jones	1.25	.35
❑ 47 Andruw Jones	.50	.15
❑ 48 Gary Sheffield	.50	.15
❑ 49 Geoff Jenkins	.50	.15
❑ 50 Richie Sexson	.50	.15
❑ 51 Ben Sheets	.50	.15
❑ 52 Albert Pujols	2.50	.75
❑ 53 J.D. Drew	.50	.15
❑ 54 Jim Edmonds	.50	.15
❑ 55 Sammy Sosa	2.00	.60
❑ 56 Moises Alou	.50	.15
❑ 57 Kerry Wood	1.25	.35
❑ 58 Jon Lieber	.50	.15
❑ 59 Fred McGriff	.75	.23
❑ 60 Randy Johnson	1.25	.35
❑ 61 Luis Gonzalez	.50	.15
❑ 62 Curt Schilling	.50	.15
❑ 63 Kevin Brown	.50	.15
❑ 64 Hideo Nomo	1.25	.35
❑ 65 Shawn Green	.50	.15
❑ 66 Vladimir Guerrero	1.25	.35
❑ 67 Jose Vidro	.50	.15
❑ 68 Barry Bonds	3.00	.90
❑ 69 Jeff Kent	.50	.15
❑ 70 Rich Aurilia	.50	.15
❑ 71 Cliff Floyd	.50	.15
❑ 72 Josh Beckett	.50	.15
❑ 73 Preston Wilson	.50	.15
❑ 74 Mike Piazza	2.00	.60
❑ 75 Mo Vaughn	.50	.15
❑ 76 Jeromy Burnitz	.50	.15
❑ 77 Roberto Alomar	.75	.23
❑ 78 Phil Nevin	.50	.15
❑ 79 Ryan Klesko	.50	.15
❑ 80 Scott Rolen	1.25	.35
❑ 81 Bobby Abreu	.50	.15
❑ 82 Jimmy Rollins	.50	.15
❑ 83 Brian Giles	.50	.15
❑ 84 Aramis Ramirez	.50	.15
❑ 85 Ken Griffey Jr.	2.00	.60
❑ 86 Sean Casey	.50	.15
❑ 87 Barry Larkin	.75	.23
❑ 88 Mike Hampton	.50	.15
❑ 89 Larry Walker	.75	.23
❑ 90 Todd Helton	.75	.23
❑ 91A Ron Calloway YS RC	8.00	2.40
❑ 91P Ron Calloway YS RC	8.00	2.40
❑ 92A Joe Orloski YS RC	8.00	2.40
❑ 92P Joe Orloski YS RC	8.00	2.40
❑ 93A An. Machado YS RC	8.00	2.40
❑ 93P An. Machado YS RC	8.00	2.40
❑ 94A Eric Good YS RC	8.00	2.40
❑ 94P Eric Good YS RC	8.00	2.40
❑ 95A Reed Johnson YS RC	10.00	3.00
❑ 95P Reed Johnson YS RC	10.00	3.00
❑ 96A Brendan Donnelly YS RC	8.00	2.40
❑ 96P Brendan Donnelly YS RC	8.00	2.40
❑ 97A Chris Baker YS RC	8.00	2.40
❑ 97P Chris Baker YS RC	8.00	2.40
❑ 98A Wilson Valdez YS RC	8.00	2.40
❑ 98P Wilson Valdez YS RC	8.00	2.40
❑ 99A Scotty Layfield YS RC	8.00	2.40
❑ 99P Scotty Layfield YS RC	8.00	2.40
❑ 100A P.J. Bevis YS RC	8.00	2.40
❑ 100P P.J. Bevis YS RC	8.00	2.40
❑ 101A Edwin Almonte YS RC	8.00	2.40
❑ 101P Edwin Almonte YS RC	8.00	2.40
❑ 102A Francis Beltran YS RC	8.00	2.40
❑ 102P Francis Beltran YS RC	8.00	2.40
❑ 103A Val Pascucci YS	8.00	2.40
❑ 103P Val Pascucci YS	8.00	2.40
❑ 104A Nelson Castro YS RC	8.00	2.40
❑ 104P Nelson Castro YS RC	8.00	2.40
❑ 105A Michael Crudale YS RC	8.00	2.40
❑ 105P Michael Crudale YS RC	8.00	2.40
❑ 106A Colin Young YS RC	8.00	2.40
❑ 106P Colin Young YS RC	8.00	2.40
❑ 107A Todd Donovan YS RC	8.00	2.40
❑ 107P Todd Donovan YS RC	8.00	2.40
❑ 108A Felix Escalona YS RC	8.00	2.40
❑ 108P Felix Escalona YS RC	8.00	2.40
❑ 109A Brandon Backe YS RC	10.00	3.00
❑ 109P Brandon Backe YS RC	10.00	3.00
❑ 110A Corey Thurman YS RC	8.00	2.40
❑ 110P Corey Thurman YS RC	8.00	2.40
❑ 111A Kyle Kane YS RC	8.00	2.40
❑ 111P Kyle Kane YS RC	8.00	2.40
❑ 112A Allan Simpson YS RC	8.00	2.40
❑ 112P Allan Simpson YS RC	8.00	2.40
❑ 113A Jose Valverde YS RC	10.00	3.00
❑ 113P Jose Valverde YS RC	10.00	3.00
❑ 114A Chris Booker YS RC	8.00	2.40
❑ 114P Chris Booker YS RC	8.00	2.40
❑ 115A Brandon Puffer YS RC	8.00	2.40
❑ 115P Brandon Puffer YS RC	8.00	2.40
❑ 116A John Foster YS RC	8.00	2.40
❑ 116P John Foster YS RC	8.00	2.40
❑ 117A Cliff Bartosh YS RC	8.00	2.40
❑ 117P Cliff Bartosh YS RC	8.00	2.40
❑ 118A Gustavo Chacin YS RC	10.00	3.00
❑ 118P Gustavo Chacin YS RC	10.00	3.00
❑ 119A Steve Kent YS RC	8.00	2.40
❑ 119P Steve Kent YS RC	8.00	2.40
❑ 120A Nate Field YS RC	8.00	2.40
❑ 120P Nate Field YS RC	8.00	2.40
❑ 121 Victor Alvarez AU RC	10.00	3.00
❑ 122 Steve Bechler AU RC	10.00	3.00
❑ 123 Adrian Burnside AU RC	10.00	3.00
❑ 124 Marlon Byrd AU	15.00	4.50
❑ 125 Jaime Cerda AU RC	10.00	3.00
❑ 126 Brandon Claussen AU	15.00	4.50
❑ 127 Mark Corey AU RC	10.00	3.00
❑ 128 Doug Devore AU RC	10.00	3.00
❑ 129 Kazuhisa Ishii AU SP RC	100.00	30.00
❑ 130 John Ennis AU RC	10.00	3.00
❑ 131 Kevin Frederick AU RC	10.00	3.00
❑ 132 Josh Hancock AU RC	10.00	3.00
❑ 133 Ben Howard AU RC	10.00	3.00
❑ 134 Orlando Hudson AU	15.00	4.50
❑ 135 Hansel Izquierdo AU RC	10.00	3.00
❑ 136 Eric Junge AU RC	10.00	3.00
❑ 137 Austin Kearns AU	25.00	7.50
❑ 138 Victor Martinez AU	40.00	12.00
❑ 139 Luis Martinez AU RC	10.00	3.00
❑ 140 Danny Mota AU RC	10.00	3.00
❑ 141 Jorge Padilla AU RC	10.00	3.00
❑ 142 Andy Pratt AU RC	10.00	3.00
❑ 143 Rene Reyes AU RC	10.00	3.00
❑ 144 Rodrigo Rosario AU RC	10.00	3.00
❑ 145 Tom Shearn AU RC	10.00	3.00
❑ 146 So Taguchi AU SP RC	40.00	12.00
❑ 147 Dennis Tankersley AU	15.00	4.50
❑ 148 Matt Thornton AU RC	10.00	3.00
❑ 149 Jeremy Ward AU RC	10.00	3.00
❑ 150 Mitch Wylie AU RC	10.00	3.00
❑ 151 Pedro Martinez JSY/800	10.00	3.00
❑ 152 Cal Ripken JSY/800	40.00	12.00
❑ 153 Roger Clemens JSY/800	25.00	7.50
❑ 154 Bernie Williams JSY/800	10.00	3.00
❑ 155 Jason Giambi JSY/700	8.00	2.40
❑ 156 Robin Ventura JSY/800	8.00	2.40
❑ 157 Carlos Delgado JSY/800	8.00	2.40
❑ 158 Frank Thomas JSY/800	10.00	3.00
❑ 159 Mag. Ordonez JSY/800	8.00	2.40
❑ 160 Jim Thome JSY/800	10.00	3.00
❑ 161 Darin Erstad JSY/800	8.00	2.40
❑ 162 Tim Salmon JSY/800	10.00	3.00
❑ 163 Tim Hudson JSY/800	8.00	2.40
❑ 164 Barry Zito JSY/800	8.00	2.40
❑ 165 Ichiro Suzuki JSY/800	40.00	12.00
❑ 166 Edgar Martinez JSY/800	10.00	3.00
❑ 167 Alex Rodriguez JSY/800	20.00	6.00
❑ 168 Ivan Rodriguez JSY/800	10.00	3.00
❑ 169 Juan Gonzalez JSY/800	10.00	3.00
❑ 170 Greg Maddux JSY/800	15.00	4.50
❑ 171 Chipper Jones JSY/800	10.00	3.00
❑ 172 Andruw Jones JSY/800	8.00	2.40
❑ 173 Tom Glavine JSY/800	10.00	3.00
❑ 174 Mike Piazza JSY/800	15.00	4.50
❑ 175 Roberto Alomar JSY/800	10.00	3.00
❑ 176 Scott Rolen JSY/800	10.00	3.00
❑ 177 Sammy Sosa JSY/800	20.00	6.00
❑ 178 Moises Alou JSY/800	8.00	2.40
❑ 179 Ken Griffey Jr. JSY/700	20.00	6.00
❑ 180 Jeff Bagwell JSY/800	10.00	3.00
❑ 181 Jim Edmonds JSY/800	8.00	2.40
❑ 182 J.D. Drew JSY/800	8.00	2.40
❑ 183 Brian Giles JSY/800	8.00	2.40
❑ 184 Randy Johnson JSY/800	10.00	3.00
❑ 185 Curt Schilling JSY/800	8.00	2.40
❑ 186 Luis Gonzalez JSY/800	8.00	2.40
❑ 187 Todd Helton JSY/800	10.00	3.00
❑ 188 Shawn Green JSY/800	8.00	2.40
❑ 189 David Wells JSY/800	8.00	2.40
❑ 190 Jeff Kent JSY/800	8.00	2.40
❑ 191 Tom Glavine	1.25	.35
❑ 192 Cliff Floyd	.75	.23
❑ 193 Mark Prior	3.00	.90
❑ 194 Corey Patterson	.75	.23
❑ 195 Paul Konerko	.75	.23
❑ 196 Adam Dunn	1.25	.35
❑ 197 Joe Borchard	.75	.23
❑ 198 Carlos Pena	.75	.23
❑ 199 Juan Encarnacion	.75	.23
❑ 200 Luis Castillo	.75	.23
❑ 201 Torii Hunter	.75	.23
❑ 202 Hee Seop Choi	.75	.23
❑ 203 Bartolo Colon	.75	.23
❑ 204 Raul Mondesi	.75	.23
❑ 205 Jeff Weaver	.75	.23
❑ 206 Eric Munson	.75	.23
❑ 207 Alfonso Soriano	1.25	.35
❑ 208 Ray Durham	.75	.23
❑ 209 Eric Chavez	.75	.23
❑ 210 Brett Myers	.75	.23
❑ 211 Jeremy Giambi	.75	.23
❑ 212 Vicente Padilla	.75	.23
❑ 213 Felipe Lopez	.75	.23
❑ 214 Sean Burroughs	.75	.23
❑ 215 Kenny Lofton	.75	.23
❑ 216 Scott Rolen	2.00	.60
❑ 217 Carl Crawford	.75	.23
❑ 218 Juan Gonzalez	1.25	.35

❑ 219 Orlando Hudson	.75	.23
❑ 220 Eric Hinske	.75	.23
❑ 221 Adam Walker AU RC	10.00	3.00
❑ 222 Aaron Cook AU RC	10.00	3.00
❑ 223 Cam Esslinger AU RC	10.00	3.00
❑ 224 Kirk Saarloos AU RC	10.00	3.00
❑ 225 Jose Diaz AU RC	10.00	3.00
❑ 226 David Ross AU RC	10.00	3.00
❑ 227 Jayson Durocher AU RC	10.00	3.00
❑ 228 Brian Mallette AU RC	10.00	3.00
❑ 229 Aaron Guiel AU RC	10.00	3.00
❑ 230 Jorge Nunez AU RC	10.00	3.00
❑ 231 Satoru Komiyama AU RC	25.00	7.50
❑ 232 Tyler Yates AU RC	15.00	4.50
❑ 233 Pete Zamora AU RC	10.00	3.00
❑ 234 Mike Gonzalez AU RC	10.00	3.00
❑ 235 Oliver Perez AU RC	50.00	15.00
❑ 236 Julius Matos AU RC	10.00	3.00
❑ 237 Andy Shibilo AU RC	10.00	3.00
❑ 238 J.Simontacchi AU RC	10.00	3.00
❑ 239 Ron Chiavacci AU	10.00	3.00
❑ 240 Deivis Santos AU	10.00	3.00
❑ 241 Travis Driskill AU RC	10.00	3.00
❑ 242 Jorge De La Rosa AU RC	10.00	3.00
❑ 243 An. Martinez AU RC	10.00	3.00
❑ 244 Earl Snyder AU RC	15.00	4.50
❑ 245 Freddy Sanchez AU RC	10.00	3.00
❑ 246 Miguel Asencio AU RC	10.00	3.00
❑ 247 Juan Brito AU RC	10.00	3.00
❑ 248 Franklyn German AU RC	10.00	3.00
❑ 249 Chris Snelling AU RC	10.00	3.00
❑ 250 Ken Huckaby AU RC	10.00	3.00

2003 SPx

	MINT	NRMT
COMP.LO SET w/o SP's (100)	25.00	11.00
COMP.LO SET w/ SP's (125)	100.00	45.00
COMMON CARD (1-125)	.50	.23
COMMON SP (1-125)	4.00	1.80
COMMON CARD (126-160)	8.00	3.60
COMMON CARD (163-178)	15.00	6.75
163-178 PRINT RUN 1224 SERIAL #'d SETS		.00
126-178 RANDOM INSERTS IN SPx PACKS		.00
COMMON CARD (179-193)	15.00	6.75
COMMON CARD (381-387)	20.00	9.00

❑ 1 Darin Erstad	.50	.23
❑ 2 Garret Anderson	.50	.23
❑ 3 Tim Salmon	.75	.35
❑ 4 Troy Glaus SP	4.00	1.80
❑ 5 Luis Gonzalez	.50	.23
❑ 6 Randy Johnson	1.25	.55
❑ 7 Curt Schilling	.50	.23
❑ 8 Lyle Overbay	.50	.23
❑ 9 Andruw Jones SP	4.00	1.80
❑ 10 Gary Sheffield	.50	.23
❑ 11 Rafael Furcal	.50	.23
❑ 12 Greg Maddux	2.00	.90
❑ 13 Chipper Jones SP	5.00	2.20
❑ 14 Tony Batista	.50	.23
❑ 15 Rodrigo Lopez	.50	.23
❑ 16 Jay Gibbons	.50	.23
❑ 17 Byung-Hyun Kim	.50	.23
❑ 18 Johnny Damon	1.25	.55
❑ 19 Derek Lowe	.50	.23
❑ 20 Nomar Garciaparra SP	8.00	3.60
❑ 21 Pedro Martinez	1.25	.55
❑ 22 Manny Ramirez SP	4.00	1.80
❑ 23 Mark Prior	1.25	.55
❑ 24 Kerry Wood	1.25	.55
❑ 25 Corey Patterson	.50	.23
❑ 26 Sammy Sosa SP	8.00	3.60
❑ 27 Moises Alou	.50	.23
❑ 28 Magglio Ordonez	.50	.23
❑ 29 Frank Thomas	1.25	.55
❑ 30 Paul Konerko	.50	.23
❑ 31 Bartolo Colon	.50	.23
❑ 32 Adam Dunn	.75	.35
❑ 33 Austin Kearns	.50	.23
❑ 34 Aaron Boone	.50	.23
❑ 35 Ken Griffey Jr. SP	8.00	3.60
❑ 36 Omar Vizquel	.75	.35
❑ 37 C.C. Sabathia	.50	.23
❑ 38 Jason Davis	.50	.23
❑ 39 Travis Hafner	.50	.23
❑ 40 Brandon Phillips	.50	.23
❑ 41 Larry Walker	.75	.35
❑ 42 Preston Wilson	.50	.23
❑ 43 Jay Payton	.50	.23
❑ 44 Todd Helton	.75	.35
❑ 45 Carlos Pena	.50	.23
❑ 46 Eric Munson	.50	.23
❑ 47 Ivan Rodriguez	1.25	.55
❑ 48 Josh Beckett	.50	.23
❑ 49 Alex Gonzalez	.50	.23
❑ 50 Roy Oswalt	.50	.23
❑ 51 Craig Biggio	.75	.35
❑ 52 Jeff Bagwell	.75	.35
❑ 53 Dontrelle Willis SP	4.00	1.80
❑ 54 Mike Sweeney	.50	.23
❑ 55 Carlos Beltran	.75	.35
❑ 56 Brent Mayne	.50	.23
❑ 57 Hideo Nomo	1.25	.55
❑ 58 Rickey Henderson	1.25	.55
❑ 59 Adrian Beltre	.75	.35
❑ 60 Miguel Cabrera SP	5.00	2.20
❑ 61 Kazuhisa Ishii	.50	.23
❑ 62 Ben Sheets	.50	.23
❑ 63 Richie Sexson	.50	.23
❑ 64 Torii Hunter SP	4.00	1.80
❑ 65 Jacque Jones	.50	.23
❑ 66 Joe Mays	.50	.23
❑ 67 Corey Koskie	.50	.23
❑ 68 A.J. Pierzynski	.50	.23
❑ 69 Jose Vidro	.50	.23
❑ 70 Vladimir Guerrero SP	5.00	2.20
❑ 71 Tom Glavine	.75	.35
❑ 72 Jose Reyes SP	4.00	1.80
❑ 73 Aaron Heilman	.50	.23
❑ 74 Mike Piazza	2.00	.90
❑ 75 Jorge Posada	.75	.35
❑ 76 Mike Mussina	.75	.35
❑ 77 Robin Ventura	.50	.23
❑ 78 Mariano Rivera	.75	.35
❑ 79 Roger Clemens SP	10.00	4.50
❑ 80 Jason Giambi	.50	.23
❑ 81 Bernie Williams	.75	.35
❑ 82 Alfonso Soriano SP	4.00	1.80
❑ 83 Derek Jeter SP	12.00	5.50
❑ 84 Miguel Tejada SP	4.00	1.80
❑ 85 Eric Chavez	.50	.23
❑ 86 Tim Hudson	.50	.23
❑ 87 Barry Zito	.50	.23
❑ 88 Mark Mulder	.50	.23
❑ 89 Erubiel Durazo	.50	.23
❑ 90 Pat Burrell	.50	.23
❑ 91 Jim Thome SP	5.00	2.20
❑ 92 Bobby Abreu	.50	.23
❑ 93 Brian Giles	.50	.23
❑ 94 Reggie Sanders SP	4.00	1.80
❑ 95 Kenny Lofton	.50	.23
❑ 96 Ryan Klesko	.50	.23
❑ 97 Sean Burroughs	.50	.23
❑ 98 Edgardo Alfonzo	.50	.23
❑ 99 Rich Aurilia	.50	.23
❑ 100 Jose Cruz Jr.	.50	.23
❑ 101 Barry Bonds SP	12.00	5.50
❑ 102 Mike Cameron	.50	.23
❑ 103 Kazuhiro Sasaki	.50	.23
❑ 104 Bret Boone	.50	.23
❑ 105 Ichiro Suzuki SP	8.00	3.60
❑ 106 J.D. Drew	.50	.23
❑ 107 Jim Edmonds	.50	.23
❑ 108 Scott Rolen SP	5.00	2.20
❑ 109 Matt Morris	.50	.23
❑ 110 Tino Martinez	.75	.35
❑ 111 Albert Pujols SP	10.00	4.50
❑ 112 Damian Rolls	.50	.23
❑ 113 Carl Crawford	.50	.23
❑ 114 Rocco Baldelli SP	4.00	1.80
❑ 115 Hank Blalock	.75	.35
❑ 116 Alex Rodriguez SP	8.00	3.60
❑ 117 Kevin Mench	.50	.23
❑ 118 Rafael Palmeiro	.75	.35
❑ 119 Mark Teixeira	.50	.23
❑ 120 Shannon Stewart	.50	.23
❑ 121 Vernon Wells	.50	.23
❑ 122 Josh Phelps	.50	.23
❑ 123 Eric Hinske	.50	.23
❑ 124 Orlando Hudson	.50	.23
❑ 125 Carlos Delgado SP	4.00	1.80
❑ 126 Jason Roach ROO RC	8.00	3.60
❑ 127 Dan Haren ROO RC	10.00	4.50
❑ 128 Luis Ayala ROO RC	8.00	3.60
❑ 129 Bo Hart ROO RC	10.00	4.50
❑ 130 Wil. Ledezma ROO RC	10.00	4.50
❑ 131 Rick Roberts ROO RC	8.00	3.60
❑ 132 Miguel Ojeda ROO RC	8.00	3.60
❑ 133 Aquilino Lopez ROO RC	8.00	3.60
❑ 134 Roger Deago ROO RC	8.00	3.60
❑ 135 Arnie Munoz ROO RC	8.00	3.60
❑ 136 Brent Hoard ROO RC	8.00	3.60
❑ 137 Terrmel Sledge ROO RC	10.00	4.50
❑ 138 Ryan Cameron ROO RC	8.00	3.60
❑ 139 Pr. Redman ROO RC	8.00	3.60
❑ 140 Clint Barmes ROO RC	10.00	4.50
❑ 141 Jeremy Griffiths ROO RC	10.00	4.50
❑ 142 Jon Leicester ROO RC	8.00	3.60
❑ 143 Brandon Webb ROO RC	10.00	4.50
❑ 144 T.Wellemeyer ROO RC	10.00	4.50
❑ 145 Felix Sanchez ROO RC	8.00	3.60
❑ 146 Anthony Ferrari ROO RC	8.00	3.60
❑ 147 Ian Ferguson ROO RC	8.00	3.60
❑ 148 Mi. Nakamura ROO RC	8.00	3.60
❑ 149 Lew Ford ROO RC	10.00	4.50
❑ 150 Nate Bland ROO RC	8.00	3.60
❑ 151 David Matranga ROO RC	8.00	3.60
❑ 152 Edgar Gonzalez ROO RC	8.00	3.60
❑ 153 Carlos Mendez ROO RC	8.00	3.60
❑ 154 Jason Gilfillan ROO RC	8.00	3.60
❑ 155 Mike Neu ROO RC	8.00	3.60
❑ 156 Jason Shiell ROO RC	8.00	3.60
❑ 157 Jeff Duncan ROO RC	10.00	4.50
❑ 158 Oscar Villarreal ROO RC	8.00	3.60
❑ 159 D.Markwell ROO RC	8.00	3.60
❑ 160 Joe Valentine ROO RC	8.00	3.60
❑ 161 H.Matsui AU JSY RC	300.00	135.00
❑ 162 Jose Contreras AU RC	40.00	18.00
❑ 163 Willie Eyre AU JSY RC	15.00	6.75
❑ 164 Matt Bruback AU JSY RC	15.00	6.75
❑ 165 Rett Johnson AU JSY RC	25.00	11.00
❑ 166 Jeremy Griffiths AU JSY	25.00	11.00
❑ 167 Fran Cruceta AU JSY RC	15.00	6.75
❑ 168 Fern Cabrera AU JSY RC	15.00	6.75
❑ 169 J.Peralta AU JSY	15.00	6.75
❑ 170 S.Bazzell AU JSY RC	15.00	6.75
❑ 171 B.Madritsch AU JSY RC	50.00	22.00
❑ 172 Phil Seibel AU JSY RC	15.00	6.75
❑ 173 J.Willingham AU JSY RC	25.00	11.00
❑ 174 R.Hammock AU JSY RC	25.00	11.00
❑ 175 A.Machado AU JSY RC	15.00	6.75
❑ 176 D.Sanders AU JSY RC	15.00	6.75
❑ 177 Matt Kata AU JSY RC	25.00	11.00
❑ 178 Heath Bell AU JSY RC	15.00	6.75
❑ 179 Chad Gaudin ROO RC	15.00	6.75
❑ 180 Chris Capuano ROO RC	15.00	6.75
❑ 181 Danny Garcia ROO RC	15.00	6.75
❑ 182 Delmon Young ROO	50.00	22.00
❑ 183 Edwin Jackson ROO RC	40.00	18.00
❑ 184 Greg Jones ROO RC	15.00	6.75
❑ 185 Jeremy Bonderman ROO RC	20.00	9.00
❑ 186 Jorge DePaula ROO	15.00	6.75
❑ 187 Khalil Greene ROO	40.00	18.00
❑ 188 Chad Cordero ROO RC	15.00	6.75
❑ 189 Miguel Cabrera ROO	20.00	9.00
❑ 190 Rich Harden ROO	20.00	9.00
❑ 191 Rickie Weeks ROO	40.00	18.00
❑ 192 Rosman Garcia ROO RC	15.00	6.75
❑ 193 Tom Gregorio ROO RC	15.00	6.75

		Nm-Mt	Ex-Mt
❑ 381	Andrew Brown AU JSY RC	25.00	11.00
❑ 382	Delm Young AU JSY RC	180.00	80.00
❑ 383	Colin Porter AU JSY RC	20.00	9.00
❑ 385	Rickie Weeks AU JSY RC	100.00	45.00
❑ 386	David Matranga AU JSY RC	20.00	9.00
❑ 387	Bo Hart AU JSY	25.00	11.00

1992 Stadium Club Dome

		Nm-Mt	Ex-Mt
COMP.FACT.SET (200)		15.00	4.50
❑ 1	Terry Adams RC	.50	.15
❑ 2	Tommy Adams RC	.25	.07
❑ 3	Rick Aguilera	.15	.04
❑ 4	Ron Allen RC	.25	.07
❑ 5	Roberto Alomar	.25	.07
❑ 6	Sandy Alomar Jr.	.10	.03
❑ 7	Greg Anthony RC	.25	.07
❑ 8	James Austin RC	.25	.07
❑ 9	Steve Avery	.10	.03
❑ 10	Harold Baines	.15	.04
❑ 11	Brian Barber RC	.25	.07
❑ 12	Jon Barnes RC	.25	.07
❑ 13	George Bell	.10	.03
❑ 14	Doug Bennett RC	.25	.07
❑ 15	Sean Bergman RC	.50	.15
❑ 16	Craig Biggio	.25	.07
❑ 17	Bill Bliss RC	.25	.07
❑ 18	Wade Boggs	.25	.07
❑ 19	Bobby Bonilla	.15	.04
❑ 20	Russell Brock RC	.25	.07
❑ 21	Tarrik Brock RC	.25	.07
❑ 22	Tom Browning	.10	.03
❑ 23	Brett Butler	.15	.04
❑ 24	Ivan Calderon	.10	.03
❑ 25	Joe Carter	.15	.04
❑ 26	Joe Caruso RC	.25	.07
❑ 27	Dan Cholowsky RC	.25	.07
❑ 28	Will Clark	.50	.15
❑ 29	Roger Clemens	1.00	.30
❑ 30	Shawn Curran RC	.25	.07
❑ 31	Chris Curtis RC	.25	.07
❑ 32	Chili Davis	.15	.04
❑ 33	Andre Dawson	.15	.04
❑ 34	Joe DeBerry RC	.25	.07
❑ 35	John Dettmer	.10	.03
❑ 36	Rob Dibble	.15	.04
❑ 37	John Donati RC	.25	.07
❑ 38	Dave Doorneweerd RC	.25	.07
❑ 39	Darren Dreifort	.10	.03
❑ 40	Mike Durant RC	.25	.07
❑ 41	Chris Durkin RC	.25	.07
❑ 42	Dennis Eckersley	.15	.04
❑ 43	Brian Edmondson RC	.25	.07
❑ 44	Vaughn Eshelman RC	.25	.07
❑ 45	Shawn Estes RC	.50	.15
❑ 46	Jorge Fabregas RC	.50	.15
❑ 47	Jon Farrell RC	.25	.07
❑ 48	Cecil Fielder	.15	.04
❑ 49	Carlton Fisk	.25	.07
❑ 50	Tim Flannelly RC	.25	.07
❑ 51	Cliff Floyd RC	.75	.23
❑ 52	Julio Franco	.15	.04
❑ 53	Greg Gagne	.10	.03
❑ 54	Chris Gambs RC	.25	.07
❑ 55	Ron Gant	.15	.04
❑ 56	Brent Gates RC	.25	.07
❑ 57	Dwayne Gerald RC	.25	.07
❑ 58	Jason Giambi	1.00	.30
❑ 59	Benji Gil RC	.50	.15
❑ 60	Mark Gipner RC	.25	.07
❑ 61	Danny Gladden	.10	.03
❑ 62	Tom Glavine	.25	.07
❑ 63	Jimmy Gonzalez RC	.25	.07
❑ 64	Jeff Granger	.10	.03
❑ 65	Dan Grapenthien RC	.25	.07
❑ 66	Dennis Gray RC	.25	.07
❑ 67	Shawn Green RC	4.00	1.20
❑ 68	Tyler Green RC	.25	.07
❑ 69	Todd Greene	.10	.03
❑ 70	Ken Griffey Jr.	.75	.23
❑ 71	Kelly Gruber	.10	.03
❑ 72	Ozzie Guillen	.10	.03
❑ 73	Tony Gwynn	.60	.18
❑ 74	Shane Halter RC	.25	.07
❑ 75	Jeffrey Hammonds	.15	.04
❑ 76	Larry Hanlon RC	.25	.07
❑ 77	Pete Harnisch	.10	.03
❑ 78	Mike Harrison RC	.25	.07
❑ 79	Bryan Harvey	.10	.03
❑ 80	Scott Hatteberg RC	.50	.15
❑ 81	Rick Helling	.10	.03
❑ 82	Dave Henderson	.10	.03
❑ 83	Rickey Henderson	.50	.15
❑ 84	Tyrone Hill RC	.25	.07
❑ 85	T.Hollandsworth RC	.50	.15
❑ 86	Brian Holliday RC	.25	.07
❑ 87	Terry Horn RC	.25	.07
❑ 88	Jeff Hostetler RC	.25	.07
❑ 89	Kent Hrbek	.15	.04
❑ 90	Mark Hubbard RC	.25	.07
❑ 91	Charles Johnson	.15	.04
❑ 92	Howard Johnson	.10	.03
❑ 93	Todd Johnson	.10	.03
❑ 94	Bobby Jones RC	.50	.15
❑ 95	Dan Jones RC	.25	.07
❑ 96	Felix Jose	.10	.03
❑ 97	David Justice	.10	.03
❑ 98	Jimmy Key	.15	.04
❑ 99	Marc Kroon RC	.25	.07
❑ 100	John Kruk	.15	.04
❑ 101	Mark Langston	.10	.03
❑ 102	Barry Larkin	.25	.07
❑ 103	Mike LaValliere	.10	.03
❑ 104	Scott Leius	.10	.03
❑ 105	Mark Lemke	.10	.03
❑ 106	Donnie Leshnock	.10	.03
❑ 107	Jimmy Lewis RC	.25	.07
❑ 108	Shane Livesy RC	.25	.07
❑ 109	Ryan Long RC	.25	.07
❑ 110	Trevor Mallory RC	.25	.07
❑ 111	Dennis Martinez	.15	.04
❑ 112	Justin Mashore RC	.25	.07
❑ 113	Jason McDonald	.10	.03
❑ 114	Jack McDowell	.10	.03
❑ 115	Tom McKinnon RC	.25	.07
❑ 116	Billy McMillon	.10	.03
❑ 117	Buck McNabb RC	.25	.07
❑ 118	Jim Mecir RC	.25	.07
❑ 119	Dan Melendez	.25	.07
❑ 120	Shawn Miller RC	.25	.07
❑ 121	Trever Miller RC	.25	.07
❑ 122	Paul Molitor	.25	.07
❑ 123	Vincent Moore RC	.25	.07
❑ 124	Mike Morgan	.10	.03
❑ 125	Jack Morris WS	.10	.03
❑ 126	Jack Morris AS	.10	.03
❑ 127	Sean Mulligan RC	.25	.07
❑ 128	Eddie Murray AS	.50	.15
❑ 129	Mike Neill RC	.50	.15
❑ 130	Phil Nevin	1.00	.30
❑ 131	Mark O'Brien RC	.25	.07
❑ 132	Alex Ochoa RC	.50	.15
❑ 133	Chad Ogea RC	.25	.07
❑ 134	Greg Olson	.10	.03
❑ 135	Paul O'Neill	.25	.07
❑ 136	Jared Osentowski RC	.25	.07
❑ 137	Mike Pagliarulo	.10	.03
❑ 138	Rafael Palmeiro	.25	.07
❑ 139	Rodney Pedraza RC	.25	.07
❑ 140	Tony Phillips (P)	.10	.03
❑ 141	Scott Pisciotta RC	.25	.07
❑ 142	C.Pritchett RC	.25	.07
❑ 143	Jason Pruitt RC	.25	.07
❑ 144	K.Puckett WS UER Championship series AB and BA is wrong	.50	.15
❑ 145	Kirby Puckett AS	.50	.15
❑ 146	Manny Ramirez RC	4.00	1.20
❑ 147	Eddie Ramos RC	.25	.07
❑ 148	Mark Ratekin RC	.25	.07
❑ 149	Jeff Reardon	.15	.04
❑ 150	Sean Rees RC	.25	.07
❑ 151	Pokey Reese RC	.75	.23
❑ 152	Desmond Relaford RC	.50	.15
❑ 153	Eric Richardson RC	.25	.07
❑ 154	Cal Ripken	1.50	.45
❑ 155	Chris Roberts	.10	.03
❑ 156	Mike Robertson RC	.25	.07
❑ 157	Steve Rodriguez	.10	.03
❑ 158	Mike Rossiter RC	.25	.07
❑ 159	Scott Ruffcorn RC	.25	.07
❑ 160	Chris Sabo	.10	.03
❑ 161	Juan Samuel	.10	.03
❑ 162	Ryne Sandberg UER (On 5th line, prior misspelled as prilor)	.75	.23
❑ 163	Scott Sanderson	.10	.03
❑ 164	Benny Santiago	.15	.04
❑ 165	Gene Schall RC	.25	.07
❑ 166	Chad Schoenvogel RC	.25	.07
❑ 167	Chris Seelbach RC	.25	.07
❑ 168	Aaron Sele RC	.75	.23
❑ 169	Basil Shabazz RC	.25	.07
❑ 170	Al Shirley RC	.25	.07
❑ 171	Paul Shuey	.10	.03
❑ 172	Ruben Sierra	.10	.03
❑ 173	John Smiley	.10	.03
❑ 174	Lee Smith	.15	.04
❑ 175	Ozzie Smith	.75	.23
❑ 176	Tim Smith RC	.25	.07
❑ 177	Zane Smith	.10	.03
❑ 178	John Smoltz	.25	.07
❑ 179	Scott Stahoviak RC	.25	.07
❑ 180	Kennie Steenstra	.10	.03
❑ 181	Kevin Stocker RC	.25	.07
❑ 182	Chris Stynes RC	.50	.15
❑ 183	Danny Tartabull	.10	.03
❑ 184	Brien Taylor RC	.50	.15
❑ 185	Todd Taylor	.10	.03
❑ 186	Larry Thomas RC	.25	.07
❑ 187	Ozzie Timmons RC (See also 188)	.25	.07
❑ 188	David Tuttle UER (Mistakenly numbered as 187 on card)	.10	.03
❑ 189	Andy Van Slyke	.15	.04
❑ 190	Frank Viola	.15	.04
❑ 191	Michael Walkden RC	.25	.07
❑ 192	Jeff Ware	.10	.03
❑ 193	Allen Watson RC	.25	.07
❑ 194	Steve Whitaker RC	.25	.07
❑ 195	Jerry Willard	.10	.03
❑ 196	Craig Wilson	.10	.03
❑ 197	Chris Wimmer	.10	.03
❑ 198	S.Wojciechowski RC	.25	.07
❑ 199	Joel Wolfe RC	.25	.07
❑ 200	Ivan Zweig	.10	.03

1993 Stadium Club Murphy

	Nm-Mt	Ex-Mt
COMP.FACT.SET (212)	40.00	12.00
COMPLETE SET (200)	25.00	7.50
COMMON CARD (1-200)	.15	.04
COMMON RC	.15	.04
❑ 1 Dave Winfield	.15	.04
❑ 2 Juan Guzman	.15	.04
❑ 3 Tony Gwynn	1.00	.30
❑ 4 Chris Roberts	.15	.04
❑ 5 Benny Santiago	.30	.09
❑ 6 Sherard Clinkscales RC	.15	.04
❑ 7 Jon Nunnally RC	.50	.15
❑ 8 Chuck Knoblauch	.30	.09
❑ 9 Bob Wolcott RC	.15	.04
❑ 10 Steve Rodriguez	.15	.04
❑ 11 Mark Williams RC	.15	.04
❑ 12 Danny Clyburn RC	.15	.04
❑ 13 Darren Dreifort	.15	.04
❑ 14 Andy Van Slyke	.30	.09
❑ 15 Wade Boggs	.50	.15
❑ 16 Scott Patton RC	.15	.04
❑ 17 Gary Sheffield	.30	.09
❑ 18 Ron Villone	.15	.04
❑ 19 Roberto Alomar	.50	.15
❑ 20 Marc Valdes	.15	.04
❑ 21 Daron Kirkreit	.15	.04
❑ 22 Jeff Granger	.15	.04
❑ 23 Levon Largusa RC	.15	.04
❑ 24 Jimmy Key	.30	.09
❑ 25 Kevin Pearson RC	.15	.04
❑ 26 Michael Moore RC	.15	.04
❑ 27 Preston Wilson RC	1.50	.45
❑ 28 Kirby Puckett	.75	.23
❑ 29 Tim Crabtree RC	.15	.04
❑ 30 Bip Roberts	.15	.04
❑ 31 Kelly Gruber	.15	.04
❑ 32 Tony Fernandez	.15	.04
❑ 33 Jason Angel RC	.15	.04
❑ 34 Calvin Murray	.15	.04
❑ 35 Chad McConnell	.15	.04
❑ 36 Jason Moler	.15	.04
❑ 37 Mark Lemke	.15	.04
❑ 38 Tom Knauss RC	.15	.04
❑ 39 Larry Mitchell RC	.15	.04
❑ 40 Doug Mirabelli RC	.50	.15
❑ 41 Everett Stull II RC	.15	.04
❑ 42 Chris Wimmer	.15	.04
❑ 43 Dan Serafini RC	.15	.04
❑ 44 Ryne Sandberg	1.25	.35
❑ 45 Steve Lyons RC	.15	.04
❑ 46 Ryan Freeburg RC	.15	.04
❑ 47 Ruben Sierra	.15	.04
❑ 48 David Mysel RC	.15	.04
❑ 49 Joe Hamilton RC	.15	.04
❑ 50 Steve Rodriguez	.15	.04
❑ 51 Tim Wakefield	.75	.23
❑ 52 Scott Gentile RC	.15	.04
❑ 53 Doug Jones	.15	.04
❑ 54 Willie Brown RC	.15	.04
❑ 55 Chad Mottola RC	.50	.15
❑ 56 Ken Griffey Jr.	1.25	.35
❑ 57 Jon Lieber RC	1.00	.30
❑ 58 Dennis Martinez	.30	.09
❑ 59 Joe Petcka RC	.15	.04
❑ 60 Benji Simonton RC	.15	.04
❑ 61 Brett Backlund RC	.15	.04
❑ 62 Damon Berryhill	.15	.04
❑ 63 Juan Guzman	.15	.04
❑ 64 Doug Hecker RC	.15	.04
❑ 65 Jamie Arnold RC	.15	.04
❑ 66 Bob Tewksbury	.15	.04
❑ 67 Tim Leger RC	.15	.04
❑ 68 Todd Etler RC	.15	.04
❑ 69 Lloyd McClendon	.15	.04
❑ 70 Kurt Ehmann RC	.15	.04
❑ 71 Rick Magdaleno RC	.15	.04
❑ 72 Tom Pagnozzi	.15	.04
❑ 73 Jeffrey Hammonds	.15	.04
❑ 74 Joe Carter	.30	.09
❑ 75 Chris Holt RC	.30	.09
❑ 76 Charles Johnson	.30	.09
❑ 77 Bob Walk	.15	.04
❑ 78 Fred McGriff	.50	.15
❑ 79 Tom Evans RC	.15	.04
❑ 80 Scott Klingenbeck RC	.15	.04
❑ 81 Chad McConnell	.15	.04
❑ 82 Chris Eddy RC	.15	.04
❑ 83 Phil Nevin	.30	.09
❑ 84 John Kruk	.30	.09
❑ 85 Tony Sheffield RC	.15	.04
❑ 86 John Smoltz	.50	.15
❑ 87 Trevor Humphry RC	.15	.04
❑ 88 Charles Nagy	.15	.04
❑ 89 Sean Runyan RC	.15	.04
❑ 90 Mike Gulan RC	.15	.04
❑ 91 Darren Daulton	.30	.09
❑ 92 Otis Nixon	.15	.04
❑ 93 Nomar Garciaparra	15.00	4.50
❑ 94 Larry Walker	.50	.15
❑ 95 Hut Smith RC	.15	.04
❑ 96 Rick Helling	.15	.04
❑ 97 Roger Clemens	1.50	.45
❑ 98 Ron Gant	.30	.09
❑ 99 Kenny Felder RC	.15	.04
❑ 100 Steve Murphy RC	.15	.04
❑ 101 Mike Smith RC	.15	.04
❑ 102 Terry Pendleton	.30	.09
❑ 103 Tim Davis	.15	.04
❑ 104 Jeff Patzke RC	.15	.04
❑ 105 Craig Wilson	.15	.04
❑ 106 Tom Glavine	.50	.15
❑ 107 Mark Langston	.15	.04
❑ 108 Mark Thompson RC	.15	.04
❑ 109 Eric Owens RC	.50	.15
❑ 110 Keith Johnson RC	.15	.04
❑ 111 Robin Ventura	.30	.09
❑ 112 Ed Sprague	.15	.04
❑ 113 Jeff Schmidt RC	.15	.04
❑ 114 Don Wengert RC	.15	.04
❑ 115 Craig Biggio	.50	.15
❑ 116 Kenny Carlyle RC	.15	.04
❑ 117 Derek Jeter RC	20.00	6.00
❑ 118 Manuel Lee	.15	.04
❑ 119 Jeff Haas RC	.15	.04
❑ 120 Roger Bailey RC	.15	.04
❑ 121 Sean Lowe RC	.15	.04
❑ 122 Rick Aguilera	.15	.04
❑ 123 Sandy Alomar Jr.	.15	.04
❑ 124 Derek Wallace RC	.15	.04
❑ 125 B.J. Wallace	.15	.04
❑ 126 Greg Maddux	1.25	.35
❑ 127 Tim Moore RC	.15	.04
❑ 128 Lee Smith	.30	.09
❑ 129 Todd Steverson RC	.15	.04
❑ 130 Chris Widger RC	.50	.15
❑ 131 Paul Molitor	.50	.15
❑ 132 Chris Smith RC	.15	.04
❑ 133 Chris Gomez RC	.50	.15
❑ 134 Jimmy Baron RC	.15	.04
❑ 135 John Smoltz	.50	.15
❑ 136 Pat Borders	.15	.04
❑ 137 Donnie Leshnock	.15	.04
❑ 138 Gus Gandarillos RC	.15	.04
❑ 139 Will Clark	.75	.23
❑ 140 Ryan Luzinski RC	.15	.04
❑ 141 Cal Ripken	2.50	.75
❑ 142 B.J. Wallace	.15	.04
❑ 143 Trey Beamon RC	.50	.15
❑ 144 Norm Charlton	.15	.04
❑ 145 Mike Mussina	.50	.15
❑ 146 Billy Owens RC	.15	.04
❑ 147 Ozzie Smith	1.25	.35
❑ 148 Jason Kendall RC	1.50	.45
❑ 149 Mike Matthews RC	.15	.04
❑ 150 David Spykstra RC	.15	.04
❑ 151 Benji Grigsby RC	.15	.04
❑ 152 Sean Smith RC	.15	.04
❑ 153 Mark McGwire	2.00	.60
❑ 154 David Cone	.30	.09
❑ 155 Shon Walker RC	.15	.04
❑ 156 Jason Giambi	1.00	.30
❑ 157 Jack McDowell	.15	.04
❑ 158 Paxton Briley RC	.15	.04
❑ 159 Edgar Martinez	.50	.15
❑ 160 Brian Sackinsky RC	.15	.04
❑ 161 Barry Bonds	2.00	.60
❑ 162 Roberto Kelly	.15	.04
❑ 163 Jeff Alkire	.15	.04
❑ 164 Mike Sharperson	.15	.04
❑ 165 Jamie Taylor RC	.15	.04
❑ 166 John Saffer UER RC	.15	.04
❑ 167 Jerry Browne	.15	.04
❑ 168 Travis Fryman	.30	.09
❑ 169 Brady Anderson	.30	.09
❑ 170 Chris Roberts	.15	.04
❑ 171 Lloyd Peever RC	.15	.04
❑ 172 Francisco Cabrera	.15	.04
❑ 173 Ramiro Martinez RC	.15	.04
❑ 174 Jeff Alkire	.15	.04
❑ 175 Ivan Rodriguez	.75	.23
❑ 176 Kevin Brown	.30	.09
❑ 177 Chad Roper RC	.15	.04
❑ 178 Rod Henderson RC	.15	.04
❑ 179 Dennis Eckersley	.30	.09
❑ 180 Shannon Stewart RC	1.50	.45
❑ 181 DeShawn Warren RC	.15	.04
❑ 182 Lonnie Smith	.15	.04
❑ 183 Willie Adams	.15	.04
❑ 184 Jeff Montgomery	.15	.04
❑ 185 Damon Hollins RC	.15	.04
❑ 186 Byron Mathews RC	.15	.04
❑ 187 Harold Baines	.30	.09
❑ 188 Rick Greene	.15	.04
❑ 189 Carlos Baerga	.15	.04
❑ 190 Brandon Cromer RC	.15	.04
❑ 191 Roberto Alomar	.50	.15
❑ 192 Rich Ireland RC	.15	.04
❑ 193 S.Montgomery RC	.15	.04
❑ 194 Brant Brown RC	.15	.04
❑ 195 Ritchie Moody RC	.15	.04
❑ 196 Michael Tucker	.30	.09
❑ 197 Jason Varitek	3.00	.90
❑ 198 David Manning RC	.15	.04
❑ 199 Marquis Riley RC	.15	.04
❑ 200 Jason Giambi	1.00	.30

2001 Studio

	Nm-Mt	Ex-Mt
COMP.SET w/o SP's (150)	40.00	12.00
COMMON CARD (1-150)	.50	.15
COMMON (151-200)	8.00	2.40
❑ 1 Alex Rodriguez	2.00	.60
❑ 2 Barry Bonds	3.00	.90
❑ 3 Cal Ripken	4.00	1.20
❑ 4 Chipper Jones	1.25	.35
❑ 5 Derek Jeter	3.00	.90
❑ 6 Troy Glaus	.50	.15
❑ 7 Frank Thomas	1.25	.35
❑ 8 Greg Maddux	2.00	.60
❑ 9 Ivan Rodriguez	1.25	.35
❑ 10 Jeff Bagwell	.75	.23
❑ 11 Mark Quinn	.50	.15
❑ 12 Todd Helton	.75	.23
❑ 13 Ken Griffey Jr.	2.00	.60
❑ 14 Manny Ramirez	.75	.23
❑ 15 Mark McGwire	3.00	.90
❑ 16 Mike Piazza	2.00	.60
❑ 17 Nomar Garciaparra	2.00	.60
❑ 18 Robin Ventura	.50	.15
❑ 19 Aramis Ramirez	.50	.15
❑ 20 J.T. Snow	.50	.15
❑ 21 Pat Burrell	.50	.15
❑ 22 Curt Schilling	.50	.15
❑ 23 Carlos Delgado	.50	.15
❑ 24 J.D. Drew	.50	.15
❑ 25 Cliff Floyd	.50	.15
❑ 26 Brian Jordan	.50	.15

- ❑ 27 Roberto Alomar .75 .23
- ❑ 28 Barry Zito .75 .23
- ❑ 29 Harold Baines .50 .15
- ❑ 30 Brad Penny .50 .15
- ❑ 31 Jose Cruz Jr. .50 .15
- ❑ 32 Andy Pettitte .75 .23
- ❑ 33 Jim Edmonds .50 .15
- ❑ 34 Darin Erstad .50 .15
- ❑ 35 Jason Giambi .50 .15
- ❑ 36 Tom Glavine .75 .23
- ❑ 37 Juan Gonzalez .75 .23
- ❑ 38 Mark Grace .75 .23
- ❑ 39 Shawn Green .50 .15
- ❑ 40 Tim Hudson .50 .15
- ❑ 41 Andruw Jones .50 .15
- ❑ 42 Jeff Kent .50 .15
- ❑ 43 Barry Larkin .75 .23
- ❑ 44 Rafael Furcal .50 .15
- ❑ 45 Mike Mussina .75 .23
- ❑ 46 Hideo Nomo 1.25 .35
- ❑ 47 Rafael Palmeiro .75 .23
- ❑ 48 Scott Rolen 1.25 .35
- ❑ 49 Gary Sheffield .50 .15
- ❑ 50 Bernie Williams .75 .23
- ❑ 51 Bob Abreu .50 .15
- ❑ 52 Edgardo Alfonzo .50 .15
- ❑ 53 Edgar Martinez .75 .23
- ❑ 54 Magglio Ordonez .50 .15
- ❑ 55 Kerry Wood 1.25 .35
- ❑ 56 Matt Morris .50 .15
- ❑ 57 Lance Berkman .50 .15
- ❑ 58 Kevin Brown .50 .15
- ❑ 59 Sean Casey .50 .15
- ❑ 60 Eric Chavez .50 .15
- ❑ 61 Bartolo Colon .50 .15
- ❑ 62 Johnny Damon .75 .23
- ❑ 63 Jermaine Dye .50 .15
- ❑ 64 Juan Encarnacion .50 .15
- ❑ 65 Carl Everett .50 .15
- ❑ 66 Brian Giles .50 .15
- ❑ 67 Mike Hampton .50 .15
- ❑ 68 Richard Hidalgo .50 .15
- ❑ 69 Geoff Jenkins .50 .15
- ❑ 70 Jacque Jones .50 .15
- ❑ 71 Jason Kendall .50 .15
- ❑ 72 Ryan Klesko .50 .15
- ❑ 73 Chan Ho Park .50 .15
- ❑ 74 Richie Sexson .50 .15
- ❑ 75 Mike Sweeney .50 .15
- ❑ 76 Fernando Tatis .50 .15
- ❑ 77 Miguel Tejada .50 .15
- ❑ 78 Jose Vidro .50 .15
- ❑ 79 Larry Walker 2.00 .60
- ❑ 80 Preston Wilson .50 .15
- ❑ 81 Craig Biggio .75 .23
- ❑ 82 Fred McGriff .75 .23
- ❑ 83 Jim Thome 1.25 .35
- ❑ 84 Garret Anderson .50 .15
- ❑ 85 Mark Mulder .50 .15
- ❑ 86 Tony Batista .50 .15
- ❑ 87 Terrence Long .50 .15
- ❑ 88 Brad Fullmer .50 .15
- ❑ 89 Rusty Greer .50 .15
- ❑ 90 Orlando Hernandez .50 .15
- ❑ 91 Gabe Kapler .50 .15
- ❑ 92 Paul Konerko .50 .15
- ❑ 93 Carlos Lee .50 .15
- ❑ 94 Kenny Lofton .50 .15
- ❑ 95 Raul Mondesi .50 .15
- ❑ 96 Jorge Posada .75 .23
- ❑ 97 Tim Salmon .75 .23
- ❑ 98 Greg Vaughn .50 .15
- ❑ 99 Mo Vaughn .50 .15
- ❑ 100 Omar Vizquel .75 .23
- ❑ 101 Ben Grieve .50 .15
- ❑ 102 Luis Gonzalez .50 .15
- ❑ 103 Ray Durham .50 .15
- ❑ 104 Ryan Dempster .50 .15
- ❑ 105 Eric Karros .50 .15
- ❑ 106 David Justice .50 .15
- ❑ 107 Pedro Martinez 1.25 .35
- ❑ 108 Randy Johnson 1.25 .35
- ❑ 109 Rick Ankiel .50 .15
- ❑ 110 Rickey Henderson 1.25 .35
- ❑ 111 Roger Clemens 2.50 .75
- ❑ 112 Sammy Sosa 2.00 .60
- ❑ 113 Tony Gwynn 1.50 .45
- ❑ 114 Vladimir Guerrero 1.25 .35
- ❑ 115 Kazuhiro Sasaki .50 .15
- ❑ 116 Phil Nevin .50 .15
- ❑ 117 Ruben Mateo .50 .15
- ❑ 118 Shannon Stewart .50 .15
- ❑ 119 Matt Williams .50 .15
- ❑ 120 Tino Martinez .75 .23
- ❑ 121 Ken Caminiti .50 .15
- ❑ 122 Edgar Renteria .50 .15
- ❑ 123 Charles Johnson .50 .15
- ❑ 124 Aaron Sele .50 .15
- ❑ 125 Javy Lopez .50 .15
- ❑ 126 Mariano Rivera .75 .23
- ❑ 127 Shea Hillenbrand .50 .15
- ❑ 128 Jeff D'Amico .50 .15
- ❑ 129 Brady Anderson .50 .15
- ❑ 130 Kevin Millwood .50 .15
- ❑ 131 Trot Nixon .50 .15
- ❑ 132 Mike Lieberthal .50 .15
- ❑ 133 Juan Pierre .50 .15
- ❑ 134 Russ Ortiz .50 .15
- ❑ 135 Jose Macias .50 .15
- ❑ 136 John Smoltz .75 .23
- ❑ 137 Jason Varitek .75 .23
- ❑ 138 Dean Palmer .50 .15
- ❑ 139 Jeff Cirillo .50 .15
- ❑ 140 Paul O'Neill .75 .23
- ❑ 141 Andres Galarraga .50 .15
- ❑ 142 David Wells .50 .15
- ❑ 143 Brad Radke .50 .15
- ❑ 144 Wade Miller .50 .15
- ❑ 145 John Olerud .50 .15
- ❑ 146 Moises Alou .50 .15
- ❑ 147 Carlos Beltran .75 .23
- ❑ 148 Jeromy Burnitz .50 .15
- ❑ 149 Steve Finley .50 .15
- ❑ 150 Joe Mays .50 .15
- ❑ 151 Alex Escobar ROO 8.00 2.40
- ❑ 152 J. Estrada ROO RC 10.00 3.00
- ❑ 153 Pedro Feliz ROO 8.00 2.40
- ❑ 154 Nate Frese ROO RC 8.00 2.40
- ❑ 155 Dee Brown ROO 8.00 2.40
- ❑ 156 B. Larson ROO RC 8.00 2.40
- ❑ 157 A. Gomez ROO RC 8.00 2.40
- ❑ 158 Jason Hart ROO 8.00 2.40
- ❑ 159 C.C. Sabathia ROO 8.00 2.40
- ❑ 160 Josh Towers ROO RC 8.00 2.40
- ❑ 161 C. Parker ROO RC 8.00 2.40
- ❑ 162 J. Melian ROO RC 8.00 2.40
- ❑ 163 Joe Kennedy ROO RC 10.00 3.00
- ❑ 164 A. Hernandez ROO RC 8.00 2.40
- ❑ 165 Jimmy Rollins ROO 8.00 2.40
- ❑ 166 Jose Mieses ROO RC 8.00 2.40
- ❑ 167 Roy Oswalt ROO 10.00 3.00
- ❑ 168 Eric Munson ROO 8.00 2.40
- ❑ 169 Xavier Nady ROO 8.00 2.40
- ❑ 170 H. Ramirez ROO RC 10.00 3.00
- ❑ 171 Abraham Nunez ROO 8.00 2.40
- ❑ 172 Jose Ortiz ROO 8.00 2.40
- ❑ 173 Jeremy Owens ROO RC UER 8.00 2.40
  Eric Owens pictured on front
- ❑ 174 C. Vargas ROO RC 8.00 2.40
- ❑ 175 Corey Patterson ROO 8.00 2.40
- ❑ 176 Carlos Pena ROO 8.00 2.40
- ❑ 177 Bud Smith ROO RC 8.00 2.40
- ❑ 178 Adam Dunn ROO 10.00 3.00
- ❑ 179 A. Pettyjohn ROO RC 8.00 2.40
- ❑ 180 E. Guzman ROO RC 8.00 2.40
- ❑ 181 Jay Gibbons ROO RC 10.00 3.00
- ❑ 182 Wilkin Ruan ROO RC 8.00 2.40
- ❑ 183 T. Shinjo ROO RC 10.00 3.00
- ❑ 184 Alfonso Soriano ROO 10.00 3.00
- ❑ 185 Marcus Giles ROO 8.00 2.40
- ❑ 186 Ichiro Suzuki ROO RC 80.00 24.00
- ❑ 187 Juan Uribe ROO RC 10.00 3.00
- ❑ 188 D. Williams ROO RC 8.00 2.40
- ❑ 189 Carlos Valderrama ROO RC 8.00 2.40
- ❑ 190 Matt White ROO RC 8.00 2.40
- ❑ 191 Albert Pujols ROO RC 120.00 36.00
- ❑ 192 D. Mendez ROO RC 8.00 2.40
- ❑ 193 C. Aldridge ROO RC 8.00 2.40
- ❑ 194 Endy Chavez ROO RC 8.00 2.40
- ❑ 195 Josh Beckett ROO 8.00 2.40
- ❑ 196 W. Betemit ROO RC 8.00 2.40
- ❑ 197 Ben Sheets ROO 10.00 3.00
- ❑ 198 A. Torres ROO RC 8.00 2.40
- ❑ 199 Aubrey Huff ROO 8.00 2.40
- ❑ 200 Jack Wilson ROO RC 12.00 3.60

2002 Studio

	Nm-Mt	Ex-Mt
COMP.LOW SET w/o SP's (200)	50.00	15.00
COMMON CARD (1-200)	.50	.15
COMMON ROOKIE (1-200)	.50	.15
COMMON CARD (201-275)	4.00	1.20

- ❑ 1 Vladimir Guerrero 1.25 .35
- ❑ 2 Chipper Jones 1.25 .35
- ❑ 3 Bob Abreu .50 .15
- ❑ 4 Barry Zito .50 .15
- ❑ 5 Larry Walker .75 .23
- ❑ 6 Miguel Tejada .50 .15
- ❑ 7 Mike Sweeney .50 .15
- ❑ 8 Shannon Stewart .50 .15
- ❑ 9 Sammy Sosa 2.00 .60
- ❑ 10 Bud Smith .50 .15
- ❑ 11 Wilson Betemit .50 .15
- ❑ 12 Kevin Brown .50 .15
- ❑ 13 Ellis Burks .50 .15
- ❑ 14 Pat Burrell .50 .15
- ❑ 15 Cliff Floyd .50 .15
- ❑ 16 Marcus Giles .50 .15
- ❑ 17 Troy Glaus .50 .15
- ❑ 18 Barry Larkin .75 .23
- ❑ 19 Carlos Lee .50 .15
- ❑ 20 Brian Lawrence .50 .15
- ❑ 21 Paul Lo Duca .50 .15
- ❑ 22 Ben Grieve .50 .15
- ❑ 23 Shawn Green .50 .15
- ❑ 24 Mike Cameron .50 .15
- ❑ 25 Roger Clemens 2.50 .75
- ❑ 26 Joe Crede .50 .15
- ❑ 27 Jose Cruz Jr. .50 .15
- ❑ 28 Jeremy Affeldt .50 .15
- ❑ 29 Adrian Beltre .75 .23
- ❑ 30 Josh Beckett .50 .15
- ❑ 31 Roberto Alomar .75 .23
- ❑ 32 Toby Hall .50 .15
- ❑ 33 Mike Hampton .50 .15
- ❑ 34 Eric Milton .50 .15
- ❑ 35 Eric Munson .50 .15
- ❑ 36 Trot Nixon .50 .15
- ❑ 37 Roy Oswalt .50 .15
- ❑ 38 Chan Ho Park .50 .15
- ❑ 39 Charles Johnson .50 .15
- ❑ 40 Nick Johnson .50 .15
- ❑ 41 Tim Hudson .50 .15
- ❑ 42 Cristian Guzman .50 .15
- ❑ 43 Drew Henson .50 .15
- ❑ 44 Mark Grace .75 .23
- ❑ 45 Luis Gonzalez .50 .15
- ❑ 46 Pedro Martinez 1.25 .35
- ❑ 47 Joe Mays .50 .15
- ❑ 48 Jorge Posada .75 .23
- ❑ 49 Aramis Ramirez .50 .15
- ❑ 50 Kip Wells .50 .15
- ❑ 51 Moises Alou .50 .15
- ❑ 52 Omar Vizquel .75 .23
- ❑ 53 Ichiro Suzuki 2.00 .60
- ❑ 54 Jimmy Rollins .50 .15
- ❑ 55 Freddy Garcia .50 .15

	No.	Player	Nm-Mt	Ex-Mt
❑	56	Steve Green	.50	.15
❑	57	Brian Jordan	.50	.15
❑	58	Paul Konerko	.50	.15
❑	59	Jack Cust	.50	.15
❑	60	Sean Casey	.50	.15
❑	61	Bret Boone	.50	.15
❑	62	Hideo Nomo	1.25	.35
❑	63	Magglio Ordonez	.50	.15
❑	64	Frank Thomas	1.25	.35
❑	65	Josh Towers	.50	.15
❑	66	Javier Vazquez	.50	.15
❑	67	Robin Ventura	.50	.15
❑	68	Aubrey Huff	.50	.15
❑	69	Richard Hidalgo	.50	.15
❑	70	Brandon Claussen	.50	.15
❑	71	Bartolo Colon	.50	.15
❑	72	John Buck	.50	.15
❑	73	Dee Brown	.50	.15
❑	74	Barry Bonds	3.00	.90
❑	75	Jason Giambi	.50	.15
❑	76	Erick Almonte	.50	.15
❑	77	Ryan Dempster	.50	.15
❑	78	Jim Edmonds	.50	.15
❑	79	Jay Gibbons	.50	.15
❑	80	Shigetoshi Hasegawa	.50	.15
❑	81	Todd Helton	.75	.23
❑	82	Erik Bedard	.50	.15
❑	83	Carlos Beltran	.75	.23
❑	84	Rafael Soriano	.50	.15
❑	85	Gary Sheffield	.50	.15
❑	86	Richie Sexson	.50	.15
❑	87	Mike Rivera	.50	.15
❑	88	Jose Ortiz	.50	.15
❑	89	Abraham Nunez	.50	.15
❑	90	Dave Williams	.50	.15
❑	91	Preston Wilson	.50	.15
❑	92	Jason Jennings	.50	.15
❑	93	Juan Diaz	.50	.15
❑	94	Steve Smyth	.50	.15
❑	95	Phil Nevin	.50	.15
❑	96	John Olerud	.50	.15
❑	97	Brad Penny	.50	.15
❑	98	Andy Pettitte	.75	.23
❑	99	Juan Pierre	.50	.15
❑	100	Manny Ramirez	.75	.23
❑	101	Edgardo Alfonzo	.50	.15
❑	102	Michael Cuddyer	.50	.15
❑	103	Johnny Damon Sox	1.25	.35
❑	104	Carlos Zambrano	.50	.15
❑	105	Jose Vidro	.50	.15
❑	106	Tsuyoshi Shinjo	.50	.15
❑	107	Ed Rogers	.50	.15
❑	108	Scott Rolen	1.25	.35
❑	109	Mariano Rivera	.75	.23
❑	110	Tim Redding	.50	.15
❑	111	Josh Phelps	.50	.15
❑	112	Gabe Kapler	.50	.15
❑	113	Edgar Martinez	.75	.23
❑	114	Fred McGriff	.75	.23
❑	115	Raul Mondesi	.50	.15
❑	116	Wade Miller	.50	.15
❑	117	Mike Mussina	.75	.23
❑	118	Rafael Palmeiro	.75	.23
❑	119	Adam Johnson	.50	.15
❑	120	Rickey Henderson	1.25	.35
❑	121	Bill Hall	.50	.15
❑	122	Ken Griffey Jr.	2.00	.60
❑	123	Geronimo Gil	.50	.15
❑	124	Robert Fick	.50	.15
❑	125	Darin Erstad	.50	.15
❑	126	Brandon Duckworth	.50	.15
❑	127	Garret Anderson	.50	.15
❑	128	Pedro Feliz	.50	.15
❑	129	Jeff Cirillo	.50	.15
❑	130	Brian Giles	.50	.15
❑	131	Craig Biggio	.75	.23
❑	132	Willie Harris	.50	.15
❑	133	Doug Davis	.50	.15
❑	134	Jeff Kent	.50	.15
❑	135	Terrence Long	.50	.15
❑	136	Carlos Delgado	.50	.15
❑	137	Tino Martinez	.75	.23
❑	138	Donaldo Mendez	.50	.15
❑	139	Sean Douglass	.50	.15
❑	140	Eric Chavez	.50	.15
❑	141	Rick Ankiel	.50	.15
❑	142	Jeremy Giambi	.50	.15
❑	143	Juan Pena	.50	.15
❑	144	Bernie Williams	.75	.23
❑	145	Craig Wilson	.50	.15
❑	146	Ricardo Rodriguez	.50	.15
❑	147	Albert Pujols	2.50	.75
❑	148	Antonio Perez	.50	.15
❑	149	Russ Ortiz	.50	.15
❑	150	Corky Miller	.50	.15
❑	151	Rich Aurilia	.50	.15
❑	152	Kerry Wood	1.25	.35
❑	153	Joe Thurston	.50	.15
❑	154	Jeff Deardorff	.50	.15
❑	155	Jermaine Dye	.50	.15
❑	156	Andruw Jones	.50	.15
❑	157	Victor Martinez	1.25	.35
❑	158	Nick Neugebauer	.50	.15
❑	159	Matt Morris	.50	.15
❑	160	Casey Fossum	.50	.15
❑	161	J.D. Drew	.50	.15
❑	162	Matt Childers	.50	.15
❑	163	Mark Buehrle	.50	.15
❑	164	Jeff Bagwell	.75	.23
❑	165	Kazuhiro Sasaki	.50	.15
❑	166	Ben Sheets	.50	.15
❑	167	Alex Rodriguez	2.00	.60
❑	168	Adam Pettyjohn	.50	.15
❑	169	Chris Snelling RC	.50	.15
❑	170	Robert Person	.50	.15
❑	171	Juan Uribe	.50	.15
❑	172	Mo Vaughn	.50	.15
❑	173	Alfredo Amezaga	.50	.15
❑	174	Ryan Drese	.50	.15
❑	175	Corey Thurman RC	.50	.15
❑	176	Jim Thome	1.25	.35
❑	177	Orlando Cabrera	.50	.15
❑	178	Eric Cyr	.50	.15
❑	179	Greg Maddux	2.00	.60
❑	180	Earl Snyder RC	.75	.23
❑	181	C.C. Sabathia	.50	.15
❑	182	Mark Mulder	.50	.15
❑	183	Jose Mieses	.50	.15
❑	184	Joe Kennedy	.50	.15
❑	185	Randy Johnson	1.25	.35
❑	186	Tom Glavine	.75	.23
❑	187	Eric Junge RC	.50	.15
❑	188	Mike Piazza	2.00	.60
❑	189	Corey Patterson	.50	.15
❑	190	Carlos Pena	.50	.15
❑	191	Curt Schilling	.50	.15
❑	192	Nomar Garciaparra	2.00	.60
❑	193	Lance Berkman	.50	.15
❑	194	Ryan Klesko	.50	.15
❑	195	Ivan Rodriguez	1.25	.35
❑	196	Alfonso Soriano	.75	.23
❑	197	Derek Jeter	3.00	.90
❑	198	David Justice	.50	.15
❑	199	Juan Gonzalez	.75	.23
❑	200	Adam Dunn	.75	.23
❑	201	Victor Alvarez ROO RC	4.00	1.20
❑	202	Miguel Asencio ROO RC	4.00	1.20
❑	203	Brandon Backe ROO RC	5.00	1.50
❑	204	Chris Baker ROO RC	4.00	1.20
❑	205	Steve Bechler ROO RC	4.00	1.20
❑	206	Francis Beltran ROO RC	4.00	1.20
❑	207	Angel Berroa ROO	4.00	1.20
❑	208	Hank Blalock ROO	5.00	1.50
❑	209	Dewon Brazelton ROO	4.00	1.20
❑	210	Sean Burroughs ROO	4.00	1.20
❑	211	Marlon Byrd ROO	4.00	1.20
❑	212	Raul Chavez ROO RC	4.00	1.20
❑	213	Juan Cruz ROO	4.00	1.20
❑	214	J.De La Rosa ROO RC	4.00	1.20
❑	215	Doug Devore ROO RC	4.00	1.20
❑	216	John Ennis ROO RC	4.00	1.20
❑	217	Felix Escalona ROO RC	4.00	1.20
❑	218	Morgan Ensberg ROO	4.00	1.20
❑	219	Cam Esslinger ROO RC	4.00	1.20
❑	220	Kevin Frederick ROO RC	4.00	1.20
❑	221	Fr.German ROO RC	4.00	1.20
❑	222	Eric Hinske ROO	4.00	1.20
❑	223	Ben Howard ROO RC	4.00	1.20
❑	224	Orlando Hudson ROO	4.00	1.20
❑	225	Travis Hughes ROO RC	4.00	1.20
❑	226	Kazuhisa Ishii ROO RC	10.00	3.00
❑	227	Ryan Jamison ROO	4.00	1.20
❑	228	Reed Johnson ROO RC	5.00	1.50
❑	229	Kyle Kane ROO RC	4.00	1.20
❑	230	Austin Kearns ROO	4.00	1.20
❑	231	Sat.Komiyama ROO RC	4.00	1.20
❑	232	Jason Lane ROO	4.00	1.20
❑	233	Jeremy Lambert ROO RC	4.00	1.20
❑	234	And. Machado ROO RC	4.00	1.20
❑	235	Brian Mallette ROO RC	4.00	1.20
❑	236	Tak. Nomura ROO RC	4.00	1.20
❑	237	Jorge Padilla ROO RC	4.00	1.20
❑	238	Luis Ugueto ROO RC	4.00	1.20
❑	239	Mark Prior ROO	12.00	3.60
❑	240	Rene Reyes ROO RC	4.00	1.20
❑	241	Deivis Santos ROO	4.00	1.20
❑	242	Elio Serrano ROO RC	4.00	1.20
❑	243	Tom Shearn ROO RC	4.00	1.20
❑	244	Allan Simpson ROO RC	4.00	1.20
❑	245	So Taguchi ROO RC	5.00	1.50
❑	246	Dennis Tankersley ROO	4.00	1.20
❑	247	Mark Teixeira ROO	5.00	1.50
❑	248	Matt Thornton ROO RC	4.00	1.20
❑	249	Bobby Hill ROO	4.00	1.20
❑	250	Ramon Vazquez ROO	4.00	1.20
❑	251	Freddy Sanchez ROO RC	4.00	1.20
❑	252	Josh Bard ROO RC	4.00	1.20
❑	253	Trey Hodges ROO RC	4.00	1.20
❑	254	Jorge Sosa ROO RC	4.00	1.20
❑	255	Ben Kozlowski ROO RC	4.00	1.20
❑	256	Eric Good ROO RC	4.00	1.20
❑	257	Brian Tallet ROO RC	4.00	1.20
❑	258	P.J. Bevis ROO RC	4.00	1.20
❑	259	Rodrigo Rosario ROO RC	4.00	1.20
❑	260	Kirk Saarloos ROO RC	4.00	1.20
❑	261	Run. Hernandez ROO RC	4.00	1.20
❑	262	Josh Hancock ROO RC	4.00	1.20
❑	263	Tim Kalita ROO RC	4.00	1.20
❑	264	J.Simontacchi ROO RC	4.00	1.20
❑	265	Clay Condrey ROO RC	4.00	1.20
❑	266	Cliff Lee ROO RC	5.00	1.50
❑	267	Aaron Guiel ROO RC	4.00	1.20
❑	268	Andy Pratt ROO RC	4.00	1.20
❑	269	Wilson Valdez ROO RC	4.00	1.20
❑	270	Oliver Perez ROO RC	10.00	3.00
❑	271	Joe Borchard ROO	4.00	1.20
❑	272	J.Robertson ROO RC	4.00	1.20
❑	273	Aaron Cook ROO RC	4.00	1.20
❑	274	Kevin Cash ROO RC	4.00	1.20
❑	275	Chone Figgins ROO RC	5.00	1.50

2003 Studio

	Nm-Mt	Ex-Mt
COMP.LO SET (200)	50.00	15.00
COMMON CARD (1-190)	.50	.15
COMMON RC (1-190)	.60	.18
COMMON CARD (191-200)	1.00	.30
COMMON CARD (201-211)	4.00	1.20

	No.	Player	Nm-Mt	Ex-Mt
❑	1	Darin Erstad	.50	.15
❑	2	David Eckstein	.50	.15
❑	3	Garret Anderson	.50	.15
❑	4	Jarrod Washburn	.50	.15
❑	5	Tim Salmon	.75	.23
❑	6	Troy Glaus	.50	.15
❑	7	Jay Gibbons	.50	.15
❑	8	Melvin Mora	.50	.15
❑	9	Rodrigo Lopez	.50	.15
❑	10	Tony Batista	.50	.15

❑ 11 Freddy Sanchez .50 .15
❑ 12 Derek Lowe .50 .15
❑ 13 Johnny Damon 1.25 .35
❑ 14 Manny Ramirez .75 .23
❑ 15 Nomar Garciaparra 2.00 .60
❑ 16 Pedro Martinez 1.25 .35
❑ 17 Rickey Henderson 1.25 .35
❑ 18 Shea Hillenbrand .50 .15
❑ 19 Carlos Lee .50 .15
❑ 20 Frank Thomas 1.25 .35
❑ 21 Magglio Ordonez .50 .15
❑ 22 Bartolo Colon .50 .15
❑ 23 Paul Konerko .50 .15
❑ 24 Josh Stewart RC .60 .18
❑ 25 C.C. Sabathia .50 .15
❑ 26 Jeremy Guthrie .50 .15
❑ 27 Ellis Burks .50 .15
❑ 28 Omar Vizquel .75 .23
❑ 29 Victor Martinez .75 .23
❑ 30 Cliff Lee .50 .15
❑ 31 Jhonny Peralta .50 .15
❑ 32 Brian Tallet .50 .15
❑ 33 Bobby Higginson .50 .15
❑ 34 Carlos Pena .50 .15
❑ 35 Nook Logan RC .60 .18
❑ 36 Steve Sparks .50 .15
❑ 37 Travis Chapman .50 .15
❑ 38 Carlos Beltran .75 .23
❑ 39 Joe Randa .50 .15
❑ 40 Mike Sweeney .50 .15
❑ 41 Jimmy Gobble .50 .15
❑ 42 Michael Tucker .50 .15
❑ 43 Runelvys Hernandez .50 .15
❑ 44 Brad Radke .50 .15
❑ 45 Corey Koskie .50 .15
❑ 46 Cristian Guzman .50 .15
❑ 47 J.C. Romero .50 .15
❑ 48 Doug Mientkiewicz .50 .15
❑ 49 Lew Ford RC 2.00 .60
❑ 50 Jacque Jones .50 .15
❑ 51 Torii Hunter .50 .15
❑ 52 Alfonso Soriano .75 .23
❑ 53 Nick Johnson .50 .15
❑ 54 Bernie Williams .75 .23
❑ 55 Jose Contreras RC 2.00 .60
❑ 56 Derek Jeter 3.00 .90
❑ 57 Jason Giambi .50 .15
❑ 58 Brandon Claussen .50 .15
❑ 59 Jorge Posada .75 .23
❑ 60 Mike Mussina .75 .23
❑ 61 Roger Clemens 2.50 .75
❑ 62 Hideki Matsui RC 5.00 1.50
❑ 63 Barry Zito .50 .15
❑ 64 Adam Morrissey .50 .15
❑ 65 Eric Chavez .50 .15
❑ 66 Jermaine Dye .50 .15
❑ 67 Mark Mulder .50 .15
❑ 68 Miguel Tejada .50 .15
❑ 69 Joe Valentine RC .60 .18
❑ 70 Tim Hudson .50 .15
❑ 71 Bret Boone .50 .15
❑ 72 Chris Snelling .50 .15
❑ 73 Edgar Martinez .75 .23
❑ 74 Freddy Garcia .50 .15
❑ 75 Ichiro Suzuki 2.00 .60
❑ 76 Jamie Moyer .50 .15
❑ 77 John Olerud .50 .15
❑ 78 Kazuhiro Sasaki .50 .15
❑ 79 Aubrey Huff .50 .15
❑ 80 Joe Kennedy .50 .15
❑ 81 Dewon Brazelton .50 .15
❑ 82 Pete LaForest RC 1.00 .30
❑ 83 Alex Rodriguez 2.00 .60
❑ 84 Chan Ho Park .50 .15
❑ 85 Hank Blalock .75 .23
❑ 86 Juan Gonzalez .75 .23
❑ 87 Kevin Mench .50 .15
❑ 88 Rafael Palmeiro .75 .23
❑ 89 Carlos Delgado .50 .15
❑ 90 Eric Hinske .50 .15
❑ 91 Josh Phelps .50 .15
❑ 92 Roy Halladay .50 .15
❑ 93 Shannon Stewart .50 .15
❑ 94 Vernon Wells .50 .15
❑ 95 Vinny Chulk .50 .15
❑ 96 Curt Schilling .50 .15
❑ 97 Junior Spivey .50 .15
❑ 98 Luis Gonzalez .50 .15
❑ 99 Mark Grace .75 .23
❑ 100 Randy Johnson 1.25 .35
❑ 101 Andruw Jones .50 .15
❑ 102 Chipper Jones 1.25 .35
❑ 103 Gary Sheffield .50 .15
❑ 104 Greg Maddux 2.00 .60
❑ 105 John Smoltz .75 .23
❑ 106 Mike Hampton .50 .15
❑ 107 Adam LaRoche .50 .15
❑ 108 Michael Hessman RC .60 .18
❑ 109 Corey Patterson .50 .15
❑ 110 Kerry Wood 1.25 .35
❑ 111 Mark Prior 1.25 .35
❑ 112 Moises Alou .50 .15
❑ 113 Sammy Sosa 2.00 .60
❑ 114 Adam Dunn .75 .23
❑ 115 Austin Kearns .50 .15
❑ 116 Barry Larkin .75 .23
❑ 117 Ken Griffey Jr. 2.00 .60
❑ 118 Sean Casey .50 .15
❑ 119 Jason Jennings .50 .15
❑ 120 Jay Payton .50 .15
❑ 121 Larry Walker .75 .23
❑ 122 Todd Helton .75 .23
❑ 123 Jeff Baker .50 .15
❑ 124 Clint Barmes RC 1.00 .30
❑ 125 Ivan Rodriguez 1.25 .35
❑ 126 Josh Beckett .50 .15
❑ 127 Juan Encarnacion .50 .15
❑ 128 Mike Lowell .50 .15
❑ 129 Craig Biggio .75 .23
❑ 130 Jason Lane .50 .15
❑ 131 Jeff Bagwell .75 .23
❑ 132 Lance Berkman .50 .15
❑ 133 Roy Oswalt .50 .15
❑ 134 Jeff Kent .50 .15
❑ 135 Hideo Nomo 1.25 .35
❑ 136 Kazuhisa Ishii .50 .15
❑ 137 Kevin Brown .50 .15
❑ 138 Odalis Perez .50 .15
❑ 139 Paul Lo Duca .50 .15
❑ 140 Shawn Green .50 .15
❑ 141 Adrian Beltre .75 .23
❑ 142 Ben Sheets .50 .15
❑ 143 Bill Hall .50 .15
❑ 144 Jeffrey Hammonds .50 .15
❑ 145 Richie Sexson .50 .15
❑ 146 Terrmel Sledge RC 1.00 .30
❑ 147 Brad Wilkerson .50 .15
❑ 148 Javier Vazquez .50 .15
❑ 149 Jose Vidro .50 .15
❑ 150 Michael Barrett .50 .15
❑ 151 Vladimir Guerrero 1.25 .35
❑ 152 Al Leiter .50 .15
❑ 153 Mike Piazza 2.00 .60
❑ 154 Mo Vaughn .50 .15
❑ 155 Cliff Floyd .50 .15
❑ 156 Roberto Alomar .75 .23
❑ 157 Roger Cedeno .50 .15
❑ 158 Tom Glavine .75 .23
❑ 159 Prentice Redman RC .60 .18
❑ 160 Bobby Abreu .50 .15
❑ 161 Jimmy Rollins .50 .15
❑ 162 Mike Lieberthal .50 .15
❑ 163 Pat Burrell .50 .15
❑ 164 Vicente Padilla .50 .15
❑ 165 Jim Thome 1.25 .35
❑ 166 Kevin Millwood .50 .15
❑ 167 Aramis Ramirez .50 .15
❑ 168 Brian Giles .50 .15
❑ 169 Jason Kendall .50 .15
❑ 170 Josh Fogg .50 .15
❑ 171 Kip Wells .50 .15
❑ 172 Jose Castillo .50 .15
❑ 173 Mark Kotsay .50 .15
❑ 174 Oliver Perez .50 .15
❑ 175 Phil Nevin .50 .15
❑ 176 Ryan Klesko .50 .15
❑ 177 Sean Burroughs .50 .15
❑ 178 Brian Lawrence .50 .15
❑ 179 Shane Victorino RC .60 .18
❑ 180 Barry Bonds 3.00 .90
❑ 181 Benito Santiago .50 .15
❑ 182 Ray Durham .50 .15
❑ 183 Rich Aurilia .50 .15
❑ 184 Damian Moss .50 .15
❑ 185 Albert Pujols 2.50 .75
❑ 186 J.D. Drew .50 .15
❑ 187 Jim Edmonds .50 .15
❑ 188 Matt Morris .50 .15
❑ 189 Tino Martinez .75 .23
❑ 190 Scott Rolen 1.25 .35
❑ 191 Troy Glaus 1.50 .45
Tim Salmon
❑ 192 Sean Casey 1.00 .30
Corky Miller
❑ 193 Carlos Lee 1.50 .45
Frank Thomas
❑ 194 Lance Berkman 1.00 .30
Jeff Kent
❑ 195 Jose Contreras 1.50 .45
Mariano Rivera
❑ 196 Alex Rodriguez 1.50 .45
Juan Gonzalez
❑ 197 Andy Pettitte 1.50 .45
David Wells
❑ 198 Shawn Green 1.00 .30
Dave Roberts
❑ 199 Mike Lieberthal 1.00 .30
Jimmy Rollins
❑ 200 Mike Mussina 2.00 .60
Hideki Matsui
❑ 201 Adam Loewen ROO RC 5.00 1.50
❑ 202 Jeremy Bonderman ROO RC 5.00 1.50
❑ 203 Brandon Webb ROO RC 5.00 1.50
❑ 204 Chien-Ming Wang ROO RC 5.00 1.50
❑ 205 Chad Gaudin ROO RC 4.00 1.20
❑ 206 Ryan Wagner ROO RC 5.00 1.50
❑ 207 Hong-Chih Kuo ROO RC 5.00 1.50
❑ 208 Dan Haren ROO RC 5.00 1.50
❑ 209 Rickie Weeks ROO RC 8.00 2.40
❑ 210 Ramon Nivar ROO RC 5.00 1.50
❑ 211 Delmon Young ROO RC 10.00 3.00

2004 Studio

	Nm-Mt	Ex-Mt
COMP.SET w/o SP's (200)	50.00	15.00
COMMON ACTIVE (1-200)	.40	.12
COMMON RETIRED (1-200)	.50	.15
COMMON RC (1-200)	.40	.12

AU'S RANDOM INSERTS IN PACKS
AU PRINT RUNS B/WN 400-800 COPIES PER

COMMON CARD (226-241)	3.00	.90
COMMON CARD (242-275)	3.00	.90

226-275 ODDS 1:23 '05 DONRUSS
CARDS 220/222-225 DO NOT EXIST

❑ 1 Bartolo Colon .40 .12
❑ 2 Garret Anderson .40 .12
❑ 3 Tim Salmon .60 .18
❑ 4 Troy Glaus .40 .12
❑ 5 Vladimir Guerrero 1.00 .30
❑ 6 Brandon Webb .40 .12
❑ 7 Brian Bruney .40 .12
❑ 8 Casey Fossum .40 .12
❑ 9 Luis Gonzalez .40 .12
❑ 10 Randy Johnson 1.00 .30
❑ 11 Richie Sexson .40 .12
❑ 12 Robby Hammock .40 .12
❑ 13 Roberto Alomar .60 .18

- ❑ 14 Shea Hillenbrand .40 .12
- ❑ 15 Steve Finley .40 .12
- ❑ 16 Adam LaRoche .40 .12
- ❑ 17 Andruw Jones .40 .12
- ❑ 18 Bubba Nelson .40 .12
- ❑ 19 Chipper Jones 1.00 .30
- ❑ 20 Dale Murphy .60 .18
- ❑ 21 J.D. Drew .40 .12
- ❑ 22 Marcus Giles .40 .12
- ❑ 23 Michael Hessman .40 .12
- ❑ 24 Rafael Furcal .40 .12
- ❑ 25 Warren Spahn .60 .18
- ❑ 26 Adam Loewen .40 .12
- ❑ 27 Cal Ripken 4.00 1.20
- ❑ 28 Javy Lopez .40 .12
- ❑ 29 Jay Gibbons .40 .12
- ❑ 30 Luis Matos .40 .12
- ❑ 31 Miguel Tejada .40 .12
- ❑ 32 Rafael Palmeiro .60 .18
- ❑ 33 Curt Schilling 1.00 .30
- ❑ 34 Jason Varitek .60 .18
- ❑ 35 Kevin Youkilis .40 .12
- ❑ 36 Manny Ramirez .60 .18
- ❑ 37 Nomar Garciaparra 1.50 .45
- ❑ 38 Pedro Martinez 1.00 .30
- ❑ 39 Trot Nixon .40 .12
- ❑ 40 Aramis Ramirez .40 .12
- ❑ 41 Brendan Harris .40 .12
- ❑ 42 Derrek Lee .40 .12
- ❑ 43 Ernie Banks 1.25 .35
- ❑ 44 Greg Maddux 1.50 .45
- ❑ 45 Kerry Wood 1.00 .30
- ❑ 46 Mark Prior 1.00 .30
- ❑ 47 Ryne Sandberg 2.50 .75
- ❑ 48 Sammy Sosa 1.50 .45
- ❑ 49 Todd Wellemeyer .40 .12
- ❑ 50 Carlos Lee .40 .12
- ❑ 51 Edwin Almonte .40 .12
- ❑ 52 Frank Thomas 1.00 .30
- ❑ 53 Joe Borchard .40 .12
- ❑ 54 Joe Crede .40 .12
- ❑ 55 Magglio Ordonez .40 .12
- ❑ 56 Adam Dunn .40 .12
- ❑ 57 Austin Kearns .40 .12
- ❑ 58 Barry Larkin .60 .18
- ❑ 59 Brandon Larson .40 .12
- ❑ 60 Ken Griffey Jr. 1.50 .45
- ❑ 61 Ryan Wagner .40 .12
- ❑ 62 Sean Casey .40 .12
- ❑ 63 Brian Tallet .40 .12
- ❑ 64 C.C. Sabathia .40 .12
- ❑ 65 Jeremy Guthrie .40 .12
- ❑ 66 Jody Gerut .40 .12
- ❑ 67 Travis Hafner .40 .12
- ❑ 68 Clint Barmes .40 .12
- ❑ 69 Jeff Baker .40 .12
- ❑ 70 Joe Kennedy .40 .12
- ❑ 71 Larry Walker .60 .18
- ❑ 72 Preston Wilson .40 .12
- ❑ 73 Todd Helton .60 .18
- ❑ 74 Dmitri Young .40 .12
- ❑ 75 Ivan Rodriguez 1.00 .30
- ❑ 76 Jeremy Bonderman .40 .12
- ❑ 77 Preston Larrison .40 .12
- ❑ 78 Dontrelle Willis .40 .12
- ❑ 79 Josh Beckett .40 .12
- ❑ 80 Juan Pierre .40 .12
- ❑ 81 Luis Castillo .40 .12
- ❑ 82 Miguel Cabrera .60 .18
- ❑ 83 Mike Lowell .40 .12
- ❑ 84 Andy Pettitte .60 .18
- ❑ 85 Chris Burke .40 .12
- ❑ 86 Craig Biggio .60 .18
- ❑ 87 Jeff Bagwell .60 .18
- ❑ 88 Jeff Kent .40 .12
- ❑ 89 Lance Berkman .40 .12
- ❑ 90 Morgan Ensberg .40 .12
- ❑ 91 Richard Hidalgo .40 .12
- ❑ 92 Roger Clemens 2.00 .60
- ❑ 93 Roy Oswalt .40 .12
- ❑ 94 Wade Miller .40 .12
- ❑ 95 Angel Berroa .40 .12
- ❑ 96 Byron Gettis .40 .12
- ❑ 97 Carlos Beltran .60 .18
- ❑ 98 Juan Gonzalez .60 .18
- ❑ 99 Mike Sweeney .40 .12
- ❑ 100 Duke Snider .75 .23
- ❑ 101 Edwin Jackson .40 .12
- ❑ 102 Eric Gagne 1.00 .30
- ❑ 103 Hideo Nomo 1.00 .30
- ❑ 104 Hong-Chih Kuo .40 .12
- ❑ 105 Kazuhisa Ishii .40 .12
- ❑ 106 Paul Lo Duca .40 .12
- ❑ 107 Robin Ventura .40 .12
- ❑ 108 Shawn Green .40 .12
- ❑ 109 Junior Spivey .40 .12
- ❑ 110 Lyle Overbay .40 .12
- ❑ 111 Rickie Weeks .40 .12
- ❑ 112 Scott Podsednik .40 .12
- ❑ 113 J.D. Durbin .40 .12
- ❑ 114 Jacque Jones .40 .12
- ❑ 115 Jason Kubel .40 .12
- ❑ 116 Johan Santana .60 .18
- ❑ 117 Shannon Stewart .40 .12
- ❑ 118 Torii Hunter .40 .12
- ❑ 119 Brad Wilkerson .40 .12
- ❑ 120 Jose Vidro .40 .12
- ❑ 121 Nick Johnson .40 .12
- ❑ 122 Orlando Cabrera .40 .12
- ❑ 123 Zach Day .40 .12
- ❑ 124 Gary Carter .50 .15
- ❑ 125 Jae Weong Seo .40 .12
- ❑ 126 Kazuo Matsui RC 2.50 .75
- ❑ 127 Mike Piazza 1.50 .45
- ❑ 128 Tom Glavine .60 .18
- ❑ 129 Alex Rodriguez Yanks 1.50 .45
- ❑ 130 Bernie Williams .60 .18
- ❑ 131 Chien-Ming Wang .40 .12
- ❑ 132 Derek Jeter 2.00 .60
- ❑ 133 Don Mattingly 2.50 .75
- ❑ 134 Gary Sheffield .40 .12
- ❑ 135 Hideki Matsui 1.50 .45
- ❑ 136 Jason Giambi .40 .12
- ❑ 137 Javier Vazquez .40 .12
- ❑ 138 Jorge Posada .60 .18
- ❑ 139 Jose Contreras .40 .12
- ❑ 140 Kevin Brown .40 .12
- ❑ 141 Mariano Rivera .60 .18
- ❑ 142 Mike Mussina .60 .18
- ❑ 143 Whitey Ford .75 .23
- ❑ 144 Barry Zito .40 .12
- ❑ 145 Eric Chavez .40 .12
- ❑ 146 Mark Mulder .40 .12
- ❑ 147 Rich Harden .40 .12
- ❑ 148 Tim Hudson .40 .12
- ❑ 149 Bobby Abreu .40 .12
- ❑ 150 Jim Thome 1.00 .30
- ❑ 151 Kevin Millwood .40 .12
- ❑ 152 Marlon Byrd .40 .12
- ❑ 153 Mike Schmidt 2.50 .75
- ❑ 154 Ryan Howard .40 .12
- ❑ 155 Jack Wilson .40 .12
- ❑ 156 Jason Kendall .40 .12
- ❑ 157 Akinori Otsuka RC .40 .12
- ❑ 158 Brian Giles .40 .12
- ❑ 159 David Wells .40 .12
- ❑ 160 Jay Payton .40 .12
- ❑ 161 Phil Nevin .40 .12
- ❑ 162 Ryan Klesko .40 .12
- ❑ 163 Sean Burroughs .40 .12
- ❑ 164 A.J. Pierzynski .40 .12
- ❑ 165 J.T. Snow .40 .12
- ❑ 166 Jason Schmidt .40 .12
- ❑ 167 Jerome Williams .40 .12
- ❑ 168 Merkin Valdez RC 1.25 .35
- ❑ 169 Will Clark 1.25 .35
- ❑ 170 Bret Boone .40 .12
- ❑ 171 Chris Snelling .40 .12
- ❑ 172 Edgar Martinez .60 .18
- ❑ 173 Ichiro Suzuki 1.50 .45
- ❑ 174 Jamie Moyer .40 .12
- ❑ 175 Randy Winn .40 .12
- ❑ 176 Rich Aurilia .40 .12
- ❑ 177 Shigetoshi Hasegawa .40 .12
- ❑ 178 Albert Pujols 2.00 .60
- ❑ 179 Dan Haren .40 .12
- ❑ 180 Edgar Renteria .40 .12
- ❑ 181 Jim Edmonds .40 .12
- ❑ 182 Matt Morris .40 .12
- ❑ 183 Scott Rolen 1.00 .30
- ❑ 184 Stan Musial 2.00 .60
- ❑ 185 Aubrey Huff .40 .12
- ❑ 186 Chad Gaudin .40 .12
- ❑ 187 Delmon Young .60 .18
- ❑ 188 Fred McGriff .60 .18
- ❑ 189 Rocco Baldelli .40 .12
- ❑ 190 Alfonso Soriano .60 .18
- ❑ 191 Hank Blalock .40 .12
- ❑ 192 Mark Teixeira .40 .12
- ❑ 193 Nolan Ryan 3.00 .90
- ❑ 194 Alexis Rios .40 .12
- ❑ 195 Carlos Delgado .40 .12
- ❑ 196 Dustin McGowan .40 .12
- ❑ 197 Guillermo Quiroz .40 .12
- ❑ 198 Josh Phelps .40 .12
- ❑ 199 Roy Halladay .40 .12
- ❑ 200 Vernon Wells .40 .12
- ❑ 201 Mike Gosling AU/400 RC 10.00 3.00
- ❑ 202 Ronny Cedeno AU/766 RC 8.00 2.40
- ❑ 203 Ron Belisario AU/400 RC 10.00 3.00
- ❑ 204 Justin Hampson AU/800 RC 8.00 2.40
- ❑ 205 Carlos Vasquez AU/800 RC 8.00 2.40
- ❑ 206 Linc.Holdzkom AU/800 RC 8.00 2.40
- ❑ 207 Casey Daigle AU/550 RC 10.00 3.00
- ❑ 208 Jason Bartlett AU/800 RC 10.00 3.00
- ❑ 209 Mariano Gomez AU/800 RC 8.00 2.40
- ❑ 210 Mike Rouse AU/800 RC 8.00 2.40
- ❑ 211 Chris Shelton AU/800 RC 10.00 3.00
- ❑ 212 Dennis Sarfate AU/800 RC 8.00 2.40
- ❑ 213 Shingo Takatsu AU/400 RC 40.00 12.00
- ❑ 214 Justin Leone AU/800 RC 10.00 3.00
- ❑ 215 Cory Sullivan AU/800 RC 8.00 2.40
- ❑ 216 Michael Wuertz AU/800 RC 10.00 3.00
- ❑ 217 Tim Bausher AU/800 RC 8.00 2.40
- ❑ 218 Jesse Harper AU/800 RC 8.00 2.40
- ❑ 219 Ryan Meaux AU/800 RC 8.00 2.40
- ❑ 220 Does Not Exist
- ❑ 221 Kevin Cave AU/800 RC 10.00 3.00
- ❑ 222 Does Not Exist
- ❑ 223 Does Not Exist
- ❑ 224 Does Not Exist
- ❑ 225 Does Not Exist
- ❑ 226 Abe Alvarez XRC 8.00 2.40
- ❑ 227 Carlos Hines XRC 5.00 1.50
- ❑ 228 Charles Thomas XRC 8.00 2.40
- ❑ 229 Frankie Francisco XRC 5.00 1.50
- ❑ 230 Greg Dobbs XRC 5.00 1.50
- ❑ 231 Hector Gimenez XRC 3.00 .90
- ❑ 232 Jesse Crain XRC 8.00 2.40
- ❑ 233 Joey Gathright XRC 8.00 2.40
- ❑ 234 Justin Knoedler XRC 5.00 1.50
- ❑ 235 Kazuhito Tadano XRC 8.00 2.40
- ❑ 236 Lance Cormier XRC 5.00 1.50
- ❑ 237 Scott Proctor XRC 8.00 2.40
- ❑ 238 Tim Bittner XRC 5.00 1.50
- ❑ 239 Travis Blackley XRC 8.00 2.40
- ❑ 240 Mike Johnston XRC 5.00 1.50
- ❑ 241 Yadier Molina XRC 8.00 2.40
- ❑ 242 B.J. Upton 8.00 2.40
- ❑ 243 Ben Sheets 5.00 1.50
- ❑ 244 Bobby Crosby 8.00 2.40
- ❑ 245 Brad Penny 3.00 .90
- ❑ 246 Carl Crawford 5.00 1.50
- ❑ 247 Carlos Beltran 8.00 2.40
- ❑ 248 Carlos Guillen 5.00 1.50
- ❑ 249 Carlos Zambrano 5.00 1.50
- ❑ 250 Casey Kotchman 8.00 2.40
- ❑ 251 Chase Utley 5.00 1.50
- ❑ 252 Craig Wilson 5.00 1.50
- ❑ 253 Danny Graves 3.00 .90
- ❑ 254 Danny Kolb 3.00 .90
- ❑ 255 David Wright 20.00 6.00
- ❑ 256 Eric Milton 3.00 .90
- ❑ 257 Esteban Loaiza 3.00 .90
- ❑ 258 Francisco Cordero 3.00 .90
- ❑ 259 Francisco Rodriguez 5.00 1.50
- ❑ 260 Jake Peavy 5.00 1.50
- ❑ 261 Jason Bay 5.00 1.50
- ❑ 262 Jermaine Dye 5.00 1.50
- ❑ 263 Joe Nathan 5.00 1.50
- ❑ 264 John Lackey 3.00 .90
- ❑ 265 Ken Harvey 3.00 .90
- ❑ 266 Khalil Greene 8.00 2.40
- ❑ 267 Lew Ford 5.00 1.50
- ❑ 268 Livan Hernandez 3.00 .90
- ❑ 269 Milton Bradley 5.00 1.50
- ❑ 270 Nomar Garciaparra 10.00 3.00
- ❑ 271 Orlando Cabrera Sox 8.00 2.40

Card	Nm-Mt	Ex-Mt
❑ 272 Paul Lo Duca	5.00	1.50
❑ 273 Richard Hidalgo	3.00	.90
❑ 274 Steve Finley	5.00	1.50
❑ 275 Victor Martinez	5.00	1.50

2001 Sweet Spot

	Nm-Mt	Ex-Mt
COMP.BASIC w/o SP's (60)	25.00	7.50
COMP.UPDATE w/o SP's (30)	10.00	3.00
COMMON CARD (1-60)	.40	.12
COMMON CARD (61-90)	10.00	3.00
COMMON CARD (91-120)	.60	.18
COMMON (121-150)	5.00	1.50
❑ 1 Troy Glaus	.40	.12
❑ 2 Darin Erstad	.40	.12
❑ 3 Jason Giambi	.40	.12
❑ 4 Tim Hudson	.40	.12
❑ 5 Ben Grieve	.40	.12
❑ 6 Carlos Delgado	.40	.12
❑ 7 David Wells	.40	.12
❑ 8 Greg Vaughn	.40	.12
❑ 9 Roberto Alomar	.60	.18
❑ 10 Jim Thome	1.00	.30
❑ 11 John Olerud	.40	.12
❑ 12 Edgar Martinez	.60	.18
❑ 13 Cal Ripken	3.00	.90
❑ 14 Albert Belle	.40	.12
❑ 15 Ivan Rodriguez	1.00	.30
❑ 16 Alex Rodriguez Rangers	3.00	.90
❑ 17 Pedro Martinez	1.00	.30
❑ 18 Nomar Garciaparra	1.50	.45
❑ 19 Manny Ramirez	.60	.18
❑ 20 Jermaine Dye	.40	.12
❑ 21 Juan Gonzalez	.60	.18
❑ 22 Dean Palmer	.40	.12
❑ 23 Matt Lawton	.40	.12
❑ 24 Eric Milton	.40	.12
❑ 25 Frank Thomas	1.00	.30
❑ 26 Magglio Ordonez	.40	.12
❑ 27 Derek Jeter	2.50	.75
❑ 28 Bernie Williams	.60	.18
❑ 29 Roger Clemens	2.00	.60
❑ 30 Jeff Bagwell	.60	.18
❑ 31 Richard Hidalgo	.40	.12
❑ 32 Chipper Jones	1.00	.30
❑ 33 Greg Maddux	1.50	.45
❑ 34 Richie Sexson	.40	.12
❑ 35 Jeromy Burnitz	.40	.12
❑ 36 Mark McGwire	2.50	.75
❑ 37 Jim Edmonds	.40	.12
❑ 38 Sammy Sosa	1.50	.45
❑ 39 Randy Johnson	1.00	.30
❑ 40 Steve Finley	.40	.12
❑ 41 Gary Sheffield	.40	.12
❑ 42 Shawn Green	.40	.12
❑ 43 Vladimir Guerrero	1.00	.30
❑ 44 Jose Vidro	.40	.12
❑ 45 Barry Bonds	2.50	.75
❑ 46 Jeff Kent	.40	.12
❑ 47 Preston Wilson	.40	.12
❑ 48 Luis Castillo	.40	.12
❑ 49 Mike Piazza	1.50	.45
❑ 50 Edgardo Alfonzo	.40	.12
❑ 51 Tony Gwynn	1.25	.35
❑ 52 Ryan Klesko	.40	.12
❑ 53 Scott Rolen	1.00	.30
❑ 54 Bob Abreu	.40	.12
❑ 55 Jason Kendall	.40	.12
❑ 56 Brian Giles	.40	.12
❑ 57 Ken Griffey Jr.	1.50	.45
❑ 58 Barry Larkin	.60	.18
❑ 59 Todd Helton	.60	.18
❑ 60 Mike Hampton Card back has batting header lines UER	.40	.12
❑ 61 Corey Patterson SB	10.00	3.00
❑ 62 Ichiro Suzuki SB RC	175.00	52.50
❑ 63 Jason Grilli SB	10.00	3.00
❑ 64 Brian Cole SB	10.00	3.00
❑ 65 Juan Pierre SB	10.00	3.00
❑ 66 Matt Ginter SB	10.00	3.00
❑ 67 Jimmy Rollins SB	10.00	3.00
❑ 68 Jason Smith SB RC	10.00	3.00
❑ 69 Israel Alcantara SB	10.00	3.00
❑ 70 Adam Pettyjohn SB RC	10.00	3.00
❑ 71 Luke Prokopec SB	10.00	3.00
❑ 72 Barry Zito SB	12.00	3.60
❑ 73 Keith Ginter SB	10.00	3.00
❑ 74 Sun Woo Kim SB	10.00	3.00
❑ 75 Ross Gload SB	10.00	3.00
❑ 76 Matt Wise SB	10.00	3.00
❑ 77 Aubrey Huff SB	10.00	3.00
❑ 78 Ryan Franklin SB	10.00	3.00
❑ 79 Brandon Inge SB	10.00	3.00
❑ 80 Wes Helms SB	10.00	3.00
❑ 81 Junior Spivey SB RC	12.00	3.60
❑ 82 Ryan Vogelsong SB	10.00	3.00
❑ 83 John Parrish SB	10.00	3.00
❑ 84 Joe Crede SB	10.00	3.00
❑ 85 Damian Rolls SB	10.00	3.00
❑ 86 Esix Snead SB RC	10.00	3.00
❑ 87 Rocky Biddle SB	10.00	3.00
❑ 88 Brady Clark SB	10.00	3.00
❑ 89 Timo Perez SB	10.00	3.00
❑ 90 Jay Spurgeon SB	10.00	3.00
❑ 91 Garret Anderson	.60	.18
❑ 92 Jermaine Dye	.60	.18
❑ 93 Shannon Stewart	.60	.18
❑ 94 Ben Grieve	.60	.18
❑ 95 Juan Gonzalez	1.00	.30
❑ 96 Brett Boone	.60	.18
❑ 97 Tony Batista	.60	.18
❑ 98 Rafael Palmeiro	1.00	.30
❑ 99 Carl Everett	.60	.18
❑ 100 Mike Sweeney	.60	.18
❑ 101 Tony Clark	.60	.18
❑ 102 Doug Mientkiewicz	.60	.18
❑ 103 Jose Canseco	1.50	.45
❑ 104 Mike Mussina	1.00	.30
❑ 105 Lance Berkman	.60	.18
❑ 106 Andruw Jones	.60	.18
❑ 107 Geoff Jenkins	.60	.18
❑ 108 Matt Morris	.60	.18
❑ 109 Fred McGriff	1.00	.30
❑ 110 Luis Gonzalez	.60	.18
❑ 111 Kevin Brown	.60	.18
❑ 112 Tony Armas Jr.	.60	.18
❑ 113 John Vander Wal	.60	.18
❑ 114 Cliff Floyd	.60	.18
❑ 115 Matt Lawton	.60	.18
❑ 116 Phil Nevin	.60	.18
❑ 117 Pat Burrell	.60	.18
❑ 118 Aramis Ramirez	.60	.18
❑ 119 Sean Casey	.60	.18
❑ 120 Larry Walker	1.00	.30
❑ 121 Albert Pujols SB RC	120.00	36.00
❑ 122 J.Estrada SB RC	8.00	2.40
❑ 123 Wilson Betemit SB RC	5.00	1.50
❑ 124 A.Hernandez SB RC	5.00	1.50
❑ 125 M.Ensberg SB RC	8.00	2.40
❑ 126 H.Ramirez SB RC	5.00	1.50
❑ 127 Josh Towers SB RC	5.00	1.50
❑ 128 Juan Uribe SB RC	5.00	1.50
❑ 129 Wilken Ruan SB RC	5.00	1.50
❑ 130 Andres Torres SB RC	5.00	1.50
❑ 131 B.Lawrence SB RC	5.00	1.50
❑ 132 Ryan Freel SB RC	5.00	1.50
❑ 133 B.Duckworth SB RC	5.00	1.50
❑ 134 Juan Diaz SB RC	5.00	1.50
❑ 135 Rafael Soriano SB RC	5.00	1.50
❑ 136 R.Rodriguez SB RC	5.00	1.50
❑ 137 Bud Smith SB RC	5.00	1.50
❑ 138 Mark Teixeira SB RC	40.00	12.00
❑ 139 Mark Prior SB RC	80.00	24.00
❑ 140 J.Melian SB RC	5.00	1.50
❑ 141 D.Brazelton SB RC	5.00	1.50
❑ 142 Greg Miller SB RC	5.00	1.50
❑ 143 Billy Sylvester SB RC	5.00	1.50
❑ 144 E.Guzman SB RC	5.00	1.50
❑ 145 Jack Wilson SB RC	10.00	3.00
❑ 146 Jose Mieses SB RC	5.00	1.50
❑ 147 Brandon Lyon SB RC	5.00	1.50
❑ 148 T.Shinjo SB RC	5.00	1.50
❑ 149 Juan Cruz SB RC	5.00	1.50
❑ 150 Jay Gibbons SB RC	8.00	2.40

2002 Sweet Spot

	Nm-Mt	Ex-Mt
COMP.SET w/o SP's (90)	25.00	7.50
COMMON CARD (1-90)	.40	.12
COMMON CARD (91-130)	4.00	1.20
COMMON TIER 1 AU (131-145)	15.00	4.50
COMMON TIER 2 AU (131-145)	25.00	7.50
COMMON CARD (146-175)	10.00	3.00
❑ 1 Troy Glaus	.40	.12
❑ 2 Darin Erstad	.40	.12
❑ 3 Tim Hudson	.40	.12
❑ 4 Eric Chavez	.40	.12
❑ 5 Barry Zito	.40	.12
❑ 6 Miguel Tejada	.40	.12
❑ 7 Carlos Delgado	.40	.12
❑ 8 Eric Hinske	.40	.12
❑ 9 Ben Grieve	.40	.12
❑ 10 Jim Thome	1.00	.30
❑ 11 C.C. Sabathia	.40	.12
❑ 12 Omar Vizquel	.60	.18
❑ 13 Ichiro Suzuki	1.50	.45
❑ 14 Edgar Martinez	.60	.18
❑ 15 Bret Boone	.40	.12
❑ 16 Freddy Garcia	.40	.12
❑ 17 Tony Batista	.40	.12
❑ 18 Geronimo Gil	.40	.12
❑ 19 Alex Rodriguez	1.50	.45
❑ 20 Rafael Palmeiro	.60	.18
❑ 21 Ivan Rodriguez	1.00	.30
❑ 22 Hank Blalock	1.00	.30
❑ 23 Juan Gonzalez	.60	.18
❑ 24 Nomar Garciaparra	1.50	.45
❑ 25 Pedro Martinez	1.00	.30
❑ 26 Manny Ramirez	.60	.18
❑ 27 Mike Sweeney	.40	.12
❑ 28 Carlos Beltran	.60	.18
❑ 29 Dmitri Young	.40	.12
❑ 30 Torii Hunter	.40	.12
❑ 31 Eric Milton	.40	.12
❑ 32 Corey Koskie	.40	.12
❑ 33 Frank Thomas	1.00	.30
❑ 34 Mark Buehrle	.40	.12
❑ 35 Magglio Ordonez	.40	.12
❑ 36 Roger Clemens	2.00	.60
❑ 37 Derek Jeter	2.50	.75
❑ 38 Jason Giambi	.40	.12
❑ 39 Alfonso Soriano	.60	.18
❑ 40 Bernie Williams	.60	.18
❑ 41 Jeff Bagwell	.60	.18
❑ 42 Roy Oswalt	.40	.12
❑ 43 Lance Berkman	.40	.12
❑ 44 Greg Maddux	1.50	.45
❑ 45 Chipper Jones	1.00	.30

❑ 46 Gary Sheffield .40 .12
❑ 47 Andruw Jones .40 .12
❑ 48 Richie Sexson .40 .12
❑ 49 Ben Sheets .40 .12
❑ 50 Albert Pujols 2.00 .60
❑ 51 Matt Morris .40 .12
❑ 52 J.D. Drew .40 .12
❑ 53 Sammy Sosa 1.50 .45
❑ 54 Kerry Wood 1.00 .30
❑ 55 Mark Prior 1.50 .45
❑ 56 Moises Alou .40 .12
❑ 57 Corey Patterson .40 .12
❑ 58 Randy Johnson 1.00 .30
❑ 59 Luis Gonzalez .40 .12
❑ 60 Curt Schilling .40 .12
❑ 61 Shawn Green .40 .12
❑ 62 Kevin Brown .40 .12
❑ 63 Paul Lo Duca .40 .12
❑ 64 Adrian Beltre .60 .18
❑ 65 Vladimir Guerrero 1.00 .30
❑ 66 Jose Vidro .40 .12
❑ 67 Javier Vazquez .40 .12
❑ 68 Barry Bonds 2.50 .75
❑ 69 Jeff Kent .40 .12
❑ 70 Rich Aurilia .40 .12
❑ 71 Mike Lowell .40 .12
❑ 72 Josh Beckett .40 .12
❑ 73 Brad Penny .40 .12
❑ 74 Roberto Alomar .60 .18
❑ 75 Mike Piazza 1.50 .45
❑ 76 Jeromy Burnitz .40 .12
❑ 77 Mo Vaughn .40 .12
❑ 78 Phil Nevin .40 .12
❑ 79 Sean Burroughs .40 .12
❑ 80 Jeremy Giambi .40 .12
❑ 81 Bobby Abreu .40 .12
❑ 82 Jimmy Rollins .40 .12
❑ 83 Pat Burrell .40 .12
❑ 84 Brian Giles .40 .12
❑ 85 Aramis Ramirez .40 .12
❑ 86 Ken Griffey Jr. 1.50 .45
❑ 87 Adam Dunn .60 .18
❑ 88 Austin Kearns .40 .12
❑ 89 Todd Helton .60 .18
❑ 90 Larry Walker .60 .18
❑ 91 Earl Snyder SB RC 5.00 1.50
❑ 92 Jorge Padilla SB RC 4.00 1.20
❑ 93 Felix Escalona SB RC 4.00 1.20
❑ 94 John Foster SB RC 4.00 1.20
❑ 95 Brandon Puffer SB RC 4.00 1.20
❑ 96 Steve Bechler SB RC 4.00 1.20
❑ 97 Hansel Izquierdo SB RC 4.00 1.20
❑ 98 Chris Baker SB RC 4.00 1.20
❑ 99 Jeremy Ward SB RC 4.00 1.20
❑ 100 Kevin Frederick SB RC 4.00 1.20
❑ 101 Josh Hancock SB RC 4.00 1.20
❑ 102 Allan Simpson SB RC 4.00 1.20
❑ 103 Mitch Wylie SB RC 4.00 1.20
❑ 104 Mark Corey SB RC 4.00 1.20
❑ 105 Victor Alvarez SB RC 4.00 1.20
❑ 106 Todd Donovan SB RC 4.00 1.20
❑ 107 Nelson Castro SB RC 4.00 1.20
❑ 108 Chris Booker SB RC 4.00 1.20
❑ 109 Corey Thurman SB RC 4.00 1.20
❑ 110 Kirk Saarloos SB RC 4.00 1.20
❑ 111 Michael Crudale SB RC 4.00 1.20
❑ 112 J.Simontacchi SB RC 4.00 1.20
❑ 113 Ron Calloway SB RC 4.00 1.20
❑ 114 Brandon Backe SB RC 5.00 1.50
❑ 115 Tom Shearn SB RC 4.00 1.20
❑ 116 Oliver Perez SB RC 10.00 3.00
❑ 117 Kyle Kane SB RC 4.00 1.20
❑ 118 Francis Beltran SB RC 4.00 1.20
❑ 119 So Taguchi SB RC 5.00 1.50
❑ 120 Doug Devore SB RC 4.00 1.20
❑ 121 Juan Brito SB RC 4.00 1.20
❑ 122 Cliff Bartosh SB RC 4.00 1.20
❑ 123 Eric Junge SB RC 4.00 1.20
❑ 124 Joe Orloski SB RC 4.00 1.20
❑ 125 Scotty Layfield SB RC 4.00 1.20
❑ 126 Jorge Sosa SB RC 4.00 1.20
❑ 127 Satoru Komiyama SB RC 4.00 1.20
❑ 128 Edwin Almonte SB RC 4.00 1.20
❑ 129 Takahito Nomura SB RC 4.00 1.20
❑ 130 John Ennis SB RC 4.00 1.20
❑ 131 Kazuhisa Ishii T2 AU RC 120.00 36.00
❑ 132 Ben Howard T2 AU RC 25.00 7.50
❑ 133 Aaron Cook T1 AU RC 15.00 4.50
❑ 134 Andy Machado T1 AU RC 15.00 4.50
❑ 135 Luis Ugueto T1 AU RC 15.00 4.50
❑ 136 Tyler Yates T1 AU RC 25.00 7.50
❑ 137 Rod. Rosario T1 AU RC 15.00 4.50
❑ 138 Jaime Cerda T1 AU RC 15.00 4.50
❑ 139 Luis Martinez T1 AU RC 15.00 4.50
❑ 140 Rene Reyes T1 AU RC 15.00 4.50
❑ 141 Eric Good T1 AU RC 15.00 4.50
❑ 142 Matt Thornton T2 AU RC 25.00 7.50
❑ 143 Steve Kent T1 AU RC 15.00 4.50
❑ 144 Jose Valverde T1 AU RC 25.00 7.50
❑ 145 A.Burnside T1 AU RC 15.00 4.50
❑ 146 Barry Bonds GF 25.00 7.50
❑ 147 Ken Griffey Jr. GF 15.00 4.50
❑ 148 Alex Rodriguez GF 15.00 4.50
❑ 149 Jason Giambi GF 4.00 1.20
❑ 150 Chipper Jones GF 10.00 3.00
❑ 151 Nomar Garciaparra GF 15.00 4.50
❑ 152 Mike Piazza GF 15.00 4.50
❑ 153 Sammy Sosa GF 15.00 4.50
❑ 154 Derek Jeter GF 25.00 7.50
❑ 155 Jeff Bagwell GF 10.00 3.00
❑ 156 Albert Pujols GF 20.00 6.00
❑ 157 Ichiro Suzuki GF 15.00 4.50
❑ 158 Randy Johnson GF 10.00 3.00
❑ 159 Frank Thomas GF 10.00 3.00
❑ 160 Greg Maddux GF 15.00 4.50
❑ 161 Jim Thome GF 10.00 3.00
❑ 162 Scott Rolen GF 10.00 3.00
❑ 163 Shawn Green GF 10.00 3.00
❑ 164 Vladimir Guerrero GF 10.00 3.00
❑ 165 Troy Glaus GF 10.00 3.00
❑ 166 Carlos Delgado GF 10.00 3.00
❑ 167 Luis Gonzalez GF 10.00 3.00
❑ 168 Roger Clemens GF 20.00 6.00
❑ 169 Todd Helton GF 10.00 3.00
❑ 170 Eric Chavez GF 10.00 3.00
❑ 171 Rafael Palmeiro GF 10.00 3.00
❑ 172 Pedro Martinez GF 10.00 3.00
❑ 173 Lance Berkman GF 10.00 3.00
❑ 174 Josh Beckett GF 10.00 3.00
❑ 175 Sean Burroughs GF 10.00 3.00
❑ MM Mark McGwire .00 .00
AU EXCH/100

2003 Sweet Spot

	MINT	NRMT
COMP.SET w/o SP's (100)	25.00	11.00
COMP.SET w/SP's (130)	120.00	55.00
COMMON CARD (1-130)	.50	.23
COMMON SP (1-130)	3.00	1.35
COMMON CARD (131-190)	3.00	1.35

131-190 PRINT RUN 2003 SERIAL #'d SETS
COMMON P1 (191-232) 4.00 1.80
P1 191-232 PRINT RUN 500 SERIAL #'d SETS.00
COMMON P2-P3 (191-232) 3.00 1.35
P2 191-232 PRINT RUN 1200 SERIAL #'d SETS
P3 191-232 PRINT RUN 1430 SERIAL #'d SETS

❑ 1 Darin Erstad .50 .23
❑ 2 Garret Anderson .50 .23
❑ 3 Tim Salmon .75 .35
❑ 4 Troy Glaus .50 .23
❑ 5 Luis Gonzalez .50 .23
❑ 6 Randy Johnson 1.25 .55
❑ 7 Curt Schilling .50 .23
❑ 8 Lyle Overbay .50 .23
❑ 9 Andruw Jones SP 3.00 1.35
❑ 10 Gary Sheffield SP 3.00 1.35
❑ 11 Rafael Furcal SP 3.00 1.35
❑ 12 Greg Maddux SP 6.00 2.70
❑ 13 Chipper Jones SP 4.00 1.80
❑ 14 Tony Batista .50 .23
❑ 15 Rodrigo Lopez .50 .23
❑ 16 Jay Gibbons .50 .23
❑ 17 Jason Johnson .50 .23
❑ 18 Byung-Hyun Kim SP 3.00 1.35
❑ 19 Johnny Damon SP 4.00 1.80
❑ 20 Derek Lowe SP 3.00 1.35
❑ 21 Nomar Garciaparra SP 6.00 2.70
❑ 22 Pedro Martinez SP 4.00 1.80
❑ 23 Manny Ramirez SP 4.00 1.80
❑ 24 Mark Prior 1.25 .55
❑ 25 Kerry Wood 1.25 .55
❑ 26 Corey Patterson .50 .23
❑ 27 Sammy Sosa 2.00 .90
❑ 28 Moises Alou .50 .23
❑ 29 Magglio Ordonez .50 .23
❑ 30 Frank Thomas 1.25 .55
❑ 31 Paul Konerko .50 .23
❑ 32 Roberto Alomar .75 .35
❑ 33 Adam Dunn .75 .35
❑ 34 Austin Kearns .50 .23
❑ 35 Ryan Wagner RC .75 .35
❑ 36 Ken Griffey Jr. 2.00 .90
❑ 37 Sean Casey .50 .23
❑ 38 Omar Vizquel .75 .35
❑ 39 C.C. Sabathia .50 .23
❑ 40 Jason Davis .50 .23
❑ 41 Travis Hafner .50 .23
❑ 42 Brandon Phillips .50 .23
❑ 43 Larry Walker .75 .35
❑ 44 Preston Wilson .50 .23
❑ 45 Jay Payton .50 .23
❑ 46 Todd Helton .75 .35
❑ 47 Carlos Pena .50 .23
❑ 48 Eric Munson .50 .23
❑ 49 Ivan Rodriguez 1.25 .55
❑ 50 Josh Beckett .50 .23
❑ 51 Alex Gonzalez .50 .23
❑ 52 Roy Oswalt .50 .23
❑ 53 Craig Biggio .75 .35
❑ 54 Jeff Bagwell .75 .35
❑ 55 Lance Berkman .50 .23
❑ 56 Mike Sweeney .50 .23
❑ 57 Carlos Beltran .75 .35
❑ 58 Brent Mayne .50 .23
❑ 59 Mike MacDougal .50 .23
❑ 60 Hideo Nomo 1.25 .55
❑ 61 Dave Roberts .50 .23
❑ 62 Adrian Beltre .75 .35
❑ 63 Shawn Green .50 .23
❑ 64 Kazuhisa Ishii .50 .23
❑ 65 Rickey Henderson 1.25 .55
❑ 66 Richie Sexson .50 .23
❑ 67 Torii Hunter .50 .23
❑ 68 Jacque Jones .50 .23
❑ 69 Joe Mays .50 .23
❑ 70 Corey Koskie .50 .23
❑ 71 A.J. Pierzynski .50 .23
❑ 72 Jose Vidro .50 .23
❑ 73 Vladimir Guerrero 1.25 .55
❑ 74 Tom Glavine .75 .35
❑ 75 Mike Piazza 2.00 .90
❑ 76 Jose Reyes .50 .23
❑ 77 Jae Weong Seo .50 .23
❑ 78 Jorge Posada SP 4.00 1.80
❑ 79 Mike Mussina SP 4.00 1.80
❑ 80 Robin Ventura SP 3.00 1.35
❑ 81 Mariano Rivera SP 4.00 1.80
❑ 82 Roger Clemens SP 8.00 3.60
❑ 83 Jason Giambi SP 3.00 1.35
❑ 84 Bernie Williams SP 4.00 1.80
❑ 85 Alfonso Soriano SP 4.00 1.80
❑ 86 Derek Jeter 3.00 1.35
❑ 87 Miguel Tejada .50 .23
❑ 88 Eric Chavez .50 .23
❑ 89 Tim Hudson .50 .23
❑ 90 Barry Zito .50 .23
❑ 91 Mark Mulder .50 .23
❑ 92 Erubiel Durazo .50 .23

❑ 93 Pat Burrell .50 .23
❑ 94 Jim Thome 1.25 .55
❑ 95 Bobby Abreu .50 .23
❑ 96 Brian Giles .50 .23
❑ 97 Reggie Sanders .50 .23
❑ 98 Jose Hernandez .50 .23
❑ 99 Ryan Klesko .50 .23
❑ 100 Sean Burroughs .50 .23
❑ 101 Edgardo Alfonzo SP 3.00 1.35
❑ 102 Rich Aurilia SP 3.00 1.35
❑ 103 Jose Cruz Jr. SP 3.00 1.35
❑ 104 Barry Bonds SP 10.00 4.50
❑ 105 Andres Galarraga SP 3.00 1.35
❑ 106 Mike Cameron .50 .23
❑ 107 Kazuhiro Sasaki .50 .23
❑ 108 Bret Boone .50 .23
❑ 109 Ichiro Suzuki 2.00 .90
❑ 110 John Olerud .50 .23
❑ 111 J.D. Drew SP 3.00 1.35
❑ 112 Jim Edmonds SP 3.00 1.35
❑ 113 Scott Rolen SP 4.00 1.80
❑ 114 Matt Morris SP 3.00 1.35
❑ 115 Tino Martinez SP 4.00 1.80
❑ 116 Albert Pujols SP 8.00 3.60
❑ 117 Jared Sandberg .50 .23
❑ 118 Carl Crawford .50 .23
❑ 119 Rafael Palmeiro .75 .35
❑ 120 Hank Blalock .75 .35
❑ 121 Alex Rodriguez SP 6.00 2.70
❑ 122 Kevin Mench .50 .23
❑ 123 Juan Gonzalez .75 .35
❑ 124 Mark Teixeira .50 .23
❑ 125 Shannon Stewart .50 .23
❑ 126 Vernon Wells .50 .23
❑ 127 Josh Phelps .50 .23
❑ 128 Eric Hinske .50 .23
❑ 129 Orlando Hudson .50 .23
❑ 130 Carlos Delgado .50 .23
❑ 131 Jason Shiell SB RC 3.00 1.35
❑ 132 Kevin Tolar SB RC 3.00 1.35
❑ 133 Nathan Bland SB RC 3.00 1.35
❑ 134 Brent Hoard SB RC 3.00 1.35
❑ 135 Jon Pridie SB RC 3.00 1.35
❑ 136 Mike Ryan SB RC 4.00 1.80
❑ 137 Francisco Rosario SB RC 3.00 1.35
❑ 138 Runelvys Hernandez SB 3.00 1.35
❑ 139 Guillermo Quiroz SB RC 4.00 1.80
❑ 140 Chin-Hui Tsao SB 3.00 1.35
❑ 141 Rett Johnson SB RC 4.00 1.80
❑ 142 Colin Porter SB RC 3.00 1.35
❑ 143 Jose Castillo SB 3.00 1.35
❑ 144 Chris Waters SB RC 3.00 1.35
❑ 145 Jeremy Guthrie SB 3.00 1.35
❑ 146 Pedro Liriano SB 3.00 1.35
❑ 147 Joe Borowski SB 3.00 1.35
❑ 148 Felix Sanchez SB RC 3.00 1.35
❑ 149 Todd Wellemeyer SB RC 4.00 1.80
❑ 150 Gerald Laird SB 3.00 1.35
❑ 151 Brandon Webb SB RC 5.00 2.20
❑ 152 Tommy Whiteman SB 3.00 1.35
❑ 153 Carlos Rivera SB 3.00 1.35
❑ 154 Rick Roberts SB RC 3.00 1.35
❑ 155 Terrmel Sledge SB RC 4.00 1.80
❑ 156 Jeff Duncan SB RC 4.00 1.80
❑ 157 Craig Brazell SB RC 4.00 1.80
❑ 158 Bernie Castro SB RC 3.00 1.35
❑ 159 Cory Stewart SB RC 3.00 1.35
❑ 160 Brandon Villafuerte SB 3.00 1.35
❑ 161 Tommy Phelps SB 3.00 1.35
❑ 162 Josh Hall SB RC 4.00 1.80
❑ 163 Ryan Cameron SB RC 3.00 1.35
❑ 164 Garret Atkins SB 3.00 1.35
❑ 165 Brian Stokes SB RC 3.00 1.35
❑ 166 Rafael Betancourt SB RC 4.00 1.80
❑ 167 Jaime Cerda SB 3.00 1.35
❑ 168 D.J. Carrasco SB RC 3.00 1.35
❑ 169 Ian Ferguson SB RC 3.00 1.35
❑ 170 Jorge Cordova SB RC 3.00 1.35
❑ 171 Eric Munson SB 3.00 1.35
❑ 172 Nook Logan SB RC 3.00 1.35
❑ 173 Jeremy Bonderman SB RC 4.00 1.80
❑ 174 Kyle Snyder SB 3.00 1.35
❑ 175 Rich Harden SB 4.00 1.80
❑ 176 Kevin Ohme SB RC 3.00 1.35
❑ 177 Roger Deago SB RC 3.00 1.35
❑ 178 Marlon Byrd SB 3.00 1.35
❑ 179 Dontrelle Willis SB 4.00 1.80
❑ 180 Bobby Hill SB 3.00 1.35
❑ 181 Jesse Foppert SB 3.00 1.35
❑ 182 Andrew Good SB 3.00 1.35
❑ 183 Chase Utley SB 3.00 1.35
❑ 184 Bo Hart SB RC 4.00 1.80
❑ 185 Dan Haren SB RC 4.00 1.80
❑ 186 Tim Olson SB RC 4.00 1.80
❑ 187 Joe Thurston SB 3.00 1.35
❑ 188 Jason Anderson SB 3.00 1.35
❑ 189 Jason Gilfillan SB RC 3.00 1.35
❑ 190 Rickie Weeks SB RC 10.00 4.50
❑ 191 Hideki Matsui SB P1 RC 25.00 11.00
❑ 192 J.Contreras SB P3 RC 8.00 3.60
❑ 193 Willie Eyre SB P3 RC 3.00 1.35
❑ 194 Matt Bruback SB P3 RC 3.00 1.35
❑ 195 Heath Bell SB P3 RC 3.00 1.35
❑ 196 Lew Ford SB P3 RC 8.00 3.60
❑ 197 J.Griffiths SB P3 RC 4.00 1.80
❑ 198 O.Villarreal SB P1 RC 4.00 1.80
❑ 199 Fr. Cruceta SB P3 RC 3.00 1.35
❑ 200 Fern Cabrera SB P3 RC 3.00 1.35
❑ 201 Jhonny Peralta SB P3 3.00 1.35
❑ 202 Shane Bazzell SB P3 RC 3.00 1.35
❑ 203 B.Madritsch SB P1 RC 25.00 11.00
❑ 204 Phil Seibel SB P3 RC 3.00 1.35
❑ 205 J.Willingham SB P3 RC 4.00 1.80
❑ 206 Rob Hammock SB P1 RC 5.00 2.20
❑ 207 Al. Machado SB P3 RC 3.00 1.35
❑ 208 David Sanders SB P3 RC 3.00 1.35
❑ 209 Mike Neu SB P1 RC 4.00 1.80
❑ 210 Andrew Brown SB P3 RC 4.00 1.80
❑ 211 N. Robertson SB P3 RC 10.00 4.50
❑ 212 Miguel Ojeda SB P3 RC 3.00 1.35
❑ 213 Beau Kemp SB P3 RC 3.00 1.35
❑ 214 Aaron Looper SB P3 RC 3.00 1.35
❑ 215 Alf.Gonzalez SB P3 RC 3.00 1.35
❑ 216 Rich Fischer SB P1 RC 4.00 1.80
❑ 218 Jeremy Wedel SB P3 RC 3.00 1.35
❑ 219 Pr.Redman SB P3 RC 3.00 1.35
❑ 220 Mi.Hernandez SB P3 RC 3.00 1.35
❑ 221 Rocco Baldelli SB P1 4.00 1.80
❑ 222 Luis Ayala SB P3 RC 3.00 1.35
❑ 223 Arnaldo Munoz SB P3 RC 3.00 1.35
❑ 224 Wil.Ledezma SB P3 RC 4.00 1.80
❑ 225 Chris Capuano SB P3 RC 3.00 1.35
❑ 226 Aquilino Lopez SB P3 RC 3.00 1.35
❑ 227 Joe Valentine SB P1 RC 4.00 1.80
❑ 228 Matt Kata SB P2 RC 4.00 1.80
❑ 229 D.Markwell SB P2 RC 3.00 1.35
❑ 230 Clint Barmes SB P2 RC 4.00 1.80
❑ 231 Mike Nicolas SB P1 RC 4.00 1.80
❑ 232 Jon Leicester SB P2 RC 3.00 1.35

2004 Sweet Spot

	Nm-Mt	Ex-Mt
COMP.SET w/o SP's (90)	25.00	7.50
COMMON CARD (1-90)	.50	.15
COMMON (91-170/261-262)	4.00	1.20
91-170/261-262 STATED ODDS 1:12		
COMMON CARD (171-230)	4.00	1.20
171-230 PRINT RUN 399 SERIAL #'d SETS		
COMMON CARD (231-250)	4.00	1.20
231-250 PRINT RUN 299 SERIAL #'d SETS		
COMMON CARD (251-260)	6.00	1.80
251-260 PRINT RUN 199 SERIAL #'d SETS		
171-260/Ltd 10/W99 OVERALL ODDS 1:12		

OVERALL PLATES ODDS 1:360 HOBBY
PLATES PRINT RUN 1 SET PER COLOR
BLACK-CYAN-MAGENTA-YELLOW ISSUED
NO PLATES PRICING DUE TO SCARCITY

❑ 1 Albert Pujols 2.50 .75
❑ 2 Alex Rodriguez 2.00 .60
❑ 3 Alfonso Soriano .75 .23
❑ 4 Andruw Jones .50 .15
❑ 5 Andy Pettitte .75 .23
❑ 6 Aubrey Huff .50 .15
❑ 7 Austin Kearns .50 .15
❑ 8 Barry Zito .50 .15
❑ 9 Bobby Abreu .50 .15
❑ 10 Brandon Webb .50 .15
❑ 11 Bret Boone .50 .15
❑ 12 Brian Giles .50 .15
❑ 13 C.C. Sabathia .50 .15
❑ 14 Carlos Beltran .75 .23
❑ 15 Carlos Delgado .50 .15
❑ 16 Chipper Jones 1.25 .35
❑ 17 Cliff Floyd .50 .15
❑ 18 Curt Schilling 1.25 .35
❑ 19 Delmon Young .75 .23
❑ 20 Derek Jeter 2.50 .75
❑ 21 Dontrelle Willis .50 .15
❑ 22 Edgar Martinez .75 .23
❑ 23 Edgar Renteria .50 .15
❑ 24 Eric Chavez .50 .15
❑ 25 Eric Gagne 1.25 .35
❑ 26 Frank Thomas 1.25 .35
❑ 27 Garret Anderson .50 .15
❑ 28 Gary Sheffield .50 .15
❑ 29 Geoff Jenkins .50 .15
❑ 30 Greg Maddux 2.00 .60
❑ 31 Hank Blalock .50 .15
❑ 32 Hideo Nomo 1.25 .35
❑ 33 Ichiro Suzuki 2.00 .60
❑ 34 Ivan Rodriguez 1.25 .35
❑ 35 Jacque Jones .50 .15
❑ 36 Jason Giambi .50 .15
❑ 37 Jason Schmidt .50 .15
❑ 38 Javier Vazquez .50 .15
❑ 39 Javy Lopez .50 .15
❑ 40 Jeff Bagwell .75 .23
❑ 41 Jim Edmonds .50 .15
❑ 42 Jim Thome 1.25 .35
❑ 43 Joe Mauer .75 .23
❑ 44 John Smoltz .50 .15
❑ 45 Jose Cruz Jr. .50 .15
❑ 46 Jose Reyes .50 .15
❑ 47 Jose Vidro .50 .15
❑ 48 Josh Beckett .50 .15
❑ 49 Ken Griffey Jr. 2.00 .60
❑ 50 Kerry Wood 1.25 .35
❑ 51 Kevin Brown .50 .15
❑ 52 Larry Walker .75 .23
❑ 53 Magglio Ordonez .50 .15
❑ 54 Manny Ramirez .75 .23
❑ 55 Mark Mulder .50 .15
❑ 56 Mark Prior 1.25 .35
❑ 57 Mark Teixeira .50 .15
❑ 58 Miguel Cabrera .75 .23
❑ 59 Miguel Tejada .50 .15
❑ 60 Mike Lowell .50 .15
❑ 61 Mike Mussina .75 .23
❑ 62 Mike Piazza 2.00 .60
❑ 63 Nomar Garciaparra 2.00 .60
❑ 64 Orlando Cabrera .50 .15
❑ 65 Pat Burrell .50 .15
❑ 66 Pedro Martinez 1.25 .35
❑ 67 Phil Nevin .50 .15
❑ 68 Preston Wilson .50 .15
❑ 69 Rafael Furcal .50 .15
❑ 70 Rafael Palmeiro .75 .23
❑ 71 Randy Johnson 1.25 .35
❑ 72 Craig Wilson .50 .15
❑ 73 Rich Harden .50 .15
❑ 74 Richie Sexson .50 .15
❑ 75 Rickie Weeks .50 .15
❑ 76 Rocco Baldelli .50 .15
❑ 77 Roger Clemens 2.50 .75
❑ 78 Roy Halladay .50 .15
❑ 79 Roy Oswalt .50 .15
❑ 80 Ryan Klesko .50 .15
❑ 81 Sammy Sosa 2.00 .60

❑ 82 Scott Podsednik .50 .15
❑ 83 Scott Rolen 1.25 .35
❑ 84 Shawn Green .50 .15
❑ 85 Tim Hudson .50 .15
❑ 86 Todd Helton .75 .23
❑ 87 Torii Hunter .50 .15
❑ 88 Troy Glaus .50 .15
❑ 89 Vernon Wells .50 .15
❑ 90 Vladimir Guerrero 1.25 .35
❑ 91 Aarom Baldiris SB RC 5.00 1.50
❑ 92 Akinori Otsuka SB RC 4.00 1.20
❑ 93 Andres Blanco SB RC 4.00 1.20
❑ 94 Angel Chavez SB RC 4.00 1.20
❑ 95 Brian Dallimore SB RC 4.00 1.20
❑ 96 Carlos Hines SB RC 4.00 1.20
❑ 97 Carlos Vasquez SB RC 5.00 1.50
❑ 98 Casey Daigle SB RC 4.00 1.20
❑ 99 Chad Bentz SB RC 4.00 1.20
❑ 100 Chris Aguila SB RC 4.00 1.20
❑ 101 Chris Oxspring SB RC 5.00 1.50
❑ 102 Chris Saenz SB RC 4.00 1.20
❑ 103 Chris Shelton SB RC 5.00 1.50
❑ 104 Colby Miller SB RC 4.00 1.20
❑ 105 Dave Crouthers SB RC 4.00 1.20
❑ 106 David Aardsma SB RC 4.00 1.20
❑ 107 Dennis Sarfate SB RC 4.00 1.20
❑ 108 Donnie Kelly SB RC 4.00 1.20
❑ 109 Eddy Rodriguez SB RC 5.00 1.50
❑ 110 Eduardo Villacis SB RC 4.00 1.20
❑ 111 Edwin Moreno SB RC 5.00 1.50
❑ 112 Enemencio Pacheco SB RC 4.00 1.20
❑ 113 Fernando Nieve SB RC 4.00 1.20
❑ 114 Franklyn Gracesqui SB RC 4.00 1.20
❑ 115 Freddy Guzman SB RC 4.00 1.20
❑ 116 Greg Dobbs SB RC 4.00 1.20
❑ 117 Hector Gimenez SB RC 4.00 1.20
❑ 118 Ian Snell SB RC 5.00 1.50
❑ 119 Ivan Ochoa SB RC 4.00 1.20
❑ 120 Jake Woods SB RC 4.00 1.20
❑ 121 Jamie Brown SB RC 4.00 1.20
❑ 122 Jason Bartlett SB RC 5.00 1.50
❑ 123 Jason Frasor SB RC 4.00 1.20
❑ 124 Jeff Bennett SB RC 4.00 1.20
❑ 125 Jerome Gamble SB RC 4.00 1.20
❑ 126 Jerry Gil SB RC 4.00 1.20
❑ 127 Brandon Medders SB RC 4.00 1.20
❑ 128 Ryan Meaux SB RC 4.00 1.20
❑ 129 John Gall SB RC 5.00 1.50
❑ 130 Jorge Sequea SB RC 4.00 1.20
❑ 131 Jorge Vasquez SB RC 4.00 1.20
❑ 132 Jose Capellan SB RC 8.00 2.40
❑ 133 Josh Labandeira SB RC 4.00 1.20
❑ 134 Justin Germano SB RC 4.00 1.20
❑ 135 Justin Hampson SB RC 4.00 1.20
❑ 136 Justin Huisman SB RC 4.00 1.20
❑ 137 Justin Knoedler SB RC 4.00 1.20
❑ 138 Justin Leone SB RC 5.00 1.50
❑ 139 Kazuhito Tadano SB RC 5.00 1.50
❑ 140 Kazuo Matsui SB RC 8.00 2.40
❑ 141 Kevin Cave SB RC 5.00 1.50
❑ 142 Lincoln Holdzkom SB RC 4.00 1.20
❑ 143 Lino Urdaneta SB RC 4.00 1.20
❑ 144 Luis A. Gonzalez SB RC 4.00 1.20
❑ 145 Mariano Gomez SB RC 4.00 1.20
❑ 146 Merkin Valdez SB RC 5.00 1.50
❑ 147 Michael Vento SB RC 5.00 1.50
❑ 148 Michael Wuertz SB RC 5.00 1.50
❑ 149 Mike Gosling SB RC 4.00 1.20
❑ 150 Mike Johnston SB RC 4.00 1.20
❑ 151 Mike Rouse SB RC 4.00 1.20
❑ 152 Nick Regilio SB RC 4.00 1.20
❑ 153 Onil Joseph SB RC 4.00 1.20
❑ 154 Orlando Rodriguez SB RC 4.00 1.20
❑ 155 Ramon Ramirez SB RC 4.00 1.20
❑ 156 Renyel Pinto SB RC 5.00 1.50
❑ 157 Roberto Novoa SB RC 5.00 1.50
❑ 158 Roman Colon SB RC 4.00 1.20
❑ 159 Ronald Belisario SB RC 4.00 1.20
❑ 160 Ronny Cedeno SB RC 4.00 1.20
❑ 161 Rusty Tucker SB RC 5.00 1.50
❑ 162 Ryan Wing SB RC 4.00 1.20
❑ 163 Scott Dohmann SB RC 4.00 1.20
❑ 164 Scott Proctor SB RC 5.00 1.50
❑ 165 Sean Henn SB RC 4.00 1.20
❑ 166 Shawn Camp SB RC 4.00 1.20
❑ 167 Shawn Hill SB RC 4.00 1.20
❑ 168 Shingo Takatsu SB RC 5.00 1.50
❑ 169 Tim Hamulack SB RC 4.00 1.20
❑ 170 William Bergolla SB RC 4.00 1.20
❑ 171 Adam Dunn SF 5.00 1.50
❑ 172 Albert Pujols SF 10.00 3.00
❑ 173 Alex Rodriguez SF 8.00 2.40
❑ 174 Alfonso Soriano SF 5.00 1.50
❑ 175 Andruw Jones SF 4.00 1.20
❑ 176 Bret Boone SF 4.00 1.20
❑ 177 Brian Giles SF 4.00 1.20
❑ 178 Carlos Delgado SF 4.00 1.20
❑ 179 Derrek Lee SF 4.00 1.20
❑ 180 Eric Chavez SF 4.00 1.20
❑ 181 Frank Thomas SF 5.00 1.50
❑ 182 Garret Anderson SF 4.00 1.20
❑ 183 Gary Sheffield SF 4.00 1.20
❑ 184 Hank Blalock SF 4.00 1.20
❑ 185 Jason Giambi SF 4.00 1.20
❑ 186 Javy Lopez SF 4.00 1.20
❑ 187 Jeff Bagwell SF 5.00 1.50
❑ 188 Jim Edmonds SF 4.00 1.20
❑ 189 Jim Thome SF 5.00 1.50
❑ 190 Ken Griffey Jr. SF 8.00 2.40
❑ 191 Lance Berkman SF 4.00 1.20
❑ 192 Magglio Ordonez SF 4.00 1.20
❑ 193 Manny Ramirez SF 5.00 1.50
❑ 194 Mike Lowell SF 4.00 1.20
❑ 195 Mike Piazza SF 8.00 2.40
❑ 196 Preston Wilson SF 4.00 1.20
❑ 197 Rafael Palmeiro SF 5.00 1.50
❑ 198 Richie Sexson SF 4.00 1.20
❑ 199 Sammy Sosa SF 8.00 2.40
❑ 200 Scott Rolen SF 5.00 1.50
❑ 201 Shawn Green SF 4.00 1.20
❑ 202 Todd Helton SF 5.00 1.50
❑ 203 Troy Glaus SF 4.00 1.20
❑ 204 Vernon Wells SF 4.00 1.20
❑ 205 Vladimir Guerrero SF 5.00 1.50
❑ 206 Garret Anderson 5.00 1.50
Vladimir Guerrero SL
❑ 207 Luis Gonzalez 4.00 1.20
Richie Sexson SL
❑ 208 Andruw Jones 5.00 1.50
Chipper Jones SL
❑ 209 Javy Lopez 4.00 1.20
Miguel Tejada SL
❑ 210 Manny Ramirez 5.00 1.50
David Ortiz SL
❑ 211 Derrek Lee 8.00 2.40
Sammy Sosa SL
❑ 212 Frank Thomas 5.00 1.50
Magglio Ordonez SL
❑ 213 Austin Kearns 8.00 2.40
Ken Griffey Jr. SL
❑ 214 Preston Wilson 5.00 1.50
Todd Helton SL
❑ 215 Dmitri Young 5.00 1.50
Ivan Rodriguez SL
❑ 216 Miguel Cabrera 5.00 1.50
Mike Lowell SL
❑ 217 Jeff Bagwell 5.00 1.50
Lance Berkman SL
❑ 218 Lyle Overbay 4.00 1.20
Geoff Jenkins SL
❑ 219 Adrian Beltre 5.00 1.50
Shawn Green SL
❑ 220 Jacque Jones 4.00 1.20
Torii Hunter SL
❑ 221 Jose Vidro 4.00 1.20
Nick Johnson SL
❑ 222 Kazuo Matsui 8.00 2.40
Mike Piazza SL
❑ 223 Alex Rodriguez 8.00 2.40
Jason Giambi SL
❑ 224 Eric Chavez 4.00 1.20
Jermaine Dye SL
❑ 225 Jim Thome 5.00 1.50
Pat Burrell SL
❑ 226 Brian Giles 4.00 1.20
Phil Nevin SL
❑ 227 Bret Boone 8.00 2.40
Ichiro Suzuki SL
❑ 228 Albert Pujols 10.00 3.00
Scott Rolen SL
❑ 229 Hank Blalock 4.00 1.20
Mark Teixeira SL
❑ 230 Carlos Delgado 4.00 1.20
Vernon Wells SL
❑ 231 Albert Pujols PD 10.00 3.00
❑ 232 Alex Rodriguez PD 8.00 2.40
❑ 233 Chipper Jones PD 5.00 1.50
❑ 234 Craig Biggio PD 5.00 1.50
❑ 235 Curt Schilling PD 5.00 1.50
❑ 236 Derek Jeter PD 10.00 3.00
❑ 237 Ivan Rodriguez PD 5.00 1.50
❑ 238 Jeff Bagwell PD 5.00 1.50
❑ 239 Jim Edmonds PD 4.00 1.20
❑ 240 Jim Thome PD 5.00 1.50
❑ 241 Josh Beckett PD 4.00 1.20
❑ 242 Kerry Wood PD 5.00 1.50
❑ 243 Kevin Brown PD 4.00 1.20
❑ 244 Mark Prior PD 5.00 1.50
❑ 245 Miguel Tejada PD 4.00 1.20
❑ 246 Mike Mussina PD 5.00 1.50
❑ 247 Nomar Garciaparra PD 8.00 2.40
❑ 248 Pedro Martinez PD 5.00 1.50
❑ 249 Randy Johnson PD 5.00 1.50
❑ 250 Roger Clemens PD 10.00 3.00
❑ 251 Alex Rodriguez 15.00 4.50
Derek Jeter DD
❑ 252 Alfonso Soriano 8.00 2.40
Hank Blalock DD
❑ 253 Bobby Abreu 6.00 1.80
Pat Burrell DD
❑ 254 Edgar Renteria 8.00 2.40
Scott Rolen DD
❑ 255 Garret Anderson 8.00 2.40
Vladimir Guerrero DD
❑ 256 Jeff Bagwell 8.00 2.40
Jeff Kent DD
❑ 257 Jose Reyes 10.00 3.00
Kazuo Matsui DD
❑ 258 Khalil Greene 8.00 2.40
Sean Burroughs DD
❑ 259 Marcus Giles 6.00 1.80
Rafael Furcal DD
❑ 260 Manny Ramirez 8.00 2.40
Johnny Damon DD
❑ 261 Tim Bausher SB RC 4.00 1.20
❑ 262 Tim Bittner SB RC 4.00 1.20

2003 Sweet Spot Classics

	Nm-Mt	Ex-Mt
COMP.SET w/o SP's (89)	40.00	12.00
COMMON (1-74/76-90)	.75	.23
COMMON CARD (91-120)	8.00	2.40
COMMON CARD (121-150)	5.00	1.50

❑ 1 Al Hrabosky .75 .23
❑ 2 Al Lopez .75 .23
❑ 3 Andre Dawson .75 .23
❑ 4 Bill Buckner .75 .23
❑ 5 Billy Williams .75 .23
❑ 6 Bob Feller .75 .23
❑ 7 Bob Lemon .75 .23
❑ 8 Bobby Doerr .75 .23
❑ 9 Cecil Cooper .75 .23
❑ 10 Cal Ripken 6.00 1.80
❑ 11 Carlton Fisk 1.25 .35
❑ 12 Catfish Hunter 1.25 .35
❑ 13 Chris Chambliss .75 .23
❑ 14 Dale Murphy 2.00 .60

❑ 15 Gaylord Perry .75 .23
❑ 16 Dave Kingman .75 .23
❑ 17 Dave Parker .75 .23
❑ 18 Dave Stewart .75 .23
❑ 19 David Cone .75 .23
❑ 20 Dennis Eckersley .75 .23
❑ 21 Don Baylor .75 .23
❑ 22 Don Sutton .75 .23
❑ 23 Duke Snider 1.25 .35
❑ 24 Dwight Evans .75 .23
❑ 25 Dwight Gooden .75 .23
❑ 26 Earl Weaver MG .75 .23
❑ 27 Early Wynn .75 .23
❑ 28 Eddie Mathews 2.00 .60
❑ 29 Enos Slaughter .75 .23
❑ 30 Ernie Banks 2.00 .60
❑ 31 Fred Lynn .75 .23
❑ 32 Fred Stanley .75 .23
❑ 33 Gary Carter .75 .23
❑ 34 George Foster .75 .23
❑ 35 Hal Newhouser .75 .23
❑ 36 George Kell .75 .23
❑ 37 Harmon Killebrew 2.00 .60
❑ 38 Hoyt Wilhelm .75 .23
❑ 39 Jack Morris .75 .23
❑ 40 Jim Bunning .75 .23
❑ 41 Jim Gilliam .75 .23
❑ 42 Jim Leyritz .75 .23
❑ 43 Jimmy Key .75 .23
❑ 44 Joe Carter .75 .23
❑ 45 Joe Morgan .75 .23
❑ 46 John Montefusco .75 .23
❑ 47 Johnny Bench 2.00 .60
❑ 48 Johnny Podres .75 .23
❑ 49 Jose Canseco 2.00 .60
❑ 50 Juan Marichal .75 .23
❑ 51 Keith Hernandez .75 .23
❑ 52 Ken Griffey Sr. .75 .23
❑ 53 Kirby Puckett 2.00 .60
❑ 54 Kirk Gibson .75 .23
❑ 55 Larry Doby .75 .23
❑ 56 Lee May .75 .23
❑ 57 Lee Mazzilli .75 .23
❑ 58 Lou Boudreau .75 .23
❑ 59 Mark McGwire 5.00 1.50
❑ 60 Maury Wills .75 .23
❑ 61 Mike Pagliarulo .75 .23
❑ 62 Monte Irvin .75 .23
❑ 63 Nolan Ryan 5.00 1.50
❑ 64 Orlando Cepeda .75 .23
❑ 65 Ozzie Smith 3.00 .90
❑ 66 Paul O'Neill 1.25 .35
❑ 67 Pee Wee Reese 1.25 .35
❑ 68 Phil Niekro .75 .23
❑ 69 Ralph Kiner .75 .23
❑ 70 Red Schoendienst .75 .23
❑ 71 Richie Ashburn 1.25 .35
❑ 72 Rick Ferrell .75 .23
❑ 73 Robin Roberts .75 .23
❑ 74 Robin Yount 3.00 .90
❑ 75 Hideki Matsui/1999 XRC 10.00 3.00
❑ 75B Rod Carew ERR .00
Not Intended for Public Release
❑ 76 Rollie Fingers .75 .23
❑ 77 Ron Cey .75 .23
❑ 78 Tom Seaver 1.25 .35
❑ 79 Sparky Anderson MG .75 .23
❑ 80 Stan Musial 3.00 .90
❑ 81 Steve Garvey .75 .23
❑ 82 Ted Williams 4.00 1.20
❑ 83 Tommy Lasorda .75 .23
❑ 84 Tony Gwynn 2.50 .75
❑ 85 Tony Perez .75 .23
❑ 86 Vida Blue .75 .23
❑ 87 Warren Spahn 1.25 .35
❑ 88 Bob Gibson 1.25 .35
❑ 89 Willie McCovey .75 .23
❑ 90 Willie Stargell 1.25 .35
❑ 91 Ted Williams TB 8.00 2.40
❑ 92 Ted Williams TB 8.00 2.40
❑ 93 Ted Williams TB 8.00 2.40
❑ 94 Ted Williams TB 8.00 2.40
❑ 95 Ted Williams TB 8.00 2.40
❑ 96 Ted Williams TB 8.00 2.40
❑ 97 Ted Williams TB 8.00 2.40
❑ 98 Ted Williams TB 8.00 2.40
❑ 99 Ted Williams TB 8.00 2.40
❑ 100 Ted Williams TB 8.00 2.40
❑ 101 Ted Williams TB 8.00 2.40
❑ 102 Ted Williams TB 8.00 2.40
❑ 103 Ted Williams TB 8.00 2.40
❑ 104 Ted Williams TB 8.00 2.40
❑ 105 Ted Williams TB 8.00 2.40
❑ 106 Ted Williams TB 8.00 2.40
❑ 107 Ted Williams TB 8.00 2.40
❑ 108 Ted Williams TB 8.00 2.40
❑ 109 Ted Williams TB 8.00 2.40
❑ 110 Ted Williams TB 8.00 2.40
❑ 111 Ted Williams TB 8.00 2.40
❑ 112 Ted Williams TB 8.00 2.40
❑ 113 Ted Williams TB 8.00 2.40
❑ 114 Ted Williams TB 8.00 2.40
❑ 115 Ted Williams TB 8.00 2.40
❑ 116 Ted Williams TB 8.00 2.40
❑ 117 Ted Williams TB 8.00 2.40
❑ 118 Ted Williams TB 8.00 2.40
❑ 119 Ted Williams TB 8.00 2.40
❑ 120 Ted Williams TB 8.00 2.40
❑ 121 Babe Ruth YH 15.00 4.50
❑ 122 Bucky Dent YH 5.00 1.50
❑ 123 Casey Stengel YH 5.00 1.50
❑ 124 Dave Righetti YH 5.00 1.50
❑ 125 Dave Winfield YH 5.00 1.50
❑ 126 Dick Tidrow YH 5.00 1.50
❑ 127 Dock Ellis YH 5.00 1.50
❑ 128 Don Mattingly YH 15.00 4.50
❑ 129 Hank Bauer YH 5.00 1.50
❑ 130 Jim Bouton YH 5.00 1.50
❑ 131 Jim Kaat YH 5.00 1.50
❑ 132 Joe DiMaggio YH 10.00 3.00
❑ 133 Joe Torre YH 8.00 2.40
❑ 134 Lou Piniella YH 5.00 1.50
❑ 135 Mel Stottlemyre YH 5.00 1.50
❑ 136 Mickey Mantle YH 20.00 6.00
❑ 137 Mickey Rivers YH 5.00 1.50
❑ 138 Phil Rizzuto YH 5.00 1.50
❑ 139 Ralph Branca YH 5.00 1.50
❑ 140 Ralph Houk YH 5.00 1.50
❑ 141 Roger Maris YH 8.00 2.40
❑ 142 Ron Guidry YH 5.00 1.50
❑ 143 Ruben Amaro Sr. YH 5.00 1.50
❑ 144 Sparky Lyle YH 5.00 1.50
❑ 145 Thurman Munson YH 8.00 2.40
❑ 146 Tommy Henrich YH 5.00 1.50
❑ 147 Tommy John YH 5.00 1.50
❑ 148 Tony Kubek YH 5.00 1.50
❑ 149 Whitey Ford YH 5.00 1.50
❑ 150 Yogi Berra YH 8.00 2.40

2004 Sweet Spot Classic

	Nm-Mt	Ex-Mt
COMP.SET w/o SP'S (90)	40.00	12.00
COMMON CARD (1-90)	.75	.23
COMMON CARD (91-161)	5.00	1.50
91-161 STATED ODDS 1:3	.00	

❑ 1 Al Kaline 2.00 .60
❑ 2 Andre Dawson .75 .23
❑ 3 Bert Blyleven .75 .23
❑ 4 Bill Dickey 1.25 .35
❑ 5 Bill Mazeroski 1.25 .35
❑ 6 Billy Martin 1.25 .35
❑ 7 Bob Feller .75 .23
❑ 8 Bob Gibson 1.25 .35
❑ 9 Bob Lemon .75 .23
❑ 10 George Kell .75 .23
❑ 11 Bobby Doerr .75 .23
❑ 12 Brooks Robinson 1.25 .35
❑ 13 Cal Ripken 6.00 1.80
❑ 14 Carl Hubbell 1.25 .35
❑ 15 Carl Yastrzemski 3.00 .90
❑ 16 Charlie Keller .75 .23
❑ 17 Chuck Dressen .75 .23
❑ 18 Cy Young 2.00 .60
❑ 19 Dave Winfield .75 .23
❑ 20 Dizzy Dean 1.25 .35
❑ 21 Don Drysdale 2.00 .60
❑ 22 Don Larsen .75 .23
❑ 23 Don Mattingly 5.00 1.50
❑ 24 Don Newcombe .75 .23
❑ 25 Duke Snider 1.25 .35
❑ 26 Early Wynn .75 .23
❑ 27 Eddie Mathews 2.00 .60
❑ 28 Elston Howard .75 .23
❑ 29 Frank Robinson .75 .23
❑ 30 Gary Carter .75 .23
❑ 31 Gil Hodges 1.25 .35
❑ 32 Gil McDougald 1.25 .35
❑ 33 Hank Greenberg 2.00 .60
❑ 34 Harmon Killebrew 2.00 .60
❑ 35 Harry Caray .75 .23
❑ 36 Honus Wagner 2.00 .60
❑ 37 Hoyt Wilhelm .75 .23
❑ 38 Jackie Robinson 2.00 .60
❑ 39 Jim Bunning .75 .23
❑ 40 Jim Palmer .75 .23
❑ 41 Jimmie Foxx 2.00 .60
❑ 42 Jimmy Wynn .75 .23
❑ 43 Joe DiMaggio 4.00 1.20
❑ 44 Joe Torre 1.25 .35
❑ 45 Johnny Mize .75 .23
❑ 46 Juan Marichal .75 .23
❑ 47 Larry Doby .75 .23
❑ 48 Lefty Gomez 1.25 .35
❑ 49 Lefty Grove 1.25 .35
❑ 50 Leo Durocher .75 .23
❑ 51 Lou Boudreau .75 .23
❑ 52 Lou Brock 1.25 .35
❑ 53 Lou Gehrig 4.00 1.20
❑ 54 Luis Aparicio .75 .23
❑ 55 Maury Wills .75 .23
❑ 56 Mel Allen .75 .23
❑ 57 Mel Ott 2.00 .60
❑ 58 Mickey Cochrane .75 .23
❑ 59 Mickey Mantle 8.00 2.40
❑ 60 Mike Schmidt 4.00 1.20
❑ 61 Monte Irvin .75 .23
❑ 62 Nolan Ryan 5.00 1.50
❑ 63 Pee Wee Reese 1.25 .35
❑ 64 Phil Rizzuto 1.25 .35
❑ 65 Ralph Kiner .75 .23
❑ 66 Richie Ashburn 1.25 .35
❑ 67 Rick Ferrell .75 .23
❑ 68 Roberto Clemente 5.00 1.50
❑ 69 Robin Roberts .75 .23
❑ 70 Robin Yount 3.00 .90
❑ 71 Rogers Hornsby 2.00 .60
❑ 72 Rollie Fingers .75 .23
❑ 73 Roy Campanella 2.00 .60
❑ 74 Ryne Sandberg 4.00 1.20
❑ 75 Tony Gwynn 2.50 .75
❑ 76 Satchel Paige 2.00 .60
❑ 77 Shoeless Joe Jackson 3.00 .90
❑ 78 Stan Musial 3.00 .90
❑ 79 Ted Williams 4.00 1.20
❑ 80 Thurman Munson 2.00 .60
❑ 81 Tom Seaver 1.25 .35
❑ 82 Tommy Henrich .75 .23
❑ 83 Tony Perez .75 .23
❑ 84 Tris Speaker 1.25 .35
❑ 85 Vida Blue .75 .23
❑ 86 Wade Boggs 1.25 .35
❑ 87 Walter Johnson 2.00 .60
❑ 88 Warren Spahn 1.25 .35
❑ 89 Whitey Ford 1.25 .35
❑ 90 Willie McCovey .75 .23
❑ 91 Andre Dawson FF/1987 5.00 1.50
❑ 92 Andre Dawson FF/1990 5.00 1.50
❑ 93 Ernie Banks FF/1958 8.00 2.40

❑ 94 Bob Lemon FF/1948	5.00	1.50
❑ 95 Cal Ripken FF/1982	15.00	4.50
❑ 96 Cal Ripken FF/1995	15.00	4.50
❑ 97 Carl Yastrzemski FF/1979	8.00	2.40
❑ 98 Carlton Fisk FF/1972	8.00	2.40
❑ 99 Cy Young FF/1910	8.00	2.40
❑ 100 Don Larsen FF/1956	5.00	1.50
❑ 101 Don Newcombe FF/1949	5.00	1.50
❑ 102 Don Newcombe FF/1956	5.00	1.50
❑ 103 Dwight Evans FF/1986	8.00	2.40
❑ 104 Elston Howard FF/1955	5.00	1.50
❑ 105 Frank Robinson FF/1956	5.00	1.50
❑ 106 Frank Robinson FF/1966	5.00	1.50
❑ 107 Frank Robinson FF/1973	5.00	1.50
❑ 108 Gil McDougald FF/1951	8.00	2.40
❑ 109 Hank Greenberg FF/1941	8.00	2.40
❑ 110 Harmon Killebrew FF/1964	8.00	2.40
❑ 111 Hoyt Wilhelm FF/1952	5.00	1.50
❑ 112 Hoyt Wilhelm FF/1958	5.00	1.50
❑ 113 Jackie Robinson FF/1946	8.00	2.40
❑ 114 J.Robinson FF Black/1947	8.00	2.40
❑ 115 J.Robinson FF ROY/1947	8.00	2.40
❑ 116 Jackie Robinson FF/1997	8.00	2.40
❑ 117 Jim Bunning FF/1964	5.00	1.50
❑ 118 J.DiMaggio FF Bench/1950	10.00	3.00
❑ 119 Joe Morgan FF/1976	5.00	1.50
❑ 120 Johnny Mize FF/1939	5.00	1.50
❑ 121 Johnny Mize FF/1947	5.00	1.50
❑ 122 Juan Marichal FF/1968	5.00	1.50
❑ 123 Ken Griffey Sr. FF/1990	5.00	1.50
❑ 124 Larry Doby FF/1947	5.00	1.50
❑ 125 Lefty Gomez FF/1933	8.00	2.40
❑ 126 Lou Boudreau FF/1946	5.00	1.50
❑ 127 Lou Gehrig FF Lineup/1939	10.00	3.00
❑ 128 Lou Gehrig FF Number/1939	10.00	3.00
❑ 129 Mark McGwire FF/1989	12.00	3.60
❑ 130 Mark McGwire FF/1998	12.00	3.60
❑ 131 Maury Wills FF/1962	5.00	1.50
❑ 132 Mel Ott FF/1946	8.00	2.40
❑ 133 Mike Schmidt FF/1980	10.00	3.00
❑ 134 Nolan Ryan FF/1973	12.00	3.60
❑ 135 Nolan Ryan FF/1989	12.00	3.60
❑ 136 Pee Wee Reese FF/1955	8.00	2.40
❑ 137 Nolan Ryan FF/1979	12.00	3.60
❑ 138 Richie Ashburn FF/1962	8.00	2.40
❑ 139 Roberto Clemente FF/1971	12.00	3.60
❑ 140 Roberto Clemente FF/1973	12.00	3.60
❑ 141 Robin Roberts FF/1956	5.00	1.50
❑ 142 Robin Yount FF/1982	8.00	2.40
❑ 143 Does Not Exist	.00	
❑ 144 Rollie Fingers FF/1975	5.00	1.50
❑ 145 Rollie Fingers FF/1981	5.00	1.50
❑ 146 Roy Campanella FF/1953	8.00	2.40
❑ 147 Ryne Sandberg FF/1990	10.00	3.00
❑ 148 Does Not Exist	.00	
❑ 149 Satchel Paige FF/1948	8.00	2.40
❑ 150 Stan Musial FF/1952	8.00	2.40
❑ 151 Stan Musial FF/1954	8.00	2.40
❑ 152 Stan Musial FF/1963	8.00	2.40
❑ 153 Ted Williams FF/1947	10.00	3.00
❑ 154 Ted Williams FF/1957	10.00	3.00
❑ 155 Tom Seaver FF/1970	8.00	2.40
❑ 156 Tom Seaver FF/1975	8.00	2.40
❑ 157 Wade Boggs FF/1999	8.00	2.40
❑ 158 Warren Spahn FF/1957	8.00	2.40
❑ 159 Warren Spahn FF/1958	8.00	2.40
❑ 160 Joe DiMaggio FF AS/1950	10.00	3.00
❑ 161 Yogi Berra FF/1947	8.00	2.40

1911 T205

	Ex-Mt	VG
COMPLETE SET (218)	35000.00	17500.00
COMMON (1-186)	100.00	50.00
COMMON (187-198)	200.00	100.00
❑ 1 Ed Abbaticchio	100.00	50.00
❑ 2 Red Ames	100.00	50.00
❑ 3 Jimmy Archer	100.00	50.00
❑ 4 Jimmy Austin	100.00	50.00
❑ 5 Bill Bailey	100.00	50.00
❑ 6 Frank "Homerun" Baker	400.00	200.00
❑ 7 Neal Ball	100.00	50.00
❑ 8A Cy Barger	100.00	50.00
(Full B)		
❑ 8B Cy Barger	300.00	150.00
Part B		
❑ 9 Jack Barry	100.00	50.00
❑ 10 Johnny Bates	100.00	50.00
❑ 11 Fred Beck	100.00	50.00
❑ 12 Beals Becker	100.00	50.00
❑ 13 George Bell	100.00	50.00
❑ 14 Chief Bender	250.00	125.00
❑ 15 Bill Bergen	100.00	50.00
❑ 16 Bob Bescher	100.00	50.00
❑ 17 Joe Birmingham	100.00	50.00
❑ 18 Russ Blackburne	100.00	50.00
❑ 19 Kitty Bransfield	100.00	50.00
❑ 20A Roger Bresnahan	250.00	125.00
(Mouth closed)		
❑ 20B Roger Bresnahan	400.00	200.00
(Mouth open)		
❑ 21 Al Bridwell	100.00	50.00
❑ 22 Mordecai Brown	400.00	200.00
❑ 23 Bobby Byrne	100.00	50.00
❑ 24 Howie Camnitz	100.00	50.00
❑ 25 Bill Carrigan	100.00	50.00
❑ 26 Frank Chance	300.00	150.00
❑ 27A Hal Chase	300.00	150.00
(Chase only)		
❑ 27B Hal Chase	150.00	75.00
(Hal Chase)		
❑ 28 Eddie Cicotte	200.00	100.00
❑ 29 Fred Clarke	400.00	200.00
❑ 30 Ty Cobb	5000.00	2500.00
❑ 31A Edward T. Collins	300.00	150.00
(Mouth closed)		
❑ 31B Edward T. Collins	500.00	250.00
(Mouth open)		
❑ 32 Frank Corridon	100.00	50.00
❑ 33A Otis Crandall	100.00	50.00
T Crossed in name		
❑ 33B Otis Crandall	100.00	50.00
T Not Crossed in Name		
❑ 34 Lou Criger	100.00	50.00
❑ 35 Bill Dahlen	150.00	75.00
❑ 36 Jake Daubert	100.00	50.00
❑ 37 Jim Delahanty	100.00	50.00
❑ 38 Art Devlin	100.00	50.00
❑ 39 Josh Devore	100.00	50.00
❑ 40 Walt Dickson	100.00	50.00
❑ 41 Jiggs Donahue UER	150.00	75.00
(Misspelled Donohue on card)		
❑ 42 Red Dooin	100.00	50.00
❑ 43 Mickey Doolan	100.00	50.00
❑ 44A Patsy Dougherty	150.00	75.00
(White stocking)		
❑ 44B Patsy Dougherty	100.00	50.00
(Red stocking)		
❑ 45 Tom Downey	100.00	50.00
❑ 46 Larry Doyle	100.00	50.00
❑ 47 Hugh Duffy	300.00	150.00
❑ 48 Jimmy Dygert	100.00	50.00
❑ 49 Dick Egan	100.00	50.00
❑ 50 Kid Elberfeld	100.00	50.00
❑ 51 Clyde Engle	100.00	50.00
❑ 52 Steve Evans	100.00	50.00
❑ 53 Johnny Evers	250.00	125.00
❑ 54 Bob Ewing	100.00	50.00
❑ 55 George Ferguson	100.00	50.00
❑ 56 Ray Fisher	150.00	75.00
❑ 57 Art Fletcher	100.00	50.00
❑ 58 John Flynn	100.00	50.00
❑ 59A Russell Ford	100.00	50.00
(Dark cap)		
❑ 59B Russell Ford	150.00	75.00
(Light cap)		
❑ 60 Bill Foxen	100.00	50.00
❑ 61 Art Fromme	100.00	50.00
❑ 62 Earl Gardner	100.00	50.00
❑ 63 Harry Gaspar	100.00	50.00
❑ 64 George Gibson	100.00	50.00
❑ 65 Wilbur Good	100.00	50.00
❑ 66A George F. Graham	100.00	50.00
(Boston Rustlers)		
❑ 66B George F. Graham	400.00	200.00
(Chicago Cubs)		
❑ 67 Eddie Grant	150.00	75.00
❑ 68A Dolly Gray	100.00	50.00
No stats on back		
❑ 68B Dolly Gray	400.00	200.00
Stats on Back		
❑ 69 Clark Griffith	300.00	150.00
❑ 70 Bob Groom	100.00	50.00
❑ 71A Robert Harmon	100.00	50.00
(Both ears)		
❑ 71B Robert Harmon	300.00	150.00
(Left ear only)		
❑ 72 Topsy Hartsel	100.00	50.00
❑ 73 Arnold Hauser	100.00	50.00
❑ 74 Charlie Hemphill	100.00	50.00
❑ 75 Buck Herzog	100.00	50.00
❑ 76A Dick Hoblitzell	10000.00	5000.00
No Stats		
❑ 76B Dick Hoblitzell	100.00	50.00
No CIN after second 1908		
❑ 76C Dick Hoblitzell	150.00	75.00
CIN after second 1908		
❑ 76D Dick Hoblitzell	100.00	50.00
sic.Hoblitzel		
❑ 77 Danny Hoffman	100.00	50.00
❑ 78 Miller Huggins	400.00	200.00
❑ 79 John Hummell	100.00	50.00
❑ 80 Fred Jacklitsch	100.00	50.00
❑ 81 Hughie Jennings	300.00	150.00
❑ 82 Walter Johnson	2000.00	1000.00
❑ 83 Davy Jones	100.00	50.00
❑ 84 Tom Jones	100.00	50.00
❑ 85 Addie Joss	700.00	350.00
❑ 86 Ed Karger	150.00	75.00
❑ 87 Ed Killian	100.00	50.00
❑ 88 Red Kleinow	150.00	75.00
❑ 89 John Kling	100.00	50.00
❑ 90 John Knight	100.00	50.00
❑ 91 Ed Konetchy	100.00	50.00
❑ 92 Harry Krause	100.00	50.00
❑ 93 Rube Kroh	100.00	50.00
❑ 94 Frank Lang	100.00	50.00
❑ 95 Frank LaPorte	100.00	50.00
❑ 96A Arlie Latham	100.00	50.00
Back says W.A. Latham		
❑ 96B Arlie Latham	100.00	50.00
A. Latham on back		
❑ 97 Tommy Leach	100.00	50.00
❑ 98 Sam Leever	100.00	50.00
❑ 99A Lefty Leifield	100.00	50.00
A.Leifield on front		
❑ 99B Lefty Leifield	100.00	50.00
A.P.Leifield on front		
❑ 100 Ed Lennox	100.00	50.00
❑ 101 Paddy Livingston	100.00	50.00
❑ 102 Hans Lobert	100.00	50.00
❑ 103 Bris Lord	100.00	50.00
❑ 104 Harry Lord	100.00	50.00
❑ 105 John Lush	100.00	50.00
❑ 106 Nick Maddox	100.00	50.00
❑ 107 Sherry Magee	100.00	50.00
❑ 108 Rube Marquard	400.00	200.00
❑ 109 Christy Mathewson	2000.00	1000.00
❑ 110 Al Mattern	100.00	50.00
❑ 111 George McBride	100.00	50.00
❑ 112 Amby McConnell	100.00	50.00
❑ 113 Pryor McElveen	100.00	50.00
❑ 114 John McGraw MG	400.00	200.00
❑ 115 Harry McIntire	100.00	50.00
❑ 116 Matty McIntyre	100.00	50.00
❑ 117 Larry McLean	100.00	50.00
❑ 118 Fred Merkle	100.00	50.00
❑ 119 Chief Meyers	100.00	50.00
❑ 120 Clyde Milan	100.00	50.00
❑ 121 Dots Miller	100.00	50.00
❑ 122 Mike Mitchell	100.00	50.00

❑ 123A	Pat Moran	300.00	150.00
	Extra Stat Line on Card		
❑ 123B	Pat Moran	100.00	50.00
❑ 124	George Moriarity	100.00	50.00
❑ 125	George Mullin	100.00	50.00
❑ 126	Danny Murphy	100.00	50.00
❑ 127	Red Murray	100.00	50.00
❑ 128	Tom Needham	100.00	50.00
❑ 129	Rebel Oakes	100.00	50.00
❑ 130	Rube Oldring	100.00	50.00
❑ 131	Charley O'Leary	100.00	50.00
❑ 132	Fred Olmstead	100.00	50.00
❑ 133	Orval Overall	100.00	50.00
❑ 134	Freddy Parent	100.00	50.00
❑ 135	Dode Paskert	100.00	50.00
❑ 136	Fred Payne	100.00	50.00
❑ 137	Barney Pelty	100.00	50.00
❑ 138	Jack Pfiester	100.00	50.00
❑ 139	Ed Phelps	100.00	50.00
❑ 140	Decon Phillippe	100.00	50.00
❑ 141	Jack Quinn	100.00	50.00
❑ 142	Bugs Raymond	150.00	75.00
❑ 143	Ed Reulbach	100.00	50.00
❑ 144	Lewis Richie	100.00	50.00
❑ 145	Jack Rowan	150.00	75.00
❑ 146	Nap Rucker	100.00	50.00
❑ 147	Doc Scanlan	150.00	75.00
❑ 148	Germany Schaefer	100.00	50.00
❑ 149	Admiral Schlei	100.00	50.00
❑ 150	Boss Schmidt	100.00	50.00
❑ 151	Wildfire Schulte	100.00	50.00
❑ 152	Jim Scott	100.00	50.00
❑ 153	Bayard Sharpe	100.00	50.00
❑ 154A	David Shean	100.00	50.00
	(Boston Rustlers)		
❑ 154B	David Shean	400.00	200.00
	(Chicago Cubs)		
❑ 155	Jimmy Sheckard	100.00	50.00
❑ 156	Hack Simmons	100.00	50.00
❑ 157	Tony Smith	100.00	50.00
❑ 158	Fred Snodgrass	100.00	50.00
❑ 159	Tris Speaker	1000.00	500.00
❑ 160	Jake Stahl	100.00	50.00
❑ 161	Oscar Stanage	100.00	50.00
❑ 162	Harry Steinfeldt	100.00	50.00
❑ 163	George Stone	100.00	50.00
❑ 164	George Stovall	100.00	50.00
❑ 165	Gabby Street	100.00	50.00
❑ 166	George Suggs	150.00	75.00
❑ 167	Ed Summers	100.00	50.00
❑ 168	Jeff Sweeney	150.00	75.00
❑ 169	Lee Tannehill	100.00	50.00
❑ 170	Ira Thomas	100.00	50.00
❑ 171	Joe Tinker	600.00	300.00
❑ 172	John Titus	100.00	50.00
❑ 173	Terry Turner	300.00	150.00
❑ 174	Hippo Vaughn	150.00	75.00
❑ 175	Heinie Wagner	150.00	75.00
❑ 176A	Bobby Wallace	250.00	125.00
	(With cap)		
❑ 176B	Bobby Wallace	500.00	250.00
	(Without cap)		
❑ 176C	Bobby Wallace	300.00	150.00
	no cap 2/1910		
❑ 177	Ed Walsh	500.00	250.00
❑ 178	Zach Wheat	300.00	150.00
❑ 179	Doc White	100.00	50.00
❑ 180	Kirby White	150.00	75.00
❑ 181	Kaiser Wilhelm	150.00	75.00
❑ 182	Ed Willett	100.00	50.00
❑ 183A	Hooks Wiltse	100.00	50.00
	(Both ears)		
❑ 183B	Hooks Wiltse	300.00	150.00
	(Right ear only)		
❑ 184	Owen Wilson	100.00	50.00
❑ 185	Harry Wolter	100.00	50.00
❑ 186	Cy Young	2000.00	1000.00
❑ 187	Dr.Merle T. Adkins:	200.00	100.00
	Baltimore		
❑ 188	Jack Dunn	250.00	125.00
❑ 189	George Merritt	200.00	100.00
❑ 190	Charles Hanford	200.00	100.00
❑ 191	Hick Cady	200.00	100.00
❑ 192	James Frick	200.00	100.00
❑ 193	Wyatt Lee	200.00	100.00
❑ 194	Lewis McAllister	200.00	100.00
❑ 195	John Nee	200.00	100.00
❑ 196	Jimmy Collins	500.00	250.00
❑ 197	James Phelan	200.00	100.00
❑ 198	Emil Batch	200.00	100.00

1909 T206

		Ex-Mt	VG
COMPLETE SET (520)		55000.00	27500.00
COMMON (1-389)		60.00	30.00
COMMON (390-475)		50.00	25.00
COMMON (476-523)		125.00	60.00
❑ 1	Ed Abbaticchio:	60.00	30.00
	Pitt		
	Batting follow thru		
❑ 2	Ed Abbaticchio:	75.00	38.00
	Pitt.		
	Batting waiting pitch		
❑ 3	Bill Abstein	60.00	30.00
❑ 4	Whitey Alperman	75.00	38.00
❑ 5	Red Ames: N.Y. NL	75.00	38.00
	Portrait		
❑ 6	Red Ames: N.Y. NL	60.00	30.00
	Hands over head		
❑ 7	Red Ames: N.Y. NL	75.00	38.00
	Hands in front of chest		
❑ 8	Frank Arellanes	60.00	30.00
❑ 9	Jake Atz	60.00	30.00
❑ 10	Frank Baker	400.00	150.00
❑ 11	Neal Ball: N.Y. AL	75.00	38.00
❑ 12	Neal Ball: Cleveland	60.00	30.00
❑ 13	Jap Barbeau	60.00	30.00
❑ 14	Jack Barry	60.00	30.00
❑ 15	Johnny Bates	75.00	38.00
❑ 16	Ginger Beaumont	75.00	38.00
❑ 17	Fred Beck	60.00	30.00
❑ 18	Beals Becker	60.00	30.00
❑ 19	George Bell:	60.00	30.00
	Brooklyn		
	pitching follow thru		
❑ 20	George Bell:	75.00	38.00
	Brooklyn		
	Hands		
	over head		
❑ 21	Chief Bender	500.00	200.00
	Phila. AL		
	Portrait		
❑ 22	Chief Bender	500.00	250.00
	Phila. AL		
	pitching, trees		
❑ 23	Chief Bender	400.00	200.00
	Phila AL		
	pitching, no trees		
❑ 24	Bill Bergen:	60.00	30.00
	Brooklyn		
	Catching		
❑ 25	Bill Bergen:	75.00	38.00
	Brooklyn		
	Batting		
❑ 26	Heinie Berger	60.00	30.00
❑ 27	Bob Bescher: Cinc.	60.00	30.00
	Catching fly ball		
❑ 28	Bob Bescher: Cinc.	60.00	30.00
	Portrait		
❑ 29	Joe Birmingham	75.00	38.00
❑ 30	Jack Bliss	60.00	30.00
❑ 31	Frank Bowerman	75.00	38.00
❑ 32	Bill Bradley:	75.00	38.00
	Cleveland		
	Portrait		
❑ 33	Bill Bradley:	60.00	30.00
	Cleveland		
	Batting		
❑ 34	Kitty Bransfield	75.00	38.00
❑ 35	Roger Bresnahan:	300.00	125.00
	St.L. NL		
	Portrait		
❑ 36	Roger Bresnahan:	300.00	100.00
	St.L. NL		
	Batting		
❑ 37	Al Bridwell	75.00	38.00
	N.Y. NL		
	Portrait		
❑ 38	Al Bridwell	60.00	30.00
	N.Y. NL		
	Wearing sweater		
❑ 39	George Brown:	125.00	60.00
	Chicago NL		
	Sic, Browne		
❑ 40	George Brown:	400.00	200.00
	Washington		
	Sic, Browne		
❑ 41	Mordecai Brown:	500.00	250.00
	Chicago NL		
	Portrait		
❑ 42	Mordecai Brown:	500.00	250.00
	Chicago NL		
	Chicago down front of shirt		
❑ 43	Mordecai Brown:	500.00	250.00
	Chicago NL		
	Cubs Shirt		
❑ 44	Al Burch: Brooklyn	60.00	30.00
	Fielding		
❑ 45	Al Burch: Brooklyn	125.00	60.00
	Batting		
❑ 46	Bill Burns	60.00	30.00
❑ 47	Donie Bush	75.00	38.00
❑ 48	Bobby Byrne	60.00	30.00
❑ 49	Howie Camnitz:	75.00	38.00
	Pitt		
	Arms folded over chest		
❑ 50	Howie Camnitz:	60.00	30.00
	Pitt		
	Hands over head		
❑ 51	Howie Camnitz:	60.00	30.00
	Pitt.		
	Throwing		
❑ 52	Billy Campbell	60.00	30.00
❑ 53	Bill Carrigan	60.00	30.00
❑ 54	Frank Chance:	500.00	200.00
	Chicago NL		
	Cubs across chest		
❑ 55	Frank Chance:	500.00	200.00
	Chicago NL		
	Chicago down front of shirt		
❑ 56	Frank Chance:	400.00	150.00
	Chicago NL		
	Batting		
❑ 57	Chappy Charles	60.00	30.00
❑ 58	Hal Chase	125.00	60.00
	N.Y. AL		
	Port. blue bkgd.		
❑ 59	Hal Chase	200.00	100.00
	N.Y. AL		
	Port., pink bkgd.		
❑ 60	Hal Chase	125.00	60.00
	N.Y. AL		
	Holding cup		
❑ 61	Hal Chase	125.00	60.00
	N.Y. AL		
	Throwing, dark cap		
❑ 62	Hal Chase	150.00	75.00
	N.Y. AL		
	Throwing, white cap		
❑ 63	Jack Chesbro	250.00	125.00
❑ 64	Eddie Cicotte	200.00	100.00
❑ 65	Fred Clarke: Pitt.	200.00	100.00
	Portrait		
❑ 66	Fred Clarke: Pitt.	200.00	100.00

❑ 67	Nig Clarke	75.00	38.00
❑ 68	Ty Cobb: Detroit Port., red bkgd.	2500.00	1250.00
❑ 69	Ty Cobb: Detroit Port., green background	3500.00	1800.00
❑ 70	Ty Cobb: Detroit Bat on shoulder	2500.00	1250.00
❑ 71	Ty Cobb: Detroit Bat away from shoulder	2500.00	1250.00
❑ 72	Eddie Collins: Phila. AL	400.00	150.00
❑ 73	Wid Conroy: Washington Fielding	75.00	38.00
❑ 74	Wid Conroy Washington Bat on shoulder	60.00	30.00
❑ 75	Harry Covaleski: Phila. NL	75.00	38.00
❑ 76	Doc Crandall N.Y. NL, without cap	60.00	30.00
❑ 77	Doc Crandall N.Y. NL sweater and cap	60.00	30.00
❑ 78	Sam Crawford: Detroit, Batting	500.00	200.00
❑ 79	Sam Crawford: Detroit, Throwing	500.00	200.00
❑ 80	Birdie Cree	60.00	30.00
❑ 81	Lou Criger	75.00	38.00
❑ 82	Dode Criss	75.00	38.00
❑ 83	Bill Dahlen: Boston NL	125.00	60.00
❑ 84	Bill Dahlen: Brooklyn	200.00	100.00
❑ 85	George Davis	200.00	100.00
❑ 86	Harry Davis Phila. AL Davis on card	60.00	30.00
❑ 87	Harry Davis Phila. AL H.Davis on card	75.00	38.00
❑ 88	Jim Delehanty Sic, Delahanty	75.00	38.00
❑ 89	Ray Demmitt St.L. AL	5000.00	2200.00
❑ 90	Ray Demmitt N.Y. AL	75.00	38.00
❑ 91	Art Devlin	75.00	38.00
❑ 92	Josh Devore	60.00	30.00
❑ 93	Bill Dineen	60.00	30.00
❑ 94	Mike Donlin N.Y. NL Fielding	125.00	60.00
❑ 95	Mike Donlin N.Y. NL Sitting	125.00	60.00
❑ 96	Mike Donlin N.Y. NL Batting	75.00	38.00
❑ 97	Jiggs Donohue	75.00	38.00
❑ 98	Bill Donovan: Detroit Portrait	75.00	38.00
❑ 99	Bill Donovan: Detroit Throwing	60.00	30.00
❑ 100	Red Dooin	75.00	38.00
❑ 101	Mickey Doolan: Phila. NL Fielding	60.00	30.00
❑ 102	Mickey Doolan: Phila. NL Batting	60.00	30.00
❑ 103	Mickey Doolin (Sic, Doolan): Phila. NL	75.00	38.00
❑ 104	Patsy Dougherty: Chicago AL Portrait	75.00	38.00
❑ 105	Patsy Dougherty: Chicago AL Fielding	60.00	30.00
❑ 106	Tom Downey: Cinc. Batting	60.00	30.00
❑ 107	Tom Downey: Cinc. Fielding	60.00	30.00
❑ 108A	Joe Doyle: N.Y. Hands over head	125.00	60.00
❑ 108B	Joe Doyle: N.Y. NAT'L hands over head)	60000.00	30000.00
❑ 109	Larry Doyle: N.Y. NL Sweater	75.00	38.00
❑ 110	Larry Doyle: N.Y. NL Throwing	125.00	60.00
❑ 111	Larry Doyle: N.Y. NL Bat on shoulder	75.00	38.00
❑ 112	Jean Dubuc	60.00	30.00
❑ 113	Hugh Duffy	400.00	150.00
❑ 114	Joe Dunn	60.00	30.00
❑ 115	Bull Durham	75.00	38.00
❑ 116	Jimmy Dygert	60.00	30.00
❑ 117	Ted Easterly	60.00	30.00
❑ 118	Dick Egan	60.00	30.00
❑ 119	Kid Elberfeld Wash. Fielding	60.00	30.00
❑ 120	Kid Elberfeld Wash. Portrait	1000.00	500.00
❑ 121	Kid Elberfeld N.Y. AL Portrait	75.00	38.00
❑ 122	Clyde Engle	60.00	30.00
❑ 123	Steve Evans	60.00	30.00
❑ 124	Johnny Evers: Chicago NL Portrait	600.00	250.00
❑ 125	Johnny Evers: Chicago NL Cubs across chest	500.00	150.00
❑ 126	Johnny Evers: Chicago NL Chicago down front of shirt	500.00	150.00
❑ 127	Bob Ewing	75.00	38.00
❑ 128	George Ferguson	60.00	30.00
❑ 129	Hobe Ferris	75.00	38.00
❑ 130	Lou Fiene Chicago AL Portrait	60.00	30.00
❑ 131	Lou Fiene Chicago AL Throwing	60.00	30.00
❑ 132	Art Fletcher	60.00	30.00
❑ 133	Elmer Flick	300.00	150.00
❑ 134	Russ Ford	60.00	30.00
❑ 135	John Frill	60.00	30.00
❑ 136	Art Fromme	60.00	30.00
❑ 137	Chick Gandil	250.00	125.00
❑ 138	Bob Ganley	75.00	38.00
❑ 139	Harry Gasper	60.00	30.00
❑ 140	Rube Geyer	60.00	30.00
❑ 141	George Gibson	75.00	38.00
❑ 142	Billy Gilbert	75.00	38.00
❑ 143	Wilbur Goode Sic, Good	75.00	38.00
❑ 144	Bill Graham	60.00	30.00
❑ 145	Peaches Graham	60.00	30.00
❑ 146	Dolly Gray	75.00	38.00
❑ 147	Clark Griffith: Cinc. Portrait	250.00	125.00
❑ 148	Clark Griffith: Cinc. Batting	250.00	125.00
❑ 149	Bob Groom	60.00	30.00
❑ 150	Ed Hahn	75.00	38.00
❑ 151	Topsy Hartsel	60.00	30.00
❑ 152	Charlie Hemphill	75.00	38.00
❑ 153	Buck Herzog N.Y. NL	75.00	38.00
❑ 154	Buck Herzog Boston NL	60.00	30.00
❑ 155	Bill Hinchman	75.00	38.00
❑ 156	Doc Hoblitzell	60.00	30.00
❑ 157	Danny Hoffman	60.00	30.00
❑ 158	Solly Hofman	60.00	30.00
❑ 159	Del Howard	60.00	30.00
❑ 160	Harry Howell St.L. AL Portrait	60.00	30.00
❑ 161	Harry Howell St.L. AL Left hand on hip	60.00	30.00
❑ 162	Miller Huggins: Cinc. Portrait	400.00	200.00
❑ 163	Miller Huggins: Cinc. Hands to Mouth	400.00	200.00
❑ 164	Rudy Hulswitt	60.00	30.00
❑ 165	John Hummel	60.00	30.00
❑ 166	George Hunter	60.00	30.00
❑ 167	Frank Isbell	75.00	38.00
❑ 168	Fred Jacklitsch	75.00	38.00
❑ 169	Hughie Jennings MG: Detroit Portrait	400.00	200.00
❑ 170	Hughie Jennings MG: Detroit One	400.00	200.00
❑ 171	Hughie Jennings MG: Detroit Both	400.00	200.00
❑ 172	Walter Johnson: Washington Portrait	1500.00	750.00
❑ 173	Walter Johnson: Washington Hands at Chest	1200.00	600.00
❑ 174	Davy Jones	60.00	30.00
❑ 175	Fielder Jones Chic. AL Portrait	75.00	38.00
❑ 176	Fielder Jones Chic AL Hands on hips	75.00	38.00
❑ 177	Tom Jones	75.00	38.00
❑ 178	Tim Jordan: Brooklyn Portrait	75.00	38.00
❑ 179	Tim Jordan: Brooklyn Batting	60.00	30.00
❑ 180	Addie Joss: Cleveland Portrait	600.00	250.00
❑ 181	Addie Joss: Cleveland Ready to pitch	500.00	200.00
❑ 182	Ed Karger	75.00	38.00
❑ 183	Willie Keeler N.Y. AL Portrait	600.00	250.00
❑ 184	Willie Keeler N.Y. AL Batting	500.00	200.00
❑ 185	Ed Killian: Detroit Portrait	75.00	38.00
❑ 186	Ed Killian: Detroit Pitching	60.00	30.00
❑ 187	Red Kleinow N.Y. AL Batting	75.00	38.00
❑ 188	Red Kleinow N.Y. AL Catching	60.00	30.00
❑ 189	Red Kleinow Boston AL Catching	1000.00	400.00
❑ 190	Johnny Kling: Chicago NL	75.00	38.00
❑ 191	Otto Knabe	60.00	30.00
❑ 192	John Knight N.Y. AL Portrait	60.00	30.00
❑ 193	John Knight N.Y. AL Batting	60.00	30.00
❑ 194	Ed Konetchy St.L. NL Awaiting low ball	60.00	30.00
❑ 195	Ed Konetchy	75.00	38.00

St.L. NL
Glove above head
❑ 196 Harry Krause 60.00 30.00
Phila. AL
Portrait
❑ 197 Harry Krause 60.00 30.00
Phila. AL
Pitching
❑ 198 Rube Kroh 60.00 30.00
❑ 199 Nap Lajoie: 800.00 400.00
Cleveland
Portrait
❑ 200 Nap Lajoie: 600.00 300.00
Cleveland
Batting
❑ 201 Nap Lajoie: 600.00 300.00
Cleveland
Throwing
❑ 202 Joe Lake 75.00 38.00
N.Y. AL
❑ 203 Joe Lake 60.00 30.00
St.L. AL
Hands over head
❑ 204 Joe Lake 60.00 30.00
St.L. AL
Throwing
❑ 205 Frank LaPorte 60.00 30.00
❑ 206 Arlie Latham 75.00 38.00
❑ 207 Tommy Leach: Pitt. 75.00 38.00
Portrait
❑ 208 Tommy Leach: Pitt. 60.00 30.00
In fielding position
❑ 209 Lefty Leifield:............... 60.00 30.00
Pitt.
Batting
❑ 210 Lefty Leifield:............... 75.00 38.00
Pitt.
Hands behind head
❑ 211 Ed Lennox 60.00 30.00
❑ 212 Glenn Liebhardt........... 75.00 38.00
❑ 213 Vive Lindaman 125.00 60.00
❑ 214 Paddy Livingstone....... 60.00 30.00
❑ 215 Hans Lobert................. 75.00 38.00
❑ 216 Harry Lord................... 60.00 30.00
❑ 217 Harry Lumley............... 75.00 38.00
❑ 218 Carl Lundgren 300.00 150.00
❑ 219 Nick Maddox. 60.00 30.00
❑ 220 Sherry Magee 125.00 60.00
Phila. NL
Portrait
❑ 221 Sherry Magee 60.00 30.00
Phila. NL
Batting
❑ 222 Sherry Magie......... 15000.00 7500.00
Phila. NL
Sic, Magee
Portrait,
name misspelled
❑ 223 Rube Manning............. 75.00 38.00
N.Y. AL
Batting
❑ 224 Rube Manning............. 60.00 30.00
N.Y. AL
Hands over head
❑ 225 Rube Marquard 500.00 200.00
N.Y. NL
Portrait
❑ 226 Rube Marquard 400.00 150.00
N.Y. NL
Pitching
❑ 227 Rube Marquard 400.00 150.00
N.Y. NL
Standing
❑ 228 Doc Marshall................ 60.00 30.00
❑ 229 Christy Mathewson: 2000.00 750.00
N.Y. NL
Portrait
❑ 230 Christy Mathewson: 1500.00 600.00
N.Y. NL
Pitching, white cap
❑ 231 Christy Mathewson: 1500.00 600.00
N.Y. NL
Pitching, dark cap
❑ 232 Al Mattern 60.00 30.00
❑ 233 Jack McAleese 60.00 30.00
❑ 234 George McBride 60.00 30.00
❑ 235 Moose McCormick 60.00 30.00
❑ 236 Pryor McElveen............ 60.00 30.00
❑ 237 John McGraw 500.00 200.00
N.Y. NL
Portrait, no cap
❑ 238 John McGraw 500.00 200.00
N.Y. NL
w/Cap
❑ 239 John McGraw 500.00 200.00
N.Y. NL
Finger
❑ 240 John McGraw 500.00 200.00
N.Y. NL
Glove on hip
❑ 241 Matty McIntyre:........... 75.00 38.00
Brooklyn
❑ 242 Matty McIntyre:........... 60.00 30.00
Brooklyn and
Chicago NL
❑ 243 Mike McIntyre: 60.00 30.00
Detroit
❑ 244 Larry McLean 60.00 30.00
❑ 245 George McQuillan: 75.00 38.00
Phila. NL
Throwing
❑ 246 George McQuillan: 60.00 30.00
Phila. NL
Batting
❑ 247 Fred Merkle.............. 125.00 60.00
N.Y. NL
Portrait
❑ 248 Fred Merkle.............. 125.00 60.00
N.Y. NL
Throwing
❑ 249 Chief Meyers............... 60.00 30.00
❑ 250 Chief Meyers............... 60.00 30.00
Sic, Myers)
N.Y. NL
Fielding
❑ 251 Chief Meyers............... 75.00 38.00
Sic, Myers)
N.Y. NL
Batting
❑ 252 Clyde Milan................. 60.00 30.00
❑ 253 Dots Miller 60.00 30.00
❑ 254 Mike Mitchell 60.00 30.00
❑ 255 Pat Moran 60.00 30.00
❑ 256 George Moriarty 60.00 30.00
❑ 257 Mike Mowrey 60.00 30.00
❑ 258 George Mullin: 60.00 30.00
Detroit
Sic, Mullen
❑ 259 George Mullin: 75.00 38.00
Detroit
Throwing
❑ 260 George Mullin: 60.00 30.00
Detroit
Batting
❑ 261 Danny Murphy 75.00 38.00
Phila. AL
Throwing
❑ 262 Danny Murphy 60.00 30.00
Phila. AL
Bat on shoulder
❑ 263 Red Murray 60.00 30.00
N.Y. NL
Sweater
❑ 264 Red Murray 60.00 30.00
N.Y. NL
Bat on shoulder
❑ 265 Tom Needham............. 60.00 30.00
❑ 266 Simon Nicholls 75.00 38.00
Phila AL
❑ 267 Simon Nicholls 60.00 30.00
Sic, Nichols:
Phila. AL
❑ 268 Harry Niles 75.00 38.00
❑ 269 Rebel Oakes 60.00 30.00
❑ 270 Bill O'Hara: N.Y. NL 60.00 30.00
❑ 271 Bill O'Hara: 5000.00 2500.00
St. Louis NL
❑ 272 Rube Oldring............... 75.00 38.00
Phila. AL
Fielding
❑ 273 Rube Oldring............... 75.00 38.00
Phila. AL
Bat on shoulder
❑ 274 Charley O'Leary: 75.00 38.00
Detroit
Portrait
❑ 275 Charley O'Leary: 60.00 30.00
Detroit
Hands on knees
❑ 276 Orval Overall: 75.00 38.00
Chicago NL
Portrait
❑ 277 Orval Overall: 60.00 30.00
Chicago NL
Pitching follow thru
❑ 278 Orval Overall: 60.00 30.00
Chicago NL,
Pitching hiding
ball in glove
❑ 279 Frank Owen 75.00 38.00
Chicago AL
Sic, Owens)
❑ 280 Freddy Parent 75.00 38.00
❑ 281 Dode Paskert............... 60.00 30.00
❑ 282 Jim Pastorius 75.00 38.00
❑ 283 Harry Pattee.............. 150.00 75.00
❑ 284 Fred Payne 60.00 30.00
❑ 285 Barney Pelty 125.00 60.00
St.L. AL
HOR
❑ 286 Barney Pelty 60.00 30.00
St.L. AL
VERT
❑ 287 George Perring 60.00 30.00
❑ 288 Jeff Pfeffer.................. 60.00 30.00
❑ 289 Jack Pfeister 60.00 30.00
Chic. NL
Sitting
❑ 290 Jack Pfeister 60.00 30.00
Chic. NL
Pitching
❑ 291 Ed Phelps 60.00 30.00
❑ 292 Deacon Phillippe. 125.00 60.00
❑ 293 Eddie Plank........... 30000.00 15000.00
❑ 294 Jack Powell 75.00 38.00
❑ 295 Mike Powers 125.00 60.00
❑ 296 Billy Purtell 60.00 30.00
❑ 297 Jack Quinn 60.00 30.00
❑ 298 Bugs Raymond 75.00 38.00
❑ 299 Ed Reulbach 125.00 60.00
Chicago NL
Pitching
❑ 300 Ed Reulbach 125.00 60.00
Chicago NL
Hands at side
❑ 301 Bob Rhoades............... 60.00 30.00
sic,Rhoads
Cleveland
Hand in air
❑ 302 Bob Rhoades............... 60.00 30.00
sic, Rhoads
Cleveland
Ready to pitch
❑ 303 Charlie Rhodes 60.00 30.00
❑ 304 Claude Ritchey 75.00 38.00
❑ 305 Claude Rossman......... 60.00 30.00
❑ 306 Nap Rucker:.............. 125.00 60.00
Brooklyn
Portrait
❑ 307 Nap Rucker:................. 75.00 38.00
Brooklyn
Pitching
❑ 308 Germany Schaefer: 75.00 38.00
Washington
❑ 309 Germany Schaefer: 75.00 38.00
Detroit
❑ 310 Admiral Schlei............. 60.00 30.00
N.Y. NL
Sweater
❑ 311 Admiral Schlei............. 60.00 30.00
N.Y. NL
Batting
❑ 312 Admiral Schlei............. 75.00 38.00
N.Y. NL
Fielding
❑ 313 Boss Schmidt:............. 60.00 30.00
Detroit
Portrait

❑	314 Boss Schmidt:	75.00	38.00
	Detroit		
	Throwing		
❑	315 Frank Schulte:	60.00	30.00
	Chicago NL		
	Batting, back turned		
❑	316 Frank Schulte:	75.00	38.00
	Chicago NL		
	Batting, front pose		
❑	317 Jim Scott	60.00	30.00
❑	318 Cy Seymour	60.00	30.00
	N.Y. NL		
	Portrait		
❑	319 Cy Seymour	60.00	30.00
	N.Y. NL		
	Throwing		
❑	320 Cy Seymour	75.00	38.00
	N.Y. NL		
	Batting		
❑	321 Al Shaw	75.00	38.00
❑	322 Jimmy Sheckard:	60.00	30.00
	Chicago NL		
	Throwing		
❑	323 Jimmy Sheckard:	75.00	38.00
	Chicago NL		
	Side view		
❑	324 Bill Shipke	75.00	38.00
❑	325 Frank Smith	60.00	30.00
	Chicago AL		
	Listed as Smith		
❑	326 Frank Smith	400.00	200.00
	Chicago and Boston AL		
❑	327 Frank Smith	75.00	38.00
	Chicago AL		
	Listed as F.Smith		
❑	328 Happy Smith	60.00	30.00
❑	329 Fred Snodgrass	75.00	38.00
	N.Y. NL		
	Batting		
❑	329A Fred Snodgrass	3000.00	1500.00
	N.Y., Battting		
	Card spelled Nodgrass		
	Due to a printing glitch		
❑	330 Fred Snodgrass	75.00	38.00
	N.Y. NL		
	Catching		
❑	331 Bob Spade	75.00	38.00
❑	332 Tris Speaker	1000.00	400.00
❑	333 Tubby Spencer	75.00	38.00
❑	334 Jake Stahl:	75.00	38.00
	Boston AL		
	Catching fly ball		
❑	335 Jake Stahl:	75.00	38.00
	Boston AL		
	Standing, arms down		
❑	336 Oscar Stanage	60.00	30.00
❑	337 Charlie Starr	60.00	30.00
❑	338 Harry Steinfeldt:	125.00	60.00
	Chicago NL		
	Portrait		
❑	339 Harry Steinfeldt:	75.00	38.00
	Chicago NL		
	Batting		
❑	340 Jim Stephens	60.00	30.00
❑	341 George Stone	75.00	38.00
❑	342 George Stovall:	75.00	38.00
	Cleveland		
	Portrait		
❑	343 George Stovall:	60.00	30.00
	Cleveland		
	Batting		
❑	344 Gabby Street:	75.00	38.00
	Washington		
	Portrait		
❑	345 Gabby Street:	60.00	30.00
	Washington		
	Catching		
❑	346 Billy Sullivan	75.00	38.00
❑	347 Ed Summers	60.00	30.00
❑	348 Jeff Sweeney	60.00	30.00
❑	349 Bill Sweeney	60.00	30.00
❑	350 Jesse Tannehill	60.00	30.00
❑	351 Lee Tannehill:	75.00	38.00
	Chicago AL		
	Listed as L.Tannehill		
❑	352 Lee Tannehill:	60.00	30.00
	Chicago AL		
	Listed as Tannehill		
❑	353 Fred Tenney	75.00	38.00
❑	354 Ira Thomas	60.00	30.00
❑	355 Joe Tinker	600.00	300.00
	Chicago NL		
	Bat Off Shoulder		
❑	356 Joe Tinker	600.00	300.00
	Chicago NL		
	Bat on Shoulder		
❑	357 Joe Tinker	800.00	300.00
	Chicago NL		
	Portrait		
❑	358 Joe Tinker	600.00	300.00
	Chicago NL		
	Hands on knees		
❑	359 John Titus	60.00	30.00
❑	360 Terry Turner	75.00	38.00
❑	361 Bob Unglaub	60.00	30.00
❑	362 Rube Waddell	600.00	250.00
	St.L. AL		
	Portrait		
❑	363 Rube Waddell	500.00	200.00
	St.L. AL		
	Pitching		
❑	364 Heinie Wagner:	125.00	60.00
	Boston AL		
	Bat on left shoulder		
❑	365 Heinie Wagner:	75.00	38.00
	Boston AL		
	Bat on right shoulder		
❑	366 Honus Wagner	400000.00	200000.00
❑	367 Bobby Wallace	400.00	150.00
❑	368 Ed Walsh	600.00	250.00
❑	369 Jack Warhop: N.Y. AL	60.00	30.00
❑	370 Jake Weimer: N.Y. NL	75.00	38.00
❑	371 Zach Wheat	300.00	150.00
❑	372 Doc White	75.00	38.00
	Chicago AL		
	Portrait		
❑	373 Doc White	60.00	30.00
	Chicago AL		
	Pitching		
❑	374 Kaiser Wilhelm:	60.00	30.00
	Brooklyn		
	Batting		
❑	375 Kaiser Wilhelm:	75.00	38.00
	Brooklyn		
	Hands to chest		
❑	376 Ed Willett: Detroit	60.00	30.00
	Batting		
❑	377 Ed Willett	60.00	30.00
	Sic, Willetts		
	Detroit		
	Pitching		
❑	378 Jimmy Williams	75.00	38.00
❑	379 Vic Willis: Pitt.	250.00	125.00
❑	380 Vic Willis	200.00	100.00
	St.L. NL		
	Pitching		
❑	381 Vic Willis	200.00	100.00
	St.L. NL		
	Batting		
❑	382 Chief Wilson	60.00	30.00
❑	383 Hooks Wiltse	75.00	38.00
	N.Y. NL		
	Portrait		
❑	384 Hooks Wiltse	60.00	30.00
	N.Y.NL		
	Sweater		
❑	385 Hooks Wiltse	60.00	30.00
	N.Y. NL		
	Pitching		
❑	386 Cy Young	2000.00	600.00
	Cleveland		
	Portrait		
❑	387 Cy Young	1500.00	500.00
	Cleveland		
	Pitch, front view		
❑	388 Cy Young	1500.00	500.00
	Cleveland		
	Pitch, side view		
❑	389 Heinie Zimmerman:	60.00	30.00
❑	390 Fred Abbott	50.00	25.00
❑	391 Merle(Doc) Adkins	50.00	25.00
❑	392 John Anderson	50.00	25.00
❑	393 Herman Armbruster	50.00	25.00
❑	394 Harry Arndt	50.00	25.00
❑	395 Cy Barger	60.00	30.00
❑	396 John Barry	50.00	25.00
❑	397 Emil H. Batch	50.00	25.00
❑	398 Jake Beckley	250.00	125.00
❑	399 Lena Blackburne	75.00	38.00
❑	400 David Brain	50.00	25.00
❑	401 Roy Brashear	50.00	25.00
❑	402 Fred Burchell	50.00	25.00
❑	403 Jimmy Burke	50.00	25.00
❑	404 John Butler	50.00	25.00
❑	405 Charles Carr	50.00	25.00
❑	406 Doc Casey	50.00	25.00
❑	407 Peter Cassidy	50.00	25.00
❑	408 Wm. Chappelle	60.00	30.00
❑	409 Wm. Clancy	50.00	25.00
❑	410 Joshua Clarke	50.00	25.00
	Sic, Clark		
❑	411 William Clymer	50.00	25.00
❑	412 Jimmy Collins	400.00	200.00
❑	413 Bunk Congalton	50.00	25.00
❑	414 Gavvy Cravath	125.00	60.00
❑	415 Monte Cross	60.00	30.00
❑	416 Paul Davidson	50.00	25.00
❑	417 Frank Delehanty	75.00	38.00
	Sic, Delahanty		
❑	418 Rube Dessau	50.00	25.00
❑	419 Gus Dorner	50.00	25.00
❑	420 Jerome Downs	50.00	25.00
❑	421 Jack Dunn	75.00	38.00
❑	422 James Flanagan	50.00	25.00
❑	423 James Freeman	50.00	25.00
❑	424 John Ganzel	50.00	25.00
❑	425 Myron Grimshaw	50.00	25.00
❑	426 Robert Hall	50.00	25.00
❑	427 William Hallman	60.00	30.00
❑	428 John Hannifan	50.00	25.00
❑	429 Jack Hayden	50.00	25.00
❑	430 Harry Hinchman	50.00	25.00
❑	431 Harry C. Hoffman	50.00	25.00
❑	432 James B. Jackson	60.00	30.00
❑	433 Joe Kelley	250.00	125.00
❑	434 Rube Kissinger	60.00	30.00
	Sic, Kisinger		
❑	435 Otto Krueger	50.00	25.00
	Sic, Kruger		
❑	436 Wm. Lattimore	50.00	25.00
❑	437 James Lavender	50.00	25.00
❑	438 Carl Lundgren	50.00	25.00
❑	439 Wm. Malarkey	60.00	30.00
❑	440 Wm. Maloney	50.00	25.00
❑	441 Dennis McGann	50.00	25.00
❑	442 James McGinley	50.00	25.00
❑	443 Joe McGinnity	250.00	125.00
❑	444 Ulysses McGlynn	50.00	25.00
❑	445 George Merritt	50.00	25.00
❑	446 Wm. Milligan	50.00	25.00
❑	447 Fred Mitchell.	50.00	25.00
❑	448 Dan Moeller	50.00	25.00
❑	449 Joseph H. Moran	50.00	25.00
❑	450 Wm. Nattress	50.00	25.00
❑	451 Frank Oberlin	50.00	25.00
❑	452 Peter O'Brien	50.00	25.00
❑	453 Wm. O'Neil	50.00	25.00
❑	454 James Phelan	50.00	25.00
❑	455 Oliver Pickering	50.00	25.00
❑	456 Philip Poland	50.00	25.00
❑	457 Ambrose Puttman	50.00	25.00
❑	458 Lee Quillen	50.00	25.00
❑	459 Newton Randall	50.00	25.00
❑	460 Louis Ritter	50.00	25.00
❑	461 Dick Rudolph	50.00	25.00
❑	462 George Schirm	50.00	25.00
❑	463 Larry Schlafly	50.00	25.00
❑	464 Ossie Schreckengost	60.00	30.00
	Sic Schreck		
❑	465 William Shannon	50.00	25.00
❑	466 Bayard Sharpe	50.00	25.00
❑	466A Bayard Sharpe	500.00	250.00
	Name is spelled Shappe on front		
❑	467 Royal Shaw	50.00	25.00
❑	468 James Slagle	50.00	25.00
❑	469 George Henry Smith	50.00	25.00
❑	470 Samuel Strang	50.00	25.00
❑	471 Dummy Taylor	125.00	60.00

❑ 472 John Thielman 50.00 25.00
❑ 473 John F. White 50.00 25.00
❑ 474 William Wright 50.00 25.00
❑ 475 Irving M. Young 60.00 30.00
❑ 476 Jack Bastian 125.00 60.00
❑ 477 Harry Bay 125.00 60.00
❑ 478 Wm. Bernhard 125.00 60.00
❑ 479 Ted Breitenstein 125.00 60.00
❑ 480 Scoops Carey 125.00 60.00
❑ 481 Cad Coles 125.00 60.00
❑ 482 Wm. Cranston 125.00 60.00
❑ 483 Roy Ellam 125.00 60.00
❑ 484 Edward Foster 125.00 60.00
❑ 485 Charles Fritz 125.00 60.00
❑ 486 Ed Greminger 125.00 60.00
❑ 487 Guiheen 125.00 60.00
❑ 488 William F. Hart 125.00 60.00
❑ 489 James Henry Hart 125.00 60.00
❑ 490 J.R. Helm 125.00 60.00
❑ 491 Gordon Hickman 125.00 60.00
❑ 492 Buck Hooker 125.00 60.00
❑ 493 Ernie Howard 125.00 60.00
❑ 494 A.O. Jordan 125.00 60.00
❑ 495 J.F. Kiernan 125.00 60.00
❑ 496 Frank King 125.00 60.00
❑ 497 James LaFitte 125.00 60.00
❑ 498 Harry Sentz 125.00 60.00
Sic, Lentz
❑ 499 Perry Lipe 125.00 60.00
❑ 500 George Manion 125.00 60.00
❑ 501 McCauley 125.00 60.00
❑ 502 Charles B. Miller 125.00 60.00
❑ 503 Carlton Molesworth 125.00 60.00
❑ 504 Dominic Mullaney 125.00 60.00
❑ 505 Albert Orth 125.00 60.00
❑ 506 William Otey 125.00 60.00
❑ 507 George Paige 125.00 60.00
❑ 508 Hub Perdue. 150.00 75.00
❑ 509 Archie Persons 125.00 60.00
❑ 510 Edward Reagan 125.00 60.00
❑ 511 R.H. Revelle 125.00 60.00
❑ 512 Isaac Rockenfeld 125.00 60.00
❑ 513 Ray Ryan 125.00 60.00
❑ 514 Charles Seitz 125.00 60.00
❑ 515 Frank "Shag" Shaughnessy 150.00 75.00
❑ 516 Carlos Smith 125.00 60.00
❑ 517 Sid Smith 125.00 60.00
❑ 518 Dolly Stark 150.00 75.00
❑ 519 Tony Thebo 125.00 60.00
❑ 520 Woodie Thornton 125.00 60.00
❑ 521 Juan Viola 125.00 60.00
Sic, Violat
❑ 522 James Westlake 125.00 60.00
❑ 523 Foley White 125.00 60.00

2004 Throwback Threads

	Nm-Mt	Ex-Mt
COMP.SET w/o SP's (200)	40.00	12.00
COMMON CARD (1-200)	.30	.09
COMMON RETIRED (201-224)	2.00	.60
COMMON ROOKIE (225-250)	3.00	.90

❑ 1 Bartolo Colon .30 .09
❑ 2 Darin Erstad .30 .09
❑ 3 David Eckstein .30 .09
❑ 4 Garret Anderson .30 .09
❑ 5 Tim Salmon .50 .15
❑ 6 Troy Glaus .30 .09
❑ 7 Vladimir Guerrero .75 .23
❑ 8 Brandon Webb .30 .09
❑ 9 Luis Gonzalez .30 .09
❑ 10 Randy Johnson .75 .23
❑ 11 Richie Sexson .30 .09
❑ 12 Roberto Alomar .50 .15
❑ 13 Shea Hillenbrand .30 .09
❑ 14 Steve Finley .30 .09
❑ 15 Adam LaRoche .30 .09
❑ 16 Andruw Jones .30 .09
❑ 17 Chipper Jones .75 .23
❑ 18 J.D. Drew .30 .09
❑ 19 John Smoltz .50 .15
❑ 20 Rafael Furcal .30 .09
❑ 21 Russ Ortiz .30 .09
❑ 22 Javy Lopez .30 .09
❑ 23 Jay Gibbons .30 .09
❑ 24 Larry Bigbie .30 .09
❑ 25 Luis Matos .30 .09
❑ 26 Melvin Mora .30 .09
❑ 27 Miguel Tejada .30 .09
❑ 28 Rafael Palmeiro .50 .15
❑ 29 Curt Schilling .75 .23
❑ 30 David Ortiz .75 .23
❑ 31 Derek Lowe .30 .09
❑ 32 Jason Varitek .50 .15
❑ 33 Johnny Damon .75 .23
❑ 34 Manny Ramirez .50 .15
❑ 35 Nomar Garciaparra 1.25 .35
❑ 36 Pedro Martinez .75 .23
❑ 37 Trot Nixon .30 .09
❑ 38 Aramis Ramirez .30 .09
❑ 39 Corey Patterson .30 .09
❑ 40 Derrek Lee .30 .09
❑ 41 Greg Maddux 1.25 .35
❑ 42 Kerry Wood .75 .23
❑ 43 Mark Prior .75 .23
❑ 44 Sammy Sosa 1.25 .35
❑ 45 Carlos Lee .30 .09
❑ 46 Esteban Loaiza .30 .09
❑ 47 Frank Thomas .75 .23
❑ 48 Joe Borchard .30 .09
❑ 49 Magglio Ordonez .30 .09
❑ 50 Mark Buehrle .30 .09
❑ 51 Paul Konerko .30 .09
❑ 52 Adam Dunn .50 .15
❑ 53 Austin Kearns .30 .09
❑ 54 Barry Larkin .50 .15
❑ 55 Brandon Larson .30 .09
❑ 56 Ken Griffey Jr. 1.25 .35
❑ 57 Ryan Wagner .30 .09
❑ 58 Sean Casey .30 .09
❑ 59 C.C. Sabathia .30 .09
❑ 60 Jody Gerut .30 .09
❑ 61 Omar Vizquel .50 .15
❑ 62 Travis Hafner .30 .09
❑ 63 Victor Martinez .30 .09
❑ 64 Charles Johnson .30 .09
❑ 65 Garrett Atkins .30 .09
❑ 66 Jason Jennings .30 .09
❑ 67 Joe Kennedy .30 .09
❑ 68 Larry Walker .50 .15
❑ 69 Preston Wilson .30 .09
❑ 70 Todd Helton .50 .15
❑ 71 Ivan Rodriguez .75 .23
❑ 72 Jeremy Bonderman .30 .09
❑ 73 A.J. Burnett .30 .09
❑ 74 Brad Penny .30 .09
❑ 75 Dontrelle Willis .30 .09
❑ 76 Josh Beckett .30 .09
❑ 77 Juan Pierre .30 .09
❑ 78 Luis Castillo .30 .09
❑ 79 Miguel Cabrera .50 .15
❑ 80 Mike Lowell .30 .09
❑ 81 Andy Pettitte .50 .15
❑ 82 Craig Biggio .50 .15
❑ 83 Jeff Bagwell .50 .15
❑ 84 Jeff Kent .30 .09
❑ 85 Lance Berkman .30 .09
❑ 86 Morgan Ensberg .30 .09
❑ 87 Richard Hidalgo .30 .09
❑ 88 Roger Clemens 1.50 .45
❑ 89 Roy Oswalt .30 .09
❑ 90 Wade Miller .30 .09
❑ 91 Angel Berroa .30 .09
❑ 92 Carlos Beltran .50 .15
❑ 93 Juan Gonzalez .50 .15
❑ 94 Ken Harvey .30 .09
❑ 95 Mike Sweeney .30 .09
❑ 96 Runelvys Hernandez .30 .09
❑ 97 Adrian Beltre .50 .15
❑ 98 Edwin Jackson .30 .09
❑ 99 Eric Gagne .75 .23
❑ 100 Hideo Nomo .75 .23
❑ 101 Hong-Chih Kuo .30 .09
❑ 102 Kazuhisa Ishii .30 .09
❑ 103 Paul Lo Duca .30 .09
❑ 104 Shawn Green .30 .09
❑ 105 Ben Sheets .30 .09
❑ 106 Geoff Jenkins .30 .09
❑ 107 Junior Spivey .30 .09
❑ 108 Rickie Weeks .30 .09
❑ 109 Scott Podsednik .30 .09
❑ 110 Corey Koskie .30 .09
❑ 111 Doug Mientkiewicz .30 .09
❑ 112 Jacque Jones .30 .09
❑ 113 Joe Mays .30 .09
❑ 114 Johan Santana .50 .15
❑ 115 Shannon Stewart .30 .09
❑ 116 Torii Hunter .30 .09
❑ 117 Brad Wilkerson .30 .09
❑ 118 Carl Everett .30 .09
❑ 119 Chad Cordero .30 .09
❑ 120 Jose Vidro .30 .09
❑ 121 Nick Johnson .30 .09
❑ 122 Orlando Cabrera .30 .09
❑ 123 Al Leiter .30 .09
❑ 124 Cliff Floyd .30 .09
❑ 125 Jae Weong Seo .30 .09
❑ 126 Jose Reyes .30 .09
❑ 127 Mike Cameron .30 .09
❑ 128 Mike Piazza 1.25 .35
❑ 129 Tom Glavine .50 .15
❑ 130 Alex Rodriguez 1.25 .35
❑ 131 Bernie Williams .50 .15
❑ 132 Chien-Ming Wang .30 .09
❑ 133 Derek Jeter 1.50 .45
❑ 134 Gary Sheffield .30 .09
❑ 135 Hideki Matsui 1.25 .35
❑ 136 Jason Giambi .30 .09
❑ 137 Javier Vazquez .30 .09
❑ 138 Jorge Posada .50 .15
❑ 139 Jose Contreras .30 .09
❑ 140 Kevin Brown .30 .09
❑ 141 Mariano Rivera .50 .15
❑ 142 Mike Mussina .50 .15
❑ 143 Barry Zito .30 .09
❑ 144 Bobby Crosby .50 .15
❑ 145 Eric Chavez .30 .09
❑ 146 Erubiel Durazo .30 .09
❑ 147 Jermaine Dye .30 .09
❑ 148 Mark Kotsay .30 .09
❑ 149 Mark Mulder .30 .09
❑ 150 Rich Harden .30 .09
❑ 151 Tim Hudson .30 .09
❑ 152 Billy Wagner .30 .09
❑ 153 Bobby Abreu .30 .09
❑ 154 Brett Myers .30 .09
❑ 155 Jim Thome .75 .23
❑ 156 Jimmy Rollins .30 .09
❑ 157 Kevin Millwood .30 .09
❑ 158 Marlon Byrd .30 .09
❑ 159 Pat Burrell .30 .09
❑ 160 Jason Bay .30 .09
❑ 161 Jason Kendall .30 .09
❑ 162 Brian Giles .30 .09
❑ 163 Jay Payton .30 .09
❑ 164 Ryan Klesko .30 .09
❑ 165 Edgardo Alfonzo .30 .09
❑ 166 Jason Schmidt .30 .09
❑ 167 Jerome Williams .30 .09
❑ 168 Todd Linden .30 .09
❑ 169 Bret Boone .30 .09
❑ 170 Edgar Martinez .50 .15
❑ 171 Freddy Garcia .30 .09
❑ 172 Ichiro Suzuki 1.25 .35
❑ 173 Jamie Moyer .30 .09
❑ 174 John Olerud .30 .09
❑ 175 Shigetoshi Hasegawa .30 .09
❑ 176 Albert Pujols 1.50 .45
❑ 177 Dan Haren .30 .09
❑ 178 Edgar Renteria .30 .09
❑ 179 Jim Edmonds .30 .09
❑ 180 Matt Morris .30 .09
❑ 181 Scott Rolen .75 .23
❑ 182 Aubrey Huff .30 .09

Card	Nm-Mt	Ex-Mt
❑ 183 Carl Crawford	.30	.09
❑ 184 Chad Gaudin	.30	.09
❑ 185 Delmon Young	.50	.15
❑ 186 Dewon Brazelton	.30	.09
❑ 187 Fred McGriff	.50	.15
❑ 188 Rocco Baldelli	.30	.09
❑ 189 Alfonso Soriano	.50	.15
❑ 190 Hank Blalock	.30	.09
❑ 191 Laynce Nix	.30	.09
❑ 192 Mark Teixeira	.30	.09
❑ 193 Michael Young	.30	.09
❑ 194 Carlos Delgado	.30	.09
❑ 195 Eric Hinske	.30	.09
❑ 196 Frank Catalanotto	.30	.09
❑ 197 Josh Phelps	.30	.09
❑ 198 Orlando Hudson	.30	.09
❑ 199 Roy Halladay	.30	.09
❑ 200 Vernon Wells	.30	.09
❑ 201 Dale Murphy RET	3.00	.90
❑ 202 Cal Ripken RET	12.00	3.60
❑ 203 Fred Lynn RET	2.00	.60
❑ 204 Wade Boggs RET	3.00	.90
❑ 205 Nolan Ryan RET	8.00	2.40
❑ 206 Rod Carew RET	3.00	.90
❑ 207 Andre Dawson RET	2.00	.60
❑ 208 Ernie Banks RET	3.00	.90
❑ 209 Ryne Sandberg RET	6.00	1.80
❑ 210 Bo Jackson RET	3.00	.90
❑ 211 Carlton Fisk RET	3.00	.90
❑ 212 Dave Concepcion RET	2.00	.60
❑ 213 Alan Trammell RET	2.00	.60
❑ 214 George Brett RET	6.00	1.80
❑ 215 Robin Yount RET	5.00	1.50
❑ 216 Gary Carter RET	2.00	.60
❑ 217 Darryl Strawberry RET	2.00	.60
❑ 218 Dwight Gooden RET	2.00	.60
❑ 219 Babe Ruth RET	6.00	1.80
❑ 220 Don Mattingly RET	6.00	1.80
❑ 221 Reggie Jackson RET	3.00	.90
❑ 222 Mike Schmidt RET	6.00	1.80
❑ 223 Tony Gwynn RET	5.00	1.50
❑ 224 Keith Hernandez RET	2.00	.60
❑ 225 Hector Gimenez ROO RC	3.00	.90
❑ 226 Graham Koonce ROO	3.00	.90
❑ 227 John Gall ROO RC	5.00	1.50
❑ 228 Jerry Gil ROO RC	3.00	.90
❑ 229 Jason Frasor ROO RC	3.00	.90
❑ 230 Justin Knoedler ROO RC	3.00	.90
❑ 231 Ivan Ochoa ROO RC	3.00	.90
❑ 232 Greg Dobbs ROO RC	3.00	.90
❑ 233 Ronald Belisario ROO RC	3.00	.90
❑ 234 Jerome Gamble ROO RC	3.00	.90
❑ 235 Roberto Novoa ROO RC	3.00	.90
❑ 236 Sean Henn ROO RC	3.00	.90
❑ 237 Willy Taveras ROO RC	5.00	1.50
❑ 238 Ramon Ramirez ROO RC	3.00	.90
❑ 239 Kazuo Matsui ROO RC	8.00	2.40
❑ 240 Akinori Otsuka ROO RC	3.00	.90
❑ 241 Jason Bartlett ROO RC	5.00	1.50
❑ 242 Fernando Nieve ROO RC	3.00	.90
❑ 243 Freddy Guzman ROO RC	3.00	.90
❑ 244 Aarom Baldiris ROO RC	5.00	1.50
❑ 245 Merkin Valdez ROO RC	5.00	1.50
❑ 246 Mike Gosling ROO RC	3.00	.90
❑ 247 Shingo Takatsu ROO RC	5.00	1.50
❑ 248 William Bergolla ROO RC	3.00	.90
❑ 249 Shawn Hill ROO RC	3.00	.90
❑ 250 Justin Germano ROO RC	3.00	.90

2003 Timeless Treasures

STATED PRINT RUN 900 SERIAL #'d SETS
PRODUCED BY DONRUSS/PLAYOFF

Card	Nm-Mt	Ex-Mt
❑ 1 Adam Dunn	4.00	1.20
❑ 2 Al Kaline	5.00	1.50
❑ 3 Alan Trammell	4.00	1.20
❑ 4 Albert Pujols	8.00	2.40
❑ 5 Alex Rodriguez	6.00	1.80
❑ 6 Alfonso Soriano	4.00	1.20
❑ 7 Andre Dawson	4.00	1.20
❑ 8 Andruw Jones	4.00	1.20
❑ 9 Austin Kearns	4.00	1.20
❑ 10 Babe Ruth	10.00	3.00
❑ 11 Barry Bonds	10.00	3.00
❑ 12 Barry Larkin	4.00	1.20
❑ 13 Barry Zito	4.00	1.20
❑ 14 Bernie Williams	4.00	1.20
❑ 15 Bo Jackson	5.00	1.50
❑ 16 Brooks Robinson	4.00	1.20
❑ 17 Cal Ripken	12.00	3.60
❑ 18 Carlton Fisk	4.00	1.20
❑ 19 Chipper Jones	5.00	1.50
❑ 20 Curt Schilling	4.00	1.20
❑ 21 Dale Murphy	5.00	1.50
❑ 22 Derek Jeter	10.00	3.00
❑ 23 Don Mattingly	10.00	3.00
❑ 24 Duke Snider	4.00	1.20
❑ 25 Eddie Mathews	5.00	1.50
❑ 26 Frank Robinson	4.00	1.20
❑ 27 Frank Thomas	5.00	1.50
❑ 28 Garret Anderson	4.00	1.20
❑ 29 Gary Carter	4.00	1.20
❑ 30 George Brett	10.00	3.00
❑ 31 Greg Maddux	6.00	1.80
❑ 32 Harmon Killebrew	5.00	1.50
❑ 33 Hideki Matsui RC	10.00	3.00
❑ 34 Hideo Nomo	5.00	1.50
❑ 35 Ichiro Suzuki	6.00	1.80
❑ 36 Ivan Rodriguez	5.00	1.50
❑ 37 Jackie Robinson	5.00	1.50
❑ 38 Jason Giambi	4.00	1.20
❑ 39 Jeff Bagwell	4.00	1.20
❑ 40 Jim Edmonds	4.00	1.20
❑ 41 Jim Palmer	4.00	1.20
❑ 42 Jim Thome	5.00	1.50
❑ 43 Joe Morgan	4.00	1.20
❑ 44 Jorge Posada	4.00	1.20
❑ 45 Jose Contreras RC	5.00	1.50
❑ 46 Juan Gonzalez	4.00	1.20
❑ 47 Kazuhisa Ishii	4.00	1.20
❑ 48 Ken Griffey Jr.	6.00	1.80
❑ 49 Kerry Wood	5.00	1.50
❑ 50 Kirby Puckett	5.00	1.50
❑ 51 Lance Berkman	4.00	1.20
❑ 52 Larry Walker	4.00	1.20
❑ 53 Lou Brock	4.00	1.20
❑ 54 Lou Gehrig	6.00	1.80
❑ 55 Magglio Ordonez	4.00	1.20
❑ 56 Mark Prior	5.00	1.50
❑ 57 Miguel Tejada	4.00	1.20
❑ 58 Mike Mussina	4.00	1.20
❑ 59 Mike Piazza	6.00	1.80
❑ 60 Mike Schmidt	8.00	2.40
❑ 61 Nolan Ryan	10.00	3.00
❑ 62 Nomar Garciaparra	6.00	1.80
❑ 63 Ozzie Smith	6.00	1.80
❑ 64 Pat Burrell	4.00	1.20
❑ 65 Pedro Martinez	5.00	1.50
❑ 66 Pee Wee Reese	4.00	1.20
❑ 67 Phil Rizzuto	4.00	1.20
❑ 68 Rafael Palmeiro	4.00	1.20
❑ 69 Randy Johnson	5.00	1.50
❑ 70 Reggie Jackson	4.00	1.20
❑ 71 Richie Ashburn	4.00	1.20
❑ 72 Rickey Henderson	5.00	1.50
❑ 73 Roberto Alomar	4.00	1.20
❑ 74 Roberto Clemente	8.00	2.40
❑ 75 Robin Yount	6.00	1.80
❑ 76 Rod Carew	4.00	1.20
❑ 77 Roger Clemens	8.00	2.40
❑ 78 Rogers Hornsby	5.00	1.50
❑ 79 Roy Oswalt	4.00	1.20
❑ 80 Ryan Klesko	4.00	1.20
❑ 81 Ryne Sandberg	8.00	2.40
❑ 82 Sammy Sosa	6.00	1.80
❑ 83 Scott Rolen	5.00	1.50
❑ 84 Shawn Green	4.00	1.20
❑ 85 Stan Musial	6.00	1.80
❑ 86 Steve Carlton	4.00	1.20
❑ 87 Thurman Munson	5.00	1.50
❑ 88 Todd Helton	4.00	1.20
❑ 89 Tom Glavine	4.00	1.20
❑ 90 Tom Seaver	4.00	1.20
❑ 91 Tony Gwynn	5.00	1.50
❑ 92 Tony Perez	4.00	1.20
❑ 93 Torii Hunter	4.00	1.20
❑ 94 Troy Glaus	4.00	1.20
❑ 95 Ty Cobb	6.00	1.80
❑ 96 Vernon Wells	4.00	1.20
❑ 97 Vladimir Guerrero	5.00	1.50
❑ 98 Warren Spahn	4.00	1.20
❑ 99 Willie McCovey	4.00	1.20
❑ 100 Yogi Berra	5.00	1.50

2004 Timeless Treasures

	Nm-Mt	Ex-Mt
COMPLETE SET (100)	250.00	75.00

STATED PRINT RUN 999 SERIAL #'d SETS

Card	Nm-Mt	Ex-Mt
❑ 1 Albert Pujols	6.00	1.80
❑ 2 Garret Anderson	4.00	1.20
❑ 3 Randy Johnson	4.00	1.20
❑ 4 Alex Rodriguez Yanks	6.00	1.80
❑ 5 Manny Ramirez	4.00	1.20
❑ 6 Mark Prior	4.00	1.20
❑ 7 Roberto Alomar	4.00	1.20
❑ 8 Barry Larkin	4.00	1.20
❑ 9 Todd Helton	4.00	1.20
❑ 10 Ivan Rodriguez	4.00	1.20
❑ 11 Jacque Jones	4.00	1.20
❑ 12 Jeff Kent	4.00	1.20
❑ 13 Mike Sweeney	4.00	1.20
❑ 14 Shawn Green	4.00	1.20
❑ 15 Richie Sexson	4.00	1.20
❑ 16 Mike Piazza	5.00	1.50
❑ 17 Vladimir Guerrero	4.00	1.20
❑ 18 Mike Mussina	4.00	1.20
❑ 19 Barry Zito	4.00	1.20
❑ 20 Don Mattingly	8.00	2.40
❑ 21 Ichiro Suzuki	5.00	1.50
❑ 22 Rocco Baldelli	4.00	1.20
❑ 23 Rafael Palmeiro	4.00	1.20
❑ 24 Carlos Delgado	4.00	1.20
❑ 25 Roger Clemens	6.00	1.80
❑ 26 Luis Gonzalez	4.00	1.20
❑ 27 Gary Sheffield	4.00	1.20
❑ 28 Jay Gibbons	4.00	1.20
❑ 29 Nomar Garciaparra	5.00	1.50
❑ 30 Aramis Ramirez	4.00	1.20
❑ 31 Frank Thomas	4.00	1.20
❑ 32 Ryan Wagner	4.00	1.20
❑ 33 Preston Wilson	4.00	1.20
❑ 34 Hideki Matsui	5.00	1.50
❑ 35 Roy Oswalt	4.00	1.20
❑ 36 Angel Berroa	4.00	1.20
❑ 37 Kazuhisa Ishii	4.00	1.20
❑ 38 Scott Podsednik	4.00	1.20
❑ 39 Torii Hunter	4.00	1.20
❑ 40 Tom Glavine	4.00	1.20
❑ 41 Jason Giambi	4.00	1.20

	NM	Ex
❑ 42 Eric Chavez	4.00	1.20
❑ 43 Jim Thome	4.00	1.20
❑ 44 Tony Gwynn	4.00	1.20
❑ 45 Edgar Martinez	4.00	1.20
❑ 46 Jim Edmonds	4.00	1.20
❑ 47 Delmon Young	4.00	1.20
❑ 48 Hank Blalock	4.00	1.20
❑ 49 Vernon Wells	4.00	1.20
❑ 50 Curt Schilling	4.00	1.20
❑ 51 Chipper Jones	4.00	1.20
❑ 52 Cal Ripken	10.00	3.00
❑ 53 Jason Varitek	4.00	1.20
❑ 54 Kerry Wood	4.00	1.20
❑ 55 Magglio Ordonez	4.00	1.20
❑ 56 Adam Dunn	4.00	1.20
❑ 57 Jay Payton	4.00	1.20
❑ 58 Josh Beckett	4.00	1.20
❑ 59 Jeff Bagwell	4.00	1.20
❑ 60 Carlos Beltran	4.00	1.20
❑ 61 Hideo Nomo	4.00	1.20
❑ 62 Rickie Weeks	4.00	1.20
❑ 63 Alfonso Soriano	4.00	1.20
❑ 64 Miguel Tejada	4.00	1.20
❑ 65 Bret Boone	4.00	1.20
❑ 66 Scott Rolen	4.00	1.20
❑ 67 Aubrey Huff	4.00	1.20
❑ 68 Juan Gonzalez	4.00	1.20
❑ 69 Roy Halladay	4.00	1.20
❑ 70 Brandon Webb	4.00	1.20
❑ 71 Andruw Jones	4.00	1.20
❑ 72 Pedro Martinez	4.00	1.20
❑ 73 Carlos Lee	4.00	1.20
❑ 74 Lance Berkman	4.00	1.20
❑ 75 Paul LoDuca	4.00	1.20
❑ 76 Jorge Posada	4.00	1.20
❑ 77 Tim Hudson	4.00	1.20
❑ 78 Stan Musial	5.00	1.50
❑ 79 Mark Teixeira	4.00	1.20
❑ 80 Trot Nixon	4.00	1.20
❑ 81 Fred McGriff	4.00	1.20
❑ 82 Nick Johnson	4.00	1.20
❑ 83 Nolan Ryan	8.00	2.40
❑ 84 Ken Griffey Jr.	5.00	1.50
❑ 85 Mariano Rivera	4.00	1.20
❑ 86 Mark Mulder	4.00	1.20
❑ 87 Bob Gibson	4.00	1.20
❑ 88 Dale Murphy UER	4.00	1.20
❑ 89 Bernie Williams	4.00	1.20
❑ 90 Carl Yastrzemski	5.00	1.50
❑ 91 Sammy Sosa	5.00	1.50
❑ 92 Miguel Cabrera	4.00	1.20
❑ 93 Craig Biggio	4.00	1.20
❑ 94 George Brett	8.00	2.40
❑ 95 Rickey Henderson	4.00	1.20
❑ 96 Derek Jeter	6.00	1.80
❑ 97 Greg Maddux	5.00	1.50
❑ 98 Bob Abreu	4.00	1.20
❑ 99 Troy Glaus	4.00	1.20
❑ 100 Dontrelle Willis	4.00	1.20

1952 Topps

	NM	Ex
COMP.MASTER SET (487)	80000.00	40000.00
COMPLETE SET (407)	65000.00	32500.00
COMMON CARD (1-80)	60.00	30.00
COMMON CARD (81-250)	40.00	20.00
COMMON (251-310)	50.00	25.00
COMMON (311-407)	250.00	125.00
WRAPPER (1-cent)	250.00	125.00
WRAPPER (5-cent)	100.00	50.00

	NM	Ex
❑ 1 Andy Pafko	5000.00	500.00
❑ 1A Andy Pafko Black	3000.00	300.00
❑ 2 Pete Runnels RC	250.00	125.00
❑ 2A Pete Runnells RC Black	250.00	125.00
❑ 3 Hank Thompson	70.00	35.00
❑ 3A Hank Thompson Black	70.00	35.00
❑ 4 Don Lenhardt	60.00	30.00
❑ 4A Don Lenhardt Black	60.00	30.00
❑ 5 Larry Jansen	70.00	35.00
❑ 5A Larry Jansen Black	70.00	35.00
❑ 6 Grady Hatton	60.00	30.00
❑ 6A Grady Hatton Black	60.00	30.00
❑ 7 Wayne Terwilliger	60.00	30.00
❑ 7A W. Terwilliger Black	60.00	30.00
❑ 8 Fred Marsh	60.00	30.00
❑ 8A Fred Marsh Black	60.00	30.00
❑ 9 Robert Hogue	60.00	30.00
❑ 9A Robert Hogue Black	60.00	30.00
❑ 10 Al Rosen	70.00	35.00
❑ 10A Al Rosen Black	70.00	35.00
❑ 11 Phil Rizzuto	400.00	200.00
❑ 11A Phil Rizzuto Black	350.00	180.00
❑ 12 Monty Basgall	60.00	30.00
❑ 12A Monty Basgall Black	60.00	30.00
❑ 13 Johnny Wyrostek	60.00	30.00
❑ 13A J. Wyrostek Black	60.00	30.00
❑ 14 Bob Elliott	70.00	35.00
❑ 14A Bob Elliott Black	70.00	35.00
❑ 15 Johnny Pesky	70.00	35.00
❑ 15A Johnny Pesky Black	70.00	35.00
❑ 16 Gene Hermanski	60.00	30.00
❑ 16A G. Hermanski Black	60.00	30.00
❑ 17 Jim Hegan	70.00	35.00
❑ 17A Jim Hegan Black	70.00	35.00
❑ 18 Merrill Combs	60.00	30.00
❑ 18A Merrill Combs Black	60.00	30.00
❑ 19 Johnny Bucha	60.00	30.00
❑ 19A Johnny Bucha Black	60.00	30.00
❑ 20 Billy Loes RC	125.00	60.00
❑ 20A Billy Loes RC Black	125.00	60.00
❑ 21 Ferris Fain	70.00	35.00
❑ 21A Ferris Fain Black	70.00	35.00
❑ 22 Dom DiMaggio	100.00	50.00
❑ 22A Dom DiMaggio Black	100.00	50.00
❑ 23 Billy Goodman	70.00	35.00
❑ 23A Billy Goodman Black	70.00	35.00
❑ 24 Luke Easter	80.00	40.00
❑ 24A Luke Easter Black	80.00	40.00
❑ 25 Johnny Groth	60.00	30.00
❑ 25A Johnny Groth Black	60.00	30.00
❑ 26 Monte Irvin	150.00	75.00
❑ 26A Monte Irvin Black	125.00	60.00
❑ 27 Sam Jethroe	70.00	35.00
❑ 27A Sam Jethroe Black	70.00	35.00
❑ 28 Jerry Priddy	60.00	30.00
❑ 28A Jerry Priddy Black	60.00	30.00
❑ 29 Ted Kluszewski	125.00	60.00
❑ 29A Ted Kluszewski Black	125.00	60.00
❑ 30 Mel Parnell	70.00	35.00
❑ 30A Mel Parnell Black	70.00	35.00
❑ 31 Gus Zernial Posed with seven baseballs	80.00	40.00
❑ 31A Gus Zernial Black Posed with seven baseballs	80.00	40.00
❑ 32 Eddie Robinson	60.00	30.00
❑ 32A Eddie Robinson Black	60.00	30.00
❑ 33 Warren Spahn	300.00	150.00
❑ 33A Warren Spahn Black	250.00	125.00
❑ 34 Elmer Valo	60.00	30.00
❑ 34A Elmer Valo Black	60.00	30.00
❑ 35 Hank Sauer	70.00	35.00
❑ 35A Hank Sauer Black	70.00	35.00
❑ 36 Gil Hodges	300.00	150.00
❑ 36A Gil Hodges Black	250.00	125.00
❑ 37 Duke Snider	500.00	250.00
❑ 37A Duke Snider Black	400.00	200.00
❑ 38 Wally Westlake	60.00	30.00
❑ 38A Wally Westlake Black	60.00	30.00
❑ 39 Dizzy Trout	70.00	35.00
❑ 39A Dizzy Trout Black	70.00	35.00
❑ 40 Irv Noren	70.00	35.00
❑ 40A Irv Noren Black	70.00	35.00
❑ 41 Bob Wellman	60.00	30.00
❑ 41A Bob Wellman Black	60.00	30.00
❑ 42 Lou Kretlow	60.00	30.00
❑ 42A Lou Kretlow Black	60.00	30.00
❑ 43 Ray Scarborough	60.00	30.00
❑ 43A R. Scarbourough Black	60.00	30.00
❑ 44 Con Dempsey	60.00	30.00
❑ 44A Con Dempsey Black	60.00	30.00
❑ 45 Eddie Joost	60.00	30.00
❑ 45A Eddie Joost Black	60.00	30.00
❑ 46 Gordon Goldsberry	60.00	30.00
❑ 46A G. Goldsberry Black	60.00	30.00
❑ 47 Willie Jones	70.00	35.00
❑ 47A Willie Jones Black	70.00	35.00
❑ 48A Joe Page ERR Bio for Sain Black Back	400.00	200.00
❑ 48B Joe Page COR Black Back	125.00	60.00
❑ 48C Joe Page COR Red Back	125.00	60.00
❑ 49A John Sain ERR Bio for Page Black Back	400.00	200.00
❑ 49B John Sain COR Black Back	125.00	60.00
❑ 49C John Sain COR Red Back	125.00	60.00
❑ 50 Marv Rickert	60.00	30.00
❑ 50A Marv Richert Black	60.00	30.00
❑ 51 Jim Russell	60.00	30.00
❑ 51A Jim Russell Black	60.00	30.00
❑ 52 Don Mueller	70.00	35.00
❑ 52A Don Mueller Black	70.00	35.00
❑ 53 Chris Van Cuyk	60.00	30.00
❑ 53A Chris Van Cuyk Black	60.00	30.00
❑ 54 Leo Kiely	60.00	30.00
❑ 54A Leo Kiely Black	60.00	30.00
❑ 55 Ray Boone	80.00	40.00
❑ 55A Ray Boone Black	80.00	40.00
❑ 56 Tommy Glaviano	60.00	30.00
❑ 56A T. Glaviano Black	60.00	30.00
❑ 57 Ed Lopat	100.00	50.00
❑ 57A Ed Lopat Black	100.00	50.00
❑ 58 Bob Mahoney	60.00	30.00
❑ 58A Bob Mahoney Black	60.00	30.00
❑ 59 Robin Roberts	175.00	90.00
❑ 59A Robin Roberts Black	175.00	90.00
❑ 60 Sid Hudson	60.00	30.00
❑ 60A Sid Hudson Black	60.00	30.00
❑ 61 Tookie Gilbert	60.00	30.00
❑ 61A Tookie Gilbert Black	60.00	30.00
❑ 62 Chuck Stobbs	60.00	30.00
❑ 62A Chuck Stobbs Black	60.00	30.00
❑ 63 Howie Pollet	60.00	30.00
❑ 63A Howie Pollet Black	60.00	30.00
❑ 64 Roy Sievers	70.00	35.00
❑ 64A Roy Sievers Black	70.00	35.00
❑ 65 Enos Slaughter	175.00	90.00
❑ 65A Enos Slaughter Black	175.00	90.00
❑ 66 Preacher Roe	100.00	50.00
❑ 66A Preacher Roe Black	100.00	50.00
❑ 67 Allie Reynolds	125.00	60.00
❑ 67A Allie Reynolds Black	100.00	50.00
❑ 68 Cliff Chambers	60.00	30.00
❑ 68A Cliff Chambers Black	60.00	30.00
❑ 69 Virgil Stallcup	60.00	30.00
❑ 69A Virgil Stallcup Black	60.00	30.00
❑ 70 Al Zarilla	60.00	30.00
❑ 70A Al Zarilla Black	60.00	30.00
❑ 71 Tom Upton	60.00	30.00
❑ 71A Tom Upton Black	60.00	30.00
❑ 72 Karl Olson	60.00	30.00
❑ 72A Karl Olson Black	60.00	30.00
❑ 73 Bill Werle	60.00	30.00
❑ 73A Bill Werle Black	60.00	30.00
❑ 74 Andy Hansen	60.00	30.00
❑ 74A Andy Hansen Black	60.00	30.00
❑ 75 Wes Westrum	70.00	35.00
❑ 75A Wes Westrum Black	70.00	35.00
❑ 76 Eddie Stanky	70.00	35.00
❑ 76A Eddie Stanky Black	70.00	35.00
❑ 77 Bob Kennedy	70.00	35.00
❑ 77A Bob Kennedy Black	70.00	35.00
❑ 78 Ellis Kinder	60.00	30.00
❑ 78A Ellis Kinder Black	60.00	30.00

❑ 79 Gerry Staley 60.00 30.00
❑ 79A Gerry Staley Black 60.00 30.00
❑ 80 Herman Wehmeier 80.00 40.00
❑ 80A H. Wehmeier Black 80.00 40.00
❑ 81 Vernon Law 80.00 40.00
❑ 82 Duane Pillette 40.00 20.00
❑ 83 Billy Johnson 40.00 20.00
❑ 84 Vern Stephens 50.00 25.00
❑ 85 Bob Kuzava 50.00 25.00
❑ 86 Ted Gray 40.00 20.00
❑ 87 Dale Coogan 40.00 20.00
❑ 88 Bob Feller 250.00 125.00
❑ 89 Johnny Lipon 40.00 20.00
❑ 90 Mickey Grasso 40.00 20.00
❑ 91 Red Schoendienst 100.00 50.00
❑ 92 Dale Mitchell 50.00 25.00
❑ 93 Al Sima 40.00 20.00
❑ 94 Sam Mele 40.00 20.00
❑ 95 Ken Holcombe 40.00 20.00
❑ 96 Willard Marshall 40.00 20.00
❑ 97 Earl Torgeson 40.00 20.00
❑ 98 Billy Pierce 50.00 25.00
❑ 99 Gene Woodling 60.00 30.00
❑ 100 Del Rice 40.00 20.00
❑ 101 Max Lanier 40.00 20.00
❑ 102 Bill Kennedy 40.00 20.00
❑ 103 Cliff Mapes 40.00 20.00
❑ 104 Don Kolloway 40.00 20.00
❑ 105 Johnny Pramesa 40.00 20.00
❑ 106 Mickey Vernon 60.00 30.00
❑ 107 Connie Ryan 40.00 20.00
❑ 108 Jim Konstanty 60.00 30.00
❑ 109 Ted Wilks 40.00 20.00
❑ 110 Dutch Leonard 40.00 20.00
❑ 111 Peanuts Lowrey 40.00 20.00
❑ 112 Hank Majeski 40.00 20.00
❑ 113 Dick Sisler 50.00 25.00
❑ 114 Willard Ramsdell 40.00 20.00
❑ 115 George Munger 40.00 20.00
❑ 116 Carl Scheib 40.00 20.00
❑ 117 Sherm Lollar 50.00 25.00
❑ 118 Ken Raffensberger 40.00 20.00
❑ 119 Mickey McDermott 40.00 20.00
❑ 120 Bob Chakales 40.00 20.00
❑ 121 Gus Niarhos 40.00 20.00
❑ 122 Jackie Jensen 80.00 40.00
❑ 123 Eddie Yost 50.00 25.00
❑ 124 Monte Kennedy 40.00 20.00
❑ 125 Bill Rigney 40.00 20.00
❑ 126 Fred Hutchinson 50.00 25.00
❑ 127 Paul Minner 40.00 20.00
❑ 128 Don Bollweg 40.00 20.00
❑ 129 Johnny Mize 150.00 75.00
❑ 130 Sheldon Jones 40.00 20.00
❑ 131 Morrie Martin 40.00 20.00
❑ 132 Clyde Kluttz 40.00 20.00
❑ 133 Al Widmar 40.00 20.00
❑ 134 Joe Tipton 40.00 20.00
❑ 135 Dixie Howell 40.00 20.00
❑ 136 Johnny Schmitz 40.00 20.00
❑ 137 Roy McMillan RC 50.00 25.00
❑ 138 Bill MacDonald 40.00 20.00
❑ 139 Ken Wood 40.00 20.00
❑ 140 Johnny Antonelli 60.00 30.00
❑ 141 Clint Hartung 40.00 20.00
❑ 142 Harry Perkowski 40.00 20.00
❑ 143 Les Moss 40.00 20.00
❑ 144 Ed Blake 40.00 20.00
❑ 145 Joe Haynes 40.00 20.00
❑ 146 Frank House 40.00 20.00
❑ 147 Bob Young 40.00 20.00
❑ 148 Johnny Klippstein 40.00 20.00
❑ 149 Dick Kryhoski 40.00 20.00
❑ 150 Ted Beard 40.00 20.00
❑ 151 Wally Post RC 50.00 25.00
❑ 152 Al Evans 40.00 20.00
❑ 153 Bob Rush 40.00 20.00
❑ 154 Joe Muir 40.00 20.00
❑ 155 Frank Overmire 40.00 20.00
❑ 156 Frank Hiller 40.00 20.00
❑ 157 Bob Usher 40.00 20.00
❑ 158 Eddie Waitkus 40.00 20.00
❑ 159 Saul Rogovin 40.00 20.00
❑ 160 Owen Friend 40.00 20.00
❑ 161 Bud Byerly 40.00 20.00
❑ 162 Del Crandall 50.00 25.00
❑ 163 Stan Rojek 40.00 20.00
❑ 164 Walt Dubiel 40.00 20.00
❑ 165 Eddie Kazak 40.00 20.00
❑ 166 Paul LaPalme 40.00 20.00
❑ 167 Bill Howerton 40.00 20.00
❑ 168 Charlie Silvera RC 60.00 30.00
❑ 169 Howie Judson 40.00 20.00
❑ 170 Gus Bell 50.00 25.00
❑ 171 Ed Erautt 40.00 20.00
❑ 172 Eddie Miksis 40.00 20.00
❑ 173 Roy Smalley 40.00 20.00
❑ 174 Clarence Marshall 60.00 30.00
❑ 175 Billy Martin RC 500.00 250.00
❑ 176 Hank Edwards 40.00 20.00
❑ 177 Bill Wight 40.00 20.00
❑ 178 Cass Michaels 40.00 20.00
❑ 179 Frank Smith 40.00 20.00
❑ 180 Charlie Maxwell RC 50.00 25.00
❑ 181 Bob Swift 40.00 20.00
❑ 182 Billy Hitchcock 40.00 20.00
❑ 183 Erv Dusak 40.00 20.00
❑ 184 Bob Ramazzotti 40.00 20.00
❑ 185 Bill Nicholson 50.00 25.00
❑ 186 Walt Masterson 40.00 20.00
❑ 187 Bob Miller 40.00 20.00
❑ 188 Clarence Podbielan 40.00 20.00
❑ 189 Pete Reiser 60.00 30.00
❑ 190 Don Johnson 40.00 20.00
❑ 191 Yogi Berra 800.00 400.00
❑ 192 Myron Ginsberg 40.00 20.00
❑ 193 Harry Simpson 50.00 25.00
❑ 194 Joe Hatton 40.00 20.00
❑ 195 Minnie Minoso RC 150.00 75.00
❑ 196 Solly Hemus RC 60.00 30.00
❑ 197 George Strickland 40.00 20.00
❑ 198 Phil Haugstad 40.00 20.00
❑ 199 George Zuverink 40.00 20.00
❑ 200 Ralph Houk RC 80.00 40.00
❑ 201 Alex Kellner 40.00 20.00
❑ 202 Joe Collins RC 60.00 30.00
❑ 203 Curt Simmons 60.00 30.00
❑ 204 Ron Northey 40.00 20.00
❑ 205 Clyde King 60.00 30.00
❑ 206 Joe Ostrowski 40.00 20.00
❑ 207 Mickey Harris 40.00 20.00
❑ 208 Marlin Stuart 40.00 20.00
❑ 209 Howie Fox 40.00 20.00
❑ 210 Dick Fowler 40.00 20.00
❑ 211 Ray Coleman 40.00 20.00
❑ 212 Ned Garver 40.00 20.00
❑ 213 Nippy Jones 40.00 20.00
❑ 214 Johnny Hopp 50.00 25.00
❑ 215 Hank Bauer 100.00 50.00
❑ 216 Richie Ashburn 250.00 125.00
❑ 217 Snuffy Stirnweiss 50.00 25.00
❑ 218 Clyde McCullough 40.00 20.00
❑ 219 Bobby Shantz 60.00 30.00
❑ 220 Joe Presko 40.00 20.00
❑ 221 Granny Hamner 40.00 20.00
❑ 222 Hoot Evers 40.00 20.00
❑ 223 Del Ennis 50.00 25.00
❑ 224 Bruce Edwards 40.00 20.00
❑ 225 Frank Baumholtz 40.00 20.00
❑ 226 Dave Philley 40.00 20.00
❑ 227 Joe Garagiola 80.00 40.00
❑ 228 Al Brazle 40.00 20.00
❑ 229 Gene Bearden UER 40.00 20.00
(Misspelled Beardon)
❑ 230 Matt Batts 40.00 20.00
❑ 231 Sam Zoldak 40.00 20.00
❑ 232 Billy Cox 50.00 25.00
❑ 233 Bob Friend RC 80.00 40.00
❑ 234 Steve Souchock 40.00 20.00
❑ 235 Walt Dropo 40.00 20.00
❑ 236 Ed Fitzgerald 40.00 20.00
❑ 237 Jerry Coleman 60.00 30.00
❑ 238 Art Houtteman 40.00 20.00
❑ 239 Rocky Bridges 50.00 25.00
❑ 240 Jack Phillips 40.00 20.00
❑ 241 Tommy Byrne 40.00 20.00
❑ 242 Tom Poholsky 40.00 20.00
❑ 243 Larry Doby 80.00 40.00
❑ 244 Vic Wertz 40.00 20.00
❑ 245 Sherry Robertson 40.00 20.00
❑ 246 George Kell 80.00 40.00
❑ 247 Randy Gumpert 40.00 20.00
❑ 248 Frank Shea 40.00 20.00
❑ 249 Bobby Adams 40.00 20.00
❑ 250 Carl Erskine 100.00 50.00
❑ 251 Chico Carrasquel 50.00 25.00
❑ 252 Vern Bickford 50.00 25.00
❑ 253 Johnny Berardino 100.00 50.00
❑ 254 Joe Dobson 50.00 25.00
❑ 255 Clyde Vollmer 50.00 25.00
❑ 256 Pete Suder 50.00 25.00
❑ 257 Bobby Avila 60.00 30.00
❑ 258 Steve Gromek 60.00 30.00
❑ 259 Bob Addis 50.00 25.00
❑ 260 Pete Castiglione 50.00 25.00
❑ 261 Willie Mays 3000.00 1500.00
❑ 262 Virgil Trucks 60.00 30.00
❑ 263 Harry Brecheen 60.00 30.00
❑ 264 Roy Hartsfield 50.00 25.00
❑ 265 Chuck Diering 50.00 25.00
❑ 266 Murry Dickson 50.00 25.00
❑ 267 Sid Gordon 60.00 30.00
❑ 268 Bob Lemon 150.00 75.00
❑ 269 Willard Nixon 50.00 25.00
❑ 270 Lou Brissie 50.00 25.00
❑ 271 Jim Delsing 60.00 30.00
❑ 272 Mike Garcia 80.00 40.00
❑ 273 Erv Palica 50.00 25.00
❑ 274 Ralph Branca 125.00 60.00
❑ 275 Pat Mullin 50.00 25.00
❑ 276 Jim Wilson RC 50.00 25.00
❑ 277 Early Wynn 175.00 90.00
❑ 278 Allie Clark 50.00 25.00
❑ 279 Eddie Stewart 50.00 25.00
❑ 280 Cloyd Boyer 80.00 40.00
❑ 281 Tommy Brown SP 80.00 40.00
❑ 282 Birdie Tebbetts SP 80.00 40.00
❑ 283 Phil Masi SP 60.00 30.00
❑ 284 Hank Arft SP 60.00 30.00
❑ 285 Cliff Fannin SP 60.00 30.00
❑ 286 Joe DeMaestri SP 60.00 30.00
❑ 287 Steve Bilko SP 60.00 30.00
❑ 288 Chet Nichols SP 80.00 40.00
❑ 289 Tommy Holmes SP 100.00 50.00
❑ 290 Joe Astroth SP 60.00 30.00
❑ 291 Gil Coan SP 60.00 30.00
❑ 292 Floyd Baker SP 60.00 30.00
❑ 293 Sibby Sisti SP 60.00 30.00
❑ 294 Walker Cooper SP 60.00 30.00
❑ 295 Phil Cavarretta SP 80.00 40.00
❑ 296 Red Rolfe MG SP 60.00 30.00
❑ 297 Andy Seminick SP 60.00 30.00
❑ 298 Bob Ross SP 60.00 30.00
❑ 299 Ray Murray SP 80.00 40.00
❑ 300 Barney McCosky SP 80.00 40.00
❑ 301 Bob Porterfield 50.00 25.00
❑ 302 Max Surkont 50.00 25.00
❑ 303 Harry Dorish 50.00 25.00
❑ 304 Sam Dente 50.00 25.00
❑ 305 Paul Richards MG 60.00 30.00
❑ 306 Lou Sleater 50.00 25.00
❑ 307 Frank Campos 50.00 25.00
❑ 307A Frank Campos
Black Star on Back
❑ 308 Luis Aloma 50.00 25.00
❑ 309 Jim Busby 60.00 30.00
❑ 310 George Metkovich 100.00 50.00
❑ 311 Mickey Mantle DP 18000.00 9000.00
❑ 312 Jackie Robinson DP 2000.00 1000.00
❑ 313 Bobby Thomson DP 350.00 180.00
❑ 314 Roy Campanella 2500.00 1250.00
❑ 315 Leo Durocher MG 600.00 300.00
❑ 316 Dave Williams RC 300.00 150.00
❑ 317 Conrado Marrero 300.00 150.00
❑ 318 Harold Gregg 300.00 150.00
❑ 319 Rube Walker 250.00 125.00
❑ 320 John Rutherford RC 300.00 150.00
❑ 321 Joe Black RC 350.00 180.00
❑ 322 Randy Jackson 300.00 150.00
❑ 323 Bubba Church 250.00 125.00
❑ 324 Warren Hacker 250.00 125.00
❑ 325 Bill Serena 300.00 150.00
❑ 326 George Shuba RC 400.00 200.00
❑ 327 Al Wilson 250.00 125.00
❑ 328 Bob Borkowski 300.00 150.00
❑ 329 Ike Delock 300.00 150.00
❑ 330 Turk Lown 300.00 150.00
❑ 331 Tom Morgan 300.00 150.00

Card	NM	Ex
❑ 332 Anthony Bartirome	300.00	150.00
❑ 333 Pee Wee Reese	1800.00	900.00
❑ 334 Wilmer Mizell RC	300.00	150.00
❑ 335 Ted Lepcio	250.00	125.00
❑ 336 Dave Koslo	250.00	125.00
❑ 337 Jim Hearn	300.00	150.00
❑ 338 Sal Yvars	300.00	150.00
❑ 339 Russ Meyer	300.00	150.00
❑ 340 Bob Hooper	300.00	150.00
❑ 341 Hal Jeffcoat	300.00	150.00
❑ 342 Clem Labine RC	400.00	200.00
❑ 343 Dick Gernert	250.00	125.00
❑ 344 Ewell Blackwell	300.00	150.00
❑ 345 Sammy White	250.00	125.00
❑ 346 George Spencer	250.00	125.00
❑ 347 Joe Adcock	400.00	200.00
❑ 348 Robert Kelly	250.00	125.00
❑ 349 Bob Cain	300.00	150.00
❑ 350 Cal Abrams	300.00	150.00
❑ 351 Alvin Dark	300.00	150.00
❑ 352 Karl Drews	300.00	150.00
❑ 353 Bobby Del Greco	300.00	150.00
❑ 354 Fred Hatfield	300.00	150.00
❑ 355 Bobby Morgan	300.00	150.00
❑ 356 Toby Atwell	300.00	150.00
❑ 357 Smoky Burgess	300.00	150.00
❑ 358 John Kucab	300.00	150.00
❑ 359 Dee Fondy	250.00	125.00
❑ 360 George Crowe RC	300.00	150.00
❑ 361 William Posedel CO	250.00	125.00
❑ 362 Ken Heintzelman	300.00	150.00
❑ 363 Dick Rozek	300.00	150.00
❑ 364 Clyde Sukeforth CO	300.00	150.00
❑ 365 Cookie Lavagetto CO	400.00	200.00
❑ 366 Dave Madison	250.00	125.00
❑ 367 Ben Thorpe	300.00	150.00
❑ 368 Ed Wright	300.00	150.00
❑ 369 Dick Groat RC	400.00	200.00
❑ 370 Billy Hoeft RC	300.00	150.00
❑ 371 Bobby Hofman	250.00	125.00
❑ 372 Gil McDougald RC	500.00	250.00
❑ 373 Jim Turner CO RC	400.00	200.00
❑ 374 John Benton	250.00	125.00
❑ 375 John Merson	250.00	125.00
❑ 376 Faye Throneberry	250.00	125.00
❑ 377 Chuck Dressen MG	400.00	200.00
❑ 378 Leroy Fusselman	300.00	150.00
❑ 379 Joe Rossi	250.00	125.00
❑ 380 Clem Koshorek	250.00	125.00
❑ 381 Milton Stock CO	300.00	150.00
❑ 382 Sam Jones RC	350.00	180.00
❑ 383 Del Wilber	250.00	125.00
❑ 384 Frank Crosetti CO	500.00	250.00
❑ 385 H.Franks CO RC	250.00	125.00
❑ 386 John Yuhas	300.00	150.00
❑ 387 Billy Meyer MG	250.00	125.00
❑ 388 Bob Chipman	250.00	125.00
❑ 389 Ben Wade	300.00	150.00
❑ 390 Rocky Nelson	300.00	150.00
❑ 391 B.Chapman UER CO Photo actually Sam Chapman	250.00	125.00
❑ 392 Hoyt Wilhelm RC	800.00	400.00
❑ 393 Ebba St.Claire	300.00	150.00
❑ 394 Billy Herman CO	600.00	300.00
❑ 395 Jake Pitler CO	300.00	150.00
❑ 396 Dick Williams RC	400.00	200.00
❑ 397 Forrest Main	250.00	125.00
❑ 398 Hal Rice	250.00	125.00
❑ 399 Jim Fridley	250.00	125.00
❑ 400 Bill Dickey CO	1000.00	500.00
❑ 401 Bob Schultz	300.00	150.00
❑ 402 Earl Harrist	300.00	150.00
❑ 403 Bill Miller	300.00	150.00
❑ 404 Dick Brodowski	300.00	150.00
❑ 405 Eddie Pellagrini	300.00	150.00
❑ 406 Joe Nuxhall RC	400.00	200.00
❑ 407 Eddie Mathews RC	12000.00	2500.00

1953 Topps

	NM	Ex
COMPLETE SET (274)	15000.00	7500.00
COMMON CARD (1-165)	30.00	15.00
COMMON (166-220)	25.00	12.50
COMMON DP (1-220)	15.00	7.50
COMMON (221-280)	100.00	50.00
NOT ISSUED (253/261/267)		
NOT ISSUED (268/271/275)		
WRAP.(1-CENT, DATED)	200.00	100.00
WRAP.(1-CENT, UNDATED)	300.00	150.00
WRAP.(5-CENT, DATED)	400.00	200.00
WRAP.(5-CENT, UNDATED)	350.00	180.00

Card	NM	Ex
❑ 1 Jackie Robinson DP	800.00	220.00
❑ 2 Luke Easter DP	20.00	10.00
❑ 3 George Crowe	40.00	20.00
❑ 4 Ben Wade	30.00	15.00
❑ 5 Joe Dobson	30.00	15.00
❑ 6 Sam Jones	40.00	20.00
❑ 7 Bob Borkowski DP	15.00	7.50
❑ 8 Clem Koshorek DP	15.00	7.50
❑ 9 Joe Collins	60.00	30.00
❑ 10 Smoky Burgess SP	80.00	40.00
❑ 11 Sal Yvars	30.00	15.00
❑ 12 Howie Judson DP	15.00	7.50
❑ 13 Conrado Marrero DP	15.00	7.50
❑ 14 Clem Labine DP	20.00	10.00
❑ 15 Bobo Newsom DP	20.00	10.00
❑ 16 Peanuts Lowrey DP	15.00	7.50
❑ 17 Billy Hitchcock	30.00	15.00
❑ 18 Ted Lepcio DP	15.00	7.50
❑ 19 Mel Parnell DP	20.00	10.00
❑ 20 Hank Thompson	40.00	20.00
❑ 21 Billy Johnson	30.00	15.00
❑ 22 Howie Fox	30.00	15.00
❑ 23 Toby Atwell DP	15.00	7.50
❑ 24 Ferris Fain	40.00	20.00
❑ 25 Ray Boone	40.00	20.00
❑ 26 Dale Mitchell DP	20.00	10.00
❑ 27 Roy Campanella DP	300.00	150.00
❑ 28 Eddie Pellagrini	30.00	15.00
❑ 29 Hal Jeffcoat	30.00	15.00
❑ 30 Willard Nixon	30.00	15.00
❑ 31 Ewell Blackwell	60.00	30.00
❑ 32 Clyde Vollmer	30.00	15.00
❑ 33 Bob Kennedy DP	15.00	7.50
❑ 34 George Shuba	40.00	20.00
❑ 35 Irv Noren DP	15.00	7.50
❑ 36 Johnny Groth DP	15.00	7.50
❑ 37 Eddie Mathews DP	250.00	125.00
❑ 38 Jim Hearn DP	15.00	7.50
❑ 39 Eddie Miksis	30.00	15.00
❑ 40 John Lipon	30.00	15.00
❑ 41 Enos Slaughter	80.00	40.00
❑ 42 Gus Zernial DP	20.00	10.00
❑ 43 Gil McDougald	60.00	30.00
❑ 44 Ellis Kinder SP	50.00	25.00
❑ 45 Grady Hatton DP	15.00	7.50
❑ 46 Johnny Klippstein DP	15.00	7.50
❑ 47 Bubba Church DP	15.00	7.50
❑ 48 Bob Del Greco DP	15.00	7.50
❑ 49 Faye Throneberry DP	15.00	7.50
❑ 50 Chuck Dressen MG DP	20.00	10.00
❑ 51 Frank Campos DP	15.00	7.50
❑ 52 Ted Gray DP	15.00	7.50
❑ 53 Sherm Lollar DP	20.00	10.00
❑ 54 Bob Feller DP	150.00	75.00
❑ 55 Maurice McDermott DP	15.00	7.50
❑ 56 Gerry Staley DP	15.00	7.50
❑ 57 Carl Scheib	30.00	15.00
❑ 58 George Metkovich	30.00	15.00
❑ 59 Karl Drews DP	15.00	7.50
❑ 60 Cloyd Boyer DP	15.00	7.50
❑ 61 Early Wynn SP	125.00	60.00
❑ 62 Monte Irvin DP	50.00	25.00
❑ 63 Gus Niarhos DP	15.00	7.50
❑ 64 Dave Philley	30.00	15.00
❑ 65 Earl Harrist	30.00	15.00
❑ 66 Minnie Minoso	60.00	30.00
❑ 67 Roy Sievers DP	20.00	10.00
❑ 68 Del Rice	30.00	15.00
❑ 69 Dick Brodowski	30.00	15.00
❑ 70 Ed Yuhas	30.00	15.00
❑ 71 Tony Bartirome	30.00	15.00
❑ 72 F.Hutchinson MG SP	50.00	25.00
❑ 73 Eddie Robinson	30.00	15.00
❑ 74 Joe Rossi	30.00	15.00
❑ 75 Mike Garcia	40.00	20.00
❑ 76 Pee Wee Reese	175.00	90.00
❑ 77 Johnny Mize DP	80.00	40.00
❑ 78 Red Schoendienst	80.00	40.00
❑ 79 Johnny Wyrostek	30.00	15.00
❑ 80 Jim Hegan	40.00	20.00
❑ 81 Joe Black SP	80.00	40.00
❑ 82 Mickey Mantle	3000.00	1800.00
❑ 83 Howie Pollet	30.00	15.00
❑ 84 Bob Hooper DP	15.00	7.50
❑ 85 Bobby Morgan DP	15.00	7.50
❑ 86 Billy Martin	125.00	60.00
❑ 87 Ed Lopat	60.00	30.00
❑ 88 Willie Jones DP	15.00	7.50
❑ 89 Chuck Stobbs DP	15.00	7.50
❑ 90 Hank Edwards DP	15.00	7.50
❑ 91 Ebba St.Claire DP	15.00	7.50
❑ 92 Paul Minner DP	15.00	7.50
❑ 93 Hal Rice DP	15.00	7.50
❑ 94 Bill Kennedy DP	15.00	7.50
❑ 95 Willard Marshall DP	15.00	7.50
❑ 96 Virgil Trucks	40.00	20.00
❑ 97 Don Kolloway DP	15.00	7.50
❑ 98 Cal Abrams DP	15.00	7.50
❑ 99 Dave Madison	30.00	15.00
❑ 100 Bill Miller	30.00	15.00
❑ 101 Ted Wilks	30.00	15.00
❑ 102 Connie Ryan DP	15.00	7.50
❑ 103 Joe Astroth DP	15.00	7.50
❑ 104 Yogi Berra	300.00	150.00
❑ 105 Joe Nuxhall DP	20.00	10.00
❑ 106 Johnny Antonelli	40.00	20.00
❑ 107 Danny O'Connell DP	15.00	7.50
❑ 108 Bob Porterfield DP	15.00	7.50
❑ 109 Alvin Dark	60.00	30.00
❑ 110 Herman Wehmeier DP	15.00	7.50
❑ 111 Hank Sauer DP	15.00	7.50
❑ 112 Ned Garver DP	15.00	7.50
❑ 113 Jerry Priddy	30.00	15.00
❑ 114 Phil Rizzuto	250.00	125.00
❑ 115 George Spencer	30.00	15.00
❑ 116 Frank Smith DP	15.00	7.50
❑ 117 Sid Gordon DP	15.00	7.50
❑ 118 Gus Bell DP	20.00	10.00
❑ 119 Johnny Sain SP	60.00	30.00
❑ 120 Davey Williams	40.00	20.00
❑ 121 Walt Dropo	40.00	20.00
❑ 122 Elmer Valo	30.00	15.00
❑ 123 Tommy Byrne DP	15.00	7.50
❑ 124 Sibby Sisti DP	15.00	7.50
❑ 125 Dick Williams DP	20.00	10.00
❑ 126 Bill Connelly DP	15.00	7.50
❑ 127 Clint Courtney DP	15.00	7.50
❑ 128 Wilmer Mizell DP (Inconsistent design, logo on front with black birds)	20.00	10.00
❑ 129 Keith Thomas	30.00	15.00
❑ 130 Turk Lown DP	15.00	7.50
❑ 131 Harry Byrd DP	15.00	7.50
❑ 132 Tom Morgan	30.00	15.00
❑ 133 Gil Coan	30.00	15.00
❑ 134 Rube Walker	40.00	20.00
❑ 135 Al Rosen DP	20.00	10.00
❑ 136 Ken Heintzelman DP	15.00	7.50
❑ 137 John Rutherford DP	15.00	7.50
❑ 138 George Kell	80.00	40.00
❑ 139 Sammy White	30.00	15.00
❑ 140 Tommy Glaviano	30.00	15.00
❑ 141 Allie Reynolds DP	50.00	25.00
❑ 142 Vic Wertz	40.00	20.00
❑ 143 Billy Pierce	60.00	30.00

Card	NM	Ex
❑ 144 Bob Schultz DP	15.00	7.50
❑ 145 Harry Dorish DP	15.00	7.50
❑ 146 Granny Hamner	30.00	15.00
❑ 147 Warren Spahn	175.00	90.00
❑ 148 Mickey Grasso	30.00	15.00
❑ 149 Dom DiMaggio DP	50.00	25.00
❑ 150 Harry Simpson DP	15.00	7.50
❑ 151 Hoyt Wilhelm	100.00	50.00
❑ 152 Bob Adams DP	15.00	7.50
❑ 153 Andy Seminick DP	15.00	7.50
❑ 154 Dick Groat	40.00	20.00
❑ 155 Dutch Leonard	30.00	15.00
❑ 156 Jim Rivera DP	20.00	10.00
❑ 157 Bob Addis DP	15.00	7.50
❑ 158 Johnny Logan RC	40.00	20.00
❑ 159 Wayne Terwilliger DP	15.00	7.50
❑ 160 Bob Young	30.00	15.00
❑ 161 Vern Bickford DP	15.00	7.50
❑ 162 Ted Kluszewski	60.00	30.00
❑ 163 Fred Hatfield DP	15.00	7.50
❑ 164 Frank Shea DP	15.00	7.50
❑ 165 Billy Hoeft	30.00	15.00
❑ 166 Billy Hunter	25.00	12.50
❑ 167 Art Schult	25.00	12.50
❑ 168 Willard Schmidt	25.00	12.50
❑ 169 Dizzy Trout	30.00	15.00
❑ 170 Bill Werle	25.00	12.50
❑ 171 Bill Glynn	25.00	12.50
❑ 172 Rip Repulski	25.00	12.50
❑ 173 Preston Ward	25.00	12.50
❑ 174 Billy Loes	30.00	15.00
❑ 175 Ron Kline	25.00	12.50
❑ 176 Don Hoak RC	40.00	20.00
❑ 177 Jim Dyck	25.00	12.50
❑ 178 Jim Waugh	25.00	12.50
❑ 179 Gene Hermanski	25.00	12.50
❑ 180 Virgil Stallcup	25.00	12.50
❑ 181 Al Zarilla	25.00	12.50
❑ 182 Bobby Hofman	25.00	12.50
❑ 183 Stu Miller RC	40.00	20.00
❑ 184 Hal Brown	25.00	12.50
❑ 185 Jim Pendleton	25.00	12.50
❑ 186 Charlie Bishop	25.00	12.50
❑ 187 Jim Fridley	25.00	12.50
❑ 188 Andy Carey RC	40.00	20.00
❑ 189 Ray Jablonski	25.00	12.50
❑ 190 Dixie Walker CO	30.00	15.00
❑ 191 Ralph Kiner	80.00	40.00
❑ 192 Wally Westlake	25.00	12.50
❑ 193 Mike Clark	25.00	12.50
❑ 194 Eddie Kazak	25.00	12.50
❑ 195 Ed McGhee	25.00	12.50
❑ 196 Bob Keegan	25.00	12.50
❑ 197 Del Crandall	40.00	20.00
❑ 198 Forrest Main	25.00	12.50
❑ 199 Marion Fricano	25.00	12.50
❑ 200 Gordon Goldsberry	25.00	12.50
❑ 201 Paul LaPalme	25.00	12.50
❑ 202 Carl Sawatski	25.00	12.50
❑ 203 Cliff Fannin	25.00	12.50
❑ 204 Dick Bokelman	25.00	12.50
❑ 205 Vern Benson	25.00	12.50
❑ 206 Ed Bailey RC	30.00	15.00
❑ 207 Whitey Ford	200.00	100.00
❑ 208 Jim Wilson	25.00	12.50
❑ 209 Jim Greengrass	25.00	12.50
❑ 210 Bob Cerv RC	40.00	20.00
❑ 211 J.W. Porter	25.00	12.50
❑ 212 Jack Dittmer	25.00	12.50
❑ 213 Ray Scarborough	25.00	12.50
❑ 214 Bill Bruton RC	40.00	20.00
❑ 215 Gene Conley RC	30.00	15.00
❑ 216 Jim Hughes	25.00	12.50
❑ 217 Murray Wall	25.00	12.50
❑ 218 Les Fusselman	25.00	12.50
❑ 219 Pete Runnels UER (Photo actually Don Johnson)	30.00	15.00
❑ 220 Satchel Paige UER (Misspelled Satchell on card front)	600.00	300.00
❑ 221 Bob Milliken	100.00	50.00
❑ 222 Vic Janowicz DP RC	60.00	30.00
❑ 223 Johnny O'Brien DP	50.00	25.00
❑ 224 Lou Sleater DP	50.00	25.00
❑ 225 Bobby Shantz	125.00	60.00
❑ 226 Ed Erautt	100.00	50.00
❑ 227 Morrie Martin	100.00	50.00
❑ 228 Hal Newhouser	150.00	75.00
❑ 229 Rocky Krsnich	100.00	50.00
❑ 230 Johnny Lindell DP	50.00	25.00
❑ 231 Solly Hemus DP	50.00	25.00
❑ 232 Dick Kokos	100.00	50.00
❑ 233 Al Aber	100.00	50.00
❑ 234 Ray Murray DP	50.00	25.00
❑ 235 John Hetki DP	50.00	25.00
❑ 236 Harry Perkowski DP	50.00	25.00
❑ 237 Bud Podbielan DP	50.00	25.00
❑ 238 Cal Hogue DP	50.00	25.00
❑ 239 Jim Delsing	100.00	50.00
❑ 240 Fred Marsh	100.00	50.00
❑ 241 Al Sima DP	50.00	25.00
❑ 242 Charlie Silvera	125.00	60.00
❑ 243 Carlos Bernier DP	50.00	25.00
❑ 244 Willie Mays	2500.00	1250.00
❑ 245 Bill Norman CO	100.00	50.00
❑ 246 Roy Face DP RC	80.00	40.00
❑ 247 Mike Sandlock DP	50.00	25.00
❑ 248 Gene Stephens DP	50.00	25.00
❑ 249 Eddie O'Brien	100.00	50.00
❑ 250 Bob Wilson	100.00	50.00
❑ 251 Sid Hudson	100.00	50.00
❑ 252 Hank Foiles	100.00	50.00
❑ 253 Does not exist		
❑ 254 Preacher Roe DP	80.00	40.00
❑ 255 Dixie Howell	100.00	50.00
❑ 256 Les Peden	100.00	50.00
❑ 257 Bob Boyd	100.00	50.00
❑ 258 Jim Gilliam RC	400.00	200.00
❑ 259 Roy McMillan DP	50.00	25.00
❑ 260 Sam Calderone	100.00	50.00
❑ 261 Does not exist		
❑ 262 Bob Oldis	100.00	50.00
❑ 263 Johnny Podres RC	300.00	150.00
❑ 264 Gene Woodling DP	60.00	30.00
❑ 265 Jackie Jensen	125.00	60.00
❑ 266 Bob Cain	100.00	50.00
❑ 267 Does not exist		
❑ 268 Does not exist		
❑ 269 Duane Pillette	100.00	50.00
❑ 270 Vern Stephens	125.00	60.00
❑ 271 Does not exist		
❑ 272 Bill Antonello	100.00	50.00
❑ 273 Harvey Haddix RC	150.00	75.00
❑ 274 John Riddle CO	100.00	50.00
❑ 275 Does not exist		
❑ 276 Ken Raffensberger	100.00	50.00
❑ 277 Don Lund	100.00	50.00
❑ 278 Willie Miranda	100.00	50.00
❑ 279 Joe Coleman DP	50.00	25.00
❑ 280 Milt Bolling RC	350.00	57.50

1954 Topps

	NM	Ex
COMPLETE SET (250)	8000.00	4000.00
COMMON (1-50/76-250)	15.00	7.50
COMMON CARD (51-75)	25.00	12.50
WRAP.(1-CENT, DATED)	200.00	100.00
WRAP.(1-CENT, UNDATED)	150.00	75.00
WRAP.(5-CENT, DATED)	300.00	150.00
WRAP.(5-CENT, UNDATED)	250.00	125.00
❑ 1 Ted Williams	800.00	275.00
❑ 2 Gus Zernial	25.00	12.50
❑ 3 Monte Irvin	50.00	25.00
❑ 4 Hank Sauer	25.00	12.50
❑ 5 Ed Lopat	25.00	12.50
❑ 6 Pete Runnels	25.00	12.50
❑ 7 Ted Kluszewski	50.00	25.00
❑ 8 Bob Young	15.00	7.50
❑ 9 Harvey Haddix	25.00	12.50
❑ 10 Jackie Robinson	400.00	200.00
❑ 11 Paul Leslie Smith	15.00	7.50
❑ 12 Del Crandall	25.00	12.50
❑ 13 Billy Martin	100.00	50.00
❑ 14 Preacher Roe UER (February is misspelled)	25.00	12.50
❑ 15 Al Rosen	25.00	12.50
❑ 16 Vic Janowicz	25.00	12.50
❑ 17 Phil Rizzuto	125.00	60.00
❑ 18 Walt Dropo	25.00	12.50
❑ 19 Johnny Lipon (Orioles Team Name on Front; White Sox team on Back; Wearing a Red Sox cap)	15.00	7.50
❑ 20 Warren Spahn	125.00	60.00
❑ 21 Bobby Shantz	25.00	12.50
❑ 22 Jim Greengrass	15.00	7.50
❑ 23 Luke Easter	25.00	12.50
❑ 24 Granny Hamner	15.00	7.50
❑ 25 Harvey Kuenn RC	40.00	20.00
❑ 26 Ray Jablonski	15.00	7.50
❑ 27 Ferris Fain	25.00	12.50
❑ 28 Paul Minner	15.00	7.50
❑ 29 Jim Hegan	25.00	12.50
❑ 30 Eddie Mathews	100.00	50.00
❑ 31 Johnny Klippstein	15.00	7.50
❑ 32 Duke Snider	200.00	100.00
❑ 33 Johnny Schmitz	15.00	7.50
❑ 34 Jim Rivera	15.00	7.50
❑ 35 Jim Gilliam	50.00	25.00
❑ 36 Hoyt Wilhelm	50.00	25.00
❑ 37 Whitey Ford	200.00	100.00
❑ 38 Eddie Stanky MG	25.00	12.50
❑ 39 Sherm Lollar	25.00	12.50
❑ 40 Mel Parnell	25.00	12.50
❑ 41 Willie Jones	15.00	7.50
❑ 42 Don Mueller	25.00	12.50
❑ 43 Dick Groat	25.00	12.50
❑ 44 Ned Garver	15.00	7.50
❑ 45 Richie Ashburn	80.00	40.00
❑ 46 Ken Raffensberger	15.00	7.50
❑ 47 Ellis Kinder	15.00	7.50
❑ 48 Billy Hunter	25.00	12.50
❑ 49 Ray Murray	15.00	7.50
❑ 50 Yogi Berra	250.00	125.00
❑ 51 Johnny Lindell	25.00	12.50
❑ 52 Vic Power RC	30.00	15.00
❑ 53 Jack Dittmer	25.00	12.50
❑ 54 Vern Stephens	30.00	15.00
❑ 55 Phil Cavarretta MG	30.00	15.00
❑ 56 Willie Miranda	25.00	12.50
❑ 57 Luis Aloma	25.00	12.50
❑ 58 Bob Wilson	25.00	12.50
❑ 59 Gene Conley	30.00	15.00
❑ 60 Frank Baumholtz	25.00	12.50
❑ 61 Bob Cain	25.00	12.50
❑ 62 Eddie Robinson	25.00	12.50
❑ 63 Johnny Pesky	30.00	15.00
❑ 64 Hank Thompson	25.00	12.50
❑ 65 Bob Swift CO	25.00	12.50
❑ 66 Ted Lepcio	25.00	12.50
❑ 67 Jim Willis	25.00	12.50
❑ 68 Sam Calderone	25.00	12.50
❑ 69 Bud Podbielan	25.00	12.50
❑ 70 Larry Doby	60.00	30.00
❑ 71 Frank Smith	25.00	12.50
❑ 72 Preston Ward	25.00	12.50
❑ 73 Wayne Terwilliger	25.00	12.50
❑ 74 Bill Taylor	25.00	12.50
❑ 75 Fred Haney MG	25.00	12.50
❑ 76 Bob Scheffing CO	15.00	7.50
❑ 77 Ray Boone	25.00	12.50
❑ 78 Ted Kazanski	15.00	7.50
❑ 79 Andy Pafko	25.00	12.50
❑ 80 Jackie Jensen	25.00	12.50
❑ 81 Dave Hoskins	15.00	7.50
❑ 82 Milt Bolling	15.00	7.50
❑ 83 Joe Collins	25.00	12.50

❑ 84 Dick Cole	15.00	7.50
❑ 85 Bob Turley RC	40.00	20.00
❑ 86 Billy Herman CO	25.00	12.50
❑ 87 Roy Face	25.00	12.50
❑ 88 Matt Batts	15.00	7.50
❑ 89 Howie Pollet	15.00	7.50
❑ 90 Willie Mays	800.00	400.00
❑ 91 Bob Oldis	15.00	7.50
❑ 92 Wally Westlake	15.00	7.50
❑ 93 Sid Hudson	15.00	7.50
❑ 94 Ernie Banks RC	1200.00	500.00
❑ 95 Hal Rice	15.00	7.50
❑ 96 Charlie Silvera	25.00	12.50
❑ 97 Jerald Hal Lane	15.00	7.50
❑ 98 Joe Black	40.00	20.00
❑ 99 Bobby Hofman	15.00	7.50
❑ 100 Bob Keegan	15.00	7.50
❑ 101 Gene Woodling	25.00	12.50
❑ 102 Gil Hodges	80.00	40.00
❑ 103 Jim Lemon RC	15.00	7.50
❑ 104 Mike Sandlock	15.00	7.50
❑ 105 Andy Carey	25.00	12.50
❑ 106 Dick Kokos	15.00	7.50
❑ 107 Duane Pillette	15.00	7.50
❑ 108 Thornton Kipper	15.00	7.50
❑ 109 Bill Bruton	25.00	12.50
❑ 110 Harry Dorish	15.00	7.50
❑ 111 Jim Delsing	15.00	7.50
❑ 112 Bill Renna	15.00	7.50
❑ 113 Bob Boyd	15.00	7.50
❑ 114 Dean Stone	15.00	7.50
❑ 115 Rip Repulski	15.00	7.50
❑ 116 Steve Bilko	15.00	7.50
❑ 117 Solly Hemus	15.00	7.50
❑ 118 Carl Scheib	15.00	7.50
❑ 119 Johnny Antonelli	25.00	12.50
❑ 120 Roy McMillan	25.00	12.50
❑ 121 Clem Labine	25.00	12.50
❑ 122 Johnny Logan	25.00	12.50
❑ 123 Bobby Adams	15.00	7.50
❑ 124 Marion Fricano	15.00	7.50
❑ 125 Harry Perkowski	15.00	7.50
❑ 126 Ben Wade	15.00	7.50
❑ 127 Steve O'Neill MG	15.00	7.50
❑ 128 Hank Aaron RC	1800.00	750.00
❑ 129 Forrest Jacobs	15.00	7.50
❑ 130 Hank Bauer	25.00	12.50
❑ 131 Reno Bertoia	25.00	12.50
❑ 132 Tommy Lasorda RC	250.00	125.00
❑ 133 Del Baker CO	15.00	7.50
❑ 134 Cal Hogue	15.00	7.50
❑ 135 Joe Presko	15.00	7.50
❑ 136 Connie Ryan	15.00	7.50
❑ 137 Wally Moon RC	40.00	20.00
❑ 138 Bob Borkowski	15.00	7.50
❑ 139 The O'Briens Johnny O'Brien Eddie O'Brien	50.00	25.00
❑ 140 Tom Wright	15.00	7.50
❑ 141 Joey Jay RC	25.00	12.50
❑ 142 Tom Poholsky	15.00	7.50
❑ 143 Rollie Hemsley CO	15.00	7.50
❑ 144 Bill Werle	15.00	7.50
❑ 145 Elmer Valo	15.00	7.50
❑ 146 Don Johnson	15.00	7.50
❑ 147 Johnny Riddle CO	15.00	7.50
❑ 148 Bob Trice	15.00	7.50
❑ 149 Al Robertson	15.00	7.50
❑ 150 Dick Kryhoski	15.00	7.50
❑ 151 Alex Grammas	15.00	7.50
❑ 152 Michael Blyzka	15.00	7.50
❑ 153 Al Walker	25.00	12.50
❑ 154 Mike Fornieles	15.00	7.50
❑ 155 Bob Kennedy	25.00	12.50
❑ 156 Joe Coleman	25.00	12.50
❑ 157 Don Lenhardt	25.00	12.50
❑ 158 Peanuts Lowrey	15.00	7.50
❑ 159 Dave Philley	15.00	7.50
❑ 160 Ralph Kress CO	15.00	7.50
❑ 161 John Hetki	15.00	7.50
❑ 162 Herman Wehmeier	15.00	7.50
❑ 163 Frank House	15.00	7.50
❑ 164 Stu Miller	25.00	12.50
❑ 165 Jim Pendleton	15.00	7.50
❑ 166 Johnny Podres	40.00	20.00
❑ 167 Don Lund	15.00	7.50
❑ 168 Morrie Martin	25.00	12.50
❑ 169 Jim Hughes	40.00	20.00
❑ 170 Dusty Rhodes RC	25.00	12.50
❑ 171 Leo Kiely	15.00	7.50
❑ 172 Harold Brown	15.00	7.50
❑ 173 Jack Harshman	15.00	7.50
❑ 174 Tom Qualters	15.00	7.50
❑ 175 Frank Leja RC	25.00	12.50
❑ 176 Robert Keely CO	15.00	7.50
❑ 177 Bob Milliken	15.00	7.50
❑ 178 Bill Glynn UER Spelled Gylnn on the front	15.00	7.50
❑ 179 Gair Allie	15.00	7.50
❑ 180 Wes Westrum	25.00	12.50
❑ 181 Mel Roach	15.00	7.50
❑ 182 Chuck Harmon	15.00	7.50
❑ 183 Earle Combs CO	25.00	12.50
❑ 184 Ed Bailey	15.00	7.50
❑ 185 Chuck Stobbs	15.00	7.50
❑ 186 Karl Olson	15.00	7.50
❑ 187 Heinie Manush CO	25.00	12.50
❑ 188 Dave Jolly	15.00	7.50
❑ 189 Bob Ross	15.00	7.50
❑ 190 Ray Herbert	15.00	7.50
❑ 191 John(Dick) Schofield RC	25.00	12.50
❑ 192 Ellis Deal CO	15.00	7.50
❑ 193 Johnny Hopp CO	25.00	12.50
❑ 194 Bill Sarni	15.00	7.50
❑ 195 Billy Consolo RC	15.00	7.50
❑ 196 Stan Jok	15.00	7.50
❑ 197 Lynwood Rowe CO ("Schoolboy")	25.00	12.50
❑ 198 Carl Sawatski	15.00	7.50
❑ 199 Glenn(Rocky) Nelson	15.00	7.50
❑ 200 Larry Jansen	25.00	12.50
❑ 201 Al Kaline RC	700.00	350.00
❑ 202 Bob Purkey RC	25.00	12.50
❑ 203 Harry Brecheen CO	25.00	12.50
❑ 204 Angel Scull	15.00	7.50
❑ 205 Johnny Sain	40.00	20.00
❑ 206 Ray Crone	15.00	7.50
❑ 207 Tom Oliver CO	15.00	7.50
❑ 208 Grady Hatton	15.00	7.50
❑ 209 Chuck Thompson	15.00	7.50
❑ 210 Bob Buhl RC	25.00	12.50
❑ 211 Don Hoak	25.00	12.50
❑ 212 Bob Micelotta	15.00	7.50
❑ 213 Johnny Fitzpatrick CO	15.00	7.50
❑ 214 Arnie Portocarrero	15.00	7.50
❑ 215 Ed McGhee	25.00	12.50
❑ 216 Al Sima	15.00	7.50
❑ 217 Paul Schreiber CO	15.00	7.50
❑ 218 Fred Marsh	15.00	7.50
❑ 219 Chuck Kress	15.00	7.50
❑ 220 Ruben Gomez	25.00	12.50
❑ 221 Dick Brodowski	15.00	7.50
❑ 222 Bill Wilson	15.00	7.50
❑ 223 Joe Haynes CO	15.00	7.50
❑ 224 Dick Weik	15.00	7.50
❑ 225 Don Liddle	15.00	7.50
❑ 226 Jehosie Heard	25.00	12.50
❑ 227 Buster Mills CO	15.00	7.50
❑ 228 Gene Hermanski	15.00	7.50
❑ 229 Bob Talbot	15.00	7.50
❑ 230 Bob Kuzava	25.00	12.50
❑ 231 Roy Smalley	15.00	7.50
❑ 232 Lou Limmer	15.00	7.50
❑ 233 Augie Galan CO	15.00	7.50
❑ 234 Jerry Lynch RC	15.00	7.50
❑ 235 Vern Law	25.00	12.50
❑ 236 Paul Penson	15.00	7.50
❑ 237 Mike Ryba CO	15.00	7.50
❑ 238 Al Aber	15.00	7.50
❑ 239 Bill Skowron RC	100.00	50.00
❑ 240 Sam Mele	25.00	12.50
❑ 241 Robert Miller	15.00	7.50
❑ 242 Curt Roberts	15.00	7.50
❑ 243 Ray Blades CO	15.00	7.50
❑ 244 Leroy Wheat	15.00	7.50
❑ 245 Roy Sievers	25.00	12.50
❑ 246 Howie Fox	15.00	7.50
❑ 247 Ed Mayo CO	15.00	7.50
❑ 248 Al Smith RC	25.00	12.50
❑ 249 Wilmer Mizell	25.00	12.50
❑ 250 Ted Williams	800.00	325.00

1955 Topps

	NM	Ex
COMPLETE SET (206)	8000.00	4000.00
COMMON CARD (1-150)	12.00	6.00
COMMON (151-160)	20.00	10.00
COMMON (161-210)	30.00	15.00
NOT ISSUED (175/186/203/209)		
WRAP.(1-CENT, DATED)	150.00	75.00
WRAP.(1-CENT, UNDATED)	50.00	25.00
WRAP.(5-CENT, DATED)	150.00	75.00
WRAP.(5-CENT, DATED)	100.00	50.00
❑ 1 Dusty Rhodes	125.00	25.00
❑ 2 Ted Williams	600.00	300.00
❑ 3 Art Fowler	15.00	7.50
❑ 4 Al Kaline	150.00	75.00
❑ 5 Jim Gilliam	40.00	20.00
❑ 6 Stan Hack MG	25.00	12.50
❑ 7 Jim Hegan	15.00	7.50
❑ 8 Harold Smith	12.00	6.00
❑ 9 Robert Miller	12.00	6.00
❑ 10 Bob Keegan	12.00	6.00
❑ 11 Ferris Fain	15.00	7.50
❑ 12 Vernon(Jake) Thies	12.00	6.00
❑ 13 Fred Marsh	12.00	6.00
❑ 14 Jim Finigan	12.00	6.00
❑ 15 Jim Pendleton	12.00	6.00
❑ 16 Roy Sievers	15.00	7.50
❑ 17 Bobby Hofman	12.00	6.00
❑ 18 Russ Kemmerer	12.00	6.00
❑ 19 Billy Herman CO	15.00	7.50
❑ 20 Andy Carey	15.00	7.50
❑ 21 Alex Grammas	12.00	6.00
❑ 22 Bill Skowron	40.00	20.00
❑ 23 Jack Parks	12.00	6.00
❑ 24 Hal Newhouser	40.00	20.00
❑ 25 Johnny Podres	25.00	12.50
❑ 26 Dick Groat	15.00	7.50
❑ 27 Billy Gardner RC	15.00	7.50
❑ 28 Ernie Banks	200.00	100.00
❑ 29 Herman Wehmeier	12.00	6.00
❑ 30 Vic Power	15.00	7.50
❑ 31 Warren Spahn	100.00	50.00
❑ 32 Warren McGhee	12.00	6.00
❑ 33 Tom Qualters	12.00	6.00
❑ 34 Wayne Terwilliger	12.00	6.00
❑ 35 Dave Jolly	12.00	6.00
❑ 36 Leo Kiely	12.00	6.00
❑ 37 Joe Cunningham RC	15.00	7.50
❑ 38 Bob Turley	15.00	7.50
❑ 39 Bill Glynn	12.00	6.00
❑ 40 Don Hoak	15.00	7.50
❑ 41 Chuck Stobbs	12.00	6.00
❑ 42 John(Windy) McCall	12.00	6.00
❑ 43 Harvey Haddix	15.00	7.50
❑ 44 Harold Valentine	12.00	6.00
❑ 45 Hank Sauer	15.00	7.50
❑ 46 Ted Kazanski	12.00	6.00
❑ 47 Hank Aaron UER (Birth incorrectly listed as 2/10)	400.00	200.00
❑ 48 Bob Kennedy	15.00	7.50
❑ 49 J.W. Porter	12.00	6.00
❑ 50 Jackie Robinson	500.00	250.00
❑ 51 Jim Hughes	15.00	7.50
❑ 52 Bill Tremel	12.00	6.00
❑ 53 Bill Taylor	12.00	6.00
❑ 54 Lou Limmer	12.00	6.00
❑ 55 Rip Repulski	12.00	6.00
❑ 56 Ray Jablonski	12.00	6.00

Card	NM	Ex
❑ 57 Billy O'Dell	12.00	6.00
❑ 58 Jim Rivera	12.00	6.00
❑ 59 Gair Allie	12.00	6.00
❑ 60 Dean Stone	12.00	6.00
❑ 61 Forrest Jacobs	12.00	6.00
❑ 62 Thornton Kipper	12.00	6.00
❑ 63 Joe Collins	15.00	7.50
❑ 64 Gus Triandos RC	15.00	7.50
❑ 65 Ray Boone	15.00	7.50
❑ 66 Ron Jackson RC	12.00	6.00
❑ 67 Wally Moon	15.00	7.50
❑ 68 Jim Davis	12.00	6.00
❑ 69 Ed Bailey	15.00	7.50
❑ 70 Al Rosen	15.00	7.50
❑ 71 Ruben Gomez	12.00	6.00
❑ 72 Karl Olson	12.00	6.00
❑ 73 Jack Shepard	12.00	6.00
❑ 74 Bob Borkowski	12.00	6.00
❑ 75 Sandy Amoros RC	40.00	20.00
❑ 76 Howie Pollet	12.00	6.00
❑ 77 Arnie Portocarrero	12.00	6.00
❑ 78 Gordon Jones	12.00	6.00
❑ 79 Clyde(Danny) Schell	12.00	6.00
❑ 80 Bob Grim RC	15.00	7.50
❑ 81 Gene Conley	15.00	7.50
❑ 82 Chuck Harmon	12.00	6.00
❑ 83 Tom Brewer	12.00	6.00
❑ 84 Camilo Pascual RC	15.00	7.50
❑ 85 Don Mossi RC	25.00	12.50
❑ 86 Bill Wilson	12.00	6.00
❑ 87 Frank House	12.00	6.00
❑ 88 Bob Skinner RC	15.00	7.50
❑ 89 Joe Frazier	15.00	7.50
❑ 90 Karl Spooner RC	15.00	7.50
❑ 91 Milt Bolling	12.00	6.00
❑ 92 Don Zimmer RC	25.00	12.50
❑ 93 Steve Bilko	12.00	6.00
❑ 94 Reno Bertoia	12.00	6.00
❑ 95 Preston Ward	12.00	6.00
❑ 96 Chuck Bishop	12.00	6.00
❑ 97 Carlos Paula	12.00	6.00
❑ 98 John Riddle CO	12.00	6.00
❑ 99 Frank Leja	12.00	6.00
❑ 100 Monte Irvin	40.00	20.00
❑ 101 Johnny Gray	12.00	6.00
❑ 102 Wally Westlake	12.00	6.00
❑ 103 Chuck White	12.00	6.00
❑ 104 Jack Harshman	12.00	6.00
❑ 105 Chuck Diering	12.00	6.00
❑ 106 Frank Sullivan	12.00	6.00
❑ 107 Curt Roberts	12.00	6.00
❑ 108 Rube Walker	15.00	7.50
❑ 109 Ed Lopat	15.00	7.50
❑ 110 Gus Zernial	15.00	7.50
❑ 111 Bob Milliken	15.00	7.50
❑ 112 Nelson King	12.00	6.00
❑ 113 Harry Brecheen CO	15.00	7.50
❑ 114 Louis Ortiz	12.00	6.00
❑ 115 Ellis Kinder	12.00	6.00
❑ 116 Tom Hurd	12.00	6.00
❑ 117 Mel Roach	12.00	6.00
❑ 118 Bob Purkey	12.00	6.00
❑ 119 Bob Lennon	12.00	6.00
❑ 120 Ted Kluszewski	80.00	40.00
❑ 121 Bill Renna	12.00	6.00
❑ 122 Carl Sawatski	12.00	6.00
❑ 123 Sandy Koufax RC	800.00	400.00
❑ 124 Harmon Killebrew RC	250.00	125.00
❑ 125 Ken Boyer RC	80.00	40.00
❑ 126 Dick Hall	12.00	6.00
❑ 127 Dale Long RC	15.00	7.50
❑ 128 Ted Lepcio	12.00	6.00
❑ 129 Elvin Tappe	15.00	7.50
❑ 130 Mayo Smith MG	12.00	6.00
❑ 131 Grady Hatton	12.00	6.00
❑ 132 Bob Trice	12.00	6.00
❑ 133 Dave Hoskins	12.00	6.00
❑ 134 Joey Jay	15.00	7.50
❑ 135 Johnny O'Brien	15.00	7.50
❑ 136 Veston(Bunky)Stewart	12.00	6.00
❑ 137 Harry Elliott	12.00	6.00
❑ 138 Ray Herbert	12.00	6.00
❑ 139 Steve Kraly	12.00	6.00
❑ 140 Mel Parnell	15.00	7.50
❑ 141 Tom Wright	12.00	6.00
❑ 142 Jerry Lynch	15.00	7.50
❑ 143 John(Dick) Schofield	15.00	7.50
❑ 144 John(Joe) Amalfitano RC	12.00	6.00
❑ 145 Elmer Valo	12.00	6.00
❑ 146 Dick Donovan RC	12.00	6.00
❑ 147 Hugh Pepper	12.00	6.00
❑ 148 Hector Brown	12.00	6.00
❑ 149 Ray Crone	12.00	6.00
❑ 150 Mike Higgins MG	12.00	6.00
❑ 151 Ralph Kress CO	20.00	10.00
❑ 152 Harry Agganis RC	100.00	50.00
❑ 153 Bud Podbielan	25.00	12.50
❑ 154 Willie Miranda	20.00	10.00
❑ 155 Eddie Mathews	200.00	60.00
❑ 156 Joe Black	50.00	25.00
❑ 157 Robert Miller	20.00	10.00
❑ 158 Tommy Carroll	25.00	12.50
❑ 159 Johnny Schmitz	20.00	10.00
❑ 160 Ray Narleski RC	20.00	10.00
❑ 161 Chuck Tanner RC	40.00	20.00
❑ 162 Joe Coleman	30.00	15.00
❑ 163 Faye Throneberry	30.00	15.00
❑ 164 Roberto Clemente RC	2000.00	1000.00
❑ 165 Don Johnson	30.00	15.00
❑ 166 Hank Bauer	80.00	40.00
❑ 167 Tom Casagrande	30.00	15.00
❑ 168 Duane Pillette	30.00	15.00
❑ 169 Bob Oldis	40.00	20.00
❑ 170 Jim Pearce DP	15.00	7.50
❑ 171 Dick Brodowski	30.00	15.00
❑ 172 Frank Baumholtz DP	15.00	7.50
❑ 173 Bob Kline	30.00	15.00
❑ 174 Rudy Minarcin	30.00	15.00
❑ 175 Does not exist		
❑ 176 Norm Zauchin	30.00	15.00
❑ 177 Al Robertson	30.00	15.00
❑ 178 Bobby Adams	30.00	15.00
❑ 179 Jim Bolger	30.00	15.00
❑ 180 Clem Labine	60.00	30.00
❑ 181 Roy McMillan	40.00	20.00
❑ 182 Humberto Robinson	30.00	15.00
❑ 183 Anthony Jacobs	30.00	15.00
❑ 184 Harry Perkowski DP	15.00	7.50
❑ 185 Don Ferrarese	30.00	15.00
❑ 186 Does not exist		
❑ 187 Gil Hodges	175.00	90.00
❑ 188 Charlie Silvera DP	15.00	7.50
❑ 189 Phil Rizzuto	175.00	90.00
❑ 190 Gene Woodling	40.00	20.00
❑ 191 Eddie Stanky MG	40.00	20.00
❑ 192 Jim Delsing	40.00	20.00
❑ 193 Johnny Sain	60.00	30.00
❑ 194 Willie Mays	600.00	300.00
❑ 195 Ed Roebuck RC	60.00	30.00
❑ 196 Gale Wade	30.00	15.00
❑ 197 Al Smith	60.00	30.00
❑ 198 Yogi Berra	300.00	150.00
❑ 199 Bert Hamric	40.00	20.00
❑ 200 Jackie Jensen	60.00	30.00
❑ 201 Sherman Lollar	40.00	20.00
❑ 202 Jim Owens	30.00	15.00
❑ 203 Does not exist		
❑ 204 Frank Smith	30.00	15.00
❑ 205 Gene Freese RC	40.00	20.00
❑ 206 Pete Daley	30.00	15.00
❑ 207 Billy Consolo	30.00	15.00
❑ 208 Ray Moore	40.00	20.00
❑ 209 Does not exist		
❑ 210 Duke Snider	600.00	180.00

1956 Topps

	NM	Ex
COMPLETE SET (340)	8000.00	4000.00
COMMON CARD (1-100)	10.00	5.00
COMMON (101-180)	12.00	6.00
COMMON (261-340)	12.00	6.00
COMMON (181-260)	15.00	7.50
WRAPPER (1-CENT)	250.00	125.00
WRAP.(1-CENT, REPEAT)	100.00	50.00
WRAPPER (5-CENT)	200.00	100.00
❑ 1 Will Harridge PRES	125.00	35.00
❑ 2 W. Giles PRES RC DP	50.00	25.00
❑ 3 Elmer Valo	15.00	7.50
❑ 4 Carlos Paula	15.00	7.50
❑ 5 Ted Williams	500.00	250.00
❑ 6 Ray Boone	25.00	12.50
❑ 7 Ron Negray	10.00	5.00
❑ 8 Walter Alston MG RC	40.00	20.00
❑ 9 Ruben Gomez DP	10.00	5.00
❑ 10 Warren Spahn	100.00	50.00
❑ 11A Chicago Cubs (Centered)	30.00	15.00
❑ 11B Cubs Team (Dated 1955)	80.00	40.00
❑ 11C Cubs Team (Name at far left)	30.00	15.00
❑ 12 Andy Carey	15.00	7.50
❑ 13 Roy Face	15.00	7.50
❑ 14 Ken Boyer DP	15.00	7.50
❑ 15 Ernie Banks DP	100.00	50.00
❑ 16 Hector Lopez RC	15.00	7.50
❑ 17 Gene Conley	15.00	7.50
❑ 18 Dick Donovan	10.00	5.00
❑ 19 Chuck Diering DP	10.00	5.00
❑ 20 Al Kaline	125.00	60.00
❑ 21 Joe Collins DP	15.00	7.50
❑ 22 Jim Finigan	10.00	5.00
❑ 23 Fred Marsh	10.00	5.00
❑ 24 Dick Groat	15.00	7.50
❑ 25 Ted Kluszewski	80.00	40.00
❑ 26 Grady Hatton	10.00	5.00
❑ 27 Nelson Burbrink DP	10.00	5.00
❑ 28 Bobby Hofman	10.00	5.00
❑ 29 Jack Harshman	10.00	5.00
❑ 30 Jackie Robinson DP	250.00	125.00
❑ 31 Hank Aaron UER DP (Small photo actually Willie Mays)	350.00	180.00
❑ 32 Frank House	10.00	5.00
❑ 33 Roberto Clemente	400.00	200.00
❑ 34 Tom Brewer DP	10.00	5.00
❑ 35 Al Rosen	15.00	7.50
❑ 36 Rudy Minarcin	15.00	7.50
❑ 37 Alex Grammas	10.00	5.00
❑ 38 Bob Kennedy	15.00	7.50
❑ 39 Don Mossi	15.00	7.50
❑ 40 Bob Turley	15.00	7.50
❑ 41 Hank Sauer	15.00	7.50
❑ 42 Sandy Amoros	25.00	12.50
❑ 43 Ray Moore	10.00	5.00
❑ 44 Windy McCall	10.00	5.00
❑ 45 Gus Zernial	15.00	7.50
❑ 46 Gene Freese DP	10.00	5.00
❑ 47 Art Fowler	10.00	5.00
❑ 48 Jim Hegan	15.00	7.50
❑ 49 Pedro Ramos	10.00	5.00
❑ 50 Dusty Rhodes DP	15.00	7.50
❑ 51 Ernie Oravetz	10.00	5.00
❑ 52 Bob Grim DP	15.00	7.50
❑ 53 Arnie Portocarrero	10.00	5.00
❑ 54 Bob Keegan	10.00	5.00
❑ 55 Wally Moon	15.00	7.50
❑ 56 Dale Long	15.00	7.50
❑ 57 Duke Maas	10.00	5.00
❑ 58 Ed Roebuck	25.00	12.50
❑ 59 Jose Santiago	10.00	5.00
❑ 60 Mayo Smith MG DP	10.00	5.00
❑ 61 Bill Skowron	25.00	12.50
❑ 62 Hal Smith	15.00	7.50
❑ 63 Roger Craig RC	40.00	20.00
❑ 64 Luis Arroyo RC	10.00	5.00
❑ 65 Johnny O'Brien	15.00	7.50
❑ 66 Bob Speake DP	10.00	5.00
❑ 67 Vic Power	15.00	7.50
❑ 68 Chuck Stobbs	10.00	5.00
❑ 69 Chuck Tanner	15.00	7.50

❑ 70 Jim Rivera	10.00	5.00
❑ 71 Frank Sullivan	10.00	5.00
❑ 72A Phillies Team	30.00	15.00
(Centered)		
❑ 72B Phillies Team	80.00	40.00
(Dated 1955)		
❑ 72C Phillies Team DP	30.00	15.00
(Name at far left)		
❑ 73 Wayne Terwilliger	10.00	5.00
❑ 74 Jim King	10.00	5.00
❑ 75 Roy Sievers DP	15.00	7.50
❑ 76 Ray Crone	10.00	5.00
❑ 77 Harvey Haddix	15.00	7.50
❑ 78 Herman Wehmeier	10.00	5.00
❑ 79 Sandy Koufax	300.00	180.00
❑ 80 Gus Triandos DP	10.00	5.00
❑ 81 Wally Westlake	10.00	5.00
❑ 82 Bill Renna DP	10.00	5.00
❑ 83 Karl Spooner	15.00	7.50
❑ 84 Babe Birrer	10.00	5.00
❑ 85A Cleveland Indians	30.00	15.00
(Centered)		
❑ 85B Indians Team	80.00	40.00
(Dated 1955)		
❑ 85C Indians Team	30.00	15.00
(Name at far left)		
❑ 86 Ray Jablonski DP	10.00	5.00
❑ 87 Dean Stone	10.00	5.00
❑ 88 Johnny Kucks RC	15.00	7.50
❑ 89 Norm Zauchin	10.00	5.00
❑ 90A Cincinnati Redlegs	30.00	15.00
Team (Centered)		
❑ 90B Reds Team	80.00	40.00
(Dated 1955)		
❑ 90C Reds Team	30.00	15.00
(Name at far left)		
❑ 91 Gail Harris	10.00	5.00
❑ 92 Bob(Red) Wilson	10.00	5.00
❑ 93 George Susce	10.00	5.00
❑ 94 Ron Kline	10.00	5.00
❑ 95A Milwaukee Braves	40.00	20.00
Team (Centered)		
❑ 95B Braves Team	80.00	40.00
(Dated 1955)		
❑ 95C Braves Team	40.00	20.00
(Name at far left)		
❑ 96 Bill Tremel	10.00	5.00
❑ 97 Jerry Lynch	15.00	7.50
❑ 98 Camilo Pascual	15.00	7.50
❑ 99 Don Zimmer	25.00	12.50
❑ 100A Baltimore Orioles	40.00	20.00
Team (centered)		
❑ 100B Orioles Team	80.00	40.00
(Dated 1955)		
❑ 100C Orioles Team	40.00	20.00
(Name at far left)		
❑ 101 Roy Campanella	150.00	75.00
❑ 102 Jim Davis	12.00	6.00
❑ 103 Willie Miranda	12.00	6.00
❑ 104 Bob Lennon	12.00	6.00
❑ 105 Al Smith	12.00	6.00
❑ 106 Joe Astroth	12.00	6.00
❑ 107 Eddie Mathews	100.00	50.00
❑ 108 Laurin Pepper	12.00	6.00
❑ 109 Enos Slaughter	40.00	20.00
❑ 110 Yogi Berra	175.00	90.00
❑ 111 Boston Red Sox	40.00	20.00
Team Card		
❑ 112 Dee Fondy	12.00	6.00
❑ 113 Phil Rizzuto	150.00	75.00
❑ 114 Jim Owens	15.00	7.50
❑ 115 Jackie Jensen	15.00	7.50
❑ 116 Eddie O'Brien	12.00	6.00
❑ 117 Virgil Trucks	15.00	7.50
❑ 118 Nellie Fox	80.00	40.00
❑ 119 Larry Jackson RC	15.00	7.50
❑ 120 Richie Ashburn	60.00	30.00
❑ 121 Pittsburgh Pirates	40.00	20.00
Team Card		
❑ 122 Willard Nixon	12.00	6.00
❑ 123 Roy McMillan	15.00	7.50
❑ 124 Don Kaiser	12.00	6.00
❑ 125 Minnie Minoso	40.00	20.00
❑ 126 Jim Brady	12.00	6.00
❑ 127 Willie Jones	15.00	7.50
❑ 128 Eddie Yost	15.00	7.50
❑ 129 Jake Martin	12.00	6.00
❑ 130 Willie Mays	300.00	150.00
❑ 131 Bob Roselli	12.00	6.00
❑ 132 Bobby Avila	12.00	6.00
❑ 133 Ray Narleski	12.00	6.00
❑ 134 St. Louis Cardinals	40.00	20.00
Team Card		
❑ 135 Mickey Mantle	1500.00	750.00
❑ 136 Johnny Logan	15.00	7.50
❑ 137 Al Silvera	12.00	6.00
❑ 138 Johnny Antonelli	15.00	7.50
❑ 139 Tommy Carroll	15.00	7.50
❑ 140 Herb Score RC	60.00	30.00
❑ 141 Joe Frazier	12.00	6.00
❑ 142 Gene Baker	12.00	6.00
❑ 143 Jim Piersall	15.00	7.50
❑ 144 Leroy Powell	12.00	6.00
❑ 145 Gil Hodges	60.00	30.00
❑ 146 Washington Nationals	40.00	20.00
Team Card		
❑ 147 Earl Torgeson	12.00	6.00
❑ 148 Alvin Dark	15.00	7.50
❑ 149 Dixie Howell	12.00	6.00
❑ 150 Duke Snider	125.00	60.00
❑ 151 Spook Jacobs	15.00	7.50
❑ 152 Billy Hoeft	15.00	7.50
❑ 153 Frank Thomas	15.00	7.50
❑ 154 Dave Pope	12.00	6.00
❑ 155 Harvey Kuenn	15.00	7.50
❑ 156 Wes Westrum	15.00	7.50
❑ 157 Dick Brodowski	12.00	6.00
❑ 158 Wally Post	15.00	7.50
❑ 159 Clint Courtney	12.00	6.00
❑ 160 Billy Pierce	15.00	7.50
❑ 161 Joe DeMaestri	12.00	6.00
❑ 162 Dave(Gus) Bell	15.00	7.50
❑ 163 Gene Woodling	15.00	7.50
❑ 164 Harmon Killebrew	100.00	50.00
❑ 165 Red Schoendienst	40.00	20.00
❑ 166 Brooklyn Dodgers	200.00	100.00
Team Card		
❑ 167 Harry Dorish	12.00	6.00
❑ 168 Sammy White	12.00	6.00
❑ 169 Bob Nelson	12.00	6.00
❑ 170 Bill Virdon	15.00	7.50
❑ 171 Jim Wilson	12.00	6.00
❑ 172 Frank Torre RC	15.00	7.50
❑ 173 Johnny Podres	25.00	12.50
❑ 174 Glen Gorbous	12.00	6.00
❑ 175 Del Crandall	15.00	7.50
❑ 176 Alex Kellner	12.00	6.00
❑ 177 Hank Bauer	25.00	12.50
❑ 178 Joe Black	15.00	7.50
❑ 179 Harry Chiti	12.00	6.00
❑ 180 Robin Roberts	50.00	25.00
❑ 181 Billy Martin	125.00	50.00
❑ 182 Paul Minner	15.00	7.50
❑ 183 Stan Lopata	20.00	10.00
❑ 184 Don Bessent	20.00	10.00
❑ 185 Bill Bruton	20.00	10.00
❑ 186 Ron Jackson	15.00	7.50
❑ 187 Early Wynn	50.00	25.00
❑ 188 Chicago White Sox	50.00	25.00
Team Card		
❑ 189 Ned Garver	15.00	7.50
❑ 190 Carl Furillo	30.00	15.00
❑ 191 Frank Lary	20.00	10.00
❑ 192 Smoky Burgess	20.00	10.00
❑ 193 Wilmer Mizell	20.00	10.00
❑ 194 Monte Irvin	30.00	15.00
❑ 195 George Kell	30.00	15.00
❑ 196 Tom Poholsky	15.00	7.50
❑ 197 Granny Hamner	15.00	7.50
❑ 198 Ed Fitzgerald	15.00	7.50
❑ 199 Hank Thompson	20.00	10.00
❑ 200 Bob Feller	125.00	60.00
❑ 201 Rip Repulski	15.00	7.50
❑ 202 Jim Hearn	15.00	7.50
❑ 203 Bill Tuttle	15.00	7.50
❑ 204 Art Swanson	15.00	7.50
❑ 205 Whitey Lockman	20.00	10.00
❑ 206 Erv Palica	15.00	7.50
❑ 207 Jim Small	15.00	7.50
❑ 208 Elston Howard	60.00	30.00
❑ 209 Max Surkont	15.00	7.50
❑ 210 Mike Garcia	20.00	10.00
❑ 211 Murry Dickson	15.00	7.50
❑ 212 Johnny Temple	15.00	7.50
❑ 213 Detroit Tigers	60.00	30.00
Team Card		
❑ 214 Bob Rush	15.00	7.50
❑ 215 Tommy Byrne	20.00	10.00
❑ 216 Jerry Schoonmaker	15.00	7.50
❑ 217 Billy Klaus	15.00	7.50
❑ 218 Joe Nuxhall UER	20.00	10.00
(Misspelled Nuxall)		
❑ 219 Lew Burdette	20.00	10.00
❑ 220 Del Ennis	20.00	10.00
❑ 221 Bob Friend	20.00	10.00
❑ 222 Dave Philley	15.00	7.50
❑ 223 Randy Jackson	15.00	7.50
❑ 224 Bud Podbielan	15.00	7.50
❑ 225 Gil McDougald	50.00	25.00
❑ 226 New York Giants	80.00	40.00
Team Card		
❑ 227 Russ Meyer	15.00	7.50
❑ 228 Mickey Vernon	20.00	10.00
❑ 229 Harry Brecheen CO	20.00	10.00
❑ 230 Chico Carrasquel	15.00	7.50
❑ 231 Bob Hale	15.00	7.50
❑ 232 Toby Atwell	15.00	7.50
❑ 233 Carl Erskine	30.00	15.00
❑ 234 Pete Runnels	15.00	7.50
❑ 235 Don Newcombe	50.00	25.00
❑ 236 Kansas City Athletics	40.00	20.00
Team Card		
❑ 237 Jose Valdivielso	15.00	7.50
❑ 238 Walt Dropo	20.00	10.00
❑ 239 Harry Simpson	15.00	7.50
❑ 240 Whitey Ford	125.00	60.00
❑ 241 Don Mueller UER	20.00	10.00
6" tall		
❑ 242 Hershell Freeman	15.00	7.50
❑ 243 Sherm Lollar	20.00	10.00
❑ 244 Bob Buhl	30.00	15.00
❑ 245 Billy Goodman	20.00	10.00
❑ 246 Tom Gorman	15.00	7.50
❑ 247 Bill Sarni	15.00	7.50
❑ 248 Bob Porterfield	15.00	7.50
❑ 249 Johnny Klippstein	15.00	7.50
❑ 250 Larry Doby	30.00	15.00
❑ 251 New York Yankees	250.00	125.00
Team Card UER		
(Don Larsen misspelled		
as Larson on front)		
❑ 252 Vern Law	20.00	10.00
❑ 253 Irv Noren	30.00	15.00
❑ 254 George Crowe	15.00	7.50
❑ 255 Bob Lemon	50.00	25.00
❑ 256 Tom Hurd	15.00	7.50
❑ 257 Bobby Thomson	30.00	15.00
❑ 258 Art Ditmar	15.00	7.50
❑ 259 Sam Jones	20.00	10.00
❑ 260 Pee Wee Reese	150.00	75.00
❑ 261 Bobby Shantz	15.00	7.50
❑ 262 Howie Pollet	12.00	6.00
❑ 263 Bob Miller	12.00	6.00
❑ 264 Ray Monzant	12.00	6.00
❑ 265 Sandy Consuegra	12.00	6.00
❑ 266 Don Ferrarese	12.00	6.00
❑ 267 Bob Nieman	12.00	6.00
❑ 268 Dale Mitchell	15.00	7.50
❑ 269 Jack Meyer	12.00	6.00
❑ 270 Billy Loes	15.00	7.50
❑ 271 Foster Castleman	12.00	6.00
❑ 272 Danny O'Connell	12.00	6.00
❑ 273 Walker Cooper	12.00	6.00
❑ 274 Frank Baumholtz	12.00	6.00
❑ 275 Jim Greengrass	12.00	6.00
❑ 276 George Zuverink	12.00	6.00
❑ 277 Daryl Spencer	12.00	6.00
❑ 278 Chet Nichols	12.00	6.00
❑ 279 Johnny Groth	12.00	6.00
❑ 280 Jim Gilliam	40.00	20.00
❑ 281 Art Houtteman	12.00	6.00
❑ 282 Warren Hacker	12.00	6.00
❑ 283 Hal Smith RC	15.00	7.50
❑ 284 Ike Delock	12.00	6.00
❑ 285 Eddie Miksis	12.00	6.00
❑ 286 Bill Wight	12.00	6.00
❑ 287 Bobby Adams	12.00	6.00
❑ 288 Bob Cerv	40.00	20.00

#	Player	NM	Ex
289	Hal Jeffcoat	12.00	6.00
290	Curt Simmons	15.00	7.50
291	Frank Kellert	12.00	6.00
292	Luis Aparicio RC	150.00	75.00
293	Stu Miller	25.00	12.50
294	Ernie Johnson	15.00	7.50
295	Clem Labine	15.00	7.50
296	Andy Seminick	12.00	6.00
297	Bob Skinner	15.00	7.50
298	Johnny Schmitz	12.00	6.00
299	Charlie Neal	40.00	20.00
300	Vic Wertz	15.00	7.50
301	Marv Grissom	12.00	6.00
302	Eddie Robinson	12.00	6.00
303	Jim Dyck	12.00	6.00
304	Frank Malzone	15.00	7.50
305	Brooks Lawrence	12.00	6.00
306	Curt Roberts	12.00	6.00
307	Hoyt Wilhelm	40.00	20.00
308	Chuck Harmon	12.00	6.00
309	Don Blasingame RC	15.00	7.50
310	Steve Gromek	12.00	6.00
311	Hal Naragon	12.00	6.00
312	Andy Pafko	15.00	7.50
313	Gene Stephens	12.00	6.00
314	Hobie Landrith	12.00	6.00
315	Milt Bolling	12.00	6.00
316	Jerry Coleman	15.00	7.50
317	Al Aber	12.00	6.00
318	Fred Hatfield	12.00	6.00
319	Jack Crimian	12.00	6.00
320	Joe Adcock	15.00	7.50
321	Jim Konstanty	15.00	7.50
322	Karl Olson	12.00	6.00
323	Willard Schmidt	12.00	6.00
324	Rocky Bridges	15.00	7.50
325	Don Liddle	12.00	6.00
326	Connie Johnson	12.00	6.00
327	Bob Wiesler	12.00	6.00
328	Preston Ward	12.00	6.00
329	Lou Berberet	12.00	6.00
330	Jim Busby	15.00	7.50
331	Dick Hall	12.00	6.00
332	Don Larsen	60.00	30.00
333	Rube Walker	12.00	6.00
334	Bob Miller	15.00	7.50
335	Don Hoak	15.00	7.50
336	Ellis Kinder	12.00	6.00
337	Bobby Morgan	12.00	6.00
338	Jim Delsing	12.00	6.00
339	Rance Pless	12.00	6.00
340	Mickey McDermott	60.00	12.00
NNO	Checklist 1/3	300.00	95.00
NNO	Checklist 2/4	300.00	95.00

1957 Topps

	NM	Ex
COMPLETE SET (407)	10000.00	5000.00
COMMON CARD (1-88)	10.00	5.00
COMMON CARD (89-176)	8.00	4.00
COMMON (177-264)	8.00	4.00
COMMON (265-352)	20.00	10.00
COMMON (353-407)	8.00	4.00
COMMON DP (265-352)	12.00	6.00
WRAPPER (1-CENT)	300.00	150.00
WRAPPER (5-CENT)	200.00	100.00

#	Player	NM	Ex
1	Ted Williams	600.00	150.00
2	Yogi Berra	200.00	100.00
3	Dale Long	20.00	10.00
4	Johnny Logan	20.00	10.00
5	Sal Maglie	20.00	10.00
6	Hector Lopez	15.00	7.50
7	Luis Aparicio	30.00	15.00
8	Don Mossi	15.00	7.50
9	Johnny Temple	15.00	7.50
10	Willie Mays	300.00	125.00
11	George Zuverink	10.00	5.00
12	Dick Groat	20.00	10.00
13	Wally Burnette	10.00	5.00
14	Bob Nieman	10.00	5.00
15	Robin Roberts	30.00	15.00
16	Walt Moryn	10.00	5.00
17	Billy Gardner	10.00	5.00
18	Don Drysdale RC	250.00	125.00
19	Bob Wilson	10.00	5.00
20	Hank Aaron UER (Reverse negative photo on front)	300.00	150.00
21	Frank Sullivan	10.00	5.00
22	Jerry Snyder UER Photo actually Ed Fitzgerald	10.00	5.00
23	Sherm Lollar	15.00	7.50
24	Bill Mazeroski RC	80.00	40.00
25	Whitey Ford	150.00	75.00
26	Bob Boyd	10.00	5.00
27	Ted Kazanski	10.00	5.00
28	Gene Conley	15.00	7.50
29	Whitey Herzog RC	30.00	15.00
30	Pee Wee Reese	80.00	40.00
31	Ron Northey	10.00	5.00
32	Hershell Freeman	10.00	5.00
33	Jim Small	10.00	5.00
34	Tom Sturdivant	15.00	7.50
35	Frank Robinson RC	300.00	125.00
36	Bob Grim	10.00	5.00
37	Frank Torre	15.00	7.50
38	Nellie Fox	50.00	25.00
39	Al Worthington	10.00	5.00
40	Early Wynn	30.00	15.00
41	Hal W. Smith	10.00	5.00
42	Dee Fondy	10.00	5.00
43	Connie Johnson	10.00	5.00
44	Joe DeMaestri	10.00	5.00
45	Carl Furillo	30.00	15.00
46	Robert J. Miller	10.00	5.00
47	Don Blasingame	10.00	5.00
48	Bill Bruton	15.00	7.50
49	Daryl Spencer	10.00	5.00
50	Herb Score	30.00	15.00
51	Clint Courtney	10.00	5.00
52	Lee Walls	10.00	5.00
53	Clem Labine	20.00	10.00
54	Elmer Valo	10.00	5.00
55	Ernie Banks	125.00	60.00
56	Dave Sisler	10.00	5.00
57	Jim Lemon	15.00	7.50
58	Ruben Gomez	10.00	5.00
59	Dick Williams	15.00	7.50
60	Billy Hoeft	15.00	7.50
61	Dusty Rhodes	15.00	7.50
62	Billy Martin	60.00	30.00
63	Ike Delock	10.00	5.00
64	Pete Runnels	15.00	7.50
65	Wally Moon	15.00	7.50
66	Brooks Lawrence	10.00	5.00
67	Chico Carrasquel	10.00	5.00
68	Ray Crone	10.00	5.00
69	Roy McMillan	15.00	7.50
70	Richie Ashburn	50.00	25.00
71	Murry Dickson	10.00	5.00
72	Bill Tuttle	10.00	5.00
73	George Crowe	10.00	5.00
74	Vito Valentinetti	10.00	5.00
75	Jimmy Piersall	15.00	7.50
76	Roberto Clemente	300.00	150.00
77	Paul Foytack	10.00	5.00
78	Vic Wertz	15.00	7.50
79	Lindy McDaniel RC	15.00	7.50
80	Gil Hodges	50.00	25.00
81	Herman Wehmeier	10.00	5.00
82	Elston Howard	30.00	15.00
83	Lou Skizas	10.00	5.00
84	Moe Drabowsky	15.00	7.50
85	Larry Doby	30.00	15.00
86	Bill Sarni	10.00	5.00
87	Tom Gorman	10.00	5.00
88	Harvey Kuenn	15.00	7.50
89	Roy Sievers	15.00	7.50
90	Warren Spahn	80.00	40.00
91	Mack Burk	8.00	4.00
92	Mickey Vernon	15.00	7.50
93	Hal Jeffcoat	8.00	4.00
94	Bobby Del Greco	8.00	4.00
95	Mickey Mantle	1000.00	600.00
96	Hank Aguirre	8.00	4.00
97	New York Yankees Team Card	100.00	50.00
98	Alvin Dark	15.00	7.50
99	Bob Keegan	8.00	4.00
100	Warren Giles PRES Will Harridge PRES	15.00	7.50
101	Chuck Stobbs	8.00	4.00
102	Ray Boone	15.00	7.50
103	Joe Nuxhall	15.00	7.50
104	Hank Foiles	8.00	4.00
105	Johnny Antonelli	15.00	7.50
106	Ray Moore	8.00	4.00
107	Jim Rivera	8.00	4.00
108	Tommy Byrne	15.00	7.50
109	Hank Thompson	8.00	4.00
110	Bill Virdon	15.00	7.50
111	Hal R. Smith	8.00	4.00
112	Tom Brewer	8.00	4.00
113	Wilmer Mizell	15.00	7.50
114	Milwaukee Braves Team Card	20.00	10.00
115	Jim Gilliam	15.00	7.50
116	Mike Fornieles	8.00	4.00
117	Joe Adcock	20.00	10.00
118	Bob Porterfield	8.00	4.00
119	Stan Lopata	8.00	4.00
120	Bob Lemon	30.00	15.00
121	Clete Boyer RC	30.00	15.00
122	Ken Boyer	20.00	10.00
123	Steve Ridzik	8.00	4.00
124	Dave Philley	8.00	4.00
125	Al Kaline	100.00	50.00
126	Bob Wiesler	8.00	4.00
127	Bob Buhl	15.00	7.50
128	Ed Bailey	15.00	7.50
129	Saul Rogovin	8.00	4.00
130	Don Newcombe	20.00	10.00
131	Milt Bolling	8.00	4.00
132	Art Ditmar	15.00	7.50
133	Del Crandall	15.00	7.50
134	Don Kaiser	8.00	4.00
135	Bill Skowron	20.00	10.00
136	Jim Hegan	15.00	7.50
137	Bob Rush	8.00	4.00
138	Minnie Minoso	20.00	10.00
139	Lou Kretlow	8.00	4.00
140	Frank Thomas	15.00	7.50
141	Al Aber	8.00	4.00
142	Charley Thompson	8.00	4.00
143	Andy Pafko	15.00	7.50
144	Ray Narleski	8.00	4.00
145	Al Smith	8.00	4.00
146	Don Ferrarese	8.00	4.00
147	Al Walker	8.00	4.00
148	Don Mueller	15.00	7.50
149	Bob Kennedy	15.00	7.50
150	Bob Friend	15.00	7.50
151	Willie Miranda	8.00	4.00
152	Jack Harshman	8.00	4.00
153	Karl Olson	8.00	4.00
154	Red Schoendienst	30.00	15.00
155	Jim Brosnan	15.00	7.50
156	Gus Triandos	15.00	7.50
157	Wally Post	15.00	7.50
158	Curt Simmons	15.00	7.50
159	Solly Drake	8.00	4.00
160	Billy Pierce	15.00	7.50
161	Pittsburgh Pirates Team Card	15.00	7.50
162	Jack Meyer	8.00	4.00
163	Sammy White	8.00	4.00
164	Tommy Carroll	8.00	4.00
165	Ted Kluszewski	100.00	50.00

❑ 166	Roy Face	15.00	7.50
❑ 167	Vic Power	15.00	7.50
❑ 168	Frank Lary	15.00	7.50
❑ 169	Herb Plews	8.00	4.00
❑ 170	Duke Snider	125.00	60.00
❑ 171	Boston Red Sox Team Card	15.00	7.50
❑ 172	Gene Woodling	15.00	7.50
❑ 173	Roger Craig	15.00	7.50
❑ 174	Willie Jones	8.00	4.00
❑ 175	Don Larsen	30.00	15.00
❑ 176A	Gene Baker ERR (Misspelled Bakep on card back)	350.00	180.00
❑ 176B	Gene Baker COR	15.00	7.50
❑ 177	Eddie Yost	15.00	7.50
❑ 178	Don Bessent	8.00	4.00
❑ 179	Ernie Oravetz	8.00	4.00
❑ 180	Gus Bell	15.00	7.50
❑ 181	Dick Donovan	8.00	4.00
❑ 182	Hobie Landrith	8.00	4.00
❑ 183	Chicago Cubs Team Card	15.00	7.50
❑ 184	Tito Francona RC	8.00	4.00
❑ 185	Johnny Kucks	15.00	7.50
❑ 186	Jim King	15.00	7.50
❑ 187	Virgil Trucks	15.00	7.50
❑ 188	Felix Mantilla RC	15.00	7.50
❑ 189	Willard Nixon	8.00	4.00
❑ 190	Randy Jackson	8.00	4.00
❑ 191	Joe Margoneri	8.00	4.00
❑ 192	Jerry Coleman	15.00	7.50
❑ 193	Del Rice	8.00	4.00
❑ 194	Hal Brown	8.00	4.00
❑ 195	Bobby Avila	8.00	4.00
❑ 196	Larry Jackson	15.00	7.50
❑ 197	Hank Sauer	15.00	7.50
❑ 198	Detroit Tigers Team Card	15.00	7.50
❑ 199	Vern Law	15.00	7.50
❑ 200	Gil McDougald	15.00	7.50
❑ 201	Sandy Amoros	15.00	7.50
❑ 202	Dick Gernert	8.00	4.00
❑ 203	Hoyt Wilhelm	30.00	15.00
❑ 204	Kansas City Athletics Team Card	15.00	7.50
❑ 205	Charlie Maxwell	15.00	7.50
❑ 206	Willard Schmidt	8.00	4.00
❑ 207	Gordon(Billy) Hunter	8.00	4.00
❑ 208	Lou Burdette	15.00	7.50
❑ 209	Bob Skinner	15.00	7.50
❑ 210	Roy Campanella	150.00	75.00
❑ 211	Camilo Pascual	15.00	7.50
❑ 212	Rocky Colavito RC	125.00	60.00
❑ 213	Les Moss	8.00	4.00
❑ 214	Philadelphia Phillies Team Card	15.00	7.50
❑ 215	Enos Slaughter	30.00	15.00
❑ 216	Marv Grissom	8.00	4.00
❑ 217	Gene Stephens	8.00	4.00
❑ 218	Ray Jablonski	8.00	4.00
❑ 219	Tom Acker	8.00	4.00
❑ 220	Jackie Jensen	20.00	10.00
❑ 221	Dixie Howell	8.00	4.00
❑ 222	Alex Grammas	8.00	4.00
❑ 223	Frank House	8.00	4.00
❑ 224	Marv Blaylock	8.00	4.00
❑ 225	Harry Simpson	8.00	4.00
❑ 226	Preston Ward	8.00	4.00
❑ 227	Gerry Staley	8.00	4.00
❑ 228	Smoky Burgess UER (Misspelled Smokey on card back)	15.00	7.50
❑ 229	George Susce	8.00	4.00
❑ 230	George Kell	30.00	15.00
❑ 231	Solly Hemus	8.00	4.00
❑ 232	Whitey Lockman	15.00	7.50
❑ 233	Art Fowler	8.00	4.00
❑ 234	Dick Cole	8.00	4.00
❑ 235	Tom Poholsky	8.00	4.00
❑ 236	Joe Ginsberg	8.00	4.00
❑ 237	Foster Castleman	8.00	4.00
❑ 238	Eddie Robinson	8.00	4.00
❑ 239	Tom Morgan	8.00	4.00
❑ 240	Hank Bauer	15.00	7.50
❑ 241	Joe Lonnett	8.00	4.00
❑ 242	Charlie Neal	15.00	7.50
❑ 243	St. Louis Cardinals Team Card	15.00	7.50
❑ 244	Billy Loes	15.00	7.50
❑ 245	Rip Repulski	8.00	4.00
❑ 246	Jose Valdivielso	8.00	4.00
❑ 247	Turk Lown	8.00	4.00
❑ 248	Jim Finigan	8.00	4.00
❑ 249	Dave Pope	8.00	4.00
❑ 250	Eddie Mathews	50.00	25.00
❑ 251	Baltimore Orioles Team Card	15.00	7.50
❑ 252	Carl Erskine	15.00	7.50
❑ 253	Gus Zernial	15.00	7.50
❑ 254	Ron Negray	8.00	4.00
❑ 255	Charlie Silvera	15.00	7.50
❑ 256	Ron Kline	8.00	4.00
❑ 257	Walt Dropo	8.00	4.00
❑ 258	Steve Gromek	8.00	4.00
❑ 259	Eddie O'Brien	8.00	4.00
❑ 260	Del Ennis	15.00	7.50
❑ 261	Bob Chakales	8.00	4.00
❑ 262	Bobby Thomson	15.00	7.50
❑ 263	George Strickland	8.00	4.00
❑ 264	Bob Turley	15.00	7.50
❑ 265	Harvey Haddix DP	12.00	6.00
❑ 266	Ken Kuhn DP	12.00	6.00
❑ 267	Danny Kravitz	20.00	10.00
❑ 268	Jack Collum	20.00	10.00
❑ 269	Bob Cerv	30.00	15.00
❑ 270	Washington Senators Team Card	60.00	30.00
❑ 271	Danny O'Connell DP	12.00	6.00
❑ 272	Bobby Shantz	30.00	15.00
❑ 273	Jim Davis	20.00	10.00
❑ 274	Don Hoak	15.00	7.50
❑ 275	Cleveland Indians Team Card UER (Text on back credits Tribe with winning AL title in '28. The Yankees won that year.)	60.00	30.00
❑ 276	Jim Pyburn	20.00	10.00
❑ 277	Johnny Podres DP	40.00	20.00
❑ 278	Fred Hatfield DP	12.00	6.00
❑ 279	Bob Thurman	20.00	10.00
❑ 280	Alex Kellner	20.00	10.00
❑ 281	Gail Harris	20.00	10.00
❑ 282	Jack Dittmer DP	12.00	6.00
❑ 283	Wes Covington DP	12.00	6.00
❑ 284	Don Zimmer	40.00	20.00
❑ 285	Ned Garver	20.00	10.00
❑ 286	Bobby Richardson RC	125.00	60.00
❑ 287	Sam Jones	20.00	10.00
❑ 288	Ted Lepcio	20.00	10.00
❑ 289	Jim Bolger DP	12.00	6.00
❑ 290	Andy Carey DP	40.00	20.00
❑ 291	Windy McCall	20.00	10.00
❑ 292	Billy Klaus	20.00	10.00
❑ 293	Ted Abernathy	20.00	10.00
❑ 294	Rocky Bridges DP	12.00	6.00
❑ 295	Joe Collins DP	40.00	20.00
❑ 296	Johnny Klippstein	20.00	10.00
❑ 297	Jack Crimian	20.00	10.00
❑ 298	Irv Noren DP	12.00	6.00
❑ 299	Chuck Harmon	20.00	10.00
❑ 300	Mike Garcia	30.00	15.00
❑ 301	Sammy Esposito DP	20.00	10.00
❑ 302	Sandy Koufax DP	350.00	150.00
❑ 303	Billy Goodman	30.00	15.00
❑ 304	Joe Cunningham	30.00	15.00
❑ 305	Chico Fernandez	20.00	10.00
❑ 306	Darrell Johnson DP	12.00	6.00
❑ 307	Jack D. Phillips DP	12.00	6.00
❑ 308	Dick Hall	20.00	10.00
❑ 309	Jim Busby DP	12.00	6.00
❑ 310	Max Surkont DP	12.00	6.00
❑ 311	Al Pilarcik DP	12.00	6.00
❑ 312	Tony Kubek DP RC	100.00	50.00
❑ 313	Mel Parnell	15.00	7.50
❑ 314	Ed Bouchee DP	12.00	6.00
❑ 315	Lou Berberet DP	12.00	6.00
❑ 316	Billy O'Dell	20.00	10.00
❑ 317	New York Giants Team Card	80.00	40.00
❑ 318	Mickey McDermott	20.00	10.00
❑ 319	Gino Cimoli RC	20.00	10.00
❑ 320	Neil Chrisley	20.00	10.00
❑ 321	John(Red) Murff	20.00	10.00
❑ 322	Cincinnati Reds Team Card	80.00	40.00
❑ 323	Wes Westrum	30.00	15.00
❑ 324	Brooklyn Dodgers Team Card	150.00	75.00
❑ 325	Frank Bolling	20.00	10.00
❑ 326	Pedro Ramos	20.00	10.00
❑ 327	Jim Pendleton	20.00	10.00
❑ 328	Brooks Robinson RC	400.00	200.00
❑ 329	Chicago White Sox Team Card	60.00	30.00
❑ 330	Jim Wilson	20.00	10.00
❑ 331	Ray Katt	20.00	10.00
❑ 332	Bob Bowman	20.00	10.00
❑ 333	Ernie Johnson	20.00	10.00
❑ 334	Jerry Schoonmaker	20.00	10.00
❑ 335	Granny Hamner	20.00	10.00
❑ 336	Haywood Sullivan RC	40.00	20.00
❑ 337	Rene Valdes	20.00	10.00
❑ 338	Jim Bunning RC	150.00	75.00
❑ 339	Bob Speake	20.00	10.00
❑ 340	Bill Wight	20.00	10.00
❑ 341	Don Gross	20.00	10.00
❑ 342	Gene Mauch	30.00	15.00
❑ 343	Taylor Phillips	15.00	7.50
❑ 344	Paul LaPalme	20.00	10.00
❑ 345	Paul Smith	20.00	10.00
❑ 346	Dick Littlefield	20.00	10.00
❑ 347	Hal Naragon	20.00	10.00
❑ 348	Jim Hearn	20.00	10.00
❑ 349	Nellie King	20.00	10.00
❑ 350	Eddie Miksis	20.00	10.00
❑ 351	Dave Hillman	20.00	10.00
❑ 352	Ellis Kinder	20.00	10.00
❑ 353	Cal Neeman	8.00	4.00
❑ 354	Rip Coleman	8.00	4.00
❑ 355	Frank Malzone	15.00	7.50
❑ 356	Faye Throneberry	8.00	4.00
❑ 357	Earl Torgeson	8.00	4.00
❑ 358	Jerry Lynch	15.00	7.50
❑ 359	Tom Cheney	8.00	4.00
❑ 360	Johnny Groth	8.00	4.00
❑ 361	Curt Barclay	8.00	4.00
❑ 362	Roman Mejias	15.00	7.50
❑ 363	Eddie Kasko	8.00	4.00
❑ 364	Cal McLish	15.00	7.50
❑ 365	Ozzie Virgil	8.00	4.00
❑ 366	Ken Lehman	8.00	4.00
❑ 367	Ed Fitzgerald	8.00	4.00
❑ 368	Bob Purkey	8.00	4.00
❑ 369	Milt Graff	8.00	4.00
❑ 370	Warren Hacker	8.00	4.00
❑ 371	Bob Lennon	8.00	4.00
❑ 372	Norm Zauchin	8.00	4.00
❑ 373	Pete Whisenant	8.00	4.00
❑ 374	Don Cardwell	8.00	4.00
❑ 375	Jim Landis	15.00	7.50
❑ 376	Don Elston	8.00	4.00
❑ 377	Andre Rodgers	8.00	4.00
❑ 378	Elmer Singleton	8.00	4.00
❑ 379	Don Lee	8.00	4.00
❑ 380	Walker Cooper	8.00	4.00
❑ 381	Dean Stone	8.00	4.00
❑ 382	Jim Brideweser	8.00	4.00
❑ 383	Juan Pizarro	8.00	4.00
❑ 384	Bobby G. Smith	8.00	4.00
❑ 385	Art Houtteman	8.00	4.00
❑ 386	Lyle Luttrell	8.00	4.00
❑ 387	Jack Sanford RC	15.00	7.50
❑ 388	Pete Daley	8.00	4.00
❑ 389	Dave Jolly	8.00	4.00
❑ 390	Reno Bertoia	8.00	4.00
❑ 391	Ralph Terry RC	15.00	7.50
❑ 392	Chuck Tanner	15.00	7.50
❑ 393	Raul Sanchez	8.00	4.00
❑ 394	Luis Arroyo	15.00	7.50
❑ 395	Bubba Phillips	8.00	4.00
❑ 396	Casey Wise	8.00	4.00
❑ 397	Roy Smalley	8.00	4.00
❑ 398	Al Cicotte	15.00	7.50
❑ 399	Billy Consolo	8.00	4.00
❑ 400	Carl Furillo Gil Hodges Roy Campanella	250.00	125.00

Duke Snider
❑ 401 Earl Battey RC 15.00 7.50
❑ 402 Jim Pisoni 8.00 4.00
❑ 403 Dick Hyde 8.00 4.00
❑ 404 Harry Anderson 8.00 4.00
❑ 405 Duke Maas 8.00 4.00
❑ 406 Bob Hale 8.00 4.00
❑ 407 Mickey Mantle 500.00 150.00
Yogi Berra
❑ CC1 Contest Card 100.00 25.00
Saturday, May 4th
Boston Red Sox
vs. Cleveland Indians
Cincinnati Redlegs
vs. New York Giants
❑ CC2 Contest Card 100.00 25.00
Saturday, May 25th
Detroit Tigers
vs. Kansas City Athletics
Pittsburgh Pirates
vs. Philadelphia Phillies
❑ CC3 Contest Card 125.00 31.00
Saturday, June 22nd
Brooklyn Dodgers
vs. St. Louis Cardinals
Chicago White Sox
vs. New York Yankees
❑ CC4 Contest Card 125.00 31.00
Saturday, July 19th
Milwaukee Braves
vs. New York Giants
Baltimore Orioles
vs. Kansas City Athletics
❑ NNO Checklist 1/2 250.00 75.00
Bazooka Back
❑ NNO Checklist 1/2 250.00 125.00
Blony Back
❑ NNO Checklist 2/3 400.00 100.00
Bazooka Back
❑ NNO Checklist 2/3 400.00 200.00
Blony Back
❑ NNO Checklist 3/4 800.00 190.00
Bazooka Back
❑ NNO Checklist 3/4 600.00 300.00
Blony Back
❑ NNO Checklist 4/5 1000.00 220.00
Bazooka Back
❑ NNO Checklist 4/5 800.00 400.00
Blony Back
❑ NNO Lucky Penny Charm 100.00 50.00
and Key Chain
offer card

1958 Topps

	NM	Ex
COMP. MASTER (534)	12000.00	6000.00
COMPLETE SET (494)	6000.00	3000.00
COMMON CARD (1-110)	12.00	6.00
COMMON (111-495)	8.00	4.00
WRAPPER (1-CENT)	100.00	50.00
WRAPPER (5-CENT)	125.00	60.00

❑ 1 Ted Williams 600.00 210.00
❑ 2A Bob Lemon 30.00 15.00
❑ 2B Bob Lemon YT 60.00 30.00
❑ 3 Alex Kellner 12.00 6.00
❑ 4 Hank Foiles 12.00 6.00
❑ 5 Willie Mays 300.00 150.00
❑ 6 George Zuverink 12.00 6.00
❑ 7 Dale Long 15.00 7.50
❑ 8A Eddie Kasko 12.00 6.00
❑ 8B Eddie Kasko YN 40.00 20.00
❑ 9 Hank Bauer 20.00 10.00
❑ 10 Lou Burdette 20.00 10.00
❑ 11A Jim Rivera 12.00 6.00
❑ 11B Jim Rivera YT 40.00 20.00
❑ 12 George Crowe 12.00 6.00
❑ 13A Billy Hoeft 12.00 6.00
❑ 13B Billy Hoeft YN 40.00 20.00
❑ 14 Rip Repulski 12.00 6.00
❑ 15 Jim Lemon 15.00 7.50
❑ 16 Charlie Neal 15.00 7.50
❑ 17 Felix Mantilla 12.00 6.00
❑ 18 Frank Sullivan 12.00 6.00
❑ 19 Giants Team Card CL 40.00 8.00
❑ 20A Gil McDougald 20.00 10.00
❑ 20B Gil McDougald YN 60.00 30.00
❑ 21 Curt Barclay 12.00 6.00
❑ 22 Hal Naragon 12.00 6.00
❑ 23A Bill Tuttle 12.00 6.00
❑ 23B Bill Tuttle YN 40.00 20.00
❑ 24A Hobie Landrith 12.00 6.00
❑ 24B Hobie Landrith YN 40.00 20.00
❑ 25 Don Drysdale 100.00 50.00
❑ 26 Ron Jackson 12.00 6.00
❑ 27 Bud Freeman 12.00 6.00
❑ 28 Jim Busby 12.00 6.00
❑ 29 Ted Lepcio 12.00 6.00
❑ 30A Hank Aaron 200.00 100.00
❑ 30B Hank Aaron YN 500.00 250.00
❑ 31 Tex Clevenger 12.00 6.00
❑ 32A J.W. Porter 12.00 6.00
❑ 32B J.W. Porter YN 40.00 20.00
❑ 33A Cal Neeman 12.00 6.00
❑ 33B Cal Neeman YT 40.00 20.00
❑ 34 Bob Thurman 12.00 6.00
❑ 35A Don Mossi 15.00 7.50
❑ 35B Don Mossi YT 40.00 20.00
❑ 36 Ted Kazanski 12.00 6.00
❑ 37 Mike McCormick RC 15.00 7.50
UER Photo actually
Ray Monzant
❑ 38 Dick Gernert 12.00 6.00
❑ 39 Bob Martyn 12.00 6.00
❑ 40 George Kell 30.00 15.00
❑ 41 Dave Hillman 12.00 6.00
❑ 42 John Roseboro RC 30.00 15.00
❑ 43 Sal Maglie 15.00 7.50
❑ 44 Washington Senators 20.00 4.00
Team Card CL
❑ 45 Dick Groat 15.00 7.50
❑ 46A Lou Sleater 12.00 6.00
❑ 46B Lou Sleater YN 40.00 20.00
❑ 47 Roger Maris RC 500.00 250.00
❑ 48 Chuck Harmon 12.00 6.00
❑ 49 Smoky Burgess 15.00 7.50
❑ 50A Billy Pierce 15.00 7.50
❑ 50B Billy Pierce YT 40.00 20.00
❑ 51 Del Rice 12.00 6.00
❑ 52A Roberto Clemente 300.00 150.00
❑ 52B Roberto Clemente YT 500.00 250.00
❑ 53A Morrie Martin 12.00 6.00
❑ 53B Morrie Martin YN 40.00 20.00
❑ 54 Norm Siebern RC 20.00 10.00
❑ 55 Chico Carrasquel 12.00 6.00
❑ 56 Bill Fischer 12.00 6.00
❑ 57A Tim Thompson 12.00 6.00
❑ 57B Tim Thompson YN 40.00 20.00
❑ 58A Art Schult 12.00 6.00
❑ 58B Art Schult YT 40.00 20.00
❑ 59 Dave Sisler 12.00 6.00
❑ 60A Del Ennis 15.00 7.50
❑ 60B Del Ennis YN 40.00 20.00
❑ 61A Darrell Johnson 12.00 6.00
❑ 61B Darrell Johnson YN 40.00 20.00
❑ 62 Joe DeMaestri 12.00 6.00
❑ 63 Joe Nuxhall 15.00 7.50
❑ 64 Joe Lonnett 12.00 6.00
❑ 65A Von McDaniel RC 12.00 6.00
❑ 65B Von McDaniel YL RC 40.00 20.00
❑ 66 Lee Walls 12.00 6.00
❑ 67 Joe Ginsberg 12.00 6.00
❑ 68 Daryl Spencer 12.00 6.00
❑ 69 Wally Burnette 12.00 6.00
❑ 70A Al Kaline 100.00 50.00
❑ 70B Al Kaline YN 250.00 125.00
❑ 71 Dodgers Team CL 60.00 12.00
❑ 72 Bud Byerly 12.00 6.00
❑ 73 Pete Daley 12.00 6.00
❑ 74 Roy Face 15.00 7.50
❑ 75 Gus Bell 15.00 7.50
❑ 76A Dick Farrell 12.00 6.00
❑ 76B Dick Farrell YT 40.00 20.00
❑ 77A Don Zimmer 15.00 7.50
❑ 77B Don Zimmer YT 40.00 20.00
❑ 78A Ernie Johnson 15.00 7.50
❑ 78B Ernie Johnson YN 40.00 20.00
❑ 79A Dick Williams 15.00 7.50
❑ 79B Dick Williams YT 40.00 20.00
❑ 80 Dick Drott 12.00 6.00
❑ 81A Steve Boros RC 12.00 6.00
❑ 81B Steve Boros YT RC 40.00 20.00
❑ 82 Ron Kline 12.00 6.00
❑ 83 Bob Hazle RC 12.00 6.00
❑ 84 Billy O'Dell 12.00 6.00
❑ 85A Luis Aparicio 30.00 15.00
❑ 85B Luis Aparicio YT 80.00 40.00
❑ 86 Valmy Thomas 12.00 6.00
❑ 87 Johnny Kucks 12.00 6.00
❑ 88 Duke Snider 80.00 40.00
❑ 89 Billy Klaus 12.00 6.00
❑ 90 Robin Roberts 30.00 15.00
❑ 91 Chuck Tanner 15.00 7.50
❑ 92A Clint Courtney 12.00 6.00
❑ 92B Clint Courtney YN 40.00 20.00
❑ 93 Sandy Amoros 15.00 7.50
❑ 94 Bob Skinner 15.00 7.50
❑ 95 Frank Bolling 12.00 6.00
❑ 96 Joe Durham 12.00 6.00
❑ 97A Larry Jackson 12.00 6.00
❑ 97B Larry Jackson YN 40.00 20.00
❑ 98A Billy Hunter 12.00 6.00
❑ 98B Billy Hunter YN 40.00 20.00
❑ 99 Bobby Adams 12.00 6.00
❑ 100A Early Wynn 30.00 15.00
❑ 100B Early Wynn YT 80.00 40.00
❑ 101A Bobby Richardson 30.00 15.00
❑ 101B B.Richardson YN 60.00 30.00
❑ 102 George Strickland 12.00 6.00
❑ 103 Jerry Lynch 15.00 7.50
❑ 104 Jim Pendleton 12.00 6.00
❑ 105 Billy Gardner 12.00 6.00
❑ 106 Dick Schofield 15.00 7.50
❑ 107 Ossie Virgil 12.00 6.00
❑ 108A Jim Landis 12.00 6.00
❑ 108B Jim Landis YT 40.00 20.00
❑ 109 Herb Plews 12.00 6.00
❑ 110 Johnny Logan 15.00 7.50
❑ 111 Stu Miller 10.00 5.00
❑ 112 Gus Zernial 10.00 5.00
❑ 113 Jerry Walker RC 8.00 4.00
❑ 114 Irv Noren 10.00 5.00
❑ 115 Jim Bunning 30.00 15.00
❑ 116 Dave Philley 8.00 4.00
❑ 117 Frank Torre 10.00 5.00
❑ 118 Harvey Haddix 10.00 5.00
❑ 119 Harry Chiti 8.00 4.00
❑ 120 Johnny Podres 10.00 5.00
❑ 121 Eddie Miksis 8.00 4.00
❑ 122 Walt Moryn 8.00 4.00
❑ 123 Dick Tomanek 8.00 4.00
❑ 124 Bobby Usher 8.00 4.00
❑ 125 Alvin Dark 10.00 5.00
❑ 126 Stan Palys 8.00 4.00
❑ 127 Tom Sturdivant 10.00 5.00
❑ 128 Willie Kirkland 8.00 4.00
❑ 129 Jim Derrington 8.00 4.00
❑ 130 Jackie Jensen 10.00 5.00
❑ 131 Bob Henrich 8.00 4.00
❑ 132 Vern Law 10.00 5.00
❑ 133 Russ Nixon RC 8.00 4.00
❑ 134 Philadelphia Phillies 15.00 3.00
Team Card CL
❑ 135 Mike(Moe)Drabowsky 10.00 5.00
❑ 136 Jim Finigan 8.00 4.00
❑ 137 Russ Kemmerer 8.00 4.00
❑ 138 Earl Torgeson 8.00 4.00
❑ 139 George Brunet 8.00 4.00
❑ 140 Wes Covington 10.00 5.00

❑ 141 Ken Lehman 8.00 4.00
❑ 142 Enos Slaughter 25.00 12.50
❑ 143 Billy Muffett RC 8.00 4.00
❑ 144 Bobby Morgan 8.00 4.00
❑ 145 Never issued
❑ 146 Dick Gray 8.00 4.00
❑ 147 Don McMahon RC 8.00 4.00
❑ 148 Billy Consolo 8.00 4.00
❑ 149 Tom Acker 8.00 4.00
❑ 150 Mickey Mantle 800.00 400.00
❑ 151 Buddy Pritchard 8.00 4.00
❑ 152 Johnny Antonelli 10.00 5.00
❑ 153 Les Moss 8.00 4.00
❑ 154 Harry Byrd 8.00 4.00
❑ 155 Hector Lopez 10.00 5.00
❑ 156 Dick Hyde 8.00 4.00
❑ 157 Dee Fondy 8.00 4.00
❑ 158 Cleveland Indians 15.00 3.00
Team Card CL
❑ 159 Taylor Phillips 8.00 4.00
❑ 160 Don Hoak 10.00 5.00
❑ 161 Don Larsen 15.00 7.50
❑ 162 Gil Hodges 40.00 20.00
❑ 163 Jim Wilson 8.00 4.00
❑ 164 Bob Taylor 8.00 4.00
❑ 165 Bob Nieman 8.00 4.00
❑ 166 Danny O'Connell 8.00 4.00
❑ 167 Frank Baumann 8.00 4.00
❑ 168 Joe Cunningham 8.00 4.00
❑ 169 Ralph Terry 10.00 5.00
❑ 170 Vic Wertz 10.00 5.00
❑ 171 Harry Anderson 8.00 4.00
❑ 172 Don Gross 8.00 4.00
❑ 173 Eddie Yost 8.00 4.00
❑ 174 K.C. Athletics Team CL 15.00 3.00
❑ 175 Marv Throneberry RC 15.00 7.50
❑ 176 Bob Buhl 10.00 5.00
❑ 177 Al Smith 8.00 4.00
❑ 178 Ted Kluszewski 25.00 12.50
❑ 179 Willie Miranda 8.00 4.00
❑ 180 Lindy McDaniel 10.00 5.00
❑ 181 Willie Jones 8.00 4.00
❑ 182 Joe Caffie 8.00 4.00
❑ 183 Dave Jolly 8.00 4.00
❑ 184 Elvin Tappe 8.00 4.00
❑ 185 Ray Boone 10.00 5.00
❑ 186 Jack Meyer 8.00 4.00
❑ 187 Sandy Koufax 200.00 100.00
❑ 188 Milt Bolling UER 8.00 4.00
(Photo actually
Lou Berberet)
❑ 189 George Susce 8.00 4.00
❑ 190 Red Schoendienst 25.00 12.50
❑ 191 Art Ceccarelli 8.00 4.00
❑ 192 Milt Graff 8.00 4.00
❑ 193 Jerry Lumpe RC 8.00 4.00
❑ 194 Roger Craig 10.00 5.00
❑ 195 Whitey Lockman 10.00 5.00
❑ 196 Mike Garcia 10.00 5.00
❑ 197 Haywood Sullivan 10.00 5.00
❑ 198 Bill Virdon 10.00 5.00
❑ 199 Don Blasingame 8.00 4.00
❑ 200 Bob Keegan 8.00 4.00
❑ 201 Jim Bolger 8.00 4.00
❑ 202 Woody Held RC 8.00 4.00
❑ 203 Al Walker 8.00 4.00
❑ 204 Leo Kiely 8.00 4.00
❑ 205 Johnny Temple 10.00 5.00
❑ 206 Bob Shaw RC 8.00 4.00
❑ 207 Solly Hemus 8.00 4.00
❑ 208 Cal McLish 8.00 4.00
❑ 209 Bob Anderson 8.00 4.00
❑ 210 Wally Moon 10.00 5.00
❑ 211 Pete Burnside 8.00 4.00
❑ 212 Bubba Phillips 8.00 4.00
❑ 213 Red Wilson 8.00 4.00
❑ 214 Willard Schmidt 8.00 4.00
❑ 215 Jim Gilliam 15.00 7.50
❑ 216 St. Louis Cardinals 15.00 3.00
Team Card CL
❑ 217 Jack Harshman 8.00 4.00
❑ 218 Dick Rand 8.00 4.00
❑ 219 Camilo Pascual 10.00 5.00
❑ 220 Tom Brewer 8.00 4.00
❑ 221 Jerry Kindall RC 8.00 4.00
❑ 222 Bud Daley 8.00 4.00
❑ 223 Andy Pafko 10.00 5.00
❑ 224 Bob Grim 10.00 5.00
❑ 225 Billy Goodman 10.00 5.00
❑ 226 Bob Smith 8.00 4.00
❑ 227 Gene Stephens 8.00 4.00
❑ 228 Duke Maas 8.00 4.00
❑ 229 Frank Zupo 8.00 4.00
❑ 230 Richie Ashburn 40.00 20.00
❑ 231 Lloyd Merritt 8.00 4.00
❑ 232 Reno Bertoia 8.00 4.00
❑ 233 Mickey Vernon 10.00 5.00
❑ 234 Carl Sawatski 8.00 4.00
❑ 235 Tom Gorman 8.00 4.00
❑ 236 Ed Fitzgerald 8.00 4.00
❑ 237 Bill Wight 8.00 4.00
❑ 238 Bill Mazeroski 30.00 15.00
❑ 239 Chuck Stobbs 8.00 4.00
❑ 240 Bill Skowron 25.00 12.50
❑ 241 Dick Littlefield 8.00 4.00
❑ 242 Johnny Klippstein 8.00 4.00
❑ 243 Larry Raines 8.00 4.00
❑ 244 Don Demeter 8.00 4.00
❑ 245 Frank Lary 10.00 5.00
❑ 246 New York Yankees 100.00 20.00
Team Card CL
❑ 247 Casey Wise 8.00 4.00
❑ 248 Herman Wehmeier 8.00 4.00
❑ 249 Ray Moore 8.00 4.00
❑ 250 Roy Sievers 10.00 5.00
❑ 251 Warren Hacker 8.00 4.00
❑ 252 Bob Trowbridge 8.00 4.00
❑ 253 Don Mueller 10.00 5.00
❑ 254 Alex Grammas 8.00 4.00
❑ 255 Bob Turley 10.00 5.00
❑ 256 Chicago White Sox 15.00 3.00
Team Card CL
❑ 257 Hal Smith 8.00 4.00
❑ 258 Carl Erskine 15.00 7.50
❑ 259 Al Pilarcik 8.00 4.00
❑ 260 Frank Malzone 10.00 5.00
❑ 261 Turk Lown 8.00 4.00
❑ 262 Johnny Groth 8.00 4.00
❑ 263 Eddie Bressoud 10.00 5.00
❑ 264 Jack Sanford 10.00 5.00
❑ 265 Pete Runnels 10.00 5.00
❑ 266 Connie Johnson 8.00 4.00
❑ 267 Sherm Lollar 10.00 5.00
❑ 268 Granny Hamner 8.00 4.00
❑ 269 Paul Smith 8.00 4.00
❑ 270 Warren Spahn 60.00 30.00
❑ 271 Billy Martin 40.00 20.00
❑ 272 Ray Crone 8.00 4.00
❑ 273 Hal Smith 8.00 4.00
❑ 274 Rocky Bridges 8.00 4.00
❑ 275 Elston Howard 15.00 7.50
❑ 276 Bobby Avila 8.00 4.00
❑ 277 Virgil Trucks 10.00 5.00
❑ 278 Mack Burk 8.00 4.00
❑ 279 Bob Boyd 8.00 4.00
❑ 280 Jim Piersall 10.00 5.00
❑ 281 Sammy Taylor 8.00 4.00
❑ 282 Paul Foytack 8.00 4.00
❑ 283 Ray Shearer 8.00 4.00
❑ 284 Ray Katt 8.00 4.00
❑ 285 Frank Robinson 100.00 50.00
❑ 286 Gino Cimoli 8.00 4.00
❑ 287 Sam Jones 10.00 5.00
❑ 288 Harmon Killebrew 100.00 50.00
❑ 289 Lou Burdette 10.00 5.00
Bobby Shantz
❑ 290 Dick Donovan 8.00 4.00
❑ 291 Don Landrum 8.00 4.00
❑ 292 Ned Garver 8.00 4.00
❑ 293 Gene Freese 8.00 4.00
❑ 294 Hal Jeffcoat 8.00 4.00
❑ 295 Minnie Minoso 25.00 12.50
❑ 296 Ryne Duren RC 15.00 7.50
❑ 297 Don Buddin 8.00 4.00
❑ 298 Jim Hearn 8.00 4.00
❑ 299 Harry Simpson 8.00 4.00
❑ 300 Will Harridge PRES 15.00 7.50
Warren Giles
❑ 301 Randy Jackson 8.00 4.00
❑ 302 Mike Baxes 8.00 4.00
❑ 303 Neil Chrisley 8.00 4.00
❑ 304 Harvey Kuenn 25.00 12.50
Al Kaline
❑ 305 Clem Labine 10.00 5.00
❑ 306 Whammy Douglas 8.00 4.00
❑ 307 Brooks Robinson 100.00 50.00
❑ 308 Paul Giel 10.00 5.00
❑ 309 Gail Harris 8.00 4.00
❑ 310 Ernie Banks 100.00 50.00
❑ 311 Bob Purkey 8.00 4.00
❑ 312 Boston Red Sox 15.00 3.00
Team Card CL
❑ 313 Bob Rush 8.00 4.00
❑ 314 Duke Snider 50.00 25.00
Walt Alston MG
❑ 315 Bob Friend 10.00 5.00
❑ 316 Tito Francona 10.00 5.00
❑ 317 Albie Pearson 10.00 5.00
❑ 318 Frank House 8.00 4.00
❑ 319 Lou Skizas 8.00 4.00
❑ 320 Whitey Ford 60.00 30.00
❑ 321 Ted Kluszewski 100.00 50.00
Ted Williams
❑ 322 Harding Peterson 10.00 5.00
❑ 323 Elmer Valo 8.00 4.00
❑ 324 Hoyt Wilhelm 25.00 12.50
❑ 325 Joe Adcock 10.00 5.00
❑ 326 Bob Miller 8.00 4.00
❑ 327 Chicago Cubs 15.00 3.00
Team Card CL
❑ 328 Ike Delock 8.00 4.00
❑ 329 Bob Cerv 10.00 5.00
❑ 330 Ed Bailey 10.00 5.00
❑ 331 Pedro Ramos 8.00 4.00
❑ 332 Jim King 8.00 4.00
❑ 333 Andy Carey 10.00 5.00
❑ 334 Bob Friend 10.00 5.00
Billy Pierce
❑ 335 Ruben Gomez 8.00 4.00
❑ 336 Bert Hamric 8.00 4.00
❑ 337 Hank Aguirre 8.00 4.00
❑ 338 Walt Dropo 10.00 5.00
❑ 339 Fred Hatfield 8.00 4.00
❑ 340 Don Newcombe 15.00 7.50
❑ 341 Pittsburgh Pirates 15.00 3.00
Team Card CL
❑ 342 Jim Brosnan 10.00 5.00
❑ 343 Orlando Cepeda RC 100.00 50.00
❑ 344 Bob Porterfield 8.00 4.00
❑ 345 Jim Hegan 10.00 5.00
❑ 346 Steve Bilko 8.00 4.00
❑ 347 Don Rudolph 8.00 4.00
❑ 348 Chico Fernandez 8.00 4.00
❑ 349 Murry Dickson 8.00 4.00
❑ 350 Ken Boyer 25.00 12.50
❑ 351 Del Crandall 40.00 20.00
Eddie Mathews
Hank Aaron
Joe Adcock
❑ 352 Herb Score 15.00 7.50
❑ 353 Stan Lopata 8.00 4.00
❑ 354 Art Ditmar 10.00 5.00
❑ 355 Bill Bruton 10.00 5.00
❑ 356 Bob Malkmus 8.00 4.00
❑ 357 Danny McDevitt 8.00 4.00
❑ 358 Gene Baker 8.00 4.00
❑ 359 Billy Loes 10.00 5.00
❑ 360 Roy McMillan 10.00 5.00
❑ 361 Mike Fornieles 8.00 4.00
❑ 362 Ray Jablonski 8.00 4.00
❑ 363 Don Elston 8.00 4.00
❑ 364 Earl Battey 8.00 4.00
❑ 365 Tom Morgan 8.00 4.00
❑ 366 Gene Green 8.00 4.00
❑ 367 Jack Urban 8.00 4.00
❑ 368 Rocky Colavito 50.00 25.00
❑ 369 Ralph Lumenti 8.00 4.00
❑ 370 Yogi Berra 100.00 50.00
❑ 371 Marty Keough 8.00 4.00
❑ 372 Don Cardwell 8.00 4.00
❑ 373 Joe Pignatano 8.00 4.00
❑ 374 Brooks Lawrence 8.00 4.00
❑ 375 Pee Wee Reese 80.00 40.00
❑ 376 Charley Rabe 8.00 4.00
❑ 377A Milwaukee Braves 15.00 7.50
Team Card
(Alphabetical)
❑ 377B Milwaukee Team 100.00 20.00

numerical checklist
❑ 378 Hank Sauer 10.00 5.00
❑ 379 Ray Herbert 8.00 4.00
❑ 380 Charlie Maxwell 10.00 5.00
❑ 381 Hal Brown 8.00 4.00
❑ 382 Al Cicotte 8.00 4.00
❑ 383 Lou Berberet 8.00 4.00
❑ 384 John Goryl 8.00 4.00
❑ 385 Wilmer Mizell 10.00 5.00
❑ 386 Ed Bailey 15.00 7.50
Birdie Tebbetts MG
Frank Robinson
❑ 387 Wally Post 10.00 5.00
❑ 388 Billy Moran 8.00 4.00
❑ 389 Bill Taylor 8.00 4.00
❑ 390 Del Crandall 10.00 5.00
❑ 391 Dave Melton 8.00 4.00
❑ 392 Bennie Daniels 8.00 4.00
❑ 393 Tony Kubek 30.00 15.00
❑ 394 Jim Grant RC 8.00 4.00
❑ 395 Willard Nixon 8.00 4.00
❑ 396 Dutch Dotterer 8.00 4.00
❑ 397A Detroit Tigers 15.00 7.50
Team Card
(Alphabetical)
❑ 397B Detroit Team 100.00 20.00
numerical checklist
❑ 398 Gene Woodling 10.00 5.00
❑ 399 Marv Grissom 8.00 4.00
❑ 400 Nellie Fox 40.00 20.00
❑ 401 Don Bessent 8.00 4.00
❑ 402 Bobby Gene Smith 8.00 4.00
❑ 403 Steve Korcheck 8.00 4.00
❑ 404 Curt Simmons 10.00 5.00
❑ 405 Ken Aspromonte 8.00 4.00
❑ 406 Vic Power 10.00 5.00
❑ 407 Carlton Willey 10.00 5.00
❑ 408A Baltimore Orioles 15.00 7.50
Team Card
(Alphabetical)
❑ 408B Baltimore Team 100.00 20.00
numerical checklist
❑ 409 Frank Thomas 10.00 5.00
❑ 410 Murray Wall 8.00 4.00
❑ 411 Tony Taylor RC 10.00 5.00
❑ 412 Gerry Staley 8.00 4.00
❑ 413 Jim Davenport RC 8.00 4.00
❑ 414 Sammy White 8.00 4.00
❑ 415 Bob Bowman 8.00 4.00
❑ 416 Foster Castleman 8.00 4.00
❑ 417 Carl Furillo 15.00 7.50
❑ 418 Mickey Mantle 400.00 200.00
Hank Aaron
❑ 419 Bobby Shantz 10.00 5.00
❑ 420 Vada Pinson RC 40.00 20.00
❑ 421 Dixie Howell 8.00 4.00
❑ 422 Norm Zauchin 8.00 4.00
❑ 423 Phil Clark 8.00 4.00
❑ 424 Larry Doby 25.00 12.50
❑ 425 Sammy Esposito 8.00 4.00
❑ 426 Johnny O'Brien 10.00 5.00
❑ 427 Al Worthington 8.00 4.00
❑ 428A Cincinnati Reds 15.00 7.50
Team Card
(Alphabetical)
❑ 428B Cincinnati Team 100.00 20.00
numerical checklist
❑ 429 Gus Triandos 10.00 5.00
❑ 430 Bobby Thomson 10.00 5.00
❑ 431 Gene Conley 10.00 5.00
❑ 432 John Powers 8.00 4.00
❑ 433A Pancho Herrer ERR 600.00 300.00
❑ 433B Pancho Herrera COR 10.00 5.00
❑ 434 Harvey Kuenn 10.00 5.00
❑ 435 Ed Roebuck 10.00 5.00
❑ 436 Willie Mays 100.00 50.00
Duke Snider
❑ 437 Bob Speake 8.00 4.00
❑ 438 Whitey Herzog 10.00 5.00
❑ 439 Ray Narleski 8.00 4.00
❑ 440 Eddie Mathews 80.00 40.00
❑ 441 Jim Marshall 10.00 5.00
❑ 442 Phil Paine 8.00 4.00
❑ 443 Billy Harrell SP 20.00 10.00
❑ 444 Danny Kravitz 8.00 4.00
❑ 445 Bob Smith 8.00 4.00
❑ 446 Carroll Hardy SP 20.00 10.00
❑ 447 Ray Monzant 8.00 4.00
❑ 448 Charlie Lau RC 10.00 5.00
❑ 449 Gene Fodge 8.00 4.00
❑ 450 Preston Ward SP 20.00 10.00
❑ 451 Joe Taylor 8.00 4.00
❑ 452 Roman Mejias 8.00 4.00
❑ 453 Tom Qualters 8.00 4.00
❑ 454 Harry Hanebrink 8.00 4.00
❑ 455 Hal Griggs 8.00 4.00
❑ 456 Dick Brown 8.00 4.00
❑ 457 Milt Pappas RC 10.00 5.00
❑ 458 Julio Becquer 8.00 4.00
❑ 459 Ron Blackburn 8.00 4.00
❑ 460 Chuck Essegian 8.00 4.00
❑ 461 Ed Mayer 8.00 4.00
❑ 462 Gary Geiger SP 20.00 10.00
❑ 463 Vito Valentinetti 8.00 4.00
❑ 464 Curt Flood RC 30.00 15.00
❑ 465 Arnie Portocarrero 8.00 4.00
❑ 466 Pete Whisenant 8.00 4.00
❑ 467 Glen Hobbie 8.00 4.00
❑ 468 Bob Schmidt 8.00 4.00
❑ 469 Don Ferrarese 8.00 4.00
❑ 470 R.C. Stevens 8.00 4.00
❑ 471 Lenny Green 8.00 4.00
❑ 472 Joey Jay 10.00 5.00
❑ 473 Bill Renna 8.00 4.00
❑ 474 Roman Semproch 8.00 4.00
❑ 475 Fred Haney AS MG 25.00 7.50
Casey Stengel AS MG CL
❑ 476 Stan Musial AS TP 50.00 25.00
❑ 477 Bill Skowron AS 10.00 5.00
❑ 478 J.Temple AS UER 8.00 4.00
Card says record vs American League
Temple was NL AS
❑ 479 Nellie Fox AS 15.00 7.50
❑ 480 Eddie Mathews AS 30.00 15.00
❑ 481 Frank Malzone AS 8.00 4.00
❑ 482 Ernie Banks AS 40.00 20.00
❑ 483 Luis Aparicio AS 15.00 7.50
❑ 484 Frank Robinson AS 40.00 20.00
❑ 485 Ted Williams AS 150.00 75.00
❑ 486 Willie Mays AS 60.00 30.00
❑ 487 Mickey Mantle AS TP 200.00 90.00
❑ 488 Hank Aaron AS 60.00 30.00
❑ 489 Jackie Jensen AS 10.00 5.00
❑ 490 Ed Bailey AS 8.00 4.00
❑ 491 Sherm Lollar AS 8.00 4.00
❑ 492 Bob Friend AS 8.00 4.00
❑ 493 Bob Turley AS 10.00 5.00
❑ 494 Warren Spahn AS 25.00 12.50
❑ 495 Herb Score AS 15.00 3.00
❑ NNO Contest Cards 40.00 20.00

1959 Topps

	NM	Ex
COMPLETE SET (572)	5000.00	2500.00
COMMON CARD (1-110)	6.00	3.00
COMMON (111-506)	4.00	2.00
COMMON (507-572)	15.00	7.50
WRAPPER (1-CENT)	125.00	60.00
WRAPPER (5-CENT)	100.00	50.00

❑ 1 Ford Frick COMM 60.00 16.50
❑ 2 Eddie Yost 8.00 4.00
❑ 3 Don McMahon 8.00 4.00
❑ 4 Albie Pearson 8.00 4.00
❑ 5 Dick Donovan 8.00 4.00
❑ 6 Alex Grammas 6.00 3.00
❑ 7 Al Pilarcik 6.00 3.00
❑ 8 Phillies Team CL 80.00 16.00
❑ 9 Paul Giel 8.00 4.00
❑ 10 Mickey Mantle 800.00 350.00
❑ 11 Billy Hunter 8.00 4.00
❑ 12 Vern Law 8.00 4.00
❑ 13 Dick Gernert 6.00 3.00
❑ 14 Pete Whisenant 6.00 3.00
❑ 15 Dick Drott 6.00 3.00
❑ 16 Joe Pignatano 6.00 3.00
❑ 17 Frank Thomas 8.00 4.00
Danny Murtaugh MG
Ted Kluszewski
❑ 18 Jack Urban 6.00 3.00
❑ 19 Eddie Bressoud 6.00 3.00
❑ 20 Duke Snider 60.00 30.00
❑ 21 Connie Johnson 6.00 3.00
❑ 22 Al Smith 8.00 4.00
❑ 23 Murry Dickson 8.00 4.00
❑ 24 Red Wilson 6.00 3.00
❑ 25 Don Hoak 8.00 4.00
❑ 26 Chuck Stobbs 6.00 3.00
❑ 27 Andy Pafko 8.00 4.00
❑ 28 Al Worthington 6.00 3.00
❑ 29 Jim Bolger 6.00 3.00
❑ 30 Nellie Fox 30.00 15.00
❑ 31 Ken Lehman 6.00 3.00
❑ 32 Don Buddin 6.00 3.00
❑ 33 Ed Fitzgerald 6.00 3.00
❑ 34 Al Kaline 20.00 10.00
Charley Maxwell
❑ 35 Ted Kluszewski 12.00 6.00
❑ 36 Hank Aguirre 6.00 3.00
❑ 37 Gene Green 6.00 3.00
❑ 38 Morrie Martin 6.00 3.00
❑ 39 Ed Bouchee 6.00 3.00
❑ 40A Warren Spahn ERR 80.00 40.00
(Born 1931)
❑ 40B Warren Spahn ERR 100.00 50.00
(Born 1931, but three
is partially obscured)
❑ 40C Warren Spahn COR 60.00 30.00
(Born 1921)
❑ 41 Bob Martyn 6.00 3.00
❑ 42 Murray Wall 6.00 3.00
❑ 43 Steve Bilko 6.00 3.00
❑ 44 Vito Valentinetti 6.00 3.00
❑ 45 Andy Carey 8.00 4.00
❑ 46 Bill R. Henry 6.00 3.00
❑ 47 Jim Finigan 6.00 3.00
❑ 48 Orioles Team CL 25.00 5.00
❑ 49 Bill Hall 6.00 3.00
❑ 50 Willie Mays 150.00 75.00
❑ 51 Rip Coleman 6.00 3.00
❑ 52 Coot Veal 6.00 3.00
❑ 53 Stan Williams RC 8.00 4.00
❑ 54 Mel Roach 6.00 3.00
❑ 55 Tom Brewer 6.00 3.00
❑ 56 Carl Sawatski 6.00 3.00
❑ 57 Al Cicotte 6.00 3.00
❑ 58 Eddie Miksis 6.00 3.00
❑ 59 Irv Noren 8.00 4.00
❑ 60 Bob Turley 8.00 4.00
❑ 61 Dick Brown 6.00 3.00
❑ 62 Tony Taylor 8.00 4.00
❑ 63 Jim Hearn 6.00 3.00
❑ 64 Joe DeMaestri 6.00 3.00
❑ 65 Frank Torre 8.00 4.00
❑ 66 Joe Ginsberg 6.00 3.00
❑ 67 Brooks Lawrence 6.00 3.00
❑ 68 Dick Schofield 8.00 4.00
❑ 69 Giants Team CL 25.00 5.00
❑ 70 Harvey Kuenn 8.00 4.00
❑ 71 Don Bessent 6.00 3.00
❑ 72 Bill Renna 6.00 3.00
❑ 73 Ron Jackson 8.00 4.00
❑ 74 Jim Lemon 8.00 4.00
Cookie Lavagetto MG
Roy Sievers
❑ 75 Sam Jones 8.00 4.00
❑ 76 Bobby Richardson 20.00 10.00
❑ 77 John Goryl 6.00 3.00
❑ 78 Pedro Ramos 6.00 3.00

❑ 79 Harry Chiti 6.00 3.00
❑ 80 Minnie Minoso 12.00 6.00
❑ 81 Hal Jeffcoat 6.00 3.00
❑ 82 Bob Boyd 6.00 3.00
❑ 83 Bob Smith 6.00 3.00
❑ 84 Reno Bertoia 6.00 3.00
❑ 85 Harry Anderson 6.00 3.00
❑ 86 Bob Keegan 8.00 4.00
❑ 87 Danny O'Connell 6.00 3.00
❑ 88 Herb Score 12.00 6.00
❑ 89 Billy Gardner 6.00 3.00
❑ 90 Bill Skowron 12.00 6.00
❑ 91 Herb Moford 6.00 3.00
❑ 92 Dave Philley 6.00 3.00
❑ 93 Julio Becquer 6.00 3.00
❑ 94 White Sox Team CL 40.00 8.00
❑ 95 Carl Willey 6.00 3.00
❑ 96 Lou Berberet 6.00 3.00
❑ 97 Jerry Lynch 8.00 4.00
❑ 98 Arnie Portocarrero 6.00 3.00
❑ 99 Ted Kazanski 6.00 3.00
❑ 100 Bob Cerv 8.00 4.00
❑ 101 Alex Kellner 6.00 3.00
❑ 102 Felipe Alou RC 30.00 15.00
❑ 103 Billy Goodman 8.00 4.00
❑ 104 Del Rice 8.00 4.00
❑ 105 Lee Walls 6.00 3.00
❑ 106 Hal Woodeshick 6.00 3.00
❑ 107 Norm Larker 8.00 4.00
❑ 108 Zack Monroe 8.00 4.00
❑ 109 Bob Schmidt 6.00 3.00
❑ 110 George Witt 8.00 4.00
❑ 111 Redlegs Team CL 15.00 3.00
❑ 112 Billy Consolo 4.00 2.00
❑ 113 Taylor Phillips 4.00 2.00
❑ 114 Earl Battey 8.00 4.00
❑ 115 Mickey Vernon 8.00 4.00
❑ 116 Bob Allison RP RC 12.00 6.00
❑ 117 J.Blanchard RP RC 12.00 6.00
❑ 118 John Buzhardt RP 5.00 2.50
❑ 119 John Callison RP RC 12.00 6.00
❑ 120 Chuck Coles RP 5.00 2.50
❑ 121 Bob Conley RP 5.00 2.50
❑ 122 Bennie Daniels RP 5.00 2.50
❑ 123 Don Dillard RP 5.00 2.50
❑ 124 Dan Dobbek RP 5.00 2.50
❑ 125 Ron Fairly RP RC 12.00 6.00
❑ 126 Eddie Haas RP 5.00 2.50
❑ 127 Kent Hadley RP 5.00 2.50
❑ 128 Bob Hartman RP 5.00 2.50
❑ 129 Frank Herrera RP 5.00 2.50
❑ 130 Lou Jackson RP 5.00 2.50
❑ 131 Deron Johnson RP RC 12.00 6.00
❑ 132 Don Lee RP 5.00 2.50
❑ 133 Bob Lillis RP RC 5.00 2.50
❑ 134 Jim McDaniel RP 5.00 2.50
❑ 135 Gene Oliver RP 5.00 2.50
❑ 136 Jim O'Toole RP RC 5.00 2.50
❑ 137 Dick Ricketts RP 5.00 2.50
❑ 138 John Romano RP RC 5.00 2.50
❑ 139 Ed Sadowski RP 5.00 2.50
❑ 140 Charlie Secrest RP 5.00 2.50
❑ 141 Joe Shipley RP 5.00 2.50
❑ 142 Dick Stigman RP 5.00 2.50
❑ 143 Willie Tasby RP RC 5.00 2.50
❑ 144 Jerry Walker RP 5.00 2.50
❑ 145 Dom Zanni RP 5.00 2.50
❑ 146 Jerry Zimmerman RP 5.00 2.50
❑ 147 Dale Long 30.00 15.00
Ernie Banks
Walt Moryn
❑ 148 Mike McCormick 8.00 4.00
❑ 149 Jim Bunning 20.00 10.00
❑ 150 Stan Musial 125.00 60.00
❑ 151 Bob Malkmus 4.00 2.00
❑ 152 Johnny Klippstein 4.00 2.00
❑ 153 Jim Marshall 4.00 2.00
❑ 154 Ray Herbert 4.00 2.00
❑ 155 Enos Slaughter 20.00 10.00
❑ 156 Billy Pierce 12.00 6.00
Robin Roberts
❑ 157 Felix Mantilla 4.00 2.00
❑ 158 Walt Dropo 4.00 2.00
❑ 159 Bob Shaw 8.00 4.00
❑ 160 Dick Groat 8.00 4.00
❑ 161 Frank Baumann 4.00 2.00
❑ 162 Bobby G. Smith 4.00 2.00
❑ 163 Sandy Koufax 150.00 75.00
❑ 164 Johnny Groth 4.00 2.00
❑ 165 Bill Bruton 4.00 2.00
❑ 166 Minnie Minoso 30.00 15.00
Rocky Colavito
(Misspelled Colovito
on card back)
Larry Doby
❑ 167 Duke Maas 4.00 2.00
❑ 168 Carroll Hardy 4.00 2.00
❑ 169 Ted Abernathy 4.00 2.00
❑ 170 Gene Woodling 8.00 4.00
❑ 171 Willard Schmidt 4.00 2.00
❑ 172 Athletics Team CL 15.00 3.00
❑ 173 Bill Monbouquette 8.00 4.00
❑ 174 Jim Pendleton 4.00 2.00
❑ 175 Dick Farrell 8.00 4.00
❑ 176 Preston Ward 4.00 2.00
❑ 177 John Briggs 4.00 2.00
❑ 178 Ruben Amaro RC 12.00 6.00
❑ 179 Don Rudolph 4.00 2.00
❑ 180 Yogi Berra 80.00 40.00
❑ 181 Bob Porterfield 4.00 2.00
❑ 182 Milt Graff 4.00 2.00
❑ 183 Stu Miller 8.00 4.00
❑ 184 Harvey Haddix 8.00 4.00
❑ 185 Jim Busby 4.00 2.00
❑ 186 Mudcat Grant 8.00 4.00
❑ 187 Bubba Phillips 8.00 4.00
❑ 188 Juan Pizarro 4.00 2.00
❑ 189 Neil Chrisley 4.00 2.00
❑ 190 Bill Virdon 8.00 4.00
❑ 191 Russ Kemmerer 4.00 2.00
❑ 192 Charlie Beamon 4.00 2.00
❑ 193 Sammy Taylor 4.00 2.00
❑ 194 Jim Brosnan 8.00 4.00
❑ 195 Rip Repulski 4.00 2.00
❑ 196 Billy Moran 4.00 2.00
❑ 197 Ray Semproch 4.00 2.00
❑ 198 Jim Davenport 8.00 4.00
❑ 199 Leo Kiely 4.00 2.00
❑ 200 W.Giles NL PRES 8.00 4.00
❑ 201 Tom Acker 4.00 2.00
❑ 202 Roger Maris 125.00 60.00
❑ 203 Ossie Virgil 4.00 2.00
❑ 204 Casey Wise 4.00 2.00
❑ 205 Don Larsen 8.00 4.00
❑ 206 Carl Furillo 12.00 6.00
❑ 207 George Strickland 4.00 2.00
❑ 208 Willie Jones 4.00 2.00
❑ 209 Lenny Green 4.00 2.00
❑ 210 Ed Bailey 4.00 2.00
❑ 211 Bob Blaylock 4.00 2.00
❑ 212 Hank Aaron 80.00 40.00
Eddie Mathews
❑ 213 Jim Rivera 8.00 4.00
❑ 214 Marcelino Solis 4.00 2.00
❑ 215 Jim Lemon 8.00 4.00
❑ 216 Andre Rodgers 4.00 2.00
❑ 217 Carl Erskine 12.00 6.00
❑ 218 Roman Mejias 4.00 2.00
❑ 219 George Zuverink 4.00 2.00
❑ 220 Frank Malzone 8.00 4.00
❑ 221 Bob Bowman 4.00 2.00
❑ 222 Bobby Shantz 8.00 4.00
❑ 223 Cardinals Team CL 15.00 3.00
❑ 224 Claude Osteen RC 8.00 4.00
❑ 225 Johnny Logan 8.00 4.00
❑ 226 Art Ceccarelli 4.00 2.00
❑ 227 Hal W. Smith 4.00 2.00
❑ 228 Don Gross 4.00 2.00
❑ 229 Vic Power 8.00 4.00
❑ 230 Bill Fischer 4.00 2.00
❑ 231 Ellis Burton 4.00 2.00
❑ 232 Eddie Kasko 4.00 2.00
❑ 233 Paul Foytack 4.00 2.00
❑ 234 Chuck Tanner 8.00 4.00
❑ 235 Valmy Thomas 4.00 2.00
❑ 236 Ted Bowsfield 4.00 2.00
❑ 237 Gil McDougald 12.00 6.00
Bob Turley
Bobby Richardson
❑ 238 Gene Baker 4.00 2.00
❑ 239 Bob Trowbridge 4.00 2.00
❑ 240 Hank Bauer 12.00 6.00
❑ 241 Billy Muffett 4.00 2.00
❑ 242 Ron Samford 4.00 2.00
❑ 243 Marv Grissom 4.00 2.00
❑ 244 Ted Gray 4.00 2.00
❑ 245 Ned Garver 4.00 2.00
❑ 246 J.W. Porter 4.00 2.00
❑ 247 Don Ferrarese 4.00 2.00
❑ 248 Red Sox Team CL 15.00 3.00
❑ 249 Bobby Adams 4.00 2.00
❑ 250 Billy O'Dell 4.00 2.00
❑ 251 Clete Boyer 12.00 6.00
❑ 252 Ray Boone 8.00 4.00
❑ 253 Seth Morehead 4.00 2.00
❑ 254 Zeke Bella 4.00 2.00
❑ 255 Del Ennis 8.00 4.00
❑ 256 Jerry Davie 4.00 2.00
❑ 257 Leon Wagner RC 8.00 4.00
❑ 258 Fred Kipp 4.00 2.00
❑ 259 Jim Pisoni 4.00 2.00
❑ 260 Early Wynn UER 20.00 10.00
1957 Cleevland
❑ 261 Gene Stephens 4.00 2.00
❑ 262 Johnny Podres 12.00 6.00
Clem Labine
Don Drysdale
❑ 263 Bud Daley 4.00 2.00
❑ 264 Chico Carrasquel 4.00 2.00
❑ 265 Ron Kline 4.00 2.00
❑ 266 Woody Held 4.00 2.00
❑ 267 John Romonosky 4.00 2.00
❑ 268 Tito Francona 8.00 4.00
❑ 269 Jack Meyer 4.00 2.00
❑ 270 Gil Hodges 30.00 15.00
❑ 271 Orlando Pena 4.00 2.00
❑ 272 Jerry Lumpe 4.00 2.00
❑ 273 Joey Jay 8.00 4.00
❑ 274 Jerry Kindall 8.00 4.00
❑ 275 Jack Sanford 8.00 4.00
❑ 276 Pete Daley 4.00 2.00
❑ 277 Turk Lown 8.00 4.00
❑ 278 Chuck Essegian 4.00 2.00
❑ 279 Ernie Johnson 4.00 2.00
❑ 280 Frank Bolling 4.00 2.00
❑ 281 Walt Craddock 4.00 2.00
❑ 282 R.C. Stevens 4.00 2.00
❑ 283 Russ Heman 4.00 2.00
❑ 284 Steve Korcheck 4.00 2.00
❑ 285 Joe Cunningham 4.00 2.00
❑ 286 Dean Stone 4.00 2.00
❑ 287 Don Zimmer 12.00 6.00
❑ 288 Dutch Dotterer 4.00 2.00
❑ 289 Johnny Kucks 8.00 4.00
❑ 290 Wes Covington 4.00 2.00
❑ 291 Pedro Ramos 4.00 2.00
Camilo Pascual
❑ 292 Dick Williams 8.00 4.00
❑ 293 Ray Moore 4.00 2.00
❑ 294 Hank Foiles 4.00 2.00
❑ 295 Billy Martin 30.00 15.00
❑ 296 Ernie Broglio RC 4.00 2.00
❑ 297 Jackie Brandt 4.00 2.00
❑ 298 Tex Clevenger 4.00 2.00
❑ 299 Billy Klaus 4.00 2.00
❑ 300 Richie Ashburn 30.00 15.00
❑ 301 Earl Averill 4.00 2.00
❑ 302 Don Mossi 8.00 4.00
❑ 303 Marty Keough 4.00 2.00
❑ 304 Cubs Team CL 15.00 3.00
❑ 305 Curt Raydon 4.00 2.00
❑ 306 Jim Gilliam 8.00 4.00
❑ 307 Curt Barclay 4.00 2.00
❑ 308 Norm Siebern 4.00 2.00
❑ 309 Sal Maglie 8.00 4.00
❑ 310 Luis Aparicio 20.00 10.00
❑ 311 Norm Zauchin 4.00 2.00
❑ 312 Don Newcombe 8.00 4.00
❑ 313 Frank House 4.00 2.00
❑ 314 Don Cardwell 4.00 2.00
❑ 315 Joe Adcock 8.00 4.00
❑ 316A Ralph Lumenti UER 4.00 2.00
(Option)
(Photo actually
Camilo Pascual)
❑ 316B Ralph Lumenti UER 80.00 40.00
(No option)
(Photo actually

Camilo Pascual)
❑ 317 Willie Mays 80.00 40.00
Richie Ashburn
❑ 318 Rocky Bridges 4.00 2.00
❑ 319 Dave Hillman 4.00 2.00
❑ 320 Bob Skinner 8.00 4.00
❑ 321A Bob Giallombardo 8.00 4.00
(Option)
❑ 321B Bob Giallombardo 80.00 40.00
(No option)
❑ 322A Harry Hanebrink 8.00 4.00
(Traded)
❑ 322B Harry Hanebrink 80.00 40.00
(No trade)
❑ 323 Frank Sullivan 4.00 2.00
❑ 324 Don Demeter 4.00 2.00
❑ 325 Ken Boyer 12.00 6.00
❑ 326 Marv Throneberry 8.00 4.00
❑ 327 Gary Bell 4.00 2.00
❑ 328 Lou Skizas 4.00 2.00
❑ 329 Tigers Team CL 15.00 3.00
❑ 330 Gus Triandos 8.00 4.00
❑ 331 Steve Boros 4.00 2.00
❑ 332 Ray Monzant 4.00 2.00
❑ 333 Harry Simpson 4.00 2.00
❑ 334 Glen Hobbie 4.00 2.00
❑ 335 Johnny Temple 8.00 4.00
❑ 336A Billy Loes 8.00 4.00
(With traded line)
❑ 336B Billy Loes 80.00 40.00
(No trade)
❑ 337 George Crowe 4.00 2.00
❑ 338 Sparky Anderson RC 60.00 30.00
❑ 339 Roy Face 8.00 4.00
❑ 340 Roy Sievers 8.00 4.00
❑ 341 Tom Qualters 4.00 2.00
❑ 342 Ray Jablonski 4.00 2.00
❑ 343 Billy Hoeft 4.00 2.00
❑ 344 Russ Nixon 4.00 2.00
❑ 345 Gil McDougald 12.00 6.00
❑ 346 Dave Sisler 4.00 2.00
Tom Brewer
❑ 347 Bob Buhl 4.00 2.00
❑ 348 Ted Lepcio 4.00 2.00
❑ 349 Hoyt Wilhelm 20.00 10.00
❑ 350 Ernie Banks 80.00 40.00
❑ 351 Earl Torgeson 4.00 2.00
❑ 352 Robin Roberts 20.00 10.00
❑ 353 Curt Flood 8.00 4.00
❑ 354 Pete Burnside 4.00 2.00
❑ 355 Jimmy Piersall 8.00 4.00
❑ 356 Bob Mabe 4.00 2.00
❑ 357 Dick Stuart RC 8.00 4.00
❑ 358 Ralph Terry 8.00 4.00
❑ 359 Bill White RC 20.00 10.00
❑ 360 Al Kaline 60.00 30.00
❑ 361 Willard Nixon 4.00 2.00
❑ 362A Dolan Nichols 4.00 2.00
(With option line)
❑ 362B Dolan Nichols 80.00 40.00
(No option)
❑ 363 Bobby Avila 4.00 2.00
❑ 364 Danny McDevitt 4.00 2.00
❑ 365 Gus Bell 8.00 4.00
❑ 366 Humberto Robinson 4.00 2.00
❑ 367 Cal Neeman 4.00 2.00
❑ 368 Don Mueller 8.00 4.00
❑ 369 Dick Tomanek 4.00 2.00
❑ 370 Pete Runnels 8.00 4.00
❑ 371 Dick Brodowski 4.00 2.00
❑ 372 Jim Hegan 8.00 4.00
❑ 373 Herb Plews 4.00 2.00
❑ 374 Art Ditmar 8.00 4.00
❑ 375 Bob Nieman 4.00 2.00
❑ 376 Hal Naragon 4.00 2.00
❑ 377 John Antonelli 8.00 4.00
❑ 378 Gail Harris 4.00 2.00
❑ 379 Bob Miller 4.00 2.00
❑ 380 Hank Aaron 150.00 60.00
❑ 381 Mike Baxes 4.00 2.00
❑ 382 Curt Simmons 8.00 4.00
❑ 383 Don Larsen 12.00 6.00
Casey Stengel MG
❑ 384 Dave Sisler 4.00 2.00
❑ 385 Sherm Lollar 8.00 4.00
❑ 386 Jim Delsing 4.00 2.00
❑ 387 Don Drysdale 50.00 25.00
❑ 388 Bob Will 4.00 2.00
❑ 389 Joe Nuxhall 8.00 4.00
❑ 390 Orlando Cepeda 20.00 10.00
❑ 391 Milt Pappas 8.00 4.00
❑ 392 Whitey Herzog 8.00 4.00
❑ 393 Frank Lary 8.00 4.00
❑ 394 Randy Jackson 4.00 2.00
❑ 395 Elston Howard 12.00 6.00
❑ 396 Bob Rush 4.00 2.00
❑ 397 Senators Team CL 15.00 3.00
❑ 398 Wally Post 8.00 4.00
❑ 399 Larry Jackson 4.00 2.00
❑ 400 Jackie Jensen 8.00 4.00
❑ 401 Ron Blackburn 4.00 2.00
❑ 402 Hector Lopez 8.00 4.00
❑ 403 Clem Labine 8.00 4.00
❑ 404 Hank Sauer 8.00 4.00
❑ 405 Roy McMillan 8.00 4.00
❑ 406 Solly Drake 4.00 2.00
❑ 407 Moe Drabowsky 8.00 4.00
❑ 408 Nellie Fox 40.00 20.00
Luis Aparicio
❑ 409 Gus Zernial 8.00 4.00
❑ 410 Billy Pierce 8.00 4.00
❑ 411 Whitey Lockman 8.00 4.00
❑ 412 Stan Lopata 4.00 2.00
❑ 413 Camilo Pascual UER 8.00 4.00
(Listed as Camillo
on front and Pasqual
on back)
❑ 414 Dale Long 8.00 4.00
❑ 415 Bill Mazeroski 12.00 6.00
❑ 416 Haywood Sullivan 8.00 4.00
❑ 417 Virgil Trucks 8.00 4.00
❑ 418 Gino Cimoli 4.00 2.00
❑ 419 Braves Team CL 15.00 3.00
❑ 420 Rocky Colavito 30.00 15.00
❑ 421 Herman Wehmeier 4.00 2.00
❑ 422 Hobie Landrith 4.00 2.00
❑ 423 Bob Grim 8.00 4.00
❑ 424 Ken Aspromonte 4.00 2.00
❑ 425 Del Crandall 8.00 4.00
❑ 426 Gerry Staley 8.00 4.00
❑ 427 Charlie Neal 8.00 4.00
❑ 428 Ron Kline 4.00 2.00
Bob Friend
Vernon Law
Roy Face
❑ 429 Bobby Thomson 8.00 4.00
❑ 430 Whitey Ford 60.00 30.00
❑ 431 Whammy Douglas 4.00 2.00
❑ 432 Smoky Burgess 8.00 4.00
❑ 433 Billy Harrell 4.00 2.00
❑ 434 Hal Griggs 4.00 2.00
❑ 435 Frank Robinson 50.00 25.00
❑ 436 Granny Hamner 4.00 2.00
❑ 437 Ike Delock 4.00 2.00
❑ 438 Sammy Esposito 4.00 2.00
❑ 439 Brooks Robinson 50.00 25.00
❑ 440 Lou Burdette 8.00 4.00
(Posing as if
lefthanded)
❑ 441 John Roseboro 8.00 4.00
❑ 442 Ray Narleski 4.00 2.00
❑ 443 Daryl Spencer 4.00 2.00
❑ 444 Ron Hansen RC 8.00 4.00
❑ 445 Cal McLish 4.00 2.00
❑ 446 Rocky Nelson 4.00 2.00
❑ 447 Bob Anderson 4.00 2.00
❑ 448 Vada Pinson UER 12.00 6.00
(Born: 8/8/38
should be 8/11/38)
❑ 449 Tom Gorman 4.00 2.00
❑ 450 Eddie Mathews 40.00 20.00
❑ 451 Jimmy Constable 4.00 2.00
❑ 452 Chico Fernandez 4.00 2.00
❑ 453 Les Moss 4.00 2.00
❑ 454 Phil Clark 4.00 2.00
❑ 455 Larry Doby 12.00 6.00
❑ 456 Jerry Casale 4.00 2.00
❑ 457 Dodgers Team CL 30.00 6.00
❑ 458 Gordon Jones 4.00 2.00
❑ 459 Bill Tuttle 4.00 2.00
❑ 460 Bob Friend 8.00 4.00
❑ 461 Mickey Mantle HL 125.00 60.00
❑ 462 Rocky Colavito HL 12.00 6.00
❑ 463 Al Kaline HL 30.00 15.00
❑ 464 Willie Mays HL 40.00 20.00
54 World Series Catch
❑ 465 Roy Sievers HL 8.00 4.00
❑ 466 Billy Pierce HL 8.00 4.00
❑ 467 Hank Aaron HL 40.00 20.00
❑ 468 Duke Snider HL 20.00 10.00
❑ 469 Ernie Banks HL 20.00 10.00
❑ 470 Stan Musial HL 30.00 15.00
3,000 Hits
❑ 471 Tom Sturdivant 4.00 2.00
❑ 472 Gene Freese 4.00 2.00
❑ 473 Mike Fornieles 4.00 2.00
❑ 474 Moe Thacker 4.00 2.00
❑ 475 Jack Harshman 4.00 2.00
❑ 476 Indians Team CL 15.00 3.00
❑ 477 Barry Latman 4.00 2.00
❑ 478 Roberto Clemente 175.00 90.00
❑ 479 Lindy McDaniel 8.00 4.00
❑ 480 Red Schoendienst 12.00 6.00
❑ 481 Charlie Maxwell 8.00 4.00
❑ 482 Russ Meyer 4.00 2.00
❑ 483 Clint Courtney 4.00 2.00
❑ 484 Willie Kirkland 4.00 2.00
❑ 485 Ryne Duren 8.00 4.00
❑ 486 Sammy White 4.00 2.00
❑ 487 Hal Brown 4.00 2.00
❑ 488 Walt Moryn 4.00 2.00
❑ 489 John Powers 4.00 2.00
❑ 490 Frank Thomas 8.00 4.00
❑ 491 Don Blasingame 4.00 2.00
❑ 492 Gene Conley 8.00 4.00
❑ 493 Jim Landis 8.00 4.00
❑ 494 Don Pavletich 4.00 2.00
❑ 495 Johnny Podres 12.00 6.00
❑ 496 W.Terwilliger UER 4.00 2.00
Athlftics on front
❑ 497 Hal R. Smith 4.00 2.00
❑ 498 Dick Hyde 4.00 2.00
❑ 499 Johnny O'Brien 8.00 4.00
❑ 500 Vic Wertz 8.00 4.00
❑ 501 Bob Tiefenauer 4.00 2.00
❑ 502 Alvin Dark 8.00 4.00
❑ 503 Jim Owens 4.00 2.00
❑ 504 Ossie Alvarez 4.00 2.00
❑ 505 Tony Kubek 12.00 6.00
❑ 506 Bob Purkey 4.00 2.00
❑ 507 Bob Hale 15.00 7.50
❑ 508 Art Fowler 15.00 7.50
❑ 509 Norm Cash RC 80.00 40.00
❑ 510 Yankees Team CL 125.00 25.00
❑ 511 George Susce 15.00 7.50
❑ 512 George Altman 15.00 7.50
❑ 513 Tommy Carroll 15.00 7.50
❑ 514 Bob Gibson RC 250.00 125.00
❑ 515 Harmon Killebrew 125.00 60.00
❑ 516 Mike Garcia 20.00 10.00
❑ 517 Joe Koppe 15.00 7.50
❑ 518 Mike Cueller UER RC 30.00 15.00
Sic, Cuellar
❑ 519 Pete Runnels 20.00 10.00
Dick Gernert
Frank Malzone
❑ 520 Don Elston 15.00 7.50
❑ 521 Gary Geiger 15.00 7.50
❑ 522 Gene Snyder 15.00 7.50
❑ 523 Harry Bright 15.00 7.50
❑ 524 Larry Osborne 15.00 7.50
❑ 525 Jim Coates 20.00 10.00
❑ 526 Bob Speake 15.00 7.50
❑ 527 Solly Hemus 15.00 7.50
❑ 528 Pirates Team CL 80.00 16.00
❑ 529 G.Bamberger RC 20.00 10.00
❑ 530 Wally Moon 20.00 10.00
❑ 531 Ray Webster 15.00 7.50
❑ 532 Mark Freeman 15.00 7.50
❑ 533 Darrell Johnson 20.00 10.00
❑ 534 Faye Throneberry 15.00 7.50
❑ 535 Ruben Gomez 15.00 7.50
❑ 536 Danny Kravitz 15.00 7.50
❑ 537 Rudolph Arias 15.00 7.50
❑ 538 Chick King 15.00 7.50
❑ 539 Gary Blaylock 15.00 7.50
❑ 540 Willie Miranda 15.00 7.50
❑ 541 Bob Thurman 15.00 7.50

Card	NM	Ex
❑ 542 Jim Perry RC	30.00	15.00
❑ 543 Bob Skinner	125.00	60.00
Bill Virdon		
Roberto Clemente		
❑ 544 Lee Tate	15.00	7.50
❑ 545 Tom Morgan	15.00	7.50
❑ 546 Al Schroll	15.00	7.50
❑ 547 Jim Baxes	15.00	7.50
❑ 548 Elmer Singleton	15.00	7.50
❑ 549 Howie Nunn	15.00	7.50
❑ 550 Roy Campanella	150.00	75.00
(Symbol of Courage)		
❑ 551 Fred Haney AS MG	15.00	7.50
❑ 552 Casey Stengel AS MG	30.00	15.00
❑ 553 Orlando Cepeda AS	30.00	15.00
❑ 554 Bill Skowron AS	20.00	10.00
❑ 555 Bill Mazeroski AS	30.00	15.00
❑ 556 Nellie Fox AS	40.00	20.00
❑ 557 Ken Boyer AS	30.00	15.00
❑ 558 Frank Malzone AS	15.00	7.50
❑ 559 Ernie Banks AS	60.00	30.00
❑ 560 Luis Aparicio AS	40.00	20.00
❑ 561 Hank Aaron AS	125.00	60.00
❑ 562 Al Kaline AS	60.00	30.00
❑ 563 Willie Mays AS	125.00	60.00
❑ 564 Mickey Mantle AS	300.00	150.00
❑ 565 Wes Covington AS	20.00	10.00
❑ 566 Roy Sievers AS	15.00	7.50
❑ 567 Del Crandall AS	15.00	7.50
❑ 568 Gus Triandos AS	15.00	7.50
❑ 569 Bob Friend AS	15.00	7.50
❑ 570 Bob Turley AS	15.00	7.50
❑ 571 Warren Spahn AS	50.00	25.00
❑ 572 Billy Pierce AS	40.00	13.00

1960 Topps

	NM	Ex
COMPLETE SET (572)	5000.00	2000.00
COMMON CARD (1-440)	4.00	1.60
COMMON (441-506)	8.00	3.20
COMMON (507-572)	15.00	6.00
WRAPPER (1-CENT)	900.00	350.00
WRAP. (1-CENT REPEAT)	500.00	200.00
WRAPPER (5-CENT)	40.00	16.00

Card	NM	Ex
❑ 1 Early Wynn	40.00	10.00
❑ 2 Roman Mejias	4.00	1.60
❑ 3 Joe Adcock	6.00	2.40
❑ 4 Bob Purkey	4.00	1.60
❑ 5 Wally Moon	6.00	2.40
❑ 6 Lou Berberet	4.00	1.60
❑ 7 Willie Mays	25.00	10.00
Bill Rigney MG		
❑ 8 Bud Daley	4.00	1.60
❑ 9 Faye Throneberry	4.00	1.60
❑ 10 Ernie Banks	50.00	20.00
❑ 11 Norm Siebern	4.00	1.60
❑ 12 Milt Pappas	6.00	2.40
❑ 13 Wally Post	6.00	2.40
❑ 14 Jim Grant	6.00	2.40
❑ 15 Pete Runnels	6.00	2.40
❑ 16 Ernie Broglio	6.00	2.40
❑ 17 Johnny Callison	6.00	2.40
❑ 18 Dodgers Team CL	50.00	10.00
❑ 19 Felix Mantilla	4.00	1.60
❑ 20 Roy Face	6.00	2.40
❑ 21 Dutch Dotterer	4.00	1.60
❑ 22 Rocky Bridges	4.00	1.60
❑ 23 Eddie Fisher	4.00	1.60
❑ 24 Dick Gray	4.00	1.60
❑ 25 Roy Sievers	6.00	2.40
❑ 26 Wayne Terwilliger	4.00	1.60
❑ 27 Dick Drott	4.00	1.60
❑ 28 Brooks Robinson	50.00	20.00
❑ 29 Clem Labine	6.00	2.40
❑ 30 Tito Francona	4.00	1.60
❑ 31 Sammy Esposito	4.00	1.60
❑ 32 Jim O'Toole	4.00	1.60
Vada Pinson		
❑ 33 Tom Morgan	4.00	1.60
❑ 34 Sparky Anderson	15.00	6.00
❑ 35 Whitey Ford	50.00	20.00
❑ 36 Russ Nixon	4.00	1.60
❑ 37 Bill Bruton	4.00	1.60
❑ 38 Jerry Casale	4.00	1.60
❑ 39 Earl Averill	4.00	1.60
❑ 40 Joe Cunningham	4.00	1.60
❑ 41 Barry Latman	4.00	1.60
❑ 42 Hobie Landrith	4.00	1.60
❑ 43 Senators Team CL	10.00	2.00
❑ 44 Bobby Locke	4.00	1.60
❑ 45 Roy McMillan	6.00	2.40
❑ 46 Jerry Fisher	4.00	1.60
❑ 47 Don Zimmer	6.00	2.40
❑ 48 Hal W. Smith	4.00	1.60
❑ 49 Curt Raydon	4.00	1.60
❑ 50 Al Kaline	50.00	20.00
❑ 51 Jim Coates	6.00	2.40
❑ 52 Dave Philley	4.00	1.60
❑ 53 Jackie Brandt	4.00	1.60
❑ 54 Mike Fornieles	4.00	1.60
❑ 55 Bill Mazeroski	15.00	6.00
❑ 56 Steve Korcheck	4.00	1.60
❑ 57 Turk Lown	4.00	1.60
Gerry Staley		
❑ 58 Gino Cimoli	4.00	1.60
❑ 58A Gino Cimoli	.00	
Cardinals Team Logo		
❑ 59 Juan Pizarro	4.00	1.60
❑ 60 Gus Triandos	6.00	2.40
❑ 61 Eddie Kasko	4.00	1.60
❑ 62 Roger Craig	6.00	2.40
❑ 63 George Strickland	4.00	1.60
❑ 64 Jack Meyer	4.00	1.60
❑ 65 Elston Howard	6.00	2.40
❑ 66 Bob Trowbridge	4.00	1.60
❑ 67 Jose Pagan	4.00	1.60
❑ 68 Dave Hillman	4.00	1.60
❑ 69 Billy Goodman	6.00	2.40
❑ 70 Lew Burdette	6.00	2.40
Card spelled as Lou on front and back		
❑ 71 Marty Keough	4.00	1.60
❑ 72 Tigers Team CL	25.00	5.00
❑ 73 Bob Gibson	50.00	20.00
❑ 74 Walt Moryn	4.00	1.60
❑ 75 Vic Power	6.00	2.40
❑ 76 Bill Fischer	4.00	1.60
❑ 77 Hank Foiles	4.00	1.60
❑ 78 Bob Grim	4.00	1.60
❑ 79 Walt Dropo	4.00	1.60
❑ 80 Johnny Antonelli	6.00	2.40
❑ 81 Russ Snyder	4.00	1.60
❑ 82 Ruben Gomez	4.00	1.60
❑ 83 Tony Kubek	15.00	6.00
❑ 84 Hal R. Smith	4.00	1.60
❑ 85 Frank Lary	6.00	2.40
❑ 86 Dick Gernert	4.00	1.60
❑ 87 John Romonosky	4.00	1.60
❑ 88 John Roseboro	6.00	2.40
❑ 89 Hal Brown	4.00	1.60
❑ 90 Bobby Avila	4.00	1.60
❑ 91 Bennie Daniels	4.00	1.60
❑ 92 Whitey Herzog	6.00	2.40
❑ 93 Art Schult	4.00	1.60
❑ 94 Leo Kiely	4.00	1.60
❑ 95 Frank Thomas	6.00	2.40
❑ 96 Ralph Terry	6.00	2.40
❑ 97 Ted Lepcio	4.00	1.60
❑ 98 Gordon Jones	4.00	1.60
❑ 99 Lenny Green	4.00	1.60
❑ 100 Nellie Fox	20.00	8.00
❑ 101 Bob Miller	4.00	1.60
❑ 102 Kent Hadley	4.00	1.60
❑ 102A Kent Hadley	.00	
Athletics Team Logo		
❑ 103 Dick Farrell	6.00	2.40
❑ 104 Dick Schofield	6.00	2.40
❑ 105 Larry Sherry RC	6.00	2.40
❑ 106 Billy Gardner	4.00	1.60
❑ 107 Carlton Willey	4.00	1.60
❑ 108 Pete Daley	4.00	1.60
❑ 109 Clete Boyer	15.00	6.00
❑ 110 Cal McLish	4.00	1.60
❑ 111 Vic Wertz	6.00	2.40
❑ 112 Jack Harshman	4.00	1.60
❑ 113 Bob Skinner	4.00	1.60
❑ 114 Ken Aspromonte	4.00	1.60
❑ 115 Roy Face	6.00	2.40
Hoyt Wilhelm		
❑ 116 Jim Rivera	4.00	1.60
❑ 117 Tom Borland RP	4.00	1.60
❑ 118 Bob Bruce RP	4.00	1.60
❑ 119 Chico Cardenas RP	6.00	2.40
❑ 120 Duke Carmel RP	4.00	1.60
❑ 121 Camilo Carreon RP	4.00	1.60
❑ 122 Don Dillard RP	4.00	1.60
❑ 123 Dan Dobbek RP	4.00	1.60
❑ 124 Jim Donohue RP	4.00	1.60
❑ 125 Dick Ellsworth RP RC	6.00	2.40
❑ 126 Chuck Estrada RP RC	4.00	1.60
❑ 127 Ron Hansen RP	6.00	2.40
❑ 128 Bill Harris RP	4.00	1.60
❑ 129 Bob Hartman RP	4.00	1.60
❑ 130 Frank Herrera RP	4.00	1.60
❑ 131 Ed Hobaugh RP	4.00	1.60
❑ 132 Frank Howard RP RC	25.00	10.00
❑ 133 Manuel Javier RC RP	6.00	2.40
(Sic, Julian)		
❑ 134 Deron Johnson RP	6.00	2.40
❑ 135 Ken Johnson RP	4.00	1.60
❑ 136 Jim Kaat RP RC	40.00	16.00
❑ 137 Lou Klimchock RP	4.00	1.60
❑ 138 Art Mahaffey RP RC	6.00	2.40
❑ 139 Carl Mathias RP	4.00	1.60
❑ 140 Julio Navarro RP RC	4.00	1.60
❑ 141 Jim Proctor RP	4.00	1.60
❑ 142 Bill Short RP	4.00	1.60
❑ 143 Al Spangler RP	4.00	1.60
❑ 144 Al Stieglitz RP	4.00	1.60
❑ 145 Jim Umbricht RP	4.00	1.60
❑ 146 Ted Wieand RP	4.00	1.60
❑ 147 Bob Will RP	4.00	1.60
❑ 148 C.Yastrzemski RP RC	175.00	70.00
❑ 149 Bob Nieman	4.00	1.60
❑ 150 Billy Pierce	6.00	2.40
❑ 151 Giants Team CL	10.00	2.00
❑ 152 Gail Harris	4.00	1.60
❑ 153 Bobby Thomson	6.00	2.40
❑ 154 Jim Davenport	6.00	2.40
❑ 155 Charlie Neal	6.00	2.40
❑ 156 Art Ceccarelli	4.00	1.60
❑ 157 Rocky Nelson	6.00	2.40
❑ 158 Wes Covington	6.00	2.40
❑ 159 Jim Piersall	6.00	2.40
❑ 160 Mickey Mantle	125.00	50.00
Ken Boyer		
❑ 161 Ray Narleski	4.00	1.60
❑ 162 Sammy Taylor	4.00	1.60
❑ 163 Hector Lopez	6.00	2.40
❑ 164 Reds Team CL	10.00	2.00
❑ 165 Jack Sanford	6.00	2.40
❑ 166 Chuck Essegian	4.00	1.60
❑ 167 Valmy Thomas	4.00	1.60
❑ 168 Alex Grammas	4.00	1.60
❑ 169 Jake Striker	4.00	1.60
❑ 170 Del Crandall	6.00	2.40
❑ 171 Johnny Groth	4.00	1.60
❑ 172 Willie Kirkland	4.00	1.60
❑ 173 Billy Martin	20.00	8.00
❑ 174 Indians Team CL	10.00	2.00
❑ 175 Pedro Ramos	4.00	1.60
❑ 176 Vada Pinson	6.00	2.40
❑ 177 Johnny Kucks	4.00	1.60
❑ 178 Woody Held	4.00	1.60
❑ 179 Rip Coleman	4.00	1.60
❑ 180 Harry Simpson	4.00	1.60
❑ 181 Billy Loes	6.00	2.40
❑ 182 Glen Hobbie	4.00	1.60
❑ 183 Eli Grba	4.00	1.60

❑	184	Gary Geiger	4.00	1.60
❑	185	Jim Owens	4.00	1.60
❑	186	Dave Sisler	4.00	1.60
❑	187	Jay Hook	4.00	1.60
❑	188	Dick Williams	6.00	2.40
❑	189	Don McMahon	4.00	1.60
❑	190	Gene Woodling	6.00	2.40
❑	191	Johnny Klippstein	4.00	1.60
❑	192	Danny O'Connell	4.00	1.60
❑	193	Dick Hyde	4.00	1.60
❑	194	Bobby Gene Smith	4.00	1.60
❑	195	Lindy McDaniel	6.00	2.40
❑	196	Andy Carey	6.00	2.40
❑	197	Ron Kline	4.00	1.60
❑	198	Jerry Lynch	6.00	2.40
❑	199	Dick Donovan	6.00	2.40
❑	200	Willie Mays	125.00	50.00
❑	201	Larry Osborne	4.00	1.60
❑	202	Fred Kipp	4.00	1.60
❑	203	Sammy White	4.00	1.60
❑	204	Ryne Duren	6.00	2.40
❑	205	Johnny Logan	6.00	2.40
❑	206	Claude Osteen	6.00	2.40
❑	207	Bob Boyd	4.00	1.60
❑	208	White Sox Team CL	10.00	2.00
❑	209	Ron Blackburn	4.00	1.60
❑	210	Harmon Killebrew	40.00	16.00
❑	211	Taylor Phillips	4.00	1.60
❑	212	Walter Alston MG	10.00	4.00
❑	213	Chuck Dressen MG	6.00	2.40
❑	214	Jimmy Dykes MG	6.00	2.40
❑	215	Bob Elliott MG	6.00	2.40
❑	216	Joe Gordon MG	6.00	2.40
❑	217	Charlie Grimm MG	6.00	2.40
❑	218	Solly Hemus MG	4.00	1.60
❑	219	Fred Hutchinson MG	6.00	2.40
❑	220	Billy Jurges MG	4.00	1.60
❑	221	Cookie Lavagetto MG	4.00	1.60
❑	222	Al Lopez MG	10.00	4.00
❑	223	Danny Murtaugh MG	6.00	2.40
❑	224	Paul Richards MG	6.00	2.40
❑	225	Bill Rigney MG	4.00	1.60
❑	226	Eddie Sawyer MG	4.00	1.60
❑	227	Casey Stengel MG	15.00	6.00
❑	228	Ernie Johnson	6.00	2.40
❑	229	Joe M. Morgan	4.00	1.60
❑	230	Lou Burdette Warren Spahn Bob Buhl	10.00	4.00
❑	231	Hal Naragon	4.00	1.60
❑	232	Jim Busby	4.00	1.60
❑	233	Don Elston	4.00	1.60
❑	234	Don Demeter	4.00	1.60
❑	235	Gus Bell	6.00	2.40
❑	236	Dick Ricketts	4.00	1.60
❑	237	Elmer Valo	4.00	1.60
❑	238	Danny Kravitz	4.00	1.60
❑	239	Joe Shipley	4.00	1.60
❑	240	Luis Aparicio	15.00	6.00
❑	241	Albie Pearson	6.00	2.40
❑	242	Cardinals Team CL	10.00	2.00
❑	243	Bubba Phillips	4.00	1.60
❑	244	Hal Griggs	4.00	1.60
❑	245	Eddie Yost	6.00	2.40
❑	246	Lee Maye	6.00	2.40
❑	247	Gil McDougald	10.00	4.00
❑	248	Del Rice	4.00	1.60
❑	249	Earl Wilson RC	6.00	2.40
❑	250	Stan Musial	100.00	40.00
❑	251	Bob Malkmus	4.00	1.60
❑	252	Ray Herbert	4.00	1.60
❑	253	Eddie Bressoud	4.00	1.60
❑	254	Arnie Portocarrero	4.00	1.60
❑	255	Jim Gilliam	6.00	2.40
❑	256	Dick Brown	4.00	1.60
❑	257	Gordy Coleman RC	4.00	1.60
❑	258	Dick Groat	6.00	2.40
❑	259	George Altman	4.00	1.60
❑	260	Rocky Colavito Tito Francona	15.00	6.00
❑	261	Pete Burnside	4.00	1.60
❑	262	Hank Bauer	6.00	2.40
❑	263	Darrell Johnson	4.00	1.60
❑	264	Robin Roberts	15.00	6.00
❑	265	Rip Repulski	4.00	1.60
❑	266	Joey Jay	6.00	2.40
❑	267	Jim Marshall	4.00	1.60
❑	268	Al Worthington	4.00	1.60
❑	269	Gene Green	4.00	1.60
❑	270	Bob Turley	6.00	2.40
❑	271	Julio Becquer	4.00	1.60
❑	272	Fred Green	6.00	2.40
❑	273	Neil Chrisley	4.00	1.60
❑	274	Tom Acker	4.00	1.60
❑	275	Curt Flood	6.00	2.40
❑	276	Ken McBride	4.00	1.60
❑	277	Harry Bright	4.00	1.60
❑	278	Stan Williams	6.00	2.40
❑	279	Chuck Tanner	6.00	2.40
❑	280	Frank Sullivan	4.00	1.60
❑	281	Ray Boone	6.00	2.40
❑	282	Joe Nuxhall	6.00	2.40
❑	283	John Blanchard	6.00	2.40
❑	284	Don Gross	4.00	1.60
❑	285	Harry Anderson	4.00	1.60
❑	286	Ray Semproch	4.00	1.60
❑	287	Felipe Alou	6.00	2.40
❑	288	Bob Mabe	4.00	1.60
❑	289	Willie Jones	4.00	1.60
❑	290	Jerry Lumpe	4.00	1.60
❑	291	Bob Keegan	4.00	1.60
❑	292	Joe Pignatano John Roseboro	6.00	2.40
❑	293	Gene Conley	6.00	2.40
❑	294	Tony Taylor	6.00	2.40
❑	295	Gil Hodges	25.00	10.00
❑	296	Nelson Chittum	4.00	1.60
❑	297	Reno Bertoia	4.00	1.60
❑	298	George Witt	4.00	1.60
❑	299	Earl Torgeson	4.00	1.60
❑	300	Hank Aaron	125.00	50.00
❑	301	Jerry Davie	4.00	1.60
❑	302	Phillies Team CL	10.00	2.00
❑	303	Billy O'Dell	4.00	1.60
❑	304	Joe Ginsberg	4.00	1.60
❑	305	Richie Ashburn	20.00	8.00
❑	306	Frank Baumann	4.00	1.60
❑	307	Gene Oliver	4.00	1.60
❑	308	Dick Hall	4.00	1.60
❑	309	Bob Hale	4.00	1.60
❑	310	Frank Malzone	6.00	2.40
❑	311	Raul Sanchez	4.00	1.60
❑	312	Charley Lau	6.00	2.40
❑	313	Turk Lown	4.00	1.60
❑	314	Chico Fernandez	4.00	1.60
❑	315	Bobby Shantz	10.00	4.00
❑	316	Willie McCovey RC	125.00	50.00
❑	317	Pumpsie Green	6.00	2.40
❑	318	Jim Baxes	6.00	2.40
❑	319	Joe Koppe	6.00	2.40
❑	320	Bob Allison	6.00	2.40
❑	321	Ron Fairly	6.00	2.40
❑	322	Willie Tasby	6.00	2.40
❑	323	John Romano	6.00	2.40
❑	324	Jim Perry	6.00	2.40
❑	325	Jim O'Toole	6.00	2.40
❑	326	Roberto Clemente	175.00	70.00
❑	327	Ray Sadecki RC	4.00	1.60
❑	328	Earl Battey	4.00	1.60
❑	329	Zack Monroe	4.00	1.60
❑	330	Harvey Kuenn	6.00	2.40
❑	331	Henry Mason	4.00	1.60
❑	332	Yankees Team CL	80.00	16.00
❑	333	Danny McDevitt	4.00	1.60
❑	334	Ted Abernathy	4.00	1.60
❑	335	Red Schoendienst	15.00	6.00
❑	336	Ike Delock	4.00	1.60
❑	337	Cal Neeman	4.00	1.60
❑	338	Ray Monzant	4.00	1.60
❑	339	Harry Chiti	4.00	1.60
❑	340	Harvey Haddix	6.00	2.40
❑	341	Carroll Hardy	4.00	1.60
❑	342	Casey Wise	4.00	1.60
❑	343	Sandy Koufax	125.00	50.00
❑	344	Clint Courtney	4.00	1.60
❑	345	Don Newcombe	6.00	2.40
❑	346	J.C. Martin UER (Face actually Gary Peters)	6.00	2.40
❑	347	Ed Bouchee	4.00	1.60
❑	348	Barry Shetrone	4.00	1.60
❑	349	Moe Drabowsky	6.00	2.40
❑	350	Mickey Mantle	500.00	200.00
❑	351	Don Nottebart	4.00	1.60
❑	352	Gus Bell Frank Robinson Jerry Lynch	10.00	4.00
❑	353	Don Larsen	6.00	2.40
❑	354	Bob Lillis	4.00	1.60
❑	355	Bill White	6.00	2.40
❑	356	Joe Amalfitano	4.00	1.60
❑	357	Al Schroll	4.00	1.60
❑	358	Joe DeMaestri	4.00	1.60
❑	359	Buddy Gilbert	4.00	1.60
❑	360	Herb Score	6.00	2.40
❑	361	Bob Oldis	6.00	2.40
❑	362	Russ Kemmerer	4.00	1.60
❑	363	Gene Stephens	4.00	1.60
❑	364	Paul Foytack	4.00	1.60
❑	365	Minnie Minoso	10.00	4.00
❑	366	Dallas Green RC	10.00	4.00
❑	367	Bill Tuttle	4.00	1.60
❑	368	Daryl Spencer	4.00	1.60
❑	369	Billy Hoeft	4.00	1.60
❑	370	Bill Skowron	10.00	4.00
❑	371	Bud Byerly	4.00	1.60
❑	372	Frank House	4.00	1.60
❑	373	Don Hoak	6.00	2.40
❑	374	Bob Buhl	6.00	2.40
❑	375	Dale Long	10.00	4.00
❑	376	John Briggs	4.00	1.60
❑	377	Roger Maris	100.00	40.00
❑	378	Stu Miller	6.00	2.40
❑	379	Red Wilson	4.00	1.60
❑	380	Bob Shaw	4.00	1.60
❑	381	Braves Team CL	10.00	2.00
❑	382	Ted Bowsfield	4.00	1.60
❑	383	Leon Wagner	4.00	1.60
❑	384	Don Cardwell	4.00	1.60
❑	385	Charlie Neal WS	8.00	3.20
❑	386	Charlie Neal WS	8.00	3.20
❑	387	Carl Furillo WS	8.00	3.20
❑	388	Gil Hodges WS	10.00	4.00
❑	389	Luis Aparicio WS Maury Wills	12.00	4.80
❑	390	World Series Game 6	8.00	3.20
❑	391	WS Summary The Champs Celebrate	8.00	3.20
❑	392	Tex Clevenger	4.00	1.60
❑	393	Smoky Burgess	6.00	2.40
❑	394	Norm Larker	6.00	2.40
❑	395	Hoyt Wilhelm	15.00	6.00
❑	396	Steve Bilko	4.00	1.60
❑	397	Don Blasingame	4.00	1.60
❑	398	Mike Cuellar	6.00	2.40
❑	399	Milt Pappas Jack Fisher Jerry Walker	6.00	2.40
❑	400	Rocky Colavito	20.00	8.00
❑	401	Bob Duliba	4.00	1.60
❑	402	Dick Stuart	15.00	6.00
❑	403	Ed Sadowski	4.00	1.60
❑	404	Bob Rush	4.00	1.60
❑	405	Bobby Richardson	15.00	6.00
❑	406	Billy Klaus	4.00	1.60
❑	407	Gary Peters RC UER (Face actually J.C. Martin)	6.00	2.40
❑	408	Carl Furillo	10.00	4.00
❑	409	Ron Samford	4.00	1.60
❑	410	Sam Jones	6.00	2.40
❑	411	Ed Bailey	4.00	1.60
❑	412	Bob Anderson	4.00	1.60
❑	413	Athletics Team CL	10.00	2.00
❑	414	Don Williams	4.00	1.60
❑	415	Bob Cerv	4.00	1.60
❑	416	Humberto Robinson	4.00	1.60
❑	417	Chuck Cottier RC	4.00	1.60
❑	418	Don Mossi	6.00	2.40
❑	419	George Crowe	4.00	1.60
❑	420	Eddie Mathews	40.00	16.00
❑	421	Duke Maas	4.00	1.60
❑	422	John Powers	4.00	1.60
❑	423	Ed Fitzgerald	4.00	1.60
❑	424	Pete Whisenant	4.00	1.60
❑	425	Johnny Podres	6.00	2.40
❑	426	Ron Jackson	4.00	1.60
❑	427	Al Grunwald	4.00	1.60

		NM	Ex
❑ 428	Al Smith	4.00	1.60
❑ 429	Nellie Fox Harvey Kuenn	10.00	4.00
❑ 430	Art Ditmar	4.00	1.60
❑ 431	Andre Rodgers	4.00	1.60
❑ 432	Chuck Stobbs	4.00	1.60
❑ 433	Irv Noren	4.00	1.60
❑ 434	Brooks Lawrence	6.00	2.40
❑ 435	Gene Freese	4.00	1.60
❑ 436	Marv Throneberry	6.00	2.40
❑ 437	Bob Friend	6.00	2.40
❑ 438	Jim Coker	4.00	1.60
❑ 439	Tom Brewer	4.00	1.60
❑ 440	Jim Lemon	6.00	2.40
❑ 441	Gary Bell	10.00	4.00
❑ 442	Joe Pignatano	8.00	3.20
❑ 443	Charlie Maxwell	8.00	3.20
❑ 444	Jerry Kindall	8.00	3.20
❑ 445	Warren Spahn	50.00	20.00
❑ 446	Ellis Burton	8.00	3.20
❑ 447	Ray Moore	8.00	3.20
❑ 448	Jim Gentile RC	15.00	6.00
❑ 449	Jim Brosnan	8.00	3.20
❑ 450	Orlando Cepeda	25.00	10.00
❑ 451	Curt Simmons	8.00	3.20
❑ 452	Ray Webster	8.00	3.20
❑ 453	Vern Law	25.00	10.00
❑ 454	Hal Woodeshick	8.00	3.20
❑ 455	Eddie Robinson CO Harry Brecheen CO Luman Harris CO	8.00	3.20
❑ 456	Rudy York CO Billy Herman CO Sal Maglie CO Del Baker CO	10.00	4.00
❑ 457	Charlie Root CO Lou Klein CO Elvin Tappe CO	8.00	3.20
❑ 458	Johnny Cooney CO Don Gutteridge CO Tony Cuccinello CO Ray Berres CO	8.00	3.20
❑ 459	Reggie Otero CO Cot Deal CO Wally Moses CO	8.00	3.20
❑ 460	Mel Harder CO Jo-Jo White CO Bob Lemon CO Ralph(Red) Kress CO	15.00	6.00
❑ 461	Tom Ferrick CO Luke Appling CO Billy Hitchcock CO	10.00	4.00
❑ 462	Fred Fitzsimmons CO Don Heffner CO Walker Cooper CO	8.00	3.20
❑ 463	Bobby Bragan CO Pete Reiser CO Joe Becker CO Greg Mulleavy CO	8.00	3.20
❑ 464	Bob Scheffing CO Whitlow Wyatt CO Andy Pafko CO George Myatt CO	8.00	3.20
❑ 465	Bill Dickey CO Ralph Houk CO Frank Crosetti CO Ed Lopat CO	25.00	10.00
❑ 466	Ken Silvestri CO Dick Carter CO Andy Cohen CO	8.00	3.20
❑ 467	Mickey Vernon CO Frank Oceak CO Sam Narron CO Bill Burwell CO	8.00	3.20
❑ 468	Johnny Keane CO Howie Pollet CO Ray Katt CO Harry Walker CO	8.00	3.20
❑ 469	Wes Westrum CO Salty Parker CO Bill Posedel CO	8.00	3.20
❑ 470	Bob Swift CO Ellis Clary CO Sam Mele CO	8.00	3.20
❑ 471	Ned Garver	8.00	3.20
❑ 472	Alvin Dark	8.00	3.20
❑ 473	Al Cicotte	8.00	3.20
❑ 474	Haywood Sullivan	8.00	3.20
❑ 475	Don Drysdale	40.00	16.00
❑ 476	Lou Johnson	8.00	3.20
❑ 477	Don Ferrarese	8.00	3.20
❑ 478	Frank Torre	8.00	3.20
❑ 479	Georges Maranda	8.00	3.20
❑ 480	Yogi Berra	80.00	32.00
❑ 481	Wes Stock	8.00	3.20
❑ 482	Frank Bolling	8.00	3.20
❑ 483	Camilo Pascual	8.00	3.20
❑ 484	Pirates Team CL	40.00	8.00
❑ 485	Ken Boyer	15.00	6.00
❑ 486	Bobby Del Greco	8.00	3.20
❑ 487	Tom Sturdivant	8.00	3.20
❑ 488	Norm Cash Shown with Indians Cap but listed as a Tiger	25.00	10.00
❑ 489	Steve Ridzik	8.00	3.20
❑ 490	Frank Robinson	50.00	20.00
❑ 491	Mel Roach	8.00	3.20
❑ 492	Larry Jackson	8.00	3.20
❑ 493	Duke Snider	50.00	20.00
❑ 494	Orioles Team CL	25.00	5.00
❑ 495	Sherm Lollar	8.00	3.20
❑ 496	Bill Virdon	10.00	4.00
❑ 497	John Tsitouris	8.00	3.20
❑ 498	Al Pilarcik	8.00	3.20
❑ 499	Johnny James	10.00	4.00
❑ 500	Johnny Temple	8.00	3.20
❑ 501	Bob Schmidt	8.00	3.20
❑ 502	Jim Bunning	25.00	10.00
❑ 503	Don Lee	8.00	3.20
❑ 504	Seth Morehead	8.00	3.20
❑ 505	Ted Kluszewski	25.00	10.00
❑ 506	Lee Walls	8.00	3.20
❑ 507	Dick Stigman	15.00	6.00
❑ 508	Billy Consolo	15.00	6.00
❑ 509	Tommy Davis RC	25.00	10.00
❑ 510	Gerry Staley	15.00	6.00
❑ 511	Ken Walters	15.00	6.00
❑ 512	Joe Gibbon	15.00	6.00
❑ 513	Chicago Cubs Team Card CL	30.00	6.00
❑ 514	Steve Barber RC	15.00	6.00
❑ 515	Stan Lopata	15.00	6.00
❑ 516	Marty Kutyna	15.00	6.00
❑ 517	Charlie James	25.00	10.00
❑ 518	Tony Gonzalez	15.00	6.00
❑ 519	Ed Roebuck	15.00	6.00
❑ 520	Don Buddin	15.00	6.00
❑ 521	Mike Lee	15.00	6.00
❑ 522	Ken Hunt	30.00	12.00
❑ 523	Clay Dalrymple	15.00	6.00
❑ 524	Bill Henry	15.00	6.00
❑ 525	Marv Breeding	15.00	6.00
❑ 526	Paul Giel	25.00	10.00
❑ 527	Jose Valdivielso	25.00	10.00
❑ 528	Ben Johnson	15.00	6.00
❑ 529	Norm Sherry RC	20.00	8.00
❑ 530	Mike McCormick	15.00	6.00
❑ 531	Sandy Amoros	20.00	8.00
❑ 532	Mike Garcia	20.00	8.00
❑ 533	Lu Clinton	15.00	6.00
❑ 534	Ken MacKenzie	15.00	6.00
❑ 535	Whitey Lockman	15.00	6.00
❑ 536	Wynn Hawkins	15.00	6.00
❑ 537	Boston Red Sox Team Card CL	30.00	6.00
❑ 538	Frank Barnes	15.00	6.00
❑ 539	Gene Baker	15.00	6.00
❑ 540	Jerry Walker	15.00	6.00
❑ 541	Tony Curry	15.00	6.00
❑ 542	Ken Hamlin	15.00	6.00
❑ 543	Elio Chacon	15.00	6.00
❑ 544	Bill Monbouquette	20.00	8.00
❑ 545	Carl Sawatski	15.00	6.00
❑ 546	Hank Aguirre	15.00	6.00
❑ 547	Bob Aspromonte	20.00	8.00
❑ 548	Don Mincher	15.00	6.00
❑ 549	John Buzhardt	15.00	6.00
❑ 550	Jim Landis	15.00	6.00
❑ 551	Ed Rakow	15.00	6.00
❑ 552	Walt Bond	15.00	6.00
❑ 553	Bill Skowron AS	20.00	8.00
❑ 554	Willie McCovey AS	40.00	16.00
❑ 555	Nellie Fox AS	30.00	12.00
❑ 556	Charlie Neal AS	15.00	6.00
❑ 557	Frank Malzone AS	15.00	6.00
❑ 558	Eddie Mathews AS	40.00	16.00
❑ 559	Luis Aparicio AS	30.00	12.00
❑ 560	Ernie Banks AS	60.00	24.00
❑ 561	Al Kaline AS	60.00	24.00
❑ 562	Joe Cunningham AS	15.00	6.00
❑ 563	Mickey Mantle AS	250.00	100.00
❑ 564	Willie Mays AS	100.00	40.00
❑ 565	Roger Maris AS	100.00	40.00
❑ 566	Hank Aaron AS	100.00	40.00
❑ 567	Sherm Lollar AS	15.00	6.00
❑ 568	Del Crandall AS	15.00	6.00
❑ 569	Camilo Pascual AS	15.00	6.00
❑ 570	Don Drysdale AS	40.00	16.00
❑ 571	Billy Pierce AS	15.00	6.00
❑ 572	Johnny Antonelli AS	30.00	9.00
❑ NNO	Iron-on team transfer	5.00	2.00

1961 Topps

	NM	Ex
COMPLETE SET (587)	7000.00	2800.00
COMMON CARD (1-370)	3.00	1.20
COMMON (371-446)	4.00	1.60
COMMON (447-522)	8.00	3.20
COMMON (523-589)	30.00	12.00
NOT ISSUED (587/588)		
WRAPPER (1-CENT)	200.00	80.00
WRAP.(1-CENT, REPEAT)	100.00	40.00
WRAPPER (5-CENT)	40.00	16.00

		NM	Ex
❑ 1	Dick Groat	30.00	6.00
❑ 2	Roger Maris	200.00	80.00
❑ 3	John Buzhardt	3.00	1.20
❑ 4	Lenny Green	3.00	1.20
❑ 5	John Romano	3.00	1.20
❑ 6	Ed Roebuck	3.00	1.20
❑ 7	White Sox Team	8.00	3.20
❑ 8	Dick Williams	6.00	2.40
❑ 9	Bob Purkey	3.00	1.20
❑ 10	Brooks Robinson	50.00	20.00
❑ 11	Curt Simmons	6.00	2.40
❑ 12	Moe Thacker	3.00	1.20
❑ 13	Chuck Cottier	3.00	1.20
❑ 14	Don Mossi	6.00	2.40
❑ 15	Willie Kirkland	3.00	1.20
❑ 16	Billy Muffett	3.00	1.20
❑ 17	Checklist 1	10.00	2.00
❑ 18	Jim Grant	6.00	2.40
❑ 19	Clete Boyer	8.00	3.20
❑ 20	Robin Roberts	15.00	6.00
❑ 21	Zorro Versalles UER RC First name should be Zoilo	8.00	3.20
❑ 22	Clem Labine	6.00	2.40
❑ 23	Don Demeter	3.00	1.20
❑ 24	Ken Johnson	6.00	2.40
❑ 25	Vada Pinson Gus Bell Frank Robinson	8.00	3.20
❑ 26	Wes Stock	3.00	1.20
❑ 27	Jerry Kindall	3.00	1.20
❑ 28	Hector Lopez	6.00	2.40
❑ 29	Don Nottebart	3.00	1.20
❑ 30	Nellie Fox	15.00	6.00

❑ 31	Bob Schmidt	3.00	1.20
❑ 32	Ray Sadecki	3.00	1.20
❑ 33	Gary Geiger	3.00	1.20
❑ 34	Wynn Hawkins	3.00	1.20
❑ 35	Ron Santo RC	40.00	16.00
❑ 36	Jack Kralick	3.00	1.20
❑ 37	Charley Maxwell	6.00	2.40
❑ 38	Bob Lillis	3.00	1.20
❑ 39	Leo Posada	3.00	1.20
❑ 40	Bob Turley	6.00	2.40
❑ 41	Dick Groat Norm Larker Willie Mays Roberto Clemente LL	40.00	16.00
❑ 42	Pete Runnels Al Smith Minnie Minoso Bill Skowron LL	8.00	3.20
❑ 43	Ernie Banks Hank Aaron Ed Mathews Ken Boyer LL	30.00	12.00
❑ 44	Mickey Mantle Roger Maris Jim Lemon Rocky Colavito LL	80.00	32.00
❑ 45	Mike McCormick Ernie Broglio Don Drysdale Bob Friend Stan Williams LL	8.00	3.20
❑ 46	Frank Baumann Jim Bunning Art Ditmar Hal Brown LL	8.00	3.20
❑ 47	Ernie Broglio Warren Spahn Vern Law Lou Burdette LL	8.00	3.20
❑ 48	Chuck Estrada Jim Perry UER (Listed as an Oriole) Bud Daley Art Ditmar Frank Lary Milt Pappas LL	8.00	3.20
❑ 49	Don Drysdale Sandy Koufax Sam Jones Ernie Broglio LL	20.00	8.00
❑ 50	Jim Bunning Pedro Ramos Early Wynn Frank Lary LL	8.00	3.20
❑ 51	Detroit Tigers Team Card	8.00	3.20
❑ 52	George Crowe	3.00	1.20
❑ 53	Russ Nixon	3.00	1.20
❑ 54	Earl Francis	3.00	1.20
❑ 55	Jim Davenport	6.00	2.40
❑ 56	Russ Kemmerer	3.00	1.20
❑ 57	Marv Throneberry	6.00	2.40
❑ 58	Joe Schaffernoth	3.00	1.20
❑ 59	Jim Woods	3.00	1.20
❑ 60	Woody Held	3.00	1.20
❑ 61	Ron Piche	3.00	1.20
❑ 62	Al Pilarcik	3.00	1.20
❑ 63	Jim Kaat	8.00	3.20
❑ 64	Alex Grammas	3.00	1.20
❑ 65	Ted Kluszewski	8.00	3.20
❑ 66	Bill Henry	3.00	1.20
❑ 67	Ossie Virgil	3.00	1.20
❑ 68	Deron Johnson	6.00	2.40
❑ 69	Earl Wilson	6.00	2.40
❑ 70	Bill Virdon	6.00	2.40
❑ 71	Jerry Adair	3.00	1.20
❑ 72	Stu Miller	6.00	2.40
❑ 73	Al Spangler	3.00	1.20
❑ 74	Joe Pignatano	3.00	1.20
❑ 75	Lindy McDaniel Larry Jackson	6.00	2.40
❑ 76	Harry Anderson	3.00	1.20
❑ 77	Dick Stigman	3.00	1.20
❑ 78	Lee Walls	6.00	2.40
❑ 79	Joe Ginsberg	3.00	1.20
❑ 80	Harmon Killebrew	20.00	8.00
❑ 81	Tracy Stallard	3.00	1.20
❑ 82	Joe Christopher	3.00	1.20
❑ 83	Bob Bruce	3.00	1.20
❑ 84	Lee Maye	3.00	1.20
❑ 85	Jerry Walker	3.00	1.20
❑ 86	Los Angeles Dodgers Team Card	8.00	3.20
❑ 87	Joe Amalfitano	3.00	1.20
❑ 88	Richie Ashburn	15.00	6.00
❑ 89	Billy Martin	15.00	6.00
❑ 90	Gerry Staley	3.00	1.20
❑ 91	Walt Moryn	3.00	1.20
❑ 92	Hal Naragon	3.00	1.20
❑ 93	Tony Gonzalez	3.00	1.20
❑ 94	Johnny Kucks	3.00	1.20
❑ 95	Norm Cash	8.00	3.20
❑ 96	Billy O'Dell	3.00	1.20
❑ 97	Jerry Lynch	6.00	2.40
❑ 98A	Checklist 2 (Red "Checklist" 98 black on white)	10.00	2.00
❑ 98B	Checklist 2 (Yellow "Checklist" 98 black on white)	10.00	2.00
❑ 98C	Checklist 2 (Yellow "Checklist" 98 white on black no copyright)	10.00	2.00
❑ 99	Don Buddin UER (66 HR's)	3.00	1.20
❑ 100	Harvey Haddix	6.00	2.40
❑ 101	Bubba Phillips	3.00	1.20
❑ 102	Gene Stephens	3.00	1.20
❑ 103	Ruben Amaro	3.00	1.20
❑ 104	John Blanchard	8.00	3.20
❑ 105	Carl Willey	3.00	1.20
❑ 106	Whitey Herzog	3.00	1.20
❑ 107	Seth Morehead	3.00	1.20
❑ 108	Dan Dobbek	3.00	1.20
❑ 109	Johnny Podres	8.00	3.20
❑ 110	Vada Pinson	8.00	3.20
❑ 111	Jack Meyer	3.00	1.20
❑ 112	Chico Fernandez	3.00	1.20
❑ 113	Mike Fornieles	3.00	1.20
❑ 114	Hobie Landrith	3.00	1.20
❑ 115	Johnny Antonelli	6.00	2.40
❑ 116	Joe DeMaestri	3.00	1.20
❑ 117	Dale Long	6.00	2.40
❑ 118	Chris Cannizzaro	3.00	1.20
❑ 119	Norm Siebern Hank Bauer Jerry Lumpe	6.00	2.40
❑ 120	Eddie Mathews	30.00	12.00
❑ 121	Eli Grba	6.00	2.40
❑ 122	Chicago Cubs Team Card	8.00	3.20
❑ 123	Billy Gardner	3.00	1.20
❑ 124	J.C. Martin	3.00	1.20
❑ 125	Steve Barber	3.00	1.20
❑ 126	Dick Stuart	6.00	2.40
❑ 127	Ron Kline	3.00	1.20
❑ 128	Rip Repulski	3.00	1.20
❑ 129	Ed Hobaugh	3.00	1.20
❑ 130	Norm Larker	3.00	1.20
❑ 131	Paul Richards MG	6.00	2.40
❑ 132	Al Lopez MG	8.00	3.20
❑ 133	Ralph Houk MG	6.00	2.40
❑ 134	Mickey Vernon MG	6.00	2.40
❑ 135	Fred Hutchinson MG	6.00	2.40
❑ 136	Walter Alston MG	8.00	3.20
❑ 137	Chuck Dressen MG	6.00	2.40
❑ 138	Danny Murtaugh MG	6.00	2.40
❑ 139	Solly Hemus MG	6.00	2.40
❑ 140	Gus Triandos	6.00	2.40
❑ 141	Billy Williams RC	60.00	24.00
❑ 142	Luis Arroyo	6.00	2.40
❑ 143	Russ Snyder	3.00	1.20
❑ 144	Jim Coker	3.00	1.20
❑ 145	Bob Buhl	6.00	2.40
❑ 146	Marty Keough	3.00	1.20
❑ 147	Ed Rakow	3.00	1.20
❑ 148	Julian Javier	6.00	2.40
❑ 149	Bob Oldis	3.00	1.20
❑ 150	Willie Mays	100.00	40.00
❑ 151	Jim Donohue	3.00	1.20
❑ 152	Earl Torgeson	3.00	1.20
❑ 153	Don Lee	3.00	1.20
❑ 154	Bobby Del Greco	3.00	1.20
❑ 155	Johnny Temple	6.00	2.40
❑ 156	Ken Hunt	6.00	2.40
❑ 157	Cal McLish	3.00	1.20
❑ 158	Pete Daley	3.00	1.20
❑ 159	Orioles Team	8.00	3.20
❑ 160	Whitey Ford UER Incorrectly listed as 5'0" tall	50.00	20.00
❑ 161	Sherman Jones UER (Photo actually Eddie Fisher)	3.00	1.20
❑ 162	Jay Hook	3.00	1.20
❑ 163	Ed Sadowski	3.00	1.20
❑ 164	Felix Mantilla	3.00	1.20
❑ 165	Gino Cimoli	3.00	1.20
❑ 166	Danny Kravitz	3.00	1.20
❑ 167	San Francisco Giants Team Card	8.00	3.20
❑ 168	Tommy Davis	8.00	3.20
❑ 169	Don Elston	3.00	1.20
❑ 170	Al Smith	3.00	1.20
❑ 171	Paul Foytack	3.00	1.20
❑ 172	Don Dillard	3.00	1.20
❑ 173	Frank Malzone Vic Wertz Jackie Jensen	6.00	2.40
❑ 174	Ray Semproch	3.00	1.20
❑ 175	Gene Freese	3.00	1.20
❑ 176	Ken Aspromonte	3.00	1.20
❑ 177	Don Larsen	6.00	2.40
❑ 178	Bob Nieman	3.00	1.20
❑ 179	Joe Koppe	3.00	1.20
❑ 180	Bobby Richardson	12.00	4.80
❑ 181	Fred Green	3.00	1.20
❑ 182	Dave Nicholson	3.00	1.20
❑ 183	Andre Rodgers	3.00	1.20
❑ 184	Steve Bilko	6.00	2.40
❑ 185	Herb Score	6.00	2.40
❑ 186	Elmer Valo	6.00	2.40
❑ 187	Billy Klaus	3.00	1.20
❑ 188	Jim Marshall	3.00	1.20
❑ 189A	Checklist 3 (Copyright symbol almost adjacent to 263 Ken Hamlin)	10.00	2.00
❑ 189B	Checklist 3 (Copyright symbol adjacent to 264 Glen Hobbie)	10.00	2.00
❑ 190	Stan Williams	6.00	2.40
❑ 191	Mike de la Hoz	3.00	1.20
❑ 192	Dick Brown	3.00	1.20
❑ 193	Gene Conley	6.00	2.40
❑ 194	Gordy Coleman	6.00	2.40
❑ 195	Jerry Casale	3.00	1.20
❑ 196	Ed Bouchee	3.00	1.20
❑ 197	Dick Hall	3.00	1.20
❑ 198	Carl Sawatski	3.00	1.20
❑ 199	Bob Boyd	3.00	1.20
❑ 200	Warren Spahn	40.00	16.00
❑ 201	Pete Whisenant	3.00	1.20
❑ 202	Al Neiger	3.00	1.20
❑ 203	Eddie Bressoud	3.00	1.20
❑ 204	Bob Skinner	6.00	2.40
❑ 205	Billy Pierce	6.00	2.40
❑ 206	Gene Green	3.00	1.20
❑ 207	Sandy Koufax Johnny Podres	30.00	12.00
❑ 208	Larry Osborne	3.00	1.20
❑ 209	Ken McBride	3.00	1.20
❑ 210	Pete Runnels	6.00	2.40
❑ 211	Bob Gibson	40.00	16.00
❑ 212	Haywood Sullivan	6.00	2.40
❑ 213	Bill Stafford	3.00	1.20
❑ 214	Danny Murphy	6.00	2.40
❑ 215	Gus Bell	6.00	2.40
❑ 216	Ted Bowsfield	3.00	1.20
❑ 217	Mel Roach	3.00	1.20
❑ 218	Hal Brown	3.00	1.20
❑ 219	Gene Mauch MG	6.00	2.40
❑ 220	Alvin Dark MG	6.00	2.40
❑ 221	Mike Higgins MG	3.00	1.20
❑ 222	Jimmy Dykes MG	6.00	2.40
❑ 223	Bob Scheffing MG	3.00	1.20

❑ 224 Joe Gordon MG 6.00 2.40
❑ 225 Bill Rigney MG 6.00 2.40
❑ 226 Cookie Lavagetto MG 6.00 2.40
❑ 227 Juan Pizarro 3.00 1.20
❑ 228 New York Yankees 60.00 24.00
Team Card
❑ 229 Rudy Hernandez 3.00 1.20
❑ 230 Don Hoak 6.00 2.40
❑ 231 Dick Drott 3.00 1.20
❑ 232 Bill White 6.00 2.40
❑ 233 Joey Jay 6.00 2.40
❑ 234 Ted Lepcio 3.00 1.20
❑ 235 Camilo Pascual 6.00 2.40
❑ 236 Don Gile 3.00 1.20
❑ 237 Billy Loes 6.00 2.40
❑ 238 Jim Gilliam 6.00 2.40
❑ 239 Dave Sisler 3.00 1.20
❑ 240 Ron Hansen 3.00 1.20
❑ 241 Al Cicotte 3.00 1.20
❑ 242 Hal Smith 3.00 1.20
❑ 243 Frank Lary 6.00 2.40
❑ 244 Chico Cardenas 6.00 2.40
❑ 245 Joe Adcock 6.00 2.40
❑ 246 Bob Davis 3.00 1.20
❑ 247 Billy Goodman 6.00 2.40
❑ 248 Ed Keegan 3.00 1.20
❑ 249 Cincinnati Reds 8.00 3.20
Team Card
❑ 250 Vern Law 6.00 2.40
Roy Face
❑ 251 Bill Bruton 3.00 1.20
❑ 252 Bill Short 3.00 1.20
❑ 253 Sammy Taylor 3.00 1.20
❑ 254 Ted Sadowski 6.00 2.40
❑ 255 Vic Power 6.00 2.40
❑ 256 Billy Hoeft 3.00 1.20
❑ 257 Carroll Hardy 3.00 1.20
❑ 258 Jack Sanford 6.00 2.40
❑ 259 John Schaive 3.00 1.20
❑ 260 Don Drysdale 30.00 12.00
❑ 261 Charlie Lau 6.00 2.40
❑ 262 Tony Curry 3.00 1.20
❑ 263 Ken Hamlin 3.00 1.20
❑ 264 Glen Hobbie 3.00 1.20
❑ 265 Tony Kubek 12.00 4.80
❑ 266 Lindy McDaniel 6.00 2.40
❑ 267 Norm Siebern 3.00 1.20
❑ 268 Ike Delock 3.00 1.20
❑ 269 Harry Chiti 3.00 1.20
❑ 270 Bob Friend 6.00 2.40
❑ 271 Jim Landis 3.00 1.20
❑ 272 Tom Morgan 3.00 1.20
❑ 273A Checklist 4 15.00 3.00
(Copyright symbol
adjacent to
336 Don Mincher)
❑ 273B Checklist 4 10.00 2.00
(Copyright symbol
adjacent to
339 Gene Baker)
❑ 274 Gary Bell 3.00 1.20
❑ 275 Gene Woodling 6.00 2.40
❑ 276 Ray Rippelmeyer 3.00 1.20
❑ 277 Hank Foiles 3.00 1.20
❑ 278 Don McMahon 3.00 1.20
❑ 279 Jose Pagan 3.00 1.20
❑ 280 Frank Howard 8.00 3.20
❑ 281 Frank Sullivan 3.00 1.20
❑ 282 Faye Throneberry 3.00 1.20
❑ 283 Bob Anderson 3.00 1.20
❑ 284 Dick Gernert 3.00 1.20
❑ 285 Sherm Lollar 6.00 2.40
❑ 286 George Witt 3.00 1.20
❑ 287 Carl Yastrzemski 50.00 20.00
❑ 288 Albie Pearson 6.00 2.40
❑ 289 Ray Moore 3.00 1.20
❑ 290 Stan Musial 100.00 40.00
❑ 291 Tex Clevenger 3.00 1.20
❑ 292 Jim Baumer 3.00 1.20
❑ 293 Tom Sturdivant 3.00 1.20
❑ 294 Don Blasingame 3.00 1.20
❑ 295 Milt Pappas 6.00 2.40
❑ 296 Wes Covington 6.00 2.40
❑ 297 Athletics Team 8.00 3.20
❑ 298 Jim Golden 3.00 1.20
❑ 299 Clay Dalrymple 3.00 1.20
❑ 300 Mickey Mantle 500.00 160.00
❑ 301 Chet Nichols 3.00 1.20
❑ 302 Al Heist 3.00 1.20
❑ 303 Gary Peters 6.00 2.40
❑ 304 Rocky Nelson 3.00 1.20
❑ 305 Mike McCormick 6.00 2.40
❑ 306 Bill Virdon WS 10.00 4.00
❑ 307 Mickey Mantle WS 80.00 32.00
❑ 308 B.Richardson WS 12.00 4.80
❑ 309 Gino Cimoli WS 10.00 4.00
❑ 310 Roy Face WS 10.00 4.00
❑ 311 Whitey Ford WS 15.00 6.00
❑ 312 Bill Mazeroski WS 20.00 8.00
Mazeroski Homer Wins it
❑ 313 WS Summary 15.00 6.00
Pirates Celebrate
❑ 314 Bob Miller 3.00 1.20
❑ 315 Earl Battey 6.00 2.40
❑ 316 Bobby Gene Smith 3.00 1.20
❑ 317 Jim Brewer 3.00 1.20
❑ 318 Danny O'Connell 3.00 1.20
❑ 319 Valmy Thomas 3.00 1.20
❑ 320 Lou Burdette 6.00 2.40
❑ 321 Marv Breeding 3.00 1.20
❑ 322 Bill Kunkel 6.00 2.40
❑ 323 Sammy Esposito 3.00 1.20
❑ 324 Hank Aguirre 3.00 1.20
❑ 325 Wally Moon 6.00 2.40
❑ 326 Dave Hillman 3.00 1.20
❑ 327 Matty Alou RC 12.00 4.80
❑ 328 Jim O'Toole 6.00 2.40
❑ 329 Julio Becquer 3.00 1.20
❑ 330 Rocky Colavito 20.00 8.00
❑ 331 Ned Garver 3.00 1.20
❑ 332 Dutch Dotterer UER 3.00 1.20
(Photo actually
Tommy Dotterer
Dutch's brother)
❑ 333 Fritz Brickell 3.00 1.20
❑ 334 Walt Bond 3.00 1.20
❑ 335 Frank Bolling 3.00 1.20
❑ 336 Don Mincher 6.00 2.40
❑ 337 Early Wynn 8.00 3.20
Al Lopez
Herb Score
❑ 338 Don Landrum 3.00 1.20
❑ 339 Gene Baker 3.00 1.20
❑ 340 Vic Wertz 6.00 2.40
❑ 341 Jim Owens 3.00 1.20
❑ 342 Clint Courtney 3.00 1.20
❑ 343 Earl Robinson 3.00 1.20
❑ 344 Sandy Koufax 100.00 40.00
❑ 345 Jimmy Piersall 8.00 3.20
❑ 346 Howie Nunn 3.00 1.20
❑ 347 St. Louis Cardinals 8.00 3.20
Team Card
❑ 348 Steve Boros 3.00 1.20
❑ 349 Danny McDevitt 3.00 1.20
❑ 350 Ernie Banks 40.00 16.00
❑ 351 Jim King 3.00 1.20
❑ 352 Bob Shaw 3.00 1.20
❑ 353 Howie Bedell 3.00 1.20
❑ 354 Billy Harrell 6.00 2.40
❑ 355 Bob Allison 8.00 3.20
❑ 356 Ryne Duren 3.00 1.20
❑ 357 Daryl Spencer 3.00 1.20
❑ 358 Earl Averill 6.00 2.40
❑ 359 Dallas Green 3.00 1.20
❑ 360 Frank Robinson 40.00 16.00
❑ 361A Checklist 5 15.00 3.00
(No ad on back)
❑ 361B Checklist 5 15.00 3.00
(Special Feature
ad on back)
❑ 362 Frank Funk 3.00 1.20
❑ 363 John Roseboro 6.00 2.40
❑ 364 Moe Drabowsky 6.00 2.40
❑ 365 Jerry Lumpe 3.00 1.20
❑ 366 Eddie Fisher 3.00 1.20
❑ 367 Jim Rivera 3.00 1.20
❑ 368 Bennie Daniels 3.00 1.20
❑ 369 Dave Philley 3.00 1.20
❑ 370 Roy Face 6.00 2.40
❑ 371 Bill Skowron SP 50.00 20.00
❑ 372 Bob Hendley 4.00 1.60
❑ 373 Boston Red Sox 8.00 3.20
Team Card
❑ 374 Paul Giel 4.00 1.60
❑ 375 Ken Boyer 12.00 4.80
❑ 376 Mike Roarke RC 6.00 2.40
❑ 377 Ruben Gomez 4.00 1.60
❑ 378 Wally Post 6.00 2.40
❑ 379 Bobby Shantz 4.00 1.60
❑ 380 Minnie Minoso 8.00 3.20
❑ 381 Dave Wickersham 4.00 1.60
❑ 382 Frank Thomas 6.00 2.40
❑ 383 Mike McCormick 6.00 2.40
Jack Sanford
Billy O'Dell
❑ 384 Chuck Essegian 4.00 1.60
❑ 385 Jim Perry 6.00 2.40
❑ 386 Joe Hicks 4.00 1.60
❑ 387 Duke Maas 4.00 1.60
❑ 388 Roberto Clemente 125.00 50.00
❑ 389 Ralph Terry 6.00 2.40
❑ 390 Del Crandall 8.00 3.20
❑ 391 Winston Brown 4.00 1.60
❑ 392 Reno Bertoia 4.00 1.60
❑ 393 Don Cardwell 4.00 1.60
Glen Hobbie
❑ 394 Ken Walters 4.00 1.60
❑ 395 Chuck Estrada 6.00 2.40
❑ 396 Bob Aspromonte 4.00 1.60
❑ 397 Hal Woodeshick 4.00 1.60
❑ 398 Hank Bauer 6.00 2.40
❑ 399 Cliff Cook 4.00 1.60
❑ 400 Vern Law 6.00 2.40
❑ 401 Babe Ruth HL 60.00 24.00
60th HR
❑ 402 Don Larsen HL SP 25.00 10.00
WS Perfect Game
❑ 403 Joe Oeschger HL 8.00 3.20
Leon Cadore
26 Inning Tie
❑ 404 Rogers Hornsby HL 12.00 4.80
.424 Season BA
❑ 405 Lou Gehrig HL 80.00 32.00
Consecutive Game Streak
❑ 406 Mickey Mantle HL 100.00 40.00
565 foot HR
❑ 407 Jack Chesbro HL 8.00 3.20
41 victories
❑ 408 C. Mathewson HL SP 20.00 8.00
267 Strikeouts
❑ 409 Walter Johnson SL 12.00 4.80
3 Shutouts in 4 days
❑ 410 Harvey Haddix HL 8.00 3.20
12 Perfect Innings
❑ 411 Tony Taylor 6.00 2.40
❑ 412 Larry Sherry 6.00 2.40
❑ 413 Eddie Yost 6.00 2.40
❑ 414 Dick Donovan 6.00 2.40
❑ 415 Hank Aaron 125.00 50.00
❑ 416 Dick Howser RC 8.00 3.20
❑ 417 Juan Marichal SP RC 100.00 40.00
❑ 418 Ed Bailey 6.00 2.40
❑ 419 Tom Borland 4.00 1.60
❑ 420 Ernie Broglio 6.00 2.40
❑ 421 Ty Cline SP 20.00 8.00
❑ 422 Bud Daley 4.00 1.60
❑ 423 Charlie Neal SP 20.00 8.00
❑ 424 Turk Lown 4.00 1.60
❑ 425 Yogi Berra 80.00 32.00
❑ 426 Milwaukee Braves 12.00 4.80
Team Card
(Back numbered 463)
❑ 427 Dick Ellsworth 6.00 2.40
❑ 428 Ray Barker SP 20.00 8.00
❑ 429 Al Kaline 50.00 20.00
❑ 430 Bill Mazeroski SP 50.00 20.00
❑ 431 Chuck Stobbs 4.00 1.60
❑ 432 Coot Veal 6.00 2.40
❑ 433 Art Mahaffey 4.00 1.60
❑ 434 Tom Brewer 4.00 1.60
❑ 435 Orlando Cepeda UER 12.00 4.80
(San Francis on
card front)
❑ 436 Jim Maloney SP RC 20.00 8.00
❑ 437A Checklist 6 15.00 3.00
440 Louis Aparicio
❑ 437B Checklist 6 15.00 3.00
440 Luis Aparicio

Card	NM	Ex
❑ 438 Curt Flood	8.00	3.20
❑ 439 Phil Regan RC	6.00	2.40
❑ 440 Luis Aparicio	12.00	4.80
❑ 441 Dick Bertell	4.00	1.60
❑ 442 Gordon Jones	4.00	1.60
❑ 443 Duke Snider	50.00	20.00
❑ 444 Joe Nuxhall	6.00	2.40
❑ 445 Frank Malzone	6.00	2.40
❑ 446 Bob Taylor	4.00	1.60
❑ 447 Harry Bright	8.00	3.20
❑ 448 Del Rice	15.00	6.00
❑ 449 Bob Bolin	8.00	3.20
❑ 450 Jim Lemon	8.00	3.20
❑ 451 Daryl Spencer	8.00	3.20
Bill White		
Ernie Broglio		
❑ 452 Bob Allen	8.00	3.20
❑ 453 Dick Schofield	8.00	3.20
❑ 454 Pumpsie Green	8.00	3.20
❑ 455 Early Wynn	15.00	6.00
❑ 456 Hal Bevan	8.00	3.20
❑ 457 Johnny James	8.00	3.20
(Listed as Angel,		
but wearing Yankee		
uniform and cap)		
❑ 458 Willie Tasby	8.00	3.20
❑ 459 Terry Fox RC	10.00	4.00
❑ 460 Gil Hodges	25.00	10.00
❑ 461 Smoky Burgess	15.00	6.00
❑ 462 Lou Klimchock	8.00	3.20
❑ 463 Jack Fisher	8.00	3.20
(See also 426)		
❑ 464 Lee Thomas RC	10.00	4.00
(Pictured with Yankee		
cap but listed as		
Los Angeles Angel)		
❑ 465 Roy McMillan	15.00	6.00
❑ 466 Ron Moeller	8.00	3.20
❑ 467 Cleveland Indians	12.00	4.80
Team Card		
❑ 468 John Callison	10.00	4.00
❑ 469 Ralph Lumenti	8.00	3.20
❑ 470 Roy Sievers	10.00	4.00
❑ 471 Phil Rizzuto MVP	25.00	10.00
❑ 472 Yogi Berra MVP	50.00	20.00
❑ 473 Bob Shantz MVP	8.00	3.20
❑ 474 Al Rosen MVP	10.00	4.00
❑ 475 Mickey Mantle MVP	200.00	80.00
❑ 476 Jackie Jensen MVP	10.00	4.00
❑ 477 Nellie Fox MVP	15.00	6.00
❑ 478 Roger Maris MVP	60.00	24.00
❑ 479 Jim Konstanty MVP	8.00	3.20
❑ 480 Roy Campanella MVP	40.00	16.00
❑ 481 Hank Sauer MVP	8.00	3.20
❑ 482 Willie Mays MVP	50.00	20.00
❑ 483 Don Newcombe MVP	10.00	4.00
❑ 484 Hank Aaron MVP	50.00	20.00
❑ 485 Ernie Banks MVP	40.00	16.00
❑ 486 Dick Groat MVP	10.00	4.00
❑ 487 Gene Oliver	8.00	3.20
❑ 488 Joe McClain	10.00	4.00
❑ 489 Walt Dropo	8.00	3.20
❑ 490 Jim Bunning	25.00	10.00
❑ 491 Philadelphia Phillies	12.00	4.80
Team Card		
❑ 492 Ron Fairly	10.00	4.00
❑ 493 Don Zimmer UER	10.00	4.00
(Brooklyn A.L.)		
❑ 494 Tom Cheney	15.00	6.00
❑ 495 Elston Howard	10.00	4.00
❑ 496 Ken MacKenzie	8.00	3.20
❑ 497 Willie Jones	8.00	3.20
❑ 498 Ray Herbert	8.00	3.20
❑ 499 Chuck Schilling RC	8.00	3.20
❑ 500 Harvey Kuenn	10.00	4.00
❑ 501 John DeMerit	8.00	3.20
❑ 502 Clarence Coleman RC	10.00	4.00
❑ 503 Tito Francona	8.00	3.20
❑ 504 Billy Consolo	8.00	3.20
❑ 505 Red Schoendienst	15.00	6.00
❑ 506 Willie Davis RC	15.00	6.00
❑ 507 Pete Burnside	8.00	3.20
❑ 508 Rocky Bridges	8.00	3.20
❑ 509 Camilo Carreon	8.00	3.20
❑ 510 Art Ditmar	8.00	3.20
❑ 511 Joe M. Morgan	8.00	3.20
❑ 512 Bob Will	8.00	3.20
❑ 513 Jim Brosnan	8.00	3.20
❑ 514 Jake Wood	8.00	3.20
❑ 515 Jackie Brandt	8.00	3.20
❑ 516 Checklist 7	15.00	3.00
❑ 517 Willie McCovey	40.00	16.00
❑ 518 Andy Carey	8.00	3.20
❑ 519 Jim Pagliaroni	8.00	3.20
❑ 520 Joe Cunningham	8.00	3.20
❑ 521 Norm Sherry	8.00	3.20
Larry Sherry		
❑ 522 Dick Farrell UER	15.00	6.00
(Phillies cap but		
listed on Dodgers)		
❑ 523 Joe Gibbon	30.00	12.00
❑ 524 Johnny Logan	30.00	12.00
❑ 525 Ron Perranoski RC	60.00	24.00
❑ 526 R.C. Stevens	30.00	12.00
❑ 527 Gene Leek	30.00	12.00
❑ 528 Pedro Ramos	30.00	12.00
❑ 529 Bob Roselli	30.00	12.00
❑ 530 Bob Malkmus	30.00	12.00
❑ 531 Jim Coates	50.00	20.00
❑ 532 Bob Hale	30.00	12.00
❑ 533 Jack Curtis	30.00	12.00
❑ 534 Eddie Kasko	40.00	16.00
❑ 535 Larry Jackson	30.00	12.00
❑ 536 Bill Tuttle	30.00	12.00
❑ 537 Bobby Locke	30.00	12.00
❑ 538 Chuck Hiller	30.00	12.00
❑ 539 Johnny Klippstein	30.00	12.00
❑ 540 Jackie Jensen	40.00	16.00
❑ 541 Roland Sheldon RC	50.00	20.00
❑ 542 Minnesota Twins	60.00	24.00
Team Card		
❑ 543 Roger Craig	40.00	16.00
❑ 544 George Thomas	50.00	20.00
❑ 545 Hoyt Wilhelm	60.00	24.00
❑ 546 Marty Kutyna	30.00	12.00
❑ 547 Leon Wagner	30.00	12.00
❑ 548 Ted Wills	30.00	12.00
❑ 549 Hal R. Smith	30.00	12.00
❑ 550 Frank Baumann	30.00	12.00
❑ 551 George Altman	40.00	16.00
❑ 552 Jim Archer	30.00	12.00
❑ 553 Bill Fischer	30.00	12.00
❑ 554 Pittsburgh Pirates	80.00	32.00
Team Card		
❑ 555 Sam Jones	30.00	12.00
❑ 556 Ken R. Hunt	30.00	12.00
❑ 557 Jose Valdivielso	30.00	12.00
❑ 558 Don Ferrarese	30.00	12.00
❑ 559 Jim Gentile	60.00	24.00
❑ 560 Barry Latman	40.00	16.00
❑ 561 Charley James	30.00	12.00
❑ 562 Bill Monbouquette	30.00	12.00
❑ 563 Bob Cerv	60.00	24.00
❑ 564 Don Cardwell	30.00	12.00
❑ 565 Felipe Alou	50.00	20.00
❑ 566 Paul Richards AS MG	30.00	12.00
❑ 567 D.Murtaugh AS MG	30.00	12.00
❑ 568 Bill Skowron AS	50.00	20.00
❑ 569 Frank Herrera AS	40.00	16.00
❑ 570 Nellie Fox AS	60.00	24.00
❑ 571 Bill Mazeroski AS	60.00	24.00
❑ 572 Brooks Robinson AS	80.00	32.00
❑ 573 Ken Boyer AS	50.00	20.00
❑ 574 Luis Aparicio AS	60.00	24.00
❑ 575 Ernie Banks AS	80.00	32.00
❑ 576 Roger Maris AS	175.00	70.00
❑ 577 Hank Aaron AS	150.00	60.00
❑ 578 Mickey Mantle AS	400.00	160.00
❑ 579 Willie Mays AS	150.00	60.00
❑ 580 Al Kaline AS	80.00	32.00
❑ 581 Frank Robinson AS	80.00	32.00
❑ 582 Earl Battey AS	30.00	12.00
❑ 583 Del Crandall AS	30.00	12.00
❑ 584 Jim Perry AS	30.00	12.00
❑ 585 Bob Friend AS	30.00	12.00
❑ 586 Whitey Ford AS	100.00	40.00
❑ 589 Warren Spahn AS	100.00	30.00

1962 Topps

	NM	Ex
COMP. MASTER (688)	7000.00	2800.00
COMPLETE SET (598)	6000.00	2400.00
COMMON CARD (1-370)	5.00	2.00
COMMON (371-446)	6.00	2.40
COMMON (447-522)	12.00	4.80
COMMON (523-598)	20.00	8.00
WRAPPER (1-CENT)	100.00	40.00
WRAPPER (5-CENT)	30.00	12.00

Card	NM	Ex
❑ 1 Roger Maris	300.00	75.00
❑ 2 Jim Brosnan	5.00	2.00
❑ 3 Pete Runnels	5.00	2.00
❑ 4 John DeMerit	8.00	3.20
❑ 5 Sandy Koufax UER	150.00	60.00
Struck ou 18		
❑ 6 Marv Breeding	5.00	2.00
❑ 7 Frank Thomas	10.00	4.00
❑ 8 Ray Herbert	5.00	2.00
❑ 9 Jim Davenport	8.00	3.20
❑ 10 Roberto Clemente	175.00	70.00
❑ 11 Tom Morgan	5.00	2.00
❑ 12 Harry Craft MG	8.00	3.20
❑ 13 Dick Howser	8.00	3.20
❑ 14 Bill White	8.00	3.20
❑ 15 Dick Donovan	5.00	2.00
❑ 16 Darrell Johnson	5.00	2.00
❑ 17 Johnny Callison	8.00	3.20
❑ 18 Mickey Mantle	175.00	70.00
Willie Mays		
❑ 19 Ray Washburn	5.00	2.00
❑ 20 Rocky Colavito	15.00	6.00
❑ 21 Jim Kaat	8.00	3.20
❑ 22A Checklist 1 ERR	12.00	2.40
(121-176 on back)		
❑ 22B Checklist 1 COR	12.00	2.40
❑ 23 Norm Larker	5.00	2.00
❑ 24 Tigers Team	10.00	4.00
❑ 25 Ernie Banks	50.00	20.00
❑ 26 Chris Cannizzaro	8.00	3.20
❑ 27 Chuck Cottier	5.00	2.00
❑ 28 Minnie Minoso	10.00	4.00
❑ 29 Casey Stengel MG	20.00	8.00
❑ 30 Eddie Mathews	40.00	16.00
❑ 31 Tom Tresh RC	15.00	6.00
❑ 32 John Roseboro	8.00	3.20
❑ 33 Don Larsen	8.00	3.20
❑ 34 Johnny Temple	8.00	3.20
❑ 35 Don Schwall	10.00	4.00
❑ 36 Don Leppert	5.00	2.00
❑ 37 Barry Latman	5.00	2.00
Dick Stigman		
Jim Perry		
❑ 38 Gene Stephens	5.00	2.00
❑ 39 Joe Koppe	5.00	2.00
❑ 40 Orlando Cepeda	15.00	6.00
❑ 41 Cliff Cook	5.00	2.00
❑ 42 Jim King	5.00	2.00
❑ 43 Los Angeles Dodgers	10.00	4.00
Team Card		
❑ 44 Don Taussig	5.00	2.00
❑ 45 Brooks Robinson	50.00	20.00
❑ 46 Jack Baldschun	5.00	2.00
❑ 47 Bob Will	5.00	2.00
❑ 48 Ralph Terry	8.00	3.20
❑ 49 Hal Jones	5.00	2.00
❑ 50 Stan Musial	100.00	40.00
❑ 51 Norm Cash	8.00	3.20
Jim Piersall		
Al Kaline		
Elston Howard LL		
❑ 52 Roberto Clemente	20.00	8.00

Vada Pinson
Ken Boyer
Wally Moon LL
❑ 53 Roger Maris 100.00 40.00
Mickey Mantle
Jim Gentile
Harmon Killebrew LL
❑ 54 Orlando Cepeda 20.00 8.00
Willie Mays
Frank Robinson LL
❑ 55 Dick Donovan 8.00 3.20
Bill Stafford
Don Mossi
Milt Pappas LL
❑ 56 Warren Spahn 8.00 3.20
Jim O'Toole
Curt Simmons
Mike McCormick LL
❑ 57 Whitey Ford 8.00 3.20
Frank Lary
Steve Barber
Jim Bunning LL
❑ 58 Warren Spahn 8.00 3.20
Joe Jay
Jim O'Toole LL
❑ 59 Camilo Pascual 8.00 3.20
Whitey Ford
Jim Bunning
Juan Pizzaro LL
❑ 60 Sandy Koufax 20.00 8.00
Stan Williams
Don Drysdale
Jim O'Toole LL
❑ 61 Cardinals Team 10.00 4.00
❑ 62 Steve Boros 5.00 2.00
❑ 63 Tony Cloninger RC 8.00 3.20
❑ 64 Russ Snyder 5.00 2.00
❑ 65 Bobby Richardson 10.00 4.00
❑ 66 Cuno Barragan 5.00 2.00
❑ 67 Harvey Haddix 8.00 3.20
❑ 68 Ken Hunt 5.00 2.00
❑ 69 Phil Ortega 5.00 2.00
❑ 70 Harmon Killebrew 25.00 10.00
❑ 71 Dick LeMay 5.00 2.00
❑ 72 Steve Boros 5.00 2.00
Bob Scheffing MG
Jake Wood
❑ 73 Nellie Fox 20.00 8.00
❑ 74 Bob Lillis 8.00 3.20
❑ 75 Milt Pappas 8.00 3.20
❑ 76 Howie Bedell 5.00 2.00
❑ 77 Tony Taylor 8.00 3.20
❑ 78 Gene Green 5.00 2.00
❑ 79 Ed Hobaugh 5.00 2.00
❑ 80 Vada Pinson 8.00 3.20
❑ 81 Jim Pagliaroni 5.00 2.00
❑ 82 Deron Johnson 8.00 3.20
❑ 83 Larry Jackson 5.00 2.00
❑ 84 Lenny Green 5.00 2.00
❑ 85 Gil Hodges 20.00 8.00
❑ 86 Donn Clendenon RC 8.00 3.20
❑ 87 Mike Roarke 5.00 2.00
❑ 88 Ralph Houk MG 8.00 3.20
(Berra in background)
❑ 89 Barney Schultz 5.00 2.00
❑ 90 Jimmy Piersall 8.00 3.20
❑ 91 J.C. Martin 5.00 2.00
❑ 92 Sam Jones 5.00 2.00
❑ 93 John Blanchard 8.00 3.20
❑ 94 Jay Hook 8.00 3.20
❑ 95 Don Hoak 8.00 3.20
❑ 96 Eli Grba 5.00 2.00
❑ 97 Tito Francona 5.00 2.00
❑ 98 Checklist 2 .... 12.00 2.40
❑ 99 John (Boog) Powell RC .. 30.00 12.00
❑ 100 Warren Spahn 40.00 16.00
❑ 101 Carroll Hardy 5.00 2.00
❑ 102 Al Schroll 5.00 2.00
❑ 103 Don Blasingame 5.00 2.00
❑ 104 Ted Savage 5.00 2.00
❑ 105 Don Mossi 8.00 3.20
❑ 106 Carl Sawatski 5.00 2.00
❑ 107 Mike McCormick 8.00 3.20
❑ 108 Willie Davis 8.00 3.20
❑ 109 Bob Shaw 5.00 2.00
❑ 110 Bill Skowron 8.00 3.20
❑ 110A Bill Skowron 8.00 3.20
Green Tint
❑ 111 Dallas Green 8.00 3.20
❑ 111A Dallas Green 8.00 3.20
Green Tint
❑ 112 Hank Foiles 5.00 2.00
❑ 112A Hank Foiles 5.00 2.00
Green Tint
❑ 113 Chicago White Sox 10.00 4.00
Team Card
❑ 113A Chicago White Sox 10.00 4.00
Team Card
Green Tint
❑ 114 Howie Koplitz 5.00 2.00
❑ 114A Howie Koplitz 5.00 2.00
Green Tint
❑ 115 Bob Skinner 8.00 3.20
❑ 115A Bob Skinner 8.00 3.20
Green Tint
❑ 116 Herb Score 8.00 3.20
❑ 116A Herb Score 8.00 3.20
Green Tint
❑ 117 Gary Geiger 8.00 3.20
❑ 117A Gary Geiger 8.00 3.20
Green Tint
❑ 118 Julian Javier 8.00 3.20
❑ 118A Julian Javier 8.00 3.20
Green Tint
❑ 119 Danny Murphy 5.00 2.00
❑ 119A Danny Murphy 5.00 2.00
Green Tint
❑ 120 Bob Purkey 5.00 2.00
❑ 120A Bob Purkey 5.00 2.00
Green Tint
❑ 121 Billy Hitchcock MG 5.00 2.00
❑ 121A Billy Hitchcock 5.00 2.00
Green Tint
❑ 122 Norm Bass 5.00 2.00
❑ 122A Norm Bass 5.00 2.00
Green Tint
❑ 123 Mike de la Hoz 5.00 2.00
❑ 123A Mike de la Hoz 5.00 2.00
Green Tint
❑ 124 Bill Pleis 5.00 2.00
❑ 124A Bill Pleis 5.00 2.00
Green Tint
❑ 125 Gene Woodling 8.00 3.20
❑ 125A Gene Woodling 8.00 3.20
Green Tint
❑ 126 Al Cicotte 5.00 2.00
❑ 126A Al Cicotte 5.00 2.00
Green Tint
❑ 127 Norm Siebern 5.00 2.00
Hank Bauer MG
Jerry Lumpe
❑ 127A Norm Siebern 5.00 2.00
Hank Bauer MG
Jerry Lumpe
Green Tint
❑ 128 Art Fowler 5.00 2.00
❑ 128A Art Fowler 5.00 2.00
Green Tint
❑ 129A Lee Walls 5.00 2.00
(Facing right)
❑ 129B Lee Walls 30.00 12.00
(Facing left)
❑ 130 Frank Bolling 5.00 2.00
❑ 130A Frank Bolling 5.00 2.00
Green Tint
❑ 131 Pete Richert 5.00 2.00
❑ 131A Pete Richert 5.00 2.00
Green Tint
❑ 132A Angels Team 10.00 4.00
(Without photo)
❑ 132B Angels Team 30.00 12.00
(With photo)
❑ 133 Felipe Alou 8.00 3.20
❑ 133A Felipe Alou 8.00 3.20
Green Tint
❑ 134A Billy Hoeft 5.00 2.00
❑ 134B Billy Hoeft 30.00 12.00
Green Tint
❑ 135 Babe Ruth Special 1 .... 20.00 8.00
Babe as a Boy
❑ 135A Babe Ruth Special 20.00 8.00
Base as a Boy
❑ 136 Babe Ruth Special 2 .... 20.00 8.00
Jacob Ruppert OWN
Babe Joins Yanks
❑ 136A Babe Ruth Special 20.00 8.00
Jacob Ruppert OWN
Babe Joins Yanks
Green Tint
❑ 137 Babe Ruth Special 3 .... 20.00 8.00
With Miller Huggins
❑ 137A Babe Ruth Special 20.00 8.00
With Miller Huggins
Green Tint
❑ 138 Babe Ruth Special 4 .... 20.00 8.00
Famous Slugger
❑ 138A Babe Ruth Special 20.00 8.00
Famous Slugger
Green Tint
❑ 139A Babe Ruth Special 5 .. 30.00 12.00
Babe Hits 60
❑ 139B Hal Reniff PORT RC .. 15.00 6.00
❑ 139C Hal Reniff RC 60.00 24.00
Pitching
❑ 140 Babe Ruth Special 6 .... 60.00 24.00
With Lou Gehrig
❑ 140A Babe Ruth Special 60.00 24.00
Lou Gehrig
Green Tint
❑ 141 Babe Ruth Special 7 .... 20.00 8.00
Twilight Years
❑ 141A Babe Ruth Special 20.00 8.00
Twilight Years
Green Tint
❑ 142 Babe Ruth Special 8 .... 20.00 8.00
Coaching Dodgers
❑ 142A Babe Ruth Special 20.00 8.00
Coaching Dodgers
Green Tint
❑ 143 Babe Ruth Special 9 .... 20.00 8.00
Greatest Sports Hero
❑ 143A Babe Ruth Special 20.00 8.00
Greatest Sports Hero
Green Tint
❑ 144 Babe Ruth Special 10 .. 20.00 8.00
Farewell Speech
❑ 144A Babe Ruth Special 20.00 8.00
Babe Ruth Special
Farewell Speech
❑ 145 Barry Latman 5.00 2.00
❑ 145A Barry Latman 5.00 2.00
Green Tint
❑ 146 Don Demeter 5.00 2.00
❑ 146A Don Demeter 5.00 2.00
Green Tint
❑ 147A Bill Kunkel PORT 5.00 2.00
❑ 147B Bill Kunkel 30.00 12.00
(Pitching pose)
❑ 148 Wally Post 5.00 2.00
❑ 148A Wally Post 5.00 2.00
Green Tint
❑ 149 Bob Duliba 5.00 2.00
❑ 149A Bob Duliba 5.00 2.00
Green Tint
❑ 150 Al Kaline 50.00 20.00
❑ 150A Al Kaline 50.00 20.00
Green Tint
❑ 151 Johnny Klippstein 5.00 2.00
❑ 151A Johnny Klippstein 5.00 2.00
Green Tint
❑ 152 Mickey Vernon MG 8.00 3.20
❑ 152A Mickey Vernon MG 8.00 3.20
Green Tint
❑ 153 Pumpsie Green 6.00 2.40
❑ 153A Pumpsie Green 6.00 2.40
Green Tint
❑ 154 Lee Thomas 6.00 2.40
❑ 154A Lee Thomas 6.00 2.40
Green Tint
❑ 155 Stu Miller 6.00 2.40
❑ 155A Stu Miller 6.00 2.40
Green Tint
❑ 156 Merritt Ranew 5.00 2.00
❑ 156A Merritt Ranew 5.00 2.00
Green Tint
❑ 157 Wes Covington 8.00 3.20
❑ 157A Wes Covington 8.00 3.20
Green Tint

❑ 158 Braves Team	10.00	4.00
❑ 158A Braves Team	15.00	6.00
Green Tint		
❑ 159 Hal Reniff RC	8.00	3.20
❑ 160 Dick Stuart	8.00	3.20
❑ 160A Dick Stuart	8.00	3.20
Green Tint		
❑ 161 Frank Baumann	5.00	2.00
❑ 161A Frank Baumann	5.00	2.00
Green Tint		
❑ 162 Sammy Drake	5.00	2.00
❑ 162A Sammy Drake	5.00	2.00
Green Tint		
❑ 163 Billy Gardner	8.00	3.20
Cletis Boyer		
❑ 163A Billy Gardner	8.00	3.20
Clete Boyer		
Green Tint		
❑ 164 Hal Naragon	5.00	2.00
❑ 164A Hal Naragon	5.00	2.00
Green Tint		
❑ 165 Jackie Brandt	5.00	2.00
❑ 165A Jackie Brandt	5.00	2.00
Green Tint		
❑ 166 Don Lee	5.00	2.00
❑ 166A Don Lee	5.00	2.00
Green Tint		
❑ 167 Tim McCarver RC	30.00	12.00
❑ 167A Tim McCarver RC	30.00	12.00
Green Tint		
❑ 168 Leo Posada	5.00	2.00
❑ 168A Leo Posada	5.00	2.00
Green Tint		
❑ 169 Bob Cerv	10.00	4.00
❑ 169A Bob Cerv	10.00	4.00
Green Tint		
❑ 170 Ron Santo	15.00	6.00
❑ 170A Ron Santo	15.00	6.00
Green Tint		
❑ 171 Dave Sisler	5.00	2.00
❑ 171A Dave Sisler	5.00	2.00
Green Tint		
❑ 172 Fred Hutchinson MG	8.00	3.20
❑ 172A Fred Hutchinson MG	8.00	3.20
Green Tint		
❑ 173 Chico Fernandez	5.00	2.00
❑ 173A Chico Fernandez	5.00	2.00
Green Tint		
❑ 174A Carl Willey	5.00	2.00
(Capless)		
❑ 174B Carl Willey	30.00	12.00
(With cap)		
❑ 175 Frank Howard	10.00	4.00
❑ 175A Frank Howard	10.00	4.00
Green Tint		
❑ 176A Eddie Yost PORT	5.00	2.00
❑ 176B Eddie Yost BATTING	30.00	12.00
❑ 177 Bobby Shantz	8.00	3.20
❑ 177A Bobby Shantz	8.00	3.20
Green Tint		
❑ 178 Camilo Carreon	5.00	2.00
❑ 178A Camilo Carreon	5.00	2.00
Green Tint		
❑ 179 Tom Sturdivant	5.00	2.00
❑ 179A Tom Sturdivant	5.00	2.00
Green Tint		
❑ 180 Bob Allison	10.00	4.00
❑ 180A Bob Allison	10.00	4.00
Green Tint		
❑ 181 Paul Brown	5.00	2.00
❑ 181A Paul Brown	5.00	2.00
Green Tint		
❑ 182 Bob Nieman	5.00	2.00
❑ 182A Bob Nieman	5.00	2.00
Green Tint		
❑ 183 Roger Craig	8.00	3.20
❑ 183A Roger Craig	8.00	3.20
Green Tint		
❑ 184 Haywood Sullivan	8.00	3.20
❑ 184A Haywood Sullivan	8.00	3.20
Green Tint		
❑ 185 Roland Sheldon	10.00	4.00
❑ 185A Roland Sheldon	10.00	4.00
Green Tint		
❑ 186 Mack Jones	5.00	2.00
❑ 186A Mack Jones	5.00	2.00
Green Tint		
❑ 187 Gene Conley	5.00	2.00
❑ 187A Gene Conley	5.00	2.00
Green Tint		
❑ 188 Chuck Hiller	5.00	2.00
❑ 188A Chuck Hiller	5.00	2.00
Green Tint		
❑ 189 Dick Hall	5.00	2.00
❑ 189A Dick Hall	5.00	2.00
Green Tint		
❑ 190A Wally Moon PORT	8.00	3.20
❑ 190B W.Moon BATTING	30.00	12.00
❑ 191 Jim Brewer	5.00	2.00
❑ 191A Jim Brewer	5.00	2.00
Green Tint		
❑ 192A Checklist 3	12.00	2.40
(Without comma)		
❑ 192B Checklist 3	15.00	3.00
(Comma after		
Checklist)		
❑ 193 Eddie Kasko	5.00	2.00
❑ 193A Eddie Kasko	5.00	2.00
Green Tint		
❑ 194 Dean Chance RC	8.00	3.20
❑ 194A Dean Chance RC	8.00	3.20
Green Tint		
❑ 195 Joe Cunningham	5.00	2.00
❑ 195A Joe Cunningham	5.00	2.00
Green Tint		
❑ 196 Terry Fox	5.00	2.00
❑ 196A Terry Fox	5.00	2.00
Green Tint		
❑ 197 Daryl Spencer	5.00	2.00
❑ 198 Johnny Keane MG	5.00	2.00
❑ 199 Gaylord Perry RC	80.00	32.00
❑ 200 Mickey Mantle	600.00	200.00
❑ 201 Ike Delock	5.00	2.00
❑ 202 Carl Warwick	5.00	2.00
❑ 203 Jack Fisher	5.00	2.00
❑ 204 Johnny Weekly	5.00	2.00
❑ 205 Gene Freese	5.00	2.00
❑ 206 Senators Team	10.00	4.00
❑ 207 Pete Burnside	5.00	2.00
❑ 208 Billy Martin	20.00	8.00
❑ 209 Jim Fregosi RC	15.00	6.00
❑ 210 Roy Face	8.00	3.20
❑ 211 Frank Bolling	5.00	2.00
Roy McMillan		
❑ 212 Jim Owens	5.00	2.00
❑ 213 Richie Ashburn	20.00	8.00
❑ 214 Dom Zanni	5.00	2.00
❑ 215 Woody Held	5.00	2.00
❑ 216 Ron Kline	5.00	2.00
❑ 217 Walter Alston MG	10.00	4.00
❑ 218 Joe Torre RC	40.00	16.00
❑ 219 Al Downing RC	8.00	3.20
❑ 220 Roy Sievers	8.00	3.20
❑ 221 Bill Short	5.00	2.00
❑ 222 Jerry Zimmerman	5.00	2.00
❑ 223 Alex Grammas	5.00	2.00
❑ 224 Don Rudolph	5.00	2.00
❑ 225 Frank Malzone	8.00	3.20
❑ 226 San Francisco Giants	10.00	4.00
Team Card		
❑ 227 Bob Tiefenauer	5.00	2.00
❑ 228 Dale Long	10.00	4.00
❑ 229 Jesus McFarlane	5.00	2.00
❑ 230 Camilo Pascual	8.00	3.20
❑ 231 Ernie Bowman	5.00	2.00
❑ 232 World Series Game 1	10.00	4.00
Yanks win opener		
❑ 233 Joey Jay WS	10.00	4.00
❑ 234 Roger Maris WS	25.00	10.00
❑ 235 Whitey Ford WS	15.00	6.00
sets new mark		
❑ 236 World Series Game 5	10.00	4.00
Yanks crush Reds		
❑ 237 WS Summary	10.00	4.00
Yanks celebrate		
❑ 238 Norm Sherry	5.00	2.00
❑ 239 Cecil Butler	5.00	2.00
❑ 240 George Altman	5.00	2.00
❑ 241 Johnny Kucks	5.00	2.00
❑ 242 Mel McGaha MG	5.00	2.00
❑ 243 Robin Roberts	15.00	6.00
❑ 244 Don Gile	5.00	2.00
❑ 245 Ron Hansen	5.00	2.00
❑ 246 Art Ditmar	5.00	2.00
❑ 247 Joe Pignatano	5.00	2.00
❑ 248 Bob Aspromonte	8.00	3.20
❑ 249 Ed Keegan	5.00	2.00
❑ 250 Norm Cash	10.00	4.00
❑ 251 New York Yankees	50.00	20.00
Team Card		
❑ 252 Earl Francis	5.00	2.00
❑ 253 Harry Chiti CO	5.00	2.00
❑ 254 Gordon Windhorn	5.00	2.00
❑ 255 Juan Pizarro	5.00	2.00
❑ 256 Elio Chacon	8.00	3.20
❑ 257 Jack Spring	5.00	2.00
❑ 258 Marty Keough	5.00	2.00
❑ 259 Lou Klimchock	5.00	2.00
❑ 260 Billy Pierce	8.00	3.20
❑ 261 George Alusik	5.00	2.00
❑ 262 Bob Schmidt	5.00	2.00
❑ 263 Bob Purkey	5.00	2.00
Jim Turner CO		
Joe Jay		
❑ 264 Dick Ellsworth	8.00	3.20
❑ 265 Joe Adcock	8.00	3.20
❑ 266 John Anderson	5.00	2.00
❑ 267 Dan Dobbek	5.00	2.00
❑ 268 Ken McBride	5.00	2.00
❑ 269 Bob Oldis	5.00	2.00
❑ 270 Dick Groat	8.00	3.20
❑ 271 Ray Rippelmeyer	5.00	2.00
❑ 272 Earl Robinson	5.00	2.00
❑ 273 Gary Bell	5.00	2.00
❑ 274 Sammy Taylor	5.00	2.00
❑ 275 Norm Siebern	5.00	2.00
❑ 276 Hal Kolstad	5.00	2.00
❑ 277 Checklist 4	15.00	3.00
❑ 278 Ken Johnson	8.00	3.20
❑ 279 Hobie Landrith UER	8.00	3.20
(Wrong birthdate)		
❑ 280 Johnny Podres	8.00	3.20
❑ 281 Jake Gibbs	10.00	4.00
❑ 282 Dave Hillman	5.00	2.00
❑ 283 Charlie Smith	5.00	2.00
❑ 284 Ruben Amaro	5.00	2.00
❑ 285 Curt Simmons	8.00	3.20
❑ 286 Al Lopez MG	10.00	4.00
❑ 287 George Witt	5.00	2.00
❑ 288 Billy Williams	30.00	12.00
❑ 289 Mike Krsnich	5.00	2.00
❑ 290 Jim Gentile	8.00	3.20
❑ 291 Hal Stowe	5.00	2.00
❑ 292 Jerry Kindall	5.00	2.00
❑ 293 Bob Miller	8.00	3.20
❑ 294 Phillies Team	10.00	4.00
❑ 295 Vern Law	8.00	3.20
❑ 296 Ken Hamlin	5.00	2.00
❑ 297 Ron Perranoski	8.00	3.20
❑ 298 Bill Tuttle	5.00	2.00
❑ 299 Don Wert	5.00	2.00
❑ 300 Willie Mays	250.00	80.00
❑ 301 Galen Cisco RC	5.00	2.00
❑ 302 Johnny Edwards	5.00	2.00
❑ 303 Frank Torre	8.00	3.20
❑ 304 Dick Farrell	8.00	3.20
❑ 305 Jerry Lumpe	5.00	2.00
❑ 306 Lindy McDaniel	5.00	2.00
Larry Jackson		
❑ 307 Jim Grant	8.00	3.20
❑ 308 Neil Chrisley	8.00	3.20
❑ 309 Moe Morhardt	5.00	2.00
❑ 310 Whitey Ford	50.00	20.00
❑ 311 Tony Kubek IA	8.00	3.20
❑ 312 Warren Spahn IA	15.00	6.00
❑ 313 Roger Maris IA	80.00	32.00
Blasts 61th		
❑ 314 Rocky Colavito IA	8.00	3.20
❑ 315 Whitey Ford IA	15.00	6.00
❑ 316 Harmon Killebrew IA	15.00	6.00
❑ 317 Stan Musial IA	20.00	8.00
❑ 318 Mickey Mantle IA	150.00	60.00
❑ 319 Mike McCormick IA	5.00	2.00
❑ 320 Hank Aaron	150.00	60.00
❑ 321 Lee Stange	5.00	2.00
❑ 322 Alvin Dark MG	8.00	3.20
❑ 323 Don Landrum	5.00	2.00
❑ 324 Joe McClain	5.00	2.00

325	Luis Aparicio	15.00	6.00
326	Tom Parsons	5.00	2.00
327	Ozzie Virgil	5.00	2.00
328	Ken Walters	5.00	2.00
329	Bob Bolin	5.00	2.00
330	John Romano	5.00	2.00
331	Moe Drabowsky	8.00	3.20
332	Don Buddin	5.00	2.00
333	Frank Cipriani	5.00	2.00
334	Boston Red Sox Team Card	10.00	4.00
335	Bill Bruton	5.00	2.00
336	Billy Muffett	5.00	2.00
337	Jim Marshall	8.00	3.20
338	Billy Gardner	5.00	2.00
339	Jose Valdivielso	5.00	2.00
340	Don Drysdale	50.00	20.00
341	Mike Hershberger	5.00	2.00
342	Ed Rakow	5.00	2.00
343	Albie Pearson	8.00	3.20
344	Ed Bauta	5.00	2.00
345	Chuck Schilling	5.00	2.00
346	Jack Kralick	5.00	2.00
347	Chuck Hinton	5.00	2.00
348	Larry Burright	8.00	3.20
349	Paul Foytack	5.00	2.00
350	Frank Robinson	50.00	20.00
351	Joe Torre Del Crandall	8.00	3.20
352	Frank Sullivan	5.00	2.00
353	Bill Mazeroski	15.00	6.00
354	Roman Mejias	8.00	3.20
355	Steve Barber	5.00	2.00
356	Tom Haller RC	5.00	2.00
357	Jerry Walker	5.00	2.00
358	Tommy Davis	8.00	3.20
359	Bobby Locke	5.00	2.00
360	Yogi Berra	80.00	32.00
361	Bob Hendley	5.00	2.00
362	Ty Cline	5.00	2.00
363	Bob Roselli	5.00	2.00
364	Ken Hunt	5.00	2.00
365	Charlie Neal	8.00	3.20
366	Phil Regan	8.00	3.20
367	Checklist 5	15.00	3.00
368	Bob Tillman	5.00	2.00
369	Ted Bowsfield	5.00	2.00
370	Ken Boyer	10.00	4.00
371	Earl Battey	6.00	2.40
372	Jack Curtis	6.00	2.40
373	Al Heist	6.00	2.40
374	Gene Mauch MG	10.00	4.00
375	Ron Fairly	10.00	4.00
376	Bud Daley	8.00	3.20
377	John Orsino	6.00	2.40
378	Bennie Daniels	6.00	2.40
379	Chuck Essegian	6.00	2.40
380	Lou Burdette	10.00	4.00
381	Chico Cardenas	10.00	4.00
382	Dick Williams	8.00	3.20
383	Ray Sadecki	6.00	2.40
384	K.C. Athletics Team Card	10.00	4.00
385	Early Wynn	15.00	6.00
386	Don Mincher	8.00	3.20
387	Lou Brock RC	125.00	50.00
388	Ryne Duren	8.00	3.20
389	Smoky Burgess	10.00	4.00
390	Orlando Cepeda AS	10.00	4.00
391	Bill Mazeroski AS	10.00	4.00
392	Ken Boyer AS UER Batting Average mistakenly listed as .392	8.00	3.20
393	Roy McMillan AS	6.00	2.40
394	Hank Aaron AS	50.00	20.00
395	Willie Mays AS	50.00	20.00
396	Frank Robinson AS	15.00	6.00
397	John Roseboro AS	6.00	2.40
398	Don Drysdale AS	15.00	6.00
399	Warren Spahn AS	15.00	6.00
400	Elston Howard	10.00	4.00
401	Roger Maris Orlando Cepeda	60.00	24.00
402	Gino Cimoli	6.00	2.40
403	Chet Nichols	6.00	2.40
404	Tim Harkness	8.00	3.20

405	Jim Perry	8.00	3.20
406	Bob Taylor	6.00	2.40
407	Hank Aguirre	6.00	2.40
408	Gus Bell	8.00	3.20
409	Pittsburgh Pirates Team Card	10.00	4.00
410	Al Smith	6.00	2.40
411	Danny O'Connell	6.00	2.40
412	Charlie James	6.00	2.40
413	Matty Alou	10.00	4.00
414	Joe Gaines	6.00	2.40
415	Bill Virdon	10.00	4.00
416	Bob Scheffing MG	6.00	2.40
417	Joe Azcue	6.00	2.40
418	Andy Carey	6.00	2.40
419	Bob Bruce	8.00	3.20
420	Gus Triandos	8.00	3.20
421	Ken MacKenzie	8.00	3.20
422	Steve Bilko	6.00	2.40
423	Roy Face Hoyt Wilhelm	10.00	4.00
424	Al McBean RC	6.00	2.40
425	Carl Yastrzemski	125.00	50.00
426	Bob Farley	6.00	2.40
427	Jake Wood	6.00	2.40
428	Joe Hicks	6.00	2.40
429	Billy O'Dell	6.00	2.40
430	Tony Kubek	15.00	6.00
431	Bob Rodgers RC	8.00	3.20
432	Jim Pendleton	6.00	2.40
433	Jim Archer	6.00	2.40
434	Clay Dalrymple	6.00	2.40
435	Larry Sherry	8.00	3.20
436	Felix Mantilla	8.00	3.20
437	Ray Moore	6.00	2.40
438	Dick Brown	6.00	2.40
439	Jerry Buchek	6.00	2.40
440	Joey Jay	6.00	2.40
441	Checklist 6	15.00	6.00
442	Wes Stock	6.00	2.40
443	Del Crandall	8.00	3.20
444	Ted Wills	6.00	2.40
445	Vic Power	8.00	3.20
446	Don Elston	6.00	2.40
447	Willie Kirkland	12.00	4.80
448	Joe Gibbon	12.00	4.80
449	Jerry Adair	12.00	4.80
450	Jim O'Toole	15.00	6.00
451	Jose Tartabull RC	15.00	6.00
452	Earl Averill Jr.	12.00	4.80
453	Cal McLish	12.00	4.80
454	Floyd Robinson	12.00	4.80
455	Luis Arroyo	15.00	6.00
456	Joe Amalfitano	15.00	6.00
457	Lou Clinton	12.00	4.80
458A	Bob Buhl (Braves emblem on cap)	15.00	6.00
458B	Bob Buhl (No emblem on cap)	50.00	20.00
459	Ed Bailey	12.00	4.80
460	Jim Bunning	20.00	8.00
461	Ken Hubbs RC	30.00	12.00
462A	Willie Tasby (Senators emblem on cap)	12.00	4.80
462B	Willie Tasby (No emblem on cap)	50.00	20.00
463	Hank Bauer MG	15.00	6.00
464	Al Jackson RC	12.00	4.80
465	Reds Team	20.00	8.00
466	Norm Cash AS	15.00	6.00
467	Chuck Schilling AS	12.00	4.80
468	Brooks Robinson AS	25.00	10.00
469	Luis Aparicio AS	15.00	6.00
470	Al Kaline AS	25.00	10.00
471	Mickey Mantle AS	200.00	80.00
472	Rocky Colavito AS	15.00	6.00
473	Elston Howard AS	15.00	6.00
474	Frank Lary AS	12.00	4.80
475	Whitey Ford AS	20.00	8.00
476	Orioles Team	20.00	8.00
477	Andre Rodgers	12.00	4.80
478	Don Zimmer Shown with Mets cap, but listed with Cincinnati	20.00	8.00
479	Joel Horlen RC	12.00	4.80
480	Harvey Kuenn	15.00	6.00
481	Vic Wertz	15.00	6.00

482	Sam Mele MG	12.00	4.80
483	Don McMahon	12.00	4.80
484	Dick Schofield	12.00	4.80
485	Pedro Ramos	12.00	4.80
486	Jim Gilliam	15.00	6.00
487	Jerry Lynch	12.00	4.80
488	Hal Brown	12.00	4.80
489	Julio Gotay	12.00	4.80
490	Clete Boyer UER Reversed Negative	15.00	6.00
491	Leon Wagner	12.00	4.80
492	Hal W. Smith	15.00	6.00
493	Danny McDevitt	12.00	4.80
494	Sammy White	12.00	4.80
495	Don Cardwell	12.00	4.80
496	Wayne Causey	12.00	4.80
497	Ed Bouchee	15.00	6.00
498	Jim Donohue	12.00	4.80
499	Zoilo Versalles	15.00	6.00
500	Duke Snider	60.00	24.00
501	Claude Osteen	15.00	6.00
502	Hector Lopez	15.00	6.00
503	Danny Murtaugh MG	15.00	6.00
504	Eddie Bressoud	12.00	4.80
505	Juan Marichal	40.00	16.00
506	Charlie Maxwell	15.00	6.00
507	Ernie Broglio	15.00	6.00
508	Gordy Coleman	15.00	6.00
509	Dave Giusti RC	15.00	6.00
510	Jim Lemon	12.00	4.80
511	Bubba Phillips	12.00	4.80
512	Mike Fornieles	12.00	4.80
513	Whitey Herzog	15.00	6.00
514	Sherm Lollar	15.00	6.00
515	Stan Williams	15.00	6.00
516A	Checklist 7 White Boxes	15.00	3.00
516B	Checklist 7 Yellow Boxes	15.00	6.00
517	Dave Wickersham	12.00	4.80
518	Lee Maye	12.00	4.80
519	Bob Johnson	12.00	4.80
520	Bob Friend	15.00	6.00
521	Jacke Davis UER (Listed as OF on front and P on back)	12.00	4.80
522	Lindy McDaniel	15.00	6.00
523	Russ Nixon SP	30.00	12.00
524	Howie Nunn SP	30.00	12.00
525	George Thomas	20.00	8.00
526	Hal Woodeshick SP	30.00	12.00
527	Dick McAuliffe RC	30.00	12.00
528	Turk Lown	20.00	8.00
529	John Schaive SP	30.00	12.00
530	Bob Gibson SP	125.00	50.00
531	Bobby G. Smith	20.00	8.00
532	Dick Stigman	20.00	8.00
533	Charley Lau SP	30.00	12.00
534	Tony Gonzalez SP	30.00	12.00
535	Ed Roebuck	20.00	8.00
536	Dick Gernert	20.00	8.00
537	Cleveland Indians Team Card	50.00	20.00
538	Jack Sanford	20.00	8.00
539	Billy Moran	20.00	8.00
540	Jim Landis SP	30.00	12.00
541	Don Nottebart SP	30.00	12.00
542	Dave Philley	20.00	8.00
543	Bob Allen SP	30.00	12.00
544	Willie McCovey SP	125.00	50.00
545	Hoyt Wilhelm SP	50.00	20.00
546	Moe Thacker SP	30.00	12.00
547	Don Ferrarese	20.00	8.00
548	Bobby Del Greco	20.00	8.00
549	Bill Rigney MG SP	30.00	12.00
550	Art Mahaffey SP	30.00	12.00
551	Harry Bright	20.00	8.00
552	Chicago Cubs SP Team Card	50.00	20.00
553	Jim Coates	30.00	12.00
554	Bubba Morton SP	30.00	12.00
555	John Buzhardt SP	30.00	12.00
556	Al Spangler	20.00	8.00
557	Bob Anderson SP	30.00	12.00
558	John Goryl	20.00	8.00
559	Mike Higgins MG	20.00	8.00
560	Chuck Estrada SP	30.00	12.00

❑ 561 Gene Oliver SP 30.00 12.00
❑ 562 Bill Henry 20.00 8.00
❑ 563 Ken Aspromonte 20.00 8.00
❑ 564 Bob Grim...................... 20.00 8.00
❑ 565 Jose Pagan 20.00 8.00
❑ 566 Marty Kutyna SP 30.00 12.00
❑ 567 Tracy Stallard SP.......... 30.00 12.00
❑ 568 Jim Golden 20.00 8.00
❑ 569 Ed Sadowski SP 30.00 12.00
❑ 570 Bill Stafford SP 30.00 12.00
❑ 571 Billy Klaus SP 30.00 12.00
❑ 572 Bob G. Miller SP 30.00 12.00
❑ 573 Johnny Logan 20.00 8.00
❑ 574 Dean Stone 20.00 8.00
❑ 575 Red Schoendienst SP .. 50.00 20.00
❑ 576 Russ Kemmerer SP 30.00 12.00
❑ 577 Dave Nicholson SP 30.00 12.00
❑ 578 Jim Duffalo 20.00 8.00
❑ 579 Jim Schaffer SP............ 30.00 12.00
❑ 580 Bill Monbouquette........ 20.00 8.00
❑ 581 Mel Roach..................... 20.00 8.00
❑ 582 Ron Piche 20.00 8.00
❑ 583 Larry Osborne 20.00 8.00
❑ 584 Minnesota Twins SP 60.00 24.00
Team Card
❑ 585 Glen Hobbie SP............ 30.00 12.00
❑ 586 Sammy Esposito SP 30.00 12.00
❑ 587 Frank Funk SP.............. 30.00 12.00
❑ 588 Birdie Tebbetts MG 20.00 8.00
❑ 589 Bob Turley.................... 30.00 12.00
❑ 590 Curt Flood.................... 30.00 12.00
❑ 591 Sam McDowell RC 80.00 32.00
Ron Taylor
Ron Nischwitz
Art Quirk
Dick Radatz SP
❑ 592 Dan Pfister 80.00 32.00
Bo Belinsky
Dave Stenhouse
Jim Bouton RC
Joe Bonikowski SP
❑ 593 Jack Lamabe 50.00 20.00
Craig Anderson
Jack Hamilton
Bob Moorhead
Bob Veale SP
❑ 594 Doc Edwards................ 80.00 32.00
Ken Retzer
Bob Uecker RC
Doug Camilli
Don Pavletich SP
❑ 595 Bob Sadowski 50.00 20.00
Felix Torres
Marlan Coughtry
Ed Charles SP
❑ 596 Bernie Allen................. 80.00 32.00
Joe Pepitone RC
Phil Linz
Rich Rollins SP
❑ 597 Jim McKnight 50.00 20.00
Rod Kanehl
Amado Samuel
Denis Menke RC SP
❑ 598 Al Luplow 80.00 23.00
Manny Jimenez
Howie Goss
Jim Hickman
Ed Olivares SP

1963 Topps

	NM	Ex
COMPLETE SET (576)	5000.00	2000.00
COMMON CARD (1-196)............	4.00	1.60
COMMON (197-283)	5.00	2.00
COMMON (284-370)	5.00	2.00
COMMON (371-446)	5.00	2.00
COMMON (447-522)	25.00	10.00
COMMON (523-576)	15.00	6.00
WRAPPER (1-CENT)..................	40.00	16.00
WRAPPER (5-CENT)..................	30.00	12.00

❑ 1 Tommy Davis 40.00 8.00
Frank Robinson
Stan Musial
Hank Aaron
Bill White LL
❑ 2 Pete Runnels.................... 50.00 20.00
Mickey Mantle
Floyd Robinson
Norm Siebern
Chuck Hinton LL
❑ 3 Willie Mays...................... 40.00 16.00
Hank Aaron
Frank Robinson
Orlando Cepeda
Ernie Banks LL
❑ 4 Harmon Killebrew 20.00 8.00
Norm Cash
Rocky Colavito
Roger Maris
Jim Gentile
Leon Wagner LL
❑ 5 Sandy Koufax 25.00 10.00
Bob Shaw
Bob Purkey
Bob Gibson
Don Drysdale LL
❑ 6 Hank Aguirre.................... 10.00 4.00
Robin Roberts
Whitey Ford
Eddie Fisher
Dean Chance LL
❑ 7 Don Drysdale 10.00 4.00
Jack Sanford
Bob Purkey
Billy O'Dell
Art Mahaffey
Joe Jay LL
❑ 8 Ralph Terry 8.00 3.20
Dick Donovan
Ray Herbert
Jim Bunning
Camilo Pascual LL
❑ 9 Don Drysdale 30.00 12.00
Sandy Koufax
Bob Gibson
Billy O'Dell
Dick Farrell LL
❑ 10 Camilo Pascual 8.00 3.20
Jim Bunning
Ralph Terry
Juan Pizarro
Jim Kaat LL
❑ 11 Lee Walls 4.00 1.60
❑ 12 Steve Barber 4.00 1.60
❑ 13 Philadelphia Phillies 8.00 3.20
Team Card
❑ 14 Pedro Ramos.................... 4.00 1.60
❑ 15 Ken Hubbs UER.............. 10.00 4.00
(No position listed
on front of card)
❑ 16 Al Smith 4.00 1.60
❑ 17 Ryne Duren 8.00 3.20
❑ 18 Smoky Burgess.............. 80.00 32.00
Dick Stuart
Bob Clemente
Bob Skinner
❑ 19 Pete Burnside 4.00 1.60
❑ 20 Tony Kubek 10.00 4.00
❑ 21 Marty Keough 4.00 1.60
❑ 22 Curt Simmons.................. 8.00 3.20
❑ 23 Ed Lopat MG 8.00 3.20
❑ 24 Bob Bruce 4.00 1.60
❑ 25 Al Kaline 50.00 20.00
❑ 26 Ray Moore........................ 4.00 1.60
❑ 27 Choo Choo Coleman........ 8.00 3.20
❑ 28 Mike Fornieles 4.00 1.60
❑ 29A 1962 Rookie Stars........ 10.00 4.00
Sammy Ellis
Ray Culp
John Boozer
Jesse Gonder
❑ 29B 1963 Rookie Stars.......... 4.00 1.60
Sammy Ellis
Ray Culp
John Boozer
Jesse Gonder
❑ 30 Harvey Kuenn 8.00 3.20
❑ 31 Cal Koonce 4.00 1.60
❑ 32 Tony Gonzalez.................. 4.00 1.60
❑ 33 Bo Belinsky...................... 8.00 3.20
❑ 34 Dick Schofield.................. 4.00 1.60
❑ 35 John Buzhardt.................. 4.00 1.60
❑ 36 Jerry Kindall 4.00 1.60
❑ 37 Jerry Lynch 4.00 1.60
❑ 38 Bud Daley 8.00 3.20
❑ 39 Angels Team 8.00 3.20
❑ 40 Vic Power 8.00 3.20
❑ 41 Charley Lau...................... 8.00 3.20
❑ 42 Stan Williams 8.00 3.20
(Listed as Yankee on
card but LA cap)
❑ 43 Casey Stengel MG............ 8.00 3.20
Gene Woodling
❑ 44 Terry Fox.......................... 4.00 1.60
❑ 45 Bob Aspromonte 4.00 1.60
❑ 46 Tommie Aaron RC............ 8.00 3.20
❑ 47 Don Lock.......................... 4.00 1.60
❑ 48 Birdie Tebbetts MG 8.00 3.20
❑ 49 Dal Maxvill RC 8.00 3.20
❑ 50 Billy Pierce 8.00 3.20
❑ 51 George Alusik 4.00 1.60
❑ 52 Chuck Schilling................ 4.00 1.60
❑ 53 Joe Moeller 8.00 3.20
❑ 54A 1962 Rookie Stars........ 15.00 6.00
Nelson Mathews
Harry Fanok
Jack Cullen
Dave DeBusschere RC
❑ 54B 1963 Rookie Stars.......... 8.00 3.20
Nelson Mathews
Harry Fanok
Jack Cullen
Dave DeBusschere RC
❑ 55 Bill Virdon........................ 8.00 3.20
❑ 56 Dennis Bennett 4.00 1.60
❑ 57 Billy Moran 4.00 1.60
❑ 58 Bob Will 4.00 1.60
❑ 59 Craig Anderson 4.00 1.60
❑ 60 Elston Howard.................. 8.00 3.20
❑ 61 Ernie Bowman.................. 4.00 1.60
❑ 62 Bob Hendley 4.00 1.60
❑ 63 Reds Team 8.00 3.20
❑ 64 Dick McAuliffe.................. 8.00 3.20
❑ 65 Jackie Brandt.................. 4.00 1.60
❑ 66 Mike Joyce 4.00 1.60
❑ 67 Ed Charles........................ 4.00 1.60
❑ 68 Duke Snider 25.00 10.00
Gil Hodges
❑ 69 Bud Zipfel 4.00 1.60
❑ 70 Jim O'Toole...................... 8.00 3.20
❑ 71 Bobby Wine...................... 8.00 3.20
❑ 72 Johnny Romano 4.00 1.60
❑ 73 Bobby Bragan MG RC 8.00 3.20
❑ 74 Denny Lemaster 4.00 1.60
❑ 75 Bob Allison 8.00 3.20
❑ 76 Earl Wilson 8.00 3.20
❑ 77 Al Spangler 4.00 1.60
❑ 78 Marv Throneberry 8.00 3.20
❑ 79 Checklist 1 .... 12.00 2.40
❑ 80 Jim Gilliam 8.00 3.20
❑ 81 Jim Schaffer 4.00 1.60
❑ 82 Ed Rakow 4.00 1.60
❑ 83 Charley James.................. 4.00 1.60
❑ 84 Ron Kline 4.00 1.60
❑ 85 Tom Haller 8.00 3.20
❑ 86 Charley Maxwell 8.00 3.20
❑ 87 Bob Veale 8.00 3.20
❑ 88 Ron Hansen...................... 4.00 1.60
❑ 89 Dick Stigman.................... 4.00 1.60
❑ 90 Gordy Coleman 8.00 3.20
❑ 91 Dallas Green 8.00 3.20

❑ 92	Hector Lopez	8.00	3.20
❑ 93	Galen Cisco	4.00	1.60
❑ 94	Bob Schmidt	4.00	1.60
❑ 95	Larry Jackson	4.00	1.60
❑ 96	Lou Clinton	4.00	1.60
❑ 97	Bob Duliba	4.00	1.60
❑ 98	George Thomas	4.00	1.60
❑ 99	Jim Umbricht	4.00	1.60
❑ 100	Joe Cunningham	4.00	1.60
❑ 101	Joe Gibbon	4.00	1.60
❑ 102A	Checklist 2 (Red on yellow)	12.00	2.40
❑ 102B	Checklist 2 (White on red)	12.00	2.40
❑ 103	Chuck Essegian	4.00	1.60
❑ 104	Lew Krausse	4.00	1.60
❑ 105	Ron Fairly	8.00	3.20
❑ 106	Bobby Bolin	4.00	1.60
❑ 107	Jim Hickman	8.00	3.20
❑ 108	Hoyt Wilhelm	10.00	4.00
❑ 109	Lee Maye	4.00	1.60
❑ 110	Rich Rollins	8.00	3.20
❑ 111	Al Jackson	4.00	1.60
❑ 112	Dick Brown	4.00	1.60
❑ 113	Don Landrum UER (Photo actually Ron Santo)	4.00	1.60
❑ 114	Dan Osinski	4.00	1.60
❑ 115	Carl Yastrzemski	40.00	16.00
❑ 116	Jim Brosnan	8.00	3.20
❑ 117	Jacke Davis	4.00	1.60
❑ 118	Sherm Lollar	4.00	1.60
❑ 119	Bob Lillis	4.00	1.60
❑ 120	Roger Maris	80.00	32.00
❑ 121	Jim Hannan	4.00	1.60
❑ 122	Julio Gotay	4.00	1.60
❑ 123	Frank Howard	8.00	3.20
❑ 124	Dick Howser	8.00	3.20
❑ 125	Robin Roberts	15.00	6.00
❑ 126	Bob Uecker	15.00	6.00
❑ 127	Bill Tuttle	4.00	1.60
❑ 128	Matty Alou	8.00	3.20
❑ 129	Gary Bell	4.00	1.60
❑ 130	Dick Groat	8.00	3.20
❑ 131	Washington Senators Team Card	8.00	3.20
❑ 132	Jack Hamilton	4.00	1.60
❑ 133	Gene Freese	4.00	1.60
❑ 134	Bob Scheffing MG	4.00	1.60
❑ 135	Richie Ashburn	20.00	8.00
❑ 136	Ike Delock	4.00	1.60
❑ 137	Mack Jones	4.00	1.60
❑ 138	Willie Mays Stan Musial	80.00	32.00
❑ 139	Earl Averill	4.00	1.60
❑ 140	Frank Lary	8.00	3.20
❑ 141	Manny Mota RC	8.00	3.20
❑ 142	Whitey Ford WS	10.00	4.00
❑ 143	Jack Sanford WS	8.00	3.20
❑ 144	Roger Maris WS	15.00	6.00
❑ 145	Chuck Hiller WS	8.00	3.20
❑ 146	Tom Tresh WS	8.00	3.20
❑ 147	Billy Pierce WS	8.00	3.20
❑ 148	Ralph Terry WS	8.00	3.20
❑ 149	Marv Breeding	4.00	1.60
❑ 150	Johnny Podres	8.00	3.20
❑ 151	Pirates Team	8.00	3.20
❑ 152	Ron Nischwitz	4.00	1.60
❑ 153	Hal Smith	4.00	1.60
❑ 154	Walter Alston MG	8.00	3.20
❑ 155	Bill Stafford	4.00	1.60
❑ 156	Roy McMillan	8.00	3.20
❑ 157	Diego Segui RC	8.00	3.20
❑ 158	Rogelio Alvares Dave Roberts Tommy Harper RC Bob Saverine	8.00	3.20
❑ 159	Jim Pagliaroni	4.00	1.60
❑ 160	Juan Pizarro	4.00	1.60
❑ 161	Frank Torre	8.00	3.20
❑ 162	Twins Team	8.00	3.20
❑ 163	Don Larsen	8.00	3.20
❑ 164	Bubba Morton	4.00	1.60
❑ 165	Jim Kaat	8.00	3.20
❑ 166	Johnny Keane MG	4.00	1.60
❑ 167	Jim Fregosi	8.00	3.20
❑ 168	Russ Nixon	4.00	1.60
❑ 169	Dick Egan Julio Navarro Tommie Sisk Gaylord Perry	25.00	10.00
❑ 170	Joe Adcock	8.00	3.20
❑ 171	Steve Hamilton	4.00	1.60
❑ 172	Gene Oliver	4.00	1.60
❑ 173	Tom Tresh Mickey Mantle Bobby Richardson	150.00	60.00
❑ 174	Larry Burright	4.00	1.60
❑ 175	Bob Buhl	8.00	3.20
❑ 176	Jim King	4.00	1.60
❑ 177	Bubba Phillips	4.00	1.60
❑ 178	Johnny Edwards	4.00	1.60
❑ 179	Ron Piche	4.00	1.60
❑ 180	Bill Skowron	8.00	3.20
❑ 181	Sammy Esposito	4.00	1.60
❑ 182	Albie Pearson	8.00	3.20
❑ 183	Joe Pepitone	8.00	3.20
❑ 184	Vern Law	8.00	3.20
❑ 185	Chuck Hiller	4.00	1.60
❑ 186	Jerry Zimmerman	4.00	1.60
❑ 187	Willie Kirkland	4.00	1.60
❑ 188	Eddie Bressoud	4.00	1.60
❑ 189	Dave Giusti	8.00	3.20
❑ 190	Minnie Minoso	8.00	3.20
❑ 191	Checklist 3	12.00	2.40
❑ 192	Clay Dalrymple	4.00	1.60
❑ 193	Andre Rodgers	4.00	1.60
❑ 194	Joe Nuxhall	8.00	3.20
❑ 195	Manny Jimenez	4.00	1.60
❑ 196	Doug Camilli	4.00	1.60
❑ 197	Roger Craig	8.00	3.20
❑ 198	Lenny Green	5.00	2.00
❑ 199	Joe Amalfitano	5.00	2.00
❑ 200	Mickey Mantle	500.00	200.00
❑ 201	Cecil Butler	5.00	2.00
❑ 202	Boston Red Sox Team Card	8.00	3.20
❑ 203	Chico Cardenas	8.00	3.20
❑ 204	Don Nottebart	5.00	2.00
❑ 205	Luis Aparicio	15.00	6.00
❑ 206	Ray Washburn	5.00	2.00
❑ 207	Ken Hunt	5.00	2.00
❑ 208	Ron Herbel John Miller Wally Wolf Ron Taylor	5.00	2.00
❑ 209	Hobie Landrith	5.00	2.00
❑ 210	Sandy Koufax	150.00	60.00
❑ 211	Fred Whitfield	5.00	2.00
❑ 212	Glen Hobbie	5.00	2.00
❑ 213	Billy Hitchcock MG	5.00	2.00
❑ 214	Orlando Pena	5.00	2.00
❑ 215	Bob Skinner	8.00	3.20
❑ 216	Gene Conley	8.00	3.20
❑ 217	Joe Christopher	5.00	2.00
❑ 218	Frank Lary Don Mossi Jim Bunning	8.00	3.20
❑ 219	Chuck Cottier	5.00	2.00
❑ 220	Camilo Pascual	8.00	3.20
❑ 221	Cookie Rojas RC	8.00	3.20
❑ 222	Cubs Team	8.00	3.20
❑ 223	Eddie Fisher	5.00	2.00
❑ 224	Mike Roarke	5.00	2.00
❑ 225	Joey Jay	5.00	2.00
❑ 226	Julian Javier	8.00	3.20
❑ 227	Jim Grant	8.00	3.20
❑ 228	Max Alvis Bob Bailey Tony Oliva (Listed as Pedro) Ed Kranepool RC	50.00	20.00
❑ 229	Willie Davis	8.00	3.20
❑ 230	Pete Runnels	8.00	3.20
❑ 231	Eli Grba UER (Large photo is Ryne Duren)	5.00	2.00
❑ 232	Frank Malzone	8.00	3.20
❑ 233	Casey Stengel MG	20.00	8.00
❑ 234	Dave Nicholson	5.00	2.00
❑ 235	Billy O'Dell	5.00	2.00
❑ 236	Bill Bryan	5.00	2.00
❑ 237	Jim Coates	8.00	3.20
❑ 238	Lou Johnson	5.00	2.00
❑ 239	Harvey Haddix	8.00	3.20
❑ 240	Rocky Colavito	15.00	6.00
❑ 241	Bob Smith	5.00	2.00
❑ 242	Ernie Banks Hank Aaron	60.00	24.00
❑ 243	Don Leppert	5.00	2.00
❑ 244	John Tsitouris	5.00	2.00
❑ 245	Gil Hodges	20.00	8.00
❑ 246	Lee Stange	5.00	2.00
❑ 247	Yankees Team	50.00	20.00
❑ 248	Tito Francona	5.00	2.00
❑ 249	Leo Burke	5.00	2.00
❑ 250	Stan Musial	100.00	40.00
❑ 251	Jack Lamabe	5.00	2.00
❑ 252	Ron Santo	10.00	4.00
❑ 253	Len Gabrielson Pete Jernigan John Wojcik Deacon Jones	5.00	2.00
❑ 254	Mike Hershberger	5.00	2.00
❑ 255	Bob Shaw	5.00	2.00
❑ 256	Jerry Lumpe	5.00	2.00
❑ 257	Hank Aguirre	5.00	2.00
❑ 258	Alvin Dark MG	8.00	3.20
❑ 259	Johnny Logan	8.00	3.20
❑ 260	Jim Gentile	8.00	3.20
❑ 261	Bob Miller	5.00	2.00
❑ 262	Ellis Burton	5.00	2.00
❑ 263	Dave Stenhouse	5.00	2.00
❑ 264	Phil Linz	5.00	2.00
❑ 265	Vada Pinson	8.00	3.20
❑ 266	Bob Allen	5.00	2.00
❑ 267	Carl Sawatski	5.00	2.00
❑ 268	Don Demeter	5.00	2.00
❑ 269	Don Mincher	5.00	2.00
❑ 270	Felipe Alou	8.00	3.20
❑ 271	Dean Stone	5.00	2.00
❑ 272	Danny Murphy	5.00	2.00
❑ 273	Sammy Taylor	5.00	2.00
❑ 274	Checklist 4	12.00	2.40
❑ 275	Eddie Mathews	30.00	12.00
❑ 276	Barry Shetrone	5.00	2.00
❑ 277	Dick Farrell	5.00	2.00
❑ 278	Chico Fernandez	5.00	2.00
❑ 279	Wally Moon	8.00	3.20
❑ 280	Bob Rodgers	5.00	2.00
❑ 281	Tom Sturdivant	5.00	2.00
❑ 282	Bobby Del Greco	5.00	2.00
❑ 283	Roy Sievers	8.00	3.20
❑ 284	Dave Sisler	5.00	2.00
❑ 285	Dick Stuart	8.00	3.20
❑ 286	Stu Miller	8.00	3.20
❑ 287	Dick Bertell	5.00	2.00
❑ 288	Chicago White Sox Team Card	10.00	4.00
❑ 289	Hal Brown	5.00	2.00
❑ 290	Bill White	8.00	3.20
❑ 291	Don Rudolph	5.00	2.00
❑ 292	Pumpsie Green	8.00	3.20
❑ 293	Bill Pleis	5.00	2.00
❑ 294	Bill Rigney MG	5.00	2.00
❑ 295	Ed Roebuck	5.00	2.00
❑ 296	Doc Edwards	5.00	2.00
❑ 297	Jim Golden	5.00	2.00
❑ 298	Don Dillard	5.00	2.00
❑ 299	Dave Morehead Bob Dustal Tom Butters Dan Schneider	8.00	3.20
❑ 300	Willie Mays	150.00	60.00
❑ 301	Bill Fischer	5.00	2.00
❑ 302	Whitey Herzog	8.00	3.20
❑ 303	Earl Francis	5.00	2.00
❑ 304	Harry Bright	5.00	2.00
❑ 305	Don Hoak	5.00	2.00
❑ 306	Earl Battey Elston Howard	10.00	4.00
❑ 307	Chet Nichols	5.00	2.00
❑ 308	Camilo Carreon	5.00	2.00
❑ 309	Jim Brewer	5.00	2.00
❑ 310	Tommy Davis	8.00	3.20
❑ 311	Joe McClain	5.00	2.00
❑ 312	Houston Colts Team Card	25.00	10.00

- ❑ 313 Ernie Broglio 5.00 2.00
- ❑ 314 John Goryl 5.00 2.00
- ❑ 315 Ralph Terry 8.00 3.20
- ❑ 316 Norm Sherry 8.00 3.20
- ❑ 317 Sam McDowell 8.00 3.20
- ❑ 318 Gene Mauch MG 8.00 3.20
- ❑ 319 Joe Gaines 5.00 2.00
- ❑ 320 Warren Spahn 60.00 24.00
- ❑ 321 Gino Cimoli 5.00 2.00
- ❑ 322 Bob Turley 8.00 3.20
- ❑ 323 Bill Mazeroski 15.00 6.00
- ❑ 324 George Williams 8.00 3.20
  Pete Ward
  Phil Roof
  Vic Davalillo
- ❑ 325 Jack Sanford 5.00 2.00
- ❑ 326 Hank Foiles 5.00 2.00
- ❑ 327 Paul Foytack 5.00 2.00
- ❑ 328 Dick Williams 8.00 3.20
- ❑ 329 Lindy McDaniel 8.00 3.20
- ❑ 330 Chuck Hinton 5.00 2.00
- ❑ 331 Bill Stafford 8.00 3.20
  Bill Pierce
- ❑ 332 Joel Horlen 8.00 3.20
- ❑ 333 Carl Warwick 5.00 2.00
- ❑ 334 Wynn Hawkins 5.00 2.00
- ❑ 335 Leon Wagner 5.00 2.00
- ❑ 336 Ed Bauta 5.00 2.00
- ❑ 337 Dodgers Team 25.00 10.00
- ❑ 338 Russ Kemmerer 5.00 2.00
- ❑ 339 Ted Bowsfield 5.00 2.00
- ❑ 340 Yogi Berra P/CO 100.00 40.00
- ❑ 341 Jack Baldschun 5.00 2.00
- ❑ 342 Gene Woodling 8.00 3.20
- ❑ 343 Johnny Pesky MG 8.00 3.20
- ❑ 344 Don Schwall 5.00 2.00
- ❑ 345 Brooks Robinson 60.00 24.00
- ❑ 346 Billy Hoeft 5.00 2.00
- ❑ 347 Joe Torre 15.00 6.00
- ❑ 348 Vic Wertz 8.00 3.20
- ❑ 349 Zoilo Versalles 8.00 3.20
- ❑ 350 Bob Purkey 5.00 2.00
- ❑ 351 Al Luplow 5.00 2.00
- ❑ 352 Ken Johnson 5.00 2.00
- ❑ 353 Billy Williams 30.00 12.00
- ❑ 354 Dom Zanni 5.00 2.00
- ❑ 355 Dean Chance 8.00 3.20
- ❑ 356 John Schaive 5.00 2.00
- ❑ 357 George Altman 5.00 2.00
- ❑ 358 Milt Pappas 8.00 3.20
- ❑ 359 Haywood Sullivan 8.00 3.20
- ❑ 360 Don Drysdale 60.00 24.00
- ❑ 361 Clete Boyer 10.00 4.00
- ❑ 362 Checklist 5 12.00 2.40
- ❑ 363 Dick Radatz 8.00 3.20
- ❑ 364 Howie Goss 5.00 2.00
- ❑ 365 Jim Bunning 20.00 8.00
- ❑ 366 Tony Taylor 8.00 3.20
- ❑ 367 Tony Cloninger 5.00 2.00
- ❑ 368 Ed Bailey 5.00 2.00
- ❑ 369 Jim Lemon 5.00 2.00
- ❑ 370 Dick Donovan 5.00 2.00
- ❑ 371 Rod Kanehl 8.00 3.20
- ❑ 372 Don Lee 5.00 2.00
- ❑ 373 Jim Campbell 5.00 2.00
- ❑ 374 Claude Osteen 8.00 3.20
- ❑ 375 Ken Boyer 15.00 6.00
- ❑ 376 John Wyatt 5.00 2.00
- ❑ 377 Baltimore Orioles 10.00 4.00
  Team Card
- ❑ 378 Bill Henry 5.00 2.00
- ❑ 379 Bob Anderson 5.00 2.00
- ❑ 380 Ernie Banks UER 100.00 40.00
  (Back has career Major
  and Minor, but he
  never played in Minors)
- ❑ 381 Frank Baumann 5.00 2.00
- ❑ 382 Ralph Houk MG 10.00 4.00
- ❑ 383 Pete Richert 5.00 2.00
- ❑ 384 Bob Tillman 5.00 2.00
- ❑ 385 Art Mahaffey 5.00 2.00
- ❑ 386 Ed Kirkpatrick 5.00 2.00
  John Bateman RC
  Larry Bearnarth
  Garry Roggenburk
- ❑ 387 Al McBean 5.00 2.00
- ❑ 388 Jim Davenport 8.00 3.20
- ❑ 389 Frank Sullivan 5.00 2.00
- ❑ 390 Hank Aaron 150.00 60.00
- ❑ 391 Bill Dailey 5.00 2.00
- ❑ 392 Johnny Romano 5.00 2.00
  Tito Francona
- ❑ 393 Ken MacKenzie 8.00 3.20
- ❑ 394 Tim McCarver 15.00 6.00
- ❑ 395 Don McMahon 5.00 2.00
- ❑ 396 Joe Koppe 5.00 2.00
- ❑ 397 Kansas City Athletics 10.00 4.00
  Team Card
- ❑ 398 Boog Powell 25.00 10.00
- ❑ 399 Dick Ellsworth 5.00 2.00
- ❑ 400 Frank Robinson 60.00 24.00
- ❑ 401 Jim Bouton 15.00 6.00
- ❑ 402 Mickey Vernon MG 8.00 3.20
- ❑ 403 Ron Perranoski 8.00 3.20
- ❑ 404 Bob Oldis 5.00 2.00
- ❑ 405 Floyd Robinson 5.00 2.00
- ❑ 406 Howie Koplitz 5.00 2.00
- ❑ 407 Frank Kostro 8.00 3.20
  Chico Ruiz
  Larry Elliot
  Dick Simpson
- ❑ 408 Billy Gardner 5.00 2.00
- ❑ 409 Roy Face 8.00 3.20
- ❑ 410 Earl Battey 5.00 2.00
- ❑ 411 Jim Constable 5.00 2.00
- ❑ 412 Johnny Podres 50.00 20.00
  Don Drysdale
  Sandy Koufax
- ❑ 413 Jerry Walker 5.00 2.00
- ❑ 414 Ty Cline 5.00 2.00
- ❑ 415 Bob Gibson 60.00 24.00
- ❑ 416 Alex Grammas 5.00 2.00
- ❑ 417 Giants Team 10.00 4.00
- ❑ 418 John Orsino 5.00 2.00
- ❑ 419 Tracy Stallard 5.00 2.00
- ❑ 420 Bobby Richardson 15.00 6.00
- ❑ 421 Tom Morgan 5.00 2.00
- ❑ 422 Fred Hutchinson MG 8.00 3.20
- ❑ 423 Ed Hobaugh 5.00 2.00
- ❑ 424 Charlie Smith 5.00 2.00
- ❑ 425 Smoky Burgess 8.00 3.20
- ❑ 426 Barry Latman 5.00 2.00
- ❑ 427 Bernie Allen 5.00 2.00
- ❑ 428 Carl Boles 5.00 2.00
- ❑ 429 Lou Burdette 8.00 3.20
- ❑ 430 Norm Siebern 5.00 2.00
- ❑ 431A Checklist 6 12.00 2.40
  (White on red)
- ❑ 431B Checklist 6 30.00 6.00
  (Black on orange)
- ❑ 432 Roman Mejias 5.00 2.00
- ❑ 433 Denis Menke 5.00 2.00
- ❑ 434 John Callison 8.00 3.20
- ❑ 435 Woody Held 5.00 2.00
- ❑ 436 Tim Harkness 8.00 3.20
- ❑ 437 Bill Bruton 5.00 2.00
- ❑ 438 Wes Stock 5.00 2.00
- ❑ 439 Don Zimmer 8.00 3.20
- ❑ 440 Juan Marichal 30.00 12.00
- ❑ 441 Lee Thomas 8.00 3.20
- ❑ 442 J.C. Hartman 5.00 2.00
- ❑ 443 Jimmy Piersall 8.00 3.20
- ❑ 444 Jim Maloney 8.00 3.20
- ❑ 445 Norm Cash 10.00 4.00
- ❑ 446 Whitey Ford 60.00 24.00
- ❑ 447 Felix Mantilla 25.00 10.00
- ❑ 448 Jack Kralick 25.00 10.00
- ❑ 449 Jose Tartabull 25.00 10.00
- ❑ 450 Bob Friend 30.00 12.00
- ❑ 451 Indians Team 40.00 16.00
- ❑ 452 Barney Schultz 25.00 10.00
- ❑ 453 Jake Wood 25.00 10.00
- ❑ 454A Art Fowler 25.00 10.00
  (Card number on
  white background)
- ❑ 454B Art Fowler 30.00 12.00
  (Card number on
  orange background)
- ❑ 455 Ruben Amaro 25.00 10.00
- ❑ 456 Jim Coker 25.00 10.00
- ❑ 457 Tex Clevenger 25.00 10.00
- ❑ 458 Al Lopez MG 30.00 12.00
- ❑ 459 Dick LeMay 25.00 10.00
- ❑ 460 Del Crandall 30.00 12.00
- ❑ 461 Norm Bass 25.00 10.00
- ❑ 462 Wally Post 25.00 10.00
- ❑ 463 Joe Schaffernoth 25.00 10.00
- ❑ 464 Ken Aspromonte 25.00 10.00
- ❑ 465 Chuck Estrada 25.00 10.00
- ❑ 466 Nate Oliver 60.00 24.00
  Tony Martinez
  Bill Freehan RC
  Jerry Robinson SP
- ❑ 467 Phil Ortega 25.00 10.00
- ❑ 468 Carroll Hardy 30.00 12.00
- ❑ 469 Jay Hook 30.00 12.00
- ❑ 470 Tom Tresh SP 60.00 24.00
- ❑ 471 Ken Retzer 25.00 10.00
- ❑ 472 Lou Brock 80.00 32.00
- ❑ 473 New York Mets 100.00 40.00
  Team Card
- ❑ 474 Jack Fisher 25.00 10.00
- ❑ 475 Gus Triandos 30.00 12.00
- ❑ 476 Frank Funk 25.00 10.00
- ❑ 477 Donn Clendenon 30.00 12.00
- ❑ 478 Paul Brown 25.00 10.00
- ❑ 479 Ed Brinkman 25.00 10.00
- ❑ 480 Bill Monbouquette 25.00 10.00
- ❑ 481 Bob Taylor 25.00 10.00
- ❑ 482 Felix Torres 25.00 10.00
- ❑ 483 Jim Owens UER 25.00 10.00
  (Stat column for Wins
  has an R instead)
- ❑ 484 Dale Long SP 30.00 12.00
- ❑ 485 Jim Landis 25.00 10.00
- ❑ 486 Ray Sadecki 25.00 10.00
- ❑ 487 John Roseboro 30.00 12.00
- ❑ 488 Jerry Adair 25.00 10.00
- ❑ 489 Paul Toth 25.00 10.00
- ❑ 490 Willie McCovey 100.00 40.00
- ❑ 491 Harry Craft MG 25.00 10.00
- ❑ 492 Dave Wickersham 25.00 10.00
- ❑ 493 Walt Bond 25.00 10.00
- ❑ 494 Phil Regan 25.00 10.00
- ❑ 495 Frank Thomas SP 30.00 12.00
- ❑ 496 Steve Dalkowski RC 30.00 12.00
  Fred Newman
  Jack Smith
  Carl Bouldin
- ❑ 497 Bennie Daniels 25.00 10.00
- ❑ 498 Eddie Kasko 25.00 10.00
- ❑ 499 J.C. Martin 25.00 10.00
- ❑ 500 Harmon Killebrew SP 150.00 60.00
- ❑ 501 Joe Azcue 25.00 10.00
- ❑ 502 Daryl Spencer 25.00 10.00
- ❑ 503 Braves Team 40.00 16.00
- ❑ 504 Bob Johnson 25.00 10.00
- ❑ 505 Curt Flood 40.00 16.00
- ❑ 506 Gene Green 25.00 10.00
- ❑ 507 Roland Sheldon 30.00 12.00
- ❑ 508 Ted Savage 25.00 10.00
- ❑ 509A Checklist 7 30.00 6.00
  (Copyright centered)
- ❑ 509B Checklist 7 30.00 6.00
  (Copyright to right)
- ❑ 510 Ken McBride 25.00 10.00
- ❑ 511 Charlie Neal 30.00 12.00
- ❑ 512 Cal McLish 25.00 10.00
- ❑ 513 Gary Geiger 25.00 10.00
- ❑ 514 Larry Osborne 25.00 10.00
- ❑ 515 Don Elston 25.00 10.00
- ❑ 516 Purnell Goldy 25.00 10.00
- ❑ 517 Hal Woodeshick 25.00 10.00
- ❑ 518 Don Blasingame 25.00 10.00
- ❑ 519 Claude Raymond RC 25.00 10.00
- ❑ 520 Orlando Cepeda 40.00 16.00
- ❑ 521 Dan Pfister 25.00 10.00
- ❑ 522 Mel Nelson 30.00 12.00
  Gary Peters
  Jim Roland
  Art Quirk
- ❑ 523 Bill Kunkel 15.00 6.00
- ❑ 524 Cardinals Team 30.00 12.00
- ❑ 525 Nellie Fox 50.00 20.00
- ❑ 526 Dick Hall 15.00 6.00
- ❑ 527 Ed Sadowski 15.00 6.00
- ❑ 528 Carl Willey 15.00 6.00
- ❑ 529 Wes Covington 15.00 6.00

Card	Player	NM	Ex
❑ 530	Don Mossi	20.00	8.00
❑ 531	Sam Mele MG	15.00	6.00
❑ 532	Steve Boros	15.00	6.00
❑ 533	Bobby Shantz	20.00	8.00
❑ 534	Ken Walters	15.00	6.00
❑ 535	Jim Perry	20.00	8.00
❑ 536	Norm Larker	15.00	6.00
❑ 537	Pedro Gonzalez	800.00	325.00
	Ken McMullen		
	Al Weis		
	Pete Rose RC		
❑ 538	George Brunet	15.00	6.00
❑ 539	Wayne Causey	15.00	6.00
❑ 540	Roberto Clemente	250.00	100.00
❑ 541	Ron Moeller	15.00	6.00
❑ 542	Lou Klimchock	15.00	6.00
❑ 543	Russ Snyder	15.00	6.00
❑ 544	Duke Carmel	50.00	20.00
	Bill Haas		
	Rusty Staub RC		
	Dick Phillips		
❑ 545	Jose Pagan	15.00	6.00
❑ 546	Hal Reniff	20.00	8.00
❑ 547	Gus Bell	15.00	6.00
❑ 548	Tom Satriano	15.00	6.00
❑ 549	Marcelino Lopez	15.00	6.00
	Pete Lovrich		
	Paul Ratliff		
	Elmo Plaskett		
❑ 550	Duke Snider	80.00	32.00
❑ 551	Billy Klaus	15.00	6.00
❑ 552	Detroit Tigers	50.00	20.00
	Team Card		
❑ 553	Brock Davis	125.00	50.00
	Jim Gosger		
	Willie Stargell RC		
	John Herrnstein		
❑ 554	Hank Fischer	15.00	6.00
❑ 555	John Blanchard	20.00	8.00
❑ 556	Al Worthington	15.00	6.00
❑ 557	Cuno Barragan	15.00	6.00
❑ 558	Bill Faul	20.00	8.00
	Ron Hunt RC		
	Al Moran		
	Bob Lipski		
❑ 559	Danny Murtaugh MG	15.00	6.00
❑ 560	Ray Herbert	15.00	6.00
❑ 561	Mike De La Hoz	15.00	6.00
❑ 562	Randy Cardinal	30.00	12.00
	Dave McNally RC		
	Ken Rowe		
	Don Rowe		
❑ 563	Mike McCormick	15.00	6.00
❑ 564	George Banks	15.00	6.00
❑ 565	Larry Sherry	15.00	6.00
❑ 566	Cliff Cook	15.00	6.00
❑ 567	Jim Duffalo	15.00	6.00
❑ 568	Bob Sadowski	15.00	6.00
❑ 569	Luis Arroyo	20.00	8.00
❑ 570	Frank Bolling	15.00	6.00
❑ 571	Johnny Klippstein	15.00	6.00
❑ 572	Jack Spring	15.00	6.00
❑ 573	Coot Veal	15.00	6.00
❑ 574	Hal Kolstad	15.00	6.00
❑ 575	Don Cardwell	15.00	6.00
❑ 576	Johnny Temple	30.00	11.00

1964 Topps

	NM	Ex
COMPLETE SET (587)	3500.00	1800.00
COMMON CARD (1-196)	3.00	1.20
COMMON (197-370)	4.00	1.60
COMMON (371-522)	8.00	3.20
COMMON (523-587)	15.00	6.00
WRAPPER (1-CENT)	100.00	40.00
WRAP. (1-CENT, REPEAT)	125.00	50.00
WRAPPER (5-CENT)	30.00	12.00
WRAP.(5-CENT, COIN)	40.00	16.00

Card	Player	NM	Ex
❑ 1	Sandy Koufax	30.00	9.00
	Dick Ellsworth		
	Bob Friend LL		
❑ 2	Gary Peters	8.00	3.20
	Juan Pizarro		
	Camilo Pascual LL		
❑ 3	Sandy Koufax	20.00	8.00
	Juan Marichal		
	Warren Spahn		
	Jim Maloney LL		
❑ 4	Whitey Ford	8.00	3.20
	Camilo Pascual		
	Jim Bouton LL		
❑ 5	Sandy Koufax	15.00	6.00
	Jim Maloney		
	Don Drysdale LL		
❑ 6	Camilo Pascual	8.00	3.20
	Jim Bunning		
	Dick Stigman LL		
❑ 7	Tommy Davis	20.00	8.00
	Roberto Clemente		
	Dick Groat		
	Hank Aaron LL		
❑ 8	Carl Yastrzemski	15.00	6.00
	Al Kaline		
	Rich Rollins LL		
❑ 9	Hank Aaron	30.00	12.00
	Willie McCovey		
	Willie Mays		
	Orlando Cepeda LL		
❑ 10	Harmon Killebrew	8.00	3.20
	Dick Stuart		
	Bob Allison LL		
❑ 11	Hank Aaron	15.00	6.00
	Ken Boyer		
	Bill White LL		
❑ 12	Dick Stuart	8.00	3.20
	Al Kaline		
	Harmon Killebrew LL		
❑ 13	Hoyt Wilhelm	12.00	4.80
❑ 14	Dick Nen RC	3.00	1.20
	Nick Willhite		
❑ 15	Zoilo Versalles	6.00	2.40
❑ 16	John Boozer	3.00	1.20
❑ 17	Willie Kirkland	3.00	1.20
❑ 18	Billy O'Dell	3.00	1.20
❑ 19	Don Wert	3.00	1.20
❑ 20	Bob Friend	6.00	2.40
❑ 21	Yogi Berra MG	40.00	16.00
❑ 22	Jerry Adair	3.00	1.20
❑ 23	Chris Zachary	3.00	1.20
❑ 24	Carl Sawatski	3.00	1.20
❑ 25	Bill Monbouquette	3.00	1.20
❑ 26	Gino Cimoli	3.00	1.20
❑ 27	New York Mets	8.00	3.20
	Team Card		
❑ 28	Claude Osteen	6.00	2.40
❑ 29	Lou Brock	40.00	16.00
❑ 30	Ron Perranoski	6.00	2.40
❑ 31	Dave Nicholson	3.00	1.20
❑ 32	Dean Chance	6.00	2.40
❑ 33	Sammy Ellis	6.00	2.40
	Mel Queen		
❑ 34	Jim Perry	6.00	2.40
❑ 35	Eddie Mathews	20.00	8.00
❑ 36	Hal Reniff	3.00	1.20
❑ 37	Smoky Burgess	6.00	2.40
❑ 38	Jim Wynn RC	8.00	3.20
❑ 39	Hank Aguirre	3.00	1.20
❑ 40	Dick Groat	6.00	2.40
❑ 41	Willie McCovey	8.00	3.20
	Leon Wagner		
❑ 42	Moe Drabowsky	6.00	2.40
❑ 43	Roy Sievers	6.00	2.40
❑ 44	Duke Carmel	3.00	1.20
❑ 45	Milt Pappas	6.00	2.40
❑ 46	Ed Brinkman	3.00	1.20
❑ 47	Jesus Alou RC	6.00	2.40
	Ron Herbel		
❑ 48	Bob Perry	3.00	1.20
❑ 49	Bill Henry	3.00	1.20
❑ 50	Mickey Mantle	350.00	120.00
❑ 51	Pete Richert	3.00	1.20
❑ 52	Chuck Hinton	3.00	1.20
❑ 53	Denis Menke	3.00	1.20
❑ 54	Sam Mele MG	3.00	1.20
❑ 55	Ernie Banks	40.00	16.00
❑ 56	Hal Brown	3.00	1.20
❑ 57	Tim Harkness	6.00	2.40
❑ 58	Don Demeter	6.00	2.40
❑ 59	Ernie Broglio	3.00	1.20
❑ 60	Frank Malzone	6.00	2.40
❑ 61	Bob Rodgers	6.00	2.40
	Ed Sadowski		
❑ 62	Ted Savage	3.00	1.20
❑ 63	John Orsino	3.00	1.20
❑ 64	Ted Abernathy	3.00	1.20
❑ 65	Felipe Alou	6.00	2.40
❑ 66	Eddie Fisher	3.00	1.20
❑ 67	Tigers Team	6.00	2.40
❑ 68	Willie Davis	6.00	2.40
❑ 69	Clete Boyer	6.00	2.40
❑ 70	Joe Torre	8.00	3.20
❑ 71	Jack Spring	3.00	1.20
❑ 72	Chico Cardenas	6.00	2.40
❑ 73	Jimmie Hall	8.00	3.20
❑ 74	Bob Priddy	3.00	1.20
	Tom Butters		
❑ 75	Wayne Causey	3.00	1.20
❑ 76	Checklist 1	10.00	2.00
❑ 77	Jerry Walker	3.00	1.20
❑ 78	Merritt Ranew	3.00	1.20
❑ 79	Bob Heffner	3.00	1.20
❑ 80	Vada Pinson	8.00	3.20
❑ 81	Nellie Fox	12.00	4.80
	Harmon Killebrew		
❑ 82	Jim Davenport	6.00	2.40
❑ 83	Gus Triandos	6.00	2.40
❑ 84	Carl Willey	3.00	1.20
❑ 85	Pete Ward	3.00	1.20
❑ 86	Al Downing	6.00	2.40
❑ 87	St. Louis Cardinals	6.00	2.40
	Team Card		
❑ 88	John Roseboro	6.00	2.40
❑ 89	Boog Powell	6.00	2.40
❑ 90	Earl Battey	3.00	1.20
❑ 91	Bob Bailey	6.00	2.40
❑ 92	Steve Ridzik	3.00	1.20
❑ 93	Gary Geiger	3.00	1.20
❑ 94	Jim Britton	3.00	1.20
	Larry Maxie		
❑ 95	George Altman	3.00	1.20
❑ 96	Bob Buhl	6.00	2.40
❑ 97	Jim Fregosi	6.00	2.40
❑ 98	Bill Bruton	3.00	1.20
❑ 99	Al Stanek	3.00	1.20
❑ 100	Elston Howard	6.00	2.40
❑ 101	Walt Alston MG	8.00	3.20
❑ 102	Checklist 2	10.00	2.00
❑ 103	Curt Flood	6.00	2.40
❑ 104	Art Mahaffey	6.00	2.40
❑ 105	Woody Held	3.00	1.20
❑ 106	Joe Nuxhall	6.00	2.40
❑ 107	Bruce Howard	3.00	1.20
	Frank Kreutzer		
❑ 108	John Wyatt	3.00	1.20
❑ 109	Rusty Staub	6.00	2.40
❑ 110	Albie Pearson	6.00	2.40
❑ 111	Don Elston	3.00	1.20
❑ 112	Bob Tillman	3.00	1.20
❑ 113	Grover Powell	6.00	2.40
❑ 114	Don Lock	3.00	1.20
❑ 115	Frank Bolling	3.00	1.20
❑ 116	Jay Ward	12.00	4.80
	Tony Oliva		
❑ 117	Earl Francis	3.00	1.20
❑ 118	John Blanchard	6.00	2.40
❑ 119	Gary Kolb	3.00	1.20
❑ 120	Don Drysdale	20.00	8.00
❑ 121	Pete Runnels	6.00	2.40
❑ 122	Don McMahon	3.00	1.20

❑ 123 Jose Pagan 3.00 1.20
❑ 124 Orlando Pena 3.00 1.20
❑ 125 Pete Rose UER 250.00 100.00
Born in 1942
❑ 126 Russ Snyder 3.00 1.20
❑ 127 Aubrey Gatewood 3.00 1.20
Dick Simpson
❑ 128 Mickey Lolich RC 20.00 8.00
❑ 129 Amado Samuel 3.00 1.20
❑ 130 Gary Peters 6.00 2.40
❑ 131 Steve Boros 3.00 1.20
❑ 132 Braves Team 6.00 2.40
❑ 133 Jim Grant 6.00 2.40
❑ 134 Don Zimmer 6.00 2.40
❑ 135 Johnny Callison 6.00 2.40
❑ 136 Sandy Koufax WS 20.00 8.00
strikes out 15
❑ 137 Willie Davis WS 8.00 3.20
❑ 138 Ron Fairly WS 8.00 3.20
❑ 139 Frank Howard WS 8.00 3.20
❑ 140 WS Summary 8.00 3.20
Dodgers celebrate
❑ 141 Danny Murtaugh MG 6.00 2.40
❑ 142 John Bateman 3.00 1.20
❑ 143 Bubba Phillips 3.00 1.20
❑ 144 Al Worthington 3.00 1.20
❑ 145 Norm Siebern 3.00 1.20
❑ 146 Tommy John RC 30.00 12.00
Bob Chance
❑ 147 Ray Sadecki 3.00 1.20
❑ 148 J.C. Martin 3.00 1.20
❑ 149 Paul Foytack 3.00 1.20
❑ 150 Willie Mays 125.00 50.00
❑ 151 Athletics Team 6.00 2.40
❑ 152 Denny Lemaster 3.00 1.20
❑ 153 Dick Williams 6.00 2.40
❑ 154 Dick Tracewski RC 6.00 2.40
❑ 155 Duke Snider 30.00 12.00
❑ 156 Bill Dailey 3.00 1.20
❑ 157 Gene Mauch MG 6.00 2.40
❑ 158 Ken Johnson 3.00 1.20
❑ 159 Charlie Dees 3.00 1.20
❑ 160 Ken Boyer 6.00 2.40
❑ 161 Dave McNally 6.00 2.40
❑ 162 Dick Sisler CO 6.00 2.40
Vada Pinson
❑ 163 Donn Clendenon 6.00 2.40
❑ 164 Bud Daley 3.00 1.20
❑ 165 Jerry Lumpe 3.00 1.20
❑ 166 Marty Keough 3.00 1.20
❑ 167 Mike Brumley 30.00 12.00
Lou Piniella RC
❑ 168 Al Weis 3.00 1.20
❑ 169 Del Crandall 6.00 2.40
❑ 170 Dick Radatz 6.00 2.40
❑ 171 Ty Cline 3.00 1.20
❑ 172 Indians Team 6.00 2.40
❑ 173 Ryne Duren 6.00 2.40
❑ 174 Doc Edwards 3.00 1.20
❑ 175 Billy Williams 12.00 4.80
❑ 176 Tracy Stallard 3.00 1.20
❑ 177 Harmon Killebrew 20.00 8.00
❑ 178 Hank Bauer MG 6.00 2.40
❑ 179 Carl Warwick 3.00 1.20
❑ 180 Tommy Davis 6.00 2.40
❑ 181 Dave Wickersham 3.00 1.20
❑ 182 Carl Yastrzemski 15.00 6.00
Chuck Schilling
❑ 183 Ron Taylor 3.00 1.20
❑ 184 Al Luplow 3.00 1.20
❑ 185 Jim O'Toole 6.00 2.40
❑ 186 Roman Mejias 3.00 1.20
❑ 187 Ed Roebuck 3.00 1.20
❑ 188 Checklist 3 10.00 2.00
❑ 189 Bob Hendley 3.00 1.20
❑ 190 Bobby Richardson 8.00 3.20
❑ 191 Clay Dalrymple 6.00 2.40
❑ 192 John Boccabella 3.00 1.20
Billy Cowan
❑ 193 Jerry Lynch 3.00 1.20
❑ 194 John Goryl 3.00 1.20
❑ 195 Floyd Robinson 3.00 1.20
❑ 196 Jim Gentile 3.00 1.20
❑ 197 Frank Lary 6.00 2.40
❑ 198 Len Gabrielson 4.00 1.60
❑ 199 Joe Azcue 4.00 1.60

❑ 200 Sandy Koufax 100.00 40.00
❑ 201 Sam Bowens 6.00 2.40
Wally Bunker
❑ 202 Galen Cisco 6.00 2.40
❑ 203 John Kennedy 6.00 2.40
❑ 204 Matty Alou 6.00 2.40
❑ 205 Nellie Fox 12.00 4.80
❑ 206 Steve Hamilton 6.00 2.40
❑ 207 Fred Hutchinson MG 6.00 2.40
❑ 208 Wes Covington 6.00 2.40
❑ 209 Bob Allen 4.00 1.60
❑ 210 Carl Yastrzemski 40.00 16.00
❑ 211 Jim Coker 4.00 1.60
❑ 212 Pete Lovrich 4.00 1.60
❑ 213 Angels Team 6.00 2.40
❑ 214 Ken McMullen 6.00 2.40
❑ 215 Ray Herbert 4.00 1.60
❑ 216 Mike de la Hoz 4.00 1.60
❑ 217 Jim King 4.00 1.60
❑ 218 Hank Fischer 4.00 1.60
❑ 219 Al Downing 6.00 2.40
Jim Bouton
❑ 220 Dick Ellsworth 6.00 2.40
❑ 221 Bob Saverine 4.00 1.60
❑ 222 Billy Pierce 6.00 2.40
❑ 223 George Banks 4.00 1.60
❑ 224 Tommie Sisk 4.00 1.60
❑ 225 Roger Maris 60.00 24.00
❑ 226 Jerry Grote RC 6.00 2.40
Larry Yellen
❑ 227 Barry Latman 4.00 1.60
❑ 228 Felix Mantilla 4.00 1.60
❑ 229 Charley Lau 6.00 2.40
❑ 230 Brooks Robinson 40.00 16.00
❑ 231 Dick Calmus 4.00 1.60
❑ 232 Al Lopez MG 8.00 3.20
❑ 233 Hal Smith 4.00 1.60
❑ 234 Gary Bell 4.00 1.60
❑ 235 Ron Hunt 4.00 1.60
❑ 236 Bill Faul 4.00 1.60
❑ 237 Cubs Team 6.00 2.40
❑ 238 Roy McMillan 6.00 2.40
❑ 239 Herm Starrette 4.00 1.60
❑ 240 Bill White 6.00 2.40
❑ 241 Jim Owens 4.00 1.60
❑ 242 Harvey Kuenn 6.00 2.40
❑ 243 Richie Allen RC 30.00 12.00
John Herrnstein
❑ 244 Tony LaRussa RC 30.00 12.00
❑ 245 Dick Stigman 4.00 1.60
❑ 246 Manny Mota 6.00 2.40
❑ 247 Dave DeBusschere 6.00 2.40
❑ 248 Johnny Pesky MG 6.00 2.40
❑ 249 Doug Camilli 4.00 1.60
❑ 250 Al Kaline 40.00 16.00
❑ 251 Choo Choo Coleman 6.00 2.40
❑ 252 Ken Aspromonte 4.00 1.60
❑ 253 Wally Post 6.00 2.40
❑ 254 Don Hoak 6.00 2.40
❑ 255 Lee Thomas 6.00 2.40
❑ 256 Johnny Weekly 4.00 1.60
❑ 257 San Francisco Giants 6.00 2.40
Team Card
❑ 258 Garry Roggenburk 4.00 1.60
❑ 259 Harry Bright 4.00 1.60
❑ 260 Frank Robinson 40.00 16.00
❑ 261 Jim Hannan 4.00 1.60
❑ 262 Mike Shannon RC 8.00 3.20
Harry Fanok
❑ 263 Chuck Estrada 4.00 1.60
❑ 264 Jim Landis 4.00 1.60
❑ 265 Jim Bunning 12.00 4.80
❑ 266 Gene Freese 4.00 1.60
❑ 267 Wilbur Wood RC 6.00 2.40
❑ 268 Danny Murtaugh MG 6.00 2.40
Bill Virdon
❑ 269 Ellis Burton 4.00 1.60
❑ 270 Rich Rollins 6.00 2.40
❑ 271 Bob Sadowski 4.00 1.60
❑ 272 Jake Wood 4.00 1.60
❑ 273 Mel Nelson 4.00 1.60
❑ 274 Checklist 4 10.00 2.00
❑ 275 John Tsitouris 4.00 1.60
❑ 276 Jose Tartabull 6.00 2.40
❑ 277 Ken Retzer 4.00 1.60
❑ 278 Bobby Shantz 6.00 2.40

❑ 279 Joe Koppe UER 4.00 1.60
(Glove on wrong hand)
❑ 280 Juan Marichal 15.00 6.00
❑ 281 Jake Gibbs 6.00 2.40
Tom Metcalf
❑ 282 Bob Bruce 4.00 1.60
❑ 283 Tom McCraw RC 4.00 1.60
❑ 284 Dick Schofield 4.00 1.60
❑ 285 Robin Roberts 15.00 6.00
❑ 286 Don Landrum 4.00 1.60
❑ 287 Tony Conigliaro RC 50.00 20.00
Bill Spanswick
❑ 288 Al Moran 4.00 1.60
❑ 289 Frank Funk 4.00 1.60
❑ 290 Bob Allison 6.00 2.40
❑ 291 Phil Ortega 4.00 1.60
❑ 292 Mike Roarke 4.00 1.60
❑ 293 Phillies Team 6.00 2.40
❑ 294 Ken L. Hunt 4.00 1.60
❑ 295 Roger Craig 6.00 2.40
❑ 296 Ed Kirkpatrick 4.00 1.60
❑ 297 Ken MacKenzie 4.00 1.60
❑ 298 Harry Craft MG 4.00 1.60
❑ 299 Bill Stafford 4.00 1.60
❑ 300 Hank Aaron 100.00 40.00
❑ 301 Larry Brown 4.00 1.60
❑ 302 Dan Pfister 4.00 1.60
❑ 303 Jim Campbell 4.00 1.60
❑ 304 Bob Johnson 4.00 1.60
❑ 305 Jack Lamabe 4.00 1.60
❑ 306 Willie Mays 40.00 16.00
Orlando Cepeda
❑ 307 Joe Gibbon 4.00 1.60
❑ 308 Gene Stephens 4.00 1.60
❑ 309 Paul Toth 4.00 1.60
❑ 310 Jim Gilliam 6.00 2.40
❑ 311 Tom Brown RC 6.00 2.40
❑ 312 Fritz Fisher 4.00 1.60
Fred Gladding
❑ 313 Chuck Hiller 4.00 1.60
❑ 314 Jerry Buchek 4.00 1.60
❑ 315 Bo Belinsky 6.00 2.40
❑ 316 Gene Oliver 4.00 1.60
❑ 317 Al Smith 4.00 1.60
❑ 318 Minnesota Twins 6.00 2.40
Team Card
❑ 319 Paul Brown 4.00 1.60
❑ 320 Rocky Colavito 12.00 4.80
❑ 321 Bob Lillis 4.00 1.60
❑ 322 George Brunet 4.00 1.60
❑ 323 John Buzhardt 4.00 1.60
❑ 324 Casey Stengel MG 15.00 6.00
❑ 325 Hector Lopez 6.00 2.40
❑ 326 Ron Brand 4.00 1.60
❑ 327 Don Blasingame 4.00 1.60
❑ 328 Bob Shaw 4.00 1.60
❑ 329 Russ Nixon 4.00 1.60
❑ 330 Tommy Harper 6.00 2.40
❑ 331 Roger Maris 150.00 60.00
Norm Cash
Mickey Mantle
Al Kaline
❑ 332 Ray Washburn 4.00 1.60
❑ 333 Billy Moran 4.00 1.60
❑ 334 Lew Krausse 4.00 1.60
❑ 335 Don Mossi 6.00 2.40
❑ 336 Andre Rodgers 4.00 1.60
❑ 337 Al Ferrara 6.00 2.40
Jeff Torborg RC
❑ 338 Jack Kralick 4.00 1.60
❑ 339 Walt Bond 4.00 1.60
❑ 340 Joe Cunningham 4.00 1.60
❑ 341 Jim Roland 4.00 1.60
❑ 342 Willie Stargell 30.00 12.00
❑ 343 Senators Team 6.00 2.40
❑ 344 Phil Linz 6.00 2.40
❑ 345 Frank Thomas 8.00 3.20
❑ 346 Joey Jay 4.00 1.60
❑ 347 Bobby Wine 6.00 2.40
❑ 348 Ed Lopat MG 6.00 2.40
❑ 349 Art Fowler 4.00 1.60
❑ 350 Willie McCovey 25.00 10.00
❑ 351 Dan Schneider 4.00 1.60
❑ 352 Eddie Bressoud 4.00 1.60
❑ 353 Wally Moon 6.00 2.40
❑ 354 Dave Giusti 4.00 1.60

❑ 355 Vic Power 6.00 2.40
❑ 356 Bill McCool 6.00 2.40
Chico Ruiz
❑ 357 Charley James 4.00 1.60
❑ 358 Ron Kline 4.00 1.60
❑ 359 Jim Schaffer 4.00 1.60
❑ 360 Joe Pepitone 12.00 4.80
❑ 361 Jay Hook 4.00 1.60
❑ 362 Checklist 5 .... 10.00 2.00
❑ 363 Dick McAuliffe 6.00 2.40
❑ 364 Joe Gaines 4.00 1.60
❑ 365 Cal McLish 6.00 2.40
❑ 366 Nelson Mathews 4.00 1.60
❑ 367 Fred Whitfield 4.00 1.60
❑ 368 Fritz Ackley 6.00 2.40
Don Buford RC
❑ 369 Jerry Zimmerman 4.00 1.60
❑ 370 Hal Woodeshick 4.00 1.60
❑ 371 Frank Howard 8.00 3.20
❑ 372 Howie Koplitz 8.00 3.20
❑ 373 Pirates Team 12.00 4.80
❑ 374 Bobby Bolin 8.00 3.20
❑ 375 Ron Santo 10.00 4.00
❑ 376 Dave Morehead 8.00 3.20
❑ 377 Bob Skinner 8.00 3.20
❑ 378 Woody Woodward RC .. 10.00 4.00
Jack Smith
❑ 379 Tony Gonzalez 8.00 3.20
❑ 380 Whitey Ford 40.00 16.00
❑ 381 Bob Taylor 8.00 3.20
❑ 382 Wes Stock 8.00 3.20
❑ 383 Bill Rigney MG 8.00 3.20
❑ 384 Ron Hansen 8.00 3.20
❑ 385 Curt Simmons 10.00 4.00
❑ 386 Lenny Green 8.00 3.20
❑ 387 Terry Fox 8.00 3.20
❑ 388 John O'Donoghue RC .. 10.00 4.00
George Williams
❑ 389 Jim Umbricht 10.00 4.00
(Card back mentions
his death)
❑ 390 Orlando Cepeda 25.00 10.00
❑ 391 Sam McDowell 10.00 4.00
❑ 392 Jim Pagliaroni 8.00 3.20
❑ 393 Casey Stengel MG 15.00 6.00
Ed Kranepool
❑ 394 Bob Miller 8.00 3.20
❑ 395 Tom Tresh 10.00 4.00
❑ 396 Dennis Bennett 8.00 3.20
❑ 397 Chuck Cottier 8.00 3.20
❑ 398 Bill Haas 10.00 4.00
Dick Smith
❑ 399 Jackie Brandt 8.00 3.20
❑ 400 Warren Spahn 40.00 16.00
❑ 401 Charlie Maxwell 8.00 3.20
❑ 402 Tom Sturdivant 8.00 3.20
❑ 403 Reds Team 12.00 4.80
❑ 404 Tony Martinez 8.00 3.20
❑ 405 Ken McBride 8.00 3.20
❑ 406 Al Spangler 8.00 3.20
❑ 407 Bill Freehan 10.00 4.00
❑ 408 Jim Stewart 8.00 3.20
Fred Burdette
❑ 409 Bill Fischer 8.00 3.20
❑ 410 Dick Stuart 10.00 4.00
❑ 411 Lee Walls 8.00 3.20
❑ 412 Ray Culp 10.00 4.00
❑ 413 Johnny Keane MG 8.00 3.20
❑ 414 Jack Sanford 8.00 3.20
❑ 415 Tony Kubek 15.00 6.00
❑ 416 Lee Maye 8.00 3.20
❑ 417 Don Cardwell 8.00 3.20
❑ 418 Darold Knowles 10.00 4.00
Buster Narum
❑ 419 Ken Harrelson RC 15.00 6.00
❑ 420 Jim Maloney 10.00 4.00
❑ 421 Camilo Carreon 8.00 3.20
❑ 422 Jack Fisher 8.00 3.20
❑ 423 Hank Aaron 125.00 50.00
Willie Mays
❑ 424 Dick Bertell 8.00 3.20
❑ 425 Norm Cash 10.00 4.00
❑ 426 Bob Rodgers 8.00 3.20
❑ 427 Don Rudolph 8.00 3.20
❑ 428 Archie Skeen 8.00 3.20
Pete Smith
(Back states Archie
has retired)
❑ 429 Tim McCarver 10.00 4.00
❑ 430 Juan Pizarro 8.00 3.20
❑ 431 George Alusik 8.00 3.20
❑ 432 Ruben Amaro 10.00 4.00
❑ 433 Yankees Team 40.00 16.00
❑ 434 Don Nottebart 8.00 3.20
❑ 435 Vic Davalillo 8.00 3.20
❑ 436 Charlie Neal 10.00 4.00
❑ 437 Ed Bailey 8.00 3.20
❑ 438 Checklist 6 .... 15.00 3.00
❑ 439 Harvey Haddix 10.00 4.00
❑ 440 R.Clemente UER 250.00 100.00
1960 Pittsburfh
❑ 441 Bob Duliba 8.00 3.20
❑ 442 Pumpsie Green 10.00 4.00
❑ 443 Chuck Dressen MG 10.00 4.00
❑ 444 Larry Jackson 8.00 3.20
❑ 445 Bill Skowron 10.00 4.00
❑ 446 Julian Javier 15.00 6.00
❑ 447 Ted Bowsfield 8.00 3.20
❑ 448 Cookie Rojas 10.00 4.00
❑ 449 Deron Johnson 10.00 4.00
❑ 450 Steve Barber 8.00 3.20
❑ 451 Joe Amalfitano 8.00 3.20
❑ 452 Gil Garrido 10.00 4.00
Jim Ray Hart RC
❑ 453 Frank Baumann 8.00 3.20
❑ 454 Tommie Aaron 10.00 4.00
❑ 455 Bernie Allen 8.00 3.20
❑ 456 Wes Parker RC 10.00 4.00
John Werhas
❑ 457 Jesse Gonder 8.00 3.20
❑ 458 Ralph Terry 10.00 4.00
❑ 459 Pete Charton 8.00 3.20
Dalton Jones
❑ 460 Bob Gibson 40.00 16.00
❑ 461 George Thomas 8.00 3.20
❑ 462 Birdie Tebbetts MG 8.00 3.20
❑ 463 Don Leppert 8.00 3.20
❑ 464 Dallas Green 15.00 6.00
❑ 465 Mike Hershberger 8.00 3.20
❑ 466 Dick Green 10.00 4.00
Aurelio Monteagudo
❑ 467 Bob Aspromonte 8.00 3.20
❑ 468 Gaylord Perry 40.00 16.00
❑ 469 Fred Norman 10.00 4.00
Sterling Slaughter
❑ 470 Jim Bouton 10.00 4.00
❑ 471 Gates Brown RC 10.00 4.00
❑ 472 Vern Law 10.00 4.00
❑ 473 Baltimore Orioles 12.00 4.80
Team Card
❑ 474 Larry Sherry 10.00 4.00
❑ 475 Ed Charles 8.00 3.20
❑ 476 Rico Carty RC 15.00 6.00
Dick Kelley
❑ 477 Mike Joyce 8.00 3.20
❑ 478 Dick Howser 10.00 4.00
❑ 479 Dave Bakenhaster 8.00 3.20
Johnny Lewis
❑ 480 Bob Purkey 8.00 3.20
❑ 481 Chuck Schilling 8.00 3.20
❑ 482 John Briggs 10.00 4.00
Danny Cater
❑ 483 Fred Valentine 8.00 3.20
❑ 484 Bill Pleis 8.00 3.20
❑ 485 Tom Haller 8.00 3.20
❑ 486 Bob Kennedy MG 8.00 3.20
❑ 487 Mike McCormick 10.00 4.00
❑ 488 Pete Mikkelsen 15.00 6.00
Bob Meyer
❑ 489 Julio Navarro 8.00 3.20
❑ 490 Ron Fairly 10.00 4.00
❑ 491 Ed Rakow 8.00 3.20
❑ 492 Jim Beauchamp RC 8.00 3.20
Mike White
❑ 493 Don Lee 8.00 3.20
❑ 494 Al Jackson 8.00 3.20
❑ 495 Bill Virdon 10.00 4.00
❑ 496 White Sox Team 12.00 4.80
❑ 497 Jeoff Long 8.00 3.20
❑ 498 Dave Stenhouse 8.00 3.20
❑ 499 Chico Salmon 8.00 3.20
Gordon Seyfried
❑ 500 Camilo Pascual 10.00 4.00
❑ 501 Bob Veale 10.00 4.00
❑ 502 Bobby Knoop RC 8.00 3.20
Bob Lee
❑ 503 Earl Wilson 8.00 3.20
❑ 504 Claude Raymond 8.00 3.20
❑ 505 Stan Williams 8.00 3.20
❑ 506 Bobby Bragan MG 8.00 3.20
❑ 507 Johnny Edwards 8.00 3.20
❑ 508 Diego Segui 8.00 3.20
❑ 509 Gene Alley RC 10.00 4.00
Orlando McFarlane
❑ 510 Lindy McDaniel 10.00 4.00
❑ 511 Lou Jackson 10.00 4.00
❑ 512 Willie Horton RC 15.00 6.00
Joe Sparma
❑ 513 Don Larsen 10.00 4.00
❑ 514 Jim Hickman 10.00 4.00
❑ 515 Johnny Romano 8.00 3.20
❑ 516 Jerry Arrigo 8.00 3.20
Dwight Siebler
❑ 517A Checklist 7 ERR 25.00 5.00
(Incorrect numbering
sequence on back)
❑ 517B Checklist 7 COR 15.00 3.00
(Correct numbering
on back)
❑ 518 Carl Bouldin 8.00 3.20
❑ 519 Charlie Smith 8.00 3.20
❑ 520 Jack Baldschun 10.00 4.00
❑ 521 Tom Satriano 8.00 3.20
❑ 522 Bob Tiefenauer 8.00 3.20
❑ 523 Lou Burdette UER 20.00 8.00
(Pitching lefty)
❑ 524 Jim Dickson 15.00 6.00
Bobby Klaus
❑ 525 Al McBean 15.00 6.00
❑ 526 Lou Clinton 15.00 6.00
❑ 527 Larry Bearnarth 15.00 6.00
❑ 528 Dave Duncan RC 20.00 8.00
Tommie Reynolds
❑ 529 Alvin Dark MG 20.00 8.00
❑ 530 Leon Wagner 15.00 6.00
❑ 531 Los Angeles Dodgers .. 25.00 10.00
Team Card
❑ 532 Bud Bloomfield 15.00 6.00
(Bloomfield photo
actually Jay Ward)
Joe Nossek RC
❑ 533 Johnny Klippstein 15.00 6.00
❑ 534 Gus Bell 15.00 6.00
❑ 535 Phil Regan 15.00 6.00
❑ 536 Larry Elliot 15.00 6.00
John Stephenson
❑ 537 Dan Osinski 15.00 6.00
❑ 538 Minnie Minoso 20.00 8.00
❑ 539 Roy Face 20.00 8.00
❑ 540 Luis Aparicio 40.00 16.00
❑ 541 Phil Roof 80.00 32.00
Phil Niekro RC
❑ 542 Don Mincher 15.00 6.00
❑ 543 Bob Uecker 40.00 16.00
❑ 544 Steve Hertz 15.00 6.00
Joe Hoerner
❑ 545 Max Alvis 15.00 6.00
❑ 546 Joe Christopher 15.00 6.00
❑ 547 Gil Hodges MG 30.00 12.00
❑ 548 Wayne Schurr 20.00 8.00
Paul Speckenbach
❑ 549 Joe Moeller 15.00 6.00
❑ 550 Ken Hubbs MEM 40.00 16.00
❑ 551 Billy Hoeft 15.00 6.00
❑ 552 Tom Kelley 15.00 6.00
Sonny Siebert
❑ 553 Jim Brewer 15.00 6.00
❑ 554 Hank Foiles 15.00 6.00
❑ 555 Lee Stange 15.00 6.00
❑ 556 Steve Dillon 15.00 6.00
Ron Locke
❑ 557 Leo Burke 15.00 6.00
❑ 558 Don Schwall 15.00 6.00
❑ 559 Dick Phillips 15.00 6.00
❑ 560 Dick Farrell 15.00 6.00
❑ 561 Dave Bennett UER 20.00 8.00
(19 ... is 18)
Rick Wise RC

Card	NM	Ex
❑ 562 Pedro Ramos	15.00	6.00
❑ 563 Dal Maxvill	20.00	8.00
❑ 564 Joe McCabe Jerry McNertney	20.00	8.00
❑ 565 Stu Miller	15.00	6.00
❑ 566 Ed Kranepool	20.00	8.00
❑ 567 Jim Kaat	20.00	8.00
❑ 568 Phil Gagliano Cap Peterson	15.00	6.00
❑ 569 Fred Newman	15.00	6.00
❑ 570 Bill Mazeroski	40.00	16.00
❑ 571 Gene Conley	15.00	6.00
❑ 572 Dave Gray Dick Egan	15.00	6.00
❑ 573 Jim Duffalo	15.00	6.00
❑ 574 Manny Jimenez	15.00	6.00
❑ 575 Tony Cloninger	15.00	6.00
❑ 576 Jerry Hinsley Bill Wakefield	15.00	6.00
❑ 577 Gordy Coleman	15.00	6.00
❑ 578 Glen Hobbie	15.00	6.00
❑ 579 Red Sox Team	25.00	10.00
❑ 580 Johnny Podres	20.00	8.00
❑ 581 Pedro Gonzalez Archie Moore	20.00	8.00
❑ 582 Rod Kanehl	20.00	8.00
❑ 583 Tito Francona	15.00	6.00
❑ 584 Joel Horlen	15.00	6.00
❑ 585 Tony Taylor	20.00	8.00
❑ 586 Jimmy Piersall	20.00	8.00
❑ 587 Bennie Daniels	20.00	8.00

1965 Topps

	NM	Ex
COMPLETE SET (598)	4000.00	1800.00
COMMON CARD (1-196)	2.00	.80
COMMON (197-283)	2.50	1.00
COMMON (284-370)	4.00	1.60
COMMON (371-598)	8.00	3.20
WRAPPER (1-CENT)	125.00	50.00
WRAPPER (5-CENT)	100.00	40.00

Card	NM	Ex
❑ 1 Tony Oliva Elston Howard Brooks Robinson LL	20.00	6.00
❑ 2 Roberto Clemente Hank Aaron Rico Carty LL	25.00	10.00
❑ 3 Harmon Killebrew Mickey Mantle Boog Powell LL	50.00	20.00
❑ 4 Willie Mays Billy Williams Jim Ray Hart Orlando Cepeda Johnny Callison LL	15.00	6.00
❑ 5 Brooks Robinson Harmon Killebrew Mickey Mantle Dick Stuart LL	40.00	16.00
❑ 6 Ken Boyer Willie Mays Ron Santo LL	12.00	4.80
❑ 7 Dean Chance Joel Horlen LL	5.00	2.00
❑ 8 Sandy Koufax Don Drysdale LL	20.00	8.00
❑ 9 Dean Chance Gary Peters Dave Wickersham Juan Pizarro Wally Bunker LL	5.00	2.00
❑ 10 Larry Jackson Ray Sadecki Juan Marichal LL	5.00	2.00
❑ 11 Al Downing Dean Chance Camilo Pascual LL	5.00	2.00
❑ 12 Bob Veale Don Drysdale Bob Gibson LL	10.00	4.00
❑ 13 Pedro Ramos	4.00	1.60
❑ 14 Len Gabrielson	2.00	.80
❑ 15 Robin Roberts	10.00	4.00
❑ 16 Joe Morgan RC Sonny Jackson DP	60.00	24.00
❑ 17 Johnny Romano	2.00	.80
❑ 18 Bill McCool	2.00	.80
❑ 19 Gates Brown	4.00	1.60
❑ 20 Jim Bunning	10.00	4.00
❑ 21 Don Blasingame	2.00	.80
❑ 22 Charlie Smith	2.00	.80
❑ 23 Bob Tiefenauer	2.00	.80
❑ 24 Minnesota Twins Team Card	6.00	2.40
❑ 25 Al McBean	2.00	.80
❑ 26 Bobby Knoop	2.00	.80
❑ 27 Dick Bertell	2.00	.80
❑ 28 Barney Schultz	2.00	.80
❑ 29 Felix Mantilla	2.00	.80
❑ 30 Jim Bouton	6.00	2.40
❑ 31 Mike White	2.00	.80
❑ 32 Herman Franks MG	2.00	.80
❑ 33 Jackie Brandt	2.00	.80
❑ 34 Cal Koonce	2.00	.80
❑ 35 Ed Charles	2.00	.80
❑ 36 Bobby Wine	2.00	.80
❑ 37 Fred Gladding	2.00	.80
❑ 38 Jim King	2.00	.80
❑ 39 Gerry Arrigo	2.00	.80
❑ 40 Frank Howard	6.00	2.40
❑ 41 Bruce Howard Marv Staehle	2.00	.80
❑ 42 Earl Wilson	4.00	1.60
❑ 43 Mike Shannon (Name in red, other Cardinals in yellow)	4.00	1.60
❑ 44 Wade Blasingame	2.00	.80
❑ 45 Roy McMillan	4.00	1.60
❑ 46 Bob Lee	2.00	.80
❑ 47 Tommy Harper	4.00	1.60
❑ 48 Claude Raymond	4.00	1.60
❑ 49 Curt Blefary RC John Miller	4.00	1.60
❑ 50 Juan Marichal	10.00	4.00
❑ 51 Bill Bryan	2.00	.80
❑ 52 Ed Roebuck	2.00	.80
❑ 53 Dick McAuliffe	4.00	1.60
❑ 54 Joe Gibbon	2.00	.80
❑ 55 Tony Conigliaro	15.00	6.00
❑ 56 Ron Kline	2.00	.80
❑ 57 Cardinals Team	6.00	2.40
❑ 58 Fred Talbot	2.00	.80
❑ 59 Nate Oliver	2.00	.80
❑ 60 Jim O'Toole	4.00	1.60
❑ 61 Chris Cannizzaro	2.00	.80
❑ 62 Jim Kaat UER DP (Misspelled Katt)	6.00	2.40
❑ 63 Ty Cline	2.00	.80
❑ 64 Lou Burdette	4.00	1.60
❑ 65 Tony Kubek	10.00	4.00
❑ 66 Bill Rigney MG	2.00	.80
❑ 67 Harvey Haddix	4.00	1.60
❑ 68 Del Crandall	4.00	1.60
❑ 69 Bill Virdon	4.00	1.60
❑ 70 Bill Skowron	6.00	2.40
❑ 71 John O'Donoghue	2.00	.80
❑ 72 Tony Gonzalez	2.00	.80
❑ 73 Dennis Ribant	2.00	.80
❑ 74 Rico Petrocelli RC Jerry Stephenson	10.00	4.00
❑ 75 Deron Johnson	4.00	1.60
❑ 76 Sam McDowell	6.00	2.40
❑ 77 Doug Camilli	2.00	.80
❑ 78 Dal Maxvill	2.00	.80
❑ 79A Checklist 1 (61 Cannizzaro)	10.00	2.00
❑ 79B Checklist 1 (61 C.Cannizzaro)	10.00	2.00
❑ 80 Turk Farrell	2.00	.80
❑ 81 Don Buford	4.00	1.60
❑ 82 Santos Alomar RC John Braun	6.00	2.40
❑ 83 George Thomas	2.00	.80
❑ 84 Ron Herbel	2.00	.80
❑ 85 Willie Smith	2.00	.80
❑ 86 Buster Narum	2.00	.80
❑ 87 Nelson Mathews	2.00	.80
❑ 88 Jack Lamabe	2.00	.80
❑ 89 Mike Hershberger	2.00	.80
❑ 90 Rich Rollins	4.00	1.60
❑ 91 Cubs Team	6.00	2.40
❑ 92 Dick Howser	4.00	1.60
❑ 93 Jack Fisher	2.00	.80
❑ 94 Charlie Lau	4.00	1.60
❑ 95 Bill Mazeroski DP	6.00	2.40
❑ 96 Sonny Siebert	4.00	1.60
❑ 97 Pedro Gonzalez	2.00	.80
❑ 98 Bob Miller	2.00	.80
❑ 99 Gil Hodges MG	6.00	2.40
❑ 100 Ken Boyer	10.00	4.00
❑ 101 Fred Newman	2.00	.80
❑ 102 Steve Boros	2.00	.80
❑ 103 Harvey Kuenn	4.00	1.60
❑ 104 Checklist 2	10.00	2.00
❑ 105 Chico Salmon	2.00	.80
❑ 106 Gene Oliver	2.00	.80
❑ 107 Pat Corrales RC Costen Shockley	4.00	1.60
❑ 108 Don Mincher	2.00	.80
❑ 109 Walt Bond	2.00	.80
❑ 110 Ron Santo	6.00	2.40
❑ 111 Lee Thomas	4.00	1.60
❑ 112 Derrell Griffith	2.00	.80
❑ 113 Steve Barber	2.00	.80
❑ 114 Jim Hickman	4.00	1.60
❑ 115 Bobby Richardson	10.00	4.00
❑ 116 Dave Dowling Bob Tolan RC	4.00	1.60
❑ 117 Wes Stock	2.00	.80
❑ 118 Hal Lanier	4.00	1.60
❑ 119 John Kennedy	2.00	.80
❑ 120 Frank Robinson	40.00	16.00
❑ 121 Gene Alley	4.00	1.60
❑ 122 Bill Pleis	2.00	.80
❑ 123 Frank Thomas	4.00	1.60
❑ 124 Tom Satriano	2.00	.80
❑ 125 Juan Pizarro	2.00	.80
❑ 126 Dodgers Team	6.00	2.40
❑ 127 Frank Lary	2.00	.80
❑ 128 Vic Davalillo	2.00	.80
❑ 129 Bennie Daniels	2.00	.80
❑ 130 Al Kaline	40.00	16.00
❑ 131 Johnny Keane MG	2.00	.80
❑ 132 Mike Shannon WS	10.00	4.00
❑ 133 Mel Stottlemyre WS	6.00	2.40
❑ 134 Mickey Mantle WS Mantle's Clutch HR UER Mantle is shown wearing a road uni form That game was played in New York	80.00	32.00
❑ 135 Ken Boyer WS	10.00	4.00
❑ 136 Tim McCarver WS	6.00	2.40
❑ 137 Jim Bouton WS	6.00	2.40
❑ 138 Bob Gibson WS	12.00	4.80
❑ 139 WS Summary Cards celebrate	6.00	2.40
❑ 140 Dean Chance	4.00	1.60
❑ 141 Charlie James	2.00	.80
❑ 142 Bill Monbouquette	2.00	.80
❑ 143 John Gelnar Jerry May	2.00	.80
❑ 144 Ed Kranepool	4.00	1.60
❑ 145 Luis Tiant RC	10.00	4.00
❑ 146 Ron Hansen	2.00	.80
❑ 147 Dennis Bennett	2.00	.80
❑ 148 Willie Kirkland	2.00	.80
❑ 149 Wayne Schurr	2.00	.80
❑ 150 Brooks Robinson	40.00	16.00

❑ 151 Athletics Team 6.00 2.40
❑ 152 Phil Ortega 2.00 .80
❑ 153 Norm Cash 6.00 2.40
❑ 154 Bob Humphreys 2.00 .80
❑ 155 Roger Maris 60.00 24.00
❑ 156 Bob Sadowski 2.00 .80
❑ 157 Zoilo Versalles 4.00 1.60
❑ 158 Dick Sisler 2.00 .80
❑ 159 Jim Duffalo 2.00 .80
❑ 160 R.Clemente UER 175.00 70.00
1960 Pittsburfh
❑ 161 Frank Baumann 2.00 .80
❑ 162 Russ Nixon 2.00 .80
❑ 163 Johnny Briggs 2.00 .80
❑ 164 Al Spangler 2.00 .80
❑ 165 Dick Ellsworth 2.00 .80
❑ 166 George Culver 4.00 1.60
Tommie Agee RC
❑ 167 Bill Wakefield 2.00 .80
❑ 168 Dick Green 2.00 .80
❑ 169 Dave Vineyard 2.00 .80
❑ 170 Hank Aaron 125.00 50.00
❑ 171 Jim Roland 2.00 .80
❑ 172 Jimmy Piersall 6.00 2.40
❑ 173 Detroit Tigers 6.00 2.40
Team Card
❑ 174 Joey Jay 2.00 .80
❑ 175 Bob Aspromonte 2.00 .80
❑ 176 Willie McCovey 20.00 8.00
❑ 177 Pete Mikkelsen 2.00 .80
❑ 178 Dalton Jones 2.00 .80
❑ 179 Hal Woodeshick 2.00 .80
❑ 180 Bob Allison 4.00 1.60
❑ 181 Don Loun 2.00 .80
Joe McCabe
❑ 182 Mike de la Hoz 2.00 .80
❑ 183 Dave Nicholson 2.00 .80
❑ 184 John Boozer 2.00 .80
❑ 185 Max Alvis 2.00 .80
❑ 186 Billy Cowan 2.00 .80
❑ 187 Casey Stengel MG 15.00 6.00
❑ 188 Sam Bowens 2.00 .80
❑ 189 Checklist 3 10.00 2.00
❑ 190 Bill White 6.00 2.40
❑ 191 Phil Regan 4.00 1.60
❑ 192 Jim Coker 2.00 .80
❑ 193 Gaylord Perry 15.00 6.00
❑ 194 Bill Kelso 2.00 .80
Rick Reichardt
❑ 195 Bob Veale 4.00 1.60
❑ 196 Ron Fairly 4.00 1.60
❑ 197 Diego Segui 2.50 1.00
❑ 198 Smoky Burgess 4.00 1.60
❑ 199 Bob Heffner 2.50 1.00
❑ 200 Joe Torre 6.00 2.40
❑ 201 Sandy Valdespino 4.00 1.60
Cesar Tovar RC
❑ 202 Leo Burke 2.50 1.00
❑ 203 Dallas Green 4.00 1.60
❑ 204 Russ Snyder 2.50 1.00
❑ 205 Warren Spahn 30.00 12.00
❑ 206 Willie Horton 4.00 1.60
❑ 207 Pete Rose 175.00 70.00
❑ 208 Tommy John 6.00 2.40
❑ 209 Pirates Team 6.00 2.40
❑ 210 Jim Fregosi 4.00 1.60
❑ 211 Steve Ridzik 2.50 1.00
❑ 212 Ron Brand 2.50 1.00
❑ 213 Jim Davenport 2.50 1.00
❑ 214 Bob Purkey 2.50 1.00
❑ 215 Pete Ward 2.50 1.00
❑ 216 Al Worthington 2.50 1.00
❑ 217 Walter Alston MG 6.00 2.40
❑ 218 Dick Schofield 2.50 1.00
❑ 219 Bob Meyer 2.50 1.00
❑ 220 Billy Williams 10.00 4.00
❑ 221 John Tsitouris 2.50 1.00
❑ 222 Bob Tillman 2.50 1.00
❑ 223 Dan Osinski 2.50 1.00
❑ 224 Bob Chance 2.50 1.00
❑ 225 Bo Belinsky 4.00 1.60
❑ 226 Elvio Jimenez 6.00 2.40
Jake Gibbs
❑ 227 Bobby Klaus 2.50 1.00
❑ 228 Jack Sanford 2.50 1.00
❑ 229 Lou Clinton 2.50 1.00

❑ 230 Ray Sadecki 2.50 1.00
❑ 231 Jerry Adair 2.50 1.00
❑ 232 Steve Blass RC 4.00 1.60
❑ 233 Don Zimmer 4.00 1.60
❑ 234 White Sox Team 6.00 2.40
❑ 235 Chuck Hinton 2.50 1.00
❑ 236 Denny McLain RC 25.00 10.00
❑ 237 Bernie Allen 2.50 1.00
❑ 238 Joe Moeller 2.50 1.00
❑ 239 Doc Edwards 2.50 1.00
❑ 240 Bob Bruce 2.50 1.00
❑ 241 Mack Jones 2.50 1.00
❑ 242 George Brunet 2.50 1.00
❑ 243 Ted Davidson 4.00 1.60
Tommy Helms RC
❑ 244 Lindy McDaniel 4.00 1.60
❑ 245 Joe Pepitone 6.00 2.40
❑ 246 Tom Butters 4.00 1.60
❑ 247 Wally Moon 4.00 1.60
❑ 248 Gus Triandos 4.00 1.60
❑ 249 Dave McNally 4.00 1.60
❑ 250 Willie Mays 150.00 60.00
❑ 251 Billy Herman MG 4.00 1.60
❑ 252 Pete Richert 2.50 1.00
❑ 253 Danny Cater 2.50 1.00
❑ 254 Roland Sheldon 2.50 1.00
❑ 255 Camilo Pascual 4.00 1.60
❑ 256 Tito Francona 2.50 1.00
❑ 257 Jim Wynn 4.00 1.60
❑ 258 Larry Bearnarth 2.50 1.00
❑ 259 Jim Northrup RC 6.00 2.40
Ray Oyler
❑ 260 Don Drysdale 20.00 8.00
❑ 261 Duke Carmel 2.50 1.00
❑ 262 Bud Daley 2.50 1.00
❑ 263 Marty Keough 2.50 1.00
❑ 264 Bob Buhl 4.00 1.60
❑ 265 Jim Pagliaroni 2.50 1.00
❑ 266 Bert Campaneris RC 10.00 4.00
❑ 267 Senators Team 6.00 2.40
❑ 268 Ken McBride 2.50 1.00
❑ 269 Frank Bolling 2.50 1.00
❑ 270 Milt Pappas 4.00 1.60
❑ 271 Don Wert 4.00 1.60
❑ 272 Chuck Schilling 2.50 1.00
❑ 273 Checklist 4 10.00 2.00
❑ 274 Lum Harris MG 2.50 1.00
❑ 275 Dick Groat 6.00 2.40
❑ 276 Hoyt Wilhelm 10.00 4.00
❑ 277 Johnny Lewis 2.50 1.00
❑ 278 Ken Retzer 2.50 1.00
❑ 279 Dick Tracewski 2.50 1.00
❑ 280 Dick Stuart 4.00 1.60
❑ 281 Bill Stafford 2.50 1.00
❑ 282 Dick Estelle 40.00 16.00
Masanori Murakami RC
❑ 283 Fred Whitfield 2.50 1.00
❑ 284 Nick Willhite 4.00 1.60
❑ 285 Ron Hunt 4.00 1.60
❑ 286 Jim Dickson 4.00 1.60
Aurelio Monteagudo
❑ 287 Gary Kolb 4.00 1.60
❑ 288 Jack Hamilton 4.00 1.60
❑ 289 Gordy Coleman 6.00 2.40
❑ 290 Wally Bunker 6.00 2.40
❑ 291 Jerry Lynch 4.00 1.60
❑ 292 Larry Yellen 4.00 1.60
❑ 293 Angels Team 6.00 2.40
❑ 294 Tim McCarver 10.00 4.00
❑ 295 Dick Radatz 6.00 2.40
❑ 296 Tony Taylor 6.00 2.40
❑ 297 Dave DeBusschere 10.00 4.00
❑ 298 Jim Stewart 4.00 1.60
❑ 299 Jerry Zimmerman 4.00 1.60
❑ 300 Sandy Koufax 100.00 40.00
❑ 301 Birdie Tebbetts MG 6.00 2.40
❑ 302 Al Stanek 4.00 1.60
❑ 303 John Orsino 4.00 1.60
❑ 304 Dave Stenhouse 4.00 1.60
❑ 305 Rico Carty 6.00 2.40
❑ 306 Bubba Phillips 4.00 1.60
❑ 307 Barry Latman 4.00 1.60
❑ 308 Cleon Jones RC 6.00 2.40
Tom Parsons
❑ 309 Steve Hamilton 6.00 2.40
❑ 310 Johnny Callison 6.00 2.40

❑ 311 Orlando Pena 4.00 1.60
❑ 312 Joe Nuxhall 4.00 1.60
❑ 313 Jim Schaffer 4.00 1.60
❑ 314 Sterling Slaughter 4.00 1.60
❑ 315 Frank Malzone 6.00 2.40
❑ 316 Reds Team 6.00 2.40
❑ 317 Don McMahon 4.00 1.60
❑ 318 Matty Alou 6.00 2.40
❑ 319 Ken McMullen 4.00 1.60
❑ 320 Bob Gibson 50.00 20.00
❑ 321 Rusty Staub 10.00 4.00
❑ 322 Rick Wise 6.00 2.40
❑ 323 Hank Bauer MG 6.00 2.40
❑ 324 Bobby Locke 4.00 1.60
❑ 325 Donn Clendenon 6.00 2.40
❑ 326 Dwight Siebler 4.00 1.60
❑ 327 Denis Menke 4.00 1.60
❑ 328 Eddie Fisher 4.00 1.60
❑ 329 Hawk Taylor 4.00 1.60
❑ 330 Whitey Ford 40.00 16.00
❑ 331 Al Ferrara 6.00 2.40
John Purdin
❑ 332 Ted Abernathy 4.00 1.60
❑ 333 Tom Reynolds 4.00 1.60
❑ 334 Vic Roznovsky 4.00 1.60
❑ 335 Mickey Lolich 6.00 2.40
❑ 336 Woody Held 4.00 1.60
❑ 337 Mike Cuellar 6.00 2.40
❑ 338 Philadelphia Phillies 6.00 2.40
Team Card
❑ 339 Ryne Duren 6.00 2.40
❑ 340 Tony Oliva 20.00 8.00
❑ 341 Bob Bolin 4.00 1.60
❑ 342 Bob Rodgers 6.00 2.40
❑ 343 Mike McCormick 6.00 2.40
❑ 344 Wes Parker 6.00 2.40
❑ 345 Floyd Robinson 4.00 1.60
❑ 346 Bobby Bragan MG 4.00 1.60
❑ 347 Roy Face 6.00 2.40
❑ 348 George Banks 4.00 1.60
❑ 349 Larry Miller 4.00 1.60
❑ 350 Mickey Mantle 500.00 200.00
❑ 351 Jim Perry 6.00 2.40
❑ 352 Alex Johnson RC 6.00 2.40
❑ 353 Jerry Lumpe 4.00 1.60
❑ 354 Billy Ott 4.00 1.60
Jack Warner
❑ 355 Vada Pinson 10.00 4.00
❑ 356 Bill Spanswick 4.00 1.60
❑ 357 Carl Warwick 4.00 1.60
❑ 358 Albie Pearson 6.00 2.40
❑ 359 Ken Johnson 4.00 1.60
❑ 360 Orlando Cepeda 15.00 6.00
❑ 361 Checklist 5 12.00 2.40
❑ 362 Don Schwall 4.00 1.60
❑ 363 Bob Johnson 4.00 1.60
❑ 364 Galen Cisco 4.00 1.60
❑ 365 Jim Gentile 6.00 2.40
❑ 366 Dan Schneider 4.00 1.60
❑ 367 Leon Wagner 4.00 1.60
❑ 368 Ken Berry 6.00 2.40
Joel Gibson
❑ 369 Phil Linz 6.00 2.40
❑ 370 Tommy Davis 6.00 2.40
❑ 371 Frank Kreutzer 8.00 3.20
❑ 372 Clay Dalrymple 8.00 3.20
❑ 373 Curt Simmons 8.00 3.20
❑ 374 Jose Cardenal RC 8.00 3.20
Dick Simpson
❑ 375 Dave Wickersham 8.00 3.20
❑ 376 Jim Landis 8.00 3.20
❑ 377 Willie Stargell 25.00 10.00
❑ 378 Chuck Estrada 8.00 3.20
❑ 379 Giants Team 8.00 3.20
❑ 380 Rocky Colavito 25.00 10.00
❑ 381 Al Jackson 8.00 3.20
❑ 382 J.C. Martin 8.00 3.20
❑ 383 Felipe Alou 15.00 6.00
❑ 384 Johnny Klippstein 8.00 3.20
❑ 385 Carl Yastrzemski 60.00 24.00
❑ 386 Paul Jaeckel 8.00 3.20
Fred Norman
❑ 387 Johnny Podres 15.00 6.00
❑ 388 John Blanchard 15.00 6.00
❑ 389 Don Larsen 15.00 6.00
❑ 390 Bill Freehan 15.00 6.00

❑ 391	Mel McGaha MG	8.00	3.20
❑ 392	Bob Friend	15.00	6.00
❑ 393	Ed Kirkpatrick	8.00	3.20
❑ 394	Jim Hannan	8.00	3.20
❑ 395	Jim Ray Hart	8.00	3.20
❑ 396	Frank Bertaina	8.00	3.20
❑ 397	Jerry Buchek	8.00	3.20
❑ 398	Dan Neville	15.00	6.00
	Art Shamsky		
❑ 399	Ray Herbert	8.00	3.20
❑ 400	Harmon Killebrew	50.00	20.00
❑ 401	Carl Willey	8.00	3.20
❑ 402	Joe Amalfitano	8.00	3.20
❑ 403	Boston Red Sox	8.00	3.20
	Team Card		
❑ 404	Stan Williams	8.00	3.20
	(Listed as Indian		
	but Yankee cap)		
❑ 405	John Roseboro	20.00	8.00
❑ 406	Ralph Terry	15.00	6.00
❑ 407	Lee Maye	8.00	3.20
❑ 408	Larry Sherry	8.00	3.20
❑ 409	Jim Beauchamp	15.00	6.00
	Larry Dierker RC		
❑ 410	Luis Aparicio	25.00	10.00
❑ 411	Roger Craig	15.00	6.00
❑ 412	Bob Bailey	8.00	3.20
❑ 413	Hal Reniff	8.00	3.20
❑ 414	Al Lopez MG	15.00	6.00
❑ 415	Curt Flood	15.00	6.00
❑ 416	Jim Brewer	8.00	3.20
❑ 417	Ed Brinkman	8.00	3.20
❑ 418	Johnny Edwards	8.00	3.20
❑ 419	Ruben Amaro	8.00	3.20
❑ 420	Larry Jackson	8.00	3.20
❑ 421	Gary Dotter	8.00	3.20
	Jay Ward		
❑ 422	Aubrey Gatewood	8.00	3.20
❑ 423	Jesse Gonder	8.00	3.20
❑ 424	Gary Bell	8.00	3.20
❑ 425	Wayne Causey	8.00	3.20
❑ 426	Braves Team	8.00	3.20
❑ 427	Bob Saverine	8.00	3.20
❑ 428	Bob Shaw	8.00	3.20
❑ 429	Don Demeter	8.00	3.20
❑ 430	Gary Peters	8.00	3.20
❑ 431	Nelson Briles RC	15.00	6.00
	Wayne Spiezio		
❑ 432	Jim Grant	15.00	6.00
❑ 433	John Bateman	8.00	3.20
❑ 434	Dave Morehead	8.00	3.20
❑ 435	Willie Davis	15.00	6.00
❑ 436	Don Elston	8.00	3.20
❑ 437	Chico Cardenas	15.00	6.00
❑ 438	Harry Walker MG	8.00	3.20
❑ 439	Moe Drabowsky	15.00	6.00
❑ 440	Tom Tresh	15.00	6.00
❑ 441	Denny Lemaster	8.00	3.20
❑ 442	Vic Power	8.00	3.20
❑ 443	Checklist 6	12.00	2.40
❑ 444	Bob Hendley	8.00	3.20
❑ 445	Don Lock	8.00	3.20
❑ 446	Art Mahaffey	8.00	3.20
❑ 447	Julian Javier	15.00	6.00
❑ 448	Lee Stange	8.00	3.20
❑ 449	Jerry Hinsley	15.00	6.00
	Gary Kroll		
❑ 450	Elston Howard	15.00	6.00
❑ 451	Jim Owens	8.00	3.20
❑ 452	Gary Geiger	8.00	3.20
❑ 453	Willie Crawford	15.00	6.00
	John Werhas		
❑ 454	Ed Rakow	8.00	3.20
❑ 455	Norm Siebern	8.00	3.20
❑ 456	Bill Henry	8.00	3.20
❑ 457	Bob Kennedy MG	15.00	6.00
❑ 458	John Buzhardt	8.00	3.20
❑ 459	Frank Kostro	8.00	3.20
❑ 460	Richie Allen	40.00	16.00
❑ 461	Clay Carroll RC	50.00	20.00
	Phil Niekro		
❑ 462	Lew Krausse UER	8.00	3.20
	(Photo actually		
	Pete Lovrich)		
❑ 463	Manny Mota	15.00	6.00
❑ 464	Ron Piche	8.00	3.20
❑ 465	Tom Haller	15.00	6.00
❑ 466	Pete Craig	8.00	3.20
	Dick Nen		
❑ 467	Ray Washburn	8.00	3.20
❑ 468	Larry Brown	8.00	3.20
❑ 469	Don Nottebart	8.00	3.20
❑ 470	Yogi Berra P/CO	50.00	20.00
❑ 471	Billy Hoeft	8.00	3.20
❑ 472	Don Pavletich UER	8.00	3.20
	Listed as a pitcher		
❑ 473	Paul Blair	15.00	6.00
	Davey Johnson RC		
❑ 474	Cookie Rojas	15.00	6.00
❑ 475	Clete Boyer	15.00	6.00
❑ 476	Billy O'Dell	8.00	3.20
❑ 477	Fritz Ackley	150.00	60.00
	Steve Carlton RC		
❑ 478	Wilbur Wood	15.00	6.00
❑ 479	Ken Harrelson	15.00	6.00
❑ 480	Joel Horlen	8.00	3.20
❑ 481	Cleveland Indians	10.00	4.00
	Team Card		
❑ 482	Bob Priddy	8.00	3.20
❑ 483	George Smith	8.00	3.20
❑ 484	Ron Perranoski	20.00	8.00
❑ 485	Nellie Fox P/CO	25.00	10.00
❑ 486	Tom Egan	8.00	3.20
	Pat Rogan		
❑ 487	Woody Woodward	15.00	6.00
❑ 488	Ted Wills	8.00	3.20
❑ 489	Gene Mauch MG	15.00	6.00
❑ 490	Earl Battey	8.00	3.20
❑ 491	Tracy Stallard	8.00	3.20
❑ 492	Gene Freese	8.00	3.20
❑ 493	Bill Roman	8.00	3.20
	Bruce Brubaker		
❑ 494	Jay Ritchie	8.00	3.20
❑ 495	Joe Christopher	8.00	3.20
❑ 496	Joe Cunningham	8.00	3.20
❑ 497	Ken Henderson	15.00	6.00
	Jack Hiatt		
❑ 498	Gene Stephens	8.00	3.20
❑ 499	Stu Miller	15.00	6.00
❑ 500	Eddie Mathews	40.00	16.00
❑ 501	Ralph Gagliano	8.00	3.20
	Jim Rittwage		
❑ 502	Don Cardwell	8.00	3.20
❑ 503	Phil Gagliano	8.00	3.20
❑ 504	Jerry Grote	15.00	6.00
❑ 505	Ray Culp	8.00	3.20
❑ 506	Sam Mele MG	8.00	3.20
❑ 507	Sammy Ellis	8.00	3.20
❑ 508	Checklist 7	12.00	2.40
❑ 509	Bob Guindon	8.00	3.20
	Gerry Vezendy		
❑ 510	Ernie Banks	80.00	32.00
❑ 511	Ron Locke	8.00	3.20
❑ 512	Cap Peterson	8.00	3.20
❑ 513	New York Yankees	40.00	16.00
	Team Card		
❑ 514	Joe Azcue	8.00	3.20
❑ 515	Vern Law	15.00	6.00
❑ 516	Al Weis	8.00	3.20
❑ 517	Paul Schaal	15.00	6.00
	Jack Warner		
❑ 518	Ken Rowe	8.00	3.20
❑ 519	Bob Uecker UER	30.00	12.00
	(Posing as a left-		
	handed batter)		
❑ 520	Tony Cloninger	8.00	3.20
❑ 521	Dave Bennett	8.00	3.20
	Morrie Stevens		
❑ 522	Hank Aguirre	8.00	3.20
❑ 523	Mike Brumley SP	12.00	4.80
❑ 524	Dave Giusti SP	12.00	4.80
❑ 525	Eddie Bressoud	8.00	3.20
❑ 526	Rene Lachemann	80.00	32.00
	Johnny Odom		
	Jim Hunter RC UER		
	(Tim on back)		
	Skip Lockwood SP		
❑ 527	Jeff Torborg SP	12.00	4.80
❑ 528	George Altman	8.00	3.20
❑ 529	Jerry Fosnow SP	12.00	4.80
❑ 530	Jim Maloney	15.00	6.00
❑ 531	Chuck Hiller	8.00	3.20
❑ 532	Hector Lopez	15.00	6.00
❑ 533	Dan Napoleon	25.00	10.00
	Ron Swoboda RC		
	Tug McGraw RC		
	Jim Bethke SP		
❑ 534	John Herrnstein	8.00	3.20
❑ 535	Jack Kralick SP	12.00	4.80
❑ 536	Andre Rodgers SP	12.00	4.80
❑ 537	Marcelino Lopez	8.00	3.20
	Phil Roof		
	Rudy May RC		
❑ 538	C.Dressen SP MG	12.00	4.80
❑ 539	Herm Starrette	8.00	3.20
❑ 540	Lou Brock SP	50.00	20.00
❑ 541	Greg Bollo	8.00	3.20
	Bob Locker		
❑ 542	Lou Klimchock	8.00	3.20
❑ 543	Ed Connolly SP	12.00	4.80
❑ 544	Howie Reed	8.00	3.20
❑ 545	Jesus Alou SP	15.00	6.00
❑ 546	Bill Davis	8.00	3.20
	Mike Hedlund		
	Ray Barker		
	Floyd Weaver		
❑ 547	Jake Wood SP	12.00	4.80
❑ 548	Dick Stigman	8.00	3.20
❑ 549	Roberto Pena	20.00	8.00
	Glenn Beckert RC		
❑ 550	Mel Stottlemyre SP RC	30.00	12.00
❑ 551	New York Mets SP	30.00	12.00
	Team Card		
❑ 552	Julio Gotay	8.00	3.20
❑ 553	Dan Coombs	8.00	3.20
	Gene Ratliff		
	Jack McClure		
❑ 554	Chico Ruiz SP	12.00	4.80
❑ 555	Jack Baldschun SP	12.00	4.80
❑ 556	Red Schoendienst	25.00	10.00
	SP MG		
❑ 557	Jose Santiago	8.00	3.20
❑ 558	Tommie Sisk	8.00	3.20
❑ 559	Ed Bailey SP	12.00	4.80
❑ 560	Boog Powell SP	25.00	10.00
❑ 561	Dennis Daboll	15.00	6.00
	Mike Kekich		
	Hector Valle		
	Jim Lefebvre RC		
❑ 562	Billy Moran	8.00	3.20
❑ 563	Julio Navarro	8.00	3.20
❑ 564	Mel Nelson	8.00	3.20
❑ 565	Ernie Broglio SP	12.00	4.80
❑ 566	Gil Blanco	12.00	4.80
	Ross Moschitto		
	Art Lopez SP		
❑ 567	Tommie Aaron	8.00	3.20
❑ 568	Ron Taylor SP	12.00	4.80
❑ 569	Gino Cimoli SP	12.00	4.80
❑ 570	Claude Osteen SP	15.00	6.00
❑ 571	Ossie Virgil SP	12.00	4.80
❑ 572	Baltimore Orioles SP	25.00	10.00
	Team Card		
❑ 573	Jim Lonborg RC	25.00	10.00
	Gerry Moses		
	Bill Schlesinger		
	Mike Ryan SP		
❑ 574	Roy Sievers	15.00	6.00
❑ 575	Jose Pagan	8.00	3.20
❑ 576	Terry Fox SP	12.00	4.80
❑ 577	Darold Knowles	12.00	4.80
	Don Buschhorn		
	Richie Scheinblum SP		
❑ 578	Camilo Carreon SP	12.00	4.80
❑ 579	Dick Smith SP	12.00	4.80
❑ 580	Jimmie Hall SP	12.00	4.80
❑ 581	Tony Perez RC	80.00	32.00
	Dave Ricketts		
	Kevin Collins SP		
❑ 582	Bob Schmidt SP	12.00	4.80
❑ 583	Wes Covington SP	12.00	4.80
❑ 584	Harry Bright	15.00	6.00
❑ 585	Hank Fischer	8.00	3.20
❑ 586	Tom McCraw SP	12.00	4.80
❑ 587	Joe Sparma	8.00	3.20
❑ 588	Lenny Green	8.00	3.20
❑ 589	Frank Linzy	12.00	4.80
	Bob Schroder SP		

		NM	Ex
❑ 590	John Wyatt	8.00	3.20
❑ 591	Bob Skinner SP	12.00	4.80
❑ 592	Frank Bork SP	12.00	4.80
❑ 593	Jackie Moore RC	12.00	4.80
	John Sullivan SP		
❑ 594	Joe Gaines	8.00	3.20
❑ 595	Don Lee	8.00	3.20
❑ 596	Don Landrum SP	12.00	4.80
❑ 597	Joe Nossek	8.00	3.20
	John Sevcik		
	Dick Reese		
❑ 598	Al Downing SP	25.00	7.50

1966 Topps

	NM	Ex
COMPLETE SET (598)	4000.00	1600.00
COMMON CARD (1-109)	1.50	.60
COMMON (110-283)	2.00	.80
COMMON (284-370)	3.00	1.20
COMMON (371-446)	5.00	2.00
COMMON (447-522)	10.00	4.00
COMMON (523-598)	15.00	6.00
COMMON SP (523-598)	30.00	12.00
WRAPPER (5-CENT)	25.00	10.00

		NM	Ex
❑ 1	Willie Mays	250.00	95.00
❑ 2	Ted Abernathy	1.50	.60
❑ 3	Sam Mele MG	1.50	.60
❑ 4	Ray Culp	1.50	.60
❑ 5	Jim Fregosi	2.00	.80
❑ 6	Chuck Schilling	1.50	.60
❑ 7	Tracy Stallard	1.50	.60
❑ 8	Floyd Robinson	1.50	.60
❑ 9	Clete Boyer	2.00	.80
❑ 10	Tony Cloninger	1.50	.60
❑ 11	Brant Alyea	1.50	.60
	Pete Craig		
❑ 12	John Tsitouris	1.50	.60
❑ 13	Lou Johnson	2.00	.80
❑ 14	Norm Siebern	1.50	.60
❑ 15	Vern Law	2.00	.80
❑ 16	Larry Brown	1.50	.60
❑ 17	John Stephenson	1.50	.60
❑ 18	Roland Sheldon	1.50	.60
❑ 19	San Francisco Giants	5.00	2.00
	Team Card		
❑ 20	Willie Horton	2.00	.80
❑ 21	Don Nottebart	1.50	.60
❑ 22	Joe Nossek	1.50	.60
❑ 23	Jack Sanford	1.50	.60
❑ 24	Don Kessinger RC	4.00	1.60
❑ 25	Pete Ward	1.50	.60
❑ 26	Ray Sadecki	1.50	.60
❑ 27	Darold Knowles	1.50	.60
	Andy Etchebarren		
❑ 28	Phil Niekro	20.00	8.00
❑ 29	Mike Brumley	1.50	.60
❑ 30	Pete Rose DP UER	100.00	40.00
	1963 Hit total is wrong		
❑ 31	Jack Cullen	2.00	.80
❑ 32	Adolfo Phillips	1.50	.60
❑ 33	Jim Pagliaroni	1.50	.60
❑ 34	Checklist 1	8.00	1.60
❑ 35	Ron Swoboda	4.00	1.60
❑ 36	Jim Hunter UER	20.00	8.00
	Stats say 1963 and 1964 should be 1964 and 1965		
❑ 37	Billy Herman MG	2.00	.80
❑ 38	Ron Nischwitz	1.50	.60
❑ 39	Ken Henderson	1.50	.60
❑ 40	Jim Grant	1.50	.60
❑ 41	Don LeJohn	1.50	.60
❑ 42	Aubrey Gatewood	1.50	.60
❑ 43A	Don Landrum	2.00	.80
	(Dark button on pants showing)		
❑ 43B	Don Landrum	20.00	8.00
	(Button on pants partially airbrushed)		
❑ 43C	Don Landrum	2.00	.80
	(Button on pants not showing)		
❑ 44	Bill Davis	1.50	.60
	Tom Kelley		
❑ 45	Jim Gentile	2.00	.80
❑ 46	Howie Koplitz	1.50	.60
❑ 47	J.C. Martin	1.50	.60
❑ 48	Paul Blair	2.00	.80
❑ 49	Woody Woodward	2.00	.80
❑ 50	Mickey Mantle DP	300.00	100.00
❑ 51	Gordon Richardson	1.50	.60
❑ 52	Wes Covington	4.00	1.60
	Johnny Callison		
❑ 53	Bob Duliba	1.50	.60
❑ 54	Jose Pagan	1.50	.60
❑ 55	Ken Harrelson	2.00	.80
❑ 56	Sandy Valdespino	1.50	.60
❑ 57	Jim Lefebvre	2.00	.80
❑ 58	Dave Wickersham	1.50	.60
❑ 59	Reds Team	5.00	2.00
❑ 60	Curt Flood	4.00	1.60
❑ 61	Bob Bolin	1.50	.60
❑ 62A	Merritt Ranew	2.00	.80
	(With sold line)		
❑ 62B	Merritt Ranew	30.00	12.00
	(Without sold line)		
❑ 63	Jim Stewart	1.50	.60
❑ 64	Bob Bruce	1.50	.60
❑ 65	Leon Wagner	1.50	.60
❑ 66	Al Weis	1.50	.60
❑ 67	Cleon Jones	4.00	1.60
	Dick Selma		
❑ 68	Hal Reniff	1.50	.60
❑ 69	Ken Hamlin	1.50	.60
❑ 70	Carl Yastrzemski	30.00	12.00
❑ 71	Frank Carpin	1.50	.60
❑ 72	Tony Perez	25.00	10.00
❑ 73	Jerry Zimmerman	1.50	.60
❑ 74	Don Mossi	2.00	.80
❑ 75	Tommy Davis	2.00	.80
❑ 76	Red Schoendienst MG	4.00	1.60
❑ 77	John Orsino	1.50	.60
❑ 78	Frank Linzy	1.50	.60
❑ 79	Joe Pepitone	4.00	1.60
❑ 80	Richie Allen	6.00	2.40
❑ 81	Ray Oyler	1.50	.60
❑ 82	Bob Hendley	1.50	.60
❑ 83	Albie Pearson	2.00	.80
❑ 84	Jim Beauchamp	1.50	.60
	Dick Kelley		
❑ 85	Eddie Fisher	1.50	.60
❑ 86	John Bateman	1.50	.60
❑ 87	Dan Napoleon	1.50	.60
❑ 88	Fred Whitfield	1.50	.60
❑ 89	Ted Davidson	1.50	.60
❑ 90	Luis Aparicio	8.00	3.20
❑ 91A	Bob Uecker TR	10.00	4.00
❑ 91B	Bob Uecker NTR	40.00	16.00
❑ 92	Yankees Team	15.00	6.00
❑ 93	Jim Lonborg	2.00	.80
❑ 94	Matty Alou	2.00	.80
❑ 95	Pete Richert	1.50	.60
❑ 96	Felipe Alou	4.00	1.60
❑ 97	Jim Merritt	1.50	.60
❑ 98	Don Demeter	1.50	.60
❑ 99	Willie Stargell	6.00	2.40
	Donn Clendenon		
❑ 100	Sandy Koufax	100.00	32.00
❑ 101A	Checklist 2	15.00	3.00
	(115 W. Spahn) ERR		
❑ 101B	Checklist 2	10.00	2.00
	(115 Bill Henry) COR		
❑ 102	Ed Kirkpatrick	1.50	.60
❑ 103A	Dick Groat TR	2.00	.80
❑ 103B	Dick Groat NTR	40.00	16.00
❑ 104A	Alex Johnson TR	2.00	.80
❑ 104B	Alex Johnson NTR	30.00	12.00
❑ 105	Milt Pappas	2.00	.80
❑ 106	Rusty Staub	4.00	1.60
❑ 107	Larry Stahl	1.50	.60
	Ron Tompkins		
❑ 108	Bobby Klaus	1.50	.60
❑ 109	Ralph Terry	2.00	.80
❑ 110	Ernie Banks	30.00	12.00
❑ 111	Gary Peters	2.00	.80
❑ 112	Manny Mota	4.00	1.60
❑ 113	Hank Aguirre	2.00	.80
❑ 114	Jim Gosger	2.00	.80
❑ 115	Bill Henry	2.00	.80
❑ 116	Walter Alston MG	6.00	2.40
❑ 117	Jake Gibbs	2.00	.80
❑ 118	Mike McCormick	2.00	.80
❑ 119	Art Shamsky	2.00	.80
❑ 120	Harmon Killebrew	15.00	6.00
❑ 121	Ray Herbert	2.00	.80
❑ 122	Joe Gaines	2.00	.80
❑ 123	Frank Bork	2.00	.80
	Jerry May		
❑ 124	Tug McGraw	4.00	1.60
❑ 125	Lou Brock	20.00	8.00
❑ 126	Jim Palmer RC UER	100.00	40.00
	Described as a lefthander on card back		
❑ 127	Ken Berry	2.00	.80
❑ 128	Jim Landis	2.00	.80
❑ 129	Jack Kralick	2.00	.80
❑ 130	Joe Torre	6.00	2.40
❑ 131	Angels Team	5.00	2.00
❑ 132	Orlando Cepeda	8.00	3.20
❑ 133	Don McMahon	2.00	.80
❑ 134	Wes Parker	4.00	1.60
❑ 135	Dave Morehead	2.00	.80
❑ 136	Woody Held	2.00	.80
❑ 137	Pat Corrales	2.00	.80
❑ 138	Roger Repoz	2.00	.80
❑ 139	Byron Browne	2.00	.80
	Don Young		
❑ 140	Jim Maloney	4.00	1.60
❑ 141	Tom McCraw	2.00	.80
❑ 142	Don Dennis	2.00	.80
❑ 143	Jose Tartabull	4.00	1.60
❑ 144	Don Schwall	2.00	.80
❑ 145	Bill Freehan	4.00	1.60
❑ 146	George Altman	2.00	.80
❑ 147	Lum Harris MG	2.00	.80
❑ 148	Bob Johnson	2.00	.80
❑ 149	Dick Nen	2.00	.80
❑ 150	Rocky Colavito	8.00	3.20
❑ 151	Gary Wagner	2.00	.80
❑ 152	Frank Malzone	4.00	1.60
❑ 153	Rico Carty	4.00	1.60
❑ 154	Chuck Hiller	2.00	.80
❑ 155	Marcelino Lopez	2.00	.80
❑ 156	Dick Schofield	2.00	.80
	Hal Lanier		
❑ 157	Rene Lachemann	2.00	.80
❑ 158	Jim Brewer	2.00	.80
❑ 159	Chico Ruiz	2.00	.80
❑ 160	Whitey Ford	30.00	12.00
❑ 161	Jerry Lumpe	2.00	.80
❑ 162	Lee Maye	2.00	.80
❑ 163	Tito Francona	2.00	.80
❑ 164	Tommie Agee	4.00	1.60
	Marv Staehle		
❑ 165	Don Lock	2.00	.80
❑ 166	Chris Krug	2.00	.80
❑ 167	Boog Powell	6.00	2.40
❑ 168	Dan Osinski	2.00	.80
❑ 169	Duke Sims	2.00	.80
❑ 170	Cookie Rojas	4.00	1.60
❑ 171	Nick Willhite	2.00	.80
❑ 172	Mets Team	5.00	2.00
❑ 173	Al Spangler	2.00	.80
❑ 174	Ron Taylor	2.00	.80
❑ 175	Bert Campaneris	4.00	1.60
❑ 176	Jim Davenport	2.00	.80
❑ 177	Hector Lopez	2.00	.80
❑ 178	Bob Tillman	2.00	.80

❑ 179 Dennis Aust	4.00	1.60
Bob Tolan		
❑ 180 Vada Pinson	4.00	1.60
❑ 181 Al Worthington	2.00	.80
❑ 182 Jerry Lynch	2.00	.80
❑ 183A Checklist 3	8.00	1.60
(Large print on front)		
❑ 183B Checklist 3	8.00	1.60
(Small print on front)		
❑ 184 Denis Menke	2.00	.80
❑ 185 Bob Buhl	4.00	1.60
❑ 186 Ruben Amaro	2.00	.80
❑ 187 Chuck Dressen MG	4.00	1.60
❑ 188 Al Luplow	2.00	.80
❑ 189 John Roseboro	4.00	1.60
❑ 190 Jimmie Hall	2.00	.80
❑ 191 Darrell Sutherland	2.00	.80
❑ 192 Vic Power	4.00	1.60
❑ 193 Dave McNally	4.00	1.60
❑ 194 Senators Team	5.00	2.00
❑ 195 Joe Morgan	15.00	6.00
❑ 196 Don Pavletich	2.00	.80
❑ 197 Sonny Siebert	2.00	.80
❑ 198 Mickey Stanley RC	6.00	2.40
❑ 199 Bill Skowron	4.00	1.60
Johnny Romano		
Floyd Robinson		
❑ 200 Eddie Mathews	15.00	6.00
❑ 201 Jim Dickson	2.00	.80
❑ 202 Clay Dalrymple	2.00	.80
❑ 203 Jose Santiago	2.00	.80
❑ 204 Cubs Team	5.00	2.00
❑ 205 Tom Tresh	4.00	1.60
❑ 206 Al Jackson	2.00	.80
❑ 207 Frank Quilici	2.00	.80
❑ 208 Bob Miller	2.00	.80
❑ 209 Fritz Fisher	4.00	1.60
John Hiller RC		
❑ 210 Bill Mazeroski	8.00	3.20
❑ 211 Frank Kreutzer	2.00	.80
❑ 212 Ed Kranepool	4.00	1.60
❑ 213 Fred Newman	2.00	.80
❑ 214 Tommy Harper	4.00	1.60
❑ 215 Bob Clemente	50.00	20.00
Hank Aaron		
Willie Mays LL		
❑ 216 Tony Oliva	5.00	2.00
Carl Yastrzemski		
Vic Davalillo LL		
❑ 217 Willie Mays	20.00	8.00
Willie McCovey		
Billy Williams LL		
❑ 218 Tony Conigliaro	5.00	2.00
Norm Cash		
Willie Horton LL		
❑ 219 Deron Johnson	12.00	4.80
Frank Robinson		
Willie Mays LL		
❑ 220 Rocky Colavito	5.00	2.00
Willie Horton		
Tony Oliva LL		
❑ 221 Sandy Koufax	12.00	4.80
Juan Marichal		
Vern Law LL		
❑ 222 Sam McDowell	5.00	2.00
Eddie Fisher		
Sonny Siebert LL		
❑ 223 Sandy Koufax	12.00	4.80
Tony Cloninger		
Don Drysdale LL		
❑ 224 Jim Grant	5.00	2.00
Mel Stottlemyre		
Jim Kaat LL		
❑ 225 Sandy Koufax	12.00	4.80
Bob Veale		
Bob Gibson LL		
❑ 226 Sam McDowell	5.00	2.00
Mickey Lolich		
Dennis McLain		
Sonny Siebert LL		
❑ 227 Russ Nixon	2.00	.80
❑ 228 Larry Dierker	4.00	1.60
❑ 229 Hank Bauer MG	4.00	1.60
❑ 230 Johnny Callison	4.00	1.60
❑ 231 Floyd Weaver	2.00	.80
❑ 232 Glenn Beckert	4.00	1.60
❑ 233 Dom Zanni	2.00	.80
❑ 234 Rich Beck	8.00	3.20
Roy White RC		
❑ 235 Don Cardwell	2.00	.80
❑ 236 Mike Hershberger	2.00	.80
❑ 237 Billy O'Dell	2.00	.80
❑ 238 Dodgers Team	5.00	2.00
❑ 239 Orlando Pena	2.00	.80
❑ 240 Earl Battey	2.00	.80
❑ 241 Dennis Ribant	2.00	.80
❑ 242 Jesus Alou	2.00	.80
❑ 243 Nelson Briles	4.00	1.60
❑ 244 Chuck Harrison	2.00	.80
Sonny Jackson		
❑ 245 John Buzhardt	2.00	.80
❑ 246 Ed Bailey	2.00	.80
❑ 247 Carl Warwick	2.00	.80
❑ 248 Pete Mikkelsen	2.00	.80
❑ 249 Bill Rigney MG	2.00	.80
❑ 250 Sammy Ellis	2.00	.80
❑ 251 Ed Brinkman	2.00	.80
❑ 252 Denny Lemaster	2.00	.80
❑ 253 Don Wert	2.00	.80
❑ 254 Fergie Jenkins RC	60.00	24.00
Bill Sorrell		
❑ 255 Willie Stargell	20.00	8.00
❑ 256 Lew Krausse	2.00	.80
❑ 257 Jeff Torborg	4.00	1.60
❑ 258 Dave Giusti	2.00	.80
❑ 259 Boston Red Sox	5.00	2.00
Team Card		
❑ 260 Bob Shaw	2.00	.80
❑ 261 Ron Hansen	2.00	.80
❑ 262 Jack Hamilton	2.00	.80
❑ 263 Tom Egan	2.00	.80
❑ 264 Andy Kosco	2.00	.80
Ted Uhlaender		
❑ 265 Stu Miller	4.00	1.60
❑ 266 Pedro Gonzalez UER	2.00	.80
(Misspelled Gonzales on card back)		
❑ 267 Joe Sparma	2.00	.80
❑ 268 John Blanchard	2.00	.80
❑ 269 Don Heffner MG	2.00	.80
❑ 270 Claude Osteen	4.00	1.60
❑ 271 Hal Lanier	2.00	.80
❑ 272 Jack Baldschun	2.00	.80
❑ 273 Bob Aspromonte	4.00	1.60
Rusty Staub		
❑ 274 Buster Narum	2.00	.80
❑ 275 Tim McCarver	4.00	1.60
❑ 276 Jim Bouton	4.00	1.60
❑ 277 George Thomas	2.00	.80
❑ 278 Cal Koonce	2.00	.80
❑ 279A Checklist 4	8.00	1.60
(Player's cap black)		
❑ 279B Checklist 4	8.00	1.60
(Player's cap red)		
❑ 280 Bobby Knoop	2.00	.80
❑ 281 Bruce Howard	2.00	.80
❑ 282 Johnny Lewis	2.00	.80
❑ 283 Jim Perry	4.00	1.60
❑ 284 Bobby Wine	3.00	1.20
❑ 285 Luis Tiant	5.00	2.00
❑ 286 Gary Geiger	3.00	1.20
❑ 287 Jack Aker	3.00	1.20
❑ 288 Bill Singer	60.00	20.00
Don Sutton RC		
❑ 289 Larry Sherry	3.00	1.20
❑ 290 Ron Santo	5.00	2.00
❑ 291 Moe Drabowsky	5.00	2.00
❑ 292 Jim Coker	3.00	1.20
❑ 293 Mike Shannon	5.00	2.00
❑ 294 Steve Ridzik	3.00	1.20
❑ 295 Jim Ray Hart	5.00	2.00
❑ 296 Johnny Keane MG	5.00	2.00
❑ 297 Jim Owens	3.00	1.20
❑ 298 Rico Petrocelli	5.00	2.00
❑ 299 Lou Burdette	5.00	2.00
❑ 300 Bob Clemente	150.00	60.00
❑ 301 Greg Bollo	3.00	1.20
❑ 302 Ernie Bowman	3.00	1.20
❑ 303 Cleveland Indians	5.00	2.00
Team Card		
❑ 304 John Herrnstein	3.00	1.20
❑ 305 Camilo Pascual	5.00	2.00
❑ 306 Ty Cline	3.00	1.20
❑ 307 Clay Carroll	5.00	2.00
❑ 308 Tom Haller	5.00	2.00
❑ 309 Diego Segui	3.00	1.20
❑ 310 Frank Robinson	40.00	16.00
❑ 311 Tommy Helms	5.00	2.00
Dick Simpson		
❑ 312 Bob Saverine	3.00	1.20
❑ 313 Chris Zachary	3.00	1.20
❑ 314 Hector Valle	3.00	1.20
❑ 315 Norm Cash	5.00	2.00
❑ 316 Jack Fisher	3.00	1.20
❑ 317 Dalton Jones	3.00	1.20
❑ 318 Harry Walker MG	3.00	1.20
❑ 319 Gene Freese	3.00	1.20
❑ 320 Bob Gibson	25.00	10.00
❑ 321 Rick Reichardt	3.00	1.20
❑ 322 Bill Faul	3.00	1.20
❑ 323 Ray Barker	3.00	1.20
❑ 324 John Boozer	3.00	1.20
❑ 325 Vic Davalillo	3.00	1.20
❑ 326 Braves Team	5.00	2.00
❑ 327 Bernie Allen	3.00	1.20
❑ 328 Jerry Grote	5.00	2.00
❑ 329 Pete Charton	3.00	1.20
❑ 330 Ron Fairly	5.00	2.00
❑ 331 Ron Herbel	3.00	1.20
❑ 332 Bill Bryan	3.00	1.20
❑ 333 Joe Coleman RC	3.00	1.20
Jim French		
❑ 334 Marty Keough	3.00	1.20
❑ 335 Juan Pizarro	3.00	1.20
❑ 336 Gene Alley	5.00	2.00
❑ 337 Fred Gladding	3.00	1.20
❑ 338 Dal Maxvill	3.00	1.20
❑ 339 Del Crandall	5.00	2.00
❑ 340 Dean Chance	5.00	2.00
❑ 341 Wes Westrum MG	5.00	2.00
❑ 342 Bob Humphreys	3.00	1.20
❑ 343 Joe Christopher	3.00	1.20
❑ 344 Steve Blass	5.00	2.00
❑ 345 Bob Allison	5.00	2.00
❑ 346 Mike de la Hoz	3.00	1.20
❑ 347 Phil Regan	5.00	2.00
❑ 348 Orioles Team	8.00	3.20
❑ 349 Cap Peterson	3.00	1.20
❑ 350 Mel Stottlemyre	8.00	3.20
❑ 351 Fred Valentine	3.00	1.20
❑ 352 Bob Aspromonte	3.00	1.20
❑ 353 Al McBean	3.00	1.20
❑ 354 Smoky Burgess	5.00	2.00
❑ 355 Wade Blasingame	3.00	1.20
❑ 356 Owen Johnson	3.00	1.20
Ken Sanders		
❑ 357 Gerry Arrigo	3.00	1.20
❑ 358 Charlie Smith	3.00	1.20
❑ 359 Johnny Briggs	3.00	1.20
❑ 360 Ron Hunt	3.00	1.20
❑ 361 Tom Satriano	3.00	1.20
❑ 362 Gates Brown	5.00	2.00
❑ 363 Checklist 5	10.00	2.00
❑ 364 Nate Oliver	3.00	1.20
❑ 365 Roger Maris UER	50.00	20.00
Wrong birth year listed on card		
❑ 366 Wayne Causey	3.00	1.20
❑ 367 Mel Nelson	3.00	1.20
❑ 368 Charlie Lau	5.00	2.00
❑ 369 Jim King	3.00	1.20
❑ 370 Chico Cardenas	3.00	1.20
❑ 371 Lee Stange	5.00	2.00
❑ 372 Harvey Kuenn	8.00	3.20
❑ 373 Jack Hiatt	8.00	3.20
Dick Estelle		
❑ 374 Bob Locker	5.00	2.00
❑ 375 Donn Clendenon	8.00	3.20
❑ 376 Paul Schaal	5.00	2.00
❑ 377 Turk Farrell	5.00	2.00
❑ 378 Dick Tracewski	5.00	2.00
❑ 379 Cardinal Team	10.00	4.00
❑ 380 Tony Conigliaro	10.00	4.00
❑ 381 Hank Fischer	5.00	2.00
❑ 382 Phil Roof	5.00	2.00
❑ 383 Jackie Brandt	5.00	2.00
❑ 384 Al Downing	8.00	3.20

❑ 385	Ken Boyer	10.00	4.00
❑ 386	Gil Hodges MG	8.00	3.20
❑ 387	Howie Reed	5.00	2.00
❑ 388	Don Mincher	5.00	2.00
❑ 389	Jim O'Toole	8.00	3.20
❑ 390	Brooks Robinson	50.00	20.00
❑ 391	Chuck Hinton	5.00	2.00
❑ 392	Bill Hands	8.00	3.20
	Randy Hundley RC		
❑ 393	George Brunet	5.00	2.00
❑ 394	Ron Brand	5.00	2.00
❑ 395	Len Gabrielson	5.00	2.00
❑ 396	Jerry Stephenson	5.00	2.00
❑ 397	Bill White	8.00	3.20
❑ 398	Danny Cater	5.00	2.00
❑ 399	Ray Washburn	5.00	2.00
❑ 400	Zoilo Versalles	8.00	3.20
❑ 401	Ken McMullen	5.00	2.00
❑ 402	Jim Hickman	5.00	2.00
❑ 403	Fred Talbot	5.00	2.00
❑ 404	Pittsburgh Pirates	10.00	4.00
	Team Card		
❑ 405	Elston Howard	8.00	3.20
❑ 406	Joey Jay	5.00	2.00
❑ 407	John Kennedy	5.00	2.00
❑ 408	Lee Thomas	8.00	3.20
❑ 409	Billy Hoeft	5.00	2.00
❑ 410	Al Kaline	40.00	16.00
❑ 411	Gene Mauch MG	5.00	2.00
❑ 412	Sam Bowens	5.00	2.00
❑ 413	Johnny Romano	5.00	2.00
❑ 414	Dan Coombs	5.00	2.00
❑ 415	Max Alvis	5.00	2.00
❑ 416	Phil Ortega	5.00	2.00
❑ 417	Jim McGlothlin	5.00	2.00
	Ed Sukla		
❑ 418	Phil Gagliano	5.00	2.00
❑ 419	Mike Ryan	5.00	2.00
❑ 420	Juan Marichal	15.00	6.00
❑ 421	Roy McMillan	8.00	3.20
❑ 422	Ed Charles	5.00	2.00
❑ 423	Ernie Broglio	5.00	2.00
❑ 424	Lee May RC	10.00	4.00
	Darrell Osteen		
❑ 425	Bob Veale	8.00	3.20
❑ 426	White Sox Team	10.00	4.00
❑ 427	John Miller	5.00	2.00
❑ 428	Sandy Alomar	5.00	2.00
❑ 429	Bill Monbouquette	5.00	2.00
❑ 430	Don Drysdale	20.00	8.00
❑ 431	Walt Bond	5.00	2.00
❑ 432	Bob Heffner	5.00	2.00
❑ 433	Alvin Dark MG	8.00	3.20
❑ 434	Willie Kirkland	5.00	2.00
❑ 435	Jim Bunning	15.00	6.00
❑ 436	Julian Javier	8.00	3.20
❑ 437	Al Stanek	5.00	2.00
❑ 438	Willie Smith	5.00	2.00
❑ 439	Pedro Ramos	5.00	2.00
❑ 440	Deron Johnson	8.00	3.20
❑ 441	Tommie Sisk	5.00	2.00
❑ 442	Ed Barnowski	5.00	2.00
	Eddie Watt		
❑ 443	Bill Wakefield	3.00	1.20
❑ 444	Checklist 6	10.00	2.00
❑ 445	Jim Kaat	10.00	4.00
❑ 446	Mack Jones	5.00	2.00
❑ 447	Dick Ellsworth UER	15.00	6.00
	(Photo actually		
	Ken Hubbs)		
❑ 448	Eddie Stanky MG	10.00	4.00
❑ 449	Joe Moeller	10.00	4.00
❑ 450	Tony Oliva	15.00	6.00
❑ 451	Barry Latman	10.00	4.00
❑ 452	Joe Azcue	10.00	4.00
❑ 453	Ron Kline	10.00	4.00
❑ 454	Jerry Buchek	10.00	4.00
❑ 455	Mickey Lolich	15.00	6.00
❑ 456	Darrell Brandon	10.00	4.00
	Joe Foy		
❑ 457	Joe Gibbon	10.00	4.00
❑ 458	Manny Jiminez	10.00	4.00
❑ 459	Bill McCool	10.00	4.00
❑ 460	Curt Blefary	10.00	4.00
❑ 461	Roy Face	15.00	6.00
❑ 462	Bob Rodgers	10.00	4.00
❑ 463	Philadelphia Phillies	15.00	6.00
	Team Card		
❑ 464	Larry Bearnarth	10.00	4.00
❑ 465	Don Buford	10.00	4.00
❑ 466	Ken Johnson	10.00	4.00
❑ 467	Vic Roznovsky	10.00	4.00
❑ 468	Johnny Podres	15.00	6.00
❑ 469	Bobby Murcer RC	30.00	12.00
	Dooley Womack		
❑ 470	Sam McDowell	15.00	6.00
❑ 471	Bob Skinner	10.00	4.00
❑ 472	Terry Fox	10.00	4.00
❑ 473	Rich Rollins	10.00	4.00
❑ 474	Dick Schofield	10.00	4.00
❑ 475	Dick Radatz	10.00	4.00
❑ 476	Bobby Bragan MG	10.00	4.00
❑ 477	Steve Barber	10.00	4.00
❑ 478	Tony Gonzalez	10.00	4.00
❑ 479	Jim Hannan	10.00	4.00
❑ 480	Dick Stuart	10.00	4.00
❑ 481	Bob Lee	10.00	4.00
❑ 482	John Boccabella	10.00	4.00
	Dave Dowling		
❑ 483	Joe Nuxhall	10.00	4.00
❑ 484	Wes Covington	10.00	4.00
❑ 485	Bob Bailey	10.00	4.00
❑ 486	Tommy John	15.00	6.00
❑ 487	Al Ferrara	10.00	4.00
❑ 488	George Banks	10.00	4.00
❑ 489	Curt Simmons	10.00	4.00
❑ 490	Bobby Richardson	25.00	10.00
❑ 491	Dennis Bennett	10.00	4.00
❑ 492	Athletics Team	15.00	6.00
❑ 493	Johnny Klippstein	10.00	4.00
❑ 494	Gordy Coleman	10.00	4.00
❑ 495	Dick McAuliffe	15.00	6.00
❑ 496	Lindy McDaniel	10.00	4.00
❑ 497	Chris Cannizzaro	10.00	4.00
❑ 498	Luke Walker	10.00	4.00
	Woody Fryman		
❑ 499	Wally Bunker	10.00	4.00
❑ 500	Hank Aaron	125.00	50.00
❑ 501	John O'Donoghue	10.00	4.00
❑ 502	Lenny Green UER	10.00	4.00
	Born: aJn. 6, 1933		
❑ 503	Steve Hamilton	15.00	6.00
❑ 504	Grady Hatton MG	10.00	4.00
❑ 505	Jose Cardenal	10.00	4.00
❑ 506	Bo Belinsky	15.00	6.00
❑ 507	Johnny Edwards	10.00	4.00
❑ 508	Steve Hargan RC	15.00	6.00
❑ 509	Jake Wood	10.00	4.00
❑ 510	Hoyt Wilhelm	25.00	10.00
❑ 511	Bob Barton	10.00	4.00
	Tito Fuentes RC		
❑ 512	Dick Stigman	10.00	4.00
❑ 513	Camilo Carreon	10.00	4.00
❑ 514	Hal Woodeshick	10.00	4.00
❑ 515	Frank Howard	15.00	6.00
❑ 516	Eddie Bressoud	10.00	4.00
❑ 517A	Checklist 7	15.00	3.00
	529 White Sox Rookies		
	544 Cardinals Rookies		
❑ 517B	Checklist 7	15.00	3.00
	529 W. Sox Rookies		
	544 Cards Rookies		
❑ 518	Herb Hippauf	10.00	4.00
	Arnie Umbach		
❑ 519	Bob Friend	15.00	6.00
❑ 520	Jim Wynn	15.00	6.00
❑ 521	John Wyatt	10.00	4.00
❑ 522	Phil Linz	10.00	4.00
❑ 523	Bob Sadowski	10.00	4.00
❑ 524	Ollie Brown	30.00	12.00
	Don Mason SP		
❑ 525	Gary Bell SP	30.00	12.00
❑ 526	Twins Team SP	100.00	40.00
❑ 527	Julio Navarro	15.00	6.00
❑ 528	Jesse Gonder SP	30.00	12.00
❑ 529	Lee Elia	15.00	6.00
	Dennis Higgins		
	Bill Voss		
❑ 530	Robin Roberts	50.00	20.00
❑ 531	Joe Cunningham	15.00	6.00
❑ 532	A.Monteagudo SP	30.00	12.00
❑ 533	Jerry Adair SP	30.00	12.00
❑ 534	Dave Eilers	15.00	6.00
	Rob Gardner		
❑ 535	Willie Davis SP	40.00	16.00
❑ 536	Dick Egan	15.00	6.00
❑ 537	Herman Franks MG	15.00	6.00
❑ 538	Bob Allen SP	30.00	12.00
❑ 539	Bill Heath	25.00	10.00
	Carroll Sembera		
❑ 540	Denny McLain SP	60.00	24.00
❑ 541	Gene Oliver SP	30.00	12.00
❑ 542	George Smith	15.00	6.00
❑ 543	Roger Craig SP	30.00	12.00
❑ 544	Joe Hoerner	30.00	12.00
	George Kernek		
	Jimy Williams RC UER SP		
	(Misspelled Jimmy		
	on card)		
❑ 545	Dick Green SP	30.00	12.00
❑ 546	Dwight Siebler	25.00	10.00
❑ 547	Horace Clarke RC SP	40.00	16.00
❑ 548	Gary Kroll SP	30.00	12.00
❑ 549	Al Closter	15.00	6.00
	Casey Cox		
❑ 550	Willie McCovey SP	100.00	40.00
❑ 551	Bob Purkey SP	30.00	12.00
❑ 552	Birdie Tebbetts	30.00	12.00
	MG SP		
❑ 553	Pat Garrett	15.00	6.00
	Jackie Warner		
❑ 554	Jim Northrup SP	30.00	12.00
❑ 555	Ron Perranoski SP	30.00	12.00
❑ 556	Mel Queen SP	30.00	12.00
❑ 557	Felix Mantilla SP	30.00	12.00
❑ 558	Guido Grilli	20.00	8.00
	Pete Magrini		
	George Scott RC		
❑ 559	Roberto Pena SP	30.00	12.00
❑ 560	Joel Horlen	15.00	6.00
❑ 561	Choo Choo Coleman SP	30.00	12.00
❑ 562	Russ Snyder	25.00	10.00
❑ 563	Pete Cimino	15.00	6.00
	Cesar Tovar		
❑ 564	Bob Chance SP	30.00	12.00
❑ 565	Jimmy Piersall SP	40.00	16.00
❑ 566	Mike Cuellar SP	30.00	12.00
❑ 567	Dick Howser SP	40.00	16.00
❑ 568	Paul Lindblad	15.00	6.00
	Ron Stone		
❑ 569	Orlando McFarlane SP	30.00	12.00
❑ 570	Art Mahaffey SP	30.00	12.00
❑ 571	Dave Roberts SP	30.00	12.00
❑ 572	Bob Priddy	15.00	6.00
❑ 573	Derrell Griffith	15.00	6.00
❑ 574	Bill Hepler	15.00	6.00
	Bill Murphy		
❑ 575	Earl Wilson	15.00	6.00
❑ 576	Dave Nicholson SP	30.00	12.00
❑ 577	Jack Lamabe SP	30.00	12.00
❑ 578	Chi Chi Olivo SP	30.00	12.00
❑ 579	Frank Bertaina	20.00	8.00
	Gene Brabender		
	Dave Johnson		
❑ 580	Billy Williams SP	60.00	24.00
❑ 581	Tony Martinez	15.00	6.00
❑ 582	Garry Roggenburk	15.00	6.00
❑ 583	Tigers Team SP UER	125.00	50.00
	Text on back states Tigers		
	finished third in 1965 instead		
	of fourth		
❑ 584	Frank Fernandez	15.00	6.00
	Fritz Peterson		
❑ 585	Tony Taylor	25.00	10.00
❑ 586	Claude Raymond SP	30.00	12.00
❑ 587	Dick Bertell	15.00	6.00
❑ 588	Chuck Dobson	15.00	6.00
	Ken Suarez		
❑ 589	Lou Klimchock SP	30.00	12.00
❑ 590	Bill Skowron SP	40.00	16.00
❑ 591	Bart Shirley	40.00	16.00
	Grant Jackson RC SP		
❑ 592	Andre Rodgers	15.00	6.00
❑ 593	Doug Camilli SP	30.00	12.00
❑ 594	Chico Salmon	15.00	6.00
❑ 595	Larry Jackson	15.00	6.00
❑ 596	Nate Colbert RC	30.00	12.00
	Greg Sims SP		

		NM	Ex
❑ 597	John Sullivan	15.00	6.00
❑ 598	Gaylord Perry SP	175.00	50.00

1967 Topps

	NM	Ex
COMPLETE SET (609)	5000.00	2000.00
COMMON CARD (1-109)	1.50	.60
COMMON (110-283)	2.00	.80
COMMON (284-370)	2.50	1.00
COMMON (371-457)	4.00	1.60
COMMON (458-533)	6.00	2.40
COMMON (534-609)	15.00	6.00
COMMON DP (534-609)	8.00	3.20
WRAPPER (5-CENT)	25.00	10.00

		NM	Ex
❑ 1	Frank Robinson	25.00	7.50
	Hank Bauer MG		
	Brooks Robinson DP		
❑ 2	Jack Hamilton	1.50	.60
❑ 3	Duke Sims	1.50	.60
❑ 4	Hal Lanier	1.50	.60
❑ 5	Whitey Ford UER	20.00	8.00
	(1953 listed as		
	1933 in stats on back)		
❑ 6	Dick Simpson	1.50	.60
❑ 7	Don McMahon	1.50	.60
❑ 8	Chuck Harrison	1.50	.60
❑ 9	Ron Hansen	1.50	.60
❑ 10	Matty Alou	4.00	1.60
❑ 11	Barry Moore	1.50	.60
❑ 12	Jim Campanis	4.00	1.60
	Bill Singer		
❑ 13	Joe Sparma	1.50	.60
❑ 14	Phil Linz	4.00	1.60
❑ 15	Earl Battey	1.50	.60
❑ 16	Bill Hands	1.50	.60
❑ 17	Jim Gosger	1.50	.60
❑ 18	Gene Oliver	1.50	.60
❑ 19	Jim McGlothlin	1.50	.60
❑ 20	Orlando Cepeda	8.00	3.20
❑ 21	Dave Bristol MG	1.50	.60
❑ 22	Gene Brabender	1.50	.60
❑ 23	Larry Elliot	1.50	.60
❑ 24	Bob Allen	1.50	.60
❑ 25	Elston Howard	4.00	1.60
❑ 26A	Bob Priddy NTR	30.00	12.00
❑ 26B	Bob Priddy TR	4.00	1.60
❑ 27	Bob Saverine	1.50	.60
❑ 28	Barry Latman	1.50	.60
❑ 29	Tom McCraw	1.50	.60
❑ 30	Al Kaline DP	20.00	8.00
❑ 31	Jim Brewer	1.50	.60
❑ 32	Bob Bailey	4.00	1.60
❑ 33	Sal Bando RC	6.00	2.40
	Randy Schwartz		
❑ 34	Pete Cimino	1.50	.60
❑ 35	Rico Carty	4.00	1.60
❑ 36	Bob Tillman	1.50	.60
❑ 37	Rick Wise	4.00	1.60
❑ 38	Bob Johnson	1.50	.60
❑ 39	Curt Simmons	4.00	1.60
❑ 40	Rick Reichardt	1.50	.60
❑ 41	Joe Hoerner	1.50	.60
❑ 42	Mets Team	10.00	4.00
❑ 43	Chico Salmon	1.50	.60
❑ 44	Joe Nuxhall	4.00	1.60
❑ 45	Roger Maris	50.00	20.00
❑ 45A	Roger Maris	1000.00	400.00
	Yankees listed as team		
	Blank Back		
❑ 46	Lindy McDaniel	4.00	1.60
❑ 47	Ken McMullen	1.50	.60
❑ 48	Bill Freehan	4.00	1.60
❑ 49	Roy Face	4.00	1.60
❑ 50	Tony Oliva	6.00	2.40
❑ 51	Dave Adlesh	1.50	.60
	Wes Bales		
❑ 52	Dennis Higgins	1.50	.60
❑ 53	Clay Dalrymple	1.50	.60
❑ 54	Dick Green	1.50	.60
❑ 55	Don Drysdale	15.00	6.00
❑ 56	Jose Tartabull	4.00	1.60
❑ 57	Pat Jarvis RC	4.00	1.60
❑ 58A	Paul Schaal	20.00	8.00
	Green Bat		
❑ 58B	Paul Schaal	1.50	.60
	Normal Colored Bat		
❑ 59	Ralph Terry	4.00	1.60
❑ 60	Luis Aparicio	8.00	3.20
❑ 61	Gordy Coleman	1.50	.60
❑ 62	Frank Robinson CL	8.00	1.60
❑ 63	Lou Brock	8.00	3.20
	Curt Flood		
❑ 64	Fred Valentine	1.50	.60
❑ 65	Tom Haller	4.00	1.60
❑ 66	Manny Mota	4.00	1.60
❑ 67	Ken Berry	1.50	.60
❑ 68	Bob Buhl	4.00	1.60
❑ 69	Vic Davalillo	1.50	.60
❑ 70	Ron Santo	6.00	2.40
❑ 71	Camilo Pascual	4.00	1.60
❑ 72	George Korince	1.50	.60
	(Photo actually		
	James Murray Brown)		
	John (Tom) Matchick		
❑ 73	Rusty Staub	6.00	2.40
❑ 74	Wes Stock	1.50	.60
❑ 75	George Scott	4.00	1.60
❑ 76	Jim Barbieri	1.50	.60
❑ 77	Dooley Womack	4.00	1.60
❑ 78	Pat Corrales	1.50	.60
❑ 79	Bubba Morton	1.50	.60
❑ 80	Jim Maloney	4.00	1.60
❑ 81	Eddie Stanky MG	4.00	1.60
❑ 82	Steve Barber	1.50	.60
❑ 83	Ollie Brown	1.50	.60
❑ 84	Tommie Sisk	1.50	.60
❑ 85	Johnny Callison	4.00	1.60
❑ 86A	Mike McCormick NTR	30.00	12.00
	(Senators on front		
	and Senators on back)		
❑ 86B	Mike McCormick TR	4.00	1.60
	(Traded line		
	at end of bio;		
	Senators on front,		
	but Giants on back)		
❑ 87	George Altman	1.50	.60
❑ 88	Mickey Lolich	4.00	1.60
❑ 89	Felix Millan	4.00	1.60
❑ 90	Jim Nash	1.50	.60
❑ 91	Johnny Lewis	1.50	.60
❑ 92	Ray Washburn	1.50	.60
❑ 93	Stan Bahnsen RC	4.00	1.60
	Bobby Murcer		
❑ 94	Ron Fairly	4.00	1.60
❑ 95	Sonny Siebert	1.50	.60
❑ 96	Art Shamsky	1.50	.60
❑ 97	Mike Cuellar	4.00	1.60
❑ 98	Rich Rollins	1.50	.60
❑ 99	Lee Stange	1.50	.60
❑ 100	Frank Robinson DP	15.00	6.00
❑ 101	Ken Johnson	1.50	.60
❑ 102	Philadelphia Phillies	4.00	1.60
	Team Card		
❑ 103	Mickey Mantle CL	20.00	4.00
❑ 104	Minnie Rojas	1.50	.60
❑ 105	Ken Boyer	6.00	2.40
❑ 106	Randy Hundley	4.00	1.60
❑ 107	Joel Horlen	1.50	.60
❑ 108	Alex Johnson	4.00	1.60
❑ 109	Rocky Colavito	6.00	2.40
	Leon Wagner		
❑ 110	Jack Aker	4.00	1.60
❑ 111	John Kennedy	2.00	.80
❑ 112	Dave Wickersham	2.00	.80
❑ 113	Dave Nicholson	2.00	.80
❑ 114	Jack Baldschun	2.00	.80
❑ 115	Paul Casanova	2.00	.80
❑ 116	Herman Franks MG	2.00	.80
❑ 117	Darrell Brandon	2.00	.80
❑ 118	Bernie Allen	2.00	.80
❑ 119	Wade Blasingame	2.00	.80
❑ 120	Floyd Robinson	2.00	.80
❑ 121	Eddie Bressoud	2.00	.80
❑ 122	George Brunet	2.00	.80
❑ 123	Jim Price	4.00	1.60
	Luke Walker		
❑ 124	Jim Stewart	2.00	.80
❑ 125	Moe Drabowsky	4.00	1.60
❑ 126	Tony Taylor	2.00	.80
❑ 127	John O'Donoghue	2.00	.80
❑ 128	Ed Spiezio	2.00	.80
❑ 129	Phil Roof	2.00	.80
❑ 130	Phil Regan	4.00	1.60
❑ 131	Yankees Team	10.00	4.00
❑ 132	Ozzie Virgil	2.00	.80
❑ 133	Ron Kline	2.00	.80
❑ 134	Gates Brown	6.00	2.40
❑ 135	Deron Johnson	4.00	1.60
❑ 136	Carroll Sembera	2.00	.80
❑ 137	Ron Clark	2.00	.80
	Jim Ollum		
❑ 138	Dick Kelley	2.00	.80
❑ 139	Dalton Jones	4.00	1.60
❑ 140	Willie Stargell	20.00	8.00
❑ 141	John Miller	2.00	.80
❑ 142	Jackie Brandt	2.00	.80
❑ 143	Pete Ward	2.00	.80
	Don Buford		
❑ 144	Bill Hepler	2.00	.80
❑ 145	Larry Brown	2.00	.80
❑ 146	Steve Carlton	50.00	20.00
❑ 147	Tom Egan	2.00	.80
❑ 148	Adolfo Phillips	2.00	.80
❑ 149	Joe Moeller	2.00	.80
❑ 150	Mickey Mantle	300.00	100.00
❑ 151	Moe Drabowsky WS	5.00	2.00
❑ 152	Jim Palmer WS	8.00	3.20
❑ 153	Paul Blair WS	5.00	2.00
❑ 154	Brooks Robinson WS	5.00	2.00
	Dave McNally		
❑ 155	WS Summary	5.00	2.00
	Winners celebrate		
❑ 156	Ron Herbel	2.00	.80
❑ 157	Danny Cater	2.00	.80
❑ 158	Jimmie Coker	2.00	.80
❑ 159	Bruce Howard	2.00	.80
❑ 160	Willie Davis	4.00	1.60
❑ 161	Dick Williams MG	4.00	1.60
❑ 162	Billy O'Dell	2.00	.80
❑ 163	Vic Roznovsky	2.00	.80
❑ 164	Dwight Siebler UER	2.00	.80
	(Last line of stats		
	shows 1960 Minnesota)		
❑ 165	Cleon Jones	4.00	1.60
❑ 166	Eddie Mathews	15.00	6.00
❑ 167	Joe Coleman	2.00	.80
	Tim Cullen		
❑ 168	Ray Culp	2.00	.80
❑ 169	Horace Clarke	4.00	1.60
❑ 170	Dick McAuliffe	4.00	1.60
❑ 171	Cal Koonce	2.00	.80
❑ 172	Bill Heath	2.00	.80
❑ 173	St. Louis Cardinals	4.00	1.60
	Team Card		
❑ 174	Dick Radatz	4.00	1.60
❑ 175	Bobby Knoop	2.00	.80
❑ 176	Sammy Ellis	2.00	.80
❑ 177	Tito Fuentes	1.50	.60
❑ 178	John Buzhardt	2.00	.80
❑ 179	Charles Vaughan	4.00	1.60
	Cecil Upshaw		
❑ 180	Curt Blefary	2.00	.80
❑ 181	Terry Fox	2.00	.80
❑ 182	Ed Charles	2.00	.80
❑ 183	Jim Pagliaroni	2.00	.80
❑ 184	George Thomas	2.00	.80
❑ 185	Ken Holtzman RC	4.00	1.60
❑ 186	Ed Kranepool	4.00	1.60

Ron Swoboda
❑ 187 Pedro Ramos 2.00 .80
❑ 188 Ken Harrelson 4.00 1.60
❑ 189 Chuck Hinton 2.00 .80
❑ 190 Turk Farrell 2.00 .80
❑ 191A Willie Mays CL 10.00 2.00
214 Tom Kelley
❑ 191B Willie Mays CL 12.00 2.40
214 Dick Kelley
❑ 192 Fred Gladding 2.00 .80
❑ 193 Jose Cardenal 4.00 1.60
❑ 194 Bob Allison 4.00 1.60
❑ 195 Al Jackson 2.00 .80
❑ 196 Johnny Romano 2.00 .80
❑ 197 Ron Perranoski 4.00 1.60
❑ 198 Chuck Hiller 2.00 .80
❑ 199 Billy Hitchcock MG 2.00 .80
❑ 200 Willie Mays UER 100.00 40.00
('63 Sna Francisco
on card back stats)
❑ 201 Hal Reniff 4.00 1.60
❑ 202 Johnny Edwards 2.00 .80
❑ 203 Al McBean 2.00 .80
❑ 204 Mike Epstein 6.00 2.40
Tom Phoebus
❑ 205 Dick Groat 4.00 1.60
❑ 206 Dennis Bennett 2.00 .80
❑ 207 John Orsino 2.00 .80
❑ 208 Jack Lamabe 2.00 .80
❑ 209 Joe Nossek 2.00 .80
❑ 210 Bob Gibson 20.00 8.00
❑ 211 Twins Team 4.00 1.60
❑ 212 Chris Zachary 2.00 .80
❑ 213 Jay Johnstone RC 4.00 1.60
❑ 214 Dick Kelley 2.00 .80
❑ 215 Ernie Banks 20.00 8.00
❑ 216 Norm Cash 8.00 3.20
Al Kaline
❑ 217 Rob Gardner 2.00 .80
❑ 218 Wes Parker 4.00 1.60
❑ 219 Clay Carroll 4.00 1.60
❑ 220 Jim Ray Hart 4.00 1.60
❑ 221 Woody Fryman 4.00 1.60
❑ 222 Darrell Osteen 4.00 1.60
Lee May
❑ 223 Mike Ryan 4.00 1.60
❑ 224 Walt Bond 2.00 .80
❑ 225 Mel Stottlemyre 6.00 2.40
❑ 226 Julian Javier 4.00 1.60
❑ 227 Paul Lindblad 2.00 .80
❑ 228 Gil Hodges MG 6.00 2.40
❑ 229 Larry Jackson 2.00 .80
❑ 230 Boog Powell 6.00 2.40
❑ 231 John Bateman 2.00 .80
❑ 232 Don Buford 2.00 .80
❑ 233 Gary Peters 4.00 1.60
Joel Horlen
Steve Hargan LL
❑ 234 Sandy Koufax 15.00 6.00
Mike Cuellar
Juan Marichal LL
❑ 235 Jim Kaat 6.00 2.40
Denny McLain
Earl Wilson LL
❑ 236 Sandy Koufax 25.00 10.00
Juan Marichal
Bob Gibson
Gaylord Perry LL
❑ 237 Sam McDowell 6.00 2.40
Jim Kaat
Earl Wilson LL
❑ 238 Sandy Koufax 12.00 4.80
Jim Bunning
Bob Veale LL
❑ 239 Frank Robinson 10.00 4.00
Tony Oliva
Al Kaline LL
❑ 240 Matty Alou 6.00 2.40
Felipe Alou
Rico Carty LL
❑ 241 Frank Robinson 10.00 4.00
Harmon Killebrew
Boog Powell LL
❑ 242 Hank Aaron 25.00 10.00
Bob Clemente
Richie Allen LL
❑ 243 Frank Robinson 10.00 4.00
Harmon Killebrew
Boog Powell LL
❑ 244 Hank Aaron 20.00 8.00
Richie Allen
Willie Mays LL
❑ 245 Curt Flood 6.00 2.40
❑ 246 Jim Perry 4.00 1.60
❑ 247 Jerry Lumpe 2.00 .80
❑ 248 Gene Mauch MG 4.00 1.60
❑ 249 Nick Willhite 2.00 .80
❑ 250 Hank Aaron UER 80.00 32.00
(Second 1961 in stats
should be 1962)
❑ 251 Woody Held 2.00 .80
❑ 252 Bob Bolin 2.00 .80
❑ 253 Bill Davis 2.00 .80
Gus Gil
❑ 254 Milt Pappas 4.00 1.60
(No facsimile auto-
graph on card front)
❑ 255 Frank Howard 4.00 1.60
❑ 256 Bob Hendley 2.00 .80
❑ 257 Charlie Smith 2.00 .80
❑ 258 Lee Maye 2.00 .80
❑ 259 Don Dennis 2.00 .80
❑ 260 Jim Lefebvre 4.00 1.60
❑ 261 John Wyatt 2.00 .80
❑ 262 Athletics Team 4.00 1.60
❑ 263 Hank Aguirre 2.00 .80
❑ 264 Ron Swoboda 4.00 1.60
❑ 265 Lou Burdette 4.00 1.60
❑ 266 Willie Stargell 4.00 1.60
Donn Clendenon
❑ 267 Don Schwall 2.00 .80
❑ 268 Johnny Briggs 2.00 .80
❑ 269 Don Nottebart 2.00 .80
❑ 270 Zoilo Versalles 2.00 .80
❑ 271 Eddie Watt 2.00 .80
❑ 272 Bill Connors RC 4.00 1.60
Dave Dowling
❑ 273 Dick Lines 2.00 .80
❑ 274 Bob Aspromonte 2.00 .80
❑ 275 Fred Whitfield 2.00 .80
❑ 276 Bruce Brubaker 2.00 .80
❑ 277 Steve Whitaker 6.00 2.40
❑ 278 Jim Kaat CL 8.00 1.60
❑ 279 Frank Linzy 2.00 .80
❑ 280 Tony Conigliaro 8.00 3.20
❑ 281 Bob Rodgers 2.00 .80
❑ 282 John Odom 2.00 .80
❑ 283 Gene Alley 4.00 1.60
❑ 284 Johnny Podres 4.00 1.60
❑ 285 Lou Brock 20.00 8.00
❑ 286 Wayne Causey 2.50 1.00
❑ 287 Greg Goossen 2.50 1.00
Bart Shirley
❑ 288 Denny Lemaster 2.50 1.00
❑ 289 Tom Tresh 5.00 2.00
❑ 290 Bill White 5.00 2.00
❑ 291 Jim Hannan 2.50 1.00
❑ 292 Don Pavletich 2.50 1.00
❑ 293 Ed Kirkpatrick 2.50 1.00
❑ 294 Walter Alston MG 8.00 3.20
❑ 295 Sam McDowell 5.00 2.00
❑ 296 Glenn Beckert 5.00 2.00
❑ 297 Dave Morehead 5.00 2.00
❑ 298 Ron Davis 2.50 1.00
❑ 299 Norm Siebern 2.50 1.00
❑ 300 Jim Kaat 5.00 2.00
❑ 301 Jesse Gonder 2.50 1.00
❑ 302 Orioles Team 8.00 3.20
❑ 303 Gil Blanco 2.50 1.00
❑ 304 Phil Gagliano 2.50 1.00
❑ 305 Earl Wilson 5.00 2.00
❑ 306 Bud Harrelson RC 5.00 2.00
❑ 307 Jim Beauchamp 2.50 1.00
❑ 308 Al Downing 5.00 2.00
❑ 309 Johnny Callison 5.00 2.00
Richie Allen
❑ 310 Gary Peters 2.50 1.00
❑ 311 Ed Brinkman 2.50 1.00
❑ 312 Don Mincher 2.50 1.00
❑ 313 Bob Lee 2.50 1.00
❑ 314 Mike Andrews 8.00 3.20
Reggie Smith RC
❑ 315 Billy Williams 15.00 6.00
❑ 316 Jack Kralick 2.50 1.00
❑ 317 Cesar Tovar 2.50 1.00
❑ 318 Dave Giusti 2.50 1.00
❑ 319 Paul Blair 5.00 2.00
❑ 320 Gaylord Perry 15.00 6.00
❑ 321 Mayo Smith MG 2.50 1.00
❑ 322 Jose Pagan 2.50 1.00
❑ 323 Mike Hershberger 2.50 1.00
❑ 324 Hal Woodeshick 2.50 1.00
❑ 325 Chico Cardenas 5.00 2.00
❑ 326 Bob Uecker 10.00 4.00
❑ 327 California Angels 8.00 3.20
Team Card
❑ 328 Clete Boyer UER 5.00 2.00
(Stats only go up
through 1965)
❑ 329 Charlie Lau 5.00 2.00
❑ 330 Claude Osteen 5.00 2.00
❑ 331 Joe Foy 5.00 2.00
❑ 332 Jesus Alou 2.50 1.00
❑ 333 Fergie Jenkins 20.00 8.00
❑ 334 Bob Allison 10.00 4.00
Harmon Killebrew
❑ 335 Bob Veale 5.00 2.00
❑ 336 Joe Azcue 2.50 1.00
❑ 337 Joe Morgan 15.00 6.00
❑ 338 Bob Locker 2.50 1.00
❑ 339 Chico Ruiz 2.50 1.00
❑ 340 Joe Pepitone 8.00 3.20
❑ 341 Dick Dietz 2.50 1.00
Bill Sorrell
❑ 342 Hank Fischer 2.50 1.00
❑ 343 Tom Satriano 2.50 1.00
❑ 344 Ossie Chavarria 2.50 1.00
❑ 345 Stu Miller 5.00 2.00
❑ 346 Jim Hickman 2.50 1.00
❑ 347 Grady Hatton MG 2.50 1.00
❑ 348 Tug McGraw 5.00 2.00
❑ 349 Bob Chance 2.50 1.00
❑ 350 Joe Torre 8.00 3.20
❑ 351 Vern Law 5.00 2.00
❑ 352 Ray Oyler 2.50 1.00
❑ 353 Bill McCool 2.50 1.00
❑ 354 Cubs Team 8.00 3.20
❑ 355 Carl Yastrzemski 60.00 24.00
❑ 356 Larry Jaster 2.50 1.00
❑ 357 Bill Skowron 5.00 2.00
❑ 358 Ruben Amaro 2.50 1.00
❑ 359 Dick Ellsworth 2.50 1.00
❑ 360 Leon Wagner 2.50 1.00
❑ 361 Roberto Clemente CL 15.00 3.00
❑ 362 Darold Knowles 2.50 1.00
❑ 363 Davey Johnson 5.00 2.00
❑ 364 Claude Raymond 2.50 1.00
❑ 365 John Roseboro 5.00 2.00
❑ 366 Andy Kosco 2.50 1.00
❑ 367 Bill Kelso 2.50 1.00
Don Wallace
❑ 368 Jack Hiatt 2.50 1.00
❑ 369 Jim Hunter 15.00 6.00
❑ 370 Tommy Davis 5.00 2.00
❑ 371 Jim Lonborg 8.00 3.20
❑ 372 Mike de la Hoz 4.00 1.60
❑ 373 Duane Josephson 4.00 1.60
Fred Klages DP
❑ 374A Mel Queen ERR DP 20.00 8.00
(Incomplete stat
line on back)
❑ 374B Mel Queen COR DP 4.00 1.60
(Complete stat
line on back)
❑ 375 Jake Gibbs 8.00 3.20
❑ 376 Don Lock DP 4.00 1.60
❑ 377 Luis Tiant 8.00 3.20
❑ 378 Detroit Tigers 8.00 3.20
Team Card UER
(Willie Horton with
262 RBI's in 1966)
❑ 379 Jerry May DP 4.00 1.60
❑ 380 Dean Chance DP 4.00 1.60
❑ 381 Dick Schofield DP 4.00 1.60
❑ 382 Dave McNally 8.00 3.20
❑ 383 Ken Henderson DP 4.00 1.60
❑ 384 Jim Cosman 4.00 1.60
Dick Hughes

❑ 385 Jim Fregosi 8.00 3.20
(Batting wrong)
❑ 386 Dick Selma DP 4.00 1.60
❑ 387 Cap Peterson DP 4.00 1.60
❑ 388 Arnold Earley DP 4.00 1.60
❑ 389 Alvin Dark MG DP 8.00 3.20
❑ 390 Jim Wynn DP 8.00 3.20
❑ 391 Wilbur Wood DP 8.00 3.20
❑ 392 Tommy Harper DP 8.00 3.20
❑ 393 Jim Bouton DP 8.00 3.20
❑ 394 Jake Wood DP 4.00 1.60
❑ 395 Chris Short 8.00 3.20
❑ 396 Denis Menke 4.00 1.60
Tony Cloninger
❑ 397 Willie Smith DP 4.00 1.60
❑ 398 Jeff Torborg 8.00 3.20
❑ 399 Al Worthington DP 4.00 1.60
❑ 400 Bob Clemente DP 100.00 40.00
❑ 401 Jim Coates 4.00 1.60
❑ 402A Phillies Rookies DP .. 20.00 8.00
Grant Jackson
Billy Wilson
Incomplete stat line
❑ 402B Phillies Rookies DP 8.00 3.20
Grant Jackson
Billy Wilson
❑ 403 Dick Nen 4.00 1.60
❑ 404 Nelson Briles 8.00 3.20
❑ 405 Russ Snyder 4.00 1.60
❑ 406 Lee Elia DP 4.00 1.60
❑ 407 Reds Team 8.00 3.20
❑ 408 Jim Northrup DP 8.00 3.20
❑ 409 Ray Sadecki 4.00 1.60
❑ 410 Lou Johnson DP 4.00 1.60
❑ 411 Dick Howser DP 4.00 1.60
❑ 412 Norm Miller 8.00 3.20
Doug Rader RC
❑ 413 Jerry Grote 4.00 1.60
❑ 414 Casey Cox 4.00 1.60
❑ 415 Sonny Jackson 4.00 1.60
❑ 416 Roger Repoz 4.00 1.60
❑ 417A Bob Bruce ERR DP 30.00 12.00
(RBAVES on back)
❑ 417B Bob Bruce COR DP 4.00 1.60
❑ 418 Sam Mele MG 4.00 1.60
❑ 419 Don Kessinger DP 8.00 3.20
❑ 420 Denny McLain 12.00 4.80
❑ 421 Dal Maxvill DP 4.00 1.60
❑ 422 Hoyt Wilhelm 15.00 6.00
❑ 423 Willie Mays 25.00 10.00
Willie McCovey DP
❑ 424 Pedro Gonzalez 4.00 1.60
❑ 425 Pete Mikkelsen 4.00 1.60
❑ 426 Lou Clinton 4.00 1.60
❑ 427A R.Gomez ERR DP 20.00 8.00
Incomplete stat
line on back
❑ 427B R.Gomez COR DP 4.00 1.60
Complete stat
line on back
❑ 428 Tom Hutton RC 8.00 3.20
Gene Michael DP
❑ 429 Garry Roggenburk DP 4.00 1.60
❑ 430 Pete Rose 100.00 40.00
❑ 431 Ted Uhlaender 4.00 1.60
❑ 432 Jimmie Hall DP 4.00 1.60
❑ 433 Al Luplow DP 4.00 1.60
❑ 434 Eddie Fisher DP 4.00 1.60
❑ 435 Mack Jones DP 4.00 1.60
❑ 436 Pete Ward 4.00 1.60
❑ 437 Senators Team 8.00 3.20
❑ 438 Chuck Dobson 4.00 1.60
❑ 439 Byron Browne 4.00 1.60
❑ 440 Steve Hargan 4.00 1.60
❑ 441 Jim Davenport 4.00 1.60
❑ 442 Bill Robinson RC 8.00 3.20
Joe Verbanic DP
❑ 443 Tito Francona DP 4.00 1.60
❑ 444 George Smith 4.00 1.60
❑ 445 Don Sutton 25.00 10.00
❑ 446 Russ Nixon DP 4.00 1.60
❑ 447A Bo Belinsky ERR DP 5.00 2.00
(Incomplete stat
line on back)
❑ 447B Bo Belinsky COR DP.... 8.00 3.20
(Complete stat
line on back)
❑ 448 Harry Walker DP MG 4.00 1.60
❑ 449 Orlando Pena 4.00 1.60
❑ 450 Richie Allen 8.00 3.20
❑ 451 Fred Newman DP 4.00 1.60
❑ 452 Ed Kranepool 8.00 3.20
❑ 453 A.Monteagudo DP 4.00 1.60
❑ 454A Juan Marichal CL 12.00 2.40
Missing left ear
❑ 454B Juan Marichal CL 12.00 2.40
left ear showing
❑ 455 Tommie Agee 8.00 3.20
❑ 456 Phil Niekro 15.00 6.00
❑ 457 Andy Etchebarren DP 8.00 3.20
❑ 458 Lee Thomas 6.00 2.40
❑ 459 Dick Bosman RC 6.00 2.40
Pete Craig
❑ 460 Harmon Killebrew 60.00 24.00
❑ 461 Bob Miller 12.00 4.80
❑ 462 Bob Barton 6.00 2.40
❑ 463 Sam McDowell 12.00 4.80
Sonny Siebert
❑ 464 Dan Coombs 6.00 2.40
❑ 465 Willie Horton 12.00 4.80
❑ 466 Bobby Wine 6.00 2.40
❑ 467 Jim O'Toole 6.00 2.40
❑ 468 Ralph Houk MG 6.00 2.40
❑ 469 Len Gabrielson 6.00 2.40
❑ 470 Bob Shaw 6.00 2.40
❑ 471 Rene Lachemann 6.00 2.40
❑ 472 John Gelnar 6.00 2.40
George Spriggs
❑ 473 Jose Santiago 6.00 2.40
❑ 474 Bob Tolan 6.00 2.40
❑ 475 Jim Palmer 80.00 32.00
❑ 476 Tony Perez SP 60.00 24.00
❑ 477 Braves Team 15.00 6.00
❑ 478 Bob Humphreys 6.00 2.40
❑ 479 Gary Bell 6.00 2.40
❑ 480 Willie McCovey 40.00 16.00
❑ 481 Leo Durocher MG 20.00 8.00
❑ 482 Bill Monbouquette 6.00 2.40
❑ 483 Jim Landis 6.00 2.40
❑ 484 Jerry Adair 6.00 2.40
❑ 485 Tim McCarver 25.00 10.00
❑ 486 Rich Reese 6.00 2.40
Bill Whitby
❑ 487 Tommie Reynolds 6.00 2.40
❑ 488 Gerry Arrigo 6.00 2.40
❑ 489 Doug Clemens 6.00 2.40
❑ 490 Tony Cloninger 6.00 2.40
❑ 491 Sam Bowens 6.00 2.40
❑ 492 Pittsburgh Pirates 15.00 6.00
Team Card
❑ 493 Phil Ortega 6.00 2.40
❑ 494 Bill Rigney MG 6.00 2.40
❑ 495 Fritz Peterson 6.00 2.40
❑ 496 Orlando McFarlane 6.00 2.40
❑ 497 Ron Campbell 6.00 2.40
❑ 498 Larry Dierker 12.00 4.80
❑ 499 George Culver 6.00 2.40
Jose Vidal
❑ 500 Juan Marichal 25.00 10.00
❑ 501 Jerry Zimmerman 6.00 2.40
❑ 502 Derrell Griffith 6.00 2.40
❑ 503 Los Angeles Dodgers .. 20.00 8.00
Team Card
❑ 504 Orlando Martinez 6.00 2.40
❑ 505 Tommy Helms 12.00 4.80
❑ 506 Smoky Burgess 6.00 2.40
❑ 507 Ed Barnowski 6.00 2.40
Larry Haney RC
❑ 508 Dick Hall 6.00 2.40
❑ 509 Jim King 6.00 2.40
❑ 510 Bill Mazeroski 25.00 10.00
❑ 511 Don Wert 6.00 2.40
❑ 512 Red Schoendienst MG.. 25.00 10.00
❑ 513 Marcelino Lopez 6.00 2.40
❑ 514 John Werhas 6.00 2.40
❑ 515 Bert Campaneris 12.00 4.80
❑ 516 Giants Team 15.00 6.00
❑ 517 Fred Talbot 12.00 4.80
❑ 518 Denis Menke 6.00 2.40
❑ 519 Ted Davidson 6.00 2.40
❑ 520 Max Alvis 6.00 2.40
❑ 521 Boog Powell 12.00 4.80
Curt Blefary
❑ 522 John Stephenson 6.00 2.40
❑ 523 Jim Merritt 6.00 2.40
❑ 524 Felix Mantilla 6.00 2.40
❑ 525 Ron Hunt 6.00 2.40
❑ 526 Pat Dobson RC 6.00 2.40
George Korince
(See 67T-72)
❑ 527 Dennis Ribant 6.00 2.40
❑ 528 Rico Petrocelli 20.00 8.00
❑ 529 Gary Wagner 6.00 2.40
❑ 530 Felipe Alou 12.00 4.80
❑ 531 Brooks Robinson CL 15.00 3.00
❑ 532 Jim Hicks 6.00 2.40
❑ 533 Jack Fisher 6.00 2.40
❑ 534 Hank Bauer MG DP 8.00 3.20
❑ 535 Donn Clendenon 25.00 10.00
❑ 536 Joe Niekro RC 50.00 20.00
Paul Popovich
❑ 537 Chuck Estrada DP 8.00 3.20
❑ 538 J.C. Martin 15.00 6.00
❑ 539 Dick Egan DP 8.00 3.20
❑ 540 Norm Cash 50.00 20.00
❑ 541 Joe Gibbon 15.00 6.00
❑ 542 Rick Monday RC 15.00 6.00
Tony Pierce DP
❑ 543 Dan Schneider 15.00 6.00
❑ 544 Cleveland Indians 30.00 12.00
Team Card
❑ 545 Jim Grant 25.00 10.00
❑ 546 Woody Woodward 25.00 10.00
❑ 547 Russ Gibson 8.00 3.20
Bill Rohr DP
❑ 548 Tony Gonzalez DP 8.00 3.20
❑ 549 Jack Sanford 15.00 6.00
❑ 550 Vada Pinson DP 10.00 4.00
❑ 551 Doug Camilli DP 8.00 3.20
❑ 552 Ted Savage 25.00 10.00
❑ 553 Mike Hegan RC 40.00 16.00
Thad Tillotson
❑ 554 Andre Rodgers DP 8.00 3.20
❑ 555 Don Cardwell 25.00 10.00
❑ 556 Al Weis DP 8.00 3.20
❑ 557 Al Ferrara 25.00 10.00
❑ 558 Mark Belanger RC 50.00 20.00
Bill Dillman
❑ 559 Dick Tracewski DP 8.00 3.20
❑ 560 Jim Bunning 60.00 24.00
❑ 561 Sandy Alomar 40.00 16.00
❑ 562 Steve Blass DP 8.00 3.20
❑ 563 Joe Adcock 40.00 16.00
❑ 564 Alonzo Harris 8.00 3.20
Aaron Pointer
❑ 565 Lew Krausse 25.00 10.00
❑ 566 Gary Geiger DP 8.00 3.20
❑ 567 Steve Hamilton 40.00 16.00
❑ 568 John Sullivan 40.00 16.00
❑ 569 Rod Carew RC 250.00 80.00
Hank Allen DP
❑ 570 Maury Wills 80.00 32.00
❑ 571 Larry Sherry 25.00 10.00
❑ 572 Don Demeter 25.00 10.00
❑ 573 Chicago White Sox 30.00 12.00
Team Card UER
(Indians team
stats on back)
❑ 574 Jerry Buchek 25.00 10.00
❑ 575 Dave Boswell 15.00 6.00
❑ 576 Ramon Hernandez 40.00 16.00
Norm Gigon RC
❑ 577 Bill Short 15.00 6.00
❑ 578 John Boccabella 15.00 6.00
❑ 579 Bill Henry 15.00 6.00
❑ 580 Rocky Colavito 125.00 50.00
❑ 581 Bill Denehy 500.00 200.00
Tom Seaver RC
❑ 582 Jim Owens DP 8.00 3.20
❑ 583 Ray Barker 40.00 16.00
❑ 584 Jimmy Piersall 40.00 16.00
❑ 585 Wally Bunker 25.00 10.00
❑ 586 Manny Jimenez 15.00 6.00
❑ 587 Don Shaw 40.00 16.00
Gary Sutherland RC
❑ 588 Johnny Klippstein DP 8.00 3.20
❑ 589 Dave Ricketts DP 8.00 3.20
❑ 590 Pete Richert 15.00 6.00

Card	NM	Ex
❑ 591 Ty Cline	25.00	10.00
❑ 592 Jim Shellenback	25.00	10.00
Ron Willis RC		
❑ 593 Wes Westrum MG	50.00	20.00
❑ 594 Dan Osinski	40.00	16.00
❑ 595 Cookie Rojas	25.00	10.00
❑ 596 Galen Cisco DP	8.00	3.20
❑ 597 Ted Abernathy	15.00	6.00
❑ 598 Walt Williams	25.00	10.00
Ed Stroud		
❑ 599 Bob Duliba DP	8.00	3.20
❑ 600 Brooks Robinson	250.00	100.00
❑ 601 Bill Bryan DP	8.00	3.20
❑ 602 Juan Pizarro	40.00	16.00
❑ 603 Tim Talton	25.00	10.00
Ramon Webster		
❑ 604 Red Sox Team	125.00	50.00
❑ 605 Mike Shannon	50.00	20.00
❑ 606 Ron Taylor	25.00	10.00
❑ 607 Mickey Stanley	50.00	20.00
❑ 608 Rich Nye	8.00	3.20
John Upham DP		
❑ 609 Tommy John	80.00	27.00

1968 Topps

	NM	Ex
COMPLETE SET (598)	3000.00	1200.00
COMMON CARD (1-457)	2.00	.80
COMMON (458-598)	4.00	1.60
WRAPPER (5-CENT)	25.00	10.00

Card	NM	Ex
❑ 1 Roberto Clemente	30.00	12.00
Tony Gonzalez		
Matty Alou LL		
❑ 2 Carl Yastrzemski	15.00	6.00
Frank Robinson		
Al Kaline LL		
❑ 3 Orlando Cepeda	20.00	8.00
Roberto Clemente		
Hank Aaron LL		
❑ 4 Carl Yastrzemski	15.00	6.00
Harmon Killebrew		
Frank Robinson LL		
❑ 5 Hank Aaron	8.00	3.20
Jim Wynn		
Ron Santo		
Willie McCovey LL		
❑ 6 Carl Yastrzemski	8.00	3.20
Harmon Killebrew		
Frank Howard LL		
❑ 7 Phil Niekro	4.00	1.60
Jim Bunning		
Chris Short LL		
❑ 8 Joel Horlen	4.00	1.60
Gary Peters		
Sonny Siebert LL		
❑ 9 Mike McCormick	4.00	1.60
Ferguson Jenkins		
Jim Bunning		
Claude Osteen LL		
❑ 10A Jim Lonborg ERR	4.00	1.60
(Misspelled Lonberg		
on card back)		
Earl Wilson		
Dean Chance LL		
❑ 10B Jim Lonborg COR	4.00	1.60
Earl Wilson		
Dean Chance LL		
❑ 11 Jim Bunning	6.00	2.40
Ferguson Jenkins		
Gaylord Perry LL		
❑ 12 Jim Lonborg UER	4.00	1.60
(Misspelled Longberg		
on card back)		
Sam McDowell		
Dean Chance LL		
❑ 13 Chuck Hartenstein	2.00	.80
❑ 14 Jerry McNertney	2.00	.80
❑ 15 Ron Hunt	2.00	.80
❑ 16 Lou Piniella	6.00	2.40
Richie Scheinblum		
❑ 17 Dick Hall	2.00	.80
❑ 18 Mike Hershberger	2.00	.80
❑ 19 Juan Pizarro	2.00	.80
❑ 20 Brooks Robinson	25.00	10.00
❑ 21 Ron Davis	2.00	.80
❑ 22 Pat Dobson	4.00	1.60
❑ 23 Chico Cardenas	4.00	1.60
❑ 24 Bobby Locke	2.00	.80
❑ 25 Julian Javier	4.00	1.60
❑ 26 Darrell Brandon	2.00	.80
❑ 27 Gil Hodges MG	8.00	3.20
❑ 28 Ted Uhlaender	2.00	.80
❑ 29 Joe Verbanic	2.00	.80
❑ 30 Joe Torre	6.00	2.40
❑ 31 Ed Stroud	2.00	.80
❑ 32 Joe Gibbon	2.00	.80
❑ 33 Pete Ward	2.00	.80
❑ 34 Al Ferrara	2.00	.80
❑ 35 Steve Hargan	2.00	.80
❑ 36 Bob Moose	4.00	1.60
Bob Robertson		
❑ 37 Billy Williams	8.00	3.20
❑ 38 Tony Pierce	2.00	.80
❑ 39 Cookie Rojas	2.00	.80
❑ 40 Denny McLain	8.00	3.20
❑ 41 Julio Gotay	2.00	.80
❑ 42 Larry Haney	2.00	.80
❑ 43 Gary Bell	2.00	.80
❑ 44 Frank Kostro	2.00	.80
❑ 45 Tom Seaver	50.00	20.00
❑ 46 Dave Ricketts	2.00	.80
❑ 47 Ralph Houk MG	4.00	1.60
❑ 48 Ted Davidson	2.00	.80
❑ 49A Eddie Brinkman	2.00	.80
(White team name)		
❑ 49B Eddie Brinkman	50.00	20.00
(Yellow team name)		
❑ 50 Willie Mays	60.00	24.00
❑ 51 Bob Locker	2.00	.80
❑ 52 Hawk Taylor	2.00	.80
❑ 53 Gene Alley	4.00	1.60
❑ 54 Stan Williams	2.00	.80
❑ 55 Felipe Alou	4.00	1.60
❑ 56 Dave Leonhard	2.00	.80
Dave May RC		
❑ 57 Dan Schneider	2.00	.80
❑ 58 Eddie Mathews	15.00	6.00
❑ 59 Don Lock	2.00	.80
❑ 60 Ken Holtzman	4.00	1.60
❑ 61 Reggie Smith	4.00	1.60
❑ 62 Chuck Dobson	2.00	.80
❑ 63 Dick Kenworthy	2.00	.80
❑ 64 Jim Merritt	2.00	.80
❑ 65 John Roseboro	4.00	1.60
❑ 66A Casey Cox	2.00	.80
(White team name)		
❑ 66B Casey Cox	100.00	40.00
(Yellow team name)		
❑ 67 Jim Kaat CL	6.00	1.20
❑ 68 Ron Willis	2.00	.80
❑ 69 Tom Tresh	4.00	1.60
❑ 70 Bob Veale	4.00	1.60
❑ 71 Vern Fuller	2.00	.80
❑ 72 Tommy John	6.00	2.40
❑ 73 Jim Ray Hart	4.00	1.60
❑ 74 Milt Pappas	4.00	1.60
❑ 75 Don Mincher	2.00	.80
❑ 76 Jim Britton	4.00	1.60
Ron Reed		
❑ 77 Don Wilson	4.00	1.60
❑ 78 Jim Northrup	6.00	2.40
❑ 79 Ted Kubiak	2.00	.80
❑ 80 Rod Carew	50.00	20.00
❑ 81 Larry Jackson	2.00	.80
❑ 82 Sam Bowens	2.00	.80
❑ 83 John Stephenson	2.00	.80
❑ 84 Bob Tolan	2.00	.80
❑ 85 Gaylord Perry	8.00	3.20
❑ 86 Willie Stargell	8.00	3.20
❑ 87 Dick Williams MG	4.00	1.60
❑ 88 Phil Regan	4.00	1.60
❑ 89 Jake Gibbs	4.00	1.60
❑ 90 Vada Pinson	4.00	1.60
❑ 91 Jim Ollom	2.00	.80
❑ 92 Ed Kranepool	4.00	1.60
❑ 93 Tony Cloninger	2.00	.80
❑ 94 Lee Maye	2.00	.80
❑ 95 Bob Aspromonte	2.00	.80
❑ 96 Frank Coggins	2.00	.80
Dick Nold		
❑ 97 Tom Phoebus	2.00	.80
❑ 98 Gary Sutherland	2.00	.80
❑ 99 Rocky Colavito	8.00	3.20
❑ 100 Bob Gibson	25.00	10.00
❑ 101 Glenn Beckert	4.00	1.60
❑ 102 Jose Cardenal	4.00	1.60
❑ 103 Don Sutton	8.00	3.20
❑ 104 Dick Dietz	2.00	.80
❑ 105 Al Downing	4.00	1.60
❑ 106 Dalton Jones	2.00	.80
❑ 107A Juan Marichal CL	6.00	1.20
Tan wide mesh		
❑ 107B Juan Marichal CL	6.00	1.20
Brown fine mesh		
❑ 108 Don Pavletich	2.00	.80
❑ 109 Bert Campaneris	4.00	1.60
❑ 110 Hank Aaron	60.00	24.00
❑ 111 Rich Reese	2.00	.80
❑ 112 Woody Fryman	2.00	.80
❑ 113 Tom Matchick	4.00	1.60
Daryl Patterson		
❑ 114 Ron Swoboda	4.00	1.60
❑ 115 Sam McDowell	4.00	1.60
❑ 116 Ken McMullen	2.00	.80
❑ 117 Larry Jaster	2.00	.80
❑ 118 Mark Belanger	4.00	1.60
❑ 119 Ted Savage	2.00	.80
❑ 120 Mel Stottlemyre	4.00	1.60
❑ 121 Jimmie Hall	2.00	.80
❑ 122 Gene Mauch MG	4.00	1.60
❑ 123 Jose Santiago	2.00	.80
❑ 124 Nate Oliver	2.00	.80
❑ 125 Joel Horlen	2.00	.80
❑ 126 Bobby Etheridge	2.00	.80
❑ 127 Paul Lindblad	2.00	.80
❑ 128 Tom Dukes	2.00	.80
Alonzo Harris		
❑ 129 Mickey Stanley	6.00	2.40
❑ 130 Tony Perez	8.00	3.20
❑ 131 Frank Bertaina	2.00	.80
❑ 132 Bud Harrelson	4.00	1.60
❑ 133 Fred Whitfield	2.00	.80
❑ 134 Pat Jarvis	2.00	.80
❑ 135 Paul Blair	4.00	1.60
❑ 136 Randy Hundley	4.00	1.60
❑ 137 Twins Team	4.00	1.60
❑ 138 Ruben Amaro	2.00	.80
❑ 139 Chris Short	2.00	.80
❑ 140 Tony Conigliaro	8.00	3.20
❑ 141 Dal Maxvill	2.00	.80
❑ 142 Buddy Bradford	2.00	.80
Bill Voss		
❑ 143 Pete Cimino	2.00	.80
❑ 144 Joe Morgan	12.00	4.80
❑ 145 Don Drysdale	12.00	4.80
❑ 146 Sal Bando	4.00	1.60
❑ 147 Frank Linzy	2.00	.80
❑ 148 Dave Bristol MG	2.00	.80
❑ 149 Bob Saverine	2.00	.80
❑ 150 Roberto Clemente	80.00	32.00
❑ 151 Lou Brock WS	10.00	4.00
❑ 152 Carl Yastrzemski WS	10.00	4.00
❑ 153 Nellie Briles WS	5.00	2.00
❑ 154 Bob Gibson WS	10.00	4.00
❑ 155 Jim Lonborg WS	5.00	2.00
❑ 156 Rico Petrocelli WS	5.00	2.00
❑ 157 World Series Game 7	5.00	2.00
St. Louis wins it		

❑ 158 WS Summary 5.00 2.00
Cardinals celebrate
❑ 159 Don Kessinger 4.00 1.60
❑ 160 Earl Wilson 4.00 1.60
❑ 161 Norm Miller 2.00 .80
❑ 162 Hal Gilson 4.00 1.60
Mike Torrez
❑ 163 Gene Brabender 2.00 .80
❑ 164 Ramon Webster 2.00 .80
❑ 165 Tony Oliva 6.00 2.40
❑ 166 Claude Raymond 2.00 .80
❑ 167 Elston Howard 6.00 2.40
❑ 168 Dodgers Team 4.00 1.60
❑ 169 Bob Bolin 2.00 .80
❑ 170 Jim Fregosi 4.00 1.60
❑ 171 Don Nottebart 2.00 .80
❑ 172 Walt Williams 2.00 .80
❑ 173 John Boozer 2.00 .80
❑ 174 Bob Tillman 2.00 .80
❑ 175 Maury Wills 6.00 2.40
❑ 176 Bob Allen 2.00 .80
❑ 177 Jerry Koosman RC 500.00 200.00
Nolan Ryan RC
❑ 178 Don Wert 4.00 1.60
❑ 179 Bill Stoneman 2.00 .80
❑ 180 Curt Flood 6.00 2.40
❑ 181 Jerry Zimmerman 2.00 .80
❑ 182 Dave Giusti 2.00 .80
❑ 183 Bob Kennedy MG 4.00 1.60
❑ 184 Lou Johnson 2.00 .80
❑ 185 Tom Haller 2.00 .80
❑ 186 Eddie Watt 2.00 .80
❑ 187 Sonny Jackson 2.00 .80
❑ 188 Cap Peterson 2.00 .80
❑ 189 Bill Landis 2.00 .80
❑ 190 Bill White 4.00 1.60
❑ 191 Dan Frisella 2.00 .80
❑ 192A Carl Yastrzemski CL 8.00 1.60
Special Baseball Playing Card
❑ 192B Carl Yastrzemski CL 8.00 1.60
Special Baseball
Playing Card Game
❑ 193 Jack Hamilton 2.00 .80
❑ 194 Don Buford 2.00 .80
❑ 195 Joe Pepitone 4.00 1.60
❑ 196 Gary Nolan 4.00 1.60
❑ 197 Larry Brown 2.00 .80
❑ 198 Roy Face 4.00 1.60
❑ 199 Roberto Rodriquez 2.00 .80
Darrell Osteen
❑ 200 Orlando Cepeda 8.00 3.20
❑ 201 Mike Marshall RC 4.00 1.60
❑ 202 Adolfo Phillips 2.00 .80
❑ 203 Dick Kelley 2.00 .80
❑ 204 Andy Etchebarren 2.00 .80
❑ 205 Juan Marichal 8.00 3.20
❑ 206 Cal Ermer MG 2.00 .80
❑ 207 Carroll Sembera 2.00 .80
❑ 208 Willie Davis 4.00 1.60
❑ 209 Tim Cullen 2.00 .80
❑ 210 Gary Peters 2.00 .80
❑ 211 J.C. Martin 2.00 .80
❑ 212 Dave Morehead 2.00 .80
❑ 213 Chico Ruiz 2.00 .80
❑ 214 Stan Bahnsen 4.00 1.60
Frank Fernandez
❑ 215 Jim Bunning 8.00 3.20
❑ 216 Bubba Morton 2.00 .80
❑ 217 Dick Farrell 2.00 .80
❑ 218 Ken Suarez 2.00 .80
❑ 219 Rob Gardner 2.00 .80
❑ 220 Harmon Killebrew 15.00 6.00
❑ 221 Braves Team 4.00 1.60
❑ 222 Jim Hardin 2.00 .80
❑ 223 Ollie Brown 2.00 .80
❑ 224 Jack Aker 2.00 .80
❑ 225 Richie Allen 6.00 2.40
❑ 226 Jimmie Price 2.00 .80
❑ 227 Joe Hoerner 2.00 .80
❑ 228 Jack Billingham 4.00 1.60
Jim Fairey
❑ 229 Fred Klages 2.00 .80
❑ 230 Pete Rose 60.00 24.00
❑ 231 Dave Baldwin 2.00 .80
❑ 232 Denis Menke 2.00 .80
❑ 233 George Scott 4.00 1.60
❑ 234 Bill Monbouquette 2.00 .80
❑ 235 Ron Santo 8.00 3.20
❑ 236 Tug McGraw 6.00 2.40
❑ 237 Alvin Dark MG 4.00 1.60
❑ 238 Tom Satriano 2.00 .80
❑ 239 Bill Henry 2.00 .80
❑ 240 Al Kaline 40.00 16.00
❑ 241 Felix Millan 2.00 .80
❑ 242 Moe Drabowsky 4.00 1.60
❑ 243 Rich Rollins 2.00 .80
❑ 244 John Donaldson 2.00 .80
❑ 245 Tony Gonzalez 2.00 .80
❑ 246 Fritz Peterson 4.00 1.60
❑ 247 Johnny Bench RC 125.00 50.00
Ron Tompkins
❑ 248 Fred Valentine 2.00 .80
❑ 249 Bill Singer 2.00 .80
❑ 250 Carl Yastrzemski 30.00 12.00
❑ 251 Manny Sanguillen RC 6.00 2.40
❑ 252 Angels Team 4.00 1.60
❑ 253 Dick Hughes 2.00 .80
❑ 254 Cleon Jones 4.00 1.60
❑ 255 Dean Chance 4.00 1.60
❑ 256 Norm Cash 6.00 2.40
❑ 257 Phil Niekro 8.00 3.20
❑ 258 Jose Arcia 2.00 .80
Bill Schlesinger
❑ 259 Ken Boyer 6.00 2.40
❑ 260 Jim Wynn 4.00 1.60
❑ 261 Dave Duncan 4.00 1.60
❑ 262 Rick Wise 4.00 1.60
❑ 263 Horace Clarke 4.00 1.60
❑ 264 Ted Abernathy 2.00 .80
❑ 265 Tommy Davis 4.00 1.60
❑ 266 Paul Popovich 2.00 .80
❑ 267 Herman Franks MG 2.00 .80
❑ 268 Bob Humphreys 2.00 .80
❑ 269 Bob Tiefenauer 2.00 .80
❑ 270 Matty Alou 4.00 1.60
❑ 271 Bobby Knoop 2.00 .80
❑ 272 Ray Culp 2.00 .80
❑ 273 Dave Johnson 4.00 1.60
❑ 274 Mike Cuellar 4.00 1.60
❑ 275 Tim McCarver 6.00 2.40
❑ 276 Jim Roland 2.00 .80
❑ 277 Jerry Buchek 2.00 .80
❑ 278 Orlando Cepeda CL 6.00 1.20
❑ 279 Bill Hands 2.00 .80
❑ 280 Mickey Mantle 250.00 100.00
❑ 281 Jim Campanis 2.00 .80
❑ 282 Rick Monday 4.00 1.60
❑ 283 Mel Queen 2.00 .80
❑ 284 Johnny Briggs 2.00 .80
❑ 285 Dick McAuliffe 6.00 2.40
❑ 286 Cecil Upshaw 2.00 .80
❑ 287 Mickey Abarbanel 2.00 .80
Cisco Carlos
❑ 288 Dave Wickersham 2.00 .80
❑ 289 Woody Held 2.00 .80
❑ 290 Willie McCovey 12.00 4.80
❑ 291 Dick Lines 2.00 .80
❑ 292 Art Shamsky 2.00 .80
❑ 293 Bruce Howard 2.00 .80
❑ 294 Red Schoendienst MG 6.00 2.40
❑ 295 Sonny Siebert 2.00 .80
❑ 296 Byron Browne 2.00 .80
❑ 297 Russ Gibson 2.00 .80
❑ 298 Jim Brewer 2.00 .80
❑ 299 Gene Michael 4.00 1.60
❑ 300 Rusty Staub 4.00 1.60
❑ 301 George Mitterwald 2.00 .80
Rick Renick
❑ 302 Gerry Arrigo 2.00 .80
❑ 303 Dick Green 4.00 1.60
❑ 304 Sandy Valdespino 2.00 .80
❑ 305 Minnie Rojas 2.00 .80
❑ 306 Mike Ryan 2.00 .80
❑ 307 John Hiller 4.00 1.60
❑ 308 Pirates Team 4.00 1.60
❑ 309 Ken Henderson 2.00 .80
❑ 310 Luis Aparicio 8.00 3.20
❑ 311 Jack Lamabe 2.00 .80
❑ 312 Curt Blefary 2.00 .80
❑ 313 Al Weis 2.00 .80
❑ 314 Bill Rohr 2.00 .80
George Spriggs
❑ 315 Zoilo Versalles 2.00 .80
❑ 316 Steve Barber 2.00 .80
❑ 317 Ron Brand 2.00 .80
❑ 318 Chico Salmon 2.00 .80
❑ 319 George Culver 2.00 .80
❑ 320 Frank Howard 4.00 1.60
❑ 321 Leo Durocher MG 6.00 2.40
❑ 322 Dave Boswell 2.00 .80
❑ 323 Deron Johnson 4.00 1.60
❑ 324 Jim Nash 2.00 .80
❑ 325 Manny Mota 4.00 1.60
❑ 326 Dennis Ribant 2.00 .80
❑ 327 Tony Taylor 4.00 1.60
❑ 328 Chuck Vinson 2.00 .80
Jim Weaver
❑ 329 Duane Josephson 2.00 .80
❑ 330 Roger Maris 50.00 20.00
❑ 331 Dan Osinski 2.00 .80
❑ 332 Doug Rader 4.00 1.60
❑ 333 Ron Herbel 2.00 .80
❑ 334 Orioles Team 4.00 1.60
❑ 335 Bob Allison 4.00 1.60
❑ 336 John Purdin 2.00 .80
❑ 337 Bill Robinson 4.00 1.60
❑ 338 Bob Johnson 2.00 .80
❑ 339 Rich Nye 2.00 .80
❑ 340 Max Alvis 2.00 .80
❑ 341 Jim Lemon MG 2.00 .80
❑ 342 Ken Johnson 2.00 .80
❑ 343 Jim Gosger 2.00 .80
❑ 344 Donn Clendenon 4.00 1.60
❑ 345 Bob Hendley 2.00 .80
❑ 346 Jerry Adair 2.00 .80
❑ 347 George Brunet 2.00 .80
❑ 348 Larry Colton 2.00 .80
Dick Thoenen
❑ 349 Ed Spiezio 4.00 1.60
❑ 350 Hoyt Wilhelm 8.00 3.20
❑ 351 Bob Barton 2.00 .80
❑ 352 Jackie Hernandez 2.00 .80
❑ 353 Mack Jones 2.00 .80
❑ 354 Pete Richert 2.00 .80
❑ 355 Ernie Banks 25.00 10.00
❑ 356A Ken Holtzman CL 6.00 1.20
Head centered within circle
❑ 356B Ken Holtzman 6.00 1.20
Head shifted right
within circle
❑ 357 Len Gabrielson 2.00 .80
❑ 358 Mike Epstein 2.00 .80
❑ 359 Joe Moeller 2.00 .80
❑ 360 Willie Horton 6.00 2.40
❑ 361 Harmon Killebrew AS 8.00 3.20
❑ 362 Orlando Cepeda AS 6.00 2.40
❑ 363 Rod Carew AS 8.00 3.20
❑ 364 Joe Morgan AS 8.00 3.20
❑ 365 Brooks Robinson AS 8.00 3.20
❑ 366 Ron Santo AS 6.00 2.40
❑ 367 Jim Fregosi AS 4.00 1.60
❑ 368 Gene Alley AS 4.00 1.60
❑ 369 Carl Yastrzemski AS 10.00 4.00
❑ 370 Hank Aaron AS 20.00 8.00
❑ 371 Tony Oliva AS 6.00 2.40
❑ 372 Lou Brock AS 8.00 3.20
❑ 373 Frank Robinson AS 8.00 3.20
❑ 374 Bob Clemente AS 30.00 12.00
❑ 375 Bill Freehan AS 4.00 1.60
❑ 376 Tim McCarver AS 4.00 1.60
❑ 377 Joel Horlen AS 4.00 1.60
❑ 378 Bob Gibson AS 8.00 3.20
❑ 379 Gary Peters AS 4.00 1.60
❑ 380 Ken Holtzman AS 4.00 1.60
❑ 381 Boog Powell 4.00 1.60
❑ 382 Ramon Hernandez 2.00 .80
❑ 383 Steve Whitaker 2.00 .80
❑ 384 Bill Henry 6.00 2.40
Hal McRae RC
❑ 385 Jim Hunter 10.00 4.00
❑ 386 Greg Goossen 2.00 .80
❑ 387 Joe Foy 2.00 .80
❑ 388 Ray Washburn 2.00 .80
❑ 389 Jay Johnstone 4.00 1.60
❑ 390 Bill Mazeroski 8.00 3.20
❑ 391 Bob Priddy 2.00 .80
❑ 392 Grady Hatton MG 2.00 .80
❑ 393 Jim Perry 4.00 1.60

No.	Player	NM	Ex
❑ 394	Tommie Aaron	6.00	2.40
❑ 395	Camilo Pascual	4.00	1.60
❑ 396	Bobby Wine	2.00	.80
❑ 397	Vic Davalillo	2.00	.80
❑ 398	Jim Grant	2.00	.80
❑ 399	Ray Oyler	4.00	1.60
❑ 400A	Mike McCormick (Yellow letters)	4.00	1.60
❑ 400B	Mike McCormick (Team name in white letters)	150.00	60.00
❑ 401	Mets Team	4.00	1.60
❑ 402	Mike Hegan	4.00	1.60
❑ 403	John Buzhardt	2.00	.80
❑ 404	Floyd Robinson	2.00	.80
❑ 405	Tommy Helms	4.00	1.60
❑ 406	Dick Ellsworth	2.00	.80
❑ 407	Gary Kolb	2.00	.80
❑ 408	Steve Carlton	30.00	12.00
❑ 409	Frank Peters / Ron Stone	2.00	.80
❑ 410	Ferguson Jenkins	10.00	4.00
❑ 411	Ron Hansen	2.00	.80
❑ 412	Clay Carroll	4.00	1.60
❑ 413	Tom McCraw	2.00	.80
❑ 414	Mickey Lolich	8.00	3.20
❑ 415	Johnny Callison	4.00	1.60
❑ 416	Bill Rigney MG	2.00	.80
❑ 417	Willie Crawford	2.00	.80
❑ 418	Eddie Fisher	2.00	.80
❑ 419	Jack Hiatt	2.00	.80
❑ 420	Cesar Tovar	2.00	.80
❑ 421	Ron Taylor	2.00	.80
❑ 422	Rene Lachemann	2.00	.80
❑ 423	Fred Gladding	2.00	.80
❑ 424	Chicago White Sox Team Card	4.00	1.60
❑ 425	Jim Maloney	4.00	1.60
❑ 426	Hank Allen	2.00	.80
❑ 427	Dick Calmus	2.00	.80
❑ 428	Vic Roznovsky	2.00	.80
❑ 429	Tommie Sisk	2.00	.80
❑ 430	Rico Petrocelli	4.00	1.60
❑ 431	Dooley Womack	2.00	.80
❑ 432	Bill Davis / Jose Vidal	2.00	.80
❑ 433	Bob Rodgers	2.00	.80
❑ 434	Ricardo Joseph	2.00	.80
❑ 435	Ron Perranoski	4.00	1.60
❑ 436	Hal Lanier	2.00	.80
❑ 437	Don Cardwell	2.00	.80
❑ 438	Lee Thomas	4.00	1.60
❑ 439	Lum Harris MG	2.00	.80
❑ 440	Claude Osteen	4.00	1.60
❑ 441	Alex Johnson	4.00	1.60
❑ 442	Dick Bosman	2.00	.80
❑ 443	Joe Azcue	2.00	.80
❑ 444	Jack Fisher	2.00	.80
❑ 445	Mike Shannon	4.00	1.60
❑ 446	Ron Kline	2.00	.80
❑ 447	George Korince / Fred Lasher	4.00	1.60
❑ 448	Gary Wagner	2.00	.80
❑ 449	Gene Oliver	2.00	.80
❑ 450	Jim Kaat	6.00	2.40
❑ 451	Al Spangler	2.00	.80
❑ 452	Jesus Alou	2.00	.80
❑ 453	Sammy Ellis	2.00	.80
❑ 454A	Frank Robinson CL Cap complete within circle	8.00	1.60
❑ 454B	Frank Robinson CL Cap partially within circle	8.00	1.60
❑ 455	Rico Carty	4.00	1.60
❑ 456	John O'Donoghue	2.00	.80
❑ 457	Jim Lefebvre	4.00	1.60
❑ 458	Lew Krausse	6.00	2.40
❑ 459	Dick Simpson	4.00	1.60
❑ 460	Jim Lonborg	6.00	2.40
❑ 461	Chuck Hiller	4.00	1.60
❑ 462	Barry Moore	4.00	1.60
❑ 463	Jim Schaffer	4.00	1.60
❑ 464	Don McMahon	4.00	1.60
❑ 465	Tommie Agee	10.00	4.00
❑ 466	Bill Dillman	4.00	1.60
❑ 467	Dick Howser	10.00	4.00
❑ 468	Larry Sherry	4.00	1.60
❑ 469	Ty Cline	4.00	1.60
❑ 470	Bill Freehan	10.00	4.00
❑ 471	Orlando Pena	4.00	1.60
❑ 472	Walter Alston MG	6.00	2.40
❑ 473	Al Worthington	4.00	1.60
❑ 474	Paul Schaal	4.00	1.60
❑ 475	Joe Niekro	6.00	2.40
❑ 476	Woody Woodward	4.00	1.60
❑ 477	Philadelphia Phillies Team Card	8.00	3.20
❑ 478	Dave McNally	6.00	2.40
❑ 479	Phil Gagliano	6.00	2.40
❑ 480	Tony Oliva / Chico Cardenas / Bob Clemente	80.00	32.00
❑ 481	John Wyatt	4.00	1.60
❑ 482	Jose Pagan	4.00	1.60
❑ 483	Darold Knowles	4.00	1.60
❑ 484	Phil Roof	4.00	1.60
❑ 485	Ken Berry	6.00	2.40
❑ 486	Cal Koonce	4.00	1.60
❑ 487	Lee May	10.00	4.00
❑ 488	Dick Tracewski	6.00	2.40
❑ 489	Wally Bunker	4.00	1.60
❑ 490	Harmon Killebrew / Willie Mays / Mickey Mantle	150.00	60.00
❑ 491	Denny Lemaster	4.00	1.60
❑ 492	Jeff Torborg	6.00	2.40
❑ 493	Jim McGlothlin	4.00	1.60
❑ 494	Ray Sadecki	4.00	1.60
❑ 495	Leon Wagner	4.00	1.60
❑ 496	Steve Hamilton	6.00	2.40
❑ 497	Cardinals Team	8.00	3.20
❑ 498	Bill Bryan	6.00	2.40
❑ 499	Steve Blass	6.00	2.40
❑ 500	Frank Robinson	30.00	12.00
❑ 501	John Odom	6.00	2.40
❑ 502	Mike Andrews	4.00	1.60
❑ 503	Al Jackson	6.00	2.40
❑ 504	Russ Snyder	4.00	1.60
❑ 505	Joe Sparma	10.00	4.00
❑ 506	Clarence Jones RC	4.00	1.60
❑ 507	Wade Blasingame	4.00	1.60
❑ 508	Duke Sims	4.00	1.60
❑ 509	Dennis Higgins	4.00	1.60
❑ 510	Ron Fairly	10.00	4.00
❑ 511	Bill Kelso	4.00	1.60
❑ 512	Grant Jackson	4.00	1.60
❑ 513	Hank Bauer MG	6.00	2.40
❑ 514	Al McBean	4.00	1.60
❑ 515	Russ Nixon	4.00	1.60
❑ 516	Pete Mikkelsen	4.00	1.60
❑ 517	Diego Segui	6.00	2.40
❑ 518A	Clete Boyer CL ERR 539 AL Rookies	12.00	2.40
❑ 518B	Clete Boyer CL COR 539 ML Rookies	12.00	2.40
❑ 519	Jerry Stephenson	4.00	1.60
❑ 520	Lou Brock	25.00	10.00
❑ 521	Don Shaw	4.00	1.60
❑ 522	Wayne Causey	4.00	1.60
❑ 523	John Tsitouris	4.00	1.60
❑ 524	Andy Kosco	6.00	2.40
❑ 525	Jim Davenport	4.00	1.60
❑ 526	Bill Denehy	4.00	1.60
❑ 527	Tito Francona	4.00	1.60
❑ 528	Tigers Team	60.00	24.00
❑ 529	Bruce Von Hoff	4.00	1.60
❑ 530	Brooks Robinson / Frank Robinson	40.00	16.00
❑ 531	Chuck Hinton	4.00	1.60
❑ 532	Luis Tiant	6.00	2.40
❑ 533	Wes Parker	6.00	2.40
❑ 534	Bob Miller	6.00	2.40
❑ 535	Danny Cater	6.00	2.40
❑ 536	Bill Short	4.00	1.60
❑ 537	Norm Siebern	6.00	2.40
❑ 538	Manny Jimenez	6.00	2.40
❑ 539	Jim Ray / Mike Ferraro	4.00	1.60
❑ 540	Nelson Briles	6.00	2.40
❑ 541	Sandy Alomar	6.00	2.40
❑ 542	John Boccabella	4.00	1.60
❑ 543	Bob Lee	4.00	1.60
❑ 544	Mayo Smith MG	12.00	4.80
❑ 545	Lindy McDaniel	6.00	2.40
❑ 546	Roy White	6.00	2.40
❑ 547	Dan Coombs	4.00	1.60
❑ 548	Bernie Allen	4.00	1.60
❑ 549	Curt Motton / Roger Nelson	4.00	1.60
❑ 550	Clete Boyer	6.00	2.40
❑ 551	Darrell Sutherland	4.00	1.60
❑ 552	Ed Kirkpatrick	4.00	1.60
❑ 553	Hank Aguirre	4.00	1.60
❑ 554	A's Team	10.00	4.00
❑ 555	Jose Tartabull	6.00	2.40
❑ 556	Dick Selma	4.00	1.60
❑ 557	Frank Quilici	6.00	2.40
❑ 558	Johnny Edwards	4.00	1.60
❑ 559	Carl Taylor / Luke Walker	4.00	1.60
❑ 560	Paul Casanova	4.00	1.60
❑ 561	Lee Elia	4.00	1.60
❑ 562	Jim Bouton	6.00	2.40
❑ 563	Ed Charles	4.00	1.60
❑ 564	Eddie Stanky MG	6.00	2.40
❑ 565	Larry Dierker	6.00	2.40
❑ 566	Ken Harrelson	6.00	2.40
❑ 567	Clay Dalrymple	4.00	1.60
❑ 568	Willie Smith	4.00	1.60
❑ 569	Ivan Murrell / Les Rohr	4.00	1.60
❑ 570	Rick Reichardt	4.00	1.60
❑ 571	Tony LaRussa	12.00	4.80
❑ 572	Don Bosch	4.00	1.60
❑ 573	Joe Coleman	4.00	1.60
❑ 574	Cincinnati Reds Team Card	10.00	4.00
❑ 575	Jim Palmer	40.00	16.00
❑ 576	Dave Adlesh	4.00	1.60
❑ 577	Fred Talbot	4.00	1.60
❑ 578	Orlando Martinez	4.00	1.60
❑ 579	Larry Hisle RC / Mike Lum	10.00	4.00
❑ 580	Bob Bailey	4.00	1.60
❑ 581	Garry Roggenburk	4.00	1.60
❑ 582	Jerry Grote	10.00	4.00
❑ 583	Gates Brown	10.00	4.00
❑ 584	Larry Shepard MG	4.00	1.60
❑ 585	Wilbur Wood	6.00	2.40
❑ 586	Jim Pagliaroni	6.00	2.40
❑ 587	Roger Repoz	4.00	1.60
❑ 588	Dick Schofield	4.00	1.60
❑ 589	Ron Clark / Moe Ogier	4.00	1.60
❑ 590	Tommy Harper	6.00	2.40
❑ 591	Dick Nen	4.00	1.60
❑ 592	John Bateman	4.00	1.60
❑ 593	Lee Stange	4.00	1.60
❑ 594	Phil Linz	6.00	2.40
❑ 595	Phil Ortega	4.00	1.60
❑ 596	Charlie Smith	4.00	1.60
❑ 597	Bill McCool	4.00	1.60
❑ 598	Jerry May	6.00	1.85

1969 Topps

	NM	Ex
COMP. MASTER (695)	5000.00	2000.00
COMPLETE SET (664)	2800.00	1100.00
COMMON (1-218/328-512)	1.50	.60
COMMON (219-327)	2.50	1.00

COMMON (513-588) 2.00 .80
COMMON (589-664) 3.00 1.20
WRAPPER (5-CENT) 20.00 8.00

❑ 1 Carl Yastrzemski 15.00 5.25
Danny Cater
Tony Oliva LL
❑ 2 Pete Rose 8.00 3.20
Matty Alou
Felipe Alou LL
❑ 3 Ken Harrelson 4.00 1.60
Frank Howard
Jim Northrup LL
❑ 4 Willie McCovey 6.00 2.40
Ron Santo
Billy Williams LL
❑ 5 Frank Howard 4.00 1.60
Willie Horton
Ken Harrelson LL
❑ 6 Willie McCovey 6.00 2.40
Richie Allen
Ernie Banks LL
❑ 7 Luis Tiant 4.00 1.60
Sam McDowell
Dave McNally LL
❑ 8 Bob Gibson 6.00 2.40
Bobby Bolin
Bob Veale LL
❑ 9 Denny McLain 4.00 1.60
Dave McNally
Luis Tiant
Mel Stottlemyre LL
❑ 10 Juan Marichal 8.00 3.20
Bob Gibson
Fergie Jenkins LL
❑ 11 Sam McDowell 4.00 1.60
Denny McLain
Luis Tiant LL
❑ 12 Bob Gibson 4.00 1.60
Fergie Jenkins
Bill Singer LL
❑ 13 Mickey Stanley 2.50 1.00
❑ 14 Al McBean 1.50 .60
❑ 15 Boog Powell 4.00 1.60
❑ 16 Cesar Gutierrez 1.50 .60
Rich Robertson
❑ 17 Mike Marshall 2.50 1.00
❑ 18 Dick Schofield 1.50 .60
❑ 19 Ken Suarez 1.50 .60
❑ 20 Ernie Banks 20.00 8.00
❑ 21 Jose Santiago 1.50 .60
❑ 22 Jesus Alou 2.50 1.00
❑ 23 Lew Krausse 1.50 .60
❑ 24 Walt Alston MG 4.00 1.60
❑ 25 Roy White 2.50 1.00
❑ 26 Clay Carroll 2.50 1.00
❑ 27 Bernie Allen 1.50 .60
❑ 28 Mike Ryan 1.50 .60
❑ 29 Dave Morehead 1.50 .60
❑ 30 Bob Allison 2.50 1.00
❑ 31 Gary Gentry RC 2.50 1.00
Amos Otis RC
❑ 32 Sammy Ellis 1.50 .60
❑ 33 Wayne Causey 1.50 .60
❑ 34 Gary Peters 1.50 .60
❑ 35 Joe Morgan 10.00 4.00
❑ 36 Luke Walker 1.50 .60
❑ 37 Curt Motton 1.50 .60
❑ 38 Zoilo Versalles 2.50 1.00
❑ 39 Dick Hughes 1.50 .60
❑ 40 Mayo Smith MG 1.50 .60
❑ 41 Bob Barton 1.50 .60
❑ 42 Tommy Harper 2.50 1.00
❑ 43 Joe Niekro 2.50 1.00
❑ 44 Danny Cater 1.50 .60
❑ 45 Maury Wills 2.50 1.00
❑ 46 Fritz Peterson 2.50 1.00
❑ 47A Paul Popovich 2.50 1.00
No helmet emblem, thick airbrushing
❑ 47B Paul Popovich 2.50 1.00
No helmet emblem, light airbrushing
❑ 47C Paul Popovich 25.00 10.00
(C emblem on helmet)
❑ 48 Brant Alyea 1.50 .60
❑ 49A Royals Rookies ERR 25.00 10.00
Steve Jones
E. Rodriquez
❑ 49B Royals Rookies COR 1.50 .60
Steve Jones
E. Rodriguez
❑ 50 Roberto Clemente UER 60.00 24.00
Bats Right listed twice
❑ 51 Woody Fryman 2.50 1.00
❑ 52 Mike Andrews 1.50 .60
❑ 53 Sonny Jackson 1.50 .60
❑ 54 Cisco Carlos 1.50 .60
❑ 55 Jerry Grote 2.50 1.00
❑ 56 Rich Reese 1.50 .60
❑ 57 Denny McLain CL 6.00 1.20
❑ 58 Fred Gladding 1.50 .60
❑ 59 Jay Johnstone 2.50 1.00
❑ 60 Nelson Briles 2.50 1.00
❑ 61 Jimmie Hall 1.50 .60
❑ 62 Chico Salmon 1.50 .60
❑ 63 Jim Hickman 2.50 1.00
❑ 64 Bill Monbouquette 1.50 .60
❑ 65 Willie Davis 2.50 1.00
❑ 66 Mike Adamson 1.50 .60
Merv Rettenmund
❑ 67 Bill Stoneman 2.50 1.00
❑ 68 Dave Duncan 2.50 1.00
❑ 69 Steve Hamilton 2.50 1.00
❑ 70 Tommy Helms 2.50 1.00
❑ 71 Steve Whitaker 2.50 1.00
❑ 72 Ron Taylor 1.50 .60
❑ 73 Johnny Briggs 1.50 .60
❑ 74 Preston Gomez MG 2.50 1.00
❑ 75 Luis Aparicio 6.00 2.40
❑ 76 Norm Miller 1.50 .60
❑ 77A Ron Perranoski 2.50 1.00
(No emblem on cap)
❑ 77B Ron Perranoski 25.00 10.00
(LA on cap)
❑ 78 Tom Satriano 1.50 .60
❑ 79 Milt Pappas 2.50 1.00
❑ 80 Norm Cash 2.50 1.00
❑ 81 Mel Queen 1.50 .60
❑ 82 Rich Hebner RC 8.00 3.20
Al Oliver RC
❑ 83 Mike Ferraro 2.50 1.00
❑ 84 Bob Humphreys 1.50 .60
❑ 85 Lou Brock 20.00 8.00
❑ 86 Pete Richert 1.50 .60
❑ 87 Horace Clarke 2.50 1.00
❑ 88 Rich Nye 1.50 .60
❑ 89 Russ Gibson 1.50 .60
❑ 90 Jerry Koosman 2.50 1.00
❑ 91 Alvin Dark MG 2.50 1.00
❑ 92 Jack Billingham 2.50 1.00
❑ 93 Joe Foy 2.50 1.00
❑ 94 Hank Aguirre 1.50 .60
❑ 95 Johnny Bench 50.00 20.00
❑ 96 Denny Lemaster 1.50 .60
❑ 97 Buddy Bradford 1.50 .60
❑ 98 Dave Giusti 1.50 .60
❑ 99A Twins Rookies 15.00 6.00
Danny Morris
Graig Nettles RC
(No loop)
❑ 99B Twins Rookies 15.00 6.00
Danny Morris
Graig Nettles RC
(Errant loop in
upper left corner
of obverse)
❑ 100 Hank Aaron 50.00 20.00
❑ 101 Daryl Patterson 1.50 .60
❑ 102 Jim Davenport 1.50 .60
❑ 103 Roger Repoz 1.50 .60
❑ 104 Steve Blass 1.50 .60
❑ 105 Rick Monday 2.50 1.00
❑ 106 Jim Hannan 1.50 .60
❑ 107A Bob Gibson CL ERR 6.00 1.20
161 Jim Purdin
❑ 107B Bob Gibson CL COR 8.00 1.60
161 John Purdin
❑ 108 Tony Taylor 2.50 1.00
❑ 109 Jim Lonborg 2.50 1.00
❑ 110 Mike Shannon 2.50 1.00
❑ 111 John Morris RC 1.50 .60
❑ 112 J.C. Martin 2.50 1.00
❑ 113 Dave May 1.50 .60
❑ 114 Alan Closter 2.50 1.00
John Cumberland
❑ 115 Bill Hands 1.50 .60
❑ 116 Chuck Harrison 1.50 .60
❑ 117 Jim Fairey 2.50 1.00
❑ 118 Stan Williams 1.50 .60
❑ 119 Doug Rader 2.50 1.00
❑ 120 Pete Rose 50.00 20.00
❑ 121 Joe Grzenda 1.50 .60
❑ 122 Ron Fairly 2.50 1.00
❑ 123 Wilbur Wood 2.50 1.00
❑ 124 Hank Bauer MG 2.50 1.00
❑ 125 Ray Sadecki 1.50 .60
❑ 126 Dick Tracewski 1.50 .60
❑ 127 Kevin Collins 2.50 1.00
❑ 128 Tommie Aaron 2.50 1.00
❑ 129 Bill McCool 1.50 .60
❑ 130 Carl Yastrzemski 20.00 8.00
❑ 131 Chris Cannizzaro 1.50 .60
❑ 132 Dave Baldwin 1.50 .60
❑ 133 Johnny Callison 2.50 1.00
❑ 134 Jim Weaver 1.50 .60
❑ 135 Tommy Davis 2.50 1.00
❑ 136 Steve Huntz 1.50 .60
Mike Torrez
❑ 137 Wally Bunker 1.50 .60
❑ 138 John Bateman 1.50 .60
❑ 139 Andy Kosco 1.50 .60
❑ 140 Jim Lefebvre 2.50 1.00
❑ 141 Bill Dillman 1.50 .60
❑ 142 Woody Woodward 1.50 .60
❑ 143 Joe Nossek 1.50 .60
❑ 144 Bob Hendley 2.50 1.00
❑ 145 Max Alvis 1.50 .60
❑ 146 Jim Perry 2.50 1.00
❑ 147 Leo Durocher MG 4.00 1.60
❑ 148 Lee Stange 1.50 .60
❑ 149 Ollie Brown 2.50 1.00
❑ 150 Denny McLain 4.00 1.60
❑ 151A Clay Dalrymple 1.50 .60
Portrait, Orioles
❑ 151B Clay Dalrymple 15.00 6.00
Catching, Phillies
❑ 152 Tommie Sisk 1.50 .60
❑ 153 Ed Brinkman 1.50 .60
❑ 154 Jim Britton 1.50 .60
❑ 155 Pete Ward 1.50 .60
❑ 156 Hal Gilson 1.50 .60
Leon McFadden
❑ 157 Bob Rodgers 2.50 1.00
❑ 158 Joe Gibbon 1.50 .60
❑ 159 Jerry Adair 1.50 .60
❑ 160 Vada Pinson 2.50 1.00
❑ 161 John Purdin 1.50 .60
❑ 162 Bob Gibson WS 8.00 3.20
Fans 17
❑ 163 Willie Horton WS 6.00 2.40
❑ 164 Tim McCarver WS 12.00 4.80
Roger Maris
❑ 165 Lou Brock WS 8.00 3.20
❑ 166 Al Kaline WS 8.00 3.20
❑ 167 Jim Northrup WS 6.00 2.40
❑ 168 Mickey Lolich WS 8.00 3.20
Bob Gibson
❑ 169 Dick McAuliffe WS 6.00 2.40
Denny McLain
Willie Horton
❑ 170 Frank Howard 2.50 1.00
❑ 171 Glenn Beckert 2.50 1.00
❑ 172 Jerry Stephenson 1.50 .60
❑ 173 Bob Christian 1.50 .60
Gerry Nyman
❑ 174 Grant Jackson 1.50 .60
❑ 175 Jim Bunning 6.00 2.40
❑ 176 Joe Azcue 1.50 .60
❑ 177 Ron Reed 1.50 .60
❑ 178 Ray Oyler 2.50 1.00
❑ 179 Don Pavletich 1.50 .60
❑ 180 Willie Horton 2.50 1.00
❑ 181 Mel Nelson 1.50 .60
❑ 182 Bill Rigney MG 1.50 .60
❑ 183 Don Shaw 2.50 1.00
❑ 184 Roberto Pena 1.50 .60
❑ 185 Tom Phoebus 1.50 .60
❑ 186 Johnny Edwards 1.50 .60
❑ 187 Leon Wagner 1.50 .60

❑ 188 Rick Wise 2.50 1.00
❑ 189 Joe Lahoud 1.50 .60
John Thibodeau
❑ 190 Willie Mays 80.00 32.00
❑ 191 Lindy McDaniel 2.50 1.00
❑ 192 Jose Pagan 1.50 .60
❑ 193 Don Cardwell 2.50 1.00
❑ 194 Ted Uhlaender 1.50 .60
❑ 195 John Odom 1.50 .60
❑ 196 Lum Harris MG 1.50 .60
❑ 197 Dick Selma 1.50 .60
❑ 198 Willie Smith 1.50 .60
❑ 199 Jim French 1.50 .60
❑ 200 Bob Gibson 12.00 4.80
❑ 201 Russ Snyder 1.50 .60
❑ 202 Don Wilson 2.50 1.00
❑ 203 Dave Johnson 2.50 1.00
❑ 204 Jack Hiatt 1.50 .60
❑ 205 Rick Reichardt 1.50 .60
❑ 206 Larry Hisle 2.50 1.00
Barry Lersch
❑ 207 Roy Face 2.50 1.00
❑ 208A Donn Clendenon 2.50 1.00
Houston
❑ 208B Donn Clendenon 15.00 6.00
Expos
❑ 209 Larry Haney UER 1.50 .60
(Reverse negative)
❑ 210 Felix Millan 1.50 .60
❑ 211 Galen Cisco 1.50 .60
❑ 212 Tom Tresh 2.50 1.00
❑ 213 Gerry Arrigo 1.50 .60
❑ 214 Checklist 3 6.00 1.20
With 69T deckle CL
on back (no player)
❑ 215 Rico Petrocelli 2.50 1.00
❑ 216 Don Sutton 6.00 2.40
❑ 217 John Donaldson 1.50 .60
❑ 218 John Roseboro 2.50 1.00
❑ 219 Freddie Patek RC 4.00 1.60
❑ 220 Sam McDowell 4.00 1.60
❑ 221 Art Shamsky 4.00 1.60
❑ 222 Duane Josephson 2.50 1.00
❑ 223 Tom Dukes 4.00 1.60
❑ 224 Bill Harrelson 2.50 1.00
Steve Kealey
❑ 225 Don Kessinger 4.00 1.60
❑ 226 Bruce Howard 2.50 1.00
❑ 227 Frank Johnson 2.50 1.00
❑ 228 Dave Leonhard 2.50 1.00
❑ 229 Don Lock 2.50 1.00
❑ 230 Rusty Staub UER 4.00 1.60
For 1966 stats, Houston spelled
Huoston
❑ 231 Pat Dobson 4.00 1.60
❑ 232 Dave Ricketts 2.50 1.00
❑ 233 Steve Barber 4.00 1.60
❑ 234 Dave Bristol MG 2.50 1.00
❑ 235 Jim Hunter 10.00 4.00
❑ 236 Manny Mota 4.00 1.60
❑ 237 Bobby Cox RC 10.00 4.00
❑ 238 Ken Johnson 2.50 1.00
❑ 239 Bob Taylor 4.00 1.60
❑ 240 Ken Harrelson 4.00 1.60
❑ 241 Jim Brewer 2.50 1.00
❑ 242 Frank Kostro 2.50 1.00
❑ 243 Ron Kline 2.50 1.00
❑ 244 Ray Fosse RC 4.00 1.60
George Woodson
❑ 245 Ed Charles 4.00 1.60
❑ 246 Joe Coleman 2.50 1.00
❑ 247 Gene Oliver 2.50 1.00
❑ 248 Bob Priddy 2.50 1.00
❑ 249 Ed Spiezio 4.00 1.60
❑ 250 Frank Robinson 20.00 8.00
❑ 251 Ron Herbel 2.50 1.00
❑ 252 Chuck Cottier 2.50 1.00
❑ 253 Jerry Johnson 2.50 1.00
❑ 254 Joe Schultz MG 4.00 1.60
❑ 255 Steve Carlton 30.00 12.00
❑ 256 Gates Brown 4.00 1.60
❑ 257 Jim Ray 2.50 1.00
❑ 258 Jackie Hernandez 4.00 1.60
❑ 259 Bill Short 2.50 1.00
❑ 260 Reggie Jackson RC 250.00 80.00
❑ 261 Bob Johnson 2.50 1.00
❑ 262 Mike Kekich 4.00 1.60
❑ 263 Jerry May 2.50 1.00
❑ 264 Bill Landis 2.50 1.00
❑ 265 Chico Cardenas 4.00 1.60
❑ 266 Tom Hutton 4.00 1.60
Alan Foster
❑ 267 Vicente Romo 2.50 1.00
❑ 268 Al Spangler 2.50 1.00
❑ 269 Al Weis 4.00 1.60
❑ 270 Mickey Lolich 4.00 1.60
❑ 271 Larry Stahl 4.00 1.60
❑ 272 Ed Stroud 2.50 1.00
❑ 273 Ron Willis 2.50 1.00
❑ 274 Clyde King MG 2.50 1.00
❑ 275 Vic Davalillo 2.50 1.00
❑ 276 Gary Wagner 2.50 1.00
❑ 277 Elrod Hendricks RC 2.50 1.00
❑ 278 Gary Geiger UER 2.50 1.00
(Batting wrong)
❑ 279 Roger Nelson 4.00 1.60
❑ 280 Alex Johnson 4.00 1.60
❑ 281 Ted Kubiak 2.50 1.00
❑ 282 Pat Jarvis 2.50 1.00
❑ 283 Sandy Alomar 4.00 1.60
❑ 284 Jerry Robertson 4.00 1.60
Mike Wegener
❑ 285 Don Mincher 4.00 1.60
❑ 286 Dock Ellis RC 4.00 1.60
❑ 287 Jose Tartabull 4.00 1.60
❑ 288 Ken Holtzman 4.00 1.60
❑ 289 Bart Shirley 2.50 1.00
❑ 290 Jim Kaat 4.00 1.60
❑ 291 Vern Fuller 2.50 1.00
❑ 292 Al Downing 4.00 1.60
❑ 293 Dick Dietz 2.50 1.00
❑ 294 Jim Lemon MG 2.50 1.00
❑ 295 Tony Perez 12.00 4.80
❑ 296 Andy Messersmith RC 4.00 1.60
❑ 297 Deron Johnson 2.50 1.00
❑ 298 Dave Nicholson 4.00 1.60
❑ 299 Mark Belanger 4.00 1.60
❑ 300 Felipe Alou 4.00 1.60
❑ 301 Darrell Brandon 4.00 1.60
❑ 302 Jim Pagliaroni 2.50 1.00
❑ 303 Cal Koonce 4.00 1.60
❑ 304 Bill Davis 6.00 2.40
Clarence Gaston RC
❑ 305 Dick McAuliffe 4.00 1.60
❑ 306 Jim Grant 4.00 1.60
❑ 307 Gary Kolb 2.50 1.00
❑ 308 Wade Blasingame 2.50 1.00
❑ 309 Walt Williams 2.50 1.00
❑ 310 Tom Haller 2.50 1.00
❑ 311 Sparky Lyle RC 10.00 4.00
❑ 312 Lee Elia 2.50 1.00
❑ 313 Bill Robinson 4.00 1.60
❑ 314 Don Drysdale CL 6.00 1.20
❑ 315 Eddie Fisher 2.50 1.00
❑ 316 Hal Lanier 2.50 1.00
❑ 317 Bruce Look 2.50 1.00
❑ 318 Jack Fisher 2.50 1.00
❑ 319 Ken McMullen UER 2.50 1.00
(Headings on back
are for a pitcher)
❑ 320 Dal Maxvill 2.50 1.00
❑ 321 Jim McAndrew 4.00 1.60
❑ 322 Jose Vidal 4.00 1.60
❑ 323 Larry Miller 2.50 1.00
❑ 324 Les Cain 4.00 1.60
Dave Campbell RC
❑ 325 Jose Cardenal 4.00 1.60
❑ 326 Gary Sutherland 4.00 1.60
❑ 327 Willie Crawford 2.50 1.00
❑ 328 Joel Horlen 1.50 .60
❑ 329 Rick Joseph 1.50 .60
❑ 330 Tony Conigliaro 4.00 1.60
❑ 331 Gil Garrido 2.50 1.00
Tom House RC
❑ 332 Fred Talbot 1.50 .60
❑ 333 Ivan Murrell 1.50 .60
❑ 334 Phil Roof 1.50 .60
❑ 335 Bill Mazeroski 6.00 2.40
❑ 336 Jim Roland 1.50 .60
❑ 337 Marty Martinez 1.50 .60
❑ 338 Del Unser 1.50 .60
❑ 339 Steve Mingori 1.50 .60
Jose Pena
❑ 340 Dave McNally 2.50 1.00
❑ 341 Dave Adlesh 1.50 .60
❑ 342 Bubba Morton 1.50 .60
❑ 343 Dan Frisella 1.50 .60
❑ 344 Tom Matchick 1.50 .60
❑ 345 Frank Linzy 1.50 .60
❑ 346 Wayne Comer 1.50 .60
❑ 347 Randy Hundley 2.50 1.00
❑ 348 Steve Hargan 1.50 .60
❑ 349 Dick Williams MG 2.50 1.00
❑ 350 Richie Allen 4.00 1.60
❑ 351 Carroll Sembera 1.50 .60
❑ 352 Paul Schaal 2.50 1.00
❑ 353 Jeff Torborg 2.50 1.00
❑ 354 Nate Oliver 1.50 .60
❑ 355 Phil Niekro 6.00 2.40
❑ 356 Frank Quilici 1.50 .60
❑ 357 Carl Taylor 1.50 .60
❑ 358 George Lauzerique 1.50 .60
Roberto Rodriquez
❑ 359 Dick Kelley 1.50 .60
❑ 360 Jim Wynn 2.50 1.00
❑ 361 Gary Holman 1.50 .60
❑ 362 Jim Maloney 2.50 1.00
❑ 363 Russ Nixon 1.50 .60
❑ 364 Tommie Agee 4.00 1.60
❑ 365 Jim Fregosi 2.50 1.00
❑ 366 Bo Belinsky 2.50 1.00
❑ 367 Lou Johnson 2.50 1.00
❑ 368 Vic Roznovsky 1.50 .60
❑ 369 Bob Skinner MG 2.50 1.00
❑ 370 Juan Marichal 8.00 3.20
❑ 371 Sal Bando 2.50 1.00
❑ 372 Adolfo Phillips 1.50 .60
❑ 373 Fred Lasher 1.50 .60
❑ 374 Bob Tillman 1.50 .60
❑ 375 Harmon Killebrew 15.00 6.00
❑ 376 Mike Fiore 1.50 .60
Jim Rooker RC
❑ 377 Gary Bell 2.50 1.00
❑ 378 Jose Herrera 1.50 .60
❑ 379 Ken Boyer 2.50 1.00
❑ 380 Stan Bahnsen 2.50 1.00
❑ 381 Ed Kranepool 2.50 1.00
❑ 382 Pat Corrales 2.50 1.00
❑ 383 Casey Cox 1.50 .60
❑ 384 Larry Shepard MG 1.50 .60
❑ 385 Orlando Cepeda 6.00 2.40
❑ 386 Jim McGlothlin 1.50 .60
❑ 387 Bobby Klaus 1.50 .60
❑ 388 Tom McCraw 1.50 .60
❑ 389 Dan Coombs 1.50 .60
❑ 390 Bill Freehan 2.50 1.00
❑ 391 Ray Culp 1.50 .60
❑ 392 Bob Burda 1.50 .60
❑ 393 Gene Brabender 2.50 1.00
❑ 394 Lou Piniella 6.00 2.40
Marv Staehle
❑ 395 Chris Short 1.50 .60
❑ 396 Jim Campanis 1.50 .60
❑ 397 Chuck Dobson 1.50 .60
❑ 398 Tito Francona 1.50 .60
❑ 399 Bob Bailey 2.50 1.00
❑ 400 Don Drysdale 15.00 6.00
❑ 401 Jake Gibbs 2.50 1.00
❑ 402 Ken Boswell 2.50 1.00
❑ 403 Bob Miller 1.50 .60
❑ 404 Vic LaRose 2.50 1.00
Gary Ross
❑ 405 Lee May 2.50 1.00
❑ 406 Phil Ortega 1.50 .60
❑ 407 Tom Egan 1.50 .60
❑ 408 Nate Colbert 1.50 .60
❑ 409 Bob Moose 1.50 .60
❑ 410 Al Kaline 25.00 10.00
❑ 411 Larry Dierker 2.50 1.00
❑ 412 Mickey Mantle CL DP 15.00 3.00
❑ 413 Roland Sheldon 2.50 1.00
❑ 414 Duke Sims 1.50 .60
❑ 415 Ray Washburn 1.50 .60
❑ 416 Willie McCovey AS 8.00 3.20
❑ 417 Ken Harrelson AS 3.00 1.20
❑ 418 Tommy Helms AS 3.00 1.20
❑ 419 Rod Carew AS 10.00 4.00
❑ 420 Ron Santo AS 4.00 1.60

❑ 421 Brooks Robinson AS 8.00 3.20
❑ 422 Don Kessinger AS 3.00 1.20
❑ 423 Bert Campaneris AS 4.00 1.60
❑ 424 Pete Rose AS 15.00 6.00
❑ 425 Carl Yastrzemski AS 10.00 4.00
❑ 426 Curt Flood AS 4.00 1.60
❑ 427 Tony Oliva AS 4.00 1.60
❑ 428 Lou Brock AS 6.00 2.40
❑ 429 Willie Horton AS 3.00 1.20
❑ 430 Johnny Bench AS 10.00 4.00
❑ 431 Bill Freehan AS 4.00 1.60
❑ 432 Bob Gibson AS 6.00 2.40
❑ 433 Denny McLain AS 3.00 1.20
❑ 434 Jerry Koosman AS 3.00 1.20
❑ 435 Sam McDowell AS 2.50 1.00
❑ 436 Gene Alley 2.50 1.00
❑ 437 Luis Alcaraz 1.50 .60
❑ 438 Gary Waslewski 1.50 .60
❑ 439 Ed Herrmann 1.50 .60
Dan Lazar
❑ 440A Willie McCovey 15.00 6.00
❑ 440B Willie McCovey WL 100.00 40.00
(McCovey white)
❑ 441A Dennis Higgins 1.50 .60
❑ 441B Dennis Higgins WL 25.00 10.00
(Higgins white)
❑ 442 Ty Cline 1.50 .60
❑ 443 Don Wert 1.50 .60
❑ 444A Joe Moeller 1.50 .60
❑ 444B Joe Moeller WL 25.00 10.00
(Moeller white)
❑ 445 Bobby Knoop 1.50 .60
❑ 446 Claude Raymond 1.50 .60
❑ 447A Ralph Houk MG 2.50 1.00
❑ 447B Ralph Houk WL 25.00 10.00
MG (Houk white)
❑ 448 Bob Tolan 2.50 1.00
❑ 449 Paul Lindblad 1.50 .60
❑ 450 Billy Williams 8.00 3.20
❑ 451A Rich Rollins 2.50 1.00
❑ 451B Rich Rollins WL 25.00 10.00
(Rich and 3B white)
❑ 452A Al Ferrara 1.50 .60
❑ 452B Al Ferrara WL 25.00 10.00
(Al and OF white)
❑ 453 Mike Cuellar 2.50 1.00
❑ 454A Phillies Rookies 2.50 1.00
Larry Colton
Don Money
❑ 454B Phillies Rookies WL 25.00 10.00
Larry Colton
Don Money
(Names in white)
❑ 455 Sonny Siebert 1.50 .60
❑ 456 Bud Harrelson 2.50 1.00
❑ 457 Dalton Jones 1.50 .60
❑ 458 Curt Blefary 1.50 .60
❑ 459 Dave Boswell 1.50 .60
❑ 460 Joe Torre 4.00 1.60
❑ 461A Mike Epstein 1.50 .60
❑ 461B Mike Epstein WL 25.00 10.00
(Epstein white)
❑ 462 Red Schoendienst 2.50 1.00
MG
❑ 463 Dennis Ribant 1.50 .60
❑ 464A Dave Marshall 1.50 .60
❑ 464B Dave Marshall WL 25.00 10.00
(Marshall white)
❑ 465 Tommy John 4.00 1.60
❑ 466 John Boccabella 2.50 1.00
❑ 467 Tommie Reynolds 1.50 .60
❑ 468A Pirates Rookies 1.50 .60
Bruce Dal Canton
Bob Robertson
❑ 468B Pirates Rookies WL 25.00 10.00
Bruce Dal Canton
Bob Robertson
(Names in white)
❑ 469 Chico Ruiz 1.50 .60
❑ 470A Mel Stottlemyre 2.50 1.00
❑ 470B Mel Stottlemyre WL 30.00 12.00
(Stottlemyre white)
❑ 471A Ted Savage 1.50 .60
❑ 471B Ted Savage WL 25.00 10.00
(Savage white)
❑ 472 Jim Price 1.50 .60
❑ 473A Jose Arcia 1.50 .60
❑ 473B Jose Arcia WL 25.00 10.00
(Jose and 2B white)
❑ 474 Tom Murphy 1.50 .60
❑ 475 Tim McCarver 4.00 1.60
❑ 476A Boston Rookies 3.00 1.20
Ken Brett RC
Gerry Moses
❑ 476B Boston Rookies WL 30.00 12.00
Ken Brett RC
Gerry Moses
(Names in white)
❑ 477 Jeff James 1.50 .60
❑ 478 Don Buford 1.50 .60
❑ 479 Richie Scheinblum 1.50 .60
❑ 480 Tom Seaver 80.00 32.00
❑ 481 Bill Melton 2.50 1.00
❑ 482A Jim Gosger 1.50 .60
❑ 482B Jim Gosger WL 25.00 10.00
(Jim and OF white)
❑ 483 Ted Abernathy 1.50 .60
❑ 484 Joe Gordon MG 2.50 1.00
❑ 485A Gaylord Perry 10.00 4.00
❑ 485B Gaylord Perry WL 80.00 32.00
(Perry white)
❑ 486A Paul Casanova 1.50 .60
❑ 486B Paul Casanova WL 25.00 10.00
(Casanova white)
❑ 487 Denis Menke 1.50 .60
❑ 488 Joe Sparma 1.50 .60
❑ 489 Clete Boyer 2.50 1.00
❑ 490 Matty Alou 2.50 1.00
❑ 491A Twins Rookies 1.50 .60
Jerry Crider
George Mitterwald
❑ 491B Twins Rookies WL 25.00 10.00
Jerry Crider
George Mitterwald
(Names in white)
❑ 492 Tony Cloninger 1.50 .60
❑ 493A Wes Parker 2.50 1.00
❑ 493B Wes Parker WL 25.00 10.00
(Parker white)
❑ 494 Ken Berry 1.50 .60
❑ 495 Bert Campaneris 2.50 1.00
❑ 496 Larry Jaster 1.50 .60
❑ 497 Julian Javier 2.50 1.00
❑ 498 Juan Pizarro 2.50 1.00
❑ 499 Don Bryant 1.50 .60
Steve Shea
❑ 500A Mickey Mantle UER 300.00 120.00
(No Topps copy-
right on card back)
❑ 500B Mickey Mantle WL 2000.00 800.00
(Mantle in white;
no Topps copyright
on card back) UER
❑ 501A Tony Gonzalez 2.50 1.00
❑ 501B Tony Gonzalez WL 25.00 10.00
(Tony and OF white)
❑ 502 Minnie Rojas 1.50 .60
❑ 503 Larry Brown 1.50 .60
❑ 504 Brooks Robinson CL 8.00 1.60
❑ 505A Bobby Bolin 1.50 .60
❑ 505B Bobby Bolin WL 25.00 10.00
(Bolin white)
❑ 506 Paul Blair 2.50 1.00
❑ 507 Cookie Rojas 2.50 1.00
❑ 508 Moe Drabowsky 2.50 1.00
❑ 509 Manny Sanguillen 2.50 1.00
❑ 510 Rod Carew 40.00 16.00
❑ 511A Diego Segui 2.50 1.00
❑ 511B Diego Segui WL 25.00 10.00
(Diego and P white)
❑ 512 Cleon Jones 2.50 1.00
❑ 513 Camilo Pascual 3.00 1.20
❑ 514 Mike Lum 2.00 .80
❑ 515 Dick Green 2.00 .80
❑ 516 Earl Weaver RC MG 20.00 8.00
❑ 517 Mike McCormick 3.00 1.20
❑ 518 Fred Whitfield 2.00 .80
❑ 519 Jerry Kenney 2.00 .80
Len Boehmer
❑ 520 Bob Veale 3.00 1.20
❑ 521 George Thomas 2.00 .80
❑ 522 Joe Hoerner 2.00 .80
❑ 523 Bob Chance 2.00 .80
❑ 524 Jose Laboy 3.00 1.20
Floyd Wicker
❑ 525 Earl Wilson 3.00 1.20
❑ 526 Hector Torres 2.00 .80
❑ 527 Al Lopez MG 5.00 2.00
❑ 528 Claude Osteen 3.00 1.20
❑ 529 Ed Kirkpatrick 3.00 1.20
❑ 530 Cesar Tovar 2.00 .80
❑ 531 Dick Farrell 2.00 .80
❑ 532 Tom Phoebus 3.00 1.20
Jim Hardin
Dave McNally
Mike Cuellar
❑ 533 Nolan Ryan 200.00 100.00
❑ 534 Jerry McNertney 3.00 1.20
❑ 535 Phil Regan 3.00 1.20
❑ 536 Danny Breeden 2.00 .80
Dave Roberts
❑ 537 Mike Paul 2.00 .80
❑ 538 Charlie Smith 2.00 .80
❑ 539 Mike Epstein 12.00 4.80
Ted Williams MG
❑ 540 Curt Flood 3.00 1.20
❑ 541 Joe Verbanic 2.00 .80
❑ 542 Bob Aspromonte 2.00 .80
❑ 543 Fred Newman 2.00 .80
❑ 544 Mike Kilkenny 2.00 .80
Ron Woods
❑ 545 Willie Stargell 12.00 4.80
❑ 546 Jim Nash 2.00 .80
❑ 547 Billy Martin MG 5.00 2.00
❑ 548 Bob Locker 2.00 .80
❑ 549 Ron Brand 2.00 .80
❑ 550 Brooks Robinson 30.00 12.00
❑ 551 Wayne Granger 2.00 .80
❑ 552 Ted Sizemore RC 3.00 1.20
Bill Sudakis
❑ 553 Ron Davis 2.00 .80
❑ 554 Frank Bertaina 2.00 .80
❑ 555 Jim Ray Hart 3.00 1.20
❑ 556 Sal Bando 3.00 1.20
Bert Campaneris
Danny Cater
❑ 557 Frank Fernandez 2.00 .80
❑ 558 Tom Burgmeier 3.00 1.20
❑ 559 Joe Hague 2.00 .80
Jim Hicks
❑ 560 Luis Tiant 3.00 1.20
❑ 561 Ron Clark 2.00 .80
❑ 562 Bob Watson RC 8.00 3.20
❑ 563 Marty Pattin 3.00 1.20
❑ 564 Gil Hodges MG 10.00 4.00
❑ 565 Hoyt Wilhelm 8.00 3.20
❑ 566 Ron Hansen 2.00 .80
❑ 567 Elvio Jimenez 2.00 .80
Jim Shellenback
❑ 568 Cecil Upshaw 2.00 .80
❑ 569 Billy Harris 1.50 .60
❑ 570 Ron Santo 8.00 3.20
❑ 571 Cap Peterson 2.00 .80
❑ 572 Willie McCovey 15.00 6.00
Juan Marichal
❑ 573 Jim Palmer 30.00 12.00
❑ 574 George Scott 3.00 1.20
❑ 575 Bill Singer 3.00 1.20
❑ 576 Ron Stone 2.00 .80
Bill Wilson
❑ 577 Mike Hegan 3.00 1.20
❑ 578 Don Bosch 2.00 .80
❑ 579 Dave Nelson 2.00 .80
❑ 580 Jim Northrup 3.00 1.20
❑ 581 Gary Nolan 3.00 1.20
❑ 582A Tony Oliva CL 6.00 1.20
White circle on back
❑ 582B Tony Oliva CL 8.00 1.60
Red circle on back
❑ 583 Clyde Wright 2.00 .80
❑ 584 Don Mason 2.00 .80
❑ 585 Ron Swoboda 3.00 1.20
❑ 586 Tim Cullen 2.00 .80
❑ 587 Joe Rudi RC 8.00 3.20
❑ 588 Bill White 3.00 1.20
❑ 589 Joe Pepitone 5.00 2.00
❑ 590 Rico Carty 5.00 2.00
❑ 591 Mike Hedlund 3.00 1.20

❑ 592 Rafael Robles 5.00 2.00
Al Santorini
❑ 593 Don Nottebart 3.00 1.20
❑ 594 Dooley Womack 3.00 1.20
❑ 595 Lee Maye 3.00 1.20
❑ 596 Chuck Hartenstein 3.00 1.20
❑ 597 Bob Floyd 40.00 16.00
Larry Burchart
Rollie Fingers RC
❑ 598 Ruben Amaro 3.00 1.20
❑ 599 John Boozer 3.00 1.20
❑ 600 Tony Oliva 8.00 3.20
❑ 601 Tug McGraw 8.00 3.20
❑ 602 Alec Distaso 5.00 2.00
Don Young
Jim Qualls
❑ 603 Joe Keough 3.00 1.20
❑ 604 Bobby Etheridge 3.00 1.20
❑ 605 Dick Ellsworth 3.00 1.20
❑ 606 Gene Mauch MG 5.00 2.00
❑ 607 Dick Bosman 3.00 1.20
❑ 608 Dick Simpson 3.00 1.20
❑ 609 Phil Gagliano 3.00 1.20
❑ 610 Jim Hardin 3.00 1.20
❑ 611 Bob Didier 5.00 2.00
Walt Hriniak RC
Gary Neibauer
❑ 612 Jack Aker 5.00 2.00
❑ 613 Jim Beauchamp 3.00 1.20
❑ 614 Tom Griffin 3.00 1.20
Skip Guinn
❑ 615 Len Gabrielson 3.00 1.20
❑ 616 Don McMahon 3.00 1.20
❑ 617 Jesse Gonder 3.00 1.20
❑ 618 Ramon Webster 3.00 1.20
❑ 619 Bill Butler 5.00 2.00
Pat Kelly
Juan Rios
❑ 620 Dean Chance 5.00 2.00
❑ 621 Bill Voss 3.00 1.20
❑ 622 Dan Osinski 3.00 1.20
❑ 623 Hank Allen 3.00 1.20
❑ 624 Darrel Chaney 5.00 2.00
Duffy Dyer RC
Terry Harmon
❑ 625 Mack Jones UER 5.00 2.00
(Batting wrong)
❑ 626 Gene Michael 5.00 2.00
❑ 627 George Stone 3.00 1.20
❑ 628 Bill Conigliaro RC 5.00 2.00
Syd O'Brien
Fred Wenz
❑ 629 Jack Hamilton 3.00 1.20
❑ 630 Bobby Bonds RC 30.00 12.00
❑ 631 John Kennedy 5.00 2.00
❑ 632 Jon Warden 3.00 1.20
❑ 633 Harry Walker MG 3.00 1.20
❑ 634 Andy Etchebarren 3.00 1.20
❑ 635 George Culver 3.00 1.20
❑ 636 Woody Held 3.00 1.20
❑ 637 Jerry DaVanon 5.00 2.00
Frank Reberger
Clay Kirby
❑ 638 Ed Sprague RC 3.00 1.20
❑ 639 Barry Moore 3.00 1.20
❑ 640 Ferguson Jenkins 20.00 8.00
❑ 641 Bobby Darwin 5.00 2.00
John Miller
Tommy Dean
❑ 642 John Hiller 3.00 1.20
❑ 643 Billy Cowan 3.00 1.20
❑ 644 Chuck Hinton 3.00 1.20
❑ 645 George Brunet 3.00 1.20
❑ 646 Dan McGinn 5.00 2.00
Carl Morton
❑ 647 Dave Wickersham 3.00 1.20
❑ 648 Bobby Wine 5.00 2.00
❑ 649 Al Jackson 3.00 1.20
❑ 650 Ted Williams MG 20.00 8.00
❑ 651 Gus Gil 5.00 2.00
❑ 652 Eddie Watt 3.00 1.20
❑ 653 A.Rodriguez RC UER 5.00 2.00
Photo actually
Angels' batboy
❑ 654 Carlos May RC 5.00 2.00
Don Secrist
Rich Morales
❑ 655 Mike Hershberger 3.00 1.20
❑ 656 Dan Schneider 3.00 1.20
❑ 657 Bobby Murcer 8.00 3.20
❑ 658 Tom Hall 3.00 1.20
Bill Burbach
Jim Miles
❑ 659 Johnny Podres 5.00 2.00
❑ 660 Reggie Smith 5.00 2.00
❑ 661 Jim Merritt 3.00 1.20
❑ 662 Dick Drago 5.00 2.00
George Spriggs
Bob Oliver
❑ 663 Dick Radatz 5.00 2.00
❑ 664 Ron Hunt 5.00 1.35

1970 Topps

	NM	Ex
COMPLETE SET (720)	2000.00	1000.00
COMMON CARD (1-132)	.75	.30
COMMON (373-459)	1.00	.40
COMMON CARD (373-459)	1.50	.60
COMMON (460-546)	2.00	.80
COMMON (547-633)	4.00	1.60
COMMON (634-720)	10.00	4.00
WRAPPER (10-CENT)	20.00	8.00

❑ 1 New York Mets 30.00 9.50
Team Card
❑ 2 Diego Segui 1.00 .40
❑ 3 Darrel Chaney .75 .30
❑ 4 Tom Egan .75 .30
❑ 5 Wes Parker 1.00 .40
❑ 6 Grant Jackson .75 .30
❑ 7 Gary Boyd .75 .30
Russ Nagelson
❑ 8 Jose Martinez .75 .30
❑ 9 Checklist 1 12.00 2.40
❑ 10 Carl Yastrzemski 20.00 8.00
❑ 11 Nate Colbert .75 .30
❑ 12 John Hiller .75 .30
❑ 13 Jack Hiatt .75 .30
❑ 14 Hank Allen .75 .30
❑ 15 Larry Dierker .75 .30
❑ 16 Charlie Metro MG .75 .30
❑ 17 Hoyt Wilhelm 4.00 1.60
❑ 18 Carlos May 1.00 .40
❑ 19 John Boccabella .75 .30
❑ 20 Dave McNally 1.00 .40
❑ 21 Vida Blue RC 4.00 1.60
Gene Tenace RC
❑ 22 Ray Washburn .75 .30
❑ 23 Bill Robinson 1.00 .40
❑ 24 Dick Selma .75 .30
❑ 25 Cesar Tovar .75 .30
❑ 26 Tug McGraw 2.00 .80
❑ 27 Chuck Hinton .75 .30
❑ 28 Billy Wilson .75 .30
❑ 29 Sandy Alomar 1.00 .40
❑ 30 Matty Alou 1.00 .40
❑ 31 Marty Pattin 1.00 .40
❑ 32 Harry Walker MG .75 .30
❑ 33 Don Wert .75 .30
❑ 34 Willie Crawford .75 .30
❑ 35 Joel Horlen .75 .30
❑ 36 Danny Breeden 1.00 .40
Bernie Carbo
❑ 37 Dick Drago .75 .30
❑ 38 Mack Jones .75 .30
❑ 39 Mike Nagy .75 .30
❑ 40 Rich Allen 2.00 .80
❑ 41 George Lauzerique .75 .30
❑ 42 Tito Fuentes .75 .30
❑ 43 Jack Aker .75 .30
❑ 44 Roberto Pena .75 .30
❑ 45 Dave Johnson 1.00 .40
❑ 46 Ken Rudolph .75 .30
❑ 47 Bob Miller .75 .30
❑ 48 Gil Garrido .75 .30
❑ 49 Tim Cullen .75 .30
❑ 50 Tommie Agee 1.00 .40
❑ 51 Bob Christian .75 .30
❑ 52 Bruce Dal Canton .75 .30
❑ 53 John Kennedy .75 .30
❑ 54 Jeff Torborg 1.00 .40
❑ 55 John Odom .75 .30
❑ 56 Joe Lis .75 .30
Scott Reid
❑ 57 Pat Kelly .75 .30
❑ 58 Dave Marshall .75 .30
❑ 59 Dick Ellsworth .75 .30
❑ 60 Jim Wynn 1.00 .40
❑ 61 Pete Rose 12.00 4.80
Bob Clemente
Cleon Jones LL
❑ 62 Rod Carew 2.00 .80
Reggie Smith
Tony Oliva LL
❑ 63 Willie McCovey 2.00 .80
Ron Santo
Tony Perez LL
❑ 64 Harmon Killebrew 4.00 1.60
Boog Powell
Reggie Jackson LL
❑ 65 Willie McCovey 4.00 1.60
Hank Aaron
Lee May LL
❑ 66 Harmon Killebrew 4.00 1.60
Frank Howard
Reggie Jackson LL
❑ 67 Juan Marichal 4.00 1.60
Steve Carlton
Bob Gibson LL
❑ 68 Dick Bosman 1.00 .40
Jim Palmer
Mike Cuellar LL
❑ 69 Tom Seaver 4.00 1.60
Phil Niekro
Fergie Jenkins
Juan Marichal LL
❑ 70 Dennis McLain 1.00 .40
Mike Cuellar
Dave Boswell
Dave McNally
Jim Perry
Mel Stottlemyre LL
❑ 71 Fergie Jenkins 2.00 .80
Bob Gibson
Bill Singer LL
❑ 72 Sam McDowell 1.00 .40
Mickey Lolich
Andy Messersmith LL
❑ 73 Wayne Granger .75 .30
❑ 74 Greg Washburn .75 .30
Wally Wolf
❑ 75 Jim Kaat 1.00 .40
❑ 76 Carl Taylor .75 .30
❑ 77 Frank Linzy .75 .30
❑ 78 Joe Lahoud .75 .30
❑ 79 Clay Kirby .75 .30
❑ 80 Don Kessinger 1.00 .40
❑ 81 Dave May .75 .30
❑ 82 Frank Fernandez .75 .30
❑ 83 Don Cardwell .75 .30
❑ 84 Paul Casanova .75 .30
❑ 85 Max Alvis .75 .30
❑ 86 Lum Harris MG .75 .30
❑ 87 Steve Renko RC .75 .30
❑ 88 Miguel Fuentes 1.00 .40
Dick Baney
❑ 89 Juan Rios .75 .30
❑ 90 Tim McCarver 1.00 .40
❑ 91 Rich Morales .75 .30

❑ 92 George Culver .75 .30
❑ 93 Rick Renick .75 .30
❑ 94 Freddie Patek 1.00 .40
❑ 95 Earl Wilson 1.00 .40
❑ 96 Leron Lee 1.00 .40
Jerry Reuss RC
❑ 97 Joe Moeller .75 .30
❑ 98 Gates Brown 1.00 .40
❑ 99 Bobby Pfeil .75 .30
❑ 100 Mel Stottlemyre 1.00 .40
❑ 101 Bobby Floyd .75 .30
❑ 102 Joe Rudi 1.00 .40
❑ 103 Frank Reberger .75 .30
❑ 104 Gerry Moses .75 .30
❑ 105 Tony Gonzalez .75 .30
❑ 106 Darold Knowles .75 .30
❑ 107 Bobby Etheridge .75 .30
❑ 108 Tom Burgmeier .75 .30
❑ 109 Garry Jestadt .75 .30
Carl Morton
❑ 110 Bob Moose .75 .30
❑ 111 Mike Hegan 1.00 .40
❑ 112 Dave Nelson .75 .30
❑ 113 Jim Ray .75 .30
❑ 114 Gene Michael 1.00 .40
❑ 115 Alex Johnson 1.00 .40
❑ 116 Sparky Lyle 1.00 .40
❑ 117 Don Young .75 .30
❑ 118 George Mitterwald .75 .30
❑ 119 Chuck Taylor .75 .30
❑ 120 Sal Bando 1.00 .40
❑ 121 Fred Beene .75 .30
Terry Crowley
❑ 122 George Stone .75 .30
❑ 123 Don Gutteridge MG .75 .30
❑ 124 Larry Jaster .75 .30
❑ 125 Deron Johnson .75 .30
❑ 126 Marty Martinez .75 .30
❑ 127 Joe Coleman .75 .30
❑ 128A Checklist 2 ERR 6.00 1.20
(226 R Perranoski)
❑ 128B Checklist 2 COR 6.00 1.20
(226 R. Perranoski)
❑ 129 Jimmie Price .75 .30
❑ 130 Ollie Brown .75 .30
❑ 131 Ray Lamb .75 .30
Bob Stinson
❑ 132 Jim McGlothlin .75 .30
❑ 133 Clay Carroll 1.00 .40
❑ 134 Danny Walton 1.00 .40
❑ 135 Dick Dietz 1.00 .40
❑ 136 Steve Hargan 1.00 .40
❑ 137 Art Shamsky 1.00 .40
❑ 138 Joe Foy 1.00 .40
❑ 139 Rich Nye 1.00 .40
❑ 140 Reggie Jackson 50.00 20.00
❑ 141 Dave Cash RC 1.50 .60
Johnny Jeter
❑ 142 Fritz Peterson 1.00 .40
❑ 143 Phil Gagliano 1.00 .40
❑ 144 Ray Culp 1.00 .40
❑ 145 Rico Carty 1.50 .60
❑ 146 Danny Murphy 1.00 .40
❑ 147 Angel Hermoso 1.00 .40
❑ 148 Earl Weaver MG 3.00 1.20
❑ 149 Billy Champion 1.00 .40
❑ 150 Harmon Killebrew 8.00 3.20
❑ 151 Dave Roberts 1.00 .40
❑ 152 Ike Brown 1.00 .40
❑ 153 Gary Gentry 1.00 .40
❑ 154 Jim Miles 1.00 .40
Jan Dukes
❑ 155 Denis Menke 1.00 .40
❑ 156 Eddie Fisher 1.00 .40
❑ 157 Manny Mota 1.50 .60
❑ 158 Jerry McNertney 1.50 .60
❑ 159 Tommy Helms 1.50 .60
❑ 160 Phil Niekro 5.00 2.00
❑ 161 Richie Scheinblum 1.00 .40
❑ 162 Jerry Johnson 1.00 .40
❑ 163 Syd O'Brien 1.00 .40
❑ 164 Ty Cline 1.00 .40
❑ 165 Ed Kirkpatrick 1.00 .40
❑ 166 Al Oliver 3.00 1.20
❑ 167 Bill Burbach 1.00 .40
❑ 168 Dave Watkins 1.00 .40
❑ 169 Tom Hall 1.00 .40
❑ 170 Billy Williams 5.00 2.00
❑ 171 Jim Nash 1.00 .40
❑ 172 Garry Hill 1.50 .60
Ralph Garr RC
❑ 173 Jim Hicks 1.00 .40
❑ 174 Ted Sizemore 1.50 .60
❑ 175 Dick Bosman 1.00 .40
❑ 176 Jim Ray Hart 1.50 .60
❑ 177 Jim Northrup 1.50 .60
❑ 178 Denny Lemaster 1.00 .40
❑ 179 Ivan Murrell 1.00 .40
❑ 180 Tommy John 1.50 .60
❑ 181 Sparky Anderson MG 5.00 2.00
❑ 182 Dick Hall 1.00 .40
❑ 183 Jerry Grote 1.50 .60
❑ 184 Ray Fosse 1.00 .40
❑ 185 Don Mincher 1.50 .60
❑ 186 Rick Joseph 1.00 .40
❑ 187 Mike Hedlund 1.00 .40
❑ 188 Manny Sanguillen 1.50 .60
❑ 189 Thurman Munson RC 80.00 32.00
Dave McDonald
❑ 190 Joe Torre 3.00 1.20
❑ 191 Vicente Romo 1.00 .40
❑ 192 Jim Qualls 1.00 .40
❑ 193 Mike Wegener 1.00 .40
❑ 194 Chuck Manuel 1.00 .40
❑ 195 Tom Seaver NLCS 15.00 6.00
❑ 196 Ken Boswell NLCS 2.00 .80
❑ 197 Nolan Ryan NLCS 30.00 12.00
❑ 198 NL Playoff Summary 15.00 6.00
Mets celebrate
(Nolan Ryan)
❑ 199 Mike Cuellar ALCS 2.00 .80
❑ 200 Boog Powell ALCS 3.00 1.20
❑ 201 Boog Powell ALCS 2.00 .80
Andy Etchebarren)
❑ 202 AL Playoff Summary 2.00 .80
Orioles celebrate
❑ 203 Rudy May 1.00 .40
❑ 204 Len Gabrielson 1.00 .40
❑ 205 Bert Campaneris 1.50 .60
❑ 206 Clete Boyer 1.50 .60
❑ 207 Norman McRae 1.00 .40
Bob Reed
❑ 208 Fred Gladding 1.00 .40
❑ 209 Ken Suarez 1.00 .40
❑ 210 Juan Marichal 5.00 2.00
❑ 211 Ted Williams MG UER 15.00 6.00
Throwing information on back incorrect
❑ 212 Al Santorini 1.00 .40
❑ 213 Andy Etchebarren 1.00 .40
❑ 214 Ken Boswell 1.00 .40
❑ 215 Reggie Smith 1.50 .60
❑ 216 Chuck Hartenstein 1.00 .40
❑ 217 Ron Hansen 1.00 .40
❑ 218 Ron Stone 1.00 .40
❑ 219 Jerry Kenney 1.00 .40
❑ 220 Steve Carlton 15.00 6.00
❑ 221 Ron Brand 1.00 .40
❑ 222 Jim Rooker 1.00 .40
❑ 223 Nate Oliver 1.00 .40
❑ 224 Steve Barber 1.50 .60
❑ 225 Lee May 1.50 .60
❑ 226 Ron Perranoski 1.00 .40
❑ 227 John Mayberry RC 1.50 .60
Bob Watkins
❑ 228 Aurelio Rodriguez 1.00 .40
❑ 229 Rich Robertson 1.00 .40
❑ 230 Brooks Robinson 15.00 6.00
❑ 231 Luis Tiant 1.50 .60
❑ 232 Bob Didier 1.00 .40
❑ 233 Lew Krausse 1.00 .40
❑ 234 Tommy Dean 1.00 .40
❑ 235 Mike Epstein 1.00 .40
❑ 236 Bob Veale 1.00 .40
❑ 237 Russ Gibson 1.00 .40
❑ 238 Jose Laboy 1.00 .40
❑ 239 Ken Berry 1.00 .40
❑ 240 Ferguson Jenkins 5.00 2.00
❑ 241 Al Fitzmorris 1.00 .40
Scott Northey
❑ 242 Walter Alston MG 3.00 1.20
❑ 243 Joe Sparma 1.00 .40
❑ 244A Checklist 3 6.00 1.20
(Red bat on front)
❑ 244B Checklist 3 6.00 1.20
(Brown bat on front)
❑ 245 Leo Cardenas 1.00 .40
❑ 246 Jim McAndrew 1.00 .40
❑ 247 Lou Klimchock 1.00 .40
❑ 248 Jesus Alou 1.00 .40
❑ 249 Bob Locker 1.00 .40
❑ 250 Willie McCovey UER 10.00 4.00
(1963 San Francisci)
❑ 251 Dick Schofield 1.00 .40
❑ 252 Lowell Palmer 1.00 .40
❑ 253 Ron Woods 1.00 .40
❑ 254 Camilo Pascual 1.00 .40
❑ 255 Jim Spencer 1.00 .40
❑ 256 Vic Davalillo 1.00 .40
❑ 257 Dennis Higgins 1.00 .40
❑ 258 Paul Popovich 1.00 .40
❑ 259 Tommie Reynolds 1.00 .40
❑ 260 Claude Osteen 1.00 .40
❑ 261 Curt Motton 1.00 .40
❑ 262 Jerry Morales 1.00 .40
Jim Williams
❑ 263 Duane Josephson 1.00 .40
❑ 264 Rich Hebner 1.00 .40
❑ 265 Randy Hundley 1.00 .40
❑ 266 Wally Bunker 1.00 .40
❑ 267 Herman Hill 1.00 .40
Paul Ratliff
❑ 268 Claude Raymond 1.00 .40
❑ 269 Cesar Gutierrez 1.00 .40
❑ 270 Chris Short 1.00 .40
❑ 271 Greg Goossen 1.50 .60
❑ 272 Hector Torres 1.00 .40
❑ 273 Ralph Houk MG 1.50 .60
❑ 274 Gerry Arrigo 1.00 .40
❑ 275 Duke Sims 1.00 .40
❑ 276 Ron Hunt 1.00 .40
❑ 277 Paul Doyle 1.00 .40
❑ 278 Tommie Aaron 1.00 .40
❑ 279 Bill Lee RC 1.50 .60
❑ 280 Donn Clendenon 1.50 .60
❑ 281 Casey Cox 1.00 .40
❑ 282 Steve Huntz 1.00 .40
❑ 283 Angel Bravo 1.00 .40
❑ 284 Jack Baldschun 1.00 .40
❑ 285 Paul Blair 1.50 .60
❑ 286 Jack Jenkins 5.00 2.00
Bill Buckner RC
❑ 287 Fred Talbot 1.00 .40
❑ 288 Larry Hisle 1.50 .60
❑ 289 Gene Brabender 1.00 .40
❑ 290 Rod Carew 15.00 6.00
❑ 291 Leo Durocher MG 3.00 1.20
❑ 292 Eddie Leon 1.00 .40
❑ 293 Bob Bailey 1.50 .60
❑ 294 Jose Azcue 1.00 .40
❑ 295 Cecil Upshaw 1.00 .40
❑ 296 Woody Woodward 1.00 .40
❑ 297 Curt Blefary 1.00 .40
❑ 298 Ken Henderson 1.00 .40
❑ 299 Buddy Bradford 1.00 .40
❑ 300 Tom Seaver 30.00 12.00
❑ 301 Chico Salmon 1.00 .40
❑ 302 Jeff James 1.00 .40
❑ 303 Brant Alyea 1.00 .40
❑ 304 Bill Russell RC 5.00 2.00
❑ 305 Don Buford WS 4.00 1.60
❑ 306 Donn Clendenon WS 4.00 1.60
❑ 307 Tommie Agee WS 4.00 1.60
❑ 308 J.C. Martin WS 4.00 1.60
❑ 309 Jerry Koosman WS 4.00 1.60
❑ 310 WS Summary 5.00 2.00
Mets whoop it up
❑ 311 Dick Green 1.00 .40
❑ 312 Mike Torrez 1.00 .40
❑ 313 Mayo Smith MG 1.00 .40
❑ 314 Bill McCool 1.00 .40
❑ 315 Luis Aparicio 5.00 2.00
❑ 316 Skip Guinn 1.00 .40
❑ 317 Billy Conigliaro 1.50 .60
Luis Alvarado
❑ 318 Willie Smith 1.00 .40
❑ 319 Clay Dalrymple 1.00 .40
❑ 320 Jim Maloney 1.50 .60
❑ 321 Lou Piniella 1.50 .60

❑ 322	Luke Walker	1.00	.40
❑ 323	Wayne Comer	1.00	.40
❑ 324	Tony Taylor	1.50	.60
❑ 325	Dave Boswell	1.00	.40
❑ 326	Bill Voss	1.00	.40
❑ 327	Hal King	1.00	.40
❑ 328	George Brunet	1.00	.40
❑ 329	Chris Cannizzaro	1.00	.40
❑ 330	Lou Brock	10.00	4.00
❑ 331	Chuck Dobson	1.00	.40
❑ 332	Bobby Wine	1.00	.40
❑ 333	Bobby Murcer	1.50	.60
❑ 334	Phil Regan	1.00	.40
❑ 335	Bill Freehan	1.50	.60
❑ 336	Del Unser	1.00	.40
❑ 337	Mike McCormick	1.50	.60
❑ 338	Paul Schaal	1.00	.40
❑ 339	Johnny Edwards	1.00	.40
❑ 340	Tony Conigliaro	3.00	1.20
❑ 341	Bill Sudakis	1.00	.40
❑ 342	Wilbur Wood	1.50	.60
❑ 343A	Checklist 4	6.00	1.20
	(Red bat on front)		
❑ 343B	Checklist 4	6.00	1.20
	(Brown bat on front)		
❑ 344	Marcelino Lopez	1.00	.40
❑ 345	Al Ferrara	1.00	.40
❑ 346	Red Schoendienst MG	1.50	.60
❑ 347	Russ Snyder	1.00	.40
❑ 348	Mike Jorgensen	1.50	.60
	Jesse Hudson		
❑ 349	Steve Hamilton	1.00	.40
❑ 350	Roberto Clemente	60.00	24.00
❑ 351	Tom Murphy	1.00	.40
❑ 352	Bob Barton	1.00	.40
❑ 353	Stan Williams	1.00	.40
❑ 354	Amos Otis	1.50	.60
❑ 355	Doug Rader	1.00	.40
❑ 356	Fred Lasher	1.00	.40
❑ 357	Bob Burda	1.00	.40
❑ 358	Pedro Borbon RC	1.50	.60
❑ 359	Phil Roof	1.00	.40
❑ 360	Curt Flood	1.50	.60
❑ 361	Ray Jarvis	1.00	.40
❑ 362	Joe Hague	1.00	.40
❑ 363	Tom Shopay	1.00	.40
❑ 364	Dan McGinn	1.00	.40
❑ 365	Zoilo Versalles	1.00	.40
❑ 366	Barry Moore	1.00	.40
❑ 367	Mike Lum	1.00	.40
❑ 368	Ed Herrmann	1.00	.40
❑ 369	Alan Foster	1.00	.40
❑ 370	Tommy Harper	1.50	.60
❑ 371	Rod Gaspar	1.00	.40
❑ 372	Dave Giusti	1.00	.40
❑ 373	Roy White	2.00	.80
❑ 374	Tommie Sisk	1.50	.60
❑ 375	Johnny Callison	2.00	.80
❑ 376	Lefty Phillips MG	1.50	.60
❑ 377	Bill Butler	1.50	.60
❑ 378	Jim Davenport	1.50	.60
❑ 379	Tom Tischinski	1.50	.60
❑ 380	Tony Perez	6.00	2.40
❑ 381	Bobby Brooks	1.50	.60
	Mike Olivo		
❑ 382	Jack DiLauro	1.50	.60
❑ 383	Mickey Stanley	2.00	.80
❑ 384	Gary Neibauer	1.50	.60
❑ 385	George Scott	2.00	.80
❑ 386	Bill Dillman	1.50	.60
❑ 387	Baltimore Orioles	3.00	1.20
	Team Card		
❑ 388	Byron Browne	1.50	.60
❑ 389	Jim Shellenback	1.50	.60
❑ 390	Willie Davis	2.00	.80
❑ 391	Larry Brown	1.50	.60
❑ 392	Walt Hriniak	2.00	.80
❑ 393	John Gelnar	1.50	.60
❑ 394	Gil Hodges MG	4.00	1.60
❑ 395	Walt Williams	1.50	.60
❑ 396	Steve Blass	2.00	.80
❑ 397	Roger Repoz	1.50	.60
❑ 398	Bill Stoneman	1.50	.60
❑ 399	New York Yankees	3.00	1.20
	Team Card		
❑ 400	Denny McLain	4.00	1.60
❑ 401	John Harrell	1.50	.60
	Bernie Williams		
❑ 402	Ellie Rodriguez	1.50	.60
❑ 403	Jim Bunning	6.00	2.40
❑ 404	Rich Reese	1.50	.60
❑ 405	Bill Hands	1.50	.60
❑ 406	Mike Andrews	1.50	.60
❑ 407	Bob Watson	2.00	.80
❑ 408	Paul Lindblad	1.50	.60
❑ 409	Bob Tolan	1.50	.60
❑ 410	Boog Powell	4.00	1.60
❑ 411	Los Angeles Dodgers	3.00	1.20
	Team Card		
❑ 412	Larry Burchart	1.50	.60
❑ 413	Sonny Jackson	1.50	.60
❑ 414	Paul Edmondson	1.50	.60
❑ 415	Julian Javier	2.00	.80
❑ 416	Joe Verbanic	1.50	.60
❑ 417	John Bateman	1.50	.60
❑ 418	John Donaldson	1.50	.60
❑ 419	Ron Taylor	1.50	.60
❑ 420	Ken McMullen	2.00	.80
❑ 421	Pat Dobson	2.00	.80
❑ 422	Royals Team	3.00	1.20
❑ 423	Jerry May	1.50	.60
❑ 424	Mike Kilkenny	1.50	.60
	(Inconsistent design card number in white circle)		
❑ 425	Bobby Bonds	6.00	2.40
❑ 426	Bill Rigney MG	1.50	.60
❑ 427	Fred Norman	1.50	.60
❑ 428	Don Buford	1.50	.60
❑ 429	Randy Bobb	1.50	.60
	Jim Cosman		
❑ 430	Andy Messersmith	2.00	.80
❑ 431	Ron Swoboda	2.00	.80
❑ 432A	Checklist 5	6.00	1.20
	(Baseball in yellow letters)		
❑ 432B	Checklist 5	6.00	1.20
	(Baseball in white letters)		
❑ 433	Ron Bryant	1.50	.60
❑ 434	Felipe Alou	2.00	.80
❑ 435	Nelson Briles	2.00	.80
❑ 436	Philadelphia Phillies	3.00	1.20
	Team Card		
❑ 437	Danny Cater	1.50	.60
❑ 438	Pat Jarvis	1.50	.60
❑ 439	Lee Maye	1.50	.60
❑ 440	Bill Mazeroski	6.00	2.40
❑ 441	John O'Donoghue	1.50	.60
❑ 442	Gene Mauch MG	2.00	.80
❑ 443	Al Jackson	1.50	.60
❑ 444	Billy Farmer	1.50	.60
	John Matias		
❑ 445	Vada Pinson	2.00	.80
❑ 446	Billy Grabarkewitz	1.50	.60
❑ 447	Lee Stange	1.50	.60
❑ 448	Houston Astros	3.00	1.20
	Team Card		
❑ 449	Jim Palmer	12.00	4.80
❑ 450	Willie McCovey AS	6.00	2.40
❑ 451	Boog Powell AS	4.00	1.60
❑ 452	Felix Millan AS	2.00	.80
❑ 453	Rod Carew AS	6.00	2.40
❑ 454	Ron Santo AS	4.00	1.60
❑ 455	Brooks Robinson AS	6.00	2.40
❑ 456	Don Kessinger AS	2.00	.80
❑ 457	Rico Petrocelli AS	4.00	1.60
❑ 458	Pete Rose AS	15.00	6.00
❑ 459	Reggie Jackson AS	12.00	4.80
❑ 460	Matty Alou AS	3.00	1.20
❑ 461	Carl Yastrzemski AS	10.00	4.00
❑ 462	Hank Aaron AS	15.00	6.00
❑ 463	Frank Robinson AS	8.00	3.20
❑ 464	Johnny Bench AS	15.00	6.00
❑ 465	Bill Freehan AS	3.00	1.20
❑ 466	Juan Marichal AS	5.00	2.00
❑ 467	Denny McLain AS	3.00	1.20
❑ 468	Jerry Koosman AS	3.00	1.20
❑ 469	Sam McDowell AS	3.00	1.20
❑ 470	Willie Stargell	10.00	4.00
❑ 471	Chris Zachary	2.00	.80
❑ 472	Braves Team	4.00	1.60
❑ 473	Don Bryant	2.00	.80
❑ 474	Dick Kelley	2.00	.80
❑ 475	Dick McAuliffe	3.00	1.20
❑ 476	Don Shaw	2.00	.80
❑ 477	Al Severinsen	2.00	.80
	Roger Freed		
❑ 478	Bobby Heise	2.00	.80
❑ 479	Dick Woodson	2.00	.80
❑ 480	Glenn Beckert	3.00	1.20
❑ 481	Jose Tartabull	2.00	.80
❑ 482	Tom Hilgendorf	2.00	.80
❑ 483	Gail Hopkins	2.00	.80
❑ 484	Gary Nolan	3.00	1.20
❑ 485	Jay Johnstone	3.00	1.20
❑ 486	Terry Harmon	2.00	.80
❑ 487	Cisco Carlos	2.00	.80
❑ 488	J.C. Martin	2.00	.80
❑ 489	Eddie Kasko MG	2.00	.80
❑ 490	Bill Singer	3.00	1.20
❑ 491	Graig Nettles	5.00	2.00
❑ 492	Keith Lampard	2.00	.80
	Scipio Spinks		
❑ 493	Lindy McDaniel	3.00	1.20
❑ 494	Larry Stahl	2.00	.80
❑ 495	Dave Morehead	2.00	.80
❑ 496	Steve Whitaker	2.00	.80
❑ 497	Eddie Watt	2.00	.80
❑ 498	Al Weis	2.00	.80
❑ 499	Skip Lockwood	3.00	1.20
❑ 500	Hank Aaron	50.00	20.00
❑ 501	Chicago White Sox	4.00	1.60
	Team Card		
❑ 502	Rollie Fingers	10.00	4.00
❑ 503	Dal Maxvill	2.00	.80
❑ 504	Don Pavletich	2.00	.80
❑ 505	Ken Holtzman	3.00	1.20
❑ 506	Ed Stroud	2.00	.80
❑ 507	Pat Corrales	2.00	.80
❑ 508	Joe Niekro	3.00	1.20
❑ 509	Montreal Expos	4.00	1.60
	Team Card		
❑ 510	Tony Oliva	5.00	2.00
❑ 511	Joe Hoerner	2.00	.80
❑ 512	Billy Harris	2.00	.80
❑ 513	Preston Gomez MG	2.00	.80
❑ 514	Steve Hovley	2.00	.80
❑ 515	Don Wilson	3.00	1.20
❑ 516	John Ellis	2.00	.80
	Jim Lyttle		
❑ 517	Joe Gibbon	2.00	.80
❑ 518	Bill Melton	2.00	.80
❑ 519	Don McMahon	2.00	.80
❑ 520	Willie Horton	3.00	1.20
❑ 521	Cal Koonce	2.00	.80
❑ 522	Angels Team	4.00	1.60
❑ 523	Jose Pena	2.00	.80
❑ 524	Alvin Dark MG	3.00	1.20
❑ 525	Jerry Adair	2.00	.80
❑ 526	Ron Herbel	2.00	.80
❑ 527	Don Bosch	2.00	.80
❑ 528	Elrod Hendricks	2.00	.80
❑ 529	Bob Aspromonte	2.00	.80
❑ 530	Bob Gibson	15.00	6.00
❑ 531	Ron Clark	2.00	.80
❑ 532	Danny Murtaugh MG	3.00	1.20
❑ 533	Buzz Stephen	2.00	.80
❑ 534	Minnesota Twins	4.00	1.60
	Team Card		
❑ 535	Andy Kosco	2.00	.80
❑ 536	Mike Kekich	2.00	.80
❑ 537	Joe Morgan	10.00	4.00
❑ 538	Bob Humphreys	2.00	.80
❑ 539	Denny Doyle	8.00	3.20
	Larry Bowa RC		
❑ 540	Gary Peters	2.00	.80
❑ 541	Bill Heath	2.00	.80
❑ 542	Checklist 6	6.00	1.20
❑ 543	Clyde Wright	2.00	.80
❑ 544	Cincinnati Reds	4.00	1.60
	Team Card		
❑ 545	Ken Harrelson	3.00	1.20
❑ 546	Ron Reed	2.00	.80
❑ 547	Rick Monday	6.00	2.40
❑ 548	Howie Reed	4.00	1.60
❑ 549	St. Louis Cardinals	6.00	2.40
	Team Card		

Card	Player	NM	Ex
❑ 550	Frank Howard	6.00	2.40
❑ 551	Dock Ellis	6.00	2.40
❑ 552	Don O'Riley Dennis Paepke Fred Rico	4.00	1.60
❑ 553	Jim Lefebvre	6.00	2.40
❑ 554	Tom Timmermann	4.00	1.60
❑ 555	Orlando Cepeda	12.00	4.80
❑ 556	Dave Bristol MG	6.00	2.40
❑ 557	Ed Kranepool	6.00	2.40
❑ 558	Vern Fuller	4.00	1.60
❑ 559	Tommy Davis	6.00	2.40
❑ 560	Gaylord Perry	12.00	4.80
❑ 561	Tom McCraw	4.00	1.60
❑ 562	Ted Abernathy	4.00	1.60
❑ 563	Boston Red Sox Team Card	6.00	2.40
❑ 564	Johnny Briggs	4.00	1.60
❑ 565	Jim Hunter	12.00	4.80
❑ 566	Gene Alley	6.00	2.40
❑ 567	Bob Oliver	4.00	1.60
❑ 568	Stan Bahnsen	6.00	2.40
❑ 569	Cookie Rojas	6.00	2.40
❑ 570	Jim Fregosi White Chevy Pick-Up in Background	6.00	2.40
❑ 571	Jim Brewer	4.00	1.60
❑ 572	Frank Quilici	4.00	1.60
❑ 573	Mike Corkins Rafael Robles Ron Slocum	4.00	1.60
❑ 574	Bobby Bolin	6.00	2.40
❑ 575	Cleon Jones	6.00	2.40
❑ 576	Milt Pappas	6.00	2.40
❑ 577	Bernie Allen	4.00	1.60
❑ 578	Tom Griffin	4.00	1.60
❑ 579	Detroit Tigers Team Card	6.00	2.40
❑ 580	Pete Rose	60.00	24.00
❑ 581	Tom Satriano	4.00	1.60
❑ 582	Mike Paul	4.00	1.60
❑ 583	Hal Lanier	4.00	1.60
❑ 584	Al Downing	6.00	2.40
❑ 585	Rusty Staub	8.00	3.20
❑ 586	Rickey Clark	4.00	1.60
❑ 587	Jose Arcia	4.00	1.60
❑ 588A	Checklist 7 ERR (666 Adolfo)	8.00	1.60
❑ 588B	Checklist 7 COR (666 Adolpho)	6.00	1.20
❑ 589	Joe Keough	4.00	1.60
❑ 590	Mike Cuellar	6.00	2.40
❑ 591	Mike Ryan UER (Pitching Record header on card back)	4.00	1.60
❑ 592	Daryl Patterson	4.00	1.60
❑ 593	Chicago Cubs Team Card	8.00	3.20
❑ 594	Jake Gibbs	4.00	1.60
❑ 595	Maury Wills	8.00	3.20
❑ 596	Mike Hershberger	6.00	2.40
❑ 597	Sonny Siebert	4.00	1.60
❑ 598	Joe Pepitone	6.00	2.40
❑ 599	Dick Stelmaszek Gene Martin Dick Such	4.00	1.60
❑ 600	Willie Mays	80.00	32.00
❑ 601	Pete Richert	4.00	1.60
❑ 602	Ted Savage	4.00	1.60
❑ 603	Ray Oyler	4.00	1.60
❑ 604	Clarence Gaston	6.00	2.40
❑ 605	Rick Wise	6.00	2.40
❑ 606	Chico Ruiz	4.00	1.60
❑ 607	Gary Waslewski	4.00	1.60
❑ 608	Pittsburgh Pirates Team Card	6.00	2.40
❑ 609	Buck Martinez RC (Inconsistent design card number in white circle)	6.00	2.40
❑ 610	Jerry Koosman	8.00	3.20
❑ 611	Norm Cash	6.00	2.40
❑ 612	Jim Hickman	6.00	2.40
❑ 613	Dave Baldwin	6.00	2.40
❑ 614	Mike Shannon	6.00	2.40
❑ 615	Mark Belanger	6.00	2.40
❑ 616	Jim Merritt	4.00	1.60
❑ 617	Jim French	4.00	1.60
❑ 618	Billy Wynne	4.00	1.60
❑ 619	Norm Miller	4.00	1.60
❑ 620	Jim Perry	6.00	2.40
❑ 621	Mike McQueen Darrell Evans RC Rick Kester	12.00	4.80
❑ 622	Don Sutton	12.00	4.80
❑ 623	Horace Clarke	6.00	2.40
❑ 624	Clyde King MG	4.00	1.60
❑ 625	Dean Chance	4.00	1.60
❑ 626	Dave Ricketts	4.00	1.60
❑ 627	Gary Wagner	4.00	1.60
❑ 628	Wayne Garrett	4.00	1.60
❑ 629	Merv Rettenmund	4.00	1.60
❑ 630	Ernie Banks	50.00	20.00
❑ 631	Oakland Athletics Team Card	6.00	2.40
❑ 632	Gary Sutherland	4.00	1.60
❑ 633	Roger Nelson	4.00	1.60
❑ 634	Bud Harrelson	15.00	6.00
❑ 635	Bob Allison	15.00	6.00
❑ 636	Jim Stewart	10.00	4.00
❑ 637	Cleveland Indians Team Card	12.00	4.80
❑ 638	Frank Bertaina	10.00	4.00
❑ 639	Dave Campbell	15.00	6.00
❑ 640	Al Kaline	50.00	20.00
❑ 641	Al McBean	10.00	4.00
❑ 642	Greg Garrett Gordon Lund Jarvis Tatum	10.00	4.00
❑ 643	Jose Pagan	10.00	4.00
❑ 644	Gerry Nyman	10.00	4.00
❑ 645	Don Money	15.00	6.00
❑ 646	Jim Britton	10.00	4.00
❑ 647	Tom Matchick	10.00	4.00
❑ 648	Larry Haney	10.00	4.00
❑ 649	Jimmie Hall	10.00	4.00
❑ 650	Sam McDowell	15.00	6.00
❑ 651	Jim Gosger	10.00	4.00
❑ 652	Rich Rollins	15.00	6.00
❑ 653	Moe Drabowsky	10.00	4.00
❑ 654	Oscar Gamble RC Boots Day Angel Mangual	15.00	6.00
❑ 655	John Roseboro	15.00	6.00
❑ 656	Jim Hardin	10.00	4.00
❑ 657	San Diego Padres Team Card	12.00	4.80
❑ 658	Ken Tatum	10.00	4.00
❑ 659	Pete Ward	10.00	4.00
❑ 660	Johnny Bench	80.00	32.00
❑ 661	Jerry Robertson	10.00	4.00
❑ 662	Frank Lucchesi MG	10.00	4.00
❑ 663	Tito Francona	10.00	4.00
❑ 664	Bob Robertson	10.00	4.00
❑ 665	Jim Lonborg	15.00	6.00
❑ 666	Adolpho Phillips	10.00	4.00
❑ 667	Bob Meyer	15.00	6.00
❑ 668	Bob Tillman	10.00	4.00
❑ 669	Bart Johnson Dan Lazar Mickey Scott	10.00	4.00
❑ 670	Ron Santo	15.00	6.00
❑ 671	Jim Campanis	10.00	4.00
❑ 672	Leon McFadden	10.00	4.00
❑ 673	Ted Uhlaender	10.00	4.00
❑ 674	Dave Leonhard	10.00	4.00
❑ 675	Jose Cardenal	15.00	6.00
❑ 676	Washington Senators Team Card	12.00	4.80
❑ 677	Woodie Fryman	10.00	4.00
❑ 678	Dave Duncan	15.00	6.00
❑ 679	Ray Sadecki	10.00	4.00
❑ 680	Rico Petrocelli	15.00	6.00
❑ 681	Bob Garibaldi	10.00	4.00
❑ 682	Dalton Jones	10.00	4.00
❑ 683	Vern Geishert Hal McRae Wayne Simpson	15.00	6.00
❑ 684	Jack Fisher	10.00	4.00
❑ 685	Tom Haller	10.00	4.00
❑ 686	Jackie Hernandez	10.00	4.00
❑ 687	Bob Priddy	10.00	4.00
❑ 688	Ted Kubiak	15.00	6.00
❑ 689	Frank Tepedino	15.00	6.00
❑ 690	Ron Fairly	15.00	6.00
❑ 691	Joe Grzenda	10.00	4.00
❑ 692	Duffy Dyer	10.00	4.00
❑ 693	Bob Johnson	10.00	4.00
❑ 694	Gary Ross	10.00	4.00
❑ 695	Bobby Knoop	10.00	4.00
❑ 696	San Francisco Giants Team Card	12.00	4.80
❑ 697	Jim Hannan	10.00	4.00
❑ 698	Tom Tresh	15.00	6.00
❑ 699	Hank Aguirre	10.00	4.00
❑ 700	Frank Robinson	50.00	20.00
❑ 701	Jack Billingham	10.00	4.00
❑ 702	Bob Johnson Ron Klimkowski Bill Zepp	10.00	4.00
❑ 703	Lou Marone	10.00	4.00
❑ 704	Frank Baker	10.00	4.00
❑ 705	Tony Cloninger UER (Batter headings on card back)	10.00	4.00
❑ 706	John McNamara MG	10.00	4.00
❑ 707	Kevin Collins	10.00	4.00
❑ 708	Jose Santiago	10.00	4.00
❑ 709	Mike Fiore	10.00	4.00
❑ 710	Felix Millan	10.00	4.00
❑ 711	Ed Brinkman	10.00	4.00
❑ 712	Nolan Ryan	200.00	80.00
❑ 713	Seattle Pilots Team Card	25.00	10.00
❑ 714	Al Spangler	10.00	4.00
❑ 715	Mickey Lolich	15.00	6.00
❑ 716	Sal Campisi Reggie Cleveland Santiago Guzman	15.00	6.00
❑ 717	Tom Phoebus	10.00	4.00
❑ 718	Ed Spiezio	10.00	4.00
❑ 719	Jim Roland	10.00	4.00
❑ 720	Rick Reichardt	15.00	5.00

1971 Topps

	NM	Ex
COMPLETE SET (752)	2500.00	1000.00
COMMON CARD (1-393)	1.50	.60
COMMON (394-523)	2.50	1.00
COMMON (524-643)	4.00	1.60
COMMON (644-752)	8.00	3.20
COMMON SP (644-752)	12.00	4.80
WRAPPER (10-CENT)	15.00	6.00

Card	Player	NM	Ex
❑ 1	Baltimore Orioles Team Card	20.00	6.75
❑ 2	Dock Ellis	1.50	.60
❑ 3	Dick McAuliffe	2.00	.80
❑ 4	Vic Davalillo	1.50	.60
❑ 5	Thurman Munson	100.00	24.00
❑ 6	Ed Spiezio	1.50	.60
❑ 7	Jim Holt	1.50	.60
❑ 8	Mike McQueen	1.50	.60
❑ 9	George Scott	2.00	.80
❑ 10	Claude Osteen	2.00	.80
❑ 11	Elliott Maddox	1.50	.60
❑ 12	Johnny Callison	2.00	.80
❑ 13	Charlie Brinkman Dick Moloney	1.50	.60
❑ 14	Dave Concepcion RC	15.00	6.00

❑ 15 Andy Messersmith .... 2.00 .80
❑ 16 Ken Singleton RC 4.00 1.60
❑ 17 Billy Sorrell .... 1.50 .60
❑ 18 Norm Miller .... 1.50 .60
❑ 19 Skip Pitlock .... 1.50 .60
❑ 20 Reggie Jackson 50.00 20.00
❑ 21 Dan McGinn .... 1.50 .60
❑ 22 Phil Roof .... 1.50 .60
❑ 23 Oscar Gamble .... 1.50 .60
❑ 24 Rich Hand .... 1.50 .60
❑ 25 Clarence Gaston .... 2.00 .80
❑ 26 Bert Blyleven RC 20.00 8.00
❑ 27 Fred Cambria .... 1.50 .60
Gene Clines
❑ 28 Ron Klimkowski .... 1.50 .60
❑ 29 Don Buford .... 1.50 .60
❑ 30 Phil Niekro 6.00 2.40
❑ 31 Eddie Kasko MG .... 1.50 .60
❑ 32 Jerry DaVanon .... 1.50 .60
❑ 33 Del Unser .... 1.50 .60
❑ 34 Sandy Vance .... 1.50 .60
❑ 35 Lou Piniella .... 2.00 .80
❑ 36 Dean Chance .... 2.00 .80
❑ 37 Rich McKinney .... 1.50 .60
❑ 38 Jim Colborn .... 1.50 .60
❑ 39 Lerrin LaGrow .... 2.00 .80
Gene Lamont RC
❑ 40 Lee May .... 2.00 .80
❑ 41 Rick Austin .... 1.50 .60
❑ 42 Boots Day .... 1.50 .60
❑ 43 Steve Kealey .... 1.50 .60
❑ 44 Johnny Edwards .... 1.50 .60
❑ 45 Jim Hunter 6.00 2.40
❑ 46 Dave Campbell .... 2.00 .80
❑ 47 Johnny Jeter .... 1.50 .60
❑ 48 Dave Baldwin .... 1.50 .60
❑ 49 Don Money .... 1.50 .60
❑ 50 Willie McCovey 10.00 4.00
❑ 51 Steve Kline .... 1.50 .60
❑ 52 Oscar Brown .... 1.50 .60
Earl Williams RC
❑ 53 Paul Blair .... 2.00 .80
❑ 54 Checklist 1 .... 10.00 2.00
❑ 55 Steve Carlton 20.00 8.00
❑ 56 Duane Josephson .... 1.50 .60
❑ 57 Von Joshua .... 1.50 .60
❑ 58 Bill Lee .... 2.00 .80
❑ 59 Gene Mauch MG .... 2.00 .80
❑ 60 Dick Bosman .... 1.50 .60
❑ 61 Alex Johnson 4.00 1.60
Carl Yastrzemski
Tony Oliva LL
❑ 62 Rico Carty .... 2.00 .80
Joe Torre
Manny Sanguillen LL
❑ 63 Frank Howard 4.00 1.60
Tony Conigliaro
Boog Powell LL
❑ 64 Johnny Bench 6.00 2.40
Tony Perez
Billy Williams LL
❑ 65 Frank Howard 4.00 1.60
Harmon Killebrew
Carl Yastrzemski LL
❑ 66 Johnny Bench 6.00 2.40
Billy Williams
Tony Perez LL
❑ 67 Diego Segui 4.00 1.60
Jim Palmer
Clyde Wright LL
❑ 68 Tom Seaver 4.00 1.60
Wayne Simpson
Luke Walker LL
❑ 69 Mike Cuellar .... 2.00 .80
Dave McNally
Jim Perry LL
❑ 70 Bob Gibson 6.00 2.40
Gaylord Perry
Fergie Jenkins LL
❑ 71 Sam McDowell .... 2.00 .80
Mickey Lolich
Bob Johnson LL
❑ 72 Tom Seaver 6.00 2.40
Bob Gibson
Fergie Jenkins LL
❑ 73 George Brunet .... 1.50 .60
❑ 74 Pete Hamm .... 1.50 .60
Jim Nettles
❑ 75 Gary Nolan .... 2.00 .80
❑ 76 Ted Savage .... 1.50 .60
❑ 77 Mike Compton .... 1.50 .60
❑ 78 Jim Spencer .... 1.50 .60
❑ 79 Wade Blasingame .... 1.50 .60
❑ 80 Bill Melton .... 1.50 .60
❑ 81 Felix Millan .... 1.50 .60
❑ 82 Casey Cox .... 1.50 .60
❑ 83 Tim Foli RC .... 2.00 .80
Randy Bobb
❑ 84 Marcel Lachemann RC .... 1.50 .60
❑ 85 Billy Grabarkewitz .... 1.50 .60
❑ 86 Mike Kilkenny .... 1.50 .60
❑ 87 Jack Heidemann .... 1.50 .60
❑ 88 Hal King .... 1.50 .60
❑ 89 Ken Brett .... 1.50 .60
❑ 90 Joe Pepitone .... 2.00 .80
❑ 91 Bob Lemon MG .... 2.00 .80
❑ 92 Fred Wenz .... 1.50 .60
❑ 93 Norm McRae .... 1.50 .60
Denny Riddleberger
❑ 94 Don Hahn .... 1.50 .60
❑ 95 Luis Tiant .... 2.00 .80
❑ 96 Joe Hague .... 1.50 .60
❑ 97 Floyd Wicker .... 1.50 .60
❑ 98 Joe Decker .... 1.50 .60
❑ 99 Mark Belanger .... 2.00 .80
❑ 100 Pete Rose 80.00 32.00
❑ 101 Les Cain .... 1.50 .60
❑ 102 Ken Forsch .... 2.00 .80
Larry Howard
❑ 103 Rich Severson .... 1.50 .60
❑ 104 Dan Frisella .... 1.50 .60
❑ 105 Tony Conigliaro .... 2.00 .80
❑ 106 Tom Dukes .... 1.50 .60
❑ 107 Roy Foster .... 1.50 .60
❑ 108 John Cumberland .... 1.50 .60
❑ 109 Steve Hovley .... 1.50 .60
❑ 110 Bill Mazeroski 6.00 2.40
❑ 111 Loyd Colson .... 1.50 .60
Bobby Mitchell
❑ 112 Manny Mota .... 2.00 .80
❑ 113 Jerry Crider .... 1.50 .60
❑ 114 Billy Conigliaro .... 2.00 .80
❑ 115 Donn Clendenon .... 2.00 .80
❑ 116 Ken Sanders .... 1.50 .60
❑ 117 Ted Simmons RC 8.00 3.20
❑ 118 Cookie Rojas .... 2.00 .80
❑ 119 Frank Lucchesi MG .... 1.50 .60
❑ 120 Willie Horton .... 2.00 .80
❑ 121 Jim Dunegan .... 1.50 .60
Roe Skidmore
❑ 122 Eddie Watt .... 1.50 .60
❑ 123A Checklist 2 .... 10.00 2.00
(Card number
at bottom right)
❑ 123B Checklist 2 .... 10.00 2.00
(Card number
centered)
❑ 124 Don Gullett RC .... 2.00 .80
❑ 125 Ray Fosse .... 1.50 .60
❑ 126 Danny Coombs .... 1.50 .60
❑ 127 Danny Thompson .... 2.00 .80
❑ 128 Frank Johnson .... 1.50 .60
❑ 129 Aurelio Monteagudo .... 1.50 .60
❑ 130 Denis Menke .... 1.50 .60
❑ 131 Curt Blefary .... 1.50 .60
❑ 132 Jose Laboy .... 1.50 .60
❑ 133 Mickey Lolich .... 2.00 .80
❑ 134 Jose Arcia .... 1.50 .60
❑ 135 Rick Monday .... 2.00 .80
❑ 136 Duffy Dyer .... 1.50 .60
❑ 137 Marcelino Lopez .... 1.50 .60
❑ 138 Joe Lis .... 2.00 .80
Willie Montanez
❑ 139 Paul Casanova .... 1.50 .60
❑ 140 Gaylord Perry 6.00 2.40
❑ 141 Frank Quilici .... 1.50 .60
❑ 142 Mack Jones .... 1.50 .60
❑ 143 Steve Blass .... 2.00 .80
❑ 144 Jackie Hernandez .... 1.50 .60
❑ 145 Bill Singer .... 2.00 .80
❑ 146 Ralph Houk MG .... 2.00 .80
❑ 147 Bob Priddy .... 1.50 .60
❑ 148 John Mayberry .... 2.00 .80
❑ 149 Mike Hershberger .... 1.50 .60
❑ 150 Sam McDowell .... 2.00 .80
❑ 151 Tommy Davis .... 2.00 .80
❑ 152 Lloyd Allen .... 1.50 .60
Winston Llenas
❑ 153 Gary Ross .... 1.50 .60
❑ 154 Cesar Gutierrez .... 1.50 .60
❑ 155 Ken Henderson .... 1.50 .60
❑ 156 Bart Johnson .... 1.50 .60
❑ 157 Bob Bailey .... 2.00 .80
❑ 158 Jerry Reuss .... 2.00 .80
❑ 159 Jarvis Tatum .... 1.50 .60
❑ 160 Tom Seaver 30.00 12.00
❑ 161 Coin Checklist 10.00 2.00
❑ 162 Jack Billingham .... 1.50 .60
❑ 163 Buck Martinez .... 2.00 .80
❑ 164 Frank Duffy .... 2.00 .80
Milt Wilcox
❑ 165 Cesar Tovar .... 1.50 .60
❑ 166 Joe Hoerner .... 1.50 .60
❑ 167 Tom Grieve RC .... 2.00 .80
❑ 168 Bruce Dal Canton .... 1.50 .60
❑ 169 Ed Herrmann .... 1.50 .60
❑ 170 Mike Cuellar .... 2.00 .80
❑ 171 Bobby Wine .... 1.50 .60
❑ 172 Duke Sims .... 1.50 .60
❑ 173 Gil Garrido .... 1.50 .60
❑ 174 Dave LaRoche .... 1.50 .60
❑ 175 Jim Hickman .... 1.50 .60
❑ 176 Bob Montgomery RC .... 2.00 .80
Doug Griffin
❑ 177 Hal McRae .... 2.00 .80
❑ 178 Dave Duncan .... 2.00 .80
❑ 179 Mike Corkins .... 1.50 .60
❑ 180 Al Kaline UER 20.00 8.00
(Home instead
of Birth)
❑ 181 Hal Lanier .... 1.50 .60
❑ 182 Al Downing .... 2.00 .80
❑ 183 Gil Hodges MG 4.00 1.60
❑ 184 Stan Bahnsen .... 1.50 .60
❑ 185 Julian Javier .... 1.50 .60
❑ 186 Bob Spence .... 1.50 .60
❑ 187 Ted Abernathy .... 1.50 .60
❑ 188 Bob Valentine RC 6.00 2.40
Mike Strahler
❑ 189 George Mitterwald .... 1.50 .60
❑ 190 Bob Tolan .... 1.50 .60
❑ 191 Mike Andrews .... 1.50 .60
❑ 192 Billy Wilson .... 1.50 .60
❑ 193 Bob Grich RC 4.00 1.60
❑ 194 Mike Lum .... 1.50 .60
❑ 195 Boog Powell ALCS .... 2.00 .80
❑ 196 Dave McNally ALCS .... 2.00 .80
❑ 197 Jim Palmer ALCS 4.00 1.60
❑ 198 AL Playoff Summary .... 2.00 .80
Orioles celebrate
❑ 199 Ty Cline NLCS .... 2.00 .80
❑ 200 Bobby Tolan NLCS .... 2.00 .80
❑ 201 Ty Cline NLCS .... 2.00 .80
❑ 202 NL Playoff Summary .... 2.00 .80
Reds celebrate
❑ 203 Larry Gura .... 2.00 .80
❑ 204 Bernie Smith .... 1.50 .60
George Kopacz
❑ 205 Gerry Moses .... 1.50 .60
❑ 206 Checklist 3 .... 10.00 2.00
❑ 207 Alan Foster .... 1.50 .60
❑ 208 Billy Martin MG 4.00 1.60
❑ 209 Steve Renko .... 1.50 .60
❑ 210 Rod Carew 15.00 6.00
❑ 211 Phil Hennigan .... 1.50 .60
❑ 212 Rich Hebner .... 2.00 .80
❑ 213 Frank Baker .... 1.50 .60
❑ 214 Al Ferrara .... 1.50 .60
❑ 215 Diego Segui .... 1.50 .60
❑ 216 Reggie Cleveland .... 1.50 .60
Luis Melendez
❑ 217 Ed Stroud .... 1.50 .60
❑ 218 Tony Cloninger .... 1.50 .60
❑ 219 Elrod Hendricks .... 1.50 .60
❑ 220 Ron Santo 4.00 1.60
❑ 221 Dave Morehead .... 1.50 .60
❑ 222 Bob Watson .... 2.00 .80
❑ 223 Cecil Upshaw .... 1.50 .60

❑ 224	Alan Gallagher	1.50	.60
❑ 225	Gary Peters	1.50	.60
❑ 226	Bill Russell	2.00	.80
❑ 227	Floyd Weaver	1.50	.60
❑ 228	Wayne Garrett	1.50	.60
❑ 229	Jim Hannan	1.50	.60
❑ 230	Willie Stargell	15.00	6.00
❑ 231	Vince Colbert	2.00	.80
	John Lowenstein RC		
❑ 232	John Strohmayer	1.50	.60
❑ 233	Larry Bowa	2.00	.80
❑ 234	Jim Lyttle	1.50	.60
❑ 235	Nate Colbert	1.50	.60
❑ 236	Bob Humphreys	1.50	.60
❑ 237	Cesar Cedeno RC	2.00	.80
❑ 238	Chuck Dobson	1.50	.60
❑ 239	Red Schoendienst MG	2.00	.80
❑ 240	Clyde Wright	1.50	.60
❑ 241	Dave Nelson	1.50	.60
❑ 242	Jim Ray	1.50	.60
❑ 243	Carlos May	1.50	.60
❑ 244	Bob Tillman	1.50	.60
❑ 245	Jim Kaat	2.00	.80
❑ 246	Tony Taylor	1.50	.60
❑ 247	Jerry Cram	2.00	.80
	Paul Splittorff		
❑ 248	Hoyt Wilhelm	6.00	2.40
❑ 249	Chico Salmon	1.50	.60
❑ 250	Johnny Bench	50.00	20.00
❑ 251	Frank Reberger	1.50	.60
❑ 252	Eddie Leon	1.50	.60
❑ 253	Bill Sudakis	1.50	.60
❑ 254	Cal Koonce	1.50	.60
❑ 255	Bob Robertson	2.00	.80
❑ 256	Tony Gonzalez	1.50	.60
❑ 257	Nelson Briles	2.00	.80
❑ 258	Dick Green	1.50	.60
❑ 259	Dave Marshall	1.50	.60
❑ 260	Tommy Harper	2.00	.80
❑ 261	Darold Knowles	1.50	.60
❑ 262	Jim Williams	1.50	.60
	Dave Robinson		
❑ 263	John Ellis	1.50	.60
❑ 264	Joe Morgan	8.00	3.20
❑ 265	Jim Northrup	2.00	.80
❑ 266	Bill Stoneman	1.50	.60
❑ 267	Rich Morales	1.50	.60
❑ 268	Philadelphia Phillies	4.00	1.60
	Team Card		
❑ 269	Gail Hopkins	1.50	.60
❑ 270	Rico Carty	2.00	.80
❑ 271	Bill Zepp	1.50	.60
❑ 272	Tommy Helms	2.00	.80
❑ 273	Pete Richert	1.50	.60
❑ 274	Ron Slocum	1.50	.60
❑ 275	Vada Pinson	2.00	.80
❑ 276	Mike Davison	8.00	3.20
	George Foster RC		
❑ 277	Gary Waslewski	1.50	.60
❑ 278	Jerry Grote	2.00	.80
❑ 279	Lefty Phillips MG	1.50	.60
❑ 280	Ferguson Jenkins	6.00	2.40
❑ 281	Danny Walton	1.50	.60
❑ 282	Jose Pagan	1.50	.60
❑ 283	Dick Such	1.50	.60
❑ 284	Jim Gosger	1.50	.60
❑ 285	Sal Bando	2.00	.80
❑ 286	Jerry McNertney	1.50	.60
❑ 287	Mike Fiore	1.50	.60
❑ 288	Joe Moeller	1.50	.60
❑ 289	Chicago White Sox	4.00	1.60
	Team Card		
❑ 290	Tony Oliva	4.00	1.60
❑ 291	George Culver	1.50	.60
❑ 292	Jay Johnstone	2.00	.80
❑ 293	Pat Corrales	2.00	.80
❑ 294	Steve Dunning	1.50	.60
❑ 295	Bobby Bonds	4.00	1.60
❑ 296	Tom Timmermann	1.50	.60
❑ 297	Johnny Briggs	1.50	.60
❑ 298	Jim Nelson	1.50	.60
❑ 299	Ed Kirkpatrick	1.50	.60
❑ 300	Brooks Robinson	20.00	8.00
❑ 301	Earl Wilson	1.50	.60
❑ 302	Phil Gagliano	1.50	.60
❑ 303	Lindy McDaniel	2.00	.80
❑ 304	Ron Brand	1.50	.60
❑ 305	Reggie Smith	2.00	.80
❑ 306	Jim Nash	1.50	.60
❑ 307	Don Wert	1.50	.60
❑ 308	St. Louis Cardinals	4.00	1.60
	Team Card		
❑ 309	Dick Ellsworth	1.50	.60
❑ 310	Tommie Agee	2.00	.80
❑ 311	Lee Stange	1.50	.60
❑ 312	Harry Walker MG	1.50	.60
❑ 313	Tom Hall	1.50	.60
❑ 314	Jeff Torborg	2.00	.80
❑ 315	Ron Fairly	2.00	.80
❑ 316	Fred Scherman	1.50	.60
❑ 317	Jim Driscoll	1.50	.60
	Angel Mangual		
❑ 318	Rudy May	1.50	.60
❑ 319	Ty Cline	1.50	.60
❑ 320	Dave McNally	2.00	.80
❑ 321	Tom Matchick	1.50	.60
❑ 322	Jim Beauchamp	1.50	.60
❑ 323	Billy Champion	1.50	.60
❑ 324	Graig Nettles	2.00	.80
❑ 325	Juan Marichal	8.00	3.20
❑ 326	Richie Scheinblum	1.50	.60
❑ 327	Boog Powell WS	2.00	.80
❑ 328	Don Buford WS	2.00	.80
❑ 329	Frank Robinson WS	4.00	1.60
❑ 330	World Series Game 4	2.00	.80
	Reds stay alive		
❑ 331	Brooks Robinson WS	6.00	2.40
	commits robbery		
❑ 332	WS Summary	2.00	.80
	Orioles celebrate		
❑ 333	Clay Kirby	1.50	.60
❑ 334	Roberto Pena	1.50	.60
❑ 335	Jerry Koosman	2.00	.80
❑ 336	Detroit Tigers	4.00	1.60
	Team Card		
❑ 337	Jesus Alou	1.50	.60
❑ 338	Gene Tenace	2.00	.80
❑ 339	Wayne Simpson	1.50	.60
❑ 340	Rico Petrocelli	2.00	.80
❑ 341	Steve Garvey RC	40.00	16.00
❑ 342	Frank Tepedino	2.00	.80
❑ 343	Ed Acosta	2.00	.80
	Milt May RC		
❑ 344	Ellie Rodriguez	1.50	.60
❑ 345	Joel Horlen	1.50	.60
❑ 346	Lum Harris MG	1.50	.60
❑ 347	Ted Uhlaender	1.50	.60
❑ 348	Fred Norman	1.50	.60
❑ 349	Rich Reese	1.50	.60
❑ 350	Billy Williams	6.00	2.40
❑ 351	Jim Shellenback	1.50	.60
❑ 352	Denny Doyle	1.50	.60
❑ 353	Carl Taylor	1.50	.60
❑ 354	Don McMahon	1.50	.60
❑ 355	Bud Harrelson	4.00	1.60
	(Nolan Ryan in photo)		
❑ 356	Bob Locker	1.50	.60
❑ 357	Cincinnati Reds	4.00	1.60
	Team Card		
❑ 358	Danny Cater	1.50	.60
❑ 359	Ron Reed	1.50	.60
❑ 360	Jim Fregosi	2.00	.80
❑ 361	Don Sutton	6.00	2.40
❑ 362	Mike Adamson	1.50	.60
	Roger Freed		
❑ 363	Mike Nagy	1.50	.60
❑ 364	Tommy Dean	1.50	.60
❑ 365	Bob Johnson	1.50	.60
❑ 366	Ron Stone	1.50	.60
❑ 367	Dalton Jones	1.50	.60
❑ 368	Bob Veale	2.00	.80
❑ 369	Checklist 4	10.00	2.00
❑ 370	Joe Torre	4.00	1.60
❑ 371	Jack Hiatt	1.50	.60
❑ 372	Lew Krausse	1.50	.60
❑ 373	Tom McCraw	1.50	.60
❑ 374	Clete Boyer	2.00	.80
❑ 375	Steve Hargan	1.50	.60
❑ 376	Clyde Mashore	1.50	.60
	Ernie McAnally		
❑ 377	Greg Garrett	1.50	.60
❑ 378	Tito Fuentes	1.50	.60
❑ 379	Wayne Granger	1.50	.60
❑ 380	Ted Williams MG	12.00	4.80
❑ 381	Fred Gladding	1.50	.60
❑ 382	Jake Gibbs	1.50	.60
❑ 383	Rod Gaspar	1.50	.60
❑ 384	Rollie Fingers	6.00	2.40
❑ 385	Maury Wills	4.00	1.60
❑ 386	Boston Red Sox	2.00	.80
	Team Card		
❑ 387	Ron Herbel	1.50	.60
❑ 388	Al Oliver	4.00	1.60
❑ 389	Ed Brinkman	1.50	.60
❑ 390	Glenn Beckert	2.00	.80
❑ 391	Steve Brye	2.00	.80
	Cotton Nash		
❑ 392	Grant Jackson	1.50	.60
❑ 393	Merv Rettenmund	2.00	.80
❑ 394	Clay Carroll	2.50	1.00
❑ 395	Roy White	4.00	1.60
❑ 396	Dick Schofield	2.50	1.00
❑ 397	Alvin Dark MG	4.00	1.60
❑ 398	Howie Reed	2.50	1.00
❑ 399	Jim French	2.50	1.00
❑ 400	Hank Aaron	60.00	24.00
❑ 401	Tom Murphy	2.50	1.00
❑ 402	Los Angeles Dodgers	6.00	2.40
	Team Card		
❑ 403	Joe Coleman	2.50	1.00
❑ 404	Buddy Harris	2.50	1.00
	Roger Metzger		
❑ 405	Leo Cardenas	2.50	1.00
❑ 406	Ray Sadecki	2.50	1.00
❑ 407	Joe Rudi	4.00	1.60
❑ 408	Rafael Robles	2.50	1.00
❑ 409	Don Pavletich	2.50	1.00
❑ 410	Ken Holtzman	4.00	1.60
❑ 411	George Spriggs	2.50	1.00
❑ 412	Jerry Johnson	2.50	1.00
❑ 413	Pat Kelly	2.50	1.00
❑ 414	Woodie Fryman	2.50	1.00
❑ 415	Mike Hegan	2.50	1.00
❑ 416	Gene Alley	2.50	1.00
❑ 417	Dick Hall	2.50	1.00
❑ 418	Adolfo Phillips	2.50	1.00
❑ 419	Ron Hansen	2.50	1.00
❑ 420	Jim Merritt	2.50	1.00
❑ 421	John Stephenson	2.50	1.00
❑ 422	Frank Bertaina	2.50	1.00
❑ 423	Dennis Saunders	2.50	1.00
	Tim Marting		
❑ 424	Roberto Rodriquez	2.50	1.00
❑ 425	Doug Rader	4.00	1.60
❑ 426	Chris Cannizzaro	2.50	1.00
❑ 427	Bernie Allen	2.50	1.00
❑ 428	Jim McAndrew	2.50	1.00
❑ 429	Chuck Hinton	2.50	1.00
❑ 430	Wes Parker	4.00	1.60
❑ 431	Tom Burgmeier	2.50	1.00
❑ 432	Bob Didier	2.50	1.00
❑ 433	Skip Lockwood	2.50	1.00
❑ 434	Gary Sutherland	2.50	1.00
❑ 435	Jose Cardenal	4.00	1.60
❑ 436	Wilbur Wood	4.00	1.60
❑ 437	Danny Murtaugh MG	4.00	1.60
❑ 438	Mike McCormick	4.00	1.60
❑ 439	Greg Luzinski RC	6.00	2.40
	Scott Reid		
❑ 440	Bert Campaneris	4.00	1.60
❑ 441	Milt Pappas	4.00	1.60
❑ 442	California Angels	4.00	1.60
	Team Card		
❑ 443	Rich Robertson	2.50	1.00
❑ 444	Jimmie Price	2.50	1.00
❑ 445	Art Shamsky	2.50	1.00
❑ 446	Bobby Bolin	2.50	1.00
❑ 447	Cesar Geronimo	4.00	1.60
❑ 448	Dave Roberts	2.50	1.00
❑ 449	Brant Alyea	2.50	1.00
❑ 450	Bob Gibson	15.00	6.00
❑ 451	Joe Keough	2.50	1.00
❑ 452	John Boccabella	2.50	1.00
❑ 453	Terry Crowley	2.50	1.00
❑ 454	Mike Paul	2.50	1.00
❑ 455	Don Kessinger	4.00	1.60
❑ 456	Bob Meyer	2.50	1.00
❑ 457	Willie Smith	2.50	1.00

❑	458	Ron Lolich	2.50	1.00
		Dave Lemonds		
❑	459	Jim Lefebvre	2.50	1.00
❑	460	Fritz Peterson	2.50	1.00
❑	461	Jim Ray Hart	2.50	1.00
❑	462	Washington Senators	6.00	2.40
		Team Card		
❑	463	Tom Kelley	2.50	1.00
❑	464	Aurelio Rodriguez	2.50	1.00
❑	465	Tim McCarver	6.00	2.40
❑	466	Ken Berry	2.50	1.00
❑	467	Al Santorini	2.50	1.00
❑	468	Frank Fernandez	2.50	1.00
❑	469	Bob Aspromonte	2.50	1.00
❑	470	Bob Oliver	2.50	1.00
❑	471	Tom Griffin	2.50	1.00
❑	472	Ken Rudolph	2.50	1.00
❑	473	Gary Wagner	2.50	1.00
❑	474	Jim Fairey	2.50	1.00
❑	475	Ron Perranoski	2.50	1.00
❑	476	Dal Maxvill	2.50	1.00
❑	477	Earl Weaver MG	6.00	2.40
❑	478	Bernie Carbo	2.50	1.00
❑	479	Dennis Higgins	2.50	1.00
❑	480	Manny Sanguillen	4.00	1.60
❑	481	Daryl Patterson	2.50	1.00
❑	482	San Diego Padres	6.00	2.40
		Team Card		
❑	483	Gene Michael	2.50	1.00
❑	484	Don Wilson	2.50	1.00
❑	485	Ken McMullen	2.50	1.00
❑	486	Steve Huntz	2.50	1.00
❑	487	Paul Schaal	2.50	1.00
❑	488	Jerry Stephenson	2.50	1.00
❑	489	Luis Alvarado	2.50	1.00
❑	490	Deron Johnson	2.50	1.00
❑	491	Jim Hardin	2.50	1.00
❑	492	Ken Boswell	2.50	1.00
❑	493	Dave May	2.50	1.00
❑	494	Ralph Garr	4.00	1.60
		Rick Kester		
❑	495	Felipe Alou	4.00	1.60
❑	496	Woody Woodward	2.50	1.00
❑	497	Horacio Pina	2.50	1.00
❑	498	John Kennedy	2.50	1.00
❑	499	Checklist 5	10.00	2.00
❑	500	Jim Perry	4.00	1.60
❑	501	Andy Etchebarren	2.50	1.00
❑	502	Chicago Cubs	6.00	2.40
		Team Card		
❑	503	Gates Brown	4.00	1.60
❑	504	Ken Wright	2.50	1.00
❑	505	Ollie Brown	2.50	1.00
❑	506	Bobby Knoop	2.50	1.00
❑	507	George Stone	2.50	1.00
❑	508	Roger Repoz	2.50	1.00
❑	509	Jim Grant	2.50	1.00
❑	510	Ken Harrelson	4.00	1.60
❑	511	Chris Short	4.00	1.60
		(Pete Rose leading off second)		
❑	512	Dick Mills	2.50	1.00
		Mike Garman		
❑	513	Nolan Ryan	150.00	60.00
❑	514	Ron Woods	2.50	1.00
❑	515	Carl Morton	2.50	1.00
❑	516	Ted Kubiak	2.50	1.00
❑	517	Charlie Fox MG	2.50	1.00
❑	518	Joe Grzenda	2.50	1.00
❑	519	Willie Crawford	2.50	1.00
❑	520	Tommy John	6.00	2.40
❑	521	Leron Lee	2.50	1.00
❑	522	Minnesota Twins	6.00	2.40
		Team Card		
❑	523	John Odom	2.50	1.00
❑	524	Mickey Stanley	6.00	2.40
❑	525	Ernie Banks	50.00	20.00
❑	526	Ray Jarvis	4.00	1.60
❑	527	Cleon Jones	6.00	2.40
❑	528	Wally Bunker	4.00	1.60
❑	529	Enzo Hernandez	6.00	2.40
		Bill Buckner		
		Marty Perez		
❑	530	Carl Yastrzemski	30.00	12.00
❑	531	Mike Torrez	4.00	1.60
❑	532	Bill Rigney MG	4.00	1.60
❑	533	Mike Ryan	4.00	1.60
❑	534	Luke Walker	4.00	1.60
❑	535	Curt Flood	6.00	2.40
❑	536	Claude Raymond	4.00	1.60
❑	537	Tom Egan	4.00	1.60
❑	538	Angel Bravo	4.00	1.60
❑	539	Larry Brown	4.00	1.60
❑	540	Larry Dierker	6.00	2.40
❑	541	Bob Burda	4.00	1.60
❑	542	Bob Miller	4.00	1.60
❑	543	New York Yankees	10.00	4.00
		Team Card		
❑	544	Vida Blue	6.00	2.40
❑	545	Dick Dietz	4.00	1.60
❑	546	John Matias	4.00	1.60
❑	547	Pat Dobson	6.00	2.40
❑	548	Don Mason	4.00	1.60
❑	549	Jim Brewer	6.00	2.40
❑	550	Harmon Killebrew	25.00	10.00
❑	551	Frank Linzy	4.00	1.60
❑	552	Buddy Bradford	4.00	1.60
❑	553	Kevin Collins	4.00	1.60
❑	554	Lowell Palmer	4.00	1.60
❑	555	Walt Williams	4.00	1.60
❑	556	Jim McGlothlin	4.00	1.60
❑	557	Tom Satriano	4.00	1.60
❑	558	Hector Torres	4.00	1.60
❑	559	Terry Cox	4.00	1.60
		Bill Gogolewski		
		Gary Jones		
❑	560	Rusty Staub	6.00	2.40
❑	561	Syd O'Brien	4.00	1.60
❑	562	Dave Giusti	4.00	1.60
❑	563	San Francisco Giants	8.00	3.20
		Team Card		
❑	564	Al Fitzmorris	4.00	1.60
❑	565	Jim Wynn	6.00	2.40
❑	566	Tim Cullen	4.00	1.60
❑	567	Walt Alston MG	8.00	3.20
❑	568	Sal Campisi	4.00	1.60
❑	569	Ivan Murrell	4.00	1.60
❑	570	Jim Palmer	30.00	12.00
❑	571	Ted Sizemore	4.00	1.60
❑	572	Jerry Kenney	4.00	1.60
❑	573	Ed Kranepool	6.00	2.40
❑	574	Jim Bunning	8.00	3.20
❑	575	Bill Freehan	6.00	2.40
❑	576	Adrian Garrett	4.00	1.60
		Brock Davis		
		Garry Jestadt		
❑	577	Jim Lonborg	6.00	2.40
❑	578	Ron Hunt	4.00	1.60
❑	579	Marty Pattin	4.00	1.60
❑	580	Tony Perez	20.00	8.00
❑	581	Roger Nelson	4.00	1.60
❑	582	Dave Cash	6.00	2.40
❑	583	Ron Cook	4.00	1.60
❑	584	Cleveland Indians	8.00	3.20
		Team Card		
❑	585	Willie Davis	6.00	2.40
❑	586	Dick Woodson	4.00	1.60
❑	587	Sonny Jackson	4.00	1.60
❑	588	Tom Bradley	4.00	1.60
❑	589	Bob Barton	4.00	1.60
❑	590	Alex Johnson	6.00	2.40
❑	591	Jackie Brown	4.00	1.60
❑	592	Randy Hundley	6.00	2.40
❑	593	Jack Aker	4.00	1.60
❑	594	Bob Chlupsa	6.00	2.40
		Bob Stinson		
		Al Hrabosky RC		
❑	595	Dave Johnson	6.00	2.40
❑	596	Mike Jorgensen	4.00	1.60
❑	597	Ken Suarez	4.00	1.60
❑	598	Rick Wise	6.00	2.40
❑	599	Norm Cash	6.00	2.40
❑	600	Willie Mays	100.00	40.00
❑	601	Ken Tatum	4.00	1.60
❑	602	Marty Martinez	4.00	1.60
❑	603	Pittsburgh Pirates	8.00	3.20
		Team Card		
❑	604	John Gelnar	4.00	1.60
❑	605	Orlando Cepeda	8.00	3.20
❑	606	Chuck Taylor	4.00	1.60
❑	607	Paul Ratliff	4.00	1.60
❑	608	Mike Wegener	4.00	1.60
❑	609	Leo Durocher MG	8.00	3.20
❑	610	Amos Otis	6.00	2.40
❑	611	Tom Phoebus	4.00	1.60
❑	612	Lou Camilli	4.00	1.60
		Ted Ford		
		Steve Mingori		
❑	613	Pedro Borbon	4.00	1.60
❑	614	Billy Cowan	4.00	1.60
❑	615	Mel Stottlemyre	6.00	2.40
❑	616	Larry Hisle	6.00	2.40
❑	617	Clay Dalrymple	4.00	1.60
❑	618	Tug McGraw	6.00	2.40
❑	619A	Checklist 6 ERR	10.00	2.00
		(No copyright)		
❑	619B	Checklist 6 COR	6.00	1.20
		(Copyright on back)		
❑	620	Frank Howard	6.00	2.40
❑	621	Ron Bryant	4.00	1.60
❑	622	Joe Lahoud	4.00	1.60
❑	623	Pat Jarvis	4.00	1.60
❑	624	Oakland Athletics	8.00	3.20
		Team Card		
❑	625	Lou Brock	30.00	12.00
❑	626	Freddie Patek	6.00	2.40
❑	627	Steve Hamilton	4.00	1.60
❑	628	John Bateman	4.00	1.60
❑	629	John Hiller	6.00	2.40
❑	630	Roberto Clemente	150.00	60.00
❑	631	Eddie Fisher	4.00	1.60
❑	632	Darrel Chaney	4.00	1.60
❑	633	Bobby Brooks	4.00	1.60
		Pete Koegel		
		Scott Northey		
❑	634	Phil Regan	4.00	1.60
❑	635	Bobby Murcer	6.00	2.40
❑	636	Denny Lemaster	4.00	1.60
❑	637	Dave Bristol MG	4.00	1.60
❑	638	Stan Williams	4.00	1.60
❑	639	Tom Haller	4.00	1.60
❑	640	Frank Robinson	40.00	16.00
❑	641	New York Mets	15.00	6.00
		Team Card		
❑	642	Jim Roland	4.00	1.60
❑	643	Rick Reichardt	4.00	1.60
❑	644	Jim Stewart SP	12.00	4.80
❑	645	Jim Maloney SP	15.00	6.00
❑	646	Bobby Floyd SP	12.00	4.80
❑	647	Juan Pizarro	8.00	3.20
❑	648	Rich Folkers	25.00	10.00
		Ted Martinez		
		John Matlack RC SP		
❑	649	Sparky Lyle SP	15.00	6.00
❑	650	Rich Allen SP	30.00	12.00
❑	651	Jerry Robertson SP	12.00	4.80
❑	652	Atlanta Braves	12.00	4.80
		Team Card		
❑	653	Russ Snyder SP	12.00	4.80
❑	654	Don Shaw SP	12.00	4.80
❑	655	Mike Epstein SP	12.00	4.80
❑	656	Gerry Nyman SP	12.00	4.80
❑	657	Jose Azcue	8.00	3.20
❑	658	Paul Lindblad SP	12.00	4.80
❑	659	Byron Browne SP	12.00	4.80
❑	660	Ray Culp	8.00	3.20
❑	661	Chuck Tanner MG SP	15.00	6.00
❑	662	Mike Hedlund SP	12.00	4.80
❑	663	Marv Staehle	8.00	3.20
❑	664	Archie Reynolds	12.00	4.80
		Bob Reynolds		
		Ken Reynolds SP		
❑	665	Ron Swoboda SP	15.00	6.00
❑	666	Gene Brabender SP	12.00	4.80
❑	667	Pete Ward	8.00	3.20
❑	668	Gary Neibauer	8.00	3.20
❑	669	Ike Brown SP	12.00	4.80
❑	670	Bill Hands	8.00	3.20
❑	671	Bill Voss SP	12.00	4.80
❑	672	Ed Crosby SP	12.00	4.80
❑	673	Gerry Janeski SP	12.00	4.80
❑	674	Montreal Expos	12.00	4.80
		Team Card		
❑	675	Dave Boswell	8.00	3.20
❑	676	Tommie Reynolds	8.00	3.20
❑	677	Jack DiLauro SP	12.00	4.80
❑	678	George Thomas	8.00	3.20
❑	679	Don O'Riley	8.00	3.20
❑	680	Don Mincher SP	12.00	4.80

Card	NM	Ex
❑ 681 Bill Butler	8.00	3.20
❑ 682 Terry Harmon	8.00	3.20
❑ 683 Bill Burbach SP	12.00	4.80
❑ 684 Curt Motton	8.00	3.20
❑ 685 Moe Drabowsky	8.00	3.20
❑ 686 Chico Ruiz SP	12.00	4.80
❑ 687 Ron Taylor SP	12.00	4.80
❑ 688 S.Anderson MG SP	30.00	12.00
❑ 689 Frank Baker	8.00	3.20
❑ 690 Bob Moose	8.00	3.20
❑ 691 Bobby Heise	8.00	3.20
❑ 692 Hal Haydel Rogelio Moret Wayne Twitchell SP	12.00	4.80
❑ 693 Jose Pena SP	12.00	4.80
❑ 694 Rick Renick SP	12.00	4.80
❑ 695 Joe Niekro	12.00	4.80
❑ 696 Jerry Morales	8.00	3.20
❑ 697 Rickey Clark SP	12.00	4.80
❑ 698 M. Brewers SP Team Card	20.00	8.00
❑ 699 Jim Britton	8.00	3.20
❑ 700 Boog Powell SP	25.00	10.00
❑ 701 Bob Garibaldi	8.00	3.20
❑ 702 Milt Ramirez	8.00	3.20
❑ 703 Mike Kekich	8.00	3.20
❑ 704 J.C. Martin SP	12.00	4.80
❑ 705 Dick Selma SP	12.00	4.80
❑ 706 Joe Foy SP	12.00	4.80
❑ 707 Fred Lasher	8.00	3.20
❑ 708 Russ Nagelson SP	12.00	4.80
❑ 709 Dusty Baker RC Don Baylor RC Tom Paciorek RC SP	80.00	32.00
❑ 710 Sonny Siebert	8.00	3.20
❑ 711 Larry Stahl SP	12.00	4.80
❑ 712 Jose Martinez	8.00	3.20
❑ 713 Mike Marshall SP	15.00	6.00
❑ 714 Dick Williams MG SP	15.00	6.00
❑ 715 Horace Clarke SP	15.00	6.00
❑ 716 Dave Leonhard	8.00	3.20
❑ 717 Tommie Aaron SP	12.00	4.80
❑ 718 Billy Wynne	8.00	3.20
❑ 719 Jerry May SP	12.00	4.80
❑ 720 Matty Alou	12.00	4.80
❑ 721 John Morris	8.00	3.20
❑ 722 Houston Astros SP Team Card	20.00	8.00
❑ 723 Vicente Romo SP	12.00	4.80
❑ 724 Tom Tischinski SP	12.00	4.80
❑ 725 Gary Gentry SP	12.00	4.80
❑ 726 Paul Popovich	8.00	3.20
❑ 727 Ray Lamb SP	12.00	4.80
❑ 728 Wayne Redmond Keith Lampard Bernie Williams	8.00	3.20
❑ 729 Dick Billings	8.00	3.20
❑ 730 Jim Rooker	8.00	3.20
❑ 731 Jim Qualls SP	12.00	4.80
❑ 732 Bob Reed	8.00	3.20
❑ 733 Lee Maye SP	12.00	4.80
❑ 734 Rob Gardner SP	12.00	4.80
❑ 735 Mike Shannon SP	15.00	6.00
❑ 736 Mel Queen SP	12.00	4.80
❑ 737 P.Gomez SP MG	12.00	4.80
❑ 738 Russ Gibson SP	12.00	4.80
❑ 739 Barry Lersch SP	12.00	4.80
❑ 740 Luis Aparicio SP UER (Led AL in steals from 1965 to 1964, should be 1956 to 1964)	30.00	12.00
❑ 741 Skip Guinn	8.00	3.20
❑ 742 Kansas City Royals Team Card	12.00	4.80
❑ 743 John O'Donoghue SP	12.00	4.80
❑ 744 Chuck Manuel SP	12.00	4.80
❑ 745 Sandy Alomar SP	12.00	4.80
❑ 746 Andy Kosco	8.00	3.20
❑ 747 Al Severinsen Scipio Spinks Balor Moore	8.00	3.20
❑ 748 John Purdin SP	12.00	4.80
❑ 749 Ken Szotkiewicz	8.00	3.20
❑ 750 Denny McLain SP	25.00	10.00
❑ 751 Al Weis SP	15.00	6.00
❑ 752 Dick Drago	12.00	2.90

1972 Topps

	NM	Ex
COMPLETE SET (787)	1500.00	700.00
COMMON CARD (1-132)	.60	.24
COMMON (133-263)	1.00	.40
COMMON (264-394)	1.25	.50
COMMON (395-525)	1.50	.60
COMMON (526-656)	4.00	1.60
COMMON (657-787)	12.00	4.80
WRAPPER (10-CENT)	15.00	6.00
❑ 1 Pittsburgh Pirates Team Card	8.00	2.90
❑ 2 Ray Culp	.60	.24
❑ 3 Bob Tolan	.60	.24
❑ 4 Checklist 1-132	6.00	1.20
❑ 5 John Bateman	.60	.24
❑ 6 Fred Scherman	.60	.24
❑ 7 Enzo Hernandez	.60	.24
❑ 8 Ron Swoboda	1.25	.50
❑ 9 Stan Williams	.60	.24
❑ 10 Amos Otis	1.25	.50
❑ 11 Bobby Valentine	1.25	.50
❑ 12 Jose Cardenal	.60	.24
❑ 13 Joe Grzenda	.60	.24
❑ 14 Pete Koegel Mike Anderson Wayne Twitchell	.60	.24
❑ 15 Walt Williams	.60	.24
❑ 16 Mike Jorgensen	.60	.24
❑ 17 Dave Duncan	1.25	.50
❑ 18A Juan Pizarro (Yellow underline C and S of Cubs)	.60	.24
❑ 18B Juan Pizarro (Green underline C and S of Cubs)	5.00	2.00
❑ 19 Billy Cowan	.60	.24
❑ 20 Don Wilson	.60	.24
❑ 21 Atlanta Braves Team Card	1.50	.60
❑ 22 Rob Gardner	.60	.24
❑ 23 Ted Kubiak	.60	.24
❑ 24 Ted Ford	.60	.24
❑ 25 Bill Singer	.60	.24
❑ 26 Andy Etchebarren	.60	.24
❑ 27 Bob Johnson	.60	.24
❑ 28 Bob Gebhard Steve Brye Hal Haydel	.60	.24
❑ 29A Bill Bonham (Yellow underline C and S of Cubs)	.60	.24
❑ 29B Bill Bonham (Green underline C and S of Cubs)	5.00	2.00
❑ 30 Rico Petrocelli	1.25	.50
❑ 31 Cleon Jones	1.25	.50
❑ 32 Cleon Jones IA	.60	.24
❑ 33 Billy Martin MG	4.00	1.60
❑ 34 Billy Martin IA	2.50	1.00
❑ 35 Jerry Johnson	.60	.24
❑ 36 Jerry Johnson IA	.60	.24
❑ 37 Carl Yastrzemski	10.00	4.00
❑ 38 Carl Yastrzemski IA	8.00	2.40
❑ 39 Bob Barton	.60	.24
❑ 40 Bob Barton IA	.60	.24
❑ 41 Tommy Davis	1.25	.50
❑ 42 Tommy Davis IA	.60	.24
❑ 43 Rick Wise	1.25	.50
❑ 44 Rick Wise IA	.60	.24
❑ 45A Glenn Beckert (Yellow underline C and S of Cubs)	1.25	.50
❑ 45B Glenn Beckert (Green underline C and S of Cubs)	5.00	2.00
❑ 46 Glenn Beckert IA	.60	.24
❑ 47 John Ellis	.60	.24
❑ 48 John Ellis IA	.60	.24
❑ 49 Willie Mays	40.00	16.00
❑ 50 Willie Mays IA	20.00	8.00
❑ 51 Harmon Killebrew	8.00	3.20
❑ 52 Harmon Killebrew IA	4.00	1.60
❑ 53 Bud Harrelson	1.25	.50
❑ 54 Bud Harrelson IA	.60	.24
❑ 55 Clyde Wright	.60	.24
❑ 56 Rich Chiles	.60	.24
❑ 57 Bob Oliver	.60	.24
❑ 58 Ernie McAnally	.60	.24
❑ 59 Fred Stanley	.60	.24
❑ 60 Manny Sanguillen	1.25	.50
❑ 61 Burt Hooton RC Gene Hiser Earl Stephenson	1.25	.50
❑ 62 Angel Mangual	.60	.24
❑ 63 Duke Sims	.60	.24
❑ 64 Pete Broberg	.60	.24
❑ 65 Cesar Cedeno	1.25	.50
❑ 66 Ray Corbin	.60	.24
❑ 67 Red Schoendienst MG	2.50	1.00
❑ 68 Jim York	.60	.24
❑ 69 Roger Freed	.60	.24
❑ 70 Mike Cuellar	1.25	.50
❑ 71 California Angels Team Card	1.50	.60
❑ 72 Bruce Kison RC	.60	.24
❑ 73 Steve Huntz	.60	.24
❑ 74 Cecil Upshaw	.60	.24
❑ 75 Bert Campaneris	1.25	.50
❑ 76 Don Carrithers	.60	.24
❑ 77 Ron Theobald	.60	.24
❑ 78 Steve Arlin	.60	.24
❑ 79 Mike Garman Cecil Cooper RC Carlton Fisk RC	50.00	20.00
❑ 80 Tony Perez	4.00	1.60
❑ 81 Mike Hedlund	.60	.24
❑ 82 Ron Woods	.60	.24
❑ 83 Dalton Jones	.60	.24
❑ 84 Vince Colbert	.60	.24
❑ 85 Joe Torre Ralph Garr Glenn Beckert LL	2.50	1.00
❑ 86 Tony Oliva Bobby Murcer Merv Rettenmund LL	2.50	1.00
❑ 87 Joe Torre Willie Stargell Hank Aaron LL	4.00	1.60
❑ 88 Harmon Killebrew Frank Robinson Reggie Smith LL	4.00	1.60
❑ 89 Willie Stargell Hank Aaron Lee May LL	2.50	1.00
❑ 90 Bill Melton Norm Cash Reggie Jackson LL	2.50	1.00
❑ 91 Tom Seaver Dave Roberts UER (Photo actually Danny Coombs) Don Wilson LL	2.50	1.00
❑ 92 Vida Blue Wilbur Wood Jim Palmer LL	2.50	1.00
❑ 93 Fergie Jenkins Steve Carlton Al Downing Tom Seaver LL	4.00	1.60
❑ 94 Mickey Lolich Vida Blue	2.50	1.00

Wilbur Wood LL
❑ 95 Tom Seaver 4.00 1.60
Fergie Jenkins
Bill Stoneman LL
❑ 96 Mickey Lolich 2.50 1.00
Vida Blue
Joe Coleman LL
❑ 97 Tom Kelley .60 .24
❑ 98 Chuck Tanner MG 1.25 .50
❑ 99 Ross Grimsley .60 .24
❑ 100 Frank Robinson 8.00 3.20
❑ 101 Bill Greif 2.50 1.00
J.R. Richard RC
Ray Busse
❑ 102 Lloyd Allen .60 .24
❑ 103 Checklist 133-263 6.00 1.20
❑ 104 Toby Harrah RC 1.25 .50
❑ 105 Gary Gentry .60 .24
❑ 106 Milwaukee Brewers 1.50 .60
Team Card
❑ 107 Jose Cruz RC 1.25 .50
❑ 108 Gary Waslewski .60 .24
❑ 109 Jerry May .60 .24
❑ 110 Ron Hunt .60 .24
❑ 111 Jim Grant .60 .24
❑ 112 Greg Luzinski 1.25 .50
❑ 113 Rogelio Moret .60 .24
❑ 114 Bill Buckner 1.25 .50
❑ 115 Jim Fregosi 1.25 .50
❑ 116 Ed Farmer .60 .24
❑ 117A Cleo James .60 .24
(Yellow underline
C and S of Cubs)
❑ 117B Cleo James 5.00 2.00
(Green underline
C and S of Cubs)
❑ 118 Skip Lockwood .60 .24
❑ 119 Marty Perez .60 .24
❑ 120 Bill Freehan 1.25 .50
❑ 121 Ed Sprague .60 .24
❑ 122 Larry Biittner .60 .24
❑ 123 Ed Acosta .60 .24
❑ 124 Alan Closter .60 .24
Rusty Torres
Roger Hambright
❑ 125 Dave Cash 1.25 .50
❑ 126 Bart Johnson .60 .24
❑ 127 Duffy Dyer .60 .24
❑ 128 Eddie Watt .60 .24
❑ 129 Charlie Fox MG .60 .24
❑ 130 Bob Gibson 8.00 3.20
❑ 131 Jim Nettles .60 .24
❑ 132 Joe Morgan 6.00 2.40
❑ 133 Joe Keough 1.00 .40
❑ 134 Carl Morton 1.00 .40
❑ 135 Vada Pinson 2.00 .80
❑ 136 Darrel Chaney 1.00 .40
❑ 137 Dick Williams MG 2.00 .80
❑ 138 Mike Kekich 1.00 .40
❑ 139 Tim McCarver 2.00 .80
❑ 140 Pat Dobson 2.00 .80
❑ 141 Buzz Capra 2.00 .80
Lee Stanton
Jon Matlack
❑ 142 Chris Chambliss RC 4.00 1.60
❑ 143 Garry Jestadt 1.00 .40
❑ 144 Marty Pattin 1.00 .40
❑ 145 Don Kessinger 2.00 .80
❑ 146 Steve Kealey 1.00 .40
❑ 147 Dave Kingman RC 6.00 2.40
❑ 148 Dick Billings 1.00 .40
❑ 149 Gary Neibauer 1.00 .40
❑ 150 Norm Cash 2.00 .80
❑ 151 Jim Brewer 1.00 .40
❑ 152 Gene Clines 1.00 .40
❑ 153 Rick Auerbach 1.00 .40
❑ 154 Ted Simmons 4.00 1.60
❑ 155 Larry Dierker 1.00 .40
❑ 156 Minnesota Twins 2.00 .80
Team Card
❑ 157 Don Gullett 1.00 .40
❑ 158 Jerry Kenney 1.00 .40
❑ 159 John Boccabella 1.00 .40
❑ 160 Andy Messersmith 2.00 .80
❑ 161 Brock Davis 1.00 .40
❑ 162 Jerry Bell 2.00 .80
Darrell Porter RC
Bob Reynolds UER
(Porter and Bell
photos switched)
❑ 163 Tug McGraw 4.00 1.60
❑ 164 Tug McGraw IA 2.00 .80
❑ 165 Chris Speier RC 2.00 .80
❑ 166 Chris Speier IA 1.00 .40
❑ 167 Deron Johnson 1.00 .40
❑ 168 Deron Johnson IA 1.00 .40
❑ 169 Vida Blue 4.00 1.60
❑ 170 Vida Blue IA 2.00 .80
❑ 171 Darrell Evans 4.00 1.60
❑ 172 Darrell Evans IA 2.00 .80
❑ 173 Clay Kirby 1.00 .40
❑ 174 Clay Kirby IA 1.00 .40
❑ 175 Tom Haller 1.00 .40
❑ 176 Tom Haller IA 1.00 .40
❑ 177 Paul Schaal 1.00 .40
❑ 178 Paul Schaal IA 1.00 .40
❑ 179 Dock Ellis 1.00 .40
❑ 180 Dock Ellis IA 1.00 .40
❑ 181 Ed Kranepool 2.00 .80
❑ 182 Ed Kranepool IA 1.00 .40
❑ 183 Bill Melton 1.00 .40
❑ 184 Bill Melton IA 1.00 .40
❑ 185 Ron Bryant 1.00 .40
❑ 186 Ron Bryant IA 1.00 .40
❑ 187 Gates Brown 1.00 .40
❑ 188 Frank Lucchesi MG 1.00 .40
❑ 189 Gene Tenace 2.00 .80
❑ 190 Dave Giusti 1.00 .40
❑ 191 Jeff Burroughs RC 4.00 1.60
❑ 192 Chicago Cubs 2.00 .80
Team Card
❑ 193 Kurt Bevacqua 1.00 .40
❑ 194 Fred Norman 1.00 .40
❑ 195 Orlando Cepeda 6.00 2.40
❑ 196 Mel Queen 1.00 .40
❑ 197 Johnny Briggs 1.00 .40
❑ 198 Charlie Hough RC 6.00 2.40
Bob O'Brien
Mike Strahler
❑ 199 Mike Fiore 1.00 .40
❑ 200 Lou Brock 8.00 3.20
❑ 201 Phil Roof 1.00 .40
❑ 202 Scipio Spinks 1.00 .40
❑ 203 Ron Blomberg 1.00 .40
❑ 204 Tommy Helms 1.00 .40
❑ 205 Dick Drago 1.00 .40
❑ 206 Dal Maxvill 1.00 .40
❑ 207 Tom Egan 1.00 .40
❑ 208 Milt Pappas 2.00 .80
❑ 209 Joe Rudi 2.00 .80
❑ 210 Denny McLain 2.00 .80
❑ 211 Gary Sutherland 1.00 .40
❑ 212 Grant Jackson 1.00 .40
❑ 213 Billy Parker 1.00 .40
Art Kusnyer
Tom Silverio
❑ 214 Mike McQueen 1.00 .40
❑ 215 Alex Johnson 2.00 .80
❑ 216 Joe Niekro 2.00 .80
❑ 217 Roger Metzger 1.00 .40
❑ 218 Eddie Kasko MG 1.00 .40
❑ 219 Rennie Stennett 2.00 .80
❑ 220 Jim Perry 2.00 .80
❑ 221 NL Playoffs 2.00 .80
Bucs champs
❑ 222 Br. Robinson ALCS 4.00 1.60
❑ 223 Dave McNally WS 2.00 .80
❑ 224 Dave Johnson WS 2.00 .80
Mark Belanger
❑ 225 Manny Sanguillen WS 2.00 .80
❑ 226 Roberto Clemente WS 8.00 3.20
❑ 227 Nellie Briles WS 2.00 .80
❑ 228 Frank Robinson WS 2.00 .80
Manny Sanguillen
❑ 229 Steve Blass WS 2.00 .80
❑ 230 WS Summary 2.00 .80
Pirates celebrate
❑ 231 Casey Cox 1.00 .40
❑ 232 Chris Arnold 1.00 .40
Jim Barr
Dave Rader
❑ 233 Jay Johnstone 2.00 .80
❑ 234 Ron Taylor 1.00 .40
❑ 235 Merv Rettenmund 1.00 .40
❑ 236 Jim McGlothlin 1.00 .40
❑ 237 New York Yankees 2.00 .80
Team Card
❑ 238 Leron Lee 1.00 .40
❑ 239 Tom Timmermann 1.00 .40
❑ 240 Rich Allen 2.00 .80
❑ 241 Rollie Fingers 6.00 2.40
❑ 242 Don Mincher 1.00 .40
❑ 243 Frank Linzy 1.00 .40
❑ 244 Steve Braun 1.00 .40
❑ 245 Tommie Agee 2.00 .80
❑ 246 Tom Burgmeier 1.00 .40
❑ 247 Milt May 1.00 .40
❑ 248 Tom Bradley 1.00 .40
❑ 249 Harry Walker MG 1.00 .40
❑ 250 Boog Powell 2.00 .80
❑ 251 Checklist 264-394 6.00 1.20
❑ 252 Ken Reynolds 1.00 .40
❑ 253 Sandy Alomar 2.00 .80
❑ 254 Boots Day 1.00 .40
❑ 255 Jim Lonborg 2.00 .80
❑ 256 George Foster 2.00 .80
❑ 257 Jim Foor 1.00 .40
Tim Hosley
Paul Jata
❑ 258 Randy Hundley 1.00 .40
❑ 259 Sparky Lyle 2.00 .80
❑ 260 Ralph Garr 2.00 .80
❑ 261 Steve Mingori 1.00 .40
❑ 262 San Diego Padres 2.00 .80
Team Card
❑ 263 Felipe Alou 2.00 .80
❑ 264 Tommy John 2.00 .80
❑ 265 Wes Parker 2.00 .80
❑ 266 Bobby Bolin 1.25 .50
❑ 267 Dave Concepcion 4.00 1.60
❑ 268 Dwain Anderson 1.25 .50
Chris Floethe
❑ 269 Don Hahn 1.25 .50
❑ 270 Jim Palmer 8.00 3.20
❑ 271 Ken Rudolph 1.25 .50
❑ 272 Mickey Rivers RC 2.00 .80
❑ 273 Bobby Floyd 1.25 .50
❑ 274 Al Severinsen 1.25 .50
❑ 275 Cesar Tovar 1.25 .50
❑ 276 Gene Mauch MG 2.00 .80
❑ 277 Elliott Maddox 1.25 .50
❑ 278 Dennis Higgins 1.25 .50
❑ 279 Larry Brown 1.25 .50
❑ 280 Willie McCovey 6.00 2.40
❑ 281 Bill Parsons 1.25 .50
❑ 282 Houston Astros 2.00 .80
Team Card
❑ 283 Darrell Brandon 1.25 .50
❑ 284 Ike Brown 1.25 .50
❑ 285 Gaylord Perry 6.00 2.40
❑ 286 Gene Alley 1.25 .50
❑ 287 Jim Hardin 1.25 .50
❑ 288 Johnny Jeter 1.25 .50
❑ 289 Syd O'Brien 1.25 .50
❑ 290 Sonny Siebert 1.25 .50
❑ 291 Hal McRae 2.00 .80
❑ 292 Hal McRae IA 1.25 .50
❑ 293 Dan Frisella 1.25 .50
❑ 294 Dan Frisella IA 1.25 .50
❑ 295 Dick Dietz 1.25 .50
❑ 296 Dick Dietz IA 1.25 .50
❑ 297 Claude Osteen 2.00 .80
❑ 298 Claude Osteen IA 1.25 .50
❑ 299 Hank Aaron 40.00 16.00
❑ 300 Hank Aaron IA 20.00 8.00
❑ 301 George Mitterwald 1.25 .50
❑ 302 George Mitterwald IA 1.25 .50
❑ 303 Joe Pepitone 2.00 .80
❑ 304 Joe Pepitone IA 1.25 .50
❑ 305 Ken Boswell 1.25 .50
❑ 306 Ken Boswell IA 1.25 .50
❑ 307 Steve Renko 1.25 .50
❑ 308 Steve Renko IA 1.25 .50
❑ 309 Roberto Clemente 50.00 20.00
❑ 310 Roberto Clemente IA 25.00 10.00
❑ 311 Clay Carroll 1.25 .50
❑ 312 Clay Carroll IA 1.25 .50
❑ 313 Luis Aparicio 6.00 2.40

❑ 314	Luis Aparicio IA	2.00	.80
❑ 315	Paul Splittorff	1.25	.50
❑ 316	Jim Bibby	2.00	.80
	Jorge Roque		
	Santiago Guzman		
❑ 317	Rich Hand	1.25	.50
❑ 318	Sonny Jackson	1.25	.50
❑ 319	Aurelio Rodriguez	1.25	.50
❑ 320	Steve Blass	2.00	.80
❑ 321	Joe Lahoud	1.25	.50
❑ 322	Jose Pena	1.25	.50
❑ 323	Earl Weaver MG	4.00	1.60
❑ 324	Mike Ryan	1.25	.50
❑ 325	Mel Stottlemyre	2.00	.80
❑ 326	Pat Kelly	1.25	.50
❑ 327	Steve Stone RC	2.00	.80
❑ 328	Boston Red Sox	2.00	.80
	Team Card		
❑ 329	Roy Foster	1.25	.50
❑ 330	Jim Hunter	6.00	2.40
❑ 331	Stan Swanson	1.25	.50
❑ 332	Buck Martinez	1.25	.50
❑ 333	Steve Barber	1.25	.50
❑ 334	Bill Fahey	1.25	.50
	Jim Mason		
	Tom Ragland		
❑ 335	Bill Hands	1.25	.50
❑ 336	Marty Martinez	1.25	.50
❑ 337	Mike Kilkenny	1.25	.50
❑ 338	Bob Grich	2.00	.80
❑ 339	Ron Cook	1.25	.50
❑ 340	Roy White	2.00	.80
❑ 341	Joe Torre KP	1.25	.50
❑ 342	Wilbur Wood KP	1.25	.50
❑ 343	Willie Stargell KP	2.00	.80
❑ 344	Dave McNally KP	1.25	.50
❑ 345	Rick Wise KP	1.25	.50
❑ 346	Jim Fregosi KP	1.25	.50
❑ 347	Tom Seaver KP	4.00	1.60
❑ 348	Sal Bando KP	1.25	.50
❑ 349	Al Fitzmorris	1.25	.50
❑ 350	Frank Howard	2.00	.80
❑ 351	Tom House	2.00	.80
	Rick Kester		
	Jimmy Britton		
❑ 352	Dave LaRoche	1.25	.50
❑ 353	Art Shamsky	1.25	.50
❑ 354	Tom Murphy	1.25	.50
❑ 355	Bob Watson	2.00	.80
❑ 356	Gerry Moses	1.25	.50
❑ 357	Woody Fryman	1.25	.50
❑ 358	Sparky Anderson MG	4.00	1.60
❑ 359	Don Pavletich	1.25	.50
❑ 360	Dave Roberts	1.25	.50
❑ 361	Mike Andrews	1.25	.50
❑ 362	New York Mets	2.00	.80
	Team Card		
❑ 363	Ron Klimkowski	1.25	.50
❑ 364	Johnny Callison	2.00	.80
❑ 365	Dick Bosman	2.00	.80
❑ 366	Jimmy Rosario	1.25	.50
❑ 367	Ron Perranoski	1.25	.50
❑ 368	Danny Thompson	1.25	.50
❑ 369	Jim Lefebvre	2.00	.80
❑ 370	Don Buford	1.25	.50
❑ 371	Denny Lemaster	1.25	.50
❑ 372	Lance Clemons	1.25	.50
	Monty Montgomery		
❑ 373	John Mayberry	2.00	.80
❑ 374	Jack Heidemann	1.25	.50
❑ 375	Reggie Cleveland	1.25	.50
❑ 376	Andy Kosco	1.25	.50
❑ 377	Terry Harmon	1.25	.50
❑ 378	Checklist 395-525	6.00	1.20
❑ 379	Ken Berry	1.25	.50
❑ 380	Earl Williams	1.25	.50
❑ 381	Chicago White Sox	2.00	.80
	Team Card		
❑ 382	Joe Gibbon	1.25	.50
❑ 383	Brant Alyea	1.25	.50
❑ 384	Dave Campbell	2.00	.80
❑ 385	Mickey Stanley	2.00	.80
❑ 386	Jim Colborn	1.25	.50
❑ 387	Horace Clarke	2.00	.80
❑ 388	Charlie Williams	1.25	.50
❑ 389	Bill Rigney MG	1.25	.50
❑ 390	Willie Davis	2.00	.80
❑ 391	Ken Sanders	1.25	.50
❑ 392	Fred Cambria	2.00	.80
	Richie Zisk RC		
❑ 393	Curt Motton	1.25	.50
❑ 394	Ken Forsch	2.00	.80
❑ 395	Matty Alou	2.00	.80
❑ 396	Paul Lindblad	1.50	.60
❑ 397	Philadelphia Phillies	2.00	.80
	Team Card		
❑ 398	Larry Hisle	2.00	.80
❑ 399	Milt Wilcox	2.00	.80
❑ 400	Tony Oliva	4.00	1.60
❑ 401	Jim Nash	1.50	.60
❑ 402	Bobby Heise	1.50	.60
❑ 403	John Cumberland	1.50	.60
❑ 404	Jeff Torborg	2.00	.80
❑ 405	Ron Fairly	2.00	.80
❑ 406	George Hendrick RC	2.00	.80
❑ 407	Chuck Taylor	1.50	.60
❑ 408	Jim Northrup	2.00	.80
❑ 409	Frank Baker	1.50	.60
❑ 410	Ferguson Jenkins	6.00	2.40
❑ 411	Bob Montgomery	1.50	.60
❑ 412	Dick Kelley	1.50	.60
❑ 413	Don Eddy	1.50	.60
	Dave Lemonds		
❑ 414	Bob Miller	1.50	.60
❑ 415	Cookie Rojas	2.00	.80
❑ 416	Johnny Edwards	1.50	.60
❑ 417	Tom Hall	1.50	.60
❑ 418	Tom Shopay	1.50	.60
❑ 419	Jim Spencer	1.50	.60
❑ 420	Steve Carlton	20.00	8.00
❑ 421	Ellie Rodriguez	1.50	.60
❑ 422	Ray Lamb	1.50	.60
❑ 423	Oscar Gamble	2.00	.80
❑ 424	Bill Gogolewski	1.50	.60
❑ 425	Ken Singleton	2.00	.80
❑ 426	Ken Singleton IA	1.50	.60
❑ 427	Tito Fuentes	1.50	.60
❑ 428	Tito Fuentes IA	1.50	.60
❑ 429	Bob Robertson	1.50	.60
❑ 430	Bob Robertson IA	1.50	.60
❑ 431	Clarence Gaston	2.00	.80
❑ 432	Clarence Gaston IA	2.00	.80
❑ 433	Johnny Bench	25.00	10.00
❑ 434	Johnny Bench IA	15.00	6.00
❑ 435	Reggie Jackson	30.00	12.00
❑ 436	Reggie Jackson IA	12.00	4.80
❑ 437	Maury Wills	2.00	.80
❑ 438	Maury Wills IA	2.00	.80
❑ 439	Billy Williams	6.00	2.40
❑ 440	Billy Williams IA	4.00	1.60
❑ 441	Thurman Munson	15.00	6.00
❑ 442	Thurman Munson IA	8.00	3.20
❑ 443	Ken Henderson	1.50	.60
❑ 444	Ken Henderson IA	1.50	.60
❑ 445	Tom Seaver	30.00	12.00
❑ 446	Tom Seaver IA	15.00	6.00
❑ 447	Willie Stargell	8.00	3.20
❑ 448	Willie Stargell IA	4.00	1.60
❑ 449	Bob Lemon MG	2.00	.80
❑ 450	Mickey Lolich	2.00	.80
❑ 451	Tony LaRussa	4.00	1.60
❑ 452	Ed Herrmann	1.50	.60
❑ 453	Barry Lersch	1.50	.60
❑ 454	Oakland A's	2.00	.80
	Team Card		
❑ 455	Tommy Harper	2.00	.80
❑ 456	Mark Belanger	2.00	.80
❑ 457	Darcy Fast	1.50	.60
	Derrel Thomas		
	Mike Ivie		
❑ 458	Aurelio Monteagudo	1.50	.60
❑ 459	Rick Renick	1.50	.60
❑ 460	Al Downing	1.50	.60
❑ 461	Tim Cullen	1.50	.60
❑ 462	Rickey Clark	1.50	.60
❑ 463	Bernie Carbo	1.50	.60
❑ 464	Jim Roland	1.50	.60
❑ 465	Gil Hodges MG	4.00	1.60
❑ 466	Norm Miller	1.50	.60
❑ 467	Steve Kline	1.50	.60
❑ 468	Richie Scheinblum	1.50	.60
❑ 469	Ron Herbel	1.50	.60
❑ 470	Ray Fosse	1.50	.60
❑ 471	Luke Walker	1.50	.60
❑ 472	Phil Gagliano	1.50	.60
❑ 473	Dan McGinn	1.50	.60
❑ 474	Don Baylor	15.00	6.00
	Roric Harrison		
	Johnny Oates RC		
❑ 475	Gary Nolan	2.00	.80
❑ 476	Lee Richard	1.50	.60
❑ 477	Tom Phoebus	1.50	.60
❑ 478	Checklist 526-656	6.00	1.20
❑ 479	Don Shaw	1.50	.60
❑ 480	Lee May	2.00	.80
❑ 481	Billy Conigliaro	2.00	.80
❑ 482	Joe Hoerner	1.50	.60
❑ 483	Ken Suarez	1.50	.60
❑ 484	Lum Harris MG	1.50	.60
❑ 485	Phil Regan	2.00	.80
❑ 486	John Lowenstein	1.50	.60
❑ 487	Detroit Tigers	2.00	.80
	Team Card		
❑ 488	Mike Nagy	1.50	.60
❑ 489	Terry Humphrey	1.50	.60
	Keith Lampard		
❑ 490	Dave McNally	2.00	.80
❑ 491	Lou Piniella KP	2.00	.80
❑ 492	Mel Stottlemyre KP	2.00	.80
❑ 493	Bob Bailey KP	2.00	.80
❑ 494	Willie Horton KP	2.00	.80
❑ 495	Bill Melton KP	2.00	.80
❑ 496	Bud Harrelson KP	2.00	.80
❑ 497	Jim Perry KP	2.00	.80
❑ 498	Brooks Robinson KP	4.00	1.60
❑ 499	Vicente Romo	1.50	.60
❑ 500	Joe Torre	4.00	1.60
❑ 501	Pete Hamm	1.50	.60
❑ 502	Jackie Hernandez	1.50	.60
❑ 503	Gary Peters	1.50	.60
❑ 504	Ed Spiezio	1.50	.60
❑ 505	Mike Marshall	2.00	.80
❑ 506	Terry Ley	1.50	.60
	Jim Moyer		
	Dick Tidrow RC		
❑ 507	Fred Gladding	1.50	.60
❑ 508	Elrod Hendricks	1.50	.60
❑ 509	Don McMahon	1.50	.60
❑ 510	Ted Williams MG	12.00	4.80
❑ 511	Tony Taylor	2.00	.80
❑ 512	Paul Popovich	1.50	.60
❑ 513	Lindy McDaniel	2.00	.80
❑ 514	Ted Sizemore	1.50	.60
❑ 515	Bert Blyleven	4.00	1.60
❑ 516	Oscar Brown	1.50	.60
❑ 517	Ken Brett	1.50	.60
❑ 518	Wayne Garrett	1.50	.60
❑ 519	Ted Abernathy	1.50	.60
❑ 520	Larry Bowa	2.00	.80
❑ 521	Alan Foster	1.50	.60
❑ 522	Los Angeles Dodgers	2.00	.80
	Team Card		
❑ 523	Chuck Dobson	1.50	.60
❑ 524	Ed Armbrister	1.50	.60
	Mel Behney		
❑ 525	Carlos May	2.00	.80
❑ 526	Bob Bailey	6.00	2.40
❑ 527	Dave Leonhard	4.00	1.60
❑ 528	Ron Stone	4.00	1.60
❑ 529	Dave Nelson	6.00	2.40
❑ 530	Don Sutton	12.00	4.80
❑ 531	Freddie Patek	6.00	2.40
❑ 532	Fred Kendall	4.00	1.60
❑ 533	Ralph Houk MG	6.00	2.40
❑ 534	Jim Hickman	6.00	2.40
❑ 535	Ed Brinkman	4.00	1.60
❑ 536	Doug Rader	6.00	2.40
❑ 537	Bob Locker	4.00	1.60
❑ 538	Charlie Sands	4.00	1.60
❑ 539	Terry Forster RC	6.00	2.40
❑ 540	Felix Millan	4.00	1.60
❑ 541	Roger Repoz	4.00	1.60
❑ 542	Jack Billingham	4.00	1.60
❑ 543	Duane Josephson	4.00	1.60
❑ 544	Ted Martinez	4.00	1.60
❑ 545	Wayne Granger	4.00	1.60
❑ 546	Joe Hague	4.00	1.60
❑ 547	Cleveland Indians	8.00	3.20

Team Card
❑ 548 Frank Reberger 4.00 1.60
❑ 549 Dave May 4.00 1.60
❑ 550 Brooks Robinson 25.00 10.00
❑ 551 Ollie Brown 4.00 1.60
❑ 552 Ollie Brown IA 4.00 1.60
❑ 553 Wilbur Wood 6.00 2.40
❑ 554 Wilbur Wood IA 4.00 1.60
❑ 555 Ron Santo 8.00 3.20
❑ 556 Ron Santo IA 6.00 2.40
❑ 557 John Odom 4.00 1.60
❑ 558 John Odom IA 4.00 1.60
❑ 559 Pete Rose 50.00 20.00
❑ 560 Pete Rose IA 25.00 10.00
❑ 561 Leo Cardenas 4.00 1.60
❑ 562 Leo Cardenas IA 4.00 1.60
❑ 563 Ray Sadecki 4.00 1.60
❑ 564 Ray Sadecki IA 4.00 1.60
❑ 565 Reggie Smith 6.00 2.40
❑ 566 Reggie Smith IA 4.00 1.60
❑ 567 Juan Marichal 12.00 4.80
❑ 568 Juan Marichal IA 6.00 2.40
❑ 569 Ed Kirkpatrick 4.00 1.60
❑ 570 Ed Kirkpatrick IA 4.00 1.60
❑ 571 Nate Colbert 4.00 1.60
❑ 572 Nate Colbert IA 4.00 1.60
❑ 573 Fritz Peterson 4.00 1.60
❑ 574 Fritz Peterson IA 4.00 1.60
❑ 575 Al Oliver 8.00 3.20
❑ 576 Leo Durocher MG 6.00 2.40
❑ 577 Mike Paul 6.00 2.40
❑ 578 Billy Grabarkewitz 4.00 1.60
❑ 579 Doyle Alexander RC 6.00 2.40
❑ 580 Lou Piniella 6.00 2.40
❑ 581 Wade Blasingame 4.00 1.60
❑ 582 Montreal Expos 8.00 3.20
Team Card
❑ 583 Darold Knowles 4.00 1.60
❑ 584 Jerry McNertney 4.00 1.60
❑ 585 George Scott 6.00 2.40
❑ 586 Denis Menke 4.00 1.60
❑ 587 Billy Wilson 4.00 1.60
❑ 588 Jim Holt 4.00 1.60
❑ 589 Hal Lanier 4.00 1.60
❑ 590 Graig Nettles 8.00 3.20
❑ 591 Paul Casanova 4.00 1.60
❑ 592 Lew Krausse 4.00 1.60
❑ 593 Rich Morales 4.00 1.60
❑ 594 Jim Beauchamp 4.00 1.60
❑ 595 Nolan Ryan 80.00 40.00
❑ 596 Manny Mota 6.00 2.40
❑ 597 Jim Magnuson 4.00 1.60
❑ 598 Hal King 6.00 2.40
❑ 599 Billy Champion 4.00 1.60
❑ 600 Al Kaline 25.00 10.00
❑ 601 George Stone 4.00 1.60
❑ 602 Dave Bristol MG 4.00 1.60
❑ 603 Jim Ray 4.00 1.60
❑ 604A Checklist 657-787 12.00 2.40
(Copyright on back bottom right)
❑ 604B Checklist 657-787 12.00 2.40
(Copyright on back bottom left)
❑ 605 Nelson Briles 6.00 2.40
❑ 606 Luis Melendez 4.00 1.60
❑ 607 Frank Duffy 4.00 1.60
❑ 608 Mike Corkins 4.00 1.60
❑ 609 Tom Grieve 6.00 2.40
❑ 610 Bill Stoneman 6.00 2.40
❑ 611 Rich Reese 4.00 1.60
❑ 612 Joe Decker 4.00 1.60
❑ 613 Mike Ferraro 4.00 1.60
❑ 614 Ted Uhlaender 4.00 1.60
❑ 615 Steve Hargan 4.00 1.60
❑ 616 Joe Ferguson RC 6.00 2.40
❑ 617 Kansas City Royals 8.00 3.20
Team Card
❑ 618 Rich Robertson 4.00 1.60
❑ 619 Rich McKinney 4.00 1.60
❑ 620 Phil Niekro 12.00 4.80
❑ 621 Comm. Award 8.00 3.20
❑ 622 MVP Award 8.00 3.20
❑ 623 Cy Young Award 8.00 3.20
❑ 624 Minor League Player 8.00 3.20
of the Year
❑ 625 Rookie of the Year 8.00 3.20
❑ 626 Babe Ruth Award 8.00 3.20
❑ 627 Moe Drabowsky 4.00 1.60
❑ 628 Terry Crowley 4.00 1.60
❑ 629 Paul Doyle 4.00 1.60
❑ 630 Rich Hebner 6.00 2.40
❑ 631 John Strohmayer 4.00 1.60
❑ 632 Mike Hegan 4.00 1.60
❑ 633 Jack Hiatt 4.00 1.60
❑ 634 Dick Woodson 4.00 1.60
❑ 635 Don Money 6.00 2.40
❑ 636 Bill Lee 6.00 2.40
❑ 637 Preston Gomez MG 4.00 1.60
❑ 638 Ken Wright 4.00 1.60
❑ 639 J.C. Martin 4.00 1.60
❑ 640 Joe Coleman 4.00 1.60
❑ 641 Mike Lum 4.00 1.60
❑ 642 Dennis Riddleberger 4.00 1.60
❑ 643 Russ Gibson 4.00 1.60
❑ 644 Bernie Allen 4.00 1.60
❑ 645 Jim Maloney 6.00 2.40
❑ 646 Chico Salmon 4.00 1.60
❑ 647 Bob Moose 4.00 1.60
❑ 648 Jim Lyttle 4.00 1.60
❑ 649 Pete Richert 4.00 1.60
❑ 650 Sal Bando 6.00 2.40
❑ 651 Cincinnati Reds 8.00 3.20
Team Card
❑ 652 Marcelino Lopez 4.00 1.60
❑ 653 Jim Fairey 4.00 1.60
❑ 654 Horacio Pina 6.00 2.40
❑ 655 Jerry Grote 4.00 1.60
❑ 656 Rudy May 4.00 1.60
❑ 657 Bobby Wine 12.00 4.80
❑ 658 Steve Dunning 12.00 4.80
❑ 659 Bob Aspromonte 12.00 4.80
❑ 660 Paul Blair 15.00 6.00
❑ 661 Bill Virdon MG 12.00 4.80
❑ 662 Stan Bahnsen 12.00 4.80
❑ 663 Fran Healy 15.00 6.00
❑ 664 Bobby Knoop 12.00 4.80
❑ 665 Chris Short 12.00 4.80
❑ 666 Hector Torres 12.00 4.80
❑ 667 Ray Newman 12.00 4.80
❑ 668 Texas Rangers 30.00 12.00
Team Card
❑ 669 Willie Crawford 12.00 4.80
❑ 670 Ken Holtzman 15.00 6.00
❑ 671 Donn Clendenon 15.00 6.00
❑ 672 Archie Reynolds 12.00 4.80
❑ 673 Dave Marshall 12.00 4.80
❑ 674 John Kennedy 12.00 4.80
❑ 675 Pat Jarvis 12.00 4.80
❑ 676 Danny Cater 12.00 4.80
❑ 677 Ivan Murrell 12.00 4.80
❑ 678 Steve Luebber 12.00 4.80
❑ 679 Bob Fenwick 12.00 4.80
Bob Stinson
❑ 680 Dave Johnson 15.00 6.00
❑ 681 Bobby Pfeil 12.00 4.80
❑ 682 Mike McCormick 15.00 6.00
❑ 683 Steve Hovley 12.00 4.80
❑ 684 Hal Breeden 12.00 4.80
❑ 685 Joel Horlen 12.00 4.80
❑ 686 Steve Garvey 40.00 16.00
❑ 687 Del Unser 12.00 4.80
❑ 688 St. Louis Cardinals 20.00 8.00
Team Card
❑ 689 Eddie Fisher 12.00 4.80
❑ 690 Willie Montanez 15.00 6.00
❑ 691 Curt Blefary 12.00 4.80
❑ 692 Curt Blefary IA 12.00 4.80
❑ 693 Alan Gallagher 12.00 4.80
❑ 694 Alan Gallagher IA 12.00 4.80
❑ 695 Rod Carew 50.00 20.00
❑ 696 Rod Carew IA 30.00 12.00
❑ 697 Jerry Koosman 15.00 6.00
❑ 698 Jerry Koosman IA 15.00 6.00
❑ 699 Bobby Murcer 15.00 6.00
❑ 700 Bobby Murcer IA 15.00 6.00
❑ 701 Jose Pagan 12.00 4.80
❑ 702 Jose Pagan IA 12.00 4.80
❑ 703 Doug Griffin 12.00 4.80
❑ 704 Doug Griffin IA 12.00 4.80
❑ 705 Pat Corrales 15.00 6.00
❑ 706 Pat Corrales IA 12.00 4.80
❑ 707 Tim Foli 12.00 4.80
❑ 708 Tim Foli IA 12.00 4.80
❑ 709 Jim Kaat 15.00 6.00
❑ 710 Jim Kaat IA 15.00 6.00
❑ 711 Bobby Bonds 20.00 8.00
❑ 712 Bobby Bonds IA 15.00 6.00
❑ 713 Gene Michael 20.00 8.00
❑ 714 Gene Michael IA 15.00 6.00
❑ 715 Mike Epstein 12.00 4.80
❑ 716 Jesus Alou 12.00 4.80
❑ 717 Bruce Dal Canton 12.00 4.80
❑ 718 Del Rice MG 12.00 4.80
❑ 719 Cesar Geronimo 12.00 4.80
❑ 720 Sam McDowell 15.00 6.00
❑ 721 Eddie Leon 12.00 4.80
❑ 722 Bill Sudakis 12.00 4.80
❑ 723 Al Santorini 12.00 4.80
❑ 724 John Curtis 12.00 4.80
Rich Hinton
Mickey Scott RC
❑ 725 Dick McAuliffe 15.00 6.00
❑ 726 Dick Selma 12.00 4.80
❑ 727 Jose Laboy 12.00 4.80
❑ 728 Gail Hopkins 12.00 4.80
❑ 729 Bob Veale 15.00 6.00
❑ 730 Rick Monday 15.00 6.00
❑ 731 Baltimore Orioles 20.00 8.00
Team Card
❑ 732 George Culver 12.00 4.80
❑ 733 Jim Ray Hart 15.00 6.00
❑ 734 Bob Burda 12.00 4.80
❑ 735 Diego Segui 12.00 4.80
❑ 736 Bill Russell 15.00 6.00
❑ 737 Len Randle 15.00 6.00
❑ 738 Jim Merritt 12.00 4.80
❑ 739 Don Mason 12.00 4.80
❑ 740 Rico Carty 15.00 6.00
❑ 741 Tom Hutton 15.00 6.00
John Milner
Rick Miller RC
❑ 742 Jim Rooker 12.00 4.80
❑ 743 Cesar Gutierrez 12.00 4.80
❑ 744 Jim Slaton 12.00 4.80
❑ 745 Julian Javier 15.00 6.00
❑ 746 Lowell Palmer 12.00 4.80
❑ 747 Jim Stewart 12.00 4.80
❑ 748 Phil Hennigan 12.00 4.80
❑ 749 Walter Alston MG 20.00 8.00
❑ 750 Willie Horton 15.00 6.00
❑ 751 Steve Carlton TR 40.00 16.00
❑ 752 Joe Morgan TR 40.00 16.00
❑ 753 Denny McLain TR 20.00 8.00
❑ 754 Frank Robinson TR 40.00 16.00
❑ 755 Jim Fregosi TR 15.00 6.00
❑ 756 Rick Wise TR 15.00 6.00
❑ 757 Jose Cardenal TR 15.00 6.00
❑ 758 Gil Garrido 12.00 4.80
❑ 759 Chris Cannizzaro 12.00 4.80
❑ 760 Bill Mazeroski 25.00 10.00
❑ 761 Ben Oglivie RC 25.00 10.00
Ron Cey RC
Bernie Williams
❑ 762 Wayne Simpson 12.00 4.80
❑ 763 Ron Hansen 12.00 4.80
❑ 764 Dusty Baker 20.00 8.00
❑ 765 Ken McMullen 12.00 4.80
❑ 766 Steve Hamilton 12.00 4.80
❑ 767 Tom McCraw 15.00 6.00
❑ 768 Denny Doyle 12.00 4.80
❑ 769 Jack Aker 12.00 4.80
❑ 770 Jim Wynn 15.00 6.00
❑ 771 San Francisco Giants 20.00 8.00
Team Card
❑ 772 Ken Tatum 12.00 4.80
❑ 773 Ron Brand 12.00 4.80
❑ 774 Luis Alvarado 12.00 4.80
❑ 775 Jerry Reuss 15.00 6.00
❑ 776 Bill Voss 12.00 4.80
❑ 777 Hoyt Wilhelm 25.00 10.00
❑ 778 Vic Albury 20.00 8.00
Rick Dempsey RC
Jim Strickland
❑ 779 Tony Cloninger 12.00 4.80
❑ 780 Dick Green 12.00 4.80
❑ 781 Jim McAndrew 12.00 4.80
❑ 782 Larry Stahl 12.00 4.80

Card	NM	Ex
❑ 783 Les Cain	12.00	4.80
❑ 784 Ken Aspromonte	12.00	4.80
❑ 785 Vic Davalillo	12.00	4.80
❑ 786 Chuck Brinkman	12.00	4.80
❑ 787 Ron Reed	15.00	5.25

1973 Topps

	NM	Ex
COMPLETE SET (660)	700.00	275.00
COMMON CARD (1-264)	.50	.20
COMMON (265-396)	.75	.30
COMMON (397-528)	1.25	.50
COMMON (529-660)	3.00	1.20
WRAP. (10-CENT, BAT)	15.00	6.00
WRAPPER (10-CENT)	15.00	6.00

Card	NM	Ex
❑ 1 Babe Ruth 714	40.00	11.50
Hank Aaron 673		
Willie Mays 654 ATL		
❑ 2 Rich Hebner	1.50	.60
❑ 3 Jim Lonborg	1.50	.60
❑ 4 John Milner	.50	.20
❑ 5 Ed Brinkman	.50	.20
❑ 6 Mac Scarce	.50	.20
❑ 7 Texas Rangers	2.00	.80
Team Card		
❑ 8 Tom Hall	.50	.20
❑ 9 Johnny Oates	1.50	.60
❑ 10 Don Sutton	4.00	1.60
❑ 11 Chris Chambliss	1.50	.60
❑ 12A Don Zimmer MG	3.00	1.20
Dave Garcia CO		
Johnny Podres CO		
Bob Skinner CO		
Whitey Wietelmann CO		
(Podres no right ear)		
❑ 12B Padres Leaders	.75	.30
(Podres has right ear)		
❑ 13 George Hendrick	1.50	.60
❑ 14 Sonny Siebert	.50	.20
❑ 15 Ralph Garr	1.50	.60
❑ 16 Steve Braun	.50	.20
❑ 17 Fred Gladding	.50	.20
❑ 18 Leroy Stanton	.50	.20
❑ 19 Tim Foli	.50	.20
❑ 20 Stan Bahnsen	.50	.20
❑ 21 Randy Hundley	1.50	.60
❑ 22 Ted Abernathy	.50	.20
❑ 23 Dave Kingman	1.50	.60
❑ 24 Al Santorini	.50	.20
❑ 25 Roy White	1.50	.60
❑ 26 Pittsburgh Pirates	2.00	.80
Team Card		
❑ 27 Bill Gogolewski	.50	.20
❑ 28 Hal McRae	1.50	.60
❑ 29 Tony Taylor	1.50	.60
❑ 30 Tug McGraw	1.50	.60
❑ 31 Buddy Bell RC	2.50	1.00
❑ 32 Fred Norman	.50	.20
❑ 33 Jim Breazeale	.50	.20
❑ 34 Pat Dobson	.50	.20
❑ 35 Willie Davis	1.50	.60
❑ 36 Steve Barber	.50	.20
❑ 37 Bill Robinson	1.50	.60
❑ 38 Mike Epstein	.50	.20
❑ 39 Dave Roberts	.50	.20
❑ 40 Reggie Smith	1.50	.60
❑ 41 Tom Walker	.50	.20
❑ 42 Mike Andrews	.50	.20
❑ 43 Randy Moffitt	.50	.20
❑ 44 Rick Monday	1.50	.60
❑ 45 Ellie Rodriguez UER	.50	.20
(Photo actually		
John Felske)		
❑ 46 Lindy McDaniel	1.50	.60
❑ 47 Luis Melendez	.50	.20
❑ 48 Paul Splittorff	.50	.20
❑ 49A Frank Quilici MG	3.00	1.20
Vern Morgan CO		
Bob Rodgers CO		
Ralph Rowe CO		
Al Worthington CO		
(Solid backgrounds)		
❑ 49B Twins Leaders	.75	.30
(Natural backgrounds)		
❑ 50 Roberto Clemente	40.00	16.00
❑ 51 Chuck Seelbach	.50	.20
❑ 52 Denis Menke	.50	.20
❑ 53 Steve Dunning	.50	.20
❑ 54 Checklist 1-132	3.00	.60
❑ 55 Jon Matlack	1.50	.60
❑ 56 Merv Rettenmund	.50	.20
❑ 57 Derrel Thomas	.50	.20
❑ 58 Mike Paul	.50	.20
❑ 59 Steve Yeager RC	1.50	.60
❑ 60 Ken Holtzman	1.50	.60
❑ 61 Billy Williams	2.50	1.00
Rod Carew LL		
❑ 62 Johnny Bench	2.50	1.00
Dick Allen LL		
Home Run Leaders		
❑ 63 Johnny Bench	2.50	1.00
Dick Allen		
RBI Leaders		
❑ 64 Lou Brock	1.50	.60
Bert Campaneris LL		
❑ 65 Steve Carlton	1.50	.60
Luis Tiant LL		
❑ 66 Steve Carlton	1.50	.60
Gaylord Perry		
Wilbur Wood LL		
❑ 67 Steve Carlton	25.00	10.00
Nolan Ryan LL		
❑ 68 Clay Carroll	1.50	.60
Sparky Lyle LL		
❑ 69 Phil Gagliano	.50	.20
❑ 70 Milt Pappas	1.50	.60
❑ 71 Johnny Briggs	.50	.20
❑ 72 Ron Reed	.50	.20
❑ 73 Ed Herrmann	.50	.20
❑ 74 Billy Champion	.50	.20
❑ 75 Vada Pinson	1.50	.60
❑ 76 Doug Rader	.50	.20
❑ 77 Mike Torrez	1.50	.60
❑ 78 Richie Scheinblum	.50	.20
❑ 79 Jim Willoughby	.50	.20
❑ 80 Tony Oliva UER	2.50	1.00
(Minnseota on front)		
❑ 81A Whitey Lockman MG	1.50	.60
Hank Aguirre CO		
Ernie Banks CO		
Larry Jansen CO		
Pete Reiser CO		
(Solid backgrounds)		
❑ 81B Cubs Leaders	1.50	.60
(Natural backgrounds)		
❑ 82 Fritz Peterson	.50	.20
❑ 83 Leron Lee	.50	.20
❑ 84 Rollie Fingers	4.00	1.60
❑ 85 Ted Simmons	1.50	.60
❑ 86 Tom McCraw	.50	.20
❑ 87 Ken Boswell	.50	.20
❑ 88 Mickey Stanley	1.50	.60
❑ 89 Jack Billingham	.50	.20
❑ 90 Brooks Robinson	8.00	3.20
❑ 91 Los Angeles Dodgers	2.00	.80
Team Card		
❑ 92 Jerry Bell	.50	.20
❑ 93 Jesus Alou	.50	.20
❑ 94 Dick Billings	.50	.20
❑ 95 Steve Blass	1.50	.60
❑ 96 Doug Griffin	.50	.20
❑ 97 Willie Montanez	1.50	.60
❑ 98 Dick Woodson	.50	.20
❑ 99 Carl Taylor	.50	.20
❑ 100 Hank Aaron	40.00	16.00
❑ 101 Ken Henderson	.50	.20
❑ 102 Rudy May	.50	.20
❑ 103 Celerino Sanchez	.50	.20
❑ 104 Reggie Cleveland	.50	.20
❑ 105 Carlos May	.50	.20
❑ 106 Terry Humphrey	.50	.20
❑ 107 Phil Hennigan	.50	.20
❑ 108 Bill Russell	1.50	.60
❑ 109 Doyle Alexander	1.50	.60
❑ 110 Bob Watson	1.50	.60
❑ 111 Dave Nelson	.50	.20
❑ 112 Gary Ross	.50	.20
❑ 113 Jerry Grote	1.50	.60
❑ 114 Lynn McGlothen	.50	.20
❑ 115 Ron Santo	1.50	.60
❑ 116A Ralph Houk MG	3.00	1.20
Jim Hegan CO		
Elston Howard CO		
Dick Howser CO		
Jim Turner CO		
(Solid backgrounds)		
❑ 116B Yankees Leaders	.75	.30
(Natural backgrounds)		
❑ 117 Ramon Hernandez	.50	.20
❑ 118 John Mayberry	1.50	.60
❑ 119 Larry Bowa	1.50	.60
❑ 120 Joe Coleman	.50	.20
❑ 121 Dave Rader	.50	.20
❑ 122 Jim Strickland	.50	.20
❑ 123 Sandy Alomar	1.50	.60
❑ 124 Jim Hardin	.50	.20
❑ 125 Ron Fairly	1.50	.60
❑ 126 Jim Brewer	.50	.20
❑ 127 Milwaukee Brewers	2.00	.80
Team Card		
❑ 128 Ted Sizemore	.50	.20
❑ 129 Terry Forster	1.50	.60
❑ 130 Pete Rose	30.00	12.00
❑ 131A Eddie Kasko MG	3.00	1.20
Doug Camilli CO		
Don Lenhardt CO		
Eddie Popowski CO		
(No right ear)		
Lee Stange CO		
❑ 131B Red Sox Leaders	1.50	.60
(Popowski has right		
ear showing)		
❑ 132 Matty Alou	1.50	.60
❑ 133 Dave Roberts RC	.50	.20
❑ 134 Milt Wilcox	.50	.20
❑ 135 Lee May UER	1.50	.60
(Career average .000)		
❑ 136A Earl Weaver MG	2.00	.80
George Bamberger CO		
Jim Frey CO		
Billy Hunter CO		
George Staller CO		
(Orange backgrounds)		
❑ 136B Orioles Leaders	3.00	1.20
(Dark pale		
backgrounds)		
❑ 137 Jim Beauchamp	.50	.20
❑ 138 Horacio Pina	.50	.20
❑ 139 Carmen Fanzone	.50	.20
❑ 140 Lou Piniella	2.50	1.00
❑ 141 Bruce Kison	.50	.20
❑ 142 Thurman Munson	8.00	3.20
❑ 143 John Curtis	.50	.20
❑ 144 Marty Perez	.50	.20
❑ 145 Bobby Bonds	2.50	1.00
❑ 146 Woodie Fryman	.50	.20
❑ 147 Mike Anderson	.50	.20
❑ 148 Dave Goltz	.50	.20
❑ 149 Ron Hunt	.50	.20
❑ 150 Wilbur Wood	1.50	.60
❑ 151 Wes Parker	1.50	.60
❑ 152 Dave May	.50	.20
❑ 153 Al Hrabosky	1.50	.60
❑ 154 Jeff Torborg	1.50	.60
❑ 155 Sal Bando	1.50	.60
❑ 156 Cesar Geronimo	.50	.20
❑ 157 Denny Riddleberger	.50	.20
❑ 158 Houston Astros	2.00	.80

Team Card
❑ 159 Clarence Gaston 1.50 .60
❑ 160 Jim Palmer 6.00 2.40
❑ 161 Ted Martinez .50 .20
❑ 162 Pete Broberg .50 .20
❑ 163 Vic Davalillo .50 .20
❑ 164 Monty Montgomery .50 .20
❑ 165 Luis Aparicio 4.00 1.60
❑ 166 Terry Harmon .50 .20
❑ 167 Steve Stone 1.50 .60
❑ 168 Jim Northrup 1.50 .60
❑ 169 Ron Schueler RC 1.50 .60
❑ 170 Harmon Killebrew 5.00 2.00
❑ 171 Bernie Carbo .50 .20
❑ 172 Steve Kline .50 .20
❑ 173 Hal Breeden .50 .20
❑ 174 Goose Gossage RC 6.00 2.40
❑ 175 Frank Robinson 6.00 2.40
❑ 176 Chuck Taylor .50 .20
❑ 177 Bill Plummer .50 .20
❑ 178 Don Rose .50 .20
❑ 179A Dick Williams MG 4.00 1.60
Jerry Adair CO
Vern Hoscheit CO
Irv Noren CO
Wes Stock CO
(Hoscheit left ear
showing)
❑ 179B A's Leaders 1.50 .60
(Hoscheit left ear
not showing)
❑ 180 Ferguson Jenkins 4.00 1.60
❑ 181 Jack Brohamer .50 .20
❑ 182 Mike Caldwell RC 1.50 .60
❑ 183 Don Buford .50 .20
❑ 184 Jerry Koosman 1.50 .60
❑ 185 Jim Wynn 1.50 .60
❑ 186 Bill Fahey .50 .20
❑ 187 Luke Walker .50 .20
❑ 188 Cookie Rojas 1.50 .60
❑ 189 Greg Luzinski 2.50 1.00
❑ 190 Bob Gibson 8.00 3.20
❑ 191 Detroit Tigers 2.50 1.00
Team Card
❑ 192 Pat Jarvis .50 .20
❑ 193 Carlton Fisk 10.00 4.00
❑ 194 Jorge Orta .50 .20
❑ 195 Clay Carroll .50 .20
❑ 196 Ken McMullen .50 .20
❑ 197 Ed Goodson .50 .20
❑ 198 Horace Clarke .50 .20
❑ 199 Bert Blyleven 2.50 1.00
❑ 200 Billy Williams 4.00 1.60
❑ 201 G. Hendrick ALCS 1.50 .60
❑ 202 George Foster NLCS 1.50 .60
❑ 203 Gene Tenace WS 1.50 .60
❑ 204 World Series Game 2 1.50 .60
A's two straight
❑ 205 Tony Perez WS 2.50 1.00
❑ 206 Gene Tenace WS 1.50 .60
❑ 207 Blue Moon Odom WS 1.50 .60
❑ 208 Johnny Bench WS6 5.00 2.00
❑ 209 Bert Campaneris WS 1.50 .60
❑ 210 W.S. Summary .50 .20
World champions:
A's Win
❑ 211 Balor Moore .50 .20
❑ 212 Joe Lahoud .50 .20
❑ 213 Steve Garvey 5.00 2.00
❑ 214 Dave Hamilton .50 .20
❑ 215 Dusty Baker 2.50 1.00
❑ 216 Toby Harrah 1.50 .60
❑ 217 Don Wilson .50 .20
❑ 218 Aurelio Rodriguez .50 .20
❑ 219 St. Louis Cardinals 2.50 1.00
Team Card
❑ 220 Nolan Ryan 50.00 24.00
❑ 221 Fred Kendall .50 .20
❑ 222 Rob Gardner .50 .20
❑ 223 Bud Harrelson 1.50 .60
❑ 224 Bill Lee 1.50 .60
❑ 225 Al Oliver 1.50 .60
❑ 226 Ray Fosse .50 .20
❑ 227 Wayne Twitchell .50 .20
❑ 228 Bobby Darwin .50 .20
❑ 229 Roric Harrison .50 .20
❑ 230 Joe Morgan 6.00 2.40
❑ 231 Bill Parsons .50 .20
❑ 232 Ken Singleton 1.50 .60
❑ 233 Ed Kirkpatrick .50 .20
❑ 234 Bill North .50 .20
❑ 235 Jim Hunter 4.00 1.60
❑ 236 Tito Fuentes .50 .20
❑ 237A Eddie Mathews MG 2.00 .80
Lew Burdette CO
Jim Busby CO
Roy Hartsfield CO
Ken Silvestri CO
(Burdette right ear
showing)
❑ 237B Braves Leaders 3.00 1.20
(Burdette right ear
not showing)
❑ 238 Tony Muser .50 .20
❑ 239 Pete Richert .50 .20
❑ 240 Bobby Murcer 1.50 .60
❑ 241 Dwain Anderson .50 .20
❑ 242 George Culver .50 .20
❑ 243 California Angels 2.50 1.00
Team Card
❑ 244 Ed Acosta .50 .20
❑ 245 Carl Yastrzemski 10.00 4.00
❑ 246 Ken Sanders .50 .20
❑ 247 Del Unser .50 .20
❑ 248 Jerry Johnson .50 .20
❑ 249 Larry Biittner .50 .20
❑ 250 Manny Sanguillen 1.50 .60
❑ 251 Roger Nelson .50 .20
❑ 252A Charlie Fox MG 4.00 1.60
Joe Amalfitano CO
Andy Gilbert CO
Don McMahon CO
John McNamara CO
(Orange backgrounds)
❑ 252B Giants Leaders 1.50 .60
(Dark pale
backgrounds)
❑ 253 Mark Belanger 1.50 .60
❑ 254 Bill Stoneman .50 .20
❑ 255 Reggie Jackson 15.00 6.00
❑ 256 Chris Zachary .50 .20
❑ 257A Yogi Berra MG 3.00 1.20
Roy McMillan CO
Joe Pignatano CO
Rube Walker CO
Eddie Yost CO
(Orange backgrounds)
❑ 257B Mets Leaders 5.00 2.00
(Dark pale
backgrounds)
❑ 258 Tommy John 1.50 .60
❑ 259 Jim Holt .50 .20
❑ 260 Gary Nolan 1.50 .60
❑ 261 Pat Kelly .50 .20
❑ 262 Jack Aker .50 .20
❑ 263 George Scott 1.50 .60
❑ 264 Checklist 133-264 3.00 .60
❑ 265 Gene Michael 1.50 .60
❑ 266 Mike Lum .75 .30
❑ 267 Lloyd Allen .75 .30
❑ 268 Jerry Morales .75 .30
❑ 269 Tim McCarver 1.50 .60
❑ 270 Luis Tiant 1.50 .60
❑ 271 Tom Hutton .75 .30
❑ 272 Ed Farmer .75 .30
❑ 273 Chris Speier .75 .30
❑ 274 Darold Knowles .75 .30
❑ 275 Tony Perez 4.00 1.60
❑ 276 Joe Lovitto .75 .30
❑ 277 Bob Miller .75 .30
❑ 278 Baltimore Orioles 1.50 .60
Team Card
❑ 279 Mike Strahler .75 .30
❑ 280 Al Kaline 8.00 3.20
❑ 281 Mike Jorgensen .75 .30
❑ 282 Steve Hovley .75 .30
❑ 283 Ray Sadecki .75 .30
❑ 284 Glenn Borgmann .75 .30
❑ 285 Don Kessinger 1.50 .60
❑ 286 Frank Linzy .75 .30
❑ 287 Eddie Leon .75 .30
❑ 288 Gary Gentry .75 .30
❑ 289 Bob Oliver .75 .30
❑ 290 Cesar Cedeno 1.50 .60
❑ 291 Rogelio Moret .75 .30
❑ 292 Jose Cruz 1.50 .60
❑ 293 Bernie Allen .75 .30
❑ 294 Steve Arlin .75 .30
❑ 295 Bert Campaneris 1.50 .60
❑ 296 Sparky Anderson MG 2.50 1.00
Alex Grammas CO
Ted Kluszewski CO
George Scherger CO
Larry Shepard CO
❑ 297 Walt Williams .75 .30
❑ 298 Ron Bryant .75 .30
❑ 299 Ted Ford .75 .30
❑ 300 Steve Carlton 10.00 4.00
❑ 301 Billy Grabarkewitz .75 .30
❑ 302 Terry Crowley .75 .30
❑ 303 Nelson Briles .75 .30
❑ 304 Duke Sims .75 .30
❑ 305 Willie Mays 40.00 16.00
❑ 306 Tom Burgmeier .75 .30
❑ 307 Boots Day .75 .30
❑ 308 Skip Lockwood .75 .30
❑ 309 Paul Popovich .75 .30
❑ 310 Dick Allen 1.50 .60
❑ 311 Joe Decker .75 .30
❑ 312 Oscar Brown .75 .30
❑ 313 Jim Ray .75 .30
❑ 314 Ron Swoboda 1.50 .60
❑ 315 John Odom .75 .30
❑ 316 San Diego Padres 1.50 .60
Team Card
❑ 317 Danny Cater .75 .30
❑ 318 Jim McGlothlin .75 .30
❑ 319 Jim Spencer .75 .30
❑ 320 Lou Brock 8.00 3.20
❑ 321 Rich Hinton .75 .30
❑ 322 Garry Maddox RC 1.50 .60
❑ 323 Billy Martin MG 1.50 .60
Art Fowler CO
Charlie Silvera CO
Dick Tracewski CO
Joe Schultz CO ERR
Schult's name not printed on card
❑ 324 Al Downing .75 .30
❑ 325 Boog Powell 1.50 .60
❑ 326 Darrell Brandon .75 .30
❑ 327 John Lowenstein .75 .30
❑ 328 Bill Bonham .75 .30
❑ 329 Ed Kranepool 1.50 .60
❑ 330 Rod Carew 8.00 3.20
❑ 331 Carl Morton .75 .30
❑ 332 John Felske .75 .30
❑ 333 Gene Clines .75 .30
❑ 334 Freddie Patek .75 .30
❑ 335 Bob Tolan .75 .30
❑ 336 Tom Bradley .75 .30
❑ 337 Dave Duncan 1.50 .60
❑ 338 Checklist 265-396 3.00 .60
❑ 339 Dick Tidrow .75 .30
❑ 340 Nate Colbert .75 .30
❑ 341 Jim Palmer KP 2.50 1.00
❑ 342 Sam McDowell KP .75 .30
❑ 343 Bobby Murcer KP .75 .30
❑ 344 Jim Hunter KP 2.50 1.00
❑ 345 Chris Speier KP .75 .30
❑ 346 Gaylord Perry KP 1.50 .60
❑ 347 Kansas City Royals 1.50 .60
Team Card
❑ 348 Rennie Stennett .75 .30
❑ 349 Dick McAuliffe .75 .30
❑ 350 Tom Seaver 12.00 4.80
❑ 351 Jimmy Stewart .75 .30
❑ 352 Don Stanhouse .75 .30
❑ 353 Steve Brye .75 .30
❑ 354 Billy Parker .75 .30
❑ 355 Mike Marshall 1.50 .60
❑ 356 Chuck Tanner MG 4.00 1.60
Joe Lonnett CO
Jim Mahoney CO
Al Monchak CO
Johnny Sain CO
❑ 357 Ross Grimsley .75 .30
❑ 358 Jim Nettles .75 .30
❑ 359 Cecil Upshaw .75 .30

❑ 360 Joe Rudi UER 1.50 .60
(Photo actually
Gene Tenace)
❑ 361 Fran Healy .75 .30
❑ 362 Eddie Watt .75 .30
❑ 363 Jackie Hernandez .75 .30
❑ 364 Rick Wise .75 .30
❑ 365 Rico Petrocelli 1.50 .60
❑ 366 Brock Davis .75 .30
❑ 367 Burt Hooton 1.50 .60
❑ 368 Bill Buckner 1.50 .60
❑ 369 Lerrin LaGrow .75 .30
❑ 370 Willie Stargell 5.00 2.00
❑ 371 Mike Kekich .75 .30
❑ 372 Oscar Gamble .75 .30
❑ 373 Clyde Wright .75 .30
❑ 374 Darrell Evans 1.50 .60
❑ 375 Larry Dierker 1.50 .60
❑ 376 Frank Duffy .75 .30
❑ 377 Gene Mauch MG 4.00 1.60
Dave Bristol CO
Larry Doby CO
Cal McLish CO
Jerry Zimmerman CO
❑ 378 Len Randle .75 .30
❑ 379 Cy Acosta .75 .30
❑ 380 Johnny Bench 12.00 4.80
❑ 381 Vicente Romo .75 .30
❑ 382 Mike Hegan .75 .30
❑ 383 Diego Segui .75 .30
❑ 384 Don Baylor 4.00 1.60
❑ 385 Jim Perry 1.50 .60
❑ 386 Don Money .75 .30
❑ 387 Jim Barr .75 .30
❑ 388 Ben Oglivie 1.50 .60
❑ 389 New York Mets 4.00 1.60
Team Card
❑ 390 Mickey Lolich 1.50 .60
❑ 391 Lee Lacy RC 1.50 .60
❑ 392 Dick Drago .75 .30
❑ 393 Jose Cardenal .75 .30
❑ 394 Sparky Lyle 1.50 .60
❑ 395 Roger Metzger .75 .30
❑ 396 Grant Jackson .75 .30
❑ 397 Dave Cash 1.25 .50
❑ 398 Rich Hand 1.25 .50
❑ 399 George Foster 2.00 .80
❑ 400 Gaylord Perry 5.00 2.00
❑ 401 Clyde Mashore 1.25 .50
❑ 402 Jack Hiatt 1.25 .50
❑ 403 Sonny Jackson 1.25 .50
❑ 404 Chuck Brinkman 1.25 .50
❑ 405 Cesar Tovar 1.25 .50
❑ 406 Paul Lindblad 1.25 .50
❑ 407 Felix Millan 1.25 .50
❑ 408 Jim Colborn 1.25 .50
❑ 409 Ivan Murrell 1.25 .50
❑ 410 Willie McCovey 6.00 2.40
(Bench behind plate)
❑ 411 Ray Corbin 1.25 .50
❑ 412 Manny Mota 2.00 .80
❑ 413 Tom Timmermann 1.25 .50
❑ 414 Ken Rudolph 1.25 .50
❑ 415 Marty Pattin 1.25 .50
❑ 416 Paul Schaal 1.25 .50
❑ 417 Scipio Spinks 1.25 .50
❑ 418 Bob Grich 2.00 .80
❑ 419 Casey Cox 1.25 .50
❑ 420 Tommie Agee 1.25 .50
❑ 421A Bobby Winkles MG 1.50 .60
Tom Morgan CO
Salty Parker CO
Jimmie Reese CO
John Roseboro CO
(Orange backgrounds)
❑ 421B Angels Leaders 3.00 1.20
(Dark pale
backgrounds)
❑ 422 Bob Robertson 1.25 .50
❑ 423 Johnny Jeter 1.25 .50
❑ 424 Denny Doyle 1.25 .50
❑ 425 Alex Johnson 1.25 .50
❑ 426 Dave LaRoche 1.25 .50
❑ 427 Rick Auerbach 1.25 .50
❑ 428 Wayne Simpson 1.25 .50
❑ 429 Jim Fairey 1.25 .50
❑ 430 Vida Blue 2.00 .80
❑ 431 Gerry Moses 1.25 .50
❑ 432 Dan Frisella 1.25 .50
❑ 433 Willie Horton 2.00 .80
❑ 434 San Francisco Giants 3.00 1.20
Team Card
❑ 435 Rico Carty 2.00 .80
❑ 436 Jim McAndrew 1.25 .50
❑ 437 John Kennedy 1.25 .50
❑ 438 Enzo Hernandez 1.25 .50
❑ 439 Eddie Fisher 1.25 .50
❑ 440 Glenn Beckert 1.25 .50
❑ 441 Gail Hopkins 1.25 .50
❑ 442 Dick Dietz 1.25 .50
❑ 443 Danny Thompson 1.25 .50
❑ 444 Ken Brett 1.25 .50
❑ 445 Ken Berry 1.25 .50
❑ 446 Jerry Reuss 2.00 .80
❑ 447 Joe Hague 1.25 .50
❑ 448 John Hiller 1.25 .50
❑ 449A Ken Aspromonte MG 4.00 1.60
Rocky Colavito CO
Joe Lutz CO
Warren Spahn CO
(Spahn's right
ear pointed)
❑ 449B Indians Leaders 4.00 1.60
(Spahn's right
ear round)
❑ 450 Joe Torre 3.00 1.20
❑ 451 John Vukovich 1.25 .50
❑ 452 Paul Casanova 1.25 .50
❑ 453 Checklist 397-528 3.00 .60
❑ 454 Tom Haller 1.25 .50
❑ 455 Bill Melton 1.25 .50
❑ 456 Dick Green 1.25 .50
❑ 457 John Strohmayer 1.25 .50
❑ 458 Jim Mason 1.25 .50
❑ 459 Jimmy Howarth 1.25 .50
❑ 460 Bill Freehan 2.00 .80
❑ 461 Mike Corkins 1.25 .50
❑ 462 Ron Blomberg 1.25 .50
❑ 463 Ken Tatum 1.25 .50
❑ 464 Chicago Cubs 3.00 1.20
Team Card
❑ 465 Dave Giusti 1.25 .50
❑ 466 Jose Arcia 1.25 .50
❑ 467 Mike Ryan 1.25 .50
❑ 468 Tom Griffin 1.25 .50
❑ 469 Dan Monzon 1.25 .50
❑ 470 Mike Cuellar 2.00 .80
❑ 471 Ty Cobb ATL 10.00 4.00
4191 Hits
❑ 472 Lou Gehrig ATL 15.00 6.00
23 Grand Slams
❑ 473 Hank Aaron ATL 10.00 4.00
6172 Total Bases
❑ 474 Babe Ruth ATL 20.00 8.00
2209 RBI
❑ 475 Ty Cobb ATL 8.00 3.20
.367 Batting Average
❑ 476 Walter Johnson ATL 3.00 1.20
113 Shutouts
❑ 477 Cy Young ATL 3.00 1.20
511 Victories
❑ 478 Walter Johnson ATL 3.00 1.20
3508 Strikeouts
❑ 479 Hal Lanier 1.25 .50
❑ 480 Juan Marichal 5.00 2.00
❑ 481 Chicago White Sox 3.00 1.20
Team Card
❑ 482 Rick Reuschel RC 3.00 1.20
❑ 483 Dal Maxvill 1.25 .50
❑ 484 Ernie McAnally 1.25 .50
❑ 485 Norm Cash 2.00 .80
❑ 486A Danny Ozark MG 1.50 .60
Carroll Beringer CO
Billy DeMars CO
Ray Rippelmeyer CO
Bobby Wine CO
(Orange backgrounds)
❑ 486B Phillies Leaders 3.00 1.20
(Dark pale
backgrounds)
❑ 487 Bruce Dal Canton 1.25 .50
❑ 488 Dave Campbell 2.00 .80
❑ 489 Jeff Burroughs 2.00 .80
❑ 490 Claude Osteen 2.00 .80
❑ 491 Bob Montgomery 1.25 .50
❑ 492 Pedro Borbon 1.25 .50
❑ 493 Duffy Dyer 1.25 .50
❑ 494 Rich Morales 1.25 .50
❑ 495 Tommy Helms 1.25 .50
❑ 496 Ray Lamb 1.25 .50
❑ 497A Red Schoendienst MG 2.00 .80
Vern Benson CO
George Kissell CO
Barney Schultz CO
(Orange backgrounds)
❑ 497B Cardinals Leaders 3.00 1.20
(Dark pale
backgrounds)
❑ 498 Graig Nettles 3.00 1.20
❑ 499 Bob Moose 1.25 .50
❑ 500 Oakland A's 3.00 1.20
Team Card
❑ 501 Larry Gura 1.25 .50
❑ 502 Bobby Valentine 3.00 1.20
❑ 503 Phil Niekro 5.00 2.00
❑ 504 Earl Williams 1.25 .50
❑ 505 Bob Bailey 1.25 .50
❑ 506 Bart Johnson 1.25 .50
❑ 507 Darrel Chaney 1.25 .50
❑ 508 Gates Brown 1.25 .50
❑ 509 Jim Nash 1.25 .50
❑ 510 Amos Otis 2.00 .80
❑ 511 Sam McDowell 2.00 .80
❑ 512 Dalton Jones 1.25 .50
❑ 513 Dave Marshall 1.25 .50
❑ 514 Jerry Kenney 1.25 .50
❑ 515 Andy Messersmith 2.00 .80
❑ 516 Danny Walton 1.25 .50
❑ 517A Bill Virdon MG 1.50 .60
Don Leppert CO
Bill Mazeroski CO
Dave Ricketts CO
Mel Wright CO
(Mazeroski has
no right ear)
❑ 517B Pirates Leaders 3.00 1.20
(Mazeroski has
right ear)
❑ 518 Bob Veale 1.25 .50
❑ 519 Johnny Edwards 1.25 .50
❑ 520 Mel Stottlemyre 2.00 .80
❑ 521 Atlanta Braves 3.00 1.20
Team Card
❑ 522 Leo Cardenas 1.25 .50
❑ 523 Wayne Granger 1.25 .50
❑ 524 Gene Tenace 2.00 .80
❑ 525 Jim Fregosi 2.00 .80
❑ 526 Ollie Brown 1.25 .50
❑ 527 Dan McGinn 1.25 .50
❑ 528 Paul Blair 1.25 .50
❑ 529 Milt May 3.00 1.20
❑ 530 Jim Kaat 5.00 2.00
❑ 531 Ron Woods 3.00 1.20
❑ 532 Steve Mingori 3.00 1.20
❑ 533 Larry Stahl 3.00 1.20
❑ 534 Dave Lemonds 3.00 1.20
❑ 535 Johnny Callison 5.00 2.00
❑ 536 Philadelphia Phillies 6.00 2.40
Team Card
❑ 537 Bill Slayback 3.00 1.20
❑ 538 Jim Ray Hart 5.00 2.00
❑ 539 Tom Murphy 3.00 1.20
❑ 540 Cleon Jones 5.00 2.00
❑ 541 Bob Bolin 3.00 1.20
❑ 542 Pat Corrales 5.00 2.00
❑ 543 Alan Foster 3.00 1.20
❑ 544 Von Joshua 3.00 1.20
❑ 545 Orlando Cepeda 8.00 3.20
❑ 546 Jim York 3.00 1.20
❑ 547 Bobby Heise 3.00 1.20
❑ 548 Don Durham 3.00 1.20
❑ 549 Whitey Herzog MG 5.00 2.00
Chuck Estrada CO
Chuck Hiller CO
Jackie Moore CO
❑ 550 Dave Johnson 5.00 2.00
❑ 551 Mike Kilkenny 3.00 1.20
❑ 552 J.C. Martin 3.00 1.20

No.	Card	NM	Ex
553	Mickey Scott	3.00	1.20
554	Dave Concepcion	5.00	2.00
555	Bill Hands	3.00	1.20
556	New York Yankees Team Card	8.00	3.20
557	Bernie Williams	3.00	1.20
558	Jerry May	3.00	1.20
559	Barry Lersch	3.00	1.20
560	Frank Howard	5.00	2.00
561	Jim Geddes	3.00	1.20
562	Wayne Garrett	3.00	1.20
563	Larry Haney	3.00	1.20
564	Mike Thompson	3.00	1.20
565	Jim Hickman	3.00	1.20
566	Lew Krausse	3.00	1.20
567	Bob Fenwick	3.00	1.20
568	Ray Newman	3.00	1.20
569	Walt Alston MG Red Adams CO Monty Basgall CO Jim Gilliam CO Tom Lasorda CO	8.00	3.20
570	Bill Singer	5.00	2.00
571	Rusty Torres	3.00	1.20
572	Gary Sutherland	3.00	1.20
573	Fred Beene	3.00	1.20
574	Bob Didier	3.00	1.20
575	Dock Ellis	3.00	1.20
576	Montreal Expos Team Card	6.00	2.40
577	Eric Soderholm	3.00	1.20
578	Ken Wright	3.00	1.20
579	Tom Grieve	5.00	2.00
580	Joe Pepitone	5.00	2.00
581	Steve Kealey	3.00	1.20
582	Darrell Porter	5.00	2.00
583	Bill Grief	3.00	1.20
584	Chris Arnold	3.00	1.20
585	Joe Niekro	5.00	2.00
586	Bill Sudakis	3.00	1.20
587	Rich McKinney	3.00	1.20
588	Checklist 529-660	20.00	4.00
589	Ken Forsch	3.00	1.20
590	Deron Johnson	3.00	1.20
591	Mike Hedlund	3.00	1.20
592	John Boccabella	3.00	1.20
593	Jack McKeon MG Galen Cisco CO Harry Dunlop CO Charlie Lau CO	4.00	1.60
594	Vic Harris	3.00	1.20
595	Don Gullett	5.00	2.00
596	Boston Red Sox Team Card	6.00	2.40
597	Mickey Rivers	5.00	2.00
598	Phil Roof	3.00	1.20
599	Ed Crosby	3.00	1.20
600	Dave McNally	5.00	2.00
601	Sergio Robles George Pena Rick Stelmaszek	5.00	2.00
602	Mel Behney Ralph Garcia Doug Rau	5.00	2.00
603	Terry Hughes Bill McNulty Ken Reitz RC	5.00	2.00
604	Jesse Jefferson Dennis O'Toole Bob Strampe	5.00	2.00
605	Enos Cabell RC Pat Bourque Gonzalo Marquez	5.00	2.00
606	Gary Matthews RC Tom Paciorek Jorge Roque	5.00	2.00
607	Pepe Frias Ray Busse Mario Guerrero	5.00	2.00
608	Steve Busby RC Dick Colpaert George Medich RC	5.00	2.00
609	Larvell Blanks Pedro Garcia Dave Lopes RC	5.00	2.00
610	Jimmy Freeman Charlie Hough Hank Webb	5.00	2.00
611	Rich Coggins Jim Wohlford Richie Zisk	5.00	2.00
612	Steve Lawson Bob Reynolds Brent Strom	5.00	2.00
613	Bob Boone RC Skip Jutze Mike Ivie	15.00	6.00
614	Al Bumbry RC Dwight Evans RC Charlie Spikes	20.00	8.00
615	Ron Cey John Hilton Mike Schmidt RC	150.00	60.00
616	Norm Angelini Steve Blateric Mike Garman	5.00	2.00
617	Rich Chiles	3.00	1.20
618	Andy Etchebarren	3.00	1.20
619	Billy Wilson	3.00	1.20
620	Tommy Harper	5.00	2.00
621	Joe Ferguson	5.00	2.00
622	Larry Hisle	5.00	2.00
623	Steve Renko	3.00	1.20
624	Leo Durocher MG Preston Gomez CO Grady Hatton CO Hub Kittle CO Jim Owens CO	5.00	2.00
625	Angel Mangual	3.00	1.20
626	Bob Barton	3.00	1.20
627	Luis Alvarado	3.00	1.20
628	Jim Slaton	3.00	1.20
629	Cleveland Indians Team Card	6.00	2.40
630	Denny McLain	8.00	3.20
631	Tom Matchick	3.00	1.20
632	Dick Selma	3.00	1.20
633	Ike Brown	3.00	1.20
634	Alan Closter	3.00	1.20
635	Gene Alley	5.00	2.00
636	Rickey Clark	3.00	1.20
637	Norm Miller	3.00	1.20
638	Ken Reynolds	3.00	1.20
639	Willie Crawford	3.00	1.20
640	Dick Bosman	3.00	1.20
641	Cincinnati Reds Team Card	6.00	2.40
642	Jose Laboy	3.00	1.20
643	Al Fitzmorris	3.00	1.20
644	Jack Heidemann	3.00	1.20
645	Bob Locker	3.00	1.20
646	Del Crandall MG Harvey Kuenn CO Joe Nossek CO Bob Shaw CO Jim Walton CO	4.00	1.60
647	George Stone	3.00	1.20
648	Tom Egan	3.00	1.20
649	Rich Folkers	3.00	1.20
650	Felipe Alou	5.00	2.00
651	Don Carrithers	3.00	1.20
652	Ted Kubiak	3.00	1.20
653	Joe Hoerner	3.00	1.20
654	Minnesota Twins Team Card	6.00	2.40
655	Clay Kirby	3.00	1.20
656	John Ellis	3.00	1.20
657	Bob Johnson	3.00	1.20
658	Elliott Maddox	3.00	1.20
659	Jose Pagan	3.00	1.20
660	Fred Scherman	5.00	1.95

1974 Topps

	NM	Ex
COMPLETE SET (660)	400.00	160.00
COMP.FACT.SET (660)	600.00	240.00
WRAPPERS (10-CENTS)	10.00	4.00

No.	Card	NM	Ex
1	Hank Aaron 715	40.00	12.00
2	Hank Aaron 54-57	8.00	3.20
3	Hank Aaron 58-61	8.00	3.20
4	Hank Aaron 62-65	8.00	3.20
5	Hank Aaron 66-69	8.00	3.20
6	Hank Aaron 70-73	8.00	3.20
7	Jim Hunter	4.00	1.60
8	George Theodore	.50	.20
9	Mickey Lolich	1.00	.40
10	Johnny Bench	15.00	6.00
11	Jim Bibby	.50	.20
12	Dave May	.50	.20
13	Tom Hilgendorf	.50	.20
14	Paul Popovich	.50	.20
15	Joe Torre	2.00	.80
16	Baltimore Orioles Team Card	1.00	.40
17	Doug Bird	.50	.20
18	Gary Thomasson	.50	.20
19	Gerry Moses	.50	.20
20	Nolan Ryan	40.00	16.00
21	Bob Gallagher	.50	.20
22	Cy Acosta	.50	.20
23	Craig Robinson	.50	.20
24	John Hiller	1.00	.40
25	Ken Singleton	1.00	.40
26	Bill Campbell	.50	.20
27	George Scott	1.00	.40
28	Manny Sanguillen	1.00	.40
29	Phil Niekro	3.00	1.20
30	Bobby Bonds	2.00	.80
31	Preston Gomez MG Roger Craig CO Hub Kittle CO Grady Hatton CO Bob Lillis CO	1.00	.40
32A	Johnny Grubb SD	1.00	.40
32B	Johnny Grubb WASH	4.00	1.60
33	Don Newhauser	.50	.20
34	Andy Kosco	.50	.20
35	Gaylord Perry	3.00	1.20
36	St. Louis Cardinals Team Card	1.00	.40
37	Dave Sells	.50	.20
38	Don Kessinger	1.00	.40
39	Ken Suarez	.50	.20
40	Jim Palmer	8.00	3.20
41	Bobby Floyd	.50	.20
42	Claude Osteen	1.00	.40
43	Jim Wynn	1.00	.40
44	Mel Stottlemyre	1.00	.40
45	Dave Johnson	1.00	.40
46	Pat Kelly	.50	.20
47	Dick Ruthven	.50	.20
48	Dick Sharon	.50	.20
49	Steve Renko	.50	.20
50	Rod Carew	8.00	3.20
51	Bobby Heise	.50	.20
52	Al Oliver	1.00	.40
53A	Fred Kendall SD	1.00	.40
53B	Fred Kendall WASH	4.00	1.60
54	Elias Sosa	.50	.20
55	Frank Robinson	8.00	3.20
56	New York Mets Team Card	1.00	.40
57	Darold Knowles	.50	.20
58	Charlie Spikes	.50	.20
59	Ross Grimsley	.50	.20
60	Lou Brock	6.00	2.40
61	Luis Aparicio	3.00	1.20
62	Bob Locker	.50	.20
63	Bill Sudakis	.50	.20
64	Doug Rau	.50	.20
65	Amos Otis	1.00	.40
66	Sparky Lyle	1.00	.40
67	Tommy Helms	.50	.20
68	Grant Jackson	.50	.20

❑ 69 Del Unser	.50	.20
❑ 70 Dick Allen	2.00	.80
❑ 71 Dan Frisella	.50	.20
❑ 72 Aurelio Rodriguez	.50	.20
❑ 73 Mike Marshall	2.00	.80
❑ 74 Minnesota Twins Team Card	1.00	.40
❑ 75 Jim Colborn	.50	.20
❑ 76 Mickey Rivers	1.00	.40
❑ 77A Rich Troedson SD	1.00	.40
❑ 77B Rich Troedson WASH	4.00	1.60
❑ 78 Charlie Fox MG	1.00	.40
John McNamara CO		
Joe Amalfitano CO		
Andy Gilbert CO		
Don McMahon CO		
❑ 79 Gene Tenace	1.00	.40
❑ 80 Tom Seaver	12.00	4.80
❑ 81 Frank Duffy	.50	.20
❑ 82 Dave Giusti	.50	.20
❑ 83 Orlando Cepeda	3.00	1.20
❑ 84 Rick Wise	.50	.20
❑ 85 Joe Morgan	8.00	3.20
❑ 86 Joe Ferguson	1.00	.40
❑ 87 Fergie Jenkins	3.00	1.20
❑ 88 Freddie Patek	1.00	.40
❑ 89 Jackie Brown	.50	.20
❑ 90 Bobby Murcer	1.00	.40
❑ 91 Ken Forsch	.50	.20
❑ 92 Paul Blair	1.00	.40
❑ 93 Rod Gilbreath	.50	.20
❑ 94 Detroit Tigers Team Card	1.00	.40
❑ 95 Steve Carlton	8.00	3.20
❑ 96 Jerry Hairston	.50	.20
❑ 97 Bob Bailey	.50	.20
❑ 98 Bert Blyleven	2.00	.80
❑ 99 Del Crandall MG	1.00	.40
Harvey Kuenn CO		
Joe Nossek CO		
Jim Walton CO		
Al Widmar CO		
❑ 100 Willie Stargell	6.00	2.40
❑ 101 Bobby Valentine	1.00	.40
❑ 102A Bill Greif SD	1.00	.40
❑ 102B Bill Greif WASH	4.00	1.60
❑ 103 Sal Bando	1.00	.40
❑ 104 Ron Bryant	.50	.20
❑ 105 Carlton Fisk	12.00	4.80
❑ 106 Harry Parker	.50	.20
❑ 107 Alex Johnson	.50	.20
❑ 108 Al Hrabosky	1.00	.40
❑ 109 Bob Grich	1.00	.40
❑ 110 Billy Williams	3.00	1.20
❑ 111 Clay Carroll	.50	.20
❑ 112 Dave Lopes	2.00	.80
❑ 113 Dick Drago	.50	.20
❑ 114 Angels Team	1.00	.40
❑ 115 Willie Horton	1.00	.40
❑ 116 Jerry Reuss	1.00	.40
❑ 117 Ron Blomberg	.50	.20
❑ 118 Bill Lee	1.00	.40
❑ 119 Danny Ozark MG	1.00	.40
Ray Ripplemeyer CO		
Bobby Wine CO		
Carroll Beringer CO		
Billy DeMars CO		
❑ 120 Wilbur Wood	.50	.20
❑ 121 Larry Lintz	.50	.20
❑ 122 Jim Holt	.50	.20
❑ 123 Nelson Briles	1.00	.40
❑ 124 Bobby Coluccio	.50	.20
❑ 125A Nate Colbert SD	1.00	.40
❑ 125B Nate Colbert WASH	4.00	1.60
❑ 126 Checklist 1-132	3.00	.60
❑ 127 Tom Paciorek	1.00	.40
❑ 128 John Ellis	.50	.20
❑ 129 Chris Speier	.50	.20
❑ 130 Reggie Jackson	15.00	6.00
❑ 131 Bob Boone	2.00	.80
❑ 132 Felix Millan	.50	.20
❑ 133 David Clyde	1.00	.40
❑ 134 Denis Menke	.50	.20
❑ 135 Roy White	1.00	.40
❑ 136 Rick Reuschel	1.00	.40
❑ 137 Al Bumbry	1.00	.40
❑ 138 Eddie Brinkman	.50	.20
❑ 139 Aurelio Monteagudo	.50	.20
❑ 140 Darrell Evans	2.00	.80
❑ 141 Pat Bourque	.50	.20
❑ 142 Pedro Garcia	.50	.20
❑ 143 Dick Woodson	.50	.20
❑ 144 Walter Alston MG	3.00	1.20
Tom Lasorda CO		
Jim Gilliam CO		
Red Adams CO		
Monty Basgall CO		
❑ 145 Dock Ellis	.50	.20
❑ 146 Ron Fairly	1.00	.40
❑ 147 Bart Johnson	.50	.20
❑ 148A Dave Hilton SD	1.00	.40
❑ 148B Dave Hilton WASH	4.00	1.60
❑ 149 Mac Scarce	.50	.20
❑ 150 John Mayberry	1.00	.40
❑ 151 Diego Segui	.50	.20
❑ 152 Oscar Gamble	1.00	.40
❑ 153 Jon Matlack	1.00	.40
❑ 154 Houston Astros Team Card	1.00	.40
❑ 155 Bert Campaneris	1.00	.40
❑ 156 Randy Moffitt	.50	.20
❑ 157 Vic Harris	.50	.20
❑ 158 Jack Billingham	.50	.20
❑ 159 Jim Ray Hart	.50	.20
❑ 160 Brooks Robinson	8.00	3.20
❑ 161 Ray Burris UER (Card number is printed sideways)	1.00	.40
❑ 162 Bill Freehan	1.00	.40
❑ 163 Ken Berry	.50	.20
❑ 164 Tom House	.50	.20
❑ 165 Willie Davis	1.00	.40
❑ 166 Jack McKeon MG	1.00	.40
Charlie Lau CO		
Harry Dunlop CO		
Galen Cisco CO		
❑ 167 Luis Tiant	2.00	.80
❑ 168 Danny Thompson	.50	.20
❑ 169 Steve Rogers RC	2.00	.80
❑ 170 Bill Melton	.50	.20
❑ 171 Eduardo Rodriguez	.50	.20
❑ 172 Gene Clines	.50	.20
❑ 173A Randy Jones SD RC	2.00	.80
❑ 173B Randy Jones WASH	5.00	2.00
❑ 174 Bill Robinson	1.00	.40
❑ 175 Reggie Cleveland	.50	.20
❑ 176 John Lowenstein	.50	.20
❑ 177 Dave Roberts	.50	.20
❑ 178 Garry Maddox	1.00	.40
❑ 179 Yogi Berra MG	5.00	2.00
Rube Walker CO		
Eddie Yost CO		
Roy McMillan CO		
Joe Pignatano CO		
❑ 180 Ken Holtzman	1.00	.40
❑ 181 Cesar Geronimo	.50	.20
❑ 182 Lindy McDaniel	1.00	.40
❑ 183 Johnny Oates	1.00	.40
❑ 184 Texas Rangers Team Card	1.00	.40
❑ 185 Jose Cardenal	.50	.20
❑ 186 Fred Scherman	.50	.20
❑ 187 Don Baylor	2.00	.80
❑ 188 Rudy Meoli	.50	.20
❑ 189 Jim Brewer	.50	.20
❑ 190 Tony Oliva	2.00	.80
❑ 191 Al Fitzmorris	.50	.20
❑ 192 Mario Guerrero	.50	.20
❑ 193 Tom Walker	.50	.20
❑ 194 Darrell Porter	1.00	.40
❑ 195 Carlos May	.50	.20
❑ 196 Jim Fregosi	1.00	.40
❑ 197A Vicente Romo SD	1.00	.40
❑ 197B V.Romo WASH	4.00	1.60
❑ 198 Dave Cash	.50	.20
❑ 199 Mike Kekich	.50	.20
❑ 200 Cesar Cedeno	1.00	.40
❑ 201 Rod Carew	6.00	2.40
Pete Rose LL		
❑ 202 Reggie Jackson	5.00	2.00
Willie Stargell LL		
❑ 203 Reggie Jackson	5.00	2.00
Willie Stargell LL		
❑ 204 Tommy Harper	2.00	.80
Lou Brock LL		
❑ 205 Wilbur Wood	1.00	.40
Ron Bryant LL		
❑ 206 Jim Palmer	5.00	2.00
Tom Seaver LL		
❑ 207 Nolan Ryan	12.00	4.80
Tom Seaver LL		
❑ 208 John Hiller	1.00	.40
Mike Marshall LL		
❑ 209 Ted Sizemore	.50	.20
❑ 210 Bill Singer	.50	.20
❑ 211 Chicago Cubs Team Card	1.00	.40
❑ 212 Rollie Fingers	3.00	1.20
❑ 213 Dave Rader	.50	.20
❑ 214 Billy Grabarkewitz	.50	.20
❑ 215 Al Kaline UER (No copyright on back)	10.00	4.00
❑ 216 Ray Sadecki	.50	.20
❑ 217 Tim Foli	.50	.20
❑ 218 Johnny Briggs	.50	.20
❑ 219 Doug Griffin	.50	.20
❑ 220 Don Sutton	3.00	1.20
❑ 221 Chuck Tanner MG	1.00	.40
Jim Mahoney CO		
Alex Monchak CO		
Johnny Sain CO		
Joe Lonnett CO		
❑ 222 Ramon Hernandez	.50	.20
❑ 223 Jeff Burroughs	2.00	.80
❑ 224 Roger Metzger	.50	.20
❑ 225 Paul Splittorff	.50	.20
❑ 226A San Diego Padres Team Card San Diego Variation	2.00	.80
❑ 226B San Diego Padres Team Card Washington Variation	8.00	3.20
❑ 227 Mike Lum	.50	.20
❑ 228 Ted Kubiak	.50	.20
❑ 229 Fritz Peterson	.50	.20
❑ 230 Tony Perez	4.00	1.60
❑ 231 Dick Tidrow	.50	.20
❑ 232 Steve Brye	.50	.20
❑ 233 Jim Barr	.50	.20
❑ 234 John Milner	.50	.20
❑ 235 Dave McNally	1.00	.40
❑ 236 Red Schoendienst MG	3.00	1.20
Barney Schultz CO		
George Kissell CO		
Johnny Lewis CO		
Vern Benson CO		
❑ 237 Ken Brett	.50	.20
❑ 238 Fran Healy HOR (Munson sliding in background)	.50	.20
❑ 239 Bill Russell	1.00	.40
❑ 240 Joe Coleman	.50	.20
❑ 241A Glenn Beckert SD	1.00	.40
❑ 241B G.Beckert WASH	4.00	1.60
❑ 242 Bill Gogolewski	.50	.20
❑ 243 Bob Oliver	.50	.20
❑ 244 Carl Morton	.50	.20
❑ 245 Cleon Jones	.50	.20
❑ 246 Oakland Athletics Team Card	2.00	.80
❑ 247 Rick Miller	.50	.20
❑ 248 Tom Hall	.50	.20
❑ 249 George Mitterwald	.50	.20
❑ 250A Willie McCovey SD	8.00	3.20
❑ 250B W.McCovey WASH	25.00	10.00
❑ 251 Graig Nettles	2.00	.80
❑ 252 Dave Parker RC	10.00	4.00
❑ 253 John Boccabella	.50	.20
❑ 254 Stan Bahnsen	.50	.20
❑ 255 Larry Bowa	1.00	.40
❑ 256 Tom Griffin	.50	.20
❑ 257 Buddy Bell	2.00	.80
❑ 258 Jerry Morales	.50	.20
❑ 259 Bob Reynolds	.50	.20
❑ 260 Ted Simmons	2.00	.80
❑ 261 Jerry Bell	.50	.20
❑ 262 Ed Kirkpatrick	.50	.20
❑ 263 Checklist 133-264	3.00	.60
❑ 264 Joe Rudi	1.00	.40
❑ 265 Tug McGraw	2.00	.80

266	Jim Northrup	1.00	.40
267	Andy Messersmith	1.00	.40
268	Tom Grieve	1.00	.40
269	Bob Johnson	.50	.20
270	Ron Santo	2.00	.80
271	Bill Hands	.50	.20
272	Paul Casanova	.50	.20
273	Checklist 265-396	3.00	.60
274	Fred Beene	.50	.20
275	Ron Hunt	.50	.20
276	Bobby Winkles MG John Roseboro CO Tom Morgan CO Jimmie Reese CO Salty Parker CO	1.00	.40
277	Gary Nolan	1.00	.40
278	Cookie Rojas	1.00	.40
279	Jim Crawford	.50	.20
280	Carl Yastrzemski	12.00	4.80
281	San Francisco Giants Team Card	1.00	.40
282	Doyle Alexander	1.00	.40
283	Mike Schmidt	20.00	8.00
284	Dave Duncan	1.00	.40
285	Reggie Smith	1.00	.40
286	Tony Muser	.50	.20
287	Clay Kirby	.50	.20
288	Gorman Thomas RC	2.00	.80
289	Rick Auerbach	.50	.20
290	Vida Blue	1.00	.40
291	Don Hahn	.50	.20
292	Chuck Seelbach	.50	.20
293	Milt May	.50	.20
294	Steve Foucault	.50	.20
295	Rick Monday	1.00	.40
296	Ray Corbin	.50	.20
297	Hal Breeden	.50	.20
298	Roric Harrison	.50	.20
299	Gene Michael	.50	.20
300	Pete Rose	25.00	10.00
301	Bob Montgomery	.50	.20
302	Rudy May	.50	.20
303	George Hendrick	1.00	.40
304	Don Wilson	.50	.20
305	Tito Fuentes	.50	.20
306	Earl Weaver MG Jim Frey CO George Bamberger CO Billy Hunter CO George Staller CO	3.00	1.20
307	Luis Melendez	.50	.20
308	Bruce Dal Canton	.50	.20
309A	Dave Roberts SD	1.00	.40
309B	Dave Roberts WASH	6.00	2.40
310	Terry Forster	1.00	.40
311	Jerry Grote	1.00	.40
312	Deron Johnson	.50	.20
313	Barry Lersch	.50	.20
314	Milwaukee Brewers Team Card	1.00	.40
315	Ron Cey	2.00	.80
316	Jim Perry	1.00	.40
317	Richie Zisk	1.00	.40
318	Jim Merritt	.50	.20
319	Randy Hundley	.50	.20
320	Dusty Baker	2.00	.80
321	Steve Braun	.50	.20
322	Ernie McAnally	.50	.20
323	Richie Scheinblum	.50	.20
324	Steve Kline	.50	.20
325	Tommy Harper	1.00	.40
326	Sparky Anderson MG Larry Shepard CO George Scherger CO Alex Grammas CO Ted Kluszewski CO	3.00	1.20
327	Tom Timmermann	.50	.20
328	Skip Jutze	.50	.20
329	Mark Belanger	1.00	.40
330	Juan Marichal	5.00	2.00
331	Carlton Fisk Johnny Bench AS	5.00	2.00
332	Dick Allen Hank Aaron AS	8.00	3.20
333	Rod Carew Joe Morgan AS	4.00	1.60
334	Brooks Robinson Ron Santo AS	2.00	.80
335	Bert Campaneris Chris Speier AS	1.00	.40
336	Bobby Murcer Pete Rose AS	5.00	2.00
337	Amos Otis Cesar Cedeno AS	1.00	.40
338	Reggie Jackson Billy Williams AS	5.00	2.00
339	Jim Hunter Rick Wise AS	3.00	1.20
340	Thurman Munson	8.00	3.20
341	Dan Driessen RC	1.00	.40
342	Jim Lonborg	1.00	.40
343	Royals Team	1.00	.40
344	Mike Caldwell	.50	.20
345	Bill North	.50	.20
346	Ron Reed	.50	.20
347	Sandy Alomar	1.00	.40
348	Pete Richert	.50	.20
349	John Vukovich	.50	.20
350	Bob Gibson	8.00	3.20
351	Dwight Evans	3.00	1.20
352	Bill Stoneman	.50	.20
353	Rich Coggins	.50	.20
354	Whitey Lockman MG J.C. Martin CO Hank Aguirre CO Al Spangler CO Jim Marshall CO	1.00	.40
355	Dave Nelson	.50	.20
356	Jerry Koosman	1.00	.40
357	Buddy Bradford	.50	.20
358	Dal Maxvill	.50	.20
359	Brent Strom	.50	.20
360	Greg Luzinski	2.00	.80
361	Don Carrithers	.50	.20
362	Hal King	.50	.20
363	New York Yankees Team Card	2.00	.80
364A	Cito Gaston SD	2.00	.80
364B	Cito Gaston WASH	8.00	3.20
365	Steve Busby	1.00	.40
366	Larry Hisle	1.00	.40
367	Norm Cash	2.00	.80
368	Manny Mota	1.00	.40
369	Paul Lindblad	.50	.20
370	Bob Watson	1.00	.40
371	Jim Slaton	.50	.20
372	Ken Reitz	.50	.20
373	John Curtis	.50	.20
374	Marty Perez	.50	.20
375	Earl Williams	.50	.20
376	Jorge Orta	.50	.20
377	Ron Woods	.50	.20
378	Burt Hooton	1.00	.40
379	Billy Martin MG Frank Lucchesi CO Art Fowler CO Charlie Silvera CO Jackie Moore CO	2.00	.80
380	Bud Harrelson	1.00	.40
381	Charlie Sands	.50	.20
382	Bob Moose	.50	.20
383	Philadelphia Phillies Team Card	1.00	.40
384	Chris Chambliss	1.00	.40
385	Don Gullett	1.00	.40
386	Gary Matthews	2.00	.80
387A	Rich Morales SD	1.00	.40
387B	Rich Morales WASH	6.00	2.40
388	Phil Roof	.50	.20
389	Gates Brown	.50	.20
390	Lou Piniella	2.00	.80
391	Billy Champion	.50	.20
392	Dick Green	.50	.20
393	Orlando Pena	.50	.20
394	Ken Henderson	.50	.20
395	Doug Rader	.50	.20
396	Tommy Davis	1.00	.40
397	George Stone	.50	.20
398	Duke Sims	.50	.20
399	Mike Paul	.50	.20
400	Harmon Killebrew	6.00	2.40
401	Elliott Maddox	.50	.20
402	Jim Rooker	.50	.20
403	Darrell Johnson MG Eddie Popowski CO Lee Stange CO Don Zimmer CO Don Bryant CO	1.00	.40
404	Jim Howarth	.50	.20
405	Ellie Rodriguez	.50	.20
406	Steve Arlin	.50	.20
407	Jim Wohlford	.50	.20
408	Charlie Hough	1.00	.40
409	Ike Brown	.50	.20
410	Pedro Borbon	.50	.20
411	Frank Baker	.50	.20
412	Chuck Taylor	.50	.20
413	Don Money	1.00	.40
414	Checklist 397-528	3.00	.60
415	Gary Gentry	.50	.20
416	Chicago White Sox Team Card	1.00	.40
417	Rich Folkers	.50	.20
418	Walt Williams	.50	.20
419	Wayne Twitchell	.50	.20
420	Ray Fosse	.50	.20
421	Dan Fife	.50	.20
422	Gonzalo Marquez	.50	.20
423	Fred Stanley	.50	.20
424	Jim Beauchamp	.50	.20
425	Pete Broberg	.50	.20
426	Rennie Stennett	.50	.20
427	Bobby Bolin	.50	.20
428	Gary Sutherland	.50	.20
429	Dick Lange	.50	.20
430	Matty Alou	1.00	.40
431	Gene Garber RC	1.00	.40
432	Chris Arnold	.50	.20
433	Lerrin LaGrow	.50	.20
434	Ken McMullen	.50	.20
435	Dave Concepcion	2.00	.80
436	Don Hood	.50	.20
437	Jim Lyttle	.50	.20
438	Ed Herrmann	.50	.20
439	Norm Miller	.50	.20
440	Jim Kaat	2.00	.80
441	Tom Ragland	.50	.20
442	Alan Foster	.50	.20
443	Tom Hutton	.50	.20
444	Vic Davalillo	.50	.20
445	George Medich	.50	.20
446	Len Randle	.50	.20
447	Frank Quilici MG Ralph Rowe CO Bob Rodgers CO Vern Morgan CO	1.00	.40
448	Ron Hodges	.50	.20
449	Tom McCraw	.50	.20
450	Rich Hebner	1.00	.40
451	Tommy John	2.00	.80
452	Gene Hiser	.50	.20
453	Balor Moore	.50	.20
454	Kurt Bevacqua	.50	.20
455	Tom Bradley	.50	.20
456	Dave Winfield RC	40.00	16.00
457	Chuck Goggin	.50	.20
458	Jim Ray	.50	.20
459	Cincinnati Reds Team Card	2.00	.80
460	Boog Powell	2.00	.80
461	John Odom	.50	.20
462	Luis Alvarado	.50	.20
463	Pat Dobson	.50	.20
464	Jose Cruz	2.00	.80
465	Dick Bosman	.50	.20
466	Dick Billings	.50	.20
467	Winston Llenas	.50	.20
468	Pepe Frias	.50	.20
469	Joe Decker	.50	.20
470	Reggie Jackson ALCS	5.00	2.00
471	Jon Matlack NLCS	1.00	.40
472	Darold Knowles WS1	1.00	.40
473	Willie Mays WS	8.00	3.20
474	Bert Campaneris WS3	1.00	.40
475	Rusty Staub WS4	1.00	.40
476	Cleon Jones WS5	1.00	.40
477	Reggie Jackson WS	5.00	2.00
478	Bert Campaneris WS7	1.00	.40

❑ 479 WS Summary	1.00	.40
A's celebrate; win		
2nd consecutive		
championship		
❑ 480 Willie Crawford	.50	.20
❑ 481 Jerry Terrell	.50	.20
❑ 482 Bob Didier	.50	.20
❑ 483 Atlanta Braves	1.00	.40
Team Card		
❑ 484 Carmen Fanzone	.50	.20
❑ 485 Felipe Alou	2.00	.80
❑ 486 Steve Stone	1.00	.40
❑ 487 Ted Martinez	.50	.20
❑ 488 Andy Etchebarren	.50	.20
❑ 489 Danny Murtaugh MG	1.00	.40
Don Osborn CO		
Don Leppert CO		
Bill Mazeroski CO		
Bob Skinner CO		
❑ 490 Vada Pinson	2.00	.80
❑ 491 Roger Nelson	.50	.20
❑ 492 Mike Rogodzinski	.50	.20
❑ 493 Joe Hoerner	.50	.20
❑ 494 Ed Goodson	.50	.20
❑ 495 Dick McAuliffe	1.00	.40
❑ 496 Tom Murphy	.50	.20
❑ 497 Bobby Mitchell	.50	.20
❑ 498 Pat Corrales	.50	.20
❑ 499 Rusty Torres	.50	.20
❑ 500 Lee May	1.00	.40
❑ 501 Eddie Leon	.50	.20
❑ 502 Dave LaRoche	.50	.20
❑ 503 Eric Soderholm	.50	.20
❑ 504 Joe Niekro	1.00	.40
❑ 505 Bill Buckner	1.00	.40
❑ 506 Ed Farmer	.50	.20
❑ 507 Larry Stahl	.50	.20
❑ 508 Montreal Expos	1.00	.40
Team Card		
❑ 509 Jesse Jefferson	.50	.20
❑ 510 Wayne Garrett	.50	.20
❑ 511 Toby Harrah	1.00	.40
❑ 512 Joe Lahoud	.50	.20
❑ 513 Jim Campanis	.50	.20
❑ 514 Paul Schaal	.50	.20
❑ 515 Willie Montanez	.50	.20
❑ 516 Horacio Pina	.50	.20
❑ 517 Mike Hegan	.50	.20
❑ 518 Derrel Thomas	.50	.20
❑ 519 Bill Sharp	.50	.20
❑ 520 Tim McCarver	2.00	.80
❑ 521 Ken Aspromonte MG	1.00	.40
Clay Bryant CO		
Tony Pacheco CO		
❑ 522 J.R. Richard	2.00	.80
❑ 523 Cecil Cooper	2.00	.80
❑ 524 Bill Plummer	.50	.20
❑ 525 Clyde Wright	.50	.20
❑ 526 Frank Tepedino	1.00	.40
❑ 527 Bobby Darwin	.50	.20
❑ 528 Bill Bonham	.50	.20
❑ 529 Horace Clarke	1.00	.40
❑ 530 Mickey Stanley	1.00	.40
❑ 531 Gene Mauch MG	1.00	.40
Dave Bristol CO		
Cal McLish CO		
Larry Doby CO		
Jerry Zimmerman CO		
❑ 532 Skip Lockwood	.50	.20
❑ 533 Mike Phillips	.50	.20
❑ 534 Eddie Watt	.50	.20
❑ 535 Bob Tolan	.50	.20
❑ 536 Duffy Dyer	.50	.20
❑ 537 Steve Mingori	.50	.20
❑ 538 Cesar Tovar	.50	.20
❑ 539 Lloyd Allen	.50	.20
❑ 540 Bob Robertson	.50	.20
❑ 541 Cleveland Indians	1.00	.40
Team Card		
❑ 542 Goose Gossage	2.00	.80
❑ 543 Danny Cater	.50	.20
❑ 544 Ron Schueler	.50	.20
❑ 545 Billy Conigliaro	1.00	.40
❑ 546 Mike Corkins	.50	.20
❑ 547 Glenn Borgmann	.50	.20
❑ 548 Sonny Siebert	.50	.20
❑ 549 Mike Jorgensen	.50	.20
❑ 550 Sam McDowell	1.00	.40
❑ 551 Von Joshua	.50	.20
❑ 552 Denny Doyle	.50	.20
❑ 553 Jim Willoughby	.50	.20
❑ 554 Tim Johnson	.50	.20
❑ 555 Woodie Fryman	.50	.20
❑ 556 Dave Campbell	1.00	.40
❑ 557 Jim McGlothlin	.50	.20
❑ 558 Bill Fahey	.50	.20
❑ 559 Darrel Chaney	.50	.20
❑ 560 Mike Cuellar	1.00	.40
❑ 561 Ed Kranepool	1.00	.40
❑ 562 Jack Aker	.50	.20
❑ 563 Hal McRae	1.00	.40
❑ 564 Mike Ryan	.50	.20
❑ 565 Milt Wilcox	.50	.20
❑ 566 Jackie Hernandez	.50	.20
❑ 567 Boston Red Sox	1.00	.40
Team Card		
❑ 568 Mike Torrez	1.00	.40
❑ 569 Rick Dempsey	1.00	.40
❑ 570 Ralph Garr	1.00	.40
❑ 571 Rich Hand	.50	.20
❑ 572 Enzo Hernandez	.50	.20
❑ 573 Mike Adams	.50	.20
❑ 574 Bill Parsons	.50	.20
❑ 575 Steve Garvey	3.00	1.20
❑ 576 Scipio Spinks	.50	.20
❑ 577 Mike Sadek	.50	.20
❑ 578 Ralph Houk MG	1.00	.40
❑ 579 Cecil Upshaw	.50	.20
❑ 580 Jim Spencer	.50	.20
❑ 581 Fred Norman	.50	.20
❑ 582 Bucky Dent RC	5.00	2.00
❑ 583 Marty Pattin	.50	.20
❑ 584 Ken Rudolph	.50	.20
❑ 585 Merv Rettenmund	.50	.20
❑ 586 Jack Brohamer	.50	.20
❑ 587 Larry Christenson	.50	.20
❑ 588 Hal Lanier	.50	.20
❑ 589 Boots Day	.50	.20
❑ 590 Roger Moret	.50	.20
❑ 591 Sonny Jackson	.50	.20
❑ 592 Ed Bane	.50	.20
❑ 593 Steve Yeager	1.00	.40
❑ 594 Leroy Stanton	.50	.20
❑ 595 Steve Blass	1.00	.40
❑ 596 Wayne Garland	.50	.20
Fred Holdsworth		
Mark Littell		
Dick Pole		
❑ 597 Dave Chalk	1.00	.40
John Gamble		
Pete MacKanin		
Manny Trillo RC		
❑ 598 Dave Augustine	12.00	4.80
Ken Griffey RC		
Steve Ontiveros		
Jim Tyrone		
❑ 599A Rookie Pitchers WAS	2.00	.80
Ron Diorio		
Dave Freisleben		
Frank Riccelli		
Greg Shanahan		
❑ 599B Rookie Pitchers SD	3.00	1.20
(SD in large print)		
❑ 599C Rookie Pitchers SD	6.00	2.40
(SD in small print)		
❑ 600 Ron Cash	5.00	2.00
Jim Cox		
Bill Madlock RC		
Reggie Sanders		
❑ 601 Ed Armbrister	3.00	1.20
Rich Bladt		
Brian Downing RC		
Bake McBride RC		
❑ 602 Glen Abbott	1.00	.40
Rick Henninger		
Craig Swan		
Dan Vossler		
❑ 603 Barry Foote	1.00	.40
Tom Lundstedt		
Charlie Moore RC		
Sergio Robles		
❑ 604 Terry Hughes	5.00	2.00
John Knox		
Andre Thornton RC		
Frank White RC		
❑ 605 Vic Albury	4.00	1.60
Ken Frailing		
Kevin Kobel		
Frank Tanana RC		
❑ 606 Jim Fuller	1.00	.40
Wilbur Howard		
Tommy Smith		
Otto Velez		
❑ 607 Leo Foster	1.00	.40
Tom Heintzelman		
Dave Rosello		
Frank Taveras RC		
❑ 608A Rookie Pitchers ERR	2.00	.80
Bob Apodaco (sic)		
Dick Baney		
John D'Acquisto		
Mike Wallace		
❑ 608B Rookie Pitchers COR	1.00	.40
Bob Apodaca		
Dick Baney		
John D'Acquisto		
Mike Wallace		
❑ 609 Rico Petrocelli	1.00	.40
❑ 610 Dave Kingman	2.00	.80
❑ 611 Rich Stelmaszek	.50	.20
❑ 612 Luke Walker	.50	.20
❑ 613 Dan Monzon	.50	.20
❑ 614 Adrian Devine	.50	.20
❑ 615 Johnny Jeter UER	.50	.20
(Misspelled Johnnie		
on card back)		
❑ 616 Larry Gura	.50	.20
❑ 617 Ted Ford	.50	.20
❑ 618 Jim Mason	.50	.20
❑ 619 Mike Anderson	.50	.20
❑ 620 Al Downing	.50	.20
❑ 621 Bernie Carbo	.50	.20
❑ 622 Phil Gagliano	.50	.20
❑ 623 Celerino Sanchez	.50	.20
❑ 624 Bob Miller	.50	.20
❑ 625 Ollie Brown	.50	.20
❑ 626 Pittsburgh Pirates	1.00	.40
Team Card		
❑ 627 Carl Taylor	.50	.20
❑ 628 Ivan Murrell	.50	.20
❑ 629 Rusty Staub	2.00	.80
❑ 630 Tommie Agee	1.00	.40
❑ 631 Steve Barber	.50	.20
❑ 632 George Culver	.50	.20
❑ 633 Dave Hamilton	.50	.20
❑ 634 Eddie Mathews MG	3.00	1.20
Herm Starrette CO		
Connie Ryan CO		
Jim Busby CO		
Ken Silvestri CO		
❑ 635 Johnny Edwards	.50	.20
❑ 636 Dave Goltz	.50	.20
❑ 637 Checklist 529-660	3.00	.60
❑ 638 Ken Sanders	.50	.20
❑ 639 Joe Lovitto	.50	.20
❑ 640 Milt Pappas	1.00	.40
❑ 641 Chuck Brinkman	.50	.20
❑ 642 Terry Harmon	.50	.20
❑ 643 Dodgers Team	1.00	.40
❑ 644 Wayne Granger	.50	.20
❑ 645 Ken Boswell	.50	.20
❑ 646 George Foster	2.00	.80
❑ 647 Juan Beniquez	.50	.20
❑ 648 Terry Crowley	.50	.20
❑ 649 Fernando Gonzalez RC	.50	.20
❑ 650 Mike Epstein	.50	.20
❑ 651 Leron Lee	.50	.20
❑ 652 Gail Hopkins	.50	.20
❑ 653 Bob Stinson	.50	.20
❑ 654A Jesus Alou ERR	4.00	1.60
(No position)		
❑ 654B Jesus Alou COR	1.00	.40
(Outfield)		
❑ 655 Mike Tyson	.50	.20
❑ 656 Adrian Garrett	.50	.20
❑ 657 Jim Shellenback	.50	.20
❑ 658 Lee Lacy	.50	.20
❑ 659 Joe Lis	.50	.20
❑ 660 Larry Dierker	2.00	.50

1975 Topps

	NM	Ex
COMPLETE SET (660)	500.00	200.00
WRAPPER (15-CENT)	8.00	3.20
❑ 1 Hank Aaron HL	30.00	10.00
❑ 2 Lou Brock HL	3.00	1.20
❑ 3 Bob Gibson HL	3.00	1.20
❑ 4 Al Kaline HL	6.00	2.40
❑ 5 Nolan Ryan HL	15.00	6.00
❑ 6 Mike Marshall HL	1.00	.40
❑ 7 Steve Busby HL	8.00	3.20
Dick Bosman		
Nolan Ryan		
❑ 8 Rogelio Moret	.50	.20
❑ 9 Frank Tepedino	1.00	.40
❑ 10 Willie Davis	1.00	.40
❑ 11 Bill Melton	.50	.20
❑ 12 David Clyde	.50	.20
❑ 13 Gene Locklear RC	1.00	.40
❑ 14 Milt Wilcox	.50	.20
❑ 15 Jose Cardenal	1.00	.40
❑ 16 Frank Tanana	2.00	.80
❑ 17 Dave Concepcion	2.00	.80
❑ 18 Tigers Team CL	2.00	.40
Ralph Houk MG		
❑ 19 Jerry Koosman	1.00	.40
❑ 20 Thurman Munson	8.00	3.20
❑ 21 Rollie Fingers	3.00	1.20
❑ 22 Dave Cash	.50	.20
❑ 23 Bill Russell	1.00	.40
❑ 24 Al Fitzmorris	.50	.20
❑ 25 Lee May	1.00	.40
❑ 26 Dave McNally	1.00	.40
❑ 27 Ken Reitz	.50	.20
❑ 28 Tom Murphy	.50	.20
❑ 29 Dave Parker	3.00	1.20
❑ 30 Bert Blyleven	2.00	.80
❑ 31 Dave Rader	.50	.20
❑ 32 Reggie Cleveland	.50	.20
❑ 33 Dusty Baker	2.00	.80
❑ 34 Steve Renko	.50	.20
❑ 35 Ron Santo	1.00	.40
❑ 36 Joe Lovitto	.50	.20
❑ 37 Dave Freisleben	.50	.20
❑ 38 Buddy Bell	2.00	.80
❑ 39 Andre Thornton	1.00	.40
❑ 40 Bill Singer	.50	.20
❑ 41 Cesar Geronimo	1.00	.40
❑ 42 Joe Coleman	.50	.20
❑ 43 Cleon Jones	1.00	.40
❑ 44 Pat Dobson	.50	.20
❑ 45 Joe Rudi	1.00	.40
❑ 46 Phillies Team CL	2.00	.40
Danny Ozark MG UER		
Terry Harmon listed as 339		
instead of 399		
❑ 47 Tommy John	2.00	.80
❑ 48 Freddie Patek	1.00	.40
❑ 49 Larry Dierker	1.00	.40
❑ 50 Brooks Robinson	8.00	3.20
❑ 51 Bob Forsch RC	1.00	.40
❑ 52 Darrell Porter	1.00	.40
❑ 53 Dave Giusti	.50	.20
❑ 54 Eric Soderholm	.50	.20
❑ 55 Bobby Bonds	2.00	.80
❑ 56 Rick Wise	1.00	.40
❑ 57 Dave Johnson	1.00	.40
❑ 58 Chuck Taylor	.50	.20
❑ 59 Ken Henderson	.50	.20
❑ 60 Fergie Jenkins	3.00	1.20
❑ 61 Dave Winfield	15.00	6.00
❑ 62 Fritz Peterson	.50	.20
❑ 63 Steve Swisher	.50	.20
❑ 64 Dave Chalk	.50	.20
❑ 65 Don Gullett	1.00	.40
❑ 66 Willie Horton	1.00	.40
❑ 67 Tug McGraw	1.00	.40
❑ 68 Ron Blomberg	.50	.20
❑ 69 John Odom	.50	.20
❑ 70 Mike Schmidt	20.00	8.00
❑ 71 Charlie Hough	1.00	.40
❑ 72 Royals Team CL	2.00	.40
Jack McKeon MG		
❑ 73 J.R. Richard	1.00	.40
❑ 74 Mark Belanger	1.00	.40
❑ 75 Ted Simmons	2.00	.80
❑ 76 Ed Sprague	.50	.20
❑ 77 Richie Zisk	1.00	.40
❑ 78 Ray Corbin	.50	.20
❑ 79 Gary Matthews	1.00	.40
❑ 80 Carlton Fisk	8.00	3.20
❑ 81 Ron Reed	.50	.20
❑ 82 Pat Kelly	.50	.20
❑ 83 Jim Merritt	.50	.20
❑ 84 Enzo Hernandez	.50	.20
❑ 85 Bill Bonham	.50	.20
❑ 86 Joe Lis	.50	.20
❑ 87 George Foster	2.00	.80
❑ 88 Tom Egan	.50	.20
❑ 89 Jim Ray	.50	.20
❑ 90 Rusty Staub	2.00	.80
❑ 91 Dick Green	.50	.20
❑ 92 Cecil Upshaw	.50	.20
❑ 93 Dave Lopes	2.00	.80
❑ 94 Jim Lonborg	1.00	.40
❑ 95 John Mayberry	1.00	.40
❑ 96 Mike Cosgrove	.50	.20
❑ 97 Earl Williams	.50	.20
❑ 98 Rich Folkers	.50	.20
❑ 99 Mike Hegan	.50	.20
❑ 100 Willie Stargell	4.00	1.60
❑ 101 Expos Team CL	2.00	.40
Gene Mauch MG		
❑ 102 Joe Decker	.50	.20
❑ 103 Rick Miller	.50	.20
❑ 104 Bill Madlock	2.00	.80
❑ 105 Buzz Capra	.50	.20
❑ 106 M. Hargrove RC UER	3.00	1.20
Gastonia At-bats are wrong		
❑ 107 Jim Barr	.50	.20
❑ 108 Tom Hall	.50	.20
❑ 109 George Hendrick	1.00	.40
❑ 110 Wilbur Wood	.50	.20
❑ 111 Wayne Garrett	.50	.20
❑ 112 Larry Hardy	.50	.20
❑ 113 Elliott Maddox	.50	.20
❑ 114 Dick Lange	.50	.20
❑ 115 Joe Ferguson	.50	.20
❑ 116 Lerrin LaGrow	.50	.20
❑ 117 Orioles Team CL	3.00	.60
Earl Weaver MG		
❑ 118 Mike Anderson	.50	.20
❑ 119 Tommy Helms	.50	.20
❑ 120 Steve Busby UER	1.00	.40
(Photo actually		
Fran Healy)		
❑ 121 Bill North	.50	.20
❑ 122 Al Hrabosky	1.00	.40
❑ 123 Johnny Briggs	.50	.20
❑ 124 Jerry Reuss	1.00	.40
❑ 125 Ken Singleton	1.00	.40
❑ 126 Checklist 1-132	3.00	.60
❑ 127 Glenn Borgmann	.50	.20
❑ 128 Bill Lee	1.00	.40
❑ 129 Rick Monday	1.00	.40
❑ 130 Phil Niekro	3.00	1.20
❑ 131 Toby Harrah	1.00	.40
❑ 132 Randy Moffitt	.50	.20
❑ 133 Dan Driessen	1.00	.40
❑ 134 Ron Hodges	.50	.20
❑ 135 Charlie Spikes	.50	.20
❑ 136 Jim Mason	.50	.20
❑ 137 Terry Forster	1.00	.40
❑ 138 Del Unser	.50	.20
❑ 139 Horacio Pina	.50	.20
❑ 140 Steve Garvey	3.00	1.20
❑ 141 Mickey Stanley	1.00	.40
❑ 142 Bob Reynolds	.50	.20
❑ 143 Cliff Johnson	1.00	.40
❑ 144 Jim Wohlford	.50	.20
❑ 145 Ken Holtzman	1.00	.40
❑ 146 Padres Team CL	2.00	.40
John McNamara MG		
❑ 147 Pedro Garcia	.50	.20
❑ 148 Jim Rooker	.50	.20
❑ 149 Tim Foli	.50	.20
❑ 150 Bob Gibson	6.00	2.40
❑ 151 Steve Brye	.50	.20
❑ 152 Mario Guerrero	.50	.20
❑ 153 Rick Reuschel	1.00	.40
❑ 154 Mike Lum	.50	.20
❑ 155 Jim Bibby	.50	.20
❑ 156 Dave Kingman	2.00	.80
❑ 157 Pedro Borbon	1.00	.40
❑ 158 Jerry Grote	.50	.20
❑ 159 Steve Arlin	.50	.20
❑ 160 Graig Nettles	2.00	.80
❑ 161 Stan Bahnsen	.50	.20
❑ 162 Willie Montanez	.50	.20
❑ 163 Jim Brewer	.50	.20
❑ 164 Mickey Rivers	1.00	.40
❑ 165 Doug Rader	1.00	.40
❑ 166 Woodie Fryman	.50	.20
❑ 167 Rich Coggins	.50	.20
❑ 168 Bill Greif	.50	.20
❑ 169 Cookie Rojas	.50	.20
❑ 170 Bert Campaneris	1.00	.40
❑ 171 Ed Kirkpatrick	.50	.20
❑ 172 Red Sox Team CL	3.00	.60
Darrell Johnson MG		
❑ 173 Steve Rogers	1.00	.40
❑ 174 Bake McBride	1.00	.40
❑ 175 Don Money	1.00	.40
❑ 176 Burt Hooton	1.00	.40
❑ 177 Vic Correll	.50	.20
❑ 178 Cesar Tovar	.50	.20
❑ 179 Tom Bradley	.50	.20
❑ 180 Joe Morgan	6.00	2.40
❑ 181 Fred Beene	.50	.20
❑ 182 Don Hahn	.50	.20
❑ 183 Mel Stottlemyre	1.00	.40
❑ 184 Jorge Orta	.50	.20
❑ 185 Steve Carlton	8.00	3.20
❑ 186 Willie Crawford	.50	.20
❑ 187 Denny Doyle	.50	.20
❑ 188 Tom Griffin	.50	.20
❑ 189 Larry (Yogi) Berra	4.00	1.60
Roy Campanella MVP		
Campanella card never issued		
❑ 190 Bobby Shantz	2.00	.80
Hank Sauer MVP		
❑ 191 Al Rosen	2.00	.80
Roy Campanella MVP		
❑ 192 Yogi Berra	4.00	1.60
Willie Mays MVP		
❑ 193 Yogi Berra	3.00	1.20
Roy Campanella MVP		
Campanella card never issued		
he is pictured with LA cap		
❑ 194 Mickey Mantle	10.00	4.00
Don Newcombe MVP		
❑ 195 Mickey Mantle	12.00	4.80
Hank Aaron MVP		
❑ 196 Jackie Jensen	3.00	1.20
Ernie Banks MVP		
❑ 197 Nellie Fox	2.00	.80
Ernie Banks MVP		
❑ 198 Roger Maris	2.00	.80
Dick Groat MVP		
❑ 199 Roger Maris	3.00	1.20
Frank Robinson MVP		
❑ 200 Mickey Mantle	10.00	4.00
Maury Wills MVP		
(Wills card never issued)		
❑ 201 Elston Howard	2.00	.80
Sandy Koufax MVP		
❑ 202 Brooks Robinson	1.00	.40
Ken Boyer MVP		

❑ 203 Zoilo Versalles .... 2.00 .80
Willie Mays MVP
❑ 204 Frank Robinson 6.00 2.40
Bob Clemente MVP
❑ 205 Carl Yastrzemski .... 2.00 .80
Orlando Cepeda MVP
❑ 206 Denny McLain UER .... 2.00 .80
Bob Gibson MVP
On the back McLain is spelled McClain
❑ 207 Harmon Killebrew .... 1.00 .40
Willie McCovey MVP
❑ 208 Boog Powell .... 2.00 .80
Johnny Bench MVP
❑ 209 Vida Blue .... 2.00 .80
Joe Torre MVP
❑ 210 Rich Allen .... 2.00 .80
Johnny Bench MVP
❑ 211 Reggie Jackson 5.00 2.00
Pete Rose MVP
❑ 212 Jeff Burroughs .... 2.00 .80
Steve Garvey MVP
❑ 213 Oscar Gamble .... 1.00 .40
❑ 214 Harry Parker .... .50 .20
❑ 215 Bobby Valentine .... 1.00 .40
❑ 216 Giants Team CL .... 2.00 .40
Wes Westrum MG
❑ 217 Lou Piniella .... 2.00 .80
❑ 218 Jerry Johnson .... .50 .20
❑ 219 Ed Herrmann .... .50 .20
❑ 220 Don Sutton 3.00 1.20
❑ 221 Aurelio Rodriguez .... .50 .20
❑ 222 Dan Spillner .... .50 .20
❑ 223 Robin Yount RC 50.00 20.00
❑ 224 Ramon Hernandez .... .50 .20
❑ 225 Bob Grich .... 1.00 .40
❑ 226 Bill Campbell .... .50 .20
❑ 227 Bob Watson .... 1.00 .40
❑ 228 George Brett RC 80.00 32.00
❑ 229 Barry Foote .... .50 .20
❑ 230 Jim Hunter 4.00 1.60
❑ 231 Mike Tyson .... .50 .20
❑ 232 Diego Segui .... .50 .20
❑ 233 Billy Grabarkewitz .... .50 .20
❑ 234 Tom Grieve .... 1.00 .40
❑ 235 Jack Billingham .... 1.00 .40
❑ 236 Angels Team CL .... 2.00 .40
Dick Williams MG
❑ 237 Carl Morton .... 1.00 .40
❑ 238 Dave Duncan .... 1.00 .40
❑ 239 George Stone .... .50 .20
❑ 240 Garry Maddox .... 1.00 .40
❑ 241 Dick Tidrow .... .50 .20
❑ 242 Jay Johnstone .... 1.00 .40
❑ 243 Jim Kaat .... 2.00 .80
❑ 244 Bill Buckner .... 1.00 .40
❑ 245 Mickey Lolich .... 2.00 .80
❑ 246 Cardinals Team CL .... 2.00 .40
Red Schoendienst MG
❑ 247 Enos Cabell .... .50 .20
❑ 248 Randy Jones .... 2.00 .80
❑ 249 Danny Thompson .... .50 .20
❑ 250 Ken Brett .... .50 .20
❑ 251 Fran Healy .... .50 .20
❑ 252 Fred Scherman .... .50 .20
❑ 253 Jesus Alou .... .50 .20
❑ 254 Mike Torrez .... 1.00 .40
❑ 255 Dwight Evans .... 2.00 .80
❑ 256 Billy Champion .... .50 .20
❑ 257 Checklist: 133-264 .... 3.00 .60
❑ 258 Dave LaRoche .... .50 .20
❑ 259 Len Randle .... .50 .20
❑ 260 Johnny Bench 15.00 6.00
❑ 261 Andy Hassler .... .50 .20
❑ 262 Rowland Office .... .50 .20
❑ 263 Jim Perry .... 1.00 .40
❑ 264 John Milner .... .50 .20
❑ 265 Ron Bryant .... .50 .20
❑ 266 Sandy Alomar .... 1.00 .40
❑ 267 Dick Ruthven .... .50 .20
❑ 268 Hal McRae .... 1.00 .40
❑ 269 Doug Rau .... .50 .20
❑ 270 Ron Fairly .... 1.00 .40
❑ 271 Gerry Moses .... .50 .20
❑ 272 Lynn McGlothen .... .50 .20
❑ 273 Steve Braun .... .50 .20
❑ 274 Vicente Romo .... .50 .20
❑ 275 Paul Blair .... 1.00 .40
❑ 276 White Sox Team CL .... 2.00 .40
Chuck Tanner MG
❑ 277 Frank Taveras .... .50 .20
❑ 278 Paul Lindblad .... .50 .20
❑ 279 Milt May .... .50 .20
❑ 280 Carl Yastrzemski 12.00 4.80
❑ 281 Jim Slaton .... .50 .20
❑ 282 Jerry Morales .... .50 .20
❑ 283 Steve Foucault .... .50 .20
❑ 284 Ken Griffey 4.00 1.60
❑ 285 Ellie Rodriguez .... .50 .20
❑ 286 Mike Jorgensen .... .50 .20
❑ 287 Roric Harrison .... .50 .20
❑ 288 Bruce Ellingsen .... .50 .20
❑ 289 Ken Rudolph .... .50 .20
❑ 290 Jon Matlack .... .50 .20
❑ 291 Bill Sudakis .... .50 .20
❑ 292 Ron Schueler .... .50 .20
❑ 293 Dick Sharon .... .50 .20
❑ 294 Geoff Zahn .... .50 .20
❑ 295 Vada Pinson .... 2.00 .80
❑ 296 Alan Foster .... .50 .20
❑ 297 Craig Kusick .... .50 .20
❑ 298 Johnny Grubb .... .50 .20
❑ 299 Bucky Dent .... 2.00 .80
❑ 300 Reggie Jackson 15.00 6.00
❑ 301 Dave Roberts .... .50 .20
❑ 302 Rick Burleson .... 1.00 .40
❑ 303 Grant Jackson .... .50 .20
❑ 304 Pirates Team CL .... 2.00 .40
Danny Murtaugh MG
❑ 305 Jim Colborn .... .50 .20
❑ 306 Rod Carew .... 2.00 .80
Ralph Garr LL
❑ 307 Dick Allen 4.00 1.60
Mike Schmidt LL
❑ 308 Jeff Burroughs .... 2.00 .80
Johnny Bench LL
❑ 309 Bill North .... 2.00 .80
Lou Brock LL
❑ 310 Jim Hunter .... 2.00 .80
Fergie Jenkins
Andy Messersmith
Phil Niekro LL
❑ 311 Jim Hunter .... 2.00 .80
Buzz Capra LL
❑ 312 Nolan Ryan 12.00 4.80
Steve Carlton LL
❑ 313 Terry Forster .... 1.00 .40
Mike Marshall LL
❑ 314 Buck Martinez .... .50 .20
❑ 315 Don Kessinger .... 1.00 .40
❑ 316 Jackie Brown .... .50 .20
❑ 317 Joe Lahoud .... .50 .20
❑ 318 Ernie McAnally .... .50 .20
❑ 319 Johnny Oates .... 1.00 .40
❑ 320 Pete Rose 30.00 12.00
❑ 321 Rudy May .... .50 .20
❑ 322 Ed Goodson .... .50 .20
❑ 323 Fred Holdsworth .... .50 .20
❑ 324 Ed Kranepool .... 1.00 .40
❑ 325 Tony Oliva .... 2.00 .80
❑ 326 Wayne Twitchell .... .50 .20
❑ 327 Jerry Hairston .... .50 .20
❑ 328 Sonny Siebert .... .50 .20
❑ 329 Ted Kubiak .... .50 .20
❑ 330 Mike Marshall .... 1.00 .40
❑ 331 Indians Team CL .... 2.00 .40
Frank Robinson MG
❑ 332 Fred Kendall .... .50 .20
❑ 333 Dick Drago .... .50 .20
❑ 334 Greg Gross .... .50 .20
❑ 335 Jim Palmer 6.00 2.40
❑ 336 Rennie Stennett .... .50 .20
❑ 337 Kevin Kobel .... .50 .20
❑ 338 Rich Stelmaszek .... .50 .20
❑ 339 Jim Fregosi .... 1.00 .40
❑ 340 Paul Splittorff .... .50 .20
❑ 341 Hal Breeden .... .50 .20
❑ 342 Leroy Stanton .... .50 .20
❑ 343 Danny Frisella .... .50 .20
❑ 344 Ben Oglivie .... 1.00 .40
❑ 345 Clay Carroll .... 1.00 .40
❑ 346 Bobby Darwin .... .50 .20
❑ 347 Mike Caldwell .... .50 .20
❑ 348 Tony Muser .... .50 .20
❑ 349 Ray Sadecki .... .50 .20
❑ 350 Bobby Murcer .... 1.00 .40
❑ 351 Bob Boone .... 2.00 .80
❑ 352 Darold Knowles .... .50 .20
❑ 353 Luis Melendez .... .50 .20
❑ 354 Dick Bosman .... .50 .20
❑ 355 Chris Cannizzaro .... .50 .20
❑ 356 Rico Petrocelli .... 1.00 .40
❑ 357 Ken Forsch UER .... .50 .20
Forsch is misspelled in blurb
❑ 358 Al Bumbry .... 1.00 .40
❑ 359 Paul Popovich .... .50 .20
❑ 360 George Scott .... 1.00 .40
❑ 361 Dodgers Team CL .... 2.00 .40
Walter Alston MG
❑ 362 Steve Hargan .... .50 .20
❑ 363 Carmen Fanzone .... .50 .20
❑ 364 Doug Bird .... .50 .20
❑ 365 Bob Bailey .... .50 .20
❑ 366 Ken Sanders .... .50 .20
❑ 367 Craig Robinson .... .50 .20
❑ 368 Vic Albury .... .50 .20
❑ 369 Merv Rettenmund .... .50 .20
❑ 370 Tom Seaver 12.00 4.80
❑ 371 Gates Brown .... .50 .20
❑ 372 John D'Acquisto .... .50 .20
❑ 373 Bill Sharp .... .50 .20
❑ 374 Eddie Watt .... .50 .20
❑ 375 Roy White .... 1.00 .40
❑ 376 Steve Yeager .... 1.00 .40
❑ 377 Tom Hilgendorf .... .50 .20
❑ 378 Derrel Thomas .... .50 .20
❑ 379 Bernie Carbo .... .50 .20
❑ 380 Sal Bando .... 1.00 .40
❑ 381 John Curtis .... .50 .20
❑ 382 Don Baylor .... 2.00 .80
❑ 383 Jim York .... .50 .20
❑ 384 Brewers Team .... 2.00 .40
Del Crandall MG
❑ 385 Dock Ellis .... .50 .20
❑ 386 Checklist: 265-396 UER 3.00 .60
Dick Sharon's name is misspelled
❑ 387 Jim Spencer .... .50 .20
❑ 388 Steve Stone .... 1.00 .40
❑ 389 Tony Solaita .... .50 .20
❑ 390 Ron Cey .... 2.00 .80
❑ 391 Don DeMola .... .50 .20
❑ 392 Bruce Bochte RC .... 1.00 .40
❑ 393 Gary Gentry .... .50 .20
❑ 394 Larvell Blanks .... .50 .20
❑ 395 Bud Harrelson .... 1.00 .40
❑ 396 Fred Norman .... 1.00 .40
❑ 397 Bill Freehan .... 1.00 .40
❑ 398 Elias Sosa .... .50 .20
❑ 399 Terry Harmon .... .50 .20
❑ 400 Dick Allen .... 2.00 .80
❑ 401 Mike Wallace .... .50 .20
❑ 402 Bob Tolan .... .50 .20
❑ 403 Tom Buskey .... .50 .20
❑ 404 Ted Sizemore .... .50 .20
❑ 405 John Montague .... .50 .20
❑ 406 Bob Gallagher .... .50 .20
❑ 407 Herb Washington RC .... 2.00 .80
❑ 408 Clyde Wright UER .... .50 .20
Listed with wrong 1974 team
❑ 409 Bob Robertson .... .50 .20
❑ 410 Mike Cueller UER .... 1.00 .40
Sic, Cuellar
❑ 411 George Mitterwald .... .50 .20
❑ 412 Bill Hands .... .50 .20
❑ 413 Marty Pattin .... .50 .20
❑ 414 Manny Mota .... 1.00 .40
❑ 415 John Hiller .... 1.00 .40
❑ 416 Larry Lintz .... .50 .20
❑ 417 Skip Lockwood .... .50 .20
❑ 418 Leo Foster .... .50 .20
❑ 419 Dave Goltz .... .50 .20
❑ 420 Larry Bowa .... 2.00 .80
❑ 421 Mets Team CL .... 3.00 .60
Yogi Berra MG
❑ 422 Brian Downing .... 1.00 .40
❑ 423 Clay Kirby .... .50 .20
❑ 424 John Lowenstein .... .50 .20
❑ 425 Tito Fuentes .... .50 .20
❑ 426 George Medich .... .50 .20

❑ 427 Clarence Gaston .... 1.00 .40
❑ 428 Dave Hamilton .... .50 .20
❑ 429 Jim Dwyer .... .50 .20
❑ 430 Luis Tiant .... 2.00 .80
❑ 431 Rod Gilbreath .... .50 .20
❑ 432 Ken Berry .... .50 .20
❑ 433 Larry Demery .... .50 .20
❑ 434 Bob Locker .... .50 .20
❑ 435 Dave Nelson .... .50 .20
❑ 436 Ken Frailing .... .50 .20
❑ 437 Al Cowens .... 1.00 .40
❑ 438 Don Carrithers .... .50 .20
❑ 439 Ed Brinkman .... .50 .20
❑ 440 Andy Messersmith .... 1.00 .40
❑ 441 Bobby Heise .... .50 .20
❑ 442 Maximino Leon .... .50 .20
❑ 443 Twins Team CL .... 2.00 .40
Frank Quilici MG
❑ 444 Gene Garber .... 1.00 .40
❑ 445 Felix Millan .... .50 .20
❑ 446 Bart Johnson .... .50 .20
❑ 447 Terry Crowley .... .50 .20
❑ 448 Frank Duffy .... .50 .20
❑ 449 Charlie Williams .... .50 .20
❑ 450 Willie McCovey 6.00 2.40
❑ 451 Rick Dempsey .... 1.00 .40
❑ 452 Angel Mangual .... .50 .20
❑ 453 Claude Osteen .... 1.00 .40
❑ 454 Doug Griffin .... .50 .20
❑ 455 Don Wilson .... .50 .20
❑ 456 Bob Coluccio .... .50 .20
❑ 457 Mario Mendoza .... .50 .20
❑ 458 Ross Grimsley .... .50 .20
❑ 459 1974 AL Champs .... 1.00 .40
A's over Orioles
(Second base action
pictured)
❑ 460 Steve Garvey NLCS .... 2.00 .80
Frank Taveras
❑ 461 Reggie Jackson WS 5.00 2.00
❑ 462 World Series Game 2 .... 1.00 .40
(Dodger dugout)
❑ 463 Rollie Fingers WS .... 2.00 .80
❑ 464 World Series Game 4 .... 1.00 .40
(A's batter)
❑ 465 Joe Rudi WS5 .... 1.00 .40
❑ 466 WS Summary .... 2.00 .80
A's do it again;
win third straight
A's group picture
❑ 467 Ed Halicki .... .50 .20
❑ 468 Bobby Mitchell .... .50 .20
❑ 469 Tom Dettore .... .50 .20
❑ 470 Jeff Burroughs .... 1.00 .40
❑ 471 Bob Stinson .... .50 .20
❑ 472 Bruce Dal Canton .... .50 .20
❑ 473 Ken McMullen .... .50 .20
❑ 474 Luke Walker .... .50 .20
❑ 475 Darrell Evans .... 1.00 .40
❑ 476 Ed Figueroa .... .50 .20
❑ 477 Tom Hutton .... .50 .20
❑ 478 Tom Burgmeier .... .50 .20
❑ 479 Ken Boswell .... .50 .20
❑ 480 Carlos May .... .50 .20
❑ 481 Will McEnaney .... 1.00 .40
❑ 482 Tom McCraw .... .50 .20
❑ 483 Steve Ontiveros .... .50 .20
❑ 484 Glenn Beckert .... 1.00 .40
❑ 485 Sparky Lyle .... 1.00 .40
❑ 486 Ray Fosse .... .50 .20
❑ 487 Astros Team CL .... 2.00 .40
Preston Gomez MG
❑ 488 Bill Travers .... .50 .20
❑ 489 Cecil Cooper .... 2.00 .80
❑ 490 Reggie Smith .... 1.00 .40
❑ 491 Doyle Alexander .... 1.00 .40
❑ 492 Rich Hebner .... 1.00 .40
❑ 493 Don Stanhouse .... .50 .20
❑ 494 Pete LaCock .... .50 .20
❑ 495 Nelson Briles .... 1.00 .40
❑ 496 Pepe Frias .... .50 .20
❑ 497 Jim Nettles .... .50 .20
❑ 498 Al Downing .... .50 .20
❑ 499 Marty Perez .... .50 .20
❑ 500 Nolan Ryan 50.00 20.00
❑ 501 Bill Robinson .... 1.00 .40
❑ 502 Pat Bourque .... .50 .20
❑ 503 Fred Stanley .... .50 .20
❑ 504 Buddy Bradford .... .50 .20
❑ 505 Chris Speier .... .50 .20
❑ 506 Leron Lee .... .50 .20
❑ 507 Tom Carroll .... .50 .20
❑ 508 Bob Hansen .... .50 .20
❑ 509 Dave Hilton .... .50 .20
❑ 510 Vida Blue .... 1.00 .40
❑ 511 Rangers Team CL .... 2.00 .40
Billy Martin MG
❑ 512 Larry Milbourne .... .50 .20
❑ 513 Dick Pole .... .50 .20
❑ 514 Jose Cruz .... 2.00 .80
❑ 515 Manny Sanguillen .... 1.00 .40
❑ 516 Don Hood .... .50 .20
❑ 517 Checklist: 397-528 .... 3.00 .60
❑ 518 Leo Cardenas .... .50 .20
❑ 519 Jim Todd .... .50 .20
❑ 520 Amos Otis .... 1.00 .40
❑ 521 Dennis Blair .... .50 .20
❑ 522 Gary Sutherland .... .50 .20
❑ 523 Tom Paciorek .... 1.00 .40
❑ 524 John Doherty .... .50 .20
❑ 525 Tom House .... .50 .20
❑ 526 Larry Hisle .... 1.00 .40
❑ 527 Mac Scarce .... .50 .20
❑ 528 Eddie Leon .... .50 .20
❑ 529 Gary Thomasson .... .50 .20
❑ 530 Gaylord Perry 3.00 1.20
❑ 531 Reds Team CL 5.00 1.00
Sparky Anderson MG
❑ 532 Gorman Thomas .... 1.00 .40
❑ 533 Rudy Meoli .... .50 .20
❑ 534 Alex Johnson .... .50 .20
❑ 535 Gene Tenace .... 1.00 .40
❑ 536 Bob Moose .... .50 .20
❑ 537 Tommy Harper .... 1.00 .40
❑ 538 Duffy Dyer .... .50 .20
❑ 539 Jesse Jefferson .... .50 .20
❑ 540 Lou Brock 6.00 2.40
❑ 541 Roger Metzger .... .50 .20
❑ 542 Pete Broberg .... .50 .20
❑ 543 Larry Biittner .... .50 .20
❑ 544 Steve Mingori .... .50 .20
❑ 545 Billy Williams 3.00 1.20
❑ 546 John Knox .... .50 .20
❑ 547 Von Joshua .... .50 .20
❑ 548 Charlie Sands .... .50 .20
❑ 549 Bill Butler .... .50 .20
❑ 550 Ralph Garr .... 1.00 .40
❑ 551 Larry Christenson .... .50 .20
❑ 552 Jack Brohamer .... .50 .20
❑ 553 John Boccabella .... .50 .20
❑ 554 Goose Gossage .... 2.00 .80
❑ 555 Al Oliver .... 2.00 .80
❑ 556 Tim Johnson .... .50 .20
❑ 557 Larry Gura .... .50 .20
❑ 558 Dave Roberts .... .50 .20
❑ 559 Bob Montgomery .... .50 .20
❑ 560 Tony Perez 4.00 1.60
❑ 561 A's Team CL .... 2.00 .40
Alvin Dark MG
❑ 562 Gary Nolan .... 1.00 .40
❑ 563 Wilbur Howard .... .50 .20
❑ 564 Tommy Davis .... 1.00 .40
❑ 565 Joe Torre .... 2.00 .80
❑ 566 Ray Burris .... .50 .20
❑ 567 Jim Sundberg RC .... 2.00 .80
❑ 568 Dale Murray .... .50 .20
❑ 569 Frank White .... 1.00 .40
❑ 570 Jim Wynn .... 1.00 .40
❑ 571 Dave Lemanczyk .... .50 .20
❑ 572 Roger Nelson .... .50 .20
❑ 573 Orlando Pena .... .50 .20
❑ 574 Tony Taylor .... .50 .20
❑ 575 Gene Clines .... .50 .20
❑ 576 Phil Roof .... .50 .20
❑ 577 John Morris .... .50 .20
❑ 578 Dave Tomlin .... .50 .20
❑ 579 Skip Pitlock .... .50 .20
❑ 580 Frank Robinson 6.00 2.40
❑ 581 Darrel Chaney .... .50 .20
❑ 582 Eduardo Rodriguez .... .50 .20
❑ 583 Andy Etchebarren .... .50 .20
❑ 584 Mike Garman .... .50 .20
❑ 585 Chris Chambliss .... 1.00 .40
❑ 586 Tim McCarver .... 2.00 .80
❑ 587 Chris Ward .... .50 .20
❑ 588 Rick Auerbach .... .50 .20
❑ 589 Braves Team CL .... 2.00 .40
Clyde King MG
❑ 590 Cesar Cedeno .... 1.00 .40
❑ 591 Glenn Abbott .... .50 .20
❑ 592 Balor Moore .... .50 .20
❑ 593 Gene Lamont .... .50 .20
❑ 594 Jim Fuller .... .50 .20
❑ 595 Joe Niekro .... 1.00 .40
❑ 596 Ollie Brown .... .50 .20
❑ 597 Winston Llenas .... .50 .20
❑ 598 Bruce Kison .... .50 .20
❑ 599 Nate Colbert .... .50 .20
❑ 600 Rod Carew 8.00 3.20
❑ 601 Juan Beniquez .... .50 .20
❑ 602 John Vukovich .... .50 .20
❑ 603 Lew Krausse .... .50 .20
❑ 604 Oscar Zamora .... .50 .20
❑ 605 John Ellis .... .50 .20
❑ 606 Bruce Miller .... .50 .20
❑ 607 Jim Holt .... .50 .20
❑ 608 Gene Michael .... .50 .20
❑ 609 Elrod Hendricks .... .50 .20
❑ 610 Ron Hunt .... .50 .20
❑ 611 Yankees Team CL .... 2.00 .40
Bill Virdon MG
❑ 612 Terry Hughes .... .50 .20
❑ 613 Bill Parsons .... .50 .20
❑ 614 Jack Kucek .... 1.00 .40
Dyar Miller
Vern Ruhle
Paul Siebert
❑ 615 Pat Darcy .... 2.00 .80
Dennis Leonard RC
Tom Underwood
Hank Webb
❑ 616 Dave Augustine 15.00 6.00
Pepe Mangual
Jim Rice RC
John Scott
❑ 617 Mike Cubbage .... 2.00 .80
Doug DeCinces RC
Reggie Sanders
Manny Trillo
❑ 618 Jamie Easterly .... 1.00 .40
Tom Johnson
Scott McGregor RC
Rick Rhoden RC
❑ 619 Benny Ayala .... 1.00 .40
Nyls Nyman
Tommy Smith
Jerry Turner
❑ 620 Gary Carter RC 15.00 6.00
Marc Hill
Danny Meyer
Leon Roberts
❑ 621 John Denny RC .... 2.00 .80
Rawly Eastwick
Jim Kern
Juan Veintidos
❑ 622 Ed Armbrister 8.00 3.20
Fred Lynn RC
Tom Poquette
Terry Whitfield UER
(Listed as Ney York)
❑ 623 Phil Garner 10.00 4.00
Keith Hernandez RC UER
(Sic, bats right)
Bob Sheldon
Tom Veryzer
❑ 624 Doug Konieczny .... 1.00 .40
Gary Lavelle
Jim Otten
Eddie Solomon
❑ 625 Boog Powell .... 2.00 .80
❑ 626 Larry Haney UER .... .50 .20
Photo actually
Dave Duncan
❑ 627 Tom Walker .... .50 .20
❑ 628 Ron LeFlore RC .... 1.00 .40
❑ 629 Joe Hoerner .... .50 .20
❑ 630 Greg Luzinski .... 2.00 .80
❑ 631 Lee Lacy .... .50 .20

	No.	Player	NM	Ex
❑	632	Morris Nettles	.50	.20
❑	633	Paul Casanova	.50	.20
❑	634	Cy Acosta	.50	.20
❑	635	Chuck Dobson	.50	.20
❑	636	Charlie Moore	.50	.20
❑	637	Ted Martinez	.50	.20
❑	638	Cubs Team CL	2.00	.40
		Jim Marshall MG		
❑	639	Steve Kline	.50	.20
❑	640	Harmon Killebrew	6.00	2.40
❑	641	Jim Northrup	1.00	.40
❑	642	Mike Phillips	.50	.20
❑	643	Brent Strom	.50	.20
❑	644	Bill Fahey	.50	.20
❑	645	Danny Cater	.50	.20
❑	646	Checklist: 529-660	3.00	.60
❑	647	Cl. Washington RC	2.00	.80
❑	648	Dave Pagan	.50	.20
❑	649	Jack Heidemann	.50	.20
❑	650	Dave May	.50	.20
❑	651	John Morlan	.50	.20
❑	652	Lindy McDaniel	1.00	.40
❑	653	Lee Richard UER	.50	.20
		(Listed as Richards		
		on card front)		
❑	654	Jerry Terrell	.50	.20
❑	655	Rico Carty	1.00	.40
❑	656	Bill Plummer	.50	.20
❑	657	Bob Oliver	.50	.20
❑	658	Vic Harris	.50	.20
❑	659	Bob Apodaca	.50	.20
❑	660	Hank Aaron	30.00	9.00

1976 Topps

	No.	Player	NM	Ex
		COMPLETE SET (660)	250.00	100.00
❑	1	Hank Aaron RB	15.00	4.70
❑	2	Bobby Bonds RB	1.50	.60
❑	3	Mickey Lolich RB	.75	.30
❑	4	Dave Lopes RB	.75	.30
❑	5	Tom Seaver RB	5.00	2.00
❑	6	Rennie Stennett RB	.75	.30
❑	7	Jim Umbarger	.40	.16
❑	8	Tito Fuentes	.40	.16
❑	9	Paul Lindblad	.40	.16
❑	10	Lou Brock	5.00	2.00
❑	11	Jim Hughes	.40	.16
❑	12	Richie Zisk	.75	.30
❑	13	John Wockenfuss	.40	.16
❑	14	Gene Garber	.75	.30
❑	15	George Scott	.75	.30
❑	16	Bob Apodaca	.40	.16
❑	17	New York Yankees	1.50	.30
		Team Card CL		
		Billy Martin MG		
❑	18	Dale Murray	.40	.16
❑	19	George Brett	30.00	12.00
❑	20	Bob Watson	.75	.30
❑	21	Dave LaRoche	.40	.16
❑	22	Bill Russell	.75	.30
❑	23	Brian Downing	.40	.16
❑	24	Cesar Geronimo	.75	.30
❑	25	Mike Torrez	.75	.30
❑	26	Andre Thornton	.75	.30
❑	27	Ed Figueroa	.40	.16
❑	28	Dusty Baker	1.50	.60
❑	29	Rick Burleson	.75	.30
❑	30	John Montefusco	.75	.30
❑	31	Len Randle	.40	.16
❑	32	Danny Frisella	.40	.16
❑	33	Bill North	.40	.16
❑	34	Mike Garman	.40	.16
❑	35	Tony Oliva	1.50	.60
❑	36	Frank Taveras	.40	.16
❑	37	John Hiller	.75	.30
❑	38	Garry Maddox	.75	.30
❑	39	Pete Broberg	.40	.16
❑	40	Dave Kingman	1.50	.60
❑	41	Tippy Martinez	.75	.30
❑	42	Barry Foote	.40	.16
❑	43	Paul Splittorff	.40	.16
❑	44	Doug Rader	.75	.30
❑	45	Boog Powell	1.50	.60
❑	46	Los Angeles Dodgers	1.50	.30
		Team Card CL		
		Walter Alston MG		
❑	47	Jesse Jefferson	.40	.16
❑	48	Dave Concepcion	1.50	.60
❑	49	Dave Duncan	.75	.30
❑	50	Fred Lynn	1.50	.60
❑	51	Ray Burris	.40	.16
❑	52	Dave Chalk	.40	.16
❑	53	Mike Beard	.40	.16
❑	54	Dave Rader	.40	.16
❑	55	Gaylord Perry	2.50	1.00
❑	56	Bob Tolan	.40	.16
❑	57	Phil Garner	.75	.30
❑	58	Ron Reed	.40	.16
❑	59	Larry Hisle	.75	.30
❑	60	Jerry Reuss	.75	.30
❑	61	Ron LeFlore	.75	.30
❑	62	Johnny Oates	.75	.30
❑	63	Bobby Darwin	.40	.16
❑	64	Jerry Koosman	.75	.30
❑	65	Chris Chambliss	.75	.30
❑	66	Gus Bell FS	.75	.30
		Buddy Bell		
❑	67	Ray Boone FS	.75	.30
		Bob Boone		
❑	68	Joe Coleman FS	.40	.16
		Joe Coleman Jr.		
❑	69	Jim Hegan FS	.40	.16
		Mike Hegan		
❑	70	Roy Smalley FS	.75	.30
		Roy Smalley Jr.		
❑	71	Steve Rogers	.75	.30
❑	72	Hal McRae	.75	.30
❑	73	Baltimore Orioles	1.50	.30
		Team Card CL		
		Earl Weaver MG		
❑	74	Oscar Gamble	.75	.30
❑	75	Larry Dierker	.75	.30
❑	76	Willie Crawford	.40	.16
❑	77	Pedro Borbon	.75	.30
❑	78	Cecil Cooper	.75	.30
❑	79	Jerry Morales	.40	.16
❑	80	Jim Kaat	1.50	.60
❑	81	Darrell Evans	.75	.30
❑	82	Von Joshua	.40	.16
❑	83	Jim Spencer	.40	.16
❑	84	Brent Strom	.40	.16
❑	85	Mickey Rivers	.75	.30
❑	86	Mike Tyson	.40	.16
❑	87	Tom Burgmeier	.40	.16
❑	88	Duffy Dyer	.40	.16
❑	89	Vern Ruhle	.40	.16
❑	90	Sal Bando	.75	.30
❑	91	Tom Hutton	.40	.16
❑	92	Eduardo Rodriguez	.40	.16
❑	93	Mike Phillips	.40	.16
❑	94	Jim Dwyer	.40	.16
❑	95	Brooks Robinson	6.00	2.40
❑	96	Doug Bird	.40	.16
❑	97	Wilbur Howard	.40	.16
❑	98	Dennis Eckersley RC	25.00	10.00
❑	99	Lee Lacy	.40	.16
❑	100	Jim Hunter	3.00	1.20
❑	101	Pete LaCock	.40	.16
❑	102	Jim Willoughby	.40	.16
❑	103	Biff Pocoroba	.40	.16
❑	104	Cincinnati Reds	2.50	.50
		Team Card CL		
		Sparky Anderson MG		
❑	105	Gary Lavelle	.40	.16
❑	106	Tom Grieve	.75	.30
❑	107	Dave Roberts	.40	.16
❑	108	Don Kirkwood	.40	.16
❑	109	Larry Lintz	.40	.16
❑	110	Carlos May	.40	.16
❑	111	Danny Thompson	.40	.16
❑	112	Kent Tekulve RC	1.50	.60
❑	113	Gary Sutherland	.40	.16
❑	114	Jay Johnstone	.75	.30
❑	115	Ken Holtzman	.75	.30
❑	116	Charlie Moore	.40	.16
❑	117	Mike Jorgensen	.40	.16
❑	118	Boston Red Sox	1.50	.30
		Team Card CL		
		Darrell Johnson MG		
❑	119	Checklist 1-132	1.50	.30
❑	120	Rusty Staub	.75	.30
❑	121	Tony Solaita	.40	.16
❑	122	Mike Cosgrove	.40	.16
❑	123	Walt Williams	.40	.16
❑	124	Doug Rau	.40	.16
❑	125	Don Baylor	1.50	.60
❑	126	Tom Dettore	.40	.16
❑	127	Larvell Blanks	.40	.16
❑	128	Ken Griffey Sr.	2.50	1.00
❑	129	Andy Etchebarren	.40	.16
❑	130	Luis Tiant	1.50	.60
❑	131	Bill Stein	.40	.16
❑	132	Don Hood	.40	.16
❑	133	Gary Matthews	.75	.30
❑	134	Mike Ivie	.40	.16
❑	135	Bake McBride	.75	.30
❑	136	Dave Goltz	.40	.16
❑	137	Bill Robinson	.75	.30
❑	138	Lerrin LaGrow	.40	.16
❑	139	Gorman Thomas	.75	.30
❑	140	Vida Blue	.75	.30
❑	141	Larry Parrish RC	1.50	.60
❑	142	Dick Drago	.40	.16
❑	143	Jerry Grote	.40	.16
❑	144	Al Fitzmorris	.40	.16
❑	145	Larry Bowa	.75	.30
❑	146	George Medich	.40	.16
❑	147	Houston Astros	1.50	.30
		Team Card CL		
		Bill Virdon MG		
❑	148	Stan Thomas	.40	.16
❑	149	Tommy Davis	.75	.30
❑	150	Steve Garvey	2.50	1.00
❑	151	Bill Bonham	.40	.16
❑	152	Leroy Stanton	.40	.16
❑	153	Buzz Capra	.40	.16
❑	154	Bucky Dent	.75	.30
❑	155	Jack Billingham	.75	.30
❑	156	Rico Carty	.75	.30
❑	157	Mike Caldwell	.40	.16
❑	158	Ken Reitz	.40	.16
❑	159	Jerry Terrell	.40	.16
❑	160	Dave Winfield	10.00	4.00
❑	161	Bruce Kison	.40	.16
❑	162	Jack Pierce	.40	.16
❑	163	Jim Slaton	.40	.16
❑	164	Pepe Mangual	.40	.16
❑	165	Gene Tenace	.75	.30
❑	166	Skip Lockwood	.40	.16
❑	167	Freddie Patek	.75	.30
❑	168	Tom Hilgendorf	.40	.16
❑	169	Graig Nettles	1.50	.60
❑	170	Rick Wise	.40	.16
❑	171	Greg Gross	.40	.16
❑	172	Texas Rangers	1.50	.30
		Team Card CL		
		Frank Lucchesi MG		
❑	173	Steve Swisher	.40	.16
❑	174	Charlie Hough	.75	.30
❑	175	Ken Singleton	.75	.30
❑	176	Dick Lange	.40	.16
❑	177	Marty Perez	.40	.16
❑	178	Tom Buskey	.40	.16
❑	179	George Foster	1.50	.60
❑	180	Goose Gossage	1.50	.60
❑	181	Willie Montanez	.40	.16
❑	182	Harry Rasmussen	.40	.16
❑	183	Steve Braun	.40	.16

❑	184	Bill Greif	.40	.16
❑	185	Dave Parker	1.50	.60
❑	186	Tom Walker	.40	.16
❑	187	Pedro Garcia	.40	.16
❑	188	Fred Scherman	.40	.16
❑	189	Claudell Washington	.75	.30
❑	190	Jon Matlack	.40	.16
❑	191	Bill Madlock	.75	.30
		Ted Simmons		
		Manny Sanguillen LL		
❑	192	Rod Carew	2.50	1.00
		Fred Lynn		
		Thurman Munson LL		
❑	193	Mike Schmidt	3.00	1.20
		Dave Kingman		
		Greg Luzinski LL		
❑	194	Reggie Jackson	3.00	1.20
		George Scott		
		John Mayberry LL		
❑	195	Greg Luzinski	1.50	.60
		Johnny Bench		
		Tony Perez LL		
❑	196	George Scott	.75	.30
		John Mayberry		
		Fred Lynn LL		
❑	197	Dave Lopes	1.50	.60
		Joe Morgan		
		Lou Brock LL		
❑	198	Mickey Rivers	.75	.30
		Claudell Washington		
		Amos Otis LL		
❑	199	Tom Seaver	2.50	1.00
		Randy Jones		
		Andy Messersmith LL		
❑	200	Jim Hunter	1.50	.60
		Jim Palmer		
		Vida Blue LL		
❑	201	Randy Jones	1.50	.60
		Andy Messersmith		
		Tom Seaver LL		
❑	202	Jim Palmer	3.00	1.20
		Jim Hunter		
		Dennis Eckersley LL		
❑	203	Tom Seaver	2.50	1.00
		John Montefusco		
		Andy Messersmith LL		
❑	204	Frank Tanana	.75	.30
		Bert Blyleven		
		Gaylord Perry LL		
❑	205	Al Hrabosky	.75	.30
		Rich Gossage LL		
❑	206	Manny Trillo	.40	.16
❑	207	Andy Hassler	.40	.16
❑	208	Mike Lum	.40	.16
❑	209	Alan Ashby	.75	.30
❑	210	Lee May	.75	.30
❑	211	Clay Carroll	.75	.30
❑	212	Pat Kelly	.40	.16
❑	213	Dave Heaverlo	.40	.16
❑	214	Eric Soderholm	.40	.16
❑	215	Reggie Smith	.75	.30
❑	216	Montreal Expos	1.50	.30
		Team Card CL		
		Karl Kuehl MG		
❑	217	Dave Freisleben	.40	.16
❑	218	John Knox	.40	.16
❑	219	Tom Murphy	.40	.16
❑	220	Manny Sanguillen	.75	.30
❑	221	Jim Todd	.40	.16
❑	222	Wayne Garrett	.40	.16
❑	223	Ollie Brown	.40	.16
❑	224	Jim York	.40	.16
❑	225	Roy White	.75	.30
❑	226	Jim Sundberg	.75	.30
❑	227	Oscar Zamora	.40	.16
❑	228	John Hale	.40	.16
❑	229	Jerry Remy	.40	.16
❑	230	Carl Yastrzemski	10.00	4.00
❑	231	Tom House	.40	.16
❑	232	Frank Duffy	.40	.16
❑	233	Grant Jackson	.40	.16
❑	234	Mike Sadek	.40	.16
❑	235	Bert Blyleven	1.50	.60
❑	236	Kansas City Royals	1.50	.30
		Team Card CL		
		Whitey Herzog MG		
❑	237	Dave Hamilton	.40	.16
❑	238	Larry Biittner	.40	.16
❑	239	John Curtis	.40	.16
❑	240	Pete Rose	25.00	10.00
❑	241	Hector Torres	.40	.16
❑	242	Dan Meyer	.40	.16
❑	243	Jim Rooker	.40	.16
❑	244	Bill Sharp	.40	.16
❑	245	Felix Millan	.40	.16
❑	246	Cesar Tovar	.40	.16
❑	247	Terry Harmon	.40	.16
❑	248	Dick Tidrow	.40	.16
❑	249	Cliff Johnson	.75	.30
❑	250	Fergie Jenkins	2.50	1.00
❑	251	Rick Monday	.75	.30
❑	252	Tim Nordbrook	.40	.16
❑	253	Bill Buckner	.75	.30
❑	254	Rudy Meoli	.40	.16
❑	255	Fritz Peterson	.40	.16
❑	256	Rowland Office	.40	.16
❑	257	Ross Grimsley	.40	.16
❑	258	Nyls Nyman	.40	.16
❑	259	Darrel Chaney	.40	.16
❑	260	Steve Busby	.40	.16
❑	261	Gary Thomasson	.40	.16
❑	262	Checklist 133-264	1.50	.30
❑	263	Lyman Bostock RC	1.50	.60
❑	264	Steve Renko	.40	.16
❑	265	Willie Davis	.75	.30
❑	266	Alan Foster	.40	.16
❑	267	Aurelio Rodriguez	.40	.16
❑	268	Del Unser	.40	.16
❑	269	Rick Austin	.40	.16
❑	270	Willie Stargell	3.00	1.20
❑	271	Jim Lonborg	.75	.30
❑	272	Rick Dempsey	.75	.30
❑	273	Joe Niekro	.75	.30
❑	274	Tommy Harper	.75	.30
❑	275	Rick Manning	.40	.16
❑	276	Mickey Scott	.40	.16
❑	277	Chicago Cubs	1.50	.30
		Team Card CL		
		Jim Marshall MG		
❑	278	Bernie Carbo	.40	.16
❑	279	Roy Howell	.40	.16
❑	280	Burt Hooton	.75	.30
❑	281	Dave May	.40	.16
❑	282	Dan Osborn	.40	.16
❑	283	Merv Rettenmund	.40	.16
❑	284	Steve Ontiveros	.40	.16
❑	285	Mike Cuellar	.75	.30
❑	286	Jim Wohlford	.40	.16
❑	287	Pete Mackanin	.40	.16
❑	288	Bill Campbell	.40	.16
❑	289	Enzo Hernandez	.40	.16
❑	290	Ted Simmons	.75	.30
❑	291	Ken Sanders	.40	.16
❑	292	Leon Roberts	.40	.16
❑	293	Bill Castro	.40	.16
❑	294	Ed Kirkpatrick	.40	.16
❑	295	Dave Cash	.40	.16
❑	296	Pat Dobson	.40	.16
❑	297	Roger Metzger	.40	.16
❑	298	Dick Bosman	.40	.16
❑	299	Champ Summers	.40	.16
❑	300	Johnny Bench	12.00	4.80
❑	301	Jackie Brown	.40	.16
❑	302	Rick Miller	.40	.16
❑	303	Steve Foucault	.40	.16
❑	304	California Angels	1.50	.30
		Team Card CL		
		Dick Williams MG		
❑	305	Andy Messersmith	.75	.30
❑	306	Rod Gilbreath	.40	.16
❑	307	Al Bumbry	.75	.30
❑	308	Jim Barr	.40	.16
❑	309	Bill Melton	.40	.16
❑	310	Randy Jones	.75	.30
❑	311	Cookie Rojas	.40	.16
❑	312	Don Carrithers	.40	.16
❑	313	Dan Ford	.40	.16
❑	314	Ed Kranepool	.40	.16
❑	315	Al Hrabosky	.75	.30
❑	316	Robin Yount	15.00	6.00
❑	317	John Candelaria RC	1.50	.60
❑	318	Bob Boone	1.50	.60
❑	319	Larry Gura	.40	.16
❑	320	Willie Horton	.75	.30
❑	321	Jose Cruz	1.50	.60
❑	322	Glenn Abbott	.40	.16
❑	323	Rob Sperring	.40	.16
❑	324	Jim Bibby	.40	.16
❑	325	Tony Perez	3.00	1.20
❑	326	Dick Pole	.40	.16
❑	327	Dave Moates	.40	.16
❑	328	Carl Morton	.40	.16
❑	329	Joe Ferguson	.40	.16
❑	330	Nolan Ryan	25.00	10.00
❑	331	San Diego Padres	1.50	.30
		Team Card CL		
		John McNamara MG		
❑	332	Charlie Williams	.40	.16
❑	333	Bob Coluccio	.40	.16
❑	334	Dennis Leonard	.75	.30
❑	335	Bob Grich	.75	.30
❑	336	Vic Albury	.40	.16
❑	337	Bud Harrelson	.75	.30
❑	338	Bob Bailey	.40	.16
❑	339	John Denny	.75	.30
❑	340	Jim Rice	4.00	1.60
❑	341	Lou Gehrig ATG	12.00	4.80
❑	342	Rogers Hornsby ATG	3.00	1.20
❑	343	Pie Traynor ATG	1.50	.60
❑	344	Honus Wagner ATG	5.00	2.00
❑	345	Babe Ruth ATG	15.00	6.00
❑	346	Ty Cobb ATG	12.00	4.80
❑	347	Ted Williams ATG	12.00	4.80
❑	348	Mickey Cochrane ATG	1.50	.60
❑	349	Walter Johnson ATG	5.00	2.00
❑	350	Lefty Grove ATG	1.50	.60
❑	351	Randy Hundley	.75	.30
❑	352	Dave Giusti	.40	.16
❑	353	Sixto Lezcano	.75	.30
❑	354	Ron Blomberg	.40	.16
❑	355	Steve Carlton	6.00	2.40
❑	356	Ted Martinez	.40	.16
❑	357	Ken Forsch	.40	.16
❑	358	Buddy Bell	.75	.30
❑	359	Rick Reuschel	.75	.30
❑	360	Jeff Burroughs	.75	.30
❑	361	Detroit Tigers	1.50	.30
		Team Card CL		
		Ralph Houk MG		
❑	362	Will McEnaney	.75	.30
❑	363	Dave Collins RC	.75	.30
❑	364	Elias Sosa	.40	.16
❑	365	Carlton Fisk	6.00	2.40
❑	366	Bobby Valentine	.75	.30
❑	367	Bruce Miller	.40	.16
❑	368	Wilbur Wood	.40	.16
❑	369	Frank White	.75	.30
❑	370	Ron Cey	.75	.30
❑	371	Elrod Hendricks	.40	.16
❑	372	Rick Baldwin	.40	.16
❑	373	Johnny Briggs	.40	.16
❑	374	Dan Warthen	.40	.16
❑	375	Ron Fairly	.75	.30
❑	376	Rich Hebner	.75	.30
❑	377	Mike Hegan	.40	.16
❑	378	Steve Stone	.75	.30
❑	379	Ken Boswell	.40	.16
❑	380	Bobby Bonds	1.50	.60
❑	381	Denny Doyle	.40	.16
❑	382	Matt Alexander	.40	.16
❑	383	John Ellis	.40	.16
❑	384	Philadelphia Phillies	1.50	.30
		Team Card CL		
		Danny Ozark MG		
❑	385	Mickey Lolich	.75	.30
❑	386	Ed Goodson	.40	.16
❑	387	Mike Miley	.40	.16
❑	388	Stan Perzanowski	.40	.16
❑	389	Glenn Adams	.40	.16
❑	390	Don Gullett	.75	.30
❑	391	Jerry Hairston	.40	.16
❑	392	Checklist 265-396	1.50	.30
❑	393	Paul Mitchell	.40	.16
❑	394	Fran Healy	.40	.16
❑	395	Jim Wynn	.75	.30
❑	396	Bill Lee	.40	.16
❑	397	Tim Foli	.40	.16
❑	398	Dave Tomlin	.40	.16

No.	Card	NrMT	VG-E
❑ 399	Luis Melendez	.40	.16
❑ 400	Rod Carew	6.00	2.40
❑ 401	Ken Brett	.40	.16
❑ 402	Don Money	.75	.30
❑ 403	Geoff Zahn	.40	.16
❑ 404	Enos Cabell	.40	.16
❑ 405	Rollie Fingers	2.50	1.00
❑ 406	Ed Herrmann	.40	.16
❑ 407	Tom Underwood	.40	.16
❑ 408	Charlie Spikes	.40	.16
❑ 409	Dave Lemanczyk	.40	.16
❑ 410	Ralph Garr	.75	.30
❑ 411	Bill Singer	.40	.16
❑ 412	Toby Harrah	.75	.30
❑ 413	Pete Varney	.40	.16
❑ 414	Wayne Garland	.40	.16
❑ 415	Vada Pinson	1.50	.60
❑ 416	Tommy John	1.50	.60
❑ 417	Gene Clines	.40	.16
❑ 418	Jose Morales RC	.40	.16
❑ 419	Reggie Cleveland	.40	.16
❑ 420	Joe Morgan	5.00	2.00
❑ 421	Oakland A's	1.50	.30
	Team Card CL		
	(No MG on front)		
❑ 422	Johnny Grubb	.40	.16
❑ 423	Ed Halicki	.40	.16
❑ 424	Phil Roof	.40	.16
❑ 425	Rennie Stennett	.40	.16
❑ 426	Bob Forsch	.40	.16
❑ 427	Kurt Bevacqua	.40	.16
❑ 428	Jim Crawford	.40	.16
❑ 429	Fred Stanley	.40	.16
❑ 430	Jose Cardenal	.75	.30
❑ 431	Dick Ruthven	.40	.16
❑ 432	Tom Veryzer	.40	.16
❑ 433	Rick Waits	.40	.16
❑ 434	Morris Nettles	.40	.16
❑ 435	Phil Niekro	2.50	1.00
❑ 436	Bill Fahey	.40	.16
❑ 437	Terry Forster	.40	.16
❑ 438	Doug DeCinces	.75	.30
❑ 439	Rick Rhoden	.75	.30
❑ 440	John Mayberry	.75	.30
❑ 441	Gary Carter	4.00	1.60
❑ 442	Hank Webb	.40	.16
❑ 443	San Francisco Giants	1.50	.30
	Team Card CL		
	(No MG on front)		
❑ 444	Gary Nolan	.75	.30
❑ 445	Rico Petrocelli	.75	.30
❑ 446	Larry Haney	.40	.16
❑ 447	Gene Locklear	.75	.30
❑ 448	Tom Johnson	.40	.16
❑ 449	Bob Robertson	.40	.16
❑ 450	Jim Palmer	5.00	2.00
❑ 451	Buddy Bradford	.40	.16
❑ 452	Tom Hausman	.40	.16
❑ 453	Lou Piniella	1.50	.60
❑ 454	Tom Griffin	.40	.16
❑ 455	Dick Allen	1.50	.60
❑ 456	Joe Coleman	.40	.16
❑ 457	Ed Crosby	.40	.16
❑ 458	Earl Williams	.40	.16
❑ 459	Jim Brewer	.40	.16
❑ 460	Cesar Cedeno	.75	.30
❑ 461	NL and AL Champs	.75	.30
	Reds sweep Bucs,		
	Bosox surprise A's		
❑ 462	'75 World Series	.75	.30
	Reds Champs		
❑ 463	Steve Hargan	.40	.16
❑ 464	Ken Henderson	.40	.16
❑ 465	Mike Marshall	.75	.30
❑ 466	Bob Stinson	.40	.16
❑ 467	Woodie Fryman	.40	.16
❑ 468	Jesus Alou	.40	.16
❑ 469	Rawly Eastwick	.75	.30
❑ 470	Bobby Murcer	.75	.30
❑ 471	Jim Burton	.40	.16
❑ 472	Bob Davis	.40	.16
❑ 473	Paul Blair	.75	.30
❑ 474	Ray Corbin	.40	.16
❑ 475	Joe Rudi	.75	.30
❑ 476	Bob Moose	.40	.16
❑ 477	Cleveland Indians	1.50	.30
	Team Card CL		
	Frank Robinson MG		
❑ 478	Lynn McGlothen	.40	.16
❑ 479	Bobby Mitchell	.40	.16
❑ 480	Mike Schmidt	15.00	6.00
❑ 481	Rudy May	.40	.16
❑ 482	Tim Hosley	.40	.16
❑ 483	Mickey Stanley	.40	.16
❑ 484	Eric Raich	.40	.16
❑ 485	Mike Hargrove	.75	.30
❑ 486	Bruce Dal Canton	.40	.16
❑ 487	Leron Lee	.40	.16
❑ 488	Claude Osteen	.75	.30
❑ 489	Skip Jutze	.40	.16
❑ 490	Frank Tanana	.75	.30
❑ 491	Terry Crowley	.40	.16
❑ 492	Marty Pattin	.40	.16
❑ 493	Derrel Thomas	.40	.16
❑ 494	Craig Swan	.75	.30
❑ 495	Nate Colbert	.40	.16
❑ 496	Juan Beniquez	.40	.16
❑ 497	Joe McIntosh	.40	.16
❑ 498	Glenn Borgmann	.40	.16
❑ 499	Mario Guerrero	.40	.16
❑ 500	Reggie Jackson	12.00	4.80
❑ 501	Billy Champion	.40	.16
❑ 502	Tim McCarver	1.50	.60
❑ 503	Elliott Maddox	.40	.16
❑ 504	Pittsburgh Pirates	1.50	.30
	Team Card CL		
	Danny Murtaugh MG		
❑ 505	Mark Belanger	.75	.30
❑ 506	George Mitterwald	.40	.16
❑ 507	Ray Bare	.40	.16
❑ 508	Duane Kuiper	.40	.16
❑ 509	Bill Hands	.40	.16
❑ 510	Amos Otis	.75	.30
❑ 511	Jamie Easterley	.40	.16
❑ 512	Ellie Rodriguez	.40	.16
❑ 513	Bart Johnson	.40	.16
❑ 514	Dan Driessen	.75	.30
❑ 515	Steve Yeager	.75	.30
❑ 516	Wayne Granger	.40	.16
❑ 517	John Milner	.40	.16
❑ 518	Doug Flynn	.40	.16
❑ 519	Steve Brye	.40	.16
❑ 520	Willie McCovey	5.00	2.00
❑ 521	Jim Colborn	.40	.16
❑ 522	Ted Sizemore	.40	.16
❑ 523	Bob Montgomery	.40	.16
❑ 524	Pete Falcone	.40	.16
❑ 525	Billy Williams	2.50	1.00
❑ 526	Checklist 397-528	1.50	.30
❑ 527	Mike Anderson	.40	.16
❑ 528	Dock Ellis	.40	.16
❑ 529	Deron Johnson	.40	.16
❑ 530	Don Sutton	2.50	1.00
❑ 531	New York Mets	1.50	.30
	Team Card CL		
	Joe Frazier MG		
❑ 532	Milt May	.40	.16
❑ 533	Lee Richard	.40	.16
❑ 534	Stan Bahnsen	.40	.16
❑ 535	Dave Nelson	.40	.16
❑ 536	Mike Thompson	.40	.16
❑ 537	Tony Muser	.40	.16
❑ 538	Pat Darcy	.40	.16
❑ 539	John Balaz	.40	.16
❑ 540	Bill Freehan	.75	.30
❑ 541	Steve Mingori	.40	.16
❑ 542	Keith Hernandez	.75	.30
❑ 543	Wayne Twitchell	.40	.16
❑ 544	Pepe Frias	.40	.16
❑ 545	Sparky Lyle	.75	.30
❑ 546	Dave Rosello	.40	.16
❑ 547	Roric Harrison	.40	.16
❑ 548	Manny Mota	.75	.30
❑ 549	Randy Tate	.40	.16
❑ 550	Hank Aaron	25.00	10.00
❑ 551	Jerry DaVanon	.40	.16
❑ 552	Terry Humphrey	.40	.16
❑ 553	Randy Moffitt	.40	.16
❑ 554	Ray Fosse	.40	.16
❑ 555	Dyar Miller	.40	.16
❑ 556	Minnesota Twins	1.50	.30
	Team Card CL		
	Gene Mauch MG		
❑ 557	Dan Spillner	.40	.16
❑ 558	Clarence Gaston	.75	.30
❑ 559	Clyde Wright	.40	.16
❑ 560	Jorge Orta	.40	.16
❑ 561	Tom Carroll	.40	.16
❑ 562	Adrian Garrett	.40	.16
❑ 563	Larry Demery	.40	.16
❑ 564	Bubble Gum Champ	1.50	.60
	Kurt Bevacqua		
❑ 565	Tug McGraw	.75	.30
❑ 566	Ken McMullen	.40	.16
❑ 567	George Stone	.40	.16
❑ 568	Rob Andrews	.40	.16
❑ 569	Nelson Briles	.75	.30
❑ 570	George Hendrick	.75	.30
❑ 571	Don DeMola	.40	.16
❑ 572	Rich Coggins	.40	.16
❑ 573	Bill Travers	.40	.16
❑ 574	Don Kessinger	.75	.30
❑ 575	Dwight Evans	1.50	.60
❑ 576	Maximino Leon	.40	.16
❑ 577	Marc Hill	.40	.16
❑ 578	Ted Kubiak	.40	.16
❑ 579	Clay Kirby	.40	.16
❑ 580	Bert Campaneris	.75	.30
❑ 581	St. Louis Cardinals	1.50	.30
	Team Card CL		
	Red Schoendienst MG		
❑ 582	Mike Kekich	.40	.16
❑ 583	Tommy Helms	.40	.16
❑ 584	Stan Wall	.40	.16
❑ 585	Joe Torre	1.50	.60
❑ 586	Ron Schueler	.40	.16
❑ 587	Leo Cardenas	.40	.16
❑ 588	Kevin Kobel	.40	.16
❑ 589	Santo Alcala	1.50	.60
	Mike Flanagan RC		
	Joe Pactwa		
	Pablo Torrealba		
❑ 590	Henry Cruz	.75	.30
	Chet Lemon RC		
	Ellis Valentine		
	Terry Whitfield		
❑ 591	Steve Grilli	.75	.30
	Craig Mitchell		
	Jose Sosa		
	George Throop		
❑ 592	Willie Randolph RC	5.00	2.00
	Dave McKay		
	Jerry Royster		
	Roy Staiger		
❑ 593	Larry Anderson	.75	.30
	Ken Crosby		
	Mark Littell		
	Butch Metzger		
❑ 594	Andy Merchant	.75	.30
	Ed Ott		
	Royle Stillman		
	Jerry White		
❑ 595	Art DeFillipis	.75	.30
	Randy Lerch		
	Sid Monge		
	Steve Barr		
❑ 596	Craig Reynolds	.75	.30
	Lamar Johnson		
	Johnnie LeMaster		
	Jerry Manuel RC		
❑ 597	Don Aase	.75	.30
	Jack Kucek		
	Frank LaCorte		
	Mike Pazik		
❑ 598	Hector Cruz	.75	.30
	Jamie Quirk		
	Jerry Turner		
	Joe Wallis		
❑ 599	Rob Dressler	8.00	3.20
	Ron Guidry RC		
	Bob McClure		
	Pat Zachry		
❑ 600	Tom Seaver	10.00	4.00
❑ 601	Ken Rudolph	.40	.16
❑ 602	Doug Konieczny	.40	.16
❑ 603	Jim Holt	.40	.16
❑ 604	Joe Lovitto	.40	.16
❑ 605	Al Downing	.40	.16

Card	NM	Ex
❑ 606 Milwaukee Brewers	1.50	.30
Team Card CL		
Alex Grammas MG		
❑ 607 Rich Hinton	.40	.16
❑ 608 Vic Correll	.40	.16
❑ 609 Fred Norman	.40	.16
❑ 610 Greg Luzinski	1.50	.60
❑ 611 Rich Folkers	.40	.16
❑ 612 Joe Lahoud	.40	.16
❑ 613 Tim Johnson	.40	.16
❑ 614 Fernando Arroyo	.40	.16
❑ 615 Mike Cubbage	.40	.16
❑ 616 Buck Martinez	.40	.16
❑ 617 Darold Knowles	.40	.16
❑ 618 Jack Brohamer	.40	.16
❑ 619 Bill Butler	.40	.16
❑ 620 Al Oliver	.75	.30
❑ 621 Tom Hall	.40	.16
❑ 622 Rick Auerbach	.40	.16
❑ 623 Bob Allietta	.40	.16
❑ 624 Tony Taylor	.40	.16
❑ 625 J.R. Richard	.75	.30
❑ 626 Bob Sheldon	.40	.16
❑ 627 Bill Plummer	.40	.16
❑ 628 John D'Acquisto	.40	.16
❑ 629 Sandy Alomar	.75	.30
❑ 630 Chris Speier	.40	.16
❑ 631 Atlanta Braves	1.50	.30
Team Card CL		
Dave Bristol MG		
❑ 632 Rogelio Moret	.40	.16
❑ 633 John Stearns RC	.75	.30
❑ 634 Larry Christenson	.40	.16
❑ 635 Jim Fregosi	.75	.30
❑ 636 Joe Decker	.40	.16
❑ 637 Bruce Bochte	.40	.16
❑ 638 Doyle Alexander	.75	.30
❑ 639 Fred Kendall	.40	.16
❑ 640 Bill Madlock	1.50	.60
❑ 641 Tom Paciorek	.75	.30
❑ 642 Dennis Blair	.40	.16
❑ 643 Checklist 529-660	1.50	.30
❑ 644 Tom Bradley	.40	.16
❑ 645 Darrell Porter	.75	.30
❑ 646 John Lowenstein	.40	.16
❑ 647 Ramon Hernandez	.40	.16
❑ 648 Al Cowens	.40	.16
❑ 649 Dave Roberts	.40	.16
❑ 650 Thurman Munson	6.00	2.40
❑ 651 John Odom	.40	.16
❑ 652 Ed Armbrister	.40	.16
❑ 653 Mike Norris RC	.75	.30
❑ 654 Doug Griffin	.40	.16
❑ 655 Mike Vail	.40	.16
❑ 656 Chicago White Sox	1.50	.30
Team Card CL		
Chuck Tanner MG		
❑ 657 Roy Smalley RC	.75	.30
❑ 658 Jerry Johnson	.40	.16
❑ 659 Ben Oglivie	.75	.30
❑ 660 Dave Lopes	1.50	.30

1977 Topps

	NM	Ex
COMPLETE SET (660)	225.00	90.00
❑ 1 George Brett	8.00	2.30
Bill Madlock LL		
❑ 2 Graig Nettles	2.50	1.00
Mike Schmidt LL		
❑ 3 Lee May	1.50	.60
George Foster LL		
❑ 4 Bill North	.75	.30
Dave Lopes LL		
❑ 5 Jim Palmer	1.50	.60
Randy Jones LL		
❑ 6 Nolan Ryan	15.00	6.00
Tom Seaver LL		
❑ 7 Mark Fidrych	.75	.30
John Denny LL		
❑ 8 Bill Campbell	.75	.30
Rawly Eastwick LL		
❑ 9 Doug Rader	.30	.12
❑ 10 Reggie Jackson	10.00	4.00
❑ 11 Rob Dressler	.30	.12
❑ 12 Larry Haney	.30	.12
❑ 13 Luis Gomez	.30	.12
❑ 14 Tommy Smith	.30	.12
❑ 15 Don Gullett	.75	.30
❑ 16 Bob Jones	.30	.12
❑ 17 Steve Stone	.75	.30
❑ 18 Indians Team CL	1.50	.30
Frank Robinson MG		
❑ 19 John D'Acquisto	.30	.12
❑ 20 Graig Nettles	1.50	.60
❑ 21 Ken Forsch	.30	.12
❑ 22 Bill Freehan	.75	.30
❑ 23 Dan Driessen	.30	.12
❑ 24 Carl Morton	.30	.12
❑ 25 Dwight Evans	1.50	.60
❑ 26 Ray Sadecki	.30	.12
❑ 27 Bill Buckner	.75	.30
❑ 28 Woodie Fryman	.30	.12
❑ 29 Bucky Dent	.75	.30
❑ 30 Greg Luzinski	1.50	.60
❑ 31 Jim Todd	.30	.12
❑ 32 Checklist 1-132	1.50	.30
❑ 33 Wayne Garland	.30	.12
❑ 34 Angels Team CL	1.50	.30
Norm Sherry MG		
❑ 35 Rennie Stennett	.30	.12
❑ 36 John Ellis	.30	.12
❑ 37 Steve Hargan	.30	.12
❑ 38 Craig Kusick	.30	.12
❑ 39 Tom Griffin	.30	.12
❑ 40 Bobby Murcer	.75	.30
❑ 41 Jim Kern	.30	.12
❑ 42 Jose Cruz	.75	.30
❑ 43 Ray Bare	.30	.12
❑ 44 Bud Harrelson	.75	.30
❑ 45 Rawly Eastwick	.30	.12
❑ 46 Buck Martinez	.30	.12
❑ 47 Lynn McGlothen	.30	.12
❑ 48 Tom Paciorek	.75	.30
❑ 49 Grant Jackson	.30	.12
❑ 50 Ron Cey	.75	.30
❑ 51 Brewers Team CL	1.50	.30
Alex Grammas MG		
❑ 52 Ellis Valentine	.30	.12
❑ 53 Paul Mitchell	.30	.12
❑ 54 Sandy Alomar	.75	.30
❑ 55 Jeff Burroughs	.75	.30
❑ 56 Rudy May	.30	.12
❑ 57 Marc Hill	.30	.12
❑ 58 Chet Lemon	.75	.30
❑ 59 Larry Christenson	.30	.12
❑ 60 Jim Rice	2.50	1.00
❑ 61 Manny Sanguillen	.75	.30
❑ 62 Eric Raich	.30	.12
❑ 63 Tito Fuentes	.30	.12
❑ 64 Larry Biittner	.30	.12
❑ 65 Skip Lockwood	.30	.12
❑ 66 Roy Smalley	.75	.30
❑ 67 Joaquin Andujar RC	.75	.30
❑ 68 Bruce Bochte	.30	.12
❑ 69 Jim Crawford	.30	.12
❑ 70 Johnny Bench	10.00	4.00
❑ 71 Dock Ellis	.30	.12
❑ 72 Mike Anderson	.30	.12
❑ 73 Charlie Williams	.30	.12
❑ 74 A's Team CL	1.50	.30
Jack McKeon MG		
❑ 75 Dennis Leonard	.75	.30
❑ 76 Tim Foli	.30	.12
❑ 77 Dyar Miller	.30	.12
❑ 78 Bob Davis	.30	.12
❑ 79 Don Money	.75	.30
❑ 80 Andy Messersmith	.75	.30
❑ 81 Juan Beniquez	.30	.12
❑ 82 Jim Rooker	.30	.12
❑ 83 Kevin Bell	.30	.12
❑ 84 Ollie Brown	.30	.12
❑ 85 Duane Kuiper	.30	.12
❑ 86 Pat Zachry	.30	.12
❑ 87 Glenn Borgmann	.30	.12
❑ 88 Stan Wall	.30	.12
❑ 89 Butch Hobson RC	.75	.30
❑ 90 Cesar Cedeno	.75	.30
❑ 91 John Verhoeven	.30	.12
❑ 92 Dave Rosello	.30	.12
❑ 93 Tom Poquette	.30	.12
❑ 94 Craig Swan	.30	.12
❑ 95 Keith Hernandez	.75	.30
❑ 96 Lou Piniella	.75	.30
❑ 97 Dave Heaverlo	.30	.12
❑ 98 Milt May	.30	.12
❑ 99 Tom Hausman	.30	.12
❑ 100 Joe Morgan	4.00	1.60
❑ 101 Dick Bosman	.30	.12
❑ 102 Jose Morales	.30	.12
❑ 103 Mike Bacsik	.30	.12
❑ 104 Omar Moreno	.75	.30
❑ 105 Steve Yeager	.75	.30
❑ 106 Mike Flanagan	.75	.30
❑ 107 Bill Melton	.30	.12
❑ 108 Alan Foster	.30	.12
❑ 109 Jorge Orta	.30	.12
❑ 110 Steve Carlton	5.00	2.00
❑ 111 Rico Petrocelli	.75	.30
❑ 112 Bill Greif	.30	.12
❑ 113 Blue Jays Leaders	1.50	.30
Roy Hartsfield MG		
Don Leppert CO		
Bob Miller CO		
Jackie Moore CO		
Harry Warner CO		
❑ 114 Bruce Dal Canton	.30	.12
❑ 115 Rick Manning	.30	.12
❑ 116 Joe Niekro	.75	.30
❑ 117 Frank White	.75	.30
❑ 118 Rick Jones	.30	.12
❑ 119 John Stearns	.30	.12
❑ 120 Rod Carew	5.00	2.00
❑ 121 Gary Nolan	.30	.12
❑ 122 Ben Oglivie	.75	.30
❑ 123 Fred Stanley	.30	.12
❑ 124 George Mitterwald	.30	.12
❑ 125 Bill Travers	.30	.12
❑ 126 Rod Gilbreath	.30	.12
❑ 127 Ron Fairly	.75	.30
❑ 128 Tommy John	1.50	.60
❑ 129 Mike Sadek	.30	.12
❑ 130 Al Oliver	.75	.30
❑ 131 Orlando Ramirez	.30	.12
❑ 132 Chip Lang	.30	.12
❑ 133 Ralph Garr	.75	.30
❑ 134 Padres Team CL	1.50	.30
John McNamara MG		
❑ 135 Mark Belanger	.75	.30
❑ 136 Jerry Mumphrey	.75	.30
❑ 137 Jeff Terpko	.30	.12
❑ 138 Bob Stinson	.30	.12
❑ 139 Fred Norman	.30	.12
❑ 140 Mike Schmidt	12.00	4.80
❑ 141 Mark Littell	.30	.12
❑ 142 Steve Dillard	.30	.12
❑ 143 Ed Herrmann	.30	.12
❑ 144 Bruce Sutter RC	5.00	2.00
❑ 145 Tom Veryzer	.30	.12
❑ 146 Dusty Baker	1.50	.60
❑ 147 Jackie Brown	.30	.12
❑ 148 Fran Healy	.30	.12
❑ 149 Mike Cubbage	.30	.12
❑ 150 Tom Seaver	8.00	3.20
❑ 151 Johnny LeMaster	.30	.12
❑ 152 Gaylord Perry	2.50	1.00
❑ 153 Ron Jackson RC	.30	.12
❑ 154 Dave Giusti	.30	.12
❑ 155 Joe Rudi	.75	.30

- ❑ 156 Pete Mackanin .30 .12
- ❑ 157 Ken Brett .30 .12
- ❑ 158 Ted Kubiak .30 .12
- ❑ 159 Bernie Carbo .30 .12
- ❑ 160 Will McEnaney .30 .12
- ❑ 161 Garry Templeton RC 1.50 .60
- ❑ 162 Mike Cuellar .75 .30
- ❑ 163 Dave Hilton .30 .12
- ❑ 164 Tug McGraw .75 .30
- ❑ 165 Jim Wynn .75 .30
- ❑ 166 Bill Campbell .30 .12
- ❑ 167 Rich Hebner .75 .30
- ❑ 168 Charlie Spikes .30 .12
- ❑ 169 Darold Knowles .30 .12
- ❑ 170 Thurman Munson 5.00 2.00
- ❑ 171 Ken Sanders .30 .12
- ❑ 172 John Milner .30 .12
- ❑ 173 Chuck Scrivener .30 .12
- ❑ 174 Nelson Briles .75 .30
- ❑ 175 Butch Wynegar .75 .30
- ❑ 176 Bob Robertson .30 .12
- ❑ 177 Bart Johnson .30 .12
- ❑ 178 Bombo Rivera .30 .12
- ❑ 179 Paul Hartzell .30 .12
- ❑ 180 Dave Lopes .75 .30
- ❑ 181 Ken McMullen .30 .12
- ❑ 182 Dan Spillner .30 .12
- ❑ 183 Cardinals Team CL 1.50 .30
  Vern Rapp MG
- ❑ 184 Bo McLaughlin .30 .12
- ❑ 185 Sixto Lezcano .30 .12
- ❑ 186 Doug Flynn .30 .12
- ❑ 187 Dick Pole .30 .12
- ❑ 188 Bob Tolan .30 .12
- ❑ 189 Rick Dempsey .75 .30
- ❑ 190 Ray Burris .30 .12
- ❑ 191 Doug Griffin .30 .12
- ❑ 192 Clarence Gaston .75 .30
- ❑ 193 Larry Gura .30 .12
- ❑ 194 Gary Matthews .75 .30
- ❑ 195 Ed Figueroa .30 .12
- ❑ 196 Len Randle .30 .12
- ❑ 197 Ed Ott .30 .12
- ❑ 198 Wilbur Wood .30 .12
- ❑ 199 Pepe Frias .30 .12
- ❑ 200 Frank Tanana .75 .30
- ❑ 201 Ed Kranepool .30 .12
- ❑ 202 Tom Johnson .30 .12
- ❑ 203 Ed Armbrister .30 .12
- ❑ 204 Jeff Newman .30 .12
- ❑ 205 Pete Falcone .30 .12
- ❑ 206 Boog Powell 1.50 .60
- ❑ 207 Glenn Abbott .30 .12
- ❑ 208 Checklist 133-264 1.50 .30
- ❑ 209 Rob Andrews .30 .12
- ❑ 210 Fred Lynn .75 .15
- ❑ 211 Giants Team CL 1.50 .60
  Joe Altobelli MG
- ❑ 212 Jim Mason .30 .12
- ❑ 213 Maximino Leon .30 .12
- ❑ 214 Darrell Porter .75 .30
- ❑ 215 Butch Metzger .30 .12
- ❑ 216 Doug DeCinces .75 .30
- ❑ 217 Tom Underwood .30 .12
- ❑ 218 John Wathan RC .75 .30
- ❑ 219 Joe Coleman .30 .12
- ❑ 220 Chris Chambliss .75 .30
- ❑ 221 Bob Bailey .30 .12
- ❑ 222 Francisco Barrios .30 .12
- ❑ 223 Earl Williams .30 .12
- ❑ 224 Rusty Torres .30 .12
- ❑ 225 Bob Apodaca .30 .12
- ❑ 226 Leroy Stanton .75 .30
- ❑ 227 Joe Sambito .30 .12
- ❑ 228 Twins Team CL 1.50 .30
  Gene Mauch MG
- ❑ 229 Don Kessinger .75 .30
- ❑ 230 Vida Blue .75 .30
- ❑ 231 George Brett RB 8.00 3.20
- ❑ 232 Minnie Minoso RB .75 .30
- ❑ 233 Jose Morales RB .30 .12
- ❑ 234 Nolan Ryan RB 15.00 6.00
- ❑ 235 Cecil Cooper .75 .30
- ❑ 236 Tom Buskey .30 .12
- ❑ 237 Gene Clines .30 .12
- ❑ 238 Tippy Martinez .30 .12
- ❑ 239 Bill Plummer .30 .12
- ❑ 240 Ron LeFlore .75 .30
- ❑ 241 Dave Tomlin .30 .12
- ❑ 242 Ken Henderson .30 .12
- ❑ 243 Ron Reed .30 .12
- ❑ 244 John Mayberry .75 .30
  (Cartoon mentions T206 Wagner)
- ❑ 245 Rick Rhoden .75 .30
- ❑ 246 Mike Vail .30 .12
- ❑ 247 Chris Knapp .30 .12
- ❑ 248 Wilbur Howard .30 .12
- ❑ 249 Pete Redfern .30 .12
- ❑ 250 Bill Madlock .75 .30
- ❑ 251 Tony Muser .30 .12
- ❑ 252 Dale Murray .30 .12
- ❑ 253 John Hale .30 .12
- ❑ 254 Doyle Alexander .30 .12
- ❑ 255 George Scott .75 .30
- ❑ 256 Joe Hoerner .30 .12
- ❑ 257 Mike Miley .30 .12
- ❑ 258 Luis Tiant .75 .30
- ❑ 259 Mets Team CL 1.50 .30
  Joe Frazier MG
- ❑ 260 J.R. Richard .75 .30
- ❑ 261 Phil Garner .75 .30
- ❑ 262 Al Cowens .30 .12
- ❑ 263 Mike Marshall .75 .30
- ❑ 264 Tom Hutton .30 .12
- ❑ 265 Mark Fidrych RC 3.00 1.20
- ❑ 266 Derrel Thomas .30 .12
- ❑ 267 Ray Fosse .30 .12
- ❑ 268 Rick Sawyer .30 .12
- ❑ 269 Joe Lis .30 .12
- ❑ 270 Dave Parker 1.50 .60
- ❑ 271 Terry Forster .30 .12
- ❑ 272 Lee Lacy .30 .12
- ❑ 273 Eric Soderholm .30 .12
- ❑ 274 Don Stanhouse .30 .12
- ❑ 275 Mike Hargrove .75 .30
- ❑ 276 C.Chambliss ALCS 1.50 .60
  homer decides it
- ❑ 277 Pete Rose NLCS 5.00 2.00
- ❑ 278 Danny Frisella .30 .12
- ❑ 279 Joe Wallis .30 .12
- ❑ 280 Jim Hunter 2.50 1.00
- ❑ 281 Roy Staiger .30 .12
- ❑ 282 Sid Monge .30 .12
- ❑ 283 Jerry DaVanon .30 .12
- ❑ 284 Mike Norris .30 .12
- ❑ 285 Brooks Robinson 5.00 2.00
- ❑ 286 Johnny Grubb .30 .06
- ❑ 287 Reds Team CL 1.50 .60
  Sparky Anderson MG
- ❑ 288 Bob Montgomery .30 .12
- ❑ 289 Gene Garber .75 .30
- ❑ 290 Amos Otis .75 .30
- ❑ 291 Jason Thompson RC .75 .30
- ❑ 292 Rogelio Moret .30 .12
- ❑ 293 Jack Brohamer .30 .12
- ❑ 294 George Medich .30 .12
- ❑ 295 Gary Carter 2.50 1.00
- ❑ 296 Don Hood .30 .12
- ❑ 297 Ken Reitz .30 .12
- ❑ 298 Charlie Hough .75 .30
- ❑ 299 Otto Velez .75 .30
- ❑ 300 Jerry Koosman .75 .30
- ❑ 301 Toby Harrah .75 .30
- ❑ 302 Mike Garman .30 .12
- ❑ 303 Gene Tenace .75 .30
- ❑ 304 Jim Hughes .30 .12
- ❑ 305 Mickey Rivers .75 .30
- ❑ 306 Rick Waits .30 .12
- ❑ 307 Gary Sutherland .30 .12
- ❑ 308 Gene Pentz .30 .12
- ❑ 309 Red Sox Team CL 1.50 .30
  Don Zimmer MG
- ❑ 310 Larry Bowa .75 .30
- ❑ 311 Vern Ruhle .30 .12
- ❑ 312 Rob Belloir .30 .12
- ❑ 313 Paul Blair .75 .30
- ❑ 314 Steve Mingori .30 .12
- ❑ 315 Dave Chalk .30 .12
- ❑ 316 Steve Rogers .30 .12
- ❑ 317 Kurt Bevacqua .30 .12
- ❑ 318 Duffy Dyer .30 .12
- ❑ 319 Goose Gossage 1.50 .60
- ❑ 320 Ken Griffey Sr. 1.50 .60
- ❑ 321 Dave Goltz .30 .12
- ❑ 322 Bill Russell .75 .30
- ❑ 323 Larry Lintz .30 .12
- ❑ 324 John Curtis .30 .12
- ❑ 325 Mike Ivie .30 .12
- ❑ 326 Jesse Jefferson .30 .12
- ❑ 327 Astros Team CL 1.50 .30
  Bill Virdon MG
- ❑ 328 Tommy Boggs .30 .12
- ❑ 329 Ron Hodges .30 .12
- ❑ 330 George Hendrick .75 .30
- ❑ 331 Jim Colborn .30 .12
- ❑ 332 Elliott Maddox .30 .12
- ❑ 333 Paul Reuschel .30 .12
- ❑ 334 Bill Stein .30 .12
- ❑ 335 Bill Robinson .75 .30
- ❑ 336 Denny Doyle .30 .12
- ❑ 337 Ron Schueler .30 .12
- ❑ 338 Dave Duncan .75 .30
- ❑ 339 Adrian Devine .30 .12
- ❑ 340 Hal McRae .75 .30
- ❑ 341 Joe Kerrigan .30 .12
- ❑ 342 Jerry Remy .30 .12
- ❑ 343 Ed Halicki .30 .12
- ❑ 344 Brian Downing .75 .30
- ❑ 345 Reggie Smith .75 .30
- ❑ 346 Bill Singer .30 .12
- ❑ 347 George Foster 1.50 .60
- ❑ 348 Brent Strom .30 .12
- ❑ 349 Jim Holt .30 .12
- ❑ 350 Larry Dierker .75 .30
- ❑ 351 Jim Sundberg .75 .30
- ❑ 352 Mike Phillips .30 .12
- ❑ 353 Stan Thomas .30 .12
- ❑ 354 Pirates Team CL 1.50 .30
  Chuck Tanner MG
- ❑ 355 Lou Brock 4.00 1.60
- ❑ 356 Checklist 265-396 1.50 .30
- ❑ 357 Tim McCarver 1.50 .60
- ❑ 358 Tom House .30 .12
- ❑ 359 Willie Randolph 1.50 .60
- ❑ 360 Rick Monday .75 .30
- ❑ 361 Eduardo Rodriguez .30 .12
- ❑ 362 Tommy Davis .75 .30
- ❑ 363 Dave Roberts .30 .12
- ❑ 364 Vic Correll .30 .12
- ❑ 365 Mike Torrez .75 .30
- ❑ 366 Ted Sizemore .30 .12
- ❑ 367 Dave Hamilton .30 .12
- ❑ 368 Mike Jorgensen .30 .12
- ❑ 369 Terry Humphrey .30 .12
- ❑ 370 John Montefusco .30 .12
- ❑ 371 Royals Team CL 1.50 .30
  Whitey Herzog MG
- ❑ 372 Rich Folkers .30 .12
- ❑ 373 Bert Campaneris .75 .30
- ❑ 374 Kent Tekulve .75 .30
- ❑ 375 Larry Hisle .75 .30
- ❑ 376 Nino Espinosa .30 .12
- ❑ 377 Dave McKay .30 .12
- ❑ 378 Jim Umbarger .30 .12
- ❑ 379 Larry Cox .30 .12
- ❑ 380 Lee May .75 .30
- ❑ 381 Bob Forsch .30 .12
- ❑ 382 Charlie Moore .30 .12
- ❑ 383 Stan Bahnsen .30 .12
- ❑ 384 Darrel Chaney .30 .12
- ❑ 385 Dave LaRoche .30 .12
- ❑ 386 Manny Mota .75 .30
- ❑ 387 Yankees Team CL 2.50 .50
  Billy Martin MG
- ❑ 388 Terry Harmon .30 .12
- ❑ 389 Ken Kravec .30 .12
- ❑ 390 Dave Winfield 6.00 2.40
- ❑ 391 Dan Warthen .30 .12
- ❑ 392 Phil Roof .30 .12
- ❑ 393 John Lowenstein .30 .12
- ❑ 394 Bill Laxton .30 .12
- ❑ 395 Manny Trillo .30 .12
- ❑ 396 Tom Murphy .30 .12
- ❑ 397 Larry Herndon RC .75 .30
- ❑ 398 Tom Burgmeier .30 .12
- ❑ 399 Bruce Boisclair .30 .12
- ❑ 400 Steve Garvey 2.50 1.00

❑ 401 Mickey Scott .30 .12
❑ 402 Tommy Helms .30 .12
❑ 403 Tom Grieve .75 .30
❑ 404 Eric Rasmussen .30 .12
❑ 405 Claudell Washington .75 .30
❑ 406 Tim Johnson .30 .12
❑ 407 Dave Freisleben .30 .12
❑ 408 Cesar Tovar .30 .12
❑ 409 Pete Broberg .30 .12
❑ 410 Willie Montanez .30 .12
❑ 411 Joe Morgan WS 2.50 1.00
Johnny Bench
❑ 412 Johnny Bench WS 2.50 1.00
❑ 413 WS Summary .75 .30
Cincy wins 2nd
straight series
❑ 414 Tommy Harper .75 .30
❑ 415 Jay Johnstone .75 .30
❑ 416 Chuck Hartenstein .30 .12
❑ 417 Wayne Garrett .30 .12
❑ 418 White Sox Team CL 1.50 .30
Bob Lemon MG
❑ 419 Steve Swisher .30 .12
❑ 420 Rusty Staub 1.50 .60
❑ 421 Doug Rau .30 .12
❑ 422 Freddie Patek .75 .30
❑ 423 Gary Lavelle .30 .12
❑ 424 Steve Brye .30 .12
❑ 425 Joe Torre 1.50 .60
❑ 426 Dick Drago .30 .12
❑ 427 Dave Rader .30 .12
❑ 428 Rangers Team CL 1.50 .30
Frank Lucchesi
❑ 429 Ken Boswell .30 .12
❑ 430 Fergie Jenkins 2.50 1.00
❑ 431 Dave Collins UER .75 .30
(Photo actually
Bobby Jones)
❑ 432 Buzz Capra .30 .12
❑ 433 Nate Colbert TBC .30 .12
(5 HR, 13 RBI)
❑ 434 Carl Yastrzemski TBC 1.50 .60
'67 Triple Crown
❑ 435 Maury Wills TBC .75 .30
104 steals
❑ 436 Bob Keegan TBC .30 .12
Majors' only no-hitter
❑ 437 Ralph Kiner TBC 1.50 .60
Leads NL in HR's
7th straight year
❑ 438 Marty Perez .30 .12
❑ 439 Gorman Thomas .75 .30
❑ 440 Jon Matlack .30 .12
❑ 441 Larvell Blanks .30 .12
❑ 442 Braves Team CL 1.50 .30
Dave Bristol MG
❑ 443 Lamar Johnson .30 .12
❑ 444 Wayne Twitchell .30 .12
❑ 445 Ken Singleton .75 .30
❑ 446 Bill Bonham .30 .12
❑ 447 Jerry Turner .30 .12
❑ 448 Ellie Rodriguez .30 .12
❑ 449 Al Fitzmorris .30 .12
❑ 450 Pete Rose 20.00 8.00
❑ 451 Checklist 397-528 1.50 .30
❑ 452 Mike Caldwell .30 .12
❑ 453 Pedro Garcia .30 .12
❑ 454 Andy Etchebarren .30 .12
❑ 455 Rick Wise .30 .12
❑ 456 Leon Roberts .30 .12
❑ 457 Steve Luebber .30 .12
❑ 458 Leo Foster .30 .12
❑ 459 Steve Foucault .30 .12
❑ 460 Willie Stargell 2.50 1.00
❑ 461 Dick Tidrow .30 .12
❑ 462 Don Baylor 1.50 .60
❑ 463 Jamie Quirk .30 .12
❑ 464 Randy Moffitt .30 .12
❑ 465 Rico Carty .75 .30
❑ 466 Fred Holdsworth .30 .12
❑ 467 Phillies Team CL 1.50 .30
Danny Ozark MG
❑ 468 Ramon Hernandez .30 .12
❑ 469 Pat Kelly .30 .12
❑ 470 Ted Simmons .75 .30
❑ 471 Del Unser .30 .12
❑ 472 Don Aase .30 .12
Bob McClure
Gil Patterson
Dave Wehrmeister
Sheldon Gill pictured instead of Gil Patterson
❑ 473 Andre Dawson RC 20.00 8.00
Gene Richards
John Scott
Denny Walling
❑ 474 Bob Bailor .75 .30
Kiko Garcia
Craig Reynolds
Alex Taveras
❑ 475 Chris Batton .75 .30
Rick Camp
Scott McGregor
Manny Sarmiento
❑ 476 Gary Alexander 20.00 8.00
Rick Cerone
Dale Murphy RC
Kevin Pasley
❑ 477 Doug Ault .75 .30
Rich Dauer
Orlando Gonzalez
Phil Mankowski
❑ 478 Jim Gideon .75 .30
Leon Hooten
Dave Johnson
Mark Lemongello
❑ 479 Brian Asselstine .75 .30
Wayne Gross
Sam Mejias
Alvis Woods
❑ 480 Carl Yastrzemski 8.00 3.20
❑ 481 Roger Metzger .30 .12
❑ 482 Tony Solaita .30 .12
❑ 483 Richie Zisk .30 .12
❑ 484 Burt Hooton .75 .30
❑ 485 Roy White .75 .30
❑ 486 Ed Bane .30 .12
❑ 487 Larry Anderson .75 .30
Ed Glynn
Joe Henderson
Greg Terlecky
❑ 488 Jack Clark RC 3.00 1.20
Ruppert Jones RC
Lee Mazzilli RC
Dan Thomas
❑ 489 Len Barker RC .75 .30
Randy Lerch
Greg Minton
Mike Overy
❑ 490 Billy Almon .75 .30
Mickey Klutts
Tommy McMillan
Mark Wagner
❑ 491 Mike Dupree 3.00 1.20
Dennis Martinez RC
Craig Mitchell
Bob Sykes
❑ 492 Tony Armas RC .75 .30
Steve Kemp RC
Carlos Lopez
Gary Woods
❑ 493 Mike Krukow .75 .30
Jim Otten
Gary Wheelock
Mike Willis
❑ 494 Juan Bernhardt 1.50 .60
Mike Champion
Jim Gantner RC
Bump Wills
❑ 495 Al Hrabosky .30 .12
❑ 496 Gary Thomasson .30 .12
❑ 497 Clay Carroll .30 .12
❑ 498 Sal Bando .75 .30
❑ 499 Pablo Torrealba .30 .12
❑ 500 Dave Kingman 1.50 .60
❑ 501 Jim Bibby .30 .12
❑ 502 Randy Hundley .30 .12
❑ 503 Bill Lee .30 .12
❑ 504 Dodgers Team CL 1.50 .30
Tom Lasorda MG
❑ 505 Oscar Gamble .75 .30
❑ 506 Steve Grilli .30 .12
❑ 507 Mike Hegan .30 .12
❑ 508 Dave Pagan .30 .12
❑ 509 Cookie Rojas .75 .30
❑ 510 John Candelaria .30 .12
❑ 511 Bill Fahey .30 .12
❑ 512 Jack Billingham .30 .12
❑ 513 Jerry Terrell .30 .12
❑ 514 Cliff Johnson .30 .12
❑ 515 Chris Speier .30 .12
❑ 516 Bake McBride .75 .30
❑ 517 Pete Vuckovich RC .75 .30
❑ 518 Cubs Team CL 1.50 .30
Herman Franks MG
❑ 519 Don Kirkwood .30 .12
❑ 520 Garry Maddox .30 .12
❑ 521 Bob Grich .75 .30
Only card in set with no date of birth
❑ 522 Enzo Hernandez .30 .12
❑ 523 Rollie Fingers 2.50 1.00
❑ 524 Rowland Office .30 .12
❑ 525 Dennis Eckersley 5.00 2.00
❑ 526 Larry Parrish .75 .30
❑ 527 Dan Meyer .75 .30
❑ 528 Bill Castro .30 .12
❑ 529 Jim Essian .30 .12
❑ 530 Rick Reuschel .75 .30
❑ 531 Lyman Bostock .75 .30
❑ 532 Jim Willoughby .30 .12
❑ 533 Mickey Stanley .30 .12
❑ 534 Paul Splittorff .30 .12
❑ 535 Cesar Geronimo .30 .12
❑ 536 Vic Albury .30 .12
❑ 537 Dave Roberts .30 .12
❑ 538 Frank Taveras .30 .12
❑ 539 Mike Wallace .30 .12
❑ 540 Bob Watson .75 .30
❑ 541 John Denny .75 .30
❑ 542 Frank Duffy .30 .12
❑ 543 Ron Blomberg .30 .12
❑ 544 Gary Ross .30 .12
❑ 545 Bob Boone .75 .30
❑ 546 Oriole Team CL 1.50 .30
Earl Weaver MG
❑ 547 Willie McCovey 4.00 1.60
❑ 548 Joel Youngblood .30 .12
❑ 549 Jerry Royster .30 .12
❑ 550 Randy Jones .30 .12
❑ 551 Bill North .30 .12
❑ 552 Pepe Mangual .30 .12
❑ 553 Jack Heidemann .30 .12
❑ 554 Bruce Kimm .30 .12
❑ 555 Dan Ford .30 .12
❑ 556 Doug Bird .30 .12
❑ 557 Jerry White .30 .12
❑ 558 Elias Sosa .30 .12
❑ 559 Alan Bannister .30 .12
❑ 560 Dave Concepcion 1.50 .60
❑ 561 Pete LaCock .30 .12
❑ 562 Checklist 529-660 1.50 .30
❑ 563 Bruce Kison .30 .12
❑ 564 Alan Ashby .75 .30
❑ 565 Mickey Lolich .75 .30
❑ 566 Rick Miller .30 .12
❑ 567 Enos Cabell .30 .12
❑ 568 Carlos May .30 .12
❑ 569 Jim Lonborg .75 .30
❑ 570 Bobby Bonds 1.50 .60
❑ 571 Darrell Evans .75 .30
❑ 572 Ross Grimsley .30 .12
❑ 573 Joe Ferguson .30 .12
❑ 574 Aurelio Rodriguez .30 .12
❑ 575 Dick Ruthven .30 .12
❑ 576 Fred Kendall .30 .12
❑ 577 Jerry Augustine .30 .12
❑ 578 Bob Randall .30 .12
❑ 579 Don Carrithers .30 .12
❑ 580 George Brett 15.00 6.00
❑ 581 Pedro Borbon .30 .12
❑ 582 Ed Kirkpatrick .30 .12
❑ 583 Paul Lindblad .30 .12
❑ 584 Ed Goodson .30 .12
❑ 585 Rick Burleson .75 .30
❑ 586 Steve Renko .30 .12
❑ 587 Rick Baldwin .30 .12
❑ 588 Dave Moates .30 .12
❑ 589 Mike Cosgrove .30 .12

Card	NM	Ex
❑ 590 Buddy Bell	.75	.30
❑ 591 Chris Arnold	.30	.12
❑ 592 Dan Briggs	.30	.12
❑ 593 Dennis Blair	.30	.12
❑ 594 Biff Pocoroba	.30	.12
❑ 595 John Hiller	.30	.12
❑ 596 Jerry Martin	.30	.12
❑ 597 Mariners Leaders CL	1.50	.30
Darrell Johnson MG		
Don Bryant CO		
Jim Busby CO		
Vada Pinson CO		
Wes Stock CO		
❑ 598 Sparky Lyle	.75	.30
❑ 599 Mike Tyson	.30	.12
❑ 600 Jim Palmer	4.00	1.60
❑ 601 Mike Lum	.30	.12
❑ 602 Andy Hassler	.30	.12
❑ 603 Willie Davis	.75	.30
❑ 604 Jim Slaton	.30	.12
❑ 605 Felix Millan	.30	.12
❑ 606 Steve Braun	.30	.12
❑ 607 Larry Demery	.30	.12
❑ 608 Roy Howell	.30	.12
❑ 609 Jim Barr	.30	.12
❑ 610 Jose Cardenal	.75	.30
❑ 611 Dave Lemanczyk	.30	.12
❑ 612 Barry Foote	.30	.12
❑ 613 Reggie Cleveland	.30	.12
❑ 614 Greg Gross	.30	.12
❑ 615 Phil Niekro	2.50	1.00
❑ 616 Tommy Sandt	.30	.12
❑ 617 Bobby Darwin	.30	.12
❑ 618 Pat Dobson	.30	.12
❑ 619 Johnny Oates	.75	.30
❑ 620 Don Sutton	2.50	1.00
❑ 621 Tigers Team CL	1.50	.30
Ralph Houk MG		
❑ 622 Jim Wohlford	.30	.12
❑ 623 Jack Kucek	.30	.12
❑ 624 Hector Cruz	.30	.12
❑ 625 Ken Holtzman	.75	.30
❑ 626 Al Bumbry	.75	.30
❑ 627 Bob Myrick	.30	.12
❑ 628 Mario Guerrero	.30	.12
❑ 629 Bobby Valentine	.75	.30
❑ 630 Bert Blyleven	1.50	.60
❑ 631 George Brett	6.00	2.40
Ken Brett		
❑ 632 Bob Forsch	.75	.30
Ken Forsch		
❑ 633 Lee May	.75	.30
Carlos May		
❑ 634 Paul Reuschel	.75	.30
Rick Reuschel UER		
(Photos switched)		
❑ 635 Robin Yount	8.00	3.20
❑ 636 Santo Alcala	.30	.12
❑ 637 Alex Johnson	.30	.12
❑ 638 Jim Kaat	1.50	.60
❑ 639 Jerry Morales	.30	.12
❑ 640 Carlton Fisk	5.00	2.00
❑ 641 Dan Larson	.30	.12
❑ 642 Willie Crawford	.30	.12
❑ 643 Mike Pazik	.30	.12
❑ 644 Matt Alexander	.30	.12
❑ 645 Jerry Reuss	.75	.30
❑ 646 Andres Mora	.30	.12
❑ 647 Expos Team CL	1.50	.30
Dick Williams MG		
❑ 648 Jim Spencer	.30	.12
❑ 649 Dave Cash	.30	.12
❑ 650 Nolan Ryan	30.00	12.00
❑ 651 Von Joshua	.30	.12
❑ 652 Tom Walker	.30	.12
❑ 653 Diego Segui	.75	.30
❑ 654 Ron Pruitt	.30	.12
❑ 655 Tony Perez	2.50	1.00
❑ 656 Ron Guidry	1.50	.60
❑ 657 Mick Kelleher	.30	.12
❑ 658 Marty Pattin	.30	.12
❑ 659 Merv Rettenmund	.30	.12
❑ 660 Willie Horton	1.50	.30

1978 Topps

	NM	Ex
COMPLETE SET (726)	200.00	80.00
COMMON CARD (1-726)	.25	.10
COMMON CARD DP	.15	.06

Card	NM	Ex
❑ 1 Lou Brock RB	3.00	.90
❑ 2 Sparky Lyle RB	.60	.24
❑ 3 Willie McCovey RB	2.50	1.00
❑ 4 Brooks Robinson RB	1.25	.50
❑ 5 Pete Rose RB	8.00	3.20
❑ 6 Nolan Ryan RB	15.00	6.00
❑ 7 Reggie Jackson RB	4.00	1.60
❑ 8 Mike Sadek	.25	.10
❑ 9 Doug DeCinces	.60	.24
❑ 10 Phil Niekro	2.50	1.00
❑ 11 Rick Manning	.25	.10
❑ 12 Don Aase	.25	.10
❑ 13 Art Howe RC	.60	.24
❑ 14 Lerrin LaGrow	.25	.10
❑ 15 Tony Perez DP	1.25	.50
❑ 16 Roy White	.60	.24
❑ 17 Mike Krukow	.25	.10
❑ 18 Bob Grich	.60	.24
❑ 19 Darrell Porter	.60	.24
❑ 20 Pete Rose DP	12.00	4.80
❑ 21 Steve Kemp	.25	.10
❑ 22 Charlie Hough	.60	.24
❑ 23 Bump Wills	.25	.10
❑ 24 Don Money DP	.15	.06
❑ 25 Jon Matlack	.25	.10
❑ 26 Rich Hebner	.60	.24
❑ 27 Geoff Zahn	.25	.10
❑ 28 Ed Ott	.25	.10
❑ 29 Bob Lacey	.25	.10
❑ 30 George Hendrick	.60	.24
❑ 31 Glenn Abbott	.25	.10
❑ 32 Garry Templeton	.60	.24
❑ 33 Dave Lemanczyk	.25	.10
❑ 34 Willie McCovey	3.00	1.20
❑ 35 Sparky Lyle	.60	.24
❑ 36 Eddie Murray RC	60.00	24.00
❑ 37 Rick Waits	.25	.10
❑ 38 Willie Montanez	.25	.10
❑ 39 Floyd Bannister RC	.25	.10
❑ 40 Carl Yastrzemski	6.00	2.40
❑ 41 Burt Hooton	.60	.24
❑ 42 Jorge Orta	.25	.10
❑ 43 Bill Atkinson	.25	.10
❑ 44 Toby Harrah	.60	.24
❑ 45 Mark Fidrych	2.50	1.00
❑ 46 Al Cowens	.25	.10
❑ 47 Jack Billingham	.25	.10
❑ 48 Don Baylor	1.25	.50
❑ 49 Ed Kranepool	.60	.24
❑ 50 Rick Reuschel	.60	.24
❑ 51 Charlie Moore DP	.15	.06
❑ 52 Jim Lonborg	.60	.24
❑ 53 Phil Garner DP	.25	.10
❑ 54 Tom Johnson	.25	.10
❑ 55 Mitchell Page	.25	.10
❑ 56 Randy Jones	.25	.10
❑ 57 Dan Meyer	.25	.10
❑ 58 Bob Forsch	.25	.10
❑ 59 Otto Velez	.25	.10
❑ 60 Thurman Munson	4.00	1.60
❑ 61 Larvell Blanks	.25	.10
❑ 62 Jim Barr	.25	.10
❑ 63 Don Zimmer MG	.60	.24
❑ 64 Gene Pentz	.25	.10
❑ 65 Ken Singleton	.60	.24
❑ 66 Chicago White Sox	1.25	.25
Team Card CL		
❑ 67 Claudell Washington	.60	.24
❑ 68 Steve Foucault DP	.15	.06
❑ 69 Mike Vail	.25	.10
❑ 70 Goose Gossage	1.25	.50
❑ 71 Terry Humphrey	.25	.10
❑ 72 Andre Dawson	4.00	1.60
❑ 73 Andy Hassler	.25	.10
❑ 74 Checklist 1-121	1.25	.25
❑ 75 Dick Ruthven	.25	.10
❑ 76 Steve Ontiveros	.25	.10
❑ 77 Ed Kirkpatrick	.25	.10
❑ 78 Pablo Torrealba	.25	.10
❑ 79 Da.Johnson DP MG	.15	.06
❑ 80 Ken Griffey Sr.	1.25	.50
❑ 81 Pete Redfern	.25	.10
❑ 82 San Francisco Giants	1.25	.25
Team Card CL		
❑ 83 Bob Montgomery	.25	.10
❑ 84 Kent Tekulve	.60	.24
❑ 85 Ron Fairly	.60	.24
❑ 86 Dave Tomlin	.25	.10
❑ 87 John Lowenstein	.25	.10
❑ 88 Mike Phillips	.25	.10
❑ 89 Ken Clay	.25	.10
❑ 90 Larry Bowa	1.25	.50
❑ 91 Oscar Zamora	.25	.10
❑ 92 Adrian Devine	.25	.10
❑ 93 Bobby Cox DP	.15	.06
❑ 94 Chuck Scrivener	.25	.10
❑ 95 Jamie Quirk	.25	.10
❑ 96 Baltimore Orioles	1.25	.25
Team Card CL		
❑ 97 Stan Bahnsen	.25	.10
❑ 98 Jim Essian	.60	.24
❑ 99 Willie Hernandez RC	1.25	.50
❑ 100 George Brett	15.00	6.00
❑ 101 Sid Monge	.25	.10
❑ 102 Matt Alexander	.25	.10
❑ 103 Tom Murphy	.25	.10
❑ 104 Lee Lacy	.25	.10
❑ 105 Reggie Cleveland	.25	.10
❑ 106 Bill Plummer	.25	.10
❑ 107 Ed Halicki	.25	.10
❑ 108 Von Joshua	.25	.10
❑ 109 Joe Torre MG	.60	.24
❑ 110 Richie Zisk	.25	.10
❑ 111 Mike Tyson	.25	.10
❑ 112 Houston Astros	1.25	.25
Team Card CL		
❑ 113 Don Carrithers	.25	.10
❑ 114 Paul Blair	.60	.24
❑ 115 Gary Nolan	.25	.10
❑ 116 Tucker Ashford	.25	.10
❑ 117 John Montague	.25	.10
❑ 118 Terry Harmon	.25	.10
❑ 119 Dennis Martinez	2.50	1.00
❑ 120 Gary Carter	2.50	1.00
❑ 121 Alvis Woods	.25	.10
❑ 122 Dennis Eckersley	3.00	1.20
❑ 123 Manny Trillo	.25	.10
❑ 124 Dave Rozema RC	.25	.10
❑ 125 George Scott	.60	.24
❑ 126 Paul Moskau	.25	.10
❑ 127 Chet Lemon	.60	.24
❑ 128 Bill Russell	.60	.24
❑ 129 Jim Colborn	.25	.10
❑ 130 Jeff Burroughs	.60	.24
❑ 131 Bert Blyleven	1.25	.50
❑ 132 Enos Cabell	.25	.10
❑ 133 Jerry Augustine	.25	.10
❑ 134 Steve Henderson	.25	.10
❑ 135 Ron Guidry DP	1.25	.50
❑ 136 Ted Sizemore	.25	.10
❑ 137 Craig Kusick	.25	.10
❑ 138 Larry Demery	.25	.10
❑ 139 Wayne Gross	.25	.10
❑ 140 Rollie Fingers	2.50	1.00
❑ 141 Ruppert Jones	.25	.10
❑ 142 John Montefusco	.25	.10
❑ 143 Keith Hernandez	.60	.24

❑ 144 Jesse Jefferson .25 .10
❑ 145 Rick Monday .60 .24
❑ 146 Doyle Alexander .60 .24
❑ 147 Lee Mazzilli .25 .10
❑ 148 Andre Thornton .60 .24
❑ 149 Dale Murray .25 .10
❑ 150 Bobby Bonds 1.25 .50
❑ 151 Milt Wilcox .25 .10
❑ 152 Ivan DeJesus .25 .10
❑ 153 Steve Stone .60 .24
❑ 154 Cecil Cooper DP .25 .10
❑ 155 Butch Hobson .25 .10
❑ 156 Andy Messersmith .60 .24
❑ 157 Pete LaCock DP .15 .06
❑ 158 Joaquin Andujar .60 .24
❑ 159 Lou Piniella .60 .24
❑ 160 Jim Palmer 3.00 1.20
❑ 161 Bob Boone 1.25 .50
❑ 162 Paul Thormodsgard .25 .10
❑ 163 Bill North .25 .10
❑ 164 Bob Owchinko .25 .10
❑ 165 Rennie Stennett .25 .10
❑ 166 Carlos Lopez .25 .10
❑ 167 Tim Foli .25 .10
❑ 168 Reggie Smith .60 .24
❑ 169 Jerry Johnson .25 .10
❑ 170 Lou Brock 3.00 1.20
❑ 171 Pat Zachry .25 .10
❑ 172 Mike Hargrove .60 .24
❑ 173 Robin Yount UER 5.00 2.00
(Played for Newark
in 1973, not 1971)
❑ 174 Wayne Garland .25 .10
❑ 175 Jerry Morales .25 .10
❑ 176 Milt May .25 .10
❑ 177 Gene Garber DP .25 .10
❑ 178 Dave Chalk .25 .10
❑ 179 Dick Tidrow .25 .10
❑ 180 Dave Concepcion 1.25 .50
❑ 181 Ken Forsch .25 .10
❑ 182 Jim Spencer .25 .10
❑ 183 Doug Bird .25 .10
❑ 184 Checklist 122-242 1.25 .25
❑ 185 Ellis Valentine .25 .10
❑ 186 Bob Stanley DP .15 .06
❑ 187 Jerry Royster DP .15 .06
❑ 188 Al Bumbry .60 .24
❑ 189 Tom Lasorda MG 2.50 1.00
❑ 190 John Candelaria .60 .24
❑ 191 Rodney Scott .25 .10
❑ 192 San Diego Padres 1.25 .25
Team Card CL
❑ 193 Rich Chiles .25 .10
❑ 194 Derrel Thomas .25 .10
❑ 195 Larry Dierker .60 .24
❑ 196 Bob Bailor .25 .10
❑ 197 Nino Espinosa .25 .10
❑ 198 Ron Pruitt .25 .10
❑ 199 Craig Reynolds .25 .10
❑ 200 Reggie Jackson 8.00 3.20
❑ 201 Dave Parker 1.25 .50
Rod Carew LL
❑ 202 George Foster .60 .24
Jim Rice LL DP
❑ 203 George Foster .60 .24
Larry Hisle LL
❑ 204 Frank Taveras .25 .10
Freddie Patek LL DP
❑ 205 Steve Carlton 2.50 1.00
Dave Goltz
Dennis Leonard
Jim Palmer LL
❑ 206 Phil Niekro 6.00 2.40
Nolan Ryan LL DP
❑ 207 John Candelaria .60 .24
Frank Tanana LL DP
❑ 208 Rollie Fingers 1.25 .50
Bill Campbell LL
❑ 209 Dock Ellis .25 .10
❑ 210 Jose Cardenal .25 .10
❑ 211 Earl Weaver MG DP 1.25 .50
❑ 212 Mike Caldwell .25 .10
❑ 213 Alan Bannister .25 .10
❑ 214 California Angels 1.25 .25
Team Card CL
❑ 215 Darrell Evans .60 .24
❑ 216 Mike Paxton .25 .10
❑ 217 Rod Gilbreath .25 .10
❑ 218 Marty Pattin .25 .10
❑ 219 Mike Cubbage .25 .10
❑ 220 Pedro Borbon .25 .10
❑ 221 Chris Speier .25 .10
❑ 222 Jerry Martin .25 .10
❑ 223 Bruce Kison .25 .10
❑ 224 Jerry Tabb .25 .10
❑ 225 Don Gullett DP .25 .10
❑ 226 Joe Ferguson .25 .10
❑ 227 Al Fitzmorris .25 .10
❑ 228 Manny Mota DP .25 .10
❑ 229 Leo Foster .25 .10
❑ 230 Al Hrabosky .25 .10
❑ 231 Wayne Nordhagen .25 .10
❑ 232 Mickey Stanley .25 .10
❑ 233 Dick Pole .25 .10
❑ 234 Herman Franks MG .25 .10
❑ 235 Tim McCarver .60 .24
❑ 236 Terry Whitfield .25 .10
❑ 237 Rich Dauer .25 .10
❑ 238 Juan Beniquez .25 .10
❑ 239 Dyar Miller .25 .10
❑ 240 Gene Tenace .60 .24
❑ 241 Pete Vuckovich .60 .24
❑ 242 Barry Bonnell DP .15 .06
❑ 243 Bob McClure .25 .10
❑ 244 Montreal Expos .60 .12
Team Card CL DP
❑ 245 Rick Burleson .60 .24
❑ 246 Dan Driessen .25 .10
❑ 247 Larry Christenson .25 .10
❑ 248 Frank White DP .60 .24
❑ 249 Dave Goltz DP .15 .06
❑ 250 Graig Nettles DP .60 .24
❑ 251 Don Kirkwood .25 .10
❑ 252 Steve Swisher DP .15 .06
❑ 253 Jim Kern .25 .10
❑ 254 Dave Collins .60 .24
❑ 255 Jerry Reuss .60 .24
❑ 256 Joe Altobelli MG .25 .10
❑ 257 Hector Cruz .25 .10
❑ 258 John Hiller .25 .10
❑ 259 Los Angeles Dodgers 1.25 .25
Team Card CL
❑ 260 Bert Campaneris .60 .24
❑ 261 Tim Hosley .25 .10
❑ 262 Rudy May .25 .10
❑ 263 Danny Walton .25 .10
❑ 264 Jamie Easterly .25 .10
❑ 265 Sal Bando DP .60 .24
❑ 266 Bob Shirley .25 .10
❑ 267 Doug Ault .25 .10
❑ 268 Gil Flores .25 .10
❑ 269 Wayne Twitchell .25 .10
❑ 270 Carlton Fisk 4.00 1.60
❑ 271 Randy Lerch DP .15 .06
❑ 272 Royle Stillman .25 .10
❑ 273 Fred Norman .25 .10
❑ 274 Freddie Patek .60 .24
❑ 275 Dan Ford .25 .10
❑ 276 Bill Bonham DP .15 .06
❑ 277 Bruce Boisclair .25 .10
❑ 278 Enrique Romo .25 .10
❑ 279 Bill Virdon MG .25 .10
❑ 280 Buddy Bell .60 .24
❑ 281 Eric Rasmussen DP .15 .06
❑ 282 New York Yankees 2.50 .50
Team Card CL
❑ 283 Omar Moreno .25 .10
❑ 284 Randy Moffitt .25 .10
❑ 285 Steve Yeager DP .60 .24
❑ 286 Ben Oglivie .60 .24
❑ 287 Kiko Garcia .25 .10
❑ 288 Dave Hamilton .25 .10
❑ 289 Checklist 243-363 1.25 .25
❑ 290 Willie Horton .60 .24
❑ 291 Gary Ross .25 .10
❑ 292 Gene Richards .25 .10
❑ 293 Mike Willis .25 .10
❑ 294 Larry Parrish .60 .24
❑ 295 Bill Lee .25 .10
❑ 296 Biff Pocoroba .25 .10
❑ 297 Warren Brusstar DP .15 .06
❑ 298 Tony Armas .60 .24
❑ 299 Whitey Herzog MG .60 .24
❑ 300 Joe Morgan 3.00 1.20
❑ 301 Buddy Schultz .25 .10
❑ 302 Chicago Cubs 1.25 .25
Team Card CL
❑ 303 Sam Hinds .25 .10
❑ 304 John Milner .25 .10
❑ 305 Rico Carty .60 .24
❑ 306 Joe Niekro .60 .24
❑ 307 Glenn Borgmann .25 .10
❑ 308 Jim Rooker .25 .10
❑ 309 Cliff Johnson .25 .10
❑ 310 Don Sutton 2.50 1.00
❑ 311 Jose Baez DP .15 .06
❑ 312 Greg Minton .25 .10
❑ 313 Andy Etchebarren .25 .10
❑ 314 Paul Lindblad .25 .10
❑ 315 Mark Belanger .60 .24
❑ 316 Henry Cruz DP .15 .06
❑ 317 Dave Johnson .25 .10
❑ 318 Tom Griffin .25 .10
❑ 319 Alan Ashby .25 .10
❑ 320 Fred Lynn .60 .24
❑ 321 Santo Alcala .25 .10
❑ 322 Tom Paciorek .60 .24
❑ 323 Jim Fregosi DP .25 .10
❑ 324 Vern Rapp MG .25 .10
❑ 325 Bruce Sutter 1.25 .50
❑ 326 Mike Lum DP .15 .06
❑ 327 Rick Langford DP .15 .06
❑ 328 Milwaukee Brewers 1.25 .25
Team Card CL
❑ 329 John Verhoeven .25 .10
❑ 330 Bob Watson .60 .24
❑ 331 Mark Littell .25 .10
❑ 332 Duane Kuiper .25 .10
❑ 333 Jim Todd .25 .10
❑ 334 John Stearns .25 .10
❑ 335 Bucky Dent .60 .24
❑ 336 Steve Busby .25 .10
❑ 337 Tom Grieve .60 .24
❑ 338 Dave Heaverlo .25 .10
❑ 339 Mario Guerrero .25 .10
❑ 340 Bake McBride .60 .24
❑ 341 Mike Flanagan .60 .24
❑ 342 Aurelio Rodriguez .25 .10
❑ 343 John Wathan DP .15 .06
❑ 344 Sam Ewing .25 .10
❑ 345 Luis Tiant .60 .24
❑ 346 Larry Biittner .25 .10
❑ 347 Terry Forster .25 .10
❑ 348 Del Unser .25 .10
❑ 349 Rick Camp DP .15 .06
❑ 350 Steve Garvey 2.50 1.00
❑ 351 Jeff Torborg .60 .24
❑ 352 Tony Scott .25 .10
❑ 353 Doug Bair .25 .10
❑ 354 Cesar Geronimo .25 .10
❑ 355 Bill Travers .25 .10
❑ 356 New York Mets 1.25 .25
Team Card CL
❑ 357 Tom Poquette .25 .10
❑ 358 Mark Lemongello .25 .10
❑ 359 Marc Hill .25 .10
❑ 360 Mike Schmidt 10.00 4.00
❑ 361 Chris Knapp .25 .10
❑ 362 Dave May .25 .10
❑ 363 Bob Randall .25 .10
❑ 364 Jerry Turner .25 .10
❑ 365 Ed Figueroa .25 .10
❑ 366 Larry Milbourne DP .15 .06
❑ 367 Rick Dempsey .60 .24
❑ 368 Balor Moore .25 .10
❑ 369 Tim Nordbrook .25 .10
❑ 370 Rusty Staub 1.25 .50
❑ 371 Ray Burris .25 .10
❑ 372 Brian Asselstine .25 .10
❑ 373 Jim Willoughby .25 .10
❑ 374 Jose Morales .25 .10
❑ 375 Tommy John 1.25 .50
❑ 376 Jim Wohlford .25 .10
❑ 377 Manny Sarmiento .25 .10
❑ 378 Bobby Winkles MG .25 .10
❑ 379 Skip Lockwood .25 .10
❑ 380 Ted Simmons .60 .24
❑ 381 Philadelphia Phillies 1.25 .25

Team Card CL
❑ 382 Joe Lahoud .25 .10
❑ 383 Mario Mendoza .25 .10
❑ 384 Jack Clark 1.25 .50
❑ 385 Tito Fuentes .25 .10
❑ 386 Bob Gorinski .25 .10
❑ 387 Ken Holtzman .60 .24
❑ 388 Bill Fahey DP .15 .06
❑ 389 Julio Gonzalez .25 .10
❑ 390 Oscar Gamble .60 .24
❑ 391 Larry Haney .25 .10
❑ 392 Billy Almon .25 .10
❑ 393 Tippy Martinez .60 .24
❑ 394 Roy Howell DP .15 .06
❑ 395 Jim Hughes .25 .10
❑ 396 Bob Stinson DP .15 .06
❑ 397 Greg Gross .25 .10
❑ 398 Don Hood .25 .10
❑ 399 Pete Mackanin .25 .10
❑ 400 Nolan Ryan 25.00 10.00
❑ 401 Sparky Anderson MG .60 .24
❑ 402 Dave Campbell .25 .10
❑ 403 Bud Harrelson .60 .24
❑ 404 Detroit Tigers 1.25 .25
Team Card CL
❑ 405 Rawly Eastwick .25 .10
❑ 406 Mike Jorgensen .25 .10
❑ 407 Odell Jones .25 .10
❑ 408 Joe Zdeb .25 .10
❑ 409 Ron Schueler .25 .10
❑ 410 Bill Madlock .60 .24
❑ 411 Mickey Rivers ALCS .60 .24
❑ 412 Davey Lopes NLCS .60 .24
❑ 413 Reggie Jackson WS 4.00 1.60
❑ 414 Darold Knowles DP .15 .06
❑ 415 Ray Fosse .25 .10
❑ 416 Jack Brohamer .25 .10
❑ 417 Mike Garman DP .15 .06
❑ 418 Tony Muser .25 .10
❑ 419 Jerry Garvin .25 .10
❑ 420 Greg Luzinski 1.25 .50
❑ 421 Junior Moore .25 .10
❑ 422 Steve Braun .25 .10
❑ 423 Dave Rosello .25 .10
❑ 424 Boston Red Sox 1.25 .25
Team Card CL
❑ 425 Steve Rogers DP .25 .10
❑ 426 Fred Kendall .25 .10
❑ 427 Mario Soto RC .60 .24
❑ 428 Joel Youngblood .25 .10
❑ 429 Mike Barlow .25 .10
❑ 430 Al Oliver .60 .24
❑ 431 Butch Metzger .25 .10
❑ 432 Terry Bulling .25 .10
❑ 433 Fernando Gonzalez .25 .10
❑ 434 Mike Norris .25 .10
❑ 435 Checklist 364-484 1.25 .25
❑ 436 Vic Harris DP .15 .06
❑ 437 Bo McLaughlin .25 .10
❑ 438 John Ellis .25 .10
❑ 439 Ken Kravec .25 .10
❑ 440 Dave Lopes .60 .24
❑ 441 Larry Gura .25 .10
❑ 442 Elliott Maddox .25 .10
❑ 443 Darrel Chaney .25 .10
❑ 444 Roy Hartsfield MG .25 .10
❑ 445 Mike Ivie .25 .10
❑ 446 Tug McGraw .60 .24
❑ 447 Leroy Stanton .25 .10
❑ 448 Bill Castro .25 .10
❑ 449 Tim Blackwell DP .15 .06
❑ 450 Tom Seaver 6.00 2.40
❑ 451 Minnesota Twins 1.25 .25
Team Card CL
❑ 452 Jerry Mumphrey .25 .10
❑ 453 Doug Flynn .25 .10
❑ 454 Dave LaRoche .25 .10
❑ 455 Bill Robinson .60 .24
❑ 456 Vern Ruhle .25 .10
❑ 457 Bob Bailey .25 .10
❑ 458 Jeff Newman .25 .10
❑ 459 Charlie Spikes .25 .10
❑ 460 Jim Hunter 2.50 1.00
❑ 461 Rob Andrews DP .15 .06
❑ 462 Rogelio Moret .25 .10
❑ 463 Kevin Bell .25 .10
❑ 464 Jerry Grote .25 .10
❑ 465 Hal McRae .60 .24
❑ 466 Dennis Blair .25 .10
❑ 467 Alvin Dark MG .60 .24
❑ 468 Warren Cromartie RC .60 .24
❑ 469 Rick Cerone .60 .24
❑ 470 J.R. Richard .60 .24
❑ 471 Roy Smalley .60 .24
❑ 472 Ron Reed .25 .10
❑ 473 Bill Buckner .60 .24
❑ 474 Jim Slaton .25 .10
❑ 475 Gary Matthews .60 .24
❑ 476 Bill Stein .25 .10
❑ 477 Doug Capilla .25 .10
❑ 478 Jerry Remy .25 .10
❑ 479 St. Louis Cardinals 1.25 .25
Team Card CL
❑ 480 Ron LeFlore .60 .24
❑ 481 Jackson Todd .25 .10
❑ 482 Rick Miller .25 .10
❑ 483 Ken Macha RC .25 .10
❑ 484 Jim Norris .25 .10
❑ 485 Chris Chambliss .60 .24
❑ 486 John Curtis .25 .10
❑ 487 Jim Tyrone .25 .10
❑ 488 Dan Spillner .25 .10
❑ 489 Rudy Meoli .25 .10
❑ 490 Amos Otis .60 .24
❑ 491 Scott McGregor .60 .24
❑ 492 Jim Sundberg .60 .24
❑ 493 Steve Renko .25 .10
❑ 494 Chuck Tanner MG .60 .24
❑ 495 Dave Cash .25 .10
❑ 496 Jim Clancy DP .15 .06
❑ 497 Glenn Adams .25 .10
❑ 498 Joe Sambito .25 .10
❑ 499 Seattle Mariners 1.25 .25
Team Card CL
❑ 500 George Foster 1.25 .50
❑ 501 Dave Roberts .25 .10
❑ 502 Pat Rockett .25 .10
❑ 503 Ike Hampton .25 .10
❑ 504 Roger Freed .25 .10
❑ 505 Felix Millan .25 .10
❑ 506 Ron Blomberg .25 .10
❑ 507 Willie Crawford .25 .10
❑ 508 Johnny Oates .60 .24
❑ 509 Brent Strom .25 .10
❑ 510 Willie Stargell 2.50 1.00
❑ 511 Frank Duffy .25 .10
❑ 512 Larry Herndon .25 .10
❑ 513 Barry Foote .25 .10
❑ 514 Rob Sperring .25 .10
❑ 515 Tim Corcoran .25 .10
❑ 516 Gary Beare .25 .10
❑ 517 Andres Mora .25 .10
❑ 518 Tommy Boggs DP .15 .06
❑ 519 Brian Downing .60 .24
❑ 520 Larry Hisle .25 .10
❑ 521 Steve Staggs .25 .10
❑ 522 Dick Williams MG .60 .24
❑ 523 Donnie Moore RC .25 .10
❑ 524 Bernie Carbo .25 .10
❑ 525 Jerry Terrell .25 .10
❑ 526 Cincinnati Reds 1.25 .25
Team Card CL
❑ 527 Vic Correll .25 .10
❑ 528 Rob Picciolo .25 .10
❑ 529 Paul Hartzell .25 .10
❑ 530 Dave Winfield 4.00 1.60
❑ 531 Tom Underwood .25 .10
❑ 532 Skip Jutze .25 .10
❑ 533 Sandy Alomar .60 .24
❑ 534 Wilbur Howard .25 .10
❑ 535 Checklist 485-605 1.25 .25
❑ 536 Roric Harrison .25 .10
❑ 537 Bruce Bochte .25 .10
❑ 538 Johnny LeMaster .25 .10
❑ 539 Vic Davalillo DP .15 .06
❑ 540 Steve Carlton 4.00 1.60
❑ 541 Larry Cox .25 .10
❑ 542 Tim Johnson .25 .10
❑ 543 Larry Harlow DP .15 .06
❑ 544 Len Randle DP .15 .06
❑ 545 Bill Campbell .25 .10
❑ 546 Ted Martinez .25 .10
❑ 547 John Scott .25 .10
❑ 548 Billy Hunter DP MG .15 .06
❑ 549 Joe Kerrigan .25 .10
❑ 550 John Mayberry .60 .24
❑ 551 Atlanta Braves 1.25 .25
Team Card CL
❑ 552 Francisco Barrios .25 .10
❑ 553 Terry Puhl .60 .24
❑ 554 Joe Coleman .25 .10
❑ 555 Butch Wynegar .25 .10
❑ 556 Ed Armbrister .25 .10
❑ 557 Tony Solaita .25 .10
❑ 558 Paul Mitchell .25 .10
❑ 559 Phil Mankowski .25 .10
❑ 560 Dave Parker 1.25 .50
❑ 561 Charlie Williams .25 .10
❑ 562 Glenn Burke .25 .10
❑ 563 Dave Rader .25 .10
❑ 564 Mick Kelleher .25 .10
❑ 565 Jerry Koosman .60 .24
❑ 566 Merv Rettenmund .25 .10
❑ 567 Dick Drago .25 .10
❑ 568 Tom Hutton .25 .10
❑ 569 Lary Sorensen .25 .10
❑ 570 Dave Kingman 1.25 .50
❑ 571 Buck Martinez .25 .10
❑ 572 Rick Wise .25 .10
❑ 573 Luis Gomez .25 .10
❑ 574 Bob Lemon MG 1.25 .50
❑ 575 Pat Dobson .25 .10
❑ 576 Sam Mejias .25 .10
❑ 577 Oakland A's 1.25 .25
Team Card CL
❑ 578 Buzz Capra .25 .10
❑ 579 Rance Mulliniks .25 .10
❑ 580 Rod Carew 4.00 1.60
❑ 581 Lynn McGlothen .25 .10
❑ 582 Fran Healy .25 .10
❑ 583 George Medich .25 .10
❑ 584 John Hale .25 .10
❑ 585 Woodie Fryman DP .15 .06
❑ 586 Ed Goodson .25 .10
❑ 587 John Urrea .25 .10
❑ 588 Jim Mason .25 .10
❑ 589 Bob Knepper .25 .10
❑ 590 Bobby Murcer .60 .24
❑ 591 George Zeber .25 .10
❑ 592 Bob Apodaca .25 .10
❑ 593 Dave Skaggs .25 .10
❑ 594 Dave Freisleben .25 .10
❑ 595 Sixto Lezcano .25 .10
❑ 596 Gary Wheelock .25 .10
❑ 597 Steve Dillard .25 .10
❑ 598 Eddie Solomon .25 .10
❑ 599 Gary Woods .25 .10
❑ 600 Frank Tanana .60 .24
❑ 601 Gene Mauch MG .60 .24
❑ 602 Eric Soderholm .25 .10
❑ 603 Will McEnaney .25 .10
❑ 604 Earl Williams .25 .10
❑ 605 Rick Rhoden .60 .24
❑ 606 Pittsburgh Pirates 1.25 .25
Team Card CL
❑ 607 Fernando Arroyo .25 .10
❑ 608 Johnny Grubb .25 .10
❑ 609 John Denny .25 .10
❑ 610 Garry Maddox .60 .24
❑ 611 Pat Scanlon .25 .10
❑ 612 Ken Henderson .25 .10
❑ 613 Marty Perez .25 .10
❑ 614 Joe Wallis .25 .10
❑ 615 Clay Carroll .25 .10
❑ 616 Pat Kelly .25 .10
❑ 617 Joe Nolan .25 .10
❑ 618 Tommy Helms .25 .10
❑ 619 Thad Bosley DP .15 .06
❑ 620 Willie Randolph 1.25 .50
❑ 621 Craig Swan DP .15 .06
❑ 622 Champ Summers .25 .10
❑ 623 Eduardo Rodriguez .25 .10
❑ 624 Gary Alexander DP .15 .06
❑ 625 Jose Cruz .60 .24
❑ 626 Toronto Blue Jays 1.25 .25
Team Card CL DP
❑ 627 David Johnson .25 .10
❑ 628 Ralph Garr .60 .24

Card	NM	Ex
❑ 629 Don Stanhouse	.25	.10
❑ 630 Ron Cey	1.25	.50
❑ 631 Danny Ozark MG	.25	.10
❑ 632 Rowland Office	.25	.10
❑ 633 Tom Veryzer	.25	.10
❑ 634 Len Barker	.25	.10
❑ 635 Joe Rudi	.60	.24
❑ 636 Jim Bibby	.25	.10
❑ 637 Duffy Dyer	.25	.10
❑ 638 Paul Splittorff	.25	.10
❑ 639 Gene Clines	.25	.10
❑ 640 Lee May DP	.25	.10
❑ 641 Doug Rau	.25	.10
❑ 642 Denny Doyle	.25	.10
❑ 643 Tom House	.25	.10
❑ 644 Jim Dwyer	.25	.10
❑ 645 Mike Torrez	.60	.24
❑ 646 Rick Auerbach DP	.15	.06
❑ 647 Steve Dunning	.25	.10
❑ 648 Gary Thomasson	.25	.10
❑ 649 Moose Haas	.25	.10
❑ 650 Cesar Cedeno	.60	.24
❑ 651 Doug Rader	.25	.10
❑ 652 Checklist 606-726	1.25	.25
❑ 653 Ron Hodges DP	.15	.06
❑ 654 Pepe Frias	.25	.10
❑ 655 Lyman Bostock	.60	.24
❑ 656 Dave Garcia MG	.25	.10
❑ 657 Bombo Rivera	.25	.10
❑ 658 Manny Sanguillen	.60	.24
❑ 659 Texas Rangers Team Card CL	1.25	.25
❑ 660 Jason Thompson	.60	.24
❑ 661 Grant Jackson	.25	.10
❑ 662 Paul Dade	.25	.10
❑ 663 Paul Reuschel	.25	.10
❑ 664 Fred Stanley	.25	.10
❑ 665 Dennis Leonard	.60	.24
❑ 666 Billy Smith RC	.25	.10
❑ 667 Jeff Byrd	.25	.10
❑ 668 Dusty Baker	1.25	.50
❑ 669 Pete Falcone	.25	.10
❑ 670 Jim Rice	1.25	.50
❑ 671 Gary Lavelle	.25	.10
❑ 672 Don Kessinger	.60	.24
❑ 673 Steve Brye	.25	.10
❑ 674 Ray Knight RC	2.50	1.00
❑ 675 Jay Johnstone	.60	.24
❑ 676 Bob Myrick	.25	.10
❑ 677 Ed Herrmann	.25	.10
❑ 678 Tom Burgmeier	.25	.10
❑ 679 Wayne Garrett	.25	.10
❑ 680 Vida Blue	.60	.24
❑ 681 Rob Belloir	.25	.10
❑ 682 Ken Brett	.25	.10
❑ 683 Mike Champion	.25	.10
❑ 684 Ralph Houk MG	.60	.24
❑ 685 Frank Taveras	.25	.10
❑ 686 Gaylord Perry	2.50	1.00
❑ 687 Julio Cruz RC	.25	.10
❑ 688 George Mitterwald	.25	.10
❑ 689 Cleveland Indians Team Card CL	1.25	.25
❑ 690 Mickey Rivers	.60	.24
❑ 691 Ross Grimsley	.25	.10
❑ 692 Ken Reitz	.25	.10
❑ 693 Lamar Johnson	.25	.10
❑ 694 Elias Sosa	.25	.10
❑ 695 Dwight Evans	1.25	.50
❑ 696 Steve Mingori	.25	.10
❑ 697 Roger Metzger	.25	.10
❑ 698 Juan Bernhardt	.25	.10
❑ 699 Jackie Brown	.25	.10
❑ 700 Johnny Bench	8.00	3.20
❑ 701 Tom Hume Larry Landreth Steve McCatty Bruce Taylor	.60	.24
❑ 702 Bill Nahorodny Kevin Pasley Rick Sweet Don Werner	.60	.24
❑ 703 Larry Andersen Tim Jones Mickey Mahler Jack Morris RC DP	5.00	2.00
❑ 704 Garth Iorg Dave Oliver Sam Perlozzo Lou Whitaker RC	8.00	3.20
❑ 705 Dave Bergman Miguel Dilone Clint Hurdle Willie Norwood	1.25	.50
❑ 706 Wayne Cage Ted Cox Pat Putnam Dave Revering	.60	.24
❑ 707 Mickey Klutts Paul Molitor RC Alan Trammell RC U.L. Washington	50.00	20.00
❑ 708 Bo Diaz Dale Murphy Lance Parrish RC Ernie Whitt	4.00	1.60
❑ 709 Steve Burke Matt Keough Lance Rautzhan Dan Schatzeder	.60	.24
❑ 710 Dell Alston Rick Bosetti Mike Easler RC Keith Smith	1.25	.50
❑ 711 Cardell Camper Dennis Lamp Craig Mitchell Roy Thomas DP	.25	.10
❑ 712 Bobby Valentine	.60	.24
❑ 713 Bob Davis	.25	.10
❑ 714 Mike Anderson	.25	.10
❑ 715 Jim Kaat	1.25	.50
❑ 716 Clarence Gaston	.60	.24
❑ 717 Nelson Briles	.25	.10
❑ 718 Ron Jackson	.25	.10
❑ 719 Randy Elliott	.25	.10
❑ 720 Fergie Jenkins	2.50	1.00
❑ 721 Billy Martin MG	1.25	.50
❑ 722 Pete Broberg	.25	.10
❑ 723 John Wockenfuss	.25	.10
❑ 724 Kansas City Royals Team Card CL	1.25	.25
❑ 725 Kurt Bevacqua	.25	.10
❑ 726 Wilbur Wood	1.25	.30

1979 Topps

	NM	Ex
COMPLETE SET (726)	175.00	70.00
COMMON CARD (1-726)	.25	.10
COMMON CARD DP	.15	.06

Card	NM	Ex
❑ 1 Rod Carew Dave Parker LL	2.50	.50
❑ 2 Jim Rice George Foster LL	1.00	.40
❑ 3 Jim Rice George Foster LL	1.00	.40
❑ 4 Ron LeFlore Omar Moreno LL	.50	.20
❑ 5 Ron Guidry Gaylord Perry LL	.50	.20
❑ 6 Nolan Ryan J.R. Richard LL	5.00	2.00
❑ 7 Ron Guidry Craig Swan LL	.50	.20
❑ 8 Rich Gossage Rollie Fingers LL	1.00	.40
❑ 9 Dave Campbell	.25	.10
❑ 10 Lee May	.50	.20
❑ 11 Marc Hill	.25	.10
❑ 12 Dick Drago	.25	.10
❑ 13 Paul Dade	.25	.10
❑ 14 Rafael Landestoy	.25	.10
❑ 15 Ross Grimsley	.25	.10
❑ 16 Fred Stanley	.25	.10
❑ 17 Donnie Moore	.25	.10
❑ 18 Tony Solaita	.25	.10
❑ 19 Larry Gura DP	.15	.06
❑ 20 Joe Morgan DP	2.00	.80
❑ 21 Kevin Kobel	.25	.10
❑ 22 Mike Jorgensen	.25	.10
❑ 23 Terry Forster	.25	.10
❑ 24 Paul Molitor	10.00	4.00
❑ 25 Steve Carlton	3.00	1.20
❑ 26 Jamie Quirk	.25	.10
❑ 27 Dave Goltz	.25	.10
❑ 28 Steve Brye	.25	.10
❑ 29 Rick Langford	.25	.10
❑ 30 Dave Winfield	4.00	1.60
❑ 31 Tom House DP	.15	.06
❑ 32 Jerry Mumphrey	.25	.10
❑ 33 Dave Rozema	.25	.10
❑ 34 Rob Andrews	.25	.10
❑ 35 Ed Figueroa	.25	.10
❑ 36 Alan Ashby	.25	.10
❑ 37 Joe Kerrigan DP	.15	.06
❑ 38 Bernie Carbo	.25	.10
❑ 39 Dale Murphy	3.00	1.20
❑ 40 Dennis Eckersley	2.00	.80
❑ 41 Twins Team CL Gene Mauch MG	1.00	.20
❑ 42 Ron Blomberg	.25	.10
❑ 43 Wayne Twitchell	.25	.10
❑ 44 Kurt Bevacqua	.25	.10
❑ 45 Al Hrabosky	.25	.10
❑ 46 Ron Hodges	.25	.10
❑ 47 Fred Norman	.25	.10
❑ 48 Merv Rettenmund	.25	.10
❑ 49 Vern Ruhle	.25	.10
❑ 50 Steve Garvey DP	1.00	.40
❑ 51 Ray Fosse DP	.15	.06
❑ 52 Randy Lerch	.25	.10
❑ 53 Mick Kelleher	.25	.10
❑ 54 Dell Alston DP	.15	.06
❑ 55 Willie Stargell	2.00	.80
❑ 56 John Hale	.25	.10
❑ 57 Eric Rasmussen	.25	.10
❑ 58 Bob Randall DP	.15	.06
❑ 59 John Denny DP	.25	.10
❑ 60 Mickey Rivers	.50	.20
❑ 61 Bo Diaz	.25	.10
❑ 62 Randy Moffitt	.25	.10
❑ 63 Jack Brohamer	.25	.10
❑ 64 Tom Underwood	.25	.10
❑ 65 Mark Belanger	.50	.20
❑ 66 Tigers Team CL Les Moss MG	1.00	.20
❑ 67 Jim Mason DP	.15	.06
❑ 68 Joe Niekro DP	.25	.10
❑ 69 Elliott Maddox	.25	.10
❑ 70 John Candelaria	.50	.20
❑ 71 Brian Downing	.50	.20
❑ 72 Steve Mingori	.25	.10
❑ 73 Ken Henderson	.25	.10
❑ 74 Shane Rawley	.25	.10
❑ 75 Steve Yeager	.50	.20
❑ 76 Warren Cromartie	.50	.20
❑ 77 Dan Briggs DP	.15	.06
❑ 78 Elias Sosa	.25	.10
❑ 79 Ted Cox	.25	.10
❑ 80 Jason Thompson	.50	.20
❑ 81 Roger Erickson	.25	.10
❑ 82 Mets Team CL Joe Torre MG	1.00	.20
❑ 83 Fred Kendall	.25	.10
❑ 84 Greg Minton	.25	.10
❑ 85 Gary Matthews	.50	.20
❑ 86 Rodney Scott	.25	.10
❑ 87 Pete Falcone	.25	.10

❑ 88 Bob Molinaro	.25	.10
❑ 89 Dick Tidrow	.25	.10
❑ 90 Bob Boone	1.00	.40
❑ 91 Terry Crowley	.25	.10
❑ 92 Jim Bibby	.25	.10
❑ 93 Phil Mankowski	.25	.10
❑ 94 Len Barker	.25	.10
❑ 95 Robin Yount	5.00	2.00
❑ 96 Indians Team CL	1.00	.20
Jeff Torborg		
❑ 97 Sam Mejias	.25	.10
❑ 98 Ray Burris	.25	.10
❑ 99 John Wathan	.50	.20
❑ 100 Tom Seaver DP	4.00	1.60
❑ 101 Roy Howell	.25	.10
❑ 102 Mike Anderson	.25	.10
❑ 103 Jim Todd	.25	.10
❑ 104 Johnny Oates DP	.25	.10
❑ 105 Rick Camp DP	.15	.06
❑ 106 Frank Duffy	.25	.10
❑ 107 Jesus Alou DP	.15	.06
❑ 108 Eduardo Rodriguez	.25	.10
❑ 109 Joel Youngblood	.25	.10
❑ 110 Vida Blue	.50	.20
❑ 111 Roger Freed	.25	.10
❑ 112 Phillies Team	1.00	.20
Danny Ozark MG		
❑ 113 Pete Redfern	.25	.10
❑ 114 Cliff Johnson	.25	.10
❑ 115 Nolan Ryan	20.00	8.00
❑ 116 Ozzie Smith RC	60.00	24.00
❑ 117 Grant Jackson	.25	.10
❑ 118 Bud Harrelson	.50	.20
❑ 119 Don Stanhouse	.25	.10
❑ 120 Jim Sundberg	.50	.20
❑ 121 Checklist 1-121 DP	.50	.10
❑ 122 Mike Paxton	.25	.10
❑ 123 Lou Whitaker	2.50	1.00
❑ 124 Dan Schatzeder	.25	.10
❑ 125 Rick Burleson	.25	.10
❑ 126 Doug Bair	.25	.10
❑ 127 Thad Bosley	.25	.10
❑ 128 Ted Martinez	.25	.10
❑ 129 Marty Pattin DP	.15	.06
❑ 130 Bob Watson DP	.25	.10
❑ 131 Jim Clancy	.25	.10
❑ 132 Rowland Office	.25	.10
❑ 133 Bill Castro	.25	.10
❑ 134 Alan Bannister	.25	.10
❑ 135 Bobby Murcer	.50	.20
❑ 136 Jim Kaat	.50	.20
❑ 137 Larry Wolfe DP	.15	.06
❑ 138 Mark Lee RC	.25	.10
❑ 139 Luis Pujols	.25	.10
❑ 140 Don Gullett	.50	.20
❑ 141 Tom Paciorek	.50	.20
❑ 142 Charlie Williams	.25	.10
❑ 143 Tony Scott	.25	.10
❑ 144 Sandy Alomar	.25	.10
❑ 145 Rick Rhoden	.25	.10
❑ 146 Duane Kuiper	.25	.10
❑ 147 Dave Hamilton	.25	.10
❑ 148 Bruce Boisclair	.25	.10
❑ 149 Manny Sarmiento	.25	.10
❑ 150 Wayne Cage	.25	.10
❑ 151 John Hiller	.25	.10
❑ 152 Rick Cerone	.25	.10
❑ 153 Dennis Lamp	.25	.10
❑ 154 Jim Gantner DP	.25	.10
❑ 155 Dwight Evans	1.00	.40
❑ 156 Buddy Solomon	.25	.10
❑ 157 U.L. Washington UER	.25	.10
(Sic, bats left, should be right)		
❑ 158 Joe Sambito	.25	.10
❑ 159 Roy White	.50	.20
❑ 160 Mike Flanagan	1.00	.40
❑ 161 Barry Foote	.25	.10
❑ 162 Tom Johnson	.25	.10
❑ 163 Glenn Burke	.25	.10
❑ 164 Mickey Lolich	.50	.20
❑ 165 Frank Taveras	.25	.10
❑ 166 Leon Roberts	.25	.10
❑ 167 Roger Metzger DP	.15	.06
❑ 168 Dave Freisleben	.25	.10
❑ 169 Bill Nahorodny	.25	.10
❑ 170 Don Sutton	2.00	.80
❑ 171 Gene Clines	.25	.10
❑ 172 Mike Bruhert	.25	.10
❑ 173 John Lowenstein	.25	.10
❑ 174 Rick Auerbach	.25	.10
❑ 175 George Hendrick	1.00	.40
❑ 176 Aurelio Rodriguez	.25	.10
❑ 177 Ron Reed	.25	.10
❑ 178 Alvis Woods	.25	.10
❑ 179 Jim Beattie DP	.15	.06
❑ 180 Larry Hisle	.25	.10
❑ 181 Mike Garman	.25	.10
❑ 182 Tim Johnson	.25	.10
❑ 183 Paul Splittorff	.25	.10
❑ 184 Darrel Chaney	.25	.10
❑ 185 Mike Torrez	.50	.20
❑ 186 Eric Soderholm	.25	.10
❑ 187 Mark Lemongello	.25	.10
❑ 188 Pat Kelly	.25	.10
❑ 189 Eddie Whitson RC	.25	.10
❑ 190 Ron Cey	.50	.20
❑ 191 Mike Norris	.25	.10
❑ 192 Cardinals Team CL	1.00	.20
Ken Boyer MG		
❑ 193 Glenn Adams	.25	.10
❑ 194 Randy Jones	.25	.10
❑ 195 Bill Madlock	.50	.20
❑ 196 Steve Kemp DP	.25	.10
❑ 197 Bob Apodaca	.25	.10
❑ 198 Johnny Grubb	.25	.10
❑ 199 Larry Milbourne	.25	.10
❑ 200 Johnny Bench DP	5.00	2.00
❑ 201 Mike Edwards RB	.25	.10
❑ 202 Ron Guidry RB	.50	.20
❑ 203 J.R. Richard RB	.25	.10
❑ 204 Pete Rose RB	5.00	2.00
❑ 205 John Stearns RB	.25	.10
❑ 206 Sammy Stewart RB	.25	.10
❑ 207 Dave Lemanczyk	.25	.10
❑ 208 Clarence Gaston	.25	.10
❑ 209 Reggie Cleveland	.25	.10
❑ 210 Larry Bowa	.50	.20
❑ 211 Denny Martinez	2.00	.80
❑ 212 Carney Lansford RC	1.00	.40
❑ 213 Bill Travers	.25	.10
❑ 214 Red Sox Team CL	1.00	.20
Don Zimmer MG		
❑ 215 Willie McCovey	2.50	1.00
❑ 216 Wilbur Wood	.25	.10
❑ 217 Steve Dillard	.25	.10
❑ 218 Dennis Leonard	.50	.20
❑ 219 Roy Smalley	.50	.20
❑ 220 Cesar Geronimo	.25	.10
❑ 221 Jesse Jefferson	.25	.10
❑ 222 Bob Beall	.25	.10
❑ 223 Kent Tekulve	.50	.20
❑ 224 Dave Revering	.25	.10
❑ 225 Goose Gossage	1.00	.40
❑ 226 Ron Pruitt	.25	.10
❑ 227 Steve Stone	.50	.20
❑ 228 Vic Davalillo	.25	.10
❑ 229 Doug Flynn	.25	.10
❑ 230 Bob Forsch	.25	.10
❑ 231 John Wockenfuss	.25	.10
❑ 232 Jimmy Sexton	.25	.10
❑ 233 Paul Mitchell	.25	.10
❑ 234 Toby Harrah	.50	.20
❑ 235 Steve Rogers	.25	.10
❑ 236 Jim Dwyer	.25	.10
❑ 237 Billy Smith	.25	.10
❑ 238 Balor Moore	.25	.10
❑ 239 Willie Horton	.50	.20
❑ 240 Rick Reuschel	.50	.20
❑ 241 Checklist 122-242 DP	.50	.10
❑ 242 Pablo Torrealba	.25	.10
❑ 243 Buck Martinez DP	.15	.06
❑ 244 Pirates Team CL	1.00	.20
Chuck Tanner MG		
❑ 245 Jeff Burroughs	.50	.20
❑ 246 Darrell Jackson	.25	.10
❑ 247 Tucker Ashford DP	.15	.06
❑ 248 Pete LaCock	.25	.10
❑ 249 Paul Thormodsgard	.25	.10
❑ 250 Willie Randolph	.50	.20
❑ 251 Jack Morris	2.00	.80
❑ 252 Bob Stinson	.25	.10
❑ 253 Rick Wise	.25	.10
❑ 254 Luis Gomez	.25	.10
❑ 255 Tommy John	1.00	.40
❑ 256 Mike Sadek	.25	.10
❑ 257 Adrian Devine	.25	.10
❑ 258 Mike Phillips	.25	.10
❑ 259 Reds Team CL	1.00	.20
Sparky Anderson MG		
❑ 260 Richie Zisk	.25	.10
❑ 261 Mario Guerrero	.25	.10
❑ 262 Nelson Briles	.25	.10
❑ 263 Oscar Gamble	.50	.20
❑ 264 Don Robinson RC	.25	.10
❑ 265 Don Money	.25	.10
❑ 266 Jim Willoughby	.25	.10
❑ 267 Joe Rudi	.50	.20
❑ 268 Julio Gonzalez	.25	.10
❑ 269 Woodie Fryman	.25	.10
❑ 270 Butch Hobson	.50	.20
❑ 271 Rawly Eastwick	.25	.10
❑ 272 Tim Corcoran	.25	.10
❑ 273 Jerry Terrell	.25	.10
❑ 274 Willie Norwood	.25	.10
❑ 275 Junior Moore	.25	.10
❑ 276 Jim Colborn	.25	.10
❑ 277 Tom Grieve	.50	.20
❑ 278 Andy Messersmith	.50	.20
❑ 279 Jerry Grote DP	.15	.06
❑ 280 Andre Thornton	.50	.20
❑ 281 Vic Correll DP	.15	.06
❑ 282 Blue Jays Team CL	.50	.10
Roy Hartsfield MG		
❑ 283 Ken Kravec	.25	.10
❑ 284 Johnnie LeMaster	.25	.10
❑ 285 Bobby Bonds	1.00	.40
❑ 286 Duffy Dyer	.25	.10
❑ 287 Andres Mora	.25	.10
❑ 288 Milt Wilcox	.25	.10
❑ 289 Jose Cruz	1.00	.40
❑ 290 Dave Lopes	.50	.20
❑ 291 Tom Griffin	.25	.10
❑ 292 Don Reynolds	.25	.10
❑ 293 Jerry Garvin	.25	.10
❑ 294 Pepe Frias	.25	.10
❑ 295 Mitchell Page	.25	.10
❑ 296 Preston Hanna	.25	.10
❑ 297 Ted Sizemore	.25	.10
❑ 298 Rich Gale	.25	.10
❑ 299 Steve Ontiveros	.25	.10
❑ 300 Rod Carew	3.00	1.20
❑ 301 Tom Hume	.25	.10
❑ 302 Braves Team CL	1.00	.20
Bobby Cox MG		
❑ 303 Lary Sorensen DP	.15	.06
❑ 304 Steve Swisher	.25	.10
❑ 305 Willie Montanez	.25	.10
❑ 306 Floyd Bannister	.25	.10
❑ 307 Larvell Blanks	.25	.10
❑ 308 Bert Blyleven	1.00	.40
❑ 309 Ralph Garr	.50	.20
❑ 310 Thurman Munson	3.00	1.20
❑ 311 Gary Lavelle	.25	.10
❑ 312 Bob Robertson	.25	.10
❑ 313 Dyar Miller	.25	.10
❑ 314 Larry Harlow	.25	.10
❑ 315 Jon Matlack	.25	.10
❑ 316 Milt May	.25	.10
❑ 317 Jose Cardenal	.50	.20
❑ 318 Bob Welch RC	2.00	.80
❑ 319 Wayne Garrett	.25	.10
❑ 320 Carl Yastrzemski	5.00	2.00
❑ 321 Gaylord Perry	2.00	.80
❑ 322 Danny Goodwin	.25	.10
❑ 323 Lynn McGlothen	.25	.10
❑ 324 Mike Tyson	.25	.10
❑ 325 Cecil Cooper	.50	.20
❑ 326 Pedro Borbon	.25	.10
❑ 327 Art Howe DP	.25	.10
❑ 328 A's Team CL	1.00	.20
Jack McKeon MG		
❑ 329 Joe Coleman	.25	.10
❑ 330 George Brett	10.00	4.00
❑ 331 Mickey Mahler	.25	.10
❑ 332 Gary Alexander	.25	.10
❑ 333 Chet Lemon	.50	.20
❑ 334 Craig Swan	.25	.10

❑ 335 Chris Chambliss .50 .20
❑ 336 Bobby Thompson .25 .10
❑ 337 John Montague .25 .10
❑ 338 Vic Harris .25 .10
❑ 339 Ron Jackson .25 .10
❑ 340 Jim Palmer 2.50 1.00
❑ 341 Willie Upshaw .50 .20
❑ 342 Dave Roberts .25 .10
❑ 343 Ed Glynn .25 .10
❑ 344 Jerry Royster .25 .10
❑ 345 Tug McGraw .50 .20
❑ 346 Bill Buckner .50 .20
❑ 347 Doug Rau .25 .10
❑ 348 Andre Dawson 3.00 1.20
❑ 349 Jim Wright .25 .10
❑ 350 Garry Templeton .50 .20
❑ 351 Wayne Nordhagen DP .15 .06
❑ 352 Steve Renko .25 .10
❑ 353 Checklist 243-363 1.00 .20
❑ 354 Bill Bonham .25 .10
❑ 355 Lee Mazzilli .25 .10
❑ 356 Giants Team CL 1.00 .20
Joe Altobelli MG
❑ 357 Jerry Augustine .25 .10
❑ 358 Alan Trammell 3.00 1.20
❑ 359 Dan Spillner DP .15 .06
❑ 360 Amos Otis .50 .20
❑ 361 Tom Dixon .25 .10
❑ 362 Mike Cubbage .25 .10
❑ 363 Craig Skok .25 .10
❑ 364 Gene Richards .25 .10
❑ 365 Sparky Lyle .50 .20
❑ 366 Juan Bernhardt .25 .10
❑ 367 Dave Skaggs .25 .10
❑ 368 Don Aase .25 .10
❑ 369A Bump Wills ERR 3.00 1.20
(Blue Jays)
❑ 369B Bump Wills COR 3.00 1.20
(Rangers)
❑ 370 Dave Kingman 1.00 .40
❑ 371 Jeff Holly .25 .10
❑ 372 Lamar Johnson .25 .10
❑ 373 Lance Rautzhan .25 .10
❑ 374 Ed Herrmann .25 .10
❑ 375 Bill Campbell .25 .10
❑ 376 Gorman Thomas .50 .20
❑ 377 Paul Moskau .25 .10
❑ 378 Rob Picciolo DP .15 .06
❑ 379 Dale Murray .25 .10
❑ 380 John Mayberry .50 .20
❑ 381 Astros Team CL 1.00 .20
Bill Virdon MG
❑ 382 Jerry Martin .25 .10
❑ 383 Phil Garner .50 .20
❑ 384 Tommy Boggs .25 .10
❑ 385 Dan Ford .25 .10
❑ 386 Francisco Barrios .25 .10
❑ 387 Gary Thomasson .25 .10
❑ 388 Jack Billingham .25 .10
❑ 389 Joe Zdeb .25 .10
❑ 390 Rollie Fingers 2.00 .80
❑ 391 Al Oliver .50 .20
❑ 392 Doug Ault .25 .10
❑ 393 Scott McGregor .50 .20
❑ 394 Randy Stein .25 .10
❑ 395 Dave Cash .25 .10
❑ 396 Bill Plummer .25 .10
❑ 397 Sergio Ferrer .25 .10
❑ 398 Ivan DeJesus .25 .10
❑ 399 David Clyde .25 .10
❑ 400 Jim Rice 1.00 .40
❑ 401 Ray Knight .50 .20
❑ 402 Paul Hartzell .25 .10
❑ 403 Tim Foli .25 .10
❑ 404 White Sox Team CL 1.00 .20
Don Kessinger MG
❑ 405 Butch Wynegar DP .15 .06
❑ 406 Joe Wallis DP .15 .06
❑ 407 Pete Vuckovich .50 .20
❑ 408 Charlie Moore DP .15 .06
❑ 409 Willie Wilson RC 1.00 .40
❑ 410 Darrell Evans 1.00 .40
❑ 411 George Sisler ATL 2.50 1.00
Ty Cobb
❑ 412 Hack Wilson ATL 2.50 1.00
Hank Aaron
❑ 413 Roger Maris ATL 4.00 1.60
Hank Aaron
❑ 414 Rogers Hornsby ATL 2.50 1.00
Ty Cobb
❑ 415 Lou Brock ATL 1.00 .40
❑ 416 Jack Chesbro ATL .50 .20
Cy Young
❑ 417 Nolan Ryan ATL DP 5.00 2.00
Walter Johnson
❑ 418 D.Leonard ATL DP .25 .10
Walter Johnson
❑ 419 Dick Ruthven .25 .10
❑ 420 Ken Griffey Sr. .50 .20
❑ 421 Doug DeCinces .50 .20
❑ 422 Ruppert Jones .25 .10
❑ 423 Bob Montgomery .25 .10
❑ 424 Angels Team CL 1.00 .20
Jim Fregosi MG
❑ 425 Rick Manning .25 .10
❑ 426 Chris Speier .25 .10
❑ 427 Andy Replogle .25 .10
❑ 428 Bobby Valentine .50 .20
❑ 429 John Urrea DP .15 .06
❑ 430 Dave Parker .50 .20
❑ 431 Glenn Borgmann .25 .10
❑ 432 Dave Heaverlo .25 .10
❑ 433 Larry Biittner .25 .10
❑ 434 Ken Clay .25 .10
❑ 435 Gene Tenace .50 .20
❑ 436 Hector Cruz .25 .10
❑ 437 Rick Williams .25 .10
❑ 438 Horace Speed .25 .10
❑ 439 Frank White .50 .20
❑ 440 Rusty Staub 1.00 .40
❑ 441 Lee Lacy .25 .10
❑ 442 Doyle Alexander .25 .10
❑ 443 Bruce Bochte .25 .10
❑ 444 Aurelio Lopez .25 .10
❑ 445 Steve Henderson .25 .10
❑ 446 Jim Lonborg .50 .20
❑ 447 Manny Sanguillen .50 .20
❑ 448 Moose Haas .25 .10
❑ 449 Bombo Rivera .25 .10
❑ 450 Dave Concepcion 1.00 .40
❑ 451 Royals Team CL 1.00 .20
Whitey Herzog MG
❑ 452 Jerry Morales .25 .10
❑ 453 Chris Knapp .25 .10
❑ 454 Len Randle .25 .10
❑ 455 Bill Lee DP .15 .06
❑ 456 Chuck Baker .25 .10
❑ 457 Bruce Sutter .50 .20
❑ 458 Jim Essian .25 .10
❑ 459 Sid Monge .25 .10
❑ 460 Graig Nettles 1.00 .40
❑ 461 Jim Barr DP .15 .06
❑ 462 Otto Velez .25 .10
❑ 463 Steve Comer .25 .10
❑ 464 Joe Nolan .25 .10
❑ 465 Reggie Smith .50 .20
❑ 466 Mark Littell .25 .10
❑ 467 Don Kessinger DP .25 .10
❑ 468 Stan Bahnsen DP .15 .06
❑ 469 Lance Parrish 1.00 .40
❑ 470 Garry Maddox DP .25 .10
❑ 471 Joaquin Andujar .50 .20
❑ 472 Craig Kusick .25 .10
❑ 473 Dave Roberts .25 .10
❑ 474 Dick Davis .25 .10
❑ 475 Dan Driessen .25 .10
❑ 476 Tom Poquette .25 .10
❑ 477 Bob Grich .50 .20
❑ 478 Juan Beniquez .25 .10
❑ 479 Padres Team CL 1.00 .20
Roger Craig MG
❑ 480 Fred Lynn .50 .20
❑ 481 Skip Lockwood .25 .10
❑ 482 Craig Reynolds .25 .10
❑ 483 Checklist 364-484 DP .50 .10
❑ 484 Rick Waits .25 .10
❑ 485 Bucky Dent .50 .20
❑ 486 Bob Knepper .25 .10
❑ 487 Miguel Dilone .25 .10
❑ 488 Bob Owchinko .25 .10
❑ 489 Larry Cox UER .25 .10
(Photo actually
Dave Rader)
❑ 490 Al Cowens .25 .10
❑ 491 Tippy Martinez .25 .10
❑ 492 Bob Bailor .25 .10
❑ 493 Larry Christenson .25 .10
❑ 494 Jerry White .25 .10
❑ 495 Tony Perez 2.00 .80
❑ 496 Barry Bonnell DP .15 .06
❑ 497 Glenn Abbott .25 .10
❑ 498 Rich Chiles .25 .10
❑ 499 Rangers Team CL 1.00 .20
Pat Corrales MG
❑ 500 Ron Guidry .50 .20
❑ 501 Junior Kennedy .25 .10
❑ 502 Steve Braun .25 .10
❑ 503 Terry Humphrey .25 .10
❑ 504 Larry McWilliams .25 .10
❑ 505 Ed Kranepool .25 .10
❑ 506 John D'Acquisto .25 .10
❑ 507 Tony Armas .50 .20
❑ 508 Charlie Hough .50 .20
❑ 509 Mario Mendoza UER .25 .10
(Career BA .278,
should say .204)
❑ 510 Ted Simmons 1.00 .40
❑ 511 Paul Reuschel DP .15 .06
❑ 512 Jack Clark .50 .20
❑ 513 Dave Johnson .50 .20
❑ 514 Mike Proly .25 .10
❑ 515 Enos Cabell .25 .10
❑ 516 Champ Summers DP .15 .06
❑ 517 Al Bumbry .50 .20
❑ 518 Jim Umbarger .25 .10
❑ 519 Ben Oglivie .50 .20
❑ 520 Gary Carter 1.00 .40
❑ 521 Sam Ewing .25 .10
❑ 522 Ken Holtzman .50 .20
❑ 523 John Milner .25 .10
❑ 524 Tom Burgmeier .25 .10
❑ 525 Freddie Patek .25 .10
❑ 526 Dodgers Team CL 1.00 .20
Tom Lasorda MG
❑ 527 Lerrin LaGrow .25 .10
❑ 528 Wayne Gross DP .15 .06
❑ 529 Brian Asselstine .25 .10
❑ 530 Frank Tanana .50 .20
❑ 531 Fernando Gonzalez .25 .10
❑ 532 Buddy Schultz .25 .10
❑ 533 Leroy Stanton .25 .10
❑ 534 Ken Forsch .25 .10
❑ 535 Ellis Valentine .25 .10
❑ 536 Jerry Reuss .50 .20
❑ 537 Tom Veryzer .25 .10
❑ 538 Mike Ivie DP .15 .06
❑ 539 John Ellis .25 .10
❑ 540 Greg Luzinski .50 .20
❑ 541 Jim Slaton .25 .10
❑ 542 Rick Bosetti .25 .10
❑ 543 Kiko Garcia .25 .10
❑ 544 Fergie Jenkins 2.00 .80
❑ 545 John Stearns .25 .10
❑ 546 Bill Russell .50 .20
❑ 547 Clint Hurdle .25 .10
❑ 548 Enrique Romo .25 .10
❑ 549 Bob Bailey .25 .10
❑ 550 Sal Bando .50 .20
❑ 551 Cubs Team CL 1.00 .20
Herman Franks MG
❑ 552 Jose Morales .25 .10
❑ 553 Denny Walling .25 .10
❑ 554 Matt Keough .25 .10
❑ 555 Biff Pocoroba .25 .10
❑ 556 Mike Lum .25 .10
❑ 557 Ken Brett .25 .10
❑ 558 Jay Johnstone .50 .20
❑ 559 Greg Pryor .25 .10
❑ 560 John Montefusco .25 .10
❑ 561 Ed Ott .25 .10
❑ 562 Dusty Baker 1.00 .40
❑ 563 Roy Thomas .25 .10
❑ 564 Jerry Turner .25 .10
❑ 565 Rico Carty .50 .20
❑ 566 Nino Espinosa .25 .10
❑ 567 Richie Hebner .50 .20
❑ 568 Carlos Lopez .25 .10
❑ 569 Bob Sykes .25 .10

❑ 570 Cesar Cedeno	.50	.20
❑ 571 Darrell Porter	.50	.20
❑ 572 Rod Gilbreath	.25	.10
❑ 573 Jim Kern	.25	.10
❑ 574 Claudell Washington	.50	.20
❑ 575 Luis Tiant	.50	.20
❑ 576 Mike Parrott	.25	.10
❑ 577 Brewers Team CL	1.00	.20
George Bamberger MG		
❑ 578 Pete Broberg	.25	.10
❑ 579 Greg Gross	.25	.10
❑ 580 Ron Fairly	.50	.20
❑ 581 Darold Knowles	.25	.10
❑ 582 Paul Blair	.50	.20
❑ 583 Julio Cruz	.25	.10
❑ 584 Jim Rooker	.25	.10
❑ 585 Hal McRae	1.00	.40
❑ 586 Bob Horner RC	1.00	.40
❑ 587 Ken Reitz	.25	.10
❑ 588 Tom Murphy	.25	.10
❑ 589 Terry Whitfield	.25	.10
❑ 590 J.R. Richard	.50	.20
❑ 591 Mike Hargrove	.50	.20
❑ 592 Mike Krukow	.25	.10
❑ 593 Rick Dempsey	.50	.20
❑ 594 Bob Shirley	.25	.10
❑ 595 Phil Niekro	2.00	.80
❑ 596 Jim Wohlford	.25	.10
❑ 597 Bob Stanley	.25	.10
❑ 598 Mark Wagner	.25	.10
❑ 599 Jim Spencer	.25	.10
❑ 600 George Foster	.50	.20
❑ 601 Dave LaRoche	.25	.10
❑ 602 Checklist 485-605	1.00	.20
❑ 603 Rudy May	.25	.10
❑ 604 Jeff Newman	.25	.10
❑ 605 Rick Monday DP	.25	.10
❑ 606 Expos Team CL	1.00	.20
Dick Williams MG		
❑ 607 Omar Moreno	.25	.10
❑ 608 Dave McKay	.25	.10
❑ 609 Silvio Martinez	.25	.10
❑ 610 Mike Schmidt	8.00	3.20
❑ 611 Jim Norris	.25	.10
❑ 612 Rick Honeycutt RC	.50	.20
❑ 613 Mike Edwards	.25	.10
❑ 614 Willie Hernandez	.50	.20
❑ 615 Ken Singleton	.50	.20
❑ 616 Billy Almon	.25	.10
❑ 617 Terry Puhl	.25	.10
❑ 618 Jerry Remy	.25	.10
❑ 619 Ken Landreaux	.50	.20
❑ 620 Bert Campaneris	.50	.20
❑ 621 Pat Zachry	.25	.10
❑ 622 Dave Collins	.50	.20
❑ 623 Bob McClure	.25	.10
❑ 624 Larry Herndon	.25	.10
❑ 625 Mark Fidrych	2.00	.80
❑ 626 Yankees Team CL	1.00	.20
Bob Lemon MG		
❑ 627 Gary Serum	.25	.10
❑ 628 Del Unser	.25	.10
❑ 629 Gene Garber	.50	.20
❑ 630 Bake McBride	.50	.20
❑ 631 Jorge Orta	.25	.10
❑ 632 Don Kirkwood	.25	.10
❑ 633 Rob Wilfong DP	.15	.06
❑ 634 Paul Lindblad	.25	.10
❑ 635 Don Baylor	1.00	.40
❑ 636 Wayne Garland	.25	.10
❑ 637 Bill Robinson	.50	.20
❑ 638 Al Fitzmorris	.25	.10
❑ 639 Manny Trillo	.25	.10
❑ 640 Eddie Murray	12.00	4.80
❑ 641 Bobby Castillo	.25	.10
❑ 642 Wilbur Howard DP	.15	.06
❑ 643 Tom Hausman	.25	.10
❑ 644 Manny Mota	.50	.20
❑ 645 George Scott DP	.25	.10
❑ 646 Rick Sweet	.25	.10
❑ 647 Bob Lacey	.25	.10
❑ 648 Lou Piniella	.50	.20
❑ 649 John Curtis	.25	.10
❑ 650 Pete Rose	12.00	4.80
❑ 651 Mike Caldwell	.25	.10
❑ 652 Stan Papi	.25	.10
❑ 653 Warren Brusstar DP	.15	.06
❑ 654 Rick Miller	.25	.10
❑ 655 Jerry Koosman	.50	.20
❑ 656 Hosken Powell	.25	.10
❑ 657 George Medich	.25	.10
❑ 658 Taylor Duncan	.25	.10
❑ 659 Mariners Team CL	1.00	.20
Darrell Johnson MG		
❑ 660 Ron LeFlore DP	.25	.10
❑ 661 Bruce Kison	.25	.10
❑ 662 Kevin Bell	.25	.10
❑ 663 Mike Vail	.25	.10
❑ 664 Doug Bird	.25	.10
❑ 665 Lou Brock	2.50	1.00
❑ 666 Rich Dauer	.25	.10
❑ 667 Don Hood	.25	.10
❑ 668 Bill North	.25	.10
❑ 669 Checklist 606-726	1.00	.20
❑ 670 Jim Hunter DP	1.00	.40
❑ 671 Joe Ferguson DP	.15	.06
❑ 672 Ed Halicki	.25	.10
❑ 673 Tom Hutton	.25	.10
❑ 674 Dave Tomlin	.25	.10
❑ 675 Tim McCarver	1.00	.40
❑ 676 Johnny Sutton	.25	.10
❑ 677 Larry Parrish	.50	.20
❑ 678 Geoff Zahn	.25	.10
❑ 679 Derrel Thomas	.25	.10
❑ 680 Carlton Fisk	3.00	1.20
❑ 681 John Henry Johnson	.25	.10
❑ 682 Dave Chalk	.25	.10
❑ 683 Dan Meyer DP	.15	.06
❑ 684 Jamie Easterly DP	.15	.06
❑ 685 Sixto Lezcano	.25	.10
❑ 686 Ron Schueler DP	.15	.06
❑ 687 Rennie Stennett	.25	.10
❑ 688 Mike Willis	.25	.10
❑ 689 Orioles Team CL	1.00	.20
Earl Weaver MG		
❑ 690 Buddy Bell DP	.25	.10
❑ 691 Dock Ellis DP	.15	.06
❑ 692 Mickey Stanley	.25	.10
❑ 693 Dave Rader	.25	.10
❑ 694 Burt Hooton	.50	.20
❑ 695 Keith Hernandez	.50	.20
❑ 696 Andy Hassler	.25	.10
❑ 697 Dave Bergman	.25	.10
❑ 698 Bill Stein	.25	.10
❑ 699 Hal Dues	.25	.10
❑ 700 Reggie Jackson DP	5.00	2.00
❑ 701 Mark Corey	.50	.20
John Flinn		
Sammy Stewart		
❑ 702 Joel Finch	.50	.20
Garry Hancock		
Allen Ripley		
❑ 703 Jim Anderson	.50	.20
Dave Frost		
Bob Slater		
❑ 704 Ross Baumgarten	.50	.20
Mike Colbern		
Mike Squires		
❑ 705 Alfredo Griffin RC	1.00	.40
Tim Norrid		
Dave Oliver		
❑ 706 Dave Stegman	.50	.20
Dave Tobik		
Kip Young		
❑ 707 Randy Bass RC	1.00	.40
Jim Gaudet		
Randy McGilberry		
❑ 708 Kevin Bass RC	1.00	.40
Eddie Romero		
Ned Yost RC		
❑ 709 Sam Perlozzo	.50	.20
Rick Sofield		
Kevin Stanfield		
❑ 710 Brian Doyle	.50	.20
Mike Heath		
Dave Rajsich		
❑ 711 Dwayne Murphy RC	1.00	.40
Bruce Robinson		
Alan Wirth		
❑ 712 Bud Anderson	.50	.20
Greg Biercevicz		
Byron McLaughlin		
❑ 713 Danny Darwin RC	1.00	.40
Pat Putnam		
Billy Sample		
❑ 714 Victor Cruz	.50	.20
Pat Kelly		
Ernie Whitt		
❑ 715 Bruce Benedict	1.00	.40
Glenn Hubbard RC		
Larry Whisenton		
❑ 716 Dave Geisel	.50	.20
Karl Pagel		
Scot Thompson		
❑ 717 Mike LaCoss	.50	.20
Ron Oester RC		
Harry Spilman		
❑ 718 Bruce Bochy	.50	.20
Mike Fischlin		
Don Pisker		
❑ 719 Pedro Guerrero RC	1.00	.40
Rudy Law		
Joe Simpson		
❑ 720 Jerry Fry	1.00	.40
Jerry Pirtle		
Scott Sanderson RC		
❑ 721 Juan Berenguer	.50	.20
Dwight Bernard		
Dan Norman		
❑ 722 Jim Morrison	1.00	.40
Lonnie Smith RC		
Jim Wright		
❑ 723 Dale Berra RC	.50	.20
Eugenio Cotes		
Ben Wiltbank		
❑ 724 Tom Bruno	1.00	.40
George Frazier		
Terry Kennedy RC		
❑ 725 Jim Beswick	.50	.20
Steve Mura		
Broderick Perkins		
❑ 726 Greg Johnston	.50	.10
Joe Strain		
John Tamargo		

1980 Topps

	NM	Ex
COMPLETE SET (726)	120.00	47.50
COMMON CARD (1-726)	.25	.10
COMMON DP	.25	.10
❑ 1 Lou Brock HL	2.50	.50
Carl Yastrzemski		
❑ 2 Willie McCovey HL	.75	.30
❑ 3 Manny Mota HL	.25	.10
❑ 4 Pete Rose HL	3.00	1.20
❑ 5 Garry Templeton HL	.25	.10
❑ 6 Del Unser HL	.25	.10
❑ 7 Mike Lum	.25	.10
❑ 8 Craig Swan	.25	.10
❑ 9 Steve Braun	.25	.10
❑ 10 Dennis Martinez	.75	.30
❑ 11 Jimmy Sexton	.25	.10
❑ 12 John Curtis DP	.25	.10
❑ 13 Ron Pruitt	.25	.10
❑ 14 Dave Cash	.75	.30
❑ 15 Bill Campbell	.25	.10
❑ 16 Jerry Narron	.25	.10
❑ 17 Bruce Sutter	.75	.30

❑ 18 Ron Jackson .25 .10
❑ 19 Balor Moore .25 .10
❑ 20 Dan Ford .25 .10
❑ 21 Manny Sarmiento .25 .10
❑ 22 Pat Putnam .25 .10
❑ 23 Derrel Thomas .25 .10
❑ 24 Jim Slaton .25 .10
❑ 25 Lee Mazzilli .75 .30
❑ 26 Marty Pattin .25 .10
❑ 27 Del Unser .25 .10
❑ 28 Bruce Kison .25 .10
❑ 29 Mark Wagner .25 .10
❑ 30 Vida Blue .75 .30
❑ 31 Jay Johnstone .25 .10
❑ 32 Julio Cruz DP .25 .10
❑ 33 Tony Scott .25 .10
❑ 34 Jeff Newman DP .25 .10
❑ 35 Luis Tiant .75 .30
❑ 36 Rusty Torres .25 .10
❑ 37 Kiko Garcia .25 .10
❑ 38 Dan Spillner DP .25 .10
❑ 39 Rowland Office .25 .10
❑ 40 Carlton Fisk 2.50 1.00
❑ 41 Rangers Team CL .75 .15
Pat Corrales MG
❑ 42 David Palmer .25 .10
❑ 43 Bombo Rivera .25 .10
❑ 44 Bill Fahey .25 .10
❑ 45 Frank White .75 .30
❑ 46 Rico Carty .75 .30
❑ 47 Bill Bonham DP .25 .10
❑ 48 Rick Miller .25 .10
❑ 49 Mario Guerrero .25 .10
❑ 50 J.R. Richard .75 .30
❑ 51 Joe Ferguson DP .25 .10
❑ 52 Warren Brusstar .25 .10
❑ 53 Ben Oglivie .75 .30
❑ 54 Dennis Lamp .25 .10
❑ 55 Bill Madlock .75 .30
❑ 56 Bobby Valentine .75 .30
❑ 57 Pete Vuckovich .25 .10
❑ 58 Doug Flynn .25 .10
❑ 59 Eddy Putman .25 .10
❑ 60 Bucky Dent .75 .30
❑ 61 Gary Serum .25 .10
❑ 62 Mike Ivie .25 .10
❑ 63 Bob Stanley .25 .10
❑ 64 Joe Nolan .25 .10
❑ 65 Al Bumbry .75 .30
❑ 66 Royals Team CL .75 .15
Jim Frey MG
❑ 67 Doyle Alexander .25 .10
❑ 68 Larry Harlow .25 .10
❑ 69 Rick Williams .25 .10
❑ 70 Gary Carter 1.50 .60
❑ 71 John Milner DP .25 .10
❑ 72 Fred Howard DP .25 .10
❑ 73 Dave Collins .25 .10
❑ 74 Sid Monge .25 .10
❑ 75 Bill Russell .75 .30
❑ 76 John Stearns .25 .10
❑ 77 Dave Stieb RC 1.50 .60
❑ 78 Ruppert Jones .25 .10
❑ 79 Bob Owchinko .25 .10
❑ 80 Ron LeFlore .75 .30
❑ 81 Ted Sizemore .25 .10
❑ 82 Astros Team CL .75 .15
Bill Virdon MG
❑ 83 Steve Trout .25 .10
❑ 84 Gary Lavelle .25 .10
❑ 85 Ted Simmons .75 .30
❑ 86 Dave Hamilton .25 .10
❑ 87 Pepe Frias .25 .10
❑ 88 Ken Landreaux .25 .10
❑ 89 Don Hood .25 .10
❑ 90 Manny Trillo .75 .30
❑ 91 Rick Dempsey .75 .30
❑ 92 Rick Rhoden .25 .10
❑ 93 Dave Roberts DP .25 .10
❑ 94 Neil Allen .25 .10
❑ 95 Cecil Cooper .75 .30
❑ 96 A's Team CL .75 .15
Jim Marshall MG
❑ 97 Bill Lee .75 .30
❑ 98 Jerry Terrell .25 .10
❑ 99 Victor Cruz .25 .10
❑ 100 Johnny Bench 3.00 1.20
❑ 101 Aurelio Lopez .25 .10
❑ 102 Rich Dauer .25 .10
❑ 103 Bill Caudill .25 .10
❑ 104 Manny Mota .75 .30
❑ 105 Frank Tanana .75 .30
❑ 106 Jeff Leonard RC 1.50 .60
❑ 107 Francisco Barrios .25 .10
❑ 108 Bob Horner .75 .30
❑ 109 Bill Travers .25 .10
❑ 110 Fred Lynn DP .50 .20
❑ 111 Bob Knepper .25 .10
❑ 112 White Sox Team CL .75 .15
Tony LaRussa MG
❑ 113 Geoff Zahn .25 .10
❑ 114 Juan Beniquez .25 .10
❑ 115 Sparky Lyle .75 .30
❑ 116 Larry Cox .25 .10
❑ 117 Dock Ellis .75 .30
❑ 118 Phil Garner .75 .30
❑ 119 Sammy Stewart .25 .10
❑ 120 Greg Luzinski .75 .30
❑ 121 Checklist 1-121 .75 .15
❑ 122 Dave Rosello DP .25 .10
❑ 123 Lynn Jones .25 .10
❑ 124 Dave Lemanczyk .25 .10
❑ 125 Tony Perez .75 .30
❑ 126 Dave Tomlin .25 .10
❑ 127 Gary Thomasson .25 .10
❑ 128 Tom Burgmeier .25 .10
❑ 129 Craig Reynolds .25 .10
❑ 130 Amos Otis .75 .30
❑ 131 Paul Mitchell .25 .10
❑ 132 Biff Pocoroba .25 .10
❑ 133 Jerry Turner .25 .10
❑ 134 Matt Keough .25 .10
❑ 135 Bill Buckner .75 .30
❑ 136 Dick Ruthven .25 .10
❑ 137 John Castino .25 .10
❑ 138 Ross Baumgarten .25 .10
❑ 139 Dane Iorg .25 .10
❑ 140 Rich Gossage .75 .30
❑ 141 Gary Alexander .25 .10
❑ 142 Phil Huffman .25 .10
❑ 143 Bruce Bochte DP .25 .10
❑ 144 Steve Comer .25 .10
❑ 145 Darrell Evans .75 .30
❑ 146 Bob Welch .75 .30
❑ 147 Terry Puhl .25 .10
❑ 148 Manny Sanguillen .75 .30
❑ 149 Tom Hume .25 .10
❑ 150 Jason Thompson .25 .10
❑ 151 Tom Hausman DP .25 .10
❑ 152 John Fulgham .25 .10
❑ 153 Tim Blackwell .25 .10
❑ 154 Lary Sorensen .25 .10
❑ 155 Jerry Remy .25 .10
❑ 156 Tony Brizzolara .25 .10
❑ 157 Willie Wilson DP .50 .20
❑ 158 Rob Picciolo DP .25 .10
❑ 159 Ken Clay .25 .10
❑ 160 Eddie Murray 5.00 2.00
❑ 161 Larry Christenson .25 .10
❑ 162 Bob Randall .25 .10
❑ 163 Steve Swisher .25 .10
❑ 164 Greg Pryor .25 .10
❑ 165 Omar Moreno .25 .10
❑ 166 Glenn Abbott .25 .10
❑ 167 Jack Clark .75 .30
❑ 168 Rick Waits .25 .10
❑ 169 Luis Gomez .25 .10
❑ 170 Burt Hooton .75 .30
❑ 171 Fernando Gonzalez .25 .10
❑ 172 Ron Hodges .25 .10
❑ 173 John Henry Johnson .25 .10
❑ 174 Ray Knight .75 .30
❑ 175 Rick Reuschel .75 .30
❑ 176 Champ Summers .25 .10
❑ 177 Dave Heaverlo .25 .10
❑ 178 Tim McCarver .75 .30
❑ 179 Ron Davis .25 .10
❑ 180 Warren Cromartie .25 .10
❑ 181 Moose Haas .25 .10
❑ 182 Ken Reitz .25 .10
❑ 183 Jim Anderson DP .25 .10
❑ 184 Steve Renko DP .25 .10
❑ 185 Hal McRae .75 .30
❑ 186 Junior Moore .25 .10
❑ 187 Alan Ashby .25 .10
❑ 188 Terry Crowley .25 .10
❑ 189 Kevin Kobel .25 .10
❑ 190 Buddy Bell .75 .30
❑ 191 Ted Martinez .25 .10
❑ 192 Braves Team CL .75 .15
Bobby Cox MG
❑ 193 Dave Goltz .25 .10
❑ 194 Mike Easler .25 .10
❑ 195 John Montefusco .75 .30
❑ 196 Lance Parrish .75 .30
❑ 197 Byron McLaughlin .25 .10
❑ 198 Dell Alston DP .25 .10
❑ 199 Mike LaCoss .25 .10
❑ 200 Jim Rice .75 .30
❑ 201 Keith Hernandez .75 .30
Fred Lynn LL
❑ 202 Dave Kingman 1.50 .60
Gorman Thomas LL
❑ 203 Dave Winfield 1.50 .60
Don Baylor LL
❑ 204 Omar Moreno .75 .30
Willie Wilson LL
❑ 205 Joe Niekro .75 .30
Phil Niekro
Mike Flanagan LL
❑ 206 J.R. Richard 5.00 2.00
Nolan Ryan LL
❑ 207 J.R. Richard .75 .30
Ron Guidry LL
❑ 208 Wayne Cage .25 .10
❑ 209 Von Joshua .25 .10
❑ 210 Steve Carlton 1.50 .60
❑ 211 Dave Skaggs DP .25 .10
❑ 212 Dave Roberts .25 .10
❑ 213 Mike Jorgensen DP .25 .10
❑ 214 Angels Team CL .75 .15
Jim Fregosi MG
❑ 215 Sixto Lezcano .25 .10
❑ 216 Phil Mankowski .25 .10
❑ 217 Ed Halicki .25 .10
❑ 218 Jose Morales .25 .10
❑ 219 Steve Mingori .25 .10
❑ 220 Dave Concepcion .75 .30
❑ 221 Joe Cannon .25 .10
❑ 222 Ron Hassey .25 .10
❑ 223 Bob Sykes .25 .10
❑ 224 Willie Montanez .25 .10
❑ 225 Lou Piniella .75 .30
❑ 226 Bill Stein .25 .10
❑ 227 Len Barker .75 .30
❑ 228 Johnny Oates .75 .30
❑ 229 Jim Bibby .25 .10
❑ 230 Dave Winfield 1.50 .60
❑ 231 Steve McCatty .25 .10
❑ 232 Alan Trammell 1.50 .60
❑ 233 LaRue Washington .25 .10
❑ 234 Vern Ruhle .25 .10
❑ 235 Andre Dawson 1.50 .60
❑ 236 Marc Hill .25 .10
❑ 237 Scott McGregor .75 .30
❑ 238 Rob Wilfong .25 .10
❑ 239 Don Aase .25 .10
❑ 240 Dave Kingman .75 .30
❑ 241 Checklist 122-242 .75 .15
❑ 242 Lamar Johnson .25 .10
❑ 243 Jerry Augustine .25 .10
❑ 244 Cardinals Team CL .75 .15
Ken Boyer MG
❑ 245 Phil Niekro .75 .30
❑ 246 Tim Foli DP .25 .10
❑ 247 Frank Riccelli .25 .10
❑ 248 Jamie Quirk .25 .10
❑ 249 Jim Clancy .25 .10
❑ 250 Jim Kaat .75 .30
❑ 251 Kip Young .25 .10
❑ 252 Ted Cox .25 .10
❑ 253 John Montague .25 .10
❑ 254 Paul Dade DP .25 .10
❑ 255 Dusty Baker DP .50 .20
❑ 256 Roger Erickson .25 .10
❑ 257 Larry Herndon .25 .10
❑ 258 Paul Moskau .25 .10
❑ 259 Mets Team CL 1.50 .30

Joe Torre MG
❑ 260 Al Oliver .75 .30
❑ 261 Dave Chalk .25 .10
❑ 262 Benny Ayala .25 .10
❑ 263 Dave LaRoche DP .25 .10
❑ 264 Bill Robinson .25 .10
❑ 265 Robin Yount 3.00 1.20
❑ 266 Bernie Carbo .25 .10
❑ 267 Dan Schatzeder .25 .10
❑ 268 Rafael Landestoy .25 .10
❑ 269 Dave Tobik .25 .10
❑ 270 Mike Schmidt DP 3.00 1.20
❑ 271 Dick Drago DP .25 .10
❑ 272 Ralph Garr .75 .30
❑ 273 Eduardo Rodriguez .25 .10
❑ 274 Dale Murphy 2.50 1.00
❑ 275 Jerry Koosman .75 .30
❑ 276 Tom Veryzer .25 .10
❑ 277 Rick Bosetti .25 .10
❑ 278 Jim Spencer .25 .10
❑ 279 Rob Andrews .25 .10
❑ 280 Gaylord Perry .75 .30
❑ 281 Paul Blair .75 .30
❑ 282 Mariners Team CL .75 .15
Darrell Johnson MG
❑ 283 John Ellis .25 .10
❑ 284 Larry Murray DP .25 .10
❑ 285 Don Baylor .75 .30
❑ 286 Darold Knowles DP .25 .10
❑ 287 John Lowenstein .25 .10
❑ 288 Dave Rozema .25 .10
❑ 289 Bruce Bochy .25 .10
❑ 290 Steve Garvey 1.50 .60
❑ 291 Randy Scarberry .25 .10
❑ 292 Dale Berra .25 .10
❑ 293 Elias Sosa .25 .10
❑ 294 Charlie Spikes .25 .10
❑ 295 Larry Gura .25 .10
❑ 296 Dave Rader .25 .10
❑ 297 Tim Johnson .25 .10
❑ 298 Ken Holtzman .75 .30
❑ 299 Steve Henderson .25 .10
❑ 300 Ron Guidry .75 .30
❑ 301 Mike Edwards .25 .10
❑ 302 Dodgers Team CL 1.50 .30
Tom Lasorda MG
❑ 303 Bill Castro .25 .10
❑ 304 Butch Wynegar .25 .10
❑ 305 Randy Jones .75 .30
❑ 306 Denny Walling .25 .10
❑ 307 Rick Honeycutt .25 .10
❑ 308 Mike Hargrove .75 .30
❑ 309 Larry McWilliams .25 .10
❑ 310 Dave Parker .75 .30
❑ 311 Roger Metzger .25 .10
❑ 312 Mike Barlow .25 .10
❑ 313 Johnny Grubb .25 .10
❑ 314 Tim Stoddard .25 .10
❑ 315 Steve Kemp .75 .30
❑ 316 Bob Lacey .25 .10
❑ 317 Mike Anderson DP .25 .10
❑ 318 Jerry Reuss .75 .30
❑ 319 Chris Speier .25 .10
❑ 320 Dennis Eckersley 1.50 .60
❑ 321 Keith Hernandez .75 .30
❑ 322 Claudell Washington .25 .10
❑ 323 Mick Kelleher .25 .10
❑ 324 Tom Underwood .25 .10
❑ 325 Dan Driessen .25 .10
❑ 326 Bo McLaughlin .25 .10
❑ 327 Ray Fosse DP .50 .20
❑ 328 Twins Team CL .75 .15
Gene Mauch MG
❑ 329 Bert Roberge .25 .10
❑ 330 Al Cowens .25 .10
❑ 331 Richie Hebner .25 .10
❑ 332 Enrique Romo .25 .10
❑ 333 Jim Norris DP .25 .10
❑ 334 Jim Beattie .25 .10
❑ 335 Willie McCovey 1.50 .60
❑ 336 George Medich .25 .10
❑ 337 Carney Lansford .75 .30
❑ 338 John Wockenfuss .25 .10
❑ 339 John D'Acquisto .25 .10
❑ 340 Ken Singleton .75 .30
❑ 341 Jim Essian .25 .10
❑ 342 Odell Jones .25 .10
❑ 343 Mike Vail .25 .10
❑ 344 Randy Lerch .25 .10
❑ 345 Larry Parrish .75 .30
❑ 346 Buddy Solomon .25 .10
❑ 347 Harry Chappas .25 .10
❑ 348 Checklist 243-363 .75 .15
❑ 349 Jack Brohamer .25 .10
❑ 350 George Hendrick .75 .30
❑ 351 Bob Davis .25 .10
❑ 352 Dan Briggs .25 .10
❑ 353 Andy Hassler .25 .10
❑ 354 Rick Auerbach .25 .10
❑ 355 Gary Matthews .75 .30
❑ 356 Padres Team CL .75 .15
Jerry Coleman MG
❑ 357 Bob McClure .25 .10
❑ 358 Lou Whitaker .75 .30
❑ 359 Randy Moffitt .25 .10
❑ 360 Darrell Porter DP .50 .20
❑ 361 Wayne Garland .25 .10
❑ 362 Danny Goodwin .25 .10
❑ 363 Wayne Gross .25 .10
❑ 364 Ray Burris .25 .10
❑ 365 Bobby Murcer .75 .30
❑ 366 Rob Dressler .25 .10
❑ 367 Billy Smith .25 .10
❑ 368 Willie Aikens .25 .10
❑ 369 Jim Kern .25 .10
❑ 370 Cesar Cedeno .75 .30
❑ 371 Jack Morris .75 .30
❑ 372 Joel Youngblood .25 .10
❑ 373 Dan Petry DP RC .75 .30
❑ 374 Jim Gantner .75 .30
❑ 375 Ross Grimsley .25 .10
❑ 376 Gary Allenson .25 .10
❑ 377 Junior Kennedy .25 .10
❑ 378 Jerry Mumphrey .25 .10
❑ 379 Kevin Bell .25 .10
❑ 380 Garry Maddox .75 .30
❑ 381 Cubs Team CL .75 .15
Preston Gomez MG
❑ 382 Dave Freisleben .25 .10
❑ 383 Ed Ott .25 .10
❑ 384 Joey McLaughlin .25 .10
❑ 385 Enos Cabell .25 .10
❑ 386 Darrell Jackson .25 .10
❑ 387A Fred Stanley YL 2.00 .80
❑ 387B Fred Stanley .25 .10
(Red name on front)
❑ 388 Mike Paxton .25 .10
❑ 389 Pete LaCock .25 .10
❑ 390 Fergie Jenkins .75 .30
❑ 391 Tony Armas DP .50 .20
❑ 392 Milt Wilcox .25 .10
❑ 393 Ozzie Smith 10.00 4.00
❑ 394 Reggie Cleveland .25 .10
❑ 395 Ellis Valentine .25 .10
❑ 396 Dan Meyer .25 .10
❑ 397 Roy Thomas DP .25 .10
❑ 398 Barry Foote .25 .10
❑ 399 Mike Proly DP .25 .10
❑ 400 George Foster .75 .30
❑ 401 Pete Falcone .25 .10
❑ 402 Merv Rettenmund .25 .10
❑ 403 Pete Redfern DP .25 .10
❑ 404 Orioles Team CL .75 .15
Earl Weaver MG
❑ 405 Dwight Evans .75 .30
❑ 406 Paul Molitor 4.00 1.60
❑ 407 Tony Solaita .25 .10
❑ 408 Bill North .25 .10
❑ 409 Paul Splittorff .25 .10
❑ 410 Bobby Bonds .75 .30
❑ 411 Frank LaCorte .25 .10
❑ 412 Thad Bosley .25 .10
❑ 413 Allen Ripley .25 .10
❑ 414 George Scott .75 .30
❑ 415 Bill Atkinson .25 .10
❑ 416 Tom Brookens .25 .10
❑ 417 Craig Chamberlain DP .25 .10
❑ 418 Roger Freed DP .25 .10
❑ 419 Vic Correll .25 .10
❑ 420 Butch Hobson .25 .10
❑ 421 Doug Bird .25 .10
❑ 422 Larry Milbourne .25 .10
❑ 423 Dave Frost .25 .10
❑ 424 Yankees Team CL .75 .15
Dick Howser MG
❑ 424A Yankees Team CL
Billy Martin MG
Card is believed to be a pre-production issue
❑ 425 Mark Belanger .75 .30
❑ 426 Grant Jackson .25 .10
❑ 427 Tom Hutton DP .25 .10
❑ 428 Pat Zachry .25 .10
❑ 429 Duane Kuiper .25 .10
❑ 430 Larry Hisle DP .25 .10
❑ 431 Mike Krukow .25 .10
❑ 432 Willie Norwood .25 .10
❑ 433 Rich Gale .25 .10
❑ 434 Johnnie LeMaster .25 .10
❑ 435 Don Gullett .75 .30
❑ 436 Billy Almon .25 .10
❑ 437 Joe Niekro .75 .30
❑ 438 Dave Revering .25 .10
❑ 439 Mike Phillips .25 .10
❑ 440 Don Sutton .75 .30
❑ 441 Eric Soderholm .25 .10
❑ 442 Jorge Orta .25 .10
❑ 443 Mike Parrott .25 .10
❑ 444 Alvis Woods .25 .10
❑ 445 Mark Fidrych .75 .30
❑ 446 Duffy Dyer .25 .10
❑ 447 Nino Espinosa .25 .10
❑ 448 Jim Wohlford .25 .10
❑ 449 Doug Bair .25 .10
❑ 450 George Brett 8.00 3.20
❑ 451 Indians Team CL .75 .15
Dave Garcia MG
❑ 452 Steve Dillard .25 .10
❑ 453 Mike Bacsik .25 .10
❑ 454 Tom Donohue .25 .10
❑ 455 Mike Torrez .75 .30
❑ 456 Frank Taveras .25 .10
❑ 457 Bert Blyleven .75 .30
❑ 458 Billy Sample .25 .10
❑ 459 Mickey Lolich DP .50 .20
❑ 460 Willie Randolph .75 .30
❑ 461 Dwayne Murphy .25 .10
❑ 462 Mike Sadek DP .25 .10
❑ 463 Jerry Royster .25 .10
❑ 464 John Denny .75 .30
❑ 465 Rick Monday .75 .30
❑ 466 Mike Squires .25 .10
❑ 467 Jesse Jefferson .25 .10
❑ 468 Aurelio Rodriguez .25 .10
❑ 469 Randy Niemann DP .25 .10
❑ 470 Bob Boone .75 .30
❑ 471 Hosken Powell DP .25 .10
❑ 472 Willie Hernandez .75 .30
❑ 473 Bump Wills .25 .10
❑ 474 Steve Busby .25 .10
❑ 475 Cesar Geronimo .75 .30
❑ 476 Bob Shirley .25 .10
❑ 477 Buck Martinez .25 .10
❑ 478 Gil Flores .25 .10
❑ 479 Expos Team CL .75 .15
Dick Williams MG
❑ 480 Bob Watson .75 .30
❑ 481 Tom Paciorek .75 .30
❑ 482 R.Henderson RC UER .. 60.00 24.00
7 steals at Modesto,
should be at Fresno
❑ 483 Bo Diaz .25 .10
❑ 484 Checklist 364-484 .75 .15
❑ 485 Mickey Rivers .75 .30
❑ 486 Mike Tyson DP .25 .10
❑ 487 Wayne Nordhagen .25 .10
❑ 488 Roy Howell .25 .10
❑ 489 Preston Hanna DP .25 .10
❑ 490 Lee May .75 .30
❑ 491 Steve Mura DP .25 .10
❑ 492 Todd Cruz .25 .10
❑ 493 Jerry Martin .25 .10
❑ 494 Craig Minetto .25 .10
❑ 495 Bake McBride .75 .30
❑ 496 Silvio Martinez .25 .10
❑ 497 Jim Mason .25 .10
❑ 498 Danny Darwin .25 .10
❑ 499 Giants Team CL .75 .15

Dave Bristol MG
❑ 500 Tom Seaver 3.00 1.20
❑ 501 Rennie Stennett .25 .10
❑ 502 Rich Wortham DP .25 .10
❑ 503 Mike Cubbage .25 .10
❑ 504 Gene Garber .25 .10
❑ 505 Bert Campaneris .75 .30
❑ 506 Tom Buskey .25 .10
❑ 507 Leon Roberts .25 .10
❑ 508 U.L. Washington .25 .10
❑ 509 Ed Glynn .25 .10
❑ 510 Ron Cey .75 .30
❑ 511 Eric Wilkins .25 .10
❑ 512 Jose Cardenal .25 .10
❑ 513 Tom Dixon DP .25 .10
❑ 514 Steve Ontiveros .25 .10
❑ 515 Mike Caldwell UER .25 .10
1979 loss total reads
96 instead of 6
❑ 516 Hector Cruz .25 .10
❑ 517 Don Stanhouse .25 .10
❑ 518 Nelson Norman .25 .10
❑ 519 Steve Nicosia .25 .10
❑ 520 Steve Rogers .75 .30
❑ 521 Ken Brett .25 .10
❑ 522 Jim Morrison .25 .10
❑ 523 Ken Henderson .25 .10
❑ 524 Jim Wright DP .25 .10
❑ 525 Clint Hurdle .25 .10
❑ 526 Phillies Team CL .75 .15
Dallas Green MG
❑ 527 Doug Rau DP .25 .10
❑ 528 Adrian Devine .25 .10
❑ 529 Jim Barr .25 .10
❑ 530 Jim Sundberg DP .50 .20
❑ 531 Eric Rasmussen .25 .10
❑ 532 Willie Horton .75 .30
❑ 533 Checklist 485-605 .75 .15
❑ 534 Andre Thornton .75 .30
❑ 535 Bob Forsch .25 .10
❑ 536 Lee Lacy .25 .10
❑ 537 Alex Trevino .25 .10
❑ 538 Joe Strain .25 .10
❑ 539 Rudy May .25 .10
❑ 540 Pete Rose 8.00 3.20
❑ 541 Miguel Dilone .25 .10
❑ 542 Joe Coleman .25 .10
❑ 543 Pat Kelly .25 .10
❑ 544 Rick Sutcliffe RC 1.50 .60
❑ 545 Jeff Burroughs .75 .30
❑ 546 Rick Langford .25 .10
❑ 547 John Wathan .25 .10
❑ 548 Dave Rajsich .25 .10
❑ 549 Larry Wolfe .25 .10
❑ 550 Ken Griffey Sr. .75 .30
❑ 551 Pirates Team CL .75 .15
Chuck Tanner MG
❑ 552 Bill Nahorodny .25 .10
❑ 553 Dick Davis .25 .10
❑ 554 Art Howe .75 .30
❑ 555 Ed Figueroa .25 .10
❑ 556 Joe Rudi .75 .30
❑ 557 Mark Lee .25 .10
❑ 558 Alfredo Griffin .25 .10
❑ 559 Dale Murray .25 .10
❑ 560 Dave Lopes .75 .30
❑ 561 Eddie Whitson .25 .10
❑ 562 Joe Wallis .25 .10
❑ 563 Will McEnaney .25 .10
❑ 564 Rick Manning .25 .10
❑ 565 Dennis Leonard .25 .10
❑ 566 Bud Harrelson .75 .30
❑ 567 Skip Lockwood .25 .10
❑ 568 Gary Roenicke .25 .10
❑ 569 Terry Kennedy .25 .10
❑ 570 Roy Smalley .75 .30
❑ 571 Joe Sambito .25 .10
❑ 572 Jerry Morales DP .25 .10
❑ 573 Kent Tekulve .75 .30
❑ 574 Scot Thompson .25 .10
❑ 575 Ken Kravec .25 .10
❑ 576 Jim Dwyer .25 .10
❑ 577 Blue Jays Team CL .75 .15
Bobby Mattick MG
❑ 578 Scott Sanderson .25 .10
❑ 579 Charlie Moore .25 .10
❑ 580 Nolan Ryan 15.00 6.00
❑ 581 Bob Bailor .25 .10
❑ 582 Brian Doyle .25 .10
❑ 583 Bob Stinson .25 .10
❑ 584 Kurt Bevacqua .25 .10
❑ 585 Al Hrabosky .75 .30
❑ 586 Mitchell Page .25 .10
❑ 587 Garry Templeton .75 .30
❑ 588 Greg Minton .25 .10
❑ 589 Chet Lemon .75 .30
❑ 590 Jim Palmer 1.50 .60
❑ 591 Rick Cerone .25 .10
❑ 592 Jon Matlack .75 .30
❑ 593 Jesus Alou .25 .10
❑ 594 Dick Tidrow .25 .10
❑ 595 Don Money .25 .10
❑ 596 Rick Matula .25 .10
❑ 597 Tom Poquette .25 .10
❑ 598 Fred Kendall DP .25 .10
❑ 599 Mike Norris .25 .10
❑ 600 Reggie Jackson 3.00 1.20
❑ 601 Buddy Schultz .25 .10
❑ 602 Brian Downing .75 .30
❑ 603 Jack Billingham DP .25 .10
❑ 604 Glenn Adams .25 .10
❑ 605 Terry Forster .75 .30
❑ 606 Reds Team CL .75 .15
John McNamara MG
❑ 607 Woodie Fryman .25 .10
❑ 608 Alan Bannister .25 .10
❑ 609 Ron Reed .25 .10
❑ 610 Willie Stargell 1.50 .60
❑ 611 Jerry Garvin DP .25 .10
❑ 612 Cliff Johnson .25 .10
❑ 613 Randy Stein .25 .10
❑ 614 John Hiller .25 .10
❑ 615 Doug DeCinces .75 .30
❑ 616 Gene Richards .25 .10
❑ 617 Joaquin Andujar .75 .30
❑ 618 Bob Montgomery DP .25 .10
❑ 619 Sergio Ferrer .25 .10
❑ 620 Richie Zisk .75 .30
❑ 621 Bob Grich .75 .30
❑ 622 Mario Soto .75 .30
❑ 623 Gorman Thomas .75 .30
❑ 624 Lerrin LaGrow .25 .10
❑ 625 Chris Chambliss .75 .30
❑ 626 Tigers Team CL .75 .15
Sparky Anderson MG
❑ 627 Pedro Borbon .25 .10
❑ 628 Doug Capilla .25 .10
❑ 629 Jim Todd .25 .10
❑ 630 Larry Bowa .75 .30
❑ 631 Mark Littell .25 .10
❑ 632 Barry Bonnell .25 .10
❑ 633 Bob Apodaca .25 .10
❑ 634 Glenn Borgmann DP .25 .10
❑ 635 John Candelaria .75 .30
❑ 636 Toby Harrah .75 .30
❑ 637 Joe Simpson .25 .10
❑ 638 Mark Clear .25 .10
❑ 639 Larry Biittner .25 .10
❑ 640 Mike Flanagan .75 .30
❑ 641 Ed Kranepool .75 .30
❑ 642 Ken Forsch DP .25 .10
❑ 643 John Mayberry .75 .30
❑ 644 Charlie Hough .75 .30
❑ 645 Rick Burleson .75 .30
❑ 646 Checklist 606-726 .75 .15
❑ 647 Milt May .25 .10
❑ 648 Roy White .75 .30
❑ 649 Tom Griffin .25 .10
❑ 650 Joe Morgan 1.50 .60
❑ 651 Rollie Fingers .75 .30
❑ 652 Mario Mendoza .25 .10
❑ 653 Stan Bahnsen .25 .10
❑ 654 Bruce Boisclair DP .25 .10
❑ 655 Tug McGraw .75 .30
❑ 656 Larvell Blanks .25 .10
❑ 657 Dave Edwards .25 .10
❑ 658 Chris Knapp .25 .10
❑ 659 Brewers Team CL .75 .15
George Bamberger MG
❑ 660 Rusty Staub .75 .30
❑ 661 Mark Corey .25 .10
Dave Ford
Wayne Krenchicki
❑ 662 Joel Finch .25 .10
Mike O'Berry
Chuck Rainey
❑ 663 Ralph Botting .75 .30
Bob Clark
Dickie Thon RC
❑ 664 Mike Colbern .25 .10
Guy Hoffman
Dewey Robinson
❑ 665 Larry Andersen .25 .10
Bobby Cuellar
Sandy Wihtol
❑ 666 Mike Chris .25 .10
Al Greene
Bruce Robbins
❑ 667 Renie Martin .75 .30
Bill Paschall
Dan Quisenberry RC
❑ 668 Danny Boitano .25 .10
Willie Mueller
Lenn Sakata
❑ 669 Dan Graham .75 .30
Rick Sofield
Gary Ward RC
❑ 670 Bobby Brown .25 .10
Brad Gulden
Darryl Jones
❑ 671 Derek Bryant .75 .30
Brian Kingman
Mike Morgan RC
❑ 672 Charlie Beamon .25 .10
Rodney Craig
Rafael Vasquez
❑ 673 Brian Allard .25 .10
Jerry Don Gleaton
Greg Mahlberg
❑ 674 Butch Edge .25 .10
Pat Kelly
Ted Wilborn
❑ 675 Bruce Benedict .25 .10
Larry Bradford
Eddie Miller
❑ 676 Dave Geisel .25 .10
Steve Macko
Karl Pagel
❑ 677 Art DeFreites .25 .10
Frank Pastore
Harry Spilman
❑ 678 Reggie Baldwin .25 .10
Alan Knicely
Pete Ladd
❑ 679 Joe Beckwith .75 .30
Mickey Hatcher RC
Dave Patterson
❑ 680 Tony Bernazard .25 .10
Randy Miller
John Tamargo
❑ 681 Dan Norman 1.50 .60
Jesse Orosco RC
Mike Scott RC
❑ 682 Ramon Aviles .25 .10
Dickie Noles
Kevin Saucier
❑ 683 Dorian Boyland .25 .10
Alberto Lois
Harry Saferight
❑ 684 George Frazier .75 .30
Tom Herr RC
Dan O'Brien
❑ 685 Tim Flannery .25 .10
Brian Greer
Jim Wilhelm
❑ 686 Greg Johnston .25 .10
Dennis Littlejohn
Phil Nastu
❑ 687 Mike Heath DP .25 .10
❑ 688 Steve Stone .75 .30
❑ 689 Red Sox Team CL .75 .15
Don Zimmer MG
❑ 690 Tommy John .75 .30
❑ 691 Ivan DeJesus .25 .10
❑ 692 Rawly Eastwick DP .50 .20
❑ 693 Craig Kusick .25 .10
❑ 694 Jim Rooker .25 .10
❑ 695 Reggie Smith .75 .30

❑ 696 Julio Gonzalez .25 .10
❑ 697 David Clyde .25 .10
❑ 698 Oscar Gamble .75 .30
❑ 699 Floyd Bannister .25 .10
❑ 700 Rod Carew DP .75 .30
❑ 701 Ken Oberkfell .25 .10
❑ 702 Ed Farmer .25 .10
❑ 703 Otto Velez .25 .10
❑ 704 Gene Tenace .75 .30
❑ 705 Freddie Patek .75 .30
❑ 706 Tippy Martinez .25 .10
❑ 707 Elliott Maddox .25 .10
❑ 708 Bob Tolan .25 .10
❑ 709 Pat Underwood .25 .10
❑ 710 Graig Nettles .75 .30
❑ 711 Bob Galasso .25 .10
❑ 712 Rodney Scott .25 .10
❑ 713 Terry Whitfield .25 .10
❑ 714 Fred Norman .25 .10
❑ 715 Sal Bando .75 .30
❑ 716 Lynn McGlothen .25 .10
❑ 717 Mickey Klutts DP .25 .10
❑ 718 Greg Gross .25 .10
❑ 719 Don Robinson .75 .30
❑ 720 Carl Yastrzemski DP 2.00 .80
❑ 721 Paul Hartzell .25 .10
❑ 722 Jose Cruz .75 .30
❑ 723 Shane Rawley .25 .10
❑ 724 Jerry White .25 .10
❑ 725 Rick Wise .25 .10
❑ 726 Steve Yeager .75 .15

1981 Topps

	Nm-Mt	Ex-Mt
COMPLETE SET (726)	50.00	20.00
COMMON CARD (1-726)	.15	.06
COMMON CARD DP	.15	.06

❑ 1 George Brett 3.00 1.20
Bill Buckner LL
❑ 2 Reggie Jackson 1.50 .60
Ben Oglivie
Mike Schmidt LL
❑ 3 Cecil Cooper 1.50 .60
Mike Schmidt LL
❑ 4 Rickey Henderson 3.00 1.20
Ron LeFlore LL
❑ 5 Steve Stone .40 .16
Steve Carlton LL
❑ 6 Len Barker .40 .16
Steve Carlton LL
❑ 7 Rudy May .40 .16
Don Sutton LL
❑ 8 Dan Quisenberry .40 .16
Rollie Fingers
Tom Hume LL
❑ 9 Pete LaCock DP .15 .06
❑ 10 Mike Flanagan .15 .06
❑ 11 Jim Wohlford DP .15 .06
❑ 12 Mark Clear .15 .06
❑ 13 Joe Charboneau RC 1.50 .60
❑ 14 John Tudor RC 1.50 .60
❑ 15 Larry Parrish .15 .06
❑ 16 Ron Davis .15 .06
❑ 17 Cliff Johnson .15 .06
❑ 18 Glenn Adams .15 .06
❑ 19 Jim Clancy .15 .06
❑ 20 Jeff Burroughs .40 .16
❑ 21 Ron Oester .15 .06
❑ 22 Danny Darwin .15 .06
❑ 23 Alex Trevino .15 .06
❑ 24 Don Stanhouse .15 .06
❑ 25 Sixto Lezcano .15 .06
❑ 26 U.L. Washington .15 .06
❑ 27 Champ Summers DP .15 .06
❑ 28 Enrique Romo .15 .06
❑ 29 Gene Tenace .40 .16
❑ 30 Jack Clark .40 .16
❑ 31 Checklist 1-121 DP .25 .10
❑ 32 Ken Oberkfell .15 .06
❑ 33 Rick Honeycutt .15 .06
❑ 34 Aurelio Rodriguez .15 .06
❑ 35 Mitchell Page .15 .06
❑ 36 Ed Farmer .15 .06
❑ 37 Gary Roenicke .15 .06
❑ 38 Win Remmerswaal .15 .06
❑ 39 Tom Veryzer .15 .06
❑ 40 Tug McGraw .40 .16
❑ 41 Bob Babcock .25 .10
John Butcher
Jerry Don Gleaton
❑ 42 Jerry White DP .15 .06
❑ 43 Jose Morales .15 .06
❑ 44 Larry McWilliams .15 .06
❑ 45 Enos Cabell .15 .06
❑ 46 Rick Bosetti .15 .06
❑ 47 Ken Brett .15 .06
❑ 48 Dave Skaggs .15 .06
❑ 49 Bob Shirley .15 .06
❑ 50 Dave Lopes .40 .16
❑ 51 Bill Robinson DP .15 .06
❑ 52 Hector Cruz .15 .06
❑ 53 Kevin Saucier .15 .06
❑ 54 Ivan DeJesus .15 .06
❑ 55 Mike Norris .15 .06
❑ 56 Buck Martinez .15 .06
❑ 57 Dave Roberts .15 .06
❑ 58 Joel Youngblood .15 .06
❑ 59 Dan Petry .15 .06
❑ 60 Willie Randolph .40 .16
❑ 61 Butch Wynegar .15 .06
❑ 62 Joe Pettini .15 .06
❑ 63 Steve Renko DP .15 .06
❑ 64 Brian Asselstine .15 .06
❑ 65 Scott McGregor .15 .06
❑ 66 Manny Castillo .25 .10
Tim Ireland
Mike Jones
❑ 67 Ken Kravec .15 .06
❑ 68 Matt Alexander DP .15 .06
❑ 69 Ed Halicki .15 .06
❑ 70 Al Oliver DP .25 .10
❑ 71 Hal Dues .15 .06
❑ 72 Barry Evans DP .15 .06
❑ 73 Doug Bair .15 .06
❑ 74 Mike Hargrove .15 .06
❑ 75 Reggie Smith .40 .16
❑ 76 Mario Mendoza .15 .06
❑ 77 Mike Barlow .15 .06
❑ 78 Steve Dillard .15 .06
❑ 79 Bruce Robbins .15 .06
❑ 80 Rusty Staub .40 .16
❑ 81 Dave Stapleton .15 .06
❑ 82 Danny Heep .25 .10
Alan Knicely
Bobby Sprowl
❑ 83 Mike Proly .15 .06
❑ 84 Johnnie LeMaster .15 .06
❑ 85 Mike Caldwell .15 .06
❑ 86 Wayne Gross .15 .06
❑ 87 Rick Camp .15 .06
❑ 88 Joe Lefebvre .15 .06
❑ 89 Darrell Jackson .15 .06
❑ 90 Bake McBride .40 .16
❑ 91 Tim Stoddard DP .15 .06
❑ 92 Mike Easler .15 .06
❑ 93 Ed Glynn DP .15 .06
❑ 94 Harry Spilman DP .15 .06
❑ 95 Jim Sundberg .40 .16
❑ 96 Dave Beard .25 .10
Ernie Camacho
Pat Dempsey
❑ 97 Chris Speier .15 .06
❑ 98 Clint Hurdle .15 .06
❑ 99 Eric Wilkins .15 .06
❑ 100 Rod Carew .75 .30
❑ 101 Benny Ayala .15 .06
❑ 102 Dave Tobik .15 .06
❑ 103 Jerry Martin .15 .06
❑ 104 Terry Forster .40 .16
❑ 105 Jose Cruz .40 .16
❑ 106 Don Money .15 .06
❑ 107 Rich Wortham .15 .06
❑ 108 Bruce Benedict .15 .06
❑ 109 Mike Scott .40 .16
❑ 110 Carl Yastrzemski 2.50 1.00
❑ 111 Greg Minton .15 .06
❑ 112 Rusty Kuntz .25 .10
Fran Mullins
Leo Sutherland
❑ 113 Mike Phillips .15 .06
❑ 114 Tom Underwood .15 .06
❑ 115 Roy Smalley .40 .16
❑ 116 Joe Simpson .15 .06
❑ 117 Pete Falcone .15 .06
❑ 118 Kurt Bevacqua .15 .06
❑ 119 Tippy Martinez .15 .06
❑ 120 Larry Bowa .40 .16
❑ 121 Larry Harlow .15 .06
❑ 122 John Denny .15 .06
❑ 123 Al Cowens .15 .06
❑ 124 Jerry Garvin .15 .06
❑ 125 Andre Dawson .75 .30
❑ 126 Charlie Leibrandt RC .75 .30
❑ 127 Rudy Law .15 .06
❑ 128 Gary Allenson DP .15 .06
❑ 129 Art Howe .15 .06
❑ 130 Larry Gura .15 .06
❑ 131 Keith Moreland .15 .06
❑ 132 Tommy Boggs .15 .06
❑ 133 Jeff Cox .15 .06
❑ 134 Steve Mura .15 .06
❑ 135 Gorman Thomas .40 .16
❑ 136 Doug Capilla .15 .06
❑ 137 Hosken Powell .15 .06
❑ 138 Rich Dotson DP .15 .06
❑ 139 Oscar Gamble .15 .06
❑ 140 Bob Forsch .15 .06
❑ 141 Miguel Dilone .15 .06
❑ 142 Jackson Todd .15 .06
❑ 143 Dan Meyer .15 .06
❑ 144 Allen Ripley .15 .06
❑ 145 Mickey Rivers .15 .06
❑ 146 Bobby Castillo .15 .06
❑ 147 Dale Berra .15 .06
❑ 148 Randy Niemann .15 .06
❑ 149 Joe Nolan .15 .06
❑ 150 Mark Fidrych .40 .16
❑ 151 Claudell Washington .15 .06
❑ 152 John Urrea .15 .06
❑ 153 Tom Poquette .15 .06
❑ 154 Rick Langford .15 .06
❑ 155 Chris Chambliss .40 .16
❑ 156 Bob McClure .15 .06
❑ 157 John Wathan .15 .06
❑ 158 Fergie Jenkins .40 .16
❑ 159 Brian Doyle .15 .06
❑ 160 Garry Maddox .15 .06
❑ 161 Dan Graham .15 .06
❑ 162 Doug Corbett .15 .06
❑ 163 Bill Almon .15 .06
❑ 164 LaMarr Hoyt RC .75 .30
❑ 165 Tony Scott .15 .06
❑ 166 Floyd Bannister .15 .06
❑ 167 Terry Whitfield .15 .06
❑ 168 Don Robinson DP .15 .06
❑ 169 John Mayberry .15 .06
❑ 170 Ross Grimsley .15 .06
❑ 171 Gene Richards .15 .06
❑ 172 Gary Woods .15 .06
❑ 173 Bump Wills .15 .06
❑ 174 Doug Rau .15 .06
❑ 175 Dave Collins .15 .06
❑ 176 Mike Krukow .15 .06
❑ 177 Rick Peters .15 .06
❑ 178 Jim Essian DP .15 .06
❑ 179 Rudy May .15 .06
❑ 180 Pete Rose 5.00 2.00
❑ 181 Elias Sosa .15 .06

❑ 182 Bob Grich .40 .16
❑ 183 Dick Davis DP .15 .06
❑ 184 Jim Dwyer .15 .06
❑ 185 Dennis Leonard .15 .06
❑ 186 Wayne Nordhagen .15 .06
❑ 187 Mike Parrott .15 .06
❑ 188 Doug DeCinces .15 .06
❑ 189 Craig Swan .15 .06
❑ 190 Cesar Cedeno .40 .16
❑ 191 Rick Sutcliffe .40 .16
❑ 192 Terry Harper .25 .10
Ed Miller
Rafael Ramirez
❑ 193 Pete Vuckovich .15 .06
❑ 194 Rod Scurry .15 .06
❑ 195 Rich Murray .15 .06
❑ 196 Duffy Dyer .15 .06
❑ 197 Jim Kern .15 .06
❑ 198 Jerry Dybzinski .15 .06
❑ 199 Chuck Rainey .15 .06
❑ 200 George Foster .40 .16
❑ 201 Johnny Bench RB .75 .30
❑ 202 Steve Carlton RB .40 .16
❑ 203 Bill Gullickson RB .15 .06
❑ 204 Ron LeFlore RB .40 .16
Rodney Scott
❑ 205 Pete Rose RB 1.50 .60
❑ 206 Mike Schmidt RB 1.50 .60
❑ 207 Ozzie Smith RB 2.00 .80
❑ 208 Willie Wilson RB .15 .06
❑ 209 Dickie Thon DP .15 .06
❑ 210 Jim Palmer .75 .30
❑ 211 Derrel Thomas .15 .06
❑ 212 Steve Nicosia .15 .06
❑ 213 Al Holland .15 .06
❑ 214 Ralph Botting .25 .10
Jim Dorsey
John Harris
❑ 215 Larry Hisle .15 .06
❑ 216 John Henry Johnson .15 .06
❑ 217 Rich Hebner .15 .06
❑ 218 Paul Splittorff .15 .06
❑ 219 Ken Landreaux .15 .06
❑ 220 Tom Seaver 1.50 .60
❑ 221 Bob Davis .15 .06
❑ 222 Jorge Orta .15 .06
❑ 223 Roy Lee Jackson .15 .06
❑ 224 Pat Zachry .15 .06
❑ 225 Ruppert Jones .15 .06
❑ 226 Manny Sanguillen DP .25 .10
❑ 227 Fred Martinez .15 .06
❑ 228 Tom Paciorek .15 .06
❑ 229 Rollie Fingers .40 .16
❑ 230 George Hendrick .40 .16
❑ 231 Joe Beckwith .15 .06
❑ 232 Mickey Klutts .15 .06
❑ 233 Skip Lockwood .15 .06
❑ 234 Lou Whitaker .75 .30
❑ 235 Scott Sanderson .15 .06
❑ 236 Mike Ivie .15 .06
❑ 237 Charlie Moore .15 .06
❑ 238 Willie Hernandez .15 .06
❑ 239 Rick Miller DP .15 .06
❑ 240 Nolan Ryan 8.00 3.20
❑ 241 Checklist 122-242 DP .25 .10
❑ 242 Chet Lemon .40 .16
❑ 243 Sal Butera .15 .06
❑ 244 Tito Landrum .25 .10
Al Olmsted
Andy Rincon
❑ 245 Ed Figueroa .15 .06
❑ 246 Ed Ott DP .15 .06
❑ 247 Glenn Hubbard DP .15 .06
❑ 248 Joey McLaughlin .15 .06
❑ 249 Larry Cox .15 .06
❑ 250 Ron Guidry .40 .16
❑ 251 Tom Brookens .15 .06
❑ 252 Victor Cruz .15 .06
❑ 253 Dave Bergman .15 .06
❑ 254 Ozzie Smith 5.00 2.00
❑ 255 Mark Littell .15 .06
❑ 256 Bombo Rivera .15 .06
❑ 257 Rennie Stennett .15 .06
❑ 258 Joe Price .15 .06
❑ 259 Juan Berenguer 2.50 1.00
Hubie Brooks RC
Mookie Wilson
❑ 260 Ron Cey .40 .16
❑ 261 Rickey Henderson 10.00 4.00
❑ 262 Sammy Stewart .15 .06
❑ 263 Brian Downing .40 .16
❑ 264 Jim Norris .15 .06
❑ 265 John Candelaria .40 .16
❑ 266 Tom Herr .15 .06
❑ 267 Stan Bahnsen .15 .06
❑ 268 Jerry Royster .15 .06
❑ 269 Ken Forsch .15 .06
❑ 270 Greg Luzinski .40 .16
❑ 271 Bill Castro .15 .06
❑ 272 Bruce Kimm .15 .06
❑ 273 Stan Papi .15 .06
❑ 274 Craig Chamberlain .15 .06
❑ 275 Dwight Evans .75 .30
❑ 276 Dan Spillner .15 .06
❑ 277 Alfredo Griffin .15 .06
❑ 278 Rick Sofield .15 .06
❑ 279 Bob Knepper .15 .06
❑ 280 Ken Griffey .40 .16
❑ 281 Fred Stanley .15 .06
❑ 282 Rick Anderson .25 .10
Greg Biercevicz
Rodney Craig
❑ 283 Billy Sample .15 .06
❑ 284 Brian Kingman .15 .06
❑ 285 Jerry Turner .15 .06
❑ 286 Dave Frost .15 .06
❑ 287 Lenn Sakata .15 .06
❑ 288 Bob Clark .15 .06
❑ 289 Mickey Hatcher .15 .06
❑ 290 Bob Boone DP .25 .10
❑ 291 Aurelio Lopez .15 .06
❑ 292 Mike Squires .15 .06
❑ 293 Charlie Lea .15 .06
❑ 294 Mike Tyson DP .15 .06
❑ 295 Hal McRae .40 .16
❑ 296 Bill Nahorodny DP .15 .06
❑ 297 Bob Bailor .15 .06
❑ 298 Buddy Solomon .15 .06
❑ 299 Elliott Maddox .15 .06
❑ 300 Paul Molitor 1.50 .60
❑ 301 Matt Keough .15 .06
❑ 302 Jack Perconte 5.00 2.00
Mike Scioscia RC
Fernando Valenzuela RC
❑ 303 Johnny Oates .40 .16
❑ 304 John Castino .15 .06
❑ 305 Ken Clay .15 .06
❑ 306 Juan Beniquez DP .15 .06
❑ 307 Gene Garber .15 .06
❑ 308 Rick Manning .15 .06
❑ 309 Luis Salazar RC .75 .30
❑ 310 Vida Blue DP .25 .10
❑ 311 Freddie Patek .15 .06
❑ 312 Rick Rhoden .15 .06
❑ 313 Luis Pujols .15 .06
❑ 314 Rich Dauer .15 .06
❑ 315 Kirk Gibson RC 3.00 1.20
❑ 316 Craig Minetto .15 .06
❑ 317 Lonnie Smith .40 .16
❑ 318 Steve Yeager .40 .16
❑ 319 Rowland Office .15 .06
❑ 320 Tom Burgmeier .15 .06
❑ 321 Leon Durham RC .75 .30
❑ 322 Neil Allen .15 .06
❑ 323 Jim Morrison DP .15 .06
❑ 324 Mike Willis .15 .06
❑ 325 Ray Knight .40 .16
❑ 326 Biff Pocoroba .15 .06
❑ 327 Moose Haas .15 .06
❑ 328 Dave Engle .25 .10
Greg Johnston
Gary Ward
❑ 329 Joaquin Andujar .40 .16
❑ 330 Frank White .40 .16
❑ 331 Dennis Lamp .15 .06
❑ 332 Lee Lacy DP .15 .06
❑ 333 Sid Monge .15 .06
❑ 334 Dane Iorg .15 .06
❑ 335 Rick Cerone .15 .06
❑ 336 Eddie Whitson .15 .06
❑ 337 Lynn Jones .15 .06
❑ 338 Checklist 243-363 .40 .16
❑ 339 John Ellis .15 .06
❑ 340 Bruce Kison .15 .06
❑ 341 Dwayne Murphy .15 .06
❑ 342 Eric Rasmussen DP .15 .06
❑ 343 Frank Taveras .15 .06
❑ 344 Byron McLaughlin .15 .06
❑ 345 Warren Cromartie .15 .06
❑ 346 Larry Christenson DP .15 .06
❑ 347 Harold Baines RC 5.00 2.00
❑ 348 Bob Sykes .15 .06
❑ 349 Glenn Hoffman .15 .06
❑ 350 J.R. Richard .40 .16
❑ 351 Otto Velez .15 .06
❑ 352 Dick Tidrow DP .15 .06
❑ 353 Terry Kennedy .15 .06
❑ 354 Mario Soto .40 .16
❑ 355 Bob Horner .40 .16
❑ 356 George Stablein .25 .10
Craig Stimac
Tom Tellmann
❑ 357 Jim Slaton .15 .06
❑ 358 Mark Wagner .15 .06
❑ 359 Tom Hausman .15 .06
❑ 360 Willie Wilson .40 .16
❑ 361 Joe Strain .15 .06
❑ 362 Bo Diaz .15 .06
❑ 363 Geoff Zahn .15 .06
❑ 364 Mike Davis RC .25 .10
❑ 365 Graig Nettles DP .25 .10
❑ 366 Mike Ramsey RC .25 .10
❑ 367 Dennis Martinez .40 .16
❑ 368 Leon Roberts .15 .06
❑ 369 Frank Tanana .40 .16
❑ 370 Dave Winfield .75 .30
❑ 371 Charlie Hough .40 .16
❑ 372 Jay Johnstone .15 .06
❑ 373 Pat Underwood .15 .06
❑ 374 Tommy Hutton .15 .06
❑ 375 Dave Concepcion .40 .16
❑ 376 Ron Reed .15 .06
❑ 377 Jerry Morales .15 .06
❑ 378 Dave Rader .15 .06
❑ 379 Lary Sorensen .15 .06
❑ 380 Willie Stargell .75 .30
❑ 381 Carlos Lezcano .25 .10
Steve Macko
Randy Martz
❑ 382 Paul Mirabella .15 .06
❑ 383 Eric Soderholm DP .15 .06
❑ 384 Mike Sadek .15 .06
❑ 385 Joe Sambito .15 .06
❑ 386 Dave Edwards .15 .06
❑ 387 Phil Niekro .40 .16
❑ 388 Andre Thornton .40 .16
❑ 389 Marty Pattin .15 .06
❑ 390 Cesar Geronimo .15 .06
❑ 391 Dave Lemanczyk DP .15 .06
❑ 392 Lance Parrish .40 .16
❑ 393 Broderick Perkins .15 .06
❑ 394 Woodie Fryman .15 .06
❑ 395 Scot Thompson .15 .06
❑ 396 Bill Campbell .15 .06
❑ 397 Julio Cruz .15 .06
❑ 398 Ross Baumgarten .15 .06
❑ 399 Mike Boddicker RC 1.50 .60
Mark Corey
Floyd Rayford
❑ 400 Reggie Jackson 1.50 .60
❑ 401 George Brett ALCS 2.50 1.00
❑ 402 NL Champs .75 .30
Phillies squeak
past Astros
(Phillies celebrating)
❑ 403 Larry Bowa WS .75 .30
❑ 404 Tug McGraw WS .75 .30
❑ 405 Nino Espinosa .15 .06
❑ 406 Dickie Noles .15 .06
❑ 407 Ernie Whitt .15 .06
❑ 408 Fernando Arroyo .15 .06
❑ 409 Larry Herndon .15 .06
❑ 410 Bert Campaneris .40 .16
❑ 411 Terry Puhl .15 .06
❑ 412 Britt Burns .15 .06
❑ 413 Tony Bernazard .15 .06
❑ 414 John Pacella DP .15 .06
❑ 415 Ben Oglivie .40 .16

❑ 416 Gary Alexander .15 .06
❑ 417 Dan Schatzeder .15 .06
❑ 418 Bobby Brown .15 .06
❑ 419 Tom Hume .15 .06
❑ 420 Keith Hernandez .40 .16
❑ 421 Bob Stanley .15 .06
❑ 422 Dan Ford .15 .06
❑ 423 Shane Rawley .15 .06
❑ 424 Tim Lollar .25 .10
Bruce Robinson
Dennis Werth
❑ 425 Al Bumbry .15 .06
❑ 426 Warren Brusstar .15 .06
❑ 427 John D'Acquisto .15 .06
❑ 428 John Stearns .15 .06
❑ 429 Mick Kelleher .15 .06
❑ 430 Jim Bibby .15 .06
❑ 431 Dave Roberts .15 .06
❑ 432 Len Barker .40 .16
❑ 433 Rance Mulliniks .15 .06
❑ 434 Roger Erickson .15 .06
❑ 435 Jim Spencer .15 .06
❑ 436 Gary Lucas .15 .06
❑ 437 Mike Heath DP .15 .06
❑ 438 John Montefusco .15 .06
❑ 439 Denny Walling .15 .06
❑ 440 Jerry Reuss .15 .06
❑ 441 Ken Reitz .15 .06
❑ 442 Ron Pruitt .15 .06
❑ 443 Jim Beattie DP .15 .06
❑ 444 Garth Iorg .15 .06
❑ 445 Ellis Valentine .15 .06
❑ 446 Checklist 364-484 .40 .16
❑ 447 Junior Kennedy DP .15 .06
❑ 448 Tim Corcoran .15 .06
❑ 449 Paul Mitchell .15 .06
❑ 450 Dave Kingman DP .25 .10
❑ 451 Chris Bando .25 .10
Tom Brennan
Sandy Wihtol
❑ 452 Renie Martin .15 .06
❑ 453 Rob Wilfong DP .15 .06
❑ 454 Andy Hassler .15 .06
❑ 455 Rick Burleson .15 .06
❑ 456 Jeff Reardon RC 1.50 .60
❑ 457 Mike Lum .15 .06
❑ 458 Randy Jones .40 .16
❑ 459 Greg Gross .15 .06
❑ 460 Rich Gossage .40 .16
❑ 461 Dave McKay .15 .06
❑ 462 Jack Brohamer .15 .06
❑ 463 Milt May .15 .06
❑ 464 Adrian Devine .15 .06
❑ 465 Bill Russell .40 .16
❑ 466 Bob Molinaro .15 .06
❑ 467 Dave Stieb .40 .16
❑ 468 John Wockenfuss .15 .06
❑ 469 Jeff Leonard .40 .16
❑ 470 Manny Trillo .15 .06
❑ 471 Mike Vail .15 .06
❑ 472 Dyar Miller DP .15 .06
❑ 473 Jose Cardenal .15 .06
❑ 474 Mike LaCoss .15 .06
❑ 475 Buddy Bell .40 .16
❑ 476 Jerry Koosman .40 .16
❑ 477 Luis Gomez .15 .06
❑ 478 Juan Eichelberger .15 .06
❑ 479 Tim Raines RC 2.50 1.00
Roberto Ramos
Bobby Pate
❑ 480 Carlton Fisk .75 .30
❑ 481 Bob Lacey DP .15 .06
❑ 482 Jim Gantner .15 .06
❑ 483 Mike Griffin RC .25 .10
❑ 484 Max Venable DP .15 .06
❑ 485 Garry Templeton .40 .16
❑ 486 Marc Hill .15 .06
❑ 487 Dewey Robinson .15 .06
❑ 488 Damaso Garcia .15 .06
❑ 489 John Littlefield .15 .06
Photo on card believed to be Mark Riggins
❑ 490 Eddie Murray 2.50 1.00
❑ 491 Gordy Pladson .15 .06
❑ 492 Barry Foote .15 .06
❑ 493 Dan Quisenberry .15 .06
❑ 494 Bob Walk RC .75 .30
❑ 495 Dusty Baker .40 .16
❑ 496 Paul Dade .15 .06
❑ 497 Fred Norman .15 .06
❑ 498 Pat Putnam .15 .06
❑ 499 Frank Pastore .15 .06
❑ 500 Jim Rice .40 .16
❑ 501 Tim Foli DP .15 .06
❑ 502 Chris Bourjos .25 .10
Al Hargesheimer
Mike Rowland
❑ 503 Steve McCatty .15 .06
❑ 504 Dale Murphy .75 .30
❑ 505 Jason Thompson .15 .06
❑ 506 Phil Huffman .15 .06
❑ 507 Jamie Quirk .15 .06
❑ 508 Rob Dressler .15 .06
❑ 509 Pete Mackanin .15 .06
❑ 510 Lee Mazzilli .40 .16
❑ 511 Wayne Garland .15 .06
❑ 512 Gary Thomasson .15 .06
❑ 513 Frank LaCorte .15 .06
❑ 514 George Riley .15 .06
❑ 515 Robin Yount 2.50 1.00
❑ 516 Doug Bird .15 .06
❑ 517 Richie Zisk .15 .06
❑ 518 Grant Jackson .15 .06
❑ 519 John Tamargo DP .15 .06
❑ 520 Steve Stone .15 .06
❑ 521 Sam Mejias .15 .06
❑ 522 Mike Colbern .15 .06
❑ 523 John Fulgham .15 .06
❑ 524 Willie Aikens .15 .06
❑ 525 Mike Torrez .15 .06
❑ 526 Marty Bystrom .25 .10
Jay Loviglio
Jim Wright
❑ 527 Danny Goodwin .15 .06
❑ 528 Gary Matthews .40 .16
❑ 529 Dave LaRoche .15 .06
❑ 530 Steve Garvey .75 .30
❑ 531 John Curtis .15 .06
❑ 532 Bill Stein .15 .06
❑ 533 Jesus Figueroa .15 .06
❑ 534 Dave Smith RC .75 .30
❑ 535 Omar Moreno .15 .06
❑ 536 Bob Owchinko DP .15 .06
❑ 537 Ron Hodges .15 .06
❑ 538 Tom Griffin .15 .06
❑ 539 Rodney Scott .15 .06
❑ 540 Mike Schmidt DP 2.00 .80
❑ 541 Steve Swisher .15 .06
❑ 542 Larry Bradford DP .15 .06
❑ 543 Terry Crowley .15 .06
❑ 544 Rich Gale .15 .06
❑ 545 Johnny Grubb .15 .06
❑ 546 Paul Moskau .15 .06
❑ 547 Mario Guerrero .15 .06
❑ 548 Dave Goltz .15 .06
❑ 549 Jerry Remy .15 .06
❑ 550 Tommy John .40 .16
❑ 551 Vance Law 1.50 .60
Tony Pena RC
Pascual Perez RC
❑ 552 Steve Trout .15 .06
❑ 553 Tim Blackwell .15 .06
❑ 554 Bert Blyleven UER .40 .16
(1 is missing from 1980 on card back)
❑ 555 Cecil Cooper .40 .16
❑ 556 Jerry Mumphrey .15 .06
❑ 557 Chris Knapp .15 .06
❑ 558 Barry Bonnell .15 .06
❑ 559 Willie Montanez .15 .06
❑ 560 Joe Morgan .75 .30
❑ 561 Dennis Littlejohn .15 .06
❑ 562 Checklist 485-605 .40 .16
❑ 563 Jim Kaat .40 .16
❑ 564 Ron Hassey DP .15 .06
❑ 565 Burt Hooton .15 .06
❑ 566 Del Unser .15 .06
❑ 567 Mark Bomback .15 .06
❑ 568 Dave Revering .15 .06
❑ 569 Al Williams DP .15 .06
❑ 570 Ken Singleton .40 .16
❑ 571 Todd Cruz .15 .06
❑ 572 Jack Morris .75 .30
❑ 573 Phil Garner .40 .16
❑ 574 Bill Caudill .15 .06
❑ 575 Tony Perez .75 .30
❑ 576 Reggie Cleveland .15 .06
❑ 577 Luis Leal .25 .10
Brian Milner
Ken Schrom
❑ 578 Bill Gullickson RC .75 .30
❑ 579 Tim Flannery .15 .06
❑ 580 Don Baylor .40 .16
❑ 581 Roy Howell .15 .06
❑ 582 Gaylord Perry .40 .16
❑ 583 Larry Milbourne .15 .06
❑ 584 Randy Lerch .15 .06
❑ 585 Amos Otis .40 .16
❑ 586 Silvio Martinez .15 .06
❑ 587 Jeff Newman .15 .06
❑ 588 Gary Lavelle .15 .06
❑ 589 Lamar Johnson .15 .06
❑ 590 Bruce Sutter .40 .16
❑ 591 John Lowenstein .15 .06
❑ 592 Steve Comer .15 .06
❑ 593 Steve Kemp .15 .06
❑ 594 Preston Hanna DP .15 .06
❑ 595 Butch Hobson .15 .06
❑ 596 Jerry Augustine .15 .06
❑ 597 Rafael Landestoy .15 .06
❑ 598 George Vukovich DP .15 .06
❑ 599 Dennis Kinney .15 .06
❑ 600 Johnny Bench 1.50 .60
❑ 601 Don Aase .15 .06
❑ 602 Bobby Murcer .40 .16
❑ 603 John Verhoeven .15 .06
❑ 604 Rob Picciolo .15 .06
❑ 605 Don Sutton .40 .16
❑ 606 Bruce Berenyi .25 .10
Geoff Combe
Paul Householder
❑ 607 David Palmer .15 .06
❑ 608 Greg Pryor .15 .06
❑ 609 Lynn McGlothen .15 .06
❑ 610 Darrell Porter .15 .06
❑ 611 Rick Matula DP .15 .06
❑ 612 Duane Kuiper .15 .06
❑ 613 Jim Anderson .15 .06
❑ 614 Dave Rozema .15 .06
❑ 615 Rick Dempsey .15 .06
❑ 616 Rick Wise .15 .06
❑ 617 Craig Reynolds .15 .06
❑ 618 John Milner .15 .06
❑ 619 Steve Henderson .15 .06
❑ 620 Dennis Eckersley .75 .30
❑ 621 Tom Donohue .15 .06
❑ 622 Randy Moffitt .15 .06
❑ 623 Sal Bando .40 .16
❑ 624 Bob Welch .40 .16
❑ 625 Bill Buckner .40 .16
❑ 626 Dave Steffen .25 .10
Jerry Ujdur
Roger Weaver
❑ 627 Luis Tiant .40 .16
❑ 628 Vic Correll .15 .06
❑ 629 Tony Armas .40 .16
❑ 630 Steve Carlton .75 .30
❑ 631 Ron Jackson .15 .06
❑ 632 Alan Bannister .15 .06
❑ 633 Bill Lee .40 .16
❑ 634 Doug Flynn .15 .06
❑ 635 Bobby Bonds .40 .16
❑ 636 Al Hrabosky .40 .16
❑ 637 Jerry Narron .15 .06
❑ 638 Checklist 606-726 .40 .16
❑ 639 Carney Lansford .40 .16
❑ 640 Dave Parker .40 .16
❑ 641 Mark Belanger .15 .06
❑ 642 Vern Ruhle .15 .06
❑ 643 Lloyd Moseby RC .75 .30
❑ 644 Ramon Aviles DP .15 .06
❑ 645 Rick Reuschel .40 .16
❑ 646 Marvis Foley .15 .06
❑ 647 Dick Drago .15 .06
❑ 648 Darrell Evans .40 .16
❑ 649 Manny Sarmiento .15 .06
❑ 650 Bucky Dent .40 .16
❑ 651 Pedro Guerrero .40 .16

Card	Nm-Mt	Ex-Mt
❑ 652 John Montague	.15	.06
❑ 653 Bill Fahey	.15	.06
❑ 654 Ray Burris	.15	.06
❑ 655 Dan Driessen	.15	.06
❑ 656 Jon Matlack	.15	.06
❑ 657 Mike Cubbage DP	.15	.06
❑ 658 Milt Wilcox	.15	.06
❑ 659 John Flinn Ed Romero Ned Yost	.75	.30
❑ 660 Gary Carter	.75	.30
❑ 661 Orioles Team CL Earl Weaver MG	.40	.16
❑ 662 Red Sox Team CL Ralph Houk MG	.40	.16
❑ 663 Angels Team CL Jim Fregosi MG	.40	.16
❑ 664 White Sox CL Tony LaRussa MG	.40	.16
❑ 665 Indians Team CL Dave Garcia MG	.40	.16
❑ 666 Tigers Team CL Sparky Anderson MG	.40	.16
❑ 667 Royals Team CL Jim Frey MG	.40	.16
❑ 668 Brewers Team CL Bob Rodgers MG	.40	.16
❑ 669 Twins Team CL John Goryl MG	.40	.16
❑ 670 Yankees Team CL Gene Michael MG	.40	.16
❑ 671 A's Team CL Billy Martin MG	.75	.30
❑ 672 Mariners Team CL Maury Wills MG	.40	.16
❑ 673 Rangers Team CL Don Zimmer MG	.40	.16
❑ 674 Blue Jays Team CL Bobby Mattick MG	.40	.16
❑ 675 Braves Team CL Bobby Cox MG	.40	.16
❑ 676 Cubs Team CL Joe Amalfitano MG	.40	.16
❑ 677 Reds Team CL John McNamara MG	.40	.16
❑ 678 Astros Team CL Bill Virdon MG	.40	.16
❑ 679 Dodgers Team CL Tom Lasorda MG	.75	.30
❑ 680 Expos Team CL Dick Williams MG	.40	.16
❑ 681 Mets Team CL Joe Torre MG	.75	.30
❑ 682 Phillies Team CL Dallas Green MG	.40	.16
❑ 683 Pirates Team CL Chuck Tanner MG	.40	.16
❑ 684 Cardinals Team CL Whitey Herzog MG	.40	.16
❑ 685 Padres Team CL Frank Howard MG	.40	.16
❑ 686 Giants Team CL Dave Bristol MG	.40	.16
❑ 687 Jeff Jones	.15	.06
❑ 688 Kiko Garcia	.15	.06
❑ 689 Bruce Hurst RC Keith MacWhorter Reid Nichols	1.50	.60
❑ 690 Bob Watson	.15	.06
❑ 691 Dick Ruthven	.15	.06
❑ 692 Lenny Randle	.15	.06
❑ 693 Steve Howe RC	.25	.10
❑ 694 Bud Harrelson DP	.25	.10
❑ 695 Kent Tekulve	.15	.06
❑ 696 Alan Ashby	.15	.06
❑ 697 Rick Waits	.15	.06
❑ 698 Mike Jorgensen	.15	.06
❑ 699 Glenn Abbott	.15	.06
❑ 700 George Brett	4.00	1.60
❑ 701 Joe Rudi	.40	.16
❑ 702 George Medich	.15	.06
❑ 703 Alvis Woods	.15	.06
❑ 704 Bill Travers DP	.15	.06
❑ 705 Ted Simmons	.40	.16
❑ 706 Dave Ford	.15	.06
❑ 707 Dave Cash	.15	.06
❑ 708 Doyle Alexander	.15	.06
❑ 709 Alan Trammell DP	.50	.20
❑ 710 Ron LeFlore DP	.25	.10
❑ 711 Joe Ferguson	.15	.06
❑ 712 Bill Bonham	.15	.06
❑ 713 Bill North	.15	.06
❑ 714 Pete Redfern	.15	.06
❑ 715 Bill Madlock	.40	.16
❑ 716 Glenn Borgmann	.15	.06
❑ 717 Jim Barr DP	.15	.06
❑ 718 Larry Biittner	.15	.06
❑ 719 Sparky Lyle	.40	.16
❑ 720 Fred Lynn	.40	.16
❑ 721 Toby Harrah	.40	.16
❑ 722 Joe Niekro	.15	.06
❑ 723 Bruce Bochte	.15	.06
❑ 724 Lou Piniella	.40	.16
❑ 725 Steve Rogers	.40	.16
❑ 726 Rick Monday	.40	.16

1981 Topps Traded

	Nm-Mt	Ex-Mt
COMP.FACT.SET (132)	25.00	10.00
❑ 727 Danny Ainge XRC	3.00	1.20
❑ 728 Doyle Alexander	.25	.10
❑ 729 Gary Alexander	.25	.10
❑ 730 Bill Almon	.25	.10
❑ 731 Joaquin Andujar	1.00	.40
❑ 732 Bob Bailor	.25	.10
❑ 733 Juan Beniquez	.25	.10
❑ 734 Dave Bergman	.25	.10
❑ 735 Tony Bernazard	.25	.10
❑ 736 Larry Biittner	.25	.10
❑ 737 Doug Bird	.25	.10
❑ 738 Bert Blyleven	1.00	.40
❑ 739 Mark Bomback	.25	.10
❑ 740 Bobby Bonds	1.00	.40
❑ 741 Rick Bosetti	.25	.10
❑ 742 Hubie Brooks	2.00	.80
❑ 743 Rick Burleson	.25	.10
❑ 744 Ray Burris	.25	.10
❑ 745 Jeff Burroughs	1.00	.40
❑ 746 Enos Cabell	.25	.10
❑ 747 Ken Clay	.25	.10
❑ 748 Mark Clear	.25	.10
❑ 749 Larry Cox	.25	.10
❑ 750 Hector Cruz	.25	.10
❑ 751 Victor Cruz	.25	.10
❑ 752 Mike Cubbage	.25	.10
❑ 753 Dick Davis	.25	.10
❑ 754 Brian Doyle	.25	.10
❑ 755 Dick Drago	.25	.10
❑ 756 Leon Durham	1.00	.40
❑ 757 Jim Dwyer	.25	.10
❑ 758 Dave Edwards UER No birthdate on card	.25	.10
❑ 759 Jim Essian	.25	.10
❑ 760 Bill Fahey	.25	.10
❑ 761 Rollie Fingers	1.00	.40
❑ 762 Carlton Fisk	2.00	.80
❑ 763 Barry Foote	.25	.10
❑ 764 Ken Forsch	.25	.10
❑ 765 Kiko Garcia	.25	.10
❑ 766 Cesar Geronimo	.25	.10
❑ 767 Gary Gray	.25	.10
❑ 768 Mickey Hatcher	.25	.10
❑ 769 Steve Henderson	.25	.10
❑ 770 Marc Hill	.25	.10
❑ 771 Butch Hobson	.25	.10
❑ 772 Rick Honeycutt	.25	.10
❑ 773 Roy Howell	.25	.10
❑ 774 Mike Ivie	.25	.10
❑ 775 Roy Lee Jackson	.25	.10
❑ 776 Cliff Johnson	.25	.10
❑ 777 Randy Jones	1.00	.40
❑ 778 Ruppert Jones	.25	.10
❑ 779 Mick Kelleher	.25	.10
❑ 780 Terry Kennedy	.25	.10
❑ 781 Dave Kingman	1.00	.40
❑ 782 Bob Knepper	.25	.10
❑ 783 Ken Kravec	.25	.10
❑ 784 Bob Lacey	.25	.10
❑ 785 Dennis Lamp	.25	.10
❑ 786 Rafael Landestoy	.25	.10
❑ 787 Ken Landreaux	.25	.10
❑ 788 Carney Lansford	1.00	.40
❑ 789 Dave LaRoche	.25	.10
❑ 790 Joe Lefebvre	.25	.10
❑ 791 Ron LeFlore	1.00	.40
❑ 792 Randy Lerch	.25	.10
❑ 793 Sixto Lezcano	.25	.10
❑ 794 John Littlefield	.25	.10
❑ 795 Mike Lum	.25	.10
❑ 796 Greg Luzinski	1.00	.40
❑ 797 Fred Lynn	1.00	.40
❑ 798 Jerry Martin	.25	.10
❑ 799 Buck Martinez	.25	.10
❑ 800 Gary Matthews	1.00	.40
❑ 801 Mario Mendoza	.25	.10
❑ 802 Larry Milbourne	.25	.10
❑ 803 Rick Miller	.25	.10
❑ 804 John Montefusco	.25	.10
❑ 805 Jerry Morales	.25	.10
❑ 806 Jose Morales	.25	.10
❑ 807 Joe Morgan	2.00	.80
❑ 808 Jerry Mumphrey	.25	.10
❑ 809 Gene Nelson	.25	.10
❑ 810 Ed Ott	.25	.10
❑ 811 Bob Owchinko	.25	.10
❑ 812 Gaylord Perry	1.00	.40
❑ 813 Mike Phillips	.25	.10
❑ 814 Darrell Porter	.25	.10
❑ 815 Mike Proly	.25	.10
❑ 816 Tim Raines	3.00	1.20
❑ 817 Lenny Randle	.25	.10
❑ 818 Doug Rau	.25	.10
❑ 819 Jeff Reardon	2.00	.80
❑ 820 Ken Reitz	.25	.10
❑ 821 Steve Renko	.25	.10
❑ 822 Rick Reuschel	1.00	.40
❑ 823 Dave Revering	.25	.10
❑ 824 Dave Roberts	.25	.10
❑ 825 Leon Roberts	.25	.10
❑ 826 Joe Rudi	1.00	.40
❑ 827 Kevin Saucier	.25	.10
❑ 828 Tony Scott	.25	.10
❑ 829 Bob Shirley	.25	.10
❑ 830 Ted Simmons	1.00	.40
❑ 831 Lary Sorensen	.25	.10
❑ 832 Jim Spencer	.25	.10
❑ 833 Harry Spilman	.25	.10
❑ 834 Fred Stanley	.25	.10
❑ 835 Rusty Staub	1.00	.40
❑ 836 Bill Stein	.25	.10
❑ 837 Joe Strain	.25	.10
❑ 838 Bruce Sutter	1.00	.40
❑ 839 Don Sutton	1.00	.40
❑ 840 Steve Swisher	.25	.10
❑ 841 Frank Tanana	1.00	.40
❑ 842 Gene Tenace	1.00	.40
❑ 843 Jason Thompson	.25	.10
❑ 844 Dickie Thon	.25	.10
❑ 845 Bill Travers	.25	.10
❑ 846 Tom Underwood	.25	.10
❑ 847 John Urrea	.25	.10
❑ 848 Mike Vail	.25	.10
❑ 849 Ellis Valentine	.25	.10
❑ 850 Fernando Valenzuela	5.00	2.00
❑ 851 Pete Vuckovich	.25	.10
❑ 852 Mark Wagner	.25	.10
❑ 853 Bob Walk	1.00	.40
❑ 854 Claudell Washington	.25	.10

❑ 855 Dave Winfield 2.00 .80
❑ 856 Geoff Zahn .25 .10
❑ 857 Richie Zisk .25 .10
❑ 858 Checklist 727-858 .25 .10

1982 Topps

	Nm-Mt	Ex-Mt
COMPLETE SET (792)	80.00	32.00

❑ 1 Steve Carlton HL .30 .12
❑ 2 Ron Davis HL .15 .06
❑ 3 Tim Raines HL .30 .12
❑ 4 Pete Rose HL .60 .24
❑ 5 Nolan Ryan HL 3.00 1.20
❑ 6 Fernando Valenzuela HL .60 .24
❑ 7 Scott Sanderson .15 .06
❑ 8 Rich Dauer .15 .06
❑ 9 Ron Guidry .30 .12
❑ 10 Ron Guidry SA .15 .06
❑ 11 Gary Alexander .15 .06
❑ 12 Moose Haas .15 .06
❑ 13 Lamar Johnson .15 .06
❑ 14 Steve Howe .15 .06
❑ 15 Ellis Valentine .15 .06
❑ 16 Steve Comer .15 .06
❑ 17 Darrell Evans .30 .12
❑ 18 Fernando Arroyo .15 .06
❑ 19 Ernie Whitt .15 .06
❑ 20 Garry Maddox .15 .06
❑ 21 Bob Bonner 50.00 20.00
Cal Ripken RC
Jeff Schneider
Birthdate for Jeff Scheider is wrong
❑ 22 Jim Beattie .15 .06
❑ 23 Willie Hernandez .15 .06
❑ 24 Dave Frost .15 .06
❑ 25 Jerry Remy .15 .06
❑ 26 Jorge Orta .15 .06
❑ 27 Tom Herr .15 .06
❑ 28 John Urrea .15 .06
❑ 29 Dwayne Murphy .15 .06
❑ 30 Tom Seaver 1.25 .50
❑ 31 Tom Seaver SA .30 .12
❑ 32 Gene Garber .15 .06
❑ 33 Jerry Morales .15 .06
❑ 34 Joe Sambito .15 .06
❑ 35 Willie Aikens .15 .06
❑ 36 Al Oliver .60 .24
Doc Medich TL
❑ 37 Dan Graham .15 .06
❑ 38 Charlie Lea .15 .06
❑ 39 Lou Whitaker .30 .12
❑ 40 Dave Parker .30 .12
❑ 41 Dave Parker SA .15 .06
❑ 42 Rick Sofield .15 .06
❑ 43 Mike Cubbage .15 .06
❑ 44 Britt Burns .15 .06
❑ 45 Rick Cerone .15 .06
❑ 46 Jerry Augustine .15 .06
❑ 47 Jeff Leonard .15 .06
❑ 48 Bobby Castillo .15 .06
❑ 49 Alvis Woods .15 .06
❑ 50 Buddy Bell .30 .12
❑ 51 Jay Howell RC .75 .30
Carlos Lezcano
Ty Waller
❑ 52 Larry Andersen .15 .06
❑ 53 Greg Gross .15 .06
❑ 54 Ron Hassey .15 .06
❑ 55 Rick Burleson .15 .06
❑ 56 Mark Littell .15 .06
❑ 57 Craig Reynolds .15 .06
❑ 58 John D'Acquisto .15 .06
❑ 59 Rich Gedman .75 .30
❑ 60 Tony Armas .30 .12
❑ 61 Tommy Boggs .15 .06
❑ 62 Mike Tyson .15 .06
❑ 63 Mario Soto .30 .12
❑ 64 Lynn Jones .15 .06
❑ 65 Terry Kennedy .15 .06
❑ 66 Art Howe 2.00 .80
Nolan Ryan TL
❑ 67 Rich Gale .15 .06
❑ 68 Roy Howell .15 .06
❑ 69 Al Williams .15 .06
❑ 70 Tim Raines .60 .24
❑ 71 Roy Lee Jackson .15 .06
❑ 72 Rick Auerbach .15 .06
❑ 73 Buddy Solomon .15 .06
❑ 74 Bob Clark .15 .06
❑ 75 Tommy John .30 .12
❑ 76 Greg Pryor .15 .06
❑ 77 Miguel Dilone .15 .06
❑ 78 George Medich .15 .06
❑ 79 Bob Bailor .15 .06
❑ 80 Jim Palmer .30 .12
❑ 81 Jim Palmer SA .15 .06
❑ 82 Bob Welch .30 .12
❑ 83 Steve Balboni RC .75 .30
Andy McGaffigan
Andre Robertson
❑ 84 Rennie Stennett .15 .06
❑ 85 Lynn McGlothen .15 .06
❑ 86 Dane Iorg .15 .06
❑ 87 Matt Keough .15 .06
❑ 88 Biff Pocoroba .15 .06
❑ 89 Steve Henderson .15 .06
❑ 90 Nolan Ryan 6.00 2.40
❑ 91 Carney Lansford .30 .12
❑ 92 Brad Havens .15 .06
❑ 93 Larry Hisle .15 .06
❑ 94 Andy Hassler .15 .06
❑ 95 Ozzie Smith 2.50 1.00
❑ 96 George Brett 1.25 .50
Larry Gura TL
❑ 97 Paul Moskau .15 .06
❑ 98 Terry Bulling .15 .06
❑ 99 Barry Bonnell .15 .06
❑ 100 Mike Schmidt 3.00 1.20
❑ 101 Mike Schmidt SA 1.25 .50
❑ 102 Dan Briggs .15 .06
❑ 103 Bob Lacey .15 .06
❑ 104 Rance Mulliniks .15 .06
❑ 105 Kirk Gibson 1.25 .50
❑ 106 Enrique Romo .15 .06
❑ 107 Wayne Krenchicki .15 .06
❑ 108 Bob Sykes .15 .06
❑ 109 Dave Revering .15 .06
❑ 110 Carlton Fisk .60 .24
❑ 111 Carlton Fisk SA .30 .12
❑ 112 Billy Sample .15 .06
❑ 113 Steve McCatty .15 .06
❑ 114 Ken Landreaux .15 .06
❑ 115 Gaylord Perry .30 .12
❑ 116 Jim Wohlford .15 .06
❑ 117 Rawly Eastwick .30 .12
❑ 118 Terry Francona RC 2.50 1.00
Brad Mills
Bryn Smith RC
❑ 119 Joe Pittman .15 .06
❑ 120 Gary Lucas .15 .06
❑ 121 Ed Lynch .15 .06
❑ 122 Jamie Easterly UER .15 .06
(Photo actually
Reggie Cleveland)
❑ 123 Danny Goodwin .15 .06
❑ 124 Reid Nichols .15 .06
❑ 125 Danny Ainge .30 .12
❑ 126 Claudell Washington .60 .24
Rick Mahler TL
❑ 127 Lonnie Smith .15 .06
❑ 128 Frank Pastore .15 .06
❑ 129 Checklist 1-132 .30 .12
❑ 130 Julio Cruz .15 .06
❑ 131 Stan Bahnsen .15 .06
❑ 132 Lee May .15 .06
❑ 133 Pat Underwood .15 .06
❑ 134 Dan Ford .15 .06
❑ 135 Andy Rincon .15 .06
❑ 136 Lenn Sakata .15 .06
❑ 137 George Cappuzzello .15 .06
❑ 138 Tony Pena .30 .12
❑ 139 Jeff Jones .15 .06
❑ 140 Ron LeFlore .30 .12
❑ 141 Chris Bando .75 .30
Tom Brennan
Von Hayes RC
❑ 142 Dave LaRoche .15 .06
❑ 143 Mookie Wilson .30 .12
❑ 144 Fred Breining .15 .06
❑ 145 Bob Horner .30 .12
❑ 146 Mike Griffin .15 .06
❑ 147 Denny Walling .15 .06
❑ 148 Mickey Klutts .15 .06
❑ 149 Pat Putnam .15 .06
❑ 150 Ted Simmons .30 .12
❑ 151 Dave Edwards .15 .06
❑ 152 Ramon Aviles .15 .06
❑ 153 Roger Erickson .15 .06
❑ 154 Dennis Werth .15 .06
❑ 155 Otto Velez .15 .06
❑ 156 Rickey Henderson 1.25 .50
Steve McCatty TL
❑ 157 Steve Crawford .15 .06
❑ 158 Brian Downing .30 .12
❑ 159 Larry Biittner .15 .06
❑ 160 Luis Tiant .30 .12
❑ 161 Bill Madlock .30 .12
Carney Lansford LL
❑ 162 Mike Schmidt 1.25 .50
Tony Armas
Dwight Evans
Bobby Grich
Eddie Murray LL
❑ 163 Mike Schmidt 1.25 .50
Eddie Murray LL
❑ 164 Tim Raines 1.25 .50
Rickey Henderson LL
❑ 165 Tom Seaver .30 .12
Denny Martinez
Steve McCatty
Jack Morris
Pete Vuckovich LL
❑ 166 Fernando Valenzuela .30 .12
Len Barker LL
❑ 167 Nolan Ryan 2.00 .80
Steve McCatty LL
❑ 168 Bruce Sutter .30 .12
Rollie Fingers LL
❑ 169 Charlie Leibrandt .15 .06
❑ 170 Jim Bibby .15 .06
❑ 171 Bob Brenly RC 1.50 .60
Chili Davis RC
Bob Tufts
❑ 172 Bill Gullickson .15 .06
❑ 173 Jamie Quirk .15 .06
❑ 174 Dave Ford .15 .06
❑ 175 Jerry Mumphrey .15 .06
❑ 176 Dewey Robinson .15 .06
❑ 177 John Ellis .15 .06
❑ 178 Dyar Miller .15 .06
❑ 179 Steve Garvey .30 .12
❑ 180 Steve Garvey SA .15 .06
❑ 181 Silvio Martinez .15 .06
❑ 182 Larry Herndon .15 .06
❑ 183 Mike Proly .15 .06
❑ 184 Mick Kelleher .15 .06
❑ 185 Phil Niekro .30 .12
❑ 186 Keith Hernandez .30 .12
Bob Forsch TL
❑ 187 Jeff Newman .15 .06
❑ 188 Randy Martz .15 .06
❑ 189 Glenn Hoffman .15 .06
❑ 190 J.R. Richard .30 .12
❑ 191 Tim Wallach RC 1.50 .60
❑ 192 Broderick Perkins .15 .06
❑ 193 Darrell Jackson .15 .06
❑ 194 Mike Vail .15 .06
❑ 195 Paul Molitor .60 .24

❑ 196 Willie Upshaw .75 .30
❑ 197 Shane Rawley .15 .06
❑ 198 Chris Speier .15 .06
❑ 199 Don Aase .15 .06
❑ 200 George Brett 3.00 1.20
❑ 201 George Brett SA 1.50 .60
❑ 202 Rick Manning .15 .06
❑ 203 Jesse Barfield RC 1.50 .60
Brian Milner
Boomer Wells
❑ 204 Gary Roenicke .15 .06
❑ 205 Neil Allen .15 .06
❑ 206 Tony Bernazard .15 .06
❑ 207 Rod Scurry .15 .06
❑ 208 Bobby Murcer .30 .12
❑ 209 Gary Lavelle .15 .06
❑ 210 Keith Hernandez .30 .12
❑ 211 Dan Petry .15 .06
❑ 212 Mario Mendoza .15 .06
❑ 213 Dave Stewart RC 2.50 1.00
❑ 214 Brian Asselstine .15 .06
❑ 215 Mike Krukow .15 .06
❑ 216 Chet Lemon .60 .24
Dennis Lamp TL
❑ 217 Bo McLaughlin .15 .06
❑ 218 Dave Roberts .15 .06
❑ 219 John Curtis .15 .06
❑ 220 Manny Trillo .15 .06
❑ 221 Jim Slaton .15 .06
❑ 222 Butch Wynegar .15 .06
❑ 223 Lloyd Moseby .15 .06
❑ 224 Bruce Bochte .15 .06
❑ 225 Mike Torrez .15 .06
❑ 226 Checklist 133-264 .60 .24
❑ 227 Ray Burris .15 .06
❑ 228 Sam Mejias .15 .06
❑ 229 Geoff Zahn .15 .06
❑ 230 Willie Wilson .30 .12
❑ 231 Mark Davis RC .75 .30
Bob Dernier
Ozzie Virgil
❑ 232 Terry Crowley .15 .06
❑ 233 Duane Kuiper .15 .06
❑ 234 Ron Hodges .15 .06
❑ 235 Mike Easler .15 .06
❑ 236 John Martin RC .25 .10
❑ 237 Rusty Kuntz .15 .06
❑ 238 Kevin Saucier .15 .06
❑ 239 Jon Matlack .15 .06
❑ 240 Bucky Dent .30 .12
❑ 241 Bucky Dent SA .15 .06
❑ 242 Milt May .15 .06
❑ 243 Bob Owchinko .15 .06
❑ 244 Rufino Linares .15 .06
❑ 245 Ken Reitz .15 .06
❑ 246 Hubie Brooks .60 .24
Mike Scott TL
❑ 247 Pedro Guerrero .30 .12
❑ 248 Frank LaCorte .15 .06
❑ 249 Tim Flannery .15 .06
❑ 250 Tug McGraw .30 .12
❑ 251 Fred Lynn .30 .12
❑ 252 Fred Lynn SA .15 .06
❑ 253 Chuck Baker .15 .06
❑ 254 Jorge Bell RC 1.50 .60
❑ 255 Tony Perez .60 .24
❑ 256 Tony Perez SA .30 .12
❑ 257 Larry Harlow .15 .06
❑ 258 Bo Diaz .15 .06
❑ 259 Rodney Scott .15 .06
❑ 260 Bruce Sutter .30 .12
❑ 261 Howard Bailey .15 .06
Marty Castillo
Dave Rucker UER
(Rucker photo actually Roger Weaver)
❑ 262 Doug Bair .15 .06
❑ 263 Victor Cruz .15 .06
❑ 264 Dan Quisenberry .15 .06
❑ 265 Al Bumbry .15 .06
❑ 266 Rick Leach .15 .06
❑ 267 Kurt Bevacqua .15 .06
❑ 268 Rickey Keeton .15 .06
❑ 269 Jim Essian .15 .06
❑ 270 Rusty Staub .30 .12
❑ 271 Larry Bradford .15 .06
❑ 272 Bump Wills .15 .06
❑ 273 Doug Bird .15 .06
❑ 274 Bob Ojeda RC .75 .30
❑ 275 Bob Watson .15 .06
❑ 276 Rod Carew .60 .24
Ken Forsch TL
❑ 277 Terry Puhl .15 .06
❑ 278 John Littlefield .15 .06
❑ 279 Bill Russell .30 .12
❑ 280 Ben Oglivie .30 .12
❑ 281 John Verhoeven .15 .06
❑ 282 Ken Macha .15 .06
❑ 283 Brian Allard .15 .06
❑ 284 Bobby Grich .30 .12
❑ 285 Sparky Lyle .30 .12
❑ 286 Bill Fahey .15 .06
❑ 287 Alan Bannister .15 .06
❑ 288 Garry Templeton .30 .12
❑ 289 Bob Stanley .15 .06
❑ 290 Ken Singleton .30 .12
❑ 291 Vance Law .30 .12
Bob Long
Johnny Ray RC
❑ 292 David Palmer .15 .06
❑ 293 Rob Picciolo .15 .06
❑ 294 Mike LaCoss .15 .06
❑ 295 Jason Thompson .15 .06
❑ 296 Bob Walk .15 .06
❑ 297 Clint Hurdle .15 .06
❑ 298 Danny Darwin .15 .06
❑ 299 Steve Trout .15 .06
❑ 300 Reggie Jackson .60 .24
❑ 301 Reggie Jackson SA .30 .12
❑ 302 Doug Flynn .15 .06
❑ 303 Bill Caudill .15 .06
❑ 304 Johnnie LeMaster .15 .06
❑ 305 Don Sutton .30 .12
❑ 306 Don Sutton SA .15 .06
❑ 307 Randy Bass RC .75 .30
❑ 308 Charlie Moore .15 .06
❑ 309 Pete Redfern .15 .06
❑ 310 Mike Hargrove .15 .06
❑ 311 Dusty Baker .30 .12
Burt Hooton TL
❑ 312 Lenny Randle .15 .06
❑ 313 John Harris .15 .06
❑ 314 Buck Martinez .15 .06
❑ 315 Burt Hooton .15 .06
❑ 316 Steve Braun .15 .06
❑ 317 Dick Ruthven .15 .06
❑ 318 Mike Heath .15 .06
❑ 319 Dave Rozema .15 .06
❑ 320 Chris Chambliss .30 .12
❑ 321 Chris Chambliss SA .15 .06
❑ 322 Garry Hancock .15 .06
❑ 323 Bill Lee .30 .12
❑ 324 Steve Dillard .15 .06
❑ 325 Jose Cruz .30 .12
❑ 326 Pete Falcone .15 .06
❑ 327 Joe Nolan .15 .06
❑ 328 Ed Farmer .15 .06
❑ 329 U.L. Washington .15 .06
❑ 330 Rick Wise .15 .06
❑ 331 Benny Ayala .15 .06
❑ 332 Don Robinson .15 .06
❑ 333 Frank DiPino .15 .06
Marshall Edwards
Chuck Porter
❑ 334 Aurelio Rodriguez .15 .06
❑ 335 Jim Sundberg .30 .12
❑ 336 Tom Paciorek .60 .24
Glenn Abbott TL
❑ 337 Pete Rose AS .60 .24
❑ 338 Dave Lopes AS .15 .06
❑ 339 Mike Schmidt AS 1.25 .50
❑ 340 Dave Concepcion AS .15 .06
❑ 341 Andre Dawson AS .15 .06
❑ 342A George Foster AS .30 .12
(With autograph)
❑ 342B George Foster AS 1.25 .50
(W/o autograph)
❑ 343 Dave Parker AS .15 .06
❑ 344 Gary Carter AS .15 .06
❑ 345 F. Valenzuela AS .60 .24
❑ 346 Tom Seaver AS ERR .30 .12
("t ed")
❑ 346B Tom Seaver AS COR .30 .12
("tied")
❑ 347 Bruce Sutter AS .15 .06
❑ 348 Derrel Thomas .15 .06
❑ 349 George Frazier .15 .06
❑ 350 Thad Bosley .15 .06
❑ 351 Scott Brown .15 .06
Geoff Combe
Paul Householder
❑ 352 Dick Davis .15 .06
❑ 353 Jack O'Connor .15 .06
❑ 354 Roberto Ramos .15 .06
❑ 355 Dwight Evans .30 .12
❑ 356 Denny Lewallyn .15 .06
❑ 357 Butch Hobson .15 .06
❑ 358 Mike Parrott .15 .06
❑ 359 Jim Dwyer .15 .06
❑ 360 Len Barker .15 .06
❑ 361 Rafael Landestoy .15 .06
❑ 362 Jim Wright UER .15 .06
(Wrong Jim Wright pictured)
❑ 363 Bob Molinaro .15 .06
❑ 364 Doyle Alexander .15 .06
❑ 365 Bill Madlock .30 .12
❑ 366 Luis Salazar .60 .24
Juan Eichelberger TL
❑ 367 Jim Kaat .30 .12
❑ 368 Alex Trevino .15 .06
❑ 369 Champ Summers .15 .06
❑ 370 Mike Norris .15 .06
❑ 371 Jerry Don Gleaton .15 .06
❑ 372 Luis Gomez .15 .06
❑ 373 Gene Nelson .15 .06
❑ 374 Tim Blackwell .15 .06
❑ 375 Dusty Baker .30 .12
❑ 376 Chris Welsh .15 .06
❑ 377 Kiko Garcia .15 .06
❑ 378 Mike Caldwell .15 .06
❑ 379 Rob Wilfong .15 .06
❑ 380 Dave Stieb .30 .12
❑ 381 Bruce Hurst .15 .06
Dave Schmidt
Julio Valdez
❑ 382 Joe Simpson .15 .06
❑ 383A Pascual Perez ERR 40.00 16.00
(No position on front)
❑ 383B Pascual Perez COR .30 .12
❑ 384 Keith Moreland .15 .06
❑ 385 Ken Forsch .15 .06
❑ 386 Jerry White .15 .06
❑ 387 Tom Veryzer .15 .06
❑ 388 Joe Rudi .30 .12
❑ 389 George Vukovich .15 .06
❑ 390 Eddie Murray 1.25 .50
❑ 391 Dave Tobik .15 .06
❑ 392 Rick Bosetti .15 .06
❑ 393 Al Hrabosky .15 .06
❑ 394 Checklist 265-396 .60 .24
❑ 395 Omar Moreno .15 .06
❑ 396 John Castino .60 .24
Fernando Arroyo TL
❑ 397 Ken Brett .15 .06
❑ 398 Mike Squires .15 .06
❑ 399 Pat Zachry .15 .06
❑ 400 Johnny Bench 1.25 .50
❑ 401 Johnny Bench SA .60 .24
❑ 402 Bill Stein .15 .06
❑ 403 Jim Tracy .30 .12
❑ 404 Dickie Thon .15 .06
❑ 405 Rick Reuschel .30 .12
❑ 406 Al Holland .15 .06
❑ 407 Danny Boone .15 .06
❑ 408 Ed Romero .15 .06
❑ 409 Don Cooper .15 .06
❑ 410 Ron Cey .30 .12
❑ 411 Ron Cey SA .15 .06
❑ 412 Luis Leal .15 .06
❑ 413 Dan Meyer .15 .06
❑ 414 Elias Sosa .15 .06
❑ 415 Don Baylor .30 .12
❑ 416 Marty Bystrom .15 .06
❑ 417 Pat Kelly .15 .06
❑ 418 John Butcher .15 .06
Bobby Johnson

		Dave Schmidt		
❑	419	Steve Stone	.15	.06
❑	420	George Hendrick	.30	.12
❑	421	Mark Clear	.15	.06
❑	422	Cliff Johnson	.15	.06
❑	423	Stan Papi	.15	.06
❑	424	Bruce Benedict	.15	.06
❑	425	John Candelaria	.15	.06
❑	426	Eddie Murray	.60	.24
		Sammy Stewart		
❑	427	Ron Oester	.15	.06
❑	428	LaMarr Hoyt	.15	.06
❑	429	John Wathan	.15	.06
❑	430	Vida Blue	.30	.12
❑	431	Vida Blue SA	.15	.06
❑	432	Mike Scott	.30	.12
❑	433	Alan Ashby	.15	.06
❑	434	Joe Lefebvre	.15	.06
❑	435	Robin Yount	2.00	.80
❑	436	Joe Strain	.15	.06
❑	437	Juan Berenguer	.15	.06
❑	438	Pete Mackanin	.15	.06
❑	439	Dave Righetti RC	2.50	1.00
❑	440	Jeff Burroughs	.15	.06
❑	441	Danny Heep	.15	.06
		Billy Smith		
		Bobby Sprowl		
❑	442	Bruce Kison	.15	.06
❑	443	Mark Wagner	.15	.06
❑	444	Terry Forster	.30	.12
❑	445	Larry Parrish	.15	.06
❑	446	Wayne Garland	.15	.06
❑	447	Darrell Porter	.15	.06
❑	448	Darrell Porter SA	.15	.06
❑	449	Luis Aguayo	.15	.06
❑	450	Jack Morris	.30	.12
❑	451	Ed Miller	.15	.06
❑	452	Lee Smith RC	3.00	1.20
❑	453	Art Howe	.15	.06
❑	454	Rick Langford	.15	.06
❑	455	Tom Burgmeier	.15	.06
❑	456	Bill Buckner	.30	.12
		Randy Martz TL		
❑	457	Tim Stoddard	.15	.06
❑	458	Willie Montanez	.15	.06
❑	459	Bruce Berenyi	.15	.06
❑	460	Jack Clark	.30	.12
❑	461	Rich Dotson	.15	.06
❑	462	Dave Chalk	.15	.06
❑	463	Jim Kern	.15	.06
❑	464	Juan Bonilla RC	.25	.10
❑	465	Lee Mazzilli	.30	.12
❑	466	Randy Lerch	.15	.06
❑	467	Mickey Hatcher	.15	.06
❑	468	Floyd Bannister	.15	.06
❑	469	Ed Ott	.15	.06
❑	470	John Mayberry	.15	.06
❑	471	Atlee Hammaker	.15	.06
		Mike Jones		
		Darryl Motley		
❑	472	Oscar Gamble	.15	.06
❑	473	Mike Stanton	.15	.06
❑	474	Ken Oberkfell	.15	.06
❑	475	Alan Trammell	.30	.12
❑	476	Brian Kingman	.15	.06
❑	477	Steve Yeager	.30	.12
❑	478	Ray Searage	.15	.06
❑	479	Rowland Office	.15	.06
❑	480	Steve Carlton	.60	.24
❑	481	Steve Carlton SA	.30	.12
❑	482	Glenn Hubbard	.15	.06
❑	483	Gary Woods	.15	.06
❑	484	Ivan DeJesus	.15	.06
❑	485	Kent Tekulve	.15	.06
❑	486	Jerry Mumphrey	.30	.12
		Tommy John TL		
❑	487	Bob McClure	.15	.06
❑	488	Ron Jackson	.15	.06
❑	489	Rick Dempsey	.15	.06
❑	490	Dennis Eckersley	.60	.24
❑	491	Checklist 397-528	.60	.24
❑	492	Joe Price	.15	.06
❑	493	Chet Lemon	.30	.12
❑	494	Hubie Brooks	.15	.06
❑	495	Dennis Leonard	.15	.06
❑	496	Johnny Grubb	.15	.06
❑	497	Jim Anderson	.15	.06
❑	498	Dave Bergman	.15	.06
❑	499	Paul Mirabella	.15	.06
❑	500	Rod Carew	.60	.24
❑	501	Rod Carew SA	.30	.12
❑	502	Steve Bedrosian RC UER	1.50	.60
		Photo actually Larry Owen)		
		Brett Butler RC		
		Larry Owen		
❑	503	Julio Gonzalez	.15	.06
❑	504	Rick Peters	.15	.06
❑	505	Graig Nettles	.30	.12
❑	506	Graig Nettles SA	.15	.06
❑	507	Terry Harper	.15	.06
❑	508	Jody Davis	.15	.06
❑	509	Harry Spilman	.15	.06
❑	510	Fernando Valenzuela	1.25	.50
❑	511	Ruppert Jones	.15	.06
❑	512	Jerry Dybzinski	.15	.06
❑	513	Rick Rhoden	.15	.06
❑	514	Joe Ferguson	.15	.06
❑	515	Larry Bowa	.30	.12
❑	516	Larry Bowa SA	.15	.06
❑	517	Mark Brouhard	.15	.06
❑	518	Garth Iorg	.15	.06
❑	519	Glenn Adams	.15	.06
❑	520	Mike Flanagan	.15	.06
❑	521	Bill Almon	.15	.06
❑	522	Chuck Rainey	.15	.06
❑	523	Gary Gray	.15	.06
❑	524	Tom Hausman	.15	.06
❑	525	Ray Knight	.30	.12
❑	526	Warren Cromartie	.60	.24
		Bill Gullickson TL		
❑	527	John Henry Johnson	.15	.06
❑	528	Matt Alexander	.15	.06
❑	529	Allen Ripley	.15	.06
❑	530	Dickie Noles	.15	.06
❑	531	Rich Bordi	.15	.06
		Mark Budaska		
		Kelvin Moore		
❑	532	Toby Harrah	.30	.12
❑	533	Joaquin Andujar	.30	.12
❑	534	Dave McKay	.15	.06
❑	535	Lance Parrish	.30	.12
❑	536	Rafael Ramirez	.15	.06
❑	537	Doug Capilla	.15	.06
❑	538	Lou Piniella	.30	.12
❑	539	Vern Ruhle	.15	.06
❑	540	Andre Dawson	.30	.12
❑	541	Barry Evans	.15	.06
❑	542	Ned Yost	.15	.06
❑	543	Bill Robinson	.15	.06
❑	544	Larry Christenson	.15	.06
❑	545	Reggie Smith	.30	.12
❑	546	Reggie Smith SA	.15	.06
❑	547	Rod Carew AS	.30	.12
❑	548	Willie Randolph AS	.15	.06
❑	549	George Brett AS	1.50	.60
❑	550	Bucky Dent AS	.15	.06
❑	551	Reggie Jackson AS	.30	.12
❑	552	Ken Singleton AS	.15	.06
❑	553	Dave Winfield AS	.15	.06
❑	554	Carlton Fisk AS	.30	.12
❑	555	Scott McGregor AS	.15	.06
❑	556	Jack Morris AS	.15	.06
❑	557	Rich Gossage AS	.15	.06
❑	558	John Tudor	.30	.12
❑	559	Mike Hargrove	.30	.12
		Bert Blyleven TL		
❑	560	Doug Corbett	.15	.06
❑	561	Glenn Brummer	.15	.06
		Luis DeLeon		
		Gene Roof		
❑	562	Mike O'Berry	.15	.06
❑	563	Ross Baumgarten	.15	.06
❑	564	Doug DeCinces	.15	.06
❑	565	Jackson Todd	.15	.06
❑	566	Mike Jorgensen	.15	.06
❑	567	Bob Babcock	.15	.06
❑	568	Joe Pettini	.15	.06
❑	569	Willie Randolph	.30	.12
❑	570	Willie Randolph SA	.15	.06
❑	571	Glenn Abbott	.15	.06
❑	572	Juan Beniquez	.15	.06
❑	573	Rick Waits	.15	.06
❑	574	Mike Ramsey	.15	.06
❑	575	Al Cowens	.15	.06
❑	576	Milt May	.60	.24
		Vida Blue TL		
❑	577	Rick Monday	.30	.12
❑	578	Shooty Babitt	.15	.06
❑	579	Rick Mahler	.15	.06
❑	580	Bobby Bonds	.30	.12
❑	581	Ron Reed	.15	.06
❑	582	Luis Pujols	.15	.06
❑	583	Tippy Martinez	.15	.06
❑	584	Hosken Powell	.15	.06
❑	585	Rollie Fingers	.30	.12
❑	586	Rollie Fingers SA	.15	.06
❑	587	Tim Lollar	.15	.06
❑	588	Dale Berra	.15	.06
❑	589	Dave Stapleton	.15	.06
❑	590	Al Oliver	.30	.12
❑	591	Al Oliver SA	.15	.06
❑	592	Craig Swan	.15	.06
❑	593	Billy Smith	.15	.06
❑	594	Renie Martin	.15	.06
❑	595	Dave Collins	.15	.06
❑	596	Damaso Garcia	.15	.06
❑	597	Wayne Nordhagen	.15	.06
❑	598	Bob Galasso	.15	.06
❑	599	Jay Loviglio	.15	.06
		Reggie Patterson		
		Leo Sutherland		
❑	600	Dave Winfield	.30	.12
❑	601	Sid Monge	.15	.06
❑	602	Freddie Patek	.15	.06
❑	603	Rich Hebner	.15	.06
❑	604	Orlando Sanchez	.15	.06
❑	605	Steve Rogers	.30	.12
❑	606	John Mayberry	.30	.12
		Dave Stieb TL		
❑	607	Leon Durham	.15	.06
❑	608	Jerry Royster	.15	.06
❑	609	Rick Sutcliffe	.30	.12
❑	610	Rickey Henderson	4.00	1.60
❑	611	Joe Niekro	.15	.06
❑	612	Gary Ward	.15	.06
❑	613	Jim Gantner	.15	.06
❑	614	Juan Eichelberger	.15	.06
❑	615	Bob Boone	.30	.12
❑	616	Bob Boone SA	.15	.06
❑	617	Scott McGregor	.15	.06
❑	618	Tim Foli	.15	.06
❑	619	Bill Campbell	.15	.06
❑	620	Ken Griffey	.30	.12
❑	621	Ken Griffey SA	.15	.06
❑	622	Dennis Lamp	.15	.06
❑	623	Ron Gardenhire RC	.75	.30
		Terry Leach		
		Tim Leary RC		
❑	624	Fergie Jenkins	.30	.12
❑	625	Hal McRae	.30	.12
❑	626	Randy Jones	.15	.06
❑	627	Enos Cabell	.15	.06
❑	628	Bill Travers	.15	.06
❑	629	John Wockenfuss	.15	.06
❑	630	Joe Charboneau	.30	.12
❑	631	Gene Tenace	.30	.12
❑	632	Bryan Clark RC	.25	.10
❑	633	Mitchell Page	.15	.06
❑	634	Checklist 529-660	.60	.24
❑	635	Ron Davis	.15	.06
❑	636	Pete Rose	1.25	.50
		Steve Carlton TL		
❑	637	Rick Camp	.15	.06
❑	638	John Milner	.15	.06
❑	639	Ken Kravec	.15	.06
❑	640	Cesar Cedeno	.30	.12
❑	641	Steve Mura	.15	.06
❑	642	Mike Scioscia	.30	.12
❑	643	Pete Vuckovich	.15	.06
❑	644	John Castino	.15	.06
❑	645	Frank White	.30	.12
❑	646	Frank White SA	.15	.06
❑	647	Warren Brusstar	.15	.06
❑	648	Jose Morales	.15	.06
❑	649	Ken Clay	.15	.06
❑	650	Carl Yastrzemski	2.00	.80
❑	651	Carl Yastrzemski SA	1.25	.50
❑	652	Steve Nicosia	.15	.06

❑	653 Tom Brunansky RC	1.50	.60
	Luis Sanchez		
	Daryl Sconiers		
❑	654 Jim Morrison	.15	.06
❑	655 Joel Youngblood	.15	.06
❑	656 Eddie Whitson	.15	.06
❑	657 Tom Poquette	.15	.06
❑	658 Tito Landrum	.15	.06
❑	659 Fred Martinez	.15	.06
❑	660 Dave Concepcion	.30	.12
❑	661 Dave Concepcion SA	.15	.06
❑	662 Luis Salazar	.15	.06
❑	663 Hector Cruz	.15	.06
❑	664 Dan Spillner	.15	.06
❑	665 Jim Clancy	.15	.06
❑	666 Steve Kemp	.60	.24
	Dan Petry TL		
❑	667 Jeff Reardon	.30	.12
❑	668 Dale Murphy	.60	.24
❑	669 Larry Milbourne	.15	.06
❑	670 Steve Kemp	.15	.06
❑	671 Mike Davis	.15	.06
❑	672 Bob Knepper	.15	.06
❑	673 Keith Drumwright	.15	.06
❑	674 Dave Goltz	.15	.06
❑	675 Cecil Cooper	.30	.12
❑	676 Sal Butera	.15	.06
❑	677 Alfredo Griffin	.15	.06
❑	678 Tom Paciorek	.15	.06
❑	679 Sammy Stewart	.15	.06
❑	680 Gary Matthews	.30	.12
❑	681 Mike Marshall RC	1.50	.60
	Ron Roenicke		
	Steve Sax RC		
❑	682 Jesse Jefferson	.15	.06
❑	683 Phil Garner	.30	.12
❑	684 Harold Baines	.30	.12
❑	685 Bert Blyleven	.30	.12
❑	686 Gary Allenson	.15	.06
❑	687 Greg Minton	.15	.06
❑	688 Leon Roberts	.15	.06
❑	689 Lary Sorensen	.15	.06
❑	690 Dave Kingman	.30	.12
❑	691 Dan Schatzeder	.15	.06
❑	692 Wayne Gross	.15	.06
❑	693 Cesar Geronimo	.15	.06
❑	694 Dave Wehrmeister	.15	.06
❑	695 Warren Cromartie	.15	.06
❑	696 Bill Madlock	.60	.24
	Eddie Solomon TL		
❑	697 John Montefusco	.15	.06
❑	698 Tony Scott	.15	.06
❑	699 Dick Tidrow	.15	.06
❑	700 George Foster	.30	.12
❑	701 George Foster SA	.15	.06
❑	702 Steve Renko	.15	.06
❑	703 Cecil Cooper	.60	.24
	Pete Vuckovich TL		
❑	704 Mickey Rivers	.15	.06
❑	705 Mickey Rivers SA	.15	.06
❑	706 Barry Foote	.15	.06
❑	707 Mark Bomback	.15	.06
❑	708 Gene Richards	.15	.06
❑	709 Don Money	.15	.06
❑	710 Jerry Reuss	.15	.06
❑	711 Dave Edler	.75	.30
	Dave Henderson RC		
	Reggie Walton		
❑	712 Dennis Martinez	.30	.12
❑	713 Del Unser	.15	.06
❑	714 Jerry Koosman	.30	.12
❑	715 Willie Stargell	.60	.24
❑	716 Willie Stargell SA	.30	.12
❑	717 Rick Miller	.15	.06
❑	718 Charlie Hough	.30	.12
❑	719 Jerry Narron	.15	.06
❑	720 Greg Luzinski	.30	.12
❑	721 Greg Luzinski SA	.15	.06
❑	722 Jerry Martin	.15	.06
❑	723 Junior Kennedy	.15	.06
❑	724 Dave Rosello	.15	.06
❑	725 Amos Otis	.30	.12
❑	726 Amos Otis SA	.15	.06
❑	727 Sixto Lezcano	.15	.06
❑	728 Aurelio Lopez	.15	.06
❑	729 Jim Spencer	.15	.06
❑	730 Gary Carter	.30	.12
❑	731 Mike Armstrong	.15	.06
	Doug Gwosdz		
	Fred Kuhaulua		
❑	732 Mike Lum	.15	.06
❑	733 Larry McWilliams	.15	.06
❑	734 Mike Ivie	.15	.06
❑	735 Rudy May	.15	.06
❑	736 Jerry Turner	.15	.06
❑	737 Reggie Cleveland	.15	.06
❑	738 Dave Engle	.15	.06
❑	739 Joey McLaughlin	.15	.06
❑	740 Dave Lopes	.30	.12
❑	741 Dave Lopes SA	.15	.06
❑	742 Dick Drago	.15	.06
❑	743 John Stearns	.15	.06
❑	744 Mike Witt	.75	.30
❑	745 Bake McBride	.30	.12
❑	746 Andre Thornton	.15	.06
❑	747 John Lowenstein	.15	.06
❑	748 Marc Hill	.15	.06
❑	749 Bob Shirley	.15	.06
❑	750 Jim Rice	.30	.12
❑	751 Rick Honeycutt	.15	.06
❑	752 Lee Lacy	.15	.06
❑	753 Tom Brookens	.15	.06
❑	754 Joe Morgan	.30	.12
❑	755 Joe Morgan SA	.15	.06
❑	756 Ken Griffey	.30	.12
	Tom Seaver TL		
❑	757 Tom Underwood	.15	.06
❑	758 Claudell Washington	.15	.06
❑	759 Paul Splittorff	.15	.06
❑	760 Bill Buckner	.30	.12
❑	761 Dave Smith	.15	.06
❑	762 Mike Phillips	.15	.06
❑	763 Tom Hume	.15	.06
❑	764 Steve Swisher	.15	.06
❑	765 Gorman Thomas	.30	.12
❑	766 Lenny Faedo	1.50	.60
	Kent Hrbek RC		
	Tim Laudner		
❑	767 Roy Smalley	.15	.06
❑	768 Jerry Garvin	.15	.06
❑	769 Richie Zisk	.15	.06
❑	770 Rich Gossage	.30	.12
❑	771 Rich Gossage SA	.15	.06
❑	772 Bert Campaneris	.30	.12
❑	773 John Denny	.15	.06
❑	774 Jay Johnstone	.15	.06
❑	775 Bob Forsch	.15	.06
❑	776 Mark Belanger	.15	.06
❑	777 Tom Griffin	.15	.06
❑	778 Kevin Hickey RC	.25	.10
❑	779 Grant Jackson	.15	.06
❑	780 Pete Rose	4.00	1.60
❑	781 Pete Rose SA	1.25	.50
❑	782 Frank Taveras	.15	.06
❑	783 Greg Harris RC	.25	.10
❑	784 Milt Wilcox	.15	.06
❑	785 Dan Driessen	.15	.06
❑	786 Carney Lansford	.60	.24
	Mike Torrez TL		
❑	787 Fred Stanley	.15	.06
❑	788 Woodie Fryman	.15	.06
❑	789 Checklist 661-792	.60	.24
❑	790 Larry Gura	.15	.06
❑	791 Bobby Brown	.15	.06
❑	792 Frank Tanana	.30	.12

1982 Topps Traded

		Nm-Mt	Ex-Mt
	COMP.FACT.SET (132)	150.00	60.00
❑	1T Doyle Alexander	.50	.20
❑	2T Jesse Barfield	3.00	1.20
❑	3T Ross Baumgarten	.50	.20
❑	4T Steve Bedrosian	1.50	.60
❑	5T Mark Belanger	.50	.20
❑	6T Kurt Bevacqua	.50	.20
❑	7T Tim Blackwell	.50	.20
❑	8T Vida Blue	1.00	.40
❑	9T Bob Boone	1.00	.40
❑	10T Larry Bowa	1.00	.40
❑	11T Dan Briggs	.50	.20
❑	12T Bobby Brown	.50	.20
❑	13T Tom Brunansky	3.00	1.20
❑	14T Jeff Burroughs	.50	.20
❑	15T Enos Cabell	.50	.20
❑	16T Bill Campbell	.50	.20
❑	17T Bobby Castillo	.50	.20
❑	18T Bill Caudill	.50	.20
❑	19T Cesar Cedeno	1.00	.40
❑	20T Dave Collins	.50	.20
❑	21T Doug Corbett	.50	.20
❑	22T Al Cowens	.50	.20
❑	23T Chili Davis	3.00	1.20
❑	24T Dick Davis	.50	.20
❑	25T Ron Davis	.50	.20
❑	26T Doug DeCinces	.50	.20
❑	27T Ivan DeJesus	.50	.20
❑	28T Bob Dernier	.50	.20
❑	29T Bo Diaz	.50	.20
❑	30T Roger Erickson	.50	.20
❑	31T Jim Essian	.50	.20
❑	32T Ed Farmer	.50	.20
❑	33T Doug Flynn	.50	.20
❑	34T Tim Foli	.50	.20
❑	35T Dan Ford	.50	.20
❑	36T George Foster	1.00	.40
❑	37T Dave Frost	.50	.20
❑	38T Rich Gale	.50	.20
❑	39T Ron Gardenhire	1.50	.60
❑	40T Ken Griffey	1.00	.40
❑	41T Greg Harris	.50	.20
❑	42T Von Hayes	1.50	.60
❑	43T Larry Herndon	.50	.20
❑	44T Kent Hrbek	3.00	1.20
❑	45T Mike Ivie	.50	.20
❑	46T Grant Jackson	.50	.20
❑	47T Reggie Jackson	2.00	.80
❑	48T Ron Jackson	.50	.20
❑	49T Fergie Jenkins	1.00	.40
❑	50T Lamar Johnson	.50	.20
❑	51T Randy Johnson	.50	.20
❑	52T Jay Johnstone	.50	.20
❑	53T Mick Kelleher	.50	.20
❑	54T Steve Kemp	.50	.20
❑	55T Junior Kennedy	.50	.20
❑	56T Jim Kern	.50	.20
❑	57T Ray Knight	1.00	.40
❑	58T Wayne Krenchicki	.50	.20
❑	59T Mike Krukow	.50	.20
❑	60T Duane Kuiper	.50	.20
❑	61T Mike LaCoss	.50	.20
❑	62T Chet Lemon	1.00	.40
❑	63T Sixto Lezcano	.50	.20
❑	64T Dave Lopes	1.00	.40
❑	65T Jerry Martin	.50	.20
❑	66T Renie Martin	.50	.20
❑	67T John Mayberry	.50	.20
❑	68T Lee Mazzilli	1.00	.40
❑	69T Bake McBride	1.00	.40
❑	70T Dan Meyer	.50	.20
❑	71T Larry Milbourne	.50	.20
❑	72T Eddie Milner	.50	.20
❑	73T Sid Monge	.50	.20
❑	74T John Montefusco	.50	.20
❑	75T Jose Morales	.50	.20
❑	76T Keith Moreland	.50	.20
❑	77T Jim Morrison	.50	.20
❑	78T Rance Mulliniks	.50	.20
❑	79T Steve Mura	.50	.20
❑	80T Gene Nelson	.50	.20
❑	81T Joe Nolan	.50	.20
❑	82T Dickie Noles	.50	.20
❑	83T Al Oliver	1.00	.40

❑ 84T Jorge Orta .50 .20
❑ 85T Tom Paciorek .50 .20
❑ 86T Larry Parrish .50 .20
❑ 87T Jack Perconte .50 .20
❑ 88T Gaylord Perry 1.00 .40
❑ 89T Rob Picciolo .50 .20
❑ 90T Joe Pittman .50 .20
❑ 91T Hosken Powell .50 .20
❑ 92T Mike Proly .50 .20
❑ 93T Greg Pryor .50 .20
❑ 94T Charlie Puleo .50 .20
❑ 95T Shane Rawley .50 .20
❑ 96T Johnny Ray XRC 1.50 .60
❑ 97T Dave Revering .50 .20
❑ 98T Cal Ripken 120.00 47.50
❑ 99T Allen Ripley .50 .20
❑ 100T Bill Robinson .50 .20
❑ 101T Aurelio Rodriguez .50 .20
❑ 102T Joe Rudi 1.00 .40
❑ 103T Steve Sax 3.00 1.20
❑ 104T Dan Schatzeder .50 .20
❑ 105T Bob Shirley .50 .20
❑ 106T Eric Show XRC 1.50 .60
❑ 107T Roy Smalley .50 .20
❑ 108T Lonnie Smith .50 .20
❑ 109T Ozzie Smith 15.00 6.00
❑ 110T Reggie Smith 1.00 .40
❑ 111T Lary Sorensen .50 .20
❑ 112T Elias Sosa .50 .20
❑ 113T Mike Stanton .50 .20
❑ 114T Steve Stroughter .50 .20
❑ 115T Champ Summers .50 .20
❑ 116T Rick Sutcliffe 1.00 .40
❑ 117T Frank Tanana 1.00 .40
❑ 118T Frank Taveras .50 .20
❑ 119T Garry Templeton 1.00 .40
❑ 120T Alex Trevino .50 .20
❑ 121T Jerry Turner .50 .20
❑ 122T Ed VandeBerg .50 .20
❑ 123T Tom Veryzer .50 .20
❑ 124T Ron Washington .50 .20
❑ 125T Bob Watson .50 .20
❑ 126T Dennis Werth .50 .20
❑ 127T Eddie Whitson .50 .20
❑ 128T Rob Wilfong .50 .20
❑ 129T Bump Wills .50 .20
❑ 130T Gary Woods .50 .20
❑ 131T Butch Wynegar .50 .20
❑ 132T Checklist: 1-132 .50 .20

1983 Topps

	Nm-Mt	Ex-Mt
COMPLETE SET (792)	80.00	32.00

❑ 1 Tony Armas RB .30 .12
❑ 2 Rickey Henderson RB 1.25 .50
❑ 3 Greg Minton RB .15 .06
❑ 4 Lance Parrish RB .15 .06
❑ 5 Manny Trillo RB .15 .06
❑ 6 John Wathan RB .15 .06
❑ 7 Gene Richards .15 .06
❑ 8 Steve Balboni .15 .06
❑ 9 Joey McLaughlin .15 .06
❑ 10 Gorman Thomas .30 .12
❑ 11 Billy Gardner MG .15 .06
❑ 12 Paul Mirabella .15 .06
❑ 13 Larry Herndon .15 .06
❑ 14 Frank LaCorte .15 .06
❑ 15 Ron Cey .30 .12
❑ 16 George Vukovich .15 .06
❑ 17 Kent Tekulve .15 .06
❑ 18 Kent Tekulve SV .15 .06
❑ 19 Oscar Gamble .15 .06
❑ 20 Carlton Fisk .60 .24
❑ 21 Eddie Murray .60 .24
Jim Palmer TL
❑ 22 Randy Martz .15 .06
❑ 23 Mike Heath .15 .06
❑ 24 Steve Mura .15 .06
❑ 25 Hal McRae .30 .12
❑ 26 Jerry Royster .15 .06
❑ 27 Doug Corbett .15 .06
❑ 28 Bruce Bochte .15 .06
❑ 29 Randy Jones .15 .06
❑ 30 Jim Rice .30 .12
❑ 31 Bill Gullickson .15 .06
❑ 32 Dave Bergman .15 .06
❑ 33 Jack O'Connor .15 .06
❑ 34 Paul Householder .15 .06
❑ 35 Rollie Fingers .30 .12
❑ 36 Rollie Fingers SV .15 .06
❑ 37 Darrell Johnson MG .15 .06
❑ 38 Tim Flannery .15 .06
❑ 39 Terry Puhl .15 .06
❑ 40 Fernando Valenzuela .30 .12
❑ 41 Jerry Turner .15 .06
❑ 42 Dale Murray .15 .06
❑ 43 Bob Dernier .15 .06
❑ 44 Don Robinson .15 .06
❑ 45 John Mayberry .15 .06
❑ 46 Richard Dotson .15 .06
❑ 47 Dave McKay .15 .06
❑ 48 Lary Sorensen .15 .06
❑ 49 Willie McGee RC 1.50 .60
❑ 50 Bob Horner UER .30 .12
('82 RBI total 7)
❑ 51 Leon Durham .15 .06
Fergie Jenkins TL
❑ 52 Onix Concepcion .15 .06
❑ 53 Mike Witt .15 .06
❑ 54 Jim Maler .15 .06
❑ 55 Mookie Wilson .30 .12
❑ 56 Chuck Rainey .15 .06
❑ 57 Tim Blackwell .15 .06
❑ 58 Al Holland .15 .06
❑ 59 Benny Ayala .15 .06
❑ 60 Johnny Bench 1.25 .50
❑ 61 Johnny Bench SV .60 .24
❑ 62 Bob McClure .15 .06
❑ 63 Rick Monday .30 .12
❑ 64 Bill Stein .15 .06
❑ 65 Jack Morris .30 .12
❑ 66 Bob Lillis MG .15 .06
❑ 67 Sal Butera .15 .06
❑ 68 Eric Show RC .75 .30
❑ 69 Lee Lacy .15 .06
❑ 70 Steve Carlton .60 .24
❑ 71 Steve Carlton SV .30 .12
❑ 72 Tom Paciorek .15 .06
❑ 73 Allen Ripley .15 .06
❑ 74 Julio Gonzalez .15 .06
❑ 75 Amos Otis .30 .12
❑ 76 Rick Mahler .15 .06
❑ 77 Hosken Powell .15 .06
❑ 78 Bill Caudill .15 .06
❑ 79 Mick Kelleher .15 .06
❑ 80 George Foster .30 .12
❑ 81 Jerry Mumphrey .30 .12
Dave Righetti TL
❑ 82 Bruce Hurst .15 .06
❑ 83 Ryne Sandberg RC 15.00 6.00
❑ 84 Milt May .15 .06
❑ 85 Ken Singleton .30 .12
❑ 86 Tom Hume .15 .06
❑ 87 Joe Rudi .30 .12
❑ 88 Jim Gantner .15 .06
❑ 89 Leon Roberts .15 .06
❑ 90 Jerry Reuss .15 .06
❑ 91 Larry Milbourne .15 .06
❑ 92 Mike LaCoss .15 .06
❑ 93 John Castino .15 .06
❑ 94 Dave Edwards .15 .06
❑ 95 Alan Trammell .30 .12
❑ 96 Dick Howser MG .15 .06
❑ 97 Ross Baumgarten .15 .06
❑ 98 Vance Law .15 .06
❑ 99 Dickie Noles .15 .06
❑ 100 Pete Rose 4.00 1.60
❑ 101 Pete Rose SV 1.25 .50
❑ 102 Dave Beard .15 .06
❑ 103 Darrell Porter .15 .06
❑ 104 Bob Walk .15 .06
❑ 105 Don Baylor .30 .12
❑ 106 Gene Nelson .15 .06
❑ 107 Mike Jorgensen .15 .06
❑ 108 Glenn Hoffman .15 .06
❑ 109 Luis Leal .15 .06
❑ 110 Ken Griffey .30 .12
❑ 111 Al Oliver .30 .12
Steve Rogers TL
❑ 112 Bob Shirley .15 .06
❑ 113 Ron Roenicke .15 .06
❑ 114 Jim Slaton .15 .06
❑ 115 Chili Davis .30 .12
❑ 116 Dave Schmidt .15 .06
❑ 117 Alan Knicely .15 .06
❑ 118 Chris Welsh .15 .06
❑ 119 Tom Brookens .15 .06
❑ 120 Len Barker .15 .06
❑ 121 Mickey Hatcher .15 .06
❑ 122 Jimmy Smith .15 .06
❑ 123 George Frazier .15 .06
❑ 124 Marc Hill .15 .06
❑ 125 Leon Durham .15 .06
❑ 126 Joe Torre MG .60 .24
❑ 127 Preston Hanna .15 .06
❑ 128 Mike Ramsey .15 .06
❑ 129 Checklist: 1-132 .30 .12
❑ 130 Dave Stieb .30 .12
❑ 131 Ed Ott .15 .06
❑ 132 Todd Cruz .15 .06
❑ 133 Jim Barr .15 .06
❑ 134 Hubie Brooks .15 .06
❑ 135 Dwight Evans .30 .12
❑ 136 Willie Aikens .15 .06
❑ 137 Woodie Fryman .15 .06
❑ 138 Rick Dempsey .15 .06
❑ 139 Bruce Berenyi .15 .06
❑ 140 Willie Randolph .30 .12
❑ 141 Toby Harrah .30 .12
Rick Sutcliffe TL
❑ 142 Mike Caldwell .15 .06
❑ 143 Joe Pettini .15 .06
❑ 144 Mark Wagner .15 .06
❑ 145 Don Sutton .30 .12
❑ 146 Don Sutton SV .15 .06
❑ 147 Rick Leach .15 .06
❑ 148 Dave Roberts .15 .06
❑ 149 Johnny Ray .15 .06
❑ 150 Bruce Sutter .30 .12
❑ 151 Bruce Sutter SV .15 .06
❑ 152 Jay Johnstone .15 .06
❑ 153 Jerry Koosman .30 .12
❑ 154 Johnnie LeMaster .15 .06
❑ 155 Dan Quisenberry .15 .06
❑ 156 Billy Martin MG .60 .24
❑ 157 Steve Bedrosian .15 .06
❑ 158 Rob Wilfong .15 .06
❑ 159 Mike Stanton .15 .06
❑ 160 Dave Kingman .30 .12
❑ 161 Dave Kingman SV .15 .06
❑ 162 Mark Clear .15 .06
❑ 163 Cal Ripken 10.00 4.00
❑ 164 David Palmer .15 .06
❑ 165 Dan Driessen .15 .06
❑ 166 John Pacella .15 .06
❑ 167 Mark Brouhard .15 .06
❑ 168 Juan Eichelberger .15 .06
❑ 169 Doug Flynn .15 .06
❑ 170 Steve Howe .15 .06
❑ 171 Joe Morgan .30 .12
Bill Laskey TL
❑ 172 Vern Ruhle .15 .06
❑ 173 Jim Morrison .15 .06
❑ 174 Jerry Ujdur .15 .06
❑ 175 Bo Diaz .15 .06
❑ 176 Dave Righetti .30 .12
❑ 177 Harold Baines .30 .12
❑ 178 Luis Tiant .30 .12

- ❑ 179 Luis Tiant SV .15 .06
- ❑ 180 Rickey Henderson 2.50 1.00
- ❑ 181 Terry Felton .15 .06
- ❑ 182 Mike Fischlin .15 .06
- ❑ 183 Ed VandeBerg .15 .06
- ❑ 184 Bob Clark .15 .06
- ❑ 185 Tim Lollar .15 .06
- ❑ 186 Whitey Herzog MG .30 .12
- ❑ 187 Terry Leach .15 .06
- ❑ 188 Rick Miller .15 .06
- ❑ 189 Dan Schatzeder .15 .06
- ❑ 190 Cecil Cooper .30 .12
- ❑ 191 Joe Price .15 .06
- ❑ 192 Floyd Rayford .15 .06
- ❑ 193 Harry Spilman .15 .06
- ❑ 194 Cesar Geronimo .15 .06
- ❑ 195 Bob Stoddard .15 .06
- ❑ 196 Bill Fahey .15 .06
- ❑ 197 Jim Eisenreich RC .75 .30
- ❑ 198 Kiko Garcia .15 .06
- ❑ 199 Marty Bystrom .15 .06
- ❑ 200 Rod Carew .60 .24
- ❑ 201 Rod Carew SV .30 .12
- ❑ 202 Damaso Garcia .30 .12
  Dave Stieb TL
- ❑ 203 Mike Morgan .15 .06
- ❑ 204 Junior Kennedy .15 .06
- ❑ 205 Dave Parker .30 .12
- ❑ 206 Ken Oberkfell .15 .06
- ❑ 207 Rick Camp .15 .06
- ❑ 208 Dan Meyer .15 .06
- ❑ 209 Mike Moore RC .75 .30
- ❑ 210 Jack Clark .30 .12
- ❑ 211 John Denny .15 .06
- ❑ 212 John Stearns .15 .06
- ❑ 213 Tom Burgmeier .15 .06
- ❑ 214 Jerry White .15 .06
- ❑ 215 Mario Soto .30 .12
- ❑ 216 Tony LaRussa MG .30 .12
- ❑ 217 Tim Stoddard .15 .06
- ❑ 218 Roy Howell .15 .06
- ❑ 219 Mike Armstrong .15 .06
- ❑ 220 Dusty Baker .30 .12
- ❑ 221 Joe Niekro .15 .06
- ❑ 222 Damaso Garcia .15 .06
- ❑ 223 John Montefusco .15 .06
- ❑ 224 Mickey Rivers .15 .06
- ❑ 225 Enos Cabell .15 .06
- ❑ 226 Enrique Romo .15 .06
- ❑ 227 Chris Bando .15 .06
- ❑ 228 Joaquin Andujar .30 .12
- ❑ 229 Bo Diaz .15 .06
  Steve Carlton TL
- ❑ 230 Fergie Jenkins .30 .12
- ❑ 231 Fergie Jenkins SV .15 .06
- ❑ 232 Tom Brunansky .30 .12
- ❑ 233 Wayne Gross .15 .06
- ❑ 234 Larry Andersen .15 .06
- ❑ 235 Claudell Washington .15 .06
- ❑ 236 Steve Renko .15 .06
- ❑ 237 Dan Norman .15 .06
- ❑ 238 Bud Black RC .75 .30
- ❑ 239 Dave Stapleton .15 .06
- ❑ 240 Rich Gossage .30 .12
- ❑ 241 Rich Gossage SV .15 .06
- ❑ 242 Joe Nolan .15 .06
- ❑ 243 Duane Walker .15 .06
- ❑ 244 Dwight Bernard .15 .06
- ❑ 245 Steve Sax .30 .12
- ❑ 246 G.Bamberger MG .15 .06
- ❑ 247 Dave Smith .15 .06
- ❑ 248 Bake McBride .30 .12
- ❑ 249 Checklist: 133-264 .30 .12
- ❑ 250 Bill Buckner .30 .12
- ❑ 251 Alan Wiggins .15 .06
- ❑ 252 Luis Aguayo .15 .06
- ❑ 253 Larry McWilliams .15 .06
- ❑ 254 Rick Cerone .15 .06
- ❑ 255 Gene Garber .15 .06
- ❑ 256 Gene Garber SV .15 .06
- ❑ 257 Jesse Barfield .30 .12
- ❑ 258 Manny Castillo .15 .06
- ❑ 259 Jeff Jones .15 .06
- ❑ 260 Steve Kemp .15 .06
- ❑ 261 Larry Herndon .30 .12
  Dan Petry TL
- ❑ 262 Ron Jackson .15 .06
- ❑ 263 Renie Martin .15 .06
- ❑ 264 Jamie Quirk .15 .06
- ❑ 265 Joel Youngblood .15 .06
- ❑ 266 Paul Boris .15 .06
- ❑ 267 Terry Francona .30 .12
- ❑ 268 Storm Davis RC .75 .30
- ❑ 269 Ron Oester .15 .06
- ❑ 270 Dennis Eckersley .60 .24
- ❑ 271 Ed Romero .15 .06
- ❑ 272 Frank Tanana .30 .12
- ❑ 273 Mark Belanger .15 .06
- ❑ 274 Terry Kennedy .15 .06
- ❑ 275 Ray Knight .30 .12
- ❑ 276 Gene Mauch MG .15 .06
- ❑ 277 Rance Mulliniks .15 .06
- ❑ 278 Kevin Hickey .15 .06
- ❑ 279 Greg Gross .15 .06
- ❑ 280 Bert Blyleven .30 .12
- ❑ 281 Andre Robertson .15 .06
- ❑ 282 Reggie Smith 1.25 .50
  (Ryne Sandberg
  ducking back)
- ❑ 283 Reggie Smith SV .15 .06
- ❑ 284 Jeff Lahti .15 .06
- ❑ 285 Lance Parrish .30 .12
- ❑ 286 Rick Langford .15 .06
- ❑ 287 Bobby Brown .15 .06
- ❑ 288 Joe Cowley .15 .06
- ❑ 289 Jerry Dybzinski .15 .06
- ❑ 290 Jeff Reardon .30 .12
- ❑ 291 Bill Madlock .30 .12
  John Candelaria TL
- ❑ 292 Craig Swan .15 .06
- ❑ 293 Glenn Gulliver .15 .06
- ❑ 294 Dave Engle .15 .06
- ❑ 295 Jerry Remy .15 .06
- ❑ 296 Greg Harris .15 .06
- ❑ 297 Ned Yost .15 .06
- ❑ 298 Floyd Chiffer .15 .06
- ❑ 299 George Wright RC .75 .30
- ❑ 300 Mike Schmidt 3.00 1.20
- ❑ 301 Mike Schmidt SV 1.25 .50
- ❑ 302 Ernie Whitt .15 .06
- ❑ 303 Miguel Dilone .15 .06
- ❑ 304 Dave Rucker .15 .06
- ❑ 305 Larry Bowa .30 .12
- ❑ 306 Tom Lasorda MG .60 .24
- ❑ 307 Lou Piniella .30 .12
- ❑ 308 Jesus Vega .15 .06
- ❑ 309 Jeff Leonard .15 .06
- ❑ 310 Greg Luzinski .30 .12
- ❑ 311 Glenn Brummer .15 .06
- ❑ 312 Brian Kingman .15 .06
- ❑ 313 Gary Gray .15 .06
- ❑ 314 Ken Dayley .15 .06
- ❑ 315 Rick Burleson .15 .06
- ❑ 316 Paul Splittorff .15 .06
- ❑ 317 Gary Rajsich .15 .06
- ❑ 318 John Tudor .30 .12
- ❑ 319 Lenn Sakata .15 .06
- ❑ 320 Steve Rogers .30 .12
- ❑ 321 Robin Yount 1.25 .50
  Pete Vuckovich TL
- ❑ 322 Dave Van Gorder .15 .06
- ❑ 323 Luis DeLeon .15 .06
- ❑ 324 Mike Marshall .15 .06
- ❑ 325 Von Hayes .15 .06
- ❑ 326 Garth Iorg .15 .06
- ❑ 327 Bobby Castillo .15 .06
- ❑ 328 Craig Reynolds .15 .06
- ❑ 329 Randy Niemann .15 .06
- ❑ 330 Buddy Bell .30 .12
- ❑ 331 Mike Krukow .15 .06
- ❑ 332 Glenn Wilson .75 .30
- ❑ 333 Dave LaRoche .15 .06
- ❑ 334 Dave LaRoche SV .15 .06
- ❑ 335 Steve Henderson .15 .06
- ❑ 336 Rene Lachemann MG .15 .06
- ❑ 337 Tito Landrum .15 .06
- ❑ 338 Bob Owchinko .15 .06
- ❑ 339 Terry Harper .15 .06
- ❑ 340 Larry Gura .15 .06
- ❑ 341 Doug DeCinces .15 .06
- ❑ 342 Atlee Hammaker .15 .06
- ❑ 343 Bob Bailor .15 .06
- ❑ 344 Roger LaFrancois .15 .06
- ❑ 345 Jim Clancy .15 .06
- ❑ 346 Joe Pittman .15 .06
- ❑ 347 Sammy Stewart .15 .06
- ❑ 348 Alan Bannister .15 .06
- ❑ 349 Checklist: 265-396 .30 .12
- ❑ 350 Robin Yount 2.00 .80
- ❑ 351 Cesar Cedeno .30 .12
  Mario Soto TL
- ❑ 352 Mike Scioscia .30 .12
- ❑ 353 Steve Comer .15 .06
- ❑ 354 Randy Johnson .15 .06
- ❑ 355 Jim Bibby .15 .06
- ❑ 356 Gary Woods .15 .06
- ❑ 357 Len Matuszek .15 .06
- ❑ 358 Jerry Garvin .15 .06
- ❑ 359 Dave Collins .15 .06
- ❑ 360 Nolan Ryan 6.00 2.40
- ❑ 361 Nolan Ryan SV 3.00 1.20
- ❑ 362 Bill Almon .15 .06
- ❑ 363 John Stuper .15 .06
- ❑ 364 Brett Butler .30 .12
- ❑ 365 Dave Lopes .30 .12
- ❑ 366 Dick Williams MG .15 .06
- ❑ 367 Bud Anderson .15 .06
- ❑ 368 Richie Zisk .15 .06
- ❑ 369 Jesse Orosco .15 .06
- ❑ 370 Gary Carter .30 .12
- ❑ 371 Mike Richardt .15 .06
- ❑ 372 Terry Crowley .15 .06
- ❑ 373 Kevin Saucier .15 .06
- ❑ 374 Wayne Krenchicki .15 .06
- ❑ 375 Pete Vuckovich .15 .06
- ❑ 376 Ken Landreaux .15 .06
- ❑ 377 Lee May .15 .06
- ❑ 378 Lee May SV .15 .06
- ❑ 379 Guy Sularz .15 .06
- ❑ 380 Ron Davis .15 .06
- ❑ 381 Jim Rice .30 .12
  Bob Stanley TL
- ❑ 382 Bob Knepper .15 .06
- ❑ 383 Ozzie Virgil .15 .06
- ❑ 384 Dave Dravecky RC 1.50 .60
- ❑ 385 Mike Easler .15 .06
- ❑ 386 Rod Carew AS .30 .12
- ❑ 387 Bob Grich AS .15 .06
- ❑ 388 George Brett AS 1.50 .60
- ❑ 389 Robin Yount AS 1.25 .50
- ❑ 390 Reggie Jackson AS .30 .12
- ❑ 391 Rickey Henderson AS 1.25 .50
- ❑ 392 Fred Lynn AS .15 .06
- ❑ 393 Carlton Fisk AS .30 .12
- ❑ 394 Pete Vuckovich AS .15 .06
- ❑ 395 Larry Gura AS .15 .06
- ❑ 396 Dan Quisenberry AS .15 .06
- ❑ 397 Pete Rose AS .60 .24
- ❑ 398 Manny Trillo AS .15 .06
- ❑ 399 Mike Schmidt AS 1.25 .50
- ❑ 400 Dave Concepcion AS .15 .06
- ❑ 401 Dale Murphy AS .30 .12
- ❑ 402 Andre Dawson AS .15 .06
- ❑ 403 Tim Raines AS .15 .06
- ❑ 404 Gary Carter AS .15 .06
- ❑ 405 Steve Rogers AS .15 .06
- ❑ 406 Steve Carlton AS .30 .12
- ❑ 407 Bruce Sutter AS .15 .06
- ❑ 408 Rudy May .15 .06
- ❑ 409 Marvis Foley .15 .06
- ❑ 410 Phil Niekro .30 .12
- ❑ 411 Phil Niekro SV .15 .06
- ❑ 412 Buddy Bell .30 .12
  Charlie Hough TL
- ❑ 413 Matt Keough .15 .06
- ❑ 414 Julio Cruz .15 .06
- ❑ 415 Bob Forsch .15 .06
- ❑ 416 Joe Ferguson .15 .06
- ❑ 417 Tom Hausman .15 .06
- ❑ 418 Greg Pryor .15 .06
- ❑ 419 Steve Crawford .15 .06
- ❑ 420 Al Oliver .30 .12
- ❑ 421 Al Oliver SV .15 .06
- ❑ 422 George Cappuzzello .15 .06
- ❑ 423 Tom Lawless .15 .06
- ❑ 424 Jerry Augustine .15 .06
- ❑ 425 Pedro Guerrero .30 .12
- ❑ 426 Earl Weaver MG .30 .12

❑ 427 Roy Lee Jackson .15 .06
❑ 428 Champ Summers .15 .06
❑ 429 Eddie Whitson .15 .06
❑ 430 Kirk Gibson .30 .12
❑ 431 Gary Gaetti RC 1.50 .60
❑ 432 Porfirio Altamirano .15 .06
❑ 433 Dale Berra .15 .06
❑ 434 Dennis Lamp .15 .06
❑ 435 Tony Armas .30 .12
❑ 436 Bill Campbell .15 .06
❑ 437 Rick Sweet .15 .06
❑ 438 Dave LaPoint .15 .06
❑ 439 Rafael Ramirez .15 .06
❑ 440 Ron Guidry .30 .12
❑ 441 Ray Knight .30 .12
Joe Niekro TL
❑ 442 Brian Downing .30 .12
❑ 443 Don Hood .15 .06
❑ 444 Wally Backman .15 .06
❑ 445 Mike Flanagan .15 .06
❑ 446 Reid Nichols .15 .06
❑ 447 Bryn Smith .15 .06
❑ 448 Darrell Evans .30 .12
❑ 449 Eddie Milner .15 .06
❑ 450 Ted Simmons .30 .12
❑ 451 Ted Simmons SV .15 .06
❑ 452 Lloyd Moseby .15 .06
❑ 453 Lamar Johnson .15 .06
❑ 454 Bob Welch .30 .12
❑ 455 Sixto Lezcano .15 .06
❑ 456 Lee Elia MG .15 .06
❑ 457 Milt Wilcox .15 .06
❑ 458 Ron Washington .15 .06
❑ 459 Ed Farmer .15 .06
❑ 460 Roy Smalley .15 .06
❑ 461 Steve Trout .15 .06
❑ 462 Steve Nicosia .15 .06
❑ 463 Gaylord Perry .30 .12
❑ 464 Gaylord Perry SV .15 .06
❑ 465 Lonnie Smith .15 .06
❑ 466 Tom Underwood .15 .06
❑ 467 Rufino Linares .15 .06
❑ 468 Dave Goltz .15 .06
❑ 469 Ron Gardenhire .15 .06
❑ 470 Greg Minton .15 .06
❑ 471 Willie Wilson .30 .12
Vida Blue TL
❑ 472 Gary Allenson .15 .06
❑ 473 John Lowenstein .15 .06
❑ 474 Ray Burris .15 .06
❑ 475 Cesar Cedeno .30 .12
❑ 476 Rob Picciolo .15 .06
❑ 477 Tom Niedenfuer .15 .06
❑ 478 Phil Garner .30 .12
❑ 479 Charlie Hough .30 .12
❑ 480 Toby Harrah .30 .12
❑ 481 Scot Thompson .15 .06
❑ 482 Tony Gwynn UER RC 25.00 10.00
No Topps logo under
card number on back
❑ 483 Lynn Jones .15 .06
❑ 484 Dick Ruthven .15 .06
❑ 485 Omar Moreno .15 .06
❑ 486 Clyde King MG .15 .06
❑ 487 Jerry Hairston .15 .06
❑ 488 Alfredo Griffin .15 .06
❑ 489 Tom Herr .15 .06
❑ 490 Jim Palmer .30 .12
❑ 491 Jim Palmer SV .15 .06
❑ 492 Paul Serna .15 .06
❑ 493 Steve McCatty .15 .06
❑ 494 Bob Brenly .15 .06
❑ 495 Warren Cromartie .15 .06
❑ 496 Tom Veryzer .15 .06
❑ 497 Rick Sutcliffe .30 .12
❑ 498 Wade Boggs RC 12.00 4.80
❑ 499 Jeff Little .15 .06
❑ 500 Reggie Jackson .60 .24
❑ 501 Reggie Jackson SV .30 .12
❑ 502 Dale Murphy .60 .24
Phil Niekro TL
❑ 503 Moose Haas .15 .06
❑ 504 Don Werner .15 .06
❑ 505 Garry Templeton .30 .12
❑ 506 Jim Gott RC .75 .30
❑ 507 Tony Scott .15 .06
❑ 508 Tom Filer .15 .06
❑ 509 Lou Whitaker .30 .12
❑ 510 Tug McGraw .30 .12
❑ 511 Tug McGraw SV .15 .06
❑ 512 Doyle Alexander .15 .06
❑ 513 Fred Stanley .15 .06
❑ 514 Rudy Law .15 .06
❑ 515 Gene Tenace .30 .12
❑ 516 Bill Virdon MG .15 .06
❑ 517 Gary Ward .15 .06
❑ 518 Bill Laskey .15 .06
❑ 519 Terry Bulling .15 .06
❑ 520 Fred Lynn .30 .12
❑ 521 Bruce Benedict .15 .06
❑ 522 Pat Zachry .15 .06
❑ 523 Carney Lansford .30 .12
❑ 524 Tom Brennan .15 .06
❑ 525 Frank White .30 .12
❑ 526 Checklist: 397-528 .30 .12
❑ 527 Larry Biittner .15 .06
❑ 528 Jamie Easterly .15 .06
❑ 529 Tim Laudner .15 .06
❑ 530 Eddie Murray 1.25 .50
❑ 531 Rickey Henderson 1.25 .50
Rick Langford TL
❑ 532 Dave Stewart .30 .12
❑ 533 Luis Salazar .15 .06
❑ 534 John Butcher .15 .06
❑ 535 Manny Trillo .15 .06
❑ 536 John Wockenfuss .15 .06
❑ 537 Rod Scurry .15 .06
❑ 538 Danny Heep .15 .06
❑ 539 Roger Erickson .15 .06
❑ 540 Ozzie Smith 2.00 .80
❑ 541 Britt Burns .15 .06
❑ 542 Jody Davis .15 .06
❑ 543 Alan Fowlkes .15 .06
❑ 544 Larry Whisenton .15 .06
❑ 545 Floyd Bannister .15 .06
❑ 546 Dave Garcia MG .15 .06
❑ 547 Geoff Zahn .15 .06
❑ 548 Brian Giles .15 .06
❑ 549 Charlie Puleo .15 .06
❑ 550 Carl Yastrzemski 2.00 .80
❑ 551 Carl Yastrzemski SV 1.25 .50
❑ 552 Tim Wallach .30 .12
❑ 553 Dennis Martinez .30 .12
❑ 554 Mike Vail .15 .06
❑ 555 Steve Yeager .30 .12
❑ 556 Willie Upshaw .15 .06
❑ 557 Rick Honeycutt .15 .06
❑ 558 Dickie Thon .15 .06
❑ 559 Pete Redfern .15 .06
❑ 560 Ron LeFlore .30 .12
❑ 561 Lonnie Smith .30 .12
Joaquin Andujar TL
❑ 562 Dave Rozema .15 .06
❑ 563 Juan Bonilla .15 .06
❑ 564 Sid Monge .15 .06
❑ 565 Bucky Dent .30 .12
❑ 566 Manny Sarmiento .15 .06
❑ 567 Joe Simpson .15 .06
❑ 568 Willie Hernandez .15 .06
❑ 569 Jack Perconte .15 .06
❑ 570 Vida Blue .30 .12
❑ 571 Mickey Klutts .15 .06
❑ 572 Bob Watson .15 .06
❑ 573 Andy Hassler .15 .06
❑ 574 Glenn Adams .15 .06
❑ 575 Neil Allen .15 .06
❑ 576 Frank Robinson MG .60 .24
❑ 577 Luis Aponte .15 .06
❑ 578 David Green RC .75 .30
❑ 579 Rich Dauer .15 .06
❑ 580 Tom Seaver 1.25 .50
❑ 581 Tom Seaver SV .30 .12
❑ 582 Marshall Edwards .15 .06
❑ 583 Terry Forster .30 .12
❑ 584 Dave Hostetler .15 .06
❑ 585 Jose Cruz .30 .12
❑ 586 Frank Viola RC 2.50 1.00
❑ 587 Ivan DeJesus .15 .06
❑ 588 Pat Underwood .15 .06
❑ 589 Alvis Woods .15 .06
❑ 590 Tony Pena .15 .06
❑ 591 Greg Luzinski .30 .12
LaMarr Hoyt TL
❑ 592 Shane Rawley .15 .06
❑ 593 Broderick Perkins .15 .06
❑ 594 Eric Rasmussen .15 .06
❑ 595 Tim Raines .30 .12
❑ 596 Randy Johnson .15 .06
❑ 597 Mike Proly .15 .06
❑ 598 Dwayne Murphy .15 .06
❑ 599 Don Aase .15 .06
❑ 600 George Brett 3.00 1.20
❑ 601 Ed Lynch .15 .06
❑ 602 Rich Gedman .15 .06
❑ 603 Joe Morgan .30 .12
❑ 604 Joe Morgan SV .15 .06
❑ 605 Gary Roenicke .15 .06
❑ 606 Bobby Cox MG .30 .12
❑ 607 Charlie Leibrandt .15 .06
❑ 608 Don Money .15 .06
❑ 609 Danny Darwin .15 .06
❑ 610 Steve Garvey .30 .12
❑ 611 Bert Roberge .15 .06
❑ 612 Steve Swisher .15 .06
❑ 613 Mike Ivie .15 .06
❑ 614 Ed Glynn .15 .06
❑ 615 Garry Maddox .15 .06
❑ 616 Bill Nahorodny .15 .06
❑ 617 Butch Wynegar .15 .06
❑ 618 LaMarr Hoyt .15 .06
❑ 619 Keith Moreland .15 .06
❑ 620 Mike Norris .15 .06
❑ 621 Mookie Wilson .30 .12
Craig Swan TL
❑ 622 Dave Edler .15 .06
❑ 623 Luis Sanchez .15 .06
❑ 624 Glenn Hubbard .15 .06
❑ 625 Ken Forsch .15 .06
❑ 626 Jerry Martin .15 .06
❑ 627 Doug Bair .15 .06
❑ 628 Julio Valdez .15 .06
❑ 629 Charlie Lea .15 .06
❑ 630 Paul Molitor .60 .24
❑ 631 Tippy Martinez .15 .06
❑ 632 Alex Trevino .15 .06
❑ 633 Vicente Romo .15 .06
❑ 634 Max Venable .15 .06
❑ 635 Graig Nettles .30 .12
❑ 636 Graig Nettles SV .15 .06
❑ 637 Pat Corrales MG .15 .06
❑ 638 Dan Petry .15 .06
❑ 639 Art Howe .15 .06
❑ 640 Andre Thornton .15 .06
❑ 641 Billy Sample .15 .06
❑ 642 Checklist: 529-660 .30 .12
❑ 643 Bump Wills .15 .06
❑ 644 Joe Lefebvre .15 .06
❑ 645 Bill Madlock .30 .12
❑ 646 Jim Essian .15 .06
❑ 647 Bobby Mitchell .15 .06
❑ 648 Jeff Burroughs .15 .06
❑ 649 Tommy Boggs .15 .06
❑ 650 George Hendrick .30 .12
❑ 651 Rod Carew .30 .12
Mike Witt TL
❑ 652 Butch Hobson .15 .06
❑ 653 Ellis Valentine .15 .06
❑ 654 Bob Ojeda .15 .06
❑ 655 Al Bumbry .15 .06
❑ 656 Dave Frost .15 .06
❑ 657 Mike Gates .15 .06
❑ 658 Frank Pastore .15 .06
❑ 659 Charlie Moore .15 .06
❑ 660 Mike Hargrove .15 .06
❑ 661 Bill Russell .30 .12
❑ 662 Joe Sambito .15 .06
❑ 663 Tom O'Malley .15 .06
❑ 664 Bob Molinaro .15 .06
❑ 665 Jim Sundberg .30 .12
❑ 666 Sparky Anderson MG .30 .12
❑ 667 Dick Davis .15 .06
❑ 668 Larry Christenson .15 .06
❑ 669 Mike Squires .15 .06
❑ 670 Jerry Mumphrey .15 .06
❑ 671 Lenny Faedo .15 .06
❑ 672 Jim Kaat .30 .12
❑ 673 Jim Kaat SV .15 .06
❑ 674 Kurt Bevacqua .15 .06

- ❑ 675 Jim Beattie .15 .06
- ❑ 676 Biff Pocoroba .15 .06
- ❑ 677 Dave Revering .15 .06
- ❑ 678 Juan Beniquez .15 .06
- ❑ 679 Mike Scott .30 .12
- ❑ 680 Andre Dawson .30 .12
- ❑ 681 Pedro Guerrero .30 .12
  Fernando Valenzuela TL
- ❑ 682 Bob Stanley .15 .06
- ❑ 683 Dan Ford .15 .06
- ❑ 684 Rafael Landestoy .15 .06
- ❑ 685 Lee Mazzilli .30 .12
- ❑ 686 Randy Lerch .15 .06
- ❑ 687 U.L. Washington .15 .06
- ❑ 688 Jim Wohlford .15 .06
- ❑ 689 Ron Hassey .15 .06
- ❑ 690 Kent Hrbek .30 .12
- ❑ 691 Dave Tobik .15 .06
- ❑ 692 Denny Walling .15 .06
- ❑ 693 Sparky Lyle .30 .12
- ❑ 694 Sparky Lyle SV .15 .06
- ❑ 695 Ruppert Jones .15 .06
- ❑ 696 Chuck Tanner MG .15 .06
- ❑ 697 Barry Foote .15 .06
- ❑ 698 Tony Bernazard .15 .06
- ❑ 699 Lee Smith .60 .24
- ❑ 700 Keith Hernandez .30 .12
- ❑ 701 Willie Wilson .30 .12
  Al Oliver LL
- ❑ 702 Reggie Jackson .30 .12
  Gorman Thomas
  Dave Kingman LL
- ❑ 703 Hal McRae .60 .24
  Dale Murphy
  Al Oliver LL
- ❑ 704 Rickey Henderson 1.25 .50
  Tim Raines LL
- ❑ 705 LaMarr Hoyt .30 .12
  Steve Carlton LL
- ❑ 706 Floyd Bannister .30 .12
  Steve Carlton LL
- ❑ 707 Rick Sutcliffe .30 .12
  Steve Rogers LL
- ❑ 708 Dan Quisenberry .30 .12
  Bruce Sutter LL
- ❑ 709 Jimmy Sexton .15 .06
- ❑ 710 Willie Wilson .30 .12
- ❑ 711 Bruce Bochte .30 .12
  Jim Beattie TL
- ❑ 712 Bruce Kison .15 .06
- ❑ 713 Ron Hodges .15 .06
- ❑ 714 Wayne Nordhagen .15 .06
- ❑ 715 Tony Perez .60 .24
- ❑ 716 Tony Perez SV .30 .12
- ❑ 717 Scott Sanderson .15 .06
- ❑ 718 Jim Dwyer .15 .06
- ❑ 719 Rich Gale .15 .06
- ❑ 720 Dave Concepcion .30 .12
- ❑ 721 John Martin .15 .06
- ❑ 722 Jorge Orta .15 .06
- ❑ 723 Randy Moffitt .15 .06
- ❑ 724 Johnny Grubb .15 .06
- ❑ 725 Dan Spillner .15 .06
- ❑ 726 Harvey Kuenn MG .15 .06
- ❑ 727 Chet Lemon .30 .12
- ❑ 728 Ron Reed .15 .06
- ❑ 729 Jerry Morales .15 .06
- ❑ 730 Jason Thompson .15 .06
- ❑ 731 Al Williams .15 .06
- ❑ 732 Dave Henderson .15 .06
- ❑ 733 Buck Martinez .15 .06
- ❑ 734 Steve Braun .15 .06
- ❑ 735 Tommy John .30 .12
- ❑ 736 Tommy John SV .15 .06
- ❑ 737 Mitchell Page .15 .06
- ❑ 738 Tim Foli .15 .06
- ❑ 739 Rick Ownbey .15 .06
- ❑ 740 Rusty Staub .30 .12
- ❑ 741 Rusty Staub SV .15 .06
- ❑ 742 Terry Kennedy .30 .12
  Tim Lollar
- ❑ 743 Mike Torrez .15 .06
- ❑ 744 Brad Mills .15 .06
- ❑ 745 Scott McGregor .15 .06
- ❑ 746 John Wathan .15 .06
- ❑ 747 Fred Breining .15 .06
- ❑ 748 Derrel Thomas .15 .06
- ❑ 749 Jon Matlack .15 .06
- ❑ 750 Ben Oglivie .30 .12
- ❑ 751 Brad Havens .15 .06
- ❑ 752 Luis Pujols .15 .06
- ❑ 753 Elias Sosa .15 .06
- ❑ 754 Bill Robinson .15 .06
- ❑ 755 John Candelaria .15 .06
- ❑ 756 Russ Nixon MG .15 .06
- ❑ 757 Rick Manning .15 .06
- ❑ 758 Aurelio Rodriguez .15 .06
- ❑ 759 Doug Bird .15 .06
- ❑ 760 Dale Murphy .60 .24
- ❑ 761 Gary Lucas .15 .06
- ❑ 762 Cliff Johnson .15 .06
- ❑ 763 Al Cowens .15 .06
- ❑ 764 Pete Falcone .15 .06
- ❑ 765 Bob Boone .30 .12
- ❑ 766 Barry Bonnell .15 .06
- ❑ 767 Duane Kuiper .15 .06
- ❑ 768 Chris Speier .15 .06
- ❑ 769 Checklist: 661-792 .30 .12
- ❑ 770 Dave Winfield .30 .12
- ❑ 771 Kent Hrbek .30 .12
  Bobby Castillo TL
- ❑ 772 Jim Kern .15 .06
- ❑ 773 Larry Hisle .15 .06
- ❑ 774 Alan Ashby .15 .06
- ❑ 775 Burt Hooton .15 .06
- ❑ 776 Larry Parrish .15 .06
- ❑ 777 John Curtis .15 .06
- ❑ 778 Rich Hebner .15 .06
- ❑ 779 Rick Waits .15 .06
- ❑ 780 Gary Matthews .30 .12
- ❑ 781 Rick Rhoden .15 .06
- ❑ 782 Bobby Murcer .30 .12
- ❑ 783 Bobby Murcer SV .15 .06
- ❑ 784 Jeff Newman .15 .06
- ❑ 785 Dennis Leonard .15 .06
- ❑ 786 Ralph Houk MG .15 .06
- ❑ 787 Dick Tidrow .15 .06
- ❑ 788 Dane Iorg .15 .06
- ❑ 789 Bryan Clark .15 .06
- ❑ 790 Bob Grich .30 .12
- ❑ 791 Gary Lavelle .15 .06
- ❑ 792 Chris Chambliss .30 .12
- ❑ XX Game Insert Card .10 .04

1983 Topps Traded

	Nm-Mt	Ex-Mt
COMP.FACT.SET (132)	40.00	16.00

- ❑ 1T Neil Allen .25 .10
- ❑ 2T Bill Almon .25 .10
- ❑ 3T Joe Altobelli MG .25 .10
- ❑ 4T Tony Armas 1.00 .40
- ❑ 5T Doug Bair .25 .10
- ❑ 6T Steve Baker .25 .10
- ❑ 7T Floyd Bannister .25 .10
- ❑ 8T Don Baylor 1.00 .40
- ❑ 9T Tony Bernazard .25 .10
- ❑ 10T Larry Biittner .25 .10
- ❑ 11T Dann Bilardello .25 .10
- ❑ 12T Doug Bird .25 .10
- ❑ 13T Steve Boros MG .25 .10
- ❑ 14T Greg Brock .25 .10
- ❑ 15T Mike C. Brown .25 .10
- ❑ 16T Tom Burgmeier .25 .10
- ❑ 17T Randy Bush .25 .10
- ❑ 18T Bert Campaneris 1.00 .40
- ❑ 19T Ron Cey 1.00 .40
- ❑ 20T Chris Codiroli .25 .10
- ❑ 21T Dave Collins .25 .10
- ❑ 22T Terry Crowley .25 .10
- ❑ 23T Julio Cruz .25 .10
- ❑ 24T Mike Davis .25 .10
- ❑ 25T Frank DiPino .25 .10
- ❑ 26T Bill Doran XRC 1.00 .40
- ❑ 27T Jerry Dybzinski .25 .10
- ❑ 28T Jamie Easterly .25 .10
- ❑ 29T Juan Eichelberger .25 .10
- ❑ 30T Jim Essian .25 .10
- ❑ 31T Pete Falcone .25 .10
- ❑ 32T Mike Ferraro MG .25 .10
- ❑ 33T Terry Forster 1.00 .40
- ❑ 34T Julio Franco XRC 4.00 1.60
- ❑ 35T Rich Gale .25 .10
- ❑ 36T Kiko Garcia .25 .10
- ❑ 37T Steve Garvey 1.00 .40
- ❑ 38T Johnny Grubb .25 .10
- ❑ 39T Mel Hall XRC* 1.00 .40
- ❑ 40T Von Hayes .25 .10
- ❑ 41T Danny Heep .25 .10
- ❑ 42T Steve Henderson .25 .10
- ❑ 43T Keith Hernandez 1.00 .40
- ❑ 44T Leo Hernandez .25 .10
- ❑ 45T Willie Hernandez .25 .10
- ❑ 46T Al Holland .25 .10
- ❑ 47T Frank Howard MG 1.00 .40
- ❑ 48T Bobby Johnson .25 .10
- ❑ 49T Cliff Johnson .25 .10
- ❑ 50T Odell Jones .25 .10
- ❑ 51T Mike Jorgensen .25 .10
- ❑ 52T Bob Kearney .25 .10
- ❑ 53T Steve Kemp .25 .10
- ❑ 54T Matt Keough .25 .10
- ❑ 55T Ron Kittle XRC* 2.00 .80
- ❑ 56T Mickey Klutts .25 .10
- ❑ 57T Alan Knicely .25 .10
- ❑ 58T Mike Krukow .25 .10
- ❑ 59T Rafael Landestoy .25 .10
- ❑ 60T Carney Lansford 1.00 .40
- ❑ 61T Joe Lefebvre .25 .10
- ❑ 62T Bryan Little .25 .10
- ❑ 63T Aurelio Lopez .25 .10
- ❑ 64T Mike Madden .25 .10
- ❑ 65T Rick Manning .25 .10
- ❑ 66T Billy Martin MG 2.00 .80
- ❑ 67T Lee Mazzilli 1.00 .40
- ❑ 68T Andy McGaffigan .25 .10
- ❑ 69T Craig McMurtry .25 .10
- ❑ 70T John McNamara MG .25 .10
- ❑ 71T Orlando Mercado .25 .10
- ❑ 72T Larry Milbourne .25 .10
- ❑ 73T Randy Moffitt .25 .10
- ❑ 74T Sid Monge .25 .10
- ❑ 75T Jose Morales .25 .10
- ❑ 76T Omar Moreno .25 .10
- ❑ 77T Joe Morgan 1.00 .40
- ❑ 78T Mike Morgan .25 .10
- ❑ 79T Dale Murray .25 .10
- ❑ 80T Jeff Newman .25 .10
- ❑ 81T Pete O'Brien XRC 1.00 .40
- ❑ 82T Jorge Orta .25 .10
- ❑ 83T Alejandro Pena XRC 2.00 .80
- ❑ 84T Pascual Perez .25 .10
- ❑ 85T Tony Perez 2.00 .80
- ❑ 86T Broderick Perkins .25 .10
- ❑ 87T Tony Phillips XRC 2.00 .80
- ❑ 88T Charlie Puleo .25 .10
- ❑ 89T Pat Putnam .25 .10
- ❑ 90T Jamie Quirk .25 .10
- ❑ 91T Doug Rader MG .25 .10
- ❑ 92T Chuck Rainey .25 .10
- ❑ 93T Bobby Ramos .25 .10
- ❑ 94T Gary Redus XRC 1.00 .40
- ❑ 95T Steve Renko .25 .10
- ❑ 96T Leon Roberts .25 .10
- ❑ 97T Aurelio Rodriguez .25 .10
- ❑ 98T Dick Ruthven .25 .10
- ❑ 99T Daryl Sconiers .25 .10
- ❑ 100T Mike Scott 1.00 .40
- ❑ 101T Tom Seaver 2.00 .80

❑ 102T John Shelby .25 .10
❑ 103T Bob Shirley .25 .10
❑ 104T Joe Simpson .25 .10
❑ 105T Doug Sisk .25 .10
❑ 106T Mike Smithson .25 .10
❑ 107T Elias Sosa .25 .10
❑ 108T D.Strawberry XRC 10.00 4.00
❑ 109T Tom Tellmann .25 .10
❑ 110T Gene Tenace 1.00 .40
❑ 111T Gorman Thomas 1.00 .40
❑ 112T Dick Tidrow .25 .10
❑ 113T Dave Tobik .25 .10
❑ 114T Wayne Tolleson .25 .10
❑ 115T Mike Torrez .25 .10
❑ 116T Manny Trillo .25 .10
❑ 117T Steve Trout .25 .10
❑ 118T Lee Tunnell .25 .10
❑ 119T Mike Vail .25 .10
❑ 120T Ellis Valentine .25 .10
❑ 121T Tom Veryzer .25 .10
❑ 122T George Vukovich .25 .10
❑ 123T Rick Waits .25 .10
❑ 124T Greg Walker 1.00 .40
❑ 125T Chris Welsh .25 .10
❑ 126T Len Whitehouse .25 .10
❑ 127T Eddie Whitson .25 .10
❑ 128T Jim Wohlford .25 .10
❑ 129T Matt Young XRC 1.00 .40
❑ 130T Joel Youngblood .25 .10
❑ 131T Pat Zachry .25 .10
❑ 132T Checklist 1T-132T .25 .10

1984 Topps

	Nm-Mt	Ex-Mt
COMPLETE SET (792)	50.00	20.00

❑ 1 Steve Carlton HL .25 .10
❑ 2 Rickey Henderson HL .60 .24
❑ 3 Dan Quisenberry HL .15 .06
❑ 4 Nolan Ryan HL 1.00 .40
Steve Carlton
Gaylord Perry
❑ 5 Dave Righetti HL .25 .10
Bob Forsch
Mike Warren
❑ 6 Johnny Bench HL .40 .16
Gaylord Perry
Carl Yastrzemski
❑ 7 Gary Lucas .15 .06
❑ 8 Don Mattingly RC 15.00 6.00
❑ 9 Jim Gott .15 .06
❑ 10 Robin Yount 1.00 .40
❑ 11 Kent Hrbek .25 .10
Ken Schrom TL
❑ 12 Billy Sample .15 .06
❑ 13 Scott Holman .15 .06
❑ 14 Tom Brookens .25 .10
❑ 15 Burt Hooton .15 .06
❑ 16 Omar Moreno .15 .06
❑ 17 John Denny .15 .06
❑ 18 Dale Berra .15 .06
❑ 19 Ray Fontenot .15 .06
❑ 20 Greg Luzinski .25 .10
❑ 21 Joe Altobelli MG .15 .06
❑ 22 Bryan Clark .15 .06
❑ 23 Keith Moreland .15 .06
❑ 24 John Martin .15 .06
❑ 25 Glenn Hubbard .15 .06
❑ 26 Bud Black .15 .06
❑ 27 Daryl Sconiers .15 .06
❑ 28 Frank Viola .40 .16
❑ 29 Danny Heep .15 .06
❑ 30 Wade Boggs 1.50 .60
❑ 31 Andy McGaffigan .15 .06
❑ 32 Bobby Ramos .15 .06
❑ 33 Tom Burgmeier .15 .06
❑ 34 Eddie Milner .15 .06
❑ 35 Don Sutton .25 .10
❑ 36 Denny Walling .15 .06
❑ 37 Buddy Bell .25 .10
Rick Honeycutt TL
❑ 38 Luis DeLeon .15 .06
❑ 39 Garth Iorg .15 .06
❑ 40 Dusty Baker .25 .10
❑ 41 Tony Bernazard .15 .06
❑ 42 Johnny Grubb .15 .06
❑ 43 Ron Reed .15 .06
❑ 44 Jim Morrison .15 .06
❑ 45 Jerry Mumphrey .15 .06
❑ 46 Ray Smith .15 .06
❑ 47 Rudy Law .15 .06
❑ 48 Julio Franco .40 .16
❑ 49 John Stuper .15 .06
❑ 50 Chris Chambliss .25 .10
❑ 51 Jim Frey MG .15 .06
❑ 52 Paul Splittorff .15 .06
❑ 53 Juan Beniquez .15 .06
❑ 54 Jesse Orosco .15 .06
❑ 55 Dave Concepcion .25 .10
❑ 56 Gary Allenson .15 .06
❑ 57 Dan Schatzeder .15 .06
❑ 58 Max Venable .15 .06
❑ 59 Sammy Stewart .15 .06
❑ 60 Paul Molitor UER .40 .16
('83 stats .272, 613, 167; should be .270, 608, 164)
❑ 61 Chris Codiroli .15 .06
❑ 62 Dave Hostetler .15 .06
❑ 63 Ed VandeBerg .15 .06
❑ 64 Mike Scioscia .25 .10
❑ 65 Kirk Gibson .25 .10
❑ 66 Jose Cruz 1.00 .40
Nolan Ryan TL
❑ 67 Gary Ward .15 .06
❑ 68 Luis Salazar .15 .06
❑ 69 Rod Scurry .15 .06
❑ 70 Gary Matthews .25 .10
❑ 71 Leo Hernandez .15 .06
❑ 72 Mike Squires .15 .06
❑ 73 Jody Davis .15 .06
❑ 74 Jerry Martin .15 .06
❑ 75 Bob Forsch .15 .06
❑ 76 Alfredo Griffin .15 .06
❑ 77 Brett Butler .25 .10
❑ 78 Mike Torrez .15 .06
❑ 79 Rob Wilfong .15 .06
❑ 80 Steve Rogers .25 .10
❑ 81 Billy Martin MG .40 .16
❑ 82 Doug Bird .15 .06
❑ 83 Richie Zisk .15 .06
❑ 84 Lenny Faedo .15 .06
❑ 85 Atlee Hammaker .15 .06
❑ 86 John Shelby .15 .06
❑ 87 Frank Pastore .15 .06
❑ 88 Rob Picciolo .15 .06
❑ 89 Mike Smithson .15 .06
❑ 90 Pedro Guerrero .25 .10
❑ 91 Dan Spillner .15 .06
❑ 92 Lloyd Moseby .15 .06
❑ 93 Bob Knepper .15 .06
❑ 94 Mario Ramirez .15 .06
❑ 95 Aurelio Lopez .25 .10
❑ 96 Hal McRae .25 .10
Larry Gura TL
❑ 97 LaMarr Hoyt .15 .06
❑ 98 Steve Nicosia .15 .06
❑ 99 Craig Lefferts RC .15 .06
❑ 100 Reggie Jackson .40 .16
❑ 101 Porfirio Altamirano .15 .06
❑ 102 Ken Oberkfell .15 .06
❑ 103 Dwayne Murphy .15 .06
❑ 104 Ken Dayley .15 .06
❑ 105 Tony Armas .25 .10
❑ 106 Tim Stoddard .15 .06
❑ 107 Ned Yost .15 .06
❑ 108 Randy Moffitt .15 .06
❑ 109 Brad Wellman .15 .06
❑ 110 Ron Guidry .25 .10
❑ 111 Bill Virdon MG .15 .06
❑ 112 Tom Niedenfuer .15 .06
❑ 113 Kelly Paris .15 .06
❑ 114 Checklist 1-132 .25 .10
❑ 115 Andre Thornton .15 .06
❑ 116 George Bjorkman .15 .06
❑ 117 Tom Veryzer .15 .06
❑ 118 Charlie Hough .25 .10
❑ 119 John Wockenfuss .15 .06
❑ 120 Keith Hernandez .25 .10
❑ 121 Pat Sheridan .15 .06
❑ 122 Cecilio Guante .15 .06
❑ 123 Butch Wynegar .15 .06
❑ 124 Damaso Garcia .15 .06
❑ 125 Britt Burns .15 .06
❑ 126 Dale Murphy .40 .16
Craig McMurtry TL
❑ 127 Mike Madden .15 .06
❑ 128 Rick Manning .15 .06
❑ 129 Bill Laskey .15 .06
❑ 130 Ozzie Smith 1.00 .40
❑ 131 Bill Madlock .60 .24
Wade Boggs LL
❑ 132 Mike Schmidt .60 .24
Jim Rice LL
❑ 133 Dale Murphy .40 .16
Cecil Cooper
Jim Rice LL
❑ 134 Tim Raines .60 .24
Rickey Henderson LL
❑ 135 John Denny .60 .24
LaMarr Hoyt LL
❑ 136 Steve Carlton .25 .10
Jack Morris LL
❑ 137 Atlee Hammaker .25 .10
Rick Honeycutt LL
❑ 138 Al Holland .25 .10
Dan Quisenberry LL
❑ 139 Bert Campaneris .25 .10
❑ 140 Storm Davis .15 .06
❑ 141 Pat Corrales MG .15 .06
❑ 142 Rich Gale .15 .06
❑ 143 Jose Morales .15 .06
❑ 144 Brian Harper RC .40 .16
❑ 145 Gary Lavelle .15 .06
❑ 146 Ed Romero .15 .06
❑ 147 Dan Petry .25 .10
❑ 148 Joe Lefebvre .15 .06
❑ 149 Jon Matlack .15 .06
❑ 150 Dale Murphy .40 .16
❑ 151 Steve Trout .15 .06
❑ 152 Glenn Brummer .15 .06
❑ 153 Dick Tidrow .15 .06
❑ 154 Dave Henderson .25 .10
❑ 155 Frank White .25 .10
❑ 156 Rickey Henderson .60 .24
Tim Conroy TL
❑ 157 Gary Gaetti .40 .16
❑ 158 John Curtis .15 .06
❑ 159 Darryl Cias .15 .06
❑ 160 Mario Soto .25 .10
❑ 161 Junior Ortiz .15 .06
❑ 162 Bob Ojeda .15 .06
❑ 163 Lorenzo Gray .15 .06
❑ 164 Scott Sanderson .15 .06
❑ 165 Ken Singleton .25 .10
❑ 166 Jamie Nelson .15 .06
❑ 167 Marshall Edwards .15 .06
❑ 168 Juan Bonilla .15 .06
❑ 169 Larry Parrish .15 .06
❑ 170 Jerry Reuss .15 .06
❑ 171 Frank Robinson MG .40 .16
❑ 172 Frank DiPino .15 .06
❑ 173 Marvell Wynne .40 .16
❑ 174 Juan Berenguer .15 .06
❑ 175 Graig Nettles .25 .10
❑ 176 Lee Smith .25 .10
❑ 177 Jerry Hairston .15 .06
❑ 178 Bill Krueger RC .15 .06
❑ 179 Buck Martinez .15 .06

❑ 180	Manny Trillo	.15	.06
❑ 181	Roy Thomas	.15	.06
❑ 182	Darryl Strawberry RC	2.00	.80
❑ 183	Al Williams	.15	.06
❑ 184	Mike O'Berry	.15	.06
❑ 185	Sixto Lezcano	.15	.06
❑ 186	Lonnie Smith	.25	.10
	John Stuper TL		
❑ 187	Luis Aponte	.15	.06
❑ 188	Bryan Little	.15	.06
❑ 189	Tim Conroy	.15	.06
❑ 190	Ben Oglivie	.25	.10
❑ 191	Mike Boddicker	.15	.06
❑ 192	Nick Esasky	.15	.06
❑ 193	Darrell Brown	.15	.06
❑ 194	Domingo Ramos	.15	.06
❑ 195	Jack Morris	.25	.10
❑ 196	Don Slaught	.25	.10
❑ 197	Garry Hancock	.15	.06
❑ 198	Bill Doran RC*	.40	.16
❑ 199	Willie Hernandez	.15	.06
❑ 200	Andre Dawson	.25	.10
❑ 201	Bruce Kison	.15	.06
❑ 202	Bobby Cox MG	.25	.10
❑ 203	Matt Keough	.15	.06
❑ 204	Bobby Meacham	.15	.06
❑ 205	Greg Minton	.15	.06
❑ 206	Andy Van Slyke RC	.75	.30
❑ 207	Donnie Moore	.15	.06
❑ 208	Jose Oquendo RC	.40	.16
❑ 209	Manny Sarmiento	.15	.06
❑ 210	Joe Morgan	.25	.10
❑ 211	Rick Sweet	.15	.06
❑ 212	Broderick Perkins	.15	.06
❑ 213	Bruce Hurst	.15	.06
❑ 214	Paul Householder	.15	.06
❑ 215	Tippy Martinez	.15	.06
❑ 216	Carlton Fisk	.25	.10
	Richard Dotson TL		
❑ 217	Alan Ashby	.15	.06
❑ 218	Rick Waits	.15	.06
❑ 219	Joe Simpson	.15	.06
❑ 220	Fernando Valenzuela	.25	.10
❑ 221	Cliff Johnson	.15	.06
❑ 222	Rick Honeycutt	.15	.06
❑ 223	Wayne Krenchicki	.15	.06
❑ 224	Sid Monge	.15	.06
❑ 225	Lee Mazzilli	.25	.10
❑ 226	Juan Eichelberger	.15	.06
❑ 227	Steve Braun	.15	.06
❑ 228	John Rabb	.15	.06
❑ 229	Paul Owens MG	.15	.06
❑ 230	Rickey Henderson	1.00	.40
❑ 231	Gary Woods	.15	.06
❑ 232	Tim Wallach	.15	.06
❑ 233	Checklist 133-264	.25	.10
❑ 234	Rafael Ramirez	.15	.06
❑ 235	Matt Young RC	.40	.16
❑ 236	Ellis Valentine	.15	.06
❑ 237	John Castino	.15	.06
❑ 238	Reid Nichols	.15	.06
❑ 239	Jay Howell	.15	.06
❑ 240	Eddie Murray	.60	.24
❑ 241	Bill Almon	.15	.06
❑ 242	Alex Trevino	.15	.06
❑ 243	Pete Ladd	.15	.06
❑ 244	Candy Maldonado	.15	.06
❑ 245	Rick Sutcliffe	.25	.10
❑ 246	Mookie Wilson	.25	.10
	Tom Seaver TL		
❑ 247	Onix Concepcion	.15	.06
❑ 248	Bill Dawley	.15	.06
❑ 249	Jay Johnstone	.15	.06
❑ 250	Bill Madlock	.25	.10
❑ 251	Tony Gwynn	2.50	1.00
❑ 252	Larry Christenson	.15	.06
❑ 253	Jim Wohlford	.15	.06
❑ 254	Shane Rawley	.15	.06
❑ 255	Bruce Benedict	.15	.06
❑ 256	Dave Geisel	.15	.06
❑ 257	Julio Cruz	.15	.06
❑ 258	Luis Sanchez	.15	.06
❑ 259	Sparky Anderson MG	.25	.10
❑ 260	Scott McGregor	.15	.06
❑ 261	Bobby Brown	.15	.06
❑ 262	Tom Candiotti RC	.75	.30
❑ 263	Jack Fimple	.15	.06
❑ 264	Doug Frobel RC	.15	.06
❑ 265	Donnie Hill	.15	.06
❑ 266	Steve Lubratich	.15	.06
❑ 267	Carmelo Martinez	.15	.06
❑ 268	Jack O'Connor	.15	.06
❑ 269	Aurelio Rodriguez	.15	.06
❑ 270	Jeff Russell RC	.40	.16
❑ 271	Moose Haas	.15	.06
❑ 272	Rick Dempsey	.15	.06
❑ 273	Charlie Puleo	.15	.06
❑ 274	Rick Monday	.25	.10
❑ 275	Len Matuszek	.15	.06
❑ 276	Rod Carew	.25	.10
	Geoff Zahn TL		
❑ 277	Eddie Whitson	.15	.06
❑ 278	Jorge Bell	.25	.10
❑ 279	Ivan DeJesus	.15	.06
❑ 280	Floyd Bannister	.15	.06
❑ 281	Larry Milbourne	.15	.06
❑ 282	Jim Barr	.15	.06
❑ 283	Larry Biittner	.15	.06
❑ 284	Howard Bailey	.15	.06
❑ 285	Darrell Porter	.15	.06
❑ 286	Lary Sorensen	.15	.06
❑ 287	Warren Cromartie	.15	.06
❑ 288	Jim Beattie	.15	.06
❑ 289	Randy Johnson	.15	.06
❑ 290	Dave Dravecky	.15	.06
❑ 291	Chuck Tanner MG	.15	.06
❑ 292	Tony Scott	.15	.06
❑ 293	Ed Lynch	.15	.06
❑ 294	U.L. Washington	.15	.06
❑ 295	Mike Flanagan	.15	.06
❑ 296	Jeff Newman	.15	.06
❑ 297	Bruce Berenyi	.15	.06
❑ 298	Jim Gantner	.15	.06
❑ 299	John Butcher	.15	.06
❑ 300	Pete Rose	2.00	.80
❑ 301	Frank LaCorte	.15	.06
❑ 302	Barry Bonnell	.15	.06
❑ 303	Marty Castillo	.15	.06
❑ 304	Warren Brusstar	.15	.06
❑ 305	Roy Smalley	.15	.06
❑ 306	Pedro Guerrero	.25	.10
	Bob Welch TL		
❑ 307	Bobby Mitchell	.15	.06
❑ 308	Ron Hassey	.15	.06
❑ 309	Tony Phillips RC	.75	.30
❑ 310	Willie McGee	.25	.10
❑ 311	Jerry Koosman	.25	.10
❑ 312	Jorge Orta	.15	.06
❑ 313	Mike Jorgensen	.15	.06
❑ 314	Orlando Mercado	.15	.06
❑ 315	Bobby Grich	.25	.10
❑ 316	Mark Bradley	.15	.06
❑ 317	Greg Pryor	.15	.06
❑ 318	Bill Gullickson	.15	.06
❑ 319	Al Bumbry	.15	.06
❑ 320	Bob Stanley	.15	.06
❑ 321	Harvey Kuenn MG	.15	.06
❑ 322	Ken Schrom	.15	.06
❑ 323	Alan Knicely	.15	.06
❑ 324	Alejandro Pena RC*	.75	.30
❑ 325	Darrell Evans	.25	.10
❑ 326	Bob Kearney	.15	.06
❑ 327	Ruppert Jones	.15	.06
❑ 328	Vern Ruhle	.15	.06
❑ 329	Pat Tabler	.15	.06
❑ 330	John Candelaria	.15	.06
❑ 331	Bucky Dent	.25	.10
❑ 332	Kevin Gross RC	.40	.16
❑ 333	Larry Herndon	.25	.10
❑ 334	Chuck Rainey	.15	.06
❑ 335	Don Baylor	.25	.10
❑ 336	Pat Putnam	.25	.10
	Matt Young TL		
❑ 337	Kevin Hagen	.15	.06
❑ 338	Mike Warren	.15	.06
❑ 339	Roy Lee Jackson	.15	.06
❑ 340	Hal McRae	.25	.10
❑ 341	Dave Tobik	.15	.06
❑ 342	Tim Foli	.15	.06
❑ 343	Mark Davis	.15	.06
❑ 344	Rick Miller	.15	.06
❑ 345	Kent Hrbek	.25	.10
❑ 346	Kurt Bevacqua	.15	.06
❑ 347	Allan Ramirez	.15	.06
❑ 348	Toby Harrah	.25	.10
❑ 349	Bob L. Gibson RC	.15	.06
❑ 350	George Foster	.25	.10
❑ 351	Russ Nixon MG	.15	.06
❑ 352	Dave Stewart	.25	.10
❑ 353	Jim Anderson	.15	.06
❑ 354	Jeff Burroughs	.15	.06
❑ 355	Jason Thompson	.15	.06
❑ 356	Glenn Abbott	.15	.06
❑ 357	Ron Cey	.25	.10
❑ 358	Bob Dernier	.15	.06
❑ 359	Jim Acker	.15	.06
❑ 360	Willie Randolph	.25	.10
❑ 361	Dave Smith	.15	.06
❑ 362	David Green	.15	.06
❑ 363	Tim Laudner	.15	.06
❑ 364	Scott Fletcher	.15	.06
❑ 365	Steve Bedrosian	.15	.06
❑ 366	Terry Kennedy	.25	.10
	Dave Dravecky TL		
❑ 367	Jamie Easterly	.15	.06
❑ 368	Hubie Brooks	.15	.06
❑ 369	Steve McCatty	.15	.06
❑ 370	Tim Raines	.25	.10
❑ 371	Dave Gumpert	.15	.06
❑ 372	Gary Roenicke	.15	.06
❑ 373	Bill Scherrer	.15	.06
❑ 374	Don Money	.15	.06
❑ 375	Dennis Leonard	.15	.06
❑ 376	Dave Anderson RC	.15	.06
❑ 377	Danny Darwin	.15	.06
❑ 378	Bob Brenly	.15	.06
❑ 379	Checklist 265-396	.25	.10
❑ 380	Steve Garvey	.25	.10
❑ 381	Ralph Houk MG	.15	.06
❑ 382	Chris Nyman	.15	.06
❑ 383	Terry Puhl	.15	.06
❑ 384	Lee Tunnell	.15	.06
❑ 385	Tony Perez	.40	.16
❑ 386	George Hendrick AS	.15	.06
❑ 387	Johnny Ray AS	.15	.06
❑ 388	Mike Schmidt AS	.60	.24
❑ 389	Ozzie Smith AS	.60	.24
❑ 390	Tim Raines AS	.15	.06
❑ 391	Dale Murphy AS	.25	.10
❑ 392	Andre Dawson AS	.15	.06
❑ 393	Gary Carter AS	.15	.06
❑ 394	Steve Rogers AS	.15	.06
❑ 395	Steve Carlton AS	.25	.10
❑ 396	Jesse Orosco AS	.15	.06
❑ 397	Eddie Murray AS	.40	.16
❑ 398	Lou Whitaker AS	.15	.06
❑ 399	George Brett AS	.60	.24
❑ 400	Cal Ripken AS	2.00	.80
❑ 401	Jim Rice AS	.15	.06
❑ 402	Dave Winfield AS	.15	.06
❑ 403	Lloyd Moseby AS	.15	.06
❑ 404	Ted Simmons AS	.15	.06
❑ 405	LaMarr Hoyt AS	.15	.06
❑ 406	Ron Guidry AS	.15	.06
❑ 407	Dan Quisenberry AS	.15	.06
❑ 408	Lou Piniella	.25	.10
❑ 409	Juan Agosto	.15	.06
❑ 410	Claudell Washington	.15	.06
❑ 411	Houston Jimenez	.15	.06
❑ 412	Doug Rader MG	.15	.06
❑ 413	Spike Owen RC	.40	.16
❑ 414	Mitchell Page	.15	.06
❑ 415	Tommy John	.25	.10
❑ 416	Dane Iorg	.15	.06
❑ 417	Mike Armstrong	.15	.06
❑ 418	Ron Hodges	.15	.06
❑ 419	John Henry Johnson	.15	.06
❑ 420	Cecil Cooper	.25	.10
❑ 421	Charlie Lea	.15	.06
❑ 422	Jose Cruz	.25	.10
❑ 423	Mike Morgan	.15	.06
❑ 424	Dann Bilardello	.15	.06
❑ 425	Steve Howe	.15	.06
❑ 426	Cal Ripken	1.50	.60
	Mike Boddicker TL		
❑ 427	Rick Leach	.15	.06
❑ 428	Fred Breining	.15	.06
❑ 429	Randy Bush	.15	.06

❑	430	Rusty Staub	.25	.10
❑	431	Chris Bando	.15	.06
❑	432	Charles Hudson	.15	.06
❑	433	Rich Hebner	.15	.06
❑	434	Harold Baines	.25	.10
❑	435	Neil Allen	.15	.06
❑	436	Rick Peters	.15	.06
❑	437	Mike Proly	.15	.06
❑	438	Biff Pocoroba	.15	.06
❑	439	Bob Stoddard	.15	.06
❑	440	Steve Kemp	.15	.06
❑	441	Bob Lillis MG	.15	.06
❑	442	Byron McLaughlin	.15	.06
❑	443	Benny Ayala	.15	.06
❑	444	Steve Renko	.15	.06
❑	445	Jerry Remy	.15	.06
❑	446	Luis Pujols	.15	.06
❑	447	Tom Brunansky	.15	.06
❑	448	Ben Hayes	.15	.06
❑	449	Joe Pettini	.15	.06
❑	450	Gary Carter	.25	.10
❑	451	Bob Jones	.15	.06
❑	452	Chuck Porter	.15	.06
❑	453	Willie Upshaw	.15	.06
❑	454	Joe Beckwith	.15	.06
❑	455	Terry Kennedy	.15	.06
❑	456	Keith Moreland Fergie Jenkins TL	.15	.06
❑	457	Dave Rozema	.15	.06
❑	458	Kiko Garcia	.15	.06
❑	459	Kevin Hickey	.15	.06
❑	460	Dave Winfield	.25	.10
❑	461	Jim Maler	.15	.06
❑	462	Lee Lacy	.15	.06
❑	463	Dave Engle	.15	.06
❑	464	Jeff A. Jones	.15	.06
❑	465	Mookie Wilson	.25	.10
❑	466	Gene Garber	.15	.06
❑	467	Mike Ramsey	.15	.06
❑	468	Geoff Zahn	.15	.06
❑	469	Tom O'Malley	.15	.06
❑	470	Nolan Ryan	3.00	1.20
❑	471	Dick Howser MG	.15	.06
❑	472	Mike G. Brown RC	.15	.06
❑	473	Jim Dwyer	.15	.06
❑	474	Greg Bargar	.15	.06
❑	475	Gary Redus RC*	.40	.16
❑	476	Tom Tellmann	.15	.06
❑	477	Rafael Landestoy	.15	.06
❑	478	Alan Bannister	.15	.06
❑	479	Frank Tanana	.25	.10
❑	480	Ron Kittle	.15	.06
❑	481	Mark Thurmond	.15	.06
❑	482	Enos Cabell	.15	.06
❑	483	Fergie Jenkins	.25	.10
❑	484	Ozzie Virgil	.15	.06
❑	485	Rick Rhoden	.15	.06
❑	486	Don Baylor Ron Guidry TL	.25	.10
❑	487	Ricky Adams	.15	.06
❑	488	Jesse Barfield	.25	.10
❑	489	Dave Von Ohlen	.15	.06
❑	490	Cal Ripken	4.00	1.60
❑	491	Bobby Castillo	.15	.06
❑	492	Tucker Ashford	.15	.06
❑	493	Mike Norris	.15	.06
❑	494	Chili Davis	.25	.10
❑	495	Rollie Fingers	.25	.10
❑	496	Terry Francona	.25	.10
❑	497	Bud Anderson	.15	.06
❑	498	Rich Gedman	.15	.06
❑	499	Mike Witt	.15	.06
❑	500	George Brett	1.50	.60
❑	501	Steve Henderson	.15	.06
❑	502	Joe Torre MG	.40	.16
❑	503	Elias Sosa	.15	.06
❑	504	Mickey Rivers	.15	.06
❑	505	Pete Vuckovich	.15	.06
❑	506	Ernie Whitt	.15	.06
❑	507	Mike LaCoss	.15	.06
❑	508	Mel Hall	.25	.10
❑	509	Brad Havens	.15	.06
❑	510	Alan Trammell	.25	.10
❑	511	Marty Bystrom	.15	.06
❑	512	Oscar Gamble	.15	.06
❑	513	Dave Beard	.15	.06
❑	514	Floyd Rayford	.15	.06
❑	515	Gorman Thomas	.25	.10
❑	516	Al Oliver Charlie Lea TL	.25	.10
❑	517	John Moses	.15	.06
❑	518	Greg Walker	.40	.16
❑	519	Ron Davis	.15	.06
❑	520	Bob Boone	.25	.10
❑	521	Pete Falcone	.15	.06
❑	522	Dave Bergman	.15	.06
❑	523	Glenn Hoffman	.15	.06
❑	524	Carlos Diaz	.15	.06
❑	525	Willie Wilson	.25	.10
❑	526	Ron Oester	.15	.06
❑	527	Checklist 397-528	.25	.10
❑	528	Mark Brouhard	.15	.06
❑	529	Keith Atherton	.15	.06
❑	530	Dan Ford	.15	.06
❑	531	Steve Boros MG	.15	.06
❑	532	Eric Show	.15	.06
❑	533	Ken Landreaux	.15	.06
❑	534	Pete O'Brien RC*	.40	.16
❑	535	Bo Diaz	.15	.06
❑	536	Doug Bair	.15	.06
❑	537	Johnny Ray	.15	.06
❑	538	Kevin Bass	.15	.06
❑	539	George Frazier	.15	.06
❑	540	George Hendrick	.25	.10
❑	541	Dennis Lamp	.15	.06
❑	542	Duane Kuiper	.15	.06
❑	543	Craig McMurtry	.15	.06
❑	544	Cesar Geronimo	.15	.06
❑	545	Bill Buckner	.25	.10
❑	546	Mike Hargrove Lary Sorensen TL	.25	.10
❑	547	Mike Moore	.15	.06
❑	548	Ron Jackson	.15	.06
❑	549	Walt Terrell	.15	.06
❑	550	Jim Rice	.25	.10
❑	551	Scott Ullger	.15	.06
❑	552	Ray Burris	.15	.06
❑	553	Joe Nolan	.15	.06
❑	554	Ted Power	.15	.06
❑	555	Greg Brock	.15	.06
❑	556	Joey McLaughlin	.15	.06
❑	557	Wayne Tolleson	.15	.06
❑	558	Mike Davis	.15	.06
❑	559	Mike Scott	.25	.10
❑	560	Carlton Fisk	.40	.16
❑	561	Whitey Herzog MG	.25	.10
❑	562	Manny Castillo	.15	.06
❑	563	Glenn Wilson	.25	.10
❑	564	Al Holland	.15	.06
❑	565	Leon Durham	.15	.06
❑	566	Jim Bibby	.15	.06
❑	567	Mike Heath	.15	.06
❑	568	Pete Filson	.15	.06
❑	569	Bake McBride	.25	.10
❑	570	Dan Quisenberry	.15	.06
❑	571	Bruce Bochy	.15	.06
❑	572	Jerry Royster	.15	.06
❑	573	Dave Kingman	.25	.10
❑	574	Brian Downing	.25	.10
❑	575	Jim Clancy	.15	.06
❑	576	Jeff Leonard Atlee Hammaker TL	.25	.10
❑	577	Mark Clear	.15	.06
❑	578	Lenn Sakata	.15	.06
❑	579	Bob James	.15	.06
❑	580	Lonnie Smith	.15	.06
❑	581	Jose DeLeon RC	.40	.16
❑	582	Bob McClure	.15	.06
❑	583	Derrel Thomas	.15	.06
❑	584	Dave Schmidt	.15	.06
❑	585	Dan Driessen	.15	.06
❑	586	Joe Niekro	.15	.06
❑	587	Von Hayes	.15	.06
❑	588	Milt Wilcox	.15	.06
❑	589	Mike Easler	.15	.06
❑	590	Dave Stieb	.25	.10
❑	591	Tony LaRussa MG	.25	.10
❑	592	Andre Robertson	.15	.06
❑	593	Jeff Lahti	.15	.06
❑	594	Gene Richards	.15	.06
❑	595	Jeff Reardon	.25	.10
❑	596	Ryne Sandberg	2.50	1.00
❑	597	Rick Camp	.15	.06
❑	598	Rusty Kuntz	.15	.06
❑	599	Doug Sisk	.15	.06
❑	600	Rod Carew	.40	.16
❑	601	John Tudor	.25	.10
❑	602	John Wathan	.15	.06
❑	603	Renie Martin	.15	.06
❑	604	John Lowenstein	.15	.06
❑	605	Mike Caldwell	.15	.06
❑	606	Lloyd Moseby Dave Stieb TL	.25	.10
❑	607	Tom Hume	.15	.06
❑	608	Bobby Johnson	.15	.06
❑	609	Dan Meyer	.15	.06
❑	610	Steve Sax	.15	.06
❑	611	Chet Lemon	.25	.10
❑	612	Harry Spilman	.15	.06
❑	613	Greg Gross	.15	.06
❑	614	Len Barker	.15	.06
❑	615	Garry Templeton	.25	.10
❑	616	Don Robinson	.15	.06
❑	617	Rick Cerone	.15	.06
❑	618	Dickie Noles	.15	.06
❑	619	Jerry Dybzinski	.15	.06
❑	620	Al Oliver	.25	.10
❑	621	Frank Howard MG	.25	.10
❑	622	Al Cowens	.15	.06
❑	623	Ron Washington	.15	.06
❑	624	Terry Harper	.15	.06
❑	625	Larry Gura	.15	.06
❑	626	Bob Clark	.15	.06
❑	627	Dave LaPoint	.15	.06
❑	628	Ed Jurak	.15	.06
❑	629	Rick Langford	.15	.06
❑	630	Ted Simmons	.25	.10
❑	631	Dennis Martinez	.25	.10
❑	632	Tom Foley	.15	.06
❑	633	Mike Krukow	.15	.06
❑	634	Mike Marshall	.15	.06
❑	635	Dave Righetti	.25	.10
❑	636	Pat Putnam	.15	.06
❑	637	Gary Matthews John Denny TL	.25	.10
❑	638	George Vukovich	.15	.06
❑	639	Rick Lysander	.15	.06
❑	640	Lance Parrish	.40	.16
❑	641	Mike Richardt	.15	.06
❑	642	Tom Underwood	.15	.06
❑	643	Mike C. Brown	.15	.06
❑	644	Tim Lollar	.15	.06
❑	645	Tony Pena	.15	.06
❑	646	Checklist 529-660	.25	.10
❑	647	Ron Roenicke	.15	.06
❑	648	Len Whitehouse	.15	.06
❑	649	Tom Herr	.15	.06
❑	650	Phil Niekro	.25	.10
❑	651	John McNamara MG	.15	.06
❑	652	Rudy May	.15	.06
❑	653	Dave Stapleton	.15	.06
❑	654	Bob Bailor	.15	.06
❑	655	Amos Otis	.25	.10
❑	656	Bryn Smith	.15	.06
❑	657	Thad Bosley	.15	.06
❑	658	Jerry Augustine	.15	.06
❑	659	Duane Walker	.15	.06
❑	660	Ray Knight	.25	.10
❑	661	Steve Yeager	.25	.10
❑	662	Tom Brennan	.15	.06
❑	663	Johnnie LeMaster	.15	.06
❑	664	Dave Stegman	.15	.06
❑	665	Buddy Bell	.25	.10
❑	666	Lou Whitaker Jack Morris TL	.25	.10
❑	667	Vance Law	.15	.06
❑	668	Larry McWilliams	.15	.06
❑	669	Dave Lopes	.25	.10
❑	670	Rich Gossage	.25	.10
❑	671	Jamie Quirk	.15	.06
❑	672	Ricky Nelson	.15	.06
❑	673	Mike Walters	.15	.06
❑	674	Tim Flannery	.15	.06
❑	675	Pascual Perez	.15	.06
❑	676	Brian Giles	.15	.06
❑	677	Doyle Alexander	.15	.06
❑	678	Chris Speier	.15	.06
❑	679	Art Howe	.15	.06

❑ 680 Fred Lynn .25 .10
❑ 681 Tom Lasorda MG .40 .16
❑ 682 Dan Morogiello .15 .06
❑ 683 Marty Barrett RC .40 .16
❑ 684 Bob Shirley .15 .06
❑ 685 Willie Aikens .15 .06
❑ 686 Joe Price .15 .06
❑ 687 Roy Howell .15 .06
❑ 688 George Wright .15 .06
❑ 689 Mike Fischlin .15 .06
❑ 690 Jack Clark .25 .10
❑ 691 Steve Lake .15 .06
❑ 692 Dickie Thon .15 .06
❑ 693 Alan Wiggins .15 .06
❑ 694 Mike Stanton .15 .06
❑ 695 Lou Whitaker .25 .10
❑ 696 Bill Madlock .25 .10
Rick Rhoden TL
❑ 697 Dale Murray .15 .06
❑ 698 Marc Hill .15 .06
❑ 699 Dave Rucker .15 .06
❑ 700 Mike Schmidt 1.50 .60
❑ 701 Bill Madlock .60 .24
Pete Rose
Dave Parker LL
❑ 702 Pete Rose .60 .24
Rusty Staub
Tony Perez LL
❑ 703 Mike Schmidt .60 .24
Tony Perez
Dave Kingman LL
❑ 704 Tony Perez .25 .10
Rusty Staub
Al Oliver LL
❑ 705 Joe Morgan .40 .16
Cesar Cedeno
Larry Bowa LL
❑ 706 Steve Carlton .25 .10
Fergie Jenkins
Tom Seaver LL
❑ 707 Steve Carlton 1.50 .60
Nolan Ryan
Tom Seaver LL
❑ 708 Tom Seaver .25 .10
Steve Carlton
Steve Rogers LL
❑ 709 Bruce Sutter .25 .10
Tug McGraw
Gene Garber LL
❑ 710 Rod Carew .40 .16
George Brett
Cecil Cooper LL
❑ 711 Rod Carew .25 .10
Bert Campaneris
Reggie Jackson LL
❑ 712 Reggie Jackson .25 .10
Graig Nettles
Greg Luzinski LL
❑ 713 Reggie Jackson .25 .10
Ted Simmons
Graig Nettles LL
❑ 714 Bert Campaneris .25 .10
Dave Lopes
Omar Moreno LL
❑ 715 Jim Palmer .25 .10
Don Sutton
Tommy John LL
❑ 716 Don Sutton .40 .16
Bert Blyleven
Jerry Koosman LL
❑ 717 Jim Palmer .25 .10
Rollie Fingers
Ron Guidry LL
❑ 718 Rollie Fingers .25 .10
Rich Gossage
Dan Quisenberry LL
❑ 719 Andy Hassler .15 .06
❑ 720 Dwight Evans .25 .10
❑ 721 Del Crandall MG .15 .06
❑ 722 Bob Welch .25 .10
❑ 723 Rich Dauer .15 .06
❑ 724 Eric Rasmussen .15 .06
❑ 725 Cesar Cedeno .25 .10
❑ 726 Ted Simmons .25 .10
Moose Haas TL
❑ 727 Joel Youngblood .15 .06
❑ 728 Tug McGraw .25 .10
❑ 729 Gene Tenace .25 .10
❑ 730 Bruce Sutter .25 .10
❑ 731 Lynn Jones .15 .06
❑ 732 Terry Crowley .15 .06
❑ 733 Dave Collins .15 .06
❑ 734 Odell Jones .15 .06
❑ 735 Rick Burleson .15 .06
❑ 736 Dick Ruthven .15 .06
❑ 737 Jim Essian .15 .06
❑ 738 Bill Schroeder .15 .06
❑ 739 Bob Watson .15 .06
❑ 740 Tom Seaver .60 .24
❑ 741 Wayne Gross .15 .06
❑ 742 Dick Williams MG .15 .06
❑ 743 Don Hood .15 .06
❑ 744 Jamie Allen .15 .06
❑ 745 Dennis Eckersley .40 .16
❑ 746 Mickey Hatcher .15 .06
❑ 747 Pat Zachry .15 .06
❑ 748 Jeff Leonard .15 .06
❑ 749 Doug Flynn .15 .06
❑ 750 Jim Palmer .25 .10
❑ 751 Charlie Moore .15 .06
❑ 752 Phil Garner .25 .10
❑ 753 Doug Gwosdz .15 .06
❑ 754 Kent Tekulve .15 .06
❑ 755 Garry Maddox .15 .06
❑ 756 Ron Oester .25 .10
Mario Soto TL
❑ 757 Larry Bowa .25 .10
❑ 758 Bill Stein .15 .06
❑ 759 Richard Dotson .15 .06
❑ 760 Bob Horner .25 .10
❑ 761 John Montefusco .15 .06
❑ 762 Rance Mulliniks .15 .06
❑ 763 Craig Swan .15 .06
❑ 764 Mike Hargrove .15 .06
❑ 765 Ken Forsch .15 .06
❑ 766 Mike Vail .15 .06
❑ 767 Carney Lansford .25 .10
❑ 768 Champ Summers .15 .06
❑ 769 Bill Caudill .15 .06
❑ 770 Ken Griffey .25 .10
❑ 771 Billy Gardner MG .15 .06
❑ 772 Jim Slaton .15 .06
❑ 773 Todd Cruz .15 .06
❑ 774 Tom Gorman .15 .06
❑ 775 Dave Parker .25 .10
❑ 776 Craig Reynolds .15 .06
❑ 777 Tom Paciorek .15 .06
❑ 778 Andy Hawkins .15 .06
❑ 779 Jim Sundberg .25 .10
❑ 780 Steve Carlton .40 .16
❑ 781 Checklist 661-792 .25 .10
❑ 782 Steve Balboni .15 .06
❑ 783 Luis Leal .15 .06
❑ 784 Leon Roberts .15 .06
❑ 785 Joaquin Andujar .25 .10
❑ 786 Wade Boggs .40 .16
Bob Ojeda TL
❑ 787 Bill Campbell .15 .06
❑ 788 Milt May .15 .06
❑ 789 Bert Blyleven .25 .10
❑ 790 Doug DeCinces .15 .06
❑ 791 Terry Forster .25 .10
❑ 792 Bill Russell .25 .10

1984 Topps Traded

	Nm-Mt	Ex-Mt
COMP.FACT.SET (132)	30.00	12.00
❑ 1T Willie Aikens	.40	.16
❑ 2T Luis Aponte	.40	.16
❑ 3T Mike Armstrong	.40	.16
❑ 4T Bob Bailor	.40	.16
❑ 5T Dusty Baker	.60	.24
❑ 6T Steve Balboni	.40	.16
❑ 7T Alan Bannister	.40	.16
❑ 8T Dave Beard	.40	.16
❑ 9T Joe Beckwith	.40	.16
❑ 10T Bruce Berenyi	.40	.16
❑ 11T Dave Bergman	.40	.16
❑ 12T Tony Bernazard	.40	.16
❑ 13T Yogi Berra MG	1.50	.60
❑ 14T Barry Bonnell	.40	.16
❑ 15T Phil Bradley	1.00	.40
❑ 16T Fred Breining	.40	.16
❑ 17T Bill Buckner	.60	.24
❑ 18T Ray Burris	.40	.16
❑ 19T John Butcher	.40	.16
❑ 20T Brett Butler	.60	.24
❑ 21T Enos Cabell	.40	.16
❑ 22T Bill Campbell	.40	.16
❑ 23T Bill Caudill	.40	.16
❑ 24T Bob Clark	.40	.16
❑ 25T Bryan Clark	.40	.16
❑ 26T Jaime Cocanower	.40	.16
❑ 27T Ron Darling XRC*	2.00	.80
❑ 28T Alvin Davis XRC	1.00	.40
❑ 29T Ken Dayley	.40	.16
❑ 30T Jeff Dedmon	.40	.16
❑ 31T Bob Dernier	.40	.16
❑ 32T Carlos Diaz	.40	.16
❑ 33T Mike Easler	.40	.16
❑ 34T Dennis Eckersley	1.00	.40
❑ 35T Jim Essian	.40	.16
❑ 36T Darrell Evans	.60	.24
❑ 37T Mike Fitzgerald	.40	.16
❑ 38T Tim Foli	.40	.16
❑ 39T George Frazier	.40	.16
❑ 40T Rich Gale	.40	.16
❑ 41T Barbaro Garbey	.40	.16
❑ 42T Dwight Gooden XRC	5.00	2.00
❑ 43T Rich Gossage	.60	.24
❑ 44T Wayne Gross	.40	.16
❑ 45T Mark Gubicza XRC	1.00	.40
❑ 46T Jackie Gutierrez	.40	.16
❑ 47T Mel Hall	.60	.24
❑ 48T Toby Harrah	.60	.24
❑ 49T Ron Hassey	.40	.16
❑ 50T Rich Hebner	.40	.16
❑ 51T Willie Hernandez	.40	.16
❑ 52T Ricky Horton	.40	.16
❑ 53T Art Howe	.40	.16
❑ 54T Dane Iorg	.40	.16
❑ 55T Brook Jacoby	1.00	.40
❑ 56T Mike Jeffcoat XRC	.50	.20
❑ 57T Dave Johnson MG	.40	.16
❑ 58T Lynn Jones	.40	.16
❑ 59T Ruppert Jones	.40	.16
❑ 60T Mike Jorgensen	.40	.16
❑ 61T Bob Kearney	.40	.16
❑ 62T Jimmy Key XRC	2.00	.80
❑ 63T Dave Kingman	.60	.24
❑ 64T Jerry Koosman	.60	.24
❑ 65T Wayne Krenchicki	.40	.16
❑ 66T Rusty Kuntz	.40	.16
❑ 67T Rene Lachemann MG	.40	.16
❑ 68T Frank LaCorte	.40	.16
❑ 69T Dennis Lamp	.40	.16
❑ 70T Mark Langston XRC	2.00	.80
❑ 71T Rick Leach	.40	.16
❑ 72T Craig Lefferts	.50	.20
❑ 73T Gary Lucas	.40	.16
❑ 74T Jerry Martin	.40	.16
❑ 75T Carmelo Martinez	.40	.16
❑ 76T Mike Mason XRC	.50	.20
❑ 77T Gary Matthews	.60	.24
❑ 78T Andy McGaffigan	.40	.16
❑ 79T Larry Milbourne	.40	.16
❑ 80T Sid Monge	.40	.16
❑ 81T Jackie Moore MG	.40	.16
❑ 82T Joe Morgan	.60	.24
❑ 83T Graig Nettles	.60	.24

❑ 84T Phil Niekro	.60	.24
❑ 85T Ken Oberkfell	.40	.16
❑ 86T Mike O'Berry	.40	.16
❑ 87T Al Oliver	.60	.24
❑ 88T Jorge Orta	.40	.16
❑ 89T Amos Otis	.60	.24
❑ 90T Dave Parker	.60	.24
❑ 91T Tony Perez	1.00	.40
❑ 92T Gerald Perry	1.00	.40
❑ 93T Gary Pettis	.40	.16
❑ 94T Rob Picciolo	.40	.16
❑ 95T Vern Rapp MG	.40	.16
❑ 96T Floyd Rayford	.40	.16
❑ 97T Randy Ready XRC	1.00	.40
❑ 98T Ron Reed	.40	.16
❑ 99T Gene Richards	.40	.16
❑ 100T Jose Rijo XRC	2.00	.80
❑ 101T Jeff D. Robinson	.40	.16
❑ 102T Ron Romanick	.40	.16
❑ 103T Pete Rose	5.00	2.00
❑ 104T B.Saberhagen XRC	3.00	1.20
❑ 105T Juan Samuel XRC*	2.00	.80
❑ 106T Scott Sanderson	.40	.16
❑ 107T Dick Schofield XRC*	1.00	.40
❑ 108T Tom Seaver	1.50	.60
❑ 109T Jim Slaton	.40	.16
❑ 110T Mike Smithson	.40	.16
❑ 111T Lary Sorensen	.40	.16
❑ 112T Tim Stoddard	.40	.16
❑ 113T Champ Summers	.40	.16
❑ 114T Jim Sundberg	.60	.24
❑ 115T Rick Sutcliffe	.60	.24
❑ 116T Craig Swan	.40	.16
❑ 117T Tim Teufel XRC*	1.00	.40
❑ 118T Derrel Thomas	.40	.16
❑ 119T Gorman Thomas	.60	.24
❑ 120T Alex Trevino	.40	.16
❑ 121T Manny Trillo	.40	.16
❑ 122T John Tudor	.60	.24
❑ 123T Tom Underwood	.40	.16
❑ 124T Mike Vail	.40	.16
❑ 125T Tom Waddell	.40	.16
❑ 126T Gary Ward	.40	.16
❑ 127T Curtis Wilkerson	.40	.16
❑ 128T Frank Williams	.40	.16
❑ 129T Glenn Wilson	.60	.24
❑ 130T John Wockenfuss	.40	.16
❑ 131T Ned Yost	.40	.16
❑ 132T Checklist 1T-132T	.40	.16

1985 Topps

	Nm-Mt	Ex-Mt
COMPLETE SET (792)	100.00	40.00
COMP.FACT.SET (792)	150.00	60.00

❑ 1 Carlton Fisk RB	.25	.10
❑ 2 Steve Garvey RB	.15	.06
❑ 3 Dwight Gooden RB	.60	.24
❑ 4 Cliff Johnson RB	.15	.06
❑ 5 Joe Morgan RB	.15	.06
❑ 6 Pete Rose RB	.40	.16
❑ 7 Nolan Ryan RB	1.50	.60
❑ 8 Juan Samuel RB	.15	.06
❑ 9 Bruce Sutter RB	.15	.06
❑ 10 Don Sutton RB	.15	.06
❑ 11 Ralph Houk MG	.15	.06
❑ 12 Dave Lopes	.25	.10
❑ 13 Tim Lollar	.15	.06
❑ 14 Chris Bando	.15	.06
❑ 15 Jerry Koosman	.25	.10
❑ 16 Bobby Meacham	.15	.06
❑ 17 Mike Scott	.25	.10
❑ 18 Mickey Hatcher	.15	.06
❑ 19 George Frazier	.15	.06
❑ 20 Chet Lemon	.25	.10
❑ 21 Lee Tunnell	.15	.06
❑ 22 Duane Kuiper	.15	.06
❑ 23 Bret Saberhagen RC	1.00	.40
❑ 24 Jesse Barfield	.25	.10
❑ 25 Steve Bedrosian	.15	.06
❑ 26 Roy Smalley	.15	.06
❑ 27 Bruce Berenyi	.15	.06
❑ 28 Dann Bilardello	.15	.06
❑ 29 Odell Jones	.15	.06
❑ 30 Cal Ripken	2.50	1.00
❑ 31 Terry Whitfield	.15	.06
❑ 32 Chuck Porter	.15	.06
❑ 33 Tito Landrum	.15	.06
❑ 34 Ed Nunez	.15	.06
❑ 35 Graig Nettles	.25	.10
❑ 36 Fred Breining	.15	.06
❑ 37 Reid Nichols	.15	.06
❑ 38 Jackie Moore MG	.15	.06
❑ 39 John Wockenfuss	.15	.06
❑ 40 Phil Niekro	.25	.10
❑ 41 Mike Fischlin	.15	.06
❑ 42 Luis Sanchez	.15	.06
❑ 43 Andre David	.15	.06
❑ 44 Dickie Thon	.15	.06
❑ 45 Greg Minton	.15	.06
❑ 46 Gary Woods	.15	.06
❑ 47 Dave Rozema	.15	.06
❑ 48 Tony Fernandez	.25	.10
❑ 49 Butch Davis	.15	.06
❑ 50 John Candelaria	.15	.06
❑ 51 Bob Watson	.15	.06
❑ 52 Jerry Dybzinski	.15	.06
❑ 53 Tom Gorman	.15	.06
❑ 54 Cesar Cedeno	.25	.10
❑ 55 Frank Tanana	.25	.10
❑ 56 Jim Dwyer	.15	.06
❑ 57 Pat Zachry	.15	.06
❑ 58 Orlando Mercado	.15	.06
❑ 59 Rick Waits	.15	.06
❑ 60 George Hendrick	.25	.10
❑ 61 Curt Kaufman	.15	.06
❑ 62 Mike Ramsey	.15	.06
❑ 63 Steve McCatty	.15	.06
❑ 64 Mark Bailey	.15	.06
❑ 65 Bill Buckner	.25	.10
❑ 66 Dick Williams MG	.15	.06
❑ 67 Rafael Santana	.15	.06
❑ 68 Von Hayes	.15	.06
❑ 69 Jim Winn	.15	.06
❑ 70 Don Baylor	.25	.10
❑ 71 Tim Laudner	.15	.06
❑ 72 Rick Sutcliffe	.25	.10
❑ 73 Rusty Kuntz	.15	.06
❑ 74 Mike Krukow	.15	.06
❑ 75 Willie Upshaw	.15	.06
❑ 76 Alan Bannister	.15	.06
❑ 77 Joe Beckwith	.15	.06
❑ 78 Scott Fletcher	.15	.06
❑ 79 Rick Mahler	.15	.06
❑ 80 Keith Hernandez	.25	.10
❑ 81 Lenn Sakata	.15	.06
❑ 82 Joe Price	.15	.06
❑ 83 Charlie Moore	.15	.06
❑ 84 Spike Owen	.15	.06
❑ 85 Mike Marshall	.15	.06
❑ 86 Don Aase	.15	.06
❑ 87 David Green	.15	.06
❑ 88 Bryn Smith	.15	.06
❑ 89 Jackie Gutierrez	.15	.06
❑ 90 Rich Gossage	.25	.10
❑ 91 Jeff Burroughs	.15	.06
❑ 92 Paul Owens MG	.15	.06
❑ 93 Don Schulze	.15	.06
❑ 94 Toby Harrah	.25	.10
❑ 95 Jose Cruz	.25	.10
❑ 96 Johnny Ray	.15	.06
❑ 97 Pete Filson	.15	.06
❑ 98 Steve Lake	.15	.06
❑ 99 Milt Wilcox	.15	.06
❑ 100 George Brett	1.50	.60
❑ 101 Jim Acker	.15	.06
❑ 102 Tommy Dunbar	.15	.06
❑ 103 Randy Lerch	.15	.06
❑ 104 Mike Fitzgerald	.15	.06
❑ 105 Ron Kittle	.15	.06
❑ 106 Pascual Perez	.15	.06
❑ 107 Tom Foley	.15	.06
❑ 108 Darnell Coles	.15	.06
❑ 109 Gary Roenicke	.15	.06
❑ 110 Alejandro Pena	.15	.06
❑ 111 Doug DeCinces	.15	.06
❑ 112 Tom Tellmann	.15	.06
❑ 113 Tom Herr	.15	.06
❑ 114 Bob James	.15	.06
❑ 115 Rickey Henderson	.75	.30
❑ 116 Dennis Boyd	.15	.06
❑ 117 Greg Gross	.15	.06
❑ 118 Eric Show	.15	.06
❑ 119 Pat Corrales MG	.15	.06
❑ 120 Steve Kemp	.15	.06
❑ 121 Checklist: 1-132	.15	.06
❑ 122 Tom Brunansky	.15	.06
❑ 123 Dave Smith	.15	.06
❑ 124 Rich Hebner	.15	.06
❑ 125 Kent Tekulve	.15	.06
❑ 126 Ruppert Jones	.15	.06
❑ 127 Mark Gubicza RC*	.40	.16
❑ 128 Ernie Whitt	.15	.06
❑ 129 Gene Garber	.15	.06
❑ 130 Al Oliver	.25	.10
❑ 131 Buddy Bell FS Gus Bell	.25	.10
❑ 132 Dale Berra FS Yogi Berra	.60	.24
❑ 133 Bob Boone FS Ray Boone	.15	.06
❑ 134 Terry Francona FS Tito Francona	.25	.10
❑ 135 Terry Kennedy FS Bob Kennedy	.15	.06
❑ 136 Jeff Kunkel FS Bill Kunkel	.15	.06
❑ 137 Vance Law FS Vern Law	.25	.10
❑ 138 Dick Schofield FS Dick Schofield	.15	.06
❑ 139 Joel Skinner FS Bob Skinner	.15	.06
❑ 140 Roy Smalley Jr. FS Roy Smalley	.15	.06
❑ 141 Mike Stenhouse FS Dave Stenhouse	.15	.06
❑ 142 Steve Trout FS Dizzy Trout	.15	.06
❑ 143 Ozzie Virgil FS Ossie Virgil	.15	.06
❑ 144 Ron Gardenhire	.15	.06
❑ 145 Alvin Davis RC*	.40	.16
❑ 146 Gary Redus	.15	.06
❑ 147 Bill Swaggerty	.15	.06
❑ 148 Steve Yeager	.25	.10
❑ 149 Dickie Noles	.15	.06
❑ 150 Jim Rice	.25	.10
❑ 151 Moose Haas	.15	.06
❑ 152 Steve Braun	.15	.06
❑ 153 Frank LaCorte	.15	.06
❑ 154 Angel Salazar	.15	.06
❑ 155 Yogi Berra MG	.60	.24
❑ 156 Craig Reynolds	.15	.06
❑ 157 Tug McGraw	.25	.10
❑ 158 Pat Tabler	.15	.06
❑ 159 Carlos Diaz	.15	.06
❑ 160 Lance Parrish	.25	.10
❑ 161 Ken Schrom	.15	.06
❑ 162 Benny Distefano	.15	.06
❑ 163 Dennis Eckersley	.40	.16
❑ 164 Jorge Orta	.15	.06
❑ 165 Dusty Baker	.25	.10
❑ 166 Keith Atherton	.15	.06
❑ 167 Rufino Linares	.15	.06
❑ 168 Garth Iorg	.15	.06
❑ 169 Dan Spillner	.15	.06
❑ 170 George Foster	.25	.10
❑ 171 Bill Stein	.15	.06

❑ 172 Jack Perconte .15 .06
❑ 173 Mike Young .15 .06
❑ 174 Rick Honeycutt .15 .06
❑ 175 Dave Parker .25 .10
❑ 176 Bill Schroeder .15 .06
❑ 177 Dave Von Ohlen .15 .06
❑ 178 Miguel Dilone .15 .06
❑ 179 Tommy John .25 .10
❑ 180 Dave Winfield .25 .10
❑ 181 Roger Clemens RC 25.00 10.00
❑ 182 Tim Flannery .15 .06
❑ 183 Larry McWilliams .15 .06
❑ 184 Carmen Castillo .15 .06
❑ 185 Al Holland .15 .06
❑ 186 Bob Lillis MG .15 .06
❑ 187 Mike Walters .15 .06
❑ 188 Greg Pryor .15 .06
❑ 189 Warren Brusstar .15 .06
❑ 190 Rusty Staub .25 .10
❑ 191 Steve Nicosia .15 .06
❑ 192 Howard Johnson .25 .10
❑ 193 Jimmy Key RC .75 .30
❑ 194 Dave Stegman .15 .06
❑ 195 Glenn Hubbard .15 .06
❑ 196 Pete O'Brien .15 .06
❑ 197 Mike Warren .15 .06
❑ 198 Eddie Milner .15 .06
❑ 199 Dennis Martinez .25 .10
❑ 200 Reggie Jackson .40 .16
❑ 201 Burt Hooton .15 .06
❑ 202 Gorman Thomas .25 .10
❑ 203 Bob McClure .15 .06
❑ 204 Art Howe .15 .06
❑ 205 Steve Rogers .25 .10
❑ 206 Phil Garner .25 .10
❑ 207 Mark Clear .15 .06
❑ 208 Champ Summers .15 .06
❑ 209 Bill Campbell .15 .06
❑ 210 Gary Matthews .25 .10
❑ 211 Clay Christiansen .15 .06
❑ 212 George Vukovich .15 .06
❑ 213 Billy Gardner MG .15 .06
❑ 214 John Tudor .25 .10
❑ 215 Bob Brenly .15 .06
❑ 216 Jerry Don Gleaton .15 .06
❑ 217 Leon Roberts .15 .06
❑ 218 Doyle Alexander .15 .06
❑ 219 Gerald Perry .15 .06
❑ 220 Fred Lynn .25 .10
❑ 221 Ron Reed .15 .06
❑ 222 Hubie Brooks .15 .06
❑ 223 Tom Hume .15 .06
❑ 224 Al Cowens .15 .06
❑ 225 Mike Boddicker .15 .06
❑ 226 Juan Beniquez .15 .06
❑ 227 Danny Darwin .15 .06
❑ 228 Dion James .15 .06
❑ 229 Dave LaPoint .15 .06
❑ 230 Gary Carter .25 .10
❑ 231 Dwayne Murphy .15 .06
❑ 232 Dave Beard .15 .06
❑ 233 Ed Jurak .15 .06
❑ 234 Jerry Narron .15 .06
❑ 235 Garry Maddox .15 .06
❑ 236 Mark Thurmond .15 .06
❑ 237 Julio Franco .25 .10
❑ 238 Jose Rijo RC .75 .30
❑ 239 Tim Teufel .15 .06
❑ 240 Dave Stieb .25 .10
❑ 241 Jim Frey MG .15 .06
❑ 242 Greg Harris .15 .06
❑ 243 Barbaro Garbey .15 .06
❑ 244 Mike Jones .15 .06
❑ 245 Chili Davis .25 .10
❑ 246 Mike Norris .15 .06
❑ 247 Wayne Tolleson .15 .06
❑ 248 Terry Forster .25 .10
❑ 249 Harold Baines .25 .10
❑ 250 Jesse Orosco .15 .06
❑ 251 Brad Gulden .15 .06
❑ 252 Dan Ford .15 .06
❑ 253 Sid Bream RC .40 .16
❑ 254 Pete Vuckovich .15 .06
❑ 255 Lonnie Smith .15 .06
❑ 256 Mike Stanton .15 .06
❑ 257 Bryan Little UER .15 .06
Name spelled Brian on front
❑ 258 Mike C. Brown .15 .06
❑ 259 Gary Allenson .15 .06
❑ 260 Dave Righetti .25 .10
❑ 261 Checklist: 133-264 .15 .06
❑ 262 Greg Booker .15 .06
❑ 263 Mel Hall .15 .06
❑ 264 Joe Sambito .15 .06
❑ 265 Juan Samuel .15 .06
❑ 266 Frank Viola .25 .10
❑ 267 Henry Cotto RC .15 .06
❑ 268 Chuck Tanner MG .15 .06
❑ 269 Doug Baker .15 .06
❑ 270 Dan Quisenberry .15 .06
❑ 271 Tim Foli FDP .15 .06
❑ 272 Jeff Burroughs FDP .15 .06
❑ 273 Bill Almon FDP .15 .06
❑ 274 F.Bannister FDP76 .15 .06
❑ 275 Harold Baines FDP77 .15 .06
❑ 276 Bob Horner FDP .15 .06
❑ 277 Al Chambers FDP .15 .06
❑ 278 Darryl Strawberry FDP80 .40 .16
❑ 279 Mike Moore FDP .15 .06
❑ 280 S.Dunston FDP82 RC .75 .30
❑ 281 T.Belcher RC FDP83 .40 .16
❑ 282 Shawn Abner FDP RC .15 .06
❑ 283 Fran Mullins .15 .06
❑ 284 Marty Bystrom .15 .06
❑ 285 Dan Driessen .15 .06
❑ 286 Rudy Law .15 .06
❑ 287 Walt Terrell .15 .06
❑ 288 Jeff Kunkel .15 .06
❑ 289 Tom Underwood .15 .06
❑ 290 Cecil Cooper .25 .10
❑ 291 Bob Welch .25 .10
❑ 292 Brad Komminsk .15 .06
❑ 293 Curt Young .15 .06
❑ 294 Tom Nieto .15 .06
❑ 295 Joe Niekro .15 .06
❑ 296 Ricky Nelson .15 .06
❑ 297 Gary Lucas .15 .06
❑ 298 Marty Barrett .15 .06
❑ 299 Andy Hawkins .15 .06
❑ 300 Rod Carew .40 .16
❑ 301 John Montefusco .15 .06
❑ 302 Tim Corcoran .15 .06
❑ 303 Mike Jeffcoat .15 .06
❑ 304 Gary Gaetti .25 .10
❑ 305 Dale Berra .15 .06
❑ 306 Rick Reuschel .25 .10
❑ 307 Sparky Anderson MG .25 .10
❑ 308 John Wathan .15 .06
❑ 309 Mike Witt .15 .06
❑ 310 Manny Trillo .15 .06
❑ 311 Jim Gott .15 .06
❑ 312 Marc Hill .15 .06
❑ 313 Dave Schmidt .15 .06
❑ 314 Ron Oester .15 .06
❑ 315 Doug Sisk .15 .06
❑ 316 John Lowenstein .15 .06
❑ 317 Jack Lazorko .15 .06
❑ 318 Ted Simmons .25 .10
❑ 319 Jeff Jones .15 .06
❑ 320 Dale Murphy .40 .16
❑ 321 Ricky Horton .15 .06
❑ 322 Dave Stapleton .15 .06
❑ 323 Andy McGaffigan .15 .06
❑ 324 Bruce Bochy .15 .06
❑ 325 John Denny .15 .06
❑ 326 Kevin Bass .15 .06
❑ 327 Brook Jacoby .15 .06
❑ 328 Bob Shirley .15 .06
❑ 329 Ron Washington .15 .06
❑ 330 Leon Durham .15 .06
❑ 331 Bill Laskey .15 .06
❑ 332 Brian Harper .15 .06
❑ 333 Willie Hernandez .15 .06
❑ 334 Dick Howser MG .15 .06
❑ 335 Bruce Benedict .15 .06
❑ 336 Rance Mulliniks .15 .06
❑ 337 Billy Sample .15 .06
❑ 338 Britt Burns .15 .06
❑ 339 Danny Heep .15 .06
❑ 340 Robin Yount 1.00 .40
❑ 341 Floyd Rayford .15 .06
❑ 342 Ted Power .15 .06
❑ 343 Bill Russell .25 .10
❑ 344 Dave Henderson .15 .06
❑ 345 Charlie Lea .15 .06
❑ 346 Terry Pendleton RC .75 .30
❑ 347 Rick Langford .15 .06
❑ 348 Bob Boone .25 .10
❑ 349 Domingo Ramos .15 .06
❑ 350 Wade Boggs .60 .24
❑ 351 Juan Agosto .15 .06
❑ 352 Joe Morgan .25 .10
❑ 353 Julio Solano .15 .06
❑ 354 Andre Robertson .15 .06
❑ 355 Bert Blyleven .25 .10
❑ 356 Dave Meier .15 .06
❑ 357 Rich Bordi .15 .06
❑ 358 Tony Pena .15 .06
❑ 359 Pat Sheridan .15 .06
❑ 360 Steve Carlton .25 .10
❑ 361 Alfredo Griffin .15 .06
❑ 362 Craig McMurtry .15 .06
❑ 363 Ron Hodges .15 .06
❑ 364 Richard Dotson .15 .06
❑ 365 Danny Ozark MG .15 .06
❑ 366 Todd Cruz .15 .06
❑ 367 Keefe Cato .15 .06
❑ 368 Dave Bergman .15 .06
❑ 369 R.J. Reynolds .15 .06
❑ 370 Bruce Sutter .25 .10
❑ 371 Mickey Rivers .15 .06
❑ 372 Roy Howell .15 .06
❑ 373 Mike Moore .15 .06
❑ 374 Brian Downing .25 .10
❑ 375 Jeff Reardon .25 .10
❑ 376 Jeff Newman .15 .06
❑ 377 Checklist: 265-396 .15 .06
❑ 378 Alan Wiggins .15 .06
❑ 379 Charles Hudson .15 .06
❑ 380 Ken Griffey .25 .10
❑ 381 Roy Smith .15 .06
❑ 382 Denny Walling .15 .06
❑ 383 Rick Lysander .15 .06
❑ 384 Jody Davis .15 .06
❑ 385 Jose DeLeon .15 .06
❑ 386 Dan Gladden RC .40 .16
❑ 387 Buddy Biancalana .15 .06
❑ 388 Bert Roberge .15 .06
❑ 389 Rod Dedeaux OLY CO .25 .10
❑ 390 Sid Akins OLY RC .15 .06
❑ 391 Flavio Alfaro OLY RC .15 .06
❑ 392 Don August OLY RC .15 .06
❑ 393 S.Bankhead RC OLY .15 .06
❑ 394 Bob Caffrey OLY RC .15 .06
❑ 395 Mike Dunne OLY RC .15 .06
❑ 396 Gary Green OLY RC .15 .06
❑ 397 John Hoover OLY RC .15 .06
❑ 398 Shane Mack RC OLY .40 .16
❑ 399 John Marzano OLY RC .15 .06
❑ 400 O.McDowell RC OLY .40 .16
❑ 401 M.McGwire OLY RC 40.00 16.00
❑ 402 Pat Pacillo OLY RC .15 .06
❑ 403 Cory Snyder OLY RC .75 .30
❑ 404 Billy Swift OLY RC .40 .16
❑ 405 Tom Veryzer .15 .06
❑ 406 Len Whitehouse .15 .06
❑ 407 Bobby Ramos .15 .06
❑ 408 Sid Monge .15 .06
❑ 409 Brad Wellman .15 .06
❑ 410 Bob Horner .25 .10
❑ 411 Bobby Cox MG .25 .10
❑ 412 Bud Black .15 .06
❑ 413 Vance Law .15 .06
❑ 414 Gary Ward .15 .06
❑ 415 Ron Darling UER .25 .10
(No trivia answer)
❑ 416 Wayne Gross .15 .06
❑ 417 John Franco RC .75 .30
❑ 418 Ken Landreaux .15 .06
❑ 419 Mike Caldwell .15 .06
❑ 420 Andre Dawson .25 .10
❑ 421 Dave Rucker .15 .06
❑ 422 Carney Lansford .25 .10
❑ 423 Barry Bonnell .15 .06
❑ 424 Al Nipper .15 .06
❑ 425 Mike Hargrove .15 .06
❑ 426 Vern Ruhle .15 .06

❑	427	Mario Ramirez	.15	.06
❑	428	Larry Andersen	.15	.06
❑	429	Rick Cerone	.15	.06
❑	430	Ron Davis	.15	.06
❑	431	U.L. Washington	.15	.06
❑	432	Thad Bosley	.15	.06
❑	433	Jim Morrison	.15	.06
❑	434	Gene Richards	.15	.06
❑	435	Dan Petry	.15	.06
❑	436	Willie Aikens	.15	.06
❑	437	Al Jones	.15	.06
❑	438	Joe Torre MG	.40	.16
❑	439	Junior Ortiz	.15	.06
❑	440	Fernando Valenzuela	.25	.10
❑	441	Duane Walker	.15	.06
❑	442	Ken Forsch	.15	.06
❑	443	George Wright	.15	.06
❑	444	Tony Phillips	.15	.06
❑	445	Tippy Martinez	.15	.06
❑	446	Jim Sundberg	.25	.10
❑	447	Jeff Lahti	.15	.06
❑	448	Derrel Thomas	.15	.06
❑	449	Phil Bradley	.40	.16
❑	450	Steve Garvey	.25	.10
❑	451	Bruce Hurst	.15	.06
❑	452	John Castino	.15	.06
❑	453	Tom Waddell	.15	.06
❑	454	Glenn Wilson	.15	.06
❑	455	Bob Knepper	.15	.06
❑	456	Tim Foli	.15	.06
❑	457	Cecilio Guante	.15	.06
❑	458	Randy Johnson	.15	.06
❑	459	Charlie Leibrandt	.15	.06
❑	460	Ryne Sandberg	1.25	.50
❑	461	Marty Castillo	.15	.06
❑	462	Gary Lavelle	.15	.06
❑	463	Dave Collins	.15	.06
❑	464	Mike Mason RC	.15	.06
❑	465	Bobby Grich	.25	.10
❑	466	Tony LaRussa MG	.25	.10
❑	467	Ed Lynch	.15	.06
❑	468	Wayne Krenchicki	.15	.06
❑	469	Sammy Stewart	.15	.06
❑	470	Steve Sax	.15	.06
❑	471	Pete Ladd	.15	.06
❑	472	Jim Essian	.15	.06
❑	473	Tim Wallach	.15	.06
❑	474	Kurt Kepshire	.15	.06
❑	475	Andre Thornton	.15	.06
❑	476	Jeff Stone	.15	.06
❑	477	Bob Ojeda	.15	.06
❑	478	Kurt Bevacqua	.15	.06
❑	479	Mike Madden	.15	.06
❑	480	Lou Whitaker	.25	.10
❑	481	Dale Murray	.15	.06
❑	482	Harry Spilman	.15	.06
❑	483	Mike Smithson	.15	.06
❑	484	Larry Bowa	.25	.10
❑	485	Matt Young	.15	.06
❑	486	Steve Balboni	.15	.06
❑	487	Frank Williams	.15	.06
❑	488	Joel Skinner	.15	.06
❑	489	Bryan Clark	.15	.06
❑	490	Jason Thompson	.15	.06
❑	491	Rick Camp	.15	.06
❑	492	Dave Johnson MG	.15	.06
❑	493	Orel Hershiser RC	1.00	.40
❑	494	Rich Dauer	.15	.06
❑	495	Mario Soto	.25	.10
❑	496	Donnie Scott	.15	.06
❑	497	Gary Pettis UER (Photo actually Gary's little brother Lynn)	.15	.06
❑	498	Ed Romero	.15	.06
❑	499	Danny Cox	.15	.06
❑	500	Mike Schmidt	1.50	.60
❑	501	Dan Schatzeder	.15	.06
❑	502	Rick Miller	.15	.06
❑	503	Tim Conroy	.15	.06
❑	504	Jerry Willard	.15	.06
❑	505	Jim Beattie	.15	.06
❑	506	Franklin Stubbs	.15	.06
❑	507	Ray Fontenot	.15	.06
❑	508	John Shelby	.15	.06
❑	509	Milt May	.15	.06
❑	510	Kent Hrbek	.25	.10
❑	511	Lee Smith	.25	.10
❑	512	Tom Brookens	.15	.06
❑	513	Lynn Jones	.15	.06
❑	514	Jeff Cornell	.15	.06
❑	515	Dave Concepcion	.25	.10
❑	516	Roy Lee Jackson	.15	.06
❑	517	Jerry Martin	.15	.06
❑	518	Chris Chambliss	.25	.10
❑	519	Doug Rader MG	.15	.06
❑	520	LaMarr Hoyt	.15	.06
❑	521	Rick Dempsey	.15	.06
❑	522	Paul Molitor	.40	.16
❑	523	Candy Maldonado	.15	.06
❑	524	Rob Wilfong	.15	.06
❑	525	Darrell Porter	.15	.06
❑	526	David Palmer	.15	.06
❑	527	Checklist: 397-528	.15	.06
❑	528	Bill Krueger	.15	.06
❑	529	Rich Gedman	.15	.06
❑	530	Dave Dravecky	.15	.06
❑	531	Joe Lefebvre	.15	.06
❑	532	Frank DiPino	.15	.06
❑	533	Tony Bernazard	.15	.06
❑	534	Brian Dayett	.15	.06
❑	535	Pat Putnam	.15	.06
❑	536	Kirby Puckett RC	5.00	2.00
❑	537	Don Robinson	.15	.06
❑	538	Keith Moreland	.15	.06
❑	539	Aurelio Lopez	.15	.06
❑	540	Claudell Washington	.15	.06
❑	541	Mark Davis	.15	.06
❑	542	Don Slaught	.15	.06
❑	543	Mike Squires	.15	.06
❑	544	Bruce Kison	.15	.06
❑	545	Lloyd Moseby	.15	.06
❑	546	Brent Gaff	.15	.06
❑	547	Pete Rose MG	.40	.16
❑	548	Larry Parrish	.15	.06
❑	549	Mike Scioscia	.25	.10
❑	550	Scott McGregor	.15	.06
❑	551	Andy Van Slyke	.25	.10
❑	552	Chris Codiroli	.15	.06
❑	553	Bob Clark	.15	.06
❑	554	Doug Flynn	.15	.06
❑	555	Bob Stanley	.15	.06
❑	556	Sixto Lezcano	.15	.06
❑	557	Len Barker	.15	.06
❑	558	Carmelo Martinez	.15	.06
❑	559	Jay Howell	.15	.06
❑	560	Bill Madlock	.25	.10
❑	561	Darryl Motley	.15	.06
❑	562	Houston Jimenez	.15	.06
❑	563	Dick Ruthven	.15	.06
❑	564	Alan Ashby	.15	.06
❑	565	Kirk Gibson	.25	.10
❑	566	Ed VandeBerg	.15	.06
❑	567	Joel Youngblood	.15	.06
❑	568	Cliff Johnson	.15	.06
❑	569	Ken Oberkfell	.15	.06
❑	570	Darryl Strawberry	.60	.24
❑	571	Charlie Hough	.25	.10
❑	572	Tom Paciorek	.15	.06
❑	573	Jay Tibbs	.15	.06
❑	574	Joe Altobelli MG	.15	.06
❑	575	Pedro Guerrero	.25	.10
❑	576	Jaime Cocanower	.15	.06
❑	577	Chris Speier	.15	.06
❑	578	Terry Francona	.25	.10
❑	579	Ron Romanick	.15	.06
❑	580	Dwight Evans	.25	.10
❑	581	Mark Wagner	.15	.06
❑	582	Ken Phelps	.15	.06
❑	583	Bobby Brown	.15	.06
❑	584	Kevin Gross	.15	.06
❑	585	Butch Wynegar	.15	.06
❑	586	Bill Scherrer	.15	.06
❑	587	Doug Frobel	.15	.06
❑	588	Bobby Castillo	.15	.06
❑	589	Bob Dernier	.15	.06
❑	590	Ray Knight	.25	.10
❑	591	Larry Herndon	.15	.06
❑	592	Jeff D. Robinson	.15	.06
❑	593	Rick Leach	.15	.06
❑	594	Curt Wilkerson	.15	.06
❑	595	Larry Gura	.15	.06
❑	596	Jerry Hairston	.15	.06
❑	597	Brad Lesley	.15	.06
❑	598	Jose Oquendo	.15	.06
❑	599	Storm Davis	.15	.06
❑	600	Pete Rose	1.50	.60
❑	601	Tom Lasorda MG	.40	.16
❑	602	Jeff Dedmon	.15	.06
❑	603	Rick Manning	.15	.06
❑	604	Daryl Sconiers	.15	.06
❑	605	Ozzie Smith	1.00	.40
❑	606	Rich Gale	.15	.06
❑	607	Bill Almon	.15	.06
❑	608	Craig Lefferts	.15	.06
❑	609	Broderick Perkins	.15	.06
❑	610	Jack Morris	.25	.10
❑	611	Ozzie Virgil	.15	.06
❑	612	Mike Armstrong	.15	.06
❑	613	Terry Puhl	.15	.06
❑	614	Al Williams	.15	.06
❑	615	Marvell Wynne	.15	.06
❑	616	Scott Sanderson	.15	.06
❑	617	Willie Wilson	.25	.10
❑	618	Pete Falcone	.15	.06
❑	619	Jeff Leonard	.15	.06
❑	620	Dwight Gooden RC	1.25	.50
❑	621	Marvis Foley	.15	.06
❑	622	Luis Leal	.15	.06
❑	623	Greg Walker	.15	.06
❑	624	Benny Ayala	.15	.06
❑	625	Mark Langston RC	.75	.30
❑	626	German Rivera	.15	.06
❑	627	Eric Davis RC	1.00	.40
❑	628	Rene Lachemann MG	.15	.06
❑	629	Dick Schofield	.15	.06
❑	630	Tim Raines	.25	.10
❑	631	Bob Forsch	.15	.06
❑	632	Bruce Bochte	.15	.06
❑	633	Glenn Hoffman	.15	.06
❑	634	Bill Dawley	.15	.06
❑	635	Terry Kennedy	.15	.06
❑	636	Shane Rawley	.15	.06
❑	637	Brett Butler	.25	.10
❑	638	Mike Pagliarulo	.15	.06
❑	639	Ed Hodge	.15	.06
❑	640	Steve Henderson	.15	.06
❑	641	Rod Scurry	.15	.06
❑	642	Dave Owen	.15	.06
❑	643	Johnny Grubb	.15	.06
❑	644	Mark Huismann	.15	.06
❑	645	Damaso Garcia	.15	.06
❑	646	Scot Thompson	.15	.06
❑	647	Rafael Ramirez	.15	.06
❑	648	Bob Jones	.15	.06
❑	649	Sid Fernandez	.25	.10
❑	650	Greg Luzinski	.25	.10
❑	651	Jeff Russell	.15	.06
❑	652	Joe Nolan	.15	.06
❑	653	Mark Brouhard	.15	.06
❑	654	Dave Anderson	.15	.06
❑	655	Joaquin Andujar	.25	.10
❑	656	Chuck Cottier MG	.15	.06
❑	657	Jim Slaton	.15	.06
❑	658	Mike Stenhouse	.15	.06
❑	659	Checklist: 529-660	.15	.06
❑	660	Tony Gwynn	1.25	.50
❑	661	Steve Crawford	.15	.06
❑	662	Mike Heath	.15	.06
❑	663	Luis Aguayo	.15	.06
❑	664	Steve Farr RC	.40	.16
❑	665	Don Mattingly	2.50	1.00
❑	666	Mike LaCoss	.15	.06
❑	667	Dave Engle	.15	.06
❑	668	Steve Trout	.15	.06
❑	669	Lee Lacy	.15	.06
❑	670	Tom Seaver	.40	.16
❑	671	Dane Iorg	.15	.06
❑	672	Juan Berenguer	.15	.06
❑	673	Buck Martinez	.15	.06
❑	674	Atlee Hammaker	.15	.06
❑	675	Tony Perez	.40	.16
❑	676	Albert Hall	.15	.06
❑	677	Wally Backman	.15	.06
❑	678	Joey McLaughlin	.15	.06
❑	679	Bob Kearney	.15	.06
❑	680	Jerry Reuss	.15	.06
❑	681	Ben Oglivie	.25	.10

Card	Player	Nm-Mt	Ex-Mt
☐ 682	Doug Corbett	.15	.06
☐ 683	Whitey Herzog MG	.25	.10
☐ 684	Bill Doran	.15	.06
☐ 685	Bill Caudill	.15	.06
☐ 686	Mike Easler	.15	.06
☐ 687	Bill Gullickson	.15	.06
☐ 688	Len Matuszek	.15	.06
☐ 689	Luis DeLeon	.15	.06
☐ 690	Alan Trammell	.25	.10
☐ 691	Dennis Rasmussen	.15	.06
☐ 692	Randy Bush	.15	.06
☐ 693	Tim Stoddard	.15	.06
☐ 694	Joe Carter	.60	.24
☐ 695	Rick Rhoden	.15	.06
☐ 696	John Rabb	.15	.06
☐ 697	Onix Concepcion	.15	.06
☐ 698	Jorge Bell	.25	.10
☐ 699	Donnie Moore	.15	.06
☐ 700	Eddie Murray	.60	.24
☐ 701	Eddie Murray AS	.40	.16
☐ 702	Damaso Garcia AS	.15	.06
☐ 703	George Brett AS	.60	.24
☐ 704	Cal Ripken AS	1.50	.60
☐ 705	Dave Winfield AS	.15	.06
☐ 706	Rickey Henderson AS	.40	.16
☐ 707	Tony Armas AS	.15	.06
☐ 708	Lance Parrish AS	.15	.06
☐ 709	Mike Boddicker AS	.15	.06
☐ 710	Frank Viola AS	.15	.06
☐ 711	Dan Quisenberry AS	.15	.06
☐ 712	Keith Hernandez AS	.15	.06
☐ 713	Ryne Sandberg AS	.60	.24
☐ 714	Mike Schmidt AS	.60	.24
☐ 715	Ozzie Smith AS	.60	.24
☐ 716	Dale Murphy AS	.25	.10
☐ 717	Tony Gwynn AS	1.00	.40
☐ 718	Jeff Leonard AS	.15	.06
☐ 719	Gary Carter AS	.15	.06
☐ 720	Rick Sutcliffe AS	.15	.06
☐ 721	Bob Knepper AS	.15	.06
☐ 722	Bruce Sutter AS	.15	.06
☐ 723	Dave Stewart	.25	.10
☐ 724	Oscar Gamble	.15	.06
☐ 725	Floyd Bannister	.15	.06
☐ 726	Al Bumbry	.15	.06
☐ 727	Frank Pastore	.15	.06
☐ 728	Bob Bailor	.15	.06
☐ 729	Don Sutton	.25	.10
☐ 730	Dave Kingman	.25	.10
☐ 731	Neil Allen	.15	.06
☐ 732	John McNamara MG	.15	.06
☐ 733	Tony Scott	.15	.06
☐ 734	John Henry Johnson	.15	.06
☐ 735	Garry Templeton	.25	.10
☐ 736	Jerry Mumphrey	.15	.06
☐ 737	Bo Diaz	.15	.06
☐ 738	Omar Moreno	.15	.06
☐ 739	Ernie Camacho	.15	.06
☐ 740	Jack Clark	.25	.10
☐ 741	John Butcher	.15	.06
☐ 742	Ron Hassey	.15	.06
☐ 743	Frank White	.25	.10
☐ 744	Doug Bair	.15	.06
☐ 745	Buddy Bell	.25	.10
☐ 746	Jim Clancy	.15	.06
☐ 747	Alex Trevino	.15	.06
☐ 748	Lee Mazzilli	.25	.10
☐ 749	Julio Cruz	.15	.06
☐ 750	Rollie Fingers	.25	.10
☐ 751	Kelvin Chapman	.15	.06
☐ 752	Bob Owchinko	.15	.06
☐ 753	Greg Brock	.15	.06
☐ 754	Larry Milbourne	.15	.06
☐ 755	Ken Singleton	.25	.10
☐ 756	Rob Picciolo	.15	.06
☐ 757	Willie McGee	.25	.10
☐ 758	Ray Burris	.15	.06
☐ 759	Jim Fanning MG	.15	.06
☐ 760	Nolan Ryan	3.00	1.20
☐ 761	Jerry Remy	.15	.06
☐ 762	Eddie Whitson	.15	.06
☐ 763	Kiko Garcia	.15	.06
☐ 764	Jamie Easterly	.15	.06
☐ 765	Willie Randolph	.25	.10
☐ 766	Paul Mirabella	.15	.06
☐ 767	Darrell Brown	.15	.06
☐ 768	Ron Cey	.25	.10
☐ 769	Joe Cowley	.15	.06
☐ 770	Carlton Fisk	.40	.16
☐ 771	Geoff Zahn	.15	.06
☐ 772	Johnnie LeMaster	.15	.06
☐ 773	Hal McRae	.25	.10
☐ 774	Dennis Lamp	.15	.06
☐ 775	Mookie Wilson	.25	.10
☐ 776	Jerry Royster	.15	.06
☐ 777	Ned Yost	.15	.06
☐ 778	Mike Davis	.15	.06
☐ 779	Nick Esasky	.15	.06
☐ 780	Mike Flanagan	.15	.06
☐ 781	Jim Gantner	.15	.06
☐ 782	Tom Niedenfuer	.15	.06
☐ 783	Mike Jorgensen	.15	.06
☐ 784	Checklist: 661-792	.15	.06
☐ 785	Tony Armas	.25	.10
☐ 786	Enos Cabell	.15	.06
☐ 787	Jim Wohlford	.15	.06
☐ 788	Steve Comer	.15	.06
☐ 789	Luis Salazar	.15	.06
☐ 790	Ron Guidry	.25	.10
☐ 791	Ivan DeJesus	.15	.06
☐ 792	Darrell Evans	.25	.10

1986 Topps

VINCE COLEMAN

	Nm-Mt	Ex-Mt
COMPLETE SET (792)	25.00	10.00
COMP.X-MAS.SET (792)	120.00	47.50

Card	Player	Nm-Mt	Ex-Mt
☐ 1	Pete Rose	2.00	.80
☐ 2	Pete Rose 63-66	.25	.10
☐ 3	Pete Rose 67-70	.25	.10
☐ 4	Pete Rose 71-74	.25	.10
☐ 5	Pete Rose 75-78	.25	.10
☐ 6	Pete Rose 79-82	.25	.10
☐ 7	Pete Rose 83-85	.25	.10
☐ 8	Dwayne Murphy	.10	.04
☐ 9	Roy Smith	.10	.04
☐ 10	Tony Gwynn	.60	.24
☐ 11	Bob Ojeda	.10	.04
☐ 12	Jose Uribe	.10	.04
☐ 13	Bob Kearney	.10	.04
☐ 14	Julio Cruz	.10	.04
☐ 15	Eddie Whitson	.10	.04
☐ 16	Rick Schu	.10	.04
☐ 17	Mike Stenhouse	.10	.04
☐ 18	Brent Gaff	.10	.04
☐ 19	Rich Hebner	.10	.04
☐ 20	Lou Whitaker	.15	.06
☐ 21	George Bamberger MG	.10	.04
☐ 22	Duane Walker	.10	.04
☐ 23	Manny Lee RC*	.10	.04
☐ 24	Len Barker	.10	.04
☐ 25	Willie Wilson	.15	.06
☐ 26	Frank DiPino	.10	.04
☐ 27	Ray Knight	.15	.06
☐ 28	Eric Davis	.25	.10
☐ 29	Tony Phillips	.10	.04
☐ 30	Eddie Murray	.40	.16
☐ 31	Jamie Easterly	.10	.04
☐ 32	Steve Yeager	.15	.06
☐ 33	Jeff Lahti	.10	.04
☐ 34	Ken Phelps	.10	.04
☐ 35	Jeff Reardon	.15	.06
☐ 36	Lance Parrish TL	.15	.06
☐ 37	Mark Thurmond	.10	.04
☐ 38	Glenn Hoffman	.10	.04
☐ 39	Dave Rucker	.10	.04
☐ 40	Ken Griffey	.15	.06
☐ 41	Brad Wellman	.10	.04
☐ 42	Geoff Zahn	.10	.04
☐ 43	Dave Engle	.10	.04
☐ 44	Lance McCullers	.10	.04
☐ 45	Damaso Garcia	.10	.04
☐ 46	Billy Hatcher	.10	.04
☐ 47	Juan Berenguer	.10	.04
☐ 48	Bill Almon	.10	.04
☐ 49	Rick Manning	.10	.04
☐ 50	Dan Quisenberry	.10	.04
☐ 51	Bobby Wine MG ERR (Number of card on back is actually 57)	.10	.04
☐ 52	Chris Welsh	.10	.04
☐ 53	Len Dykstra RC	.75	.30
☐ 54	John Franco	.15	.06
☐ 55	Fred Lynn	.15	.06
☐ 56	Tom Niedenfuer	.10	.04
☐ 57	Bill Doran (See also 51)	.10	.04
☐ 58	Bill Krueger	.10	.04
☐ 59	Andre Thornton	.10	.04
☐ 60	Dwight Evans	.15	.06
☐ 61	Karl Best	.10	.04
☐ 62	Bob Boone	.15	.06
☐ 63	Ron Roenicke	.10	.04
☐ 64	Floyd Bannister	.10	.04
☐ 65	Dan Driessen	.10	.04
☐ 66	Bob Forsch TL	.10	.04
☐ 67	Carmelo Martinez	.10	.04
☐ 68	Ed Lynch	.10	.04
☐ 69	Luis Aguayo	.10	.04
☐ 70	Dave Winfield	.15	.06
☐ 71	Ken Schrom	.10	.04
☐ 72	Shawon Dunston	.15	.06
☐ 73	Randy O'Neal	.10	.04
☐ 74	Rance Mulliniks	.10	.04
☐ 75	Jose DeLeon	.10	.04
☐ 76	Dion James	.10	.04
☐ 77	Charlie Leibrandt	.10	.04
☐ 78	Bruce Benedict	.10	.04
☐ 79	Dave Schmidt	.10	.04
☐ 80	Darryl Strawberry	.25	.10
☐ 81	Gene Mauch MG	.10	.04
☐ 82	Tippy Martinez	.10	.04
☐ 83	Phil Garner	.15	.06
☐ 84	Curt Young	.10	.04
☐ 85	Tony Perez (Eric Davis also shown on card)	.15	.06
☐ 86	Tom Waddell	.10	.04
☐ 87	Candy Maldonado	.10	.04
☐ 88	Tom Nieto	.10	.04
☐ 89	Randy St.Claire	.10	.04
☐ 90	Garry Templeton	.15	.06
☐ 91	Steve Crawford	.10	.04
☐ 92	Al Cowens	.10	.04
☐ 93	Scot Thompson	.10	.04
☐ 94	Rich Bordi	.10	.04
☐ 95	Ozzie Virgil	.10	.04
☐ 96	Jim Clancy TL	.10	.04
☐ 97	Gary Gaetti	.15	.06
☐ 98	Dick Ruthven	.10	.04
☐ 99	Buddy Biancalana	.10	.04
☐ 100	Nolan Ryan	2.00	.80
☐ 101	Dave Bergman	.10	.04
☐ 102	Joe Orsulak RC*	.25	.10
☐ 103	Luis Salazar	.10	.04
☐ 104	Sid Fernandez	.10	.04
☐ 105	Gary Ward	.10	.04
☐ 106	Ray Burris	.10	.04
☐ 107	Rafael Ramirez	.10	.04
☐ 108	Ted Power	.10	.04
☐ 109	Len Matuszek	.10	.04
☐ 110	Scott McGregor	.10	.04
☐ 111	Roger Craig MG	.15	.06
☐ 112	Bill Campbell	.10	.04
☐ 113	U.L. Washington	.10	.04
☐ 114	Mike C. Brown	.10	.04
☐ 115	Jay Howell	.10	.04
☐ 116	Brook Jacoby	.10	.04
☐ 117	Bruce Kison	.10	.04

❑ 118 Jerry Royster .10 .04
❑ 119 Barry Bonnell .10 .04
❑ 120 Steve Carlton .15 .06
❑ 121 Nelson Simmons .10 .04
❑ 122 Pete Filson .10 .04
❑ 123 Greg Walker .10 .04
❑ 124 Luis Sanchez .10 .04
❑ 125 Dave Lopes .15 .06
❑ 126 Mookie Wilson TL .10 .04
❑ 127 Jack Howell .10 .04
❑ 128 John Wathan .10 .04
❑ 129 Jeff Dedmon .10 .04
❑ 130 Alan Trammell .15 .06
❑ 131 Checklist: 1-132 .15 .06
❑ 132 Razor Shines .10 .04
❑ 133 Andy McGaffigan .10 .04
❑ 134 Carney Lansford .15 .06
❑ 135 Joe Niekro .10 .04
❑ 136 Mike Hargrove .10 .04
❑ 137 Charlie Moore .10 .04
❑ 138 Mark Davis .10 .04
❑ 139 Daryl Boston .10 .04
❑ 140 John Candelaria .10 .04
❑ 141 Chuck Cottier MG .10 .04
See also 171
❑ 142 Bob Jones .10 .04
❑ 143 Dave Van Gorder .10 .04
❑ 144 Doug Sisk .10 .04
❑ 145 Pedro Guerrero .15 .06
❑ 146 Jack Perconte .10 .04
❑ 147 Larry Sheets .10 .04
❑ 148 Mike Heath .10 .04
❑ 149 Brett Butler .15 .06
❑ 150 Joaquin Andujar .15 .06
❑ 151 Dave Stapleton .10 .04
❑ 152 Mike Morgan .10 .04
❑ 153 Ricky Adams .10 .04
❑ 154 Bert Roberge .10 .04
❑ 155 Bobby Grich .15 .06
❑ 156 Richard Dotson TL .10 .04
❑ 157 Ron Hassey .10 .04
❑ 158 Derrel Thomas .10 .04
❑ 159 Orel Hershiser UER .25 .10
(82 Alburquerque)
❑ 160 Chet Lemon .15 .06
❑ 161 Lee Tunnell .10 .04
❑ 162 Greg Gagne .10 .04
❑ 163 Pete Ladd .10 .04
❑ 164 Steve Balboni .10 .04
❑ 165 Mike Davis .10 .04
❑ 166 Dickie Thon .10 .04
❑ 167 Zane Smith .10 .04
❑ 168 Jeff Burroughs .10 .04
❑ 169 George Wright .10 .04
❑ 170 Gary Carter .15 .06
❑ 171 Bob Rodgers MG ERR .10 .04
(Number of card on
back actually 141)
❑ 172 Jerry Reed .10 .04
❑ 173 Wayne Gross .10 .04
❑ 174 Brian Snyder .10 .04
❑ 175 Steve Sax .10 .04
❑ 176 Jay Tibbs .10 .04
❑ 177 Joel Youngblood .10 .04
❑ 178 Ivan DeJesus .10 .04
❑ 179 Stu Cliburn .10 .04
❑ 180 Don Mattingly 1.25 .50
❑ 181 Al Nipper .10 .04
❑ 182 Bobby Brown .10 .04
❑ 183 Larry Andersen .10 .04
❑ 184 Tim Laudner .10 .04
❑ 185 Rollie Fingers .15 .06
❑ 186 Jose Cruz TL .10 .04
❑ 187 Scott Fletcher .10 .04
❑ 188 Bob Dernier .10 .04
❑ 189 Mike Mason .10 .04
❑ 190 George Hendrick .15 .06
❑ 191 Wally Backman .10 .04
❑ 192 Milt Wilcox .10 .04
❑ 193 Daryl Sconiers .10 .04
❑ 194 Craig McMurtry .10 .04
❑ 195 Dave Concepcion .15 .06
❑ 196 Doyle Alexander .10 .04
❑ 197 Enos Cabell .10 .04
❑ 198 Ken Dixon .10 .04
❑ 199 Dick Howser MG .10 .04
❑ 200 Mike Schmidt 1.00 .40
❑ 201 Vince Coleman RB .15 .06
❑ 202 Dwight Gooden RB .25 .10
❑ 203 Keith Hernandez RB .10 .04
❑ 204 Phil Niekro RB .15 .06
❑ 205 Tony Perez RB .15 .06
❑ 206 Pete Rose RB .40 .16
❑ 207 F. Valenzuela RB .10 .04
❑ 208 Ramon Romero .10 .04
❑ 209 Randy Ready .10 .04
❑ 210 Calvin Schiraldi .10 .04
❑ 211 Ed Wojna .10 .04
❑ 212 Chris Speier .10 .04
❑ 213 Bob Shirley .10 .04
❑ 214 Randy Bush .10 .04
❑ 215 Frank White .15 .06
❑ 216 Dwayne Murphy TL .10 .04
❑ 217 Bill Scherrer .10 .04
❑ 218 Randy Hunt .10 .04
❑ 219 Dennis Lamp .10 .04
❑ 220 Bob Horner .15 .06
❑ 221 Dave Henderson .10 .04
❑ 222 Craig Gerber .10 .04
❑ 223 Atlee Hammaker .10 .04
❑ 224 Cesar Cedeno .15 .06
❑ 225 Ron Darling .15 .06
❑ 226 Lee Lacy .10 .04
❑ 227 Al Jones .10 .04
❑ 228 Tom Lawless .10 .04
❑ 229 Bill Gullickson .10 .04
❑ 230 Terry Kennedy .10 .04
❑ 231 Jim Frey MG .10 .04
❑ 232 Rick Rhoden .10 .04
❑ 233 Steve Lyons .10 .04
❑ 234 Doug Corbett .10 .04
❑ 235 Butch Wynegar .10 .04
❑ 236 Frank Eufemia .10 .04
❑ 237 Ted Simmons .15 .06
❑ 238 Larry Parrish .10 .04
❑ 239 Joel Skinner .10 .04
❑ 240 Tommy John .15 .06
❑ 241 Tony Fernandez .10 .04
❑ 242 Rich Thompson .10 .04
❑ 243 Johnny Grubb .10 .04
❑ 244 Craig Lefferts .10 .04
❑ 245 Jim Sundberg .15 .06
❑ 246 Steve Carlton TL .10 .04
❑ 247 Terry Harper .10 .04
❑ 248 Spike Owen .10 .04
❑ 249 Rob Deer .10 .04
❑ 250 Dwight Gooden .40 .16
❑ 251 Rich Dauer .10 .04
❑ 252 Bobby Castillo .10 .04
❑ 253 Dann Bilardello .10 .04
❑ 254 Ozzie Guillen RC* .25 .10
❑ 255 Tony Armas .15 .06
❑ 256 Kurt Kepshire .10 .04
❑ 257 Doug DeCinces .10 .04
❑ 258 Tim Burke .10 .04
❑ 259 Dan Pasqua .10 .04
❑ 260 Tony Pena .10 .04
❑ 261 Bobby Valentine MG .15 .06
❑ 262 Mario Ramirez .10 .04
❑ 263 Checklist: 133-264 .15 .06
❑ 264 Darren Daulton RC .50 .20
❑ 265 Ron Davis .10 .04
❑ 266 Keith Moreland .10 .04
❑ 267 Paul Molitor .25 .10
❑ 268 Mike Scott .15 .06
❑ 269 Dane Iorg .10 .04
❑ 270 Jack Morris .15 .06
❑ 271 Dave Collins .10 .04
❑ 272 Tim Tolman .10 .04
❑ 273 Jerry Willard .10 .04
❑ 274 Ron Gardenhire .10 .04
❑ 275 Charlie Hough .15 .06
❑ 276 Willie Randolph TL .15 .06
❑ 277 Jaime Cocanower .10 .04
❑ 278 Sixto Lezcano .10 .04
❑ 279 Al Pardo .10 .04
❑ 280 Tim Raines .15 .06
❑ 281 Steve Mura .10 .04
❑ 282 Jerry Mumphrey .10 .04
❑ 283 Mike Fischlin .10 .04
❑ 284 Brian Dayett .10 .04
❑ 285 Buddy Bell .15 .06
❑ 286 Luis DeLeon .10 .04
❑ 287 John Christensen .10 .04
❑ 288 Don Aase .10 .04
❑ 289 Johnnie LeMaster .10 .04
❑ 290 Carlton Fisk .25 .10
❑ 291 Tom Lasorda MG .25 .10
❑ 292 Chuck Porter .10 .04
❑ 293 Chris Chambliss .15 .06
❑ 294 Danny Cox .10 .04
❑ 295 Kirk Gibson .15 .06
❑ 296 Geno Petralli .10 .04
❑ 297 Tim Lollar .10 .04
❑ 298 Craig Reynolds .10 .04
❑ 299 Bryn Smith .10 .04
❑ 300 George Brett 1.00 .40
❑ 301 Dennis Rasmussen .10 .04
❑ 302 Greg Gross .10 .04
❑ 303 Curt Wardle .10 .04
❑ 304 Mike Gallego RC .10 .04
❑ 305 Phil Bradley .10 .04
❑ 306 Terry Kennedy TL .10 .04
❑ 307 Dave Sax .10 .04
❑ 308 Ray Fontenot .10 .04
❑ 309 John Shelby .10 .04
❑ 310 Greg Minton .10 .04
❑ 311 Dick Schofield .10 .04
❑ 312 Tom Filer .10 .04
❑ 313 Joe DeSa .10 .04
❑ 314 Frank Pastore .10 .04
❑ 315 Mookie Wilson .15 .06
❑ 316 Sammy Khalifa .10 .04
❑ 317 Ed Romero .10 .04
❑ 318 Terry Whitfield .10 .04
❑ 319 Rick Camp .10 .04
❑ 320 Jim Rice .15 .06
❑ 321 Earl Weaver MG .15 .06
❑ 322 Bob Forsch .10 .04
❑ 323 Jerry Davis .10 .04
❑ 324 Dan Schatzeder .10 .04
❑ 325 Juan Beniquez .10 .04
❑ 326 Kent Tekulve .10 .04
❑ 327 Mike Pagliarulo .10 .04
❑ 328 Pete O'Brien .10 .04
❑ 329 Kirby Puckett .75 .30
❑ 330 Rick Sutcliffe .15 .06
❑ 331 Alan Ashby .10 .04
❑ 332 Darryl Motley .10 .04
❑ 333 Tom Henke .15 .06
❑ 334 Ken Oberkfell .10 .04
❑ 335 Don Sutton .15 .06
❑ 336 Andre Thornton TL .15 .06
❑ 337 Darnell Coles .10 .04
❑ 338 Jorge Bell .15 .06
❑ 339 Bruce Berenyi .10 .04
❑ 340 Cal Ripken 1.50 .60
❑ 341 Frank Williams .10 .04
❑ 342 Gary Redus .10 .04
❑ 343 Carlos Diaz .10 .04
❑ 344 Jim Wohlford .10 .04
❑ 345 Donnie Moore .10 .04
❑ 346 Bryan Little .10 .04
❑ 347 Teddy Higuera RC* .25 .10
❑ 348 Cliff Johnson .10 .04
❑ 349 Mark Clear .10 .04
❑ 350 Jack Clark .15 .06
❑ 351 Chuck Tanner MG .10 .04
❑ 352 Harry Spilman .10 .04
❑ 353 Keith Atherton .10 .04
❑ 354 Tony Bernazard .10 .04
❑ 355 Lee Smith .15 .06
❑ 356 Mickey Hatcher .10 .04
❑ 357 Ed VandeBerg .10 .04
❑ 358 Rick Dempsey .10 .04
❑ 359 Mike LaCoss .10 .04
❑ 360 Lloyd Moseby .10 .04
❑ 361 Shane Rawley .10 .04
❑ 362 Tom Paciorek .10 .04
❑ 363 Terry Forster .15 .06
❑ 364 Reid Nichols .10 .04
❑ 365 Mike Flanagan .10 .04
❑ 366 Dave Concepcion TL .15 .06
❑ 367 Aurelio Lopez .10 .04
❑ 368 Greg Brock .10 .04
❑ 369 Al Holland .10 .04
❑ 370 Vince Coleman RC* .50 .20
❑ 371 Bill Stein .10 .04

❑ 372	Ben Oglivie	.15	.06
❑ 373	Urbano Lugo	.10	.04
❑ 374	Terry Francona	.15	.06
❑ 375	Rich Gedman	.10	.04
❑ 376	Bill Dawley	.10	.04
❑ 377	Joe Carter	.15	.06
❑ 378	Bruce Bochte	.10	.04
❑ 379	Bobby Meacham	.10	.04
❑ 380	LaMarr Hoyt	.10	.04
❑ 381	Ray Miller MG	.10	.04
❑ 382	Ivan Calderon RC*	.25	.10
❑ 383	Chris Brown	.10	.04
❑ 384	Steve Trout	.10	.04
❑ 385	Cecil Cooper	.15	.06
❑ 386	Cecil Fielder RC	.75	.30
❑ 387	Steve Kemp	.10	.04
❑ 388	Dickie Noles	.10	.04
❑ 389	Glenn Davis	.10	.04
❑ 390	Tom Seaver	.25	.10
❑ 391	Julio Franco	.15	.06
❑ 392	John Russell	.10	.04
❑ 393	Chris Pittaro	.10	.04
❑ 394	Checklist: 265-396	.15	.06
❑ 395	Scott Garrelts	.10	.04
❑ 396	Dwight Evans TL	.15	.06
❑ 397	Steve Buechele RC	.25	.10
❑ 398	Earnie Riles	.10	.04
❑ 399	Bill Swift	.10	.04
❑ 400	Rod Carew	.25	.10
❑ 401	Fernando Valenzuela TBC '81	.10	.04
❑ 402	Tom Seaver TBC '76	.15	.06
❑ 403	Willie Mays TBC '71	.40	.16
❑ 404	Frank Robinson TBC '66	.15	.06
❑ 405	Roger Maris TBC '61	.40	.16
❑ 406	Scott Sanderson	.10	.04
❑ 407	Sal Butera	.10	.04
❑ 408	Dave Smith	.10	.04
❑ 409	Paul Runge RC	.10	.04
❑ 410	Dave Kingman	.15	.06
❑ 411	Sparky Anderson MG	.15	.06
❑ 412	Jim Clancy	.10	.04
❑ 413	Tim Flannery	.10	.04
❑ 414	Tom Gorman	.10	.04
❑ 415	Hal McRae	.15	.06
❑ 416	Dennis Martinez	.15	.06
❑ 417	R.J. Reynolds	.10	.04
❑ 418	Alan Knicely	.10	.04
❑ 419	Frank Wills	.10	.04
❑ 420	Von Hayes	.10	.04
❑ 421	David Palmer	.10	.04
❑ 422	Mike Jorgensen	.10	.04
❑ 423	Dan Spillner	.10	.04
❑ 424	Rick Miller	.10	.04
❑ 425	Larry McWilliams	.10	.04
❑ 426	Charlie Moore TL	.10	.04
❑ 427	Joe Cowley	.10	.04
❑ 428	Max Venable	.10	.04
❑ 429	Greg Booker	.10	.04
❑ 430	Kent Hrbek	.15	.06
❑ 431	George Frazier	.10	.04
❑ 432	Mark Bailey	.10	.04
❑ 433	Chris Codiroli	.10	.04
❑ 434	Curt Wilkerson	.10	.04
❑ 435	Bill Caudill	.10	.04
❑ 436	Doug Flynn	.10	.04
❑ 437	Rick Mahler	.10	.04
❑ 438	Clint Hurdle	.10	.04
❑ 439	Rick Honeycutt	.10	.04
❑ 440	Alvin Davis	.10	.04
❑ 441	Whitey Herzog MG	.25	.10
❑ 442	Ron Robinson	.10	.04
❑ 443	Bill Buckner	.15	.06
❑ 444	Alex Trevino	.10	.04
❑ 445	Bert Blyleven	.15	.06
❑ 446	Lenn Sakata	.10	.04
❑ 447	Jerry Don Gleaton	.10	.04
❑ 448	Herm Winningham	.10	.04
❑ 449	Rod Scurry	.10	.04
❑ 450	Graig Nettles	.15	.06
❑ 451	Mark Brown	.10	.04
❑ 452	Bob Clark	.10	.04
❑ 453	Steve Jeltz	.10	.04
❑ 454	Burt Hooton	.10	.04
❑ 455	Willie Randolph	.15	.06
❑ 456	Dale Murphy TL	.25	.10
❑ 457	Mickey Tettleton RC	.25	.10
❑ 458	Kevin Bass	.10	.04
❑ 459	Luis Leal	.10	.04
❑ 460	Leon Durham	.10	.04
❑ 461	Walt Terrell	.10	.04
❑ 462	Domingo Ramos	.10	.04
❑ 463	Jim Gott	.10	.04
❑ 464	Ruppert Jones	.10	.04
❑ 465	Jesse Orosco	.10	.04
❑ 466	Tom Foley	.10	.04
❑ 467	Bob James	.10	.04
❑ 468	Mike Scioscia	.15	.06
❑ 469	Storm Davis	.10	.04
❑ 470	Bill Madlock	.15	.06
❑ 471	Bobby Cox MG	.15	.06
❑ 472	Joe Hesketh	.10	.04
❑ 473	Mark Brouhard	.10	.04
❑ 474	John Tudor	.15	.06
❑ 475	Juan Samuel	.10	.04
❑ 476	Ron Mathis	.10	.04
❑ 477	Mike Easler	.10	.04
❑ 478	Andy Hawkins	.10	.04
❑ 479	Bob Melvin	.10	.04
❑ 480	Oddibe McDowell	.10	.04
❑ 481	Scott Bradley	.10	.04
❑ 482	Rick Lysander	.10	.04
❑ 483	George Vukovich	.10	.04
❑ 484	Donnie Hill	.10	.04
❑ 485	Gary Matthews	.15	.06
❑ 486	Bobby Grich TL	.10	.04
❑ 487	Bret Saberhagen	.15	.06
❑ 488	Lou Thornton	.10	.04
❑ 489	Jim Winn	.10	.04
❑ 490	Jeff Leonard	.10	.04
❑ 491	Pascual Perez	.10	.04
❑ 492	Kelvin Chapman	.10	.04
❑ 493	Gene Nelson	.10	.04
❑ 494	Gary Roenicke	.10	.04
❑ 495	Mark Langston	.15	.06
❑ 496	Jay Johnstone	.10	.04
❑ 497	John Stuper	.10	.04
❑ 498	Tito Landrum	.10	.04
❑ 499	Bob L. Gibson	.10	.04
❑ 500	Rickey Henderson	.40	.16
❑ 501	Dave Johnson MG	.10	.04
❑ 502	Glen Cook	.10	.04
❑ 503	Mike Fitzgerald	.10	.04
❑ 504	Denny Walling	.10	.04
❑ 505	Jerry Koosman	.15	.06
❑ 506	Bill Russell	.15	.06
❑ 507	Steve Ontiveros RC	.10	.04
❑ 508	Alan Wiggins	.10	.04
❑ 509	Ernie Camacho	.10	.04
❑ 510	Wade Boggs	.25	.10
❑ 511	Ed Nunez	.10	.04
❑ 512	Thad Bosley	.10	.04
❑ 513	Ron Washington	.10	.04
❑ 514	Mike Jones	.10	.04
❑ 515	Darrell Evans	.15	.06
❑ 516	Greg Minton TL	.10	.04
❑ 517	Milt Thompson RC	.25	.10
❑ 518	Buck Martinez	.10	.04
❑ 519	Danny Darwin	.10	.04
❑ 520	Keith Hernandez	.15	.06
❑ 521	Nate Snell	.10	.04
❑ 522	Bob Bailor	.10	.04
❑ 523	Joe Price	.10	.04
❑ 524	Darrell Miller	.10	.04
❑ 525	Marvell Wynne	.10	.04
❑ 526	Charlie Lea	.10	.04
❑ 527	Checklist: 397-528	.15	.06
❑ 528	Terry Pendleton	.15	.06
❑ 529	Marc Sullivan	.10	.04
❑ 530	Rich Gossage	.15	.06
❑ 531	Tony LaRussa MG	.15	.06
❑ 532	Don Carman	.10	.04
❑ 533	Billy Sample	.10	.04
❑ 534	Jeff Calhoun	.10	.04
❑ 535	Toby Harrah	.15	.06
❑ 536	Jose Rijo	.15	.06
❑ 537	Mark Salas	.10	.04
❑ 538	Dennis Eckersley	.25	.10
❑ 539	Glenn Hubbard	.10	.04
❑ 540	Dan Petry	.10	.04
❑ 541	Jorge Orta	.10	.04
❑ 542	Don Schulze	.10	.04
❑ 543	Jerry Narron	.10	.04
❑ 544	Eddie Milner	.10	.04
❑ 545	Jimmy Key	.15	.06
❑ 546	Dave Henderson TL	.10	.04
❑ 547	Roger McDowell RC*	.25	.10
❑ 548	Mike Young	.10	.04
❑ 549	Bob Welch	.15	.06
❑ 550	Tom Herr	.10	.04
❑ 551	Dave LaPoint	.10	.04
❑ 552	Marc Hill	.10	.04
❑ 553	Jim Morrison	.10	.04
❑ 554	Paul Householder	.10	.04
❑ 555	Hubie Brooks	.10	.04
❑ 556	John Denny	.10	.04
❑ 557	Gerald Perry	.10	.04
❑ 558	Tim Stoddard	.10	.04
❑ 559	Tommy Dunbar	.10	.04
❑ 560	Dave Righetti	.15	.06
❑ 561	Bob Lillis MG	.10	.04
❑ 562	Joe Beckwith	.10	.04
❑ 563	Alejandro Sanchez	.10	.04
❑ 564	Warren Brusstar	.10	.04
❑ 565	Tom Brunansky	.10	.04
❑ 566	Alfredo Griffin	.10	.04
❑ 567	Jeff Barkley	.10	.04
❑ 568	Donnie Scott	.10	.04
❑ 569	Jim Acker	.10	.04
❑ 570	Rusty Staub	.15	.06
❑ 571	Mike Jeffcoat	.10	.04
❑ 572	Paul Zuvella	.10	.04
❑ 573	Tom Hume	.10	.04
❑ 574	Ron Kittle	.10	.04
❑ 575	Mike Boddicker	.10	.04
❑ 576	Andre Dawson TL	.10	.04
❑ 577	Jerry Reuss	.10	.04
❑ 578	Lee Mazzilli	.15	.06
❑ 579	Jim Slaton	.10	.04
❑ 580	Willie McGee	.15	.06
❑ 581	Bruce Hurst	.10	.04
❑ 582	Jim Gantner	.10	.04
❑ 583	Al Bumbry	.10	.04
❑ 584	Brian Fisher RC	.10	.04
❑ 585	Garry Maddox	.10	.04
❑ 586	Greg Harris	.10	.04
❑ 587	Rafael Santana	.10	.04
❑ 588	Steve Lake	.10	.04
❑ 589	Sid Bream	.10	.04
❑ 590	Bob Knepper	.10	.04
❑ 591	Jackie Moore MG	.10	.04
❑ 592	Frank Tanana	.15	.06
❑ 593	Jesse Barfield	.15	.06
❑ 594	Chris Bando	.10	.04
❑ 595	Dave Parker	.15	.06
❑ 596	Onix Concepcion	.10	.04
❑ 597	Sammy Stewart	.10	.04
❑ 598	Jim Presley	.10	.04
❑ 599	Rick Aguilera RC	.25	.10
❑ 600	Dale Murphy	.25	.10
❑ 601	Gary Lucas	.10	.04
❑ 602	Mariano Duncan RC*	.25	.10
❑ 603	Bill Laskey	.10	.04
❑ 604	Gary Pettis	.10	.04
❑ 605	Dennis Boyd	.10	.04
❑ 606	Hal McRae TL	.15	.06
❑ 607	Ken Dayley	.10	.04
❑ 608	Bruce Bochy	.10	.04
❑ 609	Barbaro Garbey	.10	.04
❑ 610	Ron Guidry	.15	.06
❑ 611	Gary Woods	.10	.04
❑ 612	Richard Dotson	.10	.04
❑ 613	Roy Smalley	.10	.04
❑ 614	Rick Waits	.10	.04
❑ 615	Johnny Ray	.10	.04
❑ 616	Glenn Brummer	.10	.04
❑ 617	Lonnie Smith	.10	.04
❑ 618	Jim Pankovits	.10	.04
❑ 619	Danny Heep	.10	.04
❑ 620	Bruce Sutter	.15	.06
❑ 621	John Felske MG	.10	.04
❑ 622	Gary Lavelle	.10	.04
❑ 623	Floyd Rayford	.10	.04
❑ 624	Steve McCatty	.10	.04
❑ 625	Bob Brenly	.10	.04
❑ 626	Roy Thomas	.10	.04
❑ 627	Ron Oester	.10	.04

❑ 628 Kirk McCaskill RC	.25	.10
❑ 629 Mitch Webster	.10	.04
❑ 630 Fernando Valenzuela	.15	.06
❑ 631 Steve Braun	.10	.04
❑ 632 Dave Von Ohlen	.10	.04
❑ 633 Jackie Gutierrez	.10	.04
❑ 634 Roy Lee Jackson	.10	.04
❑ 635 Jason Thompson	.10	.04
❑ 636 Lee Smith TL	.10	.04
❑ 637 Rudy Law	.10	.04
❑ 638 John Butcher	.10	.04
❑ 639 Bo Diaz	.10	.04
❑ 640 Jose Cruz	.15	.06
❑ 641 Wayne Tolleson	.10	.04
❑ 642 Ray Searage	.10	.04
❑ 643 Tom Brookens	.10	.04
❑ 644 Mark Gubicza	.10	.04
❑ 645 Dusty Baker	.15	.06
❑ 646 Mike Moore	.10	.04
❑ 647 Mel Hall	.10	.04
❑ 648 Steve Bedrosian	.10	.04
❑ 649 Ronn Reynolds	.10	.04
❑ 650 Dave Stieb	.15	.06
❑ 651 Billy Martin MG	.25	.10
❑ 652 Tom Browning	.10	.04
❑ 653 Jim Dwyer	.10	.04
❑ 654 Ken Howell	.10	.04
❑ 655 Manny Trillo	.10	.04
❑ 656 Brian Harper	.10	.04
❑ 657 Juan Agosto	.10	.04
❑ 658 Rob Wilfong	.10	.04
❑ 659 Checklist: 529-660	.15	.06
❑ 660 Steve Garvey	.15	.06
❑ 661 Roger Clemens	1.50	.60
❑ 662 Bill Schroeder	.10	.04
❑ 663 Neil Allen	.10	.04
❑ 664 Tim Corcoran	.10	.04
❑ 665 Alejandro Pena	.10	.04
❑ 666 Charlie Hough TL	.15	.06
❑ 667 Tim Teufel	.10	.04
❑ 668 Cecilio Guante	.10	.04
❑ 669 Ron Cey	.15	.06
❑ 670 Willie Hernandez	.10	.04
❑ 671 Lynn Jones	.10	.04
❑ 672 Rob Picciolo	.10	.04
❑ 673 Ernie Whitt	.10	.04
❑ 674 Pat Tabler	.10	.04
❑ 675 Claudell Washington	.10	.04
❑ 676 Matt Young	.10	.04
❑ 677 Nick Esasky	.10	.04
❑ 678 Dan Gladden	.10	.04
❑ 679 Britt Burns	.10	.04
❑ 680 George Foster	.15	.06
❑ 681 Dick Williams MG	.10	.04
❑ 682 Junior Ortiz	.10	.04
❑ 683 Andy Van Slyke	.15	.06
❑ 684 Bob McClure	.10	.04
❑ 685 Tim Wallach	.10	.04
❑ 686 Jeff Stone	.10	.04
❑ 687 Mike Trujillo	.10	.04
❑ 688 Larry Herndon	.10	.04
❑ 689 Dave Stewart	.15	.06
❑ 690 Ryne Sandberg UER (No Topps logo on front)	.75	.30
❑ 691 Mike Madden	.10	.04
❑ 692 Dale Berra	.10	.04
❑ 693 Tom Tellmann	.10	.04
❑ 694 Garth Iorg	.10	.04
❑ 695 Mike Smithson	.10	.04
❑ 696 Bill Russell TL	.15	.06
❑ 697 Bud Black	.10	.04
❑ 698 Brad Komminsk	.10	.04
❑ 699 Pat Corrales MG	.10	.04
❑ 700 Reggie Jackson	.25	.10
❑ 701 Keith Hernandez AS	.10	.04
❑ 702 Tom Herr AS	.10	.04
❑ 703 Tim Wallach AS	.10	.04
❑ 704 Ozzie Smith AS	.40	.16
❑ 705 Dale Murphy AS	.15	.06
❑ 706 Pedro Guerrero AS	.10	.04
❑ 707 Willie McGee AS	.10	.04
❑ 708 Gary Carter AS	.10	.04
❑ 709 Dwight Gooden AS	.25	.10
❑ 710 John Tudor AS	.10	.04
❑ 711 Jeff Reardon AS	.10	.04
❑ 712 Don Mattingly AS	.60	.24
❑ 713 Damaso Garcia AS	.10	.04
❑ 714 George Brett AS	.40	.16
❑ 715 Cal Ripken AS	.40	.16
❑ 716 Rickey Henderson AS	.25	.10
❑ 717 Dave Winfield AS	.10	.04
❑ 718 George Bell AS	.10	.04
❑ 719 Carlton Fisk AS	.15	.06
❑ 720 Bret Saberhagen AS	.10	.04
❑ 721 Ron Guidry AS	.10	.04
❑ 722 Dan Quisenberry AS	.10	.04
❑ 723 Marty Bystrom	.10	.04
❑ 724 Tim Hulett	.10	.04
❑ 725 Mario Soto	.15	.06
❑ 726 Rick Dempsey TL	.15	.06
❑ 727 David Green	.10	.04
❑ 728 Mike Marshall	.10	.04
❑ 729 Jim Beattie	.10	.04
❑ 730 Ozzie Smith	.60	.24
❑ 731 Don Robinson	.10	.04
❑ 732 Floyd Youmans	.10	.04
❑ 733 Ron Romanick	.10	.04
❑ 734 Marty Barrett	.10	.04
❑ 735 Dave Dravecky	.10	.04
❑ 736 Glenn Wilson	.10	.04
❑ 737 Pete Vuckovich	.10	.04
❑ 738 Andre Robertson	.10	.04
❑ 739 Dave Rozema	.10	.04
❑ 740 Lance Parrish	.15	.06
❑ 741 Pete Rose MG	.40	.16
❑ 742 Frank Viola	.15	.06
❑ 743 Pat Sheridan	.10	.04
❑ 744 Lary Sorensen	.10	.04
❑ 745 Willie Upshaw	.10	.04
❑ 746 Denny Gonzalez	.10	.04
❑ 747 Rick Cerone	.10	.04
❑ 748 Steve Henderson	.10	.04
❑ 749 Ed Jurak	.10	.04
❑ 750 Gorman Thomas	.15	.06
❑ 751 Howard Johnson	.15	.06
❑ 752 Mike Krukow	.10	.04
❑ 753 Dan Ford	.10	.04
❑ 754 Pat Clements	.10	.04
❑ 755 Harold Baines	.15	.06
❑ 756 Rick Rhoden TL	.10	.04
❑ 757 Darrell Porter	.10	.04
❑ 758 Dave Anderson	.10	.04
❑ 759 Moose Haas	.10	.04
❑ 760 Andre Dawson	.15	.06
❑ 761 Don Slaught	.10	.04
❑ 762 Eric Show	.10	.04
❑ 763 Terry Puhl	.10	.04
❑ 764 Kevin Gross	.10	.04
❑ 765 Don Baylor	.15	.06
❑ 766 Rick Langford	.10	.04
❑ 767 Jody Davis	.10	.04
❑ 768 Vern Ruhle	.10	.04
❑ 769 Harold Reynolds RC	.75	.30
❑ 770 Vida Blue	.15	.06
❑ 771 John McNamara MG	.10	.04
❑ 772 Brian Downing	.15	.06
❑ 773 Greg Pryor	.10	.04
❑ 774 Terry Leach	.10	.04
❑ 775 Al Oliver	.15	.06
❑ 776 Gene Garber	.10	.04
❑ 777 Wayne Krenchicki	.10	.04
❑ 778 Jerry Hairston	.10	.04
❑ 779 Rick Reuschel	.15	.06
❑ 780 Robin Yount	.60	.24
❑ 781 Joe Nolan	.10	.04
❑ 782 Ken Landreaux	.10	.04
❑ 783 Ricky Horton	.10	.04
❑ 784 Alan Bannister	.10	.04
❑ 785 Bob Stanley	.10	.04
❑ 786 Mickey Hatcher TL	.10	.04
❑ 787 Vance Law	.10	.04
❑ 788 Marty Castillo	.10	.04
❑ 789 Kurt Bevacqua	.10	.04
❑ 790 Phil Niekro	.15	.06
❑ 791 Checklist: 661-792	.15	.06
❑ 792 Charles Hudson	.10	.04

1986 Topps Traded

	Nm-Mt	Ex-Mt
COMP.FACT.SET (132)	50.00	20.00
❑ 1T Andy Allanson	.10	.04
❑ 2T Neil Allen	.10	.04
❑ 3T Joaquin Andujar	.15	.06
❑ 4T Paul Assenmacher	.25	.10
❑ 5T Scott Bailes	.10	.04

	Nm-Mt	Ex-Mt
❑ 6T Don Baylor	.15	.06
❑ 7T Steve Bedrosian	.10	.04
❑ 8T Juan Beniquez	.10	.04
❑ 9T Juan Berenguer	.10	.04
❑ 10T Mike Bielecki	.10	.04
❑ 11T Barry Bonds XRC	40.00	16.00
❑ 12T Bobby Bonilla XRC	.50	.20
❑ 13T Juan Bonilla	.10	.04
❑ 14T Rich Bordi	.10	.04
❑ 15T Steve Boros MG	.10	.04
❑ 16T Rick Burleson	.10	.04
❑ 17T Bill Campbell	.10	.04
❑ 18T Tom Candiotti	.10	.04
❑ 19T John Cangelosi	.10	.04
❑ 20T Jose Canseco XRC	1.50	.60
❑ 21T Carmen Castillo	.10	.04
❑ 22T Rick Cerone	.10	.04
❑ 23T John Cerutti	.10	.04
❑ 24T Will Clark XRC	1.50	.60
❑ 25T Mark Clear	.10	.04
❑ 26T Darnell Coles	.10	.04
❑ 27T Dave Collins	.10	.04
❑ 28T Tim Conroy	.10	.04
❑ 29T Joe Cowley	.10	.04
❑ 30T Joel Davis	.10	.04
❑ 31T Rob Deer	.10	.04
❑ 32T John Denny	.10	.04
❑ 33T Mike Easler	.10	.04
❑ 34T Mark Eichhorn	.10	.04
❑ 35T Steve Farr	.10	.04
❑ 36T Scott Fletcher	.10	.04
❑ 37T Terry Forster	.15	.06
❑ 38T Terry Francona	.15	.06
❑ 39T Jim Fregosi MG	.10	.04
❑ 40T Andres Galarraga XRC	.75	.30
❑ 41T Ken Griffey	.15	.06
❑ 42T Bill Gullickson	.10	.04
❑ 43T Jose Guzman XRC *	.10	.04
❑ 44T Moose Haas	.10	.04
❑ 45T Billy Hatcher	.10	.04
❑ 46T Mike Heath	.10	.04
❑ 47T Tom Hume	.10	.04
❑ 48T Pete Incaviglia XRC	.25	.10
❑ 49T Dane Iorg	.10	.04
❑ 50T Bo Jackson XRC	1.50	.60
❑ 51T Wally Joyner XRC	.50	.20
❑ 52T Charlie Kerfeld	.10	.04
❑ 53T Eric King	.10	.04
❑ 54T Bob Kipper	.10	.04
❑ 55T Wayne Krenchicki	.10	.04
❑ 56T John Kruk XRC	.75	.30
❑ 57T Mike LaCoss	.10	.04
❑ 58T Pete Ladd	.10	.04
❑ 59T Mike Laga	.10	.04
❑ 60T Hal Lanier MG	.10	.04
❑ 61T Dave LaPoint	.10	.04
❑ 62T Rudy Law	.10	.04
❑ 63T Rick Leach	.10	.04
❑ 64T Tim Leary	.10	.04
❑ 65T Dennis Leonard	.10	.04
❑ 66T Jim Leyland MG XRC	.25	.10
❑ 67T Steve Lyons	.10	.04
❑ 68T Mickey Mahler	.10	.04
❑ 69T Candy Maldonado	.10	.04
❑ 70T Roger Mason XRC *	.10	.04
❑ 71T Bob McClure	.10	.04
❑ 72T Andy McGaffigan	.10	.04
❑ 73T Gene Michael MG	.10	.04

❑ 74T Kevin Mitchell XRC .50 .20
❑ 75T Omar Moreno .10 .04
❑ 76T Jerry Mumphrey .10 .04
❑ 77T Phil Niekro .15 .06
❑ 78T Randy Niemann .10 .04
❑ 79T Juan Nieves .10 .04
❑ 80T Otis Nixon XRC* .25 .10
❑ 81T Bob Ojeda .10 .04
❑ 82T Jose Oquendo .10 .04
❑ 83T Tom Paciorek .10 .04
❑ 84T David Palmer .10 .04
❑ 85T Frank Pastore .10 .04
❑ 86T Lou Piniella MG .15 .06
❑ 87T Dan Plesac .25 .10
❑ 88T Darrell Porter .10 .04
❑ 89T Rey Quinones .10 .04
❑ 90T Gary Redus .10 .04
❑ 91T Bip Roberts XRC .25 .10
❑ 92T Billy Joe Robidoux .10 .04
❑ 93T Jeff D. Robinson .10 .04
❑ 94T Gary Roenicke .10 .04
❑ 95T Ed Romero .10 .04
❑ 96T Angel Salazar .10 .04
❑ 97T Joe Sambito .10 .04
❑ 98T Billy Sample .10 .04
❑ 99T Dave Schmidt .10 .04
❑ 100T Ken Schrom .10 .04
❑ 101T Tom Seaver .25 .10
❑ 102T Ted Simmons .15 .06
❑ 103T Sammy Stewart .10 .04
❑ 104T Kurt Stillwell .10 .04
❑ 105T Franklin Stubbs .10 .04
❑ 106T Dale Sveum .10 .04
❑ 107T Chuck Tanner MG .10 .04
❑ 108T Danny Tartabull .15 .06
❑ 109T Tim Teufel .10 .04
❑ 110T Bob Tewksbury XRC .25 .10
❑ 111T Andres Thomas .10 .04
❑ 112T Milt Thompson .25 .10
❑ 113T R.Thompson XRC .25 .10
❑ 114T Jay Tibbs .10 .04
❑ 115T Wayne Tolleson .10 .04
❑ 116T Alex Trevino .10 .04
❑ 117T Manny Trillo .10 .04
❑ 118T Ed VandeBerg .10 .04
❑ 119T Ozzie Virgil .10 .04
❑ 120T Bob Walk .10 .04
❑ 121T Gene Walter .10 .04
❑ 122T Claudell Washington .10 .04
❑ 123T Bill Wegman XRC * .10 .04
❑ 124T Dick Williams MG .10 .04
❑ 125T Mitch Williams XRC .25 .10
❑ 126T Bobby Witt XRC .25 .10
❑ 127T Todd Worrell XRC * .25 .10
❑ 128T George Wright .10 .04
❑ 129T Ricky Wright .10 .04
❑ 130T Steve Yeager .15 .06
❑ 131T Paul Zuvella .10 .04
❑ 132T Checklist 1T-132T .10 .04

1987 Topps

	Nm-Mt	Ex-Mt
COMPLETE SET (792)	25.00	10.00
COMP.FACT SET (792)	25.00	10.00
COMP.HOBBY SET (792)	40.00	16.00
COMP.X-MAS.SET (792)	40.00	16.00

❑ 1 Roger Clemens RB .25 .10
❑ 2 Jim Deshaies RB .05 .02
❑ 3 Dwight Evans RB .10 .04
❑ 4 Davey Lopes RB .05 .02
❑ 5 Dave Righetti RB .05 .02
❑ 6 Ruben Sierra RB .25 .10
❑ 7 Todd Worrell RB .05 .02
❑ 8 Terry Pendleton .10 .04
❑ 9 Jay Tibbs .05 .02
❑ 10 Cecil Cooper .10 .04
❑ 11 Indians Team .05 .02
(Mound conference)
❑ 12 Jeff Sellers .05 .02
❑ 13 Nick Esasky .05 .02
❑ 14 Dave Stewart .10 .04
❑ 15 Claudell Washington .05 .02
❑ 16 Pat Clements .05 .02
❑ 17 Pete O'Brien .05 .02
❑ 18 Dick Howser MG .05 .02
❑ 19 Matt Young .05 .02
❑ 20 Gary Carter .10 .04
❑ 21 Mark Davis .05 .02
❑ 22 Doug DeCinces .05 .02
❑ 23 Lee Smith .10 .04
❑ 24 Tony Walker .05 .02
❑ 25 Bert Blyleven .10 .04
❑ 26 Greg Brock .05 .02
❑ 27 Joe Cowley .05 .02
❑ 28 Rick Dempsey .05 .02
❑ 29 Jimmy Key .10 .04
❑ 30 Tim Raines .10 .04
❑ 31 Braves Team .05 .02
(Glenn Hubbard and
Rafael Ramirez)
❑ 32 Tim Leary .05 .02
❑ 33 Andy Van Slyke .10 .04
❑ 34 Jose Rijo .10 .04
❑ 35 Sid Bream .05 .02
❑ 36 Eric King .05 .02
❑ 37 Marvell Wynne .05 .02
❑ 38 Dennis Leonard .05 .02
❑ 39 Marty Barrett .05 .02
❑ 40 Dave Righetti .10 .04
❑ 41 Bo Diaz .05 .02
❑ 42 Gary Redus .05 .02
❑ 43 Gene Michael MG .05 .02
❑ 44 Greg Harris .05 .02
❑ 45 Jim Presley .05 .02
❑ 46 Dan Gladden .05 .02
❑ 47 Dennis Powell .05 .02
❑ 48 Wally Backman .05 .02
❑ 49 Terry Harper .05 .02
❑ 50 Dave Smith .05 .02
❑ 51 Mel Hall .05 .02
❑ 52 Keith Atherton .05 .02
❑ 53 Ruppert Jones .05 .02
❑ 54 Bill Dawley .05 .02
❑ 55 Tim Wallach .05 .02
❑ 56 Brewers Team .05 .02
(Mound conference)
❑ 57 Scott Nielsen .05 .02
❑ 58 Thad Bosley .05 .02
❑ 59 Ken Dayley .05 .02
❑ 60 Tony Pena .05 .02
❑ 61 Bobby Thigpen RC .25 .10
❑ 62 Bobby Meacham .05 .02
❑ 63 Fred Toliver .05 .02
❑ 64 Harry Spilman .05 .02
❑ 65 Tom Browning .05 .02
❑ 66 Marc Sullivan .05 .02
❑ 67 Bill Swift .05 .02
❑ 68 Tony LaRussa MG .10 .04
❑ 69 Lonnie Smith .05 .02
❑ 70 Charlie Hough .10 .04
❑ 71 Mike Aldrete .05 .02
❑ 72 Walt Terrell .05 .02
❑ 73 Dave Anderson .05 .02
❑ 74 Dan Pasqua .05 .02
❑ 75 Ron Darling .10 .04
❑ 76 Rafael Ramirez .05 .02
❑ 77 Bryan Oelkers .05 .02
❑ 78 Tom Foley .05 .02
❑ 79 Juan Nieves .05 .02
❑ 80 Wally Joyner RC .40 .16
❑ 81 Padres Team .05 .02
(Andy Hawkins and
Terry Kennedy)
❑ 82 Rob Murphy .05 .02
❑ 83 Mike Davis .05 .02
❑ 84 Steve Lake .05 .02
❑ 85 Kevin Bass .05 .02
❑ 86 Nate Snell .05 .02
❑ 87 Mark Salas .05 .02
❑ 88 Ed Wojna .05 .02
❑ 89 Ozzie Guillen .05 .02
❑ 90 Dave Stieb .10 .04
❑ 91 Harold Reynolds .10 .04
❑ 92A Urbano Lugo .15 .06
ERR (no trademark)
❑ 92B Urbano Lugo COR .05 .02
❑ 93 Jim Leyland MG/TC RC* .25 .10
❑ 94 Calvin Schiraldi .05 .02
❑ 95 Oddibe McDowell .05 .02
❑ 96 Frank Williams .05 .02
❑ 97 Glenn Wilson .05 .02
❑ 98 Bill Scherrer .05 .02
❑ 99 Darryl Motley .05 .02
(Now with Braves
on card front)
❑ 100 Steve Garvey .10 .04
❑ 101 Carl Willis RC .10 .04
❑ 102 Paul Zuvella .05 .02
❑ 103 Rick Aguilera .05 .02
❑ 104 Billy Sample .05 .02
❑ 105 Floyd Youmans .05 .02
❑ 106 Blue Jays Team .05 .02
(George Bell and
Jesse Barfield)
❑ 107 John Butcher .05 .02
❑ 108 Jim Gantner UER .05 .02
(Brewers logo
reversed)
❑ 109 R.J. Reynolds .05 .02
❑ 110 John Tudor .10 .04
❑ 111 Alfredo Griffin .05 .02
❑ 112 Alan Ashby .05 .02
❑ 113 Neil Allen .05 .02
❑ 114 Billy Beane .10 .04
❑ 115 Donnie Moore .05 .02
❑ 116 Bill Russell .10 .04
❑ 117 Jim Beattie .05 .02
❑ 118 Bobby Valentine MG .10 .04
❑ 119 Ron Robinson .05 .02
❑ 120 Eddie Murray .25 .10
❑ 121 Kevin Romine .05 .02
❑ 122 Jim Clancy .05 .02
❑ 123 John Kruk RC* .50 .20
❑ 124 Ray Fontenot .05 .02
❑ 125 Bob Brenly .05 .02
❑ 126 Mike Loynd RC .10 .04
❑ 127 Vance Law .05 .02
❑ 128 Checklist 1-132 .05 .02
❑ 129 Rick Cerone .05 .02
❑ 130 Dwight Gooden .10 .04
❑ 131 Pirates Team .05 .02
(Sid Bream and
Tony Pena)
❑ 132 Paul Assenmacher .25 .10
❑ 133 Jose Oquendo .05 .02
❑ 134 Rich Yett .05 .02
❑ 135 Mike Easler .05 .02
❑ 136 Ron Romanick .05 .02
❑ 137 Jerry Willard .05 .02
❑ 138 Roy Lee Jackson .05 .02
❑ 139 Devon White RC .40 .16
❑ 140 Bret Saberhagen .10 .04
❑ 141 Herm Winningham .05 .02
❑ 142 Rick Sutcliffe .10 .04
❑ 143 Steve Boros MG .05 .02
❑ 144 Mike Scioscia .10 .04
❑ 145 Charlie Kerfeld .05 .02
❑ 146 Tracy Jones .05 .02
❑ 147 Randy Niemann .05 .02
❑ 148 Dave Collins .05 .02
❑ 149 Ray Searage .05 .02
❑ 150 Wade Boggs .15 .06
❑ 151 Mike LaCoss .05 .02
❑ 152 Toby Harrah .10 .04
❑ 153 Duane Ward RC * .25 .10
❑ 154 Tom O'Malley .05 .02
❑ 155 Eddie Whitson .05 .02
❑ 156 Mariners Team .05 .02

		(Mound conference)		
❑	157	Danny Darwin	.05	.02
❑	158	Tim Teufel	.05	.02
❑	159	Ed Olwine	.05	.02
❑	160	Julio Franco	.10	.04
❑	161	Steve Ontiveros	.05	.02
❑	162	Mike LaValliere RC *	.25	.10
❑	163	Kevin Gross	.05	.02
❑	164	Sammy Khalifa	.05	.02
❑	165	Jeff Reardon	.10	.04
❑	166	Bob Boone	.10	.04
❑	167	Jim Deshaies RC *	.10	.04
❑	168	Lou Piniella MG	.10	.04
❑	169	Ron Washington	.05	.02
❑	170	Bo Jackson RC	1.00	.40
❑	171	Chuck Cary	.05	.02
❑	172	Ron Oester	.05	.02
❑	173	Alex Trevino	.05	.02
❑	174	Henry Cotto	.05	.02
❑	175	Bob Stanley	.05	.02
❑	176	Steve Buechele	.05	.02
❑	177	Keith Moreland	.05	.02
❑	178	Cecil Fielder	.10	.04
❑	179	Bill Wegman	.05	.02
❑	180	Chris Brown	.05	.02
❑	181	Cardinals Team	.05	.02
		(Mound conference)		
❑	182	Lee Lacy	.05	.02
❑	183	Andy Hawkins	.05	.02
❑	184	Bobby Bonilla RC	.40	.16
❑	185	Roger McDowell	.05	.02
❑	186	Bruce Benedict	.05	.02
❑	187	Mark Huismann	.05	.02
❑	188	Tony Phillips	.05	.02
❑	189	Joe Hesketh	.05	.02
❑	190	Jim Sundberg	.10	.04
❑	191	Charles Hudson	.05	.02
❑	192	Cory Snyder	.05	.02
❑	193	Roger Craig MG	.10	.04
❑	194	Kirk McCaskill	.05	.02
❑	195	Mike Pagliarulo	.05	.02
❑	196	Randy O'Neal UER	.05	.02
		(Wrong ML career W-L totals)		
❑	197	Mark Bailey	.05	.02
❑	198	Lee Mazzilli	.10	.04
❑	199	Mariano Duncan	.05	.02
❑	200	Pete Rose	.60	.24
❑	201	John Cangelosi	.05	.02
❑	202	Ricky Wright	.05	.02
❑	203	Mike Kingery RC	.10	.04
❑	204	Sammy Stewart	.05	.02
❑	205	Graig Nettles	.10	.04
❑	206	Twins Team	.05	.02
		(Frank Viola and Tim Laudner)		
❑	207	George Frazier	.05	.02
❑	208	John Shelby	.05	.02
❑	209	Rick Schu	.05	.02
❑	210	Lloyd Moseby	.05	.02
❑	211	John Morris	.05	.02
❑	212	Mike Fitzgerald	.05	.02
❑	213	Randy Myers RC	.40	.16
❑	214	Omar Moreno	.05	.02
❑	215	Mark Langston	.05	.02
❑	216	B.J. Surhoff RC	.40	.16
❑	217	Chris Codiroli	.05	.02
❑	218	Sparky Anderson MG	.10	.04
❑	219	Cecilio Guante	.05	.02
❑	220	Joe Carter	.10	.04
❑	221	Vern Ruhle	.05	.02
❑	222	Denny Walling	.05	.02
❑	223	Charlie Leibrandt	.05	.02
❑	224	Wayne Tolleson	.05	.02
❑	225	Mike Smithson	.05	.02
❑	226	Max Venable	.05	.02
❑	227	Jamie Moyer RC	.50	.20
❑	228	Curt Wilkerson	.05	.02
❑	229	Mike Birkbeck	.10	.04
❑	230	Don Baylor	.10	.04
❑	231	Giants Team	.05	.02
		(Bob Brenly and Jim Gott)		
❑	232	Reggie Williams	.05	.02
❑	233	Russ Morman	.05	.02
❑	234	Pat Sheridan	.05	.02
❑	235	Alvin Davis	.05	.02
❑	236	Tommy John	.10	.04
❑	237	Jim Morrison	.05	.02
❑	238	Bill Krueger	.05	.02
❑	239	Juan Espino	.05	.02
❑	240	Steve Balboni	.05	.02
❑	241	Danny Heep	.05	.02
❑	242	Rick Mahler	.05	.02
❑	243	Whitey Herzog MG	.10	.04
❑	244	Dickie Noles	.05	.02
❑	245	Willie Upshaw	.05	.02
❑	246	Jim Dwyer	.05	.02
❑	247	Jeff Reed	.05	.02
❑	248	Gene Walter	.05	.02
❑	249	Jim Pankovits	.05	.02
❑	250	Teddy Higuera	.05	.02
❑	251	Rob Wilfong	.05	.02
❑	252	Dennis Martinez	.10	.04
❑	253	Eddie Milner	.05	.02
❑	254	Bob Tewksbury RC *	.25	.10
❑	255	Juan Samuel	.05	.02
❑	256	Royals Team	.15	.06
		(George Brett and Frank White)		
❑	257	Bob Forsch	.05	.02
❑	258	Steve Yeager	.10	.04
❑	259	Mike Greenwell RC	.25	.10
❑	260	Vida Blue	.10	.04
❑	261	Ruben Sierra RC	.50	.20
❑	262	Jim Winn	.05	.02
❑	263	Stan Javier	.05	.02
❑	264	Checklist 133-264	.05	.02
❑	265	Darrell Evans	.10	.04
❑	266	Jeff Hamilton	.05	.02
❑	267	Howard Johnson	.10	.04
❑	268	Pat Corrales MG	.05	.02
❑	269	Cliff Speck	.05	.02
❑	270	Jody Davis	.05	.02
❑	271	Mike G. Brown	.05	.02
❑	272	Andres Galarraga	.10	.04
❑	273	Gene Nelson	.05	.02
❑	274	Jeff Hearron UER	.05	.02
		(Duplicate 1986 stat line on back)		
❑	275	LaMarr Hoyt	.05	.02
❑	276	Jackie Gutierrez	.05	.02
❑	277	Juan Agosto	.05	.02
❑	278	Gary Pettis	.05	.02
❑	279	Dan Plesac	.05	.02
❑	280	Jeff Leonard	.05	.02
❑	281	Reds Team	.25	.10
		Pete Rose, Bo Diaz and Bill Gullickson		
❑	282	Jeff Calhoun	.05	.02
❑	283	Doug Drabek RC*	.40	.16
❑	284	John Moses	.05	.02
❑	285	Dennis Boyd	.05	.02
❑	286	Mike Woodard	.05	.02
❑	287	Dave Von Ohlen	.05	.02
❑	288	Tito Landrum	.05	.02
❑	289	Bob Kipper	.05	.02
❑	290	Leon Durham	.05	.02
❑	291	Mitch Williams RC *	.25	.10
❑	292	Franklin Stubbs	.05	.02
❑	293	Bob Rodgers MG	.05	.02
❑	294	Steve Jeltz	.05	.02
❑	295	Len Dykstra	.10	.04
❑	296	Andres Thomas	.05	.02
❑	297	Don Schulze	.05	.02
❑	298	Larry Herndon	.05	.02
❑	299	Joel Davis	.05	.02
❑	300	Reggie Jackson	.15	.06
❑	301	Luis Aquino UER	.05	.02
		(No trademark never corrected)		
❑	302	Bill Schroeder	.05	.02
❑	303	Juan Berenguer	.05	.02
❑	304	Phil Garner	.10	.04
❑	305	John Franco	.10	.04
❑	306	Red Sox Team	.10	.04
		(Tom Seaver, John McNamara MG, and Rich Gedman)		
❑	307	Lee Guetterman	.05	.02
❑	308	Don Slaught	.05	.02
❑	309	Mike Young	.05	.02
❑	310	Frank Viola	.10	.04
❑	311	Rickey Henderson	.15	.06
		TBC '82		
❑	312	Reggie Jackson	.10	.04
		TBC '77		
❑	313	Roberto Clemente	.25	.10
		TBC '72		
❑	314	Carl Yastrzemski UER	.25	.10
		TBC '67 (Sic, 112 RBI's on back)		
❑	315	Maury Wills TBC '62	.10	.04
❑	316	Brian Fisher	.05	.02
❑	317	Clint Hurdle	.05	.02
❑	318	Jim Fregosi MG	.05	.02
❑	319	Greg Swindell RC	.25	.10
❑	320	Barry Bonds RC	15.00	6.00
❑	321	Mike Laga	.05	.02
❑	322	Chris Bando	.05	.02
❑	323	Al Newman	.05	.02
❑	324	David Palmer	.05	.02
❑	325	Garry Templeton	.10	.04
❑	326	Mark Gubicza	.05	.02
❑	327	Dale Sveum	.05	.02
❑	328	Bob Welch	.10	.04
❑	329	Ron Roenicke	.05	.02
❑	330	Mike Scott	.10	.04
❑	331	Mets Team	.10	.04
		(Gary Carter and Darryl Strawberry)		
❑	332	Joe Price	.05	.02
❑	333	Ken Phelps	.05	.02
❑	334	Ed Correa	.05	.02
❑	335	Candy Maldonado	.05	.02
❑	336	Allan Anderson	.05	.02
❑	337	Darrell Miller	.05	.02
❑	338	Tim Conroy	.05	.02
❑	339	Donnie Hill	.05	.02
❑	340	Roger Clemens	.50	.20
❑	341	Mike C. Brown	.05	.02
❑	342	Bob James	.05	.02
❑	343	Hal Lanier MG	.05	.02
❑	344A	Joe Niekro	.05	.02
		(Copyright inside righthand border)		
❑	344B	Joe Niekro	.05	.02
		(Copyright outside righthand border)		
❑	345	Andre Dawson	.10	.04
❑	346	Shawon Dunston	.05	.02
❑	347	Mickey Brantley	.05	.02
❑	348	Carmelo Martinez	.05	.02
❑	349	Storm Davis	.05	.02
❑	350	Keith Hernandez	.10	.04
❑	351	Gene Garber	.05	.02
❑	352	Mike Felder	.05	.02
❑	353	Ernie Camacho	.05	.02
❑	354	Jamie Quirk	.05	.02
❑	355	Don Carman	.05	.02
❑	356	White Sox Team	.05	.02
		(Mound conference)		
❑	357	Steve Fireovid	.05	.02
❑	358	Sal Butera	.05	.02
❑	359	Doug Corbett	.05	.02
❑	360	Pedro Guerrero	.10	.04
❑	361	Mark Thurmond	.05	.02
❑	362	Luis Quinones	.05	.02
❑	363	Jose Guzman	.05	.02
❑	364	Randy Bush	.05	.02
❑	365	Rick Rhoden	.05	.02
❑	366	Mark McGwire	4.00	1.60
❑	367	Jeff Lahti	.05	.02
❑	368	John McNamara MG	.05	.02
❑	369	Brian Dayett	.05	.02
❑	370	Fred Lynn	.10	.04
❑	371	Mark Eichhorn	.05	.02
❑	372	Jerry Mumphrey	.05	.02
❑	373	Jeff Dedmon	.05	.02
❑	374	Glenn Hoffman	.05	.02
❑	375	Ron Guidry	.10	.04
❑	376	Scott Bradley	.05	.02
❑	377	John Henry Johnson	.05	.02
❑	378	Rafael Santana	.05	.02
❑	379	John Russell	.05	.02
❑	380	Rich Gossage	.10	.04
❑	381	Expos Team	.05	.02
		(Mound conference)		

❑ 382 Rudy Law .05 .02
❑ 383 Ron Davis .05 .02
❑ 384 Johnny Grubb .05 .02
❑ 385 Orel Hershiser .10 .04
❑ 386 Dickie Thon .05 .02
❑ 387 T.R. Bryden .05 .02
❑ 388 Geno Petralli .05 .02
❑ 389 Jeff D. Robinson .05 .02
❑ 390 Gary Matthews .10 .04
❑ 391 Jay Howell .05 .02
❑ 392 Checklist 265-396 .05 .02
❑ 393 Pete Rose MG .15 .06
❑ 394 Mike Bielecki .05 .02
❑ 395 Damaso Garcia .05 .02
❑ 396 Tim Lollar .05 .02
❑ 397 Greg Walker .05 .02
❑ 398 Brad Havens .05 .02
❑ 399 Curt Ford .05 .02
❑ 400 George Brett .60 .24
❑ 401 Billy Joe Robidoux .05 .02
❑ 402 Mike Trujillo .05 .02
❑ 403 Jerry Royster .05 .02
❑ 404 Doug Sisk .05 .02
❑ 405 Brook Jacoby .05 .02
❑ 406 Yankees Team .50 .20
(Rickey Henderson and
Don Mattingly)
❑ 407 Jim Acker .05 .02
❑ 408 John Mizerock .05 .02
❑ 409 Milt Thompson .05 .02
❑ 410 Fernando Valenzuela .10 .04
❑ 411 Darnell Coles .05 .02
❑ 412 Eric Davis .15 .06
❑ 413 Moose Haas .05 .02
❑ 414 Joe Orsulak .05 .02
❑ 415 Bobby Witt RC .25 .10
❑ 416 Tom Nieto .05 .02
❑ 417 Pat Perry .05 .02
❑ 418 Dick Williams MG .05 .02
❑ 419 Mark Portugal RC * .25 .10
❑ 420 Will Clark RC 1.00 .40
❑ 421 Jose DeLeon .05 .02
❑ 422 Jack Howell .05 .02
❑ 423 Jaime Cocanower .05 .02
❑ 424 Chris Speier .05 .02
❑ 425 Tom Seaver UER .15 .06
Earned Runs amount is wrong
For 86 Red Sox and Career
Also the ERA is wrong for 86 and
career
❑ 426 Floyd Rayford .05 .02
❑ 427 Edwin Nunez .05 .02
❑ 428 Bruce Bochy .05 .02
❑ 429 Tim Pyznarski .05 .02
❑ 430 Mike Schmidt .50 .20
❑ 431 Dodgers Team .05 .02
(Mound conference)
❑ 432 Jim Slaton .05 .02
❑ 433 Ed Hearn .05 .02
❑ 434 Mike Fischlin .05 .02
❑ 435 Bruce Sutter .10 .04
❑ 436 Andy Allanson .05 .02
❑ 437 Ted Power .05 .02
❑ 438 Kelly Downs RC .10 .04
❑ 439 Karl Best .05 .02
❑ 440 Willie McGee .10 .04
❑ 441 Dave Leiper .05 .02
❑ 442 Mitch Webster .05 .02
❑ 443 John Felske MG .05 .02
❑ 444 Jeff Russell .05 .02
❑ 445 Dave Lopes .10 .04
❑ 446 Chuck Finley RC .40 .16
❑ 447 Bill Almon .05 .02
❑ 448 Chris Bosio RC .25 .10
❑ 449 Pat Dodson .10 .04
❑ 450 Kirby Puckett .25 .10
❑ 451 Joe Sambito .05 .02
❑ 452 Dave Henderson .05 .02
❑ 453 Scott Terry RC .10 .04
❑ 454 Luis Salazar .05 .02
❑ 455 Mike Boddicker .05 .02
❑ 456 A's Team .05 .02
(Mound conference)
❑ 457 Len Matuszek .05 .02
❑ 458 Kelly Gruber .05 .02
❑ 459 Dennis Eckersley .15 .06
❑ 460 Darryl Strawberry .10 .04
❑ 461 Craig McMurtry .05 .02
❑ 462 Scott Fletcher .05 .02
❑ 463 Tom Candiotti .05 .02
❑ 464 Butch Wynegar .05 .02
❑ 465 Todd Worrell .05 .02
❑ 466 Kal Daniels .05 .02
❑ 467 Randy St.Claire .05 .02
❑ 468 G.Bamberger MG .05 .02
❑ 469 Mike Diaz .05 .02
❑ 470 Dave Dravecky .05 .02
❑ 471 Ronn Reynolds .05 .02
❑ 472 Bill Doran .05 .02
❑ 473 Steve Farr .05 .02
❑ 474 Jerry Narron .05 .02
❑ 475 Scott Garrelts .05 .02
❑ 476 Danny Tartabull .05 .02
❑ 477 Ken Howell .05 .02
❑ 478 Tim Laudner .05 .02
❑ 479 Bob Sebra .05 .02
❑ 480 Jim Rice .10 .04
❑ 481 Phillies Team .05 .02
(Glenn Wilson
Juan Samuel and
Von Hayes)
❑ 482 Daryl Boston .05 .02
❑ 483 Dwight Lowry .05 .02
❑ 484 Jim Traber .05 .02
❑ 485 Tony Fernandez .05 .02
❑ 486 Otis Nixon .05 .02
❑ 487 Dave Gumpert .05 .02
❑ 488 Ray Knight .10 .04
❑ 489 Bill Gullickson .05 .02
❑ 490 Dale Murphy .15 .06
❑ 491 Ron Karkovice RC .25 .10
❑ 492 Mike Heath .05 .02
❑ 493 Tom Lasorda MG .15 .06
❑ 494 Barry Jones .05 .02
❑ 495 Gorman Thomas .10 .04
❑ 496 Bruce Bochte .05 .02
❑ 497 Dale Mohorcic .05 .02
❑ 498 Bob Kearney .05 .02
❑ 499 Bruce Ruffin RC .10 .04
❑ 500 Don Mattingly .60 .24
❑ 501 Craig Lefferts .05 .02
❑ 502 Dick Schofield .05 .02
❑ 503 Larry Andersen .05 .02
❑ 504 Mickey Hatcher .05 .02
❑ 505 Bryn Smith .05 .02
❑ 506 Orioles Team .05 .02
(Mound conference)
❑ 507 Dave L. Stapleton .05 .02
❑ 508 Scott Bankhead .05 .02
❑ 509 Enos Cabell .05 .02
❑ 510 Tom Henke .05 .02
❑ 511 Steve Lyons .05 .02
❑ 512 Dave Magadan RC .25 .10
❑ 513 Carmen Castillo .05 .02
❑ 514 Orlando Mercado .05 .02
❑ 515 Willie Hernandez .05 .02
❑ 516 Ted Simmons .10 .04
❑ 517 Mario Soto .10 .04
❑ 518 Gene Mauch MG .05 .02
❑ 519 Curt Young .05 .02
❑ 520 Jack Clark .10 .04
❑ 521 Rick Reuschel .10 .04
❑ 522 Checklist 397-528 .05 .02
❑ 523 Earnie Riles .05 .02
❑ 524 Bob Shirley .05 .02
❑ 525 Phil Bradley .05 .02
❑ 526 Roger Mason .05 .02
❑ 527 Jim Wohlford .05 .02
❑ 528 Ken Dixon .05 .02
❑ 529 Alvaro Espinoza RC .10 .04
❑ 530 Tony Gwynn .30 .12
❑ 531 Astros Team .10 .04
(Yogi Berra conference)
❑ 532 Jeff Stone .05 .02
❑ 533 Angel Salazar .05 .02
❑ 534 Scott Sanderson .05 .02
❑ 535 Tony Armas .10 .04
❑ 536 Terry Mulholland RC .25 .10
❑ 537 Rance Mulliniks .05 .02
❑ 538 Tom Niedenfuer .05 .02
❑ 539 Reid Nichols .05 .02
❑ 540 Terry Kennedy .05 .02
❑ 541 Rafael Belliard RC .25 .10
❑ 542 Ricky Horton .05 .02
❑ 543 Dave Johnson MG .05 .02
❑ 544 Zane Smith .05 .02
❑ 545 Buddy Bell .10 .04
❑ 546 Mike Morgan .05 .02
❑ 547 Rob Deer .05 .02
❑ 548 Bill Mooneyham .05 .02
❑ 549 Bob Melvin .05 .02
❑ 550 Pete Incaviglia RC * .25 .10
❑ 551 Frank Wills .05 .02
❑ 552 Larry Sheets .05 .02
❑ 553 Mike Maddux .05 .02
❑ 554 Buddy Biancalana .05 .02
❑ 555 Dennis Rasmussen .05 .02
❑ 556 Angels Team .05 .02
(Rene Lachemann CO,
Mike Witt, and
Bob Boone)
❑ 557 John Cerutti .05 .02
❑ 558 Greg Gagne .05 .02
❑ 559 Lance McCullers .05 .02
❑ 560 Glenn Davis .05 .02
❑ 561 Rey Quinones .05 .02
❑ 562 Bryan Clutterbuck .05 .02
❑ 563 John Stefero .05 .02
❑ 564 Larry McWilliams .05 .02
❑ 565 Dusty Baker .10 .04
❑ 566 Tim Hulett .05 .02
❑ 567 Greg Mathews .05 .02
❑ 568 Earl Weaver MG .10 .04
❑ 569 Wade Rowdon .05 .02
❑ 570 Sid Fernandez .05 .02
❑ 571 Ozzie Virgil .05 .02
❑ 572 Pete Ladd .05 .02
❑ 573 Hal McRae .10 .04
❑ 574 Manny Lee .05 .02
❑ 575 Pat Tabler .05 .02
❑ 576 Frank Pastore .05 .02
❑ 577 Dann Bilardello .05 .02
❑ 578 Billy Hatcher .05 .02
❑ 579 Rick Burleson .05 .02
❑ 580 Mike Krukow .05 .02
❑ 581 Cubs Team .05 .02
(Ron Cey and
Steve Trout)
❑ 582 Bruce Berenyi .05 .02
❑ 583 Junior Ortiz .05 .02
❑ 584 Ron Kittle .05 .02
❑ 585 Scott Bailes .05 .02
❑ 586 Ben Oglivie .10 .04
❑ 587 Eric Plunk .05 .02
❑ 588 Wallace Johnson .05 .02
❑ 589 Steve Crawford .05 .02
❑ 590 Vince Coleman .05 .02
❑ 591 Spike Owen .05 .02
❑ 592 Chris Welsh .05 .02
❑ 593 Chuck Tanner MG .05 .02
❑ 594 Rick Anderson .05 .02
❑ 595 Keith Hernandez AS .05 .02
❑ 596 Steve Sax AS .05 .02
❑ 597 Mike Schmidt AS .25 .10
❑ 598 Ozzie Smith AS .25 .10
❑ 599 Tony Gwynn AS .15 .06
❑ 600 Dave Parker AS .05 .02
❑ 601 Darryl Strawberry AS .05 .02
❑ 602 Gary Carter AS .05 .02
❑ 603A D.Gooden AS .05 .02
ERR no trademark
❑ 603B D.Gooden AS COR .05 .02
❑ 604 F.Valenzuela AS .05 .02
❑ 605 Todd Worrell AS .05 .02
❑ 606 D.Mattingly AS COR .30 .12
❑ 606A Don Mattingly AS 1.00 .40
ERR (no trademark)
❑ 607 Tony Bernazard AS .05 .02
❑ 608 Wade Boggs AS .10 .04
❑ 609 Cal Ripken AS .25 .10
❑ 610 Jim Rice AS .05 .02
❑ 611 Kirby Puckett AS .15 .06
❑ 612 George Bell AS .05 .02
❑ 613 Lance Parrish AS UER .05 .02
(Pitcher heading
on back)
❑ 614 Roger Clemens AS .25 .10
❑ 615 Teddy Higuera AS .05 .02

❑ 616 Dave Righetti AS .05 .02
❑ 617 Al Nipper .05 .02
❑ 618 Tom Kelly MG .05 .02
❑ 619 Jerry Reed .05 .02
❑ 620 Jose Canseco .25 .10
❑ 621 Danny Cox .05 .02
❑ 622 Glenn Braggs RC .10 .04
❑ 623 Kurt Stillwell .05 .02
❑ 624 Tim Burke .05 .02
❑ 625 Mookie Wilson .10 .04
❑ 626 Joel Skinner .05 .02
❑ 627 Ken Oberkfell .05 .02
❑ 628 Bob Walk .05 .02
❑ 629 Larry Parrish .05 .02
❑ 630 John Candelaria .05 .02
❑ 631 Tigers Team .05 .02
(Mound conference)
❑ 632 Rob Woodward .05 .02
❑ 633 Jose Uribe .05 .02
❑ 634 Rafael Palmeiro RC 2.00 .80
❑ 635 Ken Schrom .05 .02
❑ 636 Darren Daulton .10 .04
❑ 637 Bip Roberts RC* .25 .10
❑ 638 Rich Bordi .05 .02
❑ 639 Gerald Perry .05 .02
❑ 640 Mark Clear .05 .02
❑ 641 Domingo Ramos .05 .02
❑ 642 Al Pulido .05 .02
❑ 643 Ron Shepherd .05 .02
❑ 644 John Denny .05 .02
❑ 645 Dwight Evans .10 .04
❑ 646 Mike Mason .05 .02
❑ 647 Tom Lawless .05 .02
❑ 648 Barry Larkin RC 1.00 .40
❑ 649 Mickey Tettleton .05 .02
❑ 650 Hubie Brooks .05 .02
❑ 651 Benny Distefano .05 .02
❑ 652 Terry Forster .10 .04
❑ 653 Kevin Mitchell RC * .40 .16
❑ 654 Checklist 529-660 .10 .04
❑ 655 Jesse Barfield .10 .04
❑ 656 Rangers Team .05 .02
(Bobby Valentine MG
and Ricky Wright)
❑ 657 Tom Waddell .05 .02
❑ 658 R.Thompson RC* .25 .10
❑ 659 Aurelio Lopez .05 .02
❑ 660 Bob Horner .10 .04
❑ 661 Lou Whitaker .10 .04
❑ 662 Frank DiPino .05 .02
❑ 663 Cliff Johnson .05 .02
❑ 664 Mike Marshall .05 .02
❑ 665 Rod Scurry .05 .02
❑ 666 Von Hayes .05 .02
❑ 667 Ron Hassey .05 .02
❑ 668 Juan Bonilla .05 .02
❑ 669 Bud Black .05 .02
❑ 670 Jose Cruz .10 .04
❑ 671A Ray Soff ERR .05 .02
(No D* before
copyright line)
❑ 671B Ray Soff COR .05 .02
(D* before
copyright line)
❑ 672 Chili Davis .10 .04
❑ 673 Don Sutton .10 .04
❑ 674 Bill Campbell .05 .02
❑ 675 Ed Romero .05 .02
❑ 676 Charlie Moore .05 .02
❑ 677 Bob Grich .10 .04
❑ 678 Carney Lansford .10 .04
❑ 679 Kent Hrbek .10 .04
❑ 680 Ryne Sandberg .40 .16
❑ 681 George Bell .10 .04
❑ 682 Jerry Reuss .05 .02
❑ 683 Gary Roenicke .05 .02
❑ 684 Kent Tekulve .05 .02
❑ 685 Jerry Hairston .05 .02
❑ 686 Doyle Alexander .05 .02
❑ 687 Alan Trammell .10 .04
❑ 688 Juan Beniquez .05 .02
❑ 689 Darrell Porter .05 .02
❑ 690 Dane Iorg .05 .02
❑ 691 Dave Parker .10 .04
❑ 692 Frank White .10 .04
❑ 693 Terry Puhl .05 .02
❑ 694 Phil Niekro .10 .04
❑ 695 Chico Walker .05 .02
❑ 696 Gary Lucas .05 .02
❑ 697 Ed Lynch .05 .02
❑ 698 Ernie Whitt .05 .02
❑ 699 Ken Landreaux .05 .02
❑ 700 Dave Bergman .05 .02
❑ 701 Willie Randolph .10 .04
❑ 702 Greg Gross .05 .02
❑ 703 Dave Schmidt .05 .02
❑ 704 Jesse Orosco .05 .02
❑ 705 Bruce Hurst .05 .02
❑ 706 Rick Manning .05 .02
❑ 707 Bob McClure .05 .02
❑ 708 Scott McGregor .05 .02
❑ 709 Dave Kingman .10 .04
❑ 710 Gary Gaetti .10 .04
❑ 711 Ken Griffey .10 .04
❑ 712 Don Robinson .05 .02
❑ 713 Tom Brookens .05 .02
❑ 714 Dan Quisenberry .05 .02
❑ 715 Bob Dernier .05 .02
❑ 716 Rick Leach .05 .02
❑ 717 Ed VandeBerg .05 .02
❑ 718 Steve Carlton .10 .04
❑ 719 Tom Hume .05 .02
❑ 720 Richard Dotson .05 .02
❑ 721 Tom Herr .05 .02
❑ 722 Bob Knepper .05 .02
❑ 723 Brett Butler .10 .04
❑ 724 Greg Minton .05 .02
❑ 725 George Hendrick .10 .04
❑ 726 Frank Tanana .10 .04
❑ 727 Mike Moore .05 .02
❑ 728 Tippy Martinez .05 .02
❑ 729 Tom Paciorek .05 .02
❑ 730 Eric Show .05 .02
❑ 731 Dave Concepcion .10 .04
❑ 732 Manny Trillo .05 .02
❑ 733 Bill Caudill .05 .02
❑ 734 Bill Madlock .10 .04
❑ 735 Rickey Henderson .25 .10
❑ 736 Steve Bedrosian .05 .02
❑ 737 Floyd Bannister .05 .02
❑ 738 Jorge Orta .05 .02
❑ 739 Chet Lemon .10 .04
❑ 740 Rich Gedman .05 .02
❑ 741 Paul Molitor .15 .06
❑ 742 Andy McGaffigan .05 .02
❑ 743 Dwayne Murphy .05 .02
❑ 744 Roy Smalley .05 .02
❑ 745 Glenn Hubbard .05 .02
❑ 746 Bob Ojeda .05 .02
❑ 747 Johnny Ray .05 .02
❑ 748 Mike Flanagan .05 .02
❑ 749 Ozzie Smith .40 .16
❑ 750 Steve Trout .05 .02
❑ 751 Garth Iorg .05 .02
❑ 752 Dan Petry .05 .02
❑ 753 Rick Honeycutt .05 .02
❑ 754 Dave LaPoint .05 .02
❑ 755 Luis Aguayo .05 .02
❑ 756 Carlton Fisk .15 .06
❑ 757 Nolan Ryan 1.00 .40
❑ 758 Tony Bernazard .05 .02
❑ 759 Joel Youngblood .05 .02
❑ 760 Mike Witt .05 .02
❑ 761 Greg Pryor .05 .02
❑ 762 Gary Ward .05 .02
❑ 763 Tim Flannery .05 .02
❑ 764 Bill Buckner .10 .04
❑ 765 Kirk Gibson .10 .04
❑ 766 Don Aase .05 .02
❑ 767 Ron Cey .10 .04
❑ 768 Dennis Lamp .05 .02
❑ 769 Steve Sax .05 .02
❑ 770 Dave Winfield .10 .04
❑ 771 Shane Rawley .05 .02
❑ 772 Harold Baines .10 .04
❑ 773 Robin Yount .40 .16
❑ 774 Wayne Krenchicki .05 .02
❑ 775 Joaquin Andujar .10 .04
❑ 776 Tom Brunansky .05 .02
❑ 777 Chris Chambliss .10 .04
❑ 778 Jack Morris .10 .04
❑ 779 Craig Reynolds .05 .02
❑ 780 Andre Thornton .05 .02
❑ 781 Atlee Hammaker .05 .02
❑ 782 Brian Downing .10 .04
❑ 783 Willie Wilson .10 .04
❑ 784 Cal Ripken .75 .30
❑ 785 Terry Francona .10 .04
❑ 786 Jimy Williams MG .05 .02
❑ 787 Alejandro Pena .05 .02
❑ 788 Tim Stoddard .05 .02
❑ 789 Dan Schatzeder .05 .02
❑ 790 Julio Cruz .05 .02
❑ 791 Lance Parrish .10 .04
❑ 792 Checklist 661-792 .05 .02

1987 Topps Traded

	Nm-Mt	Ex-Mt
COMP.FACT.SET (132)	10.00	4.00

❑ 1T Bill Almon .05 .02
❑ 2T Scott Bankhead .05 .02
❑ 3T Eric Bell .10 .04
❑ 4T Juan Beniquez .05 .02
❑ 5T Juan Berenguer .05 .02
❑ 6T Greg Booker .05 .02
❑ 7T Thad Bosley .05 .02
❑ 8T Larry Bowa MG .10 .04
❑ 9T Greg Brock .05 .02
❑ 10T Bob Brower .05 .02
❑ 11T Jerry Browne .10 .04
❑ 12T Ralph Bryant .05 .02
❑ 13T DeWayne Buice .05 .02
❑ 14T Ellis Burks XRC .50 .20
❑ 15T Ivan Calderon .05 .02
❑ 16T Jeff Calhoun .05 .02
❑ 17T Casey Candaele .05 .02
❑ 18T John Cangelosi .05 .02
❑ 19T Steve Carlton .10 .04
❑ 20T Juan Castillo .10 .04
❑ 21T Rick Cerone .05 .02
❑ 22T Ron Cey .10 .04
❑ 23T John Christensen .05 .02
❑ 24T David Cone XRC .75 .30
❑ 25T Chuck Crim .05 .02
❑ 26T Storm Davis .05 .02
❑ 27T Andre Dawson .10 .04
❑ 28T Rick Dempsey .05 .02
❑ 29T Doug Drabek .50 .20
❑ 30T Mike Dunne .05 .02
❑ 31T Dennis Eckersley .15 .06
❑ 32T Lee Elia MG .05 .02
❑ 33T Brian Fisher .05 .02
❑ 34T Terry Francona .10 .04
❑ 35T Willie Fraser .10 .04
❑ 36T Billy Gardner MG .05 .02
❑ 37T Ken Gerhart .05 .02
❑ 38T Dan Gladden .05 .02
❑ 39T Jim Gott .05 .02
❑ 40T Cecilio Guante .05 .02
❑ 41T Albert Hall .05 .02
❑ 42T Terry Harper .05 .02
❑ 43T Mickey Hatcher .05 .02
❑ 44T Brad Havens .05 .02
❑ 45T Neal Heaton .05 .02
❑ 46T Mike Henneman XRC .25 .10
❑ 47T Donnie Hill .05 .02
❑ 48T Guy Hoffman .05 .02
❑ 49T Brian Holton .05 .02

Card	Player	Nm-Mt	Ex-Mt
❑ 50T	Charles Hudson	.05	.02
❑ 51T	Danny Jackson	.05	.02
❑ 52T	Reggie Jackson	.15	.06
❑ 53T	Chris James XRC *	.10	.04
❑ 54T	Dion James	.05	.02
❑ 55T	Stan Jefferson	.05	.02
❑ 56T	Joe Johnson	.05	.02
❑ 57T	Terry Kennedy	.05	.02
❑ 58T	Mike Kingery	.10	.04
❑ 59T	Ray Knight	.10	.04
❑ 60T	Gene Larkin XRC	.25	.10
❑ 61T	Mike LaValliere	.25	.10
❑ 62T	Jack Lazorko	.05	.02
❑ 63T	Terry Leach	.05	.02
❑ 64T	Tim Leary	.05	.02
❑ 65T	Jim Lindeman	.10	.04
❑ 66T	Steve Lombardozzi	.05	.02
❑ 67T	Bill Long	.05	.02
❑ 68T	Barry Lyons	.05	.02
❑ 69T	Shane Mack	.05	.02
❑ 70T	Greg Maddux XRC	5.00	2.00
❑ 71T	Bill Madlock	.10	.04
❑ 72T	Joe Magrane XRC	.10	.04
❑ 73T	Dave Martinez XRC *	.25	.10
❑ 74T	Fred McGriff	.60	.24
❑ 75T	Mark McLemore	.10	.04
❑ 76T	Kevin McReynolds	.05	.02
❑ 77T	Dave Meads	.05	.02
❑ 78T	Eddie Milner	.05	.02
❑ 79T	Greg Minton	.05	.02
❑ 80T	John Mitchell XRC	.10	.04
❑ 81T	Kevin Mitchell	.15	.06
❑ 82T	Charlie Moore	.05	.02
❑ 83T	Jeff Musselman	.05	.02
❑ 84T	Gene Nelson	.05	.02
❑ 85T	Graig Nettles	.10	.04
❑ 86T	Al Newman	.05	.02
❑ 87T	Reid Nichols	.05	.02
❑ 88T	Tom Niedenfuer	.05	.02
❑ 89T	Joe Niekro	.05	.02
❑ 90T	Tom Nieto	.05	.02
❑ 91T	Matt Nokes XRC	.25	.10
❑ 92T	Dickie Noles	.05	.02
❑ 93T	Pat Pacillo	.05	.02
❑ 94T	Lance Parrish	.10	.04
❑ 95T	Tony Pena	.05	.02
❑ 96T	Luis Polonia XRC	.25	.10
❑ 97T	Randy Ready	.05	.02
❑ 98T	Jeff Reardon	.10	.04
❑ 99T	Gary Redus	.05	.02
❑ 100T	Jeff Reed	.05	.02
❑ 101T	Rick Rhoden	.05	.02
❑ 102T	Cal Ripken Sr. MG	.05	.02
❑ 103T	Wally Ritchie	.05	.02
❑ 104T	Jeff M. Robinson	.05	.02
❑ 105T	Gary Roenicke	.05	.02
❑ 106T	Jerry Royster	.05	.02
❑ 107T	Mark Salas	.05	.02
❑ 108T	Luis Salazar	.05	.02
❑ 109T	Benny Santiago	.10	.04
❑ 110T	Dave Schmidt	.05	.02
❑ 111T	Kevin Seitzer XRC*	.25	.10
❑ 112T	John Shelby	.05	.02
❑ 113T	Steve Shields	.05	.02
❑ 114T	John Smiley XRC	.25	.10
❑ 115T	Chris Speier	.05	.02
❑ 116T	Mike Stanley XRC*	.25	.10
❑ 117T	Terry Steinbach XRC	.50	.20
❑ 118T	Les Straker	.05	.02
❑ 119T	Jim Sundberg	.10	.04
❑ 120T	Danny Tartabull	.05	.02
❑ 121T	Tom Trebelhorn MG	.05	.02
❑ 122T	Dave Valle XRC **	.10	.04
❑ 123T	Ed VandeBerg	.05	.02
❑ 124T	Andy Van Slyke	.10	.04
❑ 125T	Gary Ward	.05	.02
❑ 126T	Alan Wiggins	.05	.02
❑ 127T	Bill Wilkinson	.05	.02
❑ 128T	Frank Williams	.05	.02
❑ 129T	Matt Williams XRC	1.00	.40
❑ 130T	Jim Winn	.05	.02
❑ 131T	Matt Young	.05	.02
❑ 132T	Checklist 1T-132T	.05	.02

1988 Topps

	Nm-Mt	Ex-Mt
COMPLETE SET (792)	15.00	6.00
COMP.FACT SET (792)	15.00	6.00
COMP.X-MAS.SET (792)	40.00	16.00

Card	Player	Nm-Mt	Ex-Mt
❑ 1	Vince Coleman RB	.05	.02
❑ 2	Don Mattingly RB	.30	.12
❑ 3	Mark McGwire RB Rookie Homer Record (No white spot)	.75	.30
❑ 3A	Mark McGwire RB Rookie Homer Record (White spot behind left foot)	.20	.08
❑ 4	Eddie Murray RB Switch Home Runs, Two Straight Games (No caption on front)	.15	.06
❑ 4A	Eddie Murray RB Switch Home Runs, Two Straight Games (Caption in box on card front)	.50	.20
❑ 5	Phil Niekro Joe Niekro RB	.10	.04
❑ 6	Nolan Ryan RB	.40	.16
❑ 7	Benito Santiago RB	.05	.02
❑ 8	Kevin Elster	.05	.02
❑ 9	Andy Hawkins	.05	.02
❑ 10	Ryne Sandberg	.40	.16
❑ 11	Mike Young	.05	.02
❑ 12	Bill Schroeder	.05	.02
❑ 13	Andres Thomas	.05	.02
❑ 14	Sparky Anderson MG	.10	.04
❑ 15	Chili Davis	.10	.04
❑ 16	Kirk McCaskill	.05	.02
❑ 17	Ron Oester	.05	.02
❑ 18A	Al Leiter RC ERR (Photo actually Steve George, right ear visible)	.50	.20
❑ 18B	Al Leiter RC COR (Left ear visible)	.50	.20
❑ 19	Mark Davidson	.05	.02
❑ 20	Kevin Gross	.05	.02
❑ 21	Wade Boggs Spike Owen TL	.10	.04
❑ 22	Greg Swindell	.05	.02
❑ 23	Ken Landreaux	.05	.02
❑ 24	Jim Deshaies	.05	.02
❑ 25	Andres Galarraga	.10	.04
❑ 26	Mitch Williams	.05	.02
❑ 27	R.J. Reynolds	.05	.02
❑ 28	Jose Nunez	.05	.02
❑ 29	Angel Salazar	.05	.02
❑ 30	Sid Fernandez	.05	.02
❑ 31	Bruce Bochy	.05	.02
❑ 32	Mike Morgan	.05	.02
❑ 33	Rob Deer	.05	.02
❑ 34	Ricky Horton	.05	.02
❑ 35	Harold Baines	.10	.04
❑ 36	Jamie Moyer	.10	.04
❑ 37	Ed Romero	.05	.02
❑ 38	Jeff Calhoun	.05	.02
❑ 39	Gerald Perry	.05	.02
❑ 40	Orel Hershiser	.10	.04
❑ 41	Bob Melvin	.05	.02
❑ 42	Bill Landrum	.05	.02
❑ 43	Dick Schofield	.05	.02
❑ 44	Lou Piniella MG	.10	.04
❑ 45	Kent Hrbek	.10	.04
❑ 46	Darnell Coles	.05	.02
❑ 47	Joaquin Andujar	.10	.04
❑ 48	Alan Ashby	.05	.02
❑ 49	Dave Clark	.05	.02
❑ 50	Hubie Brooks	.05	.02
❑ 51	Eddie Murray Cal Ripken TL	.40	.16
❑ 52	Don Robinson	.05	.02
❑ 53	Curt Wilkerson	.05	.02
❑ 54	Jim Clancy	.05	.02
❑ 55	Phil Bradley	.05	.02
❑ 56	Ed Hearn	.05	.02
❑ 57	Tim Crews RC	.25	.10
❑ 58	Dave Magadan	.05	.02
❑ 59	Danny Cox	.05	.02
❑ 60	Rickey Henderson	.20	.08
❑ 61	Mark Knudson	.05	.02
❑ 62	Jeff Hamilton	.05	.02
❑ 63	Jimmy Jones	.05	.02
❑ 64	Ken Caminiti RC	.75	.30
❑ 65	Leon Durham	.05	.02
❑ 66	Shane Rawley	.05	.02
❑ 67	Ken Oberkfell	.05	.02
❑ 68	Dave Dravecky	.05	.02
❑ 69	Mike Hart	.05	.02
❑ 70	Roger Clemens	.50	.20
❑ 71	Gary Pettis	.05	.02
❑ 72	Dennis Eckersley	.15	.06
❑ 73	Randy Bush	.05	.02
❑ 74	Tom Lasorda MG	.15	.06
❑ 75	Joe Carter	.10	.04
❑ 76	Dennis Martinez	.10	.04
❑ 77	Tom O'Malley	.05	.02
❑ 78	Dan Petry	.05	.02
❑ 79	Ernie Whitt	.05	.02
❑ 80	Mark Langston	.05	.02
❑ 81	Ron Robinson John Franco TL	.05	.02
❑ 82	Darrel Akerfelds	.05	.02
❑ 83	Jose Oquendo	.05	.02
❑ 84	Cecilio Guante	.05	.02
❑ 85	Howard Johnson	.10	.04
❑ 86	Ron Karkovice	.05	.02
❑ 87	Mike Mason	.05	.02
❑ 88	Earnie Riles	.05	.02
❑ 89	Gary Thurman	.05	.02
❑ 90	Dale Murphy	.15	.06
❑ 91	Joey Cora RC	.25	.10
❑ 92	Len Matuszek	.05	.02
❑ 93	Bob Sebra	.05	.02
❑ 94	Chuck Jackson	.05	.02
❑ 95	Lance Parrish	.10	.04
❑ 96	Todd Benzinger RC*	.25	.10
❑ 97	Scott Garrelts	.05	.02
❑ 98	Rene Gonzales RC	.10	.04
❑ 99	Chuck Finley	.10	.04
❑ 100	Jack Clark	.10	.04
❑ 101	Allan Anderson	.05	.02
❑ 102	Barry Larkin	.15	.06
❑ 103	Curt Young	.05	.02
❑ 104	Dick Williams MG	.05	.02
❑ 105	Jesse Orosco	.05	.02
❑ 106	Jim Walewander	.05	.02
❑ 107	Scott Bailes	.05	.02
❑ 108	Steve Lyons	.05	.02
❑ 109	Joel Skinner	.05	.02
❑ 110	Teddy Higuera	.05	.02
❑ 111	Hubie Brooks Vance Law TL	.05	.02
❑ 112	Les Lancaster	.05	.02
❑ 113	Kelly Gruber	.05	.02
❑ 114	Jeff Russell	.05	.02
❑ 115	Johnny Ray	.05	.02
❑ 116	Jerry Don Gleaton	.05	.02
❑ 117	James Steels	.05	.02
❑ 118	Bob Welch	.10	.04
❑ 119	Robbie Wine	.05	.02
❑ 120	Kirby Puckett	.20	.08
❑ 121	Checklist 1-132	.05	.02
❑ 122	Tony Bernazard	.05	.02
❑ 123	Tom Candiotti	.05	.02

❑ 124 Ray Knight .10 .04
❑ 125 Bruce Hurst .05 .02
❑ 126 Steve Jeltz .05 .02
❑ 127 Jim Gott .05 .02
❑ 128 Johnny Grubb .05 .02
❑ 129 Greg Minton .05 .02
❑ 130 Buddy Bell .10 .04
❑ 131 Don Schulze .05 .02
❑ 132 Donnie Hill .05 .02
❑ 133 Greg Mathews .05 .02
❑ 134 Chuck Tanner MG .05 .02
❑ 135 Dennis Rasmussen .05 .02
❑ 136 Brian Dayett .05 .02
❑ 137 Chris Bosio .05 .02
❑ 138 Mitch Webster .05 .02
❑ 139 Jerry Browne .05 .02
❑ 140 Jesse Barfield .10 .04
❑ 141 George Brett .20 .08
Bret Saberhagen TL
❑ 142 Andy Van Slyke .10 .04
❑ 143 Mickey Tettleton .05 .02
❑ 144 Don Gordon .05 .02
❑ 145 Bill Madlock .10 .04
❑ 146 Donell Nixon .05 .02
❑ 147 Bill Buckner .10 .04
❑ 148 Carmelo Martinez .05 .02
❑ 149 Ken Howell .05 .02
❑ 150 Eric Davis .10 .04
❑ 151 Bob Knepper .05 .02
❑ 152 Jody Reed RC .25 .10
❑ 153 John Habyan .05 .02
❑ 154 Jeff Stone .05 .02
❑ 155 Bruce Sutter .10 .04
❑ 156 Gary Matthews .10 .04
❑ 157 Atlee Hammaker .05 .02
❑ 158 Tim Hulett .05 .02
❑ 159 Brad Arnsberg .05 .02
❑ 160 Willie McGee .10 .04
❑ 161 Bryn Smith .05 .02
❑ 162 Mark McLemore .05 .02
❑ 163 Dale Mohorcic .05 .02
❑ 164 Dave Johnson MG .05 .02
❑ 165 Robin Yount .30 .12
❑ 166 Rick Rodriquez .05 .02
❑ 167 Rance Mulliniks .05 .02
❑ 168 Barry Jones .05 .02
❑ 169 Ross Jones .05 .02
❑ 170 Rich Gossage .10 .04
❑ 171 Shawon Dunston .05 .02
Manny Trillo TL
❑ 172 Lloyd McClendon RC .25 .10
❑ 173 Eric Plunk .05 .02
❑ 174 Phil Garner .10 .04
❑ 175 Kevin Bass .05 .02
❑ 176 Jeff Reed .05 .02
❑ 177 Frank Tanana .10 .04
❑ 178 Dwayne Henry .05 .02
❑ 179 Charlie Puleo .05 .02
❑ 180 Terry Kennedy .05 .02
❑ 181 David Cone .10 .04
❑ 182 Ken Phelps .05 .02
❑ 183 Tom Lawless .05 .02
❑ 184 Ivan Calderon .05 .02
❑ 185 Rick Rhoden .05 .02
❑ 186 Rafael Palmeiro .40 .16
❑ 187 Steve Kiefer .05 .02
❑ 188 John Russell .05 .02
❑ 189 Wes Gardner .05 .02
❑ 190 Candy Maldonado .05 .02
❑ 191 John Cerutti .05 .02
❑ 192 Devon White .10 .04
❑ 193 Brian Fisher .05 .02
❑ 194 Tom Kelly MG .05 .02
❑ 195 Dan Quisenberry .05 .02
❑ 196 Dave Engle .05 .02
❑ 197 Lance McCullers .05 .02
❑ 198 Franklin Stubbs .05 .02
❑ 199 Dave Meads .05 .02
❑ 200 Wade Boggs .15 .06
❑ 201 Bobby Valentine MG .05 .02
Pete O'Brien
Pete Incaviglia
Steve Buechele TL
❑ 202 Glenn Hoffman .05 .02
❑ 203 Fred Toliver .05 .02
❑ 204 Paul O'Neill .15 .06
❑ 205 Nelson Liriano .05 .02
❑ 206 Domingo Ramos .05 .02
❑ 207 John Mitchell RC .10 .04
❑ 208 Steve Lake .05 .02
❑ 209 Richard Dotson .05 .02
❑ 210 Willie Randolph .10 .04
❑ 211 Frank DiPino .05 .02
❑ 212 Greg Brock .05 .02
❑ 213 Albert Hall .05 .02
❑ 214 Dave Schmidt .05 .02
❑ 215 Von Hayes .05 .02
❑ 216 Jerry Reuss .05 .02
❑ 217 Harry Spilman .05 .02
❑ 218 Dan Schatzeder .05 .02
❑ 219 Mike Stanley .05 .02
❑ 220 Tom Henke .05 .02
❑ 221 Rafael Belliard .05 .02
❑ 222 Steve Farr .05 .02
❑ 223 Stan Jefferson .05 .02
❑ 224 Tom Trebelhorn MG .05 .02
❑ 225 Mike Scioscia .10 .04
❑ 226 Dave Lopes .10 .04
❑ 227 Ed Correa .05 .02
❑ 228 Wallace Johnson .05 .02
❑ 229 Jeff Musselman .05 .02
❑ 230 Pat Tabler .05 .02
❑ 231 Barry Bonds .50 .20
Bobby Bonilla TL
❑ 232 Bob James .05 .02
❑ 233 Rafael Santana .05 .02
❑ 234 Ken Dayley .05 .02
❑ 235 Gary Ward .05 .02
❑ 236 Ted Power .05 .02
❑ 237 Mike Heath .05 .02
❑ 238 Luis Polonia RC* .25 .10
❑ 239 Roy Smalley .05 .02
❑ 240 Lee Smith .10 .04
❑ 241 Damaso Garcia .05 .02
❑ 242 Tom Niedenfuer .05 .02
❑ 243 Mark Ryal .05 .02
❑ 244 Jeff D. Robinson .05 .02
❑ 245 Rich Gedman .05 .02
❑ 246 Mike Campbell .05 .02
❑ 247 Thad Bosley .05 .02
❑ 248 Storm Davis .05 .02
❑ 249 Mike Marshall .05 .02
❑ 250 Nolan Ryan 1.00 .40
❑ 251 Tom Foley .05 .02
❑ 252 Bob Brower .05 .02
❑ 253 Checklist 133-264 .05 .02
❑ 254 Lee Elia MG .05 .02
❑ 255 Mookie Wilson .10 .04
❑ 256 Ken Schrom .05 .02
❑ 257 Jerry Royster .05 .02
❑ 258 Ed Nunez .05 .02
❑ 259 Ron Kittle .05 .02
❑ 260 Vince Coleman .05 .02
❑ 261 Giants TL .05 .02
(Five players)
❑ 262 Drew Hall .05 .02
❑ 263 Glenn Braggs .05 .02
❑ 264 Les Straker .05 .02
❑ 265 Bo Diaz .05 .02
❑ 266 Paul Assenmacher .05 .02
❑ 267 Billy Bean RC .10 .04
❑ 268 Bruce Ruffin .05 .02
❑ 269 Ellis Burks RC .40 .16
❑ 270 Mike Witt .05 .02
❑ 271 Ken Gerhart .05 .02
❑ 272 Steve Ontiveros .05 .02
❑ 273 Garth Iorg .05 .02
❑ 274 Junior Ortiz .05 .02
❑ 275 Kevin Seitzer .05 .02
❑ 276 Luis Salazar .05 .02
❑ 277 Alejandro Pena .05 .02
❑ 278 Jose Cruz .10 .04
❑ 279 Randy St.Claire .05 .02
❑ 280 Pete Incaviglia .05 .02
❑ 281 Jerry Hairston .05 .02
❑ 282 Pat Perry .05 .02
❑ 283 Phil Lombardi .05 .02
❑ 284 Larry Bowa MG .10 .04
❑ 285 Jim Presley .05 .02
❑ 286 Chuck Crim .05 .02
❑ 287 Manny Trillo .05 .02
❑ 288 Pat Pacillo .05 .02
(Chris Sabo in
background of photo)
❑ 289 Dave Bergman .05 .02
❑ 290 Tony Fernandez .05 .02
❑ 291 Billy Hatcher .05 .02
Kevin Bass TL
❑ 292 Carney Lansford .10 .04
❑ 293 Doug Jones RC .25 .10
❑ 294 Al Pedrique .05 .02
❑ 295 Bert Blyleven .10 .04
❑ 296 Floyd Rayford .05 .02
❑ 297 Zane Smith .05 .02
❑ 298 Milt Thompson .05 .02
❑ 299 Steve Crawford .05 .02
❑ 300 Don Mattingly .60 .24
❑ 301 Bud Black .05 .02
❑ 302 Jose Uribe .05 .02
❑ 303 Eric Show .05 .02
❑ 304 George Hendrick .10 .04
❑ 305 Steve Sax .05 .02
❑ 306 Billy Hatcher .05 .02
❑ 307 Mike Trujillo .05 .02
❑ 308 Lee Mazzilli .10 .04
❑ 309 Bill Long .05 .02
❑ 310 Tom Herr .05 .02
❑ 311 Scott Sanderson .05 .02
❑ 312 Joey Meyer .05 .02
❑ 313 Bob McClure .05 .02
❑ 314 Jimy Williams MG .05 .02
❑ 315 Dave Parker .10 .04
❑ 316 Jose Rijo .10 .04
❑ 317 Tom Nieto .05 .02
❑ 318 Mel Hall .05 .02
❑ 319 Mike Loynd .05 .02
❑ 320 Alan Trammell .10 .04
❑ 321 Harold Baines .10 .04
Carlton Fisk TL
❑ 322 Vicente Palacios .05 .02
❑ 323 Rick Leach .05 .02
❑ 324 Danny Jackson .05 .02
❑ 325 Glenn Hubbard .05 .02
❑ 326 Al Nipper .05 .02
❑ 327 Larry Sheets .05 .02
❑ 328 Greg Cadaret .05 .02
❑ 329 Chris Speier .05 .02
❑ 330 Eddie Whitson .05 .02
❑ 331 Brian Downing .10 .04
❑ 332 Jerry Reed .05 .02
❑ 333 Wally Backman .05 .02
❑ 334 Dave LaPoint .05 .02
❑ 335 Claudell Washington .05 .02
❑ 336 Ed Lynch .05 .02
❑ 337 Jim Gantner .05 .02
❑ 338 Brian Holton UER .05 .02
1987 ERA .389,
should be 3.89
❑ 339 Kurt Stillwell .05 .02
❑ 340 Jack Morris .10 .04
❑ 341 Carmen Castillo .05 .02
❑ 342 Larry Andersen .05 .02
❑ 343 Greg Gagne .05 .02
❑ 344 Tony LaRussa MG .10 .04
❑ 345 Scott Fletcher .05 .02
❑ 346 Vance Law .05 .02
❑ 347 Joe Johnson .05 .02
❑ 348 Jim Eisenreich .05 .02
❑ 349 Bob Walk .05 .02
❑ 350 Will Clark .20 .08
❑ 351 Red Schoendienst CO .10 .04
Tony Pena TL
❑ 352 Bill Ripken RC* .05 .02
❑ 353 Ed Olwine .05 .02
❑ 354 Marc Sullivan .05 .02
❑ 355 Roger McDowell .05 .02
❑ 356 Luis Aguayo .05 .02
❑ 357 Floyd Bannister .05 .02
❑ 358 Rey Quinones .05 .02
❑ 359 Tim Stoddard .05 .02
❑ 360 Tony Gwynn .30 .12
❑ 361 Greg Maddux 1.00 .40
❑ 362 Juan Castillo .05 .02
❑ 363 Willie Fraser .05 .02
❑ 364 Nick Esasky .05 .02
❑ 365 Floyd Youmans .05 .02
❑ 366 Chet Lemon .10 .04
❑ 367 Tim Leary .05 .02

No.	Card	Price	Price
368	Gerald Young	.05	.02
369	Greg Harris	.05	.02
370	Jose Canseco	.20	.08
371	Joe Hesketh	.05	.02
372	Matt Williams RC	.75	.30
373	Checklist 265-396	.05	.02
374	Doc Edwards MG	.05	.02
375	Tom Brunansky	.05	.02
376	Bill Wilkinson	.05	.02
377	Sam Horn RC	.10	.04
378	Todd Frohwirth	.05	.02
379	Rafael Ramirez	.05	.02
380	Joe Magrane RC*	.05	.02
381	Wally Joyner Jack Howell TL	.10	.04
382	Keith A. Miller RC	.25	.10
383	Eric Bell	.05	.02
384	Neil Allen	.05	.02
385	Carlton Fisk	.15	.06
386	Don Mattingly AS	.30	.12
387	Willie Randolph AS	.05	.02
388	Wade Boggs AS	.10	.04
389	Alan Trammell AS	.05	.02
390	George Bell AS	.05	.02
391	Kirby Puckett AS	.15	.06
392	Dave Winfield AS	.05	.02
393	Matt Nokes AS	.05	.02
394	Roger Clemens AS	.20	.08
395	Jimmy Key AS	.05	.02
396	Tom Henke AS	.05	.02
397	Jack Clark AS	.05	.02
398	Juan Samuel AS	.05	.02
399	Tim Wallach AS	.05	.02
400	Ozzie Smith AS	.20	.08
401	Andre Dawson AS	.05	.02
402	Tony Gwynn AS	.15	.06
403	Tim Raines AS	.05	.02
404	Benny Santiago AS	.05	.02
405	Dwight Gooden AS	.05	.02
406	Shane Rawley AS	.05	.02
407	Steve Bedrosian AS	.05	.02
408	Dion James	.05	.02
409	Joel McKeon	.05	.02
410	Tony Pena	.05	.02
411	Wayne Tolleson	.05	.02
412	Randy Myers	.10	.04
413	John Christensen	.05	.02
414	John McNamara MG	.05	.02
415	Don Carman	.05	.02
416	Keith Moreland	.05	.02
417	Mark Ciardi	.05	.02
418	Joel Youngblood	.05	.02
419	Scott McGregor	.05	.02
420	Wally Joyner	.10	.04
421	Ed VandeBerg	.05	.02
422	Dave Concepcion	.10	.04
423	John Smiley RC*	.25	.10
424	Dwayne Murphy	.05	.02
425	Jeff Reardon	.10	.04
426	Randy Ready	.05	.02
427	Paul Kilgus	.05	.02
428	John Shelby	.05	.02
429	Alan Trammell Kirk Gibson TL	.10	.04
430	Glenn Davis	.05	.02
431	Casey Candaele	.05	.02
432	Mike Moore	.05	.02
433	Bill Pecota RC*	.05	.02
434	Rick Aguilera	.05	.02
435	Mike Pagliarulo	.05	.02
436	Mike Bielecki	.05	.02
437	Fred Manrique	.05	.02
438	Rob Ducey	.05	.02
439	Dave Martinez	.05	.02
440	Steve Bedrosian	.05	.02
441	Rick Manning	.05	.02
442	Tom Bolton	.05	.02
443	Ken Griffey	.10	.04
444	C.Ripken Sr. MG UER two copyrights	.05	.02
445	Mike Krukow	.05	.02
446	Doug DeCinces (Now with Cardinals on card front)	.05	.02
447	Jeff Montgomery RC	.25	.10
448	Mike Davis	.05	.02
449	Jeff M. Robinson	.05	.02
450	Barry Bonds	2.00	.80
451	Keith Atherton	.05	.02
452	Willie Wilson	.10	.04
453	Dennis Powell	.05	.02
454	Marvell Wynne	.05	.02
455	Shawn Hillegas	.05	.02
456	Dave Anderson	.05	.02
457	Terry Leach	.05	.02
458	Ron Hassey	.05	.02
459	Dave Winfield Willie Randolph TL	.05	.02
460	Ozzie Smith	.30	.12
461	Danny Darwin	.05	.02
462	Don Slaught	.05	.02
463	Fred McGriff	.20	.08
464	Jay Tibbs	.05	.02
465	Paul Molitor	.15	.06
466	Jerry Mumphrey	.05	.02
467	Don Aase	.05	.02
468	Darren Daulton	.10	.04
469	Jeff Dedmon	.05	.02
470	Dwight Evans	.10	.04
471	Donnie Moore	.05	.02
472	Robby Thompson	.05	.02
473	Joe Niekro	.05	.02
474	Tom Brookens	.05	.02
475	Pete Rose MG	.50	.20
476	Dave Stewart	.10	.04
477	Jamie Quirk	.05	.02
478	Sid Bream	.05	.02
479	Brett Butler	.10	.04
480	Dwight Gooden	.10	.04
481	Mariano Duncan	.05	.02
482	Mark Davis	.05	.02
483	Rod Booker	.05	.02
484	Pat Clements	.05	.02
485	Harold Reynolds	.10	.04
486	Pat Keedy	.05	.02
487	Jim Pankovits	.05	.02
488	Andy McGaffigan	.05	.02
489	Pedro Guerrero Fernando Valenzuela TL	.05	.02
490	Larry Parrish	.05	.02
491	B.J. Surhoff	.10	.04
492	Doyle Alexander	.05	.02
493	Mike Greenwell	.05	.02
494	Wally Ritchie	.05	.02
495	Eddie Murray	.20	.08
496	Guy Hoffman	.05	.02
497	Kevin Mitchell	.10	.04
498	Bob Boone	.10	.04
499	Eric King	.05	.02
500	Andre Dawson	.10	.04
501	Tim Birtsas	.05	.02
502	Dan Gladden	.05	.02
503	Junior Noboa	.05	.02
504	Bob Rodgers MG	.05	.02
505	Willie Upshaw	.05	.02
506	John Cangelosi	.05	.02
507	Mark Gubicza	.05	.02
508	Tim Teufel	.05	.02
509	Bill Dawley	.05	.02
510	Dave Winfield	.10	.04
511	Joel Davis	.05	.02
512	Alex Trevino	.05	.02
513	Tim Flannery	.05	.02
514	Pat Sheridan	.05	.02
515	Juan Nieves	.05	.02
516	Jim Sundberg	.10	.04
517	Ron Robinson	.05	.02
518	Greg Gross	.05	.02
519	Harold Reynolds Phil Bradley TL	.05	.02
520	Dave Smith	.05	.02
521	Jim Dwyer	.05	.02
522	Bob Patterson	.05	.02
523	Gary Roenicke	.05	.02
524	Gary Lucas	.05	.02
525	Marty Barrett	.05	.02
526	Juan Berenguer	.05	.02
527	Steve Henderson	.05	.02
528A	Checklist 397-528 ERR (455 S. Carlton)	.15	.06
528B	Checklist 397-528 COR (455 S. Hillegas)	.10	.04
529	Tim Burke	.05	.02
530	Gary Carter	.10	.04
531	Rich Yett	.05	.02
532	Mike Kingery	.05	.02
533	John Farrell RC	.10	.04
534	John Wathan MG	.05	.02
535	Ron Guidry	.10	.04
536	John Morris	.05	.02
537	Steve Buechele	.05	.02
538	Bill Wegman	.05	.02
539	Mike LaValliere	.05	.02
540	Bret Saberhagen	.10	.04
541	Juan Beniquez	.05	.02
542	Paul Noce	.05	.02
543	Kent Tekulve	.05	.02
544	Jim Traber	.05	.02
545	Don Baylor	.10	.04
546	John Candelaria	.05	.02
547	Felix Fermin	.05	.02
548	Shane Mack	.05	.02
549	Albert Hall Dale Murphy Ken Griffey Dion James TL	.10	.04
550	Pedro Guerrero	.10	.04
551	Terry Steinbach	.10	.04
552	Mark Thurmond	.05	.02
553	Tracy Jones	.05	.02
554	Mike Smithson	.05	.02
555	Brook Jacoby	.05	.02
556	Stan Clarke	.05	.02
557	Craig Reynolds	.05	.02
558	Bob Ojeda	.05	.02
559	Ken Williams RC	.05	.02
560	Tim Wallach	.05	.02
561	Rick Cerone	.05	.02
562	Jim Lindeman	.05	.02
563	Jose Guzman	.05	.02
564	Frank Lucchesi MG	.05	.02
565	Lloyd Moseby	.05	.02
566	Charlie O'Brien	.05	.02
567	Mike Diaz	.05	.02
568	Chris Brown	.05	.02
569	Charlie Leibrandt	.05	.02
570	Jeffrey Leonard	.05	.02
571	Mark Williamson	.05	.02
572	Chris James	.05	.02
573	Bob Stanley	.05	.02
574	Graig Nettles	.10	.04
575	Don Sutton	.10	.04
576	Tommy Hinzo	.05	.02
577	Tom Browning	.05	.02
578	Gary Gaetti	.10	.04
579	Gary Carter Kevin McReynolds TL	.05	.02
580	Mark McGwire	1.50	.60
581	Tito Landrum	.05	.02
582	Mike Henneman RC*	.25	.10
583	Dave Valle	.05	.02
584	Steve Trout	.05	.02
585	Ozzie Guillen	.05	.02
586	Bob Forsch	.05	.02
587	Terry Puhl	.05	.02
588	Jeff Parrett	.05	.02
589	Geno Petralli	.05	.02
590	George Bell	.10	.04
591	Doug Drabek	.05	.02
592	Dale Sveum	.05	.02
593	Bob Tewksbury	.05	.02
594	Bobby Valentine MG	.10	.04
595	Frank White	.10	.04
596	John Kruk	.10	.04
597	Gene Garber	.05	.02
598	Lee Lacy	.05	.02
599	Calvin Schiraldi	.05	.02
600	Mike Schmidt	.50	.20
601	Jack Lazorko	.05	.02
602	Mike Aldrete	.05	.02
603	Rob Murphy	.05	.02
604	Chris Bando	.05	.02
605	Kirk Gibson	.20	.08
606	Moose Haas	.05	.02
607	Mickey Hatcher	.05	.02
608	Charlie Kerfeld	.05	.02
609	Gary Gaetti Kent Hrbek TL	.10	.04

❑ 610 Keith Hernandez .10 .04
❑ 611 Tommy John .10 .04
❑ 612 Curt Ford .05 .02
❑ 613 Bobby Thigpen .05 .02
❑ 614 Herm Winningham .05 .02
❑ 615 Jody Davis .05 .02
❑ 616 Jay Aldrich .05 .02
❑ 617 Oddibe McDowell .05 .02
❑ 618 Cecil Fielder .10 .04
❑ 619 Mike Dunne .05 .02
Inconsistent design, black name on front
❑ 620 Cory Snyder .05 .02
❑ 621 Gene Nelson .05 .02
❑ 622 Kal Daniels .05 .02
❑ 623 Mike Flanagan .05 .02
❑ 624 Jim Leyland MG .10 .04
❑ 625 Frank Viola .10 .04
❑ 626 Glenn Wilson .05 .02
❑ 627 Joe Boever .05 .02
❑ 628 Dave Henderson .05 .02
❑ 629 Kelly Downs .05 .02
❑ 630 Darrell Evans .10 .04
❑ 631 Jack Howell .05 .02
❑ 632 Steve Shields .05 .02
❑ 633 Barry Lyons .05 .02
❑ 634 Jose DeLeon .05 .02
❑ 635 Terry Pendleton .10 .04
❑ 636 Charles Hudson .05 .02
❑ 637 Jay Bell RC .40 .16
❑ 638 Steve Balboni .05 .02
❑ 639 Glenn Braggs .05 .02
Tony Muser CO TL
❑ 640 Garry Templeton .10 .04
(Inconsistent design, green border)
❑ 641 Rick Honeycutt .05 .02
❑ 642 Bob Dernier .05 .02
❑ 643 Rocky Childress .05 .02
❑ 644 Terry McGriff .05 .02
❑ 645 Matt Nokes RC* .25 .10
❑ 646 Checklist 529-660 .05 .02
❑ 647 Pascual Perez .05 .02
❑ 648 Al Newman .05 .02
❑ 649 DeWayne Buice .05 .02
❑ 650 Cal Ripken .75 .30
❑ 651 Mike Jackson RC* .25 .10
❑ 652 Bruce Benedict .05 .02
❑ 653 Jeff Sellers .05 .02
❑ 654 Roger Craig MG .10 .04
❑ 655 Len Dykstra .10 .04
❑ 656 Lee Guetterman .05 .02
❑ 657 Gary Redus .05 .02
❑ 658 Tim Conroy .05 .02
(Inconsistent design, name in white)
❑ 659 Bobby Meacham .05 .02
❑ 660 Rick Reuschel .10 .04
❑ 661 Nolan Ryan TBC '83 .50 .20
❑ 662 Jim Rice TBC .05 .02
❑ 663 Ron Blomberg TBC .05 .02
❑ 664 Bob Gibson TBC '68 .25 .10
❑ 665 Stan Musial TBC '63 .20 .08
❑ 666 Mario Soto .10 .04
❑ 667 Luis Quinones .05 .02
❑ 668 Walt Terrell .05 .02
❑ 669 Lance Parrish .05 .02
Mike Ryan CO TL
❑ 670 Dan Plesac .05 .02
❑ 671 Tim Laudner .05 .02
❑ 672 John Davis .05 .02
❑ 673 Tony Phillips .05 .02
❑ 674 Mike Fitzgerald .05 .02
❑ 675 Jim Rice .10 .04
❑ 676 Ken Dixon .05 .02
❑ 677 Eddie Milner .05 .02
❑ 678 Jim Acker .05 .02
❑ 679 Darrell Miller .05 .02
❑ 680 Charlie Hough .10 .04
❑ 681 Bobby Bonilla .10 .04
❑ 682 Jimmy Key .10 .04
❑ 683 Julio Franco .10 .04
❑ 684 Hal Lanier MG .05 .02
❑ 685 Ron Darling .10 .04
❑ 686 Terry Francona .10 .04
❑ 687 Mickey Brantley .05 .02
❑ 688 Jim Winn .05 .02
❑ 689 Tom Pagnozzi RC .10 .04
❑ 690 Jay Howell .05 .02
❑ 691 Dan Pasqua .05 .02
❑ 692 Mike Birkbeck .05 .02
❑ 693 Benito Santiago .10 .04
❑ 694 Eric Nolte .05 .02
❑ 695 Shawon Dunston .05 .02
❑ 696 Duane Ward .05 .02
❑ 697 Steve Lombardozzi .05 .02
❑ 698 Brad Havens .05 .02
❑ 699 Benito Santiago .10 .04
Tony Gwynn TL
❑ 700 George Brett .50 .20
❑ 701 Sammy Stewart .05 .02
❑ 702 Mike Gallego .05 .02
❑ 703 Bob Brenly .05 .02
❑ 704 Dennis Boyd .05 .02
❑ 705 Juan Samuel .05 .02
❑ 706 Rick Mahler .05 .02
❑ 707 Fred Lynn .10 .04
❑ 708 Gus Polidor .05 .02
❑ 709 George Frazier .05 .02
❑ 710 Darryl Strawberry .10 .04
❑ 711 Bill Gullickson .05 .02
❑ 712 John Moses .05 .02
❑ 713 Willie Hernandez .05 .02
❑ 714 Jim Fregosi MG .05 .02
❑ 715 Todd Worrell .05 .02
❑ 716 Lenn Sakata .05 .02
❑ 717 Jay Baller .05 .02
❑ 718 Mike Felder .05 .02
❑ 719 Denny Walling .05 .02
❑ 720 Tim Raines .10 .04
❑ 721 Pete O'Brien .05 .02
❑ 722 Manny Lee .05 .02
❑ 723 Bob Kipper .05 .02
❑ 724 Danny Tartabull .05 .02
❑ 725 Mike Boddicker .05 .02
❑ 726 Alfredo Griffin .05 .02
❑ 727 Greg Booker .05 .02
❑ 728 Andy Allanson .05 .02
❑ 729 George Bell .10 .04
Fred McGriff TL
❑ 730 John Franco .10 .04
❑ 731 Rick Schu .05 .02
❑ 732 David Palmer .05 .02
❑ 733 Spike Owen .05 .02
❑ 734 Craig Lefferts .05 .02
❑ 735 Kevin McReynolds .05 .02
❑ 736 Matt Young .05 .02
❑ 737 Butch Wynegar .05 .02
❑ 738 Scott Bankhead .05 .02
❑ 739 Daryl Boston .05 .02
❑ 740 Rick Sutcliffe .10 .04
❑ 741 Mike Easler .05 .02
❑ 742 Mark Clear .05 .02
❑ 743 Larry Herndon .05 .02
❑ 744 Whitey Herzog MG .10 .04
❑ 745 Bill Doran .05 .02
❑ 746 Gene Larkin RC* .25 .10
❑ 747 Bobby Witt .05 .02
❑ 748 Reid Nichols .05 .02
❑ 749 Mark Eichhorn .05 .02
❑ 750 Bo Jackson .20 .08
❑ 751 Jim Morrison .05 .02
❑ 752 Mark Grant .05 .02
❑ 753 Danny Heep .05 .02
❑ 754 Mike LaCoss .05 .02
❑ 755 Ozzie Virgil .05 .02
❑ 756 Mike Maddux .05 .02
❑ 757 John Marzano .05 .02
❑ 758 Eddie Williams RC .10 .04
❑ 759 Mark McGwire .75 .30
Jose Canseco TL UER (two copyrights)
❑ 760 Mike Scott .10 .04
❑ 761 Tony Armas .10 .04
❑ 762 Scott Bradley .05 .02
❑ 763 Doug Sisk .05 .02
❑ 764 Greg Walker .05 .02
❑ 765 Neal Heaton .05 .02
❑ 766 Henry Cotto .05 .02
❑ 767 Jose Lind RC .25 .10
❑ 768 Dickie Noles .05 .02
(Now with Tigers on card front)
❑ 769 Cecil Cooper .10 .04
❑ 770 Lou Whitaker .10 .04
❑ 771 Ruben Sierra .10 .04
❑ 772 Sal Butera .05 .02
❑ 773 Frank Williams .05 .02
❑ 774 Gene Mauch MG .05 .02
❑ 775 Dave Stieb .10 .04
❑ 776 Checklist 661-792 .05 .02
❑ 777 Lonnie Smith .05 .02
❑ 778A Keith Comstock ERR 2.00 .80
(White "Padres")
❑ 778B Keith Comstock COR .05 .02
(Blue "Padres")
❑ 779 Tom Glavine RC 1.50 .60
❑ 780 Fernando Valenzuela .10 .04
❑ 781 Keith Hughes .05 .02
❑ 782 Jeff Ballard .05 .02
❑ 783 Ron Roenicke .05 .02
❑ 784 Joe Sambito .05 .02
❑ 785 Alvin Davis .05 .02
❑ 786 Joe Price .05 .02
Inconsistent design, orange team name
❑ 787 Bill Almon .05 .02
❑ 788 Ray Searage .05 .02
❑ 789 Joe Carter .05 .02
Cory Snyder TL
❑ 790 Dave Righetti .10 .04
❑ 791 Ted Simmons .10 .04
❑ 792 John Tudor .10 .04

1988 Topps Traded

	Nm-Mt	Ex-Mt
COMP.FACT.SET (132)	8.00	3.20
❑ 1T Jim Abbott OLY XRC	1.00	.40
❑ 2T Juan Agosto	.10	.04
❑ 3T Luis Alicea XRC	.50	.20
❑ 4T Roberto Alomar XRC	2.00	.80
❑ 5T Brady Anderson XRC	.75	.30
❑ 6T Jack Armstrong XRC	.50	.20
❑ 7T Don August	.10	.04
❑ 8T Floyd Bannister	.10	.04
❑ 9T Bret Barberie OLY XRC	.25	.10
❑ 10T Jose Bautista XRC	.25	.10
❑ 11T Don Baylor	.20	.08
❑ 12T Tim Belcher	.10	.04
❑ 13T Buddy Bell	.20	.08
❑ 14T Andy Benes OLY XRC	.75	.30
❑ 15T Damon Berryhill XRC	.50	.20
❑ 16T Bud Black	.10	.04
❑ 17T Pat Borders XRC	.50	.20
❑ 18T Phil Bradley	.10	.04
❑ 19T J.Branson XRC OLY	.50	.20
❑ 20T Tom Brunansky	.10	.04
❑ 21T Jay Buhner XRC	1.00	.40
❑ 22T Brett Butler	.20	.08
❑ 23T Jim Campanis OLY	.10	.04
❑ 24T Sil Campusano	.10	.04
❑ 25T John Candelaria	.10	.04
❑ 26T Jose Cecena	.10	.04
❑ 27T Rick Cerone	.10	.04
❑ 28T Jack Clark	.20	.08
❑ 29T Kevin Coffman	.10	.04
❑ 30T Pat Combs OLY XRC	.25	.10
❑ 31T Henry Cotto	.10	.04

Card	Nm-Mt	Ex-Mt
❑ 32T Chili Davis	.20	.08
❑ 33T Mike Davis	.10	.04
❑ 34T Jose DeLeon	.10	.04
❑ 35T Richard Dotson	.10	.04
❑ 36T Cecil Espy	.10	.04
❑ 37T Tom Filer	.10	.04
❑ 38T Mike Fiore OLY	.10	.04
❑ 39T Ron Gant XRC	.75	.30
❑ 40T Kirk Gibson	.50	.20
❑ 41T Rich Gossage	.20	.08
❑ 42T Mark Grace XRC	1.50	.60
❑ 43T Alfredo Griffin	.10	.04
❑ 44T Ty Griffin OLY	.10	.04
❑ 45T Bryan Harvey XRC	.50	.20
❑ 46T Ron Hassey	.10	.04
❑ 47T Ray Hayward	.10	.04
❑ 48T Dave Henderson	.10	.04
❑ 49T Tom Herr	.10	.04
❑ 50T Bob Horner	.20	.08
❑ 51T Ricky Horton	.10	.04
❑ 52T Jay Howell	.10	.04
❑ 53T Glenn Hubbard	.10	.04
❑ 54T Jeff Innis	.10	.04
❑ 55T Danny Jackson	.10	.04
❑ 56T Darrin Jackson XRC*	.25	.10
❑ 57T Roberto Kelly XRC*	.50	.20
❑ 58T Ron Kittle	.10	.04
❑ 59T Ray Knight	.20	.08
❑ 60T Vance Law	.10	.04
❑ 61T Jeffrey Leonard	.10	.04
❑ 62T Mike Macfarlane XRC	.50	.20
❑ 63T Scotti Madison	.10	.04
❑ 64T Kirt Manwaring	.10	.04
❑ 65T M.Marquess OLY CO	.10	.04
❑ 66T T.Martinez OLY XRC	1.50	.60
❑ 67T Billy Masse OLY XRC	.25	.10
❑ 68T Jack McDowell XRC	.75	.30
❑ 69T Jack McKeon MG	.20	.08
❑ 70T Larry McWilliams	.10	.04
❑ 71T M.Morandini OLY XRC	.50	.20
❑ 72T Keith Moreland	.10	.04
❑ 73T Mike Morgan	.10	.04
❑ 74T C.Nagy OLY XRC	.50	.20
❑ 75T Al Nipper	.10	.04
❑ 76T Russ Nixon MG	.10	.04
❑ 77T Jesse Orosco	.10	.04
❑ 78T Joe Orsulak	.10	.04
❑ 79T Dave Palmer	.10	.04
❑ 80T Mark Parent	.10	.04
❑ 81T Dave Parker	.20	.08
❑ 82T Dan Pasqua	.10	.04
❑ 83T Melido Perez XRC*	.50	.20
❑ 84T Steve Peters	.10	.04
❑ 85T Dan Petry	.10	.04
❑ 86T Gary Pettis	.10	.04
❑ 87T Jeff Pico	.10	.04
❑ 88T Jim Poole OLY XRC	.25	.10
❑ 89T Ted Power	.10	.04
❑ 90T Rafael Ramirez	.10	.04
❑ 91T Dennis Rasmussen	.10	.04
❑ 92T Jose Rijo	.20	.08
❑ 93T Ernie Riles	.10	.04
❑ 94T Luis Rivera	.10	.04
❑ 95T D.Robbins XRC OLY	.25	.10
❑ 96T Frank Robinson MG	.30	.12
❑ 97T Cookie Rojas MG	.10	.04
❑ 98T Chris Sabo XRC	.75	.30
❑ 99T Mark Salas	.10	.04
❑ 100T Luis Salazar	.10	.04
❑ 101T Rafael Santana	.10	.04
❑ 102T Nelson Santovenia	.10	.04
❑ 103T Mackey Sasser XRC	.50	.20
❑ 104T Calvin Schiraldi	.10	.04
❑ 105T Mike Schooler	.10	.04
❑ 106T S.Servais XRC OLY	.50	.20
❑ 107T D.Silvestri XRC OLY	.25	.10
❑ 108T Don Slaught	.10	.04
❑ 109T J.Slusarski XRC OLY	.25	.10
❑ 110T Lee Smith	.20	.08
❑ 111T Pete Smith XRC*	.25	.10
❑ 112T Jim Snyder MG	.10	.04
❑ 113T E.Sprague OLY XRC	.50	.20
❑ 114T Pete Stanicek	.10	.04
❑ 115T Kurt Stillwell	.10	.04
❑ 116T T.Stottlemyre XRC	.50	.20
❑ 117T Bill Swift	.10	.04
❑ 118T Pat Tabler	.10	.04
❑ 119T Scott Terry	.10	.04
❑ 120T Mickey Tettleton	.10	.04
❑ 121T Dickie Thon	.10	.04
❑ 122T Jeff Treadway XRC*	.50	.20
❑ 123T Willie Upshaw	.10	.04
❑ 124T R.Ventura OLY XRC	1.50	.60
❑ 125T Ron Washington	.10	.04
❑ 126T Walt Weiss XRC*	.75	.30
❑ 127T Bob Welch	.20	.08
❑ 128T David Wells XRC	1.50	.60
❑ 129T Glenn Wilson	.10	.04
❑ 130T Ted Wood OLY XRC	.25	.10
❑ 131T Don Zimmer MG	.20	.08
❑ 132T Checklist 1T-132T	.10	.04

1989 Topps

	Nm-Mt	Ex-Mt
COMPLETE SET (792)	20.00	8.00
COMP.FACT SET (792)	20.00	8.00
COMP.X-MAS.SET (792)	25.00	10.00

Card	Nm-Mt	Ex-Mt
❑ 1 George Bell RB Slams 3 HR on Opening Day	.05	.02
❑ 2 Wade Boggs RB	.10	.04
❑ 3 Gary Carter RB Sets Record for Career Putouts	.05	.02
❑ 4 Andre Dawson RB Logs Double Figures in HR and SB	.05	.02
❑ 5 Orel Hershiser RB Pitches 59 Scoreless Innings	.05	.02
❑ 6 Doug Jones RB UER Earns His 15th Straight Save Photo actually Chris Codiroli	.05	.02
❑ 7 Kevin McReynolds RB Steals 21 Without Being Caught	.05	.02
❑ 8 Dave Eiland	.05	.02
❑ 9 Tim Teufel	.05	.02
❑ 10 Andre Dawson	.10	.04
❑ 11 Bruce Sutter	.10	.04
❑ 12 Dale Sveum	.05	.02
❑ 13 Doug Sisk	.05	.02
❑ 14 Tom Kelly MG	.05	.02
❑ 15 Robby Thompson	.05	.02
❑ 16 Ron Robinson	.05	.02
❑ 17 Brian Downing	.10	.04
❑ 18 Rick Rhoden	.05	.02
❑ 19 Greg Gagne	.05	.02
❑ 20 Steve Bedrosian	.05	.02
❑ 21 Greg Walker TL	.05	.02
❑ 22 Tim Crews	.05	.02
❑ 23 Mike Fitzgerald	.05	.02
❑ 24 Larry Andersen	.05	.02
❑ 25 Frank White	.10	.04
❑ 26 Dale Mohorcic	.05	.02
❑ 27A Orestes Destrade (F* next to copyright) RC*	.10	.04
❑ 27B Orestes Destrade (E*F* next to copyright) RC*	.10	.04
❑ 28 Mike Moore	.05	.02
❑ 29 Kelly Gruber	.05	.02
❑ 30 Dwight Gooden	.10	.04
❑ 31 Terry Francona	.10	.04
❑ 32 Dennis Rasmussen	.05	.02
❑ 33 B.J. Surhoff	.10	.04
❑ 34 Ken Williams	.05	.02
❑ 35 John Tudor UER (With Red Sox in '84,should be Pirates)	.10	.04
❑ 36 Mitch Webster	.05	.02
❑ 37 Bob Stanley	.05	.02
❑ 38 Paul Runge	.05	.02
❑ 39 Mike Maddux	.05	.02
❑ 40 Steve Sax	.05	.02
❑ 41 Terry Mulholland	.05	.02
❑ 42 Jim Eppard	.05	.02
❑ 43 Guillermo Hernandez	.05	.02
❑ 44 Jim Snyder MG	.05	.02
❑ 45 Kal Daniels	.05	.02
❑ 46 Mark Portugal	.05	.02
❑ 47 Carney Lansford	.10	.04
❑ 48 Tim Burke	.05	.02
❑ 49 Craig Biggio RC	.75	.30
❑ 50 George Bell	.10	.04
❑ 51 Mark McLemore TL	.05	.02
❑ 52 Bob Brenly	.05	.02
❑ 53 Ruben Sierra	.05	.02
❑ 54 Steve Trout	.05	.02
❑ 55 Julio Franco	.10	.04
❑ 56 Pat Tabler	.05	.02
❑ 57 Alejandro Pena	.05	.02
❑ 58 Lee Mazzilli	.10	.04
❑ 59 Mark Davis	.05	.02
❑ 60 Tom Brunansky	.05	.02
❑ 61 Neil Allen	.05	.02
❑ 62 Alfredo Griffin	.05	.02
❑ 63 Mark Clear	.05	.02
❑ 64 Alex Trevino	.05	.02
❑ 65 Rick Reuschel	.10	.04
❑ 66 Manny Trillo	.05	.02
❑ 67 Dave Palmer	.05	.02
❑ 68 Darrell Miller	.05	.02
❑ 69 Jeff Ballard	.05	.02
❑ 70 Mark McGwire	1.00	.40
❑ 71 Mike Boddicker	.05	.02
❑ 72 John Moses	.05	.02
❑ 73 Pascual Perez	.05	.02
❑ 74 Nick Leyva MG	.05	.02
❑ 75 Tom Henke	.05	.02
❑ 76 Terry Blocker	.05	.02
❑ 77 Doyle Alexander	.05	.02
❑ 78 Jim Sundberg	.10	.04
❑ 79 Scott Bankhead	.05	.02
❑ 80 Cory Snyder	.05	.02
❑ 81 Tim Raines TL	.05	.02
❑ 82 Dave Leiper	.05	.02
❑ 83 Jeff Blauser	.05	.02
❑ 84 Bill Bene FDP	.05	.02
❑ 85 Kevin McReynolds	.05	.02
❑ 86 Al Nipper	.05	.02
❑ 87 Larry Owen	.05	.02
❑ 88 Darryl Hamilton RC *	.25	.10
❑ 89 Dave LaPoint	.05	.02
❑ 90 Vince Coleman UER (Wrong birth year)	.05	.02
❑ 91 Floyd Youmans	.05	.02
❑ 92 Jeff Kunkel	.05	.02
❑ 93 Ken Howell	.05	.02
❑ 94 Chris Speier	.05	.02
❑ 95 Gerald Young	.05	.02
❑ 96 Rick Cerone	.05	.02
❑ 97 Greg Mathews	.05	.02
❑ 98 Larry Sheets	.05	.02
❑ 99 Sherman Corbett	.05	.02
❑ 100 Mike Schmidt	.50	.20
❑ 101 Les Straker	.05	.02
❑ 102 Mike Gallego	.05	.02
❑ 103 Tim Birtsas	.05	.02
❑ 104 Dallas Green MG	.05	.02
❑ 105 Ron Darling	.10	.04
❑ 106 Willie Upshaw	.05	.02
❑ 107 Jose DeLeon	.05	.02
❑ 108 Fred Manrique	.05	.02
❑ 109 Hipolito Pena	.05	.02
❑ 110 Paul Molitor	.15	.06
❑ 111 Eric Davis TL	.05	.02

❑ 112 Jim Presley .05 .02
❑ 113 Lloyd Moseby .05 .02
❑ 114 Bob Kipper .05 .02
❑ 115 Jody Davis .05 .02
❑ 116 Jeff Montgomery .05 .02
❑ 117 Dave Anderson .05 .02
❑ 118 Checklist 1-132 .05 .02
❑ 119 Terry Puhl .05 .02
❑ 120 Frank Viola .10 .04
❑ 121 Garry Templeton .10 .04
❑ 122 Lance Johnson .05 .02
❑ 123 Spike Owen .05 .02
❑ 124 Jim Traber .05 .02
❑ 125 Mike Krukow .05 .02
❑ 126 Sid Bream .05 .02
❑ 127 Walt Terrell .05 .02
❑ 128 Milt Thompson .05 .02
❑ 129 Terry Clark .05 .02
❑ 130 Gerald Perry .05 .02
❑ 131 Dave Otto .05 .02
❑ 132 Curt Ford .05 .02
❑ 133 Bill Long .05 .02
❑ 134 Don Zimmer MG .10 .04
❑ 135 Jose Rijo .10 .04
❑ 136 Joey Meyer .05 .02
❑ 137 Geno Petralli .05 .02
❑ 138 Wallace Johnson .05 .02
❑ 139 Mike Flanagan .05 .02
❑ 140 Shawon Dunston .05 .02
❑ 141 Brook Jacoby TL .05 .02
❑ 142 Mike Diaz .05 .02
❑ 143 Mike Campbell .05 .02
❑ 144 Jay Bell .10 .04
❑ 145 Dave Stewart .10 .04
❑ 146 Gary Pettis .05 .02
❑ 147 DeWayne Buice .05 .02
❑ 148 Bill Pecota .05 .02
❑ 149 Doug Dascenzo .05 .02
❑ 150 Fernando Valenzuela .10 .04
❑ 151 Terry McGriff .05 .02
❑ 152 Mark Thurmond .05 .02
❑ 153 Jim Pankovits .05 .02
❑ 154 Don Carman .05 .02
❑ 155 Marty Barrett .05 .02
❑ 156 Dave Gallagher .05 .02
❑ 157 Tom Glavine .25 .10
❑ 158 Mike Aldrete .05 .02
❑ 159 Pat Clements .05 .02
❑ 160 Jeffrey Leonard .05 .02
❑ 161 G. Olson RC FDP UER .25 .10
Born Scribner, NE,
should be Omaha, NE
❑ 162 John Davis .05 .02
❑ 163 Bob Forsch .05 .02
❑ 164 Hal Lanier MG .05 .02
❑ 165 Mike Dunne .05 .02
❑ 166 Doug Jennings .05 .02
❑ 167 Steve Searcy FS .05 .02
❑ 168 Willie Wilson .10 .04
❑ 169 Mike Jackson .05 .02
❑ 170 Tony Fernandez .05 .02
❑ 171 Andres Thomas TL .05 .02
❑ 172 Frank Williams .05 .02
❑ 173 Mel Hall .05 .02
❑ 174 Todd Burns .05 .02
❑ 175 John Shelby .05 .02
❑ 176 Jeff Parrett .05 .02
❑ 177 Monty Fariss FDP .05 .02
❑ 178 Mark Grant .05 .02
❑ 179 Ozzie Virgil .05 .02
❑ 180 Mike Scott .10 .04
❑ 181 Craig Worthington .05 .02
❑ 182 Bob McClure .05 .02
❑ 183 Oddibe McDowell .05 .02
❑ 184 John Costello .05 .02
❑ 185 Claudell Washington .05 .02
❑ 186 Pat Perry .05 .02
❑ 187 Darren Daulton .10 .04
❑ 188 Dennis Lamp .05 .02
❑ 189 Kevin Mitchell .10 .04
❑ 190 Mike Witt .05 .02
❑ 191 Sil Campusano .05 .02
❑ 192 Paul Mirabella .05 .02
❑ 193 Sparky Anderson MG .10 .04
UER (553 Salazer)
❑ 194 Greg W. Harris RC .10 .04
❑ 195 Ozzie Guillen .05 .02
❑ 196 Denny Walling .05 .02
❑ 197 Neal Heaton .05 .02
❑ 198 Danny Heep .05 .02
❑ 199 Mike Schooler RC * .10 .04
❑ 200 George Brett .60 .24
❑ 201 Kelly Gruber TL .05 .02
❑ 202 Brad Moore .05 .02
❑ 203 Rob Ducey .05 .02
❑ 204 Brad Havens .05 .02
❑ 205 Dwight Evans .10 .04
❑ 206 Roberto Alomar .25 .10
❑ 207 Terry Leach .05 .02
❑ 208 Tom Pagnozzi .05 .02
❑ 209 Jeff Bittiger .05 .02
❑ 210 Dale Murphy .15 .06
❑ 211 Mike Pagliarulo .05 .02
❑ 212 Scott Sanderson .05 .02
❑ 213 Rene Gonzales .05 .02
❑ 214 Charlie O'Brien .05 .02
❑ 215 Kevin Gross .05 .02
❑ 216 Jack Howell .05 .02
❑ 217 Joe Price .05 .02
❑ 218 Mike LaValliere .05 .02
❑ 219 Jim Clancy .05 .02
❑ 220 Gary Gaetti .10 .04
❑ 221 Cecil Espy .05 .02
❑ 222 Mark Lewis FDP RC .25 .10
❑ 223 Jay Buhner .10 .04
❑ 224 Tony LaRussa MG .10 .04
❑ 225 Ramon Martinez RC .25 .10
❑ 226 Bill Doran .05 .02
❑ 227 John Farrell .05 .02
❑ 228 Nelson Santovenia .05 .02
❑ 229 Jimmy Key .10 .04
❑ 230 Ozzie Smith .40 .16
❑ 231 Roberto Alomar TL .25 .10
(Gary Carter at plate)
❑ 232 Ricky Horton .05 .02
❑ 233 Gregg Jefferies FS .05 .02
❑ 234 Tom Browning .05 .02
❑ 235 John Kruk .10 .04
❑ 236 Charles Hudson .05 .02
❑ 237 Glenn Hubbard .05 .02
❑ 238 Eric King .05 .02
❑ 239 Tim Laudner .05 .02
❑ 240 Greg Maddux .50 .20
❑ 241 Brett Butler .10 .04
❑ 242 Ed VandeBerg .05 .02
❑ 243 Bob Boone .10 .04
❑ 244 Jim Acker .05 .02
❑ 245 Jim Rice .10 .04
❑ 246 Rey Quinones .05 .02
❑ 247 Shawn Hillegas .05 .02
❑ 248 Tony Phillips .05 .02
❑ 249 Tim Leary .05 .02
❑ 250 Cal Ripken .75 .30
❑ 251 John Dopson .05 .02
❑ 252 Billy Hatcher .05 .02
❑ 253 Jose Alvarez RC .10 .04
❑ 254 Tom Lasorda MG .15 .06
❑ 255 Ron Guidry .10 .04
❑ 256 Benny Santiago .10 .04
❑ 257 Rick Aguilera .05 .02
❑ 258 Checklist 133-264 .05 .02
❑ 259 Larry McWilliams .05 .02
❑ 260 Dave Winfield .10 .04
❑ 261 Tom Brunansky .05 .02
Luis Alicea TL
❑ 262 Jeff Pico .05 .02
❑ 263 Mike Felder .05 .02
❑ 264 Rob Dibble RC .50 .20
❑ 265 Kent Hrbek .10 .04
❑ 266 Luis Aquino .05 .02
❑ 267 Jeff M. Robinson .05 .02
❑ 268 Keith Miller RC .25 .10
❑ 269 Tom Bolton .05 .02
❑ 270 Wally Joyner .10 .04
❑ 271 Jay Tibbs .05 .02
❑ 272 Ron Hassey .05 .02
❑ 273 Jose Lind .05 .02
❑ 274 Mark Eichhorn .05 .02
❑ 275 Danny Tartabull UER .05 .02
(Born San Juan, PR
should be Miami, FL)
❑ 276 Paul Kilgus .05 .02
❑ 277 Mike Davis .05 .02
❑ 278 Andy McGaffigan .05 .02
❑ 279 Scott Bradley .05 .02
❑ 280 Bob Knepper .05 .02
❑ 281 Gary Redus .05 .02
❑ 282 Cris Carpenter RC * .10 .04
❑ 283 Andy Allanson .05 .02
❑ 284 Jim Leyland MG .10 .04
❑ 285 John Candelaria .05 .02
❑ 286 Darrin Jackson .10 .04
❑ 287 Juan Nieves .05 .02
❑ 288 Pat Sheridan .05 .02
❑ 289 Ernie Whitt .05 .02
❑ 290 John Franco .10 .04
❑ 291 Darryl Strawberry .05 .02
Keith Hernandez
Kevin McReynolds TL
❑ 292 Jim Corsi .05 .02
❑ 293 Glenn Wilson .05 .02
❑ 294 Juan Berenguer .05 .02
❑ 295 Scott Fletcher .05 .02
❑ 296 Ron Gant .10 .04
❑ 297 Oswald Peraza .05 .02
❑ 298 Chris James .05 .02
❑ 299 Steve Ellsworth .05 .02
❑ 300 Darryl Strawberry .10 .04
❑ 301 Charlie Leibrandt .05 .02
❑ 302 Gary Ward .05 .02
❑ 303 Felix Fermin .05 .02
❑ 304 Joel Youngblood .05 .02
❑ 305 Dave Smith .05 .02
❑ 306 Tracy Woodson .05 .02
❑ 307 Lance McCullers .05 .02
❑ 308 Ron Karkovice .05 .02
❑ 309 Mario Diaz .05 .02
❑ 310 Rafael Palmeiro .25 .10
❑ 311 Chris Bosio .05 .02
❑ 312 Tom Lawless .05 .02
❑ 313 Dennis Martinez .10 .04
❑ 314 Bobby Valentine MG .10 .04
❑ 315 Greg Swindell .05 .02
❑ 316 Walt Weiss .05 .02
❑ 317 Jack Armstrong RC * .25 .10
❑ 318 Gene Larkin .05 .02
❑ 319 Greg Booker .05 .02
❑ 320 Lou Whitaker .10 .04
❑ 321 Jody Reed TL .05 .02
❑ 322 John Smiley .05 .02
❑ 323 Gary Thurman .05 .02
❑ 324 Bob Milacki .05 .02
❑ 325 Jesse Barfield .10 .04
❑ 326 Dennis Boyd .05 .02
❑ 327 Mark Lemke RC .40 .16
❑ 328 Rick Honeycutt .05 .02
❑ 329 Bob Melvin .05 .02
❑ 330 Eric Davis .10 .04
❑ 331 Curt Wilkerson .05 .02
❑ 332 Tony Armas .10 .04
❑ 333 Bob Ojeda .05 .02
❑ 334 Steve Lyons .05 .02
❑ 335 Dave Righetti .10 .04
❑ 336 Steve Balboni .05 .02
❑ 337 Calvin Schiraldi .05 .02
❑ 338 Jim Adduci .05 .02
❑ 339 Scott Bailes .05 .02
❑ 340 Kirk Gibson .10 .04
❑ 341 Jim Deshaies .05 .02
❑ 342 Tom Brookens .05 .02
❑ 343 Gary Sheffield FS RC 1.50 .60
❑ 344 Tom Trebelhorn MG .05 .02
❑ 345 Charlie Hough .10 .04
❑ 346 Rex Hudler .05 .02
❑ 347 John Cerutti .05 .02
❑ 348 Ed Hearn .05 .02
❑ 349 Ron Jones .10 .04
❑ 350 Andy Van Slyke .10 .04
❑ 351 Bob Melvin .05 .02
Bill Fahey CO TL
❑ 352 Rick Schu .05 .02
❑ 353 Marvell Wynne .05 .02
❑ 354 Larry Parrish .05 .02
❑ 355 Mark Langston .05 .02
❑ 356 Kevin Elster .05 .02
❑ 357 Jerry Reuss .05 .02
❑ 358 Ricky Jordan RC * .25 .10
❑ 359 Tommy John .10 .04

360 Ryne Sandberg	.40	.16
361 Kelly Downs	.05	.02
362 Jack Lazorko	.05	.02
363 Rich Yett	.05	.02
364 Rob Deer	.05	.02
365 Mike Henneman	.05	.02
366 Herm Winningham	.05	.02
367 Johnny Paredes	.05	.02
368 Brian Holton	.05	.02
369 Ken Caminiti	.10	.04
370 Dennis Eckersley	.15	.06
371 Manny Lee	.05	.02
372 Craig Lefferts	.05	.02
373 Tracy Jones	.05	.02
374 John Wathan MG	.05	.02
375 Terry Pendleton	.10	.04
376 Steve Lombardozzi	.05	.02
377 Mike Smithson	.05	.02
378 Checklist 265-396	.05	.02
379 Tim Flannery	.05	.02
380 Rickey Henderson	.25	.10
381 Larry Sheets TL	.05	.02
382 John Smoltz RC	1.00	.40
383 Howard Johnson	.10	.04
384 Mark Salas	.05	.02
385 Von Hayes	.05	.02
386 Andres Galarraga AS	.05	.02
387 Ryne Sandberg AS	.25	.10
388 Bobby Bonilla AS	.05	.02
389 Ozzie Smith AS	.25	.10
390 Darryl Strawberry AS	.05	.02
391 Andre Dawson AS	.05	.02
392 Andy Van Slyke AS	.05	.02
393 Gary Carter AS	.05	.02
394 Orel Hershiser AS	.05	.02
395 Danny Jackson AS	.05	.02
396 Kirk Gibson AS	.05	.02
397 Don Mattingly AS	.30	.12
398 Julio Franco AS	.05	.02
399 Wade Boggs AS	.10	.04
400 Alan Trammell AS	.05	.02
401 Jose Canseco AS	.15	.06
402 Mike Greenwell AS	.05	.02
403 Kirby Puckett AS	.15	.06
404 Bob Boone AS	.05	.02
405 Roger Clemens AS	.25	.10
406 Frank Viola AS	.05	.02
407 Dave Winfield AS	.05	.02
408 Greg Walker	.05	.02
409 Ken Dayley	.05	.02
410 Jack Clark	.10	.04
411 Mitch Williams	.05	.02
412 Barry Lyons	.05	.02
413 Mike Kingery	.05	.02
414 Jim Fregosi MG	.05	.02
415 Rich Gossage	.10	.04
416 Fred Lynn	.10	.04
417 Mike LaCoss	.05	.02
418 Bob Dernier	.05	.02
419 Tom Filer	.05	.02
420 Joe Carter	.10	.04
421 Kirk McCaskill	.05	.02
422 Bo Diaz	.05	.02
423 Brian Fisher	.05	.02
424 Luis Polonia UER	.05	.02
(Wrong birthdate)		
425 Jay Howell	.05	.02
426 Dan Gladden	.05	.02
427 Eric Show	.05	.02
428 Craig Reynolds	.05	.02
429 Greg Gagne TL	.05	.02
430 Mark Gubicza	.05	.02
431 Luis Rivera	.05	.02
432 Chad Kreuter RC	.25	.10
433 Albert Hall	.05	.02
434 Ken Patterson	.05	.02
435 Len Dykstra	.10	.04
436 Bobby Meacham	.05	.02
437 Andy Benes FDP RC	.40	.16
438 Greg Gross	.05	.02
439 Frank DiPino	.05	.02
440 Bobby Bonilla	.10	.04
441 Jerry Reed	.05	.02
442 Jose Oquendo	.05	.02
443 Rod Nichols	.05	.02
444 Moose Stubing MG	.05	.02
445 Matt Nokes	.05	.02
446 Rob Murphy	.05	.02
447 Donell Nixon	.05	.02
448 Eric Plunk	.05	.02
449 Carmelo Martinez	.05	.02
450 Roger Clemens	.50	.20
451 Mark Davidson	.05	.02
452 Israel Sanchez	.05	.02
453 Tom Prince	.05	.02
454 Paul Assenmacher	.05	.02
455 Johnny Ray	.05	.02
456 Tim Belcher	.05	.02
457 Mackey Sasser	.05	.02
458 Donn Pall	.05	.02
459 Dave Valle TL	.05	.02
460 Dave Stieb	.10	.04
461 Buddy Bell	.10	.04
462 Jose Guzman	.05	.02
463 Steve Lake	.05	.02
464 Bryn Smith	.05	.02
465 Mark Grace	.25	.10
466 Chuck Crim	.05	.02
467 Jim Walewander	.05	.02
468 Henry Cotto	.05	.02
469 Jose Bautista RC	.10	.04
470 Lance Parrish	.10	.04
471 Steve Curry	.05	.02
472 Brian Harper	.05	.02
473 Don Robinson	.05	.02
474 Bob Rodgers MG	.05	.02
475 Dave Parker	.10	.04
476 Jon Perlman	.05	.02
477 Dick Schofield	.05	.02
478 Doug Drabek	.05	.02
479 Mike Macfarlane RC *	.25	.10
480 Keith Hernandez	.10	.04
481 Chris Brown	.05	.02
482 Steve Peters	.05	.02
483 Mickey Hatcher	.05	.02
484 Steve Shields	.05	.02
485 Hubie Brooks	.05	.02
486 Jack McDowell	.10	.04
487 Scott Lusader	.05	.02
488 Kevin Coffman	.05	.02
Now with Cubs		
489 Mike Schmidt TL	.15	.06
490 Chris Sabo RC *	.40	.16
491 Mike Birkbeck	.05	.02
492 Alan Ashby	.05	.02
493 Todd Benzinger	.05	.02
494 Shane Rawley	.05	.02
495 Candy Maldonado	.05	.02
496 Dwayne Henry	.05	.02
497 Pete Stanicek	.05	.02
498 Dave Valle	.05	.02
499 Don Heinkel	.05	.02
500 Jose Canseco	.25	.10
501 Vance Law	.05	.02
502 Duane Ward	.05	.02
503 Al Newman	.05	.02
504 Bob Walk	.05	.02
505 Pete Rose MG	.50	.20
506 Kirt Manwaring	.05	.02
507 Steve Farr	.05	.02
508 Wally Backman	.05	.02
509 Bud Black	.05	.02
510 Bob Horner	.10	.04
511 Richard Dotson	.05	.02
512 Donnie Hill	.05	.02
513 Jesse Orosco	.05	.02
514 Chet Lemon	.10	.04
515 Barry Larkin	.15	.06
516 Eddie Whitson	.05	.02
517 Greg Brock	.05	.02
518 Bruce Ruffin	.05	.02
519 Willie Randolph TL	.05	.02
520 Rick Sutcliffe	.10	.04
521 Mickey Tettleton	.05	.02
522 Randy Kramer	.05	.02
523 Andres Thomas	.05	.02
524 Checklist 397-528	.05	.02
525 Chili Davis	.10	.04
526 Wes Gardner	.05	.02
527 Dave Henderson	.05	.02
528 Luis Medina	.05	.02
(Lower left front		
has white triangle)		
529 Tom Foley	.05	.02
530 Nolan Ryan	1.00	.40
531 Dave Hengel	.05	.02
532 Jerry Browne	.05	.02
533 Andy Hawkins	.05	.02
534 Doc Edwards MG	.05	.02
535 Todd Worrell UER	.05	.02
(4 wins in '88,		
should be 5)		
536 Joel Skinner	.05	.02
537 Pete Smith	.05	.02
538 Juan Castillo	.05	.02
539 Barry Jones	.05	.02
540 Bo Jackson	.25	.10
541 Cecil Fielder	.10	.04
542 Todd Frohwirth	.05	.02
543 Damon Berryhill	.05	.02
544 Jeff Sellers	.05	.02
545 Mookie Wilson	.10	.04
546 Mark Williamson	.05	.02
547 Mark McLemore	.05	.02
548 Bobby Witt	.05	.02
549 Jamie Moyer TL	.05	.02
550 Orel Hershiser	.10	.04
551 Randy Ready	.05	.02
552 Greg Cadaret	.05	.02
553 Luis Salazar	.05	.02
554 Nick Esasky	.05	.02
555 Bert Blyleven	.10	.04
556 Bruce Fields	.05	.02
557 Keith A. Miller	.05	.02
558 Dan Pasqua	.05	.02
559 Juan Agosto	.05	.02
560 Tim Raines	.10	.04
561 Luis Aguayo	.05	.02
562 Danny Cox	.05	.02
563 Bill Schroeder	.05	.02
564 Russ Nixon MG	.05	.02
565 Jeff Russell	.05	.02
566 Al Pedrique	.05	.02
567 David Wells UER	.10	.04
(Complete Pitching		
Recor)		
568 Mickey Brantley	.05	.02
569 German Jimenez	.05	.02
570 Tony Gwynn UER	.30	.12
('88 average should		
be italicized as		
league leader)		
571 Billy Ripken	.05	.02
572 Atlee Hammaker	.05	.02
573 Jim Abbott FDP RC*	.50	.20
574 Dave Clark	.05	.02
575 Juan Samuel	.05	.02
576 Greg Minton	.05	.02
577 Randy Bush	.05	.02
578 John Morris	.05	.02
579 Glenn Davis TL	.05	.02
580 Harold Reynolds	.10	.04
581 Gene Nelson	.05	.02
582 Mike Marshall	.05	.02
583 Paul Gibson	.05	.02
584 Randy Velarde UER	.05	.02
(Signed 1935,		
should be 1985)		
585 Harold Baines	.10	.04
586 Joe Boever	.05	.02
587 Mike Stanley	.05	.02
588 Luis Alicea RC *	.25	.10
589 Dave Meads	.05	.02
590 Andres Galarraga	.10	.04
591 Jeff Musselman	.05	.02
592 John Cangelosi	.05	.02
593 Drew Hall	.05	.02
594 Jimy Williams MG	.05	.02
595 Teddy Higuera	.05	.02
596 Kurt Stillwell	.05	.02
597 Terry Taylor RC	.10	.04
598 Ken Gerhart	.05	.02
599 Tom Candiotti	.05	.02
600 Wade Boggs	.15	.06
601 Dave Dravecky	.05	.02
602 Devon White	.10	.04
603 Frank Tanana	.10	.04
604 Paul O'Neill	.15	.06

- ❑ 605A Bob Welch ERR 2.00 .80
  (Missing line on back
  Complete M.L. Pitching Record)
- ❑ 605B Bob Welch COR .10 .04
- ❑ 606 Rick Dempsey .05 .02
- ❑ 607 Willie Ansley FDP RC .10 .04
- ❑ 608 Phil Bradley .05 .02
- ❑ 609 Frank Tanana .05 .02
  Alan Trammell
  Mike Heath TL
- ❑ 610 Randy Myers .10 .04
- ❑ 611 Don Slaught .05 .02
- ❑ 612 Dan Quisenberry .05 .02
- ❑ 613 Gary Varsho .05 .02
- ❑ 614 Joe Hesketh .05 .02
- ❑ 615 Robin Yount .40 .16
- ❑ 616 Steve Rosenberg .05 .02
- ❑ 617 Mark Parent .05 .02
- ❑ 618 Rance Mulliniks .05 .02
- ❑ 619 Checklist 529-660 .05 .02
- ❑ 620 Barry Bonds 1.25 .50
- ❑ 621 Rick Mahler .05 .02
- ❑ 622 Stan Javier .05 .02
- ❑ 623 Fred Toliver .05 .02
- ❑ 624 Jack McKeon MG .10 .04
- ❑ 625 Eddie Murray .25 .10
- ❑ 626 Jeff Reed .05 .02
- ❑ 627 Greg A. Harris .05 .02
- ❑ 628 Matt Williams .25 .10
- ❑ 629 Pete O'Brien .05 .02
- ❑ 630 Mike Greenwell .05 .02
- ❑ 631 Dave Bergman .05 .02
- ❑ 632 Bryan Harvey RC * .25 .10
- ❑ 633 Daryl Boston .05 .02
- ❑ 634 Marvin Freeman .05 .02
- ❑ 635 Willie Randolph .10 .04
- ❑ 636 Bill Wilkinson .05 .02
- ❑ 637 Carmen Castillo .05 .02
- ❑ 638 Floyd Bannister .05 .02
- ❑ 639 Walt Weiss TL .05 .02
- ❑ 640 Willie McGee .10 .04
- ❑ 641 Curt Young .05 .02
- ❑ 642 Angel Salazar .05 .02
- ❑ 643 Louie Meadows .05 .02
- ❑ 644 Lloyd McClendon .05 .02
- ❑ 645 Jack Morris .10 .04
- ❑ 646 Kevin Bass .05 .02
- ❑ 647 Randy Johnson RC 4.00 1.20
- ❑ 648 Sandy Alomar FS RC .40 .16
- ❑ 649 Stu Cliburn .05 .02
- ❑ 650 Kirby Puckett .25 .10
- ❑ 651 Tom Niedenfuer .05 .02
- ❑ 652 Rich Gedman .05 .02
- ❑ 653 Tommy Barrett .05 .02
- ❑ 654 Whitey Herzog MG .10 .04
- ❑ 655 Dave Magadan .05 .02
- ❑ 656 Ivan Calderon .05 .02
- ❑ 657 Joe Magrane .05 .02
- ❑ 658 R.J. Reynolds .05 .02
- ❑ 659 Al Leiter .25 .10
- ❑ 660 Will Clark .25 .10
- ❑ 661 D.Gooden TBC84 .05 .02
- ❑ 662 Lou Brock TBC79 .10 .04
- ❑ 663 Hank Aaron TBC74 .25 .10
- ❑ 664 Gil Hodges TBC 69 .10 .04
- ❑ 665A Tony Oliva TBC64 2.00 .80
  ERR (fabricated card
  is enlarged version
  of Oliva's 64T card;
  Topps copyright
  missing)
- ❑ 665B Tony Oliva TBC 64 .10 .04
  COR (fabricated
  card)
- ❑ 666 Randy St.Claire .05 .02
- ❑ 667 Dwayne Murphy .05 .02
- ❑ 668 Mike Bielecki .05 .02
- ❑ 669 Orel Hershiser .10 .04
  Mike Scioscia TL
- ❑ 670 Kevin Seitzer .05 .02
- ❑ 671 Jim Gantner .05 .02
- ❑ 672 Allan Anderson .05 .02
- ❑ 673 Don Baylor .10 .04
- ❑ 674 Otis Nixon .05 .02
- ❑ 675 Bruce Hurst .05 .02
- ❑ 676 Ernie Riles .05 .02
- ❑ 677 Dave Schmidt .05 .02
- ❑ 678 Dion James .05 .02
- ❑ 679 Willie Fraser .05 .02
- ❑ 680 Gary Carter .10 .04
- ❑ 681 Jeff D. Robinson .05 .02
- ❑ 682 Rick Leach .05 .02
- ❑ 683 Jose Cecena .05 .02
- ❑ 684 Dave Johnson MG .05 .02
- ❑ 685 Jeff Treadway .05 .02
- ❑ 686 Scott Terry .05 .02
- ❑ 687 Alvin Davis .05 .02
- ❑ 688 Zane Smith .05 .02
- ❑ 689A Stan Jefferson .05 .02
  (Pink triangle on
  front bottom left)
- ❑ 689B Stan Jefferson .05 .02
  (Violet triangle on
  front bottom left)
- ❑ 690 Doug Jones .05 .02
- ❑ 691 Roberto Kelly UER .05 .02
  (83 Oneonita)
- ❑ 692 Steve Ontiveros .05 .02
- ❑ 693 Pat Borders RC * .25 .10
- ❑ 694 Les Lancaster .05 .02
- ❑ 695 Carlton Fisk .15 .06
- ❑ 696 Don August .05 .02
- ❑ 697A Franklin Stubbs .05 .02
  (Team name on front
  in white)
- ❑ 697B Franklin Stubbs .05 .02
  (Team name on front
  in gray)
- ❑ 698 Keith Atherton .05 .02
- ❑ 699 Al Pedrique TL .05 .02
  Tony Gwynn sliding
- ❑ 700 Don Mattingly .60 .24
- ❑ 701 Storm Davis .05 .02
- ❑ 702 Jamie Quirk .05 .02
- ❑ 703 Scott Garrelts .05 .02
- ❑ 704 Carlos Quintana RC .10 .04
- ❑ 705 Terry Kennedy .05 .02
- ❑ 706 Pete Incaviglia .05 .02
- ❑ 707 Steve Jeltz .05 .02
- ❑ 708 Chuck Finley .10 .04
- ❑ 709 Tom Herr .05 .02
- ❑ 710 David Cone .10 .04
- ❑ 711 Candy Sierra .05 .02
- ❑ 712 Bill Swift .05 .02
- ❑ 713 Ty Griffin FDP .05 .02
- ❑ 714 Joe Morgan MG .10 .04
- ❑ 715 Tony Pena .05 .02
- ❑ 716 Wayne Tolleson .05 .02
- ❑ 717 Jamie Moyer .10 .04
- ❑ 718 Glenn Braggs .05 .02
- ❑ 719 Danny Darwin .05 .02
- ❑ 720 Tim Wallach .05 .02
- ❑ 721 Ron Tingley .05 .02
- ❑ 722 Todd Stottlemyre .05 .02
- ❑ 723 Rafael Belliard .05 .02
- ❑ 724 Jerry Don Gleaton .05 .02
- ❑ 725 Terry Steinbach .10 .04
- ❑ 726 Dickie Thon .05 .02
- ❑ 727 Joe Orsulak .05 .02
- ❑ 728 Charlie Puleo .05 .02
- ❑ 729 Steve Buechele TL .05 .02
  (Inconsistent design,
  team name on front
  surrounded by black,
  should be white)
- ❑ 730 Danny Jackson .05 .02
- ❑ 731 Mike Young .05 .02
- ❑ 732 Steve Buechele .05 .02
- ❑ 733 Randy Bockus .05 .02
- ❑ 734 Jody Reed .05 .02
- ❑ 735 Roger McDowell .05 .02
- ❑ 736 Jeff Hamilton .05 .02
- ❑ 737 Norm Charlton RC .25 .10
- ❑ 738 Darnell Coles .05 .02
- ❑ 739 Brook Jacoby .05 .02
- ❑ 740 Dan Plesac .05 .02
- ❑ 741 Ken Phelps .05 .02
- ❑ 742 Mike Harkey FS RC .10 .04
- ❑ 743 Mike Heath .05 .02
- ❑ 744 Roger Craig MG .10 .04
- ❑ 745 Fred McGriff .15 .06
- ❑ 746 G.Gonzalez UER .05 .02
  Wrong birthdate
- ❑ 747 Wil Tejada .05 .02
- ❑ 748 Jimmy Jones .05 .02
- ❑ 749 Rafael Ramirez .05 .02
- ❑ 750 Bret Saberhagen .10 .04
- ❑ 751 Ken Oberkfell .05 .02
- ❑ 752 Jim Gott .05 .02
- ❑ 753 Jose Uribe .05 .02
- ❑ 754 Bob Brower .05 .02
- ❑ 755 Mike Scioscia .10 .04
- ❑ 756 Scott Medvin .05 .02
- ❑ 757 Brady Anderson RC .40 .16
- ❑ 758 Gene Walter .05 .02
- ❑ 759 Rob Deer TL .05 .02
- ❑ 760 Lee Smith .10 .04
- ❑ 761 Dante Bichette RC .40 .16
- ❑ 762 Bobby Thigpen .05 .02
- ❑ 763 Dave Martinez .05 .02
- ❑ 764 Robin Ventura FDP RC .75 .30
- ❑ 765 Glenn Davis .05 .02
- ❑ 766 Cecilio Guante .05 .02
- ❑ 767 Mike Capel .05 .02
- ❑ 768 Bill Wegman .05 .02
- ❑ 769 Junior Ortiz .05 .02
- ❑ 770 Alan Trammell .10 .04
- ❑ 771 Ron Kittle .05 .02
- ❑ 772 Ron Oester .05 .02
- ❑ 773 Keith Moreland .05 .02
- ❑ 774 Frank Robinson MG .15 .06
- ❑ 775 Jeff Reardon .10 .04
- ❑ 776 Nelson Liriano .05 .02
- ❑ 777 Ted Power .05 .02
- ❑ 778 Bruce Benedict .05 .02
- ❑ 779 Craig McMurtry .05 .02
- ❑ 780 Pedro Guerrero .10 .04
- ❑ 781 Greg Briley .10 .04
- ❑ 782 Checklist 661-792 .05 .02
- ❑ 783 Trevor Wilson RC .10 .04
- ❑ 784 Steve Avery FDP RC .25 .10
- ❑ 785 Ellis Burks .10 .04
- ❑ 786 Melido Perez .05 .02
- ❑ 787 Dave West RC .10 .04
- ❑ 788 Mike Morgan .05 .02
- ❑ 789 Bo Jackson TL .25 .10
- ❑ 790 Sid Fernandez .05 .02
- ❑ 791 Jim Lindeman .05 .02
- ❑ 792 Rafael Santana .05 .02

1989 Topps Traded

	Nm-Mt	Ex-Mt
COMP.FACT.SET (132)	15.00	6.00
❑ 1T Don Aase	.05	.02
❑ 2T Jim Abbott	.25	.10
❑ 3T Kent Anderson	.05	.02
❑ 4T Keith Atherton	.05	.02
❑ 5T Wally Backman	.05	.02
❑ 6T Steve Balboni	.05	.02
❑ 7T Jesse Barfield	.10	.04
❑ 8T Steve Bedrosian	.05	.02
❑ 9T Todd Benzinger	.05	.02
❑ 10T Geronimo Berroa	.05	.02
❑ 11T Bert Blyleven	.10	.04
❑ 12T Bob Boone	.10	.04
❑ 13T Phil Bradley	.05	.02
❑ 14T Jeff Brantley RC	.25	.10
❑ 15T Kevin Brown	.25	.10

❑ 16T Jerry Browne .05 .02
❑ 17T Chuck Cary .05 .02
❑ 18T Carmen Castillo .05 .02
❑ 19T Jim Clancy .05 .02
❑ 20T Jack Clark .10 .04
❑ 21T Bryan Clutterbuck .05 .02
❑ 22T Jody Davis .05 .02
❑ 23T Mike Devereaux .05 .02
❑ 24T Frank DiPino .05 .02
❑ 25T Benny Distefano .05 .02
❑ 26T John Dopson .05 .02
❑ 27T Len Dykstra .10 .04
❑ 28T Jim Eisenreich .05 .02
❑ 29T Nick Esasky .05 .02
❑ 30T Alvaro Espinoza .05 .02
❑ 31T Darrell Evans UER .10 .04
(Stat headings on back are for a pitcher)
❑ 32T Junior Felix RC .10 .04
❑ 33T Felix Fermin .05 .02
❑ 34T Julio Franco .10 .04
❑ 35T Terry Francona .10 .04
❑ 36T Cito Gaston MG .05 .02
❑ 37T Bob Geren RC UER .05 .02
(Photo actually Mike Fennell)
❑ 38T Tom Gordon RC .40 .16
❑ 39T Tommy Gregg .05 .02
❑ 40T Ken Griffey Sr. .10 .04
❑ 41T Ken Griffey Jr. RC 8.00 3.20
❑ 42T Kevin Gross .05 .02
❑ 43T Lee Guetterman .05 .02
❑ 44T Mel Hall .05 .02
❑ 45T Erik Hanson RC .25 .10
❑ 46T Gene Harris RC .10 .04
❑ 47T Andy Hawkins .05 .02
❑ 48T Rickey Henderson .25 .10
❑ 49T Tom Herr .05 .02
❑ 50T Ken Hill RC .25 .10
❑ 51T Brian Holman RC * .10 .04
❑ 52T Brian Holton .05 .02
❑ 53T Art Howe MG .05 .02
❑ 54T Ken Howell .05 .02
❑ 55T Bruce Hurst .05 .02
❑ 56T Chris James .05 .02
❑ 57T Randy Johnson 2.50 .80
❑ 58T Jimmy Jones .05 .02
❑ 59T Terry Kennedy .05 .02
❑ 60T Paul Kilgus .05 .02
❑ 61T Eric King .05 .02
❑ 62T Ron Kittle .05 .02
❑ 63T John Kruk .10 .04
❑ 64T Randy Kutcher .05 .02
❑ 65T Steve Lake .05 .02
❑ 66T Mark Langston .05 .02
❑ 67T Dave LaPoint .05 .02
❑ 68T Rick Leach .05 .02
❑ 69T Terry Leach .05 .02
❑ 70T Jim Lefebvre MG .05 .02
❑ 71T Al Leiter .25 .10
❑ 72T Jeffrey Leonard .05 .02
❑ 73T Derek Lilliquist RC .10 .04
❑ 74T Rick Mahler .05 .02
❑ 75T Tom McCarthy .05 .02
❑ 76T Lloyd McClendon .05 .02
❑ 77T Lance McCullers .05 .02
❑ 78T Oddibe McDowell .05 .02
❑ 79T Roger McDowell .05 .02
❑ 80T Larry McWilliams .05 .02
❑ 81T Randy Milligan .05 .02
❑ 82T Mike Moore .05 .02
❑ 83T Keith Moreland .05 .02
❑ 84T Mike Morgan .05 .02
❑ 85T Jamie Moyer .10 .04
❑ 86T Rob Murphy .05 .02
❑ 87T Eddie Murray .25 .10
❑ 88T Pete O'Brien .05 .02
❑ 89T Gregg Olson .25 .10
❑ 90T Steve Ontiveros .05 .02
❑ 91T Jesse Orosco .05 .02
❑ 92T Spike Owen .05 .02
❑ 93T Rafael Palmeiro .25 .10
❑ 94T Clay Parker .05 .02
❑ 95T Jeff Parrett .05 .02
❑ 96T Lance Parrish .10 .04
❑ 97T Dennis Powell .05 .02
❑ 98T Rey Quinones .05 .02
❑ 99T Doug Rader MG .05 .02
❑ 100T Willie Randolph .10 .04
❑ 101T Shane Rawley .05 .02
❑ 102T Randy Ready .05 .02
❑ 103T Bip Roberts .05 .02
❑ 104T Kenny Rogers RC .75 .30
❑ 105T Ed Romero .05 .02
❑ 106T Nolan Ryan 1.50 .60
❑ 107T Luis Salazar .05 .02
❑ 108T Juan Samuel .05 .02
❑ 109T Alex Sanchez .05 .02
❑ 110T Deion Sanders RC 1.00 .40
❑ 111T Steve Sax .05 .02
❑ 112T Rick Schu .05 .02
❑ 113T Dwight Smith RC .25 .10
❑ 114T Lonnie Smith .05 .02
❑ 115T Billy Spiers RC .25 .10
❑ 116T Kent Tekulve .05 .02
❑ 117T Walt Terrell .05 .02
❑ 118T Milt Thompson .05 .02
❑ 119T Dickie Thon .05 .02
❑ 120T Jeff Torborg MG .05 .02
❑ 121T Jeff Treadway .05 .02
❑ 122T Omar Vizquel RC .75 .30
❑ 123T Jerome Walton RC .25 .10
❑ 124T Gary Ward .05 .02
❑ 125T Claudell Washington .05 .02
❑ 126T Curt Wilkerson .05 .02
❑ 127T Eddie Williams .05 .02
❑ 128T Frank Williams .05 .02
❑ 129T Ken Williams .05 .02
❑ 130T Mitch Williams .05 .02
❑ 131T Steve Wilson RC .10 .04
❑ 132T Checklist 1T-132T .05 .02

1990 Topps

	Nm-Mt	Ex-Mt
COMPLETE SET (792)	20.00	6.00
COMP.FACT.SET (792)	25.00	7.50
COMP.X-MAS.SET (792)	40.00	12.00

❑ 1 Nolan Ryan 1.00 .30
❑ 2 Nolan Ryan Mets .50 .15
❑ 3 Nolan Ryan Angels .50 .15
❑ 4 Nolan Ryan Astros .50 .15
❑ 5 N.Ryan Rangers UER .50 .15
(Says Texas Stadium rather than Arlington Stadium)
❑ 6 Vince Coleman RB .05 .02
❑ 7 Rickey Henderson RB .15 .04
❑ 8 Cal Ripken RB .25 .07
❑ 9 Eric Plunk .05 .02
❑ 10 Barry Larkin .15 .04
❑ 11 Paul Gibson .05 .02
❑ 12 Joe Girardi .15 .04
❑ 13 Mark Williamson .05 .02
❑ 14 Mike Fetters RC .25 .07
❑ 15 Teddy Higuera .05 .02
❑ 16 Kent Anderson .05 .02
❑ 17 Kelly Downs .05 .02
❑ 18 Carlos Quintana .05 .02
❑ 19 Al Newman .05 .02
❑ 20 Mark Gubicza .05 .02
❑ 21 Jeff Torborg MG .05 .02
❑ 22 Bruce Ruffin .05 .02
❑ 23 Randy Velarde .05 .02
❑ 24 Joe Hesketh .05 .02
❑ 25 Willie Randolph .10 .03
❑ 26 Don Slaught .05 .02
❑ 27 Rick Leach .05 .02
❑ 28 Duane Ward .05 .02
❑ 29 John Cangelosi .05 .02
❑ 30 David Cone .10 .03
❑ 31 Henry Cotto .05 .02
❑ 32 John Farrell .05 .02
❑ 33 Greg Walker .05 .02
❑ 34 Tony Fossas .05 .02
❑ 35 Benito Santiago .10 .03
❑ 36 John Costello .05 .02
❑ 37 Domingo Ramos .05 .02
❑ 38 Wes Gardner .05 .02
❑ 39 Curt Ford .05 .02
❑ 40 Jay Howell .05 .02
❑ 41 Matt Williams .10 .03
❑ 42 Jeff M. Robinson .05 .02
❑ 43 Dante Bichette .25 .07
❑ 44 Roger Salkeld FDP RC .10 .03
❑ 45 Dave Parker UER .10 .03
(Born in Jackson, not Calhoun)
❑ 46 Rob Dibble .10 .03
❑ 47 Brian Harper .05 .02
❑ 48 Zane Smith .05 .02
❑ 49 Tom Lawless .05 .02
❑ 50 Glenn Davis .05 .02
❑ 51 Doug Rader MG .05 .02
❑ 52 Jack Daugherty .05 .02
❑ 53 Mike LaCoss .05 .02
❑ 54 Joel Skinner .05 .02
❑ 55 Darrell Evans UER .10 .03
(HR total should be 414, not 424)
❑ 56 Franklin Stubbs .05 .02
❑ 57 Greg Vaughn .05 .02
❑ 58 Keith Miller .05 .02
❑ 59 Ted Power .05 .02
❑ 60 George Brett .60 .18
❑ 61 Deion Sanders .25 .07
❑ 62 Ramon Martinez .05 .02
❑ 63 Mike Pagliarulo .05 .02
❑ 64 Danny Darwin .05 .02
❑ 65 Devon White .10 .03
❑ 66 Greg Litton .05 .02
❑ 67 Scott Sanderson .05 .02
❑ 68 Dave Henderson .05 .02
❑ 69 Todd Frohwirth .05 .02
❑ 70 Mike Greenwell .05 .02
❑ 71 Allan Anderson .05 .02
❑ 72 Jeff Huson RC .10 .03
❑ 73 Bob Milacki .05 .02
❑ 74 Jeff Jackson FDP RC .10 .03
❑ 75 Doug Jones .05 .02
❑ 76 Dave Valle .05 .02
❑ 77 Dave Bergman .05 .02
❑ 78 Mike Flanagan .05 .02
❑ 79 Ron Kittle .05 .02
❑ 80 Jeff Russell .05 .02
❑ 81 Bob Rodgers MG .05 .02
❑ 82 Scott Terry .05 .02
❑ 83 Hensley Meulens .05 .02
❑ 84 Ray Searage .05 .02
❑ 85 Juan Samuel .05 .02
❑ 86 Paul Kilgus .05 .02
❑ 87 Rick Luecken .05 .02
❑ 88 Glenn Braggs .05 .02
❑ 89 Clint Zavaras .05 .02
❑ 90 Jack Clark .10 .03
❑ 91 Steve Frey .05 .02
❑ 92 Mike Stanley .05 .02
❑ 93 Shawn Hillegas .05 .02
❑ 94 Herm Winningham .05 .02
❑ 95 Todd Worrell .05 .02
❑ 96 Jody Reed .05 .02
❑ 97 Curt Schilling 1.00 .30
❑ 98 Jose Gonzalez .05 .02
❑ 99 Rich Monteleone .05 .02
❑ 100 Will Clark .25 .07
❑ 101 Shane Rawley .05 .02
❑ 102 Stan Javier .05 .02
❑ 103 Marvin Freeman .05 .02
❑ 104 Bob Knepper .05 .02

❑ 105 Randy Myers .10 .03
❑ 106 Charlie O'Brien .05 .02
❑ 107 Fred Lynn .05 .02
❑ 108 Rod Nichols .05 .02
❑ 109 Roberto Kelly .05 .02
❑ 110 Tommy Helms MG .05 .02
❑ 111 Ed Whited .05 .02
❑ 112 Glenn Wilson .05 .02
❑ 113 Manny Lee .05 .02
❑ 114 Mike Bielecki .05 .02
❑ 115 Tony Pena .05 .02
❑ 116 Floyd Bannister .05 .02
❑ 117 Mike Sharperson .05 .02
❑ 118 Erik Hanson .05 .02
❑ 119 Billy Hatcher .05 .02
❑ 120 John Franco .10 .03
❑ 121 Robin Ventura .25 .07
❑ 122 Shawn Abner .05 .02
❑ 123 Rich Gedman .05 .02
❑ 124 Dave Dravecky .10 .03
❑ 125 Kent Hrbek .10 .03
❑ 126 Randy Kramer .05 .02
❑ 127 Mike Devereaux .05 .02
❑ 128 Checklist 1 .05 .02
❑ 129 Ron Jones .05 .02
❑ 130 Bert Blyleven .10 .03
❑ 131 Matt Nokes .05 .02
❑ 132 Lance Blankenship .05 .02
❑ 133 Ricky Horton .05 .02
❑ 134 E.Cunningham FDP RC .10 .03
❑ 135 Dave Magadan .05 .02
❑ 136 Kevin Brown .10 .03
❑ 137 Marty Pevey .05 .02
❑ 138 Al Leiter .25 .07
❑ 139 Greg Brock .05 .02
❑ 140 Andre Dawson .10 .03
❑ 141 John Hart MG .05 .02
❑ 142 Jeff Wetherby .05 .02
❑ 143 Rafael Belliard .05 .02
❑ 144 Bud Black .05 .02
❑ 145 Terry Steinbach .05 .02
❑ 146 Rob Richie .05 .02
❑ 147 Chuck Finley .10 .03
❑ 148 Edgar Martinez .15 .04
❑ 149 Steve Farr .05 .02
❑ 150 Kirk Gibson .10 .03
❑ 151 Rick Mahler .05 .02
❑ 152 Lonnie Smith .05 .02
❑ 153 Randy Milligan .05 .02
❑ 154 Mike Maddux .05 .02
❑ 155 Ellis Burks .15 .04
❑ 156 Ken Patterson .05 .02
❑ 157 Craig Biggio .15 .04
❑ 158 Craig Lefferts .05 .02
❑ 159 Mike Felder .05 .02
❑ 160 Dave Righetti .05 .02
❑ 161 Harold Reynolds .10 .03
❑ 162 Todd Zeile .10 .03
❑ 163 Phil Bradley .05 .02
❑ 164 Jeff Juden FDP RC .10 .03
❑ 165 Walt Weiss .05 .02
❑ 166 Bobby Witt .05 .02
❑ 167 Kevin Appier .10 .03
❑ 168 Jose Lind .05 .02
❑ 169 Richard Dotson .05 .02
❑ 170 George Bell .05 .02
❑ 171 Russ Nixon MG .05 .02
❑ 172 Tom Lampkin .05 .02
❑ 173 Tim Belcher .05 .02
❑ 174 Jeff Kunkel .05 .02
❑ 175 Mike Moore .05 .02
❑ 176 Luis Quinones .05 .02
❑ 177 Mike Henneman .05 .02
❑ 178 Chris James .05 .02
❑ 179 Brian Holton .05 .02
❑ 180 Tim Raines .10 .03
❑ 181 Juan Agosto .05 .02
❑ 182 Mookie Wilson .10 .03
❑ 183 Steve Lake .05 .02
❑ 184 Danny Cox .05 .02
❑ 185 Ruben Sierra .05 .02
❑ 186 Dave LaPoint .05 .02
❑ 187 Rick Wrona .05 .02
❑ 188 Mike Smithson .05 .02
❑ 189 Dick Schofield .05 .02
❑ 190 Rick Reuschel .05 .02

❑ 191 Pat Borders .05 .02
❑ 192 Don August .05 .02
❑ 193 Andy Benes .10 .03
❑ 194 Glenallen Hill .05 .02
❑ 195 Tim Burke .05 .02
❑ 196 Gerald Young .05 .02
❑ 197 Doug Drabek .05 .02
❑ 198 Mike Marshall .05 .02
❑ 199 Sergio Valdez .05 .02
❑ 200 Don Mattingly .60 .18
❑ 201 Cito Gaston MG .05 .02
❑ 202 Mike Macfarlane .05 .02
❑ 203 Mike Roesler .05 .02
❑ 204 Bob Dernier .05 .02
❑ 205 Mark Davis .05 .02
❑ 206 Nick Esasky .05 .02
❑ 207 Bob Ojeda .05 .02
❑ 208 Brook Jacoby .05 .02
❑ 209 Greg Mathews .05 .02
❑ 210 Ryne Sandberg .40 .12
❑ 211 John Cerutti .05 .02
❑ 212 Joe Orsulak .05 .02
❑ 213 Scott Bankhead .05 .02
❑ 214 Terry Francona .10 .03
❑ 215 Kirk McCaskill .05 .02
❑ 216 Ricky Jordan .05 .02
❑ 217 Don Robinson .05 .02
❑ 218 Wally Backman .05 .02
❑ 219 Donn Pall .05 .02
❑ 220 Barry Bonds .60 .18
❑ 221 Gary Mielke .05 .02
❑ 222 Kurt Stillwell UER .05 .02
(Graduate misspelled as gradute)
❑ 223 Tommy Gregg .05 .02
❑ 224 Delino DeShields RC .25 .07
❑ 225 Jim Deshaies .05 .02
❑ 226 Mickey Hatcher .05 .02
❑ 227 Kevin Tapani RC .25 .07
❑ 228 Dave Martinez .05 .02
❑ 229 David Wells .10 .03
❑ 230 Keith Hernandez .10 .03
❑ 231 Jack McKeon MG .05 .02
❑ 232 Darnell Coles .05 .02
❑ 233 Ken Hill .10 .03
❑ 234 Mariano Duncan .05 .02
❑ 235 Jeff Reardon .10 .03
❑ 236 Hal Morris .05 .02
❑ 237 Kevin Ritz .05 .02
❑ 238 Felix Jose .05 .02
❑ 239 Eric Show .05 .02
❑ 240 Mark Grace .15 .04
❑ 241 Mike Krukow .05 .02
❑ 242 Fred Manrique .05 .02
❑ 243 Barry Jones .05 .02
❑ 244 Bill Schroeder .05 .02
❑ 245 Roger Clemens .50 .15
❑ 246 Jim Eisenreich .05 .02
❑ 247 Jerry Reed .05 .02
❑ 248 Dave Anderson .05 .02
❑ 249 Mike (Texas) Smith .05 .02
❑ 250 Jose Canseco .25 .07
❑ 251 Jeff Blauser .05 .02
❑ 252 Otis Nixon .05 .02
❑ 253 Mark Portugal .05 .02
❑ 254 Francisco Cabrera .05 .02
❑ 255 Bobby Thigpen .05 .02
❑ 256 Marvell Wynne .05 .02
❑ 257 Jose DeLeon .05 .02
❑ 258 Barry Lyons .05 .02
❑ 259 Lance McCullers .05 .02
❑ 260 Eric Davis .10 .03
❑ 261 Whitey Herzog MG .10 .03
❑ 262 Checklist 2 .05 .02
❑ 263 Mel Stottlemyre Jr. .05 .02
❑ 264 Bryan Clutterbuck .05 .02
❑ 265 Pete O'Brien .05 .02
❑ 266 German Gonzalez .05 .02
❑ 267 Mark Davidson .05 .02
❑ 268 Rob Murphy .05 .02
❑ 269 Dickie Thon .05 .02
❑ 270 Dave Stewart .10 .03
❑ 271 Chet Lemon .05 .02
❑ 272 Bryan Harvey .05 .02
❑ 273 Bobby Bonilla .10 .03
❑ 274 Mauro Gozzo .05 .02

❑ 275 Mickey Tettleton .05 .02
❑ 276 Gary Thurman .05 .02
❑ 277 Lenny Harris .05 .02
❑ 278 Pascual Perez .05 .02
❑ 279 Steve Buechele .05 .02
❑ 280 Lou Whitaker .10 .03
❑ 281 Kevin Bass .05 .02
❑ 282 Derek Lilliquist .05 .02
❑ 283 Joey Belle .25 .07
❑ 284 Mark Gardner RC .10 .03
❑ 285 Willie McGee .10 .03
❑ 286 Lee Guetterman .05 .02
❑ 287 Vance Law .05 .02
❑ 288 Greg Briley .05 .02
❑ 289 Norm Charlton .05 .02
❑ 290 Robin Yount .40 .12
❑ 291 Dave Johnson MG .10 .03
❑ 292 Jim Gott .05 .02
❑ 293 Mike Gallego .05 .02
❑ 294 Craig McMurtry .05 .02
❑ 295 Fred McGriff .25 .07
❑ 296 Jeff Ballard .05 .02
❑ 297 Tommy Herr .05 .02
❑ 298 Dan Gladden .05 .02
❑ 299 Adam Peterson .05 .02
❑ 300 Bo Jackson .25 .07
❑ 301 Don Aase .05 .02
❑ 302 Marcus Lawton .05 .02
❑ 303 Rick Cerone .05 .02
❑ 304 Marty Clary .05 .02
❑ 305 Eddie Murray .25 .07
❑ 306 Tom Niedenfuer .05 .02
❑ 307 Bip Roberts .05 .02
❑ 308 Jose Guzman .05 .02
❑ 309 Eric Yelding .05 .02
❑ 310 Steve Bedrosian .05 .02
❑ 311 Dwight Smith .05 .02
❑ 312 Dan Quisenberry .05 .02
❑ 313 Gus Polidor .05 .02
❑ 314 Donald Harris FDP .05 .02
❑ 315 Bruce Hurst .05 .02
❑ 316 Carney Lansford .10 .03
❑ 317 Mark Guthrie .05 .02
❑ 318 Wallace Johnson .05 .02
❑ 319 Dion James .05 .02
❑ 320 Dave Stieb .10 .03
❑ 321 Joe Morgan MG .05 .02
❑ 322 Junior Ortiz .05 .02
❑ 323 Willie Wilson .05 .02
❑ 324 Pete Harnisch .05 .02
❑ 325 Robby Thompson .05 .02
❑ 326 Tom McCarthy .05 .02
❑ 327 Ken Williams .05 .02
❑ 328 Curt Young .05 .02
❑ 329 Oddibe McDowell .05 .02
❑ 330 Ron Darling .05 .02
❑ 331 Juan Gonzalez RC 1.50 .45
❑ 332 Paul O'Neill .15 .04
❑ 333 Bill Wegman .05 .02
❑ 334 Johnny Ray .05 .02
❑ 335 Andy Hawkins .05 .02
❑ 336 Ken Griffey Jr. .75 .23
❑ 337 Lloyd McClendon .05 .02
❑ 338 Dennis Lamp .05 .02
❑ 339 Dave Clark .05 .02
❑ 340 Fernando Valenzuela .10 .03
❑ 341 Tom Foley .05 .02
❑ 342 Alex Trevino .05 .02
❑ 343 Frank Tanana .05 .02
❑ 344 George Canale .05 .02
❑ 345 Harold Baines .10 .03
❑ 346 Jim Presley .05 .02
❑ 347 Junior Felix .05 .02
❑ 348 Gary Wayne .05 .02
❑ 349 Steve Finley .10 .03
❑ 350 Bret Saberhagen .10 .03
❑ 351 Roger Craig MG .05 .02
❑ 352 Bryn Smith .05 .02
❑ 353 Sandy Alomar Jr. .10 .03
(Not listed as Jr. on card front)
❑ 354 Stan Belinda RC .10 .03
❑ 355 Marty Barrett .05 .02
❑ 356 Randy Ready .05 .02
❑ 357 Dave West .05 .02
❑ 358 Andres Thomas .05 .02

❑ 359 Jimmy Jones .05 .02
❑ 360 Paul Molitor .15 .04
❑ 361 Randy McCament .05 .02
❑ 362 Damon Berryhill .05 .02
❑ 363 Dan Petry .05 .02
❑ 364 Rolando Roomes .05 .02
❑ 365 Ozzie Guillen .05 .02
❑ 366 Mike Heath .05 .02
❑ 367 Mike Morgan .05 .02
❑ 368 Bill Doran .05 .02
❑ 369 Todd Burns .05 .02
❑ 370 Tim Wallach .05 .02
❑ 371 Jimmy Key .10 .03
❑ 372 Terry Kennedy .05 .02
❑ 373 Alvin Davis .05 .02
❑ 374 Steve Cummings RC .05 .02
❑ 375 Dwight Evans .10 .03
❑ 376 Checklist 3 UER .05 .02
(Higuera misalphabet-
ized in Brewer list)
❑ 377 Mickey Weston .05 .02
❑ 378 Luis Salazar .05 .02
❑ 379 Steve Rosenberg .05 .02
❑ 380 Dave Winfield .10 .03
❑ 381 Frank Robinson MG .15 .04
❑ 382 Jeff Musselman .05 .02
❑ 383 John Morris .05 .02
❑ 384 Pat Combs .05 .02
❑ 385 Fred McGriff AS .10 .03
❑ 386 Julio Franco AS .05 .02
❑ 387 Wade Boggs AS .10 .03
❑ 388 Cal Ripken AS .40 .12
❑ 389 Robin Yount AS .25 .07
❑ 390 Ruben Sierra AS .05 .02
❑ 391 Kirby Puckett AS .15 .04
❑ 392 Carlton Fisk AS .10 .03
❑ 393 Bret Saberhagen AS .05 .02
❑ 394 Jeff Ballard AS .05 .02
❑ 395 Jeff Russell AS .05 .02
❑ 396 A.Bartlett Giamatti .25 .07
COMM MEM
❑ 397 Will Clark AS .10 .03
❑ 398 Ryne Sandberg AS .25 .07
❑ 399 Howard Johnson AS .05 .02
❑ 400 Ozzie Smith AS .25 .07
❑ 401 Kevin Mitchell AS .05 .02
❑ 402 Eric Davis AS .05 .02
❑ 403 Tony Gwynn AS .15 .04
❑ 404 Craig Biggio AS .10 .03
❑ 405 Mike Scott AS .05 .02
❑ 406 Joe Magrane AS .05 .02
❑ 407 Mark Davis AS .05 .02
❑ 408 Trevor Wilson .05 .02
❑ 409 Tom Brunansky .05 .02
❑ 410 Joe Boever .05 .02
❑ 411 Ken Phelps .05 .02
❑ 412 Jamie Moyer .10 .03
❑ 413 Brian DuBois .05 .02
❑ 414A Frank Thomas FDP .. 500.00 150.00
ERR (Name missing
on card front)
❑ 414B F.Thomas COR RC 2.00 .60
❑ 415 Shawon Dunston .05 .02
❑ 416 Dave Johnson (P) .05 .02
❑ 417 Jim Gantner .05 .02
❑ 418 Tom Browning .05 .02
❑ 419 Beau Allred RC .05 .02
❑ 420 Carlton Fisk .15 .04
❑ 421 Greg Minton .05 .02
❑ 422 Pat Sheridan .05 .02
❑ 423 Fred Toliver .05 .02
❑ 424 Jerry Reuss .05 .02
❑ 425 Bill Landrum .05 .02
❑ 426 Jeff Hamilton UER .05 .02
(Stats say he fanned
197 times in 1987, but
he only had 147 at bats)
❑ 427 Carmen Castillo .05 .02
❑ 428 Steve Davis .05 .02
❑ 429 Tom Kelly MG .05 .02
❑ 430 Pete Incaviglia .05 .02
❑ 431 Randy Johnson .50 .12
❑ 432 Damaso Garcia .05 .02
❑ 433 Steve Olin RC .25 .07
❑ 434 Mark Carreon .05 .02
❑ 435 Kevin Seitzer .05 .02
❑ 436 Mel Hall .05 .02
❑ 437 Les Lancaster .05 .02
❑ 438 Greg Myers .05 .02
❑ 439 Jeff Parrett .05 .02
❑ 440 Alan Trammell .10 .03
❑ 441 Bob Kipper .05 .02
❑ 442 Jerry Browne .05 .02
❑ 443 Cris Carpenter .05 .02
❑ 444 Kyle Abbott FDP .05 .02
❑ 445 Danny Jackson .05 .02
❑ 446 Dan Pasqua .05 .02
❑ 447 Atlee Hammaker .05 .02
❑ 448 Greg Gagne .05 .02
❑ 449 Dennis Rasmussen .05 .02
❑ 450 Rickey Henderson .25 .07
❑ 451 Mark Lemke .05 .02
❑ 452 Luis DeLosSantos .05 .02
❑ 453 Jody Davis .05 .02
❑ 454 Jeff King .05 .02
❑ 455 Jeffrey Leonard .05 .02
❑ 456 Chris Gwynn .05 .02
❑ 457 Gregg Jefferies .10 .03
❑ 458 Bob McClure .05 .02
❑ 459 Jim Lefebvre MG .05 .02
❑ 460 Mike Scott .05 .02
❑ 461 Carlos Martinez .05 .02
❑ 462 Denny Walling .05 .02
❑ 463 Drew Hall .05 .02
❑ 464 Jerome Walton .05 .02
❑ 465 Kevin Gross .05 .02
❑ 466 Rance Mulliniks .05 .02
❑ 467 Juan Nieves .05 .02
❑ 468 Bill Ripken .05 .02
❑ 469 John Kruk .10 .03
❑ 470 Frank Viola .05 .02
❑ 471 Mike Brumley .05 .02
❑ 472 Jose Uribe .05 .02
❑ 473 Joe Price .05 .02
❑ 474 Rich Thompson .05 .02
❑ 475 Bob Welch .05 .02
❑ 476 Brad Komminsk .05 .02
❑ 477 Willie Fraser .05 .02
❑ 478 Mike LaValliere .05 .02
❑ 479 Frank White .10 .03
❑ 480 Sid Fernandez .05 .02
❑ 481 Garry Templeton .05 .02
❑ 482 Steve Carter .05 .02
❑ 483 Alejandro Pena .05 .02
❑ 484 Mike Fitzgerald .05 .02
❑ 485 John Candelaria .05 .02
❑ 486 Jeff Treadway .05 .02
❑ 487 Steve Searcy .05 .02
❑ 488 Ken Oberkfell .05 .02
❑ 489 Nick Leyva MG .05 .02
❑ 490 Dan Plesac .05 .02
❑ 491 Dave Cochrane RC .05 .02
❑ 492 Ron Oester .05 .02
❑ 493 Jason Grimsley RC .10 .03
❑ 494 Terry Puhl .05 .02
❑ 495 Lee Smith .10 .03
❑ 496 Cecil Espy UER .05 .02
('88 stats have 3
SB's, should be 33)
❑ 497 Dave Schmidt .05 .02
❑ 498 Rick Schu .05 .02
❑ 499 Bill Long .05 .02
❑ 500 Kevin Mitchell .05 .02
❑ 501 Matt Young .05 .02
❑ 502 Mitch Webster .05 .02
❑ 503 Randy St.Claire .05 .02
❑ 504 Tom O'Malley .05 .02
❑ 505 Kelly Gruber .05 .02
❑ 506 Tom Glavine .15 .04
❑ 507 Gary Redus .05 .02
❑ 508 Terry Leach .05 .02
❑ 509 Tom Pagnozzi .05 .02
❑ 510 Dwight Gooden .10 .03
❑ 511 Clay Parker .05 .02
❑ 512 Gary Pettis .05 .02
❑ 513 Mark Eichhorn .05 .02
❑ 514 Andy Allanson .05 .02
❑ 515 Len Dykstra .10 .03
❑ 516 Tim Leary .05 .02
❑ 517 Roberto Alomar .15 .04
❑ 518 Bill Krueger .05 .02
❑ 519 Bucky Dent MG .05 .02
❑ 520 Mitch Williams .05 .02
❑ 521 Craig Worthington .05 .02
❑ 522 Mike Dunne .05 .02
❑ 523 Jay Bell .10 .03
❑ 524 Daryl Boston .05 .02
❑ 525 Wally Joyner .10 .03
❑ 526 Checklist 4 .05 .02
❑ 527 Ron Hassey .05 .02
❑ 528 Kevin Wickander UER .05 .02
(Monthly scoreboard
strikeout total was 2.2,
that was his innings
pitched total)
❑ 529 Greg A. Harris .05 .02
❑ 530 Mark Langston .05 .02
❑ 531 Ken Caminiti .10 .03
❑ 532 Cecilio Guante .05 .02
❑ 533 Tim Jones .05 .02
❑ 534 Louie Meadows .05 .02
❑ 535 John Smoltz .25 .07
❑ 536 Bob Geren .05 .02
❑ 537 Mark Grant .05 .02
❑ 538 Bill Spiers UER .05 .02
(Photo actually
George Canale)
❑ 539 Neal Heaton .05 .02
❑ 540 Danny Tartabull .05 .02
❑ 541 Pat Perry .05 .02
❑ 542 Darren Daulton .10 .03
❑ 543 Nelson Liriano .05 .02
❑ 544 Dennis Boyd .05 .02
❑ 545 Kevin McReynolds .05 .02
❑ 546 Kevin Hickey .05 .02
❑ 547 Jack Howell .05 .02
❑ 548 Pat Clements .05 .02
❑ 549 Don Zimmer MG .05 .02
❑ 550 Julio Franco .10 .03
❑ 551 Tim Crews .05 .02
❑ 552 Mike(Miss.) Smith .05 .02
❑ 553 Scott Scudder UER .05 .02
(Cedar Rap1ds)
❑ 554 Jay Buhner .10 .03
❑ 555 Jack Morris .10 .03
❑ 556 Gene Larkin .05 .02
❑ 557 Jeff Innis .05 .02
❑ 558 Rafael Ramirez .05 .02
❑ 559 Andy McGaffigan .05 .02
❑ 560 Steve Sax .05 .02
❑ 561 Ken Dayley .05 .02
❑ 562 Chad Kreuter .05 .02
❑ 563 Alex Sanchez .05 .02
❑ 564 T.Houston FDP RC .25 .07
❑ 565 Scott Fletcher .05 .02
❑ 566 Mark Knudson .05 .02
❑ 567 Ron Gant .10 .03
❑ 568 John Smiley .05 .02
❑ 569 Ivan Calderon .05 .02
❑ 570 Cal Ripken .75 .23
❑ 571 Brett Butler .10 .03
❑ 572 Greg W. Harris .05 .02
❑ 573 Danny Heep .05 .02
❑ 574 Bill Swift .05 .02
❑ 575 Lance Parrish .05 .02
❑ 576 Mike Dyer RC .05 .02
❑ 577 Charlie Hayes .05 .02
❑ 578 Joe Magrane .05 .02
❑ 579 Art Howe MG .05 .02
❑ 580 Joe Carter .10 .03
❑ 581 Ken Griffey Sr. .10 .03
❑ 582 Rick Honeycutt .05 .02
❑ 583 Bruce Benedict .05 .02
❑ 584 Phil Stephenson .05 .02
❑ 585 Kal Daniels .05 .02
❑ 586 Edwin Nunez .05 .02
❑ 587 Lance Johnson .05 .02
❑ 588 Rick Rhoden .05 .02
❑ 589 Mike Aldrete .05 .02
❑ 590 Ozzie Smith .40 .12
❑ 591 Todd Stottlemyre .10 .03
❑ 592 R.J. Reynolds .05 .02
❑ 593 Scott Bradley .05 .02
❑ 594 Luis Sojo .05 .02
❑ 595 Greg Swindell .05 .02
❑ 596 Jose DeJesus .05 .02
❑ 597 Chris Bosio .05 .02
❑ 598 Brady Anderson .10 .03

❑ 599 Frank Williams .05 .02
❑ 600 Darryl Strawberry .10 .03
❑ 601 Luis Rivera .05 .02
❑ 602 Scott Garrelts .05 .02
❑ 603 Tony Armas .05 .02
❑ 604 Ron Robinson .05 .02
❑ 605 Mike Scioscia .05 .02
❑ 606 Storm Davis .05 .02
❑ 607 Steve Jeltz .05 .02
❑ 608 Eric Anthony RC .10 .03
❑ 609 Sparky Anderson MG .10 .03
❑ 610 Pedro Guerrero .05 .02
❑ 611 Walt Terrell .05 .02
❑ 612 Dave Gallagher .05 .02
❑ 613 Jeff Pico .05 .02
❑ 614 Nelson Santovenia .05 .02
❑ 615 Rob Deer .05 .02
❑ 616 Brian Holman .05 .02
❑ 617 Geronimo Berroa .05 .02
❑ 618 Ed Whitson .05 .02
❑ 619 Rob Ducey .05 .02
❑ 620 Tony Castillo .05 .02
❑ 621 Melido Perez .05 .02
❑ 622 Sid Bream .05 .02
❑ 623 Jim Corsi .05 .02
❑ 624 Darrin Jackson .05 .02
❑ 625 Roger McDowell .05 .02
❑ 626 Bob Melvin .05 .02
❑ 627 Jose Rijo .05 .02
❑ 628 Candy Maldonado .05 .02
❑ 629 Eric Hetzel .05 .02
❑ 630 Gary Gaetti .10 .03
❑ 631 John Wetteland .25 .07
❑ 632 Scott Lusader .05 .02
❑ 633 Dennis Cook .05 .02
❑ 634 Luis Polonia .05 .02
❑ 635 Brian Downing .05 .02
❑ 636 Jesse Orosco .05 .02
❑ 637 Craig Reynolds .05 .02
❑ 638 Jeff Montgomery .10 .03
❑ 639 Tony LaRussa MG .10 .03
❑ 640 Rick Sutcliffe .10 .03
❑ 641 Doug Strange .05 .02
❑ 642 Jack Armstrong .05 .02
❑ 643 Alfredo Griffin .05 .02
❑ 644 Paul Assenmacher .05 .02
❑ 645 Jose Oquendo .05 .02
❑ 646 Checklist 5 .05 .02
❑ 647 Rex Hudler .05 .02
❑ 648 Jim Clancy .05 .02
❑ 649 Dan Murphy RC .10 .03
❑ 650 Mike Witt .05 .02
❑ 651 Rafael Santana .05 .02
❑ 652 Mike Boddicker .05 .02
❑ 653 John Moses .05 .02
❑ 654 Paul Coleman FDP RC .10 .03
❑ 655 Gregg Olson .10 .03
❑ 656 Mackey Sasser .05 .02
❑ 657 Terry Mulholland .05 .02
❑ 658 Donell Nixon .05 .02
❑ 659 Greg Cadaret .05 .02
❑ 660 Vince Coleman .05 .02
❑ 661 Dick Howser TBC'85 .05 .02
UER (Seaver's 300th on 7/11/85, should be 8/4/85)
❑ 662 Mike Schmidt TBC'80 .25 .07
❑ 663 Fred Lynn TBC'75 .05 .02
❑ 664 Johnny Bench TBC'70 .15 .04
❑ 665 Sandy Koufax TBC'65 .50 .15
❑ 666 Brian Fisher .05 .02
❑ 667 Curt Wilkerson .05 .02
❑ 668 Joe Oliver .05 .02
❑ 669 Tom Lasorda MG .25 .07
❑ 670 Dennis Eckersley .10 .03
❑ 671 Bob Boone .10 .03
❑ 672 Roy Smith .05 .02
❑ 673 Joey Meyer .05 .02
❑ 674 Spike Owen .05 .02
❑ 675 Jim Abbott .15 .04
❑ 676 Randy Kutcher .05 .02
❑ 677 Jay Tibbs .05 .02
❑ 678 Kirt Manwaring UER .05 .02
('88 Phoenix stats repeated)
❑ 679 Gary Ward .05 .02
❑ 680 Howard Johnson .05 .02
❑ 681 Mike Schooler .05 .02
❑ 682 Dann Bilardello .05 .02
❑ 683 Kenny Rogers .10 .03
❑ 684 Julio Machado .05 .02
❑ 685 Tony Fernandez .05 .02
❑ 686 Carmelo Martinez .05 .02
❑ 687 Tim Birtsas .05 .02
❑ 688 Milt Thompson .05 .02
❑ 689 Rich Yett .05 .02
❑ 690 Mark McGwire .60 .18
❑ 691 Chuck Cary .05 .02
❑ 692 Sammy Sosa RC 5.00 1.50
❑ 693 Calvin Schiraldi .05 .02
❑ 694 Mike Stanton RC .25 .07
❑ 695 Tom Henke .05 .02
❑ 696 B.J. Surhoff .10 .03
❑ 697 Mike Davis .05 .02
❑ 698 Omar Vizquel .25 .07
❑ 699 Jim Leyland MG .05 .02
❑ 700 Kirby Puckett .25 .07
❑ 701 Bernie Williams RC 1.00 .30
❑ 702 Tony Phillips .05 .02
❑ 703 Jeff Brantley .05 .02
❑ 704 Chip Hale .05 .02
❑ 705 Claudell Washington .05 .02
❑ 706 Geno Petralli .05 .02
❑ 707 Luis Aquino .05 .02
❑ 708 Larry Sheets .05 .02
❑ 709 Juan Berenguer .05 .02
❑ 710 Von Hayes .05 .02
❑ 711 Rick Aguilera .10 .03
❑ 712 Todd Benzinger .05 .02
❑ 713 Tim Drummond .05 .02
❑ 714 Marquis Grissom RC .40 .12
❑ 715 Greg Maddux .40 .12
❑ 716 Steve Balboni .05 .02
❑ 717 Ron Karkovice .05 .02
❑ 718 Gary Sheffield .25 .07
❑ 719 Wally Whitehurst .05 .02
❑ 720 Andres Galarraga .10 .03
❑ 721 Lee Mazzilli .05 .02
❑ 722 Felix Fermin .05 .02
❑ 723 Jeff D. Robinson .05 .02
❑ 724 Juan Bell .05 .02
❑ 725 Terry Pendleton .10 .03
❑ 726 Gene Nelson .05 .02
❑ 727 Pat Tabler .05 .02
❑ 728 Jim Acker .05 .02
❑ 729 Bobby Valentine MG .05 .02
❑ 730 Tony Gwynn .30 .09
❑ 731 Don Carman .05 .02
❑ 732 Ernest Riles .05 .02
❑ 733 John Dopson .05 .02
❑ 734 Kevin Elster .05 .02
❑ 735 Charlie Hough .10 .03
❑ 736 Rick Dempsey .05 .02
❑ 737 Chris Sabo .05 .02
❑ 738 Gene Harris .05 .02
❑ 739 Dale Sveum .05 .02
❑ 740 Jesse Barfield .05 .02
❑ 741 Steve Wilson .05 .02
❑ 742 Ernie Whitt .05 .02
❑ 743 Tom Candiotti .05 .02
❑ 744 Kelly Mann .05 .02
❑ 745 Hubie Brooks .05 .02
❑ 746 Dave Smith .05 .02
❑ 747 Randy Bush .05 .02
❑ 748 Doyle Alexander .05 .02
❑ 749 Mark Parent UER .05 .02
('87 BA .80, should be .080)
❑ 750 Dale Murphy .25 .07
❑ 751 Steve Lyons .05 .02
❑ 752 Tom Gordon .10 .03
❑ 753 Chris Speier .05 .02
❑ 754 Bob Walk .05 .02
❑ 755 Rafael Palmeiro .15 .04
❑ 756 Ken Howell .05 .02
❑ 757 Larry Walker RC 1.00 .30
❑ 758 Mark Thurmond .05 .02
❑ 759 Tom Trebelhorn MG .05 .02
❑ 760 Wade Boggs .15 .04
❑ 761 Mike Jackson .05 .02
❑ 762 Doug Dascenzo .05 .02
❑ 763 Dennis Martinez .10 .03
❑ 764 Tim Teufel .05 .02
❑ 765 Chili Davis .10 .03
❑ 766 Brian Meyer .05 .02
❑ 767 Tracy Jones .05 .02
❑ 768 Chuck Crim .05 .02
❑ 769 Greg Hibbard RC .10 .03
❑ 770 Cory Snyder .05 .02
❑ 771 Pete Smith .05 .02
❑ 772 Jeff Reed .05 .02
❑ 773 Dave Leiper .05 .02
❑ 774 Ben McDonald RC .25 .07
❑ 775 Andy Van Slyke .10 .03
❑ 776 Charlie Leibrandt .05 .02
❑ 777 Tim Laudner .05 .02
❑ 778 Mike Jeffcoat .05 .02
❑ 779 Lloyd Moseby .05 .02
❑ 780 Orel Hershiser .10 .03
❑ 781 Mario Diaz .05 .02
❑ 782 Jose Alvarez .05 .02
❑ 783 Checklist 6 .05 .02
❑ 784 Scott Bailes .05 .02
❑ 785 Jim Rice .10 .03
❑ 786 Eric King .05 .02
❑ 787 Rene Gonzales .05 .02
❑ 788 Frank DiPino .05 .02
❑ 789 John Wathan MG .05 .02
❑ 790 Gary Carter .10 .03
❑ 791 Alvaro Espinoza .05 .02
❑ 792 Gerald Perry .05 .02
❑ XX George Bush PRES .00

1990 Topps Debut '89

	Nm-Mt	Ex-Mt
COMP.FACT.SET (152)	15.00	4.50

❑ 1 Jim Abbott .50 .15
❑ 2 Beau Allred .15 .04
❑ 3 Wilson Alvarez .25 .07
❑ 4 Kent Anderson .15 .04
❑ 5 Eric Anthony .15 .04
❑ 6 Kevin Appier .25 .07
❑ 7 Larry Arndt .15 .04
❑ 8 John Barfield .15 .04
❑ 9 Billy Bates .15 .04
❑ 10 Kevin Batiste .15 .04
❑ 11 Blaine Beatty .15 .04
❑ 12 Stan Belinda .15 .04
❑ 13 Juan Bell .15 .04
❑ 14 Joey Belle .75 .23
(Now known as Albert)
❑ 15 Andy Benes .25 .07
❑ 16 Mike Benjamin .15 .04
❑ 17 Geronimo Berroa .15 .04
❑ 18 Mike Blowers .25 .07
❑ 19 Brian Brady .15 .04
❑ 20 Francisco Cabrera .15 .04
❑ 21 George Canale .15 .04
❑ 22 Jose Cano .15 .04
❑ 23 Steve Carter .15 .04
❑ 24 Pat Combs .15 .04
❑ 25 Scott Coolbaugh .15 .04
❑ 26 Steve Cummings .15 .04
❑ 27 Pete Dalena .15 .04
❑ 28 Jeff Datz .15 .04
❑ 29 Bobby Davidson .15 .04
❑ 30 Drew Denson .15 .04
❑ 31 Gary DiSarcina .25 .07

Card	Nm-Mt	Ex-Mt
❑ 32 Brian DuBois	.15	.04
❑ 33 Mike Dyer	.15	.04
❑ 34 Wayne Edwards	.15	.04
❑ 35 Junior Felix	.15	.04
❑ 36 Mike Fetters	.15	.04
❑ 37 Steve Finley	.25	.07
❑ 38 Darrin Fletcher	.25	.07
❑ 39 LaVel Freeman	.15	.04
❑ 40 Steve Frey	.15	.04
❑ 41 Mark Gardner	.15	.04
❑ 42 Joe Girardi	.25	.07
❑ 43 Juan Gonzalez	2.50	.75
❑ 44 Goose Gozzo	.15	.04
❑ 45 Tommy Greene	.15	.04
❑ 46 Ken Griffey Jr.	5.00	1.50
❑ 47 Jason Grimsley	.15	.04
❑ 48 Marquis Grissom	.75	.23
❑ 49 Mark Guthrie	.15	.04
❑ 50 Chip Hale	.15	.04
❑ 51 Jack Hardy	.15	.04
❑ 52 Gene Harris	.15	.04
❑ 53 Mike Hartley	.15	.04
❑ 54 Scott Hemond	.15	.04
❑ 55 Xavier Hernandez	.15	.04
❑ 56 Eric Hetzel	.15	.04
❑ 57 Greg Hibbard	.15	.04
❑ 58 Mark Higgins	.15	.04
❑ 59 Glenallen Hill	.15	.04
❑ 60 Chris Hoiles	.25	.07
❑ 61 Shawn Holman	.15	.04
❑ 62 Dann Howitt	.15	.04
❑ 63 Mike Huff	.15	.04
❑ 64 Terry Jorgensen	.15	.04
❑ 65 David Justice	1.00	.30
❑ 66 Jeff King	.15	.04
❑ 67 Matt Kinzer	.15	.04
❑ 68 Joe Kraemer	.15	.04
❑ 69 Marcus Lawton	.15	.04
❑ 70 Derek Lilliquist	.15	.04
❑ 71 Scott Little	.15	.04
❑ 72 Greg Litton	.15	.04
❑ 73 Rick Luecken	.15	.04
❑ 74 Julio Machado	.15	.04
❑ 75 Tom Magrann	.15	.04
❑ 76 Kelly Mann	.15	.04
❑ 77 Randy McCament	.15	.04
❑ 78 Ben McDonald	.15	.04
❑ 79 Chuck McElroy	.15	.04
❑ 80 Jeff McKnight	.15	.04
❑ 81 Kent Mercker	.15	.04
❑ 82 Matt Merullo	.15	.04
❑ 83 Hensley Meulens	.15	.04
❑ 84 Kevin Mmahat	.15	.04
❑ 85 Mike Munoz	.15	.04
❑ 86 Dan Murphy	.15	.04
❑ 87 Jaime Navarro	.15	.04
❑ 88 Randy Nosek	.15	.04
❑ 89 John Olerud	1.00	.30
❑ 90 Steve Olin	.25	.07
❑ 91 Joe Oliver	.15	.04
❑ 92 Francisco Oliveras	.15	.04
❑ 93 Gregg Olson	.25	.07
❑ 94 John Orton	.15	.04
❑ 95 Dean Palmer	.50	.15
❑ 96 Ramon Pena	.15	.04
❑ 97 Jeff Peterek	.15	.04
❑ 98 Marty Pevey	.15	.04
❑ 99 Rusty Richards	.15	.04
❑ 100 Jeff Richardson	.15	.04
❑ 101 Rob Richie	.15	.04
❑ 102 Kevin Ritz	.15	.04
❑ 103 Rosario Rodriguez	.15	.04
❑ 104 Mike Roesler	.15	.04
❑ 105 Kenny Rogers	.25	.07
❑ 106 Bobby Rose	.15	.04
❑ 107 Alex Sanchez	.15	.04
❑ 108 Deion Sanders	.75	.23
❑ 109 Jeff Schaefer	.15	.04
❑ 110 Jeff Schulz	.15	.04
❑ 111 Mike Schwabe	.15	.04
❑ 112 Dick Scott	.15	.04
❑ 113 Scott Scudder	.15	.04
❑ 114 Rudy Seanez	.15	.04
❑ 115 Joe Skalski	.15	.04
❑ 116 Dwight Smith	.15	.04
❑ 117 Greg Smith	.15	.04
❑ 118 Mike Smith	.15	.04
❑ 119 Paul Sorrento	.25	.07
❑ 120 Sammy Sosa	8.00	2.40
❑ 121 Billy Spiers	.15	.04
❑ 122 Mike Stanton	.15	.04
❑ 123 Phil Stephenson	.15	.04
❑ 124 Doug Strange	.15	.04
❑ 125 Russ Swan	.15	.04
❑ 126 Kevin Tapani	.25	.07
❑ 127 Stu Tate	.15	.04
❑ 128 Greg Vaughn	.15	.04
❑ 129 Robin Ventura	.75	.23
❑ 130 Randy Veres	.15	.04
❑ 131 Jose Vizcaino	.25	.07
❑ 132 Omar Vizquel	.75	.23
❑ 133 Larry Walker	2.50	.75
❑ 134 Jerome Walton	.15	.04
❑ 135 Gary Wayne	.15	.04
❑ 136 Lenny Webster	.15	.04
❑ 137 Mickey Weston	.15	.04
❑ 138 Jeff Wetherby	.15	.04
❑ 139 John Wetteland	.50	.15
❑ 140 Ed Whited	.15	.04
❑ 141 Wally Whitehurst	.15	.04
❑ 142 Kevin Wickander	.15	.04
❑ 143 Dean Wilkins	.15	.04
❑ 144 Dana Williams	.15	.04
❑ 145 Paul Wilmet	.15	.04
❑ 146 Craig Wilson	.15	.04
❑ 147 Matt Winters	.15	.04
❑ 148 Eric Yelding	.15	.04
❑ 149 Clint Zavaras	.15	.04
❑ 150 Todd Zeile	.50	.15
❑ 151 Checklist Card	.15	.04
❑ 152 Checklist Card	.15	.04

1991 Topps

	Nm-Mt	Ex-Mt
COMPLETE SET (792)	20.00	6.00
COMP.FACT.SET (792)	25.00	7.50
❑ 1 Nolan Ryan	1.00	.30
❑ 2 George Brett RB	.30	.09
❑ 3 Carlton Fisk RB	.10	.03
❑ 4 Kevin Maas RB	.05	.02
❑ 5 Cal Ripken RB	.40	.12
❑ 6 Nolan Ryan RB	.50	.15
❑ 7 Ryne Sandberg RB	.25	.07
❑ 8 Bobby Thigpen RB	.05	.02
❑ 9 Darrin Fletcher	.05	.02
❑ 10 Gregg Olson	.05	.02
❑ 11 Roberto Kelly	.05	.02
❑ 12 Paul Assenmacher	.05	.02
❑ 13 Mariano Duncan	.05	.02
❑ 14 Dennis Lamp	.05	.02
❑ 15 Von Hayes	.05	.02
❑ 16 Mike Heath	.05	.02
❑ 17 Jeff Brantley	.05	.02
❑ 18 Nelson Liriano	.05	.02
❑ 19 Jeff D. Robinson	.05	.02
❑ 20 Pedro Guerrero	.10	.03
❑ 21 Joe Morgan MG	.05	.02
❑ 22 Storm Davis	.05	.02
❑ 23 Jim Gantner	.05	.02
❑ 24 Dave Martinez	.05	.02
❑ 25 Tim Belcher	.05	.02
❑ 26 Luis Sojo UER (Born in Barquisimento, not Carquis)	.05	.02
❑ 27 Bobby Witt	.05	.02
❑ 28 Alvaro Espinoza	.05	.02
❑ 29 Bob Walk	.05	.02
❑ 30 Gregg Jefferies	.05	.02
❑ 31 Colby Ward	.05	.02
❑ 32 Mike Simms	.05	.02
❑ 33 Barry Jones	.05	.02
❑ 34 Atlee Hammaker	.05	.02
❑ 35 Greg Maddux	.40	.12
❑ 36 Donnie Hill	.05	.02
❑ 37 Tom Bolton	.05	.02
❑ 38 Scott Bradley	.05	.02
❑ 39 Jim Neidlinger	.05	.02
❑ 40 Kevin Mitchell	.05	.02
❑ 41 Ken Dayley	.05	.02
❑ 42 Chris Hoiles	.05	.02
❑ 43 Roger McDowell	.05	.02
❑ 44 Mike Felder	.05	.02
❑ 45 Chris Sabo	.05	.02
❑ 46 Tim Drummond	.05	.02
❑ 47 Brook Jacoby	.05	.02
❑ 48 Dennis Boyd	.05	.02
❑ 49A Pat Borders ERR (40 steals at Kinston in '86)	.25	.07
❑ 49B Pat Borders COR (0 steals at Kinston in '86)	.05	.02
❑ 50 Bob Welch	.05	.02
❑ 51 Art Howe MG	.05	.02
❑ 52 Francisco Oliveras	.05	.02
❑ 53 Mike Sharperson UER (Born in 1961, not 1960)	.05	.02
❑ 54 Gary Mielke	.05	.02
❑ 55 Jeffrey Leonard	.05	.02
❑ 56 Jeff Parrett	.05	.02
❑ 57 Jack Howell	.05	.02
❑ 58 Mel Stottlemyre Jr.	.05	.02
❑ 59 Eric Yelding	.05	.02
❑ 60 Frank Viola	.10	.03
❑ 61 Stan Javier	.05	.02
❑ 62 Lee Guetterman	.05	.02
❑ 63 Milt Thompson	.05	.02
❑ 64 Tom Herr	.05	.02
❑ 65 Bruce Hurst	.05	.02
❑ 66 Terry Kennedy	.05	.02
❑ 67 Rick Honeycutt	.05	.02
❑ 68 Gary Sheffield	.10	.03
❑ 69 Steve Wilson	.05	.02
❑ 70 Ellis Burks	.10	.03
❑ 71 Jim Acker	.05	.02
❑ 72 Junior Ortiz	.05	.02
❑ 73 Craig Worthington	.05	.02
❑ 74 Shane Andrews RC	.25	.07
❑ 75 Jack Morris	.10	.03
❑ 76 Jerry Browne	.05	.02
❑ 77 Drew Hall	.05	.02
❑ 78 Geno Petralli	.05	.02
❑ 79 Frank Thomas	.25	.07
❑ 80A Fernando Valenzuela ERR (104 earned runs in '90 tied for league lead)	.40	.12
❑ 80B Fernando Valenzuela COR (104 earned runs in '90 led league, 20 CG's in 1986 now italicized)	.10	.03
❑ 81 Cito Gaston MG	.05	.02
❑ 82 Tom Glavine	.15	.04
❑ 83 Daryl Boston	.05	.02
❑ 84 Bob McClure	.05	.02
❑ 85 Jesse Barfield	.05	.02
❑ 86 Les Lancaster	.05	.02
❑ 87 Tracy Jones	.05	.02
❑ 88 Bob Tewksbury	.05	.02
❑ 89 Darren Daulton	.10	.03
❑ 90 Danny Tartabull	.05	.02
❑ 91 Greg Colbrunn RC	.25	.07
❑ 92 Danny Jackson	.05	.02
❑ 93 Ivan Calderon	.05	.02
❑ 94 John Dopson	.05	.02
❑ 95 Paul Molitor	.15	.04
❑ 96 Trevor Wilson	.05	.02

Card	Price	Price
❑ 97A Brady Anderson ERR (September, 2 RBI and 3 hits, should be 3 RBI and 14 hits	.40	.12
❑ 97B Brady Anderson COR	.10	.03
❑ 98 Sergio Valdez	.05	.02
❑ 99 Chris Gwynn	.05	.02
❑ 100 Don Mattingly COR (101 hits in 1990)	.60	.18
❑ 100A Don Mattingly ERR (10 hits in 1990)	2.00	.60
❑ 101 Rob Ducey	.05	.02
❑ 102 Gene Larkin	.05	.02
❑ 103 Tim Costo RC	.05	.02
❑ 104 Don Robinson	.05	.02
❑ 105 Kevin McReynolds	.05	.02
❑ 106 Ed Nunez	.05	.02
❑ 107 Luis Polonia	.05	.02
❑ 108 Matt Young	.05	.02
❑ 109 Greg Riddoch MG	.05	.02
❑ 110 Tom Henke	.05	.02
❑ 111 Andres Thomas	.05	.02
❑ 112 Frank DiPino	.05	.02
❑ 113 Carl Everett RC	.40	.12
❑ 114 Lance Dickson RC	.10	.03
❑ 115 Hubie Brooks	.05	.02
❑ 116 Mark Davis	.05	.02
❑ 117 Dion James	.05	.02
❑ 118 Tom Edens	.05	.02
❑ 119 Carl Nichols	.05	.02
❑ 120 Joe Carter	.10	.03
❑ 121 Eric King	.05	.02
❑ 122 Paul O'Neill	.15	.04
❑ 123 Greg A. Harris	.05	.02
❑ 124 Randy Bush	.05	.02
❑ 125 Steve Bedrosian	.05	.02
❑ 126 Bernard Gilkey	.05	.02
❑ 127 Joe Price	.05	.02
❑ 128 Travis Fryman (Front has SS back has SS-3B)	.10	.03
❑ 129 Mark Eichhorn	.05	.02
❑ 130 Ozzie Smith	.40	.12
❑ 131A Checklist 1 ERR 727 Phil Bradley	.25	.07
❑ 131B Checklist 1 COR 717 Phil Bradley	.05	.02
❑ 132 Jamie Quirk	.05	.02
❑ 133 Greg Briley	.05	.02
❑ 134 Kevin Elster	.05	.02
❑ 135 Jerome Walton	.05	.02
❑ 136 Dave Schmidt	.05	.02
❑ 137 Randy Ready	.05	.02
❑ 138 Jamie Moyer	.10	.03
❑ 139 Jeff Treadway	.05	.02
❑ 140 Fred McGriff	.15	.04
❑ 141 Nick Leyva MG	.05	.02
❑ 142 Curt Wilkerson	.05	.02
❑ 143 John Smiley	.05	.02
❑ 144 Dave Henderson	.05	.02
❑ 145 Lou Whitaker	.10	.03
❑ 146 Dan Plesac	.05	.02
❑ 147 Carlos Baerga	.05	.02
❑ 148 Rey Palacios	.05	.02
❑ 149 Al Osuna UER (Shown throwing right, but bio says lefty)	.10	.03
❑ 150 Cal Ripken	.75	.23
❑ 151 Tom Browning	.05	.02
❑ 152 Mickey Hatcher	.05	.02
❑ 153 Bryan Harvey	.05	.02
❑ 154 Jay Buhner	.10	.03
❑ 155A Dwight Evans ERR (Led league with 162 games in '82)	.40	.12
❑ 155B Dwight Evans COR (Tied for lead with 162 games in '82)	.10	.03
❑ 156 Carlos Martinez	.05	.02
❑ 157 John Smoltz	.15	.04
❑ 158 Jose Uribe	.05	.02
❑ 159 Joe Boever	.05	.02
❑ 160 Vince Coleman UER (Wrong birth year, born 9/22/60)	.05	.02
❑ 161 Tim Leary	.05	.02
❑ 162 Ozzie Canseco	.05	.02
❑ 163 Dave Johnson	.05	.02
❑ 164 Edgar Diaz	.05	.02
❑ 165 Sandy Alomar Jr.	.05	.02
❑ 166 Harold Baines	.10	.03
❑ 167A R.Tomlin RC ERR Harriburg	.25	.07
❑ 167B R.Tomlin RC COR Harrisburg	.10	.03
❑ 168 John Olerud	.10	.03
❑ 169 Luis Aquino	.05	.02
❑ 170 Carlton Fisk	.15	.04
❑ 171 Tony LaRussa MG	.10	.03
❑ 172 Pete Incaviglia	.05	.02
❑ 173 Jason Grimsley	.05	.02
❑ 174 Ken Caminiti	.10	.03
❑ 175 Jack Armstrong	.05	.02
❑ 176 John Orton	.05	.02
❑ 177 Reggie Harris	.05	.02
❑ 178 Dave Valle	.05	.02
❑ 179 Pete Harnisch	.05	.02
❑ 180 Tony Gwynn	.30	.09
❑ 181 Duane Ward	.05	.02
❑ 182 Junior Noboa	.05	.02
❑ 183 Clay Parker	.05	.02
❑ 184 Gary Green	.05	.02
❑ 185 Joe Magrane	.05	.02
❑ 186 Rod Booker	.05	.02
❑ 187 Greg Cadaret	.05	.02
❑ 188 Damon Berryhill	.05	.02
❑ 189 Daryl Irvine	.05	.02
❑ 190 Matt Williams	.10	.03
❑ 191 Willie Blair	.05	.02
❑ 192 Rob Deer	.05	.02
❑ 193 Felix Fermin	.05	.02
❑ 194 Xavier Hernandez	.05	.02
❑ 195 Wally Joyner	.10	.03
❑ 196 Jim Vatcher	.05	.02
❑ 197 Chris Nabholz	.05	.02
❑ 198 R.J. Reynolds	.05	.02
❑ 199 Mike Hartley	.05	.02
❑ 200 Darryl Strawberry	.10	.03
❑ 201 Tom Kelly MG	.05	.02
❑ 202 Jim Leyritz	.05	.02
❑ 203 Gene Harris	.05	.02
❑ 204 Herm Winningham	.05	.02
❑ 205 Mike Perez RC	.10	.03
❑ 206 Carlos Quintana	.05	.02
❑ 207 Gary Wayne	.05	.02
❑ 208 Willie Wilson	.05	.02
❑ 209 Ken Howell	.05	.02
❑ 210 Lance Parrish	.10	.03
❑ 211 Brian Barnes RC	.05	.02
❑ 212 Steve Finley	.10	.03
❑ 213 Frank Wills	.05	.02
❑ 214 Joe Girardi	.05	.02
❑ 215 Dave Smith	.05	.02
❑ 216 Greg Gagne	.05	.02
❑ 217 Chris Bosio	.05	.02
❑ 218 Rick Parker	.05	.02
❑ 219 Jack McDowell	.05	.02
❑ 220 Tim Wallach	.05	.02
❑ 221 Don Slaught	.05	.02
❑ 222 Brian McRae RC	.25	.07
❑ 223 Allan Anderson	.05	.02
❑ 224 Juan Gonzalez	.15	.04
❑ 225 Randy Johnson	.30	.09
❑ 226 Alfredo Griffin	.05	.02
❑ 227 Steve Avery UER (Pitched 13 games for Durham in 1989, not 2)	.05	.02
❑ 228 Rex Hudler	.05	.02
❑ 229 Rance Mulliniks	.05	.02
❑ 230 Sid Fernandez	.05	.02
❑ 231 Doug Rader MG	.05	.02
❑ 232 Jose DeJesus	.05	.02
❑ 233 Al Leiter	.10	.03
❑ 234 Scott Erickson	.05	.02
❑ 235 Dave Parker	.10	.03
❑ 236A Frank Tanana ERR (Tied for lead with 269 K's in '75)	.25	.07
❑ 236B Frank Tanana COR (Led league with 269 K's in '75)	.05	.02
❑ 237 Rick Cerone	.05	.02
❑ 238 Mike Dunne	.05	.02
❑ 239 Darren Lewis	.05	.02
❑ 240 Mike Scott	.05	.02
❑ 241 Dave Clark UER (Career totals 19 HR and 5 3B, should be 22 and 3)	.05	.02
❑ 242 Mike LaCoss	.05	.02
❑ 243 Lance Johnson	.05	.02
❑ 244 Mike Jeffcoat	.05	.02
❑ 245 Kal Daniels	.05	.02
❑ 246 Kevin Wickander	.05	.02
❑ 247 Jody Reed	.05	.02
❑ 248 Tom Gordon	.05	.02
❑ 249 Bob Melvin	.05	.02
❑ 250 Dennis Eckersley	.10	.03
❑ 251 Mark Lemke	.05	.02
❑ 252 Mel Rojas	.05	.02
❑ 253 Garry Templeton	.05	.02
❑ 254 Shawn Boskie	.05	.02
❑ 255 Brian Downing	.05	.02
❑ 256 Greg Hibbard	.05	.02
❑ 257 Tom O'Malley	.05	.02
❑ 258 Chris Hammond	.05	.02
❑ 259 Hensley Meulens	.05	.02
❑ 260 Harold Reynolds	.10	.03
❑ 261 Bud Harrelson MG	.05	.02
❑ 262 Tim Jones	.05	.02
❑ 263 Checklist 2	.05	.02
❑ 264 Dave Hollins	.05	.02
❑ 265 Mark Gubicza	.05	.02
❑ 266 Carmelo Castillo	.05	.02
❑ 267 Mark Knudson	.05	.02
❑ 268 Tom Brookens	.05	.02
❑ 269 Joe Hesketh	.05	.02
❑ 270 Mark McGwire COR (1987 Slugging Pctg. listed as .618)	.60	.18
❑ 270A Mark McGwire ERR (1987 Slugging Pctg. listed as 618)	2.00	.60
❑ 271 Omar Olivares RC	.10	.03
❑ 272 Jeff King	.05	.02
❑ 273 Johnny Ray	.05	.02
❑ 274 Ken Williams	.05	.02
❑ 275 Alan Trammell	.10	.03
❑ 276 Bill Swift	.05	.02
❑ 277 Scott Coolbaugh	.05	.02
❑ 278 Alex Fernandez UER (No '90 White Sox stats)	.05	.02
❑ 279A Jose Gonzalez ERR (Photo actually Billy Bean)	.25	.07
❑ 279B Jose Gonzalez COR	.05	.02
❑ 280 Bret Saberhagen	.10	.03
❑ 281 Larry Sheets	.05	.02
❑ 282 Don Carman	.05	.02
❑ 283 Marquis Grissom	.10	.03
❑ 284 Billy Spiers	.05	.02
❑ 285 Jim Abbott	.15	.04
❑ 286 Ken Oberkfell	.05	.02
❑ 287 Mark Grant	.05	.02
❑ 288 Derrick May	.05	.02
❑ 289 Tim Birtsas	.05	.02
❑ 290 Steve Sax	.05	.02
❑ 291 John Wathan MG	.05	.02
❑ 292 Bud Black	.05	.02
❑ 293 Jay Bell	.10	.03
❑ 294 Mike Moore	.05	.02
❑ 295 Rafael Palmeiro	.15	.04
❑ 296 Mark Williamson	.05	.02
❑ 297 Manny Lee	.05	.02
❑ 298 Omar Vizquel	.15	.04
❑ 299 Scott Radinsky	.05	.02
❑ 300 Kirby Puckett	.25	.07
❑ 301 Steve Farr	.05	.02
❑ 302 Tim Teufel	.05	.02
❑ 303 Mike Boddicker	.05	.02
❑ 304 Kevin Reimer	.05	.02
❑ 305 Mike Scioscia	.05	.02
❑ 306A Lonnie Smith ERR (136 games in '90)	.40	.12
❑ 306B Lonnie Smith COR (135 games in '90)	.05	.02
❑ 307 Andy Benes	.05	.02
❑ 308 Tom Pagnozzi	.05	.02

❑ 309 Norm Charlton .05 .02
❑ 310 Gary Carter .10 .03
❑ 311 Jeff Pico .05 .02
❑ 312 Charlie Hayes .05 .02
❑ 313 Ron Robinson .05 .02
❑ 314 Gary Pettis .05 .02
❑ 315 Roberto Alomar .15 .04
❑ 316 Gene Nelson .05 .02
❑ 317 Mike Fitzgerald .05 .02
❑ 318 Rick Aguilera .10 .03
❑ 319 Jeff McKnight .05 .02
❑ 320 Tony Fernandez .05 .02
❑ 321 Bob Rodgers MG .05 .02
❑ 322 Terry Shumpert .05 .02
❑ 323 Cory Snyder .05 .02
❑ 324A Ron Kittle ERR .40 .12
(Set another
standard ...)
❑ 324B Ron Kittle COR .05 .02
(Tied another
standard ...)
❑ 325 Brett Butler .10 .03
❑ 326 Ken Patterson .05 .02
❑ 327 Ron Hassey .05 .02
❑ 328 Walt Terrell .05 .02
❑ 329 Dave Justice UER .10 .03
(Drafted third round
on card, should say
fourth pick)
❑ 330 Dwight Gooden .10 .03
❑ 331 Eric Anthony .05 .02
❑ 332 Kenny Rogers .10 .03
❑ 333 C.Jones FDP RC 4.00 1.20
❑ 334 Todd Benzinger .05 .02
❑ 335 Mitch Williams .05 .02
❑ 336 Matt Nokes .05 .02
❑ 337A Keith Comstock ERR .25 .07
(Cubs logo on front)
❑ 337B Keith Comstock COR .05 .02
(Mariners logo on front)
❑ 338 Luis Rivera .05 .02
❑ 339 Larry Walker .25 .07
❑ 340 Ramon Martinez .05 .02
❑ 341 John Moses .05 .02
❑ 342 Mickey Morandini .05 .02
❑ 343 Jose Oquendo .05 .02
❑ 344 Jeff Russell .05 .02
❑ 345 Len Dykstra .10 .03
❑ 346 Jesse Orosco .05 .02
❑ 347 Greg Vaughn .05 .02
❑ 348 Todd Stottlemyre .05 .02
❑ 349 Dave Gallagher .05 .02
❑ 350 Glenn Davis .05 .02
❑ 351 Joe Torre MG .10 .03
❑ 352 Frank White .10 .03
❑ 353 Tony Castillo .05 .02
❑ 354 Sid Bream .05 .02
❑ 355 Chili Davis .10 .03
❑ 356 Mike Marshall .05 .02
❑ 357 Jack Savage .05 .02
❑ 358 Mark Parent .05 .02
❑ 359 Chuck Cary .05 .02
❑ 360 Tim Raines .10 .03
❑ 361 Scott Garrelts .05 .02
❑ 362 Hector Villenueva .05 .02
❑ 363 Rick Mahler .05 .02
❑ 364 Dan Pasqua .05 .02
❑ 365 Mike Schooler .05 .02
❑ 366A Checklist 3 ERR .25 .07
19 Carl Nichols
❑ 366B Checklist 3 COR .05 .02
119 Carl Nichols
❑ 367 Dave Walsh RC .05 .02
❑ 368 Felix Jose .05 .02
❑ 369 Steve Searcy .05 .02
❑ 370 Kelly Gruber .05 .02
❑ 371 Jeff Montgomery .05 .02
❑ 372 Spike Owen .05 .02
❑ 373 Darrin Jackson .05 .02
❑ 374 Larry Casian .05 .02
❑ 375 Tony Pena .05 .02
❑ 376 Mike Harkey .05 .02
❑ 377 Rene Gonzales .05 .02
❑ 378A Wilson Alvarez ERR .25 .07
('89 Port Charlotte
and '90 Birmingham
stat lines omitted)
❑ 378B Wilson Alvarez COR .05 .02
Text still says 143
K's in 1988,
whereas stats say 134
❑ 379 Randy Velarde .05 .02
❑ 380 Willie McGee .10 .03
❑ 381 Jim Leyland MG .05 .02
❑ 382 Mackey Sasser .05 .02
❑ 383 Pete Smith .05 .02
❑ 384 Gerald Perry .05 .02
❑ 385 Mickey Tettleton .05 .02
❑ 386 Cecil Fielder AS .05 .02
❑ 387 Julio Franco AS .05 .02
❑ 388 Kelly Gruber AS .05 .02
❑ 389 Alan Trammell AS .10 .03
❑ 390 Jose Canseco AS .10 .03
❑ 391 Rickey Henderson AS .15 .04
❑ 392 Ken Griffey Jr. AS .40 .12
❑ 393 Carlton Fisk AS .10 .03
❑ 394 Bob Welch AS .05 .02
❑ 395 Chuck Finley AS .05 .02
❑ 396 Bobby Thigpen AS .05 .02
❑ 397 Eddie Murray AS .15 .04
❑ 398 Ryne Sandberg AS .25 .07
❑ 399 Matt Williams AS .05 .02
❑ 400 Barry Larkin AS .10 .03
❑ 401 Barry Bonds AS .40 .12
❑ 402 Darryl Strawbery AS .05 .02
❑ 403 Bobby Bonilla AS .05 .02
❑ 404 Mike Scioscia AS .05 .02
❑ 405 Doug Drabek AS .05 .02
❑ 406 Frank Viola AS .05 .02
❑ 407 John Franco AS .05 .02
❑ 408 Earnest Riles .05 .02
❑ 409 Mike Stanley .05 .02
❑ 410 Dave Righetti .10 .03
❑ 411 Lance Blankenship .05 .02
❑ 412 Dave Bergman .05 .02
❑ 413 Terry Mulholland .05 .02
❑ 414 Sammy Sosa .50 .15
❑ 415 Rick Sutcliffe .10 .03
❑ 416 Randy Milligan .05 .02
❑ 417 Bill Krueger .05 .02
❑ 418 Nick Esasky .05 .02
❑ 419 Jeff Reed .05 .02
❑ 420 Bobby Thigpen .05 .02
❑ 421 Alex Cole .05 .02
❑ 422 Rick Reuschel .05 .02
❑ 423 Rafael Ramirez UER .05 .02
(Born 1959, not 1958)
❑ 424 Calvin Schiraldi .05 .02
❑ 425 Andy Van Slyke .10 .03
❑ 426 Joe Grahe RC .10 .03
❑ 427 Rick Dempsey .05 .02
❑ 428 John Barfield .05 .02
❑ 429 Stump Merrill MG .05 .02
❑ 430 Gary Gaetti .10 .03
❑ 431 Paul Gibson .05 .02
❑ 432 Delino DeShields .10 .03
❑ 433 Pat Tabler .05 .02
❑ 434 Julio Machado .05 .02
❑ 435 Kevin Maas .05 .02
❑ 436 Scott Bankhead .05 .02
❑ 437 Doug Dascenzo .05 .02
❑ 438 Vicente Palacios .05 .02
❑ 439 Dickie Thon .05 .02
❑ 440 George Bell .05 .02
❑ 441 Zane Smith .05 .02
❑ 442 Charlie O'Brien .05 .02
❑ 443 Jeff Innis .05 .02
❑ 444 Glenn Braggs .05 .02
❑ 445 Greg Swindell .05 .02
❑ 446 Craig Grebeck .05 .02
❑ 447 John Burkett .05 .02
❑ 448 Craig Lefferts .05 .02
❑ 449 Juan Berenguer .05 .02
❑ 450 Wade Boggs .15 .04
❑ 451 Neal Heaton .05 .02
❑ 452 Bill Schroeder .05 .02
❑ 453 Lenny Harris .05 .02
❑ 454A Kevin Appier ERR .40 .12
('90 Omaha stat
line omitted)
❑ 454B Kevin Appier COR .10 .03
❑ 455 Walt Weiss .05 .02
❑ 456 Charlie Leibrandt .05 .02
❑ 457 Todd Hundley .05 .02
❑ 458 Brian Holman .05 .02
❑ 459 T.Trebelhorn MG UER .05 .02
Pitching and batting
columns switched
❑ 460 Dave Stieb .05 .02
❑ 461 Robin Ventura .10 .03
❑ 462 Steve Frey .05 .02
❑ 463 Dwight Smith .05 .02
❑ 464 Steve Buechele .05 .02
❑ 465 Ken Griffey Sr. .10 .03
❑ 466 Charles Nagy .05 .02
❑ 467 Dennis Cook .05 .02
❑ 468 Tim Hulett .05 .02
❑ 469 Chet Lemon .05 .02
❑ 470 Howard Johnson .05 .02
❑ 471 Mike Lieberthal RC .40 .12
❑ 472 Kirt Manwaring .05 .02
❑ 473 Curt Young .05 .02
❑ 474 Phil Plantier RC .10 .03
❑ 475 Ted Higuera .05 .02
❑ 476 Glenn Wilson .05 .02
❑ 477 Mike Fetters .05 .02
❑ 478 Kurt Stillwell .05 .02
❑ 479 Bob Patterson UER .05 .02
(Has a decimal point
between 7 and 9)
❑ 480 Dave Magadan .05 .02
❑ 481 Eddie Whitson .05 .02
❑ 482 Tino Martinez .15 .04
❑ 483 Mike Aldrete .05 .02
❑ 484 Dave LaPoint .05 .02
❑ 485 Terry Pendleton .10 .03
❑ 486 Tommy Greene .05 .02
❑ 487 Rafael Belliard .05 .02
❑ 488 Jeff Manto .05 .02
❑ 489 Bobby Valentine MG .05 .02
❑ 490 Kirk Gibson .10 .03
❑ 491 Kurt Miller RC .05 .02
❑ 492 Ernie Whitt .05 .02
❑ 493 Jose Rijo .05 .02
❑ 494 Chris James .05 .02
❑ 495 Charlie Hough .10 .03
❑ 496 Marty Barrett .05 .02
❑ 497 Ben McDonald .05 .02
❑ 498 Mark Salas .05 .02
❑ 499 Melido Perez .05 .02
❑ 500 Will Clark .25 .07
❑ 501 Mike Bielecki .05 .02
❑ 502 Carney Lansford .10 .03
❑ 503 Roy Smith .05 .02
❑ 504 Julio Valera .05 .02
❑ 505 Chuck Finley .10 .03
❑ 506 Darnell Coles .05 .02
❑ 507 Steve Jeltz .05 .02
❑ 508 Mike York .05 .02
❑ 509 Glenallen Hill .05 .02
❑ 510 John Franco .10 .03
❑ 511 Steve Balboni .05 .02
❑ 512 Jose Mesa .05 .02
❑ 513 Jerald Clark .05 .02
❑ 514 Mike Stanton .05 .02
❑ 515 Alvin Davis .05 .02
❑ 516 Karl Rhodes .05 .02
❑ 517 Joe Oliver .05 .02
❑ 518 Cris Carpenter .05 .02
❑ 519 Sparky Anderson MG .10 .03
❑ 520 Mark Grace .15 .04
❑ 521 Joe Orsulak .05 .02
❑ 522 Stan Belinda .05 .02
❑ 523 Rodney McCray .05 .02
❑ 524 Darrel Akerfelds .05 .02
❑ 525 Willie Randolph .10 .03
❑ 526A Moises Alou ERR .40 .12
(37 runs in 2 games
for '90 Pirates)
❑ 526B Moises Alou COR .10 .03
(0 runs in 2 games
for '90 Pirates)
❑ 527A Checklist 4 ERR .25 .07
105 Keith Miller
719 Kevin McReynolds
❑ 527B Checklist 4 COR .05 .02
105 Kevin McReynolds
719 Keith Miller

❑ 528 Dennis Martinez .10 .03
❑ 529 Marc Newfield RC .10 .03
❑ 530 Roger Clemens .50 .15
❑ 531 Dave Rohde .05 .02
❑ 532 Kirk McCaskill .05 .02
❑ 533 Oddibe McDowell .05 .02
❑ 534 Mike Jackson .05 .02
❑ 535 Ruben Sierra UER .05 .02
(Back reads 100 Runs amd 100 RBI's)
❑ 536 Mike Witt .05 .02
❑ 537 Jose Lind .05 .02
❑ 538 Bip Roberts .05 .02
❑ 539 Scott Terry .05 .02
❑ 540 George Brett .60 .18
❑ 541 Domingo Ramos .05 .02
❑ 542 Rob Murphy .05 .02
❑ 543 Junior Felix .05 .02
❑ 544 Alejandro Pena .05 .02
❑ 545 Dale Murphy .25 .07
❑ 546 Jeff Ballard .05 .02
❑ 547 Mike Pagliarulo .05 .02
❑ 548 Jaime Navarro .05 .02
❑ 549 John McNamara MG .05 .02
❑ 550 Eric Davis .10 .03
❑ 551 Bob Kipper .05 .02
❑ 552 Jeff Hamilton .05 .02
❑ 553 Joe Klink .05 .02
❑ 554 Brian Harper .05 .02
❑ 555 Turner Ward RC .10 .03
❑ 556 Gary Ward .05 .02
❑ 557 Wally Whitehurst .05 .02
❑ 558 Otis Nixon .05 .02
❑ 559 Adam Peterson .05 .02
❑ 560 Greg Smith .05 .02
❑ 561 Tim McIntosh .05 .02
❑ 562 Jeff Kunkel .05 .02
❑ 563 Brent Knackert .05 .02
❑ 564 Dante Bichette .10 .03
❑ 565 Craig Biggio .15 .04
❑ 566 Craig Wilson .05 .02
❑ 567 Dwayne Henry .05 .02
❑ 568 Ron Karkovice .05 .02
❑ 569 Curt Schilling .25 .07
❑ 570 Barry Bonds .75 .23
❑ 571 Pat Combs .05 .02
❑ 572 Dave Anderson .05 .02
❑ 573 Rich Rodriguez UER .05 .02
(Stats say drafted 4th, but bio says 9th round)
❑ 574 John Marzano .05 .02
❑ 575 Robin Yount .40 .12
❑ 576 Jeff Kaiser .05 .02
❑ 577 Bill Doran .05 .02
❑ 578 Dave West .05 .02
❑ 579 Roger Craig MG .05 .02
❑ 580 Dave Stewart .10 .03
❑ 581 Luis Quinones .05 .02
❑ 582 Marty Clary .05 .02
❑ 583 Tony Phillips .05 .02
❑ 584 Kevin Brown .10 .03
❑ 585 Pete O'Brien .05 .02
❑ 586 Fred Lynn .05 .02
❑ 587 Jose Offerman UER .05 .02
(Text says he signed 7/24/86, but bio says 1988)
❑ 588 Mark Whiten .05 .02
❑ 589 Scott Ruskin .05 .02
❑ 590 Eddie Murray .25 .07
❑ 591 Ken Hill .05 .02
❑ 592 B.J. Surhoff .10 .03
❑ 593A Mike Walker ERR .25 .07
('90 Canton-Akron stat line omitted)
❑ 593B Mike Walker COR .05 .02
❑ 594 Rich Garces RC .10 .03
❑ 595 Bill Landrum .05 .02
❑ 596 Ronnie Walden RC .10 .03
❑ 597 Jerry Don Gleaton .05 .02
❑ 598 Sam Horn .05 .02
❑ 599A Greg Myers ERR .25 .07
('90 Syracuse stat line omitted)
❑ 599B Greg Myers COR .05 .02
❑ 600 Bo Jackson .25 .07
❑ 601 Bob Ojeda .05 .02
❑ 602 Casey Candaele .05 .02
❑ 603A W.Chamberlain RC ERR .40 .12
Photo actually Louie Meadows
❑ 603B Wes Chamberlain RC COR .10
.03
❑ 604 Billy Hatcher .05 .02
❑ 605 Jeff Reardon .10 .03
❑ 606 Jim Gott .05 .02
❑ 607 Edgar Martinez .15 .04
❑ 608 Todd Burns .05 .02
❑ 609 Jeff Torborg MG .05 .02
❑ 610 Andres Galarraga .10 .03
❑ 611 Dave Eiland .05 .02
❑ 612 Steve Lyons .05 .02
❑ 613 Eric Show .05 .02
❑ 614 Luis Salazar .05 .02
❑ 615 Bert Blyleven .10 .03
❑ 616 Todd Zeile .05 .02
❑ 617 Bill Wegman .05 .02
❑ 618 Sil Campusano .05 .02
❑ 619 David Wells .10 .03
❑ 620 Ozzie Guillen .05 .02
❑ 621 Ted Power .05 .02
❑ 622 Jack Daugherty .05 .02
❑ 623 Jeff Blauser .05 .02
❑ 624 Tom Candiotti .05 .02
❑ 625 Terry Steinbach .05 .02
❑ 626 Gerald Young .05 .02
❑ 627 Tim Layana .05 .02
❑ 628 Greg Litton .05 .02
❑ 629 Wes Gardner .05 .02
❑ 630 Dave Winfield .10 .03
❑ 631 Mike Morgan .05 .02
❑ 632 Lloyd Moseby .05 .02
❑ 633 Kevin Tapani .05 .02
❑ 634 Henry Cotto .05 .02
❑ 635 Andy Hawkins .05 .02
❑ 636 Geronimo Pena .05 .02
❑ 637 Bruce Ruffin .05 .02
❑ 638 Mike Macfarlane .05 .02
❑ 639 Frank Robinson MG .15 .04
❑ 640 Andre Dawson .10 .03
❑ 641 Mike Henneman .05 .02
❑ 642 Hal Morris .05 .02
❑ 643 Jim Presley .05 .02
❑ 644 Chuck Crim .05 .02
❑ 645 Juan Samuel .05 .02
❑ 646 Andujar Cedeno .05 .02
❑ 647 Mark Portugal .05 .02
❑ 648 Lee Stevens .05 .02
❑ 649 Bill Sampen .05 .02
❑ 650 Jack Clark .10 .03
❑ 651 Alan Mills .05 .02
❑ 652 Kevin Romine .05 .02
❑ 653 Anthony Telford .05 .02
❑ 654 Paul Sorrento .05 .02
❑ 655 Erik Hanson .05 .02
❑ 656A Checklist 5 ERR .25 .07
348 Vicente Palacios
381 Jose Lind
537 Mike LaValliere
665 Jim Leyland
❑ 656B Checklist 5 ERR .25 .07
433 Vicente Palacios
(Palacios should be 438)
537 Jose Lind
665 Mike LaValliere
381 Jim Leyland
❑ 656C Checklist 5 COR .05 .02
438 Vicente Palacios
537 Jose Lind
665 Mike LaValliere
381 Jim Leyland
❑ 657 Mike Kingery .05 .02
❑ 658 Scott Aldred .05 .02
❑ 659 Oscar Azocar .05 .02
❑ 660 Lee Smith .10 .03
❑ 661 Steve Lake .05 .02
❑ 662 Ron Dibble .10 .03
❑ 663 Greg Brock .05 .02
❑ 664 John Farrell .05 .02
❑ 665 Mike LaValliere .05 .02
❑ 666 Danny Darwin .05 .02
❑ 667 Kent Anderson .05 .02
❑ 668 Bill Long .05 .02
❑ 669 Lou Piniella MG .10 .03
❑ 670 Rickey Henderson .25 .07
❑ 671 Andy McGaffigan .05 .02
❑ 672 Shane Mack .05 .02
❑ 673 Greg Olson UER .05 .02
(6 RBI in '88 at Tidewater and 2 RBI in '87, should be 48 and 15)
❑ 674A Kevin Gross ERR .25 .07
(89 BB with Phillies in '88 tied for league lead)
❑ 674B Kevin Gross COR .05 .02
(89 BB with Phillies in '88 led league)
❑ 675 Tom Brunansky .05 .02
❑ 676 Scott Chiamparino .05 .02
❑ 677 Billy Ripken .05 .02
❑ 678 Mark Davidson .05 .02
❑ 679 Bill Bathe .05 .02
❑ 680 David Cone .10 .03
❑ 681 Jeff Schaefer .05 .02
❑ 682 Ray Lankford .05 .02
❑ 683 Derek Lilliquist .05 .02
❑ 684 Milt Cuyler .05 .02
❑ 685 Doug Drabek .05 .02
❑ 686 Mike Gallego .05 .02
❑ 687A John Cerutti ERR .25 .07
(4.46 ERA in '90)
❑ 687B John Cerutti COR .05 .02
(4.76 ERA in '90)
❑ 688 Rosario Rodriguez .05 .02
❑ 689 John Kruk .10 .03
❑ 690 Orel Hershiser .10 .03
❑ 691 Mike Blowers .05 .02
❑ 692A Efrain Valdez ERR .25 .07
(Born 6/11/66)
❑ 692B Efrain Valdez COR .05 .02
(Born 7/11/66 and two lines of text added)
❑ 693 Francisco Cabrera .05 .02
❑ 694 Randy Veres .05 .02
❑ 695 Kevin Seitzer .05 .02
❑ 696 Steve Olin .05 .02
❑ 697 Shawn Abner .05 .02
❑ 698 Mark Guthrie .05 .02
❑ 699 Jim Lefebvre MG .05 .02
❑ 700 Jose Canseco .25 .07
❑ 701 Pascual Perez .05 .02
❑ 702 Tim Naehring .05 .02
❑ 703 Juan Agosto .05 .02
❑ 704 Devon White .10 .03
❑ 705 Robby Thompson .05 .02
❑ 706A Brad Arnsberg ERR .25 .07
(68.2 IP in '90)
❑ 706B Brad Arnsberg COR .05 .02
(62.2 IP in '90)
❑ 707 Jim Eisenreich .05 .02
❑ 708 John Mitchell .05 .02
❑ 709 Matt Sinatro .05 .02
❑ 710 Kent Hrbek .10 .03
❑ 711 Jose DeLeon .05 .02
❑ 712 Ricky Jordan .05 .02
❑ 713 Scott Scudder .05 .02
❑ 714 Marvell Wynne .05 .02
❑ 715 Tim Burke .05 .02
❑ 716 Bob Geren .05 .02
❑ 717 Phil Bradley .05 .02
❑ 718 Steve Crawford .05 .02
❑ 719 Keith Miller .05 .02
❑ 720 Cecil Fielder .10 .03
❑ 721 Mark Lee RC .05 .02
❑ 722 Wally Backman .05 .02
❑ 723 Candy Maldonado .05 .02
❑ 724 David Segui .05 .02
❑ 725 Ron Gant .10 .03
❑ 726 Phil Stephenson .05 .02
❑ 727 Mookie Wilson .10 .03
❑ 728 Scott Sanderson .05 .02
❑ 729 Don Zimmer MG .10 .03
❑ 730 Barry Larkin .15 .04
❑ 731 Jeff Gray .05 .02
❑ 732 Franklin Stubbs .05 .02
❑ 733 Kelly Downs .05 .02
❑ 734 John Russell .05 .02
❑ 735 Ron Darling .05 .02
❑ 736 Dick Schofield .05 .02
❑ 737 Tim Crews .05 .02

❑ 738 Mel Hall .05 .02
❑ 739 Russ Swan .05 .02
❑ 740 Ryne Sandberg .40 .12
❑ 741 Jimmy Key .10 .03
❑ 742 Tommy Gregg .05 .02
❑ 743 Bryn Smith .05 .02
❑ 744 Nelson Santovenia .05 .02
❑ 745 Doug Jones .05 .02
❑ 746 John Shelby .05 .02
❑ 747 Tony Fossas .05 .02
❑ 748 Al Newman .05 .02
❑ 749 Greg W. Harris .05 .02
❑ 750 Bobby Bonilla .10 .03
❑ 751 Wayne Edwards .05 .02
❑ 752 Kevin Bass .05 .02
❑ 753 Paul Marak UER .05 .02
(Stats say drafted in Jan. but bio says May)
❑ 754 Bill Pecota .05 .02
❑ 755 Mark Langston .05 .02
❑ 756 Jeff Huson .05 .02
❑ 757 Mark Gardner .05 .02
❑ 758 Mike Devereaux .05 .02
❑ 759 Bobby Cox MG .05 .02
❑ 760 Benny Santiago .10 .03
❑ 761 Larry Andersen .05 .02
❑ 762 Mitch Webster .05 .02
❑ 763 Dana Kiecker .05 .02
❑ 764 Mark Carreon .05 .02
❑ 765 Shawon Dunston .05 .02
❑ 766 Jeff Robinson .05 .02
❑ 767 Dan Wilson RC .25 .07
❑ 768 Don Pall .05 .02
❑ 769 Tim Sherrill .05 .02
❑ 770 Jay Howell .05 .02
❑ 771 Gary Redus UER .05 .02
(Born in Tanner, should say Athens)
❑ 772 Kent Mercker UER .05 .02
(Born in Indianapolis, should say Dublin, Ohio)
❑ 773 Tom Foley .05 .02
❑ 774 Dennis Rasmussen .05 .02
❑ 775 Julio Franco .10 .03
❑ 776 Brent Mayne .05 .02
❑ 777 John Candelaria .05 .02
❑ 778 Dan Gladden .05 .02
❑ 779 Carmelo Martinez .05 .02
❑ 780A Randy Myers ERR .40 .12
(15 career losses)
❑ 780B Randy Myers COR .05 .02
(19 career losses)
❑ 781 Darryl Hamilton .05 .02
❑ 782 Jim Deshaies .05 .02
❑ 783 Joel Skinner .05 .02
❑ 784 Willie Fraser .05 .02
❑ 785 Scott Fletcher .05 .02
❑ 786 Eric Plunk .05 .02
❑ 787 Checklist 6 .05 .02
❑ 788 Bob Milacki .05 .02
❑ 789 Tom Lasorda MG .25 .07
❑ 790 Ken Griffey Jr. .75 .23
❑ 791 Mike Benjamin .05 .02
❑ 792 Mike Greenwell .05 .02

1991 Topps Traded

	Nm-Mt	Ex-Mt
COMPLETE SET (132)	10.00	3.00
COMP.FACT.SET (132)	10.00	3.00

❑ 1T Juan Agosto .05 .02
❑ 2T Roberto Alomar .15 .04
❑ 3T Wally Backman .05 .02
❑ 4T Jeff Bagwell RC 1.50 .45
❑ 5T Skeeter Barnes .05 .02
❑ 6T Steve Bedrosian .05 .02
❑ 7T Derek Bell .10 .03
❑ 8T George Bell .05 .02
❑ 9T Rafael Belliard .05 .02
❑ 10T Dante Bichette .10 .03
❑ 11T Bud Black .05 .02
❑ 12T Mike Boddicker .05 .02
❑ 13T Sid Bream .05 .02
❑ 14T Hubie Brooks .05 .02
❑ 15T Brett Butler .10 .03
❑ 16T Ivan Calderon .05 .02
❑ 17T John Candelaria .05 .02
❑ 18T Tom Candiotti .05 .02
❑ 19T Gary Carter .10 .03
❑ 20T Joe Carter .10 .03
❑ 21T Rick Cerone .05 .02
❑ 22T Jack Clark .10 .03
❑ 23T Vince Coleman .05 .02
❑ 24T Scott Coolbaugh .05 .02
❑ 25T Danny Cox .05 .02
❑ 26T Danny Darwin .05 .02
❑ 27T Chili Davis .10 .03
❑ 28T Glenn Davis .05 .02
❑ 29T Steve Decker .05 .02
❑ 30T Rob Deer .05 .02
❑ 31T Rich DeLucia .05 .02
❑ 32T John Dettmer USA RC .25 .07
❑ 33T Brian Downing .05 .02
❑ 34T D.Dreifort USA RC .50 .15
❑ 35T K.Dressendorfer RC .05 .02
❑ 36T Jim Essian MG .05 .02
❑ 37T Dwight Evans .10 .03
❑ 38T Steve Farr .05 .02
❑ 39T Jeff Fassero RC .25 .07
❑ 40T Junior Felix .05 .02
❑ 41T Tony Fernandez .05 .02
❑ 42T Steve Finley .10 .03
❑ 43T Jim Fregosi MG .05 .02
❑ 44T Gary Gaetti .10 .03
❑ 45T Jason Giambi USA RC 4.00 1.20
❑ 46T Kirk Gibson .10 .03
❑ 47T Leo Gomez .05 .02
❑ 48T Luis Gonzalez RC .50 .15
❑ 49T Jeff Granger USA RC .25 .07
❑ 50T Todd Greene USA RC .50 .15
❑ 51T J.Hammonds USA RC .50 .15
❑ 52T Mike Hargrove MG .05 .02
❑ 53T Pete Harnisch .05 .02
❑ 54T Rick Helling RC .50 .15
USA UER
Misspelled Hellings on card back
❑ 55T Glenallen Hill .05 .02
❑ 56T Charlie Hough .10 .03
❑ 57T Pete Incaviglia .05 .02
❑ 58T Bo Jackson .25 .07
❑ 59T Danny Jackson .05 .02
❑ 60T Reggie Jefferson .05 .02
❑ 61T C.Johnson USA RC .75 .23
❑ 62T Jeff Johnson .05 .02
❑ 63T T.Johnson USA RC .25 .07
❑ 64T Barry Jones .05 .02
❑ 65T Chris Jones RC .10 .03
❑ 66T Scott Kamieniecki RC .10 .03
❑ 67T Pat Kelly RC .10 .03
❑ 68T Darryl Kile .10 .03
❑ 69T Chuck Knoblauch .10 .03
❑ 70T Bill Krueger .05 .02
❑ 71T Scott Leius .05 .02
❑ 72T D.Leshnock USA RC .25 .07
❑ 73T Mark Lewis .05 .02
❑ 74T Candy Maldonado .05 .02
❑ 75T J.McDonald USA RC .25 .07
❑ 76T Willie McGee .10 .03
❑ 77T Fred McGriff .15 .04
❑ 78T B.McMillon USA RC .25 .07
❑ 79T Hal McRae MG .10 .03
❑ 80T D.Melendez USA RC .25 .07
❑ 81T Orlando Merced RC .10 .03
❑ 82T Jack Morris .10 .03
❑ 83T Phil Nevin USA RC 1.00 .30
❑ 84T Otis Nixon .05 .02
❑ 85T Johnny Oates MG .05 .02
❑ 86T Bob Ojeda .05 .02
❑ 87T Mike Pagliarulo .05 .02
❑ 88T Dean Palmer .10 .03
❑ 89T Dave Parker .10 .03
❑ 90T Terry Pendleton .10 .03
❑ 91T T.Phillips (P) USA RC .25 .07
❑ 92T Doug Piatt .05 .02
❑ 93T Ron Polk USA CO .25 .07
❑ 94T Tim Raines .10 .03
❑ 95T Willie Randolph .10 .03
❑ 96T Dave Righetti .10 .03
❑ 97T Ernie Riles .05 .02
❑ 98T C.Roberts USA RC .25 .07
❑ 99T Jeff D. Robinson .05 .02
❑ 100T Jeff M. Robinson .05 .02
❑ 101T Ivan Rodriguez RC 2.00 .60
❑ 102T S.Rodriguez USA RC .25 .07
❑ 103T Tom Runnells MG .05 .02
❑ 104T Scott Sanderson .05 .02
❑ 105T Bob Scanlan .05 .02
❑ 106T Pete Schourek RC .10 .03
❑ 107T Gary Scott .05 .02
❑ 108T Paul Shuey USA RC .50 .15
❑ 109T Doug Simons .05 .02
❑ 110T Dave Smith .05 .02
❑ 111T Cory Snyder .05 .02
❑ 112T Luis Sojo .05 .02
❑ 113T K.Steenstra USA RC .25 .07
❑ 114T Darryl Strawberry .10 .03
❑ 115T Franklin Stubbs .05 .02
❑ 116T Todd Taylor USA RC .25 .07
❑ 117T Wade Taylor .05 .02
❑ 118T Garry Templeton .05 .02
❑ 119T Mickey Tettleton .05 .02
❑ 120T Tim Teufel .05 .02
❑ 121T Mike Timlin RC .40 .12
❑ 122T David Tuttle USA RC .25 .07
❑ 123T Mo Vaughn .10 .03
❑ 124T Jeff Ware USA RC .25 .07
❑ 125T Devon White .10 .03
❑ 126T Mark Whiten .05 .02
❑ 127T Mitch Williams .05 .02
❑ 128T C.Wilson USA RC .25 .07
❑ 129T Willie Wilson .05 .02
❑ 130T C.Wimmer USA RC .25 .07
❑ 131T Ivan Zweig USA RC .25 .07
❑ 132T Checklist 1T-132T .05 .02

1992 Topps

	Nm-Mt	Ex-Mt
COMPLETE SET (792)	25.00	7.50
COMP.FACT.SET (802)	25.00	7.50
COMP.HOLIDAY (811)	40.00	12.00

❑ 1 Nolan Ryan 1.00 .30
❑ 2 Ricky Henderson RB .15 .04
Most career SB's
(Some cards have print marks that show 1.991 on the front)
❑ 3 Jeff Reardon RB .05 .02
❑ 4 Nolan Ryan RB .50 .15

❑ 5 Dave Winfield RB .05 .02
❑ 6 Brien Taylor RC .25 .07
❑ 7 Jim Olander .05 .02
❑ 8 Bryan Hickerson RC .10 .03
❑ 9 Jon Farrell RC .10 .03
❑ 10 Wade Boggs .15 .04
❑ 11 Jack McDowell .05 .02
❑ 12 Luis Gonzalez .10 .03
❑ 13 Mike Scioscia .05 .02
❑ 14 Wes Chamberlain .05 .02
❑ 15 Dennis Martinez .10 .03
❑ 16 Jeff Montgomery .05 .02
❑ 17 Randy Milligan .05 .02
❑ 18 Greg Cadaret .05 .02
❑ 19 Jamie Quirk .05 .02
❑ 20 Bip Roberts .05 .02
❑ 21 Buck Rodgers MG .05 .02
❑ 22 Bill Wegman .05 .02
❑ 23 Chuck Knoblauch .10 .03
❑ 24 Randy Myers .05 .02
❑ 25 Ron Gant .10 .03
❑ 26 Mike Bielecki .05 .02
❑ 27 Juan Gonzalez .15 .04
❑ 28 Mike Schooler .05 .02
❑ 29 Mickey Tettleton .05 .02
❑ 30 John Kruk .10 .03
❑ 31 Bryn Smith .05 .02
❑ 32 Chris Nabholz .05 .02
❑ 33 Carlos Baerga .05 .02
❑ 34 Jeff Juden .05 .02
❑ 35 Dave Righetti .10 .03
❑ 36 Scott Ruffcorn RC .10 .03
❑ 37 Luis Polonia .05 .02
❑ 38 Tom Candiotti .05 .02
❑ 39 Greg Olson .05 .02
❑ 40 Cal Ripken 2.00 .60
❑ 41 Craig Lefferts .05 .02
❑ 42 Mike Macfarlane .05 .02
❑ 43 Jose Lind .05 .02
❑ 44 Rick Aguilera .10 .03
❑ 45 Gary Carter .10 .03
❑ 46 Steve Farr .05 .02
❑ 47 Rex Hudler .05 .02
❑ 48 Scott Scudder .05 .02
❑ 49 Damon Berryhill .05 .02
❑ 50 Ken Griffey Jr. .40 .12
❑ 51 Tom Runnells MG .05 .02
❑ 52 Juan Bell .05 .02
❑ 53 Tommy Gregg .05 .02
❑ 54 David Wells .10 .03
❑ 55 Rafael Palmeiro .15 .04
❑ 56 Charlie O'Brien .05 .02
❑ 57 Donn Pall .05 .02
❑ 58 Brad Ausmus RC .25 .07
Jim Campanis Jr.
Dave Nilsson
Doug Robbins
❑ 59 Mo Vaughn .10 .03
❑ 60 Tony Fernandez .05 .02
❑ 61 Paul O'Neill .15 .04
❑ 62 Gene Nelson .05 .02
❑ 63 Randy Ready .05 .02
❑ 64 Bob Kipper .05 .02
❑ 65 Willie McGee .10 .03
❑ 66 Scott Stahoviak RC .10 .03
❑ 67 Luis Salazar .05 .02
❑ 68 Marvin Freeman .05 .02
❑ 69 Kenny Lofton .15 .04
❑ 70 Gary Gaetti .10 .03
❑ 71 Erik Hanson .05 .02
❑ 72 Eddie Zosky .05 .02
❑ 73 Brian Barnes .05 .02
❑ 74 Scott Leius .05 .02
❑ 75 Bret Saberhagen .10 .03
❑ 76 Mike Gallego .05 .02
❑ 77 Jack Armstrong .05 .02
❑ 78 Ivan Rodriguez .25 .07
❑ 79 Jesse Orosco .05 .02
❑ 80 David Justice .10 .03
❑ 81 Ced Landrum .05 .02
❑ 82 Doug Simons .05 .02
❑ 83 Tommy Greene .05 .02
❑ 84 Leo Gomez .05 .02
❑ 85 Jose DeLeon .05 .02
❑ 86 Steve Finley .10 .03
❑ 87 Bob MacDonald .05 .02
❑ 88 Darrin Jackson .05 .02
❑ 89 Neal Heaton .05 .02
❑ 90 Robin Yount .40 .12
❑ 91 Jeff Reed .05 .02
❑ 92 Lenny Harris .05 .02
❑ 93 Reggie Jefferson .05 .02
❑ 94 Sammy Sosa .40 .12
❑ 95 Scott Bailes .05 .02
❑ 96 Tom McKinnon RC .10 .03
❑ 97 Luis Rivera .05 .02
❑ 98 Mike Harkey .05 .02
❑ 99 Jeff Treadway .05 .02
❑ 100 Jose Canseco .25 .07
❑ 101 Omar Vizquel .15 .04
❑ 102 Scott Kamieniecki .05 .02
❑ 103 Ricky Jordan .05 .02
❑ 104 Jeff Ballard .05 .02
❑ 105 Felix Jose .05 .02
❑ 106 Mike Boddicker .05 .02
❑ 107 Dan Pasqua .05 .02
❑ 108 Mike Timlin .05 .02
❑ 109 Roger Craig MG .05 .02
❑ 110 Ryne Sandberg .40 .12
❑ 111 Mark Carreon .05 .02
❑ 112 Oscar Azocar .05 .02
❑ 113 Mike Greenwell .05 .02
❑ 114 Mark Portugal .05 .02
❑ 115 Terry Pendleton .10 .03
❑ 116 Willie Randolph .10 .03
❑ 117 Scott Terry .05 .02
❑ 118 Chili Davis .10 .03
❑ 119 Mark Gardner .05 .02
❑ 120 Alan Trammell .10 .03
❑ 121 Derek Bell .10 .03
❑ 122 Gary Varsho .05 .02
❑ 123 Bob Ojeda .05 .02
❑ 124 Shawn Livsey RC .10 .03
❑ 125 Chris Hoiles .05 .02
❑ 126 Ryan Klesko .25 .07
John Jaha RC
Rico Brogna
Dave Staton
❑ 127 Carlos Quintana .05 .02
❑ 128 Kurt Stillwell .05 .02
❑ 129 Melido Perez .05 .02
❑ 130 Alvin Davis .05 .02
❑ 131 Checklist 1-132 .05 .02
❑ 132 Eric Show .05 .02
❑ 133 Rance Mulliniks .05 .02
❑ 134 Darryl Kile .10 .03
❑ 135 Von Hayes .05 .02
❑ 136 Bill Doran .05 .02
❑ 137 Jeff D. Robinson .05 .02
❑ 138 Monty Fariss .05 .02
❑ 139 Jeff Innis .05 .02
❑ 140 Mark Grace UER .15 .04
Home Calie., should
be Calif.
❑ 141 Jim Leyland MG UER .10 .03
(No closed parenthesis
after East in 1991)
❑ 142 Todd Van Poppel .05 .02
❑ 143 Paul Gibson .05 .02
❑ 144 Bill Swift .05 .02
❑ 145 Danny Tartabull .05 .02
❑ 146 Al Newman .05 .02
❑ 147 Cris Carpenter .05 .02
❑ 148 Anthony Young .05 .02
❑ 149 Brian Bohanon .05 .02
❑ 150 Roger Clemens UER .50 .15
(League leading ERA in
1990 not italicized)
❑ 151 Jeff Hamilton .05 .02
❑ 152 Charlie Leibrandt .05 .02
❑ 153 Ron Karkovice .05 .02
❑ 154 Hensley Meulens .05 .02
❑ 155 Scott Bankhead .05 .02
❑ 156 Manny Ramirez RC 2.50 .75
❑ 157 Keith Miller .05 .02
❑ 158 Todd Frohwirth .05 .02
❑ 159 Darrin Fletcher .05 .02
❑ 160 Bobby Bonilla .10 .03
❑ 161 Casey Candaele .05 .02
❑ 162 Paul Faries .05 .02
❑ 163 Dana Kiecker .05 .02
❑ 164 Shane Mack .05 .02
❑ 165 Mark Langston .05 .02
❑ 166 Geronimo Pena .05 .02
❑ 167 Andy Allanson .05 .02
❑ 168 Dwight Smith .05 .02
❑ 169 Chuck Crim .05 .02
❑ 170 Alex Cole .05 .02
❑ 171 Bill Plummer MG .05 .02
❑ 172 Juan Berenguer .05 .02
❑ 173 Brian Downing .05 .02
❑ 174 Steve Frey .05 .02
❑ 175 Orel Hershiser .10 .03
❑ 176 Ramon Garcia .05 .02
❑ 177 Dan Gladden .05 .02
❑ 178 Jim Acker .05 .02
❑ 179 Bobby DeJardin .05 .02
Cesar Bernhardt
Armando Moreno
Andy Stankiewicz
❑ 180 Kevin Mitchell .05 .02
❑ 181 Hector Villanueva .05 .02
❑ 182 Jeff Reardon .10 .03
❑ 183 Brent Mayne .05 .02
❑ 184 Jimmy Jones .05 .02
❑ 185 Benito Santiago .10 .03
❑ 186 Cliff Floyd RC .40 .12
❑ 187 Ernie Riles .05 .02
❑ 188 Jose Guzman .05 .02
❑ 189 Junior Felix .05 .02
❑ 190 Glenn Davis .05 .02
❑ 191 Charlie Hough .10 .03
❑ 192 Dave Fleming .05 .02
❑ 193 Omar Olivares .05 .02
❑ 194 Eric Karros .10 .03
❑ 195 David Cone .10 .03
❑ 196 Frank Castillo .05 .02
❑ 197 Glenn Braggs .05 .02
❑ 198 Scott Aldred .05 .02
❑ 199 Jeff Blauser .05 .02
❑ 200 Len Dykstra .10 .03
❑ 201 B.Showalter RC MG .25 .07
❑ 202 Rick Honeycutt .05 .02
❑ 203 Greg Myers .05 .02
❑ 204 Trevor Wilson .05 .02
❑ 205 Jay Howell .05 .02
❑ 206 Luis Sojo .05 .02
❑ 207 Jack Clark .10 .03
❑ 208 Julio Machado .05 .02
❑ 209 Lloyd McClendon .05 .02
❑ 210 Ozzie Guillen .05 .02
❑ 211 Jeremy Hernandez RC .10 .03
❑ 212 Randy Velarde .05 .02
❑ 213 Les Lancaster .05 .02
❑ 214 Andy Mota .05 .02
❑ 215 Rich Gossage .10 .03
❑ 216 Brent Gates RC .10 .03
❑ 217 Brian Harper .05 .02
❑ 218 Mike Flanagan .05 .02
❑ 219 Jerry Browne .05 .02
❑ 220 Jose Rijo .05 .02
❑ 221 Skeeter Barnes .05 .02
❑ 222 Jaime Navarro .05 .02
❑ 223 Mel Hall .05 .02
❑ 224 Bret Barberie .05 .02
❑ 225 Roberto Alomar .15 .04
❑ 226 Pete Smith .05 .02
❑ 227 Daryl Boston .05 .02
❑ 228 Eddie Whitson .05 .02
❑ 229 Shawn Boskie .05 .02
❑ 230 Dick Schofield .05 .02
❑ 231 Brian Drahman .05 .02
❑ 232 John Smiley .05 .02
❑ 233 Mitch Webster .05 .02
❑ 234 Terry Steinbach .05 .02
❑ 235 Jack Morris .10 .03
❑ 236 Bill Pecota .05 .02
❑ 237 Jose Hernandez RC .40 .12
❑ 238 Greg Litton .05 .02
❑ 239 Brian Holman .05 .02
❑ 240 Andres Galarraga .10 .03
❑ 241 Gerald Young .05 .02
❑ 242 Mike Mussina .25 .07
❑ 243 Alvaro Espinoza .05 .02
❑ 244 Darren Daulton .10 .03
❑ 245 John Smoltz .15 .04
❑ 246 Jason Pruitt RC .10 .03
❑ 247 Chuck Finley .10 .03

❑ 248 Jim Gantner .05 .02
❑ 249 Tony Fossas .05 .02
❑ 250 Ken Griffey Sr. .10 .03
❑ 251 Kevin Elster .05 .02
❑ 252 Dennis Rasmussen .05 .02
❑ 253 Terry Kennedy .05 .02
❑ 254 Ryan Bowen .05 .02
❑ 255 Robin Ventura .10 .03
❑ 256 Mike Aldrete .05 .02
❑ 257 Jeff Russell .05 .02
❑ 258 Jim Lindeman .05 .02
❑ 259 Ron Darling .05 .02
❑ 260 Devon White .10 .03
❑ 261 Tom Lasorda MG .10 .03
❑ 262 Terry Lee .05 .02
❑ 263 Bob Patterson .05 .02
❑ 264 Checklist 133-264 .05 .02
❑ 265 Teddy Higuera .05 .02
❑ 266 Roberto Kelly .05 .02
❑ 267 Steve Bedrosian .05 .02
❑ 268 Brady Anderson .10 .03
❑ 269 Ruben Amaro .05 .02
❑ 270 Tony Gwynn .30 .09
❑ 271 Tracy Jones .05 .02
❑ 272 Jerry Don Gleaton .05 .02
❑ 273 Craig Grebeck .05 .02
❑ 274 Bob Scanlan .05 .02
❑ 275 Todd Zeile .05 .02
❑ 276 Shawn Green RC 1.50 .45
❑ 277 Scott Chiamparino .05 .02
❑ 278 Darryl Hamilton .05 .02
❑ 279 Jim Clancy .05 .02
❑ 280 Carlos Martinez .05 .02
❑ 281 Kevin Appier .10 .03
❑ 282 John Wehner .05 .02
❑ 283 Reggie Sanders .05 .02
❑ 284 Gene Larkin .05 .02
❑ 285 Bob Welch .05 .02
❑ 286 Gilberto Reyes .05 .02
❑ 287 Pete Schourek .05 .02
❑ 288 Andujar Cedeno .05 .02
❑ 289 Mike Morgan .05 .02
❑ 290 Bo Jackson .25 .07
❑ 291 Phil Garner MG .05 .02
❑ 292 Ray Lankford .05 .02
❑ 293 Mike Henneman .05 .02
❑ 294 Dave Valle .05 .02
❑ 295 Alonzo Powell .05 .02
❑ 296 Tom Brunansky .05 .02
❑ 297 Kevin Brown .10 .03
❑ 298 Kelly Gruber .05 .02
❑ 299 Charles Nagy .05 .02
❑ 300 Don Mattingly .60 .18
❑ 301 Kirk McCaskill .05 .02
❑ 302 Joey Cora .05 .02
❑ 303 Dan Plesac .05 .02
❑ 304 Joe Oliver .05 .02
❑ 305 Tom Glavine .15 .04
❑ 306 Al Shirley RC .10 .03
❑ 307 Bruce Ruffin .05 .02
❑ 308 Craig Shipley .05 .02
❑ 309 Dave Martinez .05 .02
❑ 310 Jose Mesa .05 .02
❑ 311 Henry Cotto .05 .02
❑ 312 Mike LaValliere .05 .02
❑ 313 Kevin Tapani .05 .02
❑ 314 Jeff Huson .05 .02
(Shows Jose Canseco
sliding into second)
❑ 315 Juan Samuel .05 .02
❑ 316 Curt Schilling .15 .04
❑ 317 Mike Bordick .05 .02
❑ 318 Steve Howe .05 .02
❑ 319 Tony Phillips .05 .02
❑ 320 George Bell .05 .02
❑ 321 Lou Piniella MG .10 .03
❑ 322 Tim Burke .05 .02
❑ 323 Milt Thompson .05 .02
❑ 324 Danny Darwin .05 .02
❑ 325 Joe Orsulak .05 .02
❑ 326 Eric King .05 .02
❑ 327 Jay Buhner .10 .03
❑ 328 Joel Johnston .05 .02
❑ 329 Franklin Stubbs .05 .02
❑ 330 Will Clark .25 .07
❑ 331 Steve Lake .05 .02
❑ 332 Chris Jones .05 .02
❑ 333 Pat Tabler .05 .02
❑ 334 Kevin Gross .05 .02
❑ 335 Dave Henderson .05 .02
❑ 336 Greg Anthony RC .10 .03
❑ 337 Alejandro Pena .05 .02
❑ 338 Shawn Abner .05 .02
❑ 339 Tom Browning .05 .02
❑ 340 Otis Nixon .05 .02
❑ 341 Bob Geren .05 .02
❑ 342 Tim Spehr .05 .02
❑ 343 John Vander Wal .05 .02
❑ 344 Jack Daugherty .05 .02
❑ 345 Zane Smith .05 .02
❑ 346 Rheal Cormier .05 .02
❑ 347 Kent Hrbek .10 .03
❑ 348 Rick Wilkins .05 .02
❑ 349 Steve Lyons .05 .02
❑ 350 Gregg Olson .05 .02
❑ 351 Greg Riddoch MG .05 .02
❑ 352 Ed Nunez .05 .02
❑ 353 Braulio Castillo .05 .02
❑ 354 Dave Bergman .05 .02
❑ 355 Warren Newson .05 .02
❑ 356 Luis Quinones .05 .02
❑ 357 Mike Witt .05 .02
❑ 358 Ted Wood .05 .02
❑ 359 Mike Moore .05 .02
❑ 360 Lance Parrish .10 .03
❑ 361 Barry Jones .05 .02
❑ 362 Javier Ortiz .05 .02
❑ 363 John Candelaria .05 .02
❑ 364 Glenallen Hill .05 .02
❑ 365 Duane Ward .05 .02
❑ 366 Checklist 265-396 .05 .02
❑ 367 Rafael Belliard .05 .02
❑ 368 Bill Krueger .05 .02
❑ 369 Steve Whitaker RC .10 .03
❑ 370 Shawon Dunston .05 .02
❑ 371 Dante Bichette .10 .03
❑ 372 Kip Gross .05 .02
❑ 373 Don Robinson .05 .02
❑ 374 Bernie Williams .15 .04
❑ 375 Bert Blyleven .10 .03
❑ 376 Chris Donnels .05 .02
❑ 377 Bob Zupcic RC .10 .03
❑ 378 Joel Skinner .05 .02
❑ 379 Steve Chitren .05 .02
❑ 380 Barry Bonds .60 .18
❑ 381 Sparky Anderson MG .10 .03
❑ 382 Sid Fernandez .05 .02
❑ 383 Dave Hollins .05 .02
❑ 384 Mark Lee .05 .02
❑ 385 Tim Wallach .05 .02
❑ 386 Will Clark AS .10 .03
❑ 387 Ryne Sandberg AS .25 .07
❑ 388 Howard Johnson AS .05 .02
❑ 389 Barry Larkin AS .10 .03
❑ 390 Barry Bonds AS .30 .09
❑ 391 Ron Gant AS .05 .02
❑ 392 Bobby Bonilla AS .05 .02
❑ 393 Craig Biggio AS .10 .03
❑ 394 Dennis Martinez AS .05 .02
❑ 395 Tom Glavine AS .10 .03
❑ 396 Lee Smith AS .05 .02
❑ 397 Cecil Fielder AS .05 .02
❑ 398 Julio Franco AS .05 .02
❑ 399 Wade Boggs AS .10 .03
❑ 400 Cal Ripken AS .40 .12
❑ 401 Jose Canseco AS .25 .07
❑ 402 Joe Carter AS .05 .02
❑ 403 Ruben Sierra AS .05 .02
❑ 404 Matt Nokes AS .05 .02
❑ 405 Roger Clemens AS .25 .07
❑ 406 Jim Abbott AS .10 .03
❑ 407 Bryan Harvey AS .05 .02
❑ 408 Bob Milacki .05 .02
❑ 409 Geno Petralli .05 .02
❑ 410 Dave Stewart .10 .03
❑ 411 Mike Jackson .05 .02
❑ 412 Luis Aquino .05 .02
❑ 413 Tim Teufel .05 .02
❑ 414 Jeff Ware .05 .02
❑ 415 Jim Deshaies .05 .02
❑ 416 Ellis Burks .10 .03
❑ 417 Allan Anderson .05 .02
❑ 418 Alfredo Griffin .05 .02
❑ 419 Wally Whitehurst .05 .02
❑ 420 Sandy Alomar Jr. .05 .02
❑ 421 Juan Agosto .05 .02
❑ 422 Sam Horn .05 .02
❑ 423 Jeff Fassero .05 .02
❑ 424 Paul McClellan .05 .02
❑ 425 Cecil Fielder .10 .03
❑ 426 Tim Raines .10 .03
❑ 427 Eddie Taubensee RC .25 .07
❑ 428 Dennis Boyd .05 .02
❑ 429 Tony LaRussa MG .10 .03
❑ 430 Steve Sax .05 .02
❑ 431 Tom Gordon .05 .02
❑ 432 Billy Hatcher .05 .02
❑ 433 Cal Eldred .05 .02
❑ 434 Wally Backman .05 .02
❑ 435 Mark Eichhorn .05 .02
❑ 436 Mookie Wilson .10 .03
❑ 437 Scott Servais .05 .02
❑ 438 Mike Maddux .05 .02
❑ 439 Chico Walker .05 .02
❑ 440 Doug Drabek .05 .02
❑ 441 Rob Deer .05 .02
❑ 442 Dave West .05 .02
❑ 443 Spike Owen .05 .02
❑ 444 Tyrone Hill RC .10 .03
❑ 445 Matt Williams .10 .03
❑ 446 Mark Lewis .05 .02
❑ 447 David Segui .05 .02
❑ 448 Tom Pagnozzi .05 .02
❑ 449 Jeff Johnson .05 .02
❑ 450 Mark McGwire .60 .18
❑ 451 Tom Henke .05 .02
❑ 452 Wilson Alvarez .05 .02
❑ 453 Gary Redus .05 .02
❑ 454 Darren Holmes .05 .02
❑ 455 Pete O'Brien .05 .02
❑ 456 Pat Combs .05 .02
❑ 457 Hubie Brooks .05 .02
❑ 458 Frank Tanana .05 .02
❑ 459 Tom Kelly MG .05 .02
❑ 460 Andre Dawson .10 .03
❑ 461 Doug Jones .05 .02
❑ 462 Rich Rodriguez .05 .02
❑ 463 Mike Simms .05 .02
❑ 464 Mike Jeffcoat .05 .02
❑ 465 Barry Larkin .15 .04
❑ 466 Stan Belinda .05 .02
❑ 467 Lonnie Smith .05 .02
❑ 468 Greg Harris .05 .02
❑ 469 Jim Eisenreich .05 .02
❑ 470 Pedro Guerrero .10 .03
❑ 471 Jose DeJesus .05 .02
❑ 472 Rich Rowland RC .10 .03
❑ 473 Frank Bolick .05 .02
Craig Paquette
Tom Redington
Paul Russo UER
(Line around top border)
❑ 474 Mike Rossiter RC .10 .03
❑ 475 Robby Thompson .05 .02
❑ 476 Randy Bush .05 .02
❑ 477 Greg Hibbard .05 .02
❑ 478 Dale Sveum .05 .02
❑ 479 Chito Martinez .05 .02
❑ 480 Scott Sanderson .05 .02
❑ 481 Tino Martinez .15 .04
❑ 482 Jimmy Key .10 .03
❑ 483 Terry Shumpert .05 .02
❑ 484 Mike Hartley .05 .02
❑ 485 Chris Sabo .05 .02
❑ 486 Bob Walk .05 .02
❑ 487 John Cerutti .05 .02
❑ 488 Scott Cooper .05 .02
❑ 489 Bobby Cox MG .10 .03
❑ 490 Julio Franco .10 .03
❑ 491 Jeff Brantley .05 .02
❑ 492 Mike Devereaux .05 .02
❑ 493 Jose Offerman .05 .02
❑ 494 Gary Thurman .05 .02
❑ 495 Carney Lansford .10 .03
❑ 496 Joe Grahe .05 .02
❑ 497 Andy Ashby .05 .02
❑ 498 Gerald Perry .05 .02
❑ 499 Dave Otto .05 .02

❑ 500 Vince Coleman .05 .02
❑ 501 Rob Mallicoat .05 .02
❑ 502 Greg Briley .05 .02
❑ 503 Pascual Perez .05 .02
❑ 504 Aaron Sele RC .40 .12
❑ 505 Bobby Thigpen .05 .02
❑ 506 Todd Benzinger .05 .02
❑ 507 Candy Maldonado .05 .02
❑ 508 Bill Gullickson .05 .02
❑ 509 Doug Dascenzo .05 .02
❑ 510 Frank Viola .10 .03
❑ 511 Kenny Rogers .10 .03
❑ 512 Mike Heath .05 .02
❑ 513 Kevin Bass .05 .02
❑ 514 Kim Batiste .05 .02
❑ 515 Delino DeShields .05 .02
❑ 516 Ed Sprague .05 .02
❑ 517 Jim Gott .05 .02
❑ 518 Jose Melendez .05 .02
❑ 519 Hal McRae MG .10 .03
❑ 520 Jeff Bagwell .25 .07
❑ 521 Joe Hesketh .05 .02
❑ 522 Milt Cuyler .05 .02
❑ 523 Shawn Hillegas .05 .02
❑ 524 Don Slaught .05 .02
❑ 525 Randy Johnson .25 .07
❑ 526 Doug Piatt .05 .02
❑ 527 Checklist 397-528 .05 .02
❑ 528 Steve Foster .05 .02
❑ 529 Joe Girardi .05 .02
❑ 530 Jim Abbott .15 .04
❑ 531 Larry Walker .15 .04
❑ 532 Mike Huff .05 .02
❑ 533 Mackey Sasser .05 .02
❑ 534 Benji Gil RC .25 .07
❑ 535 Dave Stieb .05 .02
❑ 536 Willie Wilson .05 .02
❑ 537 Mark Leiter .05 .02
❑ 538 Jose Uribe .05 .02
❑ 539 Thomas Howard .05 .02
❑ 540 Ben McDonald .05 .02
❑ 541 Jose Tolentino .05 .02
❑ 542 Keith Mitchell .05 .02
❑ 543 Jerome Walton .05 .02
❑ 544 Cliff Brantley .05 .02
❑ 545 Andy Van Slyke .10 .03
❑ 546 Paul Sorrento .05 .02
❑ 547 Herm Winningham .05 .02
❑ 548 Mark Guthrie .05 .02
❑ 549 Joe Torre MG .10 .03
❑ 550 Darryl Strawberry .10 .03
❑ 551 Wilfredo Cordero .25 .07
Chipper Jones
Manny Alexander
Alex Arias UER
(No line around
top border)
❑ 552 Dave Gallagher .05 .02
❑ 553 Edgar Martinez .15 .04
❑ 554 Donald Harris .05 .02
❑ 555 Frank Thomas .25 .07
❑ 556 Storm Davis .05 .02
❑ 557 Dickie Thon .05 .02
❑ 558 Scott Garrelts .05 .02
❑ 559 Steve Olin .05 .02
❑ 560 Rickey Henderson .25 .07
❑ 561 Jose Vizcaino .05 .02
❑ 562 Wade Taylor .05 .02
❑ 563 Pat Borders .05 .02
❑ 564 Jimmy Gonzalez RC .10 .03
❑ 565 Lee Smith .10 .03
❑ 566 Bill Sampen .05 .02
❑ 567 Dean Palmer .10 .03
❑ 568 Bryan Harvey .05 .02
❑ 569 Tony Pena .05 .02
❑ 570 Lou Whitaker .10 .03
❑ 571 Randy Tomlin .05 .02
❑ 572 Greg Vaughn .05 .02
❑ 573 Kelly Downs .05 .02
❑ 574 Steve Avery UER .05 .02
(Should be 13 games
for Durham in 1989)
❑ 575 Kirby Puckett .25 .07
❑ 576 Heathcliff Slocumb .05 .02
❑ 577 Kevin Seitzer .05 .02
❑ 578 Lee Guetterman .05 .02
❑ 579 Johnny Oates MG .05 .02
❑ 580 Greg Maddux .40 .12
❑ 581 Stan Javier .05 .02
❑ 582 Vicente Palacios .05 .02
❑ 583 Mel Rojas .05 .02
❑ 584 Wayne Rosenthal RC .10 .03
❑ 585 Lenny Webster .05 .02
❑ 586 Rod Nichols .05 .02
❑ 587 Mickey Morandini .05 .02
❑ 588 Russ Swan .05 .02
❑ 589 Mariano Duncan .05 .02
❑ 590 Howard Johnson .05 .02
❑ 591 Jeromy Burnitz .10 .03
Jacob Brumfield
Alan Cockrell
D.J. Dozier
❑ 592 Denny Neagle .10 .03
❑ 593 Steve Decker .05 .02
❑ 594 Brian Barber RC .10 .03
❑ 595 Bruce Hurst .05 .02
❑ 596 Kent Mercker .05 .02
❑ 597 Mike Magnante RC .10 .03
❑ 598 Jody Reed .05 .02
❑ 599 Steve Searcy .05 .02
❑ 600 Paul Molitor .15 .04
❑ 601 Dave Smith .05 .02
❑ 602 Mike Fetters .05 .02
❑ 603 Luis Mercedes .05 .02
❑ 604 Chris Gwynn .05 .02
❑ 605 Scott Erickson .05 .02
❑ 606 Brook Jacoby .05 .02
❑ 607 Todd Stottlemyre .05 .02
❑ 608 Scott Bradley .05 .02
❑ 609 Mike Hargrove MG .10 .03
❑ 610 Eric Davis .10 .03
❑ 611 Brian Hunter .05 .02
❑ 612 Pat Kelly .05 .02
❑ 613 Pedro Munoz .05 .02
❑ 614 Al Osuna .05 .02
❑ 615 Matt Merullo .05 .02
❑ 616 Larry Andersen .05 .02
❑ 617 Junior Ortiz .05 .02
❑ 618 Cesar Hernandez .05 .02
Steve Hosey
Jeff McNeely
Dan Peltier
❑ 619 Danny Jackson .05 .02
❑ 620 George Brett .60 .18
❑ 621 Dan Gakeler .05 .02
❑ 622 Steve Buechele .05 .02
❑ 623 Bob Tewksbury .05 .02
❑ 624 Shawn Estes RC .25 .07
❑ 625 Kevin McReynolds .05 .02
❑ 626 Chris Haney .05 .02
❑ 627 Mike Sharperson .05 .02
❑ 628 Mark Williamson .05 .02
❑ 629 Wally Joyner .10 .03
❑ 630 Carlton Fisk .15 .04
❑ 631 Armando Reynoso RC .25 .07
❑ 632 Felix Fermin .05 .02
❑ 633 Mitch Williams .05 .02
❑ 634 Manuel Lee .05 .02
❑ 635 Harold Baines .10 .03
❑ 636 Greg Harris .05 .02
❑ 637 Orlando Merced .05 .02
❑ 638 Chris Bosio .05 .02
❑ 639 Wayne Housie .05 .02
❑ 640 Xavier Hernandez .05 .02
❑ 641 David Howard .05 .02
❑ 642 Tim Crews .05 .02
❑ 643 Rick Cerone .05 .02
❑ 644 Terry Leach .05 .02
❑ 645 Deion Sanders .15 .04
❑ 646 Craig Wilson .05 .02
❑ 647 Marquis Grissom .10 .03
❑ 648 Scott Fletcher .05 .02
❑ 649 Norm Charlton .05 .02
❑ 650 Jesse Barfield .05 .02
❑ 651 Joe Slusarski .05 .02
❑ 652 Bobby Rose .05 .02
❑ 653 Dennis Lamp .05 .02
❑ 654 Allen Watson RC .10 .03
❑ 655 Brett Butler .10 .03
❑ 656 Rudy Pemberton .10 .03
Henry Rodriguez
Lee Tinsley RC
Gerald Williams
❑ 657 Dave Johnson .05 .02
❑ 658 Checklist 529-660 .05 .02
❑ 659 Brian McRae .05 .02
❑ 660 Fred McGriff .15 .04
❑ 661 Bill Landrum .05 .02
❑ 662 Juan Guzman .05 .02
❑ 663 Greg Gagne .05 .02
❑ 664 Ken Hill .05 .02
❑ 665 Dave Haas .05 .02
❑ 666 Tom Foley .05 .02
❑ 667 Roberto Hernandez .05 .02
❑ 668 Dwayne Henry .05 .02
❑ 669 Jim Fregosi MG .05 .02
❑ 670 Harold Reynolds .10 .03
❑ 671 Mark Whiten .05 .02
❑ 672 Eric Plunk .05 .02
❑ 673 Todd Hundley .05 .02
❑ 674 Mo Sanford .05 .02
❑ 675 Bobby Witt .05 .02
❑ 676 Sam Militello .25 .07
Pat Mahomes RC
Turk Wendell
Roger Salkeld
❑ 677 John Marzano .05 .02
❑ 678 Joe Klink .05 .02
❑ 679 Pete Incaviglia .05 .02
❑ 680 Dale Murphy .25 .07
❑ 681 Rene Gonzales .05 .02
❑ 682 Andy Benes .05 .02
❑ 683 Jim Poole .05 .02
❑ 684 Trever Miller RC .10 .03
❑ 685 Scott Livingstone .05 .02
❑ 686 Rich DeLucia .05 .02
❑ 687 Harvey Pulliam .05 .02
❑ 688 Tim Belcher .05 .02
❑ 689 Mark Lemke .05 .02
❑ 690 John Franco .10 .03
❑ 691 Walt Weiss .05 .02
❑ 692 Scott Ruskin .05 .02
❑ 693 Jeff King .05 .02
❑ 694 Mike Gardiner .05 .02
❑ 695 Gary Sheffield .10 .03
❑ 696 Joe Boever .05 .02
❑ 697 Mike Felder .05 .02
❑ 698 John Habyan .05 .02
❑ 699 Cito Gaston MG .05 .02
❑ 700 Ruben Sierra .05 .02
❑ 701 Scott Radinsky .05 .02
❑ 702 Lee Stevens .05 .02
❑ 703 Mark Wohlers .05 .02
❑ 704 Curt Young .05 .02
❑ 705 Dwight Evans .10 .03
❑ 706 Rob Murphy .05 .02
❑ 707 Gregg Jefferies .05 .02
❑ 708 Tom Bolton .05 .02
❑ 709 Chris James .05 .02
❑ 710 Kevin Maas .05 .02
❑ 711 Ricky Bones .05 .02
❑ 712 Curt Wilkerson .05 .02
❑ 713 Roger McDowell .05 .02
❑ 714 Pokey Reese RC .40 .12
❑ 715 Craig Biggio .15 .04
❑ 716 Kirk Dressendorfer .05 .02
❑ 717 Ken Dayley .05 .02
❑ 718 B.J. Surhoff .10 .03
❑ 719 Terry Mulholland .05 .02
❑ 720 Kirk Gibson .10 .03
❑ 721 Mike Pagliarulo .05 .02
❑ 722 Walt Terrell .05 .02
❑ 723 Jose Oquendo .05 .02
❑ 724 Kevin Morton .05 .02
❑ 725 Dwight Gooden .10 .03
❑ 726 Kirt Manwaring .05 .02
❑ 727 Chuck McElroy .05 .02
❑ 728 Dave Burba .05 .02
❑ 729 Art Howe MG .05 .02
❑ 730 Ramon Martinez .05 .02
❑ 731 Donnie Hill .05 .02
❑ 732 Nelson Santovenia .05 .02
❑ 733 Bob Melvin .05 .02
❑ 734 Scott Hatteberg RC .25 .07
❑ 735 Greg Swindell .05 .02
❑ 736 Lance Johnson .05 .02
❑ 737 Kevin Reimer .05 .02
❑ 738 Dennis Eckersley .10 .03

❑ 739 Rob Ducey .05 .02
❑ 740 Ken Caminiti .10 .03
❑ 741 Mark Gubicza .05 .02
❑ 742 Bill Spiers .05 .02
❑ 743 Darren Lewis .05 .02
❑ 744 Chris Hammond .05 .02
❑ 745 Dave Magadan .05 .02
❑ 746 Bernard Gilkey .05 .02
❑ 747 Willie Banks .05 .02
❑ 748 Matt Nokes .05 .02
❑ 749 Jerald Clark .05 .02
❑ 750 Travis Fryman .10 .03
❑ 751 Steve Wilson .05 .02
❑ 752 Billy Ripken .05 .02
❑ 753 Paul Assenmacher .05 .02
❑ 754 Charlie Hayes .05 .02
❑ 755 Alex Fernandez .05 .02
❑ 756 Gary Pettis .05 .02
❑ 757 Rob Dibble .10 .03
❑ 758 Tim Naehring .05 .02
❑ 759 Jeff Torborg MG .05 .02
❑ 760 Ozzie Smith .40 .12
❑ 761 Mike Fitzgerald .05 .02
❑ 762 John Burkett .05 .02
❑ 763 Kyle Abbott .05 .02
❑ 764 Tyler Green RC .10 .03
❑ 765 Pete Harnisch .05 .02
❑ 766 Mark Davis .05 .02
❑ 767 Kal Daniels .05 .02
❑ 768 Jim Thome .25 .07
❑ 769 Jack Howell .05 .02
❑ 770 Sid Bream .05 .02
❑ 771 Arthur Rhodes .05 .02
❑ 772 Garry Templeton UER .05 .02
(Stat heading in for pitchers)
❑ 773 Hal Morris .05 .02
❑ 774 Bud Black .05 .02
❑ 775 Ivan Calderon .05 .02
❑ 776 Doug Henry RC .10 .03
❑ 777 John Olerud .10 .03
❑ 778 Tim Leary .05 .02
❑ 779 Jay Bell .10 .03
❑ 780 Eddie Murray .25 .07
❑ 781 Paul Abbott .05 .02
❑ 782 Phil Plantier .05 .02
❑ 783 Joe Magrane .05 .02
❑ 784 Ken Patterson .05 .02
❑ 785 Albert Belle .10 .03
❑ 786 Royce Clayton .05 .02
❑ 787 Checklist 661-792 .05 .02
❑ 788 Mike Stanton .05 .02
❑ 789 Bobby Valentine MG .05 .02
❑ 790 Joe Carter .10 .03
❑ 791 Danny Cox .05 .02
❑ 792 Dave Winfield .10 .03

1992 Topps Traded

	Nm-Mt	Ex-Mt
COMP.FACT.SET (132)	60.00	18.00

❑ 1T Willie Adams USA RC .25 .07
❑ 2T Jeff Alkire USA RC .25 .07
❑ 3T Felipe Alou MG .20 .06
❑ 4T Moises Alou .20 .06
❑ 5T Ruben Amaro .10 .03
❑ 6T Jack Armstrong .10 .03
❑ 7T Scott Bankhead .10 .03
❑ 8T Tim Belcher .10 .03
❑ 9T George Bell .10 .03
❑ 10T Freddie Benavides .10 .03
❑ 11T Todd Benzinger .10 .03
❑ 12T Joe Boever .10 .03
❑ 13T Ricky Bones .10 .03
❑ 14T Bobby Bonilla .20 .06
❑ 15T Hubie Brooks .10 .03
❑ 16T Jerry Browne .10 .03
❑ 17T Jim Bullinger .10 .03
❑ 18T Dave Burba .10 .03
❑ 19T Kevin Campbell .10 .03
❑ 20T Tom Candiotti .10 .03
❑ 21T Mark Carreon .10 .03
❑ 22T Gary Carter .20 .06
❑ 23T Archi Cianfrocco RC .10 .03
❑ 24T Phil Clark .10 .03
❑ 25T Chad Curtis RC .40 .12
❑ 26T Eric Davis .20 .06
❑ 27T Tim Davis USA RC .25 .07
❑ 28T Gary DiSarcina .10 .03
❑ 29T Darren Dreifort USA .10 .03
❑ 30T Mariano Duncan .10 .03
❑ 31T Mike Fitzgerald .10 .03
❑ 32T John Flaherty .10 .03
❑ 33T Darrin Fletcher .10 .03
❑ 34T Scott Fletcher .10 .03
❑ 35T R.Fraser CO USA RC .25 .07
❑ 36T Andres Galarraga .20 .06
❑ 37T Dave Gallagher .10 .03
❑ 38T Mike Gallego .10 .03
❑ 39T Nomar Garciaparra USA RC 50.00 15.00
❑ 40T Jason Giambi USA 1.00 .30
❑ 41T Danny Gladden .10 .03
❑ 42T Rene Gonzales .10 .03
❑ 43T Jeff Granger USA .10 .03
❑ 44T Rick Greene USA RC .25 .07
❑ 45T J.Hammonds USA .20 .06
❑ 46T Charlie Hayes .10 .03
❑ 47T Von Hayes .10 .03
❑ 48T Rick Helling USA .10 .03
❑ 49T Butch Henry RC .10 .03
❑ 50T Carlos Hernandez .10 .03
❑ 51T Ken Hill .10 .03
❑ 52T Butch Hobson .10 .03
❑ 53T Vince Horsman .10 .03
❑ 54T Pete Incaviglia .10 .03
❑ 55T Gregg Jefferies .10 .03
❑ 56T Charles Johnson USA .20 .06
❑ 57T Doug Jones .10 .03
❑ 58T Brian Jordan RC .75 .23
❑ 59T Wally Joyner .20 .06
❑ 60T D.Kirkreit USA RC .25 .07
❑ 61T Bill Krueger .10 .03
❑ 62T Gene Lamont MG .10 .03
❑ 63T Jim Lefebvre MG .10 .03
❑ 64T Danny Leon .10 .03
❑ 65T Pat Listach RC .40 .12
❑ 66T Kenny Lofton .30 .09
❑ 67T Dave Martinez .10 .03
❑ 68T Derrick May .10 .03
❑ 69T Kirk McCaskill .10 .03
❑ 70T C.McConnell USA RC .25 .07
❑ 71T Kevin McReynolds .10 .03
❑ 72T Rusty Meacham .10 .03
❑ 73T Keith Miller .10 .03
❑ 74T Kevin Mitchell .10 .03
❑ 75T Jason Moler USA RC .25 .07
❑ 76T Mike Morgan .10 .03
❑ 77T Jack Morris .20 .06
❑ 78T C.Murray USA RC .75 .23
❑ 79T Eddie Murray .50 .15
❑ 80T Randy Myers .10 .03
❑ 81T Denny Neagle .20 .06
❑ 82T Phil Nevin USA .30 .09
❑ 83T Dave Nilsson .10 .03
❑ 84T Junior Ortiz .10 .03
❑ 85T Donovan Osborne .10 .03
❑ 86T Bill Pecota .10 .03
❑ 87T Melido Perez .10 .03
❑ 88T Mike Perez .10 .03
❑ 89T Hipolito Pichardo RC .10 .03
❑ 90T Willie Randolph .20 .06
❑ 91T Darren Reed .10 .03
❑ 92T Bip Roberts .10 .03
❑ 93T Chris Roberts USA .10 .03
❑ 94T Steve Rodriguez USA .10 .03
❑ 95T Bruce Ruffin .10 .03
❑ 96T Scott Ruskin .10 .03
❑ 97T Bret Saberhagen .20 .06
❑ 98T Rey Sanchez RC .40 .12
❑ 99T Steve Sax .10 .03
❑ 100T Curt Schilling .30 .09
❑ 101T Dick Schofield .10 .03
❑ 102T Gary Scott .10 .03
❑ 103T Kevin Seitzer .10 .03
❑ 104T Frank Seminara RC .10 .03
❑ 105T Gary Sheffield .20 .06
❑ 106T John Smiley .10 .03
❑ 107T Cory Snyder .10 .03
❑ 108T Paul Sorrento .10 .03
❑ 109T Sammy Sosa 1.50 .45
❑ 110T Matt Stairs RC .50 .15
❑ 111T Andy Stankiewicz .10 .03
❑ 112T Kurt Stillwell .10 .03
❑ 113T Rick Sutcliffe .20 .06
❑ 114T Bill Swift .10 .03
❑ 115T Jeff Tackett .10 .03
❑ 116T Danny Tartabull .10 .03
❑ 117T Eddie Taubensee .20 .06
❑ 118T Dickie Thon .10 .03
❑ 119T M.Tucker USA RC 1.50 .45
❑ 120T Scooter Tucker .10 .03
❑ 121T Marc Valdes USA RC .25 .07
❑ 122T Julio Valera .10 .03
❑ 123T J.Varitek USA RC 8.00 2.40
❑ 124T Ron Villone USA RC .25 .07
❑ 125T Frank Viola .20 .06
❑ 126T B.J. Wallace USA RC .25 .07
❑ 127T Dan Walters .10 .03
❑ 128T Craig Wilson USA .10 .03
❑ 129T Chris Wimmer USA .10 .03
❑ 130T Dave Winfield .20 .06
❑ 131T Herm Winningham .10 .03
❑ 132T Checklist 1T-132T .10 .03

1993 Topps

	Nm-Mt	Ex-Mt
COMPLETE SET (825)	40.00	12.00
COMP.HOBBY.SET (847)	50.00	15.00
COMP.RETAIL.SET (838)	40.00	12.00
COMP. SERIES 1 (396)	20.00	6.00
COMP.SERIES 2 (429)	20.00	6.00

❑ 1 Robin Yount .75 .23
❑ 2 Barry Bonds 1.25 .35
❑ 3 Ryne Sandberg .75 .23
❑ 4 Roger Clemens 1.00 .30
❑ 5 Tony Gwynn .60 .18
❑ 6 Jeff Tackett .10 .03
❑ 7 Pete Incaviglia .10 .03
❑ 8 Mark Wohlers .10 .03
❑ 9 Kent Hrbek .20 .06
❑ 10 Will Clark .50 .15
❑ 11 Eric Karros .20 .06
❑ 12 Lee Smith .20 .06
❑ 13 Esteban Beltre .10 .03
❑ 14 Greg Briley .10 .03
❑ 15 Marquis Grissom .20 .06
❑ 16 Dan Plesac .10 .03
❑ 17 Dave Hollins .10 .03
❑ 18 Terry Steinbach .10 .03

❑ 19 Ed Nunez .10 .03
❑ 20 Tim Salmon .30 .09
❑ 21 Luis Salazar .10 .03
❑ 22 Jim Eisenreich .10 .03
❑ 23 Todd Stottlemyre .10 .03
❑ 24 Tim Naehring .10 .03
❑ 25 John Franco .20 .06
❑ 26 Skeeter Barnes .10 .03
❑ 27 Carlos Garcia .10 .03
❑ 28 Joe Orsulak .10 .03
❑ 29 Dwayne Henry .10 .03
❑ 30 Fred McGriff .30 .09
❑ 31 Derek Lilliquist .10 .03
❑ 32 Don Mattingly 1.25 .35
❑ 33 B.J. Wallace .10 .03
❑ 34 Juan Gonzalez .30 .09
❑ 35 John Smoltz .30 .09
❑ 36 Scott Servais .10 .03
❑ 37 Lenny Webster .10 .03
❑ 38 Chris James .10 .03
❑ 39 Roger McDowell .10 .03
❑ 40 Ozzie Smith .75 .23
❑ 41 Alex Fernandez .10 .03
❑ 42 Spike Owen .10 .03
❑ 43 Ruben Amaro .10 .03
❑ 44 Kevin Seitzer .10 .03
❑ 45 Dave Fleming .10 .03
❑ 46 Eric Fox .10 .03
❑ 47 Bob Scanlan .10 .03
❑ 48 Bert Blyleven .20 .06
❑ 49 Brian McRae .10 .03
❑ 50 Roberto Alomar .30 .09
❑ 51 Mo Vaughn .20 .06
❑ 52 Bobby Bonilla .20 .06
❑ 53 Frank Tanana .10 .03
❑ 54 Mike LaValliere .10 .03
❑ 55 Mark McLemore .10 .03
❑ 56 Chad Mottola RC .10 .03
❑ 57 Norm Charlton .10 .03
❑ 58 Jose Melendez .10 .03
❑ 59 Carlos Martinez .10 .03
❑ 60 Roberto Kelly .10 .03
❑ 61 Gene Larkin .10 .03
❑ 62 Rafael Belliard .10 .03
❑ 63 Al Osuna .10 .03
❑ 64 Scott Chiamparino .10 .03
❑ 65 Brett Butler .20 .06
❑ 66 John Burkett .10 .03
❑ 67 Felix Jose .10 .03
❑ 68 Omar Vizquel .30 .09
❑ 69 John Vander Wal .10 .03
❑ 70 Roberto Hernandez .10 .03
❑ 71 Ricky Bones .10 .03
❑ 72 Jeff Grotewold .10 .03
❑ 73 Mike Moore .10 .03
❑ 74 Steve Buechele .10 .03
❑ 75 Juan Guzman .10 .03
❑ 76 Kevin Appier .20 .06
❑ 77 Junior Felix .10 .03
❑ 78 Greg W. Harris .10 .03
❑ 79 Dick Schofield .10 .03
❑ 80 Cecil Fielder .20 .06
❑ 81 Lloyd McClendon .10 .03
❑ 82 David Segui .10 .03
❑ 83 Reggie Sanders .10 .03
❑ 84 Kurt Stillwell .10 .03
❑ 85 Sandy Alomar Jr. .10 .03
❑ 86 John Habyan .10 .03
❑ 87 Kevin Reimer .10 .03
❑ 88 Mike Stanton .10 .03
❑ 89 Eric Anthony .10 .03
❑ 90 Scott Erickson .10 .03
❑ 91 Craig Colbert .10 .03
❑ 92 Tom Pagnozzi .10 .03
❑ 93 Pedro Astacio .10 .03
❑ 94 Lance Johnson .10 .03
❑ 95 Larry Walker .30 .09
❑ 96 Russ Swan .10 .03
❑ 97 Scott Fletcher .10 .03
❑ 98 Derek Jeter RC 10.00 3.00
❑ 99 Mike Williams .10 .03
❑ 100 Mark McGwire 1.25 .35
❑ 101 Jim Bullinger .10 .03
❑ 102 Brian Hunter .10 .03
❑ 103 Jody Reed .10 .03
❑ 104 Mike Butcher .10 .03
❑ 105 Gregg Jefferies .10 .03
❑ 106 Howard Johnson .10 .03
❑ 107 John Kiely .10 .03
❑ 108 Jose Lind .10 .03
❑ 109 Sam Horn .10 .03
❑ 110 Barry Larkin .30 .09
❑ 111 Bruce Hurst .10 .03
❑ 112 Brian Barnes .10 .03
❑ 113 Thomas Howard .10 .03
❑ 114 Mel Hall .10 .03
❑ 115 Robby Thompson .10 .03
❑ 116 Mark Lemke .10 .03
❑ 117 Eddie Taubensee .10 .03
❑ 118 David Hulse RC .10 .03
❑ 119 Pedro Munoz .10 .03
❑ 120 Ramon Martinez .10 .03
❑ 121 Todd Worrell .10 .03
❑ 122 Joey Cora .10 .03
❑ 123 Moises Alou .20 .06
❑ 124 Franklin Stubbs .10 .03
❑ 125 Pete O'Brien .10 .03
❑ 126 Bob Ayrault .10 .03
❑ 127 Carney Lansford .20 .06
❑ 128 Kal Daniels .10 .03
❑ 129 Joe Grahe .10 .03
❑ 130 Jeff Montgomery .10 .03
❑ 131 Dave Winfield .20 .06
❑ 132 Preston Wilson RC .50 .15
❑ 133 Steve Wilson .10 .03
❑ 134 Lee Guetterman .10 .03
❑ 135 Mickey Tettleton .10 .03
❑ 136 Jeff King .10 .03
❑ 137 Alan Mills .10 .03
❑ 138 Joe Oliver .10 .03
❑ 139 Gary Gaetti .20 .06
❑ 140 Gary Sheffield .20 .06
❑ 141 Dennis Cook .10 .03
❑ 142 Charlie Hayes .10 .03
❑ 143 Jeff Huson .10 .03
❑ 144 Kent Mercker .10 .03
❑ 145 Eric Young .10 .03
❑ 146 Scott Leius .10 .03
❑ 147 Bryan Hickerson .10 .03
❑ 148 Steve Finley .20 .06
❑ 149 Rheal Cormier .10 .03
❑ 150 Frank Thomas UER .50 .15
(Categories leading league are italicized but not printed in red)
❑ 151 Archi Cianfrocco .10 .03
❑ 152 Rich DeLucia .10 .03
❑ 153 Greg Vaughn .10 .03
❑ 154 Wes Chamberlain .10 .03
❑ 155 Dennis Eckersley .20 .06
❑ 156 Sammy Sosa .75 .23
❑ 157 Gary DiSarcina .10 .03
❑ 158 Kevin Koslofski .10 .03
❑ 159 Doug Linton .10 .03
❑ 160 Lou Whitaker .20 .06
❑ 161 Chad McConnell .10 .03
❑ 162 Joe Hesketh .10 .03
❑ 163 Tim Wakefield .50 .15
❑ 164 Leo Gomez .10 .03
❑ 165 Jose Rijo .10 .03
❑ 166 Tim Scott .10 .03
❑ 167 Steve Olin UER .10 .03
(Born 10/4/65 should say 10/10/65)
❑ 168 Kevin Maas .10 .03
❑ 169 Kenny Rogers .20 .06
❑ 170 David Justice .20 .06
❑ 171 Doug Jones .10 .03
❑ 172 Jeff Reboulet .10 .03
❑ 173 Andres Galarraga .20 .06
❑ 174 Randy Velarde .10 .03
❑ 175 Kirk McCaskill .10 .03
❑ 176 Darren Lewis .10 .03
❑ 177 Lenny Harris .10 .03
❑ 178 Jeff Fassero .10 .03
❑ 179 Ken Griffey Jr. .75 .23
❑ 180 Darren Daulton .20 .06
❑ 181 John Jaha .10 .03
❑ 182 Ron Darling .10 .03
❑ 183 Greg Maddux .75 .23
❑ 184 Damion Easley .10 .03
❑ 185 Jack Morris .20 .06
❑ 186 Mike Magnante .10 .03
❑ 187 John Dopson .10 .03
❑ 188 Sid Fernandez .10 .03
❑ 189 Tony Phillips .10 .03
❑ 190 Doug Drabek .10 .03
❑ 191 Sean Lowe RC .10 .03
❑ 192 Bob Milacki .10 .03
❑ 193 Steve Foster .10 .03
❑ 194 Jerald Clark .10 .03
❑ 195 Pete Harnisch .10 .03
❑ 196 Pat Kelly .10 .03
❑ 197 Jeff Frye .10 .03
❑ 198 Alejandro Pena .10 .03
❑ 199 Junior Ortiz .10 .03
❑ 200 Kirby Puckett .50 .15
❑ 201 Jose Uribe .10 .03
❑ 202 Mike Scioscia .10 .03
❑ 203 Bernard Gilkey .10 .03
❑ 204 Dan Pasqua .10 .03
❑ 205 Gary Carter .20 .06
❑ 206 Henry Cotto .10 .03
❑ 207 Paul Molitor .30 .09
❑ 208 Mike Hartley .10 .03
❑ 209 Jeff Parrett .10 .03
❑ 210 Mark Langston .10 .03
❑ 211 Doug Dascenzo .10 .03
❑ 212 Rick Reed .10 .03
❑ 213 Candy Maldonado .10 .03
❑ 214 Danny Darwin .10 .03
❑ 215 Pat Howell .10 .03
❑ 216 Mark Leiter .10 .03
❑ 217 Kevin Mitchell .10 .03
❑ 218 Ben McDonald .10 .03
❑ 219 Bip Roberts .10 .03
❑ 220 Benny Santiago .20 .06
❑ 221 Carlos Baerga .10 .03
❑ 222 Bernie Williams .30 .09
❑ 223 Roger Pavlik .10 .03
❑ 224 Sid Bream .10 .03
❑ 225 Matt Williams .20 .06
❑ 226 Willie Banks .10 .03
❑ 227 Jeff Bagwell .30 .09
❑ 228 Tom Goodwin .10 .03
❑ 229 Mike Perez .10 .03
❑ 230 Carlton Fisk .30 .09
❑ 231 John Wetteland .20 .06
❑ 232 Tino Martinez .30 .09
❑ 233 Rick Greene .10 .03
❑ 234 Tim McIntosh .10 .03
❑ 235 Mitch Williams .10 .03
❑ 236 Kevin Campbell .10 .03
❑ 237 Jose Vizcaino .10 .03
❑ 238 Chris Donnels .10 .03
❑ 239 Mike Boddicker .10 .03
❑ 240 John Olerud .20 .06
❑ 241 Mike Gardiner .10 .03
❑ 242 Charlie O'Brien .10 .03
❑ 243 Rob Deer .10 .03
❑ 244 Denny Neagle .20 .06
❑ 245 Chris Sabo .10 .03
❑ 246 Gregg Olson .10 .03
❑ 247 Frank Seminara UER .10 .03
(Acquired 12/3/98)
❑ 248 Scott Scudder .10 .03
❑ 249 Tim Burke .10 .03
❑ 250 Chuck Knoblauch .20 .06
❑ 251 Mike Bielecki .10 .03
❑ 252 Xavier Hernandez .10 .03
❑ 253 Jose Guzman .10 .03
❑ 254 Cory Snyder .10 .03
❑ 255 Orel Hershiser .20 .06
❑ 256 Wil Cordero .10 .03
❑ 257 Luis Alicea .10 .03
❑ 258 Mike Schooler .10 .03
❑ 259 Craig Grebeck .10 .03
❑ 260 Duane Ward .10 .03
❑ 261 Bill Wegman .10 .03
❑ 262 Mickey Morandini .10 .03
❑ 263 Vince Horsman .10 .03
❑ 264 Paul Sorrento .10 .03
❑ 265 Andre Dawson .20 .06
❑ 266 Rene Gonzales .10 .03
❑ 267 Keith Miller .10 .03
❑ 268 Derek Bell .10 .03
❑ 269 Todd Steverson RC .10 .03
❑ 270 Frank Viola .20 .06

Card	Mint	Ex
❑ 271 Wally Whitehurst	.10	.03
❑ 272 Kurt Knudsen	.10	.03
❑ 273 Dan Walters	.10	.03
❑ 274 Rick Sutcliffe	.20	.06
❑ 275 Andy Van Slyke	.20	.06
❑ 276 Paul O'Neill	.30	.09
❑ 277 Mark Whiten	.10	.03
❑ 278 Chris Nabholz	.10	.03
❑ 279 Todd Burns	.10	.03
❑ 280 Tom Glavine	.30	.09
❑ 281 Butch Henry	.10	.03
❑ 282 Shane Mack	.10	.03
❑ 283 Mike Jackson	.10	.03
❑ 284 Henry Rodriguez	.10	.03
❑ 285 Bob Tewksbury	.10	.03
❑ 286 Ron Karkovice	.10	.03
❑ 287 Mike Gallego	.10	.03
❑ 288 Dave Cochrane	.10	.03
❑ 289 Jesse Orosco	.10	.03
❑ 290 Dave Stewart	.20	.06
❑ 291 Tommy Greene	.10	.03
❑ 292 Rey Sanchez	.10	.03
❑ 293 Rob Ducey	.10	.03
❑ 294 Brent Mayne	.10	.03
❑ 295 Dave Stieb	.10	.03
❑ 296 Luis Rivera	.10	.03
❑ 297 Jeff Innis	.10	.03
❑ 298 Scott Livingstone	.10	.03
❑ 299 Bob Patterson	.10	.03
❑ 300 Cal Ripken	1.50	.45
❑ 301 Cesar Hernandez	.10	.03
❑ 302 Randy Myers	.10	.03
❑ 303 Brook Jacoby	.10	.03
❑ 304 Melido Perez	.10	.03
❑ 305 Rafael Palmeiro	.30	.09
❑ 306 Damon Berryhill	.10	.03
❑ 307 Dan Serafini RC	.10	.03
❑ 308 Darryl Kile	.20	.06
❑ 309 J.T. Bruett	.10	.03
❑ 310 Dave Righetti	.20	.06
❑ 311 Jay Howell	.10	.03
❑ 312 Geronimo Pena	.10	.03
❑ 313 Greg Hibbard	.10	.03
❑ 314 Mark Gardner	.10	.03
❑ 315 Edgar Martinez	.30	.09
❑ 316 Dave Nilsson	.10	.03
❑ 317 Kyle Abbott	.10	.03
❑ 318 Willie Wilson	.10	.03
❑ 319 Paul Assenmacher	.10	.03
❑ 320 Tim Fortugno	.10	.03
❑ 321 Rusty Meacham	.10	.03
❑ 322 Pat Borders	.10	.03
❑ 323 Mike Greenwell	.10	.03
❑ 324 Willie Randolph	.20	.06
❑ 325 Bill Gullickson	.10	.03
❑ 326 Gary Varsho	.10	.03
❑ 327 Tim Hulett	.10	.03
❑ 328 Scott Ruskin	.10	.03
❑ 329 Mike Maddux	.10	.03
❑ 330 Danny Tartabull	.10	.03
❑ 331 Kenny Lofton	.20	.06
❑ 332 Geno Petralli	.10	.03
❑ 333 Otis Nixon	.10	.03
❑ 334 Jason Kendall RC	.50	.15
❑ 335 Mark Portugal	.10	.03
❑ 336 Mike Pagliarulo	.10	.03
❑ 337 Kirt Manwaring	.10	.03
❑ 338 Bob Ojeda	.10	.03
❑ 339 Mark Clark	.10	.03
❑ 340 John Kruk	.20	.06
❑ 341 Mel Rojas	.10	.03
❑ 342 Erik Hanson	.10	.03
❑ 343 Doug Henry	.10	.03
❑ 344 Jack McDowell	.10	.03
❑ 345 Harold Baines	.20	.06
❑ 346 Chuck McElroy	.10	.03
❑ 347 Luis Sojo	.10	.03
❑ 348 Andy Stankiewicz	.10	.03
❑ 349 Hipolito Pichardo	.10	.03
❑ 350 Joe Carter	.20	.06
❑ 351 Ellis Burks	.20	.06
❑ 352 Pete Schourek	.10	.03
❑ 353 Buddy Groom	.10	.03
❑ 354 Jay Bell	.20	.06
❑ 355 Brady Anderson	.20	.06
❑ 356 Freddie Benavides	.10	.03
❑ 357 Phil Stephenson	.10	.03
❑ 358 Kevin Wickander	.10	.03
❑ 359 Mike Stanley	.10	.03
❑ 360 Ivan Rodriguez	.50	.15
❑ 361 Scott Bankhead	.10	.03
❑ 362 Luis Gonzalez	.20	.06
❑ 363 John Smiley	.10	.03
❑ 364 Trevor Wilson	.10	.03
❑ 365 Tom Candiotti	.10	.03
❑ 366 Craig Wilson	.10	.03
❑ 367 Steve Sax	.10	.03
❑ 368 Delino DeShields	.10	.03
❑ 369 Jaime Navarro	.10	.03
❑ 370 Dave Valle	.10	.03
❑ 371 Mariano Duncan	.10	.03
❑ 372 Rod Nichols	.10	.03
❑ 373 Mike Morgan	.10	.03
❑ 374 Julio Valera	.10	.03
❑ 375 Wally Joyner	.20	.06
❑ 376 Tom Henke	.10	.03
❑ 377 Herm Winningham	.10	.03
❑ 378 Orlando Merced	.10	.03
❑ 379 Mike Munoz	.10	.03
❑ 380 Todd Hundley	.10	.03
❑ 381 Mike Flanagan	.10	.03
❑ 382 Tim Belcher	.10	.03
❑ 383 Jerry Browne	.10	.03
❑ 384 Mike Benjamin	.10	.03
❑ 385 Jim Leyritz	.10	.03
❑ 386 Ray Lankford	.10	.03
❑ 387 Devon White	.20	.06
❑ 388 Jeremy Hernandez	.10	.03
❑ 389 Brian Harper	.10	.03
❑ 390 Wade Boggs	.30	.09
❑ 391 Derrick May	.10	.03
❑ 392 Travis Fryman	.20	.06
❑ 393 Ron Gant	.20	.06
❑ 394 Checklist 1-132	.10	.03
❑ 395 CL 133-264 UER	.10	.03
Eckerlsey		
❑ 396 Checklist 265-396	.10	.03
❑ 397 George Brett	1.25	.35
❑ 398 Bobby Witt	.10	.03
❑ 399 Daryl Boston	.10	.03
❑ 400 Bo Jackson	.50	.15
❑ 401 Fred McGriff	.30	.09
Frank Thomas AS		
❑ 402 Ryne Sandberg	.50	.15
Carlos Baerga AS		
❑ 403 Gary Sheffield	.20	.06
Edgar Martinez AS		
❑ 404 Barry Larkin	.20	.06
Travis Fryman AS		
❑ 405 Andy Van Slyke	.50	.15
Ken Griffey Jr. AS		
❑ 406 Larry Walker	.30	.09
Kirby Puckett AS		
❑ 407 Barry Bonds	.60	.18
Joe Carter AS		
❑ 408 Darren Daulton	.20	.06
Brian Harper AS		
❑ 409 Greg Maddux	.50	.15
Roger Clemens AS		
❑ 410 Tom Glavine	.20	.06
Dave Fleming AS		
❑ 411 Lee Smith	.20	.06
Dennis Eckersley AS		
❑ 412 Jamie McAndrew	.10	.03
❑ 413 Pete Smith	.10	.03
❑ 414 Juan Guerrero	.10	.03
❑ 415 Todd Frohwirth	.10	.03
❑ 416 Randy Tomlin	.10	.03
❑ 417 B.J. Surhoff	.20	.06
❑ 418 Jim Gott	.10	.03
❑ 419 Mark Thompson RC	.10	.03
❑ 420 Kevin Tapani	.10	.03
❑ 421 Curt Schilling	.20	.06
❑ 422 J.T. Snow RC	.40	.12
❑ 423 Ryan Klesko	.20	.06
Ivan Cruz		
Bubba Smith		
Larry Sutton RC		
❑ 424 John Valentin	.10	.03
❑ 425 Joe Girardi	.10	.03
❑ 426 Nigel Wilson	.10	.03
❑ 427 Bob MacDonald	.10	.03
❑ 428 Todd Zeile	.10	.03
❑ 429 Milt Cuyler	.10	.03
❑ 430 Eddie Murray	.50	.15
❑ 431 Rich Amaral	.10	.03
❑ 432 Pete Young	.10	.03
❑ 433 Roger Bailey RC	.10	.03
Tom Schmidt		
❑ 434 Jack Armstrong	.10	.03
❑ 435 Willie McGee	.20	.06
❑ 436 Greg W. Harris	.10	.03
❑ 437 Chris Hammond	.10	.03
❑ 438 Ritchie Moody RC	.10	.03
❑ 439 Bryan Harvey	.10	.03
❑ 440 Ruben Sierra	.10	.03
❑ 441 Don Lemon	.10	.03
Todd Pridy RC		
❑ 442 Kevin McReynolds	.10	.03
❑ 443 Terry Leach	.10	.03
❑ 444 David Nied	.10	.03
❑ 445 Dale Murphy	.50	.15
❑ 446 Luis Mercedes	.10	.03
❑ 447 Keith Shepherd RC	.10	.03
❑ 448 Ken Caminiti	.20	.06
❑ 449 Jim Austin	.10	.03
❑ 450 Darryl Strawberry	.20	.06
❑ 451 Ramon Caraballo	.25	.07
Jon Shave RC		
Brent Gates		
Quinton McCracken		
❑ 452 Bob Wickman	.10	.03
❑ 453 Victor Cole	.10	.03
❑ 454 John Johnstone RC	.10	.03
❑ 455 Chili Davis	.20	.06
❑ 456 Scott Taylor	.10	.03
❑ 457 Tracy Woodson	.10	.03
❑ 458 David Wells	.20	.06
❑ 459 Derek Wallace RC	.10	.03
❑ 460 Randy Johnson	.50	.15
❑ 461 Steve Reed RC	.10	.03
❑ 462 Felix Fermin	.10	.03
❑ 463 Scott Aldred	.10	.03
❑ 464 Greg Colbrunn	.10	.03
❑ 465 Tony Fernandez	.10	.03
❑ 466 Mike Felder	.10	.03
❑ 467 Lee Stevens	.10	.03
❑ 468 Matt Whiteside RC	.10	.03
❑ 469 Dave Hansen	.10	.03
❑ 470 Rob Dibble	.20	.06
❑ 471 Dave Gallagher	.10	.03
❑ 472 Chris Gwynn	.10	.03
❑ 473 Dave Henderson	.10	.03
❑ 474 Ozzie Guillen	.10	.03
❑ 475 Jeff Reardon	.20	.06
❑ 476 Mark Voisard	.10	.03
Will Scalzitti RC		
❑ 477 Jimmy Jones	.10	.03
❑ 478 Greg Cadaret	.10	.03
❑ 479 Todd Pratt RC	.10	.03
❑ 480 Pat Listach	.10	.03
❑ 481 Ryan Luzinski RC	.10	.03
❑ 482 Darren Reed	.10	.03
❑ 483 Brian Griffiths RC	.10	.03
❑ 484 John Wehner	.10	.03
❑ 485 Glenn Davis	.10	.03
❑ 486 Eric Wedge RC	.10	.03
❑ 487 Jesse Hollins	.10	.03
❑ 488 Manuel Lee	.10	.03
❑ 489 Scott Fredrickson RC	.10	.03
❑ 490 Omar Olivares	.10	.03
❑ 491 Shawn Hare	.10	.03
❑ 492 Tom Lampkin	.10	.03
❑ 493 Jeff Nelson	.10	.03
❑ 494 Kevin Young	.10	.03
Adell Davenport		
Eduardo Perez		
Lou Lucca RC		
❑ 495 Ken Hill	.10	.03
❑ 496 Reggie Jefferson	.10	.03
❑ 497 Matt Petersen	.10	.03
Willie Brown RC		
❑ 498 Bud Black	.10	.03
❑ 499 Chuck Crim	.10	.03
❑ 500 Jose Canseco	.50	.15
❑ 501 Johnny Oates MG	.20	.06
Bobby Cox MG		
❑ 502 Butch Hobson MG	.10	.03

	Jim Lefebvre MG		
❑ 503	Buck Rodgers MG	.20	.06
	Tony Perez MG		
❑ 504	Gene Lamont MG	.20	.06
	Don Baylor MG		
❑ 505	Mike Hargrove MG	.20	.06
	Rene Lachemann MG		
❑ 506	Sparky Anderson MG	.20	.06
	Art Howe MG		
❑ 507	Hal McRae MG	.20	.06
	Tom Lasorda MG		
❑ 508	Phil Garner MG	.20	.06
	Felipe Alou MG		
❑ 509	Tom Kelly MG	.10	.03
	Jeff Torborg MG		
❑ 510	Buck Showalter MG	.20	.06
	Jim Fregosi MG		
❑ 511	Tony LaRussa MG	.20	.06
	Jim Leyland MG		
❑ 512	Lou Piniella MG	.20	.06
	Joe Torre MG		
❑ 513	Kevin Kennedy MG	.10	.03
	Jim Riggleman MG		
❑ 514	Cito Gaston MG	.20	.06
	Dusty Baker MG		
❑ 515	Greg Swindell	.10	.03
❑ 516	Alex Arias	.10	.03
❑ 517	Bill Pecota	.10	.03
❑ 518	Benji Grigsby RC UER	.10	.03
	(Misspelled Bengi on card front)		
❑ 519	David Howard	.10	.03
❑ 520	Charlie Hough	.20	.06
❑ 521	Kevin Flora	.10	.03
❑ 522	Shane Reynolds	.10	.03
❑ 523	Doug Bochtler RC	.10	.03
❑ 524	Chris Hoiles	.10	.03
❑ 525	Scott Sanderson	.10	.03
❑ 526	Mike Sharperson	.10	.03
❑ 527	Mike Fetters	.10	.03
❑ 528	Paul Quantrill	.10	.03
❑ 529	Dave Silvestri	.50	.15
	Chipper Jones		
	Benji Gil		
	Jeff Patzke		
❑ 530	Sterling Hitchcock RC	.25	.07
❑ 531	Joe Millette	.10	.03
❑ 532	Tom Brunansky	.10	.03
❑ 533	Frank Castillo	.10	.03
❑ 534	Randy Knorr	.10	.03
❑ 535	Jose Oquendo	.10	.03
❑ 536	Dave Haas	.10	.03
❑ 537	Jason Hutchins RC	.10	.03
	Ryan Turner		
❑ 538	Jimmy Baron RC	.10	.03
❑ 539	Kerry Woodson	.10	.03
❑ 540	Ivan Calderon	.10	.03
❑ 541	Denis Boucher	.10	.03
❑ 542	Royce Clayton	.10	.03
❑ 543	Reggie Williams	.10	.03
❑ 544	Steve Decker	.10	.03
❑ 545	Dean Palmer	.20	.06
❑ 546	Hal Morris	.10	.03
❑ 547	Ryan Thompson	.10	.03
❑ 548	Lance Blankenship	.10	.03
❑ 549	Hensley Meulens	.10	.03
❑ 550	Scott Radinsky	.10	.03
❑ 551	Eric Young	.10	.03
❑ 552	Jeff Blauser	.10	.03
❑ 553	Andujar Cedeno	.10	.03
❑ 554	Arthur Rhodes	.10	.03
❑ 555	Terry Mulholland	.10	.03
❑ 556	Darryl Hamilton	.10	.03
❑ 557	Pedro Martinez	1.00	.30
❑ 558	Ryan Whitman RC	.10	.03
	Mark Skeels		
❑ 559	Jamie Arnold RC	.10	.03
❑ 560	Zane Smith	.10	.03
❑ 561	Matt Nokes	.10	.03
❑ 562	Bob Zupcic	.10	.03
❑ 563	Shawn Boskie	.10	.03
❑ 564	Mike Timlin	.10	.03
❑ 565	Jerald Clark	.10	.03
❑ 566	Rod Brewer	.10	.03
❑ 567	Mark Carreon	.10	.03
❑ 568	Andy Benes	.10	.03
❑ 569	Shawn Barton RC	.10	.03
❑ 570	Tim Wallach	.10	.03
❑ 571	Dave Mlicki	.10	.03
❑ 572	Trevor Hoffman	.20	.06
❑ 573	John Patterson	.10	.03
❑ 574	De Shawn Warren RC	.10	.03
❑ 575	Monty Fariss	.10	.03
❑ 576	Darrell Sherman	.20	.06
	Damon Buford		
	Cliff Floyd		
	Michael Moore		
❑ 577	Tim Costo	.10	.03
❑ 578	Dave Magadan	.10	.03
❑ 579	Neil Garret	.10	.03
	Jason Bates RC		
❑ 580	Walt Weiss	.10	.03
❑ 581	Chris Haney	.10	.03
❑ 582	Shawn Abner	.10	.03
❑ 583	Marvin Freeman	.10	.03
❑ 584	Casey Candaele	.10	.03
❑ 585	Ricky Jordan	.10	.03
❑ 586	Jeff Tabaka RC	.10	.03
❑ 587	Manny Alexander	.10	.03
❑ 588	Mike Trombley	.10	.03
❑ 589	Carlos Hernandez	.10	.03
❑ 590	Cal Eldred	.10	.03
❑ 591	Alex Cole	.10	.03
❑ 592	Phil Plantier	.10	.03
❑ 593	Brett Merriman RC	.10	.03
❑ 594	Jerry Nielsen	.10	.03
❑ 595	Shawon Dunston	.10	.03
❑ 596	Jimmy Key	.20	.06
❑ 597	Gerald Perry	.10	.03
❑ 598	Rico Brogna	.10	.03
❑ 599	Clemente Nunez	.10	.03
	Daniel Robinson		
❑ 600	Bret Saberhagen	.20	.06
❑ 601	Craig Shipley	.10	.03
❑ 602	Henry Mercedes	.10	.03
❑ 603	Jim Thome	.50	.15
❑ 604	Rod Beck	.10	.03
❑ 605	Chuck Finley	.20	.06
❑ 606	J. Owens RC	.10	.03
❑ 607	Dan Smith	.10	.03
❑ 608	Bill Doran	.10	.03
❑ 609	Lance Parrish	.20	.06
❑ 610	Dennis Martinez	.20	.06
❑ 611	Tom Gordon	.10	.03
❑ 612	Byron Mathews RC	.10	.03
❑ 613	Joel Adamson RC	.10	.03
❑ 614	Brian Williams	.10	.03
❑ 615	Steve Avery	.10	.03
❑ 616	Matt Mieske	.10	.03
	Tracy Sanders		
	Midre Cummings RC		
	Ryan Freeburg		
❑ 617	Craig Lefferts	.10	.03
❑ 618	Tony Pena	.10	.03
❑ 619	Billy Spiers	.10	.03
❑ 620	Todd Benzinger	.10	.03
❑ 621	Mike Kotarski	.10	.03
	Greg Boyd RC		
❑ 622	Ben Rivera	.10	.03
❑ 623	Al Martin	.10	.03
❑ 624	Sam Militello UER	.10	.03
	(Profile says drafted in 1988, bio says drafted in 1990)		
❑ 625	Rick Aguilera	.10	.03
❑ 626	Dan Gladden	.10	.03
❑ 627	Andres Berumen RC	.10	.03
❑ 628	Kelly Gruber	.10	.03
❑ 629	Cris Carpenter	.10	.03
❑ 630	Mark Grace	.30	.09
❑ 631	Jeff Brantley	.10	.03
❑ 632	Chris Widger RC	.25	.07
❑ 633	Three Russians UER	.10	.03
	Rudolf Razjigaev		
	Eugneyi Puchkov		
	Ilya Bogatyrev		
	Bogatyrev is a shortstop, card has pitching header		
❑ 634	Mo Sanford	.10	.03
❑ 635	Albert Belle	.20	.06
❑ 636	Tim Teufel	.10	.03
❑ 637	Greg Myers	.10	.03
❑ 638	Brian Bohanon	.10	.03
❑ 639	Mike Bordick	.10	.03
❑ 640	Dwight Gooden	.20	.06
❑ 641	Pat Leahy	.10	.03
	Gavin Baugh RC		
❑ 642	Milt Hill	.10	.03
❑ 643	Luis Aquino	.10	.03
❑ 644	Dante Bichette	.20	.06
❑ 645	Bobby Thigpen	.10	.03
❑ 646	Rich Scheid RC	.10	.03
❑ 647	Brian Sackinsky RC	.10	.03
❑ 648	Ryan Hawblitzel	.10	.03
❑ 649	Tom Marsh	.10	.03
❑ 650	Terry Pendleton	.20	.06
❑ 651	Rafael Bournigal	.10	.03
❑ 652	Dave West	.10	.03
❑ 653	Steve Hosey	.10	.03
❑ 654	Gerald Williams	.10	.03
❑ 655	Scott Cooper	.10	.03
❑ 656	Gary Scott	.10	.03
❑ 657	Mike Harkey	.10	.03
❑ 658	Jeromy Burnitz	.20	.06
	Melvin Nieves		
	Rich Becker		
	Shon Walker RC		
❑ 659	Ed Sprague	.10	.03
❑ 660	Alan Trammell	.20	.06
❑ 661	Garvin Alston RC	.10	.03
	Michael Case		
❑ 662	Donovan Osborne	.10	.03
❑ 663	Jeff Gardner	.10	.03
❑ 664	Calvin Jones	.10	.03
❑ 665	Darrin Fletcher	.10	.03
❑ 666	Glenallen Hill	.10	.03
❑ 667	Jim Rosenbohm RC	.10	.03
❑ 668	Scott Lewis	.10	.03
❑ 669	Kip Yaughn RC	.10	.03
❑ 670	Julio Franco	.20	.06
❑ 671	Dave Martinez	.10	.03
❑ 672	Kevin Bass	.10	.03
❑ 673	Todd Van Poppel	.10	.03
❑ 674	Mark Gubicza	.10	.03
❑ 675	Tim Raines	.20	.06
❑ 676	Rudy Seanez	.10	.03
❑ 677	Charlie Leibrandt	.10	.03
❑ 678	Randy Milligan	.10	.03
❑ 679	Kim Batiste	.10	.03
❑ 680	Craig Biggio	.30	.09
❑ 681	Darren Holmes	.10	.03
❑ 682	John Candelaria	.10	.03
❑ 683	Jerry Stafford	.10	.03
	Eddie Christian RC		
❑ 684	Pat Mahomes	.10	.03
❑ 685	Bob Walk	.10	.03
❑ 686	Russ Springer	.10	.03
❑ 687	Tony Sheffield RC	.10	.03
❑ 688	Dwight Smith	.10	.03
❑ 689	Eddie Zosky	.10	.03
❑ 690	Bien Figueroa	.10	.03
❑ 691	Jim Tatum RC	.10	.03
❑ 692	Chad Kreuter	.10	.03
❑ 693	Rich Rodriguez	.10	.03
❑ 694	Shane Turner	.10	.03
❑ 695	Kent Bottenfield	.10	.03
❑ 696	Jose Mesa	.10	.03
❑ 697	Darrell Whitmore RC	.10	.03
❑ 698	Ted Wood	.10	.03
❑ 699	Chad Curtis	.10	.03
❑ 700	Nolan Ryan	2.00	.60
❑ 701	Mike Piazza	1.50	.45
	Brook Fordyce		
	Carlos Delgado		
	Donnie Leshnock		
❑ 702	Tim Pugh RC	.10	.03
❑ 703	Jeff Kent	.50	.15
❑ 704	Jon Goodrich	.10	.03
	Danny Figueroa RC		
❑ 705	Bob Welch	.10	.03
❑ 706	S.Clinkscales RC	.10	.03
❑ 707	Donn Pall	.10	.03
❑ 708	Greg Olson	.10	.03
❑ 709	Jeff Juden	.10	.03
❑ 710	Mike Mussina	.30	.09
❑ 711	Scott Champarino	.10	.03
❑ 712	Stan Javier	.10	.03
❑ 713	John Doherty	.10	.03

❑ 714 Kevin Gross .10 .03
❑ 715 Greg Gagne .10 .03
❑ 716 Steve Cooke .10 .03
❑ 717 Steve Farr .10 .03
❑ 718 Jay Buhner .20 .06
❑ 719 Butch Henry .10 .03
❑ 720 David Cone .20 .06
❑ 721 Rick Wilkins .10 .03
❑ 722 Chuck Carr .10 .03
❑ 723 Kenny Felder RC .10 .03
❑ 724 Guillermo Velasquez .10 .03
❑ 725 Billy Hatcher .10 .03
❑ 726 Mike Veneziale RC .10 .03
Ken Kendrena
❑ 727 Jonathan Hurst .10 .03
❑ 728 Steve Frey .10 .03
❑ 729 Mark Leonard .10 .03
❑ 730 Charles Nagy .10 .03
❑ 731 Donald Harris .10 .03
❑ 732 Travis Buckley RC .10 .03
❑ 733 Tom Browning .10 .03
❑ 734 Anthony Young .10 .03
❑ 735 Steve Shifflett .10 .03
❑ 736 Jeff Russell .10 .03
❑ 737 Wilson Alvarez .10 .03
❑ 738 Lance Painter RC .10 .03
❑ 739 Dave Weathers .10 .03
❑ 740 Len Dykstra .20 .06
❑ 741 Mike Devereaux .10 .03
❑ 742 Rene Arocha .50 .15
Alan Embree
Brien Taylor
Tim Crabtree
❑ 743 Dave Landaker RC .10 .03
❑ 744 Chris George .10 .03
❑ 745 Eric Davis .20 .06
❑ 746 Mark Strittmatter .10 .03
Lamarr Rogers RC
❑ 747 Carl Willis .10 .03
❑ 748 Stan Belinda .10 .03
❑ 749 Scott Kamieniecki .10 .03
❑ 750 Rickey Henderson .50 .15
❑ 751 Eric Hillman .10 .03
❑ 752 Pat Hentgen .10 .03
❑ 753 Jim Corsi .10 .03
❑ 754 Brian Jordan .20 .06
❑ 755 Bill Swift .10 .03
❑ 756 Mike Henneman .10 .03
❑ 757 Harold Reynolds .20 .06
❑ 758 Sean Berry .10 .03
❑ 759 Charlie Hayes .10 .03
❑ 760 Luis Polonia .10 .03
❑ 761 Darrin Jackson .10 .03
❑ 762 Mark Lewis .10 .03
❑ 763 Rob Maurer .10 .03
❑ 764 Willie Greene .10 .03
❑ 765 Vince Coleman .10 .03
❑ 766 Todd Revenig .10 .03
❑ 767 Rich Ireland RC .10 .03
❑ 768 Mike Macfarlane .10 .03
❑ 769 Francisco Cabrera .10 .03
❑ 770 Robin Ventura .20 .06
❑ 771 Kevin Ritz .10 .03
❑ 772 Chito Martinez .10 .03
❑ 773 Cliff Brantley .10 .03
❑ 774 Curt Leskanic RC .10 .03
❑ 775 Chris Bosio .10 .03
❑ 776 Jose Offerman .10 .03
❑ 777 Mark Guthrie .10 .03
❑ 778 Don Slaught .10 .03
❑ 779 Rich Monteleone .10 .03
❑ 780 Jim Abbott .30 .09
❑ 781 Jack Clark .20 .06
❑ 782 Reynol Mendoza .10 .03
Dan Roman RC
❑ 783 Heathcliff Slocumb .10 .03
❑ 784 Jeff Branson .10 .03
❑ 785 Kevin Brown .20 .06
❑ 786 Mike Christopher .10 .03
Ken Ryan
Aaron Taylor
Gus Gandarillas RC
❑ 787 Mike Matthews RC .10 .03
❑ 788 Mackey Sasser .10 .03
❑ 789 Jeff Conine UER .20 .06
No inclusion of 1990
RBI stats in career total
❑ 790 George Bell .10 .03
❑ 791 Pat Rapp .10 .03
❑ 792 Joe Boever .10 .03
❑ 793 Jim Poole .10 .03
❑ 794 Andy Ashby .10 .03
❑ 795 Deion Sanders .30 .09
❑ 796 Scott Brosius .20 .06
❑ 797 Brad Pennington .10 .03
❑ 798 Greg Blosser .10 .03
❑ 799 Jim Edmonds RC 3.00 .90
❑ 800 Shawn Jeter .10 .03
❑ 801 Jesse Levis .10 .03
❑ 802 Phil Clark UER .10 .03
(Word "a" is missing in
sentence beginning
with "In 1992 ...")
❑ 803 Ed Pierce RC .10 .03
❑ 804 Jose Valentin RC .40 .12
❑ 805 Terry Jorgensen .10 .03
❑ 806 Mark Hutton .10 .03
❑ 807 Troy Neel .10 .03
❑ 808 Bret Boone .30 .09
❑ 809 Cris Colon .10 .03
❑ 810 Domingo Martinez RC .10 .03
❑ 811 Javier Lopez .30 .09
❑ 812 Matt Walbeck RC .10 .03
❑ 813 Dan Wilson .20 .06
❑ 814 Scooter Tucker .10 .03
❑ 815 Billy Ashley .10 .03
❑ 816 Tim Laker RC .10 .03
❑ 817 Bobby Jones .20 .06
❑ 818 Brad Brink .10 .03
❑ 819 William Pennyfeather .10 .03
❑ 820 Stan Royer .10 .03
❑ 821 Doug Brocail .10 .03
❑ 822 Kevin Rogers .10 .03
❑ 823 Checklist 397-540 .10 .03
❑ 824 Checklist 541-691 .10 .03
❑ 825 Checklist 692-825 .10 .03

1993 Topps Traded

	Nm-Mt	Ex-Mt
COMP.FACT.SET (132)	40.00	12.00

❑ 1T Barry Bonds 1.25 .35
❑ 2T Rich Renteria .10 .03
❑ 3T Aaron Sele .10 .03
❑ 4T C.Loewer USA RC .25 .07
❑ 5T Erik Pappas .10 .03
❑ 6T Greg McMichael RC .25 .07
❑ 7T Freddie Benavides .10 .03
❑ 8T Kirk Gibson .20 .06
❑ 9T Tony Fernandez .10 .03
❑ 10T Jay Gainer RC .25 .07
❑ 11T Orestes Destrade .10 .03
❑ 12T A.J. Hinch USA RC .50 .15
❑ 13T Bobby Munoz .10 .03
❑ 14T Tom Henke .10 .03
❑ 15T Rob Butler .10 .03
❑ 16T Gary Wayne .10 .03
❑ 17T David McCarty .10 .03
❑ 18T Walt Weiss .10 .03
❑ 19T Todd Helton USA RC 25.00 7.50
❑ 20T Mark Whiten .10 .03
❑ 21T Ricky Gutierrez .10 .03
❑ 22T D.Hermanson USA RC .50 .15
❑ 23T Sherman Obando RC .25 .07
❑ 24T Mike Piazza 1.50 .45
❑ 25T Jeff Russell .10 .03
❑ 26T Jason Bere .10 .03
❑ 27T Jack Voigt RC .25 .07
❑ 28T Chris Bosio .10 .03
❑ 29T Phil Hiatt .10 .03
❑ 30T M.Beaumont USA RC .25 .07
❑ 31T Andres Galarraga .20 .06
❑ 32T Greg Swindell .10 .03
❑ 33T Vinny Castilla .20 .06
❑ 34T P.Clougherty RC USA .25 .07
❑ 35T Greg Briley .10 .03
❑ 36T Dallas Green MG .10 .03
Davey Johnson MG
❑ 37T Tyler Green .10 .03
❑ 38T Craig Paquette .10 .03
❑ 39T Danny Sheaffer RC .25 .07
❑ 40T Jim Converse RC .25 .07
❑ 41T Terry Harvey USA RC .25 .07
❑ 42T Phil Plantier .10 .03
❑ 43T Doug Saunders RC .25 .07
❑ 44T Benny Santiago .20 .06
❑ 45T Dante Powell USA RC .25 .07
❑ 46T Jeff Parrett .10 .03
❑ 47T Wade Boggs .30 .09
❑ 48T Paul Molitor .30 .09
❑ 49T Turk Wendell .10 .03
❑ 50T David Wells .20 .06
❑ 51T Gary Sheffield .20 .06
❑ 52T Kevin Young .20 .06
❑ 53T Nelson Liriano .10 .03
❑ 54T Greg Maddux .75 .23
❑ 55T Derek Bell .10 .03
❑ 56T Matt Turner RC .25 .07
❑ 57T C.Nelson RC USA .25 .07
❑ 58T Mike Hampton .20 .06
❑ 59T Troy O'Leary RC .50 .15
❑ 60T Benji Gil .10 .03
❑ 61T Mitch Lyden RC .25 .07
❑ 62T J.T. Snow .30 .09
❑ 63T Damon Buford .10 .03
❑ 64T Gene Harris .10 .03
❑ 65T Randy Myers .10 .03
❑ 66T Felix Jose .10 .03
❑ 67T Todd Dunn USA RC .25 .07
❑ 68T Jimmy Key .20 .06
❑ 69T Pedro Castellano .10 .03
❑ 70T Mark Merila USA RC .25 .07
❑ 71T Rich Rodriguez .10 .03
❑ 72T Matt Mieske .10 .03
❑ 73T Pete Incaviglia .10 .03
❑ 74T Carl Everett .20 .06
❑ 75T Jim Abbott .30 .09
❑ 76T Luis Aquino .10 .03
❑ 77T Rene Arocha .20 .06
❑ 78T Jon Shave .10 .03
❑ 79T Todd Walker USA RC 1.00 .30
❑ 80T Jack Armstrong .10 .03
❑ 81T Jeff Richardson .10 .03
❑ 82T Blas Minor .10 .03
❑ 83T Dave Winfield .20 .06
❑ 84T Paul O'Neill .30 .09
❑ 85T Steve Reich USA RC .25 .07
❑ 86T Chris Hammond .10 .03
❑ 87T Hilly Hathaway RC .25 .07
❑ 88T Fred McGriff .30 .09
❑ 89T Dave Telgheder RC .25 .07
❑ 90T Richie Lewis RC .25 .07
❑ 91T Brent Gates .10 .03
❑ 92T Andre Dawson .20 .06
❑ 93T Andy Barkett USA RC .25 .07
❑ 94T Doug Drabek .10 .03
❑ 95T Joe Klink .10 .03
❑ 96T Willie Blair .10 .03
❑ 97T D.Graves USA RC 1.00 .30
❑ 98T Pat Meares RC .50 .15
❑ 99T Mike Lansing RC .50 .15
❑ 100T Marcos Armas RC .25 .07
❑ 101T D.Grass RC USA .25 .07
❑ 102T Chris Jones .10 .03
❑ 103T Ken Ryan RC .25 .07
❑ 104T Ellis Burks .20 .06
❑ 105T Roberto Kelly .10 .03
❑ 106T Dave Magadan .10 .03
❑ 107T Paul Wilson USA RC 1.00 .30

❑ 108T Rob Natal	.10	.03
❑ 109T Paul Wagner	.10	.03
❑ 110T Jeromy Burnitz	.20	.06
❑ 111T Monty Fariss	.10	.03
❑ 112T Kevin Mitchell	.10	.03
❑ 113T Scott Pose RC	.25	.07
❑ 114T Dave Stewart	.20	.06
❑ 115T R.Johnson USA RC	.25	.07
❑ 116T Armando Reynoso	.10	.03
❑ 117T Geronimo Berroa	.10	.03
❑ 118T Woody Williams RC	1.00	.30
❑ 119T Tim Bogar RC	.25	.07
❑ 120T Bob Scafa USA RC	.25	.07
❑ 121T Henry Cotto	.10	.03
❑ 122T Gregg Jefferies	.10	.03
❑ 123T Norm Charlton	.10	.03
❑ 124T B.Wagner USA RC	.25	.07
❑ 125T David Cone	.20	.06
❑ 126T Daryl Boston	.10	.03
❑ 127T Tim Wallach	.10	.03
❑ 128T Mike Martin USA RC	.25	.07
❑ 129T John Cummings RC	.25	.07
❑ 130T Ryan Bowen	.10	.03
❑ 131T John Powell USA RC	.25	.07
❑ 132T Checklist 1-132	.10	.03

1994 Topps

	Nm-Mt	Ex-Mt
COMPLETE SET (792)	50.00	15.00
COMP.FACT.SET (808)	60.00	18.00
COMP.BAKER SET (818)	60.00	18.00
COMP. SERIES 1 (396)	25.00	7.50
COMP. SERIES 2 (396)	25.00	7.50

Card	Nm-Mt	Ex-Mt
❑ 1 Mike Piazza	1.00	.30
❑ 2 Bernie Williams	.30	.09
❑ 3 Kevin Rogers	.10	.03
❑ 4 Paul Carey	.10	.03
❑ 5 Ozzie Guillen	.10	.03
❑ 6 Derrick May	.10	.03
❑ 7 Jose Mesa	.10	.03
❑ 8 Todd Hundley	.10	.03
❑ 9 Chris Haney	.10	.03
❑ 10 John Olerud	.20	.06
❑ 11 Andujar Cedeno	.10	.03
❑ 12 John Smiley	.10	.03
❑ 13 Phil Plantier	.10	.03
❑ 14 Willie Banks	.10	.03
❑ 15 Jay Bell	.20	.06
❑ 16 Doug Henry	.10	.03
❑ 17 Lance Blankenship	.10	.03
❑ 18 Greg W. Harris	.10	.03
❑ 19 Scott Livingstone	.10	.03
❑ 20 Bryan Harvey	.10	.03
❑ 21 Wil Cordero	.10	.03
❑ 22 Roger Pavlik	.10	.03
❑ 23 Mark Lemke	.10	.03
❑ 24 Jeff Nelson	.10	.03
❑ 25 Todd Zeile	.10	.03
❑ 26 Billy Hatcher	.10	.03
❑ 27 Joe Magrane	.10	.03
❑ 28 Tony Longmire	.10	.03
❑ 29 Omar Daal	.10	.03
❑ 30 Kirt Manwaring	.10	.03
❑ 31 Melido Perez	.10	.03
❑ 32 Tim Hulett	.10	.03
❑ 33 Jeff Schwarz	.10	.03
❑ 34 Nolan Ryan	2.00	.60
❑ 35 Jose Guzman	.10	.03
❑ 36 Felix Fermin	.10	.03
❑ 37 Jeff Innis	.10	.03
❑ 38 Brett Mayne	.10	.03
❑ 39 Huck Flener RC	.10	.03
❑ 40 Jeff Bagwell	.30	.09
❑ 41 Kevin Wickander	.10	.03
❑ 42 Ricky Gutierrez	.10	.03
❑ 43 Pat Mahomes	.10	.03
❑ 44 Jeff King	.10	.03
❑ 45 Cal Eldred	.10	.03
❑ 46 Craig Paquette	.10	.03
❑ 47 Richie Lewis	.10	.03
❑ 48 Tony Phillips	.10	.03
❑ 49 Armando Reynoso	.10	.03
❑ 50 Moises Alou	.20	.06
❑ 51 Manuel Lee	.10	.03
❑ 52 Otis Nixon	.10	.03
❑ 53 Billy Ashley	.10	.03
❑ 54 Mark Whiten	.10	.03
❑ 55 Jeff Russell	.10	.03
❑ 56 Chad Curtis	.10	.03
❑ 57 Kevin Stocker	.10	.03
❑ 58 Mike Jackson	.10	.03
❑ 59 Matt Nokes	.10	.03
❑ 60 Chris Bosio	.10	.03
❑ 61 Damon Buford	.10	.03
❑ 62 Tim Belcher	.10	.03
❑ 63 Glenallen Hill	.10	.03
❑ 64 Bill Wertz	.10	.03
❑ 65 Eddie Murray	.50	.15
❑ 66 Tom Gordon	.10	.03
❑ 67 Alex Gonzalez	.10	.03
❑ 68 Eddie Taubensee	.10	.03
❑ 69 Jacob Brumfield	.10	.03
❑ 70 Andy Benes	.10	.03
❑ 71 Rich Becker	.10	.03
❑ 72 Steve Cooke	.10	.03
❑ 73 Billy Spiers	.10	.03
❑ 74 Scott Brosius	.20	.06
❑ 75 Alan Trammell	.20	.06
❑ 76 Luis Aquino	.10	.03
❑ 77 Jerald Clark	.10	.03
❑ 78 Mel Rojas	.10	.03
❑ 79 Billy Masse	.10	.03
Stanton Cameron		
Tim Clark		
Craig McClure RC		
❑ 80 Jose Canseco	.50	.15
❑ 81 Greg McMichael	.10	.03
❑ 82 Brian Turang RC	.10	.03
❑ 83 Tom Urbani	.10	.03
❑ 84 Garret Anderson	.50	.15
❑ 85 Tony Pena	.10	.03
❑ 86 Ricky Jordan	.10	.03
❑ 87 Jim Gott	.10	.03
❑ 88 Pat Kelly	.10	.03
❑ 89 Bud Black	.10	.03
❑ 90 Robin Ventura	.20	.06
❑ 91 Rick Sutcliffe	.20	.06
❑ 92 Jose Bautista	.10	.03
❑ 93 Bob Ojeda	.10	.03
❑ 94 Phil Hiatt	.10	.03
❑ 95 Tim Pugh	.10	.03
❑ 96 Randy Knorr	.10	.03
❑ 97 Todd Jones	.10	.03
❑ 98 Ryan Thompson	.10	.03
❑ 99 Tim Mauser	.10	.03
❑ 100 Kirby Puckett	.50	.15
❑ 101 Mark Dewey	.10	.03
❑ 102 B.J. Surhoff	.20	.06
❑ 103 Sterling Hitchcock	.10	.03
❑ 104 Alex Arias	.10	.03
❑ 105 David Wells	.20	.06
❑ 106 Daryl Boston	.10	.03
❑ 107 Mike Stanton	.10	.03
❑ 108 Gary Redus	.10	.03
❑ 109 Delino DeShields	.10	.03
❑ 110 Lee Smith	.20	.06
❑ 111 Greg Litton	.10	.03
❑ 112 Frankie Rodriguez	.10	.03
❑ 113 Russ Springer	.10	.03
❑ 114 Mitch Williams	.10	.03
❑ 115 Eric Karros	.20	.06
❑ 116 Jeff Brantley	.10	.03
❑ 117 Jack Voigt	.10	.03
❑ 118 Jason Bere	.10	.03
❑ 119 Kevin Roberson	.10	.03
❑ 120 Jimmy Key	.20	.06
❑ 121 Reggie Jefferson	.10	.03
❑ 122 Jeromy Burnitz	.20	.06
❑ 123 Billy Brewer	.10	.03
❑ 124 Willie Canate	.10	.03
❑ 125 Greg Swindell	.10	.03
❑ 126 Hal Morris	.10	.03
❑ 127 Brad Ausmus	.10	.03
❑ 128 George Tsamis	.10	.03
❑ 129 Denny Neagle	.20	.06
❑ 130 Pat Listach	.10	.03
❑ 131 Steve Karsay	.10	.03
❑ 132 Bret Barberie	.10	.03
❑ 133 Mark Leiter	.10	.03
❑ 134 Greg Colbrunn	.10	.03
❑ 135 David Nied	.10	.03
❑ 136 Dean Palmer	.20	.06
❑ 137 Steve Avery	.10	.03
❑ 138 Bill Haselman	.10	.03
❑ 139 Tripp Cromer	.10	.03
❑ 140 Frank Viola	.20	.06
❑ 141 Rene Gonzales	.10	.03
❑ 142 Curt Schilling	.20	.06
❑ 143 Tim Wallach	.10	.03
❑ 144 Bobby Munoz	.10	.03
❑ 145 Brady Anderson	.20	.06
❑ 146 Rod Beck	.10	.03
❑ 147 Mike LaValliere	.10	.03
❑ 148 Greg Hibbard	.10	.03
❑ 149 Kenny Lofton	.20	.06
❑ 150 Dwight Gooden	.20	.06
❑ 151 Greg Gagne	.10	.03
❑ 152 Ray McDavid	.10	.03
❑ 153 Chris Donnels	.10	.03
❑ 154 Dan Wilson	.10	.03
❑ 155 Todd Stottlemyre	.10	.03
❑ 156 David McCarty	.10	.03
❑ 157 Paul Wagner	.10	.03
❑ 158 Orlando Miller	1.50	.45
Brandon Wilson		
Derek Jeter		
Mike Neal		
❑ 159 Mike Fetters	.10	.03
❑ 160 Scott Lydy	.10	.03
❑ 161 Darrell Whitmore	.10	.03
❑ 162 Bob MacDonald	.10	.03
❑ 163 Vinny Castilla	.20	.06
❑ 164 Denis Boucher	.10	.03
❑ 165 Ivan Rodriguez	.50	.15
❑ 166 Ron Gant	.20	.06
❑ 167 Tim Davis	.10	.03
❑ 168 Steve Dixon	.10	.03
❑ 169 Scott Fletcher	.10	.03
❑ 170 Terry Mulholland	.10	.03
❑ 171 Greg Myers	.10	.03
❑ 172 Brett Butler	.20	.06
❑ 173 Bob Wickman	.10	.03
❑ 174 Dave Martinez	.10	.03
❑ 175 Fernando Valenzuela	.20	.06
❑ 176 Craig Grebeck	.10	.03
❑ 177 Shawn Boskie	.10	.03
❑ 178 Albie Lopez	.10	.03
❑ 179 Butch Huskey	.10	.03
❑ 180 George Brett	1.25	.35
❑ 181 Juan Guzman	.10	.03
❑ 182 Eric Anthony	.10	.03
❑ 183 Rob Dibble	.20	.06
❑ 184 Craig Shipley	.10	.03
❑ 185 Kevin Tapani	.10	.03
❑ 186 Marcus Moore	.10	.03
❑ 187 Graeme Lloyd	.10	.03
❑ 188 Mike Bordick	.10	.03
❑ 189 Chris Hammond	.10	.03
❑ 190 Cecil Fielder	.20	.06
❑ 191 Curt Leskanic	.10	.03
❑ 192 Lou Frazier	.10	.03
❑ 193 Steve Dreyer RC	.10	.03
❑ 194 Javier Lopez	.20	.06
❑ 195 Edgar Martinez	.30	.09
❑ 196 Allen Watson	.10	.03
❑ 197 John Flaherty	.10	.03
❑ 198 Kurt Stillwell	.10	.03
❑ 199 Danny Jackson	.10	.03

❑ 200 Cal Ripken 1.50 .45
❑ 201 Mike Bell FDP RC .10 .03
❑ 202 Alan Benes FDP RC .25 .07
❑ 203 Matt Farner FDP RC .10 .03
❑ 204 Jeff Granger .10 .03
❑ 205 B.Kieschnick FDP RC .25 .07
❑ 206 Jeremy Lee FDP RC .10 .03
❑ 207 C.Peterson FDP RC .10 .03
❑ 208 Alan Rice FDP RC .10 .03
❑ 209 Billy Wagner FDP RC .50 .15
❑ 210 Kelly Wunsch FDP RC .25 .07
❑ 211 Tom Candiotti .10 .03
❑ 212 Domingo Jean .10 .03
❑ 213 John Burkett .10 .03
❑ 214 George Bell .10 .03
❑ 215 Dan Plesac .10 .03
❑ 216 Manny Ramirez .30 .09
❑ 217 Mike Maddux .10 .03
❑ 218 Kevin McReynolds .10 .03
❑ 219 Pat Borders .10 .03
❑ 220 Doug Drabek .10 .03
❑ 221 Larry Luebbers RC .10 .03
❑ 222 Trevor Hoffman .20 .06
❑ 223 Pat Meares .10 .03
❑ 224 Danny Miceli .10 .03
❑ 225 Greg Vaughn .10 .03
❑ 226 Scott Hemond .10 .03
❑ 227 Pat Rapp .10 .03
❑ 228 Kirk Gibson .20 .06
❑ 229 Lance Painter .10 .03
❑ 230 Larry Walker .30 .09
❑ 231 Benji Gil .10 .03
❑ 232 Mark Wohlers .10 .03
❑ 233 Rich Amaral .10 .03
❑ 234 Eric Pappas .10 .03
❑ 235 Scott Cooper .10 .03
❑ 236 Mike Butcher .10 .03
❑ 237 Curtis Pride .50 .15
Shawn Green
Mark Sweeney
Eddie Davis
❑ 238 Kim Batiste .10 .03
❑ 239 Paul Assenmacher .10 .03
❑ 240 Will Clark .50 .15
❑ 241 Jose Offerman .10 .03
❑ 242 Todd Frohwirth .10 .03
❑ 243 Tim Raines .20 .06
❑ 244 Rick Wilkins .10 .03
❑ 245 Bret Saberhagen .20 .06
❑ 246 Thomas Howard .10 .03
❑ 247 Stan Belinda .10 .03
❑ 248 Rickey Henderson .50 .15
❑ 249 Brian Williams .10 .03
❑ 250 Barry Larkin .30 .09
❑ 251 Jose Valentin .10 .03
❑ 252 Lenny Webster .10 .03
❑ 253 Blas Minor .10 .03
❑ 254 Tim Teufel .10 .03
❑ 255 Bobby Witt .10 .03
❑ 256 Walt Weiss .10 .03
❑ 257 Chad Kreuter .10 .03
❑ 258 Roberto Mejia .10 .03
❑ 259 Cliff Floyd .20 .06
❑ 260 Julio Franco .20 .06
❑ 261 Rafael Belliard .10 .03
❑ 262 Marc Newfield .10 .03
❑ 263 Gerald Perry .10 .03
❑ 264 Ken Ryan .10 .03
❑ 265 Chili Davis .20 .06
❑ 266 Dave West .10 .03
❑ 267 Royce Clayton .10 .03
❑ 268 Pedro Martinez .50 .15
❑ 269 Mark Hutton .10 .03
❑ 270 Frank Thomas .50 .15
❑ 271 Brad Pennington .10 .03
❑ 272 Mike Harkey .10 .03
❑ 273 Sandy Alomar Jr. .10 .03
❑ 274 Dave Gallagher .10 .03
❑ 275 Wally Joyner .20 .06
❑ 276 Ricky Trlicek .10 .03
❑ 277 Al Osuna .10 .03
❑ 278 Pokey Reese .10 .03
❑ 279 Kevin Higgins .10 .03
❑ 280 Rick Aguilera .10 .03
❑ 281 Orlando Merced .10 .03
❑ 282 Mike Mohler .10 .03
❑ 283 John Jaha .10 .03
❑ 284 Robb Nen .20 .06
❑ 285 Travis Fryman .20 .06
❑ 286 Mark Thompson .10 .03
❑ 287 Mike Lansing .10 .03
❑ 288 Craig Lefferts .10 .03
❑ 289 Damon Berryhill .10 .03
❑ 290 Randy Johnson .50 .15
❑ 291 Jeff Reed .10 .03
❑ 292 Danny Darwin .10 .03
❑ 293 J.T. Snow .20 .06
❑ 294 Tyler Green .10 .03
❑ 295 Chris Hoiles .10 .03
❑ 296 Roger McDowell .10 .03
❑ 297 Spike Owen .10 .03
❑ 298 Salomon Torres .10 .03
❑ 299 Wilson Alvarez .10 .03
❑ 300 Ryne Sandberg .75 .23
❑ 301 Derek Lilliquist .10 .03
❑ 302 Howard Johnson .10 .03
❑ 303 Greg Cadaret .10 .03
❑ 304 Pat Hentgen .10 .03
❑ 305 Craig Biggio .30 .09
❑ 306 Scott Service .10 .03
❑ 307 Melvin Nieves .10 .03
❑ 308 Mike Trombley .10 .03
❑ 309 Carlos Garcia .10 .03
❑ 310 Robin Yount UER .75 .23
(listed with 111 triples in
1988; should be 11)
❑ 311 Marcos Armas .10 .03
❑ 312 Rich Rodriguez .10 .03
❑ 313 Justin Thompson .10 .03
❑ 314 Danny Sheaffer .10 .03
❑ 315 Ken Hill .10 .03
❑ 316 Chad Ogea .10 .03
Duff Brumley
Terrell Wade RC
Chris Michalak
❑ 317 Cris Carpenter .10 .03
❑ 318 Jeff Blauser .10 .03
❑ 319 Ted Power .10 .03
❑ 320 Ozzie Smith .75 .23
❑ 321 John Dopson .10 .03
❑ 322 Chris Turner .10 .03
❑ 323 Pete Incaviglia .10 .03
❑ 324 Alan Mills .10 .03
❑ 325 Jody Reed .10 .03
❑ 326 Rich Monteleone .10 .03
❑ 327 Mark Carreon .10 .03
❑ 328 Donn Pall .10 .03
❑ 329 Matt Walbeck .10 .03
❑ 330 Charles Nagy .10 .03
❑ 331 Jeff McKnight .10 .03
❑ 332 Jose Lind .10 .03
❑ 333 Mike Timlin .10 .03
❑ 334 Doug Jones .10 .03
❑ 335 Kevin Mitchell .10 .03
❑ 336 Luis Lopez .10 .03
❑ 337 Shane Mack .10 .03
❑ 338 Randy Tomlin .10 .03
❑ 339 Matt Mieske .10 .03
❑ 340 Mark McGwire 1.25 .35
❑ 341 Nigel Wilson .10 .03
❑ 342 Danny Gladden .10 .03
❑ 343 Mo Sanford .10 .03
❑ 344 Sean Berry .10 .03
❑ 345 Kevin Brown .20 .06
❑ 346 Greg Olson .10 .03
❑ 347 Dave Magadan .10 .03
❑ 348 Rene Arocha .10 .03
❑ 349 Carlos Quintana .10 .03
❑ 350 Jim Abbott .30 .09
❑ 351 Gary DiSarcina .10 .03
❑ 352 Ben Rivera .10 .03
❑ 353 Carlos Hernandez .10 .03
❑ 354 Darren Lewis .10 .03
❑ 355 Harold Reynolds .20 .06
❑ 356 Scott Ruffcorn .10 .03
❑ 357 Mark Gubicza .10 .03
❑ 358 Paul Sorrento .10 .03
❑ 359 Anthony Young .10 .03
❑ 360 Mark Grace .30 .09
❑ 361 Rob Butler .10 .03
❑ 362 Kevin Bass .10 .03
❑ 363 Eric Helfand .10 .03
❑ 364 Derek Bell .10 .03
❑ 365 Scott Erickson .10 .03
❑ 366 Al Martin .10 .03
❑ 367 Ricky Bones .10 .03
❑ 368 Jeff Branson .10 .03
❑ 369 Luis Ortiz .50 .15
David Bell RC
Jason Giambi
George Arias
❑ 370 Benito Santiago .20 .06
(See also 379)
❑ 371 John Doherty .10 .03
❑ 372 Joe Girardi .10 .03
❑ 373 Tim Scott .10 .03
❑ 374 Marvin Freeman .10 .03
❑ 375 Deion Sanders .30 .09
❑ 376 Roger Salkeld .10 .03
❑ 377 Bernard Gilkey .10 .03
❑ 378 Tony Fossas .10 .03
❑ 379 Mark McLemore UER .10 .03
(Card number is 370)
❑ 380 Darren Daulton .20 .06
❑ 381 Chuck Finley .20 .06
❑ 382 Mitch Webster .10 .03
❑ 383 Gerald Williams .10 .03
❑ 384 Frank Thomas AS .30 .09
Fred McGriff AS
❑ 385 Roberto Alomar AS .20 .06
Robby Thompson AS
❑ 386 Wade Boggs AS .20 .06
Matt Williams AS
❑ 387 Cal Ripken AS .50 .15
Jeff Blauser AS
❑ 388 Ken Griffey Jr. AS .50 .15
Len Dykstra AS
❑ 389 Juan Gonzalez AS .20 .06
David Justice AS
❑ 390 George Belle AS .60 .18
Bobby Bonds AS
❑ 391 Mike Stanley AS .50 .15
Mike Piazza AS
❑ 392 Jack McDowell AS .30 .09
Greg Maddux AS
❑ 393 Jimmy Key AS .20 .06
Tom Glavine AS
❑ 394 Jeff Montgomery AS .10 .03
Randy Myers AS
❑ 395 Checklist 1-198 .10 .03
❑ 396 Checklist 199-396 .10 .03
❑ 397 Tim Salmon .30 .09
❑ 398 Todd Benzinger .10 .03
❑ 399 Frank Castillo .10 .03
❑ 400 Ken Griffey Jr. .75 .23
❑ 401 John Kruk .20 .06
❑ 402 Dave Telgheder .10 .03
❑ 403 Gary Gaetti .20 .06
❑ 404 Jim Edmonds .50 .15
❑ 405 Don Slaught .10 .03
❑ 406 Jose Oquendo .10 .03
❑ 407 Bruce Ruffin .10 .03
❑ 408 Phil Clark .10 .03
❑ 409 Joe Klink .10 .03
❑ 410 Lou Whitaker .20 .06
❑ 411 Kevin Seitzer .10 .03
❑ 412 Darrin Fletcher .10 .03
❑ 413 Kenny Rogers .20 .06
❑ 414 Bill Pecota .10 .03
❑ 415 Dave Fleming .10 .03
❑ 416 Luis Alicea .10 .03
❑ 417 Paul Quantrill .10 .03
❑ 418 Damion Easley .10 .03
❑ 419 Wes Chamberlain .10 .03
❑ 420 Harold Baines .20 .06
❑ 421 Scott Radinsky .10 .03
❑ 422 Rey Sanchez .10 .03
❑ 423 Junior Ortiz .10 .03
❑ 424 Jeff Kent .20 .06
❑ 425 Brian McRae .10 .03
❑ 426 Ed Sprague .10 .03
❑ 427 Tom Edens .10 .03
❑ 428 Willie Greene .10 .03
❑ 429 Bryan Hickerson .10 .03
❑ 430 Dave Winfield .20 .06
❑ 431 Pedro Astacio .10 .03
❑ 432 Mike Gallego .10 .03
❑ 433 Dave Burba .10 .03

❑ 434 Bob Walk	.10	.03
❑ 435 Darryl Hamilton	.10	.03
❑ 436 Vince Horsman	.10	.03
❑ 437 Bob Natal	.10	.03
❑ 438 Mike Henneman	.10	.03
❑ 439 Willie Blair	.10	.03
❑ 440 Dennis Martinez	.20	.06
❑ 441 Dan Peltier	.10	.03
❑ 442 Tony Tarasco	.10	.03
❑ 443 John Cummings	.10	.03
❑ 444 Geronimo Pena	.10	.03
❑ 445 Aaron Sele	.10	.03
❑ 446 Stan Javier	.10	.03
❑ 447 Mike Williams	.10	.03
❑ 448 Greg Pirkl Roberto Petagine D.J.Boston Shawn Wooten RC	.10	.03
❑ 449 Jim Poole	.10	.03
❑ 450 Carlos Baerga	.10	.03
❑ 451 Bob Scanlan	.10	.03
❑ 452 Lance Johnson	.10	.03
❑ 453 Eric Hillman	.10	.03
❑ 454 Keith Miller	.10	.03
❑ 455 Dave Stewart	.20	.06
❑ 456 Pete Harnisch	.10	.03
❑ 457 Roberto Kelly	.10	.03
❑ 458 Tim Worrell	.10	.03
❑ 459 Pedro Munoz	.10	.03
❑ 460 Orel Hershiser	.20	.06
❑ 461 Randy Velarde	.10	.03
❑ 462 Trevor Wilson	.10	.03
❑ 463 Jerry Goff	.10	.03
❑ 464 Bill Wegman	.10	.03
❑ 465 Dennis Eckersley	.20	.06
❑ 466 Jeff Conine	.20	.06
❑ 467 Joe Boever	.10	.03
❑ 468 Dante Bichette	.20	.06
❑ 469 Jeff Shaw	.10	.03
❑ 470 Rafael Palmeiro	.30	.09
❑ 471 Phil Leftwich RC	.10	.03
❑ 472 Jay Buhner	.20	.06
❑ 473 Bob Tewksbury	.10	.03
❑ 474 Tim Naehring	.10	.03
❑ 475 Tom Glavine	.30	.09
❑ 476 Dave Hollins	.10	.03
❑ 477 Arthur Rhodes	.10	.03
❑ 478 Joey Cora	.10	.03
❑ 479 Mike Morgan	.10	.03
❑ 480 Albert Belle	.20	.06
❑ 481 John Franco	.20	.06
❑ 482 Hipolito Pichardo	.10	.03
❑ 483 Duane Ward	.10	.03
❑ 484 Luis Gonzalez	.20	.06
❑ 485 Joe Oliver	.10	.03
❑ 486 Wally Whitehurst	.10	.03
❑ 487 Mike Benjamin	.10	.03
❑ 488 Eric Davis	.20	.06
❑ 489 Scott Kamieniecki	.10	.03
❑ 490 Kent Hrbek	.20	.06
❑ 491 John Hope RC	.10	.03
❑ 492 Jesse Orosco	.10	.03
❑ 493 Troy Neel	.10	.03
❑ 494 Ryan Bowen	.10	.03
❑ 495 Mickey Tettleton	.10	.03
❑ 496 Chris Jones	.10	.03
❑ 497 John Wetteland	.20	.06
❑ 498 David Hulse	.10	.03
❑ 499 Greg Maddux	.75	.23
❑ 500 Bo Jackson	.50	.15
❑ 501 Donovan Osborne	.10	.03
❑ 502 Mike Greenwell	.10	.03
❑ 503 Steve Frey	.10	.03
❑ 504 Jim Eisenreich	.10	.03
❑ 505 Robby Thompson	.10	.03
❑ 506 Leo Gomez	.10	.03
❑ 507 Dave Staton	.10	.03
❑ 508 Wayne Kirby	.10	.03
❑ 509 Tim Bogar	.10	.03
❑ 510 David Cone	.20	.06
❑ 511 Devon White	.20	.06
❑ 512 Xavier Hernandez	.10	.03
❑ 513 Tim Costo	.10	.03
❑ 514 Gene Harris	.10	.03
❑ 515 Jack McDowell	.10	.03
❑ 516 Kevin Gross	.10	.03
❑ 517 Scott Leius	.10	.03
❑ 518 Lloyd McClendon	.10	.03
❑ 519 Alex Diaz RC	.10	.03
❑ 520 Wade Boggs	.30	.09
❑ 521 Bob Welch	.10	.03
❑ 522 Henry Cotto	.10	.03
❑ 523 Mike Moore	.10	.03
❑ 524 Tim Laker	.10	.03
❑ 525 Andres Galarraga	.20	.06
❑ 526 Jamie Moyer	.20	.06
❑ 527 Norberto Martin Ruben Santana Jason Hardtke Chris Sexton RC	.10	.03
❑ 528 Sid Bream	.10	.03
❑ 529 Erik Hanson	.10	.03
❑ 530 Ray Lankford	.10	.03
❑ 531 Rob Deer	.10	.03
❑ 532 Rod Correia	.10	.03
❑ 533 Roger Mason	.10	.03
❑ 534 Mike Devereaux	.10	.03
❑ 535 Jeff Montgomery	.10	.03
❑ 536 Dwight Smith	.10	.03
❑ 537 Jeremy Hernandez	.10	.03
❑ 538 Ellis Burks	.20	.06
❑ 539 Bobby Jones	.10	.03
❑ 540 Paul Molitor	.30	.09
❑ 541 Jeff Juden	.10	.03
❑ 542 Chris Sabo	.10	.03
❑ 543 Larry Casian	.10	.03
❑ 544 Jeff Gardner	.10	.03
❑ 545 Ramon Martinez	.10	.03
❑ 546 Paul O'Neill	.30	.09
❑ 547 Steve Hosey	.10	.03
❑ 548 Dave Nilsson	.10	.03
❑ 549 Ron Darling	.10	.03
❑ 550 Matt Williams	.20	.06
❑ 551 Jack Armstrong	.10	.03
❑ 552 Bill Krueger	.10	.03
❑ 553 Freddie Benavides	.10	.03
❑ 554 Jeff Fassero	.10	.03
❑ 555 Chuck Knoblauch	.20	.06
❑ 556 Guillermo Velasquez	.10	.03
❑ 557 Joel Johnston	.10	.03
❑ 558 Tom Lampkin	.10	.03
❑ 559 Todd Van Poppel	.10	.03
❑ 560 Gary Sheffield	.20	.06
❑ 561 Skeeter Barnes	.10	.03
❑ 562 Darren Holmes	.10	.03
❑ 563 John Vander Wal	.10	.03
❑ 564 Mike Ignasiak	.10	.03
❑ 565 Fred McGriff	.30	.09
❑ 566 Luis Polonia	.10	.03
❑ 567 Mike Perez	.10	.03
❑ 568 John Valentin	.10	.03
❑ 569 Mike Felder	.10	.03
❑ 570 Tommy Greene	.10	.03
❑ 571 David Segui	.10	.03
❑ 572 Roberto Hernandez	.10	.03
❑ 573 Steve Wilson	.10	.03
❑ 574 Willie McGee	.20	.06
❑ 575 Randy Myers	.10	.03
❑ 576 Darrin Jackson	.10	.03
❑ 577 Eric Plunk	.10	.03
❑ 578 Mike Macfarlane	.10	.03
❑ 579 Doug Brocail	.10	.03
❑ 580 Steve Finley	.20	.06
❑ 581 John Roper	.10	.03
❑ 582 Danny Cox	.10	.03
❑ 583 Chip Hale	.10	.03
❑ 584 Scott Bullett	.10	.03
❑ 585 Kevin Reimer	.10	.03
❑ 586 Brent Gates	.10	.03
❑ 587 Matt Turner	.10	.03
❑ 588 Rich Rowland	.10	.03
❑ 589 Kent Bottenfield	.10	.03
❑ 590 Marquis Grissom	.20	.06
❑ 591 Doug Strange	.10	.03
❑ 592 Jay Howell	.10	.03
❑ 593 Omar Vizquel	.30	.09
❑ 594 Rheal Cormier	.10	.03
❑ 595 Andre Dawson	.20	.06
❑ 596 Hilly Hathaway	.10	.03
❑ 597 Todd Pratt	.10	.03
❑ 598 Mike Mussina	.30	.09
❑ 599 Alex Fernandez	.10	.03
❑ 600 Don Mattingly	1.25	.35
❑ 601 Frank Thomas MOG	.30	.09
❑ 602 Ryne Sandberg MOG	.50	.15
❑ 603 Wade Boggs MOG	.20	.06
❑ 604 Cal Ripken MOG	.75	.23
❑ 605 Barry Bonds MOG	.60	.18
❑ 606 Ken Griffey Jr. MOG	.50	.15
❑ 607 Kirby Puckett MOG	.30	.09
❑ 608 Darren Daulton MOG	.10	.03
❑ 609 Paul Molitor MOG	.20	.06
❑ 610 Terry Steinbach	.10	.03
❑ 611 Todd Worrell	.10	.03
❑ 612 Jim Thome	.50	.15
❑ 613 Chuck McElroy	.10	.03
❑ 614 John Habyan	.10	.03
❑ 615 Sid Fernandez	.10	.03
❑ 616 Eddie Zambrano Glenn Murray Chad Mottola Jermaine Allensworth RC	.10	.03
❑ 617 Steve Bedrosian	.10	.03
❑ 618 Rob Ducey	.10	.03
❑ 619 Tom Browning	.10	.03
❑ 620 Tony Gwynn	.60	.18
❑ 621 Carl Willis	.10	.03
❑ 622 Kevin Young	.10	.03
❑ 623 Rafael Novoa	.10	.03
❑ 624 Jerry Browne	.10	.03
❑ 625 Charlie Hough	.20	.06
❑ 626 Chris Gomez	.10	.03
❑ 627 Steve Reed	.10	.03
❑ 628 Kirk Rueter	.20	.06
❑ 629 Matt Whiteside	.10	.03
❑ 630 David Justice	.20	.06
❑ 631 Brad Holman	.10	.03
❑ 632 Brian Jordan	.20	.06
❑ 633 Scott Bankhead	.10	.03
❑ 634 Torey Lovullo	.10	.03
❑ 635 Len Dykstra	.20	.06
❑ 636 Ben McDonald	.10	.03
❑ 637 Steve Howe	.10	.03
❑ 638 Jose Vizcaino	.10	.03
❑ 639 Bill Swift	.10	.03
❑ 640 Darryl Strawberry	.20	.06
❑ 641 Steve Farr	.10	.03
❑ 642 Tom Kramer	.10	.03
❑ 643 Joe Orsulak	.10	.03
❑ 644 Tom Henke	.10	.03
❑ 645 Joe Carter	.20	.06
❑ 646 Ken Caminiti	.20	.06
❑ 647 Reggie Sanders	.10	.03
❑ 648 Andy Ashby	.10	.03
❑ 649 Derek Parks	.10	.03
❑ 650 Andy Van Slyke	.20	.06
❑ 651 Juan Bell	.10	.03
❑ 652 Roger Smithberg	.10	.03
❑ 653 Chuck Carr	.10	.03
❑ 654 Bill Gullickson	.10	.03
❑ 655 Charlie Hayes	.10	.03
❑ 656 Chris Nabholz	.10	.03
❑ 657 Karl Rhodes	.10	.03
❑ 658 Pete Smith	.10	.03
❑ 659 Bret Boone	.20	.06
❑ 660 Gregg Jefferies	.10	.03
❑ 661 Bob Zupcic	.10	.03
❑ 662 Steve Sax	.10	.03
❑ 663 Mariano Duncan	.10	.03
❑ 664 Jeff Tackett	.10	.03
❑ 665 Mark Langston	.10	.03
❑ 666 Steve Buechele	.10	.03
❑ 667 Candy Maldonado	.10	.03
❑ 668 Woody Williams	.20	.06
❑ 669 Tim Wakefield	.20	.06
❑ 670 Danny Tartabull	.10	.03
❑ 671 Charlie O'Brien	.10	.03
❑ 672 Felix Jose	.10	.03
❑ 673 Bobby Ayala	.10	.03
❑ 674 Scott Servais	.10	.03
❑ 675 Roberto Alomar	.30	.09
❑ 676 Pedro A.Martinez RC	.10	.03
❑ 677 Eddie Guardado	.10	.03
❑ 678 Mark Lewis	.10	.03
❑ 679 Jaime Navarro	.10	.03
❑ 680 Ruben Sierra	.10	.03
❑ 681 Rick Renteria	.10	.03
❑ 682 Storm Davis	.10	.03

❑ 683 Cory Snyder .10 .03
❑ 684 Ron Karkovice .10 .03
❑ 685 Juan Gonzalez .30 .09
❑ 686 Chris Howard .30 .09
Carlos Delgado
Jason Kendall
Paul Bako
❑ 687 John Smoltz .30 .09
❑ 688 Brian Dorsett .10 .03
❑ 689 Omar Olivares .10 .03
❑ 690 Mo Vaughn .20 .06
❑ 691 Joe Grahe .10 .03
❑ 692 Mickey Morandini .10 .03
❑ 693 Tino Martinez .30 .09
❑ 694 Brian Barnes .10 .03
❑ 695 Mike Stanley .10 .03
❑ 696 Mark Clark .10 .03
❑ 697 Dave Hansen .10 .03
❑ 698 Willie Wilson .10 .03
❑ 699 Pete Schourek .10 .03
❑ 700 Barry Bonds 1.25 .35
❑ 701 Kevin Appier .20 .06
❑ 702 Tony Fernandez .10 .03
❑ 703 Darryl Kile .20 .06
❑ 704 Archi Cianfrocco .10 .03
❑ 705 Jose Rijo .10 .03
❑ 706 Brian Harper .10 .03
❑ 707 Zane Smith .10 .03
❑ 708 Dave Henderson .10 .03
❑ 709 Angel Miranda UER .10 .03
(no Topps logo on back)
❑ 710 Orestes Destrade .10 .03
❑ 711 Greg Gohr .10 .03
❑ 712 Eric Young .10 .03
❑ 713 Todd Williams .10 .03
Ron Watson
Kirk Bullinger
Mike Welch
❑ 714 Tim Spehr .10 .03
❑ 715 Hank Aaron 715 HR .50 .15
❑ 716 Nate Minchey .10 .03
❑ 717 Mike Blowers .10 .03
❑ 718 Kent Mercker .10 .03
❑ 719 Tom Pagnozzi .10 .03
❑ 720 Roger Clemens 1.00 .30
❑ 721 Eduardo Perez .10 .03
❑ 722 Milt Thompson .10 .03
❑ 723 Gregg Olson .10 .03
❑ 724 Kirk McCaskill .10 .03
❑ 725 Sammy Sosa .75 .23
❑ 726 Alvaro Espinoza .10 .03
❑ 727 Henry Rodriguez .10 .03
❑ 728 Jim Leyritz .10 .03
❑ 729 Steve Scarsone .10 .03
❑ 730 Bobby Bonilla .20 .06
❑ 731 Chris Gwynn .10 .03
❑ 732 Al Leiter .20 .06
❑ 733 Bip Roberts .10 .03
❑ 734 Mark Portugal .10 .03
❑ 735 Terry Pendleton .20 .06
❑ 736 Dave Valle .10 .03
❑ 737 Paul Kilgus .10 .03
❑ 738 Greg A. Harris .10 .03
❑ 739 Jon Ratliff DP RC .10 .03
❑ 740 Kirk Presley DP RC .10 .03
❑ 741 Josue Estrada DP RC .10 .03
❑ 742 Wayne Gomes DP RC .10 .03
❑ 743 Pat Watkins DP RC .10 .03
❑ 744 Jamey Wright DP RC .25 .07
❑ 745 Jay Powell DP RC .10 .03
❑ 746 Ryan McGuire DP RC .10 .03
❑ 747 Marc Barcelo DP RC .10 .03
❑ 748 Sloan Smith DP RC .10 .03
❑ 749 John Wasdin DP RC .10 .03
❑ 750 Marc Vlades DP .10 .03
❑ 751 Dan Ehler DP RC .10 .03
❑ 752 Andre King DP RC .10 .03
❑ 753 Greg Keagle DP RC .10 .03
❑ 754 Jason Myers DP RC .10 .03
❑ 755 Dax Winslett DP RC .10 .03
❑ 756 Casey Whitten DP RC .10 .03
❑ 757 Tony Fuduric DP RC .10 .03
❑ 758 Greg Norton DP RC .25 .07
❑ 759 Jeff D'Amico DP RC .25 .07
❑ 760 Ryan Hancock DP RC .10 .03
❑ 761 David Cooper DP RC .10 .03
❑ 762 Kevin Orie DP RC .10 .03
❑ 763 John O'Donoghue .10 .03
Mike Oquist
❑ 764 Cory Bailey RC .10 .03
Scott Hatteberg
❑ 765 Mark Holzemer .10 .03
Paul Swingle RC
❑ 766 James Baldwin .10 .03
Rod Bolton
❑ 767 Jerry Di Poto .25 .07
Julian Tavarez RC
❑ 768 Danny Bautista .10 .03
Sean Bergman
❑ 769 Bob Hamelin .10 .03
Joe Vitiello
❑ 770 Mark Kiefer .10 .03
Troy O'Leary
❑ 771 Denny Hocking .10 .03
Oscar Munoz RC
❑ 772 Russ Davis .10 .03
Brien Taylor
❑ 773 Kyle Abbott RC .25 .07
Miguel Jimenez
❑ 774 Kevin King .10 .03
Eric Plantenberg RC
❑ 775 Jon Shave .10 .03
Desi Wilson
❑ 776 Domingo Cedeno .10 .03
Paul Spoljaric
❑ 777 Chipper Jones .50 .15
Ryan Klesko
❑ 778 Steve Trachsel .10 .03
Turk Wendell
❑ 779 Johnny Ruffin .10 .03
Jerry Spradlin RC
❑ 780 Jason Bates .10 .03
John Burke
❑ 781 Carl Everett .20 .06
Dave Weathers
❑ 782 Gary Mota .10 .03
James Mouton
❑ 783 Raul Mondesi .20 .06
Ben Van Ryn
❑ 784 Gabe White .20 .06
Rondell White
❑ 785 Brook Fordyce .20 .06
Bill Pulsipher
❑ 786 Kevin Foster RC .10 .03
Gene Schall
❑ 787 Rich Aude RC .10 .03
Midre Cummings
❑ 788 Brian Barber .10 .03
Rich Batchelor
❑ 789 Brian Johnson RC .10 .03
Scott Sanders
❑ 790 Ricky Faneyte .10 .03
J.R. Phillips
❑ 791 Checklist 3 .10 .03
❑ 792 Checklist 4 .10 .03

1994 Topps Traded

	Nm-Mt	Ex-Mt
COMP.FACT.SET (140)	30.00	9.00

❑ 1T Paul Wilson .20 .06
❑ 2T Bill Taylor RC 1.00 .30
❑ 3T Dan Wilson .10 .03
❑ 4T Mark Smith .10 .03
❑ 5T Toby Borland RC .25 .07
❑ 6T Dave Clark .10 .03
❑ 7T Dennis Martinez .20 .06
❑ 8T Dave Gallagher .10 .03
❑ 9T Josias Manzanillo .10 .03
❑ 10T Brian Anderson RC 1.00 .30
❑ 11T Damon Berryhill .10 .03
❑ 12T Alex Cole .10 .03
❑ 13T Jacob Shumate RC .25 .07
❑ 14T Oddibe McDowell .10 .03
❑ 15T Willie Banks .10 .03
❑ 16T Jerry Browne .10 .03
❑ 17T Donnie Elliott .10 .03
❑ 18T Ellis Burks .20 .06
❑ 19T Chuck McElroy .10 .03
❑ 20T Luis Polonia .10 .03
❑ 21T Brian Harper .10 .03
❑ 22T Mark Portugal .10 .03
❑ 23T Dave Henderson .10 .03
❑ 24T Mark Acre RC .25 .07
❑ 25T Julio Franco .20 .06
❑ 26T Darren Hall RC .25 .07
❑ 27T Eric Anthony .10 .03
❑ 28T Sid Fernandez .10 .03
❑ 29T Rusty Greer RC 1.50 .45
❑ 30T Riccardo Ingram RC .25 .07
❑ 31T Gabe White .10 .03
❑ 32T Tim Belcher .10 .03
❑ 33T Terrence Long RC 1.50 .45
❑ 34T Mark Dalesandro RC .25 .07
❑ 35T Mike Kelly .10 .03
❑ 36T Jack Morris .20 .06
❑ 37T Jeff Brantley .10 .03
❑ 38T Larry Barnes RC .25 .07
❑ 39T Brian R. Hunter .10 .03
❑ 40T Otis Nixon .10 .03
❑ 41T Bret Wagner .10 .03
❑ 42T Pedro Martinez TR .50 .15
Delino Deshields
❑ 43T Heathcliff Slocumb .10 .03
❑ 44T Ben Grieve RC 1.50 .45
❑ 45T John Hudek RC .25 .07
❑ 46T Shawon Dunston .10 .03
❑ 47T Greg Colbrunn .10 .03
❑ 48T Joey Hamilton .10 .03
❑ 49T Marvin Freeman .10 .03
❑ 50T Terry Mulholland .10 .03
❑ 51T Keith Mitchell .10 .03
❑ 52T Dwight Smith .10 .03
❑ 53T Shawn Boskie .10 .03
❑ 54T Kevin Witt RC 1.00 .30
❑ 55T Ron Gant .20 .06
❑ 56T Trenidad Hubbard RC 10.00 3.00
Jason Schmidt RC
Larry Sutton
Stephen Larkin RC
❑ 57T Jody Reed .10 .03
❑ 58T Rick Helling .10 .03
❑ 59T John Powell .10 .03
❑ 60T Eddie Murray .50 .15
❑ 61T Joe Hall RC .25 .07
❑ 62T Jorge Fabregas .10 .03
❑ 63T Mike Mordecai RC .25 .07
❑ 64T Ed Vosberg .10 .03
❑ 65T Rickey Henderson .50 .15
❑ 66T Tim Grieve RC .25 .07
❑ 67T Jon Lieber .10 .03
❑ 68T Chris Howard .10 .03
❑ 69T Matt Walbeck .10 .03
❑ 70T Chan Ho Park RC 1.50 .45
❑ 71T Bryan Eversgerd RC .25 .07
❑ 72T John Dettmer .10 .03
❑ 73T Erik Hanson .10 .03
❑ 74T Mike Thurman RC .25 .07
❑ 75T Bobby Ayala .10 .03
❑ 76T Rafael Palmeiro .30 .09
❑ 77T Bret Boone .20 .06
❑ 78T Paul Shuey .10 .03
❑ 79T Kevin Foster RC .25 .07
❑ 80T Dave Magadan .10 .03
❑ 81T Bip Roberts .10 .03
❑ 82T Howard Johnson .10 .03
❑ 83T Xavier Hernandez .10 .03
❑ 84T Ross Powell RC .25 .07
❑ 85T Doug Million RC .25 .07

❑ 86T Geronimo Berroa .10 .03
❑ 87T Mark Farris RC .25 .07
❑ 88T Butch Henry .10 .03
❑ 89T Junior Felix .10 .03
❑ 90T Bo Jackson .50 .15
❑ 91T Hector Carrasco .10 .03
❑ 92T Charlie O'Brien .10 .03
❑ 93T Omar Vizquel .30 .09
❑ 94T David Segui .10 .03
❑ 95T Dustin Hermanson .20 .06
❑ 96T Gar Finnvold RC .25 .07
❑ 97T Dave Stevens .10 .03
❑ 98T Corey Pointer RC .25 .07
❑ 99T Felix Fermin .10 .03
❑ 100T Lee Smith .20 .06
❑ 101T Reid Ryan RC 1.00 .30
❑ 102T Bobby Munoz .10 .03
❑ 103T Deion Sanders TR .30 .09
Roberto Kelly
❑ 104T Turner Ward .10 .03
❑ 105T W.VanLandingham RC .25 .07
❑ 106T Vince Coleman .10 .03
❑ 107T Stan Javier .10 .03
❑ 108T Darrin Jackson .10 .03
❑ 109T C.J. Nitkowski RC .25 .07
❑ 110T Anthony Young .10 .03
❑ 111T Kurt Miller .10 .03
❑ 112T Paul Konerko RC 5.00 1.50
❑ 113T Walt Weiss .10 .03
❑ 114T Daryl Boston .10 .03
❑ 115T Will Clark .50 .15
❑ 116T Matt Smith RC .25 .07
❑ 117T Mark Leiter .10 .03
❑ 118T Gregg Olson .10 .03
❑ 119T Tony Pena .10 .03
❑ 120T Jose Vizcaino .10 .03
❑ 121T Rick White RC .25 .07
❑ 122T Rich Rowland .10 .03
❑ 123T Jeff Reboulet .10 .03
❑ 124T Greg Hibbard .10 .03
❑ 125T Chris Sabo .10 .03
❑ 126T Doug Jones .10 .03
❑ 127T Tony Fernandez .10 .03
❑ 128T Carlos Reyes RC .25 .07
❑ 129T Kevin L.Brown RC 1.00 .30
❑ 130T Ryne Sandberg 1.25 .35
Farewell
❑ 131T Ryne Sandberg 1.25 .35
Farewell
❑ 132T Checklist 1-132 .10 .03

1995 Topps

	Nm-Mt	Ex-Mt
COMPLETE SET (660)	80.00	24.00
COMP.HOBBY SET (677)	120.00	36.00
COMP.RETAIL SET (677)	120.00	36.00
COMP.SERIES 1 (396)	40.00	12.00
COMP.SERIES 2 (264)	40.00	12.00

❑ 1 Frank Thomas .75 .23
❑ 2 Mickey Morandini .15 .04
❑ 3 Babe Ruth 100th B-Day 2.00 .60
❑ 4 Scott Cooper .15 .04
❑ 5 David Cone .30 .09
❑ 6 Jacob Shumate .15 .04
❑ 7 Trevor Hoffman .30 .09
❑ 8 Shane Mack .15 .04
❑ 9 Delino DeShields .15 .04
❑ 10 Matt Williams .30 .09
❑ 11 Sammy Sosa 1.25 .35
❑ 12 Gary DiSarcina .15 .04
❑ 13 Kenny Rogers .30 .09
❑ 14 Jose Vizcaino .15 .04
❑ 15 Lou Whitaker .30 .09
❑ 16 Ron Darling .15 .04
❑ 17 Dave Nilsson .15 .04
❑ 18 Chris Hammond .15 .04
❑ 19 Sid Bream .15 .04
❑ 20 Denny Martinez .30 .09
❑ 21 Orlando Merced .15 .04
❑ 22 John Wetteland .30 .09
❑ 23 Mike Devereaux .15 .04
❑ 24 Rene Arocha .15 .04
❑ 25 Jay Buhner .30 .09
❑ 26 Darren Holmes .15 .04
❑ 27 Hal Morris .15 .04
❑ 28 Brian Buchanan RC .15 .04
❑ 29 Keith Miller .15 .04
❑ 30 Paul Molitor .50 .15
❑ 31 Dave West .15 .04
❑ 32 Tony Tarasco .15 .04
❑ 33 Scott Sanders .15 .04
❑ 34 Eddie Zambrano .15 .04
❑ 35 Ricky Bones .15 .04
❑ 36 John Valentin .15 .04
❑ 37 Kevin Tapani .15 .04
❑ 38 Tim Wallach .15 .04
❑ 39 Darren Lewis .15 .04
❑ 40 Travis Fryman .30 .09
❑ 41 Mark Leiter .15 .04
❑ 42 Jose Bautista .15 .04
❑ 43 Pete Smith .15 .04
❑ 44 Bret Barberie .15 .04
❑ 45 Dennis Eckersley .30 .09
❑ 46 Ken Hill .15 .04
❑ 47 Chad Ogea .15 .04
❑ 48 Pete Harnisch .15 .04
❑ 49 James Baldwin .15 .04
❑ 50 Mike Mussina .50 .15
❑ 51 Al Martin .15 .04
❑ 52 Mark Thompson .15 .04
❑ 53 Matt Smith .15 .04
❑ 54 Joey Hamilton .15 .04
❑ 55 Edgar Martinez .50 .15
❑ 56 John Smiley .15 .04
❑ 57 Rey Sanchez .15 .04
❑ 58 Mike Timlin .15 .04
❑ 59 Ricky Bottalico .15 .04
❑ 60 Jim Abbott .50 .15
❑ 61 Mike Kelly .15 .04
❑ 62 Brian Jordan .30 .09
❑ 63 Ken Ryan .15 .04
❑ 64 Matt Mieske .15 .04
❑ 65 Rick Aguilera .15 .04
❑ 66 Ismael Valdes .15 .04
❑ 67 Royce Clayton .15 .04
❑ 68 Junior Felix .15 .04
❑ 69 Harold Reynolds .30 .09
❑ 70 Juan Gonzalez .50 .15
❑ 71 Kelly Stinnett .15 .04
❑ 72 Carlos Reyes .15 .04
❑ 73 Dave Weathers .15 .04
❑ 74 Mel Rojas .15 .04
❑ 75 Doug Drabek .15 .04
❑ 76 Charles Nagy .15 .04
❑ 77 Tim Raines .30 .09
❑ 78 Midre Cummings .15 .04
❑ 79 Gene Schall .15 .04
Scott Talanoa
Harold Williams
Ray Brown RC
❑ 80 Rafael Palmeiro .50 .15
❑ 81 Charlie Hayes .15 .04
❑ 82 Ray Lankford .15 .04
❑ 83 Tim Davis .15 .04
❑ 84 C.J. Nitkowski .15 .04
❑ 85 Andy Ashby .15 .04
❑ 86 Gerald Williams .15 .04
❑ 87 Terry Shumpert .15 .04
❑ 88 Heathcliff Slocumb .15 .04
❑ 89 Domingo Cedeno .15 .04
❑ 90 Mark Grace .50 .15
❑ 91 Brad Woodall RC .15 .04
❑ 92 Gar Finnvold .15 .04
❑ 93 Jaime Navarro .15 .04
❑ 94 Carlos Hernandez .15 .04
❑ 95 Mark Langston .15 .04
❑ 96 Chuck Carr .15 .04
❑ 97 Mike Gardiner .15 .04
❑ 98 Dave McCarty .15 .04
❑ 99 Cris Carpenter .15 .04
❑ 100 Barry Bonds 2.00 .60
❑ 101 David Segui .15 .04
❑ 102 Scott Brosius .30 .09
❑ 103 Mariano Duncan .15 .04
❑ 104 Kenny Lofton .30 .09
❑ 105 Ken Caminiti .30 .09
❑ 106 Darrin Jackson .15 .04
❑ 107 Jim Poole .15 .04
❑ 108 Wil Cordero .15 .04
❑ 109 Danny Miceli .15 .04
❑ 110 Walt Weiss .15 .04
❑ 111 Tom Pagnozzi .15 .04
❑ 112 Terrence Long .30 .09
❑ 113 Bret Boone .30 .09
❑ 114 Daryl Boston .15 .04
❑ 115 Wally Joyner .30 .09
❑ 116 Rob Butler .15 .04
❑ 117 Rafael Belliard .15 .04
❑ 118 Luis Lopez .15 .04
❑ 119 Tony Fossas .15 .04
❑ 120 Len Dykstra .30 .09
❑ 121 Mike Morgan .15 .04
❑ 122 Denny Hocking .15 .04
❑ 123 Kevin Gross .15 .04
❑ 124 Todd Benzinger .15 .04
❑ 125 John Doherty .15 .04
❑ 126 Eduardo Perez .15 .04
❑ 127 Dan Smith .15 .04
❑ 128 Joe Orsulak .15 .04
❑ 129 Brent Gates .15 .04
❑ 130 Jeff Conine .30 .09
❑ 131 Doug Henry .15 .04
❑ 132 Paul Sorrento .15 .04
❑ 133 Mike Hampton .30 .09
❑ 134 Tim Spehr .15 .04
❑ 135 Julio Franco .30 .09
❑ 136 Mike Dyer .15 .04
❑ 137 Chris Sabo .15 .04
❑ 138 Rheal Cormier .15 .04
❑ 139 Paul Konerko .30 .09
❑ 140 Dante Bichette .30 .09
❑ 141 Chuck McElroy .15 .04
❑ 142 Mike Stanley .15 .04
❑ 143 Bob Hamelin .15 .04
❑ 144 Tommy Greene .15 .04
❑ 145 John Smoltz .50 .15
❑ 146 Ed Sprague .15 .04
❑ 147 Ray McDavid .15 .04
❑ 148 Otis Nixon .15 .04
❑ 149 Turk Wendell .15 .04
❑ 150 Chris James .15 .04
❑ 151 Derek Parks .15 .04
❑ 152 Jose Offerman .15 .04
❑ 153 Tony Clark .15 .04
❑ 154 Chad Curtis .15 .04
❑ 155 Mark Portugal .15 .04
❑ 156 Bill Pulsipher .15 .04
❑ 157 Troy Neel .15 .04
❑ 158 Dave Winfield .30 .09
❑ 159 Bill Wegman .15 .04
❑ 160 Benito Santiago .30 .09
❑ 161 Jose Mesa .15 .04
❑ 162 Luis Gonzalez .30 .09
❑ 163 Alex Fernandez .15 .04
❑ 164 Freddie Benavides .15 .04
❑ 165 Ben McDonald .15 .04
❑ 166 Blas Minor .15 .04
❑ 167 Bret Wagner .15 .04
❑ 168 Mac Suzuki .15 .04
❑ 169 Roberto Mejia .15 .04
❑ 170 Wade Boggs .50 .15
❑ 171 Pokey Reese .15 .04
❑ 172 Hipolito Pichardo .15 .04
❑ 173 Kim Batiste .15 .04
❑ 174 Darren Hall .15 .04
❑ 175 Tom Glavine .50 .15
❑ 176 Phil Plantier .15 .04
❑ 177 Chris Howard .15 .04

❑ 178	Karl Rhodes	.15	.04
❑ 179	LaTroy Hawkins	.15	.04
❑ 180	Raul Mondesi	.30	.09
❑ 181	Jeff Reed	.15	.04
❑ 182	Milt Cuyler	.15	.04
❑ 183	Jim Edmonds	.50	.15
❑ 184	Hector Fajardo	.15	.04
❑ 185	Jeff Kent	.30	.09
❑ 186	Wilson Alvarez	.15	.04
❑ 187	Geronimo Berroa	.15	.04
❑ 188	Billy Spiers	.15	.04
❑ 189	Derek Lilliquist	.15	.04
❑ 190	Craig Biggio	.50	.15
❑ 191	Roberto Hernandez	.15	.04
❑ 192	Bob Natal	.15	.04
❑ 193	Bobby Ayala	.15	.04
❑ 194	Travis Miller RC	.15	.04
❑ 195	Bob Tewksbury	.15	.04
❑ 196	Rondell White	.30	.09
❑ 197	Steve Cooke	.15	.04
❑ 198	Jeff Branson	.15	.04
❑ 199	Derek Jeter	2.00	.60
❑ 200	Tim Salmon	.50	.15
❑ 201	Steve Frey	.15	.04
❑ 202	Kent Mercker	.15	.04
❑ 203	Randy Johnson	.75	.23
❑ 204	Todd Worrell	.15	.04
❑ 205	Mo Vaughn	.30	.09
❑ 206	Howard Johnson	.15	.04
❑ 207	John Wasdin	.15	.04
❑ 208	Eddie Williams	.15	.04
❑ 209	Tim Belcher	.15	.04
❑ 210	Jeff Montgomery	.15	.04
❑ 211	Kirt Manwaring	.15	.04
❑ 212	Ben Grieve	.30	.09
❑ 213	Pat Hentgen	.15	.04
❑ 214	Shawon Dunston	.15	.04
❑ 215	Mike Greenwell	.15	.04
❑ 216	Alex Diaz	.15	.04
❑ 217	Pat Mahomes	.15	.04
❑ 218	Dave Hansen	.15	.04
❑ 219	Kevin Rogers	.15	.04
❑ 220	Cecil Fielder	.30	.09
❑ 221	Andrew Lorraine	.15	.04
❑ 222	Jack Armstrong	.15	.04
❑ 223	Todd Hundley	.15	.04
❑ 224	Mark Acre	.15	.04
❑ 225	Darrell Whitmore	.15	.04
❑ 226	Randy Milligan	.15	.04
❑ 227	Wayne Kirby	.15	.04
❑ 228	Darryl Kile	.30	.09
❑ 229	Bob Zupcic	.15	.04
❑ 230	Jay Bell	.30	.09
❑ 231	Dustin Hermanson	.15	.04
❑ 232	Harold Baines	.30	.09
❑ 233	Alan Benes	.15	.04
❑ 234	Felix Fermin	.15	.04
❑ 235	Ellis Burks	.30	.09
❑ 236	Jeff Brantley	.15	.04
❑ 237	Brian Hunter	.40	.12
	Jose Malave		
	Karim Garcia RC		
	Shane Pullen		
❑ 238	Matt Nokes	.15	.04
❑ 239	Ben Rivera	.15	.04
❑ 240	Joe Carter	.30	.09
❑ 241	Jeff Granger	.15	.04
❑ 242	Terry Pendleton	.30	.09
❑ 243	Melvin Nieves	.15	.04
❑ 244	Frankie Rodriguez	.15	.04
❑ 245	Darryl Hamilton	.15	.04
❑ 246	Brooks Kieschnick	.15	.04
❑ 247	Todd Hollandsworth	.15	.04
❑ 248	Joe Rosselli	.15	.04
❑ 249	Bill Gullickson	.15	.04
❑ 250	Chuck Knoblauch	.30	.09
❑ 251	Kurt Miller	.15	.04
❑ 252	Bobby Jones	.15	.04
❑ 253	Lance Blankenship	.15	.04
❑ 254	Matt Whiteside	.15	.04
❑ 255	Darrin Fletcher	.15	.04
❑ 256	Eric Plunk	.15	.04
❑ 257	Shane Reynolds	.15	.04
❑ 258	Norberto Martin	.15	.04
❑ 259	Mike Thurman	.15	.04
❑ 260	Andy Van Slyke	.30	.09
❑ 261	Dwight Smith	.15	.04
❑ 262	Allen Watson	.15	.04
❑ 263	Dan Wilson	.15	.04
❑ 264	Brent Mayne	.15	.04
❑ 265	Bip Roberts	.15	.04
❑ 266	Sterling Hitchcock	.15	.04
❑ 267	Alex Gonzalez	.15	.04
❑ 268	Greg Harris	.15	.04
❑ 269	Ricky Jordan	.15	.04
❑ 270	Johnny Ruffin	.15	.04
❑ 271	Mike Stanton	.15	.04
❑ 272	Rich Rowland	.15	.04
❑ 273	Steve Trachsel	.15	.04
❑ 274	Pedro Munoz	.15	.04
❑ 275	Ramon Martinez	.15	.04
❑ 276	Dave Henderson	.15	.04
❑ 277	Chris Gomez	.15	.04
❑ 278	Joe Grahe	.15	.04
❑ 279	Rusty Greer	.30	.09
❑ 280	John Franco	.30	.09
❑ 281	Mike Bordick	.15	.04
❑ 282	Jeff D'Amico	.15	.04
❑ 283	Dave Magadan	.15	.04
❑ 284	Tony Pena	.15	.04
❑ 285	Greg Swindell	.15	.04
❑ 286	Doug Million	.15	.04
❑ 287	Gabe White	.15	.04
❑ 288	Trey Beamon	.15	.04
❑ 289	Arthur Rhodes	.15	.04
❑ 290	Juan Guzman	.15	.04
❑ 291	Jose Oquendo	.15	.04
❑ 292	Willie Blair	.15	.04
❑ 293	Eddie Taubensee	.15	.04
❑ 294	Steve Howe	.15	.04
❑ 295	Greg Maddux	1.25	.35
❑ 296	Mike Macfarlane	.15	.04
❑ 297	Curt Schilling	.30	.09
❑ 298	Phil Clark	.15	.04
❑ 299	Woody Williams	.15	.04
❑ 300	Jose Canseco	.75	.23
❑ 301	Aaron Sele	.15	.04
❑ 302	Carl Willis	.15	.04
❑ 303	Steve Buechele	.15	.04
❑ 304	Dave Burba	.15	.04
❑ 305	Orel Hershiser	.30	.09
❑ 306	Damion Easley	.15	.04
❑ 307	Mike Henneman	.15	.04
❑ 308	Josias Manzanillo	.15	.04
❑ 309	Kevin Seitzer	.15	.04
❑ 310	Ruben Sierra	.15	.04
❑ 311	Bryan Harvey	.15	.04
❑ 312	Jim Thome	.75	.23
❑ 313	Ramon Castro RC	.40	.12
❑ 314	Lance Johnson	.15	.04
❑ 315	Marquis Grissom	.30	.09
❑ 316	Terrell Wade	.15	.04
	Juan Acevedo		
	Matt Arrandale		
	Eddie Priest RC		
❑ 317	Paul Wagner	.15	.04
❑ 318	Jamie Moyer	.30	.09
❑ 319	Todd Zeile	.15	.04
❑ 320	Chris Bosio	.15	.04
❑ 321	Steve Reed	.15	.04
❑ 322	Erik Hanson	.15	.04
❑ 323	Luis Polonia	.15	.04
❑ 324	Ryan Klesko	.30	.09
❑ 325	Kevin Appier	.30	.09
❑ 326	Jim Eisenreich	.15	.04
❑ 327	Randy Knorr	.15	.04
❑ 328	Craig Shipley	.15	.04
❑ 329	Tim Naehring	.15	.04
❑ 330	Randy Myers	.15	.04
❑ 331	Alex Cole	.15	.04
❑ 332	Jim Gott	.15	.04
❑ 333	Mike Jackson	.15	.04
❑ 334	John Flaherty	.15	.04
❑ 335	Chili Davis	.30	.09
❑ 336	Benji Gil	.15	.04
❑ 337	Jason Jacome	.15	.04
❑ 338	Stan Javier	.15	.04
❑ 339	Mike Fetters	.15	.04
❑ 340	Rich Renteria	.15	.04
❑ 341	Kevin Witt	.15	.04
❑ 342	Scott Servais	.15	.04
❑ 343	Craig Grebeck	.15	.04
❑ 344	Kirk Rueter	.15	.04
❑ 345	Don Slaught	.15	.04
❑ 346	Armando Benitez	.30	.09
❑ 347	Ozzie Smith	1.25	.35
❑ 348	Mike Blowers	.15	.04
❑ 349	Armando Reynoso	.15	.04
❑ 350	Barry Larkin	.50	.15
❑ 351	Mike Williams	.15	.04
❑ 352	Scott Kamieniecki	.15	.04
❑ 353	Gary Gaetti	.30	.09
❑ 354	Todd Stottlemyre	.15	.04
❑ 355	Fred McGriff	.50	.15
❑ 356	Tim Mauser	.15	.04
❑ 357	Chris Gwynn	.15	.04
❑ 358	Frank Castillo	.15	.04
❑ 359	Jeff Reboulet	.15	.04
❑ 360	Roger Clemens	1.50	.45
❑ 361	Mark Carreon	.15	.04
❑ 362	Chad Kreuter	.15	.04
❑ 363	Mark Farris	.15	.04
❑ 364	Bob Welch	.15	.04
❑ 365	Dean Palmer	.30	.09
❑ 366	Jeromy Burnitz	.30	.09
❑ 367	B.J. Surhoff	.30	.09
❑ 368	Mike Butcher	.15	.04
❑ 369	Brad Clontz	.15	.04
	Steve Phoenix		
	Scott Gentile		
	Bucky Buckles RC		
❑ 370	Eddie Murray	.75	.23
❑ 371	Orlando Miller	.15	.04
❑ 372	Ron Karkovice	.15	.04
❑ 373	Richie Lewis	.15	.04
❑ 374	Lenny Webster	.15	.04
❑ 375	Jeff Tackett	.15	.04
❑ 376	Tom Urbani	.15	.04
❑ 377	Tino Martinez	.50	.15
❑ 378	Mark Dewey	.15	.04
❑ 379	Charles O'Brien	.15	.04
❑ 380	Terry Mulholland	.15	.04
❑ 381	Thomas Howard	.15	.04
❑ 382	Chris Haney	.15	.04
❑ 383	Billy Hatcher	.15	.04
❑ 384	Jeff Bagwell AS	.50	.15
	Frank Thomas AS		
❑ 385	Bret Boone AS	.30	.09
	Carlos Baerga AS		
❑ 386	Matt Williams AS	.30	.09
	Wade Boggs AS		
❑ 387	Wil Cordero AS	.75	.23
	Cal Ripken AS		
❑ 388	Barry Bonds AS	1.00	.30
	Ken Griffey AS		
❑ 389	Tony Gwynn AS	.30	.09
	Albert Belle AS		
❑ 390	Dante Bichette AS	.50	.15
	Kirby Puckett AS		
❑ 391	Mike Piazza AS	.75	.23
	Mike Stanley AS		
❑ 392	Greg Maddux AS	.75	.23
	David Cone AS		
❑ 393	Danny Jackson AS	.15	.04
	Jimmy Key AS		
❑ 394	John Franco AS	.15	.04
	Lee Smith AS		
❑ 395	Checklist 1-198	.15	.04
❑ 396	Checklist 199-396	.15	.04
❑ 397	Ken Griffey Jr.	1.25	.35
❑ 398	Rick Heiserman RC	.15	.04
❑ 399	Don Mattingly	2.00	.60
❑ 400	Henry Rodriguez	.15	.04
❑ 401	Lenny Harris	.15	.04
❑ 402	Ryan Thompson	.15	.04
❑ 403	Darren Oliver	.15	.04
❑ 404	Omar Vizquel	.50	.15
❑ 405	Jeff Bagwell	.50	.15
❑ 406	Doug Webb RC	.15	.04
❑ 407	Todd Van Poppel	.15	.04
❑ 408	Leo Gomez	.15	.04
❑ 409	Mark Whiten	.15	.04
❑ 410	Pedro A.Martinez	.15	.04
❑ 411	Reggie Sanders	.15	.04
❑ 412	Kevin Foster	.15	.04
❑ 413	Danny Tartabull	.15	.04
❑ 414	Jeff Blauser	.15	.04
❑ 415	Mike Magnante	.15	.04

❑ 416 Tom Candiotti .15 .04
❑ 417 Rod Beck .15 .04
❑ 418 Jody Reed .15 .04
❑ 419 Vince Coleman .15 .04
❑ 420 Danny Jackson .15 .04
❑ 421 Ryan Nye RC .15 .04
❑ 422 Larry Walker .50 .15
❑ 423 Russ Johnson DP .15 .04
❑ 424 Pat Borders .15 .04
❑ 425 Lee Smith .30 .09
❑ 426 Paul O'Neill .50 .15
❑ 427 Devon White .30 .09
❑ 428 Jim Bullinger .15 .04
❑ 429 Greg Hansell .15 .04
Brian Sackinsky
Carey Paige
Rob Welch RC
❑ 430 Steve Avery .15 .04
❑ 431 Tony Gwynn 1.00 .30
❑ 432 Pat Meares .15 .04
❑ 433 Bill Swift .15 .04
❑ 434 David Wells .30 .09
❑ 435 John Briscoe .15 .04
❑ 436 Roger Pavlik .15 .04
❑ 437 Jayson Peterson RC .15 .04
❑ 438 Roberto Alomar .50 .15
❑ 439 Billy Brewer .15 .04
❑ 440 Gary Sheffield .30 .09
❑ 441 Lou Frazier .15 .04
❑ 442 Terry Steinbach .15 .04
❑ 443 Jay Payton RC .75 .23
❑ 444 Jason Bere .15 .04
❑ 445 Denny Neagle .30 .09
❑ 446 Andres Galarraga .30 .09
❑ 447 Hector Carrasco .15 .04
❑ 448 Bill Risley .15 .04
❑ 449 Andy Benes .15 .04
❑ 450 Jim Leyritz .15 .04
❑ 451 Jose Oliva .15 .04
❑ 452 Greg Vaughn .15 .04
❑ 453 Rich Monteleone .15 .04
❑ 454 Tony Eusebio .15 .04
❑ 455 Chuck Finley .30 .09
❑ 456 Kevin Brown .30 .09
❑ 457 Joe Boever .15 .04
❑ 458 Bobby Munoz .15 .04
❑ 459 Bret Saberhagen .30 .09
❑ 460 Kurt Abbott .15 .04
❑ 461 Bobby Witt .15 .04
❑ 462 Cliff Floyd .30 .09
❑ 463 Mark Clark .15 .04
❑ 464 Andujar Cedeno .15 .04
❑ 465 Marvin Freeman .15 .04
❑ 466 Mike Piazza 1.25 .35
❑ 467 Willie Greene .15 .04
❑ 468 Pat Kelly .15 .04
❑ 469 Carlos Delgado .30 .09
❑ 470 Willie Banks .15 .04
❑ 471 Matt Walbeck .15 .04
❑ 472 Mark McGwire 2.00 .60
❑ 473 M.Christensen RC .15 .04
❑ 474 Alan Trammell .30 .09
❑ 475 Tom Gordon .15 .04
❑ 476 Greg Colbrunn .15 .04
❑ 477 Darren Daulton .30 .09
❑ 478 Albie Lopez .15 .04
❑ 479 Robin Ventura .30 .09
❑ 480 Eddie Perez RC .40 .12
Jason Kendall
Einar Diaz
Bret Hemphill
❑ 481 Bryan Eversgerd .15 .04
❑ 482 Dave Fleming .15 .04
❑ 483 Scott Livingstone .15 .04
❑ 484 Pete Schourek .15 .04
❑ 485 Bernie Williams .50 .15
❑ 486 Mark Lemke .15 .04
❑ 487 Eric Karros .30 .09
❑ 488 Scott Ruffcorn .15 .04
❑ 489 Billy Ashley .15 .04
❑ 490 Rico Brogna .15 .04
❑ 491 John Burkett .15 .04
❑ 492 Cade Gaspar RC .15 .04
❑ 493 Jorge Fabregas .15 .04
❑ 494 Greg Gagne .15 .04
❑ 495 Doug Jones .15 .04
❑ 496 Troy O'Leary .15 .04
❑ 497 Pat Rapp .15 .04
❑ 498 Butch Henry .15 .04
❑ 499 John Olerud .30 .09
❑ 500 John Hudek .15 .04
❑ 501 Jeff King .15 .04
❑ 502 Bobby Bonilla .30 .09
❑ 503 Albert Belle .30 .09
❑ 504 Rick Wilkins .15 .04
❑ 505 John Jaha .15 .04
❑ 506 Nigel Wilson .15 .04
❑ 507 Sid Fernandez .15 .04
❑ 508 Deion Sanders .50 .15
❑ 509 Gil Heredia .15 .04
❑ 510 Scott Elarton RC .40 .12
❑ 511 Melido Perez .15 .04
❑ 512 Greg McMichael .15 .04
❑ 513 Rusty Meacham .15 .04
❑ 514 Shawn Green .30 .09
❑ 515 Carlos Garcia .15 .04
❑ 516 Dave Stevens .15 .04
❑ 517 Eric Young .15 .04
❑ 518 Omar Daal .15 .04
❑ 519 Kirk Gibson .30 .09
❑ 520 Spike Owen .15 .04
❑ 521 Jacob Cruz RC .30 .09
❑ 522 Sandy Alomar Jr. .15 .04
❑ 523 Steve Bedrosian .15 .04
❑ 524 Ricky Gutierrez .15 .04
❑ 525 Dave Veres .15 .04
❑ 526 Gregg Jefferies .15 .04
❑ 527 Jose Valentin .15 .04
❑ 528 Robb Nen .30 .09
❑ 529 Jose Rijo .15 .04
❑ 530 Sean Berry .15 .04
❑ 531 Mike Gallego .15 .04
❑ 532 Roberto Kelly .15 .04
❑ 533 Kevin Stocker .15 .04
❑ 534 Kirby Puckett .75 .23
❑ 535 Chipper Jones .75 .23
❑ 536 Russ Davis .15 .04
❑ 537 Jon Lieber .15 .04
❑ 538 Trey Moore RC .15 .04
❑ 539 Joe Girardi .15 .04
❑ 540 Quilvio Veras .40 .12
Arquimedez Pozo
Miguel Cairo RC
Jason Camilli
❑ 541 Tony Phillips .15 .04
❑ 542 Brian Anderson .15 .04
❑ 543 Ivan Rodriguez .75 .23
❑ 544 Jeff Cirillo .15 .04
❑ 545 Joey Cora .15 .04
❑ 546 Chris Hoiles .15 .04
❑ 547 Bernard Gilkey .15 .04
❑ 548 Mike Lansing .15 .04
❑ 549 Jimmy Key .30 .09
❑ 550 Mark Wohlers .15 .04
❑ 551 Chris Clemons RC .15 .04
❑ 552 Vinny Castilla .30 .09
❑ 553 Mark Guthrie .15 .04
❑ 554 Mike Lieberthal .30 .09
❑ 555 Tommy Davis RC .15 .04
❑ 556 Robby Thompson .15 .04
❑ 557 Danny Bautista .15 .04
❑ 558 Will Clark .75 .23
❑ 559 Rickey Henderson .75 .23
❑ 560 Todd Jones .15 .04
❑ 561 Jack McDowell .15 .04
❑ 562 Carlos Rodriguez .15 .04
❑ 563 Mark Eichhorn .15 .04
❑ 564 Jeff Nelson .15 .04
❑ 565 Eric Anthony .15 .04
❑ 566 Randy Velarde .15 .04
❑ 567 Javier Lopez .30 .09
❑ 568 Kevin Mitchell .15 .04
❑ 569 Steve Karsay .15 .04
❑ 570 Brian Meadows RC .15 .04
❑ 571 Rey Ordonez RC .75 .23
Mike Metcalfe
Kevin Orie
Ray Holbert
❑ 572 John Kruk .30 .09
❑ 573 Scott Leius .15 .04
❑ 574 John Patterson .15 .04
❑ 575 Kevin Brown .30 .09
❑ 576 Mike Moore .15 .04
❑ 577 Manny Ramirez .50 .15
❑ 578 Jose Lind .15 .04
❑ 579 Derrick May .15 .04
❑ 580 Cal Eldred .15 .04
❑ 581 David Bell .75 .23
Joel Chelmis
Lino Diaz
Aaron Boone RC
❑ 582 J.T. Snow .30 .09
❑ 583 Luis Sojo .15 .04
❑ 584 Moises Alou .30 .09
❑ 585 Dave Clark .15 .04
❑ 586 Dave Hollins .15 .04
❑ 587 Nomar Garciaparra 2.00 .60
❑ 588 Cal Ripken 2.50 .75
❑ 589 Pedro Astacio .15 .04
❑ 590 J.R. Phillips .15 .04
❑ 591 Jeff Frye .15 .04
❑ 592 Bo Jackson .75 .23
❑ 593 Steve Ontiveros .15 .04
❑ 594 David Nied .15 .04
❑ 595 Brad Ausmus .15 .04
❑ 596 Carlos Baerga .15 .04
❑ 597 James Mouton .15 .04
❑ 598 Ozzie Guillen .15 .04
❑ 599 Ozzie Timmons .75 .23
Curtis Goodwin
Johnny Damon
Jeff Abbott RC
❑ 600 Yorkis Perez .15 .04
❑ 601 Rich Rodriguez .15 .04
❑ 602 Mark McLemore .15 .04
❑ 603 Jeff Fassero .15 .04
❑ 604 John Roper .15 .04
❑ 605 Mark Johnson RC .40 .12
❑ 606 Wes Chamberlain .15 .04
❑ 607 Felix Jose .15 .04
❑ 608 Tony Longmire .15 .04
❑ 609 Duane Ward .15 .04
❑ 610 Brett Butler .30 .09
❑ 611 W.VanLandingham .15 .04
❑ 612 Mickey Tettleton .15 .04
❑ 613 Brady Anderson .30 .09
❑ 614 Reggie Jefferson .15 .04
❑ 615 Mike Kingery .15 .04
❑ 616 Derek Bell .15 .04
❑ 617 Scott Erickson .15 .04
❑ 618 Bob Wickman .15 .04
❑ 619 Phil Leftwich .15 .04
❑ 620 David Justice .30 .09
❑ 621 Paul Wilson .15 .04
❑ 622 Pedro Martinez .75 .23
❑ 623 Terry Mathews .15 .04
❑ 624 Brian McRae .15 .04
❑ 625 Bruce Ruffin .15 .04
❑ 626 Steve Finley .30 .09
❑ 627 Ron Gant .30 .09
❑ 628 Rafael Bournigal .15 .04
❑ 629 Darryl Strawberry .30 .09
❑ 630 Luis Alicea .15 .04
❑ 631 Mark Smith .15 .04
Scott Klingenbeck
❑ 632 Cory Bailey .15 .04
Scott Hatteberg
❑ 633 Todd Greene .30 .09
Troy Percival
❑ 634 Rod Bolton .15 .04
Olmedo Saenz
❑ 635 Steve Kline .15 .04
Herb Perry
❑ 636 Sean Bergman .15 .04
Shannon Penn
❑ 637 Joe Randa .15 .04
Joe Vitiello
❑ 638 Jose Mercedes .15 .04
Duane Singleton
❑ 639 Marc Barcelo .15 .04
Marty Cordova
❑ 640 Andy Pettitte .30 .09
Ruben Rivera
❑ 641 Willie Adams .15 .04
Scott Spiezio
❑ 642 Eddy Diaz RC .15 .04
Desi Relaford
❑ 643 Terrell Lowery .15 .04

Jon Shave
❑ 644 Angel Martinez .... .15 .04
Paul Spoljaric
❑ 645 Tony Graffanino............... .15 .04
Damon Hollins
❑ 646 Darron Cox .... .15 .04
Doug Glanville
❑ 647 Tim Belk .... .15 .04
Pat Watkins
❑ 648 Rod Pedraza .... .15 .04
Phil Schneider
❑ 649 Vic Darensbourg .... .15 .04
Marc Valdes
❑ 650 Rick Huisman .... .15 .04
Roberto Petagine
❑ 651 Roger Cedeno .... .40 .12
Ron Coomer RC
❑ 652 Shane Andrews .... .40 .12
Carlos Perez RC
❑ 653 Jason Isringhausen .... .30 .09
Chris Roberts
❑ 654 Wayne Gomes .... .15 .04
Kevin Jordan
❑ 655 Esteban Loiaza .... .15 .04
Steve Pegues
❑ 656 Terry Bradshaw .... .15 .04
John Frascatore
❑ 657 Andres Berumen .... .15 .04
Bryce Florie
❑ 658 Dan Carlson .... .15 .04
Keith Williams
❑ 659 Checklist .... .15 .04
❑ 660 Checklist .... .15 .04

1995 Topps Traded

	Nm-Mt	Ex-Mt
COMPLETE SET (165)	60.00	18.00

❑ 1T Frank Thomas ATB .... .60 .18
❑ 2T Ken Griffey Jr. ATB .... 1.00 .30
❑ 3T Barry Bonds ATB............. 1.25 .35
❑ 4T Albert Belle ATB .... .40 .12
❑ 5T Cal Ripken ATB .... 1.50 .45
❑ 6T Mike Piazza ATB .... 1.00 .30
❑ 7T Tony Gwynn ATB............... .60 .18
❑ 8T Jeff Bagwell ATB .... .40 .12
❑ 9T Mo Vaughn ATB .... .20 .06
❑ 10T Matt Williams ATB .... .20 .06
❑ 11T Ray Durham .... .40 .12
❑ 12T Juan LeBron 10.00 3.00
Card pictures Carlos Beltran instead of Juan LeBron RC
❑ 13T Shawn Green................... .40 .12
❑ 14T Kevin Gross..................... .20 .06
❑ 15T Jon Nunnally.................... .20 .06
❑ 16T Brian Maxcy RC .... .25 .07
❑ 17T Mark Kiefer .... .20 .06
❑ 18T Carlos Beltran UER 30.00 9.00
Card pictures Juan LeBron instead of Carlos Beltran RC.
❑ 19T Mike Mimbs RC .... .25 .07
❑ 20T Larry Walker .... .60 .18
❑ 21T Chad Curtis...................... .20 .06
❑ 22T Jeff Barry.......................... .20 .06
❑ 23T Joe Oliver .... .20 .06
❑ 24T Tomas Perez RC .... .25 .07
❑ 25T Michael Barrett RC .... 1.00 .30
❑ 26T Brian McRae .... .20 .06
❑ 27T Derek Bell .... .20 .06
❑ 28T Ray Durham .... .40 .12
❑ 29T Todd Williams.................... .20 .06
❑ 30T Ryan Jaroncyk RC .... .25 .07
❑ 31T Todd Steverson .... .20 .06
❑ 32T Mike Devereaux................. .20 .06
❑ 33T Rheal Cormier .... .20 .06
❑ 34T Benny Santiago .... .40 .12
❑ 35T Bobby Higginson RC...... 1.00 .30
❑ 36T Jack McDowell .... .20 .06
❑ 37T Mike Macfarlane .... .20 .06
❑ 38T Tony McKnight RC .... .25 .07
❑ 39T Brian Hunter .... .20 .06
❑ 40T Hideo Nomo RC .... 3.00 .90
❑ 41T Brett Butler .... .40 .12
❑ 42T Donovan Osborne .... .20 .06
❑ 43T Scott Karl .... .20 .06
❑ 44T Tony Phillips .... .20 .06
❑ 45T Marty Cordova .... .20 .06
❑ 46T Dave Mlicki .... .20 .06
❑ 47T Bronson Arroyo RC 5.00 1.50
❑ 48T John Burkett .... .20 .06
❑ 49T J.D. Smart RC .... .25 .07
❑ 50T Mickey Tettleton .... .20 .06
❑ 51T Todd Stottlemyre.............. .20 .06
❑ 52T Mike Perez .... .20 .06
❑ 53T Terry Mulholland............... .20 .06
❑ 54T Edgardo Alfonzo .... .40 .12
❑ 55T Zane Smith .... .20 .06
❑ 56T Jacob Brumfield .... .20 .06
❑ 57T Andujar Cedeno .... .20 .06
❑ 58T Jose Parra .... .20 .06
❑ 59T Manny Alexander .... .20 .06
❑ 60T Tony Tarasco..................... .20 .06
❑ 61T Orel Hershiser .... .40 .12
❑ 62T Tim Scott........................... .20 .06
❑ 63T Felix Rodriguez RC .... .50 .15
❑ 64T Ken Hill .... .20 .06
❑ 65T Marquis Grissom .... .40 .12
❑ 66T Lee Smith .... .40 .12
❑ 67T Jason Bates .... .20 .06
❑ 68T Felipe Lira .... .20 .06
❑ 69T Alex Hernandez RC .... .25 .07
❑ 70T Tony Fernandez .... .20 .06
❑ 71T Scott Radinsky .... .20 .06
❑ 72T Jose Canseco .... 1.00 .30
❑ 73T Mark Grudzielanek RC...... .50 .15
❑ 74T Ben Davis RC .... .50 .15
❑ 75T Jim Abbott.......................... .60 .18
❑ 76T Roger Bailey .... .20 .06
❑ 77T Gregg Jefferies .... .20 .06
❑ 78T Erik Hanson........................ .20 .06
❑ 79T Brad Radke RC .... 1.00 .30
❑ 80T Jaime Navarro .... .20 .06
❑ 81T John Wetteland .... .40 .12
❑ 82T Chad Fonville RC .... .25 .07
❑ 83T John Mabry....................... .20 .06
❑ 84T Glenallen Hill .... .20 .06
❑ 85T Ken Caminiti .... .40 .12
❑ 86T Tom Goodwin .... .20 .06
❑ 87T Darren Bragg..................... .20 .06
❑ 88T Pat Ahearne .... .25 .07
Gary Rath
Larry Wimberly
Robbie Bell RC
❑ 89T Jeff Russell .... .20 .06
❑ 90T Dave Gallagher .... .20 .06
❑ 91T Steve Finley...................... .40 .12
❑ 92T Vaughn Eshelman .... .20 .06
❑ 93T Kevin Jarvis....................... .20 .06
❑ 94T Mark Gubicza .... .20 .06
❑ 95T Tim Wakefield .... .40 .12
❑ 96T Bob Tewksbury .... .20 .06
❑ 97T Sid Roberson RC .... .25 .07
❑ 98T Tom Henke .... .20 .06
❑ 99T Michael Tucker .... .20 .06
❑ 100T Jason Bates..................... .20 .06
❑ 101T Otis Nixon .... .20 .06
❑ 102T Mark Whiten .... .20 .06
❑ 103T Dilson Torres RC.............. .25 .07
❑ 104T Melvin Bunch RC .... .25 .07
❑ 105T Terry Pendleton............... .40 .12
❑ 106T Corey Jenkins RC .... .25 .07
❑ 107T Glenn Dishman RC .... .25 .07
Rob Grable
❑ 108T Reggie Taylor RC .... .50 .15
❑ 109T Curtis Goodwin .... .20 .06
❑ 110T David Cone .... .40 .12
❑ 111T Antonio Osuna .... .20 .06
❑ 112T Paul Shuey .... .20 .06
❑ 113T Doug Jones...................... .20 .06
❑ 114T Mark McLemore .... .20 .06
❑ 115T Kevin Ritz .... .20 .06
❑ 116T John Kruk .... .40 .12
❑ 117T Trevor Wilson .... .20 .06
❑ 118T Jerald Clark...................... .20 .06
❑ 119T Julian Tavarez .... .20 .06
❑ 120T Tim Pugh .... .20 .06
❑ 121T Todd Zeile .... .20 .06
❑ 122T Mark Sweeney UER ...... 3.00 .90
George Arias
Richie Sexson RC
Brian Schneider
❑ 123T Bobby Witt .... .20 .06
❑ 124T Hideo Nomo .... 1.00 .30
❑ 125T Joey Cora .... .20 .06
❑ 126T Jim Scharrer RC .... .25 .07
❑ 127T Paul Quantrill .... .20 .06
❑ 128T Chipper Jones ROY......... .60 .18
❑ 129T Kenny James RC .... .25 .07
❑ 130T Lyle Mouton .... .60 .18
Mariano Rivera
❑ 131T Tyler Green .... .20 .06
❑ 132T Brad Clontz .... .20 .06
❑ 133T Jon Nunnally.................... .20 .06
❑ 134T Dave Magadan .... .20 .06
❑ 135T Al Leiter............................ .40 .12
❑ 136T Bret Barberie .... .20 .06
❑ 137T Bill Swift .... .20 .06
❑ 138T Scott Cooper .... .20 .06
❑ 139T Roberto Kelly................... .20 .06
❑ 140T Charlie Hayes.................. .20 .06
❑ 141T Pete Harnisch .... .20 .06
❑ 142T Rich Amaral...................... .20 .06
❑ 143T Rudy Seanez .... .20 .06
❑ 144T Pat Listach .... .20 .06
❑ 145T Quilvio Veras.................... .20 .06
❑ 146T Jose Olmeda RC .... .25 .07
❑ 147T Roberto Petagine............. .20 .06
❑ 148T Kevin Brown .... .40 .12
❑ 149T Phil Plantier .... .20 .06
❑ 150T Carlos Perez .... .40 .12
❑ 151T Pat Borders .... .20 .06
❑ 152T Tyler Green .... .20 .06
❑ 153T Stan Belinda .... .20 .06
❑ 154T Dave Stewart .... .40 .12
❑ 155T Andre Dawson.................. .40 .12
❑ 156T Frank Thomas AS .... .60 .18
Fred McGriff UER
(McGriff's team shown as Blue Jays)
❑ 157T Carlos Baerga AS .... .40 .12
Craig Biggio
❑ 158T Wade Boggs AS .... .40 .12
Matt Williams
❑ 159T Cal Ripken AS............... 1.00 .30
Ozzie Smith
❑ 160T Ken Griffey Jr. AS .... 1.00 .30
Tony Gwynn
❑ 161T Albert Belle AS .... 1.25 .35
Barry Bonds
❑ 162T Kirby Puckett.................. .60 .18
Len Dykstra
❑ 163T Ivan Rodriguez AS....... 1.00 .30
Mike Piazza
❑ 164T Randy Johnson AS ...... 1.25 .35
Hideo Nomo
❑ 165T Checklist.......................... .20 .06

1996 Topps

	Nm-Mt	Ex-Mt
COMPLETE SET (440)	40.00	12.00
COMP.HOBBY SET (449)	40.00	12.00
COMP.CEREAL SET (444)	60.00	18.00
COMP.SERIES 1 (220)	20.00	6.00
COMP.SERIES 2 (220)	20.00	6.00
COMMON CARD (1-440)	.20	.06
COMMON RC	.25	.07

Card	Nm-Mt	Ex-Mt
❑ 1 Tony Gwynn STP	.30	.09
❑ 2 Mike Piazza STP	.50	.15
❑ 3 Greg Maddux STP	.50	.15
❑ 4 Jeff Bagwell STP	.20	.06
❑ 5 Larry Walker STP	.20	.06
❑ 6 Barry Larkin STP	.20	.06
❑ 7 Mickey Mantle	4.00	1.20
❑ 8 Tom Glavine STP UER	.20	.06
Won 21 games in June 95		
❑ 9 Craig Biggio STP	.20	.06
❑ 10 Barry Bonds STP	.50	.15
❑ 11 H.Slocumb STP	.20	.06
❑ 12 Matt Williams STP	.20	.06
❑ 13 Todd Helton	1.00	.30
❑ 14 Mark Redman	.25	.07
❑ 15 Michael Barrett	.25	.07
❑ 16 Ben Davis	.25	.07
❑ 17 Juan LeBron	.25	.07
❑ 18 Tony McKnight	.25	.07
❑ 19 Ryan Jaroncyk	.25	.07
❑ 20 Corey Jenkins	.25	.07
❑ 21 Jim Scharrer	.25	.07
❑ 22 Mark Bellhorn RC	3.00	.90
❑ 23 Jarrod Washburn RC	.60	.18
❑ 24 Geoff Jenkins RC	1.00	.30
❑ 25 Sean Casey RC	4.00	1.20
❑ 26 Brett Tomko RC	.40	.12
❑ 27 Tony Fernandez	.20	.06
❑ 28 Rich Becker	.20	.06
❑ 29 Andujar Cedeno	.20	.06
❑ 30 Paul Molitor	.30	.09
❑ 31 Brent Gates	.20	.06
❑ 32 Glenallen Hill	.20	.06
❑ 33 Mike Macfarlane	.20	.06
❑ 34 Manny Alexander	.20	.06
❑ 35 Todd Zeile	.20	.06
❑ 36 Joe Girardi	.20	.06
❑ 37 Tony Tarasco	.20	.06
❑ 38 Tim Belcher	.20	.06
❑ 39 Tom Goodwin	.20	.06
❑ 40 Orel Hershiser	.20	.06
❑ 41 Tripp Cromer	.20	.06
❑ 42 Sean Bergman	.20	.06
❑ 43 Troy Percival	.20	.06
❑ 44 Kevin Stocker	.20	.06
❑ 45 Albert Belle	.20	.06
❑ 46 Tony Eusebio	.20	.06
❑ 47 Sid Roberson	.20	.06
❑ 48 Todd Hollandsworth	.20	.06
❑ 49 Mark Wohlers	.20	.06
❑ 50 Kirby Puckett	.50	.15
❑ 51 Darren Holmes	.20	.06
❑ 52 Ron Karkovice	.20	.06
❑ 53 Al Martin	.20	.06
❑ 54 Pat Rapp	.20	.06
❑ 55 Mark Grace	.30	.09
❑ 56 Greg Gagne	.20	.06
❑ 57 Stan Javier	.20	.06
❑ 58 Scott Sanders	.20	.06
❑ 59 J.T. Snow	.20	.06
❑ 60 David Justice	.20	.06
❑ 61 Royce Clayton	.20	.06
❑ 62 Kevin Foster	.20	.06
❑ 63 Tim Naehring	.20	.06
❑ 64 Orlando Miller	.20	.06
❑ 65 Mike Mussina	.30	.09
❑ 66 Jim Eisenreich	.20	.06
❑ 67 Felix Fermin	.20	.06
❑ 68 Bernie Williams	.30	.09
❑ 69 Robb Nen	.20	.06
❑ 70 Ron Gant	.20	.06
❑ 71 Felipe Lira	.20	.06
❑ 72 Jacob Brumfield	.20	.06
❑ 73 John Mabry	.20	.06
❑ 74 Mark Carreon	.20	.06
❑ 75 Carlos Baerga	.20	.06
❑ 76 Jim Dougherty	.20	.06
❑ 77 Ryan Thompson	.20	.06
❑ 78 Scott Leius	.20	.06
❑ 79 Roger Pavlik	.20	.06
❑ 80 Gary Sheffield	.20	.06
❑ 81 Julian Tavarez	.20	.06
❑ 82 Andy Ashby	.20	.06
❑ 83 Mark Lemke	.20	.06
❑ 84 Omar Vizquel	.30	.09
❑ 85 Darren Daulton	.20	.06
❑ 86 Mike Lansing	.20	.06
❑ 87 Rusty Greer	.20	.06
❑ 88 Dave Stevens	.20	.06
❑ 89 Jose Offerman	.20	.06
❑ 90 Tom Henke	.20	.06
❑ 91 Troy O'Leary	.20	.06
❑ 92 Michael Tucker	.20	.06
❑ 93 Marvin Freeman	.20	.06
❑ 94 Alex Diaz	.20	.06
❑ 95 John Wetteland	.20	.06
❑ 96 Cal Ripken 2131	2.00	.60
❑ 97 Mike Mimbs	.20	.06
❑ 98 Bobby Higginson	.20	.06
❑ 99 Edgardo Alfonzo	.20	.06
❑ 100 Frank Thomas	.50	.15
❑ 101 Steve Gibralter	.20	.06
Bob Abreu		
❑ 102 Brian Givens	.25	.07
T.J. Mathews		
❑ 103 Chris Pritchett	.25	.07
Trenidad Hubbard		
❑ 104 Eric Owens	.25	.07
Butch Huskey		
❑ 105 Doug Drabek	.20	.06
❑ 106 Tomas Perez	.20	.06
❑ 107 Mark Leiter	.20	.06
❑ 108 Joe Oliver	.20	.06
❑ 109 Tony Castillo	.20	.06
❑ 110 Checklist (1-110)	.20	.06
❑ 111 Kevin Seitzer	.20	.06
❑ 112 Pete Schourek	.20	.06
❑ 113 Sean Berry	.20	.06
❑ 114 Todd Stottlemyre	.20	.06
❑ 115 Joe Carter	.20	.06
❑ 116 Jeff King	.20	.06
❑ 117 Dan Wilson	.20	.06
❑ 118 Kurt Abbott	.20	.06
❑ 119 Lyle Mouton	.20	.06
❑ 120 Jose Rijo	.20	.06
❑ 121 Curtis Goodwin	.20	.06
❑ 122 Jose Valentin	.20	.06
❑ 123 Ellis Burks	.20	.06
❑ 124 David Cone	.20	.06
❑ 125 Eddie Murray	.50	.15
❑ 126 Brian Jordan	.20	.06
❑ 127 Darrin Fletcher	.20	.06
❑ 128 Curt Schilling	.20	.06
❑ 129 Ozzie Guillen	.20	.06
❑ 130 Kenny Rogers	.20	.06
❑ 131 Tom Pagnozzi	.20	.06
❑ 132 Garret Anderson	.20	.06
❑ 133 Bobby Jones	.20	.06
❑ 134 Chris Gomez	.20	.06
❑ 135 Mike Stanley	.20	.06
❑ 136 Hideo Nomo	.50	.15
❑ 137 Jon Nunnally	.20	.06
❑ 138 Tim Wakefield	.20	.06
❑ 139 Steve Finley	.20	.06
❑ 140 Ivan Rodriguez	.50	.15
❑ 141 Quilvio Veras	.20	.06
❑ 142 Mike Fetters	.20	.06
❑ 143 Mike Greenwell	.20	.06
❑ 144 Bill Pulsipher	.20	.06
❑ 145 Mark McGwire	1.25	.35
❑ 146 Frank Castillo	.20	.06
❑ 147 Greg Vaughn	.20	.06
❑ 148 Pat Hentgen	.20	.06
❑ 149 Walt Weiss	.20	.06
❑ 150 Randy Johnson	.50	.15
❑ 151 David Segui	.20	.06
❑ 152 Benji Gil	.20	.06
❑ 153 Tom Candiotti	.20	.06
❑ 154 Geronimo Berroa	.20	.06
❑ 155 John Franco	.20	.06
❑ 156 Jay Bell	.20	.06
❑ 157 Mark Gubicza	.20	.06
❑ 158 Hal Morris	.20	.06
❑ 159 Wilson Alvarez	.20	.06
❑ 160 Derek Bell	.20	.06
❑ 161 Ricky Bottalico	.20	.06
❑ 162 Bret Boone	.20	.06
❑ 163 Brad Radke	.20	.06
❑ 164 John Valentin	.20	.06
❑ 165 Steve Avery	.20	.06
❑ 166 Mark McLemore	.20	.06
❑ 167 Danny Jackson	.20	.06
❑ 168 Tino Martinez	.30	.09
❑ 169 Shane Reynolds	.20	.06
❑ 170 Terry Pendleton	.20	.06
❑ 171 Jim Edmonds	.20	.06
❑ 172 Esteban Loaiza	.20	.06
❑ 173 Ray Durham	.20	.06
❑ 174 Carlos Perez	.20	.06
❑ 175 Raul Mondesi	.20	.06
❑ 176 Steve Ontiveros	.20	.06
❑ 177 Chipper Jones	.50	.15
❑ 178 Otis Nixon	.20	.06
❑ 179 John Burkett	.20	.06
❑ 180 Gregg Jefferies	.20	.06
❑ 181 Denny Martinez	.20	.06
❑ 182 Ken Caminiti	.20	.06
❑ 183 Doug Jones	.20	.06
❑ 184 Brian McRae	.20	.06
❑ 185 Don Mattingly	1.25	.35
❑ 186 Mel Rojas	.20	.06
❑ 187 Marty Cordova	.20	.06
❑ 188 Vinny Castilla	.20	.06
❑ 189 John Smoltz	.30	.09
❑ 190 Travis Fryman	.20	.06
❑ 191 Chris Hoiles	.20	.06
❑ 192 Chuck Finley	.20	.06
❑ 193 Ryan Klesko	.20	.06
❑ 194 Alex Fernandez	.20	.06
❑ 195 Dante Bichette	.20	.06
❑ 196 Eric Karros	.20	.06
❑ 197 Roger Clemens	1.00	.30
❑ 198 Randy Myers	.20	.06
❑ 199 Tony Phillips	.20	.06
❑ 200 Cal Ripken	1.50	.45
❑ 201 Rod Beck	.20	.06
❑ 202 Chad Curtis	.20	.06
❑ 203 Jack McDowell	.20	.06
❑ 204 Gary Gaetti	.20	.06
❑ 205 Ken Griffey Jr.	.75	.23
❑ 206 Ramon Martinez	.20	.06
❑ 207 Jeff Kent	.20	.06
❑ 208 Brad Ausmus	.20	.06
❑ 209 Devon White	.20	.06
❑ 210 Jason Giambi	.20	.06
❑ 211 Nomar Garciaparra	.75	.23
❑ 212 Billy Wagner	.20	.06
❑ 213 Todd Greene	.20	.06
❑ 214 Paul Wilson	.20	.06
❑ 215 Johnny Damon	.30	.09
❑ 216 Alan Benes	.20	.06
❑ 217 Karim Garcia	.20	.06
❑ 218 Dustin Hermanson	.20	.06
❑ 219 Derek Jeter	1.25	.35
❑ 220 Checklist (111-220)	.20	.06
❑ 221 Kirby Puckett STP	.30	.09
❑ 222 Cal Ripken STP	.75	.23
❑ 223 Albert Belle STP	.20	.06
❑ 224 Randy Johnson STP	.30	.09
❑ 225 Wade Boggs STP	.20	.06
❑ 226 Carlos Baerga STP	.20	.06
❑ 227 Ivan Rodriguez STP	.30	.09
❑ 228 Mike Mussina STP	.20	.06
❑ 229 Frank Thomas STP	.30	.09
❑ 230 Ken Griffey Jr. STP	.50	.15
❑ 231 Jose Mesa STP	.20	.06
❑ 232 Matt Morris RC	1.50	.45
❑ 233 Craig Wilson RC	1.50	.45
❑ 234 Alvie Shepherd	.25	.07
❑ 235 Randy Winn RC	.60	.18
❑ 236 David Yocum RC	.25	.07
❑ 237 Jason Brester RC	.25	.07
❑ 238 Shane Monahan RC	.25	.07
❑ 239 Brian McNichol RC	.25	.07
❑ 240 Reggie Taylor	.25	.07
❑ 241 Garrett Long	.25	.07
❑ 242 Jonathan Johnson	.25	.07
❑ 243 Jeff Liefer RC	.25	.07
❑ 244 Brian Powell	.25	.07

❑ 245 Brian Buchanan RC	.25	.07
❑ 246 Mike Piazza	.75	.23
❑ 247 Edgar Martinez	.30	.09
❑ 248 Chuck Knoblauch	.20	.06
❑ 249 Andres Galarraga	.20	.06
❑ 250 Tony Gwynn	.60	.18
❑ 251 Lee Smith	.20	.06
❑ 252 Sammy Sosa	.75	.23
❑ 253 Jim Thome	.50	.15
❑ 254 Frank Rodriguez	.20	.06
❑ 255 Charlie Hayes	.20	.06
❑ 256 Bernard Gilkey	.20	.06
❑ 257 John Smiley	.20	.06
❑ 258 Brady Anderson	.20	.06
❑ 259 Rico Brogna	.20	.06
❑ 260 Kirt Manwaring	.20	.06
❑ 261 Len Dykstra	.20	.06
❑ 262 Tom Glavine	.30	.09
❑ 263 Vince Coleman	.20	.06
❑ 264 John Olerud	.20	.06
❑ 265 Orlando Merced	.20	.06
❑ 266 Kent Mercker	.20	.06
❑ 267 Terry Steinbach	.20	.06
❑ 268 Brian L. Hunter	.20	.06
❑ 269 Jeff Fassero	.20	.06
❑ 270 Jay Buhner	.20	.06
❑ 271 Jeff Brantley	.20	.06
❑ 272 Tim Raines	.20	.06
❑ 273 Jimmy Key	.20	.06
❑ 274 Mo Vaughn	.20	.06
❑ 275 Andre Dawson	.20	.06
❑ 276 Jose Mesa	.20	.06
❑ 277 Brett Butler	.20	.06
❑ 278 Luis Gonzalez	.20	.06
❑ 279 Steve Sparks	.20	.06
❑ 280 Chili Davis	.20	.06
❑ 281 Carl Everett	.20	.06
❑ 282 Jeff Cirillo	.20	.06
❑ 283 Thomas Howard	.20	.06
❑ 284 Paul O'Neill	.30	.09
❑ 285 Pat Meares	.20	.06
❑ 286 Mickey Tettleton	.20	.06
❑ 287 Rey Sanchez	.20	.06
❑ 288 Bip Roberts	.20	.06
❑ 289 Roberto Alomar	.30	.09
❑ 290 Ruben Sierra	.20	.06
❑ 291 John Flaherty	.20	.06
❑ 292 Bret Saberhagen	.20	.06
❑ 293 Barry Larkin	.30	.09
❑ 294 Sandy Alomar Jr.	.20	.06
❑ 295 Ed Sprague	.20	.06
❑ 296 Gary DiSarcina	.20	.06
❑ 297 Marquis Grissom	.20	.06
❑ 298 John Frascatore	.20	.06
❑ 299 Will Clark	.50	.15
❑ 300 Barry Bonds	1.25	.35
❑ 301 Ozzie Smith UER	.75	.23
Padres is listed as Padre		
❑ 302 Dave Nilsson	.20	.06
❑ 303 Pedro Martinez	.50	.15
❑ 304 Joey Cora	.20	.06
❑ 305 Rick Aguilera	.20	.06
❑ 306 Craig Biggio	.30	.09
❑ 307 Jose Vizcaino	.20	.06
❑ 308 Jeff Montgomery	.20	.06
❑ 309 Moises Alou	.20	.06
❑ 310 Robin Ventura	.20	.06
❑ 311 David Wells	.20	.06
❑ 312 Delino DeShields	.20	.06
❑ 313 Trevor Hoffman	.20	.06
❑ 314 Andy Benes	.20	.06
❑ 315 Deion Sanders	.30	.09
❑ 316 Jim Bullinger	.20	.06
❑ 317 John Jaha	.20	.06
❑ 318 Greg Maddux	.75	.23
❑ 319 Tim Salmon	.30	.09
❑ 320 Ben McDonald	.20	.06
❑ 321 Sandy Martinez	.20	.06
❑ 322 Dan Miceli	.20	.06
❑ 323 Wade Boggs	.30	.09
❑ 324 Ismael Valdes	.20	.06
❑ 325 Juan Gonzalez	.30	.09
❑ 326 Charles Nagy	.20	.06
❑ 327 Ray Lankford	.20	.06
❑ 328 Mark Portugal	.20	.06
❑ 329 Bobby Bonilla	.20	.06

❑ 330 Reggie Sanders	.20	.06
❑ 331 Jamie Brewington RC	.25	.07
❑ 332 Aaron Sele	.20	.06
❑ 333 Pete Harnisch	.20	.06
❑ 334 Cliff Floyd	.20	.06
❑ 335 Cal Eldred	.20	.06
❑ 336 Jason Bates	.20	.06
❑ 337 Tony Clark	.20	.06
❑ 338 Jose Herrera	.20	.06
❑ 339 Alex Ochoa	.20	.06
❑ 340 Mark Loretta	.20	.06
❑ 341 Donne Wall	.20	.06
❑ 342 Jason Kendall	.20	.06
❑ 343 Shannon Stewart	.20	.06
❑ 344 Brooks Kieschnick	.20	.06
❑ 345 Chris Snopek	.20	.06
❑ 346 Ruben Rivera	.20	.06
❑ 347 Jeff Suppan	.20	.06
❑ 348 Phil Nevin	.20	.06
❑ 349 John Wasdin	.20	.06
❑ 350 Jay Payton	.20	.06
❑ 351 Tim Crabtree	.20	.06
❑ 352 Rick Krivda	.20	.06
❑ 353 Bob Wolcott	.20	.06
❑ 354 Jimmy Haynes	.20	.06
❑ 355 Herb Perry	.20	.06
❑ 356 Ryne Sandberg	.75	.23
❑ 357 Harold Baines	.20	.06
❑ 358 Chad Ogea	.20	.06
❑ 359 Lee Tinsley	.20	.06
❑ 360 Matt Williams	.20	.06
❑ 361 Randy Velarde	.20	.06
❑ 362 Jose Canseco	.50	.15
❑ 363 Larry Walker	.30	.09
❑ 364 Kevin Appier	.20	.06
❑ 365 Darryl Hamilton	.20	.06
❑ 366 Jose Lima	.20	.06
❑ 367 Javy Lopez	.20	.06
❑ 368 Dennis Eckersley	.20	.06
❑ 369 Jason Isringhausen	.20	.06
❑ 370 Mickey Morandini	.20	.06
❑ 371 Scott Cooper	.20	.06
❑ 372 Jim Abbott	.30	.09
❑ 373 Paul Sorrento	.20	.06
❑ 374 Chris Hammond	.20	.06
❑ 375 Lance Johnson	.20	.06
❑ 376 Kevin Brown	.20	.06
❑ 377 Luis Alicea	.20	.06
❑ 378 Andy Pettitte	.30	.09
❑ 379 Dean Palmer	.20	.06
❑ 380 Jeff Bagwell	.30	.09
❑ 381 Jaime Navarro	.20	.06
❑ 382 Rondell White	.20	.06
❑ 383 Erik Hanson	.20	.06
❑ 384 Pedro Munoz	.20	.06
❑ 385 Heathcliff Slocumb	.20	.06
❑ 386 Wally Joyner	.20	.06
❑ 387 Bob Tewksbury	.20	.06
❑ 388 David Bell	.20	.06
❑ 389 Fred McGriff	.30	.09
❑ 390 Mike Henneman	.20	.06
❑ 391 Robby Thompson	.20	.06
❑ 392 Norm Charlton	.20	.06
❑ 393 Cecil Fielder	.20	.06
❑ 394 Benito Santiago	.20	.06
❑ 395 Rafael Palmeiro	.30	.09
❑ 396 Ricky Bones	.20	.06
❑ 397 Rickey Henderson	.50	.15
❑ 398 C.J. Nitkowski	.20	.06
❑ 399 Shawon Dunston	.20	.06
❑ 400 Manny Ramirez	.30	.09
❑ 401 Bill Swift	.20	.06
❑ 402 Chad Fonville	.20	.06
❑ 403 Joey Hamilton	.20	.06
❑ 404 Alex Gonzalez	.20	.06
❑ 405 Roberto Hernandez	.20	.06
❑ 406 Jeff Blauser	.20	.06
❑ 407 LaTroy Hawkins	.20	.06
❑ 408 Greg Colbrunn	.20	.06
❑ 409 Todd Hundley	.20	.06
❑ 410 Glenn Dishman	.20	.06
❑ 411 Joe Vitiello	.20	.06
❑ 412 Todd Worrell	.20	.06
❑ 413 Wil Cordero	.20	.06
❑ 414 Ken Hill	.20	.06
❑ 415 Carlos Garcia	.20	.06

❑ 416 Bryan Rekar	.20	.06
❑ 417 Shawn Green	.20	.06
❑ 418 Tyler Green	.20	.06
❑ 419 Mike Blowers	.20	.06
❑ 420 Kenny Lofton	.20	.06
❑ 421 Denny Neagle	.20	.06
❑ 422 Jeff Conine	.20	.06
❑ 423 Mark Langston	.20	.06
❑ 424 Steve Cox	.40	.12
Jesse Ibarra		
Derrek Lee		
Ron Wright RC		
❑ 425 Jim Bonnici	.40	.12
Billy Owens		
Richie Sexson		
Daryle Ward RC		
❑ 426 Kevin Jordan	.25	.07
Bobby Morris		
Desi Relaford		
Adam Riggs RC		
❑ 427 Tim Harkrider	.25	.07
Rey Ordonez		
Neifi Perez		
Enrique Wilson		
❑ 428 Bartolo Colon	.20	.06
Doug Million		
Rafael Orellano		
Ray Ricken		
❑ 429 Jeff D'Amico	.25	.07
Marty Janzen RC		
Gary Rath		
Clint Sodowsky		
❑ 430 Matt Drews	.25	.07
Rich Hunter RC		
Matt Ruebel		
Bret Wagner		
❑ 431 Jaime Bluma	.25	.07
David Coggin		
Steve Montgomery		
Brandon Reed RC		
❑ 432 Mike Figga	.60	.18
Raul Ibanez		
Paul Konerko		
Julio Mosquera		
❑ 433 Brian Barber	.20	.06
Marc Kroon		
Marc Valdes		
Don Wengert		
❑ 434 George Arias	.50	.15
Chris Haas RC		
Scott Rolen		
Scott Spiezio		
❑ 435 Brian Banks	2.00	.60
Vladimir Guerrero		
Andruw Jones		
Billy McMillon		
❑ 436 Roger Cedeno	.60	.18
Derrick Gibson		
Ben Grieve		
Shane Spencer RC		
❑ 437 Anton French	.25	.07
Demond Smith		
DaRond Stovall RC		
Keith Williams		
❑ 438 Michael Coleman RC	.25	.07
Jacob Cruz		
Richard Hidalgo		
Charles Peterson		
❑ 439 Trey Beamon	.20	.06
Yamil Benitez		
Jermaine Dye		
Angel Echevarria		
❑ 440 Checklist	.20	.06
❑ F7 M.Mantle Last Day	5.00	1.50
❑ NNO Mickey Mantle TRIB.	3.00	.90
Promotes the Mantle Foundation		
Black and White Photo		

1997 Topps

	Nm-Mt	Ex-Mt
COMPLETE SET (495)	80.00	24.00
COMP.SERIES 1 (275)	40.00	12.00
COMP.SERIES 2 (220)	40.00	12.00
❑ 1 Barry Bonds	1.25	.35

❑ 2 Tom Pagnozzi .20 .06
❑ 3 Terrell Wade .20 .06
❑ 4 Jose Valentin .20 .06
❑ 5 Mark Clark .20 .06
❑ 6 Brady Anderson .20 .06
❑ 8 Wade Boggs .30 .09
❑ 9 Scott Stahoviak .20 .06
❑ 10 Andres Galarraga .20 .06
❑ 11 Steve Avery .20 .06
❑ 12 Rusty Greer .20 .06
❑ 13 Derek Jeter 1.25 .35
❑ 14 Ricky Bottalico .20 .06
❑ 15 Andy Ashby .20 .06
❑ 16 Paul Shuey .20 .06
❑ 17 F.P. Santangelo .20 .06
❑ 18 Royce Clayton .20 .06
❑ 19 Mike Mohler .20 .06
❑ 20 Mike Piazza .75 .23
❑ 21 Jaime Navarro .20 .06
❑ 22 Billy Wagner .20 .06
❑ 23 Mike Timlin .20 .06
❑ 24 Garret Anderson .20 .06
❑ 25 Ben McDonald .20 .06
❑ 26 Mel Rojas .20 .06
❑ 27 John Burkett .20 .06
❑ 28 Jeff King .20 .06
❑ 29 Reggie Jefferson .20 .06
❑ 30 Kevin Appier .20 .06
❑ 31 Felipe Lira .20 .06
❑ 32 Kevin Tapani .20 .06
❑ 33 Mark Portugal .20 .06
❑ 34 Carlos Garcia .20 .06
❑ 35 Joey Cora .20 .06
❑ 36 David Segui .20 .06
❑ 37 Mark Grace .30 .09
❑ 38 Erik Hanson .20 .06
❑ 39 Jeff D'Amico .20 .06
❑ 40 Jay Buhner .20 .06
❑ 41 B.J. Surhoff .20 .06
❑ 42 Jackie Robinson TRIB .50 .15
❑ 43 Roger Pavlik .20 .06
❑ 44 Hal Morris .20 .06
❑ 45 Mariano Duncan .20 .06
❑ 46 Harold Baines .20 .06
❑ 47 Jorge Fabregas .20 .06
❑ 48 Jose Herrera .20 .06
❑ 49 Jeff Cirillo .20 .06
❑ 50 Tom Glavine .30 .09
❑ 51 Pedro Astacio .20 .06
❑ 52 Mark Gardner .20 .06
❑ 53 Arthur Rhodes .20 .06
❑ 54 Troy O'Leary .20 .06
❑ 55 Bip Roberts .20 .06
❑ 56 Mike Lieberthal .20 .06
❑ 57 Shane Andrews .20 .06
❑ 58 Scott Karl .20 .06
❑ 59 Gary DiSarcina .20 .06
❑ 60 Andy Pettitte .30 .09
❑ 61 Kevin Elster .20 .06
❑ 61B Mike Fetters UER .20 .06
Card was intended as number 84
❑ 62 Mark McGwire 1.25 .35
❑ 63 Dan Wilson .20 .06
❑ 64 Mickey Morandini .20 .06
❑ 65 Chuck Knoblauch .20 .06
❑ 66 Tim Wakefield .20 .06
❑ 67 Raul Mondesi .20 .06
❑ 68 Todd Jones .20 .06
❑ 69 Albert Belle .20 .06
❑ 70 Trevor Hoffman .20 .06
❑ 71 Eric Young .20 .06
❑ 72 Robert Perez .20 .06
❑ 73 Butch Huskey .20 .06
❑ 74 Brian McRae .20 .06
❑ 75 Jim Edmonds .20 .06
❑ 76 Mike Henneman .20 .06
❑ 77 Frank Rodriguez .20 .06
❑ 78 Danny Tartabull .20 .06
❑ 79 Robb Nen .20 .06
❑ 80 Reggie Sanders .20 .06
❑ 81 Ron Karkovice .20 .06
❑ 82 Benito Santiago .20 .06
❑ 83 Mike Lansing .20 .06
❑ 85 Craig Biggio .30 .09
❑ 86 Mike Bordick .20 .06
❑ 87 Ray Lankford .20 .06
❑ 88 Charles Nagy .20 .06
❑ 89 Paul Wilson .20 .06
❑ 90 John Wetteland .20 .06
❑ 91 Tom Candiotti .20 .06
❑ 92 Carlos Delgado .20 .06
❑ 93 Derek Bell .20 .06
❑ 94 Mark Lemke .20 .06
❑ 95 Edgar Martinez .30 .09
❑ 96 Rickey Henderson .50 .15
❑ 97 Greg Myers .20 .06
❑ 98 Jim Leyritz .20 .06
❑ 99 Mark Johnson .20 .06
❑ 100 Dwight Gooden HL .20 .06
❑ 101 Al Leiter HL .20 .06
❑ 102 John Mabry HL .20 .06
❑ 103 Alex Ochoa HL .20 .06
❑ 104 Mike Piazza HL .50 .15
❑ 105 Jim Thome .50 .15
❑ 106 Ricky Otero .20 .06
❑ 107 Jamey Wright .20 .06
❑ 108 Frank Thomas .50 .15
❑ 109 Jody Reed .20 .06
❑ 110 Orel Hershiser .20 .06
❑ 111 Terry Steinbach .20 .06
❑ 112 Mark Loretta .20 .06
❑ 113 Turk Wendell .20 .06
❑ 114 Marvin Benard .20 .06
❑ 115 Kevin Brown .20 .06
❑ 116 Robert Person .20 .06
❑ 117 Joey Hamilton .20 .06
❑ 118 Francisco Cordova .20 .06
❑ 119 John Smiley .20 .06
❑ 120 Travis Fryman .20 .06
❑ 121 Jimmy Key .20 .06
❑ 122 Tom Goodwin .20 .06
❑ 123 Mike Greenwell .20 .06
❑ 124 Juan Gonzalez .30 .09
❑ 125 Pete Harnisch .20 .06
❑ 126 Roger Cedeno .20 .06
❑ 127 Ron Gant .20 .06
❑ 128 Mark Langston .20 .06
❑ 129 Tim Crabtree .20 .06
❑ 130 Greg Maddux .75 .23
❑ 131 W.VanLandingham .20 .06
❑ 132 Wally Joyner .20 .06
❑ 133 Randy Myers .20 .06
❑ 134 John Valentin .20 .06
❑ 135 Bret Boone .20 .06
❑ 136 Bruce Ruffin .20 .06
❑ 137 Chris Snopek .20 .06
❑ 138 Paul Molitor .30 .09
❑ 139 Mark McLemore .20 .06
❑ 140 Rafael Palmeiro .30 .09
❑ 141 Herb Perry .20 .06
❑ 142 Luis Gonzalez .20 .06
❑ 143 Doug Drabek .20 .06
❑ 144 Ken Ryan .20 .06
❑ 145 Todd Hundley .20 .06
❑ 146 Ellis Burks .20 .06
❑ 147 Ozzie Guillen .20 .06
❑ 148 Rich Becker .20 .06
❑ 149 Sterling Hitchcock .20 .06
❑ 150 Bernie Williams .30 .09
❑ 151 Mike Stanley .20 .06
❑ 152 Roberto Alomar .30 .09
❑ 153 Jose Mesa .20 .06
❑ 154 Steve Trachsel .20 .06
❑ 155 Alex Gonzalez .20 .06
❑ 156 Troy Percival .20 .06
❑ 157 John Smoltz .30 .09
❑ 158 Pedro Martinez .50 .15
❑ 159 Jeff Conine .20 .06
❑ 160 Bernard Gilkey .20 .06
❑ 161 Jim Eisenreich .20 .06
❑ 162 Mickey Tettleton .20 .06
❑ 163 Justin Thompson .20 .06
❑ 164 Jose Offerman .20 .06
❑ 165 Tony Phillips .20 .06
❑ 166 Ismael Valdes .20 .06
❑ 167 Ryne Sandberg UER .75 .23
Card has him with 252 homers in 1996
❑ 168 Matt Mieske .20 .06
❑ 169 Geronimo Berroa .20 .06
❑ 170 Otis Nixon .20 .06
❑ 171 John Mabry .20 .06
❑ 172 Shawon Dunston .20 .06
❑ 173 Omar Vizquel .30 .09
❑ 174 Chris Hoiles .20 .06
❑ 175 Dwight Gooden .20 .06
❑ 176 Wilson Alvarez .20 .06
❑ 177 Todd Hollandsworth .20 .06
❑ 178 Roger Salkeld .20 .06
❑ 179 Rey Sanchez .20 .06
❑ 180 Rey Ordonez .20 .06
❑ 181 Denny Martinez .20 .06
❑ 182 Ramon Martinez .20 .06
❑ 183 Dave Nilsson .20 .06
❑ 184 Marquis Grissom .20 .06
❑ 185 Randy Velarde .20 .06
❑ 186 Ron Coomer .20 .06
❑ 187 Tino Martinez .30 .09
❑ 188 Jeff Brantley .20 .06
❑ 189 Steve Finley .20 .06
❑ 190 Andy Benes .20 .06
❑ 191 Terry Adams .20 .06
❑ 192 Mike Blowers .20 .06
❑ 193 Russ Davis .20 .06
❑ 194 Darryl Hamilton .20 .06
❑ 195 Jason Kendall .20 .06
❑ 196 Johnny Damon .30 .09
❑ 197 Dave Martinez .20 .06
❑ 198 Mike Macfarlane .20 .06
❑ 199 Norm Charlton .20 .06
❑ 200 Doug Million RC .25 .07
Damian Moss
Bobby Rodgers
❑ 201 Geoff Jenkins .20 .06
Raul Ibanez
Mike Cameron
❑ 202 Sean Casey .20 .06
Jim Bonnici
Dmitri Young
❑ 203 Jed Hansen .20 .06
Homer Bush
Felipe Crespo
❑ 204 Kevin Orie .20 .06
Gabe Alvarez
Aaron Boone
❑ 205 Ben Davis .20 .06
Kevin Brown
Bobby Estalella
❑ 206 Billy McMillon RC .40 .12
Bubba Trammell
Dante Powell
❑ 207 Jarrod Washburn .20 .06
Marc Wilkins RC
Glendon Rusch
❑ 208 Brian Hunter .20 .06
❑ 209 Jason Giambi .20 .06
❑ 210 Henry Rodriguez .20 .06
❑ 211 Edgar Renteria .20 .06
❑ 212 Edgardo Alfonzo .20 .06
❑ 213 Fernando Vina .20 .06
❑ 214 Shawn Green .20 .06
❑ 215 Ray Durham .20 .06
❑ 216 Joe Randa .20 .06
❑ 217 Armando Reynoso .20 .06
❑ 218 Eric Davis .20 .06
❑ 219 Bob Tewksbury .20 .06
❑ 220 Jacob Cruz .20 .06
❑ 221 Glenallen Hill .20 .06
❑ 222 Gary Gaetti .20 .06
❑ 223 Donne Wall .20 .06
❑ 224 Brad Clontz .20 .06

❑ 225	Marty Janzen	.20	.06
❑ 226	Todd Worrell	.20	.06
❑ 227	John Franco	.20	.06
❑ 228	David Wells	.20	.06
❑ 229	Gregg Jefferies	.20	.06
❑ 230	Tim Naehring	.20	.06
❑ 231	Thomas Howard	.20	.06
❑ 232	Roberto Hernandez	.20	.06
❑ 233	Kevin Ritz	.20	.06
❑ 234	Julian Tavarez	.20	.06
❑ 235	Ken Hill	.20	.06
❑ 236	Greg Gagne	.20	.06
❑ 237	Bobby Chouinard	.20	.06
❑ 238	Joe Carter	.20	.06
❑ 239	Jermaine Dye	.20	.06
❑ 240	Antonio Osuna	.20	.06
❑ 241	Julio Franco	.20	.06
❑ 242	Mike Grace	.20	.06
❑ 243	Aaron Sele	.20	.06
❑ 244	David Justice	.20	.06
❑ 245	Sandy Alomar Jr.	.20	.06
❑ 246	Jose Canseco	.50	.15
❑ 247	Paul O'Neill	.30	.09
❑ 248	Sean Berry	.20	.06
❑ 249	Nick Bierbrodt	.25	.07
	Kevin Sweeney RC		
❑ 250	Larry Rodriguez RC	.25	.07
	Vladimir Nunez RC		
❑ 251	Ron Hartman	.25	.07
	David Hayman RC		
❑ 252	Alex Sanchez	.50	.15
	Matthew Quatraro RC		
❑ 253	Ronni Seberino RC	.25	.07
	Pablo Ortego RC		
❑ 254	Rex Hudler	.20	.06
❑ 255	Orlando Miller	.20	.06
❑ 256	Mariano Rivera	.30	.09
❑ 257	Brad Radke	.20	.06
❑ 258	Bobby Higginson	.20	.06
❑ 259	Jay Bell	.20	.06
❑ 260	Mark Grudzielanek	.20	.06
❑ 261	Lance Johnson	.20	.06
❑ 262	Ken Caminiti	.20	.06
❑ 263	J.T. Snow	.20	.06
❑ 264	Gary Sheffield	.20	.06
❑ 265	Darrin Fletcher	.20	.06
❑ 266	Eric Owens	.20	.06
❑ 267	Luis Castillo	.20	.06
❑ 268	Scott Rolen	.50	.15
❑ 269	Todd Noel	.25	.07
	John Oliver RC		
❑ 270	Robert Stratton RC	.40	.12
	Corey Lee RC		
❑ 271	Gil Meche RC	.50	.15
	Matt Halloran RC		
❑ 272	Eric Milton RC	.75	.23
	Dee Brown RC		
❑ 273	Josh Garrett	.25	.07
	Chris Reitsma RC		
❑ 274	A.J.Zapp RC	.75	.23
	Jason Marquis		
❑ 275	Checklist	.20	.06
❑ 276	Checklist	.20	.06
❑ 277	Chipper Jones UER	.50	.15
	incorrectly numbered 276		
❑ 278	Orlando Merced	.20	.06
❑ 279	Ariel Prieto	.20	.06
❑ 280	Al Leiter	.20	.06
❑ 281	Pat Meares	.20	.06
❑ 282	Darryl Strawberry	.20	.06
❑ 283	Jamie Moyer	.20	.06
❑ 284	Scott Servais	.20	.06
❑ 285	Delino DeShields	.20	.06
❑ 286	Danny Graves	.20	.06
❑ 287	Gerald Williams	.20	.06
❑ 288	Todd Greene	.20	.06
❑ 289	Rico Brogna	.20	.06
❑ 290	Derrick Gibson	.20	.06
❑ 291	Joe Girardi	.20	.06
❑ 292	Darren Lewis	.20	.06
❑ 293	Nomar Garciaparra	.75	.23
❑ 294	Greg Colbrunn	.20	.06
❑ 295	Jeff Bagwell	.30	.09
❑ 296	Brent Gates	.20	.06
❑ 297	Jose Vizcaino	.20	.06
❑ 298	Alex Ochoa	.20	.06
❑ 299	Sid Fernandez	.20	.06
❑ 300	Ken Griffey Jr.	.75	.23
❑ 301	Chris Gomez	.20	.06
❑ 302	Wendell Magee	.20	.06
❑ 303	Darren Oliver	.20	.06
❑ 304	Mel Nieves	.20	.06
❑ 305	Sammy Sosa	.75	.23
❑ 306	George Arias	.20	.06
❑ 307	Jack McDowell	.20	.06
❑ 308	Stan Javier	.20	.06
❑ 309	Kimera Bartee	.20	.06
❑ 310	James Baldwin	.20	.06
❑ 311	Rocky Coppinger	.20	.06
❑ 312	Keith Lockhart	.20	.06
❑ 313	C.J. Nitkowski	.20	.06
❑ 314	Allen Watson	.20	.06
❑ 315	Darryl Kile	.20	.06
❑ 316	Amaury Telemaco	.20	.06
❑ 317	Jason Isringhausen	.20	.06
❑ 318	Manny Ramirez	.30	.09
❑ 319	Terry Pendleton	.20	.06
❑ 320	Tim Salmon	.30	.09
❑ 321	Eric Karros	.20	.06
❑ 322	Mark Whiten	.20	.06
❑ 323	Rick Krivda	.20	.06
❑ 324	Brett Butler	.20	.06
❑ 325	Randy Johnson	.50	.15
❑ 326	Eddie Taubensee	.20	.06
❑ 327	Mark Leiter	.20	.06
❑ 328	Kevin Gross	.20	.06
❑ 329	Ernie Young	.20	.06
❑ 330	Pat Hentgen	.20	.06
❑ 331	Rondell White	.20	.06
❑ 332	Bobby Witt	.20	.06
❑ 333	Eddie Murray	.50	.15
❑ 334	Tim Raines	.20	.06
❑ 335	Jeff Fassero	.20	.06
❑ 336	Chuck Finley	.20	.06
❑ 337	Willie Adams	.20	.06
❑ 338	Chan Ho Park	.20	.06
❑ 339	Jay Powell	.20	.06
❑ 340	Ivan Rodriguez	.50	.15
❑ 341	Jermaine Allensworth	.20	.06
❑ 342	Jay Payton	.20	.06
❑ 343	T.J. Mathews	.20	.06
❑ 344	Tony Batista	.20	.06
❑ 345	Ed Sprague	.20	.06
❑ 346	Jeff Kent	.20	.06
❑ 347	Scott Erickson	.20	.06
❑ 348	Jeff Suppan	.20	.06
❑ 349	Pete Schourek	.20	.06
❑ 350	Kenny Lofton	.20	.06
❑ 351	Alan Benes	.20	.06
❑ 352	Fred McGriff	.30	.09
❑ 353	Charlie O'Brien	.20	.06
❑ 354	Darren Bragg	.20	.06
❑ 355	Alex Fernandez	.20	.06
❑ 356	Al Martin	.20	.06
❑ 357	Bob Wells	.20	.06
❑ 358	Chad Mottola	.20	.06
❑ 359	Devon White	.20	.06
❑ 360	David Cone	.20	.06
❑ 361	Bobby Jones	.20	.06
❑ 362	Scott Sanders	.20	.06
❑ 363	Karim Garcia	.20	.06
❑ 364	Kirt Manwaring	.20	.06
❑ 365	Chili Davis	.20	.06
❑ 366	Mike Hampton	.20	.06
❑ 367	Chad Ogea	.20	.06
❑ 368	Curt Schilling	.20	.06
❑ 369	Phil Nevin	.20	.06
❑ 370	Roger Clemens	1.00	.30
❑ 371	Willie Greene	.20	.06
❑ 372	Kenny Rogers	.20	.06
❑ 373	Jose Rijo	.20	.06
❑ 374	Bobby Bonilla	.20	.06
❑ 375	Mike Mussina	.30	.09
❑ 376	Curtis Pride	.20	.06
❑ 377	Todd Walker	.20	.06
❑ 378	Jason Bere	.20	.06
❑ 379	Heathcliff Slocumb	.20	.06
❑ 380	Dante Bichette	.20	.06
❑ 381	Carlos Baerga	.20	.06
❑ 382	Livan Hernandez	.20	.06
❑ 383	Jason Schmidt	.20	.06
❑ 384	Kevin Stocker	.20	.06
❑ 385	Matt Williams	.20	.06
❑ 386	Bartolo Colon	.20	.06
❑ 387	Will Clark	.50	.15
❑ 388	Dennis Eckersley	.20	.06
❑ 389	Brooks Kieschnick	.20	.06
❑ 390	Ryan Klesko	.20	.06
❑ 391	Mark Carreon	.20	.06
❑ 392	Tim Worrell	.20	.06
❑ 393	Dean Palmer	.20	.06
❑ 394	Wil Cordero	.20	.06
❑ 395	Javy Lopez	.20	.06
❑ 396	Rich Aurilia	.20	.06
❑ 397	Greg Vaughn	.20	.06
❑ 398	Vinny Castilla	.20	.06
❑ 399	Jeff Montgomery	.20	.06
❑ 400	Cal Ripken	1.50	.45
❑ 401	Walt Weiss	.20	.06
❑ 402	Brad Ausmus	.20	.06
❑ 403	Ruben Rivera	.20	.06
❑ 404	Mark Wohlers	.20	.06
❑ 405	Rick Aguilera	.20	.06
❑ 406	Tony Clark	.20	.06
❑ 407	Lyle Mouton	.20	.06
❑ 408	Bill Pulsipher	.20	.06
❑ 409	Jose Rosado	.20	.06
❑ 410	Tony Gwynn	.60	.18
❑ 411	Cecil Fielder	.20	.06
❑ 412	John Flaherty	.20	.06
❑ 413	Lenny Dykstra	.20	.06
❑ 414	Ugueth Urbina	.20	.06
❑ 415	Brian Jordan	.20	.06
❑ 416	Bob Abreu	.20	.06
❑ 417	Craig Paquette	.20	.06
❑ 418	Sandy Martinez	.20	.06
❑ 419	Jeff Blauser	.20	.06
❑ 420	Barry Larkin	.30	.09
❑ 421	Kevin Seitzer	.20	.06
❑ 422	Tim Belcher	.20	.06
❑ 423	Paul Sorrento	.20	.06
❑ 424	Cal Eldred	.20	.06
❑ 425	Robin Ventura	.20	.06
❑ 426	John Olerud	.20	.06
❑ 427	Bob Wolcott	.20	.06
❑ 428	Matt Lawton	.20	.06
❑ 429	Rod Beck	.20	.06
❑ 430	Shane Reynolds	.20	.06
❑ 431	Mike James	.20	.06
❑ 432	Steve Wojciechowski	.20	.06
❑ 433	Vladimir Guerrero	.50	.15
❑ 434	Dustin Hermanson	.20	.06
❑ 435	Marty Cordova	.20	.06
❑ 436	Marc Newfield	.20	.06
❑ 437	Todd Stottlemyre	.20	.06
❑ 438	Jeffrey Hammonds	.20	.06
❑ 439	Dave Stevens	.20	.06
❑ 440	Hideo Nomo	.50	.15
❑ 441	Mark Thompson	.20	.06
❑ 442	Mark Lewis	.20	.06
❑ 443	Quinton McCracken	.20	.06
❑ 444	Cliff Floyd	.20	.06
❑ 445	Denny Neagle	.20	.06
❑ 446	John Jaha	.20	.06
❑ 447	Mike Sweeney	.20	.06
❑ 448	John Wasdin	.20	.06
❑ 449	Chad Curtis	.20	.06
❑ 450	Mo Vaughn	.20	.06
❑ 451	Donovan Osborne	.20	.06
❑ 452	Ruben Sierra	.20	.06
❑ 453	Michael Tucker	.20	.06
❑ 454	Kurt Abbott	.20	.06
❑ 455	Andruw Jones UER	.20	.06
	Birthdate is incorrectly listed as 1-22-67, should be 1-22-77		
❑ 456	Shannon Stewart	.20	.06
❑ 457	Scott Brosius	.20	.06
❑ 458	Juan Guzman	.20	.06
❑ 459	Ron Villone	.20	.06
❑ 460	Moises Alou	.20	.06
❑ 461	Larry Walker	.30	.09
❑ 462	Eddie Murray SH	.30	.09
❑ 463	Paul Molitor SH	.20	.06
❑ 464	Hideo Nomo SH	.20	.06
❑ 465	Barry Bonds SH	.50	.15
❑ 466	Todd Hundley SH	.20	.06
❑ 467	Rheal Cormier	.20	.06
❑ 468	Jason Conti RC	.25	.07

Jhensy Sandoval
❑ 469 Rod Barajas 1.50 .45
Jackie Rexrode RC
❑ 470 Cedric Bowers RC .25 .07
Jared Sandberg RC
❑ 471 Chei Gunner RC .25 .07
Paul Wilder
❑ 472 Mike Decelle .25 .07
Marcus McCain RC
❑ 473 Todd Zeile .20 .06
❑ 474 Neifi Perez .20 .06
❑ 475 Jeromy Burnitz .20 .06
❑ 476 Trey Beamon .20 .06
❑ 477 Braden Looper RC .40 .12
John Patterson
❑ 478 Danny Peoples .75 .23
Jake Westbrook RC
❑ 479 Eric Chavez 1.25 .35
Adam Eaton RC
❑ 480 Joe Lawrence RC .25 .07
Pete Tucci
❑ 481 Kris Benson .75 .23
Billy Koch RC
❑ 482 John Nicholson .25 .07
Andy Prater RC
❑ 483 Mark Johnson RC .75 .23
Mark Kotsay
❑ 484 Armando Benitez .20 .06
❑ 485 Mike Matheny .20 .06
❑ 486 Jeff Reed .20 .06
❑ 487 Mark Bellhorn .20 .06
Russ Johnson
Enrique Wilson
❑ 488 Ben Grieve .20 .06
Richard Hidalgo
Scott Morgan RC
❑ 489 Paul Konerko .20 .06
Derrek Lee UER
spelled Derek on back
Ron Wright
❑ 490 Wes Helms RC 3.00 .90
Bill Mueller
Brad Seitzer
❑ 491 Jeff Abbott .20 .06
Shane Monahan
Edgard Velazquez
❑ 492 Jimmy Anderson RC .25 .07
Ron Blazier
Gerald Witasick
❑ 493 Darin Blood .75 .06
Heath Murray
Carl Pavano
❑ 494 Nelson Figueroa RC .25 .07
Mark Redman
Mike Villano
❑ 495 Checklist .20 .06
❑ 496 Checklist .20 .06
❑ NNO Derek Jeter AU 150.00 45.00

1998 Topps

	Nm-Mt	Ex-Mt
COMPLETE SET (503)	80.00	24.00
COMP.HOBBY SET (511)	100.00	30.00
COMP.RETAIL SET (511)	100.00	30.00
COMP.SERIES 1 (282)	40.00	12.00
COMP.SERIES 2 (221)	40.00	12.00

❑ 1 Tony Gwynn .60 .18
❑ 2 Larry Walker .30 .09
❑ 3 Billy Wagner .20 .06
❑ 4 Denny Neagle .20 .06
❑ 5 Vladimir Guerrero .50 .15
❑ 6 Kevin Brown .30 .09
❑ 8 Mariano Rivera .30 .09
❑ 9 Tony Clark .20 .06
❑ 10 Deion Sanders .30 .09
❑ 11 Francisco Cordova .20 .06
❑ 12 Matt Williams .20 .06
❑ 13 Carlos Baerga .20 .06
❑ 14 Mo Vaughn .20 .06
❑ 15 Bobby Witt .20 .06
❑ 16 Matt Stairs .20 .06
❑ 17 Chan Ho Park .20 .06
❑ 18 Mike Bordick .20 .06
❑ 19 Michael Tucker .20 .06
❑ 20 Frank Thomas .50 .15
❑ 21 Roberto Clemente 1.00 .30
❑ 22 Dmitri Young .20 .06
❑ 23 Steve Trachsel .20 .06
❑ 24 Jeff Kent .20 .06
❑ 25 Scott Rolen .50 .15
❑ 26 John Thomson .20 .06
❑ 27 Joe Vitiello .20 .06
❑ 28 Eddie Guardado .20 .06
❑ 29 Charlie Hayes .20 .06
❑ 30 Juan Gonzalez .30 .09
❑ 31 Garret Anderson .20 .06
❑ 32 John Jaha .20 .06
❑ 33 Omar Vizquel .30 .09
❑ 34 Brian Hunter .20 .06
❑ 35 Jeff Bagwell .30 .09
❑ 36 Mark Lemke .20 .06
❑ 37 Doug Glanville .20 .06
❑ 38 Dan Wilson .20 .06
❑ 39 Steve Cooke .20 .06
❑ 40 Chili Davis .20 .06
❑ 41 Mike Cameron .20 .06
❑ 42 F.P. Santangelo .20 .06
❑ 43 Brad Ausmus .20 .06
❑ 44 Gary DiSarcina .20 .06
❑ 45 Pat Hentgen .20 .06
❑ 46 Wilton Guerrero .20 .06
❑ 47 Devon White .20 .06
❑ 48 Danny Patterson .20 .06
❑ 49 Pat Meares .20 .06
❑ 50 Rafael Palmeiro .30 .09
❑ 51 Mark Gardner .20 .06
❑ 52 Jeff Blauser .20 .06
❑ 53 Dave Hollins .20 .06
❑ 54 Carlos Garcia .20 .06
❑ 55 Ben McDonald .20 .06
❑ 56 John Mabry .20 .06
❑ 57 Trevor Hoffman .20 .06
❑ 58 Tony Fernandez .20 .06
❑ 59 Rich Loiselle .20 .06
❑ 60 Mark Leiter .20 .06
❑ 61 Pat Kelly .20 .06
❑ 62 John Flaherty .20 .06
❑ 63 Roger Bailey .20 .06
❑ 64 Tom Gordon .20 .06
❑ 65 Ryan Klesko .20 .06
❑ 66 Darryl Hamilton .20 .06
❑ 67 Jim Eisenreich .20 .06
❑ 68 Butch Huskey .20 .06
❑ 69 Mark Grudzielanek .20 .06
❑ 70 Marquis Grissom .20 .06
❑ 71 Mark McLemore .20 .06
❑ 72 Gary Gaetti .20 .06
❑ 73 Greg Gagne .20 .06
❑ 74 Lyle Mouton .20 .06
❑ 75 Jim Edmonds .20 .06
❑ 76 Shawn Green .20 .06
❑ 77 Greg Vaughn .20 .06
❑ 78 Terry Adams .20 .06
❑ 79 Kevin Polcovich .20 .06
❑ 80 Troy O'Leary .20 .06
❑ 81 Jeff Shaw .20 .06
❑ 82 Rich Becker .20 .06
❑ 83 David Wells .20 .06
❑ 84 Steve Karsay .20 .06
❑ 85 Charles Nagy .20 .06
❑ 86 B.J. Surhoff .20 .06
❑ 87 Jamey Wright .20 .06
❑ 88 James Baldwin .20 .06
❑ 89 Edgardo Alfonzo .20 .06
❑ 90 Jay Buhner .20 .06
❑ 91 Brady Anderson .20 .06
❑ 92 Scott Servais .20 .06
❑ 93 Edgar Renteria .20 .06
❑ 94 Mike Lieberthal .20 .06
❑ 95 Rick Aguilera .20 .06
❑ 96 Walt Weiss .20 .06
❑ 97 Deivi Cruz .20 .06
❑ 98 Kurt Abbott .20 .06
❑ 99 Henry Rodriguez .20 .06
❑ 100 Mike Piazza .75 .23
❑ 101 Bill Taylor .20 .06
❑ 102 Todd Zeile .20 .06
❑ 103 Rey Ordonez .20 .06
❑ 104 Willie Greene .20 .06
❑ 105 Tony Womack .20 .06
❑ 106 Mike Sweeney .20 .06
❑ 107 Jeffrey Hammonds .20 .06
❑ 108 Kevin Orie .20 .06
❑ 109 Alex Gonzalez .20 .06
❑ 110 Jose Canseco .50 .15
❑ 111 Paul Sorrento .20 .06
❑ 112 Joey Hamilton .20 .06
❑ 113 Brad Radke .20 .06
❑ 114 Steve Avery .20 .06
❑ 115 Esteban Loaiza .20 .06
❑ 116 Stan Javier .20 .06
❑ 117 Chris Gomez .20 .06
❑ 118 Royce Clayton .20 .06
❑ 119 Orlando Merced .20 .06
❑ 120 Kevin Appier .20 .06
❑ 121 Mel Nieves .20 .06
❑ 122 Joe Girardi .20 .06
❑ 123 Rico Brogna .20 .06
❑ 124 Kent Mercker .20 .06
❑ 125 Manny Ramirez .30 .09
❑ 126 Jeromy Burnitz .20 .06
❑ 127 Kevin Foster .20 .06
❑ 128 Matt Morris .20 .06
❑ 129 Jason Dickson .20 .06
❑ 130 Tom Glavine .30 .09
❑ 131 Wally Joyner .20 .06
❑ 132 Rick Reed .20 .06
❑ 133 Todd Jones .20 .06
❑ 134 Dave Martinez .20 .06
❑ 135 Sandy Alomar Jr. .20 .06
❑ 136 Mike Lansing .20 .06
❑ 137 Sean Berry .20 .06
❑ 138 Doug Jones .20 .06
❑ 139 Todd Stottlemyre .20 .06
❑ 140 Jay Bell .20 .06
❑ 141 Jaime Navarro .20 .06
❑ 142 Chris Hoiles .20 .06
❑ 143 Joey Cora .20 .06
❑ 144 Scott Spiezio .20 .06
❑ 145 Joe Carter .20 .06
❑ 146 Jose Guillen .20 .06
❑ 147 Damion Easley .20 .06
❑ 148 Lee Stevens .20 .06
❑ 149 Alex Fernandez .20 .06
❑ 150 Randy Johnson .50 .15
❑ 151 J.T. Snow .20 .06
❑ 152 Chuck Finley .20 .06
❑ 153 Bernard Gilkey .20 .06
❑ 154 David Segui .20 .06
❑ 155 Dante Bichette .20 .06
❑ 156 Kevin Stocker .20 .06
❑ 157 Carl Everett .20 .06
❑ 158 Jose Valentin .20 .06
❑ 159 Pokey Reese .20 .06
❑ 160 Derek Jeter 1.25 .35
❑ 161 Roger Pavlik .20 .06
❑ 162 Mark Wohlers .20 .06
❑ 163 Ricky Bottalico .20 .06
❑ 164 Ozzie Guillen .20 .06
❑ 165 Mike Mussina .30 .09
❑ 166 Gary Sheffield .20 .06
❑ 167 Hideo Nomo .50 .15
❑ 168 Mark Grace .30 .09
❑ 169 Aaron Sele .20 .06
❑ 170 Darryl Kile .20 .06
❑ 171 Shawn Estes .20 .06
❑ 172 Vinny Castilla .20 .06
❑ 173 Ron Coomer .20 .06

❑ 174 Jose Rosado .20 .06
❑ 175 Kenny Lofton .20 .06
❑ 176 Jason Giambi .20 .06
❑ 177 Hal Morris .20 .06
❑ 178 Darren Bragg .20 .06
❑ 179 Orel Hershiser .20 .06
❑ 180 Ray Lankford .20 .06
❑ 181 Hideki Irabu .20 .06
❑ 182 Kevin Young .20 .06
❑ 183 Javy Lopez .20 .06
❑ 184 Jeff Montgomery .20 .06
❑ 185 Mike Holtz .20 .06
❑ 186 George Williams .20 .06
❑ 187 Cal Eldred .20 .06
❑ 188 Tom Candiotti .20 .06
❑ 189 Glenallen Hill .20 .06
❑ 190 Brian Giles .20 .06
❑ 191 Dave Mlicki .20 .06
❑ 192 Garrett Stephenson .20 .06
❑ 193 Jeff Frye .20 .06
❑ 194 Joe Oliver .20 .06
❑ 195 Bob Hamelin .20 .06
❑ 196 Luis Sojo .20 .06
❑ 197 LaTroy Hawkins .20 .06
❑ 198 Kevin Elster .20 .06
❑ 199 Jeff Reed .20 .06
❑ 200 Dennis Eckersley .20 .06
❑ 201 Bill Mueller .20 .06
❑ 202 Russ Davis .20 .06
❑ 203 Armando Benitez .20 .06
❑ 204 Quilvio Veras .20 .06
❑ 205 Tim Naehring .20 .06
❑ 206 Quinton McCracken .20 .06
❑ 207 Raul Casanova .20 .06
❑ 208 Matt Lawton .20 .06
❑ 209 Luis Alicea .20 .06
❑ 210 Luis Gonzalez .20 .06
❑ 211 Allen Watson .20 .06
❑ 212 Gerald Williams .20 .06
❑ 213 David Bell .20 .06
❑ 214 Todd Hollandsworth .20 .06
❑ 215 Wade Boggs .30 .09
❑ 216 Jose Mesa .20 .06
❑ 217 Jamie Moyer .20 .06
❑ 218 Darren Daulton .20 .06
❑ 219 Mickey Morandini .20 .06
❑ 220 Rusty Greer .20 .06
❑ 221 Jim Bullinger .20 .06
❑ 222 Jose Offerman .20 .06
❑ 223 Matt Karchner .20 .06
❑ 224 Woody Williams .20 .06
❑ 225 Mark Loretta .20 .06
❑ 226 Mike Hampton .20 .06
❑ 227 Willie Adams .20 .06
❑ 228 Scott Hatteberg .20 .06
❑ 229 Rich Amaral .20 .06
❑ 230 Terry Steinbach .20 .06
❑ 231 Glendon Rusch .20 .06
❑ 232 Bret Boone .20 .06
❑ 233 Robert Person .20 .06
❑ 234 Jose Hernandez .20 .06
❑ 235 Doug Drabek .20 .06
❑ 236 Jason McDonald .20 .06
❑ 237 Chris Widger .20 .06
❑ 238 Tom Martin .20 .06
❑ 239 Dave Burba .20 .06
❑ 240 Pete Rose Jr. .20 .06
❑ 241 Bobby Ayala .20 .06
❑ 242 Tim Wakefield .20 .06
❑ 243 Dennis Springer .20 .06
❑ 244 Tim Belcher .20 .06
❑ 245 Jon Garland .20 .06
Geoff Goetz
❑ 246 Glenn Davis .40 .12
Lance Berkman
❑ 247 Vernon Wells .30 .09
Aaron Akin
❑ 248 Adam Kennedy .20 .06
Jason Romano
❑ 249 Jason Dellaero .20 .06
Troy Cameron
❑ 250 Alex Sanchez .20 .06
Jared Sandberg
❑ 251 Pablo Ortega .20 .06
James Manias
❑ 252 Jason Conti RC .20 .06
Mike Stoner
❑ 253 John Patterson .20 .06
Larry Rodriguez
❑ 254 Adrian Beltre .50 .15
Ryan Minor RC
Aaron Boone
❑ 255 Ben Grieve .20 .06
Brian Buchanan
Dermal Brown
❑ 256 Kerry Wood .50 .15
Carl Pavano
Gil Meche
❑ 257 David Ortiz 1.00 .30
Daryle Ward
Richie Sexson
❑ 258 Randy Winn .20 .06
Juan Encarnacion
Andrew Vessel
❑ 259 Kris Benson .20 .06
Travis Smith
Courtney Duncan RC
❑ 260 Chad Hermansen .20 .06
Brent Butler
Warren Morris RC
❑ 261 Ben Davis .20 .06
Eli Marrero
Ramon Hernandez
❑ 262 Eric Chavez .30 .09
Russell Branyan
Russ Johnson
❑ 263 Todd Dunwoody RC .20 .06
John Barnes
Ryan Jackson
❑ 264 Matt Clement .20 .06
Roy Halladay
Brian Fuentes RC
❑ 265 Randy Johnson SH .30 .09
❑ 266 Kevin Brown SH .20 .06
❑ 267 Ricardo Rincon SH .20 .06
Francisco Cordova
❑ 268 N.Garciaparra SH .50 .15
❑ 269 Tino Martinez SH .20 .06
❑ 270 Chuck Knoblauch IL .20 .06
❑ 271 Pedro Martinez IL .30 .09
❑ 272 Denny Neagle IL .20 .06
❑ 273 Juan Gonzalez IL .20 .06
❑ 274 Andres Galarraga IL .20 .06
❑ 275 Checklist .20 .06
❑ 276 Checklist .20 .06
❑ 277 Moises Alou WS .20 .06
❑ 278 Sandy Alomar Jr. WS .20 .06
❑ 279 Gary Sheffield WS .20 .06
❑ 280 Matt Williams WS .20 .06
❑ 281 Livan Hernandez WS .20 .06
❑ 282 Chad Ogea WS .20 .06
❑ 283 Marlins Champs .20 .06
❑ 284 Tino Martinez .30 .09
❑ 285 Roberto Alomar .30 .09
❑ 286 Jeff King .20 .06
❑ 287 Brian Jordan .20 .06
❑ 288 Darin Erstad .20 .06
❑ 289 Ken Caminiti .20 .06
❑ 290 Jim Thome .50 .15
❑ 291 Paul Molitor .30 .09
❑ 292 Ivan Rodriguez .50 .15
❑ 293 Bernie Williams .30 .09
❑ 294 Todd Hundley .20 .06
❑ 295 Andres Galarraga .20 .06
❑ 296 Greg Maddux .75 .23
❑ 297 Edgar Martinez .30 .09
❑ 298 Ron Gant .20 .06
❑ 299 Derek Bell .20 .06
❑ 300 Roger Clemens 1.00 .30
❑ 301 Rondell White .20 .06
❑ 302 Barry Larkin .30 .09
❑ 303 Robin Ventura .20 .06
❑ 304 Jason Kendall .20 .06
❑ 305 Chipper Jones .50 .15
❑ 306 John Franco .20 .06
❑ 307 Sammy Sosa .75 .23
❑ 308 Troy Percival .20 .06
❑ 309 Chuck Knoblauch .20 .06
❑ 310 Ellis Burks .20 .06
❑ 311 Al Martin .20 .06
❑ 312 Tim Salmon .30 .09
❑ 313 Moises Alou .20 .06
❑ 314 Lance Johnson .20 .06
❑ 315 Justin Thompson .20 .06
❑ 316 Will Clark .50 .15
❑ 317 Barry Bonds 1.25 .35
❑ 318 Craig Biggio .30 .09
❑ 319 John Smoltz .30 .09
❑ 320 Cal Ripken 1.50 .45
❑ 321 Ken Griffey Jr. .75 .23
❑ 322 Paul O'Neill .30 .09
❑ 323 Todd Helton .30 .09
❑ 324 John Olerud .20 .06
❑ 325 Mark McGwire 1.25 .35
❑ 326 Jose Cruz Jr. .20 .06
❑ 327 Jeff Cirillo .20 .06
❑ 328 Dean Palmer .20 .06
❑ 329 John Wetteland .20 .06
❑ 330 Steve Finley .20 .06
❑ 331 Albert Belle .20 .06
❑ 332 Curt Schilling .20 .06
❑ 333 Raul Mondesi .20 .06
❑ 334 Andruw Jones .20 .06
❑ 335 Nomar Garciaparra .75 .23
❑ 336 David Justice .20 .06
❑ 337 Andy Pettitte .30 .09
❑ 338 Pedro Martinez .50 .15
❑ 339 Travis Miller .20 .06
❑ 340 Chris Stynes .20 .06
❑ 341 Gregg Jefferies .20 .06
❑ 342 Jeff Fassero .20 .06
❑ 343 Craig Counsell .20 .06
❑ 344 Wilson Alvarez .20 .06
❑ 345 Bip Roberts .20 .06
❑ 346 Kelvim Escobar .20 .06
❑ 347 Mark Bellhorn .20 .06
❑ 348 Cory Lidle RC .30 .09
❑ 349 Fred McGriff .30 .09
❑ 350 Chuck Carr .20 .06
❑ 351 Bob Abreu .20 .06
❑ 352 Juan Guzman .20 .06
❑ 353 Fernando Vina .20 .06
❑ 354 Andy Benes .20 .06
❑ 355 Dave Nilsson .20 .06
❑ 356 Bobby Bonilla .20 .06
❑ 357 Ismael Valdes .20 .06
❑ 358 Carlos Perez .20 .06
❑ 359 Kirk Rueter .20 .06
❑ 360 Bartolo Colon .20 .06
❑ 361 Mel Rojas .20 .06
❑ 362 Johnny Damon .30 .09
❑ 363 Geronimo Berroa .20 .06
❑ 364 Reggie Sanders .20 .06
❑ 365 Jermaine Allensworth .20 .06
❑ 366 Orlando Cabrera .20 .06
❑ 367 Jorge Fabregas .20 .06
❑ 368 Scott Stahoviak .20 .06
❑ 369 Ken Cloude .20 .06
❑ 370 Donovan Osborne .20 .06
❑ 371 Roger Cedeno .20 .06
❑ 372 Neifi Perez .20 .06
❑ 373 Chris Holt .20 .06
❑ 374 Cecil Fielder .20 .06
❑ 375 Marty Cordova .20 .06
❑ 376 Tom Goodwin .20 .06
❑ 377 Jeff Suppan .20 .06
❑ 378 Jeff Brantley .20 .06
❑ 379 Mark Langston .20 .06
❑ 380 Shane Reynolds .20 .06
❑ 381 Mike Fetters .20 .06
❑ 382 Todd Greene .20 .06
❑ 383 Ray Durham .20 .06
❑ 384 Carlos Delgado .20 .06
❑ 385 Jeff D'Amico .20 .06
❑ 386 Brian McRae .20 .06
❑ 387 Alan Benes .20 .06
❑ 388 Heathcliff Slocumb .20 .06
❑ 389 Eric Young .20 .06
❑ 390 Travis Fryman .20 .06
❑ 391 David Cone .20 .06
❑ 392 Otis Nixon .20 .06
❑ 393 Jeremi Gonzalez .20 .06
❑ 394 Jeff Juden .20 .06
❑ 395 Jose Vizcaino .20 .06
❑ 396 Ugueth Urbina .20 .06
❑ 397 Ramon Martinez .20 .06
❑ 398 Robb Nen .20 .06
❑ 399 Harold Baines .20 .06

❑ 400 Delino DeShields .20 .06
❑ 401 John Burkett .20 .06
❑ 402 Sterling Hitchcock .20 .06
❑ 403 Mark Clark .20 .06
❑ 404 Terrell Wade .20 .06
❑ 405 Scott Brosius .20 .06
❑ 406 Chad Curtis .20 .06
❑ 407 Brian Johnson .20 .06
❑ 408 Roberto Kelly .20 .06
❑ 409 Dave Dellucci RC .40 .12
❑ 410 Michael Tucker .20 .06
❑ 411 Mark Kotsay .20 .06
❑ 412 Mark Lewis .20 .06
❑ 413 Ryan McGuire .20 .06
❑ 414 Shawon Dunston .20 .06
❑ 415 Brad Rigby .20 .06
❑ 416 Scott Erickson .20 .06
❑ 417 Bobby Jones .20 .06
❑ 418 Darren Oliver .20 .06
❑ 419 John Smiley .20 .06
❑ 420 T.J. Mathews .20 .06
❑ 421 Dustin Hermanson .20 .06
❑ 422 Mike Timlin .20 .06
❑ 423 Willie Blair .20 .06
❑ 424 Manny Alexander .20 .06
❑ 425 Bob Tewksbury .20 .06
❑ 426 Pete Schourek .20 .06
❑ 427 Reggie Jefferson .20 .06
❑ 428 Ed Sprague .20 .06
❑ 429 Jeff Conine .20 .06
❑ 430 Roberto Hernandez .20 .06
❑ 431 Tom Pagnozzi .20 .06
❑ 432 Jaret Wright .20 .06
❑ 433 Livan Hernandez .20 .06
❑ 434 Andy Ashby .20 .06
❑ 435 Todd Dunn .20 .06
❑ 436 Bobby Higginson .20 .06
❑ 437 Rod Beck .20 .06
❑ 438 Jim Leyritz .20 .06
❑ 439 Matt Williams .20 .06
❑ 440 Brett Tomko .20 .06
❑ 441 Joe Randa .20 .06
❑ 442 Chris Carpenter .20 .06
❑ 443 Dennis Reyes .20 .06
❑ 444 Al Leiter .20 .06
❑ 445 Jason Schmidt .20 .06
❑ 446 Ken Hill .20 .06
❑ 447 Shannon Stewart .20 .06
❑ 448 Enrique Wilson .20 .06
❑ 449 Fernando Tatis .20 .06
❑ 450 Jimmy Key .20 .06
❑ 451 Darrin Fletcher .20 .06
❑ 452 John Valentin .20 .06
❑ 453 Kevin Tapani .20 .06
❑ 454 Eric Karros .20 .06
❑ 455 Jay Bell .20 .06
❑ 456 Walt Weiss .20 .06
❑ 457 Devon White .20 .06
❑ 458 Carl Pavano .30 .06
❑ 459 Mike Lansing .20 .06
❑ 460 John Flaherty .20 .06
❑ 461 Richard Hidalgo .20 .06
❑ 462 Quinton McCracken .20 .06
❑ 463 Karim Garcia .20 .06
❑ 464 Miguel Cairo .20 .06
❑ 465 Edwin Diaz .20 .06
❑ 466 Bobby Smith .20 .06
❑ 467 Yamil Benitez .20 .06
❑ 468 Rich Butler .20 .06
❑ 469 Ben Ford RC .20 .06
❑ 470 Bubba Trammell .20 .06
❑ 471 Brent Brede .20 .06
❑ 472 Brooks Kieschnick .20 .06
❑ 473 Carlos Castillo .20 .06
❑ 474 Brad Radke SH .20 .06
❑ 475 Roger Clemens SH .50 .15
❑ 476 Curt Schilling SH .20 .06
❑ 477 John Olerud SH .20 .06
❑ 478 Mark McGwire SH .60 .18
❑ 479 Mike Piazza .50 .15
Ken Griffey Jr. IL
❑ 480 Jeff Bagwell .30 .09
Frank Thomas IL
❑ 481 Chipper Jones .30 .09
Nomar Garciaparra IL
❑ 482 Larry Walker .20 .06
Juan Gonzalez IL
❑ 483 Gary Sheffield .20 .06
Tino Martinez IL
❑ 484 Derrick Gibson .20 .06
Michael Coleman
Norm Hutchins
❑ 485 Braden Looper .20 .06
Cliff Politte
Brian Rose
❑ 486 Eric Milton .20 .06
Jason Marquis
Corey Lee
❑ 487 A.J.Hinch .30 .09
Mark Osborne
Robert Fick RC
❑ 488 Aramis Ramirez .30 .09
Alex Gonzalez
Sean Casey
❑ 489 Donnie Bridges .20 .06
Tim Drew RC
❑ 490 Ntema Ndungidi RC .20 .06
Darnell McDonald
❑ 491 Ryan Anderson RC .30 .09
Mark Mangum
❑ 492 J.J.Davis 1.50 .45
Troy Glaus RC
❑ 493 Jayson Werth RC .20 .06
Dan Reichert
❑ 494 John Curtice RC .40 .12
Michael Cuddyer RC
❑ 495 Jack Cust RC .30 .09
Jason Standridge
❑ 496 Brian Anderson .20 .06
❑ 497 Tony Saunders .20 .06
❑ 498 Vladimir Nunez .20 .06
Jhensy Sandoval
❑ 499 Brad Penny .30 .09
Nick Bierbrodt
❑ 500 Dustin Carr .20 .06
Luis Cruz RC
❑ 501 Cedric Bowers .20 .06
Marcus McCain
❑ 502 Checklist .20 .06
❑ 503 Checklist .20 .06
❑ 504 Alex Rodriguez 2.00 .60

1999 Topps

	Nm-Mt	Ex-Mt
COMPLETE SET (462)	80.00	24.00
COMP.HOBBY SET (462)	80.00	24.00
COMP.X-MAS SET (463)	80.00	24.00
COMP. SERIES 1 (241)	40.00	12.00
COMP. SERIES 2 (221)	40.00	12.00
COMP.MAC HR SET (70)	400.00	120.00
COMP.SOSA HR SET (66)	200.00	60.00

❑ 1 Roger Clemens 1.00 .30
❑ 2 Andres Galarraga .20 .06
❑ 3 Scott Brosius .20 .06
❑ 4 John Flaherty .20 .06
❑ 5 Jim Leyritz .20 .06
❑ 6 Ray Durham .20 .06
❑ 8 Jose Vizcaino .20 .06
❑ 9 Will Clark .50 .15
❑ 10 David Wells .20 .06
❑ 11 Jose Guillen .20 .06
❑ 12 Scott Hatteberg .20 .06
❑ 13 Edgardo Alfonzo .20 .06
❑ 14 Mike Bordick .20 .06
❑ 15 Manny Ramirez .30 .09
❑ 16 Greg Maddux .75 .23
❑ 17 David Segui .20 .06
❑ 18 Darryl Strawberry .20 .06
❑ 19 Brad Radke .20 .06
❑ 20 Kerry Wood .50 .15
❑ 21 Matt Anderson .20 .06
❑ 22 Derrek Lee .20 .06
❑ 23 Mickey Morandini .20 .06
❑ 24 Paul Konerko .20 .06
❑ 25 Travis Lee .20 .06
❑ 26 Ken Hill .20 .06
❑ 27 Kenny Rogers .20 .06
❑ 28 Paul Sorrento .20 .06
❑ 29 Quilvio Veras .20 .06
❑ 30 Todd Walker .20 .06
❑ 31 Ryan Jackson .20 .06
❑ 32 John Olerud .20 .06
❑ 33 Doug Glanville .20 .06
❑ 34 Nolan Ryan 2.00 .60
❑ 35 Ray Lankford .20 .06
❑ 36 Mark Loretta .20 .06
❑ 37 Jason Dickson .20 .06
❑ 38 Sean Bergman .20 .06
❑ 39 Quinton McCracken .20 .06
❑ 40 Bartolo Colon .20 .06
❑ 41 Brady Anderson .20 .06
❑ 42 Chris Stynes .20 .06
❑ 43 Jorge Posada .30 .09
❑ 44 Justin Thompson .20 .06
❑ 45 Johnny Damon .30 .09
❑ 46 Armando Benitez .20 .06
❑ 47 Brant Brown .20 .06
❑ 48 Charlie Hayes .20 .06
❑ 49 Darren Dreifort .20 .06
❑ 50 Juan Gonzalez .30 .09
❑ 51 Chuck Knoblauch .20 .06
❑ 52 Todd Helton .30 .09
❑ 53 Rick Reed .20 .06
❑ 54 Chris Gomez .20 .06
❑ 55 Gary Sheffield .20 .06
❑ 56 Rod Beck .20 .06
❑ 57 Rey Sanchez .20 .06
❑ 58 Garret Anderson .20 .06
❑ 59 Jimmy Haynes .20 .06
❑ 60 Steve Woodard .20 .06
❑ 61 Rondell White .20 .06
❑ 62 Vladimir Guerrero .50 .15
❑ 63 Eric Karros .20 .06
❑ 64 Russ Davis .20 .06
❑ 65 Mo Vaughn .20 .06
❑ 66 Sammy Sosa .75 .23
❑ 67 Troy Percival .20 .06
❑ 68 Kenny Lofton .20 .06
❑ 69 Bill Taylor .20 .06
❑ 70 Mark McGwire 1.25 .35
❑ 71 Roger Cedeno .20 .06
❑ 72 Javy Lopez .20 .06
❑ 73 Damion Easley .20 .06
❑ 74 Andy Pettitte .30 .09
❑ 75 Tony Gwynn .60 .18
❑ 76 Ricardo Rincon .20 .06
❑ 77 F.P. Santangelo .20 .06
❑ 78 Jay Bell .20 .06
❑ 79 Scott Servais .20 .06
❑ 80 Jose Canseco .50 .15
❑ 81 Roberto Hernandez .20 .06
❑ 82 Todd Dunwoody .20 .06
❑ 83 John Wetteland .20 .06
❑ 84 Mike Caruso .20 .06
❑ 85 Derek Jeter 1.25 .35
❑ 86 Aaron Sele .20 .06
❑ 87 Jose Lima .20 .06
❑ 88 Ryan Christenson .20 .06
❑ 89 Jeff Cirillo .20 .06
❑ 90 Jose Hernandez .20 .06
❑ 91 Mark Kotsay .20 .06
❑ 92 Darren Bragg .20 .06
❑ 93 Albert Belle .20 .06
❑ 94 Matt Lawton .20 .06
❑ 95 Pedro Martinez .50 .15
❑ 96 Greg Vaughn .20 .06
❑ 97 Neifi Perez .20 .06
❑ 98 Gerald Williams .20 .06

- ❑ 99 Derek Bell .20 .06
- ❑ 100 Ken Griffey Jr. .75 .23
- ❑ 101 David Cone .20 .06
- ❑ 102 Brian Johnson .20 .06
- ❑ 103 Dean Palmer .20 .06
- ❑ 104 Javier Valentin .20 .06
- ❑ 105 Trevor Hoffman .20 .06
- ❑ 106 Butch Huskey .20 .06
- ❑ 107 Dave Martinez .20 .06
- ❑ 108 Billy Wagner .20 .06
- ❑ 109 Shawn Green .20 .06
- ❑ 110 Ben Grieve .20 .06
- ❑ 111 Tom Goodwin .20 .06
- ❑ 112 Jaret Wright .20 .06
- ❑ 113 Aramis Ramirez .20 .06
- ❑ 114 Dmitri Young .20 .06
- ❑ 115 Hideki Irabu .20 .06
- ❑ 116 Roberto Kelly .20 .06
- ❑ 117 Jeff Fassero .20 .06
- ❑ 118 Mark Clark UER .20 .06
  - 1997 and Career Victory totals are wrong
- ❑ 119 Jason McDonald .20 .06
- ❑ 120 Matt Williams .20 .06
- ❑ 121 Dave Burba .20 .06
- ❑ 122 Bret Saberhagen .20 .06
- ❑ 123 Deivi Cruz .20 .06
- ❑ 124 Chad Curtis .20 .06
- ❑ 125 Scott Rolen .50 .15
- ❑ 126 Lee Stevens .20 .06
- ❑ 127 J.T. Snow .20 .06
- ❑ 128 Rusty Greer .20 .06
- ❑ 129 Brian Meadows .20 .06
- ❑ 130 Jim Edmonds .20 .06
- ❑ 131 Ron Gant .20 .06
- ❑ 132 A.J. Hinch UER .20 .06
  - Photo is a reverse negative
- ❑ 133 Shannon Stewart .20 .06
- ❑ 134 Brad Fullmer .20 .06
- ❑ 135 Cal Eldred .20 .06
- ❑ 136 Matt Walbeck .20 .06
- ❑ 137 Carl Everett .20 .06
- ❑ 138 Walt Weiss .20 .06
- ❑ 139 Fred McGriff .30 .09
- ❑ 140 Darin Erstad .20 .06
- ❑ 141 Dave Nilsson .20 .06
- ❑ 142 Eric Young .20 .06
- ❑ 143 Dan Wilson .20 .06
- ❑ 144 Jeff Reed .20 .06
- ❑ 145 Brett Tomko .20 .06
- ❑ 146 Terry Steinbach .20 .06
- ❑ 147 Seth Greisinger .20 .06
- ❑ 148 Pat Meares .20 .06
- ❑ 149 Livan Hernandez .20 .06
- ❑ 150 Jeff Bagwell .30 .09
- ❑ 151 Bob Wickman .20 .06
- ❑ 152 Omar Vizquel .30 .09
- ❑ 153 Eric Davis .20 .06
- ❑ 154 Larry Sutton .20 .06
- ❑ 155 Magglio Ordonez .20 .06
- ❑ 156 Eric Milton .20 .06
- ❑ 157 Darren Lewis .20 .06
- ❑ 158 Rick Aguilera .20 .06
- ❑ 159 Mike Lieberthal .20 .06
- ❑ 160 Robb Nen .20 .06
- ❑ 161 Brian Giles .20 .06
- ❑ 162 Jeff Brantley .20 .06
- ❑ 163 Gary DiSarcina .20 .06
- ❑ 164 John Valentin .20 .06
- ❑ 165 David Dellucci .20 .06
- ❑ 166 Chan Ho Park .20 .06
- ❑ 167 Masato Yoshii .20 .06
- ❑ 168 Jason Schmidt .20 .06
- ❑ 169 LaTroy Hawkins .20 .06
- ❑ 170 Bret Boone .20 .06
- ❑ 171 Jerry DiPoto .20 .06
- ❑ 172 Mariano Rivera .30 .09
- ❑ 173 Mike Cameron .20 .06
- ❑ 174 Scott Erickson .20 .06
- ❑ 175 Charles Johnson .20 .06
- ❑ 176 Bobby Jones .20 .06
- ❑ 177 Francisco Cordova .20 .06
- ❑ 178 Todd Jones .20 .06
- ❑ 179 Jeff Montgomery .20 .06
- ❑ 180 Mike Mussina .30 .09
- ❑ 181 Bob Abreu .20 .06
- ❑ 182 Ismael Valdes .20 .06
- ❑ 183 Andy Fox .20 .06
- ❑ 184 Woody Williams .20 .06
- ❑ 185 Denny Neagle .20 .06
- ❑ 186 Jose Valentin .20 .06
- ❑ 187 Darrin Fletcher .20 .06
- ❑ 188 Gabe Alvarez .20 .06
- ❑ 189 Eddie Taubensee .20 .06
- ❑ 190 Edgar Martinez .30 .09
- ❑ 191 Jason Kendall .20 .06
- ❑ 192 Darryl Kile .20 .06
- ❑ 193 Jeff King .20 .06
- ❑ 194 Rey Ordonez .20 .06
- ❑ 195 Andruw Jones .20 .06
- ❑ 196 Tony Fernandez .20 .06
- ❑ 197 Jamey Wright .20 .06
- ❑ 198 B.J. Surhoff .20 .06
- ❑ 199 Vinny Castilla .20 .06
- ❑ 200 David Wells HL .20 .06
- ❑ 201 Mark McGwire HL .60 .18
- ❑ 202 Sammy Sosa HL .50 .15
- ❑ 203 Roger Clemens HL .50 .15
- ❑ 204 Kerry Wood HL .30 .09
- ❑ 205 Lance Berkman .40 .12
  - Mike Frank
  - Gabe Kapler
- ❑ 206 Alex Escobar RC .40 .12
  - Ricky Ledee
  - Mike Stoner
- ❑ 207 Peter Bergeron RC .40 .12
  - Jeremy Giambi
  - George Lombard
- ❑ 208 Michael Barrett .25 .07
  - Ben Davis
  - Robert Fick
- ❑ 209 Pat Cline .25 .07
  - Ramon Hernandez
  - Jayson Werth
- ❑ 210 Bruce Chen .25 .07
  - Chris Enochs
  - Ryan Anderson
- ❑ 211 Mike Lincoln .25 .07
  - Octavio Dotel
  - Brad Penny
- ❑ 212 Chuck Abbott RC .25 .07
  - Brent Butler
  - Danny Klassen
- ❑ 213 Chris C.Jones .25 .07
  - Jeff Urban RC
- ❑ 214 Arturo McDowell RC .25 .07
  - Tony Torcato
- ❑ 215 Josh McKinley RC .40 .12
  - Jason Tyner
- ❑ 216 Matt Burch .25 .07
  - Seth Etherton RC
  - UER back Etherton
- ❑ 217 Mamon Tucker RC .40 .12
  - Rick Elder
- ❑ 218 J.M.Gold .25 .07
  - Ryan Mills RC
- ❑ 219 Adam Brown .25 .07
  - Choo Freeman RC
- ❑ 220A Mark McGwire HR 1 40.00 12.00
- ❑ 220B Mark McGwire HR 2 15.00 4.50
- ❑ 220C Mark McGwire HR 3 15.00 4.50
- ❑ 220D Mark McGwire HR 4 15.00 4.50
- ❑ 220E Mark McGwire HR 5 15.00 4.50
- ❑ 220F Mark McGwire HR 6 15.00 4.50
- ❑ 220G Mark McGwire HR 7 15.00 4.50
- ❑ 220H Mark McGwire HR 8 15.00 4.50
- ❑ 220I Mark McGwire HR 9 15.00 4.50
- ❑ 220J M.McGwire HR 10 15.00 4.50
- ❑ 220K M.McGwire HR 11 15.00 4.50
- ❑ 220L M.McGwire HR 12 15.00 4.50
- ❑ 220M M.McGwire HR 13 15.00 4.50
- ❑ 220N M.McGwire HR 14 15.00 4.50
- ❑ 220O M.McGwire HR 15 15.00 4.50
- ❑ 220P M.McGwire HR 16 15.00 4.50
- ❑ 220Q M.McGwire HR 17 15.00 4.50
- ❑ 220R M.McGwire HR 18 15.00 4.50
- ❑ 220S M.McGwire HR 19 15.00 4.50
- ❑ 220T M.McGwire HR 20 15.00 4.50
- ❑ 220U M.McGwire HR 21 15.00 4.50
- ❑ 220V M.McGwire HR 22 15.00 4.50
- ❑ 220W M.McGwire HR 23 15.00 4.50
- ❑ 220X M.McGwire HR 24 15.00 4.50
- ❑ 220Y M.McGwire HR 25 15.00 4.50
- ❑ 220Z M.McGwire HR 26 15.00 4.50
- ❑ 220AA M.McGwire HR 27 15.00 4.50
- ❑ 220AB M.McGwire HR 28 15.00 4.50
- ❑ 220AC M.McGwire HR 29 15.00 4.50
- ❑ 220AD M.McGwire HR 30 15.00 4.50
- ❑ 220AE M.McGwire HR 31 15.00 4.50
- ❑ 220AF M.McGwire HR 32 15.00 4.50
- ❑ 220AG M.McGwire HR 33 15.00 4.50
- ❑ 220AH M.McGwire HR 34 15.00 4.50
- ❑ 220AI M.McGwire HR 35 15.00 4.50
- ❑ 220AJ M.McGwire HR 36 15.00 4.50
- ❑ 220AK M.McGwire HR 37 15.00 4.50
- ❑ 220AL M.McGwire HR 38 15.00 4.50
- ❑ 220AM M.McGwire HR 39 15.00 4.50
- ❑ 220AN M.McGwire HR 40 15.00 4.50
- ❑ 220AO M.McGwire HR 41 15.00 4.50
- ❑ 220AP M.McGwire HR 42 15.00 4.50
- ❑ 220AQ M.McGwire HR 43 15.00 4.50
- ❑ 220AR M.McGwire HR 44 15.00 4.50
- ❑ 220AS M.McGwire HR 45 15.00 4.50
- ❑ 220AT M.McGwire HR 46 15.00 4.50
- ❑ 220AU M.McGwire HR 47 15.00 4.50
- ❑ 220AV M.McGwire HR 48 15.00 4.50
- ❑ 220AW M.McGwire HR 49 15.00 4.50
- ❑ 220AX M.McGwire HR 50 15.00 4.50
- ❑ 220AY M.McGwire HR 51 15.00 4.50
- ❑ 220AZ M.McGwire HR 52 15.00 4.50
- ❑ 220BB M.McGwire HR 53 15.00 4.50
- ❑ 220CC M.McGwire HR 54 15.00 4.50
- ❑ 220DD M.McGwire HR 55 15.00 4.50
- ❑ 220EE M.McGwire HR 56 15.00 4.50
- ❑ 220FF M.McGwire HR 57 15.00 4.50
- ❑ 220GG M.McGwire HR 58 15.00 4.50
- ❑ 220HH M.McGwire HR 59 15.00 4.50
- ❑ 220II M.McGwire HR 60 15.00 4.50
- ❑ 220JJ M.McGwire HR 61 30.00 9.00
- ❑ 220KK M.McGwire HR 62 40.00 12.00
- ❑ 220LL M.McGwire HR 63 15.00 4.50
- ❑ 220MM M.McGwire HR 64 15.00 4.50
- ❑ 220NN M.McGwire HR 65 15.00 4.50
- ❑ 220OO M.McGwire HR 66 15.00 4.50
- ❑ 220PP M.McGwire HR 67 15.00 4.50
- ❑ 220QQ M.McGwire HR 68 15.00 4.50
- ❑ 220RR M.McGwire HR 69 15.00 4.50
- ❑ 220SS M.McGwire HR 70 80.00 24.00
- ❑ 221 Larry Walker LL .20 .06
- ❑ 222 Bernie Williams LL .20 .06
- ❑ 223 Mark McGwire LL .60 .18
- ❑ 224 Ken Griffey Jr. LL .50 .15
- ❑ 225 Sammy Sosa LL .50 .15
- ❑ 226 Juan Gonzalez LL .20 .06
- ❑ 227 Dante Bichette LL .20 .06
- ❑ 228 Alex Rodriguez LL .50 .15
- ❑ 229 Sammy Sosa LL .50 .15
- ❑ 230 Derek Jeter LL .60 .18
- ❑ 231 Greg Maddux LL .50 .15
- ❑ 232 Roger Clemens LL .50 .15
- ❑ 233 Ricky Ledee WS .20 .06
- ❑ 234 Chuck Knoblauch WS .20 .06
- ❑ 235 Bernie Williams WS .20 .06
- ❑ 236 Tino Martinez WS .20 .06
- ❑ 237 Orl. Hernandez WS .20 .06
- ❑ 238 Scott Brosius WS .20 .06
- ❑ 239 Andy Pettitte WS .20 .06
- ❑ 240 Mariano Rivera WS .20 .06
- ❑ 241 Checklist 1 .20 .06
- ❑ 242 Checklist 2 .20 .06
- ❑ 243 Tom Glavine .30 .09
- ❑ 244 Andy Benes .20 .06
- ❑ 245 Sandy Alomar Jr. .20 .06
- ❑ 246 Wilton Guerrero .20 .06
- ❑ 247 Alex Gonzalez .20 .06
- ❑ 248 Roberto Alomar .30 .09
- ❑ 249 Ruben Rivera .20 .06
- ❑ 250 Eric Chavez .20 .06
- ❑ 251 Ellis Burks .20 .06
- ❑ 252 Richie Sexson .20 .06
- ❑ 253 Steve Finley .20 .06
- ❑ 254 Dwight Gooden .20 .06
- ❑ 255 Dustin Hermanson .20 .06
- ❑ 256 Kirk Rueter .20 .06
- ❑ 257 Steve Trachsel .20 .06
- ❑ 258 Gregg Jefferies .20 .06
- ❑ 259 Matt Stairs .20 .06
- ❑ 260 Shane Reynolds .20 .06

❑ 261 Gregg Olson	.20	.06
❑ 262 Kevin Tapani	.20	.06
❑ 263 Matt Morris	.20	.06
❑ 264 Carl Pavano	.20	.06
❑ 265 Nomar Garciaparra	.75	.23
❑ 266 Kevin Young	.20	.06
❑ 267 Rick Helling	.20	.06
❑ 268 Matt Franco	.20	.06
❑ 269 Brian McRae	.20	.06
❑ 270 Cal Ripken	1.50	.45
❑ 271 Jeff Abbott	.20	.06
❑ 272 Tony Batista	.20	.06
❑ 273 Bill Simas	.20	.06
❑ 274 Brian Hunter	.20	.06
❑ 275 John Franco	.20	.06
❑ 276 Devon White	.20	.06
❑ 277 Rickey Henderson	.50	.15
❑ 278 Chuck Finley	.20	.06
❑ 279 Mike Blowers	.20	.06
❑ 280 Mark Grace	.30	.09
❑ 281 Randy Winn	.20	.06
❑ 282 Bobby Bonilla	.20	.06
❑ 283 David Justice	.20	.06
❑ 284 Shane Monahan	.20	.06
❑ 285 Kevin Brown	.30	.09
❑ 286 Todd Zeile	.20	.06
❑ 287 Al Martin	.20	.06
❑ 288 Troy O'Leary	.20	.06
❑ 289 Darryl Hamilton	.20	.06
❑ 290 Tino Martinez	.30	.09
❑ 291 David Ortiz	.30	.09
❑ 292 Tony Clark	.20	.06
❑ 293 Ryan Minor	.20	.06
❑ 294 Mark Leiter	.20	.06
❑ 295 Wally Joyner	.20	.06
❑ 296 Cliff Floyd	.20	.06
❑ 297 Shawn Estes	.20	.06
❑ 298 Pat Hentgen	.20	.06
❑ 299 Scott Elarton	.20	.06
❑ 300 Alex Rodriguez	.75	.23
❑ 301 Ozzie Guillen	.20	.06
❑ 302 Hideo Nomo	.50	.15
❑ 303 Ryan McGuire	.20	.06
❑ 304 Brad Ausmus	.20	.06
❑ 305 Alex Gonzalez	.20	.06
❑ 306 Brian Jordan	.20	.06
❑ 307 John Jaha	.20	.06
❑ 308 Mark Grudzielanek	.20	.06
❑ 309 Juan Guzman	.20	.06
❑ 310 Tony Womack	.20	.06
❑ 311 Dennis Reyes	.20	.06
❑ 312 Marty Cordova	.20	.06
❑ 313 Ramiro Mendoza	.20	.06
❑ 314 Robin Ventura	.20	.06
❑ 315 Rafael Palmeiro	.30	.09
❑ 316 Ramon Martinez	.20	.06
❑ 317 Pedro Astacio	.20	.06
❑ 318 Dave Hollins	.20	.06
❑ 319 Tom Candiotti	.20	.06
❑ 320 Al Leiter	.20	.06
❑ 321 Rico Brogna	.20	.06
❑ 322 Reggie Jefferson	.20	.06
❑ 323 Bernard Gilkey	.20	.06
❑ 324 Jason Giambi	.20	.06
❑ 325 Craig Biggio	.30	.09
❑ 326 Troy Glaus	.20	.06
❑ 327 Delino DeShields	.20	.06
❑ 328 Fernando Vina	.20	.06
❑ 329 John Smoltz	.30	.09
❑ 330 Jeff Kent	.20	.06
❑ 331 Roy Halladay	.20	.06
❑ 332 Andy Ashby	.20	.06
❑ 333 Tim Wakefield	.20	.06
❑ 334 Roger Clemens	1.00	.30
❑ 335 Bernie Williams	.30	.09
❑ 336 Desi Relaford	.20	.06
❑ 337 John Burkett	.20	.06
❑ 338 Mike Hampton	.20	.06
❑ 339 Royce Clayton	.20	.06
❑ 340 Mike Piazza	.75	.23
❑ 341 Jeremi Gonzalez	.20	.06
❑ 342 Mike Lansing	.20	.06
❑ 343 Jamie Moyer	.20	.06
❑ 344 Ron Coomer	.20	.06
❑ 345 Barry Larkin	.30	.09
❑ 346 Fernando Tatis	.20	.06
❑ 347 Chili Davis	.20	.06
❑ 348 Bobby Higginson	.20	.06
❑ 349 Hal Morris	.20	.06
❑ 350 Larry Walker	.30	.09
❑ 351 Carlos Guillen	.20	.06
❑ 352 Miguel Tejada	.20	.06
❑ 353 Travis Fryman	.20	.06
❑ 354 Jarrod Washburn	.20	.06
❑ 355 Chipper Jones	.50	.15
❑ 356 Todd Stottlemyre	.20	.06
❑ 357 Henry Rodriguez	.20	.06
❑ 358 Eli Marrero	.20	.06
❑ 359 Alan Benes	.20	.06
❑ 360 Tim Salmon	.30	.09
❑ 361 Luis Gonzalez	.20	.06
❑ 362 Scott Spiezio	.20	.06
❑ 363 Chris Carpenter	.20	.06
❑ 364 Bobby Howry	.20	.06
❑ 365 Raul Mondesi	.20	.06
❑ 366 Ugueth Urbina	.20	.06
❑ 367 Tom Evans	.20	.06
❑ 368 Kerry Ligtenberg RC	.25	.07
❑ 369 Adrian Beltre	.30	.09
❑ 370 Ryan Klesko	.20	.06
❑ 371 Wilson Alvarez	.20	.06
❑ 372 John Thomson	.20	.06
❑ 373 Tony Saunders	.20	.06
❑ 374 Dave Mlicki	.20	.06
❑ 375 Ken Caminiti	.20	.06
❑ 376 Jay Buhner	.20	.06
❑ 377 Bill Mueller	.20	.06
❑ 378 Jeff Blauser	.20	.06
❑ 379 Edgar Renteria	.20	.06
❑ 380 Jim Thome	.50	.15
❑ 381 Joey Hamilton	.20	.06
❑ 382 Calvin Pickering	.20	.06
❑ 383 Marquis Grissom	.20	.06
❑ 384 Omar Daal	.20	.06
❑ 385 Curt Schilling	.20	.06
❑ 386 Jose Cruz Jr.	.20	.06
❑ 387 Chris Widger	.20	.06
❑ 388 Pete Harnisch	.20	.06
❑ 389 Charles Nagy	.20	.06
❑ 390 Tom Gordon	.20	.06
❑ 391 Bobby Smith	.20	.06
❑ 392 Derrick Gibson	.20	.06
❑ 393 Jeff Conine	.20	.06
❑ 394 Carlos Perez	.20	.06
❑ 395 Barry Bonds	1.25	.35
❑ 396 Mark McLemore	.20	.06
❑ 397 Juan Encarnacion	.20	.06
❑ 398 Wade Boggs	.30	.09
❑ 399 Ivan Rodriguez	.50	.15
❑ 400 Moises Alou	.20	.06
❑ 401 Jeromy Burnitz	.20	.06
❑ 402 Sean Casey	.20	.06
❑ 403 Jose Offerman	.20	.06
❑ 404 Joe Fontenot	.20	.06
❑ 405 Kevin Millwood	.20	.06
❑ 406 Lance Johnson	.20	.06
❑ 407 Richard Hidalgo	.20	.06
❑ 408 Mike Jackson	.20	.06
❑ 409 Brian Anderson	.20	.06
❑ 410 Jeff Shaw	.20	.06
❑ 411 Preston Wilson	.20	.06
❑ 412 Todd Hundley	.20	.06
❑ 413 Jim Parque	.20	.06
❑ 414 Justin Baughman	.20	.06
❑ 415 Dante Bichette	.20	.06
❑ 416 Paul O'Neill	.30	.09
❑ 417 Miguel Cairo	.20	.06
❑ 418 Randy Johnson	.50	.15
❑ 419 Jesus Sanchez	.20	.06
❑ 420 Carlos Delgado	.20	.06
❑ 421 Ricky Ledee	.20	.06
❑ 422 Orlando Hernandez	.20	.06
❑ 423 Frank Thomas	.50	.15
❑ 424 Pokey Reese	.20	.06
❑ 425 Carlos Lee Mike Lowell Kit Pellow RC	.40	.12
❑ 426 Michael Cuddyer Mark DeRosa Jerry Hairston Jr.	.25	.07
❑ 427 Marlon Anderson Ron Belliard Orlando Cabrera	.40	.12
❑ 428 Micah Bowie Phil Norton RC Randy Wolf	.25	.07
❑ 429 Jack Cressend RC Jason Rakers John Rocker	.25	.07
❑ 430 Ruben Mateo Scott Morgan Mike Zywica RC	.25	.07
❑ 431 Jason LaRue Matt LeCroy Mitch Meluskey	.25	.07
❑ 432 Gabe Kapler Armando Rios Fernando Seguignol	.25	.07
❑ 433 Adam Kennedy Mickey Lopez RC Jackie Rexrode	.25	.07
❑ 434 Jose Fernandez RC Jeff Liefer Chris Truby	.25	.07
❑ 435 Corey Koskie Doug Mientkiewicz RC Damon Minor	.75	.23
❑ 436 Roosevelt Brown RC Dernell Stenson Vernon Wells	.40	.12
❑ 437 A.J. Burnett RC Billy Koch John Nicholson	.75	.23
❑ 438 Matt Belisle Matt Roney RC	.25	.07
❑ 439 Austin Kearns Chris George RC	2.00	.60
❑ 440 Nate Bump RC Nate Cornejo	.40	.12
❑ 441 Brad Lidge Mike Nannini RC	1.50	.45
❑ 442 Matt Holliday Jeff Winchester RC	.75	.23
❑ 443 Adam Everett Chip Ambres RC	.50	.15
❑ 444 Pat Burrell Eric Valent RC	1.25	.35
❑ 445 Roger Clemens SK	.50	.15
❑ 446 Kerry Wood SK	.30	.09
❑ 447 Curt Schilling SK	.20	.06
❑ 448 Randy Johnson SK	.30	.09
❑ 449 Pedro Martinez SK	.30	.09
❑ 450 Jeff Bagwell AT Andres Galarraga Mark McGwire	.50	.15
❑ 451 John Olerud AT Jim Thome Tino Martinez	.20	.06
❑ 452 Alex Rodriguez AT Nomar Garciaparra Derek Jeter	.60	.18
❑ 453 Vinny Castilla AT Chipper Jones Scott Rolen	.30	.09
❑ 454 Sammy Sosa AT Ken Griffey Jr. Juan Gonzalez	.50	.15
❑ 455 Barry Bonds AT Manny Ramirez Larry Walker	.50	.15
❑ 456 Frank Thomas AT Tim Salmon David Justice	.50	.15
❑ 457 Travis Lee AT Todd Helton Ben Grieve	.20	.06
❑ 458 Vladimir Guerrero AT Greg Vaughn Bernie Williams	.20	.06
❑ 459 Mike Piazza AT Ivan Rodriguez Jason Kendall	.50	.15
❑ 460 Roger Clemens AT Kerry Wood Greg Maddux	.50	.15
❑ 461A Sammy Sosa HR 1	20.00	6.00
❑ 461B Sammy Sosa HR 2	8.00	2.40
❑ 461C Sammy Sosa HR 3	8.00	2.40

Card	Nm-Mt	Ex-Mt
❑ 461D Sammy Sosa HR 4	8.00	2.40
❑ 461E Sammy Sosa HR 5	8.00	2.40
❑ 461F Sammy Sosa HR 6	8.00	2.40
❑ 461G Sammy Sosa HR 7	8.00	8.75
❑ 461H Sammy Sosa HR 8	8.00	2.40
❑ 461I Sammy Sosa HR 9	8.00	2.40
❑ 461J Sammy Sosa HR 10	8.00	2.40
❑ 461K Sammy Sosa HR 11	8.00	2.40
❑ 461L Sammy Sosa HR 12	8.00	2.40
❑ 461M Sammy Sosa HR 13	8.00	2.40
❑ 461N Sammy Sosa HR 14	8.00	2.40
❑ 461O Sammy Sosa HR 15	8.00	2.40
❑ 461P Sammy Sosa HR 16	8.00	2.40
❑ 461Q Sammy Sosa HR 17	8.00	2.40
❑ 461R Sammy Sosa HR 18	8.00	2.40
❑ 461S Sammy Sosa HR 19	8.00	2.40
❑ 461T Sammy Sosa HR 20	8.00	2.40
❑ 461U Sammy Sosa HR 21	8.00	2.40
❑ 461V Sammy Sosa HR 22	8.00	2.40
❑ 461W Sammy Sosa HR 23	8.00	2.40
❑ 461X Sammy Sosa HR 24	8.00	2.40
❑ 461Y Sammy Sosa HR 25	8.00	2.40
❑ 461Z Sammy Sosa HR 26	8.00	2.40
❑ 461AA S.Sosa HR 27	8.00	2.40
❑ 461AB S.Sosa HR 28	8.00	2.40
❑ 461AC S.Sosa HR 29	8.00	2.40
❑ 461AD S.Sosa HR 30	8.00	2.40
❑ 461AE S.Sosa HR 31	8.00	2.40
❑ 461AF S.Sosa HR 32	8.00	2.40
❑ 461AG S.Sosa HR 33	8.00	2.40
❑ 461AH S.Sosa HR 34	8.00	2.40
❑ 461AI S.Sosa HR 35	8.00	2.40
❑ 461AJ S.Sosa HR 36	8.00	2.40
❑ 461AK S.Sosa HR 37	8.00	2.40
❑ 461AL S.Sosa HR 38	8.00	2.40
❑ 461AM S.Sosa HR 39	8.00	2.40
❑ 461AN S.Sosa HR 40	8.00	2.40
❑ 461AO S.Sosa HR 41	8.00	2.40
❑ 461AP S.Sosa HR 42	8.00	2.40
❑ 461AR S.Sosa HR 43	8.00	2.40
❑ 461AS S.Sosa HR 44	8.00	2.40
❑ 461AT S.Sosa HR 45	8.00	2.40
❑ 461AU S.Sosa HR 46	8.00	2.40
❑ 461AV S.Sosa HR 47	8.00	2.40
❑ 461AW S.Sosa HR 48	8.00	2.40
❑ 461AX S.Sosa HR 49	8.00	2.40
❑ 461AY S.Sosa HR 50	8.00	2.40
❑ 461AZ S.Sosa HR 51	8.00	2.40
❑ 461BB S.Sosa HR 52	8.00	2.40
❑ 461CC S.Sosa HR 53	8.00	2.40
❑ 461DD S.Sosa HR 54	8.00	2.40
❑ 461EE S.Sosa HR 55	8.00	2.40
❑ 461FF S.Sosa HR 56	8.00	2.40
❑ 461GG S.Sosa HR 57	8.00	2.40
❑ 461HH S.Sosa HR 58	8.00	2.40
❑ 461II S.Sosa HR 59	8.00	2.40
❑ 461JJ S.Sosa HR 60	8.00	2.40
❑ 461KK S.Sosa HR 61	20.00	6.00
❑ 461LL S.Sosa HR 62	25.00	7.50
❑ 461MM S.Sosa HR 63	10.00	3.00
❑ 461NN S.Sosa HR 64	10.00	3.00
❑ 461OO S.Sosa HR 65	10.00	3.00
❑ 461PP S.Sosa HR 66	30.00	9.00
❑ 462 Checklist	.20	.06
❑ 463 Checklist	.20	.06

1999 Topps Traded

	Nm-Mt	Ex-Mt
COMP.FACT.SET (122)	40.00	12.00
COMPLETE SET (121)	25.00	7.50
❑ T1 Seth Etherton	.20	.06
❑ T2 Mark Harriger RC	.25	.07
❑ T3 Matt Wise RC	.25	.07
❑ T4 Carlos E. Hernandez RC	.25	.07
❑ T5 Julio Lugo RC	.25	.07
❑ T6 Mike Nannini	.20	.06
❑ T7 Justin Bowles RC	.25	.07
❑ T8 Mark Mulder RC	1.50	.35
❑ T9 Roberto Vaz RC	.25	.07
❑ T10 Felipe Lopez RC	.25	.07
❑ T11 Matt Belisle	.20	.06
❑ T12 Micah Bowie	.20	.06
❑ T13 Ruben Quevedo RC	.25	.07
❑ T14 Jose Garcia RC	.25	.07
❑ T15 David Kelton RC	.25	.07
❑ T16 Phil Norton	.20	.06
❑ T17 Corey Patterson RC	1.50	.45
❑ T18 Ron Walker RC	.25	.07
❑ T19 Paul Hoover RC	.25	.07
❑ T20 Ryan Rupe RC	.25	.07
❑ T21 J.D. Closser RC	.40	.12
❑ T22 Rob Ryan RC	.25	.07
❑ T23 Steve Colyer RC	.25	.07
❑ T24 Bubba Crosby RC	.40	.12
❑ T25 Luke Prokopec RC	.25	.07
❑ T26 Matt Blank RC	.25	.07
❑ T27 Josh McKinley	.20	.06
❑ T28 Nate Bump	.20	.06
❑ T29 G.Chiaramonte RC	.25	.07
❑ T30 Arturo McDowell	.20	.06
❑ T31 Tony Torcato	.20	.06
❑ T32 Dave Roberts RC	.40	.12
❑ T33 C.C. Sabathia RC	.75	.23
❑ T34 Sean Spencer RC	.25	.07
❑ T35 Chip Ambres	.20	.06
❑ T36 A.J. Burnett	.60	.18
❑ T37 Mo Bruce RC	.25	.07
❑ T38 Jason Tyner	.20	.06
❑ T39 Mamon Tucker	.20	.06
❑ T40 Sean Burroughs RC	1.00	.30
❑ T41 Kevin Eberwein RC	.25	.07
❑ T42 Junior Herndon RC	.25	.07
❑ T43 Bryan Wolff RC	.25	.07
❑ T44 Pat Burrell	1.00	.30
❑ T45 Eric Valent	.20	.06
❑ T46 Carlos Pena RC	.40	.12
❑ T47 Mike Zywica	.20	.06
❑ T48 Adam Everett	.30	.09
❑ T49 Juan Pena RC	.25	.07
❑ T50 Adam Dunn RC	3.00	.90
❑ T51 Austin Kearns	1.50	.45
❑ T52 Jacobo Sequea RC	.25	.07
❑ T53 Choo Freeman	.20	.06
❑ T54 Jeff Winchester	.20	.06
❑ T55 Matt Burch	.20	.06
❑ T56 Chris George	.20	.06
❑ T57 Scott Mullen RC	.25	.07
❑ T58 Kit Pellow	.20	.06
❑ T59 Mark Quinn RC	.25	.07
❑ T60 Nate Cornejo	.25	.07
❑ T61 Ryan Mills	.20	.06
❑ T62 Kevin Beirne RC	.25	.07
❑ T63 Kip Wells RC	.40	.12
❑ T64 Juan Rivera RC	.25	.07
❑ T65 Alfonso Soriano RC	4.00	1.20
❑ T66 Josh Hamilton RC	.40	.12
❑ T67 Josh Girdley RC	.25	.07
❑ T68 Kyle Snyder RC	.25	.07
❑ T69 Mike Paradis RC	.25	.07
❑ T70 Jason Jennings RC	.40	.12
❑ T71 David Walling RC	.25	.07
❑ T72 Omar Ortiz RC	.25	.07
❑ T73 Jay Gehrke RC	.25	.07
❑ T74 Casey Burns RC	.25	.07
❑ T75 Carl Crawford RC	1.25	.35
❑ T76 Reggie Sanders	.20	.06
❑ T77 Will Clark	.50	.15
❑ T78 David Wells	.20	.06
❑ T79 Paul Konerko	.20	.06
❑ T80 Armando Benitez	.20	.06
❑ T81 Brant Brown	.20	.06
❑ T82 Mo Vaughn	.20	.06
❑ T83 Jose Canseco	.50	.15
❑ T84 Albert Belle	.20	.06
❑ T85 Dean Palmer	.20	.06
❑ T86 Greg Vaughn	.20	.06
❑ T87 Mark Clark	.20	.06
❑ T88 Pat Meares	.20	.06
❑ T89 Eric Davis	.20	.06
❑ T90 Brian Giles	.20	.06
❑ T91 Jeff Brantley	.20	.06
❑ T92 Bret Boone	.20	.06
❑ T93 Ron Gant	.20	.06
❑ T94 Mike Cameron	.20	.06
❑ T95 Charles Johnson	.20	.06
❑ T96 Denny Neagle	.20	.06
❑ T97 Brian Hunter	.20	.06
❑ T98 Jose Hernandez	.20	.06
❑ T99 Rick Aguilera	.20	.06
❑ T100 Tony Batista	.20	.06
❑ T101 Roger Cedeno	.20	.06
❑ T102 C.Gubanich RC	.25	.07
❑ T103 Tim Belcher	.20	.06
❑ T104 Bruce Aven	.20	.06
❑ T105 Brian Daubach RC	.25	.07
❑ T106 Ed Sprague	.20	.06
❑ T107 Michael Tucker	.20	.06
❑ T108 Homer Bush	.20	.06
❑ T109 Armando Reynoso	.20	.06
❑ T110 Brook Fordyce	.20	.06
❑ T111 Matt Mantei	.20	.06
❑ T112 Dave Mlicki	.20	.06
❑ T113 Kenny Rogers	.20	.06
❑ T114 Livan Hernandez	.20	.06
❑ T115 Butch Huskey	.20	.06
❑ T116 David Segui	.20	.06
❑ T117 Darryl Hamilton	.20	.06
❑ T118 Terry Mulholland	.20	.06
❑ T119 Randy Velarde	.20	.06
❑ T120 Bill Taylor	.20	.06
❑ T121 Kevin Appier	.20	.06

2000 Topps

	Nm-Mt	Ex-Mt
COMPLETE SET (478)	50.00	15.00
COMP.HOBBY SET (478)	50.00	15.00
COMP. SERIES 1 (239)	25.00	7.50
COMP. SERIES 2 (240)	25.00	7.50
MCGWIRE MM SET (5)	12.00	3.60
AARON MM SET (5)	10.00	3.00
RIPKEN MM SET (5)	15.00	4.50
BOGGS MM SET (5)	3.00	.90
GWYNN MM SET (5)	6.00	1.80
GRIFFEY MM SET (5)	8.00	2.40
BONDS MM SET (5)	12.00	3.60
SOSA MM SET (5)	8.00	2.40
JETER MM SET (5)	12.00	3.60
A.ROD MM SET (5)	8.00	2.40
❑ 1 Mark McGwire	1.25	.35
❑ 2 Tony Gwynn	.60	.18
❑ 3 Wade Boggs	.30	.09
❑ 4 Cal Ripken	1.50	.45
❑ 5 Matt Williams	.20	.06
❑ 6 Jay Buhner	.20	.06
❑ 8 Jeff Conine	.20	.06
❑ 9 Todd Greene	.20	.06
❑ 10 Mike Lieberthal	.20	.06
❑ 11 Steve Avery	.20	.06

12	Bret Saberhagen	.20	.06
13	Magglio Ordonez	.20	.06
14	Brad Radke	.20	.06
15	Derek Jeter	1.25	.35
16	Javy Lopez	.20	.06
17	Russ Davis	.20	.06
18	Armando Benitez	.20	.06
19	B.J. Surhoff	.20	.06
20	Darryl Kile	.20	.06
21	Mark Lewis	.20	.06
22	Mike Williams	.20	.06
23	Mark McLemore	.20	.06
24	Sterling Hitchcock	.20	.06
25	Darin Erstad	.20	.06
26	Ricky Gutierrez	.20	.06
27	John Jaha	.20	.06
28	Homer Bush	.20	.06
29	Darrin Fletcher	.20	.06
30	Mark Grace	.30	.09
31	Fred McGriff	.30	.09
32	Omar Daal	.20	.06
33	Eric Karros	.20	.06
34	Orlando Cabrera	.20	.06
35	J.T. Snow	.20	.06
36	Luis Castillo	.20	.06
37	Rey Ordonez	.20	.06
38	Bob Abreu	.20	.06
39	Warren Morris	.20	.06
40	Juan Gonzalez	.30	.09
41	Mike Lansing	.20	.06
42	Chili Davis	.20	.06
43	Dean Palmer	.20	.06
44	Hank Aaron	.75	.23
45	Jeff Bagwell	.30	.09
46	Jose Valentin	.20	.06
47	Shannon Stewart	.20	.06
48	Kent Bottenfield	.20	.06
49	Jeff Shaw	.20	.06
50	Sammy Sosa	.75	.23
51	Randy Johnson	.50	.15
52	Benny Agbayani	.20	.06
53	Dante Bichette	.20	.06
54	Pete Harnisch	.20	.06
55	Frank Thomas	.50	.15
56	Jorge Posada	.30	.09
57	Todd Walker	.20	.06
58	Juan Encarnacion	.20	.06
59	Mike Sweeney	.20	.06
60	Pedro Martinez	.50	.15
61	Lee Stevens	.20	.06
62	Brian Giles	.20	.06
63	Chad Ogea	.20	.06
64	Ivan Rodriguez	.50	.15
65	Roger Cedeno	.20	.06
66	David Justice	.20	.06
67	Steve Trachsel	.20	.06
68	Eli Marrero	.20	.06
69	Dave Nilsson	.20	.06
70	Ken Caminiti	.20	.06
71	Tim Raines	.20	.06
72	Brian Jordan	.20	.06
73	Jeff Blauser	.20	.06
74	Bernard Gilkey	.20	.06
75	John Flaherty	.20	.06
76	Brent Mayne	.20	.06
77	Jose Vidro	.20	.06
78	David Bell	.20	.06
79	Bruce Aven	.20	.06
80	John Olerud	.20	.06
81	Pokey Reese	.20	.06
82	Woody Williams	.20	.06
83	Ed Sprague	.20	.06
84	Joe Girardi	.20	.06
85	Barry Larkin	.30	.09
86	Mike Caruso	.20	.06
87	Bobby Higginson	.20	.06
88	Roberto Kelly	.20	.06
89	Edgar Martinez	.30	.09
90	Mark Kotsay	.20	.06
91	Paul Sorrento	.20	.06
92	Eric Young	.20	.06
93	Carlos Delgado	.20	.06
94	Troy Glaus	.20	.06
95	Ben Grieve	.20	.06
96	Jose Lima	.20	.06
97	Garret Anderson	.20	.06
98	Luis Gonzalez	.20	.06
99	Carl Pavano	.20	.06
100	Alex Rodriguez	.75	.23
101	Preston Wilson	.20	.06
102	Ron Gant	.20	.06
103	Brady Anderson	.20	.06
104	Rickey Henderson	.50	.15
105	Gary Sheffield	.20	.06
106	Mickey Morandini	.20	.06
107	Jim Edmonds	.20	.06
108	Kris Benson	.20	.06
109	Adrian Beltre	.30	.09
110	Alex Fernandez	.20	.06
111	Dan Wilson	.20	.06
112	Mark Clark	.20	.06
113	Greg Vaughn	.20	.06
114	Neifi Perez	.20	.06
115	Paul O'Neill	.30	.09
116	Jermaine Dye	.20	.06
117	Todd Jones	.20	.06
118	Terry Steinbach	.20	.06
119	Greg Norton	.20	.06
120	Curt Schilling	.20	.06
121	Todd Zeile	.20	.06
122	Edgardo Alfonzo	.20	.06
123	Ryan McGuire	.20	.06
124	Rich Aurilia	.20	.06
125	John Smoltz	.30	.09
126	Bob Wickman	.20	.06
127	Richard Hidalgo	.20	.06
128	Chuck Finley	.20	.06
129	Billy Wagner	.20	.06
130	Todd Hundley	.20	.06
131	Dwight Gooden	.20	.06
132	Russ Ortiz	.20	.06
133	Mike Lowell	.20	.06
134	Reggie Sanders	.20	.06
135	John Valentin	.20	.06
136	Brad Ausmus	.20	.06
137	Chad Kreuter	.20	.06
138	David Cone	.20	.06
139	Brook Fordyce	.20	.06
140	Roberto Alomar	.30	.09
141	Charles Nagy	.20	.06
142	Brian Hunter	.20	.06
143	Mike Mussina	.30	.09
144	Robin Ventura	.30	.09
145	Kevin Brown	.30	.09
146	Pat Hentgen	.20	.06
147	Ryan Klesko	.20	.06
148	Derek Bell	.20	.06
149	Andy Sheets	.20	.06
150	Larry Walker	.30	.09
151	Scott Williamson	.20	.06
152	Jose Offerman	.20	.06
153	Doug Mientkiewicz	.20	.06
154	John Snyder RC	.40	.12
155	Sandy Alomar Jr.	.20	.06
156	Joe Nathan	.20	.06
157	Lance Johnson	.20	.06
158	Odalis Perez	.20	.06
159	Hideo Nomo	.50	.15
160	Steve Finley	.20	.06
161	Dave Martinez	.20	.06
162	Matt Walbeck	.20	.06
163	Bill Spiers	.20	.06
164	Fernando Tatis	.20	.06
165	Kenny Lofton	.20	.06
166	Paul Byrd	.20	.06
167	Aaron Sele	.20	.06
168	Eddie Taubensee	.20	.06
169	Reggie Jefferson	.20	.06
170	Roger Clemens	1.00	.30
171	Francisco Cordova	.20	.06
172	Mike Bordick	.20	.06
173	Wally Joyner	.20	.06
174	Marvin Benard	.20	.06
175	Jason Kendall	.20	.06
176	Mike Stanley	.20	.06
177	Chad Allen	.20	.06
178	Carlos Beltran	.30	.09
179	Deivi Cruz	.20	.06
180	Chipper Jones	.50	.15
181	Vladimir Guerrero	.50	.15
182	Dave Burba	.20	.06
183	Tom Goodwin	.20	.06
184	Brian Daubach	.20	.06
185	Jay Bell	.20	.06
186	Roy Halladay	.20	.06
187	Miguel Tejada	.20	.06
188	Armando Rios	.20	.06
189	Fernando Vina	.20	.06
190	Eric Davis	.20	.06
191	Henry Rodriguez	.20	.06
192	Joe McEwing	.20	.06
193	Jeff Kent	.20	.06
194	Mike Jackson	.20	.06
195	Mike Morgan	.20	.06
196	Jeff Montgomery	.20	.06
197	Jeff Zimmerman	.20	.06
198	Tony Fernandez	.20	.06
199	Jason Giambi	.20	.06
200	Jose Canseco	.50	.15
201	Alex Gonzalez	.20	.06
202	Jack Cust Mike Colangelo Dee Brown	.40	.12
203	Felipe Lopez Alfonso Soriano Pablo Ozuna	.50	.15
204	Erubiel Durazo Pat Burrell Nick Johnson	.40	.12
205	John Sneed RC Kip Wells Matt Blank	.40	.12
206	Josh Kalinowski Michael Tejera Chris Mears RC	.40	.12
207	Roosevelt Brown Corey Patterson Lance Berkman	.40	.12
208	Kit Pellow Kevin Barker Russ Branyan	.40	.12
209	B.J. Garbe Larry Bigbie RC	.75	.23
210	Eric Munson Bobby Bradley RC	.40	.12
211	Josh Girdley Kyle Snyder	.40	.12
212	Chance Caple RC Jason Jennings	.40	.12
213	Ryan Christianson Brett Myers RC	.50	.15
214	Jason Stumm Rob Purvis RC	.40	.12
215	David Walling Mike Paradis	.40	.12
216	Omar Ortiz Jay Gehrke	.40	.12
217	David Cone HL	.20	.06
218	Jose Jimenez HL	.20	.06
219	Chris Singleton HL	.20	.06
220	Fernando Tatis HL	.20	.06
221	Todd Helton HL	.20	.06
222	Kevin Millwood DIV	.20	.06
223	Todd Pratt DIV	.20	.06
224	Orl.Hernandez DIV	.20	.06
225	Pedro Martinez DIV	.30	.09
226	Tom Glavine LCS	.20	.06
227	Bernie Williams LCS	.20	.06
228	Mariano Rivera WS	.20	.06
229	Tony Gwynn 20CB	.60	.18
230	Wade Boggs 20CB	.30	.09
231	Lance Johnson CB	.20	.06
232	Mark McGwire 20CB	1.25	.35
233	R.Henderson 20CB	.50	.15
234	R.Henderson 20CB	.50	.15
235	Roger Clemens 20CB	1.00	.30
236A	M.McGwire MM 1st HR	3.00	.90
236B	M.McGwire MM 1987 ROY	3.00	.90
236C	M.McGwire MM 62nd HR	3.00	.90
236D	M.McGwire MM 70th HR	3.00	.90
236E	M.McGwire MM 500th HR	3.00	.90
237A	H.Aaron MM 1st Career HR	2.00	.60

❑ 237B H.Aaron MM 2.00 .60
1957 MVP
❑ 237C H.Aaron MM 2.00 .60
3000th Hit
❑ 237D H.Aaron MM 2.00 .60
715th HR
❑ 237E H.Aaron MM 2.00 .60
755th HR
❑ 238A C.Ripken MM 4.00 1.20
1982 ROY
❑ 238B C.Ripken MM 4.00 1.20
1991 MVP
❑ 238C C.Ripken MM 4.00 1.20
2131 Game
❑ 238D C.Ripken MM 4.00 1.20
Streak Ends
❑ 238E C.Ripken MM 4.00 1.20
400th HR
❑ 239A W.Boggs MM .75 .23
1983 Batting
❑ 239B W.Boggs MM .75 .23
1988 Batting
❑ 239C W.Boggs MM .75 .23
2000th Hit
❑ 239D W.Boggs MM .75 .23
1996 Champs
❑ 239E W.Boggs MM .75 .23
3000th Hit
❑ 240A T.Gwynn MM 1.50 .45
1984 Batting
❑ 240B T.Gwynn MM 1.50 .45
1984 NLCS
❑ 240C T.Gwynn MM 1.50 .45
1995 Batting
❑ 240D T.Gwynn MM 1.50 .45
1998 NLCS
❑ 240E T.Gwynn MM 1.50 .45
3000th Hit
❑ 241 Tom Glavine .30 .09
❑ 242 David Wells .20 .06
❑ 243 Kevin Appier .20 .06
❑ 244 Troy Percival .20 .06
❑ 245 Ray Lankford .20 .06
❑ 246 Marquis Grissom .20 .06
❑ 247 Randy Winn .20 .06
❑ 248 Miguel Batista .20 .06
❑ 249 Darren Dreifort .20 .06
❑ 250 Barry Bonds 1.25 .35
❑ 251 Harold Baines .20 .06
❑ 252 Cliff Floyd .20 .06
❑ 253 Freddy Garcia .20 .06
❑ 254 Kenny Rogers .20 .06
❑ 255 Ben Davis .20 .06
❑ 256 Charles Johnson .20 .06
❑ 257 Bubba Trammell .20 .06
❑ 258 Desi Relaford .20 .06
❑ 259 Al Martin .20 .06
❑ 260 Andy Pettitte .30 .09
❑ 261 Carlos Lee .20 .06
❑ 262 Matt Lawton .20 .06
❑ 263 Andy Fox .20 .06
❑ 264 Chan Ho Park .20 .06
❑ 265 Billy Koch .20 .06
❑ 266 Dave Roberts .20 .06
❑ 267 Carl Everett .20 .06
❑ 268 Orel Hershiser .20 .06
❑ 269 Trot Nixon .20 .06
❑ 270 Rusty Greer .20 .06
❑ 271 Will Clark .50 .15
❑ 272 Quilvio Veras .20 .06
❑ 273 Rico Brogna .20 .06
❑ 274 Devon White .20 .06
❑ 275 Tim Hudson .20 .06
❑ 276 Mike Hampton .20 .06
❑ 277 Miguel Cairo .20 .06
❑ 278 Darren Oliver .20 .06
❑ 279 Jeff Cirillo .20 .06
❑ 280 Al Leiter .20 .06
❑ 281 Shane Andrews .20 .06
❑ 282 Carlos Febles .20 .06
❑ 283 Pedro Astacio .20 .06
❑ 284 Juan Guzman .20 .06
❑ 285 Orlando Hernandez .20 .06
❑ 286 Paul Konerko .20 .06
❑ 287 Tony Clark .20 .06
❑ 288 Aaron Boone .20 .06
❑ 289 Ismael Valdes .20 .06
❑ 290 Moises Alou .20 .06
❑ 291 Kevin Tapani .20 .06
❑ 292 John Franco .20 .06
❑ 293 Todd Zeile .20 .06
❑ 294 Jason Schmidt .20 .06
❑ 295 Johnny Damon .30 .09
❑ 296 Scott Brosius .20 .06
❑ 297 Travis Fryman .20 .06
❑ 298 Jose Vizcaino .20 .06
❑ 299 Eric Chavez .20 .06
❑ 300 Mike Piazza .75 .23
❑ 301 Matt Clement .20 .06
❑ 302 Cristian Guzman .20 .06
❑ 303 C.J. Nitkowski .20 .06
❑ 304 Michael Tucker .20 .06
❑ 305 Brett Tomko .20 .06
❑ 306 Mike Lansing .20 .06
❑ 307 Eric Owens .20 .06
❑ 308 Livan Hernandez .20 .06
❑ 309 Rondell White .20 .06
❑ 310 Todd Stottlemyre .20 .06
❑ 311 Chris Carpenter .20 .06
❑ 312 Ken Hill .20 .06
❑ 313 Mark Loretta .20 .06
❑ 314 John Rocker .20 .06
❑ 315 Richie Sexson .20 .06
❑ 316 Ruben Mateo .20 .06
❑ 317 Joe Randa .20 .06
❑ 318 Mike Sirotka .20 .06
❑ 319 Jose Rosado .20 .06
❑ 320 Matt Mantei .20 .06
❑ 321 Kevin Millwood .20 .06
❑ 322 Gary DiSarcina .20 .06
❑ 323 Dustin Hermanson .20 .06
❑ 324 Mike Stanton .20 .06
❑ 325 Kirk Rueter .20 .06
❑ 326 Damian Miller RC .40 .12
❑ 327 Doug Glanville .20 .06
❑ 328 Scott Rolen .50 .15
❑ 329 Ray Durham .20 .06
❑ 330 Butch Huskey .20 .06
❑ 331 Mariano Rivera .30 .09
❑ 332 Darren Lewis .20 .06
❑ 333 Mike Timlin .20 .06
❑ 334 Mark Grudzielanek .20 .06
❑ 335 Mike Cameron .20 .06
❑ 336 Kelvim Escobar .20 .06
❑ 337 Bret Boone .20 .06
❑ 338 Mo Vaughn .20 .06
❑ 339 Craig Biggio .30 .09
❑ 340 Michael Barrett .20 .06
❑ 341 Marlon Anderson .20 .06
❑ 342 Bobby Jones .20 .06
❑ 343 John Halama .20 .06
❑ 344 Todd Ritchie .20 .06
❑ 345 Chuck Knoblauch .20 .06
❑ 346 Rick Reed .20 .06
❑ 347 Kelly Stinnett .20 .06
❑ 348 Tim Salmon .30 .09
❑ 349 A.J. Hinch .20 .06
❑ 350 Jose Cruz Jr. .20 .06
❑ 351 Roberto Hernandez .20 .06
❑ 352 Edgar Renteria .20 .06
❑ 353 Jose Hernandez .20 .06
❑ 354 Brad Fullmer .20 .06
❑ 355 Trevor Hoffman .20 .06
❑ 356 Troy O'Leary .20 .06
❑ 357 Justin Thompson .20 .06
❑ 358 Kevin Young .20 .06
❑ 359 Hideki Irabu .20 .06
❑ 360 Jim Thome .50 .15
❑ 361 Steve Karsay .20 .06
❑ 362 Octavio Dotel .20 .06
❑ 363 Omar Vizquel .30 .09
❑ 364 Raul Mondesi .20 .06
❑ 365 Shane Reynolds .20 .06
❑ 366 Bartolo Colon .20 .06
❑ 367 Chris Widger .20 .06
❑ 368 Gabe Kapler .20 .06
❑ 369 Bill Simas .20 .06
❑ 370 Tino Martinez .30 .09
❑ 371 John Thomson .20 .06
❑ 372 Delino DeShields .20 .06
❑ 373 Carlos Perez .20 .06
❑ 374 Eddie Perez .20 .06
❑ 375 Jeromy Burnitz .20 .06
❑ 376 Jimmy Haynes .20 .06
❑ 377 Travis Lee .20 .06
❑ 378 Darryl Hamilton .20 .06
❑ 379 Jamie Moyer .20 .06
❑ 380 Alex Gonzalez .20 .06
❑ 381 John Wetteland .20 .06
❑ 382 Vinny Castilla .20 .06
❑ 383 Jeff Suppan .20 .06
❑ 384 Jim Leyritz .20 .06
❑ 385 Robb Nen .20 .06
❑ 386 Wilson Alvarez .20 .06
❑ 387 Andres Galarraga .20 .06
❑ 388 Mike Remlinger .20 .06
❑ 389 Geoff Jenkins .20 .06
❑ 390 Matt Stairs .20 .06
❑ 391 Bill Mueller .20 .06
❑ 392 Mike Lowell .20 .06
❑ 393 Andy Ashby .20 .06
❑ 394 Ruben Rivera .20 .06
❑ 395 Todd Helton .30 .09
❑ 396 Bernie Williams .30 .09
❑ 397 Royce Clayton .20 .06
❑ 398 Manny Ramirez .30 .09
❑ 399 Kerry Wood .50 .15
❑ 400 Ken Griffey Jr. .75 .23
❑ 401 Enrique Wilson .20 .06
❑ 402 Joey Hamilton .20 .06
❑ 403 Shawn Estes .20 .06
❑ 404 Ugueth Urbina .20 .06
❑ 405 Albert Belle .20 .06
❑ 406 Rick Helling .20 .06
❑ 407 Steve Parris .20 .06
❑ 408 Eric Milton .20 .06
❑ 409 Dave Mlicki .20 .06
❑ 410 Shawn Green .20 .06
❑ 411 Jaret Wright .20 .06
❑ 412 Tony Womack .20 .06
❑ 413 Vernon Wells .20 .06
❑ 414 Ron Belliard .20 .06
❑ 415 Ellis Burks .20 .06
❑ 416 Scott Erickson .20 .06
❑ 417 Rafael Palmeiro .30 .09
❑ 418 Damion Easley .20 .06
❑ 419 Jamey Wright .20 .06
❑ 420 Corey Koskie .20 .06
❑ 421 Bobby Howry .20 .06
❑ 422 Ricky Ledee .20 .06
❑ 423 Dmitri Young .20 .06
❑ 424 Sidney Ponson .20 .06
❑ 425 Greg Maddux .75 .23
❑ 426 Jose Guillen .20 .06
❑ 427 Jon Lieber .20 .06
❑ 428 Andy Benes .20 .06
❑ 429 Randy Velarde .20 .06
❑ 430 Sean Casey .20 .06
❑ 431 Torii Hunter .20 .06
❑ 432 Ryan Rupe .20 .06
❑ 433 David Segui .20 .06
❑ 434 Todd Pratt .20 .06
❑ 435 Nomar Garciaparra .75 .23
❑ 436 Denny Neagle .20 .06
❑ 437 Ron Coomer .20 .06
❑ 438 Chris Singleton .20 .06
❑ 439 Tony Batista .20 .06
❑ 440 Andruw Jones .20 .06
❑ 441 Aubrey Huff .20 .06
Sean Burroughs
Adam Piatt
❑ 442 Rafael Furcal .40 .12
Travis Dawkins
Jason Dellaero
❑ 443 Mike Lamb RC .40 .12
Joe Crede
Wilton Veras
❑ 444 Julio Zuleta RC .40 .12
Jorge Toca
Dernell Stenson
❑ 445 Garry Maddox Jr. RC .40 .12
Gary Matthews Jr.
Tim Raines Jr.
❑ 446 Mark Mulder .40 .12
C.C. Sabathia
Matt Riley
❑ 447 Scott Downs RC .40 .12
Chris George

Matt Belisle
❑ 448 Doug Mirabelli .40 .12
Ben Petrick
Jayson Werth
❑ 449 Josh Hamilton .40 .12
Corey Myers RC
❑ 450 Ben Christensen RC .40 .12
Richard Stahl RC
❑ 451 Ben Sheets RC 2.00 .60
Barry Zito
❑ 452 Kurt Ainsworth .40 .12
Ty Howington RC
❑ 453 Vince Faison RC .40 .12
Rick Asadoorian
❑ 454 Keith Reed RC .40 .12
Jeff Heaverlo
❑ 455 Mike MacDougal .40 .12
Brad Baker RC
❑ 456 Mark McGwire SH .60 .18
❑ 457 Cal Ripken SH .75 .23
❑ 458 Wade Boggs SH .20 .06
❑ 459 Tony Gwynn SH .30 .09
❑ 460 Jesse Orosco SH .20 .06
❑ 461 Larry Walker .30 .09
Nomar Garciaparra LL
❑ 462 Ken Griffey Jr. .50 .15
Mark McGwire LL
❑ 463 Manny Ramirez .50 .15
Mark McGwire LL
❑ 464 Pedro Martinez .30 .09
Randy Johnson LL
❑ 465 Pedro Martinez .30 .09
Randy Johnson LL
❑ 466 Derek Jeter .50 .15
Luis Gonzalez LL
❑ 467 Larry Walker .20 .06
Manny Ramirez LL
❑ 468 Tony Gwynn 20CB .60 .18
❑ 469 Mark McGwire 20CB 1.25 .35
❑ 470 Frank Thomas 20CB .50 .15
❑ 471 Harold Baines 20CB .20 .06
❑ 472 Roger Clemens 20CB 1.00 .30
❑ 473 John Franco 20CB .20 .06
❑ 474 John Franco 20CB .20 .06
❑ 475A K.Griffey Jr. MM 2.00 .60
350th HR
❑ 475B K.Griffey Jr. MM 2.00 .60
1997 MVP
❑ 475C K.Griffey Jr. MM 2.00 .60
HR Dad
❑ 475D K.Griffey Jr. MM 2.00 .60
1992 AS MVP
❑ 475E K.Griffey Jr. MM 2.00 .60
50 HR 1997
❑ 476A B.Bonds MM 3.00 .90
400HR/400SB
❑ 476B B.Bonds MM 3.00 .90
40HR/40SB
❑ 476C B.Bonds MM 3.00 .90
1993 MVP
❑ 476D B.Bonds MM 3.00 .90
1990 MVP
❑ 476E B.Bonds MM 3.00 .90
1992 MVP
❑ 477A S.Sosa MM 2.00 .60
20 HR June
❑ 477B S.Sosa MM 2.00 .60
66 HR 1998
❑ 477C S.Sosa MM 2.00 .60
60 HR 1999
❑ 477D S.Sosa MM 2.00 .60
1998 MVP
❑ 477E S.Sosa MM HR's 2.00 .60
61/62
❑ 478A D.Jeter MM 3.00 .90
1996 ROY
❑ 478B D.Jeter MM 3.00 .90
Wins 1999 WS
❑ 478C D.Jeter MM 3.00 .90
Wins 1998 WS
❑ 478D D.Jeter MM 3.00 .90
Wins 1996 WS
❑ 478E D.Jeter MM 3.00 .90
17 GM Hit Streak
❑ 479A A.Rodriguez MM 2.00 .60
40HR/40SB
❑ 479B A.Rodriguez MM 2.00 .60
100th HR
❑ 479C A.Rodriguez MM 2.00 .60
1996 POY
❑ 479D A.Rodriguez MM 2.00 .60
Wins 1 Million
❑ 479E A.Rodriguez MM 2.00 .60
1996 Batting Leader
❑ NNO M. McGwire 85 Reprint 5.00 1.50

2000 Topps Traded

	Nm-Mt	Ex-Mt
COMP.FACT.SET (136)	50.00	15.00
COMPLETE SET (135)	25.00	7.50

FACT.SET PRICE IS FOR SEALED SETS

❑ T1 Mike MacDougal .30 .09
❑ T2 Andy Tracy RC .30 .09
❑ T3 Brandon Phillips RC .50 .15
❑ T4 Brandon Inge RC .30 .09
❑ T5 Robbie Morrison RC .30 .09
❑ T6 Josh Pressley RC .30 .09
❑ T7 Todd Moser RC .30 .09
❑ T8 Rob Purvis .30 .09
❑ T9 Chance Caple .20 .06
❑ T10 Ben Sheets 1.25 .35
❑ T11 Russ Jacobson RC .30 .09
❑ T12 Brian Cole RC .30 .09
❑ T13 Brad Baker .30 .09
❑ T14 Alex Cintron RC .30 .09
❑ T15 Lyle Overbay RC 1.25 .35
❑ T16 Mike Edwards RC .30 .09
❑ T17 Sean McGowan RC .30 .09
❑ T18 Jose Molina .20 .06
❑ T19 Marcos Castillo RC .30 .09
❑ T20 Josue Espada RC .30 .09
❑ T21 Alex Gordon RC .30 .09
❑ T22 Rob Pugmire RC .30 .09
❑ T23 Jason Stumm .20 .06
❑ T24 Ty Howington .30 .09
❑ T25 Brett Myers .50 .15
❑ T26 Maicer Izturis RC .50 .15
❑ T27 John McDonald .20 .06
❑ T28 W.Rodriguez RC .30 .09
❑ T29 Carlos Zambrano RC 3.00 .90
❑ T30 Alejandro Diaz RC .30 .09
❑ T31 Geraldo Guzman RC .30 .09
❑ T32 J.R. House RC .30 .09
❑ T33 Elvin Nina RC .30 .09
❑ T34 Juan Pierre RC .75 .23
❑ T35 Ben Johnson RC .30 .09
❑ T36 Jeff Bailey RC .30 .09
❑ T37 Miguel Olivo RC .50 .15
❑ T38 F.Rodriguez RC 2.00 .60
❑ T39 Tony Pena Jr. RC .30 .09
❑ T40 Miguel Cabrera RC 15.00 4.50
❑ T41 Asdrubal Oropeza RC .30 .09
❑ T42 Junior Zamora RC .30 .09
❑ T43 Jovanny Cedeno RC .30 .09
❑ T44 John Sneed .30 .09
❑ T45 Josh Kalinowski .30 .09
❑ T46 Mike Young RC 4.00 1.20
❑ T47 Rico Washington RC .30 .09
❑ T48 Chad Durbin RC .30 .09
❑ T49 Junior Brignac RC .30 .09
❑ T50 Carlos Hernandez RC .30 .09
❑ T51 Cesar Izturis RC .75 .23
❑ T52 Oscar Salazar RC .30 .09
❑ T53 Pat Strange RC .30 .09
❑ T54 Rick Asadoorian .30 .09
❑ T55 Keith Reed .30 .09
❑ T56 Leo Estrella RC .30 .09
❑ T57 Wascar Serrano RC .30 .09
❑ T58 Richard Gomez RC .30 .09
❑ T59 Ramon Santiago RC .30 .09
❑ T60 Jovanny Sosa RC .30 .09
❑ T61 Aaron Rowand RC 1.25 .35
❑ T62 Junior Guerrero RC .30 .09
❑ T63 Luis Terrero RC .75 .23
❑ T64 Brian Sanches RC .30 .09
❑ T65 Scott Sobkowiak RC .30 .09
❑ T66 Gary Majewski RC .50 .15
❑ T67 Barry Zito 1.25 .35
❑ T68 Ryan Christianson .30 .09
❑ T69 Cristian Guerrero RC .30 .09
❑ T70 T.De La Rosa RC .30 .09
❑ T71 Andrew Beinbrink RC .30 .09
❑ T72 Ryan Knox RC .30 .09
❑ T73 Alex Graman RC .30 .09
❑ T74 Juan Guzman RC .30 .09
❑ T75 Ruben Salazar RC .30 .09
❑ T76 Luis Matos RC .30 .09
❑ T77 Tony Mota RC .30 .09
❑ T78 Doug Davis .20 .06
❑ T79 Ben Christensen .20 .06
❑ T80 Mike Lamb .50 .15
❑ T81 Adrian Gonzalez RC 1.25 .35
❑ T82 Mike Stodolka RC .30 .09
❑ T83 Adam Johnson RC .30 .09
❑ T84 Matt Wheatland RC .30 .09
❑ T85 Corey Smith RC .30 .09
❑ T86 Rocco Baldelli RC 3.00 .90
❑ T87 Keith Bucktrot RC .30 .09
❑ T88 Adam Wainwright RC .75 .23
❑ T89 Scott Thorman RC .30 .09
❑ T90 Tripper Johnson RC .30 .09
❑ T91 Jim Edmonds .30 .09
❑ T92 Masato Yoshii .20 .06
❑ T93 Adam Kennedy .20 .06
❑ T94 Darryl Kile .30 .09
❑ T95 Mark McLemore .20 .06
❑ T96 Ricky Gutierrez .20 .06
❑ T97 Juan Gonzalez .50 .15
❑ T98 Melvin Mora .30 .09
❑ T99 Dante Bichette .30 .09
❑ T100 Lee Stevens .20 .06
❑ T101 Roger Cedeno .20 .06
❑ T102 John Olerud .30 .09
❑ T103 Eric Young .20 .06
❑ T104 Mickey Morandini .20 .06
❑ T105 Travis Lee .20 .06
❑ T106 Greg Vaughn .20 .06
❑ T107 Todd Zeile .30 .09
❑ T108 Chuck Finley .30 .09
❑ T109 Ismael Valdes .20 .06
❑ T110 Reggie Sanders .20 .06
❑ T111 Pat Hentgen .20 .06
❑ T112 Ryan Klesko .30 .09
❑ T113 Derek Bell .20 .06
❑ T114 Hideo Nomo .75 .23
❑ T115 Aaron Sele .20 .06
❑ T116 Fernando Vina .20 .06
❑ T117 Wally Joyner .30 .09
❑ T118 Brian Hunter .20 .06
❑ T119 Joe Girardi .20 .06
❑ T120 Omar Daal .20 .06
❑ T121 Brook Fordyce .20 .06
❑ T122 Jose Valentin .20 .06
❑ T123 Curt Schilling .30 .09
❑ T124 B.J. Surhoff .30 .09
❑ T125 Henry Rodriguez .20 .06
❑ T126 Mike Bordick .20 .06
❑ T127 David Justice .30 .09
❑ T128 Charles Johnson .30 .09
❑ T129 Will Clark .75 .23
❑ T130 Dwight Gooden .30 .09
❑ T131 David Segui .20 .06
❑ T132 Denny Neagle .30 .09
❑ T133 Jose Canseco .75 .23
❑ T134 Bruce Chen .20 .06
❑ T135 Jason Bere .20 .06

2001 Topps

	Nm-Mt	Ex-Mt
COMPLETE SET (790)	80.00	24.00
COMP.FACT.BLUE SET (795)	100.00	30.00
COMP.SERIES 1 (405)	40.00	12.00
COMP. SERIES 2 (385)	40.00	12.00
COMMON (1-6/8-791)	.20	.06
COMMON (352-376/727-751)	.25	.07

No.	Player	Nm-Mt	Ex-Mt
❑ 1	Cal Ripken	1.50	.45
❑ 2	Chipper Jones	.50	.15
❑ 3	Roger Cedeno	.20	.06
❑ 4	Garret Anderson	.20	.06
❑ 5	Robin Ventura	.20	.06
❑ 6	Daryle Ward	.20	.06
❑ 7	Does Not Exist	.00	
❑ 8	Craig Paquette	.20	.06
❑ 9	Phil Nevin	.20	.06
❑ 10	Jermaine Dye	.20	.06
❑ 11	Chris Singleton	.20	.06
❑ 12	Mike Stanton	.20	.06
❑ 13	Brian Hunter	.20	.06
❑ 14	Mike Redmond	.20	.06
❑ 15	Jim Thome	.50	.15
❑ 16	Brian Jordan	.20	.06
❑ 17	Joe Girardi	.20	.06
❑ 18	Steve Woodard	.20	.06
❑ 19	Dustin Hermanson	.20	.06
❑ 20	Shawn Green	.20	.06
❑ 21	Todd Stottlemyre	.20	.06
❑ 22	Dan Wilson	.20	.06
❑ 23	Todd Pratt	.20	.06
❑ 24	Derek Lowe	.20	.06
❑ 25	Juan Gonzalez	.30	.09
❑ 26	Clay Bellinger	.20	.06
❑ 27	Jeff Fassero	.20	.06
❑ 28	Pat Meares	.20	.06
❑ 29	Eddie Taubensee	.20	.06
❑ 30	Paul O'Neill	.30	.09
❑ 31	Jeffrey Hammonds	.20	.06
❑ 32	Pokey Reese	.20	.06
❑ 33	Mike Mussina	.30	.09
❑ 34	Rico Brogna	.20	.06
❑ 35	Jay Buhner	.20	.06
❑ 36	Steve Cox	.20	.06
❑ 37	Quilvio Veras	.20	.06
❑ 38	Marquis Grissom	.20	.06
❑ 39	Shigetoshi Hasegawa	.20	.06
❑ 40	Shane Reynolds	.20	.06
❑ 41	Adam Piatt	.20	.06
❑ 42	Luis Polonia	.20	.06
❑ 43	Brook Fordyce	.20	.06
❑ 44	Preston Wilson	.20	.06
❑ 45	Ellis Burks	.20	.06
❑ 46	Armando Rios	.20	.06
❑ 47	Chuck Finley	.20	.06
❑ 48	Dan Plesac	.20	.06
❑ 49	Shannon Stewart	.20	.06
❑ 50	Mark McGwire	1.25	.35
❑ 51	Mark Loretta	.20	.06
❑ 52	Gerald Williams	.20	.06
❑ 53	Eric Young	.20	.06
❑ 54	Peter Bergeron	.20	.06
❑ 55	Dave Hansen	.20	.06
❑ 56	Arthur Rhodes	.20	.06
❑ 57	Bobby Jones	.20	.06
❑ 58	Matt Clement	.20	.06
❑ 59	Mike Benjamin	.20	.06
❑ 60	Pedro Martinez	.50	.15
❑ 61	Jose Canseco	.50	.15
❑ 62	Matt Anderson	.20	.06
❑ 63	Torii Hunter	.20	.06
❑ 64	Carlos Lee UER 1999 Charlotte Games Played are wrong	.20	.06
❑ 65	David Cone	.20	.06
❑ 66	Rey Sanchez	.20	.06
❑ 67	Eric Chavez	.20	.06
❑ 68	Rick Helling	.20	.06
❑ 69	Manny Alexander	.20	.06
❑ 70	John Franco	.20	.06
❑ 71	Mike Bordick	.20	.06
❑ 72	Andres Galarraga	.20	.06
❑ 73	Jose Cruz Jr.	.20	.06
❑ 74	Mike Matheny	.20	.06
❑ 75	Randy Johnson	.50	.15
❑ 76	Richie Sexson	.20	.06
❑ 77	Vladimir Nunez	.20	.06
❑ 78	Harold Baines	.20	.06
❑ 79	Aaron Boone	.20	.06
❑ 80	Darin Erstad	.20	.06
❑ 81	Alex Gonzalez	.20	.06
❑ 82	Gil Heredia	.20	.06
❑ 83	Shane Andrews	.20	.06
❑ 84	Todd Hundley	.20	.06
❑ 85	Bill Mueller	.20	.06
❑ 86	Mark McLemore	.20	.06
❑ 87	Scott Spiezio	.20	.06
❑ 88	Kevin McGlinchy	.20	.06
❑ 89	Bubba Trammell	.20	.06
❑ 90	Manny Ramirez	.30	.09
❑ 91	Mike Lamb	.20	.06
❑ 92	Scott Karl	.20	.06
❑ 93	Brian Buchanan	.20	.06
❑ 94	Chris Turner	.20	.06
❑ 95	Mike Sweeney	.20	.06
❑ 96	John Wetteland	.20	.06
❑ 97	Rob Bell	.20	.06
❑ 98	Pat Rapp	.20	.06
❑ 99	John Burkett	.20	.06
❑ 100	Derek Jeter	1.25	.35
❑ 101	J.D. Drew	.20	.06
❑ 102	Jose Offerman	.20	.06
❑ 103	Rick Reed	.20	.06
❑ 104	Will Clark	.50	.15
❑ 105	Rickey Henderson	.50	.15
❑ 106	Dave Berg	.20	.06
❑ 107	Kirk Rueter	.20	.06
❑ 108	Lee Stevens	.20	.06
❑ 109	Jay Bell	.20	.06
❑ 110	Fred McGriff	.30	.09
❑ 111	Julio Zuleta	.20	.06
❑ 112	Brian Anderson	.20	.06
❑ 113	Orlando Cabrera	.20	.06
❑ 114	Alex Fernandez	.20	.06
❑ 115	Derek Bell	.20	.06
❑ 116	Eric Owens	.20	.06
❑ 117	Brian Bohanon	.20	.06
❑ 118	Dennys Reyes	.20	.06
❑ 119	Mike Stanley	.20	.06
❑ 120	Jorge Posada	.30	.09
❑ 121	Rich Becker	.20	.06
❑ 122	Paul Konerko	.20	.06
❑ 123	Mike Remlinger	.20	.06
❑ 124	Travis Lee	.20	.06
❑ 125	Ken Caminiti	.20	.06
❑ 126	Kevin Barker	.20	.06
❑ 127	Paul Quantrill	.20	.06
❑ 128	Ozzie Guillen	.20	.06
❑ 129	Kevin Tapani	.20	.06
❑ 130	Mark Johnson	.20	.06
❑ 131	Randy Wolf	.20	.06
❑ 132	Michael Tucker	.20	.06
❑ 133	Darren Lewis	.20	.06
❑ 134	Joe Randa	.20	.06
❑ 135	Jeff Cirillo	.20	.06
❑ 136	David Ortiz	.30	.09
❑ 137	Herb Perry	.20	.06
❑ 138	Jeff Nelson	.20	.06
❑ 139	Chris Stynes	.20	.06
❑ 140	Johnny Damon	.30	.09
❑ 141	Jeff Reboulet	.20	.06
❑ 142	Jason Schmidt	.20	.06
❑ 143	Charles Johnson	.20	.06
❑ 144	Pat Burrell	.20	.06
❑ 145	Gary Sheffield	.20	.06
❑ 146	Tom Glavine	.30	.09
❑ 147	Jason Isringhausen	.20	.06
❑ 148	Chris Carpenter	.20	.06
❑ 149	Jeff Suppan	.20	.06
❑ 150	Ivan Rodriguez	.50	.15
❑ 151	Luis Sojo	.20	.06
❑ 152	Ron Villone	.20	.06
❑ 153	Mike Sirotka	.20	.06
❑ 154	Chuck Knoblauch	.20	.06
❑ 155	Jason Kendall	.20	.06
❑ 156	Dennis Cook	.20	.06
❑ 157	Bobby Estalella	.20	.06
❑ 158	Jose Guillen	.20	.06
❑ 159	Thomas Howard	.20	.06
❑ 160	Carlos Delgado	.20	.06
❑ 161	Benji Gil	.20	.06
❑ 162	Tim Bogar	.20	.06
❑ 163	Kevin Elster	.20	.06
❑ 164	Einar Diaz	.20	.06
❑ 165	Andy Benes	.20	.06
❑ 166	Adrian Beltre	.30	.09
❑ 167	David Bell	.20	.06
❑ 168	Turk Wendell	.20	.06
❑ 169	Pete Harnisch	.20	.06
❑ 170	Roger Clemens	1.00	.30
❑ 171	Scott Williamson	.20	.06
❑ 172	Kevin Jordan	.20	.06
❑ 173	Brad Penny	.20	.06
❑ 174	John Flaherty	.20	.06
❑ 175	Troy Glaus	.20	.06
❑ 176	Kevin Appier	.20	.06
❑ 177	Walt Weiss	.20	.06
❑ 178	Tyler Houston	.20	.06
❑ 179	Michael Barrett	.20	.06
❑ 180	Mike Hampton	.20	.06
❑ 181	Francisco Cordova	.20	.06
❑ 182	Mike Jackson	.20	.06
❑ 183	David Segui	.20	.06
❑ 184	Carlos Febles	.20	.06
❑ 185	Roy Halladay	.20	.06
❑ 186	Seth Etherton	.20	.06
❑ 187	Charlie Hayes	.20	.06
❑ 188	Fernando Tatis	.20	.06
❑ 189	Steve Trachsel	.20	.06
❑ 190	Livan Hernandez	.20	.06
❑ 191	Joe Oliver	.20	.06
❑ 192	Stan Javier	.20	.06
❑ 193	B.J. Surhoff	.20	.06
❑ 194	Rob Ducey	.20	.06
❑ 195	Barry Larkin	.30	.09
❑ 196	Danny Patterson	.20	.06
❑ 197	Bobby Howry	.20	.06
❑ 198	Dmitri Young	.20	.06
❑ 199	Brian Hunter	.20	.06
❑ 200	Alex Rodriguez	.75	.23
❑ 201	Hideo Nomo	.50	.15
❑ 202	Luis Alicea	.20	.06
❑ 203	Warren Morris	.20	.06
❑ 204	Antonio Alfonseca	.20	.06
❑ 205	Edgardo Alfonzo	.20	.06
❑ 206	Mark Grudzielanek	.20	.06
❑ 207	Fernando Vina	.20	.06
❑ 208	Willie Greene	.20	.06
❑ 209	Homer Bush	.20	.06
❑ 210	Jason Giambi	.20	.06
❑ 211	Mike Morgan	.20	.06
❑ 212	Steve Karsay	.20	.06
❑ 213	Matt Lawton	.20	.06
❑ 214	Wendell Magee Jr.	.20	.06
❑ 215	Rusty Greer	.20	.06
❑ 216	Keith Lockhart	.20	.06
❑ 217	Billy Koch	.20	.06
❑ 218	Todd Hollandsworth	.20	.06
❑ 219	Raul Ibanez	.20	.06
❑ 220	Tony Gwynn	.60	.18
❑ 221	Carl Everett	.20	.06
❑ 222	Hector Carrasco	.20	.06
❑ 223	Jose Valentin	.20	.06
❑ 224	Deivi Cruz	.20	.06
❑ 225	Bret Boone	.20	.06
❑ 226	Kurt Abbott	.20	.06
❑ 227	Melvin Mora	.20	.06
❑ 228	Danny Graves	.20	.06

❑ 229 Jose Jimenez .20 .06
❑ 230 James Baldwin .20 .06
❑ 231 C.J. Nitkowski .20 .06
❑ 232 Jeff Zimmerman .20 .06
❑ 233 Mike Lowell .20 .06
❑ 234 Hideki Irabu .20 .06
❑ 235 Greg Vaughn .20 .06
❑ 236 Omar Daal .20 .06
❑ 237 Darren Dreifort .20 .06
❑ 238 Gil Meche .20 .06
❑ 239 Damian Jackson .20 .06
❑ 240 Frank Thomas .50 .15
❑ 241 Travis Miller .20 .06
❑ 242 Jeff Frye .20 .06
❑ 243 Dave Magadan .20 .06
❑ 244 Luis Castillo .20 .06
❑ 245 Bartolo Colon .20 .06
❑ 246 Steve Kline .20 .06
❑ 247 Shawon Dunston .20 .06
❑ 248 Rick Aguilera .20 .06
❑ 249 Omar Olivares .20 .06
❑ 250 Craig Biggio .30 .09
❑ 251 Scott Schoeneweis .20 .06
❑ 252 Dave Veres .20 .06
❑ 253 Ramon Martinez .20 .06
❑ 254 Jose Vidro .20 .06
❑ 255 Todd Helton .30 .09
❑ 256 Greg Norton .20 .06
❑ 257 Jacque Jones .20 .06
❑ 258 Jason Grimsley .20 .06
❑ 259 Dan Reichert .20 .06
❑ 260 Robb Nen .20 .06
❑ 261 Mark Clark .20 .06
❑ 262 Scott Hatteberg .20 .06
❑ 263 Doug Brocail .20 .06
❑ 264 Mark Johnson .20 .06
❑ 265 Eric Davis .20 .06
❑ 266 Terry Shumpert .20 .06
❑ 267 Kevin Millar .20 .06
❑ 268 Ismael Valdes .20 .06
❑ 269 Richard Hidalgo .20 .06
❑ 270 Randy Velarde .20 .06
❑ 271 Bengie Molina .20 .06
❑ 272 Tony Womack .20 .06
❑ 273 Enrique Wilson .20 .06
❑ 274 Jeff Brantley .20 .06
❑ 275 Rick Ankiel .20 .06
❑ 276 Terry Mulholland .20 .06
❑ 277 Ron Belliard .20 .06
❑ 278 Terrence Long .20 .06
❑ 279 Alberto Castillo .20 .06
❑ 280 Royce Clayton .20 .06
❑ 281 Joe McEwing .20 .06
❑ 282 Jason McDonald .20 .06
❑ 283 Ricky Bottalico .20 .06
❑ 284 Keith Foulke .20 .06
❑ 285 Brad Radke .20 .06
❑ 286 Gabe Kapler .20 .06
❑ 287 Pedro Astacio .20 .06
❑ 288 Armando Reynoso .20 .06
❑ 289 Darryl Kile .20 .06
❑ 290 Reggie Sanders .20 .06
❑ 291 Esteban Yan .20 .06
❑ 292 Joe Nathan .20 .06
❑ 293 Jay Payton .20 .06
❑ 294 Francisco Cordero .20 .06
❑ 295 Gregg Jefferies .20 .06
❑ 296 LaTroy Hawkins .20 .06
❑ 297 Jeff Tam RC .40 .12
❑ 298 Jacob Cruz .20 .06
❑ 299 Chris Holt .20 .06
❑ 300 Vladimir Guerrero .50 .15
❑ 301 Marvin Benard .20 .06
❑ 302 Alex Ramirez .20 .06
❑ 303 Mike Williams .20 .06
❑ 304 Sean Bergman .20 .06
❑ 305 Juan Encarnacion .20 .06
❑ 306 Russ Davis .20 .06
❑ 307 Hanley Frias .20 .06
❑ 308 Ramon Hernandez .20 .06
❑ 309 Matt Walbeck .20 .06
❑ 310 Bill Spiers .20 .06
❑ 311 Bob Wickman .20 .06
❑ 312 Sandy Alomar Jr. .20 .06
❑ 313 Eddie Guardado .20 .06
❑ 314 Shane Halter .20 .06
❑ 315 Geoff Jenkins .20 .06
❑ 316 Brian Meadows .20 .06
❑ 317 Damian Miller .20 .06
❑ 318 Darrin Fletcher .20 .06
❑ 319 Rafael Furcal .20 .06
❑ 320 Mark Grace .30 .09
❑ 321 Mark Mulder .20 .06
❑ 322 Joe Torre MG .20 .06
❑ 323 Bobby Cox MG .20 .06
❑ 324 Mike Scioscia MG .20 .06
❑ 325 Mike Hargrove MG .20 .06
❑ 326 Jimy Williams MG .20 .06
❑ 327 Jerry Manuel MG .20 .06
❑ 328 Buck Showalter MG .20 .06
❑ 329 Charlie Manuel MG .20 .06
❑ 330 Don Baylor MG .20 .06
❑ 331 Phil Garner MG .20 .06
❑ 332 Jack McKeon MG .20 .06
❑ 333 Tony Muser MG .20 .06
❑ 334 Buddy Bell MG .20 .06
❑ 335 Tom Kelly MG .20 .06
❑ 336 John Boles MG .20 .06
❑ 337 Art Howe MG .20 .06
❑ 338 Larry Dierker MG .20 .06
❑ 339 Lou Piniella MG .20 .06
❑ 340 Davey Johnson MG .20 .06
❑ 341 Larry Rothschild MG .20 .06
❑ 342 Davey Lopes MG .20 .06
❑ 343 Johnny Oates MG .20 .06
❑ 344 Felipe Alou MG .20 .06
❑ 345 Jim Fregosi MG .20 .06
❑ 346 Bobby Valentine MG .20 .06
❑ 347 Terry Francona MG .20 .06
❑ 348 Gene Lamont MG .20 .06
❑ 349 Tony LaRussa MG .20 .06
❑ 350 Bruce Bochy MG .20 .06
❑ 351 Dusty Baker MG .20 .06
❑ 352 Adrian Gonzalez .40 .12
Adam Johnson
❑ 353 Matt Wheatland .25 .07
Bryan Digby
❑ 354 Tripper Johnson .25 .07
Scott Thorman
❑ 355 Phil Dumatrait .25 .07
Adam Wainwright
❑ 356 Scott Heard .40 .12
David Parrish RC
❑ 357 Rocco Baldelli .50 .15
Mark Folsom RC
❑ 358 Dominic Rich RC .40 .12
Aaron Herr
❑ 359 Mike Stodolka .25 .07
Sean Burnett
❑ 360 Derek Thompson .25 .07
Corey Smith
❑ 361 Danny Borrell RC .40 .12
Jason Bourgeois RC
❑ 362 Chin-Feng Chen .40 .12
Corey Patterson
Josh Hamilton
❑ 363 Ryan Anderson .50 .15
Barry Zito
C.C. Sabathia
❑ 364 Scott Sobkowiak .50 .15
David Walling
Ben Sheets
❑ 365 Ty Howington .25 .07
Josh Kalinowski
Josh Girdley
❑ 366 Hee Seop Choi RC .75 .23
Aaron McNeal
Jason Hart
❑ 367 Bobby Bradley .40 .12
Kurt Ainsworth
Chin-Hui Tsao
❑ 368 Mike Glendenning .25 .07
Kenny Kelly
Juan Silvestre
❑ 369 J.R. House .25 .07
Ramon Castro
Ben Davis
❑ 370 Chance Caple .50 .15
Rafael Soriano RC
Pasqual Coco
❑ 371 Travis Hafner RC 1.50 .45
Eric Munson
Bucky Jacobsen
❑ 372 Jason Conti .25 .07
Chris Wakeland
Brian Cole
❑ 373 Scott Seabol .40 .12
Aubrey Huff
Joe Crede
❑ 374 Adam Everett .25 .07
Jose Ortiz
Keith Ginter
❑ 375 Carlos Hernandez .25 .07
Geraldo Guzman
Adam Eaton
❑ 376 Bobby Kielty .25 .07
Milton Bradley
Juan Rivera
❑ 377 Mark McGwire GM .60 .18
❑ 378 Don Larsen GM .20 .06
❑ 379 Bobby Thomson GM .20 .06
❑ 380 Bill Mazeroski GM .20 .06
❑ 381 Reggie Jackson GM .30 .09
❑ 382 Kirk Gibson GM .20 .06
❑ 383 Roger Maris GM .30 .09
❑ 384 Cal Ripken GM .75 .23
❑ 385 Hank Aaron GM .50 .15
❑ 386 Joe Carter GM .20 .06
❑ 387 Cal Ripken SH 1.50 .45
❑ 388 Randy Johnson SH .30 .09
❑ 389 Ken Griffey Jr. SH .75 .23
❑ 390 Troy Glaus SH .20 .06
❑ 391 Kazuhiro Sasaki SH .20 .06
❑ 392 Sammy Sosa LL .30 .09
Troy Glaus
❑ 393 Todd Helton LL .20 .06
Edgar Martinez
❑ 394 Todd Helton LL .50 .15
Nomar Garicaparra
❑ 395 Barry Bonds LL .50 .15
Jason Giambi
❑ 396 Todd Helton LL .20 .06
Manny Ramirez
❑ 397 Todd Helton LL .20 .06
Darin Erstad
❑ 398 Kevin Brown LL .30 .09
Pedro Martinez
❑ 399 Randy Johnson LL .30 .09
Pedro Martinez
❑ 400 Will Clark HL .50 .15
❑ 401 New York Mets HL .50 .15
❑ 402 New York Yankees HL .75 .23
❑ 403 Seattle Mariners HL .20 .06
❑ 404 Mike Hampton HL .20 .06
❑ 405 New York Yankees HL 1.00 .30
❑ 406 N.Y. Yankees Champs 2.00 .60
❑ 407 Jeff Bagwell .30 .09
❑ 408 Brant Brown .20 .06
❑ 409 Brad Fullmer .20 .06
❑ 410 Dean Palmer .20 .06
❑ 411 Greg Zaun .20 .06
❑ 412 Jose Vizcaino .20 .06
❑ 413 Jeff Abbott .20 .06
❑ 414 Travis Fryman .20 .06
❑ 415 Mike Cameron .20 .06
❑ 416 Matt Mantei .20 .06
❑ 417 Alan Benes .20 .06
❑ 418 Mickey Morandini .20 .06
❑ 419 Troy Percival .20 .06
❑ 420 Eddie Perez .20 .06
❑ 421 Vernon Wells .20 .06
❑ 422 Ricky Gutierrez .20 .06
❑ 423 Carlos Hernandez .20 .06
❑ 424 Chan Ho Park .20 .06
❑ 425 Armando Benitez .20 .06
❑ 426 Sidney Ponson .20 .06
❑ 427 Adrian Brown .20 .06
❑ 428 Ruben Mateo .20 .06
❑ 429 Alex Ochoa .20 .06
❑ 430 Jose Rosado .20 .06
❑ 431 Masato Yoshii .20 .06
❑ 432 Corey Koskie .20 .06
❑ 433 Andy Pettitte .30 .09
❑ 434 Brian Daubach .20 .06
❑ 435 Sterling Hitchcock .20 .06
❑ 436 Timo Perez .20 .06
❑ 437 Shawn Estes .20 .06
❑ 438 Tony Armas Jr. .20 .06

❑	439	Danny Bautista	.20	.06
❑	440	Randy Winn	.20	.06
❑	441	Wilson Alvarez	.20	.06
❑	442	Rondell White	.20	.06
❑	443	Jeromy Burnitz	.20	.06
❑	444	Kelvim Escobar	.20	.06
❑	445	Paul Bako	.20	.06
❑	446	Javier Vazquez	.20	.06
❑	447	Eric Gagne	.50	.15
❑	448	Kenny Lofton	.20	.06
❑	449	Mark Kotsay	.20	.06
❑	450	Jamie Moyer	.20	.06
❑	451	Delino DeShields	.20	.06
❑	452	Rey Ordonez	.20	.06
❑	453	Russ Ortiz	.20	.06
❑	454	Dave Burba	.20	.06
❑	455	Eric Karros	.20	.06
❑	456	Felix Martinez	.20	.06
❑	457	Tony Batista	.20	.06
❑	458	Bobby Higginson	.20	.06
❑	459	Jeff D'Amico	.20	.06
❑	460	Shane Spencer	.20	.06
❑	461	Brent Mayne	.20	.06
❑	462	Glendon Rusch	.20	.06
❑	463	Chris Gomez	.20	.06
❑	464	Jeff Shaw	.20	.06
❑	465	Damon Buford	.20	.06
❑	466	Mike DiFelice	.20	.06
❑	467	Jimmy Haynes	.20	.06
❑	468	Billy Wagner	.20	.06
❑	469	A.J. Hinch	.20	.06
❑	470	Gary DiSarcina	.20	.06
❑	471	Tom Lampkin	.20	.06
❑	472	Adam Eaton	.20	.06
❑	473	Brian Giles	.20	.06
❑	474	John Thomson	.20	.06
❑	475	Cal Eldred	.20	.06
❑	476	Ramiro Mendoza	.20	.06
❑	477	Scott Sullivan	.20	.06
❑	478	Scott Rolen	.50	.15
❑	479	Todd Ritchie	.20	.06
❑	480	Pablo Ozuna	.20	.06
❑	481	Carl Pavano	.20	.06
❑	482	Matt Morris	.20	.06
❑	483	Matt Stairs	.20	.06
❑	484	Tim Belcher	.20	.06
❑	485	Lance Berkman	.20	.06
❑	486	Brian Meadows	.20	.06
❑	487	Bob Abreu	.20	.06
❑	488	John VanderWal	.20	.06
❑	489	Donnie Sadler	.20	.06
❑	490	Damion Easley	.20	.06
❑	491	David Justice	.20	.06
❑	492	Ray Durham	.20	.06
❑	493	Todd Zeile	.20	.06
❑	494	Desi Relaford	.20	.06
❑	495	Cliff Floyd	.20	.06
❑	496	Scott Downs	.20	.06
❑	497	Barry Bonds	1.25	.35
❑	498	Jeff D'Amico	.20	.06
❑	499	Octavio Dotel	.20	.06
❑	500	Kent Mercker	.20	.06
❑	501	Craig Grebeck	.20	.06
❑	502	Roberto Hernandez	.20	.06
❑	503	Matt Williams	.20	.06
❑	504	Bruce Aven	.20	.06
❑	505	Brett Tomko	.20	.06
❑	506	Kris Benson	.20	.06
❑	507	Neifi Perez	.20	.06
❑	508	Alfonso Soriano	.30	.09
❑	509	Keith Osik	.20	.06
❑	510	Matt Franco	.20	.06
❑	511	Steve Finley	.20	.06
❑	512	Olmedo Saenz	.20	.06
❑	513	Esteban Loaiza	.20	.06
❑	514	Adam Kennedy	.20	.06
❑	515	Scott Elarton	.20	.06
❑	516	Moises Alou	.20	.06
❑	517	Bryan Rekar	.20	.06
❑	518	Darryl Hamilton	.20	.06
❑	519	Osvaldo Fernandez	.20	.06
❑	520	Kip Wells	.20	.06
❑	521	Bernie Williams	.30	.09
❑	522	Mike Darr	.20	.06
❑	523	Marlon Anderson	.20	.06
❑	524	Derrek Lee	.20	.06
❑	525	Ugueth Urbina	.20	.06
❑	526	Vinny Castilla	.20	.06
❑	527	David Wells	.20	.06
❑	528	Jason Marquis	.20	.06
❑	529	Orlando Palmeiro	.20	.06
❑	530	Carlos Perez	.20	.06
❑	531	J.T. Snow	.20	.06
❑	532	Al Leiter	.20	.06
❑	533	Jimmy Anderson	.20	.06
❑	534	Brett Laxton	.20	.06
❑	535	Butch Huskey	.20	.06
❑	536	Orlando Hernandez	.20	.06
❑	537	Magglio Ordonez	.20	.06
❑	538	Willie Blair	.20	.06
❑	539	Kevin Sefcik	.20	.06
❑	540	Chad Curtis	.20	.06
❑	541	John Halama	.20	.06
❑	542	Andy Fox	.20	.06
❑	543	Juan Guzman	.20	.06
❑	544	Frank Menechino RC	.20	.06
❑	545	Raul Mondesi	.20	.06
❑	546	Tim Salmon	.30	.09
❑	547	Ryan Rupe	.20	.06
❑	548	Jeff Reed	.20	.06
❑	549	Mike Mordecai	.20	.06
❑	550	Jeff Kent	.20	.06
❑	551	Wiki Gonzalez	.20	.06
❑	552	Kenny Rogers	.20	.06
❑	553	Kevin Young	.20	.06
❑	554	Brian Johnson	.20	.06
❑	555	Tom Goodwin	.20	.06
❑	556	Tony Clark UER 0 games, 208 At-Bats	.20	.06
❑	557	Mac Suzuki	.20	.06
❑	558	Brian Moehler	.20	.06
❑	559	Jim Parque	.20	.06
❑	560	Mariano Rivera	.30	.09
❑	561	Trot Nixon	.20	.06
❑	562	Mike Mussina	.30	.09
❑	563	Nelson Figueroa	.20	.06
❑	564	Alex Gonzalez	.20	.06
❑	565	Benny Agbayani	.20	.06
❑	566	Ed Sprague	.20	.06
❑	567	Scott Erickson	.20	.06
❑	568	Abraham Nunez	.20	.06
❑	569	Jerry DiPoto	.20	.06
❑	570	Sean Casey	.20	.06
❑	571	Wilton Veras	.20	.06
❑	572	Joe Mays	.20	.06
❑	573	Bill Simas	.20	.06
❑	574	Doug Glanville	.20	.06
❑	575	Scott Sauerbeck	.20	.06
❑	576	Ben Davis	.20	.06
❑	577	Jesus Sanchez	.20	.06
❑	578	Ricardo Rincon	.20	.06
❑	579	John Olerud	.20	.06
❑	580	Curt Schilling	.20	.06
❑	581	Alex Cora	.20	.06
❑	582	Pat Hentgen	.20	.06
❑	583	Javy Lopez	.20	.06
❑	584	Ben Grieve	.20	.06
❑	585	Frank Castillo	.20	.06
❑	586	Kevin Stocker	.20	.06
❑	587	Mark Sweeney	.20	.06
❑	588	Ray Lankford	.20	.06
❑	589	Turner Ward	.20	.06
❑	590	Felipe Crespo	.20	.06
❑	591	Omar Vizquel	.30	.09
❑	592	Mike Lieberthal	.20	.06
❑	593	Ken Griffey Jr.	.75	.23
❑	594	Troy O'Leary	.20	.06
❑	595	Dave Mlicki	.20	.06
❑	596	Manny Ramirez	.30	.09
❑	597	Mike Lansing	.20	.06
❑	598	Rich Aurilia	.20	.06
❑	599	Russell Branyan	.20	.06
❑	600	Russ Johnson	.20	.06
❑	601	Greg Colbrunn	.20	.06
❑	602	Andruw Jones	.20	.06
❑	603	Henry Blanco	.20	.06
❑	604	Jarrod Washburn	.20	.06
❑	605	Tony Eusebio	.20	.06
❑	606	Aaron Sele	.20	.06
❑	607	Charles Nagy	.20	.06
❑	608	Ryan Klesko	.20	.06
❑	609	Dante Bichette	.20	.06
❑	610	Bill Haselman	.20	.06
❑	611	Jerry Spradlin	.20	.06
❑	612	A. Rodriguez Rangers	.75	.23
❑	613	Jose Silva	.20	.06
❑	614	Darren Oliver	.20	.06
❑	615	Pat Mahomes	.20	.06
❑	616	Roberto Alomar	.30	.09
❑	617	Edgar Renteria	.20	.06
❑	618	Jon Lieber	.20	.06
❑	619	John Rocker	.20	.06
❑	620	Miguel Tejada	.20	.06
❑	621	Mo Vaughn	.20	.06
❑	622	Jose Lima	.20	.06
❑	623	Kerry Wood	.50	.15
❑	624	Mike Timlin	.20	.06
❑	625	Wil Cordero	.20	.06
❑	626	Albert Belle	.20	.06
❑	627	Bobby Jones	.20	.06
❑	628	Doug Mirabelli	.20	.06
❑	629	Jason Tyner	.20	.06
❑	630	Andy Ashby	.20	.06
❑	631	Jose Hernandez	.20	.06
❑	632	Devon White	.20	.06
❑	633	Ruben Rivera	.20	.06
❑	634	Steve Parris	.20	.06
❑	635	David McCarty	.20	.06
❑	636	Jose Canseco	.50	.15
❑	637	Todd Walker	.20	.06
❑	638	Stan Spencer	.20	.06
❑	639	Wayne Gomes	.20	.06
❑	640	Freddy Garcia	.20	.06
❑	641	Jeremy Giambi	.20	.06
❑	642	Luis Lopez	.20	.06
❑	643	John Smoltz	.30	.09
❑	644	Kelly Stinnett	.20	.06
❑	645	Kevin Brown	.20	.06
❑	646	Wilton Guerrero	.20	.06
❑	647	Al Martin	.20	.06
❑	648	Woody Williams	.20	.06
❑	649	Brian Rose	.20	.06
❑	650	Rafael Palmeiro	.30	.09
❑	651	Pete Schourek	.20	.06
❑	652	Kevin Jarvis	.20	.06
❑	653	Mark Redman	.20	.06
❑	654	Ricky Ledee	.20	.06
❑	655	Larry Walker	.30	.09
❑	656	Paul Byrd	.20	.06
❑	657	Jason Bere	.20	.06
❑	658	Rick White	.20	.06
❑	659	Calvin Murray	.20	.06
❑	660	Greg Maddux	.75	.23
❑	661	Ron Gant	.20	.06
❑	662	Eli Marrero	.20	.06
❑	663	Graeme Lloyd	.20	.06
❑	664	Trevor Hoffman	.20	.06
❑	665	Nomar Garciaparra	.75	.23
❑	666	Glenallen Hill	.20	.06
❑	667	Matt LeCroy	.20	.06
❑	668	Justin Thompson	.20	.06
❑	669	Brady Anderson	.20	.06
❑	670	Miguel Batista	.20	.06
❑	671	Erubiel Durazo	.20	.06
❑	672	Kevin Millwood	.20	.06
❑	673	Mitch Meluskey	.20	.06
❑	674	Luis Gonzalez	.20	.06
❑	675	Edgar Martinez	.30	.09
❑	676	Robert Person	.20	.06
❑	677	Benito Santiago	.20	.06
❑	678	Todd Jones	.20	.06
❑	679	Tino Martinez	.30	.09
❑	680	Carlos Beltran	.30	.09
❑	681	Gabe White	.20	.06
❑	682	Bret Saberhagen	.20	.06
❑	683	Jeff Conine	.20	.06
❑	684	Jaret Wright	.20	.06
❑	685	Bernard Gilkey	.20	.06
❑	686	Garrett Stephenson	.20	.06
❑	687	Jamey Wright	.20	.06
❑	688	Sammy Sosa	.75	.23
❑	689	John Jaha	.20	.06
❑	690	Ramon Martinez	.20	.06
❑	691	Robert Fick	.20	.06
❑	692	Eric Milton	.20	.06
❑	693	Denny Neagle	.20	.06
❑	694	Ron Coomer	.20	.06
❑	695	John Valentin	.20	.06

❑ 696 Placido Polanco .20 .06
❑ 697 Tim Hudson .20 .06
❑ 698 Marty Cordova .20 .06
❑ 699 Chad Kreuter .20 .06
❑ 700 Frank Catalanotto .20 .06
❑ 701 Tim Wakefield .20 .06
❑ 702 Jim Edmonds .20 .06
❑ 703 Michael Tucker .20 .06
❑ 704 Cristian Guzman .20 .06
❑ 705 Joey Hamilton .20 .06
❑ 706 Mike Piazza .75 .23
❑ 707 Dave Martinez .20 .06
❑ 708 Mike Hampton .20 .06
❑ 709 Bobby Bonilla .20 .06
❑ 710 Juan Pierre .20 .06
❑ 711 John Parrish .20 .06
❑ 712 Kory DeHaan .20 .06
❑ 713 Brian Tollberg .20 .06
❑ 714 Chris Truby .20 .06
❑ 715 Emil Brown .20 .06
❑ 716 Ryan Dempster .20 .06
❑ 717 Rich Garces .20 .06
❑ 718 Mike Myers .20 .06
❑ 719 Luis Ordaz .20 .06
❑ 720 Kazuhiro Sasaki .20 .06
❑ 721 Mark Quinn .20 .06
❑ 722 Ramon Ortiz .20 .06
❑ 723 Kerry Ligtenberg .20 .06
❑ 724 Rolando Arrojo .20 .06
❑ 725 Tsuyoshi Shinjo RC .50 .15
❑ 726 Ichiro Suzuki RC 15.00 4.50
❑ 727 Roy Oswalt .50 .15
Pat Strange
Jon Rauch
❑ 728 Phil Wilson RC 2.00 .60
Jake Peavy RC
Darwin Cubillan RC
❑ 729 Steve Smyth RC .25 .07
Mike Bynum
Nathan Haynes
❑ 730 Michael Cuddyer .25 .07
Joe Lawrence
Choo Freeman
❑ 731 Carlos Pena .25 .07
Larry Barnes
DeWayne Wise
❑ 732 Travis Dawkins .40 .12
Erick Almonte
Felipe Lopez
❑ 733 Alex Escobar .25 .07
Eric Valent
Brad Wilkerson
❑ 734 Toby Hall .25 .07
Rod Barajas
Jeff Goldbach
❑ 735 Jason Romano .40 .12
Marcus Giles
Pablo Ozuna
❑ 736 Dee Brown .40 .12
Jack Cust
Vernon Wells
❑ 737 David Espinosa .40 .12
Luis Montanez RC
❑ 738 Anthony Pluta RC .40 .12
Justin Wayne RC
❑ 739 Josh Axelson RC .40 .12
Carmen Cali RC
❑ 740 Shaun Boyd RC .40 .12
Chris Morris RC
❑ 741 Tommy Arko RC .40 .12
Dan Moylan RC
❑ 742 Luis Cotto RC .25 .07
Luis Escobar
❑ 743 Brandon Mims RC .40 .12
Blake Williams RC
❑ 744 Chris Russ RC .25 .07
Bryan Edwards
❑ 745 Joe Torres .25 .07
Ben Diggins
❑ 746 Hugh Quattlebaum RC .50 .15
Edwin Encarnacion RC
❑ 747 Brian Bass RC .40 .12
Odannis Ayala RC
❑ 748 Jason Kaanoi .25 .07
Michael Matthews RC UER
name misspelled Mathews
❑ 749 Stuart McFarland RC .40 .12
Adam Sterrett RC
❑ 750 David Krynzel .75 .23
Grady Sizemore
❑ 751 Keith Bucktrot .25 .07
Dane Sardinha
❑ 752 Anaheim Angels TC .20 .06
❑ 753 Ariz. Diamondbacks TC .20 .06
❑ 754 Atlanta Braves TC .20 .06
❑ 755 Baltimore Orioles TC .20 .06
❑ 756 Boston Red Sox TC .20 .06
❑ 757 Chicago Cubs TC .20 .06
❑ 758 Chicago White Sox TC .20 .06
❑ 759 Cincinnati Reds TC .20 .06
❑ 760 Cleveland Indians TC .20 .06
❑ 761 Colorado Rockies TC .20 .06
❑ 762 Detroit Tigers TC .20 .06
❑ 763 Florida Marlins TC .20 .06
❑ 764 Houston Astros TC .20 .06
❑ 765 K.C. Royals TC .20 .06
❑ 766 L.A. Dodgers TC .20 .06
❑ 767 Milw. Brewers TC .20 .06
❑ 768 Minnesota Twins TC .20 .06
❑ 769 Montreal Expos TC .20 .06
❑ 770 New York Mets TC .20 .06
❑ 771 New York Yankees TC 1.00 .30
❑ 772 Oakland Athletics TC .20 .06
❑ 773 Phil. Phillies TC .20 .06
❑ 774 Pittsburgh Pirates TC .20 .06
❑ 775 San Diego Padres TC .20 .06
❑ 776 San Francisco Giants TC .20 .06
❑ 777 Seattle Mariners TC .20 .06
❑ 778 St. Louis Cardinals TC .20 .06
❑ 779 T.B. Devil Rays TC .20 .06
❑ 780 Texas Rangers TC .20 .06
❑ 781 Toronto Blue Jays TC .20 .06
❑ 782 Bucky Dent GM .20 .06
❑ 783 Jackie Robinson GM .50 .15
❑ 784 Roberto Clemente GM .60 .18
❑ 785 Nolan Ryan GM .75 .23
❑ 786 Kerry Wood GM .30 .09
❑ 787 Rickey Henderson GM .20 .06
❑ 788 Lou Brock GM .30 .09
❑ 789 David Wells GM .20 .06
❑ 790 Andruw Jones GM .20 .06
❑ 791 Carlton Fisk GM .20 .06
❑ TK Bo Jackson 120.00 36.00
Deion Sanders Bat
❑ NNO Bobby Thomson 50.00 15.00
Ralph Branca
1991 Bowman Autograph

2001 Topps Traded

	Nm-Mt	Ex-Mt
COMPLETE SET (265)	100.00	30.00
COMMON (T1-T99/T145-T265)	.40	.12
COMMON (100-144)	1.00	.30

❑ T1 Sandy Alomar Jr. .40 .12
❑ T2 Kevin Appier .50 .15
❑ T3 Brad Ausmus .40 .12
❑ T4 Derek Bell .40 .12
❑ T5 Bret Boone .50 .15
❑ T6 Rico Brogna .40 .12
❑ T7 Ellis Burks .50 .15
❑ T8 Ken Caminiti .50 .15
❑ T9 Roger Cedeno .40 .12
❑ T10 Royce Clayton .40 .12
❑ T11 Enrique Wilson .40 .12
❑ T12 Rheal Cormier .40 .12
❑ T13 Eric Davis .50 .15
❑ T14 Shawon Dunston .40 .12
❑ T15 Andres Galarraga .50 .15
❑ T16 Tom Gordon .40 .12
❑ T17 Mark Grace .75 .23
❑ T18 Jeffrey Hammonds .40 .12
❑ T19 Dustin Hermanson .40 .12
❑ T20 Quinton McCracken .40 .12
❑ T21 Todd Hundley .40 .12
❑ T22 Charles Johnson .50 .15
❑ T23 Marquis Grissom .50 .15
❑ T24 Jose Mesa .40 .12
❑ T25 Brian Boehringer .40 .12
❑ T26 John Rocker .40 .12
❑ T27 Jeff Frye .40 .12
❑ T28 Reggie Sanders .40 .12
❑ T29 David Segui .40 .12
❑ T30 Mike Sirotka .40 .12
❑ T31 Fernando Tatis .40 .12
❑ T32 Steve Trachsel .40 .12
❑ T33 Ismael Valdes .40 .12
❑ T34 Randy Velarde .40 .12
❑ T35 Ryan Kohlmeier .40 .12
❑ T36 Mike Bordick .50 .15
❑ T37 Kent Bottenfield .40 .12
❑ T38 Pat Rapp .40 .12
❑ T39 Jeff Nelson .40 .12
❑ T40 Ricky Bottalico .40 .12
❑ T41 Luke Prokopec .40 .12
❑ T42 Hideo Nomo 1.25 .35
❑ T43 Bill Mueller .50 .15
❑ T44 Roberto Kelly .40 .12
❑ T45 Chris Holt .40 .12
❑ T46 Mike Jackson .40 .12
❑ T47 Devon White .50 .15
❑ T48 Gerald Williams .40 .12
❑ T49 Eddie Taubensee .40 .12
❑ T50 Brian Hunter UER .40 .12
Brian R Hunter pictured
Brian L Hunter stats
❑ T51 Nelson Cruz .40 .12
❑ T52 Jeff Fassero .40 .12
❑ T53 Bubba Trammell .40 .12
❑ T54 Bo Porter .40 .12
❑ T55 Greg Norton .40 .12
❑ T56 Benito Santiago .50 .15
❑ T57 Ruben Rivera .40 .12
❑ T58 Dee Brown .40 .12
❑ T59 Jose Canseco UER 1.25 .35
2000 strikeout totals are wrong
❑ T60 Chris Michalak .40 .12
❑ T61 Tim Worrell .40 .12
❑ T62 Matt Clement .40 .12
❑ T63 Bill Pulsipher .40 .12
❑ T64 Troy Brohawn RC .40 .12
❑ T65 Mark Kotsay .40 .12
❑ T66 Jimmy Rollins .50 .15
❑ T67 Shea Hillenbrand .50 .15
❑ T68 Ted Lilly .40 .12
❑ T69 Jermaine Dye .50 .15
❑ T70 Jerry Hairston Jr. .40 .12
❑ T71 John Mabry .40 .12
❑ T72 Kurt Abbott .40 .12
❑ T73 Eric Owens .40 .12
❑ T74 Jeff Brantley .40 .12
❑ T75 Roy Oswalt .75 .23
❑ T76 Doug Mientkiewicz .50 .15
❑ T77 Rickey Henderson 1.25 .35
❑ T78 Jason Grimsley .40 .12
❑ T79 Christian Parker RC .40 .12
❑ T80 Donne Wall .40 .12
❑ T81 Alex Arias .40 .12
❑ T82 Willis Roberts .40 .12
❑ T83 Ryan Minor .40 .12
❑ T84 Jason LaRue .40 .12
❑ T85 Ruben Sierra .40 .12
❑ T86 Johnny Damon .75 .23
❑ T87 Juan Gonzalez .75 .23
❑ T88 C.C. Sabathia .50 .15
❑ T89 Tony Batista .50 .15
❑ T90 Jay Witasick .40 .12
❑ T91 Brent Abernathy .40 .12
❑ T92 Paul LoDuca .50 .15

Card	Nm-Mt	Ex-Mt
❑ T93 Wes Helms	.40	.12
❑ T94 Mark Wohlers	.40	.12
❑ T95 Rob Bell	.40	.12
❑ T96 Tim Redding	.40	.12
❑ T97 Bud Smith RC	.40	.12
❑ T98 Adam Dunn	.75	.23
❑ T99 Ichiro Suzuki Albert Pujols ROY	20.00	6.00
❑ T100 Carlton Fisk 81	1.25	.35
❑ T101 Tim Raines 81	1.00	.30
❑ T102 Juan Marichal 74	1.00	.30
❑ T103 Dave Winfield 81	1.00	.30
❑ T104 Reggie Jackson 82	1.25	.35
❑ T105 Cal Ripken 82	6.00	1.80
❑ T106 Ozzie Smith 82	3.00	.90
❑ T107 Tom Seaver 83	1.25	.35
❑ T108 Lou Piniella 74	1.00	.30
❑ T109 Dwight Gooden 84	1.00	.30
❑ T110 Bret Saberhagen 84	1.00	.30
❑ T111 Gary Carter 85	1.00	.30
❑ T112 Jack Clark 85	1.00	.30
❑ T113 R. Henderson 85	2.00	.60
❑ T114 Barry Bonds 86	5.00	1.50
❑ T115 Bobby Bonilla 86	1.00	.30
❑ T116 Jose Canseco 86	2.00	.60
❑ T117 Will Clark 86	2.00	.60
❑ T118 Andres Galarraga 86	1.00	.30
❑ T119 Bo Jackson 86	2.00	.60
❑ T120 Wally Joyner 86	1.00	.30
❑ T121 Ellis Burks 87	1.00	.30
❑ T122 David Cone 87	1.00	.30
❑ T123 Greg Maddux 87	3.00	.90
❑ T124 Willie Randolph 76	1.00	.30
❑ T125 Dennis Eckersley 87	1.00	.30
❑ T126 Matt Williams 87	1.00	.30
❑ T127 Joe Morgan 81	1.00	.30
❑ T128 Fred McGriff 87	1.25	.35
❑ T129 Roberto Alomar 88	1.25	.35
❑ T130 Lee Smith 88	1.00	.30
❑ T131 David Wells 88	1.00	.30
❑ T132 Ken Griffey Jr. 89	3.00	.90
❑ T133 Deion Sanders 89	1.25	.35
❑ T134 Nolan Ryan 89	4.00	1.20
❑ T135 David Justice 90	1.00	.30
❑ T136 Joe Carter 91	1.00	.30
❑ T137 Jack Morris 92	1.00	.30
❑ T138 Mike Piazza 93	3.00	.90
❑ T139 Barry Bonds 93	5.00	1.50
❑ T140 Terrence Long 94	1.00	.30
❑ T141 Ben Grieve 94	1.00	.30
❑ T142 Richie Sexson 95 George Arias Mark Sweeney Brian Schneider	1.00	.30
❑ T143 Sean Burroughs 99	1.00	.30
❑ T144 Alfonso Soriano 99	1.25	.35
❑ T145 Bob Boone MG	.50	.15
❑ T146 Larry Bowa MG	.50	.15
❑ T147 Bob Brenly MG	.40	.12
❑ T148 Buck Martinez MG	.40	.12
❑ T149 L. McClendon MG	.40	.12
❑ T150 Jim Tracy MG	.40	.12
❑ T151 Jared Abruzzo RC	.40	.12
❑ T152 Kurt Ainsworth	.40	.12
❑ T153 Willie Bloomquist	.50	.15
❑ T154 Ben Broussard	.40	.12
❑ T155 Bobby Bradley	.40	.12
❑ T156 Mike Bynum	.40	.12
❑ T157 A.J. Hinch	.40	.12
❑ T158 Ryan Christianson	.40	.12
❑ T159 Carlos Silva	.40	.12
❑ T160 Joe Crede	.40	.12
❑ T161 Jack Cust	.40	.12
❑ T162 Ben Diggins	.40	.12
❑ T163 Phil Dumatrait	.40	.12
❑ T164 Alex Escobar	.40	.12
❑ T165 Miguel Olivo	.40	.12
❑ T166 Chris George	.40	.12
❑ T167 Marcus Giles	.50	.15
❑ T168 Keith Ginter	.40	.12
❑ T169 Josh Girdley	.40	.12
❑ T170 Tony Alvarez	.40	.12
❑ T171 Scott Seabol	.40	.12
❑ T172 Josh Hamilton	.40	.12
❑ T173 Jason Hart	.40	.12
❑ T174 Israel Alcantara	.40	.12
❑ T175 Jake Peavy	1.25	.35
❑ T176 Stubby Clapp RC	.40	.12
❑ T177 D'Angelo Jimenez	.40	.12
❑ T178 Nick Johnson	.40	.12
❑ T179 Ben Johnson	.40	.12
❑ T180 Larry Bigbie	.40	.12
❑ T181 Allen Levrault	.40	.12
❑ T182 Felipe Lopez	.40	.12
❑ T183 Sean Burnett	.40	.12
❑ T184 Nick Neugebauer	.40	.12
❑ T185 Austin Kearns	.50	.15
❑ T186 Corey Patterson	.50	.15
❑ T187 Carlos Pena	.40	.12
❑ T188 R. Rodriguez RC	.40	.12
❑ T189 Juan Rivera	.40	.12
❑ T190 Grant Roberts	.40	.12
❑ T191 Adam Pettyjohn RC	.40	.12
❑ T192 Jared Sandberg	.40	.12
❑ T193 Xavier Nady	.40	.12
❑ T194 Dane Sardinha	.40	.12
❑ T195 Shawn Sonnier	.40	.12
❑ T196 Rafael Soriano	.50	.15
❑ T197 Brian Specht RC	.40	.12
❑ T198 Aaron Myette	.40	.12
❑ T199 Juan Uribe RC	.50	.15
❑ T200 Jayson Werth	.40	.12
❑ T201 Brad Wilkerson	.40	.12
❑ T202 Horacio Estrada	.40	.12
❑ T203 Joel Pineiro	1.25	.35
❑ T204 Matt LeCroy	.40	.12
❑ T205 Michael Coleman	.40	.12
❑ T206 Ben Sheets	.75	.23
❑ T207 Eric Byrnes	.40	.12
❑ T208 Sean Burroughs	.50	.15
❑ T209 Ken Harvey	.40	.12
❑ T210 Travis Hafner	2.00	.60
❑ T211 Erick Almonte	.40	.12
❑ T212 Jason Belcher RC	.40	.12
❑ T213 Wilson Betemit RC	.40	.12
❑ T214 Hank Blalock RC	6.00	1.80
❑ T215 Danny Borrell	.40	.12
❑ T216 John Buck RC	.50	.15
❑ T217 Freddie Bynum RC	.40	.12
❑ T218 Noel Devarez RC	.40	.12
❑ T219 Juan Diaz RC	.40	.12
❑ T220 Felix Diaz RC	.40	.12
❑ T221 Josh Fogg RC	.40	.12
❑ T222 Matt Ford RC	.40	.12
❑ T223 Scott Heard	.40	.12
❑ T224 Ben Hendrickson RC	.50	.15
❑ T225 Cody Ross RC	.40	.12
❑ T226 A. Hernandez RC	.40	.12
❑ T227 Alfredo Amezaga RC	.40	.12
❑ T228 Bob Keppel RC	.50	.15
❑ T229 Ryan Madson RC	.75	.23
❑ T230 Octavio Martinez RC	.40	.12
❑ T231 Hee Seop Choi	.75	.23
❑ T232 Thomas Mitchell	.40	.12
❑ T233 Luis Montanez	.40	.12
❑ T234 Andy Morales RC	.40	.12
❑ T235 Justin Morneau RC	6.00	1.80
❑ T236 Toe Nash RC	.40	.12
❑ T237 V. Pascucci RC	.40	.12
❑ T238 Roy Smith RC	.40	.12
❑ T239 Antonio Perez RC	.40	.12
❑ T240 Chad Petty RC	.40	.12
❑ T241 Steve Smyth	.40	.12
❑ T242 Jose Reyes RC	3.00	.90
❑ T243 Eric Reynolds RC	.40	.12
❑ T244 Dominic Rich	.40	.12
❑ T245 J. Richardson RC	.40	.12
❑ T246 Ed Rogers RC	.40	.12
❑ T247 Albert Pujols RC	40.00	12.00
❑ T248 Esix Snead RC	.40	.12
❑ T249 Luis Torres RC	.40	.12
❑ T250 Matt White RC	.40	.12
❑ T251 Blake Williams	.40	.12
❑ T252 Chris Russ	.40	.12
❑ T253 Joe Kennedy RC	.50	.15
❑ T254 Jeff Randazzo RC	.40	.12
❑ T255 Beau Hale RC	.40	.12
❑ T256 Brad Hennessey RC	2.00	.60
❑ T257 Jake Gautreau RC	.40	.12
❑ T258 Jeff Mathis RC	1.50	.45
❑ T259 Aaron Heilman RC	.40	.12
❑ T260 B. Sardinha RC	.75	.23
❑ T261 Irvin Guzman RC	4.00	1.20
❑ T262 Gabe Gross RC	.50	.15
❑ T263 J.D. Martin RC	.40	.12
❑ T264 Chris Smith RC	.40	.12
❑ T265 Kenny Baugh RC	.40	.12

2002 Topps

	Nm-Mt	Ex-Mt
COMPLETE SET (718)	80.00	24.00
COMP.FACT.BROWN SET (723)	80.00	24.00
COMP.FACT.GREEN SET (723)	80.00	24.00
COMP. SERIES 1 (365)	40.00	12.00
COMPLETE SERIES 2 (354)	40.00	12.00
COMMON CARD (1-6/8-719)	.20	.06
COMMON (307-331)	.50	.15
COMMON CARD (332-364)	.50	.15
❑ 1 Pedro Martinez	.50	.15
❑ 2 Mike Stanton	.20	.06
❑ 3 Brad Penny	.20	.06
❑ 4 Mike Matheny	.20	.06
❑ 5 Johnny Damon	.30	.09
❑ 6 Bret Boone	.20	.06
❑ 7 Does Not Exist	.00	
❑ 8 Chris Truby	.20	.06
❑ 9 B.J. Surhoff	.20	.06
❑ 10 Mike Hampton	.20	.06
❑ 11 Juan Pierre	.20	.06
❑ 12 Mark Buehrle	.20	.06
❑ 13 Bob Abreu	.20	.06
❑ 14 David Cone	.20	.06
❑ 15 Aaron Sele UER Card lists him as being born in New Mexico He was born in Minnesota	.20	.06
❑ 16 Fernando Tatis	.20	.06
❑ 17 Bobby Jones	.20	.06
❑ 18 Rick Helling	.20	.06
❑ 19 Dmitri Young	.20	.06
❑ 20 Mike Mussina UER Career win total is wrong	.30	.09
❑ 21 Mike Sweeney	.20	.06
❑ 22 Cristian Guzman	.20	.06
❑ 23 Ryan Kohlmeier	.20	.06
❑ 24 Adam Kennedy	.20	.06
❑ 25 Larry Walker	.30	.09
❑ 26 Eric Davis UER 2000 Stolen Base totals are wrong	.20	.06
❑ 27 Jason Tyner	.20	.06
❑ 28 Eric Young	.20	.06
❑ 29 Jason Marquis	.20	.06
❑ 30 Luis Gonzalez	.20	.06
❑ 31 Kevin Tapani	.20	.06
❑ 32 Orlando Cabrera	.20	.06
❑ 33 Marty Cordova UER Career homer total, 1003	.20	.06
❑ 34 Brad Ausmus	.20	.06
❑ 35 Livan Hernandez	.20	.06
❑ 36 Alex Gonzalez	.20	.06
❑ 37 Edgar Renteria	.20	.06
❑ 38 Bengie Molina	.20	.06
❑ 39 Frank Menechino	.20	.06
❑ 40 Rafael Palmeiro	.30	.09
❑ 41 Brad Fullmer	.20	.06
❑ 42 Julio Zuleta	.20	.06
❑ 43 Darren Dreifort	.20	.06
❑ 44 Trot Nixon	.20	.06

Card	Hi	Lo
❑ 45 Trevor Hoffman	.20	.06
❑ 46 Vladimir Nunez	.20	.06
❑ 47 Mark Kotsay	.20	.06
❑ 48 Kenny Rogers	.20	.06
❑ 49 Ben Petrick	.20	.06
❑ 50 Jeff Bagwell	.30	.09
❑ 51 Juan Encarnacion	.20	.06
❑ 52 Ramiro Mendoza	.20	.06
❑ 53 Brian Meadows	.20	.06
❑ 54 Chad Curtis	.20	.06
❑ 55 Aramis Ramirez	.20	.06
❑ 56 Mark McLemore	.20	.06
❑ 57 Dante Bichette	.20	.06
❑ 58 Scott Schoeneweis	.20	.06
❑ 59 Jose Cruz Jr.	.20	.06
❑ 60 Roger Clemens	1.00	.30
❑ 61 Jose Guillen	.20	.06
❑ 62 Darren Oliver	.20	.06
❑ 63 Chris Reitsma	.20	.06
❑ 64 Jeff Abbott	.20	.06
❑ 65 Robin Ventura	.20	.06
❑ 66 Denny Neagle	.20	.06
❑ 67 Al Martin	.20	.06
❑ 68 Benito Santiago	.20	.06
❑ 69 Roy Oswalt	.20	.06
❑ 70 Juan Gonzalez	.30	.09
❑ 71 Garret Anderson	.20	.06
❑ 72 Bobby Bonilla	.20	.06
❑ 73 Danny Bautista	.20	.06
❑ 74 J.T. Snow	.20	.06
❑ 75 Derek Jeter	1.25	.35
❑ 76 John Olerud	.20	.06
❑ 77 Kevin Appier	.20	.06
❑ 78 Phil Nevin	.20	.06
❑ 79 Sean Casey	.20	.06
❑ 80 Troy Glaus	.20	.06
❑ 81 Joe Randa	.20	.06
❑ 82 Jose Valentin	.20	.06
❑ 83 Ricky Bottalico	.20	.06
❑ 84 Todd Zeile	.20	.06
❑ 85 Barry Larkin	.30	.09
❑ 86 Bob Wickman	.20	.06
❑ 87 Jeff Shaw	.20	.06
❑ 88 Greg Vaughn	.20	.06
❑ 89 Fernando Vina	.20	.06
❑ 90 Mark Mulder	.20	.06
❑ 91 Paul Bako	.20	.06
❑ 92 Aaron Boone	.20	.06
❑ 93 Esteban Loaiza	.20	.06
❑ 94 Richie Sexson	.20	.06
❑ 95 Alfonso Soriano	.30	.09
❑ 96 Tony Womack	.20	.06
❑ 97 Paul Shuey	.20	.06
❑ 98 Melvin Mora	.20	.06
❑ 99 Tony Gwynn	.60	.18
❑ 100 Vladimir Guerrero	.50	.15
❑ 101 Keith Osik	.20	.06
❑ 102 Bud Smith	.20	.06
❑ 103 Scott Williamson	.20	.06
❑ 104 Daryle Ward	.20	.06
❑ 105 Doug Mientkiewicz	.20	.06
❑ 106 Stan Javier	.20	.06
❑ 107 Russ Ortiz	.20	.06
❑ 108 Wade Miller	.20	.06
❑ 109 Luke Prokopec	.20	.06
❑ 110 Andruw Jones UER	.20	.06
Careel SB total, 1442		
❑ 111 Ron Coomer	.20	.06
❑ 112 Dan Wilson UER	.20	.06
Career SB total, 1245		
❑ 113 Luis Castillo	.20	.06
❑ 114 Derek Bell	.20	.06
❑ 115 Gary Sheffield	.20	.06
❑ 116 Ruben Rivera	.20	.06
❑ 117 Paul O'Neill	.30	.09
❑ 118 Craig Paquette	.20	.06
❑ 119 Kelvin Escobar	.20	.06
❑ 120 Brad Radke	.20	.06
❑ 121 Jorge Fabregas	.20	.06
❑ 122 Randy Winn	.20	.06
❑ 123 Tom Goodwin	.20	.06
❑ 124 Jaret Wright	.20	.06
❑ 125 Manny Ramirez	.30	.09
❑ 126 Al Leiter	.20	.06
❑ 127 Ben Davis	.20	.06
❑ 128 Frank Catalanotto	.20	.06
❑ 129 Jose Cabrera	.20	.06
❑ 130 Magglio Ordonez	.20	.06
❑ 131 Jose Macias	.20	.06
❑ 132 Ted Lilly	.20	.06
❑ 133 Chris Holt	.20	.06
❑ 134 Eric Milton	.20	.06
❑ 135 Shannon Stewart	.20	.06
❑ 136 Omar Olivares	.20	.06
❑ 137 David Segui	.20	.06
❑ 138 Jeff Nelson	.20	.06
❑ 139 Matt Williams	.20	.06
❑ 140 Ellis Burks	.20	.06
❑ 141 Jason Bere	.20	.06
❑ 142 Jimmy Haynes	.20	.06
❑ 143 Ramon Hernandez	.20	.06
❑ 144 Craig Counsell UER	.20	.06
Card pictures Greg Colbrunn		
Some vital stats are wrong as well		
❑ 145 John Smoltz	.30	.09
❑ 146 Homer Bush	.20	.06
❑ 147 Quilvio Veras	.20	.06
❑ 148 Esteban Yan	.20	.06
❑ 149 Ramon Ortiz	.20	.06
❑ 150 Carlos Delgado	.20	.06
❑ 151 Lee Stevens	.20	.06
❑ 152 Wil Cordero	.20	.06
❑ 153 Mike Bordick	.20	.06
❑ 154 John Flaherty	.20	.06
❑ 155 Omar Daal	.20	.06
❑ 156 Todd Ritchie	.20	.06
❑ 157 Carl Everett	.20	.06
❑ 158 Scott Sullivan	.20	.06
❑ 159 Deivi Cruz	.20	.06
❑ 160 Albert Pujols UER	1.00	.30
Placido Polanco pictured on back		
❑ 160A Albert Pujols	.00	
Pujols correctly pictured on back		
❑ 161 Royce Clayton	.20	.06
❑ 162 Jeff Suppan	.20	.06
❑ 163 C.C. Sabathia	.20	.06
❑ 164 Jimmy Rollins	.20	.06
❑ 165 Rickey Henderson	.50	.15
❑ 166 Rey Ordonez	.20	.06
❑ 167 Shawn Estes	.20	.06
❑ 168 Reggie Sanders	.20	.06
❑ 169 Jon Lieber	.20	.06
❑ 170 Armando Benitez	.20	.06
❑ 171 Mike Remlinger	.20	.06
❑ 172 Billy Wagner	.20	.06
❑ 173 Troy Percival	.20	.06
❑ 174 Devon White	.20	.06
❑ 175 Ivan Rodriguez	.50	.15
❑ 176 Dustin Hermanson	.20	.06
❑ 177 Brian Anderson	.20	.06
❑ 178 Graeme Lloyd	.20	.06
❑ 179 Russel Branyan	.20	.06
❑ 180 Bobby Higginson	.20	.06
❑ 181 Alex Gonzalez	.20	.06
❑ 182 John Franco	.20	.06
❑ 183 Sidney Ponson	.20	.06
❑ 184 Jose Mesa	.20	.06
❑ 185 Todd Hollandsworth	.20	.06
❑ 186 Kevin Young	.20	.06
❑ 187 Tim Wakefield	.20	.06
❑ 188 Craig Biggio	.30	.09
❑ 189 Jason Isringhausen	.20	.06
❑ 190 Mark Quinn	.20	.06
❑ 191 Glendon Rusch	.20	.06
❑ 192 Damian Miller	.20	.06
❑ 193 Sandy Alomar Jr.	.20	.06
❑ 194 Scott Brosius	.20	.06
❑ 195 Dave Martinez	.20	.06
❑ 196 Danny Graves	.20	.06
❑ 197 Shea Hillenbrand	.20	.06
❑ 198 Jimmy Anderson	.20	.06
❑ 199 Travis Lee	.20	.06
❑ 200 Randy Johnson	.50	.15
❑ 201 Carlos Beltran	.30	.09
❑ 202 Jerry Hairston	.20	.06
❑ 203 Jesus Sanchez	.20	.06
❑ 204 Eddie Taubensee	.20	.06
❑ 205 David Wells	.20	.06
❑ 206 Russ Davis	.20	.06
❑ 207 Michael Barrett	.20	.06
❑ 208 Marquis Grissom	.20	.06
❑ 209 Byung-Hyun Kim	.20	.06
❑ 210 Hideo Nomo	.50	.15
❑ 211 Ryan Rupe	.20	.06
❑ 212 Ricky Gutierrez	.20	.06
❑ 213 Darryl Kile	.20	.06
❑ 214 Rico Brogna	.20	.06
❑ 215 Terrence Long	.20	.06
❑ 216 Mike Jackson	.20	.06
❑ 217 Jamey Wright	.20	.06
❑ 218 Adrian Beltre	.30	.09
❑ 219 Benny Agbayani	.20	.06
❑ 220 Chuck Knoblauch	.20	.06
❑ 221 Randy Wolf	.20	.06
❑ 222 Andy Ashby	.20	.06
❑ 223 Corey Koskie	.20	.06
❑ 224 Roger Cedeno	.20	.06
❑ 225 Ichiro Suzuki	.75	.23
❑ 226 Keith Foulke	.20	.06
❑ 227 Ryan Minor	.20	.06
❑ 228 Shawon Dunston	.20	.06
❑ 229 Alex Cora	.20	.06
❑ 230 Jeromy Burnitz	.20	.06
❑ 231 Mark Grace	.30	.09
❑ 232 Aubrey Huff	.20	.06
❑ 233 Jeffrey Hammonds	.20	.06
❑ 234 Olmedo Saenz	.20	.06
❑ 235 Brian Jordan	.20	.06
❑ 236 Jeremy Giambi	.20	.06
❑ 237 Joe Girardi	.20	.06
❑ 238 Eric Gagne	.50	.15
❑ 239 Masato Yoshii	.20	.06
❑ 240 Greg Maddux	.75	.23
❑ 241 Bryan Rekar	.20	.06
❑ 242 Ray Durham	.20	.06
❑ 243 Torii Hunter	.20	.06
❑ 244 Derrek Lee	.20	.06
❑ 245 Jim Edmonds	.20	.06
❑ 246 Einar Diaz	.20	.06
❑ 247 Brian Bohanon	.20	.06
❑ 248 Ron Belliard	.20	.06
❑ 249 Mike Lowell	.20	.06
❑ 250 Sammy Sosa	.75	.23
❑ 251 Richard Hidalgo	.20	.06
❑ 252 Bartolo Colon	.20	.06
❑ 253 Jorge Posada	.30	.09
❑ 254 LaTroy Hawkins	.20	.06
❑ 255 Paul LoDuca	.20	.06
❑ 256 Carlos Febles	.20	.06
❑ 257 Nelson Cruz	.20	.06
❑ 258 Edgardo Alfonzo	.20	.06
❑ 259 Joey Hamilton	.20	.06
❑ 260 Cliff Floyd	.20	.06
❑ 261 Wes Helms	.20	.06
❑ 262 Jay Bell	.20	.06
❑ 263 Mike Cameron	.20	.06
❑ 264 Paul Konerko	.20	.06
❑ 265 Jeff Kent	.20	.06
❑ 266 Robert Fick	.20	.06
❑ 267 Allen Levrault	.20	.06
❑ 268 Placido Polanco	.20	.06
❑ 269 Marlon Anderson	.20	.06
❑ 270 Mariano Rivera	.30	.09
❑ 271 Chan Ho Park	.20	.06
❑ 272 Jose Vizcaino	.20	.06
❑ 273 Jeff D'Amico	.20	.06
❑ 274 Mark Gardner	.20	.06
❑ 275 Travis Fryman	.20	.06
❑ 276 Darren Lewis	.20	.06
❑ 277 Bruce Bochy MG	.20	.06
❑ 278 Jerry Manuel MG	.20	.06
❑ 279 Bob Brenly MG	.20	.06
❑ 280 Don Baylor MG	.20	.06
❑ 281 Davey Lopes MG	.20	.06
❑ 282 Jerry Narron MG	.20	.06
❑ 283 Tony Muser MG	.20	.06
❑ 284 Hal McRae MG	.20	.06
❑ 285 Bobby Cox MG	.20	.06
❑ 286 Larry Dierker MG	.20	.06
❑ 287 Phil Garner MG	.20	.06
❑ 288 Joe Kerrigan MG	.20	.06
❑ 289 Bobby Valentine MG	.20	.06
❑ 290 Dusty Baker MG	.20	.06
❑ 291 Lloyd McClendon MG	.20	.06
❑ 292 Mike Scioscia MG	.20	.06
❑ 293 Buck Martinez MG	.20	.06
❑ 294 Larry Bowa MG	.20	.06
❑ 295 Tony LaRussa MG	.20	.06

❑ 296	Jeff Torborg MG	.20	.06
❑ 297	Tom Kelly MG	.20	.06
❑ 298	Mike Hargrove MG	.20	.06
❑ 299	Art Howe MG	.20	.06
❑ 300	Lou Piniella MG	.20	.06
❑ 301	Charlie Manuel MG	.20	.06
❑ 302	Buddy Bell MG	.20	.06
❑ 303	Tony Perez MG	.20	.06
❑ 304	Bob Boone MG	.20	.06
❑ 305	Joe Torre MG	.50	.15
❑ 306	Jim Tracy MG	.20	.06
❑ 307	Jason Lane PROS	.50	.15
❑ 308	Chris George PROS	.50	.15
❑ 309	Hank Blalock PROS UER	1.00	.30
	Bio has him throwing lefty		
❑ 310	Joe Borchard PROS	.50	.15
❑ 311	Marlon Byrd PROS	.50	.15
❑ 312	R. Cabrera PROS RC	.50	.15
❑ 313	F. Sanchez PROS RC	.50	.15
❑ 314	S. Wiggins PROS RC	.50	.15
❑ 315	J. Maule PROS RC	.50	.15
❑ 316	D. Cesar PROS RC	.50	.15
❑ 317	Boof Bonser PROS	.50	.15
❑ 318	J. Tolentino PROS RC	.50	.15
❑ 319	Earl Snyder PROS RC	.50	.15
❑ 320	T. Wade PROS RC	.50	.15
❑ 321	N. Calzado PROS RC	.50	.15
❑ 322	Eric Glaser PROS RC	.50	.15
❑ 323	C. Kuzmic PROS RC	.50	.15
❑ 324	Nic Jackson PROS RC	.50	.15
❑ 325	Mike Rivera PROS	.50	.15
❑ 326	Jason Bay PROS RC	2.50	.75
❑ 327	Chris Smith DP	.50	.15
❑ 328	Jake Gautreau DP	.50	.15
❑ 329	Gabe Gross DP	.50	.15
❑ 330	Kenny Baugh DP	.50	.15
❑ 331	J.D. Martin DP	.50	.15
❑ 332	Barry Bonds HL	1.25	.35
	500th Homer		
❑ 333	Rickey Henderson HL	.50	.15
	Sets record for career walks		
❑ 334	Bud Smith HL	.50	.15
❑ 335	R. Henderson HL 3000	.50	.15
❑ 336	Barry Bonds HL	1.25	.35
	73 homers in a season		
❑ 337	Ichiro Suzuki	.50	.15
	Jason Giambi		
	Roberto Alomar LL		
❑ 338	Alex Rodriguez	.50	.15
	Ichiro Suzuki		
	Bret Boone LL		
❑ 339	Alex Rodriguez	.50	.15
	Jim Thome		
	Rafael Palmeiro LL		
❑ 340	Bret Boone	.50	.15
	Juan Gonzalez		
	Alex Rodriguez LL		
❑ 341	Freddy Garcia	.50	.15
	Mike Mussina		
	Joe Mays LL		
❑ 342	Hideo Nomo	.50	.15
	Mike Mussina		
	Roger Clemens LL		
❑ 343	Larry Walker	.50	.15
	Todd Helton		
	Moises Alou		
	Lance Berkman LL		
❑ 344	Sammy Sosa	.50	.15
	Todd Helton		
	Barry Bonds LL		
❑ 345	Barry Bonds	.50	.15
	Sammy Sosa		
	Luis Gonzalez LL		
❑ 346	Sammy Sosa	.50	.15
	Todd Helton		
	Luis Gonzalez LL		
❑ 347	Randy Johnson	.50	.15
	Curt Schilling		
	John Burkett LL		
❑ 348	Randy Johnson	.50	.15
	Curt Schilling		
	Chan Ho Park LL		
❑ 349	Seattle Mariners PB	.50	.15
❑ 350	Oakland Athletics PB	.50	.15
❑ 351	New York Yankees PB	.50	.15
❑ 352	Cleveland Indians PB	.50	.15
❑ 353	Ariz. Diamondbacks PB	.50	.15
❑ 354	Atlanta Braves PB	.50	.15
❑ 355	St. Louis Cardinals PB	.50	.15
❑ 356	Houston Astros PB	.50	.15
❑ 357	Ariz.Diamondbacks	.50	.15
	Colorado Rockies UWS		
❑ 358	Mike Piazza UWS	.50	.15
❑ 359	Braves-Phillies UWS	.50	.15
❑ 360	Curt Schilling UWS	.50	.15
❑ 361	Roger Clemens	.50	.15
	Lee Mazzilli UWS		
❑ 362	Sammy Sosa UWS	.50	.15
❑ 363	Tom Lampkin	.50	.15
	Ichiro Suzuki		
	Bret Boone UWS		
❑ 364	Barry Bonds	.50	.15
	Jeff Bagwell UWS		
❑ 365	Barry Bonds HR 1	15.00	4.50
❑ 365	Barry Bonds HR 2	10.00	3.00
❑ 365	Barry Bonds HR 3	10.00	3.00
❑ 365	Barry Bonds HR 4	10.00	3.00
❑ 365	Barry Bonds HR 5	10.00	3.00
❑ 365	Barry Bonds HR 6	10.00	3.00
❑ 365	Barry Bonds HR 7	10.00	3.00
❑ 365	Barry Bonds HR 8	10.00	3.00
❑ 365	Barry Bonds HR 9	10.00	3.00
❑ 365	Barry Bonds HR 10	10.00	3.00
❑ 365	Barry Bonds HR 11	10.00	3.00
❑ 365	Barry Bonds HR 12	10.00	3.00
❑ 365	Barry Bonds HR 13	10.00	3.00
❑ 365	Barry Bonds HR 14	10.00	3.00
❑ 365	Barry Bonds HR 15	10.00	3.00
❑ 365	Barry Bonds HR 16	10.00	3.00
❑ 365	Barry Bonds HR 17	10.00	3.00
❑ 365	Barry Bonds HR 18	10.00	3.00
❑ 365	Barry Bonds HR 19	10.00	3.00
❑ 365	Barry Bonds HR 20	10.00	3.00
❑ 365	Barry Bonds HR 21	10.00	3.00
❑ 365	Barry Bonds HR 22	10.00	3.00
❑ 365	Barry Bonds HR 23	10.00	3.00
❑ 365	Barry Bonds HR 24	10.00	3.00
❑ 365	Barry Bonds HR 25	10.00	3.00
❑ 365	Barry Bonds HR 26	10.00	3.00
❑ 365	Barry Bonds HR 27	10.00	3.00
❑ 365	Barry Bonds HR 28	10.00	3.00
❑ 365	Barry Bonds HR 29	10.00	3.00
❑ 365	Barry Bonds HR 30	10.00	3.00
❑ 365	Barry Bonds HR 31	10.00	3.00
❑ 365	Barry Bonds HR 32 UER	10.00	3.00
	No pitcher is listed on this card		
❑ 365	Barry Bonds HR 33	10.00	3.00
❑ 365	Barry Bonds HR 34	10.00	3.00
❑ 365	Barry Bonds HR 35	10.00	3.00
❑ 365	Barry Bonds HR 36	10.00	3.00
❑ 365	Barry Bonds HR 37	10.00	3.00
❑ 365	Barry Bonds HR 38	10.00	3.00
❑ 365	Barry Bonds HR 39	10.00	3.00
❑ 365	Barry Bonds HR 40	10.00	3.00
❑ 365	Barry Bonds HR 41	10.00	3.00
❑ 365	Barry Bonds HR 42	10.00	3.00
❑ 365	Barry Bonds HR 43	10.00	3.00
❑ 365	Barry Bonds HR 44	10.00	3.00
❑ 365	Barry Bonds HR 45	10.00	3.00
❑ 365	Barry Bonds HR 46	10.00	3.00
❑ 365	Barry Bonds HR 47	10.00	3.00
❑ 365	Barry Bonds HR 48	10.00	3.00
❑ 365	Barry Bonds HR 49	10.00	3.00
❑ 365	Barry Bonds HR 50	10.00	3.00
❑ 365	Barry Bonds HR 51	10.00	3.00
❑ 365	Barry Bonds HR 52	10.00	3.00
❑ 365	Barry Bonds HR 53	10.00	3.00
❑ 365	Barry Bonds HR 54	10.00	3.00
❑ 365	Barry Bonds HR 55	10.00	3.00
❑ 365	Barry Bonds HR 56	10.00	3.00
❑ 365	Barry Bonds HR 57	10.00	3.00
❑ 365	Barry Bonds HR 58	10.00	3.00
❑ 365	Barry Bonds HR 59	10.00	3.00
❑ 365	Barry Bonds HR 60	10.00	3.00
❑ 365	Barry Bonds HR 61	15.00	4.50
❑ 365	Barry Bonds HR 62	10.00	3.00
❑ 365	Barry Bonds HR 63	10.00	3.00
❑ 365	Barry Bonds HR 64	10.00	3.00
❑ 365	Barry Bonds HR 65	10.00	3.00
❑ 365	Barry Bonds HR 66	10.00	3.00
❑ 365	Barry Bonds HR 67	10.00	3.00
❑ 365	Barry Bonds HR 68	10.00	3.00
❑ 365	Barry Bonds HR 69	10.00	3.00
❑ 365	Barry Bonds HR 70	15.00	4.50
❑ 365	Barry Bonds HR 71	10.00	3.00
❑ 365	Barry Bonds HR 72	10.00	3.00
❑ 365	Barry Bonds HR 73	50.00	15.00
❑ 366	Pat Meares	.20	.06
❑ 367	Mike Lieberthal	.20	.06
❑ 368	Larry Bigbie	.20	.06
❑ 369	Ron Gant	.20	.06
❑ 370	Moises Alou	.20	.06
❑ 371	Chad Kreuter	.20	.06
❑ 372	Willis Roberts	.20	.06
❑ 373	Toby Hall	.20	.06
❑ 374	Miguel Batista	.20	.06
❑ 375	John Burkett	.20	.06
❑ 376	Cory Lidle	.20	.06
❑ 377	Nick Neugebauer	.20	.06
❑ 378	Jay Payton	.20	.06
❑ 379	Steve Karsay	.20	.06
❑ 380	Eric Chavez	.20	.06
❑ 381	Kelly Stinnett	.20	.06
❑ 382	Jarrod Washburn	.20	.06
❑ 383	Rick White	.20	.06
❑ 384	Jeff Conine	.20	.06
❑ 385	Fred McGriff	.30	.09
❑ 386	Marvin Benard	.20	.06
❑ 387	Joe Crede	.20	.06
❑ 388	Dennis Cook	.20	.06
❑ 389	Rick Reed	.20	.06
❑ 390	Tom Glavine	.30	.09
❑ 391	Rondell White	.20	.06
❑ 392	Matt Morris	.20	.06
❑ 393	Pat Rapp	.20	.06
❑ 394	Robert Person	.20	.06
❑ 395	Omar Vizquel	.30	.09
❑ 396	Jeff Cirillo	.20	.06
❑ 397	Dave Mlicki	.20	.06
❑ 398	Jose Ortiz	.20	.06
❑ 399	Ryan Dempster	.20	.06
❑ 400	Curt Schilling	.20	.06
❑ 401	Peter Bergeron	.20	.06
❑ 402	Kyle Lohse	.20	.06
❑ 403	Craig Wilson UER	.20	.06
	Homer totals are wrong		
❑ 404	David Justice	.20	.06
❑ 405	Darin Erstad	.20	.06
❑ 406	Jose Mercedes	.20	.06
❑ 407	Carl Pavano	.20	.06
❑ 408	Albie Lopez	.20	.06
❑ 409	Alex Ochoa	.20	.06
❑ 410	Chipper Jones	.50	.15
❑ 411	Tyler Houston	.20	.06
❑ 412	Dean Palmer	.20	.06
❑ 413	Damian Jackson	.20	.06
❑ 414	Josh Towers	.20	.06
❑ 415	Rafael Furcal	.20	.06
❑ 416	Mike Morgan	.20	.06
❑ 417	Herb Perry	.20	.06
❑ 418	Mike Sirotka	.20	.06
❑ 419	Mark Wohlers	.20	.06
❑ 420	Nomar Garciaparra	.75	.23
❑ 421	Felipe Lopez	.20	.06
❑ 422	Joe McEwing	.20	.06
❑ 423	Jacque Jones	.20	.06
❑ 424	Julio Franco	.20	.06
❑ 425	Frank Thomas	.50	.15
❑ 426	So Taguchi RC	.75	.23
❑ 427	Kazuhisa Ishii RC	1.50	.45
❑ 428	D'Angelo Jimenez	.20	.06
❑ 429	Chris Stynes	.20	.06
❑ 430	Kerry Wood	.50	.15
❑ 431	Chris Singleton	.20	.06
❑ 432	Erubiel Durazo	.20	.06
❑ 433	Matt Lawton	.20	.06
❑ 434	Bill Mueller	.20	.06
❑ 435	Jose Canseco	.50	.15
❑ 436	Ben Grieve	.20	.06
❑ 437	Terry Mulholland	.20	.06
❑ 438	David Bell	.20	.06
❑ 439	A.J. Pierzynski	.20	.06
❑ 440	Adam Dunn	.30	.09
❑ 441	Jon Garland	.20	.06
❑ 442	Jeff Fassero	.20	.06
❑ 443	Julio Lugo	.20	.06
❑ 444	Carlos Guillen	.20	.06
❑ 445	Orlando Hernandez	.20	.06

	Card	Price	Price
❑ 446	Mark Loretta UER	.20	.06
	Photo is Curtis Leskanic		
❑ 447	Scott Spiezio	.20	.06
❑ 448	Kevin Millwood	.20	.06
❑ 449	Jamie Moyer	.20	.06
❑ 450	Todd Helton	.30	.09
❑ 451	Todd Walker	.20	.06
❑ 452	Jose Lima	.20	.06
❑ 453	Brook Fordyce	.20	.06
❑ 454	Aaron Rowand	.20	.06
❑ 455	Barry Zito	.20	.06
❑ 456	Eric Owens	.20	.06
❑ 457	Charles Nagy	.20	.06
❑ 458	Raul Ibanez	.20	.06
❑ 459	Joe Mays	.20	.06
❑ 460	Jim Thome	.50	.15
❑ 461	Adam Eaton	.20	.06
❑ 462	Felix Martinez	.20	.06
❑ 463	Vernon Wells	.20	.06
❑ 464	Donnie Sadler	.20	.06
❑ 465	Tony Clark	.20	.06
❑ 466	Jose Hernandez	.20	.06
❑ 467	Ramon Martinez	.20	.06
❑ 468	Rusty Greer	.20	.06
❑ 469	Rod Barajas	.20	.06
❑ 470	Lance Berkman	.20	.06
❑ 471	Brady Anderson	.20	.06
❑ 472	Pedro Astacio	.20	.06
❑ 473	Shane Halter	.20	.06
❑ 474	Bret Prinz	.20	.06
❑ 475	Edgar Martinez	.30	.09
❑ 476	Steve Trachsel	.20	.06
❑ 477	Gary Matthews Jr.	.20	.06
❑ 478	Ismael Valdes	.20	.06
❑ 479	Juan Uribe	.20	.06
❑ 480	Shawn Green	.20	.06
❑ 481	Kirk Rueter	.20	.06
❑ 482	Damion Easley	.20	.06
❑ 483	Chris Carpenter	.20	.06
❑ 484	Kris Benson	.20	.06
❑ 485	Antonio Alfonseca	.20	.06
❑ 486	Kyle Farnsworth	.20	.06
❑ 487	Brandon Lyon	.20	.06
❑ 488	Hideki Irabu	.20	.06
❑ 489	David Ortiz	.30	.09
❑ 490	Mike Piazza	.75	.23
❑ 491	Derek Lowe	.20	.06
❑ 492	Chris Gomez	.20	.06
❑ 493	Mark Johnson	.20	.06
❑ 494	John Rocker	.20	.06
❑ 495	Eric Karros	.20	.06
❑ 496	Bill Haselman	.20	.06
❑ 497	Dave Veres	.20	.06
❑ 498	Pete Harnisch	.20	.06
❑ 499	Tomokazu Ohka	.20	.06
❑ 500	Barry Bonds	1.25	.35
❑ 501	David Dellucci	.20	.06
❑ 502	Wendell Magee	.20	.06
❑ 503	Tom Gordon	.20	.06
❑ 504	Javier Vazquez	.20	.06
❑ 505	Ben Sheets	.20	.06
❑ 506	Wilton Guerrero	.20	.06
❑ 507	John Halama	.20	.06
❑ 508	Mark Redman	.20	.06
❑ 509	Jack Wilson	.20	.06
❑ 510	Bernie Williams	.30	.09
❑ 511	Miguel Cairo	.20	.06
❑ 512	Denny Hocking	.20	.06
❑ 513	Tony Batista	.20	.06
❑ 514	Mark Grudzielanek	.20	.06
❑ 515	Jose Vidro	.20	.06
❑ 516	Sterling Hitchcock	.20	.06
❑ 517	Billy Koch	.20	.06
❑ 518	Matt Clement	.20	.06
❑ 519	Bruce Chen	.20	.06
❑ 520	Roberto Alomar	.30	.09
❑ 521	Orlando Palmeiro	.20	.06
❑ 522	Steve Finley	.20	.06
❑ 523	Danny Patterson	.20	.06
❑ 524	Terry Adams	.20	.06
❑ 525	Tino Martinez	.30	.09
❑ 526	Tony Armas Jr.	.20	.06
❑ 527	Geoff Jenkins	.20	.06
❑ 528	Kerry Robinson	.20	.06
❑ 529	Corey Patterson	.20	.06
❑ 530	Brian Giles	.20	.06
❑ 531	Jose Jimenez	.20	.06
❑ 532	Joe Kennedy	.20	.06
❑ 533	Armando Rios	.20	.06
❑ 534	Osvaldo Fernandez	.20	.06
❑ 535	Ruben Sierra	.20	.06
❑ 536	Octavio Dotel	.20	.06
❑ 537	Luis Sojo	.20	.06
❑ 538	Brent Butler	.20	.06
❑ 539	Pablo Ozuna UER	.20	.06
	Games played for Portland is wrong for 2002		
❑ 540	Freddy Garcia	.20	.06
❑ 541	Chad Durbin	.20	.06
❑ 542	Orlando Merced	.20	.06
❑ 543	Michael Tucker	.20	.06
❑ 544	Roberto Hernandez	.20	.06
❑ 545	Pat Burrell	.20	.06
❑ 546	A.J. Burnett	.20	.06
❑ 547	Bubba Trammell	.20	.06
❑ 548	Scott Elarton	.20	.06
❑ 549	Mike Darr	.20	.06
❑ 550	Ken Griffey Jr.	.75	.23
❑ 551	Ugueth Urbina	.20	.06
❑ 552	Todd Jones	.20	.06
❑ 553	Delino Deshields	.20	.06
❑ 554	Adam Piatt	.20	.06
❑ 555	Jason Kendall	.20	.06
❑ 556	Hector Ortiz	.20	.06
❑ 557	Turk Wendell	.20	.06
❑ 558	Rob Bell	.20	.06
❑ 559	Sun Woo Kim	.20	.06
❑ 560	Raul Mondesi	.20	.06
❑ 561	Brent Abernathy	.20	.06
❑ 562	Seth Etherton	.20	.06
❑ 563	Shawn Wooten	.20	.06
❑ 564	Jay Buhner	.20	.06
❑ 565	Andres Galarraga	.20	.06
❑ 566	Shane Reynolds	.20	.06
❑ 567	Rod Beck	.20	.06
❑ 568	Dee Brown	.20	.06
❑ 569	Pedro Feliz	.20	.06
❑ 570	Ryan Klesko	.20	.06
❑ 571	John Vander Wal UER	.20	.06
	Home Run Total in 1999 was 64		
❑ 572	Nick Bierbrodt	.20	.06
❑ 573	Joe Nathan	.20	.06
❑ 574	James Baldwin	.20	.06
❑ 575	J.D. Drew	.20	.06
❑ 576	Greg Colbrunn	.20	.06
❑ 577	Doug Glanville	.20	.06
❑ 578	Brandon Duckworth	.20	.06
❑ 579	Shawn Chacon	.20	.06
❑ 580	Rich Aurilia	.20	.06
❑ 581	Chuck Finley	.20	.06
❑ 582	Abraham Nunez	.20	.06
❑ 583	Kenny Lofton	.20	.06
❑ 584	Brian Daubach	.20	.06
❑ 585	Miguel Tejada	.20	.06
❑ 586	Nate Cornejo	.20	.06
❑ 587	Kazuhiro Sasaki	.20	.06
❑ 588	Chris Richard	.20	.06
❑ 589	Armando Reynoso	.20	.06
❑ 590	Tim Hudson	.20	.06
❑ 591	Neifi Perez	.20	.06
❑ 592	Steve Cox	.20	.06
❑ 593	Henry Blanco	.20	.06
❑ 594	Ricky Ledee	.20	.06
❑ 595	Tim Salmon	.30	.09
❑ 596	Luis Rivas	.20	.06
❑ 597	Jeff Zimmerman	.20	.06
❑ 598	Matt Stairs	.20	.06
❑ 599	Preston Wilson	.20	.06
❑ 600	Mark McGwire	1.25	.35
❑ 601	Timo Perez UER	.20	.06
	Biographical Information is that of Aaron Rowand's		
❑ 602	Matt Anderson	.20	.06
❑ 603	Todd Hundley	.20	.06
❑ 604	Rick Ankiel	.20	.06
❑ 605	Tsuyoshi Shinjo	.20	.06
❑ 606	Woody Williams	.20	.06
❑ 607	Jason LaRue	.20	.06
❑ 608	Carlos Lee	.20	.06
❑ 609	Russ Johnson	.20	.06
❑ 610	Scott Rolen	.50	.15
❑ 611	Brent Mayne	.20	.06
❑ 612	Darrin Fletcher	.20	.06
❑ 613	Ray Lankford	.20	.06
❑ 614	Troy O'Leary	.20	.06
❑ 615	Javier Lopez	.20	.06
❑ 616	Randy Velarde	.20	.06
❑ 617	Vinny Castilla	.20	.06
❑ 618	Milton Bradley	.20	.06
❑ 619	Ruben Mateo	.20	.06
❑ 620	Jason Giambi Yankees	.20	.06
❑ 621	Andy Benes	.20	.06
❑ 622	Joe Mauer RC	5.00	1.50
❑ 623	Andy Pettitte	.30	.09
❑ 624	Jose Offerman	.20	.06
❑ 625	Mo Vaughn	.20	.06
❑ 626	Steve Sparks	.20	.06
❑ 627	Mike Matthews	.20	.06
❑ 628	Robb Nen	.20	.06
❑ 629	Kip Wells	.20	.06
❑ 630	Kevin Brown	.20	.06
❑ 631	Arthur Rhodes	.20	.06
❑ 632	Gabe Kapler	.20	.06
❑ 633	Jermaine Dye	.20	.06
❑ 634	Josh Beckett	.20	.06
❑ 635	Pokey Reese	.20	.06
❑ 636	Benji Gil	.20	.06
❑ 637	Marcus Giles	.20	.06
❑ 638	Julian Tavarez	.20	.06
❑ 639	Jason Schmidt	.20	.06
❑ 640	Alex Rodriguez	.75	.23
❑ 641	Anaheim Angels TC	.20	.06
❑ 642	Arizona Diamondbacks TC	.30	.09
❑ 643	Atlanta Braves TC	.20	.06
❑ 644	Baltimore Orioles TC	.20	.06
❑ 645	Boston Red Sox TC	.20	.06
❑ 646	Chicago Cubs TC	.20	.06
❑ 647	Chicago White Sox TC	.20	.06
❑ 648	Cincinnati Reds TC	.20	.06
❑ 649	Cleveland Indians TC	.20	.06
❑ 650	Colorado Rockies TC	.20	.06
❑ 651	Detroit Tigers TC	.20	.06
❑ 652	Florida Marlins TC	.20	.06
❑ 653	Houston Astros TC	.20	.06
❑ 654	Kansas City Royals TC	.20	.06
❑ 655	Los Angeles Dodgers TC	.20	.06
❑ 656	Milwaukee Brewers TC	.20	.06
❑ 657	Minnesota Twins TC	.20	.06
❑ 658	Montreal Expos TC	.20	.06
❑ 659	New York Mets TC	.20	.06
❑ 660	New York Yankees TC	.50	.15
❑ 661	Oakland Athletics TC	.20	.06
❑ 662	Philadelphia Phillies TC	.20	.06
❑ 663	Pittsburgh Pirates TC	.20	.06
❑ 664	San Diego Padres TC	.20	.06
❑ 665	San Francisco Giants TC	.20	.06
❑ 666	Seattle Mariners TC	.30	.09
❑ 667	St. Louis Cardinals TC	.20	.06
❑ 668	T.B. Devil Rays TC	.20	.06
❑ 669	Texas Rangers TC	.20	.06
❑ 670	Toronto Blue Jays TC	.20	.06
❑ 671	Juan Cruz PROS	.50	.15
❑ 672	Kevin Cash PROS RC	.50	.15
❑ 673	Jimmy Gobble PROS RC	.75	.23
❑ 674	Mike Hill PROS RC	.50	.15
❑ 675	T.Buchholz PROS RC	.50	.15
❑ 676	Bill Hall PROS	.50	.15
❑ 677	B.Roneberg PROS RC	.50	.15
❑ 678	R.Huffman PROS RC	.50	.15
❑ 679	Chris Tritle PROS RC	.50	.15
❑ 680	Nate Espy PROS RC	.50	.15
❑ 681	Nick Alvarez PROS RC	.50	.15
❑ 682	Jason Botts PROS RC	.75	.23
❑ 683	Ryan Gripp PROS RC	.50	.15
❑ 684	Dan Phillips PROS RC	.50	.15
❑ 685	Pablo Arias PROS RC	.50	.15
❑ 686	J.Rodriguez PROS RC	.50	.15
❑ 687	Rich Harden PROS RC	4.00	1.20
❑ 688	Neal Frendling PROS RC	.50	.15
❑ 689	Rich Thompson PROS RC	.50	.15
❑ 690	G.Montalbano PROS RC	.50	.15
❑ 691	Len Dinardo DP RC	.50	.15
❑ 692	Ryan Raburn DP RC	.50	.15
❑ 693	Josh Barfield DP RC	1.50	.45
❑ 694	David Bacani DP RC	.50	.15
❑ 695	Dan Johnson DP RC	.75	.23
❑ 696	Mike Mussina GG	.20	.06
❑ 697	Ivan Rodriguez GG	.50	.15

❑ 698 Doug Mientkiewicz GG .20 .06
❑ 699 Roberto Alomar GG .20 .06
❑ 700 Eric Chavez GG .20 .06
❑ 701 Omar Vizquel GG .20 .06
❑ 702 Mike Cameron GG .20 .06
❑ 703 Torii Hunter GG .20 .06
❑ 704 Ichiro Suzuki GG .50 .15
❑ 705 Greg Maddux GG .50 .15
❑ 706 Brad Ausmus GG .20 .06
❑ 707 Todd Helton GG .20 .06
❑ 708 Fernando Vina GG .20 .06
❑ 709 Scott Rolen GG .30 .09
❑ 710 Orlando Cabrera GG .20 .06
❑ 711 Andruw Jones GG .20 .06
❑ 712 Jim Edmonds GG .20 .06
❑ 713 Larry Walker GG .20 .06
❑ 714 Roger Clemens CY .50 .15
❑ 715 Randy Johnson CY .30 .09
❑ 716 Ichiro Suzuki MVP .50 .15
❑ 717 Barry Bonds MVP .50 .15
❑ 718 Ichiro Suzuki ROY .50 .15
❑ 719 Albert Pujols ROY .50 .15

2002 Topps Traded

	Nm-Mt	Ex-Mt
COMPLETE SET (275)	180.00	55.00
COMMON CARD (T1-T110)	1.50	.45
COMMON CARD (T111-T275)	.40	.12

❑ T1 Jeff Weaver 1.50 .45
❑ T2 Jay Powell 1.50 .45
❑ T3 Alex Gonzalez 1.50 .45
❑ T4 Jason Isringhausen 1.50 .45
❑ T5 Tyler Houston 1.50 .45
❑ T6 Ben Broussard 1.50 .45
❑ T7 Chuck Knoblauch 1.50 .45
❑ T8 Brian L. Hunter 1.50 .45
❑ T9 Dustan Mohr 1.50 .45
❑ T10 Eric Hinske 1.50 .45
❑ T11 Roger Cedeno 1.50 .45
❑ T12 Eddie Perez 1.50 .45
❑ T13 Jeromy Burnitz 1.50 .45
❑ T14 Bartolo Colon 1.50 .45
❑ T15 Rick Helling 1.50 .45
❑ T16 Dan Plesac 1.50 .45
❑ T17 Scott Strickland 1.50 .45
❑ T18 Antonio Alfonseca 1.50 .45
❑ T19 Ricky Gutierrez 1.50 .45
❑ T20 John Valentin 1.50 .45
❑ T21 Raul Mondesi 1.50 .45
❑ T22 Ben Davis 1.50 .45
❑ T23 Nelson Figueroa 1.50 .45
❑ T24 Earl Snyder 1.50 .45
❑ T25 Robin Ventura 1.50 .45
❑ T26 Jimmy Haynes 1.50 .45
❑ T27 Kenny Kelly 1.50 .45
❑ T28 Morgan Ensberg 1.50 .45
❑ T29 Reggie Sanders 1.50 .45
❑ T30 Shigetoshi Hasegawa 1.50 .45
❑ T31 Mike Timlin 1.50 .45
❑ T32 Russell Branyan 1.50 .45
❑ T33 Alan Embree 1.50 .45
❑ T34 D'Angelo Jimenez 1.50 .45
❑ T35 Kent Mercker 1.50 .45
❑ T36 Jesse Orosco 1.50 .45
❑ T37 Gregg Zaun 1.50 .45
❑ T38 Reggie Taylor 1.50 .45
❑ T39 Andres Galarraga 1.50 .45
❑ T40 Chris Truby 1.50 .45
❑ T41 Bruce Chen 1.50 .45
❑ T42 Darren Lewis 1.50 .45
❑ T43 Ryan Kohlmeier 1.50 .45
❑ T44 John McDonald 1.50 .45
❑ T45 Omar Daal 1.50 .45
❑ T46 Matt Clement 1.50 .45
❑ T47 Glendon Rusch 1.50 .45
❑ T48 Chan Ho Park 1.50 .45
❑ T49 Benny Agbayani 1.50 .45
❑ T50 Juan Gonzalez 2.50 .75
❑ T51 Carlos Baerga 1.50 .45
❑ T52 Tim Raines 1.50 .45
❑ T53 Kevin Appier 1.50 .45
❑ T54 Marty Cordova 1.50 .45
❑ T55 Jeff D'Amico 1.50 .45
❑ T56 Dmitri Young 1.50 .45
❑ T57 Roosevelt Brown 1.50 .45
❑ T58 Dustin Hermanson 1.50 .45
❑ T59 Jose Rijo 1.50 .45
❑ T60 Todd Ritchie 1.50 .45
❑ T61 Lee Stevens 1.50 .45
❑ T62 Placido Polanco 1.50 .45
❑ T63 Eric Young 1.50 .45
❑ T64 Chuck Finley 1.50 .45
❑ T65 Dicky Gonzalez 1.50 .45
❑ T66 Jose Macias 1.50 .45
❑ T67 Gabe Kapler 1.50 .45
❑ T68 Sandy Alomar Jr. 1.50 .45
❑ T69 Henry Blanco 1.50 .45
❑ T70 Julian Tavarez 1.50 .45
❑ T71 Paul Bako 1.50 .45
❑ T72 Scott Rolen 4.00 1.20
❑ T73 Brian Jordan 1.50 .45
❑ T74 Rickey Henderson 4.00 1.20
❑ T75 Kevin Mench 1.50 .45
❑ T76 Hideo Nomo 4.00 1.20
❑ T77 Jeremy Giambi 1.50 .45
❑ T78 Brad Fullmer 1.50 .45
❑ T79 Carl Everett 1.50 .45
❑ T80 David Wells 1.50 .45
❑ T81 Aaron Sele 1.50 .45
❑ T82 Todd Hollandsworth 1.50 .45
❑ T83 Vicente Padilla 1.50 .45
❑ T84 Kenny Lofton 1.50 .45
❑ T85 Corky Miller 1.50 .45
❑ T86 Josh Fogg 1.50 .45
❑ T87 Cliff Floyd 1.50 .45
❑ T88 Craig Paquette 1.50 .45
❑ T89 Jay Payton 1.50 .45
❑ T90 Carlos Pena 1.50 .45
❑ T91 Juan Encarnacion 1.50 .45
❑ T92 Rey Sanchez 1.50 .45
❑ T93 Ryan Dempster 1.50 .45
❑ T94 Mario Encarnacion 1.50 .45
❑ T95 Jorge Julio 1.50 .45
❑ T96 John Mabry 1.50 .45
❑ T97 Todd Zeile 1.50 .45
❑ T98 Johnny Damon Sox 4.00 1.20
❑ T99 Deivi Cruz 1.50 .45
❑ T100 Gary Sheffield 1.50 .45
❑ T101 Ted Lilly 1.50 .45
❑ T102 Todd Van Poppel 1.50 .45
❑ T103 Shawn Estes 1.50 .45
❑ T104 Cesar Izturis 1.50 .45
❑ T105 Ron Coomer 1.50 .45
❑ T106 Grady Little MG RC 1.50 .45
❑ T107 Jimy Williams MG 1.50 .45
❑ T108 Tony Pena MG 1.50 .45
❑ T109 Frank Robinson MG 2.50 .75
❑ T110 Ron Gardenhire MG 1.50 .45
❑ T111 Dennis Tankersley .40 .12
❑ T112 Alejandro Cadena RC .40 .12
❑ T113 Justin Reid RC .40 .12
❑ T114 Nate Field RC .40 .12
❑ T115 Rene Reyes RC .40 .12
❑ T116 Nelson Castro RC .40 .12
❑ T117 Miguel Olivo .40 .12
❑ T118 David Espinosa .40 .12
❑ T119 Chris Bootcheck RC .40 .12
❑ T120 Rob Henkel RC .40 .12
❑ T121 Steve Bechler RC .40 .12
❑ T122 Mark Outlaw RC .40 .12
❑ T123 Henry Pichardo RC .40 .12
❑ T124 Michael Floyd RC .40 .12
❑ T125 Richard Lane RC .40 .12
❑ T126 Pete Zamora RC .40 .12
❑ T127 Javier Colina .40 .12
❑ T128 Greg Sain RC .50 .15
❑ T129 Ronnie Merrill .40 .12
❑ T130 Gavin Floyd RC 2.50 .75
❑ T131 Josh Bonifay RC .40 .12
❑ T132 Tommy Marx RC .40 .12
❑ T133 Gary Cates Jr. RC .40 .12
❑ T134 Neal Cotts RC 1.00 .30
❑ T135 Angel Berroa .40 .12
❑ T136 Elio Serrano RC .40 .12
❑ T137 J.J. Putz RC .40 .12
❑ T138 Ruben Gotay RC .40 .12
❑ T139 Eddie Rogers .40 .12
❑ T140 Wily Mo Pena .40 .12
❑ T141 Tyler Yates RC .50 .15
❑ T142 Colin Young RC .40 .12
❑ T143 Chance Caple .40 .12
❑ T144 Ben Howard RC .40 .12
❑ T145 Ryan Bukvich RC .40 .12
❑ T146 Cliff Bartosh RC .40 .12
❑ T147 Brandon Claussen .40 .12
❑ T148 Cristian Guerrero .40 .12
❑ T149 Derrick Lewis .40 .12
❑ T150 Eric Miller RC .40 .12
❑ T151 Justin Huber RC .75 .23
❑ T152 Adrian Gonzalez .40 .12
❑ T153 Brian West RC .40 .12
❑ T154 Chris Baker RC .40 .12
❑ T155 Drew Henson .40 .12
❑ T156 Scott Hairston RC 1.50 .45
❑ T157 Jason Simontacchi RC .40 .12
❑ T158 Jason Arnold RC .75 .23
❑ T159 Brandon Phillips .40 .12
❑ T160 Adam Roller RC .40 .12
❑ T161 Scotty Layfield RC .40 .12
❑ T162 Freddie Money RC .40 .12
❑ T163 Noochie Varner RC .40 .12
❑ T164 Terrance Hill RC .40 .12
❑ T165 Jeremy Hill RC .40 .12
❑ T166 Carlos Cabrera RC .40 .12
❑ T167 Jose Morban RC .40 .12
❑ T168 Kevin Frederick RC .40 .12
❑ T169 Mark Teixeira .60 .18
❑ T170 Brian Rogers .40 .12
❑ T171 Anastacio Martinez RC .40 .12
❑ T172 Bobby Jenks RC .75 .23
❑ T173 David Gil RC .40 .12
❑ T174 Andres Torres .40 .12
❑ T175 James Barrett RC .40 .12
❑ T176 Jimmy Journell .40 .12
❑ T177 Brett Kay RC .40 .12
❑ T178 Jason Young RC .40 .12
❑ T179 Mark Hamilton RC .40 .12
❑ T180 Jose Bautista RC .50 .15
❑ T181 Blake McGinley RC .40 .12
❑ T182 Ryan Mottl RC .40 .12
❑ T183 Jeff Austin RC .40 .12
❑ T184 Xavier Nady .40 .12
❑ T185 Kyle Kane RC .40 .12
❑ T186 Travis Foley RC .40 .12
❑ T187 Nathan Kaup RC .40 .12
❑ T188 Eric Cyr .40 .12
❑ T189 Josh Cisneros RC .40 .12
❑ T190 Brad Nelson RC 1.25 .35
❑ T191 Clint Weibl RC .40 .12
❑ T192 Ron Calloway RC .40 .12
❑ T193 Jung Bong .40 .12
❑ T194 Rolando Viera RC .40 .12
❑ T195 Jason Bulger RC .40 .12
❑ T196 Chone Figgins RC .75 .23
❑ T197 Jimmy Alvarez RC .40 .12
❑ T198 Joel Crump RC .40 .12
❑ T199 Ryan Doumit RC .50 .15
❑ T200 Demetrius Heath RC .40 .12
❑ T201 John Ennis RC .40 .12
❑ T202 Doug Sessions RC .40 .12
❑ T203 Clinton Hosford RC .40 .12
❑ T204 Chris Narveson RC .40 .12
❑ T205 Ross Peeples RC .40 .12
❑ T206 Alex Requena RC .40 .12
❑ T207 Matt Erickson RC .40 .12
❑ T208 Brian Forystek RC .40 .12
❑ T209 Dewon Brazelton .40 .12
❑ T210 Nathan Haynes .40 .12

Card	Nm-Mt	Ex-Mt
❑ T211 Jack Cust	.40	.12
❑ T212 Jesse Foppert RC	1.00	.30
❑ T213 Jesus Cota RC	.40	.12
❑ T214 Juan M. Gonzalez RC	.40	.12
❑ T215 Tim Kalita RC	.40	.12
❑ T216 Manny Delcarmen RC	.40	.12
❑ T217 Jim Kavourias RC	.40	.12
❑ T218 C.J. Wilson RC	.40	.12
❑ T219 Edwin Yan RC	.40	.12
❑ T220 Andy Van Hekken	.40	.12
❑ T221 Michael Cuddyer	.40	.12
❑ T222 Jeff Verplancke RC	.40	.12
❑ T223 Mike Wilson RC	.40	.12
❑ T224 Corwin Malone RC	.40	.12
❑ T225 Chris Snelling RC	.40	.12
❑ T226 Joe Rogers RC	.40	.12
❑ T227 Jason Bay	2.50	.75
❑ T228 Ezequiel Astacio RC	.40	.12
❑ T229 Joey Hammond RC	.40	.12
❑ T230 Chris Duffy RC	.40	.12
❑ T231 Mark Prior	2.50	.75
❑ T232 Hansel Izquierdo RC	.40	.12
❑ T233 Franklyn German RC	.40	.12
❑ T234 Alexis Gomez	.40	.12
❑ T235 Jorge Padilla RC	.40	.12
❑ T236 Ryan Snare RC	.40	.12
❑ T237 Deivis Santos	.40	.12
❑ T238 Taggert Bozied RC	.75	.23
❑ T239 Mike Peeples RC	.40	.12
❑ T240 Ronald Acuna RC	.40	.12
❑ T241 Koyie Hill	.40	.12
❑ T242 Garrett Guzman RC	.40	.12
❑ T243 Ryan Church RC	.75	.23
❑ T244 Tony Fontana RC	.40	.12
❑ T245 Keto Anderson RC	.40	.12
❑ T246 Brad Bouras RC	.40	.12
❑ T247 Jason Dubois RC	1.25	.35
❑ T248 Angel Guzman RC	3.00	.90
❑ T249 Joel Hanrahan RC	.75	.23
❑ T250 Joe Jiannetti RC	.40	.12
❑ T251 Sean Pierce RC	.40	.12
❑ T252 Jake Mauer RC	.40	.12
❑ T253 Marshall McDougall RC	.40	.12
❑ T254 Edwin Almonte RC	.40	.12
❑ T255 Shawn Riggans RC	.40	.12
❑ T256 Steven Shell RC	.40	.12
❑ T257 Kevin Hooper RC	.40	.12
❑ T258 Michael Frick RC	.40	.12
❑ T259 Travis Chapman RC	.40	.12
❑ T260 Tim Hummel RC	.40	.12
❑ T261 Adam Morrissey RC	.40	.12
❑ T262 Dontrelle Willis RC	3.00	.90
❑ T263 Justin Sherrod RC	.40	.12
❑ T264 Gerald Smiley RC	.40	.12
❑ T265 Tony Miller RC	.40	.12
❑ T266 Nolan Ryan WW	2.50	.75
❑ T267 Reggie Jackson WW	.60	.18
❑ T268 Steve Garvey WW	.40	.12
❑ T269 Wade Boggs WW	.60	.18
❑ T270 Sammy Sosa WW	1.50	.45
❑ T271 Curt Schilling WW	.40	.12
❑ T272 Mark Grace WW	.60	.18
❑ T273 Jason Giambi WW	.40	.12
❑ T274 Ken Griffey Jr. WW	1.50	.45
❑ T275 Roberto Alomar WW	.60	.18

2003 Topps

	Nm-Mt	Ex-Mt
COMPLETE SET (720)	80.00	24.00
COMPLETE SERIES 1 (366)	40.00	12.00
COMPLETE SERIES 2 (354)	40.00	12.00
COMMON CARD (1-6/8-721)	.20	.06
COMMON (292-331/660-684)	.50	.15
❑ 1 Alex Rodriguez	.75	.23
❑ 2 Dan Wilson	.20	.06
❑ 3 Jimmy Rollins	.20	.06
❑ 4 Jermaine Dye	.20	.06
❑ 5 Steve Karsay	.20	.06
❑ 6 Timo Perez	.20	.06
❑ 7 Does Not Exist	.00	
❑ 8 Jose Vidro	.20	.06
❑ 9 Eddie Guardado	.20	.06
❑ 10 Mark Prior	.50	.15
❑ 11 Curt Schilling	.20	.06
❑ 12 Dennis Cook	.20	.06
❑ 13 Andruw Jones	.20	.06
❑ 14 David Segui	.20	.06
❑ 15 Trot Nixon	.20	.06
❑ 16 Kerry Wood	.50	.15
❑ 17 Magglio Ordonez	.20	.06
❑ 18 Jason LaRue	.20	.06
❑ 19 Danys Baez	.20	.06
❑ 20 Todd Helton	.30	.09
❑ 21 Denny Neagle	.20	.06
❑ 22 Dave Mlicki	.20	.06
❑ 23 Roberto Hernandez	.20	.06
❑ 24 Odalis Perez	.20	.06
❑ 25 Nick Neugebauer	.20	.06
❑ 26 David Ortiz	.30	.09
❑ 27 Andres Galarraga	.20	.06
❑ 28 Edgardo Alfonzo	.20	.06
❑ 29 Chad Bradford	.20	.06
❑ 30 Jason Giambi	.20	.06
❑ 31 Brian Giles	.20	.06
❑ 32 Deivi Cruz	.20	.06
❑ 33 Robb Nen	.20	.06
❑ 34 Jeff Nelson	.20	.06
❑ 35 Edgar Renteria	.20	.06
❑ 36 Aubrey Huff	.20	.06
❑ 37 Brandon Duckworth	.20	.06
❑ 38 Juan Gonzalez	.30	.09
❑ 39 Sidney Ponson	.20	.06
❑ 40 Eric Hinske	.20	.06
❑ 41 Kevin Appier	.20	.06
❑ 42 Danny Bautista	.20	.06
❑ 43 Javier Lopez	.20	.06
❑ 44 Jeff Conine	.20	.06
❑ 45 Carlos Baerga	.20	.06
❑ 46 Ugueth Urbina	.20	.06
❑ 47 Mark Buehrle	.20	.06
❑ 48 Aaron Boone	.20	.06
❑ 49 Jason Simontacchi	.20	.06
❑ 50 Sammy Sosa	.75	.23
❑ 51 Jose Jimenez	.20	.06
❑ 52 Bobby Higginson	.20	.06
❑ 53 Luis Castillo	.20	.06
❑ 54 Orlando Merced	.20	.06
❑ 55 Brian Jordan	.20	.06
❑ 56 Eric Young	.20	.06
❑ 57 Bobby Kielty	.20	.06
❑ 58 Luis Rivas	.20	.06
❑ 59 Brad Wilkerson	.20	.06
❑ 60 Roberto Alomar	.30	.09
❑ 61 Roger Clemens	1.00	.30
❑ 62 Scott Hatteberg	.20	.06
❑ 63 Andy Ashby	.20	.06
❑ 64 Mike Williams	.20	.06
❑ 65 Ron Gant	.20	.06
❑ 66 Benito Santiago	.20	.06
❑ 67 Bret Boone	.20	.06
❑ 68 Matt Morris	.20	.06
❑ 69 Troy Glaus	.20	.06
❑ 70 Austin Kearns	.20	.06
❑ 71 Jim Thome	.50	.15
❑ 72 Rickey Henderson	.50	.15
❑ 73 Luis Gonzalez	.20	.06
❑ 74 Brad Fullmer	.20	.06
❑ 75 Herbert Perry	.20	.06
❑ 76 Randy Wolf	.20	.06
❑ 77 Miguel Tejada	.20	.06
❑ 78 Jimmy Anderson	.20	.06
❑ 79 Ramon Martinez	.20	.06

Card	Nm-Mt	Ex-Mt
❑ 80 Ivan Rodriguez	.50	.15
❑ 81 John Flaherty	.20	.06
❑ 82 Shannon Stewart	.20	.06
❑ 83 Orlando Palmeiro	.20	.06
❑ 84 Rafael Furcal	.20	.06
❑ 85 Kenny Rogers	.20	.06
❑ 86 Terry Adams	.20	.06
❑ 87 Mo Vaughn	.20	.06
❑ 88 Jose Cruz Jr.	.20	.06
❑ 89 Mike Matheny	.20	.06
❑ 90 Alfonso Soriano	.30	.09
❑ 91 Orlando Cabrera	.20	.06
❑ 92 Jeffrey Hammonds	.20	.06
❑ 93 Hideo Nomo	.50	.15
❑ 94 Carlos Febles	.20	.06
❑ 95 Billy Wagner	.20	.06
❑ 96 Alex Gonzalez	.20	.06
❑ 97 Todd Zeile	.20	.06
❑ 98 Omar Vizquel	.30	.09
❑ 99 Jose Rijo	.20	.06
❑ 100 Ichiro Suzuki	.75	.23
❑ 101 Steve Cox	.20	.06
❑ 102 Hideki Irabu	.20	.06
❑ 103 Roy Halladay	.20	.06
❑ 104 David Eckstein	.20	.06
❑ 105 Greg Maddux	.75	.23
❑ 106 Jay Gibbons	.20	.06
❑ 107 Travis Driskill	.20	.06
❑ 108 Fred McGriff	.30	.09
❑ 109 Frank Thomas	.50	.15
❑ 110 Shawn Green	.20	.06
❑ 111 Ruben Quevedo	.20	.06
❑ 112 Jacque Jones	.20	.06
❑ 113 Tomo Ohka	.20	.06
❑ 114 Joe McEwing	.20	.06
❑ 115 Ramiro Mendoza	.20	.06
❑ 116 Mark Mulder	.20	.06
❑ 117 Mike Lieberthal	.20	.06
❑ 118 Jack Wilson	.20	.06
❑ 119 Randall Simon	.20	.06
❑ 120 Bernie Williams	.30	.09
❑ 121 Marvin Benard	.20	.06
❑ 122 Jamie Moyer	.20	.06
❑ 123 Andy Benes	.20	.06
❑ 124 Tino Martinez	.30	.09
❑ 125 Esteban Yan	.20	.06
❑ 126 Juan Uribe	.20	.06
❑ 127 Jason Isringhausen	.20	.06
❑ 128 Chris Carpenter	.20	.06
❑ 129 Mike Cameron	.20	.06
❑ 130 Gary Sheffield	.20	.06
❑ 131 Geronimo Gil	.20	.06
❑ 132 Brian Daubach	.20	.06
❑ 133 Corey Patterson	.20	.06
❑ 134 Aaron Rowand	.20	.06
❑ 135 Chris Reitsma	.20	.06
❑ 136 Bob Wickman	.20	.06
❑ 137 Cesar Izturis	.20	.06
❑ 138 Jason Jennings	.20	.06
❑ 139 Brandon Inge	.20	.06
❑ 140 Larry Walker	.30	.09
❑ 141 Ramon Santiago	.20	.06
❑ 142 Vladimir Nunez	.20	.06
❑ 143 Jose Vizcaino	.20	.06
❑ 144 Mark Quinn	.20	.06
❑ 145 Michael Tucker	.20	.06
❑ 146 Darren Dreifort	.20	.06
❑ 147 Ben Sheets	.20	.06
❑ 148 Corey Koskie	.20	.06
❑ 149 Tony Armas Jr.	.20	.06
❑ 150 Kazuhisa Ishii	.20	.06
❑ 151 Al Leiter	.20	.06
❑ 152 Steve Trachsel	.20	.06
❑ 153 Mike Stanton	.20	.06
❑ 154 David Justice	.20	.06
❑ 155 Marlon Anderson	.20	.06
❑ 156 Jason Kendall	.20	.06
❑ 157 Brian Lawrence	.20	.06
❑ 158 J.T. Snow	.20	.06
❑ 159 Edgar Martinez	.30	.09
❑ 160 Pat Burrell	.20	.06
❑ 161 Kerry Robinson	.20	.06
❑ 162 Greg Vaughn	.20	.06
❑ 163 Carl Everett	.20	.06
❑ 164 Vernon Wells	.20	.06
❑ 165 Jose Mesa	.20	.06

❑ 166 Troy Percival .20 .06
❑ 167 Erubiel Durazo .20 .06
❑ 168 Jason Marquis .20 .06
❑ 169 Jerry Hairston Jr. .20 .06
❑ 170 Vladimir Guerrero .50 .15
❑ 171 Byung-Hyun Kim .20 .06
❑ 172 Marcus Giles .20 .06
❑ 173 Johnny Damon .50 .15
❑ 174 Jon Lieber .20 .06
❑ 175 Terrence Long .20 .06
❑ 176 Sean Casey .20 .06
❑ 177 Adam Dunn .30 .09
❑ 178 Juan Pierre .20 .06
❑ 179 Wendell Magee .20 .06
❑ 180 Barry Zito .20 .06
❑ 181 Aramis Ramirez .20 .06
❑ 182 Pokey Reese .20 .06
❑ 183 Jeff Kent .20 .06
❑ 184 Russ Ortiz .20 .06
❑ 185 Ruben Sierra .20 .06
❑ 186 Brent Abernathy .20 .06
❑ 187 Ismael Valdes UER .20 .06
Card does not include 2002 Rangers stats
❑ 188 Tom Wilson .20 .06
❑ 189 Craig Counsell .20 .06
❑ 190 Mike Mussina .30 .09
❑ 191 Ramon Hernandez .20 .06
❑ 192 Adam Kennedy .20 .06
❑ 193 Tony Womack .20 .06
❑ 194 Wes Helms .20 .06
❑ 195 Tony Batista .20 .06
❑ 196 Rolando Arrojo .20 .06
❑ 197 Kyle Farnsworth .20 .06
❑ 198 Gary Bennett .20 .06
❑ 199 Scott Sullivan .20 .06
❑ 200 Albert Pujols 1.00 .30
❑ 201 Kirk Rueter .20 .06
❑ 202 Phil Nevin .20 .06
❑ 203 Kip Wells .20 .06
❑ 204 Ron Coomer .20 .06
❑ 205 Jeromy Burnitz .20 .06
❑ 206 Kyle Lohse .20 .06
❑ 207 Mike DeJean .20 .06
❑ 208 Paul Lo Duca .20 .06
❑ 209 Carlos Beltran .30 .09
❑ 210 Roy Oswalt .20 .06
❑ 211 Mike Lowell .20 .06
❑ 212 Robert Fick .20 .06
❑ 213 Todd Jones .20 .06
❑ 214 C.C. Sabathia .20 .06
❑ 215 Danny Graves .20 .06
❑ 216 Todd Hundley .20 .06
❑ 217 Tim Wakefield .20 .06
❑ 218 Derek Lowe .20 .06
❑ 219 Kevin Millwood .20 .06
❑ 220 Jorge Posada .30 .09
❑ 221 Bobby J. Jones .20 .06
❑ 222 Carlos Guillen .20 .06
❑ 223 Fernando Vina .20 .06
❑ 224 Ryan Rupe .20 .06
❑ 225 Kelvim Escobar .20 .06
❑ 226 Ramon Ortiz .20 .06
❑ 227 Junior Spivey .20 .06
❑ 228 Juan Cruz .20 .06
❑ 229 Melvin Mora .20 .06
❑ 230 Lance Berkman .20 .06
❑ 231 Brent Butler .20 .06
❑ 232 Shane Halter .20 .06
❑ 233 Derrek Lee .20 .06
❑ 234 Matt Lawton .20 .06
❑ 235 Chuck Knoblauch .20 .06
❑ 236 Eric Gagne .50 .15
❑ 237 Alex Sanchez .20 .06
❑ 238 Denny Hocking .20 .06
❑ 239 Eric Milton .20 .06
❑ 240 Rey Ordonez .20 .06
❑ 241 Orlando Hernandez .20 .06
❑ 242 Robert Person .20 .06
❑ 243 Sean Burroughs .20 .06
❑ 244 Jeff Cirillo .20 .06
❑ 245 Mike Lamb .20 .06
❑ 246 Jose Valentin .20 .06
❑ 247 Ellis Burks .20 .06
❑ 248 Shawn Chacon .20 .06
❑ 249 Josh Beckett .20 .06
❑ 250 Nomar Garciaparra .75 .23
❑ 251 Craig Biggio .30 .09
❑ 252 Joe Randa .20 .06
❑ 253 Mark Grudzielanek .20 .06
❑ 254 Glendon Rusch .20 .06
❑ 255 Michael Barrett .20 .06
❑ 256 Omar Daal .20 .06
❑ 257 Elmer Dessens .20 .06
❑ 258 Wade Miller .20 .06
❑ 259 Adrian Beltre .30 .09
❑ 260 Vicente Padilla .20 .06
❑ 261 Kazuhiro Sasaki .20 .06
❑ 262 Mike Scioscia MG .20 .06
❑ 263 Bobby Cox MG .20 .06
❑ 264 Mike Hargrove MG .20 .06
❑ 265 Grady Little MG RC .20 .06
❑ 266 Alex Gonzalez UER .20 .06
2002 stats are listed as all zero's
❑ 267 Jerry Manuel MG .20 .06
❑ 268 Bob Boone MG .20 .06
❑ 269 Joel Skinner MG .20 .06
❑ 270 Clint Hurdle MG .20 .06
❑ 271 Miguel Batista UER .20 .06
All 2002 Stats are 0's
❑ 272 Bob Brenly MG .20 .06
❑ 273 Jeff Torborg MG .20 .06
❑ 274 Jimy Williams MG UER .20 .06
Career managerial record is wrong
❑ 275 Tony Pena MG .20 .06
❑ 276 Jim Tracy MG .20 .06
❑ 277 Jerry Royster MG .20 .06
❑ 278 Ron Gardenhire MG .20 .06
❑ 279 Frank Robinson MG .30 .09
❑ 280 John Halama .20 .06
❑ 281 Joe Torre MG .30 .09
❑ 282 Art Howe MG .20 .06
❑ 283 Larry Bowa MG .20 .06
❑ 284 Lloyd McClendon MG .20 .06
❑ 285 Bruce Bochy MG .20 .06
❑ 286 Dusty Baker MG .20 .06
❑ 287 Lou Piniella MG .20 .06
❑ 288 Tony LaRussa MG .20 .06
❑ 289 Todd Walker .20 .06
❑ 290 Jerry Narron MG .20 .06
❑ 291 Carlos Tosca MG .20 .06
❑ 292 Chris Duncan FY RC .50 .15
❑ 293 Franklin Gutierrez FY RC 2.00 .60
❑ 294 Adam LaRoche FY .50 .15
❑ 295 Manuel Ramirez FY RC .50 .15
❑ 296 Il Kim FY RC .50 .15
❑ 297 Wayne Lydon FY RC .50 .15
❑ 298 Daryl Clark FY RC .50 .15
❑ 299 Sean Pierce FY .50 .15
❑ 300 Andy Marte FY RC 2.50 .75
❑ 301 Matthew Peterson FY RC .50 .15
❑ 302 Gonzalo Lopez FY RC .50 .15
❑ 303 Bernie Castro FY RC .50 .15
❑ 304 Cliff Lee FY .50 .15
❑ 305 Jason Perry FY RC .75 .23
❑ 306 Jaime Bubela FY RC .50 .15
❑ 307 Alexis Rios FY .50 .15
❑ 308 Brendan Harris FY RC .50 .15
❑ 309 R.Nivar-Martinez FY RC .75 .23
❑ 310 Terry Tiffee FY RC .75 .23
❑ 311 Kevin Youkilis FY RC 1.50 .45
❑ 312 Ruddy Lugo FY RC .50 .15
❑ 313 C.J. Wilson FY .50 .15
❑ 314 Mike McNutt FY RC .50 .15
❑ 315 Jeff Clark FY RC .50 .15
❑ 316 Mark Malaska FY RC .50 .15
❑ 317 Doug Waechter FY RC .50 .15
❑ 318 Derell McCall FY RC .50 .15
❑ 319 Scott Tyler FY RC .50 .15
❑ 320 Craig Brazell FY RC .50 .15
❑ 321 Walter Young FY .50 .15
❑ 322 Marlon Byrd .50 .15
Jorge Padilla FS
❑ 323 Chris Snelling .50 .15
Shin-Soo Choo FS
❑ 324 Hank Blalock .50 .15
Mark Teixeira FS
❑ 325 Josh Hamilton .50 .15
Carl Crawford FS
❑ 326 Orlando Hudson .50 .15
Josh Phelps FS
❑ 327 Jack Cust .50 .15
Rene Reyes FS
❑ 328 Angel Berroa .50 .15
Alexis Gomez FS
❑ 329 Michael Cuddyer .50 .15
Michael Restovich FS
❑ 330 Juan Rivera .50 .15
Marcus Thames FS
❑ 331 Brandon Puffer .50 .15
Jung Bong FS
❑ 332 Mike Cameron SH .20 .06
❑ 333 Shawn Green SH .20 .06
❑ 334 Oakland A's SH .20 .06
❑ 335 Jason Giambi SH .20 .06
❑ 336 Derek Lowe SH .20 .06
❑ 337 Manny Ramirez .50 .15
Mike Sweeney
Bernie Williams LL
❑ 338 Alfonso Soriano .30 .09
Alex Rodriguez
Derek Jeter LL
❑ 339 Alex Rodriguez .50 .15
Jim Thome
Rafael Palmeiro LL
❑ 340 Alex Rodriguez .50 .15
Magglio Ordonez
Miguel Tejada LL
❑ 341 Pedro Martinez .20 .06
Derek Lowe
Barry Zito LL
❑ 342 Pedro Martinez .30 .09
Roger Clemens
Mike Mussina LL
❑ 343 Larry Walker .50 .15
Vladimir Guerrero
Todd Helton LL
❑ 344 Sammy Sosa .50 .15
Albert Pujols
Shawn Green LL
❑ 345 Sammy Sosa .50 .15
Lance Berkman
Shawn Green LL
❑ 346 Lance Berkman .20 .06
Albert Pujols
Pat Burrell LL
❑ 347 Randy Johnson .30 .09
Greg Maddux
Tom Glavine LL
❑ 348 Randy Johnson .30 .09
Curt Schilling
Kerry Wood LL
❑ 349 Francisco Rodriguez .20 .06
Darin Erstad
Tim Salmon
AL Division Series
❑ 350 Minnesota Twins .30 .09
St Louis Cardinals
AL and NL Division Series
❑ 351 Anaheim Angels .30 .09
San Francisco Giants
AL and NL Division Series
❑ 352 Jim Edmonds .30 .09
Scott Rolen
NL Division Series
❑ 353 Adam Kennedy ALCS .20 .06
❑ 354 J.T. Snow WS .30 .09
❑ 355 David Bell NLCS .30 .09
❑ 356 Jason Giambi AS .20 .06
❑ 357 Alfonso Soriano AS .20 .06
❑ 358 Alex Rodriguez AS .50 .15
❑ 359 Eric Chavez AS .20 .06
❑ 360 Torii Hunter AS .20 .06
❑ 361 Bernie Williams AS .20 .06
❑ 362 Garret Anderson AS .20 .06
❑ 363 Jorge Posada AS .20 .06
❑ 364 Derek Lowe AS .20 .06
❑ 365 Barry Zito AS .20 .06
❑ 366 Manny Ramirez AS .20 .06
❑ 367 Mike Scioscia AS .20 .06
❑ 368 Francisco Rodriguez .20 .06
❑ 369 Chris Hammond .20 .06
❑ 370 Chipper Jones .50 .15
❑ 371 Chris Singleton .20 .06
❑ 372 Cliff Floyd .20 .06
❑ 373 Bobby Hill .20 .06
❑ 374 Antonio Osuna .20 .06
❑ 375 Barry Larkin .30 .09

❑ 376 Charles Nagy .20 .06
❑ 377 Denny Stark .20 .06
❑ 378 Dean Palmer .20 .06
❑ 379 Eric Owens .20 .06
❑ 380 Randy Johnson .50 .15
❑ 381 Jeff Suppan .20 .06
❑ 382 Eric Karros .20 .06
❑ 383 Luis Vizcaino .20 .06
❑ 384 Johan Santana .30 .09
❑ 385 Javier Vazquez .20 .06
❑ 386 John Thomson .20 .06
❑ 387 Nick Johnson .20 .06
❑ 388 Mark Ellis .20 .06
❑ 389 Doug Glanville .20 .06
❑ 390 Ken Griffey Jr. .75 .23
❑ 391 Bubba Trammell .20 .06
❑ 392 Livan Hernandez .20 .06
❑ 393 Desi Relaford .20 .06
❑ 394 Eli Marrero .20 .06
❑ 395 Jared Sandberg .20 .06
❑ 396 Barry Bonds 1.25 .35
❑ 397 Esteban Loaiza .20 .06
❑ 398 Aaron Sele .20 .06
❑ 399 Geoff Blum .20 .06
❑ 400 Derek Jeter 1.25 .35
❑ 401 Eric Byrnes .20 .06
❑ 402 Mike Timlin .20 .06
❑ 403 Mark Kotsay .20 .06
❑ 404 Rich Aurilia .20 .06
❑ 405 Joel Pineiro .20 .06
❑ 406 Chuck Finley .20 .06
❑ 407 Bengie Molina .20 .06
❑ 408 Steve Finley .20 .06
❑ 409 Julio Franco .20 .06
❑ 410 Marty Cordova .20 .06
❑ 411 Shea Hillenbrand .20 .06
❑ 412 Mark Bellhorn .20 .06
❑ 413 Jon Garland .20 .06
❑ 414 Reggie Taylor .20 .06
❑ 415 Milton Bradley .20 .06
❑ 416 Carlos Pena .20 .06
❑ 417 Andy Fox .20 .06
❑ 418 Brad Ausmus .20 .06
❑ 419 Brent Mayne .20 .06
❑ 420 Paul Quantrill .20 .06
❑ 421 Carlos Delgado .20 .06
❑ 422 Kevin Mench .20 .06
❑ 423 Joe Kennedy .20 .06
❑ 424 Mike Crudale .20 .06
❑ 425 Mark McLemore .20 .06
❑ 426 Bill Mueller .20 .06
❑ 427 Rob Mackowiak .20 .06
❑ 428 Ricky Ledee .20 .06
❑ 429 Ted Lilly .20 .06
❑ 430 Sterling Hitchcock .20 .06
❑ 431 Scott Strickland .20 .06
❑ 432 Damion Easley .20 .06
❑ 433 Torii Hunter .20 .06
❑ 434 Brad Radke .20 .06
❑ 435 Geoff Jenkins .20 .06
❑ 436 Paul Byrd .20 .06
❑ 437 Morgan Ensberg .20 .06
❑ 438 Mike Maroth .20 .06
❑ 439 Mike Hampton .20 .06
❑ 440 Adam Hyzdu .20 .06
❑ 441 Vance Wilson .20 .06
❑ 442 Todd Ritchie .20 .06
❑ 443 Tom Gordon .20 .06
❑ 444 John Burkett .20 .06
❑ 445 Rodrigo Lopez .20 .06
❑ 446 Tim Spooneybarger .20 .06
❑ 447 Quinton Mccracken .20 .06
❑ 448 Tim Salmon .30 .09
❑ 449 Jarrod Washburn .20 .06
❑ 450 Pedro Martinez .50 .15
❑ 451 Dustan Mohr .20 .06
❑ 452 Julio Lugo .20 .06
❑ 453 Scott Stewart .20 .06
❑ 454 Armando Benitez .20 .06
❑ 455 Raul Mondesi .20 .06
❑ 456 Robin Ventura .20 .06
❑ 457 Bobby Abreu .20 .06
❑ 458 Josh Fogg .20 .06
❑ 459 Ryan Klesko .20 .06
❑ 460 Tsuyoshi Shinjo .20 .06
❑ 461 Jim Edmonds .20 .06
❑ 462 Cliff Politte .20 .06
❑ 463 Chan Ho Park .20 .06
❑ 464 John Mabry .20 .06
❑ 465 Woody Williams .20 .06
❑ 466 Jason Michaels .20 .06
❑ 467 Scott Schoeneweis .20 .06
❑ 468 Brian Anderson .20 .06
❑ 469 Brett Tomko .20 .06
❑ 470 Scott Erickson .20 .06
❑ 471 Kevin Millar Sox .20 .06
❑ 472 Danny Wright .20 .06
❑ 473 Jason Schmidt .20 .06
❑ 474 Scott Williamson .20 .06
❑ 475 Einar Diaz .20 .06
❑ 476 Jay Payton .20 .06
❑ 477 Juan Acevedo .20 .06
❑ 478 Ben Grieve .20 .06
❑ 479 Raul Ibanez .20 .06
❑ 480 Richie Sexson .20 .06
❑ 481 Rick Reed .20 .06
❑ 482 Pedro Astacio .20 .06
❑ 483 Adam Piatt .20 .06
❑ 484 Bud Smith .20 .06
❑ 485 Tomas Perez .20 .06
❑ 486 Adam Eaton .20 .06
❑ 487 Rafael Palmeiro .30 .09
❑ 488 Jason Tyner .20 .06
❑ 489 Scott Rolen .50 .15
❑ 490 Randy Winn .20 .06
❑ 491 Ryan Jensen .20 .06
❑ 492 Trevor Hoffman .20 .06
❑ 493 Craig Wilson .20 .06
❑ 494 Jeremy Giambi .20 .06
❑ 495 Daryle Ward .20 .06
❑ 496 Shane Spencer .20 .06
❑ 497 Andy Pettitte .30 .09
❑ 498 John Franco .20 .06
❑ 499 Felipe Lopez .20 .06
❑ 500 Mike Piazza .75 .23
❑ 501 Cristian Guzman .20 .06
❑ 502 Jose Hernandez .20 .06
❑ 503 Octavio Dotel .20 .06
❑ 504 Brad Penny .20 .06
❑ 505 Dave Veres .20 .06
❑ 506 Ryan Dempster .20 .06
❑ 507 Joe Crede .20 .06
❑ 508 Chad Hermansen .20 .06
❑ 509 Gary Matthews Jr. .20 .06
❑ 510 Matt Franco .20 .06
❑ 511 Ben Weber .20 .06
❑ 512 Dave Berg .20 .06
❑ 513 Michael Young .30 .09
❑ 514 Frank Catalanotto .20 .06
❑ 515 Darin Erstad .20 .06
❑ 516 Matt Williams .20 .06
❑ 517 B.J. Surhoff .20 .06
❑ 518 Kerry Ligtenberg .20 .06
❑ 519 Mike Bordick .20 .06
❑ 520 Arthur Rhodes .20 .06
❑ 521 Joe Girardi .20 .06
❑ 522 D'Angelo Jimenez .20 .06
❑ 523 Paul Konerko .20 .06
❑ 524 Jose Macias .20 .06
❑ 525 Joe Mays .20 .06
❑ 526 Marquis Grissom .20 .06
❑ 527 Neifi Perez .20 .06
❑ 528 Preston Wilson .20 .06
❑ 529 Jeff Weaver .20 .06
❑ 530 Eric Chavez .20 .06
❑ 531 Placido Polanco .20 .06
❑ 532 Matt Mantei .20 .06
❑ 533 James Baldwin .20 .06
❑ 534 Toby Hall .20 .06
❑ 535 Brendan Donnelly .20 .06
❑ 536 Benji Gil .20 .06
❑ 537 Damian Moss .20 .06
❑ 538 Jorge Julio .20 .06
❑ 539 Matt Clement .20 .06
❑ 540 Brian Moehler .20 .06
❑ 541 Lee Stevens .20 .06
❑ 542 Jimmy Haynes .20 .06
❑ 543 Terry Mulholland .20 .06
❑ 544 Dave Roberts .20 .06
❑ 545 J.C. Romero .20 .06
❑ 546 Bartolo Colon .20 .06
❑ 547 Roger Cedeno .20 .06
❑ 548 Mariano Rivera .30 .09
❑ 549 Billy Koch .20 .06
❑ 550 Manny Ramirez .30 .09
❑ 551 Travis Lee .20 .06
❑ 552 Oliver Perez .20 .06
❑ 553 Tim Worrell .20 .06
❑ 554 Rafael Soriano .20 .06
❑ 555 Damian Miller .20 .06
❑ 556 John Smoltz .30 .09
❑ 557 Willis Roberts .20 .06
❑ 558 Tim Hudson .20 .06
❑ 559 Moises Alou .20 .06
❑ 560 Gary Glover .20 .06
❑ 561 Corky Miller .20 .06
❑ 562 Ben Broussard .20 .06
❑ 563 Gabe Kapler .20 .06
❑ 564 Chris Woodward .20 .06
❑ 565 Paul Wilson .20 .06
❑ 566 Todd Hollandsworth .20 .06
❑ 567 So Taguchi .20 .06
❑ 568 John Olerud .20 .06
❑ 569 Reggie Sanders .20 .06
❑ 570 Jake Peavy .20 .06
❑ 571 Kris Benson .20 .06
❑ 572 Todd Pratt .20 .06
❑ 573 Ray Durham .20 .06
❑ 574 Boomer Wells .20 .06
❑ 575 Chris Widger .20 .06
❑ 576 Shawn Wooten .20 .06
❑ 577 Tom Glavine .30 .09
❑ 578 Antonio Alfonseca .20 .06
❑ 579 Keith Foulke .20 .06
❑ 580 Shawn Estes .20 .06
❑ 581 Mark Grace .30 .09
❑ 582 Dmitri Young .20 .06
❑ 583 A.J. Burnett .20 .06
❑ 584 Richard Hidalgo .20 .06
❑ 585 Mike Sweeney .20 .06
❑ 586 Alex Cora .20 .06
❑ 587 Matt Stairs .20 .06
❑ 588 Doug Mientkiewicz .20 .06
❑ 589 Fernando Tatis .20 .06
❑ 590 David Weathers .20 .06
❑ 591 Cory Lidle .20 .06
❑ 592 Dan Plesac .20 .06
❑ 593 Jeff Bagwell .30 .09
❑ 594 Steve Sparks .20 .06
❑ 595 Sandy Alomar Jr. .20 .06
❑ 596 John Lackey .20 .06
❑ 597 Rick Helling .20 .06
❑ 598 Mark DeRosa .20 .06
❑ 599 Carlos Lee .20 .06
❑ 600 Garret Anderson .20 .06
❑ 601 Vinny Castilla .20 .06
❑ 602 Ryan Drese .20 .06
❑ 603 LaTroy Hawkins .20 .06
❑ 604 David Bell .20 .06
❑ 605 Freddy Garcia .20 .06
❑ 606 Miguel Cairo .20 .06
❑ 607 Scott Spiezio .20 .06
❑ 608 Mike Remlinger .20 .06
❑ 609 Tony Graffanino .20 .06
❑ 610 Russell Branyan .20 .06
❑ 611 Chris Magruder .20 .06
❑ 612 Jose Contreras RC 1.00 .30
❑ 613 Carl Pavano .20 .06
❑ 614 Kevin Brown .20 .06
❑ 615 Tyler Houston .20 .06
❑ 616 A.J. Pierzynski .20 .06
❑ 617 Tony Fiore .20 .06
❑ 618 Peter Bergeron .20 .06
❑ 619 Rondell White .20 .06
❑ 620 Brett Myers .20 .06
❑ 621 Kevin Young .20 .06
❑ 622 Kenny Lofton .20 .06
❑ 623 Ben Davis .20 .06
❑ 624 J.D. Drew .20 .06
❑ 625 Chris Gomez .20 .06
❑ 626 Karim Garcia .20 .06
❑ 627 Ricky Gutierrez .20 .06
❑ 628 Mark Redman .20 .06
❑ 629 Juan Encarnacion .20 .06
❑ 630 Anaheim Angels TC .30 .09
❑ 631 Ariz.Diamondbacks TC .20 .06
❑ 632 Atlanta Braves TC .20 .06
❑ 633 Baltimore Orioles TC .20 .06

❑ 634	Boston Red Sox TC	.20	.06
❑ 635	Chicago Cubs TC	.20	.06
❑ 636	Chicago White Sox TC	.20	.06
❑ 637	Cincinnati Reds TC	.20	.06
❑ 638	Cleveland Indians TC	.20	.06
❑ 639	Colorado Rockies TC	.20	.06
❑ 640	Detroit Tigers TC	.20	.06
❑ 641	Florida Marlins TC	.20	.06
❑ 642	Houston Astros TC	.20	.06
❑ 643	Kansas City Royals TC	.20	.06
❑ 644	Los Angeles Dodgers TC	.20	.06
❑ 645	Milwaukee Brewers TC	.20	.06
❑ 646	Minnesota Twins TC	.20	.06
❑ 647	Montreal Expos TC	.20	.06
❑ 648	New York Mets TC	.20	.06
❑ 649	New York Yankees TC	.30	.09
❑ 650	Oakland Athletics TC	.20	.06
❑ 651	Philadelphia Phillies TC	.20	.06
❑ 652	Pittsburgh Pirates TC	.20	.06
❑ 653	San Diego Padres TC	.20	.06
❑ 654	San Francisco Giants TC	.20	.06
❑ 655	Seattle Mariners TC	.20	.06
❑ 656	St. Louis Cardinals TC	.20	.06
❑ 657	T.B. Devil Rays TC	.20	.06
❑ 658	Texas Rangers TC	.20	.06
❑ 659	Toronto Blue Jays TC	.20	.06
❑ 660	Bryan Bullington DP RC	1.25	.35
❑ 661	Jeremy Guthrie DP	.50	.15
❑ 662	Joey Gomes DP RC	.50	.15
❑ 663	E.Bastida-Martinez DP RC	.50	.15
❑ 664	Brian Wright DP RC	.50	.15
❑ 665	B.J. Upton DP	1.00	.30
❑ 666	Jeff Francis DP	.50	.15
❑ 667	Drew Meyer DP	.50	.15
❑ 668	Jeremy Hermida DP	.50	.15
❑ 669	Khalil Greene DP	2.00	.60
❑ 670	Darrell Rasner DP RC	.50	.15
❑ 671	Cole Hamels DP	.50	.15
❑ 672	James Loney DP	.50	.15
❑ 673	Sergio Santos DP	.50	.15
❑ 674	Jason Pridie DP	.50	.15
❑ 675	Brandon Phillips Victor Martinez	.50	.15
❑ 676	Hee Seop Choi Nic Jackson	.50	.15
❑ 677	Dontrelle Willis Jason Stokes	.50	.15
❑ 678	Chad Tracy Lyle Overbay	.50	.15
❑ 679	Joe Borchard Corwin Malone	.50	.15
❑ 680	Joe Mauer Justin Morneau	.75	.23
❑ 681	Drew Henson Brandon Claussen	.50	.15
❑ 682	Chase Utley Gavin Floyd	.50	.15
❑ 683	Taggert Bozied Xavier Nady	.50	.15
❑ 684	Aaron Heilman Jose Reyes	.50	.15
❑ 685	Kenny Rogers AW	.20	.06
❑ 686	Bengie Molina AW	.20	.06
❑ 687	John Olerud AW	.20	.06
❑ 688	Bret Boone AW	.20	.06
❑ 689	Eric Chavez AW	.20	.06
❑ 690	Alex Rodriguez AW	.50	.15
❑ 691	Darin Erstad AW	.20	.06
❑ 692	Ichiro Suzuki AW	.50	.15
❑ 693	Torii Hunter AW	.20	.06
❑ 694	Greg Maddux AW	.50	.15
❑ 695	Brad Ausmus AW	.20	.06
❑ 696	Todd Helton AW	.20	.06
❑ 697	Fernando Vina AW	.20	.06
❑ 698	Scott Rolen AW	.30	.09
❑ 699	Edgar Renteria AW	.20	.06
❑ 700	Andruw Jones AW	.20	.06
❑ 701	Larry Walker AW	.20	.06
❑ 702	Jim Edmonds AW	.20	.06
❑ 703	Barry Zito AW	.20	.06
❑ 704	Randy Johnson AW	.30	.09
❑ 705	Miguel Tejada AW	.20	.06
❑ 706	Barry Bonds AW	.60	.18
❑ 707	Eric Hinske AW	.20	.06
❑ 708	Jason Jennings AW	.20	.06
❑ 709	Todd Helton AS	.20	.06
❑ 710	Jeff Kent AS	.20	.06
❑ 711	Edgar Renteria AS	.20	.06
❑ 712	Scott Rolen AS	.30	.09
❑ 713	Barry Bonds AS	.60	.18
❑ 714	Sammy Sosa AS	.50	.15
❑ 715	Vladimir Guerrero AS	.30	.09
❑ 716	Mike Piazza AS	.50	.15
❑ 717	Curt Schilling AS	.20	.06
❑ 718	Randy Johnson AS	.30	.09
❑ 719	Bobby Cox AS	.20	.06
❑ 720	Anaheim Angels WS	.30	.09
❑ 721	Anaheim Angels WS	.50	.15

2003 Topps Traded

	MINT	NRMT
COMPLETE SET (275)	50.00	22.00
COMMON CARD (T1-T120)	.20	.09
COMMON CARD (121-165)	.40	.18

❑ T1	Juan Pierre	.20	.09
❑ T2	Mark Grudzielanek	.20	.09
❑ T3	Tanyon Sturtze	.20	.09
❑ T4	Greg Vaughn	.20	.09
❑ T5	Greg Myers	.20	.09
❑ T6	Randall Simon	.20	.09
❑ T7	Todd Hundley	.20	.09
❑ T8	Marlon Anderson	.20	.09
❑ T9	Jeff Reboulet	.20	.09
❑ T10	Alex Sanchez	.20	.09
❑ T11	Mike Rivera	.20	.09
❑ T12	Todd Walker	.20	.09
❑ T13	Ray King	.20	.09
❑ T14	Shawn Estes	.20	.09
❑ T15	Gary Matthews Jr.	.20	.09
❑ T16	Jaret Wright	.20	.09
❑ T17	Edgardo Alfonzo	.20	.09
❑ T18	Omar Daal	.20	.09
❑ T19	Ryan Rupe	.20	.09
❑ T20	Tony Clark	.20	.09
❑ T21	Jeff Suppan	.20	.09
❑ T22	Mike Stanton	.20	.09
❑ T23	Ramon Martinez	.20	.09
❑ T24	Armando Rios	.20	.09
❑ T25	Johnny Estrada	.20	.09
❑ T26	Joe Girardi	.20	.09
❑ T27	Ivan Rodriguez	.50	.23
❑ T28	Robert Fick	.20	.09
❑ T29	Rick White	.20	.09
❑ T30	Robert Person	.20	.09
❑ T31	Alan Benes	.20	.09
❑ T32	Chris Carpenter	.20	.09
❑ T33	Chris Widger	.20	.09
❑ T34	Travis Hafner	.20	.09
❑ T35	Mike Venafro	.20	.09
❑ T36	Jon Lieber	.20	.09
❑ T37	Orlando Hernandez	.20	.09
❑ T38	Aaron Myette	.20	.09
❑ T39	Paul Bako	.20	.09
❑ T40	Erubiel Durazo	.20	.09
❑ T41	Mark Guthrie	.20	.09
❑ T42	Steve Avery	.20	.09
❑ T43	Damian Jackson	.20	.09
❑ T44	Rey Ordonez	.20	.09
❑ T45	John Flaherty	.20	.09
❑ T46	Byung-Hyun Kim	.20	.09
❑ T47	Tom Goodwin	.20	.09
❑ T48	Elmer Dessens	.20	.09
❑ T49	Al Martin	.20	.09
❑ T50	Gene Kingsale	.20	.09
❑ T51	Lenny Harris	.20	.09
❑ T52	David Ortiz Sox	.50	.23
❑ T53	Jose Lima	.20	.09
❑ T54	Mike Difelice	.20	.09
❑ T55	Jose Hernandez	.20	.09
❑ T56	Todd Zeile	.20	.09
❑ T57	Roberto Hernandez	.20	.09
❑ T58	Albie Lopez	.20	.09
❑ T59	Roberto Alomar	.30	.14
❑ T60	Russ Ortiz	.20	.09
❑ T61	Brian Daubach	.20	.09
❑ T62	Carl Everett	.20	.09
❑ T63	Jeromy Burnitz	.20	.09
❑ T64	Mark Bellhorn	.20	.09
❑ T65	Ruben Sierra	.20	.09
❑ T66	Mike Fetters	.20	.09
❑ T67	Armando Benitez	.20	.09
❑ T68	Deivi Cruz	.20	.09
❑ T69	Jose Cruz Jr.	.20	.09
❑ T70	Jeremy Fikac	.20	.09
❑ T71	Jeff Kent	.20	.09
❑ T72	Andres Galarraga	.20	.09
❑ T73	Rickey Henderson	.50	.23
❑ T74	Royce Clayton	.20	.09
❑ T75	Troy O'Leary	.20	.09
❑ T76	Ron Coomer	.20	.09
❑ T77	Greg Colbrunn	.20	.09
❑ T78	Wes Helms	.20	.09
❑ T79	Kevin Millwood	.20	.09
❑ T80	Damion Easley	.20	.09
❑ T81	Bobby Kielty	.20	.09
❑ T82	Keith Osik	.20	.09
❑ T83	Ramiro Mendoza	.20	.09
❑ T84	Shea Hillenbrand	.20	.09
❑ T85	Shannon Stewart	.20	.09
❑ T86	Eddie Perez	.20	.09
❑ T87	Ugueth Urbina	.20	.09
❑ T88	Orlando Palmeiro	.20	.09
❑ T89	Graeme Lloyd	.20	.09
❑ T90	John Vander Wal	.20	.09
❑ T91	Gary Bennett	.20	.09
❑ T92	Shane Reynolds	.20	.09
❑ T93	Steve Parris	.20	.09
❑ T94	Julio Lugo	.20	.09
❑ T95	John Halama	.20	.09
❑ T96	Carlos Baerga	.20	.09
❑ T97	Jim Parque	.20	.09
❑ T98	Mike Williams	.20	.09
❑ T99	Fred McGriff	.30	.14
❑ T100	Kenny Rogers	.20	.09
❑ T101	Matt Herges	.20	.09
❑ T102	Jay Bell	.20	.09
❑ T103	Esteban Yan	.20	.09
❑ T104	Eric Owens	.20	.09
❑ T105	Aaron Fultz	.20	.09
❑ T106	Rey Sanchez	.20	.09
❑ T107	Jim Thome	.50	.23
❑ T108	Aaron Boone	.20	.09
❑ T109	Raul Mondesi	.20	.09
❑ T110	Kenny Lofton	.20	.09
❑ T111	Jose Guillen	.20	.09
❑ T112	Aramis Ramirez	.20	.09
❑ T113	Sidney Ponson	.20	.09
❑ T114	Scott Williamson	.20	.09
❑ T115	Robin Ventura	.20	.09
❑ T116	Dusty Baker MG	.20	.09
❑ T117	Felipe Alou MG	.20	.09
❑ T118	Buck Showalter MG	.20	.09
❑ T119	Jack McKeon MG	.20	.09
❑ T120	Art Howe MG	.20	.09
❑ T121	Bobby Crosby PROS	.60	.25
❑ T122	Adrian Gonzalez PROS	.40	.18
❑ T123	Kevin Cash PROS	.40	.18
❑ T124	Shin-Soo Choo PROS	.40	.18
❑ T125	Chin-Feng Chen PROS	1.00	.45
❑ T126	Miguel Cabrera PROS	1.00	.45
❑ T127	Jason Young PROS	.40	.18
❑ T128	Alex Herrera PROS	.40	.18
❑ T129	Jason Dubois PROS	.40	.18
❑ T130	Jeff Mathis PROS	.40	.18
❑ T131	Casey Kotchman PROS	.60	.25
❑ T132	Ed Rogers PROS	.40	.18
❑ T133	Wilson Betemit PROS	.40	.18
❑ T134	Jim Kavourias PROS	.40	.18

❑ T135 Taylor Buchholz PROS .. .40 .18
❑ T136 Adam LaRoche PROS .... .40 .18
❑ T137 D.McPherson PROS .... 1.00 .45
❑ T138 Jesus Cota PROS .... .40 .18
❑ T139 Clint Nageotte PROS ..... .40 .18
❑ T140 Boof Bonser PROS .... .40 .18
❑ T141 Walter Young PROS ...... .40 .18
❑ T142 Joe Crede PROS .... .40 .18
❑ T143 Denny Bautista PROS .... .40 .18
❑ T144 Victor Diaz PROS .... .40 .18
❑ T145 Chris Narveson PROS .... .40 .18
❑ T146 Gabe Gross PROS .... .40 .18
❑ T147 Jimmy Journell PROS .... .40 .18
❑ T148 Rafael Soriano PROS ..... .40 .18
❑ T149 Jerome Williams PROS .. .40 .18
❑ T150 Aaron Cook PROS .... .40 .18
❑ T151 An. Martinez PROS .... .40 .18
❑ T152 Scott Hairston PROS ..... .40 .18
❑ T153 John Buck PROS .... .40 .18
❑ T154 Ryan Ludwick PROS .... .40 .18
❑ T155 Chris Bootcheck PROS .. .40 .18
❑ T156 John Rheinecker PROS .. .40 .18
❑ T157 Jason Lane PROS .... .40 .18
❑ T158 Shelley Duncan PROS .... .40 .18
❑ T159 Adam Wainwright PROS .40 .18
❑ T160 Jason Arnold PROS .... .40 .18
❑ T161 Jonny Gomes PROS .... .40 .18
❑ T162 James Loney PROS .... .40 .18
❑ T163 Mike Fontenot PROS ...... .40 .18
❑ T164 Khalil Greene PROS .... 2.00 .90
❑ T165 Sean Burnett PROS .... .40 .18
❑ T166 David Martinez FY RC .... .40 .18
❑ T167 Felix Pie FY RC .... 2.00 .90
❑ T168 Joe Valentine FY RC ...... .40 .18
❑ T169 Brandon Webb FY RC .. 1.00 .45
❑ T170 Matt Diaz FY RC .... .50 .23
❑ T171 Lew Ford FY RC .... 1.25 .55
❑ T172 Jeremy Griffiths FY RC .. .50 .23
❑ T173 Matt Hensley FY RC ...... .40 .18
❑ T174 Charlie Manning FY RC .40 .18
❑ T175 Elizardo Ramirez FY RC.. .75 .35
❑ T176 Greg Aquino FY RC .... .40 .18
❑ T177 Felix Sanchez FY RC ...... .40 .18
❑ T178 Kelly Shoppach FY RC 1.00 .45
❑ T179 Bubba Nelson FY RC ...... .50 .23
❑ T180 Mike O'Keefe FY RC ...... .40 .18
❑ T181 Hanley Ramirez FY RC 2.00 .90
❑ T182 T.Wellemeyer FY RC ...... .50 .23
❑ T183 Dustin Moseley FY RC .. .50 .23
❑ T184 Eric Crozier FY RC .... .50 .23
❑ T185 Ryan Shealy FY RC .... .75 .35
❑ T186 Jer. Bonderman FY RC .. .75 .35
❑ T187 T.Story-Harden FY RC .... .40 .18
❑ T188 Dusty Brown FY RC .... .40 .18
❑ T189 Rob Hammock FY RC .... .50 .23
❑ T190 Jorge Piedra FY RC .... .50 .23
❑ T191 Chris De La Cruz FY RC .40 .18
❑ T192 Eli Whiteside FY RC ...... .40 .18
❑ T193 Jason Kubel FY RC ...... 2.00 .90
❑ T194 Jon Schuerholz FY RC .. .40 .18
❑ T195 St. Randolph FY RC ...... .40 .18
❑ T196 Andy Sisco FY RC .... 1.00 .45
❑ T197 Sean Smith FY RC .... .50 .23
❑ T198 Jon-Mark Sprowl FY RC .75 .35
❑ T199 Matt Kata FY RC .... .75 .35
❑ T200 Robinson Cano FY RC 1.00 .45
❑ T201 Nook Logan FY RC .... .40 .18
❑ T202 Ben Francisco FY RC .... .50 .23
❑ T203 Arnie Munoz FY RC .... .40 .18
❑ T204 Ozzie Chavez FY RC ...... .40 .18
❑ T205 Eric Riggs FY RC .... .50 .23
❑ T206 Beau Kemp FY RC .... .40 .18
❑ T207 Travis Wong FY RC .... .50 .23
❑ T208 Dustin Yount FY RC ...... .50 .23
❑ T209 Brian McCann FY RC .... .75 .35
❑ T210 Wilton Reynolds FY RC .. .50 .23
❑ T211 Matt Bruback FY RC ...... .40 .18
❑ T212 Andrew Brown FY RC .... .50 .23
❑ T213 Edgar Gonzalez FY RC .... .40 .18
❑ T214 Eider Torres FY RC .... .40 .18
❑ T215 Aquilino Lopez FY RC .... .40 .18
❑ T216 Bobby Basham FY RC .... .50 .23
❑ T217 Tim Olson FY RC .... .50 .23
❑ T218 Nathan Panther FY RC .... .75 .35
❑ T219 Bryan Grace FY RC .... .40 .18
❑ T220 Dusty Gomon FY RC ...... .50 .23
❑ T221 Wil Ledezma FY RC .... .50 .23
❑ T222 Josh Willingham FY RC .50 .23
❑ T223 David Cash FY RC .... .40 .18
❑ T224 Oscar Villarreal FY RC .... .40 .18
❑ T225 Jeff Duncan FY RC .... .50 .23
❑ T226 Kade Johnson FY RC ..... .40 .18
❑ T227 L.Steidlmayer FY RC ...... .40 .18
❑ T228 Brandon Watson FY RC .. .40 .18
❑ T229 Jose Morales FY RC .... .40 .18
❑ T230 Mike Gallo FY RC .... .40 .18
❑ T231 Tyler Adamczyk FY RC .. .40 .18
❑ T232 Adam Stern FY RC .... .40 .18
❑ T233 Brennan King FY RC ...... .40 .18
❑ T234 Dan Haren FY RC .... .75 .35
❑ T235 Mi. Hernandez FY RC .... .40 .18
❑ T236 Ben Fritz FY RC .... .40 .18
❑ T237 Clay Hensley FY RC ...... .40 .18
❑ T238 Tyler Johnson FY RC .... .40 .18
❑ T239 Pete LaForest FY RC ...... .50 .23
❑ T240 Tyler Martin FY RC .... .40 .18
❑ T241 J.D. Durbin FY RC .... .75 .35
❑ T242 Shane Victorino FY RC .. .40 .18
❑ T243 Rajai Davis FY RC .... .50 .23
❑ T244 Ismael Castro FY RC ...... .40 .18
❑ T245 C.Wang FY RC .... 1.25 .55
❑ T246 Travis Ishikawa FY RC .... .40 .18
❑ T247 Corey Shafer FY RC .... .50 .23
❑ T248 G.Schneidmiller FY RC .. .40 .18
❑ T249 Dave Pember FY RC .... .40 .18
❑ T250 Keith Stamler FY RC ...... .40 .18
❑ T251 Tyson Graham FY RC ..... .40 .18
❑ T252 Ryan Cameron FY RC .... .40 .18
❑ T253 E.Eckenstahler FY RC .... .40 .18
❑ T254 Ma. Peterson FY RC ...... .40 .18
❑ T255 D. McGowan FY RC .... .75 .35
❑ T256 Pr. Redman FY RC .... .40 .18
❑ T257 Haj Turay FY RC .... .50 .23
❑ T258 Carlos Guzman FY RC .... .50 .23
❑ T259 Matt DeMarco FY RC ..... .40 .18
❑ T260 Derek Michaelis FY RC .. .40 .18
❑ T261 Brian Burgamy FY RC .... .40 .18
❑ T262 Jay Sitzman FY RC .... .40 .18
❑ T263 Chris Fallon FY RC .... .40 .18
❑ T264 Mike Adams FY RC .... .40 .18
❑ T265 Clint Barmes FY RC .... .50 .23
❑ T266 Eric Reed FY RC .... .75 .35
❑ T267 Willie Eyre FY RC .... .40 .18
❑ T268 Carlos Duran FY RC .... .40 .18
❑ T269 Nick Trzesniak FY RC .... .40 .18
❑ T270 Ferdin Tejeda FY RC ..... .40 .18
❑ T271 Mi. Garciaparra FY RC .. .75 .35
❑ T272 Michael Hinckley FY RC 1.00 .45
❑ T273 Br. Florence FY RC .... .40 .18
❑ T274 Trent Oeltjen FY RC .... .50 .23
❑ T275 Mike Neu FY RC .... .40 .18

2004 Topps

	MINT	NRMT
COMP.HOBBY SET (737)	80.00	36.00
COMP.HOLIDAY SET (742)	80.00	36.00
COMP.RETAIL SET (737)	80.00	36.00
COMP.ASTROS SET (737)	80.00	36.00
COMP.CUBS SET (737)	80.00	36.00
COMP.RED SOX SET (737)	80.00	36.00
COMP.YANKEES SET (737)	80.00	36.00
COMPLETE SET (732)	80.00	36.00
COMPLETE SERIES 1 (366)	40.00	18.00
COMPLETE SERIES 2 (366)	40.00	18.00
COMMON CARD (1-6/8-732)	.20	.09
COMMON (297-326/668-687)......	.50	.23
COMMON (327-331/688-692)......	.50	.23

❑ 1 Jim Thome .... .50 .23
❑ 2 Reggie Sanders .... .20 .09
❑ 3 Mark Kotsay .... .20 .09
❑ 4 Edgardo Alfonzo .... .20 .09
❑ 5 Ben Davis .... .20 .09
❑ 6 Mike Matheny .... .20 .09
❑ 8 Marlon Anderson .... .20 .09
❑ 9 Chan Ho Park .... .20 .09
❑ 10 Ichiro Suzuki .... .75 .35
❑ 11 Kevin Millwood .... .20 .09
❑ 12 Bengie Molina .... .20 .09
❑ 13 Tom Glavine .... .30 .14
❑ 14 Junior Spivey .... .20 .09
❑ 15 Marcus Giles .... .20 .09
❑ 16 David Segui .... .20 .09
❑ 17 Kevin Millar .... .20 .09
❑ 18 Corey Patterson .... .20 .09
❑ 19 Aaron Rowand .... .20 .09
❑ 20 Derek Jeter .... 1.00 .45
❑ 21 Jason LaRue .... .20 .09
❑ 22 Chris Hammond .... .20 .09
❑ 23 Jay Payton .... .20 .09
❑ 24 Bobby Higginson .... .20 .09
❑ 25 Lance Berkman .... .20 .09
❑ 26 Juan Pierre .... .20 .09
❑ 27 Brent Mayne .... .20 .09
❑ 28 Fred McGriff .... .30 .14
❑ 29 Richie Sexson .... .20 .09
❑ 30 Tim Hudson .... .20 .09
❑ 31 Mike Piazza .... .75 .35
❑ 32 Brad Radke .... .20 .09
❑ 33 Jeff Weaver .... .20 .09
❑ 34 Ramon Hernandez .... .20 .09
❑ 35 David Bell .... .20 .09
❑ 36 Craig Wilson .... .20 .09
❑ 37 Jake Peavy .... .20 .09
❑ 38 Tim Worrell .... .20 .09
❑ 39 Gil Meche .... .20 .09
❑ 40 Albert Pujols .... 1.00 .45
❑ 41 Michael Young .... .20 .09
❑ 42 Josh Phelps .... .20 .09
❑ 43 Brendan Donnelly .... .20 .09
❑ 44 Steve Finley .... .20 .09
❑ 45 John Smoltz .... .30 .14
❑ 46 Jay Gibbons .... .20 .09
❑ 47 Trot Nixon .... .20 .09
❑ 48 Carl Pavano .... .20 .09
❑ 49 Frank Thomas .... .50 .23
❑ 50 Mark Prior .... .50 .23
❑ 51 Danny Graves .... .20 .09
❑ 52 Milton Bradley UER .... .20 .09
❑ 53 Jose Jimenez .... .20 .09
❑ 54 Shane Halter .... .20 .09
❑ 55 Mike Lowell .... .20 .09
❑ 56 Geoff Blum .... .20 .09
❑ 57 Michael Tucker UER .... .20 .09
Dee Brown pictured
❑ 58 Paul Lo Duca .... .20 .09
❑ 59 Vicente Padilla .... .20 .09
❑ 60 Jacque Jones .... .20 .09
❑ 61 Fernando Tatis .... .20 .09
❑ 62 Ty Wigginton .... .20 .09
❑ 63 Pedro Astacio .... .20 .09
❑ 64 Andy Pettitte .... .30 .14
❑ 65 Terrence Long .... .20 .09
❑ 66 Cliff Floyd .... .20 .09
❑ 67 Mariano Rivera .... .30 .14
❑ 68 Carlos Silva .... .20 .09
❑ 69 Marlon Byrd .... .20 .09
❑ 70 Mark Mulder .... .20 .09
❑ 71 Kerry Ligtenberg .... .20 .09
❑ 72 Carlos Guillen .... .20 .09
❑ 73 Fernando Vina .... .20 .09
❑ 74 Lance Carter .... .20 .09
❑ 75 Hank Blalock .... .20 .09
❑ 76 Jimmy Rollins .... .20 .09
❑ 77 Francisco Rodriguez .... .20 .09
❑ 78 Javy Lopez .... .20 .09
❑ 79 Jerry Hairston Jr. .... .20 .09
❑ 80 Andruw Jones .... .20 .09
❑ 81 Rodrigo Lopez .... .20 .09
❑ 82 Johnny Damon .... .50 .23

❑ 83 Hee Seop Choi .20 .09
❑ 84 Miguel Olivo .20 .09
❑ 85 Jon Garland .20 .09
❑ 86 Matt Lawton .20 .09
❑ 87 Juan Uribe .20 .09
❑ 88 Steve Sparks .20 .09
❑ 89 Tim Spooneybarger .20 .09
❑ 90 Jose Vidro .20 .09
❑ 91 Luis Rivas .20 .09
❑ 92 Hideo Nomo .50 .23
❑ 93 Javier Vazquez .20 .09
❑ 94 Al Leiter .20 .09
❑ 95 Darren Dreifort .20 .09
❑ 96 Alex Cintron .20 .09
❑ 97 Zach Day .20 .09
❑ 98 Jorge Posada .30 .14
❑ 99 John Halama .20 .09
❑ 100 Alex Rodriguez .75 .35
❑ 101 Orlando Palmeiro .20 .09
❑ 102 Dave Berg .20 .09
❑ 103 Brad Fullmer .20 .09
❑ 104 Mike Hampton .20 .09
❑ 105 Willis Roberts .20 .09
❑ 106 Ramiro Mendoza .20 .09
❑ 107 Juan Cruz .20 .09
❑ 108 Esteban Loaiza .20 .09
❑ 109 Russell Branyan .20 .09
❑ 110 Todd Helton .30 .14
❑ 111 Braden Looper .20 .09
❑ 112 Octavio Dotel .20 .09
❑ 113 Mike MacDougal .20 .09
❑ 114 Cesar Izturis .20 .09
❑ 115 Johan Santana .30 .14
❑ 116 Jose Contreras .20 .09
❑ 117 Placido Polanco .20 .09
❑ 118 Jason Phillips .20 .09
❑ 119 Adam Eaton .20 .09
❑ 120 Vernon Wells .20 .09
❑ 121 Ben Grieve .20 .09
❑ 122 Randy Winn .20 .09
❑ 123 Ismael Valdes .20 .09
❑ 124 Eric Owens .20 .09
❑ 125 Curt Schilling .20 .09
❑ 126 Russ Ortiz .20 .09
❑ 127 Mark Buehrle .20 .09
❑ 128 Danys Baez .20 .09
❑ 129 Dmitri Young .20 .09
❑ 130 Kazuhisa Ishii .20 .09
❑ 131 A.J. Pierzynski .20 .09
❑ 132 Michael Barrett .20 .09
❑ 133 Joe McEwing .20 .09
❑ 134 Alex Cora .20 .09
❑ 135 Tom Wilson .20 .09
❑ 136 Carlos Zambrano .20 .09
❑ 137 Brett Tomko .20 .09
❑ 138 Shigetoshi Hasegawa .20 .09
❑ 139 Jarrod Washburn .20 .09
❑ 140 Greg Maddux .75 .35
❑ 141 Craig Counsell .20 .09
❑ 142 Reggie Taylor .20 .09
❑ 143 Omar Vizquel .30 .14
❑ 144 Alex Gonzalez .20 .09
❑ 145 Billy Wagner .20 .09
❑ 146 Brian Jordan .20 .09
❑ 147 Wes Helms .20 .09
❑ 148 Kyle Lohse .20 .09
❑ 149 Timo Perez .20 .09
❑ 150 Jason Giambi .20 .09
❑ 151 Erubiel Durazo .20 .09
❑ 152 Mike Lieberthal .20 .09
❑ 153 Jason Kendall .20 .09
❑ 154 Xavier Nady .20 .09
❑ 155 Kirk Rueter .20 .09
❑ 156 Mike Cameron .20 .09
❑ 157 Miguel Cairo .20 .09
❑ 158 Woody Williams .20 .09
❑ 159 Toby Hall .20 .09
❑ 160 Bernie Williams .30 .14
❑ 161 Darin Erstad .20 .09
❑ 162 Matt Mantei .20 .09
❑ 163 Geronimo Gil .20 .09
❑ 164 Bill Mueller .20 .09
❑ 165 Damian Miller .20 .09
❑ 166 Tony Graffanino .20 .09
❑ 167 Sean Casey .20 .09
❑ 168 Brandon Phillips .20 .09
❑ 169 Mike Remlinger .20 .09
❑ 170 Adam Dunn .30 .14
❑ 171 Carlos Lee .20 .09
❑ 172 Juan Encarnacion .20 .09
❑ 173 Angel Berroa .20 .09
❑ 174 Desi Relaford .20 .09
❑ 175 Paul Quantrill .20 .09
❑ 176 Ben Sheets .20 .09
❑ 177 Eddie Guardado .20 .09
❑ 178 Rocky Biddle .20 .09
❑ 179 Mike Stanton .20 .09
❑ 180 Eric Chavez .20 .09
❑ 181 Jason Michaels .20 .09
❑ 182 Terry Adams .20 .09
❑ 183 Kip Wells .20 .09
❑ 184 Brian Lawrence .20 .09
❑ 185 Bret Boone .20 .09
❑ 186 Tino Martinez .30 .14
❑ 187 Aubrey Huff .20 .09
❑ 188 Kevin Mench .20 .09
❑ 189 Tim Salmon .30 .14
❑ 190 Carlos Delgado .20 .09
❑ 191 John Lackey .20 .09
❑ 192 Oscar Villarreal .20 .09
❑ 193 Luis Matos .20 .09
❑ 194 Derek Lowe .20 .09
❑ 195 Mark Grudzielanek .20 .09
❑ 196 Tom Gordon .20 .09
❑ 197 Matt Clement .20 .09
❑ 198 Byung-Hyun Kim .20 .09
❑ 199 Brandon Inge .20 .09
❑ 200 Nomar Garciaparra .75 .35
❑ 201 Antonio Osuna .20 .09
❑ 202 Jose Mesa .20 .09
❑ 203 Bo Hart .20 .09
❑ 204 Jack Wilson .20 .09
❑ 205 Ray Durham .20 .09
❑ 206 Freddy Garcia .20 .09
❑ 207 J.D. Drew .20 .09
❑ 208 Einar Diaz .20 .09
❑ 209 Roy Halladay .20 .09
❑ 210 David Eckstein UER .20 .09
Adam Kennedy pictured
❑ 211 Jason Marquis .20 .09
❑ 212 Jorge Julio .20 .09
❑ 213 Tim Wakefield .20 .09
❑ 214 Moises Alou .20 .09
❑ 215 Bartolo Colon .20 .09
❑ 216 Jimmy Haynes .20 .09
❑ 217 Preston Wilson .20 .09
❑ 218 Luis Castillo .20 .09
❑ 219 Richard Hidalgo .20 .09
❑ 220 Manny Ramirez .30 .14
❑ 221 Mike Mussina .30 .14
❑ 222 Randy Wolf .20 .09
❑ 223 Kris Benson .20 .09
❑ 224 Ryan Klesko .20 .09
❑ 225 Rich Aurilia .20 .09
❑ 226 Kelvim Escobar .20 .09
❑ 227 Francisco Cordero .20 .09
❑ 228 Kazuhiro Sasaki .20 .09
❑ 229 Danny Bautista .20 .09
❑ 230 Rafael Furcal .20 .09
❑ 231 Travis Driskill .20 .09
❑ 232 Kyle Farnsworth .20 .09
❑ 233 Jose Valentin .20 .09
❑ 234 Felipe Lopez .20 .09
❑ 235 C.C. Sabathia .20 .09
❑ 236 Brad Penny .20 .09
❑ 237 Brad Ausmus .20 .09
❑ 238 Raul Ibanez .20 .09
❑ 239 Adrian Beltre .30 .14
❑ 240 Rocco Baldelli .20 .09
❑ 241 Orlando Hudson .20 .09
❑ 242 Dave Roberts .20 .09
❑ 243 Doug Mientkiewicz .20 .09
❑ 244 Brad Wilkerson .20 .09
❑ 245 Scott Strickland .20 .09
❑ 246 Ryan Franklin .20 .09
❑ 247 Chad Bradford .20 .09
❑ 248 Gary Bennett .20 .09
❑ 249 Jose Cruz Jr. .20 .09
❑ 250 Jeff Kent .20 .09
❑ 251 Josh Beckett .20 .09
❑ 252 Ramon Ortiz .20 .09
❑ 253 Miguel Batista .20 .09
❑ 254 Jung Bong .20 .09
❑ 255 Deivi Cruz .20 .09
❑ 256 Alex Gonzalez .20 .09
❑ 257 Shawn Chacon .20 .09
❑ 258 Runelvys Hernandez .20 .09
❑ 259 Joe Mays .20 .09
❑ 260 Eric Gagne .50 .23
❑ 261 Dustan Mohr UER .20 .09
1998 Kinston stats are wrong
❑ 262 Tomokazu Ohka .20 .09
❑ 263 Eric Byrnes .20 .09
❑ 264 Frank Catalanotto .20 .09
❑ 265 Cristian Guzman .20 .09
❑ 266 Orlando Cabrera .20 .09
❑ 267A Juan Castro .20 .09
❑ 267B M.Scioscia MG UER 274 .20 .09
❑ 268 Bob Brenly MG .20 .09
❑ 269 Bobby Cox MG .20 .09
❑ 270 Mike Hargrove MG .20 .09
❑ 271 Grady Little MG .20 .09
❑ 272 Dusty Baker MG .20 .09
❑ 273 Jerry Manuel MG .20 .09
❑ 275 Eric Wedge MG .20 .09
❑ 276 Clint Hurdle MG .20 .09
❑ 277 Alan Trammell MG .20 .09
❑ 278 Jack McKeon MG .20 .09
❑ 279 Jimy Williams MG .20 .09
❑ 280 Tony Pena MG .20 .09
❑ 281 Jim Tracy MG .20 .09
❑ 282 Ned Yost MG .20 .09
❑ 283 Ron Gardenhire MG .20 .09
❑ 284 Frank Robinson MG .30 .14
❑ 285 Art Howe MG .20 .09
❑ 286 Joe Torre MG .30 .14
❑ 287 Ken Macha MG .20 .09
❑ 288 Larry Bowa MG .20 .09
❑ 289 Lloyd McClendon MG .20 .09
❑ 290 Bruce Bochy MG .20 .09
❑ 291 Felipe Alou MG .20 .09
❑ 292 Bob Melvin MG .20 .09
❑ 293 Tony LaRussa MG .20 .09
❑ 294 Lou Piniella MG .20 .09
❑ 295 Buck Showalter MG .20 .09
❑ 296 Carlos Tosca MG .20 .09
❑ 297 Anthony Acevedo FY RC .50 .23
❑ 298 Anthony Lerew FY RC .75 .35
❑ 299 Blake Hawksworth FY RC .50 .23
❑ 300 Brayan Pena FY RC .50 .23
❑ 301 Casey Myers FY RC .50 .23
❑ 302 Craig Ansman FY RC .50 .23
❑ 303 David Murphy FY RC 1.00 .45
❑ 304 Dave Crouthers FY RC .50 .23
❑ 305 Dioner Navarro FY RC 1.25 .55
❑ 306 Donald Levinski FY RC .50 .23
❑ 307 Jesse Roman FY RC .50 .23
❑ 308 Sung Jung FY RC .50 .23
❑ 309 Jon Knott FY RC .50 .23
❑ 310 Josh Labandeira FY RC .50 .23
❑ 311 Kenny Perez FY RC .50 .23
❑ 312 Khalid Ballouli FY RC .50 .23
❑ 313 Kyle Davies FY RC .75 .35
❑ 314 Marcus McBeth FY RC .50 .23
❑ 315 Matt Creighton FY RC .50 .23
❑ 316 Chris O'Riordan FY RC .50 .23
❑ 317 Mike Gosling FY RC .50 .23
❑ 318 Nic Ungs FY RC .50 .23
❑ 319 Omar Falcon FY RC .50 .23
❑ 320 Rodney Choy Foo FY RC .50 .23
❑ 321 Tim Frend FY RC .50 .23
❑ 322 Todd Self FY RC .50 .23
❑ 323 Tydus Meadows FY RC .50 .23
❑ 324 Yadier Molina FY RC 1.00 .45
❑ 325 Zach Duke FY RC 1.50 .70
❑ 326 Zach Miner FY RC .50 .23
❑ 327 Bernie Castro .50 .23
Khalil Greene FS
❑ 328 Ryan Madson .50 .23
Elizardo Ramirez FS
❑ 329 Rich Harden .50 .23
Bobby Crosby FS
❑ 330 Zack Greinke .50 .23
Jimmy Gobble FS
❑ 331 Bobby Jenks .50 .23
Casey Kotchman FS
❑ 332 Sammy Sosa HL .50 .23
❑ 333 Kevin Millwood HL .20 .09

❑ 334 Rafael Palmeiro HL .20 .09
❑ 335 Roger Clemens HL .50 .23
❑ 336 Eric Gagne HL .30 .14
❑ 337 Bill Mueller .50 .23
Manny Ramirez
Derek Jeter
AL Batting Avg LL
❑ 338 Vernon Wells .50 .23
Ichiro Suzuki
Michael Young
AL Hits LL
❑ 339 Alex Rodriguez .50 .23
Frank Thomas
Carlos Delgado
AL Home Runs LL
❑ 340 Carlos Delgado .50 .23
Alex Rodriguez
Bret Boone
AL RBI's LL
❑ 341 Pedro Martinez .30 .14
Tim Hudson
Esteban Loaiza
AL ERA LL
❑ 342 Esteban Loaiza .30 .14
Pedro Martinez
Roy Halladay
AL Strikeouts LL
❑ 343 Albert Pujols .50 .23
Todd Helton
Edgar Renteria
NL Batting Avg LL
❑ 344 Albert Pujols .50 .23
Todd Helton
Juan Pierre
NL Hits LL
❑ 345 Jim Thome .30 .14
Richie Sexson
Javy Lopez
NL Home Runs LL
❑ 346 Preston Wilson .30 .14
Gary Sheffield
Jim Thome
NL RBI's LL
❑ 347 Jason Schmidt .30 .14
Kevin Brown
Mark Prior
NL ERA LL
❑ 348 Kerry Wood .30 .14
Mark Prior
Javier Vazquez
NL Strikeouts LL
❑ 349 Roger Clemens .50 .23
David Wells ALDS
❑ 350 Kerry Wood .30 .14
Mark Prior NLDS
❑ 351 Josh Beckett .30 .14
Miguel Cabrera
Ivan Rodriguez NLCS
❑ 352 Jason Giambi .50 .23
Mariano Rivera
Aaron Boone ALCS
❑ 353 Derek Lowe .50 .23
Ivan Rodriguez AL/NLDS
❑ 354 Pedro Martinez .50 .23
Jorge Posada
Roger Clemens ALCS
❑ 355 Juan Pierre WS .20 .09
❑ 356 Carlos Delgado AS .20 .09
❑ 357 Bret Boone AS .20 .09
❑ 358 Alex Rodriguez AS .50 .23
❑ 359 Bill Mueller AS .20 .09
❑ 360 Vernon Wells AS .20 .09
❑ 361 Garret Anderson AS .20 .09
❑ 362 Magglio Ordonez AS .20 .09
❑ 363 Jorge Posada AS .20 .09
❑ 364 Roy Halladay AS .20 .09
❑ 365 Andy Pettitte AS .20 .09
❑ 366 Frank Thomas AS .30 .14
❑ 367 Jody Gerut AS .20 .09
❑ 368 Sammy Sosa .75 .35
❑ 369 Joe Crede .20 .09
❑ 370 Gary Sheffield .20 .09
❑ 371 Coco Crisp .20 .09
❑ 372 Torii Hunter .20 .09
❑ 373 Derrek Lee .20 .09
❑ 374 Adam Everett .20 .09
❑ 375 Miguel Tejada .20 .09
❑ 376 Jeremy Affeldt .20 .09
❑ 377 Robin Ventura .20 .09
❑ 378 Scott Podsednik .20 .09
❑ 379 Matthew LeCroy .20 .09
❑ 380 Vladimir Guerrero .50 .23
❑ 381 Tike Redman .20 .09
❑ 382 Jeff Nelson .20 .09
❑ 383 Cliff Lee .20 .09
❑ 384 Bobby Abreu .20 .09
❑ 385 Josh Fogg .20 .09
❑ 386 Trevor Hoffman .20 .09
❑ 387 Jesse Foppert .20 .09
❑ 388 Edgar Martinez .30 .14
❑ 389 Edgar Renteria .20 .09
❑ 390 Chipper Jones .50 .23
❑ 391 Eric Munson .20 .09
❑ 392 Dewon Brazelton .20 .09
❑ 393 John Thomson .20 .09
❑ 394 Chris Woodward .20 .09
❑ 395 Adam LaRoche .20 .09
❑ 396 Elmer Dessens .20 .09
❑ 397 Johnny Estrada .20 .09
❑ 398 Damian Moss .20 .09
❑ 399 Gabe Kapler .20 .09
❑ 400 Dontrelle Willis .20 .09
❑ 401 Troy Glaus .20 .09
❑ 402 Raul Mondesi .20 .09
❑ 403 Shane Reynolds .20 .09
❑ 404 Kurt Ainsworth .20 .09
❑ 405 Pedro Martinez .50 .23
❑ 406 Eric Karros .20 .09
❑ 407 Billy Koch .20 .09
❑ 408 Scott Schoeneweis .20 .09
❑ 409 Paul Wilson .20 .09
❑ 410 Mike Sweeney .20 .09
❑ 411 Jason Bay .20 .09
❑ 412 Mark Redman .20 .09
❑ 413 Jason Jennings .20 .09
❑ 414 Rondell White .20 .09
❑ 415 Todd Hundley .20 .09
❑ 416 Shannon Stewart .20 .09
❑ 417 Jae Weong Seo .20 .09
❑ 418 Livan Hernandez .20 .09
❑ 419 Mark Ellis .20 .09
❑ 420 Pat Burrell .20 .09
❑ 421 Mark Loretta .20 .09
❑ 422 Robb Nen .20 .09
❑ 423 Joel Pineiro .20 .09
❑ 424 Jason Simontacchi .20 .09
❑ 425 Sterling Hitchcock .20 .09
❑ 426 Rey Ordonez .20 .09
❑ 427 Greg Myers .20 .09
❑ 428 Shane Spencer .20 .09
❑ 429 Carlos Baerga .20 .09
❑ 430 Garret Anderson .20 .09
❑ 431 Horacio Ramirez .20 .09
❑ 432 Brian Roberts .20 .09
❑ 433 Damian Jackson .20 .09
❑ 434 Doug Glanville .20 .09
❑ 435 Brian Daubach .20 .09
❑ 436 Alex Escobar .20 .09
❑ 437 Alex Sanchez .20 .09
❑ 438 Jeff Bagwell .30 .14
❑ 439 Darrell May .20 .09
❑ 440 Shawn Green .20 .09
❑ 441 Geoff Jenkins .20 .09
❑ 442 Endy Chavez .20 .09
❑ 443 Nick Johnson .20 .09
❑ 444 Jose Guillen .20 .09
❑ 445 Tomas Perez .20 .09
❑ 446 Phil Nevin .20 .09
❑ 447 Jason Schmidt .20 .09
❑ 448 Julio Mateo .20 .09
❑ 449 So Taguchi .20 .09
❑ 450 Randy Johnson .50 .23
❑ 451 Paul Byrd .20 .09
❑ 452 Chone Figgins .20 .09
❑ 453 Larry Bigbie .20 .09
❑ 454 Scott Williamson .20 .09
❑ 455 Ramon Martinez .20 .09
❑ 456 Roberto Alomar .30 .14
❑ 457 Ryan Dempster .20 .09
❑ 458 Ryan Ludwick .20 .09
❑ 459 Ramon Santiago .20 .09
❑ 460 Jeff Conine .20 .09
❑ 461 Brad Lidge .20 .09
❑ 462 Ken Harvey .20 .09
❑ 463 Guillermo Mota .20 .09
❑ 464 Rick Reed .20 .09
❑ 465 Joey Eischen .20 .09
❑ 466 Wade Miller .20 .09
❑ 467 Steve Karsay .20 .09
❑ 468 Chase Utley .20 .09
❑ 469 Matt Stairs .20 .09
❑ 470 Yorvit Torrealba .20 .09
❑ 471 Joe Kennedy .20 .09
❑ 472 Reed Johnson .20 .09
❑ 473 Victor Zambrano .20 .09
❑ 474 Jeff Davanon .20 .09
❑ 475 Luis Gonzalez .20 .09
❑ 476 Eli Marrero .20 .09
❑ 477 Ray King .20 .09
❑ 478 Jack Cust .20 .09
❑ 479 Omar Daal .20 .09
❑ 480 Todd Walker .20 .09
❑ 481 Shawn Estes .20 .09
❑ 482 Chris Reitsma .20 .09
❑ 483 Jake Westbrook .20 .09
❑ 484 Jeremy Bonderman .20 .09
❑ 485 A.J. Burnett .20 .09
❑ 486 Roy Oswalt .20 .09
❑ 487 Kevin Brown .20 .09
❑ 488 Eric Milton .20 .09
❑ 489 Claudio Vargas .20 .09
❑ 490 Roger Cedeno .20 .09
❑ 491 David Wells .20 .09
❑ 492 Scott Hatteberg .20 .09
❑ 493 Ricky Ledee .20 .09
❑ 494 Eric Young .20 .09
❑ 495 Armando Benitez .20 .09
❑ 496 Dan Haren .20 .09
❑ 497 Carl Crawford .20 .09
❑ 498 Laynce Nix .20 .09
❑ 499 Eric Hinske .20 .09
❑ 500 Ivan Rodriguez .50 .23
❑ 501 Scot Shields .20 .09
❑ 502 Brandon Webb .20 .09
❑ 503 Mark DeRosa .20 .09
❑ 504 Jhonny Peralta .20 .09
❑ 505 Adam Kennedy .20 .09
❑ 506 Tony Batista .20 .09
❑ 507 Jeff Suppan .20 .09
❑ 508 Kenny Lofton .20 .09
❑ 509 Scott Sullivan .20 .09
❑ 510 Ken Griffey Jr. .75 .35
❑ 511 Billy Traber .20 .09
❑ 512 Larry Walker .30 .14
❑ 513 Mike Maroth .20 .09
❑ 514 Todd Hollandsworth .20 .09
❑ 515 Kirk Saarloos .20 .09
❑ 516 Carlos Beltran .30 .14
❑ 517 Juan Rivera .20 .09
❑ 518 Roger Clemens 1.00 .45
❑ 519 Karim Garcia .20 .09
❑ 520 Jose Reyes .20 .09
❑ 521 Brandon Duckworth .20 .09
❑ 522 Brian Giles .20 .09
❑ 523 J.T. Snow .20 .09
❑ 524 Jamie Moyer .20 .09
❑ 525 Jason Isringhausen .20 .09
❑ 526 Julio Lugo .20 .09
❑ 527 Mark Teixeira .20 .09
❑ 528 Cory Lidle .20 .09
❑ 529 Lyle Overbay .20 .09
❑ 530 Troy Percival .20 .09
❑ 531 Robby Hammock .20 .09
❑ 532 Robert Fick .20 .09
❑ 533 Jason Johnson .20 .09
❑ 534 Brandon Lyon .20 .09
❑ 535 Antonio Alfonseca .20 .09
❑ 536 Tom Goodwin .20 .09
❑ 537 Paul Konerko .20 .09
❑ 538 D'Angelo Jimenez .20 .09
❑ 539 Ben Broussard .20 .09
❑ 540 Magglio Ordonez .20 .09
❑ 541 Ellis Burks .20 .09
❑ 542 Carlos Pena .20 .09
❑ 543 Chad Fox .20 .09
❑ 544 Jeriome Robertson .20 .09
❑ 545 Travis Hafner .20 .09
❑ 546 Joe Randa .20 .09

❑ 547 Wil Cordero .20 .09
❑ 548 Brady Clark .20 .09
❑ 549 Ruben Sierra .20 .09
❑ 550 Barry Zito .20 .09
❑ 551 Brett Myers .20 .09
❑ 552 Oliver Perez .20 .09
❑ 553 Trey Hodges .20 .09
❑ 554 Benito Santiago .20 .09
❑ 555 David Ross .20 .09
❑ 556 Ramon Vazquez .20 .09
❑ 557 Joe Nathan .20 .09
❑ 558 Dan Wilson .20 .09
❑ 559 Joe Mauer .30 .14
❑ 560 Jim Edmonds .20 .09
❑ 561 Shawn Wooten .20 .09
❑ 562 Matt Kata .20 .09
❑ 563 Vinny Castilla .20 .09
❑ 564 Marty Cordova .20 .09
❑ 565 Aramis Ramirez .20 .09
❑ 566 Carl Everett .20 .09
❑ 567 Ryan Freel .20 .09
❑ 568 Jason Davis .20 .09
❑ 569 Mark Bellhorn Sox .30 .14
❑ 570 Craig Monroe .20 .09
❑ 571 Roberto Hernandez .20 .09
❑ 572 Tim Redding .20 .09
❑ 573 Kevin Appier .20 .09
❑ 574 Jeromy Burnitz .20 .09
❑ 575 Miguel Cabrera .30 .14
❑ 576 Ramon Nivar .20 .09
❑ 577 Casey Blake .20 .09
❑ 578 Aaron Boone .20 .09
❑ 579 Jermaine Dye .20 .09
❑ 580 Jerome Williams .20 .09
❑ 581 John Olerud .20 .09
❑ 582 Scott Rolen .50 .23
❑ 583 Bobby Kielty .20 .09
❑ 584 Travis Lee .20 .09
❑ 585 Jeff Cirillo .20 .09
❑ 586 Scott Spiezio .20 .09
❑ 587 Stephen Randolph .20 .09
❑ 588 Melvin Mora .20 .09
❑ 589 Mike Timlin .20 .09
❑ 590 Kerry Wood .50 .23
❑ 591 Tony Womack .20 .09
❑ 592 Jody Gerut .20 .09
❑ 593 Franklyn German .20 .09
❑ 594 Morgan Ensberg .20 .09
❑ 595 Odalis Perez .20 .09
❑ 596 Michael Cuddyer .20 .09
❑ 597 Jon Lieber .20 .09
❑ 598 Mike Williams .20 .09
❑ 599 Jose Hernandez .20 .09
❑ 600 Alfonso Soriano .30 .14
❑ 601 Marquis Grissom .20 .09
❑ 602 Matt Morris .20 .09
❑ 603 Damian Rolls .20 .09
❑ 604 Juan Gonzalez .30 .14
❑ 605 Aquilino Lopez .20 .09
❑ 606 Jose Valverde .20 .09
❑ 607 Kenny Rogers .20 .09
❑ 608 Joe Borowski .20 .09
❑ 609 Josh Bard .20 .09
❑ 610 Austin Kearns .20 .09
❑ 611 Chin-Hui Tsao .20 .09
❑ 612 Wil Ledezma .20 .09
❑ 613 Aaron Guiel .20 .09
❑ 614 LaTroy Hawkins .20 .09
❑ 615 Tony Armas Jr. .20 .09
❑ 616 Steve Trachsel .20 .09
❑ 617 Ted Lilly .20 .09
❑ 618 Todd Pratt .20 .09
❑ 619 Sean Burroughs .20 .09
❑ 620 Rafael Palmeiro .30 .14
❑ 621 Jeremi Gonzalez .20 .09
❑ 622 Quinton McCracken .20 .09
❑ 623 David Ortiz .50 .23
❑ 624 Randall Simon .20 .09
❑ 625 Wily Mo Pena .20 .09
❑ 626 Nate Cornejo .20 .09
❑ 627 Brian Anderson .20 .09
❑ 628 Corey Koskie .20 .09
❑ 629 Keith Foulke Sox .30 .14
❑ 630 Rheal Cormier .20 .09
❑ 631 Sidney Ponson .20 .09
❑ 632 Gary Matthews Jr. .20 .09
❑ 633 Herbert Perry .20 .09
❑ 634 Shea Hillenbrand .20 .09
❑ 635 Craig Biggio .30 .14
❑ 636 Barry Larkin .30 .14
❑ 637 Arthur Rhodes .20 .09
❑ 638 Anaheim Angels TC .20 .09
❑ 639 Arizona Diamondbacks TC .20 .09
❑ 640 Atlanta Braves TC .20 .09
❑ 641 Baltimore Orioles TC .20 .09
❑ 642 Boston Red Sox TC .30 .14
❑ 643 Chicago Cubs TC .20 .09
❑ 644 Chicago White Sox TC .20 .09
❑ 645 Cincinnati Reds TC .20 .09
❑ 646 Cleveland Indians TC .20 .09
❑ 647 Colorado Rockies TC .20 .09
❑ 648 Detroit Tigers TC .20 .09
❑ 649 Florida Marlins TC .20 .09
❑ 650 Houston Astros TC .20 .09
❑ 651 Kansas City Royals TC .20 .09
❑ 652 Los Angeles Dodgers TC .20 .09
❑ 653 Milwaukee Brewers TC .20 .09
❑ 654 Minnesota Twins TC .20 .09
❑ 655 Montreal Expos TC .20 .09
❑ 656 New York Mets TC .20 .09
❑ 657 New York Yankees TC .50 .23
❑ 658 Oakland Athletics TC .20 .09
❑ 659 Philadelphia Phillies TC .20 .09
❑ 660 Pittsburgh Pirates TC .20 .09
❑ 661 San Diego Padres TC .20 .09
❑ 662 San Francisco Giants TC .20 .09
❑ 663 Seattle Mariners TC .20 .09
❑ 664 St. Louis Cardinals TC .20 .09
❑ 665 Tampa Bay Devil Rays TC .20 .09
❑ 666 Texas Rangers TC .20 .09
❑ 667 Toronto Blue Jays TC .20 .09
❑ 668 Kyle Sleeth DP RC 1.00 .45
❑ 669 Bradley Sullivan DP RC .50 .23
❑ 670 Carlos Quentin DP RC 2.00 .90
❑ 671 Conor Jackson DP RC 2.00 .90
❑ 672 Jeffrey Allison DP RC .50 .23
❑ 673 Matthew Moses DP RC 1.00 .45
❑ 674 Tim Stauffer DP RC .75 .35
❑ 675 Estee Harris DP RC .50 .23
❑ 676 David Aardsma DP RC .50 .23
❑ 677 Omar Quintanilla DP RC 1.00 .45
❑ 678 Aaron Hill DP .50 .23
❑ 679 Tony Richie DP RC .50 .23
❑ 680 Lastings Milledge DP RC 2.00 .90
❑ 681 Brad Snyder DP RC 1.00 .45
❑ 682 Jason Hirsh DP RC .50 .23
❑ 683 Logan Kensing DP RC .50 .23
❑ 684 Chris Lubanski DP .50 .23
❑ 685 Ryan Harvey DP .50 .23
❑ 686 Ryan Wagner DP .50 .23
❑ 687 Rickie Weeks DP .50 .23
❑ 688 Grady Sizemore .50 .23
Jeremy Guthrie
❑ 689 Edwin Jackson .50 .23
Greg Miller
❑ 690 Jeremy Reed .50 .23
Neal Cotts
❑ 691 Adam Loewen .50 .23
Nick Markakis
❑ 692 B.J. Upton .50 .23
Delmon Young
❑ 693 Kings of New York 1.50 .70
Alex Rodriguez
Derek Jeter
❑ 694 Fan Favorites 1.00 .45
Ichiro Suzuki
Albert Pujols
❑ 695 South Philly Sluggers 1.00 .45
Jim Thome
Mike Schmidt
❑ 696 Mike Mussina GG .20 .09
❑ 697 Bengie Molina GG .20 .09
❑ 698 John Olerud GG .20 .09
❑ 699 Bret Boone GG .20 .09
❑ 700 Eric Chavez GG .20 .09
❑ 701 Alex Rodriguez GG .50 .23
❑ 702 Mike Cameron GG UER .20 .09
Pictures Randy Winn
❑ 703 Ichiro Suzuki GG .50 .23
❑ 704 Torii Hunter GG .20 .09
❑ 705 Mike Hampton GG .20 .09
❑ 706 Mike Matheny GG .20 .09
❑ 707 Derrek Lee GG .20 .09
❑ 708 Luis Castillo GG .20 .09
❑ 709 Scott Rolen GG .30 .14
❑ 710 Edgar Renteria GG .20 .09
❑ 711 Andruw Jones GG .20 .09
❑ 712 Jose Cruz Jr. GG .20 .09
❑ 713 Jim Edmonds GG .20 .09
❑ 714 Roy Halladay CY .20 .09
❑ 715 Eric Gagne CY .30 .14
❑ 716 Alex Rodriguez MVP .50 .23
❑ 717 Angel Berroa ROY .20 .09
❑ 718 Dontrelle Willis ROY .20 .09
❑ 719 Todd Helton AS .20 .09
❑ 720 Marcus Giles AS .20 .09
❑ 721 Edgar Renteria AS .20 .09
❑ 722 Scott Rolen AS .30 .14
❑ 723 Albert Pujols AS .50 .23
❑ 724 Gary Sheffield AS .20 .09
❑ 725 Javy Lopez AS .20 .09
❑ 726 Eric Gagne AS .30 .14
❑ 727 Randy Wolf AS .20 .09
❑ 728 Bobby Cox AS .20 .09
❑ 729 Scott Podsednik AS .20 .09
❑ 730 Alex Gonzalez WS .30 .14
❑ 731 Brad Penny WS .30 .14
❑ 732 Josh Beckett .30 .14
Ivan Rodriguez
Alex Gonzalez WS
❑ 733 Josh Beckett WS MVP .30 .14

2004 Topps Traded

	Nm-Mt	Ex-Mt
COMPLETE SET (220)	50.00	15.00
COMMON CARD (1-70)	.20	.06
COMMON CARD (71-90)	.50	.15
COMMON CARD (91-110)	.40	.12
COMMON CARD (111-220)	.40	.12

PLATE ODDS 1:1151 H, 1:1173 R, 1:327 HTA
PLATE PRINT RUN 1 SET PER COLOR
BLACK-CYAN-MAGENTA-YELLOW ISSUED
NO PLATE PRICING DUE TO SCARCITY

❑ T1 Pokey Reese .20 .06
❑ T2 Tony Womack .20 .06
❑ T3 Richard Hidalgo .20 .06
❑ T4 Juan Uribe .20 .06
❑ T5 J.D. Drew .20 .06
❑ T6 Alex Gonzalez .20 .06
❑ T7 Carlos Guillen .20 .06
❑ T8 Doug Mientkiewicz .20 .06
❑ T9 Fernando Vina .20 .06
❑ T10 Milton Bradley .20 .06
❑ T11 Kelvim Escobar .20 .06
❑ T12 Ben Grieve .20 .06
❑ T13 Brian Jordan .20 .06
❑ T14 A.J. Pierzynski .20 .06
❑ T15 Billy Wagner .20 .06
❑ T16 Terrence Long .20 .06
❑ T17 Carlos Beltran .30 .09
❑ T18 Carl Everett .20 .06
❑ T19 Reggie Sanders .20 .06
❑ T20 Javy Lopez .20 .06
❑ T21 Jay Payton .20 .06
❑ T22 Octavio Dotel .20 .06
❑ T23 Eddie Guardado .20 .06
❑ T24 Andy Pettitte .30 .09
❑ T25 Richie Sexson .20 .06

❑ T26 Ronnie Belliard .20 .06
❑ T27 Michael Tucker .20 .06
❑ T28 Brad Fullmer .20 .06
❑ T29 Freddy Garcia .20 .06
❑ T30 Bartolo Colon .20 .06
❑ T31 Larry Walker .30 .09
❑ T32 Mark Kotsay .20 .06
❑ T33 Jason Marquis .20 .06
❑ T34 Dustan Mohr .20 .06
❑ T35 Javier Vazquez .20 .06
❑ T36 Nomar Garciaparra .75 .23
❑ T37 Tino Martinez .30 .09
❑ T38 Hee Seop Choi .20 .06
❑ T39 Damian Miller .20 .06
❑ T40 Jose Lima .20 .06
❑ T41 Ty Wigginton .20 .06
❑ T42 Raul Ibanez .20 .06
❑ T43 Danys Baez .20 .06
❑ T44 Tony Clark .20 .06
❑ T45 Greg Maddux .75 .23
❑ T46 Victor Zambrano .20 .06
❑ T47 Orlando Cabrera Sox .20 .06
❑ T48 Jose Cruz Jr. .20 .06
❑ T49 Kris Benson .20 .06
❑ T50 Alex Rodriguez 1.00 .30
❑ T51 Steve Finley .20 .06
❑ T52 Ramon Hernandez .20 .06
❑ T53 Esteban Loaiza .20 .06
❑ T54 Ugueth Urbina .20 .06
❑ T55 Jeff Weaver .20 .06
❑ T56 Flash Gordon .20 .06
❑ T57 Jose Contreras .20 .06
❑ T58 Paul Lo Duca .20 .06
❑ T59 Junior Spivey .20 .06
❑ T60 Curt Schilling .50 .15
❑ T61 Brad Penny .20 .06
❑ T62 Braden Looper .20 .06
❑ T63 Miguel Cairo .20 .06
❑ T64 Juan Encarnacion .20 .06
❑ T65 Miguel Batista .20 .06
❑ T66 Terry Francona MG .20 .06
❑ T67 Lee Mazzilli MG .20 .06
❑ T68 Al Pedrique MG .20 .06
❑ T69 Ozzie Guillen MG .20 .06
❑ T70 Phil Garner MG .20 .06
❑ T71 Matt Bush DP RC 2.50 .75
❑ T72 Homer Bailey DP RC 2.00 .60
❑ T73 Greg Golson DP RC 1.50 .45
❑ T74 Kyle Waldrop DP RC 1.25 .35
❑ T75 Richie Robnett DP RC 1.25 .35
❑ T76 Jay Rainville DP RC 1.25 .35
❑ T77 Bill Bray DP RC .50 .15
❑ T78 Phillip Hughes DP RC 1.25 .35
❑ T79 Scott Elbert DP RC 1.25 .35
❑ T80 Josh Fields DP RC 2.00 .60
❑ T81 Justin Orenduff DP RC 1.25 .35
❑ T82 Dan Putnam DP RC 1.25 .35
❑ T83 Chris Nelson DP RC 2.50 .75
❑ T84 Blake DeWitt DP RC 2.50 .75
❑ T85 J.P. Howell DP RC 1.25 .35
❑ T86 Huston Street DP RC 1.25 .35
❑ T87 Kurt Suzuki DP RC 1.50 .45
❑ T88 Erick San Pedro DP RC .50 .15
❑ T89 Matt Tuiasosopo DP RC 4.00 1.20
❑ T90 Matt Macri DP RC 1.25 .35
❑ T91 Chad Tracy PROS .40 .12
❑ T92 Scott Hairston PROS .40 .12
❑ T93 Jonny Gomes PROS .40 .12
❑ T94 Chin-Feng Chen PROS .40 .12
❑ T95 Chien-Ming Wang PROS .40 .12
❑ T96 Dustin McGowan PROS .40 .12
❑ T97 Chris Burke PROS .40 .12
❑ T98 Denny Bautista PROS .40 .12
❑ T99 Preston Larrison PROS .40 .12
❑ T100 Kevin Youkilis PROS .40 .12
❑ T101 John Maine PROS .40 .12
❑ T102 Guillermo Quiroz PROS .40 .12
❑ T103 Dave Krynzel PROS .40 .12
❑ T104 David Kelton PROS .40 .12
❑ T105 Edwin Encarnacion PROS .40 .12
❑ T106 Chad Gaudin PROS .40 .12
❑ T107 Sergio Mitre PROS .40 .12
❑ T108 Laynce Nix PROS .40 .12
❑ T109 David Parrish PROS .40 .12
❑ T110 Brandon Claussen PROS .40 .12
❑ T111 Frank Francisco FY RC .40 .12
❑ T112 Brian Dallimore FY RC .40 .12
❑ T113 Jim Crowell FY RC .50 .15
❑ T114 Andres Blanco FY RC .40 .12
❑ T115 Eduardo Villacis FY RC .40 .12
❑ T116 Kazuhito Tadano FY RC .50 .15
❑ T117 Aarom Baldiris FY RC .50 .15
❑ T118 Justin Germano FY RC .40 .12
❑ T119 Joey Gathright FY RC 1.25 .35
❑ T120 Franklyn Gracesqui FY RC .40 .12
❑ T121 Chin-Lung Hu FY RC 1.00 .30
❑ T122 Scott Olsen FY RC 1.25 .35
❑ T123 Tyler Davidson FY RC .50 .15
❑ T124 Fausto Carmona FY RC .75 .23
❑ T125 Tim Hutting FY RC .40 .12
❑ T126 Ryan Meaux FY RC .40 .12
❑ T127 Jon Connolly FY RC 1.00 .30
❑ T128 Hector Made FY RC .75 .23
❑ T129 Jamie Brown FY RC .40 .12
❑ T130 Paul McAnulty FY RC .75 .23
❑ T131 Chris Saenz FY RC .40 .12
❑ T132 Marland Williams FY RC .50 .15
❑ T133 Mike Huggins FY RC .40 .12
❑ T134 Jesse Crain FY RC .75 .23
❑ T135 Chad Bentz FY RC .40 .12
❑ T136 Kazuo Matsui FY RC 1.50 .45
❑ T137 Paul Maholm FY RC .75 .23
❑ T138 Brock Jacobsen FY RC .40 .12
❑ T139 Casey Daigle FY RC .40 .12
❑ T140 Nyjer Morgan FY RC .40 .12
❑ T141 Tom Mastny FY RC .40 .12
❑ T142 Kody Kirkland FY RC .75 .23
❑ T143 Jose Capellan FY RC 1.50 .45
❑ T144 Felix Hernandez FY RC 3.00 .90
❑ T145 Shawn Hill FY RC .40 .12
❑ T146 Danny Gonzalez FY RC .40 .12
❑ T147 Scott Dohmann FY RC .40 .12
❑ T148 Tommy Murphy FY RC .40 .12
❑ T149 Akinori Otsuka FY RC .40 .12
❑ T150 Miguel Perez FY RC .40 .12
❑ T151 Mike Rouse FY RC .40 .12
❑ T152 Ramon Ramirez FY RC .40 .12
❑ T153 Luke Hughes FY RC .40 .12
❑ T154 Howie Kendrick FY RC .75 .23
❑ T155 Ryan Budde FY RC .40 .12
❑ T156 Charlie Zink FY RC .40 .12
❑ T157 Warner Madrigal FY RC .75 .23
❑ T158 Jason Szuminski FY RC .40 .12
❑ T159 Chad Chop FY RC .40 .12
❑ T160 Shingo Takatsu FY RC 1.00 .30
❑ T161 Matt Lemanczyk FY RC .40 .12
❑ T162 Wardell Starling FY RC .40 .12
❑ T163 Nick Gorneault FY RC .50 .15
❑ T164 Scott Proctor FY RC .50 .15
❑ T165 Brooks Conrad FY RC .50 .15
❑ T166 Hector Gimenez FY RC .40 .12
❑ T167 Kevin Howard FY RC .50 .15
❑ T168 Vince Perkins FY RC .50 .15
❑ T169 Brock Peterson FY RC .40 .12
❑ T170 Chris Shelton FY RC .75 .23
❑ T171 Erick Aybar FY RC 1.25 .35
❑ T172 Paul Bacot FY RC .50 .15
❑ T173 Matt Capps FY RC .40 .12
❑ T174 Kory Casto FY RC .40 .12
❑ T175 Juan Cedeno FY RC .40 .12
❑ T176 Vito Chiaravalloti FY RC .75 .23
❑ T177 Alec Zumwalt FY RC .40 .12
❑ T178 J.J. Furmaniak FY RC .75 .23
❑ T179 Lee Gwaltney FY RC .40 .12
❑ T180 Donald Kelly FY RC .40 .12
❑ T181 Benji DeQuin FY RC .40 .12
❑ T182 Brant Colamarino FY RC .75 .23
❑ T183 Juan Gutierrez FY RC .40 .12
❑ T184 Carl Loadenthal FY RC .50 .15
❑ T185 Ricky Nolasco FY RC .40 .12
❑ T186 Jeff Salazar FY RC 1.00 .30
❑ T187 Rob Tejeda FY RC .40 .12
❑ T188 Alex Romero FY RC .40 .12
❑ T189 Yoann Torrealba FY RC .40 .12
❑ T190 Carlos Sosa FY RC .40 .12
❑ T191 Tim Bittner FY RC .40 .12
❑ T192 Chris Aguila FY RC .40 .12
❑ T193 Jason Frasor FY RC .40 .12
❑ T194 Reid Gorecki FY RC .40 .12
❑ T195 Dustin Nippert FY RC .40 .12
❑ T196 Javier Guzman FY RC .50 .15
❑ T197 Harvey Garcia FY RC .40 .12
❑ T198 Ivan Ochoa FY RC .40 .12
❑ T199 David Wallace FY RC .50 .15
❑ T200 Joel Zumaya FY RC .75 .23
❑ T201 Casey Kopitzke FY RC .40 .12
❑ T202 Lincoln Holdzkom FY RC .40 .12
❑ T203 Chad Santos FY RC .40 .12
❑ T204 Brian Pilkington FY RC .40 .12
❑ T205 Terry Jones FY RC .50 .15
❑ T206 Jerome Gamble FY RC .40 .12
❑ T207 Brad Eldred FY RC 1.25 .35
❑ T208 David Pauley FY RC .40 .12
❑ T209 Kevin Davidson FY RC .40 .12
❑ T210 Damaso Espino FY RC .40 .12
❑ T211 Tom Farmer FY RC .40 .12
❑ T212 Michael Mooney FY RC .40 .12
❑ T213 James Tomlin FY RC .40 .12
❑ T214 Greg Thissen FY RC .40 .12
❑ T215 Calvin Hayes FY RC .50 .15
❑ T216 Fernando Cortez FY RC .40 .12
❑ T217 Sergio Silva FY RC .40 .12
❑ T218 Jon de Vries FY RC .40 .12
❑ T219 Don Sutton FY RC 1.00 .30
❑ T220 Leo Nunez FY RC .40 .12

2005 Topps

	Nm-Mt	Ex-Mt
COMPLETE SERIES 1 (367)	40.00	12.00
COMMON CARD (1-6/8-368)	.20	.06
COMMON CARD (297-326)	.50	.15
COMMON CARD (327-331)	.50	.15
COMMON (349-355/368)	1.00	.30

CARD NUMBER 7 DOES NOT EXIST
OVERALL PLATE SER.1 ODDS 1:154 HTA
PLATE PRINT RUN 1 SET PER COLOR
BLACK-CYAN-MAGENTA-YELLOW ISSUED
NO PLATE PRICING DUE TO SCARCITY

❑ 1 Alex Rodriguez .75 .23
❑ 2 Placido Polanco .20 .06
❑ 3 Torii Hunter .20 .06
❑ 4 Lyle Overbay .20 .06
❑ 5 Johnny Damon .50 .15
❑ 6 Johnny Estrada .20 .06
❑ 7 Does Not Exist .00
❑ 8 Francisco Rodriguez .20 .06
❑ 9 Jason LaRue .20 .06
❑ 10 Sammy Sosa .75 .23
❑ 11 Randy Wolf .20 .06
❑ 12 Jason Bay .20 .06
❑ 13 Tom Glavine .30 .09
❑ 14 Michael Tucker .20 .06
❑ 15 Brian Giles .20 .06
❑ 16 Dan Wilson .20 .06
❑ 17 Jim Edmonds .20 .06
❑ 18 Danys Baez .20 .06
❑ 19 Roy Halladay .20 .06
❑ 20 Hank Blalock .20 .06
❑ 21 Darin Erstad .20 .06
❑ 22 Robby Hammock .20 .06
❑ 23 Mike Hampton .20 .06
❑ 24 Mark Bellhorn .30 .09
❑ 25 Jim Thome .50 .15
❑ 26 Scott Schoeneweis .20 .06
❑ 27 Jody Gerut .20 .06
❑ 28 Vinny Castilla .20 .06
❑ 29 Luis Castillo .20 .06
❑ 30 Ivan Rodriguez .50 .15

❑ 31 Craig Biggio .30 .09
❑ 32 Joe Randa .20 .06
❑ 33 Adrian Beltre .30 .09
❑ 34 Scott Podsednik .20 .06
❑ 35 Cliff Floyd .20 .06
❑ 36 Livan Hernandez .20 .06
❑ 37 Eric Byrnes .20 .06
❑ 38 Gabe Kapler .20 .06
❑ 39 Jack Wilson .20 .06
❑ 40 Gary Sheffield .20 .06
❑ 41 Chan Ho Park .20 .06
❑ 42 Carl Crawford .20 .06
❑ 43 Miguel Batista .20 .06
❑ 44 David Bell .20 .06
❑ 45 Jeff DaVanon .20 .06
❑ 46 Brandon Webb .20 .06
❑ 47 Bronson Arroyo .20 .06
❑ 48 Melvin Mora .20 .06
❑ 49 David Ortiz .50 .15
❑ 50 Andruw Jones .20 .06
❑ 51 Chone Figgins .20 .06
❑ 52 Danny Graves .20 .06
❑ 53 Preston Wilson .20 .06
❑ 54 Jeremy Bonderman .20 .06
❑ 55 Chad Fox .20 .06
❑ 56 Dan Miceli .20 .06
❑ 57 Jimmy Gobble .20 .06
❑ 58 Darren Dreifort .20 .06
❑ 59 Matt LeCroy .20 .06
❑ 60 Jose Vidro .20 .06
❑ 61 Al Leiter .20 .06
❑ 62 Javier Vazquez .20 .06
❑ 63 Erubiel Durazo .20 .06
❑ 64 Doug Glanville .20 .06
❑ 65 Scot Shields .20 .06
❑ 66 Edgardo Alfonzo .20 .06
❑ 67 Ryan Franklin .20 .06
❑ 68 Francisco Cordero .20 .06
❑ 69 Brett Myers .20 .06
❑ 70 Curt Schilling .50 .15
❑ 71 Matt Kata .20 .06
❑ 72 Mark DeRosa .20 .06
❑ 73 Rodrigo Lopez .20 .06
❑ 74 Tim Wakefield .30 .09
❑ 75 Frank Thomas .50 .15
❑ 76 Jimmy Rollins .20 .06
❑ 77 Barry Zito .20 .06
❑ 78 Hideo Nomo .50 .15
❑ 79 Brad Wilkerson .20 .06
❑ 80 Adam Dunn .30 .09
❑ 81 Billy Traber .20 .06
❑ 82 Fernando Vina .20 .06
❑ 83 Nate Robertson .20 .06
❑ 84 Brad Ausmus .20 .06
❑ 85 Mike Sweeney .20 .06
❑ 86 Kip Wells .20 .06
❑ 87 Chris Reitsma .20 .06
❑ 88 Zach Day .20 .06
❑ 89 Tony Clark .20 .06
❑ 90 Bret Boone .20 .06
❑ 91 Mark Loretta .20 .06
❑ 92 Jerome Williams .20 .06
❑ 93 Randy Winn .20 .06
❑ 94 Marlon Anderson .20 .06
❑ 95 Aubrey Huff .20 .06
❑ 96 Kevin Mench .20 .06
❑ 97 Frank Catalanotto .20 .06
❑ 98 Flash Gordon .20 .06
❑ 99 Scott Hatteberg .20 .06
❑ 100 Albert Pujols 1.00 .30
❑ 101 Jose/Bengie Molina .20 .06
❑ 102 Oscar Villarreal .20 .06
❑ 103 Jay Gibbons .20 .06
❑ 104 Byung-Hyun Kim .20 .06
❑ 105 Joe Borowski .20 .06
❑ 106 Mark Grudzielanek .20 .06
❑ 107 Mark Buehrle .20 .06
❑ 108 Paul Wilson .20 .06
❑ 109 Ronnie Belliard .20 .06
❑ 110 Reggie Sanders .20 .06
❑ 111 Tim Redding .20 .06
❑ 112 Brian Lawrence .20 .06
❑ 113 Darrell May .20 .06
❑ 114 Jose Hernandez .20 .06
❑ 115 Ben Sheets .20 .06
❑ 116 Johan Santana .30 .09
❑ 117 Billy Wagner .20 .06
❑ 118 Mariano Rivera .30 .09
❑ 119 Steve Trachsel .20 .06
❑ 120 Akinori Otsuka .20 .06
❑ 121 Bobby Kielty .20 .06
❑ 122 Orlando Hernandez .20 .06
❑ 123 Raul Ibanez .20 .06
❑ 124 Mike Matheny .20 .06
❑ 125 Vernon Wells .20 .06
❑ 126 Jason Isringhausen .20 .06
❑ 127 Jose Guillen .20 .06
❑ 128 Danny Bautista .20 .06
❑ 129 Marcus Giles .20 .06
❑ 130 Javy Lopez .20 .06
❑ 131 Kevin Millar .30 .09
❑ 132 Kyle Farnsworth .20 .06
❑ 133 Carl Pavano .20 .06
❑ 134 D'Angelo Jimenez .20 .06
❑ 135 Casey Blake .20 .06
❑ 136 Matt Holliday .20 .06
❑ 137 Bobby Higginson .20 .06
❑ 138 Nate Field .20 .06
❑ 139 Alex Gonzalez .20 .06
❑ 140 Jeff Kent .20 .06
❑ 141 Aaron Guiel .20 .06
❑ 142 Shawn Green .20 .06
❑ 143 Bill Hall .20 .06
❑ 144 Shannon Stewart .20 .06
❑ 145 Juan Rivera .20 .06
❑ 146 Coco Crisp .20 .06
❑ 147 Mike Mussina .30 .09
❑ 148 Eric Chavez .20 .06
❑ 149 Jon Lieber .20 .06
❑ 150 Vladimir Guerrero .50 .15
❑ 151 Alex Cintron .20 .06
❑ 152 Horacio Ramirez .20 .06
❑ 153 Sidney Ponson .20 .06
❑ 154 Trot Nixon .30 .09
❑ 155 Greg Maddux .75 .23
❑ 156 Edgar Renteria .20 .06
❑ 157 Ryan Freel .20 .06
❑ 158 Matt Lawton .20 .06
❑ 159 Shawn Chacon .20 .06
❑ 160 Josh Beckett .20 .06
❑ 161 Ken Harvey .20 .06
❑ 162 Juan Cruz .20 .06
❑ 163 Juan Encarnacion .20 .06
❑ 164 Wes Helms .20 .06
❑ 165 Brad Radke .20 .06
❑ 166 Claudio Vargas .20 .06
❑ 167 Mike Cameron .20 .06
❑ 168 Billy Koch .20 .06
❑ 169 Bobby Crosby .20 .06
❑ 170 Mike Lieberthal .20 .06
❑ 171 Rob Mackowiak .20 .06
❑ 172 Sean Burroughs .20 .06
❑ 173 J.T. Snow Jr. .20 .06
❑ 174 Paul Konerko .20 .06
❑ 175 Luis Gonzalez .20 .06
❑ 176 John Lackey .20 .06
❑ 177 Antonio Alfonseca .20 .06
❑ 178 Brian Roberts .20 .06
❑ 179 Bill Mueller .30 .09
❑ 180 Carlos Lee .20 .06
❑ 181 Corey Patterson .20 .06
❑ 182 Sean Casey .20 .06
❑ 183 Cliff Lee .20 .06
❑ 184 Jason Jennings .20 .06
❑ 185 Dmitri Young .20 .06
❑ 186 Juan Uribe .20 .06
❑ 187 Andy Pettitte .30 .09
❑ 188 Juan Gonzalez .30 .09
❑ 189 Pokey Reese .20 .06
❑ 190 Jason Phillips .20 .06
❑ 191 Rocky Biddle .20 .06
❑ 192 Lew Ford .20 .06
❑ 193 Mark Mulder .20 .06
❑ 194 Bobby Abreu .20 .06
❑ 195 Jason Kendall .20 .06
❑ 196 Terrence Long .20 .06
❑ 197 A.J. Pierzynski .20 .06
❑ 198 Eddie Guardado .20 .06
❑ 199 So Taguchi .20 .06
❑ 200 Jason Giambi .20 .06
❑ 201 Tony Batista .20 .06
❑ 202 Kyle Lohse .20 .06
❑ 203 Trevor Hoffman .20 .06
❑ 204 Tike Redman .20 .06
❑ 205 Matt Herges .20 .06
❑ 206 Gil Meche .20 .06
❑ 207 Chris Carpenter .20 .06
❑ 208 Ben Broussard .20 .06
❑ 209 Eric Young .20 .06
❑ 210 Doug Waechter .20 .06
❑ 211 Jarrod Washburn .20 .06
❑ 212 Chad Tracy .20 .06
❑ 213 John Smoltz .30 .09
❑ 214 Jorge Julio .20 .06
❑ 215 Todd Walker .20 .06
❑ 216 Shingo Takatsu .20 .06
❑ 217 Jose Acevedo .20 .06
❑ 218 David Riske .20 .06
❑ 219 Shawn Estes .20 .06
❑ 220 Lance Berkman .20 .06
❑ 221 Carlos Guillen .20 .06
❑ 222 Jeremy Affeldt .20 .06
❑ 223 Cesar Izturis .20 .06
❑ 224 Scott Sullivan .20 .06
❑ 225 Kazuo Matsui .30 .09
❑ 226 Josh Fogg .20 .06
❑ 227 Jason Schmidt .20 .06
❑ 228 Jason Marquis .20 .06
❑ 229 Scott Spiezio .20 .06
❑ 230 Miguel Tejada .20 .06
❑ 231 Bartolo Colon .20 .06
❑ 232 Jose Valverde .20 .06
❑ 233 Derrek Lee .20 .06
❑ 234 Scott Williamson .20 .06
❑ 235 Joe Crede .20 .06
❑ 236 John Thomson .20 .06
❑ 237 Mike MacDougal .20 .06
❑ 238 Eric Gagne .50 .15
❑ 239 Alex Sanchez .20 .06
❑ 240 Miguel Cabrera .30 .09
❑ 241 Luis Rivas .20 .06
❑ 242 Adam Everett .20 .06
❑ 243 Jason Johnson .20 .06
❑ 244 Travis Hafner .20 .06
❑ 245 Jose Valentin .20 .06
❑ 246 Stephen Randolph .20 .06
❑ 247 Rafael Furcal .20 .06
❑ 248 Adam Kennedy .20 .06
❑ 249 Luis Matos .20 .06
❑ 250 Mark Prior .50 .15
❑ 251 Angel Berroa .20 .06
❑ 252 Phil Nevin .20 .06
❑ 253 Oliver Perez .20 .06
❑ 254 Orlando Hudson .20 .06
❑ 255 Braden Looper .20 .06
❑ 256 Khalil Greene .30 .09
❑ 257 Tim Worrell .20 .06
❑ 258 Carlos Zambrano .20 .06
❑ 259 Odalis Perez .20 .06
❑ 260 Gerald Laird .20 .06
❑ 261 Jose Cruz Jr. .20 .06
❑ 262 Michael Barrett .20 .06
❑ 263 Michael Young .20 .06
❑ 264 Toby Hall .20 .06
❑ 265 Woody Williams .20 .06
❑ 266 Rich Harden .20 .06
❑ 267 Mike Scioscia MG .20 .06
❑ 268 Al Pedrique MG .20 .06
❑ 269 Bobby Cox MG .20 .06
❑ 270 Lee Mazzilli MG .20 .06
❑ 271 Terry Francona MG .30 .09
❑ 272 Dusty Baker MG .20 .06
❑ 273 Ozzie Guillen MG .20 .06
❑ 274 Dave Miley MG .20 .06
❑ 275 Eric Wedge MG .20 .06
❑ 276 Clint Hurdle MG .20 .06
❑ 277 Alan Trammell MG .20 .06
❑ 278 Jack McKeon MG .20 .06
❑ 279 Phil Garner MG .20 .06
❑ 280 Tony Pena MG .20 .06
❑ 281 Jim Tracy MG .20 .06
❑ 282 Ned Yost MG .20 .06
❑ 283 Ron Gardenhire MG .20 .06
❑ 284 Frank Robinson MG .20 .06
❑ 285 Art Howe MG .20 .06
❑ 286 Joe Torre MG .30 .09
❑ 287 Ken Macha MG .20 .06
❑ 288 Larry Bowa MG .20 .06

❑ 289 Lloyd McClendon MG	.20	.06
❑ 290 Bruce Bochy MG	.20	.06
❑ 291 Felipe Alou MG	.20	.06
❑ 292 Bob Melvin MG	.20	.06
❑ 293 Tony LaRussa MG	.20	.06
❑ 294 Lou Piniella MG	.20	.06
❑ 295 Buck Showalter MG	.20	.06
❑ 296 John Gibbons MG	.20	.06
❑ 297 Steve Doetsch FY RC	.50	.15
❑ 298 Melky Cabrera FY RC	1.00	.30
❑ 299 Luis Ramirez FY RC	.50	.15
❑ 300 Chris Seddon FY RC	.50	.15
❑ 301 Nate Schierholtz FY	.75	.23
❑ 302 Ian Kinsler FY RC	1.00	.30
❑ 303 Brandon Moss FY RC	1.00	.30
❑ 304 Chadd Blasko FY RC	.50	.15
❑ 305 Jeremy West FY RC	1.00	.30
❑ 306 Sean Marshall FY RC	.50	.15
❑ 307 Matt DeSalvo FY RC	.50	.15
❑ 308 Ryan Sweeney FY RC	1.00	.30
❑ 309 Matthew Lindstrom FY RC	.50	.15
❑ 310 Ryan Goleski FY RC	.75	.23
❑ 311 Brett Harper FY RC	.50	.15
❑ 312 Chris Roberson FY RC	.50	.15
❑ 313 Andre Ethier FY RC	.75	.23
❑ 314 Chris Denorfia FY RC	.50	.15
❑ 315 Ian Bladergroen FY RC	1.00	.30
❑ 316 Darren Fenster FY RC	.50	.15
❑ 317 Kevin West FY RC	.75	.23
❑ 318 Chaz Lytle FY RC	.75	.23
❑ 319 James Jurries FY RC	.50	.15
❑ 320 Matt Rogelstad FY RC	.50	.15
❑ 321 Wade Robinson FY RC	.50	.15
❑ 322 Jake Dittler FY	.50	.15
❑ 323 Brian Stavisky FY RC	.50	.15
❑ 324 Kole Strayhorn FY RC	.50	.15
❑ 325 Jose Vaquedano FY RC	.50	.15
❑ 326 Elvys Quezada FY RC	.50	.15
❑ 327 John Maine	.50	.15
Val Majewski FS		
❑ 328 Rickie Weeks	.50	.15
J.J. Hardy FS		
❑ 329 Gabe Gross	.50	.15
Guillermo Quiroz FS		
❑ 330 David Wright	3.00	.90
Craig Brazell FS		
❑ 331 Dallas McPherson	.50	.15
Jeff Mathis FS		
❑ 332 Randy Johnson SH	.30	.09
❑ 333 Randy Johnson SH	.30	.09
❑ 334 Ichiro Suzuki SH	.50	.15
❑ 335 Ken Griffey Jr. SH	.50	.15
❑ 336 Greg Maddux SH	.50	.15
❑ 337 Ichiro Suzuki	.50	.15
Melvin Mora		
Vladimir Guerrero LL		
❑ 338 Ichiro Suzuki	.50	.15
Michael Young		
Vladimir Guerrero LL		
❑ 339 Manny Ramirez	.50	.15
Paul Konerko		
David Ortiz LL		
❑ 340 Miguel Tejada	.50	.15
David Ortiz		
Manny Ramirez LL		
❑ 341 Johan Santana	.50	.15
Curt Schilling		
Jake Westbrook LL		
❑ 342 Johan Santana	.50	.15
Pedro Martinez		
Curt Schilling LL		
❑ 343 Todd Helton	.30	.09
Mark Loretta		
Adrian Beltre LL		
❑ 344 Juan Pierre	.20	.06
Mark Loretta		
Jack Wilson LL		
❑ 345 Adrian Beltre	.50	.15
Adam Dunn		
Albert Pujols LL		
❑ 346 Vinny Castilla	.50	.15
Scott Rolen		
Albert Pujols LL		
❑ 347 Jake Peavy	.30	.09
Randy Johnson		
Ben Sheets LL		
❑ 348 Randy Johnson	.30	.09
Ben Sheets		
Jason Schmidt LL		
❑ 349 Alex Rodriguez	1.00	.30
Ruben Sierra ALDS		
❑ 350 Larry Walker	1.00	.30
Albert Pujols NLDS		
❑ 351 Curt Schilling	1.00	.30
David Ortiz ALDS		
❑ 352 Curt Schilling WS2	1.00	.30
❑ 353 Sox Celebration	1.00	.30
David Ortiz		
Curt Schilling ALCS		
❑ 354 Cards Celebration	1.00	.30
Albert Pujols		
Jim Edmonds NLCS		
❑ 355 Mark Bellhorn WS1	1.00	.30
❑ 356 Paul Konerko AS	.20	.06
❑ 357 Alfonso Soriano AS	.20	.06
❑ 358 Miguel Tejada AS	.20	.06
❑ 359 Melvin Mora AS	.20	.06
❑ 360 Vladimir Guerrero AS	.30	.09
❑ 361 Ichiro Suzuki AS	.50	.15
❑ 362 Manny Ramirez AS	.20	.06
❑ 363 Ivan Rodriguez AS	.30	.09
❑ 364 Johan Santana AS	.20	.06
❑ 365 Paul Konerko AS	.20	.06
❑ 366 David Ortiz AS	.30	.09
❑ 367 Bobby Crosby AS	.20	.06
❑ 368 Sox Celebration	2.00	.60
Manny Ramirez		
Derek Lowe WS4		

2003 Topps 205

	Nm-Mt	Ex-Mt
COMPLETE SERIES 1 (165)	40.00	12.00
COMPLETE SERIES 2 (175)	125.00	38.00
COMP.SERIES 2 w/o SP's (155)	40.00	12.00
COM (1-130/161-169/193-315)	.50	.15
COMMON (131-145/170-192)	.50	.15
COMMON (146-150)	1.00	.30
COMMON SP	2.50	.75
SERIES 2 SP STATED ODDS 1:5		

❑ 1A Barry Bonds w/Cap	3.00	.90
❑ 1B Barry Bonds w/Helmet	3.00	.90
❑ 2 Bret Boone	.50	.15
❑ 3A Albert Pujols Clear Logo	2.50	.75
❑ 3B Albert Pujols White Logo	2.50	.75
❑ 4 Carl Crawford	.50	.15
❑ 5 Bartolo Colon	.50	.15
❑ 6 Cliff Floyd	.50	.15
❑ 7 John Olerud	.50	.15
❑ 8A Jason Giambi Full Jkt	.50	.15
❑ 8B Jason Giambi Partial Jkt	.50	.15
❑ 9 Edgardo Alfonzo	.50	.15
❑ 10 Ivan Rodriguez	1.25	.35
❑ 11 Jim Edmonds	.50	.15
❑ 12A Mike Piazza Orange	2.00	.60
❑ 12B Mike Piazza Yellow	2.00	.60
❑ 13 Greg Maddux	2.00	.60
❑ 14 Jose Vidro	.50	.15
❑ 15A Vlad Guerrero Clear Logo	1.25	.35
❑ 15B V.Guerrero White Logo	1.25	.35
❑ 16 Bernie Williams	.75	.23
❑ 17 Roger Clemens	2.50	.75
❑ 18A Miguel Tejada Blue	.50	.15
❑ 18B Miguel Tejada Green	.50	.15
❑ 19 Carlos Delgado	.50	.15
❑ 20A Alfonso Soriano w/Bat	.75	.23
❑ 20B Alf. Soriano Sunglasses	.75	.23
❑ 21 Bobby Cox MG	.50	.15
❑ 22 Mike Scioscia	.50	.15
❑ 23 John Smoltz	.75	.23
❑ 24 Luis Gonzalez	.50	.15
❑ 25 Shawn Green	.50	.15
❑ 26 Raul Ibanez	.50	.15
❑ 27 Andruw Jones	.50	.15
❑ 28 Josh Beckett	.50	.15
❑ 29 Derek Lowe	.50	.15
❑ 30 Todd Helton	.75	.23
❑ 31 Barry Larkin	.75	.23
❑ 32 Jason Jennings	.50	.15
❑ 33 Darin Erstad	.50	.15
❑ 34 Magglio Ordonez	.50	.15
❑ 35 Mike Sweeney	.50	.15
❑ 36 Kazuhisa Ishii	.50	.15
❑ 37 Ron Gardenhire MG	.50	.15
❑ 38 Tim Hudson	.50	.15
❑ 39 Tim Salmon	.75	.23
❑ 40A Pat Burrell Black Bat	.50	.15
❑ 40B Pat Burrell Brown Bat	.50	.15
❑ 41 Manny Ramirez	.75	.23
❑ 42 Nick Johnson	.50	.15
❑ 43 Tom Glavine	.75	.23
❑ 44 Mark Mulder	.50	.15
❑ 45 Brian Jordan	.50	.15
❑ 46 Rafael Palmeiro	.75	.23
❑ 47 Vernon Wells	.50	.15
❑ 48 Bob Brenly MG	.50	.15
❑ 49 C.C. Sabathia	.50	.15
❑ 50A A.Rodriguez Look Ahead	2.00	.60
❑ 50B A.Rodriguez Look Away	2.00	.60
❑ 51A Sammy Sosa Head Duck	2.00	.60
❑ 51B Sammy Sosa Head Left	2.00	.60
❑ 52 Paul Konerko	.50	.15
❑ 53 Craig Biggio	.75	.23
❑ 54 Moises Alou	.50	.15
❑ 55 Johnny Damon	1.25	.35
❑ 56 Torii Hunter	.50	.15
❑ 57 Omar Vizquel	.75	.23
❑ 58 Orlando Hernandez	.50	.15
❑ 59 Barry Zito	.50	.15
❑ 60 Lance Berkman	.50	.15
❑ 61 Carlos Beltran	.75	.23
❑ 62 Edgar Renteria	.50	.15
❑ 63 Ben Sheets	.50	.15
❑ 64 Doug Mientkiewicz	.50	.15
❑ 65 Troy Glaus	.50	.15
❑ 66 Preston Wilson	.50	.15
❑ 67 Kerry Wood	1.25	.35
❑ 68 Frank Thomas	1.25	.35
❑ 69 Jimmy Rollins	.50	.15
❑ 70 Brian Giles	.50	.15
❑ 71 Bobby Higginson	.50	.15
❑ 72 Larry Walker	.75	.23
❑ 73 Randy Johnson	1.25	.35
❑ 74 Tony LaRussa MG	.50	.15
❑ 75A Derek Jeter w/Gold Trim	3.00	.90
❑ 75B D.Jeter w/o Gold Trim	3.00	.90
❑ 76 Bobby Abreu	.50	.15
❑ 77A A.Dunn Closed Mouth	.75	.23
❑ 77B Adam Dunn Open Mouth	.75	.23
❑ 78 Ryan Klesko	.50	.15
❑ 79 Francisco Rodriguez	.50	.15
❑ 80 Scott Rolen	1.25	.35
❑ 81 Roberto Alomar	.75	.23
❑ 82 Joe Torre MG	.75	.23
❑ 83 Jim Thome	1.25	.35
❑ 84 Kevin Millwood	.50	.15
❑ 85 J.T. Snow	.50	.15
❑ 86 Trevor Hoffman	.50	.15
❑ 87 Jay Gibbons	.50	.15
❑ 88A Mark Prior New Logo	1.25	.35
❑ 88B Mark Prior Old Logo	1.25	.35
❑ 89 Rich Aurilia	.50	.15
❑ 90 Chipper Jones	1.25	.35
❑ 91 Richie Sexson	.50	.15
❑ 92 Gary Sheffield	.50	.15
❑ 93 Pedro Martinez	1.25	.35
❑ 94 Rodrigo Lopez	.50	.15
❑ 95 Al Leiter	.50	.15
❑ 96 Jorge Posada	.75	.23

Card	Nm-Mt	Ex-Mt
❑ 97 Luis Castillo	.50	.15
❑ 98 Aubrey Huff	.50	.15
❑ 99 A.J. Pierzynski	.50	.15
❑ 100A I.Suzuki Look Ahead	2.00	.60
❑ 100B Ichiro Suzuki Look Right	2.00	.60
❑ 101 Eric Chavez	.50	.15
❑ 102 Brett Myers	.50	.15
❑ 103 Jason Kendall	.50	.15
❑ 104 Jeff Kent	.50	.15
❑ 105 Eric Hinske	.50	.15
❑ 106 Jacque Jones	.50	.15
❑ 107 Phil Nevin	.50	.15
❑ 108 Roy Oswalt	.50	.15
❑ 109 Curt Schilling	.50	.15
❑ 110A N.Garciaparra w/Gold Trim	2.00	.60
❑ 110B N.Garciaparra w/o Gold Trim	2.00	.60
❑ 111 Garret Anderson	.50	.15
❑ 112 Eric Gagne	1.25	.35
❑ 113 Javier Vazquez	.50	.15
❑ 114 Jeff Bagwell	.75	.23
❑ 115 Mike Lowell	.50	.15
❑ 116 Carlos Pena	.50	.15
❑ 117 Ken Griffey Jr.	2.00	.60
❑ 118 Tony Batista	.50	.15
❑ 119 Edgar Martinez	.75	.23
❑ 120 Austin Kearns	.50	.15
❑ 121 Jason Stokes PROS	.75	.23
❑ 122 Jose Reyes PROS	.50	.15
❑ 123 Rocco Baldelli PROS	.50	.15
❑ 124 Joe Borchard PROS	.50	.15
❑ 125 Joe Mauer PROS	1.25	.35
❑ 126 Gavin Floyd PROS	.50	.15
❑ 127 Mark Teixeira PROS	.50	.15
❑ 128 Jeremy Guthrie PROS	.50	.15
❑ 129 B.J. Upton PROS	1.50	.45
❑ 130 Khalil Greene PROS	2.50	.75
❑ 131 Hanley Ramirez FY RC	2.50	.75
❑ 132 Andy Marte FY RC	3.00	.90
❑ 133 J.D. Durbin FY RC	1.00	.30
❑ 134 Jason Kubel FY RC	2.50	.75
❑ 135 Craig Brazell FY RC	.60	.18
❑ 136 Bryan Bullington FY RC	1.50	.45
❑ 137 Jose Contreras FY RC	1.25	.35
❑ 138 Brian Burgamy FY RC	.50	.15
❑ 139 E.Bastida-Martinez FY RC	.50	.15
❑ 140 Joey Gomes FY RC	.50	.15
❑ 141 Ismael Castro FY RC	.60	.18
❑ 142 Travis Wong FY RC	.60	.18
❑ 143 Mi.Garciaparra FY RC	1.00	.30
❑ 144 Arnaldo Munoz FY RC	.50	.15
❑ 145 Louis Sockalexis FY XRC	.50	.15
❑ 146 Richard Hoblitzell REP	1.00	.30
❑ 147 George Graham REP	1.00	.30
❑ 148 Hal Chase REP	1.00	.30
❑ 149 John McGraw REP	1.50	.45
❑ 150 Bobby Wallace REP	1.00	.30
❑ 151 David Shean REP	1.00	.30
❑ 152 Richard Hoblitzell REP SP	2.50	.75
❑ 153 Hal Chase REP	1.00	.30
❑ 154 Hooks Wiltse REP	1.00	.30
❑ 155 George Brett RET	4.00	1.20
❑ 156 Willie Mays RET	3.00	.90
❑ 157 Honus Wagner RET SP	10.00	3.00
❑ 158 Nolan Ryan RET	4.00	1.20
❑ 159 Reggie Jackson RET	1.50	.45
❑ 160 Mike Schmidt RET	3.00	.90
❑ 161 Josh Barfield PROS	.50	.15
❑ 162 Grady Sizemore PROS	.50	.15
❑ 163 Justin Morneau PROS	.75	.23
❑ 164 Laynce Nix PROS	.50	.15
❑ 165 Zack Greinke PROS	.75	.23
❑ 166 Victor Martinez PROS	.75	.23
❑ 167 Jeff Mathis PROS	.50	.15
❑ 168 Casey Kotchman PROS	.75	.23
❑ 169 Gabe Gross PROS	.50	.15
❑ 170 Edwin Jackson FY RC	3.00	.90
❑ 171 Delmon Young FY SP RC	12.00	3.60
❑ 172 Eric Duncan FY SP RC	6.00	1.80
❑ 173 Brian Snyder FY SP RC	5.00	1.50
❑ 174 Chris Lubanski FY SP RC	6.00	1.80
❑ 175 Ryan Harvey FY SP RC	6.00	1.80
❑ 176 Nick Markakis FY SP RC	5.00	1.50
❑ 177 Chad Billingsley FY SP RC	6.00	1.80
❑ 178 Elizardo Ramirez FY RC	1.00	.30
❑ 179 Ben Francisco FY RC	.60	.18
❑ 180 Franklin Gutierrez FY SP RC	8.00	2.40
❑ 181 Aaron Hill FY SP RC	5.00	1.50
❑ 182 Kevin Correia FY RC	.50	.15
❑ 183 Kelly Shoppach FY RC	1.25	.35
❑ 184 Felix Pie FY SP RC	8.00	2.40
❑ 185 Adam Loewen FY SP RC	5.00	1.50
❑ 186 Danny Garcia FY RC	.50	.15
❑ 187 Rickie Weeks FY SP RC	10.00	3.00
❑ 188 Robby Hammock FY SP RC	5.00	1.50
❑ 189 Ryan Wagner FY SP RC	5.00	1.50
❑ 190 Matt Kata FY SP RC	5.00	1.50
❑ 191 Bo Hart FY SP RC	5.00	1.50
❑ 192 Brandon Webb FY SP RC	5.00	1.50
❑ 193 Bengie Molina	.50	.15
❑ 194 Junior Spivey	.50	.15
❑ 195 Gary Sheffield	.50	.15
❑ 196 Jason Johnson	.50	.15
❑ 197 David Ortiz	.75	.23
❑ 198 Roberto Alomar	.75	.23
❑ 199 Wily Mo Pena	.50	.15
❑ 200 Sammy Sosa	2.00	.60
❑ 201 Jay Payton	.50	.15
❑ 202 Dmitri Young	.50	.15
❑ 203 Derrek Lee	.50	.15
❑ 204A Jeff Bagwell w/Hat	.75	.23
❑ 204B Jeff Bagwell w/o Hat	.75	.23
❑ 205 Runelvys Hernandez	.50	.15
❑ 206 Kevin Brown	.50	.15
❑ 207 Wes Helms	.50	.15
❑ 208 Eddie Guardado	.50	.15
❑ 209 Orlando Cabrera	.50	.15
❑ 210 Alfonso Soriano	.75	.23
❑ 211 Ty Wigginton	.50	.15
❑ 212A Rich Harden Look Left	.75	.23
❑ 212B Rich Harden Look Right	.75	.23
❑ 213 Mike Lieberthal	.50	.15
❑ 214 Brian Giles	.50	.15
❑ 215 Jason Schmidt	.50	.15
❑ 216 Jamie Moyer	.50	.15
❑ 217 Matt Morris	.50	.15
❑ 218 Victor Zambrano	.50	.15
❑ 219 Roy Halladay	.50	.15
❑ 220 Mike Hampton	.50	.15
❑ 221 Kevin Millar Sox	.50	.15
❑ 222 Hideo Nomo	1.25	.35
❑ 223 Milton Bradley	.50	.15
❑ 224 Jose Guillen	.50	.15
❑ 225 Derek Jeter	3.00	.90
❑ 226 Rondell White	.50	.15
❑ 227A Hank Blalock Blue Jsy	.75	.23
❑ 227B Hank Blalock White Jsy	.75	.23
❑ 228 Shigetoshi Hasegawa	.50	.15
❑ 229 Mike Mussina	.75	.23
❑ 230 Cristian Guzman	.50	.15
❑ 231A Todd Helton Blue	.75	.23
❑ 231B Todd Helton Green	.75	.23
❑ 232 Kenny Lofton	.50	.15
❑ 233 Carl Everett	.50	.15
❑ 234 Shea Hillenbrand	.50	.15
❑ 235 Brad Fullmer	.50	.15
❑ 236 Bernie Williams	.75	.23
❑ 237 Vicente Padilla	.50	.15
❑ 238 Tim Worrell	.50	.15
❑ 239 Juan Gonzalez	.75	.23
❑ 240 Ichiro Suzuki	2.00	.60
❑ 241 Aaron Boone	.50	.15
❑ 242 Shannon Stewart	.50	.15
❑ 243A Barry Zito Blue	.50	.15
❑ 243B Barry Zito Green	.50	.15
❑ 244 Reggie Sanders	.50	.15
❑ 245 Scott Podsednik	.50	.15
❑ 246 Miguel Cabrera	1.25	.35
❑ 247 Angel Berroa	.50	.15
❑ 248 Carlos Zambrano	.50	.15
❑ 249 Marlon Byrd	.50	.15
❑ 250 Mark Prior	1.25	.35
❑ 251 Esteban Loaiza	.50	.15
❑ 252 David Eckstein	.50	.15
❑ 253 Alex Cintron	.50	.15
❑ 254 Melvin Mora	.50	.15
❑ 255 Russ Ortiz	.50	.15
❑ 256 Carlos Lee	.50	.15
❑ 257 Tino Martinez	.75	.23
❑ 258 Randy Wolf	.50	.15
❑ 259 Jason Phillips	.50	.15
❑ 260 Vladimir Guerrero	1.25	.35
❑ 261 Brad Wilkerson	.50	.15
❑ 262 Ivan Rodriguez	1.25	.35
❑ 263 Matt Lawton	.50	.15
❑ 264 Adam Dunn	.75	.23
❑ 265 Joe Borowski	.50	.15
❑ 266 Jody Gerut	.50	.15
❑ 267 Alex Rodriguez	2.00	.60
❑ 268 Brendan Donnelly	.50	.15
❑ 269A Randy Johnson Grey	1.25	.35
❑ 269B Randy Johnson Pink	1.25	.35
❑ 270 Nomar Garciaparra	2.00	.60
❑ 271 Javy Lopez	.50	.15
❑ 272 Travis Hafner	.50	.15
❑ 273 Juan Pierre	.50	.15
❑ 274 Morgan Ensberg	.50	.15
❑ 275 Albert Pujols	2.50	.75
❑ 276 Jason LaRue	.50	.15
❑ 277 Paul Lo Duca	.50	.15
❑ 278 Andy Pettitte	.75	.23
❑ 279 Mike Piazza	2.00	.60
❑ 280A Jim Thome Blue	1.25	.35
❑ 280B Jim Thome Green	1.25	.35
❑ 281 Marquis Grissom	.50	.15
❑ 282 Woody Williams	.50	.15
❑ 283A Curt Schilling Look Ahead	.50	.15
❑ 283B Curt Schilling Look Right	.50	.15
❑ 284A Chipper Jones Blue	1.25	.35
❑ 284B Chipper Jones Yellow	1.25	.35
❑ 285 Deivi Cruz	.50	.15
❑ 286 Johnny Damon	1.25	.35
❑ 287 Chin-Hui Tsao	.50	.15
❑ 288 Alex Gonzalez	.50	.15
❑ 289 Billy Wagner	.50	.15
❑ 290 Jason Giambi	.50	.15
❑ 291 Keith Foulke	.50	.15
❑ 292 Jerome Williams	.50	.15
❑ 293 Livan Hernandez	.50	.15
❑ 294 Aaron Guiel	.50	.15
❑ 295 Randall Simon	.50	.15
❑ 296 Byung-Hyun Kim	.50	.15
❑ 297 Jorge Julio	.50	.15
❑ 298 Miguel Batista	.50	.15
❑ 299 Rafael Furcal	.50	.15
❑ 300A Dontrelle Willis No Smile	.75	.23
❑ 300B Dontrelle Willis Smile SP	4.00	1.20
❑ 301 Alex Sanchez	.50	.15
❑ 302 Shawn Chacon	.50	.15
❑ 303 Matt Clement	.50	.15
❑ 304 Luis Matos	.50	.15
❑ 305 Steve Finley	.50	.15
❑ 306 Marcus Giles	.50	.15
❑ 307 Boomer Wells	.50	.15
❑ 308 Jeromy Burnitz	.50	.15
❑ 309 Mike MacDougal	.50	.15
❑ 310 Mariano Rivera	.75	.23
❑ 311 Adrian Beltre	.75	.23
❑ 312 Mark Loretta	.50	.15
❑ 313 Ugueth Urbina	.50	.15
❑ 314 Bill Mueller	.50	.15
❑ 315 Johan Santana	.75	.23
❑ NNO Vintage Buyback	.00	

2002 Topps 206

	Nm-Mt	Ex-Mt
COMPLETE SET (525)	220.00	65.00
COMPLETE SERIES 1 (180)	60.00	18.00
COMPLETE SERIES 2 (180)	60.00	18.00
COMPLETE SERIES 3 (165)	100.00	30.00

COM(1-140/181-260/308-418) .... .50 .15
COMMON (141-155/271-285)...... .50 .15
COMMON RC (308-418) .... .50 .15
COMMON SP (308-398) .... 2.00 .60
COMMON FYP SP (.............. 1.00 .30
COMMON RET SP (433-447)...... 2.00 .60

❑ 1 Vladimir Guerrero .... 1.25 .35
❑ 2 Sammy Sosa .... 2.00 .60
❑ 3 Garret Anderson .... .50 .15
❑ 4 Rafael Palmeiro .... .75 .23
❑ 5 Juan Gonzalez .... .75 .23
❑ 6 John Smoltz .... .75 .23
❑ 7 Mark Mulder .... .50 .15
❑ 8 Jon Lieber .... .50 .15
❑ 9 Greg Maddux .... 2.00 .60
❑ 10 Moises Alou .... .50 .15
❑ 11 Joe Randa .... .50 .15
❑ 12 Bobby Abreu .... .50 .15
❑ 13 Juan Pierre .... .50 .15
❑ 14 Kerry Wood .... 1.25 .35
❑ 15 Craig Biggio .... .75 .23
❑ 16 Curt Schilling .... .50 .15
❑ 17 Brian Jordan .... .50 .15
❑ 18 Edgardo Alfonzo .... .50 .15
❑ 19 Darren Dreifort .... .50 .15
❑ 20 Todd Helton .... .75 .23
❑ 21 Ramon Ortiz .... .50 .15
❑ 22 Ichiro Suzuki .... 2.00 .60
❑ 23 Jimmy Rollins .... .50 .15
❑ 24 Darin Erstad .... .50 .15
❑ 25 Shawn Green .... .50 .15
❑ 26 Tino Martinez .... .75 .23
❑ 27 Bret Boone .... .50 .15
❑ 28 Alfonso Soriano .... .75 .23
❑ 29 Chan Ho Park .... .50 .15
❑ 30 Roger Clemens .... 2.50 .75
❑ 31 Cliff Floyd .... .50 .15
❑ 32 Johnny Damon .... .75 .23
❑ 33 Frank Thomas .... 1.25 .35
❑ 34 Barry Bonds .... 3.00 .90
❑ 35 Luis Gonzalez .... .50 .15
❑ 36 Carlos Lee .... .50 .15
❑ 37 Roberto Alomar .... .75 .23
❑ 38 Carlos Delgado .... .50 .15
❑ 39 Nomar Garciaparra .... 2.00 .60
❑ 40 Jason Kendall .... .50 .15
❑ 41 Scott Rolen .... 1.25 .35
❑ 42 Tom Glavine .... .75 .23
❑ 43 Ryan Klesko .... .50 .15
❑ 44 Brian Giles .... .50 .15
❑ 45 Bud Smith .... .50 .15
❑ 46 Charles Nagy .... .50 .15
❑ 47 Tony Gwynn .... 1.50 .45
❑ 48 C.C. Sabathia UER .... .50 .15
Credited with incorrect victory total in 2001
❑ 49 Frank Catalanotto .... .50 .15
❑ 50 Jerry Hairston .... .50 .15
❑ 51 Jeromy Burnitz .... .50 .15
❑ 52 David Justice .... .50 .15
❑ 53 Bartolo Colon .... .50 .15
❑ 54 Andres Galarraga .... .50 .15
❑ 55 Jeff Weaver .... .50 .15
❑ 56 Terrence Long .... .50 .15
❑ 57 Tsuyoshi Shinjo .... .50 .15
❑ 58 Barry Zito .... .50 .15
❑ 59 Mariano Rivera .... .75 .23
❑ 60 John Olerud .... .50 .15
❑ 61 Randy Johnson .... 1.25 .35
❑ 62 Kenny Lofton .... .50 .15
❑ 63 Jermaine Dye .... .50 .15
❑ 64 Troy Glaus .... .50 .15
❑ 65 Larry Walker .... .75 .23
❑ 66 Hideo Nomo .... 1.25 .35
❑ 67 Mike Mussina .... .75 .23
❑ 68 Paul LoDuca .... .50 .15
❑ 69 Magglio Ordonez .... .50 .15
❑ 70 Paul O'Neill .... .75 .23
❑ 71 Sean Casey .... .50 .15
❑ 72 Lance Berkman .... .50 .15
❑ 73 Adam Dunn .... .75 .23
❑ 74 Aramis Ramirez .... .50 .15
❑ 75 Rafael Furcal .... .50 .15
❑ 76 Gary Sheffield .... .50 .15
❑ 77 Todd Hollandsworth .... .50 .15
❑ 78 Chipper Jones .... 1.25 .35
❑ 79 Bernie Williams .... .75 .23
❑ 80 Richard Hidalgo .... .50 .15
❑ 81 Eric Chavez .... .50 .15
❑ 82 Mike Piazza .... 2.00 .60
❑ 83 J.D. Drew .... .50 .15
❑ 84 Ken Griffey Jr. .... 2.00 .60
❑ 85 Joe Kennedy .... .50 .15
❑ 86 Joel Pineiro .... .50 .15
❑ 87 Josh Towers .... .50 .15
❑ 88 Andruw Jones .... .50 .15
❑ 89 Carlos Beltran .... .75 .23
❑ 90 Mike Cameron .... .50 .15
❑ 91 Albert Pujols .... 2.50 .75
❑ 92 Alex Rodriguez .... 2.00 .60
❑ 93 Omar Vizquel .... .75 .23
❑ 94 Juan Encarnacion .... .50 .15
❑ 95 Jeff Bagwell .... .75 .23
❑ 96 Jose Canseco .... 1.25 .35
❑ 97 Ben Sheets .... .50 .15
❑ 98 Mark Grace .... .75 .23
❑ 99 Mike Sweeney .... .50 .15
❑ 100 Mark McGwire .... 3.00 .90
❑ 101 Ivan Rodriguez .... 1.25 .35
❑ 102 Rich Aurilia .... .50 .15
❑ 103 Cristian Guzman .... .50 .15
❑ 104 Roy Oswalt .... .50 .15
❑ 105 Tim Hudson .... .50 .15
❑ 106 Brent Abernathy .... .50 .15
❑ 107 Mike Hampton .... .50 .15
❑ 108 Miguel Tejada .... .50 .15
❑ 109 Bobby Higginson .... .50 .15
❑ 110 Edgar Martinez .... .75 .23
❑ 111 Jorge Posada .... .75 .23
❑ 112 Jason Giambi Yankees .... .50 .15
❑ 113 Pedro Astacio .... .50 .15
❑ 114 Kazuhiro Sasaki .... .50 .15
❑ 115 Preston Wilson .... .50 .15
❑ 116 Jason Bere .... .50 .15
❑ 117 Mark Quinn .... .50 .15
❑ 118 Pokey Reese .... .50 .15
❑ 119 Derek Jeter .... 3.00 .90
❑ 120 Shannon Stewart .... .50 .15
❑ 121 Jeff Kent .... .50 .15
❑ 122 Jeremy Giambi .... .50 .15
❑ 123 Pat Burrell .... .50 .15
❑ 124 Jim Edmonds .... .50 .15
❑ 125 Mark Buehrle .... .50 .15
❑ 126 Kevin Brown .... .50 .15
❑ 127 Raul Mondesi .... .50 .15
❑ 128 Pedro Martinez .... 1.25 .35
❑ 129 Jim Thome .... 1.25 .35
❑ 130 Russ Ortiz .... .50 .15
❑ 131 Br.Duckworth PROS .... .50 .15
❑ 132 Ryan Jamison PROS .... .50 .15
❑ 133 Brandon Inge PROS .... .50 .15
❑ 134 Felipe Lopez PROS .... .50 .15
❑ 135 Jason Lane PROS .... .50 .15
❑ 136 F.Johnson PROS RC .... .50 .15
❑ 137 Greg Nash PROS .... .50 .15
❑ 138 Covelli Crisp PROS .... .50 .15
❑ 139 Nick Neugebauer PROS .... .50 .15
❑ 140 Dustan Mohr PROS .... .50 .15
❑ 141 Freddy Sanchez FYP RC .... .50 .15
❑ 142 Justin Backsmeyer FYP RC .50 .15
❑ 143 Jorge Julio FYP .... .50 .15
❑ 144 Ryan Mottl FYP RC .... .50 .15
❑ 145 Chris Tritle FYP RC .... .50 .15
❑ 146 Noochie Varner FYP RC .... .50 .15
❑ 147 Brian Rogers FYP .... .50 .15
❑ 148 Michael Hill FYP RC .... .50 .15
❑ 149 Luis Pineda FYP .... .50 .15
❑ 150 Rich Thompson FYP RC .... .50 .15
❑ 151 Bill Hall FYP .... .50 .15
❑ 152 Juan Dominguez FYP RC 1.00 .30
❑ 153 Justin Woodrow FYP .... .50 .15
❑ 154 Nic Jackson FYP RC .... .50 .15
❑ 155 Laynce Nix FYP RC .... 3.00 .90
❑ 156 Hank Aaron RET 5.00 1.50
❑ 157 Ernie Banks RET .... 2.50 .75
❑ 158 Johnny Bench RET .... 2.50 .75
❑ 159 George Brett RET 6.00 1.80
❑ 160 Carlton Fisk RET .... 1.50 .45
❑ 161 Bob Gibson RET .... 1.50 .45
❑ 162 Reggie Jackson RET .... 1.50 .45
❑ 163 Don Mattingly RET 6.00 1.80
❑ 164 Kirby Puckett RET .... 2.50 .75
❑ 165 Frank Robinson RET .... 1.50 .45
❑ 166 Nolan Ryan RET 6.00 1.80
❑ 167 Tom Seaver RET .... 1.50 .45
❑ 168 Mike Schmidt RET 5.00 1.50
❑ 169 Dave Winfield RET .... 1.00 .30
❑ 170 Carl Yastrzemski RET .... 3.00 .90
❑ 171 Frank Chance REP .... 1.00 .30
❑ 172 Ty Cobb REP 5.00 1.50
❑ 173 Sam Crawford REP .... 1.00 .30
❑ 174 Johnny Evers REP .... 1.00 .30
❑ 175 John McGraw REP .... 2.50 .75
❑ 176 Eddie Plank REP .... 2.50 .75
❑ 177 Tris Speaker REP .... 2.50 .75
❑ 178 Joe Tinker REP .... 1.00 .30
❑ 179 H.Wagner Orange REP .. 8.00 2.40
❑ 180 Cy Young REP .... 2.50 .75
❑ 181 Javier Vazquez .... .50 .15
❑ 182A Mark Mulder Green Jsy .. .50 .15
❑ 182B Mark Mulder White Jsy .. .50 .15
❑ 183A R.Clemens Blue Jsy .... 2.50 .75
❑ 183B R.Clemens Pinstripes .. 2.50 .75
❑ 184 Kazuhisa Ishii RC .... 1.25 .35
❑ 185 Roberto Alomar .... .75 .23
❑ 186 Lance Berkman .... .50 .15
❑ 187A A.Dunn Arms Folded ...... .75 .23
❑ 187B Adam Dunn w/Bat .... .75 .23
❑ 188A Aramis Ramirez w/Bat .... .50 .15
❑ 188B Aramis Ramirez w/o Bat .50 .15
❑ 189 Chuck Knoblauch .... .50 .15
❑ 190 Nomar Garciaparra .... 2.00 .60
❑ 191 Brad Penny .... .50 .15
❑ 192A Gary Sheffield w/Bat ...... .50 .15
❑ 192B Gary Sheffield w/o Bat .... .50 .15
❑ 193 Alfonso Soriano .... .75 .23
❑ 194 Andruw Jones .... .50 .15
❑ 195A R.Johnson Black Jsy .... 1.25 .35
❑ 195B R.Johnson Purple Jsy .. 1.25 .35
❑ 196A C.Patterson Blue Jsy ...... .50 .15
❑ 196B C.Patterson Pinstripes .. .50 .15
❑ 197 Milton Bradley .... .50 .15
❑ 198A J.Damon Blue Jsy/Cap 1.25 .35
❑ 198B J.Damon Blue Jsy/Hlmt 1.25 .35
❑ 198C J.Damon White Jsy ...... 1.25 .35
❑ 199A Paul Lo Duca Blue Jsy .. .50 .15
❑ 199B Paul Lo Duca White Jsy .50 .15
❑ 200A Albert Pujols Red Jsy .. 2.50 .75
❑ 200B Albert Pujols Running .. 2.50 .75
❑ 200C Albert Pujols w/Bat ...... 2.50 .75
❑ 201 Scott Rolen .... 1.25 .35
❑ 202A J.D. Drew Running .... .50 .15
❑ 202B J.D. Drew w/Bat .... .50 .15
❑ 202C J.D. Drew White Jsy ...... .50 .15
❑ 203 Vladimir Guerrero .... 1.25 .35
❑ 204A Jason Giambi Blue Jsy .. .50 .15
❑ 204B Jason Giambi Grey Jsy .. .50 .15
❑ 204C Jason Giambi Pinstripes .50 .15
❑ 205A Moises Alou Grey Jsy .... .50 .15
❑ 205B Moises Alou Pinstripes .. .50 .15
❑ 206A Mag. Ordonez Signing .. .50 .15
❑ 206B Magglio Ordonez w/Bat .. .50 .15
❑ 207 Carlos Febles .... .50 .15
❑ 208 So Taguchi RC .... .75 .23
❑ 209A Raf. Palmeiro One Hand .75 .23
❑ 209B Raf. Palmeiro Two Hands .75 .23
❑ 210 David Wells .... .50 .15
❑ 211 Orlando Cabrera .... .50 .15
❑ 212 Sammy Sosa .... 2.00 .60
❑ 213 Armando Benitez .... .50 .15
❑ 214 Wes Helms .... .50 .15
❑ 215A Mar. Rivera Arms Folded .75 .23
❑ 215B Mar. Rivera Holding Ball .75 .23
❑ 216 Jimmy Rollins .... .50 .15
❑ 217 Matt Lawton .... .50 .15
❑ 218A Shawn Green w/Bat .... .50 .15
❑ 218B Shawn Green w/o Bat ..... .50 .15
❑ 219A Bernie Williams w/Bat .... .75 .23
❑ 219B Bernie Williams w/o Bat .75 .23
❑ 220A Bret Boone Blue Jsy ...... .50 .15
❑ 220B Bret Boone White Jsy ..... .50 .15
❑ 221A Alex Rodriguez Blue Jsy 2.00 .60
❑ 221B Alex Rodriguez One Hand 2.00 .60
❑ 221C Alex Rodriguez Two Hands 2.00 .60
❑ 222 Roger Cedeno .... .50 .15
❑ 223 Marty Cordova .... .50 .15
❑ 224 Fred McGriff .... .75 .23

❑ 225A Chipper Jones Batting.. 1.25 .35
❑ 225B Chipper Jones Running 1.25 .35
❑ 226 Kerry Wood 1.25 .35
❑ 227A Larry Walker Grey Jsy .... .75 .23
❑ 227B Larry Walker Purple Jsy .75 .23
❑ 228 Robin Ventura .50 .15
❑ 229 Robert Fick .50 .15
❑ 230A Tino Martinez Black Glove .75 .23
❑ 230B Tino Martinez Throwing .75 .23
❑ 230C Tino Martinez w/Bat ...... .75 .23
❑ 231 Ben Petrick .50 .15
❑ 232 Neifi Perez .50 .15
❑ 233 Pedro Martinez 1.25 .35
❑ 234A Brian Jordan Grey Jsy .... .50 .15
❑ 234B Brian Jordan White Jsy .. .50 .15
❑ 235 Freddy Garcia .50 .15
❑ 236A Derek Jeter Batting ...... 3.00 .90
❑ 236B Derek Jeter Blue Jsy ...... 3.00 .90
❑ 236C Derek Jeter Kneeling .... 3.00 .90
❑ 237 Ben Grieve .50 .15
❑ 238A Barry Bonds Black Jsy 3.00 .90
❑ 238B B.Bonds w/Wrist Band 3.00 .90
❑ 238C B.Bonds w/o Wrist Band 3.00 .90
❑ 239 Luis Gonzalez .50 .15
❑ 240 Shane Halter .50 .15
❑ 241A Brian Giles Black Jsy .... .50 .15
❑ 241B Brian Giles Grey Jsy ...... .50 .15
❑ 242 Bud Smith .50 .15
❑ 243 Richie Sexson .50 .15
❑ 244A Barry Zito Green Jsy ...... .50 .15
❑ 244B Barry Zito White Jsy ...... .50 .15
❑ 245 Eric Milton .50 .15
❑ 246A Ivan Rodriguez Blue Jsy 1.25 .35
❑ 246B I.Rodriguez Grey Jsy .... 1.25 .35
❑ 246C I.Rodriguez White Jsy .. 1.25 .35
❑ 247 Toby Hall .50 .15
❑ 248A Mike Piazza Black Jsy .. 2.00 .60
❑ 248B Mike Piazza Grey Jsy .. 2.00 .60
❑ 249 Ruben Sierra .50 .15
❑ 250A Tsuyoshi Shinjo Cap...... .50 .15
❑ 250B Tsuyoshi Shinjo Helmet .50 .15
❑ 251A Jer. Dye Green Jsy .... .50 .15
❑ 251B Jermaine Dye White Jsy .50 .15
❑ 252 Roy Oswalt .50 .15
❑ 253 Todd Helton .75 .23
❑ 254 Adrian Beltre .75 .23
❑ 255 Doug Mientkiewicz .50 .15
❑ 256A Ichiro Suzuki Blue Jsy.. 2.00 .60
❑ 256B Ichiro Suzuki w/Bat ...... 2.00 .60
❑ 256C Ichiro Suzuki White Jsy 2.00 .60
❑ 257A C.C. Sabathia Blue Jsy .. .50 .15
❑ 257B C.C. Sabathia White Jsy .50 .15
❑ 258 Paul Konerko .50 .15
❑ 259 Ken Griffey Jr. 2.00 .60
❑ 260A Jeromy Burnitz w/Bat .... .50 .15
❑ 260B Jeromy Burnitz w/o Bat .. .50 .15
❑ 261 Hank Blalock PROS 1.25 .35
❑ 262 Mark Prior PROS 2.00 .60
❑ 263 Josh Beckett PROS .50 .15
❑ 264 Carlos Pena PROS .50 .15
❑ 265 Sean Burroughs PROS .... .50 .15
❑ 266 Austin Kearns PROS .... .50 .15
❑ 267 Chin-Hui Tsao PROS ...... .50 .15
❑ 268 Dewon Brazelton PROS .... .50 .15
❑ 269 J.D. Martin PROS .50 .15
❑ 270 Marlon Byrd PROS .50 .15
❑ 271 Joe Mauer FYP RC 5.00 1.50
❑ 272 Jason Botts FYP RC .... .75 .23
❑ 273 Mauricio Lara FYP RC...... .50 .15
❑ 274 Jonny Gomes FYP RC...... .75 .23
❑ 275 Gavin Floyd FYP RC ...... 2.50 .75
❑ 276 Alex Requena FYP RC .... .50 .15
❑ 277 Jimmy Gobble FYP RC .... .75 .23
❑ 278 Chris Duffy FYP RC .50 .15
❑ 279 Colt Griffin FYP RC .75 .23
❑ 280 Ryan Church FYP RC ...... .75 .23
❑ 281 Beltran Perez FYP RC ...... .50 .15
❑ 282 Clint Nageotte FYP RC .. 1.25 .35
❑ 283 Justin Schuda FYP RC .... .50 .15
❑ 284 Scott Hairston FYP RC .. 1.50 .45
❑ 285 Mario Ramos FYP RC ...... .50 .15
❑ 286 Tom Seaver White Sox RET 1.50 .45
❑ 286 Tom Seaver Mets RET .... 1.50 .45
❑ 287 H.Aaron White Jsy RET .. 5.00 1.50
❑ 287 H.Aaron Blue Jsy RET 5.00 1.50
❑ 288 Mike Schmidt RET 5.00 1.50
❑ 289A R.Yount Blue Jsy RET .. 4.00 1.20
❑ 289B R.Yount P'stripes RET .. 4.00 1.20
❑ 290 Joe Morgan RET 1.00 .30
❑ 291 Frank Robinson RET ...... 1.50 .45
❑ 292A Reggie Jackson A's RET 1.50 .45
❑ 292B Reggie Jackson Yanks RET 1.50 .45
❑ 293A Nolan Ryan Astros RET 6.00 1.80
❑ 293B N.Ryan Rangers RET 6.00 1.80
❑ 294 Dave Winfield RET 1.00 .30
❑ 295 Willie Mays RET 5.00 1.50
❑ 296 Brooks Robinson RET .... 1.50 .45
❑ 297A Mark McGwire A's RET 6.00 1.80
❑ 297B M.McGwire Cards RET 6.00 1.80
❑ 298 Honus Wagner RET 2.50 .75
❑ 299A Sherry Magee REP ...... 1.00 .30
❑ 299B Sherry Magie UER REP 1.00 .30
❑ 300 Frank Chance REP 1.00 .30
❑ 301A Joe Doyle NY REP 1.00 .30
❑ 301B Joe Doyle NY Nat'l REP 1.00 .30
❑ 302 John McGraw REP 2.50 .75
❑ 303 Jimmy Collins REP 1.00 .30
❑ 304 Buck Herzog REP 1.00 .30
❑ 305 Sam Crawford REP 1.00 .30
❑ 306 Cy Young REP 2.50 .75
❑ 307 Honus Wagner Blue REP 8.00 2.40
❑ 308A A.Rodriguez Blue Jsy SP 4.00 1.20
❑ 308B A.Rodriguez White Jsy 2.00 .60
❑ 309 Vernon Wells .50 .15
❑ 310A B.Bonds w/Elbow Pad .. 3.00 .90
❑ 310B B.Bonds w/o Elbow Pad SP 6.00 1.80
❑ 311 Vicente Padilla .50 .15
❑ 312A A.Soriano w/Wristband .. .75 .23
❑ 312B A.Soriano w/o Wristband SP 2.00 .60
❑ 313 Mike Piazza 2.00 .60
❑ 314 Jacque Jones .50 .15
❑ 315 Shawn Green SP 2.00 .60
❑ 316 Paul Byrd .50 .15
❑ 317 Lance Berkman .50 .15
❑ 318 Larry Walker .75 .23
❑ 319 Ken Griffey Jr. SP 4.00 1.20
❑ 320 Shea Hillenbrand .50 .15
❑ 321 Jay Gibbons .50 .15
❑ 322 Andruw Jones .50 .15
❑ 323 Luis Gonzalez SP 2.00 .60
❑ 324 Garret Anderson .50 .15
❑ 325 Roy Halladay .50 .15
❑ 326 Randy Winn .50 .15
❑ 327 Matt Morris .50 .15
❑ 328 Robb Nen .50 .15
❑ 329 Trevor Hoffman .50 .15
❑ 330 Kip Wells .50 .15
❑ 331 Orlando Hernandez .50 .15
❑ 332 Rey Ordonez .50 .15
❑ 333 Torii Hunter .50 .15
❑ 334 Geoff Jenkins .50 .15
❑ 335 Eric Karros .50 .15
❑ 336 Mike Lowell .50 .15
❑ 337 Nick Johnson .50 .15
❑ 338 Randall Simon .50 .15
❑ 339 Ellis Burks .50 .15
❑ 340A S.Sosa Blue Jsy SP...... 4.00 1.20
❑ 340B Sammy Sosa White Jsy 2.00 .60
❑ 341 Pedro Martinez 1.25 .35
❑ 342 Junior Spivey .50 .15
❑ 343 Vinny Castilla .50 .15
❑ 344 Randy Johnson SP 2.50 .75
❑ 345 Chipper Jones SP 2.50 .75
❑ 346 Orlando Hudson .50 .15
❑ 347 Albert Pujols SP 5.00 1.50
❑ 348 Rondell White .50 .15
❑ 349 Vladimir Guerrero 1.25 .35
❑ 350A Mark Prior Red SP 4.00 1.20
❑ 350B Mark Prior Yellow 2.00 .60
❑ 351 Eric Gagne 1.25 .35
❑ 352 Todd Zeile .50 .15
❑ 353 Manny Ramirez SP 2.00 .60
❑ 354 Kevin Millwood .50 .15
❑ 355 Troy Percival .50 .15
❑ 356A Jason Giambi Batting SP 2.00 .60
❑ 356B Jason Giambi Throwing .50 .15
❑ 357 Bartolo Colon .50 .15
❑ 358 Jeremy Giambi .50 .15
❑ 359 Jose Cruz Jr. .50 .15
❑ 360A I.Suzuki Blue Jsy SP 4.00 1.20
❑ 360B I.Suzuki White Jsy 2.00 .60
❑ 361 Eddie Guardado .50 .15
❑ 362 Ivan Rodriguez 1.25 .35
❑ 363 Carl Crawford .50 .15
❑ 364 Jason Simontacchi RC .... .50 .15
❑ 365 Kenny Lofton .50 .15
❑ 366 Raul Mondesi .50 .15
❑ 367 A.J. Pierzynski .50 .15
❑ 368 Ugueth Urbina .50 .15
❑ 369 Rodrigo Lopez .50 .15
❑ 370A N.Garciaparra One Bat SP 4.00 1.20
❑ 370B N.Garciaparra Two Bats 2.00 .60
❑ 371 Craig Counsell .50 .15
❑ 372 Barry Larkin .75 .23
❑ 373 Carlos Pena .50 .15
❑ 374 Luis Castillo .50 .15
❑ 375 Raul Ibanez .50 .15
❑ 376 Kazuhisa Ishii SP 2.50 .75
❑ 377 Derek Lowe .50 .15
❑ 378 Curt Schilling .50 .15
❑ 379 Jim Thome Phillies 1.25 .35
❑ 380A Derek Jeter Blue SP 6.00 1.80
❑ 380B Derek Jeter Seats 3.00 .90
❑ 381 Pat Burrell .50 .15
❑ 382 Jamie Moyer .50 .15
❑ 383 Eric Hinske .50 .15
❑ 384 Scott Rolen 1.25 .35
❑ 385 Miguel Tejada SP 2.00 .60
❑ 386 Andy Pettitte .75 .23
❑ 387 Mike Lieberthal .50 .15
❑ 388 Al Leiter .50 .15
❑ 389 Todd Helton SP 2.00 .60
❑ 390A Adam Dunn Bat SP ...... 2.00 .60
❑ 390B Adam Dunn Glove .75 .23
❑ 391 Cliff Floyd .50 .15
❑ 392 Tim Salmon .75 .23
❑ 393 Joe Torre MG .75 .23
❑ 394 Bobby Cox MG .50 .15
❑ 395 Tony LaRussa MG .50 .15
❑ 396 Art Howe MG .50 .15
❑ 397 Bob Brenly MG .50 .15
❑ 398 Ron Gardenhire MG .... .50 .15
❑ 399 Mike Cuddyer PROS .... .50 .15
❑ 400 Joe Mauer PROS 5.00 1.50
❑ 401 Mark Teixeira PROS .... .75 .23
❑ 402 Hee Seop Choi PROS ...... .50 .15
❑ 403 Angel Berroa PROS .50 .15
❑ 404 Jesse Foppert PROS RC 1.00 .30
❑ 405 Bobby Crosby PROS ...... 1.25 .35
❑ 406 Jose Reyes PROS .75 .23
❑ 407 C.Kotchman PROS RC .. 3.00 .90
❑ 408 Aaron Heilman PROS .50 .15
❑ 409 Adrian Gonzalez PROS ...... .50 .15
❑ 410 Delwyn Young PROS RC 1.25 .35
❑ 411 Brett Myers PROS .50 .15
❑ 412 Justin Huber PROS RC .... .75 .23
❑ 413 Drew Henson PROS .... .50 .15
❑ 414 T.Bozied PROS RC .75 .23
❑ 415 Dontrelle Willis PROS RC 3.00 .90
❑ 416 Rocco Baldelli PROS........ .50 .15
❑ 417 Jason Stokes PROS RC.. 3.00 .90
❑ 418 Brandon Phillips PROS .... .50 .15
❑ 419 Jake Blalock FYP RC...... 1.50 .45
❑ 420 Micah Schilling FYP RC 1.00 .30
❑ 421 Denard Span FYP RC .... 1.00 .30
❑ 422A J.Loney Red FYP RC .... 2.00 .60
❑ 422B J.Loney w/Sky FYP RC 2.00 .60
❑ 423A W.Bankston Blue FYP RC 1.25 .35
❑ 423B W.Bankston w/Sky FYP RC 1.25 .35
❑ 424 Jeremy Hermida FYP RC 2.00 .60
❑ 425 C.Granderson FYP RC.... 1.50 .45
❑ 426A J.Pridie Red FYP RC .... 1.00 .30
❑ 426B J.Pridie w/Sky FYP RC 1.00 .30
❑ 427 Larry Broadway FYP RC 1.00 .30
❑ 428A K.Greene Green FYP RC 10.00 3.00
❑ 428B K.Greene Red FYP RC 10.00 3.00
❑ 429 Joey Votto FYP RC 1.25 .35
❑ 430A B.Upton Grey FYP RC .. 8.00 2.40
❑ 430B B.Upton w/People FYP RC 8.00 2.40
❑ 431A S.Santos Gold FYP RC 2.00 .60
❑ 431B S.Santos Grey FYP RC 2.00 .60
❑ 432 Brian Dopirak FYP RC.... 3.00 .90
❑ 433 Ozzie Smith RET SP 4.00 1.20
❑ 434 Wade Boggs RET SP ...... 2.50 .75
❑ 435 Yogi Berra RET SP 4.00 1.20
❑ 436 Al Kaline RET SP 4.00 1.20
❑ 437 Robin Roberts RET SP.... 2.00 .60
❑ 438 Rob. Clemente RET SP .. 8.00 2.40

Card	Nm-Mt	Ex-Mt
❑ 439 Gary Carter RET SP	2.00	.60
❑ 440 Fergie Jenkins RET SP	2.00	.60
❑ 441 Orlando Cepeda RET SP	2.00	.60
❑ 442 Rod Carew RET SP	2.50	.75
❑ 443 Ha. Killebrew RET SP	4.00	1.20
❑ 444 Duke Snider RET SP	2.50	.75
❑ 445 Stan Musial RET SP	6.00	1.80
❑ 446 Hank Greenberg RET SP	4.00	1.20
❑ 447 Lou Brock RET SP	2.50	.75
❑ 448 Jim Palmer RET	1.00	.30
❑ 449 John McGraw REP	1.00	.30
❑ 450 Mordecai Brown REP	1.00	.30
❑ 451 Christy Mathewson REP	1.50	.45
❑ 452 Sam Crawford REP	1.00	.30
❑ 453 Bill O'Hara REP	1.00	.30
❑ 454 Joe Tinker REP	1.00	.30
❑ 455 Nap Lajoie REP	1.50	.45
❑ 456 Honus Wagner Red REP	8.00	2.40
❑ NNO Repurchased Tobacco Card		.00

2003 Topps All-Time Fan Favorites

	Nm-Mt	Ex-Mt
COMPLETE SET (150)	50.00	15.00
❑ 1 Willie Mays	3.00	.90
❑ 2 Whitey Ford	1.00	.30
❑ 3 Stan Musial	2.50	.75
❑ 4 Paul Blair	.60	.18
❑ 5 Harold Reynolds	.60	.18
❑ 6 Bob Friend	.60	.18
❑ 7 Rod Carew	1.00	.30
❑ 8 Kirk Gibson	.60	.18
❑ 9 Graig Nettles	.60	.18
❑ 10 Ozzie Smith	2.50	.75
❑ 11 Tony Perez	.60	.18
❑ 12 Tim Wallach	.60	.18
❑ 13 Bert Campaneris	.60	.18
❑ 14 Cory Snyder	.60	.18
❑ 15 Dave Parker	.60	.18
❑ 16 Darrell Evans	.60	.18
❑ 17 Joe Pepitone	.60	.18
❑ 18 Don Sutton	.60	.18
❑ 19 Dale Murphy	1.50	.45
❑ 20 George Brett	4.00	1.20
❑ 21 Carlton Fisk	1.00	.30
❑ 22 Bob Watson	.60	.18
❑ 23 Wally Joyner	.60	.18
❑ 24 Paul Molitor	1.00	.30
❑ 25 Keith Hernandez	.60	.18
❑ 26 Jerry Koosman	.60	.18
❑ 27 George Bell	.60	.18
❑ 28 Boog Powell	1.00	.30
❑ 29 Bruce Sutter	.60	.18
❑ 30 Ernie Banks	1.50	.45
❑ 31 Steve Lyons	.60	.18
❑ 32 Earl Weaver	.60	.18
❑ 33 Dave Stieb	.60	.18
❑ 34 Alan Trammell	.60	.18
❑ 35 Bret Saberhagen	.60	.18
❑ 36 J.R. Richard	.60	.18
❑ 37 Mickey Rivers	.60	.18
❑ 38 Juan Marichal	.60	.18
❑ 39 Gaylord Perry	.60	.18
❑ 40 Don Mattingly	4.00	1.20
❑ 41 Bob Grich	.60	.18
❑ 42 Steve Sax	.60	.18
❑ 43 Sparky Anderson	.60	.18
❑ 44 Luis Aparicio	.60	.18
❑ 45 Fergie Jenkins	.60	.18
❑ 46 Jim Palmer	.60	.18
❑ 47 Howard Johnson	.60	.18
❑ 48 Dwight Evans	.60	.18
❑ 49 Bill Buckner	.60	.18
❑ 50 Cal Ripken	5.00	1.50
❑ 51 Jose Cruz	.60	.18
❑ 52 Tony Oliva	.60	.18
❑ 53 Bobby Richardson	.60	.18
❑ 54 Luis Tiant	.60	.18
❑ 55 Warren Spahn	1.00	.30
❑ 56 Phil Rizzuto	1.00	.30
❑ 57 Eric Davis	.60	.18
❑ 58 Vida Blue	.60	.18
❑ 59 Steve Balboni	.60	.18
❑ 60 Mike Schmidt	3.00	.90
❑ 61 Ken Griffey Sr.	.60	.18
❑ 62 Jim Abbott	1.00	.30
❑ 63 Whitey Herzog	.60	.18
❑ 64 Rich Gossage	.60	.18
❑ 65 Tony Armas	.60	.18
❑ 66 Bill Skowron	1.00	.30
❑ 67 Don Newcombe	.60	.18
❑ 68 Bill Madlock	.60	.18
❑ 69 Lance Parrish	.60	.18
❑ 70 Reggie Jackson	1.00	.30
❑ 71 Willie Wilson	.60	.18
❑ 72 Terry Pendleton	.60	.18
❑ 73 Jim Piersall	.60	.18
❑ 74 George Foster	.60	.18
❑ 75 Bob Horner	.60	.18
❑ 76 Chris Sabo	.60	.18
❑ 77 Fred Lynn	.60	.18
❑ 78 Jim Rice	.60	.18
❑ 79 Maury Wills	.60	.18
❑ 80 Yogi Berra	1.50	.45
❑ 81 Johnny Sain	1.00	.30
❑ 82 Tom Lasorda	.60	.18
❑ 83 Bill Mazeroski	1.00	.30
❑ 84 John Kruk	.60	.18
❑ 85 Bob Feller	.60	.18
❑ 86 Frank Robinson	1.00	.30
❑ 87 Red Schoendienst	.60	.18
❑ 88 Gary Carter	.60	.18
❑ 89 Andre Dawson	.60	.18
❑ 90 Tim McCarver	.60	.18
❑ 91 Robin Yount	2.50	.75
❑ 92 Phil Niekro	.60	.18
❑ 93 Joe Morgan	.60	.18
❑ 94 Darren Daulton	.60	.18
❑ 95 Bobby Thomson	.60	.18
❑ 96 Alvin Davis	.60	.18
❑ 97 Robin Roberts	1.00	.30
❑ 98 Kirby Puckett	1.50	.45
❑ 99 Jack Clark	.60	.18
❑ 100 Hank Aaron	3.00	.90
❑ 101 Orlando Cepeda	.60	.18
❑ 102 Vern Law	.60	.18
❑ 103 Cecil Cooper	.60	.18
❑ 104 Don Larsen	.60	.18
❑ 105 Mario Mendoza	.60	.18
❑ 106 Tony Gwynn	2.00	.60
❑ 107 Ernie Harwell	.60	.18
❑ 108A Monte Irvin	.60	.18
❑ 108B Monte Irvin NO AU ERR	.60	.18
❑ 109 Tommy John	.60	.18
❑ 110 Rollie Fingers	.60	.18
❑ 111 Johnny Podres	.60	.18
❑ 112 Jeff Reardon	.60	.18
❑ 113 Buddy Bell	.60	.18
❑ 114 Dwight Gooden	.60	.18
❑ 115 Garry Templeton	.60	.18
❑ 116 Johnny Bench	1.50	.45
❑ 117 Joe Rudi	.60	.18
❑ 118 Ron Guidry	.60	.18
❑ 119 Vince Coleman	.60	.18
❑ 120 Al Kaline	1.50	.45
❑ 121 Carl Yastrzemski	2.50	.75
❑ 122 Hank Bauer	.60	.18
❑ 123 Mark Fidrych	.60	.18
❑ 124 Paul O'Neill	1.00	.30
❑ 125 Ron Cey	.60	.18
❑ 126 Willie McGee	.60	.18
❑ 127 Harmon Killebrew	1.50	.45
❑ 128 Dave Concepcion	.60	.18
❑ 129 Harold Baines	.60	.18
❑ 130 Lou Brock	1.00	.30
❑ 131 Lee Smith	.60	.18
❑ 132 Willie McCovey	.60	.18
❑ 133 Steve Garvey	.60	.18
❑ 134 Kent Tekulve	.60	.18
❑ 135 Tom Seaver	1.00	.30
❑ 136 Bo Jackson	1.50	.45
❑ 137 Walt Weiss	.60	.18
❑ 138 Brook Jacoby	.60	.18
❑ 139 Dennis Eckersley	.60	.18
❑ 140 Duke Snider	1.00	.30
❑ 141 Lenny Dykstra	.60	.18
❑ 142 Greg Luzinski	.60	.18
❑ 143 Jim Bunning	.60	.18
❑ 144 Jose Canseco	1.50	.45
❑ 145 Ron Santo	1.00	.30
❑ 146 Bert Blyleven	.60	.18
❑ 147 Wade Boggs	1.00	.30
❑ 148 Brooks Robinson	1.00	.30
❑ 149 Ray Knight	.60	.18
❑ 150 Nolan Ryan	4.00	1.20

2004 Topps All-Time Fan Favorites

	Nm-Mt	Ex-Mt
COMPLETE SET (150)	50.00	15.00
❑ 1 Willie Mays	3.00	.90
❑ 2 Bob Gibson	1.00	.30
❑ 3 Dave Stieb	.60	.18
❑ 4 Tim McCarver	.60	.18
❑ 5 Reggie Jackson	1.00	.30
❑ 6 John Candelaria	.60	.18
❑ 7 Lenny Dykstra	.60	.18
❑ 8 Tony Oliva	.60	.18
❑ 9 Frank Viola	.60	.18
❑ 10 Don Mattingly	4.00	1.20
❑ 11 Garry Maddox	.60	.18
❑ 12 Randy Jones	.60	.18
❑ 13 Joe Carter	.60	.18
❑ 14 Orlando Cepeda	.60	.18
❑ 15 Bob Sheppard ANC	1.00	.30
❑ 16 Bobby Grich	.60	.18
❑ 17 George Scott	.60	.18
❑ 18 Mickey Rivers	.60	.18
❑ 19 Ron Santo	1.00	.30
❑ 20 Mike Schmidt	3.00	.90
❑ 21 Luis Aparicio	.60	.18
❑ 22 Cesar Geronimo	.60	.18
❑ 23 Jack Morris	.60	.18
❑ 24 Jeffrey Loria OWNER	.60	.18
❑ 25 George Brett	4.00	1.20
❑ 26 Paul O'Neill	1.00	.30
❑ 27 Reggie Smith	.60	.18
❑ 28 Robin Yount	2.50	.75
❑ 29 Andre Dawson	.60	.18
❑ 30 Whitey Ford	1.00	.30
❑ 31 Ralph Kiner	.60	.18
❑ 32 Will Clark	1.50	.45
❑ 33 Keith Hernandez	.60	.18
❑ 34 Tony Fernandez	.60	.18
❑ 35 Willie McGee	.60	.18
❑ 36 Harmon Killebrew	1.50	.45
❑ 37 Dave Kingman	.60	.18
❑ 38 Kirk Gibson	1.00	.30
❑ 39 Terry Steinbach	.60	.18
❑ 40 Frank Robinson	.60	.18
❑ 41 Chet Lemon	.60	.18
❑ 42 Mike Cuellar	.60	.18
❑ 43 Darrell Evans	.60	.18
❑ 44 Don Kessinger	.60	.18
❑ 45 Dave Concepcion	.60	.18
❑ 46 Sparky Anderson	.60	.18
❑ 47 Bret Saberhagen	.60	.18
❑ 48 Brett Butler	.60	.18
❑ 49 Kent Hrbek	.60	.18
❑ 50 Hank Aaron	3.00	.90
❑ 51 Rudolph Giuliani	1.50	.45
❑ 52 Clete Boyer	.60	.18
❑ 53 Mookie Wilson	.60	.18
❑ 54 Dave Stewart	.60	.18
❑ 55 Gary Matthews Sr.	.60	.18

- ❑ 56 Roy Face .60 .18
- ❑ 57 Vida Blue .60 .18
- ❑ 58 Jimmy Key 1.00 .30
- ❑ 59 Al Hrabosky .60 .18
- ❑ 60 Al Kaline 1.50 .45
- ❑ 61 Mike Scott .60 .18
- ❑ 62 Jack McDowell .60 .18
- ❑ 63 Reggie Jackson 1.00 .30
- ❑ 64 Earl Weaver .60 .18
- ❑ 65 Ernie Harwell ANC 1.00 .30
- ❑ 66 David Justice .60 .18
- ❑ 67 Wilbur Wood .60 .18
- ❑ 68 Mike Boddicker .60 .18
- ❑ 69 Don Zimmer .60 .18
- ❑ 70 Jim Palmer .60 .18
- ❑ 71 Doug DeCinces .60 .18
- ❑ 72 Ryne Sandberg 3.00 .90
- ❑ 73 Don Newcombe .60 .18
- ❑ 74 Denny Martinez .60 .18
- ❑ 75 Carl Yastrzemski 2.50 .75
- ❑ 76 Bake McBride .60 .18
- ❑ 77 Andy Van Slyke .60 .18
- ❑ 78 Bruce Sutter .60 .18
- ❑ 79 Bobby Valentine .60 .18
- ❑ 80 Johnny Bench 1.50 .45
- ❑ 81 Orel Hershiser .60 .18
- ❑ 82 Cecil Fielder .60 .18
- ❑ 83 Lou Whitaker .60 .18
- ❑ 84 Alan Trammell .60 .18
- ❑ 85 Sam McDowell .60 .18
- ❑ 86 Ray Knight .60 .18
- ❑ 87 Gregg Jefferies .60 .18
- ❑ 88 Ben Oglivie .60 .18
- ❑ 89 Billy Beane .60 .18
- ❑ 90 Yogi Berra 1.50 .45
- ❑ 91 Jose Canseco 1.50 .45
- ❑ 92 Bobby Bonilla .60 .18
- ❑ 93 Darren Daulton .60 .18
- ❑ 94 Harold Reynolds .60 .18
- ❑ 95 Lou Brock 1.00 .30
- ❑ 96 Pete Incaviglia .60 .18
- ❑ 97 Eric Gregg UMP .60 .18
- ❑ 98 Devon White .60 .18
- ❑ 99 Kelly Gruber .60 .18
- ❑ 100 Nolan Ryan 4.00 1.20
- ❑ 101 Carlton Fisk 1.00 .30
- ❑ 102 George Foster .60 .18
- ❑ 103 Dennis Eckersley 1.00 .30
- ❑ 104 Rick Sutcliffe .60 .18
- ❑ 105 Cal Ripken 5.00 1.50
- ❑ 106 Norm Cash .60 .18
- ❑ 107 Charlie Hough .60 .18
- ❑ 108 Paul Molitor 1.00 .30
- ❑ 109 Maury Wills .60 .18
- ❑ 110 Tom Seaver 1.00 .30
- ❑ 111 Brooks Robinson 1.00 .30
- ❑ 112 Jim Rice .60 .18
- ❑ 113 Dwight Gooden .60 .18
- ❑ 114 Harold Baines .60 .18
- ❑ 115 Tim Raines .60 .18
- ❑ 116 Roy Smalley .60 .18
- ❑ 117 Richie Allen .60 .18
- ❑ 118 Ron Swoboda .60 .18
- ❑ 119 Ron Guidry 1.00 .30
- ❑ 120 Duke Snider 1.00 .30
- ❑ 121 Ferguson Jenkins .60 .18
- ❑ 122 Mark Fidrych UER .60 .18
  Posing as a lefty
- ❑ 123 Buddy Bell .60 .18
- ❑ 124 Bo Jackson 1.50 .45
- ❑ 125 Stan Musial 2.50 .75
- ❑ 126 Jesse Barfield .60 .18
- ❑ 127 Tony Gwynn 2.00 .60
- ❑ 128 Phil Garner .60 .18
- ❑ 129 Dale Murphy 1.00 .30
- ❑ 130 Wade Boggs 1.00 .30
- ❑ 131 Sid Fernandez .60 .18
- ❑ 132 Monte Irvin .60 .18
- ❑ 133 Peter Ueberroth COM .60 .18
- ❑ 134 Gary Gaetti .60 .18
- ❑ 135 Gorman Thomas .60 .18
- ❑ 136 Dave Lopes .60 .18
- ❑ 137 Sy Berger .60 .18
- ❑ 138 Buck O'Neil UER .60 .18
  Wrong birth year on back
- ❑ 139 Herb Score .60 .18
- ❑ 140 Rod Carew 1.00 .30
- ❑ 141 Joe Buck ANC 1.00 .30
- ❑ 142 Willie Horton .60 .18
- ❑ 143 Hal McRae .60 .18
- ❑ 144 Rollie Fingers .60 .18
- ❑ 145 Tom Brunansky .60 .18
- ❑ 146 Fay Vincent COM .60 .18
- ❑ 147 Gary Carter .60 .18
- ❑ 148 Bobby Richardson .60 .18
- ❑ 149 Steve Garvey .60 .18
- ❑ 150 Don Larsen .60 .18

1994 Topps Archives 1954

	Nm-Mt	Ex-Mt
COMPLETE SET (256)	150.00	45.00
COMMON CARD (2-249)	.15	.04
COMMON (251-258)	.15	.04

- ❑ 1 Not Issued .00 .00
- ❑ 2 Gus Zernial .30 .09
- ❑ 3 Monte Irvin .30 .09
- ❑ 4 Hank Sauer .30 .09
- ❑ 5 Ed Lopat .30 .09
- ❑ 6 Pete Runnels .30 .09
- ❑ 7 Ted Kluszewski .50 .15
- ❑ 8 Bobby Young .15 .04
- ❑ 9 Harvey Haddix .30 .09
- ❑ 10 Jackie Robinson .75 .23
- ❑ 11 Paul Smith .15 .04
- ❑ 12 Del Crandall .30 .09
- ❑ 13 Billy Martin .50 .15
- ❑ 14 Preacher Roe .30 .09
- ❑ 15 Al Rosen .30 .09
- ❑ 16 Vic Janowicz .30 .09
- ❑ 17 Phil Rizzuto .75 .23
- ❑ 18 Walt Dropo .15 .04
- ❑ 19 Johnny Lipon .15 .04
- ❑ 20 Warren Spahn .50 .15
- ❑ 21 Bobby Shantz .30 .09
- ❑ 22 Jim Greengrass .15 .04
- ❑ 23 Luke Easter .30 .09
- ❑ 24 Granny Hamner .30 .09
- ❑ 25 Harvey Kuenn .30 .09
- ❑ 26 Ray Jablonski .15 .04
- ❑ 27 Ferris Fain .15 .04
- ❑ 28 Paul Minner .15 .04
- ❑ 29 Jim Hegan .15 .04
- ❑ 30 Ed Mathews .75 .23
- ❑ 31 Johnny Klippstein .15 .04
- ❑ 32 Duke Snider .50 .15
- ❑ 33 Johnny Schmitz .15 .04
- ❑ 34 Jim Rivera .15 .04
- ❑ 35 Jim Gilliam .30 .09
- ❑ 36 Hoyt Wilhelm .30 .09
- ❑ 37 Whitey Ford .50 .15
- ❑ 38 Eddie Stanky MG .30 .09
- ❑ 39 Sherm Lollar .30 .09
- ❑ 40 Mel Parnell .15 .04
- ❑ 41 Willie Jones .15 .04
- ❑ 42 Don Mueller .15 .04
- ❑ 43 Dick Groat .30 .09
- ❑ 44 Ned Garver .15 .04
- ❑ 45 Richie Ashburn .50 .15
- ❑ 46 Ken Raffensberger .15 .04
- ❑ 47 Ellis Kinder .15 .04
- ❑ 48 Billy Hunter .15 .04
- ❑ 49 Ray Murray .15 .04
- ❑ 50 Yogi Berra 1.50 .45
- ❑ 51 Johnny Lindell .15 .04
- ❑ 52 Vic Power .15 .04
- ❑ 53 Jack Dittmer .15 .04
- ❑ 54 Vern Stephens .30 .09
- ❑ 55 Phil Cavarretta MG .30 .09
- ❑ 56 Willie Miranda .15 .04
- ❑ 57 Luis Aloma .15 .04
- ❑ 58 Bob Wilson .15 .04
- ❑ 59 Gene Conley .15 .04
- ❑ 60 Frank Baumholtz .15 .04
- ❑ 61 Bob Cain .15 .04
- ❑ 62 Eddie Robinson .15 .04
- ❑ 63 Johnny Pesky .30 .09
- ❑ 64 Hank Thompson .15 .04
- ❑ 65 Bob Swift .15 .04
- ❑ 66 Ted Lepcio .15 .04
- ❑ 67 Jim Willis .15 .04
- ❑ 68 Sammy Calderone .15 .04
- ❑ 69 Bud Podbielan .15 .04
- ❑ 70 Larry Doby .30 .09
- ❑ 71 Frank Smith .15 .04
- ❑ 72 Preston Ward .15 .04
- ❑ 73 Wayne Terwilliger .15 .04
- ❑ 74 Bill Taylor .15 .04
- ❑ 75 Fred Haney MG .15 .04
- ❑ 76 Bob Scheffing CO .15 .04
- ❑ 77 Ray Boone .15 .04
- ❑ 78 Ted Kazanski .15 .04
- ❑ 79 Andy Pafko .30 .09
- ❑ 80 Jackie Jensen .30 .09
- ❑ 81 Dave Hoskins .15 .04
- ❑ 82 Milt Bolling .15 .04
- ❑ 83 Joe Collins .30 .09
- ❑ 84 Dick Cole .15 .04
- ❑ 85 Bob Turley .30 .09
- ❑ 86 Billy Herman CO .30 .09
- ❑ 87 Roy Face .30 .09
- ❑ 88 Matt Batts .15 .04
- ❑ 89 Howie Pollet .15 .04
- ❑ 90 Willie Mays 5.00 1.50
- ❑ 91 Bob Oldis .15 .04
- ❑ 92 Wally Westlake .15 .04
- ❑ 93 Sid Hudson .15 .04
- ❑ 94 Ernie Banks 3.00 .90
- ❑ 95 Hal Rice .15 .04
- ❑ 96 Charlie Silvera .30 .09
- ❑ 97 Jerry Lane .15 .04
- ❑ 98 Joe Black .30 .09
- ❑ 99 Bob Hofman .15 .04
- ❑ 100 Bob Keegan .15 .04
- ❑ 101 Gene Woodling .30 .09
- ❑ 102 Gil Hodges .75 .23
- ❑ 103 Jim Lemon .15 .04
- ❑ 104 Mike Sandlock .15 .04
- ❑ 105 Andy Carey .30 .09
- ❑ 106 Dick Kokos .15 .04
- ❑ 107 Duane Pillette .15 .04
- ❑ 108 Thornton Kipper .15 .04
- ❑ 109 Bill Bruton .15 .04
- ❑ 110 Harry Dorish .15 .04
- ❑ 111 Jim Delsing .15 .04
- ❑ 112 Bill Renna .15 .04
- ❑ 113 Bob Boyd .15 .04
- ❑ 114 Dean Stone .15 .04
- ❑ 115 Rip Repulski .15 .04
- ❑ 116 Steve Bilko .15 .04
- ❑ 117 Solly Hemus .15 .04
- ❑ 118 Carl Scheib .15 .04
- ❑ 119 Johnny Antonelli .30 .09
- ❑ 120 Roy McMillan .30 .09
- ❑ 121 Clem Labine .50 .15
- ❑ 122 Johnny Logan .30 .09
- ❑ 123 Bobby Adams .15 .04
- ❑ 124 Marion Fricano .15 .04
- ❑ 125 Harry Perkowski .15 .04
- ❑ 126 Ben Wade .15 .04
- ❑ 127 Steve O'Neill MG .15 .04
- ❑ 128 Henry Aaron 6.00 1.80
- ❑ 129 Forrest Jacobs .15 .04
- ❑ 130 Hank Bauer .30 .09
- ❑ 131 Reno Bertoia .15 .04
- ❑ 132 Tom Lasorda .50 .15
- ❑ 133 Del Baker CO .15 .04
- ❑ 134 Cal Hogue .15 .04

No.	Player	Nm-Mt	Ex-Mt
❑ 135	Joe Presko	.15	.04
❑ 136	Connie Ryan	.15	.04
❑ 137	Wally Moon	.30	.09
❑ 138	Bob Borkowski	.15	.04
❑ 139	Ed O'Brien Johnny O'Brien	.30	.09
❑ 140	Tom Wright	.15	.04
❑ 141	Joe Jay	.15	.04
❑ 142	Tom Poholsky	.15	.04
❑ 143	Rollie Hemsley CO	.15	.04
❑ 144	Bill Werle	.15	.04
❑ 145	Elmer Valo	.15	.04
❑ 146	Don Johnson	.15	.04
❑ 147	John Riddle CO	.15	.04
❑ 148	Bob Trice	.15	.04
❑ 149	Jim Robertson	.15	.04
❑ 150	Dick Kryhoski	.15	.04
❑ 151	Alex Grammas	.15	.04
❑ 152	Mike Blyzka	.15	.04
❑ 153	Rube Walker	.15	.04
❑ 154	Mike Fornieles	.15	.04
❑ 155	Bob Kennedy	.15	.04
❑ 156	Joe Coleman	.15	.04
❑ 157	Don Lenhardt	.15	.04
❑ 158	Peanuts Lowrey	.15	.04
❑ 159	Dave Philley	.15	.04
❑ 160	Red Kress CO	.15	.04
❑ 161	John Hetki	.15	.04
❑ 162	Herman Wehmeier	.15	.04
❑ 163	Frank House	.15	.04
❑ 164	Stu Miller	.15	.04
❑ 165	Jim Pendleton	.15	.04
❑ 166	Johnny Podres	.30	.09
❑ 167	Don Lund	.15	.04
❑ 168	Morrie Martin	.15	.04
❑ 169	Jim Hughes	.15	.04
❑ 170	Dusty Rhodes	.15	.04
❑ 171	Leo Kiely	.15	.04
❑ 172	Hal Brown	.15	.04
❑ 173	Jack Harshman	.15	.04
❑ 174	Tom Qualters	.15	.04
❑ 175	Frank Leja	.15	.04
❑ 176	Bob Keely	.15	.04
❑ 177	Bob Milliken	.15	.04
❑ 178	Bill Glynn	.15	.04
❑ 179	Gair Allie	.15	.04
❑ 180	Wes Westrum	.15	.04
❑ 181	Mel Roach	.15	.04
❑ 182	Chuck Harmon	.15	.04
❑ 183	Earle Combs CO	.75	.23
❑ 184	Ed Bailey	.15	.04
❑ 185	Chuck Stobbs	.15	.04
❑ 186	Karl Olson	.15	.04
❑ 187	Heinie Manush CO	.75	.23
❑ 188	Dave Jolly	.15	.04
❑ 189	Bob Ross	.15	.04
❑ 190	Ray Herbert	.15	.04
❑ 191	Dick Schofield	.15	.04
❑ 192	Cot Deal CO	.15	.04
❑ 193	Johnny Hopp CO	.15	.04
❑ 194	Bill Sarni	.15	.04
❑ 195	Bill Consolo	.15	.04
❑ 196	Stan Jok	.15	.04
❑ 197	Schoolboy Rowe CO	.30	.09
❑ 198	Carl Sawatski	.15	.04
❑ 199	Rocky Nelson	.15	.04
❑ 200	Larry Jansen	.15	.04
❑ 201	Al Kaline	3.00	.90
❑ 202	Bob Purkey	.15	.04
❑ 203	Harry Brecheen CO	.15	.04
❑ 204	Angel Scull	.15	.04
❑ 205	Johnny Sain	.30	.09
❑ 206	Ray Crone	.15	.04
❑ 207	Tom Oliver CO	.15	.04
❑ 208	Grady Hatton	.15	.04
❑ 209	Charlie Thompson	.15	.04
❑ 210	Bob Buhl	.15	.04
❑ 211	Don Hoak	.15	.04
❑ 212	Mickey Micelotta	.15	.04
❑ 213	John Fitzpatrick CO	.15	.04
❑ 214	Arnold Portocarrero	.15	.04
❑ 215	Ed McGhee	.15	.04
❑ 216	Al Sima	.15	.04
❑ 217	Paul Schreiber CO	.15	.04
❑ 218	Fred Marsh	.15	.04
❑ 219	Charlie Kress	.15	.04
❑ 220	Ruben Gomez	.15	.04
❑ 221	Dick Brodowski	.15	.04
❑ 222	Bill Wilson	.15	.04
❑ 223	Joe Haynes CO	.15	.04
❑ 224	Dick Weik	.15	.04
❑ 225	Don Liddle	.15	.04
❑ 226	Jehosie Heard	.15	.04
❑ 227	Buster Mills CO	.15	.04
❑ 228	Gene Hermanski	.15	.04
❑ 229	Bob Talbot	.15	.04
❑ 230	Bob Kuzava	.15	.04
❑ 231	Roy Smalley	.15	.04
❑ 232	Lou Limmer	.15	.04
❑ 233	Augie Galan	.15	.04
❑ 234	Jerry Lynch	.15	.04
❑ 235	Vern Law	.15	.04
❑ 236	Paul Penson	.15	.04
❑ 237	Mike Ryba	.15	.04
❑ 238	Al Aber	.15	.04
❑ 239	Bill Skowron	.50	.15
❑ 240	Sam Mele	.15	.04
❑ 241	Bob Miller	.15	.04
❑ 242	Curt Roberts	.15	.04
❑ 243	Ray Blades CO	.15	.04
❑ 244	Leroy Wheat	.15	.04
❑ 245	Roy Sievers	.30	.09
❑ 246	Howie Fox	.15	.04
❑ 247	Eddie Mayo CO	.15	.04
❑ 248	Al Smith	.15	.04
❑ 249	Wilmer Mizell	.30	.09
❑ 250	Not Issued	.00	.00
❑ 251	Roberto Clemente	10.00	3.00
❑ 252	Bob Grim	.15	.04
❑ 253	Elston Howard	.50	.15
❑ 254	Harmon Killebrew	.75	.23
❑ 255	Camilo Pascual	.15	.04
❑ 256	Herb Score	.30	.09
❑ 257	Bill Virdon	.30	.09
❑ 258	Don Zimmer	.30	.09
❑ NNO	Hank Aaron AU	200.00	60.00
❑ NNO	Gold Redem. Card Exp.	.00	1.05

1999 Topps Chrome

	Nm-Mt	Ex-Mt
COMPLETE SET (462)	120.00	36.00
COMP. SERIES 1 (241)	60.00	18.00
COMP. SERIES 2 (221)	60.00	18.00
COMMON (1-6/8-463)	.50	.15
COMMON (205-212/425-437)	1.00	.30

No.	Player	Nm-Mt	Ex-Mt
❑ 1	Roger Clemens	4.00	1.20
❑ 2	Andres Galarraga	.75	.23
❑ 3	Scott Brosius	.75	.23
❑ 4	John Flaherty	.50	.15
❑ 5	Jim Leyritz	.50	.15
❑ 6	Ray Durham	.75	.23
❑ 8	Jose Vizcaino	.50	.15
❑ 9	Will Clark	2.00	.60
❑ 10	David Wells	.75	.23
❑ 11	Jose Guillen	.75	.23
❑ 12	Scott Hatteberg	.50	.15
❑ 13	Edgardo Alfonzo	.50	.15
❑ 14	Mike Bordick	.50	.15
❑ 15	Manny Ramirez	1.25	.35
❑ 16	Greg Maddux	3.00	.90
❑ 17	David Segui	.50	.15
❑ 18	Darryl Strawberry	.75	.23
❑ 19	Brad Radke	.75	.23
❑ 20	Kerry Wood	2.00	.60
❑ 21	Matt Anderson	.50	.15
❑ 22	Derrek Lee	.75	.23
❑ 23	Mickey Morandini	.50	.15
❑ 24	Paul Konerko	.75	.23
❑ 25	Travis Lee	.50	.15
❑ 26	Ken Hill	.50	.15
❑ 27	Kenny Rogers	.75	.23
❑ 28	Paul Sorrento	.50	.15
❑ 29	Quilvio Veras	.50	.15
❑ 30	Todd Walker	.50	.15
❑ 31	Ryan Jackson	.50	.15
❑ 32	John Olerud	.75	.23
❑ 33	Doug Glanville	.50	.15
❑ 34	Nolan Ryan	6.00	1.80
❑ 35	Ray Lankford	.50	.15
❑ 36	Mark Loretta	.75	.23
❑ 37	Jason Dickson	.50	.15
❑ 38	Sean Bergman	.50	.15
❑ 39	Quinton McCracken	.50	.15
❑ 40	Bartolo Colon	.75	.23
❑ 41	Brady Anderson	.75	.23
❑ 42	Chris Stynes	.50	.15
❑ 43	Jorge Posada	1.25	.35
❑ 44	Justin Thompson	.50	.15
❑ 45	Johnny Damon	1.25	.35
❑ 46	Armando Benitez	.50	.15
❑ 47	Brant Brown	.50	.15
❑ 48	Charlie Hayes	.50	.15
❑ 49	Darren Dreifort	.50	.15
❑ 50	Juan Gonzalez	1.25	.35
❑ 51	Chuck Knoblauch	.75	.23
❑ 52	Todd Helton	1.25	.35
❑ 53	Rick Reed	.50	.15
❑ 54	Chris Gomez	.50	.15
❑ 55	Gary Sheffield	.75	.23
❑ 56	Rod Beck	.50	.15
❑ 57	Rey Sanchez	.50	.15
❑ 58	Garret Anderson	.75	.23
❑ 59	Jimmy Haynes	.50	.15
❑ 60	Steve Woodard	.50	.15
❑ 61	Rondell White	.75	.23
❑ 62	Vladimir Guerrero	2.00	.60
❑ 63	Eric Karros	.75	.23
❑ 64	Russ Davis	.50	.15
❑ 65	Mo Vaughn	.75	.23
❑ 66	Sammy Sosa	3.00	.90
❑ 67	Troy Percival	.75	.23
❑ 68	Kenny Lofton	.75	.23
❑ 69	Bill Taylor	.50	.15
❑ 70	Mark McGwire	5.00	1.50
❑ 71	Roger Cedeno	.50	.15
❑ 72	Javy Lopez	.75	.23
❑ 73	Damion Easley	.50	.15
❑ 74	Andy Pettitte	1.25	.35
❑ 75	Tony Gwynn	2.50	.75
❑ 76	Ricardo Rincon	.50	.15
❑ 77	F.P. Santangelo	.50	.15
❑ 78	Jay Bell	.75	.23
❑ 79	Scott Servais	.50	.15
❑ 80	Jose Canseco	2.00	.60
❑ 81	Roberto Hernandez	.50	.15
❑ 82	Todd Dunwoody	.50	.15
❑ 83	John Wetteland	.75	.23
❑ 84	Mike Caruso	.50	.15
❑ 85	Derek Jeter	5.00	1.50
❑ 86	Aaron Sele	.50	.15
❑ 87	Jose Lima	.50	.15
❑ 88	Ryan Christenson	.50	.15
❑ 89	Jeff Cirillo	.50	.15
❑ 90	Jose Hernandez	.50	.15
❑ 91	Mark Kotsay	.50	.15
❑ 92	Darren Bragg	.50	.15
❑ 93	Albert Belle	.75	.23
❑ 94	Matt Lawton	.50	.15
❑ 95	Pedro Martinez	2.00	.60
❑ 96	Greg Vaughn	.50	.15
❑ 97	Neifi Perez	.50	.15
❑ 98	Gerald Williams	.50	.15
❑ 99	Derek Bell	.50	.15
❑ 100	Ken Griffey Jr.	3.00	.90
❑ 101	David Cone	.75	.23
❑ 102	Brian Johnson	.50	.15
❑ 103	Dean Palmer	.75	.23
❑ 104	Javier Valentin	.50	.15

❑ 105 Trevor Hoffman .75 .23
❑ 106 Butch Huskey .50 .15
❑ 107 Dave Martinez .50 .15
❑ 108 Billy Wagner .75 .23
❑ 109 Shawn Green .75 .23
❑ 110 Ben Grieve .50 .15
❑ 111 Tom Goodwin .50 .15
❑ 112 Jaret Wright .50 .15
❑ 113 Aramis Ramirez .75 .23
❑ 114 Dmitri Young .75 .23
❑ 115 Hideki Irabu .50 .15
❑ 116 Roberto Kelly .50 .15
❑ 117 Jeff Fassero .50 .15
❑ 118 Mark Clark .50 .15
❑ 119 Jason McDonald .50 .15
❑ 120 Matt Williams .75 .23
❑ 121 Dave Burba .50 .15
❑ 122 Bret Saberhagen .75 .23
❑ 123 Deivi Cruz .50 .15
❑ 124 Chad Curtis .50 .15
❑ 125 Scott Rolen 2.00 .60
❑ 126 Lee Stevens .50 .15
❑ 127 J.T. Snow .75 .23
❑ 128 Rusty Greer .75 .23
❑ 129 Brian Meadows .50 .15
❑ 130 Jim Edmonds .75 .23
❑ 131 Ron Gant .75 .23
❑ 132 A.J. Hinch .50 .15
❑ 133 Shannon Stewart .75 .23
❑ 134 Brad Fullmer .50 .15
❑ 135 Cal Eldred .50 .15
❑ 136 Matt Walbeck .50 .15
❑ 137 Carl Everett .75 .23
❑ 138 Walt Weiss .50 .15
❑ 139 Fred McGriff 1.25 .35
❑ 140 Darin Erstad .75 .23
❑ 141 Dave Nilsson .50 .15
❑ 142 Eric Young .50 .15
❑ 143 Dan Wilson .50 .15
❑ 144 Jeff Reed .50 .15
❑ 145 Brett Tomko .50 .15
❑ 146 Terry Steinbach .50 .15
❑ 147 Seth Greisinger .50 .15
❑ 148 Pat Meares .50 .15
❑ 149 Livan Hernandez .50 .15
❑ 150 Jeff Bagwell 1.25 .35
❑ 151 Bob Wickman .50 .15
❑ 152 Omar Vizquel 1.25 .35
❑ 153 Eric Davis .75 .23
❑ 154 Larry Sutton .50 .15
❑ 155 Magglio Ordonez .75 .23
❑ 156 Eric Milton .50 .15
❑ 157 Darren Lewis .50 .15
❑ 158 Rick Aguilera .50 .15
❑ 159 Mike Lieberthal .75 .23
❑ 160 Robb Nen .75 .23
❑ 161 Brian Giles .75 .23
❑ 162 Jeff Brantley .50 .15
❑ 163 Gary DiSarcina .50 .15
❑ 164 John Valentin .50 .15
❑ 165 Dave Dellucci .50 .15
❑ 166 Chan Ho Park .75 .23
❑ 167 Masato Yoshii .50 .15
❑ 168 Jason Schmidt .75 .23
❑ 169 LaTroy Hawkins .50 .15
❑ 170 Bret Boone .75 .23
❑ 171 Jerry DiPoto .50 .15
❑ 172 Mariano Rivera 1.25 .35
❑ 173 Mike Cameron .75 .23
❑ 174 Scott Erickson .50 .15
❑ 175 Charles Johnson .75 .23
❑ 176 Bobby Jones .50 .15
❑ 177 Francisco Cordova .50 .15
❑ 178 Todd Jones .50 .15
❑ 179 Jeff Montgomery .50 .15
❑ 180 Mike Mussina 1.25 .35
❑ 181 Bob Abreu .75 .23
❑ 182 Ismael Valdes .50 .15
❑ 183 Andy Fox .50 .15
❑ 184 Woody Williams .50 .15
❑ 185 Denny Neagle .50 .15
❑ 186 Jose Valentin .50 .15
❑ 187 Darrin Fletcher .50 .15
❑ 188 Gabe Alvarez .50 .15
❑ 189 Eddie Taubensee .50 .15
❑ 190 Edgar Martinez 1.25 .35
❑ 191 Jason Kendall .75 .23
❑ 192 Darryl Kile .75 .23
❑ 193 Jeff King .50 .15
❑ 194 Rey Ordonez .50 .15
❑ 195 Andruw Jones .75 .23
❑ 196 Tony Fernandez .50 .15
❑ 197 Jamey Wright .50 .15
❑ 198 B.J. Surhoff .75 .23
❑ 199 Vinny Castilla .75 .23
❑ 200 David Wells HL .50 .15
❑ 201 Mark McGwire HL 2.50 .75
❑ 202 Sammy Sosa HL 2.00 .60
❑ 203 Roger Clemens HL 2.00 .60
❑ 204 Kerry Wood HL 1.25 .35
❑ 205 Gabe Kapler 1.00 .30
Lance Berkman
Mike Frank
❑ 206 Alex Escobar RC 1.00 .30
Ricky Ledee
Mike Stoner
❑ 207 Peter Bergeron RC 1.00 .30
Jeremy Giambi
George Lombard
❑ 208 Michael Barrett 1.00 .30
Ben Davis
Robert Fick
❑ 209 Jayson Werth 1.00 .30
Ramon Hernandez
Pat Cline
❑ 210 Ryan Anderson 1.00 .30
Bruce Chen
Chris Enochs
❑ 211 Brad Penny 1.00 .30
Octavio Dotel
Mike Lincoln
❑ 212 Chuck Abbott RC 1.00 .30
Brent Butler
Danny Klassen
❑ 213 Chris C.Jones 1.00 .30
Jeff Urban RC
❑ 214 Arturo McDowell RC 1.00 .30
Tony Torcato
❑ 215 Josh McKinley RC 1.00 .30
Jason Tyner
❑ 216 Matt Burch 1.00 .30
Seth Etheron RC
❑ 217 Mamon Tucker RC 1.00 .30
Rick Elder
❑ 218 J.M.Gold 1.00 .30
Ryan Mills RC
❑ 219 Andy Brown 1.00 .30
Choo Freeman RC
❑ 220A Mark McGwire HR 1 50.00 15.00
❑ 220B Mark McGwire HR 2 30.00 9.00
❑ 220C Mark McGwire HR 3 30.00 9.00
❑ 220D Mark McGwire HR 4 30.00 9.00
❑ 220E Mark McGwire HR 5 30.00 9.00
❑ 220F Mark McGwire HR 6 30.00 9.00
❑ 220G Mark McGwire HR 7 30.00 9.00
❑ 220H Mark McGwire HR 8 30.00 9.00
❑ 220I Mark McGwire HR 9 30.00 9.00
❑ 220J M.McGwire HR 10 30.00 9.00
❑ 220K M.McGwire HR 11 30.00 9.00
❑ 220L M.McGwire HR 12 30.00 9.00
❑ 220M M.McGwire HR 13 30.00 9.00
❑ 220N M.McGwire HR 14 30.00 9.00
❑ 220O M.McGwire HR 15 30.00 9.00
❑ 220P M.McGwire HR 16 30.00 9.00
❑ 220Q M.McGwire HR 17 30.00 9.00
❑ 220R M.McGwire HR 18 30.00 9.00
❑ 220S M.McGwire HR 19 30.00 9.00
❑ 220T M.McGwire HR 20 30.00 9.00
❑ 220U M.McGwire HR 21 30.00 9.00
❑ 220V M.McGwire HR 22 30.00 9.00
❑ 220W M.McGwire HR 23 30.00 9.00
❑ 220X M.McGwire HR 24 30.00 9.00
❑ 220Y M.McGwire HR 25 30.00 9.00
❑ 220Z M.McGwire HR 26 30.00 9.00
❑ 220AA M.McGwire HR 27 30.00 9.00
❑ 220AB M.McGwire HR 28 30.00 9.00
❑ 220AC M.McGwire HR 29 30.00 9.00
❑ 220AD M.McGwire HR 30 30.00 9.00
❑ 220AE M.McGwire HR 31 30.00 9.00
❑ 220AF M.McGwire HR 32 30.00 9.00
❑ 220AG M.McGwire HR 33 30.00 9.00
❑ 220AH M.McGwire HR 34 30.00 9.00
❑ 220AI M.McGwire HR 35 30.00 9.00
❑ 220AJ M.McGwire HR 36 30.00 9.00
❑ 220AK M.McGwire HR 37 30.00 9.00
❑ 220AL M.McGwire HR 38 30.00 9.00
❑ 220AM M.McGwire HR 39 30.00 9.00
❑ 220AN M.McGwire HR 40 30.00 9.00
❑ 220AO M.McGwire HR 41 30.00 9.00
❑ 220AP M.McGwire HR 42 30.00 9.00
❑ 220AQ M.McGwire HR 43 30.00 9.00
❑ 220AR M.McGwire HR 44 30.00 9.00
❑ 220AS M.McGwire HR 45 30.00 9.00
❑ 220AT M.McGwire HR 46 30.00 9.00
❑ 220AU M.McGwire HR 47 30.00 9.00
❑ 220AV M.McGwire HR 48 30.00 9.00
❑ 220AW M.McGwire HR 49 30.00 9.00
❑ 220AX M.McGwire HR 50 30.00 9.00
❑ 220AY M.McGwire HR 51 30.00 9.00
❑ 220AZ M.McGwire HR 52 30.00 9.00
❑ 220BB M.McGwire HR 53 30.00 9.00
❑ 220CC M.McGwire HR 54 30.00 9.00
❑ 220DD M.McGwire HR 55 30.00 9.00
❑ 220EE M.McGwire HR 56 30.00 9.00
❑ 220FF M.McGwire HR 57 30.00 9.00
❑ 220GG M.McGwire HR 58 30.00 9.00
❑ 220HH M.McGwire HR 59 30.00 9.00
❑ 220II M.McGwire HR 60 30.00 9.00
❑ 220JJ M.McGwire HR 61 50.00 15.00
❑ 220KK M.McGwire HR 62 80.00 24.00
❑ 220LL M.McGwire HR 63 50.00 15.00
❑ 220MM M.McGwire HR 64 50.00 15.00
❑ 220NN M.McGwire HR 65 50.00 15.00
❑ 220OO M.McGwire HR 66 50.00 15.00
❑ 220PP M.McGwire HR 67 50.00 15.00
❑ 220QQ M.McGwire HR 68 50.00 15.00
❑ 220RR M.McGwire HR 69 50.00 15.00
❑ 220SS M.McGwire HR 70 150.00 45.00
❑ 221 Larry Walker LL .75 .23
❑ 222 Bernie Williams LL .75 .23
❑ 223 Mark McGwire LL 2.50 .75
❑ 224 Ken Griffey Jr. LL 2.00 .60
❑ 225 Sammy Sosa LL 2.00 .60
❑ 226 Juan Gonzalez LL .75 .23
❑ 227 Dante Bichette LL .50 .15
❑ 228 Alex Rodriguez LL 2.00 .60
❑ 229 Sammy Sosa LL 2.00 .60
❑ 230 Derek Jeter LL 2.50 .75
❑ 231 Greg Maddux LL 2.00 .60
❑ 232 Roger Clemens LL 2.00 .60
❑ 233 Ricky Ledee WS .50 .15
❑ 234 Chuck Knoblauch WS .50 .15
❑ 235 Bernie Williams WS .75 .23
❑ 236 Tino Martinez WS .75 .23
❑ 237 Orl. Hernandez WS .50 .15
❑ 238 Scott Brosius WS .50 .15
❑ 239 Andy Pettitte WS .75 .23
❑ 240 Mariano Rivera WS .75 .23
❑ 241 Checklist .50 .15
❑ 242 Checklist .50 .15
❑ 243 Tom Glavine 1.25 .35
❑ 244 Andy Benes .50 .15
❑ 245 Sandy Alomar Jr. .50 .15
❑ 246 Wilton Guerrero .50 .15
❑ 247 Alex Gonzalez .50 .15
❑ 248 Roberto Alomar 1.25 .35
❑ 249 Ruben Rivera .50 .15
❑ 250 Eric Chavez .75 .23
❑ 251 Ellis Burks .75 .23
❑ 252 Richie Sexson .75 .23
❑ 253 Steve Finley .75 .23
❑ 254 Dwight Gooden .75 .23
❑ 255 Dustin Hermanson .50 .15
❑ 256 Kirk Rueter .50 .15
❑ 257 Steve Trachsel .50 .15
❑ 258 Gregg Jefferies .50 .15
❑ 259 Matt Stairs .50 .15
❑ 260 Shane Reynolds .50 .15
❑ 261 Gregg Olson .50 .15
❑ 262 Kevin Tapani .50 .15
❑ 263 Matt Morris .75 .23
❑ 264 Carl Pavano .75 .23
❑ 265 Nomar Garciaparra 3.00 .90
❑ 266 Kevin Young .75 .23
❑ 267 Rick Helling .50 .15
❑ 268 Matt Franco .50 .15
❑ 269 Brian McRae .50 .15
❑ 270 Cal Ripken 6.00 1.80

	Card	Player	Hi	Lo
❑	271	Jeff Abbott	.50	.15
❑	272	Tony Batista	.75	.23
❑	273	Bill Simas	.50	.15
❑	274	Brian Hunter	.50	.15
❑	275	John Franco	.75	.23
❑	276	Devon White	.75	.23
❑	277	Rickey Henderson	2.00	.60
❑	278	Chuck Finley	.75	.23
❑	279	Mike Blowers	.50	.15
❑	280	Mark Grace	1.25	.35
❑	281	Randy Winn	.50	.15
❑	282	Bobby Bonilla	.75	.23
❑	283	David Justice	.75	.23
❑	284	Shane Monahan	.50	.15
❑	285	Kevin Brown	1.25	.35
❑	286	Todd Zeile	.75	.23
❑	287	Al Martin	.50	.15
❑	288	Troy O'Leary	.50	.15
❑	289	Darryl Hamilton	.50	.15
❑	290	Tino Martinez	1.25	.35
❑	291	David Ortiz	1.25	.35
❑	292	Tony Clark	.50	.15
❑	293	Ryan Minor	.50	.15
❑	294	Mark Leiter	.50	.15
❑	295	Wally Joyner	.75	.23
❑	296	Cliff Floyd	.75	.23
❑	297	Shawn Estes	.50	.15
❑	298	Pat Hentgen	.50	.15
❑	299	Scott Elarton	.50	.15
❑	300	Alex Rodriguez	3.00	.90
❑	301	Ozzie Guillen	.50	.15
❑	302	Hideo Nomo	2.00	.60
❑	303	Ryan McGuire	.50	.15
❑	304	Brad Ausmus	.50	.15
❑	305	Alex Gonzalez	.50	.15
❑	306	Brian Jordan	.75	.23
❑	307	John Jaha	.50	.15
❑	308	Mark Grudzielanek	.50	.15
❑	309	Juan Guzman	.50	.15
❑	310	Tony Womack	.50	.15
❑	311	Dennis Reyes	.50	.15
❑	312	Marty Cordova	.50	.15
❑	313	Ramiro Mendoza	.50	.15
❑	314	Robin Ventura	.75	.23
❑	315	Rafael Palmeiro	1.25	.35
❑	316	Ramon Martinez	.50	.15
❑	317	Pedro Astacio	.50	.15
❑	318	Dave Hollins	.50	.15
❑	319	Tom Candiotti	.50	.15
❑	320	Al Leiter	.75	.23
❑	321	Rico Brogna	.50	.15
❑	322	Reggie Jefferson	.50	.15
❑	323	Bernard Gilkey	.50	.15
❑	324	Jason Giambi	.75	.23
❑	325	Craig Biggio	1.25	.35
❑	326	Troy Glaus	.75	.23
❑	327	Delino DeShields	.50	.15
❑	328	Fernando Vina	.50	.15
❑	329	John Smoltz	1.25	.35
❑	330	Jeff Kent	.75	.23
❑	331	Roy Halladay	.50	.15
❑	332	Andy Ashby	.50	.15
❑	333	Tim Wakefield	.75	.23
❑	334	Roger Clemens	4.00	1.20
❑	335	Bernie Williams	1.25	.35
❑	336	Desi Relaford	.50	.15
❑	337	John Burkett	.50	.15
❑	338	Mike Hampton	.75	.23
❑	339	Royce Clayton	.50	.15
❑	340	Mike Piazza	3.00	.90
❑	341	Jeremi Gonzalez	.50	.15
❑	342	Mike Lansing	.50	.15
❑	343	Jamie Moyer	.75	.23
❑	344	Ron Coomer	.50	.15
❑	345	Barry Larkin	1.25	.35
❑	346	Fernando Tatis	.50	.15
❑	347	Chili Davis	.75	.23
❑	348	Bobby Higginson	.75	.23
❑	349	Hal Morris	.50	.15
❑	350	Larry Walker	1.25	.35
❑	351	Carlos Guillen	.75	.23
❑	352	Miguel Tejada	.75	.23
❑	353	Travis Fryman	.75	.23
❑	354	Jarrod Washburn	.50	.15
❑	355	Chipper Jones	2.00	.60
❑	356	Todd Stottlemyre	.50	.15
❑	357	Henry Rodriguez	.50	.15
❑	358	Eli Marrero	.50	.15
❑	359	Alan Benes	.50	.15
❑	360	Tim Salmon	1.25	.35
❑	361	Luis Gonzalez	.75	.23
❑	362	Scott Spiezio	.50	.15
❑	363	Chris Carpenter	.50	.15
❑	364	Bobby Howry	.50	.15
❑	365	Raul Mondesi	.75	.23
❑	366	Ugueth Urbina	.50	.15
❑	367	Tom Evans	.50	.15
❑	368	Kerry Ligtenberg RC	.75	.23
❑	369	Adrian Beltre	1.25	.35
❑	370	Ryan Klesko	.75	.23
❑	371	Wilson Alvarez	.50	.15
❑	372	John Thomson	.50	.15
❑	373	Tony Saunders	.50	.15
❑	374	Dave Mlicki	.50	.15
❑	375	Ken Caminiti	.75	.23
❑	376	Jay Buhner	.75	.23
❑	377	Bill Mueller	.75	.23
❑	378	Jeff Blauser	.50	.15
❑	379	Edgar Renteria	.75	.23
❑	380	Jim Thome	2.00	.60
❑	381	Joey Hamilton	.50	.15
❑	382	Calvin Pickering	.50	.15
❑	383	Marquis Grissom	.75	.23
❑	384	Omar Daal	.50	.15
❑	385	Curt Schilling	.75	.23
❑	386	Jose Cruz Jr.	.50	.15
❑	387	Chris Widger	.50	.15
❑	388	Pete Harnisch	.50	.15
❑	389	Charles Nagy	.50	.15
❑	390	Tom Gordon	.50	.15
❑	391	Bobby Smith	.50	.15
❑	392	Derrick Gibson	.50	.15
❑	393	Jeff Conine	.75	.23
❑	394	Carlos Perez	.50	.15
❑	395	Barry Bonds	5.00	1.50
❑	396	Mark McLemore	.50	.15
❑	397	Juan Encarnacion	.50	.15
❑	398	Wade Boggs	1.25	.35
❑	399	Ivan Rodriguez	2.00	.60
❑	400	Moises Alou	.75	.23
❑	401	Jeromy Burnitz	.75	.23
❑	402	Sean Casey	.75	.23
❑	403	Jose Offerman	.50	.15
❑	404	Joe Fontenot	.50	.15
❑	405	Kevin Millwood	.75	.23
❑	406	Lance Johnson	.50	.15
❑	407	Richard Hidalgo	.50	.15
❑	408	Mike Jackson	.50	.15
❑	409	Brian Anderson	.50	.15
❑	410	Jeff Shaw	.50	.15
❑	411	Preston Wilson	.75	.23
❑	412	Todd Hundley	.50	.15
❑	413	Jim Parque	.50	.15
❑	414	Justin Baughman	.50	.15
❑	415	Dante Bichette	.75	.23
❑	416	Paul O'Neill	1.25	.35
❑	417	Miguel Cairo	.50	.15
❑	418	Randy Johnson	2.00	.60
❑	419	Jesus Sanchez	.50	.15
❑	420	Carlos Delgado	.75	.23
❑	421	Ricky Ledee	.50	.15
❑	422	Orlando Hernandez	.50	.15
❑	423	Frank Thomas	2.00	.60
❑	424	Pokey Reese	.50	.15
❑	425	Carlos Lee Mike Lowell Kit Pellow RC	1.00	.30
❑	426	Michael Cuddyer Mark DeRosa Jerry Hairston Jr.	1.00	.30
❑	427	Marlon Anderson Ron Belliard Orlando Cabrera	1.00	.30
❑	428	Micah Bowie Phil Norton RC Randy Wolf	1.00	.30
❑	429	Jack Cressend RC Jason Rakers John Rocker	1.00	.30
❑	430	Ruben Mateo Scott Morgan Mike Zywica RC	1.00	.30
❑	431	Jason LaRue Matt LeCroy Mitch Meluskey	1.00	.30
❑	432	Gabe Kapler Armando Rios Fernando Seguignol	1.00	.30
❑	433	Adam Kennedy Mickey Lopez RC Jackie Rexrode	1.00	.30
❑	434	Jose Fernandez RC Jeff Liefer Chris Truby	1.00	.30
❑	435	Corey Koskie Doug Mientkiewicz RC Damon Minor	2.00	.60
❑	436	Roosevelt Brown RC Dernell Stenson Vernon Wells	1.00	.30
❑	437	A.J. Burnett RC Billy Koch John Nicholson	2.00	.60
❑	438	Matt Belisle Matt Roney RC	1.00	.30
❑	439	Austin Kearns Chris George RC	4.00	1.20
❑	440	Nate Bump RC Nate Cornejo	1.00	.30
❑	441	Brad Lidge Mike Nannini RC	4.00	1.20
❑	442	Matt Holliday Jeff Winchester RC	2.00	.60
❑	443	Adam Everett Chip Ambres RC	1.50	.45
❑	444	Pat Burrell Eric Valent RC	2.50	.75
❑	445	Roger Clemens SK	2.00	.60
❑	446	Kerry Wood SK	1.25	.35
❑	447	Curt Schilling SK	.50	.15
❑	448	Randy Johnson SK	1.25	.35
❑	449	Pedro Martinez SK	1.25	.35
❑	450	Jeff Bagwell AT Andres Galarraga Mark McGwire	2.00	.60
❑	451	John Olerud AT Jim Thome Tino Martinez	.75	.23
❑	452	Alex Rodriguez AT Nomar Garciaparra Derek Jeter	2.50	.75
❑	453	Vinny Castilla AT Chipper Jones Scott Rolen	1.25	.35
❑	454	Sammy Sosa AT Ken Griffey Jr. Juan Gonzalez	2.00	.60
❑	455	Barry Bonds AT Manny Ramirez Larry Walker	2.00	.60
❑	456	Frank Thomas AT Tim Salmon David Justice	2.00	.60
❑	457	Travis Lee AT Todd Helton Ben Grieve	.75	.23
❑	458	Vladimir Guerrero AT Greg Vaughn Bernie Williams	.75	.23
❑	459	Mike Piazza AT Ivan Rodriguez Jason Kendall	2.00	.60
❑	460	Roger Clemens AT Kerry Wood Greg Maddux	2.00	.60
❑	461A	Sammy Sosa HR 1	25.00	7.50
❑	461B	Sammy Sosa HR 2	15.00	4.50
❑	461C	Sammy Sosa HR 3	15.00	4.50
❑	461D	Sammy Sosa HR 4	15.00	4.50
❑	461E	Sammy Sosa HR 5	15.00	4.50
❑	461F	Sammy Sosa HR 6	15.00	4.50
❑	461G	Sammy Sosa HR 7	15.00	4.50
❑	461H	Sammy Sosa HR 8	15.00	4.50
❑	461I	Sammy Sosa HR 9	15.00	4.50
❑	461J	Sammy Sosa HR 10	15.00	4.50
❑	461K	Sammy Sosa HR 11	15.00	4.50
❑	461L	Sammy Sosa HR 12	15.00	4.50
❑	461M	Sammy Sosa HR 13	15.00	4.50

Card	Nm-Mt	Ex-Mt
❑ 461N Sammy Sosa HR 14	15.00	4.50
❑ 461O Sammy Sosa HR 15	15.00	4.50
❑ 461P Sammy Sosa HR 16	15.00	4.50
❑ 461Q Sammy Sosa HR 17	15.00	4.50
❑ 461R Sammy Sosa HR 18	15.00	4.50
❑ 461S Sammy Sosa HR 19	15.00	4.50
❑ 461T Sammy Sosa HR 20	15.00	4.50
❑ 461U Sammy Sosa HR 21	15.00	4.50
❑ 461V Sammy Sosa HR 22	15.00	4.50
❑ 461W Sammy Sosa HR 23	15.00	4.50
❑ 461X Sammy Sosa HR 24	15.00	4.50
❑ 461Y Sammy Sosa HR 25	15.00	4.50
❑ 461Z Sammy Sosa HR 26	15.00	4.50
❑ 461AA S.Sosa HR 27	15.00	4.50
❑ 461AB S.Sosa HR 28	15.00	4.50
❑ 461AC S.Sosa HR 29	15.00	4.50
❑ 461AD S.Sosa HR 30	15.00	4.50
❑ 461AE S.Sosa HR 31	15.00	4.50
❑ 461AF S.Sosa HR 32	15.00	4.50
❑ 461AG S.Sosa HR 33	15.00	4.50
❑ 461AH S.Sosa HR 34	15.00	4.50
❑ 461AI S.Sosa HR 35	15.00	4.50
❑ 461AJ S.Sosa HR 36	15.00	4.50
❑ 461AK S.Sosa HR 37	15.00	4.50
❑ 461AL S.Sosa HR 38	15.00	4.50
❑ 461AM S.Sosa HR 39	15.00	4.50
❑ 461AN S.Sosa HR 40	15.00	4.50
❑ 461AO S.Sosa HR 41	15.00	4.50
❑ 461AP S.Sosa HR 42	15.00	4.50
❑ 461AR S.Sosa HR 43	15.00	4.50
❑ 461AS S.Sosa HR 44	15.00	4.50
❑ 461AT S.Sosa HR 45	15.00	4.50
❑ 461AU S.Sosa HR 46	15.00	4.50
❑ 461AV S.Sosa HR 47	15.00	4.50
❑ 461AW S.Sosa HR 48	15.00	4.50
❑ 461AX S.Sosa HR 49	15.00	4.50
❑ 461AY S.Sosa HR 50	15.00	4.50
❑ 461AZ S.Sosa HR 51	15.00	4.50
❑ 461BB S.Sosa HR 52	15.00	4.50
❑ 461CC S.Sosa HR 53	15.00	4.50
❑ 461DD S.Sosa HR 54	15.00	4.50
❑ 461EE S.Sosa HR 55	15.00	4.50
❑ 461FF S.Sosa HR 56	15.00	4.50
❑ 461GG S.Sosa HR 57	15.00	4.50
❑ 461HH S.Sosa HR 58	15.00	4.50
❑ 461II S.Sosa HR 59	15.00	4.50
❑ 461JJ S.Sosa HR 60	15.00	4.50
❑ 461KK S.Sosa HR 61	25.00	7.50
❑ 461LL S.Sosa HR 62	40.00	12.00
❑ 461MM S.Sosa HR 63	25.00	7.50
❑ 461NN S.Sosa HR 64	25.00	7.50
❑ 461OO S.Sosa HR 65	25.00	7.50
❑ 461PP S.Sosa HR 66	80.00	24.00
❑ 462 Checklist	.50	.15
❑ 463 Checklist	.50	.15

1999 Topps Chrome Traded

	Nm-Mt	Ex-Mt
COMP.FACT SET (121)	80.00	24.00
❑ T1 Seth Etherton	.40	.12
❑ T2 Mark Harriger RC	.50	.15
❑ T3 Matt Wise RC	.50	.15
❑ T4 Carlos E. Hernandez RC	.75	.23
❑ T5 Julio Lugo RC	.75	.23
❑ T6 Mike Nannini	.40	.12
❑ T7 Justin Bowles RC	.50	.15
❑ T8 Mark Mulder RC	5.00	1.20
❑ T9 Roberto Vaz RC	.50	.15
❑ T10 Felipe Lopez RC	.75	.23
❑ T11 Matt Belisle	.40	.12
❑ T12 Micah Bowie	.40	.12
❑ T13 Ruben Quevedo RC	.50	.15
❑ T14 Jose Garcia RC	.50	.15
❑ T15 David Kelton RC	.75	.23
❑ T16 Phil Norton	.40	.12
❑ T17 Corey Patterson RC	5.00	1.50
❑ T18 Ron Walker RC	.50	.15
❑ T19 Paul Hoover RC	.50	.15
❑ T20 Ryan Rupe RC	.50	.15
❑ T21 J.D. Closser RC	1.25	.35
❑ T22 Rob Ryan RC	.50	.15
❑ T23 Steve Colyer RC	.75	.23
❑ T24 Bubba Crosby RC	1.25	.35
❑ T25 Luke Prokopec RC	.50	.15
❑ T26 Matt Blank RC	.50	.15
❑ T27 Josh McKinley	.60	.18
❑ T28 Nate Bump	.50	.15
❑ T29 G.Chiaramonte RC	.50	.15
❑ T30 Arturo McDowell	.40	.12
❑ T31 Tony Torcato	.60	.18
❑ T32 Dave Roberts RC	1.25	.35
❑ T33 C.C. Sabathia RC	2.50	.75
❑ T34 Sean Spencer RC	.50	.15
❑ T35 Chip Ambres	.40	.12
❑ T36 A.J. Burnett	1.50	.45
❑ T37 Mo Bruce RC	.50	.15
❑ T38 Jason Tyner	.40	.12
❑ T39 Mamon Tucker	.40	.12
❑ T40 Sean Burroughs RC	2.50	.75
❑ T41 Kevin Eberwein RC	.50	.15
❑ T42 Junior Herndon RC	.75	.23
❑ T43 Bryan Wolff RC	.50	.15
❑ T44 Pat Burrell	2.50	.75
❑ T45 Eric Valent	.75	.23
❑ T46 Carlos Pena RC	1.25	.35
❑ T47 Mike Zywica	.40	.12
❑ T48 Adam Everett	1.00	.30
❑ T49 Juan Pena RC	.50	.15
❑ T50 Adam Dunn RC	8.00	2.40
❑ T51 Austin Kearns	4.00	1.20
❑ T52 Jacobo Sequea RC	.50	.15
❑ T53 Choo Freeman	.60	.18
❑ T54 Jeff Winchester	.40	.12
❑ T55 Matt Burch	.50	.15
❑ T56 Chris George	.60	.18
❑ T57 Scott Mullen RC	.50	.15
❑ T58 Kit Pellow	.50	.15
❑ T59 Mark Quinn RC	.75	.23
❑ T60 Nate Cornejo	.75	.23
❑ T61 Ryan Mills	.40	.12
❑ T62 Kevin Beirne RC	.75	.23
❑ T63 Kip Wells RC	1.25	.35
❑ T64 Juan Rivera RC	.75	.23
❑ T65 Alfonso Soriano RC	10.00	3.00
❑ T66 Josh Hamilton RC	1.25	.35
❑ T67 Josh Girdley RC	.50	.15
❑ T68 Kyle Snyder RC	.50	.15
❑ T69 Mike Paradis RC	.50	.15
❑ T70 Jason Jennings RC	1.25	.35
❑ T71 David Walling RC	.50	.15
❑ T72 Omar Ortiz RC	.50	.15
❑ T73 Jay Gehrke RC	.50	.15
❑ T74 Casey Burns RC	.50	.15
❑ T75 Carl Crawford RC	3.00	.90
❑ T76 Reggie Sanders	.40	.12
❑ T77 Will Clark	1.50	.45
❑ T78 David Wells	.60	.18
❑ T79 Paul Konerko	.60	.18
❑ T80 Armando Benitez	.40	.12
❑ T81 Brant Brown	.40	.12
❑ T82 Mo Vaughn	.60	.18
❑ T83 Jose Canseco	1.50	.45
❑ T84 Albert Belle	.60	.18
❑ T85 Dean Palmer	.60	.18
❑ T86 Greg Vaughn	.40	.12
❑ T87 Mark Clark	.40	.12
❑ T88 Pat Meares	.40	.12
❑ T89 Eric Davis	.60	.18
❑ T90 Brian Giles	.60	.18
❑ T91 Jeff Brantley	.40	.12
❑ T92 Bret Boone	.60	.18
❑ T93 Ron Gant	.60	.18
❑ T94 Mike Cameron	.60	.18
❑ T95 Charles Johnson	.60	.18
❑ T96 Denny Neagle	.40	.12
❑ T97 Brian Hunter	.40	.12
❑ T98 Jose Hernandez	.40	.12
❑ T99 Rick Aguilera	.40	.12
❑ T100 Tony Batista	.60	.18
❑ T101 Roger Cedeno	.40	.12
❑ T102 C.Gubanich RC	.50	.15
❑ T103 Tim Belcher	.40	.12
❑ T104 Bruce Aven	.40	.12
❑ T105 Brian Daubach RC	.75	.23
❑ T106 Ed Sprague	.40	.12
❑ T107 Michael Tucker	.40	.12
❑ T108 Homer Bush	.40	.12
❑ T109 Armando Reynoso	.40	.12
❑ T110 Brook Fordyce	.40	.12
❑ T111 Matt Mantei	.40	.12
❑ T112 Dave Mlicki	.40	.12
❑ T113 Kenny Rogers	.60	.18
❑ T114 Livan Hernandez	.40	.12
❑ T115 Butch Huskey	.40	.12
❑ T116 David Segui	.40	.12
❑ T117 Darryl Hamilton	.40	.12
❑ T118 Terry Mulholland	.40	.12
❑ T119 Randy Velarde	.40	.12
❑ T120 Bill Taylor	.40	.12
❑ T121 Kevin Appier	.60	.18

2000 Topps Chrome Traded

	Nm-Mt	Ex-Mt
COMP.FACT.SET (135)	80.00	24.00
❑ T1 Mike MacDougal	1.00	.30
❑ T2 Andy Tracy RC	.50	.15
❑ T3 Brandon Phillips RC	1.50	.45
❑ T4 Brandon Inge RC	1.00	.30
❑ T5 Robbie Morrison RC	.50	.15
❑ T6 Josh Pressley RC	.50	.15
❑ T7 Todd Moser RC	.50	.15
❑ T8 Rob Purvis	.60	.18
❑ T9 Chance Caple	.40	.12
❑ T10 Ben Sheets	2.50	.75
❑ T11 Russ Jacobson RC	.50	.15
❑ T12 Brian Cole RC	.50	.15
❑ T13 Brad Baker	.60	.18
❑ T14 Alex Cintron RC	1.00	.30
❑ T15 Lyle Overbay RC	4.00	1.20
❑ T16 Mike Edwards RC	.50	.15
❑ T17 Sean McGowan RC	.50	.15
❑ T18 Jose Molina	.40	.12
❑ T19 Marcos Castillo RC	.50	.15
❑ T20 Josue Espada RC	.50	.15
❑ T21 Alex Gordon RC	.50	.15
❑ T22 Rob Pugmire RC	.50	.15
❑ T23 Jason Stumm	.50	.15
❑ T24 Ty Howington	.60	.18
❑ T25 Brett Myers	1.00	.30
❑ T26 Maicer Izturis RC	1.50	.45
❑ T27 John McDonald	.40	.12
❑ T28 W.Rodriguez RC	.50	.15
❑ T29 Carlos Zambrano RC	8.00	2.40
❑ T30 Alejandro Diaz RC	.50	.15
❑ T31 Geraldo Guzman RC	.50	.15
❑ T32 J.R. House RC	1.00	.30

❑ T33 Elvin Nina RC .50 .15
❑ T34 Juan Pierre RC 2.50 .75
❑ T35 Ben Johnson RC .50 .15
❑ T36 Jeff Bailey RC .50 .15
❑ T37 Miguel Olivo RC 1.50 .45
❑ T38 F.Rodriguez RC 6.00 1.80
❑ T39 Tony Pena Jr. RC 1.00 .30
❑ T40 Miguel Cabrera RC 40.00 12.00
❑ T41 Asdrubal Oropeza RC .50 .15
❑ T42 Junior Zamora RC 1.00 .30
❑ T43 Jovanny Cedeno RC .50 .15
❑ T44 John Sneed .60 .18
❑ T45 Josh Kalinowski .60 .18
❑ T46 Mike Young RC 8.00 2.40
❑ T47 Rico Washington RC .50 .15
❑ T48 Chad Durbin RC .50 .15
❑ T49 Junior Brignac RC .50 .15
❑ T50 Carlos Hernandez RC 1.00 .30
❑ T51 Cesar Izturis RC 2.50 .75
❑ T52 Oscar Salazar RC .50 .15
❑ T53 Pat Strange RC .50 .15
❑ T54 Rick Asadoorian 1.00 .30
❑ T55 Keith Reed .60 .18
❑ T56 Leo Estrella RC .50 .15
❑ T57 Wascar Serrano RC .50 .15
❑ T58 Richard Gomez RC .50 .15
❑ T59 Ramon Santiago RC 1.00 .30
❑ T60 Jovanny Sosa RC 1.00 .30
❑ T61 Aaron Rowand RC 4.00 1.20
❑ T62 Junior Guerrero RC .50 .15
❑ T63 Luis Terrero RC 2.50 .75
❑ T64 Brian Sanches RC .50 .15
❑ T65 Scott Sobkowiak RC .50 .15
❑ T66 Gary Majewski RC 1.50 .45
❑ T67 Barry Zito 2.50 .75
❑ T68 Ryan Christianson 1.00 .30
❑ T69 Cristian Guerrero RC 1.00 .30
❑ T70 T.De La Rosa RC .50 .15
❑ T71 Andrew Beinbrink RC .50 .15
❑ T72 Ryan Knox RC .50 .15
❑ T73 Alex Graman RC .50 .15
❑ T74 Juan Guzman RC .50 .15
❑ T75 Ruben Salazar RC .50 .15
❑ T76 Luis Matos RC 1.00 .30
❑ T77 Tony Mota RC .50 .15
❑ T78 Doug Davis .40 .12
❑ T79 Ben Christensen .40 .12
❑ T80 Mike Lamb 1.00 .30
❑ T81 Adrian Gonzalez RC 4.00 1.20
❑ T82 Mike Stodolka RC .50 .15
❑ T83 Adam Johnson RC 1.00 .30
❑ T84 Matt Wheatland RC .50 .15
❑ T85 Corey Smith RC 1.00 .30
❑ T86 Rocco Baldelli RC 8.00 2.40
❑ T87 Keith Bucktrot RC .50 .15
❑ T88 Adam Wainwright RC 2.50 .75
❑ T89 Scott Thorman RC 1.00 .30
❑ T90 Tripper Johnson RC 1.00 .30
❑ T91 Jim Edmonds .60 .18
❑ T92 Masato Yoshii .40 .12
❑ T93 Adam Kennedy .40 .12
❑ T94 Darryl Kile .60 .18
❑ T95 Mark McLemore .40 .12
❑ T96 Ricky Gutierrez .40 .12
❑ T97 Juan Gonzalez 1.00 .30
❑ T98 Melvin Mora .60 .18
❑ T99 Dante Bichette .60 .18
❑ T100 Lee Stevens .40 .12
❑ T101 Roger Cedeno .40 .12
❑ T102 John Olerud .60 .18
❑ T103 Eric Young .40 .12
❑ T104 Mickey Morandini .40 .12
❑ T105 Travis Lee .40 .12
❑ T106 Greg Vaughn .40 .12
❑ T107 Todd Zeile .60 .18
❑ T108 Chuck Finley .60 .18
❑ T109 Ismael Valdes .40 .12
❑ T110 Reggie Sanders .40 .12
❑ T111 Pat Hentgen .40 .12
❑ T112 Ryan Klesko .60 .18
❑ T113 Derek Bell .40 .12
❑ T114 Hideo Nomo 1.50 .45
❑ T115 Aaron Sele .40 .12
❑ T116 Fernando Vina .40 .12
❑ T117 Wally Joyner .60 .18
❑ T118 Brian Hunter .40 .12
❑ T119 Joe Girardi .40 .12
❑ T120 Omar Daal .40 .12
❑ T121 Brook Fordyce .40 .12
❑ T122 Jose Valentin .40 .12
❑ T123 Curt Schilling .60 .18
❑ T124 B.J. Surhoff .60 .18
❑ T125 Henry Rodriguez .40 .12
❑ T126 Mike Bordick .40 .12
❑ T127 David Justice .60 .18
❑ T128 Charles Johnson .60 .18
❑ T129 Will Clark 1.50 .45
❑ T130 Dwight Gooden .60 .18
❑ T131 David Segui .40 .12
❑ T132 Denny Neagle .60 .18
❑ T133 Jose Canseco 1.50 .45
❑ T134 Bruce Chen .40 .12
❑ T135 Jason Bere .40 .12

2001 Topps Chrome

	Nm-Mt	Ex-Mt
COMPLETE SET (661)	300.00	90.00
COMP. SERIES 1 (331)	150.00	45.00
COMP. SERIES 2 (330)	150.00	45.00

❑ 1 Cal Ripken 6.00 1.80
❑ 2 Chipper Jones 2.00 .60
❑ 3 Roger Cedeno .50 .15
❑ 4 Garret Anderson .75 .23
❑ 5 Robin Ventura .75 .23
❑ 6 Daryle Ward .50 .15
❑ 7 Does Not Exist .00
❑ 8 Phil Nevin .75 .23
❑ 9 Jermaine Dye .75 .23
❑ 10 Chris Singleton .50 .15
❑ 11 Mike Redmond .50 .15
❑ 12 Jim Thome 2.00 .60
❑ 13 Brian Jordan .75 .23
❑ 14 Dustin Hermanson .50 .15
❑ 15 Shawn Green .75 .23
❑ 16 Todd Stottlemyre .50 .15
❑ 17 Dan Wilson .50 .15
❑ 18 Derek Lowe .75 .23
❑ 19 Juan Gonzalez 1.25 .35
❑ 20 Pat Meares .50 .15
❑ 21 Paul O'Neill 1.25 .35
❑ 22 Jeffrey Hammonds .50 .15
❑ 23 Pokey Reese .50 .15
❑ 24 Mike Mussina 1.25 .35
❑ 25 Rico Brogna .50 .15
❑ 26 Jay Buhner .75 .23
❑ 27 Steve Cox .50 .15
❑ 28 Quilvio Veras .50 .15
❑ 29 Marquis Grissom .75 .23
❑ 30 Shigetoshi Hasegawa .75 .23
❑ 31 Shane Reynolds .50 .15
❑ 32 Adam Piatt .50 .15
❑ 33 Preston Wilson .75 .23
❑ 34 Ellis Burks .75 .23
❑ 35 Armando Rios .50 .15
❑ 36 Chuck Finley .75 .23
❑ 37 Shannon Stewart .75 .23
❑ 38 Mark McGwire 5.00 1.50
❑ 39 Gerald Williams .50 .15
❑ 40 Eric Young .50 .15
❑ 41 Peter Bergeron .50 .15
❑ 42 Arthur Rhodes .50 .15
❑ 43 Bobby Jones .50 .15
❑ 44 Matt Clement .50 .15
❑ 45 Pedro Martinez 2.00 .60
❑ 46 Jose Canseco 2.00 .60
❑ 47 Matt Anderson .50 .15
❑ 48 Torii Hunter .75 .23
❑ 49 Carlos Lee .75 .23
❑ 50 Eric Chavez .75 .23
❑ 51 Rick Helling .50 .15
❑ 52 John Franco .75 .23
❑ 53 Mike Bordick .75 .23
❑ 54 Andres Galarraga .75 .23
❑ 55 Jose Cruz Jr. .50 .15
❑ 56 Mike Matheny .75 .23
❑ 57 Randy Johnson 2.00 .60
❑ 58 Richie Sexson .75 .23
❑ 59 Vladimir Nunez .50 .15
❑ 60 Aaron Boone .75 .23
❑ 61 Darin Erstad .75 .23
❑ 62 Alex Gonzalez .50 .15
❑ 63 Gil Heredia .50 .15
❑ 64 Shane Andrews .50 .15
❑ 65 Todd Hundley .50 .15
❑ 66 Bill Mueller .75 .23
❑ 67 Mark McLemore .50 .15
❑ 68 Scott Spiezio .50 .15
❑ 69 Kevin McGlinchy .50 .15
❑ 70 Manny Ramirez 1.25 .35
❑ 71 Mike Lamb .50 .15
❑ 72 Brian Buchanan .50 .15
❑ 73 Mike Sweeney .75 .23
❑ 74 John Wetteland .75 .23
❑ 75 Rob Bell .50 .15
❑ 76 John Burkett .50 .15
❑ 77 Derek Jeter 5.00 1.50
❑ 78 J.D. Drew .75 .23
❑ 79 Jose Offerman .50 .15
❑ 80 Rick Reed .50 .15
❑ 81 Will Clark 2.00 .60
❑ 82 Rickey Henderson 2.00 .60
❑ 83 Kirk Rueter .50 .15
❑ 84 Lee Stevens .50 .15
❑ 85 Jay Bell .75 .23
❑ 86 Fred McGriff 1.25 .35
❑ 87 Julio Zuleta .50 .15
❑ 88 Brian Anderson .50 .15
❑ 89 Orlando Cabrera .75 .23
❑ 90 Alex Fernandez .50 .15
❑ 91 Derek Bell .50 .15
❑ 92 Eric Owens .50 .15
❑ 93 Dennys Reyes .50 .15
❑ 94 Mike Stanley .50 .15
❑ 95 Jorge Posada 1.25 .35
❑ 96 Paul Konerko .75 .23
❑ 97 Mike Remlinger .50 .15
❑ 98 Travis Lee .50 .15
❑ 99 Ken Caminiti .75 .23
❑ 100 Kevin Barker .50 .15
❑ 101 Ozzie Guillen .50 .15
❑ 102 Randy Wolf .50 .15
❑ 103 Michael Tucker .50 .15
❑ 104 Darren Lewis .50 .15
❑ 105 Joe Randa .50 .15
❑ 106 Jeff Cirillo .50 .15
❑ 107 David Ortiz 1.25 .35
❑ 108 Herb Perry .50 .15
❑ 109 Jeff Nelson .50 .15
❑ 110 Chris Stynes .50 .15
❑ 111 Johnny Damon 1.25 .35
❑ 112 Jason Schmidt .75 .23
❑ 113 Charles Johnson .50 .15
❑ 114 Pat Burrell .75 .23
❑ 115 Gary Sheffield .75 .23
❑ 116 Tom Glavine 1.25 .35
❑ 117 Jason Isringhausen .75 .23
❑ 118 Chris Carpenter .50 .15
❑ 119 Jeff Suppan .50 .15
❑ 120 Ivan Rodriguez 2.00 .60
❑ 121 Luis Sojo .50 .15
❑ 122 Ron Villone .50 .15
❑ 123 Mike Sirotka .50 .15
❑ 124 Chuck Knoblauch .75 .23
❑ 125 Jason Kendall .75 .23
❑ 126 Bobby Estalella .50 .15
❑ 127 Jose Guillen .75 .23
❑ 128 Carlos Delgado .75 .23
❑ 129 Benji Gil .50 .15

❑ 130	Einar Diaz	.50	.15
❑ 131	Andy Benes	.50	.15
❑ 132	Adrian Beltre	1.25	.35
❑ 133	Roger Clemens	4.00	1.20
❑ 134	Scott Williamson	.50	.15
❑ 135	Brad Penny	.50	.15
❑ 136	Troy Glaus	.75	.23
❑ 137	Kevin Appier	.75	.23
❑ 138	Walt Weiss	.50	.15
❑ 139	Michael Barrett	.50	.15
❑ 140	Mike Hampton	.75	.23
❑ 141	Francisco Cordova	.50	.15
❑ 142	David Segui	.50	.15
❑ 143	Carlos Febles	.50	.15
❑ 144	Roy Halladay	.50	.15
❑ 145	Seth Etherton	.50	.15
❑ 146	Fernando Tatis	.50	.15
❑ 147	Livan Hernandez	.50	.15
❑ 148	B.J. Surhoff	.75	.23
❑ 149	Barry Larkin	1.25	.35
❑ 150	Bobby Howry	.50	.15
❑ 151	Dmitri Young	.75	.23
❑ 152	Brian Hunter	.50	.15
❑ 153	A.Rodriguez Rangers	3.00	.90
❑ 154	Hideo Nomo	2.00	.60
❑ 155	Warren Morris	.50	.15
❑ 156	Antonio Alfonseca	.50	.15
❑ 157	Edgardo Alfonzo	.50	.15
❑ 158	Mark Grudzielanek	.50	.15
❑ 159	Fernando Vina	.50	.15
❑ 160	Homer Bush	.50	.15
❑ 161	Jason Giambi	.75	.23
❑ 162	Steve Karsay	.50	.15
❑ 163	Matt Lawton	.50	.15
❑ 164	Rusty Greer	.75	.23
❑ 165	Billy Koch	.50	.15
❑ 166	Todd Hollandsworth	.50	.15
❑ 167	Raul Ibanez	.50	.15
❑ 168	Tony Gwynn	2.50	.75
❑ 169	Carl Everett	.75	.23
❑ 170	Hector Carrasco	.50	.15
❑ 171	Jose Valentin	.50	.15
❑ 172	Deivi Cruz	.50	.15
❑ 173	Bret Boone	.75	.23
❑ 174	Melvin Mora	.75	.23
❑ 175	Danny Graves	.50	.15
❑ 176	Jose Jimenez	.50	.15
❑ 177	James Baldwin	.50	.15
❑ 178	C.J. Nitkowski	.50	.15
❑ 179	Jeff Zimmerman	.50	.15
❑ 180	Mike Lowell	.75	.23
❑ 181	Hideki Irabu	.50	.15
❑ 182	Greg Vaughn	.50	.15
❑ 183	Omar Daal	.50	.15
❑ 184	Darren Dreifort	.50	.15
❑ 185	Gil Meche	.50	.15
❑ 186	Damian Jackson	.50	.15
❑ 187	Frank Thomas	2.00	.60
❑ 188	Luis Castillo	.50	.15
❑ 189	Bartolo Colon	.75	.23
❑ 190	Craig Biggio	1.25	.35
❑ 191	Scott Schoeneweis	.50	.15
❑ 192	Dave Veres	.50	.15
❑ 193	Ramon Martinez	.50	.15
❑ 194	Jose Vidro	.50	.15
❑ 195	Todd Helton	1.25	.35
❑ 196	Greg Norton	.50	.15
❑ 197	Jacque Jones	.75	.23
❑ 198	Jason Grimsley	.50	.15
❑ 199	Dan Reichert	.50	.15
❑ 200	Robb Nen	.75	.23
❑ 201	Scott Hatteberg	.50	.15
❑ 202	Terry Shumpert	.50	.15
❑ 203	Kevin Millar	.75	.23
❑ 204	Ismael Valdes	.50	.15
❑ 205	Richard Hidalgo	.50	.15
❑ 206	Randy Velarde	.50	.15
❑ 207	Bengie Molina	.50	.15
❑ 208	Tony Womack	.50	.15
❑ 209	Enrique Wilson	.50	.15
❑ 210	Jeff Brantley	.50	.15
❑ 211	Rick Ankiel	.50	.15
❑ 212	Terry Mulholland	.50	.15
❑ 213	Ron Belliard	.50	.15
❑ 214	Terrence Long	.50	.15
❑ 215	Alberto Castillo	.50	.15
❑ 216	Royce Clayton	.50	.15
❑ 217	Joe McEwing	.50	.15
❑ 218	Jason McDonald	.50	.15
❑ 219	Ricky Bottalico	.50	.15
❑ 220	Keith Foulke	.75	.23
❑ 221	Brad Radke	.75	.23
❑ 222	Gabe Kapler	.50	.15
❑ 223	Pedro Astacio	.50	.15
❑ 224	Armando Reynoso	.50	.15
❑ 225	Darryl Kile	.75	.23
❑ 226	Reggie Sanders	.50	.15
❑ 227	Esteban Yan	.50	.15
❑ 228	Joe Nathan	.50	.15
❑ 229	Jay Payton	.50	.15
❑ 230	Francisco Cordero	.50	.15
❑ 231	Gregg Jefferies	.50	.15
❑ 232	LaTroy Hawkins	.50	.15
❑ 233	Jacob Cruz	.50	.15
❑ 234	Chris Holt	.50	.15
❑ 235	Vladimir Guerrero	2.00	.60
❑ 236	Marvin Benard	.50	.15
❑ 237	Alex Ramirez	.50	.15
❑ 238	Mike Williams	.50	.15
❑ 239	Sean Bergman	.50	.15
❑ 240	Juan Encarnacion	.50	.15
❑ 241	Russ Davis	.50	.15
❑ 242	Ramon Hernandez	.50	.15
❑ 243	Sandy Alomar Jr.	.50	.15
❑ 244	Eddie Guardado	.50	.15
❑ 245	Shane Halter	.50	.15
❑ 246	Geoff Jenkins	.75	.23
❑ 247	Brian Meadows	.50	.15
❑ 248	Damian Miller	.50	.15
❑ 249	Darrin Fletcher	.50	.15
❑ 250	Rafael Furcal	.75	.23
❑ 251	Mark Grace	1.25	.35
❑ 252	Mark Mulder	.75	.23
❑ 253	Joe Torre MG	.75	.23
❑ 254	Bobby Cox MG	.50	.15
❑ 255	Mike Scioscia MG	.50	.15
❑ 256	Mike Hargrove MG	.50	.15
❑ 257	Jimy Williams MG	.50	.15
❑ 258	Jerry Manuel MG	.50	.15
❑ 259	Charlie Manuel MG	.50	.15
❑ 260	Don Baylor MG	.75	.23
❑ 261	Phil Garner MG	.50	.15
❑ 262	Tony Muser MG	.50	.15
❑ 263	Buddy Bell MG	.75	.23
❑ 264	Tom Kelly MG	.50	.15
❑ 265	John Boles MG	.50	.15
❑ 266	Art Howe MG	.50	.15
❑ 267	Larry Dierker MG	.50	.15
❑ 268	Lou Piniella MG	.75	.23
❑ 269	Larry Rothschild MG	.50	.15
❑ 270	Davey Lopes MG	.75	.23
❑ 271	Johnny Oates MG	.50	.15
❑ 272	Felipe Alou MG	.50	.15
❑ 273	Bobby Valentine MG	.50	.15
❑ 274	Tony LaRussa MG	.50	.15
❑ 275	Bruce Bochy MG	.50	.15
❑ 276	Dusty Baker MG	.75	.23
❑ 277	Adrian Gonzalez	1.50	.45
	Adam Johnson		
❑ 278	Matt Wheatland	1.00	.30
	Bryan Digby		
❑ 279	Tripper Johnson	1.00	.30
	Scott Thorman		
❑ 280	Phil Dumatrait	1.00	.30
	Adam Wainwright		
❑ 281	Scott Heard	1.50	.45
	David Parrish RC		
❑ 282	Rocco Baldelli	2.00	.60
	Mark Folsom		
❑ 283	Dominic Rich RC	1.50	.45
	Aaron Herr		
❑ 284	Mike Stodolka	1.00	.30
	Sean Burnett		
❑ 285	Derek Thompson	1.00	.30
	Corey Smith		
❑ 286	Danny Borrell	1.50	.45
	Jason Bourgeois RC		
❑ 287	Chin-Feng Chen	1.50	.45
	Corey Patterson		
	Josh Hamilton		
❑ 288	Ryan Anderson	2.00	.60
	Barry Zito		
	C.C. Sabathia		
❑ 289	Scott Sobkowiak	2.00	.60
	David Walling		
	Ben Sheets		
❑ 290	Ty Howington	1.00	.30
	Josh Kalinowski		
	Josh Girdley		
❑ 291	Hee Seop Choi	3.00	.90
	Aaron McNeal		
	Jason Hart		
❑ 292	Bobby Bradley	1.50	.45
	Kurt Ainsworth		
	Chin-Hui Tsao		
❑ 293	Mike Glendenning	1.00	.30
	Kenny Kelly		
	Juan Silvestre		
❑ 294	J.R. House	1.00	.30
	Ramon Castro		
	Ben Davis		
❑ 295	Chance Caple	2.00	.60
	Rafael Soriano		
	Pasqual Coco		
❑ 296	Travis Hafner RC	6.00	1.80
	Eric Munson		
	Bucky Jacobsen		
❑ 297	Jason Conti	1.00	.30
	Chris Wakeland		
	Brian Cole		
❑ 298	Scott Seabol	1.50	.45
	Aubrey Huff		
	Joe Crede		
❑ 299	Adam Everett	1.00	.30
	Jose Ortiz		
	Keith Ginter		
❑ 300	Carlos Hernandez	1.00	.30
	Geraldo Guzman		
	Adam Eaton		
❑ 301	Bobby Kielty	1.00	.30
	Milton Bradley		
	Juan Rivera		
❑ 302	Mark McGwire GM	2.50	.75
❑ 303	Don Larsen GM	.75	.23
❑ 304	Bobby Thomson GM	.75	.23
❑ 305	Bill Mazeroski GM	.75	.23
❑ 306	Reggie Jackson GM	1.25	.35
❑ 307	Kirk Gibson GM	.75	.23
❑ 308	Roger Maris GM	1.25	.35
❑ 309	Cal Ripken GM	3.00	.90
❑ 310	Hank Aaron GM	2.00	.60
❑ 311	Joe Carter GM	.75	.23
❑ 312	Cal Ripken SH	3.00	.90
❑ 313	Randy Johnson SH	1.25	.35
❑ 314	Ken Griffey Jr. SH	2.00	.60
❑ 315	Troy Glaus SH	.75	.23
❑ 316	Kazuhiro Sasaki SH	.75	.23
❑ 317	Sammy Sosa	1.25	.35
	Troy Glaus LL		
❑ 318	Todd Helton	.75	.23
	Edgar Martinez LL		
❑ 319	Todd Helton	2.00	.60
	Nomar Garicaparra LL		
❑ 320	Barry Bonds	2.00	.60
	Jason Giambi LL		
❑ 321	Todd Helton	.75	.23
	Manny Ramirez LL		
❑ 322	Todd Helton	.75	.23
	Darin Erstad LL		
❑ 323	Kevin Brown	1.25	.35
	Pedro Martinez LL		
❑ 324	Randy Johnson	1.25	.35
	Pedro Martinez LL		
❑ 325	Will Clark HL	2.00	.60
❑ 326	New York Mets HL	2.00	.60
❑ 327	New York Yankees HL	3.00	.90
❑ 328	Seattle Mariners HL	.75	.23
❑ 329	Mike Hampton HL	.75	.23
❑ 330	New York Yankees HL	4.00	1.20
❑ 331	N.Y. Yankees Champs	8.00	2.40
❑ 332	Jeff Bagwell	1.25	.35
❑ 333	Andy Pettitte	1.25	.35
❑ 334	Tony Armas Jr.	.50	.15
❑ 335	Jeromy Burnitz	.75	.23
❑ 336	Javier Vazquez	.75	.23
❑ 337	Eric Karros	.75	.23
❑ 338	Brian Giles	.75	.23
❑ 339	Scott Rolen	2.00	.60

❑ 340 David Justice .75 .23
❑ 341 Ray Durham .75 .23
❑ 342 Todd Zeile .75 .23
❑ 343 Cliff Floyd .75 .23
❑ 344 Barry Bonds 5.00 1.50
❑ 345 Matt Williams .75 .23
❑ 346 Steve Finley .75 .23
❑ 347 Scott Elarton .50 .15
❑ 348 Bernie Williams 1.25 .35
❑ 349 David Wells .75 .23
❑ 350 J.T. Snow .75 .23
❑ 351 Al Leiter .75 .23
❑ 352 Magglio Ordonez .75 .23
❑ 353 Raul Mondesi .75 .23
❑ 354 Tim Salmon 1.25 .35
❑ 355 Jeff Kent .75 .23
❑ 356 Mariano Rivera 1.25 .35
❑ 357 John Olerud .75 .23
❑ 358 Javy Lopez .75 .23
❑ 359 Ben Grieve .50 .15
❑ 360 Ray Lankford .50 .15
❑ 361 Ken Griffey Jr. 3.00 .90
❑ 362 Rich Aurilia .50 .15
❑ 363 Andruw Jones .75 .23
❑ 364 Ryan Klesko .75 .23
❑ 365 Roberto Alomar 1.25 .35
❑ 366 Miguel Tejada .75 .23
❑ 367 Mo Vaughn .75 .23
❑ 368 Albert Belle .75 .23
❑ 369 Jose Canseco 2.00 .60
❑ 370 Kevin Brown .75 .23
❑ 371 Rafael Palmeiro 1.25 .35
❑ 372 Mark Redman .50 .15
❑ 373 Larry Walker 1.25 .35
❑ 374 Greg Maddux 3.00 .90
❑ 375 Nomar Garciaparra 3.00 .90
❑ 376 Kevin Millwood .75 .23
❑ 377 Edgar Martinez 1.25 .35
❑ 378 Sammy Sosa 3.00 .90
❑ 379 Tim Hudson .75 .23
❑ 380 Jim Edmonds .75 .23
❑ 381 Mike Piazza 3.00 .90
❑ 382 Brant Brown .50 .15
❑ 383 Brad Fullmer .50 .15
❑ 384 Alan Benes .50 .15
❑ 385 Mickey Morandini .50 .15
❑ 386 Troy Percival .75 .23
❑ 387 Eddie Perez .50 .15
❑ 388 Vernon Wells .75 .23
❑ 389 Ricky Gutierrez .50 .15
❑ 390 Rondell White .75 .23
❑ 391 Kelvim Escobar .50 .15
❑ 392 Tony Batista .75 .23
❑ 393 Jimmy Haynes .50 .15
❑ 394 Billy Wagner .75 .23
❑ 395 A.J. Hinch .50 .15
❑ 396 Matt Morris .75 .23
❑ 397 Lance Berkman .75 .23
❑ 398 Jeff D'Amico .50 .15
❑ 399 Octavio Dotel .50 .15
❑ 400 Olmedo Saenz .50 .15
❑ 401 Esteban Loaiza .50 .15
❑ 402 Adam Kennedy .50 .15
❑ 403 Moises Alou .75 .23
❑ 404 Orlando Palmeiro .50 .15
❑ 405 Kevin Young .50 .15
❑ 406 Tom Goodwin .50 .15
❑ 407 Mac Suzuki .75 .23
❑ 408 Pat Hentgen .50 .15
❑ 409 Kevin Stocker .50 .15
❑ 410 Mark Sweeney .75 .23
❑ 411 Tony Eusebio .50 .15
❑ 412 Edgar Renteria .75 .23
❑ 413 John Rocker .50 .15
❑ 414 Jose Lima .50 .15
❑ 415 Kerry Wood 2.00 .60
❑ 416 Mike Timlin .50 .15
❑ 417 Jose Hernandez .50 .15
❑ 418 Jeremy Giambi .50 .15
❑ 419 Luis Lopez .50 .15
❑ 420 Mitch Meluskey .50 .15
❑ 421 Garrett Stephenson .50 .15
❑ 422 Jamey Wright .50 .15
❑ 423 John Jaha .50 .15
❑ 424 Placido Polanco .50 .15
❑ 425 Marty Cordova .50 .15
❑ 426 Joey Hamilton .50 .15
❑ 427 Travis Fryman .75 .23
❑ 428 Mike Cameron .75 .23
❑ 429 Matt Mantei .50 .15
❑ 430 Chan Ho Park .75 .23
❑ 431 Shawn Estes .50 .15
❑ 432 Danny Bautista .50 .15
❑ 433 Wilson Alvarez .50 .15
❑ 434 Kenny Lofton .75 .23
❑ 435 Russ Ortiz .75 .23
❑ 436 Dave Burba .50 .15
❑ 437 Felix Martinez .50 .15
❑ 438 Jeff Shaw .50 .15
❑ 439 Mike DiFelice .50 .15
❑ 440 Roberto Hernandez .50 .15
❑ 441 Bryan Rekar .50 .15
❑ 442 Ugueth Urbina .50 .15
❑ 443 Vinny Castilla .75 .23
❑ 444 Carlos Perez .50 .15
❑ 445 Juan Guzman .50 .15
❑ 446 Ryan Rupe .50 .15
❑ 447 Mike Mordecai .50 .15
❑ 448 Ricardo Rincon .50 .15
❑ 449 Curt Schilling .75 .23
❑ 450 Alex Cora .50 .15
❑ 451 Turner Ward .50 .15
❑ 452 Omar Vizquel 1.25 .35
❑ 453 Russ Branyan .50 .15
❑ 454 Russ Johnson .50 .15
❑ 455 Greg Colbrunn .50 .15
❑ 456 Charles Nagy .50 .15
❑ 457 Wil Cordero .50 .15
❑ 458 Jason Tyner .50 .15
❑ 459 Devon White .75 .23
❑ 460 Kelly Stinnett .50 .15
❑ 461 Wilton Guerrero .50 .15
❑ 462 Jason Bere .50 .15
❑ 463 Calvin Murray .50 .15
❑ 464 Miguel Batista .50 .15
❑ 466 Luis Gonzalez .75 .23
❑ 467 Jaret Wright .50 .15
❑ 468 Chad Kreuter .50 .15
❑ 469 Armando Benitez .75 .23
❑ 470 Erubiel Durazo .50 .15
❑ 470 Sidney Ponson .50 .15
❑ 471 Adrian Brown .50 .15
❑ 472 Sterling Hitchcock .50 .15
❑ 473 Timo Perez .50 .15
❑ 474 Jamie Moyer .75 .23
❑ 475 Delino DeShields .50 .15
❑ 476 Glendon Rusch .50 .15
❑ 477 Chris Gomez .50 .15
❑ 478 Adam Eaton .50 .15
❑ 479 Pablo Ozuna .50 .15
❑ 480 Bob Abreu .75 .23
❑ 481 Kris Benson .50 .15
❑ 482 Keith Osik .50 .15
❑ 483 Darryl Hamilton .50 .15
❑ 484 Marlon Anderson .50 .15
❑ 485 Jimmy Anderson .50 .15
❑ 486 John Halama .50 .15
❑ 487 Nelson Figueroa .50 .15
❑ 488 Alex Gonzalez .50 .15
❑ 489 Benny Agbayani .50 .15
❑ 490 Ed Sprague .50 .15
❑ 491 Scott Erickson .50 .15
❑ 492 Doug Glanville .50 .15
❑ 493 Jesus Sanchez .50 .15
❑ 494 Mike Lieberthal .75 .23
❑ 495 Aaron Sele .50 .15
❑ 496 Pat Mahomes .50 .15
❑ 497 Ruben Rivera .50 .15
❑ 498 Wayne Gomes .50 .15
❑ 499 Freddy Garcia .75 .23
❑ 500 Al Martin .50 .15
❑ 501 Woody Williams .50 .15
❑ 502 Paul Byrd .50 .15
❑ 503 Rick White .50 .15
❑ 504 Trevor Hoffman .75 .23
❑ 505 Brady Anderson .75 .23
❑ 506 Robert Person .50 .15
❑ 507 Jeff Conine .75 .23
❑ 508 Chris Truby .50 .15
❑ 509 Emil Brown .50 .15
❑ 510 Ryan Dempster .50 .15
❑ 511 Ruben Mateo .50 .15
❑ 512 Alex Ochoa .50 .15
❑ 513 Jose Rosado .50 .15
❑ 514 Masato Yoshii .50 .15
❑ 515 Brian Daubach .50 .15
❑ 516 Jeff D'Amico .50 .15
❑ 517 Brent Mayne .50 .15
❑ 518 John Thomson .50 .15
❑ 519 Todd Ritchie .50 .15
❑ 520 John VanderWal .50 .15
❑ 521 Neifi Perez .50 .15
❑ 522 Chad Curtis .50 .15
❑ 523 Kenny Rogers .75 .23
❑ 524 Trot Nixon .75 .23
❑ 525 Sean Casey .75 .23
❑ 526 Wilton Veras .50 .15
❑ 527 Troy O'Leary .50 .15
❑ 528 Dante Bichette .75 .23
❑ 529 Jose Silva .50 .15
❑ 530 Darren Oliver .50 .15
❑ 531 Steve Parris .50 .15
❑ 532 David McCarty .50 .15
❑ 533 Todd Walker .50 .15
❑ 534 Brian Rose .50 .15
❑ 535 Pete Schourek .50 .15
❑ 536 Ricky Ledee .50 .15
❑ 537 Justin Thompson .50 .15
❑ 538 Benito Santiago .75 .23
❑ 539 Carlos Beltran 1.25 .35
❑ 540 Gabe White .50 .15
❑ 541 Bret Saberhagen .75 .23
❑ 542 Ramon Martinez .50 .15
❑ 543 John Valentin .50 .15
❑ 544 Frank Catalanotto .50 .15
❑ 545 Tim Wakefield .75 .23
❑ 546 Michael Tucker .50 .15
❑ 547 Juan Pierre .75 .23
❑ 548 Rich Garces .50 .15
❑ 549 Luis Ordaz .50 .15
❑ 550 Jerry Spradlin .50 .15
❑ 551 Corey Koskie .75 .23
❑ 552 Cal Eldred .50 .15
❑ 553 Alfonso Soriano 1.25 .35
❑ 554 Kip Wells .50 .15
❑ 555 Orlando Hernandez .50 .15
❑ 556 Bill Simas .50 .15
❑ 557 Jim Parque .50 .15
❑ 558 Joe Mays .50 .15
❑ 559 Tim Belcher .50 .15
❑ 560 Shane Spencer .50 .15
❑ 561 Glenallen Hill .50 .15
❑ 562 Matt LeCroy .50 .15
❑ 563 Tino Martinez 1.25 .35
❑ 564 Eric Milton .50 .15
❑ 565 Ron Coomer .50 .15
❑ 566 Cristian Guzman .50 .15
❑ 567 Kazuhiro Sasaki .75 .23
❑ 568 Mark Quinn .50 .15
❑ 569 Eric Gagne 2.00 .60
❑ 570 Kerry Ligtenberg .50 .15
❑ 571 Rolando Arrojo .50 .15
❑ 572 Jon Lieber .50 .15
❑ 573 Jose Vizcaino .50 .15
❑ 574 Jeff Abbott .50 .15
❑ 575 Carlos Hernandez .50 .15
❑ 576 Scott Sullivan .50 .15
❑ 577 Matt Stairs .50 .15
❑ 578 Tom Lampkin .50 .15
❑ 579 Donnie Sadler .50 .15
❑ 580 Desi Relaford .50 .15
❑ 581 Scott Downs .50 .15
❑ 582 Mike Mussina 1.25 .35
❑ 583 Ramon Ortiz .50 .15
❑ 584 Mike Myers .50 .15
❑ 585 Frank Castillo .50 .15
❑ 586 Manny Ramirez 1.25 .35
❑ 587 Alex Rodriguez 3.00 .90
❑ 588 Andy Ashby .50 .15
❑ 589 Felipe Crespo .50 .15
❑ 590 Bobby Bonilla .75 .23
❑ 591 Denny Neagle .50 .15
❑ 592 Dave Martinez .50 .15
❑ 593 Mike Hampton .75 .23
❑ 594 Gary DiSarcina .50 .15
❑ 595 Tsuyoshi Shinjo RC 2.00 .60
❑ 596 Albert Pujols RC 60.00 18.00
❑ 597 Roy Oswalt 2.00 .60

Pat Strange
Jon Rauch
❑ 598 Phil Wilson RC 8.00 2.40
Jake Peavy RC
Darwin Cubillan RC
❑ 599 Nathan Haynes 1.00 .30
Steve Smyth RC
Mike Bynum
❑ 600 Joe Lawrence 1.00 .30
Choo Freeman
Michael Cuddyer
❑ 601 Larry Barnes 1.00 .30
DeWayne Wise
Carlos Pena
❑ 602 Feilpe Lopez 1.50 .45
Gookie Dawkins
Eric Almonte RC
❑ 603 Brad Wilkerson 1.00 .30
Alex Escobar
Eric Valent
❑ 604 Jeff Goldbach 1.00 .30
Toby Hall
Rod Barajas
❑ 605 Marcus Giles 1.50 .45
Pablo Ozuna
Jason Romano
❑ 606 Vernon Wells 1.50 .45
Jack Cust
Dee Brown
❑ 607 Luis Montanez RC 1.50 .45
David Espinosa
❑ 608 Anthony Pluta RC 1.50 .45
Justin Wayne RC
❑ 609 Josh Axelson RC 1.50 .45
Carmen Cali RC
❑ 610 Shaun Boyd RC 1.50 .45
Chris Morris RC
❑ 611 Dan Moylan RC 1.50 .45
Tommy Arko RC
❑ 612 Luis Cotto RC 1.00 .30
Luis Escobar
❑ 613 Blake Williams RC 1.50 .45
Brandon Mims RC
❑ 614 Chris Russ RC 1.00 .30
Bryan Edwards
❑ 615 Joe Torres 1.00 .30
Ben Diggins
❑ 616 Hugh Quattlebaum RC 2.00 .60
Edwin Encarnacion RC
❑ 617 Brian Bass RC 1.50 .45
Odannis Ayala RC
❑ 618 Jason Kaanoi 1.00 .30
Michael Matthews RC UER
name misspelled Mathews
❑ 619 Stuart McFarland RC 1.50 .45
Adam Sterrett RC
❑ 620 David Krynzel 3.00 .90
Grady Sizemore
❑ 621 Keith Bucktrot 1.00 .30
Dane Sardinha
❑ 622 Anaheim Angels TC .75 .23
❑ 623 Ariz. Diamondbacks TC .75 .23
❑ 624 Atlanta Braves TC .75 .23
❑ 625 Baltimore Orioles TC .75 .23
❑ 626 Boston Red Sox TC .75 .23
❑ 627 Chicago Cubs TC .75 .23
❑ 628 Chicago White Sox TC .75 .23
❑ 629 Cincinnati Reds TC .75 .23
❑ 630 Cleveland Indians TC .75 .23
❑ 631 Colorado Rockies TC .75 .23
❑ 632 Detroit Tigers TC .75 .23
❑ 633 Florida Marlins TC .75 .23
❑ 634 Houston Astros TC .75 .23
❑ 635 K.C. Royals TC .75 .23
❑ 636 L.A. Dodgers TC .75 .23
❑ 637 Milw. Brewers TC .75 .23
❑ 638 Minnesota Twins TC .75 .23
❑ 639 Montreal Expos TC .75 .23
❑ 640 New York Mets TC .75 .23
❑ 641 New York Yankees TC 4.00 1.20
❑ 642 Oakland Athletics TC .75 .23
❑ 643 Phil. Phillies TC .75 .23
❑ 644 Pittsburgh Pirates TC .75 .23
❑ 645 San Diego Padres TC .75 .23
❑ 646 S.F. Giants TC .75 .23
❑ 647 Seattle Mariners TC .75 .23
❑ 648 St. Louis Cardinals TC .75 .23
❑ 649 T. Bay Devil Rays TC .75 .23
❑ 650 Texas Rangers TC .75 .23
❑ 651 Toronto Blue Jays TC .75 .23
❑ 652 Bucky Dent GM .50 .15
❑ 653 Jackie Robinson GM 2.00 .60
❑ 654 Roberto Clemente GM 2.50 .75
❑ 655 Nolan Ryan GM 3.00 .90
❑ 656 Kerry Wood GM 1.25 .35
❑ 657 Rickey Henderson GM 2.00 .60
❑ 658 Lou Brock GM 1.25 .35
❑ 659 David Wells GM .50 .15
❑ 660 Andruw Jones GM .50 .15
❑ 661 Carlton Fisk GM .75 .23

2001 Topps Chrome Traded

	Nm-Mt	Ex-Mt
COMPLETE SET (266)	150.00	45.00
COMMON (1-99/145-266)	.75	.23
COMMON (100-144)	1.25	.35

❑ T1 Sandy Alomar Jr. .75 .23
❑ T2 Kevin Appier 1.25 .35
❑ T3 Brad Ausmus .75 .23
❑ T4 Derek Bell .75 .23
❑ T5 Bret Boone 1.25 .35
❑ T6 Rico Brogna .75 .23
❑ T7 Ellis Burks 1.25 .35
❑ T8 Ken Caminiti 1.25 .35
❑ T9 Roger Cedeno .75 .23
❑ T10 Royce Clayton .75 .23
❑ T11 Enrique Wilson .75 .23
❑ T12 Rheal Cormier .75 .23
❑ T13 Eric Davis 1.25 .35
❑ T14 Shawon Dunston .75 .23
❑ T15 Andres Galarraga 1.25 .35
❑ T16 Tom Gordon .75 .23
❑ T17 Mark Grace 2.00 .60
❑ T18 Jeffrey Hammonds .75 .23
❑ T19 Dustin Hermanson .75 .23
❑ T20 Quinton McCracken .75 .23
❑ T21 Todd Hundley .75 .23
❑ T22 Charles Johnson 1.25 .35
❑ T23 Marquis Grissom 1.25 .35
❑ T24 Jose Mesa .75 .23
❑ T25 Brian Boehringer .75 .23
❑ T26 John Rocker .75 .23
❑ T27 Jeff Frye .75 .23
❑ T28 Reggie Sanders .75 .23
❑ T29 David Segui .75 .23
❑ T30 Mike Sirotka .75 .23
❑ T31 Fernando Tatis .75 .23
❑ T32 Steve Trachsel .75 .23
❑ T33 Ismael Valdes .75 .23
❑ T34 Randy Velarde .75 .23
❑ T35 Ryan Kohlmeier .75 .23
❑ T36 Mike Bordick 1.25 .35
❑ T37 Kent Bottenfield .75 .23
❑ T38 Pat Rapp .75 .23
❑ T39 Jeff Nelson .75 .23
❑ T40 Ricky Bottalico .75 .23
❑ T41 Luke Prokopec .75 .23
❑ T42 Hideo Nomo 3.00 .90
❑ T43 Bill Mueller 1.25 .35
❑ T44 Roberto Kelly .75 .23
❑ T45 Chris Holt .75 .23
❑ T46 Mike Jackson .75 .23
❑ T47 Devon White 1.25 .35
❑ T48 Gerald Williams .75 .23
❑ T49 Eddie Taubensee .75 .23
❑ T50 Brian Hunter UER .75 .23
Brian R Hunter pictured
Brian L Hunter stats
❑ T51 Nelson Cruz .75 .23
❑ T52 Jeff Fassero .75 .23
❑ T53 Bubba Trammell .75 .23
❑ T54 Bo Porter .75 .23
❑ T55 Greg Norton .75 .23
❑ T56 Benito Santiago 1.25 .35
❑ T57 Ruben Rivera .75 .23
❑ T58 Dee Brown .75 .23
❑ T59 Jose Canseco 3.00 .90
❑ T60 Chris Michalak .75 .23
❑ T61 Tim Worrell .75 .23
❑ T62 Matt Clement .75 .23
❑ T63 Bill Pulsipher .75 .23
❑ T64 Troy Brohawn RC 1.00 .30
❑ T65 Mark Kotsay .75 .23
❑ T66 Jimmy Rollins 1.25 .35
❑ T67 Shea Hillenbrand 1.25 .35
❑ T68 Ted Lilly .75 .23
❑ T69 Jermaine Dye 1.25 .35
❑ T70 Jerry Hairston Jr. .75 .23
❑ T71 John Mabry .75 .23
❑ T72 Kurt Abbott .75 .23
❑ T73 Eric Owens .75 .23
❑ T74 Jeff Brantley .75 .23
❑ T75 Roy Oswalt 2.00 .60
❑ T76 Doug Mientkiewicz 1.25 .35
❑ T77 Rickey Henderson 3.00 .90
❑ T78 Jason Grimsley .75 .23
❑ T79 Christian Parker RC 1.00 .30
❑ T80 Donne Wall .75 .23
❑ T81 Alex Arias .75 .23
❑ T82 Willis Roberts .75 .23
❑ T83 Ryan Minor .75 .23
❑ T84 Jason LaRue .75 .23
❑ T85 Ruben Sierra .75 .23
❑ T86 Johnny Damon 2.00 .60
❑ T87 Juan Gonzalez 2.00 .60
❑ T88 C.C. Sabathia 1.25 .35
❑ T89 Tony Batista 1.25 .35
❑ T90 Jay Witasick .75 .23
❑ T91 Brent Abernathy .75 .23
❑ T92 Paul LoDuca 1.25 .35
❑ T93 Wes Helms .75 .23
❑ T94 Mark Wohlers .75 .23
❑ T95 Rob Bell .75 .23
❑ T96 Tim Redding .75 .23
❑ T97 Bud Smith RC 1.00 .30
❑ T98 Adam Dunn 2.00 .60
❑ T99 Ichiro Suzuki 25.00 7.50
Albert Pujols ROY
❑ T100 Carlton Fisk 81 2.00 .60
❑ T101 Tim Raines 81 1.25 .35
❑ T102 Juan Marichal 74 1.25 .35
❑ T103 Dave Winfield 81 1.25 .35
❑ T104 Reggie Jackson 82 2.00 .60
❑ T105 Cal Ripken 82 10.00 3.00
❑ T106 Ozzie Smith 82 5.00 1.50
❑ T107 Tom Seaver 83 2.00 .60
❑ T108 Lou Piniella 74 1.25 .35
❑ T109 Dwight Gooden 84 1.25 .35
❑ T110 Bret Saberhagen 84 1.25 .35
❑ T111 Gary Carter 85 1.25 .35
❑ T112 Jack Clark 85 1.25 .35
❑ T113 Rickey Henderson 85 3.00 .90
❑ T114 Barry Bonds 86 8.00 2.40
❑ T115 Bobby Bonilla 86 1.25 .35
❑ T116 Jose Canseco 86 3.00 .90
❑ T117 Will Clark 86 3.00 .90
❑ T118 Andres Galarraga 86 1.25 .35
❑ T119 Bo Jackson 86 3.00 .90
❑ T120 Wally Joyner 86 1.25 .35
❑ T121 Ellis Burks 87 1.25 .35
❑ T122 David Cone 87 1.25 .35
❑ T123 Greg Maddux 87 5.00 1.50
❑ T124 Willie Randolph 76 1.25 .35
❑ T125 Dennis Eckersley 87 1.25 .35
❑ T126 Matt Williams 87 1.25 .35
❑ T127 Joe Morgan 81 1.25 .35
❑ T128 Fred McGriff 87 2.00 .60

❑ T129	Roberto Alomar 88	2.00	.60
❑ T130	Lee Smith 88	1.25	.35
❑ T131	David Wells 88	1.25	.35
❑ T132	Ken Griffey Jr. 89	5.00	1.50
❑ T133	Deion Sanders 89	2.00	.60
❑ T134	Nolan Ryan 89	8.00	2.40
❑ T135	David Justice 90	1.25	.35
❑ T136	Joe Carter 91	1.25	.35
❑ T137	Jack Morris 92	1.25	.35
❑ T138	Mike Piazza 93	5.00	1.50
❑ T139	Barry Bonds 93	8.00	2.40
❑ T140	Terrence Long 94	1.25	.35
❑ T141	Ben Grieve 94	1.25	.35
❑ T142	Richie Sexson 95 George Arias Mark Sweeney Brian Schneider	1.25	.35
❑ T143	Sean Burroughs 99	1.25	.35
❑ T144	Alfonso Soriano 99	2.00	.60
❑ T145	Bob Boone MG	1.25	.35
❑ T146	Larry Bowa MG	1.25	.35
❑ T147	Bob Brenly MG	.75	.23
❑ T148	Buck Martinez MG	.75	.23
❑ T149	L. McClendon MG	.75	.23
❑ T150	Jim Tracy MG	.75	.23
❑ T151	Jared Abruzzo RC	1.00	.30
❑ T152	Kurt Ainsworth	.75	.23
❑ T153	Willie Bloomquist	1.25	.35
❑ T154	Ben Broussard	.75	.23
❑ T155	Bobby Bradley	.75	.23
❑ T156	Mike Bynum	.75	.23
❑ T157	A.J. Hinch	.75	.23
❑ T158	Ryan Christianson	.75	.23
❑ T159	Carlos Silva	.75	.23
❑ T160	Joe Crede	.75	.23
❑ T161	Jack Cust	.75	.23
❑ T162	Ben Diggins	.75	.23
❑ T163	Phil Dumatrait	.75	.23
❑ T164	Alex Escobar	.75	.23
❑ T165	Miguel Olivo	.75	.23
❑ T166	Chris George	.75	.23
❑ T167	Marcus Giles	1.25	.35
❑ T168	Keith Ginter	.75	.23
❑ T169	Josh Girdley	.75	.23
❑ T170	Tony Alvarez	.75	.23
❑ T171	Scott Seabol	.75	.23
❑ T172	Josh Hamilton	.75	.23
❑ T173	Jason Hart	.75	.23
❑ T174	Israel Alcantara	.75	.23
❑ T175	Jake Peavy	5.00	1.50
❑ T176	Stubby Clapp RC	1.00	.30
❑ T177	D'Angelo Jimenez	.75	.23
❑ T178	Nick Johnson	.75	.23
❑ T179	Ben Johnson	.75	.23
❑ T180	Larry Bigbie	.75	.23
❑ T181	Allen Levrault	.75	.23
❑ T182	Felipe Lopez	.75	.23
❑ T183	Sean Burnett	.75	.23
❑ T184	Nick Neugebauer	.75	.23
❑ T185	Austin Kearns	1.25	.35
❑ T186	Corey Patterson	1.25	.35
❑ T187	Carlos Pena	.75	.23
❑ T188	R. Rodriguez RC	1.00	.30
❑ T189	Juan Rivera	.75	.23
❑ T190	Grant Roberts	.75	.23
❑ T191	Adam Pettyjohn RC	1.00	.30
❑ T192	Jared Sandberg	.75	.23
❑ T193	Xavier Nady	.75	.23
❑ T194	Dane Sardinha	.75	.23
❑ T195	Shawn Sonnier	.75	.23
❑ T196	Rafael Soriano	1.25	.35
❑ T197	Brian Specht RC	1.00	.30
❑ T198	Aaron Myette	.75	.23
❑ T199	Juan Uribe RC	1.25	.35
❑ T200	Jayson Werth	.75	.23
❑ T201	Brad Wilkerson	.75	.23
❑ T202	Horacio Estrada	.75	.23
❑ T203	Joel Pineiro	3.00	.90
❑ T204	Matt LeCroy	.75	.23
❑ T205	Michael Coleman	.75	.23
❑ T206	Ben Sheets	2.00	.60
❑ T207	Eric Byrnes	.75	.23
❑ T208	Sean Burroughs	1.25	.35
❑ T209	Ken Harvey	.75	.23
❑ T210	Travis Hafner	4.00	1.20
❑ T211	Erick Almonte	1.00	.30
❑ T212	Jason Belcher RC	1.00	.30
❑ T213	Wilson Betemit RC	1.00	.30
❑ T214	Hank Blalock RC	15.00	4.50
❑ T215	Danny Borrell	1.00	.30
❑ T216	John Buck RC	1.25	.35
❑ T217	Freddie Bynum RC	1.00	.30
❑ T218	Noel Devarez RC	1.00	.30
❑ T219	Juan Diaz RC	1.00	.30
❑ T220	Felix Diaz RC	1.00	.30
❑ T221	Josh Fogg RC	1.00	.30
❑ T222	Matt Ford RC	1.00	.30
❑ T223	Scott Heard	.75	.23
❑ T224	Ben Hendrickson RC	1.25	.35
❑ T225	Cody Ross RC	1.00	.30
❑ T226	A. Hernandez RC	1.00	.30
❑ T227	Alfredo Amezaga RC	1.00	.30
❑ T228	Bob Keppel RC	1.25	.35
❑ T229	Ryan Madson RC	2.00	.60
❑ T230	Octavio Martinez RC	1.00	.30
❑ T231	Hee Seop Choi	2.00	.60
❑ T232	Thomas Mitchell	.75	.23
❑ T233	Luis Montanez	1.00	.30
❑ T234	Andy Morales RC	1.00	.30
❑ T235	Justin Morneau RC	15.00	4.50
❑ T236	Toe Nash RC	1.00	.30
❑ T237	V. Pascucci RC	1.00	.30
❑ T238	Roy Smith RC	1.00	.30
❑ T239	Antonio Perez RC	1.00	.30
❑ T240	Chad Petty RC	1.00	.30
❑ T241	Steve Smyth	1.00	.30
❑ T242	Jose Reyes RC	8.00	2.40
❑ T243	Eric Reynolds RC	1.00	.30
❑ T244	Dominic Rich	1.00	.30
❑ T245	J. Richardson RC	1.00	.30
❑ T246	Ed Rogers RC	1.00	.30
❑ T247	Albert Pujols	60.00	18.00
❑ T248	Esix Snead RC	1.00	.30
❑ T249	Luis Torres RC	1.00	.30
❑ T250	Matt White RC	1.00	.30
❑ T251	Blake Williams	1.00	.30
❑ T252	Chris Russ	1.00	.30
❑ T253	Joe Kennedy RC	1.25	.35
❑ T254	Jeff Randazzo RC	1.00	.30
❑ T255	Beau Hale RC	1.00	.30
❑ T256	Brad Hennessey RC	3.00	.90
❑ T257	Jake Gautreau RC	1.00	.30
❑ T258	Jeff Mathis RC	4.00	1.20
❑ T259	Aaron Heilman RC	1.00	.30
❑ T260	B. Sardinha RC	2.00	.60
❑ T261	Irvin Guzman RC	10.00	3.00
❑ T262	Gabe Gross RC	1.25	.35
❑ T263	J.D. Martin RC	1.00	.30
❑ T264	Chris Smith RC	1.00	.30
❑ T265	Kenny Baugh RC	1.00	.30
❑ T266	Ichiro Suzuki RC	30.00	9.00

2002 Topps Chrome

	Nm-Mt	Ex-Mt
COMPLETE SET (660)	300.00	90.00
COMPLETE SERIES 1 (330)	150.00	45.00
COMPLETE SERIES 2 (330)	150.00	45.00
COMMON (1-331/366-695)	.50	.15
COMMON (307-326/671-690)	1.50	.45
COMMON (327-331/691-695)	1.50	.45

❑ 1	Pedro Martinez	2.50	.75
❑ 2	Mike Stanton	.50	.15
❑ 3	Brad Penny	.50	.15
❑ 4	Mike Matheny	1.00	.30
❑ 5	Johnny Damon	1.50	.45
❑ 6	Bret Boone	1.00	.30
❑ 7	Does Not Exist	.00	
❑ 8	Chris Truby	.50	.15
❑ 9	B.J. Surhoff	1.00	.30
❑ 10	Mike Hampton	1.00	.30
❑ 11	Juan Pierre	1.00	.30
❑ 12	Mark Buehrle	1.00	.30
❑ 13	Bob Abreu	1.00	.30
❑ 14	David Cone	1.00	.30
❑ 15	Aaron Sele	.50	.15
❑ 16	Fernando Tatis	.50	.15
❑ 17	Bobby Jones	.50	.15
❑ 18	Rick Helling	.50	.15
❑ 19	Dmitri Young	1.00	.30
❑ 20	Mike Mussina	1.50	.45
❑ 21	Mike Sweeney	1.00	.30
❑ 22	Cristian Guzman	.50	.15
❑ 23	Ryan Kohlmeier	.50	.15
❑ 24	Adam Kennedy	.50	.15
❑ 25	Larry Walker	1.50	.45
❑ 26	Eric Davis	1.00	.30
❑ 27	Jason Tyner	.50	.15
❑ 28	Eric Young	.50	.15
❑ 29	Jason Marquis	.50	.15
❑ 30	Luis Gonzalez	1.00	.30
❑ 31	Kevin Tapani	.50	.15
❑ 32	Orlando Cabrera	1.00	.30
❑ 33	Marty Cordova	.50	.15
❑ 34	Brad Ausmus	.50	.15
❑ 35	Livan Hernandez	.50	.15
❑ 36	Alex Gonzalez	.50	.15
❑ 37	Edgar Renteria	1.00	.30
❑ 38	Bengie Molina	.50	.15
❑ 39	Frank Menechino	.50	.15
❑ 40	Rafael Palmeiro	1.50	.45
❑ 41	Brad Fullmer	.50	.15
❑ 42	Julio Zuleta	.50	.15
❑ 43	Darren Dreifort	.50	.15
❑ 44	Trot Nixon	1.00	.30
❑ 45	Trevor Hoffman	1.00	.30
❑ 46	Vladimir Nunez	.50	.15
❑ 47	Mark Kotsay	.50	.15
❑ 48	Kenny Rogers	1.00	.30
❑ 49	Ben Petrick	.50	.15
❑ 50	Jeff Bagwell	1.50	.45
❑ 51	Juan Encarnacion	.50	.15
❑ 52	Ramiro Mendoza	.50	.15
❑ 53	Brian Meadows	.50	.15
❑ 54	Chad Curtis	.50	.15
❑ 55	Aramis Ramirez	1.00	.30
❑ 56	Mark McLemore	.50	.15
❑ 57	Dante Bichette	1.00	.30
❑ 58	Scott Schoeneweis	.50	.15
❑ 59	Jose Cruz Jr.	.50	.15
❑ 60	Roger Clemens	5.00	1.50
❑ 61	Jose Guillen	1.00	.30
❑ 62	Darren Oliver	.50	.15
❑ 63	Chris Reitsma	.50	.15
❑ 64	Jeff Abbott	.50	.15
❑ 65	Robin Ventura	1.00	.30
❑ 66	Denny Neagle	.50	.15
❑ 67	Al Martin	.50	.15
❑ 68	Benito Santiago	1.00	.30
❑ 69	Roy Oswalt	1.00	.30
❑ 70	Juan Gonzalez	1.50	.45
❑ 71	Garret Anderson	1.00	.30
❑ 72	Bobby Bonilla	1.00	.30
❑ 73	Danny Bautista	.50	.15
❑ 74	J.T. Snow	1.00	.30
❑ 75	Derek Jeter	6.00	1.80
❑ 76	John Olerud	1.00	.30
❑ 77	Kevin Appier	1.00	.30
❑ 78	Phil Nevin	1.00	.30
❑ 79	Sean Casey	1.00	.30
❑ 80	Troy Glaus	1.00	.30
❑ 81	Joe Randa	.50	.15
❑ 82	Jose Valentin	.50	.15
❑ 83	Ricky Bottalico	.50	.15
❑ 84	Todd Zeile	1.00	.30
❑ 85	Barry Larkin	1.50	.45
❑ 86	Bob Wickman	.50	.15
❑ 87	Jeff Shaw	.50	.15
❑ 88	Greg Vaughn	.50	.15

❑	89	Fernando Vina	.50	.15
❑	90	Mark Mulder	1.00	.30
❑	91	Paul Bako	.50	.15
❑	92	Aaron Boone	1.00	.30
❑	93	Esteban Loaiza	.50	.15
❑	94	Richie Sexson	1.00	.30
❑	95	Alfonso Soriano	1.50	.45
❑	96	Tony Womack	.50	.15
❑	97	Paul Shuey	.50	.15
❑	98	Melvin Mora	1.00	.30
❑	99	Tony Gwynn	3.00	.90
❑	100	Vladimir Guerrero	2.50	.75
❑	101	Keith Osik	.50	.15
❑	102	Bud Smith	.50	.15
❑	103	Scott Williamson	.50	.15
❑	104	Daryle Ward	.50	.15
❑	105	Doug Mientkiewicz	1.00	.30
❑	106	Stan Javier	.50	.15
❑	107	Russ Ortiz	1.00	.30
❑	108	Wade Miller	.50	.15
❑	109	Luke Prokopec	.50	.15
❑	110	Andruw Jones	1.00	.30
❑	111	Ron Coomer	.50	.15
❑	112	Dan Wilson	.50	.15
❑	113	Luis Castillo	.50	.15
❑	114	Derek Bell	.50	.15
❑	115	Gary Sheffield	1.00	.30
❑	116	Ruben Rivera	.50	.15
❑	117	Paul O'Neill	1.50	.45
❑	118	Craig Paquette	.50	.15
❑	119	Kelvim Escobar	.50	.15
❑	120	Brad Radke	1.00	.30
❑	121	Jorge Fabregas	.50	.15
❑	122	Randy Winn	.50	.15
❑	123	Tom Goodwin	.50	.15
❑	124	Jaret Wright	.50	.15
❑	125	Barry Bonds HR 73	40.00	12.00
❑	126	Al Leiter	.50	.15
❑	127	Ben Davis	.50	.15
❑	128	Frank Catalanotto	.50	.15
❑	129	Jose Cabrera	.50	.15
❑	130	Magglio Ordonez	1.00	.30
❑	131	Jose Macias	.50	.15
❑	132	Ted Lilly	.50	.15
❑	133	Chris Holt	.50	.15
❑	134	Eric Milton	.50	.15
❑	135	Shannon Stewart	1.00	.30
❑	136	Omar Olivares	.50	.15
❑	137	David Segui	.50	.15
❑	138	Jeff Nelson	.50	.15
❑	139	Matt Williams	1.00	.30
❑	140	Ellis Burks	1.00	.30
❑	141	Jason Bere	.50	.15
❑	142	Jimmy Haynes	.50	.15
❑	143	Ramon Hernandez	.50	.15
❑	144	Craig Counsell	.50	.15
❑	145	John Smoltz	1.50	.45
❑	146	Homer Bush	.50	.15
❑	147	Quilvio Veras	.50	.15
❑	148	Esteban Yan	.50	.15
❑	149	Ramon Ortiz	.50	.15
❑	150	Carlos Delgado	1.00	.30
❑	151	Lee Stevens	.50	.15
❑	152	Wil Cordero	.50	.15
❑	153	Mike Bordick	1.00	.30
❑	154	John Flaherty	.50	.15
❑	155	Omar Daal	.50	.15
❑	156	Todd Ritchie	.50	.15
❑	157	Carl Everett	1.00	.30
❑	158	Scott Sullivan	.50	.15
❑	159	Deivi Cruz	.50	.15
❑	160	Albert Pujols	5.00	1.50
❑	161	Royce Clayton	.50	.15
❑	162	Jeff Suppan	.50	.15
❑	163	C.C. Sabathia	1.00	.30
❑	164	Jimmy Rollins	1.00	.30
❑	165	Rickey Henderson	2.50	.75
❑	166	Rey Ordonez	.50	.15
❑	167	Shawn Estes	.50	.15
❑	168	Reggie Sanders	.50	.15
❑	169	Jon Lieber	.50	.15
❑	170	Armando Benitez	1.00	.30
❑	171	Mike Remlinger	.50	.15
❑	172	Billy Wagner	1.00	.30
❑	173	Troy Percival	1.00	.30
❑	174	Devon White	1.00	.30
❑	175	Ivan Rodriguez	2.50	.75
❑	176	Dustin Hermanson	.50	.15
❑	177	Brian Anderson	.50	.15
❑	178	Graeme Lloyd	.50	.15
❑	179	Russell Branyan	.50	.15
❑	180	Bobby Higginson	1.00	.30
❑	181	Alex Gonzalez	.50	.15
❑	182	John Franco	1.00	.30
❑	183	Sidney Ponson	.50	.15
❑	184	Jose Mesa	.50	.15
❑	185	Todd Hollandsworth	.50	.15
❑	186	Kevin Young	.50	.15
❑	187	Tim Wakefield	1.00	.30
❑	188	Craig Biggio	1.50	.45
❑	189	Jason Isringhausen	1.00	.30
❑	190	Mark Quinn	.50	.15
❑	191	Glendon Rusch	.50	.15
❑	192	Damian Miller	.50	.15
❑	193	Sandy Alomar Jr.	.50	.15
❑	194	Scott Brosius	1.00	.30
❑	195	Dave Martinez	.50	.15
❑	196	Danny Graves	.50	.15
❑	197	Shea Hillenbrand	1.00	.30
❑	198	Jimmy Anderson	.50	.15
❑	199	Travis Lee	.50	.15
❑	200	Randy Johnson	2.50	.75
❑	201	Carlos Beltran	1.50	.45
❑	202	Jerry Hairston	.50	.15
❑	203	Jesus Sanchez	.50	.15
❑	204	Eddie Taubensee	.50	.15
❑	205	David Wells	1.00	.30
❑	206	Russ Davis	.50	.15
❑	207	Michael Barrett	.50	.15
❑	208	Marquis Grissom	1.00	.30
❑	209	Byung-Hyun Kim	1.00	.30
❑	210	Hideo Nomo	2.50	.75
❑	211	Ryan Rupe	.50	.15
❑	212	Ricky Gutierrez	.50	.15
❑	213	Darryl Kile	1.00	.30
❑	214	Rico Brogna	.50	.15
❑	215	Terrence Long	.50	.15
❑	216	Mike Jackson	.50	.15
❑	217	Jamey Wright	.50	.15
❑	218	Adrian Beltre	1.50	.45
❑	219	Benny Agbayani	.50	.15
❑	220	Chuck Knoblauch	1.00	.30
❑	221	Randy Wolf	.50	.15
❑	222	Andy Ashby	.50	.15
❑	223	Corey Koskie	1.00	.30
❑	224	Roger Cedeno	.50	.15
❑	225	Ichiro Suzuki	4.00	1.20
❑	226	Keith Foulke	1.00	.30
❑	227	Ryan Minor	.50	.15
❑	228	Shawon Dunston	.50	.15
❑	229	Alex Cora	.50	.15
❑	230	Jeromy Burnitz	1.00	.30
❑	231	Mark Grace	1.50	.45
❑	232	Aubrey Huff	1.00	.30
❑	233	Jeffrey Hammonds	.50	.15
❑	234	Olmedo Saenz	.50	.15
❑	235	Brian Jordan	1.00	.30
❑	236	Jeremy Giambi	.50	.15
❑	237	Joe Girardi	.50	.15
❑	238	Eric Gagne	2.50	.75
❑	239	Masato Yoshii	.50	.15
❑	240	Greg Maddux	4.00	1.20
❑	241	Bryan Rekar	.50	.15
❑	242	Ray Durham	1.00	.30
❑	243	Torii Hunter	1.00	.30
❑	244	Derrek Lee	1.00	.30
❑	245	Jim Edmonds	1.00	.30
❑	246	Einar Diaz	.50	.15
❑	247	Brian Bohanon	.50	.15
❑	248	Ron Belliard	.50	.15
❑	249	Mike Lowell	1.00	.30
❑	250	Sammy Sosa	4.00	1.20
❑	251	Richard Hidalgo	.50	.15
❑	252	Bartolo Colon	1.00	.30
❑	253	Jorge Posada	1.50	.45
❑	254	Latroy Hawkins	.50	.15
❑	255	Paul LoDuca	1.00	.30
❑	256	Carlos Febles	.50	.15
❑	257	Nelson Cruz	.50	.15
❑	258	Edgardo Alfonzo	.50	.15
❑	259	Joey Hamilton	.50	.15
❑	260	Cliff Floyd	1.00	.30
❑	261	Wes Helms	.50	.15
❑	262	Jay Bell	1.00	.30
❑	263	Mike Cameron	1.00	.30
❑	264	Paul Konerko	1.00	.30
❑	265	Jeff Kent	1.00	.30
❑	266	Robert Fick	.50	.15
❑	267	Allen Levrault	.50	.15
❑	268	Placido Polanco	.50	.15
❑	269	Marlon Anderson	.50	.15
❑	270	Mariano Rivera	1.50	.45
❑	271	Chan Ho Park	1.00	.30
❑	272	Jose Vizcaino	.50	.15
❑	273	Jeff D'Amico	.50	.15
❑	274	Mark Gardner	.50	.15
❑	275	Travis Fryman	1.00	.30
❑	276	Darren Lewis	.50	.15
❑	277	Bruce Bochy MG	.50	.15
❑	278	Jerry Manuel MG	.50	.15
❑	279	Bob Brenly MG	.50	.15
❑	280	Don Baylor MG	1.00	.30
❑	281	Davey Lopes MG	1.00	.30
❑	282	Jerry Narron MG	.50	.15
❑	283	Tony Muser MG	.50	.15
❑	284	Hal McRae MG	1.00	.30
❑	285	Bobby Cox MG	.50	.15
❑	286	Larry Dierker MG	.50	.15
❑	287	Phil Garner MG	.50	.15
❑	288	Joe Kerrigan MG	.50	.15
❑	289	Bobby Valentine MG	.50	.15
❑	290	Dusty Baker MG	1.00	.30
❑	291	Lloyd McClendon MG	.50	.15
❑	292	Mike Scioscia MG	.50	.15
❑	293	Buck Martinez MG	.50	.15
❑	294	Larry Bowa MG	1.00	.30
❑	295	Tony LaRussa MG	1.00	.30
❑	296	Jeff Torborg MG	.50	.15
❑	297	Tom Kelly MG	.50	.15
❑	298	Mike Hargrove MG	.50	.15
❑	299	Art Howe MG	.50	.15
❑	300	Lou Piniella MG	1.00	.30
❑	301	Charlie Manuel MG	.50	.15
❑	302	Buddy Bell MG	1.00	.30
❑	303	Tony Perez MG	1.00	.30
❑	304	Bob Boone MG	1.00	.30
❑	305	Joe Torre MG	2.50	.75
❑	306	Jim Tracy MG	.50	.15
❑	307	Jason Lane PROS	1.50	.45
❑	308	Chris George PROS	1.50	.45
❑	309	Hank Blalock PROS	2.50	.75
❑	310	Joe Borchard PROS	1.50	.45
❑	311	Marlon Byrd PROS	1.50	.45
❑	312	Ray. Cabrera PROS RC	1.50	.45
❑	313	Fr. Sanchez PROS RC	1.50	.45
❑	314	Scott Wiggins PROS RC	1.50	.45
❑	315	Jason Maule PROS RC	1.50	.45
❑	316	Dionys Cesar PROS RC	1.50	.45
❑	317	Boof Bonser PROS	1.50	.45
❑	318	Juan Tolentino PROS RC	1.50	.45
❑	319	Earl Snyder PROS RC	2.50	.75
❑	320	Travis Wade PROS RC	1.50	.45
❑	321	Nap. Calzado PROS RC	1.50	.45
❑	322	Eric Glaser PROS	1.50	.45
❑	323	Craig Kuzmic PROS RC	1.50	.45
❑	324	Nic Jackson PROS RC	1.50	.45
❑	325	Mike Rivera PROS	1.50	.45
❑	326	Jason Bay PROS RC	6.00	1.80
❑	327	Chris Smith DP	1.50	.45
❑	328	Jake Gautreau DP	1.50	.45
❑	329	Gabe Gross DP	1.50	.45
❑	330	Kenny Baugh DP	1.50	.45
❑	331	J.D. Martin DP	1.50	.45
❑	366	Pat Meares	.50	.15
❑	367	Mike Lieberthal	1.00	.30
❑	368	Larry Bigbie	.50	.15
❑	369	Ron Gant	1.00	.30
❑	370	Moises Alou	1.00	.30
❑	371	Chad Kreuter	.50	.15
❑	372	Willis Roberts	.50	.15
❑	373	Toby Hall	.50	.15
❑	374	Miguel Batista	.50	.15
❑	375	John Burkett	.50	.15
❑	376	Cory Lidle	.50	.15
❑	377	Nick Neugebauer	.50	.15
❑	378	Jay Payton	.50	.15
❑	379	Steve Karsay	.50	.15
❑	380	Eric Chavez	1.00	.30

❑ 381 Kelly Stinnett .50 .15
❑ 382 Jarrod Washburn .50 .15
❑ 383 Rick White .50 .15
❑ 384 Jeff Conine 1.00 .30
❑ 385 Fred McGriff 1.50 .45
❑ 386 Marvin Benard .50 .15
❑ 387 Joe Crede .50 .15
❑ 388 Dennis Cook .50 .15
❑ 389 Rick Reed .50 .15
❑ 390 Tom Glavine 1.50 .45
❑ 391 Rondell White 1.00 .30
❑ 392 Matt Morris 1.00 .30
❑ 393 Pat Rapp .50 .15
❑ 394 Robert Person .50 .15
❑ 395 Omar Vizquel 1.50 .45
❑ 396 Jeff Cirillo .50 .15
❑ 397 Dave Mlicki .50 .15
❑ 398 Jose Ortiz .50 .15
❑ 399 Ryan Dempster .50 .15
❑ 400 Curt Schilling 1.00 .30
❑ 401 Peter Bergeron .50 .15
❑ 402 Kyle Lohse .50 .15
❑ 403 Craig Wilson 1.00 .30
❑ 404 David Justice 1.00 .30
❑ 405 Darin Erstad 1.00 .30
❑ 406 Jose Mercedes .50 .15
❑ 407 Carl Pavano 1.00 .30
❑ 408 Albie Lopez .50 .15
❑ 409 Alex Ochoa .50 .15
❑ 410 Chipper Jones 2.50 .75
❑ 411 Tyler Houston .50 .15
❑ 412 Dean Palmer 1.00 .30
❑ 413 Damian Jackson .50 .15
❑ 414 Josh Towers .50 .15
❑ 415 Rafael Furcal 1.00 .30
❑ 416 Mike Morgan .50 .15
❑ 417 Herb Perry .50 .15
❑ 418 Mike Sirotka .50 .15
❑ 419 Mark Wohlers .50 .15
❑ 420 Nomar Garciaparra 4.00 1.20
❑ 421 Felipe Lopez .50 .15
❑ 422 Joe McEwing .50 .15
❑ 423 Jacque Jones 1.00 .30
❑ 424 Julio Franco 1.00 .30
❑ 425 Frank Thomas 2.50 .75
❑ 426 So Taguchi RC 2.50 .75
❑ 427 Kazuhisa Ishii RC 5.00 1.50
❑ 428 D'Angelo Jimenez .50 .15
❑ 429 Chris Stynes .50 .15
❑ 430 Kerry Wood 2.50 .75
❑ 431 Chris Singleton .50 .15
❑ 432 Erubiel Durazo .50 .15
❑ 433 Matt Lawton .50 .15
❑ 434 Bill Mueller 1.00 .30
❑ 435 Jose Canseco 2.50 .75
❑ 436 Ben Grieve .50 .15
❑ 437 Terry Mulholland .50 .15
❑ 438 David Bell .50 .15
❑ 439 A.J. Pierzynski 1.00 .30
❑ 440 Adam Dunn 1.50 .45
❑ 441 Jon Garland .50 .15
❑ 442 Jeff Fassero .50 .15
❑ 443 Julio Lugo .50 .15
❑ 444 Carlos Guillen 1.00 .30
❑ 445 Orlando Hernandez .50 .15
❑ 446 Mark Loretta 1.00 .30
❑ 447 Scott Spiezio .50 .15
❑ 448 Kevin Millwood 1.00 .30
❑ 449 Jamie Moyer 1.00 .30
❑ 450 Todd Helton 1.50 .45
❑ 451 Todd Walker .50 .15
❑ 452 Jose Lima .50 .15
❑ 453 Brook Fordyce .50 .15
❑ 454 Aaron Rowand 1.00 .30
❑ 455 Barry Zito 1.00 .30
❑ 456 Eric Owens .50 .15
❑ 457 Charles Nagy .50 .15
❑ 458 Raul Ibanez .50 .15
❑ 459 Joe Mays .50 .15
❑ 460 Jim Thome 2.50 .75
❑ 461 Adam Eaton .50 .15
❑ 462 Felix Martinez .50 .15
❑ 463 Vernon Wells 1.00 .30
❑ 464 Donnie Sadler .50 .15
❑ 465 Tony Clark .50 .15
❑ 466 Jose Hernandez .50 .15
❑ 467 Ramon Martinez .50 .15
❑ 468 Rusty Greer 1.00 .30
❑ 469 Rod Barajas .50 .15
❑ 470 Lance Berkman 1.00 .30
❑ 471 Brady Anderson 1.00 .30
❑ 472 Pedro Astacio .50 .15
❑ 473 Shane Halter .50 .15
❑ 474 Bret Prinz .50 .15
❑ 475 Edgar Martinez 1.50 .45
❑ 476 Steve Trachsel .50 .15
❑ 477 Gary Matthews Jr. .50 .15
❑ 478 Ismael Valdes .50 .15
❑ 479 Juan Uribe .50 .15
❑ 480 Shawn Green 1.00 .30
❑ 481 Kirk Rueter .50 .15
❑ 482 Damion Easley .50 .15
❑ 483 Chris Carpenter .50 .15
❑ 484 Kris Benson .50 .15
❑ 485 Antonio Alfonseca .50 .15
❑ 486 Kyle Farnsworth .50 .15
❑ 487 Brandon Lyon .50 .15
❑ 488 Hideki Irabu .50 .15
❑ 489 David Ortiz 1.50 .45
❑ 490 Mike Piazza 4.00 1.20
❑ 491 Derek Lowe 1.00 .30
❑ 492 Chris Gomez .50 .15
❑ 493 Mark Johnson .50 .15
❑ 494 John Rocker .50 .15
❑ 495 Eric Karros 1.00 .30
❑ 496 Bill Haselman .50 .15
❑ 497 Dave Veres .50 .15
❑ 498 Pete Harnisch .50 .15
❑ 499 Tomokazu Ohka .50 .15
❑ 500 Barry Bonds 6.00 1.80
❑ 501 David Dellucci .50 .15
❑ 502 Wendell Magee .50 .15
❑ 503 Tom Gordon .50 .15
❑ 504 Javier Vazquez 1.00 .30
❑ 505 Ben Sheets 1.00 .30
❑ 506 Wilton Guerrero .50 .15
❑ 507 John Halama .50 .15
❑ 508 Mark Redman .50 .15
❑ 509 Jack Wilson 1.00 .30
❑ 510 Bernie Williams 1.50 .45
❑ 511 Miguel Cairo .50 .15
❑ 512 Denny Hocking .50 .15
❑ 513 Tony Batista 1.00 .30
❑ 514 Mark Grudzielanek .50 .15
❑ 515 Jose Vidro .50 .15
❑ 516 Sterling Hitchcock .50 .15
❑ 517 Billy Koch .50 .15
❑ 518 Matt Clement .50 .15
❑ 519 Bruce Chen .50 .15
❑ 520 Roberto Alomar 1.50 .45
❑ 521 Orlando Palmeiro .50 .15
❑ 522 Steve Finley 1.00 .30
❑ 523 Danny Patterson .50 .15
❑ 524 Terry Adams .50 .15
❑ 525 Tino Martinez 1.50 .45
❑ 526 Tony Armas Jr. UER .50 .15
Career stats do not include pre-2001
❑ 527 Geoff Jenkins 1.00 .30
❑ 528 Kerry Robinson .50 .15
❑ 529 Corey Patterson 1.00 .30
❑ 530 Brian Giles 1.00 .30
❑ 531 Jose Jimenez .50 .15
❑ 532 Joe Kennedy .50 .15
❑ 533 Armando Rios .50 .15
❑ 534 Osvaldo Fernandez .50 .15
❑ 535 Ruben Sierra .50 .15
❑ 536 Octavio Dotel .50 .15
❑ 537 Luis Sojo .50 .15
❑ 538 Brent Butler .50 .15
❑ 539 Pablo Ozuna .50 .15
❑ 540 Freddy Garcia 1.00 .30
❑ 541 Chad Durbin .50 .15
❑ 542 Orlando Merced .50 .15
❑ 543 Michael Tucker .50 .15
❑ 544 Roberto Hernandez .50 .15
❑ 545 Pat Burrell 1.00 .30
❑ 546 A.J. Burnett .50 .15
❑ 547 Bubba Trammell .50 .15
❑ 548 Scott Elarton .50 .15
❑ 549 Mike Darr .50 .15
❑ 550 Ken Griffey Jr. 4.00 1.20
❑ 551 Ugueth Urbina .50 .15
❑ 552 Todd Jones .50 .15
❑ 553 Delino Deshields .50 .15
❑ 554 Adam Piatt .50 .15
❑ 555 Jason Kendall 1.00 .30
❑ 556 Hector Ortiz .50 .15
❑ 557 Turk Wendell .50 .15
❑ 558 Rob Bell .50 .15
❑ 559 Sun Woo Kim .50 .15
❑ 560 Raul Mondesi 1.00 .30
❑ 561 Brent Abernathy .50 .15
❑ 562 Seth Etherton .50 .15
❑ 563 Shawn Wooten .50 .15
❑ 564 Jay Buhner 1.00 .30
❑ 565 Andres Galarraga 1.00 .30
❑ 566 Shane Reynolds .50 .15
❑ 567 Rod Beck .50 .15
❑ 568 Dee Brown .50 .15
❑ 569 Pedro Feliz .50 .15
❑ 570 Ryan Klesko 1.00 .30
❑ 571 John Vander Wal .50 .15
❑ 572 Nick Bierbrodt .50 .15
❑ 573 Joe Nathan .50 .15
❑ 574 James Baldwin .50 .15
❑ 575 J.D. Drew 1.00 .30
❑ 576 Greg Colbrunn .50 .15
❑ 577 Doug Glanville .50 .15
❑ 578 Brandon Duckworth .50 .15
❑ 579 Shawn Chacon .50 .15
❑ 580 Rich Aurilia .50 .15
❑ 581 Chuck Finley 1.00 .30
❑ 582 Abraham Nunez .50 .15
❑ 583 Kenny Lofton 1.00 .30
❑ 584 Brian Daubach .50 .15
❑ 585 Miguel Tejada 1.00 .30
❑ 586 Nate Cornejo .50 .15
❑ 587 Kazuhiro Sasaki 1.00 .30
❑ 588 Chris Richard .50 .15
❑ 589 Armando Reynoso .50 .15
❑ 590 Tim Hudson 1.00 .30
❑ 591 Neifi Perez .50 .15
❑ 592 Steve Cox .50 .15
❑ 593 Henry Blanco .50 .15
❑ 594 Ricky Ledee .50 .15
❑ 595 Tim Salmon 1.50 .45
❑ 596 Luis Rivas .50 .15
❑ 597 Jeff Zimmerman .50 .15
❑ 598 Matt Stairs .50 .15
❑ 599 Preston Wilson 1.00 .30
❑ 600 Mark McGwire 6.00 1.80
❑ 601 Timo Perez .50 .15
❑ 602 Matt Anderson .50 .15
❑ 603 Todd Hundley .50 .15
❑ 604 Rick Ankiel .50 .15
❑ 605 Tsuyoshi Shinjo 1.00 .30
❑ 606 Woody Williams .50 .15
❑ 607 Jason LaRue .50 .15
❑ 608 Carlos Lee 1.00 .30
❑ 609 Russ Johnson .50 .15
❑ 610 Scott Rolen 2.50 .75
❑ 611 Brent Mayne .50 .15
❑ 612 Darrin Fletcher .50 .15
❑ 613 Ray Lankford .50 .15
❑ 614 Troy O'Leary .50 .15
❑ 615 Javier Lopez 1.00 .30
❑ 616 Randy Velarde .50 .15
❑ 617 Vinny Castilla 1.00 .30
❑ 618 Milton Bradley 1.00 .30
❑ 619 Ruben Mateo .50 .15
❑ 620 Jason Giambi Yankees 1.00 .30
❑ 621 Andy Benes .50 .15
❑ 622 Joe Mauer RC 10.00 3.00
❑ 623 Andy Pettitte 1.50 .45
❑ 624 Jose Offerman .50 .15
❑ 625 Mo Vaughn 1.00 .30
❑ 626 Steve Sparks .50 .15
❑ 627 Mike Matthews .50 .15
❑ 628 Robb Nen 1.00 .30
❑ 629 Kip Wells .50 .15
❑ 630 Kevin Brown 1.00 .30
❑ 631 Arthur Rhodes .50 .15
❑ 632 Gabe Kapler .50 .15
❑ 633 Jermaine Dye 1.00 .30
❑ 634 Josh Beckett 1.00 .30
❑ 635 Pokey Reese .50 .15
❑ 636 Benji Gil .50 .15
❑ 637 Marcus Giles 1.00 .30

❑ 638 Julian Tavarez .50 .15
❑ 639 Jason Schmidt 1.00 .30
❑ 640 Alex Rodriguez 4.00 1.20
❑ 641 Anaheim Angels TC 1.00 .30
❑ 642 Ariz. Diamondbacks TC 1.50 .45
❑ 643 Atlanta Braves TC 1.00 .30
❑ 644 Baltimore Orioles TC 1.00 .30
❑ 645 Boston Red Sox TC 1.00 .30
❑ 646 Chicago Cubs TC 1.00 .30
❑ 647 Chicago White Sox TC 1.00 .30
❑ 648 Cincinnati Reds TC 1.00 .30
❑ 649 Cleveland Indians TC 1.00 .30
❑ 650 Colorado Rockies TC 1.00 .30
❑ 651 Detroit Tigers TC 1.00 .30
❑ 652 Florida Marlins TC 1.00 .30
❑ 653 Houston Astros TC 1.00 .30
❑ 654 Kansas City Royals TC 1.00 .30
❑ 655 Los Angeles Dodgers TC 1.00 .30
❑ 656 Milwaukee Brewers TC 1.00 .30
❑ 657 Minnesota Twins TC 1.00 .30
❑ 658 Montreal Expos TC 1.00 .30
❑ 659 New York Mets TC 1.00 .30
❑ 660 New York Yankees TC 2.50 .75
❑ 661 Oakland Athletics TC 1.00 .30
❑ 662 Philadelphia Phillies TC 1.00 .30
❑ 663 Pittsburgh Pirates TC 1.00 .30
❑ 664 San Diego Padres TC 1.00 .30
❑ 665 San Francisco Giants TC 1.00 .30
❑ 666 Seattle Mariners TC 1.50 .45
❑ 667 St. Louis Cardinals TC 1.00 .30
❑ 668 T.B. Devil Rays TC 1.00 .30
❑ 669 Texas Rangers TC 1.00 .30
❑ 670 Toronto Blue Jays TC 1.00 .30
❑ 671 Juan Cruz PROS 1.50 .45
❑ 672 Kevin Cash PROS RC 1.50 .45
❑ 673 Jimmy Gobble PROS RC 2.50 .75
❑ 674 Mike Hill PROS RC 1.50 .45
❑ 675 T.Buchholz PROS RC 1.50 .45
❑ 676 Bill Hall PROS 1.50 .45
❑ 677 B.Roneberg PROS RC 1.50 .45
❑ 678 R.Huffman PROS RC 1.50 .45
❑ 679 Chris Tritle PROS RC 1.50 .45
❑ 680 Nate Espy PROS 1.50 .45
❑ 681 Nick Alvarez PROS RC 1.50 .45
❑ 682 Jason Botts PROS RC 2.50 .75
❑ 683 Ryan Gripp PROS RC 1.50 .45
❑ 684 Dan Phillips PROS RC 1.50 .45
❑ 685 Pablo Arias PROS RC 1.50 .45
❑ 686 J.Rodriguez PROS RC 1.50 .45
❑ 687 Rich Harden PROS RC 10.00 3.00
❑ 688 Neal Frendling PROS RC 1.50 .45
❑ 689 R.Thompson PROS RC 1.50 .45
❑ 690 G.Montalbano PROS RC 1.50 .45
❑ 691 Len Dinardo DP RC 1.50 .45
❑ 692 Ryan Raburn DP RC 1.50 .45
❑ 693 Josh Barfield DP RC 4.00 1.20
❑ 694 David Bacani DP RC 1.50 .45
❑ 695 Dan Johnson DP RC 2.50 .75

2002 Topps Chrome Traded

	Nm-Mt	Ex-Mt
COMPLETE SET (275)	120.00	36.00

❑ T1 Jeff Weaver .50 .15
❑ T2 Jay Powell .50 .15
❑ T3 Alex Gonzalez .50 .15
❑ T4 Jason Isringhausen .75 .23
❑ T5 Tyler Houston .50 .15
❑ T6 Ben Broussard .50 .15
❑ T7 Chuck Knoblauch .75 .23
❑ T8 Brian L. Hunter .50 .15
❑ T9 Dustan Mohr .50 .15
❑ T10 Eric Hinske .50 .15
❑ T11 Roger Cedeno .50 .15
❑ T12 Eddie Perez .50 .15
❑ T13 Jeromy Burnitz .75 .23
❑ T14 Bartolo Colon .75 .23
❑ T15 Rick Helling .50 .15
❑ T16 Dan Plesac .50 .15
❑ T17 Scott Strickland .50 .15
❑ T18 Antonio Alfonseca .50 .15
❑ T19 Ricky Gutierrez .50 .15
❑ T20 John Valentin .50 .15
❑ T21 Raul Mondesi .75 .23
❑ T22 Ben Davis .50 .15
❑ T23 Nelson Figueroa .50 .15
❑ T24 Earl Snyder .50 .15
❑ T25 Robin Ventura .75 .23
❑ T26 Jimmy Haynes .50 .15
❑ T27 Kenny Kelly .50 .15
❑ T28 Morgan Ensberg .75 .23
❑ T29 Reggie Sanders .50 .15
❑ T30 Shigetoshi Hasegawa .75 .23
❑ T31 Mike Timlin .50 .15
❑ T32 Russell Branyan .50 .15
❑ T33 Alan Embree .50 .15
❑ T34 D'Angelo Jimenez .50 .15
❑ T35 Kent Mercker .50 .15
❑ T36 Jesse Orosco .50 .15
❑ T37 Gregg Zaun .50 .15
❑ T38 Reggie Taylor .50 .15
❑ T39 Andres Galarraga .75 .23
❑ T40 Chris Truby .50 .15
❑ T41 Bruce Chen .50 .15
❑ T42 Darren Lewis .50 .15
❑ T43 Ryan Kohlmeier .50 .15
❑ T44 John McDonald .50 .15
❑ T45 Omar Daal .50 .15
❑ T46 Matt Clement .50 .15
❑ T47 Glendon Rusch .50 .15
❑ T48 Chan Ho Park .75 .23
❑ T49 Benny Agbayani .50 .15
❑ T50 Juan Gonzalez 1.25 .35
❑ T51 Carlos Baerga .50 .15
❑ T52 Tim Raines .75 .23
❑ T53 Kevin Appier .75 .23
❑ T54 Marty Cordova .50 .15
❑ T55 Jeff D'Amico .50 .15
❑ T56 Dmitri Young .75 .23
❑ T57 Roosevelt Brown .50 .15
❑ T58 Dustin Hermanson .50 .15
❑ T59 Jose Rijo .50 .15
❑ T60 Todd Ritchie .50 .15
❑ T61 Lee Stevens .50 .15
❑ T62 Placido Polanco .50 .15
❑ T63 Eric Young .50 .15
❑ T64 Chuck Finley .75 .23
❑ T65 Dicky Gonzalez .50 .15
❑ T66 Jose Macias .50 .15
❑ T67 Gabe Kapler .50 .15
❑ T68 Sandy Alomar Jr. .50 .15
❑ T69 Henry Blanco .50 .15
❑ T70 Julian Tavarez .50 .15
❑ T71 Paul Bako .50 .15
❑ T72 Scott Rolen 2.00 .60
❑ T73 Brian Jordan .75 .23
❑ T74 Rickey Henderson 2.00 .60
❑ T75 Kevin Mench .50 .15
❑ T76 Hideo Nomo 2.00 .60
❑ T77 Jeremy Giambi .50 .15
❑ T78 Brad Fullmer .50 .15
❑ T79 Carl Everett .75 .23
❑ T80 David Wells .75 .23
❑ T81 Aaron Sele .50 .15
❑ T82 Todd Hollandsworth .50 .15
❑ T83 Vicente Padilla .50 .15
❑ T84 Kenny Lofton .75 .23
❑ T85 Corky Miller .50 .15
❑ T86 Josh Fogg .50 .15
❑ T87 Cliff Floyd .75 .23
❑ T88 Craig Paquette .50 .15
❑ T89 Jay Payton .50 .15
❑ T90 Carlos Pena .50 .15
❑ T91 Juan Encarnacion .50 .15
❑ T92 Rey Sanchez .50 .15
❑ T93 Ryan Dempster .50 .15
❑ T94 Mario Encarnacion .50 .15
❑ T95 Jorge Julio .50 .15
❑ T96 John Mabry .50 .15
❑ T97 Todd Zeile .75 .23
❑ T98 Johnny Damon 1.25 .35
❑ T99 Deivi Cruz .50 .15
❑ T100 Gary Sheffield .75 .23
❑ T101 Ted Lilly .50 .15
❑ T102 Todd Van Poppel .50 .15
❑ T103 Shawn Estes .50 .15
❑ T104 Cesar Izturis .50 .15
❑ T105 Ron Coomer .50 .15
❑ T106 Grady Little MG RC .50 .15
❑ T107 Jimy Williams MGR .50 .15
❑ T108 Tony Pena MGR .50 .15
❑ T109 Frank Robinson MGR 1.25 .35
❑ T110 Ron Gardenhire MGR .50 .15
❑ T111 Dennis Tankersley .50 .15
❑ T112 Alejandro Cadena RC 1.00 .30
❑ T113 Justin Reid RC 1.00 .30
❑ T114 Nate Field RC 1.00 .30
❑ T115 Rene Reyes RC 1.00 .30
❑ T116 Nelson Castro RC 1.00 .30
❑ T117 Miguel Olivo .50 .15
❑ T118 David Espinosa .50 .15
❑ T119 Chris Bootcheck RC 1.00 .30
❑ T120 Rob Henkel RC 1.00 .30
❑ T121 Steve Bechler RC 1.00 .30
❑ T122 Mark Outlaw RC 1.00 .30
❑ T123 Henry Pichardo RC 1.00 .30
❑ T124 Michael Floyd RC 1.00 .30
❑ T125 Richard Lane RC 1.00 .30
❑ T126 Pete Zamora RC 1.00 .30
❑ T127 Javier Colina .50 .15
❑ T128 Greg Sain RC 1.25 .35
❑ T129 Ronnie Merrill .50 .15
❑ T130 Gavin Floyd RC 6.00 1.80
❑ T131 Josh Bonifay RC 1.00 .30
❑ T132 Tommy Marx RC 1.00 .30
❑ T133 Gary Cates Jr. RC 1.00 .30
❑ T134 Neal Cotts RC 2.50 .75
❑ T135 Angel Berroa .50 .15
❑ T136 Elio Serrano RC 1.00 .30
❑ T137 J.J. Putz RC 1.00 .30
❑ T138 Ruben Gotay RC 1.00 .30
❑ T139 Eddie Rogers .50 .15
❑ T140 Wily Mo Pena .75 .23
❑ T141 Tyler Yates RC 1.25 .35
❑ T142 Colin Young RC .75 .23
❑ T143 Chance Caple .50 .15
❑ T144 Ben Howard RC 1.00 .30
❑ T145 Ryan Bukvich RC 1.00 .30
❑ T146 Cliff Bartosh RC 1.00 .30
❑ T147 Brandon Claussen .50 .15
❑ T148 Cristian Guerrero .50 .15
❑ T149 Derrick Lewis .50 .15
❑ T150 Eric Miller RC 1.00 .30
❑ T151 Justin Huber RC 2.00 .60
❑ T152 Adrian Gonzalez .75 .23
❑ T153 Brian West RC 1.00 .30
❑ T154 Chris Baker RC 1.00 .30
❑ T155 Drew Henson .75 .23
❑ T156 Scott Hairston RC 4.00 1.20
❑ T157 Jason Simontacchi RC 1.00 .30
❑ T158 Jason Arnold RC 2.00 .60
❑ T159 Brandon Phillips .50 .15
❑ T160 Adam Roller RC 1.00 .30
❑ T161 Scotty Layfield RC 1.00 .30
❑ T162 Freddie Money RC 1.00 .30
❑ T163 Noochie Varner RC 1.00 .30
❑ T164 Terrance Hill RC 1.00 .30
❑ T165 Jeremy Hill RC 1.00 .30
❑ T166 Carlos Cabrera RC 1.00 .30
❑ T167 Jose Morban RC 1.00 .30
❑ T168 Kevin Frederick RC 1.00 .30
❑ T169 Mark Teixeira 1.25 .35
❑ T170 Brian Rogers .50 .15
❑ T171 Anastacio Martinez RC 1.00 .30
❑ T172 Bobby Jenks RC 2.00 .60
❑ T173 David Gil RC 1.00 .30
❑ T174 Andres Torres .50 .15
❑ T175 James Barrett RC 1.00 .30

Card	Nm-Mt	Ex-Mt
❑ T176 Jimmy Journell	.50	.15
❑ T177 Brett Kay RC	1.00	.30
❑ T178 Jason Young RC	1.00	.30
❑ T179 Mark Hamilton RC	1.00	.30
❑ T180 Jose Bautista RC	.00	.00
❑ T181 Blake McGinley RC	1.00	.30
❑ T182 Ryan Mottl RC	1.00	.30
❑ T183 Jeff Austin RC	1.00	.30
❑ T184 Xavier Nady	.50	.15
❑ T185 Kyle Kane RC	1.00	.30
❑ T186 Travis Foley RC	1.00	.30
❑ T187 Nathan Kaup RC	1.00	.30
❑ T188 Eric Cyr	.50	.15
❑ T189 Josh Cisneros RC	1.00	.30
❑ T190 Brad Nelson RC	3.00	.90
❑ T191 Clint Weibl RC	1.00	.30
❑ T192 Ron Calloway RC	1.00	.30
❑ T193 Jung Bong	.50	.15
❑ T194 Rolando Viera RC	1.00	.30
❑ T195 Jason Bulger RC	1.00	.30
❑ T196 Chone Figgins RC	2.00	.60
❑ T197 Jimmy Alvarez RC	1.00	.30
❑ T198 Joel Crump RC	1.00	.30
❑ T199 Ryan Doumit RC	1.25	.35
❑ T200 Demetrius Heath RC	1.00	.30
❑ T201 John Ennis RC	1.00	.30
❑ T202 Doug Sessions RC	1.00	.30
❑ T203 Clinton Hosford RC	1.00	.30
❑ T204 Chris Narveson RC	1.00	.30
❑ T205 Ross Peeples RC	1.00	.30
❑ T206 Alex Requena RC	1.00	.30
❑ T207 Matt Erickson RC	1.00	.30
❑ T208 Brian Forystek RC	1.00	.30
❑ T209 Dewon Brazelton	.50	.15
❑ T210 Nathan Haynes	.50	.15
❑ T211 Jack Cust	.50	.15
❑ T212 Jesse Foppert RC	2.50	.75
❑ T213 Jesus Cota RC	1.00	.30
❑ T214 Juan M. Gonzalez RC	1.00	.30
❑ T215 Tim Kalita RC	1.00	.30
❑ T216 Manny Delcarmen RC	1.00	.30
❑ T217 Jim Kavourias RC	1.00	.30
❑ T218 C.J. Wilson RC	1.00	.30
❑ T219 Edwin Yan RC	1.00	.30
❑ T220 Andy Van Hekken	.50	.15
❑ T221 Michael Cuddyer	.50	.15
❑ T222 Jeff Verplancke RC	1.00	.30
❑ T223 Mike Wilson RC	1.00	.30
❑ T224 Corwin Malone RC	1.00	.30
❑ T225 Chris Snelling RC	1.00	.30
❑ T226 Joe Rogers RC	1.00	.30
❑ T227 Jason Bay	6.00	1.80
❑ T228 Ezequiel Astacio RC	1.00	.30
❑ T229 Joey Hammond RC	1.00	.30
❑ T230 Chris Duffy RC	1.00	.30
❑ T231 Mark Prior	3.00	.90
❑ T232 Hansel Izquierdo RC	1.00	.30
❑ T233 Franklyn German RC	1.00	.30
❑ T234 Alexis Gomez	.50	.15
❑ T235 Jorge Padilla RC	1.00	.30
❑ T236 Ryan Snare RC	1.00	.30
❑ T237 Deivis Santos	.50	.15
❑ T238 Taggert Bozied RC	2.00	.60
❑ T239 Mike Peeples RC	1.00	.30
❑ T240 Ronald Acuna RC	1.00	.30
❑ T241 Koyie Hill	.50	.15
❑ T242 Garrett Guzman RC	1.00	.30
❑ T243 Ryan Church RC	2.00	.60
❑ T244 Tony Fontana RC	1.00	.30
❑ T245 Keto Anderson RC	1.00	.30
❑ T246 Brad Bouras RC	1.00	.30
❑ T247 Jason Dubois RC	3.00	.90
❑ T248 Angel Guzman RC	8.00	2.40
❑ T249 Joel Hanrahan RC	2.00	.60
❑ T250 Joe Jiannetti RC	1.00	.30
❑ T251 Sean Pierce RC	1.00	.30
❑ T252 Jake Mauer RC	1.00	.30
❑ T253 Marshall McDougall RC	1.00	.30
❑ T254 Edwin Almonte RC	1.00	.30
❑ T255 Shawn Riggans RC	1.00	.30
❑ T256 Steven Shell RC	1.00	.30
❑ T257 Kevin Hooper RC	1.00	.30
❑ T258 Michael Frick RC	1.00	.30
❑ T259 Travis Chapman RC	1.00	.30
❑ T260 Tim Hummel RC	1.00	.30
❑ T261 Adam Morrissey RC	1.00	.30
❑ T262 Dontrelle Willis RC	8.00	2.40
❑ T263 Justin Sherrod RC	1.00	.30
❑ T264 Gerald Smiley RC	1.00	.30
❑ T265 Tony Miller RC	1.00	.30
❑ T266 Nolan Ryan WW	5.00	1.50
❑ T267 Reggie Jackson WW	1.25	.35
❑ T268 Steve Garvey WW	.75	.23
❑ T269 Wade Boggs WW	1.25	.35
❑ T270 Sammy Sosa WW	3.00	.90
❑ T271 Curt Schilling WW	.75	.23
❑ T272 Mark Grace WW	1.25	.35
❑ T273 Jason Giambi WW	.50	.15
❑ T274 Ken Griffey Jr. WW	3.00	.90
❑ T275 Roberto Alomar WW	1.25	.35

2003 Topps Chrome

	Nm-Mt	Ex-Mt
COMPLETE SET (440)	200.00	60.00
COMPLETE SERIES 1 (220)	100.00	30.00
COMPLETE SERIES 2 (220)	100.00	30.00
COMMON (1-200/221-420)	1.00	.30
COMMON (201-220/421-440)	1.50	.45

Card	Nm-Mt	Ex-Mt
❑ 1 Alex Rodriguez	4.00	1.20
❑ 2 Eddie Guardado	1.00	.30
❑ 3 Curt Schilling	1.00	.30
❑ 4 Andruw Jones	1.00	.30
❑ 5 Magglio Ordonez	1.00	.30
❑ 6 Todd Helton	1.50	.45
❑ 7 Odalis Perez	1.00	.30
❑ 8 Edgardo Alfonzo	1.00	.30
❑ 9 Eric Hinske	1.00	.30
❑ 10 Danny Bautista	1.00	.30
❑ 11 Sammy Sosa	4.00	1.20
❑ 12 Roberto Alomar	1.50	.45
❑ 13 Roger Clemens	5.00	1.50
❑ 14 Austin Kearns	1.00	.30
❑ 15 Luis Gonzalez	1.00	.30
❑ 16 Mo Vaughn	1.00	.30
❑ 17 Alfonso Soriano	1.50	.45
❑ 18 Orlando Cabrera	1.00	.30
❑ 19 Hideo Nomo	2.50	.75
❑ 20 Omar Vizquel	1.50	.45
❑ 21 Greg Maddux	4.00	1.20
❑ 22 Fred McGriff	1.50	.45
❑ 23 Frank Thomas	2.50	.75
❑ 24 Shawn Green	1.00	.30
❑ 25 Jacque Jones	1.00	.30
❑ 26 Bernie Williams	1.50	.45
❑ 27 Corey Patterson	1.00	.30
❑ 28 Cesar Izturis	1.00	.30
❑ 29 Larry Walker	1.50	.45
❑ 30 Darren Dreifort	1.00	.30
❑ 31 Al Leiter	1.00	.30
❑ 32 Jason Marquis	1.00	.30
❑ 33 Sean Casey	1.00	.30
❑ 34 Craig Counsell	1.00	.30
❑ 35 Albert Pujols	5.00	1.50
❑ 36 Kyle Lohse	1.00	.30
❑ 37 Paul Lo Duca	1.00	.30
❑ 38 Roy Oswalt	1.00	.30
❑ 39 Danny Graves	1.00	.30
❑ 40 Kevin Millwood	1.00	.30
❑ 41 Lance Berkman	1.00	.30
❑ 42 Denny Hocking	1.00	.30
❑ 43 Jose Valentin	1.00	.30
❑ 44 Josh Beckett	1.00	.30
❑ 45 Nomar Garciaparra	4.00	1.20
❑ 46 Craig Biggio	1.50	.45
❑ 47 Omar Daal	1.00	.30
❑ 48 Jimmy Rollins	1.00	.30
❑ 49 Jermaine Dye	1.00	.30
❑ 50 Edgar Renteria	1.00	.30
❑ 51 Brandon Duckworth	1.00	.30
❑ 52 Luis Castillo	1.00	.30
❑ 53 Andy Ashby	1.00	.30
❑ 54 Mike Williams	1.00	.30
❑ 55 Benito Santiago	1.00	.30
❑ 56 Bret Boone	1.00	.30
❑ 57 Randy Wolf	1.00	.30
❑ 58 Ivan Rodriguez	2.50	.75
❑ 59 Shannon Stewart	1.00	.30
❑ 60 Jose Cruz Jr.	1.00	.30
❑ 61 Billy Wagner	1.00	.30
❑ 62 Alex Gonzalez	1.00	.30
❑ 63 Ichiro Suzuki	4.00	1.20
❑ 64 Joe McEwing	1.00	.30
❑ 65 Mark Mulder	1.00	.30
❑ 66 Mike Cameron	1.00	.30
❑ 67 Corey Koskie	1.00	.30
❑ 68 Marlon Anderson	1.00	.30
❑ 69 Jason Kendall	1.00	.30
❑ 70 J.T. Snow	1.00	.30
❑ 71 Edgar Martinez	1.50	.45
❑ 72 Vernon Wells	1.00	.30
❑ 73 Vladimir Guerrero	2.50	.75
❑ 74 Adam Dunn	1.50	.45
❑ 75 Barry Zito	1.00	.30
❑ 76 Jeff Kent	1.00	.30
❑ 77 Russ Ortiz	1.00	.30
❑ 78 Phil Nevin	1.00	.30
❑ 79 Carlos Beltran	1.50	.45
❑ 80 Mike Lowell	1.00	.30
❑ 81 Bob Wickman	1.00	.30
❑ 82 Junior Spivey	1.00	.30
❑ 83 Melvin Mora	1.00	.30
❑ 84 Derrek Lee	1.00	.30
❑ 85 Chuck Knoblauch	1.00	.30
❑ 86 Eric Gagne	2.50	.75
❑ 87 Orlando Hernandez	1.00	.30
❑ 88 Robert Person	1.00	.30
❑ 89 Elmer Dessens	1.00	.30
❑ 90 Wade Miller	1.00	.30
❑ 91 Adrian Beltre	1.50	.45
❑ 92 Kazuhiro Sasaki	1.00	.30
❑ 93 Timo Perez	1.00	.30
❑ 94 Jose Vidro	1.00	.30
❑ 95 Geronimo Gil	1.00	.30
❑ 96 Trot Nixon	1.00	.30
❑ 97 Denny Neagle	1.00	.30
❑ 98 Roberto Hernandez	1.00	.30
❑ 99 David Ortiz	1.50	.45
❑ 100 Robb Nen	1.00	.30
❑ 101 Sidney Ponson	1.00	.30
❑ 102 Kevin Appier	1.00	.30
❑ 103 Javier Lopez	1.00	.30
❑ 104 Jeff Conine	1.00	.30
❑ 105 Mark Buehrle	1.00	.30
❑ 106 Jason Simontacchi	1.00	.30
❑ 107 Jose Jimenez	1.00	.30
❑ 108 Brian Jordan	1.00	.30
❑ 109 Brad Wilkerson	1.00	.30
❑ 110 Scott Hatteberg	1.00	.30
❑ 111 Matt Morris	1.00	.30
❑ 112 Miguel Tejada	1.00	.30
❑ 113 Rafael Furcal	1.00	.30
❑ 114 Steve Cox	1.00	.30
❑ 115 Roy Halladay	1.00	.30
❑ 116 David Eckstein	1.00	.30
❑ 117 Tomo Ohka	1.00	.30
❑ 118 Jack Wilson	1.00	.30
❑ 119 Randall Simon	1.00	.30
❑ 120 Jamie Moyer	1.00	.30
❑ 121 Andy Benes	1.00	.30
❑ 122 Tino Martinez	1.50	.45
❑ 123 Esteban Yan	1.00	.30
❑ 124 Jason Isringhausen	1.00	.30
❑ 125 Chris Carpenter	1.00	.30
❑ 126 Aaron Rowand	1.00	.30
❑ 127 Brandon Inge	1.00	.30
❑ 128 Jose Vizcaino	1.00	.30
❑ 129 Jose Mesa	1.00	.30
❑ 130 Troy Percival	1.00	.30

Card	Player	Price	Price
❑ 131	Jon Lieber	1.00	.30
❑ 132	Brian Giles	1.00	.30
❑ 133	Aaron Boone	1.00	.30
❑ 134	Bobby Higginson	1.00	.30
❑ 135	Luis Rivas	1.00	.30
❑ 136	Troy Glaus	1.00	.30
❑ 137	Jim Thome	2.50	.75
❑ 138	Ramon Martinez	1.00	.30
❑ 139	Jay Gibbons	1.00	.30
❑ 140	Mike Lieberthal	1.00	.30
❑ 141	Juan Uribe	1.00	.30
❑ 142	Gary Sheffield	1.00	.30
❑ 143	Ramon Santiago	1.00	.30
❑ 144	Ben Sheets	1.00	.30
❑ 145	Tony Armas Jr.	1.00	.30
❑ 146	Kazuhisa Ishii	1.00	.30
❑ 147	Erubiel Durazo	1.00	.30
❑ 148	Jerry Hairston Jr.	1.00	.30
❑ 149	Byung-Hyun Kim	1.00	.30
❑ 150	Marcus Giles	1.00	.30
❑ 151	Johnny Damon	2.50	.75
❑ 152	Terrence Long	1.00	.30
❑ 153	Juan Pierre	1.00	.30
❑ 154	Aramis Ramirez	1.00	.30
❑ 155	Brent Abernathy	1.00	.30
❑ 156	Ismael Valdes	1.00	.30
❑ 157	Mike Mussina	1.50	.45
❑ 158	Ramon Hernandez	1.00	.30
❑ 159	Adam Kennedy	1.00	.30
❑ 160	Tony Womack	1.00	.30
❑ 161	Tony Batista	1.00	.30
❑ 162	Kip Wells	1.00	.30
❑ 163	Jeromy Burnitz	1.00	.30
❑ 164	Todd Hundley	1.00	.30
❑ 165	Tim Wakefield	1.00	.30
❑ 166	Derek Lowe	1.00	.30
❑ 167	Jorge Posada	1.50	.45
❑ 168	Ramon Ortiz	1.00	.30
❑ 169	Brent Butler	1.00	.30
❑ 170	Shane Halter	1.00	.30
❑ 171	Matt Lawton	1.00	.30
❑ 172	Alex Sanchez	1.00	.30
❑ 173	Eric Milton	1.00	.30
❑ 174	Vicente Padilla	1.00	.30
❑ 175	Steve Karsay	1.00	.30
❑ 176	Mark Prior	2.50	.75
❑ 177	Kerry Wood	2.50	.75
❑ 178	Jason LaRue	1.00	.30
❑ 179	Danys Baez	1.00	.30
❑ 180	Nick Neugebauer	1.00	.30
❑ 181	Andres Galarraga	1.00	.30
❑ 182	Jason Giambi	1.00	.30
❑ 183	Aubrey Huff	1.00	.30
❑ 184	Juan Gonzalez	1.50	.45
❑ 185	Ugueth Urbina	1.00	.30
❑ 186	Rickey Henderson	2.50	.75
❑ 187	Brad Fullmer	1.00	.30
❑ 188	Todd Zeile	1.00	.30
❑ 189	Jason Jennings	1.00	.30
❑ 190	Vladimir Nunez	1.00	.30
❑ 191	David Justice	1.00	.30
❑ 192	Brian Lawrence	1.00	.30
❑ 193	Pat Burrell	1.00	.30
❑ 194	Pokey Reese	1.00	.30
❑ 195	Robert Fick	1.00	.30
❑ 196	C.C. Sabathia	1.00	.30
❑ 197	Fernando Vina	1.00	.30
❑ 198	Sean Burroughs	1.00	.30
❑ 199	Ellis Burks	1.00	.30
❑ 200	Joe Randa	1.00	.30
❑ 201	Chris Duncan FY RC	1.50	.45
❑ 202	Franklin Gutierrez FY RC	6.00	1.80
❑ 203	Adam LaRoche FY	1.50	.45
❑ 204	Manuel Ramirez FY RC	2.50	.75
❑ 205	Il Kim FY RC	1.50	.45
❑ 206	Daryl Clark FY RC	2.50	.75
❑ 207	Sean Pierce FY	1.50	.45
❑ 208	Andy Marte FY RC	8.00	2.40
❑ 209	Bernie Castro FY RC	1.50	.45
❑ 210	Jason Perry FY RC	2.50	.75
❑ 211	Jaime Bubela FY RC	1.50	.45
❑ 212	Alexis Rios FY	1.50	.45
❑ 213	Brendan Harris FY RC	2.50	.75
❑ 214	R.Nivar-Martinez FY RC	2.50	.75
❑ 215	Terry Tiffee FY RC	2.50	.75
❑ 216	Kevin Youkilis FY RC	5.00	1.50
❑ 217	Derell McCall FY RC	1.50	.45
❑ 218	Scott Tyler FY RC	2.50	.75
❑ 219	Craig Brazell FY RC	2.50	.75
❑ 220	Walter Young FY	1.50	.45
❑ 221	Francisco Rodriguez	1.00	.30
❑ 222	Chipper Jones	2.50	.75
❑ 223	Chris Singleton	1.00	.30
❑ 224	Cliff Floyd	1.00	.30
❑ 225	Bobby Hill	1.00	.30
❑ 226	Antonio Osuna	1.00	.30
❑ 227	Barry Larkin	1.50	.45
❑ 228	Dean Palmer	1.00	.30
❑ 229	Eric Owens	1.00	.30
❑ 230	Randy Johnson	2.50	.75
❑ 231	Jeff Suppan	1.00	.30
❑ 232	Eric Karros	1.00	.30
❑ 233	Johan Santana	1.50	.45
❑ 234	Javier Vazquez	1.00	.30
❑ 235	John Thomson	1.00	.30
❑ 236	Nick Johnson	1.00	.30
❑ 237	Mark Ellis	1.00	.30
❑ 238	Doug Glanville	1.00	.30
❑ 239	Ken Griffey Jr.	4.00	1.20
❑ 240	Bubba Trammell	1.00	.30
❑ 241	Livan Hernandez	1.00	.30
❑ 242	Desi Relaford	1.00	.30
❑ 243	Eli Marrero	1.00	.30
❑ 244	Jared Sandberg	1.00	.30
❑ 245	Barry Bonds	6.00	1.80
❑ 246	Aaron Sele	1.00	.30
❑ 247	Derek Jeter	6.00	1.80
❑ 248	Eric Byrnes	1.00	.30
❑ 249	Rich Aurilia	1.00	.30
❑ 250	Joel Pineiro	1.00	.30
❑ 251	Chuck Finley	1.00	.30
❑ 252	Bengie Molina	1.00	.30
❑ 253	Steve Finley	1.00	.30
❑ 254	Marty Cordova	1.00	.30
❑ 255	Shea Hillenbrand	1.00	.30
❑ 256	Milton Bradley	1.00	.30
❑ 257	Carlos Pena	1.00	.30
❑ 258	Brad Ausmus	1.00	.30
❑ 259	Carlos Delgado	1.00	.30
❑ 260	Kevin Mench	1.00	.30
❑ 261	Joe Kennedy	1.00	.30
❑ 262	Mark McLemore	1.00	.30
❑ 263	Bill Mueller	1.00	.30
❑ 264	Ricky Ledee	1.00	.30
❑ 265	Ted Lilly	1.00	.30
❑ 266	Sterling Hitchcock	1.00	.30
❑ 267	Scott Strickland	1.00	.30
❑ 268	Damion Easley	1.00	.30
❑ 269	Torii Hunter	1.00	.30
❑ 270	Brad Radke	1.00	.30
❑ 271	Geoff Jenkins	1.00	.30
❑ 272	Paul Byrd	1.00	.30
❑ 273	Morgan Ensberg	1.00	.30
❑ 274	Mike Maroth	1.00	.30
❑ 275	Mike Hampton	1.00	.30
❑ 276	Flash Gordon	1.00	.30
❑ 277	John Burkett	1.00	.30
❑ 278	Rodrigo Lopez	1.00	.30
❑ 279	Tim Spooneybarger	1.00	.30
❑ 280	Quinton McCracken	1.00	.30
❑ 281	Tim Salmon	1.50	.45
❑ 282	Jarrod Washburn	1.00	.30
❑ 283	Pedro Martinez	2.50	.75
❑ 284	Julio Lugo	1.00	.30
❑ 285	Armando Benitez	1.00	.30
❑ 286	Raul Mondesi	1.00	.30
❑ 287	Robin Ventura	1.00	.30
❑ 288	Bobby Abreu	1.00	.30
❑ 289	Josh Fogg	1.00	.30
❑ 290	Ryan Klesko	1.00	.30
❑ 291	Tsuyoshi Shinjo	1.00	.30
❑ 292	Jim Edmonds	1.00	.30
❑ 293	Chan Ho Park	1.00	.30
❑ 294	John Mabry	1.00	.30
❑ 295	Woody Williams	1.00	.30
❑ 296	Scott Schoeneweis	1.00	.30
❑ 297	Brian Anderson	1.00	.30
❑ 298	Brett Tomko	1.00	.30
❑ 299	Scott Erickson	1.00	.30
❑ 300	Kevin Millar Sox	1.00	.30
❑ 301	Danny Wright	1.00	.30
❑ 302	Jason Schmidt	1.00	.30
❑ 303	Scott Williamson	1.00	.30
❑ 304	Einar Diaz	1.00	.30
❑ 305	Jay Payton	1.00	.30
❑ 306	Juan Acevedo	1.00	.30
❑ 307	Ben Grieve	1.00	.30
❑ 308	Raul Ibanez	1.00	.30
❑ 309	Richie Sexson	1.00	.30
❑ 310	Rick Reed	1.00	.30
❑ 311	Pedro Astacio	1.00	.30
❑ 312	Bud Smith	1.00	.30
❑ 313	Tomas Perez	1.00	.30
❑ 314	Rafael Palmeiro	1.50	.45
❑ 315	Jason Tyner	1.00	.30
❑ 316	Scott Rolen	2.50	.75
❑ 317	Randy Winn	1.00	.30
❑ 318	Ryan Jensen	1.00	.30
❑ 319	Trevor Hoffman	1.00	.30
❑ 320	Craig Wilson	1.00	.30
❑ 321	Jeremy Giambi	1.00	.30
❑ 322	Andy Pettitte	1.50	.45
❑ 323	John Franco	1.00	.30
❑ 324	Felipe Lopez	1.00	.30
❑ 325	Mike Piazza	4.00	1.20
❑ 326	Cristian Guzman	1.00	.30
❑ 327	Jose Hernandez	1.00	.30
❑ 328	Octavio Dotel	1.00	.30
❑ 329	Brad Penny	1.00	.30
❑ 330	Dave Veres	1.00	.30
❑ 331	Ryan Dempster	1.00	.30
❑ 332	Joe Crede	1.00	.30
❑ 333	Chad Hermansen	1.00	.30
❑ 334	Gary Matthews Jr.	1.00	.30
❑ 335	Frank Catalanotto	1.00	.30
❑ 336	Darin Erstad	1.00	.30
❑ 337	Matt Williams	1.00	.30
❑ 338	B.J. Surhoff	1.00	.30
❑ 339	Kerry Ligtenberg	1.00	.30
❑ 340	Mike Bordick	1.00	.30
❑ 341	Joe Girardi	1.00	.30
❑ 342	D'Angelo Jimenez	1.00	.30
❑ 343	Paul Konerko	1.00	.30
❑ 344	Joe Mays	1.00	.30
❑ 345	Marquis Grissom	1.00	.30
❑ 346	Neifi Perez	1.00	.30
❑ 347	Preston Wilson	1.00	.30
❑ 348	Jeff Weaver	1.00	.30
❑ 349	Eric Chavez	1.00	.30
❑ 350	Placido Polanco	1.00	.30
❑ 351	Matt Mantei	1.00	.30
❑ 352	James Baldwin	1.00	.30
❑ 353	Toby Hall	1.00	.30
❑ 354	Benji Gil	1.00	.30
❑ 355	Damian Moss	1.00	.30
❑ 356	Jorge Julio	1.00	.30
❑ 357	Matt Clement	1.00	.30
❑ 358	Lee Stevens	1.00	.30
❑ 359	Dave Roberts	1.00	.30
❑ 360	J.C. Romero	1.00	.30
❑ 361	Bartolo Colon	1.00	.30
❑ 362	Roger Cedeno	1.00	.30
❑ 363	Mariano Rivera	1.50	.45
❑ 364	Billy Koch	1.00	.30
❑ 365	Manny Ramirez	1.50	.45
❑ 366	Travis Lee	1.00	.30
❑ 367	Oliver Perez	1.00	.30
❑ 368	Tim Worrell	1.00	.30
❑ 369	Damian Miller	1.00	.30
❑ 370	John Smoltz	1.50	.45
❑ 371	Willis Roberts	1.00	.30
❑ 372	Tim Hudson	1.00	.30
❑ 373	Moises Alou	1.00	.30
❑ 374	Corky Miller	1.00	.30
❑ 375	Ben Broussard	1.00	.30
❑ 376	Gabe Kapler	1.00	.30
❑ 377	Chris Woodward	1.00	.30
❑ 378	Todd Hollandsworth	1.00	.30
❑ 379	So Taguchi	1.00	.30
❑ 380	John Olerud	1.00	.30
❑ 381	Reggie Sanders	1.00	.30
❑ 382	Jake Peavy	1.00	.30
❑ 383	Kris Benson	1.00	.30
❑ 384	Ray Durham	1.00	.30
❑ 385	Boomer Wells	1.00	.30
❑ 386	Tom Glavine	1.50	.45
❑ 387	Antonio Alfonseca	1.00	.30
❑ 388	Keith Foulke	1.00	.30

❑ 389 Shawn Estes 1.00 .30
❑ 390 Mark Grace 1.50 .45
❑ 391 Dmitri Young 1.00 .30
❑ 392 A.J. Burnett 1.00 .30
❑ 393 Richard Hidalgo 1.00 .30
❑ 394 Mike Sweeney 1.00 .30
❑ 395 Doug Mientkiewicz 1.00 .30
❑ 396 Cory Lidle 1.00 .30
❑ 397 Jeff Bagwell 1.50 .45
❑ 398 Steve Sparks 1.00 .30
❑ 399 Sandy Alomar Jr. 1.00 .30
❑ 400 John Lackey 1.00 .30
❑ 401 Rick Helling 1.00 .30
❑ 402 Carlos Lee 1.00 .30
❑ 403 Garret Anderson 1.00 .30
❑ 404 Vinny Castilla 1.00 .30
❑ 405 David Bell 1.00 .30
❑ 406 Freddy Garcia 1.00 .30
❑ 407 Scott Spiezio 1.00 .30
❑ 408 Russell Branyan 1.00 .30
❑ 409 Jose Contreras RC 3.00 .90
❑ 410 Kevin Brown 1.00 .30
❑ 411 Tyler Houston 1.00 .30
❑ 412 A.J. Pierzynski 1.00 .30
❑ 413 Peter Bergeron 1.00 .30
❑ 414 Brett Myers 1.00 .30
❑ 415 Kenny Lofton 1.00 .30
❑ 416 Ben Davis 1.00 .30
❑ 417 J.D. Drew 1.00 .30
❑ 418 Ricky Gutierrez 1.00 .30
❑ 419 Mark Redman 1.00 .30
❑ 420 Juan Encarnacion 1.00 .30
❑ 421 Bryan Bullington DP RC 4.00 1.20
❑ 422 Jeremy Guthrie DP 1.50 .45
❑ 423 Joey Gomes DP RC 1.50 .45
❑ 424 E.Bastida-Martinez DP RC 1.50 .45
❑ 425 Brian Wright DP RC 1.50 .45
❑ 426 B.J. Upton DP 3.00 .90
❑ 427 Jeff Francis DP 1.50 .45
❑ 428 Jeremy Hermida DP 1.50 .45
❑ 429 Khalil Greene DP 5.00 1.50
❑ 430 Darrell Rasner DP RC 1.50 .45
❑ 431 Brandon Phillips 2.50 .75
Victor Martinez
❑ 432 Hee Seop Choi 1.50 .45
Nic Jackson
❑ 433 Dontrelle Willis 1.50 .45
Jason Stokes
❑ 434 Chad Tracy 1.50 .45
Lyle Overbay
❑ 435 Joe Borchard 1.50 .45
Corwin Malone
❑ 436 Joe Mauer 2.50 .75
Justin Morneau
❑ 437 Drew Henson 1.50 .45
Brandon Claussen
❑ 438 Chase Utley 1.50 .45
Gavin Floyd
❑ 439 Taggert Bozied 1.50 .45
Xavier Nady
❑ 440 Aaron Heilman 1.50 .45
Jose Reyes

2003 Topps Chrome Traded

	MINT	NRMT
COMPLETE SET (275)	120.00	55.00
COMMON CARD (1-120)	.75	.35
COMMON CARD (121-165)	1.00	.45
COMMON CARD (166-275)	1.00	.45
2 PER 2003 TOPPS TRADED HOBBY PACK		.00
2 PER 2003 TOPPS TRADED HTA PACK		.00
2 PER 2003 TOPPS TRADED RETAIL PACK		.00

❑ T1 Juan Pierre .75 .35
❑ T2 Mark Grudzielanek .75 .35
❑ T3 Tanyon Sturtze .75 .35
❑ T4 Greg Vaughn .75 .35
❑ T5 Greg Myers .75 .35
❑ T6 Randall Simon .75 .35
❑ T7 Todd Hundley .75 .35
❑ T8 Marlon Anderson .75 .35
❑ T9 Jeff Reboulet .75 .35
❑ T10 Alex Sanchez .75 .35
❑ T11 Mike Rivera .75 .35
❑ T12 Todd Walker .75 .35
❑ T13 Ray King .75 .35
❑ T14 Shawn Estes .75 .35
❑ T15 Gary Matthews Jr. .75 .35
❑ T16 Jaret Wright .75 .35
❑ T17 Edgardo Alfonzo .75 .35
❑ T18 Omar Daal .75 .35
❑ T19 Ryan Rupe .75 .35
❑ T20 Tony Clark .75 .35
❑ T21 Jeff Suppan .75 .35
❑ T22 Mike Stanton .75 .35
❑ T23 Ramon Martinez .75 .35
❑ T24 Armando Rios .75 .35
❑ T25 Johnny Estrada .75 .35
❑ T26 Joe Girardi .75 .35
❑ T27 Ivan Rodriguez 2.00 .90
❑ T28 Robert Fick .75 .35
❑ T29 Rick White .75 .35
❑ T30 Robert Person .75 .35
❑ T31 Alan Benes .75 .35
❑ T32 Chris Carpenter .75 .35
❑ T33 Chris Widger .75 .35
❑ T34 Travis Hafner .75 .35
❑ T35 Mike Venafro .75 .35
❑ T36 Jon Lieber .75 .35
❑ T37 Orlando Hernandez .75 .35
❑ T38 Aaron Myette .75 .35
❑ T39 Paul Bako .75 .35
❑ T40 Erubiel Durazo .75 .35
❑ T41 Mark Guthrie .75 .35
❑ T42 Steve Avery .75 .35
❑ T43 Damian Jackson .75 .35
❑ T44 Rey Ordonez .75 .35
❑ T45 John Flaherty .75 .35
❑ T46 Byung-Hyun Kim .75 .35
❑ T47 Tom Goodwin .75 .35
❑ T48 Elmer Dessens .75 .35
❑ T49 Al Martin .75 .35
❑ T50 Gene Kingsale .75 .35
❑ T51 Lenny Harris .75 .35
❑ T52 David Ortiz Sox 2.00 .90
❑ T53 Jose Lima .75 .35
❑ T54 Mike Difelice .75 .35
❑ T55 Jose Hernandez .75 .35
❑ T56 Todd Zeile .75 .35
❑ T57 Roberto Hernandez .75 .35
❑ T58 Albie Lopez .75 .35
❑ T59 Roberto Alomar 1.25 .55
❑ T60 Russ Ortiz .75 .35
❑ T61 Brian Daubach .75 .35
❑ T62 Carl Everett .75 .35
❑ T63 Jeromy Burnitz .75 .35
❑ T64 Mark Bellhorn .75 .35
❑ T65 Ruben Sierra .75 .35
❑ T66 Mike Fetters .75 .35
❑ T67 Armando Benitez .75 .35
❑ T68 Deivi Cruz .75 .35
❑ T69 Jose Cruz Jr. .75 .35
❑ T70 Jeremy Fikac .75 .35
❑ T71 Jeff Kent .75 .35
❑ T72 Andres Galarraga .75 .35
❑ T73 Rickey Henderson 2.00 .90
❑ T74 Royce Clayton .75 .35
❑ T75 Troy O'Leary .75 .35
❑ T76 Ron Coomer .75 .35
❑ T77 Greg Colbrunn .75 .35
❑ T78 Wes Helms .75 .35
❑ T79 Kevin Millwood .75 .35
❑ T80 Damion Easley .75 .35
❑ T81 Bobby Kielty .75 .35
❑ T82 Keith Osik .75 .35
❑ T83 Ramiro Mendoza .75 .35
❑ T84 Shea Hillenbrand .75 .35
❑ T85 Shannon Stewart .75 .35
❑ T86 Eddie Perez .75 .35
❑ T87 Ugueth Urbina .75 .35
❑ T88 Orlando Palmeiro .75 .35
❑ T89 Graeme Lloyd .75 .35
❑ T90 John Vander Wal .75 .35
❑ T91 Gary Bennett .75 .35
❑ T92 Shane Reynolds .75 .35
❑ T93 Steve Parris .75 .35
❑ T94 Julio Lugo .75 .35
❑ T95 John Halama .75 .35
❑ T96 Carlos Baerga .75 .35
❑ T97 Jim Parque .75 .35
❑ T98 Mike Williams .75 .35
❑ T99 Fred McGriff 1.25 .55
❑ T100 Kenny Rogers .75 .35
❑ T101 Matt Herges .75 .35
❑ T102 Jay Bell .75 .35
❑ T103 Esteban Yan .75 .35
❑ T104 Eric Owens .75 .35
❑ T105 Aaron Fultz .75 .35
❑ T106 Rey Sanchez .75 .35
❑ T107 Jim Thome 2.00 .90
❑ T108 Aaron Boone .75 .35
❑ T109 Raul Mondesi .75 .35
❑ T110 Kenny Lofton .75 .35
❑ T111 Jose Guillen .75 .35
❑ T112 Aramis Ramirez .75 .35
❑ T113 Sidney Ponson .75 .35
❑ T114 Scott Williamson .75 .35
❑ T115 Robin Ventura .75 .35
❑ T116 Dusty Baker MG .75 .35
❑ T117 Felipe Alou MG .75 .35
❑ T118 Buck Showalter MG .75 .35
❑ T119 Jack McKeon MG .75 .35
❑ T120 Art Howe MG .75 .35
❑ T121 Bobby Crosby PROS 1.50 .70
❑ T122 Adrian Gonzalez PROS 1.00 .45
❑ T123 Kevin Cash PROS 1.00 .45
❑ T124 Shin-Soo Choo PROS 1.00 .45
❑ T125 Chin-Feng Chen PROS 2.50 1.10
❑ T126 Miguel Cabrera PROS 2.50 1.10
❑ T127 Jason Young PROS 1.00 .45
❑ T128 Alex Herrera PROS 1.00 .45
❑ T129 Jason Dubois PROS 1.00 .45
❑ T130 Jeff Mathis PROS 1.00 .45
❑ T131 Casey Kotchman PROS 1.50 .70
❑ T132 Ed Rogers PROS 1.00 .45
❑ T133 Wilson Betemit PROS 1.00 .45
❑ T134 Jim Kavourias PROS 1.00 .45
❑ T135 Taylor Buchholz PROS 1.00 .45
❑ T136 Adam LaRoche PROS 1.00 .45
❑ T137 D.McPherson PROS 2.50 1.10
❑ T138 Jesus Cota PROS 1.00 .45
❑ T139 Clint Nageotte PROS 1.00 .45
❑ T140 Boof Bonser PROS 1.00 .45
❑ T141 Walter Young PROS 1.00 .45
❑ T142 Joe Crede PROS 1.00 .45
❑ T143 Denny Bautista PROS 1.00 .45
❑ T144 Victor Diaz PROS 1.00 .45
❑ T145 Chris Narveson PROS 1.00 .45
❑ T146 Gabe Gross PROS 1.00 .45
❑ T147 Jimmy Journell PROS 1.00 .45
❑ T148 Rafael Soriano PROS 1.00 .45
❑ T149 Jerome Williams PROS 1.00 .45
❑ T150 Aaron Cook PROS 1.00 .45
❑ T151 An. Martinez PROS 1.00 .45
❑ T152 Scott Hairston PROS 1.00 .45
❑ T153 John Buck PROS 1.00 .45
❑ T154 Ryan Ludwick PROS 1.00 .45
❑ T155 Chris Bootcheck PROS 1.00 .45
❑ T156 John Rheinecker PROS 1.00 .45
❑ T157 Jason Lane PROS 1.00 .45
❑ T158 Shelley Duncan PROS 1.00 .45
❑ T159 Adam Wainwright PROS 1.00 .45
❑ T160 Jason Arnold PROS 1.00 .45
❑ T161 Jonny Gomes PROS 1.00 .45
❑ T162 James Loney PROS 1.00 .45
❑ T163 Mike Fontenot PROS 1.00 .45
❑ T164 Khalil Greene PROS 5.00 2.20
❑ T165 Sean Burnett PROS 1.00 .45

❑ T166 David Martinez FY RC .. 1.00 .45
❑ T167 Felix Pie FY RC 5.00 2.20
❑ T168 Joe Valentine FY RC 1.00 .45
❑ T169 Brandon Webb FY RC .. 2.50 1.10
❑ T170 Matt Diaz FY RC 1.25 .55
❑ T171 Lew Ford FY RC 3.00 1.35
❑ T172 Jeremy Griffiths FY RC 1.25 .55
❑ T173 Matt Hensley FY RC 1.00 .45
❑ T174 Charlie Manning FY RC 1.00 .45
❑ T175 Elizardo Ramirez FY RC 2.00 .90
❑ T176 Greg Aquino FY RC 1.00 .45
❑ T177 Felix Sanchez FY RC 1.00 .45
❑ T178 Kelly Shoppach FY RC 2.50 1.10
❑ T179 Bubba Nelson FY RC 1.25 .55
❑ T180 Mike O'Keefe FY RC 1.00 .45
❑ T181 Hanley Ramirez FY RC 5.00 2.20
❑ T182 T.Wellemeyer FY RC 1.25 .55
❑ T183 Dustin Moseley FY RC 1.25 .55
❑ T184 Eric Crozier FY RC 1.25 .55
❑ T185 Ryan Shealy FY RC 2.00 .90
❑ T186 Jer. Bonderman FY RC 2.00 .90
❑ T187 T.Story-Harden FY RC .. 1.00 .45
❑ T188 Dusty Brown FY RC 1.00 .45
❑ T189 Rob Hammock FY RC .. 1.25 .55
❑ T190 Jorge Piedra FY RC 1.25 .55
❑ T191 Chris De La Cruz FY RC 1.00 .45
❑ T192 Eli Whiteside FY RC 1.00 .45
❑ T193 Jason Kubel FY RC 5.00 2.20
❑ T194 Jon Schuerholz FY RC 1.00 .45
❑ T195 St. Randolph FY RC 1.00 .45
❑ T196 Andy Sisco FY RC 2.50 1.10
❑ T197 Sean Smith FY RC 1.25 .55
❑ T198 Jon-Mark Sprowl FY RC 2.00 .90
❑ T199 Matt Kata FY RC 2.00 .90
❑ T200 Robinson Cano FY RC 2.50 1.10
❑ T201 Nook Logan FY RC 1.00 .45
❑ T202 Ben Francisco FY RC .. 1.25 .55
❑ T203 Arnie Munoz FY RC 1.00 .45
❑ T204 Ozzie Chavez FY RC 1.00 .45
❑ T205 Eric Riggs FY RC 1.25 .55
❑ T206 Beau Kemp FY RC 1.00 .45
❑ T207 Travis Wong FY RC 1.25 .55
❑ T208 Dustin Yount FY RC 1.25 .55
❑ T209 Brian McCann FY RC .. 2.00 .90
❑ T210 Wilton Reynolds FY RC 1.25 .55
❑ T211 Matt Bruback FY RC 1.00 .45
❑ T212 Andrew Brown FY RC .. 1.25 .55
❑ T213 Edgar Gonzalez FY RC .. 1.00 .45
❑ T214 Eider Torres FY RC 1.00 .45
❑ T215 Aquilino Lopez FY RC .. 1.00 .45
❑ T216 Bobby Basham FY RC .. 1.25 .55
❑ T217 Tim Olson FY RC 1.25 .55
❑ T218 Nathan Panther FY RC .. 2.00 .90
❑ T219 Bryan Grace FY RC 1.00 .45
❑ T220 Dusty Gomon FY RC 1.25 .55
❑ T221 Wil Ledezma FY RC 1.25 .55
❑ T222 Josh Willingham FY RC 1.25 .55
❑ T223 David Cash FY RC 1.00 .45
❑ T224 Oscar Villarreal FY RC .. 1.00 .45
❑ T225 Jeff Duncan FY RC 1.25 .55
❑ T226 Kade Johnson FY RC .. 1.00 .45
❑ T227 L.Steidlmayer FY RC 1.00 .45
❑ T228 Brandon Watson FY RC 1.00 .45
❑ T229 Jose Morales FY RC 1.00 .45
❑ T230 Mike Gallo FY RC 1.00 .45
❑ T231 Tyler Adamczyk FY RC 1.00 .45
❑ T232 Adam Stern FY RC 1.00 .45
❑ T233 Brennan King FY RC 1.00 .45
❑ T234 Dan Haren FY RC 2.00 .90
❑ T235 Mi. Hernandez FY RC .. 1.00 .45
❑ T236 Ben Fritz FY RC 1.00 .45
❑ T237 Clay Hensley FY RC 1.00 .45
❑ T238 Tyler Johnson FY RC .. 1.00 .45
❑ T239 Pete LaForest FY RC 1.25 .55
❑ T240 Tyler Martin FY RC 1.00 .45
❑ T241 J.D. Durbin FY RC 2.00 .90
❑ T242 Shane Victorino FY RC 1.00 .45
❑ T243 Rajai Davis FY RC 1.25 .55
❑ T244 Ismael Castro FY RC 1.00 .45
❑ T245 C.Wang FY RC 2.50 1.10
❑ T246 Travis Ishikawa FY RC .. 1.00 .45
❑ T247 Corey Shafer FY RC 1.25 .55
❑ T248 G.Schneidmiller FY RC 1.00 .45
❑ T249 Dave Pember FY RC 1.00 .45
❑ T250 Keith Stamler FY RC 1.00 .45
❑ T251 Tyson Graham FY RC .. 1.00 .45
❑ T252 Ryan Cameron FY RC .. 1.00 .45
❑ T253 Eric Eckenstahler FY 1.00 .45
❑ T254 Ma. Peterson FY RC 1.00 .45
❑ T255 Dustin McGowan FY RC 2.00 .90
❑ T256 Pr. Redman FY RC 1.00 .45
❑ T257 Haj Turay FY RC 1.25 .55
❑ T258 Carlos Guzman FY RC .. 1.25 .55
❑ T259 Matt DeMarco FY RC .. 1.00 .45
❑ T260 Derek Michaelis FY RC 1.00 .45
❑ T261 Brian Burgamy FY RC .. 1.00 .45
❑ T262 Jay Sitzman FY RC 1.00 .45
❑ T263 Chris Fallon FY RC 1.00 .45
❑ T264 Mike Adams FY RC 1.00 .45
❑ T265 Clint Barmes FY RC 1.25 .55
❑ T266 Eric Reed FY RC 2.00 .90
❑ T267 Willie Eyre FY RC 1.00 .45
❑ T268 Carlos Duran FY RC 1.00 .45
❑ T269 Nick Trzesniak FY RC .. 1.00 .45
❑ T270 Ferdin Tejeda FY RC 1.00 .45
❑ T271 Mi. Garciaparra FY RC 2.00 .90
❑ T272 Michael Hinckley FY RC 2.50 1.10
❑ T273 Br. Florence FY RC 1.00 .45
❑ T274 Trent Oeltjen FY RC 1.25 .55
❑ T275 Mike Neu FY RC 1.00 .45

2004 Topps Chrome

	Nm-Mt	Ex-Mt
COMP.SERIES 1 w/o SP's (220)	80.00	24.00
COMP.SERIES 2 w/o SP's (220)	80.00	24.00
COMMON (1-210/257-466)	1.00	.30
COMMON (211-220/247-256)	1.00	.30
COMMON AU (221-233)	10.00	3.00

❑ 1 Jim Thome 2.50 .75
❑ 2 Reggie Sanders 1.00 .30
❑ 3 Mark Kotsay 1.00 .30
❑ 4 Edgardo Alfonzo 1.00 .30
❑ 5 Tim Wakefield 1.00 .30
❑ 6 Moises Alou 1.00 .30
❑ 7 Jorge Julio 1.00 .30
❑ 8 Bartolo Colon 1.00 .30
❑ 9 Chan Ho Park 1.00 .30
❑ 10 Ichiro Suzuki 4.00 1.20
❑ 11 Kevin Millwood 1.00 .30
❑ 12 Preston Wilson 1.00 .30
❑ 13 Tom Glavine 1.50 .45
❑ 14 Junior Spivey 1.00 .30
❑ 15 Marcus Giles 1.00 .30
❑ 16 David Segui 1.00 .30
❑ 17 Kevin Millar 1.00 .30
❑ 18 Corey Patterson 1.00 .30
❑ 19 Aaron Rowand 1.00 .30
❑ 20 Derek Jeter 5.00 1.50
❑ 21 Luis Castillo 1.00 .30
❑ 22 Manny Ramirez 1.50 .45
❑ 23 Jay Payton 1.00 .30
❑ 24 Bobby Higginson 1.00 .30
❑ 25 Lance Berkman 1.00 .30
❑ 26 Juan Pierre 1.00 .30
❑ 27 Mike Mussina 1.50 .45
❑ 28 Fred McGriff 1.50 .45
❑ 29 Richie Sexson 1.00 .30
❑ 30 Tim Hudson 1.00 .30
❑ 31 Mike Piazza 4.00 1.20
❑ 32 Brad Radke 1.00 .30
❑ 33 Jeff Weaver 1.00 .30
❑ 34 Ramon Hernandez 1.00 .30
❑ 35 David Bell 1.00 .30
❑ 36 Randy Wolf 1.00 .30
❑ 37 Jake Peavy 1.00 .30
❑ 38 Tim Worrell 1.00 .30
❑ 39 Gil Meche 1.00 .30
❑ 40 Albert Pujols 5.00 1.50
❑ 41 Michael Young 1.00 .30
❑ 42 Josh Phelps 1.00 .30
❑ 43 Brendan Donnelly 1.00 .30
❑ 44 Steve Finley 1.00 .30
❑ 45 John Smoltz 1.50 .45
❑ 46 Jay Gibbons 1.00 .30
❑ 47 Trot Nixon 1.00 .30
❑ 48 Carl Pavano 1.00 .30
❑ 49 Frank Thomas 2.50 .75
❑ 50 Mark Prior 2.50 .75
❑ 51 Danny Graves 1.00 .30
❑ 52 Milton Bradley 1.00 .30
❑ 53 Kris Benson 1.00 .30
❑ 54 Ryan Klesko 1.00 .30
❑ 55 Mike Lowell 1.00 .30
❑ 56 Geoff Blum 1.00 .30
❑ 57 Michael Tucker 1.00 .30
❑ 58 Paul Lo Duca 1.00 .30
❑ 59 Vicente Padilla 1.00 .30
❑ 60 Jacque Jones 1.00 .30
❑ 61 Fernando Tatis 1.00 .30
❑ 62 Ty Wigginton 1.00 .30
❑ 63 Rich Aurilia 1.00 .30
❑ 64 Andy Pettitte 1.50 .45
❑ 65 Terrence Long 1.00 .30
❑ 66 Cliff Floyd 1.00 .30
❑ 67 Mariano Rivera 1.50 .45
❑ 68 Kelvim Escobar 1.00 .30
❑ 69 Marlon Byrd 1.00 .30
❑ 70 Mark Mulder 1.00 .30
❑ 71 Francisco Cordero 1.00 .30
❑ 72 Carlos Guillen 1.00 .30
❑ 73 Fernando Vina 1.00 .30
❑ 74 Lance Carter 1.00 .30
❑ 75 Hank Blalock 1.00 .30
❑ 76 Jimmy Rollins 1.00 .30
❑ 77 Francisco Rodriguez 1.00 .30
❑ 78 Javy Lopez 1.00 .30
❑ 79 Jerry Hairston Jr. 1.00 .30
❑ 80 Andruw Jones 1.00 .30
❑ 81 Rodrigo Lopez 1.00 .30
❑ 82 Johnny Damon 2.50 .75
❑ 83 Hee Seop Choi 1.00 .30
❑ 84 Kazuhiro Sasaki 1.00 .30
❑ 85 Danny Bautista 1.00 .30
❑ 86 Matt Lawton 1.00 .30
❑ 87 Juan Uribe 1.00 .30
❑ 88 Rafael Furcal 1.00 .30
❑ 89 Kyle Farnsworth 1.00 .30
❑ 90 Jose Vidro 1.00 .30
❑ 91 Luis Rivas 1.00 .30
❑ 92 Hideo Nomo 2.50 .75
❑ 93 Javier Vazquez 1.00 .30
❑ 94 Al Leiter 1.00 .30
❑ 95 Jose Valentin 1.00 .30
❑ 96 Alex Cintron 1.00 .30
❑ 97 Zach Day 1.00 .30
❑ 98 Jorge Posada 1.50 .45
❑ 99 C.C. Sabathia 1.00 .30
❑ 100 Alex Rodriguez 4.00 1.20
❑ 101 Brad Penny 1.00 .30
❑ 102 Brad Ausmus 1.00 .30
❑ 103 Raul Ibanez 1.00 .30
❑ 104 Mike Hampton 1.00 .30
❑ 105 Adrian Beltre 1.50 .45
❑ 106 Ramiro Mendoza 1.00 .30
❑ 107 Rocco Baldelli 1.00 .30
❑ 108 Esteban Loaiza 1.00 .30
❑ 109 Russell Branyan 1.00 .30
❑ 110 Todd Helton 1.50 .45
❑ 111 Braden Looper 1.00 .30
❑ 112 Octavio Dotel 1.00 .30
❑ 113 Mike MacDougal 1.00 .30
❑ 114 Cesar Izturis 1.00 .30
❑ 115 Johan Santana 1.50 .45
❑ 116 Jose Contreras 1.00 .30
❑ 117 Placido Polanco 1.00 .30
❑ 118 Jason Phillips 1.00 .30
❑ 119 Orlando Hudson 1.00 .30
❑ 120 Vernon Wells 1.00 .30
❑ 121 Ben Grieve 1.00 .30
❑ 122 Dave Roberts 1.00 .30
❑ 123 Ismael Valdes 1.00 .30
❑ 124 Eric Owens 1.00 .30
❑ 125 Curt Schilling 1.00 .30
❑ 126 Russ Ortiz 1.00 .30
❑ 127 Mark Buehrle 1.00 .30
❑ 128 Doug Mientkiewicz 1.00 .30
❑ 129 Dmitri Young 1.00 .30

No.	Player	Hi	Lo
130	Kazuhisa Ishii	1.00	.30
131	A.J. Pierzynski	1.00	.30
132	Brad Wilkerson	1.00	.30
133	Joe McEwing	1.00	.30
134	Alex Cora	1.00	.30
135	Jose Cruz Jr.	1.00	.30
136	Carlos Zambrano	1.00	.30
137	Jeff Kent	1.00	.30
138	Shigetoshi Hasegawa	1.00	.30
139	Jarrod Washburn	1.00	.30
140	Greg Maddux	4.00	1.20
141	Josh Beckett	1.00	.30
142	Miguel Batista	1.00	.30
143	Omar Vizquel	1.50	.45
144	Alex Gonzalez	1.00	.30
145	Billy Wagner	1.00	.30
146	Brian Jordan	1.00	.30
147	Wes Helms	1.00	.30
148	Deivi Cruz	1.00	.30
149	Alex Gonzalez	1.00	.30
150	Jason Giambi	1.00	.30
151	Erubiel Durazo	1.00	.30
152	Mike Lieberthal	1.00	.30
153	Jason Kendall	1.00	.30
154	Xavier Nady	1.00	.30
155	Kirk Rueter	1.00	.30
156	Mike Cameron	1.00	.30
157	Miguel Cairo	1.00	.30
158	Woody Williams	1.00	.30
159	Toby Hall	1.00	.30
160	Bernie Williams	1.50	.45
161	Darin Erstad	1.00	.30
162	Matt Mantei	1.00	.30
163	Shawn Chacon	1.00	.30
164	Bill Mueller	1.00	.30
165	Damian Miller	1.00	.30
166	Tony Graffanino	1.00	.30
167	Sean Casey	1.00	.30
168	Brandon Phillips	1.00	.30
169	Runelvys Hernandez	1.00	.30
170	Adam Dunn	1.50	.45
171	Carlos Lee	1.00	.30
172	Juan Encarnacion	1.00	.30
173	Angel Berroa	1.00	.30
174	Desi Relaford	1.00	.30
175	Joe Mays	1.00	.30
176	Ben Sheets	1.00	.30
177	Eddie Guardado	1.00	.30
178	Rocky Biddle	1.00	.30
179	Eric Gagne	2.50	.75
180	Eric Chavez	1.00	.30
181	Jason Michaels	1.00	.30
182	Dustan Mohr	1.00	.30
183	Kip Wells	1.00	.30
184	Brian Lawrence	1.00	.30
185	Bret Boone	1.00	.30
186	Tino Martinez	1.50	.45
187	Aubrey Huff	1.00	.30
188	Kevin Mench	1.00	.30
189	Tim Salmon	1.50	.45
190	Carlos Delgado	1.00	.30
191	John Lackey	1.00	.30
192	Eric Byrnes	1.00	.30
193	Luis Matos	1.00	.30
194	Derek Lowe	1.00	.30
195	Mark Grudzielanek	1.00	.30
196	Tom Gordon	1.00	.30
197	Matt Clement	1.00	.30
198	Byung-Hyun Kim	1.00	.30
199	Brandon Inge	1.00	.30
200	Nomar Garciaparra	4.00	1.20
201	Frank Catalanotto	1.00	.30
202	Cristian Guzman	1.00	.30
203	Bo Hart	1.00	.30
204	Jack Wilson	1.00	.30
205	Ray Durham	1.00	.30
206	Freddy Garcia	1.00	.30
207	J.D. Drew	1.00	.30
208	Orlando Cabrera	1.00	.30
209	Roy Halladay	1.00	.30
210	David Eckstein	1.00	.30
211	Omar Falcon FY RC	1.00	.30
212	Todd Self FY RC	1.00	.30
213	David Murphy FY RC	2.50	.75
214	Dioner Navarro FY RC	3.00	.90
215	Marcus McBeth FY RC	1.00	.30
216	Chris O'Riordan FY RC	1.00	.30
217	Rodney Choy Foo FY RC	1.00	.30
218	Tim Frend FY RC	1.00	.30
219	Yadier Molina FY RC	2.50	.75
220	Zach Duke FY RC	4.00	1.20
221	Anthony Lerew FY AU RC	15.00	4.50
222	B.Hawksworth FY AU RC	15.00	4.50
223	Brayan Pena FY AU RC	10.00	3.00
224	Craig Ansman FY AU RC	10.00	3.00
225	Jon Knott FY AU RC	10.00	3.00
226	Josh Labandeira FY AU RC	10.00	3.00
227	Khalid Ballouli FY AU RC	10.00	3.00
228	Kyle Davies FY AU RC	15.00	4.50
229	Matt Creighton FY AU RC	10.00	3.00
230	Mike Gosling FY AU RC	10.00	3.00
231	Nic Ungs FY AU RC	10.00	3.00
232	Zach Miner FY AU RC	15.00	4.50
233	Donald Levinski FY AU RC	10.00	3.00
234A	Bradley Sullivan FY AU RC	15.00	4.50
234B	B.Sullivan FY AU ERR 345	25.00	7.50
235	Carlos Quentin FY AU RC	30.00	9.00
236	Conor Jackson FY AU RC	30.00	9.00
237	Estee Harris FY AU RC	10.00	3.00
238	Jeffrey Allison FY AU RC	15.00	4.50
239	Kyle Sleeth FY AU RC	15.00	4.50
240	Matthew Moses FY AU RC	15.00	4.50
241	Tim Stauffer FY AU RC	15.00	4.50
242	Brad Snyder FY AU RC	15.00	4.50
243	Jason Hirsh FY AU RC	10.00	3.00
244	L.Milledge FY AU RC	25.00	7.50
245	Logan Kensing FY AU RC	10.00	3.00
246	Kory Casto FY AU RC	10.00	3.00
247	David Aardsma FY RC	1.00	.30
248	Omar Quintanilla FY RC	2.50	.75
249	Ervin Santana FY RC	3.00	.90
250	Merkin Valdez FY RC	2.50	.75
251	Vito Chiaravalloti FY RC	2.00	.60
252	Travis Blackley FY RC	2.00	.60
253	Chris Shelton FY RC	2.00	.60
254	Rudy Guillen FY RC	2.50	.75
255	Bobby Brownlie FY RC	2.00	.60
256	Paul Maholm FY RC	2.00	.60
257	Roger Clemens	5.00	1.50
258	Laynce Nix	1.00	.30
259	Eric Hinske	1.00	.30
260	Ivan Rodriguez	2.50	.75
261	Brandon Webb	1.00	.30
262	Jhonny Peralta	1.00	.30
263	Adam Kennedy	1.00	.30
264	Tony Batista	1.00	.30
265	Jeff Suppan	1.00	.30
266	Kenny Lofton	1.00	.30
267	Scott Sullivan	1.00	.30
268	Ken Griffey Jr.	4.00	1.20
269	Juan Rivera	1.00	.30
270	Larry Walker	1.50	.45
271	Todd Hollandsworth	1.00	.30
272	Carlos Beltran	1.50	.45
273	Carl Crawford	1.00	.30
274	Karim Garcia	1.00	.30
275	Jose Reyes	1.00	.30
276	Brandon Duckworth	1.00	.30
277	Brian Giles	1.00	.30
278	J.T. Snow	1.00	.30
279	Jamie Moyer	1.00	.30
280	Julio Lugo	1.00	.30
281	Mark Teixeira	1.00	.30
282	Cory Lidle	1.00	.30
283	Lyle Overbay	1.00	.30
284	Troy Percival	1.00	.30
285	Robby Hammock	1.00	.30
286	Jason Johnson	1.00	.30
287	Damian Rolls	1.00	.30
288	Antonio Alfonseca	1.00	.30
289	Tom Goodwin	1.00	.30
290	Paul Konerko	1.00	.30
291	D'Angelo Jimenez	1.00	.30
292	Ben Broussard	1.00	.30
293	Magglio Ordonez	1.00	.30
294	Carlos Pena	1.00	.30
295	Chad Fox	1.00	.30
296	Jeriome Robertson	1.00	.30
297	Travis Hafner	1.00	.30
298	Joe Randa	1.00	.30
299	Brady Clark	1.00	.30
300	Barry Zito	1.00	.30
301	Ruben Sierra	1.00	.30
302	Brett Myers	1.00	.30
303	Oliver Perez	1.00	.30
304	Benito Santiago	1.00	.30
305	David Ross	1.00	.30
306	Joe Nathan	1.00	.30
307	Jim Edmonds	1.00	.30
308	Matt Kata	1.00	.30
309	Vinny Castilla	1.00	.30
310	Marty Cordova	1.00	.30
311	Aramis Ramirez	1.00	.30
312	Carl Everett	1.00	.30
313	Ryan Freel	1.00	.30
314	Mark Bellhorn Sox	1.50	.45
315	Joe Mauer	1.50	.45
316	Tim Redding	1.00	.30
317	Jeromy Burnitz	1.00	.30
318	Miguel Cabrera	1.50	.45
319	Ramon Nivar	1.00	.30
320	Casey Blake	1.00	.30
321	Adam LaRoche	1.00	.30
322	Jermaine Dye	1.00	.30
323	Jerome Williams	1.00	.30
324	John Olerud	1.00	.30
325	Scott Rolen	2.50	.75
326	Bobby Kielty	1.00	.30
327	Travis Lee	1.00	.30
328	Jeff Cirillo	1.00	.30
329	Scott Spiezio	1.00	.30
330	Melvin Mora	1.00	.30
331	Mike Timlin	1.00	.30
332	Kerry Wood	2.50	.75
333	Tony Womack	1.00	.30
334	Jody Gerut	1.00	.30
335	Morgan Ensberg	1.00	.30
336	Odalis Perez	1.00	.30
337	Michael Cuddyer	1.00	.30
338	Jose Hernandez	1.00	.30
339	LaTroy Hawkins	1.00	.30
340	Marquis Grissom	1.00	.30
341	Matt Morris	1.00	.30
342	Juan Gonzalez	1.50	.45
343	Jose Valverde	1.00	.30
344	Joe Borowski	1.00	.30
345	Josh Bard	1.00	.30
346	Austin Kearns	1.00	.30
347	Chin-Hui Tsao	1.00	.30
348	Wil Ledezma	1.00	.30
349	Aaron Guiel	1.00	.30
350	Alfonso Soriano	1.50	.45
351	Ted Lilly	1.00	.30
352	Sean Burroughs	1.00	.30
353	Rafael Palmeiro	1.50	.45
354	Quinton McCracken	1.00	.30
355	David Ortiz	2.50	.75
356	Randall Simon	1.00	.30
357	Wily Mo Pena	1.00	.30
358	Brian Anderson	1.00	.30
359	Corey Koskie	1.00	.30
360	Keith Foulke Sox	1.50	.45
361	Sidney Ponson	1.00	.30
362	Gary Matthews Jr.	1.00	.30
363	Herbert Perry	1.00	.30
364	Shea Hillenbrand	1.00	.30
365	Craig Biggio	1.50	.45
366	Barry Larkin	1.50	.45
367	Arthur Rhodes	1.00	.30
368	Sammy Sosa	4.00	1.20
369	Joe Crede	1.00	.30
370	Gary Sheffield	1.00	.30
371	Coco Crisp	1.00	.30
372	Torii Hunter	1.00	.30
373	Derrek Lee	1.00	.30
374	Adam Everett	1.00	.30
375	Miguel Tejada	1.00	.30
376	Jeremy Affeldt	1.00	.30
377	Robin Ventura	1.00	.30
378	Scott Podsednik	1.00	.30
379	Matthew LeCroy	1.00	.30
380	Vladimir Guerrero	2.50	.75
381	Steve Karsay	1.00	.30
382	Jeff Nelson	1.00	.30
383	Chase Utley	1.00	.30
384	Bobby Abreu	1.00	.30
385	Josh Fogg	1.00	.30
386	Trevor Hoffman	1.00	.30
387	Matt Stairs	1.00	.30
388	Edgar Martinez	1.50	.45
389	Edgar Renteria	1.00	.30
390	Chipper Jones	2.50	.75
391	Eric Munson	1.00	.30
392	Dewon Brazelton	1.00	.30
393	John Thomson	1.00	.30
394	Chris Woodward	1.00	.30
395	Joe Kennedy	1.00	.30

	Card	Nm-Mt	Ex-Mt
❑ 396	Reed Johnson	1.00	.30
❑ 397	Johnny Estrada	1.00	.30
❑ 398	Damian Moss	1.00	.30
❑ 399	Victor Zambrano	1.00	.30
❑ 400	Dontrelle Willis	1.00	.30
❑ 401	Troy Glaus	1.00	.30
❑ 402	Raul Mondesi	1.00	.30
❑ 403	Jeff Davanon	1.00	.30
❑ 404	Kurt Ainsworth	1.00	.30
❑ 405	Pedro Martinez	2.50	.75
❑ 406	Eric Karros	1.00	.30
❑ 407	Billy Koch	1.00	.30
❑ 408	Luis Gonzalez	1.00	.30
❑ 409	Jack Cust	1.00	.30
❑ 410	Mike Sweeney	1.00	.30
❑ 411	Jason Bay	1.00	.30
❑ 412	Mark Redman	1.00	.30
❑ 413	Jason Jennings	1.00	.30
❑ 414	Rondell White	1.00	.30
❑ 415	Todd Hundley	1.00	.30
❑ 416	Shannon Stewart	1.00	.30
❑ 417	Jae Weong Seo	1.00	.30
❑ 418	Livan Hernandez	1.00	.30
❑ 419	Mark Ellis	1.00	.30
❑ 420	Pat Burrell	1.00	.30
❑ 421	Mark Loretta	1.00	.30
❑ 422	Robb Nen	1.00	.30
❑ 423	Joel Pineiro	1.00	.30
❑ 424	Todd Walker	1.00	.30
❑ 425	Jeremy Bonderman	1.00	.30
❑ 426	A.J. Burnett	1.00	.30
❑ 427	Greg Myers	1.00	.30
❑ 428	Roy Oswalt	1.00	.30
❑ 429	Carlos Baerga	1.00	.30
❑ 430	Garret Anderson	1.00	.30
❑ 431	Horacio Ramirez	1.00	.30
❑ 432	Brian Roberts	1.00	.30
❑ 433	Kevin Brown	1.00	.30
❑ 434	Eric Milton	1.00	.30
❑ 435	Ramon Vazquez	1.00	.30
❑ 436	Alex Escobar	1.00	.30
❑ 437	Alex Sanchez	1.00	.30
❑ 438	Jeff Bagwell	1.50	.45
❑ 439	Claudio Vargas	1.00	.30
❑ 440	Shawn Green	1.00	.30
❑ 441	Geoff Jenkins	1.00	.30
❑ 442	David Wells	1.00	.30
❑ 443	Nick Johnson	1.00	.30
❑ 444	Jose Guillen	1.00	.30
❑ 445	Scott Hatteberg	1.00	.30
❑ 446	Phil Nevin	1.00	.30
❑ 447	Jason Schmidt	1.00	.30
❑ 448	Ricky Ledee	1.00	.30
❑ 449	So Taguchi	1.00	.30
❑ 450	Randy Johnson	2.50	.75
❑ 451	Eric Young	1.00	.30
❑ 452	Chone Figgins	1.00	.30
❑ 453	Larry Bigbie	1.00	.30
❑ 454	Scott Williamson	1.00	.30
❑ 455	Ramon Martinez	1.00	.30
❑ 456	Roberto Alomar	1.50	.45
❑ 457	Ryan Dempster	1.00	.30
❑ 458	Ryan Ludwick	1.00	.30
❑ 459	Ramon Santiago	1.00	.30
❑ 460	Jeff Conine	1.00	.30
❑ 461	Brad Lidge	1.00	.30
❑ 462	Ken Harvey	1.00	.30
❑ 463	Guillermo Mota	1.00	.30
❑ 464	Rick Reed	1.00	.30
❑ 465	Armando Benitez	1.00	.30
❑ 466	Wade Miller	1.00	.30

2004 Topps Chrome Traded

	Nm-Mt	Ex-Mt
COMPLETE SET (220)	120.00	36.00
COMMON CARD (1-70)	.75	.23
COMMON CARD (71-90)	1.25	.35
COMMON CARD (91-110)	1.00	.30
COMMON CARD (111-220)	1.00	.30
2 PER 2004 TOPPS TRADED HOBBY PACK		.00
2 PER 2004 TOPPS TRADED HTA PACK		.00
2 PER 2004 TOPPS TRADED RETAIL PACK		.00
PLATE ODDS 1:1151 H, 1:1173 R, 1:327 HTA		.00
PLATE PRINT RUN 1 SET PER COLOR		.00
BLACK-CYAN-MAGENTA-YELLOW ISSUED		.00
NO PLATE PRICING DUE TO SCARCITY		.00

	Card	Nm-Mt	Ex-Mt
❑ T1	Pokey Reese	.75	.23
❑ T2	Tony Womack	.75	.23
❑ T3	Richard Hidalgo	.75	.23
❑ T4	Juan Uribe	.75	.23
❑ T5	J.D. Drew	.75	.23
❑ T6	Alex Gonzalez	.75	.23
❑ T7	Carlos Guillen	.75	.23
❑ T8	Doug Mientkiewicz	.75	.23
❑ T9	Fernando Vina	.75	.23
❑ T10	Milton Bradley	.75	.23
❑ T11	Kelvim Escobar	.75	.23
❑ T12	Ben Grieve	.75	.23
❑ T13	Brian Jordan	.75	.23
❑ T14	A.J. Pierzynski	.75	.23
❑ T15	Billy Wagner	.75	.23
❑ T16	Terrence Long	.75	.23
❑ T17	Carlos Beltran	1.25	.35
❑ T18	Carl Everett	.75	.23
❑ T19	Reggie Sanders	.75	.23
❑ T20	Javy Lopez	.75	.23
❑ T21	Jay Payton	.75	.23
❑ T22	Octavio Dotel	.75	.23
❑ T23	Eddie Guardado	.75	.23
❑ T24	Andy Pettitte	1.25	.35
❑ T25	Richie Sexson	.75	.23
❑ T26	Ronnie Belliard	.75	.23
❑ T27	Michael Tucker	.75	.23
❑ T28	Brad Fullmer	.75	.23
❑ T29	Freddy Garcia	.75	.23
❑ T30	Bartolo Colon	.75	.23
❑ T31	Larry Walker	1.25	.35
❑ T32	Mark Kotsay	.75	.23
❑ T33	Jason Marquis	.75	.23
❑ T34	Dustan Mohr	.75	.23
❑ T35	Javier Vazquez	.75	.23
❑ T36	Nomar Garciaparra	3.00	.90
❑ T37	Tino Martinez	1.25	.35
❑ T38	Hee Seop Choi	.75	.23
❑ T39	Damian Miller	.75	.23
❑ T40	Jose Lima	.75	.23
❑ T41	Ty Wigginton	.75	.23
❑ T42	Raul Ibanez	.75	.23
❑ T43	Danys Baez	.75	.23
❑ T44	Tony Clark	.75	.23
❑ T45	Greg Maddux	3.00	.90
❑ T46	Victor Zambrano	.75	.23
❑ T47	Orlando Cabrera Sox	.75	.23
❑ T48	Jose Cruz Jr.	.75	.23
❑ T49	Kris Benson	.75	.23
❑ T50	Alex Rodriguez	4.00	1.20
❑ T51	Steve Finley	.75	.23
❑ T52	Ramon Hernandez	.75	.23
❑ T53	Esteban Loaiza	.75	.23
❑ T54	Ugueth Urbina	.75	.23
❑ T55	Jeff Weaver	.75	.23
❑ T56	Flash Gordon	.75	.23
❑ T57	Jose Contreras	.75	.23
❑ T58	Paul Lo Duca	.75	.23
❑ T59	Junior Spivey	.75	.23
❑ T60	Curt Schilling	2.00	.60
❑ T61	Brad Penny	.75	.23
❑ T62	Braden Looper	.75	.23
❑ T63	Miguel Cairo	.75	.23
❑ T64	Juan Encarnacion	.75	.23
❑ T65	Miguel Batista	.75	.23
❑ T66	Terry Francona MG	.75	.23
❑ T67	Lee Mazzilli MG	.75	.23
❑ T68	Al Pedrique MG	.75	.23
❑ T69	Ozzie Guillen MG	.75	.23
❑ T70	Phil Garner MG	.75	.23
❑ T71	Matt Bush DP RC	6.00	1.80
❑ T72	Homer Bailey DP RC	5.00	1.50
❑ T73	Greg Golson DP RC	4.00	1.20
❑ T74	Kyle Waldrop DP RC	3.00	.90
❑ T75	Richie Robnett DP RC	3.00	.90
❑ T76	Jay Rainville DP RC	3.00	.90
❑ T77	Bill Bray DP RC	1.25	.35
❑ T78	Phillip Hughes DP RC	3.00	.90
❑ T79	Scott Elbert DP RC	3.00	.90
❑ T80	Josh Fields DP RC	5.00	1.50
❑ T81	Justin Orenduff DP RC	3.00	.90
❑ T82	Dan Putnam DP RC	3.00	.90
❑ T83	Chris Nelson DP RC	6.00	1.80
❑ T84	Blake DeWitt DP RC	6.00	1.80
❑ T85	J.P. Howell DP RC	3.00	.90
❑ T86	Huston Street DP RC	3.00	.90
❑ T87	Kurt Suzuki DP RC	4.00	1.20
❑ T88	Erick San Pedro DP RC	1.25	.35
❑ T89	Matt Tuiasosopo DP RC	8.00	2.40
❑ T90	Matt Macri DP RC	3.00	.90
❑ T91	Chad Tracy PROS	1.00	.30
❑ T92	Scott Hairston PROS	1.00	.30
❑ T93	Jonny Gomes PROS	1.00	.30
❑ T94	Chin-Feng Chen PROS	1.00	.30
❑ T95	Chien-Ming Wang PROS	1.00	.30
❑ T96	Dustin McGowan PROS	1.00	.30
❑ T97	Chris Burke PROS	1.00	.30
❑ T98	Denny Bautista PROS	1.00	.30
❑ T99	Preston Larrison PROS	1.00	.30
❑ T100	Kevin Youkilis PROS	1.00	.30
❑ T101	John Maine PROS	1.00	.30
❑ T102	Guillermo Quiroz PROS	1.00	.30
❑ T103	Dave Krynzel PROS	1.00	.30
❑ T104	David Kelton PROS	1.00	.30
❑ T105	Edwin Encarnacion PROS	1.00	.30
❑ T106	Chad Gaudin PROS	1.00	.30
❑ T107	Sergio Mitre PROS	1.00	.30
❑ T108	Laynce Nix PROS	1.00	.30
❑ T109	David Parrish PROS	1.00	.30
❑ T110	Brandon Claussen PROS	1.00	.30
❑ T111	Frank Francisco FY RC	1.00	.30
❑ T112	Brian Dallimore FY RC	1.00	.30
❑ T113	Jim Crowell FY RC	1.25	.35
❑ T114	Andres Blanco FY RC	1.00	.30
❑ T115	Eduardo Villacis FY RC	1.00	.30
❑ T116	Kazuhito Tadano FY RC	1.25	.35
❑ T117	Aarom Baldiris FY RC	1.25	.35
❑ T118	Justin Germano FY RC	1.00	.30
❑ T119	Joey Gathright FY RC	3.00	.90
❑ T120	Franklyn Gracesqui FY RC	1.00	.30
❑ T121	Chin-Lung Hu FY RC	2.50	.75
❑ T122	Scott Olsen FY RC	3.00	.90
❑ T123	Tyler Davidson FY RC	1.25	.35
❑ T124	Fausto Carmona FY RC	2.00	.60
❑ T125	Tim Hutting FY RC	1.00	.30
❑ T126	Ryan Meaux FY RC	1.00	.30
❑ T127	Jon Connolly FY RC	2.50	.75
❑ T128	Hector Made FY RC	2.00	.60
❑ T129	Jamie Brown FY RC	1.00	.30
❑ T130	Paul McAnulty FY RC	2.00	.60
❑ T131	Chris Saenz FY RC	1.00	.30
❑ T132	Marland Williams FY RC	1.25	.35
❑ T133	Mike Huggins FY RC	1.00	.30
❑ T134	Jesse Crain FY RC	2.00	.60
❑ T135	Chad Bentz FY RC	1.00	.30
❑ T136	Kazuo Matsui FY RC	4.00	1.20
❑ T137	Paul Maholm FY RC	2.00	.60
❑ T138	Brock Jacobsen FY RC	1.00	.30
❑ T139	Casey Daigle FY RC	1.00	.30
❑ T140	Nyjer Morgan FY RC	1.00	.30
❑ T141	Tom Mastny FY RC	1.00	.30
❑ T142	Kody Kirkland FY RC	2.00	.60
❑ T143	Jose Capellan FY RC	4.00	1.20
❑ T144	Felix Hernandez FY RC	8.00	2.40
❑ T145	Shawn Hill FY RC	1.00	.30
❑ T146	Danny Gonzalez FY RC	1.00	.30
❑ T147	Scott Dohmann FY RC	1.00	.30
❑ T148	Tommy Murphy FY RC	1.00	.30
❑ T149	Akinori Otsuka FY RC	1.00	.30
❑ T150	Miguel Perez FY RC	1.00	.30
❑ T151	Mike Rouse FY RC	1.00	.30
❑ T152	Ramon Ramirez FY RC	1.00	.30
❑ T153	Luke Hughes FY RC	1.00	.30
❑ T154	Howie Kendrick FY RC	2.00	.60

❑ T155 Ryan Budde FY RC ...... 1.00 .30
❑ T156 Charlie Zink FY RC ...... 1.00 .30
❑ T157 Warner Madrigal FY RC 2.00 .60
❑ T158 Jason Szuminski FY RC 1.00 .30
❑ T159 Chad Chop FY RC........ 1.00 .30
❑ T160 Shingo Takatsu FY RC 2.50 .75
❑ T161 Matt Lemanczyk FY RC 1.00 .30
❑ T162 Wardell Starling FY RC 1.00 .30
❑ T163 Nick Gorneault FY RC .. 1.25 .35
❑ T164 Scott Proctor FY RC .... 1.25 .35
❑ T165 Brooks Conrad FY RC .. 1.25 .35
❑ T166 Hector Gimenez FY RC 1.00 .30
❑ T167 Kevin Howard FY RC.... 1.25 .35
❑ T168 Vince Perkins FY RC .... 1.25 .35
❑ T169 Brock Peterson FY RC .. 1.00 .30
❑ T170 Chris Shelton FY RC .... 2.00 .60
❑ T171 Erick Aybar FY RC .... 3.00 .90
❑ T172 Paul Bacot FY RC .... 1.25 .35
❑ T173 Matt Capps FY RC........ 1.00 .30
❑ T174 Kory Casto FY RC .... 1.00 .30
❑ T175 Juan Cedeno FY RC .... 1.00 .30
❑ T176 Vito Chiaravalloti FY RC 2.00 .60
❑ T177 Alec Zumwalt FY RC .... 1.00 .30
❑ T178 J.J. Furmaniak FY RC .. 2.00 .60
❑ T179 Lee Gwaltney FY RC .... 1.00 .30
❑ T180 Donald Kelly FY RC...... 1.00 .30
❑ T181 Benji DeQuin FY RC .... 1.00 .30
❑ T182 Brant Colamarino FY RC 2.00 .60
❑ T183 Juan Gutierrez FY RC .. 1.00 .30
❑ T184 Carl Loadenthal FY RC 1.25 .35
❑ T185 Ricky Nolasco FY RC .. 1.00 .30
❑ T186 Jeff Salazar FY RC........ 2.50 .75
❑ T187 Rob Tejeda FY RC .... 1.00 .30
❑ T188 Alex Romero FY RC...... 1.00 .30
❑ T189 Yoann Torrealba FY RC 1.00 .30
❑ T190 Carlos Sosa FY RC ...... 1.00 .30
❑ T191 Tim Bittner FY RC .... 1.00 .30
❑ T192 Chris Aguila FY RC .... 1.00 .30
❑ T193 Jason Frasor FY RC .... 1.00 .30
❑ T194 Reid Gorecki FY RC...... 1.00 .30
❑ T195 Dustin Nippert FY RC .. 1.00 .30
❑ T196 Javier Guzman FY RC .. 1.25 .35
❑ T197 Harvey Garcia FY RC.... 1.00 .30
❑ T198 Ivan Ochoa FY RC .... 1.00 .30
❑ T199 David Wallace FY RC .. 1.25 .35
❑ T200 Joel Zumaya FY RC...... 2.00 .60
❑ T201 Casey Kopitzke FY RC .. 1.00 .30
❑ T202 Lincoln Holdzkom FY RC 1.00 .30
❑ T203 Chad Santos FY RC...... 1.00 .30
❑ T204 Brian Pilkington FY RC 1.00 .30
❑ T205 Terry Jones FY RC ...... 1.25 .35
❑ T206 Jerome Gamble FY RC 1.00 .30
❑ T207 Brad Eldred FY RC ...... 3.00 .90
❑ T208 David Pauley FY RC .... 1.00 .30
❑ T209 Kevin Davidson FY RC 1.00 .30
❑ T210 Damaso Espino FY RC 1.00 .30
❑ T211 Tom Farmer FY RC ...... 1.00 .30
❑ T212 Michael Mooney FY RC 1.00 .30
❑ T213 James Tomlin FY RC.... 1.00 .30
❑ T214 Greg Thissen FY RC .... 1.00 .30
❑ T215 Calvin Hayes FY RC .... 1.25 .35
❑ T216 Fernando Cortez FY RC 1.00 .30
❑ T217 Sergio Silva FY RC ...... 1.00 .30
❑ T218 Jon de Vries FY RC ...... 1.00 .30
❑ T219 Don Sutton FY RC........ 2.50 .75
❑ T220 Leo Nunez FY RC .... 1.00 .30

2004 Topps Clubhouse Relics

Nm-Mt Ex-Mt

TWO RELICS PER PACK.................
GROUP A CARDS NOT SERIAL-NUMBERED
GROUP A PRINT RUNS PROVIDED BY TOPPS

❑ AB Armando Benitez Jsy C.... 5.00 1.50
❑ AD Adam Dunn Jsy C............ 8.00 2.40
❑ AG Adrian Gonzalez Jsy C 5.00 1.50
❑ AJ Andruw Jones Jsy C 5.00 1.50
❑ AK Al Kaline Jsy E 10.00 3.00
❑ AL Al Leiter Jsy C................ 5.00 1.50
❑ AP Albert Pujols Jsy C 15.00 4.50
❑ AR Alex Rodriguez Bat C 12.00 3.60
❑ ARA Aramis Ramirez Bat B.... 5.00 1.50
❑ AS Alfonso Soriano Bat D 8.00 2.40
❑ BA Bobby Abreu Jsy D 5.00 1.50
❑ BB Bret Boone Jsy E............ 5.00 1.50
❑ BF Brad Fullmer Bat A/200.... 8.00 2.40
❑ BL Barry Larkin Bat A/200 .. 12.00 3.60
❑ BM Brett Myers Jsy D 5.00 1.50
❑ BW Bernie Williams Uni C 8.00 2.40
❑ BWA Billy Wagner Jsy C 5.00 1.50
❑ BZ Barry Zito Jsy A/230 .... 8.00 2.40
❑ CCR Carl Crawford Bat B 5.00 1.50
❑ CD Carlos Delgado Jsy A/200 8.00 2.40
❑ CE Carl Everett Bat C 5.00 1.50
❑ CFC Chin-Feng Chen Jsy E 10.00 3.00
❑ CFL Cliff Floyd Uni B............ 5.00 1.50
❑ CG Cristian Guzman Jsy B.... 5.00 1.50
❑ CJ Chipper Jones Jsy E 8.00 2.40
❑ CL Chris Lubanski Jsy A/209 8.00 2.40
❑ CP Chan Ho Park Jsy E 5.00 1.50
❑ CPA Corey Patterson Jsy A/267 8.00 2.40
❑ CR Cal Ripken Jsy E............ 25.00 7.50
❑ CS C.C. Sabathia Jsy E 5.00 1.50
❑ CSC Curt Schilling Jsy C...... 5.00 1.50
❑ CST Casey Stengel Uni A/217 15.00 4.50
❑ CY Carl Yastrzemski Jsy E .. 15.00 4.50
❑ DC Dave Concepcion Bat D .. 6.00 1.80
❑ DE Dennis Eckersley Uni E.. 10.00 3.00
❑ DJ Derek Jeter Bat C 15.00 4.50
❑ DL Derek Lowe Jsy A/200 .... 8.00 2.40
❑ DP Dave Parker Bat A/292 .. 10.00 3.00
❑ DS Duke Snider Bat C 10.00 3.00
❑ EA Edgardo Alfonzo Bat A/286 8.00 2.40
❑ EC Eric Chavez Uni E 5.00 1.50
❑ EG Eric Gagne Uni E............ 8.00 2.40
❑ EH Estee Harris Jsy A/206 RC 8.00 2.40
❑ EL Esteban Loaiza Jsy B........ 5.00 1.50
❑ EM Eddie Mathews Jsy A/174 25.00 7.50
❑ EMA Edgar Martinez Bat A/200 12.00 3.60
❑ EMU Eddie Murray Bat B 12.00 3.60
❑ FM Fred McGriff Bat E 8.00 2.40
❑ FR Frank Robinson Uni B...... 8.00 2.40
❑ FT Frank Thomas Bat C 8.00 2.40
❑ FV Fern Valenzuela Bat A/288 10.00 3.00
❑ GB George Brett Uni E 15.00 4.50
❑ GC Gary Carter Jkt A/221.... 10.00 3.00
❑ GM Greg Maddux Jsy B 12.00 3.60
❑ GS Gary Sheffield Jsy D 5.00 1.50
❑ HA Hank Aaron Bat A/113 .. 50.00 15.00
❑ HB Hank Bauer Bat B 8.00 2.40
❑ HBL Hank Blalock Jsy E........ 5.00 1.50
❑ HN Hideo Nomo Bat A/207 12.00 3.60
❑ IR Ivan Rodriguez Jsy D 8.00 2.40
❑ JB Jeff Bagwell Jsy A/200 .. 12.00 3.60
❑ JBE Johnny Bench Uni E 10.00 3.00
❑ JBU Jeromy Burnitz Bat A/208 8.00 2.40
❑ JC Jeff Cirillo Bat B 5.00 1.50
❑ JCA Joe Carter Jsy A/259 .. 10.00 3.00
❑ JF Jonathan Fulton Jsy A/200 8.00 2.40
❑ JG Jason Giambi Uni E 5.00 1.50
❑ JGO Juan Gonzalez Bat B 8.00 2.40
❑ JH James Houser Jsy A/182 8.00 2.40
❑ JKE Jeff Kent Jsy A/200 .... 8.00 2.40
❑ JL Javy Lopez Jsy D............ 5.00 1.50
❑ JO John Olerud Jsy B............ 5.00 1.50
❑ JP Jorge Posada Jsy A/264 12.00 3.60
❑ JPB Josh Beckett Jsy A/195 .. 8.00 2.40
❑ JR Jackie Robinson Bat A/262 50.00 15.00
❑ JRE Jose Reyes Jsy E............ 5.00 1.50
❑ JRO Jimmy Rollins Jsy E 5.00 1.50
❑ JS Jay Sborz Jsy A/176 .... 8.00 2.40
❑ JSM John Smoltz Jsy E 8.00 2.40
❑ JT Jim Thome Jsy C.............. 8.00 2.40
❑ JV Javier Vazquez Jsy A/283 8.00 2.40
❑ JVI Jose Vidro Jsy A/275 ...... 8.00 2.40
❑ KB Kevin Brown Uni A/168 .. 8.00 2.40
❑ KG Ken Griffey Jr. Jsy A/200 20.00 6.00
❑ KI Kazuhisa Ishii Jsy C.......... 5.00 1.50
❑ KM Kevin Millwood Jsy E 5.00 1.50
❑ LB Lance Berkman Jsy B 5.00 1.50
❑ LG Luis Gonzalez Jsy B 5.00 1.50
❑ LW Larry Walker Jsy C.......... 8.00 2.40
❑ MB Marlon Byrd Jsy B 5.00 1.50
❑ MC Miguel Cabrera Jsy B 8.00 2.40
❑ MDG Marquis Grissom Bat B 5.00 1.50
❑ MG Mark Grace Jsy E.......... 10.00 3.00
❑ MH Mickey Hall Jsy A/217.... 8.00 2.40
❑ MM Mark Mulder Uni E 5.00 1.50
❑ MO Magglio Ordonez Bat B .. 5.00 1.50
❑ MP Mike Piazza Jsy B 12.00 3.60
❑ MR Manny Ramirez Jsy A/207 12.00 3.60
❑ MRI Mariano Rivera Uni A/239 12.00 3.60
❑ MS Mike Schmidt Jsy D...... 15.00 4.50
❑ MSW Mike Sweeney Jsy E.... 5.00 1.50
❑ MT Mark Teixeira Jsy D 5.00 1.50
❑ MTE Miguel Tejada Uni B 5.00 1.50
❑ NG Nomar Garciaparra Bat B 12.00 3.60
❑ NR Nolan Ryan Uni E 20.00 6.00
❑ OC Orlando Cepeda Bat B 8.00 2.40
❑ OH Orel Hershiser Jsy E........ 6.00 1.80
❑ OHU Orlando Hudson Jsy A/200 8.00 2.40
❑ OS Ozzie Smith Jsy D.......... 12.00 3.60
❑ PB Pat Burrell Jsy E 5.00 1.50
❑ PK Paul Konerko Bat B.......... 5.00 1.50
❑ PL Paul Lo Duca Uni B.......... 5.00 1.50
❑ PM Pedro Martinez Jsy A/200 12.00 3.60
❑ PW Preston Wilson Jsy B...... 5.00 1.50
❑ RA Roberto Alomar Uni E 8.00 2.40
❑ RB Rocco Baldelli Jsy E 5.00 1.50
❑ RC Roberto Clemente Bat B 50.00 15.00
❑ RCE Ron Cey Bat B 8.00 2.40
❑ RF Rafael Furcal Jsy E 5.00 1.50
❑ RH Ramon Hernandez Jsy E .. 5.00 1.50
❑ RHE Rickey Henderson Uni E 10.00 3.00
❑ RJ Reggie Jackson Jsy D 10.00 3.00
❑ RLC Roger Cedeno Bat B 5.00 1.50
❑ RP Rafael Palmeiro Uni A/200 12.00 3.60
❑ RS Richie Sexson Bat A/200 8.00 2.40
❑ RSA Ryne Sandberg Bat E .. 15.00 4.50
❑ RSI Ruben Sierra Bat B.......... 5.00 1.50
❑ RY Robin Yount Bat B 15.00 4.50
❑ SF Steve Finley Jsy C............ 5.00 1.50
❑ SG Shawn Green Jsy C 5.00 1.50
❑ SL Steve Lerud Jsy A/213 .... 8.00 2.40
❑ SR Scott Rolen Bat B 8.00 2.40
❑ SS Sammy Sosa Jsy E 12.00 3.60
❑ TA Tony Armas Jr. Jsy C 5.00 1.50
❑ TB Tony Batista Jsy E............ 5.00 1.50
❑ TG Tom Glavine Jsy B 8.00 2.40
❑ TGL Troy Glaus Jsy E............ 5.00 1.50
❑ TGW Tony Gwynn Bat E 12.00 3.60
❑ TH Tim Hudson Uni E 5.00 1.50
❑ THE Todd Helton Bat C 8.00 2.40
❑ THU Torii Hunter Jsy E.......... 5.00 1.50
❑ TM Tino Martinez Uni E 8.00 2.40
❑ TP Tony Perez Uni B 8.00 2.40
❑ TPE Troy Percival Uni B 5.00 1.50
❑ TS Tim Salmon Uni C 8.00 2.40
❑ VG Vladimir Guerrero Jsy E .. 8.00 2.40
❑ VW Vernon Wells Bat A/200.. 8.00 2.40
❑ WB Wade Boggs Jsy A/250 15.00 4.50
❑ WC Will Clark Jsy E............ 10.00 3.00
❑ WF Whitey Ford Uni A/296 15.00 4.50
❑ WM Willie Mays Jsy D........ 40.00 12.00
❑ WP Wily Mo Pena Jsy B........ 5.00 1.50
❑ WS Willie Stargell Uni A/200 15.00 4.50
❑ YB Yogi Berra Uni B............ 12.00 3.60

2004 Topps Cracker Jack

Nm-Mt Ex-Mt

COMPLETE SET (250) 200.00 60.00
COMP.SET w/o SP's (200)........ 40.00 12.00
COMMON CARD .... .40 .12
COMMON SP 4.00 1.20
COMMON SP RC 4.00 1.20
SP STATED ODDS 1:3 ....
SP CL: 226/229B/232/236A-236B..

❑ 1 Jose Reyes SP.................... 4.00 1.20
❑ 2 Edgar Renteria........................ .40 .12
❑ 3A Albert Pujols Portrait........ 2.00 .60
❑ 3B Albert Pujols Swinging SP 8.00 2.40
❑ 4 Garret Anderson .... .40 .12

❑ 5 Bobby Abreu	.40	.12
❑ 6 Andruw Jones	.40	.12
❑ 7 Jeff Kent	.40	.12
❑ 8 Magglio Ordonez	.40	.12
❑ 9 Kris Benson	.40	.12
❑ 10 Luis Gonzalez	.40	.12
❑ 11 Corey Patterson	.40	.12
❑ 12 Connie Mack MG	.40	.12
❑ 13 Vernon Wells SP	4.00	1.20
❑ 14 Jim Edmonds	.40	.12
❑ 15 Bret Boone	.40	.12
❑ 16 Travis Lee	.40	.12
❑ 17 Alex Rodriguez Yanks SP	8.00	2.40
❑ 18 Erubiel Durazo	.40	.12
❑ 19 Brett Myers	.40	.12
❑ 20 Scott Rolen SP	5.00	1.50
❑ 21 Paul Lo Duca	.40	.12
❑ 22 Geoff Jenkins	.40	.12
❑ 23 Charles Comiskey	.40	.12
❑ 24 Cliff Floyd	.40	.12
❑ 25A Jim Thome Batting	1.00	.30
❑ 25B Jim Thome Fielding SP	5.00	1.50
❑ 26 Russ Ortiz	.40	.12
❑ 27 Bill Mueller	.40	.12
❑ 28 Kenny Lofton	.40	.12
❑ 29 Jay Gibbons	.40	.12
❑ 30 Ken Griffey Jr.	1.50	.45
❑ 31 Jeff Bagwell	.60	.18
❑ 32 Jose Lima	.40	.12
❑ 33 Brad Radke	.40	.12
❑ 34 Ramon Hernandez	.40	.12
❑ 35 Brian Giles SP	4.00	1.20
❑ 36 Jeremy Bonderman	.40	.12
❑ 37 Jerome Williams	.40	.12
❑ 38 Rafael Palmeiro	.60	.18
❑ 39 Scott Podsednik	.40	.12
❑ 40 Rafael Furcal	.40	.12
❑ 41 Roy Oswalt	.40	.12
❑ 42 Orlando Hudson	.40	.12
❑ 43 Todd Helton	.60	.18
❑ 44 Kerry Wood	1.00	.30
❑ 45 Tom Glavine	.60	.18
❑ 46 David Eckstein	.40	.12
❑ 47 Trot Nixon	.40	.12
❑ 48 Preston Wilson	.40	.12
❑ 49 Bernie Williams	.60	.18
❑ 50 Eric Gagne SP	5.00	1.50
❑ 51 Ichiro Suzuki SP	6.00	1.80
❑ 52 Juan Gonzalez	.60	.18
❑ 53 Torii Hunter	.40	.12
❑ 54 Bartolo Colon	.40	.12
❑ 55A Dick Hoblitzel ERR	.40	.12
❑ 55B Dick Hoblitzell COR	.40	.12
❑ 56 Al Leiter	.40	.12
❑ 57 Johnny Damon	1.00	.30
❑ 58 Larry Walker	.60	.18
❑ 59 Brian Jordan	.40	.12
❑ 60 Richie Sexson SP	4.00	1.20
❑ 61 Orlando Cabrera	.40	.12
❑ 62 Jason Phillips	.40	.12
❑ 63 Phil Nevin	.40	.12
❑ 64 John Olerud	.40	.12
❑ 65 Miguel Tejada	.40	.12
❑ 66A Nap La Joie ERR	1.00	.30
❑ 66B Nap Lajoie COR	1.00	.30
❑ 67 C.C. Sabathia	.40	.12
❑ 68 Ty Wigginton	.40	.12
❑ 69 Troy Glaus	.40	.12
❑ 70 Mike Piazza	1.50	.45
❑ 71 Craig Biggio	.60	.18
❑ 72 Cristian Guzman	.40	.12
❑ 73 Dmitri Young	.40	.12
❑ 74 Roger Clemens	2.00	.60
❑ 75 Runelvys Hernandez	.40	.12
❑ 76 Nomar Garciaparra	1.50	.45
❑ 77 Mark Mulder	.40	.12
❑ 78 Derek Lowe	.40	.12
❑ 79 Paul Konerko	.40	.12
❑ 80A Sammy Sosa SP	6.00	1.80
❑ 80B Felix Pie SP	4.00	1.20
❑ 81 Vladimir Guerrero	1.00	.30
❑ 82 Xavier Nady	.40	.12
❑ 83 Joel Pineiro	.40	.12
❑ 84 Chipper Jones	1.00	.30
❑ 85 Manny Ramirez	.60	.18
❑ 86A Burt Shotten ERR	.40	.12
❑ 86B Burt Shotton COR UER	.40	.12
Began his playing career in 1997; should be 1907		
❑ 87 Raul Ibanez SP	4.00	1.20
❑ 88 Eric Chavez	.40	.12
❑ 89 Frank Catalanotto	.40	.12
❑ 90 Dontrelle Willis	.40	.12
❑ 91 Roy Halladay	.40	.12
❑ 92 Jermaine Dye	.40	.12
❑ 93 Jason Kendall	.40	.12
❑ 94 Jacque Jones	.40	.12
❑ 95A Gary Sheffield Braves	.40	.12
❑ 95B Gary Sheffield Yanks SP	5.00	1.50
❑ 96 Mike Lieberthal	.40	.12
❑ 97 Adam Dunn	.60	.18
❑ 98 Carl Crawford	.40	.12
❑ 99 Reggie Sanders	.40	.12
❑ 100 Mark Prior SP	5.00	1.50
❑ 101 Luis Matos	.40	.12
❑ 102 Barry Zito	.40	.12
❑ 103 Randy Johnson	1.00	.30
❑ 104A Kevin Brown	.40	.12
❑ 104B Edwin Jackson SP	4.00	1.20
❑ 105 Pat Burrell	.40	.12
❑ 106 Steve Finley	.40	.12
❑ 107 Moises Alou	.40	.12
❑ 108 David Ortiz SP	5.00	1.50
❑ 109 Austin Kearns SP	4.00	1.20
❑ 110 Carlos Beltran	.60	.18
❑ 111 Shawn Green	.40	.12
❑ 112 Javier Vazquez	.40	.12
❑ 113 Hideo Nomo	1.00	.30
❑ 114 Kazuhisa Ishii	.40	.12
❑ 115 Corey Koskie	.40	.12
❑ 116 Kevin Millwood	.40	.12
❑ 117 Randy Wolf	.40	.12
❑ 118 Darin Erstad	.40	.12
❑ 119 Fernando Vina	.40	.12
❑ 120 Pedro Martinez	1.00	.30
❑ 121 Melvin Mora	.40	.12
❑ 122 Carl Everett	.40	.12
❑ 123 Matt Morris	.40	.12
❑ 124 Greg Maddux	1.50	.45
❑ 125 Jason Schmidt	.40	.12
❑ 126 Mark Teixeira SP	4.00	1.20
❑ 127 Randy Winn	.40	.12
❑ 128 Rich Aurilia	.40	.12
❑ 129 Vicente Padilla	.40	.12
❑ 130 Tim Hudson	.40	.12
❑ 131 Marlon Byrd	.40	.12
❑ 132 Jae Weong Seo	.40	.12
❑ 133 Branch Rickey MG	.40	.12
❑ 134 A.J. Pierzynski	.40	.12
❑ 135 Ryan Klesko	.40	.12
❑ 136 Eric Hinske	.40	.12
❑ 137 Mike Cameron	.40	.12
❑ 138 Roberto Alomar	.60	.18
❑ 139 Jarrod Washburn	.40	.12
❑ 140A Curt Schilling D'backs	.40	.12
❑ 140B Curt Schilling Sox SP	5.00	1.50
❑ 141 Omar Vizquel	.60	.18
❑ 142 Mike Sweeney	.40	.12
❑ 143 Wade Miller	.40	.12
❑ 144 Jose Vidro	.40	.12
❑ 145 Rich Harden SP	4.00	1.20
❑ 146 Eric Munson	.40	.12
❑ 147 Lance Berkman	.40	.12
❑ 148 Mark Buehrle	.40	.12
❑ 149 Carlos Delgado	.40	.12
❑ 150 Sean Burroughs	.40	.12
❑ 151 Kevin Millar	.40	.12
❑ 152 Frank Thomas	1.00	.30
❑ 153 Adrian Beltre	.60	.18
❑ 154 Shannon Stewart	.40	.12
❑ 155 Johan Santana	.60	.18
❑ 156 Edgardo Alfonzo	.40	.12
❑ 157 Jose Cruz Jr.	.40	.12
❑ 158 Sidney Ponson	.40	.12
❑ 159 Edgar Martinez	.60	.18
❑ 160 Jamie Moyer	.40	.12
❑ 161 Tony Batista	.40	.12
❑ 162 Wes Helms	.40	.12
❑ 163 Brandon Webb SP	4.00	1.20
❑ 164 Gil Meche	.40	.12
❑ 165 Marcus Giles SP	4.00	1.20
❑ 166 Angel Berroa SP	4.00	1.20
❑ 167 Rocco Baldelli SP	4.00	1.20
❑ 168 Michael Young	.40	.12
❑ 169 Esteban Loaiza	.40	.12
❑ 170 Casey Blake	.40	.12
❑ 171 Jody Gerut	.40	.12
❑ 172 Bo Hart SP	4.00	1.20
❑ 173 Kelvim Escobar	.40	.12
❑ 174 Aaron Guiel	.40	.12
❑ 175 Javy Lopez SP	4.00	1.20
❑ 176 Aubrey Huff	.40	.12
❑ 177 Hank Blalock	.40	.12
❑ 178 Edwin Jackson	.40	.12
❑ 179 Delmon Young SP	5.00	1.50
❑ 180 Bobby Jenks	.40	.12
❑ 181 Felix Pie	.40	.12
❑ 182 Jeremy Reed SP	4.00	1.20
❑ 183 Aaron Hill	.40	.12
❑ 184 Casey Kotchman SP	4.00	1.20
❑ 185 Grady Sizemore	.40	.12
❑ 186 Joe Mauer SP	5.00	1.50
❑ 187 Ryan Harvey	.40	.12
❑ 188 Neal Cotts	.40	.12
❑ 189 Victor Martinez	.40	.12
❑ 190 Rene Reyes	.40	.12
❑ 191 Eric Duncan	.40	.12
❑ 192 B.J. Upton SP	5.00	1.50
❑ 193 Khalil Greene SP	5.00	1.50
❑ 194 Bobby Crosby	.60	.18
❑ 195 Rickie Weeks SP	4.00	1.20
❑ 196 Zack Greinke SP	4.00	1.20
❑ 197 Laynce Nix	.40	.12
❑ 198 Vito Chiaravalloti SP RC	5.00	1.50
❑ 199 Estee Harris RC	.50	.15
❑ 200 Jon Knott SP RC	4.00	1.20
❑ 201 Dioner Navarro RC	1.25	.35
❑ 202 Craig Ansman RC	.50	.15
❑ 203 Travis Blackley RC	.75	.23
❑ 204 Yadier Molina RC	1.00	.30
❑ 205 Rodney Choy Foo RC	.50	.15
❑ 206 Kyle Sleeth SP RC	5.00	1.50
❑ 207 Jeff Allison RC	.75	.23
❑ 208 Josh Labandeira RC	.50	.15
❑ 209 Lastings Milledge SP RC	6.00	1.80
❑ 210 Rudy Guillen SP RC	5.00	1.50
❑ 211 Blake Hawksworth SP RC	5.00	1.50
❑ 212 David Aardsma RC	.50	.15
❑ 213 Shawn Hill RC	.50	.15
❑ 214 Erick Aybar SP RC	5.00	1.50
❑ 215 Ervin Santana RC	1.25	.35
❑ 216 Tim Stauffer SP RC	5.00	1.50
❑ 217 Merkin Valdez RC	1.00	.30
❑ 218 Jack McKeon MG	.40	.12
❑ 219 Jeff Conine	.40	.12
❑ 220 Josh Beckett SP	4.00	1.20
❑ 221 Luis Castillo	.40	.12
❑ 222 Mike Lowell	.40	.12
❑ 223 Juan Pierre	.40	.12
❑ 224A Ivan Rodriguez Marlins	1.00	.30
❑ 224B Ivan Rodriguez Tigers SP	5.00	1.50
❑ 225 A.J. Burnett	.40	.12
❑ 226 Miguel Cabrera SP	5.00	1.50
❑ 227 Jeffrey Loria	.40	.12
❑ 228 Joe Torre MG	.60	.18
❑ 229A Jason Giambi Portrait	.40	.12
❑ 229B Jason Giambi Fielding SP	4.00	1.20
❑ 230 Aaron Boone	.40	.12
❑ 231 Jose Contreras	.40	.12
❑ 232 Derek Jeter SP	8.00	2.40
❑ 233 Ruben Sierra	.40	.12
❑ 234 Mike Mussina	.60	.18
❑ 235 Mariano Rivera	.60	.18
❑ 236A Jorge Posada SP	5.00	1.50
❑ 236B Dioner Navarro SP	5.00	1.50
❑ 237 Alfonso Soriano	.60	.18
❑ NNO Alex Rodriguez Yanks	3.00	.90
❑ VB Vintage Buyback	.00	

2001 Topps Gallery

	Nm-Mt	Ex-Mt
COMPLETE SET (150)	80.00	24.00
COMP.SET w/o SP's (100)	40.00	12.00
COMMON (1-49/51-101)	.50	.15
COMMON (102-150)	3.00	.90

	Nm-Mt	Ex-Mt
❑ 1 Darin Erstad	.50	.15
❑ 2 Chipper Jones	1.25	.35
❑ 3 Nomar Garciaparra	2.00	.60
❑ 4 Fernando Vina	.50	.15
❑ 5 Bartolo Colon	.50	.15
❑ 6 Bobby Higginson	.50	.15
❑ 7 Antonio Alfonseca	.50	.15
❑ 8 Mike Sweeney	.50	.15
❑ 9 Kevin Brown	.50	.15
❑ 10 Jose Vidro	.50	.15
❑ 11 Derek Jeter	3.00	.90
❑ 12 Jason Giambi	.50	.15
❑ 13 Pat Burrell	.50	.15
❑ 14 Jeff Kent	.50	.15
❑ 15 Alex Rodriguez	2.00	.60
❑ 16 Rafael Palmeiro	.75	.23
❑ 17 Garret Anderson	.50	.15
❑ 18 Brad Fullmer	.50	.15
❑ 19 Doug Glanville	.50	.15
❑ 20 Mark Quinn	.50	.15
❑ 21 Mo Vaughn	.50	.15
❑ 22 Andruw Jones	.50	.15
❑ 23 Pedro Martinez	1.25	.35
❑ 24 Ken Griffey Jr.	2.00	.60
❑ 25 Roberto Alomar	.75	.23
❑ 26 Dean Palmer	.50	.15
❑ 27 Jeff Bagwell	.75	.23
❑ 28 Jermaine Dye	.50	.15
❑ 29 Chan Ho Park	.50	.15
❑ 30 Vladimir Guerrero	1.25	.35
❑ 31 Bernie Williams	.75	.23
❑ 32 Ben Grieve	.50	.15
❑ 33 Jason Kendall	.50	.15
❑ 34 Barry Bonds	3.00	.90
❑ 35 Jim Edmonds	.50	.15
❑ 36 Ivan Rodriguez	1.25	.35
❑ 37 Javy Lopez	.50	.15
❑ 38 J.T. Snow	.50	.15
❑ 39 Erubiel Durazo	.50	.15
❑ 40 Terrence Long	.50	.15
❑ 41 Tim Salmon	.75	.23
❑ 42 Greg Maddux	2.00	.60
❑ 43 Sammy Sosa	2.00	.60
❑ 44 Sean Casey	.50	.15
❑ 45 Jeff Cirillo	.50	.15
❑ 46 Juan Gonzalez	.75	.23
❑ 47 Richard Hidalgo	.50	.15
❑ 48 Shawn Green	.50	.15
❑ 49 Jeromy Burnitz	.50	.15
❑ 50 Willie Mays HTA N.Y. Giants	15.00	4.50
❑ 50 Willie Mays RETAIL S.F. Giants	40.00	12.00
❑ 51 David Justice	.50	.15
❑ 52 Tim Hudson	.50	.15
❑ 53 Brian Giles	.50	.15
❑ 54 Robb Nen	.50	.15
❑ 55 Fernando Tatis	.50	.15
❑ 56 Tony Batista	.50	.15
❑ 57 Pokey Reese	.50	.15
❑ 58 Ray Durham	.50	.15
❑ 59 Greg Vaughn	.50	.15
❑ 60 Kazuhiro Sasaki	.50	.15
❑ 61 Troy Glaus	.50	.15
❑ 62 Rafael Furcal	.50	.15
❑ 63 Magglio Ordonez	.50	.15
❑ 64 Jim Thome	1.25	.35
❑ 65 Todd Helton	.75	.23
❑ 66 Preston Wilson	.50	.15
❑ 67 Moises Alou	.50	.15
❑ 68 Gary Sheffield	.50	.15
❑ 69 Geoff Jenkins	.50	.15
❑ 70 Mike Piazza	2.00	.60
❑ 71 Jorge Posada	.75	.23
❑ 72 Bobby Abreu	.50	.15
❑ 73 Phil Nevin	.50	.15
❑ 74 John Olerud	.50	.15
❑ 75 Mark McGwire	3.00	.90
❑ 76 Jose Cruz Jr.	.50	.15
❑ 77 David Segui	.50	.15
❑ 78 Neifi Perez	.50	.15
❑ 79 Omar Vizquel	.75	.23
❑ 80 Rick Ankiel	.50	.15
❑ 81 Randy Johnson	1.25	.35
❑ 82 Albert Belle	.50	.15
❑ 83 Frank Thomas	1.25	.35
❑ 84 Manny Ramirez	.75	.23
❑ 85 Larry Walker	.75	.23
❑ 86 Luis Castillo	.50	.15
❑ 87 Johnny Damon	.75	.23
❑ 88 Adrian Beltre	.75	.23
❑ 89 Cristian Guzman	.50	.15
❑ 90 Jay Payton	.50	.15
❑ 91 Miguel Tejada	.50	.15
❑ 92 Scott Rolen	1.25	.35
❑ 93 Ryan Klesko	.50	.15
❑ 94 Edgar Martinez	.75	.23
❑ 95 Fred McGriff	.75	.23
❑ 96 Carlos Delgado	.50	.15
❑ 97 Barry Zito	.75	.23
❑ 98 Mike Lieberthal	.50	.15
❑ 99 Trevor Hoffman	.50	.15
❑ 100 Gabe Kapler	.50	.15
❑ 101 Edgardo Alfonzo	.50	.15
❑ 102 Corey Patterson	3.00	.90
❑ 103 Alfonso Soriano	.75	.23
❑ 104 Keith Ginter	3.00	.90
❑ 105 Keith Reed	3.00	.90
❑ 106 Nick Johnson	3.00	.90
❑ 107 Carlos Pena	3.00	.90
❑ 108 Vernon Wells	3.00	.90
❑ 109 Roy Oswalt	3.00	.90
❑ 110 Alex Escobar	3.00	.90
❑ 111 Adam Everett	3.00	.90
❑ 112 Jimmy Rollins	3.00	.90
❑ 113 Marcus Giles	3.00	.90
❑ 114 Jack Cust	3.00	.90
❑ 115 Chin-Feng Chen	3.00	.90
❑ 116 Pablo Ozuna	3.00	.90
❑ 117 Ben Sheets	3.00	.90
❑ 118 Adrian Gonzalez	3.00	.90
❑ 119 Ben Davis	3.00	.90
❑ 120 Eric Valent	3.00	.90
❑ 121 Scott Heard	3.00	.90
❑ 122 David Parrish RC	3.00	.90
❑ 123 Sean Burnett	3.00	.90
❑ 124 Derek Thompson	3.00	.90
❑ 125 Tim Christman RC	3.00	.90
❑ 126 Mike Jacobs RC	3.00	.90
❑ 127 Luis Montanez RC	3.00	.90
❑ 128 Chris Bass RC	3.00	.90
❑ 129 Will Smith RC	3.00	.90
❑ 130 Justin Wayne RC	3.00	.90
❑ 131 Shawn Fagan RC	3.00	.90
❑ 132 Chad Petty RC	3.00	.90
❑ 133 J.R. House	3.00	.90
❑ 134 Joel Pineiro	4.00	1.20
❑ 135 Albert Pujols RC	40.00	12.00
❑ 136 Carmen Cali RC	3.00	.90
❑ 137 Steve Smyth RC	3.00	.90
❑ 138 John Lackey	3.00	.90
❑ 139 Bob Keppel RC	3.00	.90
❑ 140 Dominic Rich RC	3.00	.90
❑ 141 Josh Hamilton	3.00	.90
❑ 142 Nolan Ryan	6.00	1.80
❑ 143 Tom Seaver	3.00	.90
❑ 144 Reggie Jackson	3.00	.90
❑ 145 Johnny Bench	4.00	1.20
❑ 146 Warren Spahn	3.00	.90
❑ 147 Brooks Robinson	3.00	.90
❑ 148 Carl Yastrzemski	5.00	1.50
❑ 149 Al Kaline	4.00	1.20
❑ 150 Bob Feller	3.00	.90
❑ 151A I. Suzuki English RC	25.00	7.50
❑ 151B I.Suzuki Japan RC	25.00	7.50

2001 Topps Heritage

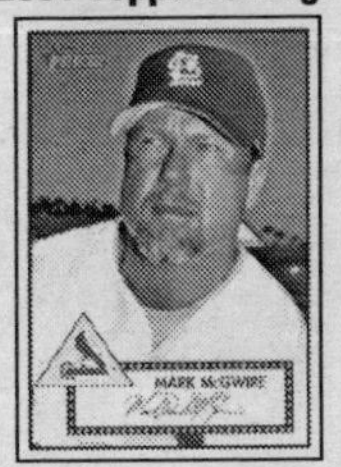

	Nm-Mt	Ex-Mt
COMP.MASTER SET (487)	400.00	120.00
COMPLETE SET (407)	300.00	90.00
COMP.SET w/o SP's (230)	60.00	18.00
COMMON CARD (81-310)	.50	.15
COMMON CARD (1-80)	2.50	.75
COMMON (311-407)	5.00	1.50

	Nm-Mt	Ex-Mt
❑ 1 Kris Benson	2.50	.75
❑ 1 Kris Benson Black	2.50	.75
❑ 2 Brian Jordan	2.50	.75
❑ 2 Brian Jordan Black	2.50	.75
❑ 3 Fernando Vina	2.50	.75
❑ 3 Fernando Vina Black	2.50	.75
❑ 4 Mike Sweeney	2.50	.75
❑ 4 Mike Sweeney Black	2.50	.75
❑ 5 Rafael Palmeiro	2.50	.75
❑ 5 Rafael Palmeiro Black	2.50	.75
❑ 6 Paul O'Neill	2.50	.75
❑ 6 Paul O'Neill Black	2.50	.75
❑ 7 Todd Helton	2.50	.75
❑ 7 Todd Helton Black	2.50	.75
❑ 8 Ramiro Mendoza	2.50	.75
❑ 8 Ramiro Mendoza Black	2.50	.75
❑ 9 Kevin Millwood	2.50	.75
❑ 9 Kevin Millwood Black	2.50	.75
❑ 10 Chuck Knoblauch	2.50	.75
❑ 10 Chuck Knoblauch Black	2.50	.75
❑ 11 Derek Jeter	10.00	3.00
❑ 11 Derek Jeter Black	10.00	3.00
❑ 12 A.Rodriguez Rangers	6.00	1.80
❑ 12 A.Rod Black Rangers	6.00	1.80
❑ 13 Geoff Jenkins	2.50	.75
❑ 13 Geoff Jenkins Black	2.50	.75
❑ 14 David Justice	2.50	.75
❑ 14 David Justice Black	2.50	.75
❑ 15 David Cone	2.50	.75
❑ 15 David Cone Black	2.50	.75
❑ 16 Andres Galarraga	2.50	.75
❑ 16 Andres Galarraga Black	2.50	.75
❑ 17 Garret Anderson	2.50	.75
❑ 17 Garret Anderson Black	2.50	.75
❑ 18 Roger Cedeno	2.50	.75
❑ 18 Roger Cedeno Black	2.50	.75
❑ 19 Randy Velarde	2.50	.75
❑ 19 Randy Velarde Black	2.50	.75
❑ 20 Carlos Delgado	2.50	.75
❑ 20 Carlos Delgado Black	2.50	.75
❑ 21 Quilvio Veras	2.50	.75
❑ 21 Quilvio Veras Black	2.50	.75
❑ 22 Jose Vidro	2.50	.75
❑ 22 Jose Vidro Black	2.50	.75
❑ 23 Corey Patterson	2.50	.75
❑ 23 Corey Patterson Black	2.50	.75
❑ 24 Jorge Posada	2.50	.75
❑ 24 Jorge Posada Black	2.50	.75

❑ 25 Eddie Perez 2.50 .75
❑ 25 Eddie Perez Black 2.50 .75
❑ 26 Jack Cust 2.50 .75
❑ 26 Jack Cust Black 2.50 .75
❑ 27 Sean Burroughs 2.50 .75
❑ 27 Sean Burroughs Black 2.50 .75
❑ 28 Randy Wolf 2.50 .75
❑ 28 Randy Wolf Black 2.50 .75
❑ 29 Mike Lamb 2.50 .75
❑ 29 Mike Lamb Black 2.50 .75
❑ 30 Rafael Furcal 2.50 .75
❑ 30 Rafael Furcal Black 2.50 .75
❑ 31 Barry Bonds 10.00 3.00
❑ 31 Barry Bonds Black 10.00 3.00
❑ 32 Tim Hudson 2.50 .75
❑ 32 Tim Hudson Black 2.50 .75
❑ 33 Tom Glavine 2.50 .75
❑ 33 Tom Glavine Black 2.50 .75
❑ 34 Javy Lopez 2.50 .75
❑ 34 Javy Lopez Black 2.50 .75
❑ 35 Aubrey Huff 2.50 .75
❑ 35 Aubrey Huff Black 2.50 .75
❑ 36 Wally Joyner 2.50 .75
❑ 36 Wally Joyner Black 2.50 .75
❑ 37 Magglio Ordonez 2.50 .75
❑ 37 Magglio Ordonez Black 2.50 .75
❑ 38 Matt Lawton 2.50 .75
❑ 38 Matt Lawton Black 2.50 .75
❑ 39 Mariano Rivera 2.50 .75
❑ 39 Mariano Rivera Black 2.50 .75
❑ 40 Andy Ashby 2.50 .75
❑ 40 Andy Ashby Black 2.50 .75
❑ 41 Mark Buehrle 2.50 .75
❑ 41 Mark Buehrle Black 2.50 .75
❑ 42 Esteban Loaiza 2.50 .75
❑ 42 Esteban Loaiza Black 2.50 .75
❑ 43 Mark Redman 2.50 .75
❑ 43 Mark Redman Black 2.50 .75
❑ 44 Mark Quinn 2.50 .75
❑ 44 Mark Quinn Black 2.50 .75
❑ 45 Tino Martinez 2.50 .75
❑ 45 Tino Martinez Black 2.50 .75
❑ 46 Joe Mays 2.50 .75
❑ 46 Joe Mays Black 2.50 .75
❑ 47 Walt Weiss 2.50 .75
❑ 47 Walt Weiss Black 2.50 .75
❑ 48 Roger Clemens 8.00 2.40
❑ 48 Roger Clemens Black 8.00 2.40
❑ 49 Greg Maddux 6.00 1.80
❑ 49 Greg Maddux Black 6.00 1.80
❑ 50 Richard Hidalgo 2.50 .75
❑ 50 Richard Hidalgo Black 2.50 .75
❑ 51 Orlando Hernandez 2.50 .75
❑ 51 O.Hernandez Black 2.50 .75
❑ 52 Chipper Jones 4.00 1.20
❑ 52 Chipper Jones Black 4.00 1.20
❑ 53 Ben Grieve 2.50 .75
❑ 53 Ben Grieve Black 2.50 .75
❑ 54 Jimmy Haynes 2.50 .75
❑ 54 Jimmy Haynes Black 2.50 .75
❑ 55 Ken Caminiti 2.50 .75
❑ 55 Ken Caminiti Black 2.50 .75
❑ 56 Tim Salmon 2.50 .75
❑ 56 Tim Salmon Black 2.50 .75
❑ 57 Andy Pettitte 2.50 .75
❑ 57 Andy Pettitte Black 2.50 .75
❑ 58 Darin Erstad 2.50 .75
❑ 58 Darin Erstad Black 2.50 .75
❑ 59 Marquis Grissom 2.50 .75
❑ 59 Marquis Grissom Black 2.50 .75
❑ 60 Raul Mondesi 2.50 .75
❑ 60 Raul Mondesi Black 2.50 .75
❑ 61 Bengie Molina 2.50 .75
❑ 61 Bengie Molina Black 2.50 .75
❑ 62 Miguel Tejada 2.50 .75
❑ 62 Miguel Tejada Black 2.50 .75
❑ 63 Jose Cruz Jr. 2.50 .75
❑ 63 Jose Cruz Jr. Black 2.50 .75
❑ 64 Billy Koch 2.50 .75
❑ 64 Billy Koch Black 2.50 .75
❑ 65 Troy Glaus 2.50 .75
❑ 65 Troy Glaus Black 2.50 .75
❑ 66 Cliff Floyd 2.50 .75
❑ 66 Cliff Floyd Black 2.50 .75
❑ 67 Tony Batista 2.50 .75
❑ 67 Tony Batista Black 2.50 .75
❑ 68 Jeff Bagwell 2.50 .75
❑ 68 Jeff Bagwell Black 2.50 .75
❑ 69 Billy Wagner 2.50 .75
❑ 69 Billy Wagner Black 2.50 .75
❑ 70 Eric Chavez 2.50 .75
❑ 70 Eric Chavez Black 2.50 .75
❑ 71 Troy Percival 2.50 .75
❑ 71 Troy Percival Black 2.50 .75
❑ 72 Andruw Jones 2.50 .75
❑ 72 Andruw Jones Black 2.50 .75
❑ 73 Shane Reynolds 2.50 .75
❑ 73 Shane Reynolds Black 2.50 .75
❑ 74 Barry Zito 2.50 .75
❑ 74 Barry Zito Black 2.50 .75
❑ 75 Roy Halladay 2.50 .75
❑ 75 Roy Halladay Black 2.50 .75
❑ 76 David Wells 2.50 .75
❑ 76 David Wells Black 2.50 .75
❑ 77 Jason Giambi 2.50 .75
❑ 77 Jason Giambi Black 2.50 .75
❑ 78 Scott Elarton 2.50 .75
❑ 78 Scott Elarton Black 2.50 .75
❑ 79 Moises Alou 2.50 .75
❑ 79 Moises Alou Black 2.50 .75
❑ 80 Adam Piatt 2.50 .75
❑ 80 Adam Piatt Black 2.50 .75
❑ 81 Wilton Veras .50 .15
❑ 82 Darryl Kile .60 .18
❑ 83 Johnny Damon 1.00 .30
❑ 84 Tony Armas Jr. .50 .15
❑ 85 Ellis Burks .60 .18
❑ 86 Jamey Wright .50 .15
❑ 87 Jose Vizcaino .50 .15
❑ 88 Bartolo Colon .60 .18
❑ 89 Carmen Cali RC .60 .18
❑ 90 Kevin Brown .60 .18
❑ 91 Josh Hamilton .50 .15
❑ 92 Jay Buhner .60 .18
❑ 93 Scott Pratt RC .60 .18
❑ 94 Alex Cora .50 .15
❑ 95 Luis Montanez RC .60 .18
❑ 96 Dmitri Young .60 .18
❑ 97 J.T. Snow .60 .18
❑ 98 Damion Easley .50 .15
❑ 99 Greg Norton .50 .15
❑ 100 Matt Wheatland .50 .15
❑ 101 Chin-Feng Chen .60 .18
❑ 102 Tony Womack .50 .15
❑ 103 Adam Kennedy Black .50 .15
❑ 104 J.D. Drew .60 .18
❑ 105 Carlos Febles .50 .15
❑ 106 Jim Thome 1.50 .45
❑ 107 Danny Graves .50 .15
❑ 108 Dave Mlicki .50 .15
❑ 109 Ron Coomer .50 .15
❑ 110 James Baldwin .50 .15
❑ 111 Shaun Boyd RC .60 .18
❑ 112 Brian Bohanon .50 .15
❑ 113 Jacque Jones .60 .18
❑ 114 Alfonso Soriano 1.00 .30
❑ 115 Tony Clark .50 .15
❑ 116 Terrence Long .50 .15
❑ 117 Todd Hundley .50 .15
❑ 118 Kazuhiro Sasaki .60 .18
❑ 119 Brian Sellier RC .60 .18
❑ 120 John Olerud .60 .18
❑ 121 Javier Vazquez .60 .18
❑ 122 Sean Burnett .50 .15
❑ 123 Matt LeCroy .50 .15
❑ 124 Erubiel Durazo .50 .15
❑ 125 Juan Encarnacion .50 .15
❑ 126 Pablo Ozuna .50 .15
❑ 127 Russ Ortiz .60 .18
❑ 128 David Segui .50 .15
❑ 129 Mark McGwire 4.00 1.20
❑ 130 Mark Grace 1.00 .30
❑ 131 Fred McGriff 1.00 .30
❑ 132 Carl Pavano .60 .18
❑ 133 Derek Thompson .50 .15
❑ 134 Shawn Green .60 .18
❑ 135 B.J. Surhoff .60 .18
❑ 136 Michael Tucker .50 .15
❑ 137 Jason Isringhausen .60 .18
❑ 138 Eric Milton .50 .15
❑ 139 Mike Stodolka .50 .15
❑ 140 Milton Bradley .60 .18
❑ 141 Curt Schilling .60 .18
❑ 142 Sandy Alomar Jr. .50 .15
❑ 143 Brent Mayne .50 .15
❑ 144 Todd Jones .50 .15
❑ 145 Charles Johnson .60 .18
❑ 146 Dean Palmer .60 .18
❑ 147 Masato Yoshii .50 .15
❑ 148 Edgar Renteria .60 .18
❑ 149 Joe Randa .50 .15
❑ 150 Adam Johnson .50 .15
❑ 151 Greg Vaughn .50 .15
❑ 152 Adrian Beltre 1.00 .30
❑ 153 Glenallen Hill .50 .15
❑ 154 David Parrish RC .60 .18
❑ 155 Neifi Perez .50 .15
❑ 156 Pete Harnisch .50 .15
❑ 157 Paul Konerko .60 .18
❑ 158 Dennys Reyes .50 .15
❑ 159 Jose Lima Black .50 .15
❑ 160 Eddie Taubensee .50 .15
❑ 161 Miguel Cairo .50 .15
❑ 162 Jeff Kent .60 .18
❑ 163 Dustin Hermanson .50 .15
❑ 164 Alex Gonzalez .50 .15
❑ 165 Hideo Nomo 1.50 .45
❑ 166 Sammy Sosa 2.50 .75
❑ 167 C.J. Nitkowski .50 .15
❑ 168 Cal Eldred .50 .15
❑ 169 Jeff Abbott .50 .15
❑ 170 Jim Edmonds .60 .18
❑ 171 Mark Mulder Black .60 .18
❑ 172 Dominic Rich RC .60 .18
❑ 173 Ray Lankford .50 .15
❑ 174 Danny Borrell RC .60 .18
❑ 175 Rick Aguilera .50 .15
❑ 176 S.Stewart Black .60 .18
❑ 177 Steve Finley .60 .18
❑ 178 Jim Parque .50 .15
❑ 179 Kevin Appier Black .60 .18
❑ 180 Adrian Gonzalez .60 .18
❑ 181 Tom Goodwin .50 .15
❑ 182 Kevin Tapani .50 .15
❑ 183 Fernando Tatis .50 .15
❑ 184 Mark Grudzielanek .50 .15
❑ 185 Ryan Anderson .50 .15
❑ 186 Jeffrey Hammonds .50 .15
❑ 187 Corey Koskie .60 .18
❑ 188 Brad Fullmer Black .50 .15
❑ 189 Rey Sanchez .50 .15
❑ 190 Michael Barrett .50 .15
❑ 191 Rickey Henderson 1.50 .45
❑ 192 Jermaine Dye .60 .18
❑ 193 Scott Brosius .60 .18
❑ 194 Matt Anderson .50 .15
❑ 195 Brian Buchanan .50 .15
❑ 196 Derrek Lee .60 .18
❑ 197 Larry Walker 1.00 .30
❑ 198 Dan Moylan RC .60 .18
❑ 199 Vinny Castilla .60 .18
❑ 200 Ken Griffey Jr. 2.50 .75
❑ 201 Matt Stairs Black .50 .15
❑ 202 Ty Howington .50 .15
❑ 203 Andy Benes .50 .15
❑ 204 Luis Gonzalez .60 .18
❑ 205 Brian Moehler .50 .15
❑ 206 Harold Baines .60 .18
❑ 207 Pedro Astacio .50 .15
❑ 208 Cristian Guzman .50 .15
❑ 209 Kip Wells .50 .15
❑ 210 Frank Thomas 1.50 .45
❑ 211 Jose Rosado .50 .15
❑ 212 Vernon Wells Black .60 .18
❑ 213 Bobby Higginson .60 .18
❑ 214 Juan Gonzalez 1.00 .30
❑ 215 Omar Vizquel 1.00 .30
❑ 216 Bernie Williams 1.00 .30
❑ 217 Aaron Sele .50 .15
❑ 218 Shawn Estes .50 .15
❑ 219 Roberto Alomar 1.00 .30
❑ 220 Rick Ankiel .50 .15
❑ 221 Josh Kalinowski .50 .15
❑ 222 David Bell .50 .15
❑ 223 Keith Foulke .60 .18
❑ 224 Craig Biggio Black 1.00 .30
❑ 225 Josh Axelson RC .60 .18
❑ 226 Scott Williamson .50 .15
❑ 227 Ron Belliard .50 .15
❑ 228 Chris Singleton .50 .15
❑ 229 Alex Serrano RC .60 .18
❑ 230 Deivi Cruz .50 .15
❑ 231 Eric Munson .50 .15
❑ 232 Luis Castillo .50 .15
❑ 233 Edgar Martinez 1.00 .30
❑ 234 Jeff Shaw .50 .15
❑ 235 Jeromy Burnitz .60 .18

❑ 236 Richie Sexson .60 .18
❑ 237 Will Clark 1.50 .45
❑ 238 Ron Villone .50 .15
❑ 239 Kerry Wood 1.50 .45
❑ 240 Rich Aurilia .50 .15
❑ 241 Mo Vaughn Black .60 .18
❑ 242 Travis Fryman .60 .18
❑ 243 M. Ramirez Red Sox 1.00 .30
❑ 244 Chris Stynes .50 .15
❑ 245 Ray Durham .60 .18
❑ 246 Juan Uribe RC 1.00 .30
❑ 247 Juan Guzman .50 .15
❑ 248 Lee Stevens .50 .15
❑ 249 Devon White .60 .18
❑ 250 Kyle Lohse RC 1.00 .30
❑ 251 Bryan Wolff .50 .15
❑ 252 Matt Galante RC .60 .18
❑ 253 Eric Young .50 .15
❑ 254 Freddy Garcia .60 .18
❑ 255 Jay Bell .60 .18
❑ 256 Steve Cox .50 .15
❑ 257 Torii Hunter .60 .18
❑ 258 Jose Canseco 1.50 .45
❑ 259 Brad Ausmus .50 .15
❑ 260 Jeff Cirillo .50 .15
❑ 261 Brad Penny .50 .15
❑ 262 Antonio Alfonseca .50 .15
❑ 263 Russ Branyan .50 .15
❑ 264 Chris Morris RC .60 .18
❑ 265 John Lackey .50 .15
❑ 266 Justin Wayne RC .60 .18
❑ 267 Brad Radke .60 .18
❑ 268 Todd Stottlemyre .50 .15
❑ 269 Mark Loretta .60 .18
❑ 270 Matt Williams .60 .18
❑ 271 Kenny Lofton .60 .18
❑ 272 Jeff D'Amico .50 .15
❑ 273 Jamie Moyer .60 .18
❑ 274 Darren Dreifort .50 .15
❑ 275 Denny Neagle .50 .15
❑ 276 Orlando Cabrera .60 .18
❑ 277 Chuck Finley .60 .18
❑ 278 Miguel Batista .60 .18
❑ 279 Carlos Beltran 1.00 .30
❑ 280 Eric Karros .60 .18
❑ 281 Mark Kotsay .50 .15
❑ 282 Ryan Dempster .50 .15
❑ 283 Barry Larkin 1.00 .30
❑ 284 Jeff Suppan .50 .15
❑ 285 Gary Sheffield .60 .18
❑ 286 Jose Valentin .50 .15
❑ 287 Robb Nen .60 .18
❑ 288 Chan Ho Park .60 .18
❑ 289 John Halama .50 .15
❑ 290 Steve Smyth RC .60 .18
❑ 291 Gerald Williams .50 .15
❑ 292 Preston Wilson .60 .18
❑ 293 Victor Hall RC .60 .18
❑ 294 Ben Sheets 1.00 .30
❑ 295 Eric Davis .60 .18
❑ 296 Kirk Rueter .50 .15
❑ 297 Chad Petty RC .60 .18
❑ 298 Kevin Millar .60 .18
❑ 299 Marvin Benard .50 .15
❑ 300 Vladimir Guerrero 1.50 .45
❑ 301 Livan Hernandez .50 .15
❑ 302 Travis Baptist RC .50 .15
❑ 303 Bill Mueller .60 .18
❑ 304 Mike Cameron .60 .18
❑ 305 Randy Johnson 1.50 .45
❑ 306 Alan Mahaffey RC .50 .15
❑ 307 Timo Perez UER .50 .15
No facsimile autograph on card
❑ 308 Pokey Reese .50 .15
❑ 309 Ryan Rupe .50 .15
❑ 310 Carlos Lee .60 .18
❑ 311 Doug Glanville SP 5.00 1.50
❑ 312 Jay Payton SP 5.00 1.50
❑ 313 Troy O'Leary SP 5.00 1.50
❑ 314 Francisco Cordero SP 5.00 1.50
❑ 315 Rusty Greer SP 5.00 1.50
❑ 316 Cal Ripken SP 25.00 7.50
❑ 317 Ricky Ledee SP 5.00 1.50
❑ 318 Brian Daubach SP 5.00 1.50
❑ 319 Robin Ventura SP 5.00 1.50
❑ 320 Todd Zeile SP 5.00 1.50
❑ 321 Francisco Cordova SP 5.00 1.50
❑ 322 Henry Rodriguez SP 5.00 1.50
❑ 323 Pat Meares SP 5.00 1.50
❑ 324 Glendon Rusch SP 5.00 1.50
❑ 325 Keith Osik SP 5.00 1.50
❑ 326 Robert Keppel SP RC 8.00 2.40
❑ 327 Bobby Jones SP 5.00 1.50
❑ 328 Alex Ramirez SP 5.00 1.50
❑ 329 Robert Person SP 5.00 1.50
❑ 330 Ruben Mateo SP 5.00 1.50
❑ 331 Rob Bell SP 5.00 1.50
❑ 332 Carl Everett SP 5.00 1.50
❑ 333 Jason Schmidt SP 5.00 1.50
❑ 334 Scott Rolen SP 8.00 2.40
❑ 335 Jimmy Anderson SP 5.00 1.50
❑ 336 Bret Boone SP 5.00 1.50
❑ 337 Delino DeShields SP 5.00 1.50
❑ 338 Trevor Hoffman SP 5.00 1.50
❑ 339 Bob Abreu SP 5.00 1.50
❑ 340 Mike Williams SP 5.00 1.50
❑ 341 Mike Hampton SP 5.00 1.50
❑ 342 John Wetteland SP 5.00 1.50
❑ 343 Scott Erickson SP 5.00 1.50
❑ 344 Enrique Wilson SP 5.00 1.50
❑ 345 Tim Wakefield SP 5.00 1.50
❑ 346 Mike Lowell SP 5.00 1.50
❑ 347 Todd Pratt SP 5.00 1.50
❑ 348 Brook Fordyce SP 5.00 1.50
❑ 349 Benny Agbayani SP 5.00 1.50
❑ 350 Gabe Kapler SP 5.00 1.50
❑ 351 Sean Casey SP 5.00 1.50
❑ 352 Darren Oliver SP 5.00 1.50
❑ 353 Todd Ritchie SP 5.00 1.50
❑ 354 Kenny Rogers SP 5.00 1.50
❑ 355 Jason Kendall SP 5.00 1.50
❑ 356 John Vander Wal SP 5.00 1.50
❑ 357 Ramon Martinez SP 5.00 1.50
❑ 358 Edgardo Alfonzo SP 5.00 1.50
❑ 359 Phil Nevin SP 5.00 1.50
❑ 360 Albert Belle SP 5.00 1.50
❑ 361 Ruben Rivera SP 5.00 1.50
❑ 362 Pedro Martinez SP 8.00 2.40
❑ 363 Derek Lowe SP 5.00 1.50
❑ 364 Pat Burrell SP 5.00 1.50
❑ 365 Mike Mussina SP 8.00 2.40
❑ 366 Brady Anderson SP 5.00 1.50
❑ 367 Darren Lewis SP 5.00 1.50
❑ 368 Sidney Ponson SP 5.00 1.50
❑ 369 Adam Eaton SP 5.00 1.50
❑ 370 Eric Owens SP 5.00 1.50
❑ 371 Aaron Boone SP 5.00 1.50
❑ 372 Matt Clement SP 5.00 1.50
❑ 373 Derek Bell SP 5.00 1.50
❑ 374 Trot Nixon SP 5.00 1.50
❑ 375 Travis Lee SP 5.00 1.50
❑ 376 Mike Benjamin SP 5.00 1.50
❑ 377 Jeff Zimmerman SP 5.00 1.50
❑ 378 Mike Lieberthal SP 5.00 1.50
❑ 379 Rick Reed SP 5.00 1.50
❑ 380 N.Garciaparra SP 12.00 3.60
❑ 381 Omar Daal SP 5.00 1.50
❑ 382 Ryan Klesko SP 5.00 1.50
❑ 383 Rey Ordonez SP 5.00 1.50
❑ 384 Kevin Young SP 5.00 1.50
❑ 385 Rick Helling SP 5.00 1.50
❑ 386 Brian Giles SP 5.00 1.50
❑ 387 Tony Gwynn SP 10.00 3.00
❑ 388 Ed Sprague SP 5.00 1.50
❑ 389 J.R. House SP 5.00 1.50
❑ 390 Scott Hatteberg SP 5.00 1.50
❑ 391 John Valentin SP 5.00 1.50
❑ 392 Melvin Mora SP 5.00 1.50
❑ 393 Royce Clayton SP 5.00 1.50
❑ 394 Jeff Fassero SP 5.00 1.50
❑ 395 Manny Alexander SP 5.00 1.50
❑ 396 John Franco SP 5.00 1.50
❑ 397 Luis Alicea SP 5.00 1.50
❑ 398 Ivan Rodriguez SP 8.00 2.40
❑ 399 Kevin Jordan SP 5.00 1.50
❑ 400 Jose Offerman SP 5.00 1.50
❑ 401 Jeff Conine SP 5.00 1.50
❑ 402 Seth Etherton SP 5.00 1.50
❑ 403 Mike Bordick SP 5.00 1.50
❑ 404 Al Leiter SP 5.00 1.50
❑ 405 Mike Piazza SP 12.00 3.60
❑ 406 Armando Benitez SP 5.00 1.50
❑ 407 Warren Morris SP 5.00 1.50
❑ NNO 1952 Card Redemption EXCH .00
❑ NNO Replica Hat-Jsy EXCH

2002 Topps Heritage

	Nm-Mt	Ex-Mt
COMPLETE SET (440)	250.00	75.00
COMP.SET w/o SP's (350)	80.00	24.00
COMMON CARD (1-363)	.50	.15
COMMON SP (364-446)	5.00	1.50

❑ 1 Ichiro Suzuki SP 12.00 3.60
❑ 2 Darin Erstad .60 .18
❑ 3 Rod Beck .60 .18
❑ 4 Doug Mientkiewicz .60 .18
❑ 5 Mike Sweeney .60 .18
❑ 6 Roger Clemens 3.00 .90
❑ 7 Jason Tyner .50 .15
❑ 8 Alex Gonzalez .50 .15
❑ 9 Eric Young .50 .15
❑ 10 Randy Johnson 1.50 .45
❑ 10N Randy Johnson Night SP 8.00 2.40
❑ 11 Aaron Sele .50 .15
❑ 12 Tony Clark .50 .15
❑ 13 C.C. Sabathia .60 .18
❑ 14 Melvin Mora .60 .18
❑ 15 Tim Hudson .60 .18
❑ 16 Ben Petrick .50 .15
❑ 17 Tom Glavine 1.00 .30
❑ 18 Jason Lane .50 .15
❑ 19 Larry Walker 1.00 .30
❑ 20 Mark Mulder .60 .18
❑ 21 Steve Finley .60 .18
❑ 22 Bengie Molina .50 .15
❑ 23 Rob Bell .50 .15
❑ 24 Nathan Haynes .50 .15
❑ 25 Rafael Furcal .60 .18
❑ 25N Rafael Furcal Night SP 5.00 1.50
❑ 26 Mike Mussina 1.00 .30
❑ 27 Paul LoDuca .60 .18
❑ 28 Torii Hunter .60 .18
❑ 29 Carlos Lee .60 .18
❑ 30 Jimmy Rollins .60 .18
❑ 31 Arthur Rhodes .50 .15
❑ 32 Ivan Rodriguez 1.50 .45
❑ 33 Wes Helms .50 .15
❑ 34 Cliff Floyd .60 .18
❑ 35 Julian Tavarez .50 .15
❑ 36 Mark McGwire 4.00 1.20
❑ 37 Chipper Jones SP 8.00 2.40
❑ 38 Denny Neagle .50 .15
❑ 39 Odalis Perez .50 .15
❑ 40 Antonio Alfonseca .50 .15
❑ 41 Edgar Renteria .60 .18
❑ 42 Troy Glaus .60 .18
❑ 43 Scott Brosius .60 .18
❑ 44 Abraham Nunez .50 .15
❑ 45 Jamey Wright .50 .15
❑ 46 Bobby Bonilla .60 .18
❑ 47 Ismael Valdes .50 .15
❑ 48 Chris Reitsma .50 .15
❑ 49 Neifi Perez .50 .15
❑ 50 Juan Cruz .50 .15
❑ 51 Kevin Brown .60 .18
❑ 52 Ben Grieve .50 .15
❑ 53 Alex Rodriguez SP 12.00 3.60
❑ 54 Charles Nagy .50 .15
❑ 55 Reggie Sanders .50 .15
❑ 56 Nelson Figueroa .50 .15
❑ 57 Felipe Lopez .50 .15
❑ 58 Bill Ortega .50 .15

❑ 59 Jeffrey Hammonds .60 .18
❑ 60 Johnny Estrada .50 .15
❑ 61 Bob Wickman .50 .15
❑ 62 Doug Glanville .50 .15
❑ 63 Jeff Cirillo .50 .15
❑ 63N Jeff Cirillo Night SP 5.00 1.50
❑ 64 Corey Patterson .60 .18
❑ 65 Aaron Myette .50 .15
❑ 66 Magglio Ordonez .60 .18
❑ 67 Ellis Burks .60 .18
❑ 68 Miguel Tejada .60 .18
❑ 69 John Olerud .60 .18
❑ 69N John Olerud Night SP 5.00 1.50
❑ 70 Greg Vaughn .50 .15
❑ 71 Andy Pettitte 1.00 .30
❑ 72 Mike Matheny .60 .18
❑ 73 Brandon Duckworth .50 .15
❑ 74 Scott Schoeneweis .50 .15
❑ 75 Mike Lowell .60 .18
❑ 76 Einar Diaz .50 .15
❑ 77 Tino Martinez 1.00 .30
❑ 78 Matt Williams .60 .18
❑ 79 Jason Young RC 1.00 .30
❑ 80 Nate Cornejo .50 .15
❑ 81 Andres Galarraga .60 .18
❑ 82 Bernie Williams SP 8.00 2.40
❑ 83 Ryan Klesko .60 .18
❑ 84 Dan Wilson .50 .15
❑ 85 Henry Pichardo RC 1.00 .30
❑ 86 Ray Durham .60 .18
❑ 87 Omar Daal .50 .15
❑ 88 Derrek Lee .60 .18
❑ 89 Al Leiter .60 .18
❑ 90 Darrin Fletcher .50 .15
❑ 91 Josh Beckett .60 .18
❑ 92 Johnny Damon 1.00 .30
❑ 92N Johnny Damon Night SP 8.00 2.40
❑ 93 Abraham Nunez .50 .15
❑ 94 Ricky Ledee .50 .15
❑ 95 Richie Sexson .60 .18
❑ 96 Adam Kennedy .50 .15
❑ 97 Raul Mondesi .60 .18
❑ 98 John Burkett .60 .18
❑ 99 Ben Sheets .60 .18
❑ 99N Ben Sheets Night SP 5.00 1.50
❑ 100 Preston Wilson .60 .18
❑ 100N Pr. Wilson Night SP 5.00 1.50
❑ 101 Boof Bonser .50 .15
❑ 102 Shigetoshi Hasegawa .60 .18
❑ 103 Carlos Febles .50 .15
❑ 104 Jorge Posada SP 8.00 2.40
❑ 105 Michael Tucker .50 .15
❑ 106 Roberto Hernandez .60 .18
❑ 107 John Rodriguez RC 1.00 .30
❑ 108 Danny Graves .50 .15
❑ 109 Rich Aurilia .50 .15
❑ 110 Jon Lieber .50 .15
❑ 111 Tim Hummel RC 1.00 .30
❑ 112 J.T. Snow .60 .18
❑ 113 Kris Benson .50 .15
❑ 114 Derek Jeter 4.00 1.20
❑ 115 John Franco .60 .18
❑ 116 Matt Stairs .50 .15
❑ 117 Ben Davis .50 .15
❑ 118 Darryl Kile .60 .18
❑ 119 Mike Peeples RC 1.00 .30
❑ 120 Kevin Tapani .50 .15
❑ 121 Armando Benitez .60 .18
❑ 122 Damian Miller .50 .15
❑ 123 Jose Jimenez .50 .15
❑ 124 Pedro Astacio .50 .15
❑ 125 Marlyn Tisdale RC 1.00 .30
❑ 126 Deivi Cruz .50 .15
❑ 127 Paul O'Neill 1.00 .30
❑ 128 Jermaine Dye .60 .18
❑ 129 Marcus Giles .60 .18
❑ 130 Mark Loretta .60 .18
❑ 131 Garret Anderson .60 .18
❑ 132 Todd Ritchie .50 .15
❑ 133 Joe Crede .50 .15
❑ 134 Kevin Millwood .60 .18
❑ 135 Shane Reynolds .50 .15
❑ 136 Mark Grace 1.00 .30
❑ 137 Shannon Stewart .60 .18
❑ 138 Nick Neugebauer .50 .15
❑ 139 Nic Jackson RC 1.00 .30
❑ 140 Robb Nen UER .60 .18
Name spelled Rob on front
❑ 141 Dmitri Young .60 .18
❑ 142 Kevin Appier .60 .18
❑ 143 Jack Cust .50 .15
❑ 144 Andres Torres .50 .15
❑ 145 Frank Thomas 1.50 .45
❑ 146 Jason Kendall .60 .18
❑ 147 Greg Maddux 2.50 .75
❑ 148 David Justice .60 .18
❑ 149 Hideo Nomo 1.50 .45
❑ 150 Bret Boone .60 .18
❑ 151 Wade Miller .50 .15
❑ 152 Jeff Kent .60 .18
❑ 153 Scott Williamson .50 .15
❑ 154 Julio Lugo .50 .15
❑ 155 Bobby Higginson .60 .18
❑ 156 Geoff Jenkins .60 .18
❑ 157 Darren Dreifort .50 .15
❑ 158 Freddy Sanchez RC 1.00 .30
❑ 159 Bud Smith .50 .15
❑ 160 Phil Nevin .60 .18
❑ 161 Cesar Izturis .50 .15
❑ 162 Sean Casey .60 .18
❑ 163 Jose Ortiz .50 .15
❑ 164 Brent Abernathy .50 .15
❑ 165 Kevin Young .50 .15
❑ 166 Daryle Ward .50 .15
❑ 167 Trevor Hoffman .60 .18
❑ 168 Rondell White .60 .18
❑ 169 Kip Wells .50 .15
❑ 170 John Vander Wal .50 .15
❑ 171 Jose Lima .50 .15
❑ 172 Wilton Guerrero .50 .15
❑ 173 Aaron Dean RC 1.00 .30
❑ 174 Rick Helling .50 .15
❑ 175 Juan Pierre .60 .18
❑ 176 Jay Bell .60 .18
❑ 177 Craig House .50 .15
❑ 178 David Bell .50 .15
❑ 179 Pat Burrell .60 .18
❑ 180 Eric Gagne 1.50 .45
❑ 181 Adam Pettyjohn .50 .15
❑ 182 Ugueth Urbina .50 .15
❑ 183 Peter Bergeron .50 .15
❑ 184 Adrian Gonzalez UER .60 .18
Birthdate is wrong
❑ 184N Adrian Gonzalez Night SP UER 5.00 1.50
Birthdate is wrong
❑ 185 Damion Easley .50 .15
❑ 186 Gookie Dawkins .50 .15
❑ 187 Matt Lawton .50 .15
❑ 188 Frank Catalanotto .50 .15
❑ 189 David Wells .60 .18
❑ 190 Roger Cedeno .50 .15
❑ 191 Brian Giles .60 .18
❑ 192 Julio Zuleta .50 .15
❑ 193 Timo Perez .50 .15
❑ 194 Billy Wagner .60 .18
❑ 195 Craig Counsell .50 .15
❑ 196 Bart Miadich .50 .15
❑ 197 Gary Sheffield .60 .18
❑ 198 Richard Hidalgo .50 .15
❑ 199 Juan Uribe .50 .15
❑ 200 Curt Schilling .60 .18
❑ 201 Javy Lopez .60 .18
❑ 202 Jimmy Haynes .50 .15
❑ 203 Jim Edmonds .60 .18
❑ 204 Pokey Reese .50 .15
❑ 204N Pokey Reese Night SP 5.00 1.50
❑ 205 Matt Clement .50 .15
❑ 206 Dean Palmer .60 .18
❑ 207 Nick Johnson .50 .15
❑ 208 Nate Espy RC 1.00 .30
❑ 209 Pedro Feliz .50 .15
❑ 210 Aaron Rowand .60 .18
❑ 211 Masato Yoshii .50 .15
❑ 212 Jose Cruz Jr. .50 .15
❑ 213 Paul Byrd .50 .15
❑ 214 Mark Phillips RC 1.00 .30
❑ 215 Benny Agbayani .50 .15
❑ 216 Frank Menechino .50 .15
❑ 217 John Flaherty .50 .15
❑ 218 Brian Boehringer .50 .15
❑ 219 Todd Hollandsworth .50 .15
❑ 220 Sammy Sosa SP 12.00 3.60
❑ 221 Steve Sparks .50 .15
❑ 222 Homer Bush .50 .15
❑ 223 Mike Hampton .60 .18
❑ 224 Bobby Abreu .60 .18
❑ 225 Barry Larkin 1.00 .30
❑ 226 Ryan Rupe .50 .15
❑ 227 Bubba Trammell .50 .15
❑ 228 Todd Zeile .60 .18
❑ 229 Jeff Shaw .50 .15
❑ 230 Alex Ochoa .50 .15
❑ 231 Orlando Cabrera .60 .18
❑ 232 Jeremy Giambi .50 .15
❑ 233 Tomo Ohka .50 .15
❑ 234 Luis Castillo .50 .15
❑ 235 Chris Holt .50 .15
❑ 236 Shawn Green .60 .18
❑ 237 Sidney Ponson .50 .15
❑ 238 Lee Stevens .50 .15
❑ 239 Hank Blalock 1.50 .45
❑ 240 Randy Winn .50 .15
❑ 241 Pedro Martinez 1.50 .45
❑ 242 Vinny Castilla .60 .18
❑ 243 Steve Karsay .50 .15
❑ 244 Barry Bonds SP 20.00 6.00
❑ 245 Jason Bere .50 .15
❑ 246 Scott Rolen 1.50 .45
❑ 246N Scott Rolen Night SP 8.00 2.40
❑ 247 Ryan Kohlmeier .50 .15
❑ 248 Kerry Wood 1.50 .45
❑ 249 Aramis Ramirez .60 .18
❑ 250 Lance Berkman .60 .18
❑ 251 Omar Vizquel 1.00 .30
❑ 252 Juan Encarnacion .50 .15
❑ 253 Does Not Exist .00
❑ 254 David Segui .50 .15
❑ 255 Brian Anderson .50 .15
❑ 256 Jay Payton .50 .15
❑ 257 Mark Grudzielanek .50 .15
❑ 258 Jimmy Anderson .50 .15
❑ 259 Eric Valent .50 .15
❑ 260 Chad Durbin .50 .15
❑ 261 Does Not Exist .00
❑ 262 Alex Gonzalez .50 .15
❑ 263 Scott Dunn .50 .15
❑ 264 Scott Elarton .50 .15
❑ 265 Tom Gordon .50 .15
❑ 266 Moises Alou .60 .18
❑ 267 Does Not Exist .00
❑ 268 Does Not Exist .00
❑ 269 Mark Buehrle .60 .18
❑ 270 Jerry Hairston .50 .15
❑ 271 Does Not Exist .00
❑ 272 Luke Prokopec .50 .15
❑ 273 Graeme Lloyd .50 .15
❑ 274 Bret Prinz .50 .15
❑ 275 Does Not Exist .00
❑ 276 Chris Carpenter .50 .15
❑ 277 Ryan Minor .50 .15
❑ 278 Jeff D'Amico .50 .15
❑ 279 Raul Ibanez .50 .15
❑ 280 Joe Mays .50 .15
❑ 281 Livan Hernandez .50 .15
❑ 282 Robin Ventura .60 .18
❑ 283 Gabe Kapler .50 .15
❑ 284 Tony Batista .60 .18
❑ 285 Ramon Hernandez .50 .15
❑ 286 Craig Paquette .50 .15
❑ 287 Mark Kotsay .50 .15
❑ 288 Mike Lieberthal .60 .18
❑ 289 Joe Borchard .50 .15
❑ 290 Cristian Guzman .50 .15
❑ 291 Craig Biggio 1.00 .30
❑ 292 Joaquin Benoit .50 .15
❑ 293 Ken Caminiti .60 .18
❑ 294 Sean Burroughs .60 .18
❑ 295 Eric Karros .60 .18
❑ 296 Eric Chavez .60 .18
❑ 297 LaTroy Hawkins .50 .15
❑ 298 Alfonso Soriano 1.00 .30
❑ 299 John Smoltz 1.00 .30
❑ 300 Adam Dunn 1.00 .30
❑ 301 Ryan Dempster .50 .15
❑ 302 Travis Hafner .60 .18
❑ 303 Russell Branyan .50 .15
❑ 304 Dustin Hermanson .50 .15
❑ 305 Jim Thome 1.50 .45
❑ 306 Carlos Beltran 1.00 .30
❑ 307 Jason Botts RC 1.00 .30

❑ 308 David Cone .60 .18
❑ 309 Ivanon Coffie .50 .15
❑ 310 Brian Jordan .60 .18
❑ 311 Todd Walker .50 .15
❑ 312 Jeromy Burnitz .60 .18
❑ 313 Tony Armas Jr. .50 .15
❑ 314 Jeff Conine .60 .18
❑ 315 Todd Jones .50 .15
❑ 316 Roy Oswalt .60 .18
❑ 317 Aubrey Huff .60 .18
❑ 318 Josh Fogg .50 .15
❑ 319 Jose Vidro .50 .15
❑ 320 Jace Brewer .50 .15
❑ 321 Mike Redmond .50 .15
❑ 322 Noochie Varner RC 1.00 .30
❑ 323 Russ Ortiz .60 .18
❑ 324 Edgardo Alfonzo .50 .15
❑ 325 Ruben Sierra .50 .15
❑ 326 Calvin Murray .50 .15
❑ 327 Marlon Anderson .50 .15
❑ 328 Albie Lopez .50 .15
❑ 329 Chris Gomez .50 .15
❑ 330 Fernando Tatis .50 .15
❑ 331 Stubby Clapp .50 .15
❑ 332 Rickey Henderson 1.50 .45
❑ 333 Brad Radke .60 .18
❑ 334 Brent Mayne .50 .15
❑ 335 Cory Lidle .50 .15
❑ 336 Edgar Martinez 1.00 .30
❑ 337 Aaron Boone .60 .18
❑ 338 Jay Witasick .50 .15
❑ 339 Benito Santiago .60 .18
❑ 340 Jose Mercedes .50 .15
❑ 341 Fernando Vina .50 .15
❑ 342 A.J. Pierzynski .60 .18
❑ 343 Jeff Bagwell 1.00 .30
❑ 344 Brian Bohanon .50 .15
❑ 345 Adrian Beltre 1.00 .30
❑ 346 Troy Percival .60 .18
❑ 347 Napoleon Calzado RC 1.00 .30
❑ 348 Ruben Rivera .50 .15
❑ 349 Rafael Soriano .50 .15
❑ 350 Damian Jackson .50 .15
❑ 351 Joe Randa .50 .15
❑ 352 Chan Ho Park .60 .18
❑ 353 Dante Bichette .60 .18
❑ 354 Bartolo Colon .60 .18
❑ 355 Jason Bay RC 3.00 .90
❑ 356 Shea Hillenbrand .60 .18
❑ 357 Matt Morris .60 .18
❑ 358 Brad Penny .50 .15
❑ 359 Mark Quinn .50 .15
❑ 360 Marquis Grissom .60 .18
❑ 361 Henry Blanco .50 .15
❑ 362 Billy Koch .50 .15
❑ 363 Mike Cameron .60 .18
❑ 364 Albert Pujols SP 15.00 4.50
❑ 365 Paul Konerko SP 5.00 1.50
❑ 366 Eric Milton SP 5.00 1.50
❑ 367 Nick Bierbrodt SP 5.00 1.50
❑ 368 Rafael Palmeiro SP 8.00 2.40
❑ 369 Jorge Padilla SP RC 5.00 1.50
❑ 370 Jason Giambi 5.00 1.50
Yankees SP
Stats on back are Jeremy Giambi's
❑ 371 Mike Piazza SP 12.00 3.60
❑ 372 Alex Cora SP 5.00 1.50
❑ 373 Todd Helton SP 8.00 2.40
❑ 374 Juan Gonzalez SP 8.00 2.40
❑ 375 Mariano Rivera SP 8.00 2.40
❑ 376 Jason LaRue SP 5.00 1.50
❑ 377 Tony Gwynn SP 10.00 3.00
❑ 378 Wilson Betemit SP 5.00 1.50
❑ 379 J.J. Trujillo SP RC 5.00 1.50
❑ 380 Brad Ausmus SP 5.00 1.50
❑ 381 Chris George SP 5.00 1.50
❑ 382 Jose Canseco SP 8.00 2.40
❑ 383 Ramon Ortiz SP 5.00 1.50
❑ 384 John Rocker SP 5.00 1.50
❑ 385 Rey Ordonez SP 5.00 1.50
❑ 386 Ken Griffey Jr. SP 12.00 3.60
❑ 387 Juan Pena SP 5.00 1.50
❑ 388 Michael Barrett SP 5.00 1.50
❑ 389 J.D. Drew SP 5.00 1.50
❑ 390 Corey Koskie SP 5.00 1.50
❑ 391 Vernon Wells SP 5.00 1.50
❑ 392 Juan Tolentino SP RC 5.00 1.50
❑ 393 Luis Gonzalez SP 5.00 1.50
❑ 394 Terrence Long SP 5.00 1.50
❑ 395 Travis Lee SP 5.00 1.50
❑ 396 Earl Snyder SP RC 8.00 2.40
❑ 397 Nomar Garciaparra SP 12.00 3.60
❑ 398 Jason Schmidt SP 5.00 1.50
❑ 399 David Espinosa SP 5.00 1.50
❑ 400 Steve Green SP 5.00 1.50
❑ 401 Jack Wilson SP 5.00 1.50
❑ 402 Chris Tritle SP RC 5.00 1.50
❑ 403 Angel Berroa SP 5.00 1.50
❑ 404 Josh Towers SP 5.00 1.50
❑ 405 Andruw Jones SP 5.00 1.50
❑ 406 Brent Butler SP 5.00 1.50
❑ 407 Craig Kuzmic SP 5.00 1.50
❑ 408 Derek Bell SP 5.00 1.50
❑ 409 Eric Glaser SP RC 5.00 1.50
❑ 410 Joel Pineiro SP 5.00 1.50
❑ 411 Alexis Gomez SP 5.00 1.50
❑ 412 Mike Rivera SP 5.00 1.50
❑ 413 Shawn Estes SP 5.00 1.50
❑ 414 Milton Bradley SP 5.00 1.50
❑ 415 Carl Everett SP 5.00 1.50
❑ 416 Kazuhiro Sasaki SP 5.00 1.50
❑ 417 Tony Fontana SP RC 5.00 1.50
❑ 418 Josh Pearce SP 5.00 1.50
❑ 419 Gary Matthews Jr. SP 5.00 1.50
❑ 420 Raymond Cabrera SP RC 5.00 1.50
❑ 421 Joe Kennedy SP 5.00 1.50
❑ 422 Jason Maule SP RC 5.00 1.50
❑ 423 Casey Fossum SP 5.00 1.50
❑ 424 Christian Parker SP 5.00 1.50
❑ 425 Layne Nix SP RC 25.00 7.50
❑ 426 Byung-Hyun Kim SP 5.00 1.50
❑ 427 Freddy Garcia SP 5.00 1.50
❑ 428 Herbert Perry SP 5.00 1.50
❑ 429 Jason Marquis SP 5.00 1.50
❑ 430 Sandy Alomar Jr. SP 5.00 1.50
❑ 431 Roberto Alomar SP 8.00 2.40
❑ 432 Tsuyoshi Shinjo SP 5.00 1.50
❑ 433 Tim Wakefield SP 5.00 1.50
❑ 434 Robert Fick SP 5.00 1.50
❑ 435 Vladimir Guerrero SP 8.00 2.40
❑ 436 Jose Mesa SP 5.00 1.50
❑ 437 Scott Spiezio SP 5.00 1.50
❑ 438 Jose Hernandez SP 5.00 1.50
❑ 439 Jose Acevedo SP 5.00 1.50
❑ 440 Brian West SP RC 5.00 1.50
❑ 441 Barry Zito SP 5.00 1.50
❑ 442 Luis Maza SP 5.00 1.50
❑ 443 Marlon Byrd SP 5.00 1.50
❑ 444 A.J. Burnett SP 5.00 1.50
❑ 445 Dee Brown SP 5.00 1.50
❑ 446 Carlos Delgado SP 5.00 1.50
❑ NNO 1953 Repurchased EXCH..

2003 Topps Heritage

	Nm-Mt	Ex-Mt
COMPLETE SET (450)	400.00	120.00
COMP.SET w/o SP's (350)	80.00	24.00
COMMON CARD	.50	.15
COMMON RC	1.00	.30
COMMON SP	5.00	1.50
COMMON SP RC	5.00	1.50

❑ 1A Alex Rodriguez Red 2.50 .75
❑ 1B Alex Rodriguez Black SP 12.00 3.60
❑ 2 Jose Cruz Jr. .50 .15
❑ 3 Ichiro Suzuki SP 12.00 3.60
❑ 4 Rich Aurilia .50 .15
❑ 5 Trevor Hoffman .60 .18
❑ 6A Brian Giles New Logo .60 .18
❑ 6B Brian Giles Old Logo SP 5.00 1.50
❑ 7A Albert Pujols Orange 3.00 .90
❑ 7B Albert Pujols Black SP 15.00 4.50
❑ 8 Vicente Padilla .50 .15
❑ 9 Bobby Crosby 1.00 .30
❑ 10A Derek Jeter New Logo 4.00 1.20
❑ 10B Derek Jeter Old Logo SP 15.00 4.50
❑ 11A Pat Burrell New Logo .60 .18
❑ 11B Pat Burrell Old Logo SP 5.00 1.50
❑ 12 Armando Benitez .60 .18
❑ 13 Javier Vazquez .60 .18
❑ 14 Justin Morneau 1.00 .30
❑ 15 Doug Mientkiewicz .60 .18
❑ 16 Kevin Brown .60 .18
❑ 17 Alexis Gomez .50 .15
❑ 18A Lance Berkman Blue .60 .18
❑ 18B Lance Berkman Black SP 5.00 1.50
❑ 19 Adrian Gonzalez .60 .18
❑ 20A Todd Helton Green 1.00 .30
❑ 20B Todd Helton Black SP 8.00 2.40
❑ 21 Carlos Pena .50 .15
❑ 22 Matt Lawton .50 .15
❑ 23 Elmer Dessens .50 .15
❑ 24 Hee Seop Choi .50 .15
❑ 25 Chris Duncan SP RC 5.00 1.50
❑ 26 Ugueth Urbina .50 .15
❑ 27A Rodrigo Lopez New Logo .50 .15
❑ 27B Ro. Lopez Old Logo SP 5.00 1.50
❑ 28 Damian Moss .50 .15
❑ 29 Steve Finley .60 .18
❑ 30A Sammy Sosa New Logo 2.50 .75
❑ 30B S.Sosa Old Logo SP 12.00 3.60
❑ 31 Kevin Cash .50 .15
❑ 32 Kenny Rogers .60 .18
❑ 33 Ben Grieve .50 .15
❑ 34 Jason Simontacchi .50 .15
❑ 35 Shin-Soo Choo .60 .18
❑ 36 Freddy Garcia .60 .18
❑ 37 Jesse Foppert .60 .18
❑ 38 Tony LaRussa MG .60 .18
❑ 39 Mark Kotsay .50 .15
❑ 40 Barry Zito .60 .18
❑ 41 Josh Fogg .50 .15
❑ 42 Marlon Byrd .50 .15
❑ 43 Marcus Thames .50 .15
❑ 44 Al Leiter .60 .18
❑ 45 Michael Barrett .50 .15
❑ 46 Jake Peavy .60 .18
❑ 47 Dustan Mohr .50 .15
❑ 48 Alex Sanchez .50 .15
❑ 49 Chin-Feng Chen .60 .18
❑ 50A Kazuhisa Ishii Blue .60 .18
❑ 50B Kazuhisa Ishii Black SP 5.00 1.50
❑ 51 Carlos Beltran 1.00 .30
❑ 52 Franklin Gutierrez RC 3.00 .90
❑ 53 Miguel Cabrera 1.50 .45
❑ 54 Roger Clemens 3.00 .90
❑ 55 Juan Cruz .50 .15
❑ 56 Jason Young .50 .15
❑ 57 Alex Herrera .50 .15
❑ 58 Aaron Boone .60 .18
❑ 59 Mark Buehrle .60 .18
❑ 60 Larry Walker 1.00 .30
❑ 61 Morgan Ensberg .50 .15
❑ 62 Barry Larkin 1.00 .30
❑ 63 Joe Borchard .50 .15
❑ 64 Jason Dubois .60 .18
❑ 65 Shea Hillenbrand .60 .18
❑ 66 Jay Gibbons .50 .15
❑ 67 Vinny Castilla .60 .18
❑ 68 Jeff Mathis .60 .18
❑ 69 Curt Schilling .60 .18
❑ 70 Garret Anderson .60 .18
❑ 71 Josh Phelps .50 .15
❑ 72 Chan Ho Park .60 .18
❑ 73 Edgar Renteria .60 .18
❑ 74 Kazuhiro Sasaki .60 .18
❑ 75 Lloyd McClendon MG .50 .15
❑ 76 Jon Lieber .50 .15
❑ 77 Rolando Viera .50 .15
❑ 78 Jeff Conine .60 .18
❑ 79 Kevin Millwood .60 .18
❑ 80A Randy Johnson Green 1.50 .45
❑ 80B Randy Johnson Black SP 12.00 3.60

❑	81	Troy Percival	.60	.18
❑	82	Cliff Floyd	.60	.18
❑	83	Tony Graffanino	.50	.15
❑	84	Austin Kearns	.60	.18
❑	85	Manuel Ramirez SP RC	8.00	2.40
❑	86	Jim Tracy MG	.50	.15
❑	87	Rondell White	.60	.18
❑	88	Trot Nixon	.60	.18
❑	89	Carlos Lee	.60	.18
❑	90	Mike Lowell	.60	.18
❑	91	Raul Ibanez	.50	.15
❑	92	Ricardo Rodriguez	.50	.15
❑	93	Ben Sheets	.60	.18
❑	94	Jason Perry SP RC	8.00	2.40
❑	95	Mark Teixeira	.60	.18
❑	96	Brad Fullmer	.50	.15
❑	97	Casey Kotchman	1.00	.30
❑	98	Craig Counsell	.50	.15
❑	99	Jason Marquis	.50	.15
❑	100A	N.Garciaparra New Logo	2.50	.75
❑	100B	N.Garciaparra Old Logo SP	12.00	3.60
❑	101	Ed Rogers	.50	.15
❑	102	Wilson Betemit	.50	.15
❑	103	Wayne Lydon RC	1.00	.30
❑	104	Jack Cust	.50	.15
❑	105	Derrek Lee	.60	.18
❑	106	Jim Kavourias	.50	.15
❑	107	Joe Randa	.50	.15
❑	108	Taylor Buchholz	.50	.15
❑	109	Gabe Kapler	.50	.15
❑	110	Preston Wilson	.60	.18
❑	111	Craig Biggio	1.00	.30
❑	112	Paul Lo Duca	.60	.18
❑	113	Eddie Guardado	.50	.15
❑	114	Andres Galarraga	1.00	.30
❑	115	Edgardo Alfonzo	.50	.15
❑	116	Robin Ventura	.60	.18
❑	117	Jeremy Giambi	.50	.15
❑	118	Ray Durham	.60	.18
❑	119	Mariano Rivera	1.00	.30
❑	120	Jimmy Rollins	.60	.18
❑	121	Dennis Tankersley	.50	.15
❑	122	Jason Schmidt	.60	.18
❑	123	Bret Boone	.60	.18
❑	124	Josh Hamilton	.50	.15
❑	125	Scott Rolen	1.50	.45
❑	126	Steve Cox	.50	.15
❑	127	Larry Bowa MG	.60	.18
❑	128	Adam LaRoche SP	5.00	1.50
❑	129	Ryan Klesko	.60	.18
❑	130	Tim Hudson	.60	.18
❑	131	Brandon Claussen	.50	.15
❑	132	Craig Brazell SP RC	8.00	2.40
❑	133	Grady Little MG	.50	.15
❑	134	Jarrod Washburn	.50	.15
❑	135	Lyle Overbay	.60	.18
❑	136	John Burkett	.50	.15
❑	137	Daryl Clark RC	1.00	.30
❑	138	Kirk Rueter	.50	.15
❑	139A	Joe Mauer Jake Mauer Green	1.50	.45
❑	139B	Joe Mauer Jake Mauer Black SP	8.00	2.40
❑	140	Troy Glaus	.60	.18
❑	141	Trey Hodges SP	5.00	1.50
❑	142	Dallas McPherson	1.50	.45
❑	143	Art Howe MG	.50	.15
❑	144	Jesus Cota	.50	.15
❑	145	J.R. House	.50	.15
❑	146	Reggie Sanders	.50	.15
❑	147	Clint Nageotte	.60	.18
❑	148	Jim Edmonds	.60	.18
❑	149	Carl Crawford	.60	.18
❑	150A	Mike Piazza Blue	2.50	.75
❑	150B	Mike Piazza Black SP	12.00	3.60
❑	151	Seung Song	.50	.15
❑	152	Roberto Hernandez	.60	.18
❑	153	Marquis Grissom	.60	.18
❑	154	Billy Wagner	.60	.18
❑	155	Josh Beckett	.60	.18
❑	156A	R.Simon New Logo	.50	.15
❑	156B	R.Simon Old Logo SP	5.00	1.50
❑	157	Ben Broussard	.50	.15
❑	158	Russell Branyan	.50	.15
❑	159	Frank Thomas	1.50	.45
❑	160	Alex Escobar	.50	.15
❑	161	Mark Bellhorn	.60	.18
❑	162	Melvin Mora	.60	.18
❑	163	Andruw Jones	.60	.18
❑	164	Danny Bautista	.50	.15
❑	165	Ramon Ortiz	.50	.15
❑	166	Wily Mo Pena	.60	.18
❑	167	Jose Jimenez	.50	.15
❑	168	Mark Redman	.50	.15
❑	169	Angel Berroa	.50	.15
❑	170	Andy Marte SP RC	15.00	4.50
❑	171	Juan Gonzalez	1.00	.30
❑	172	Fernando Vina	.50	.15
❑	173	Joel Pineiro	.60	.18
❑	174	Boof Bonser	.50	.15
❑	175	Bernie Castro SP RC	5.00	1.50
❑	176	Bobby Cox MG	.50	.15
❑	177	Jeff Kent	.60	.18
❑	178	Oliver Perez	.60	.18
❑	179	Chase Utley	.60	.18
❑	180	Mark Mulder	.60	.18
❑	181	Bobby Abreu	.60	.18
❑	182	Ramiro Mendoza	.50	.15
❑	183	Aaron Heilman	.50	.15
❑	184	A.J. Pierzynski	.60	.18
❑	185	Eric Gagne	1.50	.45
❑	186	Kirk Saarloos	.50	.15
❑	187	Ron Gardenhire MG	.50	.15
❑	188	Dmitri Young	.60	.18
❑	189	Todd Zeile	.60	.18
❑	190A	Jim Thome New Logo	1.50	.45
❑	190B	Jim Thome Old Logo SP	8.00	2.40
❑	191	Cliff Lee	.50	.15
❑	192	Matt Morris	.60	.18
❑	193	Robert Fick	.50	.15
❑	194	C.C. Sabathia	.60	.18
❑	195	Alexis Rios	1.00	.30
❑	196	D'Angelo Jimenez	.50	.15
❑	197	Edgar Martinez	1.00	.30
❑	198	Robb Nen	.60	.18
❑	199	Taggert Bozied	.50	.15
❑	200	Vladimir Guerrero SP	8.00	2.40
❑	201	Walter Young SP	5.00	1.50
❑	202	Brendan Harris RC	1.00	.30
❑	203	Mike Hargrove MG	.50	.15
❑	204	Vernon Wells	.60	.18
❑	205	Hank Blalock	1.00	.30
❑	206	Mike Cameron	.60	.18
❑	207	Tony Batista	.60	.18
❑	208	Matt Williams	.60	.18
❑	209	Tony Womack	.50	.15
❑	210	R.Nivar-Martinez RC	1.00	.30
❑	211	Aaron Sele	.50	.15
❑	212	Mark Grace	1.00	.30
❑	213	Joe Crede	.50	.15
❑	214	Ryan Dempster	.50	.15
❑	215	Omar Vizquel	1.00	.30
❑	216	Juan Pierre	.60	.18
❑	217	Denny Bautista	.50	.15
❑	218	Chuck Knoblauch	.60	.18
❑	219	Eric Karros	.60	.18
❑	220	Victor Diaz	.60	.18
❑	221	Jacque Jones	.60	.18
❑	222	Jose Vidro	.50	.15
❑	223	Joe McEwing	.50	.15
❑	224	Nick Johnson	.50	.15
❑	225	Eric Chavez	.60	.18
❑	226	Jose Mesa	.50	.15
❑	227	Aramis Ramirez	.60	.18
❑	228	John Lackey	.50	.15
❑	229	David Bell	.50	.15
❑	230	John Olerud	.60	.18
❑	231	Tino Martinez	1.00	.30
❑	232	Randy Winn	.50	.15
❑	233	Todd Hollandsworth	.50	.15
❑	234	Ruddy Lugo RC	1.00	.30
❑	235	Carlos Delgado	.60	.18
❑	236	Chris Narveson	.50	.15
❑	237	Tim Salmon	1.00	.30
❑	238	Orlando Palmeiro	.50	.15
❑	239	Jeff Clark SP RC	5.00	1.50
❑	240	Byung-Hyun Kim	.60	.18
❑	241	Mike Remlinger	.50	.15
❑	242	Johnny Damon	1.50	.45
❑	243	Corey Patterson	.60	.18
❑	244	Paul Konerko	.60	.18
❑	245	Danny Graves	.50	.15
❑	246	Ellis Burks	.60	.18
❑	247	Gavin Floyd	.60	.18
❑	248	Jaime Bubela RC	1.00	.30
❑	249	Sean Burroughs	.60	.18
❑	250	Alex Rodriguez SP	12.00	3.60
❑	251	Gabe Gross	.50	.15
❑	252	Rafael Palmeiro	1.00	.30
❑	253	Dewon Brazelton	.50	.15
❑	254	Jimmy Journell	.50	.15
❑	255	Rafael Soriano	.50	.15
❑	256	Jerome Williams	.60	.18
❑	257	Xavier Nady	.50	.15
❑	258	Mike Williams	.50	.15
❑	259	Randy Wolf	.50	.15
❑	260A	Miguel Tejada Orange	.60	.18
❑	260B	Miguel Tejada Black SP	5.00	1.50
❑	261	Juan Rivera	.50	.15
❑	262	Rey Ordonez	.50	.15
❑	263	Bartolo Colon	.60	.18
❑	264	Eric Milton	.50	.15
❑	265	Jeffrey Hammonds	.50	.15
❑	266	Odalis Perez	.50	.15
❑	267	Mike Sweeney	.60	.18
❑	268	Richard Hidalgo	.50	.15
❑	269	Alex Gonzalez	.50	.15
❑	270	Aaron Cook	.50	.15
❑	271	Earl Snyder	.50	.15
❑	272	Todd Walker	.50	.15
❑	273	Aaron Rowand	.60	.18
❑	274	Matt Clement	.50	.15
❑	275	Anastacio Martinez	.50	.15
❑	276	Mike Bordick	.60	.18
❑	277	John Smoltz	1.00	.30
❑	278	Scott Hairston	.60	.18
❑	279	David Eckstein	.50	.15
❑	280	Shannon Stewart	.60	.18
❑	281	Carl Everett	.60	.18
❑	282	Aubrey Huff	.60	.18
❑	283	Mike Mussina	1.00	.30
❑	284	Ruben Sierra	.50	.15
❑	285	Russ Ortiz	.60	.18
❑	286	Brian Lawrence	.50	.15
❑	287	Kip Wells	.50	.15
❑	288	Placido Polanco	.50	.15
❑	289	Ted Lilly	.50	.15
❑	290	Andy Pettitte	1.00	.30
❑	291	John Buck	.50	.15
❑	292	Orlando Cabrera	.60	.18
❑	293	Cristian Guzman	.50	.15
❑	294	Ruben Quevedo	.50	.15
❑	295	Cesar Izturis	.50	.15
❑	296	Ryan Ludwick	.50	.15
❑	297	Roy Oswalt	.60	.18
❑	298	Jason Stokes	1.00	.30
❑	299	Mike Hampton	.60	.18
❑	300	Pedro Martinez	1.50	.45
❑	301	Nic Jackson	.50	.15
❑	302A	Mag. Ordonez New Logo	.60	.18
❑	302B	Mag. Ordonez Old Logo SP	5.00	1.50
❑	303	Manny Ramirez	1.00	.30
❑	304	Jorge Julio	.50	.15
❑	305	Javy Lopez	.60	.18
❑	306	Roy Halladay	.50	.15
❑	307	Kevin Mench	.50	.15
❑	308	Jason Isringhausen	.60	.18
❑	309	Carlos Guillen	.60	.18
❑	310	Tsuyoshi Shinjo	.60	.18
❑	311	Phil Nevin	.60	.18
❑	312	Pokey Reese	.50	.15
❑	313	Jorge Padilla	.50	.15
❑	314	Jermaine Dye	.60	.18
❑	315	David Wells	.60	.18
❑	316	Mo Vaughn	.60	.18
❑	317	Bernie Williams	1.00	.30
❑	318	Michael Restovich	.50	.15
❑	319	Jose Hernandez	.50	.15
❑	320	Richie Sexson	.60	.18
❑	321	Daryle Ward	.50	.15
❑	322	Luis Castillo	.50	.15
❑	323	Rene Reyes	.50	.15
❑	324	Victor Martinez	1.00	.30
❑	325A	Adam Dunn New Logo	1.00	.30
❑	325B	Adam Dunn Old Logo SP	8.00	2.40
❑	326	Corwin Malone	.50	.15
❑	327	Kerry Wood	1.50	.45
❑	328	Rickey Henderson	1.50	.45
❑	329	Marty Cordova	.50	.15
❑	330	Greg Maddux	2.50	.75
❑	331	Miguel Batista	.50	.15
❑	332	Chris Bootcheck	.50	.15
❑	333	Carlos Baerga	.50	.15
❑	334	Antonio Alfonseca	.50	.15
❑	335	Shane Halter	.50	.15
❑	336	Juan Encarnacion	.50	.15
❑	337	Tom Gordon	.50	.15

❑ 338 Hideo Nomo .... 1.50 .45
❑ 339 Torii Hunter .... .60 .18
❑ 340A Alfonso Soriano Yellow 1.00 .30
❑ 340B Alf. Soriano Black SP .. 8.00 2.40
❑ 341 Roberto Alomar .... 1.00 .30
❑ 342 David Justice .... .60 .18
❑ 343 Mike Lieberthal .... .60 .18
❑ 344 Jeff Weaver .... .50 .15
❑ 345 Timo Perez .... .50 .15
❑ 346 Travis Lee .... .50 .15
❑ 347 Sean Casey .... .60 .18
❑ 348 Willie Harris .... .50 .15
❑ 349 Derek Lowe .... .60 .18
❑ 350 Tom Glavine .... 1.00 .30
❑ 351 Eric Hinske .... .50 .15
❑ 352 Rocco Baldelli .... .60 .18
❑ 353 J.D. Drew .... .60 .18
❑ 354 Jamie Moyer .... .60 .18
❑ 355 Todd Linden .... .50 .15
❑ 356 Benito Santiago .... .60 .18
❑ 357 Brad Baker .... .50 .15
❑ 358 Alex Gonzalez .... .50 .15
❑ 359 Brandon Duckworth .... .50 .15
❑ 360 John Rheinecker .... .50 .15
❑ 361 Orlando Hernandez .... .50 .15
❑ 362 Pedro Astacio .... .50 .15
❑ 363 Brad Wilkerson .... .50 .15
❑ 364 David Ortiz SP 8.00 2.40
❑ 365 Geoff Jenkins SP 5.00 1.50
❑ 366 Brian Jordan SP 5.00 1.50
❑ 367 Paul Byrd SP 5.00 1.50
❑ 368 Jason Lane SP 5.00 1.50
❑ 369 Jeff Bagwell SP 8.00 2.40
❑ 370 Bobby Higginson SP 5.00 1.50
❑ 371 Juan Uribe SP 5.00 1.50
❑ 372 Lee Stevens SP 5.00 1.50
❑ 373 Jimmy Haynes SP 5.00 1.50
❑ 374 Jose Valentin SP 5.00 1.50
❑ 375 Ken Griffey Jr. SP 12.00 3.60
❑ 376 Barry Bonds SP 20.00 6.00
❑ 377 Gary Matthews Jr. SP 5.00 1.50
❑ 378 Gary Sheffield SP 5.00 1.50
❑ 379 Rick Helling SP 5.00 1.50
❑ 380 Junior Spivey SP 5.00 1.50
❑ 381 Francisco Rodriguez SP 5.00 1.50
❑ 382 Chipper Jones SP 8.00 2.40
❑ 383 Orlando Hudson SP 5.00 1.50
❑ 384 Ivan Rodriguez SP 8.00 2.40
❑ 385 Chris Snelling SP 5.00 1.50
❑ 386 Kenny Lofton SP 5.00 1.50
❑ 387 Eric Cyr SP 5.00 1.50
❑ 388 Jason Kendall SP 5.00 1.50
❑ 389 Marlon Anderson SP 5.00 1.50
❑ 390 Billy Koch SP 5.00 1.50
❑ 391 Shelley Duncan SP 5.00 1.50
❑ 392 Jose Reyes SP 5.00 1.50
❑ 393 Fernando Tatis SP 5.00 1.50
❑ 394 Michael Cuddyer SP 5.00 1.50
❑ 395 Mark Prior SP 8.00 2.40
❑ 396 Dontrelle Willis SP 8.00 2.40
❑ 397 Jay Payton SP 5.00 1.50
❑ 398 Brandon Phillips SP 5.00 1.50
❑ 399 Dustin Moseley SP RC .. 8.00 2.40
❑ 400 Jason Giambi SP 5.00 1.50
❑ 401 John Mabry SP 5.00 1.50
❑ 402 Ron Gant SP 5.00 1.50
❑ 403 J.T. Snow SP 5.00 1.50
❑ 404 Jeff Cirillo SP 5.00 1.50
❑ 405 Darin Erstad SP 5.00 1.50
❑ 406 Luis Gonzalez SP 5.00 1.50
❑ 407 Marcus Giles SP 5.00 1.50
❑ 408 Brian Daubach SP 5.00 1.50
❑ 409 Moises Alou SP 5.00 1.50
❑ 410 Raul Mondesi SP 5.00 1.50
❑ 411 Adrian Beltre SP 8.00 2.40
❑ 412 A.J. Burnett SP 5.00 1.50
❑ 413 Jason Jennings SP 5.00 1.50
❑ 414 Edwin Almonte SP 5.00 1.50
❑ 415 Fred McGriff SP 8.00 2.40
❑ 416 Tim Raines Jr. SP 5.00 1.50
❑ 417 Rafael Furcal SP 5.00 1.50
❑ 418 Erubiel Durazo SP 5.00 1.50
❑ 419 Drew Henson SP 5.00 1.50
❑ 420 Kevin Appier SP 5.00 1.50
❑ 421 Chad Tracy SP 5.00 1.50
❑ 422 Adam Wainwright SP 5.00 1.50
❑ 423 Choo Freeman SP 5.00 1.50
❑ 424 Sandy Alomar Jr. SP 5.00 1.50
❑ 425 Corey Koskie SP 5.00 1.50
❑ 426 Jeromy Burnitz SP 5.00 1.50
❑ 427 Jorge Posada SP 8.00 2.40
❑ 428 Jason Arnold SP 5.00 1.50
❑ 429 Brett Myers SP 5.00 1.50
❑ 430 Shawn Green SP 5.00 1.50

2004 Topps Heritage

	Nm-Mt	Ex-Mt
COMPLETE SET (495)	400.00	120.00
COMP.SET w/o SP's (385)	50.00	15.00
SP STATED ODDS 1:2		

❑ 1A Jim Thome Fielding .... 1.50 .45
❑ 1B Jim Thome Hitting SP 8.00 2.40
❑ 2 Nomar Garciaparra SP 10.00 3.00
❑ 3 Aramis Ramirez .... .60 .18
❑ 4 Rafael Palmeiro SP 8.00 2.40
❑ 5 Danny Graves .... .50 .15
❑ 6 Casey Blake .... .50 .15
❑ 7 Juan Uribe .... .50 .15
❑ 8A Dmitri Young New Logo .... .60 .18
❑ 8B Dmitri Young Old Logo SP 5.00 1.50
❑ 9 Billy Wagner .... .60 .18
❑ 10A Jason Giambi Swinging .. .60 .18
❑ 10B Jason Giambi Btg Stance SP 5.00 1.50
❑ 11 Carlos Beltran .... 1.00 .30
❑ 12 Chad Hermansen .... .50 .15
❑ 13 B.J. Upton .... 1.50 .45
❑ 14 Dustan Mohr .... .50 .15
❑ 15 Endy Chavez .... .50 .15
❑ 16 Cliff Floyd .... .60 .18
❑ 17 Bernie Williams .... 1.00 .30
❑ 18 Eric Chavez .... .60 .18
❑ 19 Chase Utley .... .60 .18
❑ 20 Randy Johnson .... 1.50 .45
❑ 21 Vernon Wells .... .60 .18
❑ 22 Juan Gonzalez .... 1.00 .30
❑ 23 Joe Kennedy .... .50 .15
❑ 24 Bengie Molina .... .50 .15
❑ 25 Carlos Lee .... .60 .18
❑ 26 Horacio Ramirez .... .50 .15
❑ 27 Anthony Acevedo RC .... 1.00 .30
❑ 28 Sammy Sosa SP 10.00 3.00
❑ 29 Jon Garland .... .50 .15
❑ 30A Adam Dunn Fielding .... 1.00 .30
❑ 30B Adam Dunn Hitting SP .. 8.00 2.40
❑ 31 Aaron Rowand .... .60 .18
❑ 32 Jody Gerut .... .50 .15
❑ 33 Chin-Hui Tsao .... .60 .18
❑ 34 Alex Sanchez .... .50 .15
❑ 35 A.J. Burnett .... .50 .15
❑ 36 Brad Ausmus .... .50 .15
❑ 37 Blake Hawksworth RC .... 1.00 .30
❑ 38 Francisco Rodriguez .... .60 .18
❑ 39 Alex Cintron .... .50 .15
❑ 40A Chipper Jones Pointing .... 1.50 .45
❑ 40B Chipper Jones Fielding SP 8.00 2.40
❑ 41 Deivi Cruz .... .50 .15
❑ 42 Bill Mueller .... .60 .18
❑ 43 Joe Borowski .... .50 .15
❑ 44 Jimmy Haynes .... .50 .15
❑ 45 Mark Loretta .... .60 .18
❑ 46 Jerome Williams .... .60 .18
❑ 47 Gary Sheffield Yanks SP .. 8.00 2.40
❑ 48 Richard Hidalgo .... .50 .15
❑ 49A Jason Kendall New Logo.. .60 .18
❑ 49B Jason Kendall Old Logo SP 5.00 1.50
❑ 50 Ichiro Suzuki SP 10.00 3.00
❑ 51 Jim Edmonds .... .60 .18
❑ 52 Frank Catalanotto .... .50 .15
❑ 53 Jose Contreras .... .60 .18
❑ 54 Mo Vaughn .... .60 .18
❑ 55 Brendan Donnelly .... .50 .15
❑ 56 Luis Gonzalez .... .60 .18
❑ 57 Robert Fick .... .50 .15
❑ 58 Laynce Nix .... .60 .18
❑ 59 Johnny Damon .... 1.50 .45
❑ 60A Magglio Ordonez Running .60 .18
❑ 60B Magglio Ordonez Hitting SP 5.00 1.50
❑ 61 Matt Clement .... .50 .15
❑ 62 Ryan Ludwick .... .50 .15
❑ 63 Luis Castillo .... .50 .15
❑ 64 Dave Crouthers RC .... 1.00 .30
❑ 65 Dave Berg .... .50 .15
❑ 66 Kyle Davies RC .... 1.00 .30
❑ 67 Tim Salmon .... 1.00 .30
❑ 68 Marcus Giles .... .60 .18
❑ 69 Marty Cordova .... .50 .15
❑ 70A Todd Helton White Jsy .. 1.00 .30
❑ 70B Todd Helton Purple Jsy SP 8.00 2.40
❑ 71 Jeff Kent .... .60 .18
❑ 72 Michael Tucker .... .50 .15
❑ 73 Cesar Izturis .... .50 .15
❑ 74 Paul Quantrill .... .50 .15
❑ 75 Conor Jackson RC .... 2.00 .60
❑ 76 Placido Polanco .... .50 .15
❑ 77 Adam Eaton .... .50 .15
❑ 78 Ramon Hernandez .... .60 .18
❑ 79 Edgardo Alfonzo .... .50 .15
❑ 80 Dioner Navarro RC .... 1.25 .35
❑ 81 Woody Williams .... .50 .15
❑ 82 Rey Ordonez .... .50 .15
❑ 83 Randy Winn .... .50 .15
❑ 84 Casey Myers RC .... 1.00 .30
❑ 85A R.Choy Foo New Logo RC 1.00 .30
❑ 85B R.Choy Foo Old Logo SP 5.00 1.50
❑ 86 Ray Durham .... .60 .18
❑ 87 Sean Burroughs .... .60 .18
❑ 88 Tim Frend RC .... 1.00 .30
❑ 89 Shigetoshi Hasegawa .... .60 .18
❑ 90 Jeffrey Allison RC .... 1.00 .30
❑ 91 Orlando Hudson .... .50 .15
❑ 92 Matt Creighton SP RC 5.00 1.50
❑ 93 Tim Worrell .... .50 .15
❑ 94 Kris Benson .... .50 .15
❑ 95 Mike Lieberthal .... .60 .18
❑ 96 David Wells .... .60 .18
❑ 97 Jason Phillips .... .50 .15
❑ 98 Bobby Cox MGR .... .50 .15
❑ 99 Johan Santana .... 1.00 .30
❑ 100A Alex Rodriguez Hitting 2.50 .75
❑ 100B Alex Rodriguez Throwing SP 10.00 3.00
❑ 101 John Vander Wal .... .50 .15
❑ 102 Orlando Cabrera .... .60 .18
❑ 103 Hideo Nomo .... 1.50 .45
❑ 104 Todd Walker .... .50 .15
❑ 105 Jason Johnson .... .50 .15
❑ 106 Matt Mantei .... .50 .15
❑ 107 Jarrod Washburn .... .50 .15
❑ 108 Preston Wilson .... .60 .18
❑ 109 Carl Pavano .... .60 .18
❑ 110 Geoff Blum .... .50 .15
❑ 111 Eric Gagne .... 1.50 .45
❑ 112 Geoff Jenkins .... .60 .18
❑ 113 Joe Torre MGR .... 1.00 .30
❑ 114 Jon Knott RC .... 1.00 .30
❑ 115 Hank Blalock .... .60 .18
❑ 116 John Olerud .... .60 .18
❑ 117A Pat Burrell New Logo .... .60 .18
❑ 117B Pat Burrell Old Logo SP 5.00 1.50
❑ 118 Aaron Boone .... .60 .18
❑ 119 Zach Day .... .50 .15
❑ 120A Frank Thomas New Logo 1.50 .45
❑ 120B Frank Thomas Old Logo SP 8.00 2.40
❑ 121 Kyle Farnsworth .... .50 .15
❑ 122 Derek Lowe .... .60 .18
❑ 123 Zach Miner SP RC 8.00 2.40
❑ 124 Matthew Moses SP RC .. 8.00 2.40
❑ 125 Jesse Roman RC .... 1.00 .30
❑ 126 Josh Phelps .... .50 .15
❑ 127 Nic Ungs RC .... 1.00 .30
❑ 128 Dan Haren .... .50 .15
❑ 129 Kirk Rueter .... .50 .15

❑ 130	Jack McKeon MGR	.60	.18
❑ 131	Keith Foulke	.60	.18
❑ 132	Garrett Stephenson	.50	.15
❑ 133	Wes Helms	.50	.15
❑ 134	Raul Ibanez	.50	.15
❑ 135	Morgan Ensberg	.50	.15
❑ 136	Jay Payton	.60	.18
❑ 137	Billy Koch	.50	.15
❑ 138	Mark Grudzielanek	.50	.15
❑ 139	Rodrigo Lopez	.50	.15
❑ 140	Corey Patterson	.60	.18
❑ 141	Troy Percival	.60	.18
❑ 142	Shea Hillenbrand	.60	.18
❑ 143	Brad Fullmer	.60	.18
❑ 144	Ricky Nolasco RC	1.00	.30
❑ 145	Mark Teixeira	.60	.18
❑ 146	Tydus Meadows RC	1.00	.30
❑ 147	Toby Hall	.50	.15
❑ 148	Orlando Palmeiro	.50	.15
❑ 149	Khalid Ballouli RC	1.00	.30
❑ 150	Grady Little MGR	.50	.15
❑ 151	David Eckstein	.50	.15
❑ 152	Kenny Perez RC	1.00	.30
❑ 153	Ben Grieve	.50	.15
❑ 154	Ismael Valdes	.50	.15
❑ 155	Bret Boone	.60	.18
❑ 156	Jesse Foppert	.50	.15
❑ 157	Vicente Padilla	.50	.15
❑ 158	Bobby Abreu	.60	.18
❑ 159	Scott Hatteberg	.50	.15
❑ 160	Carlos Quentin RC	2.00	.60
❑ 161	Anthony Lerew RC	1.00	.30
❑ 162	Lance Carter	.50	.15
❑ 163	Robb Nen	.60	.18
❑ 164	Zach Duke SP RC	8.00	2.40
❑ 165	Xavier Nady	.50	.15
❑ 166	Kip Wells	.50	.15
❑ 167	Kevin Millwood	.60	.18
❑ 168	Jon Lieber	.50	.15
❑ 169	Jose Reyes	.60	.18
❑ 170	Eric Byrnes	.50	.15
❑ 171	Paul Konerko	.60	.18
❑ 172	Chris Lubanski	.60	.18
❑ 173	Jae Weong Seo	.50	.15
❑ 174	Corey Koskie	.60	.18
❑ 175	Tim Stauffer RC	1.00	.30
❑ 176	John Lackey	.50	.15
❑ 177	Danny Bautista	.50	.15
❑ 178	Shane Reynolds	.50	.15
❑ 179	Jorge Julio	.50	.15
❑ 180A	Manny Ramirez New Logo	1.00	.30
❑ 180B	Manny Ramirez Old Logo SP	8.00	2.40
❑ 181	Alex Gonzalez	.50	.15
❑ 182A	Moises Alou New Logo	.60	.18
❑ 182B	Moises Alou Old Logo SP	5.00	1.50
❑ 183	Mark Buehrle	.60	.18
❑ 184	Carlos Guillen	.60	.18
❑ 185	Nate Cornejo	.50	.15
❑ 186	Billy Traber	.50	.15
❑ 187	Jason Jennings	.50	.15
❑ 188	Eric Munson	.50	.15
❑ 189	Braden Looper	.50	.15
❑ 190	Juan Encarnacion	.50	.15
❑ 191	Dusty Baker MGR	.60	.18
❑ 192	Travis Lee	.50	.15
❑ 193	Miguel Cairo	.50	.15
❑ 194	Rich Aurilia SP	5.00	1.50
❑ 195	Tom Gordon	.50	.15
❑ 196	Freddy Garcia	.60	.18
❑ 197	Brian Lawrence	.50	.15
❑ 198	Jorge Posada SP	8.00	2.40
❑ 199	Javier Vazquez	.60	.18
❑ 200A	Albert Pujols New Logo	3.00	.90
❑ 200B	Albert Pujols Old Logo SP	12.00	3.60
❑ 201	Victor Zambrano	.50	.15
❑ 202	Eli Marrero	.50	.15
❑ 203	Joel Pineiro	.60	.18
❑ 204	Rondell White	.60	.18
❑ 205	Craig Ansman RC	1.00	.30
❑ 206	Michael Young	.60	.18
❑ 207	Carlos Baerga	.50	.15
❑ 208	Andruw Jones	.60	.18
❑ 209	Jerry Hairston Jr.	.50	.15
❑ 210	Shawn Green SP	5.00	1.50
❑ 211	Ron Gardenhire MGR	.50	.15
❑ 212	Darin Erstad	.60	.18
❑ 213A	Brandon Webb Glove Chest	.50	.15
❑ 213B	Brandon Webb Glove Out SP	5.00	1.50
❑ 214	Greg Maddux	2.50	.75
❑ 215	Reed Johnson	.50	.15
❑ 216	John Thomson	.50	.15
❑ 217	Tino Martinez	1.00	.30
❑ 218	Mike Cameron	.60	.18
❑ 219	Edgar Martinez	1.00	.30
❑ 220	Eric Young	.50	.15
❑ 221	Reggie Sanders	.50	.15
❑ 222	Randy Wolf	.50	.15
❑ 223	Erubiel Durazo	.50	.15
❑ 224	Mike Mussina	1.00	.30
❑ 225	Tom Glavine	1.00	.30
❑ 226	Troy Glaus	.60	.18
❑ 227	Oscar Villarreal	.50	.15
❑ 228	David Segui	.50	.15
❑ 229	Jeff Suppan	.50	.15
❑ 230	Kenny Lofton	.60	.18
❑ 231	Esteban Loaiza	.50	.15
❑ 232	Felipe Lopez	.50	.15
❑ 233	Matt Lawton	.50	.15
❑ 234	Mark Bellhorn	.60	.18
❑ 235	Wil Ledezma	.50	.15
❑ 236	Todd Hollandsworth	.50	.15
❑ 237	Octavio Dotel	.50	.15
❑ 238	Darren Dreifort	.50	.15
❑ 239	Paul Lo Duca	.60	.18
❑ 240	Richie Sexson	.60	.18
❑ 241	Doug Mientkiewicz	.60	.18
❑ 242	Luis Rivas	.50	.15
❑ 243	Claudio Vargas	.50	.15
❑ 244	Mark Ellis	.50	.15
❑ 245	Brett Myers	.50	.15
❑ 246	Jake Peavy	.60	.18
❑ 247	Marquis Grissom	.60	.18
❑ 248	Armando Benitez	.60	.18
❑ 249	Ryan Franklin	.50	.15
❑ 250A	Alfonso Soriano Throwing	1.00	.30
❑ 250B	Alfonso Soriano Fielding SP	8.00	2.40
❑ 251	Tim Hudson	.60	.18
❑ 252	Shannon Stewart	.60	.18
❑ 253	A.J. Pierzynski	.60	.18
❑ 254	Runelvys Hernandez	.50	.15
❑ 255	Roy Oswalt	.60	.18
❑ 256	Shawn Chacon	.50	.15
❑ 257	Tony Graffanino	.50	.15
❑ 258	Tim Wakefield	.60	.18
❑ 259	Damian Miller	.50	.15
❑ 260	Joe Crede	.50	.15
❑ 261	Jason LaRue	.50	.15
❑ 262	Jose Jimenez	.50	.15
❑ 263	Juan Pierre	.60	.18
❑ 264	Wade Miller	.50	.15
❑ 265	Odalis Perez	.50	.15
❑ 266	Eddie Guardado	.50	.15
❑ 267	Rocky Biddle	.50	.15
❑ 268	Jeff Nelson	.50	.15
❑ 269	Terrence Long	.50	.15
❑ 270	Ramon Ortiz	.50	.15
❑ 271	Raul Mondesi	.60	.18
❑ 272	Ugueth Urbina	.50	.15
❑ 273	Jeromy Burnitz	.60	.18
❑ 274	Brad Radke	.60	.18
❑ 275	Jose Vidro	.50	.15
❑ 276	Bobby Jenks	.50	.15
❑ 277	Ty Wigginton	.50	.15
❑ 278	Jose Guillen	.60	.18
❑ 279	Delmon Young	1.00	.30
❑ 280	Brian Giles	.60	.18
❑ 281	Jason Schmidt	.60	.18
❑ 282	Nick Markakis	.60	.18
❑ 283	Felipe Alou MGR	.60	.18
❑ 284	Carl Crawford	.60	.18
❑ 285	Neifi Perez	.50	.15
❑ 286	Miguel Tejada	.60	.18
❑ 287	Victor Martinez	.60	.18
❑ 288	Adam Kennedy	.50	.15
❑ 289	Kerry Ligtenberg	.50	.15
❑ 290	Scott Williamson	.50	.15
❑ 291	Tony Womack	.50	.15
❑ 292	Travis Hafner	.60	.18
❑ 293	Bobby Crosby	1.00	.30
❑ 294	Chad Billingsley	.60	.18
❑ 295	Russ Ortiz	.60	.18
❑ 296	John Burkett	.50	.15
❑ 297	Carlos Zambrano	.60	.18
❑ 298	Randall Simon	.50	.15
❑ 299	Juan Castro	.50	.15
❑ 300	Mike Lowell	.60	.18
❑ 301	Fred McGriff	1.00	.30
❑ 302	Glendon Rusch	.50	.15
❑ 303	Sung Jung RC	1.00	.30
❑ 304	Rocco Baldelli	.60	.18
❑ 305	Fernando Vina	.50	.15
❑ 306	Gil Meche	.50	.15
❑ 307	Jose Cruz Jr.	.50	.15
❑ 308	Bernie Castro	.50	.15
❑ 309	Scott Spiezio	.50	.15
❑ 310	Paul Byrd	.50	.15
❑ 311A	Jay Gibbons New Logo	.50	.15
❑ 311B	Jay Gibbons Old Logo SP	5.00	1.50
❑ 312	Trot Nixon	.60	.18
❑ 313	Chris O'Riordan RC	1.00	.30
❑ 314	Julio Lugo	.50	.15
❑ 315	Ben Davis	.50	.15
❑ 316	Mike Williams	.50	.15
❑ 317	Trevor Hoffman	.60	.18
❑ 318	Andy Pettitte	1.00	.30
❑ 319	Orlando Hernandez	.50	.15
❑ 320	Juan Rivera	.50	.15
❑ 321	Elizardo Ramirez	.50	.15
❑ 322	Junior Spivey	.50	.15
❑ 323	Tony Batista	.60	.18
❑ 324	Mike Remlinger	.50	.15
❑ 325	Alex Gonzalez	.50	.15
❑ 326	Aaron Hill	.50	.15
❑ 327	Steve Finley	.60	.18
❑ 328	Vinny Castilla	.60	.18
❑ 329	Eric Duncan	.60	.18
❑ 330	Mike Gosling RC	1.00	.30
❑ 331	Eric Hinske	.50	.15
❑ 332	Scott Rolen	1.50	.45
❑ 333	Benito Santiago	.60	.18
❑ 334	Jimmy Gobble	.50	.15
❑ 335	Bobby Higginson	.60	.18
❑ 336	Kelvim Escobar	.50	.15
❑ 337	Mike DeJean	.50	.15
❑ 338	Sidney Ponson	.50	.15
❑ 339	Todd Self RC	1.00	.30
❑ 340	Jeff Cirillo	.50	.15
❑ 341	Jimmy Rollins	.60	.18
❑ 342A	Barry Zito White Jsy	.60	.18
❑ 342B	Barry Zito Green Jsy SP	5.00	1.50
❑ 343	Felix Pie	.60	.18
❑ 344	Matt Morris	.60	.18
❑ 345	Kazuhiro Sasaki	.60	.18
❑ 346	Jack Wilson	.60	.18
❑ 347	Nick Johnson	.50	.15
❑ 348	Wil Cordero	.50	.15
❑ 349	Ryan Madson	.50	.15
❑ 350	Torii Hunter	.60	.18
❑ 351	Andy Ashby	.50	.15
❑ 352	Aubrey Huff	.60	.18
❑ 353	Brad Lidge	.60	.18
❑ 354	Derrek Lee	.60	.18
❑ 355	Yadier Molina RC	1.25	.35
❑ 356	Paul Wilson	.50	.15
❑ 357	Omar Vizquel	1.00	.30
❑ 358	Rene Reyes	.50	.15
❑ 359	Marlon Anderson	.50	.15
❑ 360	Bobby Kielty	.50	.15
❑ 361A	Ryan Wagner New Logo	.50	.15
❑ 361B	Ryan Wagner Old Logo SP	5.00	1.50
❑ 362	Justin Morneau	.60	.18
❑ 363	Shane Spencer	.50	.15
❑ 364	David Bell	.50	.15
❑ 365	Matt Stairs	.50	.15
❑ 366	Joe Borchard	.50	.15
❑ 367	Mark Redman	.50	.15
❑ 368	Dave Roberts	.50	.15
❑ 369	Desi Relaford	.50	.15
❑ 370	Rich Harden	.60	.18
❑ 371	Fernando Tatis	.50	.15
❑ 372	Eric Karros	.60	.18
❑ 373	Eric Milton	.60	.18
❑ 374	Mike Sweeney	.60	.18
❑ 375	Brian Daubach	.50	.15
❑ 376	Brian Snyder	.50	.15
❑ 377	Chris Reitsma	.50	.15
❑ 378	Kyle Lohse	.50	.15
❑ 379	Livan Hernandez	.50	.15

Card	Nm-Mt	Ex-Mt
❑ 380 Robin Ventura	.60	.18
❑ 381 Jacque Jones	.60	.18
❑ 382 Danny Kolb	.50	.15
❑ 383 Casey Kotchman	.60	.18
❑ 384 Cristian Guzman	.50	.15
❑ 385 Josh Beckett	.60	.18
❑ 386 Khalil Greene	1.50	.45
❑ 387 Greg Myers	.50	.15
❑ 388 Francisco Cordero	.50	.15
❑ 389 Donald Levinski RC	1.00	.30
❑ 390 Roy Halladay	.50	.15
❑ 391 J.D. Drew	.60	.18
❑ 392 Jamie Moyer	.60	.18
❑ 393 Ken Macha MGR	.50	.15
❑ 394 Jeff Davanon	.50	.15
❑ 395 Matt Kata	.50	.15
❑ 396 Jack Cust	.50	.15
❑ 397 Mike Timlin	.50	.15
❑ 398 Zack Greinke SP	5.00	1.50
❑ 399 Byung-Hyun Kim SP	5.00	1.50
❑ 400 Kazuhisa Ishii SP	5.00	1.50
❑ 401 Brayan Pena SP RC	5.00	1.50
❑ 402 Garret Anderson SP	5.00	1.50
❑ 403 Kyle Sleeth SP RC	8.00	2.40
❑ 404 Javy Lopez SP	5.00	1.50
❑ 405 Damian Moss SP	5.00	1.50
❑ 406 David Ortiz SP	8.00	2.40
❑ 407 Pedro Martinez SP	8.00	2.40
❑ 408 Hee Seop Choi SP	5.00	1.50
❑ 409 Carl Everett SP	5.00	1.50
❑ 410 Dontrelle Willis SP	5.00	1.50
❑ 411 Ryan Harvey SP	5.00	1.50
❑ 412 Russell Branyan SP	5.00	1.50
❑ 413 Milton Bradley SP	5.00	1.50
❑ 414 Marcus McBeth SP RC	5.00	1.50
❑ 415 Carlos Pena SP	5.00	1.50
❑ 416 Ivan Rodriguez SP	8.00	2.40
❑ 417 Craig Biggio SP	8.00	2.40
❑ 418 Angel Berroa SP	5.00	1.50
❑ 419 Brian Jordan SP	5.00	1.50
❑ 420 Scott Podsednik SP	5.00	1.50
❑ 421 Omar Falcon SP RC	5.00	1.50
❑ 422 Joe Mays SP	5.00	1.50
❑ 423 Brad Wilkerson SP	5.00	1.50
❑ 424 Al Leiter SP	5.00	1.50
❑ 425 Derek Jeter SP	12.00	3.60
❑ 426 Mark Mulder SP	5.00	1.50
❑ 427 Marlon Byrd SP	5.00	1.50
❑ 428 David Murphy SP RC	8.00	2.40
❑ 429 Phil Nevin SP	5.00	1.50
❑ 430 J.T. Snow SP	5.00	1.50
❑ 431 Brad Sullivan SP RC	8.00	2.40
❑ 432 Bo Hart SP	5.00	1.50
❑ 433 Josh Labandeira SP RC	5.00	1.50
❑ 434 Chan Ho Park SP	5.00	1.50
❑ 435 Carlos Delgado SP	5.00	1.50
❑ 436 Curt Schilling Sox SP	8.00	2.40
❑ 437 John Smoltz SP	8.00	2.40
❑ 438 Luis Matos SP	5.00	1.50
❑ 439 Mark Prior SP	8.00	2.40
❑ 440 Roberto Alomar SP	8.00	2.40
❑ 441 Coco Crisp SP	5.00	1.50
❑ 442 Austin Kearns SP	5.00	1.50
❑ 443 Larry Walker SP	8.00	2.40
❑ 444 Neal Cotts SP	5.00	1.50
❑ 445 Jeff Bagwell SP	8.00	2.40
❑ 446 Adrian Beltre SP	8.00	2.40
❑ 447 Grady Sizemore SP	5.00	1.50
❑ 448 Keith Ginter SP	5.00	1.50
❑ 449 Vladimir Guerrero SP	8.00	2.40
❑ 450 Lyle Overbay SP	5.00	1.50
❑ 451 Rafael Furcal SP	5.00	1.50
❑ 452 Melvin Mora SP	5.00	1.50
❑ 453 Kerry Wood SP	8.00	2.40
❑ 454 Jose Valentin SP	5.00	1.50
❑ 455 Ken Griffey Jr. SP	10.00	3.00
❑ 456 Brandon Phillips SP	5.00	1.50
❑ 457 Miguel Cabrera SP	8.00	2.40
❑ 458 Edwin Jackson SP	5.00	1.50
❑ 459 Eric Owens SP	5.00	1.50
❑ 460 Miguel Batista SP	5.00	1.50
❑ 461 Mike Hampton SP	5.00	1.50
❑ 462 Kevin Millar SP	5.00	1.50
❑ 463 Bartolo Colon SP	5.00	1.50
❑ 464 Sean Casey SP	5.00	1.50
❑ 465 C.C. Sabathia SP	5.00	1.50
❑ 466 Rickie Weeks SP	5.00	1.50
❑ 467 Brad Penny SP	5.00	1.50
❑ 468 Mike MacDougal SP	5.00	1.50
❑ 469 Kevin Brown SP	5.00	1.50
❑ 470 Lance Berkman SP	5.00	1.50
❑ 471 Ben Sheets SP	5.00	1.50
❑ 472 Mariano Rivera SP	8.00	2.40
❑ 473 Mike Piazza SP	10.00	3.00
❑ 474 Ryan Klesko SP	5.00	1.50
❑ 475 Edgar Renteria SP	5.00	1.50

2004 Topps Originals Signature

ONE AUTO PER PACK
PRINT RUNS B/WN 1-339 COPIES PER
NO PRICING ON QTY OF 14 OR LESS

Card	Nm-Mt	Ex-Mt
❑ AD1 Andre Dawson 77/1		
❑ AD2 Andre Dawson 79/3		
❑ AD3 Andre Dawson 80/27	30.00	9.00
❑ AD4 Andre Dawson 81/37	20.00	6.00
❑ AD5 Andre Dawson 82/55	20.00	6.00
❑ AD6 Andre Dawson 83/47	20.00	6.00
❑ AD7 Andre Dawson 84/25	30.00	9.00
❑ AD8 Andre Dawson 85/22	30.00	9.00
❑ AD9 Andre Dawson 86/24	30.00	9.00
❑ AD10 Andre Dawson 88/9		
❑ AH1 Al Hrabosky 71/1		
❑ AH2 Al Hrabosky 74/2		
❑ AH3 Al Hrabosky 75/1		
❑ AH4 Al Hrabosky 76/5		
❑ AH5 Al Hrabosky 77/5		
❑ AH6 Al Hrabosky 78/20	25.00	7.50
❑ AH7 Al Hrabosky 79/40	20.00	6.00
❑ AH8 Al Hrabosky 80/61	20.00	6.00
❑ AH9 Al Hrabosky 81/38	15.00	4.50
❑ AH10 Al Hrabosky 82/62	15.00	4.50
❑ AH11 Al Hrabosky 89 Sr./20	20.00	6.00
❑ AK1 Al Kaline 54/1		
❑ AK2 Al Kaline 59/1		
❑ AK3 Al Kaline 60/1		
❑ AK4 Al Kaline 60 AS/1		
❑ AK5 Al Kaline 61/3		
❑ AK6 Al Kaline 62/3		
❑ AK7 Al Kaline 62 AS/2		
❑ AK8 Al Kaline 64/4		
❑ AK9 Al Kaline 66/1		
❑ AK10 Al Kaline 67/18	120.00	36.00
❑ AK11 Al Kaline 68/6		
❑ AK12 Al Kaline 69/7		
❑ AK13 Al Kaline 70/3		
❑ AK14 Al Kaline 71/7		
❑ AK15 Al Kaline 72/11		
❑ AK16 Al Kaline 73/25	80.00	24.00
❑ AK17 Al Kaline 74/11		
❑ AK18 Al Kaline 75 HL/1		
❑ AO1 Al Oliver 69/1		
❑ AO2 Al Oliver 74/2		
❑ AO3 Al Oliver 75/2		
❑ AO4 Al Oliver 76/2		
❑ AO5 Al Oliver 78/3		
❑ AO6 Al Oliver 79/42	20.00	6.00
❑ AO7 Al Oliver 80/6		
❑ AO8 Al Oliver 81/54	15.00	4.50
❑ AO9 Al Oliver 82/45	15.00	4.50
❑ AO10 Al Oliver 83/50	15.00	4.50

Card	Nm-Mt	Ex-Mt
❑ AO11 Al Oliver 84/51	15.00	4.50
❑ AO12 Al Oliver 85/46	15.00	4.50
❑ AO13 Al Oliver 86/44	15.00	4.50
❑ AT1 Alan Trammell 79/12		
❑ AT2 Alan Trammell 80/17	40.00	12.00
❑ AT3 Alan Trammell 81/26	25.00	7.50
❑ AT4 Alan Trammell 82/40	20.00	6.00
❑ AT5 Alan Trammell 83/21	30.00	9.00
❑ AT6 Alan Trammell 84/57	20.00	6.00
❑ AT7 Alan Trammell 85/39	20.00	6.00
❑ AT8 Alan Trammell 86/23	30.00	9.00
❑ AT9 Alan Trammell 87/15	40.00	12.00
❑ AV1 Andy Van Slyke 84/1		
❑ AV2 Andy Van Slyke 85/35	40.00	12.00
❑ AV3 Andy Van Slyke 86/37	30.00	9.00
❑ AV4 Andy Van Slyke 87/178	25.00	7.50
❑ AV5 Andy Van Slyke 87 TR/130	25.00	7.50
❑ BB1 Buddy Bell 73/1		
❑ BB2 Buddy Bell 75/1		
❑ BB3 Buddy Bell 76/1		
❑ BB4 Buddy Bell 78/3		
❑ BB5 Buddy Bell 79/135	15.00	4.50
❑ BB6 Buddy Bell 80/10		
❑ BB7 Buddy Bell 81/11		
❑ BB8 Buddy Bell 82/34	15.00	4.50
❑ BB9 Buddy Bell 83/83	10.00	3.00
❑ BB10 Buddy Bell 84/22	20.00	6.00
❑ BB11 Buddy Bell 85/13		
❑ BB12 Buddy Bell 86/32	15.00	4.50
❑ BBL1 Bert Blyleven 71/1		
❑ BBL2 Bert Blyleven 75/1		
❑ BBL3 Bert Blyleven 76/4		
❑ BBL4 Bert Blyleven 79/45	30.00	9.00
❑ BBL5 Bert Blyleven 80/12		
❑ BBL6 Bert Blyleven 81/29	25.00	7.50
❑ BBL7 Bert Blyleven 82 NNO/51	30.00	9.00
❑ BBL8 Bert Blyleven 83/41	20.00	6.00
❑ BBL9 Bert Blyleven 84/10		
❑ BBL10 Bert Blyleven 85/40	20.00	6.00
❑ BBL11 Bert Blyleven 86/62	20.00	6.00
❑ BBL12 Bert Blyleven 87/54	20.00	6.00
❑ BC1 Bert Campaneris 65/1		
❑ BC2 Bert Campaneris 72/5		
❑ BC3 Bert Campaneris 74/1		
❑ BC4 Bert Campaneris 78/2		
❑ BC5 Bert Campaneris 79/107	15.00	4.50
❑ BC6 Bert Campaneris 80/6		
❑ BC7 Bert Campaneris 84/28	15.00	4.50
❑ BD1 Bucky Dent 74/1		
❑ BD2 Bucky Dent 78/1		
❑ BD3 Bucky Dent 79/14		
❑ BD4 Bucky Dent 80/9		
❑ BD5 Bucky Dent 81/16	40.00	12.00
❑ BD6 Bucky Dent 82/49	20.00	6.00
❑ BD7 Bucky Dent 83/92	10.00	3.00
❑ BD8 Bucky Dent 84/63	15.00	4.50
❑ BD9 Bucky Dent 90 MG/10		
❑ BG1 Bob Grich 71/1		
❑ BG2 Bob Grich 79/29	20.00	6.00
❑ BG3 Bob Grich 80/70	15.00	4.50
❑ BG4 Bob Grich 81/14		
❑ BG5 Bob Grich 82/45	15.00	4.50
❑ BG6 Bob Grich 83/85	10.00	3.00
❑ BG7 Bob Grich 84/57	15.00	4.50
❑ BG8 Bob Grich 85/36	15.00	4.50
❑ BG9 Bob Grich 86/13		
❑ BH1 Bob Horner 79/1		
❑ BH2 Bob Horner 80/14		
❑ BH3 Bob Horner 81/11		
❑ BH4 Bob Horner 82/21	30.00	9.00
❑ BH5 Bob Horner 83/69	15.00	4.50
❑ BH6 Bob Horner 84/63	20.00	6.00
❑ BH7 Bob Horner 85/15	40.00	12.00
❑ BH8 Bob Horner 86/118	15.00	4.50
❑ BH9 Bob Horner 87/38	20.00	6.00
❑ BJ1 Bo Jackson 86 TR/1		
❑ BJ2 Bo Jackson 87/100	60.00	18.00
❑ BJA1 Brook Jacoby 85/1		
❑ BJA2 Brook Jacoby 86/133	10.00	3.00
❑ BJA3 Brook Jacoby 87/191	10.00	3.00
❑ BJA4 Brook Jacoby 88/9		
❑ BM1 Bill Madlock 74/1		
❑ BM2 Bill Madlock 75/7		
❑ BM3 Bill Madlock 76/4		
❑ BM4 Bill Madlock 79/6		
❑ BM5 Bill Madlock 80/11		

❑ BM6 Bill Madlock 81/11 ....
❑ BM7 Bill Madlock 82/26 .... 15.00 4.50
❑ BM8 Bill Madlock 83/55 .... 15.00 4.50
❑ BM9 Bill Madlock 84/69 .... 10.00 3.00
❑ BM10 Bill Madlock 85/60 .. 15.00 4.50
❑ BM11 Bill Madlock 86/63 .. 15.00 4.50
❑ BM12 Bill Madlock 87/42 .. 15.00 4.50
❑ BP1 Boog Powell 62/1 ....
❑ BP2 Boog Powell 64/4 ....
❑ BP3 Boog Powell 65/7 ....
❑ BP4 Boog Powell 66/4 ....
❑ BP5 Boog Powell 67/3 ....
❑ BP6 Boog Powell 69/5 ....
❑ BP7 Boog Powell 70/6 ....
❑ BP8 Boog Powell 72/13 ....
❑ BP9 Boog Powell 73/17 ...... 40.00 12.00
❑ BP10 Boog Powell 74/7 ....
❑ BP11 Boog Powell 75/19 .... 40.00 12.00
❑ BP12 Boog Powell 76/6 ....
❑ BP13 Boog Powell 77/15 .... 40.00 12.00
❑ BR1 Brooks Robinson 57/1 ......
❑ BR2 Brooks Robinson 59/1 ......
❑ BR3 Brooks Robinson 60/2 ......
❑ BR4 Brooks Robinson 61/1 ......
❑ BR5 Brooks Robinson 69/6 ......
❑ BR6 Brooks Robinson 69 AS/2
❑ BR7 Brooks Robinson 70/8 ......
❑ BR8 Brooks Robinson 70 AS/3
❑ BR9 Brooks Robinson 72/6 ......
❑ BR10 Brooks Robinson 73/14 ..
❑ BR11 Brooks Robinson 74/20 60.00 18.00
❑ BR12 Brooks Robinson 75/10 ..
❑ BR13 Brooks Robinson 76/17 60.00 18.00
❑ BR14 Brooks Robinson 77/13 ..
❑ BS1 Bret Saberhagen 85/1 ....
❑ BS2 Bret Saberhagen 86/23 30.00 9.00
❑ BS3 Bret Saberhagen 87/230 15.00 4.50
❑ BSU1 Bruce Sutter 77/1 ....
❑ BSU2 Bruce Sutter 78/5 ....
❑ BSU3 Bruce Sutter 79/8 ....
❑ BSU4 Bruce Sutter 80/9 ....
❑ BSU5 Bruce Sutter 81/11 ....
❑ BSU6 Bruce Sutter 82/111 .. 15.00 4.50
❑ BSU7 Bruce Sutter 83/45 .... 20.00 6.00
❑ BSU8 Bruce Sutter 84/24 .... 30.00 9.00
❑ BSU9 Bruce Sutter 85/19 .... 40.00 12.00
❑ BSU10 Bruce Sutter 86/78 .. 15.00 4.50
❑ BSU11 Bruce Sutter 87/36 .. 20.00 6.00
❑ BU1 Bill Buckner 70/1 ....
❑ BU2 Bill Buckner 74/5 ....
❑ BU3 Bill Buckner 75/1 ....
❑ BU4 Bill Buckner 76/1 ....
❑ BU5 Bill Buckner 78/1 ....
❑ BU6 Bill Buckner 79/11 ....
❑ BU7 Bill Buckner 80/8 ....
❑ BU8 Bill Buckner 81/39 ...... 20.00 6.00
❑ BU9 Bill Buckner 82/38 ...... 20.00 6.00
❑ BU10 Bill Buckner 83/47 .... 20.00 6.00
❑ BU11 Bill Buckner 84/31 .... 25.00 7.50
❑ BU12 Bill Buckner 84 TR/24 30.00 9.00
❑ BU13 Bill Buckner 85/80 .... 15.00 4.50
❑ BU14 Bill Buckner 86/63 .... 20.00 6.00
❑ BW1 Bob Watson 69/1 ....
❑ BW2 Bob Watson 74/1 ....
❑ BW3 Bob Watson 79/77 ...... 15.00 4.50
❑ BW4 Bob Watson 80/8 ....
❑ BW5 Bob Watson 81/16 ...... 25.00 7.50
❑ BW6 Bob Watson 82/23 ...... 20.00 6.00
❑ BW7 Bob Watson 83/93 ...... 10.00 3.00
❑ BW8 Bob Watson 84/64 ...... 15.00 4.50
❑ BW9 Bob Watson 85/68 ...... 10.00 3.00
❑ CF1 Cecil Fielder 86/1 ....
❑ CF2 Cecil Fielder 87/208 .... 25.00 7.50
❑ CF3 Cecil Fielder 88/26 ..... 40.00 12.00
❑ CF4 Cecil Fielder 89/16 ...... 60.00 18.00
❑ CFI1 Carlton Fisk 72/1 ....
❑ CFI2 Carlton Fisk 78/3 ....
❑ CFI3 Carlton Fisk 79/24 ...... 60.00 18.00
❑ CFI4 Carlton Fisk 80/32 ...... 50.00 15.00
❑ CFI5 Carlton Fisk 81/14 ....
❑ CFI6 Carlton Fisk 82/30 ...... 40.00 12.00
❑ CG1 Cesar Geronimo 71/1 ....
❑ CG2 Cesar Geronimo 74/1 ....
❑ CG3 Cesar Geronimo 79/28 20.00 6.00
❑ CG4 Cesar Geronimo 80/11 ......
❑ CG5 Cesar Geronimo 81/21 20.00 6.00
❑ CG6 Cesar Geronimo 82/52 15.00 4.50
❑ CG7 Cesar Geronimo 83/67 10.00 3.00
❑ CG8 Cesar Geronimo 84/70 10.00 3.00
❑ CH1 Charlie Hough 72/1 ....
❑ CH2 Charlie Hough 83/19 .. 25.00 7.50
❑ CH3 Charlie Hough 84/50 .. 15.00 4.50
❑ CH4 Charlie Hough 85/57 .. 15.00 4.50
❑ CH5 Charlie Hough 86/66 .. 10.00 3.00
❑ CH6 Charlie Hough 87/46 .. 15.00 4.50
❑ CH7 Charlie Hough 88/19 .. 25.00 7.50
❑ CH8 Charlie Hough 91 TR/70 10.00 3.00
❑ CH9 Charlie Hough 92/25 .. 20.00 6.00
❑ CH10 Charlie Hough 94/8 ....
❑ CL1 Carney Lansford 79/1 ....
❑ CL2 Carney Lansford 80/12 ....
❑ CL3 Carney Lansford 81/184 10.00 3.00
❑ CL4 Carney Lansford 82/6 ....
❑ CL5 Carney Lansford 83/40 15.00 4.50
❑ CL6 Carney Lansford 85/35 15.00 4.50
❑ CL7 Carney Lansford 86/76 10.00 3.00
❑ CLE1 Chet Lemon 76/1 ....
❑ CLE2 Chet Lemon 78/3 ....
❑ CLE3 Chet Lemon 79/24 .... 25.00 7.50
❑ CLE4 Chet Lemon 80/16 .... 25.00 7.50
❑ CLE5 Chet Lemon 81/12 ....
❑ CLE6 Chet Lemon 82/23 .... 20.00 6.00
❑ CLE7 Chet Lemon 83/35 .... 15.00 4.50
❑ CLE8 Chet Lemon 84/42 .... 15.00 4.50
❑ CLE9 Chet Lemon 85/32 .... 15.00 4.50
❑ CLE10 Chet Lemon 86/136 10.00 3.00
❑ CLE11 Chet Lemon 87/27 .. 15.00 4.50
❑ CR1 Cal Ripken 82/1 ....
❑ CR2 Cal Ripken 84/10 ....
❑ CR3 Cal Ripken 85/15 ....
❑ CR4 Cal Ripken 86/74 ...... 120.00 36.00
❑ CS1 Cory Snyder 85 OLY/1 ......
❑ CS2 Cory Snyder 87/291 .... 10.00 3.00
❑ CS3 Cory Snyder 91/39 ...... 15.00 4.50
❑ CS4 Cory Snyder 91 TR/8 ....
❑ CS5 Cory Snyder 93/8 ....
❑ CS6 Cory Snyder 93 Gold/8.......
❑ CS7 Cory Snyder 94/10 ....
❑ CY1 Carl Yastrzemski 60/1 ......
❑ CY2 Carl Yastrzemski 78/3 ......
❑ CY3 Carl Yastrzemski 79/2 ......
❑ CY4 Carl Yastrzemski 80/60 100.00 30.00
❑ CY5 Carl Yastrzemski 81/35 120.00 36.00
❑ DC1 Dave Concepcion 71/1......
❑ DC2 Dave Concepcion 75/2......
❑ DC3 Dave Concepcion 76/1......
❑ DC4 Dave Concepcion 78/3......
❑ DC5 Dave Concepcion 79/3......
❑ DC6 Dave Concepcion 80/21 40.00 12.00
❑ DC7 Dave Concepcion 81/8......
❑ DC8 Dave Concepcion 82/43 20.00 6.00
❑ DC9 Dave Concepcion 83/34 25.00 7.50
❑ DC10 Dave Concepcion 84/24 30.00 9.00
❑ DC11 Dave Concepcion 85/41 20.00 6.00
❑ DC12 Dave Concepcion 86/69 15.00 4.50
❑ DD1 Darren Daulton 86/1.........
❑ DD2 Darren Daulton 87/269 10.00 3.00
❑ DD3 Darren Daulton 90/8.........
❑ DD4 Darren Daulton 92/32.. 15.00 4.50
❑ DD5 Darren Daulton 94/17.. 25.00 7.50
❑ DD6 Darren Daulton 96/22.. 20.00 6.00
❑ DDE1 Doug DeCinces 75/1 ......
❑ DDE2 Doug DeCinces 79/38 20.00 6.00
❑ DDE3 Doug DeCinces 80/24 25.00 7.50
❑ DDE4 Doug DeCinces 81/24 20.00 6.00
❑ DDE5 Doug DeCinces 82/42 15.00 4.50
❑ DDE6 Doug DeCinces 83/75 10.00 3.00
❑ DDE7 Doug DeCinces 84/19 25.00 7.50
❑ DDE8 Doug DeCinces 85/54 15.00 4.50
❑ DDE9 Doug DeCinces 86/74 10.00 3.00
❑ DE1 Dennis Eckersley 76/1 ......
❑ DE2 Dennis Eckersley 78/10 ......
❑ DE3 Dennis Eckersley 79/44 50.00 15.00
❑ DE4 Dennis Eckersley 80/40 50.00 15.00
❑ DE5 Dennis Eckersley 81/9 ......
❑ DEV1 Darrell Evans 70/1 ....
❑ DEV2 Darrell Evans 74/5 ....
❑ DEV3 Darrell Evans 75/3 ....
❑ DEV4 Darrell Evans 78/2 ....
❑ DEV5 Darrell Evans 79/19 .. 25.00 7.50
❑ DEV6 Darrell Evans 80/5 ....
❑ DEV7 Darrell Evans 81/15 .. 25.00 7.50
❑ DEV8 Darrell Evans 82/25 .. 20.00 6.00
❑ DEV9 Darrell Evans 83/63 .. 15.00 4.50
❑ DEV10 Darrell Evans 84/81 10.00 3.00
❑ DEV11 Darrell Evans 85/48 15.00 4.50
❑ DEV12 Darrell Evans 86/82 10.00 3.00
❑ DG1 Dwight Gooden 85/1 ....
❑ DG2 Dwight Gooden 86/16 60.00 18.00
❑ DG3 Dwight Gooden 87/52 30.00 9.00
❑ DG4 Dwight Gooden 89/19 60.00 18.00
❑ DJ1 David Justice 90 DB/69 15.00 4.50
❑ DJ2 David Justice 90 TR/1 ....
❑ DJ3 David Justice 93/32 .... 25.00 7.50
❑ DK1 Dave Kingman 72/1 ....
❑ DK2 Dave Kingman 79/9 ....
❑ DK3 Dave Kingman 80/8 ....
❑ DK4 Dave Kingman 81/25 .. 30.00 9.00
❑ DK5 Dave Kingman 82/5 ....
❑ DK6 Dave Kingman 83/32 .. 25.00 7.50
❑ DK7 Dave Kingman 86/25 .. 30.00 9.00
❑ DL1 Davey Lopes 73/1 ....
❑ DL2 Davey Lopes 76/1 ....
❑ DL3 Davey Lopes 78/1 ....
❑ DL4 Davey Lopes 79/71 ...... 15.00 4.50
❑ DL5 Davey Lopes 80/19 ...... 25.00 7.50
❑ DL6 Davey Lopes 81/12 ....
❑ DL7 Davey Lopes 82/17 ...... 25.00 7.50
❑ DL8 Davey Lopes 83/65 ...... 15.00 4.50
❑ DL9 Davey Lopes 84/15 ...... 25.00 7.50
❑ DL10 Davey Lopes 85/24 .... 20.00 6.00
❑ DL11 Davey Lopes 86/40 .... 15.00 4.50
❑ DL12 Davey Lopes 01 MG/67 10.00 3.00
❑ DL13 Davey Lopes 02 MG/19 25.00 7.50
❑ DM1 Don Mattingly 84/1 ....
❑ DM2 Don Mattingly 85/16 ....
❑ DM3 Don Mattingly 87/84 100.00 30.00
❑ DMU1 Dale Murphy 77/1 ....
❑ DMU2 Dale Murphy 79/38 .. 50.00 15.00
❑ DMU3 Dale Murphy 80/11 ....
❑ DMU4 Dale Murphy 82/1 ....
❑ DMU5 Dale Murphy 83/10 ....
❑ DMU6 Dale Murphy 84/29 .. 40.00 12.00
❑ DMU7 Dale Murphy 85/18 .. 60.00 18.00
❑ DMU8 Dale Murphy 86/25 .. 50.00 15.00
❑ DMU9 Dale Murphy 87/91 .. 25.00 7.50
❑ DMU10 Dale Murphy 88/11 ....
❑ DMU11 Dale Murphy 89/14 ....
❑ DP1 Dave Parker 74/1 ....
❑ DP2 Dave Parker 75/2 ....
❑ DP3 Dave Parker 79/6 ....
❑ DP4 Dave Parker 80/9 ....
❑ DP5 Dave Parker 81/19 ...... 60.00 18.00
❑ DP6 Dave Parker 82/73 ...... 25.00 7.50
❑ DP7 Dave Parker 83/30 ...... 40.00 12.00
❑ DP8 Dave Parker 84/14 ....
❑ DP9 Dave Parker 85/45 ...... 30.00 9.00
❑ DP10 Dave Parker 86/29 .... 40.00 12.00
❑ DP11 Dave Parker 87/12 ....
❑ DP12 Dave Parker 88/11 ....
❑ DS1 Duke Snider 52/1 ....
❑ DS2 Duke Snider 58/3 ....
❑ DS3 Duke Snider 59/4 ....
❑ DS4 Duke Snider 60/2 ....
❑ DS5 Duke Snider 61/13 ....
❑ DS6 Duke Snider 62/4 ....
❑ DS7 Duke Snider 63/4 ....
❑ DS8 Duke Snider 64/18 .... 120.00 36.00
❑ DSE1 Dave Stieb 80/1 ....
❑ DSE2 Dave Stieb 81/21 ...... 50.00 15.00
❑ DSE3 Dave Stieb 82/34 ...... 40.00 12.00
❑ DSE4 Dave Stieb 83/70 ...... 25.00 7.50
❑ DSE5 Dave Stieb 84/20 ...... 50.00 15.00
❑ DSE6 Dave Stieb 85/55 ...... 30.00 9.00
❑ DSE7 Dave Stieb 86/69 ...... 25.00 7.50
❑ DSE8 Dave Stieb 87/75 ...... 25.00 7.50
❑ DSE9 Dave Stieb 88/11 ....
❑ DSR1 Darryl Strawberry 84/1 ....
❑ DSR2 Darryl Strawberry 85/32 25.00 7.50
❑ DSR3 Darryl Strawberry 86/24 30.00 9.00
❑ DSR4 Darryl Strawberry 87/183 15.00 4.50
❑ DSR5 Darryl Strawberry 87 AS/110 15.00 4.50
❑ DSW1 Dave Stewart 82/1 ....
❑ DSW2 Dave Stewart 83/41 .. 15.00 4.50
❑ DSW3 Dave Stewart 84/60 .. 15.00 4.50
❑ DSW4 Dave Stewart 85/24 .. 20.00 6.00
❑ DSW5 Dave Stewart 86/53 .. 15.00 4.50
❑ DSW6 Dave Stewart 87/171 10.00 3.00
❑ EB1 Ernie Banks 54/1 ....
❑ EB2 Ernie Banks 58 AS/1 ....
❑ EB3 Ernie Banks 59/1 ....
❑ EB4 Ernie Banks 59 AS/1 ....
❑ EB5 Ernie Banks 60/2 ....
❑ EB6 Ernie Banks 61/2 ....
❑ EB7 Ernie Banks 61 MVP/7 ......
❑ EB8 Ernie Banks 62/3 ....
❑ EB9 Ernie Banks 64/5 ....

- ❑ EB10 Ernie Banks 66/7
- ❑ EB11 Ernie Banks 67/4
- ❑ EB12 Ernie Banks 68/7
- ❑ EB13 Ernie Banks 69/7
- ❑ EB14 Ernie Banks 70/2
- ❑ ED1 Eric Davis 85/1
- ❑ ED2 Eric Davis 86/13
- ❑ ED3 Eric Davis 87/336 15.00 4.50
- ❑ EW1 Earl Weaver 69 MG/1
- ❑ EW2 Earl Weaver 72 MG/1
- ❑ EW3 Earl Weaver 74 MG/1
- ❑ EW4 Earl Weaver 78 MG/52 20.00 6.00
- ❑ EW5 Earl Weaver 83 MG/38 15.00 4.50
- ❑ EW6 Earl Weaver 85 TR MG/12 .00
- ❑ EW7 Earl Weaver 86 MG/107 10.00 3.00
- ❑ EW8 Earl Weaver 87 MG/175 10.00 3.00
- ❑ FJ1 Fergie Jenkins 66/
- ❑ FJ2 Fergie Jenkins 68/2
- ❑ FJ3 Fergie Jenkins 70/1
- ❑ FJ4 Fergie Jenkins 71/1
- ❑ FJ5 Fergie Jenkins 72/4
- ❑ FJ6 Fergie Jenkins 76/10
- ❑ FJ7 Fergie Jenkins 77/11
- ❑ FJ8 Fergie Jenkins 78/17 40.00 12.00
- ❑ FJ9 Fergie Jenkins 79/9
- ❑ FJ10 Fergie Jenkins 80/37 30.00 9.00
- ❑ FJ11 Fergie Jenkins 81/32 25.00 7.50
- ❑ FJ12 Fergie Jenkins 82/65 20.00 6.00
- ❑ FJ13 Fergie Jenkins 83/22 30.00 9.00
- ❑ FJ14 Fergie Jenkins 84/42 20.00 6.00
- ❑ FR1 Frank Robinson 57/1
- ❑ FR2 Frank Robinson 63/1
- ❑ FR3 Frank Robinson 65/1
- ❑ FR4 Frank Robinson 69/4
- ❑ FR5 Frank Robinson 71/2
- ❑ FR6 Frank Robinson 72/16 60.00 18.00
- ❑ FR7 Frank Robinson 73/4
- ❑ FR8 Frank Robinson 74/4
- ❑ FR9 Frank Robinson 75/1
- ❑ FR10 Frank Robinson 83 MG/13
- ❑ FR11 Frank Robinson 84 MG/3
- ❑ FV1 Frank Viola 83/1
- ❑ FV2 Frank Viola 84/1
- ❑ FV3 Frank Viola 85/25 30.00 9.00
- ❑ FV4 Frank Viola 86/99 15.00 4.50
- ❑ FV5 Frank Viola 87/209 15.00 4.50
- ❑ FV6 Frank Viola 88/10
- ❑ GB1 George Bell 82/1
- ❑ GB2 George Bell 84/67 10.00 3.00
- ❑ GB3 George Bell 85/32 15.00 4.50
- ❑ GB4 George Bell 86/46 15.00 4.50
- ❑ GB5 George Bell 87/204 10.00 3.00
- ❑ GBR1 George Brett 75/1
- ❑ GBR2 George Brett 79/16
- ❑ GBR3 George Brett 80/9
- ❑ GBR4 George Brett 81/19
- ❑ GBR5 George Brett 82/6
- ❑ GC1 Gary Carter 75/1
- ❑ GC2 Gary Carter 78/9
- ❑ GC3 Gary Carter 79/21 40.00 12.00
- ❑ GC4 Gary Carter 80/24 40.00 12.00
- ❑ GC5 Gary Carter 81/22 30.00 9.00
- ❑ GC6 Gary Carter 82/12
- ❑ GC7 Gary Carter 83/2
- ❑ GC8 Gary Carter 84/9
- ❑ GF1 George Foster 71/1
- ❑ GF2 George Foster 74/5
- ❑ GF3 George Foster 75/3
- ❑ GF4 George Foster 76/1
- ❑ GF5 George Foster 78/3
- ❑ GF6 George Foster 79/20 25.00 7.50
- ❑ GF7 George Foster 80/7
- ❑ GF8 George Foster 81/10
- ❑ GF9 George Foster 82/14
- ❑ GF10 George Foster 83/39 15.00 4.50
- ❑ GF11 George Foster 84/112 10.00 3.00
- ❑ GF12 George Foster 85/76 10.00 3.00
- ❑ GF13 George Foster 86/64 15.00 4.50
- ❑ GL1 Greg Luzinski 71/1
- ❑ GL2 Greg Luzinski 72/5
- ❑ GL3 Greg Luzinski 75/6
- ❑ GL4 Greg Luzinski 76/1
- ❑ GL5 Greg Luzinski 78/5
- ❑ GL6 Greg Luzinski 79/14
- ❑ GL7 Greg Luzinski 80/21 40.00 12.00
- ❑ GL8 Greg Luzinski 81/11
- ❑ GL9 Greg Luzinski 82/34 25.00 7.50
- ❑ GL10 Greg Luzinski 83/75 15.00 4.50
- ❑ GL11 Greg Luzinski 84/85 15.00 4.50
- ❑ GL12 Greg Luzinski 85/92 15.00 4.50
- ❑ GM1 Gary Matthews Sr. 73/1
- ❑ GM2 Gary Matthews Sr. 82/10
- ❑ GM3 Gary Matthews Sr. 83/20 20.00 6.00
- ❑ GM4 Gary Matthews Sr. 84/43 15.00 4.50
- ❑ GM5 Gary Matthews Sr. 85/39 15.00 4.50
- ❑ GM6 Gary Matthews Sr. 86/38 15.00 4.50
- ❑ GM7 Gary Matthews Sr. 87/82 10.00 3.00
- ❑ GM8 Gary Matthews Sr. 88/30 15.00 4.50
- ❑ HA1 Hank Aaron 54/1
- ❑ HA2 Hank Aaron 58 AS/2
- ❑ HA3 Hank Aaron 59/1
- ❑ HA4 Hank Aaron 60 AS/1
- ❑ HA5 Hank Aaron 61/1
- ❑ HA6 Hank Aaron 61 MVP/1
- ❑ HA7 Hank Aaron 62 AS/1
- ❑ HA8 Hank Aaron 65/1
- ❑ HA9 Hank Aaron 68/1
- ❑ HA10 Hank Aaron 69/1
- ❑ HA11 Hank Aaron 70/6
- ❑ HA12 Hank Aaron 70 AS/3
- ❑ HA13 Hank Aaron 71/3
- ❑ HA14 Hank Aaron 72/2
- ❑ HA15 Hank Aaron 73/8
- ❑ HA16 Hank Aaron 75/5
- ❑ HA17 Hank Aaron 75 HL/1
- ❑ HA18 Hank Aaron 76/12
- ❑ HB1 Harold Baines 81/1
- ❑ HB2 Harold Baines 82/31 25.00 7.50
- ❑ HB3 Harold Baines 83/19 40.00 12.00
- ❑ HB4 Harold Baines 84/5
- ❑ HB5 Harold Baines 85/97 15.00 4.50
- ❑ HB6 Harold Baines 86/93 15.00 4.50
- ❑ HB7 Harold Baines 87/115 15.00 4.50
- ❑ HK1 Harmon Killebrew 55/1
- ❑ HK2 Harmon Killebrew 60/1
- ❑ HK3 Harmon Killebrew 61/1
- ❑ HK4 Harmon Killebrew 62/2
- ❑ HK5 Harmon Killebrew 64/2
- ❑ HK6 Harmon Killebrew 66/2
- ❑ HK7 Harmon Killebrew 68/2
- ❑ HK8 Harmon Killebrew 68 AS/2
- ❑ HK9 Harmon Killebrew 69/5
- ❑ HK10 Harmon Killebrew 70/3
- ❑ HK11 Harmon Killebrew 71/3
- ❑ HK12 Harmon Killebrew 72/12
- ❑ HK13 Harmon Killebrew 73/4
- ❑ HK14 Harmon Killebrew 74/6
- ❑ HK15 Harmon Killebrew 75/9
- ❑ HR1 Harold Reynolds 86/1
- ❑ HR2 Harold Reynolds 87/255 15.00 4.50
- ❑ JA1 Jim Abbott 88 TR/339 25.00 7.50
- ❑ JA2 Jim Abbott 89/1
- ❑ JA3 Jim Abbott 90 DB/50 30.00 9.00
- ❑ JB1 Jesse Barfield 82/1
- ❑ JB2 Jesse Barfield 83/45 15.00 4.50
- ❑ JB3 Jesse Barfield 84/12
- ❑ JB4 Jesse Barfield 85/60 15.00 4.50
- ❑ JB5 Jesse Barfield 86/37 15.00 4.50
- ❑ JB6 Jesse Barfield 87/180 10.00 3.00
- ❑ JB7 Jesse Barfield 88/10
- ❑ JBE1 Johnny Bench 68/1
- ❑ JBE2 Johnny Bench 79/14
- ❑ JBE3 Johnny Bench 80/10
- ❑ JBE4 Johnny Bench 81/8
- ❑ JBE5 Johnny Bench 82/16 80.00 24.00
- ❑ JBE6 Johnny Bench 83/2
- ❑ JC1 John Candelaria 76/1
- ❑ JC2 John Candelaria 79/77 25.00 7.50
- ❑ JC3 John Candelaria 80/8
- ❑ JC4 John Candelaria 81/19 40.00 12.00
- ❑ JC5 John Candelaria 82/42 20.00 6.00
- ❑ JC6 John Candelaria 83/77 15.00 4.50
- ❑ JC7 John Candelaria 84/18 40.00 12.00
- ❑ JC8 John Candelaria 85/61 20.00 6.00
- ❑ JC9 John Candelaria 86/36 20.00 6.00
- ❑ JC10 John Candelaria 87/13
- ❑ JCA1 Jose Canseco 86 TR/1
- ❑ JCA2 Jose Canseco 87/99 50.00 15.00
- ❑ JCR1 Joe Carter 85/1
- ❑ JCR2 Joe Carter 86/24 50.00 15.00
- ❑ JCR3 Joe Carter 87/23 50.00 15.00
- ❑ JCR4 Joe Carter 90/2
- ❑ JCU1 Jose Cruz Sr. 72/1
- ❑ JCU2 Jose Cruz Sr. 74/2
- ❑ JCU3 Jose Cruz Sr. 76/1
- ❑ JCU4 Jose Cruz Sr. 78/5
- ❑ JCU5 Jose Cruz Sr. 79/7
- ❑ JCU6 Jose Cruz Sr. 80/14
- ❑ JCU7 Jose Cruz Sr. 81/14
- ❑ JCU8 Jose Cruz Sr. 82/28 15.00 4.50
- ❑ JCU9 Jose Cruz Sr. 83/102 10.00 3.00
- ❑ JCU10 Jose Cruz Sr. 84/67 10.00 3.00
- ❑ JCU11 Jose Cruz Sr. 85/68 10.00 3.00
- ❑ JCU12 Jose Cruz Sr. 86/31 15.00 4.50
- ❑ JK1 Jimmy Key 85/1
- ❑ JK2 Jimmy Key 86/21 30.00 9.00
- ❑ JK3 Jimmy Key 87/263 15.00 4.50
- ❑ JK4 Jimmy Key 88/15 40.00 12.00
- ❑ JK5 Jimmy Key 92/37 20.00 6.00
- ❑ JK6 Jimmy Key 94/11
- ❑ JKR1 John Kruk 86 TR/1
- ❑ JKR2 John Kruk 87/214 25.00 7.50
- ❑ JKR3 John Kruk 92/22 50.00 15.00
- ❑ JKR4 John Kruk 93/13
- ❑ JL1 Jim Leyritz 90 TR/1
- ❑ JL2 Jim Leyritz 91/38 15.00 4.50
- ❑ JL3 Jim Leyritz 93/49 15.00 4.50
- ❑ JL4 Jim Leyritz 94/16 25.00 7.50
- ❑ JL5 Jim Leyritz 95/14
- ❑ JL6 Jim Leyritz 97/62 15.00 4.50
- ❑ JL7 Jim Leyritz 98/20 20.00 6.00
- ❑ JL8 Jim Leyritz 99/124 10.00 3.00
- ❑ JL9 Jim Leyritz 00/40 15.00 4.50
- ❑ JM1 Jack McDowell 88 TR/1
- ❑ JM2 Jack McDowell 89/36 15.00 4.50
- ❑ JM3 Jack McDowell 90 TR/61 15.00 4.50
- ❑ JM4 Jack McDowell 91/33 15.00 4.50
- ❑ JM5 Jack McDowell 92/38 15.00 4.50
- ❑ JM6 Jack McDowell 93/27 15.00 4.50
- ❑ JM7 Jack McDowell 94/3
- ❑ JM8 Jack McDowell 95/9
- ❑ JM9 Jack McDowell 96/15 25.00 7.50
- ❑ JM10 Jack McDowell 97/27 15.00 4.50
- ❑ JMO1 Joe Morgan 65/1
- ❑ JMO2 Joe Morgan 74/2
- ❑ JMO3 Joe Morgan 75/1
- ❑ JMO4 Joe Morgan 76/5
- ❑ JMO5 Joe Morgan 77/6
- ❑ JMO6 Joe Morgan 78/3
- ❑ JMO7 Joe Morgan 79/4
- ❑ JMO8 Joe Morgan 80/12
- ❑ JMO9 Joe Morgan 81/32 25.00 7.50
- ❑ JMO10 Joe Morgan 82/18 40.00 12.00
- ❑ JMO11 Joe Morgan 83/49 20.00 6.00
- ❑ JMO12 Joe Morgan 83 TR/4
- ❑ JMO13 Joe Morgan 84/73 15.00 4.50
- ❑ JMO14 Joe Morgan 85/40 20.00 6.00
- ❑ JP1 Jim Palmer 66/1
- ❑ JP2 Jim Palmer 79/4
- ❑ JP3 Jim Palmer 80/33 30.00 9.00
- ❑ JP4 Jim Palmer 81/23 30.00 9.00
- ❑ JP5 Jim Palmer 82/24 30.00 9.00
- ❑ JP6 Jim Palmer 83/7
- ❑ JP7 Jim Palmer 84/9
- ❑ JR1 Jim Rice 75/1
- ❑ JR2 Jim Rice 76/2
- ❑ JR3 Jim Rice 77/4
- ❑ JR4 Jim Rice 78/3
- ❑ JR5 Jim Rice 79/6
- ❑ JR6 Jim Rice 80/9
- ❑ JR7 Jim Rice 81/123 15.00 4.50
- ❑ JR8 Jim Rice 82/24 30.00 9.00
- ❑ JR9 Jim Rice 83/71 15.00 4.50
- ❑ JR10 Jim Rice 84/12
- ❑ JRU1 Joe Rudi 69/1
- ❑ JRU2 Joe Rudi 72/2
- ❑ JRU3 Joe Rudi 73/9
- ❑ JRU4 Joe Rudi 74/6
- ❑ JRU5 Joe Rudi 75/7
- ❑ JRU6 Joe Rudi 76/4
- ❑ JRU7 Joe Rudi 77/7
- ❑ JRU8 Joe Rudi 78/14
- ❑ JRU9 Joe Rudi 79/24 25.00 7.50
- ❑ JRU10 Joe Rudi 80/45 20.00 6.00
- ❑ JRU11 Joe Rudi 82/26 15.00 4.50
- ❑ JRU12 Joe Rudi 83/75 10.00 3.00
- ❑ KB1 Kevin Bass 79/1
- ❑ KB2 Kevin Bass 84/71 10.00 3.00
- ❑ KB3 Kevin Bass 85/30 15.00 4.50
- ❑ KB4 Kevin Bass 86/44 15.00 4.50
- ❑ KB5 Kevin Bass 87/74 10.00 3.00

Card	Player / Year / Print Run		
KB6	Kevin Bass 90 TR/35	15.00	4.50
KG1	Ken Griffey Sr. 74/1		
KG2	Ken Griffey Sr. 75/2		
KG3	Ken Griffey Sr. 76/2		
KG4	Ken Griffey Sr. 79/3		
KG5	Ken Griffey Sr. 80/15	40.00	12.00
KG6	Ken Griffey Sr. 81/11		
KG7	Ken Griffey Sr. 82/18	40.00	12.00
KG8	Ken Griffey Sr. 83/70	15.00	4.50
KG9	Ken Griffey Sr. 84/64	20.00	6.00
KG10	Ken Griffey Sr. 85/32	25.00	7.50
KG11	Ken Griffey Sr. 86 TR/32	25.00	7.50
KGI1	Kirk Gibson 81/1		
KGI2	Kirk Gibson 82/35	25.00	7.50
KGI3	Kirk Gibson 83/35	25.00	7.50
KGI4	Kirk Gibson 84/5		
KGI5	Kirk Gibson 85/44	20.00	6.00
KGI6	Kirk Gibson 86/44	20.00	6.00
KGI7	Kirk Gibson 87/65	20.00	6.00
KGI8	Kirk Gibson 89/14		
KGI9	Kirk Gibson 90/12		
KGU1	Kelly Gruber 87/1		
KGU2	Kelly Gruber 88/77	10.00	3.00
KGU3	Kelly Gruber 89/44	15.00	4.50
KGU4	Kelly Gruber 90/86	10.00	3.00
KGU5	Kelly Gruber 91/52	15.00	4.50
KGU6	Kelly Gruber 92/55	15.00	4.50
KGU7	Kelly Gruber 93/26	15.00	4.50
KGU8	Kelly Gruber 93 Gold/9		
KH1	Keith Hernandez 75/1		
KH2	Keith Hernandez 79/8		
KH3	Keith Hernandez 80/38	30.00	9.00
KH4	Keith Hernandez 81/19	40.00	12.00
KH5	Keith Hernandez 82/156	15.00	4.50
KH6	Keith Hernandez 83/17	40.00	12.00
KH7	Keith Hernandez 84/4		
KH8	Keith Hernandez 86/7		
KS1	Kevin Seitzer 87 TR/1		
KS2	Kevin Seitzer 88/88	10.00	3.00
KS3	Kevin Seitzer 89/39	15.00	4.50
KS4	Kevin Seitzer 90/18	25.00	7.50
KS5	Kevin Seitzer 91/39	15.00	4.50
KS6	Kevin Seitzer 92/49	15.00	4.50
KS7	Kevin Seitzer 92 Gold/2		
KS8	Kevin Seitzer 92 TR/9		
KS9	Kevin Seitzer 93/38	15.00	4.50
KS10	Kevin Seitzer 94/22	20.00	6.00
KS11	Kevin Seitzer 95/16	25.00	7.50
KS12	Kevin Seitzer 96/9		
KS13	Kevin Seitzer 97/24	20.00	6.00
KT1	Kent Tekulve 76/1		
KT2	Kent Tekulve 78/2		
KT3	Kent Tekulve 79/14		
KT4	Kent Tekulve 80/6		
KT5	Kent Tekulve 81/17	40.00	12.00
KT6	Kent Tekulve 82/36	20.00	6.00
KT7	Kent Tekulve 83/52	20.00	6.00
KT8	Kent Tekulve 84/71	15.00	4.50
KT9	Kent Tekulve 85/43	20.00	6.00
KT10	Kent Tekulve 86/57	20.00	6.00
KT11	Kent Tekulve 87/32	25.00	7.50
KT12	Kent Tekulve 88/20	30.00	9.00
LA1	Luis Aparicio 56/1		
LA2	Luis Aparicio 60/1		
LA3	Luis Aparicio 61/3		
LA4	Luis Aparicio 62/2		
LA5	Luis Aparicio 63/3		
LA6	Luis Aparicio 66/3		
LA7	Luis Aparicio 67/2		
LA8	Luis Aparicio 68/14		
LA9	Luis Aparicio 69/49	25.00	7.50
LA10	Luis Aparicio 70/2		
LA11	Luis Aparicio 71/1		
LA12	Luis Aparicio 72/15	40.00	12.00
LA13	Luis Aparicio 73/3		
LA14	Luis Aparicio 74/3		
LB1	Lou Brock 62/1		
LB2	Lou Brock 66/1		
LB3	Lou Brock 68/2		
LB4	Lou Brock 70/20	60.00	18.00
LB5	Lou Brock 71/3		
LB6	Lou Brock 72/3		
LB7	Lou Brock 73/4		
LB8	Lou Brock 74/5		
LB9	Lou Brock 75/9		
LB10	Lou Brock 76/5		
LB11	Lou Brock 77/11		
LB12	Lou Brock 78/11		
LB13	Lou Brock 79/27	50.00	15.00
LD1	Leon Durham 81/1		
LD2	Leon Durham 82/51	15.00	4.50
LD3	Leon Durham 83/52	15.00	4.50
LD4	Leon Durham 84/151	10.00	3.00
LD5	Leon Durham 85/2		
LD6	Leon Durham 86/19	25.00	7.50
LD7	Leon Durham 87/87	10.00	3.00
LDY1	Len Dykstra 86/1		
LDY2	Len Dykstra 87/200	15.00	4.50
LDY3	Len Dykstra 88/30	25.00	7.50
LDY4	Len Dykstra 89/17	40.00	12.00
LDY5	Len Dykstra 92/7		
LS1	Lee Smith 82/1		
LS2	Lee Smith 83/39	20.00	6.00
LS3	Lee Smith 84/6		
LS4	Lee Smith 85/9		
LS5	Lee Smith 86/29	25.00	7.50
LS6	Lee Smith 87/237	15.00	4.50
LS7	Lee Smith 88/27	25.00	7.50
LS8	Lee Smith 92/12		
LT1	Luis Tiant 65/1		
LT2	Luis Tiant 68/16	40.00	12.00
LT3	Luis Tiant 70/9		
LT4	Luis Tiant 71/2		
LT5	Luis Tiant 73/12		
LT6	Luis Tiant 74/19	40.00	12.00
LT7	Luis Tiant 75/10		
LT8	Luis Tiant 76/3		
LT9	Luis Tiant 77/3		
LT10	Luis Tiant 78/6		
LT11	Luis Tiant 79/22	25.00	7.50
LT12	Luis Tiant 80/23	25.00	7.50
LT13	Luis Tiant 81/20	20.00	6.00
LT14	Luis Tiant 82/51	15.00	4.50
LT15	Luis Tiant 83/58	15.00	4.50
MB1	Mike Boddicker 81/1		
MB2	Mike Boddicker 84/56	15.00	4.50
MB3	Mike Boddicker 85/139	10.00	3.00
MB4	Mike Boddicker 86/66	10.00	3.00
MB5	Mike Boddicker 87/88	10.00	3.00
MF1	Mark Fidrych 77/1		
MF2	Mark Fidrych 78/3		
MF3	Mark Fidrych 79/74	25.00	7.50
MF4	Mark Fidrych 80/16	40.00	12.00
MF5	Mark Fidrych 81/11		
MR1	Mickey Rivers 72/1		
MR2	Mickey Rivers 79/35	20.00	6.00
MR3	Mickey Rivers 80/14		
MR4	Mickey Rivers 81/13		
MR5	Mickey Rivers 82/49	15.00	4.50
MR6	Mickey Rivers 83/79	10.00	3.00
MR7	Mickey Rivers 84/91	10.00	3.00
MR8	Mickey Rivers 85/34	15.00	4.50
MS1	Mike Schmidt 73/1		
MS2	Mike Schmidt 80/100	60.00	18.00
MSC1	Mike Scott 80/1		
MSC2	Mike Scott 81/6		
MSC3	Mike Scott 82/32	15.00	4.50
MSC4	Mike Scott 83/55	15.00	4.50
MSC5	Mike Scott 84/28	15.00	4.50
MSC6	Mike Scott 86/73	10.00	3.00
MSC7	Mike Scott 87/36	15.00	4.50
MSC8	Mike Scott 88/21	20.00	6.00
MT1	Paul Molitor Alan Trammell 78/1		
MW1	Mookie Wilson 81/1		
MW2	Mookie Wilson 82/20	30.00	9.00
MW3	Mookie Wilson 83/41	20.00	6.00
MW4	Mookie Wilson 84/11		
MW5	Mookie Wilson 85/51	20.00	6.00
MW6	Mookie Wilson 86/47	20.00	6.00
MW7	Mookie Wilson 87/67	15.00	4.50
MW8	Mookie Wilson 88/12		
NR1	Nolan Ryan 68/1		
NR2	Nolan Ryan 80/10		
NR3	Nolan Ryan 81/13		
NR4	Nolan Ryan 82/11		
NR5	Nolan Ryan 83/23	175.00	52.50
NR6	Nolan Ryan 84/20	175.00	52.50
NR7	Nolan Ryan 85/4		
NR8	Nolan Ryan 86/20	175.00	52.50
OH1	Orel Hershiser 85/1		
OH2	Orel Hershiser 86/23	50.00	15.00
OH3	Orel Hershiser 87/218	25.00	7.50
OH4	Orel Hershiser 88/9		
OS1	Ozzie Smith 79/1		
OS2	Ozzie Smith 81/28	60.00	18.00
OS3	Ozzie Smith 82/27	60.00	18.00
OS4	Ozzie Smith 83/6		
OS5	Ozzie Smith 84/19	80.00	24.00
OS6	Ozzie Smith 85/16	80.00	24.00
OS7	Ozzie Smith 86/3		
PI1	Pete Incaviglia 86 TR/1		
PI2	Pete Incaviglia 87/311	10.00	3.00
PM1	Paul Molitor 79/15	60.00	18.00
PM2	Paul Molitor 80/26	50.00	15.00
PM3	Paul Molitor 81/12		
PM4	Paul Molitor 82/32	40.00	12.00
PM5	Paul Molitor 83/14		
PO1	Paul O'Neill 88/1		
PO2	Paul O'Neill 89/24	50.00	15.00
PO3	Paul O'Neill 90/18	60.00	18.00
PO4	Paul O'Neill 91/24	50.00	15.00
PO5	Paul O'Neill 97/33	40.00	12.00
RC1	Rod Carew 67/1		
RC2	Rod Carew 70/10		
RC3	Rod Carew 78/2		
RC4	Rod Carew 79/29	50.00	15.00
RC5	Rod Carew 80/10		
RC6	Rod Carew 81/21	50.00	15.00
RC7	Rod Carew 82/18	60.00	18.00
RC8	Rod Carew 84/9		
RCE1	Ron Cey 72/1		
RCE2	Ron Cey 75/4		
RCE3	Ron Cey 79/55	20.00	6.00
RCE4	Ron Cey 80/8		
RCE5	Ron Cey 81/16	25.00	7.50
RCE6	Ron Cey 82/34	15.00	4.50
RCE7	Ron Cey 83/87	10.00	3.00
RCE8	Ron Cey 83 TR/68	10.00	3.00
RCE9	Ron Cey 84/15	25.00	7.50
RCE10	Ron Cey 85/19	25.00	7.50
RCE11	Ron Cey 86/43	15.00	4.50
RD1	Ron Darling 85/1		
RD2	Ron Darling 86/12		
RD3	Ron Darling 87/224	15.00	4.50
RD4	Ron Darling 93/13		
RDI1	Rob Dibble 89/1		
RDI2	Rob Dibble 90/31	25.00	7.50
RDI3	Rob Dibble 91/62	20.00	6.00
RDI4	Rob Dibble 92/56	20.00	6.00
RDI5	Rob Dibble 92 Gold/17	40.00	12.00
RDI6	Rob Dibble 93/47	20.00	6.00
RDI7	Rob Dibble 94/37	20.00	6.00
RF1	Rollie Fingers 69/1		
RF2	Rollie Fingers 78/6		
RF3	Rollie Fingers 79/52	30.00	9.00
RF4	Rollie Fingers 80/15	40.00	12.00
RF5	Rollie Fingers 81/18	40.00	12.00
RF6	Rollie Fingers 82/8		
RG1	Rich Gossage 73/1		
RG2	Rich Gossage 74/6		
RG3	Rich Gossage 76/3		
RG4	Rich Gossage 78/2		
RG5	Rich Gossage 79/11		
RG6	Rich Gossage 80/15	40.00	12.00
RG7	Rich Gossage 81/21	20.00	6.00
RG8	Rich Gossage 82/30	25.00	7.50
RG9	Rich Gossage 83/34	25.00	7.50
RG10	Rich Gossage 84/90	15.00	4.50
RG11	Rich Gossage 85/7		
RG12	Rich Gossage 86/30	25.00	7.50
RGU1	Ron Guidry 76/1		
RGU2	Ron Guidry 78/9		
RGU3	Ron Guidry 79/10		
RGU4	Ron Guidry 80/22	40.00	12.00
RGU5	Ron Guidry 81/104	15.00	4.50
RGU6	Ron Guidry 82/53	20.00	6.00
RGU7	Ron Guidry 83/46	20.00	6.00
RGU8	Ron Guidry 84/40	20.00	6.00
RGU9	Ron Guidry 85/50	20.00	6.00
RGU10	Ron Guidry 86/15	40.00	12.00
RJ1	Reggie Jackson 69/1		
RJ2	Reggie Jackson 73/3		
RJ3	Reggie Jackson 75/1		
RJ4	Reggie Jackson 76/2		
RJ5	Reggie Jackson 79/2		
RJ6	Reggie Jackson 80/7		
RJ7	Reggie Jackson 81/12		

❑ RJ8 Reggie Jackson 82/21.. 60.00 18.00
❑ RJ9 Reggie Jackson 83/14........
❑ RJ10 Reggie Jackson 84/3........
❑ RJ11 Reggie Jackson 85/17 80.00 24.00
❑ RJ12 Reggie Jackson 86/17 80.00 24.00
❑ RK1 Ron Kittle 84/1 ....
❑ RK2 Ron Kittle 85/86 .... 10.00 3.00
❑ RK3 Ron Kittle 86/55 .... 15.00 4.50
❑ RK4 Ron Kittle 87/201 .... 10.00 3.00
❑ RKN1 Ray Knight 78/1 ....
❑ RKN2 Ray Knight 79/10 ....
❑ RKN3 Ray Knight 80/5 ....
❑ RKN4 Ray Knight 81/7 ....
❑ RKN5 Ray Knight 82/25 ...... 30.00 9.00
❑ RKN6 Ray Knight 83/36 ...... 20.00 6.00
❑ RKN7 Ray Knight 84/26 ...... 25.00 7.50
❑ RKN8 Ray Knight 85/68 ...... 15.00 4.50
❑ RKN9 Ray Knight 86/80 ...... 15.00 4.50
❑ RKN10 Ray Knight 87 TR/90 15.00 4.50
❑ RM1 Reggie Smith 67/1............
❑ RM2 Reggie Smith 69/1............
❑ RM3 Reggie Smith 73/7............
❑ RM4 Reggie Smith 74/4............
❑ RM5 Reggie Smith 75/2............
❑ RM6 Reggie Smith 76/3............
❑ RM7 Reggie Smith 77/2............
❑ RM8 Reggie Smith 79/15.... 25.00 7.50
❑ RM9 Reggie Smith 80/16.... 25.00 7.50
❑ RM10 Reggie Smith 81/14.......
❑ RM11 Reggie Smith 82/32.. 15.00 4.50
❑ RM12 Reggie Smith 83/48.. 15.00 4.50
❑ RS1 Ryne Sandberg 83/1 ....
❑ RS2 Ryne Sandberg 84/37 100.00 30.00
❑ RS3 Ryne Sandberg 85/4..........
❑ RS4 Ryne Sandberg 86/1 ....
❑ RS5 Ryne Sandberg 87/32 100.00 30.00
❑ RS6 Ryne Sandberg 88/6..........
❑ RS7 Ryne Sandberg 89/9..........
❑ RS8 Ryne Sandberg 92/10........
❑ RSA1 Ron Santo 61/1 ....
❑ RSA2 Ron Santo 67/2 ....
❑ RSA3 Ron Santo 68/6 ....
❑ RSA4 Ron Santo 69/2 ....
❑ RSA5 Ron Santo 70/1 ....
❑ RSA6 Ron Santo 70 AS/1..........
❑ RSA7 Ron Santo 71/2 ....
❑ RSA8 Ron Santo 72/2 ....
❑ RSA9 Ron Santo 72 IA/3 ....
❑ RSA10 Ron Santo 73/13 ....
❑ RSA11 Ron Santo 74/2 ....
❑ RSA12 Ron Santo 74 TR/1 ....
❑ RSA13 Ron Santo 75/12 ....
❑ RU1 Rick Sutcliffe 80/1 ....
❑ RU2 Rick Sutcliffe 81/9 ....
❑ RU3 Rick Sutcliffe 82/53 .... 15.00 4.50
❑ RU4 Rick Sutcliffe 83/43 .... 15.00 4.50
❑ RU5 Rick Sutcliffe 84/33 .... 15.00 4.50
❑ RU6 Rick Sutcliffe 85/82 .... 10.00 3.00
❑ RU7 Rick Sutcliffe 86/10 ....
❑ RU8 Rick Sutcliffe 87/19 .... 25.00 7.50
❑ RY1 Robin Yount 75/1 ....
❑ RY2 Robin Yount 77/1 ....
❑ RY3 Robin Yount 78/3 ....
❑ RY4 Robin Yount 79/1 ....
❑ RY5 Robin Yount 80/18 ...... 80.00 24.00
❑ RY6 Robin Yount 81/23 ...... 80.00 24.00
❑ RY7 Robin Yount 82/11 ....
❑ RY8 Robin Yount 83/2 ....
❑ RY9 Robin Yount 84/15 ...... 80.00 24.00
❑ RY10 Robin Yount 85/5............
❑ RY11 Robin Yount 86/21 .... 80.00 24.00
❑ SA1 Sparky Anderson 59/1 ......
❑ SA2 Sparky Anderson 60/2 ......
❑ SA3 Sparky Anderson 74 MG/3 .00
❑ SA4 Sparky Anderson 78 MG/6 .00
❑ SA5 Sparky Anderson 83 MG/67 15.00 4.50
❑ SA6 Sparky Anderson 84 MG/97 15.00 4.50
❑ SA7 Sparky Anderson 85 MG/73 15.00 4.50
❑ SA8 Sparky Anderson 86 MG/6
❑ SF1 Sid Fernandez 85/1............
❑ SF2 Sid Fernandez 86/18.... 40.00 12.00
❑ SF3 Sid Fernandez 87/211.. 15.00 4.50
❑ SF4 Sid Fernandez 93/20.... 30.00 9.00
❑ SG1 Steve Garvey 71/1 ....
❑ SG2 Steve Garvey 75/1 ....
❑ SG3 Steve Garvey 76/4 ....
❑ SG4 Steve Garvey 79/26 .... 50.00 15.00
❑ SG5 Steve Garvey 80/5 ....
❑ SG6 Steve Garvey 81/10 ....
❑ SG7 Steve Garvey 82/122 .. 25.00 7.50
❑ SG8 Steve Garvey 83/19 .... 60.00 18.00
❑ SG9 Steve Garvey 84/32 .... 40.00 12.00
❑ SG10 Steve Garvey 85/129 25.00 7.50
❑ SM1 Stan Musial 58 AS/15 150.00 45.00
❑ SM2 Stan Musial 59/1 ....
❑ SM3 Stan Musial 60/5 ....
❑ SM4 Stan Musial 61/13..............
❑ SM5 Stan Musial 62/16 .... 150.00 45.00
❑ SM6 Stan Musial 63/1 ....
❑ SS1 Steve Sax 82/1 ....
❑ SS2 Steve Sax 83/34 .... 15.00 4.50
❑ SS3 Steve Sax 84/14 ....
❑ SS4 Steve Sax 85/33 .... 15.00 4.50
❑ SS5 Steve Sax 86/45 .... 15.00 4.50
❑ SS6 Steve Sax 87/215 .... 10.00 3.00
❑ SS7 Steve Sax 88/10 ....
❑ SY1 Steve Yeager 73/1..............
❑ SY2 Steve Yeager 74/1..............
❑ SY3 Steve Yeager 76/1..............
❑ SY4 Steve Yeager 78/18...... 25.00 7.50
❑ SY5 Steve Yeager 79/23...... 25.00 7.50
❑ SY6 Steve Yeager 80/10............
❑ SY7 Steve Yeager 81/12............
❑ SY8 Steve Yeager 82/18...... 25.00 7.50
❑ SY9 Steve Yeager 83/80...... 10.00 3.00
❑ SY10 Steve Yeager 84/15.... 25.00 7.50
❑ SY11 Steve Yeager 85/4............
❑ SY12 Steve Yeager 86/47.... 15.00 4.50
❑ SY13 Steve Yeager 86 TR/100 10.00 3.00
❑ TB1 Tom Brunansky 82/1..........
❑ TB2 Tom Brunansky 83/27.. 15.00 4.50
❑ TB3 Tom Brunansky 84/62.. 15.00 4.50
❑ TB4 Tom Brunansky 85/13..........
❑ TB5 Tom Brunansky 86/28.. 15.00 4.50
❑ TB6 Tom Brunansky 87/193 10.00 3.00
❑ TB7 Tom Brunansky 88/18.. 25.00 7.50
❑ TB8 Tom Brunansky 90/8..........
❑ TF1 Tony Fernandez 85/1..........
❑ TF2 Tony Fernandez 86/41.. 15.00 4.50
❑ TF3 Tony Fernandez 87/228 10.00 3.00
❑ TF4 Tony Fernandez 88/10........
❑ TF5 Tony Fernandez 90/11........
❑ TG1 Tony Gwynn 83/1 ....
❑ TG2 Tony Gwynn 84/95 ...... 60.00 18.00
❑ TG3 Tony Gwynn 85/4 ....
❑ TH1 Tom Herr 80/1 ....
❑ TH2 Tom Herr 81/22 .... 20.00 6.00
❑ TH3 Tom Herr 82/42 .... 15.00 4.50
❑ TH4 Tom Herr 83/80 .... 10.00 3.00
❑ TH5 Tom Herr 84/30 .... 15.00 4.50
❑ TH6 Tom Herr 85/17 .... 25.00 7.50
❑ TH7 Tom Herr 86/28 .... 15.00 4.50
❑ TH8 Tom Herr 87/134 .... 10.00 3.00
❑ TM1 Tim McCarver 62/1 ....
❑ TM2 Tim McCarver 76/5 ....
❑ TM3 Tim McCarver 77/8 ....
❑ TM4 Tim McCarver 78/12 ....
❑ TM5 Tim McCarver 79/22 .. 25.00 7.50
❑ TM6 Tim McCarver 80/4 ....
❑ TO1 Tony Oliva 63/1 ....
❑ TO2 Tony Oliva 68/1 ....
❑ TO3 Tony Oliva 69/4 ....
❑ TO4 Tony Oliva 69 AS/1............
❑ TO5 Tony Oliva 70/9 ....
❑ TO6 Tony Oliva 71/2 ....
❑ TO7 Tony Oliva 72/5 ....
❑ TO8 Tony Oliva 73/18 .... 40.00 12.00
❑ TO9 Tony Oliva 74/11 ....
❑ TO10 Tony Oliva 75/10 ....
❑ TO11 Tony Oliva 76/1 ....
❑ TR1 Tim Raines 81/1 ....
❑ TR2 Tim Raines 82/43 .... 20.00 6.00
❑ TR3 Tim Raines 83/26 .... 25.00 7.50
❑ TR4 Tim Raines 84/10 ....
❑ TR5 Tim Raines 85/43 .... 20.00 6.00
❑ TR6 Tim Raines 86/21 .... 30.00 9.00
❑ TR7 Tim Raines 87/211 ...... 15.00 4.50
❑ TS1 Tom Seaver 67/1................
❑ TS2 Tom Seaver 79/44.......... 60.00 18.00
❑ TS3 Tom Seaver 80/9................
❑ TS4 Tom Seaver 81/16.......... 80.00 24.00
❑ TS5 Tom Seaver 82/25.......... 60.00 18.00
❑ TS6 Tom Seaver 83/4................
❑ TS7 Tom Seaver 85/6................
❑ TW1 Tim Wallach 82/1..............
❑ TW2 Tim Wallach 83/49...... 15.00 4.50
❑ TW3 Tim Wallach 84/13............
❑ TW4 Tim Wallach 85/46...... 15.00 4.50
❑ TW5 Tim Wallach 86/44...... 15.00 4.50
❑ TW6 Tim Wallach 87/197.... 10.00 3.00
❑ VB1 Vida Blue 70/1 ....
❑ VB2 Vida Blue 72/1 ....
❑ VB3 Vida Blue 75/1 ....
❑ VB4 Vida Blue 78/10 ....
❑ VB5 Vida Blue 79/21 .... 25.00 7.50
❑ VB6 Vida Blue 80/10 ....
❑ VB7 Vida Blue 81/227 .... 10.00 3.00
❑ VB8 Vida Blue 82/53 .... 15.00 4.50
❑ VB9 Vida Blue 83/45 .... 15.00 4.50
❑ VC1 Vince Coleman 85 TR/1 ....
❑ VC2 Vince Coleman 87/299 15.00 4.50
❑ VC3 Vince Coleman 88/34.. 25.00 7.50
❑ VC4 Vince Coleman 91 TR/23 30.00 9.00
❑ WB1 Wade Boggs 83/1 ....
❑ WB2 Wade Boggs 84/20 .... 60.00 18.00
❑ WB3 Wade Boggs 85/25 .... 60.00 18.00
❑ WB4 Wade Boggs 86/9 ....
❑ WB5 Wade Boggs 87/45 .... 50.00 15.00
❑ WF1 Whitey Ford 53/1 ....
❑ WF2 Whitey Ford 58/1 ....
❑ WF3 Whitey Ford 59/3 ....
❑ WF4 Whitey Ford 60/5 ....
❑ WF5 Whitey Ford 61/6 ....
❑ WF6 Whitey Ford 62/5 ....
❑ WF7 Whitey Ford 62 AS/2 ....
❑ WF8 Whitey Ford 62 WS/3........
❑ WF9 Whitey Ford 63/1 ....
❑ WF10 Whitey Ford 65/1 ....
❑ WF11 Whitey Ford 66/9............
❑ WF12 Whitey Ford 67/13..........
❑ WH1 Whitey Herzog 57/1..........
❑ WH2 Whitey Herzog 61/13........
❑ WH3 Whitey Herzog 62/1..........
❑ WH4 Whitey Herzog 83 MG/63 15.00 4.50
❑ WH5 Whitey Herzog 84 MG/85 10.00 3.00
❑ WH6 Whitey Herzog 85 MG/75 10.00 3.00
❑ WH7 Whitey Herzog 86 MG/66 10.00 3.00
❑ WH8 Whitey Herzog 87 MG/29 15.00 4.50
❑ WH9 Whitey Herzog 88 MG/35 15.00 4.50
❑ WJ1 Wally Joyner 86 TR/1........
❑ WJ2 Wally Joyner 87/335 .. 15.00 4.50
❑ WJ3 Wally Joyner 94/14 ....
❑ WM1 Willie Mays 52/1 ....
❑ WM2 Willie Mays 60/1 ....
❑ WM3 Willie Mays 61/3 ....
❑ WM4 Willie Mays 61 MVP/4 ....
❑ WM5 Willie Mays 62/1 ....
❑ WM6 Willie Mays 62 AS/3........
❑ WM7 Willie Mays 69/1 ....
❑ WM8 Willie Mays 70/2 ....
❑ WM9 Willie Mays 72/25 .. 300.00 90.00
❑ WM10 Willie Mays 72 IA/5 ......
❑ WM11 Willie Mays 73/5 ....
❑ WMC1 Willie McGee 83/1 ....
❑ WMC2 Willie McGee 84/66 25.00 7.50
❑ WMC3 Willie McGee 85/44 30.00 9.00
❑ WMC4 Willie McGee 86/24 50.00 15.00
❑ WMC5 Willie McGee 87/117 25.00 7.50
❑ WW1 Walt Weiss 88 TR/1 ....
❑ WW2 Walt Weiss 89/34...... 15.00 4.50
❑ WW3 Walt Weiss 91/30...... 15.00 4.50
❑ WW4 Walt Weiss 92/71...... 10.00 3.00
❑ WW5 Walt Weiss 93/10............
❑ WW6 Walt Weiss 94/21...... 20.00 6.00
❑ WW7 Walt Weiss 97/49...... 15.00 4.50
❑ WW8 Walt Weiss 98 Rockies/23 20.00 6.00
❑ WW9 Walt Weiss 98 Braves/21 20.00 6.00
❑ WW10 Walt Weiss 99/40.... 15.00 4.50
❑ WW11 Walt Weiss 01/51.... 15.00 4.50
❑ YB1 Yogi Berra 52/1 ....
❑ YB2 Yogi Berra 59/1 ....
❑ YB3 Yogi Berra 60/1 ....
❑ YB4 Yogi Berra 61/2 ....
❑ YB5 Yogi Berra 62/3 ....
❑ YB6 Yogi Berra 64 MG/3 ....
❑ YB7 Yogi Berra 65 CO/1 ....
❑ YB8 Yogi Berra 73 MG/5 ....
❑ YB9 Yogi Berra 74 MG/6 ....
❑ YB10 Yogi Berra 85 MG/27 80.00 24.00

2002 Topps Pristine

	Nm-Mt	Ex-Mt
COMMON CARD (1-140)	1.25	.35
COMMON CARD (141-150)	2.00	.60
COMMON C CARD (151-210)	1.25	.35
COMMON U CARD (151-210)	2.50	.75
COMMON R CARD (151-210)	4.00	1.20

	Nm-Mt	Ex-Mt
❑ 1 Alex Rodriguez	5.00	1.50
❑ 2 Carlos Delgado	1.25	.35
❑ 3 Jimmy Rollins	1.25	.35
❑ 4 Jason Kendall	1.25	.35
❑ 5 John Olerud	1.25	.35
❑ 6 Albert Pujols	6.00	1.80
❑ 7 Curt Schilling	1.25	.35
❑ 8 Gary Sheffield	1.25	.35
❑ 9 Johnny Damon Sox	3.00	.90
❑ 10 Ichiro Suzuki	5.00	1.50
❑ 11 Pat Burrell	1.25	.35
❑ 12 Garret Anderson	1.25	.35
❑ 13 Andruw Jones	1.25	.35
❑ 14 Kerry Wood	3.00	.90
❑ 15 Kenny Lofton	1.25	.35
❑ 16 Adam Dunn	2.00	.60
❑ 17 Juan Pierre	1.25	.35
❑ 18 Josh Beckett	1.25	.35
❑ 19 Roy Oswalt	1.25	.35
❑ 20 Derek Jeter	8.00	2.40
❑ 21 Jose Vidro	1.25	.35
❑ 22 Richie Sexson	1.25	.35
❑ 23 Mike Sweeney	1.25	.35
❑ 24 Jeff Kent	1.25	.35
❑ 25 Jason Giambi	1.25	.35
❑ 26 Bret Boone	1.25	.35
❑ 27 J.D. Drew	1.25	.35
❑ 28 Shannon Stewart	1.25	.35
❑ 29 Miguel Tejada	1.25	.35
❑ 30 Barry Bonds	8.00	2.40
❑ 31 Randy Johnson	3.00	.90
❑ 32 Pedro Martinez	3.00	.90
❑ 33 Magglio Ordonez	1.25	.35
❑ 34 Todd Helton	2.00	.60
❑ 35 Craig Biggio	2.00	.60
❑ 36 Shawn Green	1.25	.35
❑ 37 Vladimir Guerrero	3.00	.90
❑ 38 Mo Vaughn	1.25	.35
❑ 39 Alfonso Soriano	2.00	.60
❑ 40 Barry Zito	1.25	.35
❑ 41 Aramis Ramirez	1.25	.35
❑ 42 Ryan Klesko	1.25	.35
❑ 43 Ruben Sierra	1.25	.35
❑ 44 Tino Martinez	2.00	.60
❑ 45 Toby Hall	1.25	.35
❑ 46 Ivan Rodriguez	3.00	.90
❑ 47 Raul Mondesi	1.25	.35
❑ 48 Carlos Pena	1.25	.35
❑ 49 Darin Erstad	1.25	.35
❑ 50 Sammy Sosa	5.00	1.50
❑ 51 Bartolo Colon	1.25	.35
❑ 52 Robert Fick	1.25	.35
❑ 53 Cliff Floyd	1.25	.35
❑ 54 Brian Jordan	1.25	.35
❑ 55 Torii Hunter	1.25	.35
❑ 56 Roberto Alomar	2.00	.60
❑ 57 Roger Clemens	6.00	1.80
❑ 58 Mark Mulder	1.25	.35
❑ 59 Brian Giles	1.25	.35
❑ 60 Mike Piazza	5.00	1.50
❑ 61 Rich Aurilia	1.25	.35
❑ 62 Freddy Garcia	1.25	.35
❑ 63 Jim Edmonds	1.25	.35
❑ 64 Eric Hinske	1.25	.35
❑ 65 Vicente Padilla	1.25	.35
❑ 66 Javier Vazquez	1.25	.35
❑ 67 Cristian Guzman	1.25	.35
❑ 68 Paul Lo Duca	1.25	.35
❑ 69 Bobby Abreu	1.25	.35
❑ 70 Nomar Garciaparra	5.00	1.50
❑ 71 Troy Glaus	1.25	.35
❑ 72 Chipper Jones	3.00	.90
❑ 73 Scott Rolen	3.00	.90
❑ 74 Lance Berkman	1.25	.35
❑ 75 C.C. Sabathia	1.25	.35
❑ 76 Bernie Williams	2.00	.60
❑ 77 Rafael Palmeiro	2.00	.60
❑ 78 Phil Nevin	1.25	.35
❑ 79 Kazuhiro Sasaki	1.25	.35
❑ 80 Eric Chavez	1.25	.35
❑ 81 Jorge Posada	2.00	.60
❑ 82 Edgardo Alfonzo	1.25	.35
❑ 83 Geoff Jenkins	1.25	.35
❑ 84 Preston Wilson	1.25	.35
❑ 85 Jim Thome	3.00	.90
❑ 86 Frank Thomas	3.00	.90
❑ 87 Jeff Bagwell	2.00	.60
❑ 88 Greg Maddux	5.00	1.50
❑ 89 Mark Prior	6.00	1.80
❑ 90 Larry Walker	2.00	.60
❑ 91 Luis Gonzalez	1.25	.35
❑ 92 Tim Hudson	1.25	.35
❑ 93 Tsuyoshi Shinjo	1.25	.35
❑ 94 Juan Gonzalez	2.00	.60
❑ 95 Shea Hillenbrand	1.25	.35
❑ 96 Paul Konerko	1.25	.35
❑ 97 Tom Glavine	2.00	.60
❑ 98 Marty Cordova	1.25	.35
❑ 99 Moises Alou	1.25	.35
❑ 100 Ken Griffey Jr.	5.00	1.50
❑ 101 Hank Blalock	3.00	.90
❑ 102 Matt Morris	1.25	.35
❑ 103 Robb Nen	1.25	.35
❑ 104 Mike Cameron	1.25	.35
❑ 105 Mark Buehrle	1.25	.35
❑ 106 Sean Burroughs	1.25	.35
❑ 107 Orlando Cabrera	1.25	.35
❑ 108 Jeromy Burnitz	1.25	.35
❑ 109 Juan Uribe	1.25	.35
❑ 110 Eric Milton	1.25	.35
❑ 111 Carlos Lee	1.25	.35
❑ 112 Jose Mesa	1.25	.35
❑ 113 Morgan Ensberg	1.25	.35
❑ 114 Derek Lowe	1.25	.35
❑ 115 Juan Cruz	1.25	.35
❑ 116 Mike Lieberthal	1.25	.35
❑ 117 Armando Benitez	1.25	.35
❑ 118 Vinny Castilla	1.25	.35
❑ 119 Russ Ortiz	1.25	.35
❑ 120 Mike Lowell	1.25	.35
❑ 121 Corey Patterson	1.25	.35
❑ 122 Mike Mussina	2.00	.60
❑ 123 Rafael Furcal	1.25	.35
❑ 124 Mark Grace	2.00	.60
❑ 125 Ben Sheets	1.25	.35
❑ 126 John Smoltz	2.00	.60
❑ 127 Fred McGriff	2.00	.60
❑ 128 Nick Johnson	1.25	.35
❑ 129 J.T. Snow	1.25	.35
❑ 130 Jeff Cirillo	1.25	.35
❑ 131 Trevor Hoffman	1.25	.35
❑ 132 Kevin Brown	1.25	.35
❑ 133 Mariano Rivera	2.00	.60
❑ 134 Marlon Anderson	1.25	.35
❑ 135 Al Leiter	1.25	.35
❑ 136 Doug Mientkiewicz	1.25	.35
❑ 137 Eric Karros	1.25	.35
❑ 138 Bobby Higginson	1.25	.35
❑ 139 Sean Casey	1.25	.35
❑ 140 Troy Percival	1.25	.35
❑ 141 Willie Mays	6.00	1.80
❑ 142 Carl Yastrzemski	5.00	1.50
❑ 143 Stan Musial	5.00	1.50
❑ 144 Harmon Killebrew	3.00	.90
❑ 145 Mike Schmidt	6.00	1.80
❑ 146 Duke Snider	2.00	.60
❑ 147 Brooks Robinson	2.00	.60
❑ 148 Frank Robinson	2.00	.60
❑ 149 Nolan Ryan	8.00	2.40
❑ 150 Reggie Jackson	2.00	.60
❑ 151 Joe Mauer C RC	10.00	3.00
❑ 152 Joe Mauer U	20.00	6.00
❑ 153 Joe Mauer R	30.00	9.00
❑ 154 Colt Griffin C RC	2.00	.60
❑ 155 Colt Griffin U	4.00	1.20
❑ 156 Colt Griffin R	6.00	1.80
❑ 157 Jason Simontacchi C RC	1.25	.35
❑ 158 Jason Simontacchi U	2.50	.75
❑ 159 Jason Simontacchi R	4.00	1.20
❑ 160 Casey Kotchman C RC	6.00	1.80
❑ 161 Casey Kotchman U	12.00	3.60
❑ 162 Casey Kotchman R	20.00	6.00
❑ 163 Greg Sain C RC	2.00	.60
❑ 164 Greg Sain U	4.00	1.20
❑ 165 Greg Sain R	6.00	1.80
❑ 166 David Wright C RC	15.00	4.50
❑ 167 David Wright U	25.00	7.50
❑ 168 David Wright R	40.00	12.00
❑ 169 Scott Hairston C RC	3.00	.90
❑ 170 Scott Hairston U	6.00	1.80
❑ 171 Scott Hairston R	10.00	3.00
❑ 172 Rolando Viera C RC	1.25	.35
❑ 173 Rolando Viera U	2.50	.75
❑ 174 Rolando Viera R	4.00	1.20
❑ 175 Tyrell Godwin C RC	1.25	.35
❑ 176 Tyrell Godwin U	2.50	.75
❑ 177 Tyrell Godwin R	4.00	1.20
❑ 178 Jesus Cota C RC	1.25	.35
❑ 179 Jesus Cota U	2.50	.75
❑ 180 Jesus Cota R	4.00	1.20
❑ 181 Dan Johnson C RC	2.00	.60
❑ 182 Dan Johnson U	4.00	1.20
❑ 183 Dan Johnson R	6.00	1.80
❑ 184 Mario Ramos C RC	1.25	.35
❑ 185 Mario Ramos U	2.50	.75
❑ 186 Mario Ramos R	4.00	1.20
❑ 187 Jason Dubois C RC	2.50	.75
❑ 188 Jason Dubois U	5.00	1.50
❑ 189 Jason Dubois R	8.00	2.40
❑ 190 Jonny Gomes C RC	2.00	.60
❑ 191 Jonny Gomes U	4.00	1.20
❑ 192 Jonny Gomes R	6.00	1.80
❑ 193 Chris Snelling C RC	1.25	.35
❑ 194 Chris Snelling U	2.50	.75
❑ 195 Chris Snelling R	4.00	1.20
❑ 196 Hansel Izquierdo C RC	1.25	.35
❑ 197 Hansel Izquierdo U	2.50	.75
❑ 198 Hansel Izquierdo R	4.00	1.20
❑ 199 So Taguchi C RC	2.00	.60
❑ 200 So Taguchi U	4.00	1.20
❑ 201 So Taguchi R	6.00	1.80
❑ 202 Kazuhisa Ishii C RC	2.50	.75
❑ 203 Kazuhisa Ishii U	5.00	1.50
❑ 204 Kazuhisa Ishii R	8.00	2.40
❑ 205 Jorge Padilla C RC	1.25	.35
❑ 206 Jorge Padilla U	2.50	.75
❑ 207 Jorge Padilla R	4.00	1.20
❑ 208 Earl Snyder C RC	2.00	.60
❑ 209 Earl Snyder U	4.00	1.20
❑ 210 Earl Snyder R	6.00	1.80

2003 Topps Pristine

	MINT	NRMT
COMMON CARD (1-100)	1.50	.70
COMMON C (101-190)	1.25	.55
C 101-190 APPX. 2X EASIER THAN 1-100		
COMMON U (101-190)	2.50	1.10
UNCOMMON 101-190 STATED ODDS 1:2		
UNCOMMON PRINT 1499 SERIAL #'d SETS		
COMMON R (101-190)	5.00	2.20
RARE 101-190 STATED ODDS 1:6..		
RARE PRINT RUN 499 SERIAL #'d SETS		

Card	MINT	NRMT
❑ 1 Pedro Martinez	4.00	1.80
❑ 2 Derek Jeter	10.00	4.50
❑ 3 Alex Rodriguez	6.00	2.70
❑ 4 Miguel Tejada	1.50	.70
❑ 5 Nomar Garciaparra	6.00	2.70
❑ 6 Austin Kearns	1.50	.70
❑ 7 Jose Vidro	1.50	.70
❑ 8 Bret Boone	1.50	.70
❑ 9 Scott Rolen	4.00	1.80
❑ 10 Mike Sweeney	1.50	.70
❑ 11 Jason Schmidt	1.50	.70
❑ 12 Alfonso Soriano	2.50	1.10
❑ 13 Tim Hudson	1.50	.70
❑ 14 A.J. Pierzynski	1.50	.70
❑ 15 Lance Berkman	1.50	.70
❑ 16 Frank Thomas	4.00	1.80
❑ 17 Gary Sheffield	1.50	.70
❑ 18 Jarrod Washburn	1.50	.70
❑ 19 Hideo Nomo	4.00	1.80
❑ 20 Barry Zito	1.50	.70
❑ 21 Kevin Millwood	1.50	.70
❑ 22 Matt Morris	1.50	.70
❑ 23 Carl Crawford	1.50	.70
❑ 24 Carlos Delgado	1.50	.70
❑ 25 Mike Piazza	6.00	2.70
❑ 26 Brad Radke	1.50	.70
❑ 27 Richie Sexson	1.50	.70
❑ 28 Kevin Brown	1.50	.70
❑ 29 Carlos Beltran	2.50	1.10
❑ 30 Curt Schilling	1.50	.70
❑ 31 Chipper Jones	4.00	1.80
❑ 32 Paul Konerko	1.50	.70
❑ 33 Larry Walker	2.50	1.10
❑ 34 Jeff Bagwell	2.50	1.10
❑ 35 Jason Giambi	1.50	.70
❑ 36 Mark Mulder	1.50	.70
❑ 37 Vicente Padilla	1.50	.70
❑ 38 Kris Benson	1.50	.70
❑ 39 Bernie Williams	2.50	1.10
❑ 40 Jim Thome	4.00	1.80
❑ 41 Roger Clemens	8.00	3.60
❑ 42 Roberto Alomar	2.50	1.10
❑ 43 Torii Hunter	1.50	.70
❑ 44 Bobby Abreu	1.50	.70
❑ 45 Jeff Kent	1.50	.70
❑ 46 Roy Oswalt	1.50	.70
❑ 47 Bartolo Colon	1.50	.70
❑ 48 Greg Maddux	6.00	2.70
❑ 49 Tom Glavine	2.50	1.10
❑ 50 Sammy Sosa	6.00	2.70
❑ 51 Ichiro Suzuki	6.00	2.70
❑ 52 Mark Prior	4.00	1.80
❑ 53 Manny Ramirez	2.50	1.10
❑ 54 Andruw Jones	1.50	.70
❑ 55 Randy Johnson	4.00	1.80
❑ 56 Garret Anderson	1.50	.70
❑ 57 Roy Halladay	1.50	.70
❑ 58 Rafael Palmeiro	2.50	1.10
❑ 59 Rocco Baldelli	1.50	.70
❑ 60 Albert Pujols	8.00	3.60
❑ 61 Edgar Renteria	1.50	.70
❑ 62 John Olerud	1.50	.70
❑ 63 Rich Aurilia	1.50	.70
❑ 64 Ryan Klesko	1.50	.70
❑ 65 Brian Giles	1.50	.70
❑ 66 Eric Chavez	1.50	.70
❑ 67 Jorge Posada	2.50	1.10
❑ 68 Cliff Floyd	1.50	.70
❑ 69 Vladimir Guerrero	4.00	1.80
❑ 70 Cristian Guzman	1.50	.70
❑ 71 Raul Ibanez	1.50	.70
❑ 72 Paul Lo Duca	1.50	.70
❑ 73 A.J. Burnett	1.50	.70
❑ 74 Ken Griffey Jr.	6.00	2.70
❑ 75 Mark Buehrle	1.50	.70
❑ 76 Moises Alou	1.50	.70
❑ 77 Adam Dunn	2.50	1.10
❑ 78 Tony Batista	1.50	.70
❑ 79 Troy Glaus	1.50	.70
❑ 80 Luis Gonzalez	1.50	.70
❑ 81 Shea Hillenbrand	1.50	.70
❑ 82 Kerry Wood	4.00	1.80
❑ 83 Magglio Ordonez	1.50	.70
❑ 84 Omar Vizquel	2.50	1.10
❑ 85 Bobby Higginson	1.50	.70
❑ 86 Mike Lowell	1.50	.70
❑ 87 Runelvys Hernandez	1.50	.70
❑ 88 Shawn Green	1.50	.70
❑ 89 Erubiel Durazo	1.50	.70
❑ 90 Pat Burrell	1.50	.70
❑ 91 Todd Helton	2.50	1.10
❑ 92 Jim Edmonds	1.50	.70
❑ 93 Aubrey Huff	1.50	.70
❑ 94 Eric Hinske	1.50	.70
❑ 95 Barry Bonds	10.00	4.50
❑ 96 Willie Mays	8.00	3.60
❑ 97 Bo Jackson	4.00	1.80
❑ 98 Carl Yastrzemski	6.00	2.70
❑ 99 Don Mattingly	10.00	4.50
❑ 100 Gary Carter	2.50	1.10
❑ 101 Jose Contreras C RC	2.00	.90
❑ 102 Jose Contreras U	4.00	1.80
❑ 103 Jose Contreras R	8.00	3.60
❑ 104 Dan Haren C RC	2.00	.90
❑ 105 Dan Haren U	4.00	1.80
❑ 106 Dan Haren R	8.00	3.60
❑ 107 Michel Hernandez C RC	1.25	.55
❑ 108 Michel Hernandez U	2.50	1.10
❑ 109 Michel Hernandez R	5.00	2.20
❑ 110 Bobby Basham C RC	1.25	.55
❑ 111 Bobby Basham U	2.50	1.10
❑ 112 Bobby Basham R	5.00	2.20
❑ 113 Bryan Bullington C RC	2.50	1.10
❑ 114 Bryan Bullington U	5.00	2.20
❑ 115 Bryan Bullington R	10.00	4.50
❑ 116 Bernie Castro C RC	1.25	.55
❑ 117 Bernie Castro U	2.50	1.10
❑ 118 Bernie Castro R	5.00	2.20
❑ 119 Chien-Ming Wang C RC	2.00	.90
❑ 120 Chien-Ming Wang U	4.00	1.80
❑ 121 Chien-Ming Wang R	8.00	3.60
❑ 122 Eric Crozier C RC	1.25	.55
❑ 123 Eric Crozier U	2.50	1.10
❑ 124 Eric Crozier R	5.00	2.20
❑ 125 Mi. Garciaparra C RC	2.00	.90
❑ 126 Michael Garciaparra U	4.00	1.80
❑ 127 Michael Garciaparra R	8.00	3.60
❑ 128 Joey Gomes C RC	1.25	.55
❑ 129 Joey Gomes U	2.50	1.10
❑ 130 Joey Gomes R	5.00	2.20
❑ 131 Wil Ledezma C RC	1.25	.55
❑ 132 Wil Ledezma U	2.50	1.10
❑ 133 Wil Ledezma R	5.00	2.20
❑ 134 Branden Florence C RC	1.25	.55
❑ 135 Branden Florence U	2.50	1.10
❑ 136 Branden Florence R	5.00	2.20
❑ 137 Jeremy Bonderman C RC	2.00	.90
❑ 138 Jeremy Bonderman U	4.00	1.80
❑ 139 Jeremy Bonderman R	8.00	3.60
❑ 140 Travis Ishikawa C RC	1.25	.55
❑ 141 Travis Ishikawa U	2.50	1.10
❑ 142 Travis Ishikawa R	5.00	2.20
❑ 143 Ben Francisco C RC	1.25	.55
❑ 144 Ben Francisco U	2.50	1.10
❑ 145 Ben Francisco R	5.00	2.20
❑ 146 Jason Kubel C RC	4.00	1.80
❑ 147 Jason Kubel U	8.00	3.60
❑ 148 Jason Kubel R	15.00	6.75
❑ 149 Tyler Martin C RC	1.25	.55
❑ 150 Tyler Martin U	2.50	1.10
❑ 151 Tyler Martin R	5.00	2.20
❑ 152 Jason Perry C RC	2.00	.90
❑ 153 Jason Perry U	4.00	1.80
❑ 154 Jason Perry R	8.00	3.60
❑ 155 Ryan Shealy C RC	2.00	.90
❑ 156 Ryan Shealy U	4.00	1.80
❑ 157 Ryan Shealy R	8.00	3.60
❑ 158 Hanley Ramirez C RC	4.00	1.80
❑ 159 Hanley Ramirez U	8.00	3.60
❑ 160 Hanley Ramirez R	15.00	6.75
❑ 161 Rajai Davis C RC	1.25	.55
❑ 162 Rajai Davis U	2.50	1.10
❑ 163 Rajai Davis R	5.00	2.20
❑ 164 Gary Schneidmiller C RC	1.25	.55
❑ 165 Gary Schneidmiller U	2.50	1.10
❑ 166 Gary Schneidmiller R	5.00	2.20
❑ 167 Haj Turay C RC	1.25	.55
❑ 168 Haj Turay U	2.50	1.10
❑ 169 Haj Turay R	5.00	2.20
❑ 170 Kevin Youkilis C RC	3.00	1.35
❑ 171 Kevin Youkilis U	6.00	2.70
❑ 172 Kevin Youkilis R	12.00	5.50
❑ 173 Shane Bazzell C RC	1.25	.55
❑ 174 Shane Bazzell U	2.50	1.10
❑ 175 Shane Bazzell R	5.00	2.20
❑ 176 Elizardo Ramirez C RC	2.00	.90
❑ 177 Elizardo Ramirez U	4.00	1.80
❑ 178 Elizardo Ramirez R	8.00	3.60
❑ 179 Robinson Cano C RC	2.00	.90
❑ 180 Robinson Cano U	4.00	1.80
❑ 181 Robinson Cano R	8.00	3.60
❑ 182 Nook Logan C RC	1.25	.55
❑ 183 Nook Logan U	2.50	1.10
❑ 184 Nook Logan R	5.00	2.20
❑ 185 Dustin McGowan C RC	2.00	.90
❑ 186 Dustin McGowan U	4.00	1.80
❑ 187 Dustin McGowan R	8.00	3.60
❑ 188 Ryan Howard C RC	5.00	2.20
❑ 189 Ryan Howard U	10.00	4.50
❑ 190 Ryan Howard R	20.00	9.00

2004 Topps Pristine

	Nm-Mt	Ex-Mt
COMMON CARD (1-100)	1.50	.45
COMMON C (101-190)	2.00	.60
C 101-190 APPROX.EQUAL TO 1-100		
COMMON U (101-190)	3.00	.90
UNCOMMON 101-190 STATED ODDS 1:2		
UNCOMMON 101-190 PRINT 999 #'d SETS		
COMMON R (101-190)	5.00	1.50
RARE 101-190 STATED ODDS 1:4 .00		
RARE 101-190 PRINT RUN 499 #'d SETS		
OVERALL PLATES ODDS 1:52 HOBBY		
PLATE PRINT RUN 1 SET PER COLOR		
BLACK-CYAN-MAGENTA-YELLOW ISSUED		
NO PLATE PRICING DUE TO SCARCITY		

Card	Nm-Mt	Ex-Mt
❑ 1 Jim Thome	4.00	1.20
❑ 2 Ryan Klesko	1.50	.45
❑ 3 Ichiro Suzuki	6.00	1.80
❑ 4 Rocco Baldelli	1.50	.45
❑ 5 Vernon Wells	1.50	.45
❑ 6 Javier Vazquez	1.50	.45
❑ 7 Billy Wagner	1.50	.45
❑ 8 Jose Reyes	1.50	.45
❑ 9 Lance Berkman	1.50	.45
❑ 10 Alex Rodriguez	6.00	1.80
❑ 11 Pat Burrell	1.50	.45
❑ 12 Mark Mulder	1.50	.45
❑ 13 Mike Piazza	6.00	1.80
❑ 14 Miguel Cabrera	2.50	.75
❑ 15 Larry Walker	2.50	.75
❑ 16 Carlos Lee	1.50	.45
❑ 17 Mark Prior	4.00	1.20
❑ 18 Pedro Martinez	4.00	1.20
❑ 19 Melvin Mora	1.50	.45
❑ 20 Sammy Sosa	6.00	1.80
❑ 21 Bartolo Colon	1.50	.45
❑ 22 Luis Gonzalez	1.50	.45
❑ 23 Marcus Giles	1.50	.45
❑ 24 Ken Griffey Jr.	6.00	1.80
❑ 25 Ivan Rodriguez	4.00	1.20
❑ 26 Carlos Beltran	2.50	.75
❑ 27 Geoff Jenkins	1.50	.45

Card	Nm-Mt	Ex-Mt
❑ 28 Nick Johnson	1.50	.45
❑ 29 Gary Sheffield	1.50	.45
❑ 30 Alfonso Soriano	2.50	.75
❑ 31 Scott Rolen	4.00	1.20
❑ 32 Garret Anderson	1.50	.45
❑ 33 Richie Sexson	1.50	.45
❑ 34 Curt Schilling	4.00	1.20
❑ 35 Greg Maddux	6.00	1.80
❑ 36 Adam Dunn	2.50	.75
❑ 37 Preston Wilson	1.50	.45
❑ 38 Josh Beckett	1.50	.45
❑ 39 Roy Oswalt	1.50	.45
❑ 40 Derek Jeter	8.00	2.40
❑ 41 Jason Kendall	1.50	.45
❑ 42 Bret Boone	1.50	.45
❑ 43 Torii Hunter	1.50	.45
❑ 44 Roy Halladay	1.50	.45
❑ 45 Edgar Renteria	1.50	.45
❑ 46 Troy Glaus	1.50	.45
❑ 47 Chipper Jones	4.00	1.20
❑ 48 Manny Ramirez	2.50	.75
❑ 49 C.C. Sabathia	1.50	.45
❑ 50 Albert Pujols	8.00	2.40
❑ 51 Randy Wolf	1.50	.45
❑ 52 Eric Chavez	1.50	.45
❑ 53 Kevin Brown	1.50	.45
❑ 54 Cliff Floyd	1.50	.45
❑ 55 Jeff Bagwell	2.50	.75
❑ 56 Frank Thomas	4.00	1.20
❑ 57 David Ortiz	4.00	1.20
❑ 58 Rafael Palmeiro	2.50	.75
❑ 59 Randy Johnson	4.00	1.20
❑ 60 Vladimir Guerrero	4.00	1.20
❑ 61 Carlos Delgado	1.50	.45
❑ 62 Hank Blalock	1.50	.45
❑ 63 Jim Edmonds	1.50	.45
❑ 64 Jason Schmidt	1.50	.45
❑ 65 Mike Lieberthal	1.50	.45
❑ 66 Tim Hudson	1.50	.45
❑ 67 Jorge Posada	2.50	.75
❑ 68 Jose Vidro	1.50	.45
❑ 69 Eric Gagne	4.00	1.20
❑ 70 Roger Clemens	8.00	2.40
❑ 71 Mike Lowell	1.50	.45
❑ 72 Dontrelle Willis	1.50	.45
❑ 73 Austin Kearns	1.50	.45
❑ 74 Kerry Wood	4.00	1.20
❑ 75 Miguel Tejada	1.50	.45
❑ 76 Bobby Abreu	1.50	.45
❑ 77 Edgar Martinez	2.50	.75
❑ 78 Joe Mauer	2.50	.75
❑ 79 Mike Sweeney	1.50	.45
❑ 80 Jason Giambi	1.50	.45
❑ 81 Mark Teixeira	1.50	.45
❑ 82 Aubrey Huff	1.50	.45
❑ 83 Brian Giles	1.50	.45
❑ 84 Barry Zito	1.50	.45
❑ 85 Mike Mussina	2.50	.75
❑ 86 Brandon Webb	1.50	.45
❑ 87 Andruw Jones	1.50	.45
❑ 88 Javy Lopez	1.50	.45
❑ 89 Bill Mueller	1.50	.45
❑ 90 Scott Podsednik	1.50	.45
❑ 91 Moises Alou	1.50	.45
❑ 92 Esteban Loaiza	1.50	.45
❑ 93 Magglio Ordonez	1.50	.45
❑ 94 Jeff Kent	1.50	.45
❑ 95 Todd Helton	2.50	.75
❑ 96 Juan Pierre	1.50	.45
❑ 97 Jody Gerut	1.50	.45
❑ 98 Angel Berroa	1.50	.45
❑ 99 Shawn Green	1.50	.45
❑ 100 Nomar Garciaparra	6.00	1.80
❑ 101 David Aardsma C RC	2.00	.60
❑ 102 David Aardsma U	3.00	.90
❑ 103 David Aardsma R	5.00	1.50
❑ 104 Erick Aybar C RC	4.00	1.20
❑ 105 Erick Aybar U	6.00	1.80
❑ 106 Erick Aybar R	10.00	3.00
❑ 107 Chad Bentz C RC	2.00	.60
❑ 108 Chad Bentz U	3.00	.90
❑ 109 Chad Bentz R	5.00	1.50
❑ 110 Travis Blackley C RC	2.00	.60
❑ 111 Travis Blackley U	3.00	.90
❑ 112 Travis Blackley R	5.00	1.50
❑ 113 Bobby Brownlie C RC	3.00	.90
❑ 114 Bobby Brownlie U	5.00	1.50
❑ 115 Bobby Brownlie R	8.00	2.40
❑ 116 Alberto Callaspo C RC	3.00	.90
❑ 117 Alberto Callaspo U	5.00	1.50
❑ 118 Alberto Callaspo R	8.00	2.40
❑ 119 Kazuo Matsui C RC	5.00	1.50
❑ 120 Kazuo Matsui U	8.00	2.40
❑ 121 Kazuo Matsui R	12.00	3.60
❑ 122 Jesse Crain C RC	3.00	.90
❑ 123 Jesse Crain U	5.00	1.50
❑ 124 Jesse Crain R	8.00	2.40
❑ 125 Howie Kendrick C RC	3.00	.90
❑ 126 Howie Kendrick U	5.00	1.50
❑ 127 Howie Kendrick R	8.00	2.40
❑ 128 Blake Hawksworth C RC	2.00	.60
❑ 129 Blake Hawksworth U	3.00	.90
❑ 130 Blake Hawksworth R	5.00	1.50
❑ 131 Conor Jackson C RC	6.00	1.80
❑ 132 Conor Jackson U	10.00	3.00
❑ 133 Conor Jackson R	15.00	4.50
❑ 134 Paul Maholm C RC	3.00	.90
❑ 135 Paul Maholm U	5.00	1.50
❑ 136 Paul Maholm R	8.00	2.40
❑ 137 Lastings Milledge C RC	6.00	1.80
❑ 138 Lastings Milledge U	10.00	3.00
❑ 139 Lastings Milledge R	15.00	4.50
❑ 140 Matt Moses C RC	3.00	.90
❑ 141 Matt Moses U	5.00	1.50
❑ 142 Matt Moses R	8.00	2.40
❑ 143 David Murphy C RC	3.00	.90
❑ 144 David Murphy U	5.00	1.50
❑ 145 David Murphy R	8.00	2.40
❑ 146 Dioner Navarro C RC	4.00	1.20
❑ 147 Dioner Navarro U	6.00	1.80
❑ 148 Dioner Navarro R	10.00	3.00
❑ 149 Dustin Nippert C RC	2.00	.60
❑ 150 Dustin Nippert U	3.00	.90
❑ 151 Dustin Nippert R	5.00	1.50
❑ 152 Vito Chiaravalloti C RC	3.00	.90
❑ 153 Vito Chiaravalloti U	5.00	1.50
❑ 154 Vito Chiaravalloti R	8.00	2.40
❑ 155 Akinori Otsuka C RC	2.00	.60
❑ 156 Akinori Otsuka U	3.00	.90
❑ 157 Akinori Otsuka R	5.00	1.50
❑ 158 Casey Daigle C RC	2.00	.60
❑ 159 Casey Daigle U	3.00	.90
❑ 160 Casey Daigle R	5.00	1.50
❑ 161 Carlos Quentin C RC	6.00	1.80
❑ 162 Carlos Quentin U	10.00	3.00
❑ 163 Carlos Quentin R	15.00	4.50
❑ 164 Omar Quintanilla C RC	3.00	.90
❑ 165 Omar Quintanilla U	5.00	1.50
❑ 166 Omar Quintanilla R	8.00	2.40
❑ 167 Chris Saenz C RC	2.00	.60
❑ 168 Chris Saenz U	.00	.00
❑ 169 Chris Saenz R	.00	.00
❑ 170 Ervin Santana C RC	4.00	1.20
❑ 171 Ervin Santana U	6.00	1.80
❑ 172 Ervin Santana R	10.00	3.00
❑ 173 Chris Shelton C RC	3.00	.90
❑ 174 Chris Shelton U	5.00	1.50
❑ 175 Chris Shelton R	8.00	2.40
❑ 176 Kyle Sleeth C RC	3.00	.90
❑ 177 Kyle Sleeth U	5.00	1.50
❑ 178 Kyle Sleeth R	8.00	2.40
❑ 179 Brad Snyder C RC	3.00	.90
❑ 180 Brad Snyder U	5.00	1.50
❑ 181 Brad Snyder R	8.00	2.40
❑ 182 Tim Stauffer C RC	3.00	.90
❑ 183 Tim Stauffer U	5.00	1.50
❑ 184 Tim Stauffer R	8.00	2.40
❑ 185 Shingo Takatsu C RC	3.00	.90
❑ 186 Shingo Takatsu U	5.00	1.50
❑ 187 Shingo Takatsu R	8.00	2.40
❑ 188 Merkin Valdez C RC	3.00	.90
❑ 189 Merkin Valdez U	5.00	1.50
❑ 190 Merkin Valdez R	8.00	2.40

2001 Topps Reserve

	Nm-Mt	Ex-Mt
COMP.SET w/o SP's (100)	100.00	30.00
COMMON CARD (1-100)	1.00	.30
COMMON (101-151)	8.00	2.40

Card	Nm-Mt	Ex-Mt
❑ 1 Darin Erstad	1.00	.30
❑ 2 Moises Alou	1.00	.30
❑ 3 Tony Batista	1.00	.30
❑ 4 Andruw Jones	1.00	.30
❑ 5 Edgar Renteria	1.00	.30
❑ 6 Eric Young	1.00	.30
❑ 7 Steve Finley	1.00	.30
❑ 8 Adrian Beltre	1.50	.45
❑ 9 Vladimir Guerrero	2.50	.75
❑ 10 Barry Bonds	6.00	1.80
❑ 11 Juan Gonzalez	1.50	.45
❑ 12 Jay Buhner	1.00	.30
❑ 13 Luis Castillo	1.00	.30
❑ 14 Cal Ripken	8.00	2.40
❑ 15 Bob Abreu	1.00	.30
❑ 16 Ivan Rodriguez	2.50	.75
❑ 17 Nomar Garciaparra	4.00	1.20
❑ 18 Todd Helton	1.50	.45
❑ 19 Bobby Higginson	1.00	.30
❑ 20 Jorge Posada	1.50	.45
❑ 21 Tim Salmon	1.50	.45
❑ 22 Jason Giambi	1.00	.30
❑ 23 Jose Cruz Jr.	1.00	.30
❑ 24 Chipper Jones	2.50	.75
❑ 25 Jim Edmonds	1.00	.30
❑ 26 Gerald Williams	1.00	.30
❑ 27 Randy Johnson	2.50	.75
❑ 28 Gary Sheffield	1.00	.30
❑ 29 Jeff Kent	1.00	.30
❑ 30 Jim Thome	2.50	.75
❑ 31 John Olerud	1.00	.30
❑ 32 Cliff Floyd	1.00	.30
❑ 33 Mike Lowell	1.00	.30
❑ 34 Phil Nevin	1.00	.30
❑ 35 Scott Rolen	2.50	.75
❑ 36 Alex Rodriguez	4.00	1.20
❑ 37 Ken Griffey Jr.	4.00	1.20
❑ 38 Neifi Perez	1.00	.30
❑ 39 Cristian Guzman	1.00	.30
❑ 40 Mariano Rivera	1.50	.45
❑ 41 Troy Glaus	1.00	.30
❑ 42 Johnny Damon	1.50	.45
❑ 43 Rafael Furcal	1.00	.30
❑ 44 Jeromy Burnitz	1.00	.30
❑ 45 Mark McGwire	6.00	1.80
❑ 46 Fred McGriff	1.50	.45
❑ 47 Matt Williams	1.00	.30
❑ 48 Kevin Brown	1.00	.30
❑ 49 J.T. Snow	1.00	.30
❑ 50 Kenny Lofton	1.00	.30
❑ 51 Al Martin	1.00	.30
❑ 52 Antonio Alfonseca	1.00	.30
❑ 53 Edgardo Alfonzo	1.00	.30
❑ 54 Ryan Klesko	1.00	.30
❑ 55 Pat Burrell	1.00	.30
❑ 56 Rafael Palmeiro	1.50	.45
❑ 57 Sean Casey	1.00	.30
❑ 58 Jeff Cirillo	1.00	.30
❑ 59 Ray Durham	1.00	.30
❑ 60 Derek Jeter	6.00	1.80
❑ 61 Jeff Bagwell	1.50	.45
❑ 62 Carlos Delgado	1.00	.30
❑ 63 Tom Glavine	1.50	.45
❑ 64 Richie Sexson	1.00	.30
❑ 65 J.D. Drew	1.00	.30
❑ 66 Ben Grieve	1.00	.30
❑ 67 Mark Grace	1.50	.45
❑ 68 Shawn Green	1.00	.30
❑ 69 Robb Nen	1.00	.30
❑ 70 Omar Vizquel	1.50	.45
❑ 71 Edgar Martinez	1.50	.45
❑ 72 Preston Wilson	1.00	.30
❑ 73 Mike Piazza	4.00	1.20
❑ 74 Tony Gwynn	3.00	.90
❑ 75 Jason Kendall	1.00	.30

❑ 76 Manny Ramirez	1.50	.45
❑ 77 Pokey Reese	1.00	.30
❑ 78 Mike Sweeney	1.00	.30
❑ 79 Magglio Ordonez	1.00	.30
❑ 80 Bernie Williams	1.50	.45
❑ 81 Richard Hidalgo	1.00	.30
❑ 82 Brad Fullmer	1.00	.30
❑ 83 Greg Maddux	4.00	1.20
❑ 84 Geoff Jenkins	1.00	.30
❑ 85 Sammy Sosa	4.00	1.20
❑ 86 Luis Gonzalez	1.00	.30
❑ 87 Eric Karros	1.00	.30
❑ 88 Jose Vidro	1.00	.30
❑ 89 Rich Aurilia	1.00	.30
❑ 90 Roberto Alomar	1.50	.45
❑ 91 Mike Cameron	1.00	.30
❑ 92 Mike Mussina	1.50	.45
❑ 93 Barry Zito	1.50	.45
❑ 94 Mike Lieberthal	1.00	.30
❑ 95 Brian Giles	1.00	.30
❑ 96 Pedro Martinez	2.50	.75
❑ 97 Barry Larkin	1.50	.45
❑ 98 Jermaine Dye	1.00	.30
❑ 99 Frank Thomas	2.50	.75
❑ 100 David Justice	1.00	.30
❑ 101 Gary Johnson RC	8.00	2.40
❑ 102 Matt Ford RC	8.00	2.40
❑ 103 Albert Pujols RC	80.00	24.00
❑ 104 Brad Cresse	8.00	2.40
❑ 105 V. Pascucci RC	8.00	2.40
❑ 106 Bob Keppel RC	10.00	3.00
❑ 107 Luis Torres RC	8.00	2.40
❑ 108 Tony Blanco RC	10.00	3.00
❑ 109 Ronnie Corona RC	8.00	2.40
❑ 110 Phil Wilson RC	8.00	2.40
❑ 111 John Buck RC	10.00	3.00
❑ 112 Jim Journell RC	8.00	2.40
❑ 113 Victor Hall RC	8.00	2.40
❑ 114 Jeff Andra RC	8.00	2.40
❑ 115 Greg Nash RC	8.00	2.40
❑ 116 Travis Hafner RC	15.00	4.50
❑ 117 Casey Fossum RC	8.00	2.40
❑ 118 Miguel Olivo	8.00	2.40
❑ 119 Elpidio Guzman RC	8.00	2.40
❑ 120 Jason Belcher RC	8.00	2.40
❑ 121 Esix Snead RC	8.00	2.40
❑ 122 Joe Thurston RC	8.00	2.40
❑ 123 Rafael Soriano RC	10.00	3.00
❑ 124 Ed Rogers RC	8.00	2.40
❑ 125 Omar Beltre RC	8.00	2.40
❑ 126 Brett Gray RC	8.00	2.40
❑ 127 Deivi Mendez RC	8.00	2.40
❑ 128 Freddie Bynum RC	8.00	2.40
❑ 129 David Krynzel	8.00	2.40
❑ 130 Blake Williams RC	8.00	2.40
❑ 131 R. Abercrombie RC	8.00	2.40
❑ 132 Miguel Villilo RC	8.00	2.40
❑ 133 Ryan Madson RC	10.00	3.00
❑ 134 Matt Thompson RC	8.00	2.40
❑ 135 Mark Burnett RC	8.00	2.40
❑ 136 Andy Beal RC	8.00	2.40
❑ 137 Ryan Ludwick RC	8.00	2.40
❑ 138 Roberto Miniel RC	8.00	2.40
❑ 139 Steve Smyth RC	8.00	2.40
❑ 140 Ben Washburn RC	8.00	2.40
❑ 141 Marvin Seale RC	8.00	2.40
❑ 142 Reggie Griggs RC	8.00	2.40
❑ 143 Seung Song RC	10.00	3.00
❑ 144 Chad Petty RC	8.00	2.40
❑ 145 Noel Devarez RC	8.00	2.40
❑ 146 Matt Butler RC	8.00	2.40
❑ 147 Brett Evert RC	8.00	2.40
❑ 148 Cesar Izturis	8.00	2.40
❑ 149 Troy Farnsworth RC	8.00	2.40
❑ 150 Brian Schmitt RC	8.00	2.40
❑ 151 Ichiro Suzuki RC	50.00	15.00

2002 Topps Reserve

	Nm-Mt	Ex-Mt
COMP.SET w/o SP's (135)	100.00	30.00
COMMON CARD (1-135)	1.00	.30
COMMON CARD (136-150)	5.00	1.50
❑ 1 Alex Rodriguez	4.00	1.20
❑ 2 Tsuyoshi Shinjo	1.00	.30
❑ 3 Craig Biggio	1.50	.45
❑ 4 Troy Glaus	1.00	.30
❑ 5 Mike Rivera	1.00	.30
❑ 6 Curt Schilling	1.00	.30
❑ 7 Garret Anderson	1.00	.30
❑ 8 Ben Sheets	1.00	.30
❑ 9 Todd Helton	1.50	.45
❑ 10 Paul Konerko	1.00	.30
❑ 11 Sammy Sosa	4.00	1.20
❑ 12 Bud Smith	1.00	.30
❑ 13 Jeff Bagwell	1.50	.45
❑ 14 Albert Pujols	5.00	1.50
❑ 15 Jose Vidro	1.00	.30
❑ 16 Carlos Delgado	1.00	.30
❑ 17 Torii Hunter	1.00	.30
❑ 18 Jerry Hairston	1.00	.30
❑ 19 Troy Percival	1.00	.30
❑ 20 Vladimir Guerrero	2.50	.75
❑ 21 Geoff Jenkins	1.00	.30
❑ 22 Carlos Pena	1.00	.30
❑ 23 Juan Gonzalez	1.50	.45
❑ 24 Raul Mondesi	1.00	.30
❑ 25 Jimmy Rollins	1.00	.30
❑ 26 Mariano Rivera	1.50	.45
❑ 27 Jorge Posada	1.50	.45
❑ 28 Magglio Ordonez	1.00	.30
❑ 29 Roberto Alomar	1.50	.45
❑ 30 Randy Johnson	2.50	.75
❑ 31 Xavier Nady	1.00	.30
❑ 32 Terrence Long	1.00	.30
❑ 33 Chipper Jones	2.50	.75
❑ 34 Rich Aurilia	1.00	.30
❑ 35 Aramis Ramirez	1.00	.30
❑ 36 Jim Thome	2.50	.75
❑ 37 Bret Boone	1.00	.30
❑ 38 Angel Berroa	1.00	.30
❑ 39 Jeff Conine	1.00	.30
❑ 40 Cliff Floyd	1.00	.30
❑ 41 Pedro Martinez	2.50	.75
❑ 42 J.D. Drew	1.00	.30
❑ 43 Kazuhiro Sasaki	1.00	.30
❑ 44 Jon Rauch	1.00	.30
❑ 45 Orlando Hudson	1.00	.30
❑ 46 Scott Rolen	2.50	.75
❑ 47 Rafael Furcal	1.00	.30
❑ 48 Brad Penny	1.00	.30
❑ 49 Miguel Tejada	1.00	.30
❑ 50 Orlando Cabrera	1.00	.30
❑ 51 Bob Abreu	1.00	.30
❑ 52 Darin Erstad	1.00	.30
❑ 53 Edgar Martinez	1.50	.45
❑ 54 Ben Grieve	1.00	.30
❑ 55 Shawn Green	1.00	.30
❑ 56 Ivan Rodriguez	2.50	.75
❑ 57 Josh Beckett	1.00	.30
❑ 58 Ray Durham	1.00	.30
❑ 59 Jason Hart	1.00	.30
❑ 60 Nathan Haynes	1.00	.30
❑ 61 Jason Giambi	1.00	.30
❑ 62 Eric Chavez	1.00	.30
❑ 63 Matt Morris	1.00	.30
❑ 64 Lance Berkman	1.00	.30
❑ 65 Jeff Kent	1.00	.30
❑ 66 Andruw Jones	1.00	.30
❑ 67 Brian Giles	1.00	.30
❑ 68 Morgan Ensberg	1.00	.30
❑ 69 Pat Burrell	1.00	.30
❑ 70 Ken Griffey Jr.	4.00	1.20
❑ 71 Carlos Beltran	1.50	.45
❑ 72 Ichiro Suzuki	4.00	1.20
❑ 73 Larry Walker	1.50	.45
❑ 74 J.J. Putz RC	1.00	.30
❑ 75 Mike Piazza	4.00	1.20
❑ 76 Rafael Palmeiro	1.50	.45
❑ 77 Mark Prior	4.00	1.20
❑ 78 Toby Hall	1.00	.30
❑ 79 Pokey Reese	1.00	.30
❑ 80 Mike Mussina	1.50	.45
❑ 81 Omar Vizquel	1.50	.45
❑ 82 Shannon Stewart	1.00	.30
❑ 83 Jeromy Burnitz	1.00	.30
❑ 84 Bernie Williams	1.50	.45
❑ 85 C.C. Sabathia	1.00	.30
❑ 86 Mike Hampton	1.00	.30
❑ 87 Kevin Brown	1.00	.30
❑ 88 Juan Cruz	1.00	.30
❑ 89 Jeff Weaver	1.00	.30
❑ 90 Jason Lane	1.00	.30
❑ 91 Adam Dunn	1.50	.45
❑ 92 Jose Cruz Jr.	1.00	.30
❑ 93 Marlon Anderson	1.00	.30
❑ 94 Jeff Cirillo	1.00	.30
❑ 95 Mark Buehrle	1.00	.30
❑ 96 Austin Kearns	1.00	.30
❑ 97 Tim Hudson	1.00	.30
❑ 98 Brian Jordan	1.00	.30
❑ 99 Phil Nevin	1.00	.30
❑ 100 Barry Bonds	6.00	1.80
❑ 101 Derek Jeter	6.00	1.80
❑ 102 Javier Vazquez	1.00	.30
❑ 103 Jason Kendall	1.00	.30
❑ 104 Jim Edmonds	1.00	.30
❑ 105 Kenny Kelly	1.00	.30
❑ 106 Juan Pena	1.00	.30
❑ 107 Mark Grace	1.50	.45
❑ 108 Roger Clemens	5.00	1.50
❑ 109 Barry Zito	1.00	.30
❑ 110 Greg Vaughn	1.00	.30
❑ 111 Greg Maddux	4.00	1.20
❑ 112 Richie Sexson	1.00	.30
❑ 113 Jermaine Dye	1.00	.30
❑ 114 Kerry Wood	2.50	.75
❑ 115 Matt Lawton	1.00	.30
❑ 116 Sean Casey	1.00	.30
❑ 117 Gary Sheffield	1.00	.30
❑ 118 Preston Wilson	1.00	.30
❑ 119 Cristian Guzman	1.00	.30
❑ 120 Mike Sweeney	1.00	.30
❑ 121 Neifi Perez	1.00	.30
❑ 122 Paul LoDuca	1.00	.30
❑ 123 Luis Gonzalez	1.00	.30
❑ 124 Ryan Klesko	1.00	.30
❑ 125 Alfonso Soriano	1.50	.45
❑ 126 Bobby Higginson	1.00	.30
❑ 127 Juan Pierre	1.00	.30
❑ 128 Moises Alou	1.00	.30
❑ 129 Roy Oswalt	1.00	.30
❑ 130 Nomar Garciaparra	4.00	1.20
❑ 131 Fred McGriff	1.50	.45
❑ 132 Edgardo Alfonzo	1.00	.30
❑ 133 Johnny Damon Sox	2.50	.75
❑ 134 Dewon Brazelton	1.00	.30
❑ 135 Mark Mulder	1.00	.30
❑ 136 So Taguchi FYP RC	8.00	2.40
❑ 137 Mario Ramos FYP RC	5.00	1.50
❑ 138 Dan Johnson FYP RC	8.00	2.40
❑ 139 Hansel Izquierdo FYP RC	5.00	1.50
❑ 140 Kazuhisa Ishii FYP RC	12.00	3.60
❑ 141 Jon Switzer FYP RC	5.00	1.50
❑ 142 Chris Tritle FYP RC	5.00	1.50
❑ 143 Chris Snelling FYP RC	5.00	1.50
❑ 144 Chone Figgins FYP RC	8.00	2.40
❑ 145 Dan Phillips FYP RC	5.00	1.50
❑ 146 John Rodriguez FYP RC	5.00	1.50
❑ 147 Colt Griffin FYP RC	8.00	2.40
❑ 148 Jonny Gomes FYP RC	8.00	2.40
❑ 149 Josh Barfield FYP RC	10.00	3.00
❑ 150 Joe Mauer FYP RC	30.00	9.00

2003 Topps Retired Signature

	MINT	NRMT
COMPLETE SET (110)	200.00	90.00
❑ 1 Willie Mays	6.00	2.70
❑ 2 Tony Perez	1.25	.55
❑ 3 Tom Seaver	2.00	.90
❑ 4 Johnny Bench	3.00	1.35
❑ 5 Rod Carew	2.00	.90
❑ 6 Red Schoendienst	1.25	.55
❑ 7 Phil Rizzuto	2.00	.90

Card	Nm-Mt	Ex-Mt
❑ 8 Ozzie Smith	5.00	2.20
❑ 9 Maury Wills	1.25	.55
❑ 10 Hank Aaron	6.00	2.70
❑ 11 Jim Palmer	1.25	.55
❑ 12 Jose Cruz Sr.	1.25	.55
❑ 13 Dave Parker	1.25	.55
❑ 14 Don Sutton	1.25	.55
❑ 15 Brooks Robinson	2.00	.90
❑ 16 Bo Jackson	3.00	1.35
❑ 17 Andre Dawson	1.25	.55
❑ 18 Fergie Jenkins	1.25	.55
❑ 19 George Foster	1.25	.55
❑ 20 George Brett	8.00	3.60
❑ 21 Jerry Koosman	1.25	.55
❑ 22 John Kruk	1.25	.55
❑ 23 Kent Tekulve	1.25	.55
❑ 24 Lee Smith	1.25	.55
❑ 25 Nolan Ryan	8.00	3.60
❑ 26 Paul O'Neill	1.25	.55
❑ 27 Rich Gossage	1.25	.55
❑ 28 Ron Santo	1.25	.55
❑ 29 Tom Lasorda	1.25	.55
❑ 30 Tony Gwynn	4.00	1.80
❑ 31 Vida Blue	1.25	.55
❑ 32 Whitey Herzog	1.25	.55
❑ 33 Willie McGee	1.25	.55
❑ 34 Bill Mazeroski	1.25	.55
❑ 35 Al Kaline	3.00	1.35
❑ 36 Bobby Richardson	1.25	.55
❑ 37 Carlton Fisk	2.00	.90
❑ 38 Darrell Evans	1.25	.55
❑ 39 Dave Concepcion	1.25	.55
❑ 40 Cal Ripken	10.00	4.50
❑ 41 Dwight Evans	1.25	.55
❑ 42 Earl Weaver	1.25	.55
❑ 43 Fred Lynn	1.25	.55
❑ 44 Greg Luzinski	1.25	.55
❑ 45 Duke Snider	2.00	.90
❑ 46 Hank Bauer	1.25	.55
❑ 47 Jim Rice	1.25	.55
❑ 48 Johnny Sain	1.25	.55
❑ 49 Lenny Dykstra	1.25	.55
❑ 50 Mike Schmidt	6.00	2.70
❑ 51 Orlando Cepeda	1.25	.55
❑ 52 Ralph Kiner	1.25	.55
❑ 53 Robin Roberts	1.25	.55
❑ 54 Ron Guidry	1.25	.55
❑ 55 Steve Garvey	1.25	.55
❑ 56 Tony Oliva	1.25	.55
❑ 57 Whitey Ford	2.00	.90
❑ 58 Willie McCovey	1.25	.55
❑ 59 Phil Niekro	1.25	.55
❑ 60 Stan Musial	5.00	2.20
❑ 61 Rollie Fingers	1.25	.55
❑ 62 Robin Yount	5.00	2.20
❑ 63 Alan Trammell	1.25	.55
❑ 64 Bill Buckner	1.25	.55
❑ 65 Bob Feller	1.25	.55
❑ 66 Bruce Sutter	1.25	.55
❑ 67 Dale Murphy	3.00	1.35
❑ 68 Dennis Eckersley	1.25	.55
❑ 69 Don Newcombe	1.25	.55
❑ 70 Don Mattingly	8.00	3.60
❑ 71 Dwight Gooden	1.25	.55
❑ 72 Frank Robinson	2.00	.90
❑ 73 Gary Carter	1.25	.55
❑ 74 Graig Nettles	1.25	.55
❑ 75 Harmon Killebrew	3.00	1.35
❑ 76 Jim Bunning	1.25	.55
❑ 77 Joe Morgan	1.25	.55
❑ 78 Joe Rudi	1.25	.55
❑ 79 Jose Canseco	3.00	1.35
❑ 80 Ernie Banks	3.00	1.35
❑ 81 Luis Aparicio	1.25	.55
❑ 82 Luis Tiant	1.25	.55
❑ 83 Mark Fidrych	1.25	.55
❑ 84 Kirk Gibson	1.25	.55
❑ 85 Lou Brock	2.00	.90
❑ 86 Juan Marichal	1.25	.55
❑ 87 Monte Irvin	1.25	.55
❑ 88 Paul Molitor	2.00	.90
❑ 89 Tommy John	1.25	.55
❑ 90 Warren Spahn	2.00	.90
❑ 91 Wade Boggs	2.00	.90
❑ 92 Reggie Jackson	2.00	.90
❑ 93 Kirby Puckett	3.00	1.35
❑ 94 Boog Powell	2.00	.90
❑ 95 Carl Yastrzemski	5.00	2.20
❑ 96 Bobby Thomson	1.25	.55
❑ 97 Bill Skowron	1.25	.55
❑ 98 Bill Madlock	1.25	.55
❑ 99 Sparky Anderson	1.25	.55
❑ 100 Yogi Berra	3.00	1.35
❑ 101 Bobby Doerr	1.25	.55
❑ 102 Gaylord Perry	1.25	.55
❑ 103 George Kell	1.25	.55
❑ 104 Harold Reynolds	1.25	.55
❑ 105 Joe Carter	1.25	.55
❑ 106 Johnny Podres	1.25	.55
❑ 107 Ron Cey	1.25	.55
❑ 108 Tim McCarver	1.25	.55
❑ 109 Tug McGraw	1.25	.55
❑ 110 Don Larsen	1.25	.55

2004 Topps Retired Signature

	Nm-Mt	Ex-Mt
COMPLETE SET (110)	200.00	60.00
❑ 1 Willie Mays	6.00	1.80
❑ 2 Tony Gwynn	5.00	1.50
❑ 3 Dale Murphy	2.00	.60
❑ 4 Lenny Dykstra	1.25	.35
❑ 5 Johnny Bench	3.00	.90
❑ 6 Bill Buckner	1.25	.35
❑ 7 Ferguson Jenkins	1.25	.35
❑ 8 George Brett	6.00	1.80
❑ 9 Ralph Kiner	2.00	.60
❑ 10 Ernie Banks	3.00	.90
❑ 11 Hal McRae	1.25	.35
❑ 12 Lou Brock	2.00	.60
❑ 13 Keith Hernandez	1.25	.35
❑ 14 Jose Canseco	3.00	.90
❑ 15 Whitey Ford	2.00	.60
❑ 16 Dave Kingman	1.25	.35
❑ 17 Tim Raines	1.25	.35
❑ 18 Paul O'Neill	2.00	.60
❑ 19 Lou Whitaker	1.25	.35
❑ 20 Mike Schmidt	6.00	1.80
❑ 21 Wally Joyner	1.00	.30
❑ 22 Kirk Gibson	1.25	.35
❑ 23 Ryne Sandberg	6.00	1.80
❑ 24 Luis Tiant	1.25	.35
❑ 25 Al Kaline	3.00	.90
❑ 26 Brooks Robinson	2.00	.60
❑ 27 Don Zimmer	1.25	.35
❑ 28 Nolan Ryan	8.00	2.40
❑ 29 Maury Wills	1.25	.35
❑ 30 Stan Musial	5.00	1.50
❑ 31 Garry Maddox	1.00	.30
❑ 32 Tom Brunansky	1.00	.30
❑ 33 Don Mattingly	6.00	1.80
❑ 34 Earl Weaver	1.25	.35
❑ 35 Bobby Grich	1.25	.35
❑ 36 Orlando Cepeda	1.25	.35
❑ 37 Alan Trammell	1.25	.35
❑ 38 Al Hrabosky	1.00	.30
❑ 39 Dave Lopes	1.00	.30
❑ 40 Rod Carew	2.00	.60
❑ 41 Robin Yount	5.00	1.50
❑ 42 Dwight Gooden	1.25	.35
❑ 43 Andre Dawson	1.25	.35
❑ 44 Hank Aaron	6.00	1.80
❑ 45 Norm Cash	2.00	.60
❑ 46 Reggie Jackson	2.00	.60
❑ 47 Jim Rice	1.25	.35
❑ 48 Carlton Fisk	2.00	.60
❑ 49 Dave Parker	1.25	.35
❑ 50 Cal Ripken	10.00	3.00
❑ 51 Roy Face	1.00	.30
❑ 52 Bob Gibson	2.00	.60
❑ 53 Jimmy Key	1.25	.35
❑ 54 Al Oliver	1.00	.30
❑ 55 Don Larsen	1.25	.35
❑ 56 Tom Seaver	2.00	.60
❑ 57 Tony Armas	1.00	.30
❑ 58 Dave Stieb	1.25	.35
❑ 59 Will Clark	3.00	.90
❑ 60 Duke Snider	2.00	.60
❑ 61 Cesar Geronimo	1.00	.30
❑ 62 Ron Kittle	1.00	.30
❑ 63 Ron Santo	2.00	.60
❑ 64 Mickey Rivers	1.00	.30
❑ 65 Jim Piersall	1.25	.35
❑ 66 Ron Swoboda	1.25	.35
❑ 67 Kent Hrbek	1.00	.30
❑ 68 Dennis Eckersley	2.00	.60
❑ 69 Greg Luzinski	1.25	.35
❑ 70 Harmon Killebrew	3.00	.90
❑ 71 Ron Guidry	1.25	.35
❑ 72 Steve Garvey	1.25	.35
❑ 73 Andy Van Slyke	1.25	.35
❑ 74 Goose Gossage	1.25	.35
❑ 75 Ozzie Smith	5.00	1.50
❑ 76 Richie Allen	1.25	.35
❑ 77 Vida Blue	1.00	.30
❑ 78 Tony Oliva	1.25	.35
❑ 79 Darryl Strawberry	1.25	.35
❑ 80 Frank Robinson	1.25	.35
❑ 81 Bruce Sutter	1.25	.35
❑ 82 Dave Concepcion	1.25	.35
❑ 83 Darrell Evans	1.00	.30
❑ 84 Jack Morris	1.25	.35
❑ 85 Bo Jackson	3.00	.90
❑ 86 Orel Hershiser	1.25	.35
❑ 87 Rob Dibble	1.25	.35
❑ 88 Wade Boggs	2.00	.60
❑ 89 Fernando Valenzuela	1.25	.35
❑ 90 Jim Palmer	1.25	.35
❑ 91 George Foster	1.25	.35
❑ 92 Mike Scott	1.00	.30
❑ 93 Paul Molitor	2.00	.60
❑ 94 Gary Carter	1.25	.35
❑ 95 Bobby Richardson	1.25	.35
❑ 96 Rollie Fingers	1.25	.35
❑ 97 Tim McCarver	1.25	.35
❑ 98 John Candelaria	1.00	.30
❑ 99 Dave Winfield	1.25	.35
❑ 100 Yogi Berra	3.00	.90
❑ 101 Bill Madlock	1.25	.35
❑ 102 Jack McDowell	1.00	.30
❑ 103 Luis Aparicio	1.25	.35
❑ 104 Graig Nettles	1.25	.35
❑ 105 Dave Stewart	1.25	.35
❑ 106 Darren Daulton	1.25	.35
❑ 107 Gary Gaetti	1.25	.35
❑ 108 Tony Fernandez	1.00	.30
❑ 109 Buddy Bell	1.00	.30
❑ 110 Carl Yastrzemski	5.00	1.50

1997 Topps Stars

	Nm-Mt	Ex-Mt
COMPLETE SET (125)	30.00	9.00
❑ 1 Larry Walker	.50	.15
❑ 2 Tino Martinez	.50	.15
❑ 3 Cal Ripken	2.50	.75
❑ 4 Ken Griffey Jr.	1.25	.35
❑ 5 Chipper Jones	.75	.23
❑ 6 David Justice	.30	.09
❑ 7 Mike Piazza	1.25	.35
❑ 8 Jeff Bagwell	.50	.15
❑ 9 Ron Gant	.30	.09
❑ 10 Sammy Sosa	1.25	.35
❑ 11 Tony Gwynn	1.00	.30
❑ 12 Carlos Baerga	.30	.09
❑ 13 Frank Thomas	.75	.23
❑ 14 Moises Alou	.30	.09
❑ 15 Barry Larkin	.50	.15
❑ 16 Ivan Rodriguez	.75	.23
❑ 17 Greg Maddux	1.25	.35
❑ 18 Jim Edmonds	.30	.09
❑ 19 Jose Canseco	.75	.23
❑ 20 Rafael Palmeiro	.50	.15
❑ 21 Paul Molitor	.50	.15
❑ 22 Kevin Appier	.30	.09
❑ 23 Raul Mondesi	.30	.09
❑ 24 Lance Johnson	.30	.09
❑ 25 Edgar Martinez	.50	.15
❑ 26 Andres Galarraga	.30	.09
❑ 27 Mo Vaughn	.30	.09
❑ 28 Ken Caminiti	.30	.09
❑ 29 Cecil Fielder	.30	.09
❑ 30 Harold Baines	.30	.09
❑ 31 Roberto Alomar	.50	.15
❑ 32 Shawn Estes	.30	.09
❑ 33 Tom Glavine	.50	.15
❑ 34 Dennis Eckersley	.30	.09
❑ 35 Manny Ramirez	.50	.15
❑ 36 John Olerud	.30	.09
❑ 37 Juan Gonzalez	.50	.15
❑ 38 Chuck Knoblauch	.30	.09
❑ 39 Albert Belle	.30	.09
❑ 40 Vinny Castilla	.30	.09
❑ 41 John Smoltz	.50	.15
❑ 42 Barry Bonds	2.00	.60
❑ 43 Randy Johnson	.75	.23
❑ 44 Brady Anderson	.30	.09
❑ 45 Jeff Blauser	.30	.09
❑ 46 Craig Biggio	.50	.15
❑ 47 Jeff Conine	.30	.09
❑ 48 Marquis Grissom	.30	.09
❑ 49 Mark Grace	.50	.15
❑ 50 Roger Clemens	1.50	.45
❑ 51 Mark McGwire	2.00	.60
❑ 52 Fred McGriff	.50	.15
❑ 53 Gary Sheffield	.30	.09
❑ 54 Bobby Jones	.30	.09
❑ 55 Eric Young	.30	.09
❑ 56 Robin Ventura	.30	.09
❑ 57 Wade Boggs	.50	.15
❑ 58 Joe Carter	.30	.09
❑ 59 Ryne Sandberg	1.25	.35
❑ 60 Matt Williams	.30	.09
❑ 61 Todd Hundley	.30	.09
❑ 62 Dante Bichette	.30	.09
❑ 63 Chili Davis	.30	.09
❑ 64 Kenny Lofton	.30	.09
❑ 65 Jay Buhner	.30	.09
❑ 66 Will Clark	.75	.23
❑ 67 Travis Fryman	.30	.09
❑ 68 Pat Hentgen	.30	.09
❑ 69 Ellis Burks	.30	.09
❑ 70 Mike Mussina	.50	.15
❑ 71 Hideo Nomo	.75	.23
❑ 72 Sandy Alomar Jr.	.30	.09
❑ 73 Bobby Bonilla	.30	.09
❑ 74 Rickey Henderson	.75	.23
❑ 75 David Cone	.30	.09
❑ 76 Terry Steinbach	.30	.09
❑ 77 Pedro Martinez	.75	.23
❑ 78 Jim Thome	.75	.23
❑ 79 Rod Beck	.30	.09
❑ 80 Randy Myers	.30	.09
❑ 81 Charles Nagy	.30	.09
❑ 82 Mark Wohlers	.30	.09
❑ 83 Paul O'Neill	.50	.15
❑ 84 Curt Schilling	.30	.09
❑ 85 Joey Cora	.30	.09
❑ 86 John Franco	.30	.09
❑ 87 Kevin Brown	.30	.09
❑ 88 Benito Santiago	.30	.09
❑ 89 Ray Lankford	.30	.09
❑ 90 Bernie Williams	.50	.15
❑ 91 Jason Dickson	.30	.09
❑ 92 Jeff Cirillo	.30	.09
❑ 93 Nomar Garciaparra	1.25	.35
❑ 94 Mariano Rivera	.50	.15
❑ 95 Javy Lopez	.30	.09
❑ 96 Tony Womack RC	.75	.23
❑ 97 Jose Rosado	.30	.09
❑ 98 Denny Neagle	.30	.09
❑ 99 Darryl Kile	.30	.09
❑ 100 Justin Thompson	.30	.09
❑ 101 Juan Encarnacion	.30	.09
❑ 102 Brad Fullmer	.30	.09
❑ 103 Kris Benson RC	1.25	.35
❑ 104 Todd Helton	.75	.23
❑ 105 Paul Konerko	.30	.09
❑ 106 Travis Lee RC	.50	.15
❑ 107 Todd Greene	.30	.09
❑ 108 Mark Kotsay RC	1.25	.35
❑ 109 Carl Pavano	1.00	.09
❑ 110 Kerry Wood RC	10.00	3.00
❑ 111 Jason Romano RC	.30	.09
❑ 112 Geoff Goetz RC	.30	.09
❑ 113 Scott Hodges RC	.30	.09
❑ 114 Aaron Akin RC	.30	.09
❑ 115 Vernon Wells RC	2.00	.60
❑ 116 Chris Stowe RC	.30	.09
❑ 117 Brett Caradonna RC	.30	.09
❑ 118 Adam Kennedy RC	.75	.23
❑ 119 Jayson Werth RC	1.25	.35
❑ 120 Glenn Davis RC	.30	.09
❑ 121 Troy Cameron RC	.30	.09
❑ 122 J.J. Davis RC	.50	.15
❑ 123 Jason Dellaero RC	.30	.09
❑ 124 Jason Standridge RC	.50	.15
❑ 125 Lance Berkman RC	6.00	1.80
❑ NNO Checklist	.30	.09

2001 Topps Stars

	Nm-Mt	Ex-Mt
COMPLETE SET (200)	50.00	15.00
❑ 1 Darin Erstad	.50	.15
❑ 2 Luis Gonzalez	.50	.15
❑ 3 Rafael Furcal	.50	.15
❑ 4 Dante Bichette	.50	.15
❑ 5 Sammy Sosa	2.00	.60
❑ 6 Ken Griffey Jr.	2.00	.60
❑ 7 Jim Thome	1.25	.35
❑ 8 Bobby Higginson	.50	.15
❑ 9 Cliff Floyd	.50	.15
❑ 10 Lance Berkman	.50	.15
❑ 11 Eric Karros	.50	.15
❑ 12 Jeromy Burnitz	.50	.15
❑ 13 Jose Vidro	.40	.12
❑ 14 Benny Agbayani	.40	.12
❑ 15 Jorge Posada	.75	.23
❑ 16 Ramon Hernandez	.40	.12
❑ 17 Jason Kendall	.50	.15
❑ 18 Jeff Kent	.50	.15
❑ 19 John Olerud	.50	.15
❑ 20 Al Martin	.40	.12
❑ 21 Gerald Williams	.40	.12
❑ 22 Gabe Kapler	.40	.12
❑ 23 Carlos Delgado	.50	.15
❑ 24 Mariano Rivera	.75	.23
❑ 25 Javy Lopez	.50	.15
❑ 26 Paul Konerko	.50	.15
❑ 27 Daryle Ward	.40	.12
❑ 28 Mike Lieberthal	.50	.15
❑ 29 Tom Goodwin	.40	.12
❑ 30 Garret Anderson	.50	.15
❑ 31 Steve Finley	.50	.15
❑ 32 Brian Jordan	.50	.15
❑ 33 Nomar Garciaparra	2.00	.60
❑ 34 Ray Durham	.50	.15
❑ 35 Sean Casey	.50	.15
❑ 36 Kenny Lofton	.50	.15
❑ 37 Dean Palmer	.50	.15
❑ 38 Jeff Bagwell	.75	.23
❑ 39 Mike Sweeney	.50	.15
❑ 40 Adrian Beltre	.75	.23
❑ 41 Richie Sexson	.50	.15
❑ 42 Vladimir Guerrero	1.25	.35
❑ 43 Derek Jeter	3.00	.90
❑ 44 Miguel Tejada	.50	.15
❑ 45 Doug Glanville	.40	.12
❑ 46 Brian Giles	.50	.15
❑ 47 Marvin Benard	.40	.12
❑ 48 Edgar Martinez	.75	.23
❑ 49 Edgar Renteria	.50	.15
❑ 50 Fred McGriff	.75	.23
❑ 51 Ivan Rodriguez	1.25	.35
❑ 52 Brad Fullmer	.40	.12
❑ 53 Antonio Alfonseca	.40	.12
❑ 54 Tom Glavine	.75	.23
❑ 55 Warren Morris	.40	.12
❑ 56 Johnny Damon	.75	.23
❑ 57 Dmitri Young	.50	.15
❑ 58 Mo Vaughn	.50	.15
❑ 59 Randy Johnson	1.25	.35
❑ 60 Greg Maddux	2.00	.60
❑ 61 Carl Everett	.50	.15
❑ 62 Magglio Ordonez	.50	.15
❑ 63 Pokey Reese	.40	.12
❑ 64 Todd Helton	.75	.23
❑ 65 Preston Wilson	.50	.15
❑ 66 Richard Hidalgo	.40	.12
❑ 67 Jermaine Dye	.50	.15
❑ 68 Gary Sheffield	.50	.15
❑ 69 Geoff Jenkins	.50	.15
❑ 70 Edgardo Alfonzo	.40	.12
❑ 71 Paul O'Neill	.75	.23
❑ 72 Terrence Long	.40	.12
❑ 73 Bob Abreu	.50	.15
❑ 74 Kevin Young	.40	.12
❑ 75 J.T. Snow	.50	.15
❑ 76 Alex Rodriguez	2.00	.60
❑ 77 Jim Edmonds	.50	.15
❑ 78 Mark McGwire	3.00	.90
❑ 79 Tony Batista	.50	.15
❑ 80 Darrin Fletcher	.40	.12
❑ 81 Robb Nen	.50	.15
❑ 82 Jose Offerman	.40	.12
❑ 83 Travis Fryman	.50	.15
❑ 84 Joe Randa	.40	.12
❑ 85 Omar Vizquel	.75	.23
❑ 86 Tim Salmon	.75	.23

❑ 87 Andruw Jones .50 .15
❑ 88 Albert Belle .50 .15
❑ 89 Manny Ramirez .75 .23
❑ 90 Frank Thomas 1.25 .35
❑ 91 Barry Larkin .75 .23
❑ 92 Neifi Perez .40 .12
❑ 93 Luis Castillo .40 .12
❑ 94 Moises Alou .50 .15
❑ 95 Mark Quinn .40 .12
❑ 96 Kevin Brown .50 .15
❑ 97 Cristian Guzman .40 .12
❑ 98 Mike Piazza 2.00 .60
❑ 99 Bernie Williams .75 .23
❑ 100 Jason Giambi .50 .15
❑ 101 Scott Rolen 1.25 .35
❑ 102 Phil Nevin .50 .15
❑ 103 Rich Aurilia .40 .12
❑ 104 Mike Cameron .50 .15
❑ 105 Fernando Vina .40 .12
❑ 106 Greg Vaughn .40 .12
❑ 107 Jose Cruz Jr. .40 .12
❑ 108 Raul Mondesi .50 .15
❑ 109 Ben Molina .40 .12
❑ 110 Pedro Martinez 1.25 .35
❑ 111 Todd Hollandsworth .40 .12
❑ 112 Jacque Jones .50 .15
❑ 113 Rickey Henderson 1.25 .35
❑ 114 Troy Glaus .50 .15
❑ 115 Chipper Jones 1.25 .35
❑ 116 Delino DeShields .40 .12
❑ 117 Eric Young .40 .12
❑ 118 Jose Valentin .40 .12
❑ 119 Roberto Alomar .75 .23
❑ 120 Jeff Cirillo .40 .12
❑ 121 Mike Lowell .50 .15
❑ 122 Julio Lugo .40 .12
❑ 123 Shawn Green .50 .15
❑ 124 Marquis Grissom .50 .15
❑ 125 Matt Lawton .40 .12
❑ 126 Jay Payton .40 .12
❑ 127 David Justice .50 .15
❑ 128 Eric Chavez .50 .15
❑ 129 Pat Burrell .50 .15
❑ 130 Ryan Klesko .50 .15
❑ 131 Barry Bonds 3.00 .90
❑ 132 Jay Buhner .50 .15
❑ 133 J.D. Drew .50 .15
❑ 134 Rafael Palmeiro .75 .23
❑ 135 Shannon Stewart .50 .15
❑ 136 Juan Gonzalez .75 .23
❑ 137 Tony Womack .40 .12
❑ 138 Carlos Lee .50 .15
❑ 139 Derrek Lee .50 .15
❑ 140 Ben Grieve .40 .12
❑ 141 Ron Belliard .40 .12
❑ 142 Stan Musial 2.00 .60
❑ 143 Ernie Banks 1.25 .35
❑ 144 Jim Palmer .50 .15
❑ 145 Tony Perez .50 .15
❑ 146 Duke Snider .75 .23
❑ 147 Rod Carew .75 .23
❑ 148 Warren Spahn .75 .23
❑ 149 Yogi Berra 1.50 .45
❑ 150 Juan Marichal .50 .15
❑ 151 Eric Munson .40 .12
❑ 152 Carlos Pena .40 .12
❑ 153 Joe Crede .40 .12
❑ 154 Ryan Anderson .40 .12
❑ 155 Milton Bradley .50 .15
❑ 156 Sean Burroughs .50 .15
❑ 157 Corey Patterson .50 .15
❑ 158 C.C. Sabathia .50 .15
❑ 159 Ben Petrick .40 .12
❑ 160 Aubrey Huff .50 .15
❑ 161 Gookie Dawkins .40 .12
❑ 162 Ben Sheets .75 .23
❑ 163 Pablo Ozuna .40 .12
❑ 164 Eric Valent .40 .12
❑ 165 Rod Barajas .40 .12
❑ 166 Chin-Feng Chen .50 .15
❑ 167 Josh Hamilton .40 .12
❑ 168 Keith Ginter .40 .12
❑ 169 Vernon Wells .50 .15
❑ 170 Dernell Stenson .40 .12
❑ 171 Alfonso Soriano .75 .23
❑ 172 Jason Marquis .40 .12
❑ 173 Nick Johnson .40 .12
❑ 174 Adam Everett .40 .12
❑ 175 Jimmy Rollins .50 .15
❑ 176 Ben Diggins .40 .12
❑ 177 John Lackey .40 .12
❑ 178 Scott Heard .40 .12
❑ 179 Brian Hitchcox RC .60 .18
❑ 180 Odannis Ayala RC .60 .18
❑ 181 Scott Pratt RC .60 .18
❑ 182 Greg Runser RC .60 .18
❑ 183 Chris Russ RC .60 .18
❑ 184 Derek Thompson .40 .12
❑ 185 Jason Jones RC .60 .18
❑ 186 Dominic Rich RC .60 .18
❑ 187 Chad Petty RC .60 .18
❑ 188 Steve Smyth RC .60 .18
❑ 189 Bryan Hebson RC .60 .18
❑ 190 Danny Borrell RC .60 .18
❑ 191 Bob Keppel RC 1.00 .30
❑ 192 Justin Wayne RC .60 .18
❑ 193 R. Abercrombie RC .60 .18
❑ 194 Travis Baptist RC .40 .12
❑ 195 Shawn Fagan RC .60 .18
❑ 196 Jose Reyes RC 5.00 1.50
❑ 197 Chris Bass RC .60 .18
❑ 198 Albert Pujols RC 40.00 12.00
❑ 199 Luis Cotto RC .60 .18
❑ 200 Jake Peavy RC 4.00 1.20

2004 Topps Total

Nm-Mt Ex-Mt

COMPLETE SET (880) 150.00 45.00
OVERALL PRESS PLATES ODDS 1:159
PLATES PRINT RUN 1 #'d SET PER COLOR
PLATES: BLACK, CYAN, MAGENTA & YELLOW
NO PLATES PRICING DUE TO SCARCITY

❑ 1 Kevin Brown .30 .09
❑ 2 Mike Mordecai .20 .06
❑ 3 Seung Song .20 .06
❑ 4 Mike Maroth .20 .06
❑ 5 Mike Lieberthal .30 .09
❑ 6 Billy Koch .20 .06
❑ 7 Mike Stanton .20 .06
❑ 8 Brad Penny .30 .09
❑ 9 Brooks Kieschnick .20 .06
❑ 10 Carlos Delgado .30 .09
❑ 11 Brady Clark .20 .06
❑ 12 Ramon Martinez .20 .06
❑ 13 Dan Wilson .20 .06
❑ 14 Guillermo Mota .20 .06
❑ 15 Trevor Hoffman .30 .09
❑ 16 Tony Batista .30 .09
❑ 17 Rusty Greer .30 .09
❑ 18 David Weathers .20 .06
❑ 19 Horacio Ramirez .20 .06
❑ 20 Aubrey Huff .30 .09
❑ 21 Casey Blake .20 .06
❑ 22 Ryan Bukvich .20 .06
❑ 23 Garrett Atkins .20 .06
❑ 24 Jose Contreras .30 .09
❑ 25 Chipper Jones .75 .23
❑ 26 Neifi Perez .20 .06
❑ 27 Scott Linebrink .20 .06
❑ 28 Matt Kinney .20 .06
❑ 29 Michael Restovich .20 .06
❑ 30 Scott Rolen .75 .23
❑ 31 John Franco .30 .09
❑ 32 Toby Hall .20 .06
❑ 33 Wily Mo Pena .30 .09
❑ 34 Dennis Tankersley .20 .06
❑ 35 Robb Nen .30 .09
❑ 36 Jose Valverde .20 .06
❑ 37 Chin-Feng Chen .30 .09
❑ 38 Gary Knotts .20 .06
❑ 39 Mark Sweeney .20 .06
❑ 40 Bret Boone .30 .09
❑ 41 Josh Phelps .20 .06
❑ 42 Jason LaRue .20 .06
❑ 43 Tim Redding .20 .06
❑ 44 Greg Myers .20 .06
❑ 45 Darin Erstad .30 .09
❑ 46 Kip Wells .20 .06
❑ 47 Matt Ford .20 .06
❑ 48 Jerome Williams .30 .09
❑ 49 Brian Meadows .20 .06
❑ 50 Albert Pujols 1.50 .45
❑ 51 Kirk Saarloos .20 .06
❑ 52 Scott Eyre .20 .06
❑ 53 John Flaherty .20 .06
❑ 54 Rafael Soriano .20 .06
❑ 55 Shea Hillenbrand .30 .09
❑ 56 Kyle Farnsworth .20 .06
❑ 57 Nate Cornejo .20 .06
❑ 58 Julian Tavarez .20 .06
❑ 59 Ryan Vogelsong .20 .06
❑ 60 Ryan Klesko .30 .09
❑ 61 Luke Hudson .20 .06
❑ 62 Justin Morneau .30 .09
❑ 63 Frank Catalanotto .20 .06
❑ 64 Derrick Turnbow .20 .06
❑ 65 Marcus Giles .30 .09
❑ 66 Mark Mulder .30 .09
❑ 67 Matt Anderson .20 .06
❑ 68 Mike Matheny .30 .09
❑ 69 Brian Lawrence .20 .06
❑ 70 Bobby Abreu .30 .09
❑ 71 Damian Moss .20 .06
❑ 72 Richard Hidalgo .20 .06
❑ 73 Mark Kotsay .20 .06
❑ 74 Mike Cameron .30 .09
❑ 75 Troy Glaus .30 .09
❑ 76 Matt Holliday .20 .06
❑ 77 Byung-Hyun Kim .30 .09
❑ 78 Aaron Sele .20 .06
❑ 79 Danny Graves .20 .06
❑ 80 Barry Zito .30 .09
❑ 81 Matt LeCroy .20 .06
❑ 82 Jason Isringhausen .30 .09
❑ 83 Colby Lewis .20 .06
❑ 84 Franklyn German .20 .06
❑ 85 Luis Matos .20 .06
❑ 86 Mike Timlin .20 .06
❑ 87 Miguel Batista .20 .06
❑ 88 John McDonald .20 .06
❑ 89 Joey Eischen .20 .06
❑ 90 Mike Mussina .50 .15
❑ 91 Jack Wilson .30 .09
❑ 92 Aaron Cook .20 .06
❑ 93 John Parrish .20 .06
❑ 94 Jose Valentin .20 .06
❑ 95 Johnny Damon .75 .23
❑ 96 Pat Burrell .30 .09
❑ 97 Brendan Donnelly .20 .06
❑ 98 Lance Carter .20 .06
❑ 99 Omar Daal .20 .06
❑ 100 Ichiro Suzuki 1.25 .35
❑ 101 Robin Ventura .30 .09
❑ 102 Brian Shouse .20 .06
❑ 103 Kevin Jarvis .20 .06
❑ 104 Jason Young .20 .06
❑ 105 Moises Alou .30 .09
❑ 106 Wes Obermueller .20 .06
❑ 107 David Segui .20 .06
❑ 108 Mike MacDougal .20 .06
❑ 109 John Buck .20 .06
❑ 110 Gary Sheffield .30 .09
❑ 111 Yorvit Torrealba .20 .06
❑ 112 Matt Kata .20 .06
❑ 113 David Bell .20 .06
❑ 114 Juan Gonzalez .50 .15
❑ 115 Kelvim Escobar .20 .06
❑ 116 Ruben Sierra .30 .09

❑ 117	Todd Wellemeyer	.20	.06
❑ 118	Jamie Walker	.20	.06
❑ 119	Will Cunnane	.20	.06
❑ 120	Cliff Floyd	.30	.09
❑ 121	Aramis Ramirez	.30	.09
❑ 122	Damaso Marte	.20	.06
❑ 123	Juan Castro	.20	.06
❑ 124	Chris Woodward	.20	.06
❑ 125	Andruw Jones	.30	.09
❑ 126	Ben Weber	.20	.06
❑ 127	Dee Brown	.20	.06
❑ 128	Steve Reed	.20	.06
❑ 129	Gabe Kapler	.20	.06
❑ 130	Miguel Cabrera	.50	.15
❑ 131	Billy McMillon	.20	.06
❑ 132	Julio Mateo	.20	.06
❑ 133	Preston Wilson	.30	.09
❑ 134	Tony Clark	.20	.06
❑ 135	Carlos Lee	.30	.09
❑ 136	Carlos Baerga	.20	.06
❑ 137	Mike Crudale	.20	.06
❑ 138	David Ross	.20	.06
❑ 139	Josh Fogg	.20	.06
❑ 140	Dmitri Young	.30	.09
❑ 141	Cliff Lee	.20	.06
❑ 142	Mike Lowell	.30	.09
❑ 143	Jason Lane	.20	.06
❑ 144	Pedro Feliz	.20	.06
❑ 145	Ken Griffey Jr.	1.25	.35
❑ 146	Dustin Hermanson	.20	.06
❑ 147	Scott Hodges	.20	.06
❑ 148	Aquilino Lopez	.20	.06
❑ 149	Wes Helms	.20	.06
❑ 150	Jason Giambi	.30	.09
❑ 151	Erasmo Ramirez	.20	.06
❑ 152	Sean Burroughs	.30	.09
❑ 153	J.T. Snow	.30	.09
❑ 154	Eddie Guardado	.20	.06
❑ 155	C.C. Sabathia	.30	.09
❑ 156	Kyle Lohse	.20	.06
❑ 157	Roberto Hernandez	.20	.06
❑ 158	Jason Simontacchi	.20	.06
❑ 159	Tim Spooneybarger	.20	.06
❑ 160	Alfonso Soriano	.50	.15
❑ 161	Mike Gonzalez	.20	.06
❑ 162	Alex Cora	.20	.06
❑ 163	Kevin Gryboski	.20	.06
❑ 164	Mike Lincoln	.20	.06
❑ 165	Luis Castillo	.20	.06
❑ 166	Odalis Perez	.30	.09
❑ 167	Alex Sanchez	.20	.06
❑ 168	Rob Mackowiak	.20	.06
❑ 169	Francisco Rodriguez	.30	.09
❑ 170	Roy Oswalt	.30	.09
❑ 171	Omar Infante	.20	.06
❑ 172	Ryan Jensen	.20	.06
❑ 173	Ben Broussard	.20	.06
❑ 174	Mark Hendrickson	.20	.06
❑ 175	Manny Ramirez	.50	.15
❑ 176	Rob Bell	.20	.06
❑ 177	Adam Everett	.20	.06
❑ 178	Chris George	.20	.06
❑ 179	Ronnie Belliard	.20	.06
❑ 180	Eric Gagne	.75	.23
❑ 181	Scott Schoeneweis	.20	.06
❑ 182	Kris Benson	.20	.06
❑ 183	Amaury Telemaco	.20	.06
❑ 184	John Riedling	.20	.06
❑ 185	Juan Pierre	.30	.09
❑ 186	Ramon Ortiz	.20	.06
❑ 187	Luis Rivas	.20	.06
❑ 188	Larry Bigbie	.20	.06
❑ 189	Robby Hammock	.20	.06
❑ 190	Geoff Jenkins	.30	.09
❑ 191	Chad Cordero	.20	.06
❑ 192	Mark Ellis	.20	.06
❑ 193	Mark Loretta	.30	.09
❑ 194	Ryan Drese	.20	.06
❑ 195	Lance Berkman	.30	.09
❑ 196	Kevin Appier	.30	.09
❑ 197	Kiko Calero	.20	.06
❑ 198	Mickey Callaway	.20	.06
❑ 199	Chase Utley	.30	.09
❑ 200	Nomar Garciaparra	1.25	.35
❑ 201	Kevin Cash	.20	.06
❑ 202	Ramiro Mendoza	.20	.06
❑ 203	Shane Reynolds	.20	.06
❑ 204	Chris Spurling	.20	.06
❑ 205	Aaron Guiel	.20	.06
❑ 206	Mark DeRosa	.20	.06
❑ 207	Adam Kennedy	.20	.06
❑ 208	Andy Pettitte	.50	.15
❑ 209	Rafael Palmeiro	.50	.15
❑ 210	Luis Gonzalez	.30	.09
❑ 211	Ryan Franklin	.20	.06
❑ 212	Bob Wickman	.20	.06
❑ 213	Ron Calloway	.20	.06
❑ 214	Jae Weong Seo	.20	.06
❑ 215	Kazuhisa Ishii	.30	.09
❑ 216	Sterling Hitchcock	.20	.06
❑ 217	Jimmy Gobble	.20	.06
❑ 218	Chad Moeller	.20	.06
❑ 219	Jake Peavy	.30	.09
❑ 220	John Smoltz	.50	.15
❑ 221	Donovan Osborne	.20	.06
❑ 222	David Wells	.30	.09
❑ 223	Brad Lidge	.30	.09
❑ 224	Carlos Zambrano	.30	.09
❑ 225	Kerry Wood	.75	.23
❑ 226	Alex Cintron	.20	.06
❑ 227	Javier A. Lopez	.20	.06
❑ 228	Jeremy Griffiths	.20	.06
❑ 229	Jon Garland	.20	.06
❑ 230	Curt Schilling	.75	.23
❑ 231	Alex Scott Gonzalez	.20	.06
❑ 232	Jay Gibbons	.20	.06
❑ 233	Aaron Miles	.30	.09
❑ 234	Mike Gallo	.20	.06
❑ 235	Johan Santana	.50	.15
❑ 236	Jose Guillen	.30	.09
❑ 237	Jeff Conine	.30	.09
❑ 238	Matt Roney	.20	.06
❑ 239	Desi Relaford	.20	.06
❑ 240	Frank Thomas	.75	.23
❑ 241	Danny Patterson	.20	.06
❑ 242	Kevin Mench	.20	.06
❑ 243	Mike Redmond	.20	.06
❑ 244	Jeff Suppan	.20	.06
❑ 245	Carl Everett	.30	.09
❑ 246	Jack Cressend	.20	.06
❑ 247	Matt Mantei	.20	.06
❑ 248	Enrique Wilson	.20	.06
❑ 249	Craig Counsell	.20	.06
❑ 250	Mark Prior	.75	.23
❑ 251	Jared Sandberg	.20	.06
❑ 252	Scott Strickland	.20	.06
❑ 253	Lew Ford	.30	.09
❑ 254	Hee Seop Choi	.20	.06
❑ 255	Jason Phillips	.20	.06
❑ 256	Jason Jennings	.20	.06
❑ 257	Todd Pratt	.20	.06
❑ 258	Matt Herges	.20	.06
❑ 259	Kerry Ligtenberg	.20	.06
❑ 260	Austin Kearns	.30	.09
❑ 261	Jay Witasick	.20	.06
❑ 262	Tony Armas Jr.	.20	.06
❑ 263	Tom Martin	.20	.06
❑ 264	Oliver Perez	.30	.09
❑ 265	Jorge Posada	.50	.15
❑ 266	Jason Boyd	.20	.06
❑ 267	Ben Hendrickson	.20	.06
❑ 268	Reggie Sanders	.20	.06
❑ 269	Julio Lugo	.20	.06
❑ 270	Pedro Martinez	.75	.23
❑ 271	Kyle Snyder	.20	.06
❑ 272	Felipe Lopez	.20	.06
❑ 273	Kevin Millar	.30	.09
❑ 274	Travis Hafner	.30	.09
❑ 275	Magglio Ordonez	.30	.09
❑ 276	Marlon Byrd	.20	.06
❑ 277	Scott Spiezio	.20	.06
❑ 278	Mark Corey	.20	.06
❑ 279	Tim Salmon	.50	.15
❑ 280	Alex Gonzalez	.20	.06
❑ 281	Marquis Grissom	.30	.09
❑ 282	Miguel Olivo	.20	.06
❑ 283	Orlando Hudson	.20	.06
❑ 284	Rondell White	.30	.09
❑ 285	Jermaine Dye	.30	.09
❑ 286	Paul Shuey	.20	.06
❑ 287	Brandon Inge	.20	.06
❑ 288	B.J. Surhoff	.30	.09
❑ 289	Edgar Gonzalez	.20	.06
❑ 290	Angel Berroa	.20	.06
❑ 291	Claudio Vargas	.20	.06
❑ 292	Cesar Izturis	.20	.06
❑ 293	Brandon Phillips	.20	.06
❑ 294	Jeff Duncan	.20	.06
❑ 295	Randy Wolf	.20	.06
❑ 296	Barry Larkin	.50	.15
❑ 297	Felix Rodriguez	.20	.06
❑ 298	Robb Quinlan	.20	.06
❑ 299	Brian Jordan	.30	.09
❑ 300	Dontrelle Willis	.30	.09
❑ 301	Doug Davis	.20	.06
❑ 302	Ricky Stone	.20	.06
❑ 303	Travis Harper	.20	.06
❑ 304	Jaret Wright	.20	.06
❑ 305	Edgardo Alfonzo	.20	.06
❑ 306	Quinton McCracken	.20	.06
❑ 307	Jason Bay	.30	.09
❑ 308	Joe Randa	.20	.06
❑ 309	Steve Sparks	.20	.06
❑ 310	Roy Halladay	.20	.06
❑ 311	Antonio Alfonseca	.20	.06
❑ 312	Michael Cuddyer	.20	.06
❑ 313	John Patterson	.20	.06
❑ 314	Chris Widger	.20	.06
❑ 315	Shigetoshi Hasegawa	.30	.09
❑ 316	Tim Wakefield	.30	.09
❑ 317	Scott Hatteberg	.20	.06
❑ 318	Mike Remlinger	.20	.06
❑ 319	Jose Vizcaino	.20	.06
❑ 320	Rocco Baldelli	.30	.09
❑ 321	David Riske	.20	.06
❑ 322	Steve Karsay	.20	.06
❑ 323	Peter Bergeron	.20	.06
❑ 324	Jeff Weaver	.20	.06
❑ 325	Larry Walker	.50	.15
❑ 326	Jack Cust	.20	.06
❑ 327	Bo Hart	.20	.06
❑ 328	Rod Beck	.20	.06
❑ 329	Jose Acevedo	.20	.06
❑ 330	Hank Blalock	.30	.09
❑ 331	Tom Gordon	.20	.06
❑ 332	Brian Fuentes	.20	.06
❑ 333	Tomas Perez	.20	.06
❑ 334	Lenny Harris	.20	.06
❑ 335	Matt Morris	.30	.09
❑ 336	Jeremi Gonzalez	.20	.06
❑ 337	David Eckstein	.20	.06
❑ 338	Aaron Rowand	.30	.09
❑ 339	Rick Bauer	.20	.06
❑ 340	Jim Edmonds	.30	.09
❑ 341	Joe Borowski	.20	.06
❑ 342	Eric DuBose	.20	.06
❑ 343	D'Angelo Jimenez	.20	.06
❑ 344	Tomo Ohka	.20	.06
❑ 345	Victor Zambrano	.20	.06
❑ 346	Joe McEwing	.20	.06
❑ 347	Jorge Sosa	.20	.06
❑ 348	Keith Ginter	.20	.06
❑ 349	A.J. Pierzynski	.30	.09
❑ 350	Mike Sweeney	.30	.09
❑ 351	Shawn Chacon	.20	.06
❑ 352	Matt Clement	.20	.06
❑ 353	Vance Wilson	.20	.06
❑ 354	Benito Santiago	.30	.09
❑ 355	Eric Hinske	.20	.06
❑ 356	Vladimir Guerrero	.75	.23
❑ 357	Kenny Rogers	.30	.09
❑ 358	Travis Lee	.20	.06
❑ 359	Jay Powell	.20	.06
❑ 360	Phil Nevin	.30	.09
❑ 361	Willie Harris	.20	.06
❑ 362	Ty Wigginton	.20	.06
❑ 363	Chad Fox	.20	.06
❑ 364	Junior Spivey	.20	.06
❑ 365	Brandon Webb	.20	.06
❑ 366	Brett Myers	.20	.06
❑ 367	Alexis Gomez	.20	.06
❑ 368	Dave Roberts	.20	.06
❑ 369	LaTroy Hawkins	.20	.06
❑ 370	Kevin Millwood	.30	.09
❑ 371	Brian Schneider	.20	.06
❑ 372	Blaine Neal	.20	.06
❑ 373	Jeromy Burnitz	.30	.09
❑ 374	Ted Lilly	.20	.06

375	Shawn Green	.30	.09
376	Carlos Pena	.20	.06
377	Gil Meche	.20	.06
378	Jeff Bagwell	.50	.15
379	Alex Escobar	.20	.06
380	Erubiel Durazo	.20	.06
381	Cristian Guzman	.20	.06
382	Rocky Biddle	.20	.06
383	Craig Wilson	.30	.09
384	Rey Sanchez	.20	.06
385	Russ Ortiz	.30	.09
386	Freddy Garcia	.30	.09
387	Luis Vizcaino	.20	.06
388	David Ortiz	.75	.23
389	Jose Molina	.20	.06
390	Edgar Martinez	.50	.15
391	Nate Bump	.20	.06
392	Brent Mayne	.20	.06
393	Ray King	.20	.06
394	Paul Wilson	.20	.06
395	Melvin Mora	.30	.09
396	Morgan Ensberg	.20	.06
397	Ramon Hernandez	.20	.06
398	Juan Rincon	.20	.06
399	Ron Mahay	.20	.06
400	Jeff Kent	.30	.09
401	Cal Eldred	.20	.06
402	Mike Difelice	.20	.06
403	Valerio De Los Santos	.20	.06
404	Steve Finley	.30	.09
405	Trot Nixon	.30	.09
406	Akinori Otsuka RC	.40	.12
407	Ryan Freel	.20	.06
408	Ray Durham	.30	.09
409	Aaron Heilman	.20	.06
410	Edgar Renteria	.30	.09
411	Mike Hampton	.30	.09
412	Kirk Rueter	.20	.06
413	Jim Mecir	.20	.06
414	Brian Roberts	.20	.06
415	Paul Konerko	.30	.09
416	Reed Johnson	.20	.06
417	Roger Clemens	1.50	.45
418	Coco Crisp	.20	.06
419	Carlos Hernandez	.20	.06
420	Scott Podsednik	.30	.09
421	Miguel Cairo	.20	.06
422	Abraham Nunez	.20	.06
423	Endy Chavez	.20	.06
424	Eric Munson	.20	.06
425	Torii Hunter	.30	.09
426	Ben Howard	.20	.06
427	Chris Gomez	.20	.06
428	Francisco Cordero	.20	.06
429	Jeffrey Hammonds	.20	.06
430	Shannon Stewart	.30	.09
431	Einar Diaz	.20	.06
432	Eric Byrnes	.20	.06
433	Marty Cordova	.20	.06
434	Matt Ginter	.20	.06
435	Victor Martinez	.30	.09
436	Geronimo Gil	.20	.06
437	Grant Balfour	.20	.06
438	Ramon Vazquez	.20	.06
439	Jose Cruz Jr.	.20	.06
440	Orlando Cabrera	.30	.09
441	Joe Kennedy	.20	.06
442	Scott Williamson	.20	.06
443	Troy Percival	.30	.09
444	Derrek Lee	.30	.09
445	Runelvys Hernandez	.20	.06
446	Mark Grudzielanek	.20	.06
447	Trey Hodges	.20	.06
448	Jimmy Haynes	.20	.06
449	Eric Milton	.30	.09
450	Todd Helton	.50	.15
451	Greg Zaun	.20	.06
452	Woody Williams	.20	.06
453	Todd Walker	.20	.06
454	Juan Cruz	.20	.06
455	Fernando Vina	.20	.06
456	Omar Vizquel	.50	.15
457	Roberto Alomar	.50	.15
458	Bill Hall	.20	.06
459	Juan Rivera	.20	.06
460	Tom Glavine	.50	.15
461	Ramon Castro	.20	.06
462	Cory Vance	.20	.06
463	Dan Miceli	.20	.06
464	Lyle Overbay	.30	.09
465	Craig Biggio	.50	.15
466	Ricky Ledee	.20	.06
467	Michael Barrett	.20	.06
468	Jason Anderson	.20	.06
469	Matt Stairs	.20	.06
470	Jarrod Washburn	.20	.06
471	Todd Hundley	.20	.06
472	Grant Roberts	.20	.06
473	Randy Winn	.20	.06
474	Pat Hentgen	.20	.06
475	Jose Vidro	.20	.06
476	Tony Torcato	.20	.06
477	Jeremy Affeldt	.20	.06
478	Carlos Guillen	.30	.09
479	Paul Quantrill	.20	.06
480	Rafael Furcal	.30	.09
481	Adam Melhuse	.20	.06
482	Jerry Hairston Jr.	.20	.06
483	Adam Bernero	.20	.06
484	Terrence Long	.30	.09
485	Paul Lo Duca	.30	.09
486	Corey Koskie	.30	.09
487	John Lackey	.20	.06
488	Chad Zerbe	.20	.06
489	Vinny Castilla	.30	.09
490	Corey Patterson	.30	.09
491	John Olerud	.30	.09
492	Josh Bard	.20	.06
493	Darren Dreifort	.20	.06
494	Jason Standridge	.20	.06
495	Ben Sheets	.30	.09
496	Jose Castillo	.20	.06
497	Jay Payton	.20	.06
498	Rob Bowen	.20	.06
499	Bobby Higginson	.30	.09
500	Alex Rodriguez Yanks	1.25	.35
501	Octavio Dotel	.20	.06
502	Rheal Cormier	.20	.06
503	Felix Heredia	.20	.06
504	Dan Wright	.20	.06
505	Michael Young	.30	.09
506	Wilfredo Ledezma	.20	.06
507	Sun Woo Kim	.20	.06
508	Michael Tejera	.20	.06
509	Herbert Perry	.20	.06
510	Esteban Loaiza	.20	.06
511	Alan Embree	.20	.06
512	Ben Davis	.20	.06
513	Greg Colbrunn	.20	.06
514	Josh Hall	.20	.06
515	Raul Ibanez	.20	.06
516	Jason Kershner	.20	.06
517	Corky Miller	.20	.06
518	Jason Marquis	.20	.06
519	Roger Cedeno	.20	.06
520	Adam Dunn	.50	.15
521	Paul Byrd	.20	.06
522	Sandy Alomar Jr.	.20	.06
523	Salomon Torres	.20	.06
524	John Halama	.20	.06
525	Mike Piazza	1.25	.35
526	Buddy Groom	.20	.06
527	Adrian Beltre	.50	.15
528	Chad Harville	.20	.06
529	Javier Vazquez	.30	.09
530	Jody Gerut	.20	.06
531	Elmer Dessens	.20	.06
532	B.J. Ryan	.20	.06
533	Chad Durbin	.20	.06
534	Doug Mirabelli	.20	.06
535	Bernie Williams	.50	.15
536	Jeff DaVanon	.20	.06
537	Dave Berg	.20	.06
538	Geoff Blum	.20	.06
539	John Thomson	.20	.06
540	Jeremy Bonderman	.20	.06
541	Jeff Zimmerman	.20	.06
542	Derek Lowe	.30	.09
543	Scot Shields	.20	.06
544	Michael Tucker	.20	.06
545	Tim Hudson	.30	.09
546	Ryan Ludwick	.20	.06
547	Rick Reed	.20	.06
548	Placido Polanco	.20	.06
549	Tony Graffanino	.20	.06
550	Garret Anderson	.30	.09
551	Timo Perez	.20	.06
552	Jesus Colome	.20	.06
553	R.A. Dickey	.20	.06
554	Tim Worrell	.20	.06
555	Jason Kendall	.30	.09
556	Tom Goodwin	.20	.06
557	Joaquin Benoit	.20	.06
558	Stephen Randolph	.20	.06
559	Miguel Tejada	.30	.09
560	A.J. Burnett	.20	.06
561	Ben Diggins	.20	.06
562	Kent Mercker	.20	.06
563	Zach Day	.20	.06
564	Antonio Perez	.20	.06
565	Jason Schmidt	.30	.09
566	Armando Benitez	.30	.09
567	Denny Neagle	.20	.06
568	Eric Eckenstahler	.20	.06
569	Chan Ho Park	.30	.09
570	Carlos Beltran	.50	.15
571	Brett Tomko	.20	.06
572	Henry Mateo	.20	.06
573	Ken Harvey	.20	.06
574	Matt Lawton	.20	.06
575	Mariano Rivera	.50	.15
576	Darrell May	.20	.06
577	Jamie Moyer	.30	.09
578	Paul Bako	.20	.06
579	Cory Lidle	.20	.06
580	Jacque Jones	.30	.09
581	Jolbert Cabrera	.20	.06
582	Jason Grimsley	.20	.06
583	Danny Kolb	.20	.06
584	Billy Wagner	.30	.09
585	Rich Aurilia	.20	.06
586	Vicente Padilla	.20	.06
587	Oscar Villarreal	.20	.06
588	Rene Reyes	.20	.06
589	Jon Lieber	.20	.06
590	Nick Johnson	.20	.06
591	Bobby Crosby	.50	.15
592	Steve Trachsel	.20	.06
593	Brian Boehringer	.20	.06
594	Juan Uribe	.20	.06
595	Bartolo Colon	.30	.09
596	Bobby Hill	.20	.06
597	Chris Shelton RC	.75	.23
598	Carl Pavano	.30	.09
599	Kurt Ainsworth	.20	.06
600	Derek Jeter	1.50	.45
601	Doug Mientkiewicz	.30	.09
602	Orlando Palmeiro	.20	.06
603	J.C. Romero	.20	.06
604	Scott Sullivan	.20	.06
605	Brad Radke	.30	.09
606	Fernando Rodney	.20	.06
607	Jim Brower	.20	.06
608	Josh Towers	.20	.06
609	Brad Fullmer	.30	.09
610	Jose Reyes	.30	.09
611	Ryan Wagner	.20	.06
612	Joe Mays	.20	.06
613	Jung Bong	.20	.06
614	Curtis Leskanic	.20	.06
615	Al Leiter	.30	.09
616	Wade Miller	.20	.06
617	Keith Foulke Sox	.50	.15
618	Casey Fossum	.20	.06
619	Craig Monroe	.20	.06
620	Hideo Nomo	.75	.23
621	Bob File	.20	.06
622	Steve Kline	.20	.06
623	Bobby Kielty	.20	.06
624	Dewon Brazelton	.20	.06
625	Eric Chavez	.30	.09
626	Chris Carpenter	.20	.06
627	Alexis Rios	.30	.09
628	Jason Davis	.20	.06
629	Jose Jimenez	.20	.06
630	Vernon Wells	.30	.09
631	Kenny Lofton	.30	.09
632	Chad Bradford	.20	.06
633	Brad Wilkerson	.20	.06

❑ 634 Pokey Reese .20 .06
❑ 635 Richie Sexson .30 .09
❑ 636 Chin-Hui Tsao .30 .09
❑ 637 Eli Marrero .20 .06
❑ 638 Chris Reitsma .20 .06
❑ 639 Daryle Ward .20 .06
❑ 640 Mark Teixeira .30 .09
❑ 641 Corwin Malone .20 .06
❑ 642 Adam Eaton .20 .06
❑ 643 Jimmy Rollins .30 .09
❑ 644 Brian Anderson .20 .06
❑ 645 Bill Mueller .30 .09
❑ 646 Jake Westbrook .20 .06
❑ 647 Bengie Molina .20 .06
❑ 648 Jorge Julio .20 .06
❑ 649 Billy Traber .20 .06
❑ 650 Randy Johnson .75 .23
❑ 651 Javy Lopez .30 .09
❑ 652 Doug Glanville .20 .06
❑ 653 Jeff Cirillo .20 .06
❑ 654 Tino Martinez .50 .15
❑ 655 Mark Buehrle .30 .09
❑ 656 Jason Michaels .20 .06
❑ 657 Damian Rolls .20 .06
❑ 658 Rosman Garcia .20 .06
❑ 659 Scott Hairston .30 .09
❑ 660 Carl Crawford .30 .09
❑ 661 Livan Hernandez .20 .06
❑ 662 Danny Bautista .20 .06
❑ 663 Brad Ausmus .20 .06
❑ 664 Juan Acevedo .20 .06
❑ 665 Sean Casey .30 .09
❑ 666 Josh Beckett .30 .09
❑ 667 Milton Bradley .30 .09
❑ 668 Braden Looper .20 .06
❑ 669 Paul Abbott .20 .06
❑ 670 Joel Pineiro .20 .06
❑ 671 Luis Terrero .20 .06
❑ 672 Rodrigo Lopez .20 .06
❑ 673 Joe Crede .20 .06
❑ 674 Mike Koplove .20 .06
❑ 675 Brian Giles .30 .09
❑ 676 Jeff Nelson .20 .06
❑ 677 Russell Branyan .20 .06
❑ 678 Mike DeJean .20 .06
❑ 679 Brian Daubach .20 .06
❑ 680 Ellis Burks .30 .09
❑ 681 Ryan Dempster .20 .06
❑ 682 Cliff Politte .20 .06
❑ 683 Brian Reith .20 .06
❑ 684 Scott Stewart .20 .06
❑ 685 Allan Simpson .20 .06
❑ 686 Shawn Estes .20 .06
❑ 687 Jason Johnson .20 .06
❑ 688 Wil Cordero .20 .06
❑ 689 Kelly Stinnett .20 .06
❑ 690 Jose Lima .20 .06
❑ 691 Gary Bennett .20 .06
❑ 692 T.J. Tucker .20 .06
❑ 693 Shane Spencer .20 .06
❑ 694 Chris Hammond .20 .06
❑ 695 Raul Mondesi .30 .09
❑ 696 Xavier Nady .20 .06
❑ 697 Cody Ransom .20 .06
❑ 698 Ron Villone .20 .06
❑ 699 Brook Fordyce .20 .06
❑ 700 Sammy Sosa 1.25 .35
❑ 701 Terry Adams .20 .06
❑ 702 Ricardo Rincon .20 .06
❑ 703 Tike Redman .20 .06
❑ 704 Chris Stynes .20 .06
❑ 705 Mark Redman .20 .06
❑ 706 Juan Encarnacion .20 .06
❑ 707 Jhonny Peralta .30 .09
❑ 708 Denny Hocking .20 .06
❑ 709 Ivan Rodriguez .75 .23
❑ 710 Jose Hernandez .20 .06
❑ 711 Brandon Duckworth .20 .06
❑ 712 Dave Burba .20 .06
❑ 713 Joe Nathan .20 .06
❑ 714 Dan Smith .20 .06
❑ 715 Karim Garcia .20 .06
❑ 716 Arthur Rhodes .20 .06
❑ 717 Shawn Wooten .20 .06
❑ 718 Ramon Santiago .20 .06
❑ 719 Luis Ugueto .20 .06
❑ 720 Danys Baez .20 .06
❑ 721 Alfredo Amezaga PROS .20 .06
❑ 722 Sidney Ponson .20 .06
❑ 723 Joe Mauer PROS .50 .15
❑ 724 Jesse Foppert PROS .20 .06
❑ 725 Todd Greene .20 .06
❑ 726 Dan Haren PROS .20 .06
❑ 727 Brandon Larson PROS .20 .06
❑ 728 Bobby Jenks PROS .20 .06
❑ 729 Grady Sizemore PROS .30 .09
❑ 730 Ben Grieve .20 .06
❑ 731 Khalil Greene PROS .75 .23
❑ 732 Chad Gaudin PROS .20 .06
❑ 733 Johnny Estrada PROS .20 .06
❑ 734 Joe Valentine PROS .20 .06
❑ 735 Tim Raines Jr. PROS .20 .06
❑ 736 Brandon Claussen PROS .20 .06
❑ 737 Sam Marsonek PROS .20 .06
❑ 738 Delmon Young PROS .50 .15
❑ 739 David Dellucci .20 .06
❑ 740 Sergio Mitre PROS .20 .06
❑ 741 Nick Neugebauer PROS .20 .06
❑ 742 Laynce Nix PROS .30 .09
❑ 743 Joe Thurston PROS .20 .06
❑ 744 Ryan Langerhans PROS .20 .06
❑ 745 Pete LaForest PROS .20 .06
❑ 746 Arnie Munoz PROS .20 .06
❑ 747 Rickie Weeks PROS .30 .09
❑ 748 Neal Cotts PROS .20 .06
❑ 749 Jonny Gomes PROS .20 .06
❑ 750 Jim Thome .75 .23
❑ 751 Jon Rauch PROS .20 .06
❑ 752 Edwin Jackson PROS .30 .09
❑ 753 Ryan Madson PROS .20 .06
❑ 754 Andrew Good PROS .20 .06
❑ 755 Eddie Perez .20 .06
❑ 756 Joe Borchard PROS .20 .06
❑ 757 Jeremy Guthrie PROS .20 .06
❑ 758 Jose Mesa .20 .06
❑ 759 Doug Waechter PROS .20 .06
❑ 760 J.D. Drew .30 .09
❑ 761 Adam LaRoche PROS .20 .06
❑ 762 Rich Harden PROS .30 .09
❑ 763 Justin Speier .20 .06
❑ 764 Todd Zeile .20 .06
❑ 765 Turk Wendell .20 .06
❑ 766 Mark Bellhorn Sox .50 .15
❑ 767 Mike Jackson .20 .06
❑ 768 Chone Figgins .20 .06
❑ 769 Mike Neu .20 .06
❑ 770 Greg Maddux 1.25 .35
❑ 771 Frank Menechino .20 .06
❑ 772 Alec Zumwalt RC .25 .07
❑ 773 Eric Young .20 .06
❑ 774 Dustan Mohr .20 .06
❑ 775 Shane Halter .20 .06
❑ 776 Brian Buchanan .20 .06
❑ 777 So Taguchi .30 .09
❑ 778 Eric Karros .30 .09
❑ 779 Ramon Nivar .20 .06
❑ 780 Marlon Anderson .20 .06
❑ 781 Brayan Pena FY RC .40 .12
❑ 782 Chris O'Riordan FY RC .40 .12
❑ 783 Dioner Navarro FY RC 1.25 .35
❑ 784 Alberto Callaspo FY RC .75 .23
❑ 785 Hector Gimenez FY RC .25 .07
❑ 786 Yadier Molina FY RC 1.00 .30
❑ 787 Kevin Richardson FY RC .25 .07
❑ 788 Brian Pilkington FY RC .40 .12
❑ 789 Adam Greenberg FY RC .50 .15
❑ 790 Ervin Santana FY RC 1.25 .35
❑ 791 Brant Colamarino FY RC .75 .23
❑ 792 Ben Himes FY RC .25 .07
❑ 793 Todd Self FY RC .40 .12
❑ 794 Brad Vericker FY RC .40 .12
❑ 795 Donald Kelly FY RC .40 .12
❑ 796 Brock Jacobsen FY RC .25 .07
❑ 797 Brock Peterson FY RC .40 .12
❑ 798 Carlos Sosa FY RC .40 .12
❑ 799 Chad Chop FY RC .40 .12
❑ 800 Matt Moses FY RC 1.00 .30
❑ 801 Chris Aguila FY RC .40 .12
❑ 802 David Murphy FY RC 1.00 .30
❑ 803 Don Sutton FY RC 1.00 .30
❑ 804 Jereme Milons FY RC .40 .12
❑ 805 Jon Coutlangus FY RC .25 .07
❑ 806 Greg Thissen FY RC .40 .12
❑ 807 Jose Capellan FY RC 1.50 .45
❑ 808 Chad Santos FY RC .40 .12
❑ 809 Wardell Starling FY RC .40 .12
❑ 810 Kevin Kouzmanoff FY RC .75 .23
❑ 811 Kevin Davidson FY RC .25 .07
❑ 812 Michael Mooney FY RC .40 .12
❑ 813 Rodney Choy Foo FY RC .25 .07
❑ 814 Reid Gorecki FY RC .40 .12
❑ 815 Rudy Guillen FY RC 1.00 .30
❑ 816 Harvey Garcia FY RC .25 .07
❑ 817 Warner Madrigal FY RC .75 .23
❑ 818 Kenny Perez FY RC .40 .12
❑ 819 Joaquin Arias FY RC .40 .12
❑ 820 Benji DeQuin FY RC .25 .07
❑ 821 Lastings Milledge FY RC 2.00 .60
❑ 822 Blake Hawksworth FY RC .50 .15
❑ 823 Estee Harris FY RC .40 .12
❑ 824 Bobby Brownlie FY RC .75 .23
❑ 825 Wanell Severino FY RC .25 .07
❑ 826 Bobby Madritsch FY .75 .23
❑ 827 Travis Hanson FY RC .40 .12
❑ 828 Brandon Medders FY RC .25 .07
❑ 829 Kevin Howard FY RC .50 .15
❑ 830 Brian Steffek FY RC .25 .07
❑ 831 Terry Jones FY RC .50 .15
❑ 832 Anthony Acevedo FY RC .40 .12
❑ 833 Kory Casto FY RC .40 .12
❑ 834 Brooks Conrad FY RC UER .40 .12
Anthony Acevedo Pictured on front
❑ 835 Juan Gutierrez FY RC .40 .12
❑ 836 Charlie Zink FY RC .25 .07
❑ 837 David Aardsma FY RC .40 .12
❑ 838 Carl Loadenthal FY RC .50 .15
❑ 839 Donald Levinski FY RC .25 .07
❑ 840 Dustin Nippert FY RC .40 .12
❑ 841 Calvin Hayes FY RC .50 .15
❑ 842 Felix Hernandez FY RC 3.00 .90
❑ 843 Tyler Davidson FY RC .50 .15
❑ 844 George Sherrill FY RC .40 .12
❑ 845 Craig Ansman FY RC .40 .12
❑ 846 Jeff Allison FY RC .50 .15
❑ 847 Tommy Murphy FY RC .40 .12
❑ 848 Jerome Gamble FY RC .25 .07
❑ 849 Jesse English FY RC .40 .12
❑ 850 Alex Romero FY RC .40 .12
❑ 851 Joel Zumaya FY RC .75 .23
❑ 852 Carlos Quentin FY RC 2.00 .60
❑ 853 Jose Valdez FY RC .40 .12
❑ 854 J.J. Furmaniak FY RC .75 .23
❑ 855 Juan Cedeno FY RC .40 .12
❑ 856 Kyle Sleeth FY RC 1.00 .30
❑ 857 Josh Labandeira FY RC .40 .12
❑ 858 Lee Gwaltney FY RC .25 .07
❑ 859 Lincoln Holdzkom FY RC .40 .12
❑ 860 Ivan Ochoa FY RC .40 .12
❑ 861 Luke Anderson FY RC .25 .07
❑ 862 Conor Jackson FY RC 2.00 .60
❑ 863 Matt Capps FY RC .40 .12
❑ 864 Merkin Valdez FY RC 1.00 .30
❑ 865 Paul Bacot FY RC .50 .15
❑ 866 Erick Aybar FY RC 1.25 .35
❑ 867 Scott Proctor FY RC .50 .15
❑ 868 Tim Stauffer FY RC .75 .23
❑ 869 Matt Creighton FY RC .40 .12
❑ 870 Zach Miner FY RC .50 .15
❑ 871 Danny Gonzalez FY RC .25 .07
❑ 872 Tom Farmer FY RC .25 .07
❑ 873 John Santor FY RC .25 .07
❑ 874 Logan Kensing FY RC .40 .12
❑ 875 Vito Chiaravalloti FY RC .75 .23
❑ 876 Checklist .20 .06
❑ 877 Checklist .20 .06
❑ 878 Checklist .20 .06
❑ 879 Checklist .20 .06
❑ 880 Checklist .20 .06

2001 Topps Tribute

	Nm-Mt	Ex-Mt
COMPLETE SET (90)	250.00	75.00
❑ 1 Pee Wee Reese	6.00	1.80
❑ 2 Babe Ruth	20.00	6.00
❑ 3 Ralph Kiner	5.00	1.50
❑ 4 Brooks Robinson	5.00	1.50
❑ 5 Don Sutton	5.00	1.50
❑ 6 Carl Yastrzemski	10.00	3.00
❑ 7 Roger Maris	6.00	1.80
❑ 8 Andre Dawson	5.00	1.50
❑ 9 Luis Aparicio	5.00	1.50
❑ 10 Wade Boggs	5.00	1.50
❑ 11 Johnny Bench	6.00	1.80
❑ 12 Ernie Banks	6.00	1.80
❑ 13 Thurman Munson	6.00	1.80
❑ 14 Harmon Killebrew	6.00	1.80
❑ 15 Ted Kluszewski	5.00	1.50
❑ 16 Bob Feller	5.00	1.50
❑ 17 Mike Schmidt	12.00	3.60
❑ 18 Warren Spahn	5.00	1.50
❑ 19 Jim Palmer	5.00	1.50
❑ 20 Don Mattingly	15.00	4.50
❑ 21 Willie Mays	12.00	3.60
❑ 22 Gil Hodges	6.00	1.80
❑ 23 Juan Marichal	5.00	1.50
❑ 24 Robin Yount	10.00	3.00
❑ 25 Nolan Ryan Angels	15.00	4.50
❑ 26 Dave Winfield	5.00	1.50
❑ 27 Hank Greenberg	6.00	1.80
❑ 28 Honus Wagner	8.00	2.40
❑ 29 Nolan Ryan Rangers	15.00	4.50
❑ 30 Phil Niekro	5.00	1.50
❑ 31 Robin Roberts	5.00	1.50
❑ 32 Casey Stengel Yankees	5.00	1.50
❑ 33 Willie McCovey	5.00	1.50
❑ 34 Roy Campanella	6.00	1.80
❑ 35 Rollie Fingers A's	5.00	1.50
❑ 36 Tom Seaver	5.00	1.50
❑ 37 Jackie Robinson	6.00	1.80
❑ 38 Hank Aaron Braves	12.00	3.60
❑ 39 Bob Gibson	5.00	1.50
❑ 40 Carlton Fisk Red Sox	5.00	1.50
❑ 41 Hank Aaron Brewers	12.00	3.60
❑ 42 George Brett	15.00	4.50
❑ 43 Orlando Cepeda	5.00	1.50
❑ 44 Red Schoendienst	5.00	1.50
❑ 45 Don Drysdale	6.00	1.80
❑ 46 Mel Ott	6.00	1.80
❑ 47 Casey Stengel Mets	6.00	1.80
❑ 48 Al Kaline	6.00	1.80
❑ 49 Reggie Jackson	5.00	1.50
❑ 50 Tony Perez	5.00	1.50
❑ 51 Ozzie Smith	10.00	3.00
❑ 52 Billy Martin	5.00	1.50
❑ 53 Bill Dickey	5.00	1.50
❑ 54 Catfish Hunter	5.00	1.50
❑ 55 Duke Snider	5.00	1.50
❑ 56 Dale Murphy	6.00	1.80
❑ 57 Bobby Doerr	5.00	1.50
❑ 58 Earl Averill UER Card pictures Earl Averill Jr.	5.00	1.50
❑ 59 Carlton Fisk White Sox	5.00	1.50
❑ 60 Tom Lasorda	5.00	1.50
❑ 61 Lou Gehrig	12.00	3.60
❑ 62 Enos Slaughter	5.00	1.50
❑ 63 Jim Bunning	5.00	1.50
❑ 64 Rollie Fingers Brewers	5.00	1.50
❑ 65 Frank Robinson Reds	5.00	1.50
❑ 66 Earl Weaver	5.00	1.50
❑ 67 Eddie Mathews	6.00	1.80
❑ 68 Kirby Puckett	6.00	1.80
❑ 69 Phil Rizzuto	6.00	1.80
❑ 70 Lou Brock	5.00	1.50
❑ 71 Walt Alston	5.00	1.50
❑ 72 Billy Pierce	5.00	1.50
❑ 73 Joe Morgan	5.00	1.50
❑ 74 Roberto Clemente	15.00	4.50
❑ 75 Whitey Ford	5.00	1.50
❑ 76 Richie Ashburn	5.00	1.50
❑ 77 Elston Howard	5.00	1.50
❑ 78 Gary Carter	5.00	1.50
❑ 79 Carl Hubbell	5.00	1.50
❑ 80 Yogi Berra	6.00	1.80
❑ 81 Ken Boyer	5.00	1.50
❑ 82 Nolan Ryan Astros	15.00	4.50
❑ 83 Bill Mazeroski	5.00	1.50
❑ 84 Dizzy Dean	6.00	1.80
❑ 85 Nellie Fox	5.00	1.50
❑ 86 Stan Musial	10.00	3.00
❑ 87 Steve Carlton	5.00	1.50
❑ 88 Willie Stargell	5.00	1.50
❑ 89 Hal Newhouser	5.00	1.50
❑ 90 Frank Robinson Orioles	5.00	1.50
❑ NNO Mickey Mantle PSA Redemption		
❑ NNO Mickey Mantle Buyback EXCH		
❑ NNO Jackie Robinson Buyback EXCH		
❑ NNO Ted Williams Buyback EXCH		

2003 Topps Tribute Contemporary

	MINT	NRMT
COMMON CARD (1-90)	2.00	.90
COMMON CARD (91-100)	2.00	.90
COMMON CARD (101-110)	15.00	6.75
❑ 1 Jim Thome	4.00	1.80
❑ 2 Edgardo Alfonzo	2.00	.90
❑ 3 Edgar Martinez	2.50	1.10
❑ 4 Scott Rolen	4.00	1.80
❑ 5 Eric Hinske	2.00	.90
❑ 6 Mark Mulder	2.00	.90
❑ 7 Jason Giambi	2.00	.90
❑ 8 Bernie Williams	2.50	1.10
❑ 9 Cliff Floyd	2.00	.90
❑ 10 Ichiro Suzuki	6.00	2.70
❑ 11 Pat Burrell	2.00	.90
❑ 12 Garret Anderson	2.00	.90
❑ 13 Gary Sheffield	2.00	.90
❑ 14 Johnny Damon	4.00	1.80
❑ 15 Kerry Wood	4.00	1.80
❑ 16 Bartolo Colon	2.00	.90
❑ 17 Adam Dunn	2.50	1.10
❑ 18 Omar Vizquel	2.50	1.10
❑ 19 Todd Helton	2.50	1.10
❑ 20 Nomar Garciaparra	6.00	2.70
❑ 21 A.J. Burnett	2.00	.90
❑ 22 Craig Biggio	2.50	1.10
❑ 23 Carlos Beltran	2.50	1.10
❑ 24 Kazuhisa Ishii	2.00	.90
❑ 25 Vladimir Guerrero	4.00	1.80
❑ 26 Roberto Alomar	2.50	1.10
❑ 27 Roger Clemens	8.00	3.60
❑ 28 Tim Hudson	2.00	.90
❑ 29 Brian Giles	2.00	.90
❑ 30 Barry Bonds	10.00	4.50
❑ 31 Jim Edmonds	2.00	.90
❑ 32 Rafael Palmeiro	2.50	1.10
❑ 33 Francisco Rodriguez	2.00	.90
❑ 34 Andruw Jones	2.00	.90
❑ 35 Shea Hillenbrand	2.00	.90
❑ 36 Moises Alou	2.00	.90
❑ 37 Luis Gonzalez	2.00	.90
❑ 38 Darin Erstad	2.00	.90
❑ 39 John Smoltz	2.50	1.10
❑ 40 Derek Jeter	10.00	4.50
❑ 41 Aubrey Huff	2.00	.90
❑ 42 Eric Chavez	2.00	.90
❑ 43 Doug Mientkiewicz	2.00	.90
❑ 44 Lance Berkman	2.00	.90
❑ 45 Josh Beckett	2.00	.90
❑ 46 Austin Kearns	2.00	.90
❑ 47 Frank Thomas	4.00	1.80
❑ 48 Pedro Martinez	4.00	1.80
❑ 49 Tim Salmon	2.00	.90
❑ 50 Alex Rodriguez	6.00	2.70
❑ 51 Ryan Klesko	2.00	.90
❑ 52 Tom Glavine	2.50	1.10
❑ 53 Shawn Green	2.00	.90
❑ 54 Jeff Kent	2.00	.90
❑ 55 Carlos Pena	2.00	.90
❑ 56 Paul Konerko	2.00	.90
❑ 57 Troy Glaus	2.00	.90
❑ 58 Manny Ramirez	2.50	1.10
❑ 59 Jason Jennings	2.00	.90
❑ 60 Randy Johnson	4.00	1.80
❑ 61 Ivan Rodriguez	4.00	1.80
❑ 62 Roy Oswalt	2.00	.90
❑ 63 Kevin Brown	2.00	.90
❑ 64 Jose Vidro	2.00	.90
❑ 65 Jorge Posada	2.50	1.10
❑ 66 Mike Piazza	6.00	2.70
❑ 67 Bret Boone	2.00	.90
❑ 68 Carlos Delgado	2.00	.90
❑ 69 Jimmy Rollins	2.00	.90
❑ 70 Alfonso Soriano	2.50	1.10
❑ 71 Greg Maddux	6.00	2.70
❑ 72 Mark Prior	4.00	1.80
❑ 73 Jeff Bagwell	2.50	1.10
❑ 74 Richie Sexson	2.00	.90
❑ 75 Sammy Sosa	6.00	2.70
❑ 76 Curt Schilling	2.00	.90
❑ 77 Mike Sweeney	2.00	.90
❑ 78 Torii Hunter	2.00	.90
❑ 79 Larry Walker	2.50	1.10
❑ 80 Miguel Tejada	2.00	.90
❑ 81 Rich Aurilia	2.00	.90
❑ 82 Bobby Abreu	2.00	.90
❑ 83 Phil Nevin	2.00	.90
❑ 84 Rodrigo Lopez	2.00	.90
❑ 85 Chipper Jones	4.00	1.80
❑ 86 Ken Griffey Jr.	6.00	2.70
❑ 87 Mike Lowell	2.00	.90
❑ 88 Magglio Ordonez	2.00	.90
❑ 89 Barry Zito	2.00	.90
❑ 90 Albert Pujols	8.00	3.60
❑ 91 Corey Shafer FY RC	3.00	1.35
❑ 92 Dan Haren FY RC	3.00	1.35
❑ 93 Jeremy Bonderman FY RC	3.00	1.35
❑ 94 Branden Florence FY RC	2.00	.90
❑ 95 E.Bastida-Martinez FY RC	2.00	.90
❑ 96 Brian Wright FY RC	2.00	.90
❑ 97 Elizardo Ramirez FY RC	3.00	1.35
❑ 98 Mi.Garciaparra FY RC	3.00	1.35
❑ 99 Clay Hensley FY RC	2.00	.90
❑ 100 Bobby Basham FY RC	3.00	1.35
❑ 101 J.Contreras FY AU RC EXCH	25.00	11.00
❑ 102 Br. Bullington FY AU RC	25.00	11.00
❑ 103 Joey Gomes FY AU RC	15.00	6.75
❑ 104 Craig Brazell FY AU RC	15.00	6.75
❑ 105 Andy Marte FY AU RC	80.00	36.00
❑ 106 Han. Ramirez FY AU RC	50.00	22.00
❑ 107 Ryan Shealy FY AU RC	15.00	6.75
❑ 108 Daryl Clark FY AU RC	15.00	6.75
❑ 109 Tyler Johnson FY AU RC	15.00	6.75
❑ 110 Ben Francisco FY AU RC	15.00	6.75

2003 UD Authentics

	MINT	NRMT
COMP.SET w/o SP's (100)	40.00	18.00
COMMON ACTIVE (1-100)	.40	.18
COMMON RETIRED (1-100)	.50	.23
COMMON CARD (101-130)	4.00	1.80
101-130 RANDOM INSERTS IN PACKS		
101-130 PRINT RUN 999 SERIAL #'d SETS		
COMMON CARD (131-140)	8.00	3.60
131-140 RANDOM IN FINITE BONUS PACKS		
131-140 PRINT RUN 150 SERIAL #'d SETS		
❑ 1 Pee Wee Reese	.75	.35
❑ 2 Richie Ashburn	.75	.35
❑ 3 Derek Jeter	2.50	1.10
❑ 4 Alex Rodriguez	1.50	.70
❑ 5 Jose Vidro	.40	.18
❑ 6 Miguel Tejada	.40	.18
❑ 7 Nomar Garciaparra	1.50	.70
❑ 8 Pat Burrell	.40	.18
❑ 9 Albert Pujols	2.00	.90
❑ 10 Jeff Bagwell	.60	.25
❑ 11 Stan Musial	2.00	.90
❑ 12 Mickey Mantle	5.00	2.20
❑ 13 J.D. Drew	.40	.18
❑ 14 Ivan Rodriguez	1.00	.45
❑ 15 Joe Morgan	.50	.23
❑ 16 Ted Williams	2.50	1.10
❑ 17 Travis Hafner	.40	.18
❑ 18 Chipper Jones	1.00	.45
❑ 19 Hideo Nomo	1.00	.45
❑ 20 Gary Sheffield	.40	.18
❑ 21 Jacque Jones	.40	.18
❑ 22 Alfonso Soriano	.60	.25
❑ 23 Roberto Alomar	.60	.25
❑ 24 Jeff Kent	.40	.18
❑ 25 Omar Vizquel	.60	.25
❑ 26 Ernie Banks	1.25	.55
❑ 27 Shawn Green	.40	.18
❑ 28 Tim Hudson	.40	.18
❑ 29 Jim Edmonds	.40	.18
❑ 30 Brandon Larson	.40	.18
❑ 31 Doug Mientkiewicz	.40	.18
❑ 32 Darin Erstad	.40	.18
❑ 33 Bobby Hill	.40	.18
❑ 34 Todd Helton	.60	.25
❑ 35 Kazuhisa Ishii	.40	.18
❑ 36 Lance Berkman	.40	.18
❑ 37 Eric Hinske	.40	.18
❑ 38 Jason Kendall	.40	.18
❑ 39 Bob Feller	.50	.23
❑ 40 Luis Gonzalez	.40	.18
❑ 41 Sammy Sosa	1.50	.70
❑ 42 Mike Piazza	1.50	.70
❑ 43 Roger Clemens	2.00	.90
❑ 44 Jose Cruz Jr.	.40	.18
❑ 45 Mark Prior	1.00	.45
❑ 46 Mark Teixeira	.40	.18
❑ 47 Phil Nevin	.40	.18
❑ 48 Lyle Overbay	.40	.18
❑ 49 Manny Ramirez	.60	.25
❑ 50 Brian Giles	.40	.18
❑ 51 Preston Wilson	.40	.18
❑ 52 Jermaine Dye	.40	.18
❑ 53 Troy Glaus	.40	.18
❑ 54 Frank Thomas	1.00	.45
❑ 55 Jim Thome	1.00	.45
❑ 56 Barry Bonds	2.50	1.10
❑ 57 Carlos Delgado	.40	.18
❑ 58 Jason Giambi	.40	.18
❑ 59 Joe Mays	.40	.18
❑ 60 Andruw Jones	.40	.18
❑ 61 Billy Williams	.50	.23
❑ 62 Vladimir Guerrero	1.00	.45
❑ 63 Scott Rolen	1.00	.45
❑ 64 Juan Marichal	.50	.23
❑ 65 Austin Kearns	.40	.18
❑ 66 Kerry Wood	1.00	.45
❑ 67 Bret Boone	.40	.18
❑ 68 Shea Hillenbrand	.40	.18
❑ 69 Mike Sweeney	.40	.18
❑ 70 Rocco Baldelli	.40	.18
❑ 71 Ken Griffey Jr.	1.50	.70
❑ 72 Cliff Floyd	.40	.18
❑ 73 Greg Maddux	1.50	.70
❑ 74 Mike Hampton	.40	.18
❑ 75 Larry Walker	.60	.25
❑ 76 Nolan Ryan	3.00	1.35
❑ 77 Rollie Fingers	.50	.23
❑ 78 Mike Mussina	.60	.25
❑ 79 Matt Morris	.40	.18
❑ 80 Robin Roberts	.50	.23
❑ 81 Barry Zito	.40	.18
❑ 82 Curt Schilling	.40	.18
❑ 83 Ken Harvey	.40	.18
❑ 84 Troy Percival	.40	.18
❑ 85 Tom Seaver	.75	.35
❑ 86 Mariano Rivera	.60	.25
❑ 87 Raul Mondesi	.40	.18
❑ 88 Adam Dunn	.60	.25
❑ 89 Roy Oswalt	.40	.18
❑ 90 Pedro Martinez	1.00	.45
❑ 91 Andy Pettitte	.60	.25
❑ 92 Tom Glavine	.60	.25
❑ 93 Torii Hunter	.40	.18
❑ 94 Joe Thurston	.40	.18
❑ 95 Runelvys Hernandez	.40	.18
❑ 96 Randy Johnson	1.00	.45
❑ 97 Bernie Williams	.60	.25
❑ 98 Ichiro Suzuki	1.50	.70
❑ 99 C.C. Sabathia	.40	.18
❑ 100 Bobby Abreu	.40	.18
❑ 101 Jose Contreras RH RC	8.00	3.60
❑ 102 Hideki Matsui RH RC	15.00	6.75
❑ 103 Chris Capuano RH RC	4.00	1.80
❑ 104 Willie Eyre RH RC	4.00	1.80
❑ 105 Lew Ford RH RC	8.00	3.60
❑ 106 Shane Bazzell RH RC	4.00	1.80
❑ 107 Guillermo Quiroz RH RC	5.00	2.20
❑ 108 Fern. Cabrera RH RC	4.00	1.80
❑ 109 Francisco Cruceta RH RC	4.00	1.80
❑ 110 Jhonny Peralta RH	4.00	1.80
❑ 111 Bobby Madritsch RH RC	15.00	6.75
❑ 112 Diego Markwell RH RC	4.00	1.80
❑ 113 Matt Bruback RH RC	4.00	1.80
❑ 114 Matt Kata RH RC	5.00	2.20
❑ 115 Rob Hammock RH RC	5.00	2.20
❑ 116 Brandon Webb RH RC	5.00	2.20
❑ 117 Jon Leicester RH RC	4.00	1.80
❑ 118 Josh Willingham RH RC	5.00	2.20
❑ 119 Prentice Redman RH RC	4.00	1.80
❑ 120 Jeff Duncan RH RC	5.00	2.20
❑ 121 Craig Brazell RH RC	5.00	2.20
❑ 122 Jeremy Griffiths RH RC	5.00	2.20
❑ 123 Phil Seibel RH RC	4.00	1.80
❑ 124 Luis Ayala RH RC	4.00	1.80
❑ 125 Miguel Ojeda RH RC	4.00	1.80
❑ 126 Jeremy Wedel RH RC	4.00	1.80
❑ 127 Josh Hall RH RC	5.00	2.20
❑ 128 Oscar Villarreal RH RC	4.00	1.80
❑ 129 Clint Barmes RH RC	5.00	2.20
❑ 130 Nook Logan RH RC	4.00	1.80
❑ 131 Dan Haren RH RC	12.00	5.50
❑ 132 Delmon Young RH RC	25.00	11.00
❑ 133 Dontrelle Willis RH	5.00	2.20
❑ 134 Edwin Jackson RH RC	25.00	11.00
❑ 135 Jeremy Bonderman RH RC	12.00	5.50
❑ 136 Khalil Greene RH	30.00	13.50
❑ 137 Rich Harden RH	12.00	5.50
❑ 138 Rickie Weeks RH RC	20.00	9.00
❑ 139 Rosman Garcia RH RC	8.00	3.60
❑ 140 Ryan Wagner RH RC	12.00	5.50

2004 UD Diamond Pro Sigs

	Nm-Mt	Ex-Mt
COMP.SET w/o SP's (90)	15.00	4.50
COMMON CARD (1-90)	.30	.09
COMMON CARD (91-150)	4.00	1.20
91-150 STATED ODDS 1:6		
COMMON CARD (151-240)	10.00	3.00
151-240 STATED ODDS 1:24		
CARDS 160/169/174-175/177 DO NOT EXIST		
CARDS 220/224/226-228 DO NOT EXIST		
INSTANT WIN EXCH.ODDS 1:60,000		
❑ 1 Alfonso Soriano	.50	.15
❑ 2 Josh Beckett	.30	.09
❑ 3 Kerry Wood	.75	.23
❑ 4 Brandon Webb	.30	.09
❑ 5 Shannon Stewart	.30	.09
❑ 6 Larry Walker	.50	.15
❑ 7 Tim Hudson	.30	.09
❑ 8 Carlos Lee	.30	.09
❑ 9 Austin Kearns	.30	.09
❑ 10 Vernon Wells	.30	.09
❑ 11 Jeff Bagwell	.50	.15
❑ 12 Hideo Nomo	.75	.23
❑ 13 Jerome Williams	.30	.09
❑ 14 Kevin Brown	.30	.09
❑ 15 Jose Vidro	.30	.09
❑ 16 Rocco Baldelli	.30	.09
❑ 17 Frank Thomas	.75	.23
❑ 18 Albert Pujols	1.50	.45
❑ 19 Bartolo Colon	.30	.09
❑ 20 C.C. Sabathia	.30	.09
❑ 21 Andruw Jones	.30	.09
❑ 22 Reggie Sanders	.30	.09
❑ 23 Carlos Beltran	.50	.15
❑ 24 Curt Schilling	.75	.23
❑ 25 Miguel Tejada	.30	.09
❑ 26 Barry Zito	.30	.09
❑ 27 Pedro Martinez	.75	.23
❑ 28 Sean Burroughs	.30	.09
❑ 29 Sammy Sosa	1.25	.35
❑ 30 Eric Chavez	.30	.09
❑ 31 Roy Halladay	.30	.09
❑ 32 Todd Helton	.50	.15
❑ 33 Mark Prior	.75	.23
❑ 34 Mike Mussina	.50	.15
❑ 35 Alex Rodriguez Yanks	1.25	.35
❑ 36 Ivan Rodriguez	.75	.23
❑ 37 Mike Piazza	1.25	.35
❑ 38 Angel Berroa	.30	.09
❑ 39 Orlando Cabrera	.30	.09
❑ 40 Jim Thome	.75	.23
❑ 41 Brian Giles	.30	.09
❑ 42 Ichiro Suzuki	1.25	.35
❑ 43 Edgar Renteria	.30	.09
❑ 44 Eric Gagne	.75	.23
❑ 45 Gary Sheffield	.30	.09
❑ 46 Torii Hunter	.30	.09
❑ 47 Roger Clemens UER	1.50	.45
Photo on back is Curt Schilling		
❑ 48 Scott Rolen	.75	.23
❑ 49 Johan Santana	.50	.15
❑ 50 Jacque Jones	.30	.09
❑ 51 Hank Blalock	.30	.09
❑ 52 Rafael Palmeiro	.50	.15
❑ 53 Dmitri Young	.30	.09
❑ 54 Ryan Klesko	.30	.09
❑ 55 Mark Teixeira	.30	.09
❑ 56 Nomar Garciaparra	1.25	.35
❑ 57 Jose Reyes	.30	.09
❑ 58 Vladimir Guerrero	.75	.23
❑ 59 Mike Sweeney	.30	.09
❑ 60 Jorge Posada	.50	.15
❑ 61 Derek Jeter	1.50	.45
❑ 62 Milton Bradley	.30	.09
❑ 63 Bobby Abreu	.30	.09
❑ 64 Greg Maddux	1.25	.35
❑ 65 Adam Dunn	.50	.15
❑ 66 Troy Glaus	.30	.09
❑ 67 Luis Gonzalez	.30	.09
❑ 68 Shawn Green	.30	.09
❑ 69 Bret Boone	.30	.09
❑ 70 Mark Mulder	.30	.09
❑ 71 Lance Berkman	.30	.09
❑ 72 Preston Wilson	.30	.09
❑ 73 Phil Nevin	.30	.09
❑ 74 Chipper Jones	.75	.23

❑ 75 Garret Anderson .30 .09
❑ 76 Jason Giambi .30 .09
❑ 77 Magglio Ordonez .30 .09
❑ 78 Jeff Kent .30 .09
❑ 79 Richie Sexson .30 .09
❑ 80 Mike Lowell .30 .09
❑ 81 Ben Sheets .30 .09
❑ 82 Randy Johnson .75 .23
❑ 83 Dontrelle Willis .30 .09
❑ 84 Javier Vazquez .30 .09
❑ 85 Geoff Jenkins .30 .09
❑ 86 Manny Ramirez .50 .15
❑ 87 Jim Edmonds .30 .09
❑ 88 Roy Oswalt .30 .09
❑ 89 Edgar Martinez .50 .15
❑ 90 Carlos Delgado .30 .09
❑ 91 Chris Saenz FC RC 4.00 1.20
❑ 92 Justin Leone FC RC 5.00 1.50
❑ 93 Shawn Hill FC RC 4.00 1.20
❑ 94 Chad Bentz FC RC 4.00 1.20
❑ 95 Jesse Harper FC RC 4.00 1.20
❑ 96 Dave Crouthers FC RC 4.00 1.20
❑ 97 Justin Germano FC RC 4.00 1.20
❑ 98 Tim Bausher FC RC 4.00 1.20
❑ 99 Greg Dobbs FC RC 4.00 1.20
❑ 100 Enemencio Pacheco FC RC 4.00 1.20
❑ 101 Dennis Sarfate FC RC 4.00 1.20
❑ 102 Edwin Moreno FC RC 4.00 1.20
❑ 103 Colby Miller FC RC 4.00 1.20
❑ 104 Mike Rouse FC RC 4.00 1.20
❑ 105 Fernando Nieve FC RC 4.00 1.20
❑ 106 Tim Hamulack FC RC 4.00 1.20
❑ 107 Jason Frasor FC RC 4.00 1.20
❑ 108 Jose Capellan FC RC 6.00 1.80
❑ 109 Jamie Brown FC RC 4.00 1.20
❑ 110 Mariano Gomez FC RC 4.00 1.20
❑ 111 Mike Vento FC RC 5.00 1.50
❑ 112 Josh Labandeira FC RC 4.00 1.20
❑ 113 Mike Gosling FC RC 4.00 1.20
❑ 114 Shingo Takatsu FC RC 5.00 1.50
❑ 115 Justin Hampson FC RC 4.00 1.20
❑ 116 Tim Bittner FC RC 4.00 1.20
❑ 117 Jerry Gil FC RC 4.00 1.20
❑ 118 Carlos Vasquez FC RC 5.00 1.50
❑ 119 Lincoln Holdzkom FC RC 4.00 1.20
❑ 120 Mike Johnston FC RC 4.00 1.20
❑ 121 William Bergolla FC RC 4.00 1.20
❑ 122 Luis A. Gonzalez FC RC 5.00 1.50
❑ 123 Ivan Ochoa FC RC 4.00 1.20
❑ 124 Roman Colon FC RC 4.00 1.20
❑ 125 Renyel Pinto FC RC 5.00 1.50
❑ 126 Donnie Kelly FC RC 4.00 1.20
❑ 127 Chris Oxspring FC RC 5.00 1.50
❑ 128 Sean Henn FC RC 4.00 1.20
❑ 129 Ryan Meaux FC RC 4.00 1.20
❑ 130 Shawn Camp FC RC 4.00 1.20
❑ 131 Brandon Medders FC RC 4.00 1.20
❑ 132 Rusty Tucker FC RC 5.00 1.50
❑ 133 Kazuo Matsui FC RC 8.00 2.40
❑ 134 Jorge Sequea FC RC 4.00 1.20
❑ 135 Hector Gimenez FC RC 4.00 1.20
❑ 136 Casey Daigle FC RC 4.00 1.20
❑ 137 Ian Snell FC RC 5.00 1.50
❑ 138 Scott Dohmann FC RC 4.00 1.20
❑ 139 Ronny Cedeno FC RC 4.00 1.20
❑ 140 Jorge Vasquez FC RC 4.00 1.20
❑ 141 David Aardsma FC RC 4.00 1.20
❑ 142 Carlos Hines FC RC 4.00 1.20
❑ 143 Scott Proctor FC RC 5.00 1.50
❑ 144 Jerome Gamble FC RC 4.00 1.20
❑ 145 Jason Bartlett FC RC 5.00 1.50
❑ 146 Akinori Otsuka FC RC 4.00 1.20
❑ 147 Merkin Valdez FC RC 5.00 1.50
❑ 148 Jake Woods FC RC 4.00 1.20
❑ 149 Chris Aguila FC RC 4.00 1.20
❑ 150 John Gall FC RC 5.00 1.50
❑ 151 Aaron Miles AU 15.00 4.50
❑ 152 Aquilino Lopez AU 10.00 3.00
❑ 153 Bill Hall AU 10.00 3.00
❑ 154 Billy Traber AU 10.00 3.00
❑ 155 Brad Lidge AU 25.00 7.50
❑ 156 Brady Clark AU 10.00 3.00
❑ 157 Brandon Duckworth AU 10.00 3.00
❑ 158 Brett Tomko AU 10.00 3.00
❑ 159 Brian Fuentes AU 10.00 3.00
❑ 160 Does Not Exist
❑ 161 Brooks Kieshnick AU 10.00 3.00
❑ 162 Carlos Rivera AU 10.00 3.00
❑ 163 Chad Cordero AU 10.00 3.00
❑ 164 Chad Tracy AU 15.00 4.50
❑ 165 Claudio Vargas AU 10.00 3.00
❑ 166 D.J. Carrasco AU 10.00 3.00
❑ 167 Damian Rolls AU 10.00 3.00
❑ 168 David Sanders AU 10.00 3.00
❑ 169 Does Not Exist
❑ 170 Derrick Turnbow AU 10.00 3.00
❑ 171 Desi Relaford AU 10.00 3.00
❑ 172 Doug Davis AU 10.00 3.00
❑ 173 Dustan Mohr AU 10.00 3.00
❑ 174 Does Not Exist
❑ 175 Does Not Exist
❑ 176 Frank Catalanotto AU 10.00 3.00
❑ 177 Does Not Exist .00 .00
❑ 178 Franklyn German AU 10.00 3.00
❑ 179 Ron Belliard AU 10.00 3.00
❑ 180 Geoff Geary AU 10.00 3.00
❑ 181 Greg Colbrunn AU 10.00 3.00
❑ 182 Henry Mateo AU 10.00 3.00
❑ 183 Brent Mayne AU 10.00 3.00
❑ 184 Horacio Ramirez AU 10.00 3.00
❑ 185 J.C. Romero AU 10.00 3.00
❑ 186 J.J. Putz AU 10.00 3.00
❑ 187 Ferdin Tejeda AU 10.00 3.00
❑ 188 Jaime Cerda AU 10.00 3.00
❑ 189 Jason Michaels AU 10.00 3.00
❑ 190 Jason Simontacchi AU 10.00 3.00
❑ 191 Jay Witasick AU 10.00 3.00
❑ 192 Joe Valentine AU 10.00 3.00
❑ 193 Joey Eischen AU 10.00 3.00
❑ 194 Johnny Estrada AU 15.00 4.50
❑ 195 Jon Garland AU 10.00 3.00
❑ 196 Jon Switzer AU 10.00 3.00
❑ 197 Jorge Julio AU 10.00 3.00
❑ 198 Jorge Sosa AU 10.00 3.00
❑ 199 Jose Castillo AU 10.00 3.00
❑ 200 Jose Macias AU 10.00 3.00
❑ 201 Josh Bard AU 10.00 3.00
❑ 202 Juan Cruz AU 10.00 3.00
❑ 203 Juan Rivera AU 10.00 3.00
❑ 204 Ken Griffey Jr. AU 120.00 36.00
❑ 205 Kevin Hooper AU 10.00 3.00
❑ 206 Kiko Calero AU 10.00 3.00
❑ 207 Chad Gaudin AU 10.00 3.00
❑ 208 Luis Rivas AU 10.00 3.00
❑ 209 Mark Corey AU 10.00 3.00
❑ 210 Matt Ford AU 10.00 3.00
❑ 211 Matt Herges AU 10.00 3.00
❑ 212 Miguel Cairo AU 10.00 3.00
❑ 213 Fernando Cabrera AU 10.00 3.00
❑ 214 Mike MacDougal AU 10.00 3.00
❑ 215 Mike Neu AU 10.00 3.00
❑ 216 Lew Ford AU 15.00 4.50
❑ 217 Mike Wood AU 15.00 4.50
❑ 218 Nate Robertson AU 15.00 4.50
❑ 219 Nick Punto AU 10.00 3.00
❑ 220 Does Not Exist
❑ 221 Oscar Villarreal AU 10.00 3.00
❑ 222 Ramon Vazquez AU 10.00 3.00
❑ 223 Randall Simon AU 10.00 3.00
❑ 224 Does Not Exist
❑ 225 Ricky Stone AU 10.00 3.00
❑ 226 Does Not Exist
❑ 227 Does Not Exist
❑ 228 Does Not Exist
❑ 229 Ryan Drese AU 10.00 3.00
❑ 230 Ryan Ludwick AU 10.00 3.00
❑ 231 Scot Shields AU 10.00 3.00
❑ 232 Shane Nance AU 10.00 3.00
❑ 233 Steve Colyer AU 10.00 3.00
❑ 234 Tony Armas Jr. AU 10.00 3.00
❑ 235 Robby Hammock AU 10.00 3.00
❑ 236 Travis Hafner AU 15.00 4.50
❑ 237 Victor Martinez AU 15.00 4.50
❑ 238 Wilfredo Ledezma AU 10.00 3.00
❑ 239 Willie Bloomquist AU 10.00 3.00
❑ 240 Yorvit Torrealba AU 10.00 3.00
❑ NNO Instant Win Exchange

2004 UD Legends Timeless Teams

Nm-Mt Ex-Mt

COMPLETE SET (300) 50.00 15.00

❑ 1 Bob Gibson 64 1.00 .30
❑ 2 Lou Brock MM 64 1.00 .30
❑ 3 Ray Washburn 64 .40 .12
❑ 4 Tim McCarver 64 .60 .18
❑ 5 Harmon Killebrew 65 1.50 .45
❑ 6 Jim Kaat 65 .60 .18

❑ 7 Jim Perry 65 .40 .12
❑ 8 Mudcat Grant 65 .40 .12
❑ 9 Boog Powell 66 .60 .18
❑ 10 Brooks Robinson 66 1.00 .30
❑ 11 Frank Robinson MM 66 .60 .18
❑ 12 Jim Palmer 66 .60 .18
❑ 13 Carl Yastrzemski MM 67 2.50 .75
❑ 14 Jim Lonborg 67 .40 .12
❑ 15 George Scott 67 .40 .12
❑ 16 Sparky Lyle 67 .60 .18
❑ 17 Rico Petrocelli 67 .40 .12
❑ 18 Bob Gibson 67 1.00 .30
❑ 19 Julian Javier 67 .40 .12
❑ 20 Lou Brock 67 1.00 .30
❑ 21 Orlando Cepeda 67 .60 .18
❑ 22 Ray Washburn 67 .40 .12
❑ 23 Steve Carlton 67 .60 .18
❑ 24 Tim McCarver 67 .60 .18
❑ 25 Al Kaline 68 1.50 .45
❑ 26 Bill Freehan 68 .60 .18
❑ 27 Denny McLain MM 68 .60 .18
❑ 28 Dick McAuliffe 68 .40 .12
❑ 29 Jim Northrup 68 .40 .12
❑ 30 John Hiller 68 .40 .12
❑ 31 Mickey Lolich MM 68 .40 .12
❑ 32 Mickey Stanley 68 .40 .12
❑ 33 Willie Horton 68 .40 .12
❑ 34 Bob Gibson MM 68 1.00 .30
❑ 35 Julian Javier 68 .40 .12
❑ 36 Lou Brock 68 1.00 .30
❑ 37 Orlando Cepeda 68 .60 .18
❑ 38 Steve Carlton 68 .60 .18
❑ 39 Boog Powell 69 .60 .18
❑ 40 Brooks Robinson 69 1.00 .30
❑ 41 Davey Johnson 69 .40 .12
❑ 42 Merv Rettenmund 69 .40 .12
❑ 43 Eddie Watt 69 .40 .12
❑ 44 Frank Robinson 69 .60 .18
❑ 45 Jim Palmer 69 .60 .18
❑ 46 Mike Cuellar 69 .40 .12
❑ 47 Paul Blair 69 .40 .12
❑ 48 Pete Richert 69 .40 .12
❑ 49 Ellie Hendricks 69 .40 .12
❑ 50 Billy Williams 69 .60 .18
❑ 51 Randy Hundley 69 .40 .12
❑ 52 Ernie Banks 69 1.50 .45
❑ 53 Fergie Jenkins 69 .60 .18
❑ 54 Jim Hickman 69 .40 .12
❑ 55 Ken Holtzman 69 .40 .12
❑ 56 Ron Santo MM 69 1.00 .30
❑ 57 Ed Kranepool 69 .60 .18
❑ 58 Jerry Koosman MM 69 .60 .18
❑ 59 Nolan Ryan 69 4.00 1.20
❑ 60 Tom Seaver 69 1.00 .30
❑ 61 Boog Powell 70 .60 .18
❑ 62 Brooks Robinson MM 70 1.00 .30
❑ 63 Davey Johnson 70 .40 .12
❑ 64 Merv Rettenmund 70 .40 .12
❑ 65 Eddie Watt 70 .40 .12
❑ 66 Frank Robinson 70 .60 .18
❑ 67 Jim Palmer 70 .60 .18
❑ 68 Mike Cuellar 70 .40 .12
❑ 69 Paul Blair 70 .40 .12
❑ 70 Pete Richert 70 .40 .12
❑ 71 Ellie Hendricks 70 .40 .12
❑ 72 Al Kaline 72 1.50 .45
❑ 73 Bill Freehan 72 .60 .18
❑ 74 Dick McAuliffe 72 .40 .12

❑ 75 Jim Northrup 72 .40 .12
❑ 76 John Hiller 72 .40 .12
❑ 77 Mickey Lolich 72 .40 .12
❑ 78 Mickey Stanley 72 .40 .12
❑ 79 Willie Horton 72 .40 .12
❑ 80 Bert Campaneris 72 .40 .12
❑ 81 Blue Moon Odom MM 72 .40 .12
❑ 82 Sal Bando 72 .40 .12
❑ 83 Joe Rudi 72 .40 .12
❑ 84 Ken Holtzman 72 .40 .12
❑ 85 Billy North 73 .40 .12
❑ 86 Blue Moon Odom 73 .40 .12
❑ 87 Gene Tenace 73 .40 .12
❑ 88 Manny Trillo 73 .40 .12
❑ 89 Dick Green 73 .40 .12
❑ 90 Rollie Fingers 73 .60 .18
❑ 91 Sal Bando 73 .40 .12
❑ 92 Vida Blue 73 .60 .18
❑ 93 Bill Buckner 74 .60 .18
❑ 94 Davey Lopes 74 .60 .18
❑ 95 Don Sutton 74 .60 .18
❑ 96 Al Downing MM 74 .40 .12
❑ 97 Ron Cey 74 .60 .18
❑ 98 Steve Garvey 74 .60 .18
❑ 99 Tommy John 74 .60 .18
❑ 100 Bert Campaneris 74 .40 .12
❑ 101 Billy North 74 .40 .12
❑ 102 Joe Rudi MM 74 .40 .12
❑ 103 Sal Bando 74 .40 .12
❑ 104 Vida Blue 74 .60 .18
❑ 105 Carl Yastrzemski 75 2.50 .75
❑ 106 Carlton Fisk MM 75 1.00 .30
❑ 107 Cecil Cooper 75 .60 .18
❑ 108 Dwight Evans 75 .60 .18
❑ 109 Fred Lynn 75 .60 .18
❑ 110 Jim Rice 75 .60 .18
❑ 111 Luis Tiant 75 .60 .18
❑ 112 Rick Burleson 75 .40 .12
❑ 113 Rico Petrocelli 75 .40 .12
❑ 114 Pedro Borbon 75 .40 .12
❑ 115 Dave Concepcion 75 .60 .18
❑ 116 Don Gullett 75 .40 .12
❑ 117 George Foster 75 .60 .18
❑ 118 Joe Morgan MM 75 .60 .18
❑ 119 Johnny Bench 75 1.50 .45
❑ 120 Rawly Eastwick 75 .40 .12
❑ 121 Sparky Anderson 75 .60 .18
❑ 122 Tony Perez 75 .60 .18
❑ 123 Billy Williams 75 .60 .18
❑ 124 Gene Tenace 75 .40 .12
❑ 125 Jim Perry 75 .40 .12
❑ 126 Vida Blue 75 .60 .18
❑ 127 Pedro Borbon 76 .40 .12
❑ 128 Dave Concepcion 76 .60 .18
❑ 129 Don Gullett 76 .40 .12
❑ 130 George Foster 76 .60 .18
❑ 131 Joe Morgan 76 .60 .18
❑ 132 Johnny Bench MM 76 1.50 .45
❑ 133 Ken Griffey Sr. 76 .60 .18
❑ 134 Rawly Eastwick 76 .40 .12
❑ 135 Tony Perez 76 .60 .18
❑ 136 Bill Russell 77 .40 .12
❑ 137 Burt Hooton 77 .40 .12
❑ 138 Davey Lopes 77 .60 .18
❑ 139 Don Sutton 77 .60 .18
❑ 140 Dusty Baker 77 .60 .18
❑ 141 Steve Yeager 77 .40 .12
❑ 142 Ron Cey 77 .60 .18
❑ 143 Steve Garvey MM 77 .60 .18
❑ 144 Tommy John 77 .60 .18
❑ 145 Bucky Dent 77 .60 .18
❑ 146 Chris Chambliss 77 .60 .18
❑ 147 Ed Figueroa 77 .40 .12
❑ 148 Graig Nettles 77 .60 .18
❑ 149 Lou Piniella 77 .60 .18
❑ 150 Roy White 77 .40 .12
❑ 151 Don Gullett 77 .40 .12
❑ 152 Sparky Lyle 77 .60 .18
❑ 153 Brian Doyle 78 .40 .12
❑ 154 Bucky Dent MM 78 .60 .18
❑ 155 Chris Chambliss 78 .60 .18
❑ 156 Ed Figueroa 78 .40 .12
❑ 157 Graig Nettles 78 .60 .18
❑ 158 Lou Piniella 78 .60 .18
❑ 159 Roy White 78 .40 .12
❑ 160 Rich Gossage 78 .60 .18
❑ 161 Sparky Lyle 78 .60 .18
❑ 162 Bobby Grich 79 .60 .18
❑ 163 Brian Downing 79 .60 .18
❑ 164 Dan Ford 79 .40 .12
❑ 165 Nolan Ryan 79 4.00 1.20
❑ 166 Dave Concepcion 79 .60 .18
❑ 167 George Foster 79 .60 .18
❑ 168 Johnny Bench 79 1.50 .45
❑ 169 Ray Knight 79 .60 .18
❑ 170 Tom Seaver 79 1.00 .30
❑ 171 Bert Blyleven 79 .60 .18
❑ 172 Bill Madlock 79 .60 .18
❑ 173 Dave Parker MM 79 .60 .18
❑ 174 Phil Garner 79 .40 .12
❑ 175 Bill Russell 80 .40 .12
❑ 176 Steve Yeager 80 .40 .12
❑ 177 Don Sutton 80 .60 .18
❑ 178 Dusty Baker 80 .60 .18
❑ 179 Jerry Reuss 80 .40 .12
❑ 180 Mickey Hatcher 80 .40 .12
❑ 181 Pedro Guerrero 80 .40 .12
❑ 182 Ron Cey 80 .60 .18
❑ 183 Steve Garvey 80 .60 .18
❑ 184 Rudy May 80 .40 .12
❑ 185 Brian Doyle 80 .40 .12
❑ 186 Bucky Dent 80 .60 .18
❑ 187 Jim Kaat 80 .60 .18
❑ 188 Lou Piniella 80 .60 .18
❑ 189 Luis Tiant 80 .60 .18
❑ 190 Tommy John 80 .60 .18
❑ 191 Bake McBride 80 .40 .12
❑ 192 Bob Boone 80 .60 .18
❑ 193 Dickie Noles MM 80 .40 .12
❑ 194 Manny Trillo 80 .40 .12
❑ 195 Mike Schmidt 80 3.00 .90
❑ 196 Sparky Lyle 80 .60 .18
❑ 197 Steve Carlton 80 .60 .18
❑ 198 Steve Yeager 81 .40 .12
❑ 199 Burt Hooton 81 .40 .12
❑ 200 Dusty Baker 81 .60 .18
❑ 201 Jerry Reuss 81 .40 .12
❑ 202 Mike Scioscia 81 .60 .18
❑ 203 Pedro Guerrero 81 .40 .12
❑ 204 Ron Cey 81 .60 .18
❑ 205 Steve Garvey 81 .60 .18
❑ 206 Alejandro Pena 81 .40 .12
❑ 207 Steve Sax 81 .40 .12
❑ 208 Cecil Cooper 81 .60 .18
❑ 209 Gorman Thomas 81 .60 .18
❑ 210 Paul Molitor 81 1.00 .30
❑ 211 Robin Yount 81 2.50 .75
❑ 212 Rollie Fingers 81 .60 .18
❑ 213 Don Money 81 .40 .12
❑ 214 Rudy May 81 .40 .12
❑ 215 Bucky Dent 81 .60 .18
❑ 216 Dave Winfield 81 .60 .18
❑ 217 Lou Piniella 81 .60 .18
❑ 218 Rich Gossage 81 .60 .18
❑ 219 Tommy John 81 .60 .18
❑ 220 Cecil Cooper 82 .60 .18
❑ 221 Gorman Thomas 82 .60 .18
❑ 222 Paul Molitor MM 82 1.00 .30
❑ 223 Robin Yount 82 2.50 .75
❑ 224 Don Money 82 .40 .12
❑ 225 Cal Ripken MM 83 5.00 1.50
❑ 226 Dan Ford 83 .40 .12
❑ 227 Jim Palmer 83 .60 .18
❑ 228 John Shelby 83 .40 .12
❑ 229 Alan Trammell 84 .60 .18
❑ 230 Chet Lemon 84 .40 .12
❑ 231 Howard Johnson 84 .40 .12
❑ 232 Jack Morris MM 84 .60 .18
❑ 233 Kirk Gibson 84 .60 .18
❑ 234 Lou Whitaker 84 .60 .18
❑ 235 Sparky Anderson 84 .60 .18
❑ 236 Dave Winfield 85 .60 .18
❑ 237 Don Mattingly 85 3.00 .90
❑ 238 Ken Griffey Sr. 85 .60 .18
❑ 239 Phil Niekro 85 .60 .18
❑ 240 Yogi Berra 85 1.00 .30
❑ 241 Bill Buckner MM 86 .60 .18
❑ 242 Bruce Hurst 86 .40 .12
❑ 243 Dave Henderson 86 .40 .12
❑ 244 Dwight Evans 86 .60 .18
❑ 245 Jim Rice 86 .60 .18
❑ 246 Tom Seaver 86 1.00 .30
❑ 247 Wade Boggs 86 1.00 .30
❑ 248 Bob Boone 86 .60 .18
❑ 249 Bobby Grich 86 .60 .18
❑ 250 Brian Downing 86 .60 .18
❑ 251 Don Sutton 86 .60 .18
❑ 252 Terry Forster 86 .40 .12
❑ 253 Rick Burleson 86 .40 .12
❑ 254 Wally Joyner MM 86 .40 .12
❑ 255 Darryl Strawberry 86 .60 .18
❑ 256 Dwight Gooden 86 .60 .18
❑ 257 Gary Carter 86 .60 .18
❑ 258 Jesse Orosco MM 86 .40 .12
❑ 259 Keith Hernandez 86 .60 .18
❑ 260 Lenny Dykstra 86 .60 .18
❑ 261 Mookie Wilson 86 .60 .18
❑ 262 Ray Knight 86 .60 .18
❑ 263 Wally Backman 86 .40 .12
❑ 264 Sid Fernandez 86 .40 .12
❑ 265 Alan Trammell 87 .60 .18
❑ 266 Dan Petry 87 .40 .12
❑ 267 Chet Lemon 87 .40 .12
❑ 268 Sparky Anderson 87 .60 .18
❑ 269 Jack Morris 87 .60 .18
❑ 270 Kirk Gibson 87 .60 .18
❑ 271 Lou Whitaker 87 .60 .18
❑ 272 Bert Blyleven 87 .60 .18
❑ 273 Kent Hrbek MM 87 .60 .18
❑ 274 Kirby Puckett 87 1.50 .45
❑ 275 Alejandro Pena 88 .40 .12
❑ 276 Jesse Orosco 88 .40 .12
❑ 277 John Shelby 88 .40 .12
❑ 278 Kirk Gibson MM 88 .60 .18
❑ 279 Mickey Hatcher 88 .40 .12
❑ 280 Mike Scioscia 88 .60 .18
❑ 281 Steve Sax 88 .40 .12
❑ 282 Darryl Strawberry 88 .60 .18
❑ 283 Dwight Gooden 88 .60 .18
❑ 284 Gary Carter 88 .60 .18
❑ 285 Howard Johnson 88 .40 .12
❑ 286 Keith Hernandez 88 .60 .18
❑ 287 Lenny Dykstra 88 .60 .18
❑ 288 Mookie Wilson 88 .60 .18
❑ 289 Wally Backman 88 .40 .12
❑ 290 Sid Fernandez 88 .40 .12
❑ 291 Jack Morris 91 .60 .18
❑ 292 Kent Hrbek 91 .60 .18
❑ 293 Kirby Puckett MM 91 1.50 .45
❑ 294 Dave Winfield MM 92 .60 .18
❑ 295 Jack Morris 92 .60 .18
❑ 296 Joe Carter 92 .60 .18
❑ 297 Don Mattingly MM 95 3.00 .90
❑ 298 Paul O'Neill 95 1.00 .30
❑ 299 Jack McDowell 95 .40 .12
❑ 300 Wade Boggs 95 1.00 .30

2001 UD Reserve

	Nm-Mt	Ex-Mt
COMP.SET w/o SP's (180)	25.00	7.50
COMMON CARD (1-180)	.30	.09
COMMON (181-210)	4.00	1.20

❑ 1 Darin Erstad .30 .09
❑ 2 Tim Salmon .50 .15
❑ 3 Bengie Molina .30 .09
❑ 4 Troy Glaus .30 .09
❑ 5 Glenallen Hill .30 .09
❑ 6 Garret Anderson .30 .09

❑ 7 Jason Giambi .30 .09
❑ 8 Johnny Damon .50 .15
❑ 9 Eric Chavez .30 .09
❑ 10 Tim Hudson .30 .09
❑ 11 Miguel Tejada .30 .09
❑ 12 Barry Zito .50 .15
❑ 13 Jose Ortiz .30 .09
❑ 14 Tony Batista .30 .09
❑ 15 Carlos Delgado .30 .09
❑ 16 Shannon Stewart .30 .09
❑ 17 Raul Mondesi .30 .09
❑ 18 Ben Grieve .30 .09
❑ 19 Aubrey Huff .30 .09
❑ 20 Greg Vaughn .30 .09
❑ 21 Fred McGriff .50 .15
❑ 22 Gerald Williams .30 .09
❑ 23 Bartolo Colon .30 .09
❑ 24 Roberto Alomar .50 .15
❑ 25 Jim Thome .75 .23
❑ 26 Omar Vizquel .50 .15
❑ 27 Juan Gonzalez .50 .15
❑ 28 Ellis Burks .30 .09
❑ 29 Edgar Martinez .50 .15
❑ 30 Aaron Sele .30 .09
❑ 31 Jay Buhner .30 .09
❑ 32 Mike Cameron .30 .09
❑ 33 Kazuhiro Sasaki .30 .09
❑ 34 John Olerud .30 .09
❑ 35 Cal Ripken 2.50 .75
❑ 36 Brady Anderson .30 .09
❑ 37 Pat Hentgen .30 .09
❑ 38 Chris Richard .30 .09
❑ 39 Jerry Hairston Jr. .30 .09
❑ 40 Mike Bordick .30 .09
❑ 41 Ivan Rodriguez .75 .23
❑ 42 Rick Helling .30 .09
❑ 43 Rafael Palmeiro .50 .15
❑ 44 Alex Rodriguez 1.25 .35
❑ 45 Andres Galarraga .30 .09
❑ 46 Rusty Greer .30 .09
❑ 47 Ruben Mateo .30 .09
❑ 48 Ken Caminiti .30 .09
❑ 49 Nomar Garciaparra 1.25 .35
❑ 50 Pedro Martinez .75 .23
❑ 51 Manny Ramirez .50 .15
❑ 52 Carl Everett .30 .09
❑ 53 Dante Bichette .30 .09
❑ 54 Hideo Nomo .75 .23
❑ 55 Mike Sweeney .30 .09
❑ 56 Carlos Beltran .50 .15
❑ 57 Jeff Suppan .30 .09
❑ 58 Jermaine Dye .30 .09
❑ 59 Mark Quinn .30 .09
❑ 60 Joe Randa .30 .09
❑ 61 Bobby Higginson .30 .09
❑ 62 Tony Clark .30 .09
❑ 63 Brian Moehler .30 .09
❑ 64 Dean Palmer .30 .09
❑ 65 Brandon Inge .30 .09
❑ 66 Damion Easley .30 .09
❑ 67 Brad Radke .30 .09
❑ 68 Corey Koskie .30 .09
❑ 69 Cristian Guzman .30 .09
❑ 70 Eric Milton .30 .09
❑ 71 Jacque Jones .30 .09
❑ 72 Matt Lawton .30 .09
❑ 73 Frank Thomas .75 .23
❑ 74 David Wells .30 .09
❑ 75 Magglio Ordonez .30 .09
❑ 76 Paul Konerko .30 .09
❑ 77 Sandy Alomar Jr. .30 .09
❑ 78 Ray Durham .30 .09
❑ 79 Roger Clemens 1.50 .45
❑ 80 Bernie Williams .50 .15
❑ 81 Derek Jeter 2.00 .60
❑ 82 David Justice .30 .09
❑ 83 Paul O'Neill .50 .15
❑ 84 Mike Mussina .50 .15
❑ 85 Jorge Posada .50 .15
❑ 86 Jeff Bagwell .50 .15
❑ 87 Richard Hidalgo .30 .09
❑ 88 Craig Biggio .50 .15
❑ 89 Scott Elarton .30 .09
❑ 90 Moises Alou .30 .09
❑ 91 Greg Maddux 1.25 .35
❑ 92 Rafael Furcal .30 .09
❑ 93 Andruw Jones .30 .09
❑ 94 Tom Glavine .50 .15
❑ 95 Chipper Jones .75 .23
❑ 96 Javy Lopez .30 .09
❑ 97 Richie Sexson .30 .09
❑ 98 Jeromy Burnitz .30 .09
❑ 99 Jeff D'Amico .30 .09
❑ 100 Jeffrey Hammonds .30 .09
❑ 101 Geoff Jenkins .30 .09
❑ 102 Ben Sheets .50 .15
❑ 103 Mark McGwire 2.00 .60
❑ 104 Rick Ankiel .30 .09
❑ 105 Darryl Kile .30 .09
❑ 106 Edgar Renteria .30 .09
❑ 107 Jim Edmonds .30 .09
❑ 108 J.D. Drew .30 .09
❑ 109 Sammy Sosa 1.25 .35
❑ 110 Corey Patterson .30 .09
❑ 111 Kerry Wood .75 .23
❑ 112 Todd Hundley .30 .09
❑ 113 Rondell White .30 .09
❑ 114 Matt Stairs .30 .09
❑ 115 Randy Johnson .75 .23
❑ 116 Mark Grace .50 .15
❑ 117 Steve Finley .30 .09
❑ 118 Luis Gonzalez .30 .09
❑ 119 Matt Williams .30 .09
❑ 120 Curt Schilling .30 .09
❑ 121 Gary Sheffield .30 .09
❑ 122 Kevin Brown .30 .09
❑ 123 Shawn Green .30 .09
❑ 124 Eric Karros .30 .09
❑ 125 Chan Ho Park .30 .09
❑ 126 Adrian Beltre .50 .15
❑ 127 Vladimir Guerrero .75 .23
❑ 128 Fernando Tatis .30 .09
❑ 129 Lee Stevens .30 .09
❑ 130 Jose Vidro .30 .09
❑ 131 Peter Bergeron .30 .09
❑ 132 Michael Barrett .30 .09
❑ 133 Jeff Kent .30 .09
❑ 134 Russ Ortiz .30 .09
❑ 135 Barry Bonds 2.00 .60
❑ 136 J.T. Snow .30 .09
❑ 137 Livan Hernandez .30 .09
❑ 138 Rich Aurilia .30 .09
❑ 139 Preston Wilson .30 .09
❑ 140 Mike Lowell .30 .09
❑ 141 Ryan Dempster .30 .09
❑ 142 Charles Johnson .30 .09
❑ 143 Matt Clement .30 .09
❑ 144 Luis Castillo .30 .09
❑ 145 Mike Piazza UER 1.25 .35
Card lists him as a Dodger
❑ 146 Al Leiter .30 .09
❑ 147 Robin Ventura .30 .09
❑ 148 Jay Payton .30 .09
❑ 149 Todd Zeile .30 .09
❑ 150 Edgardo Alfonzo .30 .09
❑ 151 Tony Gwynn 1.00 .30
❑ 152 Ryan Klesko .30 .09
❑ 153 Phil Nevin .30 .09
❑ 154 Mark Kotsay .30 .09
❑ 155 Trevor Hoffman .30 .09
❑ 156 Damian Jackson .30 .09
❑ 157 Scott Rolen .75 .23
❑ 158 Mike Lieberthal .30 .09
❑ 159 Bruce Chen .30 .09
❑ 160 Bobby Abreu .30 .09
❑ 161 Pat Burrell .30 .09
❑ 162 Travis Lee .30 .09
❑ 163 Jason Kendall .30 .09
❑ 164 Derek Bell .30 .09
❑ 165 Kris Benson .30 .09
❑ 166 Kevin Young .30 .09
❑ 167 Brian Giles .30 .09
❑ 168 Pat Meares .30 .09
❑ 169 Sean Casey .30 .09
❑ 170 Pokey Reese .30 .09
❑ 171 Pete Harnisch .30 .09
❑ 172 Barry Larkin .50 .15
❑ 173 Ken Griffey Jr. 1.25 .35
❑ 174 Dmitri Young .30 .09
❑ 175 Mike Hampton .30 .09
❑ 176 Todd Helton .50 .15
❑ 177 Jeff Cirillo .30 .09
❑ 178 Denny Neagle .30 .09
❑ 179 Larry Walker .50 .15
❑ 180 Todd Hollandsworth .30 .09
❑ 181 Ichiro Suzuki SP RC 40.00 12.00
❑ 182 Wilson Betemit SP RC 4.00 1.20
❑ 183 A. Hernandez SP RC 4.00 1.20
❑ 184 Travis Hafner SP RC 10.00 3.00
❑ 185 Sean Douglass SP RC 4.00 1.20
❑ 186 Juan Diaz SP RC 4.00 1.20
❑ 187 H. Ramirez SP RC 5.00 1.50
❑ 188 M. Ensberg SP RC 5.00 1.50
❑ 189 B. Duckworth SP RC 4.00 1.20
❑ 190 Jack Wilson SP RC 8.00 2.40
❑ 191 Erick Almonte SP RC 4.00 1.20
❑ 192 R. Rodriguez SP RC 4.00 1.20
❑ 193 E. Guzman SP RC 4.00 1.20
❑ 194 Juan Uribe SP RC 5.00 1.50
❑ 195 Ryan Freel SP RC 4.00 1.20
❑ 196 C. Parker SP RC 4.00 1.20
❑ 197 J. Melian SP RC 4.00 1.20
❑ 198 Jose Mieses SP RC 4.00 1.20
❑ 199 Andres Torres SP RC 4.00 1.20
❑ 200 Jason Smith SP RC 4.00 1.20
❑ 201 J. Estrada SP RC 5.00 1.50
❑ 202 Cesar Crespo SP RC 4.00 1.20
❑ 203 C. Valderrama SP RC 4.00 1.20
❑ 204 Albert Pujols SP RC 50.00 15.00
❑ 205 Wilkin Ruan SP RC 4.00 1.20
❑ 206 Josh Fogg SP RC 4.00 1.20
❑ 207 Bert Snow SP RC 4.00 1.20
❑ 208 B. Lawrence SP RC 4.00 1.20
❑ 209 Esix Snead SP RC 4.00 1.20
❑ 210 T. Shinjo SP RC 5.00 1.50

2001 Ultimate Collection

	Nm-Mt	Ex-Mt
COMMON CARD (1-90)	4.00	1.20
COMMON CARD (91-100)	10.00	3.00
COMMON (101-110)	10.00	3.00
COMMON CARD (111-120)	25.00	7.50

❑ 1 Troy Glaus 4.00 1.20
❑ 2 Darin Erstad 4.00 1.20
❑ 3 Jason Giambi 4.00 1.20
❑ 4 Barry Zito 4.00 1.20
❑ 5 Tim Hudson 4.00 1.20
❑ 6 Miguel Tejada 4.00 1.20
❑ 7 Carlos Delgado 4.00 1.20
❑ 8 Shannon Stewart 4.00 1.20
❑ 9 Greg Vaughn 4.00 1.20
❑ 10 Toby Hall 4.00 1.20
❑ 11 Roberto Alomar 4.00 1.20
❑ 12 Juan Gonzalez 4.00 1.20
❑ 13 Jim Thome 6.00 1.80
❑ 14 Edgar Martinez 4.00 1.20
❑ 15 Freddy Garcia 4.00 1.20
❑ 16 Bret Boone 4.00 1.20
❑ 17 Kazuhiro Sasaki 4.00 1.20
❑ 18 Cal Ripken 20.00 6.00
❑ 19 Tim Raines Jr. 4.00 1.20
❑ 20 Alex Rodriguez 10.00 3.00
❑ 21 Ivan Rodriguez 6.00 1.80
❑ 22 Rafael Palmeiro 4.00 1.20
❑ 23 Pedro Martinez 6.00 1.80
❑ 24 Nomar Garciaparra 10.00 3.00
❑ 25 Manny Ramirez 4.00 1.20
❑ 26 Hideo Nomo 6.00 1.80
❑ 27 Mike Sweeney 4.00 1.20
❑ 28 Carlos Beltran 4.00 1.20

		Nm-Mt	Ex-Mt
❑ 29	Tony Clark	4.00	1.20
❑ 30	Dean Palmer	4.00	1.20
❑ 31	Doug Mientkiewicz	4.00	1.20
❑ 32	Cristian Guzman	4.00	1.20
❑ 33	Corey Koskie	4.00	1.20
❑ 34	Frank Thomas	6.00	1.80
❑ 35	Magglio Ordonez	4.00	1.20
❑ 36	Jose Canseco	6.00	1.80
❑ 37	Roger Clemens	12.00	3.60
❑ 38	Derek Jeter	15.00	4.50
❑ 39	Bernie Williams	4.00	1.20
❑ 40	Mike Mussina	4.00	1.20
❑ 41	Tino Martinez	4.00	1.20
❑ 42	Jeff Bagwell	4.00	1.20
❑ 43	Lance Berkman	4.00	1.20
❑ 44	Roy Oswalt	4.00	1.20
❑ 45	Chipper Jones	6.00	1.80
❑ 46	Greg Maddux	10.00	3.00
❑ 47	Andruw Jones	4.00	1.20
❑ 48	Tom Glavine	4.00	1.20
❑ 49	Richie Sexson	4.00	1.20
❑ 50	Jeromy Burnitz	4.00	1.20
❑ 51	Ben Sheets	4.00	1.20
❑ 52	Mark McGwire	15.00	4.50
❑ 53	Matt Morris	4.00	1.20
❑ 54	Jim Edmonds	4.00	1.20
❑ 55	J.D. Drew	4.00	1.20
❑ 56	Sammy Sosa	10.00	3.00
❑ 57	Fred McGriff	4.00	1.20
❑ 58	Kerry Wood	6.00	1.80
❑ 59	Randy Johnson	6.00	1.80
❑ 60	Luis Gonzalez	4.00	1.20
❑ 61	Curt Schilling	4.00	1.20
❑ 62	Shawn Green	4.00	1.20
❑ 63	Kevin Brown	4.00	1.20
❑ 64	Gary Sheffield	4.00	1.20
❑ 65	Vladimir Guerrero	6.00	1.80
❑ 66	Barry Bonds	15.00	4.50
❑ 67	Jeff Kent	4.00	1.20
❑ 68	Rich Aurilia	4.00	1.20
❑ 69	Cliff Floyd	4.00	1.20
❑ 70	Charles Johnson	4.00	1.20
❑ 71	Josh Beckett	4.00	1.20
❑ 72	Mike Piazza	10.00	3.00
❑ 73	Edgardo Alfonzo	4.00	1.20
❑ 74	Robin Ventura	4.00	1.20
❑ 75	Tony Gwynn	8.00	2.40
❑ 76	Ryan Klesko	4.00	1.20
❑ 77	Phil Nevin	4.00	1.20
❑ 78	Scott Rolen	6.00	1.80
❑ 79	Bobby Abreu	4.00	1.20
❑ 80	Jimmy Rollins	4.00	1.20
❑ 81	Brian Giles	4.00	1.20
❑ 82	Jason Kendall	4.00	1.20
❑ 83	Aramis Ramirez	4.00	1.20
❑ 84	Ken Griffey Jr.	10.00	3.00
❑ 85	Adam Dunn	4.00	1.20
❑ 86	Sean Casey	4.00	1.20
❑ 87	Barry Larkin	4.00	1.20
❑ 88	Larry Walker	4.00	1.20
❑ 89	Mike Hampton	4.00	1.20
❑ 90	Todd Helton	4.00	1.20
❑ 91	Ken Harvey T1	10.00	3.00
❑ 92	Bill Ortega T1 RC	10.00	3.00
❑ 93	Juan Diaz T1 RC	10.00	3.00
❑ 94	Greg Miller T1 RC	10.00	3.00
❑ 95	Brandon Berger T1 RC	10.00	3.00
❑ 96	Brandon Lyon T1 RC	10.00	3.00
❑ 97	Jay Gibbons T1 RC	15.00	4.50
❑ 98	Rob Mackowiak T1 RC	15.00	4.50
❑ 99	Erick Almonte T1 RC	10.00	3.00
❑ 100	J.Middlebrook T1 RC	10.00	3.00
❑ 101	Johnny Estrada T2 RC	15.00	4.50
❑ 102	Juan Uribe T2 RC	15.00	4.50
❑ 103	Travis Hafner T2 RC	25.00	7.50
❑ 104	M.Ensberg T2 RC	15.00	4.50
❑ 105	Mike Rivera T2 RC	10.00	3.00
❑ 106	Josh Towers T2 RC	10.00	3.00
❑ 107	A.Hernandez T2 RC	10.00	3.00
❑ 108	Rafael Soriano T2 RC	15.00	4.50
❑ 109	Jackson Melian T2 RC	10.00	3.00
❑ 110	Wilkin Ruan T2 RC	10.00	3.00
❑ 111	Albert Pujols T3 RC	300.00	90.00
❑ 112	T.Shinjo T3 RC	30.00	9.00
❑ 113	B.Duckworth T3 RC	25.00	7.50
❑ 114	Juan Cruz T3 RC	25.00	7.50
❑ 115	D.Brazelton T3 RC	30.00	9.00
❑ 116	Mark Prior T3 AU RC	400.00	120.00
❑ 117	Mark Teixeira T3 AU RC	250.00	75.00
❑ 118	Wilson Betemit T3 RC	25.00	7.50
❑ 119	Bud Smith T3 RC	25.00	7.50
❑ 120	I.Suzuki T3 AU RC	800.00	240.00

2002 Ultimate Collection

	Nm-Mt	Ex-Mt
COMMON CARD (1-60)	4.00	1.20
COMMON CARD (61-110)	10.00	3.00
61-110 PRINT RUN 550 SERIAL #'d SETS		.00
COMMON CARD (111-113)	25.00	7.50
COMMON CARD (114-120)	15.00	4.50

		Nm-Mt	Ex-Mt
❑ 1	Troy Glaus	4.00	1.20
❑ 2	Luis Gonzalez	4.00	1.20
❑ 3	Curt Schilling	4.00	1.20
❑ 4	Randy Johnson	6.00	1.80
❑ 5	Andruw Jones	4.00	1.20
❑ 6	Greg Maddux	10.00	3.00
❑ 7	Chipper Jones	6.00	1.80
❑ 8	Gary Sheffield	4.00	1.20
❑ 9	Cal Ripken	20.00	6.00
❑ 10	Manny Ramirez	4.00	1.20
❑ 11	Pedro Martinez	6.00	1.80
❑ 12	Nomar Garciaparra	10.00	3.00
❑ 13	Sammy Sosa	10.00	3.00
❑ 14	Kerry Wood	6.00	1.80
❑ 15	Mark Prior	10.00	3.00
❑ 16	Magglio Ordonez	4.00	1.20
❑ 17	Frank Thomas	6.00	1.80
❑ 18	Adam Dunn	4.00	1.20
❑ 19	Ken Griffey Jr.	10.00	3.00
❑ 20	Jim Thome	6.00	1.80
❑ 21	Larry Walker	4.00	1.20
❑ 22	Todd Helton	4.00	1.20
❑ 23	Nolan Ryan	15.00	4.50
❑ 24	Jeff Bagwell	4.00	1.20
❑ 25	Roy Oswalt	4.00	1.20
❑ 26	Lance Berkman	4.00	1.20
❑ 27	Mike Sweeney	4.00	1.20
❑ 28	Shawn Green	4.00	1.20
❑ 29	Hideo Nomo	6.00	1.80
❑ 30	Torii Hunter	4.00	1.20
❑ 31	Vladimir Guerrero	6.00	1.80
❑ 32	Tom Seaver	4.00	1.20
❑ 33	Mike Piazza	10.00	3.00
❑ 34	Roberto Alomar	4.00	1.20
❑ 35	Derek Jeter	15.00	4.50
❑ 36	Alfonso Soriano	4.00	1.20
❑ 37	Jason Giambi	4.00	1.20
❑ 38	Roger Clemens	12.00	3.60
❑ 39	Mike Mussina	4.00	1.20
❑ 40	Bernie Williams	4.00	1.20
❑ 41	Joe DiMaggio	12.00	3.60
❑ 42	Mickey Mantle	25.00	7.50
❑ 43	Miguel Tejada	4.00	1.20
❑ 44	Eric Chavez	4.00	1.20
❑ 45	Barry Zito	4.00	1.20
❑ 46	Pat Burrell	4.00	1.20
❑ 47	Jason Kendall	4.00	1.20
❑ 48	Brian Giles	4.00	1.20
❑ 49	Barry Bonds	15.00	4.50
❑ 50	Ichiro Suzuki	10.00	3.00
❑ 51	Stan Musial	10.00	3.00
❑ 52	J.D. Drew	4.00	1.20
❑ 53	Scott Rolen	6.00	1.80
❑ 54	Albert Pujols	12.00	3.60
❑ 55	Mark McGwire	15.00	4.50
❑ 56	Alex Rodriguez	10.00	3.00
❑ 57	Ivan Rodriguez	6.00	1.80
❑ 58	Juan Gonzalez	4.00	1.20
❑ 59	Rafael Palmeiro	4.00	1.20
❑ 60	Carlos Delgado	4.00	1.20
❑ 61	Jose Valverde UR RC	15.00	4.50
❑ 62	Doug Devore UR RC	10.00	3.00
❑ 63	John Ennis UR RC	10.00	3.00
❑ 64	Joey Dawley UR RC	10.00	3.00
❑ 65	Trey Hodges UR RC	10.00	3.00
❑ 66	Mike Mahoney UR	10.00	3.00
❑ 67	Aaron Cook UR RC	10.00	3.00
❑ 68	Rene Reyes UR RC	10.00	3.00
❑ 69	Mark Corey UR RC	10.00	3.00
❑ 70	Hansel Izquierdo UR RC	10.00	3.00
❑ 71	Brandon Puffer UR RC	10.00	3.00
❑ 72	Jeriome Robertson UR RC	10.00	3.00
❑ 73	Jose Diaz UR RC	10.00	3.00
❑ 74	David Ross UR RC	10.00	3.00
❑ 75	Jayson Durocher UR RC	10.00	3.00
❑ 76	Eric Good UR RC	10.00	3.00
❑ 77	Satoru Komiyama UR RC	10.00	3.00
❑ 78	Tyler Yates UR RC	15.00	4.50
❑ 79	Eric Junge UR RC	10.00	3.00
❑ 80	Anderson Machado UR RC	10.00	3.00
❑ 81	Adrian Burnside UR RC	10.00	3.00
❑ 82	Ben Howard UR RC	10.00	3.00
❑ 83	Clay Condrey UR RC	10.00	3.00
❑ 84	Nelson Castro UR RC	10.00	3.00
❑ 85	So Taguchi UR RC	15.00	4.50
❑ 86	Mike Crudale UR RC	10.00	3.00
❑ 87	Scotty Layfield UR RC	10.00	3.00
❑ 88	Steve Bechler UR RC	10.00	3.00
❑ 89	Travis Driskill UR RC	10.00	3.00
❑ 90	Howie Clark UR RC	10.00	3.00
❑ 91	Josh Hancock UR RC	10.00	3.00
❑ 92	Jorge De La Rosa UR RC	10.00	3.00
❑ 93	Anastacio Martinez UR RC	10.00	3.00
❑ 94	Brian Tallet UR RC	10.00	3.00
❑ 95	Carl Sadler UR RC	10.00	3.00
❑ 96	Cliff Lee UR RC	15.00	4.50
❑ 97	Josh Bard UR RC	10.00	3.00
❑ 98	Wes Obermueller UR RC	10.00	3.00
❑ 99	Juan Brito UR RC	10.00	3.00
❑ 100	Aaron Guiel UR RC	10.00	3.00
❑ 101	Jeremy Hill UR RC	10.00	3.00
❑ 102	Kevin Frederick UR RC	10.00	3.00
❑ 103	Nate Field UR RC	10.00	3.00
❑ 104	Julio Mateo UR RC	10.00	3.00
❑ 105	Chris Snelling UR RC	10.00	3.00
❑ 106	Felix Escalona UR RC	10.00	3.00
❑ 107	Reynaldo Garcia UR RC	10.00	3.00
❑ 108	Mike Smith UR RC	10.00	3.00
❑ 109	Ken Huckaby UR RC	10.00	3.00
❑ 110	Kevin Cash UR RC	10.00	3.00
❑ 111	Kazuhisa Ishii UR AU RC	50.00	15.00
❑ 112	Fr. Sanchez UR AU RC	25.00	7.50
❑ 113	J.Simontacchi UR AU RC	25.00	7.50
❑ 114	Jorge Padilla UR AU RC	15.00	4.50
❑ 115	Kirk Saarloos UR AU RC	15.00	4.50
❑ 116	Ro. Rosario UR AU RC	15.00	4.50
❑ 117	Oliver Perez UR AU RC	70.00	21.00
❑ 118	Mi. Asencio UR AU RC	15.00	4.50
❑ 119	Fr. German UR AU RC	15.00	4.50
❑ 120	Jaime Cerda UR AU RC	15.00	4.50
❑ MM	M.McGwire AU EXCH/100	.00	.00

2003 Ultimate Collection

	MINT	NRMT
COMMON CARD (1-84)	3.00	1.35
1-84 STATED ODDS TWO PER PACK		
COMMON CARD (85-117)	5.00	2.20
COMMON CARD (118-140)	5.00	2.20
118-140 PRINT RUN 399 SERIAL #'d SETS		
COMMON CARD (141-158)	6.00	2.70
COMMON CARD (159-168)	12.00	5.50
159-168 PRINT RUN 100 SERIAL #'d SETS		
85-168 STATED ODDS ONE PER PACK		
COMMON CARD (169-174)	15.00	6.75
169-174 AND ULT.SIG.OVERALL ODDS 1:4		
COMMON CARD (175-180)	15.00	6.75
175-180 AND BUYBACK OVERALL ODDS 1:8		
169-180 PRINT RUN 250 SERIAL #'d SETS		
MATSUI PART LIVE/ PART EXCH....		
EXCHANGE DEADLINE 12/17/06		

❑ 1 Ichiro Suzuki 8.00 3.60
❑ 2 Ken Griffey Jr. 8.00 3.60
❑ 3 Sammy Sosa 8.00 3.60
❑ 4 Jason Giambi 3.00 1.35
❑ 5 Mike Piazza 8.00 3.60
❑ 6 Derek Jeter 12.00 5.50
❑ 7 Randy Johnson 5.00 2.20
❑ 8 Barry Bonds 12.00 5.50
❑ 9 Carlos Delgado 3.00 1.35
❑ 10 Mark Prior 5.00 2.20
❑ 11 Vladimir Guerrero 5.00 2.20
❑ 12 Alfonso Soriano 5.00 2.20
❑ 13 Jim Thome 5.00 2.20
❑ 14 Pedro Martinez 5.00 2.20
❑ 15 Nomar Garciaparra 8.00 3.60
❑ 16 Chipper Jones 5.00 2.20
❑ 17 Rocco Baldelli 3.00 1.35
❑ 18 Dontrelle Willis 5.00 2.20
❑ 19 Garret Anderson 3.00 1.35
❑ 20 Jeff Bagwell 5.00 2.20
❑ 21 Jim Edmonds 3.00 1.35
❑ 22 Rickey Henderson 5.00 2.20
❑ 23 Torii Hunter 3.00 1.35
❑ 24 Tom Glavine 5.00 2.20
❑ 25 Hideo Nomo 5.00 2.20
❑ 26 Luis Gonzalez 3.00 1.35
❑ 27 Alex Rodriguez 8.00 3.60
❑ 28 Albert Pujols 10.00 4.50
❑ 29 Manny Ramirez 5.00 2.20
❑ 30 Rafael Palmeiro 5.00 2.20
❑ 31 Bernie Williams 5.00 2.20
❑ 32 Curt Schilling 3.00 1.35
❑ 33 Roger Clemens 10.00 4.50
❑ 34 Andruw Jones 3.00 1.35
❑ 35 J.D. Drew 3.00 1.35
❑ 36 Kerry Wood 5.00 2.20
❑ 37 Scott Rolen 5.00 2.20
❑ 38 Darin Erstad 3.00 1.35
❑ 39 Joe DiMaggio 8.00 3.60
❑ 40 Magglio Ordonez 3.00 1.35
❑ 41 Todd Helton 5.00 2.20
❑ 42 Barry Zito 3.00 1.35
❑ 43 Mickey Mantle 15.00 6.75
❑ 44 Miguel Tejada 3.00 1.35
❑ 45 Troy Glaus 3.00 1.35
❑ 46 Kazuhisa Ishii 3.00 1.35
❑ 47 Adam Dunn 5.00 2.20
❑ 48 Ted Williams 8.00 3.60
❑ 49 Mike Mussina 5.00 2.20
❑ 50 Ivan Rodriguez 5.00 2.20
❑ 51 Jacque Jones 3.00 1.35
❑ 52 Stan Musial 8.00 3.60
❑ 53 Mariano Rivera 5.00 2.20
❑ 54 Larry Walker 5.00 2.20
❑ 55 Aaron Boone 3.00 1.35
❑ 56 Hank Blalock 5.00 2.20
❑ 57 Rich Harden 5.00 2.20
❑ 58 Lance Berkman 3.00 1.35
❑ 59 Eric Chavez 3.00 1.35
❑ 60 Carlos Beltran 5.00 2.20
❑ 61 Roy Oswalt 3.00 1.35
❑ 62 Moises Alou 3.00 1.35
❑ 63 Nolan Ryan 10.00 4.50
❑ 64 Jeff Kent 3.00 1.35
❑ 65 Roberto Alomar 5.00 2.20
❑ 66 Runelvys Hernandez 3.00 1.35
❑ 67 Roy Halladay 3.00 1.35
❑ 68 Tim Hudson 3.00 1.35
❑ 69 Tom Seaver 5.00 2.20
❑ 70 Edgardo Alfonzo 3.00 1.35
❑ 71 Andy Pettitte 5.00 2.20
❑ 72 Preston Wilson 3.00 1.35
❑ 73 Frank Thomas 5.00 2.20
❑ 74 Jerome Williams 3.00 1.35
❑ 75 Shawn Green 3.00 1.35
❑ 76 David Wells 3.00 1.35
❑ 77 John Smoltz 5.00 2.20
❑ 78 Jorge Posada 5.00 2.20
❑ 79 Marlon Byrd 3.00 1.35
❑ 80 Austin Kearns 3.00 1.35
❑ 81 Bret Boone 3.00 1.35
❑ 82 Rafael Furcal 3.00 1.35
❑ 83 Jay Gibbons 3.00 1.35
❑ 84 Shane Reynolds 3.00 1.35
❑ 85 Nate Bland UR T1 RC 5.00 2.20
❑ 86 Willie Eyre UR T1 RC 5.00 2.20
❑ 87 Jeremy Guthrie UR T1 5.00 2.20
❑ 88 Jeremy Wedel UR T1 RC 5.00 2.20
❑ 89 Jhonny Peralta UR T1 5.00 2.20
❑ 90 Luis Ayala UR T1 RC 5.00 2.20
❑ 91 Michael Hessman UR T1 RC 5.00 2.20
❑ 92 Michael Nakamura UR T1 RC 5.00 2.20
❑ 93 Nook Logan UR T1 RC 5.00 2.20
❑ 94 Rett Johnson UR T1 RC 8.00 3.60
❑ 95 Josh Hall UR T1 RC 8.00 3.60
❑ 96 Julio Manon UR T1 RC 5.00 2.20
❑ 97 Heath Bell UR T1 RC 5.00 2.20
❑ 98 Ian Ferguson UR T1 RC 5.00 2.20
❑ 99 Jason Gilfillan UR T1 RC 5.00 2.20
❑ 100 Jason Roach UR T1 RC 5.00 2.20
❑ 101 Jason Shiell UR T1 RC 5.00 2.20
❑ 102 Terrmel Sledge UR T1 RC 8.00 3.60
❑ 103 Phil Seibel UR T1 RC 5.00 2.20
❑ 104 Jeff Duncan UR T1 RC 8.00 3.60
❑ 105 Mike Neu UR T1 RC 5.00 2.20
❑ 106 Colin Porter UR T1 RC 5.00 2.20
❑ 107 David Matranga UR T1 RC 5.00 2.20
❑ 108 Aaron Looper UR T1 RC 5.00 2.20
❑ 109 Jeremy Bonderman UR T1 RC 8.00 3.60
❑ 110 Miguel Ojeda UR T1 RC 5.00 2.20
❑ 111 Chad Cordero UR T1 RC 5.00 2.20
❑ 112 Shane Bazzell UR T1 RC 5.00 2.20
❑ 113 Tim Olson UR T1 RC 8.00 3.60
❑ 114 Michel Hernandez UR T1 RC 5.00 2.20
❑ 115 Chien-Ming Wang UR T1 RC 8.00 3.60
❑ 116 Josh Stewart UR T1 RC 5.00 2.20
❑ 117 Clint Barmes UR T1 RC 8.00 3.60
❑ 118 Craig Brazell UR T2 RC 8.00 3.60
❑ 119 Josh Willingham UR T2 RC 8.00 3.60
❑ 120 Brent Hoard UR T2 RC 5.00 2.20
❑ 121 Francisco Rosario UR T2 RC 5.00 2.20
❑ 122 Rick Roberts UR T2 RC 5.00 2.20
❑ 123 Geoff Geary UR T2 RC 5.00 2.20
❑ 124 Edgar Gonzalez UR T2 RC 5.00 2.20
❑ 125 Kevin Correia UR T2 RC 5.00 2.20
❑ 126 Ryan Cameron UR T2 RC 5.00 2.20
❑ 127 Beau Kemp UR T2 RC 5.00 2.20
❑ 128 Tommy Phelps UR T2 5.00 2.20
❑ 129 Mark Malaska UR T2 RC 5.00 2.20
❑ 130 Kevin Ohme UR T2 RC 5.00 2.20
❑ 131 Humberto Quintero UR T2 RC 5.00 2.20
❑ 132 Aquilino Lopez UR T2 RC 5.00 2.20
❑ 133 Andrew Brown UR T2 RC 8.00 3.60
❑ 134 Wilfredo Ledezma UR T2 RC 8.00 3.60
❑ 135 Luis De Los Santos UR T2 5.00 2.20
❑ 136 Garrett Atkins UR T2 5.00 2.20
❑ 137 Fernando Cabrera UR T2 RC 5.00 2.20
❑ 138 D.J. Carrasco UR T2 RC 5.00 2.20
❑ 139 Alfredo Gonzalez UR T2 RC 5.00 2.20
❑ 140 Alex Prieto UR T2 RC 5.00 2.20
❑ 141 Matt Kata UR T3 RC 10.00 4.50
❑ 142 Chris Capuano UR T3 RC 6.00 2.70
❑ 143 Bobby Madritsch UR T3 RC 40.00 18.00
❑ 144 Greg Jones UR T3 RC 6.00 2.70
❑ 145 Pete Zoccolillo UR T3 RC 6.00 2.70
❑ 146 Chad Gaudin UR T3 RC 6.00 2.70
❑ 147 Rosman Garcia UR T3 RC 6.00 2.70
❑ 148 Gerald Laird UR T3 6.00 2.70
❑ 149 Danny Garcia UR T3 RC 6.00 2.70
❑ 150 Stephen Randolph UR T3 RC 6.00 2.70
❑ 151 Pete LaForest UR T3 RC 10.00 4.50
❑ 152 Brian Sweeney UR T3 RC 6.00 2.70
❑ 153 Aaron Miles UR T3 RC 10.00 4.50
❑ 154 Jorge DePaula UR T3 UER 6.00 2.70
Real name is Julio DePaula
❑ 155 Graham Koonce UR T3 RC 15.00 6.75
❑ 156 Tom Gregorio UR T3 RC 6.00 2.70
❑ 157 Javier Lopez UR T3 RC 6.00 2.70
❑ 158 Oscar Villarreal UR T3 RC 6.00 2.70
❑ 159 Prentice Redman UR T4 RC 12.00 5.50
❑ 160 Francisco Cruceta UR T4 RC 12.00 5.50
❑ 161 Guillermo Quiroz UR T4 RC 20.00 9.00
❑ 162 Jeremy Griffiths UR T4 RC 20.00 9.00
❑ 163 Lew Ford UR T4 RC 25.00 11.00
❑ 164 Rob Hammock UR T4 RC 20.00 9.00
❑ 165 Todd Wellemeyer UR T4 RC 20.00 9.00
❑ 166 Ryan Wagner UR T4 RC 20.00 9.00
❑ 167 Edwin Jackson UR T4 RC 40.00 18.00
❑ 168 Dan Haren UR T4 RC 20.00 9.00
❑ 169 Hideki Matsui AU RC 300.00 135.00
❑ 170 Jose Contreras AU RC 40.00 18.00
❑ 171 Delmon Young AU RC 200.00 90.00
❑ 172 Rickie Weeks AU RC 100.00 45.00
❑ 173 Brandon Webb AU RC 30.00 13.50
❑ 174 Bo Hart AU RC 25.00 11.00
❑ 175 Rocco Baldelli YS AU 25.00 11.00
❑ 176 Jose Reyes YS AU 25.00 11.00
❑ 177 Dontrelle Willis YS AU 40.00 18.00
❑ 178 Bobby Hill YS AU 15.00 6.75
❑ 179 Jae Weong Seo YS AU 25.00 11.00
❑ 180 Jesse Foppert YS AU 25.00 11.00

1999 Ultimate Victory

	Nm-Mt	Ex-Mt
COMPLETE SET (180)	200.00	60.00
COMP.SET w/o SP's (120)	25.00	7.50
COMMON CARD (1-120)	.30	.09
COMMON SP (121-150)	2.00	.60
COMMON (151-180)	2.00	.60

❑ 1 Troy Glaus .30 .09
❑ 2 Tim Salmon .50 .15
❑ 3 Mo Vaughn .30 .09
❑ 4 Garret Anderson .30 .09
❑ 5 Darin Erstad .30 .09
❑ 6 Randy Johnson .75 .23
❑ 7 Matt Williams .30 .09
❑ 8 Travis Lee .30 .09
❑ 9 Jay Bell .30 .09
❑ 10 Steve Finley .30 .09
❑ 11 Luis Gonzalez .30 .09
❑ 12 Greg Maddux 1.25 .35
❑ 13 Chipper Jones .75 .23
❑ 14 Javy Lopez .30 .09
❑ 15 Tom Glavine .50 .15
❑ 16 John Smoltz .50 .15
❑ 17 Cal Ripken 2.50 .75
❑ 18 Charles Johnson .30 .09
❑ 19 Albert Belle .30 .09
❑ 20 Mike Mussina .50 .15
❑ 21 Pedro Martinez .75 .23
❑ 22 Nomar Garciaparra 1.25 .35
❑ 23 Jose Offerman .30 .09
❑ 24 Sammy Sosa 1.25 .35
❑ 25 Mark Grace .50 .15
❑ 26 Kerry Wood .75 .23
❑ 27 Frank Thomas .75 .23
❑ 28 Ray Durham .30 .09
❑ 29 Paul Konerko .30 .09
❑ 30 Pete Harnisch .30 .09
❑ 31 Greg Vaughn .30 .09

❑ 32 Sean Casey .30 .09
❑ 33 Manny Ramirez .50 .15
❑ 34 Jim Thome .75 .23
❑ 35 Sandy Alomar Jr. .30 .09
❑ 36 Roberto Alomar .50 .15
❑ 37 Travis Fryman .30 .09
❑ 38 Kenny Lofton .30 .09
❑ 39 Omar Vizquel .50 .15
❑ 40 Larry Walker .50 .15
❑ 41 Todd Helton .50 .15
❑ 42 Vinny Castilla .30 .09
❑ 43 Tony Clark .30 .09
❑ 44 Juan Encarnacion .30 .09
❑ 45 Dean Palmer .30 .09
❑ 46 Damion Easley .30 .09
❑ 47 Mark Kotsay .30 .09
❑ 48 Cliff Floyd .30 .09
❑ 49 Jeff Bagwell .50 .15
❑ 50 Ken Caminiti .30 .09
❑ 51 Craig Biggio .50 .15
❑ 52 Moises Alou .30 .09
❑ 53 Johnny Damon .50 .15
❑ 54 Larry Sutton .30 .09
❑ 55 Kevin Brown .50 .15
❑ 56 Adrian Beltre .50 .15
❑ 57 Raul Mondesi .30 .09
❑ 58 Gary Sheffield .30 .09
❑ 59 Jeromy Burnitz .30 .09
❑ 60 Sean Berry .30 .09
❑ 61 Jeff Cirillo .30 .09
❑ 62 Brad Radke .30 .09
❑ 63 Todd Walker .30 .09
❑ 64 Matt Lawton .30 .09
❑ 65 Vladimir Guerrero .75 .23
❑ 66 Rondell White .30 .09
❑ 67 Dustin Hermanson .30 .09
❑ 68 Mike Piazza 1.25 .35
❑ 69 Rickey Henderson .75 .23
❑ 70 Robin Ventura .30 .09
❑ 71 John Olerud .30 .09
❑ 72 Derek Jeter 2.00 .60
❑ 73 Roger Clemens 1.50 .45
❑ 74 Orlando Hernandez .30 .09
❑ 75 Paul O'Neill .50 .15
❑ 76 Bernie Williams .50 .15
❑ 77 Chuck Knoblauch .30 .09
❑ 78 Tino Martinez .50 .15
❑ 79 Jason Giambi .30 .09
❑ 80 Ben Grieve .30 .09
❑ 81 Matt Stairs .30 .09
❑ 82 Scott Rolen .75 .23
❑ 83 Ron Gant .30 .09
❑ 84 Bobby Abreu .30 .09
❑ 85 Curt Schilling .30 .09
❑ 86 Brian Giles .30 .09
❑ 87 Jason Kendall .30 .09
❑ 88 Kevin Young .30 .09
❑ 89 Mark McGwire 2.00 .60
❑ 90 Fernando Tatis .30 .09
❑ 91 Ray Lankford .30 .09
❑ 92 Eric Davis .30 .09
❑ 93 Tony Gwynn 1.00 .30
❑ 94 Reggie Sanders .30 .09
❑ 95 Wally Joyner .30 .09
❑ 96 Trevor Hoffman .30 .09
❑ 97 Robb Nen .30 .09
❑ 98 Barry Bonds 2.00 .60
❑ 99 Jeff Kent .30 .09
❑ 100 J.T. Snow .30 .09
❑ 101 Ellis Burks .30 .09
❑ 102 Ken Griffey Jr. 1.25 .35
❑ 103 Alex Rodriguez 1.25 .35
❑ 104 Jay Buhner .30 .09
❑ 105 Edgar Martinez .50 .15
❑ 106 David Bell .30 .09
❑ 107 Bobby Smith .30 .09
❑ 108 Wade Boggs .50 .15
❑ 109 Fred McGriff .50 .15
❑ 110 Rolando Arrojo .30 .09
❑ 111 Jose Canseco .75 .23
❑ 112 Ivan Rodriguez .75 .23
❑ 113 Juan Gonzalez .50 .15
❑ 114 Rafael Palmeiro .50 .15
❑ 115 Rusty Greer .30 .09
❑ 116 Todd Zeile .30 .09
❑ 117 Jose Cruz Jr. .30 .09
❑ 118 Carlos Delgado .30 .09
❑ 119 Shawn Green .30 .09
❑ 120 David Wells .30 .09
❑ 121 Eric Munson SP RC 5.00 1.50
❑ 122 Lance Berkman SP 3.00 .90
❑ 123 Ed Yarnall SP 2.00 .60
❑ 124 Jacque Jones SP 3.00 .90
❑ 125 K.Farnsworth SP RC 3.00 .90
❑ 126 Ryan Rupe SP RC 2.00 .60
❑ 127 Jeff Weaver SP RC 5.00 1.50
❑ 128 Gabe Kapler SP 2.00 .60
❑ 129 Alex Gonzalez SP 2.00 .60
❑ 130 Randy Wolf SP 2.00 .60
❑ 131 Ben Davis SP 2.00 .60
❑ 132 Carlos Beltran SP 5.00 1.50
❑ 133 Jim Morris SP RC 5.00 1.50
❑ 134 J.Zimmerman SP RC 3.00 .90
❑ 135 Bruce Aven SP 2.00 .60
❑ 136 A.Soriano SP RC 30.00 9.00
❑ 137 Tim Hudson SP RC 20.00 6.00
❑ 138 Josh Beckett SP RC 40.00 12.00
❑ 139 Michael Barrett SP 2.00 .60
❑ 140 Eric Chavez SP 3.00 .90
❑ 141 Pat Burrell SP RC 12.00 3.60
❑ 142 Kris Benson SP 2.00 .60
❑ 143 J.D. Drew SP 3.00 .90
❑ 144 Matt Clement SP 2.00 .60
❑ 145 Rick Ankiel SP RC 25.00 7.50
❑ 146 Vernon Wells SP 3.00 .90
❑ 147 Ruben Mateo SP UER 2.00 .60
Card is misnumbered
❑ 148 Roy Halladay SP 2.00 .60
❑ 149 Joe McEwing SP RC 3.00 .90
❑ 150 Freddy Garcia SP RC 8.00 2.40
❑ 151 Mark McGwire MM 2.00 .60
❑ 152 Mark McGwire MM 2.00 .60
❑ 153 Mark McGwire MM 2.00 .60
❑ 154 Mark McGwire MM 2.00 .60
❑ 155 Mark McGwire MM 2.00 .60
❑ 156 Mark McGwire MM 2.00 .60
❑ 157 Mark McGwire MM 2.00 .60
❑ 158 Mark McGwire MM 2.00 .60
❑ 159 Mark McGwire MM 2.00 .60
❑ 160 Mark McGwire MM 2.00 .60
❑ 161 Mark McGwire MM 2.00 .60
❑ 162 Mark McGwire MM 2.00 .60
❑ 163 Mark McGwire MM 2.00 .60
❑ 164 Mark McGwire MM 2.00 .60
❑ 165 Mark McGwire MM 2.00 .60
❑ 166 Mark McGwire MM 2.00 .60
❑ 167 Mark McGwire MM 2.00 .60
❑ 168 Mark McGwire MM 2.00 .60
❑ 169 Mark McGwire MM 2.00 .60
❑ 170 Mark McGwire MM 2.00 .60
❑ 171 Mark McGwire MM 2.00 .60
❑ 172 Mark McGwire MM 2.00 .60
❑ 173 Mark McGwire MM 2.00 .60
❑ 174 Mark McGwire MM 2.00 .60
❑ 175 Mark McGwire MM 2.00 .60
❑ 176 Mark McGwire MM 2.00 .60
❑ 177 Mark McGwire MM 2.00 .60
❑ 178 Mark McGwire MM 2.00 .60
❑ 179 Mark McGwire MM 2.00 .60
❑ 180 Mark McGwire MM 2.00 .60

2000 Ultimate Victory

	Nm-Mt	Ex-Mt
COMP.SET w/o SP's (90)	25.00	7.50
COMMON CARD (1-90)	.30	.09

❑ 1 Mo Vaughn .30 .09
❑ 2 Darin Erstad .30 .09
❑ 3 Troy Glaus .30 .09
❑ 4 Adam Kennedy .30 .09
❑ 5 Jason Giambi .30 .09
❑ 6 Ben Grieve .30 .09
❑ 7 Terrence Long .30 .09
❑ 8 Tim Hudson .30 .09
❑ 9 David Wells .30 .09
❑ 10 Carlos Delgado .30 .09
❑ 11 Shannon Stewart .30 .09
❑ 12 Greg Vaughn .30 .09
❑ 13 Gerald Williams .30 .09
❑ 14 Manny Ramirez .50 .15
❑ 15 Roberto Alomar .50 .15
❑ 16 Jim Thome .75 .23
❑ 17 Edgar Martinez .50 .15
❑ 18 Alex Rodriguez 1.25 .35
❑ 19 Matt Riley .30 .09
❑ 20 Cal Ripken 2.50 .75
❑ 21 Mike Mussina .50 .15
❑ 22 Albert Belle .30 .09
❑ 23 Ivan Rodriguez .75 .23
❑ 24 Rafael Palmeiro .50 .15
❑ 25 Nomar Garciaparra 1.25 .35
❑ 26 Pedro Martinez .75 .23
❑ 27 Carl Everett .30 .09
❑ 28 Tomokazu Ohka RC .30 .09
❑ 29 Jermaine Dye .30 .09
❑ 30 Johnny Damon .50 .15
❑ 31 Dean Palmer .30 .09
❑ 32 Juan Gonzalez .50 .15
❑ 33 Eric Milton .30 .09
❑ 34 Matt Lawton .30 .09
❑ 35 Frank Thomas .75 .23
❑ 36 Paul Konerko .30 .09
❑ 37 Magglio Ordonez .30 .09
❑ 38 Jon Garland .30 .09
❑ 39 Derek Jeter 2.00 .60
❑ 40 Roger Clemens 1.50 .45
❑ 41 Bernie Williams .50 .15
❑ 42 Nick Johnson .30 .09
❑ 43 Julio Lugo .30 .09
❑ 44 Jeff Bagwell .50 .15
❑ 45 Richard Hidalgo .30 .09
❑ 46 Chipper Jones .75 .23
❑ 47 Greg Maddux 1.25 .35
❑ 48 Andruw Jones .30 .09
❑ 49 Andres Galarraga .30 .09
❑ 50 Rafael Furcal .30 .09
❑ 51 Jeromy Burnitz .30 .09
❑ 52 Geoff Jenkins .30 .09
❑ 53 Mark McGwire 2.00 .60
❑ 54 Jim Edmonds .30 .09
❑ 55 Rick Ankiel .30 .09
❑ 56 Sammy Sosa 1.25 .35
❑ 57 Julio Zuleta RC .30 .09
❑ 58 Kerry Wood .75 .23
❑ 59 Randy Johnson .75 .23
❑ 60 Matt Williams .30 .09
❑ 61 Steve Finley .30 .09
❑ 62 Gary Sheffield .30 .09
❑ 63 Kevin Brown .30 .09
❑ 64 Shawn Green .30 .09
❑ 65 Milton Bradley .30 .09
❑ 66 Vladimir Guerrero .75 .23
❑ 67 Jose Vidro .30 .09
❑ 68 Barry Bonds 2.00 .60
❑ 69 Jeff Kent .30 .09
❑ 70 Preston Wilson .30 .09
❑ 71 Mike Lowell .30 .09
❑ 72 Mike Piazza 1.25 .35
❑ 73 Robin Ventura .30 .09
❑ 74 Edgardo Alfonzo .30 .09
❑ 75 Jay Payton .30 .09
❑ 76 Tony Gwynn 1.00 .30
❑ 77 Adam Eaton .30 .09
❑ 78 Phil Nevin .30 .09
❑ 79 Scott Rolen .75 .23
❑ 80 Bob Abreu .30 .09
❑ 81 Pat Burrell .30 .09
❑ 82 Brian Giles .30 .09

		Nm-Mt	Ex-Mt
❑ 83	Jason Kendall	.30	.09
❑ 84	Kris Benson	.30	.09
❑ 85	Gookie Dawkins	.30	.09
❑ 86	Ken Griffey Jr.	1.25	.35
❑ 87	Barry Larkin	.50	.15
❑ 88	Larry Walker	.50	.15
❑ 89	Todd Helton	.50	.15
❑ 90	Ben Petrick	.30	.09
❑ 91	Alex Cabrera/3500 RC	4.00	1.20
❑ 92	M.Wheatland/1000 RC	10.00	3.00
❑ 93	Joe Torres/1000 RC	10.00	3.00
❑ 94	Xavier Nady/1000 RC	15.00	4.50
❑ 95	Kenny Kelly/3500 RC	4.00	1.20
❑ 96	Matt Ginter/3500 RC	4.00	1.20
❑ 97	Ben Diggins/1000 RC	10.00	3.00
❑ 98	Danys Baez/3500 RC	4.00	1.20
❑ 99	Daylan Holt/2500 RC	5.00	1.50
❑ 100	K.Sasaki/3500 RC	5.00	1.50
❑ 101	D.Artman/2500 RC	5.00	1.50
❑ 102	Mike Tonis/1000 RC	10.00	3.00
❑ 103	Timo Perez/2500 RC	5.00	1.50
❑ 104	Barry Zito/2500 RC	10.00	3.00
❑ 105	Koyie Hill/2500 RC	5.00	1.50
❑ 106	B.Wilkerson/2500 RC	8.00	2.40
❑ 107	Juan Pierre/3500 RC	5.00	1.50
❑ 108	A.McNeal/3500 RC	4.00	1.20
❑ 109	J.Spurgeon/3500 RC	4.00	1.20
❑ 110	Sean Burnett/1000 RC	15.00	4.50
❑ 111	Luis Matos/3500 RC	4.00	1.20
❑ 112	Dave Krynzel/1000 RC	10.00	3.00
❑ 113	Scott Heard/1000 RC	10.00	3.00
❑ 114	Ben Sheets/2500 RC	10.00	3.00
❑ 115	D.Sardinha/1000 RC	10.00	3.00
❑ 116	D.Espinosa/1000 RC	10.00	3.00
❑ 117	Leo Estrella/3500 RC	4.00	1.20
❑ 118	K.Ainsworth/2500 RC	5.00	1.50
❑ 119	Jon Rauch/2500 RC	5.00	1.50
❑ 120	R.Franklin/2500 RC	5.00	1.50

1991 Ultra Update

		Nm-Mt	Ex-Mt
COMP.FACT.SET (120)		25.00	7.50
❑ 1	Dwight Evans	.50	.15
❑ 2	Chito Martinez	.25	.07
❑ 3	Bob Melvin	.25	.07
❑ 4	Mike Mussina RC	4.00	1.20
❑ 5	Jack Clark	.50	.15
❑ 6	Dana Kiecker	.25	.07
❑ 7	Steve Lyons	.25	.07
❑ 8	Gary Gaetti	.50	.15
❑ 9	Dave Gallagher	.25	.07
❑ 10	Dave Parker	.50	.15
❑ 11	Luis Polonia	.25	.07
❑ 12	Luis Sojo	.25	.07
❑ 13	Wilson Alvarez	.25	.07
❑ 14	Alex Fernandez	.25	.07
❑ 15	Craig Grebeck	.25	.07
❑ 16	Ron Karkovice	.25	.07
❑ 17	Warren Newson	.25	.07
❑ 18	Scott Radinsky	.25	.07
❑ 19	Glenallen Hill	.25	.07
❑ 20	Charles Nagy	.25	.07
❑ 21	Mark Whiten	.25	.07
❑ 22	Milt Cuyler	.25	.07
❑ 23	Paul Gibson	.25	.07
❑ 24	Mickey Tettleton	.25	.07
❑ 25	Todd Benzinger	.25	.07
❑ 26	Storm Davis	.25	.07
❑ 27	Kirk Gibson	.50	.15
❑ 28	Bill Pecota	.25	.07
❑ 29	Gary Thurman	.25	.07
❑ 30	Darryl Hamilton	.25	.07
❑ 31	Jaime Navarro	.25	.07
❑ 32	Willie Randolph	.50	.15
❑ 33	Bill Wegman	.25	.07
❑ 34	Randy Bush	.25	.07
❑ 35	Chili Davis	.50	.15
❑ 36	Scott Erickson	.25	.07
❑ 37	Chuck Knoblauch	.50	.15
❑ 38	Scott Leius	.25	.07
❑ 39	Jack Morris	.50	.15
❑ 40	John Habyan	.25	.07
❑ 41	Pat Kelly	.25	.07
❑ 42	Matt Nokes	.25	.07
❑ 43	Scott Sanderson	.25	.07
❑ 44	Bernie Williams	2.00	.60
❑ 45	Harold Baines	.50	.15
❑ 46	Brook Jacoby	.25	.07
❑ 47	Earnest Riles	.25	.07
❑ 48	Willie Wilson	.25	.07
❑ 49	Jay Buhner	.50	.15
❑ 50	Rich DeLucia	.25	.07
❑ 51	Mike Jackson	.25	.07
❑ 52	Bill Krueger	.25	.07
❑ 53	Bill Swift	.25	.07
❑ 54	Brian Downing	.25	.07
❑ 55	Juan Gonzalez	2.00	.60
❑ 56	Dean Palmer	.50	.15
❑ 57	Kevin Reimer	.25	.07
❑ 58	Ivan Rodriguez RC	10.00	3.00
❑ 59	Tom Candiotti	.25	.07
❑ 60	Juan Guzman RC	.50	.15
❑ 61	Bob MacDonald	.25	.07
❑ 62	Greg Myers	.25	.07
❑ 63	Ed Sprague	.25	.07
❑ 64	Devon White	.50	.15
❑ 65	Rafael Belliard	.25	.07
❑ 66	Juan Berenguer	.25	.07
❑ 67	Brian R. Hunter RC	.50	.15
❑ 68	Kent Mercker	.25	.07
❑ 69	Otis Nixon	.25	.07
❑ 70	Danny Jackson	.25	.07
❑ 71	Chuck McElroy	.25	.07
❑ 72	Gary Scott	.25	.07
❑ 73	Heathcliff Slocumb RC	.25	.07
❑ 74	Chico Walker	.25	.07
❑ 75	Rick Wilkins RC	.25	.07
❑ 76	Chris Hammond	.25	.07
❑ 77	Luis Quinones	.25	.07
❑ 78	Herm Winningham	.25	.07
❑ 79	Jeff Bagwell RC	8.00	2.40
❑ 80	Jim Corsi	.25	.07
❑ 81	Steve Finley	.50	.15
❑ 82	Luis Gonzalez RC	1.50	.45
❑ 83	Pete Harnisch	.25	.07
❑ 84	Darryl Kile	.50	.15
❑ 85	Brett Butler	.50	.15
❑ 86	Gary Carter	.50	.15
❑ 87	Tim Crews	.25	.07
❑ 88	Orel Hershiser	.50	.15
❑ 89	Bob Ojeda	.25	.07
❑ 90	Bret Barberie RC**	.25	.07
❑ 91	Barry Jones	.25	.07
❑ 92	Gilberto Reyes	.25	.07
❑ 93	Larry Walker	1.25	.35
❑ 94	Hubie Brooks	.25	.07
❑ 95	Tim Burke	.25	.07
❑ 96	Rick Cerone	.25	.07
❑ 97	Jeff Innis	.25	.07
❑ 98	Wally Backman	.25	.07
❑ 99	Tommy Greene	.25	.07
❑ 100	Ricky Jordan	.25	.07
❑ 101	Mitch Williams	.25	.07
❑ 102	John Smiley	.25	.07
❑ 103	Randy Tomlin RC	.25	.07
❑ 104	Gary Varsho	.25	.07
❑ 105	Cris Carpenter	.25	.07
❑ 106	Ken Hill	.25	.07
❑ 107	Felix Jose	.25	.07
❑ 108	Omar Olivares RC	.25	.07
❑ 109	Gerald Perry	.25	.07
❑ 110	Jerald Clark	.25	.07
❑ 111	Tony Fernandez	.25	.07
❑ 112	Darrin Jackson	.25	.07
❑ 113	Mike Maddux	.25	.07
❑ 114	Tim Teufel	.25	.07
❑ 115	Bud Black	.25	.07
❑ 116	Kelly Downs	.25	.07
❑ 117	Mike Felder	.25	.07
❑ 118	Willie McGee	.50	.15
❑ 119	Trevor Wilson	.25	.07
❑ 120	Checklist 1-120	.25	.07

1997 Ultra

		Nm-Mt	Ex-Mt
COMPLETE SET (553)		60.00	18.00
COMP.SERIES 1 (300)		30.00	9.00
COMP.SERIES 2 (253)		30.00	9.00
COMMON CARD (1-553)		.30	.09
COMMON RC		.40	.12
❑ 1	Roberto Alomar	.50	.15
❑ 2	Brady Anderson	.30	.09
❑ 3	Rocky Coppinger	.30	.09
❑ 4	Jeffrey Hammonds	.30	.09
❑ 5	Chris Hoiles	.30	.09
❑ 6	Eddie Murray	.75	.23
❑ 7	Mike Mussina	.50	.15
❑ 8	Jimmy Myers	.30	.09
❑ 9	Randy Myers	.30	.09
❑ 10	Arthur Rhodes	.30	.09
❑ 11	Cal Ripken	2.50	.75
❑ 12	Jose Canseco	.75	.23
❑ 13	Roger Clemens	1.50	.45
❑ 14	Tom Gordon	.30	.09
❑ 15	Jose Malave	.30	.09
❑ 16	Tim Naehring	.30	.09
❑ 17	Troy O'Leary	.30	.09
❑ 18	Bill Selby	.30	.09
❑ 19	Heathcliff Slocumb	.30	.09
❑ 20	Mike Stanley	.30	.09
❑ 21	Mo Vaughn	.30	.09
❑ 22	Garret Anderson	.30	.09
❑ 23	George Arias	.30	.09
❑ 24	Chili Davis	.30	.09
❑ 25	Jim Edmonds	.30	.09
❑ 26	Darin Erstad	.30	.09
❑ 27	Chuck Finley	.30	.09
❑ 28	Todd Greene	.30	.09
❑ 29	Troy Percival	.30	.09
❑ 30	Tim Salmon	.50	.15
❑ 31	Jeff Schmidt	.30	.09
❑ 32	Randy Velarde	.30	.09
❑ 33	Shad Williams	.30	.09
❑ 34	Wilson Alvarez	.30	.09
❑ 35	Harold Baines	.30	.09
❑ 36	James Baldwin	.30	.09
❑ 37	Mike Cameron	.30	.09
❑ 38	Ray Durham	.30	.09
❑ 39	Ozzie Guillen	.30	.09
❑ 40	Roberto Hernandez	.30	.09
❑ 41	Darren Lewis	.30	.09
❑ 42	Jose Munoz	.30	.09
❑ 43	Tony Phillips	.30	.09
❑ 44	Frank Thomas	.75	.23
❑ 45	Sandy Alomar Jr.	.30	.09
❑ 46	Albert Belle	.30	.09
❑ 47	Mark Carreon	.30	.09
❑ 48	Julio Franco	.30	.09

❑	49	Orel Hershiser	.30	.09
❑	50	Kenny Lofton	.30	.09
❑	51	Jack McDowell	.30	.09
❑	52	Jose Mesa	.30	.09
❑	53	Charles Nagy	.30	.09
❑	54	Manny Ramirez	.50	.15
❑	55	Julian Tavarez	.30	.09
❑	56	Omar Vizquel	.50	.15
❑	57	Raul Casanova	.30	.09
❑	58	Tony Clark	.30	.09
❑	59	Travis Fryman	.30	.09
❑	60	Bob Higginson	.30	.09
❑	61	Melvin Nieves	.30	.09
❑	62	Curtis Pride	.30	.09
❑	63	Justin Thompson	.30	.09
❑	64	Alan Trammell	.30	.09
❑	65	Kevin Appier	.30	.09
❑	66	Johnny Damon	.50	.15
❑	67	Keith Lockhart	.30	.09
❑	68	Jeff Montgomery	.30	.09
❑	69	Jose Offerman	.30	.09
❑	70	Bip Roberts	.30	.09
❑	71	Jose Rosado	.30	.09
❑	72	Chris Stynes	.30	.09
❑	73	Mike Sweeney	.30	.09
❑	74	Jeff Cirillo	.30	.09
❑	75	Jeff D'Amico	.30	.09
❑	76	John Jaha	.30	.09
❑	77	Scott Karl	.30	.09
❑	78	Mike Matheny	.30	.09
❑	79	Ben McDonald	.30	.09
❑	80	Matt Mieske	.30	.09
❑	81	Marc Newfield	.30	.09
❑	82	Dave Nilsson	.30	.09
❑	83	Jose Valentin	.30	.09
❑	84	Fernando Vina	.30	.09
❑	85	Rick Aguilera	.30	.09
❑	86	Marty Cordova	.30	.09
❑	87	Chuck Knoblauch	.30	.09
❑	88	Matt Lawton	.30	.09
❑	89	Pat Meares	.30	.09
❑	90	Paul Molitor	.50	.15
❑	91	Greg Myers	.30	.09
❑	92	Dan Naulty	.30	.09
❑	93	Kirby Puckett	.75	.23
❑	94	Frank Rodriguez	.30	.09
❑	95	Wade Boggs	.50	.15
❑	96	Cecil Fielder	.30	.09
❑	97	Joe Girardi	.30	.09
❑	98	Dwight Gooden	.30	.09
❑	99	Derek Jeter	2.00	.60
❑	100	Tino Martinez	.50	.15
❑	101	Ramiro Mendoza RC	.30	.09
❑	102	Andy Pettitte	.50	.15
❑	103	Mariano Rivera	.50	.15
❑	104	Ruben Rivera	.30	.09
❑	105	Kenny Rogers	.30	.09
❑	106	Darryl Strawberry	.30	.09
❑	107	Bernie Williams	.50	.15
❑	108	Tony Batista	.30	.09
❑	109	Geronimo Berroa	.30	.09
❑	110	Bobby Chouinard	.30	.09
❑	111	Brent Gates	.30	.09
❑	112	Jason Giambi	.30	.09
❑	113	Damon Mashore	.30	.09
❑	114	Mark McGwire	2.00	.60
❑	115	Scott Spiezio	.30	.09
❑	116	John Wasdin	.30	.09
❑	117	Steve Wojciechowski	.30	.09
❑	118	Ernie Young	.30	.09
❑	119	Norm Charlton	.30	.09
❑	120	Joey Cora	.30	.09
❑	121	Ken Griffey Jr.	1.25	.35
❑	122	Sterling Hitchcock	.30	.09
❑	123	Raul Ibanez	.30	.09
❑	124	Randy Johnson	.75	.23
❑	125	Edgar Martinez	.50	.15
❑	126	Alex Rodriguez	1.25	.35
❑	127	Matt Wagner	.30	.09
❑	128	Bob Wells	.30	.09
❑	129	Dan Wilson	.30	.09
❑	130	Will Clark	.75	.23
❑	131	Kevin Elster	.30	.09
❑	132	Juan Gonzalez	.50	.15
❑	133	Rusty Greer	.30	.09
❑	134	Darryl Hamilton	.30	.09
❑	135	Mike Henneman	.30	.09
❑	136	Ken Hill	.30	.09
❑	137	Mark McLemore	.30	.09
❑	138	Dean Palmer	.30	.09
❑	139	Roger Pavlik	.30	.09
❑	140	Ivan Rodriguez	.75	.23
❑	141	Joe Carter	.30	.09
❑	142	Carlos Delgado	.30	.09
❑	143	Alex Gonzalez	.30	.09
❑	144	Juan Guzman	.30	.09
❑	145	Pat Hentgen	.30	.09
❑	146	Marty Janzen	.30	.09
❑	147	Otis Nixon	.30	.09
❑	148	Charlie O'Brien	.30	.09
❑	149	John Olerud	.30	.09
❑	150	Robert Perez	.30	.09
❑	151	Jermaine Dye	.30	.09
❑	152	Tom Glavine	.50	.15
❑	153	Andruw Jones	.30	.09
❑	154	Chipper Jones	.75	.23
❑	155	Ryan Klesko	.30	.09
❑	156	Javier Lopez	.30	.09
❑	157	Greg Maddux	1.25	.35
❑	158	Fred McGriff	.50	.15
❑	159	Wonderful Monds	.30	.09
❑	160	John Smoltz	.50	.15
❑	161	Terrell Wade	.30	.09
❑	162	Mark Wohlers	.30	.09
❑	163	Brant Brown	.30	.09
❑	164	Mark Grace	.50	.15
❑	165	Tyler Houston	.30	.09
❑	166	Robin Jennings	.30	.09
❑	167	Jason Maxwell	.30	.09
❑	168	Ryne Sandberg	1.25	.35
❑	169	Sammy Sosa	1.25	.35
❑	170	Amaury Telemaco	.30	.09
❑	171	Steve Trachsel	.30	.09
❑	172	Pedro Valdes RC	.30	.09
❑	173	Tim Belk	.30	.09
❑	174	Bret Boone	.30	.09
❑	175	Jeff Brantley	.30	.09
❑	176	Eric Davis	.30	.09
❑	177	Barry Larkin	.50	.15
❑	178	Chad Mottola	.30	.09
❑	179	Mark Portugal	.30	.09
❑	180	Reggie Sanders	.30	.09
❑	181	John Smiley	.30	.09
❑	182	Eddie Taubensee	.30	.09
❑	183	Dante Bichette	.30	.09
❑	184	Ellis Burks	.30	.09
❑	185	Andres Galarraga	.30	.09
❑	186	Curt Leskanic	.30	.09
❑	187	Quinton McCracken	.30	.09
❑	188	Jeff Reed	.30	.09
❑	189	Kevin Ritz	.30	.09
❑	190	Walt Weiss	.30	.09
❑	191	Jamey Wright	.30	.09
❑	192	Eric Young	.30	.09
❑	193	Kevin Brown	.30	.09
❑	194	Luis Castillo	.30	.09
❑	195	Jeff Conine	.30	.09
❑	196	Andre Dawson	.30	.09
❑	197	Charles Johnson	.30	.09
❑	198	Al Leiter	.30	.09
❑	199	Ralph Milliard	.30	.09
❑	200	Robb Nen	.30	.09
❑	201	Edgar Renteria	.30	.09
❑	202	Gary Sheffield	.30	.09
❑	203	Bob Abreu	.30	.09
❑	204	Jeff Bagwell	.50	.15
❑	205	Derek Bell	.30	.09
❑	206	Sean Berry	.30	.09
❑	207	Richard Hidalgo	.30	.09
❑	208	Todd Jones	.30	.09
❑	209	Darryl Kile	.30	.09
❑	210	Orlando Miller	.30	.09
❑	211	Shane Reynolds	.30	.09
❑	212	Billy Wagner	.30	.09
❑	213	Donne Wall	.30	.09
❑	214	Roger Cedeno	.30	.09
❑	215	Greg Gagne	.30	.09
❑	216	Karim Garcia	.30	.09
❑	217	Wilton Guerrero	.30	.09
❑	218	Todd Hollandsworth	.30	.09
❑	219	Ramon Martinez	.30	.09
❑	220	Raul Mondesi	.30	.09
❑	221	Hideo Nomo	.75	.23
❑	222	Chan Ho Park	.30	.09
❑	223	Mike Piazza	1.25	.35
❑	224	Ismael Valdes	.30	.09
❑	225	Moises Alou	.30	.09
❑	226	Derek Aucoin	.30	.09
❑	227	Yamil Benitez	.30	.09
❑	228	Jeff Fassero	.30	.09
❑	229	Darrin Fletcher	.30	.09
❑	230	Mark Grudzielanek	.30	.09
❑	231	Barry Manuel	.30	.09
❑	232	Pedro Martinez	.75	.23
❑	233	Henry Rodriguez	.30	.09
❑	234	Ugueth Urbina	.30	.09
❑	235	Rondell White	.30	.09
❑	236	Carlos Baerga	.30	.09
❑	237	John Franco	.30	.09
❑	238	Bernard Gilkey	.30	.09
❑	239	Todd Hundley	.30	.09
❑	240	Butch Huskey	.30	.09
❑	241	Jason Isringhausen	.30	.09
❑	242	Lance Johnson	.30	.09
❑	243	Bobby Jones	.30	.09
❑	244	Alex Ochoa	.30	.09
❑	245	Rey Ordonez	.30	.09
❑	246	Paul Wilson	.30	.09
❑	247	Ron Blazier	.30	.09
❑	248	David Doster	.30	.09
❑	249	Jim Eisenreich	.30	.09
❑	250	Mike Grace	.30	.09
❑	251	Mike Lieberthal	.30	.09
❑	252	Wendell Magee	.30	.09
❑	253	Mickey Morandini	.30	.09
❑	254	Ricky Otero	.30	.09
❑	255	Scott Rolen	.75	.23
❑	256	Curt Schilling	.30	.09
❑	257	Todd Zeile	.30	.09
❑	258	Jermaine Allensworth	.30	.09
❑	259	Trey Beamon	.30	.09
❑	260	Carlos Garcia	.30	.09
❑	261	Mark Johnson	.30	.09
❑	262	Jason Kendall	.30	.09
❑	263	Jeff King	.30	.09
❑	264	Al Martin	.30	.09
❑	265	Denny Neagle	.30	.09
❑	266	Matt Ruebel	.30	.09
❑	267	Marc Wilkins	.30	.09
❑	268	Alan Benes	.30	.09
❑	269	Dennis Eckersley	.30	.09
❑	270	Ron Gant	.30	.09
❑	271	Aaron Holbert	.30	.09
❑	272	Brian Jordan	.30	.09
❑	273	Ray Lankford	.30	.09
❑	274	John Mabry	.30	.09
❑	275	T.J. Mathews	.30	.09
❑	276	Ozzie Smith	1.25	.35
❑	277	Todd Stottlemyre	.30	.09
❑	278	Mark Sweeney	.30	.09
❑	279	Andy Ashby	.30	.09
❑	280	Steve Finley	.30	.09
❑	281	John Flaherty	.30	.09
❑	282	Chris Gomez	.30	.09
❑	283	Tony Gwynn	1.00	.30
❑	284	Joey Hamilton	.30	.09
❑	285	Rickey Henderson	.75	.23
❑	286	Trevor Hoffman	.30	.09
❑	287	Jason Thompson	.30	.09
❑	288	Fernando Valenzuela	.30	.09
❑	289	Greg Vaughn	.30	.09
❑	290	Barry Bonds	2.00	.60
❑	291	Jay Canizaro	.30	.09
❑	292	Jacob Cruz	.30	.09
❑	293	Shawon Dunston	.30	.09
❑	294	Shawn Estes	.30	.09
❑	295	Mark Gardner	.30	.09
❑	296	Marcus Jensen	.30	.09
❑	297	Bill Mueller RC	3.00	.90
❑	298	Chris Singleton	.30	.09
❑	299	Allen Watson	.30	.09
❑	300	Matt Williams	.30	.09
❑	301	Rod Beck	.30	.09
❑	302	Jay Bell	.30	.09
❑	303	Shawon Dunston	.30	.09
❑	304	Reggie Jefferson	.30	.09
❑	305	Darren Oliver	.30	.09
❑	306	Benito Santiago	.30	.09
❑	307	Gerald Williams	.30	.09
❑	308	Damon Buford	.30	.09
❑	309	Jeromy Burnitz	.30	.09
❑	310	Sterling Hitchcock	.30	.09
❑	311	Dave Hollins	.30	.09
❑	312	Mel Rojas	.30	.09

❑	313	Robin Ventura	.30	.09
❑	314	David Wells	.30	.09
❑	315	Cal Eldred	.30	.09
❑	316	Gary Gaetti	.30	.09
❑	317	John Hudek	.30	.09
❑	318	Brian Johnson	.30	.09
❑	319	Denny Neagle	.30	.09
❑	320	Larry Walker	.50	.15
❑	321	Russ Davis	.30	.09
❑	322	Delino DeShields	.30	.09
❑	323	Charlie Hayes	.30	.09
❑	324	Jermaine Dye	.30	.09
❑	325	John Ericks	.30	.09
❑	326	Jeff Fassero	.30	.09
❑	327	Nomar Garciaparra	1.25	.35
❑	328	Willie Greene	.30	.09
❑	329	Greg McMichael	.30	.09
❑	330	Damion Easley	.30	.09
❑	331	Ricky Bones	.30	.09
❑	332	John Burkett	.30	.09
❑	333	Royce Clayton	.30	.09
❑	334	Greg Colbrunn	.30	.09
❑	335	Tony Eusebio	.30	.09
❑	336	Gregg Jefferies	.30	.09
❑	337	Wally Joyner	.30	.09
❑	338	Jim Leyritz	.30	.09
❑	339	Paul O'Neill	.50	.15
❑	340	Bruce Ruffin	.30	.09
❑	341	Michael Tucker	.30	.09
❑	342	Andy Benes	.30	.09
❑	343	Craig Biggio	.50	.15
❑	344	Rex Hudler	.30	.09
❑	345	Brad Radke	.30	.09
❑	346	Deion Sanders	.50	.15
❑	347	Moises Alou	.30	.09
❑	348	Brad Ausmus	.30	.09
❑	349	Armando Benitez	.30	.09
❑	350	Mark Gubicza	.30	.09
❑	351	Terry Steinbach	.30	.09
❑	352	Mark Whiten	.30	.09
❑	353	Ricky Bottalico	.30	.09
❑	354	Brian Giles RC	1.50	.45
❑	355	Eric Karros	.30	.09
❑	356	Jimmy Key	.30	.09
❑	357	Carlos Perez	.30	.09
❑	358	Alex Fernandez	.30	.09
❑	359	J.T. Snow	.30	.09
❑	360	Bobby Bonilla	.30	.09
❑	361	Scott Brosius	.30	.09
❑	362	Greg Swindell	.30	.09
❑	363	Jose Vizcaino	.30	.09
❑	364	Matt Williams	.30	.09
❑	365	Darren Daulton	.30	.09
❑	366	Shane Andrews	.30	.09
❑	367	Jim Eisenreich	.30	.09
❑	368	Ariel Prieto	.30	.09
❑	369	Bob Tewksbury	.30	.09
❑	370	Mike Bordick	.30	.09
❑	371	Rheal Cormier	.30	.09
❑	372	Cliff Floyd	.30	.09
❑	373	David Justice	.30	.09
❑	374	John Wetteland	.30	.09
❑	375	Mike Blowers	.30	.09
❑	376	Jose Canseco	.75	.23
❑	377	Roger Clemens	1.50	.45
❑	378	Kevin Mitchell	.30	.09
❑	379	Todd Zeile	.30	.09
❑	380	Jim Thome	.75	.23
❑	381	Turk Wendell	.30	.09
❑	382	Rico Brogna	.30	.09
❑	383	Eric Davis	.30	.09
❑	384	Mike Lansing	.30	.09
❑	385	Devon White	.30	.09
❑	386	Marquis Grissom	.30	.09
❑	387	Todd Worrell	.30	.09
❑	388	Jeff Kent	.30	.09
❑	389	Mickey Tettleton	.30	.09
❑	390	Steve Avery	.30	.09
❑	391	David Cone	.30	.09
❑	392	Scott Cooper	.30	.09
❑	393	Lee Stevens	.30	.09
❑	394	Kevin Elster	.30	.09
❑	395	Tom Goodwin	.30	.09
❑	396	Shawn Green	.30	.09
❑	397	Pete Harnisch	.30	.09
❑	398	Eddie Murray	.75	.23
❑	399	Joe Randa	.30	.09
❑	400	Scott Sanders	.30	.09
❑	401	John Valentin	.30	.09
❑	402	Todd Jones	.30	.09
❑	403	Terry Adams	.30	.09
❑	404	Brian Hunter	.30	.09
❑	405	Pat Listach	.30	.09
❑	406	Kenny Lofton	.30	.09
❑	407	Hal Morris	.30	.09
❑	408	Ed Sprague	.30	.09
❑	409	Rich Becker	.30	.09
❑	410	Edgardo Alfonzo	.30	.09
❑	411	Albert Belle	.30	.09
❑	412	Jeff King	.30	.09
❑	413	Kirt Manwaring	.30	.09
❑	414	Jason Schmidt	.30	.09
❑	415	Allen Watson	.30	.09
❑	416	Lee Tinsley	.30	.09
❑	417	Brett Butler	.30	.09
❑	418	Carlos Garcia	.30	.09
❑	419	Mark Lemke	.30	.09
❑	420	Jaime Navarro	.30	.09
❑	421	David Segui	.30	.09
❑	422	Ruben Sierra	.30	.09
❑	423	B.J. Surhoff	.30	.09
❑	424	Julian Tavarez	.30	.09
❑	425	Billy Taylor	.30	.09
❑	426	Ken Caminiti	.30	.09
❑	427	Chuck Carr	.30	.09
❑	428	Benji Gil	.30	.09
❑	429	Terry Mulholland	.30	.09
❑	430	Mike Stanton	.30	.09
❑	431	Wil Cordero	.30	.09
❑	432	Chili Davis	.30	.09
❑	433	Mariano Duncan	.30	.09
❑	434	Orlando Merced	.30	.09
❑	435	Kent Mercker	.30	.09
❑	436	John Olerud	.30	.09
❑	437	Quilvio Veras	.30	.09
❑	438	Mike Fetters	.30	.09
❑	439	Glenallen Hill	.30	.09
❑	440	Bill Swift	.30	.09
❑	441	Tim Wakefield	.30	.09
❑	442	Pedro Astacio	.30	.09
❑	443	Vinny Castilla	.30	.09
❑	444	Doug Drabek	.30	.09
❑	445	Alan Embree	.30	.09
❑	446	Lee Smith	.30	.09
❑	447	Darryl Hamilton	.30	.09
❑	448	Brian McRae	.30	.09
❑	449	Mike Timlin	.30	.09
❑	450	Bob Wickman	.30	.09
❑	451	Jason Dickson	.30	.09
❑	452	Chad Curtis	.30	.09
❑	453	Mark Leiter	.30	.09
❑	454	Damon Berryhill	.30	.09
❑	455	Kevin Orie	.30	.09
❑	456	Dave Burba	.30	.09
❑	457	Chris Holt	.30	.09
❑	458	Ricky Ledee RC	.40	.12
❑	459	Mike Devereaux	.30	.09
❑	460	Pokey Reese	.30	.09
❑	461	Tim Raines	.30	.09
❑	462	Ryan Jones	.30	.09
❑	463	Shane Mack	.30	.09
❑	464	Darren Dreifort	.30	.09
❑	465	Mark Parent	.30	.09
❑	466	Mark Portugal	.30	.09
❑	467	Dante Powell	.30	.09
❑	468	Craig Grebeck	.30	.09
❑	469	Ron Villone	.30	.09
❑	470	Dmitri Young	.30	.09
❑	471	Shannon Stewart	.30	.09
❑	472	Rick Helling	.30	.09
❑	473	Bill Haselman	.30	.09
❑	474	Albie Lopez	.30	.09
❑	475	Glendon Rusch	.30	.09
❑	476	Derrick May	.30	.09
❑	477	Chad Ogea	.30	.09
❑	478	Kirk Rueter	.30	.09
❑	479	Chris Hammond	.30	.09
❑	480	Russ Johnson	.30	.09
❑	481	James Mouton	.30	.09
❑	482	Mike Macfarlane	.30	.09
❑	483	Scott Ruffcorn	.30	.09
❑	484	Jeff Frye	.30	.09
❑	485	Richie Sexson	.30	.09
❑	486	Emil Brown RC	.40	.12
❑	487	Desi Wilson	.30	.09
❑	488	Brent Gates	.30	.09
❑	489	Tony Graffanino	.30	.09
❑	490	Dan Miceli	.30	.09
❑	491	Orlando Cabrera RC	1.50	.60
❑	492	Tony Womack RC	.60	.18
❑	493	Jerome Walton	.30	.09
❑	494	Mark Thompson	.30	.09
❑	495	Jose Guillen	.30	.09
❑	496	Willie Blair	.30	.09
❑	497	T.J. Staton RC	.40	.12
❑	498	Scott Kamieniecki	.30	.09
❑	499	Vince Coleman	.30	.09
❑	500	Jeff Abbott	.30	.09
❑	501	Chris Widger	.30	.09
❑	502	Kevin Tapani	.30	.09
❑	503	Carlos Castillo RC	.40	.12
❑	504	Luis Gonzalez	.30	.09
❑	505	Tim Belcher	.30	.09
❑	506	Armando Reynoso	.30	.09
❑	507	Jamie Moyer	.30	.09
❑	508	Randall Simon RC	.40	.12
❑	509	Vladimir Guerrero	.75	.23
❑	510	Wady Almonte RC	.40	.12
❑	511	Dustin Hermanson	.30	.09
❑	512	Deivi Cruz RC	.40	.12
❑	513	Luis Alicea	.30	.09
❑	514	Felix Heredia RC	.40	.12
❑	515	Don Slaught	.30	.09
❑	516	S.Hasegawa RC	1.00	.30
❑	517	Matt Walbeck	.30	.09
❑	518	David Arias-Ortiz RC	20.00	6.00
❑	519	Brady Raggio RC	.40	.12
❑	520	Rudy Pemberton	.30	.09
❑	521	Wayne Kirby	.30	.09
❑	522	Calvin Maduro	.30	.09
❑	523	Mark Lewis	.30	.09
❑	524	Mike Jackson	.30	.09
❑	525	Sid Fernandez	.30	.09
❑	526	Mike Bielecki	.30	.09
❑	527	Bubba Trammell RC	.40	.12
❑	528	Brent Brede RC	.40	.12
❑	529	Matt Morris	.30	.09
❑	530	Joe Borowski RC	.40	.12
❑	531	Orlando Miller	.30	.09
❑	532	Jim Bullinger	.30	.09
❑	533	Robert Person	.30	.09
❑	534	Doug Glanville	.30	.09
❑	535	Terry Pendleton	.30	.09
❑	536	Jorge Posada	.50	.15
❑	537	Marc Sagmoen RC	.40	.12
❑	538	Fernando Tatis RC	.40	.12
❑	539	Aaron Sele	.30	.09
❑	540	Brian Banks	.30	.09
❑	541	Derrek Lee	.30	.09
❑	542	John Wasdin	.30	.09
❑	543	Justin Towle RC	.40	.12
❑	544	Pat Cline	.30	.09
❑	545	Dave Magadan	.30	.09
❑	546	Jeff Blauser	.30	.09
❑	547	Phil Nevin	.30	.09
❑	548	Todd Walker	.30	.09
❑	549	Eli Marrero	.30	.09
❑	550	Bartolo Colon	.30	.09
❑	551	Jose Cruz Jr. RC	.60	.18
❑	552	Todd Dunwoody	.30	.09
❑	553	Hideki Irabu RC	.40	.12
❑	P11	Cal Ripken Promo Three Card Strip	2.00	.60

2001 Ultra

	Nm-Mt	Ex-Mt
COMPLETE SET (275)	120.00	36.00
COMP.SET w/o SP's (250)	25.00	7.50
COMMON CARD (1-250)	.30	.09
COMMON (251-275)	3.00	.90
COMMON (276-280)	5.00	1.50
❑ 1 Pedro Martinez	.75	.23
❑ 2 Derek Jeter	2.00	.60
❑ 3 Cal Ripken	2.50	.75
❑ 4 Alex Rodriguez	1.25	.35
❑ 5 Vladimir Guerrero	.75	.23
❑ 6 Troy Glaus	.30	.09
❑ 7 Sammy Sosa	1.25	.35
❑ 8 Mike Piazza	1.25	.35
❑ 9 Tony Gwynn	1.00	.30
❑ 10 Tim Hudson	.30	.09
❑ 11 John Flaherty	.30	.09
❑ 12 Jeff Cirillo	.30	.09
❑ 13 Ellis Burks	.30	.09
❑ 14 Carlos Lee	.30	.09
❑ 15 Carlos Beltran	.50	.15
❑ 16 Ruben Rivera	.30	.09
❑ 17 Richard Hidalgo	.30	.09
❑ 18 Omar Vizquel	.50	.15
❑ 19 Michael Barrett	.30	.09
❑ 20 Jose Canseco	.75	.23
❑ 21 Jason Giambi	.30	.09
❑ 22 Greg Maddux	1.25	.35
❑ 23 Charles Johnson	.30	.09
❑ 24 Sandy Alomar Jr.	.30	.09
❑ 25 Rick Ankiel	.30	.09
❑ 26 Richie Sexson	.30	.09
❑ 27 Matt Williams	.30	.09
❑ 28 Joe Girardi	.30	.09
❑ 29 Jason Kendall	.30	.09
❑ 30 Brad Fullmer	.30	.09
❑ 31 Alex Gonzalez	.30	.09
❑ 32 Rick Helling	.30	.09
❑ 33 Mike Mussina	.50	.15
❑ 34 Joe Randa	.30	.09
❑ 35 J.T. Snow	.30	.09
❑ 36 Edgardo Alfonzo	.30	.09
❑ 37 Dante Bichette	.30	.09
❑ 38 Brad Ausmus	.30	.09
❑ 39 Bobby Abreu	.30	.09
❑ 40 Warren Morris	.30	.09
❑ 41 Tony Womack	.30	.09
❑ 42 Russell Branyan	.30	.09
❑ 43 Mike Lowell	.30	.09
❑ 44 Mark Grace	.50	.15
❑ 45 Jeromy Burnitz	.30	.09
❑ 46 J.D. Drew	.30	.09
❑ 47 David Justice	.30	.09
❑ 48 Alex Gonzalez	.30	.09
❑ 49 Tino Martinez	.50	.15
❑ 50 Raul Mondesi	.30	.09
❑ 51 Rafael Furcal	.30	.09
❑ 52 Marquis Grissom	.30	.09
❑ 53 Kevin Young	.30	.09
❑ 54 Jon Lieber	.30	.09
❑ 55 Henry Rodriguez	.30	.09
❑ 56 Dave Burba	.30	.09
❑ 57 Shannon Stewart	.30	.09
❑ 58 Preston Wilson	.30	.09
❑ 59 Paul O'Neill	.50	.15
❑ 60 Jimmy Haynes	.30	.09
❑ 61 Darryl Kile	.30	.09
❑ 62 Bret Boone	.30	.09
❑ 63 Bartolo Colon	.30	.09
❑ 64 Andres Galarraga	.30	.09
❑ 65 Trot Nixon	.30	.09
❑ 66 Steve Finley	.30	.09
❑ 67 Shawn Green	.30	.09
❑ 68 Robert Person	.30	.09
❑ 69 Kenny Rogers	.30	.09
❑ 70 Bobby Higginson	.30	.09
❑ 71 Barry Larkin	.50	.15
❑ 72 Al Martin	.30	.09
❑ 73 Tom Glavine	.50	.15
❑ 74 Rondell White	.30	.09
❑ 75 Ray Lankford	.30	.09
❑ 76 Moises Alou	.30	.09
❑ 77 Matt Clement	.30	.09
❑ 78 Geoff Jenkins	.30	.09
❑ 79 David Wells	.30	.09
❑ 80 Chuck Finley	.30	.09
❑ 81 Andy Pettitte	.50	.15
❑ 82 Travis Fryman	.30	.09
❑ 83 Ron Coomer	.30	.09
❑ 84 Mark McGwire	2.00	.60
❑ 85 Kerry Wood	.75	.23
❑ 86 Jorge Posada	.50	.15
❑ 87 Jeff Bagwell	.50	.15
❑ 88 Andruw Jones	.30	.09
❑ 89 Ryan Klesko	.30	.09
❑ 90 Mariano Rivera	.50	.15
❑ 91 Lance Berkman	.30	.09
❑ 92 Kenny Lofton	.30	.09
❑ 93 Jacque Jones	.30	.09
❑ 94 Eric Young	.30	.09
❑ 95 Edgar Renteria	.30	.09
❑ 96 Chipper Jones	.75	.23
❑ 97 Todd Helton	.50	.15
❑ 98 Shawn Estes	.30	.09
❑ 99 Mark Mulder	.30	.09
❑ 100 Lee Stevens	.30	.09
❑ 101 Jermaine Dye	.30	.09
❑ 102 Greg Vaughn	.30	.09
❑ 103 Chris Singleton	.30	.09
❑ 104 Brady Anderson	.30	.09
❑ 105 Terrence Long	.30	.09
❑ 106 Quilvio Veras	.30	.09
❑ 107 Magglio Ordonez	.30	.09
❑ 108 Johnny Damon	.50	.15
❑ 109 Jeffrey Hammonds	.30	.09
❑ 110 Fred McGriff	.50	.15
❑ 111 Carl Pavano	.30	.09
❑ 112 Bobby Estalella	.30	.09
❑ 113 Todd Hundley	.30	.09
❑ 114 Scott Rolen	.75	.23
❑ 115 Robin Ventura	.30	.09
❑ 116 Pokey Reese	.30	.09
❑ 117 Luis Gonzalez	.30	.09
❑ 118 Jose Offerman	.30	.09
❑ 119 Edgar Martinez	.50	.15
❑ 120 Dean Palmer	.30	.09
❑ 121 David Segui	.30	.09
❑ 122 Troy O'Leary	.30	.09
❑ 123 Tony Batista	.30	.09
❑ 124 Todd Zeile	.30	.09
❑ 125 Randy Johnson	.75	.23
❑ 126 Luis Castillo	.30	.09
❑ 127 Kris Benson	.30	.09
❑ 128 John Olerud	.30	.09
❑ 129 Eric Karros	.30	.09
❑ 130 Eddie Taubensee	.30	.09
❑ 131 Neifi Perez	.30	.09
❑ 132 Matt Stairs	.30	.09
❑ 133 Luis Alicea	.30	.09
❑ 134 Jeff Kent	.30	.09
❑ 135 Javier Vazquez	.30	.09
❑ 136 Garret Anderson	.30	.09
❑ 137 Frank Thomas	.75	.23
❑ 138 Carlos Febles	.30	.09
❑ 139 Albert Belle	.30	.09
❑ 140 Tony Clark	.30	.09
❑ 141 Pat Burrell	.30	.09
❑ 142 Mike Sweeney	.30	.09
❑ 143 Jay Buhner	.30	.09
❑ 144 Gabe Kapler	.30	.09
❑ 145 Derek Bell	.30	.09
❑ 146 B.J. Surhoff	.30	.09
❑ 147 Adam Kennedy	.30	.09
❑ 148 Aaron Boone	.30	.09
❑ 149 Todd Stottlemyre	.30	.09
❑ 150 Roberto Alomar	.50	.15
❑ 151 Orlando Hernandez	.30	.09
❑ 152 Jason Varitek	.50	.15
❑ 153 Gary Sheffield	.30	.09
❑ 154 Cliff Floyd	.30	.09
❑ 155 Chad Hermansen	.30	.09
❑ 156 Carlos Delgado	.30	.09
❑ 157 Aaron Sele	.30	.09
❑ 158 Sean Casey	.30	.09
❑ 159 Ruben Mateo	.30	.09
❑ 160 Mike Bordick	.30	.09
❑ 161 Mike Cameron	.30	.09
❑ 162 Doug Glanville	.30	.09
❑ 163 Damion Easley	.30	.09
❑ 164 Carl Everett	.30	.09
❑ 165 Bengie Molina	.30	.09
❑ 166 Adrian Beltre	.50	.15
❑ 167 Tom Goodwin	.30	.09
❑ 168 Rickey Henderson	.75	.23
❑ 169 Mo Vaughn	.30	.09
❑ 170 Mike Lieberthal	.30	.09
❑ 171 Ken Griffey Jr.	1.25	.35
❑ 172 Juan Gonzalez	.50	.15
❑ 173 Ivan Rodriguez	.75	.23
❑ 174 Al Leiter	.30	.09
❑ 175 Vinny Castilla	.30	.09
❑ 176 Peter Bergeron	.30	.09
❑ 177 Pedro Astacio	.30	.09
❑ 178 Paul Konerko	.30	.09
❑ 179 Mitch Meluskey	.30	.09
❑ 180 Kevin Millwood	.30	.09
❑ 181 Ben Grieve	.30	.09
❑ 182 Barry Bonds	2.00	.60
❑ 183 Rusty Greer	.30	.09
❑ 184 Miguel Tejada	.30	.09
❑ 185 Mark Quinn	.30	.09
❑ 186 Larry Walker	.50	.15
❑ 187 Jose Valentin	.30	.09
❑ 188 Jose Vidro	.30	.09
❑ 189 Delino DeShields	.30	.09
❑ 190 Darin Erstad	.30	.09
❑ 191 Bill Mueller	.30	.09
❑ 192 Ray Durham	.30	.09
❑ 193 Ken Caminiti	.30	.09
❑ 194 Jim Thome	.75	.23
❑ 195 Javy Lopez	.30	.09
❑ 196 Fernando Vina	.30	.09
❑ 197 Eric Chavez	.30	.09
❑ 198 Eric Owens	.30	.09
❑ 199 Brad Radke	.30	.09
❑ 200 Travis Lee	.30	.09
❑ 201 Tim Salmon	.50	.15
❑ 202 Rafael Palmeiro	.50	.15
❑ 203 Nomar Garciaparra	1.25	.35
❑ 204 Mike Hampton	.30	.09
❑ 205 Kevin Brown	.30	.09
❑ 206 Juan Encarnacion	.30	.09
❑ 207 Danny Graves	.30	.09
❑ 208 Carlos Guillen	.30	.09
❑ 209 Phil Nevin	.30	.09
❑ 210 Matt Lawton	.30	.09
❑ 211 Manny Ramirez	.50	.15
❑ 212 James Baldwin	.30	.09
❑ 213 Fernando Tatis	.30	.09
❑ 214 Craig Biggio	.50	.15
❑ 215 Brian Jordan	.30	.09
❑ 216 Bernie Williams	.50	.15
❑ 217 Ryan Dempster	.30	.09
❑ 218 Roger Clemens	1.50	.45
❑ 219 Jose Cruz Jr.	.30	.09
❑ 220 John Valentin	.30	.09
❑ 221 Dmitri Young	.30	.09
❑ 222 Curt Schilling	.30	.09
❑ 223 Jim Edmonds	.30	.09
❑ 224 Chan Ho Park	.30	.09
❑ 225 Brian Giles	.30	.09
❑ 226 Jimmy Anderson Tike Redman	.30	.09
❑ 227 Adam Piatt Jose Ortiz	.30	.09
❑ 228 Kenny Kelly Aubrey Huff	.30	.09
❑ 229 Randy Choate Craig Dingman	.30	.09
❑ 230 Eric Cammack Grant Roberts	.30	.09
❑ 231 Yovanny Lara Andy Tracy	.30	.09
❑ 232 Wayne Franklin Scott Linebrink	.30	.09
❑ 233 Cameron Cairncross Chan Perry	.30	.09
❑ 234 J.C. Romero Matt LeCroy	.30	.09
❑ 235 Geraldo Guzman Jason Conti	.30	.09
❑ 236 Morgan Burkhart Paxton Crawford	.30	.09
❑ 237 Pasqual Coco Leo Estrella	.30	.09
❑ 238 John Parrish Fernando Lunar	.30	.09

❑ 239 Keith McDonald .30 .09
Justin Brunette
❑ 240 Carlos Casimiro .30 .09
Ivanon Coffie
❑ 241 Daniel Garibay .30 .09
Ruben Quevedo
❑ 242 Sang-Hoon Lee .30 .09
Tomo Ohka
❑ 243 Hector Ortiz .30 .09
Jeff D'Amico
❑ 244 Jeff Sparks .30 .09
Travis Harper
❑ 245 Jason Boyd .30 .09
David Coggin
❑ 246 Mark Buehrle .30 .09
Lorenzo Barcelo
❑ 247 Adam Melhuse .30 .09
Ben Petrick
❑ 248 Kane Davis .30 .09
Paul Rigdon
❑ 249 Mike Darr .30 .09
Kory DeHaan
❑ 250 Vicente Padilla 3.00 .90
Mark Brownson
❑ 251 Barry Zito PROS 5.00 1.50
❑ 252 Tim Drew PROS 3.00 .90
❑ 253 Luis Matos PROS 3.00 .90
❑ 254 Alex Cabrera PROS 3.00 .90
❑ 255 Jon Garland PROS 3.00 .90
❑ 256 Milton Bradley PROS 3.00 .90
❑ 257 Juan Pierre PROS 3.00 .90
❑ 258 Ismael Villegas PROS 3.00 .90
❑ 259 Eric Munson PROS 3.00 .90
❑ 260 T.De la Rosa PROS 3.00 .90
❑ 261 Chris Richard PROS 3.00 .90
❑ 262 Jason Tyner PROS 3.00 .90
❑ 263 B.J. Waszgis PROS 3.00 .90
❑ 264 Jason Marquis PROS 3.00 .90
❑ 265 Dusty Allen PROS 3.00 .90
❑ 266 C.Patterson PROS 3.00 .90
❑ 267 Eric Byrnes PROS 3.00 .90
❑ 268 Xavier Nady PROS 3.00 .90
❑ 269 G.Lombard PROS 3.00 .90
❑ 270 Timo Perez PROS 3.00 .90
❑ 271 G.Matthews Jr. PROS 3.00 .90
❑ 272 Chad Durbin PROS 3.00 .90
❑ 273 Tony Armas Jr. PROS 3.00 .90
❑ 274 F.Cordero PROS 3.00 .90
❑ 275 A.Soriano PROS 5.00 1.50
❑ 276 Junior Spivey RC 8.00 2.40
Juan Uribe RC
❑ 277 Albert Pujols RC 50.00 15.00
Bud Smith RC
❑ 278 Ichiro Suzuki RC 30.00 9.00
Tsuyoshi Shinjo RC
❑ 279 Drew Henson RC 5.00 1.50
Jackson Melian RC
❑ 280 Matt White RC 5.00 1.50
Adrian Hernandez RC

2003 Ultra

	Nm-Mt	Ex-Mt
COMP.LO SET (250)	100.00	30.00
COMP.LO SET w/o SP's (200)	25.00	7.50
COMMON CARD (201-220)	1.50	.45
COMMON CARD (221-250)	2.00	.60
COMMON CARD (251-265)	3.00	.90

❑ 1 Barry Bonds 2.00 .60
❑ 2 Derek Jeter 2.00 .60
❑ 3 Ichiro Suzuki 1.25 .35
❑ 4 Mike Lowell .30 .09
❑ 5 Hideo Nomo .75 .23
❑ 6 Javier Vazquez .30 .09
❑ 7 Jeremy Giambi .30 .09
❑ 8 Jamie Moyer .30 .09
❑ 9 Rafael Palmeiro .50 .15
❑ 10 Magglio Ordonez .30 .09
❑ 11 Trot Nixon .30 .09
❑ 12 Luis Castillo .30 .09
❑ 13 Paul Byrd .30 .09
❑ 14 Adam Kennedy .30 .09
❑ 15 Trevor Hoffman .30 .09
❑ 16 Matt Morris .30 .09
❑ 17 Nomar Garciaparra 1.25 .35
❑ 18 Matt Lawton .30 .09
❑ 19 Carlos Beltran .50 .15
❑ 20 Jason Giambi .30 .09
❑ 21 Brian Giles .30 .09
❑ 22 Jim Edmonds .30 .09
❑ 23 Garret Anderson .30 .09
❑ 24 Tony Batista .30 .09
❑ 25 Aaron Boone .30 .09
❑ 26 Mike Hampton .30 .09
❑ 27 Billy Wagner .30 .09
❑ 28 Kazuhisa Ishii .30 .09
❑ 29 Al Leiter .30 .09
❑ 30 Pat Burrell .30 .09
❑ 31 Jeff Kent .30 .09
❑ 32 Randy Johnson .75 .23
❑ 33 Ray Durham .30 .09
❑ 34 Josh Beckett .30 .09
❑ 35 Cristian Guzman .30 .09
❑ 36 Roger Clemens 1.50 .45
❑ 37 Freddy Garcia .30 .09
❑ 38 Roy Halladay .30 .09
❑ 39 David Eckstein .30 .09
❑ 40 Jerry Hairston .30 .09
❑ 41 Barry Larkin .50 .15
❑ 42 Larry Walker .50 .15
❑ 43 Craig Biggio .50 .15
❑ 44 Edgardo Alfonzo .30 .09
❑ 45 Marlon Byrd .30 .09
❑ 46 J.T. Snow .30 .09
❑ 47 Juan Gonzalez .50 .15
❑ 48 Ramon Ortiz .30 .09
❑ 49 Jay Gibbons .30 .09
❑ 50 Adam Dunn .50 .15
❑ 51 Juan Pierre .30 .09
❑ 52 Jeff Bagwell .50 .15
❑ 53 Kevin Brown .30 .09
❑ 54 Pedro Astacio .30 .09
❑ 55 Mike Lieberthal .30 .09
❑ 56 Johnny Damon .75 .23
❑ 57 Tim Salmon .50 .15
❑ 58 Mike Bordick .30 .09
❑ 59 Ken Griffey Jr. 1.25 .35
❑ 60 Jason Jennings .30 .09
❑ 61 Lance Berkman .30 .09
❑ 62 Jeromy Burnitz .30 .09
❑ 63 Jimmy Rollins .30 .09
❑ 64 Tsuyoshi Shinjo .30 .09
❑ 65 Alex Rodriguez 1.25 .35
❑ 66 Greg Maddux 1.25 .35
❑ 67 Mark Prior .75 .23
❑ 68 Mike Maroth .30 .09
❑ 69 Geoff Jenkins .30 .09
❑ 70 Tony Armas Jr. .30 .09
❑ 71 Jermaine Dye .30 .09
❑ 72 Albert Pujols 1.50 .45
❑ 73 Shannon Stewart .30 .09
❑ 74 Troy Glaus .30 .09
❑ 75 Brook Fordyce .30 .09
❑ 76 Juan Encarnacion .30 .09
❑ 77 Todd Hollandsworth .30 .09
❑ 78 Roy Oswalt .30 .09
❑ 79 Paul Lo Duca .30 .09
❑ 80 Mike Piazza 1.25 .35
❑ 81 Bobby Abreu .30 .09
❑ 82 Sean Burroughs .30 .09
❑ 83 Randy Winn .30 .09
❑ 84 Curt Schilling .30 .09
❑ 85 Chris Singleton .30 .09
❑ 86 Sean Casey .30 .09
❑ 87 Todd Zeile .30 .09
❑ 88 Richard Hidalgo .30 .09
❑ 89 Roberto Alomar .50 .15
❑ 90 Tim Hudson .30 .09
❑ 91 Ryan Klesko .30 .09
❑ 92 Greg Vaughn .30 .09
❑ 93 Tony Womack .30 .09
❑ 94 Fred McGriff .50 .15
❑ 95 Tom Glavine .50 .15
❑ 96 Todd Walker .30 .09
❑ 97 Travis Fryman .30 .09
❑ 98 Shane Reynolds .30 .09
❑ 99 Shawn Green .30 .09
❑ 100 Mo Vaughn .30 .09
❑ 101 Adam Piatt .30 .09
❑ 102 Deivi Cruz .30 .09
❑ 103 Steve Cox .30 .09
❑ 104 Luis Gonzalez .30 .09
❑ 105 Russell Branyan .30 .09
❑ 106 Daryle Ward .30 .09
❑ 107 Mariano Rivera .50 .15
❑ 108 Phil Nevin .30 .09
❑ 109 Ben Grieve .30 .09
❑ 110 Moises Alou .30 .09
❑ 111 Omar Vizquel .50 .15
❑ 112 Joe Randa .30 .09
❑ 113 Jorge Posada .50 .15
❑ 114 Mark Kotsay .30 .09
❑ 115 Ryan Rupe .30 .09
❑ 116 Javy Lopez .30 .09
❑ 117 Corey Patterson .30 .09
❑ 118 Bobby Higginson .30 .09
❑ 119 Jose Vidro .30 .09
❑ 120 Barry Zito .30 .09
❑ 121 Scott Rolen .75 .23
❑ 122 Gary Sheffield .30 .09
❑ 123 Kerry Wood .75 .23
❑ 124 Brandon Inge .30 .09
❑ 125 Jose Hernandez .30 .09
❑ 126 Michael Barrett .30 .09
❑ 127 Miguel Tejada .30 .09
❑ 128 Edgar Renteria .30 .09
❑ 129 Junior Spivey .30 .09
❑ 130 Jose Valentin .30 .09
❑ 131 Derrek Lee .30 .09
❑ 132 A.J. Pierzynski .30 .09
❑ 133 Mike Mussina .50 .15
❑ 134 Bret Boone .30 .09
❑ 135 Chan Ho Park .30 .09
❑ 136 Steve Finley .30 .09
❑ 137 Mark Buehrle .30 .09
❑ 138 A.J. Burnett .30 .09
❑ 139 Ben Sheets .30 .09
❑ 140 David Ortiz .50 .15
❑ 141 Nick Johnson .30 .09
❑ 142 Randall Simon .30 .09
❑ 143 Carlos Delgado .30 .09
❑ 144 Darin Erstad .30 .09
❑ 145 Shea Hillenbrand .30 .09
❑ 146 Todd Helton .50 .15
❑ 147 Preston Wilson .30 .09
❑ 148 Eric Gagne .75 .23
❑ 149 Vladimir Guerrero .75 .23
❑ 150 Brandon Duckworth .30 .09
❑ 151 Rich Aurilia .30 .09
❑ 152 Ivan Rodriguez .75 .23
❑ 153 Andruw Jones .30 .09
❑ 154 Carlos Lee .30 .09
❑ 155 Robert Fick .30 .09
❑ 156 Jacque Jones .30 .09
❑ 157 Bernie Williams .50 .15
❑ 158 John Olerud .30 .09
❑ 159 Eric Hinske .30 .09
❑ 160 Matt Clement .30 .09
❑ 161 Dmitri Young .30 .09
❑ 162 Torii Hunter .30 .09
❑ 163 Carlos Pena .30 .09
❑ 164 Mike Cameron .30 .09
❑ 165 Raul Mondesi .30 .09
❑ 166 Pedro Martinez .75 .23
❑ 167 Bob Wickman .30 .09
❑ 168 Mike Sweeney .30 .09
❑ 169 David Wells .30 .09
❑ 170 Jason Kendall .30 .09
❑ 171 Tino Martinez .50 .15
❑ 172 Matt Williams .50 .15

❑ 173 Frank Thomas .75 .23
❑ 174 Cliff Floyd .30 .09
❑ 175 Corey Koskie .30 .09
❑ 176 Orlando Hernandez .30 .09
❑ 177 Edgar Martinez .50 .15
❑ 178 Richie Sexson .30 .09
❑ 179 Manny Ramirez .50 .15
❑ 180 Jim Thome .75 .23
❑ 181 Andy Pettitte .50 .15
❑ 182 Aramis Ramirez .30 .09
❑ 183 J.D. Drew .30 .09
❑ 184 Brian Jordan .30 .09
❑ 185 Sammy Sosa 1.25 .35
❑ 186 Jeff Weaver .30 .09
❑ 187 Jeffrey Hammonds .30 .09
❑ 188 Eric Milton .30 .09
❑ 189 Eric Chavez .30 .09
❑ 190 Kazuhiro Sasaki .30 .09
❑ 191 Jose Cruz Jr. .30 .09
❑ 192 Derek Lowe .30 .09
❑ 193 C.C. Sabathia .30 .09
❑ 194 Adrian Beltre .50 .15
❑ 195 Alfonso Soriano .50 .15
❑ 196 Jack Wilson .30 .09
❑ 197 Fernando Vina .30 .09
❑ 198 Chipper Jones .75 .23
❑ 199 Paul Konerko .30 .09
❑ 200 Rusty Greer .30 .09
❑ 201 Jason Giambi AS 1.50 .45
❑ 202 Alfonso Soriano AS 1.50 .45
❑ 203 Shea Hillenbrand AS 1.50 .45
❑ 204 Alex Rodriguez AS 2.50 .75
❑ 205 Jorge Posada AS 1.50 .45
❑ 206 Ichiro Suzuki AS 2.50 .75
❑ 207 Manny Ramirez AS 1.50 .45
❑ 208 Torii Hunter AS 1.50 .45
❑ 209 Todd Helton AS 1.50 .45
❑ 210 Jose Vidro AS 1.50 .45
❑ 211 Scott Rolen AS 1.50 .45
❑ 212 Jimmy Rollins AS 1.50 .45
❑ 213 Mike Piazza AS 2.50 .75
❑ 214 Barry Bonds AS 4.00 1.20
❑ 215 Sammy Sosa AS 2.50 .75
❑ 216 Vladimir Guerrero AS 1.50 .45
❑ 217 Lance Berkman AS 1.50 .45
❑ 218 Derek Jeter AS 4.00 1.20
❑ 219 Nomar Garciaparra AS 2.50 .75
❑ 220 Luis Gonzalez AS 1.50 .45
❑ 221 Kazuhisa Ishii 02R 2.00 .60
❑ 222 Satoru Komiyama 02R 2.00 .60
❑ 223 So Taguchi 02R 2.00 .60
❑ 224 Jorge Padilla 02R 2.00 .60
❑ 225 Ben Howard 02R 2.00 .60
❑ 226 Jason Simontacchi 02R 2.00 .60
❑ 227 Barry Wesson 02R 2.00 .60
❑ 228 Howie Clark 02R 2.00 .60
❑ 229 Aaron Guiel 02R 2.00 .60
❑ 230 Oliver Perez 02R 2.00 .60
❑ 231 David Ross 02R 2.00 .60
❑ 232 Julius Matos 02R 2.00 .60
❑ 233 Chris Snelling 02R 2.00 .60
❑ 234 Rodrigo Lopez 02R 2.00 .60
❑ 235 Will Nieves 02R 2.00 .60
❑ 236 Joe Borchard 02R 2.00 .60
❑ 237 Aaron Cook 02R 2.00 .60
❑ 238 Anderson Machado 02R 2.00 .60
❑ 239 Corey Thurman 02R 2.00 .60
❑ 240 Tyler Yates 02R 2.00 .60
❑ 241 Coco Crisp 03R 2.00 .60
❑ 242 Andy Van Hekken 03R 2.00 .60
❑ 243 Jim Rushford 03R 2.00 .60
❑ 244 Jeriome Robertson 03R 2.00 .60
❑ 245 Shane Nance 03R 2.00 .60
❑ 246 Kevin Cash 03R 2.00 .60
❑ 247 Kirk Saarloos 03R 2.00 .60
❑ 248 Josh Bard 03R 2.00 .60
❑ 249 Dave Pember 03R RC 2.00 .60
❑ 250 Freddy Sanchez 03R 2.00 .60
❑ 251 Chien-Ming Wang PROS RC 4.00 1.20
❑ 252 Rickie Weeks PROS RC 6.00 1.80
❑ 253 Brandon Webb PROS RC 4.00 1.20
❑ 254 Hideki Matsui PROS RC 10.00 3.00
❑ 255 Michael Hessman PROS RC 3.00 .90
❑ 256 Ryan Wagner PROS RC 4.00 1.20
❑ 257 Matt Kata PROS RC 4.00 1.20
❑ 258 Edwin Jackson PROS RC 6.00 1.80
❑ 259 Jose Contreras PROS RC 3.00 .90
❑ 260 Delmon Young PROS RC 8.00 2.40
❑ 261 Bo Hart PROS RC 4.00 1.20
❑ 262 Jeff Duncan PROS RC 4.00 1.20
❑ 263 Robby Hammock PROS RC 4.00 1.20
❑ 264 Jeremy Bonderman PROS RC 4.00 1.20
❑ 265 Clint Barmes PROS RC 4.00 1.20

2004 Ultra

	MINT	NRMT
COMPLETE SERIES 1 (220)	60.00	27.00
COMP.SERIES 1 w/o SP's (200)	25.00	11.00
COMP.SERIES 2 w/o SP's (75)	25.00	11.00
COMP.SERIES 2 w/o L13 (162)	100.00	45.00
COMMON CARD (1-200)	.30	.14
COMMON CARD (201-220)	1.25	.55
201-220 APPROXIMATE ODDS 1:2 HOBBY		
201-220 RANDOM IN RETAIL PACKS		
COMMON CARD (296-382)	2.00	.90
296-382 ODDS TWO PER HOBBY/RETAIL		
COMMON CARD (383-395)	20.00	9.00
383-395 ODDS 1:28 HOBBY, 1:2000 RETAIL		
383-395 PRINT RUN 500 SERIAL #'d SETS		

❑ 1 Magglio Ordonez .30 .14
❑ 2 Bobby Abreu .30 .14
❑ 3 Eric Munson .30 .14
❑ 4 Eric Byrnes .30 .14
❑ 5 Bartolo Colon .30 .14
❑ 6 Juan Encarnacion .30 .14
❑ 7 Jody Gerut .30 .14
❑ 8 Eddie Guardado .30 .14
❑ 9 Shea Hillenbrand .30 .14
❑ 10 Andruw Jones .30 .14
❑ 11 Carlos Lee .30 .14
❑ 12 Pedro Martinez .75 .35
❑ 13 Barry Larkin .50 .23
❑ 14 Angel Berroa .30 .14
❑ 15 Edgar Martinez .50 .23
❑ 16 Sidney Ponson .30 .14
❑ 17 Mariano Rivera .50 .23
❑ 18 Richie Sexson .30 .14
❑ 19 Frank Thomas .75 .35
❑ 20 Jerome Williams .30 .14
❑ 21 Barry Zito .30 .14
❑ 22 Roberto Alomar .50 .23
❑ 23 Rocky Biddle .30 .14
❑ 24 Orlando Cabrera .30 .14
❑ 25 Placido Polanco .30 .14
❑ 26 Morgan Ensberg .30 .14
❑ 27 Jason Giambi .30 .14
❑ 28 Jim Thome .75 .35
❑ 29 Vladimir Guerrero .75 .35
❑ 30 Tim Hudson .30 .14
❑ 31 Jacque Jones .30 .14
❑ 32 Derrek Lee .30 .14
❑ 33 Rafael Palmeiro .50 .23
❑ 34 Mike Mussina .50 .23
❑ 35 Corey Patterson .30 .14
❑ 36 Mike Cameron .30 .14
❑ 37 Ivan Rodriguez .75 .35
❑ 38 Ben Sheets .30 .14
❑ 39 Woody Williams .30 .14
❑ 40 Ichiro Suzuki 1.25 .55
❑ 41 Moises Alou .30 .14
❑ 42 Craig Biggio .50 .23
❑ 43 Jorge Posada .50 .23
❑ 44 Craig Monroe .30 .14
❑ 45 Darin Erstad .30 .14
❑ 46 Jay Gibbons .30 .14
❑ 47 Aaron Guiel .30 .14
❑ 48 Travis Lee .30 .14
❑ 49 Jorge Julio .30 .14
❑ 50 Torii Hunter .30 .14
❑ 51 Luis Matos .30 .14
❑ 52 Brett Myers .30 .14
❑ 53 Sean Casey .30 .14
❑ 54 Mark Prior .75 .35
❑ 55 Alex Rodriguez 1.25 .55
❑ 56 Gary Sheffield .30 .14
❑ 57 Jason Varitek .50 .23
❑ 58 Dontrelle Willis .30 .14
❑ 59 Garret Anderson .30 .14
❑ 60 Casey Blake .30 .14
❑ 61 Jay Payton .30 .14
❑ 62 Carl Crawford .30 .14
❑ 63 Carl Everett .30 .14
❑ 64 Marcus Giles .30 .14
❑ 65 Jose Guillen .30 .14
❑ 66 Eric Karros .30 .14
❑ 67 Mike Lieberthal .30 .14
❑ 68 Hideki Matsui 1.25 .55
❑ 69 Xavier Nady .30 .14
❑ 70 Hank Blalock .30 .14
❑ 71 Albert Pujols 1.50 .70
❑ 72 Jose Cruz Jr. .30 .14
❑ 73 Randall Simon .30 .14
❑ 74 Javier Vazquez .30 .14
❑ 75 Preston Wilson .30 .14
❑ 76 Danys Baez .30 .14
❑ 77 Alex Cintron .30 .14
❑ 78 Jake Peavy .30 .14
❑ 79 Scott Rolen .75 .35
❑ 80 Robert Fick .30 .14
❑ 81 Brian Giles .30 .14
❑ 82 Roy Halladay .30 .14
❑ 83 Kazuhisa Ishii .30 .14
❑ 84 Austin Kearns .30 .14
❑ 85 Paul Lo Duca .30 .14
❑ 86 Darrell May .30 .14
❑ 87 Phil Nevin .30 .14
❑ 88 Carlos Pena .30 .14
❑ 89 Manny Ramirez .50 .23
❑ 90 C.C. Sabathia .30 .14
❑ 91 John Smoltz .50 .23
❑ 92 Jose Vidro .30 .14
❑ 93 Randy Wolf .30 .14
❑ 94 Jeff Bagwell .50 .23
❑ 95 Barry Bonds 2.00 .90
❑ 96 Frank Catalanotto .30 .14
❑ 97 Zach Day .30 .14
❑ 98 David Ortiz .75 .35
❑ 99 Troy Glaus .30 .14
❑ 100 Bo Hart .30 .14
❑ 101 Geoff Jenkins .30 .14
❑ 102 Jason Kendall .30 .14
❑ 103 Esteban Loaiza .30 .14
❑ 104 Doug Mientkiewicz .30 .14
❑ 105 Trot Nixon .30 .14
❑ 106 Troy Percival .30 .14
❑ 107 Aramis Ramirez .30 .14
❑ 108 Alex Sanchez .30 .14
❑ 109 Alfonso Soriano .50 .23
❑ 110 Omar Vizquel .50 .23
❑ 111 Kerry Wood .75 .35
❑ 112 Rocco Baldelli .30 .14
❑ 113 Bret Boone .30 .14
❑ 114 Shawn Chacon .30 .14
❑ 115 Carlos Delgado .30 .14
❑ 116 Shawn Green .30 .14
❑ 117 Tim Worrell .30 .14
❑ 118 Tom Glavine .50 .23
❑ 119 Shigetoshi Hasegawa .30 .14
❑ 120 Derek Jeter 1.50 .70
❑ 121 Jeff Kent .30 .14
❑ 122 Braden Looper .30 .14
❑ 123 Kevin Millwood .30 .14
❑ 124 Hideo Nomo .75 .35
❑ 125 Jason Phillips .30 .14
❑ 126 Tim Redding .30 .14
❑ 127 Reggie Sanders .30 .14
❑ 128 Sammy Sosa 1.25 .55
❑ 129 Billy Wagner .30 .14

❑ 130	Miguel Batista	.30	.14
❑ 131	Milton Bradley	.30	.14
❑ 132	Eric Chavez	.30	.14
❑ 133	J.D. Drew	.30	.14
❑ 134	Keith Foulke	.30	.14
❑ 135	Luis Gonzalez	.30	.14
❑ 136	LaTroy Hawkins	.30	.14
❑ 137	Randy Johnson	.75	.35
❑ 138	Byung-Hyun Kim	.30	.14
❑ 139	Javy Lopez	.30	.14
❑ 140	Melvin Mora	.30	.14
❑ 141	Aubrey Huff	.30	.14
❑ 142	Mike Piazza	1.25	.55
❑ 143	Mark Redman	.30	.14
❑ 144	Kazuhiro Sasaki	.30	.14
❑ 145	Shannon Stewart	.30	.14
❑ 146	Larry Walker	.50	.23
❑ 147	Dmitri Young	.30	.14
❑ 148	Josh Beckett	.30	.14
❑ 149	Jae Weong Seo	.30	.14
❑ 150	Hee Seop Choi	.30	.14
❑ 151	Adam Dunn	.50	.23
❑ 152	Rafael Furcal	.30	.14
❑ 153	Juan Gonzalez	.50	.23
❑ 154	Todd Helton	.50	.23
❑ 155	Carlos Zambrano	.30	.14
❑ 156	Ryan Klesko	.30	.14
❑ 157	Mike Lowell	.30	.14
❑ 158	Jamie Moyer	.30	.14
❑ 159	Russ Ortiz	.30	.14
❑ 160	Juan Pierre	.30	.14
❑ 161	Edgar Renteria	.30	.14
❑ 162	Curt Schilling	.30	.14
❑ 163	Mike Sweeney	.30	.14
❑ 164	Brandon Webb	.30	.14
❑ 165	Michael Young	.30	.14
❑ 166	Carlos Beltran	.50	.23
❑ 167	Sean Burroughs	.30	.14
❑ 168	Luis Castillo	.30	.14
❑ 169	David Eckstein	.30	.14
❑ 170	Eric Gagne	.75	.35
❑ 171	Chipper Jones	.75	.35
❑ 172	Livan Hernandez	.30	.14
❑ 173	Nick Johnson	.30	.14
❑ 174	Corey Koskie	.30	.14
❑ 175	Jason Schmidt	.30	.14
❑ 176	Bill Mueller	.30	.14
❑ 177	Steve Finley	.30	.14
❑ 178	A.J. Pierzynski	.30	.14
❑ 179	Rene Reyes	.30	.14
❑ 180	Jason Johnson	.30	.14
❑ 181	Mark Teixeira	.30	.14
❑ 182	Kip Wells	.30	.14
❑ 183	Mike MacDougal	.30	.14
❑ 184	Lance Berkman	.30	.14
❑ 185	Victor Zambrano	.30	.14
❑ 186	Roger Clemens	1.50	.70
❑ 187	Jim Edmonds	.30	.14
❑ 188	Nomar Garciaparra	1.25	.55
❑ 189	Ken Griffey Jr.	1.25	.55
❑ 190	Richard Hidalgo	.30	.14
❑ 191	Cliff Floyd	.30	.14
❑ 192	Greg Maddux	1.25	.55
❑ 193	Mark Mulder	.30	.14
❑ 194	Roy Oswalt	.30	.14
❑ 195	Marlon Byrd	.30	.14
❑ 196	Jose Reyes	.30	.14
❑ 197	Kevin Brown	.30	.14
❑ 198	Miguel Tejada	.30	.14
❑ 199	Vernon Wells	.30	.14
❑ 200	Joel Pineiro	.30	.14
❑ 201	Rickie Weeks AR	2.00	.90
❑ 202	Chad Gaudin AR	1.25	.55
❑ 203	Ryan Wagner AR	1.25	.55
❑ 204	Chris Bootcheck AR	1.25	.55
❑ 205	Koyie Hill AR	1.25	.55
❑ 206	Jeff Duncan AR	1.25	.55
❑ 207	Rich Harden AR	2.00	.90
❑ 208	Edwin Jackson AR	2.00	.90
❑ 209	Robby Hammock AR	1.25	.55
❑ 210	Khalil Greene AR	3.00	1.35
❑ 211	Chien-Ming Wang AR	2.00	.90
❑ 212	Prentice Redman AR	1.25	.55
❑ 213	Todd Wellemeyer AR	1.25	.55
❑ 214	Clint Barmes AR	1.25	.55
❑ 215	Matt Kata AR	1.25	.55
❑ 216	Jon Leicester AR	1.25	.55
❑ 217	Jeremy Guthrie AR	1.25	.55
❑ 218	Chin-Hui Tsao AR	2.00	.90
❑ 219	Dan Haren AR	1.25	.55
❑ 220	Delmon Young AR	3.00	1.35
❑ 221	Vladimir Guerrero	1.25	.55
❑ 222	Andy Pettitte	.75	.35
❑ 223	Gary Sheffield	.50	.23
❑ 224	Javier Vazquez	.50	.23
❑ 225	Alex Rodriguez	2.00	.90
❑ 226	Billy Wagner	.50	.23
❑ 227	Miguel Tejada	.50	.23
❑ 228	Greg Maddux	2.00	.90
❑ 229	Ivan Rodriguez	1.25	.55
❑ 230	Roger Clemens	2.50	1.10
❑ 231	Alfonso Soriano	.75	.35
❑ 232	Miguel Cabrera	.75	.35
❑ 233	Javy Lopez	.50	.23
❑ 234	David Wells	.50	.23
❑ 235	Eric Milton	.50	.23
❑ 236	Armando Benitez	.50	.23
❑ 237	Mike Cameron	.50	.23
❑ 238	J.D. Drew	.50	.23
❑ 239	Carlos Beltran	.75	.35
❑ 240	Bartolo Colon	.50	.23
❑ 241	Jose Guillen	.50	.23
❑ 242	Kevin Brown	.50	.23
❑ 243	Carlos Guillen	.50	.23
❑ 244	Kenny Lofton	.50	.23
❑ 245	Pokey Reese	.50	.23
❑ 246	Rafael Palmeiro	.75	.35
❑ 247	Nomar Garciaparra	2.00	.90
❑ 248	Hee Seop Choi	.50	.23
❑ 249	Juan Uribe	.50	.23
❑ 250	Nick Johnson	.50	.23
❑ 251	Scott Podsednik	.50	.23
❑ 252	Richie Sexson	.50	.23
❑ 253	Keith Foulke Sox	.75	.35
❑ 254	Jaret Wright	.50	.23
❑ 255	Johnny Estrada	.50	.23
❑ 256	Michael Barrett	.50	.23
❑ 257	Bernie Williams	.75	.35
❑ 258	Octavio Dotel	.50	.23
❑ 259	Jeromy Burnitz	.50	.23
❑ 260	Kevin Youkilis	.50	.23
❑ 261	Derrek Lee	.50	.23
❑ 262	Jack Wilson	.50	.23
❑ 263	Craig Wilson	.50	.23
❑ 264	Richard Hidalgo	.50	.23
❑ 265	Royce Clayton	.50	.23
❑ 266	Curt Schilling	1.25	.55
❑ 267	Joe Mauer	.75	.35
❑ 268	Bobby Crosby	.50	.23
❑ 269	Zack Greinke	.50	.23
❑ 270	Victor Martinez	.50	.23
❑ 271	Pedro Feliz	.50	.23
❑ 272	Tony Batista	.50	.23
❑ 273	Casey Kotchman	.50	.23
❑ 274	Freddy Garcia	.50	.23
❑ 275	Adam Everett	.50	.23
❑ 276	Alexis Rios	.50	.23
❑ 277	Lew Ford	.50	.23
❑ 278	Adam LaRoche	.50	.23
❑ 279	Lyle Overbay	.50	.23
❑ 280	Juan Gonzalez	.75	.35
❑ 281	A.J. Pierzynski	.50	.23
❑ 282	Scott Hairston	.50	.23
❑ 283	Danny Bautista	.50	.23
❑ 284	Brad Penny	.50	.23
❑ 285	Paul Konerko	.50	.23
❑ 286	Matt Lawton	.50	.23
❑ 287	Carl Pavano	.50	.23
❑ 288	Pat Burrell	.50	.23
❑ 289	Kenny Rogers	.50	.23
❑ 290	Laynce Nix	.50	.23
❑ 291	Johnny Damon	1.25	.55
❑ 292	Paul Wilson	.50	.23
❑ 293	Vinny Castilla	.50	.23
❑ 294	Aaron Miles	.50	.23
❑ 295	Ken Harvey	.50	.23
❑ 296	Onil Joseph RC	2.00	.90
❑ 297	Kazuhito Tadano RC	3.00	1.35
❑ 298	Jeff Bennett RC	2.00	.90
❑ 299	Chad Bentz RC	2.00	.90
❑ 300	Akinori Otsuka RC	2.00	.90
❑ 301	Jon Knott RC	2.00	.90
❑ 302	Ian Snell RC	3.00	1.35
❑ 303	Fernando Nieve RC	2.00	.90
❑ 304	Mike Rouse RC	2.00	.90
❑ 305	Dennis Sarfate RC	2.00	.90
❑ 306	Josh Labandeira RC	2.00	.90
❑ 307	Chris Oxspring RC	3.00	1.35
❑ 308	Alfredo Simon RC	2.00	.90
❑ 309	Rusty Tucker RC	3.00	1.35
❑ 310	Lincoln Holdzkom RC	2.00	.90
❑ 311	Justin Leone RC	3.00	1.35
❑ 312	Jorge Sequea RC	2.00	.90
❑ 313	Brian Dallimore RC	2.00	.90
❑ 314	Tim Bittner RC	2.00	.90
❑ 315	Ronny Cedeno RC	2.00	.90
❑ 316	Justin Hampson RC	2.00	.90
❑ 317	Ryan Wing RC	2.00	.90
❑ 318	Mariano Gomez RC	2.00	.90
❑ 319	Carlos Vasquez RC	3.00	1.35
❑ 320	Casey Daigle RC	2.00	.90
❑ 321	Renyel Pinto RC	3.00	1.35
❑ 322	Chris Shelton RC	3.00	1.35
❑ 323	Mike Gosling RC	2.00	.90
❑ 324	Aarom Baldiris RC	3.00	1.35
❑ 325	Ramon Ramirez RC	2.00	.90
❑ 326	Roberto Novoa RC	3.00	1.35
❑ 327	Sean Henn RC	2.00	.90
❑ 328	Nick Regilio RC	2.00	.90
❑ 329	Dave Crouthers RC	2.00	.90
❑ 330	Greg Dobbs RC	2.00	.90
❑ 331	Angel Chavez RC	2.00	.90
❑ 332	Luis A. Gonzalez RC	2.00	.90
❑ 333	Justin Knoedler RC	2.00	.90
❑ 334	Jason Frasor RC	2.00	.90
❑ 335	Jerry Gil RC	2.00	.90
❑ 336	Carlos Hines RC	2.00	.90
❑ 337	Ivan Ochoa RC	2.00	.90
❑ 338	Jose Capellan RC	3.00	1.35
❑ 339	Hector Gimenez RC	2.00	.90
❑ 340	Shawn Hill RC	2.00	.90
❑ 341	Freddy Guzman RC	2.00	.90
❑ 342	Scott Proctor RC	3.00	1.35
❑ 343	Frank Francisco RC	2.00	.90
❑ 344	Brandon Medders RC	2.00	.90
❑ 345	Andy Green RC	2.00	.90
❑ 346	Eddy Rodriguez RC	3.00	1.35
❑ 347	Tim Hamulack RC	2.00	.90
❑ 348	Michael Wuertz RC	3.00	1.35
❑ 349	Arnie Munoz	2.00	.90
❑ 350	Enemencio Pacheco RC	2.00	.90
❑ 351	Dusty Bergman RC	2.00	.90
❑ 352	Charles Thomas RC	3.00	1.35
❑ 353	William Bergolla RC	2.00	.90
❑ 354	Ramon Castro RC	2.00	.90
❑ 355	Justin Lehr RC	2.00	.90
❑ 356	Lino Urdaneta RC	2.00	.90
❑ 357	Donnie Kelly RC	2.00	.90
❑ 358	Kevin Cave RC	3.00	1.35
❑ 359	Franklyn Gracesqui RC	2.00	.90
❑ 360	Chris Aguila RC	2.00	.90
❑ 361	Jorge Vasquez RC	2.00	.90
❑ 362	Andres Blanco RC	2.00	.90
❑ 363	Orlando Rodriguez RC	2.00	.90
❑ 364	Colby Miller RC	2.00	.90
❑ 365	Shawn Camp RC	2.00	.90
❑ 366	Jake Woods RC	2.00	.90
❑ 367	George Sherrill RC	2.00	.90
❑ 368	Justin Huisman RC	2.00	.90
❑ 369	Jimmy Serrano RC	2.00	.90
❑ 370	Mike Johnston RC	2.00	.90
❑ 371	Ryan Meaux RC	2.00	.90
❑ 372	Scott Dohmann RC	2.00	.90
❑ 373	Brad Halsey RC	3.00	1.35
❑ 374	Joey Gathright RC	3.00	1.35
❑ 375	Yadier Molina RC	4.00	1.80
❑ 376	Travis Blackley RC	3.00	1.35
❑ 377	Steve Andrade RC	2.00	.90
❑ 378	Phil Stockman RC	2.00	.90
❑ 379	Roman Colon RC	2.00	.90
❑ 380	Jesse Crain RC	3.00	1.35
❑ 381	Edwardo Sierra RC	3.00	1.35
❑ 382	Justin Germano RC	2.00	.90
❑ 383	Kaz Matsui L13 RC	25.00	11.00
❑ 384	Shingo Takatsu L13 RC	25.00	11.00
❑ 385	John Gall L13 RC	20.00	9.00
❑ 386	Chris Saenz L13 RC	20.00	9.00
❑ 387	Merkin Valdez L13 RC	25.00	11.00

❑ 388 Jamie Brown L13 RC 20.00 9.00
❑ 389 Jason Bartlett L13 RC .. 20.00 9.00
❑ 390 David Aardsma L13 RC 20.00 9.00
❑ 391 Scott Kazmir L13 RC 30.00 13.50
❑ 392 David Wright L13 .... 40.00 18.00
❑ 393 Dioner Navarro L13 RC 25.00 11.00
❑ 394 B.J. Upton L13 .... 25.00 11.00
❑ 395 Gavin Floyd L13 .... 25.00 11.00

2005 Ultra

	Nm-Mt	Ex-Mt
COMPLETE SET (220)	100.00	30.00
COMP.SET w/o SP's (200)	40.00	12.00
COMMON CARD (1-200)	.30	.09
COMMON CARD (201-220)	2.00	.60

201-220 ODDS 1:4 HOBBY, 1:5 RETAIL

❑ 1 Andy Pettitte .50 .15
❑ 2 Jose Cruz Jr. .30 .09
❑ 3 Cliff Floyd .30 .09
❑ 4 Paul Konerko .30 .09
❑ 5 Joe Mauer .50 .15
❑ 6 Scott Spiezio .30 .09
❑ 7 Ben Sheets .30 .09
❑ 8 Kerry Wood .75 .23
❑ 9 Carl Pavano .30 .09
❑ 10 Matt Morris .30 .09
❑ 11 Kaz Matsui .30 .09
❑ 12 Ivan Rodriguez .75 .23
❑ 13 Victor Martinez .30 .09
❑ 14 Justin Morneau .30 .09
❑ 15 Adam Everett .30 .09
❑ 16 Carl Crawford .30 .09
❑ 17 David Ortiz .75 .23
❑ 18 Jason Giambi .30 .09
❑ 19 Derrek Lee .30 .09
❑ 20 Magglio Ordonez .30 .09
❑ 21 Bobby Abreu .30 .09
❑ 22 Milton Bradley .30 .09
❑ 23 Jeff Bagwell .50 .15
❑ 24 Jim Edmonds .30 .09
❑ 25 Garret Anderson .30 .09
❑ 26 Jacque Jones .30 .09
❑ 27 Ted Lilly .30 .09
❑ 28 Greg Maddux 1.25 .35
❑ 29 Jermaine Dye .30 .09
❑ 30 Bill Mueller .30 .09
❑ 31 Roy Oswalt .30 .09
❑ 32 Tony Womack .30 .09
❑ 33 Andruw Jones .30 .09
❑ 34 Tom Glavine .50 .15
❑ 35 Mariano Rivera .50 .15
❑ 36 Sean Casey .30 .09
❑ 37 Edgardo Alfonzo .30 .09
❑ 38 Brad Penny .30 .09
❑ 39 Johan Santana .50 .15
❑ 40 Mark Teixeira .30 .09
❑ 41 Manny Ramirez .50 .15
❑ 42 Gary Sheffield .30 .09
❑ 43 Matt Lawton .30 .09
❑ 44 Troy Percival .30 .09
❑ 45 Rocco Baldelli .30 .09
❑ 46 Doug Mientkiewicz .30 .09
❑ 47 Corey Patterson .30 .09
❑ 48 Austin Kearns .30 .09
❑ 49 Edgar Martinez .50 .15
❑ 50 Brad Radke .30 .09
❑ 51 Barry Larkin .50 .15
❑ 52 Chone Figgins .30 .09
❑ 53 Alexis Rios .30 .09
❑ 54 Alex Rodriguez 1.25 .35
❑ 55 Vinny Castilla .30 .09
❑ 56 Javier Vazquez .30 .09
❑ 57 Javy Lopez .30 .09
❑ 58 Mike Cameron .30 .09
❑ 59 Brian Giles .30 .09
❑ 60 Dontrelle Willis .30 .09
❑ 61 Rafael Furcal .30 .09
❑ 62 Trot Nixon .30 .09
❑ 63 Mark Mulder .30 .09
❑ 64 Josh Beckett .30 .09
❑ 65 J.D. Drew .30 .09
❑ 66 Brandon Webb .30 .09
❑ 67 Wade Miller .30 .09
❑ 68 Lyle Overbay .30 .09
❑ 69 Pedro Martinez .75 .23
❑ 70 Rich Harden .30 .09
❑ 71 Al Leiter .30 .09
❑ 72 Adam Eaton .30 .09
❑ 73 Mike Sweeney .30 .09
❑ 74 Steve Finley .30 .09
❑ 75 Kris Benson .30 .09
❑ 76 Jim Thome .75 .23
❑ 77 Juan Pierre .30 .09
❑ 78 Bartolo Colon .30 .09
❑ 79 Carlos Delgado .30 .09
❑ 80 Jack Wilson .30 .09
❑ 81 Ken Harvey .30 .09
❑ 82 Nomar Garciaparra 1.25 .35
❑ 83 Paul Lo Duca .30 .09
❑ 84 Cesar Izturis .30 .09
❑ 85 Adrian Beltre .50 .15
❑ 86 Brian Roberts .30 .09
❑ 87 David Eckstein .30 .09
❑ 88 Jimmy Rollins .30 .09
❑ 89 Roger Clemens 1.50 .45
❑ 90 Randy Johnson .75 .23
❑ 91 Orlando Hudson .30 .09
❑ 92 Tim Hudson .30 .09
❑ 93 Dmitri Young .30 .09
❑ 94 Chipper Jones .75 .23
❑ 95 John Smoltz .50 .15
❑ 96 Billy Wagner .30 .09
❑ 97 Hideo Nomo .75 .23
❑ 98 Sammy Sosa 1.25 .35
❑ 99 Darin Erstad .30 .09
❑ 100 Todd Helton .50 .15
❑ 101 Aubrey Huff .30 .09
❑ 102 Alfonso Soriano .50 .15
❑ 103 Jose Vidro .30 .09
❑ 104 Carlos Lee .30 .09
❑ 105 Corey Koskie .30 .09
❑ 106 Bret Boone .30 .09
❑ 107 Torii Hunter .30 .09
❑ 108 Aramis Ramirez .30 .09
❑ 109 Chase Utley .30 .09
❑ 110 Reggie Sanders .30 .09
❑ 111 Livan Hernandez .30 .09
❑ 112 Jeromy Burnitz .30 .09
❑ 113 Carlos Zambrano .30 .09
❑ 114 Hank Blalock .30 .09
❑ 115 Sidney Ponson .30 .09
❑ 116 Zack Greinke .30 .09
❑ 117 Trevor Hoffman .30 .09
❑ 118 Jeff Kent .30 .09
❑ 119 Richie Sexson .30 .09
❑ 120 Melvin Mora .30 .09
❑ 121 Eric Chavez .30 .09
❑ 122 Miguel Cabrera .50 .15
❑ 123 Ryan Freel .30 .09
❑ 124 Russ Ortiz .30 .09
❑ 125 Craig Wilson .30 .09
❑ 126 Craig Biggio .50 .15
❑ 127 Curt Schilling .75 .23
❑ 128 Kaz Ishii .30 .09
❑ 129 Marquis Grissom .30 .09
❑ 130 Bernie Williams .50 .15
❑ 131 Travis Hafner .30 .09
❑ 132 Hee Seop Choi .30 .09
❑ 133 Scott Rolen .50 .15
❑ 134 Tony Batista .30 .09
❑ 135 Frank Thomas .75 .23
❑ 136 Jason Varitek .50 .15
❑ 137 Ichiro Suzuki 1.25 .35
❑ 138 Junior Spivey .30 .09
❑ 139 Adam Dunn .50 .15
❑ 140 Jorge Posada .50 .15
❑ 141 Edgar Renteria .30 .09
❑ 142 Hideki Matsui 1.25 .35
❑ 143 Carlos Guillen .30 .09
❑ 144 Jody Gerut .30 .09
❑ 145 Wily Mo Pena .30 .09
❑ 146 Derek Jeter 1.50 .45
❑ 147 C.C. Sabathia .30 .09
❑ 148 Geoff Jenkins .30 .09
❑ 149 Albert Pujols 1.50 .45
❑ 150 Eric Munson .30 .09
❑ 151 Moises Alou .30 .09
❑ 152 Jerry Hairston .30 .09
❑ 153 Ray Durham .30 .09
❑ 154 Mike Piazza 1.25 .35
❑ 155 Omar Vizquel .30 .09
❑ 156 A.J. Pierzynski .30 .09
❑ 157 Michael Young .30 .09
❑ 158 Jason Bay .30 .09
❑ 159 Mark Loretta .30 .09
❑ 160 Shawn Green .30 .09
❑ 161 Luis Gonzalez .30 .09
❑ 162 Johnny Damon .75 .23
❑ 163 Eric Milton .30 .09
❑ 164 Mike Lowell .30 .09
❑ 165 Jose Guillen .30 .09
❑ 166 Eric Hinske .30 .09
❑ 167 Jason Kendall .30 .09
❑ 168 Carlos Beltran .50 .15
❑ 169 Johnny Estrada .30 .09
❑ 170 Scott Hatteberg .30 .09
❑ 171 Laynce Nix .30 .09
❑ 172 Eric Gagne .75 .23
❑ 173 Richard Hidalgo .30 .09
❑ 174 Bobby Crosby .30 .09
❑ 175 Woody Williams .30 .09
❑ 176 Justin Leone .30 .09
❑ 177 Orlando Cabrera .30 .09
❑ 178 Mark Prior .75 .23
❑ 179 Jorge Julio .30 .09
❑ 180 Jamie Moyer .30 .09
❑ 181 Jose Reyes .30 .09
❑ 182 Ken Griffey Jr. 1.25 .35
❑ 183 Mike Lieberthal .30 .09
❑ 184 Kenny Rogers .30 .09
❑ 185 Mike Mussina .50 .15
❑ 186 Preston Wilson .30 .09
❑ 187 Khalil Greene .75 .23
❑ 188 Angel Berroa .30 .09
❑ 189 Miguel Tejada .30 .09
❑ 190 Freddy Garcia .30 .09
❑ 191 Pat Burrell .30 .09
❑ 192 Luis Castillo .30 .09
❑ 193 Vladimir Guerrero .75 .23
❑ 194 Roy Halladay .30 .09
❑ 195 Barry Zito .30 .09
❑ 196 Lance Berkman .30 .09
❑ 197 Rafael Palmeiro .50 .15
❑ 198 Nate Robertson .30 .09
❑ 199 Jason Schmidt .30 .09
❑ 200 Scott Podsednik .30 .09
❑ 201 Casey Kotchman AR 3.00 .90
❑ 202 Scott Kazmir AR 5.00 1.50
❑ 203 Bucky Jacobsen AR 3.00 .90
❑ 204 Jeff Keppinger AR 2.00 .60
❑ 205 Dave Bush AR 3.00 .90
❑ 206 Gavin Floyd AR 3.00 .90
❑ 207 David Wright AR 8.00 2.40
❑ 208 B.J. Upton AR 5.00 1.50
❑ 209 David Aardsma AR 2.00 .60
❑ 210 Jason Bartlett AR 2.00 .60
❑ 211 Dioner Navarro AR 3.00 .90
❑ 212 Jason Kubel AR 3.00 .90
❑ 213 Ryan Howard AR 3.00 .90
❑ 214 Charles Thomas AR 2.00 .60
❑ 215 Freddy Guzman AR 2.00 .60
❑ 216 Brad Halsey AR 2.00 .60
❑ 217 Joey Gathright AR 3.00 .90
❑ 218 Jeff Francis AR 3.00 .90
❑ 219 Terry Tiffee AR 2.00 .60
❑ 220 Nick Swisher AR 5.00 .90

1989 Upper Deck

	Nm-Mt	Ex-Mt
COMPLETE SET (800)	80.00	32.00
COMP.FACT.SET (800)	100.00	40.00
COMP.HI FACT.SET (100)	10.00	4.00
❑ 1 Ken Griffey Jr. RC	50.00	20.00
❑ 2 Luis Medina RC	.25	.10
❑ 3 Tony Chance RC	.25	.10
❑ 4 Dave Otto	.25	.10
❑ 5 S.Alomar Jr. RC UER	1.00	.40
Born 6/16/66, should be 6/18/66		
❑ 6 Rolando Roomes RC	.25	.10
❑ 7 Dave West RC	.25	.10
❑ 8 Cris Carpenter RC	.25	.10
❑ 9 Gregg Jefferies	.25	.10
❑ 10 Doug Dascenzo RC	.25	.10
❑ 11 Ron Jones RC	.25	.10
❑ 12 Luis DeLosSantos RC	.25	.10
❑ 13 Gary Sheffield COR RC	6.00	2.40
❑ 13A G.Sheffield ERR RC	6.00	2.40
SS upside down on card front		
❑ 14 Mike Harkey RC	.25	.10
❑ 15 Lance Blankenship RC	.25	.10
❑ 16 William Brennan RC	.25	.10
❑ 17 John Smoltz RC	4.00	1.60
❑ 18 Ramon Martinez RC	.50	.20
❑ 19 Mark Lemke RC	1.00	.40
❑ 20 Juan Bell RC	.25	.10
❑ 21 Rey Palacios RC	.25	.10
❑ 22 Felix Jose RC	.25	.10
❑ 23 Van Snider RC	.25	.10
❑ 24 Dante Bichette RC	1.00	.40
❑ 25 Randy Johnson RC	15.00	6.00
❑ 26 Carlos Quintana RC	.25	.10
❑ 27 Star Rookie CL	.25	.10
❑ 28 Mike Schooler	.25	.10
❑ 29 Randy St.Claire	.25	.10
❑ 30 Jerald Clark RC	.25	.10
❑ 31 Kevin Gross	.25	.10
❑ 32 Dan Firova	.25	.10
❑ 33 Jeff Calhoun	.25	.10
❑ 34 Tommy Hinzo	.25	.10
❑ 35 Ricky Jordan RC	.50	.20
❑ 36 Larry Parrish	.25	.10
❑ 37 Bret Saberhagen UER	.40	.16
Hit total 931, should be 1031		
❑ 38 Mike Smithson	.25	.10
❑ 39 Dave Dravecky	.25	.10
❑ 40 Ed Romero	.25	.10
❑ 41 Jeff Musselman	.25	.10
❑ 42 Ed Hearn	.25	.10
❑ 43 Rance Mulliniks	.25	.10
❑ 44 Jim Eisenreich	.25	.10
❑ 45 Sil Campusano	.25	.10
❑ 46 Mike Krukow	.25	.10
❑ 47 Paul Gibson	.25	.10
❑ 48 Mike LaCoss	.25	.10
❑ 49 Larry Herndon	.25	.10
❑ 50 Scott Garrelts	.25	.10
❑ 51 Dwayne Henry	.25	.10
❑ 52 Jim Acker	.25	.10
❑ 53 Steve Sax	.25	.10
❑ 54 Pete O'Brien	.25	.10
❑ 55 Paul Runge	.25	.10
❑ 56 Rick Rhoden	.25	.10
❑ 57 John Dopson	.25	.10
❑ 58 Casey Candaele UER	.25	.10
(No stats for Astros for '88 season)		
❑ 59 Dave Righetti	.40	.16
❑ 60 Joe Hesketh	.25	.10
❑ 61 Frank DiPino	.25	.10
❑ 62 Tim Laudner	.25	.10
❑ 63 Jamie Moyer	.40	.16
❑ 64 Fred Toliver	.25	.10
❑ 65 Mitch Webster	.25	.10
❑ 66 John Tudor	.40	.16
❑ 67 John Cangelosi	.25	.10
❑ 68 Mike Devereaux	.25	.10
❑ 69 Brian Fisher	.25	.10
❑ 70 Mike Marshall	.25	.10
❑ 71 Zane Smith	.25	.10
❑ 72A Brian Holton ERR	1.00	.40
(Photo actually Shawn Hillegas)		
❑ 72B Brian Holton COR	.40	.16
❑ 73 Jose Guzman	.25	.10
❑ 74 Rick Mahler	.25	.10
❑ 75 John Shelby	.25	.10
❑ 76 Jim Deshaies	.25	.10
❑ 77 Bobby Meacham	.25	.10
❑ 78 Bryn Smith	.25	.10
❑ 79 Joaquin Andujar	.40	.16
❑ 80 Richard Dotson	.25	.10
❑ 81 Charlie Lea	.25	.10
❑ 82 Calvin Schiraldi	.25	.10
❑ 83 Les Straker	.25	.10
❑ 84 Les Lancaster	.25	.10
❑ 85 Allan Anderson	.25	.10
❑ 86 Junior Ortiz	.25	.10
❑ 87 Jesse Orosco	.25	.10
❑ 88 Felix Fermin	.25	.10
❑ 89 Dave Anderson	.25	.10
❑ 90 Rafael Belliard UER	.25	.10
(Born '61, not '51)		
❑ 91 Franklin Stubbs	.25	.10
❑ 92 Cecil Espy	.25	.10
❑ 93 Albert Hall	.25	.10
❑ 94 Tim Leary	.25	.10
❑ 95 Mitch Williams	.25	.10
❑ 96 Tracy Jones	.25	.10
❑ 97 Danny Darwin	.25	.10
❑ 98 Gary Ward	.25	.10
❑ 99 Neal Heaton	.25	.10
❑ 100 Jim Pankovits	.25	.10
❑ 101 Bill Doran	.25	.10
❑ 102 Tim Wallach	.25	.10
❑ 103 Joe Magrane	.25	.10
❑ 104 Ozzie Virgil	.25	.10
❑ 105 Alvin Davis	.25	.10
❑ 106 Tom Brookens	.25	.10
❑ 107 Shawon Dunston	.25	.10
❑ 108 Tracy Woodson	.25	.10
❑ 109 Nelson Liriano	.25	.10
❑ 110 Devon White UER	.40	.16
(Doubles total 46, should be 56)		
❑ 111 Steve Balboni	.25	.10
❑ 112 Buddy Bell	.40	.16
❑ 113 German Jimenez	.25	.10
❑ 114 Ken Dayley	.25	.10
❑ 115 Andres Galarraga	.40	.16
❑ 116 Mike Scioscia	.40	.16
❑ 117 Gary Pettis	.25	.10
❑ 118 Ernie Whitt	.25	.10
❑ 119 Bob Boone	.40	.16
❑ 120 Ryne Sandberg	1.50	.60
❑ 121 Bruce Benedict	.25	.10
❑ 122 Hubie Brooks	.25	.10
❑ 123 Mike Moore	.25	.10
❑ 124 Wallace Johnson	.25	.10
❑ 125 Bob Horner	.40	.16
❑ 126 Chili Davis	.40	.16
❑ 127 Manny Trillo	.25	.10
❑ 128 Chet Lemon	.40	.16
❑ 129 John Cerutti	.25	.10
❑ 130 Orel Hershiser	.40	.16
❑ 131 Terry Pendleton	.40	.16
❑ 132 Jeff Blauser	.25	.10
❑ 133 Mike Fitzgerald	.25	.10
❑ 134 Henry Cotto	.25	.10
❑ 135 Gerald Young	.25	.10
❑ 136 Luis Salazar	.25	.10
❑ 137 Alejandro Pena	.25	.10
❑ 138 Jack Howell	.25	.10
❑ 139 Tony Fernandez	.25	.10
❑ 140 Mark Grace	1.00	.40
❑ 141 Ken Caminiti	.40	.16
❑ 142 Mike Jackson	.25	.10
❑ 143 Larry McWilliams	.25	.10
❑ 144 Andres Thomas	.25	.10
❑ 145 Nolan Ryan 3X	4.00	1.60
❑ 146 Mike Davis	.25	.10
❑ 147 DeWayne Buice	.25	.10
❑ 148 Jody Davis	.25	.10
❑ 149 Jesse Barfield	.40	.16
❑ 150 Matt Nokes	.25	.10
❑ 151 Jerry Reuss	.25	.10
❑ 152 Rick Cerone	.25	.10
❑ 153 Storm Davis	.25	.10
❑ 154 Marvell Wynne	.25	.10
❑ 155 Will Clark	1.00	.40
❑ 156 Luis Aguayo	.25	.10
❑ 157 Willie Upshaw	.25	.10
❑ 158 Randy Bush	.25	.10
❑ 159 Ron Darling	.40	.16
❑ 160 Kal Daniels	.25	.10
❑ 161 Spike Owen	.25	.10
❑ 162 Luis Polonia	.25	.10
❑ 163 Kevin Mitchell UER	.40	.16
('88/total HR's 18/52, should be 19/53)		
❑ 164 Dave Gallagher	.25	.10
❑ 165 Benito Santiago	.40	.16
❑ 166 Greg Gagne	.25	.10
❑ 167 Ken Phelps	.25	.10
❑ 168 Sid Fernandez	.25	.10
❑ 169 Bo Diaz	.25	.10
❑ 170 Cory Snyder	.25	.10
❑ 171 Eric Show	.25	.10
❑ 172 Robby Thompson	.25	.10
❑ 173 Marty Barrett	.25	.10
❑ 174 Dave Henderson	.25	.10
❑ 175 Ozzie Guillen	.25	.10
❑ 176 Barry Lyons	.25	.10
❑ 177 Kelvin Torve	.25	.10
❑ 178 Don Slaught	.25	.10
❑ 179 Steve Lombardozzi	.25	.10
❑ 180 Chris Sabo RC	1.00	.40
❑ 181 Jose Uribe	.25	.10
❑ 182 Shane Mack	.25	.10
❑ 183 Ron Karkovice	.25	.10
❑ 184 Todd Benzinger	.25	.10
❑ 185 Dave Stewart	.40	.16
❑ 186 Julio Franco	.40	.16
❑ 187 Ron Robinson	.25	.10
❑ 188 Wally Backman	.25	.10
❑ 189 Randy Velarde	.25	.10
❑ 190 Joe Carter	.40	.16
❑ 191 Bob Welch	.40	.16
❑ 192 Kelly Paris	.25	.10
❑ 193 Chris Brown	.25	.10
❑ 194 Rick Reuschel	.40	.16
❑ 195 Roger Clemens	2.00	.80
❑ 196 Dave Concepcion	.40	.16
❑ 197 Al Newman	.25	.10
❑ 198 Brook Jacoby	.25	.10
❑ 199 Mookie Wilson	.40	.16
❑ 200 Don Mattingly	2.50	1.00
❑ 201 Dick Schofield	.25	.10
❑ 202 Mark Gubicza	.25	.10
❑ 203 Gary Gaetti	.40	.16
❑ 204 Dan Pasqua	.25	.10
❑ 205 Andre Dawson	.40	.16
❑ 206 Chris Speier	.25	.10
❑ 207 Kent Tekulve	.25	.10
❑ 208 Rod Scurry	.25	.10
❑ 209 Scott Bailes	.25	.10
❑ 210 R.Henderson UER	1.00	.40
Throws Right		
❑ 211 Harold Baines	.40	.16
❑ 212 Tony Armas	.40	.16
❑ 213 Kent Hrbek	.40	.16
❑ 214 Darrin Jackson	.25	.10
❑ 215 George Brett	2.50	1.00

❑ 216	Rafael Santana	.25	.10
❑ 217	Andy Allanson	.25	.10
❑ 218	Brett Butler	.40	.16
❑ 219	Steve Jeltz	.25	.10
❑ 220	Jay Buhner	.40	.16
❑ 221	Bo Jackson	1.00	.40
❑ 222	Angel Salazar	.25	.10
❑ 223	Kirk McCaskill	.25	.10
❑ 224	Steve Lyons	.25	.10
❑ 225	Bert Blyleven	.40	.16
❑ 226	Scott Bradley	.25	.10
❑ 227	Bob Melvin	.25	.10
❑ 228	Ron Kittle	.25	.10
❑ 229	Phil Bradley	.25	.10
❑ 230	Tommy John	.40	.16
❑ 231	Greg Walker	.25	.10
❑ 232	Juan Berenguer	.25	.10
❑ 233	Pat Tabler	.25	.10
❑ 234	Terry Clark	.25	.10
❑ 235	Rafael Palmeiro	1.00	.40
❑ 236	Paul Zuvella	.25	.10
❑ 237	Willie Randolph	.40	.16
❑ 238	Bruce Fields	.25	.10
❑ 239	Mike Aldrete	.25	.10
❑ 240	Lance Parrish	.40	.16
❑ 241	Greg Maddux	2.50	1.00
❑ 242	John Moses	.25	.10
❑ 243	Melido Perez	.25	.10
❑ 244	Willie Wilson	.40	.16
❑ 245	Mark McLemore	.25	.10
❑ 246	Von Hayes	.25	.10
❑ 247	Matt Williams	1.00	.40
❑ 248	John Candelaria UER Listed as Yankee for part of '87, should be Mets	.25	.10
❑ 249	Harold Reynolds	.40	.16
❑ 250	Greg Swindell	.25	.10
❑ 251	Juan Agosto	.25	.10
❑ 252	Mike Felder	.25	.10
❑ 253	Vince Coleman	.25	.10
❑ 254	Larry Sheets	.25	.10
❑ 255	George Bell	.40	.16
❑ 256	Terry Steinbach	.40	.16
❑ 257	Jack Armstrong RC	.50	.20
❑ 258	Dickie Thon	.25	.10
❑ 259	Ray Knight	.40	.16
❑ 260	Darryl Strawberry	.40	.16
❑ 261	Doug Sisk	.25	.10
❑ 262	Alex Trevino	.25	.10
❑ 263	Jeffrey Leonard	.25	.10
❑ 264	Tom Henke	.25	.10
❑ 265	Ozzie Smith	1.50	.60
❑ 266	Dave Bergman	.25	.10
❑ 267	Tony Phillips	.25	.10
❑ 268	Mark Davis	.25	.10
❑ 269	Kevin Elster	.25	.10
❑ 270	Barry Larkin	.60	.24
❑ 271	Manny Lee	.25	.10
❑ 272	Tom Brunansky	.25	.10
❑ 273	Craig Biggio RC	3.00	1.20
❑ 274	Jim Gantner	.25	.10
❑ 275	Eddie Murray	1.00	.40
❑ 276	Jeff Reed	.25	.10
❑ 277	Tim Teufel	.25	.10
❑ 278	Rick Honeycutt	.25	.10
❑ 279	Guillermo Hernandez	.25	.10
❑ 280	John Kruk	.40	.16
❑ 281	Luis Alicea RC	.50	.20
❑ 282	Jim Clancy	.25	.10
❑ 283	Billy Ripken	.25	.10
❑ 284	Craig Reynolds	.25	.10
❑ 285	Robin Yount	1.50	.60
❑ 286	Jimmy Jones	.25	.10
❑ 287	Ron Oester	.25	.10
❑ 288	Terry Leach	.25	.10
❑ 289	Dennis Eckersley	.60	.24
❑ 290	Alan Trammell	.40	.16
❑ 291	Jimmy Key	.40	.16
❑ 292	Chris Bosio	.25	.10
❑ 293	Jose DeLeon	.25	.10
❑ 294	Jim Traber	.25	.10
❑ 295	Mike Scott	.40	.16
❑ 296	Roger McDowell	.25	.10
❑ 297	Garry Templeton	.40	.16
❑ 298	Doyle Alexander	.25	.10
❑ 299	Nick Esasky	.25	.10
❑ 300	Mark McGwire UER (Doubles total 52, should be 51)	5.00	2.00
❑ 301	Darryl Hamilton RC	.50	.20
❑ 302	Dave Smith	.25	.10
❑ 303	Rick Sutcliffe	.40	.16
❑ 304	Dave Stapleton	.25	.10
❑ 305	Alan Ashby	.25	.10
❑ 306	Pedro Guerrero	.40	.16
❑ 307	Ron Guidry	.40	.16
❑ 308	Steve Farr	.25	.10
❑ 309	Curt Ford	.25	.10
❑ 310	Claudell Washington	.25	.10
❑ 311	Tom Prince	.25	.10
❑ 312	Chad Kreuter RC	.50	.20
❑ 313	Ken Oberkfell	.25	.10
❑ 314	Jerry Browne	.25	.10
❑ 315	R.J. Reynolds	.25	.10
❑ 316	Scott Bankhead	.25	.10
❑ 317	Milt Thompson	.25	.10
❑ 318	Mario Diaz	.25	.10
❑ 319	Bruce Ruffin	.25	.10
❑ 320	Dave Valle	.25	.10
❑ 321A	Gary Varsho ERR (Back photo actually Mike Bielecki bunting)	2.00	.80
❑ 321B	Gary Varsho COR (In road uniform)	.25	.10
❑ 322	Paul Mirabella	.25	.10
❑ 323	Chuck Jackson	.25	.10
❑ 324	Drew Hall	.25	.10
❑ 325	Don August	.25	.10
❑ 326	Israel Sanchez	.25	.10
❑ 327	Denny Walling	.25	.10
❑ 328	Joel Skinner	.25	.10
❑ 329	Danny Tartabull	.25	.10
❑ 330	Tony Pena	.25	.10
❑ 331	Jim Sundberg	.40	.16
❑ 332	Jeff D. Robinson	.25	.10
❑ 333	Oddibe McDowell	.25	.10
❑ 334	Jose Lind	.25	.10
❑ 335	Paul Kilgus	.25	.10
❑ 336	Juan Samuel	.25	.10
❑ 337	Mike Campbell	.25	.10
❑ 338	Mike Maddux	.25	.10
❑ 339	Darnell Coles	.25	.10
❑ 340	Bob Dernier	.25	.10
❑ 341	Rafael Ramirez	.25	.10
❑ 342	Scott Sanderson	.25	.10
❑ 343	B.J. Surhoff	.40	.16
❑ 344	Billy Hatcher	.25	.10
❑ 345	Pat Perry	.25	.10
❑ 346	Jack Clark	.40	.16
❑ 347	Gary Thurman	.25	.10
❑ 348	Tim Jones	.25	.10
❑ 349	Dave Winfield	.40	.16
❑ 350	Frank White	.40	.16
❑ 351	Dave Collins	.25	.10
❑ 352	Jack Morris	.40	.16
❑ 353	Eric Plunk	.25	.10
❑ 354	Leon Durham	.25	.10
❑ 355	Ivan DeJesus	.25	.10
❑ 356	Brian Holman RC	.25	.10
❑ 357A	Dale Murphy ERR (Front has reverse negative)	30.00	12.00
❑ 357B	Dale Murphy COR	.60	.24
❑ 358	Mark Portugal	.25	.10
❑ 359	Andy McGaffigan	.25	.10
❑ 360	Tom Glavine	1.00	.40
❑ 361	Keith Moreland	.25	.10
❑ 362	Todd Stottlemyre	.25	.10
❑ 363	Dave Leiper	.25	.10
❑ 364	Cecil Fielder	.40	.16
❑ 365	Carmelo Martinez	.25	.10
❑ 366	Dwight Evans	.40	.16
❑ 367	Kevin McReynolds	.25	.10
❑ 368	Rich Gedman	.25	.10
❑ 369	Len Dykstra	.40	.16
❑ 370	Jody Reed	.25	.10
❑ 371	Jose Canseco UER (Strikeout total 391, should be 491)	1.00	.40
❑ 372	Rob Murphy	.25	.10
❑ 373	Mike Henneman	.25	.10
❑ 374	Walt Weiss	.25	.10
❑ 375	Rob Dibble RC	1.50	.60
❑ 376	Kirby Puckett (Mark McGwire in background)	1.00	.40
❑ 377	Dennis Martinez	.40	.16
❑ 378	Ron Gant	.40	.16
❑ 379	Brian Harper	.25	.10
❑ 380	Nelson Santovenia	.25	.10
❑ 381	Lloyd Moseby	.25	.10
❑ 382	Lance McCullers	.25	.10
❑ 383	Dave Stieb	.40	.16
❑ 384	Tony Gwynn	1.25	.50
❑ 385	Mike Flanagan	.25	.10
❑ 386	Bob Ojeda	.25	.10
❑ 387	Bruce Hurst	.25	.10
❑ 388	Dave Magadan	.25	.10
❑ 389	Wade Boggs	.60	.24
❑ 390	Gary Carter	.40	.16
❑ 391	Frank Tanana	.40	.16
❑ 392	Curt Young	.25	.10
❑ 393	Jeff Treadway	.25	.10
❑ 394	Darrell Evans	.40	.16
❑ 395	Glenn Hubbard	.25	.10
❑ 396	Chuck Cary	.25	.10
❑ 397	Frank Viola	.40	.16
❑ 398	Jeff Parrett	.25	.10
❑ 399	Terry Blocker	.25	.10
❑ 400	Dan Gladden	.25	.10
❑ 401	Louie Meadows	.25	.10
❑ 402	Tim Raines	.40	.16
❑ 403	Joey Meyer	.25	.10
❑ 404	Larry Andersen	.25	.10
❑ 405	Rex Hudler	.25	.10
❑ 406	Mike Schmidt	2.00	.80
❑ 407	John Franco	.40	.16
❑ 408	Brady Anderson RC	1.00	.40
❑ 409	Don Carman	.25	.10
❑ 410	Eric Davis	.40	.16
❑ 411	Bob Stanley	.25	.10
❑ 412	Pete Smith	.25	.10
❑ 413	Jim Rice	.40	.16
❑ 414	Bruce Sutter	.40	.16
❑ 415	Oil Can Boyd	.25	.10
❑ 416	Ruben Sierra	.25	.10
❑ 417	Mike LaValliere	.25	.10
❑ 418	Steve Buechele	.25	.10
❑ 419	Gary Redus	.25	.10
❑ 420	Scott Fletcher	.25	.10
❑ 421	Dale Sveum	.25	.10
❑ 422	Bob Knepper	.25	.10
❑ 423	Luis Rivera	.25	.10
❑ 424	Ted Higuera	.25	.10
❑ 425	Kevin Bass	.25	.10
❑ 426	Ken Gerhart	.25	.10
❑ 427	Shane Rawley	.25	.10
❑ 428	Paul O'Neill	.60	.24
❑ 429	Joe Orsulak	.25	.10
❑ 430	Jackie Gutierrez	.25	.10
❑ 431	Gerald Perry	.25	.10
❑ 432	Mike Greenwell	.25	.10
❑ 433	Jerry Royster	.25	.10
❑ 434	Ellis Burks	.40	.16
❑ 435	Ed Olwine	.25	.10
❑ 436	Dave Rucker	.25	.10
❑ 437	Charlie Hough	.40	.16
❑ 438	Bob Walk	.25	.10
❑ 439	Bob Brower	.25	.10
❑ 440	Barry Bonds	5.00	2.00
❑ 441	Tom Foley	.25	.10
❑ 442	Rob Deer	.25	.10
❑ 443	Glenn Davis	.25	.10
❑ 444	Dave Martinez	.25	.10
❑ 445	Bill Wegman	.25	.10
❑ 446	Lloyd McClendon	.25	.10
❑ 447	Dave Schmidt	.25	.10
❑ 448	Darren Daulton	.40	.16
❑ 449	Frank Williams	.25	.10
❑ 450	Don Aase	.25	.10
❑ 451	Lou Whitaker	.40	.16
❑ 452	Rich Gossage	.40	.16
❑ 453	Ed Whitson	.25	.10
❑ 454	Jim Walewander	.25	.10
❑ 455	Damon Berryhill	.25	.10
❑ 456	Tim Burke	.25	.10
❑ 457	Barry Jones	.25	.10

458	Joel Youngblood	.25	.10
459	Floyd Youmans	.25	.10
460	Mark Salas	.25	.10
461	Jeff Russell	.25	.10
462	Darrell Miller	.25	.10
463	Jeff Kunkel	.25	.10
464	Sherman Corbett	.25	.10
465	Curtis Wilkerson	.25	.10
466	Bud Black	.25	.10
467	Cal Ripken	3.00	1.20
468	John Farrell	.25	.10
469	Terry Kennedy	.25	.10
470	Tom Candiotti	.25	.10
471	Roberto Alomar	1.00	.40
472	Jeff M. Robinson	.25	.10
473	Vance Law	.25	.10
474	Randy Ready UER (Strikeout total 136, should be 115)	.25	.10
475	Walt Terrell	.25	.10
476	Kelly Downs	.25	.10
477	Johnny Paredes	.25	.10
478	Shawn Hillegas	.25	.10
479	Bob Brenly	.25	.10
480	Otis Nixon	.25	.10
481	Johnny Ray	.25	.10
482	Geno Petralli	.25	.10
483	Stu Cliburn	.25	.10
484	Pete Incaviglia	.25	.10
485	Brian Downing	.40	.16
486	Jeff Stone	.25	.10
487	Carmen Castillo	.25	.10
488	Tom Niedenfuer	.25	.10
489	Jay Bell	.40	.16
490	Rick Schu	.25	.10
491	Jeff Pico	.25	.10
492	Mark Parent	.25	.10
493	Eric King	.25	.10
494	Al Nipper	.25	.10
495	Andy Hawkins	.25	.10
496	Daryl Boston	.25	.10
497	Ernie Riles	.25	.10
498	Pascual Perez	.25	.10
499	Bill Long UER (Games started total 70, should be 44)	.25	.10
500	Kirt Manwaring	.25	.10
501	Chuck Crim	.25	.10
502	Candy Maldonado	.25	.10
503	Dennis Lamp	.25	.10
504	Glenn Braggs	.25	.10
505	Joe Price	.25	.10
506	Ken Williams	.25	.10
507	Bill Pecota	.25	.10
508	Rey Quinones	.25	.10
509	Jeff Bittiger	.25	.10
510	Kevin Seitzer	.25	.10
511	Steve Bedrosian	.25	.10
512	Todd Worrell	.25	.10
513	Chris James	.25	.10
514	Jose Oquendo	.25	.10
515	David Palmer	.25	.10
516	John Smiley	.25	.10
517	Dave Clark	.25	.10
518	Mike Dunne	.25	.10
519	Ron Washington	.25	.10
520	Bob Kipper	.25	.10
521	Lee Smith	.40	.16
522	Juan Castillo	.25	.10
523	Don Robinson	.25	.10
524	Kevin Romine	.25	.10
525	Paul Molitor	.60	.24
526	Mark Langston	.25	.10
527	Donnie Hill	.25	.10
528	Larry Owen	.25	.10
529	Jerry Reed	.25	.10
530	Jack McDowell	.40	.16
531	Greg Mathews	.25	.10
532	John Russell	.25	.10
533	Dan Quisenberry	.25	.10
534	Greg Gross	.25	.10
535	Danny Cox	.25	.10
536	Terry Francona	.40	.16
537	Andy Van Slyke	.40	.16
538	Mel Hall	.25	.10
539	Jim Gott	.25	.10
540	Doug Jones	.25	.10
541	Craig Lefferts	.25	.10
542	Mike Boddicker	.25	.10
543	Greg Brock	.25	.10
544	Atlee Hammaker	.25	.10
545	Tom Bolton	.25	.10
546	Mike Macfarlane RC	.50	.20
547	Rich Renteria	.25	.10
548	John Davis	.25	.10
549	Floyd Bannister	.25	.10
550	Mickey Brantley	.25	.10
551	Duane Ward	.25	.10
552	Dan Petry	.25	.10
553	Mickey Tettleton UER (Walks total 175, should be 136)	.25	.10
554	Rick Leach	.25	.10
555	Mike Witt	.25	.10
556	Sid Bream	.25	.10
557	Bobby Witt	.25	.10
558	Tommy Herr	.25	.10
559	Randy Milligan	.25	.10
560	Jose Cecena	.25	.10
561	Mackey Sasser	.25	.10
562	Carney Lansford	.40	.16
563	Rick Aguilera	.25	.10
564	Ron Hassey	.25	.10
565	Dwight Gooden	.40	.16
566	Paul Assenmacher	.25	.10
567	Neil Allen	.25	.10
568	Jim Morrison	.25	.10
569	Mike Pagliarulo	.25	.10
570	Ted Simmons	.40	.16
571	Mark Thurmond	.25	.10
572	Fred McGriff	.60	.24
573	Wally Joyner	.40	.16
574	Jose Bautista RC	.25	.10
575	Kelly Gruber	.25	.10
576	Cecilio Guante	.25	.10
577	Mark Davidson	.25	.10
578	Bobby Bonilla UER (Total steals 2 in '87, should be 3)	.40	.16
579	Mike Stanley	.25	.10
580	Gene Larkin	.25	.10
581	Stan Javier	.25	.10
582	Howard Johnson	.40	.16
583A	Mike Gallego ERR (Front reversed negative)	1.00	.40
583B	Mike Gallego COR	1.00	.40
584	David Cone	.40	.16
585	Doug Jennings	.25	.10
586	Charles Hudson	.25	.10
587	Dion James	.25	.10
588	Al Leiter	1.00	.40
589	Charlie Puleo	.25	.10
590	Roberto Kelly	.25	.10
591	Thad Bosley	.25	.10
592	Pete Stanicek	.25	.10
593	Pat Borders RC	.50	.20
594	Bryan Harvey RC	.50	.20
595	Jeff Ballard	.25	.10
596	Jeff Reardon	.40	.16
597	Doug Drabek	.25	.10
598	Edwin Correa	.25	.10
599	Keith Atherton	.25	.10
600	Dave LaPoint	.25	.10
601	Don Baylor	.40	.16
602	Tom Pagnozzi	.25	.10
603	Tim Flannery	.25	.10
604	Gene Walter	.25	.10
605	Dave Parker	.40	.16
606	Mike Diaz	.25	.10
607	Chris Gwynn	.25	.10
608	Odell Jones	.25	.10
609	Carlton Fisk	.60	.24
610	Jay Howell	.25	.10
611	Tim Crews	.25	.10
612	Keith Hernandez	.40	.16
613	Willie Fraser	.25	.10
614	Jim Eppard	.25	.10
615	Jeff Hamilton	.25	.10
616	Kurt Stillwell	.25	.10
617	Tom Browning	.25	.10
618	Jeff Montgomery	.25	.10
619	Jose Rijo	.40	.16
620	Jamie Quirk	.25	.10
621	Willie McGee	.40	.16
622	Mark Grant UER (Glove on wrong hand)	.25	.10
623	Bill Swift	.25	.10
624	Orlando Mercado	.25	.10
625	John Costello	.25	.10
626	Jose Gonzalez	.25	.10
627A	Bill Schroeder ERR (Back photo actually Ronn Reynolds buckling shin guards)	.60	.24
627B	Bill Schroeder COR	.60	.24
628A	Fred Manrique ERR (Back photo actually Ozzie Guillen throwing)	.60	.24
628B	Fred Manrique COR (Swinging bat on back)	.25	.10
629	Ricky Horton	.25	.10
630	Dan Plesac	.25	.10
631	Alfredo Griffin	.25	.10
632	Chuck Finley	.40	.16
633	Kirk Gibson	.40	.16
634	Randy Myers	.40	.16
635	Greg Minton	.25	.10
636A	Herm Winningham ERR (W1nningham on back)	1.00	.40
636B	H.Winningham COR	.25	.10
637	Charlie Leibrandt	.25	.10
638	Tim Birtsas	.25	.10
639	Bill Buckner	.40	.16
640	Danny Jackson	.25	.10
641	Greg Booker	.25	.10
642	Jim Presley	.25	.10
643	Gene Nelson	.25	.10
644	Rod Booker	.25	.10
645	Dennis Rasmussen	.25	.10
646	Juan Nieves	.25	.10
647	Bobby Thigpen	.25	.10
648	Tim Belcher	.25	.10
649	Mike Young	.25	.10
650	Ivan Calderon	.25	.10
651	Oswald Peraza	.25	.10
652A	Pat Sheridan ERR (No position on front)	15.00	6.00
652B	Pat Sheridan COR	.25	.10
653	Mike Morgan	.25	.10
654	Mike Heath	.25	.10
655	Jay Tibbs	.25	.10
656	Fernando Valenzuela	.40	.16
657	Lee Mazzilli	.40	.16
658	Frank Viola AL CY	.25	.10
659A	J.Canseco AL MVP Eagle logo in black	.60	.24
659B	J.Canseco AL MVP Eagle logo in blue	.60	.24
660	Walt Weiss AL ROY	.25	.10
661	Orel Hershiser NL CY	.25	.10
662	Kirk Gibson NL MVP	.40	.16
663	Chris Sabo NL ROY	.40	.16
664	Dennis Eckersley ALCS MVP	.40	.16
665	Orel Hershiser NLCS MVP	.40	.16
666	Kirk Gibson WS	1.00	.40
667	O.Hershiser WS MVP	.25	.10
668	Wally Joyner TC	.25	.10
669	Nolan Ryan TC	1.25	.50
670	Jose Canseco TC	.60	.24
671	Fred McGriff TC	.40	.16
672	Dale Murphy TC	.40	.16
673	Paul Molitor TC	.40	.16
674	Ozzie Smith TC	1.00	.40
675	Ryne Sandberg TC	1.00	.40
676	Kirk Gibson TC	.25	.10
677	Andres Galarraga TC	.25	.10
678	Will Clark TC	.40	.16
679	Cory Snyder TC	.25	.10
680	Alvin Davis TC	.25	.10
681	Darryl Strawberry TC	.25	.10
682	Cal Ripken TC	1.00	.40
683	Tony Gwynn TC	.60	.24
684	Mike Schmidt TC	1.00	.40
685	A.Van Slyke TC UER	.25	.10

96 Junior Ortiz
❑ 686 Ruben Sierra TC .25 .10
❑ 687 Wade Boggs TC .40 .16
❑ 688 Eric Davis TC .25 .10
❑ 689 George Brett TC 1.00 .40
❑ 690 Alan Trammell TC .25 .10
❑ 691 Frank Viola TC .25 .10
❑ 692 Harold Baines TC .25 .10
❑ 693 Don Mattingly TC 1.00 .40
❑ 694 Checklist 1-100 .25 .10
❑ 695 Checklist 101-200 .25 .10
❑ 696 Checklist 201-300 .25 .10
❑ 697 Checklist 301-400 .25 .10
❑ 698 CL 401-500 UER .25 .10
467 Cal Ripkin Jr.
❑ 699 CL 501-600 UER .25 .10
543 Greg Booker
❑ 700 Checklist 601-700 .25 .10
❑ 701 Checklist 701-800 .25 .10
❑ 702 Jesse Barfield .40 .16
❑ 703 Walt Terrell .25 .10
❑ 704 Dickie Thon .25 .10
❑ 705 Al Leiter 1.00 .40
❑ 706 Dave LaPoint .25 .10
❑ 707 Charlie Hayes RC .50 .20
❑ 708 Andy Hawkins .25 .10
❑ 709 Mickey Hatcher .25 .10
❑ 710 Lance McCullers .25 .10
❑ 711 Ron Kittle .25 .10
❑ 712 Bert Blyleven .40 .16
❑ 713 Rick Dempsey .25 .10
❑ 714 Ken Williams .25 .10
❑ 715 Steve Rosenberg .25 .10
❑ 716 Joe Skalski .25 .10
❑ 717 Spike Owen .25 .10
❑ 718 Todd Burns .25 .10
❑ 719 Kevin Gross .25 .10
❑ 720 Tommy Herr .25 .10
❑ 721 Rob Ducey .25 .10
❑ 722 Gary Green .25 .10
❑ 723 Gregg Olson RC .50 .20
❑ 724 Greg W. Harris RC .25 .10
❑ 725 Craig Worthington .25 .10
❑ 726 Tom Howard RC .25 .10
❑ 727 Dale Mohorcic .25 .10
❑ 728 Rich Yett .25 .10
❑ 729 Mel Hall .25 .10
❑ 730 Floyd Youmans .25 .10
❑ 731 Lonnie Smith .25 .10
❑ 732 Wally Backman .25 .10
❑ 733 Trevor Wilson RC .25 .10
❑ 734 Jose Alvarez RC .25 .10
❑ 735 Bob Milacki .25 .10
❑ 736 Tom Gordon RC 1.00 .40
❑ 737 Wally Whitehurst RC .25 .10
❑ 738 Mike Aldrete .25 .10
❑ 739 Keith Miller .25 .10
❑ 740 Randy Milligan .25 .10
❑ 741 Jeff Parrett .25 .10
❑ 742 Steve Finley RC 1.50 .60
❑ 743 Junior Felix RC .25 .10
❑ 744 Pete Harnisch RC .50 .20
❑ 745 Bill Spiers RC .50 .20
❑ 746 Hensley Meulens RC .25 .10
❑ 747 Juan Bell RC .25 .10
❑ 748 Steve Sax .25 .10
❑ 749 Phil Bradley .25 .10
❑ 750 Rey Quinones .25 .10
❑ 751 Tommy Gregg .25 .10
❑ 752 Kevin Brown 1.00 .40
❑ 753 Derek Lilliquist RC .25 .10
❑ 754 Todd Zeile RC 1.00 .40
❑ 755 Jim Abbott RC 1.50 .60
Triple exposure
❑ 756 Ozzie Canseco .25 .10
❑ 757 Nick Esasky .25 .10
❑ 758 Mike Moore .25 .10
❑ 759 Rob Murphy .25 .10
❑ 760 Rick Mahler .25 .10
❑ 761 Fred Lynn .40 .16
❑ 762 Kevin Blankenship .25 .10
❑ 763 Eddie Murray 1.00 .40
❑ 764 Steve Searcy .25 .10
❑ 765 Jerome Walton RC .50 .20
❑ 766 Erik Hanson RC .50 .20
❑ 767 Bob Boone .40 .16
❑ 768 Edgar Martinez 1.00 .40
❑ 769 Jose DeJesus .25 .10
❑ 770 Greg Briley .25 .10
❑ 771 Steve Peters .25 .10
❑ 772 Rafael Palmeiro 1.00 .40
❑ 773 Jack Clark .40 .16
❑ 774 Nolan Ryan 4.00 1.60
(Throwing football)
❑ 775 Lance Parrish .40 .16
❑ 776 Joe Girardi RC 1.00 .40
❑ 777 Willie Randolph .40 .16
❑ 778 Mitch Williams .25 .10
❑ 779 Dennis Cook RC .50 .20
❑ 780 Dwight Smith RC .50 .20
❑ 781 Lenny Harris RC .50 .20
❑ 782 Torey Lovullo RC .25 .10
❑ 783 Norm Charlton RC .50 .20
❑ 784 Chris Brown .25 .10
❑ 785 Todd Benzinger .25 .10
❑ 786 Shane Rawley .25 .10
❑ 787 Omar Vizquel RC 2.00 .80
❑ 788 LaVel Freeman .25 .10
❑ 789 Jeffrey Leonard .25 .10
❑ 790 Eddie Williams .25 .10
❑ 791 Jamie Moyer .40 .16
❑ 792 Bruce Hurst UER .25 .10
(Workd Series)
❑ 793 Julio Franco .40 .16
❑ 794 Claudell Washington .25 .10
❑ 795 Jody Davis .25 .10
❑ 796 Oddibe McDowell .25 .10
❑ 797 Paul Kilgus .25 .10
❑ 798 Tracy Jones .25 .10
❑ 799 Steve Wilson .25 .10
❑ 800 Pete O'Brien .25 .10

1990 Upper Deck

	Nm-Mt	Ex-Mt
COMPLETE SET (800)	25.00	7.50
COMP.FACT.SET (800)	25.00	7.50
COMPLETE LO SET (700)	25.00	7.50
COMPLETE HI SET (100)	5.00	1.50
COMP.HI FACT.SET (100)	4.00	1.20

❑ 1 Star Rookie Checklist .10 .03
❑ 2 Randy Nosek .10 .03
❑ 3 Tom Drees UER .10 .03
(11th line, hulred, should be hurled
❑ 4 Curt Young .10 .03
❑ 5 Devon White TC .10 .03
❑ 6 Luis Salazar .10 .03
❑ 7 Von Hayes TC .10 .03
❑ 8 Jose Bautista .10 .03
❑ 9 Marquis Grissom RC .50 .15
❑ 10 Orel Hershiser TC .10 .03
❑ 11 Rick Aguilera .20 .06
❑ 12 Benito Santiago TC .10 .03
❑ 13 Deion Sanders .50 .15
❑ 14 Marvell Wynne .10 .03
❑ 15 Dave West .10 .03
❑ 16 Bobby Bonilla TC .10 .03
❑ 17 Sammy Sosa RC 5.00 1.50
❑ 18 Steve Sax TC .10 .03
❑ 19 Jack Howell .10 .03
❑ 20 Mike Schmidt Special 1.00 .30
UER (Suprising, should be surprising)
❑ 21 Robin Ventura UER .50 .15
(Samta Maria)
❑ 22 Brian Meyer .10 .03
❑ 23 Blaine Beatty .10 .03
❑ 24 Ken Griffey Jr. TC .60 .18
❑ 25 Greg Vaughn UER .10 .03
(Association misspelled as assiocation)
❑ 26 Xavier Hernandez RC .10 .03
❑ 27 Jason Grimsley RC .10 .03
❑ 28 Eric Anthony RC UER .10 .03
(Ashville, should be Asheville)
❑ 29 Tim Raines TC UER .10 .03
(Wallach listed before Walker)
❑ 30 David Wells .20 .06
❑ 31 Hal Morris .10 .03
❑ 32 Bo Jackson TC .20 .06
❑ 33 Kelly Mann .10 .03
❑ 34 Nolan Ryan Special 1.00 .30
❑ 35 Scott Service UER .10 .03
(Born Cincinatti on 7/27/67, should be Cincinnati 2/27)
❑ 36 Mark McGwire TC .60 .18
❑ 37 Tino Martinez .50 .15
❑ 38 Chili Davis .20 .06
❑ 39 Scott Sanderson .10 .03
❑ 40 Kevin Mitchell TC .10 .03
❑ 41 Lou Whitaker TC .10 .03
❑ 42 Scott Coolbaugh UER .10 .03
(Definately) RC
❑ 43 Jose Cano UER .10 .03
(Born 9/7/62, should be 3/7/62)
❑ 44 Jose Vizcaino RC .25 .07
❑ 45 Bob Hamelin RC .25 .07
❑ 46 Jose Offerman RC UER .25 .07
(Posesses)
❑ 47 Kevin Blankenship .10 .03
❑ 48 Kirby Puckett TC .30 .09
❑ 49 Tommy Greene RC UER .10 .03
(Livest, should be liveliest)
❑ 50 Will Clark Special .20 .06
UER (Perenial, should be perennial)
❑ 51 Rob Nelson .10 .03
❑ 52 C.Hammond RC UER .10 .03
Chatanooga
❑ 53 Joe Carter TC .10 .03
❑ 54A B.McDonald RC ERR 2.00 .60
No Rookie designation on card front
❑ 54B B.McDonald COR RC .25 .07
❑ 55 Andy Benes UER .20 .06
(Whichita)
❑ 56 John Olerud RC .75 .23
❑ 57 Roger Clemens TC .50 .15
❑ 58 Tony Armas .10 .03
❑ 59 George Canale .10 .03
❑ 60A Mickey Tettleton TC 2.00 .60
ERR (683 Jamie Weston)
❑ 60B Mickey Tettleton TC .10 .03
COR (683 Mickey Weston)
❑ 61 Mike Stanton RC .25 .07
❑ 62 Dwight Gooden TC .10 .03
❑ 63 Kent Mercker RC UER .25 .07
(Albuguerque)
❑ 64 Francisco Cabrera .10 .03
❑ 65 Steve Avery UER .10 .03
(Born NJ, should be MI, Merker should be Mercker
❑ 66 Jose Canseco .50 .15
❑ 67 Matt Merullo .10 .03
❑ 68 Vince Coleman TC UER .10 .03
(Guerrero)
❑ 69 Ron Karkovice .10 .03
❑ 70 Kevin Maas RC .25 .07
❑ 71 Dennis Cook UER .10 .03
(Shown with righty glove on card back)
❑ 72 Juan Gonzalez RC UER 2.50 .75
(135 games for Tulsa in '89, should be 133)

❑ 73 Andre Dawson TC .10 .03
❑ 74 Dean Palmer RC UER .25 .07
(Permanent misspelled as perminant)
❑ 75 Bo Jackson Special .20 .06
UER (Monsterous, should be monstrous)
❑ 76 Rob Richie .10 .03
❑ 77 Bobby Rose UER .10 .03
(Pickin, should be pick in)
❑ 78 Brian DuBois UER .10 .03
(Commiting)
❑ 79 Ozzie Guillen TC .10 .03
❑ 80 Gene Nelson .10 .03
❑ 81 Bob McClure .10 .03
❑ 82 Julio Franco TC .10 .03
❑ 83 Greg Minton .10 .03
❑ 84 John Smoltz TC UER .30 .09
(Oddibe not Odibbe)
❑ 85 Willie Fraser .10 .03
❑ 86 Neal Heaton .10 .03
❑ 87 Kevin Tapani RC UER .25 .07
(24th line has excpet, should be except)
❑ 88 Mike Scott TC .10 .03
❑ 89A Jim Gott ERR 2.00 .60
(Photo actually Rick Reed)
❑ 89B Jim Gott COR .10 .03
❑ 90 Lance Johnson .10 .03
❑ 91 Robin Yount TC UER .50 .15
(Checklist on back has 178 Rob Deer and 176 Mike Felder)
❑ 92 Jeff Parrett .10 .03
❑ 93 Julio Machado UER .10 .03
(Valenzuelan, should be Venezuelan)
❑ 94 Ron Jones .10 .03
❑ 95 George Bell TC .10 .03
❑ 96 Jerry Reuss .10 .03
❑ 97 Brian Fisher .10 .03
❑ 98 Kevin Ritz UER .10 .03
(Amercian)
❑ 99 Barry Larkin TC .20 .06
❑ 100 Checklist 1-100 .10 .03
❑ 101 Gerald Perry .10 .03
❑ 102 Kevin Appier .20 .06
❑ 103 Julio Franco .20 .06
❑ 104 Craig Biggio .30 .09
❑ 105 Bo Jackson UER .50 .15
('89 BA wrong, should be .256)
❑ 106 Junior Felix .10 .03
❑ 107 Mike Harkey .10 .03
❑ 108 Fred McGriff .50 .15
❑ 109 Rick Sutcliffe .20 .06
❑ 110 Pete O'Brien .10 .03
❑ 111 Kelly Gruber .10 .03
❑ 112 Dwight Evans .20 .06
❑ 113 Pat Borders .10 .03
❑ 114 Dwight Gooden .20 .06
❑ 115 Kevin Batiste .10 .03
❑ 116 Eric Davis .20 .06
❑ 117 Kevin Mitchell UER .10 .03
(Career HR total 99, should be 100)
❑ 118 Ron Oester .10 .03
❑ 119 Brett Butler .20 .06
❑ 120 Danny Jackson .10 .03
❑ 121 Tommy Gregg .10 .03
❑ 122 Ken Caminiti .20 .06
❑ 123 Kevin Brown .20 .06
❑ 124 George Brett UER 1.25 .35
(133 runs, should be 1300)
❑ 125 Mike Scott .10 .03
❑ 126 Cory Snyder .10 .03
❑ 127 George Bell .10 .03
❑ 128 Mark Grace .30 .09
❑ 129 Devon White .20 .06
❑ 130 Tony Fernandez .10 .03
❑ 131 Don Aase .10 .03
❑ 132 Rance Mulliniks .10 .03
❑ 133 Marty Barrett .10 .03
❑ 134 Nelson Liriano .10 .03
❑ 135 Mark Carreon .10 .03
❑ 136 Candy Maldonado .10 .03
❑ 137 Tim Birtsas .10 .03
❑ 138 Tom Brookens .10 .03
❑ 139 John Franco .20 .06
❑ 140 Mike LaCoss .10 .03
❑ 141 Jeff Treadway .10 .03
❑ 142 Pat Tabler .10 .03
❑ 143 Darrell Evans .20 .06
❑ 144 Rafael Ramirez .10 .03
❑ 145 O.McDowell UER .10 .03
Misspelled Odibbe
❑ 146 Brian Downing .10 .03
❑ 147 Curt Wilkerson .10 .03
❑ 148 Ernie Whitt .10 .03
❑ 149 Bill Schroeder .10 .03
❑ 150 Domingo Ramos UER .10 .03
(Says throws right, but shows him throwing lefty)
❑ 151 Rick Honeycutt .10 .03
❑ 152 Don Slaught .10 .03
❑ 153 Mitch Webster .10 .03
❑ 154 Tony Phillips .10 .03
❑ 155 Paul Kilgus .10 .03
❑ 156 Ken Griffey Jr. UER 1.50 .45
(Simultaniously)
❑ 157 Gary Sheffield .50 .15
❑ 158 Wally Backman .10 .03
❑ 159 B.J. Surhoff .20 .06
❑ 160 Louie Meadows .10 .03
❑ 161 Paul O'Neill .30 .09
❑ 162 Jeff McKnight .10 .03
❑ 163 Alvaro Espinoza .10 .03
❑ 164 Scott Scudder .10 .03
❑ 165 Jeff Reed .10 .03
❑ 166 Gregg Jefferies .20 .06
❑ 167 Barry Larkin .30 .09
❑ 168 Gary Carter .20 .06
❑ 169 Robby Thompson .10 .03
❑ 170 Rolando Roomes .10 .03
❑ 171 Mark McGwire UER 1.25 .35
(Total games 427 and hits 479, should be 467 and 427)
❑ 172 Steve Sax .10 .03
❑ 173 Mark Williamson .10 .03
❑ 174 Mitch Williams .10 .03
❑ 175 Brian Holton .10 .03
❑ 176 Rob Deer .10 .03
❑ 177 Tim Raines .20 .06
❑ 178 Mike Felder .10 .03
❑ 179 Harold Reynolds .20 .06
❑ 180 Terry Francona .20 .06
❑ 181 Chris Sabo .10 .03
❑ 182 Darryl Strawberry .20 .06
❑ 183 Willie Randolph .20 .06
❑ 184 Bill Ripken .10 .03
❑ 185 Mackey Sasser .10 .03
❑ 186 Todd Benzinger .10 .03
❑ 187 Kevin Elster UER .10 .03
(16 homers in 1989, should be 10)
❑ 188 Jose Uribe .10 .03
❑ 189 Tom Browning .10 .03
❑ 190 Keith Miller .10 .03
❑ 191 Don Mattingly 1.25 .35
❑ 192 Dave Parker .20 .06
❑ 193 Roberto Kelly UER .10 .03
(96 RBI, should be 62)
❑ 194 Phil Bradley .10 .03
❑ 195 Ron Hassey .10 .03
❑ 196 Gerald Young .10 .03
❑ 197 Hubie Brooks .10 .03
❑ 198 Bill Doran .10 .03
❑ 199 Al Newman .10 .03
❑ 200 Checklist 101-200 .10 .03
❑ 201 Terry Puhl .10 .03
❑ 202 Frank DiPino .10 .03
❑ 203 Jim Clancy .10 .03
❑ 204 Bob Ojeda .10 .03
❑ 205 Alex Trevino .10 .03
❑ 206 Dave Henderson .10 .03
❑ 207 Henry Cotto .10 .03
❑ 208 Rafael Belliard UER .10 .03
(Born 1961, not 1951)
❑ 209 Stan Javier .10 .03
❑ 210 Jerry Reed .10 .03
❑ 211 Doug Dascenzo .10 .03
❑ 212 Andres Thomas .10 .03
❑ 213 Greg Maddux .75 .23
❑ 214 Mike Schooler .10 .03
❑ 215 Lonnie Smith .10 .03
❑ 216 Jose Rijo .10 .03
❑ 217 Greg Gagne .10 .03
❑ 218 Jim Gantner .10 .03
❑ 219 Allan Anderson .10 .03
❑ 220 Rick Mahler .10 .03
❑ 221 Jim Deshaies .10 .03
❑ 222 Keith Hernandez .20 .06
❑ 223 Vince Coleman .10 .03
❑ 224 David Cone .20 .06
❑ 225 Ozzie Smith .75 .23
❑ 226 Matt Nokes .10 .03
❑ 227 Barry Bonds 1.25 .35
❑ 228 Felix Jose .10 .03
❑ 229 Dennis Powell .10 .03
❑ 230 Mike Gallego .10 .03
❑ 231 Shawon Dunston UER .10 .03
('89 stats are Andre Dawson's)
❑ 232 Ron Gant .20 .06
❑ 233 Omar Vizquel .50 .15
❑ 234 Derek Lilliquist .10 .03
❑ 235 Erik Hanson .10 .03
❑ 236 Kirby Puckett UER .50 .15
(824 games, should be 924)
❑ 237 Bill Spiers .10 .03
❑ 238 Dan Gladden .10 .03
❑ 239 Bryan Clutterbuck .10 .03
❑ 240 John Moses .10 .03
❑ 241 Ron Darling .10 .03
❑ 242 Joe Magrane .10 .03
❑ 243 Dave Magadan .10 .03
❑ 244 Pedro Guerrero UER .10 .03
(Misspelled Guererro)
❑ 245 Glenn Davis .10 .03
❑ 246 Terry Steinbach .10 .03
❑ 247 Fred Lynn .10 .03
❑ 248 Gary Redus .10 .03
❑ 249 Ken Williams .10 .03
❑ 250 Sid Bream .10 .03
❑ 251 Bob Welch UER .10 .03
(2587 career strike-outs, should be 1587)
❑ 252 Bill Buckner .10 .03
❑ 253 Carney Lansford .20 .06
❑ 254 Paul Molitor .30 .09
❑ 255 Jose DeJesus .10 .03
❑ 256 Orel Hershiser .20 .06
❑ 257 Tom Brunansky .10 .03
❑ 258 Mike Davis .10 .03
❑ 259 Jeff Ballard .10 .03
❑ 260 Scott Terry .10 .03
❑ 261 Sid Fernandez .10 .03
❑ 262 Mike Marshall .10 .03
❑ 263 Howard Johnson UER .10 .03
(192 SO, should be 592)
❑ 264 Kirk Gibson UER .20 .06
(659 runs, should be 669)
❑ 265 Kevin McReynolds .10 .03
❑ 266 Cal Ripken 1.50 .45
❑ 267 Ozzie Guillen UER .10 .03
(Career triples 27, should be 29)
❑ 268 Jim Traber .10 .03
❑ 269 Bobby Thigpen UER .10 .03
(31 saves in 1989, should be 34)
❑ 270 Joe Orsulak .10 .03
❑ 271 Bob Boone .20 .06
❑ 272 Dave Stewart UER .20 .06
(Totals wrong due to omission of '86 stats)
❑ 273 Tim Wallach .10 .03
❑ 274 Luis Aquino UER .10 .03
(Says throws lefty, but shows him throwing righty)

	No.	Player		
❑	275	Mike Moore	.10	.03
❑	276	Tony Pena	.10	.03
❑	277	Eddie Murray UER (Several typos in career total stats)	.50	.15
❑	278	Milt Thompson	.10	.03
❑	279	Alejandro Pena	.10	.03
❑	280	Ken Dayley	.10	.03
❑	281	Carmelo Castillo	.10	.03
❑	282	Tom Henke	.10	.03
❑	283	Mickey Hatcher	.10	.03
❑	284	Roy Smith	.10	.03
❑	285	Manny Lee	.10	.03
❑	286	Dan Pasqua	.10	.03
❑	287	Larry Sheets	.10	.03
❑	288	Garry Templeton	.10	.03
❑	289	Eddie Williams	.10	.03
❑	290	Brady Anderson UER (Home: Silver Springs, not Siver Springs)	.20	.06
❑	291	Spike Owen	.10	.03
❑	292	Storm Davis	.10	.03
❑	293	Chris Bosio	.10	.03
❑	294	Jim Eisenreich	.10	.03
❑	295	Don August	.10	.03
❑	296	Jeff Hamilton	.10	.03
❑	297	Mickey Tettleton	.10	.03
❑	298	Mike Scioscia	.10	.03
❑	299	Kevin Hickey	.10	.03
❑	300	Checklist 201-300	.10	.03
❑	301	Shawn Abner	.10	.03
❑	302	Kevin Bass	.10	.03
❑	303	Bip Roberts	.10	.03
❑	304	Joe Girardi	.30	.09
❑	305	Danny Darwin	.10	.03
❑	306	Mike Heath	.10	.03
❑	307	Mike Macfarlane	.10	.03
❑	308	Ed Whitson	.10	.03
❑	309	Tracy Jones	.10	.03
❑	310	Scott Fletcher	.10	.03
❑	311	Darnell Coles	.10	.03
❑	312	Mike Brumley	.10	.03
❑	313	Bill Swift	.10	.03
❑	314	Charlie Hough	.20	.06
❑	315	Jim Presley	.10	.03
❑	316	Luis Polonia	.10	.03
❑	317	Mike Morgan	.10	.03
❑	318	Lee Guetterman	.10	.03
❑	319	Jose Oquendo	.10	.03
❑	320	Wayne Tolleson	.10	.03
❑	321	Jody Reed	.10	.03
❑	322	Damon Berryhill	.10	.03
❑	323	Roger Clemens	1.00	.30
❑	324	Ryne Sandberg	.75	.23
❑	325	Benito Santiago UER (Misspelled Santago on card back)	.20	.06
❑	326	Bret Saberhagen UER (1140 hits, should be 1240; 56 CG, should be 52)	.20	.06
❑	327	Lou Whitaker	.20	.06
❑	328	Dave Gallagher	.10	.03
❑	329	Mike Pagliarulo	.10	.03
❑	330	Doyle Alexander	.10	.03
❑	331	Jeffrey Leonard	.10	.03
❑	332	Torey Lovullo	.10	.03
❑	333	Pete Incaviglia	.10	.03
❑	334	Rickey Henderson	.50	.15
❑	335	Rafael Palmeiro	.30	.09
❑	336	Ken Hill	.20	.06
❑	337	Dave Winfield UER (1418 RBI, should be 1438)	.20	.06
❑	338	Alfredo Griffin	.10	.03
❑	339	Andy Hawkins	.10	.03
❑	340	Ted Power	.10	.03
❑	341	Steve Wilson	.10	.03
❑	342	Jack Clark UER (916 BB, should be 1006; 1142 SO, should be 1130)	.20	.06
❑	343	Ellis Burks	.30	.09
❑	344	Tony Gwynn UER (Doubles stats on card back are wrong)	.60	.18
❑	345	Jerome Walton UER (Total At Bats 476, should be 475)	.10	.03
❑	346	Roberto Alomar UER (61 doubles, should be 51)	.30	.09
❑	347	Carlos Martinez UER (Born 8/11/64, should be 8/11/65)	.10	.03
❑	348	Chet Lemon	.10	.03
❑	349	Willie Wilson	.10	.03
❑	350	Greg Walker	.10	.03
❑	351	Tom Bolton	.10	.03
❑	352	German Gonzalez	.10	.03
❑	353	Harold Baines	.20	.06
❑	354	Mike Greenwell	.10	.03
❑	355	Ruben Sierra	.10	.03
❑	356	Andres Galarraga	.20	.06
❑	357	Andre Dawson	.20	.06
❑	358	Jeff Brantley	.10	.03
❑	359	Mike Bielecki	.10	.03
❑	360	Ken Oberkfell	.10	.03
❑	361	Kurt Stillwell	.10	.03
❑	362	Brian Holman	.10	.03
❑	363	Kevin Seitzer UER (Career triples total does not add up)	.10	.03
❑	364	Alvin Davis	.10	.03
❑	365	Tom Gordon	.20	.06
❑	366	Bobby Bonilla UER (Two steals in 1987, should be 3)	.20	.06
❑	367	Carlton Fisk	.30	.09
❑	368	Steve Carter UER (Charlotesville)	.10	.03
❑	369	Joel Skinner	.10	.03
❑	370	John Cangelosi	.10	.03
❑	371	Cecil Espy	.10	.03
❑	372	Gary Wayne	.10	.03
❑	373	Jim Rice	.20	.06
❑	374	Mike Dyer RC	.10	.03
❑	375	Joe Carter	.20	.06
❑	376	Dwight Smith	.10	.03
❑	377	John Wetteland	.50	.15
❑	378	Earnie Riles	.10	.03
❑	379	Otis Nixon	.10	.03
❑	380	Vance Law	.10	.03
❑	381	Dave Bergman	.10	.03
❑	382	Frank White	.20	.06
❑	383	Scott Bradley	.10	.03
❑	384	Israel Sanchez UER (Totals don't include '89 stats)	.10	.03
❑	385	Gary Pettis	.10	.03
❑	386	Donn Pall	.10	.03
❑	387	John Smiley	.10	.03
❑	388	Tom Candiotti	.10	.03
❑	389	Junior Ortiz	.10	.03
❑	390	Steve Lyons	.10	.03
❑	391	Brian Harper	.10	.03
❑	392	Fred Manrique	.10	.03
❑	393	Lee Smith	.20	.06
❑	394	Jeff Kunkel	.10	.03
❑	395	Claudell Washington	.10	.03
❑	396	John Tudor	.10	.03
❑	397	Terry Kennedy UER (Career totals all wrong)	.10	.03
❑	398	Lloyd McClendon	.10	.03
❑	399	Craig Lefferts	.10	.03
❑	400	Checklist 301-400	.10	.03
❑	401	Keith Moreland	.10	.03
❑	402	Rich Gedman	.10	.03
❑	403	Jeff D. Robinson	.10	.03
❑	404	Randy Ready	.10	.03
❑	405	Rick Cerone	.10	.03
❑	406	Jeff Blauser	.10	.03
❑	407	Larry Andersen	.10	.03
❑	408	Joe Boever	.10	.03
❑	409	Felix Fermin	.10	.03
❑	410	Glenn Wilson	.10	.03
❑	411	Rex Hudler	.10	.03
❑	412	Mark Grant	.10	.03
❑	413	Dennis Martinez	.20	.06
❑	414	Darrin Jackson	.10	.03
❑	415	Mike Aldrete	.10	.03
❑	416	Roger McDowell	.10	.03
❑	417	Jeff Reardon	.20	.06
❑	418	Darren Daulton	.20	.06
❑	419	Tim Laudner	.10	.03
❑	420	Don Carman	.10	.03
❑	421	Lloyd Moseby	.10	.03
❑	422	Doug Drabek	.10	.03
❑	423	Lenny Harris UER (Walks 2 in '89, should be 20)	.10	.03
❑	424	Jose Lind	.10	.03
❑	425	Dave Johnson (P)	.10	.03
❑	426	Jerry Browne	.10	.03
❑	427	Eric Yelding	.10	.03
❑	428	Brad Komminsk	.10	.03
❑	429	Jody Davis	.10	.03
❑	430	Mariano Duncan	.10	.03
❑	431	Mark Davis	.10	.03
❑	432	Nelson Santovenia	.10	.03
❑	433	Bruce Hurst	.10	.03
❑	434	Jeff Huson RC	.10	.03
❑	435	Chris James	.10	.03
❑	436	Mark Guthrie	.10	.03
❑	437	Charlie Hayes	.10	.03
❑	438	Shane Rawley	.10	.03
❑	439	Dickie Thon	.10	.03
❑	440	Juan Berenguer	.10	.03
❑	441	Kevin Romine	.10	.03
❑	442	Bill Landrum	.10	.03
❑	443	Todd Frohwirth	.10	.03
❑	444	Craig Worthington	.10	.03
❑	445	Fernando Valenzuela	.20	.06
❑	446	Joey Belle	.50	.15
❑	447	Ed Whited UER (Ashville, should be Asheville)	.10	.03
❑	448	Dave Smith	.10	.03
❑	449	Dave Clark	.10	.03
❑	450	Juan Agosto	.10	.03
❑	451	Dave Valle	.10	.03
❑	452	Kent Hrbek	.20	.06
❑	453	Von Hayes	.10	.03
❑	454	Gary Gaetti	.20	.06
❑	455	Greg Briley	.10	.03
❑	456	Glenn Braggs	.10	.03
❑	457	Kirt Manwaring	.10	.03
❑	458	Mel Hall	.10	.03
❑	459	Brook Jacoby	.10	.03
❑	460	Pat Sheridan	.10	.03
❑	461	Rob Murphy	.10	.03
❑	462	Jimmy Key	.20	.06
❑	463	Nick Esasky	.10	.03
❑	464	Rob Ducey	.10	.03
❑	465	Carlos Quintana UER (Internatinoal)	.10	.03
❑	466	Larry Walker RC	1.50	.45
❑	467	Todd Worrell	.10	.03
❑	468	Kevin Gross	.10	.03
❑	469	Terry Pendleton	.20	.06
❑	470	Dave Martinez	.10	.03
❑	471	Gene Larkin	.10	.03
❑	472	Len Dykstra UER ('89 and total runs understated by 10)	.20	.06
❑	473	Barry Lyons	.10	.03
❑	474	Terry Mulholland	.10	.03
❑	475	Chip Hale	.10	.03
❑	476	Jesse Barfield	.10	.03
❑	477	Dan Plesac	.10	.03
❑	478A	Scott Garrelts ERR (Photo actually Bill Bathe)	2.00	.60
❑	478B	Scott Garrelts COR	.10	.03
❑	479	Dave Righetti	.10	.03
❑	480	Gus Polidor UER Wearing 14 on front, but 10 on back	.10	.03
❑	481	Mookie Wilson	.20	.06
❑	482	Luis Rivera	.10	.03
❑	483	Mike Flanagan	.10	.03
❑	484	Dennis Boyd	.10	.03
❑	485	John Cerutti	.10	.03
❑	486	John Costello	.10	.03
❑	487	Pascual Perez	.10	.03
❑	488	Tommy Herr	.10	.03
❑	489	Tom Foley	.10	.03

❑ 490 Curt Ford .10 .03
❑ 491 Steve Lake .10 .03
❑ 492 Tim Teufel .10 .03
❑ 493 Randy Bush .10 .03
❑ 494 Mike Jackson .10 .03
❑ 495 Steve Jeltz .10 .03
❑ 496 Paul Gibson .10 .03
❑ 497 Steve Balboni .10 .03
❑ 498 Bud Black .10 .03
❑ 499 Dale Sveum .10 .03
❑ 500 Checklist 401-500 .10 .03
❑ 501 Tim Jones .10 .03
❑ 502 Mark Portugal .10 .03
❑ 503 Ivan Calderon .10 .03
❑ 504 Rick Rhoden .10 .03
❑ 505 Willie McGee .20 .06
❑ 506 Kirk McCaskill .10 .03
❑ 507 Dave LaPoint .10 .03
❑ 508 Jay Howell .10 .03
❑ 509 Johnny Ray .10 .03
❑ 510 Dave Anderson .10 .03
❑ 511 Chuck Crim .10 .03
❑ 512 Joe Hesketh .10 .03
❑ 513 Dennis Eckersley .20 .06
❑ 514 Greg Brock .10 .03
❑ 515 Tim Burke .10 .03
❑ 516 Frank Tanana .10 .03
❑ 517 Jay Bell .20 .06
❑ 518 Guillermo Hernandez .10 .03
❑ 519 Randy Kramer UER .10 .03
(Codiroli misspelled
as Codoroli)
❑ 520 Charles Hudson .10 .03
❑ 521 Jim Corsi .10 .03
Word "originally" is
misspelled on back
❑ 522 Steve Rosenberg .10 .03
❑ 523 Cris Carpenter .10 .03
❑ 524 Matt Winters .10 .03
❑ 525 Melido Perez .10 .03
❑ 526 Chris Gwynn UER .10 .03
(Albeguergue)
❑ 527 Bert Blyleven UER .20 .06
(Games career total is
wrong, should be 644)
❑ 528 Chuck Cary .10 .03
❑ 529 Daryl Boston .10 .03
❑ 530 Dale Mohorcic .10 .03
❑ 531 Geronimo Berroa .10 .03
❑ 532 Edgar Martinez .30 .09
❑ 533 Dale Murphy .50 .15
❑ 534 Jay Buhner .20 .06
❑ 535 John Smoltz UER .50 .15
(HEA Stadium)
❑ 536 Andy Van Slyke .20 .06
❑ 537 Mike Henneman .10 .03
❑ 538 Miguel Garcia .10 .03
❑ 539 Frank Williams .10 .03
❑ 540 R.J. Reynolds .10 .03
❑ 541 Shawn Hillegas .10 .03
❑ 542 Walt Weiss .10 .03
❑ 543 Greg Hibbard RC .10 .03
❑ 544 Nolan Ryan 2.00 .60
❑ 545 Todd Zeile .20 .06
❑ 546 Hensley Meulens .10 .03
❑ 547 Tim Belcher .10 .03
❑ 548 Mike Witt .10 .03
❑ 549 Greg Cadaret UER .10 .03
(Aquiring, should
be Acquiring)
❑ 550 Franklin Stubbs .10 .03
❑ 551 Tony Castillo .10 .03
❑ 552 Jeff M. Robinson .10 .03
❑ 553 Steve Olin RC .25 .07
❑ 554 Alan Trammell .20 .06
❑ 555 Wade Boggs 4X .30 .09
(Bo Jackson
in background)
❑ 556 Will Clark .50 .15
❑ 557 Jeff King .10 .03
❑ 558 Mike Fitzgerald .10 .03
❑ 559 Ken Howell .10 .03
❑ 560 Bob Kipper .10 .03
❑ 561 Scott Bankhead .10 .03
❑ 562A Jeff Innis ERR 2.00 .60
(Photo actually
David West)
❑ 562B Jeff Innis COR .10 .03
❑ 563 Randy Johnson 1.00 .23
❑ 564 Wally Whitehurst .10 .03
❑ 565 Gene Harris .10 .03
❑ 566 Norm Charlton .10 .03
❑ 567 Robin Yount UER .75 .23
(7602 career hits,
should be 2606)
❑ 568 Joe Oliver UER .10 .03
(Fl.orida)
❑ 569 Mark Parent .10 .03
❑ 570 John Farrell UER .10 .03
(Loss total added wrong)
❑ 571 Tom Glavine .30 .09
❑ 572 Rod Nichols .10 .03
❑ 573 Jack Morris .20 .06
❑ 574 Greg Swindell .10 .03
❑ 575 Steve Searcy .10 .03
❑ 576 Ricky Jordan .10 .03
❑ 577 Matt Williams .20 .06
❑ 578 Mike LaValliere .10 .03
❑ 579 Bryn Smith .10 .03
❑ 580 Bruce Ruffin .10 .03
❑ 581 Randy Myers .20 .06
❑ 582 Rick Wrona .10 .03
❑ 583 Juan Samuel .10 .03
❑ 584 Les Lancaster .10 .03
❑ 585 Jeff Musselman .10 .03
❑ 586 Rob Dibble .20 .06
❑ 587 Eric Show .10 .03
❑ 588 Jesse Orosco .10 .03
❑ 589 Herm Winningham .10 .03
❑ 590 Andy Allanson .10 .03
❑ 591 Dion James .10 .03
❑ 592 Carmelo Martinez .10 .03
❑ 593 Luis Quinones .10 .03
❑ 594 Dennis Rasmussen .10 .03
❑ 595 Rich Yett .10 .03
❑ 596 Bob Walk .10 .03
❑ 597A A.McGaffigan ERR 2.00 .60
Photo actually
Rich Thompson
❑ 597B A.McGaffigan COR .10 .03
❑ 598 Billy Hatcher .10 .03
❑ 599 Bob Knepper .10 .03
❑ 600 CL 501-600 UER .10 .03
599 Bob Kneppers
❑ 601 Joey Cora .20 .06
❑ 602 Steve Finley .20 .06
❑ 603 Kal Daniels UER .10 .03
(12 hits in '87, should
be 123; 335 runs,
should be 235)
❑ 604 Gregg Olson .20 .06
❑ 605 Dave Stieb .20 .06
❑ 606 Kenny Rogers .20 .06
(Shown catching
football)
❑ 607 Zane Smith .10 .03
❑ 608 Bob Geren UER .10 .03
(Origionally)
❑ 609 Chad Kreuter .10 .03
❑ 610 Mike Smithson .10 .03
❑ 611 Jeff Wetherby .10 .03
❑ 612 Gary Mielke .10 .03
❑ 613 Pete Smith .10 .03
❑ 614 Jack Daugherty UER .10 .03
(Born 7/30/60, should
be 7/3/60)
❑ 615 Lance McCullers .10 .03
❑ 616 Don Robinson .10 .03
❑ 617 Jose Guzman .10 .03
❑ 618 Steve Bedrosian .10 .03
❑ 619 Jamie Moyer .20 .06
❑ 620 Atlee Hammaker .10 .03
❑ 621 Rick Luecken UER .10 .03
(Innings pitched wrong)
❑ 622 Greg W. Harris .10 .03
❑ 623 Pete Harnisch .10 .03
❑ 624 Jerald Clark .10 .03
❑ 625 Jack McDowell UER .10 .03
(Career totals for Games
and GS don't include
1987 season)
❑ 626 Frank Viola .10 .03
❑ 627 Teddy Higuera .10 .03
❑ 628 Marty Pevey .10 .03
❑ 629 Bill Wegman .10 .03
❑ 630 Eric Plunk .10 .03
❑ 631 Drew Hall .10 .03
❑ 632 Doug Jones .10 .03
❑ 633 Geno Petralli UER .10 .03
(Sacremento)
❑ 634 Jose Alvarez .10 .03
❑ 635 Bob Milacki .10 .03
❑ 636 Bobby Witt .10 .03
❑ 637 Trevor Wilson .10 .03
❑ 638 Jeff Russell UER .10 .03
(Shutout stats wrong)
❑ 639 Mike Krukow .10 .03
❑ 640 Rick Leach .10 .03
❑ 641 Dave Schmidt .10 .03
❑ 642 Terry Leach .10 .03
❑ 643 Calvin Schiraldi .10 .03
❑ 644 Bob Melvin .10 .03
❑ 645 Jim Abbott .30 .09
❑ 646 Jaime Navarro .10 .03
❑ 647 Mark Langston UER .10 .03
(Several errors in
stats totals)
❑ 648 Juan Nieves .10 .03
❑ 649 Damaso Garcia .10 .03
❑ 650 Charlie O'Brien .10 .03
❑ 651 Eric King .10 .03
❑ 652 Mike Boddicker .10 .03
❑ 653 Duane Ward .10 .03
❑ 654 Bob Stanley .10 .03
❑ 655 Sandy Alomar Jr. .20 .06
❑ 656 Danny Tartabull UER .10 .03
(395 BB, should be 295)
❑ 657 Randy McCament .10 .03
❑ 658 Charlie Leibrandt .10 .03
❑ 659 Dan Quisenberry .10 .03
❑ 660 Paul Assenmacher .10 .03
❑ 661 Walt Terrell .10 .03
❑ 662 Tim Leary .10 .03
❑ 663 Randy Milligan .10 .03
❑ 664 Bo Diaz .10 .03
❑ 665 Mark Lemke UER .10 .03
(Richmond misspelled
as Richomond)
❑ 666 Jose Gonzalez .10 .03
❑ 667 Chuck Finley UER .20 .06
(Born 11/16/62, should
be 11/26/62)
❑ 668 John Kruk .20 .06
❑ 669 Dick Schofield .10 .03
❑ 670 Tim Crews .10 .03
❑ 671 John Dopson .10 .03
❑ 672 John Orton RC .10 .03
❑ 673 Eric Hetzel .10 .03
❑ 674 Lance Parrish .10 .03
❑ 675 Ramon Martinez .10 .03
❑ 676 Mark Gubicza .10 .03
❑ 677 Greg Litton .10 .03
❑ 678 Greg Mathews .10 .03
❑ 679 Dave Dravecky .20 .06
❑ 680 Steve Farr .10 .03
❑ 681 Mike Devereaux .10 .03
❑ 682 Ken Griffey Sr. .20 .06
❑ 683A Mickey Weston ERR 2.00 .60
(Listed as Jamie
on card)
❑ 683B Mickey Weston COR .10 .03
(Technically still an
error as birthdate is
listed as 3/26/81)
❑ 684 Jack Armstrong .10 .03
❑ 685 Steve Buechele .10 .03
❑ 686 Bryan Harvey .10 .03
❑ 687 Lance Blankenship .10 .03
❑ 688 Dante Bichette .50 .15
❑ 689 Todd Burns .10 .03
❑ 690 Dan Petry .10 .03
❑ 691 Kent Anderson .10 .03
❑ 692 Todd Stottlemyre .20 .06
❑ 693 Wally Joyner UER .20 .06
(Several stats errors)
❑ 694 Mike Rochford .10 .03
❑ 695 Floyd Bannister .10 .03
❑ 696 Rick Reuschel .10 .03

❑ 697 Jose DeLeon .10 .03
❑ 698 Jeff Montgomery .20 .06
❑ 699 Kelly Downs .10 .03
❑ 700A Checklist 601-700 2.00 .60
(683 Jamie Weston)
❑ 700B Checklist 601-700 .10 .03
(683 Mickey Weston)
❑ 701 Jim Gott .10 .03
❑ 702 Delino DeShields .50 .15
Marquis Grissom
Larry Walker
❑ 702A Mike Witt 10.00 3.00
Black rectangle covers much of back
❑ 703 Alejandro Pena .10 .03
❑ 704 Willie Randolph .20 .06
❑ 705 Tim Leary .10 .03
❑ 706 Chuck McElroy RC .10 .03
❑ 707 Gerald Perry .10 .03
❑ 708 Tom Brunansky .10 .03
❑ 709 John Franco .20 .06
❑ 710 Mark Davis .10 .03
❑ 711 David Justice RC .75 .23
❑ 712 Storm Davis .10 .03
❑ 713 Scott Ruskin .10 .03
❑ 714 Glenn Braggs .10 .03
❑ 715 Kevin Bearse .10 .03
❑ 716 Jose Nunez .10 .03
❑ 717 Tim Layana .10 .03
❑ 718 Greg Myers .10 .03
❑ 719 Pete O'Brien .10 .03
❑ 720 John Candelaria .10 .03
❑ 721 Craig Grebeck RC .10 .03
❑ 722 Shawn Boskie RC .10 .03
❑ 723 Jim Leyritz RC .25 .07
❑ 724 Bill Sampen .10 .03
❑ 725 Scott Radinsky RC .10 .03
❑ 726 Todd Hundley RC .25 .07
❑ 727 Scott Hemond RC .10 .03
❑ 728 Lenny Webster RC .10 .03
❑ 729 Jeff Reardon .20 .06
❑ 730 Mitch Webster .10 .03
❑ 731 Brian Bohanon RC .10 .03
❑ 732 Rick Parker .10 .03
❑ 733 Terry Shumpert .10 .03
❑ 734A Nolan Ryan 3.00 .90
6th No-Hitter
(No stripe on front)
❑ 734B Nolan Ryan 1.00 .30
6th No-Hitter
(stripe added on card
front for 300th win)
❑ 735 John Burkett .10 .03
❑ 736 Derrick May RC .10 .03
❑ 737 Carlos Baerga RC .25 .07
❑ 738 Greg Smith .10 .03
❑ 739 Scott Sanderson .10 .03
❑ 740 Joe Kraemer .10 .03
❑ 741 Hector Villanueva RC .10 .03
❑ 742 Mike Fetters RC .25 .07
❑ 743 Mark Gardner RC .10 .03
❑ 744 Matt Nokes .10 .03
❑ 745 Dave Winfield .20 .06
❑ 746 Delino DeShields RC .25 .07
❑ 747 Dann Howitt .10 .03
❑ 748 Tony Pena .10 .03
❑ 749 Oil Can Boyd .10 .03
❑ 750 Mike Benjamin .10 .03
❑ 751 Alex Cole RC .10 .03
❑ 752 Eric Gunderson .10 .03
❑ 753 Howard Farmer .10 .03
❑ 754 Joe Carter .20 .06
❑ 755 Ray Lankford RC .25 .07
❑ 756 Sandy Alomar Jr. .20 .06
❑ 757 Alex Sanchez .10 .03
❑ 758 Nick Esasky .10 .03
❑ 759 Stan Belinda RC .10 .03
❑ 760 Jim Presley .10 .03
❑ 761 Gary DiSarcina RC .25 .07
❑ 762 Wayne Edwards .10 .03
❑ 763 Pat Combs .10 .03
❑ 764 Mickey Pina .10 .03
❑ 765 Wilson Alvarez RC .25 .07
❑ 766 Dave Parker .20 .06
❑ 767 Mike Blowers RC .10 .03
❑ 768 Tony Phillips .10 .03
❑ 769 Pascual Perez .10 .03
❑ 770 Gary Pettis .10 .03
❑ 771 Fred Lynn .10 .03
❑ 772 Mel Rojas RC .10 .03
❑ 773 David Segui RC .25 .07
❑ 774 Gary Carter .20 .06
❑ 775 Rafael Valdez .10 .03
❑ 776 Glenallen Hill .10 .03
❑ 777 Keith Hernandez .20 .06
❑ 778 Billy Hatcher .10 .03
❑ 779 Marty Clary .10 .03
❑ 780 Candy Maldonado .10 .03
❑ 781 Mike Marshall .10 .03
❑ 782 Billy Joe Robidoux .10 .03
❑ 783 Mark Langston .10 .03
❑ 784 Paul Sorrento RC .25 .07
❑ 785 Dave Hollins RC .25 .07
❑ 786 Cecil Fielder .20 .06
❑ 787 Matt Young .10 .03
❑ 788 Jeff Huson .10 .03
❑ 789 Lloyd Moseby .10 .03
❑ 790 Ron Kittle .10 .03
❑ 791 Hubie Brooks .10 .03
❑ 792 Craig Lefferts .10 .03
❑ 793 Kevin Bass .10 .03
❑ 794 Bryn Smith .10 .03
❑ 795 Juan Samuel .10 .03
❑ 796 Sam Horn .10 .03
❑ 797 Randy Myers .20 .06
❑ 798 Chris James .10 .03
❑ 799 Bill Gullickson .10 .03
❑ 800 Checklist 701-800 .10 .03

1991 Upper Deck

	Nm-Mt	Ex-Mt
COMPLETE SET (800)	15.00	4.50
COMP.FACT.SET (800)	20.00	6.00
COMPLETE LO SET (700)	15.00	4.50
COMPLETE HI SET (100)	5.00	1.50

❑ 1 Star Rookie Checklist .05 .02
❑ 2 Phil Plantier RC .10 .03
❑ 3 D.J. Dozier .05 .02
❑ 4 Dave Hansen .05 .02
❑ 5 Maurice Vaughn .10 .03
❑ 6 Leo Gomez .05 .02
❑ 7 Scott Aldred .05 .02
❑ 8 Scott Chiamparino .05 .02
❑ 9 Lance Dickson RC .10 .03
❑ 10 Sean Berry RC .10 .03
❑ 11 Bernie Williams .25 .07
❑ 12 Brian Barnes UER .10 .03
(Photo either not him
or in wrong jersey)
❑ 13 Narciso Elvira .05 .02
❑ 14 Mike Gardiner .05 .02
❑ 15 Greg Colbrunn RC .25 .07
❑ 16 Bernard Gilkey .05 .02
❑ 17 Mark Lewis .05 .02
❑ 18 Mickey Morandini .05 .02
❑ 19 Charles Nagy .05 .02
❑ 20 Geronimo Pena .05 .02
❑ 21 Henry Rodriguez RC .25 .07
❑ 22 Scott Cooper .05 .02
❑ 23 Andujar Cedeno UER .05 .02
(Shown batting left,
back says right)
❑ 24 Eric Karros RC .40 .12
❑ 25 Steve Decker UER .05 .02
Lewis-Clark State
College, not Lewis
and Clark
❑ 26 Kevin Belcher .05 .02
❑ 27 Jeff Conine RC .40 .12
❑ 28 Dave Stewart TC .05 .02
❑ 29 Carlton Fisk TC .10 .03
❑ 30 Rafael Palmeiro TC .10 .03
❑ 31 Chuck Finley TC .05 .02
❑ 32 Harold Reynolds TC .05 .02
❑ 33 Bret Saberhagen TC .05 .02
❑ 34 Gary Gaetti TC .05 .02
❑ 35 Scott Leius .05 .02
❑ 36 Neal Heaton .05 .02
❑ 37 Terry Lee .05 .02
❑ 38 Gary Redus .05 .02
❑ 39 Barry Jones .05 .02
❑ 40 Chuck Knoblauch .10 .03
❑ 41 Larry Andersen .05 .02
❑ 42 Darryl Hamilton .05 .02
❑ 43 Mike Greenwell TC .05 .02
❑ 44 Kelly Gruber TC .05 .02
❑ 45 Jack Morris TC .05 .02
❑ 46 Sandy Alomar Jr. TC .05 .02
❑ 47 Gregg Olson TC .05 .02
❑ 48 Dave Parker TC .05 .02
❑ 49 Roberto Kelly TC .05 .02
❑ 50 Top Prospect Checklist .05 .02
❑ 51 Kyle Abbott .05 .02
❑ 52 Jeff Juden .05 .02
❑ 53 T.Van Poppel UER RC .25 .07
Born Arlington and
attended John Martin HS,
should say Hinsdale and
James Martin HS
❑ 54 Steve Karsay RC .25 .07
❑ 55 Chipper Jones RC 4.00 1.20
❑ 56 Chris Johnson RC UER .10 .03
(Called Tim on back)
❑ 57 John Ericks .05 .02
❑ 58 Gary Scott .05 .02
❑ 59 Kiki Jones .05 .02
❑ 60 Wil Cordero RC .10 .03
❑ 61 Royce Clayton .05 .02
❑ 62 Tim Costo RC .10 .03
❑ 63 Roger Salkeld .05 .02
❑ 64 Brook Fordyce RC .25 .07
❑ 65 Mike Mussina RC 1.25 .35
❑ 66 Dave Staton RC .10 .03
❑ 67 Mike Lieberthal RC .40 .12
❑ 68 Kurt Miller RC .05 .02
❑ 69 Dan Peltier RC .10 .03
❑ 70 Greg Blosser .05 .02
❑ 71 Reggie Sanders RC .40 .12
❑ 72 Brent Mayne .05 .02
❑ 73 Rico Brogna .05 .02
❑ 74 Willie Banks .05 .02
❑ 75 Len Brutcher .05 .02
❑ 76 Pat Kelly RC .10 .03
❑ 77 Chris Sabo TC .05 .02
❑ 78 Ramon Martinez TC .05 .02
❑ 79 Matt Williams TC .05 .02
❑ 80 Roberto Alomar TC .10 .03
❑ 81 Glenn Davis TC .05 .02
❑ 82 Ron Gant TC .05 .02
❑ 83 Cecil Fielder FEAT .05 .02
❑ 84 Orlando Merced RC .10 .03
❑ 85 Domingo Ramos .05 .02
❑ 86 Tom Bolton .05 .02
❑ 87 Andres Santana .05 .02
❑ 88 John Dopson .05 .02
❑ 89 Kenny Williams .05 .02
❑ 90 Marty Barrett .05 .02
❑ 91 Tom Pagnozzi .05 .02
❑ 92 Carmelo Martinez .05 .02
❑ 93 Bobby Thigpen SAVE .05 .02
❑ 94 Barry Bonds TC .30 .09
❑ 95 Gregg Jefferies TC .05 .02
❑ 96 Tim Wallach TC .05 .02
❑ 97 Len Dykstra TC .05 .02
❑ 98 Pedro Guerrero TC .05 .02
❑ 99 Mark Grace TC .10 .03
❑ 100 Checklist 1-100 .05 .02
❑ 101 Kevin Elster .05 .02
❑ 102 Tom Brookens .05 .02

No.	Player		
❑ 103	Mackey Sasser	.05	.02
❑ 104	Felix Fermin	.05	.02
❑ 105	Kevin McReynolds	.05	.02
❑ 106	Dave Stieb	.05	.02
❑ 107	Jeffrey Leonard	.05	.02
❑ 108	Dave Henderson	.05	.02
❑ 109	Sid Bream	.05	.02
❑ 110	Henry Cotto	.05	.02
❑ 111	Shawon Dunston	.05	.02
❑ 112	Mariano Duncan	.05	.02
❑ 113	Joe Girardi	.05	.02
❑ 114	Billy Hatcher	.05	.02
❑ 115	Greg Maddux	.40	.12
❑ 116	Jerry Browne	.05	.02
❑ 117	Juan Samuel	.05	.02
❑ 118	Steve Olin	.05	.02
❑ 119	Alfredo Griffin	.05	.02
❑ 120	Mitch Webster	.05	.02
❑ 121	Joel Skinner	.05	.02
❑ 122	Frank Viola	.10	.03
❑ 123	Cory Snyder	.05	.02
❑ 124	Howard Johnson	.05	.02
❑ 125	Carlos Baerga	.05	.02
❑ 126	Tony Fernandez	.05	.02
❑ 127	Dave Stewart	.10	.03
❑ 128	Jay Buhner	.10	.03
❑ 129	Mike LaValliere	.05	.02
❑ 130	Scott Bradley	.05	.02
❑ 131	Tony Phillips	.05	.02
❑ 132	Ryne Sandberg	.40	.12
❑ 133	Paul O'Neill	.15	.04
❑ 134	Mark Grace	.15	.04
❑ 135	Chris Sabo	.05	.02
❑ 136	Ramon Martinez	.05	.02
❑ 137	Brook Jacoby	.05	.02
❑ 138	Candy Maldonado	.05	.02
❑ 139	Mike Scioscia	.05	.02
❑ 140	Chris James	.05	.02
❑ 141	Craig Worthington	.05	.02
❑ 142	Manny Lee	.05	.02
❑ 143	Tim Raines	.10	.03
❑ 144	Sandy Alomar Jr.	.05	.02
❑ 145	John Olerud	.10	.03
❑ 146	Ozzie Canseco (With Jose)	.10	.03
❑ 147	Pat Borders	.05	.02
❑ 148	Harold Reynolds	.10	.03
❑ 149	Tom Henke	.05	.02
❑ 150	R.J. Reynolds	.05	.02
❑ 151	Mike Gallego	.05	.02
❑ 152	Bobby Bonilla	.10	.03
❑ 153	Terry Steinbach	.05	.02
❑ 154	Barry Bonds	.60	.18
❑ 155	Jose Canseco	.25	.07
❑ 156	Gregg Jefferies	.05	.02
❑ 157	Matt Williams	.10	.03
❑ 158	Craig Biggio	.15	.04
❑ 159	Daryl Boston	.05	.02
❑ 160	Ricky Jordan	.05	.02
❑ 161	Stan Belinda	.05	.02
❑ 162	Ozzie Smith	.40	.12
❑ 163	Tom Brunansky	.05	.02
❑ 164	Todd Zeile	.05	.02
❑ 165	Mike Greenwell	.05	.02
❑ 166	Kal Daniels	.05	.02
❑ 167	Kent Hrbek	.10	.03
❑ 168	Franklin Stubbs	.05	.02
❑ 169	Dick Schofield	.05	.02
❑ 170	Junior Ortiz	.05	.02
❑ 171	Hector Villanueva	.05	.02
❑ 172	Dennis Eckersley	.10	.03
❑ 173	Mitch Williams	.05	.02
❑ 174	Mark McGwire	.60	.18
❑ 175	F.Valenzuela 3X	.10	.03
❑ 176	Gary Carter	.10	.03
❑ 177	Dave Magadan	.05	.02
❑ 178	Robby Thompson	.05	.02
❑ 179	Bob Ojeda	.05	.02
❑ 180	Ken Caminiti	.10	.03
❑ 181	Don Slaught	.05	.02
❑ 182	Luis Rivera	.05	.02
❑ 183	Jay Bell	.10	.03
❑ 184	Jody Reed	.05	.02
❑ 185	Wally Backman	.05	.02
❑ 186	Dave Martinez	.05	.02
❑ 187	Luis Polonia	.05	.02
❑ 188	Shane Mack	.05	.02
❑ 189	Spike Owen	.05	.02
❑ 190	Scott Bailes	.05	.02
❑ 191	John Russell	.05	.02
❑ 192	Walt Weiss	.05	.02
❑ 193	Jose Oquendo	.05	.02
❑ 194	Carney Lansford	.10	.03
❑ 195	Jeff Huson	.05	.02
❑ 196	Keith Miller	.05	.02
❑ 197	Eric Yelding	.05	.02
❑ 198	Ron Darling	.05	.02
❑ 199	John Kruk	.10	.03
❑ 200	Checklist 101-200	.05	.02
❑ 201	John Shelby	.05	.02
❑ 202	Bob Geren	.05	.02
❑ 203	Lance McCullers	.05	.02
❑ 204	Alvaro Espinoza	.05	.02
❑ 205	Mark Salas	.05	.02
❑ 206	Mike Pagliarulo	.05	.02
❑ 207	Jose Uribe	.05	.02
❑ 208	Jim Deshaies	.05	.02
❑ 209	Ron Karkovice	.05	.02
❑ 210	Rafael Ramirez	.05	.02
❑ 211	Donnie Hill	.05	.02
❑ 212	Brian Harper	.05	.02
❑ 213	Jack Howell	.05	.02
❑ 214	Wes Gardner	.05	.02
❑ 215	Tim Burke	.05	.02
❑ 216	Doug Jones	.05	.02
❑ 217	Hubie Brooks	.05	.02
❑ 218	Tom Candiotti	.05	.02
❑ 219	Gerald Perry	.05	.02
❑ 220	Jose DeLeon	.05	.02
❑ 221	Wally Whitehurst	.05	.02
❑ 222	Alan Mills	.05	.02
❑ 223	Alan Trammell	.10	.03
❑ 224	Dwight Gooden	.10	.03
❑ 225	Travis Fryman	.10	.03
❑ 226	Joe Carter	.10	.03
❑ 227	Julio Franco	.10	.03
❑ 228	Craig Lefferts	.05	.02
❑ 229	Gary Pettis	.05	.02
❑ 230	Dennis Rasmussen	.05	.02
❑ 231A	Brian Downing ERR (No position on front)	.05	.02
❑ 231B	Brian Downing COR (DH on front)	.25	.07
❑ 232	Carlos Quintana	.05	.02
❑ 233	Gary Gaetti	.10	.03
❑ 234	Mark Langston	.05	.02
❑ 235	Tim Wallach	.05	.02
❑ 236	Greg Swindell	.05	.02
❑ 237	Eddie Murray	.25	.07
❑ 238	Jeff Manto	.05	.02
❑ 239	Lenny Harris	.05	.02
❑ 240	Jesse Orosco	.05	.02
❑ 241	Scott Lusader	.05	.02
❑ 242	Sid Fernandez	.05	.02
❑ 243	Jim Leyritz	.05	.02
❑ 244	Cecil Fielder	.10	.03
❑ 245	Darryl Strawberry	.10	.03
❑ 246	Frank Thomas UER (Comiskey Park misspelled Comisky)	.25	.07
❑ 247	Kevin Mitchell	.05	.02
❑ 248	Lance Johnson	.05	.02
❑ 249	Rick Reuschel	.05	.02
❑ 250	Mark Portugal	.05	.02
❑ 251	Derek Lilliquist	.05	.02
❑ 252	Brian Holman	.05	.02
❑ 253	Rafael Valdez UER (Born 4/17/68, should be 12/17/67)	.05	.02
❑ 254	B.J. Surhoff	.10	.03
❑ 255	Tony Gwynn	.30	.09
❑ 256	Andy Van Slyke	.10	.03
❑ 257	Todd Stottlemyre	.05	.02
❑ 258	Jose Lind	.05	.02
❑ 259	Greg Myers	.05	.02
❑ 260	Jeff Ballard	.05	.02
❑ 261	Bobby Thigpen	.05	.02
❑ 262	Jimmy Kremers	.05	.02
❑ 263	Robin Ventura	.10	.03
❑ 264	John Smoltz	.15	.04
❑ 265	Sammy Sosa	.50	.15
❑ 266	Gary Sheffield	.10	.03
❑ 267	Len Dykstra	.10	.03
❑ 268	Bill Spiers	.05	.02
❑ 269	Charlie Hayes	.05	.02
❑ 270	Brett Butler	.10	.03
❑ 271	Bip Roberts	.05	.02
❑ 272	Rob Deer	.05	.02
❑ 273	Fred Lynn	.05	.02
❑ 274	Dave Parker	.10	.03
❑ 275	Andy Benes	.05	.02
❑ 276	Glenallen Hill	.05	.02
❑ 277	Steve Howard	.05	.02
❑ 278	Doug Drabek	.05	.02
❑ 279	Joe Oliver	.05	.02
❑ 280	Todd Benzinger	.05	.02
❑ 281	Eric King	.05	.02
❑ 282	Jim Presley	.05	.02
❑ 283	Ken Patterson	.05	.02
❑ 284	Jack Daugherty	.05	.02
❑ 285	Ivan Calderon	.05	.02
❑ 286	Edgar Diaz	.05	.02
❑ 287	Kevin Bass	.05	.02
❑ 288	Don Carman	.05	.02
❑ 289	Greg Brock	.05	.02
❑ 290	John Franco	.10	.03
❑ 291	Joey Cora	.05	.02
❑ 292	Bill Wegman	.05	.02
❑ 293	Eric Show	.05	.02
❑ 294	Scott Bankhead	.05	.02
❑ 295	Garry Templeton	.05	.02
❑ 296	Mickey Tettleton	.05	.02
❑ 297	Luis Sojo	.05	.02
❑ 298	Jose Rijo	.05	.02
❑ 299	Dave Johnson	.05	.02
❑ 300	Checklist 201-300	.05	.02
❑ 301	Mark Grant	.05	.02
❑ 302	Pete Harnisch	.05	.02
❑ 303	Greg Olson	.05	.02
❑ 304	Anthony Telford	.05	.02
❑ 305	Lonnie Smith	.05	.02
❑ 306	Chris Hoiles	.05	.02
❑ 307	Bryn Smith	.05	.02
❑ 308	Mike Devereaux	.05	.02
❑ 309A	Milt Thompson ERR (Under yr information has print dot)	.25	.07
❑ 309B	Milt Thompson COR (Under yr information says 86)	.05	.02
❑ 310	Bob Melvin	.05	.02
❑ 311	Luis Salazar	.05	.02
❑ 312	Ed Whitson	.05	.02
❑ 313	Charlie Hough	.10	.03
❑ 314	Dave Clark	.05	.02
❑ 315	Eric Gunderson	.05	.02
❑ 316	Dan Petry	.05	.02
❑ 317	Dante Bichette UER (Assists misspelled as assissts)	.10	.03
❑ 318	Mike Heath	.05	.02
❑ 319	Damon Berryhill	.05	.02
❑ 320	Walt Terrell	.05	.02
❑ 321	Scott Fletcher	.05	.02
❑ 322	Dan Plesac	.05	.02
❑ 323	Jack McDowell	.05	.02
❑ 324	Paul Molitor	.15	.04
❑ 325	Ozzie Guillen	.05	.02
❑ 326	Gregg Olson	.05	.02
❑ 327	Pedro Guerrero	.10	.03
❑ 328	Bob Milacki	.05	.02
❑ 329	John Tudor UER ('90 Cardinals, should be '90 Dodgers)	.05	.02
❑ 330	Steve Finley UER (Born 3/12/65, should be 5/12)	.10	.03
❑ 331	Jack Clark	.10	.03
❑ 332	Jerome Walton	.05	.02
❑ 333	Andy Hawkins	.05	.02
❑ 334	Derrick May	.05	.02
❑ 335	Roberto Alomar	.15	.04
❑ 336	Jack Morris	.10	.03
❑ 337	Dave Winfield	.10	.03
❑ 338	Steve Searcy	.05	.02
❑ 339	Chili Davis	.10	.03
❑ 340	Larry Sheets	.05	.02
❑ 341	Ted Higuera	.05	.02

	No.	Player		
❑	342	David Segui	.05	.02
❑	343	Greg Cadaret	.05	.02
❑	344	Robin Yount	.40	.12
❑	345	Nolan Ryan	1.00	.30
❑	346	Ray Lankford	.05	.02
❑	347	Cal Ripken	.75	.23
❑	348	Lee Smith	.10	.03
❑	349	Brady Anderson	.10	.03
❑	350	Frank DiPino	.05	.02
❑	351	Hal Morris	.05	.02
❑	352	Deion Sanders	.15	.04
❑	353	Barry Larkin	.15	.04
❑	354	Don Mattingly	.60	.18
❑	355	Eric Davis	.10	.03
❑	356	Jose Offerman	.05	.02
❑	357	Mel Rojas	.05	.02
❑	358	Rudy Seanez	.05	.02
❑	359	Oil Can Boyd	.05	.02
❑	360	Nelson Liriano	.05	.02
❑	361	Ron Gant	.10	.03
❑	362	Howard Farmer	.05	.02
❑	363	David Justice	.10	.03
❑	364	Delino DeShields	.10	.03
❑	365	Steve Avery	.05	.02
❑	366	David Cone	.10	.03
❑	367	Lou Whitaker	.10	.03
❑	368	Von Hayes	.05	.02
❑	369	Frank Tanana	.05	.02
❑	370	Tim Teufel	.05	.02
❑	371	Randy Myers	.05	.02
❑	372	Roberto Kelly	.05	.02
❑	373	Jack Armstrong	.05	.02
❑	374	Kelly Gruber	.05	.02
❑	375	Kevin Maas	.05	.02
❑	376	Randy Johnson	.30	.09
❑	377	David West	.05	.02
❑	378	Brent Knackert	.05	.02
❑	379	Rick Honeycutt	.05	.02
❑	380	Kevin Gross	.05	.02
❑	381	Tom Foley	.05	.02
❑	382	Jeff Blauser	.05	.02
❑	383	Scott Ruskin	.05	.02
❑	384	Andres Thomas	.05	.02
❑	385	Dennis Martinez	.10	.03
❑	386	Mike Henneman	.05	.02
❑	387	Felix Jose	.05	.02
❑	388	Alejandro Pena	.05	.02
❑	389	Chet Lemon	.05	.02
❑	390	Craig Wilson	.05	.02
❑	391	Chuck Crim	.05	.02
❑	392	Mel Hall	.05	.02
❑	393	Mark Knudson	.05	.02
❑	394	Norm Charlton	.05	.02
❑	395	Mike Felder	.05	.02
❑	396	Tim Layana	.05	.02
❑	397	Steve Frey	.05	.02
❑	398	Bill Doran	.05	.02
❑	399	Dion James	.05	.02
❑	400	Checklist 301-400	.05	.02
❑	401	Ron Hassey	.05	.02
❑	402	Don Robinson	.05	.02
❑	403	Gene Nelson	.05	.02
❑	404	Terry Kennedy	.05	.02
❑	405	Todd Burns	.05	.02
❑	406	Roger McDowell	.05	.02
❑	407	Bob Kipper	.05	.02
❑	408	Darren Daulton	.10	.03
❑	409	Chuck Cary	.05	.02
❑	410	Bruce Ruffin	.05	.02
❑	411	Juan Berenguer	.05	.02
❑	412	Gary Ward	.05	.02
❑	413	Al Newman	.05	.02
❑	414	Danny Jackson	.05	.02
❑	415	Greg Gagne	.05	.02
❑	416	Tom Herr	.05	.02
❑	417	Jeff Parrett	.05	.02
❑	418	Jeff Reardon	.10	.03
❑	419	Mark Lemke	.05	.02
❑	420	Charlie O'Brien	.05	.02
❑	421	Willie Randolph	.10	.03
❑	422	Steve Bedrosian	.05	.02
❑	423	Mike Moore	.05	.02
❑	424	Jeff Brantley	.05	.02
❑	425	Bob Welch	.05	.02
❑	426	Terry Mulholland	.05	.02
❑	427	Willie Blair	.05	.02
❑	428	Darrin Fletcher	.05	.02
❑	429	Mike Witt	.05	.02
❑	430	Joe Boever	.05	.02
❑	431	Tom Gordon	.05	.02
❑	432	Pedro Munoz RC	.10	.03
❑	433	Kevin Seitzer	.05	.02
❑	434	Kevin Tapani	.05	.02
❑	435	Bret Saberhagen	.10	.03
❑	436	Ellis Burks	.10	.03
❑	437	Chuck Finley	.10	.03
❑	438	Mike Boddicker	.05	.02
❑	439	Francisco Cabrera	.05	.02
❑	440	Todd Hundley	.05	.02
❑	441	Kelly Downs	.05	.02
❑	442	Dann Howitt	.05	.02
❑	443	Scott Garrelts	.05	.02
❑	444	Rickey Henderson 3X	.25	.07
❑	445	Will Clark	.25	.07
❑	446	Ben McDonald	.05	.02
❑	447	Dale Murphy	.25	.07
❑	448	Dave Righetti	.10	.03
❑	449	Dickie Thon	.05	.02
❑	450	Ted Power	.05	.02
❑	451	Scott Coolbaugh	.05	.02
❑	452	Dwight Smith	.05	.02
❑	453	Pete Incaviglia	.05	.02
❑	454	Andre Dawson	.10	.03
❑	455	Ruben Sierra	.05	.02
❑	456	Andres Galarraga	.10	.03
❑	457	Alvin Davis	.05	.02
❑	458	Tony Castillo	.05	.02
❑	459	Pete O'Brien	.05	.02
❑	460	Charlie Leibrandt	.05	.02
❑	461	Vince Coleman	.05	.02
❑	462	Steve Sax	.05	.02
❑	463	Omar Olivares RC	.10	.03
❑	464	Oscar Azocar	.05	.02
❑	465	Joe Magrane	.05	.02
❑	466	Karl Rhodes	.05	.02
❑	467	Benito Santiago	.10	.03
❑	468	Joe Klink	.05	.02
❑	469	Sil Campusano	.05	.02
❑	470	Mark Parent	.05	.02
❑	471	Shawn Boskie UER (Depleted misspelled as depleated)	.05	.02
❑	472	Kevin Brown	.10	.03
❑	473	Rick Sutcliffe	.10	.03
❑	474	Rafael Palmeiro	.15	.04
❑	475	Mike Harkey	.05	.02
❑	476	Jaime Navarro	.05	.02
❑	477	Marquis Grissom UER (DeShields misspelled as DeSheilds)	.10	.03
❑	478	Marty Clary	.05	.02
❑	479	Greg Briley	.05	.02
❑	480	Tom Glavine	.15	.04
❑	481	Lee Guetterman	.05	.02
❑	482	Rex Hudler	.05	.02
❑	483	Dave LaPoint	.05	.02
❑	484	Terry Pendleton	.10	.03
❑	485	Jesse Barfield	.05	.02
❑	486	Jose DeJesus	.05	.02
❑	487	Paul Abbott RC	.25	.07
❑	488	Ken Howell	.05	.02
❑	489	Greg W. Harris	.05	.02
❑	490	Roy Smith	.05	.02
❑	491	Paul Assenmacher	.05	.02
❑	492	Geno Petralli	.05	.02
❑	493	Steve Wilson	.05	.02
❑	494	Kevin Reimer	.05	.02
❑	495	Bill Long	.05	.02
❑	496	Mike Jackson	.05	.02
❑	497	Oddibe McDowell	.05	.02
❑	498	Bill Swift	.05	.02
❑	499	Jeff Treadway	.05	.02
❑	500	Checklist 401-500	.05	.02
❑	501	Gene Larkin	.05	.02
❑	502	Bob Boone	.10	.03
❑	503	Allan Anderson	.05	.02
❑	504	Luis Aquino	.05	.02
❑	505	Mark Guthrie	.05	.02
❑	506	Joe Orsulak	.05	.02
❑	507	Dana Kiecker	.05	.02
❑	508	Dave Gallagher	.05	.02
❑	509	Greg A. Harris	.05	.02
❑	510	Mark Williamson	.05	.02
❑	511	Casey Candaele	.05	.02
❑	512	Mookie Wilson	.10	.03
❑	513	Dave Smith	.05	.02
❑	514	Chuck Carr	.05	.02
❑	515	Glenn Wilson	.05	.02
❑	516	Mike Fitzgerald	.05	.02
❑	517	Devon White	.10	.03
❑	518	Dave Hollins	.05	.02
❑	519	Mark Eichhorn	.05	.02
❑	520	Otis Nixon	.05	.02
❑	521	Terry Shumpert	.05	.02
❑	522	Scott Erickson	.05	.02
❑	523	Danny Tartabull	.05	.02
❑	524	Orel Hershiser	.10	.03
❑	525	George Brett	.60	.18
❑	526	Greg Vaughn	.05	.02
❑	527	Tim Naehring	.05	.02
❑	528	Curt Schilling	.25	.07
❑	529	Chris Bosio	.05	.02
❑	530	Sam Horn	.05	.02
❑	531	Mike Scott	.05	.02
❑	532	George Bell	.05	.02
❑	533	Eric Anthony	.05	.02
❑	534	Julio Valera	.05	.02
❑	535	Glenn Davis	.05	.02
❑	536	Larry Walker UER (Should have comma after Expos in text)	.25	.07
❑	537	Pat Combs	.05	.02
❑	538	Chris Nabholz	.05	.02
❑	539	Kirk McCaskill	.05	.02
❑	540	Randy Ready	.05	.02
❑	541	Mark Gubicza	.05	.02
❑	542	Rick Aguilera	.10	.03
❑	543	Brian McRae RC	.25	.07
❑	544	Kirby Puckett	.25	.07
❑	545	Bo Jackson	.25	.07
❑	546	Wade Boggs	.15	.04
❑	547	Tim McIntosh	.05	.02
❑	548	Randy Milligan	.05	.02
❑	549	Dwight Evans	.10	.03
❑	550	Billy Ripken	.05	.02
❑	551	Erik Hanson	.05	.02
❑	552	Lance Parrish	.10	.03
❑	553	Tino Martinez	.15	.04
❑	554	Jim Abbott	.15	.04
❑	555	Ken Griffey Jr. UER (Second most votes for 1991 All-Star Game)	.50	.15
❑	556	Milt Cuyler	.05	.02
❑	557	Mark Leonard	.05	.02
❑	558	Jay Howell	.05	.02
❑	559	Lloyd Moseby	.05	.02
❑	560	Chris Gwynn	.05	.02
❑	561	Mark Whiten	.05	.02
❑	562	Harold Baines	.10	.03
❑	563	Junior Felix	.05	.02
❑	564	Darren Lewis	.05	.02
❑	565	Fred McGriff	.15	.04
❑	566	Kevin Appier	.10	.03
❑	567	Luis Gonzalez RC	.50	.15
❑	568	Frank White	.10	.03
❑	569	Juan Agosto	.05	.02
❑	570	Mike Macfarlane	.05	.02
❑	571	Bert Blyleven	.10	.03
❑	572	Ken Griffey Sr. Ken Griffey Jr.	.25	.07
❑	573	Lee Stevens	.05	.02
❑	574	Edgar Martinez	.15	.04
❑	575	Wally Joyner	.10	.03
❑	576	Tim Belcher	.05	.02
❑	577	John Burkett	.05	.02
❑	578	Mike Morgan	.05	.02
❑	579	Paul Gibson	.05	.02
❑	580	Jose Vizcaino	.05	.02
❑	581	Duane Ward	.05	.02
❑	582	Scott Sanderson	.05	.02
❑	583	David Wells	.10	.03
❑	584	Willie McGee	.10	.03
❑	585	John Cerutti	.05	.02
❑	586	Danny Darwin	.05	.02
❑	587	Kurt Stillwell	.05	.02
❑	588	Rich Gedman	.05	.02
❑	589	Mark Davis	.05	.02
❑	590	Bill Gullickson	.05	.02

❑ 591	Matt Young	.05	.02
❑ 592	Bryan Harvey	.05	.02
❑ 593	Omar Vizquel	.15	.04
❑ 594	Scott Lewis RC	.10	.03
❑ 595	Dave Valle	.05	.02
❑ 596	Tim Crews	.05	.02
❑ 597	Mike Bielecki	.05	.02
❑ 598	Mike Sharperson	.05	.02
❑ 599	Dave Bergman	.05	.02
❑ 600	Checklist 501-600	.05	.02
❑ 601	Steve Lyons	.05	.02
❑ 602	Bruce Hurst	.05	.02
❑ 603	Donn Pall	.05	.02
❑ 604	Jim Vatcher	.05	.02
❑ 605	Dan Pasqua	.05	.02
❑ 606	Kenny Rogers	.10	.03
❑ 607	Jeff Schulz	.05	.02
❑ 608	Brad Arnsberg	.05	.02
❑ 609	Willie Wilson	.05	.02
❑ 610	Jamie Moyer	.10	.03
❑ 611	Ron Oester	.05	.02
❑ 612	Dennis Cook	.05	.02
❑ 613	Rick Mahler	.05	.02
❑ 614	Bill Landrum	.05	.02
❑ 615	Scott Scudder	.05	.02
❑ 616	Tom Edens	.05	.02
❑ 617	1917 Revisited	.10	.03
	(White Sox vintage uniforms)		
❑ 618	Jim Gantner	.05	.02
❑ 619	Darrel Akerfelds	.05	.02
❑ 620	Ron Robinson	.05	.02
❑ 621	Scott Radinsky	.05	.02
❑ 622	Pete Smith	.05	.02
❑ 623	Melido Perez	.05	.02
❑ 624	Jerald Clark	.05	.02
❑ 625	Carlos Martinez	.05	.02
❑ 626	Wes Chamberlain RC	.25	.07
❑ 627	Bobby Witt	.05	.02
❑ 628	Ken Dayley	.05	.02
❑ 629	John Barfield	.05	.02
❑ 630	Bob Tewksbury	.05	.02
❑ 631	Glenn Braggs	.05	.02
❑ 632	Jim Neidlinger	.05	.02
❑ 633	Tom Browning	.05	.02
❑ 634	Kirk Gibson	.10	.03
❑ 635	Rob Dibble	.10	.03
❑ 636	Rickey Henderson SB	.25	.07
	Lou Brock		
	May 1, 1991 on front		
❑ 636A	R.Henderson SB	.25	.07
	Lou Brock		
	no date on card		
❑ 637	Jeff Montgomery	.05	.02
❑ 638	Mike Schooler	.05	.02
❑ 639	Storm Davis	.05	.02
❑ 640	Rich Rodriguez	.05	.02
❑ 641	Phil Bradley	.05	.02
❑ 642	Kent Mercker	.05	.02
❑ 643	Carlton Fisk	.15	.04
❑ 644	Mike Bell	.05	.02
❑ 645	Alex Fernandez	.05	.02
❑ 646	Juan Gonzalez	.15	.04
❑ 647	Ken Hill	.05	.02
❑ 648	Jeff Russell	.05	.02
❑ 649	Chuck Malone	.05	.02
❑ 650	Steve Buechele	.05	.02
❑ 651	Mike Benjamin	.05	.02
❑ 652	Tony Pena	.05	.02
❑ 653	Trevor Wilson	.05	.02
❑ 654	Alex Cole	.05	.02
❑ 655	Roger Clemens	.50	.15
❑ 656	Mark McGwire BASH	.30	.09
❑ 657	Joe Grahe RC	.10	.03
❑ 658	Jim Eisenreich	.05	.02
❑ 659	Dan Gladden	.05	.02
❑ 660	Steve Farr	.05	.02
❑ 661	Bill Sampen	.05	.02
❑ 662	Dave Rohde	.05	.02
❑ 663	Mark Gardner	.05	.02
❑ 664	Mike Simms	.05	.02
❑ 665	Moises Alou	.10	.03
❑ 666	Mickey Hatcher	.05	.02
❑ 667	Jimmy Key	.10	.03
❑ 668	John Wetteland	.10	.03
❑ 669	John Smiley	.05	.02
❑ 670	Jim Acker	.05	.02
❑ 671	Pascual Perez	.05	.02
❑ 672	Reggie Harris UER	.05	.02
	(Opportunity misspelled		
	as oppurtinty)		
❑ 673	Matt Nokes	.05	.02
❑ 674	Rafael Novoa	.05	.02
❑ 675	Hensley Meulens	.05	.02
❑ 676	Jeff M. Robinson	.05	.02
❑ 677	Ground Breaking	.10	.03
	(New Comiskey Park;		
	Carlton Fisk and		
	Robin Ventura)		
❑ 678	Johnny Ray	.05	.02
❑ 679	Greg Hibbard	.05	.02
❑ 680	Paul Sorrento	.05	.02
❑ 681	Mike Marshall	.05	.02
❑ 682	Jim Clancy	.05	.02
❑ 683	Rob Murphy	.05	.02
❑ 684	Dave Schmidt	.05	.02
❑ 685	Jeff Gray	.05	.02
❑ 686	Mike Hartley	.05	.02
❑ 687	Jeff King	.05	.02
❑ 688	Stan Javier	.05	.02
❑ 689	Bob Walk	.05	.02
❑ 690	Jim Gott	.05	.02
❑ 691	Mike LaCoss	.05	.02
❑ 692	John Farrell	.05	.02
❑ 693	Tim Leary	.05	.02
❑ 694	Mike Walker	.05	.02
❑ 695	Eric Plunk	.05	.02
❑ 696	Mike Fetters	.05	.02
❑ 697	Wayne Edwards	.05	.02
❑ 698	Tim Drummond	.05	.02
❑ 699	Willie Fraser	.05	.02
❑ 700	Checklist 601-700	.05	.02
❑ 701	Mike Heath	.05	.02
❑ 702	Luis Gonzalez	1.00	.30
	Karl Rhodes		
	Jeff Bagwell		
❑ 703	Jose Mesa	.05	.02
❑ 704	Dave Smith	.05	.02
❑ 705	Danny Darwin	.05	.02
❑ 706	Rafael Belliard	.05	.02
❑ 707	Rob Murphy	.05	.02
❑ 708	Terry Pendleton	.10	.03
❑ 709	Mike Pagliarulo	.05	.02
❑ 710	Sid Bream	.05	.02
❑ 711	Junior Felix	.05	.02
❑ 712	Dante Bichette	.10	.03
❑ 713	Kevin Gross	.05	.02
❑ 714	Luis Sojo	.05	.02
❑ 715	Bob Ojeda	.05	.02
❑ 716	Julio Machado	.05	.02
❑ 717	Steve Farr	.05	.02
❑ 718	Franklin Stubbs	.05	.02
❑ 719	Mike Boddicker	.05	.02
❑ 720	Willie Randolph	.10	.03
❑ 721	Willie McGee	.10	.03
❑ 722	Chili Davis	.10	.03
❑ 723	Danny Jackson	.05	.02
❑ 724	Cory Snyder	.05	.02
❑ 725	Andre Dawson	.25	.07
	George Bell		
	Ryne Sandberg		
❑ 726	Rob Deer	.05	.02
❑ 727	Rich DeLucia	.05	.02
❑ 728	Mike Perez RC	.10	.03
❑ 729	Mickey Tettleton	.05	.02
❑ 730	Mike Blowers	.05	.02
❑ 731	Gary Gaetti	.10	.03
❑ 732	Brett Butler	.10	.03
❑ 733	Dave Parker	.10	.03
❑ 734	Eddie Zosky	.05	.02
❑ 735	Jack Clark	.10	.03
❑ 736	Jack Morris	.10	.03
❑ 737	Kirk Gibson	.10	.03
❑ 738	Steve Bedrosian	.05	.02
❑ 739	Candy Maldonado	.05	.02
❑ 740	Matt Young	.05	.02
❑ 741	Rich Garces RC	.10	.03
❑ 742	George Bell	.05	.02
❑ 743	Deion Sanders	.15	.04
❑ 744	Bo Jackson	.25	.07
❑ 745	Luis Mercedes RC	.10	.03
❑ 746	Reggie Jefferson UER	.05	.02
	(Throwing left on card;		
	back has throws right)		
❑ 747	Pete Incaviglia	.05	.02
❑ 748	Chris Hammond	.05	.02
❑ 749	Mike Stanton	.05	.02
❑ 750	Scott Sanderson	.05	.02
❑ 751	Paul Faries	.05	.02
❑ 752	Al Osuna RC	.05	.02
❑ 753	Steve Chitren	.05	.02
❑ 754	Tony Fernandez	.05	.02
❑ 755	Jeff Bagwell RC UER	1.50	.45
	(Strikeout and walk		
	totals reversed)		
❑ 756	K.Dressendorfer RC	.10	.03
❑ 757	Glenn Davis	.05	.02
❑ 758	Gary Carter	.10	.03
❑ 759	Zane Smith	.05	.02
❑ 760	Vance Law	.05	.02
❑ 761	Denis Boucher RC	.10	.03
❑ 762	Turner Ward RC	.10	.03
❑ 763	Roberto Alomar	.15	.04
❑ 764	Albert Belle	.10	.03
❑ 765	Joe Carter	.10	.03
❑ 766	Pete Schourek RC	.10	.03
❑ 767	H.Slocumb RC	.10	.03
❑ 768	Vince Coleman	.05	.02
❑ 769	Mitch Williams	.05	.02
❑ 770	Brian Downing	.05	.02
❑ 771	Dana Allison	.05	.02
❑ 772	Pete Harnisch	.05	.02
❑ 773	Tim Raines	.10	.03
❑ 774	Darryl Kile	.10	.03
❑ 775	Fred McGriff	.15	.04
❑ 776	Dwight Evans	.10	.03
❑ 777	Joe Slusarski	.05	.02
❑ 778	Dave Righetti	.10	.03
❑ 779	Jeff Hamilton	.05	.02
❑ 780	Ernest Riles	.05	.02
❑ 781	Ken Dayley	.05	.02
❑ 782	Eric King	.05	.02
❑ 783	Devon White	.10	.03
❑ 784	Beau Allred	.05	.02
❑ 785	Mike Timlin RC	.40	.12
❑ 786	Ivan Calderon	.05	.02
❑ 787	Hubie Brooks	.05	.02
❑ 788	Juan Agosto	.05	.02
❑ 789	Barry Jones	.05	.02
❑ 790	Wally Backman	.05	.02
❑ 791	Jim Presley	.05	.02
❑ 792	Charlie Hough	.10	.03
❑ 793	Larry Andersen	.05	.02
❑ 794	Steve Finley	.10	.03
❑ 795	Shawn Abner	.05	.02
❑ 796	Jeff M. Robinson	.05	.02
❑ 797	Joe Bitker	.05	.02
❑ 798	Eric Show	.05	.02
❑ 799	Bud Black	.05	.02
❑ 800	Checklist 701-800	.05	.02
❑ HH1	H.Aaron Hologram	1.50	.45
❑ SP1	Michael Jordan SP	8.00	2.40
	(Shown batting in		
	White Sox uniform)		
❑ SP2	Rickey Henderson	2.00	.60
	Nolan Ryan		
	May 1, 1991 Records		

1991 Upper Deck Final Edition

	Nm-Mt	Ex-Mt
COMP.FACT.SET (100)	10.00	3.00
❑ 1F Ryan Klesko CL	.10	.03
Reggie Sanders		
❑ 2F Pedro Martinez RC	5.00	1.50
❑ 3F Lance Dickson	.05	.02
❑ 4F Royce Clayton	.05	.02
❑ 5F Scott Bryant	.05	.02
❑ 6F Dan Wilson RC	.25	.07
❑ 7F Dmitri Young RC	.40	.12
❑ 8F Ryan Klesko RC	.50	.15
❑ 9F Tom Goodwin	.05	.02
❑ 10F Rondell White RC	.40	.12
❑ 11F Reggie Sanders	.15	.04
❑ 12F Todd Van Poppel	.05	.02
❑ 13F Arthur Rhodes RC	.25	.07
❑ 14F Eddie Zosky	.05	.02
❑ 15F Gerald Williams RC	.25	.07
❑ 16F Robert Eenhoorn RC	.10	.03
❑ 17F Jim Thome RC	2.50	.75
❑ 18F Marc Newfield RC	.10	.03
❑ 19F Kerwin Moore RC	.10	.03
❑ 20F Jeff McNeely RC	.10	.03
❑ 21F Frankie Rodriguez RC	.10	.03
❑ 22F Andy Mota	.05	.02
❑ 23F Chris Haney RC	.10	.03
❑ 24F Kenny Lofton RC	.50	.15
❑ 25F Dave Nilsson RC	.25	.07
❑ 26F Derek Bell	.10	.03
❑ 27F Frank Castillo RC	.25	.07
❑ 28F Candy Maldonado	.05	.02
❑ 29F Chuck McElroy	.05	.02
❑ 30F Chito Martinez	.05	.02
❑ 31F Steve Howe	.05	.02
❑ 32F Freddie Benavides	.05	.02
❑ 33F Scott Kamieniecki RC	.10	.03
❑ 34F Denny Neagle RC	.25	.07
❑ 35F Mike Humphreys RC	.10	.03
❑ 36F Mike Remlinger	.05	.02
❑ 37F Scott Coolbaugh	.05	.02
❑ 38F Darren Lewis	.05	.02
❑ 39F Thomas Howard	.05	.02
❑ 40F John Candelaria	.05	.02
❑ 41F Todd Benzinger	.05	.02
❑ 42F Wilson Alvarez	.05	.02
❑ 43F Patrick Lennon RC	.10	.03
❑ 44F Rusty Meacham RC	.10	.03
❑ 45F Ryan Bowen RC	.10	.03
❑ 46F Rick Wilkins RC	.10	.03
❑ 47F Ed Sprague	.05	.02
❑ 48F Bob Scanlan	.05	.02
❑ 49F Tom Candiotti	.05	.02
❑ 50F Dennis Martinez	.10	.03
(Perfecto)		
❑ 51F Oil Can Boyd	.05	.02
❑ 52F Glenallen Hill	.05	.02
❑ 53F Scott Livingstone RC	.10	.03
❑ 54F Brian R. Hunter RC	.25	.07
❑ 55F Ivan Rodriguez RC	1.50	.45
❑ 56F Keith Mitchell RC	.10	.03
❑ 57F Roger McDowell	.05	.02
❑ 58F Otis Nixon	.05	.02
❑ 59F Juan Bell	.05	.02
❑ 60F Bill Krueger	.05	.02
❑ 61F Chris Donnels	.05	.02
❑ 62F Tommy Greene	.05	.02
❑ 63F Doug Simons	.05	.02
❑ 64F Andy Ashby RC	.25	.07
❑ 65F Anthony Young RC	.10	.03
❑ 66F Kevin Morton	.05	.02
❑ 67F Bret Barberie RC**	.10	.03
❑ 68F Scott Servais RC	.25	.07
❑ 69F Ron Darling	.05	.02
❑ 70F Tim Burke	.05	.02
❑ 71F Vicente Palacios	.05	.02
❑ 72F Gerald Alexander	.05	.02
❑ 73F Reggie Jefferson	.05	.02
❑ 74F Dean Palmer	.10	.03
❑ 75F Mark Whiten	.05	.02
❑ 76F Randy Tomlin RC	.10	.03
❑ 77F Mark Wohlers RC	.25	.07
❑ 78F Brook Jacoby	.05	.02
❑ 79F Ken Griffey Jr. CL	.40	.12
Ryne Sandberg		
❑ 80F Jack Morris AS	.05	.02
❑ 81F Sandy Alomar Jr. AS	.05	.02
❑ 82F Cecil Fielder AS	.05	.02
❑ 83F Roberto Alomar AS	.10	.03
❑ 84F Wade Boggs AS	.10	.03
❑ 85F Cal Ripken AS	.40	.12
❑ 86F Rickey Henderson AS	.15	.04
❑ 87F Ken Griffey Jr. AS	.25	.07
❑ 88F Dave Henderson AS	.05	.02
❑ 89F Danny Tartabull AS	.05	.02
❑ 90F Tom Glavine AS	.10	.03
❑ 91F Benito Santiago AS	.05	.02
❑ 92F Will Clark AS	.10	.03
❑ 93F Ryne Sandberg AS	.25	.07
❑ 94F Chris Sabo AS	.05	.02
❑ 95F Ozzie Smith AS	.25	.07
❑ 96F Ivan Calderon AS	.05	.02
❑ 97F Tony Gwynn AS	.15	.04
❑ 98F Andre Dawson AS	.05	.02
❑ 99F Bobby Bonilla AS	.05	.02
❑ 100F Checklist 1-100	.05	.02

1993 Upper Deck

	Nm-Mt	Ex-Mt
COMPLETE SET (840)	40.00	12.00
COMP.FACT.SET (840)	50.00	15.00
COMP. SERIES 1 (420)	15.00	4.50
COMP. SERIES 2 (420)	25.00	7.50
❑ 1 Tim Salmon CL	.20	.06
❑ 2 Mike Piazza SR	1.50	.45
❑ 3 Rene Arocha SR RC	.50	.15
❑ 4 Willie Greene SR	.10	.03
❑ 5 Manny Alexander	.10	.03
❑ 6 Dan Wilson	.20	.06
❑ 7 Dan Smith	.10	.03
❑ 8 Kevin Rogers	.10	.03
❑ 9 Kurt Miller SR	.10	.03
❑ 10 Joe Vitko	.10	.03
❑ 11 Tim Costo	.10	.03
❑ 12 Alan Embree SR	.50	.15
❑ 13 Jim Tatum SR RC	.15	.04
❑ 14 Cris Colon	.10	.03
❑ 15 Steve Hosey	.10	.03
❑ 16 S. Hitchcock SR RC	.50	.15
❑ 17 Dave Mlicki	.10	.03
❑ 18 Jessie Hollins	.10	.03
❑ 19 Bobby Jones SR	.20	.06
❑ 20 Kurt Miller	.10	.03
❑ 21 Melvin Nieves SR	.10	.03
❑ 22 Billy Ashley SR	.10	.03
❑ 23 J.T. Snow SR RC	.75	.23
❑ 24 Chipper Jones SR	.50	.15
❑ 25 Tim Salmon SR	.30	.09
❑ 26 Tim Pugh SR RC	.15	.04
❑ 27 David Nied SR	.10	.03
❑ 28 Mike Trombley	.10	.03
❑ 29 Javier Lopez SR	.30	.09
❑ 30 Jim Abbott CH CL	.20	.06
❑ 31 Jim Abbott CH	.10	.03
❑ 32 Dale Murphy CH	.30	.09
❑ 33 Tony Pena CH	.10	.03
❑ 34 Kirby Puckett CH	.30	.09
❑ 35 Harold Reynolds CH	.10	.03
❑ 36 Cal Ripken CH	.75	.23
❑ 37 Nolan Ryan CH	1.00	.30
❑ 38 Ryne Sandberg CH	.50	.15
❑ 39 Dave Stewart CH	.10	.03
❑ 40 Dave Winfield CH	.10	.03
❑ 41 Joe Carter CL	.50	.15
Mark McGwire		
❑ 42 Joe Carter	.20	.06
Roberto Alomar		
❑ 43 Paul Molitor	.50	.15
Pat Listach		
Robin Yount		
❑ 44 Cal Ripken	.50	.15
Brady Anderson		
❑ 45 Albert Belle	.30	.09
Sandy Alomar Jr.		
Jim Thome		
Carlos Baerga		
Kenny Lofton		
❑ 46 Cecil Fielder	.10	.03
Mickey Tettleton		
❑ 47 Roberto Kelly	.60	.18
Don Mattingly		
❑ 48 Frank Viola	.50	.15
Roger Clemens		
❑ 49 Ruben Sierra	.50	.15
Mark McGwire		
❑ 50 Kent Hrbek	.30	.09
Kirby Puckett		
❑ 51 Robin Ventura	.30	.09
Frank Thomas		
❑ 52 Juan Gonzalez	.50	.15
Jose Canseco		
Ivan Rodriguez		
Rafael Palmeiro		
❑ 53 Mark Langston	.20	.06
Jim Abbott		
Chuck Finley		
❑ 54 Wally Joyner	.50	.15
Gregg Jefferies		
George Brett		
❑ 55 Kevin Mitchell	.50	.15
Ken Griffey Jr.		
Jay Buhner		
❑ 56 George Brett	1.25	.35
❑ 57 Scott Cooper	.10	.03
❑ 58 Mike Maddux	.10	.03
❑ 59 Rusty Meacham	.10	.03
❑ 60 Wil Cordero	.10	.03
❑ 61 Tim Teufel	.10	.03
❑ 62 Jeff Montgomery	.10	.03
❑ 63 Scott Livingstone	.10	.03
❑ 64 Doug Dascenzo	.10	.03
❑ 65 Bret Boone	.30	.09
❑ 66 Tim Wakefield	.50	.15
❑ 67 Curt Schilling	.20	.06
❑ 68 Frank Tanana	.10	.03
❑ 69 Len Dykstra	.20	.06
❑ 70 Derek Lilliquist	.10	.03
❑ 71 Anthony Young	.10	.03
❑ 72 Hipolito Pichardo	.10	.03
❑ 73 Rod Beck	.10	.03
❑ 74 Kent Hrbek	.20	.06
❑ 75 Tom Glavine	.30	.09
❑ 76 Kevin Brown	.20	.06
❑ 77 Chuck Finley	.20	.06
❑ 78 Bob Walk	.10	.03
❑ 79 Rheal Cormier UER	.10	.03
(Born in New Brunswick, not British Columbia)		
❑ 80 Rick Sutcliffe	.20	.06
❑ 81 Harold Baines	.20	.06
❑ 82 Lee Smith	.20	.06
❑ 83 Geno Petralli	.10	.03
❑ 84 Jose Oquendo	.10	.03
❑ 85 Mark Gubicza	.10	.03
❑ 86 Mickey Tettleton	.10	.03
❑ 87 Bobby Witt	.10	.03
❑ 88 Mark Lewis	.10	.03
❑ 89 Kevin Appier	.20	.06
❑ 90 Mike Stanton	.10	.03
❑ 91 Rafael Belliard	.10	.03
❑ 92 Kenny Rogers	.20	.06
❑ 93 Randy Velarde	.10	.03
❑ 94 Luis Sojo	.10	.03
❑ 95 Mark Leiter	.10	.03
❑ 96 Jody Reed	.10	.03
❑ 97 Pete Harnisch	.10	.03
❑ 98 Tom Candiotti	.10	.03
❑ 99 Mark Portugal	.10	.03

❑ 100 Dave Valle .10 .03
❑ 101 Shawon Dunston .10 .03
❑ 102 B.J. Surhoff .20 .06
❑ 103 Jay Bell .20 .06
❑ 104 Sid Bream .10 .03
❑ 105 Frank Thomas CL .30 .09
❑ 106 Mike Morgan .10 .03
❑ 107 Bill Doran .10 .03
❑ 108 Lance Blankenship .10 .03
❑ 109 Mark Lemke .10 .03
❑ 110 Brian Harper .10 .03
❑ 111 Brady Anderson .20 .06
❑ 112 Bip Roberts .10 .03
❑ 113 Mitch Williams .10 .03
❑ 114 Craig Biggio .30 .09
❑ 115 Eddie Murray .50 .15
❑ 116 Matt Nokes .10 .03
❑ 117 Lance Parrish .20 .06
❑ 118 Bill Swift .10 .03
❑ 119 Jeff Innis .10 .03
❑ 120 Mike LaValliere .10 .03
❑ 121 Hal Morris .10 .03
❑ 122 Walt Weiss .10 .03
❑ 123 Ivan Rodriguez .50 .15
❑ 124 Andy Van Slyke .20 .06
❑ 125 Roberto Alomar .30 .09
❑ 126 Robby Thompson .10 .03
❑ 127 Sammy Sosa .75 .23
❑ 128 Mark Langston .10 .03
❑ 129 Jerry Browne .10 .03
❑ 130 Chuck McElroy .10 .03
❑ 131 Frank Viola .20 .06
❑ 132 Leo Gomez .10 .03
❑ 133 Ramon Martinez .10 .03
❑ 134 Don Mattingly 1.25 .35
❑ 135 Roger Clemens 1.00 .30
❑ 136 Rickey Henderson .50 .15
❑ 137 Darren Daulton .20 .06
❑ 138 Ken Hill .10 .03
❑ 139 Ozzie Guillen .10 .03
❑ 140 Jerald Clark .10 .03
❑ 141 Dave Fleming .10 .03
❑ 142 Delino DeShields .10 .03
❑ 143 Matt Williams .20 .06
❑ 144 Larry Walker .30 .09
❑ 145 Ruben Sierra .10 .03
❑ 146 Ozzie Smith .75 .23
❑ 147 Chris Sabo .10 .03
❑ 148 Carlos Hernandez .10 .03
❑ 149 Pat Borders .10 .03
❑ 150 Orlando Merced .10 .03
❑ 151 Royce Clayton .10 .03
❑ 152 Kurt Stillwell .10 .03
❑ 153 Dave Hollins .10 .03
❑ 154 Mike Greenwell .10 .03
❑ 155 Nolan Ryan 2.00 .60
❑ 156 Felix Jose .10 .03
❑ 157 Junior Felix .10 .03
❑ 158 Derek Bell .10 .03
❑ 159 Steve Buechele .10 .03
❑ 160 John Burkett .10 .03
❑ 161 Pat Howell .10 .03
❑ 162 Milt Cuyler .10 .03
❑ 163 Terry Pendleton .20 .06
❑ 164 Jack Morris .20 .06
❑ 165 Tony Gwynn .60 .18
❑ 166 Deion Sanders .30 .09
❑ 167 Mike Devereaux .10 .03
❑ 168 Ron Darling .10 .03
❑ 169 Orel Hershiser .20 .06
❑ 170 Mike Jackson .10 .03
❑ 171 Doug Jones .10 .03
❑ 172 Dan Walters .10 .03
❑ 173 Darren Lewis .10 .03
❑ 174 Carlos Baerga .10 .03
❑ 175 Ryne Sandberg .75 .23
❑ 176 Gregg Jefferies .10 .03
❑ 177 John Jaha .10 .03
❑ 178 Luis Polonia .10 .03
❑ 179 Kirt Manwaring .10 .03
❑ 180 Mike Magnante .10 .03
❑ 181 Billy Ripken .10 .03
❑ 182 Mike Moore .10 .03
❑ 183 Eric Anthony .10 .03
❑ 184 Lenny Harris .10 .03
❑ 185 Tony Pena .10 .03
❑ 186 Mike Felder .10 .03
❑ 187 Greg Olson .10 .03
❑ 188 Rene Gonzales .10 .03
❑ 189 Mike Bordick .10 .03
❑ 190 Mel Rojas .10 .03
❑ 191 Todd Frohwirth .10 .03
❑ 192 Darryl Hamilton .10 .03
❑ 193 Mike Fetters .10 .03
❑ 194 Omar Olivares .10 .03
❑ 195 Tony Phillips .10 .03
❑ 196 Paul Sorrento .10 .03
❑ 197 Trevor Wilson .10 .03
❑ 198 Kevin Gross .10 .03
❑ 199 Ron Karkovice .10 .03
❑ 200 Brook Jacoby .10 .03
❑ 201 Mariano Duncan .10 .03
❑ 202 Dennis Cook .10 .03
❑ 203 Daryl Boston .10 .03
❑ 204 Mike Perez .10 .03
❑ 205 Manuel Lee .10 .03
❑ 206 Steve Olin .10 .03
❑ 207 Charlie Hough .20 .06
❑ 208 Scott Scudder .10 .03
❑ 209 Charlie O'Brien .10 .03
❑ 210 Barry Bonds CL .60 .18
❑ 211 Jose Vizcaino .10 .03
❑ 212 Scott Leius .10 .03
❑ 213 Kevin Mitchell .10 .03
❑ 214 Brian Barnes .10 .03
❑ 215 Pat Kelly .10 .03
❑ 216 Chris Hammond .10 .03
❑ 217 Rob Deer .10 .03
❑ 218 Cory Snyder .10 .03
❑ 219 Gary Carter .20 .06
❑ 220 Danny Darwin .10 .03
❑ 221 Tom Gordon .10 .03
❑ 222 Gary Sheffield .20 .06
❑ 223 Joe Carter .20 .06
❑ 224 Jay Buhner .20 .06
❑ 225 Jose Offerman .10 .03
❑ 226 Jose Rijo .10 .03
❑ 227 Mark Whiten .10 .03
❑ 228 Randy Milligan .10 .03
❑ 229 Bud Black .10 .03
❑ 230 Gary DiSarcina .10 .03
❑ 231 Steve Finley .20 .06
❑ 232 Dennis Martinez .20 .06
❑ 233 Mike Mussina .30 .09
❑ 234 Joe Oliver .10 .03
❑ 235 Chad Curtis .10 .03
❑ 236 Shane Mack .10 .03
❑ 237 Jaime Navarro .10 .03
❑ 238 Brian McRae .10 .03
❑ 239 Chili Davis .20 .06
❑ 240 Jeff King .10 .03
❑ 241 Dean Palmer .20 .06
❑ 242 Danny Tartabull .10 .03
❑ 243 Charles Nagy .10 .03
❑ 244 Ray Lankford .10 .03
❑ 245 Barry Larkin .30 .09
❑ 246 Steve Avery .10 .03
❑ 247 John Kruk .20 .06
❑ 248 Derrick May .10 .03
❑ 249 Stan Javier .10 .03
❑ 250 Roger McDowell .10 .03
❑ 251 Dan Gladden .10 .03
❑ 252 Wally Joyner .20 .06
❑ 253 Pat Listach .10 .03
❑ 254 Chuck Knoblauch .20 .06
❑ 255 Sandy Alomar Jr. .10 .03
❑ 256 Jeff Bagwell .30 .09
❑ 257 Andy Stankiewicz .10 .03
❑ 258 Darrin Jackson .10 .03
❑ 259 Brett Butler .20 .06
❑ 260 Joe Orsulak .10 .03
❑ 261 Andy Benes .10 .03
❑ 262 Kenny Lofton .20 .06
❑ 263 Robin Ventura .20 .06
❑ 264 Ron Gant .20 .06
❑ 265 Ellis Burks .20 .06
❑ 266 Juan Guzman .10 .03
❑ 267 Wes Chamberlain .10 .03
❑ 268 John Smiley .10 .03
❑ 269 Franklin Stubbs .10 .03
❑ 270 Tom Browning .10 .03
❑ 271 Dennis Eckersley .20 .06
❑ 272 Carlton Fisk .30 .09
❑ 273 Lou Whitaker .20 .06
❑ 274 Phil Plantier .10 .03
❑ 275 Bobby Bonilla .20 .06
❑ 276 Ben McDonald .10 .03
❑ 277 Bob Zupcic .10 .03
❑ 278 Terry Steinbach .10 .03
❑ 279 Terry Mulholland .10 .03
❑ 280 Lance Johnson .10 .03
❑ 281 Willie McGee .20 .06
❑ 282 Bret Saberhagen .20 .06
❑ 283 Randy Myers .10 .03
❑ 284 Randy Tomlin .10 .03
❑ 285 Mickey Morandini .10 .03
❑ 286 Brian Williams .10 .03
❑ 287 Tino Martinez .30 .09
❑ 288 Jose Melendez .10 .03
❑ 289 Jeff Huson .10 .03
❑ 290 Joe Grahe .10 .03
❑ 291 Mel Hall .10 .03
❑ 292 Otis Nixon .10 .03
❑ 293 Todd Hundley .10 .03
❑ 294 Casey Candaele .10 .03
❑ 295 Kevin Seitzer .10 .03
❑ 296 Eddie Taubensee .10 .03
❑ 297 Moises Alou .20 .06
❑ 298 Scott Radinsky .10 .03
❑ 299 Thomas Howard .10 .03
❑ 300 Kyle Abbott .10 .03
❑ 301 Omar Vizquel .30 .09
❑ 302 Keith Miller .10 .03
❑ 303 Rick Aguilera .10 .03
❑ 304 Bruce Hurst .10 .03
❑ 305 Ken Caminiti .20 .06
❑ 306 Mike Pagliarulo .10 .03
❑ 307 Frank Seminara .10 .03
❑ 308 Andre Dawson .20 .06
❑ 309 Jose Lind .10 .03
❑ 310 Joe Boever .10 .03
❑ 311 Jeff Parrett .10 .03
❑ 312 Alan Mills .10 .03
❑ 313 Kevin Tapani .10 .03
❑ 314 Darryl Kile .20 .06
❑ 315 Will Clark CL .20 .06
❑ 316 Mike Sharperson .10 .03
❑ 317 John Orton .10 .03
❑ 318 Bob Tewksbury .10 .03
❑ 319 Xavier Hernandez .10 .03
❑ 320 Paul Assenmacher .10 .03
❑ 321 John Franco .20 .06
❑ 322 Mike Timlin .10 .03
❑ 323 Jose Guzman .10 .03
❑ 324 Pedro Martinez 1.00 .30
❑ 325 Bill Spiers .10 .03
❑ 326 Melido Perez .10 .03
❑ 327 Mike Macfarlane .10 .03
❑ 328 Ricky Bones .10 .03
❑ 329 Scott Bankhead .10 .03
❑ 330 Rich Rodriguez .10 .03
❑ 331 Geronimo Pena .10 .03
❑ 332 Bernie Williams .30 .09
❑ 333 Paul Molitor .30 .09
❑ 334 Carlos Garcia .10 .03
❑ 335 David Cone .20 .06
❑ 336 Randy Johnson .50 .15
❑ 337 Pat Mahomes .10 .03
❑ 338 Erik Hanson .10 .03
❑ 339 Duane Ward .10 .03
❑ 340 Al Martin .10 .03
❑ 341 Pedro Munoz .10 .03
❑ 342 Greg Colbrunn .10 .03
❑ 343 Julio Valera .10 .03
❑ 344 John Olerud .20 .06
❑ 345 George Bell .10 .03
❑ 346 Devon White .20 .06
❑ 347 Donovan Osborne .10 .03
❑ 348 Mark Gardner .10 .03
❑ 349 Zane Smith .10 .03
❑ 350 Wilson Alvarez .10 .03
❑ 351 Kevin Koslofski .10 .03
❑ 352 Roberto Hernandez .10 .03
❑ 353 Glenn Davis .10 .03
❑ 354 Reggie Sanders .10 .03
❑ 355 Ken Griffey Jr. .75 .23
❑ 356 Marquis Grissom .20 .06
❑ 357 Jack McDowell .10 .03

❑ 358 Jimmy Key .20 .06
❑ 359 Stan Belinda .10 .03
❑ 360 Gerald Williams .10 .03
❑ 361 Sid Fernandez .10 .03
❑ 362 Alex Fernandez .10 .03
❑ 363 John Smoltz .30 .09
❑ 364 Travis Fryman .20 .06
❑ 365 Jose Canseco .50 .15
❑ 366 David Justice .20 .06
❑ 367 Pedro Astacio .10 .03
❑ 368 Tim Belcher .10 .03
❑ 369 Steve Sax .10 .03
❑ 370 Gary Gaetti .20 .06
❑ 371 Jeff Frye .10 .03
❑ 372 Bob Wickman .10 .03
❑ 373 Ryan Thompson .10 .03
❑ 374 David Hulse RC .15 .04
❑ 375 Cal Eldred .10 .03
❑ 376 Ryan Klesko .20 .06
❑ 377 Damion Easley .10 .03
❑ 378 John Kiely .10 .03
❑ 379 Jim Bullinger .10 .03
❑ 380 Brian Bohanon .10 .03
❑ 381 Rod Brewer .10 .03
❑ 382 Fernando Ramsey RC .15 .04
❑ 383 Sam Militello .10 .03
❑ 384 Arthur Rhodes .10 .03
❑ 385 Eric Karros .20 .06
❑ 386 Rico Brogna .10 .03
❑ 387 John Valentin .10 .03
❑ 388 Kerry Woodson .10 .03
❑ 389 Ben Rivera .10 .03
❑ 390 Matt Whiteside RC .15 .04
❑ 391 Henry Rodriguez .10 .03
❑ 392 John Wetteland .20 .06
❑ 393 Kent Mercker .10 .03
❑ 394 Bernard Gilkey .10 .03
❑ 395 Doug Henry .10 .03
❑ 396 Mo Vaughn .20 .06
❑ 397 Scott Erickson .10 .03
❑ 398 Bill Gullickson .10 .03
❑ 399 Mark Guthrie .10 .03
❑ 400 Dave Martinez .10 .03
❑ 401 Jeff Kent .50 .15
❑ 402 Chris Hoiles .10 .03
❑ 403 Mike Henneman .10 .03
❑ 404 Chris Nabholz .10 .03
❑ 405 Tom Pagnozzi .10 .03
❑ 406 Kelly Gruber .10 .03
❑ 407 Bob Welch .10 .03
❑ 408 Frank Castillo .10 .03
❑ 409 John Dopson .10 .03
❑ 410 Steve Farr .10 .03
❑ 411 Henry Cotto .10 .03
❑ 412 Bob Patterson .10 .03
❑ 413 Todd Stottlemyre .10 .03
❑ 414 Greg A. Harris .10 .03
❑ 415 Denny Neagle .20 .06
❑ 416 Bill Wegman .10 .03
❑ 417 Willie Wilson .10 .03
❑ 418 Terry Leach .10 .03
❑ 419 Willie Randolph .20 .06
❑ 420 Mark McGwire CL .30 .09
❑ 421 Calvin Murray CL .10 .03
❑ 422 Pete Janicki TP RC .15 .04
❑ 423 Todd Jones TP .10 .03
❑ 424 Mike Neill TP .10 .03
❑ 425 Carlos Delgado TP .50 .15
❑ 426 Jose Oliva TP .10 .03
❑ 427 Tyrone Hill TP .10 .03
❑ 428 Dmitri Young TP .20 .06
❑ 429 Derek Wallace TP RC .15 .04
❑ 430 Michael Moore TP RC .15 .04
❑ 431 Cliff Floyd TP .20 .06
❑ 432 Calvin Murray TP .10 .03
❑ 433 Manny Ramirez TP .50 .15
❑ 434 Marc Newfield TP .10 .03
❑ 435 Charles Johnson TP .20 .06
❑ 436 Butch Huskey TP .10 .03
❑ 437 Brad Pennington TP .10 .03
❑ 438 Ray McDavid TP RC .15 .04
❑ 439 Chad McConnell TP .10 .03
❑ 440 M.Cummings TP RC .15 .04
❑ 441 Benji Gil TP .10 .03
❑ 442 Frankie Rodriguez TP .10 .03
❑ 443 Chad Mottola TP RC .15 .04
❑ 444 John Burke TP RC .15 .04
❑ 445 Michael Tucker TP .20 .06
❑ 446 Rick Greene TP .10 .03
❑ 447 Rich Becker TP .10 .03
❑ 448 Mike Robertson TP .10 .03
❑ 449 Derek Jeter TP RC 10.00 3.00
❑ 450 Ivan Rodriguez CL .30 .09
David McCarty
❑ 451 Jim Abbott IN .20 .06
❑ 452 Jeff Bagwell IN .20 .06
❑ 453 Jason Bere IN .10 .03
❑ 454 Delino DeShields IN .10 .03
❑ 455 Travis Fryman IN .10 .03
❑ 456 Alex Gonzalez IN .10 .03
❑ 457 Phil Hiatt IN .10 .03
❑ 458 Dave Hollins IN .10 .03
❑ 459 Chipper Jones IN .30 .09
❑ 460 David Justice IN .10 .03
❑ 461 Ray Lankford IN .10 .03
❑ 462 David McCarty IN .10 .03
❑ 463 Mike Mussina IN .20 .06
❑ 464 Jose Offerman IN .10 .03
❑ 465 Dean Palmer IN .10 .03
❑ 466 Geronimo Pena IN .10 .03
❑ 467 Eduardo Perez IN .10 .03
❑ 468 Ivan Rodriguez IN .30 .09
❑ 469 Reggie Sanders IN .10 .03
❑ 470 Bernie Williams IN .20 .06
❑ 471 Barry Bonds CL .50 .15
Matt Williams
Will Clark
❑ 472 Greg Maddux .50 .15
Steve Avery
John Smoltz
Tom Glavine
❑ 473 Jose Rijo .20 .06
Rob Dibble
Roberto Kelly
Reggie Sanders
Barry Larkin
❑ 474 Gary Sheffield .20 .06
Phil Plantier
Tony Gwynn
Fred McGriff
❑ 475 Doug Drabek .20 .06
Craig Biggio
Jeff Bagwell
❑ 476 Will Clark .50 .15
Barry Bonds
Matt Williams
❑ 477 Eric Davis .20 .06
Darryl Strawberry
❑ 478 Dante Bichette .20 .06
David Nied
Andres Galarraga
❑ 479 Dave Magadan .10 .03
Orestes Destrade
Bret Barberie
Jeff Conine
❑ 480 Tim Wakefield .20 .06
Andy Van Slyke
Jay Bell
❑ 481 Marquis Grissom .20 .06
Delino DeShields
Dennis Martinez
Larry Walker
❑ 482 Geronimo Pena .50 .15
Ray Lankford
Ozzie Smith
Bernard Gilkey
❑ 483 Randy Myers .50 .15
Ryne Sandberg
Mark Grace
❑ 484 Eddie Murray .30 .09
Howard Johnson
Bobby Bonilla
❑ 485 John Kruk .10 .03
Dave Hollins
Darren Daulton
Len Dykstra
❑ 486 Barry Bonds AW .60 .18
❑ 487 Dennis Eckersley AW .20 .06
❑ 488 Greg Maddux AW .50 .15
❑ 489 Dennis Eckersley AW .20 .06
❑ 490 Eric Karros AW .10 .03
❑ 491 Pat Listach AW .10 .03
❑ 492 Gary Sheffield AW .10 .03
❑ 493 Mark McGwire AW .60 .18
❑ 494 Gary Sheffield AW .10 .03
❑ 495 Edgar Martinez AW .20 .06
❑ 496 Fred McGriff AW .20 .06
❑ 497 Juan Gonzalez AW .20 .06
❑ 498 Darren Daulton AW .10 .03
❑ 499 Cecil Fielder AW .10 .03
❑ 500 Brent Gates CL .10 .03
❑ 501 Tavo Alvarez DD .10 .03
❑ 502 Rod Bolton .10 .03
❑ 503 J.Cummings DD RC .15 .04
❑ 504 Brent Gates DD .10 .03
❑ 505 Tyler Green .10 .03
❑ 506 Jose Martinez DD RC .15 .04
❑ 507 Troy Percival .30 .09
❑ 508 Kevin Stocker DD .10 .03
❑ 509 Matt Walbeck DD RC .15 .04
❑ 510 Rondell White DD .20 .06
❑ 511 Billy Ripken .10 .03
❑ 512 Mike Moore .10 .03
❑ 513 Jose Lind .10 .03
❑ 514 Chito Martinez .10 .03
❑ 515 Jose Guzman .10 .03
❑ 516 Kim Batiste .10 .03
❑ 517 Jeff Tackett .10 .03
❑ 518 Charlie Hough .20 .06
❑ 519 Marvin Freeman .10 .03
❑ 520 Carlos Martinez .10 .03
❑ 521 Eric Young .10 .03
❑ 522 Pete Incaviglia .10 .03
❑ 523 Scott Fletcher .10 .03
❑ 524 Orestes Destrade .10 .03
❑ 525 Ken Griffey Jr. CL .50 .15
❑ 526 Ellis Burks .20 .06
❑ 527 Juan Samuel .10 .03
❑ 528 Dave Magadan .10 .03
❑ 529 Jeff Parrett .10 .03
❑ 530 Bill Krueger .10 .03
❑ 531 Frank Bolick .10 .03
❑ 532 Alan Trammell .20 .06
❑ 533 Walt Weiss .10 .03
❑ 534 David Cone .20 .06
❑ 535 Greg Maddux .75 .23
❑ 536 Kevin Young .20 .06
❑ 537 Dave Hansen .10 .03
❑ 538 Alex Cole .10 .03
❑ 539 Greg Hibbard .10 .03
❑ 540 Gene Larkin .10 .03
❑ 541 Jeff Reardon .20 .06
❑ 542 Felix Jose .10 .03
❑ 543 Jimmy Key .20 .06
❑ 544 Reggie Jefferson .10 .03
❑ 545 Gregg Jefferies .10 .03
❑ 546 Dave Stewart .20 .06
❑ 547 Tim Wallach .10 .03
❑ 548 Spike Owen .10 .03
❑ 549 Tommy Greene .10 .03
❑ 550 Fernando Valenzuela .20 .06
❑ 551 Rich Amaral .10 .03
❑ 552 Bret Barberie .10 .03
❑ 553 Edgar Martinez .30 .09
❑ 554 Jim Abbott .30 .09
❑ 555 Frank Thomas .50 .15
❑ 556 Wade Boggs .30 .09
❑ 557 Tom Henke .10 .03
❑ 558 Milt Thompson .10 .03
❑ 559 Lloyd McClendon .10 .03
❑ 560 Vinny Castilla .20 .06
❑ 561 Ricky Jordan .10 .03
❑ 562 Andujar Cedeno .10 .03
❑ 563 Greg Vaughn .10 .03
❑ 564 Cecil Fielder .20 .06
❑ 565 Kirby Puckett .50 .15
❑ 566 Mark McGwire 1.25 .35
❑ 567 Barry Bonds 1.25 .35
❑ 568 Jody Reed .10 .03
❑ 569 Todd Zeile .10 .03
❑ 570 Mark Carreon .10 .03
❑ 571 Joe Girardi .10 .03
❑ 572 Luis Gonzalez .20 .06
❑ 573 Mark Grace .30 .09
❑ 574 Rafael Palmeiro .30 .09
❑ 575 Darryl Strawberry .20 .06
❑ 576 Will Clark .50 .15
❑ 577 Fred McGriff .30 .09

❑ 578 Kevin Reimer .10 .03
❑ 579 Dave Righetti .20 .06
❑ 580 Juan Bell .10 .03
❑ 581 Jeff Brantley .10 .03
❑ 582 Brian Hunter .10 .03
❑ 583 Tim Naehring .10 .03
❑ 584 Glenallen Hill .10 .03
❑ 585 Cal Ripken 1.50 .45
❑ 586 Albert Belle .20 .06
❑ 587 Robin Yount .75 .23
❑ 588 Chris Bosio .10 .03
❑ 589 Pete Smith .10 .03
❑ 590 Chuck Carr .10 .03
❑ 591 Jeff Blauser .10 .03
❑ 592 Kevin McReynolds .10 .03
❑ 593 Andres Galarraga .20 .06
❑ 594 Kevin Maas .10 .03
❑ 595 Eric Davis .20 .06
❑ 596 Brian Jordan .20 .06
❑ 597 Tim Raines .20 .06
❑ 598 Rick Wilkins .10 .03
❑ 599 Steve Cooke .10 .03
❑ 600 Mike Gallego .10 .03
❑ 601 Mike Munoz .10 .03
❑ 602 Luis Rivera .10 .03
❑ 603 Junior Ortiz .10 .03
❑ 604 Brent Mayne .10 .03
❑ 605 Luis Alicea .10 .03
❑ 606 Damon Berryhill .10 .03
❑ 607 Dave Henderson .10 .03
❑ 608 Kirk McCaskill .10 .03
❑ 609 Jeff Fassero .10 .03
❑ 610 Mike Harkey .10 .03
❑ 611 Francisco Cabrera .10 .03
❑ 612 Rey Sanchez .10 .03
❑ 613 Scott Servais .10 .03
❑ 614 Darrin Fletcher .10 .03
❑ 615 Felix Fermin .10 .03
❑ 616 Kevin Seitzer .10 .03
❑ 617 Bob Scanlan .10 .03
❑ 618 Billy Hatcher .10 .03
❑ 619 John Vander Wal .10 .03
❑ 620 Joe Hesketh .10 .03
❑ 621 Hector Villanueva .10 .03
❑ 622 Randy Milligan .10 .03
❑ 623 Tony Tarasco RC .15 .04
❑ 624 Russ Swan .10 .03
❑ 625 Willie Wilson .10 .03
❑ 626 Frank Tanana .10 .03
❑ 627 Pete O'Brien .10 .03
❑ 628 Lenny Webster .10 .03
❑ 629 Mark Clark .10 .03
❑ 630 Roger Clemens CL .50 .15
❑ 631 Alex Arias .10 .03
❑ 632 Chris Gwynn .10 .03
❑ 633 Tom Bolton .10 .03
❑ 634 Greg Briley .10 .03
❑ 635 Kent Bottenfield .10 .03
❑ 636 Kelly Downs .10 .03
❑ 637 Manuel Lee .10 .03
❑ 638 Al Leiter .20 .06
❑ 639 Jeff Gardner .10 .03
❑ 640 Mike Gardiner .10 .03
❑ 641 Mark Gardner .10 .03
❑ 642 Jeff Branson .10 .03
❑ 643 Paul Wagner .10 .03
❑ 644 Sean Berry .10 .03
❑ 645 Phil Hiatt .10 .03
❑ 646 Kevin Mitchell .10 .03
❑ 647 Charlie Hayes .10 .03
❑ 648 Jim Deshaies .10 .03
❑ 649 Dan Pasqua .10 .03
❑ 650 Mike Maddux .10 .03
❑ 651 Domingo Martinez RC .15 .04
❑ 652 Greg McMichael RC .15 .04
❑ 653 Eric Wedge RC .50 .15
❑ 654 Mark Whiten .10 .03
❑ 655 Roberto Kelly .10 .03
❑ 656 Julio Franco .20 .06
❑ 657 Gene Harris .10 .03
❑ 658 Pete Schourek .10 .03
❑ 659 Mike Bielecki .10 .03
❑ 660 Ricky Gutierrez .10 .03
❑ 661 Chris Hammond .10 .03
❑ 662 Tim Scott .10 .03
❑ 663 Norm Charlton .10 .03
❑ 664 Doug Drabek .10 .03
❑ 665 Dwight Gooden .20 .06
❑ 666 Jim Gott .10 .03
❑ 667 Randy Myers .10 .03
❑ 668 Darren Holmes .10 .03
❑ 669 Tim Spehr .10 .03
❑ 670 Bruce Ruffin .10 .03
❑ 671 Bobby Thigpen .10 .03
❑ 672 Tony Fernandez .10 .03
❑ 673 Darrin Jackson .10 .03
❑ 674 Gregg Olson .10 .03
❑ 675 Rob Dibble .20 .06
❑ 676 Howard Johnson .10 .03
❑ 677 Mike Lansing RC .50 .15
❑ 678 Charlie Leibrandt .10 .03
❑ 679 Kevin Bass .10 .03
❑ 680 Hubie Brooks .10 .03
❑ 681 Scott Brosius .20 .06
❑ 682 Randy Knorr .10 .03
❑ 683 Dante Bichette .20 .06
❑ 684 Bryan Harvey .10 .03
❑ 685 Greg Gohr .10 .03
❑ 686 Willie Banks .10 .03
❑ 687 Robb Nen .20 .06
❑ 688 Mike Scioscia .10 .03
❑ 689 John Farrell .10 .03
❑ 690 John Candelaria .10 .03
❑ 691 Damon Buford .10 .03
❑ 692 Todd Worrell .10 .03
❑ 693 Pat Hentgen .10 .03
❑ 694 John Smiley .10 .03
❑ 695 Greg Swindell .10 .03
❑ 696 Derek Bell .10 .03
❑ 697 Terry Jorgensen .10 .03
❑ 698 Jimmy Jones .10 .03
❑ 699 David Wells .20 .06
❑ 700 Dave Martinez .10 .03
❑ 701 Steve Bedrosian .10 .03
❑ 702 Jeff Russell .10 .03
❑ 703 Joe Magrane .10 .03
❑ 704 Matt Mieske .10 .03
❑ 705 Paul Molitor .30 .09
❑ 706 Dale Murphy .50 .15
❑ 707 Steve Howe .10 .03
❑ 708 Greg Gagne .10 .03
❑ 709 Dave Eiland .10 .03
❑ 710 David West .10 .03
❑ 711 Luis Aquino .10 .03
❑ 712 Joe Orsulak .10 .03
❑ 713 Eric Plunk .10 .03
❑ 714 Mike Felder .10 .03
❑ 715 Joe Klink .10 .03
❑ 716 Lonnie Smith .10 .03
❑ 717 Monty Fariss .10 .03
❑ 718 Craig Lefferts .10 .03
❑ 719 John Habyan .10 .03
❑ 720 Willie Blair .10 .03
❑ 721 Darnell Coles .10 .03
❑ 722 Mark Williamson .10 .03
❑ 723 Bryn Smith .10 .03
❑ 724 Greg W. Harris .10 .03
❑ 725 Graeme Lloyd RC .50 .15
❑ 726 Cris Carpenter .10 .03
❑ 727 Chico Walker .10 .03
❑ 728 Tracy Woodson .10 .03
❑ 729 Jose Uribe .10 .03
❑ 730 Stan Javier .10 .03
❑ 731 Jay Howell .10 .03
❑ 732 Freddie Benavides .10 .03
❑ 733 Jeff Reboulet .10 .03
❑ 734 Scott Sanderson .10 .03
❑ 735 Ryne Sandberg CL .50 .15
❑ 736 Archi Cianfrocco .10 .03
❑ 737 Daryl Boston .10 .03
❑ 738 Craig Grebeck .10 .03
❑ 739 Doug Dascenzo .10 .03
❑ 740 Gerald Young .10 .03
❑ 741 Candy Maldonado .10 .03
❑ 742 Joey Cora .10 .03
❑ 743 Don Slaught .10 .03
❑ 744 Steve Decker .10 .03
❑ 745 Blas Minor .10 .03
❑ 746 Storm Davis .10 .03
❑ 747 Carlos Quintana .10 .03
❑ 748 Vince Coleman .10 .03
❑ 749 Todd Burns .10 .03
❑ 750 Steve Frey .10 .03
❑ 751 Ivan Calderon .10 .03
❑ 752 Steve Reed RC .15 .04
❑ 753 Danny Jackson .10 .03
❑ 754 Jeff Conine .20 .06
❑ 755 Juan Gonzalez .30 .09
❑ 756 Mike Kelly .10 .03
❑ 757 John Doherty .10 .03
❑ 758 Jack Armstrong .10 .03
❑ 759 John Wehner .10 .03
❑ 760 Scott Bankhead .10 .03
❑ 761 Jim Tatum .10 .03
❑ 762 Scott Pose RC .15 .04
❑ 763 Andy Ashby .10 .03
❑ 764 Ed Sprague .10 .03
❑ 765 Harold Baines .20 .06
❑ 766 Kirk Gibson .20 .06
❑ 767 Troy Neel .10 .03
❑ 768 Dick Schofield .10 .03
❑ 769 Dickie Thon .10 .03
❑ 770 Butch Henry .10 .03
❑ 771 Junior Felix .10 .03
❑ 772 Ken Ryan RC .15 .04
❑ 773 Trevor Hoffman .20 .06
❑ 774 Phil Plantier .10 .03
❑ 775 Bo Jackson .50 .15
❑ 776 Benito Santiago .20 .06
❑ 777 Andre Dawson .20 .06
❑ 778 Bryan Hickerson .10 .03
❑ 779 Dennis Moeller .10 .03
❑ 780 Ryan Bowen .10 .03
❑ 781 Eric Fox .10 .03
❑ 782 Joe Kmak .10 .03
❑ 783 Mike Hampton .20 .06
❑ 784 Darrell Sherman RC .15 .04
❑ 785 J.T. Snow .30 .09
❑ 786 Dave Winfield .20 .06
❑ 787 Jim Austin .10 .03
❑ 788 Craig Shipley .10 .03
❑ 789 Greg Myers .10 .03
❑ 790 Todd Benzinger .10 .03
❑ 791 Cory Snyder .10 .03
❑ 792 David Segui .10 .03
❑ 793 Armando Reynoso .10 .03
❑ 794 Chili Davis .20 .06
❑ 795 Dave Nilsson .10 .03
❑ 796 Paul O'Neill .30 .09
❑ 797 Jerald Clark .10 .03
❑ 798 Jose Mesa .10 .03
❑ 799 Brain Holman .10 .03
❑ 800 Jim Eisenreich .10 .03
❑ 801 Mark McLemore .10 .03
❑ 802 Luis Sojo .10 .03
❑ 803 Harold Reynolds .20 .06
❑ 804 Dan Plesac .10 .03
❑ 805 Dave Stieb .10 .03
❑ 806 Tom Brunansky .10 .03
❑ 807 Kelly Gruber .10 .03
❑ 808 Bob Ojeda .10 .03
❑ 809 Dave Burba .10 .03
❑ 810 Joe Boever .10 .03
❑ 811 Jeremy Hernandez .10 .03
❑ 812 Tim Salmon TC .20 .06
❑ 813 Jeff Bagwell TC .20 .06
❑ 814 Dennis Eckersley TC .20 .06
❑ 815 Roberto Alomar TC .20 .06
❑ 816 Steve Avery TC .10 .03
❑ 817 Pat Listach TC .10 .03
❑ 818 Gregg Jefferies TC .10 .03
❑ 819 Sammy Sosa TC .50 .15
❑ 820 Darryl Strawberry TC .10 .03
❑ 821 Dennis Martinez TC .10 .03
❑ 822 Robby Thompson TC .10 .03
❑ 823 Albert Belle TC .20 .06
❑ 824 Randy Johnson TC .30 .09
❑ 825 Nigel Wilson TC .10 .03
❑ 826 Bobby Bonilla TC .10 .03
❑ 827 Glenn Davis TC .10 .03
❑ 828 Gary Sheffield TC .10 .03
❑ 829 Darren Daulton TC .10 .03
❑ 830 Jay Bell TC .10 .03
❑ 831 Juan Gonzalez TC .20 .06
❑ 832 Andre Dawson TC .10 .03
❑ 833 Hal Morris TC .10 .03
❑ 834 David Nied TC .10 .03
❑ 835 Felix Jose TC .10 .03

❑ 836 Travis Fryman TC .10 .03
❑ 837 Shane Mack TC .10 .03
❑ 838 Robin Ventura TC .10 .03
❑ 839 Danny Tartabull TC .10 .03
❑ 840 Roberto Alomar CL .20 .06
❑ SP5 George Brett 1.00 .30
Robin Yount
❑ SP6 Nolan Ryan 2.00 .60

1994 Upper Deck

	Nm-Mt	Ex-Mt
COMPLETE SET (550)	50.00	15.00
COMP. SERIES 1 (280)	30.00	9.00
COMP. SERIES 2 (270)	20.00	6.00

❑ 1 Brian Anderson RC .40 .12
❑ 2 Shane Andrews .15 .04
❑ 3 James Baldwin .15 .04
❑ 4 Rich Becker .15 .04
❑ 5 Greg Blosser .15 .04
❑ 6 Ricky Bottalico RC .40 .12
❑ 7 Midre Cummings .15 .04
❑ 8 Carlos Delgado .50 .15
❑ 9 Steve Dreyer RC .15 .04
❑ 10 Joey Eischen .15 .04
❑ 11 Carl Everett .30 .09
❑ 12 Cliff Floyd UER .30 .09
(text indicates he throws left; should be right)
❑ 13 Alex Gonzalez .15 .04
❑ 14 Jeff Granger .15 .04
❑ 15 Shawn Green .75 .23
❑ 16 Brian L. Hunter .15 .04
❑ 17 Butch Huskey .15 .04
❑ 18 Mark Hutton .15 .04
❑ 19 Michael Jordan RC 8.00 2.40
❑ 20 Steve Karsay .15 .04
❑ 21 Jeff McNeely .15 .04
❑ 22 Marc Newfield .15 .04
❑ 23 Manny Ramirez .50 .15
❑ 24 Alex Rodriguez RC 15.00 4.50
❑ 25 Scott Ruffcorn UER .15 .04
(photo on back is Robert Ellis)
❑ 26 Paul Spoljaric UER .15 .04
(Expos logo on back)
❑ 27 Salomon Torres .15 .04
❑ 28 Steve Trachsel .15 .04
❑ 29 Chris Turner .15 .04
❑ 30 Gabe White .15 .04
❑ 31 Randy Johnson FT .50 .15
❑ 32 John Wetteland FT .15 .04
❑ 33 Mike Piazza FT .75 .23
❑ 34 Rafael Palmeiro FT .30 .09
❑ 35 Roberto Alomar FT .30 .09
❑ 36 Matt Williams FT .15 .04
❑ 37 Travis Fryman FT .15 .04
❑ 38 Barry Bonds FT 1.00 .30
❑ 39 Marquis Grissom FT .15 .04
❑ 40 Albert Belle FT .30 .09
❑ 41 Steve Avery FUT .15 .04
❑ 42 Jason Bere FUT .15 .04
❑ 43 Alex Fernandez FUT .15 .04
❑ 44 Mike Mussina FUT .30 .09
❑ 45 Aaron Sele FUT .15 .04
❑ 46 Rod Beck FUT .15 .04
❑ 47 Mike Piazza FUT .75 .23
❑ 48 John Olerud FUT .15 .04
❑ 49 Carlos Baerga FUT .15 .04
❑ 50 Gary Sheffield FUT .15 .04
❑ 51 Travis Fryman FUT .15 .04
❑ 52 Juan Gonzalez FUT .30 .09
❑ 53 Ken Griffey Jr. FUT .75 .23
❑ 54 Tim Salmon FUT .30 .09
❑ 55 Frank Thomas FUT .50 .15
❑ 56 Tony Phillips .15 .04
❑ 57 Julio Franco .30 .09
❑ 58 Kevin Mitchell .15 .04
❑ 59 Raul Mondesi .30 .09
❑ 60 Rickey Henderson .75 .23
❑ 61 Jay Buhner .30 .09
❑ 62 Bill Swift .15 .04
❑ 63 Brady Anderson .30 .09
❑ 64 Ryan Klesko .30 .09
❑ 65 Darren Daulton .30 .09
❑ 66 Damion Easley .15 .04
❑ 67 Mark McGwire 2.00 .60
❑ 68 John Roper .15 .04
❑ 69 Dave Telgheder .15 .04
❑ 70 David Nied .15 .04
❑ 71 Mo Vaughn .30 .09
❑ 72 Tyler Green .15 .04
❑ 73 Dave Magadan .15 .04
❑ 74 Chili Davis .30 .09
❑ 75 Archi Cianfrocco .15 .04
❑ 76 Joe Girardi .15 .04
❑ 77 Chris Hoiles .15 .04
❑ 78 Ryan Bowen .15 .04
❑ 79 Greg Gagne .15 .04
❑ 80 Aaron Sele .15 .04
❑ 81 Dave Winfield .30 .09
❑ 82 Chad Curtis .15 .04
❑ 83 Andy Van Slyke .30 .09
❑ 84 Kevin Stocker .15 .04
❑ 85 Deion Sanders .50 .15
❑ 86 Bernie Williams .50 .15
❑ 87 John Smoltz .50 .15
❑ 88 Ruben Santana .15 .04
❑ 89 Dave Stewart .30 .09
❑ 90 Don Mattingly 2.00 .60
❑ 91 Joe Carter .30 .09
❑ 92 Ryne Sandberg 1.25 .35
❑ 93 Chris Gomez .15 .04
❑ 94 Tino Martinez .50 .15
❑ 95 Terry Pendleton .30 .09
❑ 96 Andre Dawson .30 .09
❑ 97 Wil Cordero .15 .04
❑ 98 Kent Hrbek .30 .09
❑ 99 John Olerud .30 .09
❑ 100 Kirt Manwaring .15 .04
❑ 101 Tim Bogar .15 .04
❑ 102 Mike Mussina .50 .15
❑ 103 Nigel Wilson .15 .04
❑ 104 Ricky Gutierrez .15 .04
❑ 105 Roberto Mejia .15 .04
❑ 106 Tom Pagnozzi .15 .04
❑ 107 Mike Macfarlane .15 .04
❑ 108 Jose Bautista .15 .04
❑ 109 Luis Ortiz .15 .04
❑ 110 Brent Gates .15 .04
❑ 111 Tim Salmon .50 .15
❑ 112 Wade Boggs .50 .15
❑ 113 Tripp Cromer .15 .04
❑ 114 Denny Hocking .15 .04
❑ 115 Carlos Baerga .15 .04
❑ 116 J.R. Phillips .15 .04
❑ 117 Bo Jackson .75 .23
❑ 118 Lance Johnson .15 .04
❑ 119 Bobby Jones .15 .04
❑ 120 Bobby Witt .15 .04
❑ 121 Ron Karkovice .15 .04
❑ 122 Jose Vizcaino .15 .04
❑ 123 Danny Darwin .15 .04
❑ 124 Eduardo Perez .15 .04
❑ 125 Brian Looney RC .15 .04
❑ 126 Pat Hentgen .15 .04
❑ 127 Frank Viola .30 .09
❑ 128 Darren Holmes .15 .04
❑ 129 Wally Whitehurst .15 .04
❑ 130 Matt Walbeck .15 .04
❑ 131 Albert Belle .30 .09
❑ 132 Steve Cooke .15 .04
❑ 133 Kevin Appier .30 .09
❑ 134 Joe Oliver .15 .04
❑ 135 Benji Gil .15 .04
❑ 136 Steve Buechele .15 .04
❑ 137 Devon White .30 .09
❑ 138 S.Hitchcock UER .15 .04
two losses for career; should be four
❑ 139 Phil Leftwich RC .15 .04
❑ 140 Jose Canseco .75 .23
❑ 141 Rick Aguilera .15 .04
❑ 142 Rod Beck .15 .04
❑ 143 Jose Rijo .15 .04
❑ 144 Tom Glavine .50 .15
❑ 145 Phil Plantier .15 .04
❑ 146 Jason Bere .15 .04
❑ 147 Jamie Moyer .30 .09
❑ 148 Wes Chamberlain .15 .04
❑ 149 Glenallen Hill .15 .04
❑ 150 Mark Whiten .15 .04
❑ 151 Bret Barberie .15 .04
❑ 152 Chuck Knoblauch .30 .09
❑ 153 Trevor Hoffman .30 .09
❑ 154 Rick Wilkins .15 .04
❑ 155 Juan Gonzalez .50 .15
❑ 156 Ozzie Guillen .15 .04
❑ 157 Jim Eisenreich .15 .04
❑ 158 Pedro Astacio .15 .04
❑ 159 Joe Magrane .15 .04
❑ 160 Ryan Thompson .15 .04
❑ 161 Jose Lind .15 .04
❑ 162 Jeff Conine .30 .09
❑ 163 Todd Benzinger .15 .04
❑ 164 Roger Salkeld .15 .04
❑ 165 Gary DiSarcina .15 .04
❑ 166 Kevin Gross .15 .04
❑ 167 Charlie Hayes .15 .04
❑ 168 Tim Costo .15 .04
❑ 169 Wally Joyner .30 .09
❑ 170 Johnny Ruffin .15 .04
❑ 171 Kirk Rueter .30 .09
❑ 172 Lenny Dykstra .30 .09
❑ 173 Ken Hill .15 .04
❑ 174 Mike Bordick .15 .04
❑ 175 Billy Hall .15 .04
❑ 176 Rob Butler .15 .04
❑ 177 Jay Bell .30 .09
❑ 178 Jeff Kent .30 .09
❑ 179 David Wells .30 .09
❑ 180 Dean Palmer .30 .09
❑ 181 Mariano Duncan .15 .04
❑ 182 Orlando Merced .15 .04
❑ 183 Brett Butler .30 .09
❑ 184 Milt Thompson .15 .04
❑ 185 Chipper Jones .75 .23
❑ 186 Paul O'Neill .50 .15
❑ 187 Mike Greenwell .15 .04
❑ 188 Harold Baines .30 .09
❑ 189 Todd Stottlemyre .15 .04
❑ 190 Jeromy Burnitz .30 .09
❑ 191 Rene Arocha .15 .04
❑ 192 Jeff Fassero .15 .04
❑ 193 Robby Thompson .15 .04
❑ 194 Greg W. Harris .15 .04
❑ 195 Todd Van Poppel .15 .04
❑ 196 Jose Guzman .15 .04
❑ 197 Shane Mack .15 .04
❑ 198 Carlos Garcia .15 .04
❑ 199 Kevin Roberson .15 .04
❑ 200 David McCarty .15 .04
❑ 201 Alan Trammell .30 .09
❑ 202 Chuck Carr .15 .04
❑ 203 Tommy Greene .15 .04
❑ 204 Wilson Alvarez .15 .04
❑ 205 Dwight Gooden .30 .09
❑ 206 Tony Tarasco .15 .04
❑ 207 Darren Lewis .15 .04
❑ 208 Eric Karros .30 .09
❑ 209 Chris Hammond .15 .04
❑ 210 Jeffrey Hammonds .15 .04
❑ 211 Rich Amaral .15 .04
❑ 212 Danny Tartabull .15 .04
❑ 213 Jeff Russell .15 .04
❑ 214 Dave Staton .15 .04
❑ 215 Kenny Lofton .30 .09
❑ 216 Manuel Lee .15 .04
❑ 217 Brian Koelling .15 .04
❑ 218 Scott Lydy .15 .04

❑ 219 Tony Gwynn 1.00 .30
❑ 220 Cecil Fielder .30 .09
❑ 221 Royce Clayton .15 .04
❑ 222 Reggie Sanders .15 .04
❑ 223 Brian Jordan .30 .09
❑ 224 Ken Griffey Jr. 1.25 .35
❑ 225 Fred McGriff .50 .15
❑ 226 Felix Jose .15 .04
❑ 227 Brad Pennington .15 .04
❑ 228 Chris Bosio .15 .04
❑ 229 Mike Stanley .15 .04
❑ 230 Willie Greene .15 .04
❑ 231 Alex Fernandez .15 .04
❑ 232 Brad Ausmus .15 .04
❑ 233 Darrell Whitmore .15 .04
❑ 234 Marcus Moore .15 .04
❑ 235 Allen Watson .15 .04
❑ 236 Jose Offerman .15 .04
❑ 237 Rondell White .30 .09
❑ 238 Jeff King .15 .04
❑ 239 Luis Alicea .15 .04
❑ 240 Dan Wilson .15 .04
❑ 241 Ed Sprague .15 .04
❑ 242 Todd Hundley .15 .04
❑ 243 Al Martin .15 .04
❑ 244 Mike Lansing .15 .04
❑ 245 Ivan Rodriguez .75 .23
❑ 246 Dave Fleming .15 .04
❑ 247 John Doherty .15 .04
❑ 248 Mark McLemore .15 .04
❑ 249 Bob Hamelin .15 .04
❑ 250 Curtis Pride RC .40 .12
❑ 251 Zane Smith .15 .04
❑ 252 Eric Young .15 .04
❑ 253 Brian McRae .15 .04
❑ 254 Tim Raines .30 .09
❑ 255 Javier Lopez .30 .09
❑ 256 Melvin Nieves .15 .04
❑ 257 Randy Myers .15 .04
❑ 258 Willie McGee .30 .09
❑ 259 Jimmy Key UER .30 .09
(birthdate missing on back)
❑ 260 Tom Candiotti .15 .04
❑ 261 Eric Davis .30 .09
❑ 262 Craig Paquette .15 .04
❑ 263 Robin Ventura .30 .09
❑ 264 Pat Kelly .15 .04
❑ 265 Gregg Jefferies .15 .04
❑ 266 Cory Snyder .15 .04
❑ 267 David Justice HFA .15 .04
❑ 268 Sammy Sosa HFA .75 .23
❑ 269 Barry Larkin HFA .30 .09
❑ 270 Andres Galarraga HFA .15 .04
❑ 271 Gary Sheffield HFA .15 .04
❑ 272 Jeff Bagwell HFA .30 .09
❑ 273 Mike Piazza HFA .75 .23
❑ 274 Larry Walker HFA .15 .04
❑ 275 Bobby Bonilla HFA .15 .04
❑ 276 John Kruk HFA .15 .04
❑ 277 Jay Bell HFA .15 .04
❑ 278 Ozzie Smith HFA .75 .23
❑ 279 Tony Gwynn HFA .50 .15
❑ 280 Barry Bonds HFA 1.00 .30
❑ 281 Cal Ripken Jr. HFA 1.25 .35
❑ 282 Mo Vaughn HFA .15 .04
❑ 283 Tim Salmon HFA .30 .09
❑ 284 Frank Thomas HFA .50 .15
❑ 285 Albert Belle HFA .30 .09
❑ 286 Cecil Fielder HFA .15 .04
❑ 287 Wally Joyner HFA .15 .04
❑ 288 Greg Vaughn HFA .15 .04
❑ 289 Kirby Puckett HFA .50 .15
❑ 290 Don Mattingly HFA 1.00 .30
❑ 291 Terry Steinbach HFA .15 .04
❑ 292 Ken Griffey Jr. HFA .75 .23
❑ 293 Juan Gonzalez HFA .30 .09
❑ 294 Paul Molitor HFA .30 .09
❑ 295 Tavo Alvarez UDC .15 .04
❑ 296 Matt Brunson UDC .15 .04
❑ 297 Shawn Green UDC .30 .09
❑ 298 Alex Rodriguez UDC 5.00 1.50
❑ 299 S.Stewart UDC .75 .23
❑ 300 Frank Thomas .75 .23
❑ 301 Mickey Tettleton .15 .04
❑ 302 Pedro Munoz .15 .04
❑ 303 Jose Valentin .15 .04
❑ 304 Orestes Destrade .15 .04
❑ 305 Pat Listach .15 .04
❑ 306 Scott Brosius .30 .09
❑ 307 Kurt Miller .15 .04
❑ 308 Rob Dibble .30 .09
❑ 309 Mike Blowers .15 .04
❑ 310 Jim Abbott .50 .15
❑ 311 Mike Jackson .15 .04
❑ 312 Craig Biggio .50 .15
❑ 313 Kurt Abbott RC .40 .12
❑ 314 Chuck Finley .30 .09
❑ 315 Andres Galarraga .30 .09
❑ 316 Mike Moore .15 .04
❑ 317 Doug Strange .15 .04
❑ 318 Pedro Martinez .75 .23
❑ 319 Kevin McReynolds .15 .04
❑ 320 Greg Maddux 1.25 .35
❑ 321 Mike Henneman .15 .04
❑ 322 Scott Leius .15 .04
❑ 323 John Franco .30 .09
❑ 324 Jeff Blauser .15 .04
❑ 325 Kirby Puckett .75 .23
❑ 326 Darryl Hamilton .15 .04
❑ 327 John Smiley .15 .04
❑ 328 Derrick May .15 .04
❑ 329 Jose Vizcaino .15 .04
❑ 330 Randy Johnson .75 .23
❑ 331 Jack Morris .30 .09
❑ 332 Graeme Lloyd .15 .04
❑ 333 Dave Valle .15 .04
❑ 334 Greg Myers .15 .04
❑ 335 John Wetteland .30 .09
❑ 336 Jim Gott .15 .04
❑ 337 Tim Naehring .15 .04
❑ 338 Mike Kelly .15 .04
❑ 339 Jeff Montgomery .15 .04
❑ 340 Rafael Palmeiro .50 .15
❑ 341 Eddie Murray .75 .23
❑ 342 Xavier Hernandez .15 .04
❑ 343 Bobby Munoz .15 .04
❑ 344 Bobby Bonilla .30 .09
❑ 345 Travis Fryman .30 .09
❑ 346 Steve Finley .30 .09
❑ 347 Chris Sabo .15 .04
❑ 348 Armando Reynoso .15 .04
❑ 349 Ramon Martinez .15 .04
❑ 350 Will Clark .75 .23
❑ 351 Moises Alou .30 .09
❑ 352 Jim Thome .75 .23
❑ 353 Bob Tewksbury .15 .04
❑ 354 Andujar Cedeno .15 .04
❑ 355 Orel Hershiser .30 .09
❑ 356 Mike Devereaux .15 .04
❑ 357 Mike Perez .15 .04
❑ 358 Dennis Martinez .30 .09
❑ 359 Dave Nilsson .15 .04
❑ 360 Ozzie Smith 1.25 .35
❑ 361 Eric Anthony .15 .04
❑ 362 Scott Sanders .15 .04
❑ 363 Paul Sorrento .15 .04
❑ 364 Tim Belcher .15 .04
❑ 365 Dennis Eckersley .30 .09
❑ 366 Mel Rojas .15 .04
❑ 367 Tom Henke .15 .04
❑ 368 Randy Tomlin .15 .04
❑ 369 B.J. Surhoff .30 .09
❑ 370 Larry Walker .50 .15
❑ 371 Joey Cora .15 .04
❑ 372 Mike Harkey .15 .04
❑ 373 John Valentin .15 .04
❑ 374 Doug Jones .15 .04
❑ 375 David Justice .30 .09
❑ 376 Vince Coleman .15 .04
❑ 377 David Hulse .15 .04
❑ 378 Kevin Seitzer .15 .04
❑ 379 Pete Harnisch .15 .04
❑ 380 Ruben Sierra .15 .04
❑ 381 Mark Lewis .15 .04
❑ 382 Bip Roberts .15 .04
❑ 383 Paul Wagner .15 .04
❑ 384 Stan Javier .15 .04
❑ 385 Barry Larkin .50 .15
❑ 386 Mark Portugal .15 .04
❑ 387 Roberto Kelly .15 .04
❑ 388 Andy Benes .15 .04
❑ 389 Felix Fermin .15 .04
❑ 390 Marquis Grissom .30 .09
❑ 391 Troy Neel .15 .04
❑ 392 Chad Kreuter .15 .04
❑ 393 Gregg Olson .15 .04
❑ 394 Charles Nagy .15 .04
❑ 395 Jack McDowell .15 .04
❑ 396 Luis Gonzalez .30 .09
❑ 397 Benito Santiago .30 .09
❑ 398 Chris James .15 .04
❑ 399 Terry Mulholland .15 .04
❑ 400 Barry Bonds 2.00 .60
❑ 401 Joe Grahe .15 .04
❑ 402 Duane Ward .15 .04
❑ 403 John Burkett .15 .04
❑ 404 Scott Servais .15 .04
❑ 405 Bryan Harvey .15 .04
❑ 406 Bernard Gilkey .15 .04
❑ 407 Greg McMichael .15 .04
❑ 408 Tim Wallach .15 .04
❑ 409 Ken Caminiti .30 .09
❑ 410 John Kruk .30 .09
❑ 411 Darrin Jackson .15 .04
❑ 412 Mike Gallego .15 .04
❑ 413 David Cone .30 .09
❑ 414 Lou Whitaker .30 .09
❑ 415 Sandy Alomar Jr. .15 .04
❑ 416 Bill Wegman .15 .04
❑ 417 Pat Borders .15 .04
❑ 418 Roger Pavlik .15 .04
❑ 419 Pete Smith .15 .04
❑ 420 Steve Avery .15 .04
❑ 421 David Segui .15 .04
❑ 422 Rheal Cormier .15 .04
❑ 423 Harold Reynolds .30 .09
❑ 424 Edgar Martinez .50 .15
❑ 425 Cal Ripken Jr. 2.50 .75
❑ 426 Jaime Navarro .15 .04
❑ 427 Sean Berry .15 .04
❑ 428 Bret Saberhagen .30 .09
❑ 429 Bob Welch .15 .04
❑ 430 Juan Guzman .15 .04
❑ 431 Cal Eldred .15 .04
❑ 432 Dave Hollins .15 .04
❑ 433 Sid Fernandez .15 .04
❑ 434 Willie Banks .15 .04
❑ 435 Darryl Kile .30 .09
❑ 436 Henry Rodriguez .15 .04
❑ 437 Tony Fernandez .15 .04
❑ 438 Walt Weiss .15 .04
❑ 439 Kevin Tapani .15 .04
❑ 440 Mark Grace .50 .15
❑ 441 Brian Harper .15 .04
❑ 442 Kent Mercker .15 .04
❑ 443 Anthony Young .15 .04
❑ 444 Todd Zeile .15 .04
❑ 445 Greg Vaughn .15 .04
❑ 446 Ray Lankford .15 .04
❑ 447 Dave Weathers .15 .04
❑ 448 Bret Boone .30 .09
❑ 449 Charlie Hough .30 .09
❑ 450 Roger Clemens 1.50 .45
❑ 451 Mike Morgan .15 .04
❑ 452 Doug Drabek .15 .04
❑ 453 Danny Jackson .15 .04
❑ 454 Dante Bichette .30 .09
❑ 455 Roberto Alomar .50 .15
❑ 456 Ben McDonald .15 .04
❑ 457 Kenny Rogers .30 .09
❑ 458 Bill Gullickson .15 .04
❑ 459 Darrin Fletcher .15 .04
❑ 460 Curt Schilling .30 .09
❑ 461 Billy Hatcher .15 .04
❑ 462 Howard Johnson .15 .04
❑ 463 Mickey Morandini .15 .04
❑ 464 Frank Castillo .15 .04
❑ 465 Delino DeShields .15 .04
❑ 466 Gary Gaetti .30 .09
❑ 467 Steve Farr .15 .04
❑ 468 Roberto Hernandez .15 .04
❑ 469 Jack Armstrong .15 .04
❑ 470 Paul Molitor .50 .15
❑ 471 Melido Perez .15 .04
❑ 472 Greg Hibbard .15 .04
❑ 473 Jody Reed .15 .04
❑ 474 Tom Gordon .15 .04
❑ 475 Gary Sheffield .30 .09

	Card	Player	Nm-Mt	Ex-Mt
❑	476	John Jaha	.15	.04
❑	477	Shawon Dunston	.15	.04
❑	478	Reggie Jefferson	.15	.04
❑	479	Don Slaught	.15	.04
❑	480	Jeff Bagwell	.50	.15
❑	481	Tim Pugh	.15	.04
❑	482	Kevin Young	.15	.04
❑	483	Ellis Burks	.30	.09
❑	484	Greg Swindell	.15	.04
❑	485	Mark Langston	.15	.04
❑	486	Omar Vizquel	.50	.15
❑	487	Kevin Brown	.30	.09
❑	488	Terry Steinbach	.15	.04
❑	489	Mark Lemke	.15	.04
❑	490	Matt Williams	.30	.09
❑	491	Pete Incaviglia	.15	.04
❑	492	Karl Rhodes	.15	.04
❑	493	Shawn Green	.75	.23
❑	494	Hal Morris	.15	.04
❑	495	Derek Bell	.15	.04
❑	496	Luis Polonia	.15	.04
❑	497	Otis Nixon	.15	.04
❑	498	Ron Darling	.15	.04
❑	499	Mitch Williams	.15	.04
❑	500	Mike Piazza	1.50	.45
❑	501	Pat Meares	.15	.04
❑	502	Scott Cooper	.15	.04
❑	503	Scott Erickson	.15	.04
❑	504	Jeff Juden	.15	.04
❑	505	Lee Smith	.30	.09
❑	506	Bobby Ayala	.15	.04
❑	507	Dave Henderson	.15	.04
❑	508	Erik Hanson	.15	.04
❑	509	Bob Wickman	.15	.04
❑	510	Sammy Sosa	1.25	.35
❑	511	Hector Carrasco	.15	.04
❑	512	Tim Davis	.15	.04
❑	513	Joey Hamilton	.15	.04
❑	514	Robert Eenhoorn	.15	.04
❑	515	Jorge Fabregas	.15	.04
❑	516	Tim Hyers RC	.15	.04
❑	517	John Hudek RC	.15	.04
❑	518	James Mouton	.15	.04
❑	519	Herbert Perry RC	.40	.12
❑	520	Chan Ho Park RC	.60	.18
❑	521	W.Va Landingham RC	.15	.04
❑	522	Paul Shuey	.15	.04
❑	523	Ryan Hancock RC	.15	.04
❑	524	Billy Wagner RC	1.00	.30
❑	525	Jason Giambi	.75	.23
❑	526	Jose Silva RC	.15	.04
❑	527	Terrell Wade RC	.15	.04
❑	528	Todd Dunn	.15	.04
❑	529	Alan Benes RC	.40	.12
❑	530	B.Kieschnick RC	.40	.12
❑	531	T.Hollandsworth	.15	.04
❑	532	Brad Fullmer RC	.60	.18
❑	533	S.Soderstrom RC	.15	.04
❑	534	Daron Kirkreit	.15	.04
❑	535	Arquimedez Pozo RC	.15	.04
❑	536	Charles Johnson	.30	.09
❑	537	Preston Wilson	.30	.09
❑	538	Alex Ochoa	.15	.04
❑	539	Derrek Lee RC	1.00	.30
❑	540	Wayne Gomes RC	.15	.04
❑	541	J.Allensworth RC	.15	.04
❑	542	Mike Bell RC	.15	.04
❑	543	Trot Nixon RC	1.00	.30
❑	544	Pokey Reese	.15	.04
❑	545	Neifi Perez RC	.40	.12
❑	546	Johnny Damon	.75	.23
❑	547	Matt Brunson RC	.15	.04
❑	548	L.Hawkins RC	.60	.18
❑	549	Eddie Pearson RC	.15	.04
❑	550	Derek Jeter	2.50	.75
❑	A298	Alex Rodriguez AU	300.00	90.00
❑	P224	K.Griffey Jr. Promo	2.00	.60
❑	GM1	Ken Griffey Jr. AU	1200.00	350.00
		Mickey Mantle AU/1000		
❑	KG1	K.Griffey Jr. AU/1000	200.00	60.00
❑	MM1	M.Mantle AU/1000	500.00	150.00

1995 Upper Deck

	Nm-Mt	Ex-Mt
COMP.MASTER SET (495)	110.00	33.00
COMPLETE SET (450)	50.00	15.00
COMP. SERIES 1 (225)	25.00	7.50
COMP. SERIES 2 (225)	25.00	7.50
COMMON CARD (1-450)	.15	.04
COMP.TRADE SET (45)	60.00	18.00
COMMON (451T-495T)	1.00	.30

	Card	Player	Nm-Mt	Ex-Mt
❑	1	Ruben Rivera	.15	.04
❑	2	Bill Pulsipher	.15	.04
❑	3	Ben Grieve	.30	.09
❑	4	Curtis Goodwin	.15	.04
❑	5	Damon Hollins	.15	.04
❑	6	Todd Greene	.15	.04
❑	7	Glenn Williams	.15	.04
❑	8	Bret Wagner	.15	.04
❑	9	Karim Garcia RC	.40	.12
❑	10	Nomar Garciaparra	2.00	.60
❑	11	Raul Casanova RC	.15	.04
❑	12	Matt Smith	.15	.04
❑	13	Paul Wilson	.15	.04
❑	14	Jason Isringhausen	.30	.09
❑	15	Reid Ryan	.30	.09
❑	16	Lee Smith	.30	.09
❑	17	Chili Davis	.30	.09
❑	18	Brian Anderson	.15	.04
❑	19	Gary DiSarcina	.15	.04
❑	20	Bo Jackson	.75	.23
❑	21	Chuck Finley	.30	.09
❑	22	Darryl Kile	.30	.09
❑	23	Shane Reynolds	.15	.04
❑	24	Tony Eusebio	.15	.04
❑	25	Craig Biggio	.50	.15
❑	26	Doug Drabek	.15	.04
❑	27	Brian L. Hunter	.15	.04
❑	28	James Mouton	.15	.04
❑	29	Geronimo Berroa	.15	.04
❑	30	Rickey Henderson	.75	.23
❑	31	Steve Karsay	.15	.04
❑	32	Steve Ontiveros	.15	.04
❑	33	Ernie Young	.15	.04
❑	34	Dennis Eckersley	.30	.09
❑	35	Mark McGwire	2.00	.60
❑	36	Dave Stewart	.30	.09
❑	37	Pat Hentgen	.15	.04
❑	38	Carlos Delgado	.30	.09
❑	39	Joe Carter	.30	.09
❑	40	Roberto Alomar	.50	.15
❑	41	John Olerud	.30	.09
❑	42	Devon White	.30	.09
❑	43	Roberto Kelly	.15	.04
❑	44	Jeff Blauser	.15	.04
❑	45	Fred McGriff	.50	.15
❑	46	Tom Glavine	.50	.15
❑	47	Mike Kelly	.15	.04
❑	48	Javier Lopez	.30	.09
❑	49	Greg Maddux	1.25	.35
❑	50	Matt Mieske	.15	.04
❑	51	Troy O'Leary	.15	.04
❑	52	Jeff Cirillo	.15	.04
❑	53	Cal Eldred	.15	.04
❑	54	Pat Listach	.15	.04
❑	55	Jose Valentin	.15	.04
❑	56	John Mabry	.15	.04
❑	57	Bob Tewksbury	.15	.04
❑	58	Brian Jordan	.30	.09
❑	59	Gregg Jefferies	.15	.04
❑	60	Ozzie Smith	1.25	.35
❑	61	Geronimo Pena	.15	.04
❑	62	Mark Whiten	.15	.04
❑	63	Rey Sanchez	.15	.04
❑	64	Willie Banks	.15	.04
❑	65	Mark Grace	.50	.15
❑	66	Randy Myers	.15	.04
❑	67	Steve Trachsel	.15	.04
❑	68	Derrick May	.15	.04
❑	69	Brett Butler	.30	.09
❑	70	Eric Karros	.30	.09
❑	71	Tim Wallach	.15	.04
❑	72	Delino DeShields	.15	.04
❑	73	Darren Dreifort	.15	.04
❑	74	Orel Hershiser	.30	.09
❑	75	Billy Ashley	.15	.04
❑	76	Sean Berry	.15	.04
❑	77	Ken Hill	.15	.04
❑	78	John Wetteland	.30	.09
❑	79	Moises Alou	.30	.09
❑	80	Cliff Floyd	.30	.09
❑	81	Marquis Grissom	.30	.09
❑	82	Larry Walker	.50	.15
❑	83	Rondell White	.30	.09
❑	84	W.VanLandingham	.15	.04
❑	85	Matt Williams	.30	.09
❑	86	Rod Beck	.15	.04
❑	87	Darren Lewis	.15	.04
❑	88	Robby Thompson	.15	.04
❑	89	Darryl Strawberry	.30	.09
❑	90	Kenny Lofton	.30	.09
❑	91	Charles Nagy	.15	.04
❑	92	Sandy Alomar Jr.	.15	.04
❑	93	Mark Clark	.15	.04
❑	94	Dennis Martinez	.30	.09
❑	95	Dave Winfield	.30	.09
❑	96	Jim Thome	.75	.23
❑	97	Manny Ramirez	.50	.15
❑	98	Goose Gossage	.30	.09
❑	99	Tino Martinez	.50	.15
❑	100	Ken Griffey Jr.	1.25	.35
❑	101	Greg Maddux ANA	.75	.23
❑	102	Randy Johnson ANA	.50	.15
❑	103	Barry Bonds ANA	1.00	.30
❑	104	Juan Gonzalez ANA	.30	.09
❑	105	Frank Thomas ANA	.50	.15
❑	106	Matt Williams ANA	.15	.04
❑	107	Paul Molitor ANA	.30	.09
❑	108	Fred McGriff ANA	.30	.09
❑	109	Carlos Baerga ANA	.15	.04
❑	110	Ken Griffey Jr. ANA	.75	.23
❑	111	Reggie Jefferson	.15	.04
❑	112	Randy Johnson	.75	.23
❑	113	Marc Newfield	.15	.04
❑	114	Robb Nen	.30	.09
❑	115	Jeff Conine	.30	.09
❑	116	Kurt Abbott	.15	.04
❑	117	Charlie Hough	.30	.09
❑	118	Dave Weathers	.15	.04
❑	119	Juan Castillo	.15	.04
❑	120	Bret Saberhagen	.30	.09
❑	121	Rico Brogna	.15	.04
❑	122	John Franco	.30	.09
❑	123	Todd Hundley	.15	.04
❑	124	Jason Jacome	.15	.04
❑	125	Bobby Jones	.15	.04
❑	126	Bret Barberie	.15	.04
❑	127	Ben McDonald	.15	.04
❑	128	Harold Baines	.30	.09
❑	129	Jeffrey Hammonds	.15	.04
❑	130	Mike Mussina	.50	.15
❑	131	Chris Hoiles	.15	.04
❑	132	Brady Anderson	.30	.09
❑	133	Eddie Williams	.15	.04
❑	134	Andy Benes	.15	.04
❑	135	Tony Gwynn	1.00	.30
❑	136	Bip Roberts	.15	.04
❑	137	Joey Hamilton	.15	.04
❑	138	Luis Lopez	.15	.04
❑	139	Ray McDavid	.15	.04
❑	140	Lenny Dykstra	.30	.09
❑	141	Mariano Duncan	.15	.04
❑	142	Fernando Valenzuela	.30	.09
❑	143	Bobby Munoz	.15	.04

❑	144	Kevin Stocker	.15	.04
❑	145	John Kruk	.30	.09
❑	146	Jon Lieber	.15	.04
❑	147	Zane Smith	.15	.04
❑	148	Steve Cooke	.15	.04
❑	149	Andy Van Slyke	.30	.09
❑	150	Jay Bell	.30	.09
❑	151	Carlos Garcia	.15	.04
❑	152	John Dettmer	.15	.04
❑	153	Darren Oliver	.15	.04
❑	154	Dean Palmer	.30	.09
❑	155	Otis Nixon	.15	.04
❑	156	Rusty Greer	.30	.09
❑	157	Rick Helling	.15	.04
❑	158	Jose Canseco	.75	.23
❑	159	Roger Clemens	1.50	.45
❑	160	Andre Dawson	.30	.09
❑	161	Mo Vaughn	.30	.09
❑	162	Aaron Sele	.15	.04
❑	163	John Valentin	.15	.04
❑	164	Brian R. Hunter	.15	.04
❑	165	Bret Boone	.30	.09
❑	166	Hector Carrasco	.15	.04
❑	167	Pete Schourek	.15	.04
❑	168	Willie Greene	.15	.04
❑	169	Kevin Mitchell	.15	.04
❑	170	Deion Sanders	.50	.15
❑	171	John Roper	.15	.04
❑	172	Charlie Hayes	.15	.04
❑	173	David Nied	.15	.04
❑	174	Ellis Burks	.30	.09
❑	175	Dante Bichette	.30	.09
❑	176	Marvin Freeman	.15	.04
❑	177	Eric Young	.15	.04
❑	178	David Cone	.30	.09
❑	179	Greg Gagne	.15	.04
❑	180	Bob Hamelin	.15	.04
❑	181	Wally Joyner	.30	.09
❑	182	Jeff Montgomery	.15	.04
❑	183	Jose Lind	.15	.04
❑	184	Chris Gomez	.15	.04
❑	185	Travis Fryman	.30	.09
❑	186	Kirk Gibson	.30	.09
❑	187	Mike Moore	.15	.04
❑	188	Lou Whitaker	.30	.09
❑	189	Sean Bergman	.15	.04
❑	190	Shane Mack	.15	.04
❑	191	Rick Aguilera	.15	.04
❑	192	Denny Hocking	.15	.04
❑	193	Chuck Knoblauch	.30	.09
❑	194	Kevin Tapani	.15	.04
❑	195	Kent Hrbek	.30	.09
❑	196	Ozzie Guillen	.15	.04
❑	197	Wilson Alvarez	.15	.04
❑	198	Tim Raines	.30	.09
❑	199	Scott Ruffcorn	.15	.04
❑	200	Michael Jordan	2.50	.75
❑	201	Robin Ventura	.30	.09
❑	202	Jason Bere	.15	.04
❑	203	Darrin Jackson	.15	.04
❑	204	Russ Davis	.15	.04
❑	205	Jimmy Key	.30	.09
❑	206	Jack McDowell	.15	.04
❑	207	Jim Abbott	.50	.15
❑	208	Paul O'Neill	.50	.15
❑	209	Bernie Williams	.50	.15
❑	210	Don Mattingly	2.00	.60
❑	211	Orlando Miller	.15	.04
❑	212	Alex Gonzalez	.15	.04
❑	213	Terrell Wade	.15	.04
❑	214	Jose Oliva	.15	.04
❑	215	Alex Rodriguez	2.00	.60
❑	216	Garret Anderson	.30	.09
❑	217	Alan Benes	.15	.04
❑	218	Armando Benitez	.30	.09
❑	219	Dustin Hermanson	.15	.04
❑	220	Charles Johnson	.30	.09
❑	221	Julian Tavarez	.15	.04
❑	222	Jason Giambi	.50	.15
❑	223	LaTroy Hawkins	.15	.04
❑	224	Todd Hollandsworth	.15	.04
❑	225	Derek Jeter	2.00	.60
❑	226	Hideo Nomo RC	2.00	.60
❑	227	Tony Clark	.15	.04
❑	228	Roger Cedeno	.15	.04
❑	229	Scott Stahoviak	.15	.04
❑	230	Michael Tucker	.15	.04
❑	231	Joe Rosselli	.15	.04
❑	232	Antonio Osuna	.15	.04
❑	233	Bobby Higginson RC	.75	.23
❑	234	Mark Grudzielanek RC	.40	.12
❑	235	Ray Durham	.30	.09
❑	236	Frank Rodriguez	.15	.04
❑	237	Quilvio Veras	.15	.04
❑	238	Darren Bragg	.15	.04
❑	239	Ugueth Urbina	.15	.04
❑	240	Jason Bates	.15	.04
❑	241	David Bell	.15	.04
❑	242	Ron Villone	.15	.04
❑	243	Joe Randa	.15	.04
❑	244	Carlos Perez RC	.40	.12
❑	245	Brad Clontz	.15	.04
❑	246	Steve Rodriguez	.15	.04
❑	247	Joe Vitiello	.15	.04
❑	248	Ozzie Timmons	.15	.04
❑	249	Rudy Pemberton	.15	.04
❑	250	Marty Cordova	.15	.04
❑	251	Tony Graffanino	.15	.04
❑	252	Mark Johnson RC	.40	.12
❑	253	Tomas Perez RC	.15	.04
❑	254	Jimmy Hurst	.15	.04
❑	255	Edgardo Alfonzo	.30	.09
❑	256	Jose Malave	.15	.04
❑	257	Brad Radke RC	.75	.23
❑	258	Jon Nunnally	.15	.04
❑	259	Dilson Torres RC	.15	.04
❑	260	Esteban Loaiza	.15	.04
❑	261	Freddy Adrian Garcia RC	.15	.04
❑	262	Don Wengert	.15	.04
❑	263	Robert Person RC	.40	.12
❑	264	Tim Unroe RC	.15	.04
❑	265	Juan Acevedo RC	.15	.04
❑	266	Eduardo Perez	.15	.04
❑	267	Tony Phillips	.15	.04
❑	268	Jim Edmonds	.50	.15
❑	269	Jorge Fabregas	.15	.04
❑	270	Tim Salmon	.50	.15
❑	271	Mark Langston	.15	.04
❑	272	J.T. Snow	.30	.09
❑	273	Phil Plantier	.15	.04
❑	274	Derek Bell	.15	.04
❑	275	Jeff Bagwell	.50	.15
❑	276	Luis Gonzalez	.30	.09
❑	277	John Hudek	.15	.04
❑	278	Todd Stottlemyre	.15	.04
❑	279	Mark Acre	.15	.04
❑	280	Ruben Sierra	.15	.04
❑	281	Mike Bordick	.15	.04
❑	282	Ron Darling	.15	.04
❑	283	Brent Gates	.15	.04
❑	284	Todd Van Poppel	.15	.04
❑	285	Paul Molitor	.50	.15
❑	286	Ed Sprague	.15	.04
❑	287	Juan Guzman	.15	.04
❑	288	David Cone	.30	.09
❑	289	Shawn Green	.30	.09
❑	290	Marquis Grissom	.30	.09
❑	291	Kent Mercker	.15	.04
❑	292	Steve Avery	.15	.04
❑	293	Chipper Jones	.75	.23
❑	294	John Smoltz	.50	.15
❑	295	David Justice	.30	.09
❑	296	Ryan Klesko	.30	.09
❑	297	Joe Oliver	.15	.04
❑	298	Ricky Bones	.15	.04
❑	299	John Jaha	.15	.04
❑	300	Greg Vaughn	.15	.04
❑	301	Dave Nilsson	.15	.04
❑	302	Kevin Seitzer	.15	.04
❑	303	Bernard Gilkey	.15	.04
❑	304	Allen Battle	.15	.04
❑	305	Ray Lankford	.15	.04
❑	306	Tom Pagnozzi	.15	.04
❑	307	Allen Watson	.15	.04
❑	308	Danny Jackson	.15	.04
❑	309	Ken Hill	.15	.04
❑	310	Todd Zeile	.15	.04
❑	311	Kevin Roberson	.15	.04
❑	312	Steve Buechele	.15	.04
❑	313	Rick Wilkins	.15	.04
❑	314	Kevin Foster	.15	.04
❑	315	Sammy Sosa	1.25	.35
❑	316	Howard Johnson	.15	.04
❑	317	Greg Hansell	.15	.04
❑	318	Pedro Astacio	.15	.04
❑	319	Rafael Bournigal	.15	.04
❑	320	Mike Piazza	1.25	.35
❑	321	Ramon Martinez	.15	.04
❑	322	Raul Mondesi	.30	.09
❑	323	Ismael Valdes	.15	.04
❑	324	Wil Cordero	.15	.04
❑	325	Tony Tarasco	.15	.04
❑	326	Roberto Kelly	.15	.04
❑	327	Jeff Fassero	.15	.04
❑	328	Mike Lansing	.15	.04
❑	329	Pedro Martinez	.75	.23
❑	330	Kirk Rueter	.15	.04
❑	331	Glenallen Hill	.15	.04
❑	332	Kirt Manwaring	.15	.04
❑	333	Royce Clayton	.15	.04
❑	334	J.R. Phillips	.15	.04
❑	335	Barry Bonds	2.00	.60
❑	336	Mark Portugal	.15	.04
❑	337	Terry Mulholland	.15	.04
❑	338	Omar Vizquel	.50	.15
❑	339	Carlos Baerga	.15	.04
❑	340	Albert Belle	.30	.09
❑	341	Eddie Murray	.75	.23
❑	342	Wayne Kirby	.15	.04
❑	343	Chad Ogea	.15	.04
❑	344	Tim Davis	.15	.04
❑	345	Jay Buhner	.30	.09
❑	346	Bobby Ayala	.15	.04
❑	347	Mike Blowers	.15	.04
❑	348	Dave Fleming	.15	.04
❑	349	Edgar Martinez	.50	.15
❑	350	Andre Dawson	.30	.09
❑	351	Darrell Whitmore	.15	.04
❑	352	Chuck Carr	.15	.04
❑	353	John Burkett	.15	.04
❑	354	Chris Hammond	.15	.04
❑	355	Gary Sheffield	.30	.09
❑	356	Pat Rapp	.15	.04
❑	357	Greg Colbrunn	.15	.04
❑	358	David Segui	.15	.04
❑	359	Jeff Kent	.30	.09
❑	360	Bobby Bonilla	.30	.09
❑	361	Pete Harnisch	.15	.04
❑	362	Ryan Thompson	.15	.04
❑	363	Jose Vizcaino	.15	.04
❑	364	Brett Butler	.30	.09
❑	365	Cal Ripken Jr.	2.50	.75
❑	366	Rafael Palmeiro	.50	.15
❑	367	Leo Gomez	.15	.04
❑	368	Andy Van Slyke	.30	.09
❑	369	Arthur Rhodes	.15	.04
❑	370	Ken Caminiti	.30	.09
❑	371	Steve Finley	.30	.09
❑	372	Melvin Nieves	.15	.04
❑	373	Andujar Cedeno	.15	.04
❑	374	Trevor Hoffman	.30	.09
❑	375	Fernando Valenzuela	.30	.09
❑	376	Ricky Bottalico	.15	.04
❑	377	Dave Hollins	.15	.04
❑	378	Charlie Hayes	.15	.04
❑	379	Tommy Greene	.15	.04
❑	380	Darren Daulton	.30	.09
❑	381	Curt Schilling	.30	.09
❑	382	Midre Cummings	.15	.04
❑	383	Al Martin	.15	.04
❑	384	Jeff King	.15	.04
❑	385	Orlando Merced	.15	.04
❑	386	Denny Neagle	.30	.09
❑	387	Don Slaught	.15	.04
❑	388	Dave Clark	.15	.04
❑	389	Kevin Gross	.15	.04
❑	390	Will Clark	.75	.23
❑	391	Ivan Rodriguez	.75	.23
❑	392	Benji Gil	.15	.04
❑	393	Jeff Frye	.15	.04
❑	394	Kenny Rogers	.30	.09
❑	395	Juan Gonzalez	.50	.15
❑	396	Mike Macfarlane	.15	.04
❑	397	Lee Tinsley	.15	.04
❑	398	Tim Naehring	.15	.04
❑	399	Tim Vanegmond	.15	.04
❑	400	Mike Greenwell	.15	.04
❑	401	Ken Ryan	.15	.04

❑ 402 John Smiley .15 .04
❑ 403 Tim Pugh .15 .04
❑ 404 Reggie Sanders .15 .04
❑ 405 Barry Larkin .50 .15
❑ 406 Hal Morris .15 .04
❑ 407 Jose Rijo .15 .04
❑ 408 Lance Painter .15 .04
❑ 409 Joe Girardi .15 .04
❑ 410 Andres Galarraga .30 .09
❑ 411 Mike Kingery .15 .04
❑ 412 Roberto Mejia .15 .04
❑ 413 Walt Weiss .15 .04
❑ 414 Bill Swift .15 .04
❑ 415 Larry Walker .50 .15
❑ 416 Billy Brewer .15 .04
❑ 417 Pat Borders .15 .04
❑ 418 Tom Gordon .15 .04
❑ 419 Kevin Appier .30 .09
❑ 420 Gary Gaetti .30 .09
❑ 421 Greg Gohr .15 .04
❑ 422 Felipe Lira .15 .04
❑ 423 John Doherty .15 .04
❑ 424 Chad Curtis .15 .04
❑ 425 Cecil Fielder .30 .09
❑ 426 Alan Trammell .30 .09
❑ 427 David McCarty .15 .04
❑ 428 Scott Erickson .15 .04
❑ 429 Pat Mahomes .15 .04
❑ 430 Kirby Puckett .75 .23
❑ 431 Dave Stevens .15 .04
❑ 432 Pedro Munoz .15 .04
❑ 433 Chris Sabo .15 .04
❑ 434 Alex Fernandez .15 .04
❑ 435 Frank Thomas .75 .23
❑ 436 Roberto Hernandez .15 .04
❑ 437 Lance Johnson .15 .04
❑ 438 Jim Abbott .50 .15
❑ 439 John Wetteland .30 .09
❑ 440 Melido Perez .15 .04
❑ 441 Tony Fernandez .15 .04
❑ 442 Pat Kelly .15 .04
❑ 443 Mike Stanley .15 .04
❑ 444 Danny Tartabull .15 .04
❑ 445 Wade Boggs .50 .15
❑ 446 Robin Yount 1.25 .35
❑ 447 Ryne Sandberg 1.25 .35
❑ 448 Nolan Ryan 3.00 .90
❑ 449 George Brett 2.00 .60
❑ 450 Mike Schmidt 1.25 .35
❑ 451 Jim Abbott TRADE 2.00 .60
❑ 452 D.Tartabull TRADE 1.00 .30
❑ 453 Ariel Prieto TRADE 1.00 .30
❑ 454 Scott Cooper TRADE 1.00 .30
❑ 455 Tom Henke TRADE 1.00 .30
❑ 456 Todd Zeile TRADE 1.00 .30
❑ 457 Brian McRae TRADE 1.00 .30
❑ 458 Luis Gonzalez TRADE 1.50 .45
❑ 459 Jaime Navarro TRADE 1.00 .30
❑ 460 Todd Worrell TRADE 1.00 .30
❑ 461 Roberto Kelly TRADE 1.00 .30
❑ 462 Chad Fonville TRADE 1.00 .30
❑ 463 S.Andrews TRADE 1.00 .30
❑ 464 David Segui TRADE 1.00 .30
❑ 465 Deion Sanders TRADE 2.00 .60
❑ 466 Orel Hershiser TRADE 1.50 .45
❑ 467 Ken Hill TRADE 1.00 .30
❑ 468 Andy Benes TRADE 1.00 .30
❑ 469 T.Pendleton TRADE 1.50 .45
❑ 470 Bobby Bonilla TRADE 1.50 .45
❑ 471 Scott Erickson TRADE 1.00 .30
❑ 472 Kevin Brown TRADE 1.50 .45
❑ 473 G.Dishman TRADE 1.00 .30
❑ 474 Phil Plantier TRADE 1.00 .30
❑ 475 G.Jefferies TRADE 1.00 .30
❑ 476 Tyler Green TRADE 1.00 .30
❑ 477 H. Slocumb TRADE 1.00 .30
❑ 478 Mark Whiten TRADE 1.00 .30
❑ 479 M.Tettleton TRADE 1.00 .30
❑ 480 Tim Wakefield TRADE 1.50 .45
❑ 481 V. Eshelman TRADE 1.00 .30
❑ 482 Rick Aguilera TRADE 1.00 .30
❑ 483 Erik Hanson TRADE 1.00 .30
❑ 484 Willie McGee TRADE 1.50 .45
❑ 485 Troy O'Leary TRADE 1.00 .30
❑ 486 B.Santiago TRADE 1.50 .45
❑ 487 Darren Lewis TRADE 1.00 .30
❑ 488 Dave Burba TRADE 1.00 .30
❑ 489 Ron Gant TRADE 1.50 .45
❑ 490 B.Saberhagen TRADE 1.50 .45
❑ 491 Vinny Castilla TRADE 1.50 .45
❑ 492 F.Rodriguez TRADE 1.00 .30
❑ 493 Andy Pettitte TRADE 2.00 .60
❑ 494 Ruben Sierra TRADE 1.00 .30
❑ 495 David Cone TRADE 1.50 .45
❑ J159 R. Clemens Jumbo AU 80.00 24.00
❑ J215 A. Rodriguez Jumbo AU 80.00 24.00
❑ P100 K.Griffey Jr. Promo 2.00 .60

1999 Upper Deck

	Nm-Mt	Ex-Mt
COMPLETE SET (525)	100.00	30.00
COMP. SERIES 1 (255)	60.00	18.00
COMP. SERIES 2 (270)	40.00	12.00
COMMON (19-255/293-535)	.30	.09
COMMON SER.1 SR (1-18)	.50	.15
COMMON (266-292)	.50	.15

❑ 1 Troy Glaus SR .50 .15
❑ 2 Adrian Beltre SR .75 .23
❑ 3 Matt Anderson SR .50 .15
❑ 4 Eric Chavez SR .50 .15
❑ 5 Jin Ho Cho SR .50 .15
❑ 6 Robert Smith SR .50 .15
❑ 7 George Lombard SR .50 .15
❑ 8 Mike Kinkade SR .50 .15
❑ 9 Seth Greisinger SR .50 .15
❑ 10 J.D. Drew SR .50 .15
❑ 11 Aramis Ramirez SR .50 .15
❑ 12 Carlos Guillen SR .50 .15
❑ 13 Justin Baughman SR .50 .15
❑ 14 Jim Parque SR .50 .15
❑ 15 Ryan Jackson SR .50 .15
❑ 16 Ramon E.Martinez SR RC .50 .15
❑ 17 Orlando Hernandez SR .50 .15
❑ 18 Jeremy Giambi SR .50 .15
❑ 19 Gary DiSarcina .30 .09
❑ 20 Darin Erstad .30 .09
❑ 21 Troy Glaus .30 .09
❑ 22 Chuck Finley .30 .09
❑ 23 Dave Hollins .30 .09
❑ 24 Troy Percival .30 .09
❑ 25 Tim Salmon .50 .15
❑ 26 Brian Anderson .30 .09
❑ 27 Jay Bell .30 .09
❑ 28 Andy Benes .30 .09
❑ 29 Brent Brede .30 .09
❑ 30 David Dellucci .30 .09
❑ 31 Karim Garcia .30 .09
❑ 32 Travis Lee .30 .09
❑ 33 Andres Galarraga .30 .09
❑ 34 Ryan Klesko .30 .09
❑ 35 Keith Lockhart .30 .09
❑ 36 Kevin Millwood .30 .09
❑ 37 Denny Neagle .30 .09
❑ 38 John Smoltz .50 .15
❑ 39 Michael Tucker .30 .09
❑ 40 Walt Weiss .30 .09
❑ 41 Dennis Martinez .30 .09
❑ 42 Javy Lopez .30 .09
❑ 43 Brady Anderson .30 .09
❑ 44 Harold Baines .30 .09
❑ 45 Mike Bordick .30 .09
❑ 46 Roberto Alomar .50 .15
❑ 47 Scott Erickson .30 .09
❑ 48 Mike Mussina .50 .15
❑ 49 Cal Ripken 2.50 .75
❑ 50 Darren Bragg .30 .09
❑ 51 Dennis Eckersley .30 .09
❑ 52 Nomar Garciaparra 1.25 .35
❑ 53 Scott Hatteberg .30 .09
❑ 54 Troy O'Leary .30 .09
❑ 55 Bret Saberhagen .30 .09
❑ 56 John Valentin .30 .09
❑ 57 Rod Beck .30 .09
❑ 58 Jeff Blauser .30 .09
❑ 59 Brant Brown .30 .09
❑ 60 Mark Clark .30 .09
❑ 61 Mark Grace .50 .15
❑ 62 Kevin Tapani .30 .09
❑ 63 Henry Rodriguez .30 .09
❑ 64 Mike Cameron .30 .09
❑ 65 Mike Caruso .30 .09
❑ 66 Ray Durham .30 .09
❑ 67 Jaime Navarro .30 .09
❑ 68 Magglio Ordonez .30 .09
❑ 69 Mike Sirotka .30 .09
❑ 70 Sean Casey .30 .09
❑ 71 Barry Larkin .50 .15
❑ 72 Jon Nunnally .30 .09
❑ 73 Paul Konerko .30 .09
❑ 74 Chris Stynes .30 .09
❑ 75 Brett Tomko .30 .09
❑ 76 Dmitri Young .30 .09
❑ 77 Sandy Alomar Jr. .30 .09
❑ 78 Bartolo Colon .30 .09
❑ 79 Travis Fryman .30 .09
❑ 80 Brian Giles .30 .09
❑ 81 David Justice .30 .09
❑ 82 Omar Vizquel .50 .15
❑ 83 Jaret Wright .30 .09
❑ 84 Jim Thome .75 .23
❑ 85 Charles Nagy .30 .09
❑ 86 Pedro Astacio .30 .09
❑ 87 Todd Helton .50 .15
❑ 88 Darryl Kile .30 .09
❑ 89 Mike Lansing .30 .09
❑ 90 Neifi Perez .30 .09
❑ 91 John Thomson .30 .09
❑ 92 Larry Walker .50 .15
❑ 93 Tony Clark .30 .09
❑ 94 Deivi Cruz .30 .09
❑ 95 Damion Easley .30 .09
❑ 96 Brian L.Hunter .30 .09
❑ 97 Todd Jones .30 .09
❑ 98 Brian Moehler .30 .09
❑ 99 Gabe Alvarez .30 .09
❑ 100 Craig Counsell .30 .09
❑ 101 Cliff Floyd .30 .09
❑ 102 Livan Hernandez .30 .09
❑ 103 Andy Larkin .30 .09
❑ 104 Derrek Lee .30 .09
❑ 105 Brian Meadows .30 .09
❑ 106 Moises Alou .30 .09
❑ 107 Sean Berry .30 .09
❑ 108 Craig Biggio .50 .15
❑ 109 Ricky Gutierrez .30 .09
❑ 110 Mike Hampton .30 .09
❑ 111 Jose Lima .30 .09
❑ 112 Billy Wagner .30 .09
❑ 113 Hal Morris .30 .09
❑ 114 Johnny Damon .50 .15
❑ 115 Jeff King .30 .09
❑ 116 Jeff Montgomery .30 .09
❑ 117 Glendon Rusch .30 .09
❑ 118 Larry Sutton .30 .09
❑ 119 Bobby Bonilla .30 .09
❑ 120 Jim Eisenreich .30 .09
❑ 121 Eric Karros .30 .09
❑ 122 Matt Luke .30 .09
❑ 123 Ramon Martinez .30 .09
❑ 124 Gary Sheffield .30 .09
❑ 125 Eric Young .30 .09
❑ 126 Charles Johnson .30 .09
❑ 127 Jeff Cirillo .30 .09
❑ 128 Marquis Grissom .30 .09
❑ 129 Jeromy Burnitz .30 .09
❑ 130 Bob Wickman .30 .09
❑ 131 Scott Karl .30 .09
❑ 132 Mark Loretta .30 .09

❑ 133 Fernando Vina .30 .09
❑ 134 Matt Lawton .30 .09
❑ 135 Pat Meares .30 .09
❑ 136 Eric Milton .30 .09
❑ 137 Paul Molitor .50 .15
❑ 138 David Ortiz .50 .15
❑ 139 Todd Walker .30 .09
❑ 140 Shane Andrews .30 .09
❑ 141 Brad Fullmer .30 .09
❑ 142 Vladimir Guerrero .75 .23
❑ 143 Dustin Hermanson .30 .09
❑ 144 Ryan McGuire .30 .09
❑ 145 Ugueth Urbina .30 .09
❑ 146 John Franco .30 .09
❑ 147 Butch Huskey .30 .09
❑ 148 Bobby Jones .30 .09
❑ 149 John Olerud .30 .09
❑ 150 Rey Ordonez .30 .09
❑ 151 Mike Piazza 1.25 .35
❑ 152 Hideo Nomo .75 .23
❑ 153 Masato Yoshii .30 .09
❑ 154 Derek Jeter 2.00 .60
❑ 155 Chuck Knoblauch .30 .09
❑ 156 Paul O'Neill .50 .15
❑ 157 Andy Pettitte .50 .15
❑ 158 Mariano Rivera .50 .15
❑ 159 Darryl Strawberry .30 .09
❑ 160 David Wells .30 .09
❑ 161 Jorge Posada .50 .15
❑ 162 Ramiro Mendoza .30 .09
❑ 163 Miguel Tejada .30 .09
❑ 164 Ryan Christenson .30 .09
❑ 165 Rickey Henderson .75 .23
❑ 166 A.J. Hinch .30 .09
❑ 167 Ben Grieve .30 .09
❑ 168 Kenny Rogers .30 .09
❑ 169 Matt Stairs .30 .09
❑ 170 Bob Abreu .30 .09
❑ 171 Rico Brogna .30 .09
❑ 172 Doug Glanville .30 .09
❑ 173 Mike Grace .30 .09
❑ 174 Desi Relaford .30 .09
❑ 175 Scott Rolen .75 .23
❑ 176 Jose Guillen .30 .09
❑ 177 Francisco Cordova .30 .09
❑ 178 Al Martin .30 .09
❑ 179 Jason Schmidt .30 .09
❑ 180 Turner Ward .30 .09
❑ 181 Kevin Young .30 .09
❑ 182 Mark McGwire 2.00 .60
❑ 183 Delino DeShields .30 .09
❑ 184 Eli Marrero .30 .09
❑ 185 Tom Lampkin .30 .09
❑ 186 Ray Lankford .30 .09
❑ 187 Willie McGee .30 .09
❑ 188 Matt Morris UER .30 .09
Career strikeout totals are wrong
❑ 189 Andy Ashby .30 .09
❑ 190 Kevin Brown .50 .15
❑ 191 Ken Caminiti .30 .09
❑ 192 Trevor Hoffman .30 .09
❑ 193 Wally Joyner .30 .09
❑ 194 Greg Vaughn .30 .09
❑ 195 Danny Darwin .30 .09
❑ 196 Shawn Estes .30 .09
❑ 197 Orel Hershiser .30 .09
❑ 198 Jeff Kent .30 .09
❑ 199 Bill Mueller .30 .09
❑ 200 Robb Nen .30 .09
❑ 201 J.T. Snow .30 .09
❑ 202 Ken Cloude .30 .09
❑ 203 Russ Davis .30 .09
❑ 204 Jeff Fassero .30 .09
❑ 205 Ken Griffey Jr. 1.25 .35
❑ 206 Shane Monahan .30 .09
❑ 207 David Segui .30 .09
❑ 208 Dan Wilson .30 .09
❑ 209 Wilson Alvarez .30 .09
❑ 210 Wade Boggs .50 .15
❑ 211 Miguel Cairo .30 .09
❑ 212 Bubba Trammell .30 .09
❑ 213 Quinton McCracken .30 .09
❑ 214 Paul Sorrento .30 .09
❑ 215 Kevin Stocker .30 .09
❑ 216 Will Clark .75 .23
❑ 217 Rusty Greer .30 .09
❑ 218 Rick Helling .30 .09
❑ 219 Mark McLemore .30 .09
❑ 220 Ivan Rodriguez .75 .23
❑ 221 John Wetteland .30 .09
❑ 222 Jose Canseco .75 .23
❑ 223 Roger Clemens 1.50 .45
❑ 224 Carlos Delgado .30 .09
❑ 225 Darrin Fletcher .30 .09
❑ 226 Alex Gonzalez .30 .09
❑ 227 Jose Cruz Jr. .30 .09
❑ 228 Shannon Stewart .30 .09
❑ 229 Rolando Arrojo FF .30 .09
❑ 230 Livan Hernandez FF .30 .09
❑ 231 Orlando Hernandez FF .30 .09
❑ 232 Raul Mondesi FF .30 .09
❑ 233 Moises Alou FF .30 .09
❑ 234 Pedro Martinez FF .75 .23
❑ 235 Sammy Sosa FF 1.25 .35
❑ 236 Vladimir Guerrero FF .75 .23
❑ 237 Bartolo Colon FF .30 .09
❑ 238 Miguel Tejada FF .30 .09
❑ 239 Ismael Valdes FF .30 .09
❑ 240 Mariano Rivera FF .50 .15
❑ 241 Jose Cruz Jr. FF .30 .09
❑ 242 Juan Gonzalez FF .50 .15
❑ 243 Ivan Rodriguez FF .75 .23
❑ 244 Sandy Alomar Jr. FF .30 .09
❑ 245 Roberto Alomar FF .50 .15
❑ 246 Magglio Ordonez FF .30 .09
❑ 247 Kerry Wood SH CL .50 .15
❑ 248 Mark McGwire SH CL 2.00 .60
❑ 249 David Wells SH CL .30 .09
❑ 250 Rolando Arrojo SH CL .30 .09
❑ 251 Ken Griffey Jr. SH CL 1.25 .35
❑ 252 T.Hoffman SH CL .30 .09
❑ 253 Travis Lee SH CL .30 .09
❑ 254 R.Alomar SH CL .30 .09
❑ 255 Sammy Sosa SH CL 1.25 .35
❑ 266 Pat Burrell SR RC 1.50 .45
❑ 267 S.Hillenbrand SR RC 1.00 .30
❑ 268 Robert Fick SR .50 .15
❑ 269 Roy Halladay SR .50 .15
❑ 270 Ruben Mateo SR .50 .15
❑ 271 Bruce Chen SR .50 .15
❑ 272 Angel Pena SR .50 .15
❑ 273 Michael Barrett SR .50 .15
❑ 274 Kevin Witt SR .50 .15
❑ 275 Damon Minor SR .50 .15
❑ 276 Ryan Minor SR .50 .15
❑ 277 A.J. Pierzynski SR .50 .15
❑ 278 A.J. Burnett SR RC 1.00 .30
❑ 279 Dermal Brown SR .50 .15
❑ 280 Joe Lawrence SR .50 .15
❑ 281 Derrick Gibson SR .50 .15
❑ 282 Carlos Febles SR .50 .15
❑ 283 Chris Haas SR .50 .15
❑ 284 Cesar King SR .50 .15
❑ 285 Calvin Pickering SR .50 .15
❑ 286 Mitch Meluskey SR .50 .15
❑ 287 Carlos Beltran SR .75 .23
❑ 288 Ron Belliard SR .50 .15
❑ 289 Jerry Hairston Jr. SR .50 .15
❑ 290 F.Seguignol SR .50 .15
❑ 291 Kris Benson SR .50 .15
❑ 292 C.Hutchinson SR RC .50 .15
❑ 293 Jarrod Washburn .30 .09
❑ 294 Jason Dickson .30 .09
❑ 295 Mo Vaughn .30 .09
❑ 296 Garret Anderson .30 .09
❑ 297 Jim Edmonds .30 .09
❑ 298 Ken Hill .30 .09
❑ 299 Shigetoshi Hasegawa .30 .09
❑ 300 Todd Stottlemyre .30 .09
❑ 301 Randy Johnson .75 .23
❑ 302 Omar Daal .30 .09
❑ 303 Steve Finley .30 .09
❑ 304 Matt Williams .30 .09
❑ 305 Danny Klassen .30 .09
❑ 306 Tony Batista .30 .09
❑ 307 Brian Jordan .30 .09
❑ 308 Greg Maddux 1.25 .35
❑ 309 Chipper Jones .75 .23
❑ 310 Bret Boone .30 .09
❑ 311 Ozzie Guillen .30 .09
❑ 312 John Rocker .30 .09
❑ 313 Tom Glavine .50 .15
❑ 314 Andruw Jones .30 .09
❑ 315 Albert Belle .30 .09
❑ 316 Charles Johnson .30 .09
❑ 317 Will Clark .75 .23
❑ 318 B.J. Surhoff .30 .09
❑ 319 Delino DeShields .30 .09
❑ 320 Heathcliff Slocumb .30 .09
❑ 321 Sidney Ponson .30 .09
❑ 322 Juan Guzman .30 .09
❑ 323 Reggie Jefferson .30 .09
❑ 324 Mark Portugal .30 .09
❑ 325 Tim Wakefield .30 .09
❑ 326 Jason Varitek .50 .15
❑ 327 Jose Offerman .30 .09
❑ 328 Pedro Martinez .75 .23
❑ 329 Trot Nixon .30 .09
❑ 330 Kerry Wood .75 .23
❑ 331 Sammy Sosa 1.25 .35
❑ 332 Glenallen Hill .30 .09
❑ 333 Gary Gaetti .30 .09
❑ 334 Mickey Morandini .30 .09
❑ 335 Benito Santiago .30 .09
❑ 336 Jeff Blauser .30 .09
❑ 337 Frank Thomas .75 .23
❑ 338 Paul Konerko .30 .09
❑ 339 Jaime Navarro .30 .09
❑ 340 Carlos Lee .30 .09
❑ 341 Brian Simmons .30 .09
❑ 342 Mark Johnson .30 .09
❑ 343 Jeff Abbott .30 .09
❑ 344 Steve Avery .30 .09
❑ 345 Mike Cameron .30 .09
❑ 346 Michael Tucker .30 .09
❑ 347 Greg Vaughn .30 .09
❑ 348 Hal Morris .30 .09
❑ 349 Pete Harnisch .30 .09
❑ 350 Denny Neagle .30 .09
❑ 351 Manny Ramirez .50 .15
❑ 352 Roberto Alomar .50 .15
❑ 353 Dwight Gooden .30 .09
❑ 354 Kenny Lofton .30 .09
❑ 355 Mike Jackson .30 .09
❑ 356 Charles Nagy .30 .09
❑ 357 Enrique Wilson .30 .09
❑ 358 Russ Branyan .30 .09
❑ 359 Richie Sexson .30 .09
❑ 360 Vinny Castilla .30 .09
❑ 361 Dante Bichette .30 .09
❑ 362 Kirt Manwaring .30 .09
❑ 363 Darryl Hamilton .30 .09
❑ 364 Jamey Wright .30 .09
❑ 365 Curtis Leskanic .30 .09
❑ 366 Jeff Reed .30 .09
❑ 367 Bobby Higginson .30 .09
❑ 368 Justin Thompson .30 .09
❑ 369 Brad Ausmus .30 .09
❑ 370 Dean Palmer .30 .09
❑ 371 Gabe Kapler .30 .09
❑ 372 Juan Encarnacion .30 .09
❑ 373 Karim Garcia .30 .09
❑ 374 Alex Gonzalez .30 .09
❑ 375 Braden Looper .30 .09
❑ 376 Preston Wilson .30 .09
❑ 377 Todd Dunwoody .30 .09
❑ 378 Alex Fernandez .30 .09
❑ 379 Mark Kotsay .30 .09
❑ 380 Matt Mantei .30 .09
❑ 381 Ken Caminiti .30 .09
❑ 382 Scott Elarton .30 .09
❑ 383 Jeff Bagwell .50 .15
❑ 384 Derek Bell .30 .09
❑ 385 Ricky Gutierrez .30 .09
❑ 386 Richard Hidalgo .30 .09
❑ 387 Shane Reynolds .30 .09
❑ 388 Carl Everett .30 .09
❑ 389 Scott Service .30 .09
❑ 390 Jeff Suppan .30 .09
❑ 391 Joe Randa .30 .09
❑ 392 Kevin Appier .30 .09
❑ 393 Shane Halter .30 .09
❑ 394 Chad Kreuter .30 .09
❑ 395 Mike Sweeney .30 .09
❑ 396 Kevin Brown .50 .15
❑ 397 Devon White .30 .09
❑ 398 Todd Hollandsworth .30 .09
❑ 399 Todd Hundley .30 .09

❑ 400 Chan Ho Park .30 .09
❑ 401 Mark Grudzielanek .30 .09
❑ 402 Raul Mondesi .30 .09
❑ 403 Ismael Valdes .30 .09
❑ 404 Rafael Roque RC .30 .09
❑ 405 Sean Berry .30 .09
❑ 406 Kevin Barker .30 .09
❑ 407 Dave Nilsson .30 .09
❑ 408 Geoff Jenkins .30 .09
❑ 409 Jim Abbott .50 .15
❑ 410 Bobby Hughes .30 .09
❑ 411 Corey Koskie .30 .09
❑ 412 Rick Aguilera .30 .09
❑ 413 LaTroy Hawkins .30 .09
❑ 414 Ron Coomer .30 .09
❑ 415 Denny Hocking .30 .09
❑ 416 Marty Cordova .30 .09
❑ 417 Terry Steinbach .30 .09
❑ 418 Rondell White .30 .09
❑ 419 Wilton Guerrero .30 .09
❑ 420 Shane Andrews .30 .09
❑ 421 Orlando Cabrera .30 .09
❑ 422 Carl Pavano .30 .09
❑ 423 Javier Vazquez .30 .09
❑ 424 Chris Widger .30 .09
❑ 425 Robin Ventura .30 .09
❑ 426 Rickey Henderson .75 .23
❑ 427 Al Leiter .30 .09
❑ 428 Bobby Jones .30 .09
❑ 429 Brian McRae .30 .09
❑ 430 Roger Cedeno .30 .09
❑ 431 Bobby Bonilla .30 .09
❑ 432 Edgardo Alfonzo .30 .09
❑ 433 Bernie Williams .50 .15
❑ 434 Ricky Ledee .30 .09
❑ 435 Chili Davis .30 .09
❑ 436 Tino Martinez .50 .15
❑ 437 Scott Brosius .30 .09
❑ 438 David Cone .30 .09
❑ 439 Joe Girardi .30 .09
❑ 440 Roger Clemens 1.50 .45
❑ 441 Chad Curtis .30 .09
❑ 442 Hideki Irabu .30 .09
❑ 443 Jason Giambi .30 .09
❑ 444 Scott Spiezio .30 .09
❑ 445 Tony Phillips .30 .09
❑ 446 Ramon Hernandez .30 .09
❑ 447 Mike Macfarlane .30 .09
❑ 448 Tom Candiotti .30 .09
❑ 449 Billy Taylor .30 .09
❑ 450 Bobby Estalella .30 .09
❑ 451 Curt Schilling .30 .09
❑ 452 Carlton Loewer .30 .09
❑ 453 Marlon Anderson .30 .09
❑ 454 Kevin Jordan .30 .09
❑ 455 Ron Gant .30 .09
❑ 456 Chad Ogea .30 .09
❑ 457 Abraham Nunez .30 .09
❑ 458 Jason Kendall .30 .09
❑ 459 Pat Meares .30 .09
❑ 460 Brant Brown .30 .09
❑ 461 Brian Giles .30 .09
❑ 462 Chad Hermansen .30 .09
❑ 463 Freddy Adrian Garcia .30 .09
❑ 464 Edgar Renteria .30 .09
❑ 465 Fernando Tatis .30 .09
❑ 466 Eric Davis .30 .09
❑ 467 Darren Bragg .30 .09
❑ 468 Donovan Osborne .30 .09
❑ 469 Manny Aybar .30 .09
❑ 470 Jose Jimenez .30 .09
❑ 471 Kent Mercker .30 .09
❑ 472 Reggie Sanders .30 .09
❑ 473 Ruben Rivera .30 .09
❑ 474 Tony Gwynn 1.00 .30
❑ 475 Jim Leyritz .30 .09
❑ 476 Chris Gomez .30 .09
❑ 477 Matt Clement .30 .09
❑ 478 Carlos Hernandez .30 .09
❑ 479 Sterling Hitchcock .30 .09
❑ 480 Ellis Burks .30 .09
❑ 481 Barry Bonds 2.00 .60
❑ 482 Marvin Benard .30 .09
❑ 483 Kirk Rueter .30 .09
❑ 484 F.P. Santangelo .30 .09
❑ 485 Stan Javier .30 .09
❑ 486 Jeff Kent .30 .09
❑ 487 Alex Rodriguez 1.25 .35
❑ 488 Tom Lampkin .30 .09
❑ 489 Jose Mesa .30 .09
❑ 490 Jay Buhner .30 .09
❑ 491 Edgar Martinez .50 .15
❑ 492 Butch Huskey .30 .09
❑ 493 John Mabry .30 .09
❑ 494 Jamie Moyer .30 .09
❑ 495 Roberto Hernandez .30 .09
❑ 496 Tony Saunders .30 .09
❑ 497 Fred McGriff .50 .15
❑ 498 Dave Martinez .30 .09
❑ 499 Jose Canseco .75 .23
❑ 500 Rolando Arrojo .30 .09
❑ 501 Esteban Yan .30 .09
❑ 502 Juan Gonzalez .50 .15
❑ 503 Rafael Palmeiro .50 .15
❑ 504 Aaron Sele .30 .09
❑ 505 Royce Clayton .30 .09
❑ 506 Todd Zeile .30 .09
❑ 507 Tom Goodwin .30 .09
❑ 508 Lee Stevens .30 .09
❑ 509 Esteban Loaiza .30 .09
❑ 510 Joey Hamilton .30 .09
❑ 511 Homer Bush .30 .09
❑ 512 Willie Greene .30 .09
❑ 513 Shawn Green .30 .09
❑ 514 David Wells .30 .09
❑ 515 Kelvim Escobar .30 .09
❑ 516 Tony Fernandez .30 .09
❑ 517 Pat Hentgen .30 .09
❑ 518 Mark McGwire AR 1.00 .30
❑ 519 Ken Griffey Jr. AR .75 .23
❑ 520 Sammy Sosa AR .75 .23
❑ 521 Juan Gonzalez AR .30 .09
❑ 522 J.D. Drew AR .30 .09
❑ 523 Chipper Jones AR .50 .15
❑ 524 Alex Rodriguez AR .75 .23
❑ 525 Mike Piazza AR .75 .23
❑ 526 N.Garciaparra AR .75 .23
❑ 527 Mark McGwire SH CL 1.00 .30
❑ 528 Sammy Sosa SH CL .75 .23
❑ 529 Scott Brosius SH CL .30 .09
❑ 530 Cal Ripken SH CL 1.25 .35
❑ 531 Barry Bonds SH CL .75 .23
❑ 532 Roger Clemens SH CL .75 .23
❑ 533 Ken Griffey Jr. SH CL .75 .23
❑ 534 Alex Rodriguez SH CL .75 .23
❑ 535 Curt Schilling SH CL .30 .09
❑ NNO Ken Griffey Jr. 800.00 240.00
1989 AU/100

2001 Upper Deck

	Nm-Mt	Ex-Mt
COMPLETE SET (450)	100.00	30.00
COMP. SERIES 1 (270)	40.00	12.00
COMP. SERIES 2 (180)	60.00	18.00
COMMON (46-270/300-450)	.30	.09
COMMON SR (1-45)	.50	.15

❑ 1 Jeff DaVanon SR .50 .15
❑ 2 Aubrey Huff SR .50 .15
❑ 3 Pasqual Coco SR .50 .15
❑ 4 Barry Zito SR .60 .18
❑ 5 Augie Ojeda SR .50 .15
❑ 6 Chris Richard SR .50 .15
❑ 7 Josh Phelps SR .50 .15
❑ 8 Kevin Nicholson SR .50 .15
❑ 9 Juan Guzman SR .50 .15
❑ 10 Brandon Kolb SR .50 .15
❑ 11 Johan Santana SR 5.00 1.50
❑ 12 Josh Kalinowski SR .50 .15
❑ 13 Tike Redman SR .50 .15
❑ 14 Ivanon Coffie SR .50 .15
❑ 15 Chad Durbin SR .50 .15
❑ 16 Derrick Turnbow SR .50 .15
❑ 17 Scott Downs SR .50 .15
❑ 18 Jason Grilli SR .50 .15
❑ 19 Mark Buehrle SR .50 .15
❑ 20 Paxton Crawford SR .50 .15
❑ 21 Bronson Arroyo SR 1.00 .30
❑ 22 Tomas De la Rosa SR .50 .15
❑ 23 Paul Rigdon SR .50 .15
❑ 24 Rob Ramsay SR .50 .15
❑ 25 Damian Rolls SR .50 .15
❑ 26 Jason Conti SR .50 .15
❑ 27 John Parrish SR .50 .15
❑ 28 Geraldo Guzman SR .50 .15
❑ 29 Tony Mota SR .50 .15
❑ 30 Luis Rivas SR .50 .15
❑ 31 Brian Tollberg SR .50 .15
❑ 32 Adam Bernero SR .50 .15
❑ 33 Michael Cuddyer SR .50 .15
❑ 34 Josue Espada SR .50 .15
❑ 35 Joe Lawrence SR .50 .15
❑ 36 Chad Moeller SR .50 .15
❑ 37 Nick Bierbrodt SR .50 .15
❑ 38 DeWayne Wise SR .50 .15
❑ 39 Javier Cardona SR .50 .15
❑ 40 Hiram Bocachica SR .50 .15
❑ 41 G.Chiaramonte SR .50 .15
❑ 42 Alex Cabrera SR .50 .15
❑ 43 Jimmy Rollins SR .50 .15
❑ 44 Pat Flury SR RC .50 .15
❑ 45 Leo Estrella SR .50 .15
❑ 46 Darin Erstad .30 .09
❑ 47 Seth Etherton .30 .09
❑ 48 Troy Glaus .30 .09
❑ 49 Brian Cooper .30 .09
❑ 50 Tim Salmon .50 .15
❑ 51 Adam Kennedy .30 .09
❑ 52 Bengie Molina .30 .09
❑ 53 Jason Giambi .30 .09
❑ 54 Miguel Tejada .30 .09
❑ 55 Tim Hudson .30 .09
❑ 56 Eric Chavez .30 .09
❑ 57 Terrence Long .30 .09
❑ 58 Jason Isringhausen .30 .09
❑ 59 Ramon Hernandez .30 .09
❑ 60 Raul Mondesi .30 .09
❑ 61 David Wells .30 .09
❑ 62 Shannon Stewart .30 .09
❑ 63 Tony Batista .30 .09
❑ 64 Brad Fullmer .30 .09
❑ 65 Chris Carpenter .30 .09
❑ 66 Homer Bush .30 .09
❑ 67 Gerald Williams .30 .09
❑ 68 Miguel Cairo .30 .09
❑ 69 Ryan Rupe .30 .09
❑ 70 Greg Vaughn .30 .09
❑ 71 John Flaherty .30 .09
❑ 72 Dan Wheeler .30 .09
❑ 73 Fred McGriff .50 .15
❑ 74 Roberto Alomar .50 .15
❑ 75 Bartolo Colon .30 .09
❑ 76 Kenny Lofton .30 .09
❑ 77 David Segui .30 .09
❑ 78 Omar Vizquel .50 .15
❑ 79 Russ Branyan .30 .09
❑ 80 Chuck Finley .30 .09
❑ 81 Manny Ramirez UER .50 .15
Back pholo is of David Segui
❑ 82 Alex Rodriguez 1.25 .35
❑ 83 John Halama .30 .09
❑ 84 Mike Cameron .30 .09
❑ 85 David Bell .30 .09
❑ 86 Jay Buhner .30 .09
❑ 87 Aaron Sele .30 .09
❑ 88 Rickey Henderson .75 .23
❑ 89 Brook Fordyce .30 .09
❑ 90 Cal Ripken 2.50 .75
❑ 91 Mike Mussina .50 .15

No.	Player	Price	Price
92	Delino DeShields	.30	.09
93	Melvin Mora	.30	.09
94	Sidney Ponson	.30	.09
95	Brady Anderson	.30	.09
96	Ivan Rodriguez	.75	.23
97	Ricky Ledee	.30	.09
98	Rick Helling	.30	.09
99	Ruben Mateo	.30	.09
100	Luis Alicea	.30	.09
101	John Wetteland	.30	.09
102	Mike Lamb	.30	.09
103	Carl Everett	.30	.09
104	Troy O'Leary	.30	.09
105	Wilton Veras	.30	.09
106	Pedro Martinez	.75	.23
107	Rolando Arrojo	.30	.09
108	Scott Hatteberg	.30	.09
109	Jason Varitek	.50	.15
110	Jose Offerman	.30	.09
111	Carlos Beltran	.50	.15
112	Johnny Damon	.50	.15
113	Mark Quinn	.30	.09
114	Rey Sanchez	.30	.09
115	Mac Suzuki	.30	.09
116	Jermaine Dye	.30	.09
117	Chris Fussell	.30	.09
118	Jeff Weaver	.30	.09
119	Dean Palmer	.30	.09
120	Robert Fick	.30	.09
121	Brian Moehler	.30	.09
122	Damion Easley	.30	.09
123	Juan Encarnacion	.30	.09
124	Tony Clark	.30	.09
125	Cristian Guzman	.30	.09
126	Matt LeCroy	.30	.09
127	Eric Milton	.30	.09
128	Jay Canizaro	.30	.09
129	David Ortiz	.50	.15
130	Brad Radke	.30	.09
131	Jacque Jones	.30	.09
132	Magglio Ordonez	.30	.09
133	Carlos Lee	.30	.09
134	Mike Sirotka	.30	.09
135	Ray Durham	.30	.09
136	Paul Konerko	.30	.09
137	Charles Johnson	.30	.09
138	James Baldwin	.30	.09
139	Jeff Abbott	.30	.09
140	Roger Clemens	1.50	.45
141	Derek Jeter	2.00	.60
142	David Justice	.30	.09
143	Ramiro Mendoza	.30	.09
144	Chuck Knoblauch	.30	.09
145	Orlando Hernandez	.30	.09
146	Alfonso Soriano	.50	.15
147	Jeff Bagwell	.50	.15
148	Julio Lugo	.30	.09
149	Mitch Meluskey	.30	.09
150	Jose Lima	.30	.09
151	Richard Hidalgo	.30	.09
152	Moises Alou	.30	.09
153	Scott Elarton	.30	.09
154	Andruw Jones	.30	.09
155	Quilvio Veras	.30	.09
156	Greg Maddux	1.25	.35
157	Brian Jordan	.30	.09
158	Andres Galarraga	.30	.09
159	Kevin Millwood	.30	.09
160	Rafael Furcal	.30	.09
161	Jeromy Burnitz	.30	.09
162	Jimmy Haynes	.30	.09
163	Mark Loretta	.30	.09
164	Ron Belliard	.30	.09
165	Richie Sexson	.30	.09
166	Kevin Barker	.30	.09
167	Jeff D'Amico	.30	.09
168	Rick Ankiel	.30	.09
169	Mark McGwire	2.00	.60
170	J.D. Drew	.30	.09
171	Eli Marrero	.30	.09
172	Darryl Kile	.30	.09
173	Edgar Renteria	.30	.09
174	Will Clark	.75	.23
175	Eric Young	.30	.09
176	Mark Grace	.50	.15
177	Jon Lieber	.30	.09
178	Damon Buford	.30	.09
179	Kerry Wood	.75	.23
180	Rondell White	.30	.09
181	Joe Girardi	.30	.09
182	Curt Schilling	.30	.09
183	Randy Johnson	.75	.23
184	Steve Finley	.30	.09
185	Kelly Stinnett	.30	.09
186	Jay Bell	.30	.09
187	Matt Mantei	.30	.09
188	Luis Gonzalez	.30	.09
189	Shawn Green	.30	.09
190	Todd Hundley	.30	.09
191	Chan Ho Park	.30	.09
192	Adrian Beltre	.50	.15
193	Mark Grudzielanek	.30	.09
194	Gary Sheffield	.30	.09
195	Tom Goodwin	.30	.09
196	Lee Stevens	.30	.09
197	Javier Vazquez	.30	.09
198	Milton Bradley	.30	.09
199	Vladimir Guerrero	.75	.23
200	Carl Pavano	.30	.09
201	Orlando Cabrera	.30	.09
202	Tony Armas Jr.	.30	.09
203	Jeff Kent	.30	.09
204	Calvin Murray	.30	.09
205	Ellis Burks	.30	.09
206	Barry Bonds	2.00	.60
207	Russ Ortiz	.30	.09
208	Marvin Benard	.30	.09
209	Joe Nathan	.30	.09
210	Preston Wilson	.30	.09
211	Cliff Floyd	.30	.09
212	Mike Lowell	.30	.09
213	Ryan Dempster	.30	.09
214	Brad Penny	.30	.09
215	Mike Redmond	.30	.09
216	Luis Castillo	.30	.09
217	Derek Bell	.30	.09
218	Mike Hampton	.30	.09
219	Todd Zeile	.30	.09
220	Robin Ventura	.30	.09
221	Mike Piazza	1.25	.35
222	Al Leiter	.30	.09
223	Edgardo Alfonzo	.30	.09
224	Mike Bordick	.30	.09
225	Phil Nevin	.30	.09
226	Ryan Klesko	.30	.09
227	Adam Eaton	.30	.09
228	Eric Owens	.30	.09
229	Tony Gwynn	1.00	.30
230	Matt Clement	.30	.09
231	Wiki Gonzalez	.30	.09
232	Robert Person	.30	.09
233	Doug Glanville	.30	.09
234	Scott Rolen	.75	.23
235	Mike Lieberthal	.30	.09
236	Randy Wolf	.30	.09
237	Bob Abreu	.30	.09
238	Pat Burrell	.30	.09
239	Bruce Chen	.30	.09
240	Kevin Young	.30	.09
241	Todd Ritchie	.30	.09
242	Adrian Brown	.30	.09
243	Chad Hermansen	.30	.09
244	Warren Morris	.30	.09
245	Kris Benson	.30	.09
246	Jason Kendall	.30	.09
247	Pokey Reese	.30	.09
248	Rob Bell	.30	.09
249	Ken Griffey Jr.	1.25	.35
250	Sean Casey	.30	.09
251	Aaron Boone	.30	.09
252	Pete Harnisch	.30	.09
253	Barry Larkin	.50	.15
254	Dmitri Young	.30	.09
255	Todd Hollandsworth	.30	.09
256	Pedro Astacio	.30	.09
257	Todd Helton	.50	.15
258	Terry Shumpert	.30	.09
259	Neifi Perez	.30	.09
260	Jeffrey Hammonds	.30	.09
261	Ben Petrick	.30	.09
262	Mark McGwire SH	1.00	.30
263	Derek Jeter SH	1.00	.30
264	Sammy Sosa SH	.75	.23
265	Cal Ripken SH	1.25	.35
266	Pedro Martinez SH	.50	.15
267	Barry Bonds SH	.75	.23
268	Fred McGriff SH	.30	.09
269	Randy Johnson SH	.50	.15
270	Darin Erstad SH	.30	.09
271	Ichiro Suzuki SR RC	15.00	4.50
272	W. Betemit SR RC	.50	.15
273	Corey Patterson SR	.50	.15
274	Sean Douglass SR RC	.50	.15
275	Mike Penney SR RC	.50	.15
276	Nate Teut SR RC	.50	.15
277	R. Rodriguez SR RC	.50	.15
278	B. Duckworth SR RC	.50	.15
279	Rafael Soriano SR RC	.60	.18
280	Juan Diaz SR RC	.50	.15
281	H. Ramirez SR RC	.60	.18
282	T. Shinjo SR RC	.60	.18
283	Keith Ginter SR	.50	.15
284	Esix Snead SR RC	.50	.15
285	Erick Almonte SR RC	.50	.15
286	Travis Hafner SR RC	2.50	.75
287	Jason Smith SR RC	.50	.15
288	J. Melian SR RC	.50	.15
289	Tyler Walker SR RC	.50	.15
290	Jason Standridge SR	.50	.15
291	Juan Uribe SR RC	.60	.18
292	A. Hernandez SR RC	.50	.15
293	J. Michaels SR RC	.50	.15
294	Jason Hart SR	.50	.15
295	Albert Pujols SR RC	40.00	12.00
296	M. Ensberg SR RC	1.00	.30
297	Brandon Inge SR	.50	.15
298	Jesus Colome SR	.50	.15
299	K. Kessel SR RC UER	.50	.15
	L Missing from MLB experience		
300	Timo Perez SR	.50	.15
301	Mo Vaughn	.30	.09
302	Ismael Valdes	.30	.09
303	Glenallen Hill	.30	.09
304	Garret Anderson	.30	.09
305	Johnny Damon	.50	.15
306	Jose Ortiz	.30	.09
307	Mark Mulder	.30	.09
308	Adam Piatt	.30	.09
309	Gil Heredia	.30	.09
310	Mike Sirotka	.30	.09
311	Carlos Delgado	.30	.09
312	Alex Gonzalez	.30	.09
313	Jose Cruz Jr.	.30	.09
314	Darrin Fletcher	.30	.09
315	Ben Grieve	.30	.09
316	Vinny Castilla	.30	.09
317	Wilson Alvarez	.30	.09
318	Brent Abernathy	.30	.09
319	Ellis Burks	.30	.09
320	Jim Thome	.75	.23
321	Juan Gonzalez	.50	.15
322	Ed Taubensee	.30	.09
323	Travis Fryman	.30	.09
324	John Olerud	.30	.09
325	Edgar Martinez	.50	.15
326	Freddy Garcia	.30	.09
327	Bret Boone	.50	.15
328	Kazuhiro Sasaki	.30	.09
329	Albert Belle	.30	.09
330	Mike Bordick	.30	.09
331	David Segui	.30	.09
332	Pat Hentgen	.30	.09
333	Alex Rodriguez	1.25	.35
334	Andres Galarraga	.30	.09
335	Gabe Kapler	.30	.09
336	Ken Caminiti	.30	.09
337	Rafael Palmeiro	.50	.15
338	Manny Ramirez	.50	.15
339	David Cone	.30	.09
340	Nomar Garciaparra	1.25	.35
341	Trot Nixon	.30	.09
342	Derek Lowe	.30	.09
343	Roberto Hernandez	.30	.09
344	Mike Sweeney	.30	.09
345	Carlos Febles	.30	.09
346	Jeff Suppan	.30	.09
347	Roger Cedeno	.30	.09
348	Bobby Higginson	.30	.09

❑ 349 Deivi Cruz .30 .09
❑ 350 Mitch Meluskey .30 .09
❑ 351 Matt Lawton .30 .09
❑ 352 Mark Redman .30 .09
❑ 353 Jay Canizaro .30 .09
❑ 354 Corey Koskie .30 .09
❑ 355 Matt Kinney .30 .09
❑ 356 Frank Thomas .75 .23
❑ 357 Sandy Alomar Jr. .30 .09
❑ 358 David Wells .30 .09
❑ 359 Jim Parque .30 .09
❑ 360 Chris Singleton .30 .09
❑ 361 Tino Martinez .50 .15
❑ 362 Paul O'Neill .50 .15
❑ 363 Mike Mussina .50 .15
❑ 364 Bernie Williams .50 .15
❑ 365 Andy Pettite .50 .15
❑ 366 Mariano Rivera .50 .15
❑ 367 Brad Ausmus .30 .09
❑ 368 Craig Biggio .50 .15
❑ 369 Lance Berkman .30 .09
❑ 370 Shane Reynolds .30 .09
❑ 371 Chipper Jones .75 .23
❑ 372 Tom Glavine .50 .15
❑ 373 B.J. Surhoff .30 .09
❑ 374 John Smoltz .50 .15
❑ 375 Rico Brogna .30 .09
❑ 376 Geoff Jenkins .30 .09
❑ 377 Jose Hernandez .30 .09
❑ 378 Tyler Houston .30 .09
❑ 379 Henry Blanco .30 .09
❑ 380 Jeffrey Hammonds .30 .09
❑ 381 Jim Edmonds .30 .09
❑ 382 Fernando Vina .30 .09
❑ 383 Andy Benes .30 .09
❑ 384 Ray Lankford .30 .09
❑ 385 Dustin Hermanson .30 .09
❑ 386 Todd Hundley .30 .09
❑ 387 Sammy Sosa 1.25 .35
❑ 388 Tom Gordon .30 .09
❑ 389 Bill Mueller .30 .09
❑ 390 Ron Coomer .30 .09
❑ 391 Matt Stairs .30 .09
❑ 392 Mark Grace .50 .15
❑ 393 Matt Williams .30 .09
❑ 394 Todd Stottlemyre .30 .09
❑ 395 Tony Womack .30 .09
❑ 396 Erubiel Durazo .30 .09
❑ 397 Reggie Sanders .30 .09
❑ 398 Andy Ashby .30 .09
❑ 399 Eric Karros .30 .09
❑ 400 Kevin Brown .30 .09
❑ 401 Darren Dreifort .30 .09
❑ 402 Fernando Tatis .30 .09
❑ 403 Jose Vidro .30 .09
❑ 404 Peter Bergeron .30 .09
❑ 405 Geoff Blum .30 .09
❑ 406 J.T. Snow .30 .09
❑ 407 Livan Hernandez .30 .09
❑ 408 Robb Nen .30 .09
❑ 409 Bobby Estalella .30 .09
❑ 410 Rich Aurilia .30 .09
❑ 411 Eric Davis .30 .09
❑ 412 Charles Johnson .30 .09
❑ 413 Alex Gonzalez .30 .09
❑ 414 A.J. Burnett .30 .09
❑ 415 Antonio Alfonseca .30 .09
❑ 416 Derek Lee .30 .09
❑ 417 Jay Payton .30 .09
❑ 418 Kevin Appier .30 .09
❑ 419 Steve Trachsel .30 .09
❑ 420 Rey Ordonez .30 .09
❑ 421 Darryl Hamilton .30 .09
❑ 422 Ben Davis .30 .09
❑ 423 Damian Jackson .30 .09
❑ 424 Mark Kotsay .30 .09
❑ 425 Trevor Hoffman .30 .09
❑ 426 Travis Lee .30 .09
❑ 427 Omar Daal .30 .09
❑ 428 Paul Byrd .30 .09
❑ 429 Reggie Taylor .30 .09
❑ 430 Brian Giles .30 .09
❑ 431 Derek Bell .30 .09
❑ 432 Francisco Cordova .30 .09
❑ 433 Pat Meares .30 .09
❑ 434 Scott Williamson .30 .09
❑ 435 Jason LaRue .30 .09
❑ 436 Michael Tucker .30 .09
❑ 437 Wilton Guerrero .30 .09
❑ 438 Mike Hampton .30 .09
❑ 439 Ron Gant .30 .09
❑ 440 Jeff Cirillo .30 .09
❑ 441 Denny Neagle .30 .09
❑ 442 Larry Walker .50 .15
❑ 443 Juan Pierre .30 .09
❑ 444 Todd Walker .30 .09
❑ 445 Jason Giambi SH CL .30 .09
❑ 446 Jeff Kent SH CL .30 .09
❑ 447 Mariano Rivera SH CL .30 .09
❑ 448 Edgar Martinez SH CL .30 .09
❑ 449 Troy Glaus SH CL .30 .09
❑ 450 Alex Rodriguez SH CL .75 .23

2002 Upper Deck

	Nm-Mt	Ex-Mt
COMPLETE SET (745)	160.00	47.50
COMPLETE SERIES 1 (500)	110.00	33.00
COMPLETE SERIES 2 (245)	50.00	15.00
COMMON (51-500/546-745)	.30	.09
COMMON SR (1-50/501-545)	1.00	.30

❑ 1 Mark Prior SR 4.00 1.20
❑ 2 Mark Teixeira SR 1.50 .45
❑ 3 Brian Roberts SR 1.00 .30
❑ 4 Jason Romano SR 1.00 .30
❑ 5 Dennis Stark SR 1.00 .30
❑ 6 Oscar Salazar SR 1.00 .30
❑ 7 John Patterson SR 1.00 .30
❑ 8 Shane Loux SR 1.00 .30
❑ 9 Marcus Giles SR 1.00 .30
❑ 10 Juan Cruz SR 1.00 .30
❑ 11 Jorge Julio SR 1.00 .30
❑ 12 Adam Dunn SR 1.50 .45
❑ 13 Delvin James SR 1.00 .30
❑ 14 Jeremy Affeldt SR 1.00 .30
❑ 15 Tim Raines Jr. SR 1.00 .30
❑ 16 Luke Hudson SR 1.00 .30
❑ 17 Todd Sears SR 1.00 .30
❑ 18 George Perez SR 1.00 .30
❑ 19 Wilmy Caceres SR 1.00 .30
❑ 20 Abraham Nunez SR 1.00 .30
❑ 21 Mike Amrhein SR RC 1.00 .30
❑ 22 Carlos Hernandez SR 1.00 .30
❑ 23 Scott Hodges SR 1.00 .30
❑ 24 Brandon Knight SR 1.00 .30
❑ 25 Geoff Goetz SR 1.00 .30
❑ 26 Carlos Garcia SR 1.00 .30
❑ 27 Luis Pineda SR 1.00 .30
❑ 28 Chris Gissell SR 1.00 .30
❑ 29 Jae Weong Seo SR 1.00 .30
❑ 30 Paul Phillips SR 1.00 .30
❑ 31 Cory Aldridge SR 1.00 .30
❑ 32 Aaron Cook SR RC 1.00 .30
❑ 33 Rendy Espina SR RC 1.00 .30
❑ 34 Jason Phillips SR 1.00 .30
❑ 35 Carlos Silva SR 1.00 .30
❑ 36 Ryan Mills SR 1.00 .30
❑ 37 Pedro Santana SR 1.00 .30
❑ 38 John Grabow SR 1.00 .30
❑ 39 Cody Ransom SR 1.00 .30
❑ 40 Orlando Woodards SR 1.00 .30
❑ 41 Bud Smith SR 1.00 .30
❑ 42 Junior Guerrero SR 1.00 .30
❑ 43 David Brous SR 1.00 .30
❑ 44 Steve Green SR 1.00 .30
❑ 45 Brian Rogers SR 1.00 .30
❑ 46 Juan Figueroa SR RC 1.00 .30
❑ 47 Nick Punto SR 1.00 .30
❑ 48 Junior Herndon SR 1.00 .30
❑ 49 Justin Kaye SR 1.00 .30
❑ 50 Jason Karnuth SR 1.00 .30
❑ 51 Troy Glaus .30 .09
❑ 52 Bengie Molina .30 .09
❑ 53 Ramon Ortiz .30 .09
❑ 54 Adam Kennedy .30 .09
❑ 55 Jarrod Washburn .30 .09
❑ 56 Troy Percival .30 .09
❑ 57 David Eckstein .30 .09
❑ 58 Ben Weber .30 .09
❑ 59 Larry Barnes .30 .09
❑ 60 Ismael Valdes .30 .09
❑ 61 Benji Gil .30 .09
❑ 62 Scott Schoeneweis .30 .09
❑ 63 Pat Rapp .30 .09
❑ 64 Jason Giambi .30 .09
❑ 65 Mark Mulder .30 .09
❑ 66 Ron Gant .30 .09
❑ 67 Johnny Damon .50 .15
❑ 68 Adam Piatt .30 .09
❑ 69 Jermaine Dye .30 .09
❑ 70 Jason Hart .30 .09
❑ 71 Eric Chavez .30 .09
❑ 72 Jim Mecir .30 .09
❑ 73 Barry Zito .30 .09
❑ 74 Jason Isringhausen .30 .09
❑ 75 Jeremy Giambi .30 .09
❑ 76 Olmedo Saenz .30 .09
❑ 77 Terrence Long .30 .09
❑ 78 Ramon Hernandez .30 .09
❑ 79 Chris Carpenter .30 .09
❑ 80 Raul Mondesi .30 .09
❑ 81 Carlos Delgado .30 .09
❑ 82 Billy Koch .30 .09
❑ 83 Vernon Wells .30 .09
❑ 84 Darrin Fletcher .30 .09
❑ 85 Homer Bush .30 .09
❑ 86 Pasqual Coco .30 .09
❑ 87 Shannon Stewart .30 .09
❑ 88 Chris Woodward .30 .09
❑ 89 Joe Lawrence .30 .09
❑ 90 Esteban Loaiza .30 .09
❑ 91 Cesar Izturis .30 .09
❑ 92 Kelvim Escobar .30 .09
❑ 93 Greg Vaughn .30 .09
❑ 94 Brent Abernathy .30 .09
❑ 95 Tanyon Sturtze .30 .09
❑ 96 Steve Cox .30 .09
❑ 97 Aubrey Huff .30 .09
❑ 98 Jesus Colome .30 .09
❑ 99 Ben Grieve .30 .09
❑ 100 Esteban Yan .30 .09
❑ 101 Joe Kennedy .30 .09
❑ 102 Felix Martinez .30 .09
❑ 103 Nick Bierbrodt .30 .09
❑ 104 Damian Rolls .30 .09
❑ 105 Russ Johnson .30 .09
❑ 106 Toby Hall .30 .09
❑ 107 Roberto Alomar .50 .15
❑ 108 Bartolo Colon .30 .09
❑ 109 John Rocker .30 .09
❑ 110 Juan Gonzalez .50 .15
❑ 111 Einar Diaz .30 .09
❑ 112 Chuck Finley .30 .09
❑ 113 Kenny Lofton .30 .09
❑ 114 Danys Baez .30 .09
❑ 115 Travis Fryman .30 .09
❑ 116 C.C. Sabathia .30 .09
❑ 117 Paul Shuey .30 .09
❑ 118 Marty Cordova .30 .09
❑ 119 Ellis Burks .30 .09
❑ 120 Bob Wickman .30 .09
❑ 121 Edgar Martinez .50 .15
❑ 122 Freddy Garcia .30 .09
❑ 123 Ichiro Suzuki 1.25 .35
❑ 124 John Olerud .30 .09
❑ 125 Gil Meche .30 .09
❑ 126 Dan Wilson .30 .09
❑ 127 Aaron Sele .30 .09
❑ 128 Kazuhiro Sasaki .30 .09

❑ 129	Mark McLemore	.30	.09
❑ 130	Carlos Guillen	.30	.09
❑ 131	Al Martin	.30	.09
❑ 132	David Bell	.30	.09
❑ 133	Jay Buhner	.30	.09
❑ 134	Stan Javier	.30	.09
❑ 135	Tony Batista	.30	.09
❑ 136	Jason Johnson	.30	.09
❑ 137	Brook Fordyce	.30	.09
❑ 138	Mike Kinkade	.30	.09
❑ 139	Willis Roberts	.30	.09
❑ 140	David Segui	.30	.09
❑ 141	Josh Towers	.30	.09
❑ 142	Jeff Conine	.30	.09
❑ 143	Chris Richard	.30	.09
❑ 144	Pat Hentgen	.30	.09
❑ 145	Melvin Mora	.30	.09
❑ 146	Jerry Hairston Jr.	.30	.09
❑ 147	Calvin Maduro	.30	.09
❑ 148	Brady Anderson	.30	.09
❑ 149	Alex Rodriguez	1.25	.35
❑ 150	Kenny Rogers	.30	.09
❑ 151	Chad Curtis	.30	.09
❑ 152	Ricky Ledee	.30	.09
❑ 153	Rafael Palmeiro	.50	.15
❑ 154	Rob Bell	.30	.09
❑ 155	Rick Helling	.30	.09
❑ 156	Doug Davis	.30	.09
❑ 157	Mike Lamb	.30	.09
❑ 158	Gabe Kapler	.30	.09
❑ 159	Jeff Zimmerman	.30	.09
❑ 160	Bill Haselman	.30	.09
❑ 161	Tim Crabtree	.30	.09
❑ 162	Carlos Pena	.30	.09
❑ 163	Nomar Garciaparra	1.25	.35
❑ 164	Shea Hillenbrand	.30	.09
❑ 165	Hideo Nomo	.75	.23
❑ 166	Manny Ramirez	.50	.15
❑ 167	Jose Offerman	.30	.09
❑ 168	Scott Hatteberg	.30	.09
❑ 169	Trot Nixon	.30	.09
❑ 170	Darren Lewis	.30	.09
❑ 171	Derek Lowe	.30	.09
❑ 172	Troy O'Leary	.30	.09
❑ 173	Tim Wakefield	.30	.09
❑ 174	Chris Stynes	.30	.09
❑ 175	John Valentin	.30	.09
❑ 176	David Cone	.30	.09
❑ 177	Neifi Perez	.30	.09
❑ 178	Brent Mayne	.30	.09
❑ 179	Dan Reichert	.30	.09
❑ 180	A.J. Hinch	.30	.09
❑ 181	Chris George	.30	.09
❑ 182	Mike Sweeney	.30	.09
❑ 183	Jeff Suppan	.30	.09
❑ 184	Roberto Hernandez	.30	.09
❑ 185	Joe Randa	.30	.09
❑ 186	Paul Byrd	.30	.09
❑ 187	Luis Ordaz	.30	.09
❑ 188	Kris Wilson	.30	.09
❑ 189	Dee Brown	.30	.09
❑ 190	Tony Clark	.30	.09
❑ 191	Matt Anderson	.30	.09
❑ 192	Robert Fick	.30	.09
❑ 193	Juan Encarnacion	.30	.09
❑ 194	Dean Palmer	.30	.09
❑ 195	Victor Santos	.30	.09
❑ 196	Damion Easley	.30	.09
❑ 197	Jose Lima	.30	.09
❑ 198	Deivi Cruz	.30	.09
❑ 199	Roger Cedeno	.30	.09
❑ 200	Jose Macias	.30	.09
❑ 201	Jeff Weaver	.30	.09
❑ 202	Brandon Inge	.30	.09
❑ 203	Brian Moehler	.30	.09
❑ 204	Brad Radke	.30	.09
❑ 205	Doug Mientkiewicz	.30	.09
❑ 206	Cristian Guzman	.30	.09
❑ 207	Corey Koskie	.30	.09
❑ 208	LaTroy Hawkins	.30	.09
❑ 209	J.C. Romero	.30	.09
❑ 210	Chad Allen	.30	.09
❑ 211	Torii Hunter	.30	.09
❑ 212	Travis Miller	.30	.09
❑ 213	Joe Mays	.30	.09
❑ 214	Todd Jones	.30	.09
❑ 215	David Ortiz	.50	.15
❑ 216	Brian Buchanan	.30	.09
❑ 217	A.J. Pierzynski	.30	.09
❑ 218	Carlos Lee	.30	.09
❑ 219	Gary Glover	.30	.09
❑ 220	Jose Valentin	.30	.09
❑ 221	Aaron Rowand	.30	.09
❑ 222	Sandy Alomar Jr.	.30	.09
❑ 223	Herbert Perry	.30	.09
❑ 224	Jon Garland	.30	.09
❑ 225	Mark Buehrle	.30	.09
❑ 226	Chris Singleton	.30	.09
❑ 227	Kip Wells	.30	.09
❑ 228	Ray Durham	.30	.09
❑ 229	Joe Crede	.30	.09
❑ 230	Keith Foulke	.30	.09
❑ 231	Royce Clayton	.30	.09
❑ 232	Andy Pettitte	.50	.15
❑ 233	Derek Jeter	2.00	.60
❑ 234	Jorge Posada	.50	.15
❑ 235	Roger Clemens	1.50	.45
❑ 236	Paul O'Neill	.50	.15
❑ 237	Nick Johnson	.30	.09
❑ 238	Gerald Williams	.30	.09
❑ 239	Mariano Rivera	.50	.15
❑ 240	Alfonso Soriano	.50	.15
❑ 241	Ramiro Mendoza	.30	.09
❑ 242	Mike Mussina	.50	.15
❑ 243	Luis Sojo	.30	.09
❑ 244	Scott Brosius	.30	.09
❑ 245	David Justice	.30	.09
❑ 246	Wade Miller	.30	.09
❑ 247	Brad Ausmus	.30	.09
❑ 248	Jeff Bagwell	.50	.15
❑ 249	Daryle Ward	.30	.09
❑ 250	Shane Reynolds	.30	.09
❑ 251	Chris Truby	.30	.09
❑ 252	Billy Wagner	.30	.09
❑ 253	Craig Biggio	.50	.15
❑ 254	Moises Alou	.30	.09
❑ 255	Vinny Castilla	.30	.09
❑ 256	Tim Redding	.30	.09
❑ 257	Roy Oswalt	.30	.09
❑ 258	Julio Lugo	.30	.09
❑ 259	Chipper Jones	.75	.23
❑ 260	Greg Maddux	1.25	.35
❑ 261	Ken Caminiti	.30	.09
❑ 262	Kevin Millwood	.30	.09
❑ 263	Keith Lockhart	.30	.09
❑ 264	Rey Sanchez	.30	.09
❑ 265	Jason Marquis	.30	.09
❑ 266	Brian Jordan	.30	.09
❑ 267	Steve Karsay	.30	.09
❑ 268	Wes Helms	.30	.09
❑ 269	B.J. Surhoff	.30	.09
❑ 270	Wilson Betemit	.30	.09
❑ 271	John Smoltz	.50	.15
❑ 272	Rafael Furcal	.30	.09
❑ 273	Jeromy Burnitz	.30	.09
❑ 274	Jimmy Haynes	.30	.09
❑ 275	Mark Loretta	.30	.09
❑ 276	Jose Hernandez	.30	.09
❑ 277	Paul Rigdon	.30	.09
❑ 278	Alex Sanchez	.30	.09
❑ 279	Chad Fox	.30	.09
❑ 280	Devon White	.30	.09
❑ 281	Tyler Houston	.30	.09
❑ 282	Ronnie Belliard	.30	.09
❑ 283	Luis Lopez	.30	.09
❑ 284	Ben Sheets	.30	.09
❑ 285	Curtis Leskanic	.30	.09
❑ 286	Henry Blanco	.30	.09
❑ 287	Mark McGwire	2.00	.60
❑ 288	Edgar Renteria	.30	.09
❑ 289	Matt Morris	.30	.09
❑ 290	Gene Stechschulte	.30	.09
❑ 291	Dustin Hermanson	.30	.09
❑ 292	Eli Marrero	.30	.09
❑ 293	Albert Pujols	1.50	.45
❑ 294	Luis Saturria	.30	.09
❑ 295	Bobby Bonilla	.30	.09
❑ 296	Garrett Stephenson	.30	.09
❑ 297	Jim Edmonds	.30	.09
❑ 298	Rick Ankiel	.30	.09
❑ 299	Placido Polanco	.30	.09
❑ 300	Dave Veres	.30	.09
❑ 301	Sammy Sosa	1.25	.35
❑ 302	Eric Young	.30	.09
❑ 303	Kerry Wood	.75	.23
❑ 304	Jon Lieber	.30	.09
❑ 305	Joe Girardi	.30	.09
❑ 306	Fred McGriff	.50	.15
❑ 307	Jeff Fassero	.30	.09
❑ 308	Julio Zuleta	.30	.09
❑ 309	Kevin Tapani	.30	.09
❑ 310	Rondell White	.30	.09
❑ 311	Julian Tavarez	.30	.09
❑ 312	Tom Gordon	.30	.09
❑ 313	Corey Patterson	.30	.09
❑ 314	Bill Mueller	.30	.09
❑ 315	Randy Johnson	.75	.23
❑ 316	Chad Moeller	.30	.09
❑ 317	Tony Womack	.30	.09
❑ 318	Erubiel Durazo	.30	.09
❑ 319	Luis Gonzalez	.30	.09
❑ 320	Brian Anderson	.30	.09
❑ 321	Reggie Sanders	.30	.09
❑ 322	Greg Colbrunn	.30	.09
❑ 323	Robert Ellis	.30	.09
❑ 324	Jack Cust	.30	.09
❑ 325	Bret Prinz	.30	.09
❑ 326	Steve Finley	.30	.09
❑ 327	Byung-Hyun Kim	.30	.09
❑ 328	Albie Lopez	.30	.09
❑ 329	Gary Sheffield	.30	.09
❑ 330	Mark Grudzielanek	.30	.09
❑ 331	Paul LoDuca	.30	.09
❑ 332	Tom Goodwin	.30	.09
❑ 333	Andy Ashby	.30	.09
❑ 334	Hiram Bocachica	.30	.09
❑ 335	Dave Hansen	.30	.09
❑ 336	Kevin Brown	.30	.09
❑ 337	Marquis Grissom	.30	.09
❑ 338	Terry Adams	.30	.09
❑ 339	Chan Ho Park	.30	.09
❑ 340	Adrian Beltre	.50	.15
❑ 341	Luke Prokopec	.30	.09
❑ 342	Jeff Shaw	.30	.09
❑ 343	Vladimir Guerrero	.75	.23
❑ 344	Orlando Cabrera	.30	.09
❑ 345	Tony Armas Jr.	.30	.09
❑ 346	Michael Barrett	.30	.09
❑ 347	Geoff Blum	.30	.09
❑ 348	Ryan Minor	.30	.09
❑ 349	Peter Bergeron	.30	.09
❑ 350	Graeme Lloyd	.30	.09
❑ 351	Jose Vidro	.30	.09
❑ 352	Javier Vazquez	.30	.09
❑ 353	Matt Blank	.30	.09
❑ 354	Masato Yoshii	.30	.09
❑ 355	Carl Pavano	.30	.09
❑ 356	Barry Bonds	2.00	.60
❑ 357	Shawon Dunston	.30	.09
❑ 358	Livan Hernandez	.30	.09
❑ 359	Felix Rodriguez	.30	.09
❑ 360	Pedro Feliz	.30	.09
❑ 361	Calvin Murray	.30	.09
❑ 362	Robb Nen	.30	.09
❑ 363	Marvin Benard	.30	.09
❑ 364	Russ Ortiz	.30	.09
❑ 365	Jason Schmidt	.30	.09
❑ 366	Rich Aurilia	.30	.09
❑ 367	John Vander Wal	.30	.09
❑ 368	Benito Santiago	.30	.09
❑ 369	Ryan Dempster	.30	.09
❑ 370	Charles Johnson	.30	.09
❑ 371	Alex Gonzalez	.30	.09
❑ 372	Luis Castillo	.30	.09
❑ 373	Mike Lowell	.30	.09
❑ 374	Antonio Alfonseca	.30	.09
❑ 375	A.J. Burnett	.30	.09
❑ 376	Brad Penny	.30	.09
❑ 377	Jason Grilli	.30	.09
❑ 378	Derrek Lee	.30	.09
❑ 379	Matt Clement	.30	.09
❑ 380	Eric Owens	.30	.09
❑ 381	Vladimir Nunez	.30	.09
❑ 382	Cliff Floyd	.30	.09
❑ 383	Mike Piazza	1.25	.35
❑ 384	Lenny Harris	.30	.09
❑ 385	Glendon Rusch	.30	.09
❑ 386	Todd Zeile	.30	.09

❑ 387 Al Leiter	.30	.09
❑ 388 Armando Benitez	.30	.09
❑ 389 Alex Escobar	.30	.09
❑ 390 Kevin Appier	.30	.09
❑ 391 Matt Lawton	.30	.09
❑ 392 Bruce Chen	.30	.09
❑ 393 John Franco	.30	.09
❑ 394 Tsuyoshi Shinjo	.30	.09
❑ 395 Rey Ordonez	.30	.09
❑ 396 Joe McEwing	.30	.09
❑ 397 Ryan Klesko	.30	.09
❑ 398 Brian Lawrence	.30	.09
❑ 399 Kevin Walker	.30	.09
❑ 400 Phil Nevin	.30	.09
❑ 401 Bubba Trammell	.30	.09
❑ 402 Wiki Gonzalez	.30	.09
❑ 403 D'Angelo Jimenez	.30	.09
❑ 404 Rickey Henderson	.75	.23
❑ 405 Mike Darr	.30	.09
❑ 406 Trevor Hoffman	.30	.09
❑ 407 Damian Jackson	.30	.09
❑ 408 Santiago Perez	.30	.09
❑ 409 Cesar Crespo	.30	.09
❑ 410 Robert Person	.30	.09
❑ 411 Travis Lee	.30	.09
❑ 412 Scott Rolen	.75	.23
❑ 413 Turk Wendell	.30	.09
❑ 414 Randy Wolf	.30	.09
❑ 415 Kevin Jordan	.30	.09
❑ 416 Jose Mesa	.30	.09
❑ 417 Mike Lieberthal	.30	.09
❑ 418 Bobby Abreu	.30	.09
❑ 419 Tomas Perez	.30	.09
❑ 420 Doug Glanville	.30	.09
❑ 421 Reggie Taylor	.30	.09
❑ 422 Jimmy Rollins	.30	.09
❑ 423 Brian Giles	.30	.09
❑ 424 Rob Mackowiak	.30	.09
❑ 425 Bronson Arroyo	.30	.09
❑ 426 Kevin Young	.30	.09
❑ 427 Jack Wilson	.30	.09
❑ 428 Adrian Brown	.30	.09
❑ 429 Chad Hermansen	.30	.09
❑ 430 Jimmy Anderson	.30	.09
❑ 431 Aramis Ramirez	.30	.09
❑ 432 Todd Ritchie	.30	.09
❑ 433 Pat Meares	.30	.09
❑ 434 Warren Morris	.30	.09
❑ 435 Derek Bell	.30	.09
❑ 436 Ken Griffey Jr.	1.25	.35
❑ 437 Elmer Dessens	.30	.09
❑ 438 Ruben Rivera	.30	.09
❑ 439 Jason LaRue	.30	.09
❑ 440 Sean Casey	.30	.09
❑ 441 Pete Harnisch	.30	.09
❑ 442 Danny Graves	.30	.09
❑ 443 Aaron Boone	.30	.09
❑ 444 Dmitri Young	.30	.09
❑ 445 Brandon Larson	.30	.09
❑ 446 Pokey Reese	.30	.09
❑ 447 Todd Walker	.30	.09
❑ 448 Juan Castro	.30	.09
❑ 449 Todd Helton	.50	.15
❑ 450 Ben Petrick	.30	.09
❑ 451 Juan Pierre	.30	.09
❑ 452 Jeff Cirillo	.30	.09
❑ 453 Juan Uribe	.30	.09
❑ 454 Brian Bohanon	.30	.09
❑ 455 Terry Shumpert	.30	.09
❑ 456 Mike Hampton	.30	.09
❑ 457 Shawn Chacon	.30	.09
❑ 458 Adam Melhuse	.30	.09
❑ 459 Greg Norton	.30	.09
❑ 460 Gabe White	.30	.09
❑ 461 Ichiro Suzuki WS	.75	.23
❑ 462 Carlos Delgado WS	.30	.09
❑ 463 Manny Ramirez WS	.30	.09
❑ 464 Miguel Tejada WS	.30	.09
❑ 465 Tsuyoshi Shinjo WS	.30	.09
❑ 466 Bernie Williams WS	.30	.09
❑ 467 Juan Gonzalez WS	.30	.09
❑ 468 Andruw Jones WS	.30	.09
❑ 469 Ivan Rodriguez WS	.50	.15
❑ 470 Larry Walker WS	.50	.15
❑ 471 Hideo Nomo WS	.30	.09
❑ 472 Albert Pujols WS	.75	.23
❑ 473 Pedro Martinez WS	.50	.15
❑ 474 Vladimir Guerrero WS	.50	.15
❑ 475 Tony Batista WS	.30	.09
❑ 476 Kazuhiro Sasaki WS	.30	.09
❑ 477 Richard Hidalgo WS	.30	.09
❑ 478 Carlos Lee WS	.30	.09
❑ 479 Roberto Alomar WS	.30	.09
❑ 480 Rafael Palmeiro WS	.30	.09
❑ 481 Ken Griffey Jr. GG	.75	.23
❑ 482 Ken Griffey Jr. GG	.75	.23
❑ 483 Ken Griffey Jr. GG	.75	.23
❑ 484 Ken Griffey Jr. GG	.75	.23
❑ 485 Ken Griffey Jr. GG	.75	.23
❑ 486 Ken Griffey Jr. GG	.75	.23
❑ 487 Ken Griffey Jr. GG	.75	.23
❑ 488 Ken Griffey Jr. GG	.75	.23
❑ 489 Ken Griffey Jr. GG	.75	.23
❑ 490 Ken Griffey Jr. GG	.75	.23
❑ 491 Barry Bonds CL	.75	.23
❑ 492 Hideo Nomo CL	.30	.09
❑ 493 Ichiro Suzuki CL	.75	.23
❑ 494 Cal Ripken CL	1.25	.35
❑ 495 Tony Gwynn CL	.50	.15
❑ 496 Randy Johnson CL	.50	.15
❑ 497 A.J. Burnett CL	.30	.09
❑ 498 Rickey Henderson CL	.50	.15
❑ 499 Albert Pujols CL	.75	.23
❑ 500 Luis Gonzalez CL	.30	.09
❑ 501 Brandon Puffer SR RC	1.00	.30
❑ 502 Rodrigo Rosario SR RC	1.00	.30
❑ 503 Tom Shearn SR RC	1.00	.30
❑ 504 Reed Johnson SR RC	1.50	.45
❑ 505 Chris Baker SR RC	1.00	.30
❑ 506 John Ennis SR RC	1.00	.30
❑ 507 Luis Martinez SR RC	1.00	.30
❑ 508 So Taguchi SR RC	1.50	.45
❑ 509 Scotty Layfield SR RC	1.00	.30
❑ 510 Francis Beltran SR RC	1.00	.30
❑ 511 Brandon Backe SR RC	1.50	.45
❑ 512 Doug Devore SR RC	1.00	.30
❑ 513 Jeremy Ward SR RC	1.00	.30
❑ 514 Jose Valverde SR RC	1.50	.45
❑ 515 P.J. Bevis SR RC	1.00	.30
❑ 516 Victor Alvarez SR RC	1.00	.30
❑ 517 Kazuhisa Ishii SR RC	2.50	.75
❑ 518 Jorge Nunez SR RC	1.00	.30
❑ 519 Eric Good SR RC	1.00	.30
❑ 520 Ron Calloway SR RC	1.00	.30
❑ 521 Val Pascucci SR	1.00	.30
❑ 522 Nelson Castro SR RC	1.00	.30
❑ 523 Deivis Santos SR	1.00	.30
❑ 524 Luis Ugueto SR RC	1.00	.30
❑ 525 Matt Thornton SR RC	1.00	.30
❑ 526 Hansel Izquierdo SR RC	1.00	.30
❑ 527 Tyler Yates SR RC	1.50	.45
❑ 528 Mark Corey SR RC	1.00	.30
❑ 529 Jaime Cerda SR RC	1.00	.30
❑ 530 Satoru Komiyama SR RC	1.00	.30
❑ 531 Steve Bechler SR RC	1.00	.30
❑ 532 Ben Howard SR RC	1.00	.30
❑ 533 An. Machado SR RC	1.00	.30
❑ 534 Jorge Padilla SR RC	1.00	.30
❑ 535 Eric Junge SR RC	1.00	.30
❑ 536 Adrian Burnside SR RC	1.00	.30
❑ 537 Mike Gonzalez SR RC	1.00	.30
❑ 538 Josh Hancock SR RC	1.00	.30
❑ 539 Colin Young SR RC	1.00	.30
❑ 540 Rene Reyes SR RC	1.00	.30
❑ 541 Cam Esslinger SR RC	1.00	.30
❑ 542 Tim Kalita SR RC	1.00	.30
❑ 543 Kevin Frederick SR RC	1.00	.30
❑ 544 Kyle Kane SR RC	1.00	.30
❑ 545 Edwin Almonte SR RC	1.00	.30
❑ 546 Aaron Sele	.30	.09
❑ 547 Garret Anderson	.30	.09
❑ 548 Darin Erstad	.30	.09
❑ 549 Brad Fullmer	.30	.09
❑ 550 Kevin Appier	.30	.09
❑ 551 Tim Salmon	.50	.15
❑ 552 David Justice	.30	.09
❑ 553 Billy Koch	.30	.09
❑ 554 Scott Hatteberg	.30	.09
❑ 555 Tim Hudson	.30	.09
❑ 556 Miguel Tejada	.30	.09
❑ 557 Carlos Pena	.30	.09
❑ 558 Mike Sirotka	.30	.09
❑ 559 Jose Cruz Jr.	.30	.09
❑ 560 Josh Phelps	.30	.09
❑ 561 Brandon Lyon	.30	.09
❑ 562 Luke Prokopec	.30	.09
❑ 563 Felipe Lopez	.30	.09
❑ 564 Jason Standridge	.30	.09
❑ 565 Chris Gomez	.30	.09
❑ 566 John Flaherty	.30	.09
❑ 567 Jason Tyner	.30	.09
❑ 568 Bobby Smith	.30	.09
❑ 569 Wilson Alvarez	.30	.09
❑ 570 Matt Lawton	.30	.09
❑ 571 Omar Vizquel	.50	.15
❑ 572 Jim Thome	.75	.23
❑ 573 Brady Anderson	.30	.09
❑ 574 Alex Escobar	.30	.09
❑ 575 Russell Branyan	.30	.09
❑ 576 Bret Boone	.30	.09
❑ 577 Ben Davis	.30	.09
❑ 578 Mike Cameron	.30	.09
❑ 579 Jamie Moyer	.30	.09
❑ 580 Ruben Sierra	.30	.09
❑ 581 Jeff Cirillo	.30	.09
❑ 582 Marty Cordova	.30	.09
❑ 583 Mike Bordick	.30	.09
❑ 584 Brian Roberts	.30	.09
❑ 585 Luis Matos	.30	.09
❑ 586 Geronimo Gil	.30	.09
❑ 587 Jay Gibbons	.30	.09
❑ 588 Carl Everett	.30	.09
❑ 589 Ivan Rodriguez	.75	.23
❑ 590 Chan Ho Park	.30	.09
❑ 591 Juan Gonzalez	.50	.15
❑ 592 Hank Blalock	.75	.23
❑ 593 Todd Van Poppel	.30	.09
❑ 594 Pedro Martinez	.75	.23
❑ 595 Jason Varitek	.50	.15
❑ 596 Tony Clark	.30	.09
❑ 597 Johnny Damon Sox	.75	.23
❑ 598 Dustin Hermanson	.30	.09
❑ 599 John Burkett	.30	.09
❑ 600 Carlos Beltran	.50	.15
❑ 601 Mark Quinn	.30	.09
❑ 602 Chuck Knoblauch	.30	.09
❑ 603 Michael Tucker	.30	.09
❑ 604 Carlos Febles	.30	.09
❑ 605 Jose Rosado	.30	.09
❑ 606 Dmitri Young	.30	.09
❑ 607 Bobby Higginson	.30	.09
❑ 608 Craig Paquette	.30	.09
❑ 609 Mitch Meluskey	.30	.09
❑ 610 Wendell Magee	.30	.09
❑ 611 Mike Rivera	.30	.09
❑ 612 Jacque Jones	.30	.09
❑ 613 Luis Rivas	.30	.09
❑ 614 Eric Milton	.30	.09
❑ 615 Eddie Guardado	.30	.09
❑ 616 Matt LeCroy	.30	.09
❑ 617 Mike Jackson	.30	.09
❑ 618 Magglio Ordonez	.30	.09
❑ 619 Frank Thomas	.75	.23
❑ 620 Rocky Biddle	.30	.09
❑ 621 Paul Konerko	.30	.09
❑ 622 Todd Ritchie	.30	.09
❑ 623 Jon Rauch	.30	.09
❑ 624 John Vander Wal	.30	.09
❑ 625 Rondell White	.30	.09
❑ 626 Jason Giambi	.30	.09
❑ 627 Robin Ventura	.30	.09
❑ 628 David Wells	.30	.09
❑ 629 Bernie Williams	.50	.15
❑ 630 Lance Berkman	.30	.09
❑ 631 Richard Hidalgo	.30	.09
❑ 632 Greg Zaun	.30	.09
❑ 633 Jose Vizcaino	.30	.09
❑ 634 Octavio Dotel	.30	.09
❑ 635 Morgan Ensberg	.30	.09
❑ 636 Andruw Jones	.30	.09
❑ 637 Tom Glavine	.50	.15
❑ 638 Gary Sheffield	.30	.09
❑ 639 Vinny Castilla	.30	.09
❑ 640 Javy Lopez	.30	.09
❑ 641 Albie Lopez	.30	.09
❑ 642 Geoff Jenkins	.30	.09
❑ 643 Jeffrey Hammonds	.30	.09
❑ 644 Alex Ochoa	.30	.09

#	Player	Nm-Mt	Ex-Mt
645	Richie Sexson	.30	.09
646	Eric Young	.30	.09
647	Glendon Rusch	.30	.09
648	Tino Martinez	.50	.15
649	Fernando Vina	.30	.09
650	J.D. Drew	.30	.09
651	Woody Williams	.30	.09
652	Darryl Kile	.30	.09
653	Jason Isringhausen	.30	.09
654	Moises Alou	.30	.09
655	Alex Gonzalez	.30	.09
656	Delino DeShields	.30	.09
657	Todd Hundley	.30	.09
658	Chris Stynes	.30	.09
659	Jason Bere	.30	.09
660	Curt Schilling	.30	.09
661	Craig Counsell	.30	.09
662	Mark Grace	.50	.15
663	Matt Williams	.30	.09
664	Jay Bell	.30	.09
665	Rick Helling	.30	.09
666	Shawn Green	.30	.09
667	Eric Karros	.30	.09
668	Hideo Nomo	.75	.23
669	Omar Daal	.30	.09
670	Brian Jordan	.30	.09
671	Cesar Izturis	.30	.09
672	Fernando Tatis	.30	.09
673	Lee Stevens	.30	.09
674	Tomo Ohka	.30	.09
675	Brian Schneider	.30	.09
676	Brad Wilkerson	.30	.09
677	Bruce Chen	.30	.09
678	Tsuyoshi Shinjo	.30	.09
679	Jeff Kent	.30	.09
680	Kirk Rueter	.30	.09
681	J.T. Snow	.30	.09
682	David Bell	.30	.09
683	Reggie Sanders	.30	.09
684	Preston Wilson	.30	.09
685	Vic Darensbourg	.30	.09
686	Josh Beckett	.30	.09
687	Pablo Ozuna	.30	.09
688	Mike Redmond	.30	.09
689	Scott Strickland	.30	.09
690	Mo Vaughn	.30	.09
691	Roberto Alomar	.50	.15
692	Edgardo Alfonzo	.30	.09
693	Shawn Estes	.30	.09
694	Roger Cedeno	.30	.09
695	Jeromy Burnitz	.30	.09
696	Ray Lankford	.30	.09
697	Mark Kotsay	.30	.09
698	Kevin Jarvis	.30	.09
699	Bobby Jones	.30	.09
700	Sean Burroughs	.30	.09
701	Ramon Vazquez	.30	.09
702	Pat Burrell	.30	.09
703	Marlon Byrd	.30	.09
704	Brandon Duckworth	.30	.09
705	Marlon Anderson	.30	.09
706	Vicente Padilla	.30	.09
707	Kip Wells	.30	.09
708	Jason Kendall	.30	.09
709	Pokey Reese	.30	.09
710	Pat Meares	.30	.09
711	Kris Benson	.30	.09
712	Armando Rios	.30	.09
713	Mike Williams	.30	.09
714	Barry Larkin	.50	.15
715	Adam Dunn	.50	.15
716	Juan Encarnacion	.30	.09
717	Scott Williamson	.30	.09
718	Wilton Guerrero	.30	.09
719	Chris Reitsma	.30	.09
720	Larry Walker	.50	.15
721	Denny Neagle	.30	.09
722	Todd Zeile	.30	.09
723	Jose Ortiz	.30	.09
724	Jason Jennings	.30	.09
725	Tony Eusebio	.30	.09
726	Ichiro Suzuki YR	.75	.23
727	Barry Bonds YR	.75	.23
728	Randy Johnson YR	.50	.15
729	Albert Pujols YR	.75	.23
730	Roger Clemens YR	.75	.23
731	Sammy Sosa YR	.75	.23
732	Alex Rodriguez YR	.75	.23
733	Chipper Jones YR	.50	.15
734	Rickey Henderson YR	.50	.15
735	Ichiro Suzuki YR	.75	.23
736	Luis Gonzalez SH CL	.30	.09
737	Derek Jeter SH CL	1.00	.30
738	Ichiro Suzuki SH CL	.75	.23
739	Barry Bonds SH CL	.75	.23
740	Curt Schilling SH CL	.30	.09
741	Shawn Green SH CL	.30	.09
742	Jason Giambi SH CL	.30	.09
743	Roberto Alomar SH CL	.30	.09
744	Larry Walker SH CL	.30	.09
745	Mark McGwire SH CL	1.00	.30

2003 Upper Deck

	Nm-Mt	Ex-Mt
COMPLETE SERIES 1 (270)	50.00	15.00
COMPLETE SERIES 2 (270)	50.00	15.00
COMP.UPDATE SET (60)	20.00	6.00
COMMON (31-500/531-600)	.30	.09
COMMON (1-30/501-530)	1.00	.30
COMMON RC (541-600)	.50	.15

SR 1-30/501-530 ARE NOT SHORT PRINTS
CARD 19 DOES NOT EXIST
SCUTARO/NOMAR ARE BOTH CARD 96
541-600 ISSUED IN 04 UD1 HOBBY BOXES
UPDATE SET EXCH 1:240 '04 UD1 RETAIL
UPDATE SET EXCH.DEADLINE 11/10/06

#	Player	Nm-Mt	Ex-Mt
1	John Lackey SR	1.00	.30
2	Alex Cintron SR	1.00	.30
3	Jose Leon SR	1.00	.30
4	Bobby Hill SR	1.00	.30
5	Brandon Larson SR	1.00	.30
6	Raul Gonzalez SR	1.00	.30
7	Ben Broussard SR	1.00	.30
8	Earl Snyder SR	1.00	.30
9	Ramon Santiago SR	1.00	.30
10	Jason Lane SR	1.00	.30
11	Keith Ginter SR	1.00	.30
12	Kirk Saarloos SR	1.00	.30
13	Juan Brito SR	1.00	.30
14	Runelvys Hernandez SR	1.00	.30
15	Shawn Sedlacek SR	1.00	.30
16	Jayson Durocher SR	1.00	.30
17	Kevin Frederick SR	1.00	.30
18	Zach Day SR	1.00	.30
19	Marcos Scutaro SR UER Card number 96 on back	1.00	.30
20	Marcus Thames SR	1.00	.30
21	Esteban German SR	1.00	.30
22	Brett Myers SR	1.00	.30
23	Oliver Perez SR	1.00	.30
24	Dennis Tankersley SR	1.00	.30
25	Julius Matos SR	1.00	.30
26	Jake Peavy SR	1.00	.30
27	Eric Cyr SR	1.00	.30
28	Mike Crudale SR	1.00	.30
29	Josh Pearce SR	1.00	.30
30	Carl Crawford SR	1.00	.30
31	Tim Salmon	.50	.15
32	Troy Glaus	.30	.09
33	Adam Kennedy	.30	.09
34	David Eckstein	.30	.09
35	Ben Molina	.30	.09
36	Jarrod Washburn	.30	.09
37	Ramon Ortiz	.30	.09
38	Eric Chavez	.30	.09
39	Miguel Tejada	.30	.09
40	Adam Piatt	.30	.09
41	Jermaine Dye	.30	.09
42	Olmedo Saenz	.30	.09
43	Tim Hudson	.30	.09
44	Barry Zito	.30	.09
45	Billy Koch	.30	.09
46	Shannon Stewart	.30	.09
47	Kelvim Escobar	.30	.09
48	Jose Cruz Jr.	.30	.09
49	Vernon Wells	.30	.09
50	Roy Halladay	.30	.09
51	Esteban Loaiza	.30	.09
52	Eric Hinske	.30	.09
53	Steve Cox	.30	.09
54	Brent Abernathy	.30	.09
55	Ben Grieve	.30	.09
56	Aubrey Huff	.30	.09
57	Jared Sandberg	.30	.09
58	Paul Wilson	.30	.09
59	Tanyon Sturtze	.30	.09
60	Jim Thome	.75	.23
61	Omar Vizquel	.50	.15
62	C.C. Sabathia	.30	.09
63	Chris Magruder	.30	.09
64	Ricky Gutierrez	.30	.09
65	Einar Diaz	.30	.09
66	Danys Baez	.30	.09
67	Ichiro Suzuki	1.25	.35
68	Ruben Sierra	.30	.09
69	Carlos Guillen	.30	.09
70	Mark McLemore	.30	.09
71	Dan Wilson	.30	.09
72	Jamie Moyer	.30	.09
73	Joel Pineiro	.30	.09
74	Edgar Martinez	.50	.15
75	Tony Batista	.30	.09
76	Jay Gibbons	.30	.09
77	Chris Singleton	.30	.09
78	Melvin Mora	.30	.09
79	Geronimo Gil	.30	.09
80	Rodrigo Lopez	.30	.09
81	Jorge Julio	.30	.09
82	Rafael Palmeiro	.50	.15
83	Juan Gonzalez	.50	.15
84	Mike Young	.50	.15
85	Hideki Irabu	.30	.09
86	Chan Ho Park	.30	.09
87	Kevin Mench	.30	.09
88	Doug Davis	.30	.09
89	Pedro Martinez	.75	.23
90	Shea Hillenbrand	.30	.09
91	Derek Lowe	.30	.09
92	Jason Varitek	.50	.15
93	Tony Clark	.30	.09
94	John Burkett	.30	.09
95	Frank Castillo	.30	.09
96	Nomar Garciaparra	1.25	.35
97	Rickey Henderson	.75	.23
98	Mike Sweeney	.30	.09
99	Carlos Febles	.30	.09
100	Mark Quinn	.30	.09
101	Raul Ibanez	.30	.09
102	A.J. Hinch	.30	.09
103	Paul Byrd	.30	.09
104	Chuck Knoblauch	.30	.09
105	Dmitri Young	.30	.09
106	Randall Simon	.30	.09
107	Brandon Inge	.30	.09
108	Damion Easley	.30	.09
109	Carlos Pena	.30	.09
110	George Lombard	.30	.09
111	Juan Acevedo	.30	.09
112	Torii Hunter	.30	.09
113	Doug Mientkiewicz	.30	.09
114	David Ortiz	.50	.15
115	Eric Milton	.30	.09
116	Eddie Guardado	.30	.09
117	Cristian Guzman	.30	.09
118	Corey Koskie	.30	.09
119	Magglio Ordonez	.30	.09
120	Mark Buehrle	.30	.09
121	Todd Ritchie	.30	.09

❑ 122 Jose Valentin .30 .09
❑ 123 Paul Konerko .30 .09
❑ 124 Carlos Lee .30 .09
❑ 125 Jon Garland .30 .09
❑ 126 Jason Giambi .30 .09
❑ 127 Derek Jeter 2.00 .60
❑ 128 Roger Clemens 1.50 .45
❑ 129 Raul Mondesi .30 .09
❑ 130 Jorge Posada .50 .15
❑ 131 Rondell White .30 .09
❑ 132 Robin Ventura .30 .09
❑ 133 Mike Mussina .50 .15
❑ 134 Jeff Bagwell .50 .15
❑ 135 Craig Biggio .50 .15
❑ 136 Morgan Ensberg .30 .09
❑ 137 Richard Hidalgo .30 .09
❑ 138 Brad Ausmus .30 .09
❑ 139 Roy Oswalt .30 .09
❑ 140 Carlos Hernandez .30 .09
❑ 141 Shane Reynolds .30 .09
❑ 142 Gary Sheffield .30 .09
❑ 143 Andruw Jones .30 .09
❑ 144 Tom Glavine .50 .15
❑ 145 Rafael Furcal .30 .09
❑ 146 Javy Lopez .30 .09
❑ 147 Vinny Castilla .30 .09
❑ 148 Marcus Giles .30 .09
❑ 149 Kevin Millwood .30 .09
❑ 150 Jason Marquis .30 .09
❑ 151 Ruben Quevedo .30 .09
❑ 152 Ben Sheets .30 .09
❑ 153 Geoff Jenkins .30 .09
❑ 154 Jose Hernandez .30 .09
❑ 155 Glendon Rusch .30 .09
❑ 156 Jeffrey Hammonds .30 .09
❑ 157 Alex Sanchez .30 .09
❑ 158 Jim Edmonds .30 .09
❑ 159 Tino Martinez .50 .15
❑ 160 Albert Pujols 1.50 .45
❑ 161 Eli Marrero .30 .09
❑ 162 Woody Williams .30 .09
❑ 163 Fernando Vina .30 .09
❑ 164 Jason Isringhausen .30 .09
❑ 165 Jason Simontacchi .30 .09
❑ 166 Kerry Robinson .30 .09
❑ 167 Sammy Sosa 1.25 .35
❑ 168 Juan Cruz .30 .09
❑ 169 Fred McGriff .50 .15
❑ 170 Antonio Alfonseca .30 .09
❑ 171 Jon Lieber .30 .09
❑ 172 Mark Prior .75 .23
❑ 173 Moises Alou .30 .09
❑ 174 Matt Clement .30 .09
❑ 175 Mark Bellhorn .30 .09
❑ 176 Randy Johnson .75 .23
❑ 177 Luis Gonzalez .30 .09
❑ 178 Tony Womack .30 .09
❑ 179 Mark Grace .50 .15
❑ 180 Junior Spivey .30 .09
❑ 181 Byung Hyun Kim .30 .09
❑ 182 Danny Bautista .30 .09
❑ 183 Brian Anderson .30 .09
❑ 184 Shawn Green .30 .09
❑ 185 Brian Jordan .30 .09
❑ 186 Eric Karros .30 .09
❑ 187 Andy Ashby .30 .09
❑ 188 Cesar Izturis .30 .09
❑ 189 Dave Roberts .30 .09
❑ 190 Eric Gagne .75 .23
❑ 191 Kazuhisa Ishii .30 .09
❑ 192 Adrian Beltre .50 .15
❑ 193 Vladimir Guerrero .75 .23
❑ 194 Tony Armas Jr. .30 .09
❑ 195 Bartolo Colon .30 .09
❑ 196 Troy O'Leary .30 .09
❑ 197 Tomo Ohka .30 .09
❑ 198 Brad Wilkerson .30 .09
❑ 199 Orlando Cabrera .30 .09
❑ 200 Barry Bonds 2.00 .60
❑ 201 David Bell .30 .09
❑ 202 Tsuyoshi Shinjo .30 .09
❑ 203 Benito Santiago .30 .09
❑ 204 Livan Hernandez .30 .09
❑ 205 Jason Schmidt .30 .09
❑ 206 Kirk Rueter .30 .09
❑ 207 Ramon E. Martinez .30 .09
❑ 208 Mike Lowell .30 .09
❑ 209 Luis Castillo .30 .09
❑ 210 Derrek Lee .30 .09
❑ 211 Andy Fox .30 .09
❑ 212 Eric Owens .30 .09
❑ 213 Charles Johnson .30 .09
❑ 214 Brad Penny .30 .09
❑ 215 A.J. Burnett .30 .09
❑ 216 Edgardo Alfonzo .30 .09
❑ 217 Roberto Alomar .50 .15
❑ 218 Rey Ordonez .30 .09
❑ 219 Al Leiter .30 .09
❑ 220 Roger Cedeno .30 .09
❑ 221 Timo Perez .30 .09
❑ 222 Jeromy Burnitz .30 .09
❑ 223 Pedro Astacio .30 .09
❑ 224 Joe McEwing .30 .09
❑ 225 Ryan Klesko .30 .09
❑ 226 Ramon Vazquez .30 .09
❑ 227 Mark Kotsay .30 .09
❑ 228 Bubba Trammell .30 .09
❑ 229 Wiki Gonzalez .30 .09
❑ 230 Trevor Hoffman .30 .09
❑ 231 Ron Gant .30 .09
❑ 232 Bob Abreu .30 .09
❑ 233 Marlon Anderson .30 .09
❑ 234 Jeremy Giambi .30 .09
❑ 235 Jimmy Rollins .30 .09
❑ 236 Mike Lieberthal .30 .09
❑ 237 Vicente Padilla .30 .09
❑ 238 Randy Wolf .30 .09
❑ 239 Pokey Reese .30 .09
❑ 240 Brian Giles .30 .09
❑ 241 Jack Wilson .30 .09
❑ 242 Mike Williams .30 .09
❑ 243 Kip Wells .30 .09
❑ 244 Rob Mackowiak .30 .09
❑ 245 Craig Wilson .30 .09
❑ 246 Adam Dunn .50 .15
❑ 247 Sean Casey .30 .09
❑ 248 Todd Walker .30 .09
❑ 249 Corky Miller .30 .09
❑ 250 Ryan Dempster .30 .09
❑ 251 Reggie Taylor .30 .09
❑ 252 Aaron Boone .30 .09
❑ 253 Larry Walker .50 .15
❑ 254 Jose Ortiz .30 .09
❑ 255 Todd Zeile .30 .09
❑ 256 Bobby Estalella .30 .09
❑ 257 Juan Pierre .30 .09
❑ 258 Terry Shumpert .30 .09
❑ 259 Mike Hampton .30 .09
❑ 260 Denny Stark .30 .09
❑ 261 Shawn Green SH CL .30 .09
❑ 262 Derek Lowe SH CL .30 .09
❑ 263 Barry Bonds SH CL .75 .23
❑ 264 Mike Cameron SH CL .30 .09
❑ 265 Luis Castillo SH CL .30 .09
❑ 266 Vladimir Guerrero SH CL .50 .15
❑ 267 Jason Giambi SH CL .30 .09
❑ 268 Eric Gagne SH CL .50 .15
❑ 269 Magglio Ordonez SH CL .30 .09
❑ 270 Jim Thome SH CL .50 .15
❑ 271 Garret Anderson .30 .09
❑ 272 Troy Percival .30 .09
❑ 273 Brad Fullmer .30 .09
❑ 274 Scott Spiezio .30 .09
❑ 275 Darin Erstad .30 .09
❑ 276 Francisco Rodriguez .30 .09
❑ 277 Kevin Appier .30 .09
❑ 278 Shawn Wooten .30 .09
❑ 279 Eric Owens .30 .09
❑ 280 Scott Hatteberg .30 .09
❑ 281 Terrence Long .30 .09
❑ 282 Mark Mulder .30 .09
❑ 283 Ramon Hernandez .30 .09
❑ 284 Ted Lilly .30 .09
❑ 285 Erubiel Durazo .30 .09
❑ 286 Mark Ellis .30 .09
❑ 287 Carlos Delgado .30 .09
❑ 288 Orlando Hudson .30 .09
❑ 289 Chris Woodward .30 .09
❑ 290 Mark Hendrickson .30 .09
❑ 291 Josh Phelps .30 .09
❑ 292 Ken Huckaby .30 .09
❑ 293 Justin Miller .30 .09
❑ 294 Travis Lee .30 .09
❑ 295 Jorge Sosa .30 .09
❑ 296 Joe Kennedy .30 .09
❑ 297 Carl Crawford .30 .09
❑ 298 Toby Hall .30 .09
❑ 299 Rey Ordonez .30 .09
❑ 300 Brandon Phillips .30 .09
❑ 301 Matt Lawton .30 .09
❑ 302 Ellis Burks .30 .09
❑ 303 Bill Selby .30 .09
❑ 304 Travis Hafner .30 .09
❑ 305 Milton Bradley .30 .09
❑ 306 Karim Garcia .30 .09
❑ 307 Cliff Lee .30 .09
❑ 308 Jeff Cirillo .30 .09
❑ 309 John Olerud .30 .09
❑ 310 Kazuhiro Sasaki .30 .09
❑ 311 Freddy Garcia .30 .09
❑ 312 Bret Boone .30 .09
❑ 313 Mike Cameron .30 .09
❑ 314 Ben Davis .30 .09
❑ 315 Randy Winn .30 .09
❑ 316 Gary Matthews Jr. .30 .09
❑ 317 Jeff Conine .30 .09
❑ 318 Sidney Ponson .30 .09
❑ 319 Jerry Hairston .30 .09
❑ 320 David Segui .30 .09
❑ 321 Scott Erickson .30 .09
❑ 322 Marty Cordova .30 .09
❑ 323 Hank Blalock .50 .15
❑ 324 Herbert Perry .30 .09
❑ 325 Alex Rodriguez 1.25 .35
❑ 326 Carl Everett .30 .09
❑ 327 Einar Diaz .30 .09
❑ 328 Ugueth Urbina .30 .09
❑ 329 Mark Teixeira .30 .09
❑ 330 Manny Ramirez .50 .15
❑ 331 Johnny Damon .75 .23
❑ 332 Trot Nixon .30 .09
❑ 333 Tim Wakefield .30 .09
❑ 334 Casey Fossum .30 .09
❑ 335 Todd Walker .30 .09
❑ 336 Jeremy Giambi .30 .09
❑ 337 Bill Mueller .30 .09
❑ 338 Ramiro Mendoza .30 .09
❑ 339 Carlos Beltran .50 .15
❑ 340 Jason Grimsley .30 .09
❑ 341 Brent Mayne .30 .09
❑ 342 Angel Berroa .30 .09
❑ 343 Albie Lopez .30 .09
❑ 344 Michael Tucker .30 .09
❑ 345 Bobby Higginson .30 .09
❑ 346 Shane Halter .30 .09
❑ 347 Jeremy Bonderman RC .75 .23
❑ 348 Eric Munson .30 .09
❑ 349 Andy Van Hekken .30 .09
❑ 350 Matt Anderson .30 .09
❑ 351 Jacque Jones .30 .09
❑ 352 A.J. Pierzynski .30 .09
❑ 353 Joe Mays .30 .09
❑ 354 Brad Radke .30 .09
❑ 355 Dustan Mohr .30 .09
❑ 356 Bobby Kielty .30 .09
❑ 357 Michael Cuddyer .30 .09
❑ 358 Luis Rivas .30 .09
❑ 359 Frank Thomas .75 .23
❑ 360 Joe Borchard .30 .09
❑ 361 D'Angelo Jimenez .30 .09
❑ 362 Bartolo Colon .30 .09
❑ 363 Joe Crede .30 .09
❑ 364 Miguel Olivo .30 .09
❑ 365 Billy Koch .30 .09
❑ 366 Bernie Williams .50 .15
❑ 367 Nick Johnson .30 .09
❑ 368 Andy Pettitte .50 .15
❑ 369 Mariano Rivera .50 .15
❑ 370 Alfonso Soriano .50 .15
❑ 371 David Wells .30 .09
❑ 372 Drew Henson .30 .09
❑ 373 Juan Rivera .30 .09
❑ 374 Steve Karsay .30 .09
❑ 375 Jeff Kent .30 .09
❑ 376 Lance Berkman .30 .09
❑ 377 Octavio Dotel .30 .09
❑ 378 Julio Lugo .30 .09
❑ 379 Jason Lane .30 .09

	#	Player	Mint	NrMt
❑	380	Wade Miller	.30	.09
❑	381	Billy Wagner	.30	.09
❑	382	Brad Ausmus	.30	.09
❑	383	Mike Hampton	.30	.09
❑	384	Chipper Jones	.75	.23
❑	385	John Smoltz	.50	.15
❑	386	Greg Maddux	1.25	.35
❑	387	Javy Lopez	.30	.09
❑	388	Robert Fick	.30	.09
❑	389	Mark DeRosa	.30	.09
❑	390	Russ Ortiz	.30	.09
❑	391	Julio Franco	.30	.09
❑	392	Richie Sexson	.30	.09
❑	393	Eric Young	.30	.09
❑	394	Robert Machado	.30	.09
❑	395	Mike DeJean	.30	.09
❑	396	Todd Ritchie	.30	.09
❑	397	Royce Clayton	.30	.09
❑	398	Nick Neugebauer	.30	.09
❑	399	J.D. Drew	.30	.09
❑	400	Edgar Renteria	.30	.09
❑	401	Scott Rolen	.75	.23
❑	402	Matt Morris	.30	.09
❑	403	Garrett Stephenson	.30	.09
❑	404	Eduardo Perez	.30	.09
❑	405	Mike Matheny	.30	.09
❑	406	Miguel Cairo	.30	.09
❑	407	Brett Tomko	.30	.09
❑	408	Bobby Hill	.30	.09
❑	409	Troy O'Leary	.30	.09
❑	410	Corey Patterson	.30	.09
❑	411	Kerry Wood	.75	.23
❑	412	Eric Karros	.30	.09
❑	413	Hee Seop Choi	.30	.09
❑	414	Alex Gonzalez	.30	.09
❑	415	Matt Clement	.30	.09
❑	416	Mark Grudzielanek	.30	.09
❑	417	Curt Schilling	.30	.09
❑	418	Steve Finley	.30	.09
❑	419	Craig Counsell	.30	.09
❑	420	Matt Williams	.30	.09
❑	421	Quinton McCracken	.30	.09
❑	422	Chad Moeller	.30	.09
❑	423	Lyle Overbay	.30	.09
❑	424	Miguel Batista	.30	.09
❑	425	Paul Lo Duca	.30	.09
❑	426	Kevin Brown	.30	.09
❑	427	Hideo Nomo	.75	.23
❑	428	Fred McGriff	.50	.15
❑	429	Joe Thurston	.30	.09
❑	430	Odalis Perez	.30	.09
❑	431	Darren Dreifort	.30	.09
❑	432	Todd Hundley	.30	.09
❑	433	Dave Roberts	.30	.09
❑	434	Jose Vidro	.30	.09
❑	435	Javier Vazquez	.30	.09
❑	436	Michael Barrett	.30	.09
❑	437	Fernando Tatis	.30	.09
❑	438	Peter Bergeron	.30	.09
❑	439	Endy Chavez	.30	.09
❑	440	Orlando Hernandez	.30	.09
❑	441	Marvin Benard	.30	.09
❑	442	Rich Aurilia	.30	.09
❑	443	Pedro Feliz	.30	.09
❑	444	Robb Nen	.30	.09
❑	445	Ray Durham	.30	.09
❑	446	Marquis Grissom	.30	.09
❑	447	Damian Moss	.30	.09
❑	448	Edgardo Alfonzo	.30	.09
❑	449	Juan Pierre	.30	.09
❑	450	Braden Looper	.30	.09
❑	451	Alex Gonzalez	.30	.09
❑	452	Justin Wayne	.30	.09
❑	453	Josh Beckett	.30	.09
❑	454	Juan Encarnacion	.30	.09
❑	455	Ivan Rodriguez	.75	.23
❑	456	Todd Hollandsworth	.30	.09
❑	457	Cliff Floyd	.30	.09
❑	458	Rey Sanchez	.30	.09
❑	459	Mike Piazza	1.25	.35
❑	460	Mo Vaughn	.30	.09
❑	461	Armando Benitez	.30	.09
❑	462	Tsuyoshi Shinjo	.30	.09
❑	463	Tom Glavine	.50	.15
❑	464	David Cone	.30	.09
❑	465	Phil Nevin	.30	.09
❑	466	Sean Burroughs	.30	.09
❑	467	Jake Peavy	.30	.09
❑	468	Brian Lawrence	.30	.09
❑	469	Mark Loretta	.30	.09
❑	470	Dennis Tankersley	.30	.09
❑	471	Jesse Orosco	.30	.09
❑	472	Jim Thome	.75	.23
❑	473	Kevin Millwood	.30	.09
❑	474	David Bell	.30	.09
❑	475	Pat Burrell	.30	.09
❑	476	Brandon Duckworth	.30	.09
❑	477	Jose Mesa	.30	.09
❑	478	Marlon Byrd	.30	.09
❑	479	Reggie Sanders	.30	.09
❑	480	Jason Kendall	.30	.09
❑	481	Aramis Ramirez	.30	.09
❑	482	Kris Benson	.30	.09
❑	483	Matt Stairs	.30	.09
❑	484	Kevin Young	.30	.09
❑	485	Kenny Lofton	.30	.09
❑	486	Austin Kearns	.30	.09
❑	487	Barry Larkin	.50	.15
❑	488	Jason LaRue	.30	.09
❑	489	Ken Griffey Jr.	1.25	.35
❑	490	Danny Graves	.30	.09
❑	491	Russell Branyan	.30	.09
❑	492	Reggie Taylor	.30	.09
❑	493	Jimmy Haynes	.30	.09
❑	494	Charles Johnson	.30	.09
❑	495	Todd Helton	.50	.15
❑	496	Juan Uribe	.30	.09
❑	497	Preston Wilson	.30	.09
❑	498	Chris Stynes	.30	.09
❑	499	Jason Jennings	.30	.09
❑	500	Jay Payton	.30	.09
❑	501	Hideki Matsui SR RC	5.00	1.50
❑	502	Jose Contreras SR RC	2.00	.60
❑	503	Brandon Webb SR RC	2.00	.60
❑	504	Robby Hammock SR RC	1.50	.45
❑	505	Matt Kata SR RC	1.50	.45
❑	506	Tim Olson SR RC	1.50	.45
❑	507	Michael Hessman SR RC	1.00	.30
❑	508	Jon Leicester SR RC	1.00	.30
❑	509	Todd Wellemeyer SR RC	1.50	.45
❑	510	David Sanders SR RC	1.00	.30
❑	511	Josh Stewart SR RC	1.00	.30
❑	512	Luis Ayala SR RC	1.00	.30
❑	513	Clint Barmes SR RC	1.50	.45
❑	514	Josh Willingham SR RC	1.50	.45
❑	515	Al. Machado SR RC	1.00	.30
❑	516	Felix Sanchez SR RC	1.00	.30
❑	517	Willie Eyre SR RC	1.00	.30
❑	518	Brent Hoard SR RC	1.00	.30
❑	519	Lew Ford SR RC	2.50	.75
❑	520	Termel Sledge SR RC	1.50	.45
❑	521	Jeremy Griffiths SR RC	1.50	.45
❑	522	Phil Seibel SR RC	1.00	.30
❑	523	Craig Brazell SR RC	1.50	.45
❑	524	Prentice Redman SR RC	1.00	.30
❑	525	Jeff Duncan SR RC	1.50	.45
❑	526	Shane Bazzell SR RC	1.00	.30
❑	527	Bernie Castro SR RC	1.00	.30
❑	528	Rett Johnson SR RC	1.50	.45
❑	529	Bobby Madritsch SR RC	4.00	1.20
❑	530	Rocco Baldelli SR	1.00	.30
❑	531	Alex Rodriguez SH CL	.75	.23
❑	532	Eric Chavez SH CL	.30	.09
❑	533	Miguel Tejada SH CL	.30	.09
❑	534	Ichiro Suzuki SH CL	.75	.23
❑	535	Sammy Sosa SH CL	.75	.23
❑	536	Barry Zito SH CL	.30	.09
❑	537	Darin Erstad SH CL	.30	.09
❑	538	Alfonso Soriano SH CL	.30	.09
❑	539	Troy Glaus SH CL	.30	.09
❑	540	N.Garciaparra SH CL	.75	.23
❑	541	Bo Hart RC	.50	.15
❑	542	Dan Haren RC	.75	.23
❑	543	Ryan Wagner RC	.50	.15
❑	544	Rich Harden	.50	.15
❑	545	Dontrelle Willis	.50	.15
❑	546	Jerome Williams	.30	.09
❑	547	Bobby Crosby	.50	.15
❑	548	Greg Jones RC	.50	.15
❑	549	Todd Linden	.30	.09
❑	550	Byung-Hyun Kim	.30	.09
❑	551	Rickie Weeks RC	2.50	.75
❑	552	Jason Roach RC	.50	.15
❑	553	Oscar Villarreal RC	.50	.15
❑	554	Justin Duchscherer	.30	.09
❑	555	Chris Capuano RC	.50	.15
❑	556	Josh Hall RC	.50	.15
❑	557	Luis Matos	.30	.09
❑	558	Miguel Ojeda RC	.50	.15
❑	559	Kevin Ohme RC	.50	.15
❑	560	Julio Manon RC	.50	.15
❑	561	Kevin Correia RC	.50	.15
❑	562	Delmon Young RC	4.00	1.20
❑	563	Aaron Boone	.30	.09
❑	564	Aaron Looper RC	.50	.15
❑	565	Mike Neu RC	.50	.15
❑	566	Aquilino Lopez RC	.50	.15
❑	567	Jhonny Peralta	.50	.15
❑	568	Duaner Sanchez	.30	.09
❑	569	Stephen Randolph RC	.50	.15
❑	570	Nate Bland RC	.50	.15
❑	571	Chin-Hui Tsao	.30	.09
❑	572	Michel Hernandez RC	.50	.15
❑	573	Rocco Baldelli	.30	.09
❑	574	Robb Quinlan	.30	.09
❑	575	Aaron Heilman	.30	.09
❑	576	Jae Weong Seo	.30	.09
❑	577	Joe Borowski	.30	.09
❑	578	Chris Bootcheck	.30	.09
❑	579	Michael Ryan RC	.50	.15
❑	580	Mark Malaska RC	.50	.15
❑	581	Jose Guillen	.30	.09
❑	582	Josh Towers	.30	.09
❑	583	Tom Gregorio RC	.50	.15
❑	584	Edwin Jackson RC	2.50	.75
❑	585	Jason Anderson	.30	.09
❑	586	Jose Reyes	.30	.09
❑	587	Miguel Cabrera	.75	.23
❑	588	Nate Bump	.30	.09
❑	589	Jeromy Burnitz	.30	.09
❑	590	David Ross	.30	.09
❑	591	Chase Utley	.30	.09
❑	592	Brandon Webb	.75	.23
❑	593	Masao Kida	.30	.09
❑	594	Jimmy Journell	.30	.09
❑	595	Eric Young	.30	.09
❑	596	Tony Womack	.30	.09
❑	597	Amaury Telemaco	.30	.09
❑	598	Rickey Henderson	.75	.23
❑	599	Esteban Loaiza	.30	.09
❑	600	Sidney Ponson	.30	.09
❑	NNO	Update Set Exchange		

2004 Upper Deck

	MINT	NRMT
COMPLETE SERIES 1 (270)	50.00	22.00
COMPLETE SERIES 2 (270)	50.00	22.00
COMP.UPDATE SET (50)	15.00	6.75
COMMON (31-480/541-565)	.30	.14
COMMON (1-30/481-540)	1.00	.45
COMMON CARD (566-590)	.50	.23

541-590 ONE SET PER '05 UD1 HOBBY BOX
UPDATE SET EXCH 1:480 '05 UD1 RETAIL
UPDATE SET EXCH.DEADLINE

	#	Player	Mint	NrMt
❑	1	Dontrelle Willis SR	1.00	.45
❑	2	Edgar Gonzalez SR	1.00	.45
❑	3	Jose Reyes SR	1.00	.45
❑	4	Jae Weong Seo SR	1.00	.45

Card	Player	Price 1	Price 2
❑ 5	Miguel Cabrera SR	1.50	.70
❑ 6	Jesse Foppert SR	1.00	.45
❑ 7	Mike Neu SR	1.00	.45
❑ 8	Michael Nakamura SR	1.00	.45
❑ 9	Luis Ayala SR	1.00	.45
❑ 10	Jared Sandberg SR	1.00	.45
❑ 11	Jhonny Peralta SR	1.00	.45
❑ 12	Wil Ledezma SR	1.00	.45
❑ 13	Jason Roach SR	1.00	.45
❑ 14	Kirk Saarloos SR	1.00	.45
❑ 15	Cliff Lee SR	1.00	.45
❑ 16	Bobby Hill SR	1.00	.45
❑ 17	Lyle Overbay SR	1.00	.45
❑ 18	Josh Hall SR	1.00	.45
❑ 19	Joe Thurston SR	1.00	.45
❑ 20	Matt Kata SR	1.00	.45
❑ 21	Jeremy Bonderman SR	1.00	.45
❑ 22	Julio Manon SR	1.00	.45
❑ 23	Rodrigo Rosario SR	1.00	.45
❑ 24	Robby Hammock SR	1.00	.45
❑ 25	David Sanders SR	1.00	.45
❑ 26	Miguel Ojeda SR	1.00	.45
❑ 27	Mark Teixeira SR	1.00	.45
❑ 28	Franklyn German SR	1.00	.45
❑ 29	Ken Harvey SR	1.00	.45
❑ 30	Xavier Nady SR	1.00	.45
❑ 31	Tim Salmon	.50	.23
❑ 32	Troy Glaus	.30	.14
❑ 33	Adam Kennedy	.30	.14
❑ 34	David Eckstein	.30	.14
❑ 35	Ben Molina	.30	.14
❑ 36	Jarrod Washburn	.30	.14
❑ 37	Ramon Ortiz	.30	.14
❑ 38	Eric Chavez	.30	.14
❑ 39	Miguel Tejada	.30	.14
❑ 40	Chris Singleton	.30	.14
❑ 41	Jermaine Dye	.30	.14
❑ 42	John Halama	.30	.14
❑ 43	Tim Hudson	.30	.14
❑ 44	Barry Zito	.30	.14
❑ 45	Ted Lilly	.30	.14
❑ 46	Bobby Kielty	.30	.14
❑ 47	Kelvim Escobar	.30	.14
❑ 48	Josh Phelps	.30	.14
❑ 49	Vernon Wells	.30	.14
❑ 50	Roy Halladay	.30	.14
❑ 51	Orlando Hudson	.30	.14
❑ 52	Eric Hinske	.30	.14
❑ 53	Brandon Backe	.30	.14
❑ 54	Dewon Brazelton	.30	.14
❑ 55	Ben Grieve	.30	.14
❑ 56	Aubrey Huff	.30	.14
❑ 57	Toby Hall	.30	.14
❑ 58	Rocco Baldelli	.30	.14
❑ 59	Al Martin	.30	.14
❑ 60	Brandon Phillips	.30	.14
❑ 61	Omar Vizquel	.50	.23
❑ 62	C.C. Sabathia	.30	.14
❑ 63	Milton Bradley	.30	.14
❑ 64	Ricky Gutierrez	.30	.14
❑ 65	Matt Lawton	.30	.14
❑ 66	Danys Baez	.30	.14
❑ 67	Ichiro Suzuki	1.25	.55
❑ 68	Randy Winn	.30	.14
❑ 69	Carlos Guillen	.30	.14
❑ 70	Mark McLemore	.30	.14
❑ 71	Dan Wilson	.30	.14
❑ 72	Jamie Moyer	.30	.14
❑ 73	Joel Pineiro	.30	.14
❑ 74	Edgar Martinez	.50	.23
❑ 75	Tony Batista	.30	.14
❑ 76	Jay Gibbons	.30	.14
❑ 77	Jeff Conine	.30	.14
❑ 78	Melvin Mora	.30	.14
❑ 79	Geronimo Gil	.30	.14
❑ 80	Rodrigo Lopez	.30	.14
❑ 81	Jorge Julio	.30	.14
❑ 82	Rafael Palmeiro	.50	.23
❑ 83	Juan Gonzalez	.50	.23
❑ 84	Mike Young	.30	.14
❑ 85	Alex Rodriguez	1.25	.55
❑ 86	Einar Diaz	.30	.14
❑ 87	Kevin Mench	.30	.14
❑ 88	Hank Blalock	.30	.14
❑ 89	Pedro Martinez	.75	.35
❑ 90	Byung-Hyun Kim	.30	.14
❑ 91	Derek Lowe	.30	.14
❑ 92	Jason Varitek	.50	.23
❑ 93	Manny Ramirez	.50	.23
❑ 94	John Burkett	.30	.14
❑ 95	Todd Walker	.30	.14
❑ 96	Nomar Garciaparra	1.25	.55
❑ 97	Trot Nixon	.30	.14
❑ 98	Mike Sweeney	.30	.14
❑ 99	Carlos Febles	.30	.14
❑ 100	Mike MacDougal	.30	.14
❑ 101	Raul Ibanez	.30	.14
❑ 102	Jason Grimsley	.30	.14
❑ 103	Chris George	.30	.14
❑ 104	Brent Mayne	.30	.14
❑ 105	Dmitri Young	.30	.14
❑ 106	Eric Munson	.30	.14
❑ 107	A.J. Hinch	.30	.14
❑ 108	Andres Torres	.30	.14
❑ 109	Bobby Higginson	.30	.14
❑ 110	Shane Halter	.30	.14
❑ 111	Matt Walbeck	.30	.14
❑ 112	Torii Hunter	.30	.14
❑ 113	Doug Mientkiewicz	.30	.14
❑ 114	Lew Ford	.30	.14
❑ 115	Eric Milton	.30	.14
❑ 116	Eddie Guardado	.30	.14
❑ 117	Cristian Guzman	.30	.14
❑ 118	Corey Koskie	.30	.14
❑ 119	Magglio Ordonez	.30	.14
❑ 120	Mark Buehrle	.30	.14
❑ 121	Billy Koch	.30	.14
❑ 122	Jose Valentin	.30	.14
❑ 123	Paul Konerko	.30	.14
❑ 124	Carlos Lee	.30	.14
❑ 125	Jon Garland	.30	.14
❑ 126	Jason Giambi	.30	.14
❑ 127	Derek Jeter	1.50	.70
❑ 128	Roger Clemens	1.50	.70
❑ 129	Andy Pettitte	.50	.23
❑ 130	Jorge Posada	.50	.23
❑ 131	David Wells	.30	.14
❑ 132	Hideki Matsui	1.25	.55
❑ 133	Mike Mussina	.50	.23
❑ 134	Jeff Bagwell	.50	.23
❑ 135	Craig Biggio	.50	.23
❑ 136	Morgan Ensberg	.30	.14
❑ 137	Richard Hidalgo	.30	.14
❑ 138	Brad Ausmus	.30	.14
❑ 139	Roy Oswalt	.30	.14
❑ 140	Billy Wagner	.30	.14
❑ 141	Octavio Dotel	.30	.14
❑ 142	Gary Sheffield	.30	.14
❑ 143	Andruw Jones	.30	.14
❑ 144	John Smoltz	.50	.23
❑ 145	Rafael Furcal	.30	.14
❑ 146	Javy Lopez	.30	.14
❑ 147	Shane Reynolds	.30	.14
❑ 148	Horacio Ramirez	.30	.14
❑ 149	Mike Hampton	.30	.14
❑ 150	Jung Bong	.30	.14
❑ 151	Ruben Quevedo	.30	.14
❑ 152	Ben Sheets	.30	.14
❑ 153	Geoff Jenkins	.30	.14
❑ 154	Royce Clayton	.30	.14
❑ 155	Glendon Rusch	.30	.14
❑ 156	John Vander Wal	.30	.14
❑ 157	Scott Podsednik	.30	.14
❑ 158	Jim Edmonds	.30	.14
❑ 159	Tino Martinez	.50	.23
❑ 160	Albert Pujols	1.50	.70
❑ 161	Matt Morris	.30	.14
❑ 162	Woody Williams	.30	.14
❑ 163	Edgar Renteria	.30	.14
❑ 164	Jason Isringhausen	.30	.14
❑ 165	Jason Simontacchi	.30	.14
❑ 166	Kerry Robinson	.30	.14
❑ 167	Sammy Sosa	1.25	.55
❑ 168	Joe Borowski	.30	.14
❑ 169	Tony Womack	.30	.14
❑ 170	Antonio Alfonseca	.30	.14
❑ 171	Corey Patterson	.30	.14
❑ 172	Mark Prior	.75	.35
❑ 173	Moises Alou	.30	.14
❑ 174	Matt Clement	.30	.14
❑ 175	Randall Simon	.30	.14
❑ 176	Randy Johnson	.75	.35
❑ 177	Luis Gonzalez	.30	.14
❑ 178	Craig Counsell	.30	.14
❑ 179	Miguel Batista	.30	.14
❑ 180	Steve Finley	.30	.14
❑ 181	Brandon Webb	.30	.14
❑ 182	Danny Bautista	.30	.14
❑ 183	Oscar Villarreal	.30	.14
❑ 184	Shawn Green	.30	.14
❑ 185	Brian Jordan	.30	.14
❑ 186	Fred McGriff	.50	.23
❑ 187	Andy Ashby	.30	.14
❑ 188	Rickey Henderson	.75	.35
❑ 189	Dave Roberts	.30	.14
❑ 190	Eric Gagne	.75	.35
❑ 191	Kazuhisa Ishii	.30	.14
❑ 192	Adrian Beltre	.50	.23
❑ 193	Vladimir Guerrero	.75	.35
❑ 194	Livan Hernandez	.30	.14
❑ 195	Ron Calloway	.30	.14
❑ 196	Sun Woo Kim	.30	.14
❑ 197	Wil Cordero	.30	.14
❑ 198	Brad Wilkerson	.30	.14
❑ 199	Orlando Cabrera	.30	.14
❑ 200	Barry Bonds	2.00	.90
❑ 201	Ray Durham	.30	.14
❑ 202	Andres Galarraga	.30	.14
❑ 203	Benito Santiago	.30	.14
❑ 204	Jose Cruz Jr.	.30	.14
❑ 205	Jason Schmidt	.30	.14
❑ 206	Kirk Rueter	.30	.14
❑ 207	Felix Rodriguez	.30	.14
❑ 208	Mike Lowell	.30	.14
❑ 209	Luis Castillo	.30	.14
❑ 210	Derrek Lee	.30	.14
❑ 211	Andy Fox	.30	.14
❑ 212	Tommy Phelps	.30	.14
❑ 213	Todd Hollandsworth	.30	.14
❑ 214	Brad Penny	.30	.14
❑ 215	Juan Pierre	.30	.14
❑ 216	Mike Piazza	1.25	.55
❑ 217	Jae Weong Seo	.30	.14
❑ 218	Ty Wigginton	.30	.14
❑ 219	Al Leiter	.30	.14
❑ 220	Roger Cedeno	.30	.14
❑ 221	Timo Perez	.30	.14
❑ 222	Aaron Heilman	.30	.14
❑ 223	Pedro Astacio	.30	.14
❑ 224	Joe McEwing	.30	.14
❑ 225	Ryan Klesko	.30	.14
❑ 226	Brian Giles	.30	.14
❑ 227	Mark Kotsay	.30	.14
❑ 228	Brian Lawrence	.30	.14
❑ 229	Rod Beck	.30	.14
❑ 230	Trevor Hoffman	.30	.14
❑ 231	Sean Burroughs	.30	.14
❑ 232	Bob Abreu	.30	.14
❑ 233	Jim Thome	.75	.35
❑ 234	David Bell	.30	.14
❑ 235	Jimmy Rollins	.30	.14
❑ 236	Mike Lieberthal	.30	.14
❑ 237	Vicente Padilla	.30	.14
❑ 238	Randy Wolf	.30	.14
❑ 239	Reggie Sanders	.30	.14
❑ 240	Jason Kendall	.30	.14
❑ 241	Jack Wilson	.30	.14
❑ 242	Jose Hernandez	.30	.14
❑ 243	Kip Wells	.30	.14
❑ 244	Carlos Rivera	.30	.14
❑ 245	Craig Wilson	.30	.14
❑ 246	Adam Dunn	.50	.23
❑ 247	Sean Casey	.30	.14
❑ 248	Danny Graves	.30	.14
❑ 249	Ryan Dempster	.30	.14
❑ 250	Barry Larkin	.50	.23
❑ 251	Reggie Taylor	.30	.14
❑ 252	Wily Mo Pena	.30	.14
❑ 253	Larry Walker	.50	.23
❑ 254	Mark Sweeney	.30	.14
❑ 255	Preston Wilson	.30	.14
❑ 256	Jason Jennings	.30	.14
❑ 257	Charles Johnson	.30	.14
❑ 258	Jay Payton	.30	.14
❑ 259	Chris Stynes	.30	.14
❑ 260	Juan Uribe	.30	.14
❑ 261	Hideki Matsui SH CL	.75	.35
❑ 262	Barry Bonds SH CL	1.00	.45

No.	Player	Price	Price
263	Dontrelle Willis SH CL	.30	.14
264	Kevin Millwood SH CL	.30	.14
265	Billy Wagner SH CL	.30	.14
266	Rocco Baldelli SH CL	.30	.14
267	Roger Clemens SH CL	.75	.35
268	Rafael Palmeiro SH CL	.30	.14
269	Miguel Cabrera SH CL	.50	.23
270	Jose Contreras SH CL	.30	.14
271	Aaron Sele	.30	.14
272	Bartolo Colon	.30	.14
273	Darin Erstad	.30	.14
274	Francisco Rodriguez	.30	.14
275	Garret Anderson	.30	.14
276	Jose Guillen	.30	.14
277	Troy Percival	.30	.14
278	Alex Cintron	.30	.14
279	Casey Fossum	.30	.14
280	Elmer Dessens	.30	.14
281	Jose Valverde	.30	.14
282	Matt Mantei	.30	.14
283	Richie Sexson	.30	.14
284	Roberto Alomar	.50	.23
285	Shea Hillenbrand	.30	.14
286	Chipper Jones	.75	.35
287	Greg Maddux	1.25	.55
288	J.D. Drew	.30	.14
289	Marcus Giles	.30	.14
290	Mike Hessman	.30	.14
291	John Thomson	.30	.14
292	Russ Ortiz	.30	.14
293	Adam Loewen	.30	.14
294	Jack Cust	.30	.14
295	Jerry Hairston Jr.	.30	.14
296	Kurt Ainsworth	.30	.14
297	Luis Matos	.30	.14
298	Marty Cordova	.30	.14
299	Sidney Ponson	.30	.14
300	Bill Mueller	.30	.14
301	Curt Schilling	.30	.14
302	David Ortiz	.75	.35
303	Johnny Damon	.75	.35
304	Keith Foulke Sox	.50	.23
305	Pokey Reese	.30	.14
306	Scott Williamson	.30	.14
307	Tim Wakefield	.30	.14
308	Alex Gonzalez	.30	.14
309	Aramis Ramirez	.30	.14
310	Carlos Zambrano	.30	.14
311	Juan Cruz	.30	.14
312	Kerry Wood	.75	.35
313	Kyle Farnsworth	.30	.14
314	Aaron Rowand	.30	.14
315	Esteban Loaiza	.30	.14
316	Frank Thomas	.75	.35
317	Joe Borchard	.30	.14
318	Joe Crede	.30	.14
319	Miguel Olivo	.30	.14
320	Willie Harris	.30	.14
321	Aaron Harang	.30	.14
322	Austin Kearns	.30	.14
323	Brandon Claussen	.30	.14
324	Brandon Larson	.30	.14
325	Ryan Freel	.30	.14
326	Ken Griffey Jr.	1.25	.55
327	Ryan Wagner	.30	.14
328	Alex Escobar	.30	.14
329	Coco Crisp	.30	.14
330	David Riske	.30	.14
331	Jody Gerut	.30	.14
332	Josh Bard	.30	.14
333	Travis Hafner	.30	.14
334	Chin-Hui Tsao	.30	.14
335	Denny Stark	.30	.14
336	Jeromy Burnitz	.30	.14
337	Shawn Chacon	.30	.14
338	Todd Helton	.50	.23
339	Vinny Castilla	.30	.14
340	Alex Sanchez	.30	.14
341	Carlos Pena	.30	.14
342	Fernando Vina	.30	.14
343	Jason Johnson	.30	.14
344	Matt Anderson	.30	.14
345	Mike Maroth	.30	.14
346	Rondell White	.30	.14
347	A.J. Burnett	.30	.14
348	Alex Gonzalez	.30	.14
349	Armando Benitez	.30	.14
350	Carl Pavano	.30	.14
351	Hee Seop Choi	.30	.14
352	Ivan Rodriguez	.75	.35
353	Josh Beckett	.30	.14
354	Josh Willingham	.30	.14
355	Adam Everett	.30	.14
356	Brandon Duckworth	.30	.14
357	Jason Lane	.30	.14
358	Jeff Kent	.30	.14
359	Jeriome Robertson	.30	.14
360	Lance Berkman	.30	.14
361	Wade Miller	.30	.14
362	Aaron Guiel	.30	.14
363	Angel Berroa	.30	.14
364	Carlos Beltran	.50	.23
365	David DeJesus	.30	.14
366	Desi Relaford	.30	.14
367	Joe Randa	.30	.14
368	Runelvys Hernandez	.30	.14
369	Edwin Jackson	.30	.14
370	Hideo Nomo	.75	.35
371	Jeff Weaver	.30	.14
372	Juan Encarnacion	.30	.14
373	Odalis Perez	.30	.14
374	Paul Lo Duca	.30	.14
375	Robin Ventura	.30	.14
376	Bill Hall	.30	.14
377	Chad Moeller	.30	.14
378	Chris Capuano	.30	.14
379	Junior Spivey	.30	.14
380	Rickie Weeks	.30	.14
381	Wes Helms	.30	.14
382	Brad Radke	.30	.14
383	Jacque Jones	.30	.14
384	Joe Mays	.30	.14
385	Joe Nathan	.30	.14
386	Johan Santana	.50	.23
387	Nick Punto	.30	.14
388	Shannon Stewart	.30	.14
389	Carl Everett	.30	.14
390	Claudio Vargas	.30	.14
391	Jose Vidro	.30	.14
392	Nick Johnson	.30	.14
393	Rocky Biddle	.30	.14
394	Tony Armas Jr.	.30	.14
395	Braden Looper	.30	.14
396	Cliff Floyd	.30	.14
397	Jason Phillips	.30	.14
398	Mike Cameron	.30	.14
399	Tom Glavine	.50	.23
400	Kenny Lofton	.30	.14
401	Alfonso Soriano	.50	.23
402	Bernie Williams	.50	.23
403	Javier Vazquez	.30	.14
404	Jon Lieber	.30	.14
405	Jose Contreras	.30	.14
406	Kevin Brown	.30	.14
407	Mariano Rivera	.50	.23
408	Arthur Rhodes	.30	.14
409	Eric Byrnes	.30	.14
410	Erubiel Durazo	.30	.14
411	Graham Koonce	.30	.14
412	Marco Scutaro	.30	.14
413	Mark Mulder	.30	.14
414	Mark Redman	.30	.14
415	Rich Harden	.30	.14
416	Brett Myers	.30	.14
417	Chase Utley	.30	.14
418	Kevin Millwood	.30	.14
419	Marlon Byrd	.30	.14
420	Pat Burrell	.30	.14
421	Placido Polanco	.30	.14
422	Tim Worrell	.30	.14
423	Jason Bay	.30	.14
424	Josh Fogg	.30	.14
425	Kris Benson	.30	.14
426	Mike Gonzalez	.30	.14
427	Oliver Perez	.30	.14
428	Tike Redman	.30	.14
429	Adam Eaton	.30	.14
430	Ismael Valdes	.30	.14
431	Jake Peavy	.30	.14
432	Khalil Greene	.75	.35
433	Mark Loretta	.30	.14
434	Phil Nevin	.30	.14
435	Ramon Hernandez	.30	.14
436	A.J. Pierzynski	.30	.14
437	Edgardo Alfonzo	.30	.14
438	J.T. Snow	.30	.14
439	Jerome Williams	.30	.14
440	Marquis Grissom	.30	.14
441	Robb Nen	.30	.14
442	Bret Boone	.30	.14
443	Freddy Garcia	.30	.14
444	Gil Meche	.30	.14
445	John Olerud	.30	.14
446	Rich Aurilia	.30	.14
447	Shigetoshi Hasegawa	.30	.14
448	Bo Hart	.30	.14
449	Danny Haren	.30	.14
450	Jason Marquis	.30	.14
451	Marlon Anderson	.30	.14
452	Scott Rolen	.75	.35
453	So Taguchi	.30	.14
454	Carl Crawford	.30	.14
455	Delmon Young	.50	.23
456	Geoff Blum	.30	.14
457	Jesus Colome	.30	.14
458	Jonny Gomes	.30	.14
459	Lance Carter	.30	.14
460	Robert Fick	.30	.14
461	Chan Ho Park	.30	.14
462	Francisco Cordero	.30	.14
463	Jeff Nelson	.30	.14
464	Jeff Zimmerman	.30	.14
465	Kenny Rogers	.30	.14
466	Aquilino Lopez	.30	.14
467	Carlos Delgado	.30	.14
468	Frank Catalanotto	.30	.14
469	Reed Johnson	.30	.14
470	Pat Hentgen	.30	.14
471	Curt Schilling SH CL	.30	.14
472	Gary Sheffield SH CL	.30	.14
473	Javier Vazquez SH CL	.30	.14
474	Kazuo Matsui SH CL	1.50	.70
475	Kevin Brown SH CL	.30	.14
476	Rafael Palmeiro SH CL	.30	.14
477	Richie Sexson SH CL	.30	.14
478	Roger Clemens SH CL	.75	.35
479	Vladimir Guerrero SH CL	.50	.23
480	Alex Rodriguez SH CL	.75	.35
481	Jake Woods SR RC	1.00	.45
482	Tim Bittner SR RC	1.00	.45
483	Brandon Medders SR RC	1.00	.45
484	Casey Daigle SR RC	1.00	.45
485	Jerry Gil SR RC	1.00	.45
486	Mike Gosling SR RC	1.00	.45
487	Jose Capellan SR RC	2.50	1.10
488	Onil Joseph SR RC	1.00	.45
489	Roman Colon SR RC	1.00	.45
490	Dave Crouthers SR RC	1.00	.45
491	Eddy Rodriguez SR RC	1.50	.70
492	Franklyn Gracesqui SR RC	1.00	.45
493	Jamie Brown SR RC	1.00	.45
494	Jerome Gamble SR RC	1.00	.45
495	Tim Hamulack SR RC	1.00	.45
496	Carlos Vasquez SR RC	1.50	.70
497	Renyel Pinto SR RC	1.50	.70
498	Ronny Cedeno SR RC	1.00	.45
499	Enemencio Pacheco SR RC	1.00	.45
500	Ryan Meaux SR RC	1.00	.45
501	Ryan Wing SR RC	1.00	.45
502	Shingo Takatsu SR RC	2.00	.90
503	William Bergolla SR RC	1.00	.45
504	Ivan Ochoa SR RC	1.00	.45
505	Mariano Gomez SR RC	1.00	.45
506	Justin Hampson SR RC	1.00	.45
507	Justin Huisman SR RC	1.00	.45
508	Scott Dohmann SR RC	1.00	.45
509	Donnie Kelly SR RC	1.00	.45
510	Chris Aguila SR RC	1.00	.45
511	Lincoln Holdzkom SR RC	1.00	.45
512	Freddy Guzman SR RC	1.00	.45
513	Hector Gimenez SR RC	1.00	.45
514	Jorge Vasquez SR RC	1.00	.45
515	Jason Frasor SR RC	1.00	.45
516	Chris Saenz SR RC	1.00	.45
517	Dennis Sarfate SR RC	1.00	.45
518	Colby Miller SR RC	1.00	.45
519	Jason Bartlett SR RC	1.50	.70
520	Chad Bentz SR RC	1.00	.45
521	Josh Labandeira SR RC	1.00	.45
522	Shawn Hill SR RC	1.00	.45
523	Kazuo Matsui SR RC	3.00	1.35
524	Carlos Hines SR RC	1.00	.45
525	Mike Vento SR RC	1.50	.70
526	Scott Proctor SR RC	1.50	.70

❑ 527 Sean Henn SR RC	1.00	.45
❑ 528 David Aardsma SR RC	1.00	.45
❑ 529 Ian Snell SR RC	1.50	.70
❑ 530 Mike Johnston SR RC	1.00	.45
❑ 531 Akinori Otsuka SR RC	1.00	.45
❑ 532 Rusty Tucker SR RC	1.50	.70
❑ 533 Justin Knoedler SR RC	1.00	.45
❑ 534 Merkin Valdez SR RC	2.00	.90
❑ 535 Greg Dobbs SR RC	1.00	.45
❑ 536 Justin Leone SR RC	1.50	.70
❑ 537 Shawn Camp SR RC	1.00	.45
❑ 538 Edwin Moreno SR RC	1.00	.45
❑ 539 Angel Chavez SR RC	1.00	.45
❑ 540 Jesse Harper SR RC	1.00	.45
❑ 541 Alex Rodriguez	1.25	.55
❑ 542 Roger Clemens	1.50	.70
❑ 543 Andy Pettitte	.50	.23
❑ 544 Vladimir Guerrero	.75	.35
❑ 545 David Wells	.30	.14
❑ 546 Derrek Lee	.30	.14
❑ 547 Carlos Beltran	.50	.23
❑ 548 Orlando Cabrera Sox	.50	.23
❑ 549 Paul Lo Duca	.30	.14
❑ 550 Dave Roberts	.30	.14
❑ 551 Guillermo Mota	.30	.14
❑ 552 Steve Finley	.30	.14
❑ 553 Juan Encarnacion	.30	.14
❑ 554 Larry Walker	.50	.23
❑ 555 Ty Wigginton	.30	.14
❑ 556 Doug Mientkiewicz	.30	.14
❑ 557 Roberto Alomar	.50	.23
❑ 558 B.J. Upton	.50	.23
❑ 559 Brad Penny	.30	.14
❑ 560 Hee Seop Choi	.30	.14
❑ 561 David Wright	3.00	1.35
❑ 562 Nomar Garciaparra	1.25	.55
❑ 563 Felix Rodriguez	.30	.14
❑ 564 Victor Zambrano	.30	.14
❑ 565 Kris Benson	.30	.14
❑ 566 Aarom Baldiris SR RC	.50	.23
❑ 567 Joey Gathright SR RC	1.00	.45
❑ 568 Charles Thomas SR RC	.50	.23
❑ 569 Brian Dallimore SR RC	.50	.23
❑ 570 Chris Oxspring SR RC	.50	.23
❑ 571 Chris Shelton SR RC	.75	.35
❑ 572 Dioner Navarro SR RC	1.00	.45
❑ 573 Edwardo Sierra SR RC	.50	.23
❑ 574 Fernando Nieve SR RC	.50	.23
❑ 575 Frank Francisco SR RC	.50	.23
❑ 576 Jeff Bennett SR RC	.50	.23
❑ 577 Justin Lehr SR RC	.50	.23
❑ 578 John Gall SR RC	.50	.23
❑ 579 Jorge Sequea SR RC	.50	.23
❑ 580 Justin Germano SR RC	.50	.23
❑ 581 Kazuhito Tadano SR RC	.50	.23
❑ 582 Kevin Cave SR RC	.50	.23
❑ 583 Jesse Crain SR RC	.75	.35
❑ 584 Luis A. Gonzalez SR RC	.50	.23
❑ 585 Michael Wuertz SR RC	.50	.23
❑ 586 Orlando Rodriguez SR RC	.50	.23
❑ 587 Phil Stockman SR RC	.50	.23
❑ 588 Ramon Ramirez SR RC	.50	.23
❑ 589 Roberto Novoa SR RC	.50	.23
❑ 590 Scott Kazmir SR RC	3.00	1.35
❑ NNO Update Set Exchange Card		

2005 Upper Deck

	Nm-Mt	Ex-Mt
COMPLETE SERIES 1 (300)	50.00	15.00
COMMON (1-210/260-300)	.30	.09
COMMON CARD (211-250)	1.00	.30

OVERALL PLATES SER.1 ODDS 1:1080 H
PLATES PRINT RUN 1 #'d SET PER COLOR
BLACK-CYAN-MAGENTA-YELLOW ISSUED
NO PLATES PRICING DUE TO SCARCITY

❑ 1 Casey Kotchman	.50	.15
❑ 2 Chone Figgins	.30	.09
❑ 3 David Eckstein	.30	.09
❑ 4 Jarrod Washburn	.30	.09
❑ 5 Robb Quinlan	.30	.09
❑ 6 Troy Glaus	.30	.09
❑ 7 Vladimir Guerrero	.75	.23
❑ 8 Brandon Webb	.30	.09
❑ 9 Danny Bautista	.30	.09
❑ 10 Luis Gonzalez	.30	.09
❑ 11 Matt Kata	.30	.09
❑ 12 Randy Johnson	.75	.23
❑ 13 Robby Hammock	.30	.09
❑ 14 Shea Hillenbrand	.30	.09
❑ 15 Adam LaRoche	.30	.09
❑ 16 Andruw Jones	.30	.09
❑ 17 Horacio Ramirez	.30	.09
❑ 18 John Smoltz	.50	.15
❑ 19 Johnny Estrada	.30	.09
❑ 20 Mike Hampton	.30	.09
❑ 21 Rafael Furcal	.30	.09
❑ 22 Brian Roberts	.30	.09
❑ 23 Javy Lopez	.30	.09
❑ 24 Jay Gibbons	.30	.09
❑ 25 Jorge Julio	.30	.09
❑ 26 Melvin Mora	.30	.09
❑ 27 Miguel Tejada	.30	.09
❑ 28 Rafael Palmeiro	.50	.15
❑ 29 Derek Lowe	.30	.09
❑ 30 Jason Varitek	.50	.15
❑ 31 Kevin Youkilis	.30	.09
❑ 32 Manny Ramirez	.50	.15
❑ 33 Curt Schilling	.75	.23
❑ 34 Pedro Martinez	.75	.23
❑ 35 Trot Nixon	.30	.09
❑ 36 Corey Patterson	.30	.09
❑ 37 Derrek Lee	.30	.09
❑ 38 LaTroy Hawkins	.30	.09
❑ 39 Mark Prior	.75	.23
❑ 40 Matt Clement	.30	.09
❑ 41 Moises Alou	.30	.09
❑ 42 Sammy Sosa	1.25	.35
❑ 43 Aaron Rowand	.30	.09
❑ 44 Carlos Lee	.30	.09
❑ 45 Jose Valentin	.30	.09
❑ 46 Juan Uribe	.30	.09
❑ 47 Magglio Ordonez	.30	.09
❑ 48 Mark Buehrle	.30	.09
❑ 49 Paul Konerko	.30	.09
❑ 50 Adam Dunn	.50	.15
❑ 51 Barry Larkin	.50	.15
❑ 52 D'Angelo Jimenez	.30	.09
❑ 53 Danny Graves	.30	.09
❑ 54 Paul Wilson	.30	.09
❑ 55 Sean Casey	.30	.09
❑ 56 Wily Mo Pena	.30	.09
❑ 57 Ben Broussard	.30	.09
❑ 58 C.C. Sabathia	.30	.09
❑ 59 Casey Blake	.30	.09
❑ 60 Cliff Lee	.30	.09
❑ 61 Matt Lawton	.30	.09
❑ 62 Omar Vizquel	.30	.09
❑ 63 Victor Martinez	.30	.09
❑ 64 Charles Johnson	.30	.09
❑ 65 Joe Kennedy	.30	.09
❑ 66 Jeromy Burnitz	.30	.09
❑ 67 Matt Holliday	.30	.09
❑ 68 Preston Wilson	.30	.09
❑ 69 Royce Clayton	.30	.09
❑ 70 Shawn Estes	.30	.09
❑ 71 Bobby Higginson	.30	.09
❑ 72 Brandon Inge	.30	.09
❑ 73 Carlos Guillen	.30	.09
❑ 74 Dmitri Young	.30	.09
❑ 75 Eric Munson	.30	.09
❑ 76 Jeremy Bonderman	.30	.09
❑ 77 Ugueth Urbina	.30	.09
❑ 78 Josh Beckett	.30	.09
❑ 79 Dontrelle Willis	.30	.09
❑ 80 Jeff Conine	.30	.09
❑ 81 Juan Pierre	.30	.09
❑ 82 Luis Castillo	.30	.09
❑ 83 Miguel Cabrera	.50	.15
❑ 84 Mike Lowell	.30	.09
❑ 85 Andy Pettitte	.50	.15
❑ 86 Brad Lidge	.30	.09
❑ 87 Carlos Beltran	.50	.15
❑ 88 Craig Biggio	.50	.15
❑ 89 Jeff Bagwell	.50	.15
❑ 90 Roger Clemens	1.50	.45
❑ 91 Roy Oswalt	.30	.09
❑ 92 Benito Santiago	.30	.09
❑ 93 Jeremy Affeldt	.30	.09
❑ 94 Juan Gonzalez	.50	.15
❑ 95 Ken Harvey	.30	.09
❑ 96 Mike MacDougal	.30	.09
❑ 97 Mike Sweeney	.30	.09
❑ 98 Zach Greinke	.30	.09
❑ 99 Adrian Beltre	.50	.15
❑ 100 Alex Cora	.30	.09
❑ 101 Cesar Izturis	.30	.09
❑ 102 Eric Gagne	.75	.23
❑ 103 Kazuhisa Ishii	.30	.09
❑ 104 Milton Bradley	.30	.09
❑ 105 Shawn Green	.30	.09
❑ 106 Danny Kolb	.30	.09
❑ 107 Ben Sheets	.30	.09
❑ 108 Brooks Kieschnick	.30	.09
❑ 109 Craig Counsell	.30	.09
❑ 110 Geoff Jenkins	.30	.09
❑ 111 Lyle Overbay	.30	.09
❑ 112 Scott Podsednik	.30	.09
❑ 113 Corey Koskie	.30	.09
❑ 114 Johan Santana	.50	.15
❑ 115 Joe Mauer	.50	.15
❑ 116 Justin Morneau	.30	.09
❑ 117 Lew Ford	.30	.09
❑ 118 Matt LeCroy	.30	.09
❑ 119 Torii Hunter	.30	.09
❑ 120 Brad Wilkerson	.30	.09
❑ 121 Chad Cordero	.30	.09
❑ 122 Livan Hernandez	.30	.09
❑ 123 Jose Vidro	.30	.09
❑ 124 Termel Sledge	.30	.09
❑ 125 Tony Batista	.30	.09
❑ 126 Zach Day	.30	.09
❑ 127 Al Leiter	.30	.09
❑ 128 Jae Weong Seo	.30	.09
❑ 129 Jose Reyes	.30	.09
❑ 130 Kazuo Matsui	.30	.09
❑ 131 Mike Piazza	1.25	.35
❑ 132 Todd Zeile	.30	.09
❑ 133 Cliff Floyd	.30	.09
❑ 134 Alex Rodriguez	1.25	.35
❑ 135 Derek Jeter	1.50	.45
❑ 136 Gary Sheffield	.30	.09
❑ 137 Hideki Matsui	1.25	.35
❑ 138 Jason Giambi	.30	.09
❑ 139 Jorge Posada	.50	.15
❑ 140 Mike Mussina	.50	.15
❑ 141 Barry Zito	.30	.09
❑ 142 Bobby Crosby	.30	.09
❑ 143 Octavio Dotel	.30	.09
❑ 144 Eric Chavez	.30	.09
❑ 145 Jermaine Dye	.30	.09
❑ 146 Mark Kotsay	.30	.09
❑ 147 Tim Hudson	.30	.09
❑ 148 Billy Wagner	.30	.09
❑ 149 Bobby Abreu	.30	.09
❑ 150 David Bell	.30	.09
❑ 151 Jim Thome	.75	.23
❑ 152 Jimmy Rollins	.30	.09
❑ 153 Mike Lieberthal	.30	.09
❑ 154 Randy Wolf	.30	.09
❑ 155 Craig Wilson	.30	.09
❑ 156 Daryle Ward	.30	.09
❑ 157 Jack Wilson	.30	.09
❑ 158 Jason Kendall	.30	.09
❑ 159 Kip Wells	.30	.09
❑ 160 Oliver Perez	.30	.09
❑ 161 Rob Mackowiak	.30	.09
❑ 162 Brian Giles	.30	.09
❑ 163 Brian Lawrence	.30	.09

#	Player	Nm-Mt	Ex-Mt
164	David Wells	.30	.09
165	Jay Payton	.30	.09
166	Ryan Klesko	.30	.09
167	Sean Burroughs	.30	.09
168	Trevor Hoffman	.30	.09
169	Brett Tomko	.30	.09
170	J.T. Snow	.30	.09
171	Jason Schmidt	.30	.09
172	Kirk Rueter	.30	.09
173	A.J. Pierzynski	.30	.09
174	Pedro Feliz	.30	.09
175	Ray Durham	.30	.09
176	Eddie Guardado	.30	.09
177	Edgar Martinez	.50	.15
178	Ichiro Suzuki	1.25	.35
179	Jamie Moyer	.30	.09
180	Joel Pineiro	.30	.09
181	Randy Winn	.30	.09
182	Raul Ibanez	.30	.09
183	Albert Pujols	1.50	.45
184	Edgar Renteria	.30	.09
185	Jason Isringhausen	.30	.09
186	Jim Edmonds	.30	.09
187	Matt Morris	.30	.09
188	Reggie Sanders	.30	.09
189	Tony Womack	.30	.09
190	Aubrey Huff	.30	.09
191	Danys Baez	.30	.09
192	Carl Crawford	.30	.09
193	Jose Cruz Jr.	.30	.09
194	Rocco Baldelli	.30	.09
195	Tino Martinez	.50	.15
196	Dewon Brazelton	.30	.09
197	Alfonso Soriano	.50	.15
198	Brad Fullmer	.30	.09
199	Gerald Laird	.30	.09
200	Hank Blalock	.30	.09
201	Laynce Nix	.30	.09
202	Mark Teixeira	.30	.09
203	Michael Young	.30	.09
204	Alexis Rios	.30	.09
205	Eric Hinske	.30	.09
206	Miguel Batista	.30	.09
207	Orlando Hudson	.30	.09
208	Roy Halladay	.30	.09
209	Ted Lilly	.30	.09
210	Vernon Wells	.30	.09
211	Aarom Baldiris SR	1.00	.30
212	B.J. Upton SR	1.50	.45
213	Dallas McPherson SR	1.50	.45
214	Brian Dallimore SR	1.00	.30
215	Chris Oxspring SR	1.00	.30
216	Chris Shelton SR	1.00	.30
217	David Wright SR	2.00	.60
218	Edwardo Sierra SR	1.00	.30
219	Fernando Nieve SR	1.00	.30
220	Frank Francisco SR	1.00	.30
221	Jeff Bennett SR	1.00	.30
222	Justin Lehr SR	1.00	.30
223	John Gall SR	1.00	.30
224	Jorge Sequea SR	1.00	.30
225	Justin Germano SR	1.00	.30
226	Kazuhito Tadano SR	1.00	.30
227	Kevin Cave SR	1.00	.30
228	Joe Blanton SR	1.00	.30
229	Luis A. Gonzalez SR	1.00	.30
230	Michael Wuertz SR	1.00	.30
231	Mike Rouse SR	1.00	.30
232	Nick Regilio SR	1.00	.30
233	Orlando Rodriguez SR	1.00	.30
234	Phil Stockman SR	1.00	.30
235	Ramon Ramirez SR	1.00	.30
236	Roberto Novoa SR	1.00	.30
237	Dioner Navarro SR	1.00	.30
238	Tim Bausher SR	1.00	.30
239	Logan Kensing SR	1.00	.30
240	Andy Green SR	1.00	.30
241	Brad Halsey SR	1.00	.30
242	Charles Thomas SR	1.00	.30
243	George Sherrill SR	1.00	.30
244	Jesse Crain SR	1.00	.30
245	Jimmy Serrano SR	1.00	.30
246	Joe Horgan SR	1.00	.30
247	Chris Young SR	1.00	.30
248	Joey Gathright SR	1.00	.30
249	Gavin Floyd SR	1.00	.30
250	Ryan Howard SR	1.00	.30
251	Lance Cormier SR	1.00	.30
252	Matt Treanor SR	1.00	.30
253	Jeff Francis SR	1.00	.30
254	Nick Swisher SR	1.50	.30
255	Scott Atchison SR	1.00	.30
256	Travis Blackley SR	1.00	.30
257	Travis Smith SR	1.00	.30
258	Yadier Molina SR	1.00	.30
259	Jeff Keppinger SR	1.00	.30
260	Scott Kazmir SR	1.50	.45
261	Garret Anderson	.50	.15
	Vladimir Guerrero TL		
262	Luis Gonzalez	.50	.15
	Randy Johnson TL		
263	Andruw Jones	.50	.15
	Chipper Jones TL		
264	Miguel Tejada	.30	.09
	Rafael Palmeiro TL		
265	Curt Schilling	.75	.23
	Manny Ramirez TL		
266	Mark Prior	.75	.23
	Sammy Sosa TL		
267	Frank Thomas	.50	.15
	Maggio Ordonez TL		
268	Barry Larkin	.75	.23
	Ken Griffey Jr. TL		
269	C.C. Sabathia	.30	.09
	Victor Martinez TL		
270	Jeromy Burnitz	.30	.09
	Todd Helton TL		
271	Dmitri Young	.50	.15
	Ivan Rodriguez TL		
272	Josh Beckett	.30	.09
	Miguel Cabrera TL		
273	Jeff Bagwell	.75	.23
	Roger Clemens TL		
274	Ken Harvey	.30	.09
	Mike Sweeney TL		
275	Adrian Beltre	.30	.09
	Eric Gagne TL		
276	Ben Sheets	.30	.09
	Geoff Jenkins TL		
277	Joe Mauer	.30	.09
	Torii Hunter TL		
278	Jose Vidro	.30	.09
	Livan Hernandez TL		
279	Kazuo Matsui	.75	.23
	Mike Piazza TL		
280	Alex Rodriguez	1.50	.45
	Derek Jeter TL		
281	Eric Chavez	.30	.09
	Tim Hudson TL		
282	Bobby Abreu	.50	.15
	Jim Thome TL		
283	Craig Wilson	.30	.09
	Jason Kendall TL		
284	Brian Giles	.30	.09
	Phil Nevin TL		
285	A.J. Pierzynski	.30	.09
	Jason Schmidt TL		
286	Bret Boone	.75	.23
	Ichiro Suzuki TL		
287	Albert Pujols	.75	.23
	Scott Rolen TL		
288	Aubrey Huff	.30	.09
	Tino Martinez TL		
289	Hank Blalock	.30	.09
	Mark Teixeira TL		
290	Carlos Delgado	.30	.09
	Roy Halladay TL		
291	Vladimir Guerrero PR	.50	.15
292	Curt Schilling PR	.50	.15
293	Mark Prior PR	.50	.15
294	Josh Beckett PR	.30	.09
295	Roger Clemens PR	.75	.23
296	Derek Jeter PR	.75	.23
297	Eric Chavez PR	.30	.09
298	Jim Thome PR	.50	.15
299	Albert Pujols PR	.75	.23
300	Hank Blalock PR	.30	.09

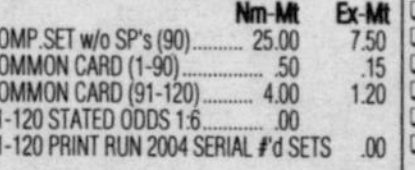

2004 Upper Deck Etchings

	Nm-Mt	Ex-Mt
COMP.SET w/o SP's (90)	25.00	7.50
COMMON CARD (1-90)	.50	.15
COMMON CARD (91-120)	4.00	1.20
91-120 STATED ODDS 1:6	.00	
91-120 PRINT RUN 2004 SERIAL #'d SETS		.00

	Nm-Mt	Ex-Mt
COMMON AUTO (121-150)	8.00	2.40
121-150 OVERALL AU ODDS 1:4		
121-150 PRINT RUN 700 SERIAL #'d SETS		

#	Player	Nm-Mt	Ex-Mt
1	Albert Pujols	2.50	.75
2	Torii Hunter	.50	.15
3	Jim Edmonds	.50	.15
4	Alex Rodriguez	2.00	.60
5	Rafael Palmeiro	.75	.23
6	Ken Griffey Jr.	2.00	.60
7	Adam Dunn	.75	.23
8	Andruw Jones	.50	.15
9	Carlos Lee	.50	.15
10	Mike Piazza	2.00	.60
11	Jeff Bagwell	.75	.23
12	Hideki Matsui	2.00	.60
13	Gary Sheffield	.50	.15
14	Edgar Renteria	.50	.15
15	Shawn Green	.50	.15
16	Kerry Wood	1.25	.35
17	Ivan Rodriguez	1.25	.35
18	Josh Beckett	.50	.15
19	Scott Rolen	1.25	.35
20	Brian Giles	.50	.15
21	Derrek Lee	.50	.15
22	Mike Lowell	.50	.15
23	Mike Mussina	.75	.23
24	Sammy Sosa	2.00	.60
25	Brandon Webb	.50	.15
26	Jacque Jones	.50	.15
27	Randy Johnson	1.25	.35
28	Luis Gonzalez	.50	.15
29	Eric Chavez	.50	.15
30	Carlos Delgado	.50	.15
31	Phil Nevin	.50	.15
32	Ichiro Suzuki	2.00	.60
33	Roy Oswalt	.50	.15
34	Tim Hudson	.50	.15
35	Juan Gonzalez	.75	.23
36	Frank Thomas	1.25	.35
37	Mark Mulder	.50	.15
38	Mark Teixeira	.50	.15
39	Miguel Tejada	.50	.15
40	Jeff Kent	.50	.15
41	Andy Pettitte	.75	.23
42	Barry Zito	.50	.15
43	Roy Halladay	.50	.15
44	Rocco Baldelli	.50	.15
45	Derek Jeter	2.50	.75
46	Corey Patterson	.50	.15
47	Javy Lopez	.50	.15
48	A.J. Burnett	.50	.15
49	Chipper Jones	1.25	.35
50	Curt Schilling	1.25	.35
51	Todd Helton	.75	.23
52	Pedro Martinez	1.25	.35
53	Hideo Nomo	1.25	.35
54	Jose Reyes	.50	.15
55	Vernon Wells	.50	.15
56	Geoff Jenkins	.50	.15
57	Troy Glaus	.50	.15
58	Greg Maddux	2.00	.60
59	Jason Schmidt	.50	.15
60	Preston Wilson	.50	.15
61	Miguel Cabrera	.75	.23
62	Hank Blalock	.50	.15
63	Rafael Furcal	.50	.15
64	Vladimir Guerrero	1.25	.35

❑ 65 Lance Berkman .50 .15
❑ 66 Javier Vazquez .50 .15
❑ 67 Bret Boone .50 .15
❑ 68 Mark Prior 1.25 .35
❑ 69 Magglio Ordonez .50 .15
❑ 70 Dontrelle Willis .50 .15
❑ 71 Richie Sexson .50 .15
❑ 72 Alfonso Soriano .75 .23
❑ 73 Edwin Jackson .50 .15
❑ 74 Jose Vidro .50 .15
❑ 75 Jason Giambi .50 .15
❑ 76 Kevin Brown .50 .15
❑ 77 Orlando Cabrera .50 .15
❑ 78 Nomar Garciaparra 2.00 .60
❑ 79 Bobby Abreu .50 .15
❑ 80 Manny Ramirez .75 .23
❑ 81 J.D. Drew .50 .15
❑ 82 Roger Clemens 2.50 .75
❑ 83 Pat Burrell .50 .15
❑ 84 Ryan Klesko .50 .15
❑ 85 Garret Anderson .50 .15
❑ 86 Johan Santana .75 .23
❑ 87 Kevin Millwood .50 .15
❑ 88 Austin Kearns .50 .15
❑ 89 Jim Thome 1.25 .35
❑ 90 Carlos Beltran .75 .23
❑ 91 Kazuo Matsui FE RC 8.00 2.40
❑ 92 Jamie Brown FE RC 4.00 1.20
❑ 93 Brandon Medders FE RC 4.00 1.20
❑ 94 Carlos Vasquez FE RC 5.00 1.50
❑ 95 Chris Aguila FE RC 4.00 1.20
❑ 96 David Aardsma FE RC 4.00 1.20
❑ 97 Justin Leone FE RC 5.00 1.50
❑ 98 Mike Johnston FE RC 4.00 1.20
❑ 99 Tim Bittner FE RC 4.00 1.20
❑ 100 Mike Rouse FE RC 4.00 1.20
❑ 101 Dennis Sarfate FE RC 4.00 1.20
❑ 102 Jason Frasor FE RC 4.00 1.20
❑ 103 Jorge Vasquez FE RC 4.00 1.20
❑ 104 Mike Gosling FE RC 4.00 1.20
❑ 105 Jake Woods FE RC 4.00 1.20
❑ 106 Akinori Otsuka FE RC 4.00 1.20
❑ 107 Lincoln Holdzkom FE RC 4.00 1.20
❑ 108 Jesse Harper FE RC 4.00 1.20
❑ 109 Edwin Moreno FE RC 4.00 1.20
❑ 110 Shingo Takatsu FE RC 5.00 1.50
❑ 111 Ryan Meaux FE RC 4.00 1.20
❑ 112 Donnie Kelly FE RC 4.00 1.20
❑ 113 Jerome Gamble FE RC 4.00 1.20
❑ 114 Josh Labandeira FE RC 4.00 1.20
❑ 115 Ian Snell FE RC 5.00 1.50
❑ 116 Michael Wuertz FE RC 5.00 1.50
❑ 117 Greg Dobbs FE RC 4.00 1.20
❑ 118 Sean Henn FE RC 4.00 1.20
❑ 119 Dave Crouthers FE RC 4.00 1.20
❑ 120 Hector Gimenez FE RC 4.00 1.20
❑ 121 Renyel Pinto FE AU RC 10.00 3.00
❑ 122 Tim Hamulack FE AU RC 8.00 2.40
❑ 123 Chris Saenz FE AU RC 8.00 2.40
❑ 124 Carlos Hines FE AU RC 8.00 2.40
❑ 125 Justin Knoedler FE AU RC 8.00 2.40
❑ 126 Onil Joseph FE AU RC 8.00 2.40
❑ 127 Ryan Wing FE AU RC 8.00 2.40
❑ 128 Scott Proctor FE AU RC 10.00 3.00
❑ 129 Rusty Tucker FE AU RC 10.00 3.00
❑ 130 Fernando Nieve FE AU RC 8.00 2.40
❑ 131 Chad Bentz FE AU RC 8.00 2.40
❑ 132 Jerry Gil FE AU RC 8.00 2.40
❑ 133 Mariano Gomez FE AU RC 8.00 2.40
❑ 134 Justin Germano FE AU RC 8.00 2.40
❑ 135 Jason Bartlett FE AU RC 10.00 3.00
❑ 136 Ronald Belisario FE AU RC 8.00 2.40
❑ 137 E.Pacheco FE AU RC 8.00 2.40
❑ 138 Justin Hampson FE AU RC 8.00 2.40
❑ 139 Mike Vento FE AU RC 10.00 3.00
❑ 140 Merkin Valdez FE AU RC 10.00 3.00
❑ 141 Casey Daigle FE AU RC 8.00 2.40
❑ 142 Eddy Rodriguez FE AU RC 10.00 3.00
❑ 143 William Bergolla FE AU RC 8.00 2.40
❑ 144 Jose Capellan FE AU RC 20.00 6.00
❑ 145 Ronny Cedeno FE AU RC 8.00 2.40
❑ 146 F.Gracesqui FE AU RC 8.00 2.40
❑ 147 Roman Colon FE AU RC 8.00 2.40
❑ 148 Roberto Novoa FE AU RC 10.00 3.00
❑ 149 Ivan Ochoa FE AU RC 8.00 2.40
❑ 150 Shawn Hill FE AU RC 8.00 2.40

2001 Upper Deck Evolution

	Nm-Mt	Ex-Mt
COMP.SET w/o SP's (90)	15.00	4.50
COMMON CARD (1-90)	.30	.09
COMMON CARD (91-120)	4.00	1.20

❑ 1 Darin Erstad .30 .09
❑ 2 Troy Glaus .30 .09
❑ 3 Jason Giambi .30 .09
❑ 4 Tim Hudson .30 .09
❑ 5 Jermaine Dye .30 .09
❑ 6 Barry Zito .50 .15
❑ 7 Carlos Delgado .30 .09
❑ 8 Shannon Stewart .30 .09
❑ 9 Jose Cruz Jr. .30 .09
❑ 10 Greg Vaughn .30 .09
❑ 11 Juan Gonzalez .50 .15
❑ 12 Roberto Alomar .50 .15
❑ 13 Omar Vizquel .50 .15
❑ 14 Jim Thome .75 .23
❑ 15 Edgar Martinez .50 .15
❑ 16 John Olerud .30 .09
❑ 17 Kazuhiro Sasaki .30 .09
❑ 18 Cal Ripken 2.50 .75
❑ 19 Alex Rodriguez 1.25 .35
❑ 20 Ivan Rodriguez .75 .23
❑ 21 Rafael Palmeiro .50 .15
❑ 22 Pedro Martinez .75 .23
❑ 23 Nomar Garciaparra 1.25 .35
❑ 24 Manny Ramirez .50 .15
❑ 25 Carl Everett .30 .09
❑ 26 Mark Quinn .30 .09
❑ 27 Mike Sweeney .30 .09
❑ 28 Neifi Perez .30 .09
❑ 29 Tony Clark .30 .09
❑ 30 Eric Milton .30 .09
❑ 31 Doug Mientkiewicz .30 .09
❑ 32 Corey Koskie .30 .09
❑ 33 Frank Thomas .75 .23
❑ 34 David Wells .30 .09
❑ 35 Magglio Ordonez .30 .09
❑ 36 Derek Jeter 2.00 .60
❑ 37 Mike Mussina .50 .15
❑ 38 Bernie Williams .50 .15
❑ 39 Roger Clemens 1.50 .45
❑ 40 David Justice .30 .09
❑ 41 Jeff Bagwell .50 .15
❑ 42 Richard Hidalgo .30 .09
❑ 43 Wade Miller .30 .09
❑ 44 Chipper Jones .75 .23
❑ 45 Greg Maddux 1.25 .35
❑ 46 Andruw Jones .30 .09
❑ 47 Rafael Furcal .30 .09
❑ 48 Geoff Jenkins .30 .09
❑ 49 Jeromy Burnitz .30 .09
❑ 50 Ben Sheets .50 .15
❑ 51 Richie Sexson .30 .09
❑ 52 Mark McGwire 2.00 .60
❑ 53 Jim Edmonds .30 .09
❑ 54 Darryl Kile .30 .09
❑ 55 J.D. Drew .30 .09
❑ 56 Sammy Sosa 1.25 .35
❑ 57 Kerry Wood .75 .23
❑ 58 Randy Johnson .75 .23
❑ 59 Luis Gonzalez .30 .09
❑ 60 Matt Williams .30 .09
❑ 61 Kevin Brown .30 .09
❑ 62 Gary Sheffield .30 .09
❑ 63 Shawn Green .30 .09
❑ 64 Chan Ho Park .30 .09
❑ 65 Vladimir Guerrero .75 .23
❑ 66 Jose Vidro .30 .09
❑ 67 Fernando Tatis .30 .09
❑ 68 Barry Bonds 2.00 .60
❑ 69 Jeff Kent .30 .09
❑ 70 Russ Ortiz .30 .09
❑ 71 Preston Wilson .30 .09
❑ 72 Ryan Dempster .30 .09
❑ 73 Charles Johnson .30 .09
❑ 74 Mike Piazza 1.25 .35
❑ 75 Edgardo Alfonzo .30 .09
❑ 76 Robin Ventura .30 .09
❑ 77 Jay Payton .30 .09
❑ 78 Tony Gwynn 1.00 .30
❑ 79 Phil Nevin .30 .09
❑ 80 Pat Burrell .30 .09
❑ 81 Scott Rolen .75 .23
❑ 82 Bob Abreu .30 .09
❑ 83 Brian Giles .30 .09
❑ 84 Jason Kendall .30 .09
❑ 85 Ken Griffey Jr. 1.25 .35
❑ 86 Barry Larkin .50 .15
❑ 87 Sean Casey .30 .09
❑ 88 Todd Helton .50 .15
❑ 89 Larry Walker .50 .15
❑ 90 Mike Hampton .30 .09
❑ 91 Ichiro Suzuki PROS RC 25.00 7.50
❑ 92 Albert Pujols PROS RC 40.00 12.00
❑ 93 W.Betemit PROS RC 4.00 1.20
❑ 94 Jay Gibbons PROS RC 5.00 1.50
❑ 95 Juan Uribe PROS RC 5.00 1.50
❑ 96 M. Ensberg PROS RC 5.00 1.50
❑ 97 C. Parker PROS RC 4.00 1.20
❑ 98 T. Shinjo PROS RC 5.00 1.50
❑ 99 Jack Wilson PROS RC 8.00 2.40
❑ 100 D. Mendez PROS RC 4.00 1.20
❑ 101 Ryan Freel PROS RC 4.00 1.20
❑ 102 Juan Diaz PROS RC 4.00 1.20
❑ 103 H. Ramirez PROS RC 5.00 1.50
❑ 104 R. Rodriguez PROS RC 4.00 1.20
❑ 105 E. Almonte PROS RC 4.00 1.20
❑ 106 J. Towers PROS RC 4.00 1.20
❑ 107 A.Hernandez PROS RC 4.00 1.20
❑ 108 B.Duckworth PROS RC 4.00 1.20
❑ 109 T. Hafner PROS RC 10.00 3.00
❑ 110 M. Vargas PROS RC 4.00 1.20
❑ 111 Kris Keller PROS RC 4.00 1.20
❑ 112 B. Lawrence PROS RC 4.00 1.20
❑ 113 Esix Snead PROS RC 4.00 1.20
❑ 114 Wilkin Ruan PROS RC 4.00 1.20
❑ 115 J. Mieses PROS RC 4.00 1.20
❑ 116 J. Estrada PROS RC 5.00 1.50
❑ 117 E. Guzman PROS RC 4.00 1.20
❑ 118 S. Douglass PROS RC 4.00 1.20
❑ 119 B. Sylvester PROS RC 4.00 1.20
❑ 120 Bret Prinz PROS RC 4.00 1.20

2003 Upper Deck Finite

	MINT	NRMT
COMMON CARD (1-100)	2.00	.90
COMMON CARD (101-150)	2.50	1.10
COMMON CARD (151-180)	4.00	1.80
COMMON CARD (181-200)	5.00	2.20

1-200 STATED ODDS TWO PER PACK		
COMMON CARD (201-300)	3.00	1.35
COMMON CARD (301-330)	5.00	2.20
301-330 PRINT RUN 599 SERIAL #'d SETS		
COMMON CARD (331-360)	10.00	4.50
331-360 PRINT RUN 299 SERIAL #'d SETS		
COMMON CARD (361-380)	15.00	6.75
361-380 PRINT RUN 150 SERIAL #'d SETS		
201-380/STARS 'N STRIPES ODDS 1:1		
❑ 1 Darin Erstad	2.00	.90
❑ 2 Garret Anderson	2.00	.90
❑ 3 Tim Salmon	2.50	1.10
❑ 4 Troy Glaus	2.00	.90
❑ 5 Luis Gonzalez	2.00	.90
❑ 6 Randy Johnson	2.50	1.10
❑ 7 Curt Schilling	2.00	.90
❑ 8 Andruw Jones	2.00	.90
❑ 9 Gary Sheffield	2.00	.90
❑ 10 Rafael Furcal	2.00	.90
❑ 11 Greg Maddux	4.00	1.80
❑ 12 Chipper Jones	2.50	1.10
❑ 13 Tony Batista	2.00	.90
❑ 14 Jay Gibbons	2.00	.90
❑ 15 Johnny Damon	2.50	1.10
❑ 16 Derek Lowe	2.00	.90
❑ 17 Nomar Garciaparra	4.00	1.80
❑ 18 Pedro Martinez	2.50	1.10
❑ 19 Manny Ramirez	2.50	1.10
❑ 20 Mark Prior	2.50	1.10
❑ 21 Kerry Wood	2.50	1.10
❑ 22 Corey Patterson	2.00	.90
❑ 23 Sammy Sosa	4.00	1.80
❑ 24 Moises Alou	2.00	.90
❑ 25 Maggiio Ordonez	2.00	.90
❑ 26 Frank Thomas	2.50	1.10
❑ 27 Paul Konerko	2.00	.90
❑ 28 Bartolo Colon	2.00	.90
❑ 29 Adam Dunn	2.50	1.10
❑ 30 Austin Kearns	2.00	.90
❑ 31 Aaron Boone	2.00	.90
❑ 32 Ken Griffey Jr.	4.00	1.80
❑ 33 Omar Vizquel	2.50	1.10
❑ 34 C.C. Sabathia	2.00	.90
❑ 35 Brandon Phillips	2.00	.90
❑ 36 Larry Walker	2.50	1.10
❑ 37 Preston Wilson	2.00	.90
❑ 38 Todd Helton	2.50	1.10
❑ 39 Eric Munson	2.00	.90
❑ 40 Ivan Rodriguez	2.50	1.10
❑ 41 Josh Beckett	2.00	.90
❑ 42 Roy Oswalt	2.00	.90
❑ 43 Craig Biggio	2.50	1.10
❑ 44 Jeff Bagwell	2.50	1.10
❑ 45 Dontrelle Willis	2.50	1.10
❑ 46 Carlos Beltran	2.50	1.10
❑ 47 Brent Mayne	2.00	.90
❑ 48 Hideo Nomo	2.50	1.10
❑ 49 Rickey Henderson	2.50	1.10
❑ 50 Adrian Beltre	2.50	1.10
❑ 51 Miguel Cabrera	2.50	1.10
❑ 52 Kazuhisa Ishii	2.00	.90
❑ 53 Richie Sexson	2.00	.90
❑ 54 Torii Hunter	2.00	.90
❑ 55 Jacque Jones	2.00	.90
❑ 56 A.J. Pierzynski	2.00	.90
❑ 57 Jose Vidro	2.00	.90
❑ 58 Vladimir Guerrero	2.50	1.10
❑ 59 Tom Glavine	2.50	1.10
❑ 60 Jose Reyes	2.00	.90
❑ 61 Mike Piazza	4.00	1.80
❑ 62 Jorge Posada	2.50	1.10
❑ 63 Mike Mussina	2.50	1.10
❑ 64 Robin Ventura	2.00	.90
❑ 65 Mariano Rivera	2.50	1.10
❑ 66 Roger Clemens	5.00	2.20
❑ 67 Jason Giambi	2.00	.90
❑ 68 Bernie Williams	2.50	1.10
❑ 69 Alfonso Soriano	2.50	1.10
❑ 70 Derek Jeter	6.00	2.70
❑ 71 Miguel Tejada	2.00	.90
❑ 72 Eric Chavez	2.00	.90
❑ 73 Tim Hudson	2.00	.90
❑ 74 Barry Zito	2.00	.90
❑ 75 Pat Burrell	2.00	.90
❑ 76 Jim Thome	2.50	1.10
❑ 77 Bobby Abreu	2.00	.90
❑ 78 Brian Giles	2.00	.90
❑ 79 Reggie Sanders	2.00	.90
❑ 80 Ryan Klesko	2.00	.90
❑ 81 Edgardo Alfonzo	2.00	.90
❑ 82 Rich Aurilia	2.00	.90
❑ 83 Barry Bonds	6.00	2.70
❑ 84 Mike Cameron	2.00	.90
❑ 85 Kazuhiro Sasaki	2.00	.90
❑ 86 Bret Boone	2.00	.90
❑ 87 Ichiro Suzuki	4.00	1.80
❑ 88 J.D. Drew	2.00	.90
❑ 89 Jim Edmonds	2.00	.90
❑ 90 Scott Rolen	2.50	1.10
❑ 91 Matt Morris	2.00	.90
❑ 92 Tino Martinez	2.50	1.10
❑ 93 Albert Pujols	5.00	2.20
❑ 94 Rocco Baldelli	2.00	.90
❑ 95 Hank Blalock	2.50	1.10
❑ 96 Alex Rodriguez	4.00	1.80
❑ 97 Rafael Palmeiro	2.50	1.10
❑ 98 Eric Hinske	2.00	.90
❑ 99 Orlando Hudson	2.00	.90
❑ 100 Carlos Delgado	2.00	.90
❑ 101 Albert Pujols MF	6.00	2.70
❑ 102 Alex Rodriguez MF	5.00	2.20
❑ 103 Alfonso Soriano MF	3.00	1.35
❑ 104 Andruw Jones MF	2.50	1.10
❑ 105 Barry Zito MF	2.50	1.10
❑ 106 Bernie Williams MF	3.00	1.35
❑ 107 Carlos Delgado MF	2.50	1.10
❑ 108 Chipper Jones MF	3.00	1.35
❑ 109 Curt Schilling MF	2.50	1.10
❑ 110 Doug Mientkiewicz MF	2.50	1.10
❑ 111 Frank Thomas MF	3.00	1.35
❑ 112 Garret Anderson MF	2.50	1.10
❑ 113 Gary Sheffield MF	2.50	1.10
❑ 114 Greg Maddux MF	5.00	2.20
❑ 115 Hank Blalock MF	3.00	1.35
❑ 116 Hideki Matsui MF	6.00	2.70
❑ 117 Hideo Nomo MF	3.00	1.35
❑ 118 Ichiro Suzuki MF	5.00	2.20
❑ 119 Ivan Rodriguez MF	3.00	1.35
❑ 120 Jason Giambi MF	2.50	1.10
❑ 121 Jeff Bagwell MF	3.00	1.35
❑ 122 Jeff Kent MF	2.50	1.10
❑ 123 Jerome Williams MF	2.50	1.10
❑ 124 Jeromy Burnitz MF	2.50	1.10
❑ 125 Jim Thome MF	3.00	1.35
❑ 126 Jose Cruz Jr. MF	2.50	1.10
❑ 127 Ken Griffey Jr. MF	5.00	2.20
❑ 128 Kerry Wood MF	3.00	1.35
❑ 129 Lance Berkman MF	2.50	1.10
❑ 130 Luis Gonzalez MF	2.50	1.10
❑ 131 Manny Ramirez MF	3.00	1.35
❑ 132 Mark Prior MF	3.00	1.35
❑ 133 Miguel Cabrera MF	3.00	1.35
❑ 134 Miguel Tejada MF	2.50	1.10
❑ 135 Mike Piazza MF	5.00	2.20
❑ 136 Pat Burrell MF	2.50	1.10
❑ 137 Pedro Martinez MF	3.00	1.35
❑ 138 Rafael Furcal MF	2.50	1.10
❑ 139 Randy Johnson MF	3.00	1.35
❑ 140 Rich Harden MF	3.00	1.35
❑ 141 Rickey Henderson MF	3.00	1.35
❑ 142 Roberto Alomar MF	3.00	1.35
❑ 143 Roger Clemens MF	6.00	2.70
❑ 144 Sammy Sosa MF	5.00	2.20
❑ 145 Shawn Green MF	2.50	1.10
❑ 146 Todd Helton MF	3.00	1.35
❑ 147 Tom Glavine MF	3.00	1.35
❑ 148 Torii Hunter MF	2.50	1.10
❑ 149 Troy Glaus MF	2.50	1.10
❑ 150 Vladimir Guerrero MF	3.00	1.35
❑ 151 Adam Dunn PP	5.00	2.20
❑ 152 Albert Pujols PP	10.00	4.50
❑ 153 Alex Rodriguez PP	8.00	3.60
❑ 154 Alfonso Soriano PP	5.00	2.20
❑ 155 Andruw Jones PP	4.00	1.80
❑ 156 Barry Bonds PP	12.00	5.50
❑ 157 Carlos Delgado PP	4.00	1.80
❑ 158 Chipper Jones PP	5.00	2.20
❑ 159 Derek Jeter PP	12.00	5.50
❑ 160 Gary Sheffield PP	4.00	1.80
❑ 161 Hank Blalock PP	5.00	2.20
❑ 162 Hideki Matsui PP	10.00	4.50
❑ 163 Ichiro Suzuki PP	8.00	3.60
❑ 164 J.D. Drew PP	4.00	1.80
❑ 165 Jason Giambi PP	4.00	1.80
❑ 166 Jeff Bagwell PP	5.00	2.20
❑ 167 Jeff Kent PP	4.00	1.80
❑ 168 Jim Edmonds PP	4.00	1.80
❑ 169 Jim Thome PP	5.00	2.20
❑ 170 Ken Griffey Jr. PP	8.00	3.60
❑ 171 Luis Gonzalez PP	4.00	1.80
❑ 172 Maggiio Ordonez PP	4.00	1.80
❑ 173 Manny Ramirez PP	5.00	2.20
❑ 174 Mike Lowell PP	4.00	1.80
❑ 175 Mike Piazza PP	8.00	3.60
❑ 176 Nomar Garciaparra PP	8.00	3.60
❑ 177 Rafael Palmeiro PP	5.00	2.20
❑ 178 Shawn Green PP	4.00	1.80
❑ 179 Troy Glaus PP	4.00	1.80
❑ 180 Vladimir Guerrero PP	5.00	2.20
❑ 181 Albert Pujols FC	12.00	5.50
❑ 182 Alex Rodriguez FC	10.00	4.50
❑ 183 Alfonso Soriano FC	6.00	2.70
❑ 184 Bernie Williams FC	6.00	2.70
❑ 185 Chipper Jones FC	6.00	2.70
❑ 186 Derek Jeter FC	15.00	6.75
❑ 187 Hideki Matsui FC	12.00	5.50
❑ 188 Ichiro Suzuki FC	10.00	4.50
❑ 189 Jim Thome FC	6.00	2.70
❑ 190 Joe DiMaggio FC	10.00	4.50
❑ 191 Ken Griffey Jr. FC	10.00	4.50
❑ 192 Mickey Mantle FC	20.00	9.00
❑ 193 Mike Piazza FC	10.00	4.50
❑ 194 Pedro Martinez FC	6.00	2.70
❑ 195 Randy Johnson FC	6.00	2.70
❑ 196 Roger Clemens FC	12.00	5.50
❑ 197 Sammy Sosa FC	10.00	4.50
❑ 198 Ted Williams FC	10.00	4.50
❑ 199 Troy Glaus FC	5.00	2.20
❑ 200 Vladimir Guerrero FC	6.00	2.70
❑ 201 Aaron Looper T1 RC	3.00	1.35
❑ 202 Alejandro Machado T1 RC	3.00	1.35
❑ 203 Alfredo Gonzalez T1 RC	3.00	1.35
❑ 204 Andrew Brown T1 RC	5.00	2.20
❑ 205 Anthony Ferrari T1 RC	3.00	1.35
❑ 206 Aquilino Lopez T1 RC	3.00	1.35
❑ 207 Beau Kemp T1 RC	3.00	1.35
❑ 208 Bernie Castro T1 RC	3.00	1.35
❑ 209 Bobby Madritsch T1 RC	15.00	6.75
❑ 210 Brandon Villafuerte T1	3.00	1.35
❑ 211 Brent Hoard T1 RC	3.00	1.35
❑ 212 Brian Stokes T1 RC	3.00	1.35
❑ 213 Carlos Mendez T1 RC	3.00	1.35
❑ 214 Chris Capuano T1 RC	3.00	1.35
❑ 215 Chris Waters T1 RC	3.00	1.35
❑ 216 Clint Barmes T1 RC	5.00	2.20
❑ 217 Colin Porter T1 RC	3.00	1.35
❑ 218 Cory Stewart T1 RC	3.00	1.35
❑ 219 Craig Brazell T1 RC	5.00	2.20
❑ 220 D.J. Carrasco T1 RC	3.00	1.35
❑ 221 Daniel Cabrera T1 RC	6.00	2.70
❑ 222 David Matranga T1 RC	3.00	1.35
❑ 223 David Sanders T1 RC	3.00	1.35
❑ 224 Diegomar Markwell T1 RC	3.00	1.35
❑ 225 Edgar Gonzalez T1 RC	3.00	1.35
❑ 226 Felix Sanchez T1 RC	3.00	1.35
❑ 227 Fernando Cabrera T1 RC	3.00	1.35
❑ 228 Francisco Cruceta T1 RC	3.00	1.35
❑ 229 Francisco Rosario T1 RC	3.00	1.35
❑ 230 Garrett Atkins T1	3.00	1.35
❑ 231 Gerald Laird T1	3.00	1.35
❑ 232 Guillermo Quiroz T1 RC	5.00	2.20
❑ 233 Heath Bell T1 RC	3.00	1.35
❑ 234 Delmon Young T1 RC	10.00	4.50
❑ 235 Jason Shiell T1 RC	3.00	1.35
❑ 236 Jeremy Bonderman T1 RC	5.00	2.20
❑ 237 Jeremy Griffiths T1 RC	5.00	2.20
❑ 238 Jeremy Guthrie T1	3.00	1.35
❑ 239 Jeremy Wedel T1 RC	3.00	1.35
❑ 240 Carlos Rivera T1	3.00	1.35
❑ 241 Joe Valentine T1 RC	3.00	1.35
❑ 242 Jon Leicester T1 RC	3.00	1.35
❑ 243 Jon Pridie T1 RC	3.00	1.35
❑ 244 Jorge Cordova T1 RC	3.00	1.35
❑ 245 Jose Castillo T1	3.00	1.35
❑ 246 Josh Hall T1 RC	5.00	2.20
❑ 247 Josh Stewart T1 RC	3.00	1.35
❑ 248 Josh Willingham T1 RC	5.00	2.20

❑ 249 Julio Manon T1 RC 3.00 1.35
❑ 250 Kevin Correia T1 RC 3.00 1.35
❑ 251 Kevin Ohme T1 RC 3.00 1.35
❑ 252 Kevin Tolar T1 RC 3.00 1.35
❑ 253 Luis De Los Santos T1 3.00 1.35
❑ 254 Jermaine Clark T1 3.00 1.35
❑ 255 Mark Malaska T1 RC 3.00 1.35
❑ 256 Juan Dominguez T1 3.00 1.35
❑ 257 Michael Hessman T1 RC 3.00 1.35
❑ 258 Michael Nakamura T1 RC 3.00 1.35
❑ 259 Miguel Ojeda T1 RC 3.00 1.35
❑ 260 Mike Gallo T1 RC 3.00 1.35
❑ 261 Edwin Jackson T1 RC 8.00 3.60
❑ 262 Mike Ryan T1 RC 5.00 2.20
❑ 263 Nate Bland T1 RC 3.00 1.35
❑ 264 Nate Robertson T1 RC 8.00 3.60
❑ 265 Nook Logan T1 RC 3.00 1.35
❑ 266 Phil Seibel T1 RC 3.00 1.35
❑ 267 Prentice Redman T1 RC 3.00 1.35
❑ 268 Rafael Betancourt T1 RC 5.00 2.20
❑ 269 Rett Johnson T1 RC 5.00 2.20
❑ 270 Richard Fischer T1 RC 3.00 1.35
❑ 271 Rick Roberts T1 RC 3.00 1.35
❑ 272 Roger Deago T1 RC 3.00 1.35
❑ 273 Ryan Cameron T1 RC 3.00 1.35
❑ 274 Shane Bazzell T1 RC 3.00 1.35
❑ 275 Erasmo Ramirez T1 3.00 1.35
❑ 276 Termel Sledge T1 RC 5.00 2.20
❑ 277 Tim Olson T1 RC 5.00 2.20
❑ 278 Tommy Phelps T1 3.00 1.35
❑ 279 Tommy Whiteman T1 3.00 1.35
❑ 280 Willie Eyre T1 RC 3.00 1.35
❑ 281 Alex Prieto T1 RC 3.00 1.35
❑ 282 Michel Hernandez T1 RC 3.00 1.35
❑ 283 Greg Jones T1 RC 3.00 1.35
❑ 284 Victor Martinez T1 5.00 2.20
❑ 285 Tom Gregorio T1 RC 3.00 1.35
❑ 286 Marcus Thames T1 3.00 1.35
❑ 287 Jorge DePaula T1 3.00 1.35
❑ 288 Aaron Miles T1 RC 5.00 2.20
❑ 289 Reynaldo Garcia T1 3.00 1.35
❑ 290 Brian Sweeney T1 RC 3.00 1.35
❑ 291 Pete LaForest T1 RC 5.00 2.20
❑ 292 Pete Zoccolillo T1 RC 3.00 1.35
❑ 293 Danny Garcia T1 RC 3.00 1.35
❑ 294 Jonny Gomes T1 3.00 1.35
❑ 295 Rosman Garcia T1 RC 3.00 1.35
❑ 296 Mike Edwards T1 3.00 1.35
❑ 297 Marlon Byrd T1 3.00 1.35
❑ 298 Khalil Greene T1 10.00 4.50
❑ 299 Jose Valverde T1 3.00 1.35
❑ 300 Drew Henson T1 3.00 1.35
❑ 301 Chris Bootcheck T2 5.00 2.20
❑ 302 Matt Belisle T2 5.00 2.20
❑ 303 Kevin Gregg T2 5.00 2.20
❑ 304 Bobby Jenks T2 5.00 2.20
❑ 305 Jason Young T2 5.00 2.20
❑ 306 Laynce Nix T2 5.00 2.20
❑ 307 Robb Quinlan T2 5.00 2.20
❑ 308 Chase Utley T2 5.00 2.20
❑ 309 Humberto Quintero T2 RC 5.00 2.20
❑ 310 Tim Raines Jr. T2 5.00 2.20
❑ 311 Stephen Smitherman T2 5.00 2.20
❑ 312 Jason Anderson T2 5.00 2.20
❑ 313 Joe Dawley T2 5.00 2.20
❑ 314 Chad Cordero T2 RC 5.00 2.20
❑ 315 Victor Alvarez T2 5.00 2.20
❑ 316 Jimmy Gobble T2 5.00 2.20
❑ 317 Jared Fernandez T2 5.00 2.20
❑ 318 Eric Bruntlett T2 5.00 2.20
❑ 319 Neal Cotts T2 5.00 2.20
❑ 320 Ryan Madson T2 5.00 2.20
❑ 321 Rocco Baldelli T2 5.00 2.20
❑ 322 Graham Koonce T2 RC 8.00 3.60
❑ 323 Bobby Crosby T2 8.00 3.60
❑ 324 Mike Wood T2 5.00 2.20
❑ 325 Jesse Garcia T2 5.00 2.20
❑ 326 Noah Lowry T2 8.00 3.60
❑ 327 Edwin Almonte T2 5.00 2.20
❑ 328 Justin Morneau T2 8.00 3.60
❑ 329 Steve Colyer T2 5.00 2.20
❑ 330 Vinnie Chulk T2 5.00 2.20
❑ 331 Brian Schmack T3 RC 10.00 4.50
❑ 332 Stephen Randolph T3 RC 10.00 4.50
❑ 333 Pedro Feliciano T3 RC 15.00 6.75
❑ 334 Koyie Hill T3 10.00 4.50
❑ 335 Geoff Geary T3 RC 10.00 4.50
❑ 336 Jon Switzer T3 10.00 4.50
❑ 337 Xavier Nady T3 10.00 4.50
❑ 338 Rich Harden T3 15.00 6.75
❑ 339 Dontrelle Willis T3 15.00 6.75
❑ 340 Angel Berroa T3 10.00 4.50
❑ 341 Jerome Williams T3 10.00 4.50
❑ 342 Brandon Claussen T3 10.00 4.50
❑ 343 Kurt Ainsworth T3 10.00 4.50
❑ 344 Horacio Ramirez T3 10.00 4.50
❑ 345 Hee Seop Choi T3 10.00 4.50
❑ 346 Billy Traber T3 10.00 4.50
❑ 347 Brandon Phillips T3 10.00 4.50
❑ 348 Jody Gerut T3 10.00 4.50
❑ 349 Mark Teixeira T3 10.00 4.50
❑ 350 Javier Lopez T3 RC 10.00 4.50
❑ 351 Miguel Cabrera T3 15.00 6.75
❑ 352 Brad Lidge T3 10.00 4.50
❑ 353 Mike MacDougal T3 10.00 4.50
❑ 354 Ken Harvey T3 10.00 4.50
❑ 355 Chien-Ming Wang T3 RC 25.00 11.00
❑ 356 Aaron Heilman T3 10.00 4.50
❑ 357 Jason Phillips T3 10.00 4.50
❑ 358 Jason Bay T3 10.00 4.50
❑ 359 Arnie Munoz T3 RC 10.00 4.50
❑ 360 Ian Ferguson T3 RC 10.00 4.50
❑ 361 Ryan Wagner T4 RC 20.00 9.00
❑ 362 Rickie Weeks T4 RC 50.00 22.00
❑ 363 Chad Gaudin T4 RC 15.00 6.75
❑ 364 Jason Gilfillan T4 RC 15.00 6.75
❑ 365 Jason Roach T4 RC 15.00 6.75
❑ 366 Jhonny Peralta T4 15.00 6.75
❑ 367 Mike Neu T4 RC 15.00 6.75
❑ 368 Jose Contreras T4 RC 20.00 9.00
❑ 369 Wilfredo Ledezma T4 RC 20.00 9.00
❑ 370 Lew Ford T4 RC 20.00 9.00
❑ 371 Luis Ayala T4 RC 15.00 6.75
❑ 372 Bo Hart T4 RC 20.00 9.00
❑ 373 Brandon Webb T4 RC 20.00 9.00
❑ 374 Dan Haren T4 RC 20.00 9.00
❑ 375 Hideki Matsui T4 RC 40.00 18.00
❑ 376 Jeff Duncan T4 RC 20.00 9.00
❑ 377 Matt Kata T4 RC 20.00 9.00
❑ 378 Oscar Villarreal T4 RC 15.00 6.75
❑ 379 Rob Hammock T4 RC 20.00 9.00
❑ 380 Todd Wellemeyer T4 RC 20.00 9.00

2003 Upper Deck Game Face

	Nm-Mt	Ex-Mt
COMP.SET w/o SP's (90)	25.00	7.50
COMMON CARD (1-120)	.50	.15
COMMON SP (1-120)	4.00	1.20
COMMON CARD (121-150)	4.00	1.20
COMMON CARD (151-171)	5.00	1.50
COMMON CARD (172-192)	5.00	1.50
COMMON CARD (193-217)	8.00	2.40

193-217 RANDOM IN FINITE BONUS PACKS
193-217 PRINT RUN 299 SERIAL #'d SETS

❑ 1 Darin Erstad .50 .15
❑ 2 Garret Anderson .50 .15
❑ 3 Tim Salmon .75 .23
❑ 4 Jarrod Washburn .50 .15
❑ 5 Troy Glaus SP 4.00 1.20
❑ 6 Luis Gonzalez .50 .15
❑ 7 Junior Spivey .50 .15
❑ 8 Randy Johnson SP 5.00 1.50
❑ 9 Curt Schilling SP 4.00 1.20
❑ 10 Andruw Jones .50 .15
❑ 11 Gary Sheffield .50 .15
❑ 12 Rafael Furcal .50 .15
❑ 13 Greg Maddux SP 8.00 2.40
❑ 14 Chipper Jones SP 5.00 1.50
❑ 15 Tony Batista .50 .15
❑ 16 Rodrigo Lopez .50 .15
❑ 17 Jay Gibbons .50 .15
❑ 18 Shea Hillenbrand .50 .15
❑ 19 Johnny Damon 1.25 .35
❑ 20 Derek Lowe .50 .15
❑ 21 Nomar Garciaparra 2.00 .60
❑ 22 Pedro Martinez SP 5.00 1.50
❑ 23 Manny Ramirez SP 5.00 1.50
❑ 24 Mark Prior 1.25 .35
❑ 25 Kerry Wood 1.25 .35
❑ 26 Corey Patterson .50 .15
❑ 27 Sammy Sosa SP 8.00 2.40
❑ 28 Magglio Ordonez .50 .15
❑ 29 Frank Thomas 1.25 .35
❑ 30 Paul Konerko .50 .15
❑ 31 Adam Dunn .75 .23
❑ 32 Austin Kearns .50 .15
❑ 33 Aaron Boone .50 .15
❑ 34 Ken Griffey Jr. SP 8.00 2.40
❑ 35 Omar Vizquel .75 .23
❑ 36 C.C. Sabathia .50 .15
❑ 37 Karim Garcia SP 4.00 1.20
❑ 38 Larry Walker .75 .23
❑ 39 Preston Wilson .50 .15
❑ 40 Jay Payton .50 .15
❑ 41 Todd Helton SP 5.00 1.50
❑ 42 Carlos Pena .50 .15
❑ 43 Eric Munson .50 .15
❑ 44 Mike Lowell .50 .15
❑ 45 Josh Beckett .50 .15
❑ 46 A.J. Burnett .50 .15
❑ 47 Roy Oswalt .50 .15
❑ 48 Craig Biggio .75 .23
❑ 49 Jeff Bagwell SP 5.00 1.50
❑ 50 Lance Berkman SP 4.00 1.20
❑ 51 Mike Sweeney .50 .15
❑ 52 Carlos Beltran .75 .23
❑ 53 Hideo Nomo 1.25 .35
❑ 54 Odalis Perez .50 .15
❑ 55 Adrian Beltre .75 .23
❑ 56 Shawn Green SP 4.00 1.20
❑ 57 Kazuhisa Ishii SP 4.00 1.20
❑ 58 Ben Sheets .50 .15
❑ 59 Richie Sexson .50 .15
❑ 60 Torii Hunter .50 .15
❑ 61 Jacque Jones .50 .15
❑ 62 Eric Milton .50 .15
❑ 63 Corey Koskie .50 .15
❑ 64 A.J. Pierzynski .50 .15
❑ 65 Jose Vidro .50 .15
❑ 66 Bartolo Colon .50 .15
❑ 67 Vladimir Guerrero SP 5.00 1.50
❑ 68 Tom Glavine .75 .23
❑ 69 Mike Piazza SP 8.00 2.40
❑ 70 Roberto Alomar SP 5.00 1.50
❑ 71 Jorge Posada .75 .23
❑ 72 Mike Mussina .75 .23
❑ 73 Robin Ventura .50 .15
❑ 74 Raul Mondesi .50 .15
❑ 75 Roger Clemens SP UER 10.00 3.00
Card mistakenly numbered as 79
❑ 76 Jason Giambi SP 4.00 1.20
❑ 77 Bernie Williams SP 5.00 1.50
❑ 78 Alfonso Soriano SP 5.00 1.50
❑ 79 Derek Jeter SP 12.00 3.60
❑ 80 Miguel Tejada .50 .15
❑ 81 Eric Chavez .50 .15
❑ 82 Tim Hudson .50 .15
❑ 83 Barry Zito .50 .15
❑ 84 Mark Mulder .50 .15
❑ 85 Pat Burrell .50 .15
❑ 86 Jim Thome 1.25 .35
❑ 87 Bobby Abreu .50 .15
❑ 88 Brian Giles .50 .15
❑ 89 Jason Kendall .50 .15
❑ 90 Aramis Ramirez .50 .15
❑ 91 Ryan Klesko .50 .15
❑ 92 Phil Nevin .50 .15

❑ 93 Sean Burroughs .... .50 .15
❑ 94 J.T. Snow .... .50 .15
❑ 95 Rich Aurilia .... .50 .15
❑ 96 Benito Santiago.................. .50 .15
❑ 97 Barry Bonds SP............ 12.00 3.60
❑ 98 Edgar Martinez .... .75 .23
❑ 99 John Olerud .... .50 .15
❑ 100 Bret Boone .... .50 .15
❑ 101 Ichiro Suzuki SP 8.00 2.40
❑ 102 J.D. Drew .... .50 .15
❑ 103 Jim Edmonds .... .50 .15
❑ 104 Scott Rolen .... 1.25 .35
❑ 105 Matt Morris .... .50 .15
❑ 106 Tino Martinez .... .75 .23
❑ 107 Albert Pujols SP 10.00 3.00
❑ 108 Aubrey Huff .... .50 .15
❑ 109 Carl Crawford .... .50 .15
❑ 110 Rafael Palmeiro .... .75 .23
❑ 111 Hank Blalock .... .75 .23
❑ 112 Alex Rodriguez SP.......... 8.00 2.40
❑ 113 Kevin Mench SP 4.00 1.20
❑ 114 Juan Gonzalez SP 5.00 1.50
❑ 115 Shannon Stewart .... .50 .15
❑ 116 Vernon Wells..................... .50 .15
❑ 117 Josh Phelps .... .50 .15
❑ 118 Eric Hinske .... .50 .15
❑ 119 Orlando Hudson .... .50 .15
❑ 120 Carlos Delgado SP 4.00 1.20
❑ 121 David Sanders FF RC 4.00 1.20
❑ 122 Rob Hammock FF RC 5.00 1.50
❑ 123 Rett Johnson FF RC 5.00 1.50
❑ 124 Mike Nicolas FF RC 4.00 1.20
❑ 125 Terrmel Sledge FF RC 5.00 1.50
❑ 126 Ryan Cameron FF RC 4.00 1.20
❑ 127 Prentice Redman FF RC 4.00 1.20
❑ 128 Clint Barmes FF RC........ 5.00 1.50
❑ 129 Brent Hoard FF RC 4.00 1.20
❑ 130 Willie Eyre FF RC 4.00 1.20
❑ 131 Phil Seibel FF RC 4.00 1.20
❑ 132 Chris Capuano FF RC 4.00 1.20
❑ 133 Bobby Madritsch FF RC 10.00 3.00
❑ 134 Shane Bazzell FF RC 4.00 1.20
❑ 135 Jeremy Griffiths FF RC .. 5.00 1.50
❑ 136 Jon Leicester FF RC 4.00 1.20
❑ 137 Brandon Webb FF RC 5.00 1.50
❑ 138 Todd Wellemeyer FF RC 5.00 1.50
❑ 139 Jose Contreras FF RC 5.00 1.50
❑ 140 Felix Sanchez FF RC 4.00 1.20
❑ 141 Arnie Munoz FF RC........ 4.00 1.20
❑ 142 Delvis Lantigua FF RC.... 4.00 1.20
❑ 143 Francisco Cruceta FF RC 4.00 1.20
❑ 144 Josh Willingham FF RC 5.00 1.50
❑ 145 Oscar Villarreal FF RC.... 4.00 1.20
❑ 146 Ian Ferguson FF RC 4.00 1.20
❑ 147 Pedro Liriano FF 4.00 1.20
❑ 148 Lew Ford FF RC 5.00 1.50
❑ 149 Jeff Duncan FF RC 5.00 1.50
❑ 150 Rich Fischer FF RC 4.00 1.20
❑ 151 Troy Glaus GF 5.00 1.50
❑ 152 Randy Johnson GF 8.00 2.40
❑ 153 Hideki Matsui GF RC.... 15.00 4.50
❑ 154 Chipper Jones GF 8.00 2.40
❑ 155 Nomar Garciaparra GF.. 15.00 4.50
❑ 156 Pedro Martinez GF 8.00 2.40
❑ 157 Ted Williams GF 20.00 6.00
❑ 158 Sammy Sosa GF 15.00 4.50
❑ 159 Ken Griffey Jr. GF 15.00 4.50
❑ 160 Vladimir Guerrero GF 8.00 2.40
❑ 161 Mike Piazza GF 12.00 3.60
❑ 162 Mickey Mantle GF........ 40.00 12.00
❑ 163 Alfonso Soriano GF........ 8.00 2.40
❑ 164 Derek Jeter GF............. 20.00 6.00
❑ 165 Roger Clemens GF 15.00 4.50
❑ 166 Jason Giambi GF........... 5.00 1.50
❑ 167 Barry Bonds GF........... 20.00 6.00
❑ 168 Ichiro Suzuki GF 12.00 3.60
❑ 169 Albert Pujols GF 15.00 4.50
❑ 170 Mark McGwire GF........ 20.00 6.00
❑ 171 Alex Rodriguez GF........ 12.00 3.60
❑ 172 Roy Oswalt 15.00 4.50
Ken Griffey Jr.
❑ 173 Barry Zito 5.00 1.50
Troy Glaus
❑ 174 Tim Hudson 15.00 4.50
Ichiro Suzuki
❑ 175 Mark Mulder 15.00 4.50
Alex Rodriguez
❑ 176 Tom Glavine 8.00 2.40
Vladimir Guerrero
❑ 177 Greg Maddux 15.00 4.50
Mike Piazza
❑ 178 Mark McGwire............. 30.00 9.00
Sammy Sosa
❑ 179 Mark Prior...................... 8.00 2.40
Lance Berkman
❑ 180 Kerry Wood 15.00 4.50
Albert Pujols
❑ 181 Randy Johnson 8.00 2.40
Jeff Bagwell
❑ 182 Curt Schilling 20.00 6.00
Derek Jeter
❑ 183 Hideo Nomo 20.00 6.00
Barry Bonds
❑ 184 Kazuhisa Ishii 5.00 1.50
Todd Helton
❑ 185 Freddy Garcia 5.00 1.50
Eric Chavez
❑ 186 Al Leiter........................ 8.00 2.40
Chipper Jones
❑ 187 Ted Williams............... 20.00 6.00
Nomar Garciaparra
❑ 188 Pedro Martinez 15.00 4.50
Hideki Matsui
❑ 189 Derek Lowe 8.00 2.40
Bernie Williams
❑ 190 Roger Clemens 20.00 6.00
Mike Piazza
❑ 191 Mike Mussina 8.00 2.40
Manny Ramirez
❑ 192 Mickey Mantle............ 30.00 9.00
Jason Giambi
❑ 193 Aaron Looper FF RC 8.00 2.40
❑ 194 Alex Prieto FF RC 8.00 2.40
❑ 195 Bo Hart FF RC 10.00 3.00
❑ 196 Chad Gaudin FF RC 8.00 2.40
❑ 197 Colin Porter FF RC 8.00 2.40
❑ 198 D.J. Carrasco FF RC 8.00 2.40
❑ 199 Dan Haren FF RC 10.00 3.00
❑ 200 Delmon Young FF RC .. 25.00 7.50
❑ 201 Dontrelle Willis FF 10.00 3.00
❑ 202 Jon Switzer FF................ 8.00 2.40
❑ 203 Edwin Jackson FF RC .. 20.00 6.00
❑ 204 Fernando Cabrera FF RC 8.00 2.40
❑ 205 Garrett Atkins FF 8.00 2.40
❑ 206 Jeremy Bonderman FF RC 10.00 3.00
❑ 207 Kevin Ohme FF RC 8.00 2.40
❑ 208 Khalil Greene FF 20.00 6.00
❑ 209 Luis Ayala FF RC............ 8.00 2.40
❑ 210 Matt Kata FF RC 10.00 3.00
❑ 211 Noah Lowry FF 10.00 3.00
❑ 212 Rich Harden FF 10.00 3.00
❑ 213 Rickie Weeks FF RC 20.00 6.00
❑ 214 Rosman Garcia FF RC.... 8.00 2.40
❑ 215 Ryan Wagner FF RC 10.00 3.00
❑ 216 Tom Gregorio FF RC 8.00 2.40
❑ 217 Wilfredo Ledezma FF RC 10.00 3.00
❑ NNO Ken Griffey Jr. Sample.. 5.00 1.50

2001 Upper Deck Gold Glove

	Nm-Mt	Ex-Mt
COMP.SET w/o SP'S (90)	15.00	4.50
COMMON CARD (1-90)...............	.60	.18
COMMON CARD (91-129).........	5.00	1.50
COMMON (130-135)	10.00	3.00

❑ 1 Troy Glaus............................ .60 .18
❑ 2 Darin Erstad .... .60 .18
❑ 3 Jason Giambi .... .60 .18
❑ 4 Tim Hudson .... .60 .18
❑ 5 Jermaine Dye .... .60 .18
❑ 6 Raul Mondesi .... .60 .18
❑ 7 Carlos Delgado .... .60 .18
❑ 8 Shannon Stewart .... .60 .18
❑ 9 Greg Vaughn .... .60 .18
❑ 10 Aubrey Huff .... .60 .18
❑ 11 Juan Gonzalez .... 1.00 .30
❑ 12 Roberto Alomar .... 1.00 .30
❑ 13 Omar Vizquel.................... 1.00 .30
❑ 14 Jim Thome .... 1.50 .45
❑ 15 John Olerud .... .60 .18
❑ 16 Edgar Martinez .... 1.00 .30
❑ 17 Kazuhiro Sasaki.................. .60 .18
❑ 18 Aaron Sele............................ .60 .18
❑ 19 Cal Ripken........................ 5.00 1.50
❑ 20 Chris Richard .... .60 .18
❑ 21 Ivan Rodriguez .... 1.50 .45
❑ 22 Rafael Palmeiro .... 1.00 .30
❑ 23 Alex Rodriguez .... 2.50 .75
❑ 24 Pedro Martinez .... 1.50 .45
❑ 25 Nomar Garciaparra .... 2.50 .75
❑ 26 Manny Ramirez .... 1.00 .30
❑ 27 Neifi Perez .... .60 .18
❑ 28 Mike Sweeney .... .60 .18
❑ 29 Bobby Higginson .... .60 .18
❑ 30 Dean Palmer .... .60 .18
❑ 31 Tony Clark .... .60 .18
❑ 32 Doug Mientkiewicz .... .60 .18
❑ 33 Brad Radke .... .60 .18
❑ 34 Joe Mays.............................. .60 .18
❑ 35 Frank Thomas .... 1.50 .45
❑ 36 Magglio Ordonez................. .60 .18
❑ 37 Carlos Lee........................... .60 .18
❑ 38 Bernie Williams................. 1.00 .30
❑ 39 Mike Mussina .... 1.00 .30
❑ 40 Derek Jeter 4.00 1.20
❑ 41 Roger Clemens .... 3.00 .90
❑ 42 Craig Biggio .... 1.00 .30
❑ 43 Jeff Bagwell .... 1.00 .30
❑ 44 Lance Berkman .... .60 .18
❑ 45 Andruw Jones .... .60 .18
❑ 46 Greg Maddux .... 2.50 .75
❑ 47 Chipper Jones.................. 1.50 .45
❑ 48 Geoff Jenkins .... .60 .18
❑ 49 Ben Sheets .... 1.00 .30
❑ 50 Jeromy Burnitz .... .60 .18
❑ 51 Jim Edmonds .... .60 .18
❑ 52 Mark McGwire.................. 4.00 1.20
❑ 53 Mike Matheny .... .60 .18
❑ 54 J.D. Drew .... .60 .18
❑ 55 Sammy Sosa.................... 2.50 .75
❑ 56 Kerry Wood .... 1.50 .45
❑ 57 Fred McGriff .... 1.00 .30
❑ 58 Randy Johnson .... 1.50 .45
❑ 59 Steve Finley......................... .60 .18
❑ 60 Mark Grace .... 1.00 .30
❑ 61 Matt Williams .... .60 .18
❑ 62 Luis Gonzalez .... .60 .18
❑ 63 Shawn Green....................... .60 .18
❑ 64 Kevin Brown .... .60 .18
❑ 65 Gary Sheffield .... .60 .18
❑ 66 Vladimir Guerrero .... 1.50 .45
❑ 67 Tony Armas Jr. .... .60 .18
❑ 68 Barry Bonds 4.00 1.20
❑ 69 J.T. Snow .... .60 .18
❑ 70 Jeff Kent .... .60 .18
❑ 71 Charles Johnson .... .60 .18
❑ 72 Preston Wilson .... .60 .18
❑ 73 Cliff Floyd .... .60 .18
❑ 74 Robin Ventura .... .60 .18
❑ 75 Mike Piazza .... 2.50 .75
❑ 76 Edgardo Alfonzo .... .60 .18
❑ 77 Tony Gwynn .... 2.00 .60
❑ 78 Ryan Klesko .... .60 .18
❑ 79 Scott Rolen .... 1.50 .45
❑ 80 Mike Lieberthal .... .60 .18
❑ 81 Pat Burrell .... .60 .18
❑ 82 Jason Kendall .... .60 .18
❑ 83 Brian Giles .... .60 .18

❑ 84 Ken Griffey Jr. 2.50 .75
❑ 85 Barry Larkin 1.00 .30
❑ 86 Pokey Reese .60 .18
❑ 87 Larry Walker 1.00 .30
❑ 88 Mike Hampton .60 .18
❑ 89 Juan Pierre .60 .18
❑ 90 Todd Helton 1.00 .30
❑ 91 Mike Penney GD RC 5.00 1.50
❑ 92 Wilkin Ruan GD RC 5.00 1.50
❑ 93 Greg Miller GD RC 5.00 1.50
❑ 94 Johnny Estrada GD RC 8.00 2.40
❑ 95 Tsuyoshi Shinjo GD RC 8.00 2.40
❑ 96 Josh Towers GD RC 5.00 1.50
❑ 97 H. Ramirez GD RC 8.00 2.40
❑ 98 Ryan Freel GD RC 5.00 1.50
❑ 99 M. Ensberg GD RC 8.00 2.40
❑ 100 A. Hernandez GD RC 5.00 1.50
❑ 101 Juan Uribe GD RC 8.00 2.40
❑ 102 Jose Mieses GD RC 5.00 1.50
❑ 103 Jack Wilson GD RC 8.00 2.40
❑ 104 Cesar Crespo GD RC 5.00 1.50
❑ 105 Bud Smith GD RC 5.00 1.50
❑ 106 Erick Almonte GD RC 5.00 1.50
❑ 107 E. Guzman GD RC 5.00 1.50
❑ 108 B. Duckworth GD RC 5.00 1.50
❑ 109 Juan Diaz GD RC 5.00 1.50
❑ 110 Kris Keller GD RC 5.00 1.50
❑ 111 J. Michaels GD RC 5.00 1.50
❑ 112 Bret Prinz GD RC 5.00 1.50
❑ 113 Henry Mateo GD RC 5.00 1.50
❑ 114 R. Rodriguez GD RC 5.00 1.50
❑ 115 Travis Hafner GD RC 10.00 3.00
❑ 116 Nate Teut GD RC 5.00 1.50
❑ 117 Alexis Gomez GD RC 5.00 1.50
❑ 118 Billy Sylvester GD RC 5.00 1.50
❑ 119 A. Pettyjohn GD RC 5.00 1.50
❑ 120 Josh Fogg GD RC 5.00 1.50
❑ 121 Juan Cruz GD RC 5.00 1.50
❑ 122 C. Valderrama GD RC 5.00 1.50
❑ 123 Jay Gibbons GD RC 8.00 2.40
❑ 124 D. Mendez GD RC 5.00 1.50
❑ 125 Bill Ortega GD RC 5.00 1.50
❑ 126 Sean Douglass GD RC 5.00 1.50
❑ 127 C. Parker GD RC 5.00 1.50
❑ 128 Grant Balfour GD RC 5.00 1.50
❑ 129 Joe Kennedy GD RC 8.00 2.40
❑ 130 Albert Pujols GD RC 80.00 24.00
❑ 131 W. Betemit GD RC 10.00 3.00
❑ 132 Mark Teixeira GD RC 30.00 9.00
❑ 133 Mark Prior GD RC 50.00 15.00
❑ 134 D. Brazelton GD RC 15.00 4.50
❑ 135 Ichiro Suzuki GD RC 50.00 15.00

2001 Upper Deck MVP

	Nm-Mt	Ex-Mt
COMPLETE SET (330)	40.00	12.00

❑ 1 Mo Vaughn .20 .06
❑ 2 Troy Percival .20 .06
❑ 3 Adam Kennedy .20 .06
❑ 4 Darin Erstad .20 .06
❑ 5 Tim Salmon .30 .09
❑ 6 Bengie Molina .20 .06
❑ 7 Troy Glaus .20 .06
❑ 8 Garret Anderson .20 .06
❑ 9 Ismael Valdes .20 .06
❑ 10 Glenallen Hill .20 .06
❑ 11 Tim Hudson .20 .06
❑ 12 Eric Chavez .20 .06
❑ 13 Johnny Damon .30 .09
❑ 14 Barry Zito .30 .09
❑ 15 Jason Giambi .20 .06
❑ 16 Terrence Long .20 .06
❑ 17 Jason Hart .20 .06
❑ 18 Jose Ortiz .20 .06
❑ 19 Miguel Tejada .20 .06
❑ 20 Jason Isringhausen .20 .06
❑ 21 Adam Piatt .20 .06
❑ 22 Jeremy Giambi .20 .06
❑ 23 Tony Batista .20 .06
❑ 24 Darrin Fletcher .20 .06
❑ 25 Mike Sirotka .20 .06
❑ 26 Carlos Delgado .20 .06
❑ 27 Billy Koch .20 .06
❑ 28 Shannon Stewart .20 .06
❑ 29 Raul Mondesi .20 .06
❑ 30 Brad Fullmer .20 .06
❑ 31 Jose Cruz Jr. .20 .06
❑ 32 Kelvim Escobar .20 .06
❑ 33 Greg Vaughn .20 .06
❑ 34 Aubrey Huff .20 .06
❑ 35 Albie Lopez .20 .06
❑ 36 Gerald Williams .20 .06
❑ 37 Ben Grieve .20 .06
❑ 38 John Flaherty .20 .06
❑ 39 Fred McGriff .30 .09
❑ 40 Ryan Rupe .20 .06
❑ 41 Travis Harper .20 .06
❑ 42 Steve Cox .20 .06
❑ 43 Roberto Alomar .30 .09
❑ 44 Jim Thome .50 .15
❑ 45 Russell Branyan .20 .06
❑ 46 Bartolo Colon .20 .06
❑ 47 Omar Vizquel .30 .09
❑ 48 Travis Fryman .20 .06
❑ 49 Kenny Lofton .20 .06
❑ 50 Chuck Finley .20 .06
❑ 51 Ellis Burks .20 .06
❑ 52 Eddie Taubensee .20 .06
❑ 53 Juan Gonzalez .30 .09
❑ 54 Edgar Martinez .30 .09
❑ 55 Aaron Sele .20 .06
❑ 56 John Olerud .20 .06
❑ 57 Jay Buhner .20 .06
❑ 58 Mike Cameron .20 .06
❑ 59 John Halama .20 .06
❑ 60 Ichiro Suzuki RC 10.00 3.00
❑ 61 David Bell .20 .06
❑ 62 Freddy Garcia .20 .06
❑ 63 Carlos Guillen .20 .06
❑ 64 Bret Boone .20 .06
❑ 65 Al Martin .20 .06
❑ 66 Cal Ripken 1.50 .45
❑ 67 Delino DeShields .20 .06
❑ 68 Chris Richard .20 .06
❑ 69 Sean Douglass RC .50 .15
❑ 70 Melvin Mora .20 .06
❑ 71 Luis Matos .20 .06
❑ 72 Sidney Ponson .20 .06
❑ 73 Mike Bordick .20 .06
❑ 74 Brady Anderson .20 .06
❑ 75 David Segui .20 .06
❑ 76 Jeff Conine .20 .06
❑ 77 Alex Rodriguez .75 .23
❑ 78 Gabe Kapler .20 .06
❑ 79 Ivan Rodriguez .50 .15
❑ 80 Rick Helling .20 .06
❑ 81 Kenny Rogers .20 .06
❑ 82 Andres Galarraga .20 .06
❑ 83 Rusty Greer .20 .06
❑ 84 Justin Thompson .20 .06
❑ 85 Ken Caminiti .20 .06
❑ 86 Rafael Palmeiro .30 .09
❑ 87 Ruben Mateo .20 .06
❑ 88 Travis Hafner RC 1.50 .45
❑ 89 Manny Ramirez .30 .09
❑ 90 Pedro Martinez .50 .15
❑ 91 Carl Everett .20 .06
❑ 92 Dante Bichette .20 .06
❑ 93 Derek Lowe .20 .06
❑ 94 Jason Varitek .30 .09
❑ 95 Nomar Garciaparra .75 .23
❑ 96 David Cone .20 .06
❑ 97 Tomokazu Ohka .20 .06
❑ 98 Troy O'Leary .20 .06
❑ 99 Trot Nixon .20 .06
❑ 100 Jermaine Dye .20 .06
❑ 101 Joe Randa .20 .06
❑ 102 Jeff Suppan .20 .06
❑ 103 Roberto Hernandez .20 .06
❑ 104 Mike Sweeney .20 .06
❑ 105 Mac Suzuki .20 .06
❑ 106 Carlos Febles .20 .06
❑ 107 Jose Rosado .20 .06
❑ 108 Mark Quinn .20 .06
❑ 109 Carlos Beltran .30 .09
❑ 110 Dean Palmer .20 .06
❑ 111 Mitch Meluskey .20 .06
❑ 112 Bobby Higginson .20 .06
❑ 113 Brandon Inge .20 .06
❑ 114 Tony Clark .20 .06
❑ 115 Brian Moehler .20 .06
❑ 116 Juan Encarnacion .20 .06
❑ 117 Damion Easley .20 .06
❑ 118 Roger Cedeno .20 .06
❑ 119 Jeff Weaver .20 .06
❑ 120 Matt Lawton .20 .06
❑ 121 Jay Canizaro .20 .06
❑ 122 Eric Milton .20 .06
❑ 123 Corey Koskie .20 .06
❑ 124 Mark Redman .20 .06
❑ 125 Jacque Jones .20 .06
❑ 126 Brad Radke .20 .06
❑ 127 Cristian Guzman .20 .06
❑ 128 Joe Mays .20 .06
❑ 129 Denny Hocking .20 .06
❑ 130 Frank Thomas .50 .15
❑ 131 David Wells .20 .06
❑ 132 Ray Durham .20 .06
❑ 133 Paul Konerko .20 .06
❑ 134 Joe Crede .20 .06
❑ 135 Jim Parque .20 .06
❑ 136 Carlos Lee .20 .06
❑ 137 Magglio Ordonez .20 .06
❑ 138 Sandy Alomar Jr. .20 .06
❑ 139 Chris Singleton .20 .06
❑ 140 Jose Valentin .20 .06
❑ 141 Roger Clemens 1.00 .30
❑ 142 Derek Jeter 1.25 .35
❑ 143 Orlando Hernandez .20 .06
❑ 144 Tino Martinez .30 .09
❑ 145 Bernie Williams .30 .09
❑ 146 Jorge Posada .30 .09
❑ 147 Mariano Rivera .30 .09
❑ 148 David Justice .20 .06
❑ 149 Paul O'Neill .30 .09
❑ 150 Mike Mussina .30 .09
❑ 151 Christian Parker RC .50 .15
❑ 152 Andy Pettitte .30 .09
❑ 153 Alfonso Soriano .30 .09
❑ 154 Jeff Bagwell .30 .09
❑ 155 Morgan Ensberg RC .75 .23
❑ 156 Daryle Ward .20 .06
❑ 157 Craig Biggio .30 .09
❑ 158 Richard Hidalgo .20 .06
❑ 159 Shane Reynolds .20 .06
❑ 160 Scott Elarton .20 .06
❑ 161 Julio Lugo .20 .06
❑ 162 Moises Alou .20 .06
❑ 163 Lance Berkman .20 .06
❑ 164 Chipper Jones .50 .15
❑ 165 Greg Maddux .75 .23
❑ 166 Javy Lopez .20 .06
❑ 167 Andruw Jones .20 .06
❑ 168 Rafael Furcal .20 .06
❑ 169 Brian Jordan .20 .06
❑ 170 Wes Helms .20 .06
❑ 171 Tom Glavine .30 .09
❑ 172 B.J. Surhoff .20 .06
❑ 173 John Smoltz .30 .09
❑ 174 Quilvio Veras .20 .06
❑ 175 Rico Brogna .20 .06
❑ 176 Jeromy Burnitz .20 .06
❑ 177 Jeff D'Amico .20 .06
❑ 178 Geoff Jenkins .20 .06
❑ 179 Henry Blanco .20 .06
❑ 180 Mark Loretta .20 .06
❑ 181 Richie Sexson .20 .06
❑ 182 Jimmy Haynes .20 .06

❑ 183 Jeffrey Hammonds .20 .06
❑ 184 Ron Belliard .20 .06
❑ 185 Tyler Houston .20 .06
❑ 186 Mark McGwire 1.25 .35
❑ 187 Rick Ankiel .20 .06
❑ 188 Darryl Kile .20 .06
❑ 189 Jim Edmonds .20 .06
❑ 190 Mike Matheny .20 .06
❑ 191 Edgar Renteria .20 .06
❑ 192 Ray Lankford .20 .06
❑ 193 Garrett Stephenson .20 .06
❑ 194 J.D. Drew .20 .06
❑ 195 Fernando Vina .20 .06
❑ 196 Dustin Hermanson .20 .06
❑ 197 Sammy Sosa .75 .23
❑ 198 Corey Patterson .20 .06
❑ 199 Jon Lieber .20 .06
❑ 200 Kerry Wood .50 .15
❑ 201 Todd Hundley .20 .06
❑ 202 Kevin Tapani .20 .06
❑ 203 Rondell White .20 .06
❑ 204 Eric Young .20 .06
❑ 205 Matt Stairs .20 .06
❑ 206 Bill Mueller .20 .06
❑ 207 Randy Johnson .50 .15
❑ 208 Mark Grace .30 .09
❑ 209 Jay Bell .20 .06
❑ 210 Curt Schilling .20 .06
❑ 211 Erubiel Durazo .20 .06
❑ 212 Luis Gonzalez .20 .06
❑ 213 Steve Finley .20 .06
❑ 214 Matt Williams .20 .06
❑ 215 Reggie Sanders .20 .06
❑ 216 Tony Womack .20 .06
❑ 217 Gary Sheffield .20 .06
❑ 218 Kevin Brown .20 .06
❑ 219 Adrian Beltre .30 .09
❑ 220 Shawn Green .20 .06
❑ 221 Darren Dreifort .20 .06
❑ 222 Chan Ho Park .20 .06
❑ 223 Eric Karros .20 .06
❑ 224 Alex Cora .20 .06
❑ 225 Mark Grudzielanek .20 .06
❑ 226 Andy Ashby .20 .06
❑ 227 Vladimir Guerrero .50 .15
❑ 228 Tony Armas Jr. .20 .06
❑ 229 Fernando Tatis .20 .06
❑ 230 Jose Vidro .20 .06
❑ 231 Javier Vazquez .20 .06
❑ 232 Lee Stevens .20 .06
❑ 233 Milton Bradley .20 .06
❑ 234 Carl Pavano .20 .06
❑ 235 Peter Bergeron .20 .06
❑ 236 Wilton Guerrero .20 .06
❑ 237 Ugueth Urbina .20 .06
❑ 238 Barry Bonds 1.25 .35
❑ 239 Livan Hernandez .20 .06
❑ 240 Jeff Kent .20 .06
❑ 241 Pedro Feliz .20 .06
❑ 242 Bobby Estalella .20 .06
❑ 243 J.T. Snow .20 .06
❑ 244 Shawn Estes .20 .06
❑ 245 Robb Nen .20 .06
❑ 246 Rich Aurilia .20 .06
❑ 247 Russ Ortiz .20 .06
❑ 248 Preston Wilson .20 .06
❑ 249 Brad Penny .20 .06
❑ 250 Cliff Floyd .20 .06
❑ 251 A.J. Burnett .20 .06
❑ 252 Mike Lowell .20 .06
❑ 253 Luis Castillo .20 .06
❑ 254 Ryan Dempster .20 .06
❑ 255 Derrek Lee .20 .06
❑ 256 Charles Johnson .20 .06
❑ 257 Pablo Ozuna .20 .06
❑ 258 Antonio Alfonseca .20 .06
❑ 259 Mike Piazza .75 .23
❑ 260 Robin Ventura .20 .06
❑ 261 Al Leiter .20 .06
❑ 262 Timo Perez .20 .06
❑ 263 Edgardo Alfonzo .20 .06
❑ 264 Jay Payton .20 .06
❑ 265 Tsuyoshi Shinjo RC .50 .15
❑ 266 Todd Zeile .20 .06
❑ 267 Armando Benitez .20 .06
❑ 268 Glendon Rusch .20 .06
❑ 269 Rey Ordonez .20 .06
❑ 270 Kevin Appier .20 .06
❑ 271 Tony Gwynn .60 .18
❑ 272 Phil Nevin .20 .06
❑ 273 Mark Kotsay .20 .06
❑ 274 Ryan Klesko .20 .06
❑ 275 Adam Eaton .20 .06
❑ 276 Mike Darr .20 .06
❑ 277 Damian Jackson .20 .06
❑ 278 Woody Williams .20 .06
❑ 279 Chris Gomez .20 .06
❑ 280 Trevor Hoffman .20 .06
❑ 281 Xavier Nady .20 .06
❑ 282 Scott Rolen .50 .15
❑ 283 Bruce Chen .20 .06
❑ 284 Pat Burrell .20 .06
❑ 285 Mike Lieberthal .20 .06
❑ 286 B. Duckworth RC .50 .15
❑ 287 Travis Lee .20 .06
❑ 288 Bobby Abreu .20 .06
❑ 289 Jimmy Rollins .20 .06
❑ 290 Robert Person .20 .06
❑ 291 Randy Wolf .20 .06
❑ 292 Jason Kendall .20 .06
❑ 293 Derek Bell .20 .06
❑ 294 Brian Giles .20 .06
❑ 295 Kris Benson .20 .06
❑ 296 John VanderWal .20 .06
❑ 297 Todd Ritchie .20 .06
❑ 298 Warren Morris .20 .06
❑ 299 Kevin Young .20 .06
❑ 300 Francisco Cordova .20 .06
❑ 301 Aramis Ramirez .20 .06
❑ 302 Ken Griffey Jr. .75 .23
❑ 303 Pete Harnisch .20 .06
❑ 304 Aaron Boone .20 .06
❑ 305 Sean Casey .20 .06
❑ 306 Jackson Melian RC .50 .15
❑ 307 Rob Bell .20 .06
❑ 308 Barry Larkin .30 .09
❑ 309 Dmitri Young .20 .06
❑ 310 Danny Graves .20 .06
❑ 311 Pokey Reese .20 .06
❑ 312 Leo Estrella .20 .06
❑ 313 Todd Helton .30 .09
❑ 314 Mike Hampton .20 .06
❑ 315 Juan Pierre .20 .06
❑ 316 Brent Mayne .20 .06
❑ 317 Larry Walker .30 .09
❑ 318 Denny Neagle .20 .06
❑ 319 Jeff Cirillo .20 .06
❑ 320 Pedro Astacio .20 .06
❑ 321 Todd Hollandsworth .20 .06
❑ 322 Neifi Perez .20 .06
❑ 323 Ron Gant .20 .06
❑ 324 Todd Walker .20 .06
❑ 325 Alex Rodriguez CL .50 .15
❑ 326 Ken Griffey Jr. CL .50 .15
❑ 327 Mark McGwire CL .60 .18
❑ 328 Pedro Martinez CL .30 .09
❑ 329 Derek Jeter CL .60 .18
❑ 330 Mike Piazza CL .50 .15

2001 Upper Deck Ovation

	Nm-Mt	Ex-Mt
COMP.SET w/o SP'S (60)	20.00	6.00
COMMON CARD (1-60)	.40	.12
COMMON WP (61-90)	5.00	1.50

❑ 1 Troy Glaus .40 .12
❑ 2 Darin Erstad .40 .12
❑ 3 Jason Giambi .40 .12
❑ 4 Tim Hudson .40 .12
❑ 5 Eric Chavez .40 .12
❑ 6 Carlos Delgado .40 .12
❑ 7 David Wells .40 .12
❑ 8 Greg Vaughn .40 .12
❑ 9 Omar Vizquel .60 .18
Travis Fryman is pictured on card front
UER
❑ 10 Jim Thome 1.00 .30
❑ 11 Roberto Alomar .60 .18
❑ 12 John Olerud .40 .12
❑ 13 Edgar Martinez .60 .18
❑ 14 Cal Ripken 3.00 .90
❑ 15 Alex Rodriguez 1.50 .45
❑ 16 Ivan Rodriguez 1.00 .30
❑ 17 Manny Ramirez .60 .18
❑ 18 Nomar Garciaparra 1.50 .45
❑ 19 Pedro Martinez 1.00 .30
❑ 20 Jermaine Dye .40 .12
❑ 21 Juan Gonzalez .60 .18
❑ 22 Matt Lawton .40 .12
❑ 23 Frank Thomas 1.00 .30
❑ 24 Magglio Ordonez .40 .12
❑ 25 Bernie Williams .60 .18
❑ 26 Derek Jeter 2.50 .75
❑ 27 Roger Clemens 2.00 .60
❑ 28 Jeff Bagwell .60 .18
❑ 29 Richard Hidalgo .40 .12
❑ 30 Chipper Jones 1.00 .30
❑ 31 Greg Maddux 1.50 .45
❑ 32 Andruw Jones .40 .12
❑ 33 Jeromy Burnitz .40 .12
❑ 34 Mark McGwire 2.50 .75
❑ 35 Jim Edmonds .40 .12
❑ 36 Sammy Sosa 1.50 .45
❑ 37 Kerry Wood 1.00 .30
❑ 38 Randy Johnson 1.00 .30
❑ 39 Steve Finley .40 .12
❑ 40 Gary Sheffield .40 .12
❑ 41 Kevin Brown .40 .12
❑ 42 Shawn Green .40 .12
❑ 43 Vladimir Guerrero 1.00 .30
❑ 44 Jose Vidro .40 .12
❑ 45 Barry Bonds 2.50 .75
❑ 46 Jeff Kent .40 .12
❑ 47 Preston Wilson .40 .12
❑ 48 Luis Castillo .40 .12
❑ 49 Mike Piazza 1.50 .45
❑ 50 Edgardo Alfonzo .40 .12
❑ 51 Tony Gwynn 1.25 .35
❑ 52 Ryan Klesko .40 .12
❑ 53 Scott Rolen 1.00 .30
❑ 54 Bob Abreu .40 .12
❑ 55 Jason Kendall .40 .12
❑ 56 Brian Giles .40 .12
❑ 57 Ken Griffey Jr. 1.50 .45
❑ 58 Barry Larkin .60 .18
❑ 59 Todd Helton .60 .18
❑ 60 Mike Hampton .40 .12
❑ 61 Corey Patterson WP 5.00 1.50
❑ 62 Timo Perez WP 5.00 1.50
❑ 63 Toby Hall WP 5.00 1.50
❑ 64 Brandon Inge WP 5.00 1.50
❑ 65 Joe Crede WP 5.00 1.50
❑ 66 Xavier Nady WP 5.00 1.50
❑ 67 A. Pettyjohn WP RC 5.00 1.50
❑ 68 Keith Ginter WP 5.00 1.50
❑ 69 Brian Cole WP 5.00 1.50
❑ 70 Tyler Walker WP RC 5.00 1.50
❑ 71 Juan Uribe WP RC 5.00 1.50
❑ 72 Alex Hernandez WP 5.00 1.50
❑ 73 Leo Estrella WP 5.00 1.50
❑ 74 Joey Nation WP 5.00 1.50
❑ 75 Aubrey Huff WP 5.00 1.50
❑ 76 Ichiro Suzuki WP RC 80.00 24.00
❑ 77 Jay Spurgeon WP 5.00 1.50
❑ 78 Sun Woo Kim WP 5.00 1.50
❑ 79 Pedro Feliz WP 5.00 1.50
❑ 80 Pablo Ozuna WP 5.00 1.50
❑ 81 Hiram Bocachica WP 5.00 1.50

❑ 82 Brad Wilkerson WP 5.00 1.50
❑ 83 Rocky Biddle WP 5.00 1.50
❑ 84 Aaron McNeal WP 5.00 1.50
❑ 85 Adam Bernero WP 5.00 1.50
❑ 86 Danys Baez WP 5.00 1.50
❑ 87 Dee Brown WP 5.00 1.50
❑ 88 Jimmy Rollins WP 5.00 1.50
❑ 89 Jason Hart WP 5.00 1.50
❑ 90 Ross Gload WP 5.00 1.50

2004 Upper Deck Play Ball

	Nm-Mt	Ex-Mt
COMP.SET w/o SP's (132)	25.00	7.50
COMP.UPDATE SET (50)	20.00	6.00
COMMON ACTIVE (1-132)	.30	.09
COMMON RETIRED (1-132)	.40	.12
COMMON CARD (133-162)	4.00	1.20
COMMON CARD (163-183)	4.00	1.20
163-183 STATED ODDS 1:24		
163-183 PRINT RUN 1999 SERIAL #'d SETS		
COMMON CARD (183-232)	.40	.12
ONE UPDATE SET PER 4 UD2 HOBBY BOXES		

❑ 1 Hideo Nomo .... .75 .23
❑ 2 Curt Schilling .... .75 .23
❑ 3 Barry Zito .... .30 .09
❑ 4 Nomar Garciaparra .... 1.25 .35
❑ 5 Yogi Berra .... 1.00 .30
❑ 6 Randy Johnson .... .75 .23
❑ 7 Jason Giambi .... .30 .09
❑ 8 Sammy Sosa .... 1.25 .35
❑ 9 David Ortiz .... .75 .23
❑ 10 Derek Jeter .... 1.50 .45
❑ 11 Warren Spahn .... .60 .18
❑ 12 Mark Prior .... .75 .23
❑ 13 Roger Clemens .... 1.50 .45
❑ 14 Mike Piazza .... 1.25 .35
❑ 15 Nolan Ryan .... 2.50 .75
❑ 16 Joe DiMaggio .... 2.00 .60
❑ 17 Alfonso Soriano .... .50 .15
❑ 18 Brandon Webb .... .30 .09
❑ 19 Shawn Green .... .30 .09
❑ 20 Bob Feller .... .40 .12
❑ 21 Mike Schmidt .... 2.00 .60
❑ 22 Mark Teixeira .... .30 .09
❑ 23 Pedro Martinez .... .75 .23
❑ 24 Vladimir Guerrero .... .75 .23
❑ 25 Rafael Furcal .... .30 .09
❑ 26 Derrek Lee .... .30 .09
❑ 27 Carlos Delgado .... .30 .09
❑ 28 Mickey Mantle 5.00 1.50
❑ 29 Dontrelle Willis .... .30 .09
❑ 30 Ted Williams .... 2.50 .75
❑ 31 Vernon Wells .... .30 .09
❑ 32 Alex Rodriguez Yanks .... 1.25 .35
❑ 33 Brooks Robinson .... .60 .18
❑ 34 Tom Seaver .... .60 .18
❑ 35 Ernie Banks .... 1.00 .30
❑ 36 Bob Gibson .... .60 .18
❑ 37 Jim Thome .... .75 .23
❑ 38 Mike Mussina .... .50 .15
❑ 39 Eric Chavez .... .30 .09
❑ 40 Roy Halladay .... .30 .09
❑ 41 Eric Gagne .... .75 .23
❑ 42 Jose Reyes .... .30 .09
❑ 43 Jeff Bagwell .... .50 .15
❑ 44 Rich Harden .... .30 .09
❑ 45 Jeff Kent .... .30 .09
❑ 46 Lance Berkman .... .30 .09
❑ 47 Adam Dunn .... .50 .15
❑ 48 Richie Sexson .... .30 .09
❑ 49 Andruw Jones .... .30 .09
❑ 50 Ichiro Suzuki .... 1.25 .35
❑ 51 Edgar Renteria .... .30 .09
❑ 52 Rocco Baldelli .... .30 .09
❑ 53 Jim Edmonds .... .30 .09
❑ 54 Magglio Ordonez .... .30 .09
❑ 55 Austin Kearns .... .30 .09
❑ 56 Garret Anderson .... .30 .09
❑ 57 Manny Ramirez .... .50 .15
❑ 58 Roy Oswalt .... .30 .09
❑ 59 Gary Sheffield .... .30 .09
❑ 60 Mark Mulder .... .30 .09
❑ 61 Ben Sheets .... .30 .09
❑ 62 Scott Rolen .... .75 .23
❑ 63 Greg Maddux .... 1.25 .35
❑ 64 Jose Contreras .... .30 .09
❑ 65 Miguel Cabrera .... .50 .15
❑ 66 Hank Blalock .... .30 .09
❑ 67 Miguel Tejada .... .30 .09
❑ 68 Albert Pujols .... 1.50 .45
❑ 69 Hideki Matsui .... 1.25 .35
❑ 70 Mike Lowell .... .30 .09
❑ 71 Tim Hudson .... .30 .09
❑ 72 Bret Boone .... .30 .09
❑ 73 Ivan Rodriguez .... .75 .23
❑ 74 Josh Beckett .... .30 .09
❑ 75 Todd Helton .... .50 .15
❑ 76 Brian Giles .... .30 .09
❑ 77 Orlando Cabrera .... .30 .09
❑ 78 Carlos Beltran .... .50 .15
❑ 79 Jason Schmidt .... .30 .09
❑ 80 Kerry Wood .... .75 .23
❑ 81 Preston Wilson .... .30 .09
❑ 82 Troy Glaus .... .30 .09
❑ 83 Kevin Brown .... .30 .09
❑ 84 Rafael Palmeiro .... .50 .15
❑ 85 Chipper Jones .... .75 .23
❑ 86 Reggie Sanders .... .30 .09
❑ 87 Cliff Floyd .... .30 .09
❑ 88 Corey Patterson .... .30 .09
❑ 89 Kevin Millwood .... .30 .09
❑ 90 Aaron Boone .... .30 .09
❑ 91 Darin Erstad .... .30 .09
❑ 92 Richard Hidalgo .... .30 .09
❑ 93 Dmitri Young .... .30 .09
❑ 94 Jeremy Bonderman .... .30 .09
❑ 95 Larry Walker .... .50 .15
❑ 96 Edgar Martinez .... .50 .15
❑ 97 Jerome Williams .... .30 .09
❑ 98 Luis Gonzalez .... .30 .09
❑ 99 Roberto Alomar .... .50 .15
❑ 100 Jerry Hairston Jr. .... .30 .09
❑ 101 Luis Matos .... .30 .09
❑ 102 Andy Pettitte .... .50 .15
❑ 103 Frank Thomas .... .75 .23
❑ 104 Rondell White .... .30 .09
❑ 105 Jody Gerut .... .30 .09
❑ 106 Bartolo Colon .... .30 .09
❑ 107 Johnny Damon .... .75 .23
❑ 108 Ryan Klesko .... .30 .09
❑ 109 Geoff Jenkins .... .30 .09
❑ 110 Jorge Posada .... .50 .15
❑ 111 Melvin Mora .... .30 .09
❑ 112 Bernie Williams .... .50 .15
❑ 113 Shannon Stewart .... .30 .09
❑ 114 Bobby Abreu .... .30 .09
❑ 115 Jose Guillen .... .30 .09
❑ 116 Brandon Phillips .... .30 .09
❑ 117 Jose Vidro .... .30 .09
❑ 118 Mike Sweeney .... .30 .09
❑ 119 Jacque Jones .... .30 .09
❑ 120 Josh Phelps .... .30 .09
❑ 121 Milton Bradley .... .30 .09
❑ 122 Torii Hunter .... .30 .09
❑ 123 Carl Crawford .... .30 .09
❑ 124 Javier Vazquez .... .30 .09
❑ 125 Juan Gonzalez .... .50 .15
❑ 126 Travis Hafner .... .30 .09
❑ 127 Ken Griffey Jr. .... 1.25 .35
❑ 128 Phil Nevin .... .30 .09
❑ 129 Trot Nixon .... .30 .09
❑ 130 Carlos Lee .... .30 .09
❑ 131 Javy Lopez .... .30 .09
❑ 132 Jay Gibbons .... .30 .09
❑ 133 Brandon Medders RP RC 4.00 1.20
❑ 134 Colby Miller RP RC 4.00 1.20
❑ 135 Dave Crouthers RP RC .. 4.00 1.20
❑ 136 Dennis Sarfate RP RC 4.00 1.20
❑ 137 Donald Kelly RP RC 4.00 1.20
❑ 138 Frank Brooks RP RC 4.00 1.20
❑ 139 Chris Aguila RP RC 4.00 1.20
❑ 140 Greg Dobbs RP RC 4.00 1.20
❑ 141 Ian Snell RP RC 5.00 1.50
❑ 142 Jake Woods RP RC 4.00 1.20
❑ 143 Jamie Brown RP RC 4.00 1.20
❑ 144 Jason Frasor RP RC 4.00 1.20
❑ 145 Jerome Gamble RP RC .. 4.00 1.20
❑ 146 Jesse Harper RP RC 4.00 1.20
❑ 147 Josh Labandeira RP RC .. 4.00 1.20
❑ 148 Justin Hampson RP RC .. 4.00 1.20
❑ 149 Justin Huisman RP RC .. 4.00 1.20
❑ 150 Justin Leone RP RC 5.00 1.50
❑ 151 Lincoln Holdzkom RP RC 4.00 1.20
❑ 152 Mike Bumatay RP RC 4.00 1.20
❑ 153 Mike Gosling RP RC 4.00 1.20
❑ 154 Mike Johnston RP RC 4.00 1.20
❑ 155 Mike Rouse RP RC 4.00 1.20
❑ 156 Nick Regilio RP RC 4.00 1.20
❑ 157 Ryan Meaux RP RC 4.00 1.20
❑ 158 Scott Dohmann RP RC .. 4.00 1.20
❑ 159 Sean Henn RP RC 4.00 1.20
❑ 160 Tim Bausher RP RC 4.00 1.20
❑ 161 Tim Bittner RP RC 4.00 1.20
❑ 162 Alec Zumwalt RP RC 4.00 1.20
❑ 163 Aaron Boone 5.00 1.50
Bret Boone
Geoff Jenkins
Mark Prior
Barry Zito CC
❑ 164 Albert Pujols 5.00 1.50
Edgar Renteria
Alex Rodriguez CC
❑ 165 Alfonso Soriano 5.00 1.50
Sammy Sosa CC
❑ 166 Bobby Abreu 5.00 1.50
Jim Thome CC
❑ 167 Bret Boone 5.00 1.50
John Olerud
Ichiro Suzuki CC
❑ 168 Derek Jeter 8.00 2.40
Alfonso Soriano CC
❑ 169 Eric Chavez 4.00 1.20
Miguel Tejada CC
❑ 170 Garret Anderson 4.00 1.20
Jim Edmonds
Troy Glaus CC
❑ 171 Hank Blalock 5.00 1.50
Alex Rodriguez CC
❑ 172 Alex Rodriguez 5.00 1.50
Mark Teixeira
Michael Young
Rafael Palmeiro CC
❑ 173 Ivan Rodriguez 5.00 1.50
Dontrelle Willis CC
❑ 174 Jason Giambi 8.00 2.40
Derek Jeter CC
❑ 175 Joe DiMaggio 10.00 3.00
Mickey Mantle CC
❑ 176 Joe DiMaggio 10.00 3.00
Mickey Mantle
Ted Williams CC
❑ 177 Joe DiMaggio 10.00 3.00
Ted Williams CC
❑ 178 Nomar Garciaparra 5.00 1.50
Alfonso Soriano CC
❑ 179 Nomar Garciaparra 5.00 1.50
Jason Giambi CC
❑ 180 Paul LoDuca 5.00 1.50
Hideo Nomo CC
❑ 181 Rafael Palmeiro 5.00 1.50
Alex Rodriguez
Michael Young CC
❑ 182 Ralph Kiner 8.00 2.40
Ted Williams CC
❑ 183 Aaron Boone 8.00 2.40
Derek Jeter CC
❑ 183 Kazuo Matsui RC 4.00 1.20

	Nm-Mt	Ex-Mt
❑ 184 Jerry Gil RC	.60	.18
❑ 185 Jose Capellan RC	3.00	.90
❑ 186 Tim Hamulack RC	.40	.12
❑ 187 Renyel Pinto RC	1.00	.30
❑ 188 Carlos Vasquez RC	.60	.18
❑ 189 Enemencio Pacheco RC	.60	.18
❑ 190 Ronny Cedeno RC	.60	.18
❑ 191 Mariano Gomez RC	1.00	.30
❑ 192 Carlos Hines RC	.60	.18
❑ 193 Mike Vento RC	1.00	.30
❑ 194 David Aardsma RC	.60	.18
❑ 195 Hector Gimenez RC	.40	.12
❑ 196 Fernando Nieve RC	.60	.18
❑ 197 Chris Saenz RC	.40	.12
❑ 198 Shawn Hill RC	.60	.18
❑ 199 Angel Chavez RC	.60	.18
❑ 200 Scott Proctor RC	1.00	.30
❑ 201 William Bergolla RC	.60	.18
❑ 202 Justin Germano RC	.60	.18
❑ 203 Onil Joseph RC	.60	.18
❑ 204 Rusty Tucker RC	1.00	.30
❑ 205 Justin Knoedler RC	.60	.18
❑ 206 Casey Daigle RC	.60	.18
❑ 207 Edwin Moreno RC	.60	.18
❑ 208 Chad Bentz RC	.60	.18
❑ 209 Ryan Wing RC	.60	.18
❑ 210 Shawn Camp RC	.40	.12
❑ 211 Eddy Rodriguez RC	1.00	.30
❑ 212 Roman Colon RC	.60	.18
❑ 213 Jason Bartlett RC	1.00	.30
❑ 214 Jorge Vasquez RC	.60	.18
❑ 215 Ivan Ochoa RC	.60	.18
❑ 216 Akinori Otsuka RC	.60	.18
❑ 217 Merkin Valdez RC	2.50	.75
❑ 218 Shingo Takatsu RC	2.50	.75
❑ 219 Chris Oxspring RC	1.00	.30
❑ 220 Kevin Cave RC	1.00	.30
❑ 221 Ramon Ramirez RC	.60	.18
❑ 222 Orlando Rodriguez RC	.60	.18
❑ 223 Lino Urdaneta RC	.60	.18
❑ 224 Franklyn Gracesqui RC	.40	.12
❑ 225 Michael Wuertz RC	1.00	.30
❑ 226 Jorge Sequea RC	.60	.18
❑ 227 Luis A. Gonzalez RC	1.00	.30
❑ 228 Jason Szuminski RC	.40	.12
❑ 229 John Gall RC	1.00	.30
❑ 230 Freddy Guzman RC	.60	.18
❑ 231 Jeff Bennett RC	.60	.18
❑ 232 Roberto Novoa RC	1.00	.30

2000 Upper Deck Pros and Prospects

	Nm-Mt	Ex-Mt
COMP.BASIC w/o SP's (90)	20.00	6.00
COMP.UPDATE w/o SP'S (30)	10.00	3.00
COMMON CARD (1-90)	.40	.12
COMMON PS (91-120)	5.00	1.50
COMMON PF (121-132)	4.00	1.20
COMMON PS (133-162)	5.00	1.50
COMMON (163-192)	.60	.18

	Nm-Mt	Ex-Mt
❑ 1 Darin Erstad	.40	.12
❑ 2 Troy Glaus	.40	.12
❑ 3 Mo Vaughn	.40	.12
❑ 4 Jason Giambi	.40	.12
❑ 5 Tim Hudson	.40	.12
❑ 6 Ben Grieve	.40	.12
❑ 7 Eric Chavez	.40	.12
❑ 8 Shannon Stewart	.40	.12
❑ 9 Raul Mondesi	.40	.12
❑ 10 Carlos Delgado	.40	.12
❑ 11 Jose Canseco	1.00	.30
❑ 12 Fred McGriff	.60	.18
❑ 13 Greg Vaughn	.40	.12
❑ 14 Manny Ramirez	.60	.18
❑ 15 Roberto Alomar	.60	.18
❑ 16 Jim Thome	1.00	.30
❑ 17 Alex Rodriguez	1.50	.45
❑ 18 Freddy Garcia	.40	.12
❑ 19 John Olerud	.40	.12
❑ 20 Cal Ripken	3.00	.90
❑ 21 Albert Belle	.40	.12
❑ 22 Mike Mussina	.60	.18
❑ 23 Ivan Rodriguez	1.00	.30
❑ 24 Rafael Palmeiro	.60	.18
❑ 25 Ruben Mateo	.40	.12
❑ 26 Gabe Kapler	.40	.12
❑ 27 Pedro Martinez	1.00	.30
❑ 28 Nomar Garciaparra	1.50	.45
❑ 29 Carl Everett	.40	.12
❑ 30 Carlos Beltran	.60	.18
❑ 31 Jermaine Dye	.40	.12
❑ 32 Johnny Damon UER Picture on front is Joe Randa	.60	.18
❑ 33 Juan Gonzalez	.60	.18
❑ 34 Juan Encarnacion	.40	.12
❑ 35 Dean Palmer	.40	.12
❑ 36 Jacque Jones	.40	.12
❑ 37 Matt Lawton	.40	.12
❑ 38 Frank Thomas	1.00	.30
❑ 39 Paul Konerko	.40	.12
❑ 40 Magglio Ordonez	.40	.12
❑ 41 Derek Jeter	2.50	.75
❑ 42 Bernie Williams	.60	.18
❑ 43 Mariano Rivera	.60	.18
❑ 44 Roger Clemens	2.00	.60
❑ 45 Jeff Bagwell	.60	.18
❑ 46 Craig Biggio	.60	.18
❑ 47 Richard Hidalgo	.40	.12
❑ 48 Chipper Jones	1.00	.30
❑ 49 Andres Galarraga	.40	.12
❑ 50 Andruw Jones	.40	.12
❑ 51 Greg Maddux	1.50	.45
❑ 52 Jeromy Burnitz	.40	.12
❑ 53 Geoff Jenkins	.40	.12
❑ 54 Mark McGwire	2.50	.75
❑ 55 Jim Edmonds	.40	.12
❑ 56 Fernando Tatis	.40	.12
❑ 57 J.D. Drew	.40	.12
❑ 58 Sammy Sosa	1.50	.45
❑ 59 Kerry Wood	1.00	.30
❑ 60 Randy Johnson	1.00	.30
❑ 61 Matt Williams	.40	.12
❑ 62 Erubiel Durazo	.40	.12
❑ 63 Shawn Green	.40	.12
❑ 64 Kevin Brown	.40	.12
❑ 65 Gary Sheffield	.40	.12
❑ 66 Adrian Beltre	.60	.18
❑ 67 Vladimir Guerrero	1.00	.30
❑ 68 Jose Vidro	.40	.12
❑ 69 Barry Bonds	2.50	.75
❑ 70 Jeff Kent	.40	.12
❑ 71 Preston Wilson	.40	.12
❑ 72 Ryan Dempster	.40	.12
❑ 73 Mike Lowell	.40	.12
❑ 74 Mike Piazza	1.50	.45
❑ 75 Robin Ventura	.40	.12
❑ 76 Edgardo Alfonzo	.40	.12
❑ 77 Derek Bell	.40	.12
❑ 78 Tony Gwynn	1.25	.35
❑ 79 Matt Clement	.40	.12
❑ 80 Scott Rolen	1.00	.30
❑ 81 Bobby Abreu	.40	.12
❑ 82 Curt Schilling	.40	.12
❑ 83 Brian Giles	.40	.12
❑ 84 Jason Kendall	.40	.12
❑ 85 Kris Benson	.40	.12
❑ 86 Ken Griffey Jr.	1.50	.45
❑ 87 Sean Casey	.40	.12
❑ 88 Pokey Reese	.40	.12
❑ 89 Larry Walker	.60	.18
❑ 90 Todd Helton	.60	.18
❑ 91 Rick Ankiel PS	5.00	1.50
❑ 92 Milton Bradley PS	5.00	1.50
❑ 93 Vernon Wells PS	5.00	1.50
❑ 94 Rafael Furcal PS	5.00	1.50
❑ 95 Kazuhiro Sasaki PS RC	8.00	2.40
❑ 96 Joe Torres PS RC	5.00	1.50
❑ 97 Adam Kennedy PS	5.00	1.50
❑ 98 Adam Piatt PS	5.00	1.50
❑ 99 Matt Wheatland PS RC	5.00	1.50
❑ 100 Alex Cabrera PS RC	5.00	1.50
❑ 101 Barry Zito PS RC	12.00	3.60
❑ 102 Mike Lamb PS RC	5.00	1.50
❑ 103 Scott Heard PS RC	5.00	1.50
❑ 104 Danys Baez PS RC	5.00	1.50
❑ 105 Matt Riley PS	5.00	1.50
❑ 106 Mark Mulder PS	5.00	1.50
❑ 107 W.Rodriguez PS RC	5.00	1.50
❑ 108 Luis Matos PS RC	5.00	1.50
❑ 109 Alfonso Soriano PS	8.00	2.40
❑ 110 Pat Burrell PS	5.00	1.50
❑ 111 Mike Tonis PS RC	5.00	1.50
❑ 112 Aaron McNeal PS RC	5.00	1.50
❑ 113 Dave Krynzel PS RC	5.00	1.50
❑ 114 Josh Beckett PS	8.00	2.40
❑ 115 Sean Burnett PS RC	8.00	2.40
❑ 116 Eric Munson PS	5.00	1.50
❑ 117 Scott Downs PS RC	5.00	1.50
❑ 118 Brian Tollberg PS RC	5.00	1.50
❑ 119 Nick Johnson PS	5.00	1.50
❑ 120 Leo Estrella PS RC	5.00	1.50
❑ 121 Ken Griffey Jr. PF	10.00	3.00
❑ 122 Frank Thomas PF	6.00	1.80
❑ 123 Cal Ripken PF	20.00	6.00
❑ 124 Ivan Rodriguez PF	6.00	1.80
❑ 125 Derek Jeter PF	15.00	4.50
❑ 126 Mark McGwire PF	15.00	4.50
❑ 127 Pedro Martinez PF	6.00	1.80
❑ 128 Chipper Jones PF	6.00	1.80
❑ 129 Sammy Sosa PF	10.00	3.00
❑ 130 Alex Rodriguez PF	10.00	3.00
❑ 131 Vladimir Guerrero PF	6.00	1.80
❑ 132 Jeff Bagwell PF	6.00	1.80
❑ 133 Dane Artman PS RC	5.00	1.50
❑ 134 Juan Pierre PS RC	8.00	2.40
❑ 135 Jace Brewer PS RC	5.00	1.50
❑ 136 Sun Woo Kim PS RC	5.00	1.50
❑ 137 Jon Rauch PS RC	5.00	1.50
❑ 138 Juan Guzman PS RC	5.00	1.50
❑ 139 Daylan Holt PS RC	5.00	1.50
❑ 140 R.Washington PS RC	5.00	1.50
❑ 141 Ben Diggins PS RC	5.00	1.50
❑ 142 Mike Meyers PS RC	5.00	1.50
❑ 143 C.Wakeland PS RC	5.00	1.50
❑ 144 Cory Vance PS RC	5.00	1.50
❑ 145 Keith Ginter PS RC	5.00	1.50
❑ 146 Koyie Hill PS RC	5.00	1.50
❑ 147 Julio Zuleta PS RC	5.00	1.50
❑ 148 G.Guzman PS RC	5.00	1.50
❑ 149 Jay Spurgeon PS RC	5.00	1.50
❑ 150 Ross Gload PS RC	5.00	1.50
❑ 151 Ben Sheets PS RC	12.00	3.60
❑ 152 J.Kalinowski PS RC	5.00	1.50
❑ 153 Kurt Ainsworth PS RC	5.00	1.50
❑ 154 P.Crawford PS RC	5.00	1.50
❑ 155 Xavier Nady PS RC	8.00	2.40
❑ 156 B.Wilkerson PS RC	8.00	2.40
❑ 157 Kris Wilson PS RC	5.00	1.50
❑ 158 Paul Rigdon PS RC	5.00	1.50
❑ 159 R.Kohlmeier PS RC	5.00	1.50
❑ 160 Dane Sardinha PS RC	5.00	1.50
❑ 161 Javier Cardona PS RC	5.00	1.50
❑ 162 Brad Cresse PS RC	5.00	1.50
❑ 163 Ron Gant	.60	.18
❑ 164 Mark Mulder	.60	.18
❑ 165 David Wells	.60	.18
❑ 166 Jason Tyner	.60	.18
❑ 167 David Segui	.60	.18
❑ 168 Al Martin	.60	.18
❑ 169 Melvin Mora	.60	.18
❑ 170 Ricky Ledee	.60	.18
❑ 171 Rolando Arrojo	.60	.18
❑ 172 Mike Sweeney	.60	.18
❑ 173 Bobby Higginson	.60	.18
❑ 174 Eric Milton	.60	.18
❑ 175 Charles Johnson	.60	.18
❑ 176 David Justice	.60	.18
❑ 177 Moises Alou	.60	.18

❑ 178 Andy Ashby	.60	.18
❑ 179 Richie Sexson	.60	.18
❑ 180 Will Clark	1.50	.45
❑ 181 Rondell White	.60	.18
❑ 182 Curt Schilling	.60	.18
❑ 183 Tom Goodwin	.60	.18
❑ 184 Lee Stevens	.60	.18
❑ 185 Ellis Burks	.60	.18
❑ 186 Henry Rodriguez	.60	.18
❑ 187 Mike Bordick	.60	.18
❑ 188 Ryan Klesko	.60	.18
❑ 189 Travis Lee	.60	.18
❑ 190 Kevin Young	.60	.18
❑ 191 Barry Larkin	1.00	.30
❑ 192 Jeff Cirillo	.60	.18

2001 Upper Deck Pros and Prospects

	Nm-Mt	Ex-Mt
COMP.SET w/o SP's (90)	15.00	4.50
COMMON CARD (1-90)	.40	.12
COMMON CARD (91-135)	5.00	1.50
COMMON (136-141)	20.00	6.00

❑ 1 Troy Glaus	.40	.12
❑ 2 Darin Erstad	.40	.12
❑ 3 Tim Hudson	.40	.12
❑ 4 Jason Giambi	.40	.12
❑ 5 Jermaine Dye	.40	.12
❑ 6 Barry Zito	.60	.18
❑ 7 Carlos Delgado	.40	.12
❑ 8 Shannon Stewart	.40	.12
❑ 9 Raul Mondesi	.40	.12
❑ 10 Greg Vaughn	.40	.12
❑ 11 Ben Grieve	.40	.12
❑ 12 Roberto Alomar	.60	.18
❑ 13 Juan Gonzalez	.60	.18
❑ 14 Jim Thome	1.00	.30
❑ 15 C.C. Sabathia	.40	.12
❑ 16 Edgar Martinez	.60	.18
❑ 17 Kazuhiro Sasaki	.40	.12
❑ 18 Aaron Sele	.40	.12
❑ 19 John Olerud	.40	.12
❑ 20 Cal Ripken	3.00	.90
❑ 21 Rafael Palmeiro	.60	.18
❑ 22 Ivan Rodriguez	1.00	.30
❑ 23 Alex Rodriguez	1.50	.45
❑ 24 Manny Ramirez	.60	.18
❑ 25 Pedro Martinez	1.00	.30
❑ 26 Carl Everett	.40	.12
❑ 27 Nomar Garciaparra	1.50	.45
❑ 28 Neifi Perez	.40	.12
❑ 29 Mike Sweeney	.40	.12
❑ 30 Bobby Higginson	.40	.12
❑ 31 Tony Clark	.40	.12
❑ 32 Doug Mientkiewicz	.40	.12
❑ 33 Cristian Guzman	.40	.12
❑ 34 Brad Radke	.40	.12
❑ 35 Magglio Ordonez	.40	.12
❑ 36 Carlos Lee	.40	.12
❑ 37 Frank Thomas	1.00	.30
❑ 38 Roger Clemens	2.00	.60
❑ 39 Bernie Williams	.60	.18
❑ 40 Derek Jeter	2.50	.75
❑ 41 Tino Martinez	.60	.18
❑ 42 Wade Miller	.40	.12
❑ 43 Jeff Bagwell	.60	.18
❑ 44 Lance Berkman	.40	.12
❑ 45 Richard Hidalgo	.40	.12
❑ 46 Greg Maddux	1.50	.45
❑ 47 Andruw Jones	.40	.12
❑ 48 Chipper Jones	1.00	.30
❑ 49 Rafael Furcal	.40	.12
❑ 50 Jeromy Burnitz	.40	.12
❑ 51 Geoff Jenkins	.40	.12
❑ 52 Ben Sheets	.60	.18
❑ 53 Mark McGwire	2.50	.75
❑ 54 Jim Edmonds	.40	.12
❑ 55 J.D. Drew	.40	.12
❑ 56 Fred McGriff	.60	.18
❑ 57 Sammy Sosa	1.50	.45
❑ 58 Kerry Wood	1.00	.30
❑ 59 Randy Johnson	1.00	.30
❑ 60 Luis Gonzalez	.40	.12
❑ 61 Curt Schilling	.40	.12
❑ 62 Kevin Brown	.40	.12
❑ 63 Shawn Green	.40	.12
❑ 64 Gary Sheffield	.40	.12
❑ 65 Vladimir Guerrero	1.00	.30
❑ 66 Jose Vidro	.40	.12
❑ 67 Barry Bonds	2.50	.75
❑ 68 Jeff Kent	.40	.12
❑ 69 Rich Aurilia	.40	.12
❑ 70 Preston Wilson	.40	.12
❑ 71 Charles Johnson	.40	.12
❑ 72 Cliff Floyd	.40	.12
❑ 73 Mike Piazza	1.50	.45
❑ 74 Al Leiter	.40	.12
❑ 75 Matt Lawton	.40	.12
❑ 76 Tony Gwynn	1.25	.35
❑ 77 Ryan Klesko	.40	.12
❑ 78 Phil Nevin	.40	.12
❑ 79 Scott Rolen	1.00	.30
❑ 80 Pat Burrell	.40	.12
❑ 81 Jimmy Rollins	.40	.12
❑ 82 Jason Kendall	.40	.12
❑ 83 Brian Giles	.40	.12
❑ 84 Aramis Ramirez	.40	.12
❑ 85 Ken Griffey Jr.	1.50	.45
❑ 86 Barry Larkin	.60	.18
❑ 87 Sean Casey	.40	.12
❑ 88 Larry Walker	.60	.18
❑ 89 Todd Helton	.60	.18
❑ 90 Mike Hampton	.40	.12
❑ 91 Juan Cruz PS RC	5.00	1.50
❑ 92 Brian Lawrence PS RC	5.00	1.50
❑ 93 Brandon Lyon PS RC	5.00	1.50
❑ 94 A.Hernandez PS RC	5.00	1.50
❑ 95 Jose Mieses PS RC	5.00	1.50
❑ 96 Juan Uribe PS RC	8.00	2.40
❑ 97 M.Ensberg PS RC	8.00	2.40
❑ 98 Wilson Betemit PS RC	5.00	1.50
❑ 99 Ryan Freel PS RC	5.00	1.50
❑ 100 Jack Wilson PS RC	10.00	3.00
❑ 101 Cesar Crespo PS RC	5.00	1.50
❑ 102 Bret Prinz PS RC	5.00	1.50
❑ 103 H.Ramirez PS RC	8.00	2.40
❑ 104 E. Guzman PS RC	5.00	1.50
❑ 105 Josh Towers PS RC	5.00	1.50
❑ 106 B. Duckworth PS RC	5.00	1.50
❑ 107 Esix Snead PS RC	5.00	1.50
❑ 108 Billy Sylvester PS RC	5.00	1.50
❑ 109 Alexis Gomez PS RC	5.00	1.50
❑ 110 J. Estrada PS RC	8.00	2.40
❑ 111 Joe Kennedy PS RC	8.00	2.40
❑ 112 Travis Hafner PS RC	12.00	3.60
❑ 113 Martin Vargas PS RC	5.00	1.50
❑ 114 Jay Gibbons PS RC	8.00	2.40
❑ 115 Andres Torres PS RC	5.00	1.50
❑ 116 Sean Douglass PS RC	5.00	1.50
❑ 117 Juan Diaz PS RC	5.00	1.50
❑ 118 Greg Miller PS RC	5.00	1.50
❑ 119 C. Valderrama PS RC	5.00	1.50
❑ 120 Bill Ortega PS RC	5.00	1.50
❑ 121 Josh Fogg PS RC	5.00	1.50
❑ 122 Wilken Ruan PS RC	5.00	1.50
❑ 123 Kris Keller PS RC	5.00	1.50
❑ 124 Erick Almonte PS RC	5.00	1.50
❑ 125 R. Rodriguez PS RC	5.00	1.50
❑ 126 Grant Balfour PS RC	5.00	1.50
❑ 127 Nick Maness PS RC	5.00	1.50
❑ 128 Jeremy Owens PS RC	5.00	1.50
❑ 129 Doug Nickle PS RC	5.00	1.50
❑ 130 Bert Snow PS RC	5.00	1.50
❑ 131 Jason Smith PS RC	5.00	1.50
❑ 132 Henry Mateo PS RC	5.00	1.50
❑ 133 Mike Penney PS RC	5.00	1.50
❑ 134 Bud Smith PS RC	5.00	1.50
❑ 135 Junior Spivey PS RC	8.00	2.40
❑ 136 Ichiro Suzuki JSY RC	100.00	30.00
❑ 137 Albert Pujols JSY RC	150.00	45.00
❑ 138 Mark Teixeira JSY RC	100.00	30.00
❑ 139 D. Brazelton JSY RC	20.00	6.00
❑ 140 Mark Prior JSY RC	100.00	30.00
❑ 141 T. Shinjo JSY RC	20.00	6.00

2001 Upper Deck Prospect Premieres

	Nm-Mt	Ex-Mt
COMP.SET w/o SP's (90)	25.00	7.50
COMMON CARD (1-90)	.40	.12
COMMON AUTO (91-102)	15.00	4.50

❑ 1 Jeff Mathis XRC	1.50	.45
❑ 2 Jake Woods XRC	.40	.12
❑ 3 Dallas McPherson XRC	6.00	1.80
❑ 4 Steven Shell XRC	.40	.12
❑ 5 Ryan Budde XRC	.40	.12
❑ 6 Kirk Saarloos XRC	.40	.12
❑ 7 Ryan Stegall XRC	.40	.12
❑ 8 Bobby Crosby XRC	4.00	1.20
❑ 9 J.T. Stotts XRC	.40	.12
❑ 10 Neal Cotts XRC	1.00	.30
❑ 11 J.Bonderman XRC	.75	.23
❑ 12 Brandon League XRC	.40	.12
❑ 13 Tyrell Godwin XRC	.40	.12
❑ 14 Gabe Gross XRC	.50	.15
❑ 15 Chris Neylan XRC	.40	.12
❑ 16 Macay McBride XRC	.40	.12
❑ 17 Josh Burrus XRC	.40	.12
❑ 18 Adam Stern XRC	.40	.12
❑ 19 Richard Lewis XRC	1.00	.30
❑ 20 Cole Barthel XRC	.40	.12
❑ 21 Mike Jones XRC	.50	.15
❑ 22 J.J. Hardy XRC	2.00	.60
❑ 23 Jon Steitz XRC	.40	.12
❑ 24 Brad Nelson XRC	1.25	.35
❑ 25 Justin Pope XRC	.40	.12
❑ 26 Dan Haren XRC UER	.75	.23
Blurb incorrectly lists him as a lefty		
❑ 27 Andy Sisco XRC	1.00	.30
❑ 28 Ryan Theriot XRC	.40	.12
❑ 29 Ricky Nolasco XRC	.40	.12
❑ 30 Jon Switzer XRC	.40	.12
❑ 31 Justin Wechsler XRC	.40	.12
❑ 32 Mike Gosling XRC	.40	.12
❑ 33 Scott Hairston XRC	1.50	.45
❑ 34 Brian Pilkington XRC	.40	.12
❑ 35 Kole Strayhorn XRC	.40	.12
❑ 36 David Taylor XRC	.40	.12
❑ 37 Donald Levinski XRC	.40	.12
❑ 38 Mike Hinckley XRC	1.00	.30
❑ 39 Nick Long XRC	.40	.12
❑ 40 Brad Hennessey XRC	.75	.23
❑ 41 Noah Lowry XRC	2.00	.60
❑ 42 Josh Cram XRC	.40	.12
❑ 43 Jesse Foppert XRC	1.00	.30
❑ 44 Julian Benavidez XRC	.40	.12
❑ 45 Dan Denham XRC	.40	.12
❑ 46 Travis Foley XRC	.40	.12

❑ 47 Mike Conroy XRC .... .40 .12
❑ 48 Jake Dittler XRC .... .75 .23
❑ 49 Rene Rivera XRC .... .40 .12
❑ 50 John Cole XRC .... .40 .12
❑ 51 Lazaro Abreu XRC .... .40 .12
❑ 52 David Wright XRC 12.00 3.60
❑ 53 Aaron Heilman XRC .... .40 .12
❑ 54 Len DiNardo XRC .... .40 .12
❑ 55 Alhaji Turay XRC .... .50 .15
❑ 56 Chris Smith XRC .... .40 .12
❑ 57 Rommie Lewis XRC .... .40 .12
❑ 58 Bryan Bass XRC .... .40 .12
❑ 59 David Crouthers XRC .... .40 .12
❑ 60 Josh Barfield XRC .... 1.50 .45
❑ 61 Jake Peavy XRC .... 2.00 .60
❑ 62 Ryan Howard XRC 4.00 1.20
❑ 63 Gavin Floyd XRC .... 2.50 .75
❑ 64 Michael Floyd XRC .... .40 .12
❑ 65 Stefan Bailie XRC .... .40 .12
❑ 66 Jon DeVries XRC .... .40 .12
❑ 67 Steve Kelly XRC .... .40 .12
❑ 68 Alan Moye XRC .... .40 .12
❑ 69 Justin Gillman XRC .... .40 .12
❑ 70 Jayson Nix XRC .... .75 .23
❑ 71 John Draper XRC .... .40 .12
❑ 72 Kenny Baugh XRC .... .40 .12
❑ 73 Michael Woods XRC .... .40 .12
❑ 74 Preston Larrison XRC .... .50 .15
❑ 75 Matt Coenen XRC .... .40 .12
❑ 76 Scott Tyler XRC .... .50 .15
❑ 77 Jose Morales XRC .... .40 .12
❑ 78 Corwin Malone XRC .... .40 .12
❑ 79 Dennis Ulacia XRC .... .50 .15
❑ 80 Andy Gonzalez XRC .... .40 .12
❑ 81 Kris Honel XRC .... 1.50 .45
❑ 82 Wyatt Allen XRC .... .40 .12
❑ 83 Ryan Wing XRC .... .40 .12
❑ 84 Sean Henn XRC .... .40 .12
❑ 85 John-Ford Griffin XRC .... .40 .12
❑ 86 Bronson Sardinha XRC .... .75 .23
❑ 87 Jon Skaggs XRC .... .40 .12
❑ 88 Shelley Duncan XRC .... .40 .12
❑ 89 Jason Arnold XRC .... .75 .23
❑ 90 Aaron Rifkin XRC .... .50 .15
❑ 91 Colt Griffin AU XRC 25.00 7.50
❑ 92 J.D. Martin AU XRC 15.00 4.50
❑ 93 Justin Wayne AU XRC 15.00 4.50
❑ 94 J.VanBenschoten AU XRC 30.00 9.00
❑ 95 Chris Burke AU XRC 25.00 7.50
❑ 96 C. Kotchman AU XRC 70.00 21.00
❑ 97 M. Garciaparra AU XRC.. 25.00 7.50
❑ 98 Jake Gautreau AU XRC .. 15.00 4.50
❑ 99 J. Williams AU XRC 40.00 12.00
❑ 100 Toe Nash AU XRC 15.00 4.50
❑ 101 Joe Borchard AU XRC .. 25.00 7.50
❑ 102 Mark Prior AU XRC 150.00 45.00

2002 Upper Deck Prospect Premieres

	Nm-Mt	Ex-Mt
COMP.SET w/o SP's (72)	25.00	7.50
COMMON CARD (1-60)	.40	.12
COMMON CARD (61-85)	5.00	1.50
COMMON CARD (86-97)	10.00	3.00
COMMON RIPKEN (98-99)	2.00	.60
COMMON MCGWIRE (100-105)	2.00	.60
COMMON DIMAGGIO (106-109)	1.50	.45

PENDER COR AVAIL.VIA MAIL EXCHANGE .00

❑ 1 Josh Rupe XRC .... .40 .12
❑ 2 Blair Johnson XRC .... .40 .12
❑ 3 Jason Pridie XRC .... .75 .23
❑ 4 Tim Gilhooly XRC .... .40 .12
❑ 5 Kennard Jones XRC .... .40 .12
❑ 6 Darrell Rasner XRC .... .40 .12
❑ 7 Adam Donachie XRC .... .40 .12
❑ 8 Josh Murray XRC .... .40 .12
❑ 9 Brian Dopirak XRC .... 2.50 .75
❑ 10 Jason Cooper XRC .... .50 .15
❑ 11 Zach Hammes XRC .... .40 .12
❑ 12 Jon Lester XRC .... .40 .12
❑ 13 Kevin Jepsen XRC .... 1.00 .30
❑ 14 Curtis Granderson XRC .... 1.25 .35
❑ 15 David Bush XRC .... .75 .23
❑ 16 Joel Guzman .... .50 .15
❑ 17A Matt Pender UER XRC...... .75 .23
Pictures Curtis Granderson
❑ 17B Matt Pender COR .... .00
❑ 18 Derick Grigsby XRC .... .40 .12
❑ 19 Jeremy Reed XRC .... 2.50 .75
❑ 20 Jonathan Broxton XRC .... .75 .23
❑ 21 Jesse Crain XRC .... .75 .23
❑ 22 Justin Jones XRC .... 1.00 .30
❑ 23 Brian Slocum XRC .... .40 .12
❑ 24 Brian McCann XRC .... .75 .23
❑ 25 Francisco Liriano XRC .... .50 .15
❑ 26 Fred Lewis XRC .... .40 .12
❑ 27 Steve Stanley XRC .... .40 .12
❑ 28 Chris Snyder XRC .... .75 .23
❑ 29 Dan Cevette XRC .... .40 .12
❑ 30 Kiel Fisher XRC .... .50 .15
❑ 31 Brandon Weeden XRC .... .40 .12
❑ 32 Pat Osborn XRC .... .40 .12
❑ 33 Taber Lee XRC .... .40 .12
❑ 34 Dan Ortmeier XRC .... .75 .23
❑ 35 Josh Johnson XRC .... .40 .12
❑ 36 Val Majewski XRC .... 1.00 .30
❑ 37 Larry Broadway XRC .... .75 .23
❑ 38 Joey Gomes XRC .... .40 .12
❑ 39 Eric Thomas XRC .... .40 .12
❑ 40 James Loney XRC .... 1.50 .45
❑ 41 Charlie Morton XRC .... .40 .12
❑ 42 Mark McLemore XRC .... .40 .12
❑ 43 Matt Craig XRC .... .50 .15
❑ 44 Ryan Rodriguez XRC .... .40 .12
❑ 45 Rich Hill XRC .... .40 .12
❑ 46 Bob Malek XRC .... .40 .12
❑ 47 Justin Maureau XRC .... .40 .12
❑ 48 Randy Braun XRC .... .40 .12
❑ 49 Brian Grant XRC .... .40 .12
❑ 50 Tyler Davidson XRC .... .50 .15
❑ 51 Travis Hanson XRC .... .40 .12
❑ 52 Kyle Boyer XRC .... .40 .12
❑ 53 James Holcomb XRC .... .40 .12
❑ 54 Ryan Williams XRC .... .40 .12
❑ 55 Ben Crockett XRC .... .40 .12
❑ 56 Adam Greenberg XRC .... .50 .15
❑ 57 John Baker XRC .... .40 .12
❑ 58 Matt Carson XRC .... .40 .12
❑ 59 Jonathan George XRC .... .40 .12
❑ 60 David Jensen XRC .... .40 .12
❑ 61 Nick Swisher JSY XRC .. 15.00 4.50
❑ 62 Br.Clevlen JSY XRC UER 8.00 2.40
Name mispelled as Cleven
❑ 63 Royce Ring JSY XRC 8.00 2.40
❑ 64 Mike Nixon JSY XRC 5.00 1.50
❑ 65 Ricky Barrett JSY XRC 5.00 1.50
❑ 66 Russ Adams JSY XRC 8.00 2.40
❑ 67 Joe Mauer JSY XRC 20.00 6.00
❑ 68 Jeff Francoeur JSY XRC 20.00 6.00
❑ 69 Joseph Blanton JSY XRC 8.00 2.40
❑ 70 Micah Schilling JSY XRC 5.00 1.50
❑ 71 John McCurdy JSY XRC .. 5.00 1.50
❑ 72 Sergio Santos JSY XRC 10.00 3.00
❑ 73 Josh Womack JSY XRC .. 5.00 1.50
❑ 74 Jared Doyle JSY XRC 5.00 1.50
❑ 75 Ben Fritz JSY XRC 5.00 1.50
❑ 76 Greg Miller JSY XRC 10.00 3.00
❑ 77 Luke Hagerty JSY XRC 5.00 1.50
❑ 78 Matt Whitney JSY XRC 8.00 2.40
❑ 79 Dan Meyer JSY XRC 8.00 2.40
❑ 80 Bill Murphy JSY XRC 8.00 2.40
❑ 81 Zach Segovia JSY XRC 8.00 2.40
❑ 82 St. Obenchain JSY XRC .. 5.00 1.50
❑ 83 Matt Clanton JSY XRC 5.00 1.50
❑ 84 Mark Teahen JSY XRC .. 10.00 3.00
❑ 85 Kyle Pawelczyk JSY XRC.. 5.00 1.50
❑ 86 Khalil Greene AU XRC 70.00 21.00
❑ 87 Joe Saunders AU XRC 10.00 3.00
❑ 88 Jeremy Hermida AU XRC 25.00 7.50
❑ 89 Drew Meyer AU XRC 10.00 3.00
❑ 90 Jeff Francis AU XRC 25.00 7.50
❑ 91 Scott Moore AU XRC 10.00 3.00
❑ 92 Prince Fielder AU XRC .. 70.00 21.00
❑ 93 Zack Greinke AU XRC 40.00 12.00
❑ 94 Chris Gruler AU XRC 10.00 3.00
❑ 95 Scott Kazmir AU XRC 70.00 21.00
❑ 96 B.J. Upton AU XRC 70.00 21.00
❑ 97 Clint Everts AU XRC 20.00 6.00
❑ 98 Cal Ripken TRIB .... 2.00 .60
❑ 99 Cal Ripken TRIB .... 2.00 .60
❑ 100 Mark McGwire TRIB .... 2.00 .60
❑ 101 Mark McGwire TRIB .... 2.00 .60
❑ 102 Mark McGwire TRIB .... 2.00 .60
❑ 103 Mark McGwire TRIB .... 2.00 .60
❑ 104 Mark McGwire TRIB .... 2.00 .60
❑ 105 Joe DiMaggio TRIB .... 1.50 .45
❑ 106 Joe DiMaggio TRIB .... 1.50 .45
❑ 107 Joe DiMaggio TRIB .... 1.50 .45
❑ 108 Joe DiMaggio TRIB .... 1.50 .45
❑ 109 Joe DiMaggio TRIB .... 1.50 .45

2003 Upper Deck Prospect Premieres

	MINT	NRMT
COMPLETE SET (90)	40.00	18.00

❑ 1 Bryan Opdyke XRC .... .40 .18
❑ 2 Gabriel Sosa XRC .... .40 .18
❑ 3 Tila Reynolds XRC .... .40 .18
❑ 4 Aaron Hill XRC .... .75 .35
❑ 5 Aaron Marsden XRC .... .50 .23
❑ 6 Abe Alvarez XRC .... .50 .23
❑ 7 Adam Jones XRC .... .60 .25
❑ 8 Adam Miller XRC .... 1.25 .55
❑ 9 Andre Ethier XRC .... .60 .25
❑ 10 Anthony Gwynn XRC .... 1.00 .45
❑ 11 Brad Snyder XRC .... .75 .35
❑ 12 Brad Sullivan XRC .... .50 .23
❑ 13 Brian Anderson XRC .... 1.50 .70
❑ 14 Brian Buscher XRC .... .40 .18
❑ 15 Brian Snyder XRC .... .50 .23
❑ 16 Carlos Quentin XRC .... 2.00 .90
❑ 17 Chad Billingsley XRC .... 1.00 .45
❑ 18 Fraser Dizard XRC .... .40 .18
❑ 19 Chris Durbin XRC .... .40 .18
❑ 20 Chris Ray XRC .... .50 .23
❑ 21 Conor Jackson XRC .... 2.00 .90
❑ 22 Kory Casto XRC .... .40 .18
❑ 23 Craig Whitaker XRC .... .50 .23
❑ 24 Daniel Moore XRC .... .40 .18
❑ 25 Daric Barton XRC .... 2.00 .90
❑ 26 Darin Downs XRC .... .50 .23
❑ 27 David Murphy XRC .... .75 .35
❑ 28 Dustin Majewski XRC .... .50 .23
❑ 29 Edgardo Baez XRC .... .50 .23
❑ 30 Jake Fox XRC .... .40 .18
❑ 31 Jake Stevens XRC .... 1.00 .45
❑ 32 Jamie D'Antona XRC .... 1.00 .45
❑ 33 James Houser XRC .... .50 .23

❑ 34 Jar. Saltalamacchia XRC .60 .25
❑ 35 Jason Hirsh XRC .40 .18
❑ 36 Javi Herrera XRC .50 .23
❑ 37 Jeff Allison XRC .50 .23
❑ 38 John Hudgins XRC .40 .18
❑ 39 Jo Jo Reyes XRC .50 .23
❑ 40 Justin James XRC .40 .18
❑ 41 Kurt Isenberg XRC .40 .18
❑ 42 Kyle Boyer XRC .40 .18
❑ 43 Lastings Milledge XRC 2.00 .90
❑ 44 Luis Atilano XRC .40 .18
❑ 45 Matt Murton XRC .40 .18
❑ 46 Matt Moses XRC .75 .35
❑ 47 Matt Harrison XRC .60 .25
❑ 48 Michael Bourn XRC .40 .18
❑ 49 Miguel Vega XRC .40 .18
❑ 50 Mitch Maier XRC .60 .25
❑ 51 Omar Quintanilla XRC .60 .25
❑ 52 Ryan Sweeney XRC 1.00 .45
❑ 53 Scott Baker XRC .40 .18
❑ 54 Sean Rodriguez XRC 1.00 .45
❑ 55 Steve Lerud XRC .60 .25
❑ 56 Thomas Pauly XRC .40 .18
❑ 57 Tom Gorzelanny XRC .60 .25
❑ 58 Tim Moss XRC .40 .18
❑ 59 Robbie Wooley XRC .50 .23
❑ 60 Trey Webb XRC .40 .18
❑ 61 Wes Littleton XRC .50 .23
❑ 62 Beau Vaughan XRC .50 .23
❑ 63 Willy Jo Ronda XRC .50 .23
❑ 64 Chris Lubanski XRC 1.25 .55
❑ 65 Ian Stewart XRC 3.00 1.35
❑ 66 John Danks XRC 1.25 .55
❑ 67 Kyle Sleeth XRC .75 .35
❑ 68 Michael Aubrey XRC 1.50 .70
❑ 69 Kevin Kouzmanoff XRC .60 .25
❑ 70 Ryan Harvey XRC 1.25 .55
❑ 71 Tim Stauffer XRC .60 .25
❑ 72 Tony Richie XRC .40 .18
❑ 73 Brandon Wood XRC .75 .35
❑ 74 David Aardsma XRC .40 .18
❑ 75 David Shinskie XRC .40 .18
❑ 76 Dennis Dove XRC .50 .23
❑ 77 Eric Sultemeier XRC .40 .18
❑ 78 Jay Sborz XRC .40 .18
❑ 79 Jimmy Barthmaier XRC .40 .18
❑ 80 Josh Whitesell XRC .40 .18
❑ 81 Josh Anderson XRC .75 .35
❑ 82 Kenny Lewis XRC .50 .23
❑ 83 Mateo Miramontes XRC .40 .18
❑ 84 Nick Markakis XRC .75 .35
❑ 85 Paul Bacot XRC .50 .23
❑ 86 Peter Stonard XRC .40 .18
❑ 87 Reggie Willits XRC .40 .18
❑ 88 Shane Costa XRC .50 .23
❑ 89 Billy Sadler XRC .40 .18
❑ 90 Delmon Young XRC 2.50 1.10

2004 Upper Deck r-class

	Nm-Mt	Ex-Mt
COMPLETE SET (180)	100.00	30.00
COMP.SET w/o SP'S (90)	20.00	6.00
COMMON CARD (1-90)	.30	.09
COMMON CARD (91-180)	1.00	.30
91-180 STATED ODDS 1:2		

❑ 1 Adam Dunn .50 .15
❑ 2 Jose Vidro .30 .09
❑ 3 Vladimir Guerrero .75 .23
❑ 4 Hideo Nomo .75 .23
❑ 5 Eric Chavez .30 .09
❑ 6 Carlos Delgado .30 .09
❑ 7 Javy Lopez .30 .09
❑ 8 Javier Vazquez .30 .09
❑ 9 Miguel Cabrera .30 .09
❑ 10 Manny Ramirez .50 .15
❑ 11 Scott Rolen .75 .23
❑ 12 Rafael Furcal .30 .09
❑ 13 Jim Thome .75 .23
❑ 14 Edgar Renteria .30 .09
❑ 15 Jason Kendall .30 .09
❑ 16 Alfonso Soriano .50 .15
❑ 17 Troy Glaus .30 .09
❑ 18 Vernon Wells .30 .09
❑ 19 Todd Helton .50 .15
❑ 20 Mark Mulder .30 .09
❑ 21 Albert Pujols 1.50 .45
❑ 22 Andy Pettitte .50 .15
❑ 23 Kevin Millwood .30 .09
❑ 24 Bret Boone .30 .09
❑ 25 Ken Griffey Jr. 1.25 .35
❑ 26 Kevin Brown .30 .09
❑ 27 J.D. Drew .30 .09
❑ 28 Corey Patterson .30 .09
❑ 29 Jason Giambi .30 .09
❑ 30 Jason Schmidt .30 .09
❑ 31 Jose Reyes .30 .09
❑ 32 Torii Hunter .30 .09
❑ 33 Brian Giles .30 .09
❑ 34 Garret Anderson .30 .09
❑ 35 Mark Teixeira .30 .09
❑ 36 Sammy Sosa 1.25 .35
❑ 37 Rocco Baldelli .30 .09
❑ 38 Jeff Bagwell .50 .15
❑ 39 Rafael Palmeiro .50 .15
❑ 40 Derrek Lee .30 .09
❑ 41 Randy Johnson .75 .23
❑ 42 Roger Clemens 1.50 .45
❑ 43 Austin Kearns .30 .09
❑ 44 Dontrelle Willis .30 .09
❑ 45 Lance Berkman .30 .09
❑ 46 Juan Gonzalez .50 .15
❑ 47 Ichiro Suzuki 1.25 .35
❑ 48 Pat Burrell .30 .09
❑ 49 Miguel Tejada .30 .09
❑ 50 Mike Piazza 1.25 .35
❑ 51 Mark Prior .75 .23
❑ 52 C.C. Sabathia .30 .09
❑ 53 Jacque Jones .30 .09
❑ 54 Carlos Beltran .50 .15
❑ 55 Mike Mussina .50 .15
❑ 56 Mike Lowell .30 .09
❑ 57 Phil Nevin .30 .09
❑ 58 Andruw Jones .30 .09
❑ 59 Barry Zito .30 .09
❑ 60 Magglio Ordonez .30 .09
❑ 61 Carlos Lee .30 .09
❑ 62 Nomar Garciaparra 1.25 .35
❑ 63 Kerry Wood .75 .23
❑ 64 Luis Gonzalez .30 .09
❑ 65 Derek Jeter 1.50 .45
❑ 66 Preston Wilson .30 .09
❑ 67 Greg Maddux 1.25 .35
❑ 68 Pedro Martinez .75 .23
❑ 69 Richie Sexson .30 .09
❑ 70 Hank Blalock .30 .09
❑ 71 Chipper Jones .75 .23
❑ 72 Ivan Rodriguez .75 .23
❑ 73 Roy Halladay .30 .09
❑ 74 Tim Hudson .30 .09
❑ 75 Ryan Klesko .30 .09
❑ 76 Hideki Matsui 1.25 .35
❑ 77 Josh Beckett .30 .09
❑ 78 Brandon Webb .30 .09
❑ 79 Alex Rodriguez 1.25 .35
❑ 80 Jim Edmonds .30 .09
❑ 81 Jeff Kent .30 .09
❑ 82 Bobby Abreu .30 .09
❑ 83 Curt Schilling .75 .23
❑ 84 Roy Oswalt .30 .09
❑ 85 Orlando Cabrera .30 .09
❑ 86 Johan Santana .50 .15
❑ 87 Geoff Jenkins .30 .09
❑ 88 Gary Sheffield .30 .09
❑ 89 Shawn Green .30 .09
❑ 90 Frank Thomas .75 .23
❑ 91 Tim Hamulack TC RC 1.00 .30
❑ 92 Shingo Takatsu TC RC 2.50 .75
❑ 93 Justin Huisman TC RC 1.00 .30
❑ 94 Sean Henn TC RC 1.00 .30
❑ 95 Jamie Brown TC RC 1.00 .30
❑ 96 Dennis Sarfate TC RC 1.00 .30
❑ 97 Lincoln Holdzkom TC RC 1.00 .30
❑ 98 Roman Colon TC RC 1.00 .30
❑ 99 Scott Dohmann TC RC 1.00 .30
❑ 100 Ivan Ochoa TC RC 1.00 .30
❑ 101 Akinori Otsuka TC RC 1.00 .30
❑ 102 Fernando Nieve TC RC 1.00 .30
❑ 103 Mike Johnston TC RC 1.00 .30
❑ 104 Mariano Gomez TC RC 1.00 .30
❑ 105 Justin Leone TC RC 1.50 .45
❑ 106 Evan Rust TC RC 1.00 .30
❑ 107 Mike Rouse TC RC 1.00 .30
❑ 108 Ian Snell TC RC 2.00 .60
❑ 109 Jason Bartlett TC RC 1.50 .45
❑ 110 Ryan Wing TC RC 1.00 .30
❑ 111 Nick Regilio TC RC 1.00 .30
❑ 112 Merkin Valdez TC RC 2.50 .75
❑ 113 Josh Labandeira TC RC 1.00 .30
❑ 114 David Aardsma TC RC 1.00 .30
❑ 115 Justin Knoedler TC RC 1.00 .30
❑ 116 Shawn Hill TC RC 1.00 .30
❑ 117 Casey Daigle TC RC 1.00 .30
❑ 118 Donnie Kelly TC RC 1.00 .30
❑ 119 Justin Germano TC RC 1.00 .30
❑ 120 Eddy Rodriguez TC RC 1.50 .45
❑ 121 Onil Joseph TC RC 1.00 .30
❑ 122 Michael Wuertz TC RC 1.50 .45
❑ 123 Roberto Novoa TC RC 1.50 .45
❑ 124 Jerome Gamble TC RC 1.00 .30
❑ 125 Justin Hampson TC RC 1.00 .30
❑ 126 Ronald Belisario TC RC 1.00 .30
❑ 127 Tim Bausher TC RC 1.00 .30
❑ 128 Chris Saenz TC RC 1.00 .30
❑ 129 Hector Gimenez TC RC 1.00 .30
❑ 130 Ronny Cedeno TC RC 1.00 .30
❑ 131 Jason Frasor TC RC 1.00 .30
❑ 132 Kazuo Matsui TC RC 4.00 1.20
❑ 133 Mike Gosling TC RC 1.00 .30
❑ 134 Jerry Gil TC RC 1.00 .30
❑ 135 Orlando Rodriguez TC RC 1.00 .30
❑ 136 Jorge Vasquez TC RC 1.00 .30
❑ 137 Chris Aguila TC RC 1.00 .30
❑ 138 Tim Bittner TC RC 1.00 .30
❑ 139 Jake Woods TC RC 1.00 .30
❑ 140 Enemencio Pacheco TC RC 1.00 .30
❑ 141 Dave Crouthers TC RC 1.00 .30
❑ 142 Jose Capellan TC RC 4.00 1.20
❑ 143 Chad Bentz TC RC 1.00 .30
❑ 144 Mike Vento TC RC 1.50 .45
❑ 145 Scott Proctor TC RC 1.50 .45
❑ 146 Edwin Moreno TC RC 1.50 .45
❑ 147 Brandon Medders TC RC 1.00 .30
❑ 148 Renyel Pinto TC RC 1.50 .45
❑ 149 Rusty Tucker TC RC 1.50 .45
❑ 150 Ryan Meaux TC RC 1.00 .30
❑ 151 William Bergolla TC RC 1.00 .30
❑ 152 Angel Chavez TC RC 1.00 .30
❑ 153 Colby Miller TC RC 1.00 .30
❑ 154 John Gall TC RC 1.50 .45
❑ 155 Carlos Hines TC RC 1.00 .30
❑ 156 Carlos Vasquez TC RC 1.50 .45
❑ 157 Justin Lehr TC RC 1.00 .30
❑ 158 Kevin Cave TC RC 1.50 .45
❑ 159 Jeff Bennett TC RC 1.00 .30
❑ 160 Greg Dobbs TC RC 1.00 .30
❑ 161 Jorge Sequea TC RC 1.00 .30
❑ 162 Chris Oxspring TC RC 1.50 .45
❑ 163 Franklyn Gracesqui TC RC 1.00 .30
❑ 164 Shawn Camp TC RC 1.00 .30
❑ 165 Lino Urdaneta TC RC 1.00 .30
❑ 166 Luis A. Gonzalez TC RC 1.00 .30
❑ 167 Ramon Ramirez TC RC 1.00 .30
❑ 168 Freddy Guzman TC RC 1.00 .30
❑ 169 Chris Shelton TC RC 2.00 .60
❑ 170 Andres Blanco TC RC 1.00 .30
❑ 171 Aarom Baldiris TC RC 1.50 .45
❑ 172 Kazuhito Tadano TC RC 1.50 .45

	Player	Nm-Mt	Ex-Mt
❑ 173	Brian Dallimore TC RC	1.00	.30
❑ 174	Eduardo Villacis TC RC	1.00	.30
❑ 175	Frank Francisco TC RC	1.00	.30
❑ 176	Edwin Jackson TC	1.00	.30
❑ 177	Bobby Crosby TC	1.50	.45
❑ 178	Joe Mauer TC	1.50	.45
❑ 179	Rickie Weeks TC	1.00	.30
❑ 180	Delmon Young TC	1.50	.45

2001 Upper Deck Victory

		Nm-Mt	Ex-Mt
COMPLETE SET (660)		50.00	15.00
❑ 1	Troy Glaus	.20	.06
❑ 2	Scott Spiezio	.20	.06
❑ 3	Gary DiSarcina	.20	.06
❑ 4	Darin Erstad	.20	.06
❑ 5	Tim Salmon	.30	.09
❑ 6	Troy Percival	.20	.06
❑ 7	Ramon Ortiz	.20	.06
❑ 8	Orlando Palmeiro	.20	.06
❑ 9	Tim Belcher	.20	.06
❑ 10	Mo Vaughn	.20	.06
❑ 11	Bengie Molina	.20	.06
❑ 12	Benji Gil	.20	.06
❑ 13	Scott Schoeneweis	.20	.06
❑ 14	Garret Anderson	.20	.06
❑ 15	Matt Wise	.20	.06
❑ 16	Adam Kennedy	.20	.06
❑ 17	Jarrod Washburn	.20	.06
❑ 18	Darin Erstad	.20	.06
	Troy Percival CL		
❑ 19	Jason Giambi	.20	.06
❑ 20	Tim Hudson	.20	.06
❑ 21	Ramon Hernandez	.20	.06
❑ 22	Eric Chavez	.20	.06
❑ 23	Gil Heredia	.20	.06
❑ 24	Jason Isringhausen	.20	.06
❑ 25	Jeremy Giambi	.20	.06
❑ 26	Miguel Tejada	.20	.06
❑ 27	Barry Zito	.30	.09
❑ 28	Terrence Long	.20	.06
❑ 29	Ryan Christenson	.20	.06
❑ 30	Mark Mulder	.20	.06
❑ 31	Olmedo Saenz	.20	.06
❑ 32	Adam Piatt	.20	.06
❑ 33	Ben Grieve	.20	.06
❑ 34	Omar Olivares	.20	.06
❑ 35	John Jaha	.20	.06
❑ 36	Jason Giambi	.20	.06
	Tim Hudson CL		
❑ 37	Carlos Delgado	.20	.06
❑ 38	Esteban Loaiza	.20	.06
❑ 39	Brad Fullmer	.20	.06
❑ 40	David Wells	.20	.06
❑ 41	Chris Woodward	.20	.06
❑ 42	Billy Koch	.20	.06
❑ 43	Shannon Stewart	.20	.06
❑ 44	Chris Carpenter	.20	.06
❑ 45	Steve Parris	.20	.06
❑ 46	Darrin Fletcher	.20	.06
❑ 47	Joey Hamilton	.20	.06
❑ 48	Jose Cruz Jr.	.20	.06
❑ 49	Vernon Wells	.20	.06
❑ 50	Raul Mondesi	.20	.06
❑ 51	Kelvim Escobar	.20	.06
❑ 52	Tony Batista	.20	.06
❑ 53	Alex Gonzalez	.20	.06
❑ 54	Carlos Delgado	.20	.06
	David Wells CL		
❑ 55	Greg Vaughn	.20	.06
❑ 56	Albie Lopez	.20	.06
❑ 57	Randy Winn	.20	.06
❑ 58	Ryan Rupe	.20	.06
❑ 59	Steve Cox	.20	.06
❑ 60	Vinny Castilla	.20	.06
❑ 61	Jose Guillen	.20	.06
❑ 62	Wilson Alvarez	.20	.06
❑ 63	Bryan Rekar	.20	.06
❑ 64	Gerald Williams	.20	.06
❑ 65	Esteban Yan	.20	.06
❑ 66	Felix Martinez	.20	.06
❑ 67	Fred McGriff	.30	.09
❑ 68	John Flaherty	.20	.06
❑ 69	Jason Tyner	.20	.06
❑ 70	Russ Johnson	.20	.06
❑ 71	Roberto Hernandez	.20	.06
❑ 72	Greg Vaughn	.20	.06
	Albie Lopez CL		
❑ 73	Eddie Taubensee	.20	.06
❑ 74	Bob Wickman	.20	.06
❑ 75	Ellis Burks	.20	.06
❑ 76	Kenny Lofton	.20	.06
❑ 77	Einar Diaz	.20	.06
❑ 78	Travis Fryman	.20	.06
❑ 79	Omar Vizquel	.30	.09
❑ 80	Jason Bere	.20	.06
❑ 81	Bartolo Colon	.20	.06
❑ 82	Jim Thome	.50	.15
❑ 83	Roberto Alomar	.30	.09
❑ 84	Chuck Finley	.20	.06
❑ 85	Steve Woodard	.20	.06
❑ 86	Russ Branyan	.20	.06
❑ 87	Dave Burba	.20	.06
❑ 88	Jaret Wright	.20	.06
❑ 89	Jacob Cruz	.20	.06
❑ 90	Steve Karsay	.20	.06
❑ 91	Manny Ramirez	.20	.06
	Bartolo Colon CL		
❑ 92	Raul Ibanez	.20	.06
❑ 93	Freddy Garcia	.20	.06
❑ 94	Edgar Martinez	.30	.09
❑ 95	Jay Buhner	.20	.06
❑ 96	Jamie Moyer	.20	.06
❑ 97	John Olerud	.20	.06
❑ 98	Aaron Sele	.20	.06
❑ 99	Kazuhiro Sasaki	.20	.06
❑ 100	Mike Cameron	.20	.06
❑ 101	John Halama	.20	.06
❑ 102	David Bell	.20	.06
❑ 103	Gil Meche	.20	.06
❑ 104	Carlos Guillen	.20	.06
❑ 105	Mark McLemore	.20	.06
❑ 106	Stan Javier	.20	.06
❑ 107	Al Martin	.20	.06
❑ 108	Dan Wilson	.20	.06
❑ 109	Alex Rodriguez	.50	.15
	Kazuhiro Sasaki CL		
❑ 110	Cal Ripken	1.50	.45
❑ 111	Delino DeShields	.20	.06
❑ 112	Sidney Ponson	.20	.06
❑ 113	Albert Belle	.20	.06
❑ 114	Jose Mercedes	.20	.06
❑ 115	Scott Erickson	.20	.06
❑ 116	Jerry Hairston Jr.	.20	.06
❑ 117	Brook Fordyce	.20	.06
❑ 118	Luis Matos	.20	.06
❑ 119	Eugene Kingsale	.20	.06
❑ 120	Jeff Conine	.20	.06
❑ 121	Chris Richard	.20	.06
❑ 122	Fernando Lunar	.20	.06
❑ 123	John Parrish	.20	.06
❑ 124	Brady Anderson	.20	.06
❑ 125	Ryan Kohlmeier	.20	.06
❑ 126	Melvin Mora	.20	.06
❑ 127	Albert Belle	.20	.06
	Jose Mercedes CL		
❑ 128	Ivan Rodriguez	.50	.15
❑ 129	Justin Thompson	.20	.06
❑ 130	Kenny Rogers	.20	.06
❑ 131	Rafael Palmeiro	.30	.09
❑ 132	Rusty Greer	.20	.06
❑ 133	Gabe Kapler	.20	.06
❑ 134	John Wetteland	.20	.06
❑ 135	Mike Lamb	.20	.06
❑ 136	Doug Davis	.20	.06
❑ 137	Ruben Mateo	.20	.06
❑ 138	A. Rodriguez Rangers	1.50	.45
❑ 139	Chad Curtis	.20	.06
❑ 140	Rick Helling	.20	.06
❑ 141	Ryan Glynn	.20	.06
❑ 142	Andres Galarraga	.20	.06
❑ 143	Ricky Ledee	.20	.06
❑ 144	Frank Catalanotto	.20	.06
❑ 145	Rafael Palmeiro	.20	.06
	Rick Helling CL		
❑ 146	Pedro Martinez	.50	.15
❑ 147	Wilton Veras	.20	.06
❑ 148	M. Ramirez Red Sox	.30	.09
❑ 149	Rolando Arrojo	.20	.06
❑ 150	Nomar Garciaparra	.75	.23
❑ 151	Darren Lewis	.20	.06
❑ 152	Troy O'Leary	.20	.06
❑ 153	Tomokazu Ohka	.20	.06
❑ 154	Carl Everett	.20	.06
❑ 155	Jason Varitek	.30	.09
❑ 156	Frank Castillo	.20	.06
❑ 157	Pete Schourek	.20	.06
❑ 158	Jose Offerman	.20	.06
❑ 159	Derek Lowe	.20	.06
❑ 160	John Valentin	.20	.06
❑ 161	Dante Bichette	.20	.06
❑ 162	Trot Nixon	.20	.06
❑ 163	Nomar Garciaparra	.50	.15
	Pedro Martinez CL		
❑ 164	Jermaine Dye	.20	.06
❑ 165	Dave McCarty	.20	.06
❑ 166	Jose Rosado	.20	.06
❑ 167	Mike Sweeney	.20	.06
❑ 168	Rey Sanchez	.20	.06
❑ 169	Jeff Suppan	.20	.06
❑ 170	Chad Durbin	.20	.06
❑ 171	Carlos Beltran	.30	.09
❑ 172	Brian Meadows	.20	.06
❑ 173	Todd Dunwoody	.20	.06
❑ 174	Johnny Damon	.30	.09
❑ 175	Blake Stein	.20	.06
❑ 176	Carlos Febles	.20	.06
❑ 177	Joe Randa	.20	.06
❑ 178	Mac Suzuki	.20	.06
❑ 179	Mark Quinn	.20	.06
❑ 180	Gregg Zaun	.20	.06
❑ 181	Mike Sweeney	.20	.06
	Jeff Suppan		
❑ 182	Juan Gonzalez	.30	.09
❑ 183	Dean Palmer	.20	.06
❑ 184	Wendell Magee	.20	.06
❑ 185	Todd Jones	.20	.06
❑ 186	Bobby Higginson	.20	.06
❑ 187	Brian Moehler	.20	.06
❑ 188	Juan Encarnacion	.20	.06
❑ 189	Tony Clark	.20	.06
❑ 190	Rich Becker	.20	.06
❑ 191	Roger Cedeno	.20	.06
❑ 192	Mitch Meluskey	.20	.06
❑ 193	Shane Halter	.20	.06
❑ 194	Jeff Weaver	.20	.06
❑ 195	Deivi Cruz	.20	.06
❑ 196	Damion Easley	.20	.06
❑ 197	Robert Fick	.20	.06
❑ 198	Matt Anderson	.20	.06
❑ 199	Bobby Higginson	.20	.06
	Brian Moehler		
❑ 200	Brad Radke	.20	.06
❑ 201	Mark Redman	.20	.06
❑ 202	Corey Koskie	.20	.06
❑ 203	Matt Lawton	.20	.06
❑ 204	Eric Milton	.20	.06
❑ 205	Chad Moeller	.20	.06
❑ 206	Jacque Jones	.20	.06
❑ 207	Matt Kinney	.20	.06
❑ 208	Jay Canizaro	.20	.06
❑ 209	Torii Hunter	.20	.06
❑ 210	Ron Coomer	.20	.06
❑ 211	Chad Allen	.20	.06
❑ 212	Denny Hocking	.20	.06
❑ 213	Cristian Guzman	.20	.06
❑ 214	LaTroy Hawkins	.20	.06

❑ 215 Joe Mays .20 .06
❑ 216 David Ortiz .30 .09
❑ 217 Matt Lawton .20 .06
Eric Milton CL
❑ 218 Frank Thomas .50 .15
❑ 219 Jose Valentin .20 .06
❑ 220 Mike Sirotka .20 .06
❑ 221 Kip Wells .20 .06
❑ 222 Magglio Ordonez .20 .06
❑ 223 Herbert Perry .20 .06
❑ 224 James Baldwin .20 .06
❑ 225 Jon Garland .20 .06
❑ 226 Sandy Alomar Jr. .20 .06
❑ 227 Chris Singleton .20 .06
❑ 228 Keith Foulke .20 .06
❑ 229 Paul Konerko .20 .06
❑ 230 Jim Parque .20 .06
❑ 231 Greg Norton .20 .06
❑ 232 Carlos Lee .20 .06
❑ 233 Cal Eldred .20 .06
❑ 234 Ray Durham .20 .06
❑ 235 Jeff Abbott .20 .06
❑ 236 Frank Thomas .30 .09
Mike Sirotka CL
❑ 237 Derek Jeter 1.25 .35
❑ 238 Glenallen Hill .20 .06
❑ 239 Roger Clemens 1.00 .30
❑ 240 Bernie Williams .30 .09
❑ 241 David Justice .20 .06
❑ 242 Luis Sojo .20 .06
❑ 243 Orlando Hernandez .20 .06
❑ 244 Mike Mussina .30 .09
❑ 245 Jorge Posada .30 .09
❑ 246 Andy Pettitte .30 .09
❑ 247 Paul O'Neill .30 .09
❑ 248 Scott Brosius .20 .06
❑ 249 Alfonso Soriano .30 .09
❑ 250 Mariano Rivera .30 .09
❑ 251 Chuck Knoblauch .20 .06
❑ 252 Ramiro Mendoza .20 .06
❑ 253 Tino Martinez .30 .09
❑ 254 David Cone .20 .06
❑ 255 Derek Jeter .60 .18
Andy Pettite CL
❑ 256 Jeff Bagwell .30 .09
❑ 257 Lance Berkman .20 .06
❑ 258 Craig Biggio .30 .09
❑ 259 Scott Elarton .20 .06
❑ 260 Bill Spiers .20 .06
❑ 261 Moises Alou .20 .06
❑ 262 Billy Wagner .20 .06
❑ 263 Shane Reynolds .20 .06
❑ 264 Tony Eusebio .20 .06
❑ 265 Julio Lugo .20 .06
❑ 266 Jose Lima .20 .06
❑ 267 Octavio Dotel .20 .06
❑ 268 Brad Ausmus .20 .06
❑ 269 Daryle Ward .20 .06
❑ 270 Glen Barker .20 .06
❑ 271 Wade Miller .20 .06
❑ 272 Richard Hidalgo .20 .06
❑ 273 Chris Truby .20 .06
❑ 274 Jeff Bagwell .20 .06
Scott Elarton CL
❑ 275 Greg Maddux .75 .23
❑ 276 Chipper Jones .50 .15
❑ 277 Tom Glavine .30 .09
❑ 278 Brian Jordan .20 .06
❑ 279 Andruw Jones .20 .06
❑ 280 Kevin Millwood .20 .06
❑ 281 Rico Brogna .20 .06
❑ 282 George Lombard .20 .06
❑ 283 Reggie Sanders .20 .06
❑ 284 John Rocker .20 .06
❑ 285 Rafael Furcal .20 .06
❑ 286 John Smoltz .30 .09
❑ 287 Javy Lopez .20 .06
❑ 288 Walt Weiss .20 .06
❑ 289 Quilvio Veras .20 .06
❑ 290 Eddie Perez .20 .06
❑ 291 B.J. Surhoff .20 .06
❑ 292 Chipper Jones .30 .09
Tom Glavine CL
❑ 293 Jeromy Burnitz .20 .06
❑ 294 Charlie Hayes .20 .06
❑ 295 Jeff D'Amico .20 .06
❑ 296 Jose Hernandez .20 .06
❑ 297 Richie Sexson .20 .06
❑ 298 Tyler Houston .20 .06
❑ 299 Paul Rigdon .20 .06
❑ 300 Jamey Wright .20 .06
❑ 301 Mark Loretta .20 .06
❑ 302 Geoff Jenkins .20 .06
❑ 303 Luis Lopez .20 .06
❑ 304 John Snyder .20 .06
❑ 305 Henry Blanco .20 .06
❑ 306 Curtis Leskanic .20 .06
❑ 307 Ron Belliard .20 .06
❑ 308 Jimmy Haynes .20 .06
❑ 309 Marquis Grissom .20 .06
❑ 310 Geoff Jenkins .20 .06
Jeff D'Amico CL
❑ 311 Mark McGwire 1.25 .35
❑ 312 Rick Ankiel .20 .06
❑ 313 Dave Veres .20 .06
❑ 314 Carlos Hernandez .20 .06
❑ 315 Jim Edmonds .20 .06
❑ 316 Andy Benes .20 .06
❑ 317 Garrett Stephenson .20 .06
❑ 318 Ray Lankford .20 .06
❑ 319 Dustin Hermanson .20 .06
❑ 320 Steve Kline .20 .06
❑ 321 Mike Matheny .20 .06
❑ 322 Edgar Renteria .20 .06
❑ 323 J.D. Drew .20 .06
❑ 324 Craig Paquette .20 .06
❑ 325 Darryl Kile .20 .06
❑ 326 Fernando Vina .20 .06
❑ 327 Eric Davis .20 .06
❑ 328 Placido Polanco .20 .06
❑ 329 Jim Edmonds .20 .06
Darryl Kile CL
❑ 330 Sammy Sosa .75 .23
❑ 331 Rick Aguilera .20 .06
❑ 332 Willie Greene .20 .06
❑ 333 Kerry Wood .50 .15
❑ 334 Todd Hundley .20 .06
❑ 335 Rondell White .20 .06
❑ 336 Julio Zuleta .20 .06
❑ 337 Jon Lieber .20 .06
❑ 338 Joe Girardi .20 .06
❑ 339 Damon Buford .20 .06
❑ 340 Kevin Tapani .20 .06
❑ 341 Ricky Gutierrez .20 .06
❑ 342 Bill Mueller .20 .06
❑ 343 Ruben Quevedo .20 .06
❑ 344 Eric Young .20 .06
❑ 345 Gary Matthews Jr. .20 .06
❑ 346 Daniel Garibay .20 .06
❑ 347 Sammy Sosa .30 .09
Jon Lieber CL
❑ 348 Randy Johnson .50 .15
❑ 349 Matt Williams .20 .06
❑ 350 Kelly Stinnett .20 .06
❑ 351 Brian Anderson .20 .06
❑ 352 Steve Finley .20 .06
❑ 353 Curt Schilling .20 .06
❑ 354 Erubiel Durazo .20 .06
❑ 355 Todd Stottlemyre .20 .06
❑ 356 Mark Grace .30 .09
❑ 357 Luis Gonzalez .20 .06
❑ 358 Danny Bautista .20 .06
❑ 359 Matt Mantei .20 .06
❑ 360 Tony Womack .20 .06
❑ 361 Armando Reynoso .20 .06
❑ 362 Greg Colbrunn .20 .06
❑ 363 Jay Bell .20 .06
❑ 364 Byung-Hyun Kim .20 .06
❑ 365 Luis Gonzalez .30 .09
Randy Johnson CL
❑ 366 Gary Sheffield .20 .06
❑ 367 Eric Karros .20 .06
❑ 368 Jeff Shaw .20 .06
❑ 369 Jim Leyritz .20 .06
❑ 370 Kevin Brown .20 .06
❑ 371 Alex Cora .20 .06
❑ 372 Andy Ashby .20 .06
❑ 373 Eric Gagne .50 .15
❑ 374 Chan Ho Park .20 .06
❑ 375 Shawn Green .20 .06
❑ 376 Kevin Elster .20 .06
❑ 377 Mark Grudzielanek .20 .06
❑ 378 Darren Dreifort .20 .06
❑ 379 Dave Hansen .20 .06
❑ 380 Bruce Aven .20 .06
❑ 381 Adrian Beltre .30 .09
❑ 382 Tom Goodwin .20 .06
❑ 383 Gary Sheffield .20 .06
Chan Ho Park CL
❑ 384 Vladimir Guerrero .50 .15
❑ 385 Ugueth Urbina .20 .06
❑ 386 Michael Barrett .20 .06
❑ 387 Geoff Blum .20 .06
❑ 388 Fernando Tatis .20 .06
❑ 389 Carl Pavano .20 .06
❑ 390 Jose Vidro .20 .06
❑ 391 Orlando Cabrera .20 .06
❑ 392 Terry Jones .20 .06
❑ 393 Mike Thurman .20 .06
❑ 394 Lee Stevens .20 .06
❑ 395 Tony Armas Jr. .20 .06
❑ 396 Wilton Guerrero .20 .06
❑ 397 Peter Bergeron .20 .06
❑ 398 Milton Bradley .20 .06
❑ 399 Javier Vazquez .20 .06
❑ 400 Fernando Seguignol .20 .06
❑ 401 Vladimir Guerrero .30 .09
Dustin Hermanson CL
❑ 402 Barry Bonds 1.25 .35
❑ 403 Russ Ortiz .20 .06
❑ 404 Calvin Murray .20 .06
❑ 405 Armando Rios .20 .06
❑ 406 Livan Hernandez .20 .06
❑ 407 Jeff Kent .20 .06
❑ 408 Bobby Estalella .20 .06
❑ 409 Felipe Crespo .20 .06
❑ 410 Shawn Estes .20 .06
❑ 411 J.T. Snow .20 .06
❑ 412 Marvin Benard .20 .06
❑ 413 Joe Nathan .20 .06
❑ 414 Robb Nen .20 .06
❑ 415 Shawon Dunston .20 .06
❑ 416 Mark Gardner .20 .06
❑ 417 Kirk Rueter .20 .06
❑ 418 Rich Aurilia .20 .06
❑ 419 Doug Mirabelli .20 .06
❑ 420 Russ Davis .20 .06
❑ 421 Barry Bonds .60 .18
Livan Hernandez CL
❑ 422 Cliff Floyd .20 .06
❑ 423 Luis Castillo .20 .06
❑ 424 Antonio Alfonseca .20 .06
❑ 425 Preston Wilson .20 .06
❑ 426 Ryan Dempster .20 .06
❑ 427 Jesus Sanchez .20 .06
❑ 428 Derrek Lee .20 .06
❑ 429 Brad Penny .20 .06
❑ 430 Mark Kotsay .20 .06
❑ 431 Alex Fernandez .20 .06
❑ 432 Mike Lowell .20 .06
❑ 433 Chuck Smith .20 .06
❑ 434 Alex Gonzalez .20 .06
❑ 435 Dave Berg .20 .06
❑ 436 A.J. Burnett .20 .06
❑ 437 Charles Johnson .20 .06
❑ 438 Reid Cornelius .20 .06
❑ 439 Mike Redmond .20 .06
❑ 440 Preston Wilson .20 .06
Ryan Dempster CL
❑ 441 Mike Piazza .75 .23
❑ 442 Kevin Appier .20 .06
❑ 443 Jay Payton .20 .06
❑ 444 Steve Trachsel .20 .06
❑ 445 Al Leiter .20 .06
❑ 446 Joe McEwing .20 .06
❑ 447 Armando Benitez .20 .06
❑ 448 Edgardo Alfonzo .20 .06
❑ 449 Glendon Rusch .20 .06
❑ 450 Mike Bordick .20 .06
❑ 451 Lenny Harris .20 .06
❑ 452 Matt Franco .20 .06
❑ 453 Darryl Hamilton .20 .06
❑ 454 Bobby Jones .20 .06
❑ 455 Robin Ventura .20 .06
❑ 456 Todd Zeile .20 .06
❑ 457 John Franco .20 .06
❑ 458 Mike Piazza .50 .15
Al Leiter CL

❑ 459 Tony Gwynn .60 .18
❑ 460 John Mabry .20 .06
❑ 461 Trevor Hoffman .20 .06
❑ 462 Phil Nevin .20 .06
❑ 463 Ryan Klesko .20 .06
❑ 464 Wiki Gonzalez .20 .06
❑ 465 Matt Clement .20 .06
❑ 466 Alex Arias .20 .06
❑ 467 Woody Williams .20 .06
❑ 468 Ruben Rivera .20 .06
❑ 469 Sterling Hitchcock .20 .06
❑ 470 Ben Davis .20 .06
❑ 471 Bubba Trammell .20 .06
❑ 472 Jay Witasick .20 .06
❑ 473 Eric Owens .20 .06
❑ 474 Damian Jackson .20 .06
❑ 475 Adam Eaton .20 .06
❑ 476 Mike Darr .20 .06
❑ 477 Phil Nevin .20 .06
Trevor Hoffman CL
❑ 478 Scott Rolen .50 .15
❑ 479 Robert Person .20 .06
❑ 480 Mike Lieberthal .20 .06
❑ 481 Reggie Taylor .20 .06
❑ 482 Paul Byrd .20 .06
❑ 483 Bruce Chen .20 .06
❑ 484 Pat Burrell .20 .06
❑ 485 Kevin Jordan .20 .06
❑ 486 Bobby Abreu .20 .06
❑ 487 Randy Wolf .20 .06
❑ 488 Kevin Selcik .20 .06
❑ 489 Brian Hunter .20 .06
❑ 490 Doug Glanville .20 .06
❑ 491 Kent Bottenfield .20 .06
❑ 492 Travis Lee .20 .06
❑ 493 Jeff Brantley .20 .06
❑ 494 Omar Daal .20 .06
❑ 495 Bobby Abreu .20 .06
Randy Wolf CL
❑ 496 Jason Kendall .20 .06
❑ 497 Adrian Brown .20 .06
❑ 498 Warren Morris .20 .06
❑ 499 Brian Giles .20 .06
❑ 500 Jimmy Anderson .20 .06
❑ 501 John VanderWal .20 .06
❑ 502 Mike Williams .20 .06
❑ 503 Aramis Ramirez .20 .06
❑ 504 Pat Meares .20 .06
❑ 505 Jason Schmidt .20 .06
❑ 506 Todd Ritchie .20 .06
❑ 507 Abraham Nunez .20 .06
❑ 508 Jose Silva .20 .06
❑ 509 Francisco Cordova .20 .06
❑ 510 Kevin Young .20 .06
❑ 511 Derek Bell .20 .06
❑ 512 Kris Benson .20 .06
❑ 513 Brian Giles .20 .06
Jose Silva CL
❑ 514 Ken Griffey Jr. .75 .23
❑ 515 Scott Williamson .20 .06
❑ 516 Dmitri Young .20 .06
❑ 517 Sean Casey .20 .06
❑ 518 Barry Larkin .30 .09
❑ 519 Juan Castro .20 .06
❑ 520 Danny Graves .20 .06
❑ 521 Aaron Boone .20 .06
❑ 522 Pokey Reese .20 .06
❑ 523 Elmer Dessens .20 .06
❑ 524 Michael Tucker .20 .06
❑ 525 Benito Santiago .20 .06
❑ 526 Pete Harnisch .20 .06
❑ 527 Alex Ochoa .20 .06
❑ 528 Gookie Dawkins .20 .06
❑ 529 Seth Etherton .20 .06
❑ 530 Rob Bell .20 .06
❑ 531 Ken Griffey Jr. .50 .15
Steve Parris CL
❑ 532 Todd Helton .30 .09
❑ 533 Jose Jimenez .20 .06
❑ 534 Todd Walker .20 .06
❑ 535 Ron Gant .20 .06
❑ 536 Neifi Perez .20 .06
❑ 537 Butch Huskey .20 .06
❑ 538 Pedro Astacio .20 .06
❑ 539 Juan Pierre .20 .06
❑ 540 Jeff Cirillo .20 .06
❑ 541 Ben Petrick .20 .06
❑ 542 Brian Bohanon .20 .06
❑ 543 Larry Walker .30 .09
❑ 544 Masato Yoshii .20 .06
❑ 545 Denny Neagle .20 .06
❑ 546 Brent Mayne .20 .06
❑ 547 Mike Hampton .20 .06
❑ 548 Todd Hollandsworth .20 .06
❑ 549 Brian Rose .20 .06
❑ 550 Todd Helton .20 .06
Pedro Astacio CL
❑ 551 Jason Hart .20 .06
❑ 552 Joe Crede .20 .06
❑ 553 Timo Perez .20 .06
❑ 554 Brady Clark .20 .06
❑ 555 Adam Pettyjohn RC .20 .06
❑ 556 Jason Grilli .20 .06
❑ 557 Paxton Crawford .20 .06
❑ 558 Jay Spurgeon .20 .06
❑ 559 Hector Ortiz .20 .06
❑ 560 Vernon Wells .20 .06
❑ 561 Aubrey Huff .20 .06
❑ 562 Xavier Nady .20 .06
❑ 563 Billy McMillon .20 .06
❑ 564 Ichiro Suzuki RC 8.00 2.40
❑ 565 Tomas De la Rosa .20 .06
❑ 566 Matt Ginter .20 .06
❑ 567 Sun Woo Kim .20 .06
❑ 568 Nick Johnson .20 .06
❑ 569 Pablo Ozuna .20 .06
❑ 570 Tike Redman .20 .06
❑ 571 Brian Cole .20 .06
❑ 572 Ross Gload .20 .06
❑ 573 Dee Brown .20 .06
❑ 574 Tony McKnight .20 .06
❑ 575 Allen Levrault .20 .06
❑ 576 Lesli Brea .20 .06
❑ 577 Adam Bernero .20 .06
❑ 578 Tom Davey .20 .06
❑ 579 Morgan Burkhart .20 .06
❑ 580 Britt Reames .20 .06
❑ 581 Dave Coggin .20 .06
❑ 582 Trey Moore .20 .06
❑ 583 Matt Kinney .20 .06
❑ 584 Pedro Feliz .20 .06
❑ 585 Brandon Inge .20 .06
❑ 586 Alex Hernandez .20 .06
❑ 587 Toby Hall .20 .06
❑ 588 Grant Roberts .20 .06
❑ 589 Brian Sikorski .20 .06
❑ 590 Aaron Myette .20 .06
❑ 591 Derek Jeter PM 1.25 .35
❑ 592 Ivan Rodriguez PM .30 .09
❑ 593 Alex Rodriguez PM .75 .23
❑ 594 Carlos Delgado PM .20 .06
❑ 595 Mark McGwire PM 1.25 .35
❑ 596 Troy Glaus PM .20 .06
❑ 597 Sammy Sosa PM .75 .23
❑ 598 Vladimir Guerrero PM .50 .15
❑ 599 Manny Ramirez PM .20 .06
❑ 600 Pedro Martinez PM .30 .09
❑ 601 Chipper Jones PM .30 .09
❑ 602 Jason Giambi PM .20 .06
❑ 603 Frank Thomas PM .30 .09
❑ 604 Ken Griffey Jr. PM .75 .23
❑ 605 Nomar Garciaparra PM .75 .23
❑ 606 Randy Johnson PM .30 .09
❑ 607 Mike Piazza PM .75 .23
❑ 608 Barry Bonds PM 1.25 .35
❑ 609 Todd Helton PM .20 .06
❑ 610 Jeff Bagwell PM .20 .06
❑ 611 Ken Griffey Jr. VB .75 .23
❑ 612 Carlos Delgado VB .20 .06
❑ 613 Jeff Bagwell VB .20 .06
❑ 614 Jason Giambi VB .20 .06
❑ 615 Cal Ripken VB 1.50 .45
❑ 616 Brian Giles VB .20 .06
❑ 617 Bernie Williams VB .20 .06
❑ 618 Greg Maddux VB .75 .23
❑ 619 Troy Glaus VB .20 .06
❑ 620 Greg Vaughn VB .20 .06
❑ 621 Sammy Sosa VB .75 .23
❑ 622 Pat Burrell VB .20 .06
❑ 623 Ivan Rodriguez VB .30 .09
❑ 624 Chipper Jones VB .30 .09
❑ 625 Barry Bonds VB 1.25 .35
❑ 626 Roger Clemens VB 1.00 .30
❑ 627 Jim Edmonds VB .20 .06
❑ 628 Nomar Garciaparra VB .75 .23
❑ 629 Frank Thomas VB .30 .09
❑ 630 Mike Piazza VB .75 .23
❑ 631 Randy Johnson VB .30 .09
❑ 632 Andruw Jones VB .20 .06
❑ 633 David Wells VB .20 .06
❑ 634 Manny Ramirez VB .20 .06
❑ 635 Preston Wilson VB .20 .06
❑ 636 Todd Helton VB .20 .06
❑ 637 Kerry Wood VB .30 .09
❑ 638 Albert Belle VB .20 .06
❑ 639 Juan Gonzalez VB .20 .06
❑ 640 Vladimir Guerrero VB .50 .15
❑ 641 Gary Sheffield VB .20 .06
❑ 642 Larry Walker VB .30 .09
❑ 643 Magglio Ordonez VB .20 .06
❑ 644 Jermaine Dye VB .20 .06
❑ 645 Scott Rolen VB .30 .09
❑ 646 Tony Gwynn VB .60 .18
❑ 647 Shawn Green VB .20 .06
❑ 648 Roberto Alomar VB .20 .06
❑ 649 Eric Milton VB .20 .06
❑ 650 Mark McGwire VB 1.25 .35
❑ 651 Tim Hudson VB .20 .06
❑ 652 Jose Canseco VB .20 .06
❑ 653 Tom Glavine VB .20 .06
❑ 654 Derek Jeter VB 1.25 .35
❑ 655 Alex Rodriguez VB .75 .23
❑ 656 Darin Erstad VB .20 .06
❑ 657 Jason Kendall VB .20 .06
❑ 658 Pedro Martinez VB .30 .09
❑ 659 Richie Sexson VB .20 .06
❑ 660 Rafael Palmeiro VB .20 .06

2001 Upper Deck Vintage

	Nm-Mt	Ex-Mt
COMPLETE SET (400)	50.00	15.00
COMMON (1-340/371-400)	.30	.09
COMMON (341-370)	.50	.15

❑ 1 Darin Erstad .30 .09
❑ 2 Seth Etherton .30 .09
❑ 3 Troy Glaus .30 .09
❑ 4 Bengie Molina .30 .09
❑ 5 Mo Vaughn .30 .09
❑ 6 Tim Salmon .50 .15
❑ 7 Ramon Ortiz .30 .09
❑ 8 Adam Kennedy .30 .09
❑ 9 Garret Anderson .30 .09
❑ 10 Troy Percival .30 .09
❑ 11 Tim Salmon .30 .09
Bengie Molina
MoVaughn
Adam Kennedy
Troy Glaus
Kevin Stocker
Darin Erstad
Garret Anderson
Ron Gant CL
❑ 12 Jason Giambi .30 .09
❑ 13 Tim Hudson .30 .09
❑ 14 Adam Piatt .30 .09
❑ 15 Miguel Tejada .30 .09
❑ 16 Mark Mulder .30 .09

❑ 17 Eric Chavez .30 .09
❑ 18 Ramon Hernandez .30 .09
❑ 19 Terrence Long .30 .09
❑ 20 Jason Isringhausen .30 .09
❑ 21 Barry Zito .50 .15
❑ 22 Ben Grieve .30 .09
❑ 23 Olmedo Saenz .30 .09
Ramon Hernandez
Jason Giambi
Randy Velarde
Eric Chavez
Miguel Tejada
Ben Grieve
Terrence Long
Adam Piatt CL
❑ 24 David Wells .30 .09
❑ 25 Raul Mondesi .30 .09
❑ 26 Darrin Fletcher .30 .09
❑ 27 Shannon Stewart .30 .09
❑ 28 Kelvim Escobar .30 .09
❑ 29 Tony Batista .30 .09
❑ 30 Carlos Delgado .30 .09
❑ 31 Brad Fullmer .30 .09
❑ 32 Billy Koch .30 .09
❑ 33 Jose Cruz Jr. .30 .09
❑ 34 Brad Fullmer .30 .09
Darrin Fletcher
Carlos Delgado
Homer Bush
Tony Batista
Alex Gonzalez
Shannon Stewart
Jose Cruz Jr.
Raul Mondesi CL
❑ 35 Greg Vaughn .30 .09
❑ 36 Roberto Hernandez .30 .09
❑ 37 Vinny Castilla .30 .09
❑ 38 Gerald Williams .30 .09
❑ 39 Aubrey Huff .30 .09
❑ 40 Bryan Rekar .30 .09
❑ 41 Albie Lopez .30 .09
❑ 42 Fred McGriff .50 .15
❑ 43 Miguel Cairo .30 .09
❑ 44 Ryan Rupe .30 .09
❑ 45 Greg Vaughn .30 .09
John Flaherty
Fred McGriff
Miguel Cairo
Vinny Castilla
Felix Martinez
Gerald Williams
Jose Guillen
Steve Cox CL
❑ 46 Jim Thome .75 .23
❑ 47 Roberto Alomar .50 .15
❑ 48 Bartolo Colon .30 .09
❑ 49 Omar Vizquel .50 .15
❑ 50 Travis Fryman .30 .09
❑ 51 Manny Ramirez UER .50 .15
Picture is of David Segui
❑ 52 Dave Burba .30 .09
❑ 53 Chuck Finley .30 .09
❑ 54 Russ Branyan .30 .09
❑ 55 Kenny Lofton .30 .09
❑ 56 Russell Branyan .30 .09
Sandy Alomar Jr.
Jim Thome
Roberto Alomar
Travis Fryman
Omar Vizquel
Wil Cordero
Kenny Lofton
Manny Ramirez
Picture is off David Segui CL UER
❑ 57 Alex Rodriguez 1.25 .35
❑ 58 Jay Buhner .30 .09
❑ 59 Aaron Sele .30 .09
❑ 60 Kazuhiro Sasaki .30 .09
❑ 61 Edgar Martinez .50 .15
❑ 62 John Halama .30 .09
❑ 63 Mike Cameron .30 .09
❑ 64 Freddy Garcia .30 .09
❑ 65 John Olerud .25 .09
❑ 66 Jamie Moyer .30 .09
❑ 67 Gil Meche .30 .09
❑ 68 Edgar Martinez .30 .09
Joe Oliver
John Olerud
David Bell
Carlos Guillen
Alex Rodriguez
Jay Buhner
Mike Cameron
Al Martin CL
❑ 69 Cal Ripken 2.50 .75
❑ 70 Sidney Ponson .30 .09
❑ 71 Chris Richard .30 .09
❑ 72 Jose Mercedes .30 .09
❑ 73 Albert Belle .30 .09
❑ 74 Mike Mussina .50 .15
❑ 75 Brady Anderson .30 .09
❑ 76 Delino DeShields .30 .09
❑ 77 Melvin Mora .30 .09
❑ 78 Luis Matos .30 .09
❑ 79 Brook Fordyce .30 .09
❑ 80 Jeff Conine .30 .09
Brook Fordyce
Chris Richard
Delino DeShields
Cal Ripken
Melvin Mora
Luis Matos
Brady Anderson
Albert Belle CL
❑ 81 Rafael Palmeiro .50 .15
❑ 82 Rick Helling .30 .09
❑ 83 Ruben Mateo .30 .09
❑ 84 Rusty Greer .30 .09
❑ 85 Ivan Rodriguez .75 .23
❑ 86 Doug Davis .30 .09
❑ 87 Gabe Kapler .30 .09
❑ 88 Mike Lamb .30 .09
❑ 89 A.Rodriguez Rangers 3.00 .90
❑ 90 Kenny Rogers .30 .09
❑ 91 David Segui .50 .15
Ivan Rodriguez
Rafael Palmeiro
Frank Catalanotto
Mike Lamb
Royce Clayton
Ruben Mateo
Gabe Kapler
Rusty Greer CL
❑ 92 Nomar Garciaparra 1.25 .35
❑ 93 Trot Nixon .30 .09
❑ 94 Tomokazu Ohka .30 .09
❑ 95 Pedro Martinez .75 .23
❑ 96 Dante Bichette .30 .09
❑ 97 Jason Varitek .50 .15
❑ 98 Rolando Arrojo .30 .09
❑ 99 Carl Everett .30 .09
❑ 100 Derek Lowe .30 .09
❑ 101 Troy O'Leary .30 .09
❑ 102 Tim Wakefield .30 .09
❑ 103 Troy O'Leary .30 .09
Jason Varitek
Jose Offerman
Mike Lansing
Wilton Veras
Nomar Garciaparra
Carl Everett
Trot Nixon
Dante Bichette CL
❑ 104 Mike Sweeney .30 .09
❑ 105 Carlos Febles .30 .09
❑ 106 Joe Randa .30 .09
❑ 107 Jeff Suppan .30 .09
❑ 108 Mac Suzuki .30 .09
❑ 109 Jermaine Dye .30 .09
❑ 110 Carlos Beltran .50 .15
❑ 111 Mark Quinn .30 .09
❑ 112 Johnny Damon .50 .15
❑ 113 Mark Quinn .30 .09
Gregg Zaun
Mike Sweeney
Carlos Febles
Joe Randa
Rey Sanchez
Carlos Beltran
Johnny Damon
Jermaine Dye CL
❑ 114 Tony Clark .30 .09
❑ 115 Dean Palmer .30 .09
❑ 116 Brian Moehler .30 .09
❑ 117 Brad Ausmus .30 .09
❑ 118 Juan Gonzalez .50 .15
❑ 119 Juan Encarnacion .30 .09
❑ 120 Jeff Weaver .30 .09
❑ 121 Bobby Higginson .30 .09
❑ 122 Todd Jones .30 .09
❑ 123 Deivi Cruz .30 .09
❑ 124 Juan Gonzalez .30 .09
Brad Ausmus
Tony Clark
Damion Easley
Dean Palmer
Deivi Cruz
Bobby Higginson
Juan Encarnacion
Rich Becker CL
❑ 125 Corey Koskie .30 .09
❑ 126 Matt Lawton .30 .09
❑ 127 Mark Redman .30 .09
❑ 128 David Ortiz .50 .15
❑ 129 Jay Canizaro .30 .09
❑ 130 Eric Milton .30 .09
❑ 131 Jacque Jones .30 .09
❑ 132 J.C. Romero .30 .09
❑ 133 Ron Coomer .30 .09
❑ 134 Brad Radke .30 .09
❑ 135 David Ortiz .50 .15
Matt LeCroy
Ron Coomer
Jay Canizaro
Corey Koskie
Cristian Guzman
Jacque Jones
Matt Lawton
Torii Hunter CL
❑ 136 Carlos Lee .30 .09
❑ 137 Frank Thomas .75 .23
❑ 138 Mike Sirotka .30 .09
❑ 139 Charles Johnson .30 .09
❑ 140 James Baldwin .30 .09
❑ 141 Magglio Ordonez .30 .09
❑ 142 Jon Garland .30 .09
❑ 143 Paul Konerko .30 .09
❑ 144 Ray Durham .30 .09
❑ 145 Keith Foulke .30 .09
❑ 146 Chris Singleton .30 .09
❑ 147 Frank Thomas .50 .15
Charles Johnson
Paul Konerko
Ray Durham
Herbert Perry
Jose Valentin
Carlos Lee
Magglio Ordonez
Chris Singleton CL
❑ 148 Bernie Williams .50 .15
❑ 149 Orlando Hernandez .30 .09
❑ 150 David Justice .30 .09
❑ 151 Andy Pettitte .50 .15
❑ 152 Mariano Rivera .50 .15
❑ 153 Derek Jeter 2.00 .60
❑ 154 Jorge Posada .50 .15
❑ 155 Jose Canseco .75 .23
❑ 156 Glenallen Hill .30 .09
❑ 157 Paul O'Neill .50 .15
❑ 158 Denny Neagle .30 .09
❑ 159 Chuck Knoblauch .30 .09
❑ 160 Roger Clemens 1.50 .45
❑ 161 Glenallen Hill .75 .23
Jorge Posada
Tino Martinez
Chuck Knoblauch
Scott Brosius
Derek Jeter
Paul O'Neill
Bernie Williams
David Justice CL
❑ 162 Jeff Bagwell .50 .15
❑ 163 Moises Alou .30 .09
❑ 164 Lance Berkman .30 .09
❑ 165 Shane Reynolds .30 .09
❑ 166 Ken Caminiti .30 .09
❑ 167 Craig Biggio .50 .15
❑ 168 Jose Lima .30 .09

❑ 169 Octavio Dotel .30 .09
❑ 170 Richard Hidalgo .30 .09
❑ 171 Scott Elarton .30 .09
❑ 172 Scott Elarton .50 .15
Mitch Meluskey
Jeff Bagwell
Craig Biggio
Bill Spiers
Julio Lugo
Moises Alou
Richard Hidalgo
Lance Berkman CL
❑ 173 Rafael Furcal .30 .09
❑ 174 Greg Maddux 1.25 .35
❑ 175 Quilvio Veras .30 .09
❑ 176 Chipper Jones .75 .23
❑ 177 Andres Galarraga .30 .09
❑ 178 Brian Jordan .30 .09
❑ 179 Tom Glavine .50 .15
❑ 180 Kevin Millwood .30 .09
❑ 181 Javier Lopez .30 .09
❑ 182 B.J. Surhoff .30 .09
❑ 183 Andruw Jones .30 .09
❑ 184 Andy Ashby .30 .09
❑ 185 Tom Glavine .30 .09
Javy Lopez
Andres Galarraga
Quilvio Veras
Chipper Jones
Rafael Furcal
Reggie Sanders
Brian Jordan
Andruw Jones CL
❑ 186 Richie Sexson .30 .09
❑ 187 Jeff D'Amico .30 .09
❑ 188 Ron Belliard .30 .09
❑ 189 Jeromy Burnitz .30 .09
❑ 190 Jimmy Haynes .30 .09
❑ 191 Marquis Grissom .30 .09
❑ 192 Jose Hernandez .30 .09
❑ 193 Geoff Jenkins .30 .09
❑ 194 Jamey Wright .30 .09
❑ 195 Mark Loretta .30 .09
❑ 196 Jeff D'Amico .30 .09
Henry Blanco
Richie Sexson
Ron Belliard
Tyler Houston
Mark Loretta
Jeromy Burnitz
Marquis Grissom
Geoff Jenkins CL
❑ 197 Rick Ankiel .30 .09
❑ 198 Mark McGwire 2.00 .60
❑ 199 Fernando Vina .30 .09
❑ 200 Edgar Renteria .30 .09
❑ 201 Darryl Kile .30 .09
❑ 202 Jim Edmonds .30 .09
❑ 203 Ray Lankford .30 .09
❑ 204 Garrett Stephenson .30 .09
❑ 205 Fernando Tatis .30 .09
❑ 206 Will Clark .75 .23
❑ 207 J.D. Drew .30 .09
❑ 208 Darryl Kile .30 .09
Mike Matheny
Mark McGwire
Fernando Vina
Fernando Tatis
Edgar Renteria
Ray Lankford
Jim Edmonds
J.D. Drew CL
❑ 209 Mark Grace .50 .15
❑ 210 Eric Young .30 .09
❑ 211 Sammy Sosa 1.25 .35
❑ 212 Jon Lieber .30 .09
❑ 213 Joe Girardi .30 .09
❑ 214 Kevin Tapani .30 .09
❑ 215 Ricky Gutierrez .30 .09
❑ 216 Kerry Wood .75 .23
❑ 217 Rondell White .30 .09
❑ 218 Damon Buford .30 .09
❑ 219 Jon Lieber .30 .09
Joe Girardi
Mark Grace
Eric Young
Willie Greene
Ricky Gutierrez
Sammy Sosa
Damon Bufford
Rondell White CL
❑ 220 Luis Gonzalez .30 .09
❑ 221 Randy Johnson .75 .23
❑ 222 Jay Bell .30 .09
❑ 223 Erubiel Durazo .30 .09
❑ 224 Matt Williams .30 .09
❑ 225 Steve Finley .30 .09
❑ 226 Curt Schilling .30 .09
❑ 227 Todd Stottlemyre .30 .09
❑ 228 Tony Womack .30 .09
❑ 229 Brian Anderson .30 .09
❑ 230 Randy Johnson .30 .09
Kelly Stinnett
Greg Colbrunn
Jay Bell
Matt Williams
Tony Womack
Luis Gonzalez
Steve Finley
Danny Bautista CL
❑ 231 Gary Sheffield .30 .09
❑ 232 Adrian Beltre .50 .15
❑ 233 Todd Hundley .30 .09
❑ 234 Chan Ho Park .30 .09
❑ 235 Shawn Green .30 .09
❑ 236 Kevin Brown .30 .09
❑ 237 Tom Goodwin .30 .09
❑ 238 Mark Grudzielanek .30 .09
❑ 239 Ismael Valdes .30 .09
❑ 240 Eric Karros .30 .09
❑ 241 Kevin Brown .30 .09
Todd Hundley
Eric Karros
Mark Grudzielanek
Adrian Beltre
Alex Cora
Gary Sheffield
Shawn Green
Tom Goodwin CL
❑ 242 Jose Vidro .30 .09
❑ 243 Javier Vazquez .30 .09
❑ 244 Orlando Cabrera .30 .09
❑ 245 Peter Bergeron .30 .09
❑ 246 Vladimir Guerrero .75 .23
❑ 247 Dustin Hermanson .30 .09
❑ 248 Tony Armas Jr. .30 .09
❑ 249 Lee Stevens .30 .09
❑ 250 Milton Bradley .30 .09
❑ 251 Carl Pavano .30 .09
❑ 252 Dustin Hermanson .30 .09
Michael Barrett
Lee Stevens
Jose Vidro
Geoff Jenkins
Orlando Cabrera
Vladimir Guerrero
Peter Bergeron
Milton Bradley CL
❑ 253 Ellis Burks .30 .09
❑ 254 Robb Nen .30 .09
❑ 255 J.T. Snow .30 .09
❑ 256 Barry Bonds 2.00 .60
❑ 257 Shawn Estes .30 .09
❑ 258 Jeff Kent .30 .09
❑ 259 Kirk Rueter .30 .09
❑ 260 Bill Mueller .30 .09
❑ 261 Livan Hernandez .30 .09
❑ 262 Rich Aurilia .30 .09
❑ 263 Livan Hernadez .30 .09
Bobby Estalella
J.T. Snow
Jeff Kent
Bill Mueller
Rich Aurilia
Barry Bonds
Marvin Benard
Ellis Burks CL
❑ 264 Ryan Dempster .30 .09
❑ 265 Cliff Floyd .30 .09
❑ 266 Mike Lowell .30 .09
❑ 267 A.J. Burnett .30 .09
❑ 268 Preston Wilson .30 .09
❑ 269 Luis Castillo .30 .09
❑ 270 Henry Rodriguez .30 .09
❑ 271 Antonio Alfonseca .30 .09
❑ 272 Derrek Lee .30 .09
❑ 273 Mark Kotsay .30 .09
❑ 274 Brad Penny .30 .09
❑ 275 Ryan Dempster .30 .09
Mike Redmond
Derrek Lee
Luis Castillo
Mike Lowell
Alex Gonzalez
Cliff Floyd
Mark Kotsay
Preston Wilson CL
❑ 276 Mike Piazza 1.25 .35
❑ 277 Jay Payton .30 .09
❑ 278 Al Leiter .30 .09
❑ 279 Mike Bordick .30 .09
❑ 280 Armando Benitez .30 .09
❑ 281 Todd Zeile .30 .09
❑ 282 Mike Hampton .30 .09
❑ 283 Edgardo Alfonzo .30 .09
❑ 284 Derek Bell .30 .09
❑ 285 Robin Ventura .30 .09
❑ 286 Mike Hampton .30 .09
Mike Piazza
Todd Zeile
Edgardo Alfonzo
Robin Ventura
Mike Bordick
Derek Bell
Jay Payton
Timo Perez CL
❑ 287 Tony Gwynn 1.00 .30
❑ 288 Trevor Hoffman .30 .09
❑ 289 Ryan Klesko .30 .09
❑ 290 Phil Nevin .30 .09
❑ 291 Matt Clement .30 .09
❑ 292 Ben Davis .30 .09
❑ 293 Ruben Rivera .30 .09
❑ 294 Bret Boone .30 .09
❑ 295 Adam Eaton .30 .09
❑ 296 Eric Owens .30 .09
❑ 297 Matt Clemente .30 .09
Ben Davis
Ryan Klesko
Bret Boone
Phil Nevin
Damian Jackson
Ruben Rivera
Eric Owens
Tony Gwynn CL
❑ 298 Bob Abreu .30 .09
❑ 299 Mike Lieberthal .30 .09
❑ 300 Robert Person .30 .09
❑ 301 Scott Rolen .75 .23
❑ 302 Randy Wolf .30 .09
❑ 303 Bruce Chen .30 .09
❑ 304 Travis Lee .30 .09
❑ 305 Kent Bottenfield .30 .09
❑ 306 Pat Burrell .30 .09
❑ 307 Doug Glanville .30 .09
❑ 308 Robert Person .30 .09
Mike Lieberthal
Pat Burrell
Kevin Jordan
Scott Rolen
Alex Arias
Bob Abreu
Doug Glanville
Travis Lee CL
❑ 309 Brian Giles .30 .09
❑ 310 Todd Ritchie .30 .09
❑ 311 Warren Morris .30 .09
❑ 312 John VanderWal .30 .09
❑ 313 Kris Benson .30 .09
❑ 314 Jason Kendall .30 .09
❑ 315 Kevin Young .30 .09
❑ 316 Francisco Cordova .30 .09
❑ 317 Jimmy Anderson .30 .09
❑ 318 Kris Benson .30 .09
Jason Kendall
Kevin Young
Warren Morris
Mike Benjamin

Pat Meares
John VanderWal
Brian Giles
Adrian Brown CL
❑ 319 Ken Griffey Jr. .... 1.25 .35
❑ 320 Pokey Reese .... .30 .09
❑ 321 Chris Stynes .... .30 .09
❑ 322 Barry Larkin..................... .50 .15
❑ 323 Steve Parris..................... .30 .09
❑ 324 Michael Tucker .... .30 .09
❑ 325 Dmitri Young..................... .30 .09
❑ 326 Pete Harnisch .... .30 .09
❑ 327 Danny Graves .... .30 .09
❑ 328 Aaron Boone .... .30 .09
❑ 329 Sean Casey .... .30 .09
❑ 330 Steve Parris...................... .30 .09
Ed Taubensee
Sean Casey
Pokey Reese
Aaron Boone
Barry Larkin
Ken Griffey Jr.
Dmitri Young
Michael Tucker CL
❑ 331 Todd Helton .... .50 .15
❑ 332 Pedro Astacio .... .30 .09
❑ 333 Larry Walker .... .50 .15
❑ 334 Ben Petrick .... .30 .09
❑ 335 Brian Bohanon .... .30 .09
❑ 336 Juan Pierre .... .30 .09
❑ 337 Jeffrey Hammonds .... .30 .09
❑ 338 Jeff Cirillo .... .30 .09
❑ 339 Todd Hollandsworth .... .30 .09
❑ 340 Pedro Astacio .... .30 .09
Brent Mayne
Todd Helton
Todd Walker
Jeff Cirillo
Neifi Perez
Larry Walker
Jeffrey Hammonds
Juan Pierre CL
❑ 341 Matt Wise .... .50 .15
Keith Luuola
Derrick Turnbow
❑ 342 Jason Hart........................ .50 .15
Jose Ortiz
Mario Encarnacion
❑ 343 Vernon Wells..................... .50 .15
Pasqual Coco
Josh Phelps
❑ 344 Travis Harper.................... .50 .15
Kenny Kelley
Toby Hall
❑ 345 Danys Baez .... .50 .15
Tim Drew
Martin Vargas
❑ 346 Ichiro Suzuki 15.00 4.50
Ryan Franklin
Ryan Christianson
❑ 347 Jay Spurgeon .... .50 .15
Lesli Brea
Carlos Casimiro
❑ 348 B.J. Waszgis .... .50 .15
Brian Sikorski
Joaquin Benoit
❑ 349 Sun-Woo Kim .... .50 .15
Paxton Crawford
Steve Lomasney
❑ 350 Kris Wilson .... .50 .15
Orber Moreno
Dee Brown
❑ 351 Mark Johnson .... .50 .15
Brandon Inge
Adam Bernero
❑ 352 Danny Ardoin .... .50 .15
Matt Kinney
Jason Ryan
❑ 353 Rocky Biddle.................... .50 .15
Joe Crede
Josh Paul
❑ 354 Nick Johnson .... .50 .15
D'Angelo Jimenez
Wily Mo Pena
❑ 355 Tony McKnight .... .50 .15
Aaron McNeal
Keith Ginter
❑ 356 Mark DeRosa.................... .30 .09
Jason Marquis
Wes Helms UER
Photos do not match the players ID'd
❑ 357 Allen Levrault .... .50 .15
Horacio Estrada
Santiago Perez
❑ 358 Luis Saturria .... .50 .15
Gene Stechschulte
Britt Reames
❑ 359 Joey Nation .... .50 .15
Corey Patterson
Cole Liniak
❑ 360 Alex Cabrera .... .50 .15
Geraldo Guzman
Nelson Figuero
❑ 361 Hiram Bocachica .... .50 .15
Mike Judd
Luke Prokopec
❑ 362 Tomas de la Rosa .... .50 .15
Yohanny Valera
Talmadge Nunnari
❑ 363 Ryan Vogelsong .... .50 .15
Juan Melo
Chad Zerbe
❑ 364 Jason Grilli .... .50 .15
Pablo Ozuna
Ramon Castro
❑ 365 Timo Perez .... .50 .15
Grant Roberts
Brian Cole
❑ 366 Tom Davey .... .50 .15
Xavier Nady
Dave Maurer
❑ 367 Jimmy Rollins................... .50 .15
Mark Brownson
Reggie Taylor
❑ 368 Alex Hernandez .... .50 .15
Adam Hyzdu
Tike Redman
❑ 369 Brady Clark .... .50 .15
John Riedling
Mike Bell
❑ 370 Giovanni Carrara .... .50 .15
Josh Kalinowski
Craig House
❑ 371 Jim Edmonds SH .... .30 .09
❑ 372 Edgar Martinez SH .... .30 .09
❑ 373 Rickey Henderson SH ...... .75 .23
❑ 374 Barry Zito SH.................... .50 .15
❑ 375 Tino Martinez SH .... .50 .15
❑ 376 J.T. Snow SH .... .30 .09
❑ 377 Bobby Jones SH .... .30 .09
❑ 378 Alex Rodriguez SH .... .75 .23
❑ 379 Mike Hampton SH............ .30 .09
❑ 380 Roger Clemens SH .... .75 .23
❑ 381 Jay Payton SH.................. .30 .09
❑ 382 John Olerud SH................ .30 .09
❑ 383 David Justice SH.............. .30 .09
❑ 384 Mike Hampton SH............ .30 .09
❑ 385 New York Yankees SH...... .75 .23
❑ 386 Jose Vizcaino SH .... .30 .09
❑ 387 Roger Clemens SH .... .75 .23
❑ 388 Todd Zeile SH .... .30 .09
❑ 389 Derek Jeter SH .... 1.00 .30
❑ 390 New York Yankees SH...... .75 .23
❑ 391 Nomar Garciaparra .... .75 .23
Darin Erstad
Manny Ramirez
Derek Jeter
Carlos Delgado LL
❑ 392 Todd Helton .... .50 .15
Luis Castillo
Jeffrey Hammonds
Vladimir Guerrero
Moises Alou LL
❑ 393 Troy Glaus........................ .75 .23
Frank Thomas
Alex Rodriguez
Jason Giambi
David Justice LL
❑ 394 Sammy Sosa..................... .50 .15
Jeff Bagwell
Barry Bonds
Vladimir Guerrero
Richard Hidalgo LL
❑ 395 Edgar Martinez .... .30 .09
Mike Sweeney
Frank Thomas
Carlos Delgado
Jason Giambi LL
❑ 396 Todd Helton .... .30 .09
Jeff Kent
Brian Giles
Sammy Sosa
Jeff Bagwell LL
❑ 397 Pedro Martinez .... .50 .15
Roger Clemens
Mike Mussina
Bartolo Colon
Mike Sirotka LL
❑ 398 Kevin Brown .... .30 .09
Randy Johnson
Jeff D'Amico
Greg Maddux
Mike Hampton LL
❑ 399 Tim Hudson .... .30 .09
David Wells
Aaron Sele
Andy Pettitte
Pedro Martinez LL
❑ 400 Tom Glavine .... .50 .15
Darryl Kile
Randy Johnson
Chan Ho Park
Greg Maddux LL
❑ S30 K.Griffey Jr. Sample ...... 1.25 .35

2004 Upper Deck Vintage

	Nm-Mt	Ex-Mt
COMP.SET w/o SP's (300)........	60.00	18.00
COMP.UPDATE SET (50)..........	15.00	4.50
COMMON CARD (1-300)............	.30	.09
301-315 STATED ODDS 1:5.........	.00	
COMMON CARD (316-325).........	2.00	.60
316-325 STATED ODDS 1:7.........	.00	
COMMON CARD (326-350).........	4.00	1.20
326-350 STATED ODDS 1:5.........	.00	
COMMON CARD (351-440)......	10.00	3.00
351-440 STATED ODDS 1:12........	.00	
COMMON CARD (441-450).........	4.00	1.20
COMMON CARD (451-465)..........	.30	.09
COMMON CARD (466-500)..........	.30	.09
ONE UPDATE SET PER 1.5 UD2 HOB.BOXES		.00

❑ 1 Albert Pujols .... 1.50 .45
❑ 2 Carlos Delgado .... .30 .09
❑ 3 Todd Helton .... .50 .15
❑ 4 Nomar Garciaparra .... 1.25 .35
❑ 5 Vladimir Guerrero .... .75 .23
❑ 6 Alfonso Soriano .... .50 .15
❑ 7 Alex Rodriguez .... 1.25 .35
❑ 8 Jason Giambi .... .30 .09
❑ 9 Derek Jeter .... 1.50 .45
❑ 10 Pedro Martinez .... .75 .23
❑ 11 Ivan Rodriguez .... .75 .23
❑ 12 Mark Prior.......................... .75 .23
❑ 13 Marquis Grissom .... .30 .09
❑ 14 Barry Zito .... .30 .09
❑ 15 Alex Cintron .... .30 .09
❑ 16 Wade Miller........................ .30 .09

❑ 17	Eric Chavez	.30	.09
❑ 18	Matt Clement	.30	.09
❑ 19	Orlando Cabrera	.30	.09
❑ 20	Odalis Perez	.30	.09
❑ 21	Lance Berkman	.30	.09
❑ 22	Keith Foulke	.30	.09
❑ 23	Shawn Green	.30	.09
❑ 24	Byung-Hyun Kim	.30	.09
❑ 25	Geoff Jenkins	.30	.09
❑ 26	Torii Hunter	.30	.09
❑ 27	Richard Hidalgo	.30	.09
❑ 28	Edgar Martinez	.50	.15
❑ 29	Placido Polanco	.30	.09
❑ 30	Brad Lidge	.30	.09
❑ 31	Alex Escobar	.30	.09
❑ 32	Garret Anderson	.30	.09
❑ 33	Larry Walker	.50	.15
❑ 34	Ken Griffey Jr.	1.25	.35
❑ 35	Junior Spivey	.30	.09
❑ 36	Carlos Beltran	.50	.15
❑ 37	Bartolo Colon	.30	.09
❑ 38	Ichiro Suzuki	1.25	.35
❑ 39	Ramon Ortiz	.30	.09
❑ 40	Roy Oswalt	.30	.09
❑ 41	Mike Piazza	1.25	.35
❑ 42	Benito Santiago	.30	.09
❑ 43	Mike Mussina	.50	.15
❑ 44	Jeff Kent	.30	.09
❑ 45	Curt Schilling	.30	.09
❑ 46	Adam Dunn	.50	.15
❑ 47	Mike Sweeney	.30	.09
❑ 48	Chipper Jones	.75	.23
❑ 49	Frank Thomas	.75	.23
❑ 50	Kerry Wood	.75	.23
❑ 51	Rod Beck	.30	.09
❑ 52	Brian Giles	.30	.09
❑ 53	Hank Blalock	.30	.09
❑ 54	Andruw Jones	.30	.09
❑ 55	Dmitri Young	.30	.09
❑ 56	Juan Pierre	.30	.09
❑ 57	Jacque Jones	.30	.09
❑ 58	Phil Nevin	.30	.09
❑ 59	Rocco Baldelli	.30	.09
❑ 60	Greg Maddux	1.25	.35
❑ 61	Eric Gagne	.75	.23
❑ 62	Tim Hudson	.30	.09
❑ 63	Brian Lawrence	.30	.09
❑ 64	Sammy Sosa	1.25	.35
❑ 65	Corey Koskie	.30	.09
❑ 66	Bobby Abreu	.30	.09
❑ 67	Preston Wilson	.30	.09
❑ 68	Jay Gibbons	.30	.09
❑ 69	Dontrelle Willis	.30	.09
❑ 70	Richie Sexson	.30	.09
❑ 71	Kevin Millwood	.30	.09
❑ 72	Randy Johnson	.75	.23
❑ 73	Jack Cust	.30	.09
❑ 74	Randy Wolf	.30	.09
❑ 75	Johan Santana	.50	.15
❑ 76	Magglio Ordonez	.30	.09
❑ 77	Sean Casey	.30	.09
❑ 78	Billy Wagner	.30	.09
❑ 79	Javier Vazquez	.30	.09
❑ 80	Jorge Posada	.50	.15
❑ 81	Jason Schmidt	.30	.09
❑ 82	Bret Boone	.30	.09
❑ 83	Jeff Bagwell	.50	.15
❑ 84	Rickie Weeks	.30	.09
❑ 85	Troy Percival	.30	.09
❑ 86	Jose Vidro	.30	.09
❑ 87	Freddy Garcia	.30	.09
❑ 88	Manny Ramirez	.50	.15
❑ 89	John Smoltz	.50	.15
❑ 90	Moises Alou	.30	.09
❑ 91	Ugueth Urbina	.30	.09
❑ 92	Bobby Hill	.30	.09
❑ 93	Marcus Giles	.30	.09
❑ 94	Aramis Ramirez	.30	.09
❑ 95	Brad Wilkerson	.30	.09
❑ 96	Ray Durham	.30	.09
❑ 97	David Wells	.30	.09
❑ 98	Paul Lo Duca	.30	.09
❑ 99	Danny Graves	.30	.09
❑ 100	Jason Kendall	.30	.09
❑ 101	Carlos Lee	.30	.09
❑ 102	Rafael Furcal	.30	.09
❑ 103	Mike Lowell	.30	.09
❑ 104	Kevin Brown	.30	.09
❑ 105	Vicente Padilla	.30	.09
❑ 106	Miguel Tejada	.30	.09
❑ 107	Bernie Williams	.50	.15
❑ 108	Octavio Dotel	.30	.09
❑ 109	Steve Finley	.30	.09
❑ 110	Lyle Overbay	.30	.09
❑ 111	Delmon Young	.50	.15
❑ 112	Bo Hart	.30	.09
❑ 113	Jason Lane	.30	.09
❑ 114	Matt Roney	.30	.09
❑ 115	Brian Roberts	.30	.09
❑ 116	Tom Glavine	.50	.15
❑ 117	Rich Aurilia	.30	.09
❑ 118	Adam Kennedy	.30	.09
❑ 119	Hee Seop Choi	.30	.09
❑ 120	Trot Nixon	.30	.09
❑ 121	Gary Sheffield	.30	.09
❑ 122	Jay Payton	.30	.09
❑ 123	Brad Penny	.30	.09
❑ 124	Garrett Atkins	.30	.09
❑ 125	Aubrey Huff	.30	.09
❑ 126	Juan Gonzalez	.50	.15
❑ 127	Jason Jennings	.30	.09
❑ 128	Luis Gonzalez	.30	.09
❑ 129	Vinny Castilla	.30	.09
❑ 130	Esteban Loaiza	.30	.09
❑ 131	Erubiel Durazo	.30	.09
❑ 132	Eric Hinske	.30	.09
❑ 133	Scott Rolen	.75	.23
❑ 134	Craig Biggio	.50	.15
❑ 135	Tim Wakefield	.30	.09
❑ 136	Darin Erstad	.30	.09
❑ 137	Denny Stark	.30	.09
❑ 138	Ben Sheets	.30	.09
❑ 139	Hideo Nomo	.75	.23
❑ 140	Derrek Lee	.30	.09
❑ 141	Matt Mantei	.30	.09
❑ 142	Reggie Sanders	.30	.09
❑ 143	Jose Guillen	.30	.09
❑ 144	Joe Mays	.30	.09
❑ 145	Jimmy Rollins	.30	.09
❑ 146	Juan Encarnacion	.30	.09
❑ 147	Joe Crede	.30	.09
❑ 148	Aaron Guiel	.30	.09
❑ 149	Mark Mulder	.30	.09
❑ 150	Travis Lee	.30	.09
❑ 151	Josh Phelps	.30	.09
❑ 152	Michael Young	.30	.09
❑ 153	Paul Konerko	.30	.09
❑ 154	John Lackey	.30	.09
❑ 155	Damian Moss	.30	.09
❑ 156	Javy Lopez	.30	.09
❑ 157	Joe Borowski	.30	.09
❑ 158	Jose Cruz Jr.	.30	.09
❑ 159	Ramon Hernandez	.30	.09
❑ 160	Raul Ibanez	.30	.09
❑ 161	Adrian Beltre	.50	.15
❑ 162	Bobby Higginson	.30	.09
❑ 163	Jorge Julio	.30	.09
❑ 164	Miguel Batista	.30	.09
❑ 165	Luis Castillo	.30	.09
❑ 166	Aaron Harang	.30	.09
❑ 167	Ken Harvey	.30	.09
❑ 168	Rocky Biddle	.30	.09
❑ 169	Mariano Rivera	.50	.15
❑ 170	Matt Morris	.30	.09
❑ 171	Laynce Nix	.30	.09
❑ 172	Mike Maroth	.30	.09
❑ 173	Francisco Rodriguez	.30	.09
❑ 174	Livan Hernandez	.30	.09
❑ 175	Aaron Heilman	.30	.09
❑ 176	Nick Johnson	.30	.09
❑ 177	Woody Williams	.30	.09
❑ 178	Joe Kennedy	.30	.09
❑ 179	Jesse Foppert	.30	.09
❑ 180	Ryan Franklin	.30	.09
❑ 181	Endy Chavez	.30	.09
❑ 182	Chin-Hui Tsao	.30	.09
❑ 183	Todd Walker	.30	.09
❑ 184	Edgardo Alfonzo	.30	.09
❑ 185	Edgar Renteria	.30	.09
❑ 186	Matt LeCroy	.30	.09
❑ 187	Carl Everett	.30	.09
❑ 188	Jeff Conine	.30	.09
❑ 189	Jason Varitek	.50	.15
❑ 190	Russ Ortiz	.30	.09
❑ 191	Melvin Mora	.30	.09
❑ 192	Mark Buehrle	.30	.09
❑ 193	Bill Mueller	.30	.09
❑ 194	Miguel Cabrera	.50	.15
❑ 195	Carlos Zambrano	.30	.09
❑ 196	Jose Valverde	.30	.09
❑ 197	Danys Baez	.30	.09
❑ 198	Mike MacDougal	.30	.09
❑ 199	Zach Day	.30	.09
❑ 200	Roy Halladay	.30	.09
❑ 201	Jerome Williams	.30	.09
❑ 202	Josh Fogg	.30	.09
❑ 203	Mark Kotsay	.30	.09
❑ 204	Pat Burrell	.30	.09
❑ 205	A.J. Pierzynski	.30	.09
❑ 206	Fred McGriff	.50	.15
❑ 207	Brandon Larson	.30	.09
❑ 208	Robb Quinlan	.30	.09
❑ 209	David Ortiz	.75	.23
❑ 210	A.J. Burnett	.30	.09
❑ 211	John Vander Wal	.30	.09
❑ 212	Jim Thome	.75	.23
❑ 213	Matt Kata	.30	.09
❑ 214	Kip Wells	.30	.09
❑ 215	Scott Podsednik	.30	.09
❑ 216	Rickey Henderson	.75	.23
❑ 217	Travis Hafner	.30	.09
❑ 218	Tony Batista	.30	.09
❑ 219	Robert Fick	.30	.09
❑ 220	Derek Lowe	.30	.09
❑ 221	Ryan Klesko	.30	.09
❑ 222	Joe Beimel	.30	.09
❑ 223	Doug Mientkiewicz	.30	.09
❑ 224	Angel Berroa	.30	.09
❑ 225	Adam Eaton	.30	.09
❑ 226	C.C. Sabathia	.30	.09
❑ 227	Wilfredo Ledezma	.30	.09
❑ 228	Jason Johnson	.30	.09
❑ 229	Ryan Wagner	.30	.09
❑ 230	Al Leiter	.30	.09
❑ 231	Joel Pineiro	.30	.09
❑ 232	Jason Isringhausen	.30	.09
❑ 233	John Olerud	.30	.09
❑ 234	Ron Calloway	.30	.09
❑ 235	Jose Reyes	.30	.09
❑ 236	J.D. Drew	.30	.09
❑ 237	Jared Sandberg	.30	.09
❑ 238	Gil Meche	.30	.09
❑ 239	Jose Contreras	.30	.09
❑ 240	Eric Milton	.30	.09
❑ 241	Jason Phillips	.30	.09
❑ 242	Luis Ayala	.30	.09
❑ 243	Bobby Kielty	.30	.09
❑ 244	Jose Lima	.30	.09
❑ 245	Brooks Kieschnick	.30	.09
❑ 246	Xavier Nady	.30	.09
❑ 247	Danny Haren	.30	.09
❑ 248	Victor Zambrano	.30	.09
❑ 249	Kelvim Escobar	.30	.09
❑ 250	Oliver Perez	.30	.09
❑ 251	Jamie Moyer	.30	.09
❑ 252	Orlando Hudson	.30	.09
❑ 253	Danny Kolb	.30	.09
❑ 254	Jake Peavy	.30	.09
❑ 255	Kris Benson	.30	.09
❑ 256	Roger Clemens	1.50	.45
❑ 257	Jim Edmonds	.30	.09
❑ 258	Rafael Palmeiro	.50	.15
❑ 259	Jae Weong Seo	.30	.09
❑ 260	Chase Utley	.30	.09
❑ 261	Rich Harden	.30	.09
❑ 262	Mark Teixeira	.30	.09

❑ 263 Johnny Damon .75 .23
❑ 264 Luis Matos .30 .09
❑ 265 Shigetoshi Hasegawa .30 .09
❑ 266 Alfredo Amezaga .30 .09
❑ 267 Tim Worrell .30 .09
❑ 268 Kazuhisa Ishii .30 .09
❑ 269 Miguel Ojeda .30 .09
❑ 270 Kazuhiro Sasaki .30 .09
❑ 271 Hideki Matsui 1.25 .35
❑ 272 Troy Glaus .30 .09
❑ 273 Michael Tucker .30 .09
❑ 274 Lew Ford .30 .09
❑ 275 Brian Jordan .30 .09
❑ 276 David Eckstein .30 .09
❑ 277 Robby Hammock .30 .09
❑ 278 Corey Patterson .30 .09
❑ 279 Wes Helms .30 .09
❑ 280 Jermaine Dye .30 .09
❑ 281 Cliff Floyd .30 .09
❑ 282 Dustan Mohr .30 .09
❑ 283 Kevin Mench .30 .09
❑ 284 Ellis Burks .30 .09
❑ 285 Jerry Hairston Jr. .30 .09
❑ 286 Tim Salmon .50 .15
❑ 287 Omar Vizquel .50 .15
❑ 288 Andy Pettitte .50 .15
❑ 289 Guillermo Mota .30 .09
❑ 290 Tino Martinez .50 .15
❑ 291 Lance Carter .30 .09
❑ 292 Francisco Cordero .30 .09
❑ 293 Robb Nen .30 .09
❑ 294 Mike Cameron .30 .09
❑ 295 Jhonny Peralta .30 .09
❑ 296 Braden Looper .30 .09
❑ 297 Jarrod Washburn .30 .09
❑ 298 Mark Prior CL .50 .15
❑ 299 Alfonso Soriano CL .30 .09
❑ 300 Rocco Baldelli CL .30 .09
❑ 301 Pedro Martinez PBP 2.50 .75
❑ 302 Mark Prior PBP 2.50 .75
❑ 303 Barry Zito PBP 2.00 .60
❑ 304 Roger Clemens PBP 5.00 1.50
❑ 305 Randy Johnson PBP 2.50 .75
❑ 306 Roy Halladay PBP 2.00 .60
❑ 307 Hideo Nomo PBP 2.50 .75
❑ 308 Roy Oswalt PBP 2.00 .60
❑ 309 Kerry Wood PBP 2.50 .75
❑ 310 Dontrelle Willis PBP 2.00 .60
❑ 311 Mark Mulder PBP 2.00 .60
❑ 312 Brandon Webb PBP 2.00 .60
❑ 313 Mike Mussina PBP 2.00 .60
❑ 314 Curt Schilling PBP 2.00 .60
❑ 315 Tim Hudson PBP 2.00 .60
❑ 316 Dontrelle Willis WSH 2.00 .60
❑ 317 Juan Pierre WSH 2.00 .60
❑ 318 Hideki Matsui WSH 4.00 1.20
❑ 319 Andy Pettitte WSH 2.00 .60
❑ 320 Mike Mussina WSH 2.00 .60
❑ 321 Roger Clemens WSH 5.00 1.50
❑ 322 Alex Gonzalez WSH 2.00 .60
❑ 323 Brad Penny WSH 2.00 .60
❑ 324 Ivan Rodriguez WSH 2.50 .75
❑ 325 Josh Beckett WSH 2.00 .60
❑ 326 Aaron Boone TR 4.00 1.20
❑ 327 Jeff Suppan TR 4.00 1.20
❑ 328 Shea Hillenbrand TR 4.00 1.20
❑ 329 Jeromy Burnitz TR 4.00 1.20
❑ 330 Sidney Ponson TR 4.00 1.20
❑ 331 Rondell White TR 4.00 1.20
❑ 332 Shannon Stewart TR 4.00 1.20
❑ 333 Armando Benitez TR 4.00 1.20
❑ 334 Roberto Alomar TR 4.00 1.20
❑ 335 Raul Mondesi TR 4.00 1.20
❑ 336 Morgan Ensberg SP1 4.00 1.20
❑ 337 Milton Bradley SP1 4.00 1.20
❑ 338 Brandon Webb SP1 4.00 1.20
❑ 339 Marlon Byrd SP1 4.00 1.20
❑ 340 Carlos Pena SP1 4.00 1.20
❑ 341 Brandon Phillips SP1 4.00 1.20
❑ 342 Josh Beckett SP1 4.00 1.20
❑ 343 Eric Munson SP1 4.00 1.20
❑ 344 Brett Myers SP1 4.00 1.20
❑ 345 Austin Kearns SP1 4.00 1.20
❑ 346 Jody Gerut SP2 4.00 1.20
❑ 347 Vernon Wells SP2 4.00 1.20
❑ 348 Jeff Duncan SP2 4.00 1.20
❑ 349 Sean Burroughs SP2 4.00 1.20
❑ 350 Jeremy Bonderman SP2 4.00 1.20
❑ 351 Hideki Matsui 3D 15.00 4.50
❑ 352 Jason Giambi 3D 10.00 3.00
❑ 353 Alfonso Soriano 3D 10.00 3.00
❑ 354 Derek Jeter 3D 20.00 6.00
❑ 355 Aaron Boone 3D 10.00 3.00
❑ 356 Jorge Posada 3D 10.00 3.00
❑ 357 Bernie Williams 3D 10.00 3.00
❑ 358 Manny Ramirez 3D 10.00 3.00
❑ 359 Nomar Garciaparra 3D 15.00 4.50
❑ 360 Johnny Damon 3D 15.00 4.50
❑ 361 Jason Varitek 3D 10.00 3.00
❑ 362 Carlos Delgado 3D 10.00 3.00
❑ 363 Vernon Wells 3D 10.00 3.00
❑ 364 Jay Gibbons 3D 10.00 3.00
❑ 365 Tony Batista 3D 10.00 3.00
❑ 366 Rocco Baldelli 3D 10.00 3.00
❑ 367 Aubrey Huff 3D 10.00 3.00
❑ 368 Carlos Beltran 3D 10.00 3.00
❑ 369 Mike Sweeney 3D 10.00 3.00
❑ 370 Magglio Ordonez 3D 10.00 3.00
❑ 371 Frank Thomas 3D 15.00 4.50
❑ 372 Carlos Lee 3D 10.00 3.00
❑ 373 Roberto Alomar 3D 10.00 3.00
❑ 374 Jacque Jones 3D 10.00 3.00
❑ 375 Torii Hunter 3D 10.00 3.00
❑ 376 Milton Bradley 3D 10.00 3.00
❑ 377 Travis Hafner 3D 10.00 3.00
❑ 378 Jody Gerut 3D 10.00 3.00
❑ 379 Dmitri Young 3D 10.00 3.00
❑ 380 Carlos Pena 3D 10.00 3.00
❑ 381 Ichiro Suzuki 3D 15.00 4.50
❑ 382 Bret Boone 3D 10.00 3.00
❑ 383 Edgar Martinez 3D 10.00 3.00
❑ 384 Eric Chavez 3D 10.00 3.00
❑ 385 Miguel Tejada 3D 10.00 3.00
❑ 386 Erubiel Durazo 3D 10.00 3.00
❑ 387 Jose Guillen 3D 10.00 3.00
❑ 388 Garret Anderson 3D 10.00 3.00
❑ 389 Troy Glaus 3D 10.00 3.00
❑ 390 Alex Rodriguez 3D 15.00 4.50
❑ 391 Rafael Palmeiro 3D 10.00 3.00
❑ 392 Hank Blalock 3D 10.00 3.00
❑ 393 Mark Teixeira 3D 10.00 3.00
❑ 394 Gary Sheffield 3D 10.00 3.00
❑ 395 Andruw Jones 3D 10.00 3.00
❑ 396 Chipper Jones 3D 15.00 4.50
❑ 397 Javy Lopez 3D 10.00 3.00
❑ 398 Marcus Giles 3D 10.00 3.00
❑ 399 Rafael Furcal 3D 10.00 3.00
❑ 400 Jim Thome 3D 15.00 4.50
❑ 401 Bobby Abreu 3D 10.00 3.00
❑ 402 Pat Burrell 3D 10.00 3.00
❑ 403 Mike Lowell 3D 10.00 3.00
❑ 404 Ivan Rodriguez 3D 15.00 4.50
❑ 405 Derrek Lee 3D 10.00 3.00
❑ 406 Miguel Cabrera 3D 10.00 3.00
❑ 407 Vladimir Guerrero 3D 15.00 4.50
❑ 408 Orlando Cabrera 3D 10.00 3.00
❑ 409 Jose Vidro 3D 10.00 3.00
❑ 410 Mike Piazza 3D 15.00 4.50
❑ 411 Cliff Floyd 3D 10.00 3.00
❑ 412 Albert Pujols 3D 20.00 6.00
❑ 413 Scott Rolen 3D 15.00 4.50
❑ 414 Jim Edmonds 3D 10.00 3.00
❑ 415 Edgar Renteria 3D 10.00 3.00
❑ 416 Lance Berkman 3D 10.00 3.00
❑ 417 Jeff Bagwell 3D 10.00 3.00
❑ 418 Jeff Kent 3D 10.00 3.00
❑ 419 Richard Hidalgo 3D 10.00 3.00
❑ 420 Morgan Ensberg 3D 10.00 3.00
❑ 421 Sammy Sosa 3D 15.00 4.50
❑ 422 Moises Alou 3D 10.00 3.00
❑ 423 Ken Griffey Jr. 3D 15.00 4.50
❑ 424 Adam Dunn 3D 10.00 3.00
❑ 425 Austin Kearns 3D 10.00 3.00
❑ 426 Richie Sexson 3D 10.00 3.00
❑ 427 Geoff Jenkins 3D 10.00 3.00
❑ 428 Brian Giles 3D 10.00 3.00
❑ 429 Reggie Sanders 3D 10.00 3.00
❑ 430 Rich Aurilia 3D 10.00 3.00
❑ 431 Jose Cruz Jr. 3D 10.00 3.00
❑ 432 Shawn Green 3D 10.00 3.00
❑ 433 Jeromy Burnitz 3D 10.00 3.00
❑ 434 Luis Gonzalez 3D 10.00 3.00
❑ 435 Todd Helton 3D 10.00 3.00
❑ 436 Preston Wilson 3D 10.00 3.00
❑ 437 Larry Walker 3D 10.00 3.00
❑ 438 Ryan Klesko 3D 10.00 3.00
❑ 439 Phil Nevin 3D 10.00 3.00
❑ 440 Sean Burroughs 3D 10.00 3.00
❑ 441 Sammy Sosa OJ 8.00 2.40
❑ 442 Albert Pujols OJ 10.00 3.00
❑ 443 Magglio Ordonez OJ 4.00 1.20
❑ 444 Vladimir Guerrero OJ 5.00 1.50
❑ 445 Todd Helton OJ 4.00 1.20
❑ 446 Jason Giambi OJ 4.00 1.20
❑ 447 Ichiro Suzuki OJ 8.00 2.40
❑ 448 Alex Rodriguez OJ 8.00 2.40
❑ 449 Carlos Delgado OJ 4.00 1.20
❑ 450 Manny Ramirez OJ 4.00 1.20
❑ 451 Alex Rodriguez 2.00 .60
❑ 452 Javy Lopez .30 .09
❑ 453 Alfonso Soriano .50 .15
❑ 454 Vladimir Guerrero .75 .23
❑ 455 Rafael Palmeiro .50 .15
❑ 456 Gary Sheffield .30 .09
❑ 457 Curt Schilling .30 .09
❑ 458 Miguel Tejada .30 .09
❑ 459 Kevin Brown .30 .09
❑ 460 Richie Sexson .30 .09
❑ 461 Roger Clemens 1.50 .45
❑ 462 Javier Vazquez .30 .09
❑ 463 Bartolo Colon .30 .09
❑ 464 Ivan Rodriguez .75 .23
❑ 465 Greg Maddux 1.25 .35
❑ 466 Jamie Brown RC .30 .09
❑ 467 Dave Crouthers RC .30 .09
❑ 468 Jason Frasor RC .50 .15
❑ 469 Greg Dobbs RC 1.25 .35
❑ 470 Jesse Harper RC .50 .15
❑ 471 Nick Regilio RC .50 .15
❑ 472 Ryan Wing RC .50 .15
❑ 473 Akinori Otsuka RC .50 .15
❑ 474 Shingo Takatsu RC 1.50 .45
❑ 475 Kazuo Matsui RC 2.50 .75
❑ 476 Mike Vento RC .75 .23
❑ 477 Mike Gosling RC .30 .09
❑ 478 Justin Huisman RC .50 .15
❑ 479 Justin Hampson RC .50 .15
❑ 480 Dennis Sarfate RC .50 .15
❑ 481 Ian Snell RC 1.25 .35
❑ 482 Tim Bausher RC .50 .15
❑ 483 Donnie Kelly RC .50 .15
❑ 484 Jerome Gamble RC .30 .09
❑ 485 Mike Rouse RC .50 .15
❑ 486 Merkin Valdez RC 2.00 .60
❑ 487 Lincoln Holdzkom RC .50 .15
❑ 488 Justin Leone RC .75 .23
❑ 489 Sean Henn RC .50 .15
❑ 490 Brandon Medders RC .30 .09
❑ 491 Mike Johnston RC .50 .15
❑ 492 Tim Bittner RC .50 .15
❑ 493 Michael Wuertz RC .75 .23
❑ 494 Chad Bentz RC .50 .15
❑ 495 Ryan Meaux RC .50 .15
❑ 496 Chris Aguila RC .50 .15
❑ 497 Jake Woods RC .50 .15
❑ 498 Scott Dohmann RC .30 .09
❑ 499 Colby Miller RC .50 .15
❑ 500 Josh Labandeira RC .50 .15

Acknowledgments

Each year we refine the process of developing the most accurate and up-to-date information for this book. I believe this year's Price Guide is our best yet. Thanks again to all the contributors nationwide (listed below) as well as our staff here in Dallas.

Those who have worked closely with us on this and many other books have again proven themselves invaluable: Ed Allan, Frank and Vivian Barning, Levi Bleam and Jim Fleck (707 Sportscards), T. Scott Brandon, Peter Brennan, Ray Bright, Card Collectors Co., Dwight Chapin, Theo Chen, Barry Colla, Bill and Diane Dodge, Brett Domue, Dan Even, David Festberg, Fleer/SkyBox (Josh Perlman), Steve Freedman, Gervise Ford, Larry and Jeff Fritsch, Tony Galovich, Georgia Music and Sports (Dick DeCourcey), Dick Gilkeson, Steve Gold (AU Sports), Bill Goodwin (St. Louis Baseball Cards), Mike and Howard Gordon, George Grauer, Steve Green (STB Sports), John Greenwald, Bill Henderson, Jerry and Etta Hersh, Mike Hersh, Neil Hoppenworth, Hunt Auction, Mike Jaspersen, Jay and Mary Kasper (Jay's Emporium), Jerry Katz, Pete Kennedy, David Kohler (SportsCards Plus), Terry Knouse (Tik and Tik), Tom Leon, Lew Lipset (Four Base Hits), Mike Livingston (U-Trading Cards), Mark Macrae, Bill Madden, Bill Mastro, Dr.William McAvoy, Michael McDonald, Mid-Atlantic Sports Cards (Bill Bossert), Gary Mills, Ernie Montella, Brian Morris, Mike Mosier (Columbia City Collectibles Co.), B.A. Murry, Ralph Nozaki, Mike O'Brien, Oldies and Goodies (Nigel Spill), Oregon Trail Auctions, Pacific Trading Cards (Mike Cramer and Mike Monson), Playoff Trading Cards (Ben Ecklar, Steve Judd, and Tracy Hackler), Jack Pollard, Jeff Prillaman, Pat Quinn, Jerald Reichstein (Fabulous Cardboard), Tom Reid, Gavin Riley, Clifton Rouse, John Rumierz, Pat Blandford, Lonn Passon and Kevin Savage (Sports Gallery), Gary Sawatski and Jim Justus (The Wizards of Odd), Mike Schechter, Bill and Darlene Shafer, Barry Sloate, John E. Spalding, Phil Spector, Murvin Sterling, Ted Taylor, Lee Temanson, Topps (Marty Appel), Treat (Harold Anderson), Ed Twombly, Upper Deck (Justin Kanoya), Wayne Varner, Rob Veres, Bill Vizas, Waukesha Sportscards, Bill Wesslund (Portland Sports Card Co.), Kit Young, Rick Young, Ted Zanidakis, Robert Zanze (Z-Cards and Sports), Bill Zimpleman, and Dean Zindler. Finally we give a special acknowledgment to the late Dennis W. Eckes, "Mr. Sport Americana." The success of the Beckett Price Guides has always been the result of a team effort.

It is very difficult to be "accurate" — one can only do one's best. But this job is especially difficult since we're shooting at a moving target: Prices are fluctuating all the time. Having several full-time pricing experts has definitely proven to be better than just one, and I thank all of them for working together to provide you, our readers, with the most accurate prices possible.

Many people have provided price input, illustrative material, checklist verifications, errata, and/or background information. We should like to individually thank AbD Cards (Dale Wesolewski), Action Card Sales, Jerry Adamic, Johnny and Sandy Adams, Mehdi Ahlei, Alex's MVP Cards & Comics, Doug Allen, Will Allison, Dennis Anderson, Ed Anderson, Shane Anderson, Ellis Anmuth, Alan Applegate, Ric Apter, Clyde Archer, Randy Archer, Burl Armstrong, Neil Armstrong, Carlos Ayala, B and J Sportscards, Jeremy Bachman, Dave Bailey, Ball Four Cards (Frank and Steve Pemper), Bob Bartosz, Bubba Bennett, Carl Berg, Beulah Sports (Jeff Blatt), B.J. Sportscollectables, David Boedicker (The Wild Pitch Inc.), Louis Bollman, Tim Bond, Andrew Bosarge, Terry Boyd, Dan Brandenberry, Jeff Breitenfield, Scott Brockleman, John Broggi, Virgil Burns, Greg Bussineau, David Byer, California Card Co., Capital Cards, Danny Cariseo, Carl Carlson (C.T.S.), Jim Carr, Ira Cetron, Sandy Chan, Ric Chandgie, Ray Cherry, Bigg Wayne Christian, Josh Chidester, Michael and Abe Citron, Dr. Jeffrey Clair, Michael Cohen, Tom Cohoon (Cardboard Dreams), Gary Collett, Rick Cosmen (RC Card Co.), Lou Costanzo (Champion Sports), Mike Coyne, Tony Craig (T.C. Card Co.), Solomon Cramer, Kevin Crane, Taylor Crane, Chad Cripe, Scott Crump, Allen Custer, Dave Dame, Scott Dantio, Dee's Baseball Cards (Dee Robinson), Joe Delgrippo, Mike DeLuca, Ken Dinerman (California Cruizers), Rob DiSalvatore, Cliff Dolgins, Discount Dorothy, Richard Dolloff (Dolloff Coin Center), Joe Donato, Jerry Dong, Pat Dorsey, Double Play Baseball Cards, Joe Drelich, Richard Duglin (Baseball Cards-N-More), The Dugout, Ken Edick (Home Plate of Utah), Brad Englehardt, Doak Ewing, Terry Falkner, Mike and Chris Fanning, Linda Ferrigno and Mark Mezzardi, Jay Finglass, Bob Flitter, Fremont Fong, Paul Franzetti, Ron Frasier, Tom Freeman, Bob Frye, Bill Fusaro, Chris Gala, Richard Galasso, David Garza, David Gaumer, Georgetown Card Exchange, David Giove, Dick Goddard, Jeff Goldstein, Ron Gomez, Rich Gove, Jay and Jan Grinsby, Bob Grissett, Gerry Guenther, Neil Gubitz (What-A-Card), Hall's Nostalgia, Hershell Hanks, Gregg Hara, Todd Harrell, Robert Harrison, Steve Hart, Floyd Haynes (H and H Baseball Cards), Kevin Heffner, Joel Hellman, Hit and Run Cards (Jon, David, and Kirk Peterson), Vinny Ho, Johnny Hustle Card Co., John Inouye, Vern Isenberg, Dale Jackson, Marshall Jackson, Mike Jardina, Paul Jastrzembski, Jeff's Sports Cards, Donn Jennings Cards, George Johnson, Craig Jones, Chuck Juliana, Nick Kardoulias, Scott Kashner, Frank and Rose Katen, Kevin's Kards, Kingdom Collectibles, Inc., John Klassnik, Steve Kluback,

Don Knutsen, Gregg Kohn, Mike Kohlhas, Bob & Bryan Kornfield, Carl and Maryanne Laron, Howard Lau, Richard S. Lawrence, William Lawrence, Brent Lee, Morley Leeking, Irv Lerner, Larry and Sally Levine, Larry Loeschen (A and J Sportscards), Neil Lopez, Kendall Loyd (Orlando Sportscards South), Steve Lowe, Jim Macie, Peter Maltin, Paul Marchant, Brian Marcy, Scott Martinez, James S. Maxwell Jr., McDag Productions Inc., Bob McDonald, Steve McHenry, Tony McLaughlin, Mendal Mearkle, Carlos Medina, Ken Melanson, William Mendel, Blake Meyer (Lone Star Sportscards), Tim Meyer, Joe Michalowicz, Lee Milazzo, Cary S. Miller, George Miller, Wayne Miller, Dick Millerd, Frank Mineo, Mitchell's Baseball Cards, John Morales, William Munn, Mark Murphy, Robert Nappe, National Sportscard Exchange, Roger Neufeldt, Steve Novella, Bud Obermeyer, John O'Hara, Glenn Olson, Scott Olson, Ron Oser, Luther Owen, Earle Parrish, Clay Pasternack, Michael Perrotta, Tom Pfirrmann, Don Phlong, Loran Pulver, Bob Ragonese, Bryan Rappaport, Don and Tom Ras, Robert M. Ray, Phil Regli, Rob Resnick, Dave Reynolds, Carson Ritchey, Bill Rodman, Craig Roehrig, Mike Sablow, Terry Sack, Thomas Salem, Barry Sanders, Jon Sands, Tony Scarpa, John Schad, Dave Schau (Baseball Cards), Masa Shinohara, Eddie Silard, Mike Slepcevic, Sam Sliheet, Art Smith, Lynn and Todd Solt, Jerry Sorice, Don Spagnolo, Sports Card Fan-Attic, The Sport Hobbyist, Norm Stapleton, Bill Steinberg, Lisa Stellato (Never Enough Cards), Rob Stenzel, Jason Stern, Andy Stoltz, Rob Stenzel, Bill Stone, Ted Straka, Tim Strandberg (East Texas Sports Cards), Edward Strauss, Strike Three, Richard Strobino, Kevin Struss, Superior Sport Card, Dr. Richard Swales, George Tahinos, Brent Thorton, Ian Taylor, The The Thirdhand Shoppe, Brent Thornton, Paul Thornton, Jim and Sally Thurtell, Bud Tompkins (Minnesota Connection), Philip J. Tremont, Ralph Triplette, Umpire's Choice Inc., Eric Unglaub, Hoyt Vanderpool, Steven Wagman, T. Wall, Gary A. Walter, Joe and John Weisenburger (The Wise Guys), Brian and Mike Wentz (BMW Sportscards), Richard West, Mike Wheat, Richard Wiercinski, Don Williams (Robin's Nest of Dolls), Jeff Williams, John Williams, Kent and Louise Williams, Craig Williamson, Rich Wojtasick, John Wolf Jr., Jay Wolt (Cavalcade of Sports), Joe Yanello, Peter Yee, Tom Zocco, Mark Zubrensky, and Tim Zwick.

Every year we make active solicitations for expert input. We are particularly appreciative of help (however extensive or cursory) provided for this volume. We receive many inquiries, comments, and questions regarding material within this book. In fact, each and every one is read and digested. Time constraints, however, prevent us from personally replying. But keep sharing your knowledge. Your letters and input are part of the "big picture" of hobby information we can pass along to readers in our books and magazines. Even though we cannot respond to each letter, you are making significant contributions to the hobby through your interest and comments.

The effort to continually refine and improve this book also involves a growing number of people and types of expertise on our home team. Our company boasts a substantial Sports Data Publishing team, which strengthens our ability to provide comprehensive analysis of the marketplace. SDP capably handled numerous technical details and provided able assistance in the preparation of this edition.

Our baseball analysts played a major part in compiling this year's book, traveling thousands of miles during the past year to attend sports card shows and visit card shops around the United States and Canada. The Beckett baseball specialists are: Gabe Harro, Rich Klein, Dave Porter, and Grant Sandground (Senior Price Guide Editor). Their pricing analysis and careful proofreading were key contributions to the accuracy of this annual.

Grant Sandground's coordination and reconciling of prices as Beckett Baseball Card Monthly Price Guide Editor helped immeasurably. Rich Klein, as research analyst, contributed detailed pricing analysis and hours of proofing.

The effort was led by Dan Hitt, the Senior Manager of Sports Data Publishing. He was ably assisted by the rest of the Price Guide analysts: Clint Hall, Keith Hower, Tony Joseph, Beverly Mills, Bill Sutherland, Tim Trout, and Joe White.

The price gathering and analytical talents of this fine group of hobbyists have helped make our Beckett team stronger, while making this guide and its companion monthly Price Guide more widely recognized as the hobby's most reliable and relied upon sources of pricing information.

The Beckett Interactive Division played a critical role in technology. They spent countless hours programming, testing, and implementing it to simplify the handling of thousands of prices that must be checked and updated for each edition.

In the years since this guide debuted, Beckett Publications has grown beyond any rational expectation. A great many talented and hard working individuals have been instrumental in this growth and success. Our whole team is to be congratulated for what we together have accomplished.

The whole Beckett Publications team has my thanks for jobs well done. Thank you, everyone.

NOTES

NOTES

NOTES

NOTES

NOTES